PURPOSE AND ORGANIZATION

Purpose

CHILDREN'S CORE COLLECTION is designed to serve a number of purposes:

As an aid in purchasing. The Core Collection is designed to assist in the selection and ordering of titles. Annotations and grade level designations are provided for each title along with information concerning the publisher, ISBN, price, and availability. Since Part 1, Classified Collection, is arranged according to the Dewey Decimal Classification, the Core Collection may be used to identify parts of the library collection that should be updated or strengthened. In evaluating the suitability of a work each library will want to consider the special character of the school and community it serves.

As an aid in user service. Every title in this Core Collection is a recommended work of its kind and can be given with confidence to a user who expresses a need based on topic, genre, etc. Reference work and user service are further aided by information about grade level, sequels, and companion volumes; by the descriptive and critical annotations; and by the series and subject headings in the Index. In addition, the Index includes entries under names of illustrators and series.

As an aid in curriculum support. The classification, subject indexing, annotations, and grade level designations are helpful in identifying materials appropriate for classroom use.

As an aid in collection maintenance. Information about titles available on a subject facilitates decisions to rebind, replace, or discard items. If a book has been deleted from the Core Collection in this edition because it is no longer in print, that deletion is not intended as a sign that the book is no longer valuable or that it should necessarily be weeded from the collection.

As an aid in professional development. The Core Collection is useful in courses that deal with children's literature and book selection, especially in the creation of bibliographies and reading lists.

Organization

CHILDREN'S CORE COLLECTION is presented in a single volume again. By enlarging the trim size of the book, we have been able to include more titles in this edition than in the two volume twenty second edition. As in previous editions, the CHILDREN'S CORE COLLECTION contains a generous selection of graphic novels. Most fiction graphic novels are in 741.5 with nonfiction either in biography, 92, or under specific Dewey headings by subject. For the comprehensive list of recommended graphic novels, refer to the GRAPHIC NOVELS CORE COLLECTION database on EBSCO*host* or the print version thereof.

The Core Collection consists of two parts: a Classified Collection, and an Author, Title, and Subject Index.

Part 1. Classified Collection

The Classified Collection is arranged with nonfiction books first, classified according to the Dewey Decimal Classification in numerical order from 000 to 999. Individual biographies are classed at 92 and precede the 920s (collective biography) in volume 1. Three sections follow nonfiction: Easy Books (E), consisting chiefly of picture books of interest to children from preschool to grade three; Fiction (Fic); and Story Collections (S C). The information supplied for each book includes bibliographic description, suggested subject headings, an annotation, and frequently, an evaluation from a quote source.

An Outline of Classification, which serves as a table of contents for the Classified Collection, is reproduced below. It should be noted that many topics can be classified in more than one discipline. If a particular title is not found where it might be expected, the Index should be consulted to determine if it is classified elsewhere.

Within classes, works are arranged alphabetically under main entry, usually the author. Works of individual biography are arranged alphabetically under the biography's subject.

Each listing consists of a full bibliographical description. Prices, which are always subject to change, have been obtained from the publisher, when available, and are as current as possible. Entries include recommended subject headings derived from the *Sears List of Subject Headings,* a suggested classification number from the *Abridged Dewey Decimal Classification and Relative Index,* a brief description of the contents, and, whenever possible, an evaluation from a quoted source. The following is an example of a typical entry and a description of its components:

> ★**Silverstein, Alvin**
> Wildfires; the science behind raging infernos; [by] Alvin and Virginia Silverstein and Laura Silverstein Nunn. Enslow Publishers 2010 48p il map (The science behind natural disasters) lib bdg $23.95
>
> Grades: 4 5 6   **634.9**
> 1. Wildfires
> ISBN 978-0-7660-2973-6 (lib bdg); 0-7660-2973-5 (lib bdg)
>   LC 2004-13282
> "Examines the science behind wildfires, including what causes them, the different types of wildfires, their devastating effects, and how to stay safe during a wildfire" Publisher's note
> "Scientific explanations are accompanied by plentiful color diagrams that will help students to grasp causes and effect.... Photos...are effective, and are sometimes turning into helpful, lively diagrams by the addition of such features as wind-direction arrows." SLJ
> Includes glossary and bibliographical references

The star at the start of the entry indicates this is a "Most Highly Recommended" title. The name of the author, Alvin Silverstein, is given in conformity with *Anglo-American Cataloguing Rules,* 2nd edition, 2002 revision. The title of the book is *Wildfires; the science behind raging infernos.* The book was published by Enslow Publishers in 2010.

The book has 48 pages and contains illustrations. It is published in the "The science behind natural disasters" series, in a library binding, and sells for $23.95. (Prices given were current when the Collection went to press.) The book is recommended for any of the following grade levels: 4 5 6.

At the end of the last line of type in the body entry is the figure 634.9 in bold face type. This is the classification number derived from the fifteenth edition of the *Abridged Dewey Decimal Classification.* The number 634.9 is the classification number for "Forestry".

The numbered term "1. Wildfires" is a recommended subject heading for this book based on *Sears List of Subject Headings.*

The ISBN (International Standard Book Number) is included to facilitate ordering. The Library of Congress control number is provided when available.

Following are three notes supplying additional information about the book. The first is a description of the book's content. The second is a critical note from *School Library Journal*. Such annotations are useful in evaluating books for selection and in determining which of several books on the same subject is best suited for the individual reader. The final note describes special features, in this case a glossary and a bibliography. Notes are also made to describe sequels and companion volumes, editions available, awards, and publication history.

Part 2. Author, Title, and Subject Index

The Index is a single alphabetical list of all the books entered in the Core Collection. Each book is entered under author; title (if distinctive); and subject. The classification number, displayed in boldface type, is the key to the location of the main entry for the book in the Classified Collection.

Appropriate added entries are made for joint authors and editors. "See" references are made from forms of names or subjects that are not used as headings. "See also" references are made to related or more specific headings.

The following are examples of Index entries for the book cited above:

Author	**Silverstein, Alvin** Wildfires	**634.9**
Title	**Wildfires;** the science behind raging infernos	**634.9**
Subject	**Wildfires** Silverstein, A. Wildfires	**634.9**
Publisher's series	**The science behind natural disasters** [series] Silverstein, A. Wildfires	**634.9**
Joint authors	**Silverstein, Virginia B.** (jt. auth) Silverstein, A. Wildfires	**634.9**

Standards Used

Anglo-American Cataloguing Rules, 2nd ed., 2002 revision, 2005 update. Chicago: American Library Association, 2005.

Dewey, Melvil. *Abridged Dewey Decimal Classification and Relative Index.* 15th ed. Edited by Joan S. Mitchell, et al. Dublin, Ohio: OCLC, 2012.

Bristow, Barbara and Christi Showman Farrar, eds. *Sears List of Subject Headings*. 21st ed. Ipswich, MA: H. W. Wilson, a division of EBSCO Information Services, 2014.

OUTLINE OF CLASSIFICATION

Reproduced below is the Second Summary of the Dewey Decimal Classification.* As Part 1 of this Core Collection is arranged according to this classification, the outline will serve as a table of contents for it. Please note, however, that the inclusion of this outline is not to be considered a substitute for consulting the Dewey Decimal Classification itself.

000 Computer science, knowledge & systems
010 Bibliographies
020 Library & information sciences
030 Encyclopedias & books of facts
040 [Unassigned]
050 Magazines, journals & serials
060 Associations, organizations & museums
070 News media, journalism & publishing
080 Quotations
090 Manuscripts & rare books

100 Philosophy
110 Metaphysics
120 Epistemology
130 Parapsychology & occultism
140 Philosophical schools of thought
150 Psychology
160 Logic
170 Ethics
180 Ancient, medieval & eastern philosophy
190 Modern western philosophy

200 Religion
210 Philosophy & theory of religion
220 The Bible
230 Christianity & Christian theology
240 Christian practice & observance
250 Christian pastoral practice & religious orders
260 Christian organization, social work & worship
270 History of Christianity
280 Christian denominations
290 Other religions

300 Social sciences, sociology & anthropology
310 Statistics
320 Political science
330 Economics
340 Law
350 Public administration & military science
360 Social problems & social services
370 Education
380 Commerce, communications & transportation
390 Customs, etiquette & folklore

400 Language
410 Linguistics
420 English & Old English languages
430 German & related languages
440 French & related languages
450 Italian, Romanian & related languages
460 Spanish & Portuguese languages
470 Latin & Italic languages
480 Classical & modern Greek languages
490 Other languages

500 Science
510 Mathematics
520 Astronomy
530 Physics
540 Chemistry
550 Earth sciences & geology
560 Fossils & prehistoric life
570 Life sciences; biology
580 Plants (Botany)
590 Animals (Zoology)

600 Technology
610 Medicine & health
620 Engineering
630 Agriculture
640 Home & family management
650 Management & public relations
660 Chemical engineering
670 Manufacturing
680 Manufacture for specific uses
690 Building & construction

700 Arts
710 Landscaping & area planning
720 Architecture
730 Sculpture, ceramics & metalwork
740 Drawing & decorative arts
750 Painting
760 Graphic arts
770 Photography & computer art
780 Music
790 Sports, games & entertainment

800 Literature, rhetoric & criticism
810 American literature in English
820 English & Old English literatures
830 German & related literatures
840 French & related literatures
850 Italian, Romanian & related literatures
860 Spanish & Portuguese literatures
870 Latin & Italian literatures
880 Classical & modern Greek literatures
890 Other literatures

900 History
910 Geography & travel
920 Biography & genealogy
930 History of ancient world (to ca. 499)
940 History of Europe
950 History of Asia
960 History of Africa
970 History of North America
980 History of South America
990 History of other areas

ACKNOWLEDGMENTS

EBSCO Information Services express special gratitude to the following librarians who both advised the company in editorial matters and assisted in the selection and weeding of titles for this Core Collection:

Advisory Board

James Bobick
Retired, Science & Technology Department Head
Carnegie Library of Pittsburgh
Pittsburgh, Pennsylvania

Julie Corsaro
Library Consultant
Williamsburg, VA

Gail de Vos
Storyteller, Author & Educator
Adjunct Associate Professor
SLIS University of Alberta
Edmonton, Alberta, Canada

Francisca Goldsmith
Library and Media Consultant
Worcester, Massachusetts

Joquetta Johnson
Library Media Specialist
Randallstown High School
Randallstown, Maryland

Angela Leeper
Director of Curriculum Materials Center
University of Richmond
Richmond, Virginia

John Meier
Science Librarian
Penn State University
University Park, Pennsylvania

Edward Sullivan
Instructor at Pellissippi State Community College
Oak Ridge, Tennessee

Linda Ward-Callaghan
Youth Services Manager
Joliet Public Library
Joliet, Illinois

The editors would like to thank EBSCO librarians Claire Fielder and Hannah Callahan as well as Emily Young, Teen Services Librarian at the San Antonio Public Library, whose help was instrumental in the creation of this collection.

CHILDREN'S CORE COLLECTION
TWENTY-THIRD EDITION
CLASSIFIED COLLECTION

000 COMPUTER SCIENCE, KNOWLEDGE & SYSTEMS

001.4 Research; statistical methods

Cefrey, Holly
★ **Researching** people, places, and events. Rosen Central 2010 48p il (Digital and information literacy) lib bdg $26.50
Grades: 5 6 7 8   **001.4**
1. Research 2. Report writing 3. Internet research
ISBN 978-1-4358-5317-1 lib bdg; 1-4358-5317-2 lib bdg
LC 2008-46785
Describes researching people, places, and events on the Internet, including using primary and secondary sources, evaluating source material, and avoiding plagiarism

"Colorful photos, diagrams, and sidebars and [a] lively [text creates an] appealing, user-friendly [presentation]. . . . Students and teachers will find [this title] useful in keeping up-to-date on and utilizing online resources and today's technology in a rapidly changing digital world." SLJ

Includes glossary and bibliographical references

Gaines, Ann
Ace your Internet research; [by] Ann Graham Gaines. Enslow Publishers 2009 48p il (Ace it! information literacy) lib bdg $23.93
Grades: 3 4 5   **001.4**
1. Internet research 2. Internet searching
ISBN 978-0-7660-3392-4 lib bdg; 0-7660-3392-9 lib bdg
LC 2008032351
"Readers will learn what the internet is, and how to do effective research while staying safe online" Publisher's note
Includes bibliographical references

Jakubiak, David J.
A **smart** kid's guide to doing Internet research. PowerKids Press 2009 24p il (Kids online) lib bdg $21.25; pa $8.25
Grades: 3 4 5 6   **001.4**
1. Internet research
ISBN 978-1-4042-8116-5 lib bdg; 1-4042-8116-9 lib bdg; 978-1-4358-3352-4 pa; 1-4358-3352-X pa
LC 2009002879
In this title "readers are shown how to read URL tags, use browsers, and develop search-term strings. Readers are told that Wikipedia is not reliable because anybody can add to it. . . . [This is a] worthwhile [purchase] for . . . updating collections in this area." SLJ
Includes glossary

Randolph, Ryan P.
New research techniques; getting the most out of search engine tools. [by] Ryan Randolph. Rosen Central 2011 48p il (Digital and information literacy) lib bdg $27.95; pa $11.75

Grades: 5 6 7 8   **001.4**
1. Internet resources 2. Internet searching 3. Web search engines
ISBN 978-1-4488-1321-6 lib bdg; 1-4488-1321-2 lib bdg; 978-1-4488-2292-8 pa; 1-4488-2292-0 pa
LC 2010016912
Explains new research techniques and tools that are available for online searching. Among the topics covered are browser tools and search engine toolbars, browser add-ons, Web mashups, e-mail and text alerts, RSS feeds and readers, Boolean operators, and refining research results.

"Color illustrations, large fonts, clearly defined sub-headings, and easy to read content encourage access to copious information. . . . Teachers and librarians should find this . . . to be a highly versatile teaching tool." Libr Media Connect

Includes glossary and bibliographical references

001.9 Controversial knowledge

Allen, Judy
Unexplained. Kingfisher 2006 144p il $19.95
Grades: 5 6 7 8   **001.9**
1. Parapsychology 2. Curiosities and wonders
ISBN 978-0-7534-5950-8; 0-7534-5950-7
This addresses such topics as ghosts, psychic phenomena, superstitions, mysterious natural phenomena, alleged monsters, disappearances, secrets and mysteries of ancient history, and possible extraterrestrials.

"A seamless combination of absorbing fact-filled text and stunning visuals in an investigation of mysteries that continue to baffle, tantalize, and spark endless debate." SLJ
Includes glossary

Arnosky, Jim
Monster hunt; exploring mysterious creatures with Jim Arnosky. Disney/Hyperion 2011 32p il $16.99
Grades: 2 3 4 5   **001.9**
1. Monsters
ISBN 978-1-4231-3028-4; 1-4231-3028-6
"Arnosky invites readers to join him on a cryptozoology adventure. . . . He compares legends to fact and asks if, for example, sharks could be the documented carcharodon from 13 millennia ago, or if the Loch Ness Monster might be a plesiosaur, thought extinct for 100 million years. The expansive format is appealing. A third of each full-page spread features accessible text, while two-thirds are given over to a painting of the subject. . . . This offers many opportunities for readers to speculate about these intriguing mysteries." Booklist

Erickson, Justin
Alien abductions. Bellwether Media 2011 24p il (Torque: The unexplained) lib bdg $15.95
Grades: 3 4 5 6   **001.9**
1. Extraterrestrial beings
ISBN 978-1-60014-582-7; 1-60014-582-5
LC 2010034773

This book explores the history of alien abduction stories, some of the commonly reported themes, and whether or not the stories could be true.

"Designed for struggling readers, this . . . combines accessible writing, dynamic illustrations, and [a] high-interest [topic]. [A] snazzy [cover] and an abundance of glossy, full-color illustrations provide appeal. . . . The writing is succinct but informative." SLJ

Includes glossary and bibliographical references

Gee, Joshua

★ **Encyclopedia** horrifica; the terrifying truth! about vampires, ghosts, monsters, and more. Scholastic Inc. 2007 129p il $14.99

Grades: 4 5 6 7   **001.9**

1. Ghosts 2. Monsters 3. Vampires

ISBN 978-0-439-92255-5; 0-439-92255-0

LC 2007061733

A visual reference contains true stories of such creatures as vampires, aliens, werewolves, and ghosts, accompanied by photographic evidence, eyewitness accounts, and original interviews.

"Each topic is replete with color illustrations and photos and is accompanied by a light, readable text that tries to separate fact from fiction." Voice Youth Advocates

Includes bibliographical references

Halls, Kelly Milner

In search of Sasquatch; an exercise in zoological evidence. Houghton Mifflin Books for Children 2011 47p il map $16.99

Grades: 4 5 6   **001.9**

1. Animals 2. Sasquatch

ISBN 978-0-547-25761-7; 0-547-25761-9

LC 2011005785

"This book does a fair job of presenting the evidence for Sasquatch through stories of people who have dedicated their lives to finding the cryptid. Evidence for its existence might leave many kids unconvinced, but they will likely be entertained anyway. Black-and-white and muted color illustrations and photos of people, lush forests, clues, and Sasquatch itself are scattered throughout." SLJ

★ **Tales** of the cryptids; mysterious creatures that may or may not exist. by Kelly Milner Halls, Rick Spears, Roxyanne Young; [illustrated by Rick Spears] Darby Creek 2006 72p il map $18.95

Grades: 4 5 6 7   **001.9**

1. Monsters

ISBN 1-58196-049-2

This considers the existence of creatures such as Bigfoot, the Loch Ness Monster, Marozi of Kenya, the Orang-pendek of Sumatra, and the Thylacine of Tasmania.

"The conversational text makes for fun reading, and a plethora of pictures . . . will prove enticing." SLJ

Helstrom, Kraig

Crop circles. Bellwether Media 2011 24p il (Torque: The unexplained) lib bdg $15.95

Grades: 3 4 5 6   **001.9**

1. Crop circles

ISBN 978-1-60014-583-4; 1-60014-583-3

LC 2010034776

This title explores the history of crop circles and looks into whether or not some could be of alien origin.

"Designed for struggling readers, this . . . combines accessible writing, dynamic illustrations, and [a] high-interest [topic]. [A] snazzy [cover] and an abundance of glossy, full-color illustrations provide appeal. . . . The writing is succinct but informative." SLJ

Includes glossary and bibliographical references

Karst, Ken

Area 51; Ken Karst. Creative Education 2014 48 p. color illustrations, map (Enduring mysteries) (hardcover : alk. paper) $35.65

Grades: 5 6 7 8   **001.9**

1. Nevada 2. Air bases 3. Unidentified flying objects 4. Area 51 (Nev.) 5. Air bases -- Nevada 6. Research aircraft -- United States 7. Unidentified flying objects -- Sightings and encounters -- Nevada

ISBN 1608183998; 9781608183999

LC 2013036073

This book, by Ken Karst, part of the "Enduring Mysteries" series, "takes an investigative approach to the curious phenomena and mysterious circumstances surrounding Area 51, from conspiracy theories to claims of extraterrestrial sightings to hard facts." (Publisher's note)

"With only the barest dashes of skepticism, these handsomely produced surveys present budding cryptozoologists and conspiracy theorists with rich arrays of historical anecdotes and encounters, supposed evidence, 'scientific' explanations of varying plausibility, and tantalizing speculations. . . . Karst goes beyond standard issue recaps—ensuring, for instance, that readers will come away from Atlantis knowing more than they did about Madame Blavatsky, as well as Mu and Lemuria, and also expanding his topics with references to, at best, tangentially relevant mysteries such as the fate of Amelia Earhart in Loch Ness Monster." SLJ

Includes bibliographical references and index

Other titles in the series are:

Atlantis (2014)

Bigfoot (2014)

Loch Ness Monster (2014)

Bermuda Triangle (2015)

Matthews, Rupert

Strange animals. QEB Pub. 2011 30p il (Unexplained) lib bdg $28.50

Grades: 4 5 6 7   **001.9**

1. Monsters

ISBN 978-1-59566-856-1; 1-59566-856-X

LC 2010017915

This discusses the possible existence of cryptids such as Bigfoot, the Loch Ness monster, the Bunyip, sea monsters, the Orang Pendek, and the Marozi.

"This well-written and thoughtfully designed [book] features [an] engrossing [topic]. . . . Though the pages are profusely illustrated with large, well-reproduced photographs and drawings, the layout is not cluttered. This [book] just might inspire kids to seek out more in-depth materials." SLJ

Includes glossary and bibliographical references

Michels, Troy

Atlantis. Bellwether Media 2011 24p il (Torque: The unexplained) lib bdg $15.95

Grades: 3 4 5 6   **001.9**

1. Atlantis

ISBN 978-1-60014-585-8; 1-60014-585-X

This book explores the story of Atlantis and the debate about the existence of this ancient civilization.

"Designed for struggling readers, this . . . combines accessible writing, dynamic illustrations, and [a] high-interest [topic]. [A] snazzy [cover] and an abundance of glossy, full-color illustrations provide appeal. . . . The writing is succinct but informative." SLJ

Includes glossary and bibliographical references

004.6 Interfacing and communications

Cornwall, Phyllis

Online etiquette and safety. Cherry Lake Pub. 2010 32p il (Super smart information strategies) lib bdg $27.07

Grades: 3 4 5 6   **004.6**

1. Etiquette 2. Internet -- Social aspects 3. Internet -- Security measures

ISBN 978-1-60279-956-1 lib bdg; 1-60279-956-3 lib bdg

LC 2010002023

This "teaches valuable lessons on why it's important to be responsible online citizens despite the misleading anonymity of the Web and offers tips on how to deal with cyberbullies and other online dangers." Booklist

Includes bibliographical references

Grayson, Robert

Managing your digital footprint. Rosen Central 2011 48p il (Digital and information literacy) lib bdg $26.50; pa $11.75

Grades: 5 6 7 8   **004.6**

1. Internet 2. Etiquette 3. Right of privacy

ISBN 978-1-4488-1319-3 lib bdg; 1-4488-1319-0 lib bdg; 978-1-4488-2290-4 pa; 1-4488-2290-4 pa

LC 2010025746

Though this "title is a broad overview of a sometimes-complex subject, the detail is significant. . . . Touches of blue enhance the clean design. . . . [This] discusses the permanence of impulsively posted material online, contrasting it with more retro forms of self-expression, such as keeping a paper diary." Booklist

Includes bibliographical references

005.1 Computer programming and programs

Bedell, Jane

So, you want to be a coder? The Ultimate Guide to a Career in Programming, Video Game Creation, Robotics, and More! Jane (J. M.) Bedell. Aladdin 2016 247 p. illustrations (hardcover) $19.99

Grades: 4 5 6 7   **005.1**

1. Robotics 2. Video games 3. Computer programming 4. Programming languages 5. Computer programming -- Vocational guidance 6. Programming languages (Electronic computers)

ISBN 1582705798; 1582705801; 9781582705798; 9781582705804

LC 2015040640

This book by Jane (J. M.) Bedell, part of the "Be What You Want" series, presents a "comprehensive guide that reveals a whole host of careers working with code. . . . Covering everything from navigating the maze of computer languages to writing code for games to cyber security and artificial intelligence, . . . [the book] debugs the secrets behind a career in the diverse and state-of-the-art industry." (Publisher's note)

"Quizzes, tech timelines, resource lists, and sidebars on related topics further round out the career advice. While it's a solid resource for any reader, the focus on female coders and innovators make it an especially apt choice for girls interested in STEM fields." Pub Wkly

Includes bibliographical references (pages 227-247)

McManus, Sean

How to Code in 10 Easy Lessons; Sean McManus. Walter Foster 2015 64 p. color illustrations $12.95

Grades: 4 5 6 7 8   **005.1**

1. Computer games 2. Computer programming

ISBN 1633220508; 9781633220508

In this book from author Sean McManus "from writing simple coding instructions using Scratch software, to learning the coding skills to create your own computer game and even design your own website, this book leads the way. By breaking this daunting subject down into the 10 'super skills' needed, young readers can get familiar with computer coding and build on their skills." (Publisher's note)

"The book is made more accessible with plenty of colorful graphics as visual references, information divided into manageable chunks, and a concluding list of useful web links. Kids will bite at this first taste of coding." Booklist

005.8 Data security

Jakubiak, David J.

A **smart** kid's guide to Internet privacy. PowerKids Press 2009 24p il (Kids online) lib bdg $21.25; pa $8.25

Grades: 3 4 5 6   **005.8**

1. Computer crimes 2. Right of privacy 3. Internet and children 4. Internet -- Security measures

ISBN 978-1-4042-8118-9 lib bdg; 1-4042-8118-5 lib bdg; 978-1-4358-3356-2 pa; 1-4358-3356-2 pa

LC 2009005369

This title "is straightforward about not sharing information without parental permission and also gives support and suggestions in case something does happen. . . . [A] worthwhile [purchase] for teaching online safety and updating collections in this area." SLJ

Includes glossary and bibliographical references

006.7 Multimedia systems

Fontichiaro, Kristin

Podcasting 101. Cherry Lake Pub. 2010 32p il (Super smart information strategies) lib bdg $27.07

Grades: 3 4 5 6   **006.7**

1. Podcasting

ISBN 978-1-60279-953-0 lib bdg; 1-60279-953-9 lib bdg

LC 2010004533

"A knockout resource for media-fair projects, Podcasting 101 doles out page after page of useful information, from the equipment required to content ideas for those who might need a creative spark to tips for structuring and adding effects to a successful podcast." Booklist

Includes bibliographical references

Rowell, Rebecca

YouTube; the company and its founders. ABDO Pub. Co. 2011 112p il (Technology pioneers) lib bdg $32.44

Grades: 5 6 7 8   **006.7**

1. Internet 2. YouTube, Inc.

ISBN 978-1-61714-813-2 lib bdg; 1-61714-813-X lib bdg; 978-1-61758-971-3 e-book

LC 2010043379

This is an introduction to YouTube and its founders.

"Written in a clear, linear fashion, this series offers vivid, well-researched details about the development of technological advancements considered essential in today's society. . . . Readers who are interested in technology and inventions will be thoroughly engrossed." SLJ

Includes glossary and bibliographical references

Selfridge, Benjamin

A **teen's** guide to creating Web pages and blogs; [by] Benjamin Selfridge, Peter Selfridge, and Jennifer Osburn. Prufrock Press 2009 148p il pa $16.95; OP

Grades: 5 6 7 8 9 10 **006.7**

1. Weblogs 2. Internet and teenagers 3. Web sites -- Design
ISBN 978-1-59363-345-5; 1-59363-345-9

LC 2008-40044

First published 2004 by Zephyr Press with title: Kid's guide to creating Web pages for home and school

"This guide begins with basic step-by-step information about HTML, fonts, images, lists, and tables. . . . The book's last half introduces more advanced techniques, such as JavaScript, functions, loops, and applications like Flash and Instant Messenger. . . . Illustrated, with references and a glossary, this attractive paperback has lots of practical content." Voice Youth Advocates

Includes glossary and bibliographical references

Truesdell, Ann

Wonderful wikis; by Ann Truesdell. Cherry Lake Publishing 2013 32 p. (Information explorer) (library) $28.50; (paperback) $14.21

Grades: 4 5 6 7 **006.7**

1. Wikis (Computer science)
ISBN 1610804805; 9781610804806; 9781610806541

LC 2012001758

This juvenile nonfiction book, by Ann Truesdell, as part of the publisher's "Explorer Library" series, presents a profile and guidelines for school children to make use of wikis online for educational purposes. Topics addressed include definitions of what a wiki is, how to contribute to them properly, and what ways they are most useful.

Includes bibliographical references and index

Woog, Adam

YouTube. Norwood House Press 2008 48p il (A great idea) lib bdg $25.27

Grades: 3 4 5 6 **006.7**

1. Internet 2. YouTube, Inc.
ISBN 978-1-59953-198-4 lib bdg; 1-59953-198-4 lib bdg

LC 2008010724

This "offers a fresh topic and handles it extremely well. . . . Woog's account is interesting and informative and written in simple yet uncondescending prose that's spot-on for the intended audience. . . . The attractive design features full-color photographs, while fast facts appear throughout the narrative in eye-catching sidebars." Booklist

Includes glossary and bibliographical references

011.6 General bibliographies and catalogs of works for young people and people with disabilities; for specific types of libraries

East, Kathy

★ **Across** cultures; a guide to multicultural literature for children. Libraries Unlimited 2007 342p il (Children's and young adult literature reference series) $55

Grades: Adult Professional **011.6**

1. Reference books 2. Multiculturalism -- Bibliography 3. Children's literature -- Bibliography
ISBN 978-1-59158-336-3; 1-59158-336-5

LC 2007013573

This is "user-friendly and extremely helpful both in terms of the choices and the descriptions." SLJ

Includes bibliographical references

Fichtelberg, Susan

★ **Primary** genreflecting; a guide to picture books and easy readers. [by] Susan Fichtelberg and Bridget Dealy Volz. Libraries Unlimited 2010 375p (Genreflecting advisory series) $48

Grades: Adult Professional **011.6**

1. Children's literature 2. Picture books for children 3. Children's literature -- Bibliography 4. Picture books for children -- Bibliography
ISBN 1-56308-907-6; 978-1-56308-907-7

LC 2010036578

This "covers picture books and easy readers for children ages three to eight. . . . Fichtelberg and Volz . . . organize 2,500 annotated titles by theme. Most titles are positively reviewed and award-winning books published between 1999 and 2009. . . . Succinct descriptions of plot and style of illustration accompany bibliographic information, awards won, and grade level." Booklist

Includes bibliographical references

Freeman, Judy

★ **Books** kids will sit still for 3; a read-aloud guide. [by] Judy Freeman; Catherine Barr, series editor. Libraries Unlimited 2006 915p il (Children's and young adult literature reference series) $70; pa $55

Grades: Adult Professional **011.6**

1. Best books 2. Reference books 3. Children's literature -- Bibliography
ISBN 1-59158-163-X; 1-59158-164-8 pa

First published 1984 by Alleyside with title: Books kids will sit still for

"This excellent resource will be a favorite with teachers who need assistance finding quality children's literature, and it will also aid librarians and media specialists." SLJ

Gillespie, John Thomas, 1928-

The **children's** and young adult literature handbook; a research and reference guide. Libraries Unlimited 2005 393p (Children's and young adult literature reference series) $55

Grades: Adult Professional **011.6**

1. Reference books 2. Children's literature -- Bibliography 3. Young adult literature -- Bibliography 4. Children's literature -- History and criticism 5. Young adult literature -- History and criticism
ISBN 1-56308-949-1

"This reference should meet the needs of librarians, teachers, and scholars." Choice

Matthew, Kathryn I.

Neal-Schuman guide to recommended children's books and media for use with every elementary subject; by Kathryn I. Matthew and Joy L. Lowe. 2nd ed; Neal-Schuman Publishers 2010 356p pa $75

Grades: Adult Professional **011.6**

1. Best books 2. Books and reading 3. Audiovisual materials -- Catalogs 4. Children's literature -- Bibliography
ISBN 978-1-55570-688-3; 1-55570-688-6

LC 2010014082

First published 2002

"Listing more than 1,000 books, videos, software, CDs, and Web sites up through early 2010, this book offers elementary (and middle-school) librarians a wonderful collection-development and collaboration tool. Each chapter covers one elementary subject area. . . . The chapters are broken down into narrower topics; each section covers the book and media choices plus ideas for exploring many of the resources listed. Each chapter begins with relevant national standards and ends with teacher resources and references including books, professional organizations, and Web sites. The annotated listings are arranged by grade level from pre–K up through middle school and include full bibliographic information." Booklist

Includes bibliographical references

Meese, Ruth Lyn
   Family matters; adoption and foster care in children's literature. Libraries Unlimited 2010 147p pa $35

Grades: Adult Professional   **011.6**
   1. Adoption -- Bibliography 2. Foster home care -- Bibliography 3. Children's literature -- Bibliography
   ISBN 978-1-59158-782-8 pa; 1-59158-782-4 pa

                      LC 2009040750
   "Meese's goal is to help adults, particularly educators, select high-quality children's books about adoption and foster care and to raise awareness about the unique issues that adoptees often face. . . . Charts, Venn diagrams, and extensive annotations supplement the annotated list of books for children in kindergarten through grade eight. Meese explains her rationale for choosing these books so that readers have the tools to evaluate other selections." SLJ

   Includes bibliographical references

Reid, Rob
   Reid's read-alouds; selections for children and teens. American Library Association 2009 xiii, 121p pa $45

Grades: Adult Professional   **011.6**
   1. Books and reading 2. Children's literature -- Bibliography 3. Young adult literature -- Bibliography
   ISBN 978-0-8389-0980-5 pa; 0-8389-0980-9 pa

                      LC 2008045376
   "Reid has collected 200 titles published between 2000 and 2008 that have both readability and general kid appeal. The titles are organized alphabetically by author, and the book includes subject and age-level indexes. Each selection has a cursory summary, grade-level range, and a suggestion for a 10-minute read-aloud, which either provides an introduction to the main characters or a glimpse into the story. . . . This last part is what makes the book so useful." SLJ

   Includes bibliographical references

   Reid's read-alouds 2; modern day classics from C.S. Lewis to Lemony Snicket. American Library Association 2011 160p

Grades: Adult Professional   **011.6**
   1. Books and reading 2. Children's literature 3. Young adult literature 4. Children's literature -- Bibliography 5. Young adult literature -- Bibliography
   ISBN 0-8389-1072-6; 978-0-8389-1072-6

                      LC 2010028985
   "The very successful first edition of Reid's Read-Alouds (ALA, 2009) profiled children's and young adult books published between the years 2000 and 2008. This companion volume showcases 200 strong titles that were published from 1950 to 1999. Reid offers a variety of genres and age levels, and a good balance between male and female protagonists. . . . The focus is on books that are great to read to groups of young people. Each entry includes a brief plot summary, suggested grade level, and Reid's signature '10 Minute Selections,' which are engaging episodes from the books that can be read in one sitting. These alone make the book a valuable resource." SLJ

   Includes bibliographical references

Safford, Barbara Ripp
   Guide to reference materials for school library media centers; 6th ed; Libraries Unlimited 2010 236p $60

Grades: Adult Professional   **011.6**
   1. Instructional materials centers 2. School libraries -- Catalogs 3.

Reference books -- Bibliography
   ISBN 978-1-59158-277-9; 1-59158-277-6

                      LC 2009-51190
   First edition by Christine Gehrt Wynar published 1973 with title: Guide to reference books for school media centers
   "This volume has been updated to include web-based reference offerings as well as listings of older sources, provided that their content is still valid. . . . This title profiles resources recommended for use by school librarians for collection management, readers' advisory, teaching, general reference materials, the social sciences and humanities, and science and technology. This volume is an excellent starting point for new school librarians, as well as for those who are building a library from scratch." SLJ

   Includes bibliographical references

Schon, Isabel
   Recommended books in Spanish for children and young adults, 2004-2008. Scarecrow Press 2009 414p $55

Grades: Adult Professional   **011.6**
   1. Reference books 2. Spanish literature -- Bibliography 3. Children's literature -- Bibliography 4. Young adult literature -- Bibliography 5. Latin American literature -- Bibliography
   ISBN 978-0-8108-6386-6; 0-8108-6386-3

                      LC 2008-33390
   "Schon evaluates 1231 reference books, fiction, and nonfiction. . . . Entries are arranged alphabetically by author and include a grade level for each book. . . . Schon examines and recommends materials based on the quality of the Spanish language, literary appeal, and the versatility of the translators, paying special attention to the effective use of Peninsular Spanish or the Spanish from the Americas. This annotated bibliography will help selectors in public libraries and media centers to develop existing Spanish-language collections." SLJ

Spiegel, Carol
   Book by book; an annotated guide to young people's literature with peacemaking and conflict resolution themes. Educators for Social Responsibility 2010 186p pa $35

Grades: Adult Professional   **011.6**
   1. Peace -- Bibliography 2. Conflict management -- Bibliography 3. Children's literature -- Bibliography 4. Young adult literature -- Bibliography
   ISBN 978-0-942349-93-1 pa; 0-942349-93-8 pa

   "More than 900 books for preschool through high school have been organized by title into two sections, picture and chapter books; described; and assigned behavioral headings. Thematic clusters include making connections, emotional literacy, caring and effective communication, cultural competence and social responsibility, and conflict management and responsible decision making. . . . Useful especially in elementary and middle schools where character education is part of the curriculum without the explicit mandate." SLJ

011.62   Works for young people

Barr, Catherine
   ★ **Best** books for children; preschool through grade 6. Catherine Barr and John T. Gillespie. 9th ed. Libraries Unlimited/ABC-CLIO 2010 xv, 1901 p.p (hardcover : acid-free paper) $95

Grades: Adult Professional   **011.62**
   1. Best books -- United States 2. Children's literature -- Bibliography 3. Children -- Books and reading -- United States
   ISBN 1591585759; 9781591585756

                      LC 2009049873
   First published 1978

Author Catherine Barr's book allows librarians to "build collections to make their young patrons--and their parents and teachers--happy." It is a "guide to the best recreational and educational reading for children in preschool through grade 6." The book "brings together information on nearly 25,000 of the best fiction and nonfiction for children in preschool through grade 6." (Publisher's note)

Hearne, Betsy Gould

Choosing books for children; a commonsense guide. [by] Betsy Hearne with Deborah Stevenson. 3rd ed; University of Ill. Press 1999 229p il hardcover o.p. OP; pa $21

Grades: Adult Professional   **011.62**

1. Reference books 2. Books and reading 3. Children's literature -- Bibliography

ISBN 0-252-02516-4; 0-252-06928-5 pa

LC 99-6144

First published 1981 by Delacorte Press

"The focus is on books since 1950; the 14 chapter-opening illustrations mainly represent books of the last decade. Chapters divide books by age and genre; one chapter considers the value of controversial books while another affectionately revisits classics." Publ Wkly

Silvey, Anita

★ **Children's** book-a-day almanac; Anita Silvey. Roaring Brook Press 2012 388 p. $19.99

Grades: Adult Professional   **011.62**

1. Children's literature 2. Children -- Books and reading 3. Almanacs 4. Best books -- United States 5. Children's literature -- Bibliography 6. Children's literature -- Stories, plots, etc 7. Children -- Books and reading -- United States

ISBN 1596437081; 9781596437081

LC 2012013301

Author Anita Silvey presents a reference book of great children's books of the past and present. "Each page features an event of the day, a children's book that relates to that event, and a list of other events that took place on that day." The almanac includes 365 books for children of various ages, from picture books to counting books and read-along books. (Publisher's note)

Includes bibliographical references

016   Bibliographies and catalogs of works on specific subjects

Al-Hazza, Tami Craft

Books about the Middle East; selecting and using them with children and adolescents. [by] Tami Craft Al-Hazza and Katherine T. Bucher. Linworth Pub. 2008 168p pa $39.95

Grades: Adult Professional   **016**

1. Reference books 2. Middle East -- Bibliography 3. Children's literature -- Bibliography 4. Young adult literature -- Bibliography

ISBN 978-1-58683-285-8; 1-58683-285-9

LC 2007-40149

"This book examines the body of literature about the diverse groups of people who inhabit the Middle East, and it also explores a variety of ways in which this literature can be used. . . . It fills a huge gap and should not be overlooked. This powerhouse book will be tremendously helpful to media specialists, educators, and public librarians." Voice Youth Advocates

Includes bibliographical references

Child Study Children's Book Committee at Bank Street

The **best** children's books of the year; selected by the Children's Book Committee at Bank Street College of Education. Teacher's College Press

Grades: Adult Professional   **016**

1. Reference books 2. Children's literature -- Bibliography

First published 1998

"This is a comprehensive annotated book list for children, aged infant--14." Publisher's note

Crew, Hilary S.

Women engaged in war in literature for youth; a guide to resources for children and young adults. Scarecrow Press 2007 303p (Literature for youth) pa $51

Grades: Adult Professional   **016**

1. Reference books 2. War -- Bibliography 3. Women -- Bibliography 4. Children's literature -- Bibliography 5. Young adult literature -- Bibliography

ISBN 978-0-8108-4929-7; 0-8108-4929-1

LC 2006-101112

"Crew's guide to print and online sources documents women's roles in wars over the centuries and throughout the world, divided by time periods. . . . This is a great addition for libraries looking for a way to move Women's Studies beyond the month of March." SLJ

Includes bibliographical references

Garcha, Rajinder

The **world** of Islam in literature for youth; a selective annotated bibliography for K-12. [by] Rajinder Garcha, Patricia Yates Russell. Scarecrow Press 2006 xx, 221p (Literature for youth) pa $35

Grades: Adult Professional   **016**

1. Reference books 2. Islam -- Bibliography 3. Children's literature -- Bibliography 4. Young adult literature -- Bibliography

ISBN 978-0-8108-5488-8; 0-8108-5488-0

LC 2005-26645

"This highly useful bibliography fills a conspicuous gap in a much-needed cultural area." Voice Youth Advocates

Includes bibliographical references

Hall, Susan

★ **Using** picture storybooks to teach literary devices; recommended books for children and young adults. Libraries Unlimited 2007 282p (Using picture books to teach) pa $42

Grades: Adult Professional   **016**

1. Literature -- Study and teaching

ISBN 978-1-59158-493-3 pa; 1-59158-493-0 pa

"This fourth volume of the series, . . . gives teachers and librarians the . . . tool to teach literary devices in grades K-12. With this volume, the author has added: colloquialism; counterpoint; solecism; archetype; and others to the list of devices. The entries have been reorganized to include all the information under the book listing itself. Each entry includes an annotation, a listing of curricular tie-ins for the book and the art style used, and a listing and explanation of all the literary devices taught by that title." Publisher's note

Includes bibliographical references

Scales, Pat R.

★ **Books** under fire; a hit list of banned and challenged children's books. Pat Scales. ALA Editions, an imprint of the American Library Association 2015 xvi, 208 p.p illustrations (pbk.) $47

Grades: Adult Professional   **016**

1. Books -- Censorship 2. Children -- Books and reading -- United States 3. School libraries -- Censorship -- United States 4. Challenged books -- United States -- Bibliography 5. Prohibited

books -- United States -- Bibliography 6. Children's literature -- Censorship -- United States

ISBN 0838911099; 9780838911099

LC 2014023945

This book on banned and challenged books, by Pat R. Scales, "covers both children's and young adult books. The main section profiles 34 books (and series such as 'Harry Potter' and 'Captain Underpants') that have recently been challenged for library or curriculum suitability in the US.... Each entry includes a... synopsis, quotations from some reviews, details of known challenges, awards/accolades, and a 'Further Reading' section." (Choice)

Includes bibliographical references and index

Thomas, Rebecca L.

★ **Popular** series fiction for K-6 readers; a reading and selection guide. [by] Rebecca L. Thomas and Catherine Barr. 2nd ed; Libraries Unlimited 2008 1002p (Children's and young adult literature reference series) $65

Grades: Adult Professional
016

1. Reference books 2. Children's literature -- Bibliography

ISBN 978-1-59158-659-3; 1-59158-659-3

LC 2008-38124

First published 2004

"Using standard review sources and bibliographies as well as author, publisher, bookseller, and library Web sites, the authors have identified nearly 2,200 in-print series appropriate for K-6 readers.... Entries are arranged by the series title and contain author, most recent publisher, grade level, notation for availability of accelerated-reader resources, genre, a descriptive three to five-sentence annotation, and a list of individual titles in the series, arranged by publication date. Following the entries are author, title, and genre/subject indexes as well as appendixes that list books for boys, girls, and reluctant readers.... [This is] essential as reference and selection tools in all school, public, and academic libraries." Booklist

Includes bibliographical references

Walter, Virginia A.

★ **War** & peace; a guide to literature and new media, grades 4-8. [by] Virginia A. Walter. Libraries Unlimited 2007 276p (Children's and young adult literature reference series) pa $40

Grades: Adult Professional
016

1. Reference books 2. War -- Bibliography 3. Peace -- Bibliography 4. Children's literature -- Bibliography 5. Young adult literature -- Bibliography

ISBN 1-59158-271-7 pa; 978-1-59158-271-7 pa

LC 2006030671

"Walter addresses the issue of war—and peace—by examining the information needs of children and how we as professionals can meet them.... The bulk of the book is the annotated listing of resources that is divided topically.... The well-annotated bibliography includes books, DVDs, Web sites, and CDs, as well as suggestions for using the materials.... This book should be a 'must purchase.'" SLJ

Includes bibliographical references

Wesson, Lindsey Patrick

Green reads; best environmental resources for youth, K-12. Libraries Unlimited 2009 219p (Children's and young adult literature reference series) $50

Grades: Adult Professional
016

1. Reference books 2. Children's literature -- Bibliography 3. Young adult literature -- Bibliography 4. Environmental protection -- Bibliography 5. Conservation of natural resources -- Bibliography

ISBN 978-1-59158-834-4; 1-59158-834-0

LC 2009-17353

"This well-organized bibliography offers 450 annotated resources that can be integrated into the classroom to introduce students to environmental concepts. The five chapters focus on global warming, pollution, the Earth's resources, recycling, and conservation. Subchapters follow a uniform organization, including fiction; DVDs and CDs; nonfiction; seminal works, which are labeled 'Recycled Favorites'; and a storytime lesson plan with a variety of activities including songs and tactile learning activities.... This reference will delight educators and professionals interested in making students aware of environmental issues and to help youngsters rediscover the outside and natural worlds around them." SLJ

Includes bibliographical references

020 Library and information sciences

Fontichiaro, Kristin

Go straight to the source. Cherry Lake Pub. 2010 32p il (Super smart information strategies) lib bdg $27.07

Grades: 3 4 5 6
020

1. Research 2. Information resources 3. History -- Sources

ISBN 978-1-60279-640-9 lib bdg; 1-60279-640-8 lib bdg

LC 2009028057

"The appealing layout includes manageable paragraphs, a variety of engaging illustrations, and examples that clearly guide reader through each topic.... [This] provides an excellent introduction to primary sources and will create enthusiasm in readers for examining old photographs and ads." SLJ

Includes glossary and bibliographical references

Gaines, Ann

Master the library and media center; [by] Ann Graham Gaines. Enslow Publishers, Inc. 2009 48p il (Ace it! information literacy) lib bdg $23.93

Grades: 3 4 5
020

1. Research 2. Libraries 3. Information literacy 4. Information resources 5. Instructional materials centers

ISBN 978-0-7660-3393-1 lib bdg; 0-7660-3393-7 lib bdg

LC 2008024886

"Readers will learn about both the regular and electronic research materials available at the library" Publisher's note

Includes bibliographical references

Kenney, Karen Latchana

Librarians at work; by Karen L. Kenney; illustrated by Brian Caleb Dumm; content consultant, Judith Stepan-Norris. Magic Wagon 2010 32p il (Meet your community workers!) lib bdg $18.95

Grades: K 1 2 3
020

1. Librarians 2. Vocational guidance

ISBN 978-1-60270-649-1 lib bdg; 1-60270-649-2 lib bdg

LC 2009-2386

This book about librarians has "an uncluttered layout and consistent organization.... Chapter headings such as 'Problems on the Job,' and 'Technology at Work,' and 'Special Skills and Training' make it easy to pinpoint specific information." SLJ

Includes glossary

Pinborough, Jan

Miss Moore thought otherwise; the story of the lady who made libraries for children. by Jan Pinborough; illustrated by Debby Atwell. Houghton Mifflin Harcourt 2013 40 p. (reinforced) $16.99

Grades: 1 2 3 4 5
020

1. Librarians 2. Children's libraries 3. New York Public Library -- Biography 4. Children's libraries -- United States -- History 5.

Children's librarians -- United States -- Biography
ISBN 054747105X; 9780547471051

LC 2012018092

This book is a biography of "children's advocate and librarian [Anne Carroll] Moore (1871-1961), celebrated for her pioneering work in making libraries and library services accessible to (and fun for) kids." Author Jan Pinborough "has selected highlights from Moore's life—her belief in letting children touch and borrow books, her ascent to the head of children's services for the New York Public Library—and streamlined them." (Publishers Weekly)

Includes bibliographical references

021　Relationships of libraries, archives, information centers

York, Sherry

Booktalking authentic multicultural literature; fiction and history for young readers. Linworth Pub. 2009 112p pa $39.95

Grades: Adult Professional　　　　　　　　　**021**

1. Book talks 2. Multicultural education 3. Youth -- Books and reading 4. Teenagers -- Books and reading 5. Multiculturalism -- Bibliography 6. Young adult literature -- Bibliography
ISBN 978-1-58683-300-8 pa; 1-58683-300-6 pa

LC 200843798

This title "highlights 101 contemporary books by a variety of U.S. authors. Arranged alphabetically by title, entries include the cultural background of author, illustrator, and translator; their Web sites when available; reading and interest levels; genre; related titles; and the single-paragraph booktalk itself. Over 20 ethnic groups are represented. . . . Librarians will find this book helpful in expanding their collections to reflect our global society." SLJ

021.2　Relationships with the community

Squires, Tasha

Library partnerships; making connections between school and public libraries. Information Today, Inc. 2009 203p pa $39.50

Grades: Adult Professional　　　　　　　　　**021.2**

1. Public libraries 2. School libraries 3. Library cooperation 4. Libraries and schools 5. Libraries and students
ISBN 978-1-57387-362-8; 1-57387-362-4

LC 2008-51647

"Squires's confident advice can get beleaguered librarians through . . . difficulties and into mutually productive partnerships." Voice Youth Advocates

Includes bibliographical references

021.7　Promotion of libraries, archives, information centers

Cole, Sonja

Booktalking around the world; great global reads for ages 9-14. Libraries Unlimited 2010 155p pa $35

Grades: Adult Professional　　　　　　　　　**021.7**

1. Book talks 2. Children's literature 3. Ethnology 4. Geography 5. World history 6. Children's literature -- Bibliography
ISBN 1-59884-613-2 pa; 978-1-59884-613-3 pa; 978-1-59884-614-0 ebook

LC 2010036580

"In this authoritative and highly readable text, [Cole] presents booktalks and reading lists of interest to children. The titles chosen are set in Africa, Asia, Europe, the Americas, Australia, New Zealand and the South Pacific Islands, and the Arctic and Antarctic. Each booktalk contains an enticing description of the book, bibliographic information, interest and reading levels, and awards. Those that have videos available are noted." SLJ

Includes bibliographical references

Keane, Nancy J.

★ The **tech**-savvy booktalker; a guide for 21st-century educators. [by] Nancy J. Keane and Terence W. Cavanaugh. Libraries Unlimited 2009 162p il pa $35

Grades: Adult Professional　　　　　　　　　**021.7**

1. Book talks 2. Information technology
ISBN 978-1-59158-637-1 pa; 1-59158-637-2 pa

LC 2008-38988

"Keane offers a way to enhance booktalks with technology and to invite students to explore new ways to talk about books using Web 2.0 tools. The volume is divided into 11 chapters from booktalking concepts to more advanced uses of technology including scanners, digital cameras, computer software, and audio recording. Also included are chapters on software programs such as PowerPoint and iMovie as well as Internet sites such as YouTube and Amazon. The sequence of chapters is designed to allow easy access to information for both novice and experienced computer users. . . . This excellent resource shows ways to use existing technology to augment booktalks and to expand the experience beyond the classroom." SLJ

Includes bibliographical references

Skaggs, Gayle

Look, it's books! marketing your library with displays and promotions. [by] Gayle Skaggs. McFarland & Co. 2008 188p il pa $45

Grades: Adult Professional　　　　　　　　　**021.7**

1. School libraries 2. Books and reading 3. Libraries -- Exhibitions
ISBN 978-0-7864-3132-8 pa; 0-7864-3132-6 pa

LC 2007049517

"A good basic resource for anyone needing ideas to promote reading to elementary students." Booklist

025.04　Information storage and retrieval systems

Bell, Suzanne S.

Librarian's guide to online searching; cultivating database skills for research and instruction. Suzanne S. Bell. 4th edition Libraries Unlimitied 2015 xvii, 320 p.p illustrations $55

Grades: Adult Professional　　　　　　　　　**025.04**

1. Internet searching 2. Librarians -- Training of
ISBN 161069998X; 9781610699983

LC 2014038457

"In its fourth edition, this work still serves as the best how-to on online searching for library degree students and those new to the profession. Bell . . . provides an updated version that includes a more thorough discussion on Google Scholar, and offers fresh discussions on discovery services and video tutorials. . . . Bell discusses the gamut of database basics, starting with database construction, moving to specialized databases by broad subject area and search strategies, and ending with advice on effectively working to engage the audience during instruction." LJ

Includes bibliographical references (pages 299-309) and index

Porterfield, Jason

★ **Conducting** basic and advanced searches. Rosen Central 2010 48p il (Digital and information literacy) lib bdg $26.50

Grades: 5 6 7 8 **025.04**
1. Internet resources 2. Internet searching
ISBN 978-1-4358-5316-4 lib bdg; 1-4358-5316-4 lib bdg
LC 2008-46783

Describes how to conduct both basic and advanced searches on the Internet, from the basics of online search engines, boolean search terms, and evaluating the content of search results

"Colorful photos, diagrams, and sidebars and [a] lively [text creates an] appealing, user-friendly [presentation]. . . . Students and teachers will find [this title] useful in keeping up-to-date on and utilizing online resources and today's technology in a rapidly changing digital world." SLJ

Includes glossary and bibliographical references

Rabbat, Suzy
Find your way online. Cherry Lake Pub. 2010 32p il (Super smart information strategies) lib bdg $27.07
Grades: 3 4 5 6 **025.04**
1. Internet searching
ISBN 978-1-60279-639-3 lib bdg; 1-60279-639-4 lib bdg
LC 2009024549

"The appealing layout includes manageable paragraphs, a variety of engaging illustrations, and examples that clearly guide readers through each topic. . . . [This] begins with keywords, narrowing the search, and search engines. Then it shows students how to 'drill down' using subject directories and databases." SLJ

Scheeren, William O.
Technology for the school librarian; theory and practice. Libraries Unlimited 2010 223p il $50
Grades: Adult Professional **025.04**
1. School libraries 2. Digital libraries 3. Information technology 4. Libraries -- Special collections
ISBN 978-1-59158-900-6; 1-59158-900-2
LC 2009-51922

"This title provides information on the practical aspects of technology in the school library as well as the theoretical framework to spark continued learning. Sharing actual case studies as well as practical tips on technology implentation and terminology, this title will be a valuable resource to any school librarian." Libr Media Connect

Includes bibliographical references

Truesdell, Ann
Find the right site. Cherry Lake Pub. 2010 32p il (Super smart information strategies) lib bdg $27.07
Grades: 3 4 5 6 **025.04**
1. Internet searching
ISBN 978-1-60279-638-6 lib bdg; 1-60279-638-6 lib bdg
LC 2009027083

"The appealing layout includes manageable paragraphs, a variety of engaging illustrations, and examples that clearly guide readers through each topic. . . . [This] is an excellent introduction to Web site evaluation and related pitfalls." SLJ

Includes glossary and bibliographical references

025.1 Administration

Farmer, Lesley S. Johnson
Neal-Schuman technology management handbook for school library media centers; by Lesley S. Johnson Farmer and Marc E. McPhee. Neal-Schuman Publishers 2010 289p il pa $59.95

Grades: Adult Professional **025.1**
1. School libraries 2. Instructional materials centers
ISBN 978-1-55570-659-3; 1-55570-659-2
LC 2010-9301

"This informative, well-researched text is perfect for those in the early stages of integrating technology into their programs. The first chapter begins with an overview of the impact technology has had on society and defines technology and its role in the library, including past, present, and possible future changes, as well as managerial roles of the librarian. Other chapters examine planning for management, assessing, researching, developing a technology plan, acquiring all types of tech resources, and managing the physical space to accommodate equipment and networking." SLJ

Includes bibliographical references

The **frugal** librarian; thriving in tough economic times. edited by Carol Smallwood. American Library Association 2011 277p il
Grades: Adult Professional **025.1**
1. Library finance 2. Libraries and community 3. Libraries -- United States
ISBN 0-8389-1075-0; 978-0-8389-1075-7
LC 2010034317

"The thirty-four chapters in Smallwood's collection address a myriad of issues faced by libraries and librarians when times get tough and money is tight. Written by practicing librarians from academic, public, and school libraries, the concise essays are easy to read, sometimes personal, and highly practical. Each chapter can stand alone, so the volume can serve as a reference tool for a librarian needing specific help; or the entire volume can be perused from start to finish." (VOYA)

Includes bibliographical references

Fullner, Sheryl Kindle
The **shoestring** library. Linworth Publishing 2010 139p il pa $30
Grades: Adult Professional **025.1**
1. Library finance
ISBN 978-1-58683-520-0 pa; 1-58683-520-3 pa
LC 2010-718

"The book is divided into two sections. 'Library Management for Tough Times' has hints for taking advantage of free continuing-education opportunities, using volunteers, networking, and more. 'The Physical Plant' contains suggestions for sprucing up the library at little or no cost (for example: request mismatched or clearance paints from paint stores; then get students to do the painting)." (Booklist)

Independent school libraries; perspectives on excellence. Dorcas Hand, editor. Libraries Unlimited 2010 369p il (Libraries Unlimited professional guides in school librarianship) pa $45
Grades: Adult Professional **025.1**
1. Private schools 2. School libraries
ISBN 978-1-59158-803-0 pa; 1-59158-803-0 pa; 978-1-59158-812-2 ebook
LC 2010-14567

"Twenty-one essays by prominent independent school librarians both address the current state of independent school librarianship in the United States and offer suggestions for the future. Pieces cover the library's role in the school, statistical comparisons, staffing, advocacy, assessment, technology, information commons, collaboration, college preparation, programming, traditions, collection development, minors' rights, budgeting, facilities, accreditation, and disaster planning. . . . Librarians from all schools will find a wealth of information here." Voice Youth Advocates

Includes bibliographical references

Johnson, Doug

★ The **indispensable** librarian; surviving and thriving in school libraries in the information age. Doug Johnson; illustrations by Brady Johnson. Linworth, an imprint of ABC-CLIO, LLC 2013 xix, 207 p.p illustrations (pbk.) $40

Grades: Adult Professional　　　　　**025.1**

1. Librarians 2. School libraries 3. School librarians -- United States 4. School libraries -- United States -- Administration

ISBN 161069239X; 9781610692397

LC 2012051394

This book, by Doug A. Johnson, "defines and clarifies the role of the school library media specialist in a technologically enhanced school, providing relevant examples and useful advice on a variety of topics; and underscores the importance of strong management skills, especially regarding collaborative planning and communications. The book is written especially for K-12 school librarians, both new and experienced, and is also suitable for pre-service librarians as a textbook." (Publisher's note)

"Johnson offers both theory and practical suggestions on ways to embed [librarians] and [their] jobs into the fabric of a school's culture and curriculum." Lib Med Con

Includes bibliographical references and index

MacDonell, Colleen

★ **Essential** documents for school libraries; 2nd ed.; Linworth 2010 xxiv, 156p il $50

Grades: Adult Professional　　　　　**025.1**

1. Libraries -- Administration

ISBN 978-1-58683-400-5

LC 2010-21241

First published 2004

"Each chapter begins with why the documents are needed, followed by practical advice for writing the documents, and examples of how the documents make an effective change in the library media program." Libr Media Connect [review of 2004 edition]

Includes bibliographical references

Martin, Barbara Stein

★ **Fundamentals** of school library media management; a how-to-do-it manual. [by] Barbara Stein Martin and Marco Zannier. Neal-Schuman Publishers 2009 172p il (How-to-do-it manuals for librarians) pa $59.95

Grades: Adult Professional　　　　　**025.1**

1. School libraries 2. Instructional materials centers

ISBN 978-1-55570-656-2; 1-55570-656-8

LC 2009-7930

This book "contains useful information to help school librarians manage a myriad of tasks and roles. . . . [The authors] have created a book that is helpful, accessible, and full of down-to-earth, concrete examples." Booklist

Includes bibliographical references

★ **School** library management; [edited by] Judi Repman and Gail Dickinson. 6th ed.; Linworth Pub. 2007 200p il pa $44.95

Grades: Adult Professional　　　　　**025.1**

1. School libraries 2. Libraries -- Administration

ISBN 1-58683-296-4; 978-1-58683-296-4

LC 2006-103468

First published 1987 with title: School library management notebook

"This collection of more than 35 articles written for Library Media Connection from 2003 to 2006 is a virtual treasure trove for library media specialists. . . . The book covers the very practical everyday issues such as scheduling and overdues, and also provides invaluable information on data gathering, facilities planning, professional development, the role of the library in the world of standardized testing, the technological future of libraries, and much more." SLJ

Includes bibliographical references

Tips and other bright ideas for elementary school libraries. Volume 4 Kate Vande Brake, editor. Linworth 2010 134p Volume 4 pa $35

Grades: Adult Professional　　　　　**025.1**

1. Elementary school libraries 2. Libraries -- Administration

ISBN 978-1-58683-416-6 pa; 1-58683-416-9 pa; 978-1-58683-417-3 ebook

LC 2010011049

This title includes "fun and informative management advice from fellow librarians. All of it has been taken from 2006-2009 Library Media Connection magazine. . . . [The introduction] reviews some of the many jobs and responsibilities in a librarian's day. Section one includes management hints to help maximize effectiveness, followed by sections on working with students, teaching skills, . . . working with teachers, technology, reading promotion, public relations, and working with helpers." SLJ

025.2　Acquisitions and collection development

Baumbach, Donna

★ **Less** is more; a practical guide to weeding school library collections. American Library Association 2006 194p il pa $32

Grades: Adult Professional　　　　　**025.2**

1. Libraries -- Collection development

ISBN 978-0-8389-0919-5; 0-8389-0919-1

LC 2006-7490

"Chapter one gives an overview for weeding school collections. Chapter two describes common weeding guidelines. Chapter three covers the where and how of the weeding process. Chapter four is the core of the book, covering 70 topics and subject areas or Dewey classifications, giving guidelines for those subjects." Lib Med Con

"This outstanding, easy-to-use guide makes weeding realistic and achievable. . . . This is an indispensable resource for every school library." Booklist

Includes bibliographical references

Brenner, Robin E.

★ **Understanding** manga and anime. Libraries Unlimited 2007 335p il pa $40

Grades: Adult Professional　　　　　**025.2**

1. Anime 2. Manga -- Study and teaching 3. Libraries -- Collection development 4. Libraries -- Special collections -- Graphic novels

ISBN 978-1-59158-332-5; 1-59158-332-2

LC 2007-9773

The author "provides thorough explanations of manga and anime vocabulary, potential censorship issues because of cultural disparities, and typical Manga conventions. . . . No professional collection could possibly be complete without this all-inclusive and exceptional work." Voice Youth Advocates

Fagan, Bryan D.

Comic book collections for libraries; [by] Bryan D. Fagan and Jody Condit Fagan; foreword by Stan Sakai; cover art by Derek Steed. Libraries Unlimited 2011 162p pa $45; e-book $45

Grades: Adult Professional　　　　　**025.2**

1. Graphic novels -- Bibliography 2. Comic books, strips, etc. -- Bibliography 3. Libraries -- Special collections -- Graphic novels

ISBN 978-1-59884-511-2 pa; 1-59884-511-X pa; 978-1-59884-512-9 e-book

LC 2010052532

"This thorough guide focuses on creating a core collection for adults, though much of it will also be useful for youth librarians. It begins with a brief history of comics, then moves on to a detailed explanation of their structure, including the arcs, crossovers, and continuity essential to understanding the Marvel and DC universes. An annotated list of major publishers, writers, artists, and terms follows, along with a breakdown of genres in the medium, covering not just superheroes and manga but also Westerns, crime, romance, and more. The authors give detailed information about creating, maintaining, cataloging, and promoting a collection; circulation policies; and sample Marc records and circulation reports." (School Library Journal)

"Armed with this book, librarian should feel confident about knowledgeably creating and maintaining a successful comic-book collection." SLJ

Includes bibliographical references

Franklin, Patricia

School library collection development; just the basics. Claire Gatrell Stephens and Patricia Franklin. Libraries Unlimited 2012 x, 71 p.p ill. (Just the basics) (paperback) $35

Grades: Adult Professional   **025.2**

1. School libraries 2. Libraries -- Collection development 3. Collection management (Libraries) -- United States 4. School libraries -- Collection development -- United States

ISBN 1598849433; 9781598849431

LC 2012016990

This book, by Claire Gatrell Stephens and Patricia Franklin, discusses collection development for school librarians. This volume offers a "manual that explains the fundamentals of purchasing, developing, and managing a collection. Containing information useful to anyone from a paraprofessional working under the guidance of a certified school librarian to a newcomer to the field to a certified media specialist, this book covers all of the basics through best practices." (Publisher's note)

Gallaway, Beth

★ **Game** on! gaming at the library. Neal-Schuman Publishers 2009 306p il pa $55

Grades: Adult Professional   **025.2**

1. Video games 2. Video games and children 3. Video games and teenagers 4. Multimedia library services 5. Electronic games -- Collections 6. Libraries -- Special collections

ISBN 1-55570-595-2; 978-1-55570-595-4

LC 2009-14110

"An essential guide for any librarian who plans on embracing the video-game phenomenon, or at the very least, understanding it. . . . [The chapters] are well organized and contain an abundance of practical information. The sections on selection, collection, and circulation of video games include relevant advice on policy, cataloging, marketing, storage, and displays. . . . The annotated list of video games for a core collection is wonderful for selection purposes." SLJ

Includes bibliographical references

Goldsmith, Francisca

The **readers'** advisory guide to graphic novels. American Library Association 2010 124p (ALA readers' advisory series) pa $45

Grades: Adult Professional   **025.2**

1. Graphic novels -- Bibliography 2. Libraries -- Special collections -- Graphic novels

ISBN 978-0-8389-1008-5; 0-8389-1008-4

LC 2009-25239

"After dispelling the two main myths that ghettoize graphic novels—they are just for adolescents and they are far less complex than texts without pictures—Goldsmith emphasizes that GNs are a format and not a genre. She suggests active and passive ways to offer readers'

advisory (RA) from face-to-face encounters with patrons to book displays and book groups and offers guidance on helping established GN readers to find new titles they might enjoy. . . . All in all it is a valuable and quite readable resource that belongs in every library's professional collection." Voice Youth Advocates

Includes glossary and bibliographical references

Graphic novels beyond the basics; insights and issues for libraries. Martha Cornog and Timothy Perper, editors. Libraries Unlimited 2009 xxx, 281p il pa $45

Grades: Adult Professional   **025.2**

1. Graphic novels -- History and criticism 2. Comic books, strips, etc. -- History and criticism 3. Libraries -- Special collections -- Graphic novels

ISBN 978-1-59158-478-0; 1-59158-478-7

LC 2009-16189

Editors Cornog and Perper have collected essays by experts Robin Brenner, Francisca Goldsmith, Trina Robbins, Michael R. Lavin, Gilles Poitras, Lorena O'English, Michael Niederhausen, Erin Byrne, and Cornog herself, all about graphic novels in libraries. Topics covered range from the appeal of superheroes to manga, the appeal of comics to women and girls, anime, independent comics, dealing with challenges to the material, and more. Appendices provide resource information on African American-interest graphic novels, Latino-Interest graphic novels, LGBT-interest graphic novels, religious-themed graphic novels, a bibliography of books about graphic novels in libraries, and online resources.

"Whether you are serious about the genre, interested in the history, or looking for ammunition, this book should be on your shelf. The wealth of knowledge and research that went into these essays is impressive, and reading this book will put you on the road to becoming an expert." Libr Media Connect

Includes bibliographical references

Herald, Nathan

Graphic novels for young readers; a genre guide for ages 4-14. Libraries Unlimited 2011 188p (Genreflecting advisory series) $40

Grades: Adult Professional   **025.2**

1. Graphic novels 2. Children's literature 3. Graphic novels -- Bibliography

ISBN 1-59884-395-8; 978-1-59884-395-8

LC 2010044947

"The annotated entries are laid out in eight chapters organized by major genre, and from action and adventure to educational. Within chapters, the titles, 600 in all, are arranged alphabetically into popular subgenres such as superheroes, mythology, sports, and many more." (School Library Journal)

"Librarians looking to beef up their graphic-novel collections will do well to get their hands on this valuable volume. The annotated entries are laid out in eight chapters organized by major genre, and from action and adventure to educational. Within chapters, the titles, 600 in all, are arranged alphabetically into popular subgenres such as superheroes, mythology, sports, and many more. . . . The intended audience for each title is clear, with bold icons providing an age range. Herald's writing style lends personality to what could easily be a dry overview. . . . A thorough, well-organized, one-stop shop for quality graphic novels." SLJ

Includes bibliographical references

★ **Intellectual** Freedom Manual; Trina Magi, Martin Garnar, Office for Intellectual Freedom of the American Library Association. 9th Edition American Library Association 2015 434 p. $70

Grades: Professional   **025.2**

1. Freedom of information -- United States -- Handbooks, manuals, etc. 2. Libraries -- Censorship -- United States -- Handbooks,

manuals, etc.

ISBN 0838912923; 9780838912928

This book by Trina Magi, Martin Garnar, and the Office for Intellectual Freedom "is more than just an invaluable compendium of guiding principles and policies. It s also an indispensable resource for day-to-day guidance on maintaining free and equal access to information for all people. Fortifying and emboldening professionals and students from across the library spectrum, this manual includes . . . 34 ALA policy statements and documents [and] explanations of legal points." (Publisher's note)

Magi, Trina

★ Intellectual Freedom Manual; Trina Magi, Martin Garnar, Office for Intellectual Freedom of the American Library Association. 9th ed. ALA Editions, An imprint of the American Library Association 2015 434 p. $70

Grades: Adult Professional **025.2**

1. Censorship 2. Library science 3. Intellectual freedom 4. Freedom of information -- United States -- Handbooks, manuals, etc. 5. Libraries -- Censorship -- United States -- Handbooks, manuals, etc.

ISBN 0838912923; 9780838912928

LC 2014037437

First published 1974

This newest edition "is more than just an invaluable compendium of guiding principles and policies. It's also an indispensable resource for day-to-day guidance on maintaining free and equal access to information for all people. Fortifying and emboldening professionals and students from across the library spectrum, this manual includes . . . 34 ALA policy statements and documents [and] explanations of legal points." (Publisher's note)

"All libraries should have a copy of this book to use when writing or revising policies; indispensable." Libr J

Includes bibliographical references and index

Mayer, Brian

Libraries got game; aligned learning through modern board games. [by] Brian Mayer and Christopher Harris. American Library Association 2010 134p il pa $45

Grades: Adult Professional **025.2**

1. Board games 2. Libraries -- Special collections

ISBN 978-0-8389-1009-2; 0-8389-1009-2

LC 2009-26839

"This is a valuable resource for K-12 librarians interested in building curriculum-aligned 'designer' game collections. The authors . . . explain how specific games enhance language-arts, social-studies, and math units, and build literacy skills. The two chapters devoted to promoting and justifying the inclusion of games in the library are well documented and a wonderful source to have to convince skeptical administrators. Suggestions for building a core collection, which highlights top recommended games for elementary school, middle school, and high school; a list of game publishers; a list of games discussed; and a glossary of terminology are included." SLJ

Includes bibliographical references

Scales, Pat R.

★ Protecting intellectual freedom in your school library; scenarios from the front lines. [by] Pat R. Scales for the Office for Intellectual Freedom. American Library Association 2009 148p (Intellectual freedom front lines) pa $55

Grades: Adult Professional **025.2**

1. School libraries 2. Intellectual freedom

ISBN 978-0-8389-3581-1; 0-8389-3581-8

LC 2008-39893

"Scales uses court opinions, federal and state laws, and ALA documents to offer solutions for responding to infringements. A broad range of potential scenarios—from challenges to materials in both the library and the classroom, the legality of film rating systems, using computerized reading programs as selection tools and labeling books by reading levels, policies for interlibrary loans and reserves to confidentiality of children's and teens' circulation records—are covered. . . . This resource should be in every school library's professional collection." Voice Youth Advocates

Includes bibliographical references

025.3   Bibliographic analysis and control

★ Cataloging correctly for kids; an introduction to the tools. edited by Sheila S. Intner, Joanna F. Fountain, and Jean Weihs. 5th ed.; Association for Library Collections and Technical Services, American Library Association 2011 224p pa $55

Grades: Adult Professional **025.3**

1. Cataloging 2. Reference books 3. Children's literature -- Cataloging

ISBN 978-0-8389-3589-7 pa; 0-8389-3589-3 pa

LC 2010012945

First published 1989 by the Cataloging for Children's Materials Committee

Among the topics discussed are: guidelines for standardized cataloging for children; how children search; using AACR2 and MARC 21; copy cataloging; using RDA; Sears List of Subject Headings; LC Children's headings; sources for Dewey numbers; cataloging nonbook materials; authority control; how the CIP program helps children; cataloging for kids in the academic library; cataloging for non-English-speaking children and preliterate children; automating the children's catalog; vendors of cataloging for children's materials.

Includes bibliographical references

025.4   Subject analysis and control

Donovan, Sandra, 1967-

Bob the Alien discovers the Dewey decimal system; by Sandy Donovan; illustrated by Martin Haake. Picture Window 2010 24p il (In the library) lib bdg $25.32

Grades: 2 3 4 **025.4**

1. Bibliographic instruction 2. Dewey Decimal Classification

ISBN 978-1-4048-5757-5 lib bdg; 1-4048-5757-5 lib bdg

Bob is from planet Plainold, where they have just discovered spiders. But planet Plainold doesn't have books, so Bob has traveled to Earth to find books about spiders. Join Allison Wonderland as she teaches Bob how to use the Dewey Decimal System to find books about spiders.

"What is wonderful about this . . . is that key terms and phrases are enlarged and placed in bold letters to stress their importance. . . . [This is a] vital resource for teaching library skills. All elementary librarians will appreciate the innovative way the author and illustrator combine their talents to create an exciting way to share specifics about libraries and books." Libr Media Connect

Bored Bella learns about fiction and nonfiction; by Sandy Donovan; illustrated by Leeza Hernandez. Picture Window 2010 24p il (In the library) lib bdg $25.32

Grades: 2 3 4 **025.4**

1. Library classification 2. Bibliographic instruction

ISBN 978-1-4048-5758-2 lib bdg; 1-4048-5758-3 lib bdg

Bored Bella thinks books are boring. When his class takes a trip to the library, Bella isn't thrilled. Join Ms. Paige Turner as she introduces fiction and nonfiction books to Bella and her class.

"What is wonderful about this . . . is that key terms and phrases are enlarged and placed in bold letters to stress their importance. . . . [This is a] vital resource for teaching library skills. All elementary librarians will appreciate the innovative way the author and illustrator combine their talents to create an exciting way to share specifics about libraries and books." Libr Media Connect

Includes glossary

★ **Sears** List of Subject Headings; Barbara A. Bristow, editor; Christi Showman Farrar, associate editor. 21st edition Grey House Publishing/H.W. Wilson 2014 946 pp. (hardcover) $165.00
Grades: Adult Professional   025.4
1. Cataloging 2. Library science 3. Subject headings
ISBN 9781619251908
                                                          LC 2013498263
This book, edited by Barbara A. Bristow and Christi Showman Farrar, presents the frameworks for the Sears List of Subject Headings cataloging system. "This resource lists subject headings used by small and medium-sized libraries, with patterns, examples, and notes on usage. The subject headings are listed alphabetically and aligned with the Dewey Decimal Classification system and include a list of canceled and replacement headings, as well as a discussion of the theoretical foundations of the list and the general principles of subject cataloging." (Book News)

025.5   Services for users

American Association of School Librarians
Standards for the 21st-century learner in action. American Association of School Librarians 2009 120p pa $39
Grades: Adult Professional   025.5
1. Information literacy 2. Libraries -- Standards
ISBN 978-0-8389-8507-6 pa; 0-8389-8507-6 pa
"Standards in Action attempts to expand upon AASL's Standards for the 21st Century Learner by providing benchmarks and action examples. The original document was a nine-page brochure that outlined nine common beliefs, four learning standards, four strands, and indicators under each strand. It was an excellent starting point, but the addition of benchmarks at grades two, five, eight, ten, and twelve helps flesh out the original vision. . . . School libraries should own a copy of this professional, which has a role within any program." Voice Youth Advocates

Includes glossary and bibliographical references

Grassian, Esther S.
★ **Information** literacy instruction; theory and practice. [by] Esther S. Grassian and Joan R. Kaplowitz. 2nd ed; Neal-Schuman Publishers 2009 xxvii, 412p pa $75
Grades: Adult Professional   025.5
1. Information literacy 2. Information literacy -- Study and teaching 3. Information retrieval -- Study and teaching 4. Bibliographic instruction -- College and university students
ISBN 978-155570-666-1; 1-55570-666-5
                                                          LC 2009-23647
First published 2001
This "is designed for anyone involved in the creation and management of information literacy programming. Sixteen well-written chapters, organized into five sections, provide both theory and practical applications, with the emphasis on the practical. . . . Several extras appear in the accompanying CD-ROM. . . . A timely, thorough, and endlessly

useful must-have title for librarians, teaching librarians, and library schools." Booklist

Includes bibliographical references

Harper, Meghan
Reference sources and services for youth. Neal-Schuman Publishers 2011 307p $65
Grades: Adult Professional   025.5
1. School libraries 2. Children's libraries 3. Young adults' libraries 4. Reference services (Libraries)
ISBN 978-1-55570-641-8; 1-55570-641-X
                                                          LC 2011004987
"The concept of school and public library collaboration is thoroughly explored in this excellent volume on providing reference services. The chapter on information literacy includes web links with information about standards, models, instruction and assessment, rubrics, web quests, graphic organizers, evaluation tools, and assessment. Additional chapters provide a discussion of online resources, government resources for youth, evaluation and marketing reference services, and managing them." SLJ

Includes bibliographical references

Intner, Carol F.
Homework help from the library; in person and online. American Library Association 2011 202p il pa $47
Grades: Adult Professional   025.5
1. Homework 2. Library resources 3. Libraries and students
ISBN 978-0-8389-1046-7; 0-8389-1046-7
                                                          LC 2010042096
"Building on the concept that information services and education converge with homework help, the author sketches in the history of youth services and current learning theories. She offers practical suggestions for needs assessment and determining a guiding philosophy. Speaking to the public librarian, Intner outlines the points to consider in designing a homework help program and training staff. Possible workshop topics include an overview of student needs and available resources, creating a comfortable and inviting space, considering the needs of different ages, understanding youth culture, and responding to various learning styles. . . . Youth librarians will want this comprehensive and practical guide within easy reach. " Voice Youth Advocates

Includes bibliographical references

Lanning, Scott
Essential reference services for today's school media specialists; [by] Scott Lanning and John Bryner. 2nd ed.; Libraries Unlimited 2010 141p il pa $45
Grades: Adult Professional   025.5
1. School libraries 2. Reference services (Libraries)
ISBN 978-1-59158-883-2; 1-59158-883-9
                                                          LC 2009-39375
"The content focuses on core reference skills, electronic resources, and leadership. The first few chapters discuss information literacy, evaluation of resources, the role of print resources, and the reference interview. These are followed by chapters on the library catalog, electronic resources, and the Web as a reference tool. Finally, there are several chapters dealing with the teacher-librarians' instructional and leadership roles. The authors use a very accessible tone while providing the basics." Booklist

Includes bibliographical references

Peck, Penny
Readers' advisory for children and 'tweens. Libraries Unlimited 2010 190p pa $36

Grades: Adult Professional　　**025.5**

1. Children's libraries 2. Children's literature 3. Young adult literature 4. Children -- Books and reading 5. Children's literature -- Bibliography

ISBN 978-1-59884-387-3 pa; 1-59884-387-7 pa

LC 2010002589

"Written for novices, this useful guide will provide many valuable suggestions to library staff unfamiliar with the literature and how to go about recommending it to their young patrons and their caregivers. The first two chapters define readers' advisory and describe how to provide it successfully. The next few chapters are divided into age categories. . . . The concluding chapters are divided by type of literature. . . . All of the chapters include helpful booklists and websites, which are great collection development tools as well. There are some tips on promoting books. . . . This title is a valuable resource." SLJ

Includes bibliographical references

Wichman, Emily T.

Librarian's guide to passive programming; easy and affordable activities for all ages. Emily T. Wichman. Libraries Unlimited Inc. 2012 xvii, 152 p.p ill. (pbk. : acid-free paper) $40

Grades: Adult Professional　　**025.5**

1. Librarians 2. Library finance 3. Library services 4. Libraries -- Activity programs -- United States

ISBN 159884895X; 9781598848953; 9781598848960

LC 2011045419

In her book, author Emily T. Wichman discusses library budget cuts, and how "librarians are seeking new ways to stretch their programming dollars and maximize staff resources. Passive programming allows libraries to inexpensively showcase their services while inviting visitors of all ages to enjoy the value that libraries bring to the community." (Publisher's note)

Includes bibliographical references and index.

025.52　Reference and information services

Becoming a media mentor; a guide for working with children and families. Claudia Haines, Cen Campbell, and the Association for Library Service to Children. ALA Editions, an imprint of the American Library Association 2016 176 p. (paperback) $48

Grades: Adult Professional　　**025.52**

1. Digital media 2. Media librarians 3. Multimedia library services 4. Application software 5. Libraries and families 6. Media librarians -- United States 7. Media literacy -- Study and teaching 8. Computer literacy -- Study and teaching 9. Children's libraries -- Activity programs 10. Multimedia library services -- United States 11. Children's digital libraries -- United States 12. Electronic information resource literacy -- Study and teaching

ISBN 9780838914632

LC 2016013272

This book, by Claudia Haines, Cen Campbell, and the Association for Library Service to Children, "empowers youth services staff to confidently assist families and caregivers as they navigate the digital world, guiding them towards digital media experiences that will translate into positive and productive lifelong learning skills, regardless of format." (Publisher's note)

Includes bibliographical references and index

027　General libraries, archives, information centers

Sawa, Maureen

The **library** book; the story of libraries from camels to computers. illustrated by Bill Slavin. Tundra Books 2006 72p il $18.95

Grades: 3 4 5 6　　**027**

1. Libraries

ISBN 0-88776-698-6

"This information-packed picture book is an excellent tribute to libraries around the world, describing the development of libraries from ancient times to today. . . . The picture-book format, filled with earth-toned illustrations, adds appeal. . . . The book is also filled with interesting sidebars and highlighted sections of information." Voice Youth Advocates

Includes bibliographical references

Trumble, Kelly

The **Library** of Alexandria; illustrated by Robina MacIntyre Marshall. Clarion Bks. 2003 72p il maps $17

Grades: 5 6 7 8　　**027**

1. Ancient civilization 2. Egypt -- Civilization 3. Alexandrian Library (Egypt)

ISBN 0-395-75832-7

LC 2003-150

An introduction to the largest and most famous library in the ancient world, discussing its construction in Alexandria, Egypt, its vast collections, rivalry with the Pergamum Library, famous scholars, and destruction by fire

This is a "well-organized and thorough resource." SLJ

Includes glossary and bibliographical references

027.4　Public libraries

King, M. G.

Librarian on the roof! a true story. illustrated by Stephen Gilpin. Albert Whitman 2010 un il $16.95

Grades: K 1 2 3　　**027.4**

1. Libraries 2. Librarians

ISBN 978-0-8075-4512-6; 0-8075-4512-0

"King's writing is clear and often witty, and she does a credible job of capturing Laurell's determined and forthright personality, as well as the drama and excitement of this unusual approach to fund-raising. Gilpin's hand-drawn, vibrantly colored cartoon illustrations enliven the story." SLJ

027.6　Libraries for special groups and organizations

Alire, Camila

★ **Serving** Latino communities; a how-to-do-it manual for librarians. [by] Camila Alire, Jacqueline Ayala. 2nd ed; Neal-Schuman Publishers 2007 229p il (How-to-do-it manuals for librarians) pa $59.95

Grades: Adult Professional　　**027.6**

1. Libraries and Hispanic Americans

ISBN 978-1-55570-606-7; 1-55570-606-1

LC 2007-7783

First published 1998

"The information covered helps library staff understand the needs of their library's Latino community; develop successful programs and services; obtain funding for projects and programs; prepare staff to work more effectively with Latinos; establish partnerships with relevant external agencies and organizations; improve collection development;

and perform effective outreach and public relations. . . . There are few resources widely available on this topic and none as complete." Libr Media Connect

Includes bibliographical references

Diamant-Cohen, Betsy

Early literacy programming en Espanol; Mother Goose on the Loose programs for bilingual learners. Neal-Schuman Publishers 2010 xxii, 177p il pa $65

Grades: Adult Professional   **027.6**

1. Nursery rhymes 2. Bilingual education 3. Children's libraries
ISBN 978-1-55570-691-3; 1-55570-691-6

LC 2009049594

"Diamant-Cohen has developed this manual to encourage librarians to present Spanish-language MGOL programs. . . . The author proposes recruiting community partners fluent in Spanish who will be trained by the children's librarian and will copresent the sessions. Five parts cover the basics on how to run the program successfully. The manual is complemented with illustrations that can be replicated and used as flannel-board figures; bibliographies, worksheets, and a CD with instructions; nursery rhymes in English and Spanish; and graphics and templates of documents. This volume is infused with enthusiasm to serve the children of Spanish-speakers. It will not only help English-speaking librarians, but also the bilingual ones to present and enjoy MGOL." SLJ

Includes bibliographical references

Klipper, Barbara

Programming for children and teens with autism spectrum disorder; Barbara Klipper. ALA Editions 2014 168 p. illustrations (pbk) $45

Grades: Adult Professional   **027.6**

1. Autism 2. Autistic children 3. Libraries and people with disabilities 4. Children's libraries -- Activity programs 5. Youth with autism spectrum disorders -- Services for 6. Children with autism spectrum disorders -- Services for
ISBN 9780838912065; 0838912060

LC 2013044207

This book, by Barbara Klipper, is "[f]or librarians who offer or are thinking about offering programming to children and/or teens with autism spectrum disorders (ASD). . . . There are storytime models; programming for school-age children, teens, and families; and program plans for school libraries. Helpful side boxes include tips on ways to supplement or adapt existing programs and library spaces. . . . The appendixes include valuable resources such as vendors, websites, and publishers." (School Library Journal)

Includes bibliographical references and index

027.62 Libraries for specific age groups

Bauer, Caroline Feller

Leading kids to books through crafts. American Lib. Assn. 2000 145p (Mighty easy motivators) pa $30

Grades: Adult Professional   **027.62**

1. Handicraft 2. Reference books 3. Books and reading 4. Children's libraries 5. Children's literature -- Bibliography
ISBN 0-8389-0769-5

LC 99-41387

"Bauer gives basic, practical information on presenting programs that introduce preschool and primary-grade youngsters to stories and poems and demonstrates related crafts that are easy to prepare and execute." SLJ

Leading kids to books through magic; illustrated by Richard Laurent. American Lib. Assn. 1996 128p il (Mighty easy motivators) pa $35

Grades: Adult Professional   **027.62**

1. Magic tricks 2. Reference books 3. Books and reading 4. Children's libraries 5. Children's literature -- Bibliography
ISBN 978-0-8389-0684-2 pa; 0-8389-0684-2 pa

LC 95-53049

The author's "concise yet thorough directions accompanied by Richard Laurent's delightful line drawings make this book a useful tool for teachers and librarians looking for ways to promote children's enthusiasm for reading." J Youth Serv Libr

Includes bibliographical references

Leading kids to books through puppets; illustrated by Richard Laurent. American Lib. Assn. 1997 156p il (Mighty easy motivators) pa $35

Grades: Adult Professional   **027.62**

1. Reference books 2. Books and reading 3. Children's libraries 4. Puppets and puppet plays 5. Children's literature -- Bibliography
ISBN 978-0-8389-0706-1 pa; 0-8389-0706-7 pa

LC 97-1357

"Even the most reluctant performer will be encouraged by this practical, concise, easy-to-use book." SLJ

Includes bibliographical references

Benton, Gail

Ready-to-go storytimes; fingerplays, scripts, patterns, music, and more. [by] Gail Benton, Trisha Waichulaitis. Neal-Schuman 2003 239p il pa $65

Grades: Adult Professional   **027.62**

1. Storytelling 2. Children's libraries
ISBN 978-1-55570-449-0 pa; 1-55570-449-2 pa

LC 2002-5806

"This resource is excellent for beginning librarians and teachers and for any professionals who seek new ideas to freshen up their repertoires." Booklist

Includes bibliographical references

Bird, Elizabeth

Children's literature gems; choosing and using them in your library career. American Library Association 2009 125p pa $45

Grades: Adult Professional   **027.62**

1. Book selection 2. Children's libraries 3. Children -- Books and reading 4. Children's literature -- Bibliography
ISBN 978-0-8389-0995-9 pa; 0-8389-0995-7 pa

LC 2009003079

"Bird writes in a chatty tone reminiscent of her popular blog, A Fuse #8 Production, and her love of children's literature shines through on every page. This slim volume is not meant to be an in-depth textbook, but rather a brief overview of the field and an introduction to the stars of children's literature. . . . Highlighted boxes throughout feature questions and answers from seasoned professionals on how they handle various parts of their collections and aspects of their work. Readers who are new to the field may find this a comforting basic guide to managing their collections." SLJ

Includes bibliographical references

Bromann, Jennifer

More storytime action! 2,000+ more ideas for making 500+ picture books interactive. Neal-Schuman Publishers 2009 326p pa $55

Grades: Adult Professional   **027.62**

1. Storytelling 2. Children's libraries 3. Picture books for children

-- Bibliography
ISBN 978-1-55570-675-3 pa; 1-55570-675-4 pa
LC 2009031724

"Bromann presents more than 2,000 activities related to more than 500 picture books published since 2003. Beginning chapters cover 10 elements of interactive stories; storytelling, including how to select and prepare stories; and how to select books for interactive storytimes, identifying clues found in reviews. . . . The final chapter lists the more than 500 books alphabetically by author with bibliographic information, summary, and storytime activities. . . . For librarians looking to hold the attention of their youngest patrons or to spice up storytime, this title will be a welcome resource." Booklist

Includes bibliographical references

Cerny, Rosanne
★ **Outstanding** library service to children; putting the core competencies to work. [by] Rosanne Cerny, Penny Markey, and Amanda Williams. American Library Association 2006 94p pa $25
Grades: Adult Professional   **027.62**
1. Children's libraries
ISBN 978-0-8389-0922-5 pa; 0-8389-0922-1 pa
"This slim volume should be required reading for all future children's services librarians." Booklist
Includes bibliiographical references

Children's services; partnerships for success. edited by Betsy Diamant-Cohen. American Library Association 2010 126p il (ALA public library handbook series) pa $50
Grades: Adult Professional   **027.62**
1. Children's libraries 2. Libraries and schools 3. Libraries and community
ISBN 978-0-8389-1044-3 pa; 0-8389-1044-0 pa
LC 2009045788
"Diamant-Cohen has created a valuable resource by providing practical examples of successful partnerships between libraries of various sizes and community organizations. Concrete scenarios include successful partnerships with law enforcement agencies, recreation departments, academic institutions, children's museums, cultural institutions, churches that attract mainly immigrant populations, businesses, and other agencies." SLJ
Includes bibliographical references

Cullum, Carolyn N.
★ The **storytime** sourcebook II; [a compendium of 3500+ new ideas and resources for storytellers] Neal-Schuman Publishers 2007 489p pa $75
Grades: Adult Professional   **027.62**
1. Storytelling 2. Children's libraries
ISBN 978-1-55570-589-3 pa; 1-55570-589-8 pa
LC 2006-35096
First published 1990 with title: The storytime sourcebook
"Each of the 146 themed programs, designed for children ages two to eight, appears on two facing pages that include appropriate calendar tie-ins, videos, books, music, movements, crafts, activities, and songs. . . . [The author] presents clear and simple directions for crafts and activities, quick and uncomplicated for librarians to prepare, and easy for children to follow. . . . This sourcebook is an essential purchase for libraries serving this audience." SLJ
Includes bibliographical references

De las Casas, Dianne
Tell along tales! playing with participation stories. illustrated by Soleil Lisette. Libraries Unlimited 2011 125p il pa $30

Grades: Adult Professional   **027.62**
1. Storytelling 2. Children's libraries
ISBN 978-1-59884-635-5; 1-59884-635-3
LC 2011000335
"In five chapters chock-full of storyteller tips and ideas, de las Casas explains various types of participation models from call-and-response to directed role-playing and covers how to direct questions to the group. She offers valuable clues for warming up an audience and for settling boisterous children back down. . . . The main body of the book contains the author's choices of suitable stories from around the world with suggested age levels and pointers for leaders. . . . Both novice and veteran storytellers will benefit from the myriad suggestions offered here." SLJ
Includes bibliographical references

Del Negro, Janice M.
Folktales aloud; practical advice for playful storytelling. Janice M. Del Negro. American Library Association 2014 212 p. (alk. paper) $47
Grades: Adult Professional   **027.62**
1. Fairy tales 2. Storytelling 3. Children's libraries -- Activity programs 4. Elementary school libraries -- Activity programs
ISBN 0838911358; 9780838911358
LC 2013028036
This book, by Janice M. Del Negro, "aims to show that storytelling is still vital in librarianship and throughout the greater community. . . . The text provides useful information for novice and seasoned storytellers alike while engaging the reader with its conversational tone. The chapters are broken down by audience age . . . and include information about audience needs and wants, stories, and resource information." (Booklist)
"Folktales are an integral part of children's literature and are the basis for many classic books librarians use daily in their work. These much loved tales are also the backbone of the art of storytelling...Del Negro leads novice tellers through the nuances of successful storytelling...Advice is offered in a very practical way on how to approach this group and suggestions are made as to how to grab and hold their interest with pacing, movement and suspense. If you have even a passing interest in the art of storytelling, this guide is not to be missed." SLJ
Includes bibliographical references and index

Diamant-Cohen, Betsy
Crash course in library services to preschool children. Libraries Unlimited 2010 137p pa $30
Grades: Adult Professional   **027.62**
1. Children's libraries
ISBN 978-1-59884-688-1 pa; 1-59884-688-4 pa
LC 2010024071
"This book presents 10 chapters to quickly immerse the librarian working with preschoolers into the field. An overview of children's services to preschoolers in public libraries is followed by chapters on programming, books, collections, reader's advisory and reference, and the children's room. . . . All librarians who deal with preschoolers, whether experienced public librarians or new school media specialist, will benefit from the ideas, concepts, and guidance provided here." SLJ
Includes bibliographical references

Ernst, Linda L.
Baby rhyming time; [by] Linda L. Ernst. Neal-Schuman Publishers 2008 235p il pa $59.95
Grades: Adult Professional   **027.62**
1. Children's libraries
ISBN 978-1-55570-540-4 pa; 1-55570-540-5 pa
LC 2007043246
"This useful resource provides background, logistics, and a wealth of practical ideas for programs. Ernst describes brain development and

language acquisition clearly, with quotes and references for support. She does a good job of tying the science to infant/toddler growth and explaining the librarian's important role in sharing the information with caregivers. She discusses broader factors to consider when planning baby-time programs, including community, facilities, staffing, and potential partnerships." SLJ

Includes bibliographical references

Fasick, Adele M.

Managing children's services in the public library; [by] Adele M. Fasick and Leslie E. Holt. 3rd ed; Libraries Unlimited 2008 248p bibl il tab pa $45

Grades: Adult Professional   **027.62**

1. Public libraries 2. Children's libraries 3. Children -- Books and reading

ISBN 978-1-59158-412-4 pa; 1-59158-412-4 pa

           LC 2007032759

First published 1991

"Excellent support for newbies and as a basis for professional development." Booklist

Includes bibliographical references

Fiore, Carole D.

Fiore's summer library reading program handbook. Neal-Schuman Publishers 2005 xxiii, 312p pa $65

Grades: Adult Professional   **027.62**

1. Books and reading 2. Children's libraries

ISBN 1-55570-513-8

           LC 2004-31104

"This research-laden handbook . . . serves as a 'comprehensive program-planning and implementation tool' for public libraries seeking to revamp, revise, or develop a summer library reading program. . . . This is an invaluable resource, both for its concrete guidance and its abstract exploration of the meaning of summer library programs." Bull Cent Child Books

Includes bibliographical references

Ghoting, Saroj Nadkarni

STEP into storytime; using storytime effective practice to strengthen the development of newborns to five-year-olds. Saroj Nadkarni Ghoting and Kathy Fling Klatt. ALA Editions, an imprint of the American Library Association 2014 368 p. illustrations $59

Grades: Professional   **027.62**

1. Storytelling 2. Early childhood education 3. Children's libraries -- Activity programs 4. Storytelling -- United States 5. Libraries and preschool children -- United States 6. Children's libraries -- Activity programs -- United States

ISBN 0838912222; 9780838912225

           LC 2014004162

This book, by Saroj Nadkarni Ghoting and Kathy Fling Klatt, focuses on "Story Time Effective Practice (STEP). . . . [It] is an approach that articulates the link between child development theory and storytimes. This important resource shows how presenters can use STEP to craft a storytime that is effective for mixed-age groups and adheres to best practices for emotional, social, physical, and cognitive support." (Publisher's note)

"It is a rare volume that could serve as both pleasure reading or as a textbook, but STEP into Storytime walks that fine line...The majority of children's librarians have studied childhood development and early literacy best practices; consider this book required reading to keep this knowledge fresh while reminding us of the importance—and delightful fun—of our work." Booklist

Includes bibliographical references and index

Kirker, Christine

Multicultural storytime magic; Kathy MacMillan and Christine Kirker. American Library Association 2012 241 p. $47

Grades: Professional   **027.62**

1. Storytelling 2. Multicultural education 3. Children's libraries -- Activity programs 4. Storytelling -- United States 5. Children's libraries -- Activity programs -- United States 6. Multicultural education -- Activity programs -- United States

ISBN 0838911420; 9780838911426

           LC 2011043434

"Authors [Kathy] MacMillan and [Christine] Kirker offer a . . . paradigm for multicultural programs, one in which diversity is woven into any and every storytime, no matter what the topic. Arranged thematically around dozens of popular storytime themes, the authors . . . offer . . . book recommendations, fingerplays, and other activities that can be integrated into existing storytimes." (Publisher's note)

Includes bibliographical references and indexes

LibrarySparks: library lessons. Upstart Bks. 2011 200p $17.95

Grades: Adult Professional   **027.62**

1. Books and reading 2. Children's libraries 3. Bibliographic instruction

ISBN 1-60213-052-3; 978-1-60213-052-4

"Compiled from the first six volumes of the magazine LibrarySparks, this book contains 24 lessons by librarians and educators attuned to the interests, needs, and learning styles of youngsters from kindergarten through fifth grade. . . . Students are challenged to access information in a variety of formats. This fine collection will provide rich and rewarding lessons all year long." SLJ

MacDonald, Margaret Read

Look back and see; twenty lively tales for gentle tellers. illustrations by Roxane Murphy. Wilson, H.W. 1991 178p il $60

Grades: Adult Professional   **027.62**

1. Folklore 2. Storytelling

ISBN 978-0-8242-0810-3; 0-8242-0810-3

           LC 91-2539

The author presents twenty non-violent folktales from around the world, with background notes and suggestions for storytelling uses

"Delightfully varied in mood, the tales range from silly and rowdy to contemplative and touching. . . . MacDonald's useful, informative, and entertaining notes follow each story. . . . The notes alone are worth the price of the book." J Youth Serv Libr

Includes bibliographical references

★ **When** the lights go out; twenty scary tales to tell. illustrations by Roxane Murphy. Wilson, H.W. 1988 176p il $70

Grades: Adult Professional   **027.62**

1. Folklore 2. Storytelling 3. Horror fiction

ISBN 0-8242-0770-X

           LC 88-14197

"Divided into six sections—Not Too Scary, Scary in the Dark, Gross Stuff, Jump Tales, Tales to Act Out, and Tales to Draw or Stir Up—the selections will be especially useful around Halloween, although, as the author points out, the book can be used year round. Following each inclusion are helpful notes on telling the stories and a section that gives sources on origins and variants. Murphy's decorative drawings introduce chapters and are scattered throughout the text. Several concluding chapters list bibliographies and provide other helpful information." Booklist

Includes bibliographical references

MacMillan, Kathy

Storytime magic; 400 fingerplays, flannelboards, and other activities. [by] Kathy MacMillan and Christine Kirker. American Library Association 2009 139p il pa $45

Grades: Adult Professional   **027.62**

1. Storytelling 2. Children's libraries

ISBN 978-0-8389-0977-5 pa; 0-8389-0977-9 pa

LC 2008030266

"Both new and veteran storytellers will appreciate this book. Sixteen chapters are arranged by themes such as 'All About Me,' 'Animals,' and 'Holidays.' Whenever a flannelboard idea is listed, a thumbnail pen-and-ink sketch of the necessary pieces is included next to a Web icon. Readers can then proceed to an ALA Web page to view the actual-sized pattern. An appendix gives further instruction on how to use other props or costumes along with a story." SLJ

Includes bibliographical references

Marino, Jane

★ Babies in the library! Scarecrow Press 2003 149p hardcover o.p. pa $32

Grades: Adult Professional   **027.62**

1. Children's libraries

ISBN 0-8108-4576-8; 0-8108-6044-9 pa

LC 2002-12022

The author presents "arguments for holding library programs specifically geared toward babies. Organizing and presenting her ideas in a thoughtful and philosophical manner, she addresses many relevant topics: making babies feel comfortable in the library, creating programs for prewalkers and walkers, handling registration, and offering suggestions for planning and executing programs. She also includes various activities that introduce books, rhymes, puppets, and other tools that enhance language skills." SLJ

Includes bibliographical references

Nichols, Judy

Storytimes for two-year-olds; [by] Judy Nichols; illustrated by Lori D. Sears. 3rd ed; American Library Association 2007 252p bibl il pa $40

Grades: Adult Professional   **027.62**

1. Storytelling 2. Children's libraries

ISBN 0-8389-0925-6 pa; 978-0-8389-0925-6 pa

LC 2006023915

First published 1987

This outlines techniques for creating library programs for two-year-olds using books, rhymes, songs, fingerplays, puppets, and crafts on such themes as farms, animals, seasons, and bedtimes.

"The variety of programs, the diverse and excellent book selections, and the other program components . . . make this book useful for librarians, nursery-school teachers, and homeschoolers." Booklist

Includes bibliographical references

Pavon, Ana-Elba

★ 25 Latino craft projects; [by] Ana-Elba Pavon, Diana Borrego. American Library Association 2003 80p il (Celebrating culture in your library) pa $35

Grades: Adult Professional   **027.62**

1. Handicraft 2. Children's libraries 3. Hispanic Americans -- Social life and customs

ISBN 978-0-8389-0833-4 pa; 0-8389-0833-0 pa

LC 2002-5750

Following a "chapter on planning, the projects are organized around important Latino holidays and are inspired by artesenias (Latino folk art). . . . For each celebration, there is a suggested program for preschoolers, after-schooler, and families; each program incorporates the craft with songs, poems, and books. Activities include making piñatas, paper flowers, sweet tamales, and salsa." SLJ

Includes glossary and bibliographical references

Peck, Penny

Crash course in storytime fundamentals. Libraries Unlimited 2009 154p (Crash course) pa $30

Grades: Adult Professional   **027.62**

1. Storytelling 2. Children's libraries

ISBN 978-1-59158-715-6 pa; 1-59158-715-8 pa

LC 2008031234

"Practical and concise, this well-organized and readable guide is for inexperienced staff members who are not necessarily children's librarians. . . . The 75 themed storytimes include different types of books and Web sites and sources for songs, musical instruments, fingerplays, games, puppets, and crafts. The author discusses best times and settings for programs; special issues, such as children's and parents' behavior; selection and training of volunteers; the 'registration' question, and more." SLJ

Includes bibliographical references

Reid, Rob

More family storytimes; twenty-four creative programs for all ages. American Library Association 2009 181p pa $45

Grades: Adult Professional   **027.62**

1. Storytelling 2. Children's libraries

ISBN 978-0-8389-0973-7

LC 2008015377

"This volume contains 24 programs, each lasting 30 minutes, that promote learning readiness and reading skills. . . . Clearly presented and easy to follow, this is an excellent resource for librarians who want to come up with winning story hours that have broad appeal." Booklist

Includes bibliographical references

Shake & shout; 16 noisy, lively story programs. Upstart Books 2008 110p il pa $17.95

Grades: Adult Professional   **027.62**

1. Dance 2. Songs 3. Storytelling 4. Children's libraries 5. Children -- Books and reading

ISBN 978-1-60213-006-7 pa; 1-60213-006-X pa

LC 2009535346

"This book centers on the idea of using one song as the jumping-off point for a thematic storytime. Each program features two to three picture books that support the theme, along with one or two movement activities. There's also a 'backup picture book' listed as well as more related songs. . . . The featured songs are listed within the programs, where recordings can be found, and are also printed at the end of the chapter with suggested guitar chords. The themes run the gamut from seasonal, to various animals and their environments, to pretend activities and emotions. This volume will spark creativity and imagination." SLJ

Includes bibliographical references

★ What's black and white and Reid all over? something hilarious happened at the library. Rob Reid. American Library Association 2012 xii, 175 p.p (softbound) $45

Grades: Adult Professional   **027.62**

1. Storytelling 2. Humorous fiction 3. Children's libraries 4. Storytelling -- United States 5. Wit and humor, Juvenile -- Bibliography 6. Children's libraries -- Activity programs -- United States

ISBN 0838911471; 9780838911471

LC 2011043233

This book presents "10 humorous story programs -- five aimed at preschoolers and five for school-aged children. . . . Each one provides read-aloud suggestions and movement activities. There are also . . . storytelling tips that include everything from how to hold the book to what props to use. . . . Reid also includes an additional list of titles that can be substituted, jokes, call-and-response chants, short storybooks, songs, and musical activities." (School Library Journal)

"Those new to interactive book talking will appreciate his instructions for hamming up particular titles. Seasoned users will be grateful for the flexibility Reid provides to tailor programs to the tastes, time slots, and collection at hand." VOYA

Includes bibliographical references and index

Sierra, Judy

The **flannel** board storytelling book; 2nd ed rev & expanded; Wilson, H.W. 1997 241p il music $65

Grades: Adult Professional   **027.62**

  1. Storytelling 2. Children's libraries

  ISBN 978-0-8242-0932-2; 0-8242-0932-X

                            LC 97-15107

First published 1987

"Fifty stories, poems, and songs and over three hundred patterns are included for presenting stories to children in a flannel board medium, including classic children's stories, nursery rhymes, folk tales, and songs. . . . Sierra's experience telling stories with children is reflected throughout her book." J Youth Serv Libr

Sima, Judy

Raising voices; creating youth storytelling groups and troupes. [by] Judy Sima, Kevin Cordi. Libraries Unlimited 2003 xxviii, 241p pa $32.50

Grades: Adult Professional   **027.62**

  1. Storytelling

  ISBN 1-56308-919-X

                          LC 2003-47631

This offers a "blueprint for beginning and sustaining a successful group or troupe of storytellers from grades 4 to 12. . . . The book includes reproducible forms that will save a lot of work and lists of valuable resources. . . . Raising Voices is the complete, and essential, handbook for this special group of storytellers." SLJ

Includes bibliographical references

Sullivan, Michael

★ **Fundamentals** of children's services; by Michael Sullivan. American Library Association 2013 xx, 359 p.p (alk. paper) $52

Grades: Professional   **027.62**

  1. Children's libraries 2. Libraries -- Collection development 3. Children's libraries -- United States

  ISBN 0838911889; 9780838911884

                        LC 2013005037

This book, by Michael Sullivan, presents a reference on children's services at libraries. It covers "both innovative and standard practices in children's services. Fundamentals such as collection development and management, programming, homework support, and reference and reader's advisory are all thoroughly updated. [It] offers an expansive view of what it means to ensure that children are well-served in light of ongoing budgetary challenges." (Publisher's note)

Includes bibliographical references (pages 327-339) and index

Walter, Virginia A.

Twenty-first-century kids, twenty-first-century librarians. American Library Association 2010 104p pa $45

Grades: Adult Professional   **027.62**

  1. Librarians 2. Children's libraries 3. Young adults' libraries

  ISBN 978-0-8389-1007-8 pa; 0-8389-1007-6 pa

                        LC 2009016972

"This volume more than updates Walter's 2001 Children and Libraries; it revisits the nature of children, addressing social changes and encouraging a new generation of children's librarians. Chapter 1 provides a fine history about U.S. library services to children, primarily in public libraries. Subsequent chapters detail six enduring core values of children's library services and add two emerging themes: the need for information (and information literacy) and collaboration. Walter's main contribution lies in her description of five models of children relative to the library: as reader, as a child of the information age, as a community member, as global, and as an empowered person. Another chapter focuses on management principals. . . . Walter's core values are worth reading and implementing." Booklist

Includes bibliographical references

027.8   School libraries

Adams, Helen R.

★ **Ensuring** intellectual freedom and access to information in the school library media program. Libraries Unlimited 2008 xxi, 254p il map pa $40

Grades: Adult Professional   **027.8**

  1. Censorship 2. School libraries 3. Freedom of information

  ISBN 978-1-59158-539-8; 1-59158-539-2

                        LC 2008-16753

This is "an extremely helpful guide for dealing with intellectual-freedom and information-access issues. In chapters geared to school situations and covering topics including selection of resources, the First Amendment, privacy, challenges to resources, the Internet, and access for students with disabilities, Adams offers background on the topic and bulleted lists of strategies for dealing with the issue. . . . This is a book that every school librarian needs to keep handy and share with administrators, colleagues, and parents." Booklist

Includes bibliographical references

Bishop, Kay

The **collection** program in schools; concepts, practices, and information sources. 4th ed. Libraries Unlimited 2007 xx, 269p il (Library and information science text series) pa $50; $65

Grades: Adult Professional   **027.8**

  1. School libraries 2. Libraries -- Collection development 3. School libraries -- Collection development 4. Children's literature -- Bibliography of bibliographies 5. Young adult literature -- Bibliography of bibliographies

  ISBN 1-59158-360-8 pa; 1-59158-583-X; 978-1-59158-360-8 pa; 978-1-59158-583-1

                        LC 2007-9005

First published 1988 under the authorship of Phyllis J. Van Orden

"Media specialists who read this book will be renewed in their quest for excellence in their collections. . . . The book covers A-Z: Acquisitions, Evaluation, Ethical Issues, Inventory, Procedure Manual, Selection, Special Groups of Students, Weeding, etc. . . . This is a must purchase for every school library media center." Libr Media Connect

Includes bibliographical references

Buzzeo, Toni

Collaborating to meet standards: teacher/librarian partnerships for K-6; [by] Toni Buzzeo. 2nd ed.; Linworth Pub. 2007 246p pa $39.95

Grades: Adult Professional   **027.8**

  1. School libraries

  ISBN 1-58683-302-2 pa; 978-1-58683-302-2 pa

                        LC 2007015406

First published 2002

This "addresses the assessment-driven educational environment of the No Child Left Behind Act. In the first section, Buzzeo focuses on the benefits of an involved school librarian to the educational process and how best to achieve this collaboration. She includes a template for collaborative planning and instruction. Sample lessons for specific grades from librarians around the United States complete the book. Practical suggestions and examples from school librarians across the country appear in separate text boxes.... Buzzeo gives worthwhile advice." SLJ

Includes bibliographical references

The **collaboration** handbook. Linworth Pub. 2008 132p il pa $42.95

Grades: Adult Professional   **027.8**
1. School libraries
ISBN 978-1-58683-298-8 pa; 1-58683-298-0 pa

LC 2008-18119

"In this succinct guide, Buzzeo paints a picture of how media specialists can use instructional collaboration to transform a media program and increase student achievement.... Those new to the field will appreciate the step-by-step approach to increasing collaboration, while experienced media specialists will likely benefit most from the chapters on data-driven collaboration and assessment. The book concludes with a substantial amount of information on how to overcome common barriers to collaboration, the role of advocacy, and the importance of integrating new technologies into collaborative projects." SLJ

Includes bibliographical references

Erikson, Rolf
Designing a school library media center for the future; [by] Rolf Erikson and Carolyn Markuson. 2nd ed; American Library Association 2007 117p il pa $45

Grades: Adult Professional   **027.8**
1. School libraries -- Design and construction 2. Instructional materials centers -- Design and construction
ISBN 978-0-8389-0945-4; 0-8389-0945-0

LC 2006-37644

First published 2000

"The first chapter offers an overview of the various steps involved in any project. Succeeding chapters cover technology planning, space allocations, furniture and placement, lighting and acoustics, ADA requirements, specifications, and bids." Booklist

Includes bibliographical references

Franklin, Patricia
Library 101; a handbook for the school library media specialist. [by] Claire Gatrell Stephens and Patricia Franklin. Libraries Unlimited 2007 233p il pa $35

Grades: Adult Professional   **027.8**
1. School libraries 2. Instructional materials centers 3. Procedure manuals 4. Libraries -- Handbooks, manuals, etc.
ISBN 1-59158-324-1; 978-1-59158-324-0

LC 2007-18420

"This handbook provides information for brand-new and inexperienced librarians preparing for a first job in a school library media center. Articles are divided into four subcategories covering day-to-day operations (library organization, circulation policies, media management, scheduling, staffing, and media center arrangement); collaboration with teachers; collection development and management; and equipment." Booklist

Includes bibliographical references

Grimes, Sharon
★ **Reading** is our business; how libraries can foster reading comprehension. American Library Association 2006 155p il pa $35

Grades: Adult Professional   **027.8**
1. School libraries 2. Books and reading 3. Reading comprehension
ISBN 0-8389-0912-4

LC 2005028263

Grimes "led a school-wide research study with classroom teachers to transform the reading program at Lansdowne Elementary School in Baltimore. The study resulted in dramatic and measurable gains in student reading achievement. This book can be used as a toolkit to duplicate those results. Grimes's work is informed by solid educational research in the field of reading comprehension. The text is lively and clearly written, accessible to teachers and librarians." SLJ

Includes bibliographical references

Harada, Violet H.
Assessing for learning; librarians and teachers as partners. [by] Violet H. Harada and Joan M. Yoshina. 2nd ed.; Libraries Unlimited 2010 242p il pa $45

Grades: Adult Professional   **027.8**
1. School libraries 2. Instructional materials centers
ISBN 978-1-59884-470-2; 1-59884-470-9
First published 2055 with title: Assessing learning

"Using assessment tools familiar to the classroom teacher, the authors show how to use them in the library setting. Starting with the challenges that face 21st century schools, the rationale for schools as learning organizations is laid out. The tools for assessment are the main points of this title and include checklists, rubrics, rating scales, conferences, logs, personal correspondence, exit passes, graphic organizers, and student portfolios.... The tools for better instruction and assessment of learning need to be used by all educators, and this title provides examples and models for all librarians." Libr Media Connect

Includes bibliographical references

Hughes-Hassell, Sandra
★ **School** reform and the school library media specialist; [by] Sandra Hughes-Hassell and Violet H. Harada. Libraries Unlimited 2007 xxiii, 204p il (Principles and practice series) pa $40

Grades: Adult Professional   **027.8**
1. School libraries
ISBN 978-1-59158-427-8; 1-59158-427-2

LC 2007-16437

"This volume covers critical issues impacting school libraries today and offers practical solutions to meet these challenges. Written by leaders in the field such as Pam Berger, Carol Gordon, Barbara Stripling, and Ross Todd, the articles expound on implications of No Child Left Behind legislation, 21st-century literacy requirements, population diversity, and professional growth.... This volume will empower current and future school librarians as they embrace its guidelines." SLJ

Morris, Betty J.
★ **Administering** the school library media center; 5th ed.; Libraries Unlimited 2010 580p il $75; pa $60

Grades: Adult Professional   **027.8**
1. School libraries 2. Instructional materials centers
ISBN 978-1-59158-685-2; 1-59158-685-2; 978-1-59158-689-0 pa; 1-59158-689-5 pa

LC 2010015939

First published 1973 under the authorship of John T. Gillespie and Diana L. Spirt with title: Creating a school media program

"This updated edition provides a comprehensive and current examination of the multiple and varied jobs media specialists do to manage today's school library media centers.... Sample job description statements, media center budgets, and budget justification tools are thorough and valuable references. Morris addresses the proactive and visible leadership role that today's media specialists must take on to remain viable and support student learning. . . . The title supports concepts on current standards. It is a forward thinking text for new or future library media specialists and a realistic, functional reference for practitioners." Libr Media Connect

Includes bibliographical references

Sykes, Judith A.

Conducting action research to evaluate your school library; Judith Anne Sykes. Libraries Unlimited, an imprint of ABC-CLIO, LLC 2013 118 p. illustrations (hard copy) $40

Grades: Adult Professional   027.8

1. School libraries 2. Librarians -- Rating 3. Educational evaluation 4. School librarians 5. Teacher-librarians 6. Action research in education 7. School libraries -- Evaluation

ISBN 161069077X; 9781610690775

                                            LC 2012051277

In this book, author Judith Anne Sykes "coalesces current expert opinions on the topic of action research in the school library environment and highlighting what other teacher librarians in the field have identified as the pros and cons of using the process. Readers are directed to focus on mitigating the 'cons' through the use of specific working pages and templates and by initially exploring 'five favorite' links." (Publisher's note)

"When budget issues hit, school librarianship can be in danger, and this text provides tools for professionals to evaluate their programs and make necessary changes to stay a vital part of their schools. . . . This purchase would be worthwhile for any teacher-librarian interested in evaluating his or her program and taking advantage of Sykes' extensive research and expertise." Booklist

Includes bibliographical references and index

028.1   Reviews

Baxter, Kathleen A.

★ **From** cover to cover; evaluating and reviewing children's books. rev ed.; Collins 2010 229p $14.99

Grades: Adult Professional   028.1

1. Books -- Reviews 2. Children's literature -- History and criticism

ISBN 978-0-06-077757-9; 0-06-077757-5

First published 1997

The author addresses the distinctions between evaluation and review, and what makes a good children's book. She discusses categories of children's books including nonfiction; traditional literature (folktales, myths, legends, etc.); poetry, verse, rhymes, and songs; picture books; easy readers and transitional books; and fiction. She then describes the process of writing a review.

This is a "very complete resource that will continue to be the venerable reference tool and required reading for education and library-science students, youth librarians, teachers, and anyone else interested in kids, reading, and children's literature." SLJ

Naidoo, Jamie Campbell

★ **Rainbow** family collections; selecting and using children's books with lesbian, gay, bisexual, transgender, and queer content. Jamie Campbell Naidoo. Libraries Unlimited, an imprint of ABC-CLIO, LLC 2012 xvii, 260 p.p ill. (hardback) $50

Grades: Adult Professional   028.1

1. Libraries and sexual minorities 2. Sexual minorities in literature 3. Libraries and sexual minorities -- United States 4. Libraries -- Special collections -- Sexual minorities 5. Sexual minorities -- Bibliography 6. Children's libraries -- Collection development -- United States 7. Children's libraries -- Services to minorities -- United States 8. Children of sexual minority parents -- Books and

reading -- United States

ISBN 1598849603; 9781598849608

                                            LC 2012008362

This book by Jamie Campbell Naidoo "highlight[s] titles for children from infancy to age 11" featuring lesbian, gay, bisexual, transgender, and queer content. It "supplies a synopsis of the title's content, lists awards it has received, cites professional reviews, and provides suggestions for librarians considering acquisition. The book also provides a brief historical overview of LGBTQ children's literature along with the major book awards for this genre." (Publisher's note)

Includes bibliographical references and index

028.5   Reading and use of other information media by young people

Allyn, Pam

What to read when; the books and stories to read with your child, and all the best times to read them. Avery 2009 318p pa $16.95

Grades: Adult Professional   028.5

1. Children -- Books and reading

ISBN 978-1-58333-334-1

                                            LC 2008-54501

The author "provides many ways to promote a love of reading to children and offers top-ten lists of reasons to read to kids that incorporate practical, easy-to-use tips to encourage literacy from a young age. . . . This is an indispensable guide to choosing age-appropriate books for children. Allyn provides a list of more than 300 titles on 50 themes including such issues as adoption, feelings about school, sharing, and coping with illness. This valuable resource for children's librarians, educators, and parents is highly recommended." Libr J

American Library Association

The **Newbery** and Caldecott awards; a guide to the medal and honor books. [by] Association for Library Service to Children. American Lib. Assn. il

Grades: Adult Professional   028.5

1. Newbery Medal 2. Caldecott Medal

Annual

"An annotated listing of winning titles since the inception of the awards (1922 and 1938 respectively). . . . Annotations serve as a reliable guide for colllection development, reader's advisory, curriculum development, and a host of other programs." (Publisher's note)

"An annotated listing of winning titles since the inception of the awards (1922 and 1938 respectively). . . . Annotations serve as a reliable guide for colllection development, reader's advisory, curriculum development, and a host of other programs." Publisher's note

Baxter, Kathleen A.

Gotcha again for guys! more nonfiction books to get boys excited about reading. [by] Kathleen A. Baxter and Marcia Agness Kochel. Libraries Unlimited 2010 248p il pa $35

Grades: Adult Professional   028.5

1. Book talks 2. Boys -- Books and reading 3. Children's literature -- Bibliography

ISBN 978-1-59884-376-7 pa; 1-59884-376-1 pa; 978-1-59884-377-4 e-book

                                            LC 2010036577

This "highlights books published mainly between 2007 and 2009. Twelve chapters cover themes such as sports, animals, gross/disgusting stuff, mysteries/disasters, and machines. Each one features anywhere from a few to two dozen ready-to-use booktalks, most aimed at grades 3-8, along with extensive bibliographies (not annotated) of other titles that have received good reviews in Booklist, Horn Book Guide, and

School Library Journal. New to this volume are enlightening interviews with male authors such as Kadir Nelson, Nic Bishop, and Seymour Simon, whose books are featured in the text. The introduction also lists ideas for promoting books to boys in public libraries and school media centers." SLJ

Includes bibliographical references

Gotcha good! nonfiction books to get kids excited about reading. [by] Kathleen A. Baxter and Marcia Agness Kochel. Libraries Unlimited 2008 259p pa $35
Grades: Adult Professional　　　　　**028.5**
　1. Books and reading　2. Children's literature -- Bibliography　3. Young adult literature -- Bibliography
　ISBN 978-1-59158-654-8 pa; 1-59158-654-2 pa
　　　　　　　　　　　　　　LC 2008010350

"In addition to annotations for over 1000 nonfiction titles, [the authors] profile eight prolific authors and provide fun top-10 features for the various subjects covered. . . . The titles chosen are truly high quality, relevant, and up-to-date, with suggested ages provided, most ranging from grades three through eight. . . . A must-have for all librarians who want to get kids excited about nonfiction." SLJ

Includes bibliographical references

Bishop, Rudine Sims
　Free within ourselves; the development of African American children's literature. Heinemann/Greenwood 2007 295p bibl il $65; pa $22
Grades: Adult Professional　　　　　**028.5**
　1. African Americans in literature　2. Children -- Books and reading　3. Children's literature -- History and criticism　4. American literature -- African American authors -- History and criticism
　ISBN 978-0-325-07135-0 Heinemann; 978-0-313-34093-2 pa Greenwood
　　　　　　　　　　　　　　LC 2007000612

"Bishop traces the evolution of fiction written for black children and by black authors and illustrators within the context of African-American social and literary history. . . . Her writing is precise and engaging, and it really comes alive when presenting primary-source material. . . . Librarians as well as teachers will be enriched by this work." SLJ

Includes bibliographical references

Brooks, Wanda M.
　Embracing, evaluating, and examining African American children's and young adult literature; edited by Wanda M. Brooks, Jonda C. McNair; foreword by Rudine Sims Bishop. Scarecrow Press 2008 251p pa $45
Grades: Adult Professional　　　　　**028.5**
　1. African Americans in literature　2. Children -- Books and reading　3. Children's literature -- History and criticism　4. Young adult literature -- History and criticism　5. American literature -- African American authors -- History and criticism
　ISBN 978-0-8108-6027-8 pa; 0-8108-6027-9 pa
　　　　　　　　　　　　　　LC 2007025703

"Brooks and McNair have compiled 12 scholarly studies about the use of books by and about African-American children and young adults in classrooms across the United States. Selections include a detailed textual analysis of the work of Arna Bontemps and Langston Hughes; a sociolinguistic perspective on readers' response to books containing African-American Vernacular English; and a detailed study of the books used as classroom read-alouds by teachers in rural schools, which found that only three percent were about African Americans. While each study is complete in and of itself, the text as a whole gives a broad picture of

what is currently being done in this field, both in K-12 classrooms and college classes that emphasize children's literature." SLJ

Includes bibliographical references

Casement, Rose
　Black history in the pages of children's literature. Scarecrow Press 2008 317p pa $55
Grades: Adult Professional　　　　　**028.5**
　1. African Americans in literature　2. Children's literature -- Bibliography　3. Children's literature -- History and criticism
　ISBN 978-0-8108-5843-5 pa; 0-8108-5843-6 pa
　　　　　　　　　　　　　　LC 2007018137

"Casement has organized her book along a time line from the initial presence of Africans in America before colonization to the present day. Each chapter begins with a brief description of important historical events that have often been left out of our history books. This is followed by an annotated bibliography that includes excerpts from each title and a description of the content. Books listed are primarily straight nonfiction but some fantasy, realistic fiction, biography, and poetry are included. The final two chapters address criteria for selecting children's literature for classroom use and introduce several talented African-American writers and illustrators. Putting this eminently accessible book into the hands of teachers should greatly increase the use of accurate books about African Americans and help to identify and pass on a more truthful historical picture than most of us were given in school." SLJ

Includes bibliographical references

Diamant-Cohen, Betsy
　Booktalking bonanza; ten ready-to-use multimedia sessions for the busy librarian. American Library Association 2009 240p il pa $40
Grades: Adult Professional　　　　　**028.5**
　1. Book talks　2. Books and reading　3. Children's literature
　ISBN 978-0-8389-0965-2; 0-8389-0965-5
　　　　　　　　　　　　　　LC 2008-15371

"This volume is a collection of scripts for multimedia-enriched booktalks. After an introductory chapter that explains the reasoning for this approach, 10 scripts are outlined. Books, music, video, and Web sites are included for each one. The programs are geared toward elementary-aged children, although suggestions for adapting them for a middle or high school audience are included." SLJ

Includes bibliographical references

Embracing, evaluating, and examining African American children's and young adult literature; edited by Wanda M. Brooks, Jonda C. McNair; foreword by Rudine Sims Bishop. Scarecrow Press 2008 251p pa $45
Grades: Adult Professional　　　　　**028.5**
　1. African Americans in literature　2. Children -- Books and reading　3. Children's literature -- History and criticism　4. Young adult literature -- History and criticism　5. American literature -- African American authors -- History and criticism
　ISBN 978-0-8108-6027-8 pa; 0-8108-6027-9 pa
　　　　　　　　　　　　　　LC 2007025703

"Brooks and McNair have compiled 12 scholarly studies about the use of books by and about African-American children and young adults in classrooms across the United States. Selections include a detailed textual analysis of the work of Arna Bontemps and Langston Hughes; a sociolinguistic perspective on readers' response to books containing African-American Vernacular English; and a detailed study of the books used as classroom read-alouds by teachers in rural schools, which found that only three percent were about African Americans. While each study is complete in and of itself, the text as a whole gives a broad picture of what is currently being done in this field, both in K-12 classrooms and college classes that emphasize children's literature." SLJ

Includes bibliographical references

Feinberg, Barbara

Welcome to Lizard Motel; children, stories, and the mystery of making things up: a memoir. Beacon Press 2004 256p $20

Grades: Adult Professional   **028.5**

1. Imagination 2. Children -- Books and reading

ISBN 0-8070-7144-7

LC 2004-710

"Feinberg, who's spent years working with children in a creativity workshop she designed, has the independence and experience to raise important questions. Her critique . . . . should stir some much-needed controversy." Publ Wkly

Includes bibliographical references

Gilmore, Barry

★ **Speaking** volumes; how to get students discussing books, and much more. Heinemann 2006 128p pa $17.95

Grades: Adult Professional   **028.5**

1. Books and reading

ISBN 978-0-325-00915-5 pa; 0-325-00915-5 pa

LC 2005-28371

"Gilmore provides practical, hands-on methods to involve students in oral and written classroom conversations that encourage reflection and ultimately polished, coherent expression. . . . Both new and seasoned discussion leaders will want a copy for repeated reference." Voice Youth Advocates

Includes bibliographical references

Gilton, Donna L.

Multicultural and ethnic children's literature in the United States; [by] Donna L. Gilton. Scarecrow Press 2007 236p pa $45

Grades: Adult Professional   **028.5**

1. Multiculturalism 2. Minorities in literature 3. Children's literature -- History and criticism

ISBN 978-0-8108-5672-1 pa; 0-8108-5672-7 pa

LC 2007006391

"Gilton writes with authority, clarity, and conviction, presenting a strong rationale for the necessity for teachers to use multicultural literature whether or not their schools and/or classrooms have diverse populations. . . . The author offers a wealth of information. . . . She gives a history of multicultural literature in the U.S. . . . Gilton addresses current issues. . . . There is ample information on how to find the best books that appropriately represent a variety of cultures. Finally, Gilton looks closely at groups that are growing in the U.S." SLJ

Includes bibliographical references

Handbook of research on children's and young adult literature; edited by Shelby A. Wolf . . . [et al.] Routledge 2010 555p $295; pa $119.95

Grades: Adult Professional   **028.5**

1. Children's literature -- History and criticism 2. Young adult literature -- History and criticism

ISBN 978-0-415-96505-7; 0-415-96505-5; 978-0-415-96506-4 pa; 0-415-96506-3 pa; 978-0-203-84354-3 e-book

LC 2010-16339

"The book examines readers, texts, and cultural contexts of children's literature and across the three intersecting disciplines of Education, English, and Library and Information Science, in an effort to model a multidisciplinary approach to children's literature research. Thirty-seven scholarly articles, by figures such as Eliza Dresang, Rudine Sims Bishop, and Roderick McGillis . . . are counterpointed by responses that often provide more personal perspectives, including insights from noted authors such as Lois Lowry, M. T. Anderson, and Markus Zusak." Bull Cent Child Books

Herb, Steven

Connecting fathers, children, and reading; a how-to-do it manual for librarians. [by] Steven Herb, Sara Willoughby-Herb. Neal-Schuman 2001 196p (How-to-do-it manuals for librarians) pa $45

Grades: Adult Professional   **028.5**

1. Fathers 2. Books and reading

ISBN 1-55570-390-9

LC 2001-18315

This "book looks at both the importance and effect of father involvement in children's reading. . . . Case studies, anecdotes, and interesting sidebars abound in this well-organized, well-written source. . . . An extensive bibliography includes more than 450 children's books about fathers and fathering." SLJ

Hey! listen to this; stories to read aloud. edited by Jim Trelease. Viking 1992 414p hardcover o.p. pa $15

Grades: Adult Professional   **028.5**

1. Authors 2. Books and reading 3. Literature -- Collections

ISBN 0-14-014653-9 pa

LC 91-37668

"Divided into categories such as 'Animal Tales,' 'Children of Courage,' or 'Classic Tales,' the forty-eight selections cover a wide spectrum from folktales to fantasy, classics to contemporary stories. More than half are complete stories, while the remainder are one or two chapters from longer books. Trelease skillfully weaves his choices into a cohesive whole. Beyond merely categorizing them, he refers to other authors or stories in the discussions that precede and follow each story." J Youth Serv Libr

Includes bibliographical references

Keane, Nancy J.

101 great, ready-to-use book lists for children; Nancy J. Keane. Libraries Unlimited, an imprint of ABC-CLIO, LLC 2012 xiv, 246 p.p (paperback) $45

Grades: Adult Professional   **028.5**

1. Best books 2. Children -- Books and reading 3. School libraries -- Book lists 4. Children's libraries -- Book lists 5. Children's literature -- Bibliography 6. Children -- Books and reading -- United States

ISBN 1610690834; 9781610690836

LC 2011051429

"Keane uses her vast knowledge of children's literature to create book lists for children K-8th grade. They are broken into seven parts that are subdivided into subject areas. . . . Each entry includes the title, author, publisher, publication date, number of pages, an annotation, Lexile level when available, and interest level by grade or age range. The easily reproducible lists will be useful for curriculum and collection development as well as for interesting book displays." SLJ

Includes bibliographical references and index

Kitain, Sandra

Shelf-esteem; [by] Sandra Kitain. Neal-Schuman Publishers 2008 183p pa $49.95

Grades: Adult Professional   **028.5**

1. Book talks 2. Reference books 3. Books and reading 4. Children's libraries 5. Children's literature -- Bibliography

ISBN 978-1-55570-568-8 pa; 1-55570-568-5 pa

LC 2007034737

"Kitain offers an array of books that 'help children relate to their personal lives and individual challenges.' Chapters are based on themes including but not limited to friendship, courage, emotions, moving, new siblings, physical challenges, and bullies. Tough subjects like alcoholism, illness and death, and homelessness are also included. . . . The quality and variety of texts are excellent. The remaining chapters of the book explore working with community partners. This text is highly recommended for all librarians, teachers, caregivers, and parents of younger readers." SLJ

Includes bibliographical references

Latrobe, Kathy Howard
The **children's** literature dictionary; definitions, resources, and teaching activities. [by] Kathy Latrobe, Carolyn S. Brodie, Maureen White. Neal-Schuman 2002 282p pa $59.95
Grades: Adult Professional   **028.5**
    1. Reference books 2. Children's literature -- Dictionaries
    ISBN 1-55570-424-7
                     LC 2001-44434

"The first section is an alphabetical dictionary of 325 terms found in reviews, lesson plans, and other resources. Definitions of terms contain meanings and examples from popular children's literature and activities related to the term. The activities descriptions provide a starting point for teaching or demonstrating the term. This reference book supports resources and materials that librarians or teachers should have in their collection." Book Rep

Lerer, Seth
   ★ **Children's** literature; a reader's history, from Aesop to Harry Potter. University of Chicago Press 2008 385p il
Grades: Adult Professional   **028.5**
    1. Books and reading 2. Children's literature -- History and criticism
    ISBN 0-226-47300-7; 978-0-226-47300-0
                     LC 2007046708

The author sets out to "chart the makings of the Western literary imagination from Aesop's fables to Mother Goose, from Alice's Adventures in Wonderland to Peter Pan, from Where the Wild Things Are to Harry Potter. Lerer here explores the iconic books, ancient and contemporary alike, that have forged a lifelong love of literature in young readers during their formative years. Along the way, Lerer also looks at the changing environments of family life and human growth, schooling and scholarship, and publishing and politics in which children found themselves changed by the books they read." (Publisher's note) Index.

"This work presents a true critical history of [children's literature], from Aesop to the present. Scholarly, erudite, and all but exhaustive, it is also entertaining and accessible. . . . [Lerer] asks important questions about writers' intentions and readers' reactions, about why some texts endure and others do not, about the influence of science and religion on children's literature, and even about the impact of libraries and literary prizes upon the genre." Libr J

Includes bibliographical references

Marks, Diana F.
Children's book award handbook. Libraries Unlimited 2006 412p bibl il tab pa $40
Grades: Adult Professional   **028.5**
    1. Children's literature -- Awards 2. Young adult literature -- Awards
    ISBN 1-59158-304-7
The author "has compiled a valuable resource that will be much appreciated by teachers and school librarians. Her handbook provides details on the history and origins of 24 major children's book awards from the Jane Addams Book Award to the Charlotte Zolotow Award and includes lesson plans and student activity sheets for 21 of them." Libr J

McDaniel, Deanna
Gentle reads; great books to warm hearts and lift spirits, grades 5-9. [by] Deanna J. McDaniel. Libraries Unlimited 2008 318p (Children's and young adult literature reference series) $45
Grades: Adult Professional   **028.5**
    1. Children's literature -- Bibliography 2. Young adult literature -- Bibliography
    ISBN 978-1-59158-491-9
                     LC 2008018878

This includes "500 recommended titles. Here readers will find books with divorce, drug use, attempted suicides, and more but they all meet the criteria the author has set by being either inspiring, heartwarming, or in some way uplifting. . . . Arranged by genres, the entries include full bibliographic information, an annotation, and a description of why the book fits the 'gentle criteria.'" SLJ

Includes bibliographical references

Nespeca, Sue McCleaf
Picture books plus; 100 extension activities in art, drama, music, math, and science. [by] Sue McCleaf Nespeca, Joan B. Reeve. American Lib. Assn. 2003 133p il pa $38
Grades: Adult Professional   **028.5**
    1. Books and reading 2. Picture books for children
    ISBN 0-8389-0840-3
                     LC 2002-11822

"This book is intended for use by teachers, librarians, and others working with children in preschool through grade three and features extension activities for use with a variety of materials. . . . Each chapter includes titles with annotations, 20 activities, and a list of resource books that will introduce readers to further activities. . . . Librarians and teachers will find many useful ideas here." Booklist

Includes bibliographical references

Reid, Rob
   ★ **Cool** story programs for the school-age crowd. American Library Association 2004 181p il pa $32
Grades: Adult Professional   **028.5**
    1. Books and reading 2. Children's literature
    ISBN 0-8389-0887-X
                     LC 2004-9933

This offers plans for story programs which incorporate poetry, picture books, chapter book excerpts, and short stories

"Eighteen well-developed plans with wacky themes that kids will love will bring literature to life with a minimum of stress for public librarians, teachers, and school media specialists. . . . A useful book with surefire suggestions for winning programs." SLJ

Includes bibliographical references

Saccardi, Marianne
Books that teach kids to write; [by] Marianne C. Saccardi. Libraries Unlimited 2011 150p pa $30; e-book $30
Grades: Adult Professional   **028.5**
    1. Creative writing 2. Books and reading 3. Literature -- Study and teaching
    ISBN 978-1-59884-451-1 pa; 978-1-59884-452-8 e-book
                     LC 2011001866

"Divided into sections such as 'Making Stories Unique,' 'Creating Memorable Characters,' and 'Putting Passion and Voice into Nonfiction Writing,' this book gives countless recommendations for teaching various skills. Saccardi offers short, annotated summaries of mentor texts and describes how they can be used to model good writing techniques. . . . After reading this resource, educators will have a long wish list of materials to purchase." SLJ

Includes bibliographical references

Sullivan, Michael

★ **Connecting** boys with books 2; closing the reading gap. American Library Association 2009 119p il pa $40

Grades: Adult Professional **028.5**

1. School libraries 2. Children's libraries 3. Young adults' libraries 4. Boys -- Books and reading

ISBN 978-0-8389-0979-9 pa; 0-8389-0979-5 pa

LC 2008-34925

"A must-read for all librarians and media specialists." SLJ

Includes bibliographical references (p. 105-110)

Raising boy readers; Michael Sullivan. Huron Street Press/ALA 2014 xiii, 193 p.p illustrations (pbk.) $19.95

Grades: Adult Professional **028.5**

1. Reading 2. Boys -- Education 3. Boys -- Books and reading 4. Reading -- Sex differences 5. Teenage boys -- Books and reading 6. Children's literature, American -- Bibliography 7. Young adult literature, American -- Bibliography

ISBN 1937589439; 9781937589431

LC 2013011537

This book, by Michael Sullivan, "conveys an understanding of the differences that are common among many boys and how these differences affect reading. It provides practical approaches to promote reading to boys, addressing physical differences, such as the different rates of early brain development between boys and girls; psychological issues, such as the outward focus of boys; and social issues, such as stress and confidence." (Publisher's note)

"So much more than just a compendium of annotated book lists (though they are here and well organized by genre and age level), Raising Boy Readers lays out the challenges of reaching reluctant readers, identifies common stumbling blocks, and systematically explores the how, when, why, what, and with whom of boys and their books." Booklist

Includes bibliographical references and index

Serving boys through readers' advisory. American Library Association 2010 152p (ALA readers' advisory series) pa $48

Grades: Adult Professional **028.5**

1. Children's literature 2. Reference services (Libraries) 3. Boys -- Books and reading 4. Boys

ISBN 978-0-8389-1022-1; 0-8389-1022-X

LC 2009-26841

"This volume was created to give a general direction when helping most boys select books. . . . Sullivan challenges us to throw out our preconceived notions about how to conduct such an interview. Methods of performing indirect readers' advisory with parents and teachers are included. The excellent booktalks for elementary, middle school, and high school boys alone make this a worthwhile purchase." SLJ

Includes bibliographical references

Temple, Charles A.

Children's books in children's hands; an introduction to their literature. [by] Charles Temple, Miriam Martinez, Junko Yokota; with contributions by Evelyn B. Freeman. 4th ed.; Pearson Allyn & Bacon 2010 572p pa $137.40

Grades: Adult Professional **028.5**

1. Books and reading 2. Children's literature -- History and criticism

ISBN 978-0-1370-7403-7 pa; 0-1370-7403-4 pa

LC 2010018237

First published 1998

The authors focus on creating an understanding of how literature works and how children respond to literature, they provide a wide range

of good books to use with children, and they suggest ways to guide children into books and help them enjoy the experience.

Includes bibliographical references

Vardell, Sylvia M.

Children's literature in action; a librarian's guide. Libraries Unlimited 2008 323p (Library and information science text series) $65; pa $50

Grades: Adult Professional **028.5**

1. Children's literature 2. Children -- Books and reading 3. Children's literature -- History and criticism 4. Children's library services -- Activity projects

ISBN 1591585570; 9781591585572; 1591586577; 9781591586579

LC 2007038012

"This excellent introduction to children's literature and its various genres and forms offers many activities and practical applications. Each chapter includes 'Action' components that highlight literature, authors, specific book titles, or history. . . . It also includes evaluation criteria, writing reviews, collection development of various genres, awards, and other programs of merit as well as additional information in numerous bibliographies and lists of recommended reading and Web sites." SLJ

Includes bibliographical references

Yolen, Jane

Touch magic; fantasy, faerie & folklore in the literature of childhood. Expanded ed; August House 2000 128p pa $11.95

Grades: Adult Professional **028.5**

1. Folklore 2. Children's literature -- History and criticism

ISBN 0-87483-591-7

LC 00-27565

First published 1981 by Philomel Bks.

The author provides perspectives on reading, appreciating, and preserving fantasy and folklore for children. Among topics discussed are the morality of fairy tales, the definition of story, and the theme of time travel

Includes bibliographical references

Zbaracki, Matthew D.

Best books for boys; a resource for educators. foreword by Jon Scieszka. Libraries Unlimited 2008 189p il (Children's and young adult literature reference series)

Grades: Adult Professional **028.5**

1. Best books 2. Children's literature 3. Young adult literature 4. Reading interests 5. Boys -- Books and reading 6. Boys 7. Children's literature -- Book lists 8. Children's literature -- Bibliography 9. Young adult literature -- Bibliography

ISBN 1-59158-599-6; 978-1-59158-599-2

LC 2007-51065

"Good source notes guide readers to additional writings on the topic and speak to the author's significant research in his field. Nicely indexed by author, title, and subject, this [is an] easy-to-navigate resource." Voice Youth Advocates

Includes bibliographical references

Zvirin, Stephanie

Read with me; best books for preschoolers. Stephanie Zvirin. Huron Street Press 2012 171 p. (pbk.) $18.95

Grades: Adult Professional **028.5**

1. Reading readiness 2. Children -- Books and reading 3. Best books -- United States 4. Reading -- Parent participation 5.

Libraries and preschool children
ISBN 193758903X; 9781937589035; 9781937589066;
9781937589073

LC 2012002405

This book, by Stephanie Zvirin, "offers more than 300 age-appropri-ate and subject-specific book selections from librarians for reading time with children. From board and picture books to hot new books, these recommendations reflect family, community, play, and the environment. Chapters include segments on reading together, friendship, places near and far, and making believe." (Publisher's note)

Includes bibliographical references and index

028.7   Use of books and other information media as sources of information

Callison, Daniel

★ The **blue** book on information age inquiry, instruction and literacy; [by] Daniel Callison and Leslie Preddy. Libraries Unlimited 2006
643p il pa $45
Grades: Adult Professional   **028.7**
  1. Information literacy
  ISBN 978-1-59158-325-7; 1-59158-325-X

LC 2006-23645

A revised edition of Key Words, Concepts and Methods for Informa-tion Age Instruction, published 2003 by LMS Associates

"Part 1 introduces the concepts of information inquiry, providing foundational documents and exploring search and use models, informa-tion literacy, standards, the instructional role of library media special-ists, online inquiry learning, and resource management. Part 2 offers concrete examples of inquiry applied to the middle-school student re-search process and supplies reproducible pages for classroom use. Part 3 discusses and defines 51 key terms. Entries here are several pages in length and include citations and references. Indispensable for all school media specialists, this book will also appeal to other readers, who will be impressed by its well-organized design, thoroughness, and practical-ity." Booklist

Includes bibliographical references

030   General encyclopedic works

Anderson, Jennifer Joline

Wikipedia; the company and its founders. ABDO Pub. Co. 2011
112p il (Technology pioneers) lib bdg $34.22
Grades: 5 6 7 8   **030**
  1. Electronic encyclopedias 2. Wikis (Computer science) 3. Wikimedia Foundation
  ISBN 978-1-61714-812-5 lib bdg; 1-61714-812-1 lib bdg; 978-1-61758-970-6 e-book

LC 2010037886

This is an introduction to Wikipedia and its founders.

"Written in a clear, linear fashion, this series offers vivid, well-re-searched details about the development of technological advancements considered essential in today's society. . . . Readers who are interested in technology and inventions will be thoroughly engrossed." SLJ

Includes glossary and bibliographical references

031   General encyclopedic works in specific languages and language families

DK Publishing, Inc.

DK children's illustrated encyclopedia; 7th ed.; DK Pub. 2010
600p il map $34.99
Grades: 4 5 6 7   **031**
  1. Encyclopedias and dictionaries
  ISBN 978-0-7566-5759-8; 0-7566-5759-8

LC 2010279636

First published 1991 with title: Random House children's encyclo-pedia; a revised edition of Dorling Kindersley's children's illustrated encyclopedia 6th ed. published 2006

A highly illustrated one-volume encyclopedia containing entries ranging from Abolitionist movement to Zoos.

"This handsome revision features more than 3000 photographs, maps, time lines, and illustrations. . . . The attractive format encourages browsing." SLJ

Guinness world records 2015; by Guinness World Records. St. Mar-tin's Press 2014 255 p. ill. (some col.) $28.95
Grades: 3 4 5 6 7 8 9 10 11 12 Adult   **031**
  1. World records 2. World records -- Periodicals 3. Curiosities and wonders -- Periodicals
  ISBN 1908843632; 9781908843630
  Published annually

This 2015 edition of the Guinness World Records book "presents thousands of new and updated records. . . . [It] showcases the very best of the most recent world records, with new subjects as diverse as castles, 3D printing, the search for alien life and the latest developments in AI and robotics. Plus, the Flashback features offer a look back at the ar-chives to bring you the best of the classic and iconic records from the past 60 years." (Publisher's note)

The **Kingfisher** children's encyclopedia. Kingfisher 2012 480 p. (hardcover) $29.99
Grades: 3 4 5 6 7 8   **031**
  1. Picture books for children 2. Encyclopedias and dictionaries
  ISBN 075346814X; 9780753468142

The entries in this updated children's encyclopedia "range from one to four pages in length each, feature full-color illustrations and photos and subheadings in a large, easy-to-read font and sidebars and fact box-es of thought-provoking information." Topics include "continents and countries, technology, transportation, animal and plant life, religion, and space." (School Library Journal)

Knowledge Encyclopedia. Dk Pub 2013 360 p. $29.99
Grades: 4 5 6 7 8   **031**
  1. Encyclopedias and dictionaries
  ISBN 1465414177; 9781465414175

This book, by the Smithsonian Institution, is a "family reference us-ing 3-D rendered images to explore the wonders of the world . . . Di-vided into six chapters . . . a wide range of topics come to life. Illustrated with fascinating facts, maps, timelines, and graphics, the Knowledge Encyclopedia makes complex subjects easy to understand and is the per-fect resource for kids, whether to help with homework or to pique their curiosity." (Publisher's note)

Turner, Tracey

World of the weird. Firefly Books 2009 144p il $14.95
Grades: 5 6 7 8   **031**
  1. Curiosities and wonders
  ISBN 978-1-55407-481-5; 1-55407-481-9

"A first-rate browsing item, from the bicycle-riding frog on the front cover to the recipe for chocolate-covered crickets at the end. . . . Turner presents barrages of snippets on extreme sports ('chessboxing'), uncommon maladies ('exploding head syndrome'), oddball festivals, bizarre beliefs ('Eating stolen bacon is a cure for constipation.' Do tell!), strange creatures real or otherwise, supernatural phenomena and . . . more. . . . Illustrated with photos that are often startling but never gory or gross, this compact page-turner will light up the imaginations of motivated young readers and jaded nonreaders alike." Kirkus

Wilkes, Angela

My world of discovery. Kingfisher 2007 192p il $14.95

Grades: 3 4 5 6 **031**

1. Reference books 2. Encyclopedias and dictionaries

ISBN 0-7534-5931-0

This "is an excellent resource for a young person developing an interest in a diverse number of science topics. Many colorful, clear illustrations accompany the text. . . . The text is easy to read and follow." Sci Books Films

The **World** Book Encyclopedia. World Book, Inc 22 v col ill, col maps

Grades: 4 5 6 7 8 9 10 11 12 Adult **031**

1. Reference books 2. Encyclopedias and dictionaries

New editions published yearly; revised frequently

"A 22-volume, highly illustrated, A-Z general encyclopedia for all ages, featuring sections on how to use World Book, other research aids, pronunciation key, a student guide to better writing, speaking, and research skills, and comprehensive index." (Publisher's note)

031.02   Books of miscellaneous facts

Aronson, Marc

For boys only; the biggest, baddest book ever. [by] Marc Aronson [and] H.P. Newquist. Feiwel and Friends 2007 157p il map $14.95

Grades: 4 5 6 7 **031.02**

1. Boys 2. Curiosities and wonders

ISBN 978-0-312-37706-9; 0-312-37706-1

LC 2007-32847

"In a tone both light and humorous, Newquist and Aronson aim to please by assembling a tantalizing miscellany—codes, puzzles, best lists, brief history and science facts, instructions for making fake blood and playing Ultimate Frisbee. . . . This offers lots of good fun." Booklist

Farndon, John

Do not open; written by John Farndon. DK Publishing 2007 256p il $24.99

Grades: 4 5 6 7 **031.02**

1. Curiosities and wonders

ISBN 978-0-7566-3205-2; 0-7566-3205-6

LC 2007300131

This encyclopedic tome catalogues "the mysterious and unusual. . . . Flaps, foldout pages and varied styles of illustration—from photomontage to digital cartoons and more conventional line art—keep the book visually fresh and ably complement the subject matter. . . . Taking in everything from weird weather like St. Elmo's fire and raining frogs to possible locations of Atlantis, the book incites curiosity—and expansively rewards it." Publ Wkly

Iggulden, Conn

The **dangerous** book for boys; [by] Conn Iggulden, Hal Iggulden. Collins 2007 270p il map $24.95

Grades: 4 5 6 7 **031.02**

1. Boys 2. Amusements 3. Recreation 4. Curiosities and wonders

ISBN 0-06-124358-2; 978-0-06-124358-5

LC 2006-491918

"This eclectic collection addresses the undeniable boy-appeal of certain facts and activities. Dozens of short chapters, in fairly random order, cover a wide range of topics in conversational prose. Simple instructions for coin tricks and paper airplanes alternate with excerpts from history such as Famous Battles and facts about ancient wonders of the world and astronomy. . . . Tongue-in-cheek humor emerges throughout." SLJ

Masoff, Joy

Oh, yuck! the encyclopedia of everything nasty. illustrated by Terry Sirrell. Workman 2000 212p il pa $14.95

Grades: 4 5 6 7 **031.02**

1. Curiosities and wonders

ISBN 0-7611-0771-1

LC 99-43603

An alphabetical collection of articles about disgusting things, from acne, ants, and bacteria to worms, x-periments, and zits

"Amusing cartoons and well-chosen, black-and-white photographs with humorous captions support the text. . . . This delightful volume will be enjoyed by fans of grossness everywhere." SLJ

Includes bibliographical references

Mills, Andrea

Strange but true! DK Publishing. DK Publishing 2015 192 p. illustrations, map $19.99

Grades: 4 5 6 7 **031.02**

1. Animals 2. Curiosities and wonders

ISBN 1465439110; 9781465439116

LC 2015487476

This book from DK Publishing is a "collection of extreme, unusual, and cryptic animals, places, and phenomena. 'Fast facts' panels on each spread provide background to the main subject or details of related cases in a stripped-down and engaging style, while the infographic spreads in each section offer even more weird facts and stories while debunking popular strange-but-untrue myths." (Publisher's note)

"Full-bleed photographs dominate the layout: up-close images provide intimate views of unusual creatures like the Satanic leaf-tailed gecko, which camouflages itself as a rotting leaf, while small sidebars augment the 70+ entries with information about the greenhouse effect, the reflexes of carnivorous plants, and more." Pub Wkly

Murrie, Steve

While You Were Sleeping; Fun Facts That Happen at Night. by Steve Murrie and Matthew Murrie; illustrated by Tom Bloom. Turtleback Books 2012 224 p. col. ill. (paperback) $9.99; (prebind) $20.85

Grades: 2 3 4 **031.02**

1. Night 2. Sleep

ISBN 0545430283; 0606267468; 9780545430289; 9780606267465

This book "provides general observations about internal biological processes associated with sleep, nocturnal animals, nighttime jobs, and wee-hours activities--interleaved with mini-disquisitions on earthquakes, Mount Rushmore, bamboo, comets, space probes, the largest Lego tower every constructed, and an array of other subjects." (Booklist)

Ripley, Catherine

How? the most awesome question and answer book about nature, animals, people, places, and you! by Catherine Ripley; illustrated by Scot Ritchie. Owlkids Books 2012 192 p. col. ill. (hardcover) $19.95

Grades: 1 2 3 **031.02**

1. Shells 2. Hamsters 3. Questions and answers 4. Children's

questions and answers
ISBN 1926973240; 9781926973241

LC 2012405052

Author Catherine Ripley uses humor to answer questions about how everyday subjects work for children. In "question-and-answer format, . . . [the questions] include how batter turns into cake and how birthday candles stay on fire, why hamsters run on wheels and why they stuff their cheeks with food, why you hear the sea in a seashell and why the ocean is salty." (Kirkus Reviews)

Shields, Amy
    Little kids first big book of why. National Geographic 2011 127p (National geographic little kids) $14.95
Grades: K 1 2 3   **031.02**
    1. Science   2. Curiosities and wonders
ISBN 978-1-4263-0793-5; 1-4263-0793-4

"Young readers will find clear answers to a variety of basic science, nature, technology, and human body questions in this random but potentially useful volume. . . . Crisp photographs illustrate the information, including brief explanations behind everything from curly hair to blue skies to purring cats to why planes fly." Horn Book Guide

Terry, Paul
    Top 10 of Everything 2015; by Paul Terry. Firefly Books Ltd 2014 320 p. ills. (color); portraits $24.95
Grades: 4 5 6 7 8   **031.02**
    1. Almanacs   2. World records
ISBN 177085469X; 9781770854697

This book, by Paul Terry, is "packed with pictures and charts and information. The 2015 edition will be bigger . . . and once again deliver the tallest . . . , scariest . . . , windiest . . . and much more! Packed with unusual comparisons, special features, awe-inspiring photographs and holographic foil histories, engineering feats, and thousands of facts and pictures." (Publisher's note)

"The sheer busyness of the design—there is not one spare micron of space for eyes to rest on—will endear the book to readers with short attention spans, who might just find themselves looking up after an hour has passed, astonished at their absorption. For fans of the form, this compendium has plenty of juice." Kirkus

Winterbottom, Julie
    Frightlopedia; An Encyclopedia of Everything Scary, Creepy, and Spine-Chilling, from Arachnids to Zombies. by Julie Winterbottom, illustrated by Stefano Tambellini. Workman Pub Co 2016 224 p. illustrations (ebook) $9.95; (paperback) $9.95
Grades: 4 5 6   **031.02**
    1. Fear -- Encyclopedias   2. Ghost stories   3. Curiosities and wonders
ISBN 9780761189640; 9780761183792; 0761183795

This children's book by Julie Winterbottom, illustrated by Stefano Tambellini "is an illustrated A-Z collection of some of the world's most frightening places, scariest stories, and gruesomest creatures, both real and imagined. Discover Borneo's Gomantong Cave, where literally millions of bats, cockroaches, spiders, and rats coexist. . . . Learn about mythical creatures like the Mongolian Death Worm--and scarily real ones like killer bees." (Publisher's note)

"A prime source of thrills and chills, equally suitable for casual browsing or quick reference." Booklist

Wonders of the world; Barron's 2016 32 p. illustrations (chiefly color) $6.99
Grades: 4 5 6 7   **031.02**
    1. Seven Wonders of the World   2. Curiosities and wonders
ISBN 1438008309; 9781438008301

LC 2015956070

In this children's book, by Toby Reynolds and Paul Calver, part of the Visual Explorers series, "learn about the biggest, oldest and most spectacular natural and man-made wonders of our world, including the Great Wall of China, Taj Mahal, Great Barrier Reef, and more. Engaging text, detailed facts, and impressive statistics give children exciting scientific insight into the many wonders of the world." (Publisher's note)

"Inexpensive and relatively sturdy, these large-format paperbacks make for a visually enticing series." Booklist

★ The **World** almanac for kids. World Almanac il maps
Grades: 4 5 6 7   **031.02**
    1. Almanacs   2. Reference books
Annual. First published 1995 for 1996

This volume contains information on animals, art, religion, sports, books, law, language, science and computers. Includes a section of full-color maps and flags. Illustrated throughout with pictures, diagrams, and charts

050   General serial publications

Botzakis, Stergios
    Pretty in print; questioning magazines. by Stergios Botzakis. Fact Finders 2007 32p il (Media literacy) lib bdg $22.60; pa $7.95
Grades: 4 5 6 7   **050**
    1. Periodicals   2. Publishers and publishing
ISBN 978-0-7368-6764-1 lib bdg; 0-7368-6764-3 lib bdg; 978-0-7368-7860-9 pa; 0-7368-7860-2 pa

LC 2006021443

This is "written in a breezy style and [has] plenty of popping colors and photos. . . . Useful and attractive." SLJ
    Includes bibliographical references

051   General serial publications in specific languages and language families

Hopkins, Lee Bennett
    ★ **Days** to celebrate; a full year of poetry, people, holidays, history, fascinating facts, and more. written and edited by Lee Bennett Hopkins; illustrated by Stephen Alcorn. Greenwillow Books 2005 112p il $17.99; lib bdg $18.89
Grades: 3 4 5   **051**
    1. Almanacs   2. Holidays   3. Reference books   4. Poetry -- Collections
ISBN 0-06-000765-6; 0-06-000766-4 lib bdg

LC 2003-49288

"The writers represented include Robert Frost, Langston Hughes, Richard Wilbur, and Gwendolyn Brooks. Alcorn's large, vibrant, whimsical artwork perfectly enhances the prose and verse to make this book a delight to the eye and the ear." SLJ

069   Museology (Museum science)

Korrell, Emily B.

Awesome adventures at the Smithsonian; the official kids guide to the Smithsonian Institution. Emily B. Korrell. Smithsonian Books 2013 127 p. ill. (chiefly col.) (paperback) $14.95

Grades: 4 5 6   **069**

1. Museums -- Guidebooks 2. National Air and Space Museum 3. Washington (D.C.) -- Guidebooks 4. National Museum of Natural History (U.S.) 5. National Museum of American History (U.S.) 6. Science museums -- Washington (D.C.) -- Guidebooks

ISBN 1588343499; 9781588343499

LC 2012029119

This "guide offers children ages 8-12 years a way to navigate the Smithsonian. Engaging maps, photographs, and illustrations present the main museum halls along with puzzles, games, mad libs, and pages for journal entries, drawings, and superlatives that will help get kids ready for their big trip to the nation's capital and keep them focused and attentive as they navigate the world's largest museum complex that is the Smithsonian Institution." (Publisher's note)

Mark, Jan

The **museum** book; a guide to strange and wonderful collections. written by Jan Mark; illustrated by Richard Holland. Candlewick Press 2007 54p il $15

Grades: 3 4 5 6   **069**

1. Museums

ISBN 978-0-7636-3370-7; 0-7636-3370-4

LC 2006-49055

Explains what a museum is, and what fascinating things you might find there.

This "tome will launch readers on a leisurely and edifying journey of discovery.... Holland ... jolts readers ... with his mixed-media collages, which sparingly employ color and liberally combine to look like Victorian engravings, pencil sketches, Gorey-like figures, and photos of various locales." Publ Wkly

070.4   Journalism

Mahoney, Ellen

Nellie Bly and investigative journalism for kids; mighty muckrakers from the golden age to today, with 21 activities. Ellen Mahoney. Chicago Review Press, Incorporated 2015 144 p. illustrations (trade paper) $16.95

Grades: 4 5 6   **070.4**

1. Journalism 2. Reporters and reporting 3. Investigative reporting

ISBN 161374997X; 9781613749975

LC 2014037538

In this children's book by Ellen Mahoney "budding reporters learn about the major figures of the muckraking era: the bold and audacious Bly, one of the most famous women in the world in her day; social reformer and photojournalist Jacob Riis; monopoly buster Ida Tarbell; antilynching crusader Ida B. Wells; and Upton Sinclair." (Publisher's note)

"With comprehensive back matter and plenty of sources for further exploration, this title is tailor-made for classroom use, though individuals will likely find it appealing as well. Pair with Sue Macy's Bylines: A Photobiography of Nellie Bly (2009) for an in-depth look at the pioneering journalist." Booklist

Includes bibliographical references and index

070.5   Publishing

Donovan, Sandra, 1967-

★ **Pingpong** Perry experiences how a book is made; by Sandy Donovan; illustrated by Martin Haake. Picture Window 2010 24p il (In the library) lib bdg $25.32

Grades: 1 2 3   **070.5**

1. Publishers and publishing

ISBN 978-1-4048-5759-9 lib bdg; 1-4048-5759-1 lib bdg

This volume "surprises and amuses with every page, while also neatly explaining the publishing process.... On the first page, Perry (digitally illustrated in an angular, retro-cool style) is clutching his own book: Perry's Practical Guide to the Pizza Picks of Popular Pingpong Players. Donovan then backtracks to relate Perry's meteoric transformation into publishing royalty.... The editing process, complete with a sample of a copyedited page, is admirably realistic, as is the portrayal of the savvy professional women Perry encounters at every turn." Booklist

Neuburger, Emily K.

Golden legacy; how Golden Books won children's hearts, changed publishing forever, and became an American icon along the way. Golden Books 2007 245p il $40

Grades: Adult Professional   **070.5**

1. Publishers and publishing 2. Golden Books Publishing Co. Inc. 3. Children's literature -- History and criticism

ISBN 978-0-375-82996-3; 0-375-82996-2

LC 2006-939312

Presents a history of Golden Books, discussing how it was founded in the midst of World War II providing quality books at inexpensive prices and used innovative writers and marketing techniques to establish itself as a highly successful publishing firm

This is a "lavishly illustrated, handsomely designed volume.... The author unearths some startling facts.... The highly readable narrative is documented with thorough and detailed footnotes.... This winning combination of nostalgia and clear-eyed, meticulously researched history breaks new ground." SLJ

★ **Minders** of make-believe; idealists, entrepreneurs, and the shaping of American children's literature. Houghton Mifflin Co. 2008 402p $28

Grades: Adult Professional   **070.5**

1. Publishers and publishing 2. Children -- Books and reading 3. Children's literature -- History and criticism

ISBN 978-0-395-67407-9; 0-395-67407-7

LC 2008-00589

"Marcus' approach and tone are always, and irresistibly, well informed, sensible, and intelligent.... It is hard to imagine any issue that he has overlooked, and the resulting book is, in word, indispensable." Booklist

Includes bibliographical references

Wickings, Ruth

Pop-up; everything you need to know to create your own pop-up book. paper engineering by Ruth Wickings; illustrated by Frances Castle. Candlewick Press 2010 un il $19.99

Grades: 3 4 5 6   **070.5**

1. Pop-up books

ISBN 978-0-7636-5056-8; 0-7636-5056-0

LC 2010-05488

"First outlining the basic building blocks of pop-up engineering (types of folds, mechanics like noisemakers and spirals), the book then uses the example of a pop-up robot to demonstrate how such components work together. The remaining sections offer four illustrated scenes, into which punch-put elements can be incorporated.... Completing the pop-ups will be tricky for younger readers (the difficulty level increases with each project) but the end result should be as gratifying as it is illuminating." Publ Wkly

081   General collections in specific languages and language families

Hudson, Wade

Powerful words; more than 200 years of extraordinary writing by African Americans. illustrated by Sean Qualls; foreword by Marian Wright Edelman. Scholastic Nonfiction 2004 178p il $19.95

Grades: 5 6 7 8   **081**

1. African Americans -- History 2. African Americans -- Biography 3. American literature -- African American authors

ISBN 0-439-40969-1

LC 2003-42792

A collection of speeches and writings by African Americans, with commentary about the time period in which each person lived, information about the speaker/writer, and public response to the words.

"Short enough to hold attention, the selections . . . are also long enough to show the writers' tone and style. Many sensitive full-page portraits are included. . . . This well-designed volume will be an excellent addition to many library collections." Booklist

Includes bibliographical references

100   PHILOSOPHY

100   Philosophy, parapsychology and occultism, psychology

Law, Stephen

Really, really big questions; about the weird, the wonderful, and everything else. illustrated by Nishant Choksi. Kingfisher 2009 62p il $16.99

Grades: 5 6 7 8   **100**

1. Philosophy

ISBN 978-0-7534-6309-3; 0-7534-6309-1

An introduction to philosophy which uses clear analogies to explore some of life's biggest moral and scientific questions, including the origins of the universe and the meaning of life

"Through a combination of vibrant colors; hip, retro illustrations; and interesting quotes, Law has produced a stimulating work for young minds that is sure to spark conversation and, of course, more questions." SLJ

133.1   Apparitions

Everett, J. H.

Haunted histories; creepy castles, dark dungeons, and powerful palaces. J. H. Everett and Marilyn Scott-Waters. 1st ed. Henry Holt and Company 2012 160 p. (hardcover) $14.99; (paperback) $5.99

Grades: 4 5 6   **133.1**

1. Castles 2. Torture 3. Historic sites 4. Ghosts 5. Haunted places

ISBN 0805089713; 9780805089714; 9781250027269

LC 2011033495

In this book, authors J.H. Everett and Marilyn Scott-Waters focus on "Virgil Dante, youngest Master Ghostorian in London," ghosts, and his raven, Thor, as they "tour history with the assistance of a cursed pocket

watch and look in on castles, dungeons, palaces and graveyards. . . . The usual suspects get the eye: The Tower of London and the Bastille figure prominently, but there are also lesser-known nests of nastiness like Himeji Castle in Japan and Castle Neuschwanstein in Bavaria." (Kirkus Reviews)

Hawes, Jason

Ghost hunt; chilling tales of the unknown. [by] Jason Hawes & Grant Wilson; with Cameron Dokey. Little Brown & Co. 2010 218p il $16.99

Grades: 4 5 6 7 8 9   **133.1**

1. Ghosts

ISBN 978-0-316-09959-2; 0-316-09959-7

"This collection of stories is based on case files from The [Atlantic] Paranormal Society, TAPS, founded by Hawes and Wilson. Each of the eight selections describes the sightings and paranormal activity from the perspective of the observer, then describes how members of TAPS researched, set up equipment, and discovered explanations for what happened. . . . The stories have enough elements of the unknown to make them spine-tingling, but they are more mystery than horror. . . . The easy-to-read format and subject matter will keep even the most reluctant of readers interested." SLJ

Followed by: Ghost hunt 2: more chilling tales of the unknown (2011)

Ghost hunt 2; more chilling tales of the unknown. by Jason Hawes and Grant Wilson; with Cameron Dokey. Little Brown & Co. 2011 297p il $16.99

Grades: 4 5 6 7 8   **133.1**

1. Ghosts

ISBN 978-0-316-09958-5; 0-316-09958-9

"From ghostly spirits roaming Alcatraz to glowing red eyes in the woods, The Atlantic Paranormal Society (aka the popular reality television series Ghost Hunters) is back with a compilation of even more chilling and terrifying tales. Selections include a restless spirit terrorizing a house-sitting victim through her dreams, ghosts reappearing in the O.K. Corral in Tombstone, AZ, and a saddened ghost revisiting a lighthouse where her family was eradicated long ago." SLJ

133.3   Divinatory arts

Doft, Tony

Nostradamus. Bellwether Media 2011 24p il (Torque: The unexplained) lib bdg $15.95

Grades: 3 4 5 6   **133.3**

1. Physicians 2. Prophecies 3. Astrologers 4. Futurologists

ISBN 978-1-60014-584-1; 1-60014-584-1

LC 2010034777

This considers the life and predictions of Nostradamus, who died in 1566.

"Designed for struggling readers, this . . . combines accessible writing, dynamic illustrations, and [a] high-interest [topic]. [A] snazzy [cover] and an abundance of glossy, full-color illustrations provide appeal. . . . The writing is succinct but informative." SLJ

Includes bibliographical references

133.4   Demonology and witchcraft

Hirschmann, Kris

Demons. ReferencePoint Press 2011 80p il (Monsters and mythical creatures) $26.95

Grades: 5 6 7 8   **133.4**

1. Demonology
ISBN 978-1-60152-147-7; 1-60152-147-2

LC 2010029905

"Beginning with an introduction that explains the origins of the devilish creatures, the book discusses demon-like entities throughout cultures and religions. . . . The book's visuals, which include contemporary photos of ceremonies and artists' rendering of demons, can be quite startling. Excellent sidebars . . . cover topics such as the number of exorcists in the Catholic Church." Booklist

Includes bibliographical references

Jackson, Shirley

The **witchcraft** of Salem Village. Random House 1987 146p hardcover o.p.; pa $5.99

Grades: 4 5 6 7   **133.4**

1. Witchcraft 2. Salem (Mass.) -- History
ISBN 0-394-89176-7 pa

LC 87-4543

A reissue of the title first published 1956

"A simple, chilling account of the witchcraft trials of 1692 and '93 when, because of testimony given by a group of little girls, twenty persons were executed as witches and others died in jail. There is good introductory background and though the story's subject is by nature horrifying the book does not play on the emotions. . . . It presents a difficult theme lucidly and without condescension." Horn Book

Kerns, Ann

Wizards and witches. Lerner Publications 2010 48p il (Fantasy chronicles) lib bdg $27.93

Grades: 4 5 6 7   **133.4**

1. Witches
ISBN 978-0-8225-9983-8 lib bdg; 0-8225-9983-X lib bdg

LC 2008050757

"The explanations and history behind . . . witches [and wizards] . . . will provide satisfaction for readers who want to know more about these familiar characters from myth, fantasy, and folk and fairy tales. Brief and concise." SLJ

Includes bibliographical references

Roach, Marilynne K.

In the days of the Salem witchcraft trials. Houghton Mifflin 1996 92p il map hardcover o.p.; pa $5.95

Grades: 4 5 6 7   **133.4**

1. Witchcraft 2. Salem (Mass.) -- History
ISBN 0-395-69704-2; 0-618-39196-7 pa

LC 94-32383

"After discussing the Salem Witchcraft trials in one short chapter, this attractive volume explores the social history of the times to show the context that made such events possible. Topics include the law and punishment, magic, social status, clothing, food, household goods, occupations, recreation, common activities, government, and the political troubles leading to widespread tension and unrest. Readers will come away with a much fuller picture of who lived in Salem and how they lived. Small ink drawings decorate the pages." Booklist

Includes bibliographical references

133.5   Astrology

Young, Ed

Cat and Rat; the legend of the Chinese zodiac. Holt & Co. 1995 un il $15.95; pa $6.95

Grades: K 1 2 3   **133.5**

1. Zodiac 2. Cats -- Folklore 3. Rats -- Folklore 4. Folklore -- China
ISBN 0-8050-2977-X; 0-8050-6049-9 pa

LC 94-49147

"Young tells the story in lively, spare prose. . . . His charcoal and pastel drawings on dark blue and buff rice paper are elegant and full of action." SLJ

152.1   Sensory perception

Cobb, Vicki

How to really fool yourself; illusions for all your senses. illustrated by Jessica Wolk-Stanley. Wiley 1999 120p il pa $12.95

Grades: 5 6 7 8   **152.1**

1. Perception 2. Optical illusions 3. Senses and sensation
ISBN 0-471-31592-3

LC 98-27723

A newly illustrated edition of the title first published 1981 by Lippincott

"The book begins with an explanation of perception and explores many different sensory aspects of it through experiments, definitions of important terms (italicized), background information and how illusions affect us in everyday life." SLJ

152.14   Visual perception

Banyai, Istvan

Zoom. Viking 1995 un il $16.99; pa $6.99

Grades: K 1 2 3   **152.14**

1. Stories without words
ISBN 0-670-85804-8; 0-14-055774-1 pa

LC 94-33181

A wordless picture book presents a series of scenes, each one from farther away, showing, for example, a girl playing with toys which is actually a picture on a magazine cover, which is part of a sign on a bus, and so on

"If the concept is not wholly new, the execution is superior. Readers are in for a perpetually surprising—and even philosophical—adventure." Publ Wkly

Brocket, Jane

Spotty, stripy, swirly; what are patterns? [written and photographed by Jane Brocket] Millbrook Press 2012 31 p. (Jane brocket's clever concepts)

Grades: PreK K 1 2   **152.14**

1. Color 2. Pattern perception
ISBN 9780761346135

LC 2011022179

This illustrated children's book, a part of Jane Brocket's Clever Concepts Series, "examines patterns from almost every conceivable angle. There are patterns determined sometimes by shape, sometimes by color, sometimes by object. They run the gamut from simple to quite complex. There are man-made patterns such as brickwork or quilts, and patterns that occur in nature, such as geranium leaves." (School Libr J) "[Brocket's] up-close photos show a wide array of objects with their own distinctive patterns, from fabrics and architectural elements to food and plants. . . . [S]he delves into the reasons for patterns. They help us identify plants, stay organized, decorate and plan, but, most of all, they are pleasing to the eye." (Kirkus)

Includes bibliographical references

Goldstone, Bruce

I see a pattern here; Bruce Goldstone. Henry Holt & Co. (BYR) 2015 32 p. (hardback) $17.99

Grades: 2 3 4 5   **152.14**

1. Pattern perception

ISBN 0805092099; 9780805092097

LC 2014028433

This juvenile book, by Bruce Goldstone, discusses patterns in nature and art. "They can be so beautiful that people come from all over the world to see them, or so familiar you hardly notice them. . . . With stunning photographs that show diverse examples from nature and artwork around the world, Bruce Goldstone reveals the secrets behind patterns--and gives you some fun ideas for making your own." (Publisher's note)

"By pointing out patterns in many disparate things, from honeycombs through beads, tires, and tiles of the Alhambra, Goldstone encourages readers to contemplate the world through an interesting lens. 'MathSpeak' sidebars explain geometric terms, such as reflection for flipping a design. Photos and sharp graphics in bright colors illustrate dozens of patterns that nicely expand the minimal but effective text. Pattern-making ideas are appended." Horn Book

Simon, Seymour

★ Now you see it, now you don't; the amazing world of optical illusions. drawings by Constance Ftera. rev ed; Morrow Junior Bks. 1998 64p il $17.99

Grades: 4 5 6 7   **152.14**

1. Optical illusions

ISBN 0-688-16152-9

LC 97-49855

First published 1976 by FourWinds Press with title: The optical illusion book

The author explains optical illusions involving lines and spaces, changeable figures, depth and distance, brightness and contrast, and color

"One of the clearest and most interesting discussions of optical illusions ever written for children." Booklist

Vry, Silke

Trick of the eye; art and illusion. Prestel 2010 89p il $14.95

Grades: 4 5 6   **152.14**

1. Art appreciation 2. Optical illusions

ISBN 978-3-7913-7026-2; 3-7913-7026-X

"From the Parthenon to the Mona Lisa to the Op-Art of the 1960s, images and text reveal the many ways our eyes play tricks on us. Perception of size and color is discussed using standard optical illusions, but this book includes much more. Anecdotes, such as the story of dueling Greek painters Zeuxis and Parrhasius, and unique reproductions, like portraits with altered facial features, lend excitement. The author has taken an interactive approach, filling the pages with questions, puzzles, and project ideas. . . . Text explains the images, which are large and clear. The broad range of styles represented and the fun of the interactive approach will no doubt appeal to young art lovers and curious kids alike." SLJ

Wick, Walter

★ Walter Wick's optical tricks; by Walter Wick. 10th anniversary edition; Cartwheel Books 2008 43p il $14.99

Grades: 4 5 6 7   **152.14**

1. Optical illusions

ISBN 978-0-439-85520-4; 0-439-85520-9

First published 1998

Presents a series of optical illustions and explains what is seen.

The author "has produced a stunning picture book of optical illusions. With crystal-clear photographs, he creates a series of scenes that fool the eye and the brain." Booklist [review of 1998 ed.]

152.4   Emotions

Aliki

★ Feelings. Greenwillow Bks. 1984 32p il $16; pa $5.95

Grades: K 1 2 3   **152.4**

1. Emotions

ISBN 0-688-03831-X; 0-688-06518-X pa

LC 84-4098

"Small pen-and-ink cartoons with vivid coloring depict boys and girls interacting and experiencing the full range of feelings which evolve in everyday settings. This creative, unique book would be ideal for parent/child interaction or use by elementary teachers in language arts classes. Children will enjoy the comic book 'frame' format." Child Book Rev Serv

Freymann, Saxton

★ How are you peeling? foods with moods. [by] Saxton Freymann and Joost Elffers. Scholastic 1999 un il $16.95; pa $6.99

Grades: PreK K 1 2 3   **152.4**

1. Emotions

ISBN 0-439-10431-9; 0-439-59841-9 pa

LC 99-18162

Brief text and photographs of carvings made from vegetables introduce the world of emotions by presenting leading questions such as "Are you feeling angry?"

"Kids will find the inherent silliness irresistible and be drawn in by the book's visual appeal: the colors are strong, the photography is excellent, and the expressions . . . are surprisingly masterful." Booklist

Graves, Sue

But what if? Sue Graves; illustrated by Desideria Guicciardini. Free Spirit Publishing 2013 25 p. $12.99

Grades: PreK K 1   **152.4**

1. Moving -- Fiction 2. Emotions -- fiction 3. Worry in children

ISBN 1575424444; 9781575424446

LC 2013012337

In this book, by Sue Graves, "Daisy's family is moving, and Daisy is very worried. What if she doesn't like her new home? What if her cat runs away? What if her new teacher isn't nice? A conversation with her grandpa helps Daisy learn that many worries don't come true--and if one does, someone will be there to help her solve the problem." (Publisher's note)

"Books in the Our Emotions and Behavior series offer young children and their caregivers help with hard-to-manage feelings and inappropriate actions...A fictional story portrays a child struggling with a particular emotion. Each story takes the main character through several misdeeds or scenarios, looking at the same theme in slightly different ways... In But What If?, Daisy worries about moving to a new house, neighborhood, and school. Bright but sometimes too intensely colored, the cartoon-style digital illustrations are generally easy to interpret. Advising adults on using the book with children, the final two-page section suggests related activities. These purposeful books will be useful in many libraries." Booklist.

But why can't I? written by Sue Graves; illustrated by Desideria Guicciardini. Free Spirit Pub. 2011 25p il (Our emotions and behavior)

Grades: PreK K 1   **152.4**

1. Etiquette 2. Conduct of life

ISBN 1-57542-376-6; 978-1-57542-376-0

LC 2011001563

This book joins Noah and his babysitter, Jenny, who shows him how rules help keep people safe, healthy, and happy.

"Short sentences and [a] simple [plotline] create [an] excellent [lead-in] to talking about making good decisions what faced with new and difficult emotions. . . . The color cartoon illustrations help make the concepts easy to grasp. . . . Discussion questions are included in the back matter." SLJ

I hate everything! Sue Graves; illustrated by Desideria Guicciardini. Free Spirit Publishing 2013 28 p. (Our emotions and behavior) $12.99
Grades: K 1 2   **152.4**
1. Emotions in children 2. Picture books for children 3. Anger 4. Anger in children
ISBN 1575424436; 9781575424439

LC 2013012336

This book by Sue Graves is part of the Our Emotions and Behavior series, which offers "young children and their caregivers help with hard-to-manage feelings and inappropriate actions. . . . A fictional story portrays a child struggling with a particular emotion. Each story takes the main character through several misdeeds or scenarios, looking at the same theme in slightly different ways." Here, "Sam has difficulty controlling his anger . . . but Aunt Meg's suggestions give him some tools to try." (Booklist)

I'm not happy; written by Sue Graves; illustrated by Desideria Guicciardini. Free Spirit Pub. 2011 25p il (Our emotions and behavior)
Grades: PreK K 1   **152.4**
1. Kindness 2. Happiness
ISBN 1-57542-373-1; 978-1-57542-373-9

LC 2011001565

Ben helps cheer up his friends and shows how kids can turn sadness into smiles.

"Short sentences and [a] simple [plotline] create [an] excellent [lead-in] to talking about making good decisions when faced with difficult emotions. . . . The color cartoon illustrations help make the concepts easy to grasp. . . . Discussion questions are included in the back matter." SLJ

Not fair, won't share; written by Sue Graves; illustrated by Desideria Guicciardini. Free Spirit Pub. 2011 25p il (Our emotions and behavior)
Grades: PreK K 1   **152.4**
1. Conduct of life 2. Interpersonal relations
ISBN 1-57542-375-8; 978-1-57542-375-3

LC 2011001566

When Nora, Dan, and Henry have trouble sharing at school, they all end up feeling mad. With the help of their teacher, the friends learn that when kids get frustrated, there are ways to calm down, share, and play fairly.

"Short sentences and [a] simple [plotline] create [an] excellent [lead-in] to talking about making good decisions when faced with difficult emotions. . . . The color cartoon illustrations help make the concepts easy to grasp. . . . Discussion questions are included in the back matter." SLJ

Take a deep breath; by Sue Graves; illustrated by Desideria Guicciardini. Free Spirit Publishing 2013 28 p. (Our emotions and behavior) $12.99
Grades: PreK K 1   **152.4**
1. Fear in children 2. Friendship -- fiction 3. Fear in children
ISBN 1575424460; 9781575424460

LC 2013012339

In this book by Sue Graves, "Lucy is afraid of dogs, Josh doesn't like to go in the pool, Dan doesn't want the nurse to touch his bruised

knee, and Ben is afraid to go on stage in front of people. Follow along as these friends learn that when something scares them, they can take a deep breath and feel brave enough to get through their ordeals." (Publisher's note)

Who feels scared? written by Sue Graves; illustrated by Desideria Guicciardini. Free Spirit Pub. 2011 25p il (Our emotions and behavior) $12.99
Grades: PreK K 1   **152.4**
1. Fear
ISBN 978-1-57542-374-6; 1-57542-374-X

LC 2011001626

Everybody feels afraid sometimes—like Jack and his friends Ravi and Kevin when they have a sleepover. This book shows children that they can cope with their fears and be brave.

"Short sentences and [a] simple [plotline] create [an] excellent [lead-in] to talking about making good decisions when faced with new and difficult emotions. . . . The color cartoon illustrations help make the concepts easy to grasp. . . . Discussion questions are included in the back matter." SLJ

153.4   Thought, thinking, reasoning, intuition, value, judgment

Kelsey, Elin
Wild ideas; Elin Kelsey; illustrated by Soyeon Kim. Owlkids Books, Inc. 2015 32 p. color illustrations $18.95
Grades: K 1 2 3 4 5   **153.4**
1. Animal behavior 2. Problem solving
ISBN 1771470623; 9781771470629

LC 2014947497

This picture book by Elin Kelsey, illustrated by Soyeon Kim, "looks deep into the forests, skies and oceans to explore how animals solve problems. Whether it's weaving a safe place to rest and reflect, blowing a fine net of bubbles to trap fish, or leaping boldly into a new situation, the animals featured (including the orangutan, humpback whale and gibbon) can teach us a lot about creative problem solving tools and strategies." (Publisher's note)

"Finding solutions to sticky problems can be a mind-expanding adventure. The creative team behind You Are Stardust (2012) again blends science with a philosophical spark that demands thoughtful inquiry. Employing well-researched facts, Kelsey focuses on the rather remarkable adaptations and achievements of animals. . . . This is a work that will be read and examined again and again, with something new to be discovered at every turn. Profound and entirely wonderful." Kirkus

Watanabe, Ken
No problem! an easy guide to getting what you want. illustrated by Elwood H. Smith; adapted by Sarah L. Thomson. Viking 2010 70p il $16.99; pa $9.99
Grades: 4 5 6   **153.4**
1. Problem solving
ISBN 978-0-670-01203-9; 0-670-01203-3; 978-0-670-01254-1 pa; 0-670-01254-8 pa
Adaptation of: Problem solving 101, published 2009 for adults

"This little gem explains how to approach intimidating goals or jobs by breaking them down into simple tasks. Realistic scenarios such as finding money for a big purchase or choosing a high school are approached with data-driven evaluation tools. The author defines the steps involved along with terms such as hypotheses, logic trees, matrixes, and evaluation charts." SLJ

153.6 Communication

Jackson, Donna M.

★ **Every** body's talking; what we say without words. by Donna M. Jackson. Twenty-First Century Books 2014 64 p. illustrations (lib. bdg. : alk. paper) $30.60

Grades: 5 6 7 8 9   **153.6**

1. Body language 2. Nonverbal communication 3. Body language

ISBN 1467708585; 9781467708586

LC 2013019674

This book, by Donna M. Jackson, "explores the complexities of body language. Discover what is really being expressed when people stand, sit, or move in certain ways and learn how you can use your body and facial expressions to communicate more effectively in a variety of situations." (Publisher's note)

"Nonverbal clues including stance, facial expression, posture, eye contact, and others add meaning to our words, or sometimes contradict them. Using second-person narration to engage readers, suggestions for interpreting body language is followed by a chapter explaining how cultural differences affect interpretations. A final chapter encourages readers to practice physical positions to increase confidence. Plentiful full-color pictures illustrate concepts." Horn Book

Includes bibliographical references and index

153.7 Perceptual processes

Hillman, Ben

How big is it? a big book all about bigness. Scholastic 2007 47p il $14.99

Grades: 3 4 5   **153.7**

1. Size

ISBN 0-439-91808-1; 978-0-439-91808-4

LC 2006050609

"This oversize picture book . . . presents 22 giant creatures, objects, and plants, prehistoric and contemporary. On each double-page spread there is a panel of chatty information next to a huge, unframed color picture, which uses digitally blended images to show comparative size. . . . These clear, astonishing pictures [are] both a magnet to browsers as well as a device to demonstrate gradations of bigness." Booklist

Miller, Margaret

★ **Big** and little. Greenwillow Bks. 1998 un il $15.99

Grades: PreK   **153.7**

1. Size

ISBN 0-688-14748-8

LC 97-17242

Photographs and easy text introduce the concepts of size and opposites

"This book uses cheerful, clear color photos of active toddlers to teach basic concepts." Booklist

155.45 Exceptional children; children by social and economic levels, by ethnic or national group

Fonseca, Christine

101 success secrets for gifted kids; the ultimate guide. Prufrock Press 2011 xi, 191p pa $14.95

Grades: 4 5 6 7 8   **155.45**

1. Gifted children

ISBN 978-1-59363-544-2; 1-59363-544-3

LC 2011004912

"Fonseca explains what it means to be labeled 'gifted,' how to cope in school, and how to interact with friends and family. Information is delivered in a friendly, conversational manner with firsthand advice from gifted kids and their parents. The myriad tips include how to deal with stress, how to complete homework assignments effectively, how to be respectful of others, how to accept oneself, and even how to deal with bullies. All are incredibly useful." SLJ

Includes bibliographical references

Gerstein, Mordicai

★ **The wild** boy; based on the true story of the Wild Boy of Aveyron. Foster Bks. 1998 39p il hardcover o.p. pa $6.95

Grades: K 1 2 3   **155.45**

1. Wild children

ISBN 0-374-38431-2; 0-374-48396-5 pa

LC 97-37246

Relates the story of a boy who grew up wild in the forests of France and was captured in 1800, studied and cared for and named Victor, but who never learned to speak

"Gerstein's prose finds power in its simplicity and emotional resonance in its declarative understatement. . . . The narrative strength and energy of the illustrations expand the inherent drama of Victor's situation. Together, Gerstein's text and pictures work to create an unforgettable story." Booklist

155.9 Environmental psychology

Brown, Laurene Krasny

When dinosaurs die; a guide to understanding death. [by] Laurie Krasny Brown and Marc Brown. Little, Brown 1996 32p il hardcover o.p. pa $5.95

Grades: K 1 2 3   **155.9**

1. Death 2. Bereavement

ISBN 0-316-10917-7; 0-316-11955-5 pa

LC 95-14511

"The text explains the inevitability of death, various reasons for death (including old age, sickness, accident, and suicide), and the difference between death and sleep; it then goes on to examine feelings about death and ways, both individual and cultural, of dealing with the loss of loved ones. . . . The simple watercolor illustrations help to make some scary situations more approachable. Quiet, respectful, and unthreatening, this will probably become a primary-grades standard on the subject." Bull Cent Child Books

Includes glossary

Krementz, Jill

How it feels when a parent dies. Knopf 1981 110p il hardcover o.p. pa $16

Grades: 4 5 6 7   **155.9**

1. Death 2. Bereavement

ISBN 0-394-75854-4 pa

LC 80-8808

This book is "a hopeful tribute to the healing power sustained by young survivors, who are competently interviewed and photographed in their widely varied reactions and situations. The subjects range in age from 7 to 16 and cope with a variety of deaths by suicide, accident, and illness. Adults helping children through a hard time will better understand their charges' problems through the honest opinions expressed here, and young readers might feel less alone." Booklist

Murphy, Patricia J.

Death; [by] Patricia J. Murphy. Heinemann Library 2008 32p il (Tough topics) lib bdg $25.36; pa $7.99

Grades: PreK K 1 2 3 **155.9**
1. Death 2. Bereavement
ISBN 978-1-4034-9778-9 lib bdg; 978-1-4034-9783-3 pa

LC 2007007230

The author "discusses what death is, how it can happen, how it affects people, funerals and memories, and different ways of coping with such loss.... The two-page chapters include full-color photos and two paragraphs of text that are frank yet sensitive in their approach." SLJ

Includes glossary and bibliographical references

Raschka, Christopher
The **purple** balloon; [by] Chris Raschka. Schwartz & Wade Books 2007 un il $16.99; lib bdg $19.99
Grades: PreK K 1 2 **155.9**
1. Death 2. Terminally ill
ISBN 978-0-375-84146-0; 0-375-84146-6; 978-0-375-94259-4 lib bdg; 0-375-94259-9 lib bdg

LC 2006-23725

"Dying is the subject of this sensitive and somber book intended for terminally ill children and their families and friends.... The focus is first on how support from those around us can help 'make dying not so hard' for an older person. The same case is then made for a child who faces death.... The illustrations are appropriately subdued, with balloons as the characters, all of them given loving and supportive faces and postures.... The book ends with suggestions on how to help a friend who is terminally ill." Booklist

Simons, Rae
Survival skills; how to handle life's catastrophes. Mason Crest Publishers 2009 128p il (Survivors: ordinary people, extraordinary circumstances) lib bdg $24.95
Grades: 5 6 7 8 **155.9**
1. Life skills 2. Survival skills
ISBN 978-1-4222-0456-6 lib bdg; 1-4222-0456-1 lib bdg

LC 2008-50320

"Begins with a brief and accessible discussion of the psychology of stress and its role in adolescence, and offers twelve pieces of advice for overcoming difficult experiences and catastrophes.... [This book features] important, and sometimes complex, information in an easy-to-read format, offering high gloss photographs, marginal glossary notes, concept definitions, a bibliography, and further reading reccommendations." Voice Youth Advocates

Includes glossary and bibliographical references

158 Applied psychology

Andrews, Linda Wasmer
Meditation; [by] Linda Wasmer Andrews. F. Watts 2004 79p (Life balance) $19.50; pa $6.95
Grades: 5 6 7 8 **158**
1. Meditation
ISBN 0-531-12219-0; 0-531-16609-0 pa

LC 2003-7153

"Andrews emphasizes that meditation is not a flaky practice, or a particularly religious one, but one that's designed to reduce stress and help individuals manage their lives. Four chapters explain the why and how of meditating.... [This offers] solid, easy-to-understand information" SLJ

Includes bibliographical references

Burstein, John
I said no! refusal skills. Crabtree Pub. Co. 2010 32p il (Slim Goodbody's life skills 101) lib bdg $26.60; pa $8.95

Grades: 1 2 3 4 5 **158**
1. Peer pressure 2. Decision making 3. Risk-taking (Psychology)
ISBN 978-0-7787-4789-5 lib bdg; 0-7787-4789-1 lib bdg; 978-0-7787-4805-2 pa; 0-7787-4805-7 pa

LC 2009022850

In this book children are taught to understand when and why they need to say "no," and how to refuse and still keep their friends

This book offers "clear and simple advice for children and [provides] adults with springboards for discussion and role-playing. [It has] appealing color photographs of a variety of types of kids, ... opening scenarios, concrete coping suggestions, and solid reasoning." SLJ

Includes bibliographical references

Crist, James J.
What to do when you're sad & lonely; a guide for kids. [by] James J. Crist. Free Spirit Pub. 2006 124p il pa $9.95
Grades: 4 5 6 7 **158**
1. Solitude 2. Depression (Psychology)
ISBN 978-1-57542-189-6 pa; 1-57542-189-5 pa

LC 2005021794

"Advising his audience to read this book and work through negative feelings with an adult, Crist describes sad and lonely feelings, distinguishes them from more serious conditions such as depression, and then suggests 'Blues Busters' and ways to ask for help.... Crist's clear explanations and simple techniques ... are relevant for both children and adults." Voice Youth Advocates

Includes bibliographical references

What to do when you're scared & worried; a guide for kids. [by] James Crist. Free Spirit Pub. 2004 128p il pa $9.95
Grades: 4 5 6 7 **158**
1. Fear 2. Worry
ISBN 1-57542-153-4

"Part one deals with normal anxiety, offering detailed steps for developing 10 coping mechanisms. Expert help is needed to deal with the more serious problems discussed in Part two (e.g., phobias, separation anxiety, obsessive-compulsive disorder). Throughout, the author provides information, case histories, and coping skills in a manner that is both reassuring and encouraging.... Illustrations lighten the tone of the subject matter." SLJ

Includes bibliographical references

Fox, Annie
Real friends vs. the other kind. Free Spirit Pub. 2009 90p il
Grades: 5 6 7 8 **158**
1. Friendship 2. Interpersonal relations
ISBN 1-57542-319-7 pa; 978-1-57542-319-7 pa

LC 2008031368

"Jack, Abby, Mateo, Jen, Chris, and Michelle are the middle school students of various ethnicities who take readers through this slim, interactive guide. Chapters cover such topics as friendship dilemmas, so-called friends, when friendships aren't working, crushes, and making new friends. Each chapter opens with a scene played out by the students in cartoon panels. Next, bits of text, along with a multitude of side boxes, address the topic at hand.... Lists of questions are offered, along with the answers. There's a lot packed into this colorful title that falls somewhere between self-help and peer advice." SLJ

McIntyre, Thomas
The **behavior** survival guide for kids; how to make good choices and stay out of trouble. [by] Thomas McIntyre. Free Spirit Pub. 2003 167p pa $14.95

Grades: 5 6 7 8 **158**
1. Conduct of life 2. Interpersonal relations
ISBN 1-57542-132-1

LC 2003-4565

"The author provides skills and activities to learn and practice so that new behaviors can replace those that have resulted in getting students into trouble. . . . Those motivated to make better choices for how they behave in school or with friends and family will find much to help them." Voice Youth Advocates

Moss, Wendy
Being me; a kid's guide to boosting confidence and self-esteem. by Wendy L. Moss. Magination Press 2010 112p il $14.95; pa $9.95
Grades: 5 6 7 8 **158**
1. Self-esteem 2. Self-confidence
ISBN 978-1-4338-0883-8; 1-4338-0883-8; 978-1-4338-0884-5 pa; 1-4338-0884-6 pa

LC 2010014384

"Moss encourages her young audience to concentrate on two areas: focusing on inner self-esteem and building social confidence. Through procedure and practice . . . Moss reminds kids that real confidence doesn't come from being the smartest, prettiest, or the most popular one in the room but from the comfort one has with him- or herself. . . . Moss' offering gives great tips for the truly interested." Booklist

Rogers, Fred
Making friends; photographs by Jim Judkis. Putnam 1987 un il hardcover o.p. pa $6.99
Grades: PreK K 1 **158**
1. Friendship
ISBN 0-698-11409-4 pa

LC 86-12353

"From its opening lines ('When people like each other and like to do things together, they're friends. Can you think of someone who's your friend?'), Rogers's inimitable voice reaches out to his small readers with understanding and reassurance. He describes the pleasures of friendship as well as potential problem areas. . . . Judkis's large color photos capture the range of emotions Rogers writes about." Publ Wkly

Seuss, Dr., 1904-1991
Oh, the places you'll go! Random House 1990 un il $17; lib bdg $20.99
Grades: PreK K 1 2 **158**
1. Stories in rhyme 2. Success
ISBN 0-679-80527-3; 0-679-90527-8 lib bdg

LC 89-36892

The author presents advice on taking the initiative in life and being successful. "Preschool to grade three." (SLJ)

"The combination of the lively text and wacky, offbeat pictures will delight both children and their parents." Child Book Rev Serv

158.2 Interpersonal relations

Brown, Laurene Krasny
How to be a friend; a guide to making friends and keeping them. [by] Laurie Krasny Brown and Marc Brown. Little, Brown 1998 31p il $15.99; pa $6.99
Grades: K 1 2 3 **158.2**
1. Friendship
ISBN 0-316-10913-4; 0-316-11153-8 pa

LC 97-10179

Dinosaur characters illustrate the value of friends, how to make friends, and how to be and not to be a good friend

"Dialogue balloons personalize, enrich, and add humor to the main text. . . . How to Be a Friend will be very useful to parents, teachers, and other caregivers of young children." Horn Book

170 Ethics (Moral philosophy)

MacGregor, Cynthia
Think for yourself; a kid's guide to solving life's dilemmas and other sticky problems. by Cynthia MacGregor; illustrator: Paula Becker. 2nd ed.; Lobster Press 2008 142p il pa $14.95
Grades: 3 4 5 6 **170**
1. Ethics 2. Conduct of life
ISBN 978-1-897073-90-2 pa; 1-897073-90-9 pa
First published 2003

This book "presents 53 real-life dilemmas that 21st century children might face. Topics range from cyberbullying, chat rooms, and online porn to situations with friends, family and adults. . . . Each dilemma is . . . followed by three questions. . . . The questions encourage readers to examine why the predicaments are dilemmas, to analyze possible solutions, and to arrive at acceptable decisions. . . . This indispensible book is recommended for school and public library collections." Libr Media Connect

Parker, Victoria
Making choices; [by] Vic Parker. Heinemann Library 2010 32p il (Exploring citizenship) $25.36; pa $7.99
Grades: 1 2 3 4 **170**
1. Decision making 2. Choice (Psychology)
ISBN 978-1-4329-3317-3; 1-4329-3317-5; 978-1-4329-3325-8 pa; 1-4329-3325-6 pa

LC 2008-55310

This describes the different choices and decisions people have to make every day and why it is important to think for yourself, what to do if you are bullied, and how to make the right choices for your health.

"The text presents a multitude of realistic situations to which young children will relate. There are 'Think About It' fact boxes and checklists that aid in understanding and that will spark discussion. All are filled with captioned, color photographs that relate to the text. The information is relevant and current. . . . Strongly consider this." Libr Media Connect
Includes glossary and bibliographical references

172 Applied ethics

Halperin, Wendy Anderson
Peace; Wendy Anderson Halperin. Atheneum Books for Young Readers 2013 40 p. $16.99
Grades: K 1 2 **172**
1. Picture books for children 2. Peace 3. Taoism 4. Peace (Philosophy)
ISBN 0689825528; 9780689825521; 9781442467873

LC 2012030589

This picture book, by Wendy Anderson Halperin, offers a "compilation of . . . illustrations and wisely chosen words [which] reveals the heart of where peace truly must originate: within ourselves. . . . Intricate artwork, with tiny, precisely rendered details of life across the globe, complements . . . text that includes quotations from famous peacemakers." (Publisher's note)

174   Occupational ethics

Hartman, Eve

Science ethics and controversies; [by] Eve Hartman and Wendy Meshbesher. Raintree 2009 48p il (Sci-hi: life science) $31.43; pa $8.99

Grades: 5 6 7 8   **174**

1. Science -- Ethical aspects
ISBN 978-1-4109-3330-0; 1-4109-3330-X; 978-1-4109-3338-6 pa; 1-4109-3338-5 pa

LC 2009003475

In this introduction to science ethics and controversies "clear language, embedded definitions, and interesting examples illustrate abstract concepts through both text and well-chosen photographs. . . . [It] discusses topics such as global warming and animal research, and their implications for decision-making by scientists, policy makers, and voters. Because so many issues are raised in this book, it will be especially useful as a research starter in both science and social-studies classes. . . . [The] book also includes suggested activities to test ideas as well as a thorough glossary and a Webliography." SLJ

Includes glossary and bibliographical references

175   Ethics of recreation, leisure, public performances, communication

Barraclough, Sue

Fair play. Heinemann Library 2010 32p il (Exploring citizenship) $25.36; pa $7.99

Grades: 1 2 3 4   **175**

1. Respect 2. Sportsmanship
ISBN 978-1-4329-3313-5; 1-4329-3313-2; 978-1-4329-3321-0 pa; 1-4329-3321-3 pa

LC 2008-55301

"The text presents a multitude of realistic situations to which young children will relate. There are 'Think About It' fact boxes and checklists that aid in understanding and that will spark discussion. All are filled with captioned, color photographs that relate to the text. The information is relevant and current. . . . Strongly consider this." Libr Media Connect

Includes glossary and bibliographical references

177   Ethics of social relations

Barraclough, Sue

Sharing. Heinemann Library 2010 32p il (Exploring citizenship) $25.36; pa $7.99

Grades: 1 2 3 4   **177**

1. Kindness 2. Etiquette
ISBN 978-1-4329-3312-8; 1-4329-3312-4; 978-1-4329-3320-3 pa; 1-4329-3320-5 pa

LC 2008-55300

"The text presents a multitude of realistic situations to which young children will relate. There are 'Think About It' fact boxes and checklists that aid in understanding and that will spark discussion. All are filled with captioned, color photographs that relate to the text. The information is relevant and current. . . . Strongly consider this." Libr Media Connect

Includes glossary and bibliographical references

Graves, Sue

I didn't do it; Sue Graves; illustrated by Desideria Guicciardini. Free Spirit Publishing 2013 28 p. (Our emotions and behavior) $12.99

Grades: PreK K 1   **177**

1. Emotions in children 2. Truthfulness and falsehood 3. Truthfulness and falsehood in children
ISBN 1575424452; 9781575424453

LC 2013012340

This book by Sue Graves is part of the Our Emotions and Behavior series, which offers "young children and their caregivers help with hard-to-manage feelings and inappropriate actions. . . . A fictional story portrays a child struggling with a particular emotion. Each story takes the main character through several misdeeds or scenarios, looking at the same theme in slightly different ways." This entry looks at lying. (Booklist)

Parker, Victoria

Good relationships. Heinemann Library 2008 32p il (Exploring citizenship) $25.36; pa $7.99

Grades: 1 2 3 4   **177**

1. Interpersonal relations
ISBN 978-1-4329-3316-6; 1-4329-3316-7; 978-1-4329-3324-1 pa; 1-4329-3324-8 pa

LC 2008-55306

This describes how important it is to get along with the people around us and what can happen when people do not try to listen to or understand each other.

"The text presents a multitude of realistic situations to which young children will relate. There are 'Think About It' fact boxes and checklists that aid in understanding and that will spark discussion. All are filled with captioned, color photographs that relate to the text. The information is relevant and current. . . . Strongly consider this." Libr Media Connect

Includes glossary and bibliographical references

Pryor, Kimberley Jane

Cooperation; by Kimberley Jane Pryor. Marshall Cavendish Benchmark 2008 32p il (Values) lib bdg $19.95

Grades: 1 2 3   **177**

1. Cooperation 2. Conduct of life
ISBN 978-0-7614-3124-4 lib bdg; 0-7614-3124-1 lib bdg

LC 2008001617

In this book "cooperation is described as following instructions, sharing, and solving problems. [This] value is considered in a direct manner, which makes the [book] useful for the younger part of the age range, while the [title] will provide springboards for discussion among the older children. The brief [text is] accompanied by attractive, captioned color photographs." SLJ

Honesty; by Kimberley Jane Pryor. Marshall Cavendish Benchmark 2008 32p il (Values) lib bdg $19.95

Grades: 1 2 3   **177**

1. Honesty 2. Conduct of life
ISBN 978-0-7614-3125-1 lib bdg; 0-7614-3125-X lib bdg

LC 2008001673

This "well-executed [book provides a] simple [definition] of [honesty], examples of how it can be demonstrated, and a breakdown of the behavior into individual actions. . . . The brief [text is] accompanied by attractive, captioned color photographs." SLJ

Kindness; by Kimberley Jane Pryor. Marshall Cavendish Benchmark 2008 32p il (Values) lib bdg $19.95

Grades: 1 2 3   **177**

1. Kindness 2. Conduct of life
ISBN 978-0-7614-3126-8 lib bdg; 0-7614-3126-8 lib bdg

LC 2008001661

This "begins with a bulleted explanation of the word 'values.'. . . The rest of the text describes [kindness]. . . . The author then goes on to discuss examples of behaviors and emotions such as being kind to family and friends, feeling sympathy, and caring. The accompanying color photographs, showing children that appear to be unposed, are age-appropriate, culturally diverse, and complement the [narrative]." SLJ

Respect; by Kimberley Jane Pryor. Marshall Cavendish Benchmark 2008 32p il (Values) lib bdg $19.95
Grades: 1 2 3   177
1. Respect 2. Conduct of life
ISBN 978-0-7614-3128-2 lib bdg; 0-7614-3128-4 lib bdg
LC 2008001669
This "begins with a bulleted explanation of the word 'values.' . . . The rest of the text describes [respect]. . . . The author then goes on to discuss examples of behaviors and emotions such as being kind to family and friends, feeling sympathy, and caring. The accompanying color photographs, showing children that appear to be unposed, are age-appropriate, culturally diverse, and complement the [narrative]." SLJ

Tolerance; by Kimberley Jane Pryor. Marshall Cavendish Benchmark 2008 32p il (Values) lib bdg $19.95
Grades: 1 2 3   177
1. Toleration 2. Conduct of life
ISBN 978-0-7614-3129-9 lib bdg; 0-7614-3129-2 lib bdg
LC 2008001672
This "begins with a bulleted explanation of the word 'values.' . . . The rest of the text describes [tolerance]. . . . The author then goes on to discuss examples of behaviors and emotions such as being kind to family and friends, feeling sympathy, and caring. The accompanying color photographs, showing children that appear to be unposed, are age-appropriate, culturally diverse, and complement the [narrative]." SLJ

Verdick, Elizabeth
Words are not for hurting; illustrated by Marieka Heinlen. Free Spirit Pub. 2004 33p il pa $11.95; bd bk $7.95
Grades: K 1 2   177
1. Etiquette 2. Conversation 3. Interpersonal relations
ISBN 1-57542-156-9 pa; 1-57542-155-0 bd bk
LC 2003-21273
Encourages toddlers and preschoolers to express themselves using helpful, not hurtful, words. Includes a note for parents and caregivers
"The brightly colored drawings, which bring the minimal text to life, are especially effective at showing the range of emotions children experience when they hear unkind language. An excellent resource for sharing at home and at preschools." Booklist

Vermond, Kira
Half-truths and Brazen Lies; An Honest Look at Lying. by Kira Vermond; illustrated by Clayton Hanmer. Owlkids Books 2016 48 p. color illustrations (hardcover) $16.95
Grades: 5 6 7 8   177
1. Truthfulness and falsehood
ISBN 9781771471466; 1771471468
This juvenile book, by Kira Vermond, illustrated by Clayton Hanmer, "answers questions like: Why do we lie? What types of lies are there? What are the consequences of lying? What methods are used to detect lies? And when is it okay or even good to lie? From forgeries and hoaxes to plagiarism and placebos, . . . [it] offers historical anecdotes, scientific studies, and sociocultural analyses to help unpack the complex world of untruths." (Publisher's note)
"Rich with evidence, explanation, and food for thought, this well-documented approach to an issue not often covered in-depth for this age group will be enjoyed for curiosity's sake as well as a resource for study." Booklist
Includes bibliographical references (page 47) and index.

179   Other ethical norms

Barraclough, Sue
Honesty. Heinemann Library 2010 32p il (Exploring citizenship) $25.36; pa $7.99
Grades: 1 2 3 4   179
1. Honesty 2. Citizenship
ISBN 978-1-4329-3311-1; 1-4329-3311-6; 978-1-4329-3319-7 pa; 1-4329-3319-1 pa
LC 2008-55297
"The text presents a multitude of realistic situations to which young children will relate. There are 'Think About It' fact boxes and checklists that aid in understanding and that will spark discussion. All are filled with captioned, color photographs that relate to the text. The information is relevant and current. . . . Strongly consider this." Libr Media Connect
Includes glossary and bibliographical references

Belanger, Jeff
What it's like; to climb Mount Everest, blast off into space, survive a tornado, and other extraordinary stories. Sterling Pub. Co. 2010 136p il pa $9.95
Grades: 5 6 7 8   179
1. Courage 2. Anecdotes 3. Adventure and adventurers
ISBN 978-1-4027-6711-1; 1-4027-6711-0
LC 2009040875
"This illustrated collection presents short, first-person accounts of high-octane adventures—and, in some cases, personal disasters—by the people who actually experienced them. . . . The stories are told in present-tense, straightforward language, filled in with many pertinent and fascinating details. . . . The exciting action and the entries' short length will draw reluctant readers, as will the many color photographs, which are imaginatively laid out. This attractive package will be an easy sell." Booklist

Burstein, John
Can we get along? dealing with differences. Crabtree Pub. Company 2010 32p il (Slim Goodbody's life skills 101) lib bdg $26.60; pa $8.95
Grades: 1 2 3 4 5   179
1. Toleration
ISBN 978-0-7787-4788-8 lib bdg; 0-7787-4788-3 lib bdg; 978-0-7787-4804-5 pa; 0-7787-4804-9 pa
LC 2009023634
This book helps students understand the need and importance for tolerance, and the steps they can take to increase peace in their lives and in the world.
These book offers "clear and simple advice for children and [provides] adults with springboards for discussion and roleplaying. All have appealing color photographs of a variety of types of kids, . . . opening scenarios, concrete coping suggestions, and solid reasoning." SLJ
Includes bibliographical references

Obama, Barack, 1961-
Of thee I sing; a letter to my daughters. illustrated by Loren Long. Alfred A. Knopf 2010 un il $17.99; lib bdg $20.99
Grades: 1 2 3 4   179
1. Conduct of life 2. Heroes and heroines 3. United States -- History
ISBN 0-375-83527-X; 0-375-93527-4 lib bdg; 978-0-375-83527-8; 978-0-375-93527-5 lib bdg
"In characteristically measured prose, the 44th President introduces 13 American icons and heroes as exemplars of personal virtues, from Georgia O'Keeffe (creativity) and Jackie Robinson (courage) to Helen Keller (strength) and Cesar Chavez (inspiration). . . . Long's superb tech-

nical gifts and gentle sense of humor shine in the pictures. . . . [This offers] thought-provoking choices and commentary. . . . This [is a] stately outing." SLJ

Parker, Victoria
  Acting responsibly; [by] Vic Parker. Heinemann Library 2010 32p il (Exploring citizenship) $25.36; pa $7.99
  Grades: 1 2 3 4   179
    1. Responsibility
  ISBN 978-1-4329-3315-9; 1-4329-3315-9; 978-1-4329-3323-4 pa; 1-4329-3323-X pa
                                                           LC 2008-55305
  This describes how and why to behave in a responsible way
  "The text presents a multitude of realistic situations to which young children will relate. There are 'Think About It' fact boxes and checklists that aid in understanding and that will spark discussion. All are filled with captioned, color photographs that relate to the text. The information is relevant and current. . . . Strongly consider this." Libr Media Connection
  Includes glossary and bibliographical references

Pryor, Kimberley Jane
  Courage; by Kimberley Jane Pryor. Marshall Cavendish Benchmark 2008 32p il (Values) lib bdg $19.95
  Grades: 1 2 3   179
    1. Courage 2. Conduct of life
  ISBN 978-0-7614-3131-2 lib bdg; 0-7614-3131-4 lib bdg
                                                           LC 2008001662
  This "well-executed [book provides a] simple [definition] of [courage], examples of how it can be demonstrated, and a breakdown of the behavior into individual actions. . . . The brief [text is] accompanied by attractive, captioned color photographs." SLJ

183   Sophistic, Socratic, related Greek philosophies

Jun Lim
  Socrates; the public conscience of Golden Age Athens. by Jun Lim. 1st ed. Rosen Pub. 2006 112 p. col. ill., col. map (library) $34.60
  Grades: 5 6 7 8   183
    1. Philosophers
  ISBN 1404205640; 9781404205642
                                                           LC 2005012259
  This book by Jun Lim is part of the Library of Greek Philosophers series and looks at Socrates. "This series introduces students to the great philosophers and mathematicians who helped shape the intellectual world in modern times." Examples are given "of the kinds of knowledge these men taught to their students. The early years, travels, and education of each man are told, and the contributions to society are detailed in the context of the times." (Library Media Connection)
  Includes bibliographical references (p. 107-108) and index.

200   RELIGION

200   Religion

Mooney, Carla
  Comparative religion; investigate the world through religious tradition. by Carla Mooney. Nomad Press 2015 120 p. col. ill., col. maps $22.95

  Grades: 5 6 7 8   200
    1. Religion
  ISBN 1619303019; 9781619303010
  In this book, by Carla Mooney, "readers seek answers . . . by comparing and contrasting the cultural, spiritual, and geographical underpinnings of five different religions. By developing a better understanding of the similarities and differences among religions of the world, readers gain a strong foothold in a dialogue that has continued for thousands of years." (Publisher's note)
  "By examining complex beliefs and doctrine in an accessible and reader-friendly format, Mooney effectively teases out the commonalities among major world religions." Booklist
  Includes bibliographical references (pages 116-117) and index.

Osborne, Mary Pope
  ★ **One** world, many religions; the ways we worship. Knopf 1996 86p il map $19.95
  Grades: 4 5 6 7   200
    1. Islam 2. Taoism 3. Judaism 4. Buddhism 5. Hinduism 6. Religions 7. Christianity 8. Confucianism
  ISBN 0-679-83930-5
                                                           LC 96-836
  "The presentation is notable for its respect to each group, succinctness, and clarity. . . . The artful, full-page, color and black-and-white photographs tell much of the story." SLJ
  Includes glossary and bibliographical references

What do you believe? religion and faith in the world today. DK Pub. 2011 96p il map $16.99
  Grades: 4 5 6 7   200
    1. Religions 2. Philosophy
  ISBN 978-0-7566-7228-7; 0-7566-7228-7
  "This extensive guidebook covers the beliefs and history of the world's major religions. Focusing in particular on Buddhism, Christianity, Hinduism, Islam, Judaism, and Sikhism, the book also explores atheism and agnosticism, indigenous belief systems, East Asian religions, philosophy, and morality. . . . The graphically bold format—which mixes photographs, cartoons, and sidebars—will keep kids' attention, whether they are seeking truth, knowledge, or more to ponder." Publ Wkly

201   Specific aspects of religion

Hamilton, Virginia
  ★ **In** the beginning; creation stories from around the world; told by Virginia Hamilton; illustrated by Barry Moser. Harcourt Brace Jovanovich 1988 161p il hardcover o.p. pa $20
  Grades: 5 6 7 8   201
    1. Creation 2. Mythology
  ISBN 0-15-238740-4; 0-15-238742-0 pa
                                                           LC 88-6211
  A Newbery Medal honor book, 1989
  "Hamilton has gathered 25 creation myths from various cultures and retold them in language true to the original. Images from the tales are captured in Moser's 42 full-page illustrations, tantalizing oil paintings that are rich with somber colors and striking compositions. Included in the collection are the familiar stories (biblical creation stories, Greek and Roman myths), and some that are not so familiar (tales from the Australian aborigines, various African and native American tribes, as well as from countries like Russia, China, and Iceland). At the end of each tale, Hamilton provides a brief commentary on the story's origin and originators." Booklist
  Includes bibliographical references

Reinhart, Matthew

Gods & heroes; [by] Matthew Reinhart and Robert Sabuda. Candlewick Press 2010 un il (Encyclopedia mythologica) $29.99

Grades: K 1 2 3   **201**

1. Mythology 2. Gods and goddesses 3. Pop-up books

ISBN 978-0-7636-3171-0; 0-7636-3171-X

                             LC 2009-15140

This is "a global tour of gods and other deities. Multiple stories unfold on each page within layered tableaus in miniature booklets, like treasures to be unveiled. . . . A fun and engaging assemblage that seamlessly marries its form and content." Publ Wkly

202.4   Creation and cosmology

Fleischman, Paul

First light, first life; a worldwide creation story. Paul Fleischman; illustrated by Julie Paschkis. Henry Holt & Co. 2016 32 p. color illustrations (hardback) $17.99

Grades: K 1 2 3 4   **202.4**

1. Creation 2. Multicultural literature 3. Mythology 4. Beginning 5. Creation -- Mythology

ISBN 9781627791014

                             LC 2015030948

In this picture book by Paul Fleischman, illustrated by Julie Paschkis, "combining elements of the creation story from different traditions, this narrative weaves together one complete picture of how the world began. It is a celebration of the many and varied peoples of the earth, of their commonalities and their differences. It is a celebration of life." (Publisher's note)

"The stories' references to weather and environment are specific, yet they share an essential understanding of humans as made by gods and at the mercy of events they can't control. Humankind really is one family, Fleischman suggests." Pub Wkly

204   Religious experience, life, practice

Pelham, Sophie

Food and faith; [by] Susan Reuben and Sophie Pelham. Frances Lincoln Children's Books 2011 45 p. ill. $18.99

Grades: 3 4 5   **204**

1. Food 2. Religions 3. Religious holidays

ISBN 1845079868; 9781845079864

Author Susan Reuben presents a cookbook for "people of various ethnic backgrounds [and religious celebrations] . . . [The book discusses] the Jewish Shabbat, as well as Chanukah, Rosh Hashanah, Yom Kippur, Purim and Passover, [in addition to] the Muslim Eid ul Fitr . . . and Christingle . . . Recipes for one representative dish per religion are included, [such as] Hinduism and Sikhism." (Kirkus)

220.5   Modern versions and translations

The **Bible**: Authorized King James Version; with an introduction and notes by Robert Carroll and Stephen Prickett. Oxford University Press 2008 lxxiv, 1039, 248, 445p il map (Oxford world's classics) pa $18.95

Grades: 5 6 7 8 9 10 11 12 Adult   **220.5**

ISBN 978-0-19-953594-1

                           LC 2008-273825

This Oxford World's Classics version first published 1997

The authorized or King James Version originally published 1611. Includes bibliographical references

The **Holy** Bible; containing the Old and New Testaments with the Apocryphal/Deuterocanonical books: New Revised Standard Version. Oxford University Press 1989 xxi, 996, 298, 284p map $29.99

Grades: 5 6 7 8 9 10 11 12 Adult   **220.5**

ISBN 0-19-528330-9; 978-0-19-528330-3

                           LC 90-222105

"Intended for public reading, congregational worship, private study, instruction, and meditation, it attempts to be as literal as possible while following standard American English usage, avoids colloquialism, and prefers simple, direct terms and phrases." Sheehy. Guide to Ref Books. 10th edition. suppl

220.8   Nonreligious subjects treated in Bible

Animals of the Bible; a picture book by Dorothy P. Lathrop; with text selected by Helen Dean Fish from the King James Bible. Harper & Row 1987 65p il $17.95; lib bdg $18.89

Grades: 1 2 3 4   **220.8**

1. Animals 2. Bible -- Natural history

ISBN 0-397-31536-8; 0-397-30047-6 lib bdg

A reissue of the title first published 1937 by Lippincott

Awarded the Caldecott Medal, 1938

"Dorothy Lathrop's love and understanding of animals, the sensitiveness and joy with which she draws them, make her the ideal artist for such a volume. It is more than a beautiful picture book, for she has studied the fauna and flora of Bible lands until each animal and bird, each flower and tree, is true to natural history." NY Times Book Rev

220.9   Geography, history, chronology, persons of Bible lands in Bible times

Barnes, Trevor

The **Kingfisher** children's illustrated Bible; illustrated by Vanessa Card . . . [et al.] 2011 256p il map $14.99

Grades: 3 4 5 6   **220.9**

1. Bible stories

ISBN 978-0-7534-6490-8; 0-7534-6490-X

"In the straightforward style of a practiced storyteller, Barnes recreates the ancient world of the Israelites peopled by patriarchs, prophets, kings, the Messiah, and his disciples. Beginning with Creation and concluding the first portion of the book with a selection of psalms and proverbs, he pays homage to key Old Testament figures. . . . The second section focuses on the New Testament stories of Jesus' life and teachings and the spread of Christianity. . . . The one to two-page stories flow together seamlessly from Genesis to Revelation. Each entry includes a citation to the corresponding scripture passages and is complemented by illustrations replete with historically correct cultural details. A supplementary reference section featuring commentary, maps, and captioned photographs puts the sacred stories in historical and geographical context." SLJ

Brown, Laaren

The **Children's** illustrated Jewish Bible; retold by Laaren Brown & Lenny Hort; illustrated by Eric Thomas. rev ed; DK Pub. 2007 192p il map $19.99

Grades: 1 2 3 4 5 6   **220.9**
  1. Bible stories
  ISBN 978-0-7566-2665-5

"This is indeed a Jewish Bible, written by Jewish authors, and successful in its inclusion of many popular stories retold in a lively, child-friendly style. Realistic and colorful pencil-drawn illustrations add to the telling, and as a treat for curious minds, the small photographs on the sidebars are really interesting." SLJ

Delval, Marie-Helene

  The **Bible** for young children; [illustrated by] Götting. Eerdmans Books for Young Readers 2010 88p il $16.50
Grades: K 1 2 3   **220.9**
  1. Bible stories
  ISBN 978-0-8028-5383-7; 0-8028-5383-8

LC 2010005164
Original French edition 2002

"This introduction to the Christian Bible uses simple format that is accessible both to younger children and new readers. Forty Bible stories are retold with just a few sentences for each story or incident. . . . The text is set in large type on the left-hand pages against an attractive corresponding illustration on the right-hand pages. The paintings used for the illustrations use a variety of perspectives and a palette of deep shades that suggests an ancient setting. The clear and simple format provides an accessible introduction to major stories and characters in the Bible." Kirkus

  Includes bibliographical references

DePaola, Tomie, 1934-

  ★ **Tomie** dePaola's book of Bible stories. Putnam 1989 127p il $24.99; pa $12.99
Grades: 2 3 4 5   **220.9**
  1. Bible stories
  ISBN 0-399-21690-1; 0-698-11923-1 pa

LC 88-26468
"A collection of 17 stories from the Old Testament, 15 from the New Testament, and 4 psalms. The text is from the New International Version. . . . De Paola uses the text as written with some abridgment to make the stories an appropriate length. Done in his typical style, the illustrations feature stylized people and objects. . . . There are several illustrations for each story, many of which are full page, and most make dramatic use of color. The large format enhances the impact of the pictures." SLJ

Lottridge, Celia Barker

  Stories from Adam and Eve to Ezekiel; retold from the Bible. by Celia Barker Lottridge; illustrated by Gary Clement. Douglas & McIntyre/Groundwood 2004 192p il $24.95
Grades: 4 5 6 7   **220.9**
  1. Bible stories
  ISBN 0-88899-490-7

"Lottridge uses her storyteller's ear to bring ancient stories from the Hebrew Bible to a young audience, tailoring them to make them more age appropriate. . . . The numerous, well-drawn ink-and-watercolor illustrations are reminiscent of Warwick Hutton's work. Some pictures . . . are quite spectacular." Booklist

Osborne, Mary Pope

  The **Random** House book of Bible stories; by Mary Pope Osborne and Natalie Pope Boyce; illustrated by Michael Welply. Random House 2009 165p il $24.99; lib bdg $27.99

Grades: 2 3 4 5   **220.9**
  1. Bible stories
  ISBN 978-0-375-82281-0; 0-375-82281-X; 978-0-375-92281-7 lib bdg; 0-375-92281-4 lib bdg

LC 2007047308
"The retellers do a credible job of adapting more than 50 Old and New Testament selections in sequential order. Each story is related in language that evokes biblical storytelling, giving the collection the feel of a real Bible with the accessibility of a shared read-aloud. . . . Welply's realistic illustrations . . . will help readers contextualize the place and time." SLJ

Pirotta, Saviour

  Children's stories from the Bible; stories retold. color art by Anne Yvonne Gilbert; monochrome art by Ian Andrew. Templar Books 2009 292p il map $19.99
Grades: 4 5 6   **220.9**
  1. Bible stories
  ISBN 978-0-7636-4551-9; 0-7636-4551-6

LC 2008944069
Recounts over seventy stories from the Bible, including "The Walls of Jericho," "The Prodigal Son," "Jesus and the Children," and "Rahab and the Spies"

"Pirotta 'adds, for example, kid-friendly details about the weather on the day Mary and Joseph travel to Bethlehem, and he resolves each story with a tidy ending. Softly textured illustrations enhance the mood of the tales." Horn Book Guide

Watts, Murray

  The **Bible** for children from Good Books; retold by Murray Watts; illustrated by Helen Cann. Good Bks. (Pa.) 2002 352p il map $23.99
Grades: 3 4 5 6   **220.9**
  1. Bible stories
  ISBN 1-56148-362-1

LC 2002-20243
A collection of approximately two hundred and fifty illustrated stories from the Old and New Testaments, retold for children

"Watts' retellings from the Old and New Testaments are vivid and evocative. . . . The handsome pictures and decorated borders employ a rich palette of colors and patterns, giving the book a contemporary look." Booklist

220.95 History

Ehrlich, Amy, 1942-

  With a mighty hand; the story of the Torah. Amy Ehrlich, Daniel Nevins. Candlewick Press 2013 224 p. $29.99
Grades: 2 3 4 5 6 7 8   **220.95**
  1. Bible 2. Bible stories 3. Picture books for children
  ISBN 0763643955; 9780763643959

LC 2012947723
This book is an interpretation of the Torah for children. Amy Ehrlich has "changed the traditional phrasing" of the Bible's first five books. She "describes Moses' basket as 'a little ark of papyrus,' reminding readers of how much danger the baby was in, floating in the middle of the Nile. . . . Not every word of the Bible has been included, the text having been pared down to a series of interconnected stories." (Kirkus Reviews)

221.9   Geography, history, chronology, persons of Old Testament lands in Old Testament times

Hanft, Joshua E.
  Miracles of the Bible; by Josh Hanft; illustrated by Seymour Chwast. Blue Apple Books 2007 un il $16.95
Grades: K 1 2   **221.9**
  1. Miracles 2. Bible stories
  ISBN 978-1-59354-617-5; 1-59354-617-3
                    LC 2007007093
  This retells "such familiar Bible stories as 'Daniel in the Lion's Den' and 'Jonah and the Fish' and 'Noah's Ark.' He also includes such dramatic episodes as the parting of the Red Sea and the conquests of Samson and David. . . . It's Chwast's full-page-and-more compositions, rendered in creamy, pastel-toned ink-and-watercolor that stand out—literally. A number of these illustrations, in Chwast's signature comics-influenced style, appear on foldout pages that boldly expand the scene, vertically or horizontally. Children will likely flock to this hands-on reading experience." Publ Wkly

Sasso, Sandy Eisenberg
  But God remembered; stories of women from creation to the promised land. illustrated by Bethanne Andersen. Jewish Lights Pub. 1995 31p il $16.95
Grades: 3 4 5   **221.9**
  1. Bible stories 2. Women in the Bible
  ISBN 1-879045-43-5
                    LC 95-3591
  "Although part of the pleasure of the book lies in its strong feminist voice, Sasso also tells good stories; and these will have even more value for the discussions they can generate. Andersen's evocative paintings are beautiful additions to this carefully designed book." Booklist

Ward, Elaine M.
  Old Testament women; [by] Elaine Ward. Enchanted Lion 2004 32p il (Art revelations) $18.95
Grades: 5 6 7 8   **221.9**
  1. Bible stories 2. Women in the Bible
  ISBN 1-59270-011-X
  These Old Testament stories about women include "explanatory paragraphs, sidebars, and captions by the author. Art masterpieces . . . illustrate each story. . . . The captions provide background on the artist and the significance of each painting or mosaic. . . . The 18 women . . . include Rachel, Leah, Ruth, and Bathsheba. . . . Bosch, Botticelli, and Poussin are among the painters whose work appears here. . . . Visually stunning." SLJ

222   Historical books of Old Testament

Feiler, Bruce S.
  ★ **Walking** the Bible; an illustrated journey for kids through the greatest stories ever told. by Bruce Feiler; illustrated by Sasha Meret. HarperCollinsPublishers 2004 108p il map $16.99; lib bdg $17.89
Grades: 5 6 7 8   **222**
  1. Bible (as subject) 2. Middle East
  ISBN 0-06-051117-6; 0-06-051118-4 lib bdg
                    LC 2003-15861
  The author describes his journey through places mentioned in the Old Testament
  "In this version of his adult book with the same title (Morrow, 2001), Feiler largely succeeds in slimming rather than dumbing down his account of his trip across the 10,000-mile setting of the earliest Bible sto-

ries. The author's unpretentious . . . tone and astute pacing help make the volume accessible, and his sincerity is palpable." SLJ

Fischer, Chuck
  ★ **In** the beginning: the art of Genesis; a pop-up book. by Chuck Fischer. Little, Brown 2008 un il $35
Grades: 5 6 7 8   **222**
  1. Bible stories 2. Religious art 3. Pop-up books 4. Bible -- O.T. -- Genesis
  ISBN 978-0-316-11842-2; 0-316-11842-7
                    LC 2007045411
  Fischer "presents an impressive, three-dimensional view of the Book of Genesis. . . . Fischer and his collaborators offer a Garden of Eden scene executed in an artistic style that recalls ancient tile work; a huge Noah's Ark landed atop a mountain; and a Tower of Babel impressively high. . . . The text, more commentary than story, is hidden in inset mini-books and is accompanied by reproductions of biblical masterpieces. . . . This book becomes more amazing as the pages are turned." Booklist

Hodges, Margaret
  ★ **Moses**; illustrated by Barry Moser. Harcourt, Inc. 2006 un il $16
Grades: 3 4 5   **222**
  1. Prophets 2. Bible stories 3. Biblical characters
  ISBN 978-0-15-200946-5; 0-15-200946-9
  Retells the story of Moses, from his birth and trip in a boat of bulrushes to his bringing of the Ten Commandments down from Mount Sinai.
  "The venerable story of Moses gets a brisk yet compelling treatment by Hodges. . . . The book is beautiful to page through, with cream-colored pages and the bordered watercolors in Moser's signature style." Booklist

Jules, Jacqueline
  Abraham's search for God; by Jacqueline Jules; illustrated by Natascia Ugliano. Kar-Ben Pub. 2007 un il lib bdg $17.95
Grades: K 1 2 3   **222**
  1. God 2. Prophets 3. Biblical characters
  ISBN 978-1-58013-243-5 lib bdg; 1-58013-243-X lib bdg
                    LC 2006027429
  "Jules retells a midrash (a legend based on biblical text) in which the youthful Abraham discovers the concept of monotheism. Rejecting worship of unresponsive idols, Abraham spends time outdoors where he senses an unseen hand directing the movements of the moon, sun, storm, and rainbow. He concludes that 'God is everywhere. God is in everything. God is something we know with our hearts.' . . . The energetic pastel illustrations are cheerful and warm. . . . This simply told tale is an excellent introduction to the concept of monotheism, and would be a great discussion starter for talking about God." SLJ
  Includes bibliographical references

  Benjamin and the silver goblet; illustrated by Natascia Ugliano. Kar-Ben Pub. 2009 un il $17.95; pa $8.95
Grades: K 1 2 3   **222**
  1. Bible stories
  ISBN 978-0-8225-8757-6; 0-8225-8757-2; 978-0-8225-8758-3 pa; 0-8225-8758-0 pa
                    LC 2007048344
  "When Jacob's sons arrive home from their travels in Egypt, they tell their father that one brother is being held as a hostage by the governor, who demands that they return with the youngest brother, Benjamin. The child, aching to see the world, is only too happy to oblige, though Jacob fears that he will lose this son the way he lost his eldest, Joseph, years before. . . . Well paced and well told, this familiar story makes itself fresh

with a folkloric feel and a satisfying ending. Ugliano's heavily textured, colorful pastel illustrations ably support and extend the text." Kirkus

Miriam in the desert; illustrated by Natascia Ugliano. Kar-Ben Pub. 2010 un il lib bdg $17.95; pa $8.95
Grades: K 1 2 3   222
    1. Bible stories 2. Biblical characters
    ISBN 978-0-7613-4494-0 lib bdg; 0-7613-4494-2 lib bdg; 978-0-7613-4496-4 pa; 0-7613-4496-9 pa
            LC 2009001874
"Miriam, Moses's sister, is featured in [this book] . . ., offering encouragement and guidance to the Israelites as they continue their seemingly endless thirst- and hunger-filled journey through the desert following their escape from Egypt. . . . Deeply colored pastel-and-acrylic double-page paintings effectively portray a legendary biblical setting in a guileless and unsophisticated style. . . . They effectively match the original and simple dialogue-driven text." Kirkus

Sarah laughs; by Jacqueline Jules; illustrated by Natascia Ugliano. Kar-Ben Pub. 2008 32p il $17.95; pa $8.95
Grades: K 1 2 3   222
    1. Prophets 2. Bible stories 3. Biblical characters
    ISBN 978-0-8225-7216-9; 0-8225-7216-8; 978-0-8225-9934-0 pa; 0-8225-9934-1 pa
            LC 2006039738
"Through poetic language and sweeping illustrations, this picture book tells the story of the biblical patriarch and matriarch Abraham and Sarah from Sarah's point of view. . . . Sarah is portrayed as graceful, loving, and faithful. However, her sadness about remaining childless through the years has made her lose her bright laughter. With the birth of Isaac, when she is gray-haired and wrinkled, she finally laughs again. . . . This lovely retelling deserves a place on the shelves of any library that collects religious materials." SLJ
    Includes bibliographical references

Kimmel, Eric A.
  ★ The **story** of Esther; retold by Eric A. Kimmel; illustrated by Jill Weber. Holiday House 2010 un il $16.95
Grades: K 1 2   222
    1. Purim 2. Queens 3. Bible stories 4. Biblical characters
    ISBN 978-0-8234-2223-4; 0-8234-2223-2
            LC 2008048490
"Kimmel and Weber turn their considerable talents to the Book of Esther and its corresponding Jewish holiday. . . . As always, Kimmel is an effortless storyteller, his learnedness leavened with an expert sense of pacing for young audiences—even the book's longer passages feel like they're exactly the right length. In vibrant mixed-media paintings, Weber proves once again that she's an excellent match for this unflashy master." Publ Wkly

Koralek, Jenny
  The **coat** of many colors; illustrated by Pauline Baynes. Eerdmans Books for Young Readers 2004 un il $16
Grades: K 1 2 3   222
    1. Bible stories 2. Biblical characters
    ISBN 0-8028-5277-7
            LC 2004-6575
This "retelling of the story from the Book of Genesis highlights the key events in the life of Joseph . . . and explores timeless themes of sibling rivalry and the power of forgiveness. . . . Baynes enhances the straightforward text with atmospheric illustrations rendered in muted desert shades. . . . This appealing rendition of a well-known tale is perfect for reading aloud." SLJ

The **story** of Queen Esther; written by Jenny Koralek; illustrated by Grizelda Holderness. Eerdmans Books for Young Readers 2008 un il $17.50
Grades: K 1 2 3   222
    1. Queens 2. Bible stories 3. Biblical characters
    ISBN 978-0-8028-5348-6; 0-8028-5348-X
            LC 2008017713
This is a "retelling of the biblical story of the Jewish queen of ancient Persia who saved her people from the plotting of the king's evil vizier, Haman. . . . The Jewish holiday of Purim, which commemorates the story of Queen Esther, is mentioned on the final spread. . . . The illustrations are the highlight of the book. Stylized, dreamy pastel spreads sing with deep color. . . . The dignified pictures support the solemn tone of the text." SLJ

Manushkin, Fran
  Miriam's cup; a Passover story. illustrated by Bob Dacey. Scholastic 1998 un il hardcover o.p. pa $6.99
Grades: K 1 2 3   222
    1. Passover 2. Bible stories 3. Biblical characters
    ISBN 0-590-67720-9; 0-439-81111-2 pa
            LC 96-2480
A Jewish mother preparing for Passover tells her young children, the story of Miriam, the Biblical woman who prophesied the birth of Moses
    "The text and the lush double-spread watercolors, which are painted to reflect a child's perspective, are framed on a papyrus background. Each illustration bursts with movement, immersing readers and prereaders alike in the sequence and drama of the story." Booklist
    Includes bibliographical references

Ray, Jane
  Adam and Eve and the Garden of Eden; written and illustrated by Jane Ray. Eerdmans Books for Young Readers 2005 un il $17
Grades: K 1 2 3   222
    1. Bible stories 2. Biblical characters
    ISBN 0-8028-5278-5
            LC 2004-6804
"Adam and Eve live harmoniously with the animals that have been named by the first man, until Eve is tempted by the serpent. In rich prose, the author describes the garden in lyrical detail. The descriptive passages are complemented by exquisite illustrations that lend a mystical aura to the narrative." SLJ

Sasso, Sandy Eisenberg
  Cain & Abel; finding the fruits of peace. illustrated by Joani Keller Rothenberg. Jewish Lights Pub. 2001 32p il $16.95
Grades: K 1 2 3   222
    1. Bible stories 2. Biblical characters
    ISBN 1-58023-123-3
            LC 2001-2206
Retells the story of two brothers who, after years of sharing everything, become angry enough to lose control and bring violence into the world
    "In this simple yet effective book, Sasso leads children to think not only about how the brothers' personal relationship failed but also about the story's connection to today's violence. The eye-catching, folk-artstyle illustrations, with thick swathes of color and inventive background designs, make as strong a statement as the text." Booklist

Spier, Peter
  ★ **Noah's** ark; illustrated by Peter Spier. Doubleday 1977 un il $16.95; pa $7.99

Grades: K 1 2   **222**
1. Noah's ark 2. Bible stories
ISBN 0-385-09473-6; 0-440-49693-8 pa
LC 76-43630

Awarded the Caldecott Medal, 1978

"A seventeenth-century Dutch poem, 'The Flood' by Jacobus Revius, opens the otherwise almost wordless book. Skillfully translated by the artist and set in a readable, appropriately archaic type, the artlessly reverent verses add an unexpected dimension to the full-color pictures. Peter Spier's characteristic panoramas are marvels of minute detail, activity, vitality, and humor." Horn Book

Stewig, John W.

The **animals** watched; by John Warren Stewig; illustrated by Rosanne Litzinger. Holiday House 2007 un il $16.95
Grades: K 1 2   **222**
1. Alphabet 2. Noah's ark
ISBN 978-0-8234-1906-7; 0-8234-1906-1
LC 2006004784

"A simple account of the story of Noah's ark. The language is easy enough for young children to understand, but remains true to the basics of the Genesis text. . . . In alphabetical order from aardvarks to jaguars to zebras, animals tell a part of the tale. . . . The appealing illustrations are done in pencil, watercolor, gouache, and colored pencil." SLJ

Wolf, Gita

The **Enduring** Ark; by Gita Wolf; illustrated by Joydeb Chitrakar. Pgw 2013 34 p. ill. (hardcover) $21.95
Grades: 1 2 3 4   **222**
1. Toy and movable books 2. Noah's Ark -- fiction
ISBN 9380340184; 9789380340180

This children's book, by Gita Wolf, illustrated by Joydeb Chitrakar, offers an "Indian version of the Biblical tale [of the Flood and Noah's Ark, which] . . . leads the reader from a deluge of water to a rainbow of hope. A book that can be leafed through in the traditional way or unfolded out as an accordion." (Publisher's note)

223 Poetic books of Old Testament

Delval, Marie-Helene

Psalms for young children; by Marie-Helene Delval; illustrated by Arno. Eerdmans Books for Young Readers 2008 un il $16
Grades: K 1 2 3   **223**
1. Bible. Old Testament 2. Bible -- O.T. -- Psalms
ISBN 978-0-8028-5322-6; 0-8028-5322-6
LC 2006031831

"Each psalm expresses feelings familiar to children: fear and uncertainty, comfort and contentment, amazement and gratitude. The sacred songs, paraphrased in simple, child-friendly language, celebrate the beautiful world, which is protected by God's all-encompassing love, and provide a sense of reassurance. . . . Organized in numerical order, the selections are printed in a large, readable font. . . . The magical paintings feature exotic settings, bold outlines, and rich hues. They are filled with images of children and the natural world." SLJ

Dillon, Leo

★ **To** every thing there is a season; verses from Ecclesiastes. illustrations by Leo and Diane Dillon. Blue Sky Press (NY) 1998 un il $16.95
Grades: 4 5 6 7 8   **223**
ISBN 0-590-47887-7
LC 97-35124

"The words of Ecclesiastes I:4 and III:1-8, adapted from the King James Version of the Bible, are . . . {illustrated here in} 16 full- and double-page paintings. . . . Kindergarten and up." (SLJ)

"The Dillons compellingly convey the relevance of the Ecclesiastes verse throughout history, via a stunning array of artwork that embraces motifs from cultures the world over." Publ Wkly

Lindbergh, Reeve

On morning wings; adapted from Psalm 139 by Reeve Lindbergh; illustrated by Holly Meade. Candlewick Press 2002 un il $15.99
Grades: K 1 2 3   **223**
1. God 2. Bible -- O.T. -- Psalms
ISBN 0-7636-1106-9
LC 2001-58169

"On morning wings" was previously published in the anthology In every tiny grain of sand: a child's book of prayers and praise, collected by Reeve Lindbergh, published by Candlewick Press, 2000

Retells, in simple words, a psalm of God's knowledge of and love for each of us

"Meade's visual story line shows four children spending an idyllic summer day together outdoors. The striking use of light, reflected in water or filtered by campfire, conveys the natural reverence of the text with seeming spontaneity." Publ Wkly

Moser, Barry

Psalm 23; illustrated by Barry Moser. Zonderkidz 2008 un il $14.99
Grades: K 1 2   **223**
1. Bible. Old Testament 2. Bible -- O.T. -- Psalms
ISBN 978-0-310-71085-1; 0-310-71085-5
LC 2006027616

"In a two-page introduction, Moser invites readers to see the venerable poem through a new prism: that of a boy tending goats and sheep on a Caribbean island such as Antigua, where the author-illustrator has spent much time. While watching the island animals, Moser says he often recited the psalm, which he writes here in simple words. . . . Moser strives to accentuate mood and nature, and the paintings in this book . . . highlight the feeling that as God watches over us, we watch over those in our charge." Booklist

226 Gospels and Acts

Warren, Rick

The **Lord's** prayer; [illustrated by] Richard Jesse Watson; commentary by Rick Warren. Zonderkidz 2011 un il (Master illustrator series) $16.99
Grades: PreK K 1 2   **226**
1. Prayer
ISBN 978-0-310-71086-8; 0-310-71086-3
LC 2009037508

"With vibrant illustrations featuring children of all ages and nationalities, Watson illuminates the message of love and worship contained within the lines of the King James Version of The Lord's Prayer. Each spread focuses on a single line, which is printed in elegant font and incorporated into the painting. Images of animals and the sun recur throughout the book. Some of the pictures are painted in rich colors while others appear to be shadowy, gray pencil sketches. . . . Warren explains the meaning behind the words Jesus taught his disciples with line-by-line commentary, teaching young readers the value of prayer. The artist also offers a reflection on what this prayer means to him. This lovely picture book is a fine choice to help parents introduce the practice of prayer into their children's daily lives." SLJ

230 Christianity

Nardo, Don

Christianity. Compass Point Books 2010 48p il map (World religions) lib bdg $27.99

Grades: 5 6 7 8   **230**

1. Christianity

ISBN 978-0-7565-4237-5 lib bdg; 0-7565-4237-5 lib bdg

LC 2009-15811

"The colorful, attractive layout includes high-quality reproductions of photographs, maps, and paintings. Students who are new to religious studies, as well as those doing reports, will find that this . . . meets their needs." SLJ

Includes glossary and bibliographical references

Self, David

★ **Christianity**; [by] David Self. World Almanac Library 2005 48p il map (Religions of the world) lib bdg $30

Grades: 5 6 7 8   **230**

1. Christianity

ISBN 0-8368-5866-2

LC 2005041712

This is a summary of the Christian religion including history, beliefs, worship, festivals, practice, and current disagreements.

"Wonderfully colorful in images, language, and fact. . . . [This is] enumerated with full-color photographs on every page, charts, maps, and tables." SLJ

Includes bibliographical references

231 Christian doctrinal theology

Delval, Marie-Helene

Images of God for young children; illustrated by Barbara Nascimbeni. Eerdmans Books for Young Readers 2011 88p il $16.50

Grades: K 1 2 3   **231**

1. God

ISBN 978-0-8028-5391-2; 0-8028-5391-9

This "sets out to explain the concept of God to children in creative, often metaphorical ways. . . . The explanatory text is written in a thoughtful, calm voice with a comforting view of God as kind, loving and all-encompassing. This modern point of view is complemented by Nascimbeni's bright, imaginative illustrations on the right-hand pages, using children and images from nature painted in a cheery surrealistically childlike style." Kirkus

231.7 Relation to the world

DePaola, Tomie, 1934-

★ **Let** the whole earth sing praise. G. P. Putnam's Sons 2011 un il $15.99

Grades: PreK K 1   **231.7**

1. Creation

ISBN 978-0-399-25478-9; 0-399-25478-1

LC 2010011565

"In this small-format book, dePaola masterfully pairs simple words and resonant images. Rendered in acrylics and inspired by the folk art of the Otomi people from Puebla, Mexico, the pictures offer primitive depictions of natural phenomena. . . . Based on two pieces of Old Testament scripture—the Canticle of the Three Young Men from the Book of Daniel and Psalm 148—dePaola's narrative bids specific creatures and forces of nature to give praise, before issuing a cumulative call-out: 'Let everything in heaven and on earth bless and praise God.' The very largeness of the loose, hand-lettered text, which appears in all caps, amplifies the message, while the joy that emanates from the cheerful spreads confirms its value." Publ Wkly

232.9 Family and life of Jesus

Castillo, Lauren

★ **Christmas** is here; words from the King James Bible; illustrated by Lauren Castillo. Simon & Schuster 2010 un il $12.99

Grades: PreK K 1 2   **232.9**

1. Christmas

ISBN 978-1-4424-0822-7; 1-4424-0822-7

"This touching interpretation of the Christmas story wordlessly follows a modern-day family as they journey through a snowy town in the evening to view a live Nativity scene. . . . The setting shifts in time and place to Bethlehem of long ago, accompanied by the traditional words from the King James Bible, before returning to the contemporary setting. Gorgeous watercolor illustrations in a subdued palette of twilight grays set off the falling snowflakes in the modern scenes, while the biblical scenes are brilliantly lit by starlight. Castillo's smudgy style infuses all with wonder." Kirkus

Crossley-Holland, Kevin

★ **How** many miles to Bethlehem? illustrated by Peter Malone. Arthur A. Levine Books 2004 un il $16.95

Grades: K 1 2 3   **232.9**

1. Jesus Christ -- Nativity 2. Christmas

ISBN 0-439-67642-8

LC 2003-28079

This is a telling of the Nativity story, told from the perspectives of Mary, the innkeeper, the ox, the donkey, the shepherds, the Wise Men, King Herod, the child, the lamb, and the angels.

"The language is both colloquial and lyrical. . . . Malone's illustrations are reminiscent of early Renaissance and medieval Eastern art in their wealth of detail and color. . . . The paintings evoke both sumptuous glory and a serene stillness." SLJ

Demi

★ **Jesus**; written and illustrated by Demi. Margaret K. McElderry Books 2005 un il $19.95

Grades: 3 4 5 6   **232.9**

1. Jesus Christ

ISBN 0-689-86905-3

LC 2004-12854

This life of Jesus is based "on Isaiah and the four Gospels from the King James version of the Bible. . . . Grades three to six." (Bull Cent Child Books)

"Brilliantly colored artwork and text based on the King James version of the Bible tell the story of the life of Jesus, beginning with the prophesies and the annunciation and ending with his ascension into Heaven. Demi's paintings are full of bright, intricate patterns, and bold touches of gold produce a feeling of awe and splendor." SLJ

Hendrix, John

Miracle man; the story of Jesus. John Hendrix. Abrams Books for Young Readers 2016 40 p. color illustrations $18.95; (ebook) $15.54

Grades: K 1 2 3   **232.9**

ISBN 9781419718991; 9781613129258

LC 2015018202

This book, by John Hendrix, "is a beautifully illustrated biography of Jesus Christ. . . . For all Christian denominations and perfect for families to share throughout the year, this book will be especially beloved by the faithful as a gift for Easter, communions, christenings, religious graduations, and all other secular holidays." (Publisher's note)

"It's an emotional and approachable account of the gospel that should have broad Christian appeal." Pub Wkly

Johnson, Pamela

The **story** of Christmas; from the King James Bible. illustrations by Pamela Dalton. Handprint Books 2011 un il $17.99

Grades: 1 2 3   **232.9**

  ISBN 978-1-4521-0470-6; 1-4521-0470-0

                   LC 2011025407

"Delicate paper-cut illustrations provide a lovely, solemn backdrop to the King James Bible's account of the Nativity story.... As shepherds, wise men, and angels gather to honor the birth of Jesus, Dalton sets her tableaus against black backgrounds, which both focus attention on the story's major players and make logical sense given the nocturnal setting of much of the story's events. The iconic nature of Dalton's scenes is ideally suited to the traditional Biblical translation used." Publ Wkly

Lottridge, Celia Barker

Stories from the life of Jesus; retold from the Bible by Celia Barker Lottridge; illustrated by Linda Wolfsgruber. Doulgas & McIntyre 2004 140p il $24.95

Grades: 4 5 6 7   **232.9**

  1. Bible stories

  ISBN 0-88899-497-4

A retelling of selected events from the life of Christ based on biblical accounts

This is an "exceptional collection.... Each story is retold in three or four pages of clear, concise prose that is meant to be read aloud.... Each selection is enhanced by dramatic and atmospheric, mixed-media illustrations that are executed in warm earth tones." SLJ

Menotti, Gian Carlo

Amahl and the night visitors; illustrated by Michèle Lemieux. Morrow 1986 64p il $21

Grades: 2 3 4   **232.9**

  1. Magi -- Fiction

  ISBN 0-688-05426-9

                   LC 84-27196

Relates how a crippled young shepherd comes to accompany the three Kings on their way to pay hommage to the newborn Jesus

"Some of the pictures, which are dominated by reddish brown, have rich tension and composition, as in the one of Amahl's mother contemplating theft, or in the portrait of Melchior describing the Christ child.... There is a great deal to look at, and the story, popular since the opera's 1951 debut, has sentimental appeal, humor, and some commanding moments." Bull Cent Child Books

Paterson, Katherine

★ The **light** of the world; the life of Jesus for children. [by] Katherine Paterson; [illustrated by] Francois Roca. Arthur A. Levine Books 2008 un il $17.99

Grades: K 1 2 3   **232.9**

  1. Jesus Christ

  ISBN 978-0-545-01172-3; 0-545-01172-8

                   LC 2007-06811

"The incisive text ... deftly moves through the story of Jesus' life and death, and also highlights several of the best-known parables.... Roca presents ... close-ups of the various people surrounding Jesus and ... handsome landscapes that give import to events." Booklist

Skevington, Andrea

The **story** of Jesus; illustrated by Angelo Ruta. Lion Children's 2009 127p il $16.95

Grades: 2 3 4 5   **232.9**

  1. Bible stories

  ISBN 978-0-7459-4982-6; 0-7459-4982-7

                   LC 2008278094

"Skevington's collection of key New Testament stories chronicles the life of Jesus beginning with his birth in a humble stable in Bethlehem and concluding with the feast of Pentecost when the Holy Spirit descends upon the disciples. Retelling stories from all four gospels, the author fictionalizes the scripture passages, adding dialogue and cultural details to enliven the characters and the setting.... Explanatory margin notes supplement the stories, and the neatly drawn illustrations portray Jesus and his followers in a palette of soft pastels." SLJ

Slegers, Liesbet

The **child** in the manger. Clavis Pub. 2010 un il $15.95

Grades: PreK K 1   **232.9**

  1. Jesus Christ -- Nativity

  ISBN 978-1-60537-084-2; 1-60537-084-3

"This is a short version of the Nativity story, told in simple language that very young children can understand. .... The cheerful, colorful paintings, rendered in primary colors with bold outlines, feature childlike animals and smiley-faced Biblical people. This is a fine choice for sharing with toddlers and preschoolers one-on-one, as well as in a religious preschool storytime." SLJ

Spirin, Gennady

★ **Jesus**; his life in verses from the King James Holy Bible. art by Gennady Spirin. Marshall Cavendish Children 2010 un il $21

Grades: 5 6 7 8   **232.9**

  1. Jesus Christ

  ISBN 978-0-7614-5630-8; 0-7614-5630-9

                   LC 2009005956

"In an unusual project, a tempera painting by Spirin has been digitally dissected to create individual images for this picture book that portrays 13 events from the life of Jesus.... Details from the larger work illustrate key moments—including the Annunciation, Jesus' baptism, and the raising of Lazarus, among others—beside passages from the King James Bible (Jesus' words are printed in red). The result is an elegant, large-format volume that offers a reverent and arresting visual interpretation of biblical events." Publ Wkly

Wildsmith, Brian

Jesus. Eerdmans Bks. for Young Readers 2000 un il $20

Grades: K 1 2 3   **232.9**

  1. Jesus Christ

  ISBN 0-8028-5212-2

                   LC 00-55126

"Wildsmith's pictures are framed in windowlike arches, set against backgrounds of pure colors. As with his other works, gold embellishments add majesty." Booklist

Williams, Sophy

The **first** Christmas; a changing picture book. Templar Books 2010 un il $12.99

Grades: PreK K 1 2   **232.9**

  1. Jesus Christ -- Nativity

  ISBN 978-0-7636-5013-1; 0-7636-5013-7

                   LC 2010004644

"This lovely presentation of the Nativity story includes four 'changing-pictures,' which are created by overlaying two images divided into vertical slats. In this case, the images change when a flap is opened. Williams's pastel illustrations are both luminous and child-centric, conveying a sense of mystery, awe, and gentle humor." SLJ

232.91 Mary, mother of Jesus

Bernier-Grand, Carmen T.

Our Lady of Guadalupe; retold by Carmen T. Bernier-Grand; illustrated by Tonya Engel. 1st ed. Marshall Cavendish Children 2012 31 p. ill. (hardcover) $17.99

Grades: 1 2 3   232.91

1. Aztecs -- Folklore 2. Religious biography 3. Guadalupe, Our Lady of

ISBN 9780761461357; 9780761461371

LC 2011016398

Author Carmen Bernier-Grand "describes the Aztec Juan Diego's three encounters with the Virgin Mary on Tepeyac Hill, near Tlatelolco (now Mexico City). Mary requests that Juan Diego tell the local bishop to build her a shrine on the hill . . . [and he] carries a sign from the Virgin to the bishop: roses in December. . . . The author concludes the tale with details on the significance of the shrine, the origins of the name 'Our Lady of Guadalupe' and other relevant historical facts and dates." (Kirkus Reivews)

Demi

Mary; written and illustrated by Demi. Margaret K. McElderry Books 2006 un il $19.95

Grades: 3 4 5 6   232.91

1. Saints 2. Mary, Blessed Virgin, Saint

ISBN 0-689-87692-0; 978-0-689-87692-9

LC 2005005844

"Demi begins her story before Mary is born, when her parents, Anna and Joachim, learn that their prayers have been heard, and that they will have a child whom they will dedicate to the service of the Lord. . . . The words simply serve as a backdrop for the glorious artwork. . . . Along with her familiar beautiful borders and diminutive characters, she incorporates many Jewish and Christian symbols that tie the religions together." SLJ

Gollogly, Eugene

Talking Eagle and the Lady of Roses; the story of Juan Diego and Our Lady of Guadalupe. illustrated by Amy Cordova; written by Amy Cordova, with Eugene Gollogly. SteinerBooks 2010 un il

Grades: K 1 2   232.91

1. Christian saints 2. Mary, Blessed Virgin, Saint

ISBN 0-88010-719-7; 978-0-88010-719-8

LC 2010032329

This "story tells of the appearance of Our Lady of Guadalupe to an indigenous healer, Talking Eagle, who had converted to Catholicism, becoming Juan Diego. . . . Rendered in dazzling jewel tones, Córdova's drawings possess a quiet radiance." Publ Wkly

232.92 Birth, infancy, childhood of Jesus

Sabuda, Robert

The **Christmas** story; Robert Sabuda. Candlewick Press 2016 12 p. color illustrations $35

Grades: K 1 2 3 4 5 6   232.92

1. Jesus Christ -- Nativity

ISBN 9780763683269

LC 2016946781

This book, by Robert Sabuda, is a "pop-up book celebrating the Nativity. Long ago in the town of Bethlehem, on a bright and starry night, a baby was born, a child who was called the son of God. Announced by an angel, born in a humble manger, laid in a bed of straw, visited by shepherds and wise men—the age-old, awe-inspiring story of the birth of Jesus is lovingly brought to life " (Publisher's note)

"This memorable interpretation will appeal to collectors of pop-up books and Christmas stories and to Christian families who would like a special version of the Nativity story to share on Christmas Eve." Kirkus

242 Devotional literature

Billingsley, Mary

The **life** of Jesus; an illustrated rosary. written and illustrated by Mary Billingsley; foreword by Benedict J. Groeschel. Eerdmans Books for Young Readers 2010 56p il $19.99

Grades: 3 4 5 6   242

1. Prayer

ISBN 978-0-8028-5362-2; 0-8028-5362-5

"Billingsley has divided this book according to the four 'Mysteries' that are emblematic of Christ's life—'Joyful,' 'Luminous,' 'Sorrowful,' and 'Glorious,' and then into subsections about each of its five parts. The book is remarkable in the accessibility it offers to readers of all ages. The introductory page provides visual instruction—a painting of a rosary with labels and arrows indicating which beads are meant for each prayer—followed by the prayers themselves. . . . Billingsley's unusual technique is what stands out; she has created 'shrines' of everyday objects, flowers, puppets, children's toys arranged in a vignette, and then reproduced them in gouache. The overall effect is child-friendly but also intensely emotionally evocative." SLJ

Brooks, Jeremy

Let there be peace; prayers from around the world. illustrated by Jude Daly. Frances Lincoln 2009 un il $16.95

Grades: PreK K 1 2 3   242

1. Peace 2. Prayers

ISBN 978-1-8450-7530-9; 1-8450-7530-7

"This picture-book collection of prayers sends universal messages of peace and global unity. Brooks . . . has pulled from diverse religious traditions. . . . Almost all of the selections are simple, immediate, and rhythmic. . . . Daly's delicately rendered, brightly hued paintings greatly increase the impact of the words. . . . Children of many backgrounds will be stirred by these prayers." Booklist

My first prayers. Albert Whitman 2009 un il $16.95

Grades: K 1 2   242

1. Prayers

ISBN 978-1-84507-535-4; 1-84507-535-8

"Brooks has collected prayers from a variety of nations including Poland, South Africa, the United States, and France, as well as several from his native England. The book features prayers of thanks, requests for guidance, blessings, and bedtime prayers. . . . Young readers will appreciate Brooks's gentle message of acceptance and inclusiveness." SLJ

A world of prayers; illustrated by Elena Gomez. Eerdmans Books for Young Readers 2006 un il $16

Grades: 1 2 3 4   242

1. Prayers

ISBN 0-8028-5285-8

LC 2004017482

"A collection of 26 prayers assembled under the headings, Prayers for the Morning, Mealtime Graces, Prayers for Nighttime, and Blessings. A brief introduction and comments at the beginning of each chapter reflect on the place of prayer in our lives. Written in simple, easy-to-read language, the entreaties are recited by children in a variety of lands. . . . Dreamlike, decorative paintings that reflect the various cultures greatly enhance the selections and emphasize the books message of inclusiveness." SLJ

A child's book of prayers; collected and illustrated by Juli Kangas. Dial Books for Young Readers 2007 un il $12.99

Grades: PreK K   242

1. Prayers

ISBN 978-0-8037-3054-0; 0-8037-3054-3

LC 2006017595

"Simple meditations, both familiar and less well known, are presented along with warmhearted illustrations for the purpose of exposing children to the spiritual benefits of prayer. The well-chosen selections begin at the start of the day and follow different youngsters and their families through school, meals, and other typical pursuits, offering prayers of blessing, thanksgiving, or praise suited to each endeavor. The pencil, watercolor, and oil-wash artwork skillfully depicts the charismatic characters, who hale from a variety of ethnic backgrounds and live in both city and rural settings." SLJ

Field, Rachel

Prayer for a child; pictures by Elizabeth Orton Jones. Diamond anniversary ed; Simon & Schuster Books for Young Readers 2004 un il $10.95

Grades: K 1 2   242

1. Prayers

ISBN 0-689-87356-5

LC 2004-5259

A reissue of the title first published 1944 by Macmillan

Awarded the Caldecott Medal, 1945

"The complete prayer, written in rhymed couplets, appears on the first page; then a few lines per page accompany serene illustrations of a girl in tender moments—stargazing out a window or smiling up at her parents. . . . This lovely book lends itself to nightly repetition (a reference to Jesus tags it for a Christian audience)." Publ Wkly

Goble, Paul

Song of creation; written and illustrated by Paul Goble. Eerdmans Books for Young Readers 2004 un il $16

Grades: K 1 2 3   242

1. Prayers 2. Creation

ISBN 0-8028-5271-8

LC 2004-6576

"In striking graphic compositions, Goble creates magical, yet concrete, scenes of birds, beasts, fish, and more, conveying a personal and a universal reverence for and connection to nature. A beautiful, praiseworthy volume that does, indeed, sing." Booklist

Jordan, Deloris

Baby blessings; a prayer for the day you are born. illustrated by James E. Ransome. Simon & Schuster Books for Young Readers 2010 un il $16.99

Grades: PreK K   242

1. Prayers

ISBN 1-4169-5362-0; 978-1-4169-5362-3

LC 2008017131

Jordan "offers a colloquial prayer to greet the newborn child, offers advice, and gives reassurance of family love and support as well as God's blessings. . . . Ransome's handsome . . . oil paintings follow an African American child growing from infancy to the start of kindergarten under the watchful eyes of his loving parents. . . . Tenderly portraying a child growing up within a warmhearted family, this appealing picture

book clearly expresses the faith, love, and hopes that surround him." Booklist

Piper, Sophie

I can say a prayer; illustrated by Emily Bolam. IPG/Lion 2011 un il $12.99

Grades: PreK   242

1. Prayers

ISBN 978-0-7459-6233-7; 0-7459-6233-5

"This collection of 12 rhyming prayers for the young child is accompanied by simple pen, ink, and watercolor illustrations that are right up preschoolers' alleys. Some of the prayers are original and some are familiar, such as the Lord's Prayer. A few are accompanied by verses from the Bible that serve to introduce that particular prayer. The prayers include familiar preschool concepts like counting, sharing, and making music. The bright, smiley illustrations, meanwhile, depict children going about their everyday activities. . . . This book does its job and does it well." Booklist

Prayers for a better world; [illustrated by] Mique Moriuchi. Lion Children's 2010 63p il $9.99

Grades: 1 2 3   242

1. Prayers 2. Religious poetry

ISBN 978-0-7459-6929-9; 0-7459-6929-1

"This brightly colored little book offers 38 short prayers in verse that reflect on the earth, its animals and plants, and living in harmony with other people and with nature. Most are original . . . while a few of the entries are attributed to other poets. The verses are lyrical and thought-provoking but still accessible to a young audience. . . . Moriuchi's naive artwork illustrates children and the natural world in joyful, colorful, and occasionally playful collages of painted papers." Booklist

Rivett, Rachel

I imagine; a child's book of prayers. illustrated by Mique Moriushi. Lion/Trafalgar 2011 il $12.99

Grades: PreK K 1   242

1. Prayers

ISBN 978-0-7459-6208-5; 0-7459-6208-4

"An unusual, whimsical collection of 12 short prayers offers an imaginative approach with a patterned text and creative responses from the children narrating the prayers. Each prayer follows a similar pattern, describing a particular circumstance or challenge familiar to young children ('if life is stormy'), followed by the child narrator's imagined action ('I imagine I'm a tree, tossed and tumbled in the wind'). In alternating spreads, there is also a comforting response from God ('you show me how my roots are getting stronger'). . . . Moriuchi's pleasing collage illustrations of chubby-cheeked children incorporate textured papers, fabrics and snippets of print along with painted elements. . . . The light, soothing atmosphere created by the well-matched prayers and illustrations is deceptively simple, effectively conveying powerful images and a strong sense of comfort." Kirkus

Rock, Lois

A child's first book of prayers; illustrated by Alison Jay. IPG/Lion 2012 il $12.99

Grades: K 1 2 3 4   242

1. Prayers

ISBN 978-0-7459-4474-6; 0-7459-4474-4

First published 2002 in the United Kingdom

"With its portable size, thick binding, comforting illustrations, and more than 150 prayers, this book is an appealing package. . . . The book's strength is that has something for everyone. The table of contents provides a quick guide, offering chapters like 'This Fragile World' and 'Prayers for Sad Times.' . . . The often attributed prayers, some of which rhyme, run the gamut from aspirational to celebratory to comforting and are uniformly short. . . . Jay's omnipresent soft watercolors add a further peacefulness." Booklist

263 Days, times, places of religious observance

Fisher, Aileen Lucia

The **story** of Easter; by Aileen Fisher; illustrated by Stefano Vitale. HarperCollins Pubs. 1997 un il hardcover o.p. pa $5.95

Grades: 3 4 5   **263**

1. Easter

ISBN 0-06-027296-1; 0-06-443490-7 pa

LC 96-17395

A newly illustrated edition of Easter published 1968 by Crowell

"This book begins with the story of Jesus' crucifixion and resurrection, but focuses on the origins of various Easter and vernal equinox traditions, with an emphasis on the history of egg decorating. . . . The folk-art illustrations are defined by strong black outlines, simple shapes, and natural colors." Horn Book Guide

264 Public worship

Alexander, Cecil Frances

★ **All** things bright and beautiful; based on the hymn by Cecil F. Alexander. Atheneum Books for Young Readers 2010 un il $16.99

Grades: PreK K 1 2 3   **264**

1. Hymns 2. Religious poetry

ISBN 978-1-4169-8939-4; 1-4169-8939-0

LC 2009032628

Bryan "interprets Cecil F. Alexander's 19th century hymn with cut-paper art defined by swirling geometrical shapes in neon hues, contributing to a pervasively jubilant atmosphere. Every spread is a riot of colors, movement, and natural splendors." Publ Wkly

Granfield, Linda

Out of slavery; the journey to Amazing Grace. illustrated by Janet Wilson. Tundra Books 2009 un il map $15.95

Grades: 4 5 6 7   **264**

1. Hymns 2. Clergy 3. Slave trade 4. Amazing grace (Hymn)

ISBN 978-0-88776-915-3; 0-88776-915-2

LC 2009502001

First published 1997 with title: Amazing Grace

This story of the hymn Amazing Grace "and its writer is beautifully written, evocative, and heart-wrenching. With an emphasis on John Newton and his years as a slave trader, Granfield shares how the events in his life led him to become an abolitionist, a pastor, and a writer of hymns. . . . Quotations from Newton's own writings are peppered throughout. Full-color, full-page illustrations add grandeur and appeal to the story. Rich in texture and color, the artwork is somber in tone and content." SLJ

266 Missions

Perritano, John

Spanish missions. Children's Press 2010 48p il map (True book) lib bdg $35; pa $6.95

Grades: 3 4 5   **266**

1. Franciscans 2. Native Americans 3. Missions 4. Southwestern

States 5. Spaniards -- United States

ISBN 978-0-531-20575-4 lib bdg; 0-531-20575-4 lib bdg; 978-0-531-21238-7 pa; 0-531-21238-6 pa

LC 2009017742

This "takes a look at the Christianity-fueled Spanish side of New World colonization. Beginning with a pithy account that delves into the conquer-and-cash-in strategy of Spanish exploration, it then nicely outlines what missions are . . . who built them . . . and why they were built. . . . With an evenhanded tone, Perritano also touches on important Spanish priests, . . . native revolts, and various missions in what is now Mexico and the southwestern U.S. . . . The colorful, amply illustrated design make for an accessible read." Booklist

Includes glossary and bibliographical references

270 History, geographic treatment, biography of Christianity; Church history; Christian denominations and sects

Demi

The **legend** of Saint Nicholas. Margaret K. McElderry Bks. 2003 un il $19.95

Grades: 3 4 5 6   **270**

1. Saints 2. Bishops 3. Santa Claus 4. Christian saints

ISBN 0-689-84681-9

LC 2002-8426

Recounts pivotal events in the history and life of Saint Nicholas, including how he came to be associated with Christmas and Santa Claus

"The gilded paintings are full of absorbing . . . details. . . . The greatest strength of this book is its straightforward, affectionate depiction of a person who, by his deep love for the young and the needy, embodies the spirit of Christmas." SLJ

270.1 Historical periods

Sabuda, Robert

Saint Valentine; retold and illustrated by Robert Sabuda. Atheneum Pubs. 1992 un il $16.95; pa $5.99

Grades: 1 2 3   **270.1**

1. Saints 2. Christian saints

ISBN 0-689-31762-X; 0-689-82429-7 pa

LC 91-25012

Recounts an incident in the life of St. Valentine, a physician who lived some 200 years after Christ, in which he treated a small child for blindness

"The fluid, straightforward retelling of the legend is accompanied by evocative, mosaiclike illustrations created from colored cut paper. Varying sizes of illustrations, careful page placement, and effective use of white space create the impression of the large-scale period mosaics. A fine melding of text and art." SLJ

271 Religious congregations and orders in church history

Kennedy, Robert Francis

Saint Francis of Assisi; a life of joy. written by Robert F. Kennedy, Jr.; illustrated by Dennis Nolan. Hyperion Books for Children 2004 31p il $18.99

Grades: 2 3 4   **271**

1. Saints 2. Christian saints 3. Writers on religion

ISBN 0-7868-1875-1

LC 2003-60420

"The book paints Francis in glowing terms . . . weaving together the major threads of his life: his early kindness to beggars in his family's fabric shop; his call to and ultimate rejection of a military career; his estrangement from his wealthy father; and his ministry to lepers, the impoverished, and animals. . . . Nolan's oil paintings render realistic figures in carefully staged scenes." SLJ

Norris, Kathleen
★ The **holy** twins: Benedict and Scholastica; written by Kathleen Norris; illustrated by Tomie De Paola. Putnam 2001 un il $16.99
Grades: 3 4 5   **271**
     1. Monks 2. Saints 3. Christian saints 4. Writers on religion
     ISBN 0-399-23424-1
                        LC 00-40294

"This fictionalized biography of Saints Benedict and Scholastica, twins who lived in sixth-century Italy, is told in a lively, authoritative manner. . . . dePaola's elegant, stylized artwork seems particularly well suited to the eternal quality of religious subjects. The framed spreads are painted in soft, warm acrylics on tea-stained watercolor paper, which gives the semblance of an old manuscript." SLJ

Visconti, Guido
Clare and Francis; text by Guido Visconti, inspired by the biographies and written works of the two saints of Assisi collected in the Franciscan Sources. Eerdmans Books for Young Readers 2004 un il $20
Grades: 4 5 6 7   **271**
     1. Nuns 2. Saints 3. Christian saints 4. Writers on religion
     ISBN 0-8028-5269-6
                      LC 2003-13441

Reviews the lives and works of two members of Assisi society, Francis and Clare, who renounced their wealth and founded religious orders dedicated to relying on God and living in peace, poverty, and humility.

"The familiar story of Francis (and to a lesser extent, Clare) is beautifully treated in this book, with luminous iconic artwork and a text that is both down-to-earth and stroking the stars." Booklist

282   Roman Catholic Church

Hawker, Frances
Christianity in Mexico; written by Frances Hawker and Noemi Paz; photography by Bruce Campbell. Crabtree Pub. Co. 2010 32p il (Families and their faiths) lib bdg $26.60; pa $8.95
Grades: 3 4 5   **282**
     1. Catholics 2. Mexico
     ISBN 978-0-7787-5007-9 lib bdg; 0-7787-5007-8 lib bdg; 978-0-7787-5024-6 pa; 0-7787-5024-8 pa
                      LC 2009-14157

This "book introduces a child who practices [Christianity]. . . . Provides a solid introduction without overwhelming readers with complex regional variations in practices and beliefs. . . . Words and phrases that are unique to the faith appear in bold font and are defined at greater length in the glossary." SLJ

Includes glossary

289.3   Latter-Day Saints (Mormons)

Bial, Raymond
Nauvoo; Mormon city on the Mississippi River. [by] Raymond Bial. Houghton Mifflin Co. 2006 44p il map $17
Grades: 5 6 7 8   **289.3**
     1. Mormons 2. Church of Jesus Christ of Latter-day Saints 3.

Illinois -- History
     ISBN 978-0-618-39685-6; 0-618-39685-3
                      LC 2005027528

"Bial introduces readers to a city that was established by the Church of Jesus Christ of Latter Day Saints in 1839. . . . This effectively written account provides a sympathetic but balanced introduction to Mormon beliefs. . . . Excellent color photographs grace almost every page." SLJ

George, Charles
What makes me a Mormon? by Charles George. KidHaven Press 2004 48p il map (What makes me a--?) $27
Grades: 3 4 5   **289.3**
     1. Mormons 2. Church of Jesus Christ of Latter-day Saints
     ISBN 978-0-7377-3083-8; 0-7377-3083-8
                      LC 2004-13636

This describes Morman origins, beliefs, practices, and holidays
"Presenting information about religion objectively for younger audiences poses a difficult challenge, but [this title does] an excellent job of it." Booklist
Includes bibliographical references

289.6   Society of Friends (Quakers)

Woog, Adam
What makes me a Quaker? by Adam Woog. KidHaven Press 2004 48p il (What makes me a--?) $27
Grades: 3 4 5   **289.6**
     1. Society of Friends
     ISBN 978-0-7377-3082-1; 0-7377-3082-X
                      LC 2004-13096

This explains Quakerism's origins, beliefs, practices, and future
"Presenting information about religion objectively for younger readers poses a difficult challenge, but [this title does] an excellent job of it." Booklist
Includes glossary and bibliographical references

292   Classical religion (Greek and Roman religion)

Aliki
★ The **gods** and goddesses of Olympus; written and illustrated by Aliki. HarperCollins Pubs. 1994 48p il $16; pa $6.95
Grades: 2 3 4 5   **292**
     1. Classical mythology
     ISBN 0-06-023530-6; 0-06-446189-0 pa
                      LC 93-17834

"This large-format book provides a quick, brightly illustrated introduction to the ancient Greek gods and goddesses." Booklist

Bryant, Megan E.
Oh my gods! a look-it-up guide to the gods of mythology. Franklin Watts 2009 128p il map (Mythlopedia) lib bdg $39; pa $13.95
Grades: 4 5 6 7   **292**
     1. Gods and goddesses 2. Classical mythology
     ISBN 978-1-60631-026-7 lib bdg; 1-60631-026-7 lib bdg; 978-1-60631-058-8 pa; 1-60631-058-5 pa
                      LC 2009-17169

Presents a guide to Greek mythology, providing profiles of gods and goddesses along with information on monsters, heroes, and the underworld.

"The book is organized around entries on major gods and titans, each with vital stats and a Top 10 Things to Know about Me, followed by a few highlights from their lore and sidebars that delve into their cultural relevance. Illustrations abound, from embellished stock images to original cartoons, and the pastel-heavy color scheme may entice readers otherwise resistant to the grays and ivories that tend to dominate classicism." Booklist

Includes glossary and bibliographical references

She's all that! a look-it-up guide to the goddesses of mythology. Franklin Watts 2009 128p il map (Mythlopedia) lib bdg $39; pa $13.95

Grades: 4 5 6 7   **292**
    1. Gods and goddesses 2. Classical mythology
    ISBN 978-1-60631-027-4 lib bdg; 1-60631-027-5 lib bdg; 978-1-60631-059-5 pa; 1-60631-059-3 pa

                            LC 2009-17168
Presents a guide to Greek mythology, providing profiles of goddesses and the myths surrounding them.

This "spices things up with sassy artwork, a pastel color scheme, and an OMG sensibility. . . . Aside from the heaps of information coming from all angles on just about every page, . . . [this] book also contains a decent family tree, a rudimentary star chart, and lists of further reading. . . . For kids unconvinced that anything so old and gray could have any bearing on their lives, . . . [this provides] a feisty . . . guide to the many cultural references lingering from antiquity." Booklist

Includes glossary and bibliographical references

Clayton, Sally Pomme
    Greek myths; stories of sun, stone, and sea. Sally Pomme Clayton; illustrated by Jan Ray. Frances Lincoln Children's Books 2012 77 p. $19.99

Grades: 2 3 4   **292**
    1. Greek mythology
    ISBN 1847802273; 9781847802279

This children's book by Sally Pomme Clayton presents a "collection of Greek myths with special emphasis on adventure and heroic quests. The ten stories include: Creation of the Gods, Pandora's Box, Atalanta, Perseus, Pegasus and Bellerophon, King Midas and the Gift of Gold, King Midas and the Donkey's Ears, How Arachne Became a Spider." (Publisher's note)

    ★ **Persephone**; a journey from winter to spring. by Sally Pomme Clayton; illustrated by Virginia Lee. Eerdmans Books for Young Readers 2009 un il $18

Grades: 2 3 4   **292**
    1. Persephone (Greek deity)
    ISBN 0-8028-5349-8; 978-0-8028-5349-3

                            LC 2008018391
"Approaching the Greek myth of Persephone with the respect that a good storyteller holds for a great story, Clayton retells the tale with drama and grace. The mixed-media artwork creates a series of scenes defined by sweeping lines, broad views, and restrained use of color." Booklist

Curlee, Lynn
    Mythological creatures; a classical bestiary: tales of strange beings, fabulous creatures, fearsome beasts, & hideous monsters from ancient Greek mythology. Atheneum Books for Young Readers 2008 35p il $17.99

Grades: 3 4 5   **292**
    1. Mythical animals 2. Classical mythology
    ISBN 978-1-4169-1453-2; 1-4169-1453-6

                            LC 2006-16980
"A proponderance of these sixteen fabulous beasts are half human (or, like Pan, minor deities). Most are monstrous in behavior as well as

body; only the purely animal Pegasus and Phoenix possess some sort of nobility. Confining each within a broad, sober border, Curlee depicts all as classically statuesque. . . . Staightforward and clean, the accompanying text outlines without dramatization what these mythical beings were and their role in Greek lore. . . . The book is an eye-catching introduction to the world of ancient myth." Horn Book

Gerstein, Mordicai, 1935-
    ★ **I** am Pan! written and illustrated by Mordicai Gerstein. Roaring Brook Press 2016 80 p. color illustrations

Grades: K 1 2 3 4 5   **292**
    1. Greek mythology 2. Gods, Greek 3. Pan (Greek deity)
    ISBN 1626720355; 9781626720350

                            LC 2014033005
In this book, by Mordicai Gerstein, "Pan, god of the wild, creates pandemonium wherever he goes. Noise and confusion follow him as he steals arrows from Artemis, conceives panic, tricks the moon into falling in love with him, and saves the world from the monster, Typhon. With panache and a wicked pair of horns, Pan spreads chaos and laughter on the way to becoming Mount Olympus's most lovable pest." (Publisher's note)

"The illustrations are fun and blend seamlessly with the text, making the story engaging. The format is perfect for packing tons of humor, whimsy, and action on every page." SLJ

Includes bibliographical references.

Karas, G. Brian
    ★ **Young** Zeus. Scholastic Press 2010 un il $17.99

Grades: 2 3 4 5   **292**
    1. Classical mythology 2. Zeus (Greek deity)
    ISBN 978-0-439-72806-5; 0-439-72806-1

                            LC 2009-10148
Karas "opens this spirited embellishment of Zeus's little-documented boyhood with an author's note explaining that he drew form early accounts of the Greek gods and 'true to the nature of myths, imagined the rest.'. . . . But Kara's imagination serves him well in making Zeus a relatable character. . . . Droll dialogue and asides mitigate the tale's dark undertones [and] . . . energetic, airy gouache and pencil cartoons playfully skew scale and also keep the tone light." Publ Wkly

Kimmel, Eric A.
    ★ The **McElderry** book of Greek myths; [by] Eric A. Kimmel; illustrated by Pep Montserrat. M.K. McElderry Books 2008 96p il $21.99

Grades: K 1 2 3   **292**
    1. Classical mythology
    ISBN 1-4169-1534-6; 978-1-4169-1534-8

                            LC 2005031010
In this collection of retellings of Greek myths "Kimmel uses spare, direct language and lots of exciting action. . . . Montserrat's stylish computer-generated artwork picks up on ancient Greek design motifs and creates memorable characters from the mythical archetypes." Booklist

Lupton, Hugh
    The **adventures** of Odysseus; [by] Hugh Lupton and Daniel Morden; [illustrated by] Christina Balit. Barefoot Books 2006 un il $19.99

Grades: 3 4 5 6   **292**
    1. Classical mythology 2. Odysseus (Greek mythology)
    ISBN 1-84148-800-3

                            LC 2005032532
This "book retells Homer's epic of Odysseus' perilous journey home in a immediate, fast-paced narrative. . . . The text is beautifully framed with crisp, brightly colored, mosaic-style illustrations of the heroes and monsters, rendered in watercolor, gouache, and gold ink." Booklist

Mayer, Marianna

★ **Pegasus**; as told by Marianna Mayer; illustrated by K. Y. Craft. Morrow Junior Bks. 1998 un il $17.99

Grades: 4 5 6   **292**

1. Classical mythology 2. Pegasus (Greek mythology)

ISBN 0-688-13382-7; 0-688-13383-5 lib bdg

LC 96-32442

Retells how Bellerophon, son of the King of Corinth, secures the help of the winged horse Pegasus in order to fight the monstrous Chimera

"Dark, painterly illustrations set in gold frames heighten the mysticism in this lyrical interpretation of the Greek myth." Horn Book Guide

McCaughrean, Geraldine

★ **Hercules**; retold by Geraldine McCaughrean. Cricket Books 2005 142p il (Heroes) $16.95

Grades: 5 6 7 8   **292**

1. Classical mythology 2. Hercules (Legendary character)

ISBN 978-0-8126-2737-4; 0-8126-2737-7

LC 2005004524

First published 2003 by Oxford University Press

This is a retelling of the twelve labors of Hercules including his battles with the Cretan Bull, the many-headed Hydra, the Nemean Lion, and the three-headed guardian of hell, Cerberus.

"This volume does a creditable job of making Hercules a dimensional character whose struggles against fate and the vindictiveness of the gods arouse readers' sympathy. . . . McCaughrean enlivens the familiar story with arresting imagery." SLJ

★ **Odysseus**; retold by Geraldine McCaughrean. Cricket Books 2004 148p il (Heroes) $16.95

Grades: 5 6 7 8   **292**

1. Classical mythology 2. Odysseus (Greek mythology)

ISBN 978-0-8126-2721-3; 0-8126-2721-0

LC 2004-10734

"With mounting suspense, wild action, and simple, rhythmic prose, this dramatic retelling of Homer's classic makes a gripping read-aloud as well as an exciting introduction to the story." Booklist

★ **Perseus**; retold by Geraldine McCaughrean. Cricket Books 2005 118p il (Heroes) $16.95

Grades: 5 6 7 8   **292**

1. Classical mythology 2. Perseus (Greek mythology)

ISBN 978-0-8126-2735-0; 0-8126-2735-0

This "makes a thrilling read-aloud. . . . McCaughrean blends the colloquial and contemporary into the heroic quest." Booklist

Osborne, Mary Pope

Favorite Greek myths; retold by Mary Pope Osborne; illustrated by Troy Howell. Scholastic 1989 81p il lib bdg $18.95

Grades: 3 4 5 6   **292**

1. Classical mythology

ISBN 0-590-41338-4

LC 87-32332

Retells twelve tales from Greek mythology, including the stories of King Midas, Echo and Narcissus, the Golden Apples, and Cupid and Psyche

"Osborne's retellings are both lively and descriptive, while Howell's full-color, often iridescent illustrations set the scene and mood at the start of each tale." Publ Wkly

Includes glossary and bibliographical references

Otfinoski, Steven

All in the family; a look-it-up guide to the in-laws, outlaws, and offspring of mythology. F. Watts 2009 128p il (Mythlopedia) lib bdg $39; pa $13.95

Grades: 4 5 6 7   **292**

1. Classical mythology

ISBN 978-1-60631-025-0 lib bdg; 1-60631-025-9 lib bdg; 978-1-60631-057-1 pa; 1-60631-057-7 pa

LC 2009-20999

"Jam-packed with trivia, brief profiles, god and goddess relationships, stories, 'Top 10 Things to Know About Me' facts, and entertaining illustrations, this title explores 20 heroes and mortals of classic Greek mythology. The selections include the well-known Achilles, Heracles, Odysseus, and Pandora and the more obscure Meleager, Orion, Atalanta, and Bellerophon; each one is given lively treatment. . . . The lighthearted style and humorous collage and cartoon illustrations may draw even the most reluctant of readers." SLJ

Includes glossary and bibliographical references

Rylant, Cynthia

The **beautiful** stories of life; six Greek myths, retold. illustrated by Carson Ellis. Harcourt 2009 71p il $16

Grades: 5 6 7 8   **292**

1. Classical mythology

ISBN 978-0-15-206184-5; 0-15-206184-3

LC 2007-34808

"Rylant retells the stories of Pandora, Persephone, Orpheus, Pygmalion, Narcissus, and Psyche in this trim, handsome book. Written in a modern style with an old-fashioned feel, the selections sit well with other titles in the genre. . . . Accompanied by full-page black-and-white illustrations and sprinkled with decorations, the whole package is nicely done." SLJ

Steer, Dugald

The **mythology** handbook; a course in ancient Greek myths. by Hestia Evans; edited by Dugald A. Steer and Clint Twist. Candlewick Press 2009 71p il map $12.99

Grades: 4 5 6 7   **292**

1. Classical mythology

ISBN 978-0-7636-4291-4

"This follow-up to Mythology (Candlewick, 2007) again uses the voice of a fictional 19th-century scholar. Here, Lady Hestia Evans offers a guide to elements of Greek myth for her two children, providing information in 'lessons' . . . with exercises based on each topic. Some of the activities encourage students to do further research . . . while others suggest that they draw new monsters, write hymns with the Muses' help, or design a new pentathlon for the Olympics. Mazes and a word search (using Greek letters) are also included. . . . The activities are engaging, and the illustrations of creatures and maps of the ancient world will add to the knowledge of even more experienced myth fans." SLJ

Townsend, Michael

Michael Townsend's amazing Greek myths of wonder and blunders. Dial Books for Young Readers 2010 160p il $14.99

Grades: 4 5 6 7   **292**

1. Greek mythology -- Graphic novels 2. Graphic novels 3. Mythology, Greek

ISBN 978-0-8037-3308-4; 0-8037-3308-9

"Ten familiar myths—the stories of Pandora, Arachne, Midas, Perseus, and others—are embellished with humor, the gory parts glossed over, and served up in blazing color for fans of either comic books or Percy Jackson, or both. . . . Conversational, up-to-date language and broad jokes help to make the stories accessible and coordinate well with the simple, cartoon illustration style." SLJ

Turnbull, Ann

★ **Greek** myths; retold by Ann Turnbull; illustrated by Sarah Young. Candlewick Press 2011 165p il

Grades: 5 6 7 8 9 10 **292**

1. Classical mythology
ISBN 0-7636-5111-7; 978-0-7636-5111-4

LC 2010-39178

Turnbull divides sixteen Greek myths "under three headings: Earth, the Heavens, and the Underworld; Monsters and Heroes; Gods and Mortals. . . . Grades five to ten." (Bull Cent Child Books)

"Sixteen Greek myths . . . are retold here with stylistic grace well matched to beautiful visual presentation. . . . Turnbull narrates with . . . vibrancy. . . . Sarah Young's mixed-media artwork—regal, yet sensuous compositions in richly textured earthtones touch[ed] with gold—is sufficiently representational to assist younger readers with context clues, and sufficiently elegant and sophisticated to satisfy seasoned readers." Bull Cent Child Books

292.1 Specific elements

Craft, Marie

★ **Cupid** and Psyche; as told by M. Charlotte Craft; illustrated by K. Y. Craft. Morrow Junior Bks. 1996 un il $16

Grades: 4 5 6 7 **292.1**

1. Classical mythology 2. Eros (Greek deity) 3. Psyche (Greek deity)
ISBN 0-688-13163-8

LC 95-14895

"In this Greek myth, Cupid falls in love with Psyche and treats her royally but does not reveal himself. When Psyche tries to discover his identity, Cupid leaves her, but she wins him back by accomplishing three difficult tasks. Recalling an earlier artistic era, the occasionally ornate romantic paintings—some of them quite dramatic—feature detailed landscapes and beautiful figures in flowing drapery." Horn Book Guide

293 Germanic religion

Fisher, Leonard Everett

Gods and goddesses of the ancient Norse. Holiday House 2001 un il $16.95

Grades: 3 4 5 6 **293**

1. Norse mythology
ISBN 0-8234-1569-4

LC 00-32040

In this guide each "double-page spread is devoted to one or two of the major gods or goddesses, accompanied by a succinct description that includes significant characteristics and responsibilities. A pronunciation guide and family tree are appended." Horn Book Guide
Includes bibliographical references

Lunge-Larsen, Lise

The **adventures** of Thor the Thunder God; retold by Lise Lunge-Larsen; illustrated by Jim Madsen. Houghton Mifflin 2007 76p il $19.95

Grades: 3 4 5 6 **293**

1. Norse mythology
ISBN 0-618-47301-7; 978-0-618-47301-4

LC 2004015765

"Madsen's . . . majestic digitally rendered illustrations bring the tales to life, echoing their humor. . . . These retellings offer an accessible and engaging doorway into the world of Norse mythology." Publ Wkly

Yasuda, Anita

Explore Norse Myths! With 25 Great Projects. Anita Yasuda, illustrated by Bryan Stone. Nomad Press 2015 96 p. col. ill., color maps (hardcover) $19.95

Grades: 3 4 5 6 **293**

1. Vikings 2. Norse mythology
ISBN 9781619303164; 9781619303201; 1619303167

This children's book, by Anita Yasuda and illustrated by Bryan Stone, part of the "Explore Your World" series, profiles Norse mythology. "Learning about Norse myths means unearthing the origin of Viking beliefs, as well as exploring their ships, tools, and other technology that flourished for nearly 450 years. Along the way, kids will read how Norse myths helped explain the natural world from thunder to the seasons, from creation to death." (Publisher's note)

"The graphics-heavy page layouts nicely balance the content, vocab explanations, cartoon illustrations... and sidebars, which makes it easy to negotiate the different categories of presentation." Booklist
Includes glossary, bibliographic references and index.

294 Religions of Indic origin

Ollhoff, Jim

Indian mythology. ABDO Pub. 2012 32 p. il map (The world of mythology) lib bdg $27.07

Grades: 5 6 7 8 **294**

1. Hinduism 2. Indic mythology 3. India -- Religion
ISBN 978-1-61714-722-7; 1-61714-722-2

LC 2010041628

'This book offers information about Indian mythology, answering questions such as "Who is Devi? What is Ganesha? Why are myths so important in our lives? Myths are a rich source of history. People use them to make sense of our world. Even before myths were written down, people told and retold the stories of the gods and goddesses of their homeland. Readers of Indian Mythology will learn the history of myths, as well as their deeper meaning." (Publisher's note) The book "introduces Brahma, Vishnu, Shiva, Kali, and other Hindu gods and goddesses while also discussing how the deities often took on different forms called avatars." (Booklist)

"Ollhoff writes in a clear and engaging fashion, presenting complex issues in a way that will be easy for youngsters to grasp. . . . The photographs and reproductions of art tie directly to the [text]." SLJ

294.3 Buddhism

Chodzin, Sherab

The **wisdom** of the crows and other Buddhist tales; retold by Sherab Chödzin & Alexandra Kohn; illustrated by Marie Cameron. Tricycle Press 1998 80p il pa $16.95

Grades: 4 5 6 7 **294.3**

1. Buddhism
ISBN 1-883672-68-6

LC 97-30441

First published 1997 in the United Kingdom with title: The Barefoot book of Buddhist tales

A collection of thirteen retold Buddhist tales from all over Asia, illustrating various aspects of Buddhist thought

"Folktale lovers will find much to like here. Marie Cameron's clear, fresh watercolors, incorporating Asian artistic motifs and bordered with waves and origami, are handsomely rendered." Booklist
Includes bibliographical references

Demi

★ **Buddha**. Holt & Co. 1996 un il $21.95

Grades: 4 5 6   **294.3**

   1. Philosophers 2. Buddhist leaders

   ISBN 0-8050-4203-2

                    LC 95-16906

Demi "uses clear, uncomplicated storytelling to present complex philosophical concepts. . . . The gilded illustrations (based, according to the jacket, on 'Indian, Chinese, Japanese, Burmese, and Indonesian paintings, sculptures, and sutra illustrations') are delicate, yet the colors and composition are bold, with central figures and action cascading beyond the careful borders." Bull Cent Child Books

   Buddha stories. Holt & Co. 1997 un il $21.95

Grades: 3 4 5 6   **294.3**

   1. Jataka stories

   ISBN 0-8050-4886-3

                    LC 96-31253

This "is a picture-book collection of eleven Jataka tales retold in a formal yet straightforward style. . . . An author's note gives the source of the tales as well as the historical basis for the design concept behind the elegantly sophisticated artwork. Both text and illustrations are done in gold ink on deep indigo paper, resulting in a striking visual impact." Bull Cent Child Books

Ganeri, Anita

   ★ **Buddhism**; [by] Anita Ganeri. World Almanac Library 2006 48p il map (Religions of the world) lib bdg $30.60

Grades: 5 6 7 8   **294.3**

   1. Buddhism

   ISBN 0-8368-5865-4

                    LC 2005041708

The author "presents a survey of Buddhist history, beliefs, sacred texts, festivals, and lifecycle events. . . . There is discussion of the art and folk literature associated with the religious tradition. Colorful photographs, illustrations, and art reproductions appear throughout." SLJ

   Includes bibliographical references

George, Charles

   What makes me a Buddhist? by Charles George. KidHaven Press 2004 48p il (What makes me a--?) $23.70

Grades: 3 4 5   **294.3**

   1. Buddhism

   ISBN 0-7377-2269-X

                    LC 2003-24344

This describes the beliefs, origins, practices, holidays and future of Buddhism.

"An attractive, colorful design is the background for a map and numerous color photographs and diagrams. But best of all is the straightforward organization and the clarity of the text." Booklist

   Includes bibliographical references

Hawker, Frances

   Buddhism in Thailand; written by Frances Hawker and Sunantha Phusomsai; photography by Bruce Campbell. Crabtree Pub. Co. 2009 32p il map (Families and their faiths) lib bdg $26.60; pa $8.95

Grades: 3 4 5   **294.3**

   1. Buddhism 2. Thailand

   ISBN 978-0-7787-5006-2 lib bdg; 0-7787-5006-X lib bdg; 978-0-7787-5023-9 pa; 0-7787-5023-X pa

                    LC 2009-14156

This "book introduces a child who practices [Buddhism]. . . . Provides a solid introduction without overwhelming readers with complex regional variations in practices and beliefs. . . . Words and phrases that are unique to the faith appear in bold font and are defined at greater length in the glossary." SLJ

   Includes glossary

Nardo, Don

   Buddhism. Compass Point Books 2009 48p il map (World religions) lib bdg $27.99

Grades: 5 6 7 8   **294.3**

   1. Buddhism

   ISBN 978-0-7565-4236-8 lib bdg; 0-7565-4236-7 lib bdg

                    LC 2009-11453

"The colorful, attractive layout includes high-quality reproductions of photographs, maps, and paintings. Students who are new to religious studies, as well as those doing reports, will find that this . . . meets their needs." SLJ

   Includes glossary and bibliographical references

Wallace, Holly

   Buddhism; by Holly Wallace. NewForest Press 2012 33 p. color illustrations library $31.35

Grades: 3 4 5 6   **294.3**

   1. Buddhism 2. Buddhism -- Customs and practices

   ISBN 9781848986152

                    LC 2012003250

Looks at the beliefs, customs, and festivals of Buddhism, with information on the clothing, traditions, food, historical writings, holy days, and holy places that define Buddhists as presented by a child who practices the religion.

294.5   Hinduism

Ganeri, Anita

   The **Ramayana** and Hinduism. Smart Apple Media 2003 30p il (Sacred texts) $27.10

Grades: 5 6 7 8 9   **294.5**

   1. Hinduism

   ISBN 1-58340-242-X

                    LC 2003-42352

Explains the history and practices of the religion of Hinduism, especially as revealed through its sacred book, the Ramayana

George, Charles

   What makes me a Hindu? by Charles George. KidHaven Press 2004 48p il map (What makes me a--?) $27

Grades: 3 4 5   **294.5**

   1. Hinduism

   ISBN 978-0-7377-2267-3; 0-7377-2267-3

                    LC 2003-24346

This describes Hindu origins, beliefs, practices, and holidays

"Presenting information about religion objectively for younger audiences poses a difficult challenge, but [this title does] an excellent job of it." Booklist

   Includes bibliographical references

Hawker, Frances

   Hinduism in Bali; written by Frances Hawker and Putu Resi; photography by Bruce Campbell. Crabtree Pub. Company 2009 32p il (Families and their faiths) lib bdg $26.60; pa $8.95

Grades: 3 4 5   **294.5**

   1. Hinduism 2. Indonesia 3. Bali Island (Indonesia)

   ISBN 978-0-7787-5008-6 lib bdg; 0-7787-5008-6 lib bdg; 978-0-7787-5008-6 pa; 0-7787-5008-6 pa

                    LC 2009-14297

This "book introduces a child who practices [Hinduism]. . . . Provides a solid introduction without overwhelming readers with complex regional variations in practices and beliefs. . . . Words and phrases that are unique to the faith appear in bold font and are defined at greater length in the glossary." SLJ

Includes glossary

Heiligman, Deborah

★ **Celebrate** Diwali; [by] Deborah Heiligman; consultant, Dr. Vasudha Narayanan. National Geographic 2006 32p il map (Holidays around the world) $15.95; lib bdg $23.90

Grades: K 1 2 3 **294.5**

1. Divali

ISBN 0-7922-5922-X; 0-7922-5923-8 lib bdg

LC 2006003426

This "focuses on the Hindu celebration in India but mentions observance by the Sikh and Jain faiths and also show customs in four other countries. . . . Each spread features up to three high-quality color photographs." SLJ

Jani, Mahendra

What you will see inside a Hindu temple; [by] Mahendra Jani and Vandana Jani; with photographs by Neirah Bhargava and Vijay Dave. Skylight Paths 2005 32p il (What you will see inside¿) $17.99

Grades: 3 4 5 6 **294.5**

1. Hinduism

ISBN 978-1-59473-116-7; 1-59473-116-0

"This introduces the beliefs and practices of the Hindu religion. The book opens with a traditional Sanskrit word of greeting . . . setting the respectful, inviting tone of the text, which leads readers into a temple. The book explains what can be seen there and discusses Hindu beliefs, worship practices, scriptures, celebrations, blessing ceremonies, and family shrines in homes. A typical double-page spread includes one large color photograph and a few small ones illustrating several paragraphs of clear, concise text." Booklist

Plum-Ucci, Carol

Celebrate Diwali; [by] Carol Plum-Ucci. Enslow Publishers 2008 128p il map (Celebrate holidays) $31.93

Grades: 5 6 7 8 **294.5**

1. Divali

ISBN 978-0-7660-2778-7; 0-7660-2778-3

LC 2006028106

This describes the history, cultural significance, customs, symbols and celebrations around the world of the Hindu holiday of Diwali.

"Captioned photographs, maps, drawings, and sidebars combine with accessible text to present a thorough discussion of [Diwali]. . . . This . . . is a useful resource." Horn Book Guide

Includes glossary and bibliographical references

Rasamandala Das

★ **Hinduism**. World Almanac Library 2006 48p il map (Religions of the world) $30.60

Grades: 5 6 7 8 **294.5**

1. Hinduism

ISBN 0-8368-5867-0

Hinduism is "explored in an accessible introductory manner, including information on [its] history, teachings, religious practices, culture and lifestyle, and the [faith's role] in today's global society. Vibrant full-color photographs are appropriately placed within the [text]. Ideal for . . . school reports or for general interest." SLJ

Includes bibliographical references

Wallace, Holly

Hinduism; Babu's story. by Holly Wallace. NewForest Press 2012 2 p. color illustrations (library bound) $31.35

Grades: 3 4 5 6 **294.5**

1. Hinduism

ISBN 9781848986169

LC 2012003252

Looks at the beliefs, customs, and festivals of Hinduism, with information on the clothing, traditions, food, historical writings, holy days, and holy places that define Hindus as presented by a girl who practices the religion.

294.6 Sikhism

Dalton, David, 1945-

Sikhism; Inderjeet's story. by David Dalton. NewForest Press 2012 32 p. color illustrations library $31.35

Grades: 3 4 5 6 **294.6**

1. Sikhism

ISBN 9781848986176

LC 2012003256

"Using a first-person narrative, explains the beliefs, customs, and festivals of Sikhism. Explains the clothing, traditions, historical writings, former leaders, and holy places that define Sikhs. Includes a map to show where Sikhism originated." (Publisher's note)

Hawker, Frances

Sikhism in India; written by Frances Hawker and Mohini Kaur Bhatia; photography by Bruce Campbell. Crabtree Pub. Company 2009 32p il (Families and their faiths) lib bdg $26.60; pa $8.95

Grades: 3 4 5 **294.6**

1. Sikhs 2. Sikhism 3. India

ISBN 978-0-7787-5011-6 lib bdg; 0-7787-5011-6 lib bdg; 978-0-7787-5028-4 pa; 0-7787-5028-0 pa

LC 2009-14160

This "book introduces a child who practices [Sikhism]. . . . Provides a solid introduction without overwhelming readers with complex regional variations in practices and beliefs. . . . Words and phrases that are unique to the faith appear in bold font and are defined at greater length in the glossary." SLJ

Includes glossary

296 Judaism

Hawker, Frances

Judaism in Israel; written by Frances Hawker and Daniel Taub; photography by Bruce Campbell. Crabtree Pub. 2010 32p il (Families and their faiths) lib bdg $26.60; pa $8.95

Grades: 3 4 5 **296**

1. Judaism 2. Israel

ISBN 978-0-7787-5010-9 lib bdg; 0-7787-5010-8 lib bdg; 978-0-7787-5027-7 pa; 0-7787-5027-2 pa

LC 2009-14159

This "book introduces a child who practices [Judaism]. . . . Provides a solid introduction without overwhelming readers with complex regional variations in practices and beliefs. . . . Words and phrases that are unique to the faith appear in bold font and are defined at greater length in the glossary." SLJ

Includes glossary

Keene, Michael

★ **Judaism**; [by] Michael Keene. World Almanac Library 2006 48p il map (Religions of the world) lib bdg $30.60

Grades: 5 6 7 8   **296**

1. Judaism

ISBN 0-8368-5869-7

LC 2005041734

This "volume presents fundamental beliefs and faith foundations, current status and practices of [Judaism] around the globe, and a time line of historically significant events. . . . The [book is] enumerated with full-color photographs on every page, charts, maps, and tables. . . . [This title] will enhance the education of diverse populations." SLJ

Includes bibliographical references

Rosinsky, Natalie M.

Judaism. Compass Point Books 2009 48p il map (World religions) lib bdg $27.99

Grades: 5 6 7 8   **296**

1. Judaism

ISBN 978-0-7565-4240-5 lib bdg; 0-7565-4240-5 lib bdg

LC 2009-15813

"The colorful, attractive layout includes high-quality reproductions of photographs, maps, and paintings. Students who are new to religious studies, as well as those doing reports, will find that this . . . meets their needs." SLJ

Includes glossary and bibliographical references

296.1   Sources

Chaikin, Miriam

Angels sweep the desert floor; Bible legends about Moses in the wilderness. illustrated by Alexander Koshkin. Clarion Bks. 2002 102p il $19

Grades: 4 5 6 7   **296.1**

1. Prophets 2. Bible stories 3. Jewish legends 4. Angels -- Fiction 5. Biblical characters

ISBN 0-395-97825-4

LC 2001-47501

A collection of eighteen stories based on the Bible which tell how angels respond to God's commands to ease the way for Moses and the Israelites as they cross the wilderness after being freed from slavery in Egypt

"The full-page watercolor, tempera, and gouache illustrations have a fanciful formality that complements the narrative. Capable of exciting the creative, as well as the spiritual imagination, these wonderful stories make great read-alouds." SLJ

Includes bibliographical references

Heiman, Diane

It's a-- it's a-- it's a mitzvah! Diane Heiman and Liz Suneby; Illustrations by Laurel Molk. Jewish Lights Publishing 2012 32 p. $18.99

Grades: PreK K 1 2   **296.1**

1. Judaism -- fiction 2. Kindness -- fiction 3. Judaism -- Customs and practices -- fiction 4. Commandments (Judaism)

ISBN 1580235093; 9781580235099

LC 2012003703

This book by Liz Suneby and Diane Heiman, illustrated by Laurel Molk, is an "introduction to the joys of doing mitzvoth. Join Mitzvah Meerkat and friends as they introduce children to the everyday kindnesses that mark the beginning of . . . a lifetime commitment to 'tikkun olam' (repairing the world). . . . Children engage with Jewish wisdom as they share in welcoming new friends, forgiving mistakes, respecting elders, sharing food with the hungry, and much, much more." (Publisher's note)

Pinsker, Marlee

In the days of sand and stars; illustrated by Fran¿cois Thisdale. Tundra Books 2006 87p il $22.95

Grades: 5 6 7 8   **296.1**

1. Bible stories 2. Jewish legends 3. Women in the Bible

ISBN 978-0-88776-724-1; 0-88776-724-9

This is a collection of stories from the Midrash about women including Eve, Naamah, Sarai, Sarah, Rebecca, Leah, Rachel, Dina, and Yocheved.

"Pinsker works like a musician, playing with words instead of notes, but the result is just as lilting and lyrical. The stories are matched by unusual illustrations. Thisdale blends traditional artwork with digital technology. Pieces of photographs mix with ancient elements, giving the pictures a fresh, compelling look." Booklist

296.4   Traditions, rites, public services

Balsley, Tilda

Maccabee! the story of Hanukkah. illustrated by David Harrington. Kar-Ben Pub. 2010 un il lib bdg $17.95; pa $7.95

Grades: K 1 2 3   **296.4**

1. Hanukkah 2. Stories in rhyme

ISBN 978-0-7613-4507-7 lib bdg; 0-7613-4507-8 lib bdg; 978-0-7613-4508-4 pa; 0-7613-4508-6 pa

LC 2009001877

Judah and his small army of Maccabees fight to free Jerusalem from the cruel King Antiochus in this rhyming version of the Hanukkah story.

"Balsley's rhythmic narration includes basic characterization and dialogue for the key players to make the story come alive. Bold opaque paintings of brave, bearded men with flowing hair . . . provide a cinematic view of this legend of heroism and determination." Kirkus

Bernhard, Durga Yael

Around the world in one Shabbat; Jewish people celebrate the Sabbath together. [by] Durga Yael Bernhard. Jewish Lights Pub. 2011 32p il $18.99

Grades: K 1 2 3   **296.4**

1. Jews 2. Sabbath

ISBN 978-1-58023-433-7; 1-58023-433-X

LC 2010041803

"Bernhard uses a global, child-centric approach to explore traditions and rituals that accompany the Sabbath. Each spread tells the story of a different child; in Buenos Aires, Alicia awakens from a nap and helps her sister braid challah, while in Istanbul Leyla joins her brother and parents around the table. . . . As Bernhard moves from France and Canada to Ethiopia and Thailand, warm, genial paintings add to an overall sense of serenity and community. The lyricism of the vignettes belies just how much information Bernhard packs into the book—it's an excellent resource." Publ Wkly

Chaikin, Miriam

★ **Menorahs**, mezuzas, and other Jewish symbols; illustrated by Erika Weihs. Clarion Bks. 1990 102p il $17; pa $5.95

Grades: 5 6 7 8   **296.4**

1. Jewish art and symbolism 2. Judaism -- Customs and practices

ISBN 0-89919-856-2; 0-618-37835-9 pa

LC 89-77719

Explains the history and significance of many Jewish symbols, such as the Shield of David, the menorah, and the mezuza, and discusses holiday symbols and rituals

"Embellished with bibliographical references as well as Weihs' simple yet elegant and wonderfully dramatic scratchboard illustrations, this smoothly woven patchwork of history and culture is a fine introduction that will attract browsers and be useful for children investigating the subject of symbolism in school." Booklist

Cooper, Ilene

★ **Jewish** holidays all year round; a family treasury. written by Ilene Cooper; illustrations by Elivia Savadier; captions by Josh Feinberg; in association with the Jewish Museum, New York. Abrams 2002 80p il $19.95

Grades: 4 5 6 7 **296.4**

1. Handicraft 2. Jewish cooking 3. Jewish holidays
ISBN 0-8109-0550-7

LC 2001-56741

As the author "explores the history and significance of the holidays and festivals of the Jewish year, she . . . links these to traditions and rituals. . . . Instructions for holiday activities (crafts, recipes, etc.) are also included. . . . Savadier's vignettes, mostly of busy, happy people, underscore the liveliness of Jewish faith." Publ Wkly

Includes bibliographical references

Had gadya; a Passover song. paintings by Seymour Chwast; afterword by Michael Strassfeld. Roaring Brook Press 2005 un il $16.95; pa $7.95

Grades: K 1 2 3 **296.4**

1. Songs 2. Passover
ISBN 1-59643-033-8; 1-59643-298-5 pa

LC 2003-17831

"The bright, acrylic folk-art paintings express the rhythm of the chant. . . . The book, complete with musical notation and Hebrew and English words, is bound to add to the pleasure of the seder." Booklist

Hanft, Josh

The **miracles** of Passover; [by] Josh Hanft; illustrated by Seymour Chwast. Blue Apple Books 2007 un il $15.95

Grades: PreK K 1 2 **296.4**

1. Passover
ISBN 978-1-59354-600-7; 1-59354-600-9

LC 2006031585

"The story of Moses, Pharaoh, the 10 plagues, and the crossing of the Red Sea is explained in child-friendly language with additional information included about the traditions of the Seder. What distinguishes this book from others of its kind is the overall excellence of the colorful artwork." SLJ

Heiligman, Deborah

★ **Celebrate** Hanukkah; [by] Deborah Heiligman; consultant, Shira Stern. National Geographic 2006 32p il (Holidays around the world) $15.95; lib bdg $23.90

Grades: K 1 2 3 **296.4**

1. Hanukkah
ISBN 0-7922-5924-6; 0-7922-5925-4 lib bdg

LC 2005032427

This "introduces children to the Jewish Festival of Lights. Heiligman recounts the holiday's history and origins and describes how it is celebrated today. . . . The main text is succinct and appropriate for reading aloud. . . . Decorating the pages are sumerous crisp, full-color photos." Booklist

Includes glossary and bibliographical references

★ **Celebrate** Passover; [by] Deborah Heiligman. National Geographic 2007 32p il (Holidays around the world) $15.95; lib bdg $23.90

Grades: K 1 2 3 **296.4**

1. Passover
ISBN 978-1-4263-0018-9; 978-1-4263-00196 lib bdg

LC 2006020676

This "begins with a short recitation of the Passover story and then moves directly into how the holiday is celebrated. . . . A concluding essay by a rabbi offers thoughts on the meaning of the holiday. The clean format evokes the spring holiday, but the book's visual emphasis is also on Jewish communities in Africa, Asia, the Middle East, and elsewhere." Booklist

Includes bibliographical references

★ **Celebrate** Rosh Hashanah and Yom Kippur; [by] Deborah Heiligman; consultant, Shira Stern. National Geographic 2007 31p il (Holidays around the world) $15.95; lib bdg $23.90

Grades: K 1 2 3 **296.4**

1. Yom Kippur 2. Rosh ha-Shanah
ISBN 978-1-4263-0076-9; 978-1-4263-0077-6 lib bdg

LC 2006100317

"Lush color photographs show the diversity of the celebrants and bring an immediacy to these observances. Clear, simple [text provides] history and background information, descriptions of customs, and basic analyses of each celebration's deeper meaning. . . . Exemplary back matter includes quick facts and extra information to provide context. There is even a map showing where all of the fascinating photos were taken." SLJ

Includes glossary and bibliographical references

Heller, Esther Susan

Menorah under the sea; photographs by David Ginsburg. Kar-Ben Pub. 2009 29p il lib bdg $17.95

Grades: K 1 2 3 **296.4**

1. Hanukkah 2. Marine biology 3. Antarctica
ISBN 978-0-8225-7386-9 lib bdg; 0-8225-7386-5 lib bdg

LC 2007043175

Describes how, while studying sea urchins in Antarctica, marine biologist David Ginsburg celebrated Hanukkah by creating his own menorah on the sea floor

"The vibrant color photography and surprising thematic juxtaposition—readers will learn as much about urchins as about the holiday—makes this a memorable selection, even for readers who don't celebrate Hanukkah." Publ Wkly

Hoffman, Lawrence A.

What you will see inside a synagogue; [by] Lawrence Hoffman and Ron Wolfson; with photographs by Bill Aron. SkyLight Paths 2004 31p il (What you will see inside--) $17.99

Grades: 3 4 5 6 **296.4**

1. Judaism
ISBN 1-59473-012-1

LC 2004-11178

"This book provides a warm and thorough welcome to the center of Jewish life. . . . Numerous clear color photos and pronunciation guides for Hebrew words are included. . . . An excellent overview." SLJ

Kimmel, Eric A.

★ **Wonders** and miracles; a Passover companion. illustrated with art spanning three thousand years; written and compiled by Eric A. Kimmel. Scholastic Press 2004 136p il $18.95

Grades: 4 5 6 7 **296.4**

1. Passover
ISBN 0-439-07175-5

LC 2002-4732

Presents the steps performed in a traditional Passover Seder, plus stories, songs, poetry, and pictures that celebrate the historical significance of this holiday to Jews all over the world.

"The marvelous selection of art—paintings, photographs, artifacts, and illustrations from historical Haggadahs—illuminates each step in the service. . . . Both the presentation of information and the overall design attest to the careful and loving attention given to every detail. This inviting, handsome, and informative compendium should find a place of honor in every library." SLJ

Includes bibliographical references

Lehman-Wilzig, Tami

Hanukkah around the world; by Tami Lehman-Wilzig; illustrated by Vicki Wehrman. Kar-Ben Pub. 2009 48p il map $16.95

Grades: 2 3 4 5   **296.4**

1. Hanukkah

ISBN 978-0-8225-8761-3; 0-8225-8761-0

LC 2008031196

"This tour of Hanukkah includes information on its historical significance and the ways in which it is celebrated in places like New York City, Turin, Sydney and Warsaw. After an introductory section about the history, terminology and customs associated with the holiday, the book features a story of a child living in each city." Publ Wkly

Melmed, Laura Krauss

Eight winter nights; a family Hanukkah book. illustrated by Elisabeth Schlossberg. Chronicle Books 2010 un il $16.99

Grades: PreK K 1   **296.4**

1. Hanukkah

ISBN 978-0-8118-5552-5; 0-8118-5552-X

LC 2009019574

Short verses describe symbols, foods, and family fun associated with the festival of Hanukkah. Includes facts about the history and traditions.

"The verse and illustrations work well together. . . . Created with pencil and pastels, the illustrations use plenty of curved lines and deep, warm colors to depict the celebrations in this lively, amiable household." Booklist

Metter, Bert

Bar mitzvah, bat mitzvah; the ceremony, the party, and how the day came to be. by Bert Metter; illustrated by Joan Reilly. Clarion Books 2007 un il $16; pa $5.95

Grades: 4 5 6 7   **296.4**

1. Bar mitzvah 2. Bat mitzvah

ISBN 978-0-618-76772-4; 0-618-76772-X; 978-0-618-76773-1 pa; 0-618-76773-8 pa

LC 2006032942

The author "describes a typical ceremony and explains how this custom began for boys during the Middle Ages and how it was adapted for girls beginning in 1922. He also discusses the recent custom of adult bar and bat mitzvahs and celebratory parties. The writing is clear and concise; ink illustrations . . . help break up the text." Booklist

Includes bibliographical references

Podwal, Mark H.

Built by angels; the story of the old-new synagogue. by Mark Podwal. Harcourt Children's Books 2009 un il $16

Grades: 1 2 3 4   **296.4**

1. Synagogues 2. Jews -- Czech Republic

ISBN 978-0-15-206678-9; 0-15-206678-0

LC 2007052091

"Legend, history and spiritual significance intertwine in Podwal's illustrated free-verse poem paying homage to Prague's Altneuschul, or Old-New Synagogue, which is the oldest in Europe, dating back to 1270,

and is treasured for its early Gothic architecture. . . . Childlike yet abstract drawings in acrylic, gouache and colored pencil-dominated by a combination of reds . . . delineate the building's history as a haven for worship throughout the centuries. . . . A beautiful, Impressionistic introduction to a portion of Judaic lore and a European architectural marvel." Kirkus

★ A **sweet** year; a taste of the Jewish holidays. [by] Mark Podwal. Doubleday Bks. for Young Readers 2003 un il hardcover o.p. lib bdg $14.99

Grades: K 1 2 3   **296.4**

1. Food 2. Jewish holidays

ISBN 0-385-74637-7; 0-385-90869-5 lib bdg

LC 2002-155442

Pictures and easy-to-read text introduce Jewish holidays, focusing on the foods associated with each

This offers "beautifully crafted poetic text and symbolic paintings in gouache and acrylics." SLJ

Includes bibliographical references

Schecter, Ellen

★ The **family** Haggadah; illustrated by Neil Waldman. Viking 1999 66p il music pa $13.99

Grades: 4 5 6 7   **296.4**

1. Passover

ISBN 0-670-88341-7

LC 98-28597

"Although really intended for parents to use with their children at a family Passover seder, this attractive book may also be useful to children wanting to plan their own model celebration." Booklist

The **story** of Hanukkah; illustrated by Jill Weber. Holiday House 2011 un il $14.95

Grades: PreK K 1 2   **296.4**

1. Hanukkah 2. Hanukkah stories

ISBN 978-0-8234-2295-1; 0-8234-2295-X

This retells the Hanukkah story of the Maccabees and the miracle that took place in the Temple in Jerusalem. Includes a recipe for latkes and directions for playing dreidel.

"The events commemorated in the holiday of Hanukkah are retold simply for young ears. . . . Weber's full-spread color illustrations, with an emphasis on traditional holiday blue, convey the epic scope of the story." Publ Wkly

Walker, Robert

Bar and bat mitzvahs; Robert Walker. Crabtree Pub. Co. 2012 32 p. (reinforced library binding : alk. paper) $26.60

Grades: 1 2 3   **296.4**

1. Bar mitzvah 2. Bat mitzvah 3. Rites and ceremonies

ISBN 0778740862; 0778740919; 1427178453; 1427179603; 9780778740865; 9780778740919; 9781427178459; 9781427179609

LC 2012004070

This book looks at bar and bat mitzvahs. Chapters explore themes including the "history of the ceremony," "the Sabbath," "important religious texts," "the Hebrew language," and how "girls get their own day." The post-ceremony reception and party is also considered. (WorldCat)

Includes bibliographical references and index

Woog, Adam

What makes me a Jew? Kidhaven Press 2004 48p il (What makes me a-- ?) $23.70

Grades: 3 4 5   **296.4**
  1. Judaism
  ISBN 0-7377-2266-5

LC 2003-20951

This describes Jewish origins, beliefs, practices, foods, and holidays. "Presenting information about religion objectively for younger audiences poses a difficult challenge, but [this title does] and excellent job of it." Booklist
  Includes bibliographical references

Ziefert, Harriet
  ★ **Hanukkah** haiku; [by] Harriet Ziefert; paintings by Karla Gudeon. Blue Apple Books 2008 un il $16.95
Grades: PreK K 1   **296.4**
  1. Haiku 2. Hanukkah
  ISBN 978-1-934706-33-6; 1-934706-33-7

LC 2008005877

"Combining festive illustrations and a playful format, this title uses haiku to celebrate the eight nights of Hanukkah. . . . Each turn of the stepped pages brings fresh excitement as another lit candle and verse are revealed. Illustrations have a lovely folkloric quality in which Chagall-like figures, surrounded by richly colored flowers and stars, float across a fibrous tan background." SLJ

  Passover; celebrating now, remembering then. paintings by Karla Gudeon. Blue Apple Books 2010 un il $17.99
Grades: PreK K 1 2 3   **296.4**
  1. Passover
  ISBN 978-1-60905-020-7; 1-60905-020-7

"Ziefert provides a simplified adaptation of Exodus, a description of holiday preparations, and a concise Haggadah, or service for this ritual meal. Throughout, Ziefert contrasts current practice . . . with ancient origins. . . . On every page, Gudeon's Chagall-like paintings exhibit a folkloric style. . . . This title is one that families with young children will appreciate and want to own." Booklist

297   Islam, Babism, Bahai Faith

Barnard, Bryn
  ★ The **genius** of Islam; how Muslims made the modern world. Alfred A. Knopf 2011 37p il map $17.99; lib bdg $20.99
Grades: 4 5 6 7   **297**
  1. Islamic civilization 2. Islam -- History
  ISBN 978-0-375-84072-2; 0-375-84072-9; 978-0-375-94072-9 lib bdg; 0-375-94072-3 lib bdg

LC 2010-12777

This is a "concise and eloquent exploration of the far-reaching influence of Islam over the centuries. Each spread is devoted to a different subject (writing, Arabic numerals, architecture, astronomy, agriculture), while captioned spot art homes in on specific inventions and innovations (the zither, the astrolabe, advanced medical knowledge)." Publ Wkly
  Includes bibliographical references

Cooper, Alison
  Facts about Islam. Rosen Central 2010 45p il map (World religions) lib bdg $26.50
Grades: 3 4 5 6   **297**
  1. Islam
  ISBN 978-1-61532-322-7 lib bdg; 1-61532-322-8 lib bdg

LC 2009052445

"This book describes who Muslims are, the beginning of Islam, beliefs and leaders, the Qur'an, Sunna, family life, worship, the Islamic calendar, Hajj, festivals, and how the religion spread. . . . Colorful pho-

tographs, maps, and illustrations appear on every chapter spread, and the language is easy to understand, making this a useful resource for children." SLJ
  Includes glossary and bibliographical references

Demi
  ★ **Muhammad**; written and illustrated by Demi. Margaret K. McElderry Bks. 2003 un il $19.95
Grades: 4 5 6 7   **297**
  1. Islam 2. Prophets 3. Islamic leaders 4. Writers on religion
  ISBN 0-689-85264-9

LC 2002-2985

"With dramatic scenes extending past the borders of the intricately patterned frames, the art will be a continual source of interest for young people. . . . [An] excellent retelling of the Prophet's life that combines beauty and scholarship." Booklist
  Includes bibliographical references

Hawker, Frances
  Islam in Turkey; written by Frances Hawker and Leyla Alicavu-soglu; photography by Bruce Campbell. Crabtree Pub. Company 2010 32p il (Families and their faiths) lib bdg $26.60; pa $8.95
Grades: 3 4 5   **297**
  1. Islam 2. Turkey
  ISBN 978-0-7787-5009-3 lib bdg; 0-7787-5009-4 lib bdg; 978-0-7787-5026-0 pa; 0-7787-5026-4 pa

LC 2009-14158

This "book introduces a child who practices [Islam]. . . . Provides a solid introduction without overwhelming readers with complex regional variations in practices and beliefs. . . . Words and phrases that are unique to the faith appear in bold font and are defined at greater length in the glossary." SLJ
  Includes glossary

Raatma, Lucia
  Islam. Compass Point Books 2010 48p il map (World religions) lib bdg $27.99
Grades: 5 6 7 8   **297**
  1. Islam
  ISBN 978-0-7565-4239-9 lib bdg; 0-7565-4239-1 lib bdg

LC 2009-15812

"The colorful, attractive layout includes high-quality reproductions of photographs, maps, and paintings. Students who are new to religious studies, as well as those doing reports, will find that this . . . meets their needs." SLJ
  Includes glossary and bibliographical references

Wallace, Holly
  Islam; Budi's story. by Holly Wallace. Barrons Eductional Series, Inc. 2006 32 p. col. ill., map;
Grades: 3 4 5 6   **297**
  1. Islam -- Doctrines .
  ISBN 9780764134753 (alk. paper); 0764134752 (alk. paper); 9780764159664; 0764159666

LC 2005939033

A twelve-year-old boy named Budi describes how his life in Indonesia follows the doctrines of Islam.

Whiting, Jim
  The **role** of religion in the early Islamic world; Jim Whiting. Crabtree Pub. Company 2012 48 p. (Life in the early islamic world) (reinforced library binding : alk. paper) $30.60

Grades: 4 5 6   **297**
1. Islam -- History 2. Picture books for children
ISBN 0778721698; 9780778721697; 9780778721765;
9781427195623; 9781427198419

LC 2012000075

This book looks at the role of religion in the early Islamic world. "Information is presented in concise chapters. . . . The main texts are supplemented with blue boxes of information, subsections, and many . . . reproductions, maps, and paintings. Each book contains time lines and short biographies of important historical figures." (School Library Journal)

297.3   Islamic worship

Brown, Tricia
   Salaam; a Muslim American boy's story. Henry Holt 2006 un il $17.95
Grades: K 1 2 3   **297.3**
  1. Islam 2. Muslims
  ISBN 978-0-8050-6538-1; 0-8050-6538-5

LC 2005013147

"A gentle and informative look at a Muslim-American boy and the way he practices his faith. The book does a good job of explaining each of the Five Pillars of Islam. . . . Good-quality black-and-white photos enhance the presentation and effectively show the warmth of Imran's family life." SLJ
  Includes glossary

Bullard, Lisa
   Rashad's Ramadan and Eid al-Fitr; by Lisa Bullard; illustrated by Holli Conger. Millbrook Press 2012 24 p. col. ill. (lib. bdg. : alk. paper) $23.93; (ebook) $35.93; (paperback) $6.95
Grades: 1 2 3   **297.3**
  1. Muslims 2. Islamic holidays 3. Picture books for children 4. Ramadan 5. Id al-Fir
  ISBN 0761350799; 9780761350798; 9780761388425; 9780761385837

LC 2011024545

Author Lisa Bullard's book focuses on Muslim holidays and celebrations. "For Muslims, Ramadan is a time for fasting, prayer, and thinking of others. Rashad tries to be good all month. When it's time for Eid al-Fitr, he feasts and plays! Find out how people celebrate this special time of year. Learn the history behind the days people celebrate in the Holidays and Special Days series, part of the Cloverleaf Books collection." (Publisher's note)

Dickmann, Nancy
   Ramadan and Id-ul-Fitr. Heinemann Library 2010 24p il (Holidays and festivals) $21.50; pa $5.99
Grades: PreK K 1   **297.3**
  1. Islam 2. Ramadan 3. Id al-Adha
  ISBN 978-1-4329-4049-2; 1-4329-4049-X; 978-1-4329-4068-3 pa; 1-4329-4068-6 pa

LC 2009054305

This is a "clear introduction to Islam's holy month. . . . Large photos dominate the top two-thirds of each page, while a single line of large-print text delivers information. . . . Even lesser known to Americans is the celebration of Id-ul-Fitr at the end of Ramadan, and it is here where the book's photographs are particularly effective." Booklist
  Includes bibliographical references

Douglass, Susan L.
   ★ **Ramadan**; illustrations by Jeni Reeves. Carolrhoda Books 2004 48p il (On my own holidays) lib bdg $23.93; pa $4.95

Grades: 1 2 3   **297.3**
  1. Islam 2. Ramadan 3. Id al-Adha
  ISBN 0-87614-932-8 lib bdg; 1-57505-584-8 pa

LC 2002-6781

An introduction to Islamic observances during the month of Ramadan and the subsequent festival of Eid-al-Fitr
  "Reeves's abundant, framed illustrations in pastel colors provide detailed windows on the observance. . . . An easy-to-read, well-organized introduction." SLJ

Heiligman, Deborah
   ★ **Celebrate** Ramadan & Eid al-Fitr; [by] Deborah Heiligman; consultant, Neguin Yavari. National Geographic 2006 31p il map (Holidays around the world) $15.95; lib bdg $23.90
Grades: K 1 2 3   **297.3**
  1. Islam 2. Ramadan 3. Id al-Adha
  ISBN 0-7922-5926-2; 0-7922-5927-0 lib bdg

LC 2006008889

"Heiligman offers a simple, accessible introduction to the traditions of this solemn month and its concluding festival. Numerous clear, expressive photos feature captions that describe the experiences of children from varying countries and cultures and how they observe Ramadan." Publ Wkly
  Includes glossary and bibliographical references

Hoyt-Goldsmith, Diane
   ★ **Celebrating** Ramadan; Ramadan al-mu'azzam. photographs by Lawrence Migdale. Holiday House 2001 32p il map $16.95
Grades: 3 4 5   **297.3**
  1. Islam 2. Ramadan
  ISBN 0-8234-1581-3

LC 2001-16643

"This picture book for older readers follows devout muslim Ibraheem, a fourth-grader living in New Jersey, through the holy month of Ramadan. . . . This is a sensitive introduction to Ramadan; the quality of the photographs and the eloquent text make the book the one of the best introductions in recent memory." Booklist

Jeffrey, Laura S.
   Celebrate Ramadan; [by] Laura S. Jeffrey. Enslow Publishers 2007 112p il (Celebrate holidays) lib bdg $31.93
Grades: 5 6 7 8   **297.3**
  1. Islam 2. Ramadan 3. Id al-Adha
  ISBN 978-0-7660-2774-9 lib bdg; 0-7660-2774-0 lib bdg

LC 2006028107

"This book opens by introducing a contemporary Muslim, Bushra, who celebrated Ramadan as a girl growing up in England [and] later immigrated to the United States. . . . An informative chapter surveys the history, beliefs, and practices of Islam. . . . The remainder of the book offers a detailed discussion of Ramadan, prayer, and spiritual awareness, and of l'Id al Fitr. . . . Punctuated by sidebars and illustrated with color photos, this clearly written book offers a good overview of how the holidays of Islam are celebrated." Booklist
  Includes glossary and bibliographical references

Khan, Aisha Karen
   What you will see inside a mosque; photographs by Aaron Pepis. Skylight Paths Pub. 2003 31p il (What you will see inside--) $16.95; pa $8.99
Grades: 3 4 5 6   **297.3**
  1. Islam 2. Mosques
  ISBN 1-893361-60-8; 1-594732-57-4 pa

LC 2002-153436

Describes what happens inside a mosque and introduces the Muslim faith

This is an "excellent introduction. . . . Full-page photographs are supplemented by smaller photos with informative captions." SLJ

Murray, Julie
Ramadan. ABDO Pub. Company 2011 24p il (Holidays) $25.26
Grades: 2 3 4   **297.3**
1. Ramadan
ISBN 978-1-61783-041-9; 1-61783-041-0
LC 2011002287

"This short, concise introduction is simple enough for the target audience, and it is accurate. Each two-page chapter introduces an aspect of Ramadan that is rooted in religious practices that are common to all Muslims: Sunnis and Shi'ites, Salafis and Sufis, liberals and conservatives. Each spread has a large, full-color picture. The publisher's website provides further reading with links to additional, credible Internet resources. This title succeeds where others have been undermined by cultural bias. An excellent addition." SLJ

Whitman, Sylvia
Under the Ramadan moon; [by] Sylvia Whitman; illustrated by Sue Williams. A. Whitman & Co. 2008 un il $15.99
Grades: PreK K 1 2   **297.3**
1. Ramadan 2. Moon
ISBN 978-0-8075-8304-3; 0-8075-8304-9
LC 2008001307

"This delightful picture book describes the month-long Muslim observance of Ramadan by a modern family. . . . The images of the waxing, full, and waning moon progress along with the spare, lyrical text. Practices such as fasting, speaking kind words, giving to the poor, decorating with bright lights, and praying all take place, 'under the moon, under the Ramadan moon.' Williams uses soft, luminous pastels in richly textured, detailed spreads." SLJ

299   Religions not provided for elsewhere

Fisher, Leonard Everett
★ The gods and goddesses of ancient China. Holiday House 2003 un il $16.95
Grades: 3 4 5 6   **299**
1. Gods and goddesses 2. China -- Religion
ISBN 0-8234-1694-1
LC 2002-68802

"Beginning with an introduction that mentions Qin Shi Huangdi, China's First Supreme Emperor, Fisher offers very brief historical and cultural background to China's deities. . . . Profiles of 17 gods and goddesses follow, each one presented on a double-page spread that includes a roughly brushed portrait opposite a few paragraphs summarizing the figure's corresponding legend. . . . Fisher combines concise, accessible language, colorful art, and exciting stories about figures that aren't often covered in books for youth." Booklist

Includes bibliographical references

Kramer, Ann
Egyptian myth; a treasury of legends, art, and history. M. E. Sharpe 2008 96p il map (The world of mythology) $35.95
Grades: 5 6 7 8   **299**
1. Egyptian art 2. Egyptian mythology 3. Egypt -- History
ISBN 978-0-7656-8105-8; 0-7656-8105-6
LC 2007005876

This "handsomely designed [book is] illustrated with works of art from the culture. [It] is a well-organized presentation that includes in-

formation and tales about the gods and the pharoahs as well as magical stories and legends, providing an excellent introduction to this fascinating culture." SLJ

Includes glossary and bibliographical references

Williams, Marcia
Ancient Egypt; tales of gods and pharaohs. Candlewick Press 2011 un il $16.99
Grades: 4 5 6   **299**
1. Egyptian mythology 2. Egypt -- Religion
ISBN 978-0-7636-5308-8; 0-7636-5308-X
LC 2010040745

"The highpoints of Egyptian mythology—creation, the divinity of Ra, the death of Osiris, and the vengeance of his son Horus—as well as the stories of four great pharaohs—are presented in this lighthearted picture book/graphic novel. . . . This book makes them all seem like fun. Williams utilizes a beautiful, sun-soaked palette of gold, turquoise, lapis, jade, and carnelian lifted right off a sarcophagus. . . . Expressive postures, smiling faces, and playful interactions among them keep readers scouring the pages for every little joke. . . . Each figure in this book . . . fairly leaps off the page in order to grab readers' attention." SLJ

299.31   Ancient Egyptian religion

Napoli, Donna Jo
★ Treasury of Egyptian Mythology; Classic Stories of Gods, Goddesses, Monsters & Mortals. by Donna Jo Napoli and illustrated by Christina Balit. National Geographic Children's books 2013 192 p. $24.95
Grades: 3 4 5 6   **299.31**
1. Egyptian mythology 2. Gods and goddesses
ISBN 1426313802; 9781426313806

Author Donna Jo Napoli presents a "tableau of Egyptian myths, including those of pharaohs, queens, the boisterous Sun God Ra, and legendary creatures like the Sphinx. The stories are embellished with sidebars that provide historical, cultural, and geographic context and a mapping feature that adds to the fun and fascination. Resource notes and ample back matter direct readers to discover more about ancient Egypt." (Publisher's note)

299.5   Religions of East and Southeast Asian origin

Demi
★ The legend of Lao Tzu and the Tao te ching. Margaret K. McElderry Books 2007 un il $21.99
Grades: 4 5 6 7   **299.5**
1. Taoism 2. Philosophers
ISBN 1-4169-1206-1; 978-1-4169-1206-4
LC 2005029695

"This is the legend of Lao Tzu . . . who may or may not have founded Taoism, one of the greatest religions of the world. Demi's elegant picture-book introduction to the legendary Chinese philosopher . . . combines nuggets of his purported life with 20 verses from the Tao Te Ching. . . . The narrative and graceful paintings are contained in a gold circular frame on each parchment shaded page." SLJ

Levin, Judith
Japanese mythology; [by] Judith Levin. The Rosen Pub. Group 2008 64p il map (Mythology around the world) $29.95
Grades: 5 6 7 8   **299.5**
1. Shinto 2. Buddhism 3. Japanese mythology 4. Japan --

Civilization
ISBN 978-1-4042-0736-3; 1-4042-0736-8
LC 2005035279

This "presents not only an introduction to Shinto and Buddhist beliefs, but also Japanese history and mythology in general. . . . The most remarkable part of [this book] . . . is the respect [it shows] for the mythological customs, treating them throughout with the same care that writers of books on major religions might offer. The illustrations show both ancient and modern incarnations of the deities and heroes." SLJ

Includes glossary and bibliographical references

299.7   Religions of North American native origin

Swamp, Jake
    Giving thanks; a Native American good morning message. by Chief Jake Swamp; illustrated by Erwin Printup, Jr. Lee & Low Bks. 1995 un il $16.95; pa $6.95
Grades: K 1 2 3   **299.7**
    1. Human ecology 2. Mohawk Indians 3. Native Americans
ISBN 1-880000-15-6; 1-880000-54-7 pa
LC 94-5955

"Its simple, timeless language bears witness to the Native American reverence for the natural world and sense of unity with all living things. . . . The gifts of the earth . . . are richly depicted in paintings of wildlife and bountiful harvests." Publ Wkly

300   SOCIAL SCIENCES, SOCIOLOGY & ANTHROPOLOGY

302.23   Media (Means of communication)

Milich, Zoran
    City signs. Kids Can Press 2002 un il $15.95; pa $6.95
Grades: PreK K 1 2   **302.23**
    1. Signs and signboards
ISBN 1-55337-003-1; 1-55337-748-6 pa

"Milich took to the streets with his camera, looking for printed words found in various outdoor environments. The 30 photographs here demonstrate that even children who can't yet read a book understand many of the words they see around them. The quality of the pictures is very good. They are nicely composed, clear, and often colorful." Booklist

302.3   Social interaction within groups

Burstein, John
    Why are you picking on me? dealing with bullies. Crabtree Pub. Company 2009 32p il (Slim Goodbody's life skills 101) lib bdg $26.60; pa $8.95
Grades: 1 2 3 4 5   **302.3**
    1. Bullies
ISBN 978-0-7787-4792-5 lib bdg; 0-7787-4792-1 lib bdg; 978-0-7787-4808-3 pa; 0-7787-4808-1 pa
LC 2009022427

This book about dealing with bullies offers "clear and simple advice for children and [provides] adults with springboards for discussion and roleplaying. All have appealing color photographs of a variety of types

of kids, . . . opening scenarios, concrete coping suggestions, and solid reasoning." SLJ

Includes bibliographical references

Ellis, Deborah
    ★ **We** want you to know; kids talk about bullying. Coteau Books 2010 120p il $19.95; pa $15.95
Grades: 5 6 7 8 9 10   **302.3**
    1. Bullies
ISBN 978-1-55050-417-0; 1-55050-417-7; 978-1-55050-463-7 pa; 1-55050-463-0

"As part of her work with an anti-bullying campaign in her local Canadian community, Ellis interviewed young people between the ages of 9 and 19 about their experiences. In honest, straightforward prose, she shares their stories, many as targets and some as perpetrators or bystanders. . . . Each story is written from the first-person point of view, some with real names and photos, providing an intimacy and immediacy that are critical with these kinds of issues. Readers will find at least one or two stories they can relate to, and educators should be able to use many of the narratives to jumpstart conversation." SLJ

Includes bibliographical references

Fox, Debbie
    Good-bye bully machine; written by Debbie Fox and Allan L. Beane; illustrated by Debbie Fox. Free Spirit Pub. 2009 39p il pa $8.95; $12.99
Grades: K 1 2 3 4 5   **302.3**
    1. Bullies
ISBN 978-1-57542-321-0 pa; 1-57542-321-9 pa; 978-1-57542-326-5; 1-57542-326-X
LC 2008-41025

Kids learn what bullying is, why it hurts, and what they can do to end it with this fresh, compelling book including contemporary collage art, lively layout, and straightforward text.

"The authors provide tips for dealing with negative behaviors and encourage readers to take a stand against bullying and unplug the bully machine. Fox's enticing, edgy, collage artwork will draw readers in. . . . This offering will be a great discussion springboard for teachers and counselors." SLJ

Jakubiak, David J.
    A **smart** kid's guide to online bullying. PowerKids Press 2009 24p il (Kids online) lib bdg $21.25; pa $8.95
Grades: 3 4 5 6   **302.3**
    1. Bullies 2. Safety education 3. Internet -- Security measures
ISBN 978-1-4042-8114-1 lib bdg; 978-1-4358-3348-7 pa
LC 2009000695

This describes how to identify bullies online, how to deal with them, and how to avoid becoming a bully.

"This . . . is easy to read, has vibrant photos on each page, and offers Tips. Additional links can be found at the publisher's portal, which is regularly updated." Libr Media Connect

Includes glossary

Kevorkian, Meline
    ★ **101** facts about bullying; what everyone should know. [by] Meline Kevorkian and Robin D'Antona. Rowman & Littlefield Pub. 2008 148p $32.95
Grades: Adult Professional   **302.3**
    1. Bullies
ISBN 978-1-57886-849-0; 1-57886-849-1

"A user-friendly, accessible, and well-organized resource. . . . The format will lend itself well to group discussions and give teachers and others who work with young people a solid basis upon which to explore the issues surrounding this prevalent problem." SLJ

Lutz, Lisa

How to negotiate everything; David Spellman with Lisa Lutz; illustrated by Jaime Temairik. Simon & Schuster Books for Young Readers 2012 32 p. (hardcover) $16.99
Grades: K 1 2 3   **302.3**
   1. Wit and humor 2. Negotiation
   ISBN 144245119X; 9781442451193

LC 2011038386

This humorous juvenile picture book, by Lisa Lutz, illustrated by Jaime Temairik, "teaches you how to get everything you want. . . . Through several simple steps, you will learn the best way to ask for what you want, how to ask for more of what you want, and the importance of not overreaching. With helpful illustrations and a complete glossary, there is no end to what these skills can get you." (Publisher's note)

Schwartz, Heather E.

Safe social networking; by Heather E. Schwartz. Capstone Press 2013 32 p. col. ill. (Fact finders. Tech safety smarts) (library) $26.65
Grades: 4 5 6 7   **302.3**
   1. Online social networks 2. Internet -- Security measures 3. Social networking 4. Social networks 5. Online social networks -- Security measures
   ISBN 1429699434; 9781429699433; 9781620658024

LC 2012026027

This children's resource book, by Heather E. Schwartz, is part of the publisher's "Fact Finders" series, providing guidance for young children to safely use and navigate online social media. "If a strange person asks to be your online friend, do you know what to do? . . . This book is here to help! Learn tech-savvy ways to keep your social networking sites safe sites without taking away all the fun!" (Publisher's note)
   Includes bibliographical references (p. 31) and index.

Shapiro, Ouisie

Bullying and me; schoolyard stories. illustrated by Steven Vote. Albert Whitman & Company 2010 un il $16.99
Grades: 4 5 6 7   **302.3**
   1. Bullies
   ISBN 978-0-8075-0921-0; 0-8075-0921-3

LC 2010000754

"Thirteen individuals, including some adults, who have been bullied at school share their painful experiences. . . . Vote's full-color portraits sensitively depict the faces at the receiving end of abuse. . . . An educational psychologist specifically addresses each individual's dilemma, but the book's strength lies in the honestly conveyed through the personal stories." Publ Wkly

303.3   Coordination and control

Barraclough, Sue

Leadership. Heinemann Library 2009 32p il (Exploring Citizenship) $25.36; pa $7.99
Grades: 1 2 3 4   **303.3**
   1. Leadership
   ISBN 978-1-4329-3314-2; 1-4329-3314-0; 978-1-4329-3322-7 pa; 1-4329-3322-1 pa

LC 2008-55302

"The text presents a multitude of realistic situations to which young children will relate. There are 'Think About It' fact boxes and checklists that aid in understanding and that will spark discussion. All are filled

with captioned, color photographs that relate to the text. The information is relevant and current. . . . Strongly consider this." Libr Media Connect
   Includes glossary and bibliographical references

303.4   Social change

Solway, Andrew

Communication; the impact of science and technology. Gareth Stevens Pub. 2010 64p il (Pros and cons) lib bdg $35
Grades: 5 6 7 8   **303.4**
   1. Communication 2. Telecommunication 3. Information technology
   ISBN 978-1-4339-1986-2 lib bdg; 1-4339-1986-9 lib bdg

LC 2009-12435

An "active layout that features color photographs, maps, graphs or charts on every spread, this . . . [book] has much to offer. . . . It conveniently outlines the range of views . . . helping students to learn how to view both sides of [the] issue[s]." SLJ
   Includes glossary and bibliographical references

303.48   Causes of change

Scandiffio, Laura

People who said no; courage against oppression. Laura Scandiffio. Annick Press 2012 168 p. $24.95
Grades: 5 6 7   **303.48**
   1. Demonstrations 2. Protest movements 3. Civil disobedience 4. Resistance to government
   ISBN 1554513839; 9781554513833

This book, by Laura Scandiffio, profiles activists who broke the law to protest injustices. "Sometimes it's okay to ignore the rules or break the law. . . . This . . . book features people who did just that: Sophie and Hans Scholl . . . and Andrei Sakharov. . . . Also included are Helen Suzman, . . . Aung San Suu Kyi, . . . and the people of Egypt, who recently brought down the repressive government of Hosni Mubarak." (Publisher's note)

Slade, Suzanne

Friends for freedom; the Story of Susan B. Anthony & Frederick Douglass. Suzanne Slade; illustrated by Nicole Tadgell. Charlesbridge 2014 40 p. color illustrations (reinforced) $16.95
Grades: 1 2 3 4   **303.48**
   1. Suffragists 2. Social problems 3. Abolitionists -- Biography 4. Social reformers -- United States -- Biography
   ISBN 1580895689; 9781607346517; 9781607347491; 9781580895682

LC 2013022795

In this children's book, by Suzanne Slade, "no one thought Susan B. Anthony and Frederick Douglass would ever become friends. The former slave and the outspoken woman came from two different worlds. But they shared deep-seated beliefs in equality and the need to fight for it. Despite naysayers, hecklers, and even arsonists, Susan and Frederick became fast friends and worked together to change America." (Publisher's note)

"Tadgell's carefully drafted and evocative watercolors capture both the past and present obstacles Anthony and Douglass faced, from Douglass's youth as a slave to rotten eggs hurled at the two when they appeared in public together and combative differences of opinion, as when the Fifteenth Amendment proposed to give voting rights to black men but not to women." Pub Wkly

303.6   Conflict and conflict resolution

Ellis, Deborah

   Off to war; voices of soldiers' children. Groundwood Books/House of Anansi Press 2008 175p il $15.95; pa $9.95

Grades: 5 6 7 8   **303.6**

   1. Children and war 2. Iraq War, 2003-2011 3. Afghanistan

   ISBN 978-0-88899-894-1; 0-88899-894-5; 978-0-88899-895-8 pa; 0-88899-895-3 pa

   The wars in Iraq and Afghanistan have impacted the children of soldiers—men and women who have been called away from their families to fight in a faraway war. In their own words, some of these children describe how their experience has marked and shaped their lives

   "Accessible and utterly readable. . . . The book is an excellent resource for opening discussions about the current events." SLJ

   Includes glossary and bibliographical references

Gilley, Jeremy

   ★ **Peace** one day; illustrated by Karen Blessen. Putnam 2005 48p il $16.99 **303.6**

   1. Peace

   ISBN 0-399-24330-5

                              LC 2004-20475

   The author "tells how he persuaded world leaders to establish World Peace Day. . . . His personal account of filming the consequences of war in several countries . . . draws attention to the issue, as do his accounts of meeting with world leaders. . . . Most powerful are the double-page collage illustrations . . . which blend some of Gilley's film images of kids caught up in war and portraits of world peace leaders with colored pencil drawings, posters, and even news headlines. [This offers] passionate prose and stirring images." Booklist

Walker, Niki

   Why do we fight? conflict, war, and peace. Niki Walker. Owlkids Books 2013 80p $16.95

Grades: 5 6 7 8   **303.6**

   1. War 2. Culture conflict 3. Conflict management

   ISBN 1926973860; 9781926973869

                              LC 2013930981

   In this book, Niki Walker explains "different types of conflict and then contemplat[es] ways conflict can escalate." (Kirkus Reviews) "Using real-world examples, such as the 1979 peace deal between Egypt and Israel or the history of Afghanistan over multiple centuries, Walker offers . . . explanations of power and resource inequities, cultural divisions, the global role of the United Nations, bias, prejudice, and more." (Publishers Weekly)

304.2   Human ecology

McCarthy, Pat

   Friends of the earth; a history of American environmentalism. Pat McCarthy. 1st ed. Chicago Review Press 2012 132 p. ill. (paperback) $16.95

Grades: 3 4 5   **304.2**

   1. Environmentalists 2. Environmental movement -- United States 3. Environmentalism -- United States -- History 4. Environmentalists -- United States -- History 5. Environmental protection -- United States -- History

   ISBN 1569767181; 9781569767184

                              LC 2012039334

   This book provides "10 profiles of American naturalists and environmentalists" that "offer a broad overview of the movement's past highlights." Also included are "photos, sidebars, resource lists, and a quick closing survey of current environmental issues." Figures mentioned include John Muir, Henry David Thoreau, and Rachel Carson. (Booklist)

Urrutia, María Cristina

   Who will save my planet? Maria Cristina Urrutia. Tundra Books of Northern New York 2012 32 p. (hardcover) $10.95

Grades: 3 4 5   **304.2**

   1. Human influence on nature

   ISBN 177049281X; 9781770492813

                              LC 2011923291

   This book by Maria Cristina Urrutia "uses striking photos to show the impact of humans on the environment. . . . On every spread we are shown a treasure that nature has given us beside a picture of how we've abused that treasure. We see a beautiful forest glade beside a devastated patch of burned-out wood, a gorgeous green parrot beside a dull-feathered caged bird, a sparkling waterfall beside a garbage-clogged river." (Publisher's note)

304.6   Population

Barber, Nicola

   Coping with population growth; Nicola Barber. Raintree 2011 48 p. col. ill.

Grades: 4 5 6 7   **304.6**

   1. Population 2. Population -- Environmental aspects

   ISBN 9781410942968; 9781410943033

                              LC 2010052702

   "Barber examines the pressures exerted on the environment and global resources due to population growth... Color photographs add interest, and helpful diagrams effectively convey statistical concepts." Horn Book

   Includes bibliographical references (p. 46-47) and index

Smith, David J.

   If the World Were a Village; 2 A Book About the World's People. by David J. Smith and illustrated by Shelagh Armstrong. Kids Can Press 2011 32 p. $18.95

Grades: 3 4 5   **304.6**

   1. Population 2. Citizenship

   ISBN 1554535956; 9781554535958

   This book, by David J. Smith and illustrated by Shelagh Armstrong, promotes "world-mindedness by imagining the world's population, all 6.8 billion of us, as a village of just 100 people. Now, 'If the World Were a Village' has been newly revised with updated statistics, several new activities and completely new material on food security, energy and health. By exploring the lives of the 100 villagers, children will discover that life in other nations is often very different from their own." (Publisher's note)

304.8   Movement of people

Kenney, Karen Latchana

   Ellis Island; illustrated by Judith A. Hunt. Magic Wagon 2011 32p il (Our nation's pride) lib bdg $28.50

Grades: 2 3 4   **304.8**

   1. Ellis Island Immigration Station 2. United States -- Immigration and emigration

   ISBN 978-1-61641-150-3; 1-61641-150-3

                              LC 2010013995

   "The author describes how the existing island was built up and expanded to accomodate the station to process immigrants coming into the United States and the various buildings that were constructed. . . . The full-color artwork not only explains the text but also gives almost photographic rendering of the [topic]." SLJ

Lawlor, Veronica

★ **I** was dreaming to come to America; memories from the Ellis Island Oral History Project. selected and illustrated by Veronica Lawlor; foreword by Rudolph W. Giuliani. Viking 1995 38p il hardcover o.p. pa $6.99

Grades: 4 5 6 7   **304.8**

   1. Ellis Island Immigration Station 2. United States -- Immigration and emigration

   ISBN 0-670-86164-2; 0-14-055622-2 pa

                                   LC 95-1281

"Begun in 1975, the Ellis Island Oral History Project is . . . {a} collection of interviews with individuals who immigrated to the U.S. through Ellis Island. Short selections—each 1 or 2 paragraphs long— from 15 of those interviews are reprinted here. The subjects were for the most part children when they arrived in the period 1900-1925. . . . Grades four to six." (SLJ)

"There is a flavor of Chagall in the peasant figures dancing above the ship or hopping ashore near the turreted towers of the huge building on Ellis Island. The elegant rendering offers a timeless view of this significant journey that is at once personal and universal." Horn Book

Ollhoff, Jim

  Exploring immigration. ABDO Pub. Co. 2011 32p il (Your family tree) $18.95

Grades: 4 5 6 7   **304.8**

   1. Genealogy 2. Immigrants 3. United States -- Immigration and emigration

   ISBN 978-1-61613-463-1; 1-61613-463-1

                       LC 2009050807

This book about immigration is "great . . . for kids interested in genealogy. [It does] a wonderful job of presenting the fundamentals of genealogical research in a clear and exciting manner. . . . Understanding and properly using primary documents is stressed throughout. . . . [An] attractive, spacious [layout]; full-color, sharp images; clearly labeled diagrams; and scattered maps add information and appeal." SLJ

   Includes glossary

305.23 Young people

★ **Children** Just Like Me; a new celebration of children around the world. 20th anniversary edition DK Pub 2016 80 p. color illustrations hbk $19.99

Grades: 3 4 5 6   **305.23**

1. Children -- Pictorial works

ISBN 9781465453921; 146545392X

"A new edition of a 1995 favorite, this volume will draw in today's children with the immediacy of its photos of 44 international children. Six sections feature, in turn, North America, South America, Europe, Africa, Asia, and Southeast Asia and Australasia. . . . Text is limited to short paragraphs and photo captions. It is the engaging photos that pop, showing children in both contemporary, Western-style dress and traditional clothes still worn for special occasions." (Kirkus Reviews)

Freedman, Russell

★ **Children** of the Great Depression. Clarion Books 2005 118p il lib bdg $20

Grades: 4 5 6 7   **305.23**

   1. Great Depression, 1929-1939 2. Children -- United States 3.

United States -- Social conditions

   ISBN 0-618-44630-3

                       LC 2005-06506

"This stirring photo-essay combines . . . unforgettable personal details with a clear historical overview of the period and black-and-white photos by Dorothea Lange, Walker Evans, and many others." Booklist

Kerley, Barbara

★ **One** world, one day. National Geographic 2009 un il map $17.95; lib bdg $26.90

Grades: PreK K 1 2   **305.23**

   1. Children -- Pictorial works

   ISBN 978-1-4263-0460-6; 1-4263-0460-9; 978-1-4263-0461-3 lib bdg; 1-4263-0461-7 lib bdg

                       LC 2008-29315

"An arresting, eye-opening compilation." Publ Wkly

Pinkney, Sandra L.

★ **Shades** of black; a celebration of our children. photographs by Myles C. Pinkney. Scholastic 2000 un il $14.95; bd bk $6.99

Grades: PreK K 1   **305.23**

   1. African Americans

   ISBN 0-439-14892-8; 0-439-80251-2 bd bk

                       LC 99-86593

Photographs and text celebrate the beauty and diversity of African American children

"Wonderful, clear, full-color photographs of youngsters illustrate a poetic, vivid text that describes a range of skin and eye colors and hair textures." SLJ

Smith, David J.

  This child, every child; a book about the world's children. written by David J. Smith; illustrated by Shelagh Armstrong. Kids Can Press 2011 36p il (CitizenKid) $18.95

Grades: 4 5 6 7   **305.23**

   1. Children

   ISBN 978-1-55453-466-1; 1-55453-466-6

This title "takes a global look at the lives of contemporary children. Balancing statistics with fictional profiles of kids, Smith's concise narrative focuses on such topics as families, homes, health, work, war, and play. Each spread contains accessible summaries of articles from 1989's United Nations Convention on the Rights of the Child, underscoring the disparity between many children's lives and that document's vision and goals. . . . Rendered in acrylics with digital textures, Armstrong's gauzy paintings sometimes span multiple cultures in a single illustration . . . reinforcing the universal nature of children's needs." Publ Wkly

Wilson, Janet

  One peace; true stories of young activists. written and illustrated by Janet Wilson. Orca Book Publishers 2008 43p il $19.95

Grades: 4 5 6 7   **305.23**

   1. Peace 2. Children and war

   ISBN 978-1-55143-892-4; 1-55143-892-5

"The stories of young people who have been refugees from war, injured by land mines, or learned about the consequences of violence through other means are interspersed with children's poems, quotes, artwork, and photographs. The brief, powerful accounts document how these children ages 8 to 15 worked for or became symbols of peace." SLJ

305.4 Women

Carosella, Melissa

Founding mothers; women who shaped America. Teacher Created Materials 2011 il (Primary source readers: focus on women in U.S. history)

Grades: 3 4 5 6   **305.4**

1. Women -- United States -- History

ISBN 143331505X; 978-1-43331505-3

"This introduction to influential women in early American history begins with the colonial period and closes with the Civil War. . . . The clear text is enhanced with archival illustrations and sidebars that highlight notable items about the women discussed in the narrative. A glossary, an index, and two suggested extension activities conclude this informative book." Booklist

Coster, Patience

A **new** deal for women; the expanding roles of women, 1938-1960. Chelsea House 2011 il (A cultural history of women in America) $35

Grades: 5 6 7 8   **305.4**

1. Feminism 2. Women -- Social conditions 3. Women -- United States -- History 4. United States -- Social conditions

ISBN 978-1-6041-3934-1; 1-6041-3934-X

LC 2010045959

An "eye-catching [layout] with good use of color, photographs, and informative sidebars, many of which use primary-source quotations, are the highlights of [this] appealing [volume]. . . . After a succinct overview of contemporary events, the chapters describe women's lives at home, at work, in education, in politics, in the arts, and their role in the general culture. . . . New opportunities for women were a part of the New Deal and World War II and together changed American culture—these topics are explored [this] volume covering the years 1938-1960." SLJ

Includes glossary and bibliographical references

Gelletly, LeeAnne

A **woman's** place in early America; LeeAnne Gelletly. Mason Crest Publishers 2013 64 p. (Finding a voice : women's fight for equality in U.S. society) (hc) $22.95

Grades: 4 5 6 7 8   **305.4**

1. Women -- United States -- History 2. United States -- Social conditions 3. United States -- Politics and government 4. Women's rights -- United States 5. Women -- United States -- History 6. United States -- Politics and government 7. United States -- Social life and customs 8. Women -- United States -- Social conditions

ISBN 1422223558; 9781422223550; 9781422223659

LC 2011043480

Author LeeAnne Gelletly's book focuses on women in Early America. "In early America, married women had no rights under law. They belonged to their husbands. Their voices were not heard in public. But with the War of Independence, women found a voice as patriots. They supported the rebellion with boycotts. During wartime, women spied on the enemy. They served as messengers. They tended the wounded. Some even served as soldiers. Women performed daring feats of bravery. And they proved they were capable of doing much more than 18-century society allowed them." (Publisher's note)

Includes bibliographical references and index

Gorman, Jacqueline Laks

The **modern** feminist movement; sisters under the skin, 1961-1979. Chelsea House 2011 il (A cultural history of women in America) $35

Grades: 5 6 7 8   **305.4**

1. Feminism 2. Women -- Social conditions 3. Women -- United

States -- History

ISBN 978-1-6041-3935-8; 1-6041-3935-8

LC 2010045990

An "eye-catching [layout] with good use of color, photographs, and informative sidebars, many of which use primary-source quotations, are the highlights of [this] appealing [volume]. . . . After a succinct overview of contemporary events, the chapters describe women's lives at home, at work, in education, in politics, in the arts, and their role in the general culture. . . . [This book] delves into the years of protest and quest for equal rights." SLJ

Includes glossary and bibliographical references

Heinemann, Sue

★ The **New** York Public Library amazing women in American history; a book of answers for kids. Wiley 1998 192p (New York Public Library answer books for kids series) pa $12.95

Grades: 5 6 7 8   **305.4**

1. Women -- United States -- History

ISBN 0-471-19216-3

LC 97-18465

Consists of short answers to questions about the roles and achievements of women in America from prehistory to the end of the twentieth century

"The text is succinct, easy to read, and informative. . . . Pertinent black-and-white photos appear throughout." SLJ

Includes glossary and bibliographical references

Stearman, Kaye

Women of today; contemporary issues and conflicts, 1980-present. [by] Kaye Stearman and Patience Coster. Chelsea House 2011 il (A cultural history of women in America) $35

Grades: 5 6 7 8   **305.4**

1. Feminism 2. Women -- United States 3. Women -- Social conditions

ISBN 978-1-6041-3936-5; 1-6041-3936-6

LC 2010046014

An "eye-catching [layout] with good use of color, photographs, and informative sidebars, many of which use primary-source quotations, are the highlights of [this] appealing [volume]. . . . After a succinct overview of contemporary events, the chapters describe women's lives at home, at work, in education, in politics, in the arts, and their role in the general culture. . . . [This book] highlights women's achievements, including U.S. Supreme Court justices, Speaker of the U.S. House of Representatives, and presidential candidates." SLJ

Includes glossary and bibliographical references

305.5 People by social and economic levels

Adler, David A.

A **picture** book of Harriet Tubman; illustrated by Samuel Byrd. Holiday House 1992 un il $17.95; pa $6.95

Grades: 1 2 3   **305.5**

1. Abolitionists 2. Underground railroad 3. African American women -- Biography

ISBN 0-8234-0926-0; 0-8234-1065-X pa

LC 91-19628

Biography of the black woman who escaped from slavery to become famous as a conductor on the Underground Railroad

This book features "brief, easy-to-read text. . . . Byrd's appealing, colorful illustrations convey the quiet dignity of a brave heroine." Booklist

A **picture** book of Sojourner Truth; illustrated by Gershom Griffith. Holiday House 1994 un il $17.95; pa $6.95

Grades: 1 2 3   **305.5**

1. Feminism 2. Abolitionists 3. Memoirists 4. African American women -- Biography

ISBN 0-8234-1072-2; 0-8234-1262-8 pa

LC 93-7478

An introduction to the life of the woman born into slavery who became a well-known abolitionist and crusader for the rights of African Americans in the United States

The author "portrays his subject in a realistic manner, discussing slavery and other issues in an easy-to-read style. The quotes, while undocumented, are simple enough for the target audience and help to place events in context. Excellent-quality watercolor illustrations capture the action and provide effective representations and details of the time period." SLJ

Horn, Geoffrey M.

Sojourner Truth; speaking up for freedom. by Geoffrey Michael Horn. Crabtree Pub. Co. 2010 64 p. ill. (some col.) (pbk. : alk. paper) $10.95

Grades: 4 5 6 7 8   **305.5**

1. Abolitionists -- United States -- Biography 2. African American women -- Biography 3. African American abolitionists -- Biography 4. Social reformers -- United States -- Biography

ISBN 0778748405; 9780778748243; 9780778748403

LC 2009022428

This children's picture book by Geoffrey M. Horn in the Voices for Freedom: Abolitionist Views series looks at abolitionist Sojourner Truth. It "relates and details Truth's life and times, from her often-brutal treatment as a slave, named Isabella at birth, to her freedom, religious influences, and self-determination . . . and path to outspoken, sometimes provocative, and influential traveling speaker on a mission to raise awareness of and support for abolitionism." (Booklist)

"Combining accessible, lively prose and abundant visuals, this title . . . offers an engaging, informative introduction to the early advocate for the rights of African Americans and women." Booklist

Schroeder, Alan

Minty: a story of young Harriet Tubman; pictures by Jerry Pinkney. Dial Bks. for Young Readers 1996 un il hardcover o.p. pa $6.99

Grades: 1 2 3 4   **305.5**

1. Abolitionists 2. Slavery -- Fiction

ISBN 0-8037-1888-8; 0-14-056196-X pa

LC 95-23499

Coretta Scott King Award for illustration

Pinkney's "paintings, done in pencil, colored-pencils, and watercolor, use light and shadow to great effect. . . . This is a dramatic story that will hold listeners' interest and may lead them to biographical material." SLJ

305.8   Ethnic and national groups

Bolden, Tonya

Tell all the children our story; memories and mementos of being young and Black in America. Abrams 2001 128p il $24.95

Grades: 5 6 7 8   **305.8**

1. African American children 2. United States -- Race relations

ISBN 0-8109-4496-0

LC 2001-1353

"This compilation of the African American experience, from colonial times through the twentieth century, reads and looks like a family scrapbook. . . . Photographs, excerpts from diaries and memoirs, and

reproductions of artwork by black artists such as Charles Altson beautifully bring the story of each generation to life. Bolden vibrantly delivers her historical message through a contemporary perspective." Booklist

Includes bibliographical references

Cha, Dia

★ **Dia's** story cloth; written by Dia Cha; stitched by Chue and Nhia Thao Cha. Lee & Low Bks. 1996 un il $15.95; pa $6.95

Grades: 3 4 5   **305.8**

1. Hmong (Asian people)

ISBN 1-880000-34-2; 1-880000-63-6 pa

LC 95-41465

The story cloth made for her by her aunt and uncle chronicles the life of the author and her family in their native Laos and their eventual emigration to the United States

"An interesting and unusual title that resists neat categorization. . . . Part autobiography, part history, part description of a changing culture adapting life and art to new circumstances, the book serves as a brief introduction to the Hmong people." SLJ

Includes bibliographical references

Lester, Julius

★ **Let's** talk about race; illustrated by Karen Barbour. HarperCollinsPublishers 2005 un il $15.99; lib bdg $16.89

Grades: K 1 2 3   **305.8**

1. Racism 2. Prejudices

ISBN 0-06-028596-6; 0-06-028598-2 lib bdg

LC 2002-10979

This "picture book introduces race as just one of many chapters in a person's story. . . . Throughout the narrative, [the author] asks questions that young readers can answer, creating a dialogue about who they are and encouraging them to tell their own tales. He also discusses 'stories' that are not always true, pointing out that we create prejudice by perceiving ourselves as better than others. . . . The pairing of text and dazzling artwork is flawless." SLJ

Myers, Walter Dean, 1937-2014

★ **Now** is your time! the African-American struggle for freedom. HarperCollins Pubs. 1991 292p il hardcover o.p. pa $14.99

Grades: 6 7 8 9   **305.8**

1. African Americans -- History

ISBN 0-06-446120-3 pa

LC 91-314

Coretta Scott King Award for text

A history of the African-American struggle for freedom and equality, beginning with the capture of Africans in 1619, continuing through the American Revolution, the Civil War, and into contemporary times

"Myers's unique episodic approach makes this history a compelling exploration of the African-American experience. . . . This fascinating book will engender pride in heritage for young African Americans and provide insight into American history for all of us." Horn Book

Includes bibliographical references

Nelson, Kadir

★ **Heart** and soul; words and paintings by Kadir Nelson. Balzer + Bray 2011 108p. col. ill. $19.99; lib bdg $20.89

Grades: 3 4 5 6   **305.8**

1. African Americans -- History

ISBN 978-0-06-173074-0; 0-06-173074-2; 978-0-06-173076-4 lib bdg; 0-06-173076-9 lib bdg

LC 2010046236

Coretta Scott King Award (Authors) (2012)

"Nelson knits together the nation's proudest moments with its most shameful, taking on the whole of African-American history, from Revolutionary-era slavery up to the election of Barack Obama. He handles this vast subject with easy grace. . . . In jaw-dropping portraits, Nelson paints heroes like Frederick Douglass and Joe Louis, conferring equal dignity on the slaves, workers, soldiers, and students. . . . A tremendous achievement." Publ Wkly

Include bibliographical references (p. 104) and index.

Petrillo, Valerie

★ A **kid's** guide to Latino history; more than 70 activities. Chicago Review Press 2009 214p il pa $14.95

Grades: 4 5 6 7   **305.8**
   1. Hispanic Americans -- History
   ISBN 978-1-55652-771-5 pa; 1-55652-771-3 pa
                        LC 2008040433

"This big, lively overview examines the history of Latinos in the U.S. . . . The chatty, informative text, presented in readable, spacious layouts, will draw kids with lots of fun, illustrated instructions for related activities. . . . The accessible facts and the individual portraits of notable authors, athletes, entertainers, and politicians portray Latinos' rich contribution to U.S. heritage, and kids will want to talk about the well-presented issues." Booklist

Includes bibliographical references

Rappaport, Doreen

★ **Free** at last! stories and songs of Emancipation. illustrated by Shane W. Evans. Candlewick Press 2004 63p il $19.99; pa $7.99

Grades: 3 4 5 6   **305.8**
   1. African Americans -- History 2. African Americans -- Civil rights 3. Southern States -- Race relations
   ISBN 0-7636-1440-8; 0-7636-3147-7 pa
                        LC 2003-43853

"Stories, poems, and songs about events from the Emancipation Proclamation of 1863 through the Brown v. Board of Education decision of 1954 are perfectly matched with vibrant oil paintings. The result is a glorious tribute to the lives of African-American heroes and heroines." SLJ

Reynolds, Jan

Only the mountains do not move; a Maasai story of culture and conservation. Lee & Low Books 2011 40p il $18.95; pa $9.95

Grades: 2 3 4   **305.8**
   1. Agriculture 2. Kenya -- Social life and customs
   ISBN 978-1-60060-333-4; 1-60060-333-5; 978-1-60060-844-5 pa; 1-60060-844-2 pa
                        LC 2010050879

"With many clear color photos and an appended glossary with pronunciation, this is an excellent addition to classroom units on Africa today." Booklist

Slade, Suzanne

Climbing Lincoln's steps; the African American journey. illustrated by Colin Bootman. Albert Whitman 2010 un il $16.99

Grades: 2 3 4 5   **305.8**
   1. United States -- Race relations 2. African Americans -- Civil rights 3. Lincoln Memorial (Washington, D.C.)
   ISBN 978-0-8075-1204-3; 0-8075-1204-4
                        LC 2010004962

"This attractive, accessible title uses the Lincoln Memorial as a vehicle to outline the history of the Civil Rights Movement from the Emancipation Proclamation to Dr. King's 'I Have a Dream' speech to the 2008 presidential election. Other pivotal moments include world-renowned singer Marian Anderson's 1939 performance at the memorial when she was barred from singing at Constitution Hall. . . . Bootman's realistic watercolor spreads are striking." SLJ

Stefoff, Rebecca, 1951-

A **different** mirror for young people; a history of multicultural America. by Ronald Takaki; adapted by Rebecca Stefoff. Seven Stories Press 2012 vi, 377 p.p ill. (paperback : alk. paper) $18.95; (hardcover : alk. paper) $40.00; (ebook) $18.95

Grades: 7 8 9 10   **305.8**
   1. Letters 2. Multiculturalism 3. United States -- History 4. United States -- Race relations 5. United States -- Ethnic relations 6. Minorities -- United States -- History 7. Cultural pluralism -- United States -- History
   ISBN 1609804163; 9781609804169; 9781609804848; 9781609804176
                        LC 2012017004

Through studies of "American ethnic history . . . multicultural studies . . . and diversity" author Ronald Takaki "brings ethnic history alive through the words of people, including teenagers, who recorded their experiences in letters, diaries, and poems." The book "offers a rich and rewarding 'people's view' perspective on the American story." (Publisher's note)

Includes bibliographical references and index.

305.896 Africans and people of African descent

King, Martin Luther, Jr., 1929-1968

★ **I** have a dream; foreword by Coretta Scott King; paintings by fifteen Coretta Scott King Award and Honor Book artists, Ashley Bryan . . . [et al.] Scholastic 1997 40p il $16.95

Grades: K 1 2 3   **305.896**
   1. Illustration of books 2. United States -- Race relations 3. African Americans -- Civil rights
   ISBN 0-590-20516-1
                        LC 95-45189

"Martin Luther King, Jr.'s classic speech is creatively illustrated by 15 Coretta Scott King Award-winning artists. Signed statements from the artists explain the emotions they were trying to capture and why and how they used certain colors and tones. . . . From cover to cover this is a beautiful book." SLJ

McKissack, Pat, 1944-

Let's clap, jump, sing, and shout; dance, spin, and turn it out! Games, Songs, and Stories from an African American Childhood. collected by Patricia C. McKissack; illustrated by Brian Pinkney. Schwartz & Wade Books 2017 184 p. color illustrations $24.99

Grades: PreK K 1 2 3 4   **305.896**
   1. African Americans -- Games 2. African Americans -- Songs and music 3. African Americans -- Social life and customs 4. African American children
   ISBN 9780375870880; 9780375970887; 9780307974952
                        LC 2016000969

This book, collected by Patricia C. McKissack, illustrated by Brian Pinkney, is a "collection of classic playtime favorites. . . . Parents and grandparents will delight in sharing this exuberant book with the children in their lives. Here is a songbook, a storybook, a poetry collection, and much more, all rolled into one. Find a partner for hand claps such as 'Eenie, Meenie, Sassafreeny,' or form a circle for games like 'Little Sally Walker.'" (Publisher's note)

"Pinkney's watercolor-and-India ink spot illustrations swirl through the pages, bursting with energy tapped from joy and rich tradition. A comprehensive treasury of memories, verbal art, and play." Kirkus

Includes bibliographical references

305.9 People by occupation and miscellaneous social statuses; people with disabilities and illnesses, gifted people

Coy, John

★ **Their** great gift; courage, sacrifice, and hope in a new land. by John Coy; photographs by Wing Young Huie. Carolrhoda Books 2016 32 p. color illustrations $19.99

Grades: K 1 2 3 4 **305.9**

1. Immigrants -- United States -- Pictorial works 2. Immigrants -- United States 3. United States -- Emigration and immigration 4. United States -- Emigration and immigration -- Pictorial works

ISBN 1467780545; 9781467780544

LC 2015024013

This children's book, by John Coy, with photography by Wing Young Huie, "explores the experiences of immigrants in the twenty-first century, focusing on the lives of children. Images of families who came to the United States from many different parts of the world celebrate the diversity of our country and contain a vision of hope for the future." (Publisher's note)

"Coy takes a simple approach with the text, employing only a few words per page, while Huie uses his mostly black-and-white photographs to illuminate the experience of coming to a new country, working hard, making mistakes, and building a new home. The images carry this volume, featuring people of various ages, occupations, and cultural backgrounds." SLJ

Includes bibliographical references and index

306.3 Economic institutions

Huey, Lois Miner

Forgotten bones; uncovering a slave cemetery. by Lois Miner Huey. Millbrook Press 2016 112 p. illustrations (library binding : alkaline paper) $30.65

Grades: 4 5 6 7 **306.3**

1. Slavery 2. Cemeteries 3. Human remains (Archeology) 4. Northeastern States -- Antiquities 5. Slaves -- Tombs -- Northeastern States 6. Slave cemeteries -- Northeastern States 7. Slaves -- Northeastern States -- History 8. African American cemeteries -- Northeastern States 9. Human remains (Archaeology) -- Northeastern States 10. African Americans -- Northeastern States -- History 11. African Americans -- Northeastern States -- Antiquities

ISBN 1467733938; 9781467733939

LC 2014009379

This children's book by Lois Miner Huey tells how "when a skeleton's head rolled off a dirt pile, all work came to a halt at a construction project in upstate New York. Archaeologists began excavating and found thirteen skeletons. Further investigation revealed that the bones were those of eighteenth-century African American slaves who had worked at the nearby Schuyler farm. Find out what these skeletons tell us about slavery and daily life long ago." (Publisher's note)

"Together with chronicles of two other noted northern slave cemeteries and full-color photos of the excavation in process, this account provides a vivid description of both the eighteenth-century slave experience and the field of archaeology." Booklist

Includes bibliographical references and index

Lester, Julius

★ **From** slave ship to freedom road; paintings by Rod Brown. Dial Bks. 1998 40p il hardcover o.p. pa $6.99

Grades: 5 6 7 8 **306.3**

1. Slavery -- United States

ISBN 0-8037-1893-4; 0-14-056669-4 pa

LC 96-44422

"Lester's impassioned questions grow from his visceral response to Brown's narrative paintings. . . . The combination of history, art, and commentary demands interaction." Booklist

306.76 Sexual orientation, transgenderism, intersexuality

Seba, Jaime

Gallup guides for youth facing persistent prejudice; The LGBT community. by Jaime Seba. Mason Crest Publishers 2013 64 p. col. ill., photographs (library) $22.95

Grades: 5 6 7 8 **306.76**

1. LGBT people -- Civil rights 2. Homophobia 3. Gay youth -- United States 4. Homophobia -- United States 5. Sexual minorities -- Civil rights -- United States

ISBN 1422224678; 9781422224670

LC 2012017108

This book by Jaime Seba on the LGBT community "discusses the history of prejudice toward this group, the laws that protect people against discrimination-and what you can do to fight the prejudice you find in the world." (Publisher's note) As part of the "Gallup Guides for Youth Facing Persistent Prejudice" series, it "emphasiz[es] recent violence and other problems, such as bullying and depression, which are, unfortunately, still routine for many LGBT youth." (Booklist)

Includes bibliographical references (p. 62) and index.

Stevenson, Robin

★ **Pride**; Celebrating Diversity & Community. by Robin Stevenson. Orca Book Pub 2016 120 p. illustrations (chiefly color) (ebook) $19.99; $24.95

Grades: 4 5 6 7 8 9 **306.76**

1. Gays 2. LGBT people

ISBN 9781459809949; 1459809939; 9781459809932

LC 2015946192

Stonewall Honor Book: Children's and Young Adult Literature (2017)

In this book, by Robin Stevenson, "for LGBTQ people and their supporters, Pride events are an opportunity to honor the past, protest injustice, and celebrate a diverse and vibrant community. The high point of Pride, the Pride Parade, is spectacular and colorful. But there is a whole lot more to Pride than rainbow flags and amazing outfits. How did Pride come to be? And what does Pride mean to the people who celebrate it?" (Publisher's note)

"This attractive work will be welcomed by readers searching for guidance and hope." Kirkus

Includes bibliographical references (pages 110-113) and index.

306.8 Marriage and family

Ajmera, Maya

Our grandparents; a global album. [by] Maya Ajmera, Sheila Kinkade, Cynthia Pon; with a foreword by Archbishop Desmond Tutu. Charlesbridge 2010 un il $16.95

Grades: PreK K 1 2 **306.8**

1. Grandparents

ISBN 978-1-57091-458-4; 1-57091-458-3

LC 2009005494

"Clear, colorful photographs show the two generations engaged in a variety of activities and invite careful observation. The pictures are clearly labeled with the name of the families' countries and highlight common threads, e.g., 'listening,' in Tibet, India, Mexico, and USA. Spare text defines the actions represented. The book concludes with 'Five Things to Do with Your Grandparents.'" SLJ

Alko, Selina

★ The **case** for loving; fighting for interracial marriage. by Selina Alko; illustrated by Sean Qualls and Selina Alko. Arthur A. Levine Books, an imprint of Scholastic Inc. 2015 40 p. illustrations (chiefly color) (jacketed hardcover : alk. paper) $18.99

Grades: K 1 2 3 4   **306.8**
    1. Family 2. Interracial marriage -- Law and legislation 3. Interracial marriage
    ISBN 0545478537; 9780545478533

                          LC 2014005329

This children's book by Selina Alko is "story of one brave family: Mildred Loving, Richard Perry Loving, and their three children. It is the story of how Mildred and Richard fell in love, and got married in Washington, D.C. But when they moved back to their hometown in Virginia, they were arrested (in dramatic fashion) for violating that state's laws against interracial marriage." (Publisher's note)

"The story of Richard and Mildred Loving, the interracial couple whose fight for the right to be married led to the Supreme Court's ruling that ended anti-miscegenation laws, is relayed here as a love story that does not sugarcoat the virulent racism of the time. . . . An author's note grounds the Lovings' story in the present as Alko recognizes that her own interracial marriage is part of the trajectory of change, which continues today in the LGBTQ community's fight for equality. Inspirational, never heavy-handed, and appropriate for just about everyone. " Booklist
    Includes bibliographical references

Crist, James J.

Siblings; you're stuck with each other so stick together. by James J. Crist & Elizabeth Verdick; illustrated by Steve Mark. Free Spirit Pub. 2010 118p il (Laugh & learn) pa $8.95

Grades: 3 4 5 6   **306.8**
    1. Siblings
    ISBN 978-1-57542-336-4 pa; 1-57542-336-7 pa

"Starting with the wry subtitle and the colorful cover cartoon of two fuming kids standing back to back, this lively title uses accessible humor to approach sibling-related topics, such as birth order, privacy, jealousy, bullying, and bonding. The authors discuss each subject in a child-centered, casual, and humorous tone. . . . The book's open design and interactive features, such as quick checklists and quizzes, help make this a great choice for kids and grownups to talk and laugh about together." Booklist
    Includes bibliographical references

Guillain, Charlotte

A **new** brother or sister. Heinemann Library 2011 24p il (Growing up) lib bdg $22; pa $6.49

Grades: PreK K 1 2   **306.8**
    1. Infants 2. Siblings
    ISBN 978-1-4329-4803-0 lib bdg; 1-4329-4803-2 lib bdg; 978-1-4329-4813-9 pa; 1-4329-4813-X pa

                          LC 2010024197

Brief text and photographs explain what happens when a new baby joins your family, the special care babies need, and how you can help take care of your new brother or sister.
    Includes bibliographical references

Hoffman, Mary

★ The **great** big book of families; pictures by Ros Asquith. Dial Books for Young Readers 2011 un il $16.99

Grades: PreK K 1 2   **306.8**
    1. Family 2. Family 3. Single-parent families
    ISBN 978-0-8037-3516-3; 0-8037-3516-2

                          LC 2010-12141

"In matter-of-fact prose and genial pen-and-ink drawings, Hoffman and Asquith reassure readers [that] . . . there's no one right way to be a family. What sets their survey of familyhood apart . . . is the collaborators' expansive take on demographics. They cover not only a wide range of parental and domestic arrangements, but also schooling, homes, consumerism, employment—or lack of it—and psychographics. . . . Asquith's spreads have a lively, encyclopedic feel, with whimsical themed borders." Publ Wkly

Konrad, Marla Stewart

Grand. Tundra Books 2010 un il (World vision early readers) $12.95

Grades: PreK K   **306.8**
    1. Grandparents
    ISBN 978-0-88776-997-9; 0-88776-997-7

This features color photographs of children around the world engaged in activities with their grandparents.

This book's "simple, sharp aesthetic will capture the imagination of a good number of children." Booklist

Mom and me. Tundra Books 2009 un il (World vision early readers) $12.95

Grades: PreK K   **306.8**
    1. Mother-child relationship
    ISBN 978-0-88776-866-8; 0-88776-866-0

"A spare easy-to-read text combined with high-quality, full-color photographs highlights youngsters and mothers throughout the world involved in universal activities such as bathing, feeding, and providing comfort and support. Each spread demonstrates strong emotions and provides evidence of the woman's love and pride in her child. The vivid photos present a variety of settings, including many different cultures, and draw viewers into the pages." SLJ

Sheldon, Annette

★ **Big** sister now; a story about me and our new baby. written by Annette Sheldon; illustrated by Karen Maizel. Magination Press 2006 32p il $14.95; pa $8.95

Grades: PreK   **306.8**
    1. Infants 2. Siblings
    ISBN 1-59147-243-1; 1-59147-244-X pa

                          LC 2005005839

"Among the flood of titles about older siblings and new babies, this book, published under the auspices of the American Psychological Association, stands out for its appealing illustrations and direct story, which wraps a clear, comforting message. . . . An appended section offers parents solid ideas for helping a child adjust to a new baby." Booklist

306.85   Family

Rotner, Shelley

Families; by Shelley Rotner and Sheila M. Kelly; photographs by Shelley Rotner. Holiday House 2015 32 p. color illustrations (hardcover) $17.95

Grades: PreK K 1 2   **306.85**
  1. Family 2. Families
  ISBN 0823430537; 9780823430536

LC 2013032957

This book, by Shelley Rotner and Sheila M. Kelly, is "a picture book for very young children about the many faces of contemporary families. . . . This inclusive look at many varieties of families will help young readers see beyond their own immediate experiences and begin to understand others." (Publisher's note)

"Rotner and Kelly describe all kinds of familial units: those with only one parent or one child, those in which the parents and children resemble one another, those with members of different races, those with same and opposite sex parents, and those with adopted children. Winsome, clear photographs are accompanied by brief, large-font text. This celebration of differences is further enhanced by the inclusion of women in head scarves, a dad in a wheelchair, and multigenerational groupings." SLJ

306.874   Parent-child relationship

Joosse, Barbara M.
  ★ **Mama,** do you love me? illustrated by Barbara Lavallee. Chronicle Bks. 1991 un il $15.99; bd bk $6.99
Grades: PreK K   **306.874**
  1. Inuit -- Fiction 2. Mother-daughter relationship -- Fiction
  ISBN 978-0-87701-759-2; 0-87701-759-X; 978-0-8118-2131-5 bd bk; 0-8118-2131-5 bd bk

LC 90-1863

"A young girl asks how much her mother loves her, even when she is naughty, and receives warm, reassuring answers. The twist on this familiar theme is that the two are Inuits, and the text and pictures draw on their unique culture. . . . Two pages of back matter define and explain the functions of various terms in Inuit life past and present. Charming, vibrant watercolor illustrations expand the simple rhythmic text, adding to the characters' personalities and to the cultural information." SLJ

Thomas, Pat
  This is my family a first look at same sex parents; a first look at same-sex parents. by Pat Thomas. 1st ed. Barron's Educational Series, Inc. 2012 29 p. ill. (A first look at) (paperback) $7.99
Grades: K 1 2   **306.874**
  1. Same-sex marriage -- fiction 2. Children of gay parents -- fiction 3. Families 4. Gay parents 5. Children of gay parents 6. Gay fathers -- Family relationships 7. Lesbian mothers -- Family relationships
  ISBN 1438001878; 9781438001876

LC 2012940639

This book by Pat Thomas is part of the "A First Look At" series, which "encourages kids of preschool through early school age to understand and overcome problems that might trouble them in social and family relationships." It "takes a child's point of view in its discussion of same-sex marriage. Its message is intended both for children of gay or lesbian parents, as well as for the kids and parents of the children's friends and playmates." (Publisher's note)

Includes bibliographical references (p. 29).

306.875   Sibling relationships

Cole, Joanna
  ★ The **new** baby at your house; photographs by Margaret Miller. rev ed; Morrow Junior Bks. 1998 un il hardcover o.p. pa $6.99

Grades: K 1 2 3   **306.875**
  1. Infants 2. Siblings
  ISBN 0-688-13897-7; 0-688-13898-5 lib bdg; 0-688-16698-9 pa

LC 97-29267

A revised and newly illustrated edition of the title first published 1985

Describes the activities and changes involved in having a new baby in the house and the feelings experienced by the older brothers and sisters

"Miller captures many intimate and touching moments with her pictures. . . . There is a good balance of families from varied ethnic backgrounds. . . . This book opens with a clear and precise note to parents that gives honest, practical advice." SLJ

Includes bibliographical references

306.89   Separation and divorce

Brown, Laurene Krasny
  ★ **Dinosaurs** divorce; a guide for changing families. [by] Laurene Krasny Brown and Marc Brown. Atlantic Monthly Press 1986 31p il $15.95; pa $7.95
Grades: K 1 2 3   **306.89**
  1. Divorce
  ISBN 0-316-11248-8; 0-316-10996-7 pa

LC 86-1079

Text and illustrations of dinosaur characters introduce aspects of divorce such as its causes and effects, living with a single parent, spending holidays in two separate households, and adjusting to a stepparent

"The picture-book, almost comic-book, format, the touches of humor, and the distancing effect of the dinosaurs as surrogate humans may make the book accessible to young or extremely anxious children. A thoughtful, useful book." Horn Book

Cook, Julia
  The "D" word; [illustrated by Phillip W. Rodgers] National Center for Youth Issues 2011 32 p. $9.95
Grades: K 1 2 3 4   **306.89**
  1. Divorce 2. Children of divorced parents
  ISBN 1931636761; 9781931636766

Otis used to have the "perfect" family. That all changed when his parents told him that they were getting a D... D... D... The "D" Word - he can't even say it! At first Otis blames himself. With the help of his Gram, Otis discovers the reasons why people get divorced.

Holyoke, Nancy
  A **smart** girl's guide to her parents' divorce; how to land on your feet when your world turns upside down. illustrated by Scott Nash. American Girl Pub. 2009 120p il pa $9.95
Grades: 3 4 5   **306.89**
  1. Divorce 2. Children of divorced parents
  ISBN 978-1-59369-488-3 pa; 1-59369-488-1 pa

"Short chapters illustrated with bright cartoon drawings cover many important concerns and offer explanations of the divorce process. Topics range from how to deal with negative emotions, family changes, and new living arrangements, to tougher issues such as violence and financial troubles. The text has a compassionate tone, and sprinkled throughout are answers to questions that readers might have as well as snippets of advice from girls who have found what works for them." SLJ

306.9   Institutions pertaining to death

Roberts, Jillian

   What happens when a loved one dies? our first talk about death. by Dr. Jillian Roberts; illustrated by Cindy Revell. Orca Book Publishers 2016 32 p. color illustrations $19.95

Grades: PreK K   **306.9**

   1. Children and death

   ISBN 1459809459; 9781459809451

                               LC 2015944498

   In this book, by Dr. Jillian Roberts, illustrated by Cindy Revell, "Whether children are experiencing grief and loss for the first time or simply curious, it can be difficult to know how to talk to them about death. Using questions posed in a child's voice and answers that start simply and become more in-depth, this book allows adults to guide the conversation to a natural and reassuring conclusion. Additional questions at the back of the book allow for further discussion." (Publisher's note)

   "Soft, pastel digital art depicts a wide variety of ethnicities, family groupings, and even animals, and gives visual suggestions about behaviors related to visiting the dying, celebrating the memory of a loved one, and even working through grief. An excellent choice for preschools as well as libraries." Booklist

Thornhill, Jan

   I found a dead bird; the kids' guide to the cycle of life & death. Maple Tree Press 2006 64p il $21.95; pa $9.95

Grades: 4 5 6   **306.9**

   1. Death 2. Bereavement

   ISBN 1-897066-70-8; 1-897066-71-6 pa

   Explores the cycle of life and death, and how the process is necessary in nature, while also commenting on how death effects people personally, and the skills they use to cope with such a trauma when it occurs.

   "This straightforward, no holds barred approach to the subject will captivate children. Chock-full of color photographs, the well-designed book contains boxes with tidbits of information on a wide variety of topics, such as death of a species, human destruction, plant decomposition, trapped in time, and learning from death." SLJ

307   Communities

Ajmera, Maya

   Be my neighbor; [by] Maya Ajmera & John D. Ivanko. Shakti for Children. Charlesbridge 2004 un il $15.95; pa $6.95

Grades: K 1 2   **307**

   1. Community life

   ISBN 1-57091-504-0; 1-57091-685-3 pa

                            LC 2003-21230

   A simple introduction to the characteristics of a neighborhood

   "This beautifully crafted book explores the concept of community, using well-chosen words from the late Mr. Rogers as a starting point. . . . Illustrated with bright, beautiful full-color photos of children around the world, the gorgeous spreads are organized by themes." SLJ

Hopkinson, Deborah

   Shutting out the sky; life in the tenements of New York, 1880-1924. Orchard Bks. 2003 134p il $17.95

Grades: 5 6 7 8 9 10   **307**

   1. Poor 2. Immigrants -- United States 3. Lower East Side (New York, N.Y.)

   ISBN 0-439-37590-8

                            LC 2002-44781

   Photographs and text document the experiences of five individuals who came to live in the Lower East Side of New York City as children or young adults from Belarus, Italy, Lithuania, and Romania at the turn of the twentieth century.

   "The text is supported by numerous tinted archival photos of living and working conditions. Although this book will appeal to students looking for material for projects, the writing lends immediacy and vivid images make it simply a fascinating read." SLJ

   Includes bibliographical references

307.76   Urban communities

Reilly, Kathleen M.

   Cities; Discover How They Work. by Kathleen M. Reilly, illustrated by Tom Casteel. Pgw 2014 128 p. $16.95

Grades: 4 5 6   **307.76**

   1. Urban ecology 2. Cities and towns 3. City planning 4. Civil engineering

   ISBN 1619302136; 1619302179; 9781619302136; 9781619302174

   This book, by Kathleen M. Reilly and illustrated by Tom Casteel, "will give kids a view into the inner functioning of . . . urban areas. They'll learn about all the parts that come together to make cities work and how they've grown and changed since the very first riverside settlements. . . . Sidebars, unique illustrations, . . . and fun . . . facts combine with age-appropriate hands-on activities to make learning about complex urban environments fun and reinforce learning." (Publisher's note)

   "According to the 2010 Census, 80% of Americans live in urban areas." But do they know what it takes to make a city run? From this well-organized and engaging text, readers will learn how cities developed and grew...The simple black-and-white illustrations are helpful, but young readers accustomed to photos might pass on it when leafing through the book. Even so, this is a worthy title for any library collection." SLJ

320   Political science (Politics and government)

Cooper, Ilene

   A woman in the House and Senate; how women came to the United States Congress, broke down barriers, and changed the country. by Ilene Cooper; illustrations by Elizabeth Baddeley; foreword by Former U.S. senator Olympia Snowe. Abrams Books for Young Readers 2014 144 p. illustrations $24.95

Grades: 5 6 7 8   **320**

   1. Women in politics -- United States 2. United States. Congress -- History 3. Women legislators -- United States -- History 4. Women -- Political activity -- United States -- History

   ISBN 9781419710360; 1419710362

                            LC 2013022201

   In this book, "beginning with the women's suffrage movement and going all the way through the results of the 2012 election, Ilene Cooper . . . covers more than a century of U.S. history in order to highlight the influential and diverse group of female leaders who opened doors for women in politics as well as the nation as a whole. Featured women include Hattie Caraway (the first woman elected to the Senate) [and] Patsy Mink (the first woman of color to serve in Congress)." (Publisher's note)

   Includes bibliographical references and index

Giesecke, Ernestine

   National government; 2nd ed; Heinemann Library 2010 32p il map (Kids' guide to government) $29.29; pa $7.99

Grades: 3 4 5   **320**
1. United States -- Politics and government
ISBN 978-1-4329-2708-0; 1-4329-2708-6; 978-1-4329-2713-4
pa; 1-4329-2713-2 pa
First published 2000
Introduces the purpose and function of national government, the significance of the Constitution, the three branches of government, how the government raises money, and how a bill becomes a law
"This . . . would be a great asset. . . . Students will learn about a different, but related government every two pages. The font is large and easy to read. The photos, diagrams, charts, maps, and illustrations supplement the text well." Libr Media Connect
Includes glossary

320.3 Comparative government

Giesecke, Ernestine
Governments around the world; 2nd ed; Heinemann Library 2010 32p il map (Kids' guide to government) $29.29; pa $7.99
Grades: 3 4 5   **320.3**
1. Comparative government
ISBN 978-1-4329-2705-9; 1-4329-2705-1; 978-1-4329-2710-3
pa; 1-4329-2710-8 pa
First published 2000
Introduces the concept of government, exploring various types of systems, including democracy, communism, and socialism, and presenting international organizations such as the UN and NATO
"This . . . would be a great asset. . . . Students will learn about a different, but related government every two pages. The font is large and easy to read. The photos, diagrams, charts, maps, and illustrations supplement the text well." Libr Media Connect
Includes glossary and bibliographical references

Who's in charge? how governments make the world go round. foreword by Andrew Marr; [editors, Alexander Cox, Deborah Lock, Fleur Star; US editor, Margaret Parrish] DK 2010 96p il $16.99
Grades: 3 4 5 6   **320.3**
1. Political science
ISBN 978-0-7566-6278-3; 0-7566-6278-8
LC 2010280417
Introduces politicians and how laws are made, what happens in government and how the reader can get involved.
"The book explains ideas like democracy, monarchy, communism, and capitalism in a way that is accessible to children. Information is presented with DK's signature bright, colorful graphics. . . . This book is a timely and useful addition." Libr Media Connect
Includes glossary

320.4 Structure and functions of government

Wyatt, Valerie
How to build your own country; written by Valerie Wyatt; illustrated by Fred Rix. Kids Can Press 2009 40p il (CitizenKid) $17.95
Grades: 3 4 5   **320.4**
1. Citizenship 2. Political science
ISBN 978-1-55453-310-7; 1-55453-310-4
"This unique, odd, and informative book offers a guide for readers to create their own personal countries. Everything from finding unclaimed land and coming up with a name . . . to holding elections and serving one's citizens is covered. Despite the silliness, useful information

is given, teaching readers about the value of diplomacy and how actual governments function." Horn Book Guide
Includes glossary

320.8 Local government

Giesecke, Ernestine
Local government; 2nd ed; Heinemann Library 2009 32p il map (Kids' guide to government) $29.29; pa $7.99
Grades: 3 4 5   **320.8**
1. Local government 2. United States -- Politics and government
ISBN 978-1-4329-2706-6; 1-4329-2706-X; 978-1-4329-2711-0
pa; 1-4329-2711-6 pa
First published 2000
Introduces the purpose and function of local governments, explores the three branches of government at the city and county level, and presents the relationships between city and suburban governments and between various governments and schools
"This . . . would be a great asset. . . . Students will learn about a different, but related government every two pages. The font is large and easy to read. The photos, diagrams, charts, maps, and illustrations supplement the text well." Libr Media Connect
Includes glossary

322.4 Political action groups

Schwartz, Heather E.
Political activism; how you can make a difference. by Heather E. Schwartz. Capstone Press 2009 32p il (Take action) lib bdg $19.99
Grades: 3 4 5 6   **322.4**
1. Lobbying 2. Social action 3. Political activists
ISBN 978-1-4296-2799-3 lib bdg; 1-4296-2799-9 lib bdg
LC 2008026939
"Whether the issue is animal rights, global warming, or student representation in government, this lively hands-on title . . . combines personal profiles of activist teens with the politics of what they are fighting for, and includes realistic advice about how to do research, set goals, ask questions, and take one step at a time to reach those in power. The open, attractive design will draw readers with color photos of young activists." Booklist
Includes bibliographical references

323 Civil and political rights

Marzollo, Jean
★ **Happy** birthday, Martin Luther King; illustrated by J. Brian Pinkney. Scholastic 1993 un il $15.95; pa $6.99
Grades: K 1 2 3   **323**
1. Clergy 2. Nonfiction writers 3. Civil rights activists 4. Nobel laureates for peace 5. African Americans -- Biography 6. African Americans -- Civil rights 7. Biography, Individual
ISBN 0590440659; 0439782244 pa
LC 91-42137
This biography of the Baptist minister discusses "his education, his life as a pastor, and his involvement in the civil rights movement. . . . Ages four to eight." (Booklist)
"This very easy biography of Martin Luther King is distinguished by its succinct explanations of King's achievements. . . . The narrative of King's life is smooth and accessible. Pinkney's scratchboard paintings are fluidly drawn, warm, and dignified." Bull Cent Child Books

National Geographic Society (U.S.)

★ Every human has rights; a photographic declaration for kids. based on the United Nations Universal Declaration of Human Rights; with poetry from the ePals community; foreword by Mary Robinson. National Geographic 2009 30p il $26.90

Grades: 4 5 6 7 8　　　　　**323**

1. Human rights

ISBN 978-1-4263-0511-5; 1-4263-0511-7

"On the sixtieth anniversary of the Universal Declaration of Human Rights, this full-color photo-essay combines prize-winning poems by young people with beautiful photographs from all over the world. . . . The stirring pictures will stimulate classroom discussion about the declaration, which is quoted in full at the back." Booklist

Thomas, William David

What are citizens' basic rights? [by] William David Thomas. Gareth Stevens Pub. 2008 32p il (My American government) lib bdg $23.93; pa $8.95

Grades: 3 4 5　　　　　**323**

1. Civil rights

ISBN 978-0-8368-8861-4 lib bdg; 0-8368-8861-8 lib bdg; 978-0-8368-8866-9 pa; 0-8368-8866-9 pa

LC 2007032425

This describes the basic legal rights of United States citizens

This book has "an accessible format and clear writing. . . . Black-and-white and full-color vintage and more recent photographs appear throughout." SLJ

Includes glossary and bibliographical references

323.1　Civil and political rights of nondominant groups

Aretha, David

Sit-ins and freedom rides. Morgan Reynolds Pub. 2009 128p il lib bdg $28.95

Grades: 5 6 7 8　　　　　**323.1**

1. African Americans -- Civil rights 2. Southern States -- Race relations

ISBN 978-1-59935-098-1 lib bdg; 1-59935-098-X lib bdg

LC 2008039600

"Aretha opens with an introduction to the four college students who orchestrated the famous sit-in at Woolworth's in Greensboro, NC, in 1960. He follows that with chapters that describe slavery, Reconstruction, and Jim Crow in terms of how they set the stage for the resistance efforts. . . . [The book] offers insight into to workings of the protests at the grassroots level. Individual anecdotes interspersed thoughout the detailed narrative provide personal and effective accounts that go beyond mere facts. Black-and-white and some color photographs appear on almost every page." SLJ

Includes bibliographical references

Bass, Hester

Seeds of freedom; the peaceful integration of Huntsville, Alabama. Hester Bass, illustrated by E.B. Lewis. Candlewick Press 2014 32 p. color illustrations $16.99

Grades: K 1 2 3　　　　　**323.1**

1. Blacks -- Segregation 2. Alabama -- Race relations 3. African Americans -- Civil rights

ISBN 0763669199; 9780763669195

LC 2013955948

This children's book by Hester Bass tells "a little-known story of the civil rights movement, in which black and white citizens in [Huntsville,] Alabama city worked together nonviolently to end segregation. Bass and illustrator E. B. Lewis show children how racial discrimination, bully-

ing, and unfairness can be faced successfully with perseverance and ingenuity." (Publisher's note)

"Capturing the period with finesse, Lewis' expressive watercolor paintings record the events and settings in beautifully composed scenes. His portrayal of people is particularly fine, conveying the personalities, attitudes, and emotions of individuals as well as the essential dignity of the nonviolent protesters." Booklist

Bausum, Ann

Freedom Riders; John Lewis and Jim Zwerg on the front lines of the civil rights movement. by Ann Bausum; forewords by Freedom Riders Congressman John Lewis and Jim Zwerg. National Geographic 2006 79p il por $18.95; lib bdg $28.90

Grades: 5 6 7 8　　　　　**323.1**

1. Members of Congress 2. Civil rights activists 3. African Americans -- Civil rights 4. Southern States -- Race relations

ISBN 0-7922-4173-8; 0-7922-4174-6 lib bdg

LC 2005012947

"Bausum's narrative style, fresh, engrossing, and at times heart-stopping, brings the story of the turbulent and often violent dismantling of segregated travel alive in vivid detail. The language, presentation of material, and pacing will draw readers in and keep them captivated." SLJ

Includes bibliographical references

Brimner, Larry Dane, 1949-

★ Birmingham Sunday. Calkins Creek 2010 48p il

Grades: 5 6 7 8　　　　　**323.1**

1. Bombings 2. Hate crimes 3. Racism 4. African Americans -- Civil rights 5. Birmingham (Ala.) -- Race relations 6. Sixteenth Street Baptist Church (Birmingham, Ala.) 7. Hate crimes -- Birmingham (Ala.) 8. Bombings -- Alabama -- Birmingham

ISBN 1590786130; 9781590786130

LC 2009035716

This book describes the bombing of the Sixteenth Street Church in 1963 by Ku Klux Klan members, which killed four girls, and discusses how the event contributed to the civil rights movement. "Grades five to eight." (Bull Cent Child Books)

"This moving photo-essay covers much more than just an account of the Birmingham, Alabama, Baptist Church bombing that killed four young girls in 1963. The detailed text, illustrated with black-and-white photos on every spacious double-page spread, sets the shocking assassination of the children within a general overview of both the racist segregation of the times and the struggle against it." Booklist

Freedman, Russell

★ Freedom walkers; the story of the Montgomery bus boycott. Holiday House 2006 114p il $18.95

Grades: 4 5 6 7　　　　　**323.1**

1. Clergy 2. Historians 3. College teachers 4. Nonfiction writers 5. Civil rights activists 6. Nobel laureates for peace 7. African Americans -- Civil rights 8. Montgomery (Ala.) -- Race relations

ISBN 978-0-8234-2031-5; 0-8234-2031-0

LC 2006-41148

This account of the Montgomery bus boycott of 1955 focuses on Jo Ann Robinson, Claudette Colvin, Rosa Parks, Martin Luther King, and other participants.

This offers "expertly paced text, balanced but impassioned. . . . The narrative arc is compelling; well-captioned black-and-white photographs enhance the impact." Horn Book

Includes bibliographical references

Holland, Leslie J.

Dr. Martin Luther King Jr.'s I have a dream speech in translation; what it really means. Capstone Press 2009 32p il (Fact finders. Kids' translations) lib bdg $23.99; pa $7.95

Grades: 3 4 5 **323.1**

1. Clergy 2. American speeches 3. Nonfiction writers 4. Civil rights activists 5. Nobel laureates for peace 6. African Americans -- Civil rights

ISBN 978-1-4296-2793-1 lib bdg; 1-4296-2793-X lib bdg; 978-1-4296-3449-6 pa; 1-4296-3449-9 pa

LC 2008-32867

"Presents Dr. Martin Luther King Jr.'s speech and explains its meaning using everyday language. Describes the events that led to the speech and its significance through history." Publisher's note

Includes glossary and bibliographical references

Kittinger, Jo S.

Rosa's bus; illustrated by Steven Walker. Boyds Mills Press 2010 un il $17.95

Grades: 1 2 3 4 **323.1**

1. Buses 2. Civil rights activists 3. African Americans -- Civil rights 4. Montgomery (Ala.) -- Race relations

ISBN 978-1-59078-722-9; 1-59078-722-6

LC 2010005091

"In an inventive approach, this handsome picture book frames the biography of Rosa Parks with the story of the bus on which she famously refused to give up her seat to a white passenger. . . . The free-verse narrative and dramatic oil paintings tell the larger story of discrimination in daily life." Booklist

Includes bibliographical references

McWhorter, Diane

★ A **dream** of freedom; the Civil Rights Movement from 1954 to 1968. foreword by Reverend Fred Shuttlesworth. Scholastic Nonfiction 2004 160p il $19.95

Grades: 5 6 7 8 **323.1**

1. United States -- Race relations 2. African Americans -- Civil rights

ISBN 0-439-57678-4

The author discusses "the national civil rights movement from Brown v. the Board of Education to the assassination of Martin Luther King Jr. . . . This account is both factual and personal. She discusses her feelings as a white child in the South, and she focuses in on the many ways in which both white and black children were involved in the movement. . . . The breadth and depth of McWhorter's book is exemplary." Booklist

Mooney, Carla

Freedom Summer, 1964; Carla Mooney. ABDO Publishing Co. 2015 48 p. color ill., color map (hardcover) $32.79

Grades: 3 4 5 6 **323.1**

1. Civil rights -- United States -- History 2. African Americans -- Civil rights

ISBN 9781624038785; 1624038786

LC 2015931579

This juvenile book, by Carla Mooney, part of the "Stories of the Civil Rights Movement" series, "will inform readers about the Freedom Summer, like where it took place, the organizers, why its purpose was to get African-Americans registered to vote, and more. Vivid details, well-chosen photographs, and primary sources bring this story and this case to life." (Publisher's note)

"Succinct and often powerful, this set is a solid purchase." SLJ

Includes bibliographical references (page 47) and index.

Pinkney, Andrea Davis

★ **Sit-in**; how four friends stood up by sitting down. [by] Andrea Davis Pinkney and Brian Pinkney. Little, Brown and Company 2010 un il $16.99

Grades: K 1 2 3 **323.1**

1. African Americans -- Civil rights 2. Southern States -- Race relations 3. Civil rights movements 4. African Americans -- Civil rights

ISBN 0316070165; 9780316070164

LC 2009-19470

Flora Stieglitz Straus Award for Nonficton 2011

"This picture book is a celebration of the 50th anniversary of the . . . Woolworth's lunch counter sit-in, when four college students staged a peaceful protest." (Publisher's note) "Grades three to five." (Bull Cent Child Books)

"This compelling picture book is based on the historic sit-in 50 years ago by four college students who tried to integrate a Woolworth's lunch counter in Greensboro, North Carolina. Food-related wordplay adds layers to free verse. . . . At the core of the exciting narrative are scenes that show the difficulty of facing hatred. . . . Even young children will grasp the powerful, elemental, and historic story." Booklist

Rappaport, Doreen

★ **Nobody** gonna turn me 'round; stories and songs of the civil rights movement. illustrated by Shane W. Evans. Candlewick Press 2006 63p il $19.99

Grades: 3 4 5 6 **323.1**

1. United States -- Race relations 2. African Americans -- Civil rights

ISBN 0-7636-1927-2; 978-0-7636-1927-5

LC 2005-53184

"Rappaport draws on songs, poems, memories, letters, court testimony, and first-person accounts to provide a moving portrayal of the experiences of African Americans from the 1955 Montgomery Bus Boycott to the Voting Rights Act in July 1965. . . . Evans's earth-toned oil paintings enhance the stories with images that are by turns poignant, sad, hurtful, resigned, determined, hopeful, and triumphant." SLJ

Includes bibliographical references

Shelton, Paula Young

★ **Child** of the civil rights movement; illustrated by Raul Colón. Schwartz & Wade Books 2010 un il $17.99; lib bdg $20.99

Grades: K 1 2 3 **323.1**

1. Clergy 2. Mayors 3. Members of Congress 4. Civil rights activists 5. United Nations officials 6. Selma (Ala.) -- Race relations 7. African Americans -- Civil rights

ISBN 978-0-375-84314-3; 0-375-84314-0; 978-0-375-95414-6 lib bdg; 0-375-95414-7 lib bdg

LC 2008045855

The daughter of Andrew Young recalls her memories of her father and other African American Civil Rights activists, including Martin Luther King Jr., Dorothy Cotton and Ralph Abernathy, and the march from Selma to Montgomery Alabama.

"Colón's . . . soft-focus art features his customarily rich textural backdrop of speckles, scratches, and waves. Both contributors evoke the drama and emotion of the times . . . and a triumphal sense of community and family." Publ Wkly

Includes bibliographical references

Watkins, Angela Farris

My Uncle Martin's words of love for America; Martin Luther King Jr.'s niece tells how he made a difference. by Angela Farris Watkins, PhD; Illustrated by Eric Velasquez. Abrams Books for Young Readers 2011 40p il

Grades: 2 3 4 **323.1**

1. Clergy 2. Nonfiction writers 3. Civil rights activists 4. Nobel laureates for peace 5. African Americans -- Civil rights

ISBN 1-4197-0022-7; 978-1-4197-0022-4

LC 2011003888

"Explaining Jim Crow laws and the Civil Rights movement to a very young audience is not easy, but Watkins and Velasquez rise to the challenge with grace and warmth. Using a childlike voice, Martin Luther King Jr.'s niece simply and clearly emphasizes themes of love, nonviolence, freedom and equality. The repetitive text instills the message 'people listened, and things changed' and focuses on the positive. While the prejudice and violence of segregation is broached, . . . the intensity and extent of that violence is omitted. . . . Though picture books about Dr. King by his family members and others abound, this stands out for its graceful, age-appropriate treatment of the Movement." Kirkus

Includes bibliographical references

Weatherford, Carole Boston

★ The **beatitudes**; from slavery to civil rights. written by Carole Boston Weatherford; illustrated by Tim Ladwig. Eerdmans Books for Young Readers 2010 un il $16.99

Grades: 1 2 3 4 **323.1**

1. African Americans -- History 2. African Americans -- Civil rights

ISBN 978-0-8028-5352-3; 0-8028-5352-8

"Using the Beatitudes of blessings found in the Sermon on the Mount as an underpinning, Weatherford . . . highlights the faith that bolstered the African American struggle for freedom and civil rights. . . . The words serve as a refrain to puncuate Ladwig's elegant watercolors and lend a dreamlike quality to the stirring depictions." Booklist

323.11 Ethnic and national groups

Rubin, Susan Goldman

Freedom Summer; the 1964 Struggle for Civil Rights in Mississippi. by Susan Rubin. Holiday House 2014 120 p. illustrations (hardcover) $18.95

Grades: 5 6 7 8 9 10 **323.11**

1. African Americans -- Civil rights 2. Mississippi Freedom Project 3. African Americans -- Suffrage 4. Civil rights workers -- Mississippi 5. Civil rights movements -- Mississippi

ISBN 0823429202; 9780823429202

LC 2013020208

"Rubin has created a narrative retelling of the events and occurrences from the summer of 1964. Chock-full of primary sources, such as photographs, memos sent to applicants regarding the growing tensions in Mississippi, and pencil drawings depicting various settings from Neshoba County, Mississippi, Freedom Summer is organized in a time-line fashion, from June 1964 until late August 1964." (VOYA)

"This work gives a real sense of the time and place, the issues and the opposing sides, and the impact on the nation. Including myriad period photos and drawings, facsimiles of reports and records, meticulous source notes, an extensive bibliography, picture credits, and an extensive index, this title is the epitome of excellent historical reporting, with the human element never forgotten." SLJ

Includes bibliographical references and index

323.3 Civil and political rights of other social groups

Rappaport, Doreen, 1939-

Elizabeth started all the trouble; by Doreen Rappaport; illustrated by Matt Faulkner. Disney-Hyperion 2015 40 p. color illustrations $17.99

Grades: 1 2 3 **323.3**

1. Suffragists 2. Women's rights -- History 3. Suffragists -- United States 4. Women's rights -- United States 5. Women social reformers -- United States

ISBN 0786851422; 9780786851423

LC 2014031824

This picture book, by Doreen Rappaport, illustrated by Matt Faulkner, focuses on Elizabeth Cady Stanton. "She called on women across the nation to stand together and demand to be treated as equal to men-and that included the right to vote. It took nearly seventy-five years and generations of women fighting for their rights through words, through action, and through pure determination . . . for things to slowly begin to change." (Publisher's note)

"Faulkner's illustrations capture the spirit of each character and of the movement itself, and primary source quotes from the likes of Sojourner Truth and Alice Paul drive home the importance of the events described." Booklist

Includes bibliographical references.

Serres, Alain

I have the right to be a child; author, Alain Serres; illustrator, Aurélia Fronty; translator, Helen Mixter. Groundwood Books 2012 48 p.

Grades: 3 4 5 6 7 **323.3**

1. Treaties 2. Human rights 3. Children -- Civil rights

ISBN 1554981492; 9781554981496

In this children's book, "a young narrator describes what it means to be a child with rights -- from the right to food, water and shelter, to the right to go to school, to the right to be free from violence, to the right to breathe clean air, and much more. The book emphasizes that these rights belong to every child on the planet. . . . A brief afterword explains that the rights outlined in the book come from the Convention on the Rights of the Child." (Publisher's note)

323.4 Specific civil rights; limitation and suspension of civil rights

King, Martin Luther, Jr., 1929-1968

I have a dream; Martin Luther King, Jr.; illustrated by Kadir Nelson. 1st ed. Schwartz & Wade Books 2012 40 p. ill. (some col.) $18.99

Grades: K 1 2 3 4 5 **323.4**

1. Freedom 2. Equality 3. Speeches 4. Picture books for children 5. African Americans -- Civil rights 6. Civil rights movements -- United States -- History

ISBN 0375858873; 9780375858871; 9780375958878

LC 2011044259

Coretta Scott King Illustrator Honor Book (2013)

This children's book celebrates Civil Rights activist Martin Luther King, Jr. "On August 28, 1963, on the steps of the Lincoln Memorial during the March on Washington, Martin Luther King [Jr.] gave one of the most powerful and memorable speeches in our nation's history. His words [are] paired with Caldecott Honor winner Kadir Nelson's . . . paintings" for this book. (Publisher's note)

323.6   Citizenship and related topics

Raatma, Lucia

   Citizenship; by Lucia Raatma. Children's Press 2012 64 p. ill. (chiefly col.), col. map (Cornerstones of freedom) (library) $30; (paperback) $8.95

Grades: 4 5 6   **323.6**

   1. Citizenship -- United States

   ISBN 0329917374; 0531230643; 0531281647; 9780329917371; 9780531230640; 9780531281642

                                           LC 2011031340

   This book on citizenship by Lucia Raatma "covers everything from basic facts about naturalization to debates over hot issues such as gun control." It is part of the "Cornerstones of Freedom" series for students in grades 4 to 6. Included are "a two-page map of 'What Happened Where?'; a two-page epilogue; glossary-style identifications of significant people; a page of primary sources; a bibliography of books; a glossary; and an index plus author bio." (Booklist)

   Includes bibliographical references (p. 61) and index.

Raum, Elizabeth

   The **Pledge** of Allegiance in translation; what it really means. by Elizabeth Raum. Capstone Press 2009 32p il map (Fact finders. Kids' translations) lib bdg $23.93; pa $7.95

Grades: 3 4 5   **323.6**

   1. Pledge of Allegiance

   ISBN 978-1-4296-1931-8 lib bdg; 1-4296-1931-7 lib bdg; 978-1-4296-2846-4 pa; 1-4296-2846-4 pa

                                           LC 2007-51304

   Provides "a nearly line-by-line translation that makes . . . the written word accessible and meaningful." SLJ

   Includes glossary and bibliographical references

324.6   Election systems and procedures; suffrage

Fritz, Jean

   You want women to vote, Lizzie Stanton? illustrated by DyAnne DiSalvo-Ryan. Putnam 1995 88p il $16.99; pa $5.99

Grades: 2 3 4   **324.6**

   1. Feminism 2. Suffragists 3. Women -- Suffrage

   ISBN 0-399-22786-5; 0-698-11764-6 pa

                                           LC 94-30018

   This is a biography of the 19th century feminist and advocate of women's suffrage

   "With remarkable clarity, sensitivity, and momentum, Fritz has captured—but never imprisoned [Stanton's] spirit in an accessible, fascinating portrait." Horn Book

   Includes bibliographical references

Hollihan, Kerrie Logan

   Rightfully ours; how women won the vote : 21 activities. Kerrie Logan Hollihan. 1st ed. Chicago Review Press 2012 xiii, 130 p.p ill. (some col.) (paperback) $16.95

Grades: 4 5 6 7 8   **324.6**

   1. Women -- Suffrage 2. Women -- United States -- History 3. Suffragists -- United States -- History 4. Women's rights -- United States -- History 5. Women -- Suffrage -- United States -- History 6. Women's rights -- Study and teaching -- Activity programs -- United States 7. Women -- Suffrage -- Study and teaching -- Activity programs -- United States

   ISBN 1883052890; 9781883052898

                                           LC 2012006044

   This book is an "account of the struggle for women's suffrage. The first three chapters focus on notable activists Lucy Stone, Elizabeth Cady Stanton, and Susan B. Anthony. [Kerrie Logan] Hollihan recounts how this battle was inexorably tied to the antislavery movement and the role played by women of color in both movements, including Harriett Tubman, Sojourner Truth, and Ida Wells-Barnett." (School Library Journal)

   Includes bibliographical references (p. 121-124) and index

Rockliff, Mara

   Around America to Win the Vote; Two Suffragists, a Kitten, and 10,000 Miles. by Mara Rockliff; illustrated by Hadley Hooper. Candlewick Press 2016 40 p. color illustrations $16.99

Grades: K 1 2 3   **324.6**

   1. Historical fiction 2. Friendship -- Fiction 3. Suffragists -- Fiction 4. Women -- Suffrage -- Fiction

   ISBN 0763678937; 9780763678937

                                           LC 2015940254

   This picture book by Mara Rockliff, illustrated by Hadley Hooper, tells "the story of two brave suffragists on a trek across America to spread the word: Votes for Women! In April 1916, Nell Richardson and Alice Burke set out from New York City. . . . The Women's suffrage movement was in full swing, and Nell and Alice would not let anything keep them from spreading the word about equal voting rights for women." (Publisher's note)

   "A lively look at the ingenuity of women suffragists near the end of their long road to the vote." Kirkus

   Includes bibliographical references (page [39]).

Van Rynbach, Iris

   The **taxing** case of the cows; a true story about suffrage. by Iris Van Rynbach and Pegi Deitz Shea; illustrated by Emily Arnold McCully. Clarion Books 2010 32p il $16.99

Grades: 1 2 3   **324.6**

   1. Cattle 2. Taxation 3. Suffragists 4. Women -- Suffrage

   ISBN 978-0-547-23631-5; 0-547-23631-X

   "This title introduces the little-known story of two elderly sisters, Abby and Julia Smith, who fought against the taxation levied upon them as nonvoting citizens in nineteenth-century Connecticut. . . . The sisters' beloved cows became pawns in the arguments, used as collateral and bargaining chips by both sides. . . . McCully's watercolor illustrations of the historical scenes enhance this account of a pivotal event in women's long struggle for equality." Booklist

Wallner, Alexandra

   Susan B. Anthony; by Alexandra Wallner. Holiday House 2011 32 p. col. ill. (hardcover) $16.95

Grades: K 1 2 3   **324.6**

   1. Women -- Suffrage 2. Picture books for children 3. Women's rights -- United States 4. Feminists -- United States -- Biography 5. Suffragists -- United States -- Biography

   ISBN 0823419533; 9780823419531

                                           LC 2009017815

   This "picture-book biography focuses on America's foremost champion for women's rights," Susan B. Anthony. It covers her life, "from her strict upbringing in Massachusetts to her death after 58 years of working for reform, and her passionate role in the women's-suffrage movement." (School Library Journal)

   Includes bibliographical references

324.7 Conduct of election campaigns

Donovan, Sandy

Getting elected; a Look at running for office. Robin Nelson and Sandy Donovan. Lerner Publications 2012 40 p. (Searchlight books. How government does works) (lib. bdg. : alk. paper) $27.93
Grades: 3 4 5 **324.7**
1. Politics 2. Elections -- United States 3. Campaign management -- United States 4. Political campaigns -- United States
ISBN 0761365192; 9780761365198

LC 2010041859

Author Robin Nelson's book focuses on information regarding elections, government, and politics in the United States. "What does it mean to be elected to political office? It means you get to decide how to make a town, a state, or even the whole country a better place to live. But how does someone get elected? And what are the challenges of running for office?" (Publisher's note)

Includes bibliographical references (p. 39) and index

324.9 History and geographic treatment of elections

Christelow, Eileen

★ **Vote!** Clarion 2003 47p il $16
Grades: K 1 2 3 **324.9**
1. Politics 2. Elections
ISBN 0-618-24754-8

LC 2002-152288

Using a campaign for mayor as an example, shows the steps involved in an election, from the candidate's speeches and rallies, to the voting booth where every vote counts, to the announcement of the winner

"It's hard to imagine a more accessible introduction to voting. The words are straightforward, the art whimsical and creative, and two darling dogs provide color commentary on the action." Booklist

Includes glossary

325 International migration and colonization

Bial, Raymond

Ellis Island; coming to the land of liberty. Houghton Mifflin Books for Children 2009 56p il $18
Grades: 4 5 6 7 **325**
1. Ellis Island Immigration Station 2. United States -- Immigration and emigration
ISBN 978-0-618-99943-9; 0-618-99943-4

LC 2008-36794

"Bial examines the history of the famed immigration station. . . . He looks at the socio-historical roots of the mass exodus to America and provides a detailed look at the immigrant experience from ship to shore, with Ellis Island in between. Primary-source quotes and period photos pair eloquently with the modern narrative voice and color photographs of the museum exhibits. . . . The generously sized period photos and Bial's museum shots tell a vivid and poignant tale." SLJ

Includes bibliographical references

Levine, Ellen

★ . . . if your name was changed at Ellis Island; illustrated by Wayne Parmenter. Scholastic 1993 80p il hardcover o.p. pa $6.99
Grades: 3 4 5 **325**
1. Immigrants -- United States 2. Ellis Island (N.J. and N.Y.) 3. Ellis Island Immigration Station 4. United States -- Immigration and emigration
ISBN 0-590-43829-8 pa

LC 92-27940

Describes, in question and answer format, the great migration of immigrants to New York's Ellis Island, from the 1880s to 1914. Features quotes from children and adults who passed through the station

The author "writes in a clear, direct style that's packed with information and lively case histories. . . . There are many illustrations, sometimes full-page, sometimes small, in acrylic earth colors . . . they are an attractive part of a clear and accessible design." Booklist

Maestro, Betsy

★ **Coming** to America: the story of immigration; illustrated by Susannah Ryan. Scholastic 1996 un il $15.95
Grades: K 1 2 3 **325**
1. Immigrants -- United States 2. Ellis Island Immigration Station 3. United States -- Immigration and emigration
ISBN 0-590-44151-5

LC 94-31110

"In an introductory look at immigration, all inhabitants of the United States are considered immigrants or descendants of immigrants, whether they crossed the land bridge from Asia, came across the oceans voluntarily, or were brought as slaves. The clear, simple text and bright, animated illustrations convey excitement and adventure as well as hardship and loss." Horn Book Guide

Solway, Andrew

Graphing immigration. Raintree 2010 32p il (Real world data) $28.21; pa $7.99
Grades: 4 5 6 7 **325**
1. Statistics 2. Graphic methods 3. Immigrants -- United States 4. United States -- Immigration and emigration
ISBN 978-1-4329-2617-5; 1-4329-2617-9; 978-1-4329-2626-7 pa; 1-4329-2626-8 pa

LC 2009001185

"A line graph in [this] title shows the estimated number of illegal immigrants in the U.S. from 1980 to 2005. Arguments about costs and benefits of all kinds of immigrants include a pie chart that shows where immigrants in the U.S. come from and pairs thoughts on why people migrate with a discussion of costs and benefits. . . . The clear design, with lots of full-color photos and sidebars, will encourage browsers as much as the up-to-date examples and the clear directions for remaining 'chart smart.'" Booklist

Includes glossary and bibliographical references

Staton, Hilarie

Ellis Island. Chelsea Clubhouse 2009 48p il (Symbols of American freedom) $30
Grades: 3 4 5 **325**
1. Immigrants -- United States 2. Ellis Island (N.J. and N.Y.) 3. New York (N.Y.) 4. Ellis Island Immigration Station 5. United States -- Immigration and emigration
ISBN 978-1-60413-519-0; 1-60413-519-0

LC 2009-12067

This book about Ellis Island Immigration Station "provides nearly as much information as a guided tour by a park ranger. [It begins] with the story of how the place came to be, and where it fits into U.S. history. Information boxes offer additional background and some surprising facts, such as the stages an immigrant would pass through at Ellis Island. . . . The final chapter shows the landmark today and includes maps and photographs of the visitors' center and some of the things individuals might see or do while visiting the site. Much information is packed into

[this] slim [book]. Excellent . . . for state reports or to complement U.S. history units." SLJ

Includes glossary

326 Slavery and emancipation

Bial, Raymond

The **Underground** Railroad. Houghton Mifflin 1995 48p il map hardcover o.p. pa $6.95

Grades: 4 5 6 7

326

1. Underground railroad 2. Slavery -- United States

ISBN 0-395-69937-1; 0-395-97915-3 pa

LC 94-19614

"Although the text covers ground often trodden by other works on this popular subject, Bial's shots of places and things which now appear tidy and innocent conjure spirits of desperate freedom-seekers as handily as do more detailed narratives." Bull Cent Child Books

Includes bibliographical references

Hamilton, Virginia

★ **Many** thousand gone; African Americans from slavery to freedom. illustrated by Leo and Diane Dillon. Knopf 1993 151p il hardcover o.p. pa $12.95

Grades: 5 6 7 8

326

1. Underground railroad 2. Slavery -- United States

ISBN 0-394-92873-3; 0-679-87936-6 pa

LC 89-19988

In this book the author tells "the story of slavery through a series of dramatic biographical vignettes. . . . Her book includes such famous historical figures as Frederick Douglass, Sojourner Truth and Harriet Tubman. She also presents some more obscure individuals. . . . All of these profiles drive home the sickening realities of slavery in a personal way. . . . These are powerful stories eloquently told." N Y Times Book Rev

Includes bibliographical references

Haskins, James

Get on board: the story of the Underground Railroad. Scholastic 1993 152p il map hardcover o.p. pa $4.50

Grades: 5 6 7 8

326

1. Slaves 2. Abolitionists 3. Underground railroad 4. Slavery -- United States

ISBN 0-590-45419-6; 0-590-45418-8 pa

LC 92-13247

"Weaving together poignant personal stories and carefully researched historical data, Haskins has produced a stirring account of the founding and the workings of the Underground Railroad." Publ Wkly

Includes bibliographical references

Heinrichs, Ann

★ The **Underground** Railroad. Compass Point Bks. 2001 48p il map (We the people) lib bdg $21.26

Grades: 2 3 4

326

1. Underground railroad 2. Slavery -- United States

ISBN 0-7565-0102-4

LC 00-11020

This book briefly describes the Underground Railroad, slavery, and important abolitionists in the U.S.

"Short chapters, succinct text, large print, and well-chosen illustrations make this book a good starting point for young readers embarking on a study of the topic." SLJ

Includes glossary and bibliographical references

Lester, Julius

★ **To** be a slave; paintings by Tom Feelings. 30th anniversary ed; Dial Bks. 1998 160p il hardcover o.p. pa $6.99

Grades: 6 7 8 9

326

1. Slavery -- United States

ISBN 0-8037-2347-4; 0-14-131001-4 pa

LC 98-5213

A reissue of the title first published 1968

"Through the words of the slave, interwoven with strongly sympathetic commentary, the reader learns what it is to be another man's property; how the slave feels about himself; and how he feels about others. Every aspect of slavery, regardless of how grim, has been painfully and unrelentingly described." Read Ladders for Hum Relat. 6th edition

Includes bibliographical references

327 International relations

Deedy, Carmen Agra

14 cows for America; [by] Carmen Agra Deedy in collaboration with Wilson Kimeli Naiyomah; illustrated by Thomas Gonzalez. Peachtree 2009 un il $17.95

Grades: K 1 2 3

327

1. Masai (African people) 2. September 11 terrorist attacks, 2001 3. Kenya

ISBN 978-1-56145-490-7; 1-56145-490-7

"A native of Kenya, Naiyomah was in New York City on September 11, 2001. In his and Deedy's . . . lyrical account, he returns to his homeland and tells the members of his Maasai tribe the story that had 'burned a hole in his heart.' . . . Featuring luminous images . . . Gonzalez's pastel, colored pencil and airbrush paintings appear almost three-dimensional in their realism. A moving tale of compassion and generosity." Publ Wkly

327.1 Foreign policy and specific topics in international relations

Kerley, Barbara

A **little** peace; by Barbara Kerley; with a note by Richard H. Solomon. National Geographic 2007 un il $16.95; lib bdg $25.90

Grades: 1 2 3 4

327.1

1. Peace

ISBN 978-1-4263-0086-8; 1-4263-0086-7; 978-1-4263-0087-5 lib bdg; 1-4263-0087-5 lib bdg

LC 2006026367

Juxtaposes photographs from around the world with a simple message about our responsibilities for making and keeping peace on the planet.

This is a "simple, beautiful photo-essay. . . . The colorful pictures are supported by limited, yet powerful text, illustrating how each person can work to achieve peace." SLJ

Includes bibliographical references

327.12 Espionage and subversion

Earnest, Peter

The **real** spy's guide to becoming a spy; by Peter Earnest and Suzanne Harper, in association with the Spy Museum. Abrams Books for Young Readers 2009 144p il $16.95

Grades: 4 5 6 7   327.12
  1. Spies 2. Espionage 3. Intelligence service
  ISBN 978-0-8109-8329-8; 0-8109-8329-X
                                                    LC 2009-00518
"This guide, written by the executive director of the International Spy Museum, gives readers a glimpse at how spies work. Along with descriptions of the different types of intelligence officers and agencies and the tasks they perform, the text includes brief stories of spies in action." Horn Book Guide

Gilbert, Adrian
  Secret agents. Firefly 2009 32p il (Spy files) pa $6.95
Grades: 3 4 5 6   327.12
  1. Spies 2. Secret service
  ISBN 978-1-55407-574-4; 1-55407-574-2
First published 2008 in the United Kingdom
Discusses American, British, and Russian spies and secret agents, and the history of espionage. Includes profiles of famous spies and double agents.
  The text's "short paragraphs and great pictures are combined in a collage style that will draw readers quickly through the information. Useful for reports and browsing." SLJ
  Includes glossary

  Spy school. Firefly 2009 32p il (Spy files) pa $6.95
Grades: 3 4 5 6   327.12
  1. Spies 2. Espionage
  ISBN 978-1-55407-575-1 pa; 1-55407-575-0 pa
"Gilbert reveals how spies are recruited and trained, discussing methods of disguise, surveillance, interrogation, evasion, and escape. . . . The [text's] short paragraphs and great pictures are combined in a collage style that will draw readers quickly through the information. Useful for reports and browsing." SLJ
  Includes glossary

Janeczko, Paul B.
  The **dark** game; true spy stories. Candlewick Press 2010 248p il $16.99
Grades: 5 6 7 8   327.12
  1. Espionage
  ISBN 978-0-7636-2915-1; 0-7636-2915-4
"From Benedict Arnold and Mata Hari to the lesser-known Elizabeth Van Lew and Juan Pujol, Janeczko delves into [spies'] stories with delicious detail, drawing readers into a world of intrigue and danger. Did you ever wonder why invisible ink works? How a code breaker deciphers a message? Or whether dentistry could affect a secret agent's success? The answers to these questions and more can be found here. Each chapter covers a historical era and chronicles the maturation of spying, while primary-source photographs are interspersed throughout, lending an authentic feel to each section." SLJ

Mitchell, Susan K.
  Spies and lies; famous and infamous spies. Enslow Publishers 2011 48p il (The secret world of spies) lib bdg $23.93
Grades: 4 5 6   327.12
  1. Spies 2. Espionage
  ISBN 978-0-7660-3713-7
                                                    LC 2010044126
"Archival photographs, sidebars, and multiple fact-filled features (sidebars, text boxes, etc.) combine with accessible texts to present a thorough (albeit busy) introduction to the history and current enterprise of spies and spying." Horn Book
  Includes glossary and bibliographical references

  Spies, double agents, and traitors. Enslow Publishers 2011 48p il (The secret world of spies) lib bdg $23.93
Grades: 4 5 6   327.12
  1. Spies 2. Espionage
  ISBN 978-0-7660-3711-3
                                                    LC 2010006178
Discusses double agents and traitors throughout history, such as Benedict Arnold, Dusan Popov, Kim Philby, and Robert Hanssen, and includes information on becoming a spy catcher (counterintelligence agent).
  Includes glossary bibliographical references

  Spy gizmos and gadgets. Enslow Publishers 2011 48p il (The secret world of spies) lib bdg $23.93
Grades: 4 5 6   327.12
  1. Espionage 2. Electronic surveillance
  ISBN 978-0-7660-3710-6
                                                    LC 2010006177
Discusses different gadgets used by spies, such as invisible ink, hidden cameras, small guns made to look like ordinary objects, and bugs, and includes career information.
  Includes glossary and bibliographical references

★ **Spyology;** the complete book of spycraft. Candlewick Press 2008 un il $22.99
Grades: 3 4 5 6   327.12
  1. Spies 2. Espionage
  ISBN 978-0-7636-4048-4; 0-7636-4048-4
This "poses as a collection of items assembled in 1958 and stored in national archives, now declassified under the 'fifty-year rule.' Agent K, a British spy, is tracking down the evil international Operation Codex, using his mission to ground a training manual for spies. Readers can match wits with Agent K as they pick up clues." Publ Wkly

328 The legislative process

Bow, James
  What is the legislative branch? by James Bow. Crabtree Publishing Company 2013 32 p. (Your guide to government) (reinforced library binding) $26.60
Grades: 4 5 6 7   328
  1. Legislative bodies 2. United States. Congress 3. United States -- Politics and government
  ISBN 0778708799; 9780778708797; 9780778709053
                                                    LC 2013001277
  This book, by James Bow "provide[s] solid introductory material about the U.S. government. [The] book discusses the purpose of [the legislative] branch; the different positions, . . . the work done; and the strengths and the challenges of each branch and how they interact." (School Library Journal)

Hamilton, John
  How a bill becomes a law; [by] John Hamilton. ABDO Pub. Co. 2004 32p il (Government in action!) lib bdg $15.95
Grades: 3 4 5   328
  1. Law 2. Legislation
  ISBN 1-59197-646-4
                                                    LC 2003-69305
  This describes the steps in passing a federal law in the United States
  This "book has an interesting assortment of vintage and recent color photos, all well captioned, and is logically arranged." SLJ

330   Economics

Hlinka, Michael

Follow Your Money; Who Gets It, Who Spends It, Where Does It Go? by Kevin Sylvester and Michael Hlinka; illustrated by Kevin Sylvester. Annick Press 2013 56 p. col. ill. (paperback) $14.95; (hardcover) $24.95

Grades: 5 6 7 8   **330**

1. Pricing 2. Money
ISBN 1554514800; 1554514819; 9781554514809; 9781554514816

This book by Kevin Sylvester and Michael Hlinka answers the questions "what happens to your money after you hand it to the cashier? Who actually pockets it or puts it into the bank? Was the price you paid fair? Why do things cost what they do? Kids will also discover the trail their money takes through advertising, banks [and] charitable giving. [It is an] introduction to the . . .people and companies that we influence and are influenced by when we pay for a product or service." (Publisher's note)

330.9   Economic situation and conditions

Heinrichs, Ann

★ The **great** recession. Children's Press 2011 il (Cornerstones of freedom) lib bdg $30; pa $8.95

Grades: 4 5 6 7   **330.9**

1. Recessions 2. Financial crises 3. Economic policy -- United States
ISBN 978-0-531-25035-8 lib bdg; 0-531-25035-0 lib bdg; 978-0-531-26560-4 pa; 0-531-26560-9 pa

LC 2011010824

This "offers simplified but not simplistic explanations of the current great recession's course and immediate causes. The . . . design has . . . visually stimulating pages that combine big color photos, boxed side essays, and blocks of large text with bright-red headers and highlights. In simple language and a judicious, matter-of-fact tone, Heinrichs describes the origins and growth of the housing bubble and the trade in mortgage-backed securities that magnified the effects of its eventual collapse; summarizes the federal government's palliative measures; surveys the effects of hard times on general patterns of living and spending; and notes the creation of a 'Generation R,' for whom high unemployment and financial insecurity are likely to become ways of life." Booklist

Includes bibliographical references

Mooney, Carla

The **Industrial** Revolution; investigate how science and technology changed the world with 25 projects. illustrated by Jen Vaughn. Nomad Press 2011 120p il (Build it yourself) $21.95; pa $15.95

Grades: 4 5 6 7   **330.9**

1. Industrial revolution
ISBN 978-1-936313-81-5; 1-936313-81-2; 978-1936313-80-8; 1-936313-80-4 pa

This "gives on overview of the era known as the Industrial Revolution as well as the consequences, good and bad, of each new development upon the average citizen. Topics covered include the transformation of textiles from homespun to manufactured, the birth of labor unions, advances in transportation and communication, the inventions of Thomas Edison, and brief profiles of 'Captains of Industry,' such as Carnegie, Vanderbilt, and Rockefeller. Each chapter ends with enticing projects related to the topic. . . . The crisp, clear format, featuring ample black-and-white sketches and diagrams and pleasingly arranged type in a large font, is in sync with the straightforward text." Booklist

331.1   Labor force and market

Lynette, Rachel

What to do when your parent is out of work. PowerKids Press 2010 24p il (Let's work it out) lib bdg $21.25; pa $8.25

Grades: 2 3 4   **331.1**

1. Unemployed
ISBN 978-1-4358-9338-2 lib bdg; 1-4358-9338-7 lib bdg; 978-1-4358-9764-9 pa; 1-4358-9764-1 pa

LC 2009-23067

A guide to unemployment, what it is, what it may mean for your family, and how you can help.

"Full-page color photographs appear opposite the [narrative], depicting multicultural children, parents, grandparents, social workers, and others, whose demeanors match the hopeful tone of the [title]. This . . . will help promote empathy and understanding for the plight of others and is a key purchase." SLJ

Includes glossary

331.3   Labor force by personal attributes

Bartoletti, Susan Campbell

★ **Growing** up in coal country. Houghton Mifflin 1996 127p il $17; pa $7.95

Grades: 5 6 7 8   **331.3**

1. Child labor 2. Coal mines and mining 3. Immigrants 4. Coal miners 5. Pennsylvania -- History
ISBN 0-395-77847-6; 0-395-97914-5 pa

LC 96-3142

This is an "account of working and living conditions in Pennsylvania coal towns. The first half of the volume . . . {describes} various duties in the mines, from jobs performed by the youngest boys to the tasks of adult miners, while the second half describes the company village, common customs and recreational activities, and the accidents and diseases that frequently beset the workers. Preceding each chapter and within the text {are} quotes from personal interviews with miners, as well as taped interviews and transcripts." (Horn Book) Bibliography. "Grade five and up." (Booklist)

"With compelling black-and-white photographs of children at work in the coal mines of northeastern Pennsylvania about 100 years ago, this handsome, spacious photo-essay will draw browsers as well as students doing research on labor and immigrant history." Booklist

Includes bibliographical references

Freedman, Russell

★ **Kids** at work; Lewis Hine and the crusade against child labor. with photographs by Lewis Hine. Clarion Bks. 1994 104p il $20; pa $9.95

Grades: 5 6 7 8   **331.3**

1. Child labor 2. Photographers
ISBN 0-395-58703-4; 0-395-79726-8 pa

LC 93-5989

Freedman "does an outstanding job of integrating historical photographs with meticulously researched and highly readable prose." Publ Wkly

Includes bibliographical references

331.4   Women workers

Colman, Penny

Rosie the riveter; women working on the home front in World War II. Crown 1995 120p il hardcover o.p. pa $10.99

Grades: 5 6 7 8   **331.4**

1. Women -- Employment 2. World War, 1939-1945 -- United States

ISBN 0-517-59790-X; 0-517-88567-0 pa

LC 94-3614

"A thoughtfully prepared look at women's history and wartime society, this dynamic book is characterized by extensive research." Horn Book

Includes bibliographical references

Warren, Sarah

Dolores Huerta; a hero to migrant workers. by Sarah E. Warren; illustrated by Robert Casilla. Marshall Cavendish Children 2012 32 p. (hardcover) $17.99

Grades: 3 4 5   **331.4**

1. Labor unions 2. Migrant labor 3. Women political activists 4. Mexican American women -- Biography 5. Women labor leaders -- United States -- Biography 6. Mexican American women labor union members -- Biography 7. Migrant agricultural laborers -- Labor unions -- United States -- History 8. Mexican American migrant agricultural laborers -- Labor unions -- Organizing -- History

ISBN 0761461078; 9780761461074; 9780761461081

LC 2011016403

This picture-book, by Sarah E. Warren, "chronicles the campaigns of the Latina activist who advocated for the rights of agricultural laborers in 1960s and '70s California. . . . Each double-page spread begins with 'Dolores is a . . . ' and adds a noun that embodies an aspect of her advocacy. . . . An appended timeline offers expanded details of Huerta's personal life and her collaboration with Cesar and Richard Chavez." (Bulletin of the Center for Children's Books)

"While the book alone will work with younger children, the backmatter makes this title an exceptional resource for both Hispanic Heritage and Woman's History months. A welcome title for children and educators alike." Kirkus

331.7   Labor by industry and occupation

Coulter, Laurie

★ **Cowboys** and coffin makers; one hundred 19th-century jobs you might have feared or fancied. by Laurie Coulter; art by Martha Newbigging. Annick Press 2007 96p il $25.95; pa $16.95

Grades: 3 4 5 6   **331.7**

1. Occupations 2. World history -- 19th century

ISBN 978-1-55451-068-9; 1-55451-068-6; 978-1-55451-067-2 pa; 1-55451-067-8 pa

"Short job descriptions, usually one or two per page, are written in an entertaining style and grouped according to headings. . . . The author considers a variety of economic and social classes, from robber barons to forced laborers and slaves, and acknowledges how locations affect available occupations. . . . Bright watercolor, cartoon-style illustrations accompany each job description." SLJ

Hopkinson, Deborah

★ **Up** before daybreak; cotton and people in America. Scholastic Nonfiction 2005 120p il $18.99

Grades: 5 6 7 8   **331.7**

1. Cotton 2. Working class 3. Textile industry -- History

ISBN 0-439-63901-8

LC 2005-8128

"From the industrial revolution to the 1950s demise of the Lowell cotton mills, Hopkinson discusses the history and sociology of king cotton, frequently emphasizing the children who labored under slave masters, endured dead-end mill jobs, or helped sharecropping parents claw out a living. . . . Stories of real people . . . sharply focus the dramatic history, as do arresting archival photos of stern youngsters manipulating hoes, cotton sags, or bobbins." Booklist

Hord, Colleen

My safe community. Rourke 2011 il (Little world social studies)

Grades: K 1 2 3   **331.7**

1. Occupations

ISBN 1-61741-795-5; 1-61741-997-4 pa; 978-1-61741-795-5 lib bdg; 978-1-61741-997-3 pa

This "introduces various community workers such as the mayor, police, or sanitation workers. . . . The [book has] minimal text but still [manages] to impart basic information and even raise questions. The full-page color photographs that face the text pages are crisp." Booklist

Miller, Margaret

★ **Guess** who? Greenwillow Bks. 1994 un il $16.99

Grades: PreK   **331.7**

1. Occupations

ISBN 0-688-12783-5

LC 93-26704

A child is asked who delivers the mail, gives haircuts, flies an airplane, and performs other important tasks. Each question has several different answers from which to choose

"Gender and ethnic representation are deftly handled. The author's sharp, clear full-color photographs are well composed, and her use of cropped photos and white space alternating with bled photos is an effective tool for involving youngsters." SLJ

Paul, Miranda

Whose hands are these? a community helper guessing book. by Miranda Paul. Millbrook Press 2016 32 p. color illustrations (lb : alk. paper) $19.99

Grades: K 1 2 3   **331.7**

1. Occupations 2. Helping behavior

ISBN 9781467752145; 9781467797269

LC 2015001721

In this children's book, by Miranda Paul, illustrated by Luciana Navarro Powell, "hands . . ., and the people attached to them, do all sorts of helpful work. And together, these helpers make their community a safe and fun place to live. As you read, keep an eye out for community members who make repeat appearances! Can you guess all the jobs based on the actions of these busy hands?" (Publisher's note)

"Care has been taken to ensure that people of all ages, races, and genders are depicted doing the work—sometimes solo, sometimes in pairs or teams. Beyond the content, the text is linguistically complex and fun, helping readers to build vocabulary with words associated with the professions." Booklist

Tsiang, Sarah

Warriors and wailers; one hundred ancient Chinese jobs you might have relished or reviled. Annick Press 2012 96 p.

Grades: 4 5 6   **331.7**

1. China -- History 2. Occupations -- History 3. Professions -- History

ISBN 155451391X; 9781554513918

This book, by Sarah Tsiang, is part of the "Jobs in History" series. "China was one of the most advanced societies in the ancient world. Whether in medicine, the arts, or education, the Chinese far outpaced the Europeans. Although most people were peasants, society included a myriad of other jobs. . . . Other jobs included wailer, . . . noodle maker, . . . or Shaolin warrior monk." (Publisher's note)

331.702   Choice of vocation

Zephaniah, Benjamin, 1958-
When I Grow Up; poems by Benjamin Zephaniah; photographs by Prodeepta Das. Pgw 2012 32 p. $17.99
Grades: 1 2 3 4 5   **331.702**
   1. Occupations 2. Vocational guidance
   ISBN 1847800599; 9781847800596
This book by Benjamin Zephaniah "takes an alternative look at 12 occupations and the people who fill them. Its aim is to open up children's imaginations to the possibility that there are many more roles open to them than they may think. It . . . depict[s] . . .broad-ranging examples of unusual people doing unusual jobs, such as Sikh lollipop man, a female clown and a black British Space Scientist." (Publisher's note)

331.8   Labor unions, labor-management bargaining and disputes

Bartoletti, Susan Campbell
★ **Kids** on strike! Houghton Mifflin 1999 208p il $20; pa $8.95
Grades: 5 6 7 8   **331.8**
   1. Strikes 2. Child labor 3. Centenarians 4. Labor leaders
   ISBN 0-395-88892-1; 0-618-36923-6 pa
                              LC 98-50575
Describes the conditions and treatment that drove workers, including many children, to various strikes, from the mill workers strikes in 1828 and 1836 and the coal strikes at the turn of the century to the work of Mother Jones on behalf of child workers
   "This well-researched and well-illustrated account creates a vivid portrait of the working conditions of many American children in the 19th and early 20th centuries." SLJ
   Includes bibliographical references

Brill, Marlene Targ
Annie Shapiro and the clothing workers' strike; illustrated by Jamel Akib. Millbrook Press 2010 48p il (History speaks: picture books plus reader's theater) lib bdg $27.93; pa $9.95
Grades: 2 3 4   **331.8**
   1. Strikes 2. Labor unions 3. Readers' theater 4. Clothing industry 5. Labor leaders
   ISBN 978-1-58013-672-3 lib bdg; 1-58013-672-9 lib bdg; 978-0-7613-6132-9 pa; 0-7613-6132-4 pa
                              LC 2009051812
"This partly fictionalized picture-book story is followed by an eight-page script for reader's theater. In 1910, Hannah 'Annie' Shapiro, a teenage Russian immigrant, led a walkout in Chicago to protest pay cuts and poor conditions in the clothing factory where she worked. . . . Dramatic double-page spreads in deep shades of red and brown focus on Annie as they show the confrontations. . . . After the story, an author's note fills in more historical facts, and a reader's theater section features roles for Annie, two narrators, and two additional readers and includes practical notes about costumes, props, and performance." Booklist
   Includes bibliographical references

331.892   Strikes

Markel, Michelle
★ **Brave** girl; Clara and the Shirtwaist Makers' Strike of 1909. written by Michelle Markel; pictures by Melissa Sweet. Balzer + Bray 2013 32 p. (hardcover bdg.) $17.99
Grades: K 1 2 3 4   **331.892**
   1. Picture books for children 2. Strikes -- United States -- History 3. Shirtwaist Makers' Strike, New York, N.Y., 1909 4. Women clothing workers -- New York (State) -- New York 5. Women in the labor movement -- New York (State) -- New York 6. Strikes and lockouts -- Clothing trade -- New York (State) -- New York
   ISBN 0061804428; 9780061804427
                              LC 2012025439
Amelia Bloomer Project (2014)
Orbis Pictus Awards Honor Book (2014)
This children's picture book offers a biography of Clara Lemlich, early 20th-century union organizer. "She not only worked to support her family in a factory that made women's clothing, but read and studied at night. When the male workers talked about a strike to protest their fearsome working conditions," Clara "called for a general strike. She was arrested 17 times and beaten, but the strike won the right to unionize for workers in many factories." (Kirkus Reviews)

332.02   Miscellany and personal finance

Brennan, Linda Crotta
Managing money; by Linda Crotta Brennan and illustrated by Rowan Barnes-Murphy. Childs World 2012 24 p. (library reinforced : alk. paper) $27.07
Grades: 2 3 4 5   **332.02**
   1. Economics 2. Personal finance
   ISBN 1614732418; 9781614732419
                              LC 2012932818
This book, by Linda Crotta Brennan and illustrated by Rowan Barnes-Murphy, "introduces money management, including how to create a budget and the importance of spending, saving, and donating. [It also] features a glossary and lists resources to explore the subject further." (Publisher's note)

332.024   Personal finance

Bochner, Rose
   The **new** totally awesome money book for kids (and their parents) [by] Arthur Bochner & Rose Bochner; foreword by Adriane G. Berg. 3rd ed., rev & updated.; Newmarket Press 2007 189p il pa $9.95
Grades: 4 5 6 7   **332.024**
   1. Personal finance
   ISBN 978-1-55704-738-0
                              LC 2006038930
First published 1993 with title: The totally awesome money book for kids (and their parents)
   An introduction to money for kids including the basics of saving, investing, working, and taxes.
   "Using an easy and comfortable style that young people will find unthreatening, the book presents a wealth of information. . . . The cute illustrations are also fun." Voice Youth Advocates
   Includes bibliographical references

Chatzky, Jean

Not your parents' money book; making, saving, and spending your own money. [by Jean Sherman Chatzky]; illustrated by Erwin Haya. Simon & Schuster Books for Young Readers 2010 162p il pa $12.99

Grades: 5 6 7 8   **332.024**

1. Money 2. Personal finance

ISBN 978-1-4169-9472-5 pa; 1-4169-9472-6 pa

LC 2010008840

"Written in a light, somewhat jocular tone and sprinkled with amusing but eye-opening and conversation-starting quotes from 12, 13, and 14-year-olds, this book is sure to hold readers' attention. The content includes how you get money, via allowances and jobs, and notes the difference between cash-only and paychecks. Tracking typical teen expenditures, both long-term and short, is juxtaposed against keeping money in checking, savings, and money-market accounts. . . . Chatzky's presentation is engaging. . . . Cartoons appear on almost every page, adding humor and some additional material." SLJ

Includes bibliographical references

Hall, Alvin

Show me the money; [by] Alvin Hall. DK 2008 96p il $15.99

Grades: 4 5 6   **332.024**

1. Money 2. Personal finance

ISBN 978-0-7566-3762-0; 0-7566-3762-7

"Four main sections cover the history of money, expenses/income, the basics of economics, and the world of work and business. Brief profiles of eight wealthy entrepreneurs and their paths to prosperity and eight significant economists and their theories are included. The lively writing features real-life examples that will be meaningful to students and is presented in a balanced, nonjudgmental style that encourages them to decide for themselves among the various ideas concerning economic policies. . . . Color photos and graphics excel at conveying the concepts presented and represent diversity well." SLJ

Includes glossary

Holyoke, Nancy

Money; how to make it, save it, and spend it. by Nancy Holyoke; illustrated by Brigette Barrager. American Girl Publishing 2014 94 p. color illustrations (A smart girl's guide) (pbk.) $12.99

Grades: 4 5 6 7   **332.024**

1. Women -- Personal finance 2. Money 3. Finance, Personal 4. Money-making projects for children 5. Teenage girls -- Finance, Personal

ISBN 1609584074; 9781609584078

LC 2013025896

In this book, by Nancy Holyoke, illustrated by Brigette Barrager, "learn how to not only spend that cash, but also how to earn it. The quizzes, tips, and helpful quotes from other girls will make learning about money management easy and fun." (Publisher's note)

Hord, Colleen

Need it or want it? Rourke 2011 il (Little world social studies) $22.79; pa $7.95

Grades: K 1 2 3   **332.024**

1. Personal finance

ISBN 978-1-61741-793-1; 1-61741-793-9; 978-1-61741-995-9 pa; 1-61741-995-8 pa

This book "brings up the provocative question of whether you desire something because it will be useful or just because it will be fun. Examples of both are given, and a page reminds readers they can give back to their communities by donating needed goods. The [book has] minimal text but still [manages] to impart basic information and even raise questions. The full-page color photographs that face the text pages are crisp." Booklist

Larson, Jennifer S.

Do I need it? or do I want it? making budget choices. Lerner 2010 32p il (Exploring economics) lib bdg $25.26; pa $7.95

Grades: K 1 2   **332.024**

1. Personal finance

ISBN 978-0-7613-3914-4 lib bdg; 0-7613-3914-0 lib bdg; 978-0-7613-5664-6 pa; 0-7613-5664-9 pa

An introduction to budgeting that explains how to make a budget and stick to it, how to decide if something is a need or a want, why it is important to have a budget, and how to save and spend money wisely.

"Clear, age-appropriate language explains new concepts well. . . . The [book's] layout is interesting and fresh, and each page features a large, well-chosen photograph with a boxed caption." SLJ

What can you do with money? earning, spending, and saving. Lerner Pub. 2010 32p il (Exploring economics) lib bdg $25.26; pa $7.95

Grades: K 1 2   **332.024**

1. Personal finance

ISBN 978-0-7613-3910-6 lib bdg; 0-7613-3910-8 lib bdg; 978-0-7613-5666-0 pa; 0-7613-5666-5 pa

Provides an introduction to earning, spending, and saving and discusses goods, services, and how people choose what to buy.

"Clear, age-appropriate language explains new concepts well. . . . The [book's] layout is interesting and fresh, and each page features a large, well-chosen photograph with a boxed caption." SLJ

Lynette, Rachel

What to do when your family has to cut costs. PowerKids Press 2010 24p il (Let's work it out) lib bdg $21.25; pa $8.25

Grades: 2 3 4   **332.024**

1. Personal finance

ISBN 978-1-4358-9340-5 lib bdg; 1-4358-9340-9 lib bdg; 978-1-4358-9768-7 pa; 1-4358-9768-4 pa

LC 2009-23737

Learn about prioritizing needs over wants and ways to be cost-conscious and frugal.

"Full-page color photographs appear opposite the [narrative], depicting multicultural children, parents, grandparents, social workers, and others, whose demeanors match the hopeful tone of the [title]. This . . . will help promote empathy and understanding for the plight of others and is a key purchase." SLJ

Includes glossary

What to do when your family is in debt. PowerKids Press 2010 24p il (Let's work it out) lib bdg $21.25; pa $8.25

Grades: 2 3 4   **332.024**

1. Debt 2. Consumer credit

ISBN 978-1-4358-9341-2 lib bdg; 1-4358-9341-7 lib bdg; 978-1-4358-9770-0 pa; 1-4358-9770-6 pa

A guide to debt, what it is, what it may mean for your family, and how you can help.

"Full-page color photographs appear opposite the [narrative], depicting multicultural children, parents, grandparents, social workers, and others, whose demeanors match the hopeful tone of the [title]. This . . . will help promote empathy and understanding for the plight of others and is a key purchase." SLJ

Includes glossary

Mitten, Ellen K.

Goods or services? Ellen K. Mitten. Rourke 2011 24 p. col. ill. (library) $22.79; $15.95; (paperback) $7.95

Grades: K 1 2 3   332.024
1. Personal finance
ISBN 9781617417917; 9781612367095; 9781617419935
LC 2011924836

In this book "the concept of different ways to use money is introduced, with pages showing how you can buy something, like an apple, or have a service provided to you, like getting a haircut. Readers are told families must make choices about how to spend their money. . . . The [book has] minimal text but still [manages] to impart basic information and even raise questions. The full-page color photographs that face the text pages are crisp." Booklist

Includes bibliographical references and index.

Morrison, Jessica

Saving. Weigl Publishers 2009 32p il (Everyday economics) lib bdg $26; pa $9.95
Grades: 5 6 7   332.024
1. Saving and investment
ISBN 978-1-60596-647-2 lib bdg; 1-60596-647-9 lib bdg; 978-1-60596-648-9 pa; 1-60596-648-7 pa
LC 2009018567

This "informative [book introduces savings in] U.S. economic theory and practices using everyday language and real-life examples. [It] includes history, a brief annotated chronology, sidebar and intext explanations of terminology, and helpful diagrams. . . . With brief paragraphs; large, captioned photographs; ample margins; and well-organized graphics, the [book's] design makes economics accessible without sacrificing content. . . . [This is] easy to navigate and full of solid information and interesting facts." SLJ

Includes glossary

Roderick, Stacey

Centsibility; the Planet Girl guide to money. [by] Stacey Roderick and Ellen Warwick; illustrated by Monika Melnychuk. Kids Can Press 2008 80p il (Planet girl) $12.95
Grades: 5 6 7 8   332.024
1. Personal finance
ISBN 978-1-55453-208-7

"This book presents handy methods for managing money. . . . Chapters are broken down into subsections . . . which are peppered with quizzes and craft projects to keep readers engaged. . . . The book's sound advice is both practical and approachable." Horn Book Guide

Schwartz, David M.

If you made a million; pictures by Steven Kellogg. Lothrop, Lee & Shepard Bks. 1989 un il hardcover o.p. pa $6.99
Grades: PreK K 1 2 3   332.024
1. Personal finance
ISBN 0-688-07017-5; 0-688-13634-6 pa
LC 88-12819

"The concepts of banks and banking . . . are all explained with absurd and humorous examples involving Ferris wheels, ogres, and rhinoceroses. . . . The best advice of all is 'Enjoying your work is more important than money.' Steven Kellogg's splendidly funny illustrations contain a troupe of two cats, one dog, numerous kids, a unicorn, and the wonderful magician Marvelosissimo." Horn Book

Scott, Elaine

Dollars and sense; A Kid's Guide to Using--Not Losing--Money. by Elaine Scott; illustrated by David Clark. Charlesbridge 2015 112 p. illustrations (reinforced for library use) $16.95
Grades: 4 5 6 7   332.024
1. Money   2. Personal finance   3. Money -- United States   4.

Finance, Personal -- United States
ISBN 9781580893961; 9781607345404; 9781607346241
LC 2013022069

This book by Elaine Scott, illustrated by David Clark, "is a basic operating instruction manual for money that will teach readers about the history of money, the way our American economy works, and how to make important decisions about personal finance. . . . An engaging and approachable guide for kids tackling how to responsibly manage their money. Included are sidebars, time lines, . . . as well as information on related topics such as the Great Recession and sequestration." (Publisher's note)

"An informative primer on how money functions that doesn't trigger the dismal science's snooze button." Kirkus

Includes bibliographical references and index.

Wiseman, Blaine

Budgeting. Weigl Publishers 2009 32p il (Everyday economics) lib bdg $26; pa $9.95
Grades: 5 6 7   332.024
1. Budget
ISBN 978-1-60596-643-4 lib bdg; 1-60596-643-6 lib bdg; 978-1-60596-644-1 pa; 1-60596-644-4 pa
LC 2009018439

This "informative [book introduces budgeting in] U.S. economic theory and practices using everyday language and real-life examples. [It] includes history, a brief annotated chronology, sidebar and intext explanations of terminology, and helpful diagrams. . . . With brief paragraphs; large, captioned photographs; ample margins; and well-organized graphics, the [book's] design makes economics accessible without sacrificing content. . . . [This is] easy to navigate and full of solid information and interesting facts." SLJ

Includes glossary

332.4   Money

Adler, David A.

★ **Money** madness; by David A. Adler; illustrated by Edward Miller. Holiday House 2009 un il $16.95
Grades: PreK K 1 2   332.4
1. Money
ISBN 978-0-8234-1474-1; 0-8234-1474-4
LC 2008004223

"This brightly illustrated picture book introduces the concept of money, first by looking at its development as an alternative to bartering and then by explaining the many forms of money, from primitive rocks, feathers, and metal lumps to the familiar coins and paper bills to alternatives such as checks, credit cards, and digital forms of payment. Adler does a particularly good job explaining the inconvenience of bartering through child-friendly examples. . . . Using flat colors and stylized designs, Miller's upbeat digital artwork helps to clarify points made in the text, while adding occasional bits of visual humor. Photos of coins and bills are incorporated where appropriate." Booklist

Blobaum, Cindy

Explore money! With 25 Great Projects. by Cindy Blobaum; illustrated by Bryan Stone. Nomad Press 2014 90 p. color illustrations $19.95
Grades: 3 4 5 6   332.4
1. Money
ISBN 1619302853; 9781619302853

In this book, by Cindy Blobaum, "young readers explore the cultural aspect of money as well as its physical properties, discovering how these properties have affected business and global relationships throughout history. Kids experiment with various substances to clean coins, scientifically test coin components, design their own currency, and plan how to allocate their own money." (Publisher's note)

Brennan, Linda Crotta

Payment methods; by Linda Crotta Brennan and illustrated by Rowan Barnes-Murphy. Childs World 2012 24 p. (library reinforced : alk. paper) $27.07

Grades: 2 3 4 5   332.4

1. Economics 2. Personal finance

ISBN 1614732426; 9781614732426

LC 2012932820

This book, by Linda Crotta Brennan and illustrated by Rowan Barnes-Murphy, "introduces payment methods including cash, checks, and credit. [It also] features a glossary and lists resources to explore the subject further." (Publisher's note)

Cleary, Brian P., 1959-

A **dollar**, a penny, how much and how many? by Brian P. Cleary; illustrated by Brian Gable. Millbrook Press 2012 31 p. col. ill. (Math is Categorical) (reinforced) $16.95

Grades: K 1 2   332.4

1. Money 2. Mathematics 3. Coins

ISBN 0822578824; 9780822578826

LC 2011045864

This nonfiction children's book was written by Brian P. Cleary. "In rhyming text young readers are introduced to the world of currency and coins, and more subtly, to the economic concepts of value and compensation. In this new series called 'Math is CATegorical,' the popular cats from the 'Words are CATegorical' series show how to combine bills and coins of various denominations in order to pay for goods and services." (Children's Literature)

★ **Eyewitness** money; written by Joe Cribb. 3rd edition DK Publishing 2016 72 p illustrations (DK Eyewitness) paperback $9.99; library $19.99

Grades: 4 5 6 7   332.4

1. Money

ISBN 9781465451781; 9781465451798; 146545179X; 1465451781

"From the earliest forms of money to the intricate banking systems we have today, currency has been around for millennia, whether made from stones and shells to the coins and paper we see today. This guide details various types of currency from both the past and present, from the sea salt money of Ethiopia to the modern Euro. Discover where the term piggy bank came from, why Ancient Greeks put coins in the mouths of dead people, and how coins and banknotes are made today. . . . . [The revised edition] retains the stunning artwork and photography from the groundbreaking original series, but the text has been reduced and re-worked to speak more clearly to younger readers." (Publisher's note)

Forest, Christopher

The **dollar** bill in translation; what it really means. Capstone Press 2009 32p il (Fact finders. Kids' translations) lib bdg $23.99; pa $7.95

Grades: 3 4 5   332.4

1. Money 2. Dollar 3. Paper money 4. Signs and symbols

ISBN 978-1-4296-2794-8 lib bdg; 1-4296-2794-8 lib bdg; 978-1-4296-3448-9 pa; 1-4296-3448-0 pa

LC 2008-28981

"Presents the dollar bill and explains its meaning and symbolism using everyday language. Describes the events that led to the creation of currency and its significance through history." Publisher's note

Includes glossary and bibliographical references

Jenkins, Martin

The **history** of money; from bartering to banking. Martin Jenkins, illustrated by Satoshi Kitamura. First U.S. Edition Candlewick Press 2014 64 p. color illustrations $16.99

Grades: 4 5 6 7 8   332.4

1. Money -- History

ISBN 0763667633; 9780763667634

LC 2013952840

"Martin Jenkins and Satoshi Kitamura take readers on a . . . . tour of the history of money. What can take the form of a stone with a hole in the middle, a string of shells, a piece of paper, or a plastic card? The answer is money, of course. But when did we start using it? And why? What does money have to do with writing? And how do taxes and interest work?" (Publisher's note)

"This cleverly designed picture book uses just the right balance of information and explanation to guide students through both the global history of currency and the application of market pressures on exchange methods." Booklist

Includes bibliographical references and index

Larson, Jennifer S.

What is money, anyway? why dollars and coins have value. Lerner Pub. 2010 32p il (Exploring economics) lib bdg $25.26

Grades: K 1 2   332.4

1. Money

ISBN 978-0-7613-3915-1 lib bdg; 0-7613-3915-9 lib bdg

An introduction to money that discusses what it is made of, the values of coins and bills, how it is used, and other related topics.

"Clear, age-appropriate language explains new concepts well. . . . The [book's] layout is interesting and fresh, and each page features a large, well-chosen photograph with a boxed caption." SLJ

Leedy, Loreen

★ **Follow** the money! written and illustrated by Loreen Leedy. Holiday House 2002 un il $16.95; pa $6.95

Grades: K 1 2 3   332.4

1. Coins 2. Money

ISBN 0-8234-1587-2; 0-8234-1794-8 pa

LC 2001-39418

A quarter describes all the ways it is used from the time it is minted until it is taken back to a bank

"Leedy includes a good deal of information, while keeping the book light, energetic, and entertaining." Booklist

Includes glossary

Orr, Tamra

Coins and other currency; a kid's guide to coin collecting. by Tamra Orr. Mitchell Lane Publishers 2009 48p il map (Money matters: a kid's guide to money) lib bdg $29.95

Grades: 4 5 6   332.4

1. Coins 2. Money

ISBN 978-1-58415-640-6 lib bdg; 1-58415-640-6 lib bdg

LC 2008-2262

"Photos feature multigenerational and diverse subjects and illustrate related locations and historical figures, while graphs and sidebars enhance the [text]. Well-documented and informative." SLJ

Includes glossary and bibliographical references

332.6 Investment

Minden, Cecilia

Investing; making your money work for you. Cherry Lake Pub. 2008 32p il (Real world math: personal finance) lib bdg $25.26

Grades: 3 4 5 6 **332.6**

1. Investments 2. Personal finance
ISBN 978-1-60279-003-2 lib bdg; 1-60279-003-5 lib bdg

LC 2007005917

This "examines the importance of short-term and long-term savings and explains the pros and cons of savings accounts, certificates of deposit, government bonds, and stocks. Engaging full-color photographs on every page feature diverse children and families, and plenty of white space." SLJ

Includes bibliographical references

Morrison, Jessica

Investing. Weigl Publishers 2009 32p il (Everyday economics) lib bdg $26; pa $9.95

Grades: 5 6 7 **332.6**

1. Investments
ISBN 978-1-60596-649-6 lib bdg; 1-60596-649-5 lib bdg; 978-1-60596-650-2 pa; 1-60596-650-9 pa

LC 2009018568

This explains the advantages of investing money, how to read a stock report, interest, and the types of investments provided by different companies.

This "informative [book introduces] U.S. economic theory and practices using everyday language and real-life examples. . . . [This is] easy to navigate and full of solid information and interesting facts." SLJ

Includes glossary

332.7 Credit

Hall, Margaret

Credit cards and checks; [by] Margaret Hall. 2nd ed.; Heinemann Library 2008 32p il (Earning, saving, spending) lib bdg $28.21; pa $7.99

Grades: 1 2 3 **332.7**

1. Debit cards 2. Credit cards 3. Personal finance
ISBN 978-1-4034-9816-8 lib bdg; 978-1-4034-9821-2 pa

LC 2007015150

First published 2000

This offers an overview of spending money without using cash, including details on credit, checkbooks, debt and interest.

"Illustrated with sharp, clear photographs, each spread presents a different concept in a logical procession. The author uses simple sentences, highlighting important words." SLJ

Includes glossary and bibliographical references

Tomljanovic, Tatiana

Borrowing. Weigl Pubs. 2009 32p il (Everyday economics) lib bdg $26; pa $9.95

Grades: 5 6 7 **332.7**

1. Credit
ISBN 978-1-60596-645-8 lib bdg; 1-60596-645-2 lib bdg; 978-1-60596-646-5 pa; 1-60596-646-0 pa

LC 2009018444

This "informative [book introduces borrowing in] U.S. economic theory and practices using everyday language and real-life examples. [It] includes history, a brief annotated chronology, sidebar and intext explanations of terminology, and helpful diagrams. . . . With brief paragraphs; large, captioned photographs; ample margins; and well-organized graphics, the [book's] design makes economics accessible without sacrificing content. . . . [This is] easy to navigate and full of solid information and interesting facts." SLJ

Includes glossary

333.7 Natural resources and energy

Gazlay, Suzy

Managing green spaces; careers in wilderness and wildlife management. Crabtree 2010 64p il (Green-collar careers) lib bdg $30.60; pa $10.95

Grades: 4 5 6 7 **333.7**

1. Wildlife 2. Wilderness areas 3. Vocational guidance
ISBN 978-0-7787-4855-7 lib bdg; 0-7787-4855-3 lib bdg; 978-0-7787-4866-3 pa; 0-7787-4866-9 pa

LC 2009-28145

"Passions often lead to professions, as this upbeat title . . . shows. . . . There is inevitable overlap among the categories: government-run parks and forestry, outdoor adventure, science, and wildlife sanctuaries. The browsable format, combining many crisp color photos with blocks of narrative texts and sidebars featuring specific ecoprofessionals, will easily lead students through the survey of nature-focused careers." Booklist

Yasuda, Anita

Explore Natural Resources! with 25 great projects. Anita Yasuda, illustrated by Jennifer Keller. Pgw 2014 96 p. illustrations pbk $13.95

Grades: 2 3 4 **333.7**

1. Science projects 2. Natural resources
ISBN 1619302233; 9781619302235

LC 2014497629

"The 25 projects inspire young readers ages 6-9 to have fun while learning why natural resources are important to all living things and how every child can take care of the earth's resources through reducing, reusing, and recycling. Kids will read about national parks and early environmentalists, Earth celebrations, and the science behind renewable and nonrenewable resources." (Publisher's note)

"Words to know, listed in the sidebar of each chapter, are boldface in the text, underscored in the illustrations, and defined in a glossary. Activities follow each chapter and include art projects, experiments, building plans, and challenges." Booklist

Includes bibliographical references and index

333.72 Conservation and protection

Black, Jess

A **year** in the life of Bindi; Australia's Favorite Wildlife Warrior. Random House Australia 2012 95 p.

Grades: 4 5 6 **333.72**

1. Wildlife
ISBN 1864718382; 9781864718386

This book gives "the inside scoop on how Bindi Irwin, daughter of Steve Irwin the Crocodile Hunter, spends her time. Appearing on 'Oprah' in Sydney one day, helping out at the Australia Zoo Wildlife Hospital the next, spending weeks croc tagging in the Cape York Peninsula--she's an Australian girl with a life like no other." (Publisher's note)

Bullard, Lisa

Earth Day every day; illustrated by Xiao Xin. Millbrook Press 2011 24p col. ill. (Planet protectors) lib bdg $23.93

Grades: K 1 2 3 **333.72**

1. Earth Day 2. Environmental protection
ISBN 978-0-7613-6109-1; 0-7613-6109-X

LC 2010053466

On Earth Day Trina plants trees with her class. She forms an Earth Day club with her friends and explains what can you do to make every day Earth Day.

"The bright colors used in the illustrations . . . will attract young readers to the environmental science content. . . . [The] facts are written in child-friendly language and the information should be attainable by young children. . . . [This book] will raise the environmental awareness of young children." Sci Books Films

Fuoco, Gina Dal

Earth. Compass Point Books 2009 40p il (Mission: science) lib bdg $26.60

Grades: 4 5 6   333.72

1. Earth

ISBN 978-0-7565-4070-8 lib bdg; 0-7565-4070-4 lib bdg

LC 2008-37575

Discusses the basic parts systems (atmosphere, hydrosphere, and geosphere) of Earth and how important it is to protect Earth's resources

Includes glossary

Hirsch, Rebecca E.

Protecting our natural resources; by Rebecca Hirsch. Cherry Lake Pub. 2010 32p il (Save the planet) lib bdg $27.07

Grades: 3 4 5 6   333.72

1. Conservation of natural resources

ISBN 978-1-60279-661-4 lib bdg; 1-60279-661-0 lib bdg

LC 2009-38097

Explains what natural resources are, how they are being exploited, and what should be done to protect them

"At the beginning of . . . [the] book, readers are given a mission and advised to be alert to the facts provided so that they can successfully answer the questions at the end. . . . Children are made to feel part of the process; suggestions for how they can become involved abound." SLJ

Includes glossary and bibliographical references

Kelsey, Elin

★ **Not** your typical book about the environment; illustrated by Clayton Hammer. Owlkids 2010 64p il $22.95; pa $10.95

Grades: 4 5 6 7   333.72

1. Environmental protection 2. Ecology 3. Sustainable living

ISBN 978-1-897349-79-3; 1-897349-79-3; 978-1-897349-84-7 pa; 1-897349-84-X pa

Written to allay children's fears about the environment, this book shows how smart technologies, innovative ideas, and a growing commitment to alternative lifestyles are exploding around the world, creating a future that will be brighter than we sometimes might think. Includes profiles of unexpected personalities.

"Imaginative, comic-booklike illustrations add to a lively layout that will keep readers moving from one paragraph to the next, and funny wordplay prevents the facts from becoming overwhelming or dry. . . . This hilarious, information-packed work is an excellent addition." SLJ

Kriesberg, Daniel A.

Think green, take action; books and activities for kids. illustrated by Kathleen A. Price. Libraries Unlimited 2010 136p il pa $30; e-book $30

Grades: Adult Professional   333.72

1. Environmental sciences -- Study and teaching

ISBN 978-1-59884-378-1 pa; 1-59884-378-8 pa; 978-1-59884-379-8 e-book

LC 2010014409

"A resource for teaching environmental understanding and activism through stewardship, this book outlines teaching strategies for ages 6-10, provides resources for understanding environmental concerns for ages 10-13, and promotes action and growth for ages 13+. Chapters focus on local ecology, endangered species, resource depletion, and pollution. Extensive annotated bibliographies of both recent and older fiction and nonfiction selections . . . supplement the activities." SLJ

Includes bibliographical references

McKay, Kim

True green kids; 100 things you can do to save the planet. [by] Kim McKay and Jenny Bonnin. National Geographic 2008 143p il $15.95

Grades: 4 5 6 7   333.72

1. Environmental protection

ISBN 978-1-4263-0442-2; 1-4263-0442-0

Presents an overview of global warming and describes 100 simple ways to be more environmentally friendly in the bedroom, in the house, at school, and on vacation.

"Accompanied by attractive, up-to-date pictures in a lively design, the one hundred suggestions are direct . . . and generally practical." Horn Book Guide

Includes glossary

Parr, Todd

The **Earth** book. Little, Brown Books for Young Readers 2010 un il $15.99

Grades: PreK K 1   333.72

1. Environmental protection

ISBN 978-0-316-04265-9; 0-316-04265-X

LC 2008047562

"With illustrations that look as though they might have been done by enthusiastic children themselves, Parr's book offers first-person advice about ways to take care of the earth. . . . The strong appeal comes from the simple artwork done in Parr's signature style, which features pure colors, objects and people outlined in thick black ink, and kids whose round faces are comprised of two dots for eyes and upturned lines for mouths. Young children will get a kick out of the vivid art." Booklist

★ **Recycle** this book; 100 top children's book authors tell you how to go green. edited by Dan Gutman. Yearling 2009 267p pa $5.99

Grades: 5 6 7 8   333.72

1. Authors 2. Recycling 3. Environmental protection

ISBN 978-0-385-73721-0 pa; 0-385-73721-1 pa

LC 2008-10800

"This lively collection of brief essays (and a poem) by 100 outstanding children's and young adult authors teaches through example. Each selection highlights a small step (or steps) taken by the writer toward a greener Earth. . . . The essays also provide insight into the lives and thoughts of many familiar and beloved authors such as Laurie Halse Anderson, Ralph Fletcher, Gary Schmidt, Lois Lowry, Susan Patron, and Rick Riordan. Several pages of Web sites offer a starting point for action and information. Highly useful for classroom and family discussions and science-project ideas." SLJ

Reilly, Kathleen M.

Planet Earth; 25 environmental projects you can build yourself. Nomad Press 2008 122p il (Projects you can build yourself) $21.95; pa $14.95

Grades: 4 5 6 7   333.72

1. Science projects 2. Environmental sciences

ISBN 978-1-934670-05-7; 1-934670-05-7; 978-1-934670-04-0 pa; 1-934670-04-9 pa

"Both comprehensive and approachable, this title . . . combines explanations of science concepts and environmental issues with hands-on projects. . . . Elementary- and middle-school students will find the succinct overview of the facts very useful, and they'll welcome the clearly presented projects." Booklist

Ride, Sally K.

Mission: save the planet; things you can do to help fight global warming. [by] Sally Ride and Tam O'Shaughnessy; illustrated by Andrew Arnold. Roaring Brook Press 2009 61p il (Sally Ride science) pa $7.99

Grades: 5 6 7 8   **333.72**
1. Environmental protection
ISBN 978-159643-379-3 pa; 1-59643-379-5 pa
LC 2009-29254
"The first chapter in this slim volume discusses our energy use, dependence on fossil fuels, and the environmental impact of these practices. The remaining chapters are packed with facts and suggestions on
reducing our carbon footprint. . . . The authors' background in science
education is evident, as the writing style is clear, precise, and kid-friendly. Black-and-white cartoon illustrations provide excellent visuals for
many of the recommendations." SLJ

Rohmer, Harriet
★ **Heroes** of the environment; true stories of people who are help-
ing to protect our planet. illustrated by Julie McLaughlin. Chronicle
Books 2009 109p il map $16.99
Grades: 4 5 6   **333.72**
1. Environmentalists
ISBN 978-0-8118-6779-5; 0-8118-6779-X
LC 2009004366
"Engaging graphics and clear writing combine to provide a compel-
ling reading experience." Sci Books Films

Smalley, Carol Parenzan
Green changes you can make around your home. Mitchell Lane
Publishers 2010 47p il (Tell your parents) lib bdg $21.50
Grades: 4 5 6 7   **333.72**
1. Environmental movement 2. Environmental protection
ISBN 978-1-58415-764-9 lib bdg; 1-58415-764-X lib bdg
LC 2009-4527
This book that explains how to be environmentally friendly "offers
numerous facts and statistics, all of which are cited. . . . Chapters cover
present-day issues and . . . are interspersed with full-color photographs
and short 'Did You Know' trivia boxes. . . . Back matter includes detailed resource lists and 'Try This!' experiments." SLJ
Includes glossary and bibliographical references

Try this at home; planet-friendly projects for kids. Jackie Farquhar,
D.I.Y. editor. Owlkids 2009 93p il pa $10.95
Grades: 5 6 7 8   **333.72**
1. Environmental protection
ISBN 978-2-89579-192-8 pa; 2-89579-192-9 pa
"Many of these projects are unique or innovative, featuring ideas
like growing your own pizza ingredients and making a foosball game
out of recycled corks, clothespins, and plastic fruit baskets. One of the
best projects provides tips on making sure a bike is road ready, offering
advice on checking the cables, gears, and oiling the chain. The book
also includes sections designed to increase environmental awareness,
including information on carbon footprint and 'eco all-stars.' Interactive
elements, like a game board, should appeal to children. Illustrations are
hip collages of full-color photographs and cartoons." SLJ
Includes bibliographical references

Walsh, Melanie
★ **10** things I can do to help my world. Candlewick Press 2008
un il $15.99
Grades: PreK K 1   **333.72**
1. Waste minimization
ISBN 978-0-7636-4144-3; 0-7636-4144-8
LC 2007051888
"A thoroughly successful presentation on how even small changes in
lifestyle can make a big difference. On each spread, a large and colorful
acrylic painting is accompanied by a sturdy die-cut flap and eco-friendly
tips. Each suggestion opens with 'I,' followed by a verb, such as 're-

member,' 'try,' and 'always.' The sentence is completed under the flap,
along with a reason why the tip is conservation friendly. The recommendations are those that children can easily relate to, such as turning
off the water while brushing your teeth, . . . using both sides of the paper,
recycling, etc. Visually appealing and effective in its presentation, this
title will serve as an introduction to environmental studies." SLJ

Wilson, Janet
★ **Our** earth; how kids are saving the planet. written and illustrated by Janet Wilson. Second Story Press 2010 un il $18.95
Grades: 2 3 4 5   **333.72**
1. Environmentalists
ISBN 978-1-897187-84-5; 1-897187-84-X
"Packed with inspiring, true-life stories on every spread, this collective biography introduces contemporary kids around the world who
have made remarkable efforts to help protect the earth. . . . The spreads
combine both paintings and photos of the young activists with brief,
lively descriptions of their environmental work, including web links
when available so that readers can learn more." Booklist

333.78 Recreational and wilderness areas

Carson, Mary Kay
The **park** scientists; Mary Kay Carson; with photographs by Tom
Uhlman. Houghton Mifflin Harcourt 2014 80 p. (Scientists in the
field) $18.99
Grades: 4 5 6 7 8 9   **333.78**
1. Science 2. National parks and reserves -- United States 3. Park
rangers -- United States 4. Interpretation of cultural and natural
resources -- United States
ISBN 0547792689; 9780547792682
LC 2013039895
Written by Mary Kay Carson and illustrated by Tom Uhlman, this
children's book describes how "America's National Parks are protected
places and have become living museums for as many as 270 million visitors per year! In addition, researchers are able to perform long term studies of a wide number of subjects from salamanders the size of thumbnails to gigantic geothermal geysers. These parks are natural laboratories
for scientists." (Publisher's note)
"The National Park System is often known as the nation's own
backyard due to the possibilities it provides for leisure, recreation, and
scientific study. This entry into the long-running Scientists in the Field
series celebrates this by focusing on three specific parks: Yellowstone,
Saguaro, and the Great Smoky Mountains... With a conservationist bent,
Carson describes just how accessible these real-life "natural laboratories
and living museums" are and how each individual can act with the same
spirit of inquiry as the scientist-explorers detailed here." Booklist

McHugh, Erin
National Parks; A Kid's Guide to America's Parks, Monuments and
Landmarks. Erin McHugh; Art by Neal Aspinall, Doug Leen, and Brian
Maebius. Black Dog & Leventhal Publishers 2012 128 p. col. ill., col.
map (hbk.) $19.95; (hbk.) $19.95
Grades: 4 5 6   **333.78**
1. National parks and reserves -- United States
ISBN 157912884X; 9781579128845
This book, "arranged alphabetically by state . . . tours more than
75 U.S. parks, monuments, and landmarks, from the rocky shores of
Maine's Acadia National Park to the ancient redwood groves of Northern California. Also included is a removable, fold-out collector map to
house" the commemorative quarters from the America the Beautiful series. (Publisher's note)

333.79　Energy

Bailey, Gerry

Out of energy. Gareth Stevens 2011 48p il (Planet SOS) lib bdg $31.95; pa $14.05

Grades: 4 5 6　　　　　　　　　　　　　　　　333.79

1. Energy resources　2. Renewable energy resources

ISBN 978-1-4339-4978-4 lib bdg; 1-4339-4978-4 lib bdg; 978-1-4339-4979-1 pa; 1-4339-4979-2 pa

LC 2010032889

This book "has separate chapters on fossil fuels, renewable energy, nuclear energy, and more. The many large, colorful photos will engage readers and assist them in understanding the important concepts introduced." SLJ

Includes glossary

Brezina, Corona

Jobs in sustainable energy. Rosen Pub. 2010 80p il (Green careers) lib bdg $30

Grades: 5 6 7 8　　　　　　　　　　　　　　　333.79

1. Vocational guidance　2. Renewable energy resources

ISBN 978-1-4358-3569-6 lib bdg; 1-4358-3569-7 lib bdg

LC 2009021855

This "well-conceived [introduction focuses] on various jobs in [sustainable energy], the education and experience required, and expected earnings. The [book is] well organized, making it easy to gain an overview of the major aspects of the work. . . . [This book] will make [a] good [addition] to career collections. Photographs from the field and website and contact information for professional organizations add value." SLJ

Includes glossary and bibliographical references

Bullard, Lisa

Go easy on energy; illustrated by Wes Thomas. Millbrook Press 2011 24p il (Planet protectors)

Grades: K 1 2 3　　　　　　　　　　　　　　　333.79

1. Energy conservation

ISBN 0-7613-6107-3; 978-0-7613-6107-7

LC 2010053302

A boy named Tyler shows how we can use energy wisely.

"The bright colors used in the illustrations . . . will attract young readers to the environmental science content. . . . [The] facts are written in child-friendly language and the information should be attainable by young children. . . . [This book] will raise the environmental awareness of young children." Sci Book Films

Includes bibliographical references

Caduto, Michael J.

Catch the wind, harness the sun; 22 super-charged science projects for kids. Storey Pub. 2011 223p il $26.95; pa $16.95

Grades: 5 6 7 8　　　　　　　　　　　　　　　333.79

1. Energy conservation　2. Renewable energy resources　3. Science -- Experiments

ISBN 978-1-60342-971-9; 1-60342-971-9; 978-1-60342-794-4 pa; 1-60342-794-5 pa; 1603427945 pa; 1603429719; 9781603427944 pa; 9781603429719

LC 2010051169

"The eco-themed activities that Caduto lays out here are only the beginning, as he embeds them in short but clear explanations of relevant scientific facts, profiles of young eco-activitists, provocative follow-up questions, photos and cartoon spot art aplenty, folktales, and other enhancements." Booklist

Farrell, Courtney

Using alternative energies. Cherry Lake Pub. 2010 32p il (Save the planet) lib bdg $27.07

Grades: 3 4 5 6　　　　　　　　　　　　　　　333.79

1. Renewable energy resources

ISBN 978-1-60279-663-8 lib bdg; 1-60279-663-7 lib bdg

Examines the climate change and the problems caused by the use of traditional fossil fuels, and looks at alternatives such wind, solar, and hydroelectric energy

"At the beginning of . . . [the] book, readers are given a mission and advised to be alert to the facts provided so that they can successfully answer the questions at the end. . . . Children are made to feel part of the process; suggestions for how they can become involved abound." SLJ

Includes glossary and bibliographical references

Gaarder-Juntti, Oona

What in the world is green energy? ABDO Pub. Company 2010 24p il (Going green) lib bdg $24.21

Grades: 1 2 3 4　　　　　　　　　　　　　　　333.79

1. Renewable energy resources

ISBN 978-1-61613-191-3 lib bdg; 1-61613-191-8 lib bdg

LC 2010004320

"The lively layout design, featuring colorful headings, short paragraphs, and attractive photographs, has a scrapbook-like quality. . . . [The title explains] how all our choices require energy and resources, and encourage readers to make changes in their lifestyles. . . . [This] . . . will inspire and empower readers to make a difference." SLJ

Includes glossary and bibliographical references

Hewitt, Sally

Using energy. Crabtree Pub. Co. 2009 32p il (Green team) $26.60; pa $8.95

Grades: 3 4 5 6　　　　　　　　　　　　　　　333.79

1. Energy resources　2. Energy conservation

ISBN 978-0-7787-4096-4; 0-7787-4096-X; 978-0-7787-4103-9 pa; 0-7787-4103-6 pa

LC 2008023288

"The color graphics and layouts are highly appealing and will definitely be attractive to young readers. . . . This . . . is an excellent resource for school libraries, science teachers, and community sponsors." Libr Media Connect

Leedy, Loreen

The shocking truth about energy; written and illustrated by Loreen Leedy. Holiday House 2010 32p il $17.95

Grades: 1 2 3　　　　　　　　　　　　　　　　333.79

1. Energy resources

ISBN 978-0-8234-2220-3; 0-8234-2220-8

An imaginary bolt of pure energy named Erg introduces the nature of energy, offers tips on how to use energy sensibly, and shows different ways energy can be harnessed.

"Leedy's experience selecting facts that are most relevant and engaging for young readers is evident, and the information is eminently digestible. The design moves from energetic to near-frenetic. Her brightly colored mixed-media illustrations are filled with animated appliances, bursts of information, and decorated fonts." Booklist

Mulder, Michelle, 1976-

Brilliant! shining a light on sustainable energy. Michelle Mulder. Orca Book Publishers 2013 48 p. (Orca footprints) (pbk.) $19.95

Grades: 4 5 6　　　　　　　　　　　　　　　　333.79

1. Energy resources　2. Energy development　3. Sustainable

development

ISBN 1459802217; 9781459802216; 9781459802223; 9781459805200

LC 2013935381

This book on sustainable energy "begins with a very basic explanation of how energy is created and transmitted, beginning with the moment a light switch is flicked. Our current dependence on fossil fuels is discussed, and the disadvantages of their use are laid out as the impetus for exploring alternative sources of energy. Environmental problems are treated as exciting opportunities for ingenuity, rather than a scary future menace." (Booklist)

Ollhoff, Jim

Geothermal, biomass, and hydrogen. ABDO Pub. 2010 32p il (Future energy) lib bdg $18.95

Grades: 3 4 5 6   333.79

1. Renewable energy resources

ISBN 978-1-60453-937-0 lib bdg; 1-60453-937-2 lib bdg

Discusses the advantages and disadvantages of alternative energy sources and the promise of harnessing other renewable energy sources, such as hydrogen fuel cells, geothermal power, and biomass.

"Liberally filled with bright photographs, the text provides examples with accurate data and narrative. . . . Inquiring readers will find this . . . valuable." Libr Media Connect

Includes glossary

Other titles in this series are:

Fossil fuels

Nuclear energy

Solar power

Wind and water

World in crisis. ABDO Pub. 2010 32p il (Future energy) lib bdg $18.95

Grades: 3 4 5 6   333.79

1. Energy policy 2. Energy resources

ISBN 978-1-60453-940-0; 1-60453-940-2

Discusses what can be done and the possible future of energy.

"Liberally filled with bright photographs, the text provides examples with accurate data and narrative. . . . Inquiring readers will find this . . . valuable." Libr Media Connect

Includes glossary

Rau, Dana Meachen

Alternative energy beyond fossil fuels. Compass Point Books 2010 64p il (Green generation) lib bdg $31.99; pa $6.95

Grades: 5 6 7 8 9   333.79

1. Energy resources 2. Renewable energy resources

ISBN 978-0-7565-4247-4 lib bdg; 0-7565-4247-2 lib bdg; 978-0-7565-4289-4 pa; 0-7565-4289-8 pa

LC 2009-08778

"This great little book introduces the topics of fossil fuel usage, the limited nature of fossil fuels, and alternative energy options. It is particularly praiseworthy for its refreshingly objective, but still enthusiastic, presentations on solar, wind, geothermal, hydro, and biomass energy. . . . Interesting, well-written, and appropriately illustrated, the book is entertaining enough for general reading, but factual enough for use as a science text." Sci Books Films

Includes glossary and bibliographical references

Sneideman, Joshua

Renewable Energy; Discover the Fuel of the Future With 20 Projects. by Joshua Sneideman and Erin Twamley; illustrated by Heather Jane Brinesh. Nomad Press 2016 128 p. color illustrations $22.95

Grades: 4 5 6 7   333.79

1. Renewable energy resources

ISBN 1619303566; 9781619303560

In this book, by Joshua Sneideman and Erin Twamley, illustrated by Heather Jane Brinesh, "readers ages 9 to 12 learn about . . . renewable energy sources and discover how sunshine can be used to power light bulbs and how the earth's natural heat can be used to warm our houses. Young readers weigh the pros and cons of different energy sources and make their own informed opinions about which resources are the best choices for different uses." (Publisher's note)

"Links to online sources couple with essential questions and writing prompts about a range of interdisciplinary topics to make this book a quality choice for both the classroom and pleasure reading." Booklist

Includes bibliographical references (pages 117-118) and index.

Vogel, Julia

Power up! Learn about energy; illustrated by Jane Yamada. The Child's World 2010 24p il (Science definitions) lib bdg $22.79

Grades: PreK K 1 2   333.79

1. Energy resources

ISBN 978-1-60253-512-1; 1-60253-512-4

LC 2010010980

This book about energy is "attractive and succinct. . . . Large, eye-catching photos cover the recto of each spread. . . . Varying, jewel-toned accents are used in headings, highlighted glossary terms, and in a sidebar on each spread." SLJ

Includes glossary

Weakland, Mark

Onion juice, poop, and other surprising sources of alternative energy. Capstone Press 2010 32p il (Fact finders. Nasty (but useful!) science) lib bdg $25.99

Grades: 3 4 5   333.79

1. Biomass energy 2. Renewable energy resources

ISBN 978-1-4296-4536-2; 1-4296-4536-9

This informative guide also explains "relevant chemical processes, medical rationales, and ecological functions in reasonably specific detail. . . . A list of relevant web resources is maintained on the publisher's page." SLJ

Includes glossary and bibliographical references

333.8 Subsurface resources

Bang, Molly

★ **Buried** sunlight; how fossil fuels have changed the Earth. by Molly Bang and Penny Chisholm. The Blue Sky Press, an imprint of Scholastic Inc. 2014 48 p. color illustrations $18.99

Grades: 2 3 4 5 6   333.8

1. Sunshine 2. Fossil fuels 3. Sunshine 4. Fossil fuels

ISBN 0545577853; 9780545577854

LC 2014000215

This children's book, by Molly Bang and Penny Chisholm, tells the "story of fossil fuels. What are fossil fuels, and how did they come to exist? This . . . book explains how coal, oil, and gas are really 'buried sunlight,' trapped beneath the surface of our planet for millions and millions of years. Now, in a very short time, we are digging them up and burning them, changing the carbon balance of our planet's air and water. What does this mean, and what should we do about it?" (Publisher's note)

"The sun serves as narrator describing the relationship between photosynthesis (plants) and respiration (animals) and energy; a slight imbalance produces fossil fuels. Bang's illustrations brilliantly represent the chemistry: bright yellow dots of energy against a deep-blue background hover over their producers." Horn Book

Hartman, Eve

Fossil fuels; [by] Eve Hartman and Wendy Meshbesher. Raintree 2010 48p il map (Sci-hi: Earth and space science) lib bdg $31.43; pa $8.99

Grades: 4 5 6 7   **333.8**

1. Coal 2. Oils and fats

ISBN 978-1-4109-3350-8 lib bdg; 1-4109-3350-4 lib bdg; 978-1-4109-3360-7 pa; 1-4109-3360-1 pa

LC 2009-3548

"Multiple colorful sidebars and large and small diagrams and photographs will help students to grasp the fundamentals being discussed, and the easy but interesting science experiments will act as further reinforcements." SLJ

Includes glossary and bibliographical references

Rice, William B.

The **story** of fossil fuels; William B. Rice. Teacher Created Materials 2016 32 p. color illustrations (pbk.) $8.99

Grades: 3 4 5   **333.8**

1. Fossil fuels 2. Energy resources 3. Natural resources

ISBN 1480746908; 9781480746909

LC 2014045213

This children's book, by WIlliam Rice, examines "how fossil fuels form and the amazing impact they have on society. To bring concepts to life, a Think Like a Scientist activity that supports STEM instruction is included at the end of the book." (Publisher's note)

"Smartly written, these innovative and imaginative volumes make learning fun." SLJ

White, Nancy

Using Earth's underground heat. Bearport Pub. 2009 32p il (Going green) lib bdg $25.27

Grades: 4 5 6 7   **333.8**

1. Geothermal resources

ISBN 978-1-59716-963-9 lib bdg; 1-59716-963-3 lib bdg

LC 2009-15119

"Color photographs (most full page) and a few diagrams accompany the informative text[s]. . . . Overall, the [book] . . . is user-friendly and covers topics that are not easily found elsewhere." SLJ

Includes glossary and bibliographical references

333.9   Other natural resources

Dobson, Clive

Wind power; 20 projects to make with paper. Firefly Books 2010 96p il $24.95; pa $12.95

Grades: 5 6 7 8   **333.9**

1. Wind power 2. Paper crafts

ISBN 978-1-55407-659-8; 1-55407-659-5; 978-1-55407-749-6 pa; 1-55407-749-4 pa

"In this informative craft book, a celebration of wind and of innovative efforts to harness its energy, Dobson describes the geometric and aerodynamic principles behind windmills, sails, and wind turbines, then implements these concepts via 20 paper projects, ranging from a two-blade pinwheel to a dramatic 'Squirrel Cage' turbine. . . . Readers should gain a more palpable understanding of the subject matter by building and watching the graceful compositions function." Publ Wkly

Drummond, Allan

★ **Energy** island; how one community harnessed the wind and changed their world. Farrar, Straus and Giroux 2011 un il $16.99

Grades: K 1 2 3   **333.9**

1. Wind power 2. Renewable energy resources 3. Denmark

ISBN 978-0-374-32184-0; 0-374-32184-1

This is an "account of how the residents of a Danish island made large and small changes to switch to renewable energy sources. . . . Now people from around the world come to Samsø to learn about ways to harness renewable energy and reduce carbon emissions. Informative sidebars supply information on global warming, renewable and nonrenewable energy, and conservation. What is most remarkable about this island . . . is how ordinary people achieved an extraordinary 140 percent reduction in carbon emissions in just 10 years. The illustrations further personalize the story with energy of their own as they bring Samsø and its residents to life." SLJ

Includes bibliographical references

333.91   Water and lands adjoining bodies of water

Bullard, Lisa

Watch over our water; illustrated by Xiao Xin. Millbrook Press 2011 il (Planet protectors) lib bdg $23.93

Grades: K 1 2 3   **333.91**

1. Water 2. Water pollution

ISBN 978-0-7613-6106-0; 0-7613-6106-5

LC 2010053299

A girl named Trina shows how to care for Earth's water.

"The bright colors used in the illustrations . . . will attract young readers to the environmental science content. . . . [The] facts are written in child-friendly language and the information should be attainable by young children. . . . [This book] will raise the environmental awareness of young children." Sci Books Films

Mulder, Michelle, 1976-

★ **Every** last drop; bringing clean water home. Michelle Mulder. Orca Book Pub 2014 48 p. illustrations (some color) (Orca footprints) (hardcover) $19.95

Grades: 4 5 6 7   **333.91**

1. Water conservation 2. Water resources development 3. Water quality management

ISBN 9781459802247; 9781459807129; 1459802233; 9781459802230

LC 2013951377

This book, by Michelle Mulder, "looks at why the world's water resources are at risk and how communities around the world are finding innovative ways to quench their thirst and water their crops. Maybe you're not ready to drink fog, as they do in Chile, or use water made from treated sewage, but you can get a low-flush toilet, plant a tree, protect a wetland or just take shorter showers." (Publisher's note)

"Divided into four chapters, this book explores the history of water use by humans; the natural cycle of water on earth; how people access, clean, and desalinate water; and ways in which we can conserve and preserve our water resources. Plenty of well-captioned photos, including some from the author's own travels, illustrate and personalize the accessible text." Horn Book

333.95   Biological resources

Arnosky, Jim

Crinkleroot's guide to giving back to nature; by Jim Arnosky. G.P. Putnam's Sons 2012 48 p. $17.99

Grades: K 1 2 **333.95**
1. Hermits -- fiction 2. Nature 3. Nature conservation
ISBN 0399255206; 9780399255205

LC 2011028758

This children's nature book, by Jim Arnosky, shows "[f]orest-dweller Crinkleroot . . . lead[ing] 21st-century readers outdoors, urging them to appreciate and give back to nature. Arnosky's bearded guide [was] inspired by 19th-century naturalist John Burroughs. . . . In this . . . title, the author focuses on things children can do on their own for their environment." (Kirkus)

Guillain, Charlotte
Caring for nature; [by] Charlotte Guillain. Heinemann Library 2008 24p il (Help the environment) $21.70; pa $5.99
Grades: PreK K 1 2 **333.95**
1. Nature conservation
ISBN 978-1-4329-0889-8; 1-4329-0889-8; 978-1-4329-0895-9 pa; 1-4329-0895-2 pa

LC 2007-41174

This book is "a great jumping–off point for a broader discussion of environmentalism. . . . The bright, vibrant photographs will grab readers' attention as they reinforce the simple sentences." Libr Media Connect
Includes glossary

Laidlaw, Rob
★ **Saving** lives & changing hearts; animal sanctuaries and rescue centres. Fitzhenry & Whiteside 2012 62 p. $19.95
Grades: 4 5 6 7 8 **333.95**
1. Wildlife refuges 2. Wildlife rehabilitation
ISBN 1554552125; 9781554552122

This book "profiles a variety of sanctuaries throughout the world and the people who work to safeguard the wildlife. . . . The author offers the . . . stories behind the founding of many of these sanctuaries and presents . . . conclusions to the many . . . stories of rescued animals. A section showing the difference between true sanctuaries and those neither meeting the needs of animals in their care nor preparing them for rehabilitation into the wild is" included. (School Library Journal)

Reptiles and amphibians; edited by Tim Harris. Brown Bear Books 2012 64 p. (Facts at your fingertips: endangered animals) (library binding) $35.65
Grades: 5 6 7 8 **333.95**
1. Reptiles 2. Amphibians 3. Endangered species 4. Rare reptiles 5. Rare amphibians
ISBN 1936333368; 9781936333363

LC 2010053968

This book "profiles a global sampling of reptiles and amphibians in various degrees of endangerment . . . . Twenty-one species are described in . . . detail that includes information on their classification, distribution, physical characteristics, habitat, diet, and reproduction." The book is part of "the 'Facts at Your Fingertips: Endangered Animals' series, which profiles various groups of endangered species from all parts of the planet." (National Science Teachers Association)
Includes bibliographical references and index

Salmansohn, Pete, 1947-
Saving birds; heroes around the world. [by] Pete Salmansohn and Stephen W. Kress. Tilbury House 2003 39p il $16.95; pa $7.95
Grades: 5 6 7 8 **333.95**
1. Endangered species 2. Wildlife conservation 3. Birds -- Protection
ISBN 0-88448-237-5; 0-88448-276-6 pa

LC 2002-6710

Profiles adults and children working in six habitats around the world to save wild birds, some of which are on the brink of extinction.
"As a teaching aid, this volume is an exceptional supplement. The six articles relating the heroic rescue of the endangered birds are accurate and enhanced by appropriate color photographs." Sci Books Films

Sheehan, Sean
Endangered species; by Sean Sheehan. Gareth Stevens Pub. 2009 48p il map (What if we do nothing?) lib bdg $31
Grades: 5 6 7 8 **333.95**
1. Endangered species
ISBN 978-1-4339-0086-0 lib bdg; 1-4339-0086-6 lib bdg

LC 2008029167

"Using intelligent, focused text; an open design; vivid photos; and excellent maps, [this] book demands attention." Booklist
Includes bibliographical references

342 Branches of law; laws, regulations, cases; law of specific jurisdictions, areas, socioeconomic regions

Cheney, Lynne V.
We the people; the story of our Constitution. by Lynne Cheney; illustrated by Greg Harlin. Simon & Schuster Books for Young Readers 2008 30p il pbk. $7.99
Grades: 3 4 5 **342**
1. United States -- Constitution 2. Constitutional history -- United States 3. United States -- Politics and government -- 1783-1809 4. United States -- Politics and government -- 1775-1783, Revolution
ISBN 9781442444225

LC 2008-8871

In May 1787 delegates from across the country—including George Washington, James Madison, and Benjamin Franklin—gathered in Philadelphia and, meeting over the course of a sweltering summer, created a new framework for governing: the Constitution of the United States
This book is written "in clear, cogent prose. . . . The vocabulary is rich, and the author incorporates fascinating details. . . . [It is illustrated with] Harlin's impressive artwork, described as being done in "various water media." The sweep of these realistic paintings across the pages highlights the drama of each situation, and the artist makes remarkable use of perspective." SLJ
Includes bibliographical references

Fritz, Jean
★ **Shh!** we're writing the Constitution; illustrated by Tomie dePaola. Putnam 1987 64p il $15.99; pa $5.99
Grades: 2 3 4 **342**
1. Constitutional history -- United States
ISBN 0-399-21403-8; 0-698-11624-0 pa

LC 86-22528

"Jean Fritz gives a vivid, vibrant picture of the 1787 Constitutional Convention. The wonderful, full-color illustrations are a perfect match for the captivating text." Child Book Rev Serv

Krull, Kathleen
A **kid's** guide to America's Bill of Rights; curfews, censorship, and the 100-pound giant. illustrated by Anna DiVito. Avon Bks. 1999 226p il $15.99
Grades: 4 5 6 7 **342**
1. Civil rights 2. United States -- Constitution -- 1st-10th amendments
ISBN 0-380-97497-5

LC 99-17324

"After describing how the first 10 amendments came to be added to the Constitution, the book considers each one from a historical point of view, examining Supreme Court cases and famous challenges, and explaining in what ways each amendment applies to children and teenagers. Anna Divito's cartoonlike drawings add a visually appealing touch." Booklist

Includes bibliographical references

Leavitt, Amie Jane

The **Bill** of Rights in translation; what it really means. by Amie Jane Leavitt. Capstone Press 2009 32p il (Fact finders. Kids' translations) lib bdg $23.93; pa $7.95

Grades: 3 4 5   **342**

1. Civil rights 2. United States -- Constitution -- 1st-10th amendments
ISBN 978-1-4296-1928-8 lib bdg; 1-4296-1928-7 lib bdg; 978-1-4296-2843-3 pa; 1-4296-2843-X pa

LC 2007-51307

Provides "a nearly line-by-line translation that makes . . . the written word accessible and meaningful." SLJ

Includes glossary and bibliographical references

Maestro, Betsy

A **more** perfect union; the story of our Constitution. illustrated by Giulio Maestro. Lothrop, Lee & Shepard Bks. 1987 48p il hardcover o.p. pa $7.99

Grades: 2 3 4   **342**

1. Constitutional history -- United States
ISBN 0-688-10192-5 pa

LC 87-4083

"A simple, straightforward account using an oversize format with full-color illustration throughout. There is an excellent, fact-filled addenda that also includes the Preamble, chronologies and summaries of the Articles of the Constitution, the Bill of Rights, the Amendments and the Connecticut Compromise. This fine book places important events in historical context." Publ Wkly

Thomas, William David

What is a constitution? [by] William David Thomas. Gareth Stevens Pub. 2008 32p il (My American government) lib bdg $23.93; pa $8.95

Grades: 3 4 5   **342**

1. Democracy 2. Constitutions 3. United States -- Constitution
ISBN 978-0-8368-8863-8 lib bdg; 0-8368-8863-4 lib bdg; 978-0-8368-8868-3 pa; 0-8368-8868-5 pa

LC 2007027281

This describes the United States constitution as well as the constitutions of state governments.

This book has "an accessible format and clear writing. . . . Black-and-white and full-color vintage and more recent photographs appear throughout." SLJ

Includes glossary and bibliographical references

342.73   Constitutional law – United States

Baxter, Roberta

The **Bill** of Rights; by Roberta Baxter. Heinemann Library 2012 48 p. (hbk) $32

Grades: 4 5 6 7   **342.73**

1. Legislation 2. United States -- Politics and government 3. Constitutional history -- United States 4. Civil rights -- United States

-- History 5. United States. Constitution. 1st-10th Amendments
ISBN 1432967517; 9781432967512; 9781432967604

LC 2011037780

In this book, Roberta Baxter, readers can "learn about the Bill of Rights, one of the most significant documents in U.S. history. [They can] find out about those who were involved in its creation and why studying this primary source is [considered] so important." (Publisher's note)

Includes bibliographical references (p. 47) and index

Sonneborn, Liz

The **Articles** of Confederation; by Liz Sonneborn. Heinemann Library 2013 48 p. (Documenting U.S. history) (hb) $32

Grades: 4 5 6 7   **342.73**

1. United States -- Politics and government -- 1775-1783, Revolution 2. Constitutional history -- United States 3. United States. Articles of Confederation 4. United States -- Politics and government -- 1775-1783
ISBN 1432967495; 9781432967499; 9781432967581

LC 2011037709

In this book, written by Liz Sonneborn, readers can "learn about the Articles of Confederation, one of the most significant documents in U.S. history. [They can] find out about those who were involved in its creation and why studying this primary source is [considering] so important." (Publisher's note)

Includes bibliographical references and index

The **United** States Constitution; by Liz Sonneborn. Heinemann-Raintree 2012 48 p. (hb) $32

Grades: 4 5 6 7   **342.73**

1. United States. Constitution 2. Constitutional law -- United States 3. United States. Constitution 4. Constitutional history -- United States
ISBN 1432967525; 9781432967529; 9781432967611

LC 2011037781

In this book, by Liz Sonneborn, readers can "learn about the United States Constitution, one of the most significant documents in U.S. history. [They can also] find out about those who were involved in its creation and why studying this primary source is [considered] so important." (Publisher's note)

Includes bibliographical references and index

344   Labor, social service, education, cultural law

Chmara, Theresa

★ **Privacy** and confidentiality issues; a guide for libraries and their lawyers. American Library Association 2009 98p pa $40

Grades: Adult Professional   **344**

1. Library services 2. Right of privacy 3. Libraries -- Law and legislation
ISBN 978-0-8389-0970-6; 0-8389-0970-1

LC 2008-34902

"This slim title is a must read. Chmara, a First Amendment attorney and litigation expert, clarifies privacy and confidentiality issues such as requests or subpoenas for patron-use records (both book and Internet), hostile-work-environment issues, state and federal privacy and confidentiality statutes, and minors' First Amendment rights and rights to privacy." Booklist

Includes bibliographical references

344.73   Legal issues – United States

Rubin, Susan Goldman

Brown v. Board of Education; a fight for simple justice. Susan Goldman Rubin. Holiday House 2016 160 p. illustrations (ebook) $18.95; (hardcover) $18.95

Grades: 5 6 7 8   **344.73**

1. Segregation in education 2. Topeka (Kan.). Board of Education -- Trials, litigation, etc. 3. African Americans -- Civil rights 4. Segregation in education -- Law and legislation -- United States

ISBN 9780823437085; 9780823436460

LC 2016004631

This book, by Susan Goldman Rubin, focuses on the Supreme Court decision that "aimed to end school segregation in the United States. Although known as Brown v. Board of Education, the ruling applied not just to the case of Linda Carol Brown, an African American third grader refused entry to an all-white Topeka, Kansas school, but to cases involving children in South Carolina, Delaware, Virginia, and Washington, DC." (Publisher's note)

"A rich, compelling story of the many people who stood up to racial inequality, risking significant danger and hardship for the cause of justice." Kirkus

Includes bibliographical references (pages 118-120) and index.

Wilson, Sharon J.

Brown vs. the Board of Education of Topeka; Sharon J. Wilson. Abdo Pub. 2016 48 p. illustrations $32.79

Grades: 3 4 5 6   **344.73**

1. Segregation in education

ISBN 1624038778; 9781624038778

LC 2015931187

This book, by Sharon J. Wilson, "will inform readers about Brown v. Board of Education of Topeka, segregation in public schools, those involved in the case, and the law applied after the ruling the fourteenth amendment. Vivid details, well-chosen photographs, and primary sources bring this story and this case to life." (Publisher's note)

"Succinct and often powerful, this set is a solid purchase." SLJ

345   Criminal law

Coleman, Wim

Racism on trial; From the Medgar Evers murder case to 'Ghosts of Mississippi' [by] Wim Coleman and Pat Perrin. Enslow Publishers 2009 112p il lib bdg $31.93

Grades: 5 6 7 8   **345**

1. Lynching 2. Trials (Homicide) 3. Murderers 4. White supremacists 5. Civil rights activists 6. Mississippi -- Race relations

ISBN 978-0-7660-3059-6; 0-7660-3059-8

LC 2008-21483

"Examines the Byron De La Beckwith murder trials, including the mistrials and his eventual conviction, key figures in the case, and the inspiration for the movie Ghosts of Mississippi." Publisher's note

346   Private law

Butler, Rebecca P.

Copyright for teachers & librarians in the 21st century. Neal-Schuman Publishers 2011 274p il pa $70

Grades: Adult Professional   **346**

1. Copyright 2. Fair use (Copyright)

ISBN 978-1-55570-738-5

LC 2011012600

First published 2004 with title: Copyright for teachers and librarians

"Library educator Rebecca Butler explains fair use, public domain, documentation and licenses, permissions, violations and penalties, policies and ethics codes, citations, creation and ownership, how to register copyrights, and gives tips for staying out of trouble." Publisher's note

Includes bibliographical references

Popek, Emily

Copyright and digital ethics. Rosen Central 2011 48p il (Digital and information literacy) lib bdg $26.50; pa $11.75

Grades: 5 6 7 8   **346**

1. Ethics 2. Internet 3. Copyright

ISBN 978-1-4488-1323-0 lib bdg; 1-4488-1323-9; 978-1-4488-2294-2 pa; 1-4488-2294-7 pa

LC 2010027018

Though this "title is a broad overview of a sometimes-complex subject, the detail is significant. . . . Touches of blue enhance the clean design. . . . [This] explains concepts like fair use and tries to persuade readers of the damage done by digital piracy and plagiarism." Booklist

Includes bibliographical references

346.04   Property

Crews, Kenneth D.

Copyright law for librarians and educators; creative strategies and practical solutions. with contributions from Dwayne K. Buttler . . . [et al.] 2nd ed; American Library Association 2012 xii, 192 p.p ill. (alk. paper) $57

Grades: Adult Professional   **346.04**

1. Copyright 2. Sound recordings 3. Fair use (Copyright) 4. Copyright -- United States 5. Fair use (Copyright) -- United States 6. Teachers -- United States -- Handbooks, manuals, etc 7. Librarians -- United States -- Handbooks, manuals, etc

ISBN 0838910920; 9780838910924

LC 2011027604

First published 2000 with title: Copyright essentials for librarians and educators

Author Kenneth D. Crews' book "allows readers to get up to speed on current interpretations of the Digital Millennium Copyright Act from a librarian-educator viewpoint." It also "draws on cutting-edge case law in 18 discrete areas of copyright, including specialized and controversial music and sound recording issues. [This guide offers] information professionals . . . the tools they need to take control of their rights and responsibilities as copyright owners and users." (Publisher's note)

The author "addresses 18 areas of copyright in 5 parts. He begins with the scope of protectable works as well as works without copyright protection. Next, he discusses the rights of ownership, including duration and exceptions. He then explains fair use and its related guidelines. Part 4 focuses on the TEACH Act, Section 108, and responsibilities and liabilities. Lastly, Crews examines special issues such as the Digital Millennium Copyright Act." Booklist

Includes bibliographical references and index.

Russell, Carrie

Complete copyright for K-12 librarians and educators; Carrie Russell. American Library Association 2012 xi, 173 p.p ill. (chiefly col.) (alk. paper) $50

Grades: Professional   **346.04**

1. Copyright 2. Fair use (Copyright) 3. Segregation -- Law and

legislation 4. Copyright -- United States 5. Fair use (Copyright) -- United States 6. Librarians -- Legal status, laws, etc. -- United States 7. School libraries -- Law and legislation -- United States
ISBN 0838910831; 9780838910832

LC 2012016674

This book by Carrie Russell "is designed as a resource for educators, offering guidance for providing material to students while carefully observing copyright law. The book offers detailed advice on distinctive issues of intellectual property in the school setting; explores scenarios often encountered by educators . . . and precisely defines 'fair use,' by showing readers exactly what's possible within the law." (Education Digest)

Includes bibliographical references and index

347 Procedure and courts

Adler, David A.
A **picture** book of Thurgood Marshall; illustrated by Robert Casilla. Holiday House 1997 un il $16.95; pa $6.95
Grades: 1 2 3   **347**
1. Judges 2. Lawyers 3. Solicitors general 4. Civil rights activists 5. Supreme Court justices 6. African Americans -- Biography 7. United States -- Supreme Court
ISBN 0-8234-1308-X; 0-823-41506-6 pa

LC 96-37248

Follows the life of the first African American to serve as a judge on the United States Supreme Court

"Adler presents the high points of Marshall's life with enough detail to humanize the man. . . . Sensitive line-and-watercolor illustrations on every page add warmth to the story as they define people and settings." Booklist

347.73 Civil procedure and courts of the United States

Rodger, Ellen
What is the judicial branch? by Ellen Rodger. Crabtree Publishing Company 2013 32 p. (Your guide to government) (reinforced library binding) $26.60
Grades: 4 5 6 7   **347.73**
1. Law -- United States 2. Courts -- United States 3. Procedure (Law) -- United States
ISBN 0778708802; 9780778708803; 9780778709060

LC 2013001275

This book, by Ellen Rodger "provide[s] solid introductory material about the U.S. government. [The] book discusses the purpose of [the judicial] branch; the different positions, . . . the work done; and the strengths and the challenges of each branch and how they interact." (School Library Journal)

351 Public administration

Bow, James
What is the executive branch? by James Bow. Crabtree Publishing Company 2013 32 p. (Your guide to government) (reinforced library binding) $26.60
Grades: 4 5 6 7   **351**
1. Presidents -- United States 2. Executive power -- United States 3. Executive departments -- United States
ISBN 0778709027; 9780778709022; 9780778709077

LC 2013001276

This book, by James Bow "provide[s] solid introductory material about the U.S. government. [The] book discusses the purpose of [the executive] branch; the different positions, . . . the work done; and the strengths and the challenges of each branch and how they interact." (School Library Journal)

352.13 Administration of subordinate jurisdictions

Giesecke, Ernestine
State government; Rev. and updated; Heinemann Library 2010 32p il map (Kids' guide to government) $29.29; pa $7.99
Grades: 3 4 5   **352.13**
1. State governments 2. United States -- Politics and government
ISBN 978-1-4329-2707-3; 1-4329-2707-8; 978-1-4329-2712-7 pa; 1-4329-2712-4 pa
First published 2000

Introduces the purpose and function of state government, the function of the three branches, how states raise money, how state government operates, and how a bill becomes a state law.

"This . . . would be a great asset. . . . Students will learn about a different, but related government every two pages. The font is large and easy to read. The photos, diagrams, charts, maps, and illustrations supplement the text well." Libr Media Connect

Includes glossary

355 Military science

Chapman, Caroline
Battles & weapons: exploring history through art; [by] Caroline Chapman. Two-Can 2007 64p il (Picture that!) $19.95
Grades: 5 6 7 8   **355**
1. War in art 2. Military history 3. Military art and science
ISBN 978-1-58728-588-2

LC 2006033229

"High quality reproductions of paintings, murals, sculptures, and artifacts show military customs and equipment over the centuries. . . . The lively, informative text creates a 'you are there' sense that will engage even reluctant readers." SLJ

Includes bibliographical references

Humphreys, Jessica Dee
Child Soldier; When Boys and Girls Are Used in War. Michel Chikwanine, Jessica Dee Humphreys; illustrated by Claudia Davila. Kids Can Press 2015 48 p. color illustrations $17.95
Grades: 5 6 7 8   **355**
1. Child soldiers
ISBN 1771381264; 9781771381260
Eisner Nominee: Best Publication for Kids (2016)

This children's book, written by Michel Chikwanine and Jessica Dee Humphreys, and illustrated by Claudia Davila, describes the experience of a child solder. "Michel Chikwanine was five years old when he was abducted from his schoolyard soccer game in the Democratic Republic of Congo and forced to become a soldier for a brutal rebel militia. Against the odds, Michel managed to escape . . . , but he was never the same again." (Publisher's note)

"Chikwanine's narration is matter of fact but never didactic, emphasizing less the gruesome details and more young Michel's emotional response and attempts to make sense of the world around him. Earthy hued and gentle, the images make a potentially disturbing topic accessible." SLJ

Murrell, Deborah Jane

Greek warrior; by Deborah Murrell. QEB Pub. 2010 32p il map (QEB warriors) lib bdg $28.50

Grades: 4 5 6 7 **355**

1. Greece -- Military history 2. Military art and science -- History

ISBN 978-1-59566-759-5 lib bdg; 1-59566-759-8 lib bdg

LC 2009-3542

"Bold, comprehensible type and full-color and black-and-white illustrations; reproductions; and photographs will make this offering a hit with its target audience, including reluctant readers." SLJ

Includes glossary

Samurai; by Deborah Murrell. QEB Pub. 2010 32p il map (QEB warriors) lib bdg $28.50

Grades: 4 5 6 7 **355**

1. Samurai 2. Military art and science

ISBN 978-1-59566-734-2 lib bdg; 1-59566-734-2 lib bdg

LC 2009-3545

"Bold, comprehensible type and full-color and black-and-white illustrations; reproductions; and photographs will make this offering a hit with its target audience, including reluctant readers." SLJ

Includes glossary

Park, Louise

The Pharaohs' armies; by Louise Park and Timothy Love. Marshall Cavendish Benchmark 2009 32p il map (Ancient and medieval people) lib bdg $28.50

Grades: 4 5 6 **355**

1. Egypt -- Civilization 2. Military art and science -- History

ISBN 978-0-7614-4451-0 lib bdg; 0-7614-4451-3 lib bdg

This title has "a simple and elegant design with the proper balance of quality writing and quantity of information. . . . Handy time lines, well-chosen photos of ruins and artifacts, quality illustrations, inset 'Quick Facts', and 'What You Should Know About' features will grab reluctant readers and captivate even those with short attention spans." SLJ

Includes glossary

Solway, Andrew

Graphing war and conflict. Raintree 2010 32p il (Real world data) $28.21; pa $7.99

Grades: 4 5 6 7 **355**

1. Graphic methods 2. Military history

ISBN 978-1-4329-2620-5; 1-4329-2620-9; 978-1-4329-2629-8 pa; 1-4329-2629-2 pa

LC 2009001188

This "uses graphs and charts to talk about global conflicts between 1990 and 2005, from guerilla warfare and civil war to nuclear attacks, with a special section on terrorism, including 9/11 and suicide bombers. . . . The clear design, with lots of full-color photos and sidebars, will encourage browsers as much as the up-to-date examples and the clear directions for remaining 'chart smart.'" Booklist

Includes glossary and bibliographical references

Souter, Janet

War in Afghanistan and Iraq; the daily life of the men and women serving in Afghanistan and Iraq. [by] Janet Souter and Gerry Souter. Carlton Books 2011 47p il map $16.95

Grades: 2 3 4 **355**

1. Afghan War, 2001- 2. Iraq War, 2003-2011

ISBN 978-1-84732-895-3; 1-84732-895-4

"An overview of these wartorn countries' physical and religious make-ups leads to the review of current political instability in the region. The discussion of combat techniques illustrates America's military power, though a nod to numerous international organizations (from NATO to ISAF) conveys the global scope. Double-page spreads address the perceived catalysts for conflict and the United States' accompanying responses (including Osama Bin Laden's recent death). . . . Despite its slimness, a remarkably effective and timely treatment." Kirkus

Inlcudes glossary

355.02 War and warfare

Benoit, Peter

The nuclear age; by Peter Benoit. Children's Press 2012 64 p. ill. (chiefly col.), col. map (Cornerstones of freedom) (library) $30.00; (paperback) $8.95

Grades: 4 5 6 **355.02**

1. Nuclear energy -- History 2. Nuclear weapons -- History

ISBN 0531230627; 0531281620; 9780531230626; 9780531281628

LC 2011031341

This book by Peter Benoit, part of the "Cornerstones of Freedom" series, "offers comprehensive coverage of all concepts related to the nuclear age beginning in the late 1800s through current times. . . . Four chapters highlight issues that emerge--birth of the new age, cold war, atom's legacy and human dilemma." Topics include "the atomic bomb, [Adolf] Hitler versus allies, international competitions, precautions, peaceful pursuits and cleaner sources of energy." (Children's Literature)

Includes bibliographical references (p. 61) and index.

355.1 Military life and customs

Biden, Jill, 1951-

Don't forget, God bless our troops; Jill Biden; illustrated by Raúl Colón. Simon & Schuster Books for Young Readers 2012 40 p. (hbk.) $16.99

Grades: K 1 2 **355.1**

1. Children and war 2. Afghan War, 2001- 3. Father-daughter relationship 4. Children of military personnel -- United States 5. Families of military personnel -- United States 6. Soldiers -- Family relationships -- United States

ISBN 144245735X; 1442457376; 9781442457355; 9781442457379

LC 2012008493

In the book by author Jill Biden, "when her father leaves for a year of being at war, Natalie knows that she will miss him. Natalie is proud of her father but there is nothing to stop her from wishing he was home. Some things do help her feel better. Natalie works with her Nana to send her dad and the other service men and women cookies and treats they have made. Natalie, her mom, and brother can see and talk to Dad over the computer, and the kindness of friends at school and at church help her feel supported and loved. But there is nothing like the day when her Dad comes home at last." (Publisher's note)

Includes bibliographical references.

Kerley, Barbara

Brave like me; Barbara Kerley. National Geographic Children's Books 2016 48 p. color illustrations, map (hardback) $17.99

Grades: PreK K 1 2 3 **355.1**

1. Separation (Psychology) 2. Children of military personnel 3. Separation (Psychology) in children 4. Children of military personnel -- United States 5. Families of military personnel -- United States

ISBN 9781426323607; 9781426323614; 1426323603

LC 2015027844

This book, by Barbara Kerley, looks at how "when someone is serving our country, far from home, everyone in their family has to be brave. Including -- and sometimes especially -- the kids. This book speaks to all kids in this situation in telling the story of a boy and a girl with parents away on duty. It captures the children's worries, fears, trials, and triumphs while waiting for their parents to return from service." (Publisher's note)

"The colorful photographs of diverse children and families personalize these points, while final pages offer suggestions, show kids' definitions of bravery, and provide additional resources. An important book for comfort, support, and education." Booklist

Includes bibliographical references

355.4   Military operations

Durman, Laura
    Siege; by Laura Durman. Arcturus Pub. 2012 32 p. col. ill. (Knights and castles) (library) $28.50
Grades: 4 5 6   **355.4**
    1. Middle Ages 2. Military art and science 3. Sieges 4. Castles 5. Siege warfare
    ISBN 1848585624; 9781848585621
                                              LC 2011051446
This book by Laura Durman is part of the Knights and Castles series and looks at sieges. In "two-page spreads filled with photos, staged reenactments, diagrams, and line drawings, Durman . . . outlines how both sides prepared and fared in a siege. Chapters on castle defense, defense tactics, and personal protection" are included as is an "in-depth look at the precision and force at work with such siege machines as the trebuchet, mangonel, battering ram, and belfry." (Children's Literature)

Includes bibliographical references (p. 31) and index.

Grayson, Robert
    Military. Marshall Cavendish Benchmark 2010 62p il (Working animals) lib bdg $28.50
Grades: 4 5 6 7   **355.4**
    1. Animals -- War use
    ISBN 978-1-60870-164-3 lib bdg; 1-60870-164-6 lib bdg
"Describes animals, including elephants, dogs, horses, mules, sea lions, dolphins, rats, and homing pigeons, which provide valuable service to the military." Publisher's note

Includes glossary and bibliographical references

Patent, Dorothy Hinshaw
    Dogs on duty; soldiers' best friends on the battlefield and beyond. by Dorothy Hinshaw Patent. Walker & Co. 2012 48 p. (hardcover) $16.99
Grades: 3 4 5 6   **355.4**
    1. Working dogs 2. Dogs -- War use 3. Dogs -- War use
    ISBN 0802728456; 9780802728456
                                              LC 2012004457
Author Dorothy Hinshaw Patent reports that "nine thousand dogs served in World War II, . . . four thousand dogs served in Vietnam, and hundreds died in combat. . . . [She] sketches the history of dogs in war from ancient times to World Wars I and II and on to modern wars--Vietnam, Iraq and Afghanistan. It's dogs' 'super senses' of sight, sound and smell, and their capacity to bond with soldiers that make them so useful in military theaters. They uncovered hidden tunnels in Vietnam, find dangerous land mines in Afghan villages, and locate weapons, explosives and drugs at home and abroad." (Kirkus Reviews)

"The straightforward text and color photographs celebrate the bonds between dogs and handlers that are so crucial in modern warfare. A sure hit with dog lovers everywhere." Kirkus

355.8   Military equipment and supplies (Materiel)

Arms & armor; written by Michèle Byam; [special photography, Dave King] Revised edition DK Publishing 2011 72 p ill. (chiefly col.) hardcover $16.99
Grades: 4 5 6 7   **355.8**
    1. Armor 2. Weapons
    ISBN 9780756689513; 9780756673192; 0756673194
    First published 1988 by Knopf
A photo essay examining the design, construction, and uses of hand weapons and armor from a Stone Age axe to the revolvers and rifles of the Wild West

Perritano, John
    Bomb squad technician; by John Perritano. Mason Crest 2016 48 p. color illustrations (Other titles in series include: FBI Agent; Dogs on Patrol; Firefighter; SWAT Team; Paramedic; Undercover Police Officer; Search and Rescue Team; Secret Service Agent.) (hardback : alk. paper) $20.95
Grades: 4 5 6 7   **355.8**
    1. Ordnance disposal units 2. Explosives -- Safety measures 3. Ordnance disposal units 4. Bombs -- Safety measures 5. Explosive ordnance disposal 6. Explosives -- Safety measures
    ISBN 9781422233917; 9781422233924
                                              LC 2015004820
This book, by John Perritano, "demonstrates the bravery and courage Bomb Squad Technicians show every time they go to work. It tells how they train their minds and bodies to handle the stress of disarming explosive devices and stay ahead of bombers." (Publisher's note)

"Excitement never flags in this book, as every chapter is accompanied by explosive stories, such as Guy Fawkes and the Boston Marathon bombing." Booklist

355.825   Ammunition

Winter, Jonah
    The **secret** project; Jonah Winter; illustrated by Jeanette Winter. Beach Lane Books 2017 40 p. color illustrations (hardcover : alk. paper) $17.99
Grades: K 1 2 3 4   **355.825**
    1. Picture books for children 2. Atomic bomb -- History 3. Manhattan Project (U.S.) -- History 4. Los Alamos (N.M.) 5. Trinity Site (N.M.) 6. Atomic bomb -- New Mexico -- Los Alamos -- History
    ISBN 9781481469135
                                              LC 2016018832
This children's nonfiction picture book by Jonah Winter, illustrated by Jeanette Winter, describes the Manhattan Project. "At a former boy's school in the remote desert of New Mexico, the world's greatest scientists have gathered to work on the 'Gadget,' an invention so dangerous and classified they cannot even call it by its real name. . . . Finally they take their creation far out into the desert to test it, and afterward the world will never be the same." (Publisher's note)

"Sure to spark conversation about ethics and the use of nuclear weaponry, this powerful book demands a wide readership." Pub Wkly

Includes bibliographical references

358.4 Air forces and warfare

Schwartz, Heather E.
 Women of the U.S. Air Force; aiming high. Capstone Press 2011 32p (Women in the U.S. Armed Forces) lib bdg $26.65
Grades: 4 5 6 7   **358.4**
 1. Women air pilots 2. Women in the armed forces 3. United States -- Air Force
 ISBN 978-1-4296-5449-4; 1-4296-5449-X
                                    LC 2010040749
Describes the past, present, and future of women in the U.S. Air Force.
 The book has "a snappy design and eye-catching photographs, and the [text is] written with struggling readers in mind. The content is engaging, the material is worthy, and the [package is] attractive." SLJ
 Includes glossary and bibliographical references

359 Sea forces and warfare

Llanas, Sheila Griffin
 Women of the U.S. Navy; making waves. Capstone Press 2011 32p il (Women in the U.S. Armed Forces) lib bdg $26.65
Grades: 4 5 6 7   **359**
 1. Sailors 2. United States -- Navy 3. Women in the armed forces
 ISBN 978-1-4296-5448-7; 1-4296-5448-1
                                    LC 2010040801
This book explains "how women's roles in the U.S. [Navy] have evolved over the years. [The] volume starts with an account of one specific servicewoman and then delves into her branch's history. [The book has] a snappy design and eye-catching photographs, and the [text is] written with struggling readers in mind. The content is engaging, the material is worthy, and the [package is] attractive." SLJ
 Includes glossary and bibliographical references

361.2 Social action

Olien, Rebecca
 Kids care! 75 ways to make a difference for people, animals & the environment. [by] Rebecca Olien; illustrations by Michael Kline. Williamson Books 2007 128p il (Williamson kids can! book) $16.99; pa $12.99
Grades: 3 4 5 6   **361.2**
 1. Social action 2. Interpersonal relations
 ISBN 978-0-8249-6793-2; 0-8249-6793-3; 978-0-8249-6792-5 pa; 0-8249-6792-5 pa
                                    LC 2006036186
"This book is filled with ideas that children can implement in order to make a positive impact on the world around them. It is divided into five sections: people, pets, wildlife, environment, and kids joining together. . . . Throughout, material is neatly organized and the book has plenty of factual insets; color cartoon illustrations appear on every spread. . . . This is an excellent resource." SLJ
 Includes bibliographical references

361.3 Social work

O'Neal, Claire
 Volunteering in your school. Mitchell Lane Publishers 2011 47p (How to help: a guide to giving back) lib bdg $29.95

Grades: 4 5 6   **361.3**
 1. Volunteer work
 ISBN 978-1-58415-920-9; 1-58415-920-0
                                    LC 2010011982
This suggests ways in which young people can volunteer to do such tasks as participating in a clean-up day, setting up a recycling center, or planting a garden to enhance and contribute to the school community.
 This "well-organized [book] will encourage children to contribute to the world around them. [The] title is filled with examples of volunteer opportunities that can be accomplished with some adult involvement and supervision to guide, steer, and maintain focus so that youngsters will have varied and successful experiences." SLJ
 Includes bibliographical references

 Ways to help in your community. Mitchell Lane 2010 47p il (How to help: a guide to giving back) lib bdg $29.95
Grades: 4 5 6   **361.3**
 1. Community life 2. Volunteer work
 ISBN 978-1-58415-921-6 lib bdg; 1-58415-921-9 lib bdg
This "well-organized [book] will encourage children to contribute to the world around them. [The] title is filled with examples of volunteer opportunities that can be accomplished with some adult involvement and supervision to guide, steer, and maintain focus so that youngsters will have varied and successful experiences. . . . [The book] offers specific examples and steps for making a neighborhood safer, organizing yard sales, spending time with an elderly person, helping at a soup kitchen, or offering to do storyhours at a library." SLJ
 Includes bibliographical references

361.7 Private action

Reusser, Kayleen
 Celebrities giving back. Mitchell Lane Publishers 2011 47p (How to help: a guide to giving back) lib bdg $29.95
Grades: 4 5 6   **361.7**
 1. Charities 2. Celebrities 3. Philanthropists
 ISBN 978-1-58415-922-3 lib bdg; 1-58415-922-7 lib bdg
                                    LC 2010014904
"Reusser writes about 17 people, including Bono and his interest in eliminating world hunger and poverty, President Carter's dreams of building homes for the homeless, and charitable works by Rihanna, Shakira, Tony Hawk, and others." SLJ
 Includes bibliographical references

Shoveller, Herb
 Ryan and Jimmy; and the well in Africa that brought them together. Kids Can Press 2006 55p il $16.95; pa $9.95
Grades: 3 4 5 6   **361.7**
 1. Wells 2. Children 3. Social action 4. International cooperation 5. Uganda 6. Humanitarians
 ISBN 978-1-55337-967-6; 1-55337-967-5; 978-1-55453-271-1 pa; 1-55453-271-X pa
This is an account of the a Canadian boy named Ryan Hreljac, whose efforts helped provide clean drinking water to a village in Uganda, and who befriended and ultimately rescued a boy named Akana Jimmy from Ugandan rebels
 "Clearly written and illustrated with full-color family photographs set against colorful backgrounds, this story is both personal and representative of the many people living in developing countries, the individuals working against all odds to help them, and the power of young people to make a difference." SLJ

362.1　People with illnesses and disabilities

Barber, Nicola
　Going to the hospital. PowerKids Press 2009 24p il (The big day!) lib bdg $21.25; pa $8.25
Grades: PreK K 1　　　　　　　　　　　**362.1**
　1. Hospitals 2. Medical care
　ISBN 978-1-4358-2840-7 lib bdg; 1-4358-2840-2 lib bdg; 978-1-4358-2896-4 pa; 1-4358-2896-8 pa
　　　　　　　　　　　　　　　　　　LC 2008025812
　"Children in kindergarten will enjoy [this book] as a read-aloud] . . . while those at the end of first grade will be able to read [it] independently. The writing is straightforward and reassuring, and the content provides a realistic view of what youngsters might experience in [a hospital]. . . . [The book] discusses sickness, admission and surroundings, fasting for surgery, and blood tests." SLJ
　Includes bibliographical references

Fleischman, John
　★ **Phineas** Gage: a gruesome but true story about brain science. Houghton Mifflin 2002 86p il $16; pa $8.95
Grades: 5 6 7 8 9　　　　　　　　　　　**362.1**
　1. Railroad workers 2. Brain -- Wounds and injuries
　ISBN 0-618-05252-6; 0-618-49478-2 pa
　　　　　　　　　　　　　　　　　　LC 2001-39253
　"The author deftly introduces readers to a diverse range of relevant scientific history as well as more specific beliefs that influenced the medical establishment's understanding of Gage, then goes on to examine subsequent neurological discoveries that have changed and enhanced our understanding of Gage's fate. The book's present-tense narrative is inviting and intimate, and the text is crisp and lucid." Bull Cent Child Books
　Includes glossary and bibliographical references

Parker, Victoria
　Going to the hospital; [by] Vic Parker. Heinemann Library 2011 24p il (Growing up) lib bdg $22; pa $6.49
Grades: PreK K 1 2　　　　　　　　　　**362.1**
　1. Hospitals 2. Medical care
　ISBN 978-1-4329-4797-2 lib bdg; 1-4329-4797-4 lib bdg; 978-1-4329-4807-8 pa; 1-4329-4807-5 pa
　　　　　　　　　　　　　　　　　　LC 2010024191
　This describes the experience of being a patient in a hospital.
　Includes bibliographical references

362.18　Emergency services

Shepherd, Jodie
　A **day** with paramedics; by Jodie Shepherd. Children's Press 2013 32 p. (pbk.) $5.95
Grades: K 1 2　　　　　　　　　　　　　**362.18**
　1. Emergency medical technicians 2. Emergency medical services 3. Emergency medical technicians
　ISBN 0531289540; 9780531289549; 9780531292549
　　　　　　　　　　　　　　　　　　LC 2012013358
　This book describes the job of paramedics. "In four short chapters dominated by photos of stretchers, oxygen masks, and neck braces . . . and a couple lines of text, [Jodie] Shepherd . . . list[s] where you find paramedics (football games, fairs) and establish[es] their professionalism: 'They work quickly and calmly.' After stating that paramedics sometimes restart hearts or lungs, we go inside the ambulance . . . before wrapping up with some odder means of rescue (skis and helicopters)." (Booklist)

362.19　Services to patients with specific conditions

Pruessen, Linda
　Saving Eyesight; Adventures of Seva Around the World. Linda Pruessen. Firefly Books Ltd 2015 64 p. color ill., color portraits $19.95
Grades: 4 5 6 7　　　　　　　　　　　**362.19**
　1. Vision 2. Medical charities
　ISBN 1770856161; 9781770856165
　　　　　　　　　　　　　　　　　　LC 2015458723
　This book, by Linda Pruessen, is a " travelogue chronicling the efforts of Seva, an international development agency. Readers will learn about how the eye works and how eye problems are corrected. Illustrations reveal how the eyes work to transmit images to the brain." (Publisher's note)
　"A good choice for youth community service groups looking for a worthy cause, this offering might even inspire a career in ophthalmology." SLJ

362.29　Substance abuse

LeVert, Suzanne
　Ecstasy; by Suzanne LeVert with Jeff Hendricks. Marshall Cavendish Benchmark 2010 32p il (Drug facts) $19.95
Grades: 4 5 6 7　　　　　　　　　　　**362.29**
　1. Drug abuse 2. Designer drugs 3. Ecstasy (Drug)
　ISBN 978-0-7614-4349-0; 0-7614-4349-5
　　　　　　　　　　　　　　　　　　LC 2008-52753
　"Provides clear explanations about effects, followed by diagrams of the body to clarify the specific organs/body systems that suffer the most damage. . . . An excellent starting point." SLJ
　Includes glossary

　Steroids; by Suzanne LeVert with Jim Whiting. Marshall Cavendish Benchmark 2010 32p il (Drug facts) $19.95
Grades: 4 5 6 7　　　　　　　　　　　**362.29**
　1. Steroids 2. Sports -- Corrupt practices
　ISBN 978-0-7614-4352-0; 0-7614-4352-5
　　　　　　　　　　　　　　　　　　LC 2008-52752
　"Provides clear explanations about effects, followed by diagrams of the body to clarify the specific organs/body systems that suffer the most damage. . . . An excellent starting point." SLJ
　Includes glossary

Menhard, Francha Roffe
　The **facts** about inhalants; by Francha Roffe Menhard with Laura Purdie Salas. Marshall Cavendish Benchmark 2010 32p il (Drug facts) $19.95
Grades: 4 5 6 7　　　　　　　　　　　**362.29**
　1. Inhalant abuse
　ISBN 978-0-7614-4350-6; 0-7614-4350-9
　　　　　　　　　　　　　　　　　　LC 2008-52739
　"Provides clear explanations about effects, followed by diagrams of the body to clarify the specific organs/body systems that suffer the most damage. . . . An excellent starting point." SLJ
　Includes glossary

362.292　Alcohol

Bjornlund, Lydia D.
　Alcohol; [by] Lydia Bjornlund. Cherry Lake Pub. 2009 32p il (Health at risk) lib bdg $27.07

Grades: 4 5 6 7

362.292

1. Alcohol 2. Alcoholism

ISBN 978-1-60279-280-7 lib bdg; 1-60279-280-1 lib bdg

LC 2008017495

This describes the effects of alcohol, the dangers of driving drunk, how to get help, and how to make good choices.

"Great for reports or reluctant readers." Booklist

Includes bibliographical references

Gottfried, Ted

Alcohol; by Ted Gottfried with Katherine Follett. Marshall Cavendish Benchmark 2010 32p il (Drug facts) $19.95

Grades: 4 5 6 7

362.292

1. Alcoholism 2. Drinking of alcoholic beverages 3. Alcohol -- Physiological effect

ISBN 978-0-7614-4348-3; 0-7614-4348-7

LC 2008-52751

"Provides clear explanations about effects, followed by diagrams of the body to clarify the specific organs/body systems that suffer the most damage. . . . An excellent starting point." SLJ

Includes glossary

362.4 People with physical disabilities

Bozzo, Linda

Guide dog heroes. Enslow Publishers 2010 48p il (Amazing working dogs with American Humane) lib bdg $23.93

Grades: 2 3 4

362.4

1. Guide dogs

ISBN 978-0-7660-3198-2; 0-7660-3198-5

This describes the work of guide dogs, the breeds that are best suited to the job, the training required, the tasks the dogs perform, and what happens to them after they retire.

"Full-color photos, some full page, appear throughout. [This book is] clearly written in a personable style, with plenty of anecdotal and factual information, which makes [it] suitable for report writing and enjoyable for general reading." SLJ

Includes glossary and bibliographical references

Service dog heroes. Enslow Publishers 2010 48p il (Amazing working dogs with American Humane) lib bdg $23.93

Grades: 2 3 4

362.4

1. Working dogs 2. Animals and people with disabilities

ISBN 978-0-7660-3199-9; 0-7660-3199-3

This describes the work of service dogs who help people with disabilities, the breeds that are best suited to the work, the training required, the tasks the dogs perform, and what happens to them after they retire.

"Full-color photos, some full page, appear throughout. [This book is] clearly written in a personable style, with plenty of anecdotal and factual information, which makes [it] suitable for report writing and enjoyable for general reading." SLJ

Includes glossary and bibliographical references

Goldish, Meish

Prison puppies. Bearport Pub. 2011 32p il (Dog heroes) lib bdg $25.27

Grades: 3 4 5

362.4

1. Prisoners 2. Animals and people with disabilities

ISBN 978-1-61772-151-9; 1-61772-151-4

LC 2010037154

In this book, "readers learn about the 'Puppies Behind Bars' program, where inmates train dogs for careers as service animals. While the future work duties of the dogs are evident, the real story here is how

they give the inmates an opportunity to contribute to society in a positive way. . . . [This book is] engaging not just because the content is so compelling, but also because the [author has] highlighted specific dogs currently working in [this field]. The use of real names and full-color photographs on every page, many contributed by the individuals who work with these dogs, makes reading [this book] a personal experience. . . . [An] excellent [introduction] to [this] new [development] in service-dog training." SLJ

Includes glossary and bibliographical references

Hoffman, Mary Ann

Helping dogs. Gareth Stevens Pub. 2011 24p il (Working dogs) lib bdg $22.60; pa $8.15

Grades: 2 3 4

362.4

1. Animals and people with disabilities

ISBN 978-1-4339-4651-6 lib bdg; 1-4339-4651-3 lib bdg; 978-1-4339-4652-3 pa; 1-4339-4652-1 pa

LC 2010035242

This describes helping "dogs and the training they receive. The short chapters, complemented by numerous color photographs, provide examples of particular breeds that do [this] job and show how their characteristics are suited for the tasks. The charts provided are especially helpful, covering commands and more specific tasks. There is enough information to make the [text] feel fresh. . . . A solid choice for readers looking for more than cute pictures." SLJ

Hopkinson, Deborah

Annie and Helen; by Deborah Hopkinson; illustrated by Raul Colón. Schwartz & Wade Books 2012 48 p. $17.99

Grades: 2 3 4 5

362.4

1. Reading 2. Female friendship 3. Deafblind women -- United States -- Biography

ISBN 0375857060; 9780375857065; 9780375957062

LC 2010031443

Author Deborah Hopkinson presents a picture-book biography on Helen Keller. "Focusing on the relationship between Helen and her teacher, Annie Sullivan, the book is interspersed with excerpts of Annie's letters home, written as she struggled with her angry, wild pupil. But slowly, with devotion and determination, Annie teaches Helen finger spelling and braille, letters, and sentences. As Helen comes to understand language and starts to communicate, she connects for the first time with her family and the world around her." (Publisher's note)

Includes bibliographical references.

Lambert, Joseph

The **Center** for Cartoon Studies presents Annie Sullivan and the trials of Helen Keller; by Joseph Lambert. Disney Hyperion Books 2012 96 p.

Grades: 5 6 7

362.4

1. Women authors -- Biography 2. Female friendship -- Graphic novels 3. People with disabilities -- Graphic novels 4. Graphic novels 5. Women -- United States -- History 6. Women -- United States -- Biography 7. Female friendship -- United States -- History

ISBN 9781423113362

LC 2011036324

This nonfiction graphic novel about Annie Sullivan and Helen Keller "focuses on the trials both Annie and Helen struggle with in their lives," particularly the incident when Helen was accused of plagiarism in her story 'The Frost King' and interrogated at the Perkins Institution. "Helen's perspective is . . . communicated in dialogue-free black panels in which she is represented as only a gray silhouette" by author/illustrator Joseph Lambert. (Kirkus) Bibliography.

Martin, Claudia
   Helpers. Marshall Cavendish Benchmark 2010 64p il (Working animals) lib bdg $28.50
Grades: 4 5 6 7   **362.4**
   1. Animals and people with disabilities
   ISBN 978-1-60870-163-6 lib bdg; 1-60870-163-8 lib bdg
   "Attractively designed and packed with information. . . . The composition of each page is attractively set up with well-selected and reproduced stock and historical photos." SLJ

Patent, Dorothy Hinshaw
   ★ The **right** dog for the job; Ira's path from service dog to guide dog. photographs by William Muñoz. Walker & Co. 2004 un il $16.95
Grades: 2 3 4   **362.4**
   1. Guide dogs 2. Animals and people with disabilities 3. Animals -- Training
   ISBN 0-8027-8914-5
                      LC 2003-65785
   This "photo-essay follows a puppy from his training to become a service dog to becoming a guide dog. . . . The author . . . manages to slip in an extraordinary amount of information about the raising and training of guide dogs. . . . Myriad full-color photographs that will capture kids' interest accompany the text." SLJ

Rappaport, Doreen, 1939-
   ★ **Helen's** big world; the life of Helen Keller. written by Doreen Rappaport; illustrated by Matt Tavares. Disney/Hyperion Books 2012 48 p. $17.99
Grades: K 1 2 3 4   **362.4**
   1. Disabilities 2. Picture books for children 3. Deafblind women -- United States -- Biography 4. Deafblind people -- United States -- Biography
   ISBN 078680890X; 9780786808908
                      LC 2011053516
   In this children's picture-book biography of Helen Keller, author Doreen Rappaport and illustrator Matt Tavares begin "when Keller was a healthy baby . . . and end . . . with her death at 87, when she had long been a national icon and social activist." Her teacher Annie Sullivan is featured throughout the book, which "conveys . . . both the catastrophic nature of Helen's disabilities and the steely will that raged to be unleashed." (Publishers Weekly)
   Includes bibliographical references.

Witter, Bret
   Tuesday tucks me in; the loyal bond between a soldier and his service dog. Luis Carlos Montalvan, Bret Witter; [photographs by] Dan Dion. Roaring Brook Press 2014 40 p. (hardback) $16.99
Grades: K 1 2 3 4   **362.4**
   1. Service dogs 2. Human-animal relationship
   ISBN 1596438916; 9781596438910
                      LC 2013032042
   Written by Luis Carlos Montalván and Bret Witter, with photography by Dan Dion, "'Tuesday Tucks Me In' is a day in the life of this service dog extraordinaire and tail-wagging ambassador for all things positive and uplifting in the world. The book takes us through a typical day of adventures, starting with Tuesday waking Luis in the morning and greeting him with dog breath in the face, and then ending with Tuesday cuddling up to Luis on their bed." (Publisher's note)
   "Montalván, the best-selling author of the adult memoir Until Tuesday: A Wounded Warrior and the Golden Retriever Who Saved Him (2011), is a 17-year army veteran and advocate for veterans with disabilities. Yet this is not his story but that of his golden retriever service dog, Tuesday...Tuesday typifies the unbreakable bond between humans and canines and in a kid-friendly way, manages to dispel some of the stigma of post-traumatic stress disorder and invisible war wounds." Booklist

362.5   Poor people

Lynette, Rachel
   What to do when your family loses its home. PowerKids Press 2010 24p il (Let's work it out) lib bdg $21.25; pa $8.25
Grades: 2 3 4   **362.5**
   1. Homeless persons
   ISBN 978-1-4358-9339-9 lib bdg; 1-4358-9339-5 lib bdg; 978-1-4358-9766-3 pa; 1-4358-9766-8 pa
   "Full-page color photographs appear opposite the [narrative], depicting multicultural children, parents, grandparents, social workers, and others, whose demeanors match the hopeful tone of the [title]. This . . . will help promote empathy and understanding for the plight of others and is a key purchase." SLJ
   Includes glossary

Mason, Paul, 1967-
   Poverty; [by] Paul Mason. Heinemann Library 2006 48p il map (Planet under pressure) lib bdg $31.43
Grades: 4 5 6 7   **362.5**
   1. Poverty
   ISBN 1-4034-7743-4
                      LC 2005017166
   "Mason presents common factors for poverty worldwide, such as lack of money and education, as well as natural disasters. He also addresses the effects of outsourcing jobs from wealthier countries to poorer ones and how poverty affects environment. The book should make the global situation clearer. [This has] numerous quality color visuals, and sidebars. Up-to-date and informative." SLJ
   Includes bibliographical references

362.7   Young people

Krementz, Jill
   How it feels to be adopted. Knopf 1982 107p il hardcover o.p. pa $15
Grades: 4 5 6 7   **362.7**
   1. Adoption
   ISBN 0-394-75853-6 pa
                      LC 82-48011
   This "is an important contribution to literature on adoption and the question of searching for biological parents." SLJ
   Includes bibliographical references

Lynette, Rachel
   What to do when your family is on welfare. PowerKids Press 2010 24p il (Let's work it out) lib bdg $21.25; pa $8.25
Grades: 2 3 4   **362.7**
   1. Public welfare
   ISBN 978-1-4358-9337-5 lib bdg; 1-4358-9337-9 lib bdg; 978-1-4358-9762-5 pa; 1-4358-9762-5 pa
                      LC 2009-19863
   "Full-page color photographs appear opposite the [narrative], depicting multicultural children, parents, grandparents, social workers, and others, whose demeanors match the hopeful tone of the [title]. This . . . will help promote empathy and understanding for the plight of others and is a key purchase." SLJ
   Includes glossary

Parr, Todd

We belong together; a book about adoption and families. Little, Brown 2007 32p il $15.99

Grades: PreK K   **362.7**

1. Family 2. Adoption

ISBN 0-316-01668-3

"Parr illustrates the rewards of family ties in this heartfelt, supportive book geared toward adopted children and their parents. In each double-page spread, Parr completes the phrase 'We belong together because . . .' with poignant explanations that touch upon basic, tangible needs . . . as well as emotional ones. . . . Cheerful, friendly artwork, with thickly outlined forms and characters and a bold rainbow palette, inclusively depicts an array of children and families—including one with a single parent and one with two dads." Booklist

Rotner, Shelley

I'm adopted! by Shelley Rotner and Sheila M. Kelly; photographs by Shelley Rotner. Holiday House 2011 un il $16.95

Grades: PreK K 1   **362.7**

1. Adoption

ISBN 978-0-8234-2294-4; 0-8234-2294-1

LC 2010029561

"This introduction to adoption for very young children stands out in its clear, accessible approach to [the] topic. . . . Engaging, full-color photos portray kids and parents of varying ethnicities and families of varying compositions. The process of adoption is explained in simple language that children understand. . . . Both domestic and international adoption are addressed, making this suitable for all kinds of adoptive families. The photo album-like design . . . adds to the appeal." Kirkus

Saul, Laya

Ways to help disadvantaged youth. Mitchell Lane Publishers 2011 47p (How to help: a guide to giving back) lib bdg $29.95

Grades: 4 5 6   **362.7**

1. Poor 2. Social action

ISBN 978-1-58415-918-6; 1-58415-918-9

LC 2010006536

This "well-organized [book] will encourage children to contribute to the world around them. [This] title is filled with examples of volunteer opportunities that can be accomplished with some adult involvement and supervision to guide, steer, and maintain focus so that youngsters will have varied and successful experiences. . . . [The book] suggests tutoring, having a toy or food drive, etc." SLJ

Includes bibliographical references

Stewart, Sheila

A **house** between homes; kids in the foster care system. by Sheila Stewart and Camden Flath. Mason Crest Publishers 2010 48p il (Kids have troubles too) lib bdg $19.95; pa $7.95

Grades: 3 4 5 6   **362.7**

1. Foster home care

ISBN 978-1-4222-1692-7 lib bdg; 1-4222-1692-6 lib bdg; 978-1-4222-1905-8 pa; 1-4222-1905-4 pa

LC 2010012756

Discusses the foster care system, including the reasons why children enter the system, what happens in foster care, the types of children, foster parents, and what happens next, and provides a story about siblings who are placed in foster care.

"The prose is respectable in its dialogue, character development, and pacing. . . . This series will be well placed in a school media center, as well as in any institution that serves high-risk children." SLJ

Includes bibliographical references

362.73 Institutional and related services

Warren, Andrea

We rode the orphan trains. Houghton Mifflin 2001 132p il $18; pa $8.95

Grades: 4 5 6 7   **362.73**

1. Orphans

ISBN 0-618-11712-1; 0-618-11712-1 pa

LC 00-47279

"This is powerful nonfiction for classroom and personal reading and for discussion." Booklist

Includes bibliographical references

362.82 Families

Stewart, Sheila

When Daddy hit Mommy; by Sheila Stewart and Rae Simons. Mason Crest Publishers 2011 48p il (Kids have troubles too) lib bdg $19.95; pa $7.95

Grades: 3 4 5   **362.82**

1. Child abuse 2. Domestic violence

ISBN 978-1-4222-1696-5 lib bdg; 1-4222-1696-9 lib bdg; 978-1-4222-1909-6 pa; 1-4222-1909-7 pa

LC 2010029346

Discusses domestic violence, including its causes, its effects on the family, how to get help, life in a shelter, and help for the abuser, and provides a story about a girl whose father gets violent.

Includes bibliographical references

363.1 Public safety programs

Aronson, Marc

★ **Trapped**; how the world rescued 33 miners from 2,000 feet below the Chilean desert. Atheneum 2011 144p il

Grades: 4 5 6 7   **363.1**

1. Rescue work 2. Gold mines and mining 3. Copper mines and mining 4. Mine accidents -- Chile

ISBN 1-4169-1397-1; 978-1-4169-1397-9

LC 2011000777

This title is about thirty-three miners trapped in a copper-gold mine in San Jose, Chile and how experts from around the world, from drillers, to astronauts, to submarine specialists, came together to make their remarkable rescue possible.

This is "a riveting, in-depth recounting of the events that held the world rapt. . . . Twelve short chapters with photos and diagrams keep the story well-paced." Publ Wkly

Includes bibliographical references

Benoit, Peter

The **Hindenburg** disaster. Children's Press 2011 48p il map (True book) lib bdg $28

Grades: 3 4 5   **363.1**

1. Airships 2. Aircraft accidents 3. Hindenburg (Airship)

ISBN 978-0-531-20626-3 lib bdg; 0-531-20626-2 lib bdg; 978-0-531-29025-5 pa; 0-531-29025-5 pa

LC 2010045931

This describes how the Hindenburg blimp crashed and burned in New Jersey on May 6, 1937.

"Benoit provides unbiased information that is on target for the intended audience. . . . The photographs and reproductions enhance the [text]. . . . [This book is] well-conceived." SLJ

Includes bibliographical references

Nuclear meltdowns. Children's Press 2011 48p il (True book: disasters) lib bdg $28; pa $6.99

Grades: 3 4 5   **363.1**

1. Chernobyl Nuclear Accident, Chernobyl, Ukraine, 1986 2. Nuclear power plants -- Security measures 3. Three Mile Island Nuclear Power Plant (Pa.)

ISBN 978-0-531-25422-6 lib bdg; 0-531-25422-4; 978-0-531-26627-4 pa; 0-531-26627-3 pa

LC 2011007142

This describes nuclear power plant accidents at Three Mile Island, Chernobyl, and in Japan.

This is "thoughtfully designed. . . . The information . . . is right on target: concise, accurate, and thorough. . . . The photographs . . . are especially effective at putting a human face on large-scale devastation." Booklist

Includes glossary and bibliographical references

363.11   Occupational and industrial hazards

Scott, Elaine

★ **Buried** alive! how 33 miners survived 69 days deep under the Chilean desert. Elaine Scott. Houghton Mifflin Harcourt 2012 80 p. col. ill., col. maps (hardcover) $17.99; (ebook) $17.99

Grades: 4 5 6 7 8   **363.11**

1. Miners 2. Disasters 3. Industrial accidents 4. San José Mine Accident, Chile, 2010 5. Mine rescue work -- Chile -- Copiapó Region 6. San José Mine Accident, Chile, 2010 7. Gold mines and mining -- Accidents -- Chile -- Copiapó Region 8. Copper mines and mining -- Accidents -- Chile -- Copiapó Region 9. Mine rescue work -- Chile -- Copiapó Region 10. Gold mines and mining -- Accidents -- Chile -- Copiapó Region 11. Copper mines and mining -- Accidents -- Chile -- Copiapó Region

ISBN 0547707789; 9780547707785; 9780547691787

LC 2011025945

Author Elaine Scott chronicles the events that took place "[o]n August 5, 2010, [when] a copper mine in Chile collapsed, trapping 33 miners nearly half a mile underground . . . [The author] describes the choices the miners' strong leader advised that prolonged their survival long enough to be rescued and the creative solutions that effected that rescue. They drilled through over 2,000 feet of especially hard rock, delivered supplies to the trapped men through a tiny bore hole and then invented a way to carry the men, one at a time, to the surface in a very small capsule." (Kirkus)

Includes bibliographical references (p. 78) and index.

363.12   Transportation hazards

Verstraete, Larry

Surviving the Hindenburg; by Larry Verstraete; illustrated by David Geister. Sleeping Bear Press 2012 32 p. col. ill.

Grades: 2 3 4   **363.12**

1. Airships 2. Aeronautics 3. Aircraft accidents 4. Hindenburg (Airship) 5. Cabin boys -- Germany -- Biography 6. Airships -- Germany -- History -- 20th century 7. Survival -- New Jersey -- History -- 20th century 8. Aircraft accident victims -- New Jersey -- Biography 9. Aircraft accidents -- New Jersey -- History -- 20th

century

ISBN 1585367877; 9781585367870

LC 2011027879

This historical story, by Larry Verstraete and David Geister, relates the story of the German airship "Hindenburg." "On May 6, 1937, the . . . airship . . . exploded. . . . 62 survived, including Werner Franz, the ship's 14-year-old cabin boy. . . . Verstrate recounts young Werner's story. . . . Through Werner's memories young readers will explore the inner workings of the giant airship . . . and hold their breath during Werner's terrifying escape from the fiery devastation." (Publisher's note)

363.2   Police services

Arroyo, Sheri L.

How crime fighters use math; math curriculum consultant: Rhea A. Stewart. Chelsea Clubhouse 2010 32p il (Math in the real world) lib bdg $28

Grades: 4 5 6   **363.2**

1. Mathematics 2. Vocational guidance 3. Criminal investigation

ISBN 978-1-60413-602-9 lib bdg; 1-60413-602-2 lib bdg

LC 2009-23330

"The layout for [this] slim [title] is bright and colorful with a photograph and a 'You Do the Math' problem to solve and large, easy-to-read text on every spread. An answer key is included in the back matter, along with a page detailing the career choices and the educational requirements. [It] touches on crime-scene grids, the importance of shoe prints in tracking a criminal, cracking secret codes, and more. . . . [This title] would be useful to supplement lessons on mathematics. [It] will also appeal to students wanting to learn more about math as it relates to specific careers." SLJ

Includes glossary and bibliographical references

Bozzo, Linda

Police dog heroes. Enslow Publishers 2010 48p il (Amazing working dogs with American Humane) lib bdg $23.93

Grades: 2 3 4   **363.2**

1. Working dogs 2. Animals in police work

ISBN 978-0-7660-3197-5; 0-7660-3197-7

LC 2008048017

"Full-color photos, some full page, appear throughout. [This book is] clearly written in a personable style, with plenty of anecdotal and factual information, which makes [it] suitable for report writing and enjoyable for general reading." SLJ

Includes glossary and bibliographical references

Graham, Ian

Forensic technology. Smart Apple Media 2011 il (New technology) lib bdg $34.25

Grades: 4 5 6 7   **363.2**

1. Forensic sciences 2. Criminal investigation

ISBN 978-1-599-20532-8; 1-599-20532-7

LC 2010044238

Describes the technology used by forensic scientists to gather and analyze evidence from crime scenes.

This "offers a fine overview for reports, and its attractive design may also entice middle-grade readers to learn more." Booklist

Hoffman, Mary Ann

Police dogs. Gareth Stevens Pub. 2011 24p il (Working dogs) lib bdg $22.60; pa $8.15

Grades: 2 3 4

363.2

1. Dogs

ISBN 978-1-4339-4659-2 lib bdg; 1-4339-4659-9 lib bdg; 978-1-4339-4660-8 pa; 1-4339-4660-2 pa

LC 2010035244

This describes police "dogs and the training they receive. The short chapters, complemented by numerous color photographs, provide examples of particular breeds that do [this] job and show how their characteristics are suited for the tasks. The charts provided are especially helpful, covering commands and more specific tasks. There is enough information to make the [text] feel fresh. . . . A solid choice for readers looking for more than cute pictures." SLJ

Jackson, Donna M.

★ The **wildlife** detectives; how forensic scientists fight crimes against nature. by Donna M. Jackson; photographs by Wendy Shattil and Bob Rozinski. Houghton Mifflin 2000 47p il $16

Grades: 4 5 6 7

363.2

1. Game protection 2. Forensic sciences 3. U.S. Fish and Wildlife Service -- Forensics Laboratory

ISBN 0-395-86976-5

LC 99-34857

Describes how the wildlife detectives at the National Fish and Wildlife Forensics Laboratory in Ashland, Oregon, analyze clues to catch and convict people responsible for crimes against animals

This book features "a smoothly written text that unfolds almost like a mystery novel. . . . Engaging full-color photographs help clarify the text and will appeal to browsers. A list of follow-up suggestions and a glossary of terms are appended. A book that will be welcomed by mystery fans and anyone who cares about animals." Booklist

Kenney, Karen Latchana

Police officers at work; by Karen L. Kenney; illustrated by Brian Caleb Dumm; content consultant: Judith Stepan-Norris. Magic Wagon 2009 32p il (Meet your community workers!) lib bdg $18.95

Grades: K 1 2 3

363.2

1. Police 2. Vocational guidance

ISBN 978-1-60270-652-1 lib bdg; 1-60270-652-2 lib bdg

LC 2009-2391

This book about police officers has "an uncluttered layout and consistent organization. . . . Chapter headings such as 'Problems on the Job,' and 'Technology at Work,' and 'Special Skills and Training' make it easy to pinpoint specific information." SLJ

Includes glossary

MacLeod, Elizabeth

Bones Never Lie; How Forensics Helps Solve History's Mysteries. Elizabeth MacLeod. Firefly Books Ltd 2013 iv, 156 p.p (hardcover) $24.95

Grades: 4 5 6 7 8

363.2

1. Forensic sciences -- Encyclopedias

ISBN 1554514835; 9781554514830

This children's book, by Elizabeth MacLeod, explores how through "forensics--the scientific way of examining physical evidence--we now know what killed Napoleon and whether Anastasia survived the massacre of the Russian royal family. Seven intriguing stories about historical royal figures whose demise was suspicious, and hard scientific facts about crime-solving techniques make each event seem like an episode of CSI rather than a history lesson." (Publisher's note)

"In real life, forensics can be slow and tedious, but MacLeod invests these high-profile deaths with considerable vim and drama. A good selection of staged and archival photographs and artwork accompany the stories. A fully fleshed and crisply told story of forensics at its romantic best." Kirkus

Mezzanotte, Jim

Police. Marshall Cavendish Benchmark 2010 64p il (Working animals) lib bdg $28.50

Grades: 4 5 6 7

363.2

1. Animals in police work

ISBN 978-1-60870-166-7 lib bdg; 1-60870-166-2 lib bdg

LC 2010007006

Describes animals, such as dogs and horses, which work with police in such areas as search-and-rescue, tracking criminals, and sniffing out explosives

"Attractively designed and packed with information. . . . The composition of each page is attractively set up with well-selected and reproduced stock and historical photos." SLJ

Spilsbury, Richard

Counterfeit! stopping fakes and forgeries. Enslow Publishers 2009 48p il (Solve that crime!) lib bdg $23.93

Grades: 5 6 7 8

363.2

1. Fraud 2. Forgery

ISBN 978-0-7660-3378-8 lib bdg; 0-7660-3378-3 lib bdg

LC 2008-33310

This "title boasts in-depth information, sidebars detailing events of true crime, and activities that will increase understanding. . . . Photographs are colorful, well-captioned, and related to the text." SLJ

Includes glossary and bibliographical references

Townsend, John

Famous forensic cases. Amicus 2011 il (Amazing crime scene science) $19.95

Grades: 4 5 6 7

363.2

1. Forensic sciences 2. Criminal investigation

ISBN 978-1-60753-169-2; 1-60753-169-0

In this book "readers will find a straight presentation of fascinating information. Loosely organized by era, the book opens with a history of fingerprinting . . . which focuses on the 1920s and 1930s. Other topics include hair science in the 1950s, voiceprints in the 1970s, and recent advancements in DNA forensics. Scatter throughout are case studies. . . . This entry features an eye-catching layout, plenty of sidebars, and well-chosen photos. . . . Kids will go for this one." Booklist

363.3 Other aspects of public safety

Nolan, Janet

★ The **firehouse** light; illustrations by Marie Lafrance. Tricycle Press 2010 un il lib bdg $18.95; $15.99

Grades: K 1 2 3

363.3

1. Electric lamps 2. Fire departments

ISBN 978-1-58246-346-9 lib bdg; 1-58246-346-8 lib bdg; 978-1-58246-298-1; 1-58246-298-4

LC 2009-7964

The true story of a lightbulb in a firehouse located in Livermore, California, that has stayed lit for more than one hundred years.

"The narrative successfully knits firefighting and history into a fast dash through the twentieth century. . . . Flat, folk-style acrylic illustrations feature fluid, sinewy human figures amid a variety of vintage fire trucks." Booklist

363.34 Disasters

Bailey, Gerry

Fragile planet. Gareth Stevens Pub. 2011 48p il map (Planet SOS) lib bdg $31.95; pa $14.05

Grades: 4 5 6   **363.34**

1. Natural disasters

ISBN 978-1-4339-4974-6 lib bdg; 1-4339-4974-1 lib bdg; 978-1-4339-4975-3 pa; 1-4339-4975-X pa

LC 2010032886

This "well-designed [book]. . . . discusses natural events and disasters, such as avalanches, earthquakes, floods, hurricanes, lightning, volcanoes, and windstorms. . . . The many large, colorful photos will engage readers and assist them in understanding the important concepts introduced." SLJ

Includes glossary

Fradin, Judith Bloom

★ **Droughts**; [by] Judy & Dennis Fradin. National Geographic 2008 48p il map (Witness to disaster) $16.95; lib bdg $20.90

Grades: 4 5 6 7   **363.34**

1. Droughts

ISBN 978-1-4263-0339-5; 1-4263-0339-4; 978-1-4263-0340-1 lib bdg; 1-4263-0340-8 lib bdg

LC 2008020424

"This book examines the lessons from the Dust Bowl droughts for farmers, including the importance of topsoil. The history of droughts around the world compares impacts on a wide variety of societies. The final chapter looks at the latest tools and technologies developed to help us survive future droughts." Publisher's note

Includes glossary and bibliographical references

Garbe, Suzanne

The **Worst** wildfires of all time; by Suzanne Garbe. Capstone Press 2013 32 p. ill. (chiefly col.), col. maps (library) $27.32

Grades: 4 5 6 7   **363.34**

1. Wildfires 2. Natural disasters

ISBN 1429684186; 9781429684187

LC 2011053150

This book by Suzanne Garbe is part of the Epic Disasters series and looks at the worst wildfires of all time. "These uncontrolled fires can strike in the blink of an eye and spread just as quickly. Put out the flames and read about the worst wildfires in history." The series allows readers to "witness the destructive power of hurricanes, earthquakes, and more." (Publisher's note)

Includes bibliographical references and index.

Gregory, Josh

The **superstorm** hurricane Sandy; Josh Gregory. Children's Press, an Imprint of Scholastic Inc. 2013 48 p. illustrations

Grades: 2 3 4   **363.34**

1. Hurricanes 2. Hurricane Sandy, 2012 3. Disaster relief -- United States 4. Hurricane damage -- United States

ISBN 9780531237502; 9780531237519

LC 2012045292

Recounts the events of superstorm Hurricane Sandy and the devastation it caused in the New York metropolitan area, discusses the long-term effects of the storm on the urban environment, and describes the rebuilding efforts.

Includes bibliographical references and index

Karwoski, Gail

Tsunami; the true story of an April Fools' Day disaster. [by] Gail Langer Karwoski; illustrated by John MacDonald. Darby Creek Pub. 2006 64p il $17.95

Grades: 4 5 6 7   **363.34**

1. Tsunamis 2. Hawaii -- History 3. Hawaii

ISBN 1581960441

The author "opens with a description of the tsunami waves that struck the northern coast of the Hawaiian Islands in 1946, destroying a school and sweeping many children and adults out to sea. The book goes on to provide broader information about tsunamis, from scientific understanding of how they occur to ongoing efforts at early warning systems. . . . Clearly written and informative." Booklist

Markle, Sandra

★ **Rescues!** Millbrook Press 2006 88p il map lib bdg $25.26

Grades: 4 5 6 7   **363.34**

1. Rescue work 2. Survival after airplane accidents, shipwrecks, etc.

ISBN 978-0-8225-3413-6 lib bdg; 0-8225-3413-4 lib bdg

LC 2005-09707

"From the collapse of a Pennsylvania coal mine in 2002 to the tsunami that struck 11 countries in 2004 to Hurricane Katrina in 2005, the 11 disasters Markle describes are straight from news headlines. In this full-color photo-essay, she uses individual experiences of rescue and survival to bring each drama close." Booklist

Includes bibliographical references

Meyer, Susan

Adapting to flooding and rising sea levels; Susan Meyer. 1st ed. Rosen Central 2012 64 p. col. ill., col. maps (Science to the rescue : Adapting to climate change) (library) $31.95

Grades: 4 5 6   **363.34**

1. Sea level 2. Climate change 3. Global warming 4. Floods

ISBN 1448868475; 9781448868476

LC 2011045624

This book is part of the Science to the Rescue: Adapting to Climate Change series. It "focuses on the devastation to coastal regions worldwide caused by storms and global warming and how those issues are being addressed in various countries. A succinct explanation of the reasons for global warming and the rising sea level is followed by a section on the methods of adaptation . . . and a rundown of the current research being conducted." (Booklist)

Includes bibliographical references and index

Reilly, Kathleen M.

Natural disasters; investigate Earth's most destructive forces. by Kathleen M. Reilly; illustrated by Tom Casteel. Nomad Press 2012 121 p. (paperback) $15.95

Grades: 4 5 6 7   **363.34**

1. Weather 2. Natural disasters

ISBN 1619301466; 9781619301467

In this book, "spiraling winds, surging waters, eruptions, blazing forests, and chilling snows are discussed." Topics include "the MMS Scale and the Enhanced Fujita Scale." In addition to an "explanation of each type of phenomenon, safety tips, historical incidences, pen-and-ink line drawings, and correlative projects using simple materials are included." (School Library Journal)

Rusch, Elizabeth

★ **Eruption!** volcanoes and the science of saving lives. text by Elizabeth Rusch; illustrated by Tom Uhlman. Houghton Mifflin Harcourt 2013 76 p. col. ill. (hardcover) $18.99

Grades: 5 6 7 8   **363.34**
1. Disaster response and recovery 2. Volcanoes 3. Natural disasters 4. Volcanic eruptions
ISBN 0547503504; 9780547503509

LC 2012034055

This book by Elizabeth Rusch contains "photographs and sidebars [which] reveals the perilous . . . life-saving work of an international volcano crisis team (VDAP) and the sleeping giants they study, from Colombia to the Philippines, from Chile to Indonesia. [It presents an] stunning account of volcanologists Andy Lockhart, John Pallister, and their group of scientists who risk their lives, investigating deadly volcanoes that remain constant threats to people around the world." (Publisher's note)
Includes bibliographical references (pages 74-75) and index.

Saul, Laya
Ways to help after a natural disaster; by Laya Saul. Mitchell Lane Publishers 2011 47 p. col. ill. (library) $29.95
Grades: 4 5 6   **363.34**
1. Volunteer work 2. Disaster relief
ISBN 1584159170; 9781584159179

LC 2010006538

"This focuses on various activities in which children can participate to help families be prepared in the event of a natural disaster or in its aftermath, when citizens experience the devastating results. The brief sections on teaching preparedness include advice for putting together supply kits and a sample list for collecting emergency numbers. The bulk of the information is sound, practical, commonsense recommendations. . . . Included are simple measures, such as offering emotional support, as well as those that are more complicated, such as organizing drives for collecting blood or food and clothing. The design is inviting, with text appealingly laid out and offset by blocks of color." Booklist
Includes bibliographical references and index.

Somervill, Barbara A.
Graphing natural disasters. Heinemann Library 2010 32p il (Real world data) $28.21; pa $7.99
Grades: 5 6 7 8   **363.34**
1. Graphic methods 2. Natural disasters
ISBN 978-1-4329-2622-9; 1-4329-2622-5; 978-1-4329-2631-1 pa; 1-4329-2631-4 pa

LC 2009001290

This describes natural disasters such as tornadoes and volcanic eruptions using graphs and charts.
The book is "colorful, easy to read, and well designed." SLJ
Includes glossary and bibliographical references

363.37   Fire hazards

Cooper, Michael L., 1950-
Fighting fire! ten of the deadliest fires in American history and how we fought them. Michael L. Cooper. Henry Holt and Co. 2014 224 p. illustrations, maps (hardback) $19.99
Grades: 5 6 7 8   **363.37**
1. Fires 2. Fire fighting 3. Fire extinction -- United States -- History
ISBN 0805097147; 9780805097146

LC 2013043580

This book, by Michael L. Cooper, "brings to life ten of the deadliest infernos . . . [the United States] has ever endured: the great fires of Boston, New York, Chicago, Baltimore, and San Francisco, the disasters of the Triangle Shirtwaist Factory, the General Slocum, and the Cocoanut

Grove nightclub, the wildfire of Witch Creek in San Diego County, and the catastrophe of 9/11." (Publisher's note)
"Throughout history, fires have wreaked destruction but have also sparked innovation and reform. The Great Chicago Fire (1871) destroyed a third of the city but brought about a new architecture style; the Triangle Shirtwaist Factory Fire (1911) killed 146 people but led to the passage of laws protecting workers. Entries are lively, with dramatic illustrations to match." Horn Book
Includes bibliographical references and index

363.6   Public utilities and related services

Brown, Cynthia Light
Discover National Monuments, National Parks; natural wonders. illustrated by Blair Shedd. Nomad Press 2009 106p il (Discover your world) pa $19.95
Grades: 5 6 7 8   **363.6**
1. National parks and reserves
ISBN 978-1-9346702-8-6 pa; 1-9346702-8-6 pa
"With an inviting, browsable design and a chatty style, this large-sized volume . . . covers 15 national monuments and parks in the U.S. that celebrate and protect natural phenomena . . . . The science will excite readers, with detailed explanations of tectonic plates, radiometric dating, and dendrochronology." Booklist

Burgan, Michael
Not a drop to drink; water for a thirsty world. Peter H. Gleick, consultant. National Geographic 2008 64p il map (National Geographic investigates) $17.95
Grades: 4 5 6 7   **363.6**
1. Water 2. Water supply
ISBN 978-1-4263-0360-9; 1-4263-0360-2
Explores the important connections between human activity and the water cycle and shows how researchers are working to understand such issues as how climate change affects water supplies and how the oceans can help solve the water crisis.

Hollyer, Beatrice
★ **Our** world of water; children and water around the world. foreword by Zadie Smith. Henry Holt and Co. 2009 47p il map $16.99
Grades: 3 4 5   **363.6**
1. Water 2. Water supply
ISBN 978-0-8050-8941-7; 0-8050-8941-1

LC 2008040596

"Seven and eight-year-olds share what water means to them by revealing their everyday uses of it. An opening spread introduces the children and their countries—Peru, Ethiopia, Mauritania, Tajikistan, Bangladesh, and the United States—on an outline world map. Locations vary from mountaintop to seaside and from scarcity to abundance. . . . There is no order to the countries and the text is matter-of-fact, leaving readers to draw their own conclusions about the subjects' varying circumstances. Several full-color, captioned photos appear on each spread. . . . Questions will inevitably arise from this revealing look at the status of water in the world." SLJ
Includes bibliographical references

Kerley, Barbara
A cool drink of water. National Geographic Soc. 2002 un il map $16.95; pa $7.95
Grades: K 1 2 3   **363.6**
1. Water 2. Water supply
ISBN 0-7922-6723-0; 0-7922-5489-9 pa

LC 2001-2479

Depicts people around the world collecting, chilling, and drinking water

"Children will be entranced by the beautiful images of a basic substance that connects us all. Excellent for cross-cultural discussions." Booklist

363.7   Environmental problems

Aitken, Stephen

Earth's fever; written and illustrated by Stephen Aitken. Magic Wagon 2011 il (Climate change) $28.50

Grades: K 1 2 3   **363.7**

1. Greenhouse effect 2. Climate -- Environmental aspects
ISBN 1-61641-670-X; 978-1-61641-670-6

LC 2011001872

This "strikes a perfect balance for young readers. Aitken presents scientific facts straightforwardly and offers practical, age-appropriate suggestions for environmentally friendly activities. . . . The earnest cartoon illustrations . . . . are generally helpful." Booklist

Albee, Sarah

★ Poop happened! a history of the world from the bottom up. illustrated by Robert Leighton. Walker 2010 170p il lib bdg $20.89; pa $15.99

Grades: 4 5 6 7   **363.7**

1. Feces 2. Toilets 3. Sanitation 4. Refuse and refuse disposal
ISBN 978-0-8027-9825-1 lib bdg; 0-8027-9825-X lib bdg; 978-0-8027-2077-1 pa; 0-8027-2077-3 pa

"Albee deposits a heaping history of human sanitation—or rather lack thereof— and its effects. . . . She pumps out a steady stream of comments on the miasmic effects of urbanization, waste disposal, and the roles of (not) bathing in ancient Greece, Rome, medieval Europe, . . . and the 'Reeking Renaissance.' She then digs into the gradual adoption of better practices in the nineteenth century. . . . The cartoon illustrations feature sludgy green highlights." Booklist

Barnham, Kay

Recycle; [by] Kay Barnham. Crabtree Pub. 2008 32p il (Environment action!) lib bdg $22.60; pa $7.95

Grades: K 1 2 3   **363.7**

1. Recycling
ISBN 978-0-7787-3659-2 lib bdg; 0-7787-3659-8 lib bdg; 978-0-7787-3669-1 pa; 0-7787-3669-5 pa

LC 2007030000

This book "exposes young children to concepts that can truly make a difference. . . . [The book has] plenty of colorful, relevant, and interesting glossy color photographs." Sci Books Films

Includes glossary

Barraclough, Sue

Reusing things; by Sue Barraclough. Sea to Sea Publications 2008 30p il (Making a difference) lib bdg $27.10

Grades: 1 2 3   **363.7**

1. Recycling 2. Environmental protection
ISBN 978-1-59771-109-8 lib bdg; 1-59771-109-8 lib bdg

LC 2006051277

This suggests ways in which people can reduce waste by reusing paper or junk, repairing or repainting old items, borrowing or giving away things, and buying or using second-hand things.

This features "clear, concise information that is simple to read and understand, alternating between giving simple facts and dispersing helpful hints and suggestions. The full-color photographs are crisp and attractive." SLJ

Benoit, Peter

The BP oil spill. Children's Press 2011 48p il map (True book) lib bdg $28; pa $6.95

Grades: 3 4 5   **363.7**

1. Gulf of Mexico oil spill, 2010 2. BP (Firm).
ISBN 978-0-531-20630-0 lib bdg; 0-531-20630-0 lib bdg; 978-0-531-28999-0 pa; 0-531-28999-0 pa

LC 2010045927

Photographs, maps, time lines, and text describe the events surrounding the 2010 British Petroleum oil spill in the Gulf of Mexico.

"Benoit provides unbiased information that is on target for the intended audience. . . . The photos are realistic and well chosen to show that current events can be examined as critically as historical events." SLJ

Includes bibliographical references

Bullard, Lisa

Power up to fight pollution; illustrated by Wes Thomas. Lerner 2011 24p il (Planet protectors) lib bdg $23.93

Grades: K 1 2 3   **363.7**

1. Pollution 2. Environmental protection
ISBN 978-0-7613-6108-4; 0-7613-6108-1

LC 2010048862

A boy named Tyler shows what makes Earth's land, air, and water dirty and ways to clean up our world.

"The bright colors used in the illustrations . . . will attract young readers to the environmental science content. . . . [The] facts are written in child-friendly language and the information should be attainable by young children. . . . [This book] will raise the environmental awareness of young children." Sci Books Films

Includes bibliographical references

Cherry, Lynne

★ How we know what we know about our changing climate; scientists and kids explore global warming. by Lynne Cherry and Gary Braasch; with a foreword by David Sobel. Dawn Publications 2008 66p il $18.95; pa $11.95

Grades: 4 5 6 7   **363.7**

1. Greenhouse effect 2. Climate -- Environmental aspects
ISBN 978-1-58469-103-7; 0-1-58469-103-4; 978-1-58469-130-3 pa; 1-58469-130-1 pa

LC 2007-37255

"The can-do emphasis helps to make the topic less depressing, and the intriguing color photographs are thoughtful and upbeat." Booklist

Cole, Joanna

The magic school bus and the climate challenge; illustrated by Bruce Degen. Scholastic 2010 37p il $16.99

Grades: 2 3 4   **363.7**

1. Environmental protection 2. Greenhouse effect 3. Climate -- Environmental aspects
ISBN 978-0-590-10826-3; 0-590-10826-3

"Ms. Frizzle and her class challenge readers to go green. After traveling in their bus-plane and showing in storyboard style example after example of the Earth's changing climate, Ms. Frizzle, reluctant traveler Arnold, new South Korean classmate Joon, and the gang ride sun rays to the Earth, and then get back on the bus as those rays (and riders) get caught by heat-trapping gases." SLJ

David, Laurie

★ The down-to-earth guide to global warming; [by] Laurie David and Cambria Gordon. Orchard Books 2007 112p il map pa $15.99

Grades: 4 5 6 7 **363.7**
1. Greenhouse effect 2. Climate -- Environmental aspects
ISBN 978-0-439-02494-5 pa; 0-439-02494-3 pa

LC 2006-35705

The authors "put forth the basics on global warming, climate change, and how readers can green up the environment. They temper the book's often troubling subject matter with kid-friendly humor, some celebrity shout-outs, and explanations of the scientific underpinnings. An amply illustrated layout, featuring attention-grabbing sidebars, dramatic photos, and diagrams, will sustain reader interest." Booklist

Includes bibliographical references

Davies, Nicola
Gaia warriors; urgent; the fight is on! with an afterword by James Lovelock. Candlewick Press 2011 192p il $14.99
Grades: 5 6 7 8 **363.7**
1. Gaia hypothesis 2. Environmental protection 3. Greenhouse effect 4. Climate -- Environmental aspects 5. Climatic changes
ISBN 978-0-7636-4808-4; 0-7636-4808-6

LC 2010-40126

This "offers a dynamic overview of global warming's causes and concerns. Davies . . . devotes half the book to exciting profiles of individuals . . . who are working to slow climate change. . . . They include scientists, rock musicians, food distributors, architects, and youth organizers, and their broad variety reinforces the sense that every creative individual effort matters. Highly browsable layouts combine color photos and quotes printed in varied, eye-catching fonts. . . . [This has a] humorous, conversational tone." Booklist

Includes glossary

Delano, Marfe Ferguson
★ **Earth** in the hot seat; bulletins from a warming world. National Geographic 2009 63p il (Preserve our planet) $19.95; lib bdg $28.90
Grades: 5 6 7 8 **363.7**
1. Greenhouse effect 2. Climate -- Environmental aspects
ISBN 978-1-4263-0434-7; 1-4263-0434-X; 978-1-4263-0435-4 lib bdg; 1-4263-0435-8 lib bdg

LC 2008029317

"This book lays out . . . the evidence for global warming and the part that human activity plays in it. Five chapters lay out the signs and evidences of a warming world. . . . Subsequent chapters of the book are devoted to what humankind can expect in a warming world and steps that must be taken to avert catastrophe for humans and the planet. . . . The illustrative photos are fully up to National Geographic high standards. This [is a] fine book, reasonably priced and carefully researched." Voice Youth Advocates

Includes bibliographical references

Farrell, Courtney
Keeping water clean. Cherry Lake Pub. 2010 32p il (Save the planet) lib bdg $27.04
Grades: 3 4 5 6 **363.7**
1. Water pollution
ISBN 978-1-60279-659-1 lib bdg; 1-60279-659-9 lib bdg

Teaches young readers the importance of unpolluted water, and describes how to keep water clean by using gray water processes, conserving drinking water, and reducing overall pollution

"At the beginning of . . . [the] book, readers are given a mission and advised to be alert to the facts provided so that they can successfully answer the questions at the end. . . . Children are made to feel part of the process; suggestions for how they can become involved abound." SLJ

Includes glossary and bibliographical references

Geiger, Beth
Clean water. Roaring Brook Press 2009 40p il (Sally Ride science) pa $7.99
Grades: 5 6 7 8 **363.7**
1. Water supply 2. Water pollution
ISBN 978-1-59643-577-3 pa; 1-59643-577-1 pa

This is a "well-written, engaging book. . . . The [book']s best feature is the conversational tone that simply and clearly conveys important, and sometimes complicated, scientific concepts. Illustrations and layout are well done, and include colorful photographs and charts. Excellent." SLJ

Gore, Al
★ An **inconvenient** truth; the crisis of global warming. adapted for young readers by Jane O'Connor. rev ed.; Viking 2007 191p il map $23; pa $16
Grades: 5 6 7 8 **363.7**
1. Greenhouse effect 2. Climate -- Environmental aspects
ISBN 978-0-670-06271-3; 978-0-670-06272-0 pa
Adapted from the title for adults published 2006 by Rodale Press

This explains what global warming is, what causes it, and explains how to take action to stop this crisis.

This is illustrated with "easy-to-grasp graphics and revealing before-and-after photos. . . . O'Connor rephrases Gore's arguments in briefer, simpler language without compromising their flow." SLJ

Guiberson, Brenda Z.
★ **Earth** feeling the heat; illustrated by Chad Wallace. Henry Holt and Company 2010 un il map $16.99
Grades: K 1 2 3 **363.7**
1. Animals 2. Greenhouse effect 3. Climate -- Environmental aspects
ISBN 978-0-8050-7719-3; 0-8050-7719-7

LC 2009012219

"This handsome picture book shows the threat of global warming, one creature at a time. . . . On each double-page spread, the detailed oil paintings pair with rhythmic text. . . . An accompanying world map shows the habitat of each creature and emphasizes the sense of global connections among living beings, while a final page features detailed suggestions for kids to practice conservation in their daily lives." Booklist

Hanel, Rachael
Climate fever; stopping global warming. Compass Point Books 2010 64p il (Green generation) lib bdg $31.99; pa $6.95
Grades: 5 6 7 8 9 **363.7**
1. Greenhouse effect 2. Climate -- Environmental aspects
ISBN 978-0-7565-4246-7 lib bdg; 0-7565-4246-4 lib bdg; 978-0-7565-4291-7 pa; 0-7565-4291-X pa

LC 2009-11448

"The cover design, layout, and graphics feel hip and of the moment. The clear writing is easy to understand and includes many concrete examples of environmentally friendly practices. . . . [A] good choice[s] for both leisure reading and reports." SLJ

Includes glossary and bibliographical references

Hunter, Nick
How carbon footprints work; Nick Hunter. Gareth Stevens Publishing 2014 32 p. (Ecoworks) (library binding) $26.60
Grades: 3 4 5 **363.7**
1. Sustainability 2. Energy conservation 3. Environmental protection 4. Sustainable living
ISBN 1433995522; 1433995530; 9781433995521; 9781433995538

LC 2012277824

This book, by Nick Hunter, explains "what exactly is a carbon footprint. . . . Content . . . takes on climate change, vehicle emissions, and wasting electricity. Practical solutions to reducing readers' carbon footprints compliment social studies and science information that augment what they encounter in the classroom." (Publisher's note)

"Carbon footprint is a term few people knew a decade ago, and now it is used constantly. But what exactly does it mean? This title from the EcoWorks series gives kids a good understanding of the term, but more importantly it shows how each individual's carbon footprint affects the environment...Illustrated with stock color photos, the text is occasionally broken up by "Eco Facts" and other sidebars. A thought-provoking overview, and the good back matter will lead kids to more." Booklist

Includes bibliographical references (page 31) and index

Other titles include:

How a solar-powered home works

How community gardens work

How electric and hybrid cars work

How recycling works

How renewable energy works

Jakab, Cheryl

Waste management. Marshall Cavendish Benchmark 2010 32p il map (Environment in focus) lib bdg $28.50

Grades: 4 5 6   363.7

1. Refuse and refuse disposal

ISBN 978-1-60870-093-6; 1-60870-093-3

"The layout gives each topic the look of a file folder, with the first spread going to a case-study problem and the second going to a 'Toward a Sustainable Future' case-study solution. . . . Photos bring home the heartbreaking litter, human-waste treatment plants, etc." Booklist

Includes glossary

Jakubiak, David J.

What can we do about acid rain? PowerKids Press 2011 24p il (Protecting our planet) lib bdg $21.25; pa $8.25

Grades: 2 3 4   363.7

1. Acid rain

ISBN 9781448849840 lib bdg; 9781448851164 pa

LC 2010053329

This explains how acid rain forms, how it affects the environment, and what can be done about it.

"Every spread has a full-page, thoughtfully captioned color photograph. . . . School and public libraries will want [this title] to round out collections or as [an update] to replace older books." SLJ

Includes glossary and bibliographical references

What can we do about nuclear waste? PowerKids Press 2011 24p il (Protecting our planet) lib bdg $21.25; pa $8.25

Grades: 2 3 4   363.7

1. Nuclear engineering 2. Radioactive waste disposal

ISBN 978-1-4488-4983-3 lib bdg; 978-1-4488-5114-0 pa

LC 2010052216

This describes nuclear waste, how nuclear energy is used, how nuclear waste is stored, and how it affects the environment.

Includes glossary

What can we do about oil spills and ocean pollution? PowerKids Press 2011 24p il (Protecting our planet) lib bdg $21.25; pa $8.25

Grades: 2 3 4   363.7

1. Oil spills 2. Marine pollution

ISBN 978-1-4488-4982-6 lib bdg; 978-1-4488-5112-6 pa

LC 2010047319

This explains the importance of oceans, how they can be polluted, and the damage caused by oil spills.

Includes glossary

What can we do about ozone loss? PowerKids Press 2011 24p il (Protecting our planet) lib bdg $21.25; pa $8.25

Grades: 2 3 4   363.7

1. Pollution 2. Ozone layer 3. Greenhouse effect

ISBN 978-1-4488-4985-7 lib bdg; 978-1-4488-5118-8 pa

LC 2011000156

This explains the depletion of the ozone layer and its affect on the environment.

Includes glossary

Landau, Elaine

★ **Oil** spill! disaster in the Gulf of Mexico. Millbrook Press 2011 32p il lib bdg $25.26

Grades: 3 4 5   363.7

1. Oil spills 2. Gulf of Mexico oil spill, 2010

ISBN 978-0-7613-7485-5; 0-7613-7485-X

LC 2010029390

"Landau documents the mind-boggling scope of the 2010 oil spill in the Gulf of Mexico, and the urgent progression of measures taken to contain the calamity. . . . Throughout, Landau applies the clearsighted, nonalarmist tone of a veteran science writer but still manages to infuse the narrative with nearly the same urgency as an edge-of-your-seat disaster flick. Diagrams and photos present a revealing look at the fascinating science and technology behind deep-sea drilling and complex, one-step-forward/two steps back cleanup efforts." Booklist

Includes glossary and bibliographical references

Martin, Laura C.

Recycled crafts box; [by] Laura C. Martin. Storey Publishing 2004 88p il $19.95; pa $10.95

Grades: 3 4 5 6   363.7

1. Recycling 2. Handicraft

ISBN 1-58017-523-6; 1-58017-522-8 pa; 9781580175227

LC 2003-16703

Discusses recycling and provides information and instructions for making art projects from a variety of recycled materials

"Illustrated with cheerful cartoon drawings and color photos of the finished projects, and bolstered by many resource lists, this is a surprisingly attractive, substantive offering." Booklist

Minden, Cecilia

Reduce, reuse, and recycle. Cherry Lake Pub. 2010 32p il (Save the planet) lib bdg $27.07

Grades: 3 4 5 6   363.7

1. Recycling 2. Waste minimization 3. Conservation of natural resources

ISBN 978-1-60279-662-1 lib bdg; 1-60279-662-9 lib bdg

Presents tips for how to reduce the amount of garbage thrown away, from buying items that have less packaging at the store to precycling and making art from trash

"At the beginning of . . . [the] book, readers are given a mission and advised to be alert to the facts provided so that they can successfully answer the questions at the end. . . . Children are made to feel part of the process; suggestions for how they can become involved abound." SLJ

Includes glossary and bibliographical references

Morgan, Sally

Pollution. Cherrytree Books 2011 30p il (Helping our planet) lib bdg $28.50

Grades: 1 2 3

363.7

1. Pollution

ISBN 978-1-84234-607-5; 1-84234-607-5

LC 2010000036

This book "discusses activities that are harming the planet and how individuals can prevent or minimize their effects. . . . The [book features] large, full-color photos with one or two paragraphs of large-print text per page. 'Find Out More' boxes scattered throughout give additional facts with related websites and 'You Choose' boxes ask students questions regarding important choices they can make. . . . [This] well-designed [book] will be useful for reports and general interest." SLJ

Includes glossary

Waste and recycling. Cherrytree Books 2010 30p il (Helping our planet) lib bdg $28.50

Grades: 1 2 3

363.7

1. Recycling 2. Refuse and refuse disposal

ISBN 978-1-84234-608-2

LC 2010000037

This book "suggests how discarded items can be reduced, reused, and recycled. The [book features] large, full-color photos with one or two paragraphs of large-print text per page. 'Find Out More' boxes scattered throughout give additional facts with related websites and 'You Choose' boxes ask students questions regarding important choices they can make. . . . [This] well-designed [book] will be useful for reports and general interest." SLJ

Includes glossary

Morris, Neil

Global warming. World Almanac Library 2007 48p il (What if we do nothing?) lib bdg $22.95; pa $11.95

Grades: 5 6 7 8

363.7

1. Greenhouse effect 2. Climate -- Environmental aspects

ISBN 978-0-8368-7755-7 lib bdg; 0-8368-7755-1 lib bdg; 978-0-8368-155-4 pa; 0-8368-8155-9 pa

LC 2006-30444

This "boasts an attractive format, with large pages that allow room for pictures, excellent charts and graphs, as well as a thoughtful, clear discussion of the topic." Booklist

Includes bibliographical references

Nardo, Don

Climate crisis; the science of global warming. by Don Nardo. Compass Point Books 2009 47p il map (Headline science) lib bdg $27.93; pa $7.95

Grades: 5 6 7

363.7

1. Greenhouse effect 2. Climate -- Environmental aspects

ISBN 978-0-7565-3571-1 lib bdg; 0-7565-3571-9 lib bdg; 978-0-7565-3948-1 pa; 0-7565-3948-X pa

LC 2008-7259

"Color photos and graphics provide visual information; a timeline is helpful to find fast facts, and the Facthound Web site provides students with additional information." Libr Media Connect

Includes glossary and bibliographical references

Oil spill; disaster. Scholastic Press 2010 31p il pa $5.99

Grades: 4 5 6 7 8

363.7

1. Oil spills 2. Gulf of Mexico oil spill, 2010

ISBN 978-0-545-31776-4; 0-545-31776-2

Explores the immediate and future consequences of the Gulf of Mexico oil spill in April 2010, when the offshore oil rig Deepwater Horizon exploded, causing major environmental and economical damage along the Gulf coast of the United States.

"While text and color photographs convey the extent of the devastation to the Gulf, the book also highlights some innovative attempts to clean up oil spills and profiles two middle school students, who researched cleaning up oil in their own neighborhood." Publ Wkly

Parker, Steve, 1952-

Population. QEB Pub. 2010 32p il (QEB changes in . . .) lib bdg $28.50

Grades: 3 4 5 6

363.7

1. Human ecology 2. Human influence on nature

ISBN 978-1-59566-774-8 lib bdg; 1-59566-774-1 lib bdg

LC 2008-56070

"The information is presented in brief paragraphs and sidebars. Suggestions for kids to help improve the planet are sprinkled throughout. . . . Students will enjoy this appealing layout and the information can spark further research on the topic[s]. . . . Either digitally or on paper, students could make fantastic presentations using a similar design." Libr Media Connect

Includes glossary

Paul, Miranda

One plastic bag; Isatou Ceesay and the recycling women of the Gambia. by Miranda Paul; illustrated by Elizabeth Zunon. Millbrook Press 2015 32 p. color illustrations, color map

Grades: K 1 2 3 4

363.7

1. Plastics 2. Recycling 3. Wolof (African people) 4. Pollution -- Africa, West 5. Plastic bags -- Africa, West 6. Plastic bag craft -- Africa, West 7. Recycling (Waste, etc.) -- Africa, West

ISBN 1467716081; 9781467716086

LC 2014009382

In this children's book by Miranda Paul, "distressed by the problem of plastic-bag disposal, a Gambian woman organizes her neighbors to turn trash into treasure. When Isatou Ceesay first discovered plastic bags in the Gambia in West Africa, in the 1980s, they seemed wonderfully useful and sturdy. But in her village, they soon became a nuisance. . . . Her solution was to collect and clean used bags, cut them into strips and crochet the strips into useful plastic purses." (Kirkus Reviews)

"One woman's efforts to rid her Gambian village of trash sparks a recycling movement in this uplifting tale inspired by true events . . . Incorporating real plastic bags into her mixed-media collages, Zunon, who grew up in West Africa, juxtaposes the brown, dusty landscape against splashes of color and vibrant printed dresses and head coverings worn by the village women. A glossary and list of suggested reading are included." PW

Potts, Aiden

The **smash!** smash! truck; recycling as you've never heard it before. by Professor Potts. David Fickling Books 2009 un il $16.99; lib bdg $19.99

Grades: PreK K 1 2

363.7

1. Recycling

ISBN 978-0-385-75143-8; 0-385-75143-5; 978-0-385-75144-5 lib bdg; 0-385-75144-3 lib bdg

"What self-respecting glass bottle would want to be trapped in a trash dump for hundreds of thousands of years, when it could be transformed over and over again into new and exciting containers? Luckily, the Smash! Smash! Truck is on hand to speed up the recycling process, making things go round faster. Professor Potts takes us all the way back to the Big Bang to look at how the earth naturally recycles its resources and ends with a series of glorious smashes as a modern recycling truck is loaded and unloaded." (Publisher's note)

Rapp, Valerie

Protecting Earth's air quality; by Valerie Rapp. Lerner Publications 2009 72p il map (Saving our living Earth) lib bdg $30.60
Grades: 5 6 7 8   **363.7**

1. Air pollution
ISBN 978-0-8225-7558-0 lib bdg; 0-8225-7558-2 lib bdg

LC 2008-907

"Provides a thorough, interesting discussion of multiple aspects of [protecting Earth's air quality], including historical origins, the current situation, and potential solutions. . . . Photos from around the world accompany discussions. . . . [This is a] solid choice to replace outdated books." SLJ

Includes glossary and bibliographical references

Rockwell, Anne F.

★ **Why** are the ice caps melting? the dangers of global warming. Written by Anne Rockwell; illustrated by Paul Meisel. HarperCollins 2006 33p il (Let's-read-and-find-out science) $15.99; pa $4.99
Grades: K 1 2 3   **363.7**

1. Greenhouse effect 2. Climate -- Environmental aspects
ISBN 0-06-054669-7; 0-06-054671-9 pa

LC 2005-17972

Tells about the greenhouse effect, recycling, and what you can do to help fight global warming

"The information is detailed, but not overwhelming. . . . Colorful illustrations provide details that support the [text]." SLJ

Silverstein, Alvin

Smog, oil spills, sewage, and more; the yucky pollution book. by Alvin Silverstein, Virginia Silverstein, and Laura Silverstein Nunn; illustrated by Gerald Kelley. Enslow Publishers 2010 48p il (Yucky science) lib bdg $23.93
Grades: 3 4 5 6   **363.7**

1. Pollution 2. Environmental protection
ISBN 978-0-7660-3313-9 lib bdg; 0-7660-3313-9 lib bdg

LC 2009021274

"With conversational prose and zany, retro-gross illustrations, . . . [this volume provides] a painless intro to . . . pollution. Filthy air, polluted water, . . . nonbiodegradable landfills, asbestos, greenhouse gases, and the scourge of 'cow farts' are all here. . . . Kelley's art . . . is a perfect fit for the material, and 'Yikes!' sidebars keep things gregariously gross." Booklist

Simon, Seymour

★ **Global** warming. Collins 2010 31p il $17.99; lib bdg $18.89
Grades: 3 4 5   **363.7**

1. Greenhouse effect 2. Climate -- Environmental aspects
ISBN 978-0-06-114250-5; 0-06-114250-6; 978-0-06-114251-2 lib bdg; 0-06-114251-4 lib bdg

LC 2009001265

This takes "on the timely matter of climate change. Informative and noncondescending, this boils down large, complex issues into understandable concepts, even as it covers the range of current understanding on how we are impacting the planet. . . . Thoughtfully chosen full-page photos complement and reflect the text." Booklist

Includes glossary, bibliographical references and index

Wells, Robert E.

Polar bear, why is your world melting? Albert Whitman & Co. 2008 un il $16.99; pa $6.99

Grades: 1 2 3 4   **363.7**

1. Ice 2. Arctic regions 3. Greenhouse effect
ISBN 978-0-8075-6598-8; 0-8075-6598-9; 978-0-8075-6599-5 pa; 0-8075-6599-7 pa

LC 2008-01308

"Two children sail in a red research vessel through the pages of this clear and simple explanation of global warming. Colorful, cartoon drawings show the youngsters rescuing a mother polar bear and her two cubs by hauling them onto their boat. Then, beginning with an explanation of the sun's effect on the Earth's atmosphere, they pursue the reasons that the Arctic ice is melting. Without oversimplifying, Wells makes the large concepts of the Greenhouse Effect and the sources of CO_2 understandable for young children. . . . An excellent introduction to the topic." SLJ

363.72   Sanitation

Richmond, Benjamin

Where do garbage trucks go? and other questions about trash and recycling. by Ben Richmond. Sterling Pub Co Inc 2016 40 p. color illustrations $12.95
Grades: 3 4 5 6   **363.72**

1. Recycling (Waste, etc.)
ISBN 1454916249; 9781454916246

LC 2016427911

This book, by Ben Richmond, focuses on trash and recycling. "What is a landfill? What makes some garbage dangerous? Why it is good to recycle—and can we recycle water? Kids see the garbage truck all the time—but this entertaining and educational book will tell them what it does and where it goes, along with other facts about the trash we create and how it affects the environment." (Publisher's note)

"Answering questions about topics such as why garbage stinks, why recycling is good, and whether we can recycle food, this book is an informative introduction to the purpose of waste management and recycling." Horn Book

Includes bibliographical references and index

363.728   Wastes

Miller, Edward

Recycling day; Edward Miller. Holiday House 2014 32 p. color illustrations (hardcover) $16.95
Grades: PreK K 1 2 3   **363.728**

1. Compost -- Fiction 2. Landfills -- Fiction 3. Animals -- Fiction 4. Recycling -- fiction
ISBN 0823424197; 9780823424191

LC 2014001893

In this children's book, by Edward Miller, "so much garbage has piled up in the vacant lot that's home to a group of bugs that revolting rats are moving in and taking over. Luckily recycling day is almost here. Volunteers swoop in to tidy up this neighborhood eyesore. As they take the ant's old bottle and the grasshopper's cardboard box, the kids explain the processes of recycling paper, glass, plastic, and metal as well as how to compost." (Publisher's note)

363.738   Pollutants

Arnold, Caroline

A **warmer** world; from polar bears to butterflies, how global warming is changing lives. Caroline Arnold; illustrated by Jamie Hogan. Charlesbridge 2012 31 p.

Grades: 3 4 5   363.738
   1. Ecology 2. Wildlife 3. Climate change 4. Global warming 5.
Adaptation (Biology)
   ISBN 9781580892667

LC 2011000811

The focus of this book is how "[a] warmer world is the new reality for many animals and plants . . . and how they are reacting to climbing temperatures. . . . [Caroline] Arnold looks at the . . . impact of melting ice on polar bears and at the broadening range of Edith's checkerspot butterflies. . . . The speed of this change is leaving many species unable to adapt, and as many as a million species are feared to face extinction. A few might actually benefit from a wider habitable range, but often at a cost to other species. Combining general information on rising seas, melting ice caps, and warmer water with specific emphasis on individual animals such as loggerhead turtles, marmots, penguins, and walruses, this book offers students the opportunity to examine a natural world in flux." (School Libr J)

Bow, James
   Earth's climate change; carbon dioxide overload. James Bow. Crabtree Publishing Company 2016 32 p. illustrations paperback $8.95; library $27.60
Grades: 5 6 7 8   363.738
   1. Climate change 2. Global warming 3. Carbon dioxide
   ISBN 9780778720010; 9780778719786

LC 2015020964

Humans "live in an energy-rich age, in which we can turn on a light with the flick of a switch or drive anywhere by turning a key. But, our vehicles, factories, and power stations, which create the electricity needed to light and heat our buildings, pump carbon dioxide into Earth's atmosphere. Carbon dioxide overload from these human activities is making our planet hotter and hotter--and is causing the Earth's climate to change." (Publisher's note)

   Includes bibliographical references and index

Sneideman, Joshua
   Climate Change; Discover How It Impacts Spaceship Earth. by Joshua Sneideman and Erin Twamley; illustrated by Mike Crosier. Nomad Press 2015 128 p. color illustrations, color map $22.95
Grades: 4 5 6 7   363.738
   1. Climate change 2. Earth sciences 3. Science projects
   ISBN 1619302691; 9781619302693

In this book on climate change, by Joshua Sneideman and Erin Twamley, illustrated by Mike Crosier, "young readers examine real studies concerning planetary science, Arctic ice bubbles, and migratory patterns. Kids explore the history of human impact from the Industrial Revolution to our modern-day technology, as well as the innovations underway around the world to address global climate change." (Publisher's note)

"This installment of the well-known series encourages students to examine the timely subject of climate change. The volume is full of questions, words to know, primary sources, and fun-filled learning activities. The introductory chapter reminds readers of the importance of taking care of the planet. . . . The text and activities work together to remind students that the future is in their hands and they can be a part of the solution." SLJ

364   Criminology

Somervill, Barbara A.
   Graphing crime. Raintree 2010 32p il (Real world data) $28.21; pa $7.99

Grades: 4 5 6 7   364
   1. Crime 2. Statistics 3. Graphic methods
   ISBN 978-1-4329-2623-6; 1-4329-2623-3; 978-1-4329-2632-8 pa; 1-4329-2632-2 pa

LC 2009001292

This "discusses juvenile offenders, drug money, terrorism, and more, and teaches readers how to evaluate statistics in the various charts, such as the difference between crimes committed and crimes reported, or between total numbers and rate per population. . . . The clear design, with lots of full-color photos and sidebars, will encourage browsers as much as the up-to-date examples and the clear directions for remaining 'chart smart.'" Booklist

   Includes glossary and bibliographical references

364.15   Offenses against the person

Schroeder, Andreas
   Robbers! true stories of the world's most notorious thieves. by Andreas Schroeder, illustrated by Remy Simard. Annick Press 2012 166 p. $21.95
Grades: 4 5 6   364.15
   1. Picture books for children 2. Crime 3. Thieves
   ISBN 155451441X; 9781554514410

This juvenile book, by Andreas Schroeder, illustrated by Remy Simard, offers true stories of historical thieves. In it accounts are given for "eight cunning master thieves, including master-of-disguise Willie Sutton, who robbed banks in costume, . . . D. B. Cooper, who hijacked a plane, demanded $200,000, and parachuted to safety, . . . [and] London's Great Train Robbers, who held up a moving train to pull off one of the largest ever hauls of banknotes." (Publisher's note)

364.16   Offenses against property

Guillain, Charlotte
   Great art thefts; by Charlotte Guillain. Capstone Raintree 2013 48 p. col. ill. (Treasure hunters) (library) $29.33; (paperback) $8.99
Grades: 5 6 7 8   364.16
   1. Theft -- History 2. Art thefts
   ISBN 1410949583; 9781410949516; 9781410949585

LC 2012012759

This book by Charlotte Guillain, part of the Treasure Hunters series, looks at art thefts. "After . . . introductions that lay foundations so children will understand why thieves might want to steal art or treasure hunters take such risks, each volume contains chapters that follow the discovery and/or quests for objects such as 'Roman Riches' or locations such as the legendary city of Troy." (School Library Journal)

   Includes bibliographical references and index.

368.3   Old-age insurance and insurance against death, illness, injury

Lynette, Rachel
   What to do when your family can't afford healthcare. PowerKids Press 2010 24p il (Let's work it out) $21.25; pa $8.25
Grades: 2 3 4   368.3
   1. Medicaid 2. Health insurance
   ISBN 978-1-4358-9342-9; 1-4358-9342-5; 978-1-4358-9772-4 pa; 1-4358-9772-2 pa

This book explains what healthcare and insurance are and why they are so crucial. It also explains the many different low-cost insurance options that are available so that every family can get the care they need.

"Full-page color photographs appear opposite the [narrative], depicting multicultural children, parents, grandparents, social workers, and others, whose demeanors match the hopeful tone of the [title]. This . . . will help promote empathy and understanding for the plight of others and is a key purchase." SLJ

Includes glossary

369.463   Girl Scouts and Girl Guides

Corey, Shana
   Here come the Girl Scouts! by Shana Corey; illustrated by Hadley Hooper. Scholastic Press 2012 40 p.
Grades: 2 3 4   **369.463**
  1. Girl Scouts -- History 2. Women -- United States -- Biography 3. Girl Scouts of the United States of America -- History
ISBN 0545342783; 9780545342780

                                LC 2011008690

This book, a "celebration of the life of [Juliette] Low, founder of the Girl Scouts, reveals a gutsy, active girl growing up in Savannah, Ga., at a time when "proper young ladies were supposed to be dainty and delicate." Low craved 'adventure and excitement,' and, as an adult, she traveled extensively and decided that she 'wanted to be useful, to make a difference in the world.' . . . [S]he launched the Girl Scouts and, at an inaugural meeting, told the girls what to expect: 'They'd hike and camp and swim! They'd do good deeds. They'd learn to tie knots and survive in the wilderness and even save lives!' [Shana Corey] . . . conveys Low's gumption and optimism, and . . . quotations from the first Girl Scout handbook impart . . . tenets for living and scouting." (Publishers Weekly)

Includes bibliographical references

370   Education

A **school** like mine; a celebration of schools around the world. 2nd edition DK Publishing 2016 77 p. color illustrations, color map hbk $19.99
Grades: 3 4 5 6   **370**
  1. Schools 2. Children
ISBN 1465451005; 9781465451002

                                LC 2016498604

Introduces children from around the world and discusses where they live, how they play, and what their schools are like.

370.1   Philosophy and theory, education for specific objectives, educational psychology

Barker, Dan
   Maybe right, maybe wrong; a guide for young thinkers. by Dan Barker; illustrated by Brian Strassburg. Prometheus Bks. 1992 76p il pa $17.98
Grades: 4 5 6   **370.1**
  1. Human rights 2. Conduct of life 3. Moral education
ISBN 978-0-87975-731-1 pa; 0-87975-731-0 pa

                                LC 92-416

Discusses learning right from wrong, stressing such aspects as the difference between rules and principles and the importance of an individual's rights

370.71   Education

Growing schools; librarians as professional developers. Debbie Abilock, Kristin Fontichiaro, and Violet H. Harada, editors. Libraries Unlimited 2012 390 p. (pbk.) $45
Grades: Professional   **370.71**
  1. Teachers -- Training 2. Educational technology 3. School libraries -- Information technology 4. Libraries and teachers -- United States -- Case studies 5. Teachers -- Training of -- United States -- Case studies 6. Educational technology -- Study and teaching -- Case studies 7. Information technology -- Study and teaching -- Case studies 8. Technological literacy -- Study and teaching -- Case studies 9. Teachers -- In-service training -- United States -- Case studies 10. School librarian participation in curriculum planning -- Case studies 11. Academic libraries -- Relations with faculty and curriculum -- Case studies
ISBN 1610690419; 9781610690416

                              LC 2012016191

In this book, "editors [Debbie] Abilock, [Kristin] Fontichiaro, and [Violet H.] Harada examine ways school librarians can act as professional developers within their pedagogical communities. Thirty-two articles in sixteen thematic chapters offer real-world examples of how teacher librarians have leveraged their skills and expertise to provide learning experiences for other teachers, community members, and students." (Voice of Youth Advocates)

"This book promotes the role of the school librarian as a leader in school, district, and online professional development in 16 essays written by school librarians, school district personnel, and professors...A rich smorgasbord of ideas, this book would be invaluable for an individual librarian looking to become a professional development leader, and for district librarians to use in planning and implementing meaningful district-wide professional development." (Library Media Connection)

Includes bibliographical references and index

McKeown, Rosalyn
   Into the classroom; a practical guide for starting student teaching. Rosalyn McKeown. University of Tennessee Press 2011 xv, 165 p.p (pbk.) $14.95
Grades: Adult Professional   **370.71**
  1. Teaching 2. Student teaching 3. Student teaching -- United States
ISBN 1572338164; 9781572338166

                              LC 2011011282

This book offers suggestions to those "just starting out in a secondary school classroom. . . . After exploring the pitfalls of inexperience and providing . . . guidance on maintaining order in the classroom, [Rosalyn] McKeown focuses on teaching skills. She advises readers on writing objectives and lesson plans, creating interesting ways to start and end class, introducing variety into the classroom, lecturing, asking meaningful questions, and using visual aids." (Amazon.com)

Includes bibliographical references and index.

370.9   History, geographic treatment, biography

Aillaud, Cindy Lou
   ★ **Recess** at 20 below. Alaska Northwest Books 2005 un il hardcover o.p. pa $8.95
Grades: K 1 2 3   **370.9**
  1. Schools -- Alaska
ISBN 0-88240-604-3; 0-88240-609-4 pa

"Aillaud, who wrote the text and took the photos here, teaches elementary physical education in Delta Junction, Alaska, a town at the end of the Alaska Highway, above the Arctic Circle. By focusing on one school activity—outdoor recess . . . she demonstrates how cold things get and how kids deal with it and still have plenty of fun. . . . Twenty-five color photographs capture marvelous details." Booklist

Ruurs, Margriet

My school in the rain forest; how children attend school around the world. Boyds Mills Press 2009 31p il map $17.95

Grades: 1 2 3 4 5 **370.9**

1. Schools 2. Students

ISBN 978-1-59078-601-7; 1-59078-601-7

LC 2009000366

"The book introduces 13 schools, including home schools in Australia and the U.S., a floating school on a Cambodian lake, a village school in Guatemala, a monastery school in Myanmar, and one operated by a global charity. Each double-page spread includes several paragraphs of text, four color photos, and fact box with information about the country, a drawing of its flag, and a map. . . . The book as a whole gives a good sense of the vastly different educational experiences of children around the world." Booklist

370.92 Education biography

Asim, Jabari

★ Fifty cents and a dream; by Jabari Asim; illustrated by Bryan Collier. Little, Brown and Co. 2012 48 p. $16.99

Grades: 2 3 4 **370.92**

1. Biography 2. United States -- History 3. Education -- United States -- History 4. African Americans -- Biography 5. Educators -- United States -- Biography

ISBN 0316086576; 9780316086578

LC 2012007265

Author Jabari Asim tells the story of Booker T. Washington. "Born into slavery, young Booker T. Washington could only dream of learning to read and write. After emancipation, Booker began a five-hundred-mile journey, mostly on foot, to Hampton Institute, taking his first of many steps towards a college degree. When he arrived, he had just fifty cents in his pocket and a dream about to come true." (Publisher's note)

McKissack, Fredrick, 1939-2013

Mary McLeod Bethune; woman of courage. Patricia and Frederick McKissack. Enslow Publishers 2013 24 p. (Famous African Americans) (library) $21.26

Grades: 1 2 3 **370.92**

1. African American women 2. African Americans -- Education 3. Teachers -- United States -- Biography 4. African American women educators -- Biography 5. African American women social reformers -- Biography

ISBN 0766041034; 9780766041035

LC 2012007620

This book, part of the Famous African Americans series, looks at Mary McLeod Bethune. She was "her parents' fifteenth child but the first born free. Determined to read the family Bible, she went to school, then college, and then, with just $1.50 in her pocket, opened the first school for black girls in Daytona Beach, Florida." (Booklist)

371 Schools and their activities; special education

Guillain, Charlotte

My first day at a new school. Heinemann Library 2011 24p il (Growing up) lib bdg $22; pa $6.49

Grades: PreK K 1 2 **371**

1. Schools

ISBN 978-1-4329-4796-5 lib bdg; 1-4329-4796-6 lib bdg; 978-1-4329-4806-1 pa; 1-4329-4806-7 pa

LC 2010024189

This book examines a "common, often scary [event] in children's lives and [guides] readers through [it] step-by-step. The [author discusses] the who, what, and why of [the] experience. . . . By confronting . . . fears head-on, children will feel 'in the know' and be prepared to experience [this first]. The text—two sentences per page in a large font and placed on white space—is accompanied by large color photos of children, families, and adults of a variety of ethnic backgrounds. [The] volume includes boldface vocabulary words, a picture glossary, and dos and don'ts." SLJ

Includes glossary and bibliographical references

Hughes, Susan

Off to class; incredible and unusual schools around the world. Owlkids Books 2011 64p il map $22.95; pa $12.95

Grades: 2 3 4 5 **371**

1. Schools 2. Students

ISBN 978-1-926818-85-6; 1-926818-85-7; 978-1-926818-86-3 pa; 1-926818-86-5 pa

"This book examines innovative schools around the world, the educators who brought them about, and the students who attend them. The book has three chapters. 'Working with the Environment' features boat schools, rainforest schools, and tent schools; 'No School? No Way!,' focuses on educational opportunities for disenfranchised populations; and 'One Size Doesn't Fit All' is about unconventional programs in nontraditional settings. Each spread is devoted to one school, with five to seven paragraphs of text, vivid full-color photographs, and a map indicating its general area of the world. The strong emphasis on humanitarianism will move, excite, and inspire those reading about Hurricane Katrina survivors planting gardens, homeless children in India hearing stories on a train platform, and Maasai girls going to school instead of being sold into marriage." SLJ

371.1 Schools and their activities

Harada, Violet H.

Inquiry learning through librarian-teacher partnerships; [by] Violet H. Harada and Joan M. Yoshina. Linworth Pub. 2004 172p il pa $39.95

Grades: Adult Professional **371.1**

1. Teaching teams 2. School libraries

ISBN 1-58683-134-8

LC 2004-662

"The authors describe what happens in an inquiry-based classroom and library media center and show teachers/librarians how to develop a curriculum that incorporates essential questions and important habits of mind, all aligned with content standards. . . . The volume contains everything a teacher-librarian team would need to create, teach, research, and assess major interdisciplinary units." SLJ

Includes bibliographical references

Houston, Gloria

My great-aunt Arizona; illustrated by Susan Condie Lamb. HarperCollins Pubs. 1992 un il $15.99; pa $6.99

Grades: K 1 2 3 **371.1**

1. Teachers 2. Appalachian region

ISBN 0-06-022606-4; 0-06-022607-2 lib bdg; 0-06-443374-9 pa

LC 90-44112

"The pleasant, conversational rhythm of the prose, the unobtrusive use of repetition, and the ability to sum up the unique quality of a life in a few telling phrases give the writing its substance. . . . Sunny and lively, the watercolor paintings have a naive quality that suits the story well." Booklist

Kenney, Karen Latchana

Teachers at work; by Karen L. Kenney; illustrated by Brian Caleb Dumm; content consultant, Judith Stepan-Norris. Magic Wagon 2009 32p il (Meet your community workers!) lib bdg $18.95

Grades: K 1 2 3   **371.1**

1. Teachers 2. Vocational guidance

ISBN 978-1-60270-653-8 lib bdg; 1-60270-653-0 lib bdg

LC 2009-2395

This book about teachers has "an uncluttered layout and consistent organization. . . . Chapter headings such as 'Problems on the Job,' and 'Technology at Work,' and 'Special Skills and Training' make it easy to pinpoint specific information." SLJ

Includes glossary

371.3   Methods of instruction and study

Fox, Janet S.

Get organized without losing it; by Janet S. Fox; edited by Pamela Espeland. Free Spirit Pub. 2006 105p il (Laugh & learn) pa $8.95

Grades: 5 6 7 8   **371.3**

1. Life skills 2. Study skills 3. Time management

ISBN 978-1-57542-193-3 pa; 1-57542-193-3 pa

LC 2005032809

"In this handbook for students, Fox uses humor to provide practical, easy-to-follow ideas for organizing desks, backpacks, and lockers; managing time for homework and after school activities; planning long-term projects; and taking better notes. . . . Fox writes in a conversational style. . . . Humorous illustrations complement the text." Voice Youth Advocates

Includes bibliographical references

Green, Julie

Write it down. Cherry Lake Pub. 2010 32p il (Super smart information strategies) lib bdg $27.07

Grades: 3 4 5 6   **371.3**

1. Note-taking

ISBN 978-1-60279-645-4 lib bdg; 1-60279-645-9 lib bdg

LC 2009024741

"The appealing layout includes manageable paragraphs, a variety of engaging illustrations, and examples that clearly guide readers through each topic. . . . Effective note taking and highlighting are the focus of [this book], but the book also suggests using sticky notes and creating diagrams and charts." SLJ

Includes glossary and bibliographical references

Kraus, Jeanne

Annie's plan; taking charge of schoolwork and homework. written by Jeanne Kraus; illustrated by Charles Beyl. Magination Press 2007 47p il $14.95; pa $8.95

Grades: 2 3 4 5   **371.3**

1. Homework 2. Study skills 3. Attention deficit disorder

ISBN 978-1-59147-481-4; 1-59147-481-7; 978-1-59147-482-1 pa; 1-59147-482-5 pa

LC 2006009948

"Annie is smart but she just can't stay focused on anything so she is always behind in class. With the help of her parents and teacher, she learns how to organize her work and is given other tips for completing her assignments. The book offers 10 easy-to-follow steps that begin with a clean, organized desk at school and a quiet, organized work space at home, and end with a signed reward contract. . . . Comical color illustrations and a conversational tone explain that a youngster with ADHD is neither dumb nor an incurable behavioral problem. . . . An extensive note for adults is included. This is an excellent resource for school libraries, professional collections, and parenting collections, and a great shared read for parent and child." SLJ

November, Alan C.

Empowering students with technology; 2nd ed.; Corwin Press 2010 115p il pa $25.95

Grades: Adult Professional   **371.3**

1. Internet in education 2. Computer-assisted instruction

ISBN 978-1-4129-7425-7; 1-4129-7425-9

LC 2009-43649

First published 2001 by Skylight Professional Development

"Discusses the relationship of technology to today's learning environment and the potential for technology to encourage students to learn collaboratively. This . . . edition emphasizes current topics such as information literacy, global connectivity, and the educational applications of utilities such as digital cameras and cell phones. The book's usefulness is as a reasource for teachers and librarians to consult in creating, planning, and assisting with school projects in all subjects." Libr Media Connect

Includes bibliographical references

Richardson, Will

Blogs, wikis, podcasts, and other powerful Web tools for classrooms; 3rd ed.; Corwin 2010 171p il pa $31.95

Grades: Adult Professional   **371.3**

1. Weblogs 2. Podcasting 3. Internet in education 4. Online social networks 5. Wikis (Computer science) 6. Teaching -- Aids and devices

ISBN 978-1-4129-7747-0; 1-4129-7747-9

LC 2009-51376

First published 2006

"The book is well-written and comprehensive. The author's engaging writing style will instill confidence in readers that they will be able to easily integrate the same technologies with the same results in their classrooms. Readers will not want to stop reading this eye-opening and inspirational book. It is jam-packed with proven ideas, and individuals, especially educators, will want to try out these technologies." Libr Media Connect

Includes bibliographical references

Superbrain; the insider's guide to getting smart. Toronto Public Library; art by Dave Whamond. Firefly Books Ltd 2015 72 p. color illustrations $19.95

Grades: 4 5 6 7   **371.3**

1. Study skills

ISBN 1554517354; 9781554517350

This book presents "a guide to research practices and intellectual property for students in the middle-grade set. Continuing the superhero theme evinced in the title, the book presents many of the explanations and tips about the appropriate use of print and Internet sources. . . . Sidebars offer portraits of diverse young people who used good research practices to change their own and others' lives." (Booklist)

Teehan, Kay

Wikis; the educator's power tool. Linworth 2010 78p il pa $30

Grades: Adult Professional   **371.3**

1. Internet in education 2. Electronic encyclopedias 3. Wikis

(Computer science) 4. Computer-assisted instruction
ISBN 978-1-58683-530-9 pa; 1-58683-530-0 pa; 978-1-58683-531-6 e-book; 1-58683-531-9 e-book

LC 2010020285

"This book breaks down three types of wikis: library wikis, which are usually content and link-to-content focused; reciprocal wikis, which are collaborative in nature; and student-produced wikis that are developed to share projects and research. . . . There is also a wiki to complement the guidelines in the book. This is a simple to use quick-start guide and a great resource for school technology teachers and librarians." Libr Media Connect

Includes bibliographical references

371.5 School discipline and related activities

Beaudoin, Marie-Nathalie
Responding to the culture of bullying and disrespect; new perspectives on collaboration, compassion, and responsibility. [by] Marie-Nathalie Beaudoin, Maureen Taylor. rev 2nd ed.; Corwin Press 2009 281p il $76.95; pa $36.95
Grades: Adult Professional   371.5
1. Bullies 2. School discipline
ISBN 978-1-4129-6853-9; 1-4129-6853-4; 978-1-4129-6854-6 pa; 1-4129-6854-2 pa

LC 2008-55933

First published 2004 with title: Breaking the culture of bullying and disrespect

"This profound resource explores the behaviors that cultivate a culture of bullying and disrespect. . . . Concrete solutions to issues are offered, and the authors make sure to load this title with practical suggestions for affecting change. They delve into ways to work directly with young people to better address their concerns. . . . This purchase is essential for any educator, counselor, or parent. It should be a staple of the school library reference collection because the information provided should be used daily. It will be a title that can be referenced for years to come and will help with adults struggling to overcome bullying." Voice Youth Advocates

Includes glossary and bibliographical references

Bott, C. J.
More bullies in more books. Scarecrow Press 2009 197p il pa $35
Grades: Adult Professional   371.5
1. Bullies 2. Reference books 3. Children's literature -- Bibliography 4. Young adult literature -- Bibliography
ISBN 978-0-8108-6654-6 pa; 0-8108-6654-4 pa

LC 2009-923

This "offers more than 350 annotated titles published since 2000 to create awareness of the many types of harassment and bullying. . . . Although the text is written for educators and librarians for use in classroom settings, the information is equally helpful for parents, caregivers, and public librarians." SLJ

Includes bibliographical references

★ **Bully;** an action plan for teachers and parents to combat the bullying crisis. edited by Lee Hirsch and Cynthia Lowen; with Dina Santorelli. Perseus Books Group 2012 viii, 295 p.p ill. $15.99
Grades: Adult Professional   371.5
1. Bullies 2. Bullying -- Prevention 3. Cyberbullying -- Prevention 4. Bullying in schools -- Prevention
ISBN 1602861846; 1602861854; 9781602861848; 9781602861855

LC 2012289039

"This companion book to the documentary film Bully was edited by filmmaker [Lee]Hirsch and writer/producer [Cynthia] Lowen, with contributing chapters by a number of celebrities, authors, experts, government officials, and educators. Part homage to the film, part resource, the book interweaves the stories of children who have been bullied with practical information and advice for parents and other readers." (Publishers Weekly)

Includes bibliographical references (p. 281-289) and index

Myers, Jill J.
Responding to cyber bullying; an action tool for school leaders. [by] Jill J. Myers, Donna S. McCaw, Leaunda S. Hemphill. Corwin Press 2011 195p pa $33.95
Grades: Adult Professional   371.5
1. Bullies 2. Cyberbullying 3. School violence
ISBN 978-1-4129-9484-2; 1-4129-9484-5

LC 2010040679

"The book's introduction addresses the nature of 'digital generation' students. The problem of cyberbullying is introduced in light of the generational reality. The book covers decisions made to resolve real-life situations, practical principles about censorship, and the capacity and limitations of school authority. Included is a matrix that serves as a decision-making tool for administration. This resource is a healthy blend of the theoretical and practical." Libr Media Connect

Includes bibliographical references

371.6 Physical plant; materials management

Gaarder-Juntti, Oona
What in the world is a green school? ABDO Pub. Company 2011 24p il (Going green) lib bdg $24.21
Grades: 1 2 3 4   371.6
1. School buildings 2. Environmental protection
ISBN 978-1-61613-190-6 lib bdg; 1-61613-190-X lib bdg

LC 2010004324

"The lively layout design, featuring colorful headings, short paragraphs, and attractive photographs, has a scrapbook-like quality. . . . [The title explains] how all our choices require energy and resources, and encourage readers to make changes in their lifestyles. . . . [This] . . . will inspire and empower readers to make a difference." SLJ

Includes glossary and bibliographical references

371.7 Student welfare

Curtis, Andrea
What's for lunch? How schoolchildren eat around the world. Andrea Curtis; Yvonne Duivenvoorden. Red Deer Press 2012 40 p. $12.95
Grades: 3 4 5   371.7
1. School children -- Food
ISBN 0889954828; 9780889954823

This book by Andrea Curtis and Yvonne Duivenvoorden "reveals the variety and inequality to be found in the food consumed by young people in typical school lunches from thirteen countries around the world, including Japan, Kenya, Russia, United States, Canada, Mexico, Brazil and Afghanistan. In some countries, the meals are nutritious and well-balanced. In others they barely satisfy basic nutrition standards." (Publisher's note)

371.82　Specific groups of students; schools for specific groups of students

Finkelstein, Norman H.

Schools of hope; the Rosenwald Schools of the American South. Norman H. Finkelstein. Calkins Creek 2014 80 p. illustrations $16.95

Grades: 5 6 7 8　　　　　　　　　　　　　**371.82**

1. African Americans -- History 2. African Americans -- Education

ISBN 1590788419; 9781590788417

LC 2013951346

"When Booker T. Washington, the famed African American educator, asked Julius Rosenwald, the wealthy president of Sears, Roebuck and Company and noted philanthropist, to help him build well-designed and fully equipped schools for black children, the face of education in the South changed for the better. . . . In this inspiring story, noted nonfiction writer Norman H. Finkelstein spotlights one man's legacy and the power of community action." (Publisher's note)

"This straightforward narrative is substantially supported with many photographs of the period, especially of the schools and the students. Source notes, a bibliography (which could have used a few more titles for the target readership), a list of websites, an index and picture credits add to its authenticity. Clean layout and design augment a quality introduction to an important chapter in the history of American education." -Kirkus

Jordan-Fenton, Christy

When I was eight; Christy Jordan-Fenton, Margaret Pokiak-Fenton, illustrated by Gabrielle Grimard. Annick Press 2013 32 p. (reinforced) $21.95

Grades: 1 2 3 4　　　　　　　　　　　　　**371.82**

1. Girls -- Education 2. Inuit -- Biography

ISBN 1554514916; 9781554514915

In this children's book, by Christy Jordan-Fenton, Margaret Pokiak-Fenton, "Olemaun is eight and knows a lot of things. But she does not know how to read. She must travel to the outsiders' school to learn. . . . The nuns at the school take her Inuit name and call her Margaret. . . . Margaret's tenacious character draws the attention of a black-cloaked nun who tries to break her spirit at every turn. But she is more determined than ever to read." (Publisher's note)

Marx, Trish

Kindergarten day USA and China; a flip-me-over book. by Trish Marx and Ellen B. Senisi. Charlesbridge 2010 un il $16.95; pa $7.95

Grades: PreK K 1　　　　　　　　　　　　**371.82**

1. Kindergarten 2. Schools -- China 3. Schools -- United States

ISBN 978-1-58089-219-3; 1-58089-219-1; 978-1-58089-220-9 pa; 1-58089-220-5 pa

"Half of this book narrates a day at a kindergarten in Schenectady, NY; when flipped, it details a day with Chinese children in Beijing. Although there are some differences between the two classes, the book focuses on illustrating their similarities. . . . Large, bright photographs and a limited number of words per page make this a good choice for storytime." SLJ

Mortenson, Greg

Listen to the wind; the story of Dr. Greg and Three Cups of Tea. by Greg Mortenson and Susan L. Roth; collages by Susan L. Roth. Dial Books for Young Readers 2009 un il $16.99

Grades: K 1 2 3　　　　　　　　　　　　　**371.82**

1. Humanitarian intervention 2. Schools -- Pakistan

ISBN 978-0-8037-3058-8; 0-8037-3058-6

LC 2008-12268

Originally published as a nonfiction memoir, Three Cups of Tea, upon which this book is based, was later accused of being fabricated all or in part.

Roth "pairs the words with her signature mixed-media collage work . . . using scraps of cloth along with a variety of papers. Her work has a welcoming, tactile dimension." Publ Wkly

Includes bibliographical references

Winter, Jeanette

★ Nasreen's secret school; a true story from Afghanistan. Beach Lane Books 2009 un il $16.99

Grades: 2 3 4　　　　　　　　　　　　　**371.82**

1. Girls -- Education 2. Schools -- Afghanistan 3. Afghanistan -- Social conditions

ISBN 978-1-4169-9437-4; 1-4169-9437-8

LC 2009-08285

"This story begins with an author's note that succinctly explains the drastic changes that occurred when the Taliban came to power in Afghanistan in 1996. The focus is primarily on the regime's impact on women, who were no longer allowed to attend school or leave home without a male chaperone, and had to cover their heads and bodies with a burqa. After Nasreen's parents disappeared, the child neither spoke nor smiled. Her grandmother, the story's narrator, took her to a secret school, where she slowly discovered a world of art, literature, and history obscured by the harsh prohibitions of the Taliban. . . . Winter manages to achieve that delicate balance that is respectful of the seriousness of the experience, yet presents it in a way that is appropriate for young children. Winter's acrylic paintings make effective use of color. . . . This is an important book that makes events in a faraway place immediate and real." SLJ

371.9　Special education

Lauren, Jill

That's like me! stories about amazing people with learning differences. foreword by Jerry Pinkney. Star Bright Books 2009 un il $17.95; pa $7.95

Grades: 3 4 5　　　　　　　　　　　　　**371.9**

1. Learning disabilities

ISBN 978-1-59572-207-2; 1-59572-207-6; 978-1-59572-208-9 pa; 1-59572-208-4 pa

LC 2009028647

"This colorful book spotlights people of different ages, backgrounds, and interests who have coped with learning disabilities and succeeded in their chosen fields. . . . Each entry includes several photos showing the person at different ages. A good resource for encouraging children with learning disabilities." Booklist

Includes bibliographical references

Stanley, Jerry

★ Children of the Dust Bowl; the true story of the school at Weedpatch Camp. Crown 1992 85p il map hardcover o.p. pa $9.95

Grades: 5 6 7 8　　　　　　　　　　　　　**371.9**

1. Migrant labor 2. Great Depression, 1929-1939 3. Education -- Social aspects

ISBN 0-517-88094-6; 0-517-58782-3 pa

LC 92-393

Describes the plight of the migrant workers who traveled from the Dust Bowl to California during the Depression and were forced to live in a federal labor camp and discusses the school that was built for their children

"Stanley's text is a compelling document. . . . The story is inspiring and disturbing, and Stanley has recorded the details with passion and dignity." Booklist

Includes bibliographical references

371.91 Students with physical disabilities

Hauser, Peter C.

★ **How** deaf children learn; what parents and teachers need to know. Marc Marschark Peter C. Hauser. Oxford University Press 2012 156 p. $26.50

Grades: Adult Professional   **371.91**

1. Teaching 2. Deaf children 3. Elementary education 4. Deaf -- Education 5. Deaf -- Means of communication

ISBN 0195389751; 9780195389753

LC 2011012553

This book is "about teaching deaf children. Written primarily for parents and teachers of deaf or hard-of-hearing children, this work covers general information about their education, gives insights into their cognitive development, and provides steps to their school success. The authors also discuss issues such as the value of cochlear implants and the debate over signing vs. speaking." (Library Journal)

Includes bibliographical references.

372 Specific levels of education

Barber, Nicola

First day of school. PowerKids Press 2009 24p il (The big day!) lib bdg $21.25; pa $8.25

Grades: PreK K 1   **372**

1. Schools

ISBN 978-1-4358-2839-1 lib bdg; 1-4358-2839-9 lib bdg; 978-1-4358-2895-7 pa; 1-4358-2895-X pa

LC 2008025816

"Children in kindergarten will enjoy [this book] as [a read-aloud] . . . while those at the end of first grade will be able to read [it] independently. The writing is straightforward and reassuring, and the content provides a realistic view of what youngsters might experience in [school]. . . .The author discusses the activities of a typical day as well as feelings of sadness or loneliness that may occur." SLJ

Includes bibliographical references

Brooks-Young, Susan

Teaching with the tools kids really use; learning with Web and mobile technologies. Corwin 2010 137p pa $26.95

Grades: Adult Professional   **372**

1. Web 2.0 2. Teachers -- Training

ISBN 978-1-4129-7275-8 pa; 1-4129-7275-2 pa

LC 2009-43856

"In this book, we see how technology can be used, but we also see the reponsibility of the educator to make sure it is done appropriately, so 21st-century skills are addressed. The author addresses technologies and applications, and also discusses their ethical uses and how to think ahead to make adjustments for the future. . . . This book will be incredibly useful for those who are unsure about Web 2.0 tools, want to explore their possibilities, and would like to educate themselves further about usage in their own schools." Libr Media Connect

Includes bibliographical references

Carlow, Regina

Exploring the connection between children's literature and music. Libraries Unlimited 2008 124p il pa $30

Grades: Adult Professional   **372**

1. Music -- Study and teaching 2. Children's literature -- Bibliography

ISBN 978-1-59158-439-1 pa; 1-59158-439-6 pa; 9780313363559

LC 2007-40134

"Carlow sees music as part of developmental human activity and issues a plea to introduce it as direct participation. . . . This collection of methods and lessons encourages adults to broaden the possibilities of interacting with music, thereby using it to introduce young children to language, literature, and culture. Text is divided into chapters on singing and other ways to be musical. . . . The succeeding chapters are devoted to specific grade levels. . . . Each chapter includes an explanation of methods appropriate for the age group, followed by numerous lesson ideas for classrooms. The organization of this book makes it a solid addition to enhance curriculum materials." SLJ

Includes bibliographical references

Gates, Pamela

Cultural Journeys; Multicultural Literature for Elementary and Middle School Students. Rowman & Littlefield Pub Inc 2010 258 p. (paperback) $29.95

Grades: Adult Professional   **372**

1. Best books 2. Multicultural literature

ISBN 144220687X; 9781442206878

This book looks at multicultural literature for elementary and middle school students. The first chapter asks "the question of 'why.' Why use multicultural literature? . . . The 'why' is further developed as the chapter continues with a definition of multicultural literature." The seventh chapter looks at "works that challenge stereotypes and go beyond the common one-dimensional diversity theme." (Alberta Journal of Educational Research)

Libresco, Andrea S.

Every book is a social studies book; how to meet standards with picture books, K-6. [by] Andrea S. Libresco, Jeannette Balantic, and Jonie C. Kipling. Libraries Unlimited 2011 269p il pa $30

Grades: Adult Professional   **372**

1. Social sciences -- Study and teaching

ISBN 978-1-59884-520-4; 1-59884-520-9

LC 2010053649

"Based on observations and instructional surveys, the authors theorize that consistent social studies instruction no longer occurs due to the time requirements of reading and math instruction. They recommend teaching reading and social studies concurrently by using trade picture books. Each of the national standards' thematic strands is featured along with essential questions to frame classroom discussion. Three representative titles are featured for each theme, followed by social studies concepts and supporting discussion questions. Thoughtful hands-on, student-centered activities are provided for each title as well as reproducibles, study sheets, and graphic organizers." Libr Media Connect

Includes bibliographical references

Lukenbill, W. Bernard

Health information in a changing world; practical approaches for teachers, schools, and school librarians. [by] W. Bernard Lukenbill and Barbara Froling Immroth. Libraries Unlimited 2010 244p il $45

Grades: Adult Professional   **372**

1. Health education 2. Youth -- Health and hygiene 3. Health

-- Information services

ISBN 978-1-59884-398-9; 1-59884-398-2

LC 2010-7505

"This is quite an impressive book and a real treasure for any professional involved with health education, whether for the classroom, public health, or personal counseling." Voice Youth Advocates

Includes bibliographical references

Mackey, Bonnie

A **librarian's** guide to cultivating an elementary school garden; [by] Bonnie Mackey and Jennifer Mackey Stewart. Linworth Pub. 2009 124p il pa $39.95

Grades: Adult Professional   **372**

1. Gardening 2. School libraries -- Activity projects

ISBN 978-1-58683-328-2 pa; 1-58683-328-6 pa

LC 2008-34963

"Its unusual topic makes this book a standout." Libr Media Connect

Includes bibliographical references

372.21   Preschool education

Howe, James

When you go to kindergarten; text by James Howe; photographs by Betsy Imershein. rev & updated ed; Morrow Junior Bks. 1994 un il hardcover o.p. pa $6.99

Grades: PreK K   **372.21**

1. Kindergarten

ISBN 0-688-12912-9; 0-688-14387-3 pa

LC 93-48152

First published 1986 by Knopf

"The author tells youngsters what school might look like and how they might get there, and describes some of the possible activities. . . . Multicultural children are welcomed and taught by both male and female teachers. Smiling, busy kids engaged in many activities portray school as an exciting, interesting, and happy place." SLJ

372.4   Reading

Grover, Sharon

Listening to learn; audiobooks supporting literacy. by Sharon Grover and Lizette D. Hannegan. American Library Association 2011 xi, 188 p.p (alk. paper) $45

Grades: Adult Professional   **372.4**

1. Literacy 2. Audiobooks 3. Educational technology 4. Reading -- United States 5. Children -- Books and reading 6. Libraries -- Special collections -- Audiobooks 7. Literacy -- Study and teaching -- United States 8. School librarian participation in curriculum planning

ISBN 0838911072; 9780838911075

LC 2011041814

Authors Sharon Grover and Lizette D. Hannegan "make the case that audiobooks not only present excellent opportunities to engage the attention of young people but also advance literacy. 'Listening to Learn' connects audiobooks with K-12 curricula and demonstrates how the format can support national learning standards and literacy skills." (Publisher's note)

"This informative resource establishes the literacy benefits of audiobooks as an alternate reading delivery method...Discussions of audiobook formats and recommended sources for building an audiobook collection are also included. The authors provide a collaborative resource that would benefit a classroom, library, or home setting." (Library Media Connection)

Includes bibliographical references (p. 175-178) and index

Hutchins, Darcy J.

Family reading night; [by] Darcy J. Hutchins, Marsha D. Greenfeld, Joyce L. Epstein. Eye on Education 2008 126p il pa $29.95

Grades: Adult Professional   **372.4**

1. Reading 2. Family literacy programs

ISBN 978-1-59667-063-1 pa; 1-59667-063-0 pa

LC 2007034492

"This guide presents clear examples of how to plan and implement thematic, monthly programs to help engage families with elementary-age children in literacy activities that they can do together. . . . This title would be an excellent tool for any school librarian, educator, or administrator working to devise a successful and strategically planned school-wide family reading program." SLJ

Moreillon, Judi

Collaborative strategies for teaching reading comprehension; maximizing your impact. [by] Judi Moreillon. American Library Association 2007 170p il $38

Grades: Adult Professional   **372.4**

1. Reading comprehension

ISBN 978-0-8389-0929-4; 0-8389-0929-9

LC 2006036132

This "begins by importance of collaboration between classroom teachers and teacher-librarians. . . . . The bulk of the book focuses on seven reading comprehension strategies and how to teach them. . . . Overall this book is a cut above other 'how-to' books with its plethora of suggestions and resources for teachers and librarians." Voice Youth Advocates

Includes glossary and bibliographical references

372.47   Reading comprehension strategies

Bradbury, Judy

The **read**-aloud scaffold; best books to enhance content area curriculum, grades pre-K-3. by Judy Bradbury. Libraries Unlimited 2011 xi, 180 p.p (pbk. : acid-free paper) $40

Grades: Adult Professional   **372.47**

1. Books and reading 2. Curriculum planning 3. Children's literature 4. Content area reading -- United States 5. Reading (Elementary) -- United States 6. Language arts (Elementary) -- United States

ISBN 1598846841; 9781598846843

LC 2011023169

This book, by Judy Bradbury, "offers teachers and librarians over 700 content area connections through carefully selected, recently published children's trade books. These selections include fiction and nonfiction titles that represent outstanding read-aloud choices that will augment the instructional curriculum, covering subjects ranging from history to holidays to special events, and from biographies and memoirs to poetry and character education." (Publisher's note)

Includes bibliographical references and indexes

372.5 The arts

Press, Judy

★ **Around**-the-world art & activities; visiting the 7 continents through craft fun. illustrations by Betsy Day. Williamson 2001 128p il (Williamson Little Hands book) pa $12.95

Grades: K 1 2   **372.5**

1. Handicraft

ISBN 1-88559-345-7

LC 00-60030

"North American totem poles, Hawaiian leis, Aboriginal bark painting, Japanese dolls in kimonos, Korean drums, egg-carton camels, Masai beaded necklaces, nesting Russian dolls, and South American gaucho belts are among the projects. While the ideas will not be new to veteran crafters, they are basic and solid for the intended audience." SLJ

372.6 Language arts (Communication skills)

Briggs, Diane

Preschool favorites; 35 storytimes kids love. [by] Diane Briggs; illustrated by Thomas Briggs. American Library Association 2007 227p bibl il pa $40

Grades: Adult Professional   **372.6**

1. Storytelling

ISBN 0-8389-0938-8 pa; 978-0-8389-0938-6 pa

LC 2006103159

"This book presents suggestions and resources for a variety of themes, from 'Animal Oddballs' to 'A Woggle of Witches.' Each session includes a variety of books and activities per topic. . . . Several fingerplays and folk rhymes per theme come with clear instructions for accompanying motions. . . . A useful discography provides sources for musical selections. Each theme also incorporates a flannel board poem, story, or song, with simple reproducible patterns and instructions on how to present them. . . . The thematic groupings and quantity of ideas should be useful to beginners and some experienced presenters looking to freshen up their programs." SLJ

Includes bibliographical references

Toddler storytimes II; [by] Diane Briggs; illustrations by Thomas Briggs. Scarecrow Press 2008 165p il pa $45

Grades: Adult Professional   **372.6**

1. Storytelling

ISBN 978-0-8108-6057-5 pa; 0-8108-6057-0 pa

LC 2008006243

"With 25 theme-based chapters, this is a handy resource. Each theme includes book recommendations, often 10 or more, with a nice mixture of classic and newer titles, and a suggestion to choose two or three per session. Words and instructions for fingerplays, rhymes, and songs are provided, while a discography provides melody sources for all songs. Each theme includes a flannel-board activity, complete with reproducible patterns and brief directions on how to present the story or song on the board." SLJ

Includes discography and bibliographical references

Cavanaugh, Terence W.

Bookmapping; lit trips and beyond. [by] Terence W. Cavanaugh, Jerome Burg. International Society for Technology in Education 2011 228p il pa $34.95

Grades: Adult Professional   **372.6**

1. Audiovisual education 2. Literature -- Study and teaching 3. Maps -- Study and teaching -- Activities and projects

ISBN 978-1-56484-283-1; 1-56484-283-5

LC 2010051664

This book "provides ideas on how teachers can use elements from different disciplines in their own classrooms. . . . Other information includes using Google Earth, sources for images, Bing maps, information on creating your own bookmaps, instruction for bookmaps done individually and in cooperation with another teacher's class or classes, how to set up mapping in the classroom, and exploring existing bookmaps available on the Web. . . . This book should be in the professional collection of every middle and high school library, preferably in every classroom." Voice Youth Advocates

Includes bibliographical references

Chatton, Barbara

Using poetry across the curriculum; learning to love language. 2nd ed; Libraries Unlimited 2010 241p pa $40

Grades: Adult Professional   **372.6**

1. Poetry -- Study and teaching

ISBN 978-1-59158-697-5; 1-59158-697-6

LC 2009-36711

First published 1993

"With the emphasis in most schools on improving literacy, fluency, and reading and writing test scores, this book is extremely valuable. Sections are divided into various curricula areas. Each section begins with the national standards for that discipline, then a few paragraphs explain how the poetry in the extensive listing can be used. . . . Because all teachers must incorporate writing into their teaching, having relevant poetry for their curriculum and ideas on how to use it, will make this book popular." Libr Media Connect

Includes bibliographical references

Greene, Ellin

Storytelling: art & technique; [by] Ellin Greene and Janice Del Negro. 4th ed.; Libraries Unlimited 2010 xxvii, 455p il $55

Grades: Adult Professional   **372.6**

1. Storytelling

ISBN 978-1-59158-600-5; 1-59158-600-3

First published 1977 by Bowker under the authorship of Augusta Baker and Ellin Greene

"The fourth edition of this storytelling standby includes a wealth of updated and new materials." Bull Cent Child Books

Includes bibliographical references

Heitman, Jane

★ **Once** upon a time; fairy tales in the library and language arts. [by] Jane Heitman. Linworth Pub. 2007 132p pa $36.95

Grades: Adult Professional   **372.6**

1. Reading 2. Fairy tales 3. Language arts

ISBN 1-58683-231-X pa; 978-1-58683-231-X pa

LC 2007006890

"Heitman presents a well-organized and comprehensive look at how fairy tales can be infused into the curriculum. . . . The book includes ways in which various lessons can be adapted for special and English-language learners, as well as numerous templates for writing, speaking, and listening activities. . . . This excellent resource deserves a place in most professional collections." SLJ

Includes bibliographical references

Hostmeyer, Phyllis

Storytelling and QAR strategies; [by] Phyllis Hostmeyer and Marilyn Adele Kinsella. Libraries Unlimited 2010 123p pa $30

Grades: Adult Professional   **372.6**

1. Storytelling

ISBN 978-1-59884-494-8 pa; 1-59884-494-6 pa; 978-1-59884-495-5 e-book

LC 2010036576

"The authors, both storytellers with backgrounds in education and library work, present 18 stories based on six aspects of character development. These selections, which include folktales, fables, and myths, are just right for youngsters in third through eighth grades. Each one is followed by telling tips, a story path, and questions using the QAR (Question-Answer Relationships) model." SLJ

Includes bibliographical references

MacDonald, Margaret Read

Shake-it-up tales! stories to sing, dance, drum, and act out. August House 2000 174p il music $24.95; pa $14.95

Grades: Adult Professional   **372.6**

1. Folklore 2. Storytelling

ISBN 0-87483-590-9; 0-87483-570-4 pa

LC 00-36228

This is a collection of "participation tales from different cultures. Each of the 20 stories is easy to learn and MacDonald provides wonderful ideas on how to inspire elementary-aged children to join in and become part of the storytelling tradition." SLJ

Includes bibliographical references

Miller, Donalyn

★ The **book** whisperer; awakening the inner reader in every child. [by] Donalyn Miller; foreword by Jeff Anderson. Jossey-Bass 2009 227p

Grades: Adult Professional   **372.6**

1. Books and reading

ISBN 0-4703-7227-3; 978-0-4703-7227-2

LC 2008055666

Donalyn Miller's approach to reading promotion "is simple yet provocative: affirm the reader in every student, allow students to choose their own books, carve out extra reading time, model authentic reading behaviors, discard time-worn reading assignments such as book reports and comprehension worksheets, and develop a classroom library filled with high-interest books. . . . Miller provides many tips for teachers and parents and includes a useful list of ultimate reading suggestions picked by her students. This outstanding contribution to the literature is highly recommended." Libr J

Includes bibliographical references

Roth, Rita

The **story** road to literacy; [by] Rita Roth. Teacher Ideas Press 2006 176p il pa $30

Grades: Adult Professional   **372.6**

1. Language arts 2. Children of immigrants 3. English language -- Study and teaching

ISBN 1-59158-323-3

LC 2005030835

"Roth advances the idea that using traditional literature with students who are learning English will help them acquire critical communication skills while tying unfamiliar new places to familiar elements of their own heritages. The author provides practical, ready-to-use lesson plans, story samples, and suggested activities." SLJ

Includes bibliographical references

Sawyer, Ruth

The **way** of the storyteller. Viking 1962 360p il hardcover o.p. pa $16

Grades: Adult Professional   **372.6**

1. Storytelling 2. Literature -- Collections

ISBN 0-14-004436-1 pa

First published 1942

"This is not primarily a book on how to tell stories; it is rather the whole philosophy of story telling as a creative art. From her own rich experience the author writes inspiringly of the background, experience, creative imagination, technique and selection essential to this art. A part of the book is devoted to a few well-loved stories with suggestions and comments." Booklist

Includes bibliographical references

Spaulding, Amy E.

The **art** of storytelling; telling truths through telling stories. Scarecrow Press, Inc. 2011 210p $49.95

Grades: Adult Professional   **372.6**

1. Storytelling

ISBN 978-0-8108-7776-4; 0-8108-7776-7; 978-0-8108-7777-1 ebook

LC 2010039697

"Spaulding's passion for storytelling is evident as she shares the skills she has learned over the years. . . . She offers practical advice on selecting and learning stories, matching the story to the audience, and avoiding common performance pitfalls. . . . The presentation is conversational, filled with personal insights, interesting quotes, and thorough documentation." SLJ

Includes bibliographical references

372.61   Grammar

Rosenthal, Betsy R.

An **ambush** of tigers; a wild gathering of collective nouns. By Betsy R. Rosenthal; Illustrated by Jago. Millbrook Press 2015 32 p. (lib. bdg. : alk. paper) $19.99

Grades: K 1 2 3 4   **372.61**

1. Animals 2. English language -- Rhymes 3. English language -- Grammar 4. English language -- Collective nouns

ISBN 146771464X; 9781467714648

LC 2014009383

This children's book, by Betsy R. Rosenthal and illustrated by Jago, "introduces collective nouns for animals through wordplay. Clever rhymes and humorous illustrations bring these collective nouns to life in funny ways, making it easy to remember which terms and animals go together." (Publisher's note)

"While several picture books have tackled collective nouns, Rosenthal and Jago's collaboration stands out for the sheer inventiveness they bring to the subject. Rosenthal frames her rhymes as rhetorical questions that often make surprising (and wonderful) interspecies connections . . . Witty delights abound as a shiver of sharks bundles up in winter knitwear and a bouquet of pheasants peers glumly out of a tall vase." Pub Wkly

372.62   Written and spoken expression

Ellis, Sarah

From reader to writer; teaching writing through classic children's books. Douglas & McIntyre 2000 176p hardcover o.p. pa $14.95

Grades: Adult Professional   **372.62**

1. Poets 2. Artists 3. Authors 4. Novelists 5. Dramatists 6. Librarians 7. Theologians 8. Illustrators 9. Mathematicians 10. Editors 11. Essayists 12. Linguists 13. Satirists 14. Biographers 15. Philologists 16. Travel writers 17. Fantasy writers 18. Literary critics 19. Children's authors 20. Nonfiction writers 21. Writers on science 22. Short story writers 23. Young adult authors 24. Science fiction writers 25. Rhetoric -- Study and teaching 26. Children's literature -- Study and teaching

ISBN 0-88899-372-2; 0-88899-440-0 pa

The author discusses the work of seventeen British, Canadian and American authors of children's literature. "With each classic book, there's a 'sneak preview' (i.e., booktalk), a suggested read-aloud, exercises to help students and adult writers find their own stories, and a short annotated bibliography of related children's books." Booklist

372.63   Spelling and handwriting

Cunha, Stephen F.

How to ace the National Geographic Bee; official study guide. by Stephen F. Cunha. 4th ed. National Geographic 2012 127 p. ill., maps (library) $18.90; (paperback) $9.95

Grades: 4 5 6 7 8   **372.63**

1. Maps 2. Geography 3. Examinations -- Study guides 4. Contests 5. Geography -- Competitions 6. School contests -- United States
ISBN 1426309856; 1426309864; 9781426309854; 9781426309861

LC 2012419185

This book "is a study guide to prepare the reader for test questions in geographic trivia. . . . The book then separates into six distinct chapters. It begins with defining geography and giving the reader an overall understanding of how the bee is conducted. Chapter 3 . . . defines the various types of maps and how they should be interpreted and also explains map features and landforms." (Voice of Youth Advocates)

Includes bibliographical references (p. 109-117).

372.64   Literature appreciation

MacDonald, Margaret Read

★ The **storyteller's** start-up book; finding, learning, performing, and using folktales including twelve tellable tales. August House 1993 215p $26.95; pa $14.95

Grades: Adult Professional   **372.64**

1. Folklore 2. Storytelling
ISBN 0-87483-304-3; 0-87483-305-1 pa

LC 93-1580

The author's advice on storytelling "covers the practical ground, from selection, learning (in one hour!), performance, and setting to classroom applications. . . . A dozen texts of proven success follow, with performance tips and source notes. Equally valuable are the selected and annotated bibliographies appended to every chapter." Libr J

Includes bibliographical references

Pellowski, Anne

★ The **storytelling** handbook; a young people's collection of unusual tales and helpful hints on how to tell them. illustrated by Martha Stoberock. Simon & Schuster Bks. for Young Readers 1995 129p il hardcover o.p. pa $7.99

Grades: Adult Professional   **372.64**

1. Storytelling
ISBN 0-689-80311-7; 978-1-4169-7598-4 pa; 1-4169-7598-5 pa

LC 95-2991

This work "addresses the young person who wants to tell stories in a public setting. It is similar in format to many adult books on storytelling how-tos, with sections on getting started and selecting and preparing stories, as well as a selection of sample tales. Pellowski's notes are extensive and will be very useful to novices looking for ways to research stories." Booklist

Includes bibliographical references

372.66   Drama (Theater)

Bany-Winters, Lisa

On stage; theater games and activities for kids. Lisa Bany-Winters. Chicago Review Press 2012 227 p. il (pbk.) $16.95

Grades: 3 4 5   **372.66**

1. Educational games 2. Drama in education 3. Play 4. Children's plays, American
ISBN 1613740735; 9781613740736

LC 2012012741

This book, by Lisa Bany-Winters, is a theater teaching resource for young actors, offering "more than 125 theater games that spark creativity, boost confidence, and encourage collaboration. They'll learn all about how to make a stage performance great with improvisational games, . . . they'll make puppets, discover makeup secrets, and design and build a set." (Publisher's note)

Includes bibliographical references

Champlin, Connie

★ **Storytelling** with puppets; 2nd ed; American Library Association 1998 249p il pa $35

Grades: Adult Professional   **372.66**

1. Storytelling 2. Puppets and puppet plays
ISBN 0-8389-0709-1

LC 97-24810

First published 1985 under the authorship of Connie Champlin and Nancy Renfro

This book covers "such topics as puppet types and styles, developing a puppet collection, participatory storytelling, and presentation formats. . . . A very useful choice for professional shelves in both school and public libraries." Booklist

Includes bibliographical references

372.7   Mathematics

Long, Ethan

★ The **Wing** Wing brothers math spectacular! Ethan Long. Holiday House 2012 32 p. (hardcover) $15.95

Grades: PreK K 1 2   **372.7**

1. Vaudeville -- Fiction 2. Mathematics 3. Numeration -- Study and teaching (Primary) 4. Numbers, Natural -- Study and teaching (Primary)
ISBN 0823423204; 9780823423200

LC 2011018256

The protagonists of this children's picture book, "Wilber, Wendell, Willy, Walter, and Woody really know how to put on a show. Five hilarious ducks juggle pies . . . spin plates . . . and show off their magic box. . . . Their slapstick routine is also a math lesson. They introduce the concepts greater than, less than, and equal to as well as addition and subtraction." (Publisher's note)

"[Long's] humorous illustrations—black pencil outlines with digital color that are reminiscent of Mo Willems' pigeon—will keep kids riveted with the birds' fantastically expressive faces. This is how learning math should be—painless, comical and, yes, spectacular." Kirkus

Long, Lynette

Measurement mania; games and activities that make math easy and fun. Wiley 2001 122p il (Magical math) pa $12.95

Grades: 3 4 5 6   **372.7**

1. Measurement
ISBN 0-471-36980-2

LC 00-43383

In this introduction to measurement "the activities range from using hands and feet to measure distance to making a sundial. . . . [This book provides] valuable activities and games to help children learn about the concepts." SLJ

VanCleave, Janice Pratt

Janice VanCleave's play and find out about math; easy activities for young children. Wiley 1998 122p il $29.95; pa $12.95

Grades: K 1 2   **372.7**

1. Mathematics

ISBN 0-471-12937-2; 0-471-12938-0 pa

LC 96-53002

"Fifty simple activities that involve basic arithmetic such as using one's fingers to do simple addition and subtraction. . . . Most procedures are between four and eight steps and are clearly written and accompanied by pencil drawings." SLJ

372.89   History and geography

Panchyk, Richard

New York City history for kids; from New Amsterdam to the Big Apple, with 21 activities. Richard Panchyk. Chicago Review Press 2012 134 p. $16.95

Grades: 4 5 6   **372.89**

1. Picture books for children 2. Historic buildings -- New York (N.Y.) 3. New York (N.Y.) -- History 4. New York (N.Y.) -- History -- Study and teaching (Primary) -- Activity programs

ISBN 1883052939; 9781883052935

LC 2012029893

"In this . . . 400-year history [of New York City, by Richard Panchyk,] kids will read about Peter Stuyvesant and the enterprising Dutch colonists, follow the . . . patriots as they rebel against the British during the American Revolution, . . . journey through the notorious Five Points slum with its tenements and street vendors, and soar to new heights with the Empire State Building and New York City's other . . . skyscrapers." (Publisher's note)

Includes bibliographical references and index

373.1   Organization and activities in secondary education

Glasser, Debbie

New kid, new scene; a guide to moving and switching schools. by Debbie Glasser and Emily Schenck. Magination Press 2012 112p il $14.95; pa 9.95

Grades: 5 6 7 8   **373.1**

1. Moving 2. Students

ISBN 978-1-4338-1039-8; 1-4338-1039-5; 978-1-4338-1038-1 pa; 1-4338-1038-7 pa

LC 2011013608

"Students making the transition to new schools, new communities, or new homes will always experience a bit of anxiety, and this self-help book offers practical advice on how to make those changes smoother. The ideas and suggestions are sound and practical. . . . The eye-catching layout will keep students flipping through the pages." SLJ

375   Curricula

Bishop, Kay

Connecting libraries with classrooms; the curricular roles of the media specialist. 2nd. ed.; Linworth 2011 122p pa $45

Grades: Adult Professional   **375**

1. Librarians 2. School libraries 3. Instructional materials centers

ISBN 978-1-59884-599-0; 1-59884-599-3

LC 2010051623

This book provides an . . . exploration of the topics that are currently relevant in K-12 curricula, including the school librarian's role in dealing with these issues, collaborating with teachers, and connecting to classrooms.

"Kay Bishop's book covers a wide range of topics and issues within the school library field. . . . Collaborative planning between classroom teacher, principal, students, and the community is also addressed. This material will be a welcome addition to the Library Media Specialist's arsenal of resources to stay current and involved." Libr Media Connect

Includes bibliographical references

379   Public policy issues in education

Morrison, Toni

Remember; the journey to school integration. Houghton Mifflin Co. 2004 78p il $18

Grades: 3 4 5   **379**

1. School integration 2. Discrimination in education 3. African Americans -- Education 4. United States -- Race relations

ISBN 978-0-618-39740-2; 0-618-39740-X

LC 2003-22884

Historical real photo/portraits combined with simple factual statement from the point of view of African American children tells the history of the school integration in this country

"The provocative, candid images and conversational text should spark questions and discussion, a respect for past sacrifices, and inspiration for facing future challenges." SLJ

Walker, Paul Robert

★ **Remember** Little Rock; the time, the people, the stories. by Paul Robert Walker. National Geographic 2008 61p il map $17.95; lib bdg $27.90

Grades: 5 6 7 8 9   **379**

1. School integration 2. Segregation in education 3. Arkansas -- Race relations 4. African Americans -- Education 5. Central High School (Little Rock, Ark.)

ISBN 978-1-4263-0402-6; 1-4263-0402-1; 978-1-4263-0403-3 lib bdg; 1-4263-0403-X lib bdg

LC 2008-24959

"The story of the battle to integrate Central High School in 1957 Little Rock, Arkansas, is presented through photographs and firsthand accounts from those who were there. . . . The multitude of eyewitness accounts, the poignant photographs, and the contextual background make this text a must-have addition to any classroom or library." Voice Youth Advocates

Includes bibliographical references

379.2   Specific policy issues in public education

Tonatiuh, Duncan

★ **Separate** is never equal; Sylvia Mendez & her family's fight for desegregation. by Duncan Tonatiuh. Abrams Books for Young Readers 2014 40 p. illustrations (hardback) $18.95

Grades: 2 3 4 5   **379.2**

1. School integration 2. Latinos (U.S.) -- History -- 20th century 3. Hispanic Americans -- Education 4. Hispanic Americans -- Civil rights 5. School integration -- United States 6. Civil rights

movements -- United States
ISBN 1419710540; 9781419710544

LC 2013032089

Pura Belpré (Illustrator) Honor Book (2015)
Robert F. Sibert Honor Book (2015)

This children's book by Duncan Tonatiuh describes how "Sylvia Mendez and her parents helped end school segregation in California. An American citizen of Mexican and Puerto Rican heritage who spoke and wrote perfect English, Mendez was denied enrollment to a 'Whites only' school. Her parents took action by organizing the Hispanic community and filing a lawsuit in federal district court. Their success eventually brought an end to the era of segregated education in California." (Publisher's note)

"Tonatiuh's multimedia artwork showcases period detail, such as the children's clothing and the differences between the school facilities, in his unique folk art style. An endnote essay recapping the events, photos of Sylvia and her schools, and a glossary and resource list for further research complete this thorough exploration of an event that is rarely taught." Booklist

Includes bibliographical references and index

381 Commerce (Trade)

Freese, Susan M.
Craigslist; the company and its founder. ABDO Pub. Co. 2011 112p il (Technology pioneers) lib bdg $34.22
Grades: 5 6 7 8   381
1. Advertising 2. Businessmen 3. Internet marketing 4. Online social networks 5. Webmasters 6. Craigslist Inc. 7. Software engineers
ISBN 978-1-61714-806-4 lib bdg; 1-61714-806-7 lib bdg; 978-1-61758-964-5 e-book

LC 2010042448

This is an introduction to Craigslist and its founder, Craig Newmark.
"Written in a clear, linear fashion, this series offers vivid, well-researched details about the development of technological advancements considered essential in today's society.... Readers who are interested in technology and inventions will be thoroughly engrossed." SLJ

Includes glossary and bibliographical references

Lanz, Helen
Shopping choices; Helen Lanz. Sea-to-Sea Publications 2012 30 p. col. ill. (Go green) (library) $28.50
Grades: 3 4 5   381
1. Commerce -- Environmental aspects 2. Shopping 3. Sustainable living 4. Shopping -- Environmental aspects
ISBN 159771304X; 9781597713047

LC 2011005509

This entry in the Go Green series "reminds readers that all goods come from a finite supply of natural resources." It looks at "where products come from and how commerce contributes to global warming and impacts forests, while also suggesting solutions like frequenting thrift stores, purchasing products made from recycled materials, and identifying items approved by the Forest Stewardship Council." (Booklist)

Larson, Jennifer S.
Who's buying? Who's selling? understanding consumers and producers. Lerner Pub. 2010 32p il (Exploring economics) lib bdg $25.26; pa $7.95
Grades: K 1 2   381
1. Commerce
ISBN 978-0-7613-3912-0 lib bdg; 0-7613-3912-4 lib bdg; 978-0-7613-5665-3 pa; 0-7613-5665-3 pa

Photographs and simple text introduce young readers to how people buy and sell goods.

"Clear, age-appropriate language explains new concepts well.... The [book's] layout is interesting and fresh, and each page features a large, well-chosen photograph with a boxed caption." SLJ

Lassieur, Allison
Trade and commerce in the early Islamic world; Allison Lassieur. Crabtree Pub. Company 2012 48 p. (Life in the early Islamic world) (reinforced library binding : alk. paper) $30.60
Grades: 4 5 6   381
1. Commerce 2. Islam -- History 3. Islamic Empire -- Commerce 4. Islamic Empire -- Economic conditions
ISBN 0778721728; 9780778721727; 9780778721796; 9781427195654; 9781427198426

LC 2012000078

This book is part of a series where "each book covers a particular aspect of life in the early Islamic world.... The main texts are supplemented with blue boxes of information, subsections, and many ... reproductions, maps, and paintings. Each book contains time lines and short biographies of important historical figures." (School Library Journal)

McClure, Nikki
★ **To** market, to market. Abrams Books for Young Readers 2011 un il $17.95
Grades: K 1 2 3   381
1. Food 2. Markets 3. Farm produce
ISBN 0-8109-9738-X; 978-0-8109-9738-7

LC 2010032946

"As a mother and son meander through the Olympia, WA, market, a full-page illustration shows them at a farmer's table while the facing page names the food sold there and briefly introduces the person who grows it. On the next page the farmer is illustrated at work and several paragraphs of elegant prose describe each process, ending with a simple 'thank you.' In this way, youngsters learn about apple-tree grafting and pruning, growing kale, beekeeping, smoking fish, baking, making batik napkins, and the art of cheese-making.... McClure's mysterious and beautiful images are cut from black paper with an X-Acto knife; the lacelike result is scanned and colored. McClure's art and life intersect in this stirring tribute to the connections among nature, people, and the food that nourishes them." SLJ

383 Communications and transportation

Brown, Craig McFarland
★ **Mule** train mail. Charlesbridge Pub. 2009 un il lib bdg $16.95; pa $7.95
Grades: 1 2 3   383
1. Grand Canyon (Ariz.) 2. Postal service -- West (U.S.)
ISBN 978-1-58089-187-5 lib bdg; 1-58089-187-X lib bdg; 978-1-58089-188-2 pa; 1-58089-188-8 pa

LC 2008007252

"Brown relates the daily trip made by Anthony the Postman from the top of the Grand Canyon to the village of Supai far below on the canyon floor.... An author's note gives additional details that children will appreciate.... He also describes the expedition he made with Anthony Paya, lead muleteer, to appreciate firsthand the journey and the rigors of the landscape. Brown's wonderful pastel and colored pencil illustrations are a testament to the time he spent on the trail.... A fascinating and informative addition." SLJ

Kay, Verla

Whatever happened to the Pony Express? illustrated by Kimberley Bulcken Root & Barry Root. G. P. Putnam's Sons 2010 un il $16.99

Grades: K 1 2 3   **383**

1. Pony express 2. Postal service 3. West (U.S.) -- History

ISBN 978-0-399-24483-4; 0-399-24483-2

"Through a series of letters between a brother and sister, Kay examines changes in mail delivery during the time period 1851-1870. . . . The rhymed text flows well. . . . While the brief phrases provide the larger historical context, the illustrations, rendered in pencil, ink, gouache, and watercolor, are crucial in developing the personal drama of the siblings and their families. . . . Libraries will want to accept delivery of this attractive and informative package." SLJ

Kenney, Karen Latchana

Mail carriers at work; by Karen L. Kenney; illustrated by Brian Caleb Dumm; content consultant: Judith Stepan-Norris. Magic Wagon 2009 32p il (Meet your community!) lib bdg $18.95

Grades: K 1 2 3   **383**

1. Letter carriers 2. Vocational guidance

ISBN 978-1-60270-650-7 lib bdg; 1-60270-650-6 lib bdg

LC 2009-2398

This book about mail carriers has "an uncluttered layout and consistent organization. . . . Chapter headings such as 'Problems on the Job,' and 'Technology at Work,' and 'Special Skills and Training' make it easy to pinpoint specific information." SLJ

Includes glossary

Spradlin, Michael P.

Off like the wind! the first ride of the pony express. illustrated by Layne Johnson. Walker Books for Young Readers 2010 un il map $17.99; lib bdg $18.89

Grades: 3 4 5   **383**

1. Pony express 2. Postal service 3. West (U.S.) -- History

ISBN 978-0-8027-9652-3; 0-8027-9652-4; 978-0-8027-9653-0 lib bdg; 0-8027-9653-2 lib bdg

LC 2009-10827

"Basing his book, as much as possible, on scanty historical records . . . Spradlin re-creates the Pony Express' first rides east from Sacramento and west from St. Joseph, Missouri—naming riders and horses when he can, and providing a composite of various Express riders' adventures. Johnson heightens the drama with evocative full-bleed oils." Booklist

Includes bibliographical references

Thompson, Gare

Riding with the mail; the story of the Pony Express. by Gare Thompson. National Geographic 2007 40p il map (National Geographic history chapters) lib bdg $17.90

Grades: 2 3 4   **383**

1. Pony express 2. West (U.S.) -- History

ISBN 978-1-4263-0192-6 lib bdg; 1-4263-0192-8 lib bdg

LC 2007007897

"After an introduction sets the historical scene, this engaging volume provides a comprehensive introduction to the rise and fall of America's first postal service, the Pony Express. . . . Archival photographs, . . . maps, and . . . sidebars extend the text." Horn Book Guide

384.55   Television

Hirschmann, Kris

HDTV; high definition television. Norwood House Press 2010 48p il (A great idea) lib bdg $25.27

Grades: 3 4 5 6   **384.55**

1. High definition television

ISBN 978-1-59953-379-7 lib bdg; 1-59953-379-0 lib bdg

LC 2010008699

This "book is peppered with clear, current photographs, useful websites, and [a] complete [index]. Students do not need prior knowledge to appreciate [this] worthy [title]." SLJ

Includes glossary and bibliographical references

385   Railroad transportation

Curlee, Lynn

★ **Trains**. Atheneum Books for Young Readers 2009 40p il $19.99

Grades: 4 5 6   **385**

1. Railroads -- History

ISBN 978-1-4169-4848-3; 1-4169-4848-1

LC 2007-40425

"Curlee illuminates . . . trains . . . with stunning, clean-lined illustrations and informative narration. He opens with a romantic reminiscence about the mighty engines that rumbled through his North Carolina hometown. . . . Launching into a chronological account of the evolution of the 'iron horse,' subsequent pages highlight major developments in (mostly American) railroad history, from the first steam engines to run on rails to the high-speed trains of Europe and Asia. Flatly styled and employing limited color palettes, several of Curlee's acrylic paintings will impress and awe readers." Publ Wkly

Floca, Brian

★ **Locomotive**; written and illustrated by Brian Floca. Atheneum Books for Young Readers 2013 64 p. ill. (hardcover) $17.99

Grades: K 1 2 3 4 5   **385**

1. Picture books for children 2. Locomotives 3. Railroads -- United States -- History -- 19th century 4. Locomotives -- United States -- History -- 19th century

ISBN 1416994157; 9781416994152; 9781442485228

LC 2012042295

Robert F. Sibert Honor Book (2014)

Caldecott Medal (2014)

Orbis Pictus Award Honor Book (2014)

In this children's picture book, Brian Richard Floca "invites readers to join a family—mother, daughter and son—on one of the first passenger trips from Omaha to Sacramento after the meeting of the Union Pacific and the Central Pacific in May 1869. . . . Floca visually documents the trip, vignettes illustrating the train's equipment as well as such . . . details as toilet and sleeping conditions." (Kirkus Reviews)

Halpern, Monica

★ **Railroad** fever; building the Transcontinental Railroad, 1830-1870. [by] Monica Halpern. National Geographic 2004 40p il map (Crossroads America) $21.90; pa $12.95

Grades: 4 5 6   **385**

1. Frontier and pioneer life 2. Railroads -- History 3. Central Pacific Railroad 4. Union Pacific Railroad Company

ISBN 0-7922-6767-2; 0-7922-6767-2 pa

LC 2003-17858

Presents a history of the building of the transcontinental railroad and its effects on American life

"This is a first-choice purchase for its visually appealing presentation and its succinct yet thorough treatment of the topic." SLJ

Includes glossary

McMahon, Peter

Ultimate trains. Kids Can Press 2010 40p il (Machines of the future) $16.95

Grades: 4 5 6 7
385

1. Railroads 2. Science -- Experiments

ISBN 978-1-55453-366-4; 1-55453-366-X

"In simple engaging text and illustrations, McMahon and Mora present a brief history of [railroads]. Integral to the book are five experiments children can create. . . . Each experiment ties in well with a particular type of train, features clear instructions, and offers safety precautions." Booklist

Includes glossary

Murphy, Jim

Across America on an emigrant train. Clarion Bks. 1993 150p il hardcover o.p. pa $10.95

Grades: 5 6 7 8
385

1. Poets 2. Authors 3. Novelists 4. Authors, Scottish 5. Essayists 6. Travel writers 7. Short story writers 8. Railroads -- History 9. United States -- Description and travel

ISBN 0-395-63390-7; 0-395-76483-1 pa

LC 92-38650

"Murphy presents a forthright and thoroughly engrossing history of the transcontinental railway, with entries from Robert Louis Stevenson's 1879 journal as he rode cross country. It's also an inviting introduction to Stevenson, with a romance in the bargain." SLJ

Includes bibliographical references

Perritano, John

The **transcontinental** railroad. Children's Press 2010 48p il map (True book) lib bdg o.p.; pa $6.95

Grades: 3 4 5
385

1. Railroads -- History 2. Central Pacific Railroad 3. West (U.S.) -- Exploration 4. Union Pacific Railroad Company

ISBN 978-0-531-20585-3 lib bdg; 978-0-531-21248-6 pa

LC 2009014185

This introduction to the history of the transcontinental railroads provides "elementary readers with clear explanations, maps, illustrations, time lines, and engaging reproductions of primary resources. [This] volume contains eye-catching quick facts; illustrations and photographs are representational of regional Native Americans, pioneers, and explorers. This is ideal material for reports on the Westward expansion." SLJ

Includes bibliographical references

Simon, Seymour

★ **Seymour** Simon's book of trains. HarperCollins Pubs. 2002 un il $16.99; lib bdg $17.89; pa $6.99

Grades: K 1 2 3
385

1. Railroads

ISBN 0-06-028475-7; 0-06-028476-5 lib bdg; 0-06-446223-4 pa

LC 2001-24020

"Each double-page spread in this picture book sets a dramatic close-up photo of a moving train opposite a few sentences about the train's source of power (steam, diesel, electric) and how it works. The full-color, close-up pictures by a number of photographers will grab even young preschoolers. . . . The astonishing facts will interest older train buffs." Booklist

Steele, Phillip W.

Legendary journeys: trains. Kingfisher 2010 30p $19.99

Grades: 3 4 5
385

1. Railroads -- History

ISBN 978-0-7534-6465-6; 0-7534-6465-9

"The squat, wide format of this book is already well-suited to its subject matter, and it becomes even more so when its trick is revealed: five pages pull out, almost tripling the scenes' width and unveiling additional railroad cars. Steele provides an informative chronology of locomotive history from the advent of steam power to the rise of luxury trains." Publ Wkly

Zimmermann, Karl R.

★ **All** aboard! passenger trains around the world. [by] Karl Zimmermann; photography by the author. Boyds Mills Press 2006 48p il $19.95

Grades: 5 6 7 8
385

1. Railroads

ISBN 1-59078-325-5

LC 2005-24990

Zimmermann "has traveled by train across six continents, and his beautiful, big color photos appear on every double-page spread of this enthusiastic account, which blends history, geography, business, and engineering with his personal focus." Booklist

Steam locomotives; whistling, chugging, smoking iron horses of the past. Boyds Mills Press 2004 48p il $19.95

Grades: 4 5 6 7
385

1. Locomotives 2. Steam engines

ISBN 1-59078-165-1

"In this photo-essay, Zimmermann shares his excitement for steam locomotives with young readers, tracing the development of the early engines and their impact on the history of the U.S. He includes a clear explanation . . . of how a steam engine works. The photographs, some archival and some from the present day, are excellent. . . . The engaging text clearly imparts the author's enthusiasm and love for the subject." SLJ

Includes glossary

386   Inland waterway and ferry transportation

Harness, Cheryl

★ The **amazing** impossible Erie Canal. Macmillan Bks. for Young Readers 1995 un il map hardcover o.p. pa $5.99

Grades: 3 4 5
386

1. Erie Canal (N.Y.)

ISBN 0-02-742641-6; 0-689-82584-6 pa

LC 94-11114

"Harness has done a wonderful job of making the history and construction of the Erie Canal come alive. . . . The narrative is matched with illustrations that cover each page." SLJ

Includes bibliographical references

Kendall, Martha E.

The **Erie** Canal; by Martha E. Kendall. National Geographic 2008 128p il $18.95; lib bdg $28.90

Grades: 4 5 6
386

1. Erie Canal (N.Y.)

ISBN 978-1-4263-0022-6; 978-1-4263-0023-3 lib bdg

LC 2007029386

"This handsomely packaged introduction to our country's first great public works project pairs plenty of period prints and photos to a fluidly written account of the canal's origins, construction, uses and the folklore surrounding it." Booklist

387.1 Ports

House, Katherine L.

Lighthouses for kids; history, science, and lore with 21 activities. [by] Katherine L. House. Chicago Review Press 2008 118p il pa $14.95

Grades: 4 5 6 7 8   **387.1**

1. Lighthouses

ISBN 978-1-55652-720-3 pa; 1-55652-720-9 pa

       LC 2007-27093

"This book is noteworthy for the way in which the activities are related to the information in the text. . . . Readers learn about the challenges of building . . . [lighthouses], inventions to make them more reliable, and how lighthouses function as historical relics today." SLJ

Includes glossary and bibliographical references

387.2 Ships

Barton, Byron

Boats. Crowell 1986 un il lib bdg $16.89; bd bk $6.99

Grades: K 1   **387.2**

1. Ships 2. Boats and boating

ISBN 0-690-04536-0 lib bdg; 0-694-01165-7 bd bk

       LC 85-47900

Depicts a variety of boats and a cruise ship docking and unloading passengers

"Thick black outlines contain vivid colors . . . clean lines, bright hues, and undemanding text." Booklist

Floca, Brian

★ **Lightship**. Atheneum Books for Young Readers 2007 un il $16.99

Grades: K 1 2   **387.2**

1. Lightships

ISBN 978-1-4169-2436-4; 1-4169-2436-1

       LC 2005-28028

"Lightships—floating lighthouses—were retired in 1983, but they live on in Floca's handsome picture book, which uses simple words and repeated phrases to emphasize the vessels' purpose and uniqueness as well as their day-to-day operation. . . . Some pictures include elements of humor, while other scenes are notable for their quiet beauty." Booklist

Lavery, Brian

Legendary journeys: ships; illustrated Sebastian Quigley. Kingfisher 2011 il $19.99

Grades: 3 4 5   **387.2**

1. Ships

ISBN 978-0-7534-6681-0; 0-7534-6681-3

"Compelling details and interactive effects appear throughout this guide to ships. . . . Recreations of Greek triremes, Viking longships, and the Titanic, among others, are enhanced by slide-out pages that double (or more) the spreads' width, providing a sense of the boats' scale. Flaps reveal cross-sections of ships' interiors, while depictions of naval, cargo, and other commercial vessels emphasize our continued reliance on ships. A thorough and well-constructed guide for boat fanatics." Publ Wkly

Zimmermann, Karl R.

★ **Ocean** liners; crossing and cruising the seven seas. photographs by the author. Boyds Mills Press 2008 48p il $17.95

Grades: 5 6 7 8   **387.2**

1. Ocean liners 2. Ocean travel

ISBN 978-1-59078-552-2; 1-59078-552-5

       LC 2007049323

This is "a comprehensive overview of ships from sail to steam to diesel, from the important modes of transportation to the modern resorts at sea. The information is organized in chapters about the history and development of the ships, the star ships of the Atlantic crossings and the conversion to modern cruising. . . . All is accompanied by photographs taken over the years by the author and supplemented by historic drawings, photos and documents. . . . A fascinating voyage." Kirkus

Includes glossary

387.7 Air transportation

Barton, Byron

★ **Airplanes**. Crowell 1986 un il lib bdg $15.89

Grades: PreK K 1   **387.7**

1. Airplanes

ISBN 0-690-04532-8

       LC 85-47899

Brief text and illustrations present a variety of airplanes and what they do, "as well as some of the usual scenes surrounding each (e.g., workers checking a passenger plane). Brightly colored illustrations outlined in heavy black convey a bold and simple first impression, yet they portray a good number of accurate details that preschoolers find so fascinating." SLJ

Other titles in this series are:

Boats

Trains

Trucks

Brown, Lisa

The **airport** book; Lisa Brown. Roaring Brook Press 2016 40 p. illustrations (hardcover) $17.99

Grades: PreK K 1 2   **387.7**

1. Air travel 2. Airports

ISBN 9781626720916

       LC 2015024467

In this children's story, by Lisa Brown, "we follow a family on its way through the complexities of a modern-day airport. From checking bags and watching them disappear on the mysterious conveyer belt, to security clearance and a seemingly endless wait at the gate to finally being airborne. But wait! There's more! The youngest family member's sock monkey has gone missing." (Publisher's note)

"Strategically placed text, with modest typeface and subtle sizing, makes the story-building straightforward and the busy pictures navigable. Instructional, comforting, and threaded with multiple air-travel story strands, this travelogue delivers at many altitudes." Kirkus

Parker, Steve

By air. Marshall Cavendish Benchmark 2011 il (Future transport)

Grades: 4 5 6   **387.7**

1. Aeronautics 2. Forecasting

ISBN 1608707776; 9781608707775

       LC 2011000998

"Beginning with a speculative illustration featuring people of the future traveling through the air in carlike personal jets, this title . . . offers a fascinating look at prototypes for all sorts of aircraft, from small planes to passenger airliners to lighter-than-air vehicles. . . . The various possibilities for future aircraft are covered in double-page spreads that are well laid out and easy to digest. Illustrated with plenty of striking, digitally enhanced color pictures, this will probably be of equal interest to those doing reports and browsers." Booklist

Includes bibliographical references

Parker, Steve, 1952-

My first trip on an airplane. Heinemann Library 2011 24p il (Growing up) lib bdg $22; pa $6.49

Grades: PreK K 1 2 **387.7**

1. Airports 2. Airplanes 3. Aeronautics

ISBN 978-1-4329-4801-6 lib bdg; 1-4329-4801-6 lib bdg; 978-1-4329-4811-5 pa; 1-4329-4811-3 pa

LC 2010024195

This book examines a "common, often scary [event] in children's lives and [guides] readers through [it] step-by-step. The [author discusses] the who, what, and why of [the] experience . . . [including] what happens before and during a flight. . . . By confronting . . . fears head-on, children will feel 'in the know' and be prepared to experience [this first]. The text—two sentences per page in a large font and placed on white space—is accompanied by large color photos of children, families, and adults of a variety of ethnic backgrounds. [The] volume includes bold-face vocabulary words, a picture glossary, and dos and don'ts." SLJ

Includes glossary and bibliographical references

388 Transportation

Bodensteiner, Peter

Supercars; Peter Bodensteiner. Black Rabbit Books 2017 (library binding) $31.35

Grades: 3 4 5 **388**

1. Automobiles

ISBN 1680720368; 9781680720365; 9781680720754

LC 2015954674

This book, by Peter Bodensteiner, focuses on supercars. "Rev up your reading engines! Gearhead Garage is ready to take you for a ride. From screaming fast F1 cars to custom choppers, get to know what's 'under the hood' of your favorite vehicles. You're in the driver's seat now. Which book will you start with?" (Publisher's note)

"Close-up looks at shiny chrome and glossy paint jobs are a visual feast and will have intermediate readers oohing and aahing from one page to the next." SLJ

Diaz, Julio

Tesla models; Julio Diaz; [edited by] Keli Sipperley. Rourke Educational Media 2016 32 p. $32.79

Grades: 4 5 6 7 8 **388**

1. Automobiles

ISBN 1681917491; 9781681917498; 9781681918501

LC 2016932712

In this middle grades book, by Julio Diaz, part of the "Vroom! Hot Cars" series, "the ground-breaking Tesla is featured in this title with information on how it is changing the automobile world." (Publisher's note)

"Some of the hottest sports car available today are highlighted in this sleek series, which delivers strong content, impressive details, and eye-popping images to young car fanatics." SLJ

Gaarder-Juntti, Oona

What in the world is green transportation? ABDO Pub. Company 2011 24p il (Going green) lib bdg $24.21

Grades: 1 2 3 4 **388**

1. Transportation -- Environmental aspects

ISBN 978-1-61613-193-7 lib bdg; 1-61613-193-4 lib bdg

LC 2010004310

"The lively layout design, featuring colorful headings, short paragraphs, and attractive photographs, has a scrapbook-like quality. . . . [The title explains] how all our choices require energy and resources,

and encourage readers to make changes in their lifestyles. . . . [This] . . . will inspire and empower readers to make a difference." SLJ

Includes glossary and bibliographical references

Mulder, Michelle, 1976-

Pedal it! how bicycles are changing the world. Michelle Mulder. Orca Book Publishers 2013 48 p. (Footprints) (hardcover) $19.95

Grades: 3 4 5 6 7 8 **388**

1. Cycling 2. Bicycles

ISBN 1459802195; 9781459802193

LC 2012953464

This book, by Michelle Mulder, "celebrates the humble bicycle--from the very first boneshakers to the sleek racing bikes of today, from handlebars to spokes to gear sprockets--and shows you why and how bikes can make the world a better place. Not only can bikes be used to power computers and generators, they can also reduce pollution, promote wellness and get a package across a crowded city--fast!" (Publisher's note)

Wooldridge, Connie Nordhielm

Just fine the way they are; from dirt roads to rail roads to interstates. illustrated by Richard Walz. Calkins Creek 2011 un il $17.95

Grades: 2 3 4 5 **388**

1. Roads 2. Transportation

ISBN 978-1-59078-710-6; 1-59078-710-2

"Wooldridge's picture book traces the development of the National Road in the United States. . . . Wooldridge interjects the public's positive and negative opinions regarding the road's development and describes how the inventions of the steam engine and automobile influenced changes in the highway, which ultimately became Route 40 and crossed the country. As the story winds down, Wooldridge raises the problem of air pollution. Her folksy, conversational writing style incorporates flavorful language. . . . Muscular horses, changing modes of transportation, and caricatured people populate the bright artwork." SLJ

Includes bibliographical references

388.4 Local transportation

Miller, Heather

★ Subway ride; illustrated by Sue Rama. Charlesbridge 2009 un il lib bdg $15.95

Grades: PreK K 1 **388.4**

1. Subways

ISBN 978-1-58089-111-0 lib bdg; 1-58089-111-X lib bdg

LC 2008-7249

"Take a ride on subway trains all around the world. Beginning in Cairo, a multicultural group of children rides the trains in ten cities, zig-zagging from stop to stop around the globe. . . . Vivid colors and blurred lines evoke a bustling cheer. Cleverly composed to suggest both depth and action, the pictures tell most of the story. . . . The offbeat idea is deftly handled and should trigger further study." Kirkus

389 Metrology and standardization

Adler, David A.

Time zones; illustrated by Edward Miller. Holiday House 2010 31p il map $16.95

Grades: 3 4 5 **389**

1. Time

ISBN 978-0-8234-2201-2; 0-8234-2201-1

LC 2009007733

"Adler offers a simple but thorough explanation of time zones and why people experience different parts of the day simultaneously depending on their location around the globe. Illustrations of an astronaut and his robot dog provide a perspective from high above Earth, which helps readers visualize the way sunlight reaches different parts of the planet as it rotates. . . . Numerous maps and diagrams help visualize these abstract boundaries, including the international date line in the Pacific. . . . Adler explains the impact of daylight savings time and includes a simple experiment for readers to see for themselves how noon and midnight occur simultaneously on opposite sides of the globe." SLJ

Bernhard, Durga

While you are sleeping; a lift-the-flap book of time around the world. Charlesbridge 2011 un il map $14.95

Grades: PreK K 1 2 3   **389**

1. Time 2. Time -- Systems and standards

ISBN 978-1-57091-473-7; 1-57091-473-7

LC 2010007589

"A clever design allows readers to travel the world, one page turn at a time. . . . The illustrations show an Alaskan child curled up in bed with a parent at 10 p.m., facing a map of Africa, Nigeria highlighted, with an inset gatefold. A flip reveals a young Nigerian girl at 9 a.m. Turning the page reveals that same Nigerian girl opposite a Japanese child . . . and so on until the circular tale returns to Alaska. Teachers will appreciate Bernhard's incorporation of 12- and 24-hour digital clocks, as well as the analog clock hiding under each gatefold. The final page is a map of the world delineated by time zone and includes thumbnails from each highlighted country. A small text block explains the reason for the time zones and tells how they work. Gorgeous illustrations combine beautiful colors with a glimpse of life in other countries." Kirkus

Murphy, Stuart J.

Mighty Maddie; comparing weights. illustrated by Bernice Lum. HarperCollins Publishers 2004 31p il (MathStart) hardcover o.p. pa $4.99

Grades: K 1 2   **389**

1. Cleanliness 2. Weights and measures

ISBN 0-06-053159-2; 0-06-053161-4 pa

LC 2003-17610

As Maddie cleans up her room, she learns how to compare the weights of various objects

"Childlike line drawings with bright colors give readers a sense of action. This appealing book has uses beyond the math concept, and offers messages about family life, self-image, and responsibility." SLJ

391 Customs

Bliss, John

Preening, painting, and piercing; body art. Raintree 2010 32p il (Culture in action) lib bdg $29

Grades: 5 6 7 8   **391**

1. Body art 2. Cosmetics 3. Tattooing 4. Theatrical makeup

ISBN 978-1-4109-3924-1; 1-4109-3924-1

LC 2009051182

"This book covers different looks achieved through makeup, body painting, tattoos, and piercing. Photographs, advertisements, paintings, and artifacts show a variety of cultures and time periods and help readers see the huge changes in the fashion of physical appearance. . . . The author does a good job of explaining that some cultures have negative stereotypes of tattooed people being criminals and some piercing can be dangerous to people with allergies. Fun activities are included. . . . This book . . . is well written and has few biases." SLJ

Includes glossary and bibliographical references

DeCarufel, Laura

Learn to speak fashion; a guide to creating, showcasing, and promoting your style. DeCarufel, Laura. Owlkids Books, Inc. 2012 96 p. (hardcover) $22.95

Grades: 4 5 6   **391**

1. Fashion 2. Fashion -- Handbooks, manuals, etc. 3. Clothing and dress

ISBN 1926973372; 9781926973371

LC 2011941966

Author Laura deCarufel "takes preteen readers with her on the 'clothes + art = fashion' formula. She starts with finding one's own style and continues with learning to see: using visual curiosity to examine design, pattern, color and so on to find what inspires. Window shopping, building a wardrobe, preparing a sketchbook and learning to sew are all part of the plan. She gives advice about runway shows, models, fashion shoots, stylists and so on." (Kirkus)

Jaber, Pamela

When royals wore ruffles; a funny & fashionable alphabet! written by Chesley McLaren and Pamela Jaber; illustrated by Chesley McLaren. Schwartz & Wade Books 2009 un il $16.99; lib bdg $19.99

Grades: K 1 2 3   **391**

1. Alphabet 2. Fashion -- History 3. Clothing and dress -- History

ISBN 978-0-375-85166-7; 0-375-85166-6; 978-0-375-95166-4 lib bdg; 0-375-95166-0 lib bdg

LC 2008017374

McLaren and "Jaber cover the fashion waterfront, enlightening readers on both history . . . and the less tangible aspects of glamour. . . . The commentary is smart and accessible. . . . Witty as the writing may be, the illustrations are irresistible. Like the best fashion, the lines and colors feel effortlessly right." Publ Wkly

Krull, Kathleen

★ **Big** wig; a little history of hair. illustrated by Peter Malone. Arthur A. Levine Books 2011 un il $18.99

Grades: 3 4 5 6   **391**

1. Hair 2. Fashion

ISBN 978-0-439-67640-3; 0-439-67640-1

LC 2010031005

"Krull delivers a fascinating and quite funny 'history' of humankind's relationship with hair, from furry prehistory to the advent of punk style. . . . Equally wonderful are Malone's gouache illustrations, rife with humor." Publ Wkly

Includes bibliographical references

Morris, Ann

Hats, hats, hats; photographs by Ken Heyman. Lothrop, Lee & Shepard Bks. 1989 un il $16; pa $4.95

Grades: PreK K 1   **391**

1. Hats

ISBN 0-688-06338-1; 0-688-12274-4 pa

LC 88-26676

This book introduces a variety of hats worn around the world

"The vivid color photographs, one or two per page, show people engaged in lively activities while . . . wearing their hats. Each picture offers a strong ethnic identity or a thought-provoking human interaction, with captions of only a few words in large print. An unusual index . . . gives background information about the pictures, citing the countries of origin and a few facts about each . . . kind of hat." SLJ

Shoes, shoes, shoes. Lothrop, Lee & Shepard Bks. 1995 32p il hardcover o.p. pa $4.95

Grades: PreK K 1 **391**
1. Shoes
ISBN 0-688-13666-4; 0-688-16166-9 pa

LC 94-46649

"Morris gives a world-tour of shoes . . . in [a] picture book illustrated by various photographers. In rhyming text, she talks about shoes for all kinds of activities. . . . [The] book includes a map and a photograph key of the places visited." Bull Cent Child Books

Platt, Richard
They wore what?! the weird history of fashion and beauty. [by] Richard Platt. Two-Can 2007 48p il $16.95; pa $9.95
Grades: 4 5 6 **391**
1. Personal appearance 2. Fashion -- History
ISBN 978-1-58728-582-0; 1-58728-582-7; 978-1-58728-584-4 pa; 1-58728-584-3 pa

LC 2006039159

Published in the United Kingdom with title: Would you believe in 1500, platform shoes were outlawed?

"Busy, colorful pages recount the historical, social, and political sides of clothing, hair, hats, and shoes, from legal and moral issues such as wearing fur to dangerous practices like cinched waists and bound feet. . . . Ever-fluctuating ideas of beauty and body image are also explored." Horn Book Guide

Includes glossary and bibliographical references

Rowland-Warne, L.
Costume; written by L. Rowland-Warne; [special photography, Liz McAulay] Dorling Kindersley 2000 63p il (DK eyewitness books) $15.99; lib bdg $19.99
Grades: 4 5 6 7 **391**
1. Costume 2. Clothing and dress 3. Fashion -- History
ISBN 0-7894-5586-2; 0-7894-6584-1 lib bdg

First published 1992 by Knopf

Photographs and text document the history and meaning of clothing, from loincloths to modern children's clothes

Swain, Ruth Freeman
Underwear; what we wear under there. by Ruth Freeman Swain; illustrated by John O'Brien. Holiday House 2008 32p il $16.95
Grades: 2 3 4 5 **391**
1. Underwear 2. Fashion -- History
ISBN 978-0-8234-1920-3; 0-8234-1920-7

LC 2008-4041

"Swain packs a lot of detail into the text as she quickly and chronologically progresses through a discussion of different types of underwear throughout the ages and how it has accommodated people's lifestyles. Children will find a multitude of interesting historical tidbits. . . . The winsome, imaginative illustrations vary in size and are rendered in watercolor over ink." SLJ

391.4 Kinds of garments; accessories; buttons

Kyi, Tanya Lloyd, 1973-
50 underwear questions; a bare-all history. by Tanya Kyi and illustrated by Ross Kinnaird. Annick Press 2011 116 p. $21.95
Grades: 4 5 6 7 **391.4**
1. Underwear 2. Clothing and dress -- History
ISBN 1554513537; 9781554513536

This book, by Tanya Kyi and illustrated by Ross Kinnaird, examines the history of underwear. "The format, as the title indicates, is question-and-answer. Beginning with 'ancient undies,' the questions cover everything from what's worn under certain kinds of dress to how the modern

bra came into being, and reasons for wearing underclothes in the first place." (Booklist)

392 Customs of life cycle and domestic life

Hepplewhite, Peter
Loos, poos, and number twos; a disgusting journey through the bowels of history! Peter Hepplewhite. Gareth Stevens Publishing 2016 32 p. color illustrations $26.60
Grades: 4 5 6 7 8 **392**
1. Sewage disposal
ISBN 9781482431186

LC 2015458295

This children's book, by Peter Hepplewhite, explores the history of the toilet "from the sewage system of ancient Athens to the muckrakers of the Middle Ages. . . . Unique information reframes common social studies topics and time periods including ancient China, Victorian times, and more." (Publisher's note)

"A lively, surprisingly informative, high-interest volume that manages to both entertain and educate." Booklist

Includes bibliographical references and index

Laroche, Giles
★ **If** you lived here; houses of the world. Houghton Mifflin Harcourt 2011 un il $16.99
Grades: K 1 2 3 **392**
1. Houses
ISBN 978-0-547-23892-0; 0-547-23892-4

LC 2010044361

"Laroche applies his signature bas-relief cut-paper collage technique to sixteen different dwellings that illustrate the range of places that people call home. . . . Each . . . is introduced with a paragraph that begins with the phrase 'If you lived here,' enticing the reader to imagine how it might be. . . . For young readers, these profiles not only provide glimpses into the lives of people who might live very differently from us but also expand and broaden their worldview." Horn Book

Lauber, Patricia
★ **What** you never knew about beds, bedrooms, and pajamas; illustrated by John Manders. Simon & Schuster Books for Young Readers 2007 un il (Around-the-house history) $16.95
Grades: 2 3 4 **392**
1. Sleeping customs
ISBN 0-689-85211-8

LC 2004-20654

"Focusing on sleeping customs through the ages, Lauber begins with the Stone Age and moves up to the 1700s, but includes some more contemporary facts as well. . . . Manders's engaging artwork varies between full-page and spot illustrations. The humorous asides from characters in the comic-style pictures will entertain youngsters." SLJ

Includes bibliographical references

393 Death customs

Carney, Elizabeth
Mummies. National Geographic 2009 31p il (National Geographic readers) lib bdg $11.90; pa $3.99

Grades: 1 2 3   **393**
1. Mummies
ISBN 978-1-4263-0529-0 lib bdg; 1-4263-0529-X lib bdg; 978-1-4263-0528-3 pa; 1-4263-0528-1 pa

LC 2009-3630

"In challenging but readable text for early independent readers, Carney highlights mummies discovered all over the world. Details such as a 2,300-year-old vegetable soup in one mummy's stomach and another's still-soft hair and skin raise the bar on an already high-interest topic. Photographs don't shy away from showing human remains." Horn Book Guide

Deem, James M.
★ **Bodies** from the ice; melting glaciers and the recovery of the past. Houghton Mifflin 2008 58p il map $17
Grades: 5 6 7 8 9 10   **393**
1. Mummies 2. Glaciers
ISBN 978-0-618-80045-2; 0-618-80045-X

LC 2008-01868

A Sibert Medal honor book, 2009

This describes the discovery of human remains preserved in glaciers in the Alps, the Andes, The Himalayas, and other places around the world and what can be learned from them

"Full-color photographs, reproductions, and maps are clearly captioned; grand images of glaciated mountain peaks span entire pages, and detailed pictures of recovered objects . . . are presented. . . . [This] is a fantastic resource. Deem superbly weaves diverse geographical settings, time periods, and climate issues into a readable work that reveals the increasing interdisciplinary dimensions of the sciences." SLJ

Includes bibliographical references

Halls, Kelly Milner
Mysteries of the mummy kids. Darby Creek Pub. 2007 72p il map $18.95
Grades: 4 5 6 7   **393**
1. Mummies
ISBN 978-1-58196-059-4; 1-58196-059-X

"Halls presents an eerily fascinating exploration of mummified children and teens found in South and North America, Europe, and Asia. . . . The writing style is plain yet absorbing, presenting scientific and historical information in simple terms." Voice Youth Advocates

Includes bibliographical references

Knapp, Ron
Mummy secrets uncovered. Enslow Publishers 2011 48p il (Bizarre science) lib bdg $23.93
Grades: 5 6 7 8   **393**
1. Mummies
ISBN 978-0-7660-3670-3; 0-7660-3670-7

LC 2010000976

First published 1996 with title: Mummies

This describes mummies such as the Iceman found in the Italian Alps in 1991, King Tut of Egypt, the people of Pompeii killed by the eruption of Mount Vesuvius, Tollund Man found in Denmark in 1950, and the Ice Maiden found in the Siberian Steppes.

"Aimed at reluctant readers, [this title is] sure to disgust and delight in equal measure. . . . [The title] will pique interest and get kids lining up at the reference desk looking for more. The text is complemented by illustrations and magnified photos of things that you would hope never to see." SLJ

Includes glossary and bibliographical references

Markle, Sandra
★ **Outside** and inside mummies. Walker & Co. 2005 40p il $17.95; lib bdg $18.85
Grades: 4 5 6 7   **393**
1. Mummies
ISBN 0-8027-8966-8; 0-8027-8967-6 lib bdg

LC 2004-66128

"Markle explores a global smorgasbord of mummy varieties, both those created by human procedures and those caused by nature. Crisp (if gruesome) color photos accompany the readable, informative text, which discusses not only the mummification process, but also the cutting-edge technologies used by forensic anthropologists and others to study the mummies themselves." SLJ

Includes glossary

Rau, Dana Meachen
Mummies. Marshall Cavendish Benchmark 2010 24p il (Surprising science) lib bdg $22.79
Grades: 2 3 4   **393**
1. Mummies
ISBN 978-0-7614-4869-3; 0-7614-4869-1

LC 2009053761

"Colorfully illustrated with photographs on each page, this . . . will be well received by elementary students and educators." Libr Media Connect

Includes glossary and bibliographical references

Robson, David
The **mummy.** ReferencePoint Press 2011 il (Monsters and mythical creatures) $27.95
Grades: 6 7 8 9   **393**
1. Mummies
ISBN 978-1-60152-182-8; 1-60152-182-0

LC 2011022437

This is "an ideal starting point for young researchers interested in the weird, mysterious, and paranormal. Using fleet, descriptive prose to communicate the impressively researched (and sourced) information, [this] medium-length [work manages] to rope in just about everything, from folklore to history to pop culture. . . . The Mummy begins with the seminal 1932 Boris Karloff film before backtracking into the worldwide 'mummy lust' that began with the 1922 discovery of King Tut's tomb and and the subsequent curses and legends. . . . The illustrations are fine and varied, the sidebars always illuminating, and the back matter robust." Booklist

Includes bibliographical references

Sloan, Christopher
Mummies. National Geographic 2010 48p il (National Geographic Kids) $17.95; lib bdg $26.90
Grades: 4 5 6 7   **393**
1. Mummies
ISBN 978-1-4263-0695-2; 1-4263-0695-4; 978-1-4263-0696-9 lib bdg; 1-4263-0696-2 lib bdg

LC 2010-08498

"A gratifyingly grisly album of choice photos accompanies Sloan's lucid, informative text as he describes not only the mummification processes but also individual mummies produced whether by intent or by chance. From the dried Beauty of Kroran in China to the bundled Lady of Cao in a Peruvian pyramid or the familiar Boy King Tut in Egypt, a global variety is offered to fascinated readers. . . . [This is a] well-written, heavily illustrated glimpse into the world of after-death preservation, either by accident or design." SLJ

Includes glossary and bibliographical references

394 General customs

Gibbons, Gail

★ **Knights** in shining armor. Little, Brown 1995 un il hardcover o.p. pa $7.99

Grades: K 1 2 3

394

1. Medieval civilization 2. Knights and knighthood

ISBN 0-316-30948-6 lib bdg; 0-316-30038-1 pa

LC 94-35525

The author "covers tournaments, chivalry, and what happened when a bad knight was caught. Legendary knights such as Sir Gawain and the knights of the Round Table are briefly described, as is St. George and the dragon, and Gibbons also discusses present-day knights. The watercolor-and-ink pictures are some of Gibbons' liveliest and most attractive." Booklist

394.1 Eating, drinking; using drugs

Ancona, George

Come and eat. Charlesbridge 2011 il $16.95; pa $7.95

Grades: K 1 2

394.1

1. Eating customs

ISBN 158089366X; 1580893678; 9781580893664; 9781580893671

LC 2010033632

"This introduces food customs around the world for younger children. As focused on culture as on food, the brief, chatty text discusses the varied ways foods are eaten. . . . The clean design features full-color photos." Booklist

Augustin, Byron

The **food** of Mexico. Marshall Cavendish Benchmark 2011 il (Flavors of the world) $21.95

Grades: 4 5 6 7

394.1

1. Mexican cooking 2. Festivals -- Mexico 3. Mexico -- Social life and customs

ISBN 978-1-6087-0237-4

LC 2010013830

"Explores the culture of Mexico through its food." (Publisher's note)

Includes bibliographical references

Ichord, Loretta Frances

★ **Double** cheeseburgers, quiche, and vegetarian burritos; American cooking from the 1920s through today. by Loretta Frances Ichord; illustrated by Jan Davey Ellis. Millbrook Press 2007 63p il (Cooking through time) lib bdg $25.26

Grades: 3 4 5 6

394.1

1. Cooking 2. Eating customs

ISBN 978-0-8225-5969-6 lib bdg; 0-8225-5969-2 lib bdg

LC 2005-24535

"Each chapter, illustrated with lighthearted drawings, presents a quick, cogent overview of an American eating trend—from the first processed foods through TV dinners, fast food, the mainstreaming of organic foods, and more—ending with the influential fad diets of the 1990s. The examples are clear and lively, and relevant recipes close each chapter." Booklist

Includes bibliographical references

Kras, Sara Louise

The **food** of Italy. Marshall Cavendish Benchmark 2011 il (Flavors of the world) $21.95

Grades: 4 5 6 7

394.1

1. Italian cooking 2. Festivals -- Italy 3. Italy -- Social life and customs

ISBN 978-1-6087-0236-7

This explores the culture, traditions, and festivals of Italy through its food.

Includes bibliographical references

Kummer, Patricia K.

The **food** of Thailand. Marshall Cavendish Benchmark 2011 il (Flavors of the world) $21.95

Grades: 4 5 6 7

394.1

1. Thai cooking 2. Festivals -- Thailand 3. Thailand -- Social life and customs

ISBN 978-1-6087-0238-1

LC 2010023508

This explores the culture, traditions, and festivals of Thailand through its food.

Includes bibliographical references

Lauber, Patricia

★ **What** you never knew about fingers, forks, & chopsticks; illustrated by John Manders. Simon & Schuster Bks. for Young Readers 1999 un il (Around-the-house history) $16

Grades: 2 3 4

394.1

1. Tableware 2. Eating customs 3. Table etiquette

ISBN 0-689-80479-2

LC 97-17041

Describes changes in eating customs throughout the centuries and the origins of table manners

"A delicious blend of humor and fascinating facts. . . . The lively, linear drawings incorporate amusing asides in dialogue balloons that will entertain readers as the text enlightens them about the subject." SLJ

Includes bibliographical references

Mogren, Molly

Andrew Zimmern's field guide to exceptionally weird, wild, & wonderful foods; an intrepid eater's digest. by Andrew Zimmern. 1st ed. Feiwel & Friends 2012 197 p. ill. (paperback) $14.99; (hardcover) $19.99

Grades: 5 6 7

394.1

1. Food 2. Cooking

ISBN 0312606613; 125001929X; 9780312606619; 9781250019295

LC 2012289475

This book is a "guide to world cuisine." The authors Andrew Zimmern and Molly Mogren "focus on 40 unusual foodstuffs including cockroaches, guinea pigs, headcheese, lutefisk, turducken, and Twinkies. Recipes, interviews, and a great many facts . . . lead to . . . digressions, including suggestions on how to survive a zombie outbreak . . . and a time line of popular dances, following a discussion of eating 'dancing' (live) shrimp." (Publishers Weekly)

Orr, Tamra

The **food** of Greece; [by] Tamra B. Orr. Marshall Cavendish Benchmark 2011 il (Flavors of the world) $21.95

Grades: 4 5 6 7

394.1

1. Greek cooking 2. Festivals -- Greece 3. Greece -- Social life and customs

ISBN 978-1-6087-0235-0; 978-1-6087-0688-4 e-book

LC 2010035820

This explores the culture, traditions, and festivals of Greece through its food.

Includes bibliographical references

Orr, Tamra B.

The **food** of China; [by] Tamra B. Orr. Marshall Cavendish Benchmark 2011 il (Flavors of the world)

Grades: 4 5 6 7   **394.1**

  1. Chinese cooking 2. Festivals -- China 3. China -- Social life and customs

  ISBN 1-608-70234-0; 978-1-608-70234-3; 978-1-608-70687-7 e-book

                LC 2010039293

This explores the culture, traditions, and festivals of China through its food.

"Numerous high-quality, close-up color photos of outdoor vegetable markets, food in various stages of preparation, and families gathering around the table will keep readers engaged (and hungry) throughout the accessible and enlightening food tour." Booklist

Includes bibliographical references

Silverstein, Alvin

Chocolate ants, maggot cheese, and more; the yucky food book. by Alvin and Virginia Silverstein and Laura Silverstein Nunn; illustrated by Gerald Kelley. Enslow Publishers 2010 48p il (Yucky science) lib bdg $23.93

Grades: 4 5 6 7   **394.1**

  1. Eating customs

  ISBN 978-0-7660-3315-3 lib bdg; 0-7660-3315-5 lib bdg

                LC 2009012283

"Written in an engaging and conversational style and full of revolting descriptions and entertaining cartoon illustrations . . . [this is] sure to turn even the strongest stomach. An introduction . . . puts 'yucky' in perspective, reminding kids that our world is diverse and that everyone has a different definition of repulsive." SLJ

Includes glossary and bibliographical references

394.2   Special occasions

Ancona, George

Powwow; photographs and text by George Ancona. Harcourt Brace Jovanovich 1993 un il hardcover o.p. pa $10

Grades: 3 4 5 6   **394.2**

  1. Crow Fair (Crow Agency, Mont.) 2. Native Americans -- Rites and ceremonies

  ISBN 0-15-263268-9; 0-15-263269-7 pa

                LC 92-15912

A photo essay on the pan-Indian celebration called a powwow, this particular one being held on the Crow Reservation in Montana

The book is "illustrated with well-placed, full-color photos that clearly reflect the text. . . . An exquisite kaleidoscope of Native American music, customs, and crafts." SLJ

Johnston, Tony

Day of the Dead; illustrated by Jeanette Winter. Harcourt Brace & Co. 1997 un il hardcover o.p. pa $6

Grades: PreK K 1 2   **394.2**

  1. Mexico -- Fiction 2. All Souls' Day -- Fiction

  ISBN 0-15-222863-2; 0-15-202446-8 pa

                LC 96-2276

Describes a Mexican family preparing for and celebrating the Day of the Dead

"Spanish phrases are a natural part of the storytelling as the children ask questions about the cooking and preparations. . . . Winter's brilliantly colored, acrylic illustratons in folk-art style express the magic realism that is part of the ceremony under the stars." Booklist

394.26   Holidays

Chocolate, Debbi

My first Kwanzaa book; illustrated by Cal Massey. Scholastic 1992 un il hardcover o.p. pa $5.99

Grades: K 1 2   **394.26**

  1. Kwanzaa 2. African Americans -- Social life and customs

  ISBN 0-590-45762-4; 0-439-12926-5 pa

                LC 92-1200

Introduces Kwanzaa, the holiday in which Afro-Americans celebrate their cultural heritage

"The book effectively conveys the spirit of the holiday through the text and the acrylic paint and colored-pencil illustrations, all outlined in a thin line of earthy brown." SLJ

Includes glossary

Craats, Rennay

Columbus Day; American celebrations. AV2 by Weigl Pubs. 2011 24p il (American celebrations) lib bdg $27.13; pa $11.95

Grades: 3 4 5   **394.26**

  1. Explorers 2. Columbus Day 3. America -- Exploration

  ISBN 978-1-60596-775-2 lib bdg; 1-60596-6775-0 lib bdg; 978-1-60596-933-6 pa; 1-60596-933-8 pa; 978-1-60596-940-4 e-book

                LC 2009050986

First published 2004

This book about Columbus Day "is well positioned to plug holes in school units on holidays, with [a] punchy, informative [entry] on the past and present [history] of [the holiday]. The colorful [layout features] an ever-shifting mix of period and modern photographs, while sidebars keep things from settling too comfortably into the organizing structure, which is: . . . introduction, history, key personalities, celebrations, symbols, and activities." Booklist

Demi

Happy, happy Chinese New Year! Crown Pubs. 2003 un il $8.95

Grades: K 1 2 3   **394.26**

  1. Chinese New Year 2. China -- Social life and customs

  ISBN 0-375-82642-4

                LC 2003-43469

First published in different form 1997 with title: Happy New Year! Kung-Hsi Fa-ts'ai!

Examines the customs, traditions, food, and lore associated with the celebration of Chinese New Year

Farmer, Jacqueline

O Christmas tree; its history and holiday traditions. illustrated by Joanne Friar. Charlesbridge 2010 un il lib bdg $16.95; pa $7.95

Grades: 1 2 3 4   **394.26**

  1. Christmas trees

  ISBN 978-1-58089-238-4 lib bdg; 1-58089-238-8 lib bdg; 978-1-58089-239-1 pa; 1-58089-239-6 pa

                LC 2009027788

"This slender but informative book traces the roots and history of the Christmas tree through pagan and Christian practices over thousands of years. . . . Then the focus shifts to Christmas tree agriculture in North America: the varieties of trees grown, the stages of growing them, and the challenges of tree farming. . . . The clearly written text shows respect for its audience by introducing some stories . . . as legends rather than history. . . . Colorful gouache paintings brighten the presentation and provide visual information that complements the text." Booklist

Includes bibliographical references

Foran, Jill

Martin Luther King, Jr. Day; American celebrations. AV2 by Weigl Pubs. 2011 24p il (American celebrations) lib bdg $27.13; pa $11.95

Grades: 3 4 5   **394.26**

1. Clergy 2. Martin Luther King Day 3. Nonfiction writers 4. Civil rights activists 5. Nobel laureates for peace

ISBN 978-1-60596-772-1 lib bdg; 1-60596-772-6 lib bdg; 978-1-60596-779-0 pa; 1-60596-779-3 pa; 978-1-60596-937-4 e-book

LC 2009050988

First published 2004

This book about Martin Luther King Day "is well positioned to plug holes in school units on holidays, with [a] punchy, informative [entry] on the past and present histories of [the holiday]. The colorful [layout features] an ever-shifting mix of period and modern photographs, while sidebars keep things from settling too comfortably into the organizing structure: . . . introduction, history, key personalities, celebrations, symbols, and activities." Booklist

Gibbons, Gail

Easter. Holiday House 1989 un il lib bdg $16.95; pa $6.95

Grades: K 1 2 3   **394.26**

1. Easter

ISBN 0-8234-0737-3 lib bdg; 0-8234-0866-3 pa

LC 88-23292

Examines the background, significance, symbols, and traditions of Easter

Gibbons "simplifies complex beliefs and traditions in a straightforward way, though transitions are occasionally abrupt. Pleasing watercolors outlined in black ink illustrate the text." Booklist

Groundhog day! shadow or no shadow? by Gail Gibbons. Holiday House 2007 32p il $16.95

Grades: K 1 2 3   **394.26**

1. Marmots 2. Groundhog Day

ISBN 978-0-8234-2003-2; 0-8234-2003-5

LC 2006003456

"A look at some fascinating facts about this red-letter day, presented in Gibbons's signature style. Readers will learn about the traditions that led to the big celebration now held each year on February 2nd in Punxsutawney, PA. The author includes tidbits about the groundhog's diet, habitat, burrows, newborns/kits and looks at past cultures that depended on hibernating animals to help them determine the arrival of spring." SLJ

Halloween is-- Holiday House 2002 un il $16.95; pa $6.95

Grades: K 1 2 3   **394.26**

1. Halloween

ISBN 0-8234-1758-1; 0-8234-1797-2 pa

LC 2001-59429

Describes the origins and history of Halloween traditions and festivities from ancient times to the present day

"The new version of Gibbons' Halloween (1984) features a larger format, new illustrations, and a revised and slightly longer text as well as the new title. . . . Libraries with multiple copies of the earlier book will still find this version useful when the holiday rush is on, and given a choice, children will reach for this bigger, brighter, new edition." Booklist

St. Patrick's Day. Holiday House 1994 un il lib bdg $16.95; pa $6.95

Grades: K 1 2 3   **394.26**

1. Saint Patrick's Day

ISBN 0-8234-1119-2 lib bdg; 0-8234-1173-7 pa

LC 93-29570

"A basic introduction to the holiday—how it began, the life and works of St. Patrick, and the various ways in which the day is celebrated. The text is clear and concise, and the pages are full of information. Gibbons's simple, clean, full-page watercolor-and-ink illustrations flow logically from one to the next." SLJ

★ **Giving** thanks; poems, prayers, and praise songs of thanksgiving. edited and with reflections by Katherine Paterson; illustrated by Pamela Dalton. Chronicle Books LLC 2013 56 p. $18.99

Grades: 3 4 5 6 7 8   **394.26**

1. Thanksgiving Day 2. Picture books for children 3. Gratitude 4. Children's poetry 5. Children -- Prayers and devotions 6. Religious poetry 7. Gratitude -- Religious aspects

ISBN 1452113394; 9781452113395

LC 2013009517

Katherine Paterson presents a collection of speeches, songs, and prayers related to giving thanks. She "offers an essay before each section: 'Gather Around the Table,' 'A Celebration of Life,' 'The Spirit Within' and 'Circle of Community.'" (Kirkus Reviews)

Hamilton, Lynn

Presidents' Day; American celebrations. AV2 by Weigl Pubs. 2011 24p il (American celebrations) lib bdg $27.13; pa $11.95

Grades: 3 4 5   **394.26**

1. Presidents' Day 2. Presidents -- United States

ISBN 978-1-60596-773-8 lib bdg; 1-60596-773-4 lib bdg; 978-1-60596-931-2 pa; 1-60596-931-1 pa; 978-1-60596-938-1 e-book

LC 2009050991

First published 2004

This book about Presidents' Day "is well positioned to plug holes in school units on holidays, with [a] punchy, informative [entry] on the past and present histories of [the holiday]. The colorful [layout features] an ever-shifting mix of period and modern photographs, while sidebars keep things from settling too comfortably into the organizing structure: . . . introduction, history, key personalities, celebrations, symbols, and activities. . . . With its fascinating account of the frequently renamed and repositioned holiday, Presidents' Day is a series standout and expands the idea of 'symbols' to include not just Mount Rushmore but also U.S. currency." Booklist

Heiligman, Deborah

★ **Celebrate** Christmas; [by] Deborah Heiligman; consultant, Reverend Father Nathan J.A. Humphrey. National Geographic 2007 31p il (Holidays around the world) $15.95; lib bdg $23.90

Grades: K 1 2 3   **394.26**

1. Christmas

ISBN 978-1-4263-0122-3; 978-1-4263-0123-0 lib bdg

LC 2007012659

"Brief text accompanies captivating and colorful photographs that demonstrate customs around the world. The use of bonfires and candles, Nativity plays, Advent wreaths, Three Kings Day, and Yule logs are among the topics touched upon. . . . A solid addition." SLJ

Includes glossary and bibliographical references

★ **Celebrate** Halloween; [by] Deborah Heiligman; consultant, Jack Santino. National Geographic Society 2007 31p il (Holidays around the world) $15.95; lib bdg $23.90

Grades: K 1 2 3 **394.26**
1. Halloween
ISBN 978-1-4263-0120-9; 978-1-4263-0121-6 lib bdg
LC 2007003121

In this introduction to Halloween "children will recognize familiar customs, such as carving pumpkins, dressing up, and hanging decorations, explained in simple, yet satisfying, text. The holiday is made accessible and inviting. . . . Lovely, well-captioned color photographs feature children around the world joyfully taking part in festivities." SLJ

Includes glossary and bibliographical references

★ **Celebrate** Independence Day; [by] Deborah Heiligman; consultant, Matthew Dennis. National Geographic 2007 31p il map (Holidays around the world) $15.95; lib bdg $23.90
Grades: K 1 2 3 **394.26**
1. Fourth of July
ISBN 978-1-4263-0074-5; 978-1-4263-0075-2 lib bdg
LC 2006100316

"Heiligman captures the festiveness of Independence Day, also reminding readers of its origin and relevence. . . . Her writing is clear and easy to read. . . . Plentiful photographs depict varied community celebrations." Horn Book Guide

Includes glossary and bibliographical references

★ **Celebrate** Thanksgiving; [by] Deborah Heiligman; consultant, Elizabeth Pleck. National Geographic 2006 32p il map (Holidays around the world) $15.95; lib bdg $23.90
Grades: K 1 2 3 **394.26**
1. Thanksgiving Day
ISBN 0-7922-5928-9; 0-7922-5929-7 lib bdg
LC 2006008685

This briefly describes the history of Thanksgiving Day and how it is celebrated.

Includes glossary and bibliographical references

Hoyt-Goldsmith, Diane
★ **Cinco** de Mayo; celebrating the traditions of Mexico. by Diane Hoyt-Goldsmith; photographs by Lawrence Migdale. Holiday House 2007 30p il $16.95
Grades: 3 4 5 **394.26**
1. Cinco de Mayo 2. Mexico -- Social life and customs
ISBN 978-0-8234-2107-7; 0-8234-2107-4
LC 2006101433

"This colorful photo-essay introduces Rosie, whose family celebrates their Mexican American traditions in California. After discussing Benito Juárez, the history of Cinco de Mayo, and three major waves of immigration from Mexico, Hoyt-Goldsmith presents elements of Rosie's heritage such as food, language, and mariachi music. . . . The clearly written text and the many fine, color photos provide readers with information as well as glimpses of the life in Rosie's community." Booklist

Includes glossary

★ **Three** Kings Day; a celebration at Christmastime. photographs by Lawrence Migdale. Holiday House 2004 30p il map $16.95
Grades: 3 4 5 **394.26**
1. Epiphany 2. Puerto Ricans -- United States
ISBN 0-8234-1839-1
LC 2003-67625

This "photo-essay introduces Three Kings Day, or Dia de los Tres Reyes, and shows the celebration as experienced by a 10-year-old girl in New York's Puerto Rican community. . . . The clearly written text conveys a good deal of information in a lively, accessible manner. The many photographs capture the joyful spirit of the holiday." Booklist

Includes glossary

Jango-Cohen, Judith
Chinese New Year; illustrations by Jason Chin. Carolrhoda Books 2005 48p il (On my own holidays) lib bdg $23.93; pa $5.95
Grades: 1 2 3 **394.26**
1. Chinese New Year
ISBN 1-57505-653-4 lib bdg; 1-57505-763-8 pa
LC 2004-4472

This "book describes the celebration of Chinese New Year. . . . Among the topics discussed are the Chinese zodiac, traditional symbols of the new year, family feasts and traditions for the holiday, and community activities, such as parades. . . . Clearly written, informative, and child-centered without talking down to children, this provides a good introduction to the holiday." Booklist

Jeffrey, Laura S.
Celebrate Martin Luther King, Jr., Day; [by] Laura S. Jeffrey. Enslow 2006 104p il (Celebrate holidays) lib bdg $31.93
Grades: 5 6 7 8 **394.26**
1. Clergy 2. Martin Luther King Day 3. Nonfiction writers 4. Civil rights activists 5. Nobel laureates for peace 6. African Americans -- Civil rights
ISBN 0-7660-2492-X
LC 2005028110

This offers a brief introduction to the life of Martin Luther King and the Civil Rights movement in the United States and how Martin Luther King Day became a holiday and is celebrated.

Includes glossary and bibliographical references

Celebrate Tet; [by] Laura S. Jeffrey. Enslow Publishers 2008 104p il map (Celebrate holidays) lib bdg $31.93
Grades: 5 6 7 8 **394.26**
1. Vietnamese New Year
ISBN 978-0-7660-2775-6 lib bdg; 0-7660-2775-9 lib bdg
LC 2006031922

"Captioned photographs, maps, drawings, and sidebars combine with an accessible text to present a thorough discussion of the Vietnamese New Year celebration. Jeffrey discusses the holiday's legendary origins and ancient traditions along with people's modern-day observances." Horn Book Guide

Includes glossary and bibliographical references

Jones, Lynda
Kids around the world celebrate! the best feasts and festivals from many lands. Wiley 1999 124p il pa $12.95
Grades: 4 5 6 **394.26**
1. Holidays 2. Festivals
ISBN 0-471-34527-X
LC 99-14639

Introduces a variety of festivals celebrated around the world. Includes recipes and hands-on activities to give a taste of what it is like to be part of a feast or ceremony in another country

Lankford, Mary D.
★ **Christmas** around the world; illustrated by Karen Dugan. Morrow Junior Bks. 1995 47p il map hardcover o.p. pa $5.95
Grades: 3 4 5 **394.26**
1. Christmas
ISBN 0-688-12166-7; 0-688-12167-5 lib bdg; 0-688-16323-8 pa
LC 93-38566

This book "looks at the rich diversity of Christmas traditions found in 12 distinctly different cultures. A small amount of pertinent background information serves as an introduction to each entry, but the majority of the text discusses the special ways each culture celebrates the holiday. The book's attractive layout effectively uses repetition of color and theme, with each double-page spread of text and art surrounded by a decorative border.... The book features a small selection of craft activities.... A helpful pronunciation guide, and an interesting selection of Christmas superstitions." Booklist

Includes bibliographical references

Lewis, Anne Margaret

What am I? Halloween; illustrated by Tom Mills. Albert Whitman 2011 un il $9.99

Grades: PreK

394.26

1. Halloween

ISBN 978-0-8075-8959-5; 0-8075-8959-4

LC 2010049643

"When looking for a simple yet entertaining introduction to Halloween for the very youngest readers, search no further.... A friendly witch, pumpkin to carve, funny bat, silly scarecrow, hooting owl, happy monster, black cat, dancing skeleton, busy spider and trick-or-treater are all included in this easy interactive guessing game.... This nonthreatening approach will surely satisfy those who wish to avoid the scary or creepy Halloween offerings that abound. A solid introduction for toddlers." Kirkus

MacMillan, Dianne M.

Diwali--Hindu festival of lights; [by] Dianne M. MacMillan. rev and updated ed.; Enslow Elementary 2008 48p il (Best holiday books) lib bdg $23.93

Grades: 2 3 4

394.26

1. Divali 2. Hindu holidays

ISBN 978-0-7660-3060-2 lib bdg; 0-7660-3060-1 lib bdg

LC 2007002420

First published 1997

This describes the history of the Hindu festival of Diwali and how it is celebrated in the United States

Includes glossary and bibliographical references

Mattern, Joanne

Celebrate Christmas; [by] Joanne Mattern. Enslow Publishers 2007 112p il (Celebrate holidays) lib bdg $31.93

Grades: 5 6 7 8

394.26

1. Christmas

ISBN 978-0-7660-2776-3 lib bdg; 0-7660-2776-7 lib bdg

LC 2006025258

The author "devotes several pages to the origins of Christmas, first as a pagan holiday, then as a celebration of Jesus' birth, and its evolution into the holiday as it is observed today. Symbols of Christmas, important people, and traditions from around the world are explored, and there is a fair amount of discussion about the commercialization of the holiday.... Full-color photos and reproductions appear throughout. There is plenty here for reports." SLJ

Includes glossary and bibliographical references

Celebrate Cinco de Mayo; [by] Joanne Mattern. Enslow Pub. 2006 104p il map (Celebrate holidays) lib bdg $31.93

Grades: 5 6 7 8

394.26

1. Cinco de Mayo 2. Mexico -- History 3. Mexico -- Social life and customs

ISBN 0-7660-2579-9

LC 2005028107

This describes the history of Cinco de Mayo and how it is celebrated.

Includes glossary and bibliographical references

Nelson, Vaunda Micheaux

★ **Juneteenth**; by Vaunda Micheaux Nelson and Drew Nelson; illustrations by Mark Schroder. Millbrook Press 2006 48p il (On my own holidays) lib bdg $23.93

Grades: 2 3 4

394.26

1. Juneteenth 2. African Americans -- Social life and customs

ISBN 978-1-57505-876-4 lib bdg; 1-57505-876-6 lib bdg

LC 2005-15334

This is an introduction to the holiday "which celebrates the belated arrival of emancipation news to Texas slaves on June 19, 1865.... [This] offers a solid introduction to the holiday for independent readers or for presenting to small groups." Booklist

Otto, Carolyn

★ **Celebrate** Chinese New Year; [by] Carolyn Otto; consultant, Haiwang Yuan. National Geographic 2008 32p il (Holidays around the world) $15.95; lib bdg $23.90

Grades: K 1 2 3

394.26

1. Chinese New Year 2. China -- Social life and customs

ISBN 978-1-4263-0381-4; 1-4263-0381-5; 978-1-4263-0382-1 lib bdg; 1-4263-0382-3 lib bdg

LC 2008024678

"Vivid, colorful photographs of fireworks, lion dancers, and food fill the pages of this introduction to Chinese New Year. The concise but informative narrative notes when the event occurs, cites a few of the countries where it is observed, and explains the reasons behind the customs and symbols, especially those traditions involving children. The well-captioned pictures capture the intense excitement and raucous exuberance of the festivities." Booklist

Includes glossary and bibliographical references

★ **Celebrate** Cinco de Mayo; [by] Carolyn Otto; consultant, Jose M. Alamillo. National Geographic 2008 32p il map (Holidays around the world) $15.95; lib bdg $23.90

Grades: K 1 2 3

394.26

1. Cinco de Mayo 2. Mexico -- Social life and customs

ISBN 978-1-4263-0215-2; 1-4263-0215-0; 978-1-4263-0216-9 lib bdg; 1-4263-0216-9 lib bdg

This "combines a clear, read-aloud-friendly text with big, beautiful color photos. After introducing Cinco de Mayo's 1862 origins, Otto shows and tells how the celebration has become an annual, joyous festival of Mexican culture, both north and south of the border.... Excellent back matter includes bibliography, recipes, a glossary and an informative afterword." Booklist

★ **Celebrate** Kwanzaa; [by] Carolyn Otto; consultant, Keith A. Mayes. National Geographic 2007 32p il (Holidays around the world) $15.95; lib bdg $23.90

Grades: K 1 2 3

394.26

1. Kwanzaa 2. African Americans -- Social life and customs

ISBN 978-1-4263-0319-7; 978-1-4263-0320-3 lib bdg

LC 2007041221

This describes the history of the African American holiday of Kwanzaa and how it is celebrated and includes a craft activity and a recipe.

Includes glossary and bibliographical references

★ **Celebrate** Valentine's Day; [by] Carolyn Otto; consultant, Jack Santino. National Geographic 2008 32p il map (Holidays around the world) $15.95; lib bdg $23.90

Grades: K 1 2 3

394.26

1. Valentine's Day

ISBN 978-1-4263-0213-8; 1-4263-0213-4; 978-1-4263-0214-5 lib bdg; 1-4263-0214-2 lib bdg

LC 2007033764

This describes how Valentine's Day is celebrated and includes a game and a recipe

Includes glossary and bibliographical references

Peppas, Lynn

Cultural traditions in Mexico; Lynn Peppas. Crabtree Publishing Company 2012 32 p. (Cultural traditions in my world) (reinforced library binding : alk. paper) $26.60

Grades: 3 4 5   **394.26**

1. Holidays 2. Festivals -- Mexico 3. Holidays -- Mexico 4. Festivals -- Mexico 5. Mexico -- Social life and customs
ISBN 0778775879; 9780778775874; 9780778775942; 9781427178664; 9781427179814

    LC 2012003079

Author Lynn Peppas's "book describes how the blending of native and Spanish traditions, beliefs, and rituals has resulted in many of the lively and colorful festivals celebrated today. . . . Mexico's culture is a unique mixture of ancient traditions passed down by the native Maya and Aztec peoples, and the religion and culture of Mexico's Spanish conquerors. . . . Young readers will also learn how the Mexican people celebrate family occasions with fiestas." (Publisher's note)

Pfeffer, Wendy

The **longest** day; celebrating the summer solstice. illustrated by Linda Bleck. Dutton Children's Books 2010 un il $17.99

Grades: K 1 2 3   **394.26**

1. Summer 2. Summer solstice
ISBN 978-0-525-42237-2; 0-525-42237-4

"Science, myth and custom merge into a celebratory introduction to the Summer Solstice. . . . Bleck's sprightly, colorful illustrations offer a visual celebration as they faithfully track the text. A comfortable, multidimensional investigation of the Summer Solstice that transcends time and place." Kirkus

A **new** beginning; celebrating the spring equinox. illustrated by Linda Bleck. Dutton Children's Books 2008 un il $17.99

Grades: K 1 2 3   **394.26**

1. Spring 2. Vernal equinox
ISBN 978-0-525-47874-4; 0-525-47874-4

    LC 2007-18123

This "covers the spring equinox and how people mark its passage in the northern hemisphere. . . . [It includes] five multicultural activities. The free-verse text is clear and simple, and the colorful illustrations blanket every page with celebrants clad in traditional, festive clothing." Booklist

Includes bibliographical references

The **shortest** day; celebrating the winter solstice. illustrated by Jesse Reisch. Dutton Children's Books 2003 un il $16.99

Grades: K 1 2 3   **394.26**

1. Winter solstice
ISBN 0-525-46968-0

    LC 2003-40811

Describes how and why daylight grows shorter as winter approaches, the effect of shorter days on animals and people, and how the winter solstice has been celebrated throughout history. Includes activities

This uses "clear, concise language. . . . Pfeffer uses an easy, comfortable tone for conveying the basic information. . . . Reisch's realistic craypas illustrations provide serviceable interpretations of the author's ideas." SLJ

Rissman, Rebecca

Martin Luther King, Jr. Day. Heinemann Library 2011 24p il (Holidays and festivals) $21.50; pa $5.99

Grades: PreK K   **394.26**

1. Clergy 2. Martin Luther King Day 3. Nonfiction writers 4. Civil rights activists 5. Nobel laureates for peace 6. African Americans -- Civil rights
ISBN 978-1-4329-4055-3; 1-4329-4055-4; 978-1-4329-4074-4 pa; 1-4329-4074-0 pa

    LC 2009052855

This introduction to Martin Luther King Day offers "large pictures on the top three-fourths of the page and a simple line or two of text below. . . . Pictures of segregation—in particular, a 'For Colored Only' water fountain—still retain their power to shock and will compel children to ask questions. Rissman uses five very short chapters to take the youngest readers through some simple facts about slavery . . . before touching on King's life. . . . This is . . . a fine introduction." Booklist

Includes bibliographical references

Simonds, Nina

★ **Moonbeams,** dumplings & dragon boats; a treasury of Chinese holiday tales, activities & recipes. [by] Nina Simonds, Leslie Swartz, & the Children's Museum of Boston; illustrated by Meilo So. Harcourt 2002 74p il $20

Grades: 4 5 6 7   **394.26**

1. Handicraft 2. Chinese cooking 3. Chinese New Year 4. Folklore -- China 5. Festivals -- China
ISBN 0-15-201983-9

    LC 2001-4280

Presents background information, related tales, and activities for celebrating five Chinese festivals—Chinese New Year, the Lantern Festival, Qing Ming, the Dragon Boat Festival, and the Moon Festival

"The ample white space surrounding the text is filled with small, whimsical watercolor illustrations. . . . [This] is a useful, visually appealing addition to any holiday collection." SLJ

Includes bibliographical references

Tait, Leia

Cinco de Mayo. AV2 by Weigl Pubs. 2011 24p il (American celebrations) lib bdg $27.13; pa $8.95

Grades: 3 4 5   **394.26**

1. Cinco de Mayo 2. Mexico -- Social life and customs 3. Mexican Americans -- Social life and customs
ISBN 978-1-6059-6776-9 lib bdg; 1-60596-776-9 lib bdg; 978-1-60596-934-3 pa; 1-60496-934-6 pa

    LC 2009050985

This book about Cinco de Mayo "is well positioned to plug holes in school units on holidays, with [a] punchy, informative [entry] on the past and present [history] of [the holiday]. The colorful [layout features] an ever-shifting mix of period and modern photographs, while sidebars keep things from settling too comfortably into the organizing structure: . . . introduction, history, key personalities, celebrations, symbols, and activities. . . . Cinco de Mayo does an admirable job explaining this all-too-infrequently-explained holiday." Booklist

Tokunbo, Dimitrea

The **sound** of Kwanzaa; illustrated by Lisa Cohen. Scholastic Press 2009 un il $16.99

Grades: PreK K 1 2   **394.26**

1. Kwanzaa 2. African Americans -- Social life and customs
ISBN 978-0-545-01865-4; 0-545-01865-X

    LC 2007025916

"This picture book provides readers with an introduction to Kwanzaa's seven principles. . . . Rhythmic text includes the definitions, pronunciations, and significances of the principles. Uncluttered, vibrantly colored illustrations extend the meanings of each of the seven candles of Kwanzaa." Horn Book Guide

Includes bibliographical references

394.261 Secular holidays

Loh-Hagan, Virginia

PoPo's lucky Chinese New Year; written by Virginia Loh-Hagan; illustrated by Renne Benoit. Sleeping Bear Press 2016 32 p. color illustrations (ebook) $16.99; $16.99

Grades: PreK K 1 2   **394.261**

1. Grandmothers 2. Chinese New Year 3. Grandmothers 4. Chinese New Year 5. China -- Social life and customs 6. United States -- Social life and customs

ISBN 9781634718868; 9781585369782

LC 2016007685

In this book, written by Virginia Loh-Hagan and illustrated by Renne Benoit, "when her Chinese grandmother comes to visit, a young Chinese-American girl learns of and participates in the customs and beliefs celebrating an authentic Chinese New Year." (Publisher's note)

"One of the best of its genre; attractive and informative, and a must for the growing Chinese New Year shelf." Kirkus

394.263 Holidays of June, July, August

DeRubertis, Barbara

Let's celebrate Constitution Day; Barbara deRubertis. The Kane Press 2015 32 p. color illustrations (library reinforced binding : alk. paper) $25.32

Grades: 2 3 4 5   **394.263**

1. Holidays 2. United States. Constitution 3. Constitutional history -- United States 4. Constitution Day and Citizenship Day (U.S.) 5. United States. Constitution -- Anniversaries, etc. 6. United States -- Politics and government -- 1783-1789

ISBN 157565749X; 9781575657493; 9781575658148

LC 2015012885

This children's book, by Barbara deRubertis, focuses on how "on September 17 every year, we remember the signing of the Constitution by our Founders who worked hard to secure our freedoms. We also celebrate those who pledge their allegiance and become U.S. citizens." (Publisher's note)

"The series combines crisp, informative texts with attractive full-color illustrations and a pleasing design." Booklist

394.264 Thanksgiving

Grace, Catherine O'Neill

★ 1621; a new look at Thanksgiving. [by] Catherine O'Neill Grace and Margaret M. Bruchac with Plimoth Plantation; photographs by Sisse Brimberg and Cotton Coulson. National Geographic Soc. 2001 47p il map $17.95; pa $7.95

Grades: 3 4 5   **394.264**

1. Thanksgiving Day 2. Wampanoag Indians 3. Pilgrims (New England colonists) 4. Plimoth Plantation, Inc. (Plymouth, Mass.)

ISBN 0-7922-7027-4; 0-7922-6139-1 pa

LC 2001-124

This is a "pictorial presentation of the reenactment of the first Thanksgiving, held at Plimoth Plantation museum in October, 2000. Countering the prevailing, traditional story of the first Thanksgiving . . . this lushly illustrated photo-essay presents a more measured, balanced,

and historically accurate version of the three-day harvest celebration in 1621." SLJ

Includes bibliographical references

395 Etiquette (Manners)

Aliki

★ Manners. Greenwillow Bks. 1990 un il $16; lib bdg $15.93; pa $5.95

Grades: K 1 2 3   **395**

1. Etiquette

ISBN 0-688-09198-9; 0-688-09199-7 lib bdg; 0-688-04579-0 pa

LC 89-34622

The author discusses etiquette and good manners

"Aliki makes manners accessible to children through colorful cartoon-style illustrations. . . . Her lively primer sparkles with examples of the proper and the poor." Booklist

Joslin, Sesyle

★ What do you do, dear? pictures by Maurice Sendak. Harper & Row 1985 un il hardcover o.p. pa $6.95

Grades: PreK K 1 2   **395**

1. Etiquette

ISBN 0-06-443113-4 pa

LC 84-43139

First published 1961 by Addison-Wesley

A "wonderful spoof on manners in a hilarious picture-book made for laughing aloud." Child Study Assoc of Am

★ What do you say, dear? pictures by Maurice Sendak. Harper & Row 1986 un il lib bdg $15.89; pa $5.95

Grades: PreK K 1 2   **395**

1. Etiquette

ISBN 0-06-023074-6 lib bdg; 0-06-443112-6 pa

LC 84-43140

First published 1958 by Addison-Wesley

A Caldecott Medal honor book, 1959

"A rollicking introduction to manners for the very young. A series of delightfully absurd situations—being introduced to a baby elephant, bumping into a crocodile, being rescued from a dragon—are posed and appropriately answered. The illustrations are among Sendak's best—and funniest." Bull Cent Child Books

★ Manners mash-up: a goofy guide to good behavior; story and pictures. featuring Tedd Arnold [et al.] Dial Books for Young Readers 2010 un il $16.99

Grades: 2 3 4 5   **395**

1. Etiquette 2. Etiquette for children and teenagers

ISBN 0-8037-3480-8; 978-0-8037-3480-7

LC 2010-11882

This "picture-book look at manners showcases the . . . [work] of fourteen illustrators, each of whom get a spread to explore a particular area of behavior. . . . Grades two to four." (Bull Cent Child Books)

"This follow-up to Why Did the Chicken Cross the Road? (2006) and Knock Knock (2007) rounds up 14 of the usual suspects—the most gifted illustrators working today—and gives them one spread to explain the hows and whys of etiquette. . . . The results are top-notch." Publ Wkly

Post, Peggy

Emily Post's table manners for kids. Collins 2009 96p $15.99

Grades: 4 5 6 7 **395**
1. Etiquette
ISBN 978-0-06-111709-1; 0-06-111709-9
LC 2008010655

"This deceptively slim guide teems with advice about everything from meal courses to table settings, from the art of conversation to dining out. The tone is measured and mildly proscriptive, offset by Bjorkman's amusing cartoons. . . . A strength: the excellent troubleshooting for specific concerns, such as eating fondue and using chopsticks." Kirkus

Emily Post's The guide to good manners for kids; by Peggy Post & Cindy Post Senning. HarperCollins 2004 144p il $15.99; lib bdg $16.89
Grades: 4 5 6 7 **395**
1. Etiquette
ISBN 0-06-057196-9; 0-06-057197-7 lib bdg
LC 2003-26426

This offers advice on etiquette at home, at school, and other places, including letter writing and on-line communication, table manners, phone answering, and behavior at social gatherings, and public places.

"The writing is clear, friendly, and sometimes clever. . . . The advice is consistently practical and simple." SLJ

Emily's everyday manners; [by] Peggy Post and Cindy Post Senning; illustrated by Steve Bjorkman. HarperCollins 2006 un il $16.99; lib bdg $17.89
Grades: PreK K 1 2 **395**
1. Etiquette
ISBN 0-06-076174-1; 0-06-076177-6 lib bdg

"Cheerful illustrations set the upbeat (and updated) tone for this introduction to manners. A succinct running text introduces young Emily and her neighbor Ethan and comments on how and why they use manners as well as how etiquette can differ according to the time and place." Booklist
Other titles in this series are:
Emily's magic words (2007)
Emily's Christmas gifts (2008)
Emily's sharing and caring book (2008)
Emily's out and about book (2009)
Emily's new friend (2010)

Emily's magic words; please, thank you, and more. by Peggy Post and Cindy Post Senning; illustrated by Leo Landry. Collins 2007 un il $15.99; lib bdg $16.89
Grades: PreK K **395**
1. Etiquette
ISBN 978-0-06-111680-3; 0-06-111680-7; 978-0-06-111681-0 lib bdg; 0-06-111681-5 lib bdg
LC 2006019582

Emily explains how just a few little words please, thank you, hello, goodbye, and excuse me can work magic!

This is a "chipper, earnest etiquette primer. . . . Landry's . . . crisp, winsome ink and watercolor spot illustrations keep the mood light. . . . Parents will welcome the useful, encouraging advice supplied in an endnote." Publ Wkly
Includes bibliographical references

Senning, Cindy Post
Emily's new friend; by Cindy Post Senning and Peggy Post; illustrated by Steve Björkman. Collins 2010 un il $16.99

Grades: PreK K **395**
1. Etiquette 2. Friendship
ISBN 978-0-06-111706-0; 0-06-111706-4
LC 2009011767

Emily and a new neighbor become friends by treating one another with generosity, kindness, and good manners. Includes a note for parents on the importance of teaching principles of etiquette at home.

"Björkman's brightly colored watercolor-and-ink illustrations add a welcome touch of levity to the . . . text; readers will especially enjoy the antics of the two dogs. Small vignettes allow the artwork to match the many activities of the characters." Kirkus

Emily's out and about book; by Cindy Post Senning and Peggy Post; illustrated by Leo Landry. Collins 2009 un il $16.99
Grades: PreK K **395**
1. Etiquette
ISBN 978-0-06-111700-8; 0-06-111700-5
LC 2008029286

"Emily and her mother visit the library and the doctor's office, eat tacos from an outdoor stand, and greet a neighbor. Along the way, Emily remembers her manners, and that helps make the day a good one for everyone. The genial story and pictures will please children who like to see their everyday activities mirrored in their books. . . . This closes with a note to parents, here encouraging them to teach preschoolers not just how to behave but why they should do so." Booklist

Emily's sharing and caring book; by Cindy Post Senning and Peggy Post; illustrated by Leo Landry. HarperCollins Children's Books 2008 un il $16.99; lib bdg $17.89
Grades: PreK K **395**
1. Etiquette 2. Interpersonal relations
ISBN 978-0-06-111697-1; 0-06-111697-1; 978-0-06-111698-8; 0-06-111698-X
LC 2006102927

"This appealing and practical picture book . . . encourages young children to share with others and to show other people that they care about them. . . . The section on sharing defines the term broadly to include sharing time or even a good mood with someone, as well as sharing toys or food. The section on caring shows young Emily and her friend thinking about others and doing things to make them feel good. The book's potentially weighty message is buoyed by the simplicity and lightness of its delivery in both the text and the inviting line-and-watercolor artwork." Booklist

Verdick, Elizabeth
Don't behave like you live in a cave. Free Spirit Pub. 2010 120p il (Laugh & learn) pa $8.95
Grades: 4 5 6 **395**
1. Etiquette 2. Child psychology
ISBN 978-1-57542-353-1 pa; 1-57542-353-7 pa
LC 2010010441

Explains how children can make smarter, more positive choices about how they behave at home and at school and, as a result, stay out of trouble, feel good about themselves, and get along better with family, friends, and teachers.

"Not only are the antics of a cartoon Cave Boy and Cave Girl used to represent bad behavior throughout the book, but they are also part of the infusion of humor that makes the tone light, accessible, and soapbox free. Verdick keeps the dialogue conversational." SLJ

395.2 Etiquette for stages in life cycle

Hoyt-Goldsmith, Diane

★ **Celebrating** a Quinceanera; a Latina's 15th birthday celebration. photographs by Lawrence Migdale. Holiday House 2002 30p il $16.95

Grades: 3 4 5   **395.2**

    1. Quinceañera (Social custom) 2. Mexican Americans -- Social life and customs

    ISBN 0-8234-1693-3

                                     LC 2001-59424

Describes the customs and traditions connected with the celebration of a Mexican-American girl's fifteenth birthday, marking her coming of age

This offers "eye-catching, full-color photos. . . . The clearly written, engaging text conveys both the social and religious significance of the event." SLJ

398 Folklore

Beeler, Selby B.

  Throw your tooth on the roof; tooth traditions from around the world. illustrated by G. Brian Karas. Houghton Mifflin 1998 un il $16; pa $6.95

Grades: K 1 2 3   **398**

    1. Teeth -- Folklore

    ISBN 0-395-89108-6; 0-618-15238-5 pa

                                      LC 97-46042

Consists of brief statements relating what children from around the world do with a tooth that has fallen out. Includes facts about teeth

"This book will be an eye-opener for young Americans who may have assumed that the Tooth Fairy holds a worldwide visa." Publ Wkly

Berk, Ariel

  Secret history of mermaids and creatures of the deep; or the Liber Aquaticum. written and collected by Ari Berk, magister and scribe; illuminated by Wayne Anderson, Gary Chalk, Matt Dangler, Virginia Lee. Candlewick Press 2009 un il $16.99

Grades: 4 5 6   **398**

    1. Mermaids and mermen

    ISBN 978-0-7636-4515-1; 0-7636-4515-X

"This volume details merfolk from tales and mythologies around the world. A wide variety of creatures, their customs, and habitats are touched on. The often ornately scripted text is accompanied by intricate illustrations and numerous foldouts." Horn Book Guide

Kallen, Stuart A.

  The **sphinx**; part of the Monsters and mythical creatures series. by Stuart A. Kallen. ReferencePoint Press 2012 80 p. ill. (chiefly col.) (Monsters and mythical creatures series) (hardback) $27.95

Grades: 4 5 6 7 8   **398**

    1. Sphinxes (Mythology)

    ISBN 1601522223; 9781601522221

                                      LC 2011026636

This book, part of the "Monsters and Mythical Creatures" series, looks at the "history . . . [and] associated mythology" of the Sphinx. (School Library Journal). It "reveals the significant symbolic role this creature has played in human civilization from ancient Egypt through classical Greece and the Renaissance into the twenty-first century. . . . The ancient mythical creature has been an inspiration for artists, writers, architects, scholars, and theologians for millennia." (Publisher's note)

"Children will get a well-rounded look at the featured subjects and how they have evolved into the creatures that still fascinate many today." SLJ

Includes bibliographical references and index

Kelly, Sophia

  What a beast! a look-it-up guide to the monsters and mutants of mythology. Scholastic 2010 128p il map (Mythlopedia) lib bdg $39; pa $13.95

Grades: 4 5 6 7   **398**

    1. Monsters 2. Classical mythology

    ISBN 978-1-60631-028-1 lib bdg; 1-60631-028-3 lib bdg; 978-1-60631-060-1 pa; 1-60631-060-7 pa

                                      LC 2009-20998

Describes some of the creatures and monsters in Greek mythology.

This "spices things up with sassy artwork, a pastel color scheme, and an OMG sensibility. . . . [This title is] loaded with information on the inspired methods with which various nasty creatures could put an end to bothersome heroes. Aside from the heaps of information coming from all angles on just about every page, . . . [the] book also contains a decent family tree, a rudimentary star chart, and lists of further reading. . . . For kids unconvinced that anything so old and gray could have any bearing on their lives, . . . [this book provides] a feisty . . . guide to the many cultural references lingering from antiquity." Booklist

Includes glossary and bibliographical references

Knudsen, Shannon

  Fairies and elves. Lerner 2010 48p il (Fantasy chronicles) lib bdg $27.93

Grades: 4 5 6 7   **398**

    1. Fairies

    ISBN 978-0-8225-9979-1 lib bdg; 0-8225-9979-1 lib bdg

                                      LC 2008050207

"The explanations and history behind . . . fairies [and elves] . . . will provide satisfaction for readers who want to know more about these familiar characters from myth, fantasy, and folk and fairy tales. Brief and concise." SLJ

Includes bibliographical references

  Fantastical creatures and magical beasts. Lerner Publications 2010 48p il (Fantasy chronicles) lib bdg $27.93

Grades: 4 5 6 7   **398**

    1. Mythical animals

    ISBN 978-0-8225-9987-6 lib bdg; 0-8225-9987-2 lib bdg

                                      LC 2009004794

This describes mythical beasts such as dragons, unicorns, Hydra, Medusa, the labyrinth, and basilisks

"The explanations and history behind well-known fantastical creatures . . . will provide satisfaction for readers who want to know more about these familiar characters from myth, fantasy, and folk and fairy tales. Brief and concise." SLJ

Includes bibliographical references

Losure, Mary

  The **Fairy** Ring, or, Elsie and Frances Fool the World; Mary Losure. Candlewick Press 2012 184 p. ill.

Grades: 5 6 7 8   **398**

    1. Deception 2. Fairies 3. Fairies -- England

    ISBN 9780763656706; 0763656704

                                      LC 2011046081

This book offers explores an event that occurred "[t]owards the end of World War I, [when] two girls in Yorkshire took photographs that purported to capture the fairies they regularly saw, and these pictures . . . became a national sensation when . . . Sir Arthur Conan Doyle . . .

championed them as authentic. . . . [The] book . . . conveys the widening of the ripples from the event and . . . the impulses behind the creation of the photographs." (Bulletin of the Center for Children's Books)

Ogburn, Jacqueline K.

A **dignity** of dragons; collective nouns for magical beasts. by Jacqueline K. Ogburn, Nicoletta Ceccoli; illustrated by Nicoletta Ceccoli. Houghton Mifflin Books for Children 2010 un il $16

Grades: 2 3 4   **398**

1. Mythical animals

ISBN 978-0-618-86254-2; 0-618-86254-4

"Gorgeous mixed-media illustrations complement dozens of inventive collective nouns. . . . These creative descriptions comprise the only text in the book. A four-page glossary defines each fantastic creature and identifies the culture(s) of its origin. Ceccoli has created a stylized and luminous fantasyland energetically inhabited by Ogburn's enchanting bestiary. Fans of mythology and fantasy as well as budding lexophiles will savor this sophisticated picture book." SLJ

Peebles, Alice

Giants and trolls; by Alice Peebles; illustrated by Nigel Chilvers. Hungry Tomato 2016 32 p. color illustrations (Mythical beasts) (pb : alk. paper) $7.99

Grades: 3 4 5   **398**

1. Giants 2. Trolls

ISBN 146777653X; 9781467763400; 9781467776530

LC 2015001593

This book by Alice Peebles and Nigel Chilvers looks at "all that the giants and trolls of mythology have in common. Some have several heads. Some have only one eye--or lots of eyes! You wouldn't want to cross paths with any of them. But what if they crossed paths with each other? Who would win in a battle? Find out about each giant or troll's features and skills, where in the world they come from, how they rank compared to one another, and how you might defeat them if you ever strayed into their remote realms." (Publisher's note)

"Probably most interesting to readers of horror, these might occasionally spark interest in mythology." SLJ

Reinhart, Matthew

★ **Dragons** & Monsters; [by] Matthew Reinhart and Robert Sabuda. Candlewick Press 2011 un il (Encyclopedia mythologica)

Grades: K 1 2 3   **398**

1. Dragons 2. Monsters 3. Pop-up books

ISBN 0-7636-3173-6; 978-0-7636-3173-4

LC 2010015485

"The pop-up book veterans continue to push the envelope in this addition to the Encyclopedia Mythologica series, with infamous figures like Medusa . . . joining more general creatures such as dragons, sea monsters, and vampires. Minibooks and sidebars profile less recognizable monsters—the golem, sharklike 'taniwha,' and 'wendigo,' known to Algonquian tribes. . . . Once again, Reinhart and Sabuda have created an offering distinguished by clever details, superb execution, and a sense of wonder." Publ Wkly

★ **Fairies** and magical creatures; [by] Matthew Reinhart and Robert Sabuda. Candlewick Press 2008 un il (Encyclopedia mythologica) $27.99

Grades: K 1 2 3   **398**

1. Fairies 2. Mythical animals 3. Pop-up books

ISBN 978-0-7636-3172-7; 0-7636-3172-8

This pop-up book depicts and describes such magical creatures as Shakespeare's fairy queen Titania, hobgoblins, trolls, a humanoid magical tree, brownies, Pegasus, satyrs, Serbian enchanted birds, and merfolk.

"A dramatic pop-up towers over each spread, surrounded by flaps and corner gatefolds that open up more surprises. . . . The paper engineering consistently enhances the text. . . . The emphasis on global legends as well as a palette heavy on blues, purples and reds widen the audience way past the girly-girl set." Publ Wkly

Scieszka, Jon

★ The **true** story of the 3 little pigs; pictures by Lane Smith. Viking Kestrel 1989 un il $16.99; pa $7.99

Grades: K 1 2 3 4   **398**

1. Pigs -- Fiction 2. Wolves -- Fiction

ISBN 0-670-82759-2; 0-14-054451-8 pa

LC 89-8953

The wolf gives his own outlandish version of what really happened when he tangled with the three little pigs

"The 'excited and funky' illustrations match the hilarious revisionist text to a standard story." N Y Times Book Rev

Sierra, Judy

The **gruesome** guide to world monsters; illustrated by Henrik Drescher. Candlewick Press 2005 63p il $18.99

Grades: 5 6 7 8   **398**

1. Folklore 2. Monsters

ISBN 0-7636-1727-X

LC 2004-57470

This presents "brief introductions to dozens of ugly customers from world folklore. . . . [The author] offers wonderfully provocative warnings against creatures as diverse as the giant skunk Aniwye, the blood-sucking bat Mansusopsop, and Bloody Mary, an evil specter who lives on the other side of mirrors." SLJ

Thong, Roseanne

Wish; wishing traditions around the world. illustrated by Elisa Kleven. Chronicle Books 2008 un il $16.99

Grades: K 1 2 3   **398**

1. Wishes

ISBN 978-0-8118-5716-1

LC 2007038299

"'The many ways to make a wish wherever home may be' come in for lighthearted yet respectful exploration in this attractive square-format book. Thong . . . entices readers with consistently well-rhymed verses . . . following up each with a brief description of a national custom. . . . Rendered in Kleven's . . . kaleidoscopic style, many of the full-bleed spreads nearly shimmer. . . . Endnotes include more information along with an invitation to find 15 lucky symbols hidden in the pictures." Publ Wkly

398.2   Folk literature

Aardema, Verna

★ **Borreguita** and the coyote; a tale from Ayutla, Mexico. retold by Verna Aardema; illustrated by Petra Mathers. Knopf 1991 un il hardcover o.p. pa $6.99

Grades: K 1 2 3   **398.2**

1. Sheep -- Folklore 2. Folklore -- Mexico 3. Coyote (Legendary character)

ISBN 0-679-88936-1 pa

LC 90-33302

A little lamb uses her clever wiles to keep a coyote from eating her up

This folk tale "is energetically told and comfortably packed with many recognizable motifs. Mathers enlarges upon the humorous elements of the story in her boldly colored paintings. . . . Aardema and

Mathers are felicitously paired in a tale of trickery rewarded that begs to be read aloud." Horn Book

Includes glossary

★ **Bringing** the rain to Kapiti Plain; a Nandi tale. retold by Verna Aardema; pictures by Beatriz Vidal. Dial Bks. for Young Readers 1981 un il $16.99; pa $5.99

Grades: K 1 2 3   **398.2**

1. Stories in rhyme 2. Folklore -- Africa 3. Droughts -- Folklore

ISBN 0-8037-0809-2; 0-8037-0904-8 pa

LC 80-25886

"Effective both in the rhythm of its metered storytelling and in the brilliance of its stylized paintings, the panoramic picture book quickly engages both eye and ear." Horn Book

Who's in Rabbit's house? a Masai tale. retold by Verna Aardema; pictures by Leo and Diane Dillon. Dial Bks. for Young Readers 1977 un il hardcover o.p. pa $6.99

Grades: K 1 2 3   **398.2**

1. Animals -- Folklore 2. Folklore -- East Africa 3. Masai (African people) -- Folklore

ISBN 0-14-054724-X pa

LC 77-71514

This "tale relates the attempts of Rabbit to regain possession of her house after it is taken over by an intruder. Rabbit's friends offer suggestions on how to solve the problem, but the solution comes from 'an unexpected source.' The story, adapted from the Masai tale 'The Long One,' uses repetition of key phrases to produce a rhythmic read-aloud text. The Dillons skillfully present their artistry in a vivid, colorful and impressive manner which contributes to the story and sets the tone." Child Book Rev Serv

★ **Why** mosquitoes buzz in people's ears; a West African tale retold. pictures by Leo and Diane Dillon. Dial Bks. for Young Readers 1975 un il $16.99; pa $6.99

Grades: K 1 2 3   **398.2**

1. Animals -- Folklore 2. Mosquitoes -- Folklore 3. Folklore -- West Africa

ISBN 0-8037-6089-2; 0-14-054905-6 pa

Awarded the Caldecott Medal, 1976

"Stunning full-color illustrations—watercolor sprayed with air gun, overlayed with pastel, cut out and repasted—give an eye-catching abstract effect and tell the story with humor and power." SLJ

Alley, Zoe B.

★ **There's** a princess in the palace; pictures by R.W. Alley. Roaring Brook Press 2010 34p il $19.99

Grades: 1 2 3 4   **398.2**

1. Graphic novels 2. Humorous graphic novels 3. Folklore -- Graphic novels 4. Princesses -- Graphic novels

ISBN 978-1-59643-471-4; 1-59643-471-6

"Within a graphic-novel format, the tales of Cinderella, Sleeping Beauty, Snow White, the Frog Prince and the Princess and the Pea develop familial and hilarious interconnections while retaining the stories' traditional structures. . . . Smartly hysterical." Kirkus

★ **There's** a wolf at the door; pictures by R. W. Alley. Roaring Brook Press 2008 40p il $19.95

Grades: K 1 2 3   **398.2**

1. Graphic novels 2. Humorous graphic novels 3. Wolves -- Folklore -- Graphic novels

ISBN 978-1-59643-275-8; 1-59643-275-6

LC 2007-44025

As his plans are spoiled over and over again, the wolf keeps trying to find his dinner, in this retelling of five well-known stories and fables.

This is a "hilarious romp. . . . Illustrated with softly colored pen-and-ink drawings, these five stories meld seamlessly together. The text is full of puns, alliteration, and occasional rhymes." SLJ

Andrews, Jan, 1942-

Rude stories; illustrations by Francis Blake. Tundra Books 2010 87p il $19.95

Grades: 3 4 5   **398.2**

1. Folklore

ISBN 978-0-88776-921-4; 0-88776-921-7

"Andrews has added her own special touches to a collection of humorous, traditional tales from cultures around the world. The rudeness in the stories takes different forms: in an original tale, two sisters compete in a belching contest. In a Swahili tale, a girl known for her kindness finally speaks her mind to her family, and in another from Japan, a man receives a magical fan from a goblin. Its special power? Waving it will increase or decrease the size of someone's bottom. . . . A selection of witty, original poems is interspersed among the stories. . . . The selections have the flavor of the oral tradition. Blake's colorful spot art and occasional full-page illustrations are a perfect match for the irreverent humor." SLJ

Includes bibliographical references

★ **When** apples grew noses and white horses flew; tales of Ti-Jean. illustrations by Dusan Petricic. Groundwood Books/House of Anansi Press 2011 67p il $16.95

Grades: 2 3 4 5   **398.2**

1. Folklore -- Canada

ISBN 978-0-88899-952-8; 0-88899-952-6

This is a retelling of three stories featuring "Quebec's traditional folktale hero, Ti-Jean. He's an endearing character who is both wise and foolish, and though he does find himself in hard situations (often of his own making), in the end, he somehow manages to do what needs to be done. In 'Ti-Jean and the Princess of Tomboso,' he outwits a greedy princess; in 'Ti-Jean the Marble Player,' he gets the best of a pint-sized scoundrel; and in 'How Ti-Jean Became a Fiddler,' he turns the tables on a too-clever-for-her-own-good seigneur's daughter, and finds true love in the process." (Publisher's note) "Ages seven to ten." (Quill Quire)

"Ti-Jean, the cheerful, hapless, ultimately triumphant stripling of French-Canadian folklore . . . makes a winning appearance in three tales of European origin lightly transposed to a New World setting. . . . These zesty, well-paced texts virtually read themselves. . . . Sly Petricic drawings underpin the fun throughout." Horn Book

The **August** House book of scary stories; spooky tales for telling out loud. edited by Liz Parkhurst. August House 2009 144p $15.95

Grades: 4 5 6 7 8   **398.2**

1. Folklore 2. Storytelling 3. Short stories 4. Horror fiction

ISBN 978-0-87483-915-9; 0-87483-915-7

LC 2009008711

An anthology of spooky stories drawn from folklore, local history, and the storytellers' imaginations, and divided into the categories "Just Desserts and Lessons Learned," "Ghostly Guardians," "Dark Humor," "Urban Legends and Jump Tales," and "Fearless Females."

"Each of these 20 chilling tales is meant to be told out loud and includes author notes about how to maximize the spooky effect. Middle schoolers will relish reading and sharing these tales, hoping to creep each other out." SLJ

Aylesworth, Jim

Goldilocks and the three bears; retold by Jim Aylesworth; illustrated by Barbara McClintock. Scholastic Press 2003 un il $15.95

Grades: K 1 2 3   **398.2**
1. Folklore 2. Bears -- Folklore
ISBN 0-439-39545-3

LC 2002-15964

A little girl walking in the woods finds the house of the three bears and helps herself to their belongings

"Aylesworth's text is faithful to the traditional elements of the original, juicing up the plot with folksy, conversational asides. . . . The artist's watercolor, sepia ink, and gouache illustrations are pastel and dainty yet full of life and action." SLJ

★ The **mitten**; retold by Jim Aylesworth; illustrated by Barbara McClintock. Scholastic Press 2009 un il $16.99
Grades: PreK K 1 2   **398.2**
1. Winter -- Folklore 2. Animals -- Folklore 3. Folklore -- Ukraine
ISBN 978-0-439-92544-0; 0-439-92544-4

LC 2006-37115

A retelling of the traditional tale of how a boy's lost mitten becomes a refuge from the cold for an increasing number of animals.

"Aylesworth's polished story together with McClintock's energetic pictures prove that The Mitten can hold one more. Aylesworth's text shows its storytelling roots with its perfect pacing, precisely chosen details, and most of all its particapatory repetition." Horn Book

Badoe, Adwoa
The **pot** of wisdom: Ananse stories; pictures by Baba Wagué Diakité. Douglas & McIntyre 2001 63p il hardcover o.p. pa $12.95
Grades: 3 4 5 6   **398.2**
1. Folklore -- West Africa 2. Anansi (Legendary character)
ISBN 0-88899-429-X; 0-88899-869-4 pa

"Badoe remembers hearing these trickster stories in her youth in Ghana, and she retells them with the freshness and verve of the spoken word. . . . Each tale is illustrated with a brilliantly colored polychrome tile by Diakite, the Mali-born illustrator. The tiles employ strong black linear motifs and sun-and-earth colors: gold, orange, brown, blue, lemon." Booklist

Barrager, Brigette
The **twelve** dancing princesses; written and illustrated by Brigette Barrager. Chronicle Books 2011 un il $16.99
Grades: K 1 2 3   **398.2**
1. Fairy tales 2. Folklore -- Germany
ISBN 978-0-8118-7696-4; 0-8118-7696-9

LC 2010011580

A retelling of the Grimm brothers' tale of twelve princesses who dance secretly all night long and how their secret is eventually discovered.

"With art resembling that of animated film and several graceful dance scenes, this story could easily be set to a sound track. The plot is true to that told by the Grimms, and nice bits of dialogue and observations by Pip thread easily through the narrative, bringing the characters to life." SLJ

Barton, Byron
★ The **little** red hen. HarperCollins Pubs. 1993 un il $15.95; lib bdg $15.89; pa $24.99; bd bk $7.99
Grades: K 1 2   **398.2**
1. Folklore 2. Chickens -- Folklore
ISBN 0-06-021675-1; 0-06-021676-X lib bdg; 0-06-443379-X pa; 0-694-00999-7 bd bk

LC 91-4051

The little red hen finds none of her lazy friends willing to help her plant, harvest, or grind wheat into flour, but all are eager to eat the bread she makes from it. "Preschool." (SLJ)

"Barton here skillfully pares down a well-known tale for the youngest readers and listeners. Vibrant hues abound in his full-page, collage-like illustrations." Publ Wkly

★ The **three** bears. HarperCollins Pubs. 1991 un il $15.95; lib bdg $15.89; bd bk $7.99
Grades: K 1   **398.2**
1. Folklore 2. Bears -- Folklore
ISBN 0-06-020423-0; 0-06-020424-9 lib bdg; 0-694-00998-9 bd bk

LC 90-43151

While the three bears are away from home, Goldilocks ventures inside their house, tastes their porridge, tries their chairs, and finally falls asleep in Baby Bear's bed. "Ages two to four." (Bull Cent Child Books)

"Here's the familiar tale of the three bears and their blond gal pal drawn for the very youngest. Byron uses large simple shapes, bright colors, and a spare text to tell his story. . . . The size of the art makes this a good choice for mother-toddler story hours." Booklist

Bateman, Teresa
The **Frog** with the Big Mouth; retold by Teresa Bateman; illustrated by Will Terry. Albert Whitman & Co. 2008 un il $16.99
Grades: K 1 2   **398.2**
1. Frogs -- Folklore 2. Folklore -- South America 3. Rain forest animals -- Folklore
ISBN 978-0-8075-2621-7; 0-8075-2621-5

LC 2007052157

An Argentine wide-mouthed frog sets out through the rain forest to brag about his fly-eating abilities and encounters a toco toucan, a coati, a capybara, and a jaguar. Includes a note about the animals.

"Terry's shiny, verdant rain forest capably offsets myriad greens with shadows of lavender, an electric-blue beetle, and wine-red berries. The spreads swirl with movement and beckon forward via fluid lines. . . . This is an inventive version of a long-favored tale." SLJ

Baynes, Pauline
Questionable creatures; a bestiary. [by] Pauline Baynes. Eerdmans Books for Young Readers 2006 47p il $18
Grades: 4 5 6 7   **398.2**
1. Bestiaries 2. Mythical animals
ISBN 978-0-8028-5284-7; 0-8028-5284-X

LC 2005033658

"Baynes introduces readers to the creatures and myths found in medieval bestiaries and explains how the books were made and how they were viewed by the general public. The rest of the volume details the commonly held beliefs that both peasants and scholars embraced about specific animals. . . . Baynes's detailed gouache and colored-pencil illustrations . . . are done in the style of medieval illuminations. . . . The artist shows great respect for the early bestiary creators while also giving the stories relevance for modern readers." SLJ

Includes bibliographical references

Berner, Rotraut Susanne
Definitely not for little ones; some very Grimm fairy-tale comics. translated by Shelley Tanaka. House of Anansi Press 2009 un il $18.95
Grades: 4 5 6   **398.2**
1. Authors 2. Folklore 3. Fairy tales 4. Folklorists 5. Philologists 6. Short story writers
ISBN 978-0-88899-957-3; 0-88899-957-7

"In a comic book format, Berner retells the Brothers Grimm tales of the Frog Prince, Mother Holle, Tom Thumb, Rapunzel, Jorinda & Jorindel, Lucky Hans, Hans the Hedgehog, and Little Red Cap, using a humorous, breezy and somewhat ironic tone. . . . Older elementary-school readers who like sneaky humor, slightly violent demises of villains, and humorous takes on familiar tales will enjoy these comics. . . . Tanaka's translation lets the narration and dialogue flow seamlessly." Booklist

Blackstone, Stella

Storytime; first tales for sharing. told by Stella Blackstone; illustrated by Anne Wilson. Barefoot Books 2005 94p il $19.99; pa $12.99

Grades: K 1   **398.2**

1. Folklore 2. Animals -- Folklore

ISBN 1-84148-345-1; 1-84686-165-9 pa

LC 2004029542

"Seven familiar nursery tales are accompanied by bright, stylized, folk-art illustrations, done in paper collage and acrylic. Selections include The Cock, the Mouse and the Little Red Hen, The Gingerbread Man, The Ugly Duckling, Goldilocks, The Timid Hare (a Henny Penny story from India), The Three Little Pigs, and Stone Soup. The retellings are straightforward; most are faithful to the most commonly known versions and retain the familiar refrains. . . . The collection as a whole is delightful; the art is fresh, vibrant, and full of child appeal." SLJ

Includes bibliographical references

Blackwood, Gary L.

Legends or lies? Marshall Cavendish Benchmark 2006 72p il (Unsolved history) lib bdg $34.21

Grades: 4 5 6 7   **398.2**

1. Legends

ISBN 978-0-7614-1891-7 lib bdg; 0-7614-1891-1 lib bdg

Describes several legends that have intrigued people for centuries: the lost civilization of Atlantis, the Amazons, King Arthur, St Brendon, Pope Joan, and El Dorado

This collection "of tidbits about lingering mysteries of the past . . . [offers] more substance than most. . . . [It offers] a full-page illustration opening each chapter; reproductions, many in color; and a generously spaced format." SLJ

Includes glossary and bibliographical references

Blia Xiong

Nine-in-one, Grr! Grr! a folktale from the Hmong people of Laos. told by Blia Xiong; adapted by Cathy Spagnoli; illustrated by Nancy Hom. Children's Bk. Press 1989 30p il hardcover o.p. pa $7.95

Grades: K 1 2   **398.2**

1. Folklore -- Laos 2. Tigers -- Folklore 3. Hmong (Asian people) -- Folklore

ISBN 0-89239-048-4; 0-89239-110-3 pa

LC 89-9891

When the great god Shao promises Tiger nine cubs each year, Bird comes up with a clever trick to prevent the land from being overrun by tigers

"Simply and eloquently told, this pourquoi tale from a minority Laotian culture is boldly illustrated in a style adapted from the multi-imaged embroidered story cloths of the Hmong people. Its rhythmic text and appealing, brightly colored pictures make it a good choice for preschool story hours." Booklist

The **Blue** fairy book; edited by Andrew Lang; with numerous illustrations by H. J. Ford and G. P. Jacomb Hood. Dover Publs. 1965 390p il pa $10.95

Grades: 4 5 6   **398.2**

1. Folklore 2. Fairy tales

ISBN 0-486-21437-0

Also available in paperback $10.95 each: The Green fairy book; The Grey fairy book; The Lilac fairy book; The Olive fairy book; The Or-

ange fairy book; The Pink fairy book; The Red fairy book; The Yellow fairy book

A reprint of the title first published 1889 by Longmans

A collection of thirty-seven fairy tales from various countries, consisting largely of old favorites from such sources as Perrault, the Brothers Grimm, Madame D'Aulnoy, Asbjörnsen and Möe, the Arabian Nights and Swift's Gulliver's travels

Brett, Jan, 1949-

Beauty and the beast; retold and illustrated by Jan Brett. Clarion Bks. 1989 un il lib bdg $16; pa $6.95

Grades: 1 2 3   **398.2**

1. Fairy tales 2. Folklore -- France

ISBN 0-89919-497-4 lib bdg; 0-395-55702-X pa

LC 88-16965

This is a retelling of the French fairy tale. Through her great capacity to love, a kind and beautiful maid releases a handsome prince from the spell which has given him the appearance of a wild beast and turned his servants into animals. "Ages four to eight." (Booklist)

"A Beauty of distinguished appearance, a delightful set of animal servants, and a suitably hideous Beast are presented in Jan Brett's distinctive, decorative style. Small details, such as tapestries mirroring the action of the tale, add to the effect of the simply written story." Horn Book Guide

Gingerbread baby. Putnam 1999 un il $16.99

Grades: K 1 2 3   **398.2**

1. Folklore

ISBN 0-399-23444-6

LC 98-52310

A young boy and his mother bake a gingerbread baby that escapes from their oven and leads a crowd on a chase

"Although the story remains true to the original tale, Brett has added her own touches and a surprise ending. . . . The illustrations are pure Brett and feature warm colors against a snow-white landscape." SLJ

Other Gingerbread baby books are:

Gingerbread friends (2008)

Gingerbread Christmas (2016)

Goldilocks and the three bears; retold and illustrated by Jan Brett. Putnam 1992 48 p. col il $17.99

Grades: PreK K 1 2   **398.2**

1. Folklore 2. Bears -- Folklore

ISBN 039922033X; 9780399220333

LC 87565

This children's story, retold and illustrated by Jan Brett, presents the classic "story of the curious little girl named Goldilocks, who made herself quite at home in the house of the three bears. Jan Brett's lavish illustrations for this classic tale, full of details and surprises, gives this edition a special flair." (Publisher's note)

"Brett's beautifully executed retelling of this classic story is distinguished by the use of luxuriant color and a wealth of visual detail...with such a display before them, readers will hardly blame Goldilocks for her lack of restraint." Publishers Weekly

The **mitten**; a Ukrainian folktale. adapted and illustrated by Jan Brett. anniversary ed.; Penguin Young Readers Group 2009 un il $17.99

Grades: K 1 2   **398.2**

1. Animals -- Folklore 2. Folklore -- Ukraine

ISBN 978-0-399-25296-9; 0-399-25296-7

First published 1989 by Putnam

After Nicki accidentally drops his mitten in the forest it becomes an object of curiosity for a mole, a rabbit, a badger, a tiny brown mouse, and a big brown bear, as they all crawl into it

"Readers will enjoy the charm and humor in the portrayal of the animals as they make room for each newcomer in the mitten and sprawl in the snow after the big sneeze." Horn Book

Who's that knocking on Christmas Eve. Putnam 2002 un il $16.99
Grades: K 1 2   **398.2**
1. Folklore -- Norway 2. Christmas -- Fiction
ISBN 0-399-23873-5

LC 2001-48253

A boy from Finnmark and his ice bear help scare away some hungry trolls so that Kyri and her father can enjoy their Christmas Eve meal

This is a "vivid, well-paced retelling of an old Norwegian folktale. . . . Gorgeous endpapers depicting night-sky constellations studded with trolls, bears, and other mythical symbols complement the exquisitely detailed winter-wonderland artistry within." Booklist

Brown, Marcia
Once a mouse; a fable cut in wood. Atheneum Pubs. 1961 un il $16; pa $5.99
Grades: K 1 2 3   **398.2**
1. Fables 2. Folklore -- India
ISBN 0-684-12662-1; 0-689-71343-6 pa
Awarded the Caldecott Medal, 1962

"The illustrations are remarkably beautiful. The emotional elements of the story . . . are conveyed with just as much intensity as the purely visual ones." New Yorker

Stone soup; an old tale. told and pictured by Marcia Brown. Scribner 1947 un il $16.95; pa $6.99
Grades: K 1 2 3   **398.2**
1. Folklore -- France
ISBN 0-684-92296-7; 0-689-71103-4 pa
A Caldecott Medal honor book, 1948

"When the people in a French village heard that three soldiers were coming, they hid all their food for they knew what soldiers are. However, when the soldiers began to make soup with water and stones the pot gradually filled with all the vegetables which had been hidden away. The simple language and quiet humour of this folktale are amplified and enriched by gay and witty drawings of clever light-hearted soldiers, and the gullible 'light-witted' peasants." Cont Libr Rev

Bruchac, James
★ The **girl** who helped thunder and other Native American folktales; retold by James Bruchac and Joseph Bruchac; illustrated by Stefano Vitale. Sterling Pub. Co. 2008 96p il (Folktales of the world) $14.95
Grades: 3 4 5 6   **398.2**
1. Native Americans -- Folklore
ISBN 978-1-4027-3263-8; 1-4027-3263-5

LC 2007-16876

"The Bruchacs retell Native North American folktales in a clear yet bold voice. The anthology is arranged geographically, a logical organization that reveals the diversity of Native peoples. . . . Descriptions of each region introduce the original inhabitants of those places, as the authors provide succinct yet enriching historical and cultural context for the stories that follow. . . . Vitale's stylized oil-on-wood illustrations vividly reveal the colorful spirit of the tales, as bright blues and reds complement the earth tones found throughout." SLJ

Bruchac, Joseph
Between earth & sky; legends of Native American sacred places. written by Joseph Bruchac; illustrated by Thomas Locker. Harcourt Brace & Co. 1996 un il map hardcover o.p. pa $7
Grades: 3 4 5   **398.2**
1. Native Americans -- Folklore
ISBN 0-15-200042-9; 0-15-202062-4 pa

LC 95-10862

"Each tale is a model of economy, gracefully distilling its message, while Locker's landscapes capture the mysticism inherent in each setting." Horn Book Guide

★ The **first** strawberries; a Cherokee story. retold by Joseph Bruchac; pictures by Anna Vojtech. Dial Bks. for Young Readers 1993 un il hardcover o.p. pa $6.99
Grades: K 1 2 3   **398.2**
1. Strawberries -- Folklore 2. Cherokee Indians -- Folklore
ISBN 0-8037-1331-2; 0-14-05409-8 pa

LC 91-31058

A quarrel between the first man and the first woman is reconciled when the Sun causes strawberries to grow out of the earth

"This retelling . . . is simply and clearly written, and as sweet as the berries the woman stops to taste. The attractive watercolors and colored-pencil illustrations show an idealized pastoral world." SLJ

How Chipmunk got his stripes; a tale of bragging and teasing. as told by Joseph Bruchac & James Bruchac; pictures by Jose Aruego & Ariane Dewey. Dial Bks. for Young Readers 2001 un il hardcover o.p. pa $6.99
Grades: K 1 2 3   **398.2**
1. Bears -- Folklore 2. Chipmunks -- Folklore 3. Squirrels -- Folklore 4. Native Americans -- Folklore
ISBN 0-8037-2404-7; 0-14-250021-6 pa

LC 99-16793

"This pourquoi story is succinctly written in simple, concrete language, and repeated chants give listeners an opportunity to participate actively in the narrative's unfolding. . . . The pictures are large enough to be seen and enjoyed by a group." Bull Cent Child Books

Thirteen moons on a turtle's back; a Native American year of moons. by Joseph Bruchac and Jonathan London; illustrated by Thomas Locker. Philomel Bks. 1992 un il $16.95; pa $5.99
Grades: K 1 2 3 4   **398.2**
1. Seasons -- Poetry 2. Native Americans -- Poetry 3. Native Americans -- Folklore 4. Poetry -- By individual authors
ISBN 0-399-22141-7; 0-698-11584-8 pa

LC 91-3961

"Locker . . . has created a dramatic oil painting for each short tale. His artwork portrays seasonal changes in the land as well as the specific seasonal activities of humans and animals. The large format with minimal text will appeal to younger children, while the alternative calendar, based on changes in nature, will interest middle readers. An unusual, easy-to-use resource for librarians, teachers, and others wishing to incorporate multicultural activites throughout the year." Booklist

Turtle's race with Beaver; a traditional Seneca story. as told by Joseph Bruchac & James Bruchac; pictures by Jose Aruego & Ariane Dewey. Dial Bks. for Young Readers 2003 un il $15.99; pa $5.99
Grades: K 1 2 3   **398.2**
1. Beavers -- Folklore 2. Turtles -- Folklore 3. Seneca Indians -- Folklore
ISBN 0-8037-2852-2; 0-14-240466-7 pa

LC 2002-4001

When Beaver challenges Turtle to a swimming race for ownership of the pond, Turtle outsmarts Beaver, and Beaver learns to share

"Done in pen and ink, gouache, and pastel, the cheerful artwork is a wonderful match for this well-told tale." SLJ

Bryan, Ashley

★ **Ashley** Bryan's African tales, uh-huh. Atheneum Bks. for Young Readers 1998 198p $22
Grades: 4 5 6   **398.2**
   1. Folklore -- Africa
   ISBN 0-689-82076-3
            LC 97-77743

This volume combines three previously published titles: The ox of the wonderful horns and other African folktales (1971), Beat the story-drum, pum-pum (1980), Lion and the ostrich chicks and other African folktales (1986)

This collection of African folktales is "told with Bryan's distinctive rhythmic word patterns and filled with humor, life lessons, and the antics of trickster Ananse. . . . Quality reproductions of the original woodcuts enrich this handsome volume." Horn Book Guide

★ **Beautiful** blackbird. Atheneum Bks. for Young Readers 2003 un il $16.95
Grades: K 1 2 3   **398.2**
   1. Birds -- Folklore 2. Folklore -- Zambia 3. Folklore -- Africa
   ISBN 0-689-84731-9
            LC 2002-5290

In a story of the Ila people, the colorful birds of Africa ask Blackbird, whom they think is the most beautiful of birds, to decorate them with some of his blackening brew. "Ages five to nine." (Bull Cent Child Books)

"Bryan employs boldly colored, cut-paper artwork to dramatize the action. The overlapping collage images fill the pages with energy. . . . Ready-made for participative storytelling." Booklist

Buehner, Caralyn

Goldilocks and the three bears; [by] Caralyn Buehner; pictures by Mark Buehner. Dial Books for Young Readers 2007 un il $16.99
Grades: PreK K 1 2   **398.2**
   1. Folklore 2. Bears -- Folklore
   ISBN 0-8037-2939-1
            LC 2005036401

In this variation on the classic folktale, a rhyming, rope-skipping, little girl rudely helps herself to the belongings of a genteel family of bears.

"This warm and pleasing retelling of the classic include a rope-jumping Goldilocks in red cowboy boots who bursts with personality. . . . The luminous oil-over-acrylic illustrations enhance the story with delightful details." SLJ

Bunting, Eve

Finn McCool and the great fish; written by Eve Bunting; illustrated by Zachary Pullen. Sleeping Bear Press 2010 un il $16.95
Grades: K 1 2 3   **398.2**
   1. Fishes -- Folklore 2. Giants -- Folklore 3. Folklore -- Ireland
   ISBN 1-58536-366-9; 978-1-58536-366-7
            LC 2009036936

Irish giant Finn McCool is told that in order to become wise he much catch and eat the salmon that possesses knowledge, but Finn finds that he cannot bring himself to kill the miraculous fish

"Bunting makes this unfamiliar story accessible to readers. The art beautifully illustrates the green Irish countryside and makes Finn a real gentle giant." SLJ

Burningham, John

Tug-of-war; John Burningham. Candlewick Press 2013 32 p. $16.99
Grades: K 1 2 3   **398.2**
   1. Tricksters -- Folklore 2. Picture books for children
   ISBN 0763665754; 9780763665753
            LC 2012947722

This children's picture book offers an illustrated retelling of a West African folktale. Hare is teased by Hippopotamus and Elephant, so "Hare is keen to defeat his tormenters using his superior wits. Hare finds Elephant in the forest, challenges him to a tug-of-war, and gives him an end of rope. Hare meets Hippopotamus at the river and gives him the other end. Sight unseen, both creatures believe Hare is pulling against them, and fail to realize their error until Hare" has disappeared. (Publishers Weekly)

Burns, Batt

★ The **king** with horse's ears and other Irish folktales; [by] Batt Burns; illustrated by Igor Oleynikov. Sterling Pub. Co. 2009 96p il (Folktales of the world) $14.95
Grades: 4 5 6 7   **398.2**
   1. Fairy tales 2. Folklore -- Ireland
   ISBN 978-1-4027-3772-5; 1-4027-3772-6
            LC 2007035258

"These 13 Irish tales retold by storyteller Burns follow fairies and warriors, heroes and clever thieves. . . . The stories are cleanly retold in contemporary, accessible language, and each is introduced with a short paragraph providing cultural or other information. . . . Oleynikov's paintings have a rough texture that suits the energy of the retellings and adds to the lively tone. This is a hearty collection, handsomely produced with Celtic-knot borders and gouache full-page and spot illustrations." Booklist

Includes glossary

Byrd, Robert, 1942-

Jason and the Argonauts; The First Great Quest in Greek Mythology. by Robert Byrd. Dial Books for Young Readers 2016 48 p. color illustrations, maps (ebook) $53.97; (hardcover) $17.99
Grades: 2 3 4 5   **398.2**
   1. Jason (Greek mythology) 2. Picture books for children 3. Argonauts (Greek mythology)
   ISBN 9780735227651; 9780803741188
            LC 2015040910

This children's book, by Robert Byrd, is "the story of Jason and the Argonauts . . . one of the earliest recorded Greek myths. . . . [It] traces each step of our hero's journey, from the Golden Fleece's origin story and Jason's childhood to his triumphant return with the prize and eventual death. Deftly designed to accommodate glorious large pictures and captioned insets, the book is not only a great story, but a wealth of information about ancient Greece." (Publisher's note)

"The endpaper maps and title-page illustration are particularly fine. This handsome book offers a colorfully illustrated retelling of Jason's adventures." Booklist

Caduto, Michael J.

Keepers of the night; Native American stories and nocturnal activities for children. [by] Michael J. Caduto and Joseph Bruchac; story illustrations by David Kanietakeron Fadden; chapter illustrations by Jo Levasseur and Carol Wood; foreword by Merlin D. Tuttle. Fulcrum 1994 146p il pa $15.95
Grades: Adult Professional   **398.2**
   1. Nature study 2. Night -- Folklore 3. Native Americans --

Folklore
ISBN 1-55591-177-3

LC 94-2602

"The well-written chapters include discussions with illuminating scientific information." Sci Books Films

Includes glossary and bibliographical references

Campoy, F. Isabel

★ **Tales** our abuelitas told; a Hispanic folktale collection. [by] F. Isabel Campoy and Alma Flor Ada; illustrated by Felipe Dávalos . . . [et al.] Simon & Schuster 2006 118p il $19.95

Grades: 3 4 5 6   **398.2**

1. Folklore -- Latin America 2. Hispanic Americans -- Folklore
ISBN 0-689-82583-5

Presents the authors' retellings of twelve traditional tales accompanied by information on origins and different versions

"All of the selections are peppered with energetic dialogue and witty detail. Children will relish their humor, especially if read aloud." SLJ

Cardenas, Teresa

Oloyou; pictures by Margarita Sada; translated by Elisa Amado. Groundwood Books 2008 un il $18.95

Grades: 2 3 4 5   **398.2**

1. Cats -- Folklore 2. Folklore -- Cuba 3. Bilingual books -- English-Spanish 4. Yoruba (African people) -- Folklore
ISBN 978-0-88899-795-1; 0-88899-795-7

"In this striking bilingual retelling of a Yoruba myth, Oloyou the Cat is the very first creature created by the Godchild while he is still too young to know what he is doing. More importantly, Oloyou becomes God's first friend. They are happy until Oloyou falls into Nothing, which is an oceanic kingdom presided over by Okun Aró. . . . The clarity of the writing makes this book suitable for reading aloud, while the complexity of the story will hold the interest of older readers. The oil-on-canvas illustrations are rich and bold with a mythic scope that incorporates the story's African-Caribbean roots." SLJ

Casey, Dawn

The **Barefoot** book of Earth tales; retold by Dawn Casey; illustrated by Anne Wilson. Barefoot Books 2009 95p il $19.99

Grades: 2 3 4 5 6   **398.2**

1. Folklore 2. Ecology -- Folklore
ISBN 978-1-84686-224-3; 1-84686-224-8

"This enchanting collection of folk tales and creation myths from different cultures encourages readers to live a more harmonious life with nature. . . . Well chosen and crafted with broad appeal, the tales are woven with subtle morals and wisdom. Each story is introduced by a brief overview about the featured locale and culture . . . and followed by a related, easy-to-replicate activity or craft. Full-page and spot illustrations and colorful decorative borders reflect the spirit and origins of each offering. Done with collaged papers with acrylic and printed backgrounds." SLJ

The **great** race; the story of the Chinese zodiac. written by Dawn Casey; illustrated by Anne Wilson. Barefoot Books 2006 un il $16.99

Grades: 1 2 3 4   **398.2**

1. Zodiac 2. Folklore -- China 3. Animals -- Folklore
ISBN 1-905236-77-8

LC 2005032544

Relates how the Jade Emperor chose twelve animals to represent the years in his calendar. Also discusses the Chinese calendar, zodiac, the qualities associated with each animal, and what animal rules the year in which the reader was born

"In this retelling of the ancient legend, Casey maintains the pace well. . . . The book is a visual treat, with illustrations in simple collage

designs on acrylic and painted backgrounds placed in such a way as to keep the eye engaged and moving." SLJ

Cech, John

Jack and the beanstalk; retold by John Cech; illustrated by Robert Mackenzie. Sterling Pub. Co. 2008 un il $14.95

Grades: 1 2 3   **398.2**

1. Fairy tales 2. Giants -- Folklore 3. Folklore -- Great Britain
ISBN 978-1-4027-3064-1; 1-4027-3064-0

LC 2007001783

A boy climbs to the top of a giant beanstalk where he uses his quick wits to outsmart an ogre and make his and his mother's fortune. Includes historical notes on versions of this tale, other heroic stories, and alternate "ascension" tales.

Cech "knits fresh strands into the . . . . story. This smoothly paced version, which begins with some hilarious wordplay, runs close to traditional tellings until the end, when the giant's wife joins Jack in his hasty escape. . . . MacKenzie ably ramps up the drama in the pencil-and-paint scenes." Booklist

Puss in boots; retold by John Cech; illustrated by Bernhard Oberdieck. Sterling Pub. 2010 un il (Classic fairy tale collection) $14.95

Grades: K 1 2 3   **398.2**

1. Fairy tales 2. Folklore -- France
ISBN 978-1-4027-4436-5; 1-4027-4436-6

LC 2008052496

A clever cat helps his poor master win fame, fortune, and the hand of a beautiful princess. Includes historical notes on versions of this tale and other fairy tales

This "offers an enjoyable retelling of the timeless story. . . . The narrative is descriptive, lively, and droll, and the colorful watercolor-and-ink illustrations, filled with period details, are intricately rendered." Booklist

Rapunzel; retold by John Cech; illustrated by Fiona Sansom. Sterling 2010 un il (Classic fairy tale collection) $14.95

Grades: K 1 2 3   **398.2**

1. Folklore 2. Fairy tales
ISBN 978-1-4027-6911-5; 1-4027-6911-3

A retelling of a folktale in which a beautiful girl with long golden hair is kept imprisoned in a lonely tower by a witch. Includes a note on the origins of the story.

"Cech employs clear, descriptive language that is fresh and appealing to modern readers, at times seeming to speak directly to his audience. Varying in size from inserts to double-page spreads, with the text often placed in frames, Sansom's lovely medieval paintings complement and enhance the text, depicting the action while concentrating on emotional content. . . . A spendid candidate for a crowd-pleasing read-aloud." Kirkus

Chase, Richard

The **Jack** tales; told by R.M. Ward and his kindred in the Beech Mountain section of western North Carolina and by other descendants of Council Harmon (1803-1896) elsewhere in the southern mountains; with three tales from Wise County, Virginia; set down from these sources and edited by Richard Chase; with an appendix compiled by Herbert Halpert; and illustrated by Berkeley Williams, Jr. Houghton Mifflin 2003 216p il pa $7.95

Grades: 5 6 7 8 Adult Professional   **398.2**

1. Folklore -- Southern States
ISBN 978-0-618-34692-9 pa; 0-618-34692-9 pa

LC 2003276676

First published 1943

A collection of folk tales from the southern Appalachians that center on a single character, the irrepressible Jack

"Humor, freshness, colorful American background, and the use of one character as a central figure in the cycle mark these 18 folk tales, told here in the dialect of the mountain country of North Carolina. A scholarly appendix by Herbert Halpert, giving sources and parallels, increases the book's value as a contribution to American folklore. Black-and-white illustrations in the spirit of the text." Booklist

Includes bibliographical references

Chichester-Clark, Emma

★ **Goldilocks** and the three bears. Candlewick Press 2010 un il $14.99

Grades: PreK K 1

    1. Folklore 2. Bears -- Folklore   **398.2**

    ISBN 978-0-7636-4680-6; 0-7636-4680-6

LC 2009-14601

A retelling of the adventures of a nosy, naughty, and sassy little girl who finds the house of the three bears and helps herself to their belongings.

"This large-format edition of the traditional story offers plenty of scope for Clark's colorful illustrations. While the plot remains the same, the telling is a little more elaborate here than in most versions, with a couple of new refrains and added dialogue. . . . The controlled profusion of patterns gives the pencil-and-acrylic illustrations a busy but cheerful look. . . . Recommended for the freshness and energy of its artwork." Booklist

Christopher, Neil

Way Back Then; by Neil Christopher; illustrated by Germaine Arnaktauyok. Inhabit Media 2015 40 p. color illustrations $16.95

Grades: K 1 2 3

    1. Inuit -- fiction 2. Giants -- fiction 3. Animals -- fiction 4. Bedtime -- fiction   **398.2**

    ISBN 1772270210; 9781772270211

This book, by Neil Christopher, illustrated by Germaine Arnaktauyok, is a "A . . . bedtime story . . . from Inuit mythology. Kudlu's children will not go to sleep until he tells them a story of long ago. Before they will shut their eyes, they want to hear about a time long before Kudlu was born, a time when the world was magic. Before they can sleep, they want to hear about giants, animals . . . little people the size of lemmings, and . . . things that existed way back then." (Publisher's note)

"A bilingual sampler—cold of setting but warm of spirit." Kirkus

Cinderella; [illustrated by K.Y. Craft] SeaStar Books 2000 32 p. col. ill. $16.99

Grades: K 1 2 3

    1. Fairy tales -- Fiction 2. Folklore 3. Fairy tales   **398.2**

    ISBN 1587170043; 9781587170041

LC 00024540

This retold fairy tale of Cinderella is illustrated by K.Y. Craft. "Inspired by the opulent styles of 17th- and 18th-century France, the paintings are confections of luxurious clothing, densely vegetated woods and regally appointed ballrooms. . . . The story, adapted from Arthur Rackham's and Andrew Lang's versions, contains pleasing touches as well as a moral." (Publishers Weekly)

"In this fresh retelling, Cinderella is tending to a wounded bird in the woods when she accidentally meets the prince for the first time. The bird later transforms into her fairy godmother and makes it possible for her to attend the ball, where she captures the prince's heart. Ornate illustrations, echoed by elaborate marginalia that swirl around the text, place the tale in seventeenth-century France." Horn Book

Clayton, Sally Pomme

Amazons! women warriors of the world. illustrated by Sophie Herxheimer. Frances Lincoln 2009 93p il $19.95

Grades: 3 4 5 6

                                            398.2

    1. Folklore 2. Women -- Folklore

    ISBN 978-1-84507-660-3; 1-84507-660-5

"This handsome collection of folktales showcases seven empowering females, each with her own unique strengths and abilities. . . . Filled with lively language and fast-paced action, the tales introduce a pleasing range of characters and moods. . . . The illustrations employ swirling lines and vibrant color washes to reflect the setting and tone of each tale. The stories are separated by two-page interludes that provide brief facts or activities." SLJ

Includes glossary

Tales told in tents; stories from central Asia. written by Sally Pomme Clayton; illustrated by Sophie Herxheimer. Frances Lincoln 2005 64p il map $16.95; pa $8.95

Grades: 2 3 4

                                            398.2

    1. Folklore -- Asia

    ISBN 978-1-84507-066-3; 1-84507-066-6; 978-1-84507-278-0 pa; 1-84507-278-2 pa

"In 12 traditional stories from the nomadic cultures of Central Asia, folklorist Clayton retells myth and folklore she heard in Kazakhstan, Afghanistan, and elsewhere. The lively tales include epic creation myths, rhyming riddles, trickster tales, songs, and stories of magic carpets and music. The large picture book is illustrated with richly colored line-and-watercolor paintings that evoke Central Asian traditional culture. . . . A rich resource, even for older readers, this anthology has stories that travel across the world." Booklist

Includes glossary

Climo, Shirley

The **Egyptian** Cinderella; illustrated by Ruth Heller. Crowell 1989 un il $15.95; pa $5.95

Grades: K 1 2 3

                                            398.2

    1. Fairy tales 2. Folklore -- Egypt

    ISBN 0-690-04822-X; 0-06-443279-3 pa

LC 88-37547

This picture book tells the legend of Rhodopis, a Greek slave who married the sixth-century B.C. pharaoh Amasis. This "is accomplished through the intercession of the great falcon, symbol of the god Horus. When the majestic bird deposits one of Rhodopis' rosy-gold slippers, a gift from her master, in the lap of the Pharaoh, he determines this to be a signal from the gods to marry the maiden whose foot it fits. . . . Kindergarten to grade three." (SLJ)

"The beauty of the language is set off to perfection by Heller's arresting full-color illustrations." SLJ

Coburn, Jewell Reinhart

Domitila; a Cinderella tale from the Mexican tradition. adapted by Jewell Reinhart Coburn; illustrated by Connie McLennan. Shen's Bks. 2000 un il $16.95

Grades: 2 3 4

                                            398.2

    1. Folklore -- Mexico

    ISBN 1-88500-813-9

LC 99-56173

By following her mother's admonition to perform every task with care and love, a poor young Mexican girl wins the devotion of the governor's son

"The full-page oil-on-cavas illustrations are bright, sumptuous, and visually enticing. The text is bordered by proverbs rendered in both Spanish and English. Well-written and strongly illustrated." SLJ

Cohen, Caron Lee

The **mud** pony; a traditional Skidi Pawnee tale. retold by Caron Lee Cohen; illustrated by Shonto Begay. Scholastic 1988 un il hardcover o.p. pa $4.99

Grades: K 1 2 3   **398.2**

1. Horses -- Folklore 2. Pawnee Indians -- Folklore

ISBN 0-590-41526-3 pa

LC 87-23451

A poor boy becomes a powerful leader when Mother Earth turns his mud pony into a real one, but after the pony turns back to mud, he must find his own strength

"The text is powerful because it is spare and unadorned. It is extended well by the softly toned, full-color, impressionistic pictures." Helbig. This land is our land

Corr, Christopher

Deep in the Woods; by Christopher Corr. Frances Lincoln Children's Books 2017 32 p. color illustrations $17.99

Grades: PreK K 1 2   **398.2**

1. Folklore -- Russia 2. Bears -- fiction 3. Forest animals -- fiction

ISBN 1847807267; 9781847807267

In this book, by Christopher Corr, "deep in the woods is a little wooden house, with nine neat windows and a red front door. When a little mouse decides it will make the perfect home, so do the other animals in the wood - including a great big bear! But will the bear be able to put everything right when their home comes tumbling down?" (Publisher's note)

Cousins, Lucy

★ **Yummy**; eight favorite fairy tales. Candlewick Press 2009 121p il $18.99

Grades: PreK K 1   **398.2**

1. Folklore 2. Fairy tales

ISBN 978-0-7636-4474-1; 0-7636-4474-9

"Beloved classics are successfully served by these bold, striking renditions. . . . Large, arresting gouache spreads in Cousins's signature style utilize saturated colors and thick, dark outlines against solid backgrounds. Expressive characters enhance the stories' shifting moods. Large type accentuates the dynamic texts, building each spare entry to its powerful climax." SLJ

Craft, Mahlon F.

Sleeping Beauty; illustrated by Kinuko Y. Craft; as retold by Mahlon F. Craft. SeaStar Bks. 2002 un il $15.95; lib bdg $16.50

Grades: 2 3 4   **398.2**

1. Fairy tales 2. Folklore -- Germany

ISBN 1-58717-120-1; 1-58717-121-X lib bdg

LC 2002-2009

A beautiful and beloved princess, cursed by the one fairy who was not invited to her christening, pricks her finger on her sixteenth birthday and falls asleep for one hundred years

"Mahlon Craft relates events in formal language, using specifics that correspond to most traditional Brothers Grimm version[s]. The lush, richly detailed, oil-on-watercolor paintings perfectly complement the text." Booklist

Crews, Nina

Jack and the beanstalk. Henry Holt 2011 32p il $16.99

Grades: K 1 2   **398.2**

1. Fairy tales 2. Giants -- Folklore 3. Folklore -- Great Britain

ISBN 978-0-8050-8765-9; 0-8050-8765-6

LC 2010026951

Photo-collage illustrations and updated text provide a new look at the traditional tale of a boy who plants magic beans, climbs the beanstalk, and is captured by a giant and his wife.

"The images are quite keen, photographs and the occasional line drawing manipulated and layered to shape the story. . . . Crews' fans will be delighted; others will be drawn in by the nifty mix of folktale and photo-collage." Kirkus

Cummings, Pat

★ **Ananse** and the lizard; a West African tale. retold and illustrated by Pat Cummings. Holt & Co. 2002 un il $16.95

Grades: K 1 2 3   **398.2**

1. Folklore -- Ghana 2. Anansi (Legendary character)

ISBN 0-8050-6476-1

LC 2001-1679

Ananse the spider thinks he will marry the daughter of the village chief, but instead he is outsmarted by Lizard

"Cummings' lively prose and humor are a perfect match for the story. The boxed text is accompanied by gorgeous watercolor, gouache, and pencil illustrations, rich in color and lively pattern." Booklist

Curry, Jane Louise

Hold up the sky: and other Native American tales from Texas and the Southern Plains; illustrated by James Watts. Margaret K. McElderry Bks. 2003 159p il $17.95

Grades: 4 5 6 7   **398.2**

1. Folklore -- Southern States 2. Native Americans -- Folklore

ISBN 0-689-85287-8

LC 2002-16519

Retells twenty-six tales from Native Americans whose traditional lands were in Texas and the Southern Plains, and provides a brief introduction to the history of each tribe

"Curry has carefully researched and sensitively retold tales from fourteen Native American nations. Attractive pencil drawings enhance the stories." Horn Book Guide

Includes bibliographical references

D'Aulaire, Ingri

The **terrible** troll-bird; [by] Ingri and Edgar Parin d'Aulaire. New York Review Books 2007 41p il $15.95

Grades: K 1 2 3   **398.2**

1. Trolls 2. Fairy tales 3. Folklore -- Norway

ISBN 978-1-59017-252-0; 1-59017-252-3

LC 2007-13020

First published 1976 by Doubleday

When four children defeat the terrible troll-bird who has terrified their Norwegian valley for years, everyone celebrates in a merry feast.

"The d'Aulaires illustrate this rousing Scandinavian folktale in exuberant pictures using both sketchy black-and-white lines and mottled color." Horn Book Guide

Dabcovich, Lydia

The **polar** bear son; an Inuit tale. retold and illustrated by Lydia Dabcovich. Clarion Bks. 1997 37p il hardcover o.p. pa $5.95

Grades: K 1 2 3   **398.2**

1. Inuit -- Folklore 2. Polar bear -- Folklore

ISBN 0-395-72766-9; 0-395-97567-0 pa

LC 96-4780

An old woman adopts and raises a polar bear cub which grows up and provides for her even after she has had to send it away to save it from the jealous men of the village

"Illustrated in muted pastel colors, the pictures capture this stark, yet beautiful, winter world." SLJ

Dayrell, Elphinstone

★ **Why** the Sun and the Moon live in the sky; an African folktale. illustrated by Blair Lent. Houghton Mifflin 1968 26p il $16; pa $6.95

Grades: K 1 2 3   398.2

1. Sun -- Folklore 2. Moon -- Folklore 3. Folklore -- Nigeria

ISBN 0-395-29609-9; 0-395-53963-3 pa

First told by the author in his book: Folk stories from Southern Nigeria, West Africa, published 1910 in England

A Caldecott Medal honor book, 1969

"The beautifully detailed and stylized art work is based on African sources; the artist uses cool colors for the water, a pale blue-grey for the moon, and shades of gold and white for the sun." Sutherland. The Best in Child Books

De las Casas, Dianne

The **gigantic** sweet potato; illustrated by Marita Gentry. Pelican Pub. Co. 2010 un il $16.99

Grades: K 1 2 3   398.2

1. Folklore -- Russia

ISBN 978-1-58980-755-6; 1-58980-755-3

LC 2010009434

Ma Farmer craves sweet potato pie but needs help to harvest a homegrown sweet potato—in this version of the Russian folktale, The Giant Turnip. Includes recipe and directions to make sweet potato pie.

"Colorful watercolors accompany the rhythmic text and add a touch of foreshadowing. . . . Children will happily join in the repetitive, cumulative text and enjoy the satisfying end. . . . This tasty selection is a solid interpretation of the classic tale, with appealing pictures and a strong female character." Kirkus

De Regniers, Beatrice Schenk

Little sister and the month brothers; retold by Beatrice Schenk de Regniers; pictures by Margot Tomes. Marshall Cavendish Children 2009 un il $17.99

Grades: K 1 2 3   398.2

1. Fairy tales 2. Slavs -- Folklore

ISBN 978-0-7614-5546-2; 0-7614-5546-9

A reissue of the title first published 1976 by Seabury Press

A retelling of the Slavic fairy tale in which the Month Brothers' magic helps Little Sister fulfill seemingly impossible tasks which prove the undoing of her greedy stepmother and stepsister.

"Tomes's intimate, unpretentious illustrations extend the text brilliantly. A timeless treasure." Horn Book Guide

Deedy, Carmen Agra

★ **Martina** the beautiful cockroach; a Cuban folktale. retold by Carmen Agra Deedy; illustrated by Michael Austin. Peachtree 2007 un il $16.95

Grades: 2 3 4 5   398.2

1. Folklore -- Cuba 2. Cockroaches -- Folklore

ISBN 978-1-56145-399-3

LC 2007003108

In this humorous retelling of a Cuban folktale, a cockroach interviews her suitors in order to decide whom to marry

"Deedy's masterful retelling . . . has a rollicking voice imbued with sly tongue-in-cheek humor. The acrylic illustrations, in a hyperrealistic style . . . are rendered in a vivid tropical palette." Booklist

Delacre, Lulu

Golden tales; myths, legends, and folktales from Latin America. [retold by] Lulu Delacre. Scholastic 1996 73p hardcover o.p. pa $5.99

Grades: 5 6 7 8   398.2

1. Folklore -- Latin America 2. Native Americans -- Folklore

ISBN 0-439-24398-X pa

LC 94-36724

This includes 12 "stories from four native cultures (Taino, Zapotec, Muisca, and Quechua), including pourquoi tales, legends of the conquistadores, and folktales from before and after the age of Columbus. . . . [The author's] . . . retellings are done in a clear and confident voice and are accompanied by her robust, colorful oil paintings. . . . This impressively presented and referenced collection will inspire readers and tellers alike." Booklist

Includes bibliographical references

Dembicki, Matt

★ **Trickster:** Native American tales; a graphic collection. edited by Matt Dembicki. Fulcrum 2010 231p il pa $22.95

Grades: 5 6 7 8   398.2

1. Graphic novels 2. Folklore -- Graphic novels 3. Native Americans -- Folklore

ISBN 978-1-55591-724-1 pa; 1-55591-724-0 pa

LC 2009-49668

"More than 40 storytellers and cartoonists have contributed to this original and provocative compendium of traditional folklore presented in authentic, colorful, and engaging sequential art. The stories are drawn from a variety of Native peoples across North America, and so the trickster character appears variously as Rabbit, a raccoon, Coyote, and in other guises; landscapes, clothing and rhythms of speech and action also vary in keeping with distinct traditions. Realistic, impressionistic, painterly, and cartoon styles of art are employed to echo and announce the tone of each tale and telling style, making this a rich visual treasure as well as cultural trove." SLJ

Demi

★ The **hungry** coat; a tale from Turkey. Margaret K. McElderry Books 2004 un il $19.95

Grades: K 1 2 3   398.2

1. Folklore -- Turkey

ISBN 0-689-84680-0

LC 2002-155129

After being forced to change to a fancy new coat to attend a party, Nasrettin Hoca tries to feed his dinner to the coat, reasoning that it was the coat that was the invited guest.

"Demi's retelling of this tale is compelling and includes many details that help bring both time and place into focus. Her paint-and-ink illustrations are resplendent with her trademark gold leaf and intricate borders." SLJ

King Midas; the golden touch. Margaret K. McElderry Bks. 2002 un il $19.95

Grades: 2 3 4   398.2

1. Midas (Legendary character)

ISBN 0-689-83297-4

LC 99-89389

A king finds himself bitterly regretting the consequences of his wish that everything he touches would turn to gold

Demi's "unsourced but briskly amusing retelling begins with the contest when Midas's preference for Pan's shrill discord so angers the great musician Apollo that he gives the king donkey's ears. . . . The gilded special effects take center stage; still, Demi's glowing colors, decorative figures, and delicate drafting are also worthy of note. . . . This handsome book breathes new life into one of the oldest of cautionary tales." Horn Book

DePaola, Tomie, 1934-

★ **Adelita**; a Mexican Cinderella story. written and illustrated by Tomie de Paola. Putnam 2002 un il hardcover o.p. pa $6.99

Grades: K 1 2 3   **398.2**

1. Fairy tales 2. Folklore -- Mexico

ISBN 0-399-23866-2; 0-14-240187-0 pa

LC 2001-57873

After the death of her mother and father, Adelita is badly mistreated by her stepmother and stepsisters until she finds her own true love at a grand fiesta

"The prose is straightforward and crisp. . . . Making perfect use of clear, warm hues, the full-color acrylic illustrations are a feast for the eye." SLJ

The **clown** of God; an old story. told and illustrated by Tomie de Paola. Harcourt Brace Jovanovich 1978 un il $16; pa $7

Grades: K 1 2 3   **398.2**

1. Legends 2. Miracles -- Folklore 3. Christmas -- Folklore

ISBN 0-15-219175-5; 0-15-618192-4 pa

LC 78-3845

An orphan whose juggling skill led him to a career as a traveling entertainer has grown old and clumsy and returns as a hungry beggar to his birthplace. On Christmas Eve in the monastery church a miracle occurs as he summons his last strength to make his only possible offering

"Mr. de Paola has written the tale with love, tenderness, and joy. He has executed authentic Renaissance illustrations that are magnificent in design and beauty." Child Book Rev Serv

Jamie O'Rourke and the big potato; an Irish folktale. retold and illustrated by Tomie dePaola. Putnam 1992 un il hardcover o.p. pa $5.99; bd bk $5.99

Grades: K 1 2 3   **398.2**

1. Folklore -- Ireland

ISBN 0-399-22257-X; 0-698-11603-8 pa; 0-448-45090-9 bd bk

LC 91-10626

The laziest man in all of Ireland catches a leprechaun, who offers a potato seed instead of a pot of gold for his freedom

"Illustrated in dePaola's signature style, this has an inviting look. Buoyant watercolors are framed by thin orange borders, but the potato simply can't be contained and bulges beyond the boundaries, graphic proof of its enormous size, an engaging read-aloud choice for Saint Patrick's Day." Booklist

★ The **legend** of the Indian paintbrush; retold and illustrated by Tomie dePaola. Putnam 1988 un il $16.99; pa $7.99

Grades: K 1 2 3   **398.2**

1. Native Americans -- Folklore

ISBN 0-399-21534-4; 0-698-11360-8 pa

LC 87-20160

"The native American motifs are rendered simply and authentically; the night sky and glorious sunset spreads are truly beautiful with line, color, and form perfectly balanced to capture the text." Horn Book

Tomie dePaola's Favorite nursery tales. Putnam 1986 127p il $24.99

Grades: K 1 2 3   **398.2**

1. Fables 2. Folklore

ISBN 0-399-21319-8

LC 85-28302

"DePaola's droll, witty, and very funny illustrations capture the essence of each story from a child's point of view. . . . The beautiful layout of these pages, in which the print and pictures are perfectly at ease with one another, invites confident new readers as well as adults for reading aloud." SLJ

DiPrimio, Pete

The **sphinx**. Mitchell Lane Publishers 2010 48p il map (Monsters in myth) lib bdg $29.95

Grades: 4 5 6 7   **398.2**

1. Sphinxes (Mythology)

ISBN 978-1-58415-931-5; 1-58415-931-6

LC 2010006560

This describes the mythic Sphinx that has appeared in both Egyptian and Greek myth.

This book is "thorough and respectful of a number of ancient and modern sources and [bends] over backward to navigate often contradictory, interlinked legends. . . . A number of paintings and photos break up the otherwise text-heavy pages, and copious chapter notes and reading suggestions conclude. This is by no means entry-level stuff, but for kids handy with the basics and ready to delve deeper, [this book] will be of great use." Booklist

Includes glossary and bibliographical references

Doherty, Berlie

Fairy tales; told by Berlie Doherty; illustrated by Jane Ray. Candlewick Press 2000 223p il $19.99

Grades: 4 5 6   **398.2**

1. Folklore 2. Fairy tales

ISBN 0-7636-0997-8

LC 99-89380

A collection of well-known fairy tales, such as Cinderella, Rapunzel, Aladdin and the enchanted lamp, and The fire-bird

These are "superb retellings on the earliest available sources in fresh versions sure to captivate readers anew. Ray's gold paint and folk art motifs prevail, but she also peppers the spreads with striking silhouette-collage compositions in a sumptuously designed volume." Publ Wkly

Downard, Barry

The **race** of the century; retold, written, and illustrated by Barry Downard. Simon & Schuster Books for Young Readers 2008 un il $15.99

Grades: 2 3 4   **398.2**

1. Fables 2. Rabbits -- Folklore 3. Turtles -- Folklore

ISBN 978-1-4169-2509-5; 1-4169-2509-0

LC 2006028791

Fed up with his incessant taunting, Tom Tortoise challenges Flash Harry Hare to the race of the century, which turns into a worldwide media event complete with television and newspaper coverage, photographers, and many other distractions.

"Digitally created photocollages of an animal cast, [the illustrations are] packed with silly exaggeration and humorous visual personification. . . . The sheer ludicrousness of this scenario will elicit snickering even in kids allergic to fables." Bull Cent Child Books

Eastman, Mary Huse

Index to fairy tales; including folklore, legends, and myths in collections. Scarecrow Press 1985 4v

Grades: Adult Professional   **398.2**

1. Fairy tales 2. Reference books 3. Legends -- Indexes 4. Folklore -- Indexes 5. Mythology -- Indexes

Volumes covering 1949-1972 and 1973-1977 first published by Faxon 1973 and 1979 respectively

"Although this is an essential reference book for the children's department, it is also a valuable source for the location of much folklore and fairy-tale material and should be available in adult book collections as well." Ref Sources for Small & Medium-sized Libr. 6th edition

Ehlert, Lois

★ **Cuckoo.** Cucu; a Mexican folktale. translated into Spanish by Gloria de Aragón Andújar. Harcourt Brace & Co. 1997 un il $16; pa $7

Grades: K 1 2 3   **398.2**
1. Mayas -- Folklore 2. Folklore -- Mexico 3. Bilingual books -- English-Spanish
ISBN 0-15-200274-X; 0-15-202428-X pa

LC 95-39560

A traditional Mayan tale which reveals how the cuckoo lost her beautiful feathers

"This tale, charmingly told in both English and Spanish, is boldly illustrated with large, brightly colored, cut-paper pictures. Inspired by folk art and crafts, the images evoke the tin work and cutout fiesta banners of Mexico." SLJ

Mole's hill; a woodland tale. Harcourt Brace & Co. 1994 un il $17; pa $7

Grades: PreK K 1 2   **398.2**
1. Moles (Animals) -- Fiction
ISBN 0-15-255116-6; 0-15-201890-5 pa

LC 93-31151

When Fox tells Mole she must move out of her tunnel to make way for a new path, Mole finds an ingenious way to save her home

"Ehlert's language is compact and telling. . . . The art . . . is dark-hued, appropriately nocturnal without losing spirit or contrast, and the beads stippled across the cutout cloth shapes lend interesting texture to the planes of color. . . . The story (which Ehlert says she based on a fragment of a Seneca tale, with source completely cited in the book) has charm and vigor." Bull Cent Child Books

Ehrlich, Amy

A **treasury** of princess stories; retold by Amy Ehrlich; illustrated by Gary Blythe; [paper engineering by Keith Finch] Candlewick Press 2009 un il lib bdg $19.99

Grades: 1 2 3   **398.2**
1. Folklore 2. Fairy tales 3. Pop-up books 4. Princesses -- Fiction
ISBN 978-0-7636-4478-9 lib bdg; 0-7636-4478-1 lib bdg

"Six fairy tales previously retold by Ehrlich are here compiled, re-packaged, and reillustrated with pop-ups. Each begins with a sort of title page/frontispiece designed to resemble a miniature book; when the cover is opened, a beautifully rendered pop-up illustration is revealed. The stories themselves are recounted faithfully and rhythmically. Each features at least two lush illustrations as well as spot decorations." Horn Book Guide

Elya, Susan Middleton, 1955-

★ **Rubia** and the three osos; illustrated by Melissa Sweet. Disney/Hyperion Books 2010 un il $15.99

Grades: PreK K 1 2   **398.2**
1. Folklore 2. Stories in rhyme 3. Bears -- Folklore 4. Spanish language -- Vocabulary
ISBN 978-1-4231-1252-5; 1-4231-1252-0

LC 2009028131

Retells the story of Goldilocks and the three bears in rhyming text interspersed with Spanish words, which are defined in a glossary.

"Pencil, watercolor and collage illustrations are packed with Southwest detail and rendered in fiesta colors, adding a Latin flair, while the overtly comic depiction of the three osos and Rubia in her red cowgirl boots contributes to the lighthearted humor." Kirkus

Emberley, Ed

★ **Chicken** Little. Roaring Brook Press 2009 un il $16.95

Grades: PreK K 1 2   **398.2**
1. Folklore 2. Animals -- Folklore
ISBN 978-1-59643-464-6; 1-59643-464-3

LC 2008-49329

A retelling of the classic story of Chicken Little, who has an acorn fall on his head and runs in a panic to his friends Henny Penny, Lucky Ducky, and Loosey Goosey, to tell them the sky is falling.

"The punchy text is perfectly complemented by high-impact illustrations in collage-like planes of electric hues. The bold splashes of countless colors, contrasted against sharp fields of white, briliantly jump out from the square pages. This is certain to become a favorite version of this story, and young readers will gleefully welcome an ending that offers no pedantic lesson." Bull Cent Child Books

★ The **red** hen; by Rebecca Emberley and Ed Emberley. Roaring Brook Press 2010 1 v. (unpaged)

Grades: PreK K 1 2   **398.2**
1. Folklore
ISBN 1596434929; 9781596434929

LC 2010284450

"When Red Hen finds a recipe for 'simply splendid cake,' she repeatedly asks the cat, the rat, and the frog for help gathering the ingredients. . . . The cat and the rat provide the familiar 'not I' but the frog croaks out a humorous 'bribbit.' . . . Set against white backgrounds, the zany characters, each with uniquely distinct eyes, pop off the pages. . . . The short, simple text allows for instant audience participation and offers a satisfying lesson on cooperation and fairness." SLJ

Endredy, James

The **journey** of Tunuri and the Blue Deer; a Huichol Indian story. illustrated by Maria Hernández de la Cruz and Casimiro de la Cruz López. Bear Cub Books 2003 32p il $15.95

Grades: 1 2 3   **398.2**
1. Native Americans -- Folklore -- Mexico
ISBN 1-59143-016-X

LC 2003-52298

Retells a traditional Huichol folktale in which the young Tunuri learns his place in the natural world when he meets the magical Blue Deer, and follows him on an enlightening journey.

"The colorful artwork is made from yarn that is applied to a piece of wood, an elaborate process that is a long-practiced art of the Huichol. The illustrations enhance the feel and authenticity of the story. Elaborate notes explain the sacred symbols, who the Huichol are, and how the art was created. A strong addition to folktale collections." SLJ

English folktales; edited by Dan Keding and Amy Douglas. Libraries Unlimited 2005 231p il map (World folklore series) $35

Grades: Adult Professional   **398.2**
1. Folklore -- Great Britain
ISBN 1-59158-260-1

LC 2005016075

"This collection of more than 50 English folktales contains a variety of stories arranged by common themes: The Fool in All His Glory, Wily Wagers and Tall Tales, Dragons and Devils, etc. The work of 22 storytellers is represented and their tellings are lively and inflected with the rhythms and speech of the regions from which their stories emanate. It is a delightful compendium for storytellers." SLJ

Ernst, Lisa Campbell

Little Red Riding Hood: a newfangled prairie tale. Simon & Schuster Bks. for Young Readers 1995 un il $16; pa $5.99

Grades: K 1 2 3   **398.2**
1. Folklore 2. Wolves -- Folklore
ISBN 0-689-80145-9; 0-689-82191-3 pa

LC 94-45723

In this "contemporary rendering of the old tale, Little Red Riding Hood wears a hooded sweatshirt and rides her bicycle, while Grandma is a robust farmer who turns the tables on the wolf. Ernst's inventive plot, enjoyable characters, and characteristic cartoon-style drawings demonstrate her mastery of the picture-book form." Horn Book Guide

Fleischman, Paul
★ **Glass** slipper, gold sandal; a worldwide Cinderella. illustrated by Julie Paschkis. Henry Holt 2007 un il $16.95
Grades: K 1 2 3 4   **398.2**
1. Folklore 2. Fairy tales
ISBN 978-0-8050-7953-1; 0-8050-7953-X

LC 2006-30615

"This inspired retelling blends many versions of Cinderella into a single, extraordinary tale. . . . As . . . Fleischman's . . . strong storytelling voice incorporates sometimes small details from different traditions, text and illustrations nimbly morph from one Cinderella story to the next, creating this brand-new version. Paschkis . . . makes use of folk art and textile patterns throughout the world in the clever background paintings behind each of her vibrant panel illustrations." Publ Wkly

Forest, Heather
The **contest** between the Sun and the Wind; an Aesop's fable. retold by Heather Forest; illustrated by Susan Gaber. August House Little Folk 2008 un il $16.95
Grades: K 1 2 3   **398.2**
1. Fables 2. Authors 3. Folklore 4. Storytellers
ISBN 978-0-87483-832-9; 0-87483-832-0

LC 2007018813

The sun and the wind test their strength by seeing which of them can cause a man to remove his coat, demonstrating the value of using gentle persuasion rather than force as a means of achieving a goal.

"Forest recasts this fable from Aesop in simple, crystalline language and occasional rhyme. . . . Gaber's wild and vivid images reflect, augment, and illuminate the story." Booklist

★ The **little** red hen; an old fable. retold by Heather Forest; illustrated by Susan Gaber. August House Little Folk 2006 un il $16.95
Grades: K 1 2 3   **398.2**
1. Folklore 2. Animals -- Folklore 3. Chickens -- Folklore
ISBN 0-87483-795-2

LC 2006040727

A rhymed retelling of the traditional tale about the industrious little red hen and her lazy friends

"Gaber's bold acrylic artwork and varied use of space . . . and the infectious, familiar refrain . . . make this an appealing storytime and readers' theater selection." SLJ

French, Vivian
Henny Penny; [by] Vivian French; illustrated by Sophie Windham. Bloomsbury Children's Books 2006 un il $16.95
Grades: PreK K 1 2   **398.2**
1. Folklore 2. Animals -- Folklore
ISBN 1-58234-706-9

LC 2005053688

Henny Penny and her barnyard friends are on their way to tell the king that the sky is falling when they meet a hungry fox, but Henny Penny's quick thinking saves the day

"A charmingly fleshed-out version of the traditional story. . . . Brightly colored and skillfully drawn illustrations balance perfectly with the delightful text and draw readers into their depths." SLJ

Galdone, Joanna
★ The **tailypo**; a ghost story. told by Joanna Galdone; illustrated by Paul Galdone. Clarion Bks. 1984 un il hardcover o.p. pa $7.95
Grades: K 1 2 3   **398.2**
1. Folklore -- United States
ISBN 0-395-30084-3 pa

LC 77-23289

First published by Seabury Press

"An old man lives in the Tennessee backwoods with his three hunting dogs. . . . The old man sees an odd animal squeezing through a crack in his cabin and grabs it. All he gets is its tail but he makes a snack of that and gets into bed with a satisfied appetite. But the dismembered [creature] wants its tail back." Publ Wkly

Galdone, Paul
The **elves** and the shoemaker; retold and illustrated by Paul Galdone. Clarion Bks. 1984 un il hardcover o.p. pa $6.95
Grades: PreK K 1 2   **398.2**
1. Fairy tales 2. Folklore -- Germany
ISBN 0-89919-422-2 pa

LC 83-14979

A pair of elves help a poor shoemaker become successful, and the shoemaker and his wife reward them with elegant outfits

"The pictures in flashing hues emphasize the secret helpers' impishness; they seem to be performing the service more for a lark than in the name of sweet charity." Publ Wkly

★ The **gingerbread** boy. Clarion Bks. 1975 un il $16; pa $6.95
Grades: PreK K 1 2   **398.2**
1. Folklore 2. Fairy tales
ISBN 0-395-28799-5; 0-89919-163-0 pa

First published by Seabury Press

"A lively version of the tale of the gingerbread boy who sprang into action as soon as he was baked and gleefully eluded all would-be captors until he was finally outwitted by a fox. The artist's gingerbread boy is a strong-legged, cocky individual, who sets out on a merry race through the countryside. The action of the tale is well-paced; large, humorous illustrations with stone fences, a covered bridge, and hearty rural folk suggest a New England background, while the triumphant fox is the epitome of all slyness." Horn Book

★ **Henny** Penny; retold and illustrated by Paul Galdone. Clarion Bks. 1968 un il $16; pa $6.95
Grades: PreK K 1 2   **398.2**
1. Folklore 2. Animals -- Folklore
ISBN 0-395-28800-2; 0-89919-225-4 pa

First published by Seabury Press

A folktale also popularly known as Chicken Little. "The simple retelling has a different ending which makes the fox seem somewhat less villainous—when Henny Penny and her credulous friends follow Foxy Loxy into the cave they are never seen again and the king is never told that the sky is falling, but Foxy Loxy, his wife, and seven little foxes (appealingly portrayed in a picture as a family group) still remember the fine feast they had that day." Booklist

★ The **little** red hen; a folk tale classic. Houghton Mifflin Harcourt 2011 un il $8.99
Grades: K 1 2 3   **398.2**
1. Folklore 2. Animals -- Folklore 3. Chickens -- Folklore
ISBN 978-0-547-37018-7; 0-547-37018-0

A reissue of the edition first published 1973 by Seabury Press

The little red hen finds none of her lazy friends willing to help her plant, harvest, or grind wheat into flour, but all are eager to eat the cake she makes from it.

Galdone's retelling is "straightforward and his unassuming loose-lined pictures provide just enough embellishment." Horn Book Guide

★ The **monkey** and the crocodile; a Jataka tale from India. Clarion Bks. 1969 un il hardcover o.p. pa $6.95

Grades: PreK K 1 2   **398.2**
1. Fables 2. Jataka stories 3. Folklore -- India 4. Monkeys -- Folklore 5. Crocodiles -- Folklore
ISBN 0-89919-524-5 pa
First published by Seabury Press

Illustrated by Galdone, this is a retelling of one of the Jataka fables about Buddha in his animal incarnations. "The crocodile wants a meal of monkey, but the intended prey is far wilier than his antagonist." SLJ

★ **Puss** in boots. Clarion Bks. 1976 un il hardcover o.p. pa $7.95

Grades: K 1 2   **398.2**
1. Fairy tales 2. Cats -- Folklore 3. Folklore -- France
ISBN 0-89919-192-4 pa
First published by Seabury Press

"Galdone follows Perrault's story line faithfully, as Puss works mischief to obtain a fortune for his master. The writing, fluid and readable, makes even this familiar tale sound fresh—no mean feat. Galdone's large, humorous caricatures—easily seen for story hour—have great gusto, and Puss is the embodiment of cleverness and knavery." SLJ

★ The **teeny**-tiny woman; a ghost story. Clarion Bks. 1984 un il $16; pa $5.95

Grades: PreK K 1 2   **398.2**
1. Ghost stories 2. Folklore -- Great Britain
ISBN 0-89919-270-X; 0-89919-463-X pa

LC 84-4311

Retold and illustrated by Galdone, this is an English folk tale about a "teeny-tiny woman who lives in a teeny-tiny house in a teeny-tiny village goes for a teeny-tiny walk, etc. Opening the gates to a churchyard, she finds a bone that will add flavor to the soup she plans for supper. Back home, she goes to bed but is alarmed by a voice . . . demanding, 'Give me back my bone!'" Publ Wkly

★ The **three** bears. Clarion Bks. 1972 un il $15; pa $6.95

Grades: PreK K 1 2   **398.2**
1. Folklore 2. Bears -- Folklore
ISBN 0-395-28811-8; 0-89919-401-X pa
First published by Seabury Press

In Galdone's illustrations for his retelling of the tale of Goldilocks, "his three bears are beautifully groomed, civilized creatures, living a life of rustic contentment in an astonishingly verdant forest, while his Goldilocks is a horrid, be-ringletted, overdressed child who rampages wantonly through the bears' tidy home." Times Lit Suppl

★ The **three** Billy Goats Gruff. Clarion Bks. 1973 un il $16; pa $6.95

Grades: PreK K 1 2   **398.2**
1. Goats -- Folklore 2. Folklore -- Norway
ISBN 0-395-28812-6; 0-89919-035-9 pa
First published by Seabury Press

In this retelling of the old Norwegian folk tale, "the goats flummox the wicked troll and send him over the rickety bridge to a watery grave." Publ Wkly

★ The **three** little pigs; a folk tale classic. Houghton Mifflin Harcourt 2011 un il $8.99

Grades: K 1 2 3   **398.2**
1. Pigs -- Folklore 2. Wolves -- Folklore
ISBN 978-0-547-37020-0; 0-547-37020-2

LC 2011281137

A reissue of the edition published 1970 by Clarion Books

Retells the fatal episodes in the lives of two foolish pigs and how the third pig managed to avoid the same pigfalls.

Galdone's retelling is "straightforward and his unassuming loose-lined pictures provide just enough embellishment." Horn Book Guide

Gavin, Jamila
Tales from India; illustrated by Amanda Hall. Candlewick Press 2011 il

Grades: 5 6 7 8   **398.2**
1. Hindu mythology 2. Folklore -- India
ISBN 0-7636-5564-3; 978-0-7636-5564-8

LC 2010047651

"Gavin, . . . presents 10 classic Hindu stories, accompanied by Hall's lush and elegant gouache illustrations. . . . Readers should be drawn toward the valor, action, and dramatic transformations in these powerful tales." Publ Wkly

Gerson, Mary-Joan
Why the sky is far away; a Nigerian folktale. retold by Mary-Joan Gerson; pictures by Carla Golembe. Little, Brown 1992 un il hardcover o.p. pa $5.95

Grades: K 1 2 3   **398.2**
1. Folklore -- Nigeria
ISBN 0-316-30874-9 pa

LC 91-24949

A revised and newly illustrated edition of the title first published 1974 by Harcourt

The sky was once so close to the Earth that people cut parts of it to eat, but their waste and greed caused the sky to move far away

"Golembe's simple, theatrical illustrations combine monotype prints and collages in brilliant colors. . . . With its playfulness and drama, this is a fine book for story hour, especially in an ecology program." Booklist

Ginsburg, Mirra
Clay boy; adapted from a Russian folk tale by Mirra Ginsburg; pictures by Jos. A. Smith. Greenwillow Bks. 1997 un il $16

Grades: K 1 2 3   **398.2**
1. Folklore -- Russia
ISBN 0-688-14409-8; 0-688-14410-1 lib bdg

LC 96-33820

Wanting a son, an old man and woman make a clay boy who comes to life and begins eating everything in sight until he meets a clever goat

"The tale is adapted from a Russian folktale, and the storytelling voice is very simple and immediate. . . . In their play with scale, the illustrations express a wonderful combination of the monstrous and the cozy." Booklist

Goble, Paul
The **girl** who loved wild horses; story and illustrations by Paul Goble. Bradbury Press 1978 un il $14.95; pa $5.99

Grades: K 1 2 3   **398.2**
1. Horses -- Folklore 2. Native Americans -- Folklore
ISBN 0-02-736570-0; 0-689-71696-6 pa

LC 77-20500

Awarded the Caldecott Medal, 1979

"Elaborate double-page spreads burst with life, revealing details of flowers and insects, animals and birds. . . . The story is told in simple language, and the author has included verses of a Navaho and Sioux song about horses. Both storytelling and art express the harmony with and the love of nature which characterize Native American culture." Horn Book

The **legend** of the White Buffalo Woman. National Geographic Soc. 1998 un il hardcover o.p. pa $7.95
Grades: 3 4 5 **398.2**
    1. Native Americans -- Folklore
    ISBN 0-7922-7074-6; 0-7922-6552-1 pa
LC 97-24086
A Lakota Indian legend in which the White Buffalo Woman presents her people with the Sacred Calf Pipe which gives them the means to pray to the Great Spirit
    "In his fluid retelling of the legend of the first peace pipe, Goble . . . handles sweeping Lakota history succinctly and assuredly, largely due to his compelling artwork." Publ Wkly
    Includes bibliographical references

The **woman** who lived with wolves, & other stories from the tipi; told and illustrated by Paul Goble; foreword by Vivian Arviso Deloria. World Wisdom, Inc. 2011 un $14.95
Grades: 3 4 5 6 **398.2**
    1. Native Americans -- Folklore
    ISBN 978-1-935493-20-4; 1-935493-20-5
LC 2010029180
    "Goble has collected and retold 27 stories, poems, and song lyrics from a variety of Native American tribes. . . . Depictions of how animals and man worked in harmony with one another permeate the stories and convey Goble's message that humans must live with tolerance and understanding of the natural world in order for both to survive. This collection is unique in its simplicity. The tales are accessible to young listeners as they beg to be read aloud. Most are only a page long. The accompanying illustrations are vintage Goble, finely detailed and painstakingly painted in rich tones of morning sky blues, orange-hued sunsets, and myriad chestnut, black, and amber horses." SLJ
    Includes bibliographical references

Goldman, Judy
    Whiskers, tails, and wings; animal folktales from Mexico. Judy Goldman; illustrated by Fabricio Vanden Broeck. Charlesbridge 2012 58 p. (reinforced for library use) $16.95
Grades: 2 3 4 5 **398.2**
    1. Native Americans -- Folklore -- Mexico 2. Native American mythology 3. Tales -- Mexico 4. Animals -- Mexico -- Folklore
    ISBN 1580893724; 9781580893725
LC 2012024636
    This book is a "selection of Mexican folktales from five indigenous groups includes trickster tales, origin stories, and brief narratives about the triumphs of unconventional heroes. In a story from the Triqui people, the God of Creation creates the irritating flea in order to prevent Man and Woman from lying about lazily; a story from the Huichol tribe tells how the opossum lost its tail hair." Glossaries are provided. (Publishers Weekly)
    Includes bibliographical references and index

Grandfather tales; American-English folk tales. selected and edited by Richard Chase; illustrated by Berkeley Williams, Jr. Houghton Mifflin 1948 239p il pa $7.95
Grades: 4 5 6 7 **398.2**
    1. Folklore -- Southern States
    ISBN 0-395-06692-1; 0-618-34690-2 pa
Folklore gathered in Alabama, "North Carolina, Virginia and Kentucky. Written down only after many tellings, these [twenty-four] humorous tales are told in the vernacular of the region with added touches

of local color provided by the storytellers as they meet together to keep Old-Christmas Eve. . . . Of special interest to storytellers." Booklist

Green, Roger Lancelyn
    King Arthur and his Knights of the Round Table; retold out of the old romances. with illustrations by Aubrey Beardsley. Knopf 1993 355p il $14.95
Grades: 5 6 7 8 **398.2**
    1. Arthurian romances 2. Kings
    ISBN 0-679-42311-7
LC 92-55073
A newly illustrated edition of the title first published 1953 in the United Kingdom
    Relates the exploits of King Arthur and his knights from the birth of Arthur to the destruction of Camelot

Gregorowski, Christopher
    Fly, eagle, fly! an African tale. retold by Christopher Gregorowski; pictures by Niki Daly. Margaret K. McElderry Bks. 2000 un il hardcover o.p. pa $12.99
Grades: K 1 2 3 **398.2**
    1. Eagles -- Folklore 2. Folklore -- Africa
    ISBN 0-689-82398-3; 1-4169-7599-3 pa
LC 98-45302
Original two-color illustrated edition published 1982 in South Africa
A farmer finds an eagle and raises it to behave like a chicken, until a friend helps the eagle learn to find its rightful place in the sky
    This "is a powerful celebration of the human spirit and its need for independence. It is beautifully complemented by watercolors, rich in the vibrant tones of earth and sky." Booklist

Grifalconi, Ann
    The **village** of round and square houses. Little, Brown 1986 un il lib bdg $16.95
Grades: K 1 2 3 **398.2**
    1. Folklore -- Africa
    ISBN 0-316-32862-6
LC 85-24150
A Caldecott Medal honor book, 1987
A grandmother explains to her listeners why in their village on the side of a volcano the men live in square houses and the women in round ones
    The author "illustrates her own tale, told to her by a young girl who grew up in Tos. The resting purple volcano, suddenly erupting into orange; the eerie orange sun; the villagers covered with ash; the fiery colored skies; the dense, lush jungles—all are captured beautifully by Grifalconi's art." Publ Wkly

Grimm, Jacob, 1785-1863
    ★ **Fairy** tales of the Brothers Grimm; edited by Noel Daniel; translated by Matthew R. Price. Taschen 2011 il $39.99
Grades: 4 5 6 **398.2**
    1. Fairy tales 2. Folklore -- Germany
    ISBN 978-3-8365-2672-2; 3-8365-2672-7
    "This gorgeous treasury pairs new translations of 27 of the Grimm brothers' fairy tales with vintage illustrations dating from the 1820s to the 1950s. Brief introductions offer insight into the symbolism, themes, and contemporary relevance of each tale. Though Price and Daniel's translations feel modern . . . they honor the darkness that characterizes 'Little Red Riding Hood,' 'Snow White,' and other tales. The images show striking range. . . . The elegant presentation should entice readers to discover the cornucopia within." Publ Wkly

Grimm's fairy tales; illustrated by Arthur Rackam. Seastar Books 2001 160p il $19.95
Grades: 4 5 6   398.2
1. Fairy tales 2. Folklore -- Germany
ISBN 978-158717-092-8; 1-58717-092-2
A collection of twenty-two favorite fairy tales from the Brothers Grimm, including "Rapunzel," "The Bremen Town Musicians," "The Valiant Tailor", "The Frog Prince," "Ashenputtel," and "The Elves and the Shoemanker."
"This handsome facsimile of the 1909 edition is illustrated with twenty-one color plates and twenty-eight black-and-white drawings with an afterword by Peter Glassman." Horn Book Guide

Little Red Riding Hood; [by] the Brothers Grimm; illustrated by Bernadette Watts. North-South 2009 un il $16.95
Grades: K 1 2 3   398.2
1. Fairy tales 2. Wolves -- Folklore 3. Folklore -- Germany
ISBN 978-0-7358-2256-6; 0-7358-2256-5
A reissue of the edition first published 1968
A sweet little girl meets a hungry wolf in the forest while on her way to visit her grandmother.
"The well-known story is told simply and without embellishment, including some violent elements (e.g., the wolf's belly is slit open and filled with stones). The expansive illustrations use Old World folk-art elements to envelope readers in the forest landscapes." Horn Book Guide

The **Original** Folk and Fairy Tales of the Brothers Grimm; the complete first edition. [Jacob Grimm, Wilhelm Grimm; translated by] Jack Zipes; [illustrated by Andrea Dezsö] Princeton University Press 2014 xliii, 519 p.p illustrations (hardback : acid-free paper) $35
Grades: Adult   398.2
1. Fairy tales 2. Folklore -- Germany 3. Tales -- Germany 4. Fairy tales -- Germany
ISBN 9780691160597
LC 2014004127
"For the very first time, 'The Original Folk and Fairy Tales of the Brothers Grimm' makes available in English all 156 stories from the 1812 and 1815 editions. These narrative gems, newly translated and brought together in one. . . book, are accompanied by . . . new illustrations from . . . artist Andrea Dezsö." (Publisher's note)
Includes bibliographical references and index

Snow White; [by] the Brothers Grimm; illustrated by Charles Santore. Sterling 2010 un il $16.95
Grades: 1 2 3   398.2
1. Fairy tales 2. Folklore -- Germany
ISBN 978-1-4027-7157-6; 1-4027-7157-6
A reissue of the edition published 1996 by Random House
Retells the tale of the beautiful princess whose lips were red as blood, skin was white as snow, and hair was black as ebony.
"Lovely, broad paintings provide a rich sense of place and characters in this faithful rendering of the well-known tale. Snow White is a pretty child, the envious queen is haughty and wonderfully wizened in her disguises, and the dwarfs are distinctive individuals." SLJ

The **story** of Little Red Riding Hood; [by] The Brothers Grimm; illustrated by Christopher Bing. Handprint Books 2010 un il $18.99
Grades: K 1 2 3   398.2
1. Folklore 2. Fairy tales 3. Wolves -- Folklore
ISBN 978-0-8118-6986-7; 0-8118-6986-5
LC 2009019577
"This newly illustrated fairy tale includes three versions of an old favorite. The first and primary telling is Grimm's story. The grandmother

and Little Red Riding Hood are consumed by the wolf, but freed by the hunter. . . . A second, lesser-known tale shows a resourceful girl who outfoxes the wolf, and all ends happily. In Perrault's shorter, darker version, which appears on the back endpaper with its original art, the old woman and girl are eaten and not saved. . . . The new, yet traditionally styled illustrations for the first two tales are well matched to the old stories. . . . [Bing] successfully takes the story back to its traditions." SLJ

Tales from the Brothers Grimm; selected & illustrated by Lisbeth Zwerger. Lisbeth Zwerger. Minedition 2013 96 p. (hbk.) $29.99
Grades: 4 5 6 7 8   398.2
1. Fairy tales 2. Fairy tales -- Germany
ISBN 9789888240531; 9888240536
In this book, Lisbeth Zwerger selects and illustrates stories "from the well-known collection of fairy tales by the Brothers Grimm. Old favorites such as 'Hansel and Gretel' and 'The Bremen Town Musicians' are included as are some lesser-known stories such as 'The Seven Ravens' and 'Hans My Hedgehog.'" (Publisher's note)
"High production values give this mix of new and recycled translations and illustrations a suitably sumptuous air. . . . Like Zwerger's figures, which are nearly all small on the page and tend to look off into the distance, Bell's translations are more often lyrical than intimate or earthy." Kirkus

The **twelve** dancing princesses; [originally] written by the Brothers Grimm; [adapted and] illustrated by Rachel Isadora. G.P. Putnam's Sons 2007 un il $16.99
Grades: K 1 2 3   398.2
1. Folklore 2. Fairy tales 3. Folklore -- Germany
ISBN 0-399-24744-0; 978-0-399-24744-6
LC 2007-08160
This is a retelling of the story of twelve princesses who dance secretly all night long and how their secret is eventually discovered. "Age four and up." (N Y Times Book Rev)
"Working in collages of painted, textured paper, Isadora evokes an archetypal African kingdom through sumptuous, kente cloth textiles and Serengenti-like landscapes that pop vibrantly agains primarily white backgrounds." Booklist

Haley, Gail E.
★ A **story,** a story; an African tale retold and illustrated by Gail E. Haley. Atheneum Pubs. 1970 un il $18; pa $7.99
Grades: K 1 2 3   398.2
1. Folklore -- Africa 2. Anansi (Legendary character)
ISBN 0-689-20511-2; 0-689-71201-4 pa
Awarded the Caldecott Medal, 1971
"The story explains the origin of that favorite African folk material, the spider tale. Here Ananse, the old spider man, wanting to buy the Sky God's stories, completes by his cleverness three seemingly impossible tasks set as the price for the golden box of stories which he takes back to earth." Sutherland. The Best in Child Books

Hamilton, Martha
The **ghost** catcher; a Bengali folktale. [by] Martha Hamilton & Mitch Weiss; illustrated by Kristen Balouch. August House Little Folk 2008 un il $16.95
Grades: PreK K 1 2   398.2
1. Folklore -- India 2. Ghosts -- Folklore
ISBN 978-0-87483-835-0; 0-87483-835-5
LC 2007-14308
A retelling of a traditional Bengali tale in which a kind and generous Indian barber, pressed by his father then his wife to earn more money, cleverly persuades a ghost to bring him riches.

"Hamilton and Weiss relate the tale with economy and wit. . . . The illustrations' lyrical lines, colorful forms, and linen-textured backdrop create a distinctive look." Booklist

Hamilton, Virginia

★ The **people** could fly: American Black folktales; told by Virginia Hamilton; illustrated by Leo and Diane Dillon. 2009 178p il $24.99; pa $13

Grades: 5 6 7 8   398.2

1. African Americans -- Folklore
ISBN 978-0-394-86925-4; 0-394-86925-7; 978-0-679-84336-8 pa; 0-679-84336-1 pa
A reissue of the title first published 1985
Coretta Scott King honor book for illustration, 1986

The author "has been successful in her efforts to write these tales in the Black English of the slave storytellers. Her scholarship is unobtrusive and intelligible. She has provided a glossary and notes concerning the origins of the tales and the different versions in other cultures. Handsomely illustrated." NY Times Book Rev

Includes bibliographical references

★ The **people** could fly: the picture book; illustrated by Leo and Diane Dillon. Knopf 2004 un il $16.95

Grades: 3 4 5 6   398.2

1. Slavery -- Folklore 2. African Americans -- Folklore
ISBN 0-375-82405-7

LC 2003-25579

This is a retelling of the story first published in the author's collection, The people could fly: American black folktales, published 1985

In this retelling of a folktale, a group of slaves, unable to bear their sadness and starvation any longer, calls upon the African magic that allows them to fly away. "Age four and up." (N Y Times Book Rev)

"Familiar as it is, we have never seen the story like this. Not with all these evocative images, vivid, bright and moving, leading us on a journey through territory we thought we knew." NY Times Book Rev

Han, Suzanne Crowder

The **rabbit's** tail; a story from Korea. illustrated by Richard Wehrman. Holt & Co. 1999 un il $16.95

Grades: K 1 2 3   398.2

1. Folklore -- Korea 2. Tigers -- Folklore 3. Rabbits -- Folklore
ISBN 0-8050-4580-5

LC 98-16627

Tiger is afraid of being eaten by a fearsome dried persimmon, but when Rabbit tries to convince him he is wrong, Rabbit loses his long tail

"The tale is vividly retold. . . . An amusing entertainment about misperceptions." SLJ

Harris, John

My **monster** notebook; [by] John Harris & Mark Todd. J. Paul Getty Museum 2011 un il $16.95

Grades: 4 5 6   398.2

1. Folklore 2. Monsters
ISBN 978-1-60606-050-6; 1-60606-050-3

LC 2010025302

"At its core, the volume is a descriptive list of mythological monsters, from the immortal half-woman, half-serpent Echidna to Python, the dangerous snake sent to kill baby Apollo. The notebook-style layout includes doodles, photographs, and scrap papers, making the book appear to be a relic unearthed from the ruins of a modern school locker." Horn Book Guide

Strong stuff; Herakles and his labors. fierce words by John Harris; powerful art by Gary Baseman. J. Paul Getty Museum 2005 un il map $16.95

Grades: 4 5 6 7   398.2

1. Classical mythology 2. Hercules (Legendary character)
ISBN 0-89236-784-9

LC 2004-7904

This is a "simplified version of the 12 labors of Hercules (Herakles as the Greeks called him). . . . Each labor is allotted a spread with bright and bold illustrations featuring Herakles locked in mortal combat with the monster of the moment, accompanied by a chatty, humorous commentary." SLJ

Hartman, Bob

The **Lion** storyteller book of animal tales; animal tales old and new especially for reading aloud. illustrated by Krisztina Kállai Nagy. Lion 2011 128p il $19.99

Grades: K 1 2 3   398.2

1. Fables 2. Folklore 3. Animals -- Fiction
ISBN 978-0-74596-131-6; 0-74596-131-2

"Hartman vibrantly retells and updates 36 animal fables hailing from ancient Greece, Africa, Japan, India, and other world cultures. The selections include trickster, morality, and animal-origin tales . . . along with a few original stories. Nagy's bright and friendly illustrations mimic Hartman's descriptive but accessible tone. A thoughtful collection that might inspire some readers to create animal stories of their own." Publ Wkly

Mr. Aesop's story shop; illustrated by Jago Silver. Lion/Trafalgar 2011 48p il $14.99

Grades: K 1 2 3   398.2

1. Fables 2. Authors 3. Storytellers
ISBN 0-7459-6915-1; 978-0-7459-6915-2

"This title re-frames 10 familiar fables . . . to add new context and setting to the stories. Each entry is narrated in first person, as if Aesop himself were speaking. . . . The introduction informs young readers about what is known, and what is not, about Aesop and defines what makes a story a fable. . . . The painterly illustrations look as if they are done on textured paper and incorporate Greek architectural details. . . . A worthwhile addition to collections." Booklist

Hausman, Gerald

Horses of myth; [by] Gerald and Loretta Hausman; pictures by Robert Florczak. Dutton Children's Books 2004 100p il $12

Grades: 4 5 6 7   398.2

1. Folklore 2. Horses -- Folklore
ISBN 0-525-46964-8

LC 2002-40809

"These five tales each feature a different type of horse, remarkable for both its individuality and the qualities representative of its breed. . . . Florczak's illustrations adapt characteristics appropriate to the locations and time periods of each selection's origins. . . . This is an attractive volume, useful to teachers and librarians for read-alouds and of interest to horse-loving youngsters." SLJ

Hayes, Joe

The **coyote** under the table; = El coyote debajo de la mesa : folktales told in Spanish and English. illustrations by Antonio Castro L. Cinco Puntos Press 2011 il $19.95; pa $12.95

Grades: 3 4 5 6   398.2

1. Folklore -- New Mexico 2. Bilingual books -- English-Spanish
ISBN 978-1-935955-21-4; 1-935955-21-7; 978-1-935955-06-1 pa; 1-935955-06-3 pa

LC 2011011430

"Eight tales of tricksters and magical transformations are given a Southwestern setting by a veteran storyteller and paired to Spanish versions on facing pages. . . . Each tale opens with a realistically detailed black-and-white scene to set the comic or dramatic mood. . . . These wise and witty tales continue to repay fresh encounters." Kirkus

Dance, Nana, dance; Cuban folktales in English and Spanish. retold by Joe Hayes; illustrated by Mauricio Trenard Sayago. Cinco Puntos Press 2008 128p il $20.95

Grades: 5 6 7 8 9   **398.2**
    1. Folklore -- Cuba 2. Bilingual books -- English-Spanish
    ISBN 978-1-933693-17-0; 1-933693-17-7
                         LC 2007-38295

A collection of stories from Cuban folklore, representing the cultures of Spain, Africa, and the Caribbean.

"Each tale is accompanied by a full-page illustration that is colorful and contributes to the text. This book is a great addition to folktale and Spanish language collections. Students will enjoy these stories that could easily be incorporated into the curriculum." Libr Media Connect

Little Gold Star; a Cinderella cuento/Estrellita de oro. retold in Spanish & English by Joe Hayes; illustrated by Gloria Osuna Perez & Lucia Angela Perez. Cinco Puntos Press 2000 30p il $15.95

Grades: K 1 2 3   **398.2**
    1. Fairy tales 2. Hispanic Americans -- Folklore 3. Bilingual books -- English-Spanish
    ISBN 0-938317-49-0
                         LC 99-57104

In this variation of the Cinderella story, coming from the Hispanic tradition in New Mexico, Arciá and her wicked stepsisters have different encounters with a magical hawk and are left physically changed in ways that will affect their meeting with the prince

"The English text, which is made full-bodied by its many details, appears with a Spanish translation. The impressive acrylic illustrations, done in a sturdy folk-art style, are thick with color and bright with humor." Booklist

Hennessy, B. G.
The **boy** who cried wolf; retold by B.G. Hennessy; illustrated by Boris Kulikov. Simon & Schuster Books for Young Readers 2006 un il $15.95

Grades: K 1 2   **398.2**
    1. Folklore 2. Sheep -- Folklore 3. Wolves -- Folklore
    ISBN 0-689-87433-2
                         LC 2004-21672

A boy tending sheep on a lonely mountainside thinks it a fine joke to cry "wolf" and watch the people come running—and then one day a wolf is really there, but no one answers his call

"The story begs to be read aloud, and the large, colorful, and amusing watercolor-and-gouache paintings are perfect for group viewing. . . . A clever take on an old favorite." SLJ

Henrichs, Wendy
I am Tama, lucky cat; a Japanese legend. illustrated by Yoshiko Jaeggi. Peachtree 2011 un il $16.95

Grades: K 1 2 3   **398.2**
    1. Cats -- Folklore 2. Folklore -- Japan
    ISBN 978-1-56145-589-8; 1-56145-589-X
                         LC 2010052072

A retelling of the traditional Japanese tale describing the origins of the beckoning cat and how it came to be a symbol of good luck.

"Evocative watercolor illustrations capture ancient Japan in this picture book retelling of the lucky-cat legend. . . . The story's tone is formal but not stilted. . . . The artist studied in Osaka and her traditional

training comes through, blending formal composition with light comic touches. . . . With its compelling story and stunning art, this is a worthy addition." SLJ

Hickox, Rebecca
The **golden** sandal; a Middle Eastern Cinderella story. illustrated by Will Hillenbrand. Holiday House 1998 un il $16.95; pa $6.95

Grades: K 1 2 3   **398.2**
    1. Fairy tales 2. Folklore -- Iraq
    ISBN 0-8234-1331-4; 0-8234-1513-9 pa
                         LC 97-5071

An Iraqi version of the Cinderella story in which a kind and beautiful girl who is mistreated by her stepmother and stepsister finds a husband with the help of a magic fish

"The story is charmingly told and illustrated with paintings on vellum, giving the pictures a soft, luxurious quality." N Y Times Book Rev

Hirsh, Marilyn
The **rabbi** and the twenty-nine witches. Marshall Cavendish Children 2009 un il $17.99

Grades: K 1 2 3   **398.2**
    1. Rain -- Fiction 2. Jews -- Folklore 3. Moon -- Folklore 4. Witches -- Folklore
    ISBN 978-0-7614-5586-8; 0-7614-5586-8
                         LC 2008022985

A reissue of the title first published 1976 by Holiday House
A wise old rabbi finally rids the village of the witches that terrorize it every night that the moon is full.

Hoberman, Mary Ann
Very short fables to read together; adapted by Mary Ann Hoberman; illustrated by Michael Emberley. Little Brown & Company 2010 32p il (You read to me, I'll read to you) $16.99

Grades: K 1 2 3   **398.2**
    1. Fables 2. Poetry -- By individual authors
    ISBN 978-0-316-04117-1; 0-316-04117-3

"The team behind the collaborative reading series turns their attention to Aesop's fables. Two readers can recite alternating passages differentiated by color, with the closing morals to be read in unison. Emberley's pencil and watercolor spot illustrations bring fresh energy to the classic tales as well as a softening tone. . . . The jaunty rhymes and theatrical element of adopting a persona should spark enthusiasm from reluctant readers." Publ Wkly

Hodges, Margaret
★ **Dick** Whittington and his cat; retold by Margaret Hodges; illustrated by Melisande Potter. Holiday House 2006 un il $16.95

Grades: K 1 2 3   **398.2**
    1. Mayors 2. Cats -- Folklore 3. Folklore -- Great Britain
    ISBN 0-8234-1987-8
                         LC 2005-46222

Retells the legend of the poor boy in medieval England who trades his beloved cat for a fortune in gold and jewels and eventually becomes Lord Mayor of London.

"In this spare retelling of the British legend, the narrative keeps buoyant with droll dialogue. The humorous illustrations, created with colorful inks and gouache, enhance the story with expressive faces and movement that delight the eye." SLJ

★ **Saint** George and the dragon; a golden legend. adapted by Margaret Hodges from Edmund Spenser's Faerie Queene; illustrated by Trina Schart Hyman. Little, Brown 1984 32p il $16.95; pa $6.95

Grades: 2 3 4 5   **398.2**
    1. Saints 2. Martyrs 3. Soldiers 4. Dragons -- Folklore 5.

Knights and knighthood -- Folklore

ISBN 0-316-36789-3; 0-316-36795-8 pa

LC 83-19980

Awarded the Caldecott Medal, 1985

Retells the segment from Spenser's The Faerie Queene, in which George, the Red Cross Knight, slays the dreadful dragon that has been terrorizing the countryside for years and brings peace and joy to the land

"Hyman's illustrations are uniquely suited to this outrageously romantic and appealing legend. . . . The paintings are richly colored, lush, detailed and dramatic. . . . This is a beautifully crafted book, a fine combination of author and illustrator." SLJ

Hogrogian, Nonny

The **contest**; adapted and illustrated by Nonny Hogrogian. Greenwillow Bks. 1976 un il lib bdg $15.89

Grades: K 1 2 3   398.2

1. Folklore -- Armenia

ISBN 0-688-84042-6

A Caldecott Medal honor book, 1977

"The symmetrical elements of the tale, which create arabesques of humor, are well-served by the full-color, full-page illustrations and by the pencil drawings scattered through the text. Some of the colored illustrations are bordered by oriental rug patterns, and all of the paintings and drawings are strong in their depiction of Armenian physiognomy." Horn Book

★ **One** fine day. Macmillan 1971 un il $16; pa $5.99

Grades: K 1 2 3   398.2

1. Foxes -- Folklore 2. Folklore -- Armenia

ISBN 0-02-744000-1; 0-02-043620-3 pa

Awarded the Caldecott Medal, 1972

When a fox drinks the milk in an old woman's jug, she chops off his tail and refuses to sew it back on unless he gives her milk back. The author-illustrator's cumulative tale, based on an Armenian folktale, tells of the many transactions the fox must go through before his tail is restored

"A charming picture book that is just right for reading aloud to small children, the scale of the pictures also appropriate for group use." Sutherland. The Best in Child Books

Huck, Charlotte S.

Princess Furball; retold by Charlotte Huck; illustrated by Anita Lobel. Greenwillow Bks. 1989 un il hardcover o.p. pa $6.99

Grades: 1 2 3   398.2

1. Fairy tales

ISBN 0-688-13107-7 pa

LC 88-18780

This book is about a "princess who rebels against her tyrannical father and makes the most of her gifts to survive in another kingdom and win the hand of the king. This narrative focuses on the ingenuity of a girl who plots her own destiny." N Y Times Book Rev

Huling, Jan

Ol' Bloo's boogie-woogie band and blues ensemble; illustrated by Henri Sorensen. Peachtree 2010 un il $16.95

Grades: 2 3 4   398.2

1. Animals -- Folklore 2. Folklore -- Germany 3. Musicians -- Folklore

ISBN 978-1-56145-436-5; 1-56145-436-2

Set in Louisiana, four aging animals who are no longer of any use to their masters find a new home after outwitting a gang of robbers.

"The story of the Bremen Town Musicians works just as well in the American South as it does in the Black Forest. . . . In contrast to the antic narration, Sørensen . . . contributes thoughtful, painterly landscapes of the tin-roofed buildings and dry scrub of the South, and realistic portraits

of the animals. . . . Small black silhouettes adjacent to the main paintings add another layer of visual interest. Read-aloud audiences will giggle at the dialect, nonstop action, and atmospheric descriptions of Huling's . . . . retelling." Publ Wkly

Hyman, Trina Schart

★ **Little** Red Riding Hood; by the Brothers Grimm retold and illustrated by Trina Schart Hyman. Holiday House 1983 un il lib bdg $16.95; pa $6.95

Grades: K 1 2   398.2

1. Wolves -- Folklore 2. Folklore -- Germany

ISBN 0-8234-0470-6 lib bdg; 0-8234-0653-9 pa

LC 82-7700

On her way to deliver a basket of food to her sick grandmother, Elisabeth encounters a sly wolf. "Grades two to four." (Bull Cent Child Books)

This retelling "basically follows the Grimm story, although the text has been fleshed out with some extraneous details (for instance, the little girl is called Elisabeth). . . . The illustrations seem to be a labor of love; richly colored paintings of the forest teem with exquisitely detailed plant and animal life, and the interior scenes, awash with atmospheric light, are beautifully composed and executed." Horn Book

Isadora, Rachel

The **fisherman** and his wife; written by the Brothers Grimm; retold and illustrated by Rachel Isadora. G. P. Putnam's Sons 2008 un il $16.99

Grades: K 1 2 3   398.2

1. Folklore 2. Fairy tales

ISBN 978-0-399-24771-2; 0-399-24771-8

LC 2007-18385

The fisherman's greedy wife is never satisfied with the wishes granted her by an enchanted fish.

"Isadora uses collages of paint-striated paper in tropical colors, plus occasional scraps of fabric, to give this familiar tale a generic African setting. . . . Compared to other retellings, dialogue here is minimal, suiting the story to listeners and beginning readers. . . . It's a handsome book, and a tale that sits comfortably in its new setting." Horn Book

Hansel and Gretel; written by the Brothers Grimm; retold and illustrated by Rachel Isadora. G.P. Putnam's Sons 2009 un il $16.99

Grades: PreK K 1 2   398.2

1. Folklore 2. Fairy tales

ISBN 978-0-399-25028-6; 0-399-25028-X

LC 2008018580

When they are left in the woods by their parents, two children find their way home despite an encounter with a wicked witch.

"Isadora's abbreviated retelling of the popular Grimm Brothers tale closely follows the original in both plot and detail while making the story more accessible to a younger audience. . . . She again sets her tale in Africa, piecing colorfully patterned and hand-painted papers together to create bold, busy eye-catching scenes with a strong ethnic feel." SLJ

Rapunzel; written by the Brothers Grimm; retold and illustrated by Rachel Isadora. G. P. Putnam's Sons 2008 un il $16.99

Grades: K 1 2 3   398.2

1. Fairy tales 2. Folklore -- Germany

ISBN 978-0-399-24772-9; 0-399-24772-6

LC 2007047104

Recasts in an African setting the familiar fairy tale in which a beautiful girl with extraordinarily long hair is imprisoned in a lonely tower by a witch.

"The story remains true to the original. . . . Colorful, vibrant oil paints and collages brighten up the story. The artwork has rich brush-strokes and is heavily patterned, and details abound." SLJ

Jacobs, Joseph

English fairy tales; with illustrations by John Batten. Knopf 1993 428p il $13.95

Grades: 4 5 6 **398.2**

1. Fairy tales 2. Folklore -- Great Britain

ISBN 0-679-42809-7

LC 93-13878

A reissue in one volume of the author's English fairy tales (1891) and More English fairy tales (1894)

A collection of more than eighty traditional stories that recount the adventures of giants, witches, princes, princesses, and animals

James, Alison

The **star** child; translated & adapted from German by J. Alison James; illustrated by Bernadette Watts. North-South 2010 un il $16.95

Grades: PreK K 1 **398.2**

1. Fairy tales 2. Folklore -- Germany

ISBN 978-0-7358-2330-3; 0-7358-2330-8

"Poor in worldly goods but possessing 'a loving and courageous heart,' orphaned Mathilde spends a day giving away her meager possessions and reaps a splendid return. The original tale is often known as 'The Shower of Gold,' but apart from the title change and naming the girl, this sunny version faithfully recounts the story and its lesson. Watts's simply drawn and warmly colored figures encounter one another in appealing rural scenes." SLJ

James, Elizabeth

The **woman** who married a bear; retold by Elizabeth James; illustrated by Atanas. Simply Read Books 2008 un il $16.95

Grades: 2 3 4 **398.2**

1. Bears -- Folklore 2. Native Americans -- Folklore

ISBN 978-1-894965-49-1; 1-894965-49-3

"In this retelling of a West Coast First Nations' myth, a young woman tells her friends that bears are ugly, filthy, dumb animals. The Chief of the Bear People wants to punish her, but his nephew asks for her as his wife. From Mouse Woman she learns that bears can transform into humans and then into bears again. . . . Atanas's exquisite watercolor illustrations capture the natural beauty of the Pacific Coast and the distinctive culture of the First Nations people. . . . This is a welcome addition to units on Native American cultures." SLJ

Jeffers, Susan

Hansel and Gretel; by Susan Jeffers. Rev. ed.; Dutton Children's Books 2011 il $17.99

Grades: 2 3 4 **398.2**

1. Fairy tales 2. Folklore -- Germany

ISBN 978-0-525-42221-1

LC 2011005246

A revised version of the edition published 1980 by Dial Press

When they are left in the woods by their parents, two children find their way home despite an encounter with a wicked witch.

"Those familiar with Jeffers's 1980 version (Dial) will notice that this edition includes a few changes in the illustrations and a simplified text. . . . The artwork, done once again in pen, ink, and dyes, is for the most part from the earlier edition. . . . The pictures are slightly more muted overall, but are still presented in Jeffers's very recognizable style." SLJ

Johnson, Paul Brett

★ **Fearless** Jack; adapted and illustrated by Paul Brett Johnson. Margaret K. McElderry Bks. 2001 un il hardcover o.p. pa $10.99

Grades: K 1 2 3 **398.2**

1. Folklore -- Appalachian Mountains

ISBN 0-689-83296-6; 1-416-96833-4 pa

LC 99-89184

In this Appalachian folktale, Jack wins fame and fortune after killing ten yellow jackets with one whack

"In an Appalachian twang, complete with distinct vocabulary and speech patterns, Johnson's colorful, comical, sturdy pictures are just as energetic as the story which is told." Booklist

★ **Jack** outwits the giants; adapted and illustrated by Paul Brett Johnson. Margaret K. McElderry Bks. 2002 un il hardcover o.p. pa $11.99

Grades: K 1 2 3 **398.2**

1. Giants -- Folklore 2. Folklore -- Appalachian Mountains

ISBN 0-689-83902-2; 1-4169-7861-5 pa

LC 2001-30811

Companion volume to Fearless Jack

In this Appalachian folktale, Jack outwits two giants who want fresh meat for breakfast

"Johnson interweaves several familiar motifs from many traditions while bringing an authentic mountain twang to his telling. Johnson's lively acrylics leave no doubt that these events are as comical as they are suspenseful; the equally lively dialogue makes this an especially good read-aloud." Horn Book Guide

Kajikawa, Kimiko

★ **Tsunami!** illustrated by Ed Young. Philomel Books 2009 un il $16.99

Grades: K 1 2 3 **398.2**

1. Folklore -- Japan 2. Tsunamis -- Folklore

ISBN 978-0-399-25006-4; 0-399-25006-9

LC 2008-25747

A wealthy man in a Japanese village, who everyone calls Ojiisan, which means grandfather, sets fire to his rice fields to warn the innocent people of an approaching tsunami.

"Kajikawa imbues the story with a sense of nobility. . . . Young's rough, impressionistic collages of handpainted papers, fabric, and organic material are dark and stirring." Booklist

Karlin, Barbara

James Marshall's Cinderella; illustrated by James Marshall; retold by Barbara Karlin. Dial Bks. for Young Readers 2001 un il hardcover o.p. pa $6.99

Grades: K 1 2 **398.2**

1. Folklore 2. Fairy tales

ISBN 0-8037-2730-5; 0-14-230048-9 pa

LC 2001-23097

This is a reissue of Barbara Karlin's Cinderella, published 1989 by Little, Brown

"Those seeking a condensed version of the classic fairy tale will find just what they want in Karlin's brief retelling; . . . James Marshall's witty, warts-and-all illustrations add the sparkle that brings out the best in Karlin's straightforward retelling." Horn Book

Keats, Ezra Jack

John Henry; an American legend. story and pictures by Ezra Jack Keats. Pantheon Bks. 1965 un il hardcover o.p. pa $5.99

Grades: K 1 2 3 **398.2**

1. Folklore -- United States 2. African Americans -- Folklore 3.

John Henry (Legendary character)
ISBN 0-394-89052-3 pa

LC 86-27453

This is a picture book retelling of the legend of the Black American folk hero who drove spikes for the railroads

"The dynamic power with which John Henry wields his hammer is matched by the strong illustrations: brilliant oranges and reds contrast with grays and blacks that are often silhouettes; unusual backgrounds produce startling effects. A good picture-story to show to a group." Horn Book

Kellogg, Steven

Chicken Little; retold & illustrated by Steven Kellogg. Morrow 1985 un il hardcover o.p. pa $5.95
Grades: K 1 2 3   398.2
1. Folklore 2. Animals -- Folklore
ISBN 0-688-07045-0 pa

LC 84-25519

In this adaptation of Joseph Jacobs' fable, Chicken Little and his feathered friends, alarmed that the sky seems to be falling, are easy prey to hungry Foxy Loxy when he poses as a police officer in hopes of tricking them into his truck. "Grades one to three." (SLJ)

"Kellogg has enlivened the text [by] giving it some modern touches (Turkey Lurkey carries golf clubs, Foxy Loxy is caught when a 'hippoliceman' tumbles out of a patrol helicopter to land him). Children have always enjoyed the repetition and cumulation of the story, as well as the silliness of the fowls who believe the sky is falling; here there's added fun." Bull Cent Child Books

★ **Paul** Bunyan; a tall tale. retold and illustrated by Steven Kellogg. Morrow 1984 un il lib bdg $16.89; pa $5.95
Grades: K 1 2 3   398.2
1. Tall tales 2. Bunyan, Paul (Legendary character)
ISBN 0-688-03850-6 lib bdg; 0-688-05800-0 pa

LC 83-26684

"Kellogg uses oversize pages for busy, detail-crowded illustrations that have vitality and humor, echoing the exaggeration and ebullience of the story." Bull Cent Child Books

Pecos Bill; a tall tale. retold and illustrated by Steven Kellogg. Morrow 1986 un il $17; pa $5.95
Grades: K 1 2 3   398.2
1. Tall tales 2. Pecos Bill (Legendary character)
ISBN 0-688-05871-X; 0-688-09924-6 pa

LC 86-784

Incidents from the life of Pecos Bill, from his childhood among the coyotes to his unusual wedding day

"Although there's a lot going on in these pictures, they're not cluttered; both the gradations of color and the page design smooth the lines of continuous action and tumult of humorous detail. Kellogg's portrayal of Pecos Bill as a perpetual boy will appeal to children. The retelling is a smooth adaptation for introducing young listeners to longer versions or to accompany storytelling sessions centered around tall-tale heroes." Bull Cent Child Books

★ **Sally** Ann Thunder Ann Whirlwind Crockett; a tall tale. retold and illustrated by Steven Kellogg. Morrow Junior Bks. 1995 un il hardcover o.p. $17
Grades: K 1 2 3   398.2
1. Tall tales
ISBN 0-688-14042-4; 0-688-14043-2 lib bdg; 0-688-17113-3 pa

LC 94-43782

Sally Ann is "Davy's wife and a match for any bear, alligator, or macho man in the West. As retold (and scrupulously sourced) by Kellogg,

Sally Ann's early life outracing and outswimming her nine big brothers and beating all comers at the state fair . . . is but a prelude to her flight to the frontier and subsequent rescue of and marriage to Davy Crockett. . . . Kellogg's characteristically energetic paintings meet their match in this story's kinetic hyperbole; the fact that his Sally Ann and Davy look like rambunctious big kids will only add to their story-hour appeal." Bull Cent Child Books

Kim, So-Un

Korean children's favorite stories; retold by Kim So-un; illustrated by Jeong Kyoung-Sim. Tuttle 2004 95p il $16.95
Grades: 3 4 5 6   398.2
1. Folklore -- Korea
ISBN 0-8048-3591-8

A newly illustrated edition of The story bag, published 1955

This collection of 13 Korean folktales "includes elements shared by many cultures, such as a flood story, and others with a unique sensibility. A variety of animals appear, including tigers, both good and bad, and snakes, depicted as dragons. The delicate watercolor illustrations make the stories accessible to children." SLJ

Kimmel, Eric A.

Anansi and the moss-covered rock; retold by Eric A. Kimmel; illustrated by Janet Stevens. Holiday House 1988 un il lib bdg $17.95
Grades: 1 2 3 4   398.2
1. Animals -- Folklore 2. Spiders -- Folklore 3. Folklore -- West Africa 4. Anansi (Legendary character)
ISBN 0-8234-0689-X

LC 87-31766

Anansi the Spider uses a strange moss-covered rock in the forest to trick all the other animals, until Little Bush Deer decides he needs to learn a lesson

"The text is rhythmic, nicely building suspense to the inevitable conclusion. Stevens' complementary, colorful illustrations add detail, humor, and movement to the text." SLJ

Anansi's party time; by Eric A. Kimmel; illustrated by Janet Stevens. Holiday House 2008 un il $16.95; pa $6.95
Grades: K 1 2 3   398.2
1. Spiders -- Folklore 2. Turtles -- Folklore 3. Folklore -- West Africa 4. Anansi (Legendary character)
ISBN 978-0-8234-1922-7; 0-8234-1922-3; 978-0-8234-2241-8 pa; 0-8234-2241-0 pa

LC 2007002206

When Anansi the spider invites Turtle to a party just to play a trick on him, Turtle gets revenge at a party of his own

"Children will delight in hearing this tale of the spider's comeuppance. . . . Almost every page, illustrated in acrylic ink and colored pencils, has some comical element." SLJ

Even higher! Holiday House 2009 un il $16.95
Grades: K 1 2 3   398.2
1. Jews -- Folklore 2. Rosh ha-Shanah -- Fiction
ISBN 978-0-8234-2020-9; 0-8234-2020-5

LC 2008019710

A skeptical visitor to the village of Nemirov finds out where its rabbi really goes just before the Jewish New Year, when the villagers claim he goes to heaven to speak to God.

"Kimmel's wise, reassuring voice embellishes the story with wonderful details. . . . while keeping the narrative taut. . . . Weber's colorful, openhearted drawings immerse readers in a lost world where piety defined life and the quest for truth was the biggest adventure of all." Publ Wkly

The **fisherman** and the turtle; adapted by Eric A. Kimmel; illustrated by Martha Aviles. Marshall Cavendish Children 2008 un il $16.99

Grades: K 1 2

398.2

1. Folklore 2. Fairy tales 3. Aztecs -- Folklore 4. Turtles -- Folklore

ISBN 978-0-7614-5387-1; 0-7614-5387-3

A retelling of the Grimm tale about the fisherman's greedy wife, set in the land of the Aztecs

"The vivid colors of the acrylic-and-watercolor illustrations and pages bordered with motifs from Aztec art give the tale an authentic flavor." Booklist

The **flying** canoe; a Christmas story. retold by Eric A. Kimmel; illustrated by Daniel San Souci and Justin San Souci. Holiday House 2011 un il $16.95

Grades: K 1 2 3

398.2

1. Folklore -- Canada 2. Christmas -- Folklore 3. French Canadians -- Folklore

ISBN 0823417301; 9780823417308; 978-0-8234-1730-8; 0-8234-1730-1

LC 2011001919

On Christmas Eve, six French-Canadian trappers meet a mysterious stranger who gives them the gift of a trip to their homes in Montreal, if only they agree not to speak until they cross their own thresholds.

"This French-Canadian folktale is brought to luminous life by the San Soucis. The atmospheric artwork, done in traditional and digital media, conveys the mystery and wonder of the snowy journey. Kimmel's storytelling is rich and straightforward." SLJ

★ **Gershon's** monster; a story for the Jewish New Year. retold by Eric A. Kimmel; illustrated by Jon J. Muth. Scholastic Press 2000 un il $16.95

Grades: K 1 2 3

398.2

1. Jews -- Folklore 2. Rosh ha-Shanah -- Fiction

ISBN 0-439-10839-X

LC 99-46986

When his sins threaten the lives of his beloved twin children, a Jewish man finally repents of his wicked ways

"This presentation of a Hasidic legend has everything a reader could want: a suspenseful story, an insightful lesson and brilliantly conceived, airy pictures that accelerate the delivery of both." Publ Wkly

★ **Hershel** and the Hanukkah goblins; written by Eric A. Kimmel; illustrated by Trina Schart Hyman. Holiday House 1989 un il $16.95; pa $6.95

Grades: K 1 2 3

398.2

1. Jews -- Fiction 2. Fairies -- Fiction 3. Hanukkah -- Fiction

ISBN 0-8234-0769-1; 0-8234-1131-1 pa

LC 89-1954

A Caldecott Medal honor book, 1990

This "will fit companionably with haunted castle variants. Hyman is at her best with windswept landscapes, dark interiors, close portraiture, and imaginatively wicked creatures. Both art and history are charged with energy." Bull Cent Child Books

Medio Pollito; a Spanish tale. adapted by Eric A. Kimmel; illustrated by Valeria DoCampo. Marshall Cavendish 2010 un il $17.99

Grades: PreK K 1 2

398.2

1. Folklore -- Spain 2. Chickens -- Folklore

ISBN 978-0-7614-5705-3; 0-7614-5705-4

In this version of the Spanish folktale, Medio Pollito, the half-chick, ventures from his safe barnyard home all the way to Madrid, aided by the friends that he helped along the way.

"Richly colored, cheerful paintings show the endearing, plucky half chick with one leg and one wing, hopping along the road." Booklist

The **runaway** tortilla; illustrated by Randy Cecil. Winslow Press (Delray Beach) 2000 un il $16.95

Grades: K 1 2 3

398.2

1. Folklore 2. Fairy tales 3. Hispanic Americans -- Folklore

ISBN 1-89081-718-X

LC 00-20487

In this Southwestern version of the Gingerbread Man, a tortilla runs away from the woman who is about to cook her. She escapes all her pursuers until she meets Coyote. "Ages four to seven." (Bull Cent Child Books)

"The primitive oil paintings feature a palette of sunset colors, a rotund Tia and Tio, and a lipsticked, scowling tortilla. . . . Kimmel's saucy story joins a swarm of similar, albeit popular, retellings of traditional tales with a Southwestern setting." SLJ

The **spider's** gift; a Ukrainian Christmas story. retold by Eric A. Kimmel; illustrated by Katya Krenina. Holiday House 2010 un il $16.95

Grades: K 1 2 3

398.2

1. Folklore -- Ukraine 2. Spiders -- Folklore 3. Christmas -- Folklore

ISBN 978-0-8234-1743-8; 0-8234-1743-3

LC 2004054162

Katrusya's family cannot afford Christmas, but they cut a small pine tree in the forest, decorate it with buttons, and, when baby spiders hatch in its branches, they especially enjoy the silvery webs that appear.

"Painterly illustrations work well with a charmingly retold text to introduce American children to this unusual yet appealing holiday fable." Booklist

Kimmelman, Leslie

★ The **Little** Red Hen and the Passover matzah; illustrated by Paul Meisel. Holiday House 2010 un il $16.95

Grades: PreK K 1 2

398.2

1. Folklore 2. Jews -- Folklore 3. Animals -- Folklore 4. Chickens -- Folklore 5. Passover -- Folklore

ISBN 978-0-8234-1952-4; 0-8234-1952-5

LC 2008-48488

No one will help the Little Red Hen make the Passover matzah, but they all want to help her eat it. Includes information about Passover, a recipe for matzah, and a glossary of Yiddish words used in the story.

"Such a clever idea! . . . By the time Kimmelman, . . . a terrifically conversational storyteller, and Meisel, . . . a slyly astute cartoonist, . . . are done, readers of all faiths will know a lot more than some emotionally evocative Yiddish words." Publ Wkly

Knutson, Barbara

Love and roast chicken; a trickster tale from the Andes. Lerner Pub. Group 2004 un il map lib bdg $16.95

Grades: K 1 2 3

398.2

1. Folklore -- Peru 2. Foxes -- Folklore 3. Guinea pigs -- Folklore 4. Native Americans -- South America -- Folklore

ISBN 1-57505-657-7

LC 2003-18045

In this folktale from the Andes, a clever guinea pig repeatedly outsmarts the fox that wants to eat him for dinner

"Knutson's boldly outlined, vibrant woodcut-and-watercolor artwork captures the mischievous nature of the guinea pig. . . . A thoroughly enjoyable tale that deserves a place in most libraries." SLJ

Kopisch, August

The **helpful** elves; illustrated by Beatrice Braun-Fock. Floris 2011 il $17.95

Grades: PreK K 1 2   **398.2**

1. Fairies -- Fiction 2. Folklore -- Germany

ISBN 978-0-86315-815-5; 0-86315-815-3

"According to legend, the city of Cologne once had tiny helpers who would sneak into homes at night and complete the daily chores while the townsfolk slept. . . . Until one day the tailor's wife grew curious to see these mysterious helpers. . . . Based on a well-known poem by Kopisch (1799-1853) and illustrated in muted tones by Braun-Fock (1898-1973), the charm of this tale lies in the tiny elf tabs found at the top of each page. Together in a row, 10 elves are perched expectantly—each made distinct with a different smile or a long white beard-forming a miniature audience to watch readers. . . . An enchanting . . . piece of German lore brought to a new audience." Kirkus

Krasno, Rena

Cloud weavers; ancient Chinese legends. [by] Rena Krasno and Yeng-Fong Chiang; illustrations from the collection of Yeng-Fong Chiang. Pacific View Press 2003 96p il $22.95

Grades: 5 6 7 8   **398.2**

1. Folklore -- China

ISBN 1-881896-26-9

LC 2002-35911

Presents legends and tales from China, including ancient folktales, stories that reflect Chinese traditions and virtues, historical tales, and selections from literature

This collection "provides a showcase for some remarkable pieces of Chinese calendar art and advertising posters from the 1920s and 1930s. . . . Prefaces provide cultural insight for some stories, and the brisk retellings weave important background unobtrusively into the narrative." Booklist

Krensky, Stephen

Anansi and the box of stories; a West African folktale. adapted by Stephen Krensky; illustrations by Jeni Reeves. Millbrook Press 2007 48p il (On my own folklore) lib bdg $25.26

Grades: 1 2 3 4   **398.2**

1. Folklore -- West Africa 2. Anansi (Legendary character)

ISBN 978-0-8225-6741-7

LC 2006037783

Long ago in Africa, the sky god Nyame keeps all of the stories to himself, but when Anansi the spider asks their price, Nyame agrees to trade his stories if Anansi can perform four seemingly impossible tasks

"Krensky's retelling is simple and fast-moving, ably supported by Reeve's illustrations." SLJ

John Henry; adapted by Stephen Krensky; illustrations by Mark Oldroyd. Millbrook Press 2007 48p il (On my own folklore) lib bdg $25.26

Grades: 1 2 3 4   **398.2**

1. Folklore -- United States 2. African Americans -- Folklore 3. John Henry (Legendary character)

ISBN 978-1-57505-887-0 lib bdg; 1-57505-887-1 lib bdg

LC 2005010187

Retells the life of the legendary African American hero who raced against a steam drill to cut through a mountain.

This is "written in a comfortably folksy tone. . . . While the narrative has its moments of understated humor, it also involves readers. . . . Full of light and movement, Oldroyd's impressionistic pictures effectively illustrate the story." Booklist

Paul Bunyan; adapted by Stephen Krensky; illustrated by Craig Orback. Millbrook Press 2007 42p il (On my own folklore) lib bdg $25.26

Grades: 1 2 3 4   **398.2**

1. Tall tales 2. Folklore -- United States 3. Bunyan, Paul (Legendary character)

ISBN 978-1-57505-888-7 lib bdg; 1-57505-888-X lib bdg

LC 2005033157

Relates some of the exploits of Paul Bunyan, a lumberjack said to be taller than the trees whose pet was a blue ox named Babe.

"With simple vocabulary and some dialogue, Krensky gives children a feeling for the characters as well as the flavor of the time and the story's setting." SLJ

Includes bibliographical references

Pecos Bill; adapted by Stephen Krensky; illustrations by Paul Tong. Millbrook Press 2007 44p il (On my own folklore) lib bdg $25.26

Grades: 1 2 3 4   **398.2**

1. Tall tales 2. Folklore -- United States 3. Pecos Bill (Legendary character)

ISBN 978-1-57505-889-4 lib bdg; 1-57505-889-8 lib bdg

LC 2005033174

Relates some of the exploits of Pecos Bill, the extraordinary cowboy who was raised by coyotes, rode a mountain lion, and used a rattle snake as a rope.

"With simple vocabulary and some dialogue, Krensky gives children a feeling for the characters as well as the flavor of the time and the story's setting." SLJ

Kurtz, Jane

Fire on the mountain; illustrated by E. B. Lewis. Simon & Schuster Bks. for Young Readers 1994 un il hardcover o.p. pa $5.99

Grades: 1 2 3 4   **398.2**

1. Folklore -- Ethiopia

ISBN 0-689-81896-3 pa

LC 93-11477

A clever young shepherd boy uses his wits to gain a fortune for himself and his sister from a haughty rich man

"Lewis uses color to achieve intriguing contrast and articulates characters' faces with expression and power. Kurtz, who heard the story as a child in Ethiopia, retells it in a strong narrative voice: her language is simple and spare yet evocative." Booklist

L'Homme, Erik

Tales of a lost kingdom; a journey into Northwest Pakistan. written by Erik L'Homme; illustrated by Francois Place; translated by Claudia Zoe Bedrick. Enchanted Lion Books 2007 47p il $17.95

Grades: 3 4 5 6   **398.2**

1. Folklore -- Pakistan

ISBN 978-1-59270-072-1; 1-59270-072-1

A collection of three authentic folktales from the ancient kingdom of Chitral at the border between Pakistan and Afghanistan. Includes a travelogue with photographs, illustrations, and a map.

"Sardonic, bittersweet, and often tragic, these three tales reflect the hardscrabble life of this country. . . . The retellings are flavored with detail and language suitable to the oral tradition. . . . Place's elegantly simple, naive watercolor and pen-and-ink illustrations add to the attractive, hand-crafted design." SLJ

Laird, Elizabeth

★ **Pea** boy; and other stories from Iran. illustrated by Shirin Adl. Frances Lincoln Children's Books 2010 61p il $22.95

Grades: 3 4 5

398.2

1. Folklore -- Iran

ISBN 978-1-84507-912-3; 1-84507-912-4

Retells folktales and fables from Iran, including the story of a mouse and a cockroach who fell in love, a foolish weaver's apprentice, and a boy with the head of a chickpea.

"Adl, who grew up in Iran, creates collages with quirky characters, a naive folk quality and a modern artistic sensibility. . . . A wonderful blend of traditional stories and original art that reflects the customs of this country." Kirkus

Lang, Andrew

The **Arabian** nights entertainments; selected and edited by Andrew Lang; with numerous illustrations by H. J. Ford. Dover Publs. 1969 424p il pa $9.95

Grades: 5 6 7 8

398.2

1. Fairy tales 2. Arabs -- Folklore

ISBN 0-486-22289-6

First published 1898 in the United Kingdom

"A collection of popular tales assembled over many centuries, and well known in Europe from the 18th cent. It contains the stories of 'Aladdin, Alibaba, and Sindbad the sailor.' . . . The framing story in which the tales are set concerns Scheherazade, who is determined to delay her royal husband's plan of killing her—he has taken to murdering his wives because the first was unfaithful to him—by telling him a story every evening. She leaves each evening's tale incomplete until the next day, so that he has to spare her life in order to hear its conclusion. He is so entertained that he finally abandons his murderous plan." Oxford Companion to Child Lit

Lee, H. Chuku

Beauty and the beast; a retelling. by H. Chuku Lee; illustrations by Pat Cummings. Harper 2014 32 p. color illustrations (hardcover bdg.) $17.99

Grades: K 1 2 3

398.2

1. Fairy tales 2. Romance fiction 3. Folklore -- France

ISBN 0688148190; 9780688148195

LC 2013021852

This book, by H. Chuku Lee and illustrated by Pat Cummings, is a retelling of the Beauty and the Beast fairy tale. The book creates a "fairy-tale world flavored by the art, architecture, and culture of West Africa. . . . When her father is taken prisoner by a fearsome Beast, Beauty begs the captor to take her instead. . . . Though he will give her whatever her heart desires . . . she is forbidden to leave. Over time, however, Beauty sees the gentler side of the Beast, and an unexpected bond forms." (Publisher's note)

"Beautifully executed full- and double-page folk-style illustrations combine the vivid hues of watercolor, the softness of pastel, and the texture of gouache. Bold African patterns; elegance in design of clothing, jewelry and coiffures; and the unique architectural style of the Beast's enchanted palace, with influences from the ancient Dogon buildings of Mali, add to the book's distinctiveness." SLJ

Lesser, Rika

★ **Hansel** and Gretel; illustrated by Paul O. Zelinsky; retold by Rika Lesser. Dutton Children's Bks. 1999 un il $16.99; pa $6.99

Grades: K 1 2 3

398.2

1. Fairy tales 2. Folklore -- Germany

ISBN 0-525-46152-3; 0-698-11407-8 pa

LC 99-10198

A reissue of the edition first published 1984 by Dodd, Mead

A Caldecott Medal honor book, 1985

A retelling of the well-known tale in which two children are left in the woods but find their way home despite an encounter with a wicked witch

"Direct and unembellished, Lesser's retelling resembles that of the earliest German edition of Grimm, published in 1812. . . . A visual feast, the illustrations frequently recall Flemish and French genre painting of the seventeenth century, while the idyllic woodland scenes reflect a later Romantic mood." Horn Book Guide

Lester, Julius

★ **John** Henry; pictures by Jerry Pinkney. Dial Bks. for Young Readers 1994 un il $17.99; pa $6.99

Grades: K 1 2 3

398.2

1. Folklore -- United States 2. African Americans -- Folklore 3. John Henry (Legendary character)

ISBN 0-8037-1606-0; 0-14-056622-8 pa

LC 93-34583

A Caldecott Medal honor book, 1995

"The original legend of John Henry and how he beat the steam drill with his sledgehammer has been enhanced and enriched, in Lester's retelling, with wonderful contemporary details and poetic similes that add humor, beauty, and strength. Pinkney's evocative illustrations—especially the landscapes, splotchy and impressionistic, yet very solid and vigorous—are little short of magnificent." Horn Book Guide

The **tales** of Uncle Remus; the adventures of Brer Rabbit. as told by Julius Lester; illustrated by Jerry Pinkney. Dial Bks. 1987 151p il $19.99; pa $8.99

Grades: 4 5 6 7

398.2

1. Animals -- Folklore 2. African Americans -- Folklore

ISBN 0-8037-0271-X; 0-14-130347-6 pa

LC 85-20449

This adaptation of 48 Brer Rabbit stories "is the work of a writer familiar with the methodology of folkloristic and historical research but also with the techniques of flavoring fiction. . . . Pinkney's illustrations—black-and-white drawings with occasional double-page spreads in full color—are well drafted, fresh, and funny." Bull Cent Child Books

★ **Uncle** Remus, the complete tales; with a new introduction. as told by Julius Lester; illustrated by Jerry Pinkney. 1999 xxi, 686p il lib bdg $35

Grades: 4 5 6 7

398.2

1. Animals -- Folklore 2. African Americans -- Folklore

ISBN 0-8037-2451-9

LC 99-17121

Reprint in one volume of works originally published separately, 1987-1994

Lester retells stories of the trickster rabbit from African American folklore collected by Joel Chandler Harris

"This is a landmark collection. . . . Lester's retellings are sharp and flavorful and grounded in the here and now." [review of book 1] Booklist

Livo, Norma J.

Tales to tickle your funny bone; humorous tales from around the world. [by] Norma J. Livo; foreward by Pat Mendoza. Libraries Unlimited 2007 xxvii, 206p il pa $30

Grades: Adult Professional

398.2

1. Folklore 2. Wit and humor

ISBN 978-1-59158-504-6

LC 2007003331

"Tall tales, noodlehead stories, urban legends, riddles, and songs fill this delightful collection of humorous tales. The selections are in shortened but lively formats for easy reading or telling. Introductory notes discuss folklore and the healing power of humor. The more than 70 stories are arranged by genre and labeled with the country of origin. . . . The bibliography includes books and Internet sources as well as VHS and DVD materials. An excellent resource for teachers, librarians, and students." SLJ

Includes bibliographical references

Louie, Ai-Ling

★ **Yeh-Shen**; a Cinderella story from China. retold by Ai-Ling Louie; illustrated by Ed Young. Philomel Bks. 1982 un il $16.99; pa $6.99

Grades: 2 3 4　　　　　　　　　　　　　　　**398.2**

1. Fairy tales 2. Folklore -- China

ISBN 0-399-20900-X; 0-698-11388-8 pa

LC 80-11745

This version of the Cinderella story, in which a young girl overcomes the wickedness of her stepsister and stepmother to become the bride of a prince, is based on ancient Chinese manuscripts written 1000 years before the earliest European version

"The reteller has cast the tale in well-cadenced prose, fleshing out the spare account with elegance and grace. In a manner reminiscent of Chinese scrolls and of decorated folding screens, the text is chiefly set within vertical panels, while the luminescent illustrations—less narrative than emotional—often increase their impact by overspreading the narrow framework or appearing on pages of their own." Horn Book

Lowery, Linda

The **tale** of La Llorona; a Mexican folktale. adapted by Linda Lowery and Richard Keep; illustrations by Janice Lee Porter. Millbrook Press 2008 48p il (On my own folklore) lib bdg $25.26

Grades: 1 2 3 4　　　　　　　　　　　　　　**398.2**

1. Ghost stories 2. Folklore -- Mexico

ISBN 978-0-8225-6378-5 lib bdg; 0-8225-6378-9 lib bdg

LC 2006005478

Expands on a popular Mexican folktale about a ghost that haunts riverbanks at night, crying as she searches for her lost children

"The illustrations are done in soft earth tones in a style reminiscent of Mexican folk art. . . . Given the limitations of the easy-reader format and the necessity of not terrifying young audiences too much, this is a creditable retelling." SLJ

Includes bibliographical references

Luna, James

The **runaway** piggy; illustrated by Laura Lacamara. Pinata Books 2010 un il

Grades: PreK K 1 2　　　　　　　　　　　　**398.2**

1. Folklore 2. Bilingual books -- English-Spanish

ISBN 1-55885-586-6; 978-1-55885-586-1

LC 2009053971

A Mexican piggy cookie escapes from the bakery before it can be eaten and eludes an ever-growing line of people pursuing it. Includes recipe for piggy cookies.

"The story of The Gingerbread Man gets a lively Mexican makeover in this bilingual tale." Publ Wkly

Lunge-Larsen, Lise

The **troll** with no heart in his body and other tales of trolls from Norway; retold by Lise Lunge-Larsen; woodcuts by Betsy Bowen. Houghton Mifflin 1999 92p il hardcover o.p. pa $7.95

Grades: 3 4 5 6　　　　　　　　　　　　　**398.2**

1. Folklore -- Norway

ISBN 0-395-91371-3; 0-618-35403-4 pa

LC 98-43244

"Lunge-Larsen presents nine Norwegian tales about the greed and foolishness of trolls in a casual style that makes these stories ripe for reading aloud and storytelling. Her liveliness of language and easy turn of phrase give these retellings a comforting tone despite the sometimes

scary events. Bowen's colored-ink woodblock prints, inspired by traditional Norwegian woodcarving and design, suit the monumental nature of the subject." Bull Cent Child Books

Includes bibliographical references

MacDonald, Margaret Read, 1940-

Bat's big game; retold by Margaret Read MacDonald; illustrated by Eugenia Nobati. Albert Whitman & Co. 2008 un il $16.95

Grades: K 1 2 3　　　　　　　　　　　　　**398.2**

1. Fables 2. Bats -- Folklore 3. Soccer -- Folkore 4. Animals -- Folklore

ISBN 978-0-8075-0587-8; 0-8075-0587-0

"In this retelling of a traditional fable, Bat cannot decide whether he wants to be on the Animals' or the Birds' soccer team. At first he chooses the Animals, but when they start to fall behind, he switches to the Birds. When they start to lose, he tries to switch back. . . . The text is compact and has an innate rhythm characteristic of a veteran storyteller. Nobati's full-page, digitally created color illustrations are highly stylized. . . . The pictures are full of action and recreate the mood of a heated soccer game." SLJ

★ The **boy** from the dragon palace; a folktale from Japan. retold by Margaret Read MacDonald; illustrated by Sachiko Yoshikawa. Albert Whitman 2011 un il

Grades: K 1 2 3　　　　　　　　　　　　　**398.2**

1. Folklore -- Japan

ISBN 0-8075-7513-5; 978-0-8075-7513-0

LC 2010045965

A magical boy grants a poor flower-seller's every wish until the greedy and ungrateful man grows tired of the boy's unpleasant behavior and sends him away.

"The digitally enhanced, watercolor collage art is typically Japanese in setting, clothing and the wide-eyed . . . boy's black topknot. The text is nicely repetitive and includes satisfyingly disgusting nose-blowing effects that children will love." Kirkus

Conejito; a folktale from Panama. illustrated by Geraldo Valério. August House 2006 un il $16.95

Grades: K 1 2 3　　　　　　　　　　　　　**398.2**

1. Folklore -- Panama 2. Rabbits -- Folklore

ISBN 0-87483-779-0

LC 2005-52567

In this folktale from Panama, a little rabbit and his Tia Monica outwit a fox, a tiger, and a lion, all of whom want to eat him for lunch.

"Rhyming refrains invite the participation of young listeners. . . . Valerio's splashy tropical colors and elongated, rubbery characters . . . capture the tale's bouncing energy." Booklist

Five-minute tales; more stories to read and tell when time is short. [by] Margaret Read MacDonald. August House Publishers 2007 159p $24.94; pa $14.95

Grades: Adult Professional　　　　　　　　**398.2**

1. Folklore 2. Storytelling

ISBN 978-0-87483-781-0; 0-87483-781-2; 978-0-87483-782-7 pa; 0-87483-782-0 pa

LC 2007014511

"Quick tales in storytellers' pockets are like money in the bank. They fill in when programs are delayed, and when class periods are cut short or interrupted so that lengthier stories are no longer suitable. . . . This collection fits the bill with participation, animal, origin, riddle, romance, strange, trickster, and moral tales from around the world and for all ages.

. . . Her practical guidance enables newer as well as veteran tellers to proceed confidently with these engaging stories." SLJ

Includes bibliographical references

Go to sleep, Gecko! a Balinese folktale. retold by Margaret Read MacDonald; illustrated by Geraldo Valério. August House Little Folk 2006 un il $16.95

Grades: K 1 2 **398.2**

1. Geckos -- Folklore 2. Folklore -- Indonesia
ISBN 978-0-87483-780-3; 0-87483-780-4

LC 2006-40748

Retells the folktale of the gecko who complains to the village chief that the fireflies keep him awake at night but then learns that in nature all things are connected

"MacDonald's lyrical language and use of repetition help bring this folktale to life. There is just the right touch of humor in both the text and the art. The pacing is perfectly matched to the richly colored acrylic illustrations." SLJ

The **great** smelly, slobbery, small-tooth dog; a folktale from Great Britain. retold by Margaret Read MacDonald; illustrated by Julie Paschkis. August House Little Folk 2007 un il $16.95

Grades: PreK K 1 2 **398.2**

1. Dogs -- Folklore 2. Folklore -- Great Britain
ISBN 978-0-87483-808-4

LC 2007005504

In this British variant of a traditional tale, a great smelly, slobbery, small-tooth dog rescues a rich man from bandits and demands that the man bring his beautiful daughter to live in his castle.

"The text is perfectly paced for interactive read-alouds . . . but the active, richly colored gouache paintings, which include beautiful details, . . . will work best with small groups." Booklist

How many donkeys? an Arabic counting tale. retold by Margaret Read MacDonald and Nadia Jameel Taibah; illustrations by Carol Liddiment. Albert Whitman 2009 un il $16.99

Grades: K 1 2 **398.2**

1. Counting 2. Arabs -- Folklore
ISBN 978-0-8075-3424-3; 0-8075-3424-2

LC 2008056047

When Jouha counts the ten donkeys carrying his dates to market, he repeatedly forgets to count the one he is riding on, causing him great consternation. Includes numbers written out in Arabic and in English transliteration, as well as the numerals one through ten, and a note on the origins and other versions of the story

"Bright, painterly illustrations depict the sunny desert setting; jewel-toned robes, turban, and blankets enliven the sandy palette. . . . A winning, witty, and surprisingly effective combination." Booklist

Little Rooster's diamond button; retold by Margaret Read MacDonald; illustrated by Will Terry. Albert Whitman 2007 un il $16.95

Grades: K 1 2 3 **398.2**

1. Folklore -- Hungary 2. Roosters -- Fiction
ISBN 0807546445; 9780807546444

LC 2006-23979

In this Hungarian folktale, a rooster with a magic stomach retrieves the diamond button which was stolen from him by a greedy king

"This fine paean to cleverness and persistence is given extra zest by Terry's acrylic illustrations, which are as colorful as sparkling gems." Booklist

Surf war! a folktale from the Marshall Islands. illustrated by Geraldo Valerio. August House LittleFolk 2009 un il $16.95

Grades: K 1 2 **398.2**

1. Ecology -- Folklore 2. Folklore -- Marshall Islands
ISBN 978-0-87483-889-3; 0-87483-889-4

LC 2008042589

A bragging contest between Whale and Sandpiper turns into a battle over the beach and sea, until both parties realize that the beach and the sea, as well as sea creatures and shorebirds, are interdependent

"The illustrations dominate the pages, with the birds and their backgrounds painted with bright shades of yellow, pink, and orange, while the sea and its creatures are deeper blues, grays, and purples. This charming story provides a moral about getting along with others and caring for the environment." SLJ

Three-minute tales; stories from around the world to tell or read when time is short. August House 2004 160p $24.95; pa $17.95 **398.2**

1. Folklore 2. Storytelling
ISBN 0-87483-728-6; 0-87483-729-4 pa

LC 2004-46257

"Easy to tell, easy to teach to children and adults, and easy to remember, the 80 very short tales in this global collection are for sharing in the classroom, library, and home and around the campfire. . . . The informal, highly practical suggestions for beginners make storytelling sound easy." Booklist

Includes bibliographical references

Too many fairies; a Celtic Tale. retold by Margaret Read MacDonald; illustrated by Susan Mitchell. Marshall Cavendish Children 2010 un il $17.99

Grades: K 1 2 3 **398.2**

1. Fairies -- Folklore 2. Folklore -- Scotland
ISBN 978-0-7614-5604-9; 0-7614-5604-X

LC 2009007128

An old woman complains about all the housework she has to do, but when some fairies come to help her she finds that they are more trouble than they are worth

"This Scottish folktale is subtle but effective in its message of humility. The illustrations are folksy and warm with amusing detail. . . . A fun read-aloud." SLJ

Tunjur! Tunjur! Tunjur! a Palestinian folktale. retold by Margaret Read MacDonald; collected by Ibrahim Muhawi and Sharif Kanaana; illustrated by Alik Arzoumanian. Marshall Cavendish Children 2006 un il $16.95

Grades: K 1 2 **398.2**

1. Theft -- Fiction 2. Palestinian Arabs -- Folklore
ISBN 978-0-7614-5225-6; 0-7614-5225-7

LC 2005009719

"In this lively Palestinian tale, a woman wishes for a child to love, 'even if it is nothing more than a cooking pot.' Voila! Her wish comes true, and red Little Pot appears. . . . Reluctantly, the mother lets her pot outdoors, and its adventures include meetings with a merchant and even the royal family. Little Pot manages to roll away from each encounter with valuable stolen goods tucked inside her lid, but after her petty thefts are discovered, she receives a stinky comeuppance that is sure to please read-aloud crowds. Folklorist MacDonald's briskly paced text brims with repetitive phrases that evoke the sounds and rhythm of Little Pot's tumbling, rolling movement, and Arzoumanian's richly hued, stylized acrylics, bordered with Islamic motifs, add subtle cultural detail." Booklist

Mahy, Margaret

★ The **seven** Chinese brothers; illustrated by Jean and Mou-Sien Tseng. Scholastic 1990 un hardcover o.p. pa $5.99

Grades: 1 2 3   398.2
1. Fairy tales 2. Folklore -- China
ISBN 0-590-42057-7 pa

LC 88-33668

A story about "seven brothers, each of whom was blessed with an extraordinary power. Together, they use their amazing talents to avoid death at the hands of Emperor Ch'in Shih Huang, while trying to help the exhausted conscripted laborers working on the Great Wall." Child Book Rev Serv

Malam, John
Fairies. QEB Pub. 2010 32p il (QEB mythologies) lib bdg $28.50
Grades: 4 5 6 7   398.2
1. Fairies
ISBN 978-1-59566-979-7; 1-59566-979-5

LC 2008-56083

"A wealth of sidebars and captions . . . adds depth to the compelling [narrative]. Supported by vibrant color illustrations, . . . [this] fascinating and well-written [tale] will integrate well with social-science curriculums." SLJ
Includes glossary

Giants. QEB Pub. 2010 32p il (QEB mythologies) lib bdg $28.50
Grades: 4 5 6 7   398.2
1. Giants -- Folklore
ISBN 978-1-59566-980-3; 1-59566-980-9

LC 2009000389

"A wealth of sidebars . . . adds depth to the compelling [narrative]. Supported by vibrant color illustrations, . . . [this] fascinating and well-written [tale] will integrate well with social-science curriculums." SLJ
Includes glossary

Monsters. QEB Pub. 2010 32p il map (QEB mythologies) $28.50
Grades: 4 5 6 7   398.2
1. Monsters
ISBN 978-1-59566-981-0; 1-59566-981-7

LC 2008056090

This "is filled with some of the weirdest creatures ever conceived. . . . Take the Hambaba (Iraqi myth), the hideous giant with a face of coiled intestines. Or the Flying Head (Iroquois folktale). . . . The layout, designed as if printed upon an ancient map or scroll, is great, and Follenn's artwork is a rousing example of graphic novel-style menace." Booklist

Mandell, Muriel, 1921-
A **donkey** reads; adapted from a Turkish folktale by Muriel Mandell from a Turkish folktale; art by André Letria. Star Bright Books 2011 un il $16.95; pa $6.95
Grades: K 1 2 3   398.2
1. Donkeys -- Fiction 2. Folklore -- Turkey 3. Books and reading -- Fiction
ISBN 978-1-59572-255-3; 1-59572-255-6; 978-1-59572-256-0 pa; 1-59572-256-4 pa

LC 2010002989

In a small village in Anatolia, even the poorest villager is expected to pay tribute to a tyrranical Mongol ruler, but the wiseman, Nasreddin Hoca, finds a way to make an aged donkey seem most valuable.
"The story's clever trickery and triumph-over-wickedness elements are satisfying. The vivid illustrations have a playful reverence. . . . The last page provides some historical context for Nasreddin." Horn Book Guide

Manna, Anthony L.
The **orphan**; a Cinderella story from Greece. [by] Anthony L. Manna and Soula Mitakidou; illustrated by Giselle Potter. Schwartz & Wade 2011 un il $16.99; lib bdg $19.99
Grades: K 1 2 3   398.2
1. Fairy tales 2. Folklore -- Greece
ISBN 978-0-375-86691-3; 0-375-86691-4; 978-0-375-96691-0 lib bdg; 0-375-96691-9 lib bdg

LC 2010044480

In this variation on the Cinderella story set in Greece, a girl mistreated by her stepmother and stepsisters manages to captivate the prince, with help from Mother Nature and her children.
"The doll-like faces and stiff limbs of Potter's naïve-style watercolor figures suit the fairy-tale setting, and the pictures of tiny tailors and jewelers fawning before the pudgy stepsisters give the otherwise earnest story mordant humor. This Cinderella somehow seems more resourceful than her French counterpart, and her happy ending more dearly earned." Publ Wkly

Marshall, James
★ **Goldilocks** and the three bears; retold and illustrated by James Marshall. Dial Bks. for Young Readers 1988 un il $15.99; pa $5.99
Grades: PreK K 1 2   398.2
1. Folklore 2. Bears -- Folklore
ISBN 0-8037-0542-5; 0-14-056366-0 pa

LC 87-32983

A Caldecott Medal honor book, 1989
Three bears return home from a walk to find a little girl asleep in baby bear's bed. "Preschool to grade two." (SLJ)
"Marshall's Goldilocks, the naughty little girl who disrupts a placid bear household, is no adorable blond moppet led more by curiosity than by mischievous intent. Instead, she is a sturdy, brazen, mini-hussy who stomps over the doorsill with a determined set to her mouth and a confident bounce in her step. . . . The big cartoonlike pictures depict a cozy modern setting for the respectable, suburban bears with snug rooms cluttered with books, bulbous upholstered furniture and a messy little bear's room. . . . The story contains a genuine enjoyment of Goldilock's adventures as they are reflected in Marshall's usual slapdash and rollicking illustrations." Horn Book

Hansel and Gretel; retold and illustrated by James Marshall. Dial Bks. for Young Readers 1990 un il hardcover o.p. pa $5.99
Grades: PreK K 1 2   398.2
1. Fairy tales 2. Folklore -- Germany
ISBN 0-14-050836-8 pa

LC 89-26011

A poor woodcutter's children, lost in the forest, come upon a house made of cookies, cakes, and candy, occupied by a wicked witch who likes to have children for dinner
'Marshall's trademark wit and slyness mark every page of this effervescent interpretation. Never has there been a more horribly magnificent witch than his—an overstuffed, cackling harridan resplendent in scarlet costume, lipstick and rouge, her hair bedecked with incongruously delicate bows." Publ Wkly

★ **Red** Riding Hood; retold and illustrated by James Marshall. Dial Bks. for Young Readers 1987 un il $15.99; pa $5.99
Grades: PreK K 1 2   398.2
1. Wolves -- Folklore 2. Folklore -- Germany
ISBN 0-8037-0344-9; 0-14-054693-6 pa

LC 86-16722

A little girl meets a hungry wolf in the forest on her way to visit her grandmother. "Preschool to grade three." (SLJ)

A "retelling of the familiar tale . . . maintaining the integrity of the Grimm Brothers' version, with both Grandma and Red Riding Hood eaten and later rescued by a hunter." SLJ

★ The **three** little pigs; retold and illustrated by James Marshall. Dial Bks. for Young Readers 1989 un il hardcover o.p. pa $6.99
Grades: PreK K 1 2
398.2
1. Pigs -- Folklore 2. Wolves -- Folklore 3. Folklore -- Great Britain
ISBN 0-8037-0591-3; 0-14-055742-3 pa
LC 88-33411

"In his spiffed-up version of the story, the three porkers follow the traditional course of straw, sticks, and bricks with the traditional results, but the players and accoutrements have a bit more zip than those in other versions. . . . The large, exuberant, cartoonlike illustrations provide much additional entertainment, jouncing readers along delightfully from one amusing scene to the next." Horn Book

Martin, Rafe
★ The **world** before this one; a novel told in legend. with paper sculpture by Calvin Nicholls. Levine Bks. 2002 195p il hardcover o.p. pa $5.99
Grades: 4 5 6 7
398.2
1. Seneca Indians -- Folklore
ISBN 0-590-37976-3; 978-0-590-37980-9 pa; 0-590-37980-1 pa
LC 2001-23403

"Written in the style of a novel, this collection of 14 Seneca tales is presented through the retelling of one central story into which all of the others are artfully woven. . . . Martin offers sources for the tales along with an introductory note by Seneca Elder Peter Jemison. Each chapter includes a painstakingly detailed white paper sculpture of a character (often an animal) from one of the stories." SLJ

Mayer, Marianna
Baba Yaga and Vasilisa the brave; as told by Marianna Mayer; illustrated by K. Y. Craft. Morrow Junior Bks. 1994 un il $16.95
Grades: 3 4 5
398.2
1. Fairy tales 2. Folklore -- Russia
ISBN 0-688-08500-8
LC 90-38514

This is a retelling of a Russian fairy tale. "After the death of her father, Vasilisa is mistreated by her stepmother and stepsisters; her only comfort is the magical doll made by her mother before she died. Sent to Baba Yaga's house to fetch a light, the girl . . . is given a series of impossible tasks to perform. With the help of her doll, she pleases the demanding hag, who sends her home with the precious light. After it destroys her stepmother and stepsisters, Vasilisa goes to live with an elderly woman and learns to spin and weave. She creates an exquisite piece of cloth that catches the attention of the tsar, . . . {who} asks for her hand in marriage." (SLJ) "Ages four to eight." (Booklist)

"Mayer's graceful prose conveys both the wonder and power of the tale. Complementing the text are Craft's illustrations done in a mixture of watercolor, gouache, and oils. The palette of red and gold set against a dark background resembles Russian folk-art paintings on black-lacquered wood." SLJ

The **twelve** dancing princesses; as told by Marianna Mayer; illustrated by K.Y. Craft. Morrow Junior Bks. 1988 [40] p. col. ill. $17.99
Grades: K 1 2 3
398.2
1. Dance -- Fiction 2. Shoes -- Fiction 3. Princesses -- Fiction 4. Fairy tales -- Fiction 5. Fairy tales
ISBN 0688020267; 0688080510; 9780688080518
LC 83001034

This children's book, by Marianna Mayer, illustrated by K.Y. Craft, tells the "enchanting story of the twelve beautiful princesses and the handsome young lad who solves the mystery of their tattered shoes." (Publisher's note)

"Craft's richly hued illustrations create a magical setting for Mayer's polished version of this romantic fairy tale... With skillful use of lighting, texture and detail and a fine sense of mood, Craft captures both the regal opulence of the King's court and the shimmery, ethereal beauty of the subterranean world of the all-night dancing, resulting in a lavish feast for the eyes and the imagination. All ages."

McCaughrean, Geraldine
★ The **epic** of Gilgamesh; retold by Geraldine McCaughrean; illustrated by David Parkins. Eerdmans Bks. for Young Readers 2003 95p il $18
Grades: 5 6 7 8
398.2
1. Gilgamesh 2. Folklore -- Iraq
ISBN 0-8028-5262-9
LC 2003-1086

A retelling, based on seventh-century B.C. Assyrian clay tablets, of the wanderings and adventures of the god king, Gilgamesh, who ruled in ancient Mesopotamia (now Iraq) in about 2700 B.C., and of his faithful companion, Enkidu

This is "clearly a telling for our time, but one that honors its source. Parkins captures the epic's primitive power and universal emotions in rough, broadly rendered portraits." Horn Book

McDermott, Gerald
★ **Anansi** the spider; a tale from the Ashanti. adapted and illustrated by Gerald McDermott. Holt & Co. 1972 un il $16.95; pa $6.95
Grades: K 1 2 3
398.2
1. Folklore -- Ghana 2. Anansi (Legendary character) 3. Ashanti (African people) -- Folklore
ISBN 0-8050-0310-X; 0-8050-0311-8 pa
A Caldecott Medal honor book, 1973

The adaptation of this traditional tale of Ghana is based on an animated film by McDermott. It tells of Anansi, a spider, who is saved from terrible fates by his six sons and is unable to decide which of them to reward. The solution to his predicament is also an explanation for how the moon was put into the sky

This offers "brief poetic text, complemented by geometric African folk-style illustrations in pure, bold colors." SLJ

★ **Arrow** to the sun; a Pueblo Indian tale. adapted and illustrated by Gerald McDermott. Viking 1974 un il $16.99; pa $6.99
Grades: K 1 2 3
398.2
1. Pueblo Indians -- Folklore
ISBN 0-670-13369-8; 0-14-050211-4 pa
Awarded the Caldecott Medal, 1975

This myth tells how Boy searches for his immortal father, the Lord of the Sun, in order to substantiate his paternal heritage. Shot as an arrow to the sun, Boy passes through the four chambers of ceremony to prove himself. Accepted by his father, he returns to earth to bring the Lord of the Sun's spirit to the world of men

"The simple, brief text—which suggests similar stories in religion and folklore—is amply illustrated in full-page and doublespread pictures. . . . The strong colors and the bold angular forms powerfully accompany the text." Horn Book

★ **Coyote:** a trickster tale from the American Southwest; told and illustrated by Gerald McDermott. Harcourt Brace & Co. 1994 un il $15; pa $6

Grades: K 1 2 3   **398.2**
1. Coyote (Legendary character) 2. Native Americans -- Folklore
ISBN 0-15-220724-4; 0-15-201958-8 pa

LC 92-32979

"Coyote persuades the crows to help him fly, but he becomes so obnoxious and boastful that they abandon him in midair, so he falls back to earth. Told with playful illustrations against the glowing orange of a desert sky, the humorous Zuni tale explains how Coyote, who once had blue fur, got his dust-colored coat and black-tippped tail." Horn Book Guide

Jabuti the tortoise; a trickster tale from the Amazon. told and illustrated by Gerald McDermott. Harcourt 2001 un il hardcover o.p. pa $7
Grades: K 1 2 3   **398.2**
1. Turtles -- Folklore 2. Native Americans -- Folklore 3. Amazon River valley -- Folklore
ISBN 0-15-200496-3; 0-15-205374-3 pa

LC 00-11977

All the birds enjoy the song-like flute music of Jabuti, the tortoise, except Vulture who, jealous because he cannot sing, tricks Jabuti into riding his back toward a festival planned by the King of Heaven

"The story succeeds by embracing what McDermott refers to as a universal trickster theme. . . . Utilizing a radiant palette to evoke the brilliance and vitality of the region, McDermott's spreads feature his familiar geometrically drawn characters that seem to vibrate against the lush-green stylized foliage set upon hot-pink backgrounds." SLJ

★ **Monkey**; a trickster tale from India. Harcourt Children's Books 2011 un il $16.99
Grades: K 1 2 3   **398.2**
1. Folklore -- India 2. Monkeys -- Folklore 3. Crocodiles -- Folklore
ISBN 978-0-15-216596-3; 0-15-216596-7

LC 2009007977

Crocodile wants to feast on Monkey's heart and Monkey must outsmart him if he is to enjoy eating mangoes all day.

"Playfully told with succinct text and illustrations, this tale will appeal to a wide audience. It is both simple and sophisticated with subtle and not-so-subtle levels of irony. The cut/torn paper illustrations are inseparable from the text." SLJ

Pig-Boy; a trickster tale from Hawai'i. Harcourt Children's Books 2009 un il $16
Grades: PreK K 1 2 3   **398.2**
1. Pigs -- Folklore 2. Folklore -- Hawaii
ISBN 978-0-15-216590-1; 0-15-216590-8

LC 2006-35426

The mischievous, shape-shifting Pig-Boy gets in trouble with both the King and Pele, the goddess of fire, but always manages to slip away as his grandmother has told him to do.

"The boldly colored art is dynamic and reflects both the humor of the sprightly text and the author/illustrator's background as an animator in its visual pacing. The tale itself has just enough folkloric elements to convey action, character and setting without bogging down in detail. . . . Good rascally fun." Kirkus

Raven; a trickster tale from the Pacific Northwest. told and illustrated by Gerald McDermott. Harcourt Brace Jovanovich 1993 un il $16; pa $7
Grades: K 1 2 3   **398.2**
1. Native Americans -- Folklore
ISBN 0-15-265661-8; 0-15-202449-2 pa

LC 91-14563

A Caldecott Medal honor book, 1994

Raven, a Pacific Coast Indian trickster, sets out to find the sun

"Raven, whether he appears as a bird or child, is always marked with a distinctive design of clear-cut red, green, and blue on black, sharply contrasting with the softer hues and forms of the backgrounds and the other characters. In this way, Raven is always recognizable, even when he shifts his shape to human form. . . . Read this picture book aloud for the full effect of its simple, rhythmic text and striking artwork." Booklist

McGill, Alice
Way up and over everything; illustrated by Jude Daly. Houghton Mifflin 2008 un il $16
Grades: 2 3 4 5   **398.2**
1. Slavery -- Folklore 2. Folklore -- United States 3. African Americans -- Folklore
ISBN 978-0-618-38796-0; 0-618-38796-X

LC 2003-19384

In this retelling of a folktale, five Africans escape the horrors of slavery by flying away

"Daly's delicate and elongated figures, small in scale against the vast watercolor landscapes of the Georgia countryside, present a bird's eye view of the story and suggest the enormity of such an escape." Booklist

McGovern, Ann
Too much noise; illustrated by Simms Taback. Houghton Mifflin 1967 44p il $16; pa $6.95
Grades: K 1 2 3   **398.2**
1. Folklore
ISBN 0-395-18110-0; 0-395-62985-3 pa

"The too crowded house of a familiar old tale becomes a too noisy house in this entertaining picture-book story. Bothered by the noises in his house, an old man follows the advice of the village wise man by first acquiring and then getting rid of a cow, donkey, sheep, hen, dog, and cat. Only then can he appreciate how quiet his house is. The simplicity and straightforwardness of the folktale are evident in both the telling of the cumulative story and in the amusing colored illustrations." Booklist

Menchu, Rigoberta
The **honey** jar; [by] Rigoberta Menchu with Dante Liano; pictures by Domi; translated by David Unger. Groundwood Books/House of Anansi Press 2006 64p il $18.95
Grades: 4 5 6   **398.2**
1. Mayas -- Folklore
ISBN 978-0-88899-670-1; 0-88899-670-5

This is a collection of 12 Mayan folktales that the author "heard as a child. The stories range from creation stories and pourquoi tales about animals to selections that reflect a distinctive worldview, a broad awareness of nature, and a sense of humor. Using vivid colors, the naturalistic, folk-art oil paintings . . . illustrate the stories in a manner that reflects the simple spirit and directness of the tellings. An expressive collection that lends insight into the Mayan culture in which Menchu grew up." Booklist

Includes glossary

The **secret** legacy; [by] Rigoberta Menchu with Dante Liano; pictures by Domi; translated by David Unger. Groundwood Books/House of Anansi Press 2008 64p il $19.95
Grades: 4 5 6 7 8   **398.2**
1. Mayas -- Folklore 2. Folklore -- Guatemala
ISBN 978-0-88899-896-5; 0-88899-896-1

"On her first day watching over her Mayan grandfather's cornfields, young Ixkem is invited by the b'e'n, spirits in the form of small humans, to visit them underground. They feed her generously and she tells them stories that explain Mayan customs and include bits of folklore. . . . The

Mexican artist Domi has provided bright paintings in a naturalistic, folk-art style. The lyrical translation preserves the storyteller's voice." SLJ

Mhlophe, Gcina

African tales; a Barefoot collection. written by Gcina Mhlophe; illustrated by Rachel Griffin. Barefoot Books 2009 95p il map
Grades: 5 6 7 8
398.2
    1. Folklore -- Africa
    ISBN 1-84686-118-7; 978-1-84686-118-5

LC 2008028042

"Each of these eight tales is preceded by information and interesting facts about the country from which it originated. A basic map of Africa helps orient readers to the location of the various countries represented. Extensive source notes are appended. . . . There are many choices that could be read aloud or told using a call-and-response format. The book design . . . is a feast for the eyes. Griffin employs a collage technique using colored beads, sewn fabric, and textured papers, and incorporates them into shapes and faces of animals and humans. . . . This compilation contains a wealth of information and will enhance folklore collections." SLJ

Includes bibliographical references

Miller, Bobbi

Davy Crockett gets hitched; retold by Bobbi Miller; illustrated by Megan Lloyd. Holiday House 2009 un il $16.95
Grades: K 1 2 3
398.2
    1. Tall tales 2. Folklore -- United States
    ISBN 978-0-8234-1837-4; 0-8234-1837-5

LC 2006050063

An accidental encounter with a thorn bush on his way to the spring dance has Davy Crockett kicking up his heels and out-dancing even the audacious Miss Sally Ann Thunder Ann Whirlwind.

"Lloyd's energetic artwork propels the narrative with effective use of light and line. . . . The text sings with rich vocabulary, making this tall tale a great choice for reading aloud." Booklist

One fine trade; retold by Bobbi Miller; illustrated by Will Hillenbrand. Holiday House 2009 un il $16.95
Grades: K 1 2 3
398.2
    1. Weddings -- Folklore 2. Folklore -- United States 3. Peddlers and peddling -- Folklore
    ISBN 978-0-8234-1836-7; 0-8234-1836-7

LC 2007-25493

Georgy Piney Woods, the best peddler who ever lived, makes several trades so his daughter can buy a wedding dress.

This is an "entertaining romp. . . . The ink and pencil scenes were scanned and digitally manipulated, with colored pencil and gouache additions to the final work. This creates a convincing depth. . . . The outlandish events and droll caricatures are supported by lively language that is full of rhythm and fun to read aloud." SLJ

Milligan, Bryce

Brigid's cloak; an ancient Irish story. written by Bryce Milligan; illustrated by Helen Cann. Eerdmans Bks. for Young Readers 2002 un il $16; pa $8
Grades: K 1 2 3
398.2
    1. Nuns 2. Saints 3. Folklore -- Ireland
    ISBN 0-8028-5224-6; 0-8028-5297-1 pa

LC 2001-40174

Relates a legend about the Irish slave girl who became Saint Brigid, beginning with a celestial song, a mysterious gift, and a prophecy on the night of her birth

"Borders of Celtic designs frame Cann's mixed-media pictures and add both authenticity and wonder to the tale." Booklist

Mitchell, Stephen

Iron Hans; a Grimm's fairy tale. retold by Stephen Mitchell; illustrated by Matt Tavares. Candlewick Press 2007 un il $16.99
Grades: K 1 2 3
398.2
    1. Fairy tales 2. Folklore -- Germany
    ISBN 978-0-7636-2160-5; 0-7636-2160-9

LC 2006047520

With the help of Iron Hans, the wild man of the forest, a young prince makes his own way in the world and wins the hand of a princess

"Clamoring knights, galloping steeds and scenes of palace splendor crowd the pages, which rise in a vertical format as if to stress Iron Hans's nine-foot stature. . . . Complex and muscular, this is a good bet for readers who demand lots of action." Publ Wkly

Mitton, Tony

The **storyteller's** secrets; illustrated by Peter Bailey. David Fickling Books 2010 118p il $15.99
Grades: 4 5 6
398.2
    1. Folklore 2. Storytelling -- Fiction
    ISBN 978-0-385-75190-2; 0-385-75190-7

"In a handsome volume profusely illustrated with a mix of silhouettes and vigorous line drawings, Mitton presents verse renditions of European tales and legends. . . . Written in ballad-style quatrains with unforced, natural sounding rhymes and cadences, the stories offer enthralling, easy-to-follow plots with clear themes. . . . Mitton links all of his selections with prose encounters between two marveling children and a mysterious old Storyteller. . . . This gathering will cast the same sort of profound spell on readers and listeners." Booklist

Moerbeek, Kees

Aesop's fables: a pop-up book of classic tales; paper engineering by Kees Moerbeek; illustrated by Chris Beatrice & Bruce Whatley. Little Simon 2011 il $27.99
Grades: K 1 2 3 4
398.2
    1. Fables 2. Folklore 3. Pop-up books
    ISBN 978-1-4169-7146-7; 1-4169-7146-7

"This book makes good use of the format to showcase 10 traditional tales. Five of the fables are presented on handsomely illustrated spreads, each including a dramatic 3D sculpture that takes center stage and two smaller foldouts embellished with movable parts that contain the bulk of the text. . . . Each centerpiece pop-up does an excellent job of grabbing readers' attention and drawing them into the story. . . . Throughout, rich earthy hues, lush forest landscapes, and vivid detail make the illustrations appealing. The straightforward text aptly conveys the gist of each tale, and a brief section offers background about Aesop." SLJ

Montes, Marisa

★ **Juan** Bobo goes to work; a Puerto Rican folktale. retold by Marisa Montes; illustrated by Joe Cepeda. HarperCollins Pubs. 2000 un il $15.95; lib bdg $15.89
Grades: K 1 2 3
398.2
    1. Folklore -- Puerto Rico
    ISBN 0-688-16233-9; 0-688-16234-7 lib bdg

LC 99-28799

Although he tries to do exactly as his mother tells him, foolish Juan Bobo keeps getting things all wrong

"The funny, well-paced retelling smoothly incorporates Spanish words and phrases. . . . Using bold, bright Caribbean colors, Cepeda's oil paintings amplify Juan's silliness and charm. Brush strokes add texture, and background details establish the Puerto Rican setting." Booklist
Includes glossary

Morales, Yuyi

★ **Just** a minute; a trickster tale and counting book. Chronicle Books 2003 un il $15.95

Grades: K 1 2 3   **398.2**

1. Counting 2. Folklore -- Mexico 3. Bilingual books -- English-Spanish
ISBN 0-8118-3758-0

LC 2002-151386

In this version of a traditional tale, Senor Calavera arrives at Grandma Beetle's door, ready to take her to the next life, but after helping her count, in English and Spanish, as she makes her birthday preparations, he changes his mind

"Like the text, the rich, lively artwork draws strongly upon Mexican culture. . . . The splendid paintings and spirited storytelling—along with useful math and multicultural elements—augur a long, full life for this original folktale." Booklist

Morpurgo, Michael

★ **Beowulf**; illustrated by Michael Foreman. Candlewick Press 2006 92p il $17.99

Grades: 5 6 7 8   **398.2**

1. Beowulf 2. Folklore -- Europe 3. Monsters -- Folklore
ISBN 978-0-7636-3206-9; 0-7636-3206-6

"Morpurgo retells the classic story of the courageous young warrior . . . who used his brute strength to save the neighboring Danes, then his own kinsmen, by slaying two horrible monsters, a sea serpent, and a massive dragon. . . . Many attractive full-page watercolor and pastel paintings illustrate important action-filled scenes. . . . This is a fine retelling." SLJ

Hansel and Gretel; retold by Michael Morpurgo; illustrated by Emma Chichester Clark. Candlewick Press 2008 un il $18.99

Grades: 2 3 4   **398.2**

1. Fairy tales 2. Folklore -- Germany
ISBN 978-0-7636-4012-5; 0-7636-4012-3

LC 2007052335

When they are left in the woods by their parents, Hansel and Gretel find their way home despite an encounter with a wicked witch

"Leaving the basic framework of the Grimm Brothers' tale intact, Morpurgo has altered details of the plot, creating a story in which strong familial bonds allow the innocent brother and sister to overcome evil. . . . Folk-art-style paintings, in watercolor with colored-pencil outlines and facial features, range in size from small decorations and vertical strips of various widths to full-page scenes." SLJ

★ The **McElderry** book of Aesop's fables; illustrations by Emma Chichester Clark. Margaret K. McElderry Books 2005 94p il $19.95

Grades: K 1 2   **398.2**

1. Fables 2. Authors 3. Storytellers
ISBN 1-4169-0290-2

LC 2004-58160

First published 2004 in the United Kingdom with title: The Orchard book of Aesop's fables

Retellings of twenty-one classic Aesop fables, including "The Hare and the Tortoise" and "Belling the Cat," in updated language.

"This large, spacious hardcover is perfectly designed for reading aloud. The text appears in big, clear type on thick paper, and Clark's gorgeous watercolors show the characters. . . . Morpurgo's adaptations of 21 short tales stay true to the tradition of humanlike animal characters and lessons that eschew heavy philosophizing in favor of warnings about ordinary folk and their foolishness." Booklist

The **Pied** Piper of Hamelin; [retold by] Michael Morpurgo; illustrated by Emma Chichester Clark. Candlewick Press 2011 il $16.99

Grades: K 1 2   **398.2**

1. Folklore -- Germany 2. Pied Piper of Hamelin
ISBN 978-0-7636-4824-4; 0-7636-4824-8

LC 2010050683

The Pied Piper pipes a village free of rats, and when the villagers refuse to pay him for the service, he pipes away their children as well.

"Chichester Clark's pencil-and-acrylic illustrations are bright and beautifully composed; the teeming rats radiate menace without being actively scary. An evocative and effective retelling of an old classic." Kirkus

★ **Sir** Gawain and the Green Knight; as told by Michael Morpurgo; illustrated by Michael Foreman. Candlewick Press 2004 114p il $18.99

Grades: 5 6 7 8   **398.2**

1. Arthurian romances 2. Gawain (Legendary character)
ISBN 0-7636-2519-1

LC 2003-65527

The quest of Sir Gawain for the Green Knight teaches him a lesson in pride, humility, and honor

"Morpurgo's sprightly writing brings out all the humor as well as the horror of the original tale, and Foreman's profuse, evocative watercolor-and-pastel illustrations highlight the drama in each scene." SLJ

Mosel, Arlene

The **funny** little woman; retold by Arlene Mosel; pictures by Blair Lent. Dutton 1972 un il hardcover o.p. pa $5.99

Grades: K 1 2   **398.2**

1. Folklore -- Japan
ISBN 0-14-054753-3 pa
Awarded the Caldecott Medal, 1973

While chasing a dumpling, a little lady is captured by wicked creatures from whom she escapes with the means of becoming the richest woman in Japan

"The tale unfolds in a simple tellable style. . . . Using elements of traditional Japanese art, the illustrator has made marvelously imaginative pictures. . . . All the inherent drama and humor of the story are manifest in the illustrations." Horn Book

Mueller, Doris L.

The **best** nest; by Doris L. Mueller; illustrated by Sherry Neidigh. Sylvan Dell 2008 un il $16.95; pa $8.95

Grades: 2 3 4   **398.2**

1. Birds -- Nests 2. Birds -- Folklore 3. Folklore -- Great Britain
ISBN 978-1-934359-09-9; 1-934359-09-2; 978-1-934359-25-9 pa; 1-934359-25-4 pa

LC 2007-935084

In this retelling of an old English folktale featuring birds native to the U.S., Magpie explains to the other birds how to build a nest. Some birds are impatient and fly off without listening to all the instructions, however. That is why, to this day, birds' nests come in different shapes and sizes

"The author provides support for additional activities, information about each bird, 'bird math' (problems based upon the number of broods and eggs for each species), bird care, and a 'match the nest' activity. Illustrations show each bird in mixed media with watercolor and pen and ink details." SLJ

Muller, Gerda

Goldilocks and the three bears. Floris 2011 il $17.95

Grades: PreK K 1 2   **398.2**

1. Bears -- Folklore
ISBN 978-0-86315-795-0

"This delicately illustrated version of this tale, first published in France, removes some of the familiar oppositions (too hard, too soft, just right) found in earlier versions and gives the heroine a contemporary backstory (she lives in a traveling circus caravan). The charm of the book lies primarily in Muller's detailed illustrations, which are set against tan backgrounds and include an inviting fairy tale woods dotted with wildflowers and a rustic abode for the bears. . . . The story's size motif is emphasized both textually and in the art, with big, medium, and small objects appearing throughout." Publ Wkly

Muth, Jon J.

★ **Stone** soup; retold and illustrated by Jon J. Muth. Scholastic Press 2003 un il $16.95

Grades: K 1 2 3   **398.2**

  1. Folklore 2. China -- Fiction

  ISBN 0-439-33909-X

LC 2002-3776

"Muth's muted blue-and-gray watercolors are ideally suited to portraying the inhospitable village. . . . His respect for Chinese people and their culture makes this serving of fusion cuisine delicious and satisfying." Horn Book

Myers, Christopher

Lies and other tall tales; collected by Zora Neale Hurston; adapted and illustrated by Christopher Myers. HarperCollins Pub. 2005 un il $15.99; lib bdg $16.89 **398.2**

  1. Authors 2. Novelists 3. Dramatists 4. Tall tales 5. Memoirists 6. Folklorists 7. Short story writers 8. African Americans -- Folklore

  ISBN 0-06-000655-2; 0-06-000656-0 lib bdg

LC 2004-22252

"Myers has adapted and illustrated some of the wild, very short, wicked stories collected by . . . Zora Neale Hurston. . . . True to the spirit of the tall-tale oral tradition, Myers' quiltlike pictures in paper and fabric collage are minimalist and exaggerated, magical and mundane. . . . Perfect for sharing with many age groups." Booklist

Myers, Tim

The **furry**-legged teapot; retold by Tim Myers; illustrated by Robert McGuire. Marshall Cavendish Children 2007 un il $16.99

Grades: 1 2 3 4   **398.2**

  1. Folklore -- Japan

  ISBN 978-0-7614-5295-9

LC 2005016935

In ancient Japan, a young tanuki, a raccoon dog that can change shapes, becomes stuck in the form of a teapot

"McGuire's acrylic spreads place the farmer's hut and monk's quarters in a lush Japanese countryside with mountains in the background. . . . Myers provides source notes for his entertaining version of the tanuki-turned-teapot story." SLJ

Naidoo, Beverley

★ **Aesop's** fables; [illustrated by] Piet Grobler. Frances Lincoln Children's Books 2011 48p il $18.95

Grades: 2 3 4 5   **398.2**

  1. Fables 2. Authors 3. Storytellers 4. Africa -- Fiction

  ISBN 978-1-84780-007-7; 1-84780-007-6

"Wearing a deliberate African patina, this refreshing collection of 16 Aesop fables takes place in the South African veld, giving these timeless moral tales a visual and verbal facelift. . . . In typical Aesop fashion, animals serve as lead characters, but Naidoo adds to the African texture by populating the tales with distinctive African animals. . . . The single-action narrative of each fable preserves the impersonal moral tone of the

originals. . . . Primitive, whimsical watercolor-and-pencil illustrations preserve the African theme." Kirkus

Who is king? ten magical stories from Africa. by Beverley Naidoo; illustrated by Piet Grobler. Motorbooks Intl 2015 69 p. color illustrations (hardcover) $22.99

Grades: 2 3 4 5   **398.2**

  1. Folklore -- Africa 2. Animals -- Folklore

  ISBN 1847805140; 9781847805140

In this children's story, by Beverley Naidoo, illustrated by Piet Grobler, "find out what happens to Lion when he challenges Elephant and discovers who is the real king of the savannah; laugh along with Tortoise as he bewitches the animals in Tiger's work-party with his irresistible music; find out why Hippo has no hair, how Elephant got his trunk, and why Cockerel crows." (Publisher's note)

Namm, Diane

Greek myths; retold from the classic originals by Diane Namm; illustrated by Eric Freeberg. Sterling 2011 152p il (Classic starts) $5.95

Grades: 2 3 4 5   **398.2**

  1. Greek mythology

  ISBN 978-1-4027-7312-9; 1-4027-7312-9

LC 2010039803

From Icarus's legendary flight to Orpheus's trip to the underworld, this introduces young readers to classic Greek myths.

"Namm retells 15 familiar myths in the simple, straightforward style that makes this series so accessible for emerging readers. . . . Motivations and feelings are described directly, allowing children to easily grasp the deeper meaning of the stories. The book ends with discussion questions and a note for parents and educators. . . . It will likely become a fixture in most libraries." SLJ

Nanji, Shenaaz

Indian tales; written by Shenaaz Nanji; illustrated by Christopher Corr. Barefoot Books 2007 92p il $19.99

Grades: 3 4 5 6   **398.2**

  1. Folklore -- India

  ISBN 978-1-846860-83-6

LC 2006100357

"This anthology presents eight fluid retellings of folktales from different Indian states. . . . An introduction offers a brief overview of the country's history. . . . Each folktale is preceded by a note with facts about the state from which it originated, including explanations of festivals or terms that appear in the text. Illustrations and page borders support the texts perfectly as the folk-style paintings reflect colors of rural life." SLJ

Napoli, Donna Jo, 1948-

★ **Tales** from the Arabian nights; Stories of Adventure, Magic, Love, and Betrayal. by Donna Jo Napoli; illustrated by Christina Balit. National Geographic Partners 2016 208 p. color ill., color map (ebook) $34.90; (hardcover : alk. paper) $24.99

Grades: 5 6 7 8   **398.2**

  1. Fairy tales 2. Arabs -- Folklore 3. Folklore -- Arab countries

  ISBN 9781426326387; 9781426325403; 9781426325410

LC 2016016718

In this book, by Donna Jo Napoli, illustrated by Christina Balit, "classic stories and dazzling illustrations of princesses, kings, sailors, and genies come to life in a stunning retelling of the Arabian folk tales from One Thousand and One Nights and other collections, including those of Aladdin, Sinbad the Sailor, and Al Baba and the Forty Thieves." (Publisher's note)

"A brilliant tapestry woven not of yarn but of stories, both fresh and faithful to its historical roots." Kirkus

★ **Treasury** of Greek mythology; classic stories of gods, goddesses, heroes & monsters. National Geographic Society 2011 191p il map $24.95; lib bdg $33.90

Grades: 5 6 7 8 **398.2**

1. Greek mythology

ISBN 978-1-4263-0844-4; 1-4263-0844-2; 978-1-4263-0845-1 lib bdg; 1-4263-0845-0 lib bdg

LC 2011024327

"Napoli presents 25 tales introducing the major players of the Greek pantheon along with an assortment of celebrated heroes and mortals. . . . At once eloquent and elemental, these lyrically written portraits deftly detail each character's origins, realm of power, and legendary story lines. Filled with sensual imagery, the language is poetic, yet balanced by amusing asides and wry observations that add a contemporary, almost conversational accessibility. . . . Stunning stylized paintings featuring luminous colors, rich patterns, and star-infused motifs add depth and drama to the text. . . . Interesting sidebars appear throughout, providing historical, scientific, and cultural information." SLJ

Nesbit, E.

Jack and the beanstalk; [by] E. Nesbit; illustrated by Matt Tavares. Candlewick Press 2006 un il $16.99

Grades: 2 3 4 **398.2**

1. Fairy tales 2. Giants -- Folklore 3. Folklore -- Great Britain

ISBN 0-7636-2124-2

LC 2005050190

After climbing to the top of a huge beanstalk, a boy uses his quick wits to outsmart a giant and gain a fortune for himself and his mother

"First published in Nesbit's The Old Nursery Stories (1908), this lively retelling adds character and wit to the timeless fairy tale, and Tavares' large pencil-and-watercolor illustrations, in shades of dusky brown and green, are a fitting accompaniment to the young boy's scary encounter with the giant." Booklist

Nishizuka, Koko

The **beckoning** cat; based on a Japanese folktale. illustrated by Rosanne Litzinger. Holiday House 2009 un il $16.95

Grades: K 1 2 3 **398.2**

1. Cats -- Folklore 2. Folklore -- Japan

ISBN 978-0-8234-2051-3; 0-8234-2051-5

LC 2008007266

A retelling of the traditional Japanese tale describing the origins of the beckoning cat and how it came to be a symbol of good luck.

Litzinger's "full-bleed pictures—a highly tactile mix of watercolor, colored pencil, ink and gouache—combine comfortably rounded, stylized forms and a gently shaded palette to evoke a contemplative mood." Publ Wkly

O'Malley, Kevin

The **great** race. Walker Books for Young Readers 2011 un il $16.99

Grades: K 1 2 **398.2**

1. Fables 2. Folklore 3. Rabbits -- Folklore 4. Turtles -- Folklore

ISBN 978-0-8027-2158-7; 0-8027-2158-3

LC 2010031075

Retells the traditional tale of the tortoise and the hare as a match between the very vain Lever Lapin and Nate Turtle, who is tired of all of the publicity Lever's speed generates.

"Working in watercolor and ink, O'Malley makes fine use of the wide trim, alternating sprawling crowd shots with extreme close-ups that really distill the mano a mano dislike brewing between the opponents. A simple tale, enjoyably told." Booklist

Oberman, Sheldon

Solomon and the ant; and other Jewish folktales. retold by Sheldon Oberman; introduction and commentary by Peninnah Schram. Boyds Mills Press 2006 165p $19.95

Grades: 5 6 7 8 **398.2**

1. Jews -- Folklore

ISBN 1-59078-307-7

LC 2005020115

"This collection of 43 traditional Jewish stories is authoritative as well as immensely entertaining. . . . The stories, from both Ashkenazi and Sephardic traditions, are arranged more or less chronologically—from biblical days through the talmudic period to more contemporary times. There are legends, medieval fables, trickster tales, and more. . . . The stories, wonderful for storytelling and sharing, are accessible even to listeners younger than the target audience, and the notes and commentary will provide older children with context and history." Booklist

Includes bibliographical references

Ollhoff, Jim

Japanese mythology. ABDO Pub. 2011 32p il lib bdg $27.07

Grades: 5 6 7 8 **398.2**

1. Japanese mythology

ISBN 978-1-61714-723-4

LC 2010042019

'This book offers information about Japanese mythology, answering questions such as "Who is Hachiman? What is the Seven Gods of Fortune? Why are myths so important in our lives? Myths are a rich source of history. People use them to make sense of our world. Even before myths were written down, people told and retold the stories of the gods and goddesses of their homeland. Readers of Japanese Mythology will learn the history of myths, as well as their deeper meaning." (Publisher's note) "A Shinto creation story forms the backbone of [this book], which also introduces the sun goddess Amaterasu; the fabled first emperor of Japan, Jimmu; and the impish Oni." (Booklist)

"Ollhoff writes in a clear and engaging fashion, presenting complex issues in a way that will be easy for youngsters to grasp. . . . The photographs and reproductions of art tie directly to the [text]." SLJ

Olson, Arielle North

Ask the bones: scary stories from around the world; selected and retold by Arielle North Olson and Howard Schwartz; illustrated by David Linn. Viking 1999 145p il hardcover o.p. pa $5.99

Grades: 4 5 6 7 **398.2**

1. Folklore

ISBN 0-670-87581-3; 0-14-230140-X pa

LC 98-19108

A collection of scary folktales from countries around the world including China, Russia, Spain, and the United States

"David Linn's bone-chilling black-and-white illustrations . . . will stay with the reader long after the book is closed. Excellent for reading aloud, this collection will satisfy even jaded genre fans." Booklist

Includes bibliographical references

More bones; scary stories from around the world. selected and retold by Arielle North Olson and Howard Schwartz; illustrated by E.M. Gist. Viking 2008 162p il $15.99

Grades: 4 5 6 7 **398.2**

1. Folklore

ISBN 978-0-670-06339-0; 0-670-06339-8

"This tour of the world's shadowy corners is full of dark wizards, unkind witches, and other untrustworthy creatures. . . . The 22 tales, as retold by Olson and Schwartz, give a vivid glimpse into unfamiliar, unnerving territory. . . . The atmospheric illustrations, while not intricately detailed, are somewhat startling in their imagery." Booklist

Onyefulu, Ifeoma

The **girl** who married a ghost; and other tales from Nigeria. illustrated by Julia Cairns. Frances Lincoln Children's 2010 109p il $15.95

Grades: 2 3 4 5 **398.2**

1. Folklore -- Nigeria

ISBN 978-1-84780-176-0; 1-84780-176-5

A collection of nine Nigerian tales from a world where spirits rule and animals talk.

"Onyefulu retells these tales in an informal, chatty style that captures the drama. . . . The stated morals are heavy. . . . But the stories and occasional, appealing pencil drawings move beyond the lessons, with surprising twists and turns and animal characters that steal, lie, and get their comeuppances." Booklist

Orgel, Doris

Doctor All-Knowing; a folk tale from the Brothers Grimm. retold by Doris Orgel; illustrated by Alexandra Boiger. Atheneum Books for Young Readers 2008 un il $16.99

Grades: PreK K 1 2 **398.2**

1. Folklore -- Germany

ISBN 978-1-4169-1246-0; 1-4169-1246-0

Desperate to provide enough food for himself and his daughter, a poor man sets himself up as Doctor All-Knowing and is soon called upon by a rich man to find a thief.

"Consistent in style, yet varied in size, composition, and perspective, the watercolor paintings use comic exaggeration to good effect. Vivid in both the telling and art." Booklist

Orr, Tamra

The **monsters** of Hercules. Mitchell Lane Publishers 2011 48p il map (Monsters in myth) lib bdg $29.95

Grades: 4 5 6 7 **398.2**

1. Monsters 2. Hercules (Legendary character)

ISBN 978-1-58415-927-8; 1-58415-927-8

LC 2010028764

This book about the monsters of Hercules is "thorough and respectful of a number of ancient and modern sources and [bends] over backward to navigate often contradictory, interlinked legends. . . . A number of paintings and photos break up the otherwise text-heavy pages, and copious chapter notes and reading suggestions conclude. This is by no means entry-level stuff, but for kids handy with the basics and ready to delve deeper, [this book] will be of great use." Booklist

Includes glossary and bibliographical references

The **sirens**. Mitchell Lane Publishers 2011 48p il map (Monsters in myth) lib bdg $29.95

Grades: 4 5 6 7 **398.2**

1. Sirens (Mythology)

ISBN 978-1-58415-930-8; 1-58415-930-8

LC 2010026965

This book examines the various stories that surround the myths of the Sirens.

This book is "thorough and respectful of a number of ancient and modern sources and [bends] over backward to navigate often contradictory, interlinked legends. . . . A number of paintings and photos break up the otherwise text-heavy pages, and copious chapter notes and reading suggestions conclude. This is by no means entry-level stuff, but for kids handy with the basics and ready to delve deeper, [this book] will be of great use." Booklist

Includes glossary and bibliographical references

Osborne, Mary Pope

★ **American** tall tales; wood engravings by Michael McCurdy. Knopf 1991 115p il map $22

Grades: 3 4 5 6 **398.2**

1. Tall tales 2. Folklore -- United States

ISBN 0-679-80089-1

LC 89-37235

A collection of tall tales about such American folk heroes as Sally Ann Thunder Ann Whirlwind, Pecos Bill, John Henry, and Paul Bunyan

"As tantalizing as Osborne's storytelling are McCurdy's . . . elaborate, full-color wood engravings, which in their robust stylization dramatically render the grandeur of these engrossing yarns." Publ Wkly

Includes bibliographical references

★ The **brave** little seamstress; written by Mary Pope Osborne; illustrated by Giselle Potter. Atheneum Bks. for Young Readers 2002 un il hardcover o.p. $16

Grades: K 1 2 3 **398.2**

1. Folklore 2. Fairy tales

ISBN 0-689-84486-7; 1-4169-1620-2 pa

LC 2001-33018

A seamstress who kills seven flies with one blow outwits the king and, with the help of a kind knight, becomes a wise and kind queen

"The whimsically perky, generous text is perfectly matched to the illustrations, in Potter's signature ink-gouache-gesso-water-colors, which affix just the right amount of sauciness to the cheeky heroine." Booklist

★ **Kate** and the beanstalk; written by Mary Pope Osborne; illustrated by Giselle Potter. Atheneum Bks. for Young Readers 2000 un il pa $7.99

Grades: K 1 2 3 **398.2**

1. Fairy tales 2. Giants -- Folklore 3. Folklore -- Great Britain

ISBN 0-689-82550-1; 1-4169-0818-8 pa

LC 99-27029

In this version of the classic tale, a girl climbs to the top of a giant beanstalk, where she uses her quick wits to outsmart a giant and make her and her mother's fortune

"The text is straightforward but punctuated by some delicious dialogue. . . . Using a variety of mediums—pencil, ink, gouache, and watercolor—the illustrations are executed in Potter's signature folk-art style. They are immediate, innovative, and just the right size for story hours." Booklist

Osborne, Will

★ **Sleeping** Bobby; [by] Will Osborne and Mary Pope Osborne; illustrated by Giselle Potter. Atheneum Books for Young Readers 2005 un il $16.95

Grades: K 1 2 3 **398.2**

1. Fairy tales 2. Folklore -- Germany

ISBN 0-689-87668-8

LC 2004-06346

A retelling of the Grimm tale featuring a handsome prince who is put into a deep sleep by a curse until he is awakened by the kiss of a brave princess.

This "is written in a breezy, readable style, and most details of the original story have been included. . . . Potter's folk-style characters are dressed in Elizabethan garb with details such as puffed sleeves, high lace collars, and ruffs." SLJ

Palatini, Margie

★ **Lousy** rotten stinkin' grapes; illustrated by Barry Moser. Simon & Schuster Books for Young Readers 2009 un il $15.99

Grades: PreK K 1 2 **398.2**

1. Fables 2. Authors 3. Folklore 4. Storytellers 5. Foxes --

Folklore
ISBN 978-0-689-80246-1; 0-689-80246-3

LC 2007015727

Retells the fable of a frustrated fox that, after many tries to reach a high bunch of grapes, decides they must be sour anyway.

"Moser's wonderful watercolor illustrations of the doubting animals executing Fox's convoluted plans are rich in humor. . . . Matched by a text that rolls off the tongue and is full of action and repetitive phrases, the book is a delight." SLJ

Paterson, Katherine
Parzival; the quest of the Grail Knight. retold by Katherine Paterson. Lodestar Bks. 1998 127p hardcover o.p. pa $5.99
Grades: 5 6 7 8   **398.2**
1. Arthurian romances
ISBN 0-525-67579-5; 0-14-130573-8 pa

LC 97-23891

A retelling of the Arthurian legend in which Parzival, unaware of his noble birth, comes of age through his quest for the Holy Grail

"Nearly 800 years old, the story has freshness, humor, grace, and depth. . . . Paterson clarifies much of the Christian doctrine that is the basis of the story, but she is never dull or pedantic." SLJ

Paye, Won-Ldy
★ **Head,** body, legs; a story from Liberia. retold by Won-Ldy Paye & Margaret H. Lippert; illustrated by Julie Paschkis. Holt & Co. 2002 un il $16.95; pa $7.95
Grades: K 1 2 3   **398.2**
1. Folklore -- Liberia
ISBN 0-8050-6570-9; 0-8050-7890-8 pa

LC 00-44856

In this tale from the Dan people of Liberia, Head, Arms, Body, and Legs learn that they do better when they work together

"This simple fable about working together is told in a straightforward text; humor is inherent in the situation. Enticing illustrations in ripe fruit colors enhance the strange, silly tale." Horn Book Guide

★ **Mrs.** Chicken and the hungry crocodile; [by] Won-Ldy Paye & Margaret H. Lippert; illustrated by Julie Paschkis. Holt & Co. 2003 un il $16.95
Grades: K 1 2 3   **398.2**
1. Folklore -- Liberia 2. Chickens -- Folklore 3. Crocodiles -- Folklore
ISBN 0-8050-7047-8

LC 2002-1755

When a crocodile captures Mrs. Chicken and takes her to an island to fatten her up, clever Mrs. Chicken claims that she can prove they are sisters and that, therefore, the crocodile shouldn't eat her

"Told in straightforward language this trickster tale is smart and funny. . . . The stylized gouache artwork is strong and streamlined. . . . The flat paintings recall folk art, and Crocodile's checkerboard skin reflects the patterns found in her home." SLJ

Perrault, Charles
Cinderella; or, The little glass slipper. a free translation from the French of Charles Perrault; with pictures by Marcia Brown. Scribner 1954 un il $16; pa $5.99
Grades: K 1 2 3   **398.2**
1. Fairy tales 2. Folklore -- France
ISBN 0-684-12676-1; 0-689-81474-7 pa
Awarded the Caldecott Medal, 1955

This is the classic story of the poor, good-natured girl who works for her selfish step-sisters until a fairy godmother transforms her into a beautiful 'princess' for just one night

"With soft, delicate colors and lines that subtly suggest, Miss Brown creates a thoroughly fairyland atmosphere, at the same time recreating the sophistication of the French Court with its golden coach, canopied bed, dazzling chandeliers, liveried footmen, curled and pompadoured ladies, and peruked (bewigged) courtiers." Libr J

Pinkney, Jerry
★ The **little** red hen. Dial Books for Young Readers 2006 un il $16.99
Grades: K 1 2 3   **398.2**
1. Folklore 2. Animals -- Folklore 3. Chickens -- Folklore
ISBN 0-8037-2935-9

LC 2005-13301

A newly illustrated edition of the classic fable of the hen who is forced to do all the work of baking bread and of the animals who learn a bitter lesson from it.

This is "a lush, light-filled rendition of a folktale staple. . . . The animal's names appear in color-coded font (red for the hen, brown for the dog, etc.), making it extra-easy even for pre-readers to chime in, and the glorious, generous paintings are a real gift." SLJ

★ **Little** Red Riding Hood; [written and illustrated by] Jerry Pinkney. Little, Brown 2007 un il $16.99
Grades: PreK K   **398.2**
1. Fairy tales 2. Wolves -- Folklore 3. Folklore -- Germany
ISBN 978-0-316-01355-0; 0-316-01355-2

LC 2006025291

This is an adaptation of the fairy tale by the Brothers Grimm. "Preschool, primary." (Horn Book)

This is a "delightful, old-fashioned version of a familiar tale. . . . With lively detail . . . and lots of pattern and colors, Pinkney's watercolors show the predator in nightcap and glasses under Grandmother's patchwork quilt." Booklist

Pirotta, Saviour
Firebird; paintings by Catherine Hyde. Candlewick Press 2010 40p il $18.99
Grades: 2 3 4 5   **398.2**
1. Fairy tales 2. Folklore -- Russia
ISBN 978-0-7636-5076-6; 0-7636-5076-5

LC 2010006608

With the aid of Gray Wolf, young Prince Ivan fulfills a series of tasks set for him by his father and two other kings, winning the legendary firebird, a magical horse, and the hand of Princess Helen by his efforts.

"Large and lavish, this handsome presentation builds nicely on European folktale elements. . . . Hyde's acrylic paintings are soft in focus and deep with luminous portrayals of the featured animals and dusky views of the nighttime and woodland journeys. The book's expansive layout nicely varies the use of white space and painting size. . . . A welcome choice for storytelling and reading aloud." SLJ

The **McElderry** book of Grimms' fairy tales; retold by Saviour Pirotta; illustrated by Emma Clark. Margaret K. McElderry Books 2006 126p il $19.95
Grades: 2 3 4   **398.2**
1. Authors 2. Fairy tales 3. Folklorists 4. Philologists 5. Folklore -- Germany 6. Short story writers
ISBN 1-4169-1798-5

First published 2002 in the United Kingdom with title: The sleeping princess and other fairy tales from Grimm

"An appealing collection of 10 fairy tales. . . . Pirotta writes like a storyteller, with great imagery and description, and the lively stories read aloud beautifully. . . . Clark's dark, twisty branches in the forest enhance the mood of this story. The large typeface, generous use of white space, and overall design make this book one children can read themselves, and the artist's expressive illustrations contribute to the appeal." SLJ

Polacco, Patricia

★ **Luba** and the wren. Philomel Bks. 1999 un il hardcover o.p. pa $6.99

Grades: K 1 2 3 **398.2**

1. Fairy tales 2. Birds -- Folklore 3. Folklore -- Russia

ISBN 0-399-23168-4; 0-698-11922-3 pa

LC 98-16353

In this variation on the story of "The Fisherman and His Wife," a young Ukrainian girl must repeatedly return to the wren she has rescued to relay her parents' increasingly greedy demands

"Polacco's signature illustrations are lush and vibrant. The regal colors of royal blue and crimson play against deep green, dappled brown, and ocher of the natural world." SLJ

Princess stories; a classic illustrated edition. compiled by Cooper Edens. Chronicle Books 2004 133p il $19.95

Grades: 2 3 4 **398.2**

1. Folklore 2. Fairy tales

ISBN 0-8118-4032-8

LC 2003-20890

"This edition of classic princess stories showcases artists from the Golden Age of Illustration, roughly the 1880s to the 1920s. . . . Arthur Rackham, Walter Crane, Jesse Wilcox Smith, Charles Robinson, Kay Nielsen, and Edmund Dulac are among the American and European artists represented. The edition is rich in language, tone, and picture and despite the disparate nature of each artist's style, it somehow comes together as a classic whole." SLJ

Pringle, Laurence P.

Imagine a dragon; [by] Laurence Pringle; illustrated by Eujin Kim Neilan. Boyds Mills Press 2008 un il $16.95

Grades: 3 4 5 **398.2**

1. Dragons

ISBN 978-1-56397-328-4; 1-56397-328-6

LC 2007017575

This is a history of dragons in various world cultures

"The book is interesting with lots of materials without being overwhelming. It provides a good introduction to dragon myths in world literature. The pictures, done in acrylic, are strong and powerful." Libr Media Connect

Puttapipat, Niroot

The **musicians** of Bremen; a brothers Grimm tale. retold and illustrated by Niroot Puttapipat. Candlewick Press 2005 un il $15.99

Grades: K 1 2 3 **398.2**

1. Animals -- Folklore 2. Folklore -- Germany

ISBN 0-7636-2758-5

LC 2005-46907

While on their way to Bremen, four aging animals who are no longer of any use to their masters find a new home after outwitting a gang of robbers

"Puttipipat makes music the strong focus of this lively version of the old Grimm folktale. . . . The dramatic ink-and-watercolor illustrations show the characters as real barnyard animals." Booklist

Ramsden, Ashley

Seven fathers; retold by Ashley Ramsden; illustrated by Ed Young. Roaring Brook Press 2011 32p il $16.99

Grades: 2 3 4 5 **398.2**

1. Fairy tales 2. Folklore -- Norway 3. Fathers -- Folklore 4. Old

age -- Folklore

ISBN 978-1-59643-544-5; 1-59643-544-5

LC 2010009674

A lone traveler, tired, hungry, and cold, finds a house and asks for a room for the night, but the old man to whom he speaks refers him to his father, and that man to his father, until he is finally rewarded for his efforts by the eldest.

"Striking collage art accompanies a fluid retelling of a lesser-known Norwegian folktale. . . . Young's minimalist yet highly expressive illustrations use a strong black line to artfully convey the wintry setting and the stranger's encounters with the fathers." SLJ

Ray, Jane

Snow White. Candlewick Press 2009 un il $19.99

Grades: 3 4 5 **398.2**

1. Fairy tales 2. Pop-up books 3. Folklore -- Germany

ISBN 978-0-7636-4473-4; 0-7636-4473-0

LC 2009007774

Retells, in six dioramas with accompanying text, the tale of the beautiful princess whose lips were red as blood, skin was white as snow, and hair was black as ebony.

"Unusual paper engineering makes this a particularly memorable version of the familiar tale. . . . Birds, squirrels, and other wildlife join viewers in looking through a die-cut screen of trees (or in interior scenes an archway) at gracefully posed, richly clad figures. The jewel-like colors, as well as Ray's almond-eyed Snow White and dusky-skinned Prince, give the tale an otherworldly air." SLJ

Robbins, Ruth

Baboushka and the three kings; illustrated by Nicolas Sidjakov; adapted from a Russian folk tale. Houghton Mifflin 1960 un il $16; pa $6.95

Grades: 1 2 3 4 **398.2**

1. Folklore -- Russia 2. Christmas -- Folklore

ISBN 0-395-27673-X; 0-395-42647-2 pa

First published by Parnassus Press

Awarded The Caldecott Medal, 1961

A retelling of the Christmas legend about the old woman who declined to accompany the three kings on their search for the Christ Child and has ever since then searched for the Child on her own. Each year as she renews her search she leaves gifts at the homes she visits, acting, in this respect, as a Russian equivalent to Santa Claus

"Mystery and dignity are in the retelling. . . . At the end of the book is the story in verse set to original music." Horn Book

Rodgers, Greg

Chukfi Rabbit's big, bad bellyache; a trickster tale. told by Greg Rodgers; illustrated by Leslie Stall Widener. Cinco Puntos Press 2014 40 p. color illustrations (hardback) $16.95

Grades: K 1 2 3 **398.2**

1. Food -- Fiction 2. Choctaw Indians -- Folklore 3. Rabbit (Legendary character) -- Legends

ISBN 1935955268; 9781935955269; 9781935955276

LC 2013010568

"Deep in Choctaw Country, Chukfi Rabbit is always figuring out some way to avoid work at all costs. When Bear, Turtle, Fox, and Beaver agree on an everybody-work-together day to build Ms. Possum a new house, Chukfi Rabbit says he's too busy to help. Until he hears there will be a feast to eat after the work is done." (Publisher's note)

"Choctaw illustrator Widener dresses her animal characters in a mélange of traditional and contemporary attire; Chula Fox and Luksi Turtle sport black, brimmed hats and tasseled belts, while Kinta Beaver wears a denim work shirt and a baseball cap. Both text and illustrations positively exude good humor." Kirkus

Rohmer, Harriet

Uncle Nacho's hat; adapted by Harriet Rohmer; illustrations by Veg Reisberg; Spanish version, Rosalma Zubizarreta. Children's Bk. Press 1989 31p il hardcover o.p. pa $7.95

Grades: K 1 2 3   **398.2**

1. Folklore -- Nicaragua 2. Bilingual books -- English-Spanish

ISBN 0-89239-112-X pa

LC 88-37090

"Adaptation of a Nicaraguan folktale.... When his niece, Ambrosia, gives Uncle Nacho a new hat, he tries unsuccessfully several times to get rid of the old, holey one. Seeing him dejected because his hat keeps coming back, Ambrosia suggests he put his mind on the new one instead. Flattened primitive paintings in brilliant, clear tropical colors and motifs enhance the fun of this comedy of errors." Helbig. This land is our land

Rumford, James

★ **Beowulf**; a hero's tale retold. Houghton Mifflin Company 2007 un il $17

Grades: 4 5 6 7   **398.2**

1. Beowulf 2. Folklore -- Europe 3. Monsters -- Folklore

ISBN 0-618-75637-X; 978-0-618-75637-7

A simplified and illustrated retelling of the exploits of the Anglo-Saxon warrior, Beowulf, and how he came to defeat the monster Grendel, Grendel's mother, and a dragon that threatened the kingdom.

"Superb on all counts—from the elegant bookmaking to the vigorous, evocative prose . . . to the pen-and-ink and watercolor illustrations that strikingly recall the work of Edmund Dulac." Horn Book

Sage, Alison

★ **Rapunzel**; [illustrations by] Sarah Gibb; based on the original story by the Brothers Grimm. Albert Whitman 2011 un il $16.99

Grades: 1 2 3 4   **398.2**

1. Folklore 2. Fairy tales

ISBN 978-0-8075-6804-0; 0-8075-6804-X

Beautiful Rapunzel is locked away in a tall, tall tower, visited only by the little creatures of the forest and the witch who has imprisoned her. Until one day a handsome prince, passing by on his horse, is transfixed by the magical sound of Rapunzel singing to her animals friends and knows he must reach her.

"Reminiscent of elaborate embroidery or tapestries, the pictures create and sustain the tale's magical atmosphere. . . . Children and adults alike will be spellbound, poring over the pages again and again, delighting each time in new details and discoveries." Kirkus

Sakade, Florence

Japanese children's favorite stories; compiled by Florence Sakade; illustrated by Yoshisuke Kurosaki. 3rd ed; Tuttle 2003 109p il $16.95

Grades: 2 3 4   **398.2**

1. Folklore -- Japan

ISBN 0-8048-3449-0

First published 1953

A collection of Japanese folktales.

"This enduring collection presents 20 stories to enchant and enlighten young readers. . . . Minor text revisions have little effect on the stories. . . . The text remains simple, clear, and accessible to beginning readers and storytellers alike. The 'sparkling new color illustrations' are simply Kurosaki's original stylized scenes, repainted in bright dabs of watercolor." SLJ

San Souci, Robert

As luck would have it; from the Brothers Grimm. [by] Robert D. San Souci; illustrated by Daniel San Souci. August House/Little Folk 2008 un il $16.95

Grades: K 1 2 3 4

1. Folklore -- Germany

ISBN 978-0-87483-833-6; 0-87483-833-9

LC 2008000965

"Lively, comical illustrations enhance the abundant droll humor in this noodle-head tale that plays off the Grimm Brothers' 'Clever Elsie.'. . . The expressive, lucent watercolors highlighted with Prismacolor pencils portray the foolish escapades adeptly, and the anthropomorphized animal characters evocatively represent human characteristics and foibles." SLJ

★ **Cendrillon**; a Caribbean Cinderella. [by] Robert D. San Souci; illustrated by Brian Pinkney. Simon & Schuster Bks. for Young Readers 1998 un il hardcover o.p. pa $8.99

Grades: K 1 2 3   **398.2**

1. Fairy tales 2. Folklore -- Martinique

ISBN 0-689-80668-X; 0-689-84888-9 pa

LC 96-53142

A Creole variant of the familiar Cinderella tale set in Martinique and narrated by the godmother who helps Cendrillon find true love

"The narrative is full of French Creole words and phrases. . . . A fruit`a pain (breadfruit) is transformed into the coach; six agoutis (a kind of rodent) become the horses. . . . Pinkney's art perfectly conveys the lush beauty and atmosphere of the island setting." SLJ

★ **Cut** from the same cloth; American women of myth, legend, and tall tale. collected and told by Robert D. San Souci; illustrated by Brian Pinkney; introduction by Jane Yolen. Philomel Bks. 1993 140p il hardcover o.p. pa $6.99

Grades: 4 5 6 7   **398.2**

1. Tall tales 2. Women -- Folklore 3. Folklore -- United States

ISBN 0-399-21987-0; 0-698-11811-1 pa

LC 92-5233

A collection of fifteen stories about legendary American women from Anglo-American, African American, and Native American folklore

"San Souci's language is vigorous and action verbs abound; Pinkney's black-and-white block prints match the strength of the telling. The inclusion of notes on the sources and a general bibliography make this an academic resource as well as a good collection of rolicking stories." Child Book Rev Serv

Little Gold Star; a Spanish American Cinderella tale. retold by Robert D. San Souci; illustrated by Sergio Martinez. HarperCollins Pubs. 2000 un il $15.95; lib bdg $15.89

Grades: 2 3 4   **398.2**

1. Fairy tales 2. Folklore -- Southern States 3. Hispanic Americans -- Folklore

ISBN 0-688-14780-1; 0-688-14781-X lib bdg

LC 99-50290

A Spanish American retelling of the familiar story of a kind girl who is mistreated by her jealous stepmother and stepsisters. In this version, the Virgin Mary replaces the traditional fairy godmother

"Martinez' watercolors depict homes with Spanish architectural influences in an arid, southwest desert landscape; his characters have lively, expressive faces and evocative body language. . . . This is effective fairy-tale magic transported to new terrain." Bull Cent Child Books

★ **Robin** Hood and the golden arrow; retold by Robert D. San Souci; illustrations by E.B. Lewis. Orchard Books 2010 un il $17.99

Grades: K 1 2 3   **398.2**

1. Folklore -- Great Britain 2. Robin Hood (Legendary character)

ISBN 978-0-439-62538-8; 0-439-62538-6

LC 2009015624

Retells, in easy text, of the Sheriff of Nottingham's plot to hold an archery contest in order to capture the outlaw Robin Hood, but Robin and his band of merry men arrive in disguise with a plan of their own.

"Lewis draws young readers in with the splendid cover image of Robin. . . . The watercolor pictures, reminiscent of both Pyle and N. C. Wyeth, are full of mottled greens and dappled light, with powerful figures running, shooting arrows or standing nobly. It is a feast to look upon." Kirkus

Short & shivery; thirty chilling tales. retold by Robert D. San Souci; illustrated by Katherine Coville. Doubleday 1987 175p il hardcover o.p. pa $5.50

Grades: 4 5 6 7 **398.2**

1. Folklore 2. Ghost stories

ISBN 0-440-41804-6 pa

LC 86-29067

"A collection of spooky stories, competently adapted and retold (sometimes quite freely) from world folklore, including Japan, Africa, and Latin America, as well as Europe and the U.S. . . . The stories drawn from collections of regional American folklore are not only the freshest, but often the scariest. Sources are fully documented. . . . There are some delicious shivers here, with plenty of fodder for an active imagination, as well as excitement." SLJ

★ **Sister** tricksters; rollicking tales of clever females. retold by Robert D. San Souci; illustrated by Daniel San Souci. August House Pubs. 2006 69p il $19.95

Grades: 3 4 5 6 **398.2**

1. Animals -- Folklore 2. Folklore -- Southern States

ISBN 978-0-87483-791-9; 0-87483-791-X

LC 2006-40793

"These eight stories, featuring characters like Molly Cottontail, Miz Grasshopper, and Miz Goose, are energetically retold from Anne Virginia Culbertsons long out-of-print At the Big House (Bobbs-Merrill, 1904). . . . Delicious dialect and expressions convey a rural Southern flavor, yet the text is never hard to read or understand. . . . Stunning, richly colored, detailed, and playful paintings showing animals dressed in lavish finery introduce each lively tale." SLJ

★ **Sukey** and the mermaid; [by] Robert D. San Souci; illustrated by Brian Pinkney. Four Winds Press 1992 un il hardcover o.p. pa $5.95

Grades: 1 2 3 4 **398.2**

1. Mermaids and mermen 2. African Americans -- Folklore

ISBN 0-02-778141-0; 0-689-80718-X pa

LC 90-24559

Unhappy with her life at home, Sukey receives kindness and wealth from Mama Jo the mermaid

San Souci "outdoes himself here with pungent, lyrical prose that reverberates with the cadences of the South Carolina islands. . . . The supple lines of Pinkney's fluid scratchboard technique capture the grace and spirit of this magical tale and serve as the perfect foil to its darker undertones." Publ Wkly

★ The **talking** eggs; a folktale from the American South. retold by Robert D. San Souci; pictures by Jerry Pinkney. Dial Bks. for Young Readers 1989 un il $16

Grades: K 1 2 3 **398.2**

1. Folklore -- Southern States

ISBN 0-8037-0619-7

LC 88-33469

A Caldecott Medal honor book, 1990

A Southern folktale in which kind Blanche, following the instructions of an old witch, gains riches, while her greedy sister makes fun of the old woman and is duly rewarded

"Adapted from a Creole folk tale originally included in a collection of Louisiana stories by folklorist Alcee Fortier, this tale captures the flavor of the nineteenth-century South in its language and story line. . . . Jerry Pinkney's watercolors are chiefly responsible for the excellence of the book; his characters convey their moods with vivid facial expressions." Horn Book

Sanfield, Steve

The **adventures** of High John the Conqueror; [illustrated by John Ward] August House 1995 113p il hardcover o.p. pa $11.95

Grades: 4 5 6 7 **398.2**

1. Folklore -- United States 2. African Americans -- Folklore

ISBN 0-87483-433-3; 0-87483-774-X pa

LC 95-35825

A reissue of the title first published 1988 by Orchard Books

A collection of folk tales about High John the Conqueror, the traditional trickster hero of blacks during and immediately after the time of slavery

"Simply told in language comprehensible to very young readers, these tales are short, funny, and entertaining. . . . Fourteen full-page black-and-white pencil drawings illustrate some of the more dramatic moments in the stories." SLJ

Includes bibliographical references

Schlitz, Laura Amy

★ The **Bearskinner**; a tale of the Brothers Grimm. retold by Laura Amy Schlitz; illustrated by Max Grafe. Candlewick Press 2007 un il $16.99

Grades: 3 4 5 6 **398.2**

1. Fairy tales 2. Folklore -- Germany

ISBN 978-0-7636-2730-0; 0-7636-2730-5

LC 2007-22787

A retelling of the Grimm fairy tale in which a despondent soldier makes a pact to do the devil's bidding for seven years in return for as much money and property as he could ever want

"Schlitz narrates with clarity, grace, and sensitivity. . . . Except for the devil's coat of darkest green, Grafe's atmospheric full-page illustrations are almost monochromatic. . . . A provocative edition that should set older children thinking about the meaning of endurance and heroism." Horn Book

Schram, Peninnah

The **magic** pomegranate; by Peninnah Schram; illustrated by Melanie Hall. Millbrook Press 2008 48p il (On my own folklore) lib bdg $25.26; pa $6.95

Grades: 1 2 3 4 **398.2**

1. Fairy tales 2. Jews -- Folklore 3. Pomegranates -- Folklore

ISBN 978-0-8225-6742-4 lib bdg; 0-8225-6742-3 lib bdg; 978-0-8225-6746-2 pa; 0-8225-6746-6 pa

LC 2006036722

Three handsome and clever brothers compete to find the world's most unusual gift. Includes a note on doing good deeds, or mitzvah, and discusses the symbolism of the pomegranate in Judaism

The "tale is paired with an illustration style that nicely reflects the culture." Horn Book Guide

Includes bibliographical references

Schwartz, Alvin, 1927-1992

★ **Ghosts!** ghostly tales from folklore. retold by Alvin Schwartz; illustrated by Victoria Chess. HarperCollins Pubs. 1991 63p il (I can read book) lib bdg $15.89; pa $3.95

Grades: K 1 2   **398.2**
1. Folklore 2. Ghost stories
ISBN 0-06-021797-9 lib bdg; 0-06-444170-9 pa

LC 90-21746

Presents seven, easy-to-read ghost stories based on traditional folk tales and legends from various countries

"All of the pen-and-watercolor illustrations are tidy and cheery and creepy. . . . Retold in a style that is simple but not choppy . . . and accompanied by a page of brief notes, all the tales will lend themselves to elaboration and innovation." Bull Cent Child Books

I saw you in the bathtub, and other folk rhymes; collected by Alvin Schwartz; pictures by Syd Hoff. Harper & Row 1989 64p il (I can read book) hardcover o.p. pa $3.99
Grades: K 1 2   **398.2**
1. Folklore
ISBN 0-06-444151-2 pa

LC 88-16111

Presents an illustrated collection of traditional folk rhymes, some composed by children

"Kids may be surprised to see their recess yells on the printed page but will relish the confirmation of significance. Hoff's full-color cartoons interpret the rhymes literally, an approach that leads to some pretty surreal results." Bull Cent Child Books

★ **In** a dark, dark room, and other scary stories; retold by Alvin Schwartz; illustrated by Dirk Zimmer. Harper & Row 1984 63p il (I can read book) $15.95; pa $3.95
Grades: K 1 2   **398.2**
1. Folklore 2. Ghost stories 3. Horror fiction
ISBN 0-06-025271-5; 0-06-444090-7 pa

LC 83-47699

This is a collection of "seven traditional tales from around the world retold in simple yet effective language. . . . The chill here springs from suspense, an eerie setting or a ghostly surprise, rather than from blood and gore. Though pared down somewhat from longer versions, the stories retain their genuine creepiness. . . . The colorfully dark illustrations are sinister without being gruesome and add a comic touch." SLJ

★ **There** is a carrot in my ear, and other noodle tales; retold by Alvin Schwartz; pictures by Karen Ann Weinhaus. Harper & Row 1982 64p il (I can read book) hardcover o.p. pa $3.95
Grades: K 1 2   **398.2**
1. Folklore 2. Wit and humor
ISBN 0-06-025234-0; 0-06-444103-2 pa

LC 80-8442

This "is a collection of six stories from sources . . . as diverse as American 'Little Moron' stories, ancient Greek tales and vaudeville pieces. Explaining in his foreword that a 'noodle is a silly person,' reteller Alvin Schwartz goes on to introduce the noodly Brown family and reveal their various foibles. . . . Most of the stories don't appear in other beginning noodle collections and will provide laughs for readers who catch the puns and absurdities the stories hinge on. The drawings by Karen Ann Weinhaus . . . show funny, pointy-proboscised folk blissfully unaware of their own goofiness." SLJ

Schwartz, Howard
A **coat** for the moon and other Jewish tales; selected and retold by Howard Schwartz and Barbara Rush; illustrated by Michael Iofin. Jewish Publ. Soc. 1999 81p il hardcover o.p. pa $13
Grades: 4 5 6 7   **398.2**
1. Jews -- Folklore
ISBN 0-8276-0596-X; 0-8276-0736-9 pa

LC 98-52704

A collection of Jewish folktales from around the world, including "The Lamp on the Mountain," "The Witch Barusha," "The Sabbath Walking Stick," and "The Fisherman and the Silver Fish"

"These tales incorporate everything from the magical to the bizarre, all the while imparting specific Jewish values that have transcended time and cultural dispersion. . . . Each retelling opens with a delightfully detailed pen-and-ink illustration encircled by a key sentence or phrase from the text that gives a hint of what's to come." SLJ

Scott, Nathan Kumar
The **sacred** banana leaf; an Indonesian trickster tale. by Nathan Kumar Scott; illustrated by Radhashyam Raut. Tara 2008 un il $16.95
Grades: 2 3 4   **398.2**
1. Animals -- Folklore 2. Folklore -- Indonesia
ISBN 978-81-86211-28-1; 81-86211-28-4

"Scott's retelling has verve and humor, and the illustrations, rendered in patachitra (a traditional style of temple painting originating in eastern India) are both accessible and graceful. Saturated colors gleam from sand-toned pages, and the patterned skins of the clearly delineated animals add texture." Booklist

Seeger, Pete
★ **Abiyoyo**; based on a South African lullaby and folk story. text by Pete Seeger; illustrations by Michael Hays. Simon & Schuster Bks. for Young Readers 2001 un il $19.95; pa $6.99
Grades: K 1 2 3   **398.2**
1. Giants -- Folklore 2. Folklore -- South Africa
ISBN 0-689-84693-2; 0-689-71810-1 pa

A reissue of the title first published 1986 by Macmillan

Banished from the town for making mischief, a little boy and his father are welcomed back when they make the giant Abiyoyo disappear

"Told in the familiar Seeger style, with brief musical phrases of the one-word song incorporated in the text and printed complete at the end, and with illustrations full of light and color, this rendering of a South African tale is a pleasure. The giant is imposing but not too scary for the youngest listener leaning over the book while a parent tells the story." N Y Times Book Rev

Shannon, George
★ **More** stories to solve; fifteen folktales from around the world. told by George Shannon; illustrated by Peter Sis. Greenwillow Bks. 1991 64p il hardcover o.p. pa $4.99
Grades: 3 4 5 6   **398.2**
1. Riddles 2. Folklore
ISBN 0-688-09161-X; 0-380-73261-0 pa

"Shannon combines the folktale and the riddle in a brief collection that brings together 15 international stories." Booklist

Includes bibliographical references

Rabbit's gift; a fable from China. told by George Shannon; illustrated by Laura Dronzek. Harcourt 2007 un il $16
Grades: PreK K 1   **398.2**
1. Fables 2. Folklore -- China 3. Animals -- Folklore 4. Rabbits -- Folklore
ISBN 978-0-15-206073-2; 0-15-206073-1

LC 2006-04789

Woodland animals, each thinking of his neighbor, share a turnip left on their doorstep.

"The uncluttered illustrations, many framed in purple to compliment the purple of the turnip, perfectly capture the action of the story. The expressive faces of the animals are charming." Booklist

★ **Stories** to solve; folktales from around the world. illustrated by Peter Sis. Greenwillow Bks. 1985 55p il hardcover o.p. pa $4.99

Grades: 3 4 5 6   **398.2**
1. Riddles 2. Folklore
ISBN 0-688-04303-8; 0-380-73260-2 pa

LC 84-18656

"Each of these 14 delightful folktales is a short puzzle to be solced through clevernes, common sense or careful observations of details in the text. . . . Sis' pointillistic pen-and-ink drawings illustrate each puzzle, and sometimes clarify the solutions." SLJ

Sharpe, Leah Marinsky
★ The **goat**-faced girl; a classic Italian folktale. retold by Leah Marinsky Sharpe; illustrated by Jane Marinsky. David R. Godine 2009 un il $16.95
Grades: K 1 2 3   **398.2**
1. Fairy tales 2. Folklore -- Italy
ISBN 978-1-56792-393-3; 1-56792-393-3

LC 2009-22383

When Isabella, a beautiful but lazy young woman, agrees to marry an equally lazy prince, the sorceress who raised her gives her the head of a goat in hopes that she will learn to do things for herself.

"Rich storytelling and intricately imagined artwork make this debut a standout. . . . Marinsky's paintings, in the chalky, sun-bleached colors of the Italian renaissance, contain many small pleasures." Publ Wkly

Shelby, Anne
The **adventures** of Molly Whuppie and other Appalachian folktales; [by] Anne Shelby; illustrations by Paula McArdle. The University of North Carolina Press 2007 88p il $14.95
Grades: 4 5 6 7   **398.2**
1. Folklore -- Appalachian Mountains
ISBN 978-0-8078-3163-2

LC 2007013789

A collection of Appalachian folktales featuring Molly Whuppie and her adventures.

"Shelby has captured the language of Appalachia. . . . Her adaptations are true to the traditional folktales. . . . Young readers and listeners will make these stories their own and enjoy retelling them." SLJ

Includes bibliographical references

Shepard, Aaron
★ The **princess** mouse; a tale of Finland. told by Aaron Shepard; illustrated by Leonid Gore. Atheneum Bks. for Young Readers 2003 un il hardcover o.p. pa $13.99
Grades: K 1 2 3   **398.2**
1. Fairy tales 2. Mice -- Folklore 3. Folklore -- Finland
ISBN 0-689-82912-4; 1-4169-8969-2 pa

LC 2001-55273

A retelling of a Finnish folk tale about a young man who plans to marry his mouse sweetheart

"Shepard's charmingly droll version of a Finnish folktale combines classic elements with unexpected, witty details. . . . The jewel-toned art has beautiful luminescence; the elongated, somewhat blocky look of the characters reinforces the fantasy; and the mice are downright irresistible." Booklist

The **sea** king's daughter; a Russian legend. retold by Aaron Shepard; illustrated by Gennady Spirin. Atheneum Bks. for Young Readers 1997 28p il pa $11.99
Grades: 3 4 5 6   **398.2**
1. Folklore -- Russia 2. Musicians -- Folklore
ISBN 0-689-80759-7; 0-689-84259-7 pa

LC 96-3391

This is a retelling of a Russian folktale. "A poor but gifted musician draws the attention of the King of the Sea, who invites him to visit his palace under the sea. The ruler then becomes so taken with the young man's music that he insists Sadko stay and marry one of his daughters. The Sea Queen, however, whispers to Sadko that if he kisses or embraces his sea-wife, he will never be able to return home again. That evening he lies next to his bride, the Princess Volkhova, but never touches her. The next morning he awakes beside the River Volkhov in his beloved city of Novgorod. He becomes a rich merchant, marries, and raises a family, but whenever he plays his music near the river, he thinks he sees the Princess Volkhova raising her head out of the water to listen. . . . Grades three to six." (SLJ)

"The telling is descriptive yet very accessible, with the art, in Spirin's majestic signature style, evoking both the mythical feel of the legend and the folk-music roots from which the story sprang." Booklist

Shulevitz, Uri
★ The **treasure**. Farrar, Straus & Giroux 1978 un il hardcover o.p. pa $6.95
Grades: K 1 2 3   **398.2**
1. Folklore
ISBN 0-374-37740-5; 0-374-47955-0 pa

A Caldecott Medal honor book, 1980

"Although the story is known in many cultures the retelling suggests the Hassidic tradition. . . . The eastern European influence is extended in the illustrations." Horn Book

Sierra, Judy
Can you guess my name? traditional tales around the world. selected and retold by Judy Sierra; illustrated by Stefano Vitale. Clarion Bks. 2002 110p il $20
Grades: 3 4 5 6   **398.2**
1. Folklore
ISBN 0-618-13328-3

LC 2002-3509

A collection of fifteen folktales from all over the world, including stories that resemble "The Three Pigs," "The Bremen Town Musicians," "Rumpelstiltskin," "The Frog Prince," and "Hansel and Gretel"

"All of the selections have dramatic dialogue and repetitive phrases and refrains, and are easy to learn. . . . Vitale's engaging folk illustrations are painted on wood. . . . This collection provides a fascinating experience with comparative literature, one that can open doors to other cultures. A must purchase for most collections." SLJ

Includes bibliographical references

The **gift** of the Crocodile; a Cinderella story. illustrated by Reynold Ruffins. Simon & Schuster Bks. for Young Readers 2000 un il $17
Grades: K 1 2 3   **398.2**
1. Fairy tales 2. Folklore -- Indonesia
ISBN 0-689-82188-3

LC 98-40592

In this Indonesian version of the Cinderella story, a girl named Damura escapes her cruel stepmother and stepsister and marries a handsome prince with the help of Grandmother Crocodile

"Sierra's unadorned retelling is straightforward. . . . Ruffins's brightly colored, patterned paintings, with their angular figures and wavy landscapes, express and evoke the story's island setting." Horn Book

★ **Nursery** tales around the world; selected and retold by Judy Sierra; illustrated by Stefano Vitale. Clarion Bks. 1996 114p il $20
Grades: K 1 2 3 4 5   **398.2**
1. Folklore
ISBN 0-395-67894-3

LC 93-2068

Presents eighteen simple stories from international folklore, grouped around six themes, such as "Runaway Cookies," "Slowpokes and

Speedsters," and "Chain Tales." Includes background information and storytelling hints

"This richly illustrated compendium of folktales does double duty as a nursery story book for lap-sharing and as a sourcebook for parents and professionals. . . . Most entries feature strong rhythms and repetition that invite audience participation and develop memory. . . . Top this engaging text with Vitale's lavish oil-on-wood ethnic borders, motif vignettes, and full-page illustrations, and you have a handsome work to be valued by readers and treasured by listeners." Bull Cent Child Books

Includes bibliographical references

Singer, Isaac Bashevis

Zlateh the goat, and other stories; pictures by Maurice Sendak; translated from the Yiddish by the author and Elizabeth Shub. Harper & Row 1966 90p il $15.95; pa $6.95

Grades: 4 5 6 7   **398.2**

1. Jews -- Folklore

ISBN 0-06-028477-3; 0-06-440147-2 pa

A Newbery Award honor book, 1967

"Seven tales drawn from middle-European Jewish village life, with illustrations which extend the humor and subtlety of the situations." Hodges. Books for Elem Sch Libr

Singh, Rina

Nearly nonsense; Hoja tales from Turkey. illustrated by Farida Zaman. Tundra Books 2011 48p il $17.95

Grades: 2 3 4 5   **398.2**

1. Folklore -- Turkey

ISBN 978-0-88776-974-0; 0-88776-974-8

"Turkey has a particularly vibrant oral tradition, and the stories of Nasrudin Hoja—a foolish/wise man—are legion and deservedly popular. . . . When he and his son take their donkey to market, they are ridiculed whether they ride, walk, or carry the animal on their backs, proving that you can't please everyone. When Hoja wears fancy clothing, he is treated more deferentially than when he wears patched clothing, so he 'feeds' his coat to show the error of his host's behavior. Lesser-known stories are also included. . . . These retellings are unembellished, but their humor and intention are clear." SLJ

Smith, Alex T.

Little Red and the very hungry lion; Alex T. Smith. Scholastic Press, an imprint of Scholastic Inc. 2016 32 p. color illustrations $17.99

Grades: PreK K 1 2   **398.2**

1. Folklore 2. Lions -- fiction 3. Grandmothers -- fiction 4. Fairy tales 5. Humorous stories 6. Little Red Riding Hood (Tale) -- Adaptations -- fiction

ISBN 9780545914383

LC 2015027660

In this book, by Alex T. Smith, "Little Red is on her way to visit Auntie Rosie with a basket of goodies and some spot medicine. Along the way she meets the Very Hungry Lion. The Lion is eager to gobble up Little Red. The Lion's plan doesn't work out the way he wanted." (Publisher's note)

"Spectacular, zingy, warm colors, an African setting, fantastic comic timing, and cartoonish, acrobatic lines infuse this updated take on a classic tale with maximum humor and energy. This hilarious retelling is destined for repeat reads." Booklist

Smith, Chris

★ **One** city, two brothers; written by Chris Smith, illustrated by Aurélia Fronty. Barefoot Books 2007 un il $16.99

Grades: 2 3 4   **398.2**

1. Brothers -- Folklore 2. Jerusalem -- Folklore 3. Folklore --

Middle East

ISBN 978-1-846860-42-3

To settle an inheritance dispute between two brothers, King Solomon tells a tale of how Jerusalem came to be founded.

"Based on a folktale told by both Jews and Arabs, this picture book beautifully captures the spirit of brotherhood. . . . The accomplished folk-style artwork, in shades of verdant green, heavenly blue, and harvest orange . . . adds an air of peace and hope." Booklist

Snyder, Dianne

The **boy** of the three-year nap; illustrated by Allen Say. Houghton Mifflin 1988 32p il $16.95; pa $6.95

Grades: 1 2 3   **398.2**

1. Folklore -- Japan

ISBN 0-395-44090-4; 0-395-66957-X pa

LC 87-30674

A Caldecott Medal honor book, 1989

"Japan's contribution to the trickster folktale, in which a lazy son cons a rich man, only to be outsmarted by his own, even trickier mother. Lilting prose and shimmering illustrations combine in perfect harmony." SLJ

Souhami, Jessica

King Pom and the fox; [by] Jessica Souhami. Frances Lincoln 2007 un il $16.95

Grades: K 1 2 3   **398.2**

1. Folklore

ISBN 978-1-84507-478-4; 1-84507-478-5

"In this Chinese version of 'Puss in Boots,' a young man is called King Pom because he owns a grand pomegranate tree. When a fox is caught stealing its fruit, he strikes a bargain. The fox arranges for King Pom to be rescued from the river and presented to the Emperor as a rich man, unfortunately attacked by robbers. . . . Souhami's bright, uncluttered collages are made of Ingres papers adorned with watercolor, ink, and pencil and lightly positioned on creamy backgrounds. . . . The spareness of the text matches the simplicity of the artwork." SLJ

The **little,** little house. Frances Lincoln 2006 32p il $15.95

Grades: K 1 2   **398.2**

1. Jews -- Folklore

ISBN 1-84507-108-5

"A delightful retelling. . . . The vibrant colors and strong contrast of the cut-paper shapes against neutral backgrounds provide great visual energy. The simple yet dramatic text makes it especially well suited to reading aloud." SLJ

Sausages. Frances Lincoln Children's Books 2006 un il hardcover o.p. pa $8.95

Grades: PreK K 1 2   **398.2**

1. Folklore

ISBN 978-1-84507-397-8; 1-84507-397-5; 978-1-84507-601-6 pa; 1-84507-601-X pa

"In this vibrant retelling of the Grimms' The Three Wishes, brilliantly designed paper collages capture every trace of humor in this cautionary tale. . . . A woodcutter rescues an elf from a rosebush and is granted three wishes. . . . The woodcutter asks for sausages. His wife responds with an angry reply that leaves the sausages stuck on his nose, and, of course, the last wish must be used to remove them. The story begs to be read aloud or told—the language is rich with sound effects." SLJ

Spirin, Gennady

Goldilocks and the three bears; retold and illustrated by Gennady Spirin. Marshall Cavendish Children 2009 un il $17.99

Grades: PreK K 1 2   **398.2**
1. Folklore 2. Bears -- Folklore
ISBN 978-0-7614-5596-7; 0-7614-5596-5

LC 2008026984

A simplified retelling of the adventures of a little girl walking in the woods who finds the house of the three bears and helps herself to their belongings. Includes a note on the history of the tale

"Spirin's version of this classic pairs a simple, straightforward re-telling with lush Renaissance costumes and elegant page designs. The bears, rendered in watercolor and colored pencil, are solid, realistic crea-tures, revealing sharp teeth and claws. . . . The setting is created with richly realized essentials: solid porridge bowls, carved chairs, ornate beds, a massive stucco and wood-trimmed dwelling. . . . This . . . will be embraced for its visual clarity and sumptuous style." SLJ

★ **Little** Red Riding Hood; adapted from the Brothers Grimm by Gennady Spirin. Marshall Cavendish 2010 un il $17.99
Grades: 2 3 4   **398.2**
1. Fairy tales 2. Wolves -- Folklore 3. Folklore -- Germany
ISBN 0761457046; 978-0-7614-5704-6

A retelling of Little Red Riding Hood's encounter with a wicked wolf while visiting her grandmother.

"This classic Grimm tale has had many interpretations over the years, but Spirin's splendid version is inspired by the lavish Dutch paint-ings of the 17th century. The jacket, with windmills and Renaissance cathedral spires in the background, sets the scene. . . . Grandmother, who is garbed in lace and flounces, and the hunters with their long rifles and Cavalier hats fit well into the setting. . . . Spirin places his characters up front on the page against plentiful white space, giving intensity to the unfolding drama. A simply retold and richly illustrated addition." SLJ

★ The **tale** of the Firebird; translated by Tatiana Popova. Philomel Bks. 2002 32p il $16.99
Grades: 2 3 4   **398.2**
1. Fairy tales 2. Birds -- Folklore 3. Folklore -- Russia
ISBN 0-399-23584-1

LC 2001-36660

When Prince Ivan sets out to find the Firebird for his father the tsar, he must complete a series of tasks before obtaining the Firebird and winning the hand of a beautiful princess. "Ages six to ten." (Bull Cent Child Books)

"The storytelling is dramatic and controlled, the language rising and falling in a cadence that encourages reading aloud. . . . Detailed and dra-matic, with a golden palette that echoes crown jewels, the illustrations have an adventurous fairy-tale sweep." Bull Cent Child Books

Steptoe, John
★ **Mufaro's** beautiful daughters; an African tale. Lothrop, Lee & Shepard Bks. 1987 un il $15.95; lib bdg $15.89
Grades: K 1 2 3   **398.2**
1. Fairy tales 2. Folklore -- Africa
ISBN 0-688-04045-4; 0-688-04046-2 lib bdg

LC 84-7158

A Caldecott Medal honor book, 1988; Coretta Scott King Award for illustration, 1988; Boston Globe-Horn Book Award, picture book 1987

Mufaro's two beautiful daughters, one bad-tempered, one kind and sweet, go before the king, who is choosing a wife

"The pace of the text matches the rhythm of the illustrations—both move in dramatic unity to the climax. By changing perspective the artist not only captures the lush, rich background but also the personalities of the characters with revealing studies of their faces." Horn Book

★ The **story** of Jumping Mouse; a native American legend. retold and illustrated by John Steptoe. Lothrop, Lee & Shepard Bks. 1984 un il $15.95; pa $5.95
Grades: 1 2 3   **398.2**
1. Mice -- Folklore 2. Native Americans -- Folklore
ISBN 0-688-01902-1; 0-688-08740-X pa

LC 82-14848

A Caldecott Medal honor book, 1985

"By keeping hope alive within himself, a mouse is successful in his quest for the far-off land. Steptoe's retelling of an unattributed tribal legend is exquisite in its use of language and in its expansive drawings which employ dazzling subtleties of light and shadow." SLJ

Steven, Kenneth C.
Stories for a fragile planet; [written by] Kenneth Steven; [illus-trated by] Jane Ray. Trafalgar Square 2011 48p il $16.99
Grades: 3 4 5 6   **398.2**
1. Folklore
ISBN 978-0-7459-6157-6; 0-7459-6157-6

"This appealing collection consists of 10 brief stories each with a nature theme. Settings include Ancient Greece, . . . Africa, . . . Green-land, . . . Russia, Asia, South America, and Ireland. . . . Although there are no source notes, each smoothly written story is preceded by a brief statement about its origins. The book is beautifully designed, with most of the stories illustrated with crisp, jewel-toned paintings in a primitive style." Booklist

Stevens, Janet
Coyote steals the blanket; an Ute tale. retold and illustrated by Janet Stevens. Holiday House 1993 un il lib bdg $17.95; pa $6.95
Grades: K 1 2 3   **398.2**
1. Ute Indians -- Folklore 2. Coyote (Legendary character)
ISBN 0-8234-0996-1 lib bdg; 0-8234-1129-X pa

LC 92-54415

"When Coyote swipes a blanket, thus angering the spirit of the des-ert, he is pursued by a rock on a rampage. This traditional trickster tale features a scraggly, scruffy yet lovable character, a narrative that will roll right off storytellers' tongues, and hilarious pictures of boastful animals trying to halt the furious boulder." SLJ

★ **Tops** and bottoms; adapted and illustrated by Janet Stevens. Harcourt Brace & Co. 1995 un il $16
Grades: K 1 2 3   **398.2**
1. Bears -- Folklore 2. Rabbits -- Folklore 3. African Americans -- Folklore
ISBN 0-15-292851-0

LC 93-19154

A Caldecott Medal honor book, 1996

"Bear agrees to enter into a farming partnership with Hare, but first Hare makes Bear choose which half he will receive at harvest time: tops or bottoms. Because Bear picks tops, Hare sows all root vegetables. For the second crop, Bear chooses bottoms; this time Hare grows lettuce, broccoli, and celery. Finally, the frustrated Bear demands tops and bot-toms from the final season's crop. But Hare is still the winner: he grows corn [and] keeps the ears 'in the middle' for his family. . . . Steven's bold, well-composed watercolor, pencil, and gesso illustrations cover every inch of each vertically oriented double-page spread. . . . The story contains enough sly humor and reassuring predictability to captivate lis-teners." Horn Book

Sturges, Philemon
★ The **Little** Red Hen (makes a pizza) retold by Philemon Stur-ges; illustrated by Amy Walrod. Dutton Children's Bks. 1999 un il $15.99

Grades: K 1 2 3   **398.2**
1. Folklore 2. Chickens -- Folklore
ISBN 0-525-45953-7

LC 99-20066

In this version of the traditional tale, the duck, the dog, and the cat refuse to help the Little Red Hen make a pizza but do get to participate when the time comes to eat it and then they wash the dishes

"There's a keen sense of the absurd here, and the hilarious cut-paper illustrations are right in tune with the zany plot." SLJ

Taback, Simms
★ **Joseph** had a little overcoat. Viking 1999 un il music $15.99
Grades: K 1 2 3   **398.2**
1. Jews 2. Coats 3. Jews -- Fiction 4. Toy and movable books 5. Folklore -- Europe, Eastern 6. Clothing and dress -- Fiction 7. Toy and movable books -- Specimens
ISBN 0-670-87855-3

LC 98-47721

A newly illustrated edition of the title first published 1977 by Random House

Awarded the Caldecott Medal, 2000

This is an "adaptation of a Yiddish folk song (a newly illustrated version of a book Taback first did in 1977). . . . {It} tells the story of resourceful Joseph, a farmer/tailor of Yehupetz, Poland, who recycles his worn overcoat into ever-smaller elements (jacket, vest, scarf, tie, handkerchief, and button)." (Horn Book) "Ages four to seven." (Booklist)

"Taback's inventive use of die-cut pages shows off his signature artwork. . . . This diverting, sequential story unravels as swiftly as the threads of Joseph's well-loved, patch-covered plaid coat." Publ Wkly

Talbott, Hudson
King Arthur and the Round Table; written and illustrated by Hudson Talbott. Books of Wonder 1995 un il $18.99
Grades: 3 4 5   **398.2**
1. Arthurian romances 2. Kings
ISBN 0-688-11340-0

LC 94-43766

"The rich watercolor tableaux . . . paint war as bloody and painful, not all glorious. The love scenes glow golden. The Round Table, huge and decorated with the signs of the zodiac, exhibits its power more than the words do. Overall, this is a rousing addition to the current pickings of Arthurian stories." SLJ

Tarnowska, Wafa'
★ **Arabian** nights; written by Wafa' Tarnowska; illustrated by Carole Hénaff. Barefoot Books 2010 125p il $24.99
Grades: 5 6 7 8   **398.2**
1. Fairy tales 2. Arabs -- Folklore
ISBN 978-1-84686-122-2; 1-84686-122-5

LC 2008028159

"With bright, lush, stylized acrylic illustrations, this collection of eight stories from A Thousand and One Nights is designed for reading aloud. . . . Throughout, the spacious paintings capture the sense of the supernatural in daily life, including magical images of people taking flight above city, trees, and desert." Booklist

Tatanka and the Lakota people; a creation story. illustrated by Donald F. Montileaux. South Dakota State Historical Society Press 2006 un il $16.95
Grades: 1 2 3 4   **398.2**
1. Creation -- Folklore 2. Teton Indians -- Folklore
ISBN 0-9749195-8-6

LC 2006016009

The transformaton of the Buffalo Nation into the Ordinary People and their salvation by Tatanka comes from this traditional creation story of the Lakota, or Sioux, Indians.

"Montileaux, an Oglala Lakota artist, illustrates the text with paintings rendered in a two-dimensional format that reflects traditional buffalo-hide paintings. The colorful, stylized images match the formal tone of the story. The English telling is clear and concise, with the corresponding Lakota text appearing alongside." SLJ

Taylor, C. J.
Spirits, fairies, and merpeople; Native stories of other worlds. Tundra Books 2009 39p il $19.95
Grades: 3 4 5 6   **398.2**
1. Native Americans -- Folklore
ISBN 978-0-88776-872-9; 0-88776-872-5

"The seven brief legends in this collection hail from a range of Native cultures. Mohawk artist/storyteller Taylor includes one from her own heritage, along with one each from the Mi'kmaq, Dakota, Coos, Ojibwa, Ute, and Cree. . . . Taylor's retellings are crisp and lend themselves well to reading aloud. Each story is accompanied by a lushly hued, surrealistic painting. The powerful images featuring fearsome creatures and tiny human figures balance the taut economy of the text." SLJ

Tchana, Katrin Hyman
Changing Woman and her sisters; stories of goddesses from around the world. retold by Katrin Hyman Tchana; illustrated by Trina Schart Hyman. Holiday House 2006 80p il $18.95
Grades: 5 6 7 8   **398.2**
1. Folklore 2. Gods and goddesses
ISBN 978-0-8234-1999-9; 0-8234-1999-1

LC 2005-52504

An illustrated collection of traditional tales which feature goddesses from different cultures, including Navajo, Mayan, and Fon. Notes explain each goddess's place in her culture, the reason for the book, and how the illustrations were developed

"This large, handsome volume assembles well-chosen, well-told stories. . . . Hyman . . . contributed distinctive portrayals of the goddesses using a technique that melded photographs and found materials into full-page ink and acrylic paintings." Booklist

Includes bibliographical references

Tonatiuh, Duncan
★ The **princess** and the warrior; A Tale of Two Volcanoes. by Duncan Tonatiuh. Abrams Books for Young Readers 2016 40 p. color illustrations (ebook) $15.54; (hardback) $16.95
Grades: 1 2 3 4   **398.2**
1. Legends -- Mexico 2. Aztecs -- Folklore 3. Nahuatl literature 4. Volcanoes -- Foklore 5. Mountains -- Folklore
ISBN 9781613129708; 1419721305; 9781419721304

LC 2015051082

Pura Belpre Illustrator Honor Book (2017)

This children's book by Duncan Tonatiuh reimagines a Mexican legend that explains the origins of two volcanoes. "The emperor promised [the warrior] Popoca [that] if he could defeat their enemy Jaguar Claw, then Popoca and [Princess] Izta could wed. When Popoca was near to defeating Jaguar Claw, his opponent sent a messenger to Izta saying Popoca was dead. Izta fell into a deep sleep and, upon his return, even Popoca could not wake her." (Publisher's note)

"The appealing story, compelling illustrations, and celebration of the Aztec culture make this a sure thing for those looking for a story, while an extensive author's note goes a step beyond, adding to the impact of the tale with a great deal of historical and cultural information." Booklist

Includes bibliographical references.

Tracy, Kathleen

Cerberus. Mitchell Lane Publishers 2011 48p il map (Monsters in myth) lib bdg $29.95

Grades: 4 5 6 7 **398.2**

1. Classical mythology

ISBN 978-1-58415-924-7; 1-58415-924-3

LC 2010026968

This describes myths of Cerberus, Hades three-headed watchdog who guarded the gates of the Greek Underworld.

This book is "thorough and respectful of a number of ancient and modern sources and [bends] over backward to navigate often contradictory, interlinked legends. . . . A number of paintings and photos break up the otherwise text-heavy pages, and copious chapter notes and reading suggestions conclude. This is by no means entry-level stuff, but for kids handy with the basics and ready to delve deeper, [this book] will be of great use." Booklist

Includes glossary and bibliographical references

Vallverdu, Josep

Aladdin and the magic lamp; from The thousand and one nights. adaptation by Josep Vallverdu; illustrated by Pep Montserrat. Chronicle Books 2006 un il $14.95; pa $6.95

Grades: K 1 2 **398.2**

1. Fairy tales 2. Arabs -- Folklore 3. Bilingual books -- English-Spanish

ISBN 0-8118-5061-7; 0-8118-5062-5 pa

Aladdin outwits an evil magician who first tries to trick him into handing over an old lamp with a genie inside and later steals Aladdin's wife and possessions.

"Told in a simple but richly descriptive style, the story is both entertaining and lends itself very well to reading out loud. . . . This is a handsomely executed English-Spanish version that will make a great addition to a child's library of favorite bedtime readings." Booklist

Wada, Stephanie

Momotaro and the island of ogres; a Japanese folktale. as told by Stephanie Wada; paintings by Kano Naganobu. George Braziller 2005 47p il $19.95

Grades: 3 4 5 6 **398.2**

1. Folklore -- Japan

ISBN 0-8076-1552-8

Found floating on the river inside a peach by an old couple, Momotaro grows up and fights the terrible demons who have terrorized the village for years.

"Nineteenth-century silk handscrolls, painted by master Naganobu and housed in the New York Public Library's Spencer Collection, illustrate this handsome retelling of a much-loved Japanese folktale." Booklist

Waldman, Debby

Clever Rachel; story by Debby Waldman; illustrations by Cindy Revell. Orca Book Publishers 2009 un il $19.95

Grades: K 1 2 3 **398.2**

1. Jews -- Folklore 2. Riddles -- Fiction

ISBN 978-1-55469-081-7; 1-55469-081-1

Retells a traditional Jewish folktale about a clever girl named Rachel who clashes with a boy named Jacob when he challenges her with his riddles, until a woman with an urgent problem shows them that they are at their best when they work together.

"The lighthearted text includes occasional Yiddish words. Energetic illustrations convey Rachel and Jacob's competitive spirits." Horn Book Guide

A **sack** full of feathers; story by Debby Waldman; illustrations by Cindy Revell. Orca Book Publishers 2006 un il $19.95

Grades: K 1 2 3 **398.2**

1. Jews -- Folklore 2. Gossip -- Folklore

ISBN 1-55143-332-X

"Yankel loves to tell stories and repeat the gossip that he hears in his father's store in the shtetl. . . . Unfortunately, Yankel only hears the bits and pieces that make trouble, not how things turn out. So the rabbi decides to teach the boy a lesson by making him see that stories spread and that they can be hurtful. The fun in this retelling of a Jewish folktale is not in the lesson, but in the setting, the people, and the stories they tell. The bright acrylic folk art shows the characters gossiping, quarreling . . . and, finally, getting together." Booklist

Wang Ping

The **dragon** emperor; a Chinese folktale. retold by Wang Ping; illustrations by Tang Ge. Millbrook Press 2008 48p il (On my own folklore) lib bdg $25.26

Grades: 1 2 3 4 **398.2**

1. Folklore -- China 2. Dragons -- Folklore

ISBN 978-0-8225-6740-0 lib bdg; 0-8225-6740-7 lib bdg

LC 2006036718

A jealous warrior challenges the leadership of the dragon emperor. End note discusses the dragon in Chinese folklore and culture.

The "tale is paired with an illustration style that nicely reflects the culture." Horn Book Guide

Wargin, Kathy-Jo

The **frog** prince; by the Brothers Grimm; as retold by Kathy-jo Wargin; illustrated by Anne Yvonne Gilbert. Mitten Press 2007 un il $18.95

Grades: K 1 2 3 **398.2**

1. Fairy tales 2. Folklore -- Germany

ISBN 978-1-58726-279-1; 1-58726-279-7

LC 2006020283

As payment for retrieving the princess's ball, the frog exacts a promise which the princess is reluctant to fulfill

"Intricate, gloriously lush illustrations highlight this retelling of the familiar tale. Wargin has preserved much of the tone of the original text while editing the length to make it more palatable for younger audiences." Booklist

Waters, Fiona

Aesop's fables; retold by Fiona Waters; illustrated by Fulvio Testa. Trafalgar Square 2011 il $24.99

Grades: 1 2 3 4 **398.2**

1. Fables

ISBN 978-1-84939-049-1; 1-84939-049-5

"Waters deftly adds a contemporary tone in description and dialogue to her smooth rendering of 60 familiar and less-well-known tales. The terse moral of each fable, concluding each one in customary style, is usually set in traditional terms. . . . Testa's pen and watercolor drawings are fun, portraying all animals with the large eyes currently popular in cartoon art. . . . With its many comic touches, this anthology presents once again the humor, folly, ingenuity, and wisdom that make Aesop so durable." SLJ

Willey, Margaret

★ The **3** bears and Goldilocks; illustrated by Heather M. Solomon. Atheneum Books for Young Readers 2008 un il $16.99

Grades: PreK K 1 2 3 **398.2**

1. Folklore 2. Bears -- Folklore

ISBN 978-1-4169-2494-4; 1-4169-2494-9

LC 2007-13857

Goldilocks, ignoring her father's warning not to rush in where she does not belong, enters a cabin in the woods, cleans it to meet her standards, plucks from the porridge items unappealing to her before eating a bowlful, and falls asleep on the bed that suits her best.

"There is a rustic feel to the illustrations, rendered in watercolor, collage, colored pencil, acrylic, and oil paint. . . . This satisfying read-aloud offers a new twist on an old favorite." SLJ

Clever Beatrice; an Upper Peninsula conte. illustrated by Heather McWhorter. Atheneum Bks. for Young Readers 2001 un il $16
Grades: K 1 2 3   **398.2**
1. Giants -- Folklore 2. Folklore -- United States
ISBN 0-689-83254-0

LC 00-42019

A small, but clever young girl outwits a rich giant and wins all his gold

"Set in Michigan's Upper Peninsula, this is a winning tale of brain vs. brawn. . . . Willey's telling is simple but spirited, and her dialogue, with its slight French-Canadian cadence, is pitch perfect. Heather Solomon's illustrations are remarkable: watercolors augmented with collage, they have unusual texture and depth." Horn Book

Other titles about Clever Beatrice by this author are:

Clever Beatrice and the best little pony (2004)

A Clever Beatrice Christmas (2006)

Wisniewski, David
Rain player; story and pictures by David Wisniewski. Clarion Bks. 1991 un il pa $7.95; $17
Grades: 1 2 3 4   **398.2**
1. Games -- Fiction 2. Mayas -- Fiction
ISBN 0-395-72083-4 pa; 0-395-55112-9

LC 90-44101

To bring rain to his thirsty village, Pik challenges the rain god to a game of pok-a-tok

"This original tale combines research on Mayan history and legend with a suspenseful sports story. . . . Intricate and dramatic cut-paper illustrations powerfully re-create the foliage, landscape, architecture, and clothing of the Mayan classical period. . . . An author's note provides fascinating background information on Mayan civilization and gives in-depth explanations of some of the words and phrases used in the text." Horn Book

Wolf, Gita
Gobble You Up! Pgw 2013 40 p. $34.95
Grades: PreK K   **398.2**
1. Jackals 2. Folk literature 3. Animals -- Fiction
ISBN 8192317145; 9788192317144

Author Gita Wolf's book "is an adaptation of an oral trickster tale from Rajasthan, north India. It is illustrated with finger painting by . . . Sunita, a young woman artist who hails from the Meena tribe. In this handmade, silkscreen printed children's book, Sunita adapts a traditional Meena art form called Mandna, which is traditionally painted by women on the walls and floors of their village homes." (Publisher's note)

Wormell, Christopher
Mice, morals, & monkey business; lively lessons from Aesop's Fables. Running Press 2005 un il $18.95
Grades: K 1 2 3   **398.2**
1. Fables 2. Authors 3. Storytellers
ISBN 0-7624-2404-4

"Wormell uses linocut prints to illuminate 21 of Aesop's famous life lessons. . . . The bold, black lines of the expertly rendered images and colorful accents primarily in earth tones create instantly recognizable

figures. The subtle use of light and shadow adds clarity, expression, and often drama without extraneous detail." SLJ

Yolen, Jane
Sister Bear; a Norse tale. adapted by Jane Yolen; illustrated by Linda Graves. Marshall Cavendish Children 2011 un il
Grades: K 1 2 3   **398.2**
1. Bears -- Folklore 2. Folklore -- Norway
ISBN 0-7614-5958-8; 978-0-7614-5958-3

LC 2010024235

Halva is traveling with her trained bear to visit the King of Denmark when they stop for the night at a cottage where, they learn, a pack of trolls is about to make its annual Christmas Eve visit, causing trouble and making a big mess. Includes author's note about the story's origins.

"There isn't a dull moment in Yolen's rousing retelling of this Norwegian folktale. . . . Grave's . . . characters have the attraction of costumed toys, and nearly every spread features a loving look at a traditional Scandinavian garment and its inticate needlework. . . . Yolen knows a good story when she sees one." Publ Wkly

Young, Ed
★ **Lon** Po Po; a Red-Riding Hood story from China. translated and illustrated by Ed Young. Philomel Bks. 1989 un il $16.99; pa $6.99
Grades: 1 2 3   **398.2**
1. Folklore -- China 2. Wolves -- Folklore
ISBN 0-399-21619-7; 0-698-11382-9 pa

LC 88-15222

Awarded the Caldecott Medal, 1990

This folktale "involves three little sisters who outsmart the wolf (lon or long in Cantonese) who has gained entry to their home under the false pretense of being their maternal grandmother (Po Po). The clever animal blows out the candle before the children can see him, and is actually in bed with them when they start asking the traditional 'Why Grandma!' questions. The eldest realizes the truth and tricks the wolf into letting them go outside to pick gingko nuts, and then lures him to his doom." (SLJ) "Ages six to nine." (Booklist)

"The text possesses that matter-of-fact veracity that characterizes the best fairy tales. The watercolor and pastel pictures are remarkable: mystically beautiful in their depiction of the Chinese countryside, menacing in the exchanges with the wolf, and positively chilling in the scenes inside the house." SLJ

★ The **sons** of the Dragon King; a Chinese legend. Atheneum Bks. for Young Readers 2004 un il $16.95
Grades: 3 4 5   **398.2**
1. Folklore -- China
ISBN 0-689-85184-7

LC 2002-154321

The nine immortal sons of the Dragon King set out to make something of themselves, and each, with help from a watchful father, finds a role that suits his individual strengths.

"The text is engrossing and includes an informative author's note. The illustrations, rendered in brush, ink, and cut paper, use softly smudged lines for the part of the story focused on the legend, and sharper, cleaner lines augmented by a minimal but dramatically effective use of color for the present-day segments. This elegant addition to folklore shelves should be a first purchase for most libraries." SLJ

Zelinsky, Paul O.
Rumpelstiltskin; from the German of the Brothers Grimm. retold & illustrated by Paul O. Zelinsky. Dutton 1986 un il lib bdg $16.99; pa $6.99

Grades: K 1 2 3   **398.2**
1. Fairy tales 2. Folklore -- Germany
ISBN 0-525-44265-0 lib bdg; 0-14-055864-0 pa

LC 86-4482

A Caldecott Medal honor book, 1987

A strange little man helps the miller's daughter spin straw into gold for the king on the condition that she will give him her first-born child. This adaptation is based mainly on the 1819 edition of the Grimm brothers' Kinder-und Hausmärchen. "Kindergarten to grade four." (SLJ)

"Zelinsky's painterly style and rich colors provide an evocative backdrop to this story. The medieval setting and costumes and the spools of gold thread which shine on the page like real gold are suggestive of an illuminated manuscript. . . . Zelinsky's smooth retelling and glowing pictures cast the story in a new and beautiful light." SLJ

Zemach, Margot
The **three** little pigs; an old story. Farrar, Straus & Giroux 1989 un il hardcover o.p. pa $5.95
Grades: K 1 2   **398.2**
1. Pigs -- Folklore 2. Wolves -- Folklore 3. Folklore -- Great Britain
ISBN 0-374-37527-5; 0-374-47717-5 pa

LC 87-73488

This is an adaptation of the traditional folktale about a hungry wolf who "attempts to wile his way to three pork chop dinners." (Horn Book) "Preschool to grade two." (SLJ)

Zemach "has brought a familiar, often-told tale to life with marvelous ink-and-watercolor illustrations. Her wolf, wearing a dapper green hat and radiating slyness with every inch of his furry self, cuts a spendidly sinister figure as he attempts to wile his way to three pork chop dinners. With simple, lively sentences Zemach has related the complete story, including the apple-picking and country fair episodes." Horn Book

Ziefert, Harriet
Little Red Riding Hood; retold by Harriet Ziefert; illustrated by Emily Bolam. Viking 2000 un il (Viking easy-to-read) hardcover o.p. pa $3.99
Grades: K 1 2   **398.2**
1. Fairy tales 2. Wolves -- Folklore 3. Folklore -- Germany
ISBN 0-670-88389-1; 0-14-056529-9 pa

LC 99-23210

A little girl meets a hungry wolf in the forest while on her way to visit her gandmother

This adaptation of the Grimm's fairy tale "tells the story in a brisk, straightforward style . . . [with] simple, colorful illustrations. . . . The vocabulary is appropriate for beginning readers. The lively illustrations and familiarity of the story should provide a successful reading experience." SLJ

398.209 History, geographic treatment, biography

Aardema, Verna
★ **Anansi** does the impossible! an Ashanti tale. retold by Verna Aardema; illustrated by Lisa Desimini. Atheneum Bks. for Young Readers 1997 un il $16; pa $5.99
Grades: K 1 2 3   **398.209**
1. Folklore -- West Africa 2. Anansi (Legendary character)
ISBN 0-689-81092-X; 0-689-83933-2 pa

LC 96-20033

"Vivid, stylized collage illustrations convey the frightening force and power of the Sky God yet also reveal Anansi's own pluck and boldness. Perfect for reading or telling aloud." Booklist

Includes glossary and bibliographical references

Beneduce, Ann
Jack and the beanstalk; retold by Ann Keay Beneduce; illustrated by Gennady Spirin. Philomel Bks. 1999 32p il $16.99
Grades: 2 3 4   **398.209**
1. Fairy tales 2. Folklore -- Great Britain
ISBN 0-399-23118-8

LC 98-5722

A boy climbs to the top of a giant beanstalk, where he uses his quick wits to outsmart an ogre and make his and his mother's fortune

"Beneduce bases her version of Jack and the Beanstalk on a Victorian version, complete with a fairy guardian. . . . Spirin contributes some glorious borders for the text as well as many impressively detailed paintings, notable for their dark muted colors and mysterious, foggy look." Booklist

Bodkin, Odds
The **crane** wife; retold by Odds Bodkin; illustrated by Gennady Spirin. Gulliver Bks. 1998 un il hardcover o.p. pa $7
Grades: 3 4 5   **398.209**
1. Folklore -- Japan
ISBN 0-15-201407-1; 0-15-216350-6 pa

LC 96-35488

A retelling of the traditional Japanese tale about a poor sail maker who gains a beautiful but mysterious wife skilled at weaving magical sails

"Capturing the tale's mystery and tragedy, Spirin's watercolor-and-gouache paintings take their inspiration from Japanese art. Delicate shades of tawny gray and burnished gold predominate in the illustrations." Booklist

Casanova, Mary
The **hunter**; a Chinese folktale. retold by Mary Casanova; illustrations by Ed Young. Atheneum Bks. for Young Readers 2000 un il $16.95
Grades: K 1 2 3   **398.209**
1. Folklore -- China
ISBN 0-689-82906-X

LC 99-32166

After learning to understand the language of animals, Hai Li Bu the hunter sacrifices himself to save his village

Casanova "tells the tale in a dignified yet moving way that is complemented by the stark artwork. Arid-looking, dun-colored paper is the background for Young's masterful brush strokes." Booklist

Craft, Charlotte
★ **King** Midas and the golden touch; as told by Charlotte Craft; illustrated by K.Y. Craft. Morrow 1999 32p il $16; pa $6.99
Grades: 2 3 4   **398.209**
1. Midas (Legendary character)
ISBN 0-688-13165-4; 0-06-054063-X pa

LC 98-24035

A king finds himself bitterly regretting the consequences of his wish that everything he touches would turn to gold

"This sophisticated retelling, set in the Middle Ages, places King Midas in a sumptuous palace. . . . The elaborate oil-over-watercolor illustrations show the wondrous, tragic effects of the golden touch." Horn Book Guide

Defelice, Cynthia
Nelly May has her say; Cynthia DeFelice; pictures by Henry Cole. Margaret Ferguson Books 2013 32 p. col. ill. $16.99
Grades: K 1 2 3   **398.209**
1. Picture books for children 2. Folklore -- England
ISBN 0374398992; 9780374398996

LC 2011018484

In this children's picture book, Nelly May Nimble leaves her childhood home and 12 siblings to work for Lord Ignasius Pinkwinkle. Lord Pinkwinkle "agrees with one condition; the master of the house has special names for things, and Nelly must use those names when she speaks to him. . . . But when Lord Pinkwinkle's 'fur-faced fluffenbarker's wigger-wagger' catches fire, Nelly has to wake him and announce the fire before the house burns down. Can she remember all those silly names?" (School Library Journal)

Demi

★ The **empty** pot. Holt & Co. 1990 un il $16.95; pa $6.95
Grades: K 1 2 3   **398.209**
    1. Folklore -- China
    ISBN 0-8050-1217-6; 0-8050-4900-2 pa

LC 89-39062

"This simple story with its clear moral is illustrated with beautiful paintings. . . . A beautifully crafted book that will be enjoyed as much for the richness of its illustrations as for the simplicity of its story." SLJ

Doyle, Malachy

Tales from old Ireland; retold by Malachy Doyle; illustrated by Niamh Sharkey. Barefoot Bks. (NY) 2000 95p il $19.99; pa $16.99
Grades: 3 4 5 6   **398.209**
    1. Folklore -- Ireland
    ISBN 978-1-902283-97-5; 1-902283-97-X; 978-1-905236-32-9 pa; 1-905236-32-8 pa
A collection of seven Irish folk tales

Doyle's "retellings are simple and economical, yet contain all the lilting rhythm and musical quality for which Irish tales are famous. Sharkey's illustrations, prepared in oil and gesso on canvas, are a perfect match." SLJ

Includes bibliographical references

Fang, Linda

The **Ch'i**-lin purse; a collection of ancient Chinese stories. retold by Linda Fang; pictures by Jeanne M. Lee. Farrar, Straus & Giroux 1994 127p il hardcover o.p. pa $5.95
Grades: 5 6 7 8   **398.209**
    1. Folklore -- China
    ISBN 0-374-31241-9; 0-374-41189-1 pa

LC 94-9909

A collection of "Chinese stories derived from the history of the Warring States Period (770-221 B.C.E.) and from operatic versions of popular tales. Retellings are vivid, lively, and read aloud well. Many have a moral, and all are entertaining. . . . The black-and-white illustrations—one per selection—are graceful, depicting widely different epochs with amazing accuracy." SLJ

Includes glossary and bibliographical references

Garland, Sherry

Children of the dragon; selected tales from Vietnam. with illustrations by Trina Schart Hyman. Harcourt 2001 58p il $18
Grades: 3 4 5 6   **398.209**
    1. Folklore -- Vietnam
    ISBN 0-15-224200-7

LC 00-8300

An illustrated collection of Vietnamese folktales with explanatory notes following each story

"This handsome volume gathers six well-told traditional tales not readily available elsewhere. . . . [The book is] greatly enhanced by Hyman's strong color work, romantic sensibility, and dramatic characterizations." SLJ

Gavin, Jamila

School for princes; stories from the Panchatantra. retold by Jamila Gavin; illustrated by Bee Willey. Reprint Frances Lincoln Children's Books 2012 64 p. ill. (hardcover) $19.99
Grades: 4 5 6   **398.209**
    1. Indic mythology 2. Indian literature (English) 3. Indic literature -- Collections 4. Conduct of life -- Literary collections
    ISBN 1845079906; 9781845079901

This children's book presents "a series of newly created stories in combination with five traditional tales to reveal the Panchatantra's themes. . . . Three arrogant princes change their tune in six short months as a sage uses stories to teach them the art of ruling. These fables have been introduced to people of all classes for generations to spread ideas of wisdom, kindness, friendship and unity, and self-control." (Kirkus Reviews)

Heo, Yumi

The **green** frogs; a Korean folktale. retold by Yumi Heo. Houghton Mifflin 1996 un il $16; pa $6.95
Grades: K 1 2 3   **398.209**
    1. Folklore -- Korea 2. Frogs -- Folklore
    ISBN 0-395-68378-5; 0-618-43228-8 pa

LC 95-19129

"Using delicate tones, flat perspectives, and somewhat abstract figures set against busy backgrounds, [Heo] creates a quaint, comic effect. . . . This is a quirkier pourquoi tale than most, but it's too mischievous to be morbid." Horn Book

Jiang, Ji-li

★ The **magical** Monkey King; mischief in heaven. classic Chinese tales retold by Ji-Li Jiang; illustrated by Hui Hui Su-Kennedy. HarperCollins Pubs. 2002 122p il hardcover o.p. pa $4.95
Grades: 3 4 5   **398.209**
    1. Folklore -- China 2. Monkeys -- Folklore
    ISBN 0-06-029544-9 lib bdg; 0-06-442149-X pa

LC 2001-39672

The mischievous Monkey King attempts to achieve immortality the easy way, gains god-like powers, and wreaks havoc in heaven

The author "provides a lively telling, and the stories move briskly. Accompanying black-and-white pictures have the look of woodcuts." Booklist

MacDonald, Margaret Read

★ **Fat** cat; a Danish folktale. retold by Margaret Read MacDonald; illustrated by Julie Paschkis. August House 2001 un il $15.95; pa $7.95
Grades: K 1 2 3   **398.209**
    1. Cats -- Folklore 2. Mice -- Folklore 3. Folklore -- Denmark
    ISBN 0-87483-616-6; 0-87483-765-0 pa

LC 00-68939

A greedy cat grows enormous as he eats everything in sight, including his friends and neighbors who call him fat

"The book's huge, bright illustrations are glorious. . . . The large, funny illustrations will carry well for a bigger crowd and, combined with refrain that invites chanting along, make this a surefire hit for reading aloud." Booklist

★ **Mabela** the clever; retold by Margaret Read MacDonald; illustrated by Tim Coffey. Whitman, A. 2001 un il music hardcover o.p. pa $6.95
Grades: K 1 2 3   **398.209**
    1. Cats -- Folklore 2. Mice -- Folklore 3. Folklore -- Africa
    ISBN 0-8075-4902-9; 0-8075-4903-7 pa

LC 00-8307

An African folktale about a mouse who pays close attention to her surroundings and avoids being tricked by the cat

"MacDonald's retelling of this Limba tale is engineered for story-time success. . . . Coffey's thatch-strewn paintings, rendered in acrylic on watercolor paper textured with gesso, feature lots of visibly clue-less, wide-eyed mice, and his cat oozes predatory shrewdness to the very end." SLJ

Napoli, Donna Jo, 1948-

Treasury of Norse mythology; stories of intrigue, trickery, love, and revenge. by Donna Jo Napoli; illustrated by Christina Balit. National Geographic 2015 191 p. color illustrations, map (hardcover : alk. paper) $24.99

Grades: 5 6 7 8   **398.209**

1. Norse legends 2. Norse mythology 3. Tales -- Scandinavia 4. Gods, Norse 5. Mythology, Norse
ISBN 9781426320989; 9781426320996

LC 2015013321

This book, by Donna Jo Napoli, illustrated by Christina Balit, is "a new look at Asgard and the timeless tales of ancient Scandinavia. Classic stories and dazzling illustrations of gods, goddesses, heroes and monsters come to life in a stunning tableau of Norse myths, including those of the thunder god Thor, the one-eyed god and Allfather Odin, and the trickster god Loki." (Publisher's note)

"Buy it, and if space is an issue, weed to make it fit." SLJ
Includes bibliographical references and index

Ollhoff, Jim

Middle Eastern Mythology; by Jim Ollhoff. ABDO Publishing Company 2011 32p il (The world of mythology) lib bdg $27.07

Grades: 5 6 7 8   **398.209**

1. Mythology 2. Middle East 3. Children -- Books and reading
ISBN 1617147257; 9781617147258; 1-61714-725-7; 978-1-61714-725-8

LC 2010042977

This describes the history of myths of the Middle East, their meaning, and their gods and goddesses including Mithra, Mot, the Mesopotamian goddess Ishtar, and the Canaanite thunder god, Baal.

"Ollhoff writes in a clear and engaging fashion, presenting complex issues in a way that will be easy for youngsters to grasp. . . . The photographs and reproductions of art tie directly to the [text]." SLJ

Tolman, Marije

The **island**; Ronald Tolman; Marije Tolman. Lemniscaat USA 2012 32 p. $17.95

Grades: PreK K   **398.209**

1. Picture books for children 2. Islands -- fiction 3. Polar bears -- fiction
ISBN 1935954199; 9781935954194

In this "wordless picture book" by Marije Tolman and Ronald Tolman "you swim along with a bear on a journey through a unique archipelago. . . . With every island lies a whole new world to discover, until the bear finds the ultimate island. Has he finally come across his home, or is he merely passing through?" (Publisher's note)

Wisniewski, David

★ **Sundiata**; lion king of Mali. story and pictures by David Wisniewski. Clarion Bks. 1992 un il hardcover o.p. pa $5.95

Grades: 1 2 3 4   **398.209**

1. Kings 2. Mali -- History
ISBN 0-395-61302-7; 0-395-76481-5 pa

LC 91-27951

The story of Sundiata, who overcame physical handicaps, social disgrace, and strong opposition to rule Mali in the thirteenth century

"Passed down through oral tradition, this historical account has the drama and depth of a folktale. The illustrations—elaborate collages inspired by the artifacts and culture of the Malinke—create a series of dramatic images. The intricacy of the paper-cuts and the richness of the colors and patterns give the artwork visual as well as narrative strength." Booklist

398.21   Tales and lore on a specific topic

Cruz, Alejandro

The **woman** who outshone the sun; the legend of Lucia Zenteno. from a poem by Alejandro Cruz Martinez; pictures by Fernando Olivera; story by Rosalma Zubizarreta, Harriet Rohmer, David Schecter. Children's Bk. Press 1991 30p hardcover o.p. pa $7.95

Grades: K 1 2 3   **398.21**

1. Zapotec Indians -- Folklore 2. Bilingual books -- English-Spanish
ISBN 0-89239-101-4; 0-89239-126-X pa

LC 91-16646

Retells the Zapotec legend of Lucia Zenteno, a beautiful woman with magical powers who is exiled from a mountain village and takes its water away in punishment

This "Hispanic folktale is skillfully told, and is solid and colorfully steeped with imagery of the earth and sky. Both the Spanish and English read gracefully, and the poetic use of language suits the story well for telling. The illustrations have a sense of volume that is reminiscent of Orozco." SLJ

Egielski, Richard

★ The **gingerbread** boy. HarperCollins Pubs. 1997 un il $15.95; pa $5.95

Grades: K 1 2 3   **398.21**

1. Folklore 2. New York (N.Y.) -- Fiction
ISBN 0-06-026030-0; 0-06-443708-6 pa

LC 95-50026

"Egielski's retelling is straightforward and retains the traditional refrain: 'Run run run as fast as you can'—it sounds just right, making a satisfying modern variation. The illustrations . . . adroitly evoke the city setting while giving a solid three-dimensionality and unique individuality to the Gingerbread Boy and his pursuers." SLJ

Hong, Lily Toy

★ **Two** of everything; a Chinese folktale. retold and illustrated by Lily Toy Hong. Whitman, A. 1993 un il $15.95

Grades: K 1 2 3   **398.21**

1. Folklore -- China
ISBN 0-8075-8157-7

LC 92-29880

A poor old Chinese farmer finds a magic brass pot that doubles or duplicates whatever is placed inside it, but his efforts to make himself wealthy lead to unexpected complications

The author "here paints with muted colors, defining rounded forms with broad outlines. Retold with verve and gentle humor, this Chinese folktale could become a read-aloud favorite." Booklist

Kellogg, Steven

Jack and the beanstalk; retold and illustrated by Steven Kellogg. Morrow Junior Bks. 1991 un il $16; lib bdg $16.89; pa $6.95

Grades: K 1 2 3   **398.21**

1. Fairy tales 2. Giants -- Folklore 3. Folklore -- Great Britain
ISBN 0-688-10250-6; 0-688-10251-4 lib bdg; 0-688-15281-3 pa

LC 90-45990

Jack climbs to the top of a giant beanstalk, where he uses his quick wits to outsmart an ogre and make his and his mother's fortune. "Kindergarten to grade three." (SLJ)

"Seldom has the ogre at the top of the beanstalk been depicted with such gusto! The warty, fanged, pug-nosed lout dressed in animal skins and a necklace of teeth is a wonder to behold. Steven Kellogg's humorous detail provides witty embellishment for savoring. His story line is quite faithful to the Joseph Jacobs version of the story, the sturdy text offering a strong framework for the energetic illustrations." Horn Book

Kimmel, Eric A.

The **gingerbread** man; retold by Eric A. Kimmel; illustrated by Megan Lloyd. Holiday House 1993 un il $16.95; pa $6.95

Grades: K 1 2   **398.21**

1. Folklore

ISBN 0-8234-0824-8; 0-8234-1137-0 pa

LC 90-33202

A freshly baked gingerbread man escapes when he is taken out of the oven and eludes a number of animals until he meets a clever fox. "Preschool." (SLJ)

"This version softens the ending with a final page of fresh, recently baked gingerbread men. This is a story that calls for energetic art, and Lloyd provides just that in warm-toned watercolors that feature the gingerbread man zipping across the pages. A compact text and suitably large pictures make this just right for groups." Booklist

Mollel, Tololwa M.

The **orphan** boy; a Maasai story. illustrated by Paul Morin. Clarion Bks. 1990 un il hardcover o.p. pa $6.95

Grades: K 1 2 3   **398.21**

1. Folklore -- Africa 2. Masai (African people) -- Folklore

ISBN 0-89919-985-2; 0-395-72079-6 pa

LC 90-2358

"Infused with an aura of mystery, Mollel's compelling story is told skillfully and dramatically. Morin's richly textured paintings, evoking in bold colors an Africa of both parched desert and lush vegetation, are worthy companions." Publ Wkly

Salley, Coleen

Epossumondas; written by Coleen Salley; illustrated by Janet Stevens. Harcourt 2002 un il $16

Grades: K 1 2 3   **398.21**

1. Opossums -- Folklore 2. Folklore -- Southern States

ISBN 0-15-216748-X

LC 2001-4906

A retelling of a classic tale in which a well-intentioned young possum continually takes his mother's instructions much too literally. "Ages four to seven." (Bull Cent Child Books)

"All of the elements of a good story are here. . . . Salley's text rolls off the page (and off the tongue) easily, and is accompanied by delightful watercolor and colored-pencil art." SLJ

Other titles about Epossumondas are:

Epossumondas saves the day (2006)

Epossumondas plays possum (2009)

Why Epossumondas has no hair on his tail (2004)

San Souci, Robert

The **faithful** friend; [by] Robert D. San Souci; illustrated by Brian Pinkney. Simon & Schuster Bks. for Young Readers 1995 un il $16; pa $5.99

Grades: 2 3 4   **398.21**

1. Folklore -- Martinique

ISBN 0-02-786131-7; 0-689-82458-0 pa

LC 93-40672

A Caldecott Medal honor book, 1996

"Pinkney's scratchboard and oil artwork switches from bright daytime hues for most of the book to purples and grays for scenes with the zombies and snakes, which are very effective. . . . This excellent title contains all the elements of a well-researched folktale, and convincingly conveys the richness of the West Indian culture." SLJ

Includes bibliographical references

Wisniewski, David

★ **Golem**; story and pictures by David Wisniewski. Clarion Bks. 1996 un il $15.95; pa $6.95

Grades: 3 4 5   **398.21**

1. Jews -- Folklore 2. Monsters -- Folklore

ISBN 0-395-72618-2; 0-618-89424-1 pa

LC 95-21777

Awarded the Caldecott Medal, 1997

"The fiery, crisply layered paper illustrations, portraying with equal drama and precision the ornamental architecture of Prague and the unearthly career of the Golem, match the specificity and splendor of the storytelling." Publ Wkly

398.22   Tales and lore of persons without paranormal powers

Hodges, Margaret

The **kitchen** knight; a tale of King Arthur. retold by Margaret Hodges and illustrated by Trina Schart Hyman. Holiday House 1990 un il $16.95

Grades: 3 4 5 6   **398.22**

1. Arthurian romances 2. Gareth (Legendary character)

ISBN 0-8234-0787-X

LC 89-11215

A retelling of the Arthurian legend of how Sir Gareth becomes a knight and rescues the lady imprisoned by the fearsome Red Knight of the Red Plain

"Hyman's richly romantic illustrations are lush watercolors, framed and broken with framed insets for closeups and framed text inside the panoramic picture. The format is horizontal, capturing the sweep of the story. While not a tale of King Arthur, it's a wonderful taste of Arthurian legend, hopefully whetting young appetites for more." SLJ

Kellogg, Steven

Mike Fink; a tall tale. retold and illustrated by Steven Kellogg. Morrow Junior Bks. 1992 un il hardcover o.p. pa $6.95

Grades: K 1 2 3   **398.22**

1. Tall tales 2. Pioneers

ISBN 0-688-07003-5; 0-688-13577-3 pa

LC 91-46014

Relates the extraordinary deeds of the frontiersman who became King of the Keelboatmen on the Mississippi River

"Steven Kellogg's ebullient retelling of Mike's tall-tale feats—illustrated with large, glowing scenes suffused with blue and yellow and with smaller vignettes emphasizing comic detail—follows Mike's prodigious childhood exploits, his teenage wrestling practice with Rocky Mountain grizzlies, and his years as King of the Keelboatmen, and closes with a final showdown with enormous steamboats taking over the river trade." Horn Book

Yolen, Jane

Not one damsel in distress; world folktales for strong girls. collected and told by Jane Yolen; with illustrations by Susan Guevara. Silver Whistle Bks. 2000 116p il $17

Grades: 4 5 6 7   398.22
1. Fairy tales 2. Women -- Folklore
ISBN 0-15-202047-0

LC 99-18509

A collection of thirteen traditional tales from various parts of the world, each of whose main character is a fearless, strong, heroic, and resourceful woman

"This is a spirited collection with a lively pace. . . . The stories sing and soar in Yolen's supple language, and each is contained enough for a read-aloud." Booklist

Includes bibliographical references

Zelinsky, Paul O.

★ **Rapunzel**; retold and illustrated by Paul O. Zelinsky. Dutton Children's Bks. 1997 un il $16.99
Grades: 3 4 5   398.22
1. Folklore 2. Fairy tales
ISBN 0-525-45607-4

LC 96-50260

Awarded the Caldecott Medal, 1998

A retelling of the folktale in which a beautiful girl with long golden hair is kept imprisoned in a lonely tower by a sorceress

"An elegant and sophisticated retelling that draws on early French and Italian versions of the tale. Masterful oil paintings capture the Renaissance setting and flesh out the tragic figures." SLJ

398.24   Tales and lore of plants and animals

Brett, Jan, 1949-

Town mouse, country mouse. Putnam 1994 un il $16.99; pa $6.99
Grades: K 1 2 3   398.24
1. Fables 2. Authors 3. Storytellers 4. Mice -- Folklore
ISBN 0-399-22622-2; 0-698-11986-X pa

LC 93-41227

"A mouse couple living in a town are enchanted by the simple life of the country, and, while on a picnic, meet a pair of local mice who long for the luxury and convenience of the city. Homes are swapped, but they find that reality is different from their expectations. Both couples end up fleeing from unfamiliar predators—a cat in town and an owl in the country—all the way home. The owl and cat collide, and . . . negotiate a territorial swap of their own. . . . Kindergarten to grade three." (SLJ)

"In Brett's version, the town mice are as charming and naive as their country cousins. . . . Brett's narrative alternates the parallel mishaps of the two sets of mice with lively, smooth writing and a deft touch of humor. . . . The illustrations are rich with meticulous detail." SLJ

DePaola, Tomie, 1934-

The **legend** of the poinsettia; retold and illustrated by Tomie de Paola. Putnam 1994 un il $16.99; pa $6.99
Grades: K 1 2 3   398.24
1. Folklore -- Mexico 2. Flowers -- Folklore 3. Christmas -- Folklore
ISBN 0-399-21692-8; 0-698-11567-8 pa

LC 92-20459

When Lucida is unable to finish her gift for the Baby Jesus in time for the Christmas procession, a miracle enables her to offer the beautiful flower we now call the poinsettia

"dePaola establishes a sense of place in his use of glowing colors and architectural details as he retells another legend of miraculous transcendence." Horn Book

Johnston, Tony

The **tale** of Rabbit and Coyote; illustrated by Tomie de Paola. Putnam 1994 un il hardcover o.p. pa $5.99
Grades: K 1 2 3   398.24
1. Zapotec Indians -- Folklore 2. Coyote (Legendary character) 3. Rabbit (Legendary character)
ISBN 0-399-22258-8; 0-698-11630-5 pa

LC 92-43652

Rabbit outwits Coyote in this Zapotec tale which explains why coyotes howl at the moon

"DePaola's vivid, spicy palette of gold, red, and turquoise tones and his use of folk-art borders evoke the desert setting and complement the broad humor of Johnston's text. A glossary of the Spanish phrases that pepper the illustrations is appended." Booklist

Kellogg, Steven

★ The **three** little pigs; retold and illustrated by Steven Kellogg. Morrow Junior Bks. 1997 un il hardcover o.p. pa $6.99
Grades: K 1 2 3   398.24
1. Folklore 2. Pigs -- Folklore 3. Wolves -- Folklore
ISBN 0-688-08731-0; 0-688-08732-9 lib bdg; 0-06-443779-5 pa

LC 96-34434

In this retelling of a well-known tale, Serafina Sow starts her own waffle-selling business in order to enable her three offspring to prepare for the future, which includes an encounter with a surly wolf

"Much of the broad humor is carried in the lively, colorful illustrations, though there's wordplay aplenty in the text and pictures too." Booklist

Kimmel, Eric A.

Anansi and the magic stick; illustrated by Janet Stevens. Holiday House 2001 un il $16.95; pa $6.95
Grades: K 1 2 3   398.24
1. Folklore -- Africa 2. Anansi (Legendary character)
ISBN 0-8234-1443-4; 0-8234-1763-8 pa

LC 00-39608

Anansi the Spider steals Hyena's magic stick so he won't have to do the chores, but when the stick's magic won't stop, he gets more than he bargained for

"Kimmel tells it with cheerful energy, and Stevens' chaotic mixed-media illustrations, with lots of bright pink and green, show Anansi's friends and neighbors . . . caught up in the mess." Booklist

Anansi and the talking melon; retold by Eric A. Kimmel; illustrated by Janet Stevens. Holiday House 1994 un il $16.95; pa $6.95
Grades: K 1 2 3   398.24
1. Folklore -- Africa 2. Anansi (Legendary character)
ISBN 0-8234-1104-4; 0-8234-1167-2 pa

LC 93-4239

In this African folktale, the trickster hero "Anansi the spider outwits all the great galumphing gullible animals, including Elephant, Hippo, Warthog, and even the stupid king. Hiding inside a melon, the wily spider tricks the animals, one by one, into believing that the melon can talk, and what he says is usually an insult. . . . Ages four to eight." (Booklist)

"The snappy narration is well suited for individual reading or group sharing. The colorful line-and-wash illustrations are filled with movement and playful energy." SLJ

★ **Anansi** goes fishing; retold by Eric A. Kimmel; illustrated by Janet Stevens. Holiday House 1992 un il $16.95; pa $6.95
Grades: K 1 2 3   398.24
1. Folklore -- Africa 2. Anansi (Legendary character)
ISBN 0-8234-0918-X; 0-8234-1022-6 pa

LC 91-17813

This is an African etiological tale explaining the origin of spider webs and playing on the motif of the trickster tricked. Anansi the spider "decides to trick turtle into catching a fish for him. But Turtle has his own plans: 'One of us can work while the other gets tired.' Anansi doesn't want to get tired, so he weaves a net, sets it in the river, and catches and cooks the fish. When the fish is ready, Turtle tells Anansi: 'One of us should eat while the other gets full.' Of course, Anansi wants to get full, so Turtle eats the whole fish. . . . {Anansi} never understands Turtle's deception; however, he does share his newly acquired weaving skills with his friends, and today spiders everywhere weave webs. . . . Ages five to eight." (Booklist)

"Children able to comprehend the wordplay will be delighted when the lazy but lovable trickster figure is outwitted by the clever turtle, and Stevens' colorful, comical illustrations are perfect for this contemporary rendition of the tale." Booklist

McDermott, Gerald
★ **Zomo** the Rabbit; a trickster tale from West Africa. told and illustrated by Gerald McDermott. Harcourt Brace Jovanovich 1992 un il $14.95; pa $6
Grades: K 1 2 3   **398.24**
1. Folklore -- Africa 2. Rabbits -- Folklore
ISBN 0-15-299967-1; 0-15-201010-6 pa
                                                  LC 91-14558
"Like the spare text, the shapes here are boldly controlled—ideal for sharing with a group of very young children. Because of their rich patterns and sharp color contrasts, the images in the gouache paintings, although simple, never become simplistic." Bull Cent Child Books

Paterson, Katherine
The **tale** of the mandarin ducks; illustrated by Leo & Diane Dillon. Lodestar Bks. 1989 un il hardcover o.p. pa $6.99
Grades: 1 2 3   **398.24**
1. Ducks -- Folklore 2. Folklore -- Japan
ISBN 0-525-67283-4; 0-14-055739-3 pa
                                                  LC 88-30484
"A Japanese fairy tale, in picture-book format, about a Mandarin duck caught and caged at the whim of a wealthy Japanese lord. Separated from his mate, the bird languishes in captivity until a compassionate servant girl sets him free. The lord sentences the girl and her beloved to death, but they in turn are freed and rewarded with happiness." Booklist

Peebles, Alice
Demons & dragons; by Alice Peebles; illustrated by Nigel Chilvers. Lerner Publications 2016 32 p. color illustrations (Mythical beasts) (pb : alk. paper) $7.99
Grades: 3 4 5   **398.24**
1. Mythical animals 2. Monsters 3. Mythology 4. Animals, Mythical
ISBN 1467776513; 9781467763417; 9781467776516
                                                  LC 2015002071
In this book, by Alice Peebles, illustrated by Nigel Chilvers,"[s]upernatural fiends and fire-breathing tormentors loom large in myth and folklore. . . . But who would be the hardest to defeat in battle? Which one reigns supreme? Find out about each demon or dragon's features and skills, where in the world they come from, how they rank compared to one another, and how you might defeat them if you ever strayed into their remote realms." (Publisher's note)

"Probably most interesting to readers of horror, these might occasionally spark interest in mythology." SLJ
Includes bibliographical references and index
Demons and dragons

Perrault, Charles
Puss in boots; illustrated by Fred Marcellino; translated by Malcolm Arthur. Farrar, Straus & Giroux 1990 un il $16; pa $8.95
Grades: K 1 2 3   **398.24**
1. Fairy tales 2. Cats -- Folklore 3. Folklore -- France
ISBN 0-374-36160-6; 0-374-46034-5 pa
                                                  LC 90-82136
A Caldecott Medal honor book, 1991
This is a new illustrated version of the French fairy tale in which a clever cat wins for his master a castle and the hand of a princess. "Ages five to nine." (Booklist)

"Opulently designed and handsomely illustrated, this picture book provides a fitting showcase for Perrault's artful tale of deceit and resourcefulness. Unsullied by type, the striking front of the book features a close-up portrait of the cat's face. Befitting a fairy tale, the artwork inside is suffused with a golden light that proclaims the story to be from a sunnier, more dreamlike world." Booklist

Taylor, Harriet Peck
Coyote places the stars; retold and illustrated by Harriet Peck Taylor. Bradbury Press 1993 un il hardcover o.p. pa $5.99
Grades: K 1 2 3   **398.24**
1. Stars -- Folklore 2. Chinook Indians -- Folklore 3. Coyote (Legendary character)
ISBN 0-689-81535-2 pa
                                                  LC 92-46431
"Taylor's batik-and-dye paintings are a good match for the casual, playful rhythm of her retelling." Booklist

Trivizas, Eugene
The **three** little wolves and the big bad pig; illustrated by Helen Oxenbury. Margaret K. McElderry Bks. 1993 un il $18.99; pa $7.99
Grades: PreK K 1 2   **398.24**
1. Fables 2. Pigs -- Fiction 3. Wolves -- Fiction
ISBN 0-689-50569-8; 0-689-81528-X pa
                                                  LC 92-24829
In this original variant on the story of the Three Little Pigs, three cuddly little wolves "go out into the world to build a house for themselves only to be menaced by a big bad pig. . . . {They} use brick, concrete, and steel constructions, but their nemesis is not called big and bad for nothing. With sledgehammer, pneumatic drill, and dynamite, the pig wrecks each structure. 'Something must be wrong with our building materials,' the wolves muse. Their final house is built from flowers, insubstantial yet beautiful. It is their lovely scent that causes the pig to change his nasty ways and all live together as friends happily ever after. . . . Preschool to grade three." (SLJ)

"Trivizas laces the text with funny, clever touches. . . . Oxenbury's watercolors capture the story's broad humor and add a wealth of supplementary details, with exquisite renderings of the wolves' comic temerity and the pig's bellicose stances." Publ Wkly

Young, Ed
Seven blind mice. Philomel Bks. 1992 un il $17.99; pa $7.99
Grades: K 1 2 3   **398.24**
1. Fables 2. Mice -- Folklore 3. Folklore -- India 4. Elephants -- Folklore
ISBN 0-399-22261-8; 0-698-11895-2 pa
                                                  LC 90-35396
A Caldecott Medal honor book, 1993
In this retelling of the "Indian folktale of the blind men and the elephant, seven blind mice approach an elephant, {and} ask what it is. . . . On Monday, Red Mouse feels the elephant's leg and proclaims 'It's a pillar.' On Tuesday, Green Mouse jumps onto the elephant's trunk and decides, 'It's a snake.' On Wednesday, Yellow Mouse checks out

the tusk and says, 'It's a spear.' But on the seventh day, White Mouse scampers all over the creature and puts all the clues together. The author offers this moral, 'Knowing in part may make a fine tale, but wisdom comes from seeing the whole.' . . . Ages three to eight." (Booklist)

"In Young's version of the familiar Indian folktale of the blind men and the elephant, seven blind mice approach an elephant, ask what it is, explore various parts of the beast, and arrive at different conclusions. . . . Many preschool and primary grade teachers will find that the book reinforces their students' learning of colors, days of the week, and ordinal numbers, while heeding the story's admonition not to lose sight of the whole in their enthusiasm for identifying the parts. Graphically, this picture book is stunning, with the cut-paper figures of the eight characters dramatically silhouetted against black backgrounds. . . . At once profound and simple, intelligent and playful." Booklist

398.245 Folklore -- Animals

Breslin, Theresa
An **Illustrated** Treasury of Scottish Mythical Creatures; Theresa Breslin; illustrated by Kate Leiper. Floris Books 2015 192 p. colour illustrations $24.95
Grades: 2 3 4 5 6   398.245
1. Monsters 2. Scotland 3. Mythology -- Encyclopedias
ISBN 1782501959; 9781782501954

In this book of Scottish mythology, "author Theresa Breslin brings together a stunning collection of tales from across Scotland. Alternately humorous, poignant and thrilling, each story is brought to life with exquisite illustrations by Scottish fine artist Kate Leiper." (Publisher's note)

"In contrast to the generous use of white space and the subdued hues used in most of the illustrations, the occasional splash of rich, brilliant colors becomes all the more vivid and dramatic. A memorable collection of Scottish tales, highly recommended for reading aloud." Booklist

Mayor, Adrienne, 1946-
The **Griffin** and the Dinosaur; How Adrienne Mayor Discovered a Fascinating Link Between Myth and Science. Natl Geographic Soc Childrens books 2014 48 p. col. ill. $18.99
Grades: 5 6 7 8   398.245
1. Griffins 2. Dinosaurs
ISBN 1426311087; 9781426311086

"Could Griffins have been real? When [author] Adrienne Mayor carefully read the ancient Greek and Roman descriptions, this mythic hybrid of a lion and an eagle sounded like something people had actually seen." Co-written by Mayor and Marc Aronson, with illustrations by Chris Muller, "Here is the story of one insightful, curious, and determined woman who solved the mystery of the Griffin, and invented a new science. Now she and others travel the world matching myths and fossils." (Publisher's note)

"With the suspense of a detective story, the narrative details Mayor's research process as she consults with experts, conducts fieldwork, and seeks out ancient documents, artifacts, and stories." - PM reviews

398.25 Ghost stories

Schwartz, Alvin, 1927-1992
★ **More** scary stories to tell in the dark; collected from folklore and retold by Alvin Schwartz; illustrated by Brett Helquist. Reillustrated Harper Trophy ed Harper 2010 111 p. ill. (hardcover) $15.99

Grades: 4 5 6 7   398.25
1. Ghost stories 2. Horror fiction 3. Folklore -- United States
ISBN 9780060835217; 0060835214
                                    LC 2010922248
Originally published in 1984 by Lippincott, with illustrations by Stephen Gammell.

This volume contains stories of ghosts, murders, graveyards and other horrors.

"Helquist's new illustrations for Schwartz's classic [collection] of ghost stories inhabit an altogether more benign universe than the nightmarish Stephen Gammell originals. [This edition is] handsome and accessible, ceding the stories themselves pride of place." Horn Book Guide
Includes bibliographical references (pages 105-111).

★ **Scary** stories 3; more tales to chill your bones. collected from folklore and retold by Alvin Schwartz; drawings by Stephen Gammell. HarperCollins Pubs. 1991 115p il music $15.99; lib bdg $16.89; pa $5.99
Grades: 4 5 6 7   398.25
1. Ghost stories 2. Horror fiction 3. Folklore -- United States
ISBN 0-06-021794-4; 0-06-021795-2 lib bdg; 0-06-440418-8 pa
                                    LC 90-47474
Traditional and modern-day stories of ghosts, haunts, superstitions, monsters, and horrible scary things

"The book is well paced and continually captivates, surprises, and entices audiences into reading just one more page. Gammell's gauzy, cobwebby, black-and-white pen-and-ink drawings help to sustain the overall creepy mood." SLJ
Includes bibliographical references

★ **Scary** stories to tell in the dark; collected from folklore by Alvin Schwartz; edited by Rachel Abrams; illustrated by Brett Helquist. Newly illustrated ed. Harper 2010 113 p. ill. (paperback) $5.99; (hardcover) $16.99
Grades: 4 5 6 7   398.25
1. Ghost stories 2. Horror fiction 3. Folklore -- United States
ISBN 9780060835200; 0060835192; 0060835206; 9780060835194
Stories of ghosts and witches, "jump" stories, scary songs, and modern-day scary stories.

"Helquist's new illustrations for Schwartz's classic [collection] of ghost stories inhabit an altogether more benign universe than the nightmarish Stephen Gammell originals. [This edition is] handsome and accessible, ceding the stories themselves pride of place." Horn Book Guide

398.8 Rhymes and rhyming games

Ada, Alma Flor
Ten little puppies; adapted from a traditional nursery rhyme in Spanish. [by] Alma Flor Ada; F. Isabel Campoy; English version by Rosalma Zubizarreta; illustrated by Ulises Wensell. Rayo 2011 un il $16.99; lib bdg $17.89
Grades: PreK   398.8
1. Counting 2. Nursery rhymes 3. Dogs -- Poetry 4. Bilingual books -- English-Spanish
ISBN 978-0-06-147043-1; 0-06-147043-0; 978-0-06-147044-8 lib bdg; 0-06-147044-9 lib bdg
                                    LC 2010015930
Ten little puppies are lost, one by one, for different reasons, until only one little puppy remains.

This is "one of the most popular counting rhymes in Spanish folklore. . . . Vibrant colored-pencil and watercolor illustrations are done in deep hues of green, pastels, and earth tones to create realistic images that capture the spontaneous, playful, and affectionate nature of the pups. The text can be sung or spoken in Spanish or English. The English translation skillfully utilizes rhyme to maintain the story's authenticity while accurately reflecting the original poem." SLJ

Cole, Joanna

Anna Banana: 101 jump-rope rhymes; compiled by Joanna Cole; illustrated by Alan Tiegreen. Morrow Junior Bks. 1989 64p il hardcover o.p. pa $7.95

Grades: 3 4 5   **398.8**

1. Games 2. Jump rope rhymes

ISBN 0-688-08809-0 pa

LC 88-29108

An illustrated collection of jump rope rhymes arranged according to the type of jumping they are meant to accompany

"Heavily inked drawings provide cartoon-style humor; sources for jump-rope rhymes and an index of first lines are appended." Booklist

Delacre, Lulu

★ **Arrorro** mi nino; Latino lullabies and gentle games. selected and illustrated by Lulu Delacre; musical arrangements by Cecilia Esqivel and Diana Sáez. Lee & Low Books 2004 un il $16.95

Grades: K 1 2 3   **398.8**

1. Lullabies 2. Finger play 3. Nursery rhymes 4. Lullabies, Spanish -- Texts 5. Nursery rhymes, Spanish American 6. Bilingual books -- English-Spanish 7. Spanish language materials -- Bilingual 8. Children's songs -- Latin America -- Texts

ISBN 1-58430-159-7

LC 2003-9234

An illustrated collection of nursery rhymes, finger play games, and lullabies from the major Latino groups living in the United States today

"The bright, beautiful oil-wash illustrations . . . reflect the diversity of the Latino experience. . . . The bilingual text appears first in Spanish, with the English translation beneath or by its side. . . . Musical notation and comments about the melodies are at the back." Booklist

Baker, Keith

★ **Big** fat hen; illustrated by Keith Baker. Harcourt Brace & Co. 1994 un il $15; pa $6; bd bk $6.95

Grades: PreK K 1 2   **398.8**

1. Counting 2. Nursery rhymes 3. Chickens -- Folklore

ISBN 0-15-200294-4; 0-15-201951-0 pa; 0-15-201331-8 bd bk

LC 93-19160

"The text is the old rhyme, 'One, two, buckle my shoe,' and the double-page spreads show the hen and her chicks (first appearing as eggs) enacting the words. . . . Children who want to skip the counting altogether can just enjoy the singsong text and the pictures executed in acrylic paints. The big fat hen is very large and quite beautiful, with iridescent green feathers accented with purple and red; her friends are just as lovely, all colors, some with delicate patterns in their feathers." Booklist

Bodden, Valerie

Nursery rhymes. Creative Education 2010 32p il (Poetry basics) $28.50

Grades: 5 6 7 8   **398.8**

1. Nursery rhymes

ISBN 978-1-58341-778-2; 1-58341-778-8

LC 2008009157

This book describes nursery rhymes' "history, characteristics, and variations. Many examples are provided as well as ideas for how children can write their own pieces. The information is accessible, and the writing is sufficiently lively to engage readers. The well-designed pages

feature a variety of art reproductions from different literary eras and some photographs." Horn Book Guide

Includes glossary and bibliographical references

Brown, Marc

Marc Brown's playtime rhymes; a treasury for families to learn and play together. by Marc Brown. Little, Brown and Co. 2013 48 p. (hc) $18

Grades: PreK K Professional   **398.8**

1. Nursery rhymes 2. Finger play 3. Children's poetry

ISBN 0316207357; 9780316207355

LC 2012048542

This book presents "a treasury of twenty favorite finger rhymes compiled and illustrated by . . . artist Marc Brown. These are rhymes to say and sing aloud, each with pictorial instructions for the correlating finger movements. 'Playtime Rhymes' [is designed to] get little hands wiggling, jiggling, pointing, pounding, bending, stretching, and dancing as children animate the rhymes, pore over the vibrant pictures, and share the fun with family and friends." (Publisher's note)

Playtime rhymes

Chapman, Jane

Sing a song of sixpence; a pocketful of nursery rhymes and tales. [by] Jane Chapman. Candlewick Press 2004 61p il $15.99

Grades: K 1   **398.8**

1. Nursery rhymes

ISBN 0-7636-2545-0

LC 2003-69565

An illustrated collection of twenty-five traditional nursery rhymes and stories, including "Jack and Jill," "Wee Willie Winkie," "Little Miss Muffet," "Three Blind Mice," "Goldilocks and the Three Bears," and "The Little Red Hen"

"With clear, bright acrylic pictures, Chapman brings an action-packed collection to preschoolers. . . . The type is large and clear, and lots of boisterous pictures decorate the big, spacious pages." Booklist

Chorao, Kay

The **Baby's** Lap Book; Kay Chorao. Dutton Children's Books 2004 58 p. color illustrations hardcover $18.99

Grades: PreK   **398.8**

1. Nursery rhymes

ISBN 9780525473305; 0525473300

Originally published 1977

"Originally published in 1977 with black-and-white art, this collection of fifty nursery rhymes was first reissued in 1990 with full-color spreads. Designed to be shared with small children, this welcome reissue abounds with mischief, humor, and spirit." (Horn Book)

Cleary, Brian P.

Six sheep sip thick shakes; and other tricky tongue twisters. illustrations by Steve Mack. Millbrook Press 2011 31p il

Grades: 1 2 3   **398.8**

1. Tongue twisters

ISBN 1580135854 lib bdg; 9781580135856 lib bdg

LC 2010014421

This is an illustrated collection of tongue twisters. "Grades two to four." (Bull Cent Child Books)

"This high-energy collection of pleasantly rhythmic tongue twisters features a screwball cast of cartoon animals rendered in digital collages. . . . An appended guide provides tips for creating effective tongue twisters-something readers are likely to try out once they master the satisfying sounds of these silly, slippery, serpentine selections." Publ Wkly

Collins, Heather

Out came the sun; a day in nursery rhymes. Kids Can Press 2007 91p il $19.95

Grades: PreK K

1. Nursery rhymes   **398.8**

ISBN 978-1-55337-881-5; 1-55337-881-4

"Collins arranges 45 mostly familiar nursery rhymes in a sun-up to sun-down romp starring a multi-species stuffed animal family. . . . Collins's watercolors display just enough verve and domestic humor to keep her subjects from turning twee. . . . The manageable size and good-natured fun make this volume stand out." Publ Wkly

Crews, Nina

★ The **neighborhood** Mother Goose; [illustrated by] Nina Crews. Greenwillow Books 2004 63p il $15.99; lib bdg $16.89

Grades: PreK K 1 2 3

1. Nursery rhymes   **398.8**

ISBN 0-06-051573-2; 0-06-051574-0 lib bdg

LC 2003-41763

"Nina Crews' urban photographs and photo montages . . . {illustrate} over forty . . . verses and chants from Mother Goose. . . . Ages two to seven." (Bull Cent Child Books)

"Nina Crews' clear, beautiful color photographs and computer manipulations bring children closeup to people like them. . . . She uses computer tools to combine photos of joyful kids in her Brooklyn neighborhood with all kinds of scenarios, realistic and wild." Booklist

DePaola, Tomie, 1934-

Tomie dePaola's Mother Goose. Putnam 1985 127p il $24.99

Grades: PreK K   **398.8**

1. Nursery rhymes

ISBN 0-399-21258-2

LC 84-26314

This "is a large, ample, unfussy edition of every child's first staple of literature. . . . The neat, flat illustrations are darkly outlined and colored generally in the illustrator's favorite palette of clear pinks, blues, and violets and surrounded with a lot of white space. Each verse is pictured in a simple and unmistakable interpretation. . . . A perfectly basic and lovely Mother Goose, lavish yet simple, and a splendid beginning for the youngest listener." Horn Book

Emberley, Barbara

Drummer Hoff; adapted by Barbara Emberley; illustrated by Ed Emberley. Simon & Schuster 1987 un il $16; pa $5.95

Grades: PreK K 1 2   **398.8**

1. Nursery rhymes

ISBN 0-671-66248-1; 0-671-66249-X pa

LC 87-35755

First published 1967 by Prentice-Hall

Awarded the Caldecott Medal, 1968

"A cumulative folk rhyme is adapted in spirited style and illustrated with arresting black woodcuts accented with brilliant color. The characters who participate in the building and firing of a cannon—'Sergeant Crowder brought the powder, Corporal Farrell brought the barrel,' etc.— are hilariously rugged characters, while 'Drummer Hoff who fired it off stands by, deadpan, waiting to touch off the marvelously satisfying explosion.'" Hodges. Books for Elem Sch Libr

Fitzgerald, Joanne, 1956-

Yum! yum!! delicious nursery rhymes. [compiled and illustrated by] Joanne Fitzgerald. Fitzhenry & Whiteside 2007 un il $18.95

Grades: PreK   **398.8**

1. Nursery rhymes 2. Food -- Poetry

ISBN 978-1-55041-888-0; 1-55041-888-2

This Mother Goose collection pairs illustrated nursery rhymes with the story of a little pig on his way to market. In addition to This Little Piggy, the rhymes include: "Little Tommy Tucker, Jack Sprat, Hey Diddle Diddle, Peter Piper, Pease Porridge Hot, I Eat My Peas with Honey, If All the World were Apple Pie, I Had a Little Nut Tree, Polly Put the Kettle On, Higgledy, Piggledy, Little Jack Horner, [and] Little Miss Muffet." (Publisher's note) "Ages two to six." (Quill Quire)

"A farmer's market is the setting for this charming story, set around 13 well-known nursery rhymes that deal with food. The characters are animals dressed in human clothes. Listeners will have fun hunting for the piggy who appears in every scene. . . . The small pictures, all in light pastels, are beautifully detailed. . . . Subtle humor abounds." SLJ

Galdone, Paul

The **cat** goes fiddle-i-fee; adapted and illustrated by Paul Galdone. Clarion Bks. 1985 un il hardcover o.p. pa $6.95

Grades: K 1   **398.8**

1. Nursery rhymes 2. Animals -- Poetry

ISBN 0-89919-705-1 pa

LC 85-2686

An old English rhyme names all the animals a farm boy feeds on his daily rounds

"Galdone's line-and-watercolor illustrations have all the verve and accessible good humor associated with his work, and the varied and irresistible rhythm of the verses carries the nonsense along at a good pace, enhancing its appeal to the very young. Whether told or sung, this is a diverting selection for preschool story times." Booklist

Three little kittens. Clarion Bks. 1986 un il $15; pa $5.95

Grades: PreK K 1 2   **398.8**

1. Nursery rhymes 2. Cats -- Poetry

ISBN 0-89919-426-5; 0-89919-796-5 pa

LC 86-2655

Three little kittens lose, find, soil, and wash their mittens

"Galdone's characteristically exuberant pen-and-wash drawings fill these pages with feline faces, first rueful then joyful, then repentant, and finally excited about the prospects of catching 'a rat close by.' This is one of those sustained nursery rhymes that initiates youngest listeners into the concentration required for stories, and there's enough dramatic movement and color contrast in the art to hold toddlers' attention." Bull Cent Child Books

Gustafson, Scott

Favorite nursery rhymes from Mother Goose; illustrated by Scott Gustafson. Greenwich Workshop Press 2007 96p il $19.95

Grades: PreK K 1   **398.8**

1. Nursery rhymes

ISBN 978-0-86713-097-3; 0-86713-097-0

This book contains forty-five nursery rhymes. "Age two and up." (N Y Times Book Rev)

"These 45 rhymes include the very well known (Itsy Bitsy Spider) and the somewhat familiar (Hickety, Pickety, My Black Hen). . . . [The illustrations include] an anthropomorphic baking bear, a pelican sea captain, and Peter Piper as a pug on two legs." Publisher's note

★ The **Helen** Oxenbury nursery collection. Alfred A. Knopf 2004 91p il $19.95; lib bdg $21.99

Grades: K 1 2 3   **398.8**

1. Nursery rhymes 2. Poetry -- Collections

ISBN 0-375-82992-X; 0-375-92992-4 lib bdg

LC 2004-58446

"The stories all feature Oxenbury's trademark winsome pencil-and-watercolor pictures. They include such favorites as 'Little Red Riding

Hood,' 'Henny-Penny,' and 'The Three Little Pigs,' and are retold with drama and humor." SLJ

Hillenbrand, Will

★ **Mother** Goose picture puzzles. Marshall Cavendish Children's Books 2011 40p il $17.99

Grades: K 1 2 3   **398.8**

1. Puzzles 2. Nursery rhymes 3. Children's poetry 4. Rebuses
ISBN 978-0-7614-5808-1; 0-7614-5808-5

LC 2010-23111

This is a "collection of nursery rhymes—jazzed up by a rebus format. . . . Playful tweaks in visually depicting both verse and action make this outing special. Each uncluttered, mixed-media spread features a rhyme . . . which appears in large font with pictures in place of some of the words. . . . Gently humorous touches abound. . . . This volume works as a nifty guessing game for early readers . . . and the beloved rhymes and detail-rich artwork should earn the project an enthusiastic audience." Publ Wkly

Hoberman, Mary Ann

Miss Mary Mack; a hand-clapping rhyme. adapted by Mary Ann Hoberman; illustrated by Nadine Bernard Westcott. Little, Brown 1998 un il music hardcover o.p. pa $6.99; bd bk $6.99

Grades: PreK K 1   **398.8**

1. Nursery rhymes
ISBN 0-316-93118-7; 0-316-07614-7 pa; 0-316-36642-0 bd bk

LC 96-34829

"In this expanded version of the popular hand-clapping rhyme, the elephant (who's 'jumped so high' . . ./ He reached the sky/) . . . lands in the middle of a picnic where Mary Mack promises him her silver buttons if he doesn't go back to the zoo. Westcott's loose and humorous illustrations add to the necessarily limited text. A melody line and instructions for hand-clapping are included on the front endpapers." Horn Book Guide

If you love a nursery rhyme; illustrated by Susanna Lockheart. Barrons Educational Series 2009 un il $18.99

Grades: PreK K   **398.8**

1. Nursery rhymes
ISBN 978-0-7641-6186-5; 0-7641-6186-5

"This large-format volume features just a dozen nursery rhymes but illustrates them with grace, style, and imaginative details. Some of the rhymes are featured on single pages, but five appear on double-page spreads accompanied with gatefold pages that, when opened out, move the vertical panels in the picture's central, cur-out oval to reveal a new scene. . . . Well designed and illustrated for active toddlers as well as older preschoolers." Booklist

Kubler, Annie

Hop a little, jump a little! illustrated by Annie Kubler. Child's Play 2010 un il bd bk $4.99

Grades: PreK   **398.8**

1. Nursery rhymes 2. Board books for children
ISBN 978-1-84643-341-2; 1-84643-341-X

"These board books are appealing introductions to nursery rhymes. Most pages or spreads have just one line of text, allowing the soft, lively watercolors to take center stage." SLJ

Pat-a-cake; illustrated by Annie Kubler. Child's Play 2010 un il bd bk $4.99

Grades: PreK   **398.8**

1. Nursery rhymes 2. Board books for children
ISBN 978-1-84643-338-2; 1-84643-338-X

"The rhymes stay true to the originals. One of the best aspects of the illustrations is that many different babies and toddlers are represented, including children with disabilities." SLJ

Lipchenko, Oleg

Humpty Dumpty and friends; nursery rhymes for the young at heart. selected and illustrated by Oleg Lipchenko. Tundra Books 2010 un $17.95

Grades: PreK K   **398.8**

1. Nursery rhymes
ISBN 978-1-77049-205-9; 1-77049-205-4

"Mother Goose rhymes are smartly paired and dreamily illustrated in this beguiling collection from Lipchenko. Each page features two poems, which often have shared elements or themes. . . . Classics are far outnumbered by rarer rhymes of equal charm. . . . The highly detailed and surreal nature of Lipchenko's illustrations will keep readers poring over the pages." Publ Wkly

Long, Sylvia

Sylvia Long's Mother Goose. Chronicle Bks. 1999 109p il $22.95

Grades: PreK   **398.8**

1. Nursery rhymes
ISBN 0-8118-2088-2

LC 98-52311

"Human beings are replaced by animals, reptiles, and insects, all elegantly dressed, in this exuberant nursery-rhyme collection, which includes 82 familiar and less familiar verses." SLJ

Morris, Jackie

★ The **cat** and the fiddle; a treasury of nursery rhymes. Francis Lincoln 2011 il $19.95

Grades: PreK K   **398.8**

1. Nursery rhymes
ISBN 978-1-84507-987-1; 1-84507-987-6

"Animals figure prominently in this collection of 40 nursery rhymes, distinguished by Morris's dreamlike watercolor illustrations. For 'Lavender's Blue' and 'Lilies Are White' a king and queen ride a polar bear, all three crowned with botanicals mentioned in the verse. Later, a woman in vibrant robes knits yarn carried 'three bags full' by her enormous, shaggy black sheep. Morris places nomadic, magisterial figures against pastoral backdrops, peppered with castles and cottages, creating moments of strange, bewitching beauty." Publ Wkly

Moses, Will

Will Moses Mother Goose. Philomel Bks. 2003 61p il $17.99

Grades: PreK K   **398.8**

1. Nursery rhymes
ISBN 0-399-23744-5

LC 2003-731

Folk art paintings accompany this compilation of over sixty of the best-loved Mother Goose rhymes

"In a marvelous match of style and content Moses's . . . sprightly folk-art oil paintings make this a 'must have' Mother Goose volume. The book's tempo is set from the first page, which intersperses thumbnail vignettes with individual rhymes. . . . A turn of the page then blends the vignettes into a full-bleed panorama of busy village life." Publ Wkly

Opie, Iona Archibald

★ **Here** comes Mother Goose; edited by Iona Opie; illustrated by Rosemary Wells. Candlewick Press 1999 107p il $21.99

Grades: PreK K 1 2   **398.8**

1. Nursery rhymes
ISBN 0-7636-0683-9

LC 99-14256

This selection presents some sixty traditional nursery rhymes, including Old Mother Hubbard, I'm a Little Teapot, and One, Two, Buckle My Shoe, accompanied by illustrations of various animals. "Age two and up." (Commonweal)

"Wells's watercolor-and-ink pictures of somersaulting guinea pigs, mischievous rabbits, and fluffy ducklings capture the sheer joy and exuberance of the rhymes. . . . Make room on the shelves for this must-have title." SLJ

I saw Esau; the schoolchild's pocket book. edited by Iona and Peter Opie; illustrated by Maurice Sendak. Candlewick Press 1992 160p il $19.99; pa $9.99

    Grades: Adult Professional   **398.8**

    1. Folklore -- Great Britain 2. English poetry -- Collections

    ISBN 1-56402-046-0; 0-7636-1199-9 pa

                  LC 91-71845

A revised and newly illustrated edition of the title first published 1947 in the United Kingdom

A collection of rhymes and riddles traditionally passed on orally from child to child

"From lamentation, pun, and insult to rebuttal, tongue-twister, and comic complaint, these schoolyard folk rhymes are vulgar, absurd, fierce, and utterly compelling. . . . [The book features] Sendak's wicked, joyful illustrations. Blending the factual and the surreal, the pictures (most in color, some in sepia or in black and white) extend the rhymes with characters and scenarios that are gross and tender. Sendak knows kids' ferocity and their fear." Booklist

Mother Goose's little treasures; [edited by] Iona Opie; illustrated by Rosemary Wells. Candlewick Press 2007 52p il $17.99

    Grades: PreK K   **398.8**

    1. Nursery rhymes

    ISBN 978-0-7636-3655-5; 0-7636-3655-X

                  LC 2007-24959

This is a collection of nursery rhymes featuring such characters as the wee melodie man and Handy Spandy, Mrs. Whirly and little bonny Button-cap. "Age three and up." (N Y Times Book Rev)

"This gem . . . shines with the charm of old-time rhymes and with Wells' beloved animal and child characters, set down in her signature style." Booklist

Over the hills and far away; a treasury of nursery rhymes from around the world. [edited by] Elizabeth Hammill. Candlewick Press 2015 160 p. color illustrations $21.99

    Grades: PreK K 1 2 3   **398.8**

    1. Nursery rhymes

    ISBN 0763677299; 9780763677299

                  LC 2014934992

This children's anthology, edited by Elizabeth Hammill, presents a "treasury of 150 classic nursery rhymes. . . . [It contains] rhymes from the English-speaking world as well as verse that entered English from Chinese, Latino, African, and other cultures. With illustrations from seventy-seven artists, many celebrated throughout the world, and some just emerging, this volume is . . . an adventure in language, image, and imagination." (Publisher's note)

"Hammill's skills as collector are especially sharp in juxtaposing cultural variants of rhymes--for example, a spread with the English Little Miss Muffet includes the Jamaican Lickle Muss Julie, the American Little Miss Tuckett and the Australian Little Miss Muffet, who gets frightened away by a pugnacious wombat rather than a spider." Kirkus

    Includes bibliographical references and index

The **Oxford** dictionary of nursery rhymes; edited by Iona and Peter Opie. 2nd ed; Oxford Univ. Press 1997 xxix, 559p il $55

    Grades: Adult Professional   **398.8**

    1. Reference books 2. Nursery rhymes -- Dictionaries

    ISBN 0-19-860088-7

                  LC 98-140995

    First published 1951

"The novice as well as the professional will find it an enjoyable read, as well as a learning experience." Am Ref Books Annu, 1999

Pinkney, J. Brian, 1961-

    Three little kittens. Dial Books for Young Readers 2010 un il

    Grades: PreK K   **398.8**

    1. Nursery rhymes

    ISBN 0803735332; 9780803735330

                  LC 2009051660

Presents the classic tale of three youngsters who are careless with their mittens, but who turn out to be good little kittens after all.

"Pinkney offers another masterful visual interpretation of a classic narrative. . . . Rendered in graphite, color pencil, and watercolor, Pinkney's sparkling-eyed young cats . . . are almost impossibly . . . cuddly and precious, exuding boundless energy and capricious emotions." Publ Wkly

★ **Pocketful** of posies; a treasury of nursery rhymes. [illustrated by] Salley Mavor. Houghton Mifflin Harcourt 2010 62p il $21.99

    Grades: PreK K   **398.8**

    1. Nursery rhymes

    ISBN 978-0-618-73740-6; 0-618-73740-5

                  LC 2009049700

    Boston Globe-Horn Book Award: Picture Book (2011)

    An illustrated collection of sixty-four traditional nursery rhymes.

"Rarely have classic childhood verses been depicted with so much care and detail—and fabric. Loosely organizing the rhymes over the course of the day . . . Mavor creates a miniature world using wood felt, various stitching techniques, and found materials like acorn caps and seashells. . . . Mavor's intricate and colorful embroidered work of art makes even the best-known childhood poems feel special and new again." Publ Wkly

Polacco, Patricia

    Babushka's Mother Goose. Philomel Bks. 1995 64p il hardcover o.p. pa $7.99

    Grades: PreK   **398.8**

    1. Nursery rhymes

    ISBN 0-399-22747-4; 0-698-11860-X pa

                  LC 94-32332

"Polacco credits her story-telling Babushka as the reshaper of many of the 24 rhymes and stories in this collection, borrowed from such sources as Aesop, Moldavian folktales, and Mother Goose. . . . Preschool to grade one." (SLJ)

"The collection includes original rhymes written by Polacco as well as Ukrainian folktales and retellings from Mother Goose and Aesop that Polacco heard as a child from her own Babushka. The distinctive and humorous folk-art illustrations and delightful verses and stories make this book a joy to share with children." Horn Book Guide

Ranson, Claire

    Sally go round the stars; favourite rhymes for an Irish childhood. compiled by Sarah Webb & Claire Ranson; illustrated by Steve McCarthy. O'Brien 2011 64 p.

Grades: PreK K 1 2 3 **398.8**
1. Nursery rhymes
ISBN 1847172113; 9781847172112

LC 2012418512

This book by Sarah Webb and Claire Ranson, illustrated by Steve McCarthy, is a "collection of favourite nursery rhymes known and loved throughout Ireland. It includes favourite international, British and Irish rhymes as well as special Irish favourites." The book "Includes Sally Go Round the Moon; Diddly, Diddle, Dumpling; Two Little Dicky Birds; Are Ye Right There, Michael?; Half a Pound of Tuppeny Rice; Adam and Eve and Pinch Me; and many, many more!" (Publisher's note)

Ross, Tony

Three little kittens and other favorite nursery rhymes; selected and illustrated by Tony Ross. Henry Holt and Co. 2009 90p il $16.95
Grades: PreK **398.8**
1. Nursery rhymes
ISBN 978-0-8050-8885-4; 0-8050-8885-7

LC 2008-925587

This is a "collection of nearly fifty classic nursery verses. . . . Illustrator Ross has sensibly taken a broad and pragmatic interpretation of the genre, so classic anonymous verse rubs shoulders with Lewis Carroll and lullabies. The presentation is invitingly simple. . . . Ross' visual style remains his usual rumply, comfortable , personable line and watercolor, his figures imbued with a gentle sense of comedy and individuality, and the illustrative vignettes are spirited and deft, sometimes approaching the masterful." Bull Cent Child Books

Schertle, Alice

★ **Pio** peep! traditional Spanish nursery rhymes. selected by Alma Flor Ada & F. Isabel Campoy; English adaptations by Alice Schertle; illustrated by Vivi Escrivá. HarperCollins Pubs. 2003 64p il $14.99; lib bdg $16.89
Grades: K 1 2 3 **398.8**
1. Nursery rhymes 2. Bilingual books -- English-Spanish
ISBN 0-688-16019-0; 0-688-16020-4 lib bdg

LC 2001-51641

A collection of more than two dozen nursery rhymes in Spanish, from Spain and Latin America, with English translations

"Deeply rhythmic verses, compelling rhyme schemes, and words that 'play trippingly on the tongue' characterize every verse. Schertle's excellent English adaptations are not literal translations but poetic recreations. They retain the rhythm, meter, and general meaning of the originals. . . . Escrivá's watercolor and colored-pencil illustrations use brilliant hues and detail to reconstruct a young child's world." SLJ

Seibold, J. Otto

Other goose; re-nurseried, and re-rhymed, re-mothered, and re-goosed . . . Chronicle Books 2010 69p il $19.99
Grades: 2 3 4 5 **398.8**
1. Nursery rhymes
ISBN 978-0-8118-6882-2; 0-8118-6882-6

"In the spirit of Mother Goose rhymes, many of which started as parodies, the funny rhymes and wild, vibrantly colored pictures in this picture-book collection bring the nonsense up to date with technological and cultural references kids will recognize and silliness that is universal. . . . Most if the farce and the wordplay are for sharing and reading aloud with older grade-schoolers, who will best appreciate the satire and puns as well as the busy, full-page computer graphics." Booklist

Taback, Simms

★ **This** is the house that Jack built. Putnam 2002 un il $15.99; pa $6.99

Grades: K 1 2 3 **398.8**
1. Nursery rhymes
ISBN 0-399-23488-8; 0-14-240200-1 pa

LC 00-28057

The cumulative nursery rhyme about the chain of events that started when Jack built a house

"Taback's version of the age-old cumulative rhyme is an explosion of color, energy, zaniness, and pore-over-able detail." Horn Book

★ **This** little piggy; lap songs, finger plays, clapping rhymes, and pantomime rhymes. edited by Jane Yolen; illustrated by Will Hillenbrand; musical arrangements by Adam Stemple. Candlewick Press 2006 80p il $19.99
Grades: PreK K 1 2 **398.8**
1. Songs 2. Finger play 3. Nursery rhymes
ISBN 0-7636-1348-7

An "anthology of approximately 60 lap rhymes, songs, clapping rhymes, and finger and foot rhymes, all presented with explanations and simple instructions for parents to play with their babies and toddlers. . . . Hillenbrand has framed the rhymes with lovely mixed-media pictures in an array of sherbet pastel colors with happy piggy families acting out the rhymes. . . . A delightful accompanying CD includes 13 songs from the text, beautifully done with vivacious accompaniment. The result is a perfect book for one-on-one sharing." SLJ

Tildes, Phyllis Limbacher

Will you be mine? a nursery rhyme romance. compiled and illustrated by Phyllis Limbacher Tildes. Charlesbridge 2011 un il lib bdg $17.95; pa $7.95
Grades: PreK K 1 **398.8**
1. Nursery rhymes
ISBN 978-1-58089-244-5 lib bdg; 1-58089-244-2; 978-1-58089-245-2 pa; 1-58089-245-0 pa

LC 2010007590

"Tildes has compiled and illustrated 18 traditional nursery rhymes that trace an 18th-century courtship to honeymoon of a farmer tabby cat and his long-lashed poodle love. The pastoral scenes of preparation for the nuptials include mice tailors, a piggy florist, and a hedgehog minister. Gouache paintings in pastel colors accompany favorites like 'Hickory, Dickory, Dock' and less-familiar poems such as 'Pretty John Watts.' . . . this picture book offers nursery rhymes in a fresh way." SLJ

Tortillitas para mama and other nursery rhymes; Spanish and English. selected and translated by Margot C. Griego . . . [et al.]; illustrated by Barbara Cooney. Holt & Co. 1981 un il hardcover o.p. pa $5.95
Grades: PreK K 1 2 **398.8**
1. Nursery rhymes 2. Folklore -- Latin America 3. Bilingual books -- English-Spanish
ISBN 0-8050-0317-7

LC 81-4823

A bilingual collection of 13 popular Latin American nursery rhymes

The purpose of this book "is to preserve a unique aspect of Hispanic culture which deserves to be passed down to all children. . . . The illustrations are strikingly beautiful, capturing the rich color and texture of some parts of South America. . . . [But their] homogenized view of Latin Americans can easily lead to the perpetuation of some familiar stereotypes." Interracial Books Child Bull

Trapani, Iza

Rufus and friends: rhyme time; traditional poems extended and illustrated by Iza Trapani. Charlesbridge 2008 33p il $16.95; pa $7.95

Grades: PreK K **398.8**
1. Nursery rhymes
ISBN 978-1-58089-206-3; 978-1-58089-207-0 pa

LC 2007026200

In this collection of tongue-twisting nursery rhymes, the reader is asked to find hidden objects in the illustrations.

"The lively artwork was created using watercolor, ink, and colored pencils. Each actor/pooch is a different breed; they all have priceless facial expressions and vary with the situations. Children will ask for repeated readings as they search for the pictures again and again." SLJ

Rufus and friends: school days; extended and illustrated by Iza Trapani. Charlesbridge 2010 35p il lib bdg $16.96; pa $7.95
Grades: PreK K **398.8**
1. Nursery rhymes
ISBN 978-1-58089-248-3; 1-58089-248-5; 978-1-58089-249-0 pa; 1-58089-249-3 pa

LC 2009-4307

A collection of traditional rhymes illustrated and adapted to a school setting, with hidden objects for the reader to find in the illustrations.

"Many of the source poems will be unfamiliar, but Trapani's inventive and precise verse allows each rhyme to stand on its own. Similarly, her illustrations, in watercolor, ink and colored pencil, are bright and distinct. . . . A winner." Kirkus

Wright, Blanche Fisher
The **real** Mother Goose; illustrated by Blanch Fisher Wright. Scholastic 1994 128p il $9.95
Grades: PreK K 1 2 **398.8**
1. Nursery rhymes
ISBN 0-590-22517-0
First published 1916 by Rand McNally

A comprehensive collection of over three-hundred traditional nursery rhymes

398.9   Proverbs

The **Night** has ears; African proverbs. selected and illustrated by Ashley Bryan. Atheneum Bks. for Young Readers 1999 un il $16
Grades: K 1 2 3 **398.9**
1. Proverbs 2. Folklore -- Africa
ISBN 0-689-82427-0

LC 98-48772

A collection of twenty-six proverbs, some serious and some humorous, from a variety of African tribes

"Illustrated in Bryan's distinctive multishape, multicolor style, the tempera-and-gouache art resembles stained glass. . . . A worthy supplement to cultural studies, this will also inspire students to write and illustrate their own proverbs." Booklist

400   LANGUAGE

401   Philosophy and theory

Lunge-Larsen, Lise
★ **Gifts** from the gods; written by Lise Lunge-Larsen; illustrated by Gareth Hinds. Houghton Mifflin Harcourt/Childrens 2011 90p. $18.99

Grades: 4 5 6 7 **401**
1. Vocabulary 2. Classical mythology
ISBN 978-0-547-15229-5; 0-547-15229-9

LC 2010031635

In this book "[Lise] Lunge-Larsen and [Gareth] Hinds explain what words like echo, grace, hypnotize, and janitor have in common, tracing the origins of common words and expressions to Greek and Roman myths. Readers may know that 'arachnid' derives from the story of Arachne and that modern-day 'sirens' have mythical antecedents, but this collection . . . [also explains] the roots of 'nemesis' (the goddess of justice) or 'tantalize,' after doomed Tantalus. Lunge-Larsen provides additional context, including dictionary definitions, and quotes from children's literature. Hinds incorporates graphic novel—style elements into his . . . illustrations, including dialogue balloons and filmic perspectives." (Publishers Weekly)

"Lunge-Larsen and Hinds explain what words like echo, grace, hypnotize, and janitor have in common, tracing the origins of common words and expressions to Greek and Roman myths. . . . Lunge-Larsen provides additional context, including dictionary definitions, and quotes from children's literature. Hinds incorporates graphic novel style elements into his dynamic illustrations, including dialogue balloons and filmic perspectives. A treat for myth lovers and language lovers alike, this smart and well-executed compilation should provide readers with a deeper understanding of the ways in which language evolves and of the surprising symbolism behind certain words." Publ Wkly

411   Writing systems of standard forms of languages

Agee, Jon
★ **Z** goes home. Hyperion Bks. for Children 2003 un il $16.95
Grades: PreK K 1 2 **411**
1. Alphabet
ISBN 0-7868-1987-1

LC 2002-114205

"The letter Z abandons its allotted spot in the City Zoo sign and heads off in Agee's innovative alphabet book. Children can track the red Z's journey past an Alien, over a Bridge, into some Cake, and over Hurdles until the red-letter moment when it finally finds its way to its similarly colored friends. . . . Each letter is exemplified by a noun . . . but to make matters more interesting, the object is also shaped like the letter. . . . Bold shapes and lines create a clean, comical look." Booklist

Bayer, Jane
A **my** name is Alice; pictures by Steven Kellogg. Dial Bks. for Young Readers 1984 un il $16.99; pa $6.99
Grades: PreK K 1 2 **411**
1. Alphabet 2. Stories in rhyme
ISBN 0-8037-0123-3; 0-14-054668-5 pa

LC 84-7059

"It is a superlative blend of visual and textual nonsense because the visual surprises keep the repetitive pattern in the text from becoming tedious. The verbal parts gradually expand in their ludicrousness, in their cataloging of zany characters and occupations." Wilson Libr Bull

Donoughue, Carol
The **story** of writing; [by] Carol Donoughue. Firefly Books 2007 48p il map $19.95
Grades: 4 5 6 7 **411**
1. Writing -- History 2. Alphabet -- History
ISBN 978-1-55407-306-1; 1-55407-306-5

This is an "introduction to the history of the Roman alphabet. . . . Beginning sections about early civilizations' alphabets, starting with Sumerian cuniforms, include a you-are-there narrative. . . . Later spreads cover European illuminated manuscripts and the development of printing technology. A final section [covers] Chinese characters. . . . Numerous carefully chosen color photos of artifacts . . . greatly enhance the book's appeal." Booklist

Includes bibliographical references

Ehlert, Lois

★ **Eating** the alphabet; fruits and vegetables from A to Z. Harcourt Brace Jovanovich 1989 un il $17; pa $7; bd bk $6.95

Grades: PreK K 1   **411**

1. Fruit 2. Alphabet 3. Vegetables

ISBN 0-15-224435-2; 0-15-224436-0 pa; 0-15-201036-X bd bk

LC 88-10906

An alphabetical tour of the world of fruits and vegetables, from apricot and artichoke to yam and zucchini

"The objects depicted, shown against a white ground, are easily identifiable for the most part, and represent the more common sounds of the letter shown. . . . Both upper- and lower-case letters are printed in large, black type. A nice added touch is the glossary which includes the pronunciation and interesting facts about the origin of each fruit and vegetable, how it grows, and its uses. An exuberant, eye-catching alphabet book." SLJ

Fleming, Denise

★ **Alphabet** under construction. Holt & Co. 2002 un il $16.95

Grades: PreK K 1 2   **411**

1. Alphabet 2. Mice -- Fiction

ISBN 0-8050-6848-1

LC 2001-5210

Companion volume to Lunch

A mouse works his way through the alphabet as he folds the "F," measures the "M," and rolls the "R"

"Fleming has poured colored cotton fiber through hand-cut stencils to make her illustrations, which are thus bold in outline and shape and vivid with an almost incandescent coloring. Although this has the simplicity of many alphabet books, it also has momentum . . . and ingenuity in its execution." Booklist

Floca, Brian

The **racecar** alphabet. Atheneum Bks. for Young Readers 2003 un il $15.95

Grades: PreK K 1 2   **411**

1. Alphabet 2. Automobile racing -- Fiction

ISBN 0-689-85091-3

LC 2002-2198

Automobile races highlight the letters of the alphabet

"The alphabetical text often uses alliterative phrases. . . . Although a single race appears to proceed throughout the book, the cars, drivers, tracks, and spectators change considerably from the book's opening in 1901 . . . to the conclusion in 2001. . . . Large in scale, the ink-and-watercolor artwork is bold enough to share with a story hour or classroom group, yet young racing fans will find the details absorbing. Floca's introductory note on the history of racing may interest them as well." Booklist

Jeffrey, Laura S.

All about Braille; reading by touch. Enslow Publishers 2004 48p il (Transportation & communication series) lib bdg $23.93

Grades: 2 3 4   **411**

1. Blind -- Books and reading

ISBN 0-7660-2184-X

LC 2003-17617

This offers a brief history of braille, describes the braille alphabet and how it is used for communication for the blind.

Includes glossary and bibliographical references

Johnson, Stephen

★ **Alphabet** city; [by] Stephen T. Johnson. Viking 1995 un il $16.99; pa $6.99

Grades: PreK K 1   **411**

1. Alphabet

ISBN 0-670-85631-2; 0-14-055904-3 pa

LC 95-12335

A Caldecott Medal honor book, 1995

"Only after careful scrutiny will viewers realize that these arresting images aren't photographs but compositions of pastels, watercolors, gouache and charcoal. A visual tour de force, Johnson's ingenious alphabet book transcends the genre by demanding close inspection of not just letters, but the world." Publ Wkly

Lobel, Anita

Alison's zinnia. Greenwillow Bks. 1990 un il hardcover o.p. pa $6.99

Grades: PreK K 1 2   **411**

1. Alphabet 2. Flowers -- Fiction

ISBN 0-688-08865-1; 0-688-14737-2 pa

LC 89-23700

Alison acquired an amaryllis for Beryl who bought a begonia for Crystal—and so on through the alphabet, as full-page illustrations are presented of each flower. "Preschool to grade two." (SLJ)

"More than two dozen little girls, a full alphabet of them, pick flowers for their friends: 'Alison acquired an Amaryllis for Beryl' and 'Nancy noticed a Narcissus for Olga' and so on till 'Zena zeroed in on a Zinnia for Alison.' Underneath each large handsome floral illustration is a smaller picture of the named child and her flower. Charming." N Y Times Book Rev

Macdonald, Suse

Alphabatics. Bradbury Press 1986 un il $19.95; pa $7.99

Grades: PreK K 1 2   **411**

1. Alphabet

ISBN 0-02-761520-0; 0-689-71625-7 pa

LC 85-31429

A Caldecott Medal honor book, 1987

In this book the letters of the alphabet are transformed and incorporated into twenty-six illustrations, so that the hole in "b" becomes a balloon and "y" turns into the head of a yak. "Ages two to five." (Christ Sci Monit)

MacDonald "maneuvers each letter to create a visual image as well as an object that begins with that letter." Child Book Rev Serv

Pelletier, David

The **graphic** alphabet. Orchard Bks. 1996 un il $17.95

Grades: PreK K 1 2   **411**

1. Alphabet

ISBN 0-531-36001-6

LC 96-4001

A Caldecott Medal honor book, 1997

For this "alphabet book, {Pelletier} decided that 'the illustration of the letterform had to retain the natural shape of the letter as well as represent the meaning of the word.'" (Publisher's note) "Ages four to eight." (N Y Times Book Rev)

In this alphabet book "a stylized letter Y, pink against a black background, is turned on its side and looks like a mouth open in a yawn. . . . The letter Q is repeated in squares, becoming a handsome quilt, and a three-dimensional golden H hovers over a darkened sky. Even for those who know their letters very well, some of the pictures demand a second look before the artist's view is clear. But that's the point; things can be more than or different from what they seem. An engaging book that will certainly have art-class relevance." Booklist

Robb, Don

★ **Ox,** house, stick; the history of our alphabet. illustrated by Anne Smith. Charlesbridge 2007 48p il $16.95; pa $7.95

Grades: 4 5 6 7   **411**

   1. Writing -- History 2. Alphabet -- History

   ISBN 978-1-57091-609-0; 978-1-57091-610-6 pa

LC 2005-06015

"Robb traces the history of each letter from its origin to its modern appearance in the Roman alphabet. He explains the birth of writing in pictogram form and the eventual transition to written symbols that stand for sounds. . . . Smith's whimsical paintings are a fitting companion to Robb's lighthearted text." SLJ

Van Allsburg, Chris

   The **Z** was zapped; a play in twenty-six acts. performed by the Caslon Players; written and directed by Chris Van Allsburg. Houghton Mifflin 1987 un il $18.95

Grades: K 1 2 3   **411**

   1. Alphabet

   ISBN 0-395-44612-0

LC 87-14988

One by one the letters of the alphabet appear on stage, where each suffers a mishap, from "A was in an avalanche" to "Z was zapped." "Ages five to eight years." (Bull Cent Child Books)

"Children can try to guess what action has occured, thereby increasing their vocabulary and the fun, or they can turn the page and read the text, or better yet—do both. This clever romp resembles old vaudeville theater, with one curious act following the next." SLJ

Werner, Sharon

   Alphabeasties and other amazing types; by Sharon Werner and Sarah Forss. Blue Apple Books 2009 un il $19.99

Grades: K 1 2 3   **411**

   1. Animals 2. Alphabet

   ISBN 978-1-934706-78-7; 1-934706-78-7

LC 2009-12599

"An alphabet of animals is presented, each one cleverly composed of its initial letter in a typeface that often suits the characteristics of that creature—a spiky alligator, shaggy sheep, etc. Foldout pages allow for the impressive height of the giraffe or the length of the alligator to be revealed. . . . Young readers will enjoy the animals while older children will have a greater appreciation for the book's artistry." SLJ

413 Dictionaries of standard forms of languages

Evans, Lezlie

   Can you greet the whole wide world? 12 common phrases in 12 different languages. by Lezlie Evans; illustrated by Denis Roche. Houghton Mifflin 2006 un il $16

Grades: K 1 2 3   **413**

   1. Vocabulary 2. Polyglot materials

   ISBN 0-618-56327-X

LC 2005020612

Introduces young readers to common phrases such as "good morning," "thank you," and "please" in German, Hebrew, Spanish, Arabic, Russian, Hindi, Chinese, Zulu, Japanese, Italian, French, and Portuguese.

"This book is a great way to introduce the many similarities and interests of children around the world. . . . Flat, cartoon-style illustrations done in bright colors reinforce action and concepts." SLJ

Includes bibliographical references

Ogburn, Jacqueline K.

   Little treasures; endearments from around the world. Houghton Mifflin 2012 il $16.99

Grades: PreK K 1 2   **413**

   1. Love 2. Polyglot materials

   ISBN 978-0-547-42862-8; 0-547-42862-6

"Ogburn and Raschka give families a whole new vocabulary with which to express their love, exploring terms of endearment used around the globe. Impish, doe-eyed figures rendered in broad, calligraphic brushstrokes wear with pride terms like 'ducky,' used in England, and 'kullanmuru,' which means 'nugget of gold' in Finland. Raschka forgoes painting his characters with black, brown, or white skin, instead using gleeful pinks, blues, teals, and greens. The phrases appear both in English and in their original languages . . . with phonetic pronunciations provided. . . . The message about familial love being a universal human trait is clearly and joyfully articulated; it's hard to imagine a sweeter concept." Publ Wkly

Padmanabhan, Manjula

   I am different; can you find me? Charlesbridge Publishing 2011 un il $16.95; pa $7.95

Grades: K 1 2 3   **413**

   1. Vocabulary 2. Picture puzzles 3. Polyglot materials 4. Language and culture

   ISBN 978-1-57091-639-7; 1-57091-639-X; 978-1-57091-640-3 pa; 1-57091-640-3 pa

LC 2010007579

First published in India

"An informational picture book presenting diverse languages to child readers, this offering . . . is a tour de force. Each page opening includes a brightly colored picture puzzle image with one item differing from the others, accompanied by the question 'Can you find me?' written in one of 16 languages from page to page and supported by phonetic pronunciation guides. Supplemental text provides information about each language, including words potentially familiar to English speakers . . . or words and phrases for readers to learn. . . . The resulting whole broadens readers' awareness of how languages evolve and adopt words from one another. . . . A substantive, engaging title." Kirkus

Park, Linda Sue

   Mung-mung! a foldout book of animal sounds. illustrated by Diane Bigda. Charlesbridge 2004 un il $9.95

Grades: K 1 2   **413**

   1. Vocabulary 2. Polyglot materials

   ISBN 1-57091-486-9

LC 2003-3765

"A multilingual guessing game for the youngest children. Each spread begins with the question, 'What kind of animal says.' and features a variety of sounds in playful handwritten typefaces. Opening a flap reveals the answer. Several languages from Europe, Asia, and the Middle East are included, as well as the sound in English to tip off youngsters. Bigda's cotton-candy-colored gouache artwork displays a lightness of line and a jazzy, freeform feel that blends well with the simple fare." SLJ

   Yum! Yuck! a foldout book of people sounds from around the world. [by] Linda Sue Park, Julia Durango; illustrated by Sue Rama. Charlesbridge 2005 un il $9.95

Grades: K 1 2 **413**
1. Vocabulary 2. Polyglot materials
ISBN 1-57091-659-4

LC 2004-18955

Presenting sounds that people make to utter or cry out abruptly in various languages to express such emotion as distaste, excitement, and surprise

"This original offering is a delightful addition to the canon of multicultural picture books and a fun read-aloud guessing game." SLJ

Stojic, Manya
Hello world! greetings in 42 languages around the globe! Scholastic 2002 38p il $14.95
Grades: K 1 2 **413**
1. Vocabulary 2. Polyglot materials
ISBN 0-439-36202-4

LC 2001-43615

Children from around the world say "hello" in forty-two languages, from Amharic to Zulu

"Greetings appear with a bold nearly full-page acrylic painting of a child. . . . This deceivingly simple book encourages interest in and awareness of other languages." SLJ

Weinstein, Ellen
Everywhere the cow says Moo! [by] Ellen Weinstein; illustrated by Kenneth Andersson. Boyds Mills Press 2008 un il $14.95
Grades: PreK K **413**
1. Vocabulary 2. Polyglot materials
ISBN 978-1-59078-458-7; 1-59078-458-8

LC 2007-17566

"Via simple text and illustrations, children are told what a dog, frog, duck, rooster, and cow say in English, Spanish, French, and Japanese. . . . Each phrase has its own page featuring the animal and an iconic item (the Eiffel Tower, a bullfighter, etc.). . . . The spare and colorful cartoon-like pictures mix the look of folk art and digital precision. Bold primary colors and heavy black lines abound. A glossary includes proper and phonetic spellings." SLJ

Includes glossary

419 Sign languages

Ault, Kelly
★ Let's sign! every baby's guide to communicating with grown-ups. written by Kelly Ault; illustrated by Leo Landry. Houghton Mifflin Co. 2005 77p il $17
Grades: PreK K 1 **419**
1. Sign language
ISBN 0-618-50774-4

"After a brief and informative introduction that details the benefits of using sign language with babies, Ault presents three simple stories: Mealtime, Playtime, and Bedtime. . . . Landry's pencil-and-watercolor illustrations are child-friendly, and his depictions of the signs are both appealing and informative. . . . The signs are well chosen to reflect a child's world." SLJ

Gordon, Jean M.
★ The Gallaudet children's dictionary of American Sign Language; Jean Gordon, editorial Consultant; color illustrations by Debbie Tilley; sign illustrations by Peggy Swartzel Lott, Daniel Renner, and Rob Hills. Gallaudet University Press 2014 384 p. illustrations (some color) (hardcover : alk. paper) $39.95
Grades: K 1 2 3 4 **419**
1. Deaf children 2. Sign language -- Dictionaries 3. American

Sign Language -- Dictionaries 4. Deaf children -- United States -- Education
ISBN 1563686317; 9781563686313

LC 2014004275

This book, Jean M. Gordon, "is a bilingual dictionary that serves a twofold purpose-to increase and improve deaf children's English vocabulary skills and to teach American Sign Language to hearing children. . . . This dictionary will help deaf children make the connections between the signs they already know and the written English words that express the same concept. . . . Hearing children will learn a new language and a new way to communicate." (Publisher's note)

"This long-anticipated and colorfully designed reference work is the first comprehensive American Sign Language dictionary for children published to date. It boasts more than 1,000 signs and includes a searchable DVD, which features young native signers demonstrating each sign and 150 of the practice sentences... The comprehensive introduction relays important information about ASL, including regional differences, and explains the arrows used to depict the motions of the signs. Highly recommended." SLJ

Children's dictionary of American Sign Language

Heller, Lora
★ Sign language for kids; a fun & easy guide to American sign language. [by] Lora Heller. Sterling 2004 95p il $14.95
Grades: 3 4 5 6 **419**
1. Sign language
ISBN 1-4027-0672-3

LC 2003-19011

Color photos illustrate sign language for numbers, letters, colors, feelings, animals, and clothes

"Clear color photos and simple text combine to form an excellent introduction to American Sign Language (ASL)." SLJ

Lowenstein, Felicia
All about sign language; talking with your hands. Enslow Publishers 2004 48p il (Transportation & communication series) lib bdg $23.93
Grades: 2 3 4 **419**
1. Sign language
ISBN 0-7660-2028-2

LC 2003-26608

This discusses "how sign language came about, the jobs where it is useful to know sign language, and people who are important to sign language. Also {includes} the manual alphabet." Publisher's note

Includes glossary and bibliographical references

Warner, Penny
Signing fun; American sign language vocabulary, phrases, games & activities. illustrated by Paula Gray. Gallaudet Univ. Press 2006 225p il pa $19.95
Grades: 4 5 6 7 8 **419**
1. Sign language
ISBN 1-56368-292-3

"This book is a great resource for readers who want to learn more signs, or for teachers and librarians looking for fun ways to share them with kids." SLJ

420 Specific languages

Dubosarsky, Ursula
The word snoop; illustrated by Tohby Riddle. Dial Books 2009 246p il $16.99

Grades: 5 6 7 8 **420**
1. English language -- History
ISBN 978-0-8037-3406-7; 0-8037-3406-9

LC 2009-8306

First published 2008 in Australia with title: The word spy

A tour of the English language from the beginning of the alphabet in 4000 BC to modern text messaging and emoticons

"Short chapters, clear explanations, and humorous examples bring the subject to life, while word puzzles and coded messages at the end of each section invite reader participation. The attractive design adds to the appeal." Booklist

422 Etymology of standard English

Baker, Rosalie F.

In a word; 750 words and their fascinating stories and origins. by Rosalie Baker; illustrated by Tom Lopes. Cobblestone Pub. 2003 221p il $17.95
Grades: 5 6 7 8 **422**
1. English language -- Etymology
ISBN 0-8126-2710-5

LC 2003-25582

"The entries in this book discuss the meanings and derivations of 750 words and phrases. . . . While exploring word origins, Baker also touches on interesting facets of European history and Greek mythology. The jaunty illustrations are reproduced in black and shades of gray. . . . This informative book fosters an appreciation for the richness of the English language." Booklist

423 Dictionaries of standard English

★ The **American** Heritage children's dictionary; by the editors of the American Heritage dictionaries. Houghton Mifflin Harcourt 2010 885 p. $19.95
Grades: 3 4 5 6 **423**
1. Vocabulary 2. Encyclopedias and dictionaries 3. English language -- Dictionaries
ISBN 0547212550; 0547659555; 9780547212555; 9780547659558

LC 2009012324

This book is a dictionary for children. It "covers all the vocabulary young readers need today. More than 2,000 new words and senses" are included. It's an "illustrated reference book including an A-Z vocabulary listing, a thesaurus, and special sections on synonyms, word histories, vocabulary builders, and phonics." (Publisher's note)

★ The **American** Heritage first dictionary; rev ed; Houghton Mifflin 2009 405p il $17.95
Grades: PreK K 1 2 **423**
1. Reference books 2. English language -- Dictionaries
ISBN 978-0-547-21597-6; 0-547-21597-5
First published 2007

This dictionary includes more than 2,000 entry words, and 850 full-color photographs and drawings

Bollard, John K.

Scholastic children's thesaurus; illustrated by Mike Reed. [new and updated ed]; Scholastic Reference 2006 240p il $16.99

Grades: 4 5 6 7 **423**
1. Reference books 2. English language -- Synonyms and antonyms
ISBN 0-43979-831-0

LC 2005050010

First published 1998

An illustrated thesaurus for young readers defines more than five hundred headwords and 2,500 synonyms, providing example sentences for each synonym and including an extensive cross-referencing index.

DK Merriam-Webster children's dictionary; rev ed; Dorling Kindersley 2005 911p il map $19.99
Grades: 3 4 5 6 **423**
1. Reference books 2. English language -- Dictionaries
ISBN 0-7566-1143-1
First published 2000

Presents definitions for over 32,000 entries and includes some 3,000 illustrations interspersed throughout the text

Foster, John

Barron's junior rhyming Dictionary; illustrated by Melanie Williamson and Rupert Van Wyk. Barron's 2006 160p il pa $12.99
Grades: 3 4 5 **423**
1. Poetics 2. Reference books 3. English language -- Rhyme
ISBN 0-7641-3424-8
First published 2005 in the United Kingdom with title: Oxford junior rhyming dictionary

"Young poets will have fun perusing this book in search of the perfect rhyme. . . . Short rhymes scattered throughout are likely to encourage and inspire readers to try their hand at creating their own poems. [Illustrated with] fanciful cartoons. . . . Tips for writing limericks, nonsense nursery rhymes, and various other rhymes are included in this useful resource." SLJ

Hellweg, Paul

★ The **American** Heritage Children's Thesaurus; by Paul Hellweg with the editors of the American Heritage dictionaries. Houghton Mifflin Harcourt 2012 280 p. il $18.95
Grades: 3 4 5 6 **423**
1. Vocabulary 2. English language -- Synonyms and antonyms
ISBN 0395849772; 0547659547; 9780547659541

LC 9712396

This book is a thesaurus for children. The "entries appear in dark purple type and are followed by the part of speech in smaller italic black type. A solid diamond then indicates in bold type the best choices of synonyms. Next, an open diamond gives other synonyms that don't fit the example sentence as well as the first group or are related words. Lastly, a sentence is given as a usage example. If a word can be more than one part of speech, each part is treated separately." (School Library Journal)

"Each entry word is printed in dark purple, followed by part of speech. Best choices are listed first, followed by other choices. . . . Homographs are entered separately and are numbered. . . . Recommended for breadth, attractiveness, and usefulness." Booklist

Hillerich, Robert L.

★ The **American** Heritage picture dictionary; illustrations by Maggie Swanson. Houghton Mifflin Harcourt 2012 138 p. col il $15.95
Grades: K 1 2 **423**
1. Picture dictionaries 2. Picture books for children 3. Encyclopedias and dictionaries 4. Picture dictionaries, English
ISBN 0547659571; 9780547659572

LC 8615279

This book was "created especially for preschoolers and children in the first years of school." This "dictionary lists 900 words, arranged alphabetically and illustrated with lively full-color drawings. The A-to-Z list is complemented by nine thematic illustrations at the back of the book that feature related vocabulary grouped in settings such as a classroom, a supermarket, and an apartment." (Publisher's note)

The **Kingfisher** children's illustrated dictionary & thesaurus; 2nd ed.; Kingfisher 2011 320p il $16.99

Grades: 2 3 4 5   **423**

1. Reference books 2. English language -- Dictionaries

ISBN 978-0-7534-6469-4; 0-7534-6469-1

First published 2003

"One of the challenges when designing books for children is to present information in a way that is appealing to them. The second edition of The Kingfisher Children's Illustrated Dictionary and Thesaurus meets this challenge. The design of the book makes it intuitive for students to use. . . . The illustrations and information on these pages will spark the imagination of the reader. . . . This book would be a good resource for elementary-school-age students and is recommended for both elementary-school and public libraries." Booklist

Kingfisher first thesaurus. Kingfisher 2004 144 p. $10.99

Grades: 1 2 3 4   **423**

1. Vocabulary 2. English language -- Synonyms and antonyms 3. English language -- Synonyms and antonyms

ISBN 075345808X; 0753465868; 9780753465868

LC 2004274244

This book is a thesaurus for young children. An "introduction gives a basic review of specific word choices and synonyms. It includes directions for using the thesaurus and clearly describes the organization by key words and cross references. A discussion of antonyms and homonyms follows with the promise of games on special topic pages." (Children's Literature)

★ **Macmillan** dictionary for children; general editor, Christopher G. Morris. [rev and updated ed.]; Simon & Schuster Books for Young Readers 2007 832p il map $19.99

Grades: 2 3 4 5   **423**

1. Reference books 2. English language -- Dictionaries

ISBN 978-1-4169-3959-7; 1-4169-3959-8

LC 2007297593

First published 1975

"With 35,000 entries and more than 3,000 full-color illustrations, this attractive dictionary is a browser's delight. An introductory section explains how to find a word and includes a helpful spelling guide. . . . Eye-catching feature panels provide detailed information about words of particular interest to children. . . . An accessible and enticing addition." SLJ

The **McGraw-Hill** children's dictionary; by the Wordsmyth Collaboratory. McGraw-Hill Children's Pub. 2003 various paging il (Wordsmyth reference series) $24.95

Grades: 4 5 6 7   **423**

1. Reference books 2. English language -- Dictionaries

ISBN 1-57768-298-X

LC 2002-18796

A dictionary with word histories, synonyms, illustrations, and spelling, grammar, and usage features

"The more than 30,000 entries are easy to read, with definitions arranged in three columns. 'Word History,' 'Homophone Note,' and 'Synonyms' boxes give extra information about some words. . . . This attractive dictionary is a fine work." Booklist

The **McGraw-Hill** children's thesaurus; by the Wordsmyth Collaboratory. McGraw-Hill Children's Pub. 2003 294p (Wordsmyth reference series) $19.95

Grades: 4 5 6 7   **423**

1. Reference books 2. English language -- Synonyms and antonyms

ISBN 1-57768-296-3

LC 2002-18797

Presents an alphabetical list of more than 3000 entries, with explanations of the different meanings of each headword and its synonyms

This is "a valuable addition to the upper elementary classroom, library, or any place where children write or do homework." Am Ref Books Annu, 2003

McIllwain, John

DK Children's illustrated dictionary. Dorling Kindersley 2009 256p il $19.99

Grades: K 1 2 3   **423**

1. Reference books 2. English language -- Dictionaries

ISBN 978-0-7566-5196-1; 0-7566-5196-4

First published 1994 with title: The Dorling Kindersley children's illustrated dictionary

This dictionary offers concise definitions with numerous illustrations, and information about abbreviations, spelling, word building, facts and figures, and countries of the world

Merriam-Webster's elementary dictionary; New and expanded ed.; Merriam-Webster 2009 24a, 824p il map $17.95

Grades: 3 4 5 6   **423**

1. English language -- Dictionaries

ISBN 978-0-87779-675-6; 0-87779-675-0

LC 2008041753

First published 1986 with title: Webster's elementary dictionary

More than 36,000 entries with expanded definitions, usage examples, and nearly 1,300 quotes from classic and contemporary children's literature.

Includes bibliographical references

Merriam-Webster's first dictionary; with illustrations by Ruth Heller. Merriam-Webster 2012 [12a], 436 p.p (alk. paper) $16.95

Grades: K 1 2 3   **423**

1. Vocabulary 2. Encyclopedias and dictionaries 3. English language -- Dictionaries

ISBN 0877792747; 9780877792741

LC 2011017950

This book is "a beginner's dictionary written for children in grades K-2, ages 5-7. Formerly Merriam-Webster's Primary Dictionary, [it] introduces young readers to almost 3,000 words using 1,000 entries—many new and revised for 2012—with hundreds of captivating illustrations by Ruth Heller." (Publisher's note)

★ **Merriam**-Webster's intermediate dictionary. Merriam-Webster 2011 18a, 1005 p.p $18.95

Grades: 5 6 7 8   **423**

1. Vocabulary 2. Encyclopedias and dictionaries 3. English language -- Dictionaries

ISBN 0877796793; 9780877796794

LC 2011534122

This dictionary is "written especially for the needs of students grades 6-8, ages 11-14" and has "nearly 70,000 entries including new words and definitions from the fields of science, technology, entertainment, and health" as well as "more than 22,000 usage examples." The book also "provides definitions, pronunciation, etymology, part of speech designation, and other appropriate information." (Publisher's note)

★ **Scholastic** children's dictionary. Scholastic Inc 2010 800p il $19.99

Grades: 3 4 5 6 **423**

1. Reference books 2. English language -- Dictionaries

ISBN 978-0-545-21858-0; 0-545-21858-6

LC 2010001521

First published 1996

Offers a dictionary that includes pronunciations, definitions, parts of speech, sample sentences, etymologies, synonyms, and cross-references

Scholastic first dictionary; updated ed; Scholastic Reference 2006 256p il $16.99

Grades: 1 2 3 **423**

1. Reference books 2. English language -- Dictionaries

ISBN 0-439-79834-5

LC 2005049911

First published 1998

This offers definitions for approximately 1,500 words, illustrated with approximately 600 full-color photographs, and includes alternate forms for nouns, verbs, and adjectives, illustrative example sentences, and a phonetic pronunciation guide for each word

Scholastic first picture dictionary; rev ed; Scholastic Reference 2009 92p il $15.99

Grades: PreK K 1 **423**

1. Reference books 2. Picture dictionaries 3. English language -- Dictionaries

ISBN 978-0-545-13769-0; 0-545-13769-1

First published 2005

This visual dictionary "features more than 700 clearly labeled images of inanimate objects, food items and living things. A section called 'The Living Room' contains common items including a remote control, telephone and DVD player.... The artwork (and assorted reader-directed questions) will engage the curious." Publ Wkly

Seuss

The **Cat** in the Hat beginner book dictionary; by the Cat himself and P. D. Eastman. Beginner Bks. 1964 133p il $21

Grades: K 1 2 3 **423**

1. Reference books 2. Picture dictionaries 3. English language -- Dictionaries

ISBN 0-394-81009-0; 978-0-394-91009-3

"This alphabetically arranged dictionary, illustrated with rollicking funny drawings, explains word meanings with sentences and pictures. It intends to help pre-schoolers 'recognize, remember, and really enjoy a basic vocabulary of 1,350 words.' Despite its age, this book will still appeal to young children." Peterson. Ref Books for Child. 4th edition

Terban, Marvin

Mad as a wet hen! and other funny idioms; illustrated by Giulio Maestro. Clarion Bks. 1987 64p il hardcover o.p. pa $7.95

Grades: 3 4 5 **423**

1. English language -- Idioms 2. English language -- Terms and phrases

ISBN 0-89919-479-6 pa

LC 86-17575

Illustrates and explains over 100 common English idioms, in categories including animals, body parts, and colors

"Maestro's two-color cartoonlike illustrations are amusing and informative themselves, providing visual clues that support the textual explanations.... Although some of the expressions included are dated, the alphabetical index enables teachers and librarians to pick and choose."

This book might be particularly beneficial in schools having a large ESL program, especially for older, more advanced students." SLJ

★ **Scholastic** dictionary of idioms; new & updated; Scholastic 2006 298p il pa $19.85

Grades: 4 5 6 7 **423**

1. Reference books 2. English language -- Idioms

ISBN 978-0-439-77083-5 pa; 0-439-77083-1 pa

First published 1996

This "introduction to American slang and phrase origins identifies and defines more than six hundred commonly used idioms, complementing the entries with .... sample sentences and . . . illustrations." Publisher's note

Webster's New World children's dictionary; editor in chief, Michael Agnes. 2nd ed., rev.; Wiley Pub. 2006 928p il map $17.95

Grades: 3 4 5 6 **423**

1. Reference books 2. English language -- Dictionaries

ISBN 978-0-471-78688-7; 0-471-78688-8

LC 2005053750

First published 1991

This dictionary includes more than 33,000 entries, more than 800 notes and tips on synonyms, homonyms, prefixes, spelling, and word histories, over 750 photographs and illustrations, a thesaurus, an album of U.S. presidents, tables of weights and measures, an atlas of the world, and an album of U.S. states

"This dictionary is almost three reference books in one. . . . [It] is enjoyable to read and makes learning easy." Libr Media Connect

425 Grammar of standard English

Cleary, Brian P.

But and for, yet and nor; what is a conjunction? illustrated by Brian Gable. Millbrook Press 2010 31p il (Words are categorical) lib bdg $15.95

Grades: 2 3 4 **425**

1. English language -- Grammar

ISBN 978-0-8225-9153-5 lib bdg; 0-8225-9153-7 lib bdg

LC 2009015861

"This colorful book offers information about conjunctions and examples of how they work, all in easy-to-read rhymes. . . . The cartoon-style artwork depicts brightly colored, catlike creatures in human dress dramatizing a variety of situations. The high-energy illustrations rev up the comic intensity of the lightly humorous verse and promise to engage children in the subject." Booklist

Pre- and re-, mis- and dis; what is a prefix? by Brian P. Cleary; Illustrated by Martin Goneau. Millbrook Press 2013 31 p. (lib. bdg. : alk. paper) $16.95

Grades: 2 3 4 **425**

1. Word skills 2. English language -- Grammar 3. Language arts (Primary) 4. English language -- Suffixes and prefixes

ISBN 0761390316; 9780761390312

LC 2013001050

This book, by Brian P. Cleary and illustrated by Martin Goneau, is part of the Words are CATegorical series. It "presents the concept of prefixes for young readers. For easy identification, key prefixes appear in color and comical cats reinforce each idea. [It] turns traditional grammar lessons on end!." (Publisher's note)

Heller, Ruth

Fantastic! wow! and unreal! a book about interjections and conjunctions. written and illustrated by Ruth Heller. Grosset & Dunlap 1998 un il hardcover o.p. pa $7.99

Grades: K 1 2   **425**

1. English language -- Grammar

ISBN 0-448-41862-2; 0-698-11875-8 pa

LC 98-36361

Rhyming text and illustrations introduce and explain various interjections and conjunctions, including "awesome," "alas," and "yet."

Lawlor, Laurie

Muddy as a duck puddle and other American similes; illustrated by Ethan Long. Holiday House 2010 un il $16.95

Grades: 1 2 3   **425**

1. Simile

ISBN 978-0-8234-2229-6; 0-8234-2229-1

LC 2009-29944

"Sly and irreverent, the folk sayings collected here, one for each letter of the alphabet, stretch back over history and reflect Americans' restlessness. . . . For each letter, big, clear, brightly colored cartoons show the literal meaning in the imagery expressed in such phrases as 'crooked as a barrel of snakes,' as well as the words' sly double meanings. . . . Kids will relish the boisterous insults and ornery frontier references in both the words and the pictures." Booklist

428   Standard English usage (Prescriptive linguistics)

Agee, Jon

Jon Agee's palindromania! Farrar, Straus & Giroux 2002 un il hardcover o.p. pa $6.96

Grades: 3 4 5 6   **428**

1. Palindromes

ISBN 0-374-35730-7; 0-374-40025-3 pa

LC 2002-101771

This "book on word play is a creative, comedic gem." Booklist

Bacon, Pamela S.

100 + literacy lifesavers; a survival guide for librarians and teachers K-12. [by] Pamela S. Bacon and Tammy K. Bacon. Libraries Unlimited 2009 363p il pa $40

Grades: Adult Professional   **428**

1. Reading 2. Teaching teams

ISBN 978-1-59158-669-2 pa; 1-59158-669-0 pa

LC 2008-45514

"This wonderful professional resource's focus is mainly school librarians and teachers, but it could be used by public librarians to generate ideas for educational programs. . . . This book is an insightful tool that provides the skills and plans for successful collaboration and evaluation of literacy efforts between teachers and librarians." Voice Youth Advocates

Includes glossary and bibliographical references

Bruno, Elsa Knight

A **punctuation** celebration! illustrated by Jenny Whitehead. Henry Holt and Co. 2009 un il $17.95

Grades: 1 2 3 4   **428**

1. Punctuation

ISBN 978-0-8050-7973-9; 0-8050-7973-4

LC 2008018337

"Young readers will receive a better-than-average introduction to punctuation marks and their uses in this cheerfully illustrated collection of poems. Each selection presents an individual punctuation mark

through rhyming verse. . . . Bruno's writing is clear and lively throughout. . . . Bright collages of children of various ethnicities engaged in diverse activities complement the text." SLJ

Budzik, Mary

Punctuation: the write stuff! [created by Basher; written by Mary Budzik] Kingfisher 2010 64p il (Basher basics) pa $7.99

Grades: 4 5 6 7   **428**

1. Punctuation

ISBN 978-0-7534-6420-5 pa; 0-7534-6420-9 pa

"This slim volume uses catchy graphic design and an informal narrative to spark interest in the subject. In a presentation reminiscent of manga and Saturday-morning cartoons, each punctuation mark is introduced as a unique character who conveys his job through chatty dialogue. . . . The book explains the various uses of each mark and some basics of sentence structure." SLJ

Includes glossary

Cleary, Brian P.

Cool! whoa! ah! and oh! what is an interjection? illustrated by Brian Gable. Millbrook Press 2010 32p il (Words are CATegorical) lib bdg $16.98

Grades: 2 3 4   **428**

1. English language -- Grammar

ISBN 978-1-58013-594-8 lib bdg; 1-58013-594-3 lib bdg

LC 2010026263

The "defines an interjection as a 'word or phrase spoken suddenly and used to show emotion,' then demonstrates its uses in a rhyming, rhythmic text. Throughout, the level of Cleary's inventive verbal humor is greatly magnified by Gable's madcap drawings of dressed animals dramatizing the sentences with cartoon-style exaggeration." Booklist

★ **Hairy,** scary, ordinary; what is an adjective? illustrated by Jenya Prosmitsky. Carolrhoda Bks. 2000 32p il (Words are categorical) hardcover o.p. $12.95

Grades: 2 3 4   **428**

1. English language -- Grammar

ISBN 1-57505-401-9; 1-57505-419-1 pa

LC 98-32132

"Descriptive words of many kinds are presented in bouncy, rhyming text. . . . The adjectives are colorfully highlighted and readers will see their function demonstrated in a wide variety of contexts. Little round cats and quirky humans, both with fat noses and wide eyes, humorously illustrate the meanings." SLJ

★ **How** much can a bare bear bear? what are homonyms and homophones? by Brian P. Cleary; illustrated by Brian Gable. Millbrook Press 2005 un il (Words are categorical) lib bdg $15.95

Grades: 2 3 4   **428**

1. English language -- Homonyms

ISBN 1-57505-824-3

LC 2004031106

"Through rhyming wordplay, Cleary explains two parts of speech that are often difficult to understand. . . . Gable took ample advantage of the pairings to create zany cartoons that provide visual clues for readers. The grouping of each set of homophones and homonyms by color is also a helpful tool." SLJ

Lazily, crazily, just a bit nasally; more about adverbs. by Brian P. Cleary; illustrations by Brian Gable. Millbrook Press 2008 31p il (Words are categorical) lib bdg $15.95

Grades: 2 3 4 **428**

1. English language -- Grammar

ISBN 978-0-8225-7848-2 lib bdg; 0-8225-7848-4 lib bdg

LC 2006033800

"A professorial feline opens this offbeat lecture with a definition of adverbs and a color-coded guide to the types found throughout the book. Readers are then drawn into another of Cleary's signature rhyming narratives, which tumbles across each page verbally and visually.... Knob-nosed felines done in a rainbow of colors mime numerous examples of actions that can be performed with adverbial panache." SLJ

The **punctuation** station; illustrations by Joanne Lew-Vriethoff. Millbrook Press 2010 37p il lib bdg $16.95

Grades: K 1 2 3 **428**

1. Punctuation

ISBN 978-0-8225-7852-9 lib bdg; 0-8225-7852-2 lib bdg

LC 2009015860

"Perky rhymes, animal characters, and a chaotic train-station setting provide an entertaining introduction to seven oft-used punctuation marks: periods, commas, apostrophes, quotation marks, question marks, hyphens, and exclamation points.... The young audience will enjoy learning the concepts as they pore over the details in the cheerful, wittily detailed cartoon art." Booklist

Quirky, jerky, extra-perky; more about adjectives. by Brian P. Cleary; illustrations by Brian Gable. Millbrook Press 2007 30p il (Words are categorical) lib bdg $15.95

Grades: 2 3 4 **428**

1. English language -- Grammar

ISBN 978-0-8225-6709-7 lib bdg; 0-8225-6709-1 lib bdg

LC 2006010756

"Cleary offers more examples of the descriptive words in this upbeat, energetically illustrated book. Beginning with a straightforward definition of the word adjective, Cleary takes off with a series of imaginative examples presented in rhythmic, rhyming verses.... Colorful, comical, cartoon-style illustrations help create the madcap quality that distinguishes the series." Booklist

Stop and go, yes and no; what is an antonym? by Brian P. Cleary; illustrations by Brian Gable. Millbrook Press 2006 un il (Words are categorical) lib bdg $15.95

Grades: 2 3 4 **428**

1. Opposites 2. English language -- Synonyms and antonyms

ISBN 978-1-57505-860-3 lib bdg; 1-57505-860-X lib bdg

LC 2005013991

"Cleary describes and illustrates antonyms from the obvious stop and go, yes and no, front and back, fast and slow, to the more obscure: excite and soothe, hefty and diminutive. He elaborates on reasons for celebrating opposites and also describes how to create them through the use of powerful prefixes such as un, dis, im, and non.... The bouncy lettering style enhances the whimsical rhymes and makes for yet another strong addition to collections of books about the English language." SLJ

Stroll and walk, babble and talk; more about synonyms. by Brian P. Cleary; illustrated by Brian Gable. Millbrook Press 2008 31p il (Words are categorical) lib bdg $15.95

Grades: 2 3 4 **428**

1. English language -- Synonyms and antonyms

ISBN 978-0-8225-7850-5 lib bdg; 0-8225-7850-6 lib bdg

LC 2007040360

This book "shows the fun of words with light nonsense rhymes and color cartoons of animal characters that brag and boast, lie and deceive. ... With all the slapstick fun, the pages show and tell about shades of meaning and the importance of choosing just the right word." Booklist

Edwards, Wallace

The **cat's** pajamas. Kids Can Press 2010 un il $18.95

Grades: 3 4 5 **428**

1. English language -- Idioms

ISBN 978-1-55453-308-4; 1-55453-308-2

"Edwards begins this picture book with a definition of 'idiom,' and English teachers will thrill to find a book that deals with this elusive idea.... Edwards's illustrations show the literal meaning, which is effective in its own way.... A list of the real meanings is provided at the end of the book. The illustrations are handsome and detailed, which adds to the ridiculous nature of the literal interpretations. This is a useful book to introduce this figure of speech." SLJ

Heinrichs, Ann

Adjectives; illustrated by Dan McGeehan and David Moore. The Child's World 2011 24p il (Language rules!) lib bdg $27.07

Grades: 2 3 4 **428**

1. English language -- Grammar

ISBN 978-1-60253-425-4; 1-60253-425-X

LC 2010011445

This explains the ways adjectives work in reading, writing, and speaking.

This "tackles the usually humdrum mechanics of grammar using fun examples, silly sentences, and cute little monster artwork.... Through humor and clear and concise examples the sometimes mysterious world of grammar becomes so much easier to understand. Illustrations complement the text well, with silly characters in bright and lively colors speaking sentences using the parts of speech." Libr Media Connect

Includes glossary and bibliographical references

Adverbs; illustrated by Dan McGeehan and David Moore. The Child's World 2011 24p il (Language rules!) lib bdg $27.07

Grades: 2 3 4 **428**

1. English language -- Grammar

ISBN 978-1-60253-426-1; 1-60253-426-8

LC 2010011456

This explains the ways adverbs work in reading, writing, and speaking.

This "tackles the usually humdrum mechanics of grammar using fun examples, silly sentences, and cute little monster artwork.... Through humor and clear and concise examples the sometimes mysterious world of grammar becomes so much easier to understand. Illustrations complement the text well, with silly characters in bright and lively colors speaking sentences using the parts of speech." Libr Media Connect

Includes glossary and bibliographical references

Interjections; written by Ann Heinrichs; illustrated by Dan McGeehan and David Moore. Child's World 2010 24p il (Language rules!) lib bdg $27.07

Grades: 2 3 4 **428**

1. English language -- Grammar

ISBN 978-1-60253-428-5 lib bdg; 1-60253-428-4 lib bdg

LC 2010011458

This explains the ways interjections work in reading, writing, and speaking.

The book is "well organized and attractive, and [injects] humor into what might overwise be [a] fairly dry [subject].... The brightly colored cartoon illustrations are amusing and clearly demonstrate ... [the] part of speech ... being explored. A purple-and-green monster levitates off his chair after spotting a mouse beneath it in Interjections —'Eek!.'" SLJ

Includes bibliographical references

Nouns; illustrated by Dan McGeehan and David Moore. Child's World 2011 24p il (Language rules!) lib bdg $27.07

Grades: 2 3 4   **428**

1. English language -- Grammar

ISBN 978-1-60253-429-2; 1-60253-429-2

LC 2010011459

This explains the ways nouns work in reading, writing, and speaking.

This "tackles the usually humdrum mechanics of grammar using fun examples, silly sentences, and cute little monster artwork. . . . Through humor and clear and concise examples the sometimes mysterious world of grammar becomes so much easier to understand. Illustrations complement the text well, with silly characters in bright and lively colors speaking sentences using the parts of speech." Libr Media Connect

Includes glossary and bibliographical references

Prefixes and suffixes; written by Ann Heinrichs; illustrated by Dan McGeehan and David Moore. Child's World 2010 24p il (Language rules!) lib bdg $27.07

Grades: 2 3 4   **428**

1. English language -- Grammar

ISBN 978-1-60253-430-8 lib bdg; 1-60253-430-6 lib bdg

LC 2010012343

This explains the ways prefixes and suffixes work in reading, writing, and speaking.

The book is "well organized and attractive, and [injects] humor into what might otherwise be [a] fairly dry [subject]. . . . The brightly colored cartoon illustrations are amusing and clearly demonstrate [prefixes and suffixes]." SLJ

Includes bibliographical references

Prepositions; written by Ann Heinrichs; illustrated by Dan McGeehan and David Moore. Child's World 2010 24p il (Language rules!) lib bdg $27.07

Grades: 2 3 4   **428**

1. English language -- Grammar

ISBN 978-1-60253-431-5 lib bdg; 1-60253-431-4 lib bdg

LC 2010011460

This explains the ways prepositions work in reading, writing, and speaking.

The book is "well organized and attractive, and [injects] humor into what might otherwise be [a] fairly dry subject. . . . The brightly colored cartoon illustrations are amusing and clearly demonstrate [prepositions]." SLJ

Includes bibliographical references

Pronouns; illustrated by Dan McGeehan and David Moore. The Child's World 2011 24p il (Language rules!) lib bdg $27.07

Grades: 2 3 4   **428**

1. English language -- Grammar

ISBN 978-1-60253-432-2; 1-60253-432-2

LC 2010011461

This explains the ways pronouns work in reading, writing, and speaking.

This "tackles the usually humdrum mechanics of grammar using fun examples, silly sentences, and cute little monster artwork. . . . Through humor and clear and concise examples the sometimes mysterious world of grammar becomes so much easier to understand. Illustrations complement the text well, with silly characters in bright and lively colors speaking sentences using the parts of speech." Libr Media Connect

Includes glossary and bibliographical references

Punctuation; illustrated by Dan McGeehan and David Moore. The Child's World 2011 24p il (Language rules!) lib bdg $27.07

Grades: 2 3 4   **428**

1. English language -- Grammar

ISBN 978-1-60253-433-9; 1-60253-433-0

LC 2010012344

This explains the proper use of punctuation and why it's important.

This "tackles the usually humdrum mechanics of grammar using fun examples, silly sentences, and cute little monster artwork. . . . Through humor and clear and concise examples the sometimes mysterious world of grammar becomes so much easier to understand. Illustrations complement the text well, with silly characters in bright and lively colors speaking sentences using the parts of speech." Libr Media Connect

Includes glossary and bibliographical references

Similes and metaphors; written by Ann Heinrichs; illustrated by Dan McGeehan and David Moore. Child's World 2010 24p il (Language rules!) lib bdg $27.07

Grades: 2 3 4   **428**

1. Simile 2. Metaphor

ISBN 978-1-60253-434-6 lib bdg; 1-60253-434-9 lib bdg

LC 2010012346

This explains the ways similies and metaphors work in reading, writing, and speaking.

The book is "well organized and attractive, and [injects] humor into what might otherwise be [a] fairly dry subject. . . . The brightly colored cartoon illustrations are amusing and clearly demonstrate [similes and metaphors]." SLJ

Includes bibliographical references

Synonyms and antonyms; illustrated by Dan McGeehan and David Moore. The Child's World 2011 24p il (Language rules!) lib bdg $27.07

Grades: 2 3 4   **428**

1. English language -- Synonyms and antonyms

ISBN 978-1-60253-435-3; 1-60253-435-7

LC 2010012347

This explains the ways synonyms and antonyms work in reading, writing, and speaking.

This "tackles the usually humdrum mechanics of grammar using fun examples, silly sentences, and cute little monster artwork. . . . Through humor and clear and concise examples the sometimes mysterious world of grammar becomes so much easier to understand. Illustrations complement the text well, with silly characters in bright and lively colors speaking sentences using the parts of speech." Libr Media Connect

Includes glossary and bibliographical references

Verbs; illustrated by Dan McGeehan and David Moore. The Child's World 2011 24p il (Language rules!) lib bdg $27.07

Grades: 2 3 4   **428**

1. English language -- Grammar

ISBN 978-1-60253-436-0; 1-60253-436-5

LC 2010011462

This explains the ways verbs work in reading, writing, and speaking.

This "tackles the usually humdrum mechanics of grammar using fun examples, silly sentences, and cute little monster artwork. . . . Through humor and clear and concise examples the sometimes mysterious world of grammar becomes so much easier to understand. Illustrations complement the text well, with silly characters in bright and lively colors speaking sentences using the parts of speech." Libr Media Connect

Includes glossary and bibliographical references

Heller, Ruth

Behind the mask; a book about prepositions. written and illustrated by Ruth Heller. Grosset & Dunlap 1995 un il hardcover o.p. pa $7.99

Grades: K 1 2 **428**
   1. English language -- Grammar
   ISBN 0-448-41123-7; 0-698-11698-4 pa

LC 95-9535

Explores through rhyming text the subject of prepositions and how they're used

"Large, colorful drawings illustrate the words imaginatively." Booklist

A **cache** of jewels and other collective nouns; written and illustrated by Ruth Heller. Grosset & Dunlap 1987 un il hardcover o.p. pa $7.99
Grades: K 1 2 **428**
   1. English language -- Grammar
   ISBN 0-448-19211-X; 0-698-11354-3 pa

LC 87-80254

"In light verse and brightly colored pictures, Heller provides an introduction to a specialized part of speech, the collective noun. She lists and depicts more than 25, including such familiar terms as 'batch of bread' and 'bunch of bananas,' as well as more unusual phrases. . . . The concept will stimulate the curiosity and imaginations of children with an ear for language. The illustrations, containing large, bold objects in simple yet striking compositions, ensure a visually inspiring exploration as well." Publ Wkly

Kites sail high: a book about verbs; written and illustrated by Ruth Heller. Grosset & Dunlap 1988 un il hardcover o.p. pa $7.99
Grades: K 1 2 **428**
   1. English language -- Grammar
   ISBN 0-448-10480-6; 0-698-11389-6 pa

LC 87-82718

This "book explicates and celebrates verbs of all kinds, in ebullient verses which themselves sail and soar. . . . The verses are accompanied by bold, gaily colored graphics that are especially striking for their skillful use of pattern and design." Publ Wkly

Many luscious lollipops: a book about adjectives; written and illustrated by Ruth Heller. Grosset & Dunlap 1989 un il hardcover o.p. pa $7.99
Grades: K 1 2 **428**
   1. English language -- Grammar
   ISBN 0-448-03151-5; 0-698-11641-0 pa

LC 88-83045

"The text begins: 'An adjective's terrific/when you want to be specific/It easily identifies/by number, color or by size/TWELVE LARGE, BLUE, GORGEOUS butterflies.' And there they are, blue and yellow, filling a double-page spread. . . . There is great diversity and technical brilliance in the art work, and the text has rhyme, rhythm, humor, and a very clear presentation of the concepts of different kinds of adjectives and what they do." Bull Cent Child Books

Merry-go-round; a book about nouns. written and illustrated by Ruth Heller. Grosset & Dunlap 1990 un il hardcover o.p. pa $7.99
Grades: K 1 2 **428**
   1. English language -- Grammar
   ISBN 0-448-40085-5; 0-698-11642-9 pa

LC 90-80645

Rhyming text and illustrations present explanations of various types of nouns and rules for their usage

"While the text will be helpful to children struggling with noun usage, the large, bountiful illustrations will appeal to everyone." Horn Book Guide

Mine, all mine; a book about pronouns. written and illustrated by Ruth Heller. Grosset & Dunlap 1997 un il hardcover o.p. pa $7.99
Grades: K 1 2 **428**
   1. English language -- Grammar
   ISBN 0-448-41606-9; 0-698-11797-2 pa

LC 97-10051

Introduces various types of pronouns, explains how and when to use them, and provides whimsical glimpses of what our language would be without them

"Heller has taken a part of speech and made its function perfectly and entertainingly clear. . . . The stylishly drawn, brilliantly colored, double-paged illustrations grab readers and don't let go. The exceptionally fluent, rhythmic text is printed in an unobtrusive font with pronouns highlighted in bright blue." SLJ

Up, up and away; a book about adverbs. written and illustrated by Ruth Heller. Grosset & Dunlap 1991 un il hardcover o.p. pa $7.99
Grades: K 1 2 **428**
   1. English language -- Grammar
   ISBN 0-448-40249-1; 0-698-11663-1 pa

LC 91-70668

"Here the author explains concisely how adverbs answer precisely the questions of How? How often? When? and Where? The adverbs, in capital letters, stand out boldly and cannot be missed. . . . In the large, appealing illustrations, her penguins stand proudly, her pandas eat daintily, and her cat stares piercingly. . . . The cheerful volume . . . offers a clever introduction to kinds of words." Booklist

Hellweg, Paul
   ★ The **American** Heritage student thesaurus; Paul Hellweg, Joyce LeBaron, Susannah LeBaron. Houghton Mifflin Harcourt 2012 vi, 378 p.p $18.95
Grades: 5 6 7 8 9 10 **428**
   1. Vocabulary 2. English language -- Synonyms and antonyms 3. English language -- Synonyms and antonyms
   ISBN 0547659164; 9780547659169

LC 2012462955

This newly updated student thesaurus "includes advice to teen writers about choosing the best word for their purpose, how synonyms are presented in the text, and the use of other words like antonyms. . . . Pages are large, with the entry word in a blue sans-serif type, while the synonyms appear in a smaller black boldface type. An even smaller type is used for each explanatory sentence, followed by antonyms (marked with a blue arrow) where appropriate." (Children's Literature)

Hoban, Tana
   ★ **Exactly** the opposite. Greenwillow Bks. 1990 un il $17.99; pa $6.99
Grades: PreK K **428**
   1. English language -- Synonyms and antonyms
   ISBN 0-688-08861-9; 0-688-15473-5 pa

LC 89-27227

"Using a variety of people, animals, and objects found in outdoor settings of both the city and the country, [the author] introduces and expands on the concept of opposites in this wordless photographic book. The photographs are clear, bright, and enticing. Pairs of opposites are presented on facing pages." SLJ

Jenkins, Emily
   Small, medium, large; a book about relative sizes. illustrated by Tomek Bogacki. Star Bright Books 2011 un il $19.95

Grades: PreK K 1 **428**
1. Size 2. Vocabulary
ISBN 978-1-59572-278-2; 1-59572-278-5

LC 2010050853

"Four colorful mouselike beings of varied sizes represent the concepts of small, medium, large, and extra large in bold, posterlike spreads rendered in black line and swathes of thick, textured paints. Similar characters, larger and smaller, join the original four to expand the notion of size at both ends of the scale (e.g., 'huge,' 'enormous,' 'colossal'; and 'tiny,' 'minuscule,' and 'itty-bitty' and demonstrate how many smaller sizes can stack up to equal one 'colossal' size in a splendid, culminating vertical gatefold. . . . The generous trim size, large font, simple ideas, and eye-popping shapes and colors add up to a cheerful concept book ideal for sharing with a group of young children or as a lapsit." SLJ

L is for lollygag; quirky words for a clever tongue. Chronicle Books 2008 125p $12.99
Grades: 4 5 6 7 **428**
1. Vocabulary
ISBN 978-0-8118-6021-5; 0-8118-6021-3

LC 2007021061

"Budding and accomplished wordsmiths will delight in this specialized dictionary showcasing oft-overlooked gems of the English language. . . . Each definition is related with humor, sometimes including word origination and listing equally interesting synonyms. . . . Black-and-white engravings juxtaposed with cartoons in Picassoesque profile give an old-fashioned yet offbeat air to this unusual compendium." SLJ
Includes bibliographical references

Leedy, Loreen
There's a frog in my throat; 440 animal sayings a little bird told me. written by Loreen Leedy & Pat Street; illustrated by Loreen Leedy. Holiday House 2003 48p il $16.95
Grades: 2 3 4 5 **428**
1. Animals -- Folklore 2. English language -- Terms and phrases
ISBN 0-8234-1774-3

LC 2002-68920

"The sayings are loosely grouped by types of animals—domestic, barnyard, winged, etc.—and each adage is accompanied by a short definition. For example, 'It's raining cats and dogs. It's raining hard.' . . . Children will pore over the pages. The collaboration of text and art makes the volume lively and humorous." SLJ

Moses, Will
Raining cats and dogs; [by] Will Moses. Philomel Books 2008 un il $17.99
Grades: 1 2 3 4 5 **428**
1. English language -- Idioms
ISBN 978-0-399-24233-5; 0-399-24233-3

LC 2008-10339

"In this highly appropriate pairing of folk art and sayings, Moses explains many common idioms. A colorful definition . . . a sample sentence, and one of Moses's old-fashioned Americana-style oil paintings accompany each phrase. The lesson is kept lighthearted through examples that play upon the literal meanings of each phrase, often to comedic effect." SLJ

National Geographic Society (U.S.)
Word book; learning the words in your world. National Geographic 2011 64p il (National Geographic little kids) $15.95; lib bdg $23.99

Grades: PreK **428**
1. Vocabulary
ISBN 978-1-4263-0789-8; 1-4263-0789-6; 978-1-4263-0790-4 lib bdg; 1-4263-0790-X lib bdg

LC 2010049462

Presents hundreds of words with images representing each word, grouped together by such themes as shapes, food, games, pets, music, and seasons.

"Small, clearly labeled photos set against single-colored squares enhance the easy-to-follow design." Horn Book Guide

O'Conner, Patricia T.
Woe is I Jr; the junior grammarphobes' guide to better English in plain English. [by] Patricia O'Conner; drawings by Tom Stiglich. G.P. Putnam's Sons 2007 152p il $16.99
Grades: 4 5 6 7 8 **428**
1. English language -- Usage 2. English language -- Grammar
ISBN 978-0-399-24331-8

LC 2006020575

An adaptation of Woe is I, published 2003 for adults by Riverhead Books
The author "covers pronouns, plurals, possessives, verb usage, subject-verb agreement, capitalization, and punctuation with jargon-free explanations and entertaining examples. . . . She knows her subject, can convey her message with wit and ease, and does it all in a compact, easy-to-read format." SLJ

Reid, Alastair
Ounce, dice, trice; drawings by Ben Shahn. New York Review Books 2009 57p il $15.95
Grades: K 1 2 3 **428**
1. Vocabulary 2. Wit and humor
ISBN 978-1-59017-320-6; 1-59017-320-1

LC 2008050325

A reissue of the title first published 1958 by Atlantic-Little
"'Words have a sound and shape, in addition to their meanings. Sometimes the sound is the meaning.' This 'odd collection of words and names' includes 'light words' (lisssom, sibilant), 'heavy words' (befuddled), and other fascinating categories. The author's poetic lists have been turned into picture-and-word amusement through collaboration with an illustrator whose Lear-like sketches have originality, joy, and absurdity." Horn Book Guide

Roy, Jennifer Rozines
You can write using good grammar; [by] Jennifer Rozines Roy. Enslow 2004 64p il (You can write) lib bdg $22.60
Grades: 4 5 6 **428**
1. English language -- Grammar
ISBN 0-7660-2084-3

LC 2002-156035

This "discusses parts of speech, punctuation, and proofreading. A list of 'Common Grammar Goofs' is appended. . . . Students will find [this book] useful." Horn Book Guide
Includes glossary and bibliographical references

Terban, Marvin
★ **Scholastic** dictionary of spelling; rev ed; Scholastic Reference 2006 272p il pa $9.99
Grades: 4 5 6 **428**
1. Spellers 2. Reference books
ISBN 978-0-439-76421-6; 0-439-76421-1
First published 1998
This spelling dictionary gives instructions for looking up a word the reader does not know how to spell, offers more than 150 memory tricks

to correct commonly misspelled words, explains general spelling rules and their exceptions, and includes sections such as "The Four Longest Words in the English Language" and "The Spelling Words That Made Kids Champions." To aid pronunciation, each word is divided into syllables with the accented syllable in boldface.

Scholastic guide to grammar; [by] Marvin Terban as Professor Grammar. Scholastic Inc. 2011 255p il pa $9.99

Grades: 4 5 6 7

1. English language -- Grammar   **428**

ISBN 978-0-545-35669-5; 0-545-35669-5

This guide to English language grammar covers the parts of speech, sentences and paragraphs, spelling, capitalization, punctuation, communicating ideas through vocabulary, homonyms, homophones, homographs, figures of speech, alliteration, hyperbole, similes, personification, and idioms, and includes a thesaurus.

Truss, Lynne

Eats, shoots & leaves; why, commas really do make a difference! illustrated by Bonnie Timmons. G.P. Putnam's Sons 2006 un il $15.99

Grades: 2 3 4   **428**

1. Punctuation

ISBN 0-399-24491-3

LC 2005-28559

This version of Truss's work on punctuation is intended for children. It includes only the section on comma usage. "Primary." (Horn Book)

"Truss's picture-book version of her adult bestseller tackles the topic of commas and what can go wrong when they are misused. . . . Versions of two identically worded sentences are presented side by side, demonstrating the difference in meaning achieved when a comma is added or subtracted. Timmons's humorous watercolor cartoons bring the point home." SLJ

The **girl's** like spaghetti; why, you can't manage without apostrophes! illustrated by Bonnie Timmons. G. P. Putnam's Sons 2007 un il $16.99

Grades: 2 3 4   **428**

1. Punctuation

ISBN 978-0-399-24706-4; 0-399-24706-8

LC 2006-34456

This is a guide to the use of the apostrophe. "Age six and up." (N Y Times Book Rev)

"This book presents readers with two identical sentences whose meaning changes with the simple placement of the apostrophe. The plural versus the possessive is depicted through lively cartoons illustrating the sentences. Truss . . . . manages to keep her lessons funny and full of kid appeal." SLJ

Twenty-odd ducks; why, every punctuation mark counts! [by] Lynne Truss; illustrated by Bonnie Timmons. G.P. Putman's Sons 2008 un il $16.99

Grades: 2 3 4   **428**

1. Punctuation

ISBN 978-0-399-25058-3; 0-399-25058-1

LC 2007045386

This "emphasizes the importance of punctuation in general. Truss . . . makes the case that careless application can dramatically change one's meaning. To prove her point, she provides contrasting examples of the same sentence, punctuated in different ways. Timmons's charming watercolors make the change in meaning clearer." SLJ

428.1 Vocabulary – English language -- usage

Cleary, Brian P., 1959-

Breezier, cheesier, newest, and bluest; what are comparatives and superlatives? by Brian P. Cleary; illustrations by Brian Gable. Millbrook Press 2013 31 p. col. ill. (Words are CATegorical) (reinforced) $16.95

Grades: 2 3 4   **428.1**

1. Picture books for children 2. English language -- Grammar 3. Comparison (Grammar) 4. Grammar, comparative and general -- Adjective

ISBN 0761353623; 9780761353621

LC 2012019105

This book is part of the Words Are CATegorical series and "presents a quick grammar lesson through a fast-paced, rhyming text and cartoon-style illustrations. The introductory page defines (in prose) the terms 'comparatives' and 'superlatives.' An appended page tells (in prose) how to form comparative and superlative adjectives. And in between come the rhyming verses, briefly explaining these parts of speech and providing . . . many examples." (Booklist)

Escoffier, Michael

Have you seen my trumpet? written by Michaël Escoffier; illustrated by Kris Di Giacomo. Enchanted Lion Books 2016 48 p. color illustrations (alk. paper) $17.95

Grades: K 1 2 3   **428.1**

1. Word games 2. Vocabulary 3. Grammar, Comparative and general -- Word formation 4. Plays on words

ISBN 9781592702015

LC 2016013955

This children's book, written by Michaël Escoffier and illustrated by Kris Di Giacomo, is the final installment of the team's "surprising, clever, and fun wordplay trilogy that includes 'Take Away the A' and 'Where's the Baboon?' Here you will find ridiculously delightful art, an engaging narrative, and wordplay that will keep even preschoolers deeply engaged." (Publisher's note)

"As with the other titles in this clever picture-book series, it works wonderfully for prereaders and readers alike, giving art and text equal footing and boasting an irresistible hook that keeps kids turning the page." Booklist

Take away the A; by Michaël Escoffier; illustrated by Kris Di Giacomo. Enchanted Lion Books 2014 56 p. color illustrations (alk. paper) $17.95

Grades: 2 3 4 5   **428.1**

1. Alphabet 2. Vocabulary 3. Wit and humor 4. Plays on words 5. Grammar, Comparative and general -- Word formation

ISBN 1592701566; 9781592701568

LC 2014014890

This juvenile book, by Michaël Escoffier and illustrated by Kris Di Giacomo "is a . . . romp through the alphabet. The idea behind the book is that within every language there are words that change and become a different word through the simple subtraction of a single letter. In other words, without the 'A,' the Beast is Best. Or, without the 'M,' a chomp becomes a chop." (Publisher's note)

"Amid the flood of alphabet books, now and then one rises to the surface. This one is a prize catch. In a distinctive, refreshing approach, the text takes a word and subtracts one letter, turning it into a different word." Kirkus

Könnecke, Ole

The big book of words and pictures; Ole Könnecke; translated by Monika Smith. Gecko Press 2012 22 p. $14.95

Grades: K 1   **428.1**

1. Children's literature   2. Picture books for children   3. Vocabulary
ISBN 187757905X; 9781877579059

This children's picture book, written and illustrated by Ole Konnecke, "is a large format board book of early concept words and pictures. . . . multiple vocabulary words and their contextual concepts are demonstrated by illustrated scenarios with animals and people, each with their own simple story to tell. (Publisher's note)

430   German and related languages

Hettinga, Donald R.

The **Brothers** Grimm; two lives, one legacy. Clarion Bks. 2001 180p il $22
Grades: 5 6 7 8   **430**

1. Authors   2. Folklorists   3. Philologists   4. Folklore -- Germany   5. Short story writers
ISBN 0-618-05599-1

                                    LC 00-65598

A biography of the brothers famous for collecting German folk tales

"No book for young readers presents the Grimms' intertwined lives against the larger background of early 19th-century Europe in such fascinating detail as this absorbing new biography. . . . Students will find it an excellent resource for term papers, yet it is written so clearly that it makes for enjoyable pleasure reading." SLJ

Includes bibliographical references

433   Dictionaries of standard German

Kudela, Katy R.

My first book of German words. Capstone Press 2010 32p il (A+ books: bilingual picture dictionaries) lib bdg $25.99
Grades: K 1 2 3   **433**

1. German language   2. Picture dictionaries
ISBN 978-1-4296-3296-6; 1-4296-3296-8

                                   LC 2009005516

Simple text paired with themed photos invite the reader to learn German vocabulary and phrases.

"Ideal for children encountering multicultural friends at school and at play. . . . [This] makes simple language exchanges fun and easy. . . . The pictures are full-bleed and have the brilliant, bright look of a catalogue. . . . [This] makes for good kindergarten ready reference." Booklist

Includes bibliographical references

439   Other Germanic languages

Sussman, Joni Kibort

My first Yiddish word book; edited by Joni Kibort Sussman; pictures by Pepi Marzel. Kar-Ben Pub. 2008 32p il $17.95
Grades: K 1 2   **439**

1. Reference books   2. Yiddish language   3. Picture dictionaries
ISBN 978-0-8225-8755-2

                                   LC 2007028347

"With this [Yiddish] picture dictionary, select vocabulary is accessible to young readers. Basic words for parts of the body, members of the family, clothing, the house, school, playground, city, grocery store, bedtime, the zoo, colors, etc., are included. All are written in block letters with English transliteration and translation. Each spread includes a large, detailed illustration with the individual items clearly identified along the bottom. The pictures are cheerful and contemporary." SLJ

443   Dictionaries of standard French

Corbeil, Jean-Claude

★ **My** first French English visual dictionary; [by] Jean-Claude Corbeil; Ariane Archambault. Firefly Books 2006 80p il $14.95
Grades: 3 4 5 6   **443**

1. Reference books   2. Picture dictionaries   3. French language -- Dictionaries
ISBN 978-1-55407-193-7; 1-55407-193-3

"There are 36 themes-among them 'Clothing,' 'Colors and Shapes,' 'Dinosaurs,' 'Space,' and 'Sports' selected to appeal to primary-age children. Each theme has a double-page spread of small to medium-sized individual illustrations of items allied to the theme. The other 1,300 illustrations are large and in full color and are accompanied by the English word in boldface letters with the word in the other language underneath. The typeface is large and uncluttered and easy to see. . . . Separate English and French indexes complete the book." Booklist

Kudela, Katy R.

My first book of French words; translator, Translations.com. Capstone Press 2009 32p il (A+ books: bilingual picture dictionaries) lib bdg $23.99
Grades: K 1 2 3   **443**

1. Picture dictionaries   2. French language -- Dictionaries
ISBN 978-1-4296-3295-9 lib bdg; 1-4296-3295-X lib bdg

                                   LC 2009005510

"This simple bilingual picture dictionary is illustrated with attractive, colorful photos. Each themed spread introduces 10 words, first in English and then in French, followed by the approximate French pronunciation. . . . The 130 words cover family, body parts, clothes, toys, bedroom, bathroom, kitchen, food, farm, garden, colors, classroom, city, numbers, and useful phrases. . . . Overall, this book is appealing, useful, and easy to comprehend." SLJ

Includes bibliographical references

463   Dictionaries of standard Spanish

Corbeil, Jean-Claude

★ **My** first Spanish English visual dictionary; [by] Jean-Claude Corbeil; Ariane Archambault. Firefly Books 2006 80p il $14.95
Grades: 3 4 5 6   **463**

1. Reference books   2. Picture dictionaries   3. Spanish language -- Dictionaries
ISBN 978-1-55407-194-4; 1-55407-194-1

A Spanish/English visual dictionary for children: 1,600 terms annotate 1,300 realistic illustrations organized in 36 themes that children experience in their lives. Two indexes, by language, and Spanish terms include gender.

Kudela, Katy R.

My first book of Spanish words. Capstone Press 2009 32p il (A+ books: bilingual picture dictionaries) lib bdg $23.99
Grades: K 1 2 3   **463**

1. Picture dictionaries   2. Spanish language -- Dictionaries
ISBN 978-1-4296-3298-0 lib bdg; 1-4296-3298-4 lib bdg

                                   LC 2009005518

This picture dictionary introduces common Spanish words with color photos.

Includes bibliographical references

492.4 Hebrew

Groner, Judyth Saypol

My first Hebrew word book; [by Judye Groner and Madeline Wikler]; pictures by Pepi Marzel. Kar-Ben Pub. 2005 32p il lib bdg $17.95

Grades: K 1 2 **492.4**

1. Hebrew language 2. Reference books 3. Picture dictionaries

ISBN 1-58013-126-3

LC 2004-13504

"Basic Hebrew words . . . are included. All are written in block letters with English transliteration and translation. Each spread includes a large, detailed illustration with the individual items clearly identified along the bottom. The color cartoon art is cheerful and contemporary. At the back of the book, a word list is organized alphabetically in English and includes the Hebrew words and corresponding page numbers. All in all, this is a wonderful resource." SLJ

493 Non-Semitic Afro-Asiatic languages

Giblin, James

★ The **riddle** of the Rosetta Stone; key to ancient Egypt. [by] James Cross Giblin. Crowell 1990 85p il hardcover o.p. pa $7.99

Grades: 5 6 7 8 **493**

1. Hieroglyphics 2. Rosetta stone 3. Egyptian language

ISBN 0-06-446137-8 pa

LC 89-29289

Describes how the discovery and deciphering of the Rosetta Stone unlocked the secret of Egyptian hieroglyphics

"Suspense keeps the reader glued to this fine piece of nonfiction as the mystery of hieroglyphs is slowly unraveled. . . . The author has done a masterful job of distilling information, citing the highlights, and fitting it all together in an interesting and enlightening look at a puzzling subject." Horn Book

Includes bibliographical references

495.1 Chinese

Kudela, Katy R.

My first book of Mandarin Chinese words. Capstone Press 2010 32p il (A+ books: bilingual picture dictionaries) lib bdg $25.99

Grades: K 1 2 3 **495.1**

1. Chinese language 2. Picture dictionaries

ISBN 978-1-4296-3297-3; 1-4296-3297-6

LC 2009005517

Simple text paired with themed photos invite the reader to learn Mandarin Chinese vocabulary and phrases.

"Ideal for children encountering multicultural friends at school and at play. . . . [This] makes simple language exchanges fun and easy. . . . The pictures are full-bleed and have the brilliant, bright look of a catalogue. . . . [This] makes for good kindergarten ready reference." Booklist

Includes bibliographical references

Lee, Huy Voun

1, 2, 3 go! Holt & Co. 2000 un il $17.95

Grades: K 1 2 3 **495.1**

1. Counting 2. Chinese language

ISBN 0-8050-6205-X

LC 99-48326

An introduction to Chinese writing describing the construction, meaning, and pronunciation of simple characters used for a variety of words and the numbers one through ten

"Lee effectively displays boldly contrasted cut-paper shapes on stark white backgrounds. . . . With masterful simplicity, Lee leads readers to a preliminary appreciation of Chinese culture." Booklist

At the beach; written and illustrated by Huy Voun Lee. Holt & Co. 1994 un il hardcover o.p. pa $7.95

Grades: K 1 2 3 **495.1**

1. Chinese language

ISBN 0-8050-2768-8; 0-8050-5822-2 pa

LC 93-25462

A mother amuses her young son at the beach by drawing in the sand Chinese characters, many of which resemble the objects they stand for

"The intricate, visually captivating cut-paper collages have borders with sea motifs. Useful for beginning language study and interesting due to its artistic innovation, the book includes a pronunciation guide." Horn Book Guide

Other titles in this series are:

In the leaves (2005)

In the park (1998)

In the snow (1995)

495.6 Japanese

Kudela, Katy R.

My first book of Japanese words. Capstone Press 2010 32p il (A+ books: bilingual picture dictionaries) lib bdg $25.99

Grades: K 1 2 3 **495.6**

1. Japanese language 2. Picture dictionaries

ISBN 978-1-4296-3916-3; 1-4296-3916-4

LC 2009028665

Simple text paired with themed photos invite the reader to learn Japanese vocabulary and phrases.

"Ideal for children encountering multicultural friends at school and at play. . . . [This] makes simple language exchanges fun and easy. . . . The pictures are full-bleed and have the brilliant, bright look of a catalogue. . . . [This] makes for good kindergarten ready reference." Booklist

Includes bibliographical references

500 SCIENCE

500 Natural sciences and mathematics

★ The **big** idea science book; incredible concepts that show how science works in the real world. editor, Matilda Gollon; consultant, Lisa Burke. DK Pub. 2010 304p il $29.99

Grades: 4 5 6 7 **500**

1. Science

ISBN 978-0-7566-6287-5; 0-7566-6287-7

LC 2010-281143

"Aimed at grabbing readers' general interest in science, this lively overview is split into sections on life, earth, and physical science; within each category, specific subjects are plainly labeled for easy reference. . . . Full-color photographs, drawings, and diagrams further inform, and readers can visit an interactive Web site for more exploration. For breadth of material and clarity, it's hard to beat." Publ Wkly

Bryson, Bill

A **really** short history of nearly everything. Delacorte Press 2009 169p il $19.99

Grades: 4 5 6 7 **500**

1. Science

ISBN 978-0-385-73810-1; 0-385-73810-2

A newly illustrated, abridged and adapted edition of A short history of nearly everything, published 2003 by Broadway Books for adults; this edition first published in the United Kingdom 2008

Bryson "whirls through mind-numbing notions such as the creation of the universe and the life span of an atom with good cheer and accessible, even exciting, writing. The two-page speads meander their way through the various recesses of science with a combination of explanatory prose, historical anecdotes, wry asides, and illustrations that range from helpful to comical." Booklist

Cobb, Vicki

What's the big idea? amazing science questions for the curious kid. Skyhorse 2010 197p il $19.95

Grades: 3 4 5 6 **500**

1. Science 2. Questions and answers

ISBN 978-1-61608-013-6; 1-61608-013-2

LC 2009-46866

"The four main topics—energy, motion, matter, and life—are presented as 'big ideas' and explained through a series of two to four-page chapters that open with a kid-friendly question designed to provide insight into some of the great scientific breakthroughs. . . . Each question is introduced with an illustrated page of four students reacting (in speech bubbles) with humor and sarcasm to the question. . . . Spots of black-line cartoon-style artwork filled with color break up most pages and keep the large-point sans-serif text from overwhelming the spreads. This will be a quality addition to any collection." SLJ

Goldsmith, Mike

Everything you need to know about science. Kingfisher 2009 160p il $18.99

Grades: 1 2 3 4 5 **500**

1. Science

ISBN 978-0-7534-6302-4; 0-7534-6302-4

"This broad, accessible encyclopedia will appeal to browsers because of the 500-plus highly realistic computer-generated illustrations, large fonts, and short paragraphs. . . . Science enthusiasts will enjoy browsing this smorgasbord of information." SLJ

Hillman, Ben

How weird is it; a freaky book all about strangeness. Scholastic 2009 47p il $15.99

Grades: 5 6 7 8 **500**

1. Science

ISBN 978-0-439-91868-8; 0-439-91868-5

LC 2008-09787

Strange but facinating facts about everyday things that turn out to be extraordinary.

"Humor adds interest to the random but readable text. Large, vivid computer-manipulated photographs illustrate the information." Horn Book Guide

Isabella, Jude

Hoaxed! fakes & mistakes in the world of science. by the editors of YES mag; illustrated by Howie Woo. Kids Can Press 2009 48p il lib bdg $16.95; pa $8.95

Grades: 5 6 7 8 **500**

1. Fraud 2. Science

ISBN 978-1-55453-206-3 lib bdg; 1-55453-206-X lib bdg; 978-1-55453-207-0 pa; 1-55453-207-8 pa

This title examines hoaxes, fakes and mistakes from the world of science, including crop circles, Bigfoot and the Loch Ness monster, and UFOs reported at Roswell, New Mexico. Index. "Ages nine to twelve." (Quill Quire)

"Piltdown man, Richard Meinertzhagen the light-fingered bird collector, 'Stone Age' Tasaday in the Philippines, crop circles in England, cold fusion energy and UFOs in Roswell, N.M., are the fakes and mistakes described in this lively introduction to fraud in science. The breezy text opens with a clear description of the scientific process of hypothesis, experiment, publication in professional magazines and replication of results before proceeding to the many colorful fakes exposed." Kirkus

Includes index.

Murphy, Glenn

Why is snot green; and other extremely important questions (and answers) Roaring Brook Press 2009 236p il pa $9.95

Grades: 4 5 6 7 **500**

1. Science 2. Technology

ISBN 978-1-59643-500-1 pa; 1-59643-500-3 pa

"Conservation, evolution, technology, animal life, space travel, physics, and much more are discussed in this lively science book. . . . [This offers] chatty questions and answers . . . with text that is compelling, never intimidating, and sometimes deliberately outrageous. . . . Children will have fun browsing the spacious pages and sharing what they read with adults." Booklist

O'Meara, Stephen James

Are you afraid yet? the science behind scary stuff; written by Stephen James O'Meara; illustrated by Jeremy Kaposy. Kids Can Press 2009 78p il $17.95; pa $9.95

Grades: 5 6 7 8 **500**

1. Science 2. Supernatural

ISBN 978-1-55453-294-0; 1-55453-294-9; 978-1-55453-295-7 pa; 1-55453-295-7 pa

"This book cleverly weaves together the supernatural and the scientific in an entertaining read that answers questions about ghosts, UFOs, vampires, werewolves, and how long a decapitated head can remain conscious. Examples depicting such things in classical fiction and popular movies are seamlessly interjected between the factual explanations. Each page is filled with detailed black-and-white illustrations, emphasizing the sometimes-humorous, yet often-macabre descriptions." SLJ

Rice, Dona

★ **What** a scientist sees; Dona Herweck Rice. Teacher Created Materials 2016 32 p. (pbk.) $8.99

Grades: 4 5 6 **500**

1. Scientists 2. Observation (Scientific method) 3. Scientists 4. Science -- Methodology

ISBN 1480746916; 9781480746916

LC 2014045214

This children's book by Dona Rice shows how "scientists see things much differently than the average person. They observe and research, create hypotheses, make predictions, and much more when conducting experiments. A Think Like a Scientist lab activity that supports STEM instruction is included at the end of the book for students to use what they learned in the text and apply that knowledge to the activity." (Publisher's note)

"Smartly written, these innovative and imaginative volumes make learning fun... First-rate nonfiction." SLJ

Richardson, Gillian

   Kaboom! explosions of all kinds. Annick Press 2009 83p il $22.95; pa $12.95

Grades: 4 5 6 7   **500**

   1. Science 2. Explosions

   ISBN 978-1-55451-204-1; 1-55451-204-2; 978-1-55451-203-4 pa; 1-55451-203-4 pa

"With comic-style sound-effect headings and fact boxes galore, Kaboom! highlights the supercharged of the natural and manmade worlds, from astronomy, geology, biology, herbology, and entomology to chemistry, mechanics, pyrotechnics, and art. Text is broken into asymmetrical panels for bite-size explanations. Some explosions are captured in sequence and detail with historical and high-speed photography and illustrations in comic-style panel frames. . . . Kaboom! is an engrossing attention-getter, effectively tapping the sensationalism of all types of blasts." SLJ

This book thinks you are a scientist; by London Science Museum, illustrated by Harriet Russell. Thames & Hudson 2016 96 p. $14.95

   Grades: 1 2 3 4   **500**

   1. Science

   ISBN 9780500650813

                LC 2016931257

This book, "developed by the Science Museum, London, as a complement to their new interactive gallery for children, explores seven key scientific areas: force and motion, electricity and magnetism, earth and space, light, matter, sound, and mathematics. Each spread centers on an open-ended question or activity, with space on the page for the child to write, draw, or interact with the book. Bend water with static power." (Publisher's note)

"With easy setups and few required tools, the activities encourage imagination, curiosity, and careful observation." Pub Wkly

Watts, Claire

   The most explosive science book in the universe; by the Brainwaves; illustrated by Lisa Swerling and Ralph Lazar; written by Claire Watts. DK Pub. 2009 60p il $19.99

Grades: 3 4 5 6   **500**

   1. Science

   ISBN 978-0-7566-5152-7; 0-7566-5152-2

The Brainwaves are pint-sized pals that explore the world of science including the building blocks of matter, chemistry, light, electricity and the future of science

"A sprawling, unique overview of the various scientific fields. Although students will have to hunt through the dense layout to find facts, they will likely encounter what they are searching for. . . . Appealing enough to inspire pleasure reading, the book will also serve those looking for scientific facts." SLJ

502   Miscellany

Murphy, Glenn

   How loud can you burp? more extremely important questions (and answers!) Roaring Book Press 2009 284p il pa $10.99

Grades: 4 5 6 7   **502**

   1. Science 2. Questions and answers

   ISBN 978-1-59643-506-3 pa; 1-59643-506-2 pa

"'Why does pollen give you hay fever?' 'Why don't big metal ships just sink?' These are but a couple of the questions that Murphy received on the Web site he set up to solicit inquiries from kids. Written in an informal, question-and-answer format, he delivers serious scientific information in an easygoing, humorous manner, with several pages dedicated to each topic. . . . A few line drawings break up the text and sidebars

highlight interesting facts or are, at times, simply funny. . . . This an entertaining, accessible approach to science that's sure to appeal to science buffs and general browsers alike." SLJ

502.8   Auxiliary techniques and procedures; apparatus, equipment, materials

Kramer, Stephen

   Hidden worlds: looking through a scientist's microscope; photographs by Dennis Kunkel. Houghton Mifflin 2001 57p il (Scientists in the field) $16; pa $5.95

Grades: 4 5 6 7   **502.8**

   1. Microscopes 2. Microscopists

   ISBN 0-618-05546-0; 0-618-35405-0 pa

                LC 00-58083

This book takes a "look at the work of a microscopist. Kunkel works with microscopes to explore science. . . . This book contains many of his photos, most taken with electron microscopes. . . . Several opening pages, along with the front and back endpapers, are visually dazzling. The heart of the book, though, is what readers learn about how Kunkel produces these images, and to what uses scientists put them. . . . This title offers a wealth of scientific information along with an insightful look at the world of an individual scientist." SLJ

   Includes bibliographical references

Levine, Shar

   ★ The **ultimate** guide to your microscope; [by] Shar Levine & Leslie Johnstone. Sterling Pub. 2008 143p il pa $9.95

Grades: 5 6 7 8 9   **502.8**

   1. Microscopes

   ISBN 978-1-4027-4329-0 pa; 1-4027-4329-7 pa

                LC 2006-100967

"Through this fun and inviting book, readers can begin to explore the world using a microscope. Students are encouraged to learn the basics in the two first chapters and then undertake the 41 hands-on activities in the next eight chapters. Activities are presented in manageable one or two-page uniformly formatted modules." SLJ

503   Dictionaries, encyclopedias, concordances

   ★ **DK** first science encyclopedia; [senior editors, Currie Love, Caroline Stamps and Ben Morgan] DK Publishing 2008 127p il map $16.99

   Grades: K 1 2 3 4   **503**

   1. Science -- Encyclopedias

   ISBN 978-0-7566-4296-9; 0-7566-4296-5

                LC 2009277384

Provides a basic reference guide to life, materials, physical, earth, and space science

"On flipping to any page, readers' first impressions will be the vibrancy and beauty of the photography, but further examination reveals a wealth of interesting facts and information about the topics presented, along with real-world context for their importance." Sci Books Films

Everything you need to know; an encyclopedia for inquiring young minds. Kingfisher 2007 320p il map $24.95

   Grades: PreK K 1 2 3 4   **503**

   1. Reference books 2. Science -- Encyclopedias 3. Technology -- Encyclopedias

   ISBN 978-0-7534-6089-4; 0-7534-6089-0

"The encyclopedia is arranged thematically into 10 sections ('Our Earth,' 'Plants,' 'Animals,' 'Dinosaurs,' 'People and Places,' 'People Through Time,' 'My Body,' 'Science,' 'Space,' and 'Machines') with between 11 and 17 topics grouped under each. Most topics are treated in two-page spreads. . . . There is plenty of worthwhile information to answer questions and spark curiosity. . . . The volume is visually appealing, with full-color illustrations." Booklist

Jakab, Cheryl

★ The **encyclopedia** of junior science; [by] Cheryl Jakab, David Keystone. Chelsea Clubhouse 2009 10v il map set $230

Grades: 4 5 6 7   **503**

1. Reference books 2. Science -- Encyclopedias
ISBN 978-1-60413-554-1 set; 1-60413-554-9 set
LC 2008-38113

"This set introduces students to basic science concepts. Approximately 270 entries are arranged alphabetically. . . . The writing is basic, and much of the information is presented in the form of charts and bulleted lists. . . . This set would be useful for school and public libraries seeking a science encyclopedia." Booklist

The **Kingfisher** science encyclopedia; general editor, Charles Taylor. 3rd ed. Kingfisher 2011 vii, 488 p.p ill. (some col.) (hardcover) $34.99

Grades: 5 6 7 8   **503**

1. Science -- Encyclopedias 2. Science
ISBN 0753466880; 9780753466889
LC 2011047026

This book is a science encyclopedia edited by Charles Taylor. The book is arranged thematically and "most topics are presented on . . . two-page spreads, with relevant charts, timelines, and other illustrations surrounding the text. In the bottom right corner of the spread is a 'See Also Pages' box that directs readers to related topics with their page numbers." (Voice of Youth Advocates)

Topical chapters present "basic surveys of physics, geology, chemistry, biology, anatomy, the environment, and space. . . . Articles are generally, though not rigidly, confined to a spread each, and all have see-also references. . . . The illustrations are a plus; they are crisply reproduced, finely detailed, and labeled, enhancing the text rather than competing with it." SLJ

507   Education, research, related topics

Glass, Susan

Analyze this! understanding the scientific method. [by] Susan Glass. Heinemann Library 2007 48p il (How to be a scientist) lib bdg $21; pa $8.99

Grades: 3 4 5 6   **507**

1. Science -- Methodology
ISBN 978-1-4034-8358-4 lib bdg; 978-1-4034-8362-1 pa
LC 2006010638

Includes bibliographical references

Prove it! the scientific method in action. [by] Susan Glass. Heinemann Library 2007 48p il (How to be a scientist) hardcover o.p. lib bdg $21

Grades: 3 4 5 6   **507**

1. Science -- Experiments 2. Science -- Methodology
ISBN 978-1-4034-8359-1 lib bdg; 978-1-4034-8363-8 pa
LC 2006010639

Includes bibliographical references

Science detectives; how scientists solved six real-life mysteries. by the editors of Yes Mag; illustrated by Rose Cowles. Kids Can Press 2006 48p il $15.95; pa $8.95

Grades: 4 5 6   **507**

1. Science -- Methodology
ISBN 978-1-55337-994-2; 1-55337-994-2; 978-1-55337-995-9; 1-55337-995-0 pa

This describes how scientists solved mysteries such as the spread of typhoid in 1906, the death of vultures in India in 1999, and the crash of a Swissair flight in 1998. Includes related projects.

507.2   Research

Rockliff, Mara

★ **Mesmerized**; How Ben Franklin Solved a Mystery That Baffled All of France. Mara Rockliff, illustrated by Iacopo Bruno. Candlewick Press 2015 48 p. col ill, col map hbk $17.99

Grades: 2 3 4   **507.2**

1. Hypnotism 2. Science -- Methodology
ISBN 0763663514; 9780763663513
LC 2014939337

Includes bibliographical references

In this book, Mara Rockliff "tells the story of how Benjamin Franklin debunked Dr. [Anton Franz] Mesmer's magical cure-all. . . . With a heavy emphasis on his use of the scientific method, Rockliff shows how Franklin's experiment--blindfolding subjects so that they don't know they're being mesmerized--led to the discovery of the placebo effect, a vital component of medical testing to this day." (Booklist)

"The tale is nicely pitched to emphasize the importance of a hypothesis, testing and verification, and several inset text boxes are used to explain these scientific tools. Rockliff points out that Franklin's blind-test technique is in use today for medical treatments, and both the placebo effect and hypnosis are studied today." Kirkus

Swanson, Diane, 1944-

Nibbling on Einstein's brain; the good, the bad & the bogus in science. by Diane Swanson; illustrated by Francis Blake. Annick Press 2009 151 p. il (pbk.) $12.95; (hbk.) $24.95

Grades: 5 6 7 8   **507.2**

1. Science -- Methodology 2. Science -- Methodology
ISBN 1554511860; 1554511879; 9781554511860; 9781554511877

This book, by Diane Swanson, illustrated by Francis Blake, presents "strategies for sorting the good from the misleading in science. Through playful scenarios and fascinating real-world examples, each chapter encourages critical thinking. You'll find tips for spotting bad science, ideas for identifying reports that misrepresent facts and ways to keep your own brain from muddling the science news you receive." (Publisher's note)

The author "discusses topics such as the difference between correlation and cause-and-effect relationships, the importance of asking the right questions about advertisers' claims, and the links between superstition, coincidence, and probability. With a highly readable text and jaunty line illustrations, the book encourages critical thinking and skepticism when evaluating science reporting and media hype." Booklist

507.21   Research methods

Rice, Dona Herweck

What the evidence shows; Dona Herweck Rice. Teacher Created Materials 2016 32 p. color illustrations (ebook) $8.99; (pbk.) $8.99

Grades: 4 5 6 **507.21**
1. Science -- Experiments 2. Scientists 3. Science -- Methodology
ISBN 9781480751286; 1480747300; 9781480747302
LC 2015003157

In this book, by Dona Herweck Rice, "learn how to navigate through the scientific inquiry journey and analyze evidence to discover truth. Fifth-grade readers will learn all about authentic scientific evidence and its role in each of the eight main science practices through this high-interest informational text filled with vibrant photographs. Aligned to the Next Generation Science Standards." (Publisher's note)

507.8 Use of apparatus and equipment in study and teaching

Austin, John
  Labcraft wizards; Magical Projects and Experiments. John Austin. Chicago Review Press 2016 256 p. illustrations (chiefly color) (paperback) $16.99; (ebook) $16.99
Grades: 4 5 6 7 **507.8**
  1. Magic 2. Handicraft 3. Science -- Experiments 4. Physics -- Experiments
ISBN 9781613736210; 9781613736227
LC 2016027300

This book, by John Austin, "provides dozens of step-by-step projects to transform everyday objects into instruments of magic, such as a sculpted magic wand, gooey ogre snot, bouncy dragon eggs, edible brewed slugs, an enchanted hourglass, and more! Through its creative activities, [it] encourages scientific observation and helps eager minds explore basic concepts in chemistry and physics through experimentation." (Publisher's note)

"Keep this one close at hand—it's screaming to be used for a Harry Potter–themed program or party and would fit well in the classroom or in a public library." Booklist

Banqueri, Eduardo
  Everyday science; 66 Experiments that explain the small and big things all around us. by Eduardo Banqueri, Joseph M. Barras and Octavi López Coronado; illustrations by Roger Zanni. Barrons Educational Series, Inc. 2016 144 p. color illustrations (paperback) $14.99
Grades: 3 4 5 6 **507.8**
  1. Science -- Experiments
ISBN 9781438008622
LC 2015951730

In this book by Eduardo Banqueri, Joseph M. Barras and Octavi López Coronado, with illustrations by Roger Zanni, "kids can learn how to find the science that exists in everyday activities. Four main chapters offer experiments in physics, chemistry, geology, and biology. Budding scientists will gain practical knowledge while learning how to: build a time machine, guess tomorrow's weather, generate salty stalactites, [and] make a rainbow disappear, [among others]." (Publisher's note)

"Lively cartoons, photographs of kids, and clear step-by-step directions make each project easy to follow, and sidebars dive into the hard science behind the complex subjects explored." Pub Wkly

Becker, Helaine
  ★ **Science** on the loose; amazing activities and science facts you'll never believe. illustrated by Claudia Dávila. Maple Tree Press 2008 64p il $22.95; pa $10.95
Grades: 3 4 5 6 **507.8**
  1. Science -- Experiments
ISBN 978-1-897349-18-2; 1-897349-18-1; 978-1-897349-19-9 pa; 1-897349-19-X pa
LC 2007939081

This "is thought provoking, imaginative, and engaging, with a wonderful blend of intelligent writing, intriguing ideas and easy-to-perform experiments. There is also plenty of humor." Sci Books Films

Bell-Rehwoldt, Sheri
  Science experiments that surprise and delight; fun projects for curious kids. Capstone Press 2011 32p il (Edge books: kitchen science) lib bdg $26.65; pa $7.95
Grades: 3 4 5 6 **507.8**
  1. Science -- Experiments
ISBN 978-1-4296-5428-9 lib bdg; 1-4296-5428-7 lib bdg; 978-1-4296-6253-6 pa; 1-4296-6253-0 pa
LC 2010025205

Provides step-by-step instructions for science projects using household materials and explains the science behind the experiments.

"Attractive, colorful, and full of photos, [this title] will appeal to a wide range of kids. . . . Anyone looking for a straightforward, fun, and easy science experiment will want [this title] close by." SLJ

Includes bibliographical references

Burke, Lisa
  Backyard; fun experiments for budding scientists. DK Pub. 2010 23p il (I'm a scientist) $12.99
Grades: K 1 2 3 **507.8**
  1. Nature 2. Science -- Experiments
ISBN 978-0-7566-6306-3; 0-7566-6306-7
LC 2010459418

"Each spread offers a science experiment with foldout flaps that demonstrate the science behind the project which introduces natural phenomena and the outside world in backyards and gardens." Publisher's note

  Kitchen. DK Pub. 2010 23p il (I'm a scientist) $12.99
Grades: K 1 2 3 **507.8**
  1. Science -- Experiments
ISBN 978-0-7566-6307-0; 0-7566-6307-5

"Each spread contains a kid-friendly science experiment for very young readers which they can perform right in their own kitchen, with foldout flaps that demonstrate the science behind the project." Publisher's note

Burns, Kylie
  What's going on? collecting and recording your data. Crabtree 2010 32p il (Step into science) lib bdg $26.60; pa $8.95
Grades: 4 5 6 **507.8**
  1. Science -- Methodology
ISBN 978-0-7787-5155-7 lib bdg; 0-7787-5155-4 lib bdg; 978-0-7787-5170-0 pa; 0-7787-5170-8 pa

This "shows the reader how to collect and record data in a journal, as well as how to organize the data by using graphs, charts, and diagrams. . . . The colorful photographs and illustrations enhance the text. A time line showing scientific discoveries and inventions, a glossary, a list of books and websites for further information, and an index are presented at the back of the book. This . . . would be a wonderful addition to a school classroom." Sci Books Films

Includes glossary and bibliographical references

Challen, Paul C.
  What just happened? reading results and making inferences. [by] Paul Challen. Crabtree 2010 32p il (Step into science) lib bdg $26.60; pa $8.95

217

Grades: 4 5 6 **507.8**
1. Science -- Methodology
ISBN 978-0-7787-5156-4 lib bdg; 0-7787-5156-2 lib bdg; 978-0-7787-5171-7 pa; 0-7787-5171-6 pa

This "shows the reader how to make sense of the data that have been collected and recorded during the experiment. . . . The examples of charts and graphs, along with colorful photographs and illustrations, enhance the text. A time line showing scientific discoveries and inventions, a glossary, a list of books, and websites for further information, and an index are presented at the back of the book. This . . . would be a wonderful addition to a school classroom." Sci Books Films

Includes glossary and bibliographical references

What's going to happen? making your hypothesis. [by] Paul Challen. Crabtree 2010 32p il (Step into science) lib bdg $26.60; pa $8.95
Grades: 4 5 6 **507.8**
1. Science -- Methodology
ISBN 978-0-7787-5157-1 lib bdg; 0-7787-5157-0 lib bdg; 978-0-7787-5172-4 pa; 0-7787-5172-4 pa

Learn how scientists make educated guesses called hypotheses to test their theories. . . . Readers will learn how to construct a measurable and focused hypothesis to test in an experiment.

"A time line showing important hypotheses, a glossary, a list of books and websites for further information, and an index are provided at the back of the book. This . . . would be a wonderful addition to a school classroom." Sci Books Films

Includes glossary and bibliographical references

Challoner, Jack
Maker Lab; 28 Super Cool Projects: Build * Invent * Create * Discover. Jack Challoner; foreword by Jack Andraka. DK Publishing 2016 160 p. color illustrations hardcover $19.99
Grades: 3 4 5 6 7 8 **507.8**
1. Science projects 2. Science -- Experiments
ISBN 9781465451354; 1465451358
LC 2016427641

This book by Jack Challoner, with foreword by Jack Andraka, "includes 28 kid-safe projects and crafts that will get young inventors' wheels turning and make science pure fun. Each step-by-step activity is appropriate for kids ages 8-12 and ranked easy, medium, or hard, with an estimated time frame for completion. Requiring only household materials, young makers can build an exploding volcano, race balloon rocket cars, construct a solar system, make a lemon battery, and more." (Publisher's note)

"Though not all projects are innovative, what sets this book apart is that each experiment is accompanied by real-world applications that tie new observations to kids' existing understanding and offer endless opportunities for STEM-related discussions. Not only are young scientists encouraged to experiment, they are challenged to apply the information gleaned to real-world problem-solving." Booklist

Cobb, Vicki
See for yourself; more than 100 amazing experiments for science fairs and school projects. illustrated by Dave Klug. 2nd ed; Skyhorse Pub. 2010 192p il pa $14.95
Grades: 4 5 6 7 **507.8**
1. Science -- Experiments
ISBN 978-1-61608-083-9; 1-61608-083-3
LC 2010020800

First published 2001 by Scholastic
This is an "accessible and often intriguing collection of activities and experiments. . . . The experiments are grouped by their source of inspiration: humans, the supermarket, the toy store, drugstore, and hard-ware and stationery stores. . . . Cartoon-style illustrations are . . . in full color." SLJ

We dare you! hundreds of science bets, challenges, and experiments you can do at home. [by] Vicki Cobb and Kathy Darling. Skyhorse Pub. 2007 321p il hardcover o.p. pa $14.94
Grades: 4 5 6 7 **507.8**
1. Science -- Experiments
ISBN 978-1-60239-225-0; 1-60239-225-0; 978-1-60239-775-0 pa; 1-60239-775-9 pa
LC 2007-51236

"Divided into chapters with titles such as 'The Human Wonder,' 'Fluid Feats,' 'Energy Entrapments,' and 'Mathematical Duplicity,' this volume has more than 200 experiments with clear how-to instructions. All of the projects are doable and the science behind them is explained in a kid-accessible manner. . . . Black-and-white line drawings add humor and clarify instructions. This is a great resource for teachers, parents, and budding scientists—and for any youngster who can't resist a challenge." SLJ

Includes bibliographical references

Connolly, Sean
The **book** of potentially catastrophic science; 50 experiments for daring young scientists. Workman Pub. 2010 305p il
Grades: 5 6 7 8 **507.8**
1. Science -- Experiments
ISBN 0-7611-5687-9; 978-0-7611-5687-1
LC 2010-07044

This book presents thirty-four experiments. "Each chapter starts with a brief outline of the scientific advances of the time, followed by a clarification of the science and then one or more hands-on experiments to illustrate the object or concept presented. . . . Grades five to eight." (Sci Books Films)

"This volume approaches science historically, spotlighting certain periods, processes, individuals, discoveries, and inventions. Each of the 34 chapters includes a discussion and one or two related activities, such as making a Stone Age tool, creating an earthquake in Jell-O, building a parachute for an egg drop, and extracting a banana's DNA. Safety concerns are addressed for each project, and adult help will be necessary to complete some of the experiments successfully. . . . Connolly's writing is engaging, and the historical approach works well, offering kids a quick introduction to science history and the opportunity to explore certain ideas along the way." Booklist

Gabrielson, Curt
Stomp rockets, catapults, and kaleidoscopes; 30+ amazing science projects you can build for less than $1. Chicago Review Press 2008 159p il $16.95
Grades: 3 4 5 6 **507.8**
1. Science projects 2. Science -- Experiments
ISBN 978-1-55652-737-1; 1-55652-737-3
LC 2007-37917

"Projects include building a working model of the human hand's muscles, bones, and tendons using drinking straws, tape, and string; using a pair of two-liter bottles and a length of rubber tubing to learn how a toilet flushes; and discovering how musical instruments make sounds by fashioning a harmonica, saxophone, drum, flute, or oboe. All devices are designed to use recycled or nearly free materials and common tools." Publisher's note

Goodstein, Madeline
Ace your sports science project; great science fair ideas. [by] Madeline Goodstein, Robert Gardner, and Barbara Gardner Conklin. Enslow

Publishers 2009 128p il (Ace your physics science project) lib bdg $31.93

Grades: 5 6 7 8   **507.8**

1. Sports 2. Physics 3. Science projects 4. Science -- Experiments

ISBN 978-0-7660-3229-3 lib bdg; 0-7660-3229-9 lib bdg

LC 2008-4689

"Presents several science experiments and project ideas dealing with the physics of sports." Publisher's note

Includes bibliographical references

Goal! science projects with soccer. Enslow Publishers 2009 104p il (Score! Sports science projects) lib bdg $31.93

Grades: 5 6 7 8   **507.8**

1. Motion 2. Soccer 3. Force and energy 4. Science projects 5. Science -- Experiments

ISBN 978-0-7660-3106-7 lib bdg; 0-7660-3106-3 lib bdg

LC 2008-2999

"Introductions include information about the history of the sport, safety steps to follow, and the scientific method. . . . Detailed diagrams help clarify many of the directions." SLJ

Includes glossary and bibliographical references

Hammond, Richard

Super science lab. DK Pub. 2009 96p il pa $8.99

Grades: 3 4 5   **507.8**

1. Science -- Experiments

ISBN 978-0-7566-5341-5 pa; 0-7566-5341-X pa

"With more than 30 scientific experiments, ranging from more traditional science-fair projects . . . this fun book has plenty of ideas to sample. Also offered are magnified images. . . . In between experiments, Hammond explores the science behind the subjects. . . . The active approach to science and scrapbook-style design, with plenty of photos, notes and asides, should win over curious kids." Publ Wkly

Hopwood, James

Cool dry ice devices; fun science projects with dry ice. [by] James Hopwood. ABDO Pub. 2008 32p il (Cool science) lib bdg $25.65

Grades: 4 5 6   **507.8**

1. Science projects 2. Science -- Experiments

ISBN 978-1-59928-907-6 lib bdg; 1-59928-907-5 lib bdg

LC 2007010257

This offers science projects using dry ice, including "Fast Frozen Confections"

The experiments "will attract boys and girls. [The] book begins with [an] upbeat introduction and three chapters about the scientific method, keeping a journal, and safety. . . . Background on the science concepts involved is presented along with a complete list of supplies. . . . The numbered instructions are easy to follow and are accompanied by small, closeup photos." SLJ

Hyde, Natalie

What's the plan? designing your experiment. Crabtree 2010 32p il (Step into science) lib bdg $26.60; pa $8.95

Grades: 4 5 6   **507.8**

1. Science -- Methodology

ISBN 978-0-7787-5154-0 lib bdg; 0-7787-5154-6 lib bdg; 978-0-7787-5169-4 pa; 0-7787-5169-4 pa

LC 2009-44172

This "shows readers how to gather materials and create a step-by-step procedure to test their hypotheses. . . . Colorful photographs and illustrations enhance the text. A time line showing scientific discoveries and inventions, a glossary, a list of books and websites for further

information, and an index are presented at the back of the book. This . . . would be a wonderful addition to a school classroom." Sci Books Films

Includes glossary and bibliographical references

Johnson, Robin R.

What do we know now? drawing conclusions and answering the question. Crabtree 2010 32p il (Step into science) lib bdg $26.60; pa $8.95

Grades: 4 5 6   **507.8**

1. Science -- Methodology

ISBN 978-0-7787-5153-3 lib bdg; 0-7787-5153-8 lib bdg; 978-0-7787-5168-7 pa; 0-7787-5168-6 pa

LC 2009-44171

This book illustrates fun and interesting ways in which to report your results, from a science fair demonstration to a written report.

"This title . . . would be a wonderful addition to a school classroom." Sci Books Films

Includes glossary and bibliographical references

Leavitt, Loralee

Candy experiments; Loralee Leavitt. Andrews McMeel Pub., LLC 2012 146 p. $14.99

Grades: 4 5 6   **507.8**

1. Candy 2. Science -- Experiments 3. Candy 4. Science -- Experiments

ISBN 1449418368; 9781449418366

LC 2011944678

This book presents science activities for children involving candy. "Grouped by physical properties that include 'Color,' 'Secret Ingredients,' and 'Sticky' or processes like 'Blow It Up,' 'Squash It,' and 'Dissolve This,' the activities begin with an introductory question and tend to flow incrementally. Each one includes the time required, a list of ingredients . . . step-by-step directions, and a discussion, including a cursory scientific explanation." (School Library Journal)

Lew, Kristi

Science experiments that fly and move; fun projects for curious kids. Capstone Press 2011 32p il (Edge books: kitchen science) lib bdg $26.65; pa $7.95

Grades: 3 4 5 6   **507.8**

1. Science -- Experiments

ISBN 978-1-4296-5426-5; 1-4296-5426-0; 978-1-4296-6252-9 pa; 1-4296-6252-2 pa

LC 2010025206

Provides step-by-step instructions for science projects using household materials and explains the science behind the experiments.

"Attractive, colorful, and full of photos, [this title] will appeal to a wide range of kids. . . . Anyone looking for a straightforward, fun, and easy science experiment will want [this title] close by." SLJ

Includes glossary and bibliographical references

Margles, Samantha

Mythbusters science fair book. Scholastic 2011 128p il pa $9.99

Grades: 4 5 6 7   **507.8**

1. Science projects 2. Science -- Experiments

ISBN 978-0-545-23745-1; 0-545-23745-9

This offers "50 original ideas for science fair projects or long, boredom-riddled summer days. Much like the popular television program on which it's based, the book stays true to the scientific method. . . . Divided into chapters on chemical reactions, temperature, energy and force, and more, the two- to three-page experiments on busily designed pages feature easy step-by-step procedures." Booklist

Murphy, Pat

Exploratopia; by Pat Murphy, Ellen Macaulay, and the staff of the Exploratorium; illustrated by Jason Gorski. Little, Brown and Co. 2006 373p il $29.99

Grades: 3 4 5 6   **507.8**

1. Science -- Experiments

ISBN 978-0-316-61281-4; 0-316-61281-2

LC 2006-40942

"Practiced young experimenters ready to strike out on their own will find enticing science demonstrations on nearly every page of this inviting collection. Each of the 21 sections contains a half dozen or more entries that feature easily gathered ingredients, clear directions, and color photos or diagrams that are not only informative but often arresting as well." SLJ

Includes bibliographical references

Science activities for all students; edited by Aviva Ebner. Facts on File 2009 2v il loose-leaf $370

Grades: Adult Professional   **507.8**

1. Science projects 2. Science -- Experiments

ISBN 978-0-8160-7396-2 loose-leaf; 0-8160-7396-1 loose-leaf

LC 2008043827

Replaces Science Projects for All Students and More Science Projects for All Students, published 1998 and 2002 respectively

These "binders enable students in grades 4 through 9 with developmental or physical challenges to join their classmates in . . . hands-on [science] activities. There are 60 experiments in each binder—designed to be as inclusive as possible—in the areas of basic skills, Earth science, weather, space science, life science, and physical science. Each binder is also enhanced by approximately 250 black-and-white line illustrations." Publisher's note

Includes glossary and bibliographical references

Shores, Lori

How to build flipsticks. Capstone Press 2011 24p il (Hands-on science fun) lib bdg $23.99; pa $6.95

Grades: PreK K 1   **507.8**

1. Science -- Experiments

ISBN 978-1-4296-5292-6 lib bdg; 1-4296-5292-6 lib bdg; 978-1-4296-6213-0 pa; 1-4296-6213-1 pa

Simple text and full-color photos instruct readers on how to make two drawings act like a cartoon and explain the science behind the activity.

"Bright, glossy photos and irresistible ideas make these science lessons effortless fun." Booklist

How to make a bouncing egg. Capstone Press 2011 24p il (Hands-on science fun) lib bdg $23.99; pa $6.95

Grades: PreK K 1   **507.8**

1. Science -- Experiments

ISBN 978-1-4296-5291-9 lib bdg; 1-4296-5291-8 lib bdg; 978-1-4296-6214-7 pa; 1-4296-6214-X pa

Simple text and full-color photos instruct readers on how to make a bouncing egg.

"Bright, glossy photos and irresistible ideas make these science lessons effortless fun." Booklist

How to make a liquid rainbow. Capstone Press 2011 24p il (Hands-on science fun) lib bdg $23.99; pa $6.95

Grades: PreK K 1   **507.8**

1. Science -- Experiments

ISBN 978-1-4296-6216-1 lib bdg; 1-4296-6216-6 lib bdg; 978-1-4296-6216-1 pa; 1-4296-6216-6 pa

Simple text and full-color photos instruct readers on how to make a rainbow in a jar.

"Bright, glossy photos and irresistible ideas make these science lessons effortless fun." Booklist

How to make a mystery smell balloon. Capstone Press 2011 24p il (Hands-on science fun) lib bdg $23.99; pa $6.95

Grades: PreK K 1   **507.8**

1. Science -- Experiments

ISBN 978-1-4296-4494-5 lib bdg; 1-4296-4494-X lib bdg; 978-1-4296-5579-8 pa; 1-4296-5579-8 pa

LC 2010009483

Simple text and full-color photos instruct readers how to make a mystery smell balloon and explain the science behind the activity.

"Bright, glossy photos and irresistible ideas make these science lessons effortless fun." Booklist

Includes bibliographical references

Spangler, Steve

Naked eggs and flying potatoes; unforgettable experiments that make science fun. Greenleaf Book Group Press 2010 155p il (Steve Spangler science) pa $14.95

Grades: 3 4 5 6   **507.8**

1. Scientific recreations 2. Science -- Experiments

ISBN 978-1-60832-0608 pa; 1-60832-060-X pa

"Spangler uses cheap, everyday materials to invent entertaining, highly kid-appealing activities. . . . Heavily illustrated with color photos and described in funny, casual prose, the experiments will easily engage a young audience, and each is followed by a succinct explanation of the science concepts at play." Booklist

Tocci, Salvatore

More simple science fair projects, grades 3-5; illustrated by Bob Wiacek. Chelsea House Pub. 2006 48p il (Scientific American winning science fair projects) $27

Grades: 3 4 5   **507.8**

1. Science projects 2. Science -- Experiments

ISBN 0-7910-9055-8

LC 2005-57097

This "begins by describing how to exhibit information on a trifold display with the following information: background, the experimental question, materials, procedures, results, and explanations. The author then describes 18 experiments following that format. The language is clear and easy to follow. Simple drawings add a great deal to the explanations." Sci Books Films

VanCleave, Janice Pratt

★ **Janice** VanCleave's 201 awesome, magical, bizarre & incredible experiments. Wiley 1994 118p pa $12.95

Grades: 4 5 6 7   **507.8**

1. Science -- Experiments

ISBN 0-471-31011-5

LC 93-29807

The experiments in this book "are organized by field: astronomy, biology, chemistry, earth science, and physics; the purpose, materials needed, procedure, results, and an explanation are included for each demonstration. The author writes in a clear, easy-to-understand style. . . . The book will be especially useful to teachers looking for ideas that can be adapted as hands-on activities." SLJ

Includes glossary

★ **Janice** VanCleave's 202 oozing, bubbling, dripping & bouncing experiments. Wiley 1996 120p pa $12.95

Grades: 4 5 6 7 **507.8**
1. Science -- Experiments
ISBN 0-471-14025-2

LC 95-46398

Provides instructions for over 200 short experiments in astronomy, biology, chemistry, earth science, and physics

"Some activities consist merely of observation, such as 'To study parts of a feather.' Some are more complex, but all are clearly and concisely explained. Many are repeats from prior VanCleave books, but 40 are supposedly new." SLJ

Includes glossary

★ **Janice** VanCleave's 203 icy, freezing, frosty, cool & wild experiments. Wiley 1999 122p pa $12.95
Grades: 4 5 6 7 **507.8**
1. Science -- Experiments
ISBN 0-471-25223-9

LC 98-49721

This includes "experiments in astronomy, biology, chemistry, earth science, and physics. . . . Each activity includes a purpose, a list of materials, a step-by-step procedure, results, and an explanation. Experiments address such topics as the Moon's 'changing' size, how environment affects body temperature, and why ice pops are softer than ice. An excellent resource." SLJ

Janice VanCleave's big book of play and find out science projects. Wiley 2007 213p il pa $19.95
Grades: K 1 2 3 **507.8**
1. Science projects 2. Science -- Experiments
ISBN 978-0-7879-8928-6 pa; 0-7879-8928-2 pa

LC 2006-52572

This "is a compilation of 56 hands-on activities based on authentic questions asked by children. The four-part book contains activities in each of the following content areas: 'Physical Science,' 'Nature,' 'Bugs,' and 'Human Body.' . . . Adults and children will likely find it a useful tool." Sci Books Films

Includes glossary and bibliographical references

Janice VanCleave's engineering for every kid; easy activities that make learning science fun. Jossey-Bass 2007 205p il (Science for every kid series) pa $14.95
Grades: 4 5 6 7 **507.8**
1. Engineering 2. Science projects 3. Science -- Experiments
ISBN 978-0-471-47182-0 pa; 0-471-47182-8 pa

LC 2006-10540

Explains some of the basic physical principles of engineering, accompanied by activities that illustrate those principles

★ **Janice** VanCleave's guide to the best science fair projects; [by] Janice VanCleave. Wiley 1997 156p il pa $14.95
Grades: 4 5 6 7 **507.8**
1. Science projects 2. Science -- Experiments
ISBN 0-471-14802-4

LC 96-27512

"In the first section, VanCleave discusses scientific methodology: how to organize a project from selecting a topic through the investigatory process, the importance of keeping records, writing a final report, and the value of a nicely crafted presentation. . . . The next section—the largest by far—presents a number of double-page projects in a variety of fields. . . . A clear and informative addition." SLJ

Includes glossary and bibliographical references

Janice VanCleave's science around the year. Wiley 2000 122p il pa $12.95

Grades: 4 5 6 7 **507.8**
1. Science -- Experiments
ISBN 0-471-33096-5

LC 99-53778

Presents experiments and activities in such fields as astronomy, biology, chemistry, earth science, and physics that are in some way related to one of the four seasons

Wheeler-Toppen, Jodi
Science experiments that explode and implode; fun projects for curious kids. Capstone Press 2011 32p il (Edge books: kitchen science) lib bdg $26.65; pa $7.95
Grades: 3 4 5 6 **507.8**
1. Explosions 2. Science -- Experiments
ISBN 978-1-4296-5427-2; 1-4296-5427-9; 978-1-4296-6250-5 pa; 1-4296-6250-6 pa

LC 2010027687

Provides step-by-step instructions for science projects using household materials and explains the science behind the experiments.

"Attractive, colorful, and full of photos, [this title] will appeal to a wide range of kids. . . . Anyone looking for a straightforward, fun, and easy science experiment will want [this title] close by." SLJ

Includes glossary and bibliographical references

Science experiments that fizz and bubble; fun projects for curious kids. Capstone Press 2011 32p il (Edge books: kitchen science) lib bdg $26.65; pa $7.95
Grades: 3 4 5 6 **507.8**
1. Gases 2. Bubbles 3. Science -- Experiments
ISBN 978-1-4296-5425-8 lib bdg; 1-4296-5425-2 lib bdg; 978-1-4296-6251-2 pa; 1-4296-6251-4 pa

LC 2010027684

Provides step-by-step instructions for science projects using household materials and explains the science behind the experiments.

"Attractive, colorful, and full of photos, [this title] will appeal to a wide range of kids. . . . Anyone looking for a straightforward, fun, and easy science experiment will want [this title] close by." SLJ

Includes glossary and bibliographical references

Williams, Jennifer
★ **Oobleck,** slime, & dancing spaghetti; twenty terrific at-home science experiments inspired by favorite children's books. by Jennifer Williams. Bright Sky Press 2009 192 p. ill. (paperback) $14.95
Grades: 4 5 6 **507.8**
1. Children's literature 2. Science -- Experiments
ISBN 1933979348; 9781933979342

LC 2009000876

This book "provides a series of science experiments designed to explore concepts and ideas that spring from various stories. At the beginning of each chapter, a children's book is . . . summarized. The author then explains a related science concept, suggests discussion questions that connect the experiment to the story, and offers ideas for taking the project further. . . . The experiments cover concepts including polymers, chemical reactions, and non-Newtonian fluids." (School Library Journal)

"Using children's literature as a springboard, this title provides a series of science experiments designed to explore concepts and ideas that spring from various stories. At the beginning of each chapter, a children's book is nicely summarized. The author then explains a related science concept, suggests discussion questions that connect the experiment to the story, and offers ideas for taking the project further. This is serious science. . . . The experiments do a really wonderful job of emphasizing the importance of observation and data collection. The writing is relatively clear. . . . This book is great choice for home use and science units." SLJ

Includes bibliographical references.

Young, Karen Romano

Experiments to do on your family; 20 projects and experiments about sisters, brothers, parents, pets, and the rest of the gang. illustrations by David Goldin. National Geographic 2010 80p il (Science fair winners) $24.90; pa $12.95

Grades: 3 4 5 6   **507.8**

1. Psychology 2. Science -- Experiments
ISBN 978-1-4263-0692-1; 1-4263-0692-X; 978-1-4263-0691-4 pa; 1-4263-0691-1 pa

This volume provides "outlines for science fair projects in the behavioral . . . sciences. The procedures include just enough structure to help novice experimenters get started. . . . Well-placed questions encourage creativity and further thinking. [The] volume includes humorous cartoon spot illustrations and a section on preparing presentations." Horn Book Guide

Junkyard science; 20 projects and experiments about junk, garbage, waste, things we don't need anymore, and ways to recycle or reuse it--or lose it. illustrations by David Goldin. National Geographic 2010 80p il (Science fair winners) $24.90; pa $12.95

Grades: 3 4 5 6   **507.8**

1. Recycling 2. Environmental sciences 3. Science -- Experiments
ISBN 978-1-4263-0690-7; 1-4263-0690-3; 978-1-4263-0689-1 pa; 1-4263-0689-X pa

This volume provides "outlines for science fair projects in the . . . environmental . . . sciences. The procedures include just enough structure to help novice experimenters get started. . . . Well-placed questions encourage creativity and further thinking. [The] volume includes humorous cartoon spot illustrations and a section on preparing presentations." Horn Book Guide

508   Natural history

Baker, Stuart

In the Antarctic. Marshall Cavendish Benchmark 2009 32p il map (Climate change) lib bdg $19.95

Grades: 5 6 7 8   **508**

1. Antarctica 2. Greenhouse effect
ISBN 978-0-7614-4438-1 lib bdg; 0-7614-4438-6 lib bdg
LC 2009-5766

The book about climate change in the Antarctic "is perfectly organized for students. . . . Unique layout features serve as signposts and will help focus readers' attention. . . . [The book] features an outstanding chart of possible effects of global warming on the area in question, listing 'Possible Event', 'Predicted Result', and 'Impact' in short, bulleted statements." SLJ

Includes glossary

In the tropics. Marshall Cavendish Benchmark 2010 32p il map (Climate change) lib bdg $19.95

Grades: 5 6 7 8   **508**

1. Tropics 2. Greenhouse effect
ISBN 978-0-7614-4440-4 lib bdg; 0-7614-4440-8 lib bdg
LC 2009-5768

The book about climate change in the Tropics "is perfectly organized for students. . . . Unique layout features serve as signposts and will help focus readers' attention. . . . [The book] features an outstanding chart of possible effects of global warming on the area in question, listing 'Pos-

sible Event', 'Predicted Result', and 'Impact' in short, bulleted statements." SLJ

Includes glossary

Banes, Graham L.

★ The **Kingfisher** encyclopedia of life; minutes, months, millennia--how long is a life on Earth? Kingfisher 2012 160 p. $19.99

Grades: 3 4 5 6   **508**

1. Biology 2. Longevity
ISBN 0753468913; 9780753468913

This book "focuses on 230 species . . . , categorizing them according to lifespan. The chapters start with 'Here today . . . ,' which includes bacteria that survive for less than an hour, and close with 'Time Is on My Side,' which mentions champions of longevity such as the Great Barrier Reef. . . . Spreads focusing on a life span or on species are interspersed with features highlighting biodiversity, habitats, genetics, and other influences on Earth's lifeforms." (School Library Journal)

Bardhan-Quallen, Sudipta

Nature science experiments; what's hopping in a dust bunny? illustrated by Edward Miller. Sterling 2010 64p il (Mad science) $12.95

Grades: 4 5 6   **508**

1. Nature study 2. Science -- Experiments
ISBN 978-1-4027-2412-1; 1-4027-2412-8

"The first chapter of this attractive book, 'The Stuff of Life,' jumps right in by outlining the materials needed and the step-by-step process to follow to collect and isolate DNA by rinsing one's mouth out with salt water. . . . Youngsters can turn to the table of contents or detailed index to choose experiments based on interest and availability of resources. . . . The chapters on bacteria and protists include color photomicrographs of the organisms, and amusing cartoon illustrations appear throughout. This exploration of the natural world will spark readers' interest in experimenting and questioning results." SLJ

Beer, Amy-Jane

Cool nature; Filled with facts & projects for kids of all ages. Amy-Jane Beer. Trafalgar Square Books 2016 111 p. color illustrations $14.99

Grades: 4 5 6 7   **508**

1. Nature 2. Natural history
ISBN 1910232254; 9781910232255

This children's book in the My Cool series by Amy-Jane Beer "contains everything . . . [a] naturalist needs to know. Meet nature's most fearsome predators, explore the wonders of the ocean, and marvel at the ability of animals to survive in the harshest environments. . . . Learn about why we should all care about endangered species, who would win in a fight between a shark and a honey badger, and where to go to see whales in the wild." (Publisher's note)

"Nature enthusiasts who enjoy learning about the life cycle of the guinea worm or understanding basic scientific principles such as photosynthesis will enjoy this colorful and informative book." SLJ

Burnie, David

The **Kingfisher** nature encyclopedia; rev ed.; Kingfisher 2010 320p il $27.99

Grades: 4 5 6 7   **508**

1. Nature 2. Natural history 3. Reference books
ISBN 978-0-7534-6503-5; 0-7534-6503-5

First published 2004 with title: The Kingfisher illustrated nature encyclopedia

"Organized into three sections—the first on our planet's origin and the evolution of life, the second surveying the five biotic kingdoms, the third taking closer looks at 14 biomes . . .—each spread offers a topical discussion that ranges in scope from 'Seasons and Weather' or 'How

Fungi Feed' to 'Protozoans' and 'Tropical Forests.' Color photos on every page add visual interest while playing supporting roles to information presented in captions and columns of lucid, not heavily technical narrative text. . . . This is a first-rate overview of its topic." SLJ

Chin, Jason

★ **Island**; a story of the Galapagos. Jason Chin. 1st ed. Roaring Brook Press 2012 40 p. (alk. paper) $16.99

Grades: 3 4 5 6   **508**

1. Birds 2. Droughts 3. Reptiles 4. Natural history -- Galapagos Islands

ISBN 1596437162; 9781596437166

LC 2011033797

The author, Jason Chin, explains "how species of reptiles and birds on the Galapagos have evolved. He begins with the birth of the islands themselves, a process in which volcanic eruptions punch successive holes in the Earth's surface as tectonic plates move over them, [and] the adaptations of the islands' animals. . . . [Chin also provides information on the] droughts [that] become more common [due to the] climate and geology." (Publishers Weekly)

Includes bibliographical references and index.

Gates, Phil

Nature got there first; 2nd ed.; Kingfisher 2010 64p il $16.99

Grades: 3 4 5 6   **508**

1. Nature 2. Inventions 3. Technology

ISBN 978-0-7534-6410-6; 0-7534-6410-1

First published 1995

"This browsable title presents fascinating facts about inventions inspired by nature, showing the similarities between the workings of I beams and the make-up of dinosaur vertebrae; the mechanics of sailboats and the physiognomy of jellyfish; and the movements of giant squids and jet engine design. . . . The well-chosen images are both inviting and clearly illustrate the points made in the text and captions. . . . This is an informative, appealing look at the connections between natural and human design." Booklist

Includes glossary

Granström, Brita

Nature adventures; [by] Mick Manning & Brita Granstr["o]m. Frances Lincoln Children's Books 48p il $18.95

Grades: 2 3 4 5   **508**

1. Nature study

ISBN 978-1-84780-088-6; 1-84780-088-2

"Highly illustrated, information-packed pages entice readers to explore nature wherever they might find themselves and to take an active look at the world around them. Chapters include 'In the Town,' 'Fresh Water,' 'Woodland,' 'Field and Hedgerow,' 'Wild Country,' 'The Seashore,' and 'Through the Seasons.' Beautifully drawn artwork in pencil and watercolor provides field-guide references for budding explorers." SLJ

Includes glossary

Kalman, Bobbie

What are opposites in nature? Crabtree Pub. Co. 2010 24p il (Looking at nature) lib bdg $21.27; pa $6.95

Grades: K 1 2   **508**

1. Opposites

ISBN 978-0-7787-3326-3 lib bdg; 0-7787-3326-2 lib bdg; 978-0-7787-3346-1 pa; 0-7787-3346-7 pa

LC 2010016399

This book explores opposites found in nature.

"Bright, colorful photographs were selected with young readers in mind, and the type is large—perfect for reading together. . . Throughout

the book are questions that challenge the reader to identify the opposites shown on the pages. . . . Parents and teachers will find . . . [this book] a great addition to a child's library." Sci Books & Films

The **Kid's** Guide to Exploring Nature; Brooklyn Botanic Garden Educators; illustrated by Laszlo; Veres. Sterling Pub Co Inc 2014 120 p. color illustrations $16.95

Grades: 3 4 5 6   **508**

1. Nature 2. Nature conservation

ISBN 1889538884; 9781889538884

AAAS/Subaru SB & F Prize in Excellence in Science Books Finalists, Hands-on Science (2014)

This children's book, by the educators of the Brooklyn Botanic Garden and illustrated by László Veres, part of the "BBG Guides for a Greener Planet" series, "will inspire kids to look closely at the world around them! . . . It teaches children how to observe environments as a naturalist does and leads them on 24 adventures that reveal the complex ecosystems of plants and animals in the woods, at the beach, and in a city park." (Publisher's note)

"This addition to the BBG Guides for a Green Planet series walks readers through the basics of becoming a naturalist. Divided by season, the chapters introduce a variety of ecosystems, such as the beach, woods, city, and meadow. Nature-themed activities appear alongside guides to the flora and fauna of the regions, scavenger hunts, naturalist careers, and introductions to concepts like symbiotic relationships, all of which encourage readers to observe the intricacies of the natural world. Despite the project's New York City origins, readers from just about any geographical location will be able to find information for identifying local wildlife." PW

Lynch, Wayne

The **Everglades**; text and photographs by Wayne Lynch. NorthWord Books for Young Readers 2007 64p il (Our wild world: ecosystems) $16.95; pa $8.95

Grades: 4 5 6 7   **508**

1. Everglades (Fla.) 2. Natural history -- Florida

ISBN 978-1-55971-970-4; 1-55971-970-2; 978-1-55971-971-1 pa; 1-55971-971-0 pa

LC 2006-101497

This "provides an up-close look at the fascinating flora and fauna of the world-famous Everglades. . . . Lynch . . . smoothly pairs engaging prose with numerous color photographs that capture the beauty of the region in both sweeping panorama and close-up detail." Booklist

Morrison, Gordon

★ **Nature** in the neighborhood; [by] Gordon Morrison. Houghton Mifflin Company 2004 32p il $16

Grades: 3 4 5 6   **508**

1. Seasons 2. Natural history

ISBN 0-618-35215-5

LC 2004-2354

"Morrison offers another quiet, layered view of a natural world that is familiar to many children. . . . His precise, pencil-and-watercolor artwork encourages viewers to look closely at common neighborhood scenes." Booklist

Potter, Jean

Nature in a nutshell for kids; over 100 activities you can do in ten minutes or less. Wiley 1995 136p il pa $12.95

Grades: 2 3 4   **508**

1. Nature study

ISBN 0-471-04444-X

LC 94-28953

"Each of the 102 experiments is easy, uses safe and mostly readily available household supplies, and is fun at the same time. Divided into seasonal sections, the activities have catchy titles, state hypotheses, list materials, lay out procedures, and finish with clear explanations. Among the noteworthy investigations are: how duck feathers react to water, how mountains are formed, what keeps a seal from freezing in icy weather, whether ants prefer sugar or aspertame, and more." SLJ

Includes glossary and bibliographical references

Rau, Dana Meachen

Day and night. Marshall Cavendish Benchmark 2010 31p il (Bookworms. Nature's cycles) lib bdg $22.79

Grades: PreK K 1   **508**

1. Day 2. Night

ISBN 978-0-7614-4094-9 lib bdg; 0-7614-4094-1 lib bdg

LC 2008-42512

"Well composed, simple sentences tie directly to colorful, carefully chosen photos [and] . . . accurate information flows naturally. . . . A great resource for sharing one-on-one with the youngest readers." Libr Media Connect

Includes glossary

Schwartz, David M.

★ What in the wild? mysteries of nature concealed and revealed: ear-tickling poems. by David M. Schwartz and Yael Schy; eye-tricking photos by Dwight Kuhn. Tricycle Press 2010 un il $16.99; lib bdg $19.99

Grades: K 1 2 3 4   **508**

1. Animals 2. Nature study 3. Nature poetry

ISBN 978-1-58246-310-0; 1-58246-310-7; 978-1-58246-359-9 lib bdg; 1-58246-359-9 lib bdg

"A nifty combo of poetry (often of the concrete variety), super color photos, scientific information, and a guessing game (complete with whole-page flaps for lifting). . . . Fun as a read-alone or for one-on-one sharing, this tidy package from a talented trio will delight children (and teachers of whole curriculum, too)." SLJ

Includes bibliographical references

Wood, A. J.

Charles Darwin and the Beagle adventure; countries visited during the voyage round the world of HMS Beagle under the command of Captain Fitzroy, Royal Navy, including extracts from the works of Charles Darwin. written by A.J. Wood & Clint Twist. Candlewick Press 2009 un il map $19.99

Grades: 4 5 6 7 8   **508**

1. Evolution 2. Naturalists 3. Travel writers 4. Writers on science 5. Beagle Expedition (1831-1836)

ISBN 978-0-7636-4538-0; 0-7636-4538-9

LC 2009-921214

"This beautifully illustrated large-format book immediately appeals to both the eye and the mind. Imitating a 19th-century scrapbook to a certain extent, including various pullouts . . . the book draws the young reader in. . . . Included are copious quotes from Darwin's journals and other writings, as well as reproductions . . . of numerous 19th-century engravings, drawings, and watercolors, some from the Beagle voyage itself. . . . Integrated into the 19th-century material are modern illustrations and well-written narratives relating background information, the story of the Beagle's voyage . . . and notes on Darwin's life and work. . . . This volume provides an excellent introduction to Darwin and his accomplishments." Sci Books Films

508.2   Seasons

Anderson, Maxine

Explore spring! 25 great ways to learn about spring. [by Maxine Anderson; illustrated by Alexis Frederick-Frost] Nomad Press 2007 92p il pa $12.95

Grades: 2 3 4 5   **508.2**

1. Spring 2. Science -- Experiments

ISBN 978-0-9785037-4-1

Explains what spring is and why it occurs. Includes projects, activities, and experiments.

"Bold, black-and-white cartoons and occasional jokes add levity to the science. . . . The information is sound, with engaging activities to test and illuminate spring events." SLJ

Includes glossary and bibliographical references

Explore winter! 25 great ways to learn about winter. [by Maxine Anderson; illustrated by Alexis Frederick-Frost] Nomad Press 2007 92p il pa $12.95

Grades: 2 3 4 5   **508.2**

1. Winter 2. Science -- Experiments

ISBN 978-0-9785037-5-8

Explains what winter is and why it occurs. Includes projects, activities, and experiments.

"Pages of basic information are interspersed with 'Wow' facts, black-and-white cartoon illustrations, and jokes. . . . Curious readers will gain a new level of understanding about winter after reading, laughing at, and experimenting with this book." SLJ

Includes glossary and bibliographical references

Branley, Franklyn Mansfield

★ Sunshine makes the seasons; illustrated by Michael Rex. newly illustrated ed; HarperCollins Pubs. 2005 31p il (Let's-read-and-find-out science) hardcover o.p. pa $4.99

Grades: K 1 2 3   **508.2**

1. Seasons

ISBN 0-06-059203-6; 0-06-059205-2 pa

LC 2003-25457

First published 1974; this is a newly illustrated edition of the text revised for the 1985 edition

Describes how sunshine and the tilt of the earth's axis are responsible for the changing seasons

Includes bibliographical references

Carter, David A.

Spring; by David Carter (Author) Harry N Abrams Inc 2016 12 p. color illustrations $14.95

Grades: PreK K   **508.2**

1. Spring -- fiction

ISBN 1419719122; 9781419719127

This is the second book in David Carter's "seasons pop-up" series. "Just in time for spring, each spread has a very brief verse and depicts common springtime flora and fauna. All things pictured are labeled (robins, water lilies, deer and fawns, cherry trees, etc.). The text is simple for very young readers to understand and enjoy." (Publisher's note)

"It's a well-executed and well-rounded exploration of the season of rebirth and renewal." Pub Wkly

Crausaz, Anne

Seasons. Kane/Miller 2011 un il $15.99

Grades: K 1 2   **508.2**

1. Seasons

ISBN 1-61067-006-X; 978-1-61067-006-7

"Spring is when everything looks green, blooming trees smell fragrant, 'blackbirds are singing about their favorite season,' a ladybug on your hand 'might tickle,' and cherries are sweet. . . . Preschool." (Horn Book)

"With an emphasis on taste, smell, and outdoor activity, Crausaz guides readers through the seasons of the year in this understated and evocative French import. Crisp, delicate digital artwork set against mostly plain backgrounds keeps the focus on the freckled, rosy-cheeked girl." Publ Wkly

Esbaum, Jill

Everything spring. National Geographic 2010 15p il (Picture the seasons) pa $5.95

Grades: PreK K 1 **508.2**

1. Spring

ISBN 978-1-4263-0607-5; 1-4263-0607-5

"These pages burst with vibrant photographs of baby animals and closeups of buds and growth. Esbaum uses poetic prose to connect children with the joy of the season." SLJ

Goldstone, Bruce

Wonderful winter; All Kinds of Winter Facts and Fun. Bruce Goldstone. Henry Holt & Co. 2016 48 p. color illustrations (hardcover) $17.99; (ebook) $60

Grades: K 1 2 3 **508.2**

1. Winter -- Pictorial works

ISBN 9780805099812; 9780805099829

LC 2015030952

In this book, by Bruce Goldstone, "winter is a season of wondering and waiting. We wonder why some trees lose their leaves while others stay green all winter long. We wait for the first snowfall—and then wonder at how amazing each snowflake is. We wonder how animals manage to live in the cold. And we can't wait to celebrate Christmas, Hanukkah, and Kwanzaa." (Publisher's note)

"With its appealing illustrations and clearly presented information, here's a fine resource for teachers discussing winter with young children. Consider multiple copies." Booklist

Lindeen, Mary

Fall; by Mary Lindeen. Norwood House Press 2015 32 p. color illustrations (library edition : alk. paper) $22.60

Grades: PreK K 1 **508.2**

1. Easy reading materials 2. Autumn

ISBN 1599536811; 9781599536811

LC 2014047649

In this juvenile book, by Mary Lindeen, part of the publisher's "Beginning-to-Read" series, describes the Autumn. "Fall is a time of change. The leaves change colors, the weather gets cooler, birds fly south, and school starts. It's also time for picking apples and Halloween. This . . . book features engaging, informative text and beautiful full-color photographs, which work together to foster independent reading." (Publisher's note)

"These books are clearly intended for instructional use or supplementary skills practice, with back matter sections for parents and teachers corresponding closely to Common Core reading standards on vocabulary, craft and structure, foundational skills, close reading, and fluency." Booklist

Rau, Dana Meachen

Seasons. Marshall Cavendish Benchmark 2009 31p il (Bookworms. Nature's cycles) lib bdg $22.79

Grades: PreK K 1 **508.2**

1. Seasons

ISBN 978-0-7614-4098-7 lib bdg; 0-7614-4098-4 lib bdg

LC 2008-42507

"Well composed, simple sentences tie directly to colorful, carefully chosen photos [and] . . . accurate information flows naturally. . . . A great resource for sharing one-on-one with the youngest readers." Libr Media Connect

Includes glossary

Rotner, Shelley

Hello spring! Shelley Rotner. Holiday House 2017 32 p. color illustrations (hardcover) $16.95

Grades: PreK K 1 **508.2**

1. Spring

ISBN 9780823437528

LC 2016032932

In this book, by Shelley Rotner, "when winter ends, spring begins! The days get longer and the air gets warmer. Trees and flowers bloom and animals have their babies. Spring is the perfect time to have fun! Preschoolers will love this lyrical yet simple introduction to the wondrous surprises brought by spring." (Publisher's note)

Rustad, Martha E. H.

Fall weather; cooler temperatures. illustrated by Amanda Enright. Millbrook Press 2011 24p il (Fall's here!) lib bdg $23.93

Grades: K 1 2 3 **508.2**

1. Autumn

ISBN 978-0-7613-5063-7; 0-7613-5063-2

LC 2010048309

This book about Fall weather is "outstanding for . . . its clear description of seasons and the word 'equinox.' . . . Colorful illustrations fill the spreads with active, cartoonlike boys and girls surrounded by the green, brown, and orange hues of autumn." SLJ

Schuette, Sarah L.

Let's look at fall; by Sarah L. Schuette. Capstone Press 2007 24p il (Investigate the seasons) $19.93

Grades: K 1 2 **508.2**

1. Autumn 2. Animal behavior

ISBN 978-0-7368-6705-4; 0-7368-6705-8

LC 2006020449

"The format consists of about three descriptive sentences per page in a large font, a vivid color photograph opposite, and colorful chapter titles in a larger typeface. . . . [This book is] excellent . . . for unit study and wonderful for sharing or browsing." SLJ

Includes bibliographical references

Let's look at spring; by Sarah L. Schuette. Capstone Press 2007 24p il (Investigate the seasons) $19.93

Grades: K 1 2 **508.2**

1. Spring 2. Animal behavior

ISBN 978-0-7368-6707-8; 0-7368-6707-4

LC 2006020451

"The format consists of about three descriptive sentences per page in a large font, a vivid color photograph opposite, and colorful chapter titles in a larger typeface. . . . [This book is] excellent . . . for unit study and wonderful for sharing or browsing." SLJ

Includes bibliographical references

Let's look at summer; by Sarah L. Schuette. Capstone Press 2007 24p il (Investigate the seasons) $19.93

Grades: K 1 2   **508.2**

1. Summer 2. Animal behavior

ISBN 978-0-7368-6708-5; 0-7368-6708-2

LC 2006020452

"The format consists of about three descriptive sentences per page in a large font, a vivid color photograph opposite, and colorful chapter titles in a larger typeface.... [This book is] excellent ... for unit study and wonderful for sharing or browsing." SLJ

Includes bibliographical references

Let's look at winter; by Sarah L. Schuette. Capstone Press 2007 24p il (Investigate the seasons) $19.93

Grades: K 1 2   **508.2**

1. Winter 2. Animal behavior

ISBN 978-0-7368-6706-1; 0-7368-6706-6

LC 2006020508

"The format consists of about three descriptive sentences per page in a large font, a vivid color photograph opposite, and colorful chapter titles in a larger typeface.... [This book is] excellent ... for unit study and wonderful for sharing or browsing." SLJ

Includes bibliographical references

Smith, Sian

Fall. Heinemann Library 2009 24p il (Seasons) lib bdg $20.71; pa $5.99

Grades: K 1   **508.2**

1. Autumn

ISBN 1-4329-2732-9 pa; 978-1-4329-2727-1 lib bdg; 1-4329-2727-2 lib bdg; 978-1-4329-2732-5 pa

LC 2008049155

This describes the clothing, weather, and human and animal activities of the Autumn.

"What distinguishes [this book] from others on the same [subject is] the vibrant, eye-catching photographs. The sentences are simple and repetitive.... Reading teachers will want to use this ... for instructional purposes while early readers will feel successful mastering the text. Students will delight in the color photographs of animals and children enjoying the activities." SLJ

Spring. Heinemann Library 2009 24p il (Seasons) lib bdg $20.71; pa $5.99

Grades: K 1   **508.2**

1. Spring

ISBN 978-1-4329-2728-8 lib bdg; 1-4329-2728-0 lib bdg; 978-1-4329-2733-2 pa; 1-4329-2733-7 pa

LC 2008049156

This describes the clothing, weather, and human and animal activities of spring

"What distinguishes [this book] from others on the same [subject is] the vibrant, eye-catching photographs. The sentences are simple and repetitive.... Reading teachers will want to use this ... for instructional purposes while early readers will feel successful mastering the text. Students will delight in the color photographs of animals and children enjoying the activities." SLJ

Summer. Heinemann Library 2009 24p il (Seasons) lib bdg $20.71; pa $5.99

Grades: K 1   **508.2**

1. Summer

ISBN 978-1-4329-2729-5 lib bdg; 1-4329-2729-9 lib bdg; 978-1-4329-2734-9 pa; 1-4329-2734-5 pa

LC 2008049157

This describes the clothing, weather, and human and animal activities of summer

"What distinguishes [this book] from others on the same [subject is] the vibrant, eye-catching photographs. The sentences are simple and repetitive.... Reading teachers will want to use this ... for instructional purposes while early readers will feel successful mastering the text. Students will delight in the color photographs of animals and children enjoying the activities." SLJ

Winter. Heinemann Library 2009 24p il (Seasons) lib bdg $20.71; pa $5.99

Grades: K 1   **508.2**

1. Winter

ISBN 978-1-4329-2730-1 lib bdg; 1-4329-2730-2 lib bdg; 978-1-4329-2735-6 pa; 1-4329-2735-3 pa

LC 2008049162

This describes the clothing, weather, and human and animal activities of winter

"What distinguishes [this book] from others on the same [subject is] the vibrant, eye-catching photographs. The sentences are simple and repetitive.... Reading teachers will want to use this ... for instructional purposes while early readers will feel successful mastering the text. Students will delight in the color photographs of animals and children enjoying the activities." SLJ

509   History, geographic treatment, biography

Beshore, George W.

★ **Science** in ancient China; [by] George Beshore. Watts 1998 63p il map (Science of the past) hardcover o.p. pa $8.95

Grades: 4 5 6 7   **509**

1. Science and civilization 2. Science -- China -- History

ISBN 0-531-11334-5 lib bdg; 0-531-15914-0 pa

LC 97-3519

First published 1988 in the First book series

Surveys the achievements of the ancient Chinese in science, medicine, astronomy, and cosmology, and describes such innovations as rockets, wells, the compass, water wheels, and movable type

Includes glossary and bibliographical references

Cole, Joanna

★ The **magic** school bus and the science fair expedition; illustrated by Bruce Degen. Scholastic Press 2006 45p il $15.99

Grades: 2 3 4   **509**

1. Scientists 2. Science -- History

ISBN 0-590-10824-7

Ms. Frizzle takes her class on a tour through the history of science so they can get ideas for their science fair

"This has all the hallmarks of the winning series: humorous cartoon speech bubbles; instructive, funny, appealing illustrations; and clear language that explains basic concepts without condescension." Booklist

Eamer, Claire

Before the World Was Ready; Stories of Daring Genius in Science. by Claire Eamer. Firefly Books Ltd 2013 125 p. (paperback) $14.95; $24.95

Grades: 5 6 7 8   **509**

1. Inventions 2. Scientists

ISBN 1554515351; 9781554515356; 9781554515363

This book looks at eight scientists and inventors. "Alfred Wegener struggled to convince geologists that the ground beneath our feet is moving.... Nikola Tesla's futuristic ideas about electricity were dismissed. Charles Darwin delayed publishing his controversial theory of evolution for decades." Also included are Charles Babbage, Ada Lovelace, Rachel Carson, and George Cayley. (Publisher's note)

Harris, Jacqueline L.

★ **Science** in ancient Rome. Watts 1998 64p il map (Science of the past) hardcover o.p. pa $8.95

Grades: 4 5 6 7   **509**

1. Science and civilization 2. Science -- Rome -- History
ISBN 0-531-20354-9; 0-531-15916-7 pa

LC 97-1901

First published 1988 in the First book series

Describes how the Romans put to use and expanded the scientific achievements of earlier civilizations

This "includes clear, easy-to-read text; simple yet effective topic headings; excellent-quality, full-color photographs and reproductions; and Internet sites." SLJ

Includes glossary and bibliographical references

Jackson, Donna M.

★ **Extreme** scientists; exploring nature's mysteries from perilous places. Houghton Mifflin Harcourt 2009 63p il (Scientists in the field) $18

Grades: 5 6 7 8   **509**

1. Botanists 2. Explorers 3. Scientists 4. Spelunkers 5. Meteorologists 6. Microbiologists 7. College teachers
ISBN 978-0-618-77706-8; 0-618-77706-7

LC 2008-36796

This volume "profiles three scientists working far out in the field. Hurricane hunter Paul Flaherty, . . . Hazel Barton, a microbiologist specializing in single-cell organisms living in extreme conditions, . . . [and] ecologist and college professor Steve Sillett, who . . . climbs into the canopies to study redwoods. While the clearly written text includes vivid passages about the dangers these scientists face, it goes on to discuss what drives them to pursue their subjects and what they have discovered along the way. . . . The many excellent color photos portray these adventures as scientists intently focused on their work." Booklist

Includes glossary and bibliographical references

Woods, Geraldine

★ **Science** in ancient Egypt. Watts 1998 64p il (Science of the past) hardcover o.p. pa $8.95

Grades: 4 5 6 7   **509**

1. Science and civilization 2. Science -- Egypt -- History
ISBN 0-531-20341-7; 0-531-15915-9 pa

LC 97-649

First published 1988 in the First book series

Discusses the achievements of the ancient Egyptians in science, mathematics, astronomy, medicine, agriculture, and technology

"Well-researched and easy-to-understand. . . . Woods offers a fascinating look at the ancient Egyptians' accomplishments." SLJ

Includes glossary and bibliographical references

509.2 Scientists

Davidson, Tish

African American scientists and inventors; by Tish Davidson. Mason Crest Publishers 2013 64 p. ill. (some col.) (Major Black contributions from Emancipation to civil rights) (library) $22.95

Grades: 4 5 6   **509.2**

1. African American inventors 2. African American scientists 3. African American inventors -- Biography 4. African American scientists -- Biography
ISBN 1422223752; 9781422223758

LC 2011051942

This book by Tish Davidson profiles African American scientists and inventors. "Some of them were elementary school dropouts. Others became medical doctors or college professors. Some were famous, while some toiled in obscurity. . . . Lewis Latimer devised a manufacturing process that made electric lights affordable for ordinary people. Charles Drew did pioneering work in blood storage, helping save countless lives. Garrett Woods figured out how to send messages from moving trains." (Publisher's note)

Includes bibliographical references (pages 60-61) and index.

Di Domenico, Kelly

Women scientists who changed the world; by Kelly Di Domenico. Rosen Pub. 2012 106 p. col. ill. (library) $34.60

Grades: 5 6 7 8   **509.2**

1. Women scientists -- Biography 2. Women in science -- Biography
ISBN 1448859999; 9781448859993

LC 2011032120

In this collective biography by Kelly Di Domenico, "readers meet eleven women scientists, whose research and discoveries are outstanding in their fields. . . . Readers are introduced to each scientist's life and work, including the obstacles each woman had to overcome to achieve success. Profiles include biologist Rachel Carson, orangutan researcher Birute Galdikas, and Nobel Prize-winning biochemist Ada Yonath." (Publisher's note)

Includes bibliographical references (p. 101) and index.

Krull, Kathleen

Lives of the scientists; experiments, explosions (and what the neighbors thought) Kathleen Krull, Illustrated by Kathryn Hewitt. Houghton Mifflin Harcourt 2013 96 p. $20.99

Grades: 4 5 6 7   **509.2**

1. Science -- History 2. Scientists -- Biography
ISBN 0152059091; 9780152059095

LC 2012953333

The author Kathleen Krull's book focuses on the history of science. "This latest in the Lives of . . . series is summed up by the subtitle's 'What the Neighbors Thought.' The authors delve into intriguing, obscure, and peculiar facts about 20 famous scientists from all fields of study, regions of the globe, and eras of history." Topics include James D. Watson, Francis Crick, Marie Curie, Edwin Hubble, Barbara McClintock, and Grace Murray Hopper." (Booklist)

Miles, Liz

Louis Pasteur; by Liz Miles. Raintree 2009 48 p. ill. (chiefly col.) (Great scientists) (library) $32.00

Grades: 4 5 6   **509.2**

1. Science -- History -- 19th century 2. Scientists -- France -- Biography 3. Microbiologists -- France -- Biography
ISBN 141093229X; 9781410932297

LC 2007050125

This book by Liz Miles is part of the Leveled Biographies series and looks at Louis Pasteur. "What is Pasteurization? How has Pasteur's work helped treat many diseases? The 'Leveled Biographies' series offers leveled, high-interest nonfiction in a range of text genres. Each title tells the story of one memorable life, using pictures, maps, sidebars, and engaging text to make each person's story come alive." (Publisher's note)

Includes bibliographical references (p. 46) and index.

Swaby, Rachel

Trailblazers; 33 Women in Science Who Changed the World. Rachel Swaby. Delacorte Press 2016 208 p. (hardcover) $15.99; (ebook) $47.97

Grades: 5 6 7 8   **509.2**

1. Women scientists 2. Women inventors -- Biography 3. Women

scientists -- Biography

ISBN 9780399553967; 9780399554162; 9780399554179

LC 2016003806

This book, by Rachel Swaby, is a "collection of profiles of some of the world's most influential women in science. . . . These women have made strides in fields including biology, medicine, astronomy, and technology. In addition, Swaby emphasizes the fact that people aren't born brilliant scientists. They observe and experiment as kids and as adults, testing ideas again and again, each time learning something new." (Publisher's note)

"Readers with scientific ambitions of their own will find much to admire in these accomplished and unconventional women." Pub Wkly

Includes bibliographical references (pages [171]-189) and index.

509.56   Science – Islamic Empire -- History

Romanek, Trudee

Science, medicine, and math in the early Islamic world; Trudee Romanek. Crabtree Pub. Company 2012 48 p. (reinforced library binding : alk. paper) $30.60

Grades: 4 5 6 7   **509.56**

1. Science -- History 2. Medicine -- History 3. Mathematics -- History 4. Islamic civilization 5. Science -- Islamic Empire -- History

ISBN 0778721701; 9780778721703; 9780778721772; 9781427195630; 9781427198402

LC 2012000077

This children's educational book, by Trudee Romanek, describes "the scientific contributions of the early Islamic empires to science, medicine, and mathematics. . . . This . . . book explores their public hospitals, libraries, and universities; their achievements in mathematics and astronomy, and the pursuit of alchemy; Arabic numbers; optics; music and musical instruments; poetry; and education." (Publisher's note)

510   Mathematics

Ball, Johnny

Go figure! Johnny Ball. Revised edition DK Publishing 2016 96p color illustrations $9.99

Grades: 3 4 5 6 7   **510**

1. Numbers 2. Mathematics

ISBN 9781465443854; 1465443851

"Discover why there are 60 minutes in an hour, why daisies have to have 34, 55, or 89 petals, and why finding a prime number could make you a millionaire." (Publisher's note)

Bodach, Vijaya

Bar graphs; by Vijaya Khisty Bodach. Capstone Press 2008 32p il (Making graphs) lib bdg $23.93; pa $7.95

Grades: K 1 2   **510**

1. Graphic methods

ISBN 978-1-4296-0040-8 lib bdg; 1-4296-0040-3 lib bdg; 978-1-4296-2870-9 pa; 1-4296-2870-7 pa

LC 2007004670

This "book illustrates how to sort items and represent quantity using horizontal and vertical bars on a graph. Toy animals, fruit, pet type, and hair color are used as examples. . . . [The] title encourages readers to create their own graphs. Large, colorful photographs depict the concepts and feature ethnically diverse children. The photos and graphs complement the controlled-vocabulary [text]." SLJ

Includes glossary and bibliographical references

Other titles in this series:

Pictographs

Pie graphs

Tally charts

Connolly, Sean

The **book** of perfectly perilous math; 24 death-defying challenges for young mathematicians. by Sean Connolly. Workman Pub. 2012 xiii, 240 p.p ill. (alk. paper) $12.95

Grades: 4 5 6   **510**

1. Mathematical recreations 2. Word problems (Mathematics) 3. Mathematics -- Study and teaching 4. Mathematics -- Problems, exercises, etc 5. Problem solving -- Problems, exercises, etc

ISBN 0761163743; 9780761163749

LC 2012003443

This children's book by Sean Connolly "blends middle school math with fantasy. . . . These word problems are perilous, do-or-die scenarios of blood-sucking vampires . . . or [of] a rowboat of 5 shipwrecked sailors with a single barrel of freshwater. . . . They test readers on fractions, algebra, geometry, probability, expressions and equations, and more." (Publisher's note)

D'Amico, Joan

The **math** chef; over 60 math activities and recipes for kids. [by] Joan D'Amico, Karen Eich Drummond; illustrations by Tina Cash-Walsh. Wiley 1997 180p il pa $12.95

Grades: 4 5 6   **510**

1. Cooking 2. Mathematics

ISBN 0-471-13813-4

LC 96-22143

Relates math and cookery by presenting math concepts and reinforcing them with recipes. Provides practice in converting from English to metric system, multiplying quantities, measuring area, estimating, and more

"The instructional value of this book is excellent. . . . The illustrations and content are accurate and very well depicted." Sci Books Films

Includes glossary

Flatt, Lizann

Sorting through spring; Lizann Flatt, Ashley Barron. Owlkids Books Inc. 2013 32 p. (Math in nature) $14.95

Grades: 1 2 3   **510**

1. Nature 2. Mathematics

ISBN 1926973593; 9781926973593

LC 2012945652

"The aim of this . . . picture book is to introduce mathematical concepts such as patterning, data management, and probability by using occurrences in nature as examples. It examines events in springtime, such as rain, bird nests, budding flowers, and baby rabbits, and asks mathematical questions about them. . . . This is the second in the 'Math in Nature' series." (Children's Literature)

Green, Dan

Math; a book you can count on! created by Basher; written by Dan Green. Kingfisher 2010 64p il $12.99; pa $7.99

Grades: 4 5 6 7   **510**

1. Mathematics

ISBN 978-0-7534-6620-9; 0-7534-6620-1; 978-0-7534-6419-9 pa; 0-7534-6419-5 pa

This "introduces basic mathematical terms such as zero, line, pi, quadrilaterals, ratio, bar graph, and x (representing unknown quantities). Each one, personified in the accompanying digital illustration, speaks for itself. . . . Reminiscent of Japanese cartoons, the colorful, iconic illustrations of the characters are appealing enough to disarm many mathphobic students, while those who love the subject will be in their element. . . . Appealing to a broad range of readers, this little book introduces plenty of ideas to build on while presenting familiar concepts in a fresh way." Booklist

Lee, Cora

The **Great** Number Rumble; a story of math in surprising places. Cora Lee & Gillian O'Reilly; illustrations by Lil Crump. 2nd edition Annick Press 2016 104 p. chiefly color illustrations pbk $12.95; hbk $19.95

Grades: 3 4 5 6   **510**

1. Mathematics

ISBN 9781554518494; 9781554518500; 1554518504

"Math can show up in the most unlikely places! When the schools in Jeremy's town ban math, all the kids cheer, all except his friend Sam, a self-proclaimed mathnik, who sets out to prove that math is not only important, but fun. Running parallel to the fictional narrative are informative sidebars that discuss the weird, puzzling, and amusing aspects of mathematics. Some topics covered are math in nature, art, music, magic and tricks, crime solving, and sports." (Publisher's note)

"This is a fun romp with lots of unexpected bits about geometry, consonance in music, geographic profiling, virtual reality, and a whole lot of other neat stuff, carefully packaged to entice readers." SLJ

Includes bibliographical references (pages 92-94) and index

McKellar, Danica

Math doesn't suck; how to survive middle school math without losing your mind or breaking a nail. [by] Danica McKellar. Hudson Street Press 2007 297p il $23.95

Grades: 5 6 7 8   **510**

1. Mathematics

ISBN 1-59463-039-9; 978-1-59463-039-2

LC 2007017091

This "covers some of the most basic ideas of middle-grade math, including concepts relating to fractions, decimals, and ratios, making each comprehensible, interesting, and fun. Using real-world constructions, such as tangled necklaces, boyfriends, and pizza, concepts are thoroughly explained." Voice Youth Advocates

Merriam, Eve

12 ways to get to 11; written by Eve Merriam; illustrated by Bernie Karlin. Simon & Schuster Bks. for Young Readers 1993 un il hardcover o.p. pa $6.99

Grades: K 1 2 3   **510**

1. Counting 2. Mathematics

ISBN 0-689-80892-5 pa

LC 91-25810

Uses ordinary experiences to present twelve combinations of numbers that add up to eleven. Example: At the circus, six peanut shells and five pieces of popcorn

"Some of the double-page spreads are simpler to solve than others, which allows children to progress as they learn more about counting. The huge, vibrant cut-paper and colored-pencil pictures make the book fun, lively, and painlessly educational." Horn Book Guide

Schwartz, David M.

★ **G** is for googol; a math alphabet book. written by David M. Schwartz; illustrated by Marissa Moss. Tricycle Press 1998 57p il $15.95

Grades: 4 5 6 7   **510**

1. Alphabet 2. Mathematics

ISBN 1-883672-58-9

LC 98-15162

Explains the meaning of mathematical terms which begin with the different letters of the alphabet from abacus, binary, and cubit to zillion

"The text is lively and clear and will appeal to even those who think math is as dull as the kitchen floor. . . . The cartoon illustrations are colorful, amusing, and informative." SLJ

Includes glossary

Tang, Greg

Math-terpieces; the art of problem-solving. illustrated by Greg Paprocki. Scholastic Press 2003 31p il $16.95

Grades: 2 3 4   **510**

1. Counting 2. Set theory 3. Art appreciation

ISBN 0-439-44388-1

LC 2002-5361

A series of rhymes about artists and their works introduces counting and grouping numbers, as well as such artistic styles as cubism, pointillism, and surrealism

"Clearly written solutions to these exercises are given at the end of the book along with art definitions and brief explanations. This mathconcept book is far more appealing than most." SLJ

511   General principles of mathematics

Cocca, Lisa Colozza

Graphing story problems; by Lisa Colozza Cocca; illustrated by Katleen Petelinsek. Cherry Lake Pub. 2013 24 p. paperback $12.79; library $29.93

Grades: 1 2 3 4   **511**

1. Mathematics -- Graphic methods   2. Word problems (Mathematics) -- Graphic methods

ISBN 9781610809641; 9781610809894; 9781610809399; 9781610809146

LC 2012033603

"Designed to introduce readers to how graphs tell stories. Readers will see bar, line, pie, and pictographs, as well as tally charts, and be encouraged to read the stories graphs tell and create their own stories. Activities build on the material presented." (Publisher's note)

Other titles in this series are:

Line graphs

Pictographs

Pie graphs

Tally charts

Murphy, Stuart J.

The **sundae** scoop; illustrated by Cynthia Jabar. HarperCollins Pubs. 2003 33p il (Mathstart) hardcover o.p. pa $4.99

Grades: 1 2 3   **511**

1. Mathematics

ISBN 0-06-028924-4; 0-06-028925-2 lib bdg; 0-06-446250-1 pa

LC 2001-24322

This "presents the concept of combinations in a story about a group of children who host an ice-cream booth at their school picnic. With two flavors of ice cream, two sauces, and two choices of toppings, the children are surprised that eight different sundaes are available. . . . Murphy easily folds the math concepts into a lively story that will capture young readers, and Jabar reinforces the lesson with colorful , whimsical drawings of delectable ice-cream scoops." Booklist

511.3 Mathematical logic (Symbolic logic)

Berry, Minta

What comes in sets? Minta Berry. Crabtree Pub. Co. 2012 24 p.
lib bdg $22.60

Grades: K 1 2   **511.3**

1. Set theory 2. Set theory
ISBN 0778752682 pa; 0778752798 lib bdg; 9780778752684
pa; 9780778752790 lib bdg; 9781427196507 e-books;
9781427198099 e-books

LC 2011040391

This children's book by Minta Berry "introduces young readers to
the concept of equal sets. Readers will learn to identify familiar things
that come in pairs, sets of threes, fours, fives, and more." (Publisher's
note) "The basic idea of sets is introduced through familiar objects:
clothing, toys, kitchen items, and body parts. The activities encourage
children to search through their homes for sets and make comparisons."
(School Library Journal)

512 Algebra

Adler, David A., 1947-

Mystery math; a first book of algebra. by David A. Adler; illustrated by Edward Miller. Holiday House 2011 1 v.

Grades: 2 3 4   **512**

1. Algebra
ISBN 0823422895; 9780823422890

LC 2010024188

Adler tackles the "topic of algebra, starting with the basics and
working up from there. . . . Easy-to-understand mathematical notations
guide readers through the solution to each problem, which are originally
posed as word problems involving two children, Mandy and Billy, and
Igor, the caretaker of a haunted house. The Halloween theme echoes the
idea of algebra as the solving of mathematical mysteries, and Miller's
digital artwork ups the ante with a palette strong on blacks, dark blues
and lime greens." Kirkus

513 Arithmetic

Adler, David A., 1947-

Fractions, decimals, and percents; illustrated by Edward Miller.
Holiday House 2010 un il $16.95

Grades: 2 3 4   **513**

1. Fractions 2. Percentage 3. Decimal fractions
ISBN 978-0-8234-2199-2; 0-8234-2199-6

LC 2008048464

"This brightly illustrated book . . . quickly presents several math
concepts related to fractions, decimals, and percents. Using a county fair
as a backdrop, Adler discusses how to change a number in one form to
its equivalent in another; and how the value of a digit depends upon its
placement in relation to a decimal point. Miller's digital artwork illustrates the ideas clearly." Booklist

Millions, billions & trillions; understanding big numbers. by David
A. Adler; illustrated by Edward Miller. 1st ed. Holiday House 2012 32
p. col. ill. (hardcover) $17.95

Grades: 2 3 4   **513**

1. Counting 2. Picture books for children 3. Number concept 4.
Billion (The number) 5. Million (The number) 6. Trillion (The

number)
ISBN 0823424030; 9780823424030

LC 2011044752

In this book, David A. Adler and Edward Miller "put giant numbers
into perspective by using familiar frames of reference and by appealing
to readers' imaginations: 'How many ice cream sundaes would one billion dollars buy? At five dollars a sundae, you could buy one thousand
sundaes every day for more than five hundred years.' Real-world examples (New York City has a population of over eight million people)
combine with more fanciful ways to conceptualize these quantities.'"
(Publishers Weekly)

Bang, Molly

★ **Ten,** nine, eight. Greenwillow Bks. 1983 un il $16.99; lib bdg
$17.89; pa $6.99; bd bk $6.99

Grades: PreK K 1   **513**

1. Counting 2. Bedtime -- Fiction
ISBN 0-688-00906-9; 0-688-00907-7 lib bdg; 0-688-10480-0 pa;
0-688-14901-4 bd bk

LC 81-20106

A Caldecott Medal honor book, 1984
"In countdown style, the text of this counting book begins with '10
small toes all washed and warm,' and ends with '1 big girl all ready
for bed.' The captions rhyme . . . and the pictures—warm, bright paintings—show a black father and child snuggling in a chair, the child yawning, and the child hugging her toy bear after some loving good night
kisses." Bull Cent Child Books

Campbell, Sarah C.

★ **Growing** patterns; Fibonacci numbers in nature. photographs
by Sarah C. Campbell and Richard P. Campbell. Boyds Mills Press
2010 32p il $17.95

Grades: 2 3 4 5   **513**

1. Numbers 2. Nature study
ISBN 978-1-59078-752-6; 1-59078-752-8

LC 2009-24075

The authors "turn their attention to the Fibonacci sequence of numbers, employing photographs from nature, basic addition, and reader-directed text to explain it. . . . Besides being eye-catching, the photographs
ought to prove invaluable for visual learners. . . . Kids should be left with
a clear understanding of the pattern and curious about its remarkable
prevalence in nature." Publ Wkly
Includes glossary

Cleary, Brian P.

A **fraction's** goal; parts of a whole. illustrated by Brian Gable.
Millbrook Press 2011 31p il (Math is categorical) lib bdg $16.95

Grades: 2 3 4 5   **513**

1. Fractions
ISBN 978-0-8225-7881-9; 0-8225-7881-6

LC 2010051518

This "title presents fractions as a way to express parts of an entity
(pizza) or group (jugglers). The rhyming lines of text bounce along in a
genial way. . . . Brightened with eye-catching color combinations, Gable's cartoon-style illustrations express the simple mathematical ideas
clearly, while his wacky critters add a good deal of humor." Booklist
Another title in this series is:
The action of subtraction

Clements, Andrew

A **million** dots; illustrated by Mike Reed. Simon & Schuster
Books for Young Readers 2006 un il $16.95

Grades: K 1 2   513
1. Million (The number)
ISBN 0-689-85824-8

LC 2004-05349

"With one million dots printed on its pages, this large-format picture book shows how big a million really is. Along the way, the text and illustrations offer plenty to look at and think about besides the rows and rows of tiny dots. On each page, Clements selects one number and connects it to a numerical fact." Booklist

Dodds, Dayle Ann

Full house; an invitation to fractions. [by] Dayle Ann Dodds; illustrated by Abby Carter. Candlewick Press 2007 un il $16.99
Grades: 1 2 3   513
1. Fractions 2. Stories in rhyme
ISBN 978-0-7636-2468-2; 0-7636-2468-3

LC 2006051847

Miss Bloom uses fractions as the six-room Strawberry Inn fills with guests and she divides her pie into sixths

"Fresh, whimsical watercolor illustrations fairly float off the pages in this title. Rhyming text invites readers to enjoy every moment at the Strawberry Inn." SLJ

Fisher, Valorie

How high can a dinosaur count? and other math mysteries. [by] Valorie Fisher. Schwartz & Wade Books 2006 un il $16.95
Grades: 1 2 3   513
1. Counting 2. Arithmetic
ISBN 0-375-83608-X

LC 2005010851

"The text for each of the 15 problems is presented on the left, using a large, clean font on a spectrum of soft pastel backgrounds. The problems are clearly explained, but lots of alliteration and some unexpected vocabulary make for interesting reading. The illustration on the right features Fisher's unique photographic technique. Richly textured patterns and hand-drawn objects are cut out and arranged, then photographed in such a way as to create whimsical tableaux with a three-dimensional feel. The characters are charming." SLJ

Fleming, Denise

★ **Count!** Holt & Co. 1992 un il $17.95; pa $7.95
Grades: PreK K 1 2   513
1. Animals 2. Counting
ISBN 0-8050-1595-7; 0-8050-4252-0 pa

LC 91-25686

The antics of lively and colorful animals present the numbers one to ten, twenty, thirty, forty, and fifty

"A fresh, upbeat concept book. Lizards, giraffes, toucans, butterflies are available for counting—if only they'll hold still long enough! Fuchsias and oranges, teals and purples, roll over the pages blending into each other in Fleming's beautiful couched paper with hand cut-stencil illustrations. Her explosions of color and motion are captivating and energizing." SLJ

Franco, Betsy

★ **Zero** is the leaves on the tree; illustrations by Shino Arihara. Tricycle Press 2009 un il $15.99
Grades: PreK K 1 2   513
1. Zero (The number)
ISBN 978-1-58246-249-3; 1-58246-249-6

LC 2008042185

Using "evocative examples from children's everyday experiences throughout the seasons, Franco explores the concept of zero. The gouache illustrations are done in soft, muted tones and have a naive charm that will have substantial child appeal." SLJ

Giganti, Paul

How many snails? a counting book. by Paul Giganti, Jr.; pictures by Donald Crews. Greenwillow Bks. 1988 un il $16.99; pa $6.99
Grades: PreK K 1 2   513
1. Counting
ISBN 0-688-06369-1; 0-688-13639-7 pa

LC 87-26281

"Instead of inviting children to count static objects, Mr. Giganti poses a series of simple, direct questions designed to encourage youngsters to determine the often subtle differences between those objects. Donald Crews . . . concentrates here on decorating each page with objects that supply the necessary links to the text. Some of the pages—depicting a collection of motley dogs at the park or beautiful toy boats and trucks, cars and airplanes at a toy store—are a joy to look at." N Y Times Book Rev

Lewis, J. Patrick

Arithme-tickle; an even number of odd riddle-rhymes. illustrated by Frank Remkiewicz. Harcourt 2002 32p il $16
Grades: 2 3 4   513
1. Arithmetic 2. Mathematical recreations
ISBN 0-15-216418-9

LC 2001-3228

"Wordplay, riddles, and math problems test readers' skill at addition, subtraction, multiplication, division, telling time, logic, and even general knowledge in this colorfully illustrated collection. Clearly meant to make math more approachable and enjoyable, this compilation includes enough genuinely complex puzzles to keep hardcore young math buffs entertained." Booklist

Long, Lynette

Marvelous multiplication; games and activities that make math easy and fun. Wiley 2000 122p il (Magical math) pa $12.95
Grades: 3 4 5 6   513
1. Multiplication
ISBN 0-471-36982-9

LC 00-20473

Presents a series of activities, arranged in order of difficulty, that teach the operation of multiplication

"The cheerful ink drawings help make the [book] more inviting." Booklist

Markel, Michelle

Tyrannosaurus math; illustrations by Doug Cushman. Tricycle Press 2009 un il $15.99
Grades: 1 2 3   513
1. Dinosaurs 2. Arithmetic 3. Mathematics
ISBN 978-1-58246-282-0; 1-58246-282-8

LC 2008042389

"From the moment he bursts out of his shell, T-Math thinks mathematically, making number sentences to express how many digits he has and the number of kids in his family. He counts footprints by twos and uses fives and tens to group and count a herd of triceratops. He checks his subtraction with addition, draws pictures to solve word problems, creates pictographs and thinks in pie graphs. And it is his estimation skills that save his sister, who gets stranded on the wrong side of a canyon after an earthquake. . . . Cushman's brightly colored acrylic illustrations nicely show readers the math involved without diminishing in any way the personalities of the dinosaurs. The ultimate melding of a topic kids love with knowledge they need." Kirkus

Mattern, Joanne

Even or odd? Rourke Pub. 2010 24p il (Little world math concepts) lib bdg $22.79; pa $7.95

Grades: PreK K   **513**

1. Number concept

ISBN 978-1-61590-292-7 lib bdg; 1-61590-292-9 lib bdg; 978-1-61590-531-7 pa; 1-61590-531-6 pa

LC 2010009893

"Aimed at both preliterate preschoolers and emerging readers, the minimal text and images present questions and answers that introduce even and odd numbers. Magnified color photos show organized groups of everyday items . . . providing numerous opportunities for young children to practice counting by twos and identify the orphans when the groups represent odd numbers. . . . This book is a focused, one-stop resource for helping young children grasp the single, essential math concept it presents." Booklist

Includes bibliographical references

Murphy, Stuart J.

★ Divide and ride; illustrated by George Ulrich. HarperCollins Pubs. 1997 32p il (MathStart) hardcover o.p. pa $4.95

Grades: 1 2 3   **513**

1. Division

ISBN 0-06-026776-3; 0-06-026777-1 lib bdg; 0-06-446710-4 pa

LC 95-26134

"Eleven friends climb aboard the Dare-Devil roller coaster and three other rides, but before each ride can begin, all of the seats must be filled. Readers follow the children as they solve each problem by dividing and then filling the empty seats with new friends. Watercolor, pen, and ink illustrations and follow-up activities accompany the story." Horn Book Guide

Other titles in this series are:

Double the ducks

Elevator magic

The Grizzly gazette

Henry the fourth

Jack the builder

Jump kangaroo jump

Less than zero

Mall mania

More or less

Slugger's car wash

Mall mania; illustrated by Renée Andriani. HarperCollins 2006 33p il (MathStart) $15.99; pa $4.99

Grades: K 1 2   **513**

1. Addition 2. Counting

ISBN 0-06-055776-1; 0-06-055776-X pa

"The 100th person to enter Parkside Mall will get lots of promotional gifts, and four kids from Wilson Elementary School's chess club are on hand to count up the shoppers and add the numbers together. . . . The counters use a variety of addition strategies and activities, as always, Murphy adds greatly to the math lesson by making it seem a part of daily life. Suggestions for follow-up activities, both complex and easy . . . are appended." Booklist

Includes bibliographical references

Nagda, Ann Whitehead

Cheetah math; learning about division from baby cheetahs. by Ann Whitehead Nagda in collaboration with the San Diego Zoo. Henry Holt 2007 29p il $16.95

Grades: 2 3 4   **513**

1. Cheetahs 2. Division

ISBN 978-0-8050-7645-5; 0-8050-7645-X

LC 2006030069

Other titles in this series are: Panda math; Polar bear math

"Each spread includes division problems that revolve around the big cats on the left and facts about the birth and development of two baby cheetahs, Majani and Kubali, on the right. The color photography is outstanding. . . . This is a wonderful cross-curricular book and an appealing way to introduce math." SLJ

Rubin, Alan

How many fish? Yellow Umbrella Bks. 2003 17p il (Yellow umbrella books for early readers) $14.60

Grades: PreK K 1 2   **513**

1. Fishes 2. Counting

ISBN 0-7368-2013-2

LC 2003-924

Introduces counting by showing different numbers of fish and other creatures swimming in the sea

"Not only can beginning readers feel successful at mastering the short, repetitive sentences, but they can also excel at counting the human feet and fish under the water. Colorful illustrations enhance the text." SLJ

Schwartz, Richard Evan

Really big numbers; Richard Evan Scwartz. AMS, American Mathematical Society 2014 192 p. color illustrations $25

Grades: 2 3 4 5   **513**

1. Number concept

ISBN 9781470414252

LC 2013404369

"The book begins with small, easily observable numbers before building up to truly gigantic ones, like a nonillion, a tredecillion, a googol, and even ones too huge for names!" (Publisher's note)

Scieszka, Jon

★ Math curse; illustrated by Lane Smith. Viking 1995 un il $16.99

Grades: 2 3 4 5   **513**

1. Mathematics -- Fiction

ISBN 0-670-86194-4

LC 95-12341

When the teacher tells her class that they can think of almost everything as a math problem, one student acquires a math anxiety which becomes a real curse

"Bold in design and often bizarre in expression, Smith's paintings clearly express the child's feelings of bemusement, frustration, and panic as well as her eventual joy when she overcomes the math curse. . . . A child-centered, witty picture book." Booklist

Slade, Suzanne

What's new at the zoo? an animal adding adventure. illustrated by Joan Waites. Sylvan Dell 2009 un il $16.95

Grades: PreK K 1 2   **513**

1. Zoos 2. Animals 3. Addition

ISBN 978-1-934359-93-8; 1-934359-93-9

"On a visit to the zoo, a young boy counts the animal babies and parents in each enclosure, the accompanying rhyme encouraging readers to do the math along with him. . . . Slade slyly sneaks in some great vocabulary, working the animal baby names into each verse. . . . Backmatter teaches two methods for adding all the numbers, a section about fact families and a matching game wherein readers can test their memories of baby names against some paragraphs of information about each animal's development. The solid math and informative backmatter make this a worthwhile addition to libraries and math programs." Kirkus

Tang, Greg

★ The **best** of times; math strategies that multiply. illustrated by Harry Briggs. Scholastic Press 2002 un il $16.95

Grades: 2 3 4   **513**
1. Multiplication
ISBN 0-439-21044-5
LC 2002-23043

Simple rhymes offer hints on how to multiply any number by zero through ten without memorizing the multiplication tables

"Encouraging rhymes and colorful, jaunty illustrations bolster the multiplication lesson." Booklist

★ **Math** fables; lessons that count. illustrated by Heather Cahoon. Scholastic Press 2004 un il $16.95

Grades: K 1 2   **513**
1. Science 2. Counting
ISBN 0-439-45399-2
LC 2002-5360

A series of rhymes about animals introduces counting and grouping numbers, as well as examples of such behaviors as cooperation, friendship, and appreciation.

"The text and perky, computer-generated cartoons show youngsters that there are many different ways of putting numbers together. . . . The enriching vocabulary is an added bonus. A fine addition to math shelves." SLJ

513.2   Arithmetic operations

Adler, David A., 1947-

Fraction fun; illustrated by Nancy Tobin. Holiday House 1996 un il $16.95; pa $6.95

Grades: 2 3 4   **513.2**
1. Fractions
ISBN 0-8234-1259-8; 0-8234-1341-1 pa
LC 96-10773

"Adler presents the concept of fractions with the tried-and-true example of dividing a pie (pizza pie, in this case), then directs readers to draw lines across paper plates and color the eight resultant wedges in various color combinations. . . . Adler doesn't shy away from correct terminology—numerators and denominators—in this primary-grade introduction. Next he launches into some hands-on experimentation. . . . Tobin supplies a jazzy, eye-popping color scheme and diagrams of exceptional clarity to illuminate the straightforward text." Bull Cent Child Books

Place value; David A. Adler; illustrated by Edward Miller. Holiday House 2016 32 p. color illustrations (hardcover) $17.95

Grades: K 1 2 3   **513.2**
1. Monkeys 2. Mathematics 3. Numeration 4. Decimal system 5. Place value (Mathematics)
ISBN 0823435504; 9780823435500
LC 2015014874

This children's book, by David A. Adler and illustrated by Edward Miller, "the monkeys . . . bake the biggest banana cupcake ever, they need to get the amounts in the recipe correct. There s a big difference between 216 eggs and 621 eggs. Place value is the key to keeping the numbers straight." (Publisher's note)

"This fun and simple explanation of place value provides a strong introduction for young readers." SLJ

Browne, Anthony

One gorilla; a counting book. Anthony Browne. Candlewick Press 2013 32 p. $16.99

Grades: PreK K 1   **513.2**
1. Counting 2. Picture books for children 3. Primates
ISBN 0763663522; 9780763663520
LC 2012942388

This children's book by Anthony Browne provides children with an "array of creatures for kids to count." The book offers a "presentation of primates from gorillas to gibbons, macaques to mandrills, ring-tailed lemurs to spider monkeys . . . [and] extends the basic number concept into a look at similarities and differences -- portraying an extended family we can count ourselves part of." (Publisher's note)

Cooper, Elisha

★ **8,** an animal alphabet; an animal alphabet. Elisha Cooper. Orchard Books, an imprint of Scholastic Inc. 2015 40 p. color illustrations $17.99

Grades: PreK K 1 2 3   **513.2**
1. Alphabet 2. Alphabet books 3. Counting 4. Animals -- Miscellanea
ISBN 0545470838; 9780545470834
LC 2014030747

In this children's alphabet book by Elisha Cooper, readers can "discover hundreds of animals, great and small. Lion and lizard, whale and wombat. Learn one wild fact about each animal. (Did you know that gorillas yawn when they are nervous?) Look carefully, because for each letter of the alphabet, one animal is pictured eight times." (Publisher's note)

"Unusual in its conception and scope and illustrated with joy, this is an alphabet book to pore over, worth adding to any collection." SLJ

Eight, an animal alphabet

Hoban, Tana

★ **Let's** count. Greenwillow Bks. 1999 un il $17.99

Grades: PreK K   **513.2**
1. Counting
ISBN 0-688-16008-5
LC 98-44739

Photographs and dots introduce the numbers one to one hundred

"Hoban brings us another dazzling picture book. . . . Her photos range from the simple—1 hen, 8 Dalmatian puppies—to the more sophisticated—6 twirling rings on the arms of a circus performer; 12 rolls of toilet paper unpacked and stored on a pantry shelf." Booklist

Leedy, Loreen

2 x 2; a set of spooky multiplication stories. written and illustrated by Loreen Leedy. Holiday House 1995 32p il $17.95; pa $6.95

Grades: K 1 2 3   **513.2**
1. Multiplication
ISBN 0-8234-1190-7; 0-8234-1272-5 pa
LC 94-46711

This is an "introduction to basic multiplication, with witches, cats, and monsters demonstrating the consequences of multiplying numbers from 0 to 5. The illustrations are done in muted, autumnal tones of black, blue, orange, and mustard, and arranged in a comic-strip format. . . . The concepts are clear and understandable. . . . Leedy's book presents an entertaining alternative to rote memorization." SLJ

Other titles in this series are:
Fraction action
Mission addition
Subtraction action

Long, Lynette

Fabulous fractions; games and activities that make math easy and fun. Wiley 2001 122p il (Magical math) pa $12.95

Grades: 3 4 5 6 **513.2**

1. Fractions

ISBN 0-471-36981-0

LC 00-43386

This introduction to fractions includes activities using such materials as sandwiches, paper plates, cards, and dominoes

This book includes "lists of the required materials, clear and complete procedures, and a black-and-white illustration." SLJ

Marzollo, Jean

Help me learn subtraction; by Jean Marzollo; photographs by Chad Phillips. 1st American ed. Holiday House 2012 32 p. col. ill. (hardcover) $15.95; (paperback) $6.99

Grades: K 1 2 **513.2**

1. Visual literacy 2. Word problems (Mathematics) 3. Mathematics -- Study and teaching 4. Subtraction 5. Counting-out rhymes

ISBN 0823424014; 9780823424016; 9780823428229

LC 2011046540

Author Jean Marzollo's book "in the photograph-based Help Me Learn series . . . uses puppets, figurines, and other playful items to demonstrate [subtraction] math equations, which are presented both numerically and in words. . . . [The book utilizes] finger puppets, pipe cleaner dogs, and other objects" to help children visualize the problems. (Publishers Weekly)

Menotti, Andrea

How many jelly beans? Andrea Menotti; illustrator, Yancey Labat. Chronicle Books 2012 28 p. ill. (hardcover) $18.99

Grades: 2 3 4 **513.2**

1. Candy 2. Numbers 3. Calendars 4. Counting 5. Jellybeans 6. Mathematics

ISBN 1452102066; 9781452102061

LC 2011030673

Author Andrea Menotti "takes on big numbers . . . [in this oversized book] using jelly beans as counters. When Emma and Aiden are asked how many jelly beans they want, they carry on a boasting match, resulting in escalating amounts of candy. . . . Five hundred beans cover a coffee table, and 1,000 beans are divided out over the days of a year on calendar pages." (Publishers Weekly)

Neuschwander, Cindy

Sir Cumference and the roundabout battle; a math adventure. Cindy Neuschwander; illustrated by Wayne Geehan. Charlesbridge 2015 32 p. color illustrations (reinforced for library use) $16.95

Grades: 2 3 4 5 **513.2**

1. Castles -- Fiction 2. Mathematics 3. Counting 4. Rounding (Numerical analysis)

ISBN 9781570917653; 9781570917660

LC 2014010499

In this children's story, by Cindy Neuschwander and illustrated by Wayne Geehan, "when Steward Edmund Rounds and Sir Cumference notice that there are strangers camped nearby, Rounds II decides to investigate despite being involved with the task of learning how to make accurate counts of the castle's stores. . . . When he reports back that an enemy is lying in wait, . . . will Rounds II be able to figure out how many bows and arrows they have to create an appropriate battle plan?" (Publisher's note)

"Complete with the illustration style and subtle puns expected of the series, this title will be enjoyed by fans of the previous books." SLJ

Pallotta, Jerry

The **butterfly** counting book; Jerry Pallotta; illustrated by Shennen Bersani. Charlesbridge 2015 32 p. (softcover) $7.95

Grades: PreK K 1 2 **513.2**

1. Counting 2. Butterflies

ISBN 157091415X; 9781570914140; 9781570914157

LC 2013049018

This picture book, written by Jerry Pallotta and illustrated by Shennen Bersani, teaches children how to "count from one to twenty-six and learn about the many different kids of butterflies in the world." (Publisher's note)

Perritano, John

Mummies in the library; divide the pages. by John Perritano and David Hughes. Norwood House Press 2012 32 p. (iMath readers) (library edition : alk. paper) $22.60

Grades: 2 3 4 **513.2**

1. Mummies 2. Division 3. Reading 4. Division

ISBN 1599535580; 9781599535586; 9781603575270

LC 2012023839

Authors John Perritano and David T. Hughes presents a "fictional story line involving a young boy's visit to the library for a book on mummies (thus the title) to introduce the concept of division. Division problems are woven into the story (for example, how many days will it take the narrator to read his 160-page book?), followed by information about Egyptian mummies and a few more division problems. The information about mummies connects a range of topics to curriculum segments." (Publisher's note)

Includes bibliographical references and index

Pistoia, Sara

Fractions; by Sara Pistoia. Child's World 2007 24 p. (Math-Books) $25.64

Grades: PreK K 1 2 **513.2**

1. Fractions 2. Mathematics -- Study and teaching

ISBN 1592966861; 1623235294; 9781623235291

LC 2005037833

This children's book on fractions, by Sara Pistoia, is part of the "Simply Math" series, which "offer[s] real-world introductions to basic math concepts suited for the youngest children." This book "uses foods, such as pie, pizza, a candy bar, fruit, a sandwich, and cookies, as well as everyday objects like traffic lights, to show how a whole can be divided into even parts. (They encourage sharing, too.)" (Booklist)

"In the first book, children are introduced to the basic concepts of counting by ones, fives, and tens, and of place values. Groups of children use familiar objects such as rocks, buttons, and jelly beans to count... Each book concludes with a short list of key words (without definitions) facing an index that duplicates these words. Appropriate additions for the earliest readers in schools or public libraries." SLJ

Other titles in the series include:

Graphs

Measurement

Patterns

Shapes

Money

Rose, Deborah Lee

★ **One** nighttime sea; an ocean counting rhyme. pictures by Steve Jenkins. Scholastic 2003 un il $16.95

Grades: PreK K 1 2 **513.2**

1. Night 2. Counting 3. Marine animals

ISBN 0-439-33906-5

LC 2002-8127

A counting book featuring nocturnal sea creatures, from one blue whale calf to ten turtle hatchlings, and back down to one seal pup. Includes facts about each of the twenty featured animals

"In a lapping, sealike rhythm, this enchanting counting book lulls its audience into the world beneath the waves. . . . Vivid cut-paper collages beautifully interplay with the rhymes." SLJ

Schmandt-Besserat, Denise

The **history** of counting; illustrated by Michael Hays. Morrow Junior Bks. 1999 45p il $17; lib bdg $16.93

Grades: 4 5 6 7   **513.2**

1. Counting 2. Mathematics

ISBN 0-688-14118-8; 0-688-14119-6 lib bdg

LC 96-35316

"Beginning with a look at primitive expressions of numbers, the text goes on to explain abstract counting and the methods used by the Sumerians, the Phoenicians, the Greeks, the Romans, and finally the Arabs, who brought Hindu numerals from India to Europe about 1,000 years ago. . . . Imaginatively conceived and well composed, Hays' acrylic paintings feature warm, harmonious colors and delicate plays of light and shadow against textured-linen backings. Cogently written and beautifully made." Booklist

Includes glossary

Weill, Cynthia

Count me in; a parade of numbers in English and Spanish. by Cynthia Weill; figurines by the Aguilar Sisters: Guillermina, Josefina, Irene and Concepción. Cinco Puntos Press 2012 32 p. (hardback : alk. paper) $14.95

Grades: PreK   **513.2**

1. Counting 2. Mexican art 3. Picture books for children 4. Parades 5. Numerals

ISBN 193595539X; 9781935955399

LC 2012004538

This children's picture book helps children "practice [their] numbers in English and Spanish when [they] count the beautiful dancers, playful musicians, and happy children of Oaxaca as the Guelaguetza parade goes by! Pronounced Gal-a-get-zah, the lively celebration—full of traditional dancing and music—takes place every July deep in the heart of southern Mexico." (Publisher's note)

Winter, Jeanette

Josefina. Harcourt Brace & Co. 1996 un il $16

Grades: PreK K 1 2   **513.2**

1. Counting 2. Mexico -- Fiction 3. Women artists -- Fiction

ISBN 0-15-201091-2

LC 95-34110

"In a sunny patio in Mexico, there is one rising sun in a sky where two angels keep watch over three houses. . . . Throughout her life—from her childhood through the deaths of her parents, her marriage to José, and the birth of their nine children, Josefina works the soft clay into figures to create this world. . . . Inspired by the painted clay figures decorating Josefina Aguilar's patio in Ocotlán, Mexico, Winter has crafted a picture-book vision of the folk artist's life that cleverly turns into a bilingual counting story. . . . Paired with a simple prose narrative, the artwork creates an effect that is both elegant and soothing." Booklist

513.5   Numeration systems

Geisert, Arthur

Roman numerals I to MM; Numerabilia romana uno ad duo mila: liber de difficillimo computando numerum. Houghton Mifflin 1996 xxxii $16

Grades: K 1 2 3   **513.5**

1. Counting 2. Roman numerals

ISBN 0-395-74519-5

LC 95-36247

"Geisert's detailed etchings reward extended perusal, and children will revel in the sheer abundance of pigs. A great lesson in Roman numerals." Publ Wkly

Giganti, Paul

★ **Each** orange had 8 slices; a counting book. by Paul Giganti, Jr.; pictures by Donald Crews. Greenwillow Bks. 1992 un il $16.99; lib bdg $17.89; pa $6.99

Grades: PreK K 1 2   **513.5**

1. Counting 2. Mathematics

ISBN 0-688-10428-2; 0-688-10429-0 lib bdg; 0-688-13985-X pa

LC 90-24167

"This bright, well-designed book challenges young children to think analytically about what's on its pages. . . . Since the objects are organized into sets and subsets, this could be used to introduce the concept of multiplication as well as counting and addition." Booklist

Schwartz, David M.

On beyond a million; an amazing math journey. illustrated by Paul Meisel. Doubleday Bks. for Young Readers 1999 un il hardcover o.p. pa $6.99

Grades: 2 3 4   **513.5**

1. Counting

ISBN 0-385-32217-8; 0-440-41177-7 pa

LC 98-52990

"The design is busy, with sidebars and balloon comments. Each double-page spread is clearly meant to be talked about, and the discussions aren't overwhelming. . . . Awesome and yet accessible." Booklist

515   Analysis

Cleary, Brian P.

A-B-A-B-A--a book of pattern play; illustrated by Brian Gable. Millbrook Press 2010 31p il (Math is categorical) lib bdg $16.95

Grades: 2 3 4 5   **515**

1. Patterns (Mathematics)

ISBN 978-0-8225-7880-2 lib bdg; 0-8225-7880-8 lib bdg

LC 2009-49386

"Through rhyming text and colorful illustrations, readers are given examples of simple visual and numerical patterns—from circle-square-circle-square to 1-3-5-7. . . . The buoyant narrative calls for reading aloud and the images are large enough for a modest group setting." SLJ

Murphy, Stuart J.

Beep beep, vroom vroom! illustrated by Chris Demarest. HarperCollins Pubs. 2000 33p il (MathStart) hardcover o.p. pa $4.95

Grades: K 1   **515**

1. Patterns (Mathematics)

ISBN 0-06-028016-6; 0-06-028017-4 lib bdg; 0-06-446728-7 pa

LC 98-51907

"Molly loves playing with cars, but her brother, Kevin, tells her she's too young. He lines up his 12 cars—four red, four green, four yellow—in special order on the shelf and tells her not to touch them while he's gone. . . . At the back are practical suggestions for adults and kids to find patterns on the pages and make their own patterns with pebbles, buttons, coins, and kitchen utensils. Demarest's clear, simple pastel pictures express the fun of playing with cars as the vrooming action reveals the patterns in everyday things." Booklist

Includes bibliographical references

516 Geometry

Adler, David A., 1947-

Perimeter, area, and volume; a monster book of dimensions. by David A. Adler; illustrated by Edward Miller. 1st ed. Holiday House 2012 32 p. col. ill. (hardcover) $16.95

Grades: 3 4 5   516

1. Mathematics 2. Measurement 3. Dimensions 4. Weights and measures 5. Dimensions 6. Weights and measures

ISBN 0823422909; 9780823422906

LC 2010048653

This educational children's book by David A. Adler, illustrated by Edward Miller, provides lessons in measurement-taking within the context of a film set crewed by monsters. The book is "aligned with the Common Core State Standards for third-grade, fourth-grade, and fifth-grade mathematics in measurement and data.... Grab your jumbo popcorn and 3-D glasses, because you're invited to the premiere of a 3-D movie! The star-studded cast of monsters will help you calculate the perimeter of the set, the area of the movie screen, and the volume of your popcorn box." (Publisher's note)

★ **Shape** up! illustrated by Nancy Tobin. Holiday House 1998 un il $16.95; pa $6.95

Grades: 2 3 4   516

1. Shape 2. Geometry

ISBN 0-8234-1346-2; 0-8234-1638-0 pa

LC 97-22236

Uses cheese slices, pretzel sticks, a slice of bread, graph paper, a pencil, and more to introduce various polygons, flat shapes with varying numbers of straight sides

"Tobin's colorful diagrams and lanky, baseball-capped tour guide make each definition and direction crystal clear, making this a useful and appealing title for extending classroom lessons or encouraging beginners to charge beyond circle-square-triangle." Bull Cent Child Books

Brocket, Jane

Circles, stars, and squares; looking for shapes. by Jane Brocket; photographs by Jane Brocket. Millbrook Press 2013 30 p. col. ill. (library) $26.60

Grades: K 1 2   516

1. Shape 2. Plane geometry 3. Shapes 4. Geometry, Plane

ISBN 0761346112; 9780761346111

LC 2011050199

This children's picture book by Jane Brocket "teaches readers about two- and three-dimensional shapes.... The first of two loose sections looks at 'flat' shapes--circles, ovals, squares, rectangles, triangles, diamonds, and a brief mention of pentagons, hexagons and octagons--the second at 'solid' shapes--spheres, cylinders, cubes, cones, rings and eggs." (Kirkus Reviews)

Caron, Lucille

Geometry smarts! [by] Lucille Caron, Philip M. St. Jacques. Enslow Publishers 2011 64p il lib bdg $27.93

Grades: 5 6 7 8   516

1. Geometry

ISBN 978-0-7660-3935-3

LC 2011008384

Reinforces classroom learning of geometry skills such as points, lines, planes, triangles, circles, quadrilaterals, perimeter, area, and circumference.

Other titles in this series are:
Fraction and decimal smarts
Percent and ratio smarts

Hoban, Tana

★ **So** many circles, so many squares. Greenwillow Bks. 1998 un il $16

Grades: PreK K   516

1. Shape

ISBN 0-688-15165-5

LC 97-10110

The geometric concepts of circles and squares are shown in photographs of wheels, signs, pots, and other familiar objects

"Teachers and young children will find plenty to talk about as they look at the colorful, well-composed, and clearly defined images." Booklist

Other titles in this series are:
Shapes, shapes, shapes
Is it larger? Is it smaller?

Leedy, Loreen

Seeing symmetry; written and illustrated by Loreen Leedy. Holiday House 2012 32 p. ill. (chiefly col.) (hardcover) $17.95

Grades: PreK K 1 2   516

1. Symmetry 2. Ratio and proportaion

ISBN 0823423603; 9780823423606

LC 2011024038

This book presents an "introduction" to the concept of symmetry, "us[ing] a host of natural and manmade objects, as well as purely geometric designs, to illustrate horizontal, vertical, and rotational symmetry." The author asks "readers to consider whether all animals are symmetrical, to examine words for different types of symmetry in their lettering, to identify rotational symmetry in a display of buildings and furniture." (Bulletin of the Center for Children's Books)

Loughrey, Anita

Circles. QEB Pub. 2010 23p il (Shapes around me) lib bdg $24.25

Grades: PreK K 1 2   516

1. Shape

ISBN 978-1-59566-918-6; 1-59566-918-3

LC 2010005380

This "has a good grasp of how children best learn new math concepts. [The] book begins with a bright illustration of the shape and asks children to trace it with a finger. Subsequent pages present the shape in a variety of colorful sizes, places where it can be found, and activities. Well-thought-out, age appropriate, and attractive." Horn Book Guide

Other titles in this series are:
Rectangles
Squares
Triangles

Murphy, Stuart J.

★ **Polly's** pen pal; illustrated by Remy Simard. HarperCollins 2005 30p il (MathStart) $15.99; pa $4.99

Grades: K 1 2 3   516

1. Measurement 2. Metric system

ISBN 0-06-053168-1; 0-06-053170-3 pa

LC 2003-27526

"Polly has an e-mail pen pal in Montreal. As Ally uses metrics to discuss height, weight, and distances, Polly learns what they mean. No comparisons to English measurements are made but the metric measurements are likened to common objects that kids will recognize. This title features colorful ... computer-generated cartoons." SLJ

Olson, Nathan

Cylinders; by Nathan Olson. Capstone Press 2008 32p il (3-D shapes) lib bdg $23.93

Grades: K 1 2 **516**
  1. Shape 2. Geometry 3. Cylinders
  ISBN 978-1-4296-0050-7 lib bdg; 1-4296-0050-0 lib bdg
LC 2006037421

"Large color photographs show real-world examples of . . . cylinders (canned goods, birthday candles). Short descriptions flank each photo. . . . A hands-on activity will appeal to kids." Horn Book Guide

Includes glossary and bibliographical references

Other titles in this series are:

Cones

Cubes

Pyramids

Spheres

Rissman, Rebecca

  ★ **Shapes** in sports. Heinemann Library 2009 24p il (Spot the shape) $14.50; pa $5.99

Grades: PreK K 1 **516**
  1. Shape 2. Sports
  ISBN 978-1-4329-2170-5; 1-4329-2176-2; 978-1-4329-2176-7 pa; 1-4329-2176-2 pa
LC 2008043208

This describes the shapes that can be found in sports.

This "is a near-perfect union of concept and execution. Using . . . vibrant photography and clarion text . . . . Rissman lays out a simple premise ('Shapes are all around us.') before introducing seven shapes to come: rectangle, square, semicircle, diamond, and so forth. . . . What is most impressive . . . . are the stunning aerial photographs that turn baseball diamonds and tennis courts into dazzling intersections of geometric patterns. This is the kind of book that will wake readers up to the complexity of everyday items." Booklist

Other titles in this series are:

Shapes in art

Shapes in buildings

Shapes in music

Shapes in the garden

Somervill, Barbara A.

  Distance, area, and volume. Heinemann Library 2010 32p il map (Measure it!) lib bdg $29; pa $7.99

Grades: 3 4 5 **516**
  1. Measurement 2. Volume (Cubic content)
  ISBN 978-1-4329-3763-8 lib bdg; 1-4329-3763-4 lib bdg; 978-1-4329-3769-0 pa; 1-4329-3769-3 pa
LC 2009-35191

"Size of text and font is suitable for this age group with uncluttered pages designed so that text is set off with the illustrations, graphs, or drawings placed vertically. Key words appear in bold." Libr Media Connect

Includes glossary and bibliographical references

VanCleave, Janice Pratt

  Janice VanCleave's geometry for every kid; easy activities that make learning geometry fun. Wiley 1994 221p il hardcover o.p. pa $12.95

Grades: 4 5 6 7 **516**
  1. Geometry
  ISBN 0-471-31142-1; 0-471-31141-3 pa
LC 93-43049

This "introductory text covers many topics in geometry, from lines, optical illusions, and art-related activities to applications with protractors and the construction of basic solids. Terms are presented in a simplified fashion and are easily understood. Graphics are clear. The

hands-on activities encourage learning, creativity, and excitement." Sci Books Films

Includes glossary

516.15   Geometric configurations

Adler, David A., 1947-

  ★ **Triangles**; by David A. Adler; illustrated by Edward Miller. Holiday House 2014 32 p. (hardcover) $17.95

Grades: 2 3 4 **516.15**
  1. Triangle
  ISBN 0823423786; 9780823423781
LC 2012037371

This children's book, written by David A. Adler and illustrated by Edward Miller, "tackle[s] questions about different kinds of triangles with . . . text and . . . illustrations starring two friendly kids and one savvy robot." (Publisher's note) "Beginning with the definition of a triangle and a breakdown of its parts--sides, angles, vertices--[David A.] Adler quickly launches into a discussion of angles, even teaching kids how they are named, measured and classified." (Kirkus Reviews)

"A straightforward and easy introduction to triangles and angles. There is a lot of repeated information, which will work well with students with different learning styles, and the bold, exciting illustrations will hold kids' attention...A recommended purchase for any math collection, this title serves as a great update on the subject." SLJ

Campbell, Sarah C.

  ★ **Mysterious** patterns; finding fractals in nature. Sarah C. Campbell. First edition Boyds Mills Press 2014 32 p. $16.95

Grades: 2 3 4 5 **516.15**
  1. Fractals 2. Mathematical models 3. Nature 4. Shapes 5. Pattern perception 6. Mathematics in nature
  ISBN 1620916274; 9781620916278
LC 2013951286

This book, by Sarah C. Campbell, is an "introduction to fractals through examples that can be seen in parks, rivers, and our very own backyards. Readers will . . . learn that broccoli florets are fractals - just like mountain ranges, river systems, and trees--and will share in the wonder of math as it is reflected in the world around us." (Publisher's note)

"Here's a clear, fluid, concise introduction to fractals, identified in 1975 by scientist Benoit Mandelbrot, who noticed that the shapes of trees, broccoli, and ferns share a common pattern: each has 'smaller parts that look like the whole shape.' Well-designed pages feature crisp, up-close photographs, which pair perfectly with the accessible text. Includes an activity and an afterword by a Mandelbrot colleague." Horn Book

Fischer, Jeremie

  Wild About Shapes; by Jeremie Fischer. Flying Eye Books 2015 70 p. chiefly color illustrations $16.99

Grades: PreK K 1 2 **516.15**
  1. Color 2. Shape 3. Animals
  ISBN 1909263389; 9781909263383

This children's book, written and illustrated by Jérémie Fischer, "is playfully designed so that animals hide and reveal themselves within pages of overlapping color and alternating pages of printed acetate. From crocodiles and giraffes to snails and mice, each page offers a fresh surprise!" (Publisher's note)

"Acetate inserts—printed with abstract shapes in pink, teal, and yellow—transform Fischer's equally abstract screen prints into animals in a process that's graceful in its execution and delightful in its simplicity. . . . Clever and rewarding, this ranks with Hervé Tullet's Press Here and Rufus Butler Seder's Scanimation series as a book whose deceptively simple interactivity creates a reading experience that's nothing short of magic." Pub Wkly

Sidman, Joyce

★ **Round;** Joyce Sidman; illustrated by Taeeun Yoo. Houghton Mifflin Harcourt 2017 32 p. color illustrations (hardcover) $17.99

    Grades: PreK K 1 2   **516.15**

    1. Picture books for children 2. Shape 3. Solid geometry 4. Shapes 5. Geometry, Solid

    ISBN 9780544387614

                       LC 2016014695

In this book, by Joyce Sidman, illustrated by Taeeun Yoo, "if you look closely, you will find that the world is bursting, swelling, budding, and ripening with round things awaiting discovery--like eggs about to hatch, sunflowers stretching toward the sun, or planets slowly spinning together for billions of years." (Publisher's note)

516.2 Euclidean geometry

Green, Dan

    Algebra & geometry; anything but square. illustrated by Simon Basher. Kingfisher 2011 il (Basher science) $14.99; pa $8.99

Grades: 4 5 6   **516.2**

    1. Algebra 2. Geometry

    ISBN 978-0-7534-6627-8; 978-0-7534-6597-4 pa

"This creative team introduces the components of algebra and geometry as cartoon-style characters. The book begins with a brief introduction to the subject of mathematics and Pythagoras. . . . Each chapter begins with an introduction and then the concepts are presented on a spread. One page features a drawing of the concept's character, while the opposing page provides a brief introduction to its characteristics and personality." (School Library Journal)

519.2 Probabilities

Aboff, Marcie

    Pigs, cows, and probability. Capstone Press 2011 24p il (First facts. Data mania) lib bdg $23.99

Grades: 3 4 5 6   **519.2**

    1. Mathematics 2. Probabilities

    ISBN 978-1-4296-4529-4; 1-4296-4529-6

                   LC 2010000551

"Information is presented in a few pages in a clear, concise manner. The definitions provided for words will help readers learn the [subject]. This is an excellent introduction to elementary statistics and statistical analysis." Libr Media Connect

    Includes glossary and bibliographical references

Goldstone, Bruce

    ★ **That's** a possibility! a book about what might happen. Bruce Goldstone. 1st ed. Henry Holt & Co 2013 32 p. ill. (hardcover) $16.99

Grades: 1 2 3 4   **519.2**

    1. Picture books for children 2. Probabilities

    ISBN 0805089985; 9780805089981

                   LC 2012036691

This children's picture book looks at probability. "Starting with basic concepts of possibility, certainty, and impossibility ('Will an elephant hatch from this egg? That's impossible!'), [Bruce Goldstone] stages highly specific situations in photographic and digital illustrations. 'Will this butterfly land on one of the purple flowers?' he asks.

'That's probable. Can you see why?' (Spiky purple thistles dwarf and outnumber two yellow flowers, helping readers make the connection.)" (Publishers Weekly)

Leedy, Loreen

    It's probably Penny; written and illustrated by Loreen Leedy. Henry Holt 2007 un il $16.95

Grades: 1 2 3   **519.2**

    1. Probabilities

    ISBN 978-0-8050-7389-8; 0-8050-7389-2

                   LC 2006-02872

"Lisa's teacher assigns the class to study probability by writing down predictions, determining results, and recording them. He demonstrates by using (and eating) jellybeans. Choosing Penny as her focal point, Lisa begins to calculate her results. . . . Leedy clearly and cleverly depicts the possibilities and choices in panels and segmented pages that feature Penny in funny poses." Booklist

519.5 Statistical mathematics

Goldstone, Bruce

    ★ **Great** estimations. H. Holt 2006 32p il $16.95

Grades: 1 2 3 4   **519.5**

    1. Approximate computation

    ISBN 978-0-8050-7446-8; 0-8050-7446-5

                   LC 2005-19776

"Laying out a mixed assemblage of toys, pipe cleaners, marbles, peanuts, and other small items, Goldstone helps viewers train themselves to estimate the size of groups of about 10 things on sight, then goes on to present similar, often fetchingly arranged, materials by hundreds and (!) thousands. He also describes 'clump counting' and 'box and count' methods. . . . This book lends itself equally well to skill building and to casual reading." Booklist

    ★ **Greater** estimations. Henry Holt and Company 2008 31p il $16.95

Grades: 1 2 3 4   **519.5**

    1. Approximate computation

    ISBN 0-8050-8315-4; 978-0-8050-8315-6

                   LC 2007-40894

"Goldstone builds on the topics introduced in Great Estimations (Holt, 2006) and also discusses how to estimate length, weight, area, and volume. He does an exceptional job of breaking down the process of so that even early elementary students can comprehend it. The author also effectively introduces different methods of estimation. . . . The vivid, eye-catching photographs are the highlight of the book. . . . This lively book would be an excellent addition." SLJ

520 Astronomy and allied sciences

Carson, Mary Kay

    ★ **Beyond** the solar system; exploring galaxies, black holes, alien planets, and more : a history with 21 activities. by Mary Kay Carson. Chicago Review Press 2013 vii, 127 p.p col. ill. (paperback) $18.95

Grades: 5 6 7 8   **520**

    1. Creative activities 2. Astronomy -- History

    ISBN 1613745443; 9781613745441

                   LC 2012046330

In this book, "Mary Kay Carson traces the evolution of humankind's astronomical knowledge, from the realization that we are not at the center of the universe to recent telescopic proof of planets orbiting stars outside our solar system. . . . This book contains 21 hands-on projects to further explore the subjects discussed" as well as "minibiographies of famous astronomers, a time line of major scientific discoveries . . .[and] a glossary of technical terms." (Publisher's note)

Includes bibliographical references (p. 121) and index.

Gifford, Clive

Astronomy, astronauts, and space exploration; Clive Gifford. Crabtree Publishing Company 2016 32 p. color illustrations (reinforced library binding : alk. paper) $27.6; (ebook) $41.40

Grades: 4 5 6   **520**

1. Outer space -- Exploration 2. Astronomy 3. Astronauts 4. Astronomical observatories 5. Observatories

ISBN 9780778720218; 9780778720256; 9781427116840

LC 2015015366

In this children's book by Clive Gifford, part of the Watch This Space! series, readers will "Uncover the amazing story of astronomy from telescopes in space to outstanding observatories. Learn about the latest space probes, how rockets lift off, and what it's like living in the weightlessness of space. And find out about the remarkable astronauts who have spacewalked their way into history." (Publisher's note)

"Like a clear night sky, the layout consists of dark backgrounds that highlight vibrant colors, computer-style fonts, and a plethora of photo reproductions and simulated models. Each page consists of multiple text boxes that group information into manageable and engaging chunks." Booklist

Includes index

Goldsmith, Mike

The **Kingfisher** space encyclopedia; Dr. Mike Goldsmith. Kingfisher 2012 159 p. (hardcover) $18.99

Grades: 4 5 6   **520**

1. Astronomy -- Encyclopedias

ISBN 0753468050; 9780753468050

In this book, "[Mike] Goldsmith skims the history of astronomy and space exploration, tours the solar system and the universe beyond, then closes with glances at dark matter and other undiscovered territory." A "spread on Global Positioning Systems" is included along with "digital images" as illustrations. (Kirkus)

Green, Dan

Astronomy; out of this world! illustrated by Simon Basher. Kingfisher 2009 128p il pa $8.95

Grades: 5 6 7 8   **520**

1. Astronomy

ISBN 978-0-7534-6290-4 pa; 0-7534-6290-7 pa

"Basher has created a portrait gallery of personified planets, comets, space probes, galaxies, several kinds of stars, and an array of other celestial bodies in a hyper-cute, pastel cartoon style. . . . Along with short bulleted lists of additional information, each figure offers a fact-based self-description. . . . Green's astro-narrative is both accurate and spiced with seldom-mentioned details." SLJ

Includes glossary

Lasky, Kathryn

★ The **librarian** who measured the earth; illustrated by Kevin Hawkes. Little, Brown 1994 48p il $16.95

Grades: 2 3 4 5   **520**

1. Astronomers 2. Geographers 3. Writers on science

ISBN 0-316-51526-4

LC 92-42656

Describes the life and work of Eratosthenes, the Greek geographer and astronomer who accurately measured the circumference of the Earth

"Illustrating the text with warmth and humor, Hawkes' acrylic paintings capture the period details of the setting and clarify the geometric concepts used in the measurement. The often dramatic compositions vary from page to page, while the sunlit reds, oranges, and yellows glow brightly against the cooler blues and greens. . . . Entertaining as well as instructional." Booklist

Includes bibliographical references

Mitchell, Chris

How Do Astronauts Wee in Space? Chris Mitchell. Trafalgar Square Books 2016 192 p. illustrations (Dr Dino's Learnatorium) $8.99

Grades: 4 5 6 7 8   **520**

1. Outer space 2. Space sciences

ISBN 1784186538; 9781784186531

LC 2016023616

In this book in Dr Dino's Learnatorium series, by Chris Mitchell, "amaze your friends with facts about planets made from diamonds, stars that could destroy our solar system, and how long humans could survive in space! This book is packed with the wildest, weirdest, funniest, filthiest, foulest, wisest, grossest, brainiest, biggest, and best facts about space and the universe." (Publisher's note)

"Frequent comic spot art keeps things light, and as for that title question? The answer is more involved than you might think." Booklist

Pinkney, Andrea Davis

★ **Dear** Benjamin Banneker; illustrated by Brian Pinkney. Harcourt Brace & Co. 1994 un il hardcover o.p. pa $7

Grades: 2 3 4   **520**

1. Astronomers 2. Mathematicians 3. Nonfiction writers 4. Clock and watch makers 5. African Americans -- Biography

ISBN 0-15-200417-3; 0-15-201892-1 pa

LC 93-31162

This offers "lucid text and striking illustrations, rendered on scratchboard and colored with oil paint." Publ Wkly

Sis, Peter, 1949-

★ **Starry** messenger; a book depicting the life of a famous scientist, mathematician, philosopher, physicist, Galileo Galilei. created and illustrated by Peter Sis. Farrar, Straus & Giroux 1996 un il $18; pa $7.99

Grades: 2 3 4 5   **520**

1. Astronomers 2. Writers on science 3. Biography, Individual

ISBN 0-374-37191-1; 0-374-47027-8 pa

LC 95-44986

A Caldecott Medal honor book, 1997

This book traces "the astronomer's life from his birth, . . . to his childhood, . . . and finally to his years as a celebrated scientist whose experiments culminated in his construction of the first complete astronomical telescope. . . . Age six and up." (N Y Times Book Rev)

"Large, beautiful drawings reflect the ideas, events, books, maps, world view, and symbolism of the times. These intricate ink drawings, idiosyncratic in concept and beautifully tinted with delicate watercolor washes, are complemented by smaller drawings and prints that illustrate a side-text of significant dates, time lines, quotations, comments, and explanations. . . . Those drawn to the book will find that it works on many levels, offering not just facts but intuitive visions of another world." Booklist

Space: a visual encyclopedia. DK Pub. 2010 254p il $24.99

Grades: 5 6 7 8   **520**

1. Astronomy 2. Astronautics 3. Space sciences

ISBN 978-0-7566-6277-6; 0-7566-6277-X

"Any reader wishing to gain a fair introductory understanding of astronomy in one concise book will find much satisfaction in this work. An abundance of fascinating information is contained within these pages, and the format is such that excellent and attractive related photographs and diagrams directly accompany the text. . . . The book is very well organized and very well written." Sci Books & Films

VanCleave, Janice Pratt, 1942-
Step-by-step science experiments in astronomy; by Janice VanCleave. Rosen Pub. 2013 80 p. col. ill. (Janice Vancleave's first-place science fair projects) (library) $33.25; (paperback) $14.15
Grades: 5 6 7 8   **520**
1. Astronomy 2. Science -- Experiments 3. Science projects
ISBN 1448869781; 9781448869787; 9781448884612
LC 2012000715
This book by Janice VanCleave presents 22 science experiments in astronomy for children. "Van Cleave states the basic goal of the experiments, followed by a list of necessary materials. . . . Step-by-step instructions are . . . accompanied by diagrams where needed. The results section states exactly what is expected to happen and the 'Why?' section explains in accessible terms why those specific results were achieved." (School Library Journal)
Includes bibliographical references (p. 77-78) and index

520.9 Astronomy -- History

Jenkins, Martin
Exploring Space; From Galileo to the Mars Rover and Beyond. by Martin Jenkins, illustrated by Stephen Biesty. Candlewick Press 2017 64 p. color illustrations $17.99
Grades: 5 6 7 8   **520.9**
1. Outer space -- Exploration 2. Outer space
ISBN 0763689319; 9780763689315
LC 2017942646
This book, by Martin Jenkins, illustrated by Stephen Biesty, is an "examination of the past, present, and future of humans in space. . . . Find out what life is like on the International Space Station, what the chances are that we will ever settle on Mars, where in the solar system we might find alien life, and why visiting other stars will almost certainly remain a dream." (Publisher's note)
"In exceptionally clear prose, Jenkins surveys the history and possible future of SPACE EXPLORATION ... The subject matter is thrilling on its own, but this expert portrayal of the facts makes it all the more captivating." Booklist
Includes bibliographical references and index

522 Techniques, procedures, apparatus, equipment, materials

Cole, Michael D.
Eye on the universe; the incredible hubble space telescope. Michael D. Cole. Enslow Publishers 2013 48 p. $23.93
Grades: 4 5 6 7 8   **522**
1. Hubble Space Telescope 2. Outer space -- Exploration 3. Picture books for children 4. Astronomy -- Research 5. Astronautics in astronomy 6. Hubble Space Telescope (Spacecraft)
ISBN 0766040771; 9780766040779
LC 2011047074
This book looks at the Hubble Space Telescope. "Orbiting high above Earth, the Hubble Telescope captures . . . wonders of space. . . . Photographs are relayed back to Earth, allowing scientists and as-

tronomers to study parts of space that were once completely unknown. Michael D. Cole explores the . . . journey of launching this telescope into space and how it has unlocked many of the . . . mysteries in the universe." (Publisher's note)
Includes bibliographical references and index

Jefferis, David
Star spotters; telescopes and observatories. Crabtree Pub. 2009 32p il (Exploring our solar system) lib bdg $26.60; pa $8.95
Grades: 3 4 5   **522**
1. Astronomy 2. Telescopes 3. Outer space -- Exploration
ISBN 978-0-7787-3725-4 lib bdg; 0-7787-3725-X lib bdg; 978-0-7787-3742-1 pa; 0-7787-3742-X pa
LC 2008-49242
"Focuses on important observatories—earthbound and orbiting—along with types of telescopes—and concludes with brief observations about binoculars and cameras. . . . [This book is] designed with easily digestible blocks of question-and-answer text sharing page space with large, sharply reproduced space photos and graphic art." SLJ
Includes glossary

Scott, Elaine
★ Space, stars, and the beginning of time; what the Hubble telescope saw. Clarion Books 2011 66p il $17.99
Grades: 5 6 7 8   **522**
1. Astronomy 2. Hubble Space Telescope 3. Outer space -- Exploration
ISBN 0-547-24189-5; 978-0-547-24189-0
LC 2010-08040
This book examines data collected from the Hubble Space Telescope. Index. "Grades four to eight." (Bull Cent Child Books)
This examines "some of the data that has been collected over the two decades of the Hubble Telescope's operation. Opening chapters discuss the satellite's instrumentation and its 2009 repairs, and then the real fun begins with sections on calculating the age of the universe and its speed of expansion; the nature of dark matter, dark energy, and black holes; star formation; and planet formation, particularly outside our solar system. . . . Gasp-worthy photographs should fire up the most sluggish imaginations." Bull Cent Child Books

523 Specific celestial bodies and phenomena

De Cristofano, Carolyn Cinami
★ The sun and the moon; by Carolyn Cinami DeCristofano; illustrated by Taia Morley. Harper, an imprint of HarperCollinsPublishers 2015 40 p. color illustrations (hardcover) $17.99; (ebook) $6.99
Grades: K 1 2 3   **523**
1. Sun 2. Moon 3. Earth (Planet)
ISBN 9780062338037; 9780062338044; 9780062446978
LC 2015018465
This book, by Carolyn Cinami Decristofano, illustrated by Taia Morley, "will guide young readers into a deeper understanding of their observations of the sun and the moon. Featuring a find-out-more section with instructions on how to keep an observation log and how to make moon ice, a glossary of new terms, and web research prompts, this book will begin children's explorations of the sun and the moon." (Publisher's note)
"Well designed, engaging, and highly recommended for children's science collections." Booklist
Includes bibliographical references

Gardner, Robert

Far-out science projects about Earth's sun and moon; illustrations by Tom Labaff. Enslow Publishers 2007 48p il (Rockin' earth science experiments) lib bdg $23.93

Grades: 3 4 5   **523**

1. Science projects 2. Sun 3. Moon 4. Science -- Experiments

ISBN 978-0-7660-2736-7 lib bdg; 0-7660-2736-8 lib bdg

LC 2006-13789

A collection of science experiments such as getting direction and time from the sun, finding locations of sunrise and sunset, measuring heat from the sun, and observing the phases of the moon

This is "just right for students with limited experience looking for projects that are fairly interesting and manageable." SLJ

Includes glossary and bibliographical references

523.1 The universe, galaxies, quasars

Asimov, Isaac

The **Milky** Way and other galaxies; by Isaac Asimov; with revisions and updating by Richard Hantula. Gareth Stevens Pub. 2005 32p (Isaac Asimov's 21st century library of the universe) lib bdg $24.67

Grades: 4 5 6   **523.1**

1. Galaxies 2. Milky Way

ISBN 0-8368-3968-4

LC 2004-58313

This "examines various galactic types, structures, and superstructures, as observed by a wide array of specialized telescopes. . . . The pictures . . . are striking. . . . [An] excellent collection [enhancer]." SLJ

Includes bibliographical references

Fox, Karen C.

Older than the stars; [by] Karen C. Fox; illustrated by Nancy Davis. Charlesbridge 2010 un il lib bdg $15.95

Grades: 2 3 4 5   **523.1**

1. Atoms 2. Cosmology 3. Big bang theory

ISBN 978-1-57091-787-5 lib bdg; 1-57091-787-6 lib bdg

LC 2009-04304

"Fox and Davis tackle the challenge of creating an engaging read-aloud about the Big Bang theory with energy and style. Employing the structure of a familiar nursery rhyme, the text takes readers through the steps of the universe's expansion. . . . A text box on each spread offers a clear, concise explanation of what happened in that particular stage of the universe. . . . Perfect for the classroom, this is an intriguing introduction to a difficult-to-understand concept." SLJ

Gibbons, Gail

Galaxies, galaxies! Holiday House 2006 32p il $16.95

Grades: K 1 2 3   **523.1**

1. Galaxies

ISBN 978-0-8234-2002-5; 0-8234-2002-7

LC 2006-02504

"Between an opening description of the Milky Way and a closing claim that galaxy formation is still going on, the author depicts ancient astronomers at work, describes several kinds of telescopes, and profiles five distinctive galactic forms, from irregular to lenticular. Pairing brief, matter-of-fact generalizations leavened with digestible doses of specific information to painted scenes that link diverse groups of human observers to galaxies seen in blobby, broadly brushed portraits, this introduction to some of the universe's largest structures will put stars in the eyes of the most Earthbound young readers." SLJ

Gifford, Clive

The **universe**, black holes, and the Big Bang; Clive Gifford. Crabtree Publishing Co. 2016 32 p. color illustrations (ebook) $41.40; (reinforced library binding : alk. paper) $27.60

Grades: 4 5 6   **523.1**

1. Cosmology 2. Black holes (Astronomy) 3. Universe 4. Cosmology 5. Expanding universe 6. Black holes (Astronomy)

ISBN 9781427116871; 0778720241; 9780778720249; 9780778720287

LC 2015015367

In this book, by Clive Gifford, "travel back in time to the big bang, and learn about the formation of the universe. Explore the baffling world of black holes, and find out how scientists are searching for alien life. Discover the strangest sights of the universe, from quirky quasars to clouds that smell like raspberries." (Publisher's note)

"Together, these books cover all aspects of space, combining pertinent facts with a cool factor." Booklist

Includes index

Goldsmith, Mike

Universe; journey into deep space. Mike Goldsmith; illustrated by Mark A. Garlick. Kingfisher 2012 48 p. (hardcover) $17.99

Grades: 4 5 6 7   **523.1**

1. Universe 2. Astronomy 3. Outer space

ISBN 075346876X; 9780753468760

This book, by Mike Goldsmith, illustrated by Mark A. Garlick, profiles "some of the Universe's most intriguing places, and along the way . . . [describes] the amazing history of the Cosmos. A series of . . . spreads give . . . snapshots of distant galactic locations as the reader journeys . . . from red cold Mars (3 light minutes away) to a massive Supernova (10,000 light years away) and beyond." (Publisher's note)

Jefferis, David

Galaxies; immense star islands. Crabtree Pub. 2009 32p il (Exploring our solar system) lib bdg $26.60; pa $8.95

Grades: 3 4 5   **523.1**

1. Galaxies 2. Milky Way

ISBN 978-0-7787-3723-0 lib bdg; 0-7787-3723-3 lib bdg; 978-0-7787-3740-7 pa; 0-7787-3740-3 pa

LC 2008-46248

This "begins with a summary look at galactic types and origins, then goes on to describe cores, halos, and other structures with special reference to the Milky Way. It closes with a smattering of advice for young sky watchers and a spread of general facts about galaxies. . . . Designed with easily digestible blocks of question-and-answer text sharing page space with large, sharply reproduced space photos and graphic art." SLJ

Includes glossary

Simon, Seymour

★ **Galaxies**. Morrow Junior Bks. 1988 un il hardcover o.p. pa $6.95

Grades: 3 4 5 6   **523.1**

1. Galaxies

ISBN 0-688-08002-2; 0-688-10992-6 pa

LC 87-23967

"This fine introduction to an awe-inspiring subject will surely stimulate interest in stargazing, further reading, and investigation." Horn Book

523.2 Planetary systems

Aguilar, David A.

13 planets; the latest view of the solar system. David A. Aguilar. National Geographic Books 2011 60 p. il $16.95

Grades: 5 6 7 8 **523.2**
1. Planets 2. Astronomy 3. Solar system
ISBN 1426307705; 1426307713; 9781426307706;
9781426307713
LC 2010032510

Updated and revised edition of: 11 planets: A new view of the Solar System (2008)

This book by David A. Aguilar is designed to "update young readers on the high-interest topic of space. Using simple text and spectacular photorealistic computer art by the author, this book profiles all 13 planets in their newly created categories--plus the sun, the Oort Cloud, comets, and other worlds being discovered." (Publisher's note)

"Aguilar offers an amended volume reflecting the findings of the International Astronomical Union, which currently classifies eight objects in the solar system as planets and, with the addition of Haumea and Makemake, five as dwarf planets. . . . Aguilar has not only added sections on Haumea and Makemake, he has also used this opportunity to rewrite portions of the text and captions throughout the book and, in some cases, to substitute new illustrations or improve old ones for the new volume. The result is a more readable, more accurate, and more handsome edition of the previous work." Booklist

Includes bibliographical references and index
Thirteen planets
Latest view of the solar system

Carson, Mary Kay
Exploring the solar system; a history with 22 activities. by Mary Kay Carson. Chicago Review Press 2008 vii, 168 p.p ill. (paperback) $17.95
Grades: 4 5 6 7 **523.2**
1. Astronomy 2. Solar system
ISBN 1556527152; 9781556527159

This book by Mary Kay Carson is a "mix of facts, history, and hands-on activities [about the solar system]. Beginning with a two-page table of contents with chapters arranged as planets in our solar system and an introductory time line, the author takes readers on a historical journey of what was known and/or discovered in each of eight time periods." (School Library Journal)

Gifford, Clive
The **Solar** System, meteors, and comets; Clive Gifford. Crabtree Publishing Company 2016 32 p. color illustrations (ebook) $41.40; (pbk. : alk. paper) $8.95
Grades: 4 5 6 **523.2**
1. Planets 2. Solar system
ISBN 9781427116864; 9780778720232; 9780778720270
LC 2015015368

Written by Clive Gifford and part of the Watch This Space! series, this children's book allows readers to "Explore our stunning solar system and learn about its eight planets, from mini Mercury to giant Jupiter. [They will] find out about marvellous moons and mighty meteorites, and discover curious comets and eccentric exoplanets." (Publisher's note)

"Together, these books cover all aspects of space, combining pertinent facts with a cool factor. " Booklist

Includes bibliographical references and index.

Goldsmith, Mike
Solar system. Kingfisher 2010 56p il (Discover science) $9.99
Grades: 1 2 3 **523.2**
1. Solar system
ISBN 978-0-7534-6447-2; 0-7534-6447-0

First published in the series Kingfisher young knowledge in 2006
"With glossy color pages, abundant visuals, and descriptive prose, this . . . title provides an accessible introduction to earth's solar system.

Printed in large font, the text is well suited to newly independent readers' abilities . . . and occasionally uses familiar comparisons to aid comprehension. . . . The visual-laden pages feature a wide range of images, from stock photos to detailed renderings of planetary surfaces." Booklist

Includes glossary and bibliographical references

Kops, Deborah
Exploring exoplanets. Lerner Publications 2011 40p il (What's amazing about space?) lib bdg $27.93
Grades: 4 5 6 **523.2**
1. Extrasolar planets
ISBN 978-0-7613-5444-4; 0-7613-5444-1
LC 2010046109

This explains how scientists have discovered other planets in the universe similar to those in our solar system.

Includes glossary and bibliographical references

Kudlinski, Kathleen V.
Boy were we wrong about the solar system! illustrated by John Rocco. Dutton Children's Books 2008 un il $15.99
Grades: K 1 2 3 **523.2**
1. Solar system
ISBN 978-0-525-46979-7; 0-525-46979-6
LC 2007-50557

This is a "debunking of such erstwhile astronomical theories as solar revolution around the Earth, concentric glass spheres dividing planetary orbits, Martian canals, and, of course, the overly elevated status of Pluto. . . . [This is illustrated with] jewel-hued, cartoonishly exaggerated paintings. . . . The concept of adults getting it dead wrong is realiably engaging." Bull Cent Child Books

Portman, Michael
Are there other Earths? Michael Portman. Gareth Stevens Publishing 2013 32 p. (Space mysteries) (library binding) $25.25
Grades: 3 4 5 **523.2**
1. Extrasolar planets 2. Solar system 3. Extrasolar planets
ISBN 1433982579; 9781433982576; 9781433982583
LC 2012019207

Author Michael Portman presents information "about the other planets that scientists have discovered through accessible text, fun fact boxes, and amazing photographs. They will be introduced to amazing scientific tools including the Kepler telescope, which has assisted in locating many planets outside of our solar system. The question of other planets sustaining life, as it is on earth, has been plaguing scientists and . . . readers will speculate whether there are habitable planets and if people could move to them or not." (Publisher's note)

Simon, Seymour
★ **Our** solar system; [by] Seymour Simon. updated ed.; Collins 2007 62p il $19.99; lib bdg $20.89
Grades: 3 4 5 6 **523.2**
1. Solar system
ISBN 978-0-06-114008-2; 0-06-114008-2; 978-0-06-114009-9 lib bdg; 0-06-114009-0 lib bdg
LC 2007279969

First published 1992

Describes the origins, characteristics, and future of the sun, planets, moons, asteroids, meteoroids, and comets

This "is a fine, comprehensive work on the solar system. . . . [The book includes] excellent photographs. Beautifully designed and a pleasure to use." Horn Book Guide

Tourville, Amanda Doering

Exploring the solar system. Rourke Pub. 2010 48p il (Let's explore science) $32.79; pa $9.95

Grades: 4 5 6 7 **523.2**

1. Solar system

ISBN 978-1-61590-323-8; 1-61590-323-2; 1-61590-562-6 pa; 9781615905621 pa

LC 2010009910

This "moves from basic definitions . . . to more technical information, such as the formula for calculating the speed of light. Also included is up-to-date coverage of Pluto's demotion from planet to plutoid, as well as a section on dwarf planets. . . . In [this] title, well-chosen boxed examples, abundant color photos, diagrams, and an appended glossary add interest and support the engaging [text]." Booklist

Includes glossary and bibliographical references

Trammel, Howard K.

★ The **solar** system. Children's Press 2009 48p il (True book) lib bdg $26; pa $6.95

Grades: 3 4 5 **523.2**

1. Solar system

ISBN 978-0-531-16898-1 lib bdg; 0-531-16898-0 lib bdg; 978-0-531-22805-0 pa; 0-531-22805-3 pa

LC 2008049376

"The Solar System begins with a lineup of the usual suspects (yes, Pluto is off the hook). The way the chapters move from inner to outer planets is no surprise, but the called-out details are cunningly illustrated and plenty fascinating. . . . Short but solid back matter closes out [this] impressive [offering]." Booklist

Wittenstein, Vicki Oransky

Planet hunter; Goeff Marcy and the search for other earths. Boyds Mills Press 2010 48p il $17.95

Grades: 5 6 7 8 **523.2**

1. Extrasolar planets 2. Life on other planets 3. Astrophysicists 4. College teachers

ISBN 978-1-59078-592-8; 1-59078-592-4

"The profound thrill of searching for (and finding!) planets orbiting stars other than our own is deftly captured in this profile of Geoff Marcy, one of the great hunt's most successful practitioners. Matched to big, sharp color photos of scientists (mostly) at work and compelling speculative views of exotic suns and landscapes, Wittenstein's matter-of-fact narrative first introduces readers to Marcy and his team on the night shift . . . at the W. M. Keck Observatory atop Hawaii's Mauna Kea. . . . This handsomely packaged introduction is just the ticket for turning earthbound (for now) children into budding skywatchers." SLJ

Includes glossary and bibliographical references

523.3 Specific parts of solar system

Carson, Mary Kay

Far-out guide to the moon. Enslow Publishers 2010 48p il (Far-out guide to the solar system) lib bdg $23.93; pa $7.95

Grades: 3 4 5 **523.3**

1. Moon 2. Solar system

ISBN 978-0-7660-3189-0 lib bdg; 0-7660-3189-6 lib bdg; 978-1-59845-184-9 pa; 1-59845-184-7 pa

LC 2009006487

"Presents information about the moon, including fast facts, history, and technology used to study it." Publisher's note

Includes glossary and bibliographical references

Gibbons, Gail

The **moon** book. Holiday House 1997 un il $16.95; pa $6.95

Grades: K 1 2 3 **523.3**

1. Moon

ISBN 0-8234-1297-0; 0-8234-1364-0 pa

LC 96-36826

Identifies the moon as our only natural satellite, describes its movement and phases, and discusses how we have observed and explored it over the years

"Gibbons presents a great deal of information in a deceptively simple format by combining inviting illustrations with clear writing." Horn Book Guide

Scott, Elaine

Our moon; new discoveries about Earth's closest companion. Elaine Scott. Clarion Books 2015 72 p. chiefly color illustrations (hardcover) $18.99

Grades: 4 5 6 7 **523.3**

1. Moon 2. Astronomy 3. Earth (Planet) 4. Moon -- Exploration 5. Space flight to the moon

ISBN 9780547483948

LC 2015006855

This children's book, by Elaine Scott, "presents a wealth of captivating, kid-friendly information, covering everything from the newest theories on how the moon formed, to the recent, startling discovery of water on its surface and the very real possibility of future moon colonies." (Publisher's note)

"Broader in focus, more detailed, and more up-to-date than most children's books on the subject, this well-designed volume will be a useful addition to astronomy collections." Booklist

Includes bibliographical references and index

Simon, Seymour

★ The **moon**; rev ed.; Simon & Schuster Bks. for Young Readers 2003 un il $17.95

Grades: 4 5 6 7 **523.3**

1. Moon 2. Moon -- Exploration

ISBN 0-689-83563-9

LC 2001-31303

First published 1984 by Four Winds Press

A basic introduction to Earth's closest neighbor, its composition, and man's missions to it

"The digitally remastered color photographs in this update are incredible. . . . The text has undergone minimal change. . . . The facts remain true and relevant, and the writing reflects the graphics: beautiful. This is a must-have for astronomy sections." SLJ

Tomecek, Steve

★ **Moon**; illustrated by Liisa Chauncy Guida. National Geographic 2005 31p il (Jump into science) $16.95; lib bdg $25.90

Grades: K 1 2 **523.3**

1. Moon

ISBN 0-7922-5123-7; 0-7922-8304-X lib bdg

LC 2004-8761

This book presents facts about the moon. "Kindergarten to grade two." (Sci Books Films)

"A cartoon cat and bug explain scientific history and concepts regarding the Earth's moon: its ever-changing appearance, composition, comparisons to Earth and the sun, Galileo's observations and discoveries in 1609, astronauts, orbits, and other topics." SLJ

523.4   Planets, asteroids, trans-Neptunian objects of solar system

Bjorklund, Ruth

Venus. Marshall Cavendish Benchmark 2009 64p il (Space!) lib bdg o.p.; ebook $33

Grades: 4 5 6 7   **523.4**

1. Venus (Planet)

ISBN 978-0-7614-4251-6; 9780761445616

LC 2009014665

"Describes Venus, including its history, its composition, and its role in the solar system." Publisher's note

Includes glossary and bibliographical references

Capaccio, George

Jupiter. Marshall Cavendish Benchmark 2009 64p il (Space!) lib bdg $22.95

Grades: 4 5 6 7   **523.4**

1. Jupiter (Planet)

ISBN 978-0-7614-4244-8 lib bdg; 0-7614-4244-8 lib bdg; 9780761445555

LC 2008037276

"Describes Jupiter, including its history, its composition, and its role in the solar system." Publisher's note

Includes glossary and bibliographical references

Mars. Marshall Cavendish Benchmark 2010 64p il (Space!) lib bdg $22.95

Grades: 4 5 6 7   **523.4**

1. Mars (Planet)

ISBN 978-0-7614-4247-9 lib bdg; 0-7614-4247-2 lib bdg; 9780761445579

LC 2008037280

Describes Mars, including its history, its composition, and its role in the solar system

Includes glossary and bibliographical references

Carson, Mary Kay

Far-out guide to asteroids and comets. Enslow Publishers 2010 48p il (Far-out guide to the solar system) lib bdg $23.93; pa $7.95

Grades: 3 4 5   **523.4**

1. Comets 2. Asteroids 3. Solar system

ISBN 978-0-7660-3188-3 lib bdg; 0-7660-3188-8 lib bdg; 978-1-59845-191-7 pa; 1-59845-191-X pa

LC 2009006484

"Lively writing with specific facts systematically presented and plenty of dramatic space art and photography add up to a winning formula. . . . Carson offers a thrillingly alarmist view . . . of the (relatively) small rocks and comets that hurtle through local space to, on occasion, collide spectacularly with Earth or other planets." SLJ

Includes glossary and bibliographical references

Far-out guide to Jupiter. Enslow Publishers 2010 48p il (Far-out guide to the solar system) lib bdg $23.93; pa $7.95

Grades: 3 4 5   **523.4**

1. Jupiter (Planet) 2. Solar system

ISBN 978-0-7660-3184-5 lib bdg; 0-7660-3184-5 lib bdg; 978-1-59845-186-3 pa; 1-59845-186-3 pa

LC 2008050036

"Presents information about Jupiter, including fast facts, history, and technology used to study the planet.' Publisher's note

Includes glossary and bibliographical references

Far-out guide to Mars. Enslow Publishers 2010 48p il (Far-out guide to the solar system) lib bdg $23.93; pa $7.95

Grades: 3 4 5   **523.4**

1. Mars (Planet) 2. Solar system

ISBN 978-0-7660-3183-8 lib bdg; 0-7660-3183-7 lib bdg; 978-1-59845-185-6 pa; 1-59845-185-5 pa

LC 2009006485

"Presents information about Mars, including fast facts, history, and technology used to study the planet." Publisher's note

Includes glossary and bibliographical references

Far-out guide to Mercury. Enslow Publishers 2010 48p il (Far-out guide to the solar system) lib bdg $23.93; pa $7.95

Grades: 3 4 5   **523.4**

1. Mercury (Planet) 2. Solar system

ISBN 978-0-7660-3180-7 lib bdg; 0-7660-3180-2 lib bdg; 978-1-59845-181-8 pa; 1-59845-181-2 pa

LC 2009006486

"Presents information about Mercury, including fast facts, history, and technology used to study the planet." Publisher's note

Far-out guide to Neptune. Enslow Publishers 2010 48p il (Far-out guide to the solar system) lib bdg $23.93; pa $7.95

Grades: 3 4 5   **523.4**

1. Neptune (Planet) 2. Solar system

ISBN 978-0-7660-3186-9 lib bdg; 0-7660-3186-1 lib bdg; 978-1-59845-189-4 pa; 1-59845-189-8 pa

LC 2008050037

"Presents information about Neptune, including fast facts, history, and technology used to study the planet." Publisher's note

Includes glossary and bibliographical references

Far-out guide to Saturn. Enslow Publishers 2010 48p il (Far-out guide to the solar system) lib bdg $23.93; pa $7.95

Grades: 3 4 5   **523.4**

1. Saturn (Planet) 2. Solar system

ISBN 978-0-7660-3178-4 lib bdg; 0-7660-3178-0 lib bdg; 978-1-59845-187-0 pa; 1-59845-187-1 pa

LC 2008050038

"Presents information about Saturn, including fast facts, history, and technology used to study the planet" Publisher's note

Includes glossary and bibliographical references

Far-out guide to the icy dwarf planets. Enslow Publishers 2010 48p il (Far-out guide to the solar system) lib bdg $23.93; pa $7.95

Grades: 3 4 5   **523.4**

1. Planets

ISBN 978-0-7660-3187-6 lib bdg; 0-7660-3187-X lib bdg; 978-1-59845-190-0 pa; 1-59845-190-1 pa

LC 2009037810

"Lively writing with specific facts systematically presented and plenty of dramatic space art and photography add up to a winning formula." SLJ

Includes glossary and bibliographical references

Far-out guide to Uranus. Enslow Publishers 2010 48p il (Far-out guide to the solar system) lib bdg $23.93; pa $7.95

Grades: 3 4 5   **523.4**

1. Uranus (Planet) 2. Solar system

ISBN 978-0-7660-3185-2 lib bdg; 0-7660-3185-3 lib bdg; 978-1-59845-188-7 pa; 1-59845-188-X pa

LC 2008050040

"Presents information about Uranus, including fast facts, history, and technology used to study the planet." Publisher's note

Includes glossary and bibliographical references

Far-out guide to Venus. Enslow Publishers 2010 48p il (Far-out guide to the solar system) lib bdg $23.93; pa $7.95

Grades: 3 4 5   **523.4**

1. Venus (Planet) 2. Solar system

ISBN 978-0-7660-3181-4 lib bdg; 0-7660-3181-0 lib bdg; 978-1-59845-182-5 pa; 1-59845-182-0 pa

LC 2008050041

"Presents information about Venus, including fast facts, history, and technology used to study the planet" Publisher's note

Includes glossary and bibliographical references

Colligan, L. H.

Mercury. Marshall Cavendish Benchmark 2009 64p il (Space!) lib bdg $22.95

Grades: 4 5 6 7   **523.4**

1. Mercury (Planet)

ISBN 0-7614-4239-1 lib bdg; 9780761442394 lib bdg; 9780761445517

LC 2008037278

"Describes Mercury, including its history, its composition, and its role in the solar system." Publisher's note

Includes glossary and bibliographical references

Hicks, Terry Allan

Saturn. Marshall Cavendish Benchmark 2010 64p il (Space!) lib bdg $22.95

Grades: 4 5 6 7   **523.4**

1. Saturn (Planet)

ISBN 978-0-7614-4249-3 lib bdg; 0-7614-4249-9 lib bdg; 9780761445593

LC 2008037453

"Describes Saturn, including its history, its composition, and its role in the solar system." Publisher's note

Includes glossary and bibliographical references

Landau, Elaine

Beyond Pluto; [by] Elaine Landau. Children's Press 2007 48p il (True book) lib bdg $26

Grades: 2 3 4   **523.4**

1. Planets

ISBN 0-531-12565-3 lib bdg; 978-0-531-12565-6 lib bdg

LC 2007012280

This "looks past Pluto into the Kuiper Belt, the Oort Cloud, and the search for extrasolar planets. . . . [This] matches a clearly reasoned, matter-of-fact text to plenty of small but sharply reproduced color photos." SLJ

Includes glossary and bibliographical references

Jupiter; [by] Elaine Landau. Children's Press 2007 48p il (True book) lib bdg $26; pa $6.95

Grades: 2 3 4   **523.4**

1. Jupiter (Planet)

ISBN 978-0-531-12559-5 lib bdg; 0-531-12559-9 lib bdg; 978-0-531-14789-4 pa; 0-531-14789-4 pa

LC 2007003869

First published 1991

This describes the atmosphere and geographic features of Jupiter and the missions which have explored the planet

This "matches a clearly reasoned, matter-of-fact text to plenty of small but sharply reproduced color photos." SLJ

Includes glossary and bibliographical references

Neptune; [by] Elaine Landau. Children's Press 2007 48p il (True book) lib bdg $26; pa $6.95

Grades: 2 3 4   **523.4**

1. Neptune (Planet)

ISBN 978-0-531-12563-2 lib bdg; 0-531-12563-7 lib bdg; 978-0-531-14793-1 pa; 0-531-14793-2 pa

LC 2007008257

This describes Neptune's place in the solar system, its atmosphere and composition

This "matches a clearly reasoned, matter-of-fact text to plenty of small but sharply reproduced color photos." SLJ

Includes glossary and bibliographical references

Pluto; from planet to dwarf. [by] Elaine Landau. Children's Press 2007 48p il (True book) lib bdg $26; pa $6.95

Grades: 2 3 4   **523.4**

1. Pluto (Dwarf planet) 2. Pluto (Planet)

ISBN 978-0-531-12566-3 lib bdg; 0-531-12566-1 lib bdg; 978-0-531-14794-8 pa; 0-531-14794-0 pa

LC 2007012279

This describes Pluto's place in the solar system, its change in status from planet to dwarf, its moons, and missions to Pluto

This "matches a clearly reasoned, matter-of-fact text to plenty of small but sharply reproduced color photos." SLJ

Includes glossary and bibliographical references

Saturn; [by] Elaine Landau. Children's Press 2007 48p il (True book) lib bdg $26; pa $6.95

Grades: 2 3 4   **523.4**

1. Saturn (Planet)

ISBN 978-0-531-12567-0 lib bdg; 0-531-12567-X lib bdg; 978-0-531-14795-5 pa; 0-531-14795-9 pa

LC 2007004181

This describes Saturn's place in the solar system, its composition, its moons and rings and missions to Saturn

This "matches a clearly reasoned, matter-of-fact text to plenty of small but sharply reproduced color photos." SLJ

Includes glossary and bibliographical references

Uranus; [by] Elaine Landau. Children's Press 2007 48p il (True book) lib bdg $26; pa $6.95

Grades: 2 3 4   **523.4**

1. Uranus (Planet)

ISBN 978-0-531-12569-4 lib bdg; 0-531-12569-6 lib bdg; 978-0-531-14797-9 pa; 0-531-14797-5 pa

LC 2007012258

This describes Uranus's place in the solar system, its atmosphere, moons, and rings, and exploration

This "matches a clearly reasoned, matter-of-fact text to plenty of small but sharply reproduced color photos." SLJ

Includes glossary and bibliographical references

Venus; [by] Elaine Landau. Children's Press 2007 48p il (True book) lib bdg $26; pa $6.95

Grades: 2 3 4   **523.4**

1. Venus (Planet)

ISBN 978-0-531-12564-9 lib bdg; 0-531-12564-5 lib bdg; 978-0-531-14798-6 pa; 0-531-14798-3 pa

LC 2007004449

This describes Venus's place in the solar system, its atmosphere and composition, and missions to Venus

This "matches a clearly reasoned, matter-of-fact text to plenty of small but sharply reproduced color photos." SLJ

Includes glossary and bibliographical references

Miller, Ron

Seven wonders of the gas giants and their moons. Twenty-First Century Books 2011 80p il (Seven wonders) lib bdg $33.26
Grades: 5 6 7 8   **523.4**
1. Planets
ISBN 978-0-7613-5449-9 lib bdg; 0-7613-5449-2 lib bdg; 9780761372813
LC 2010-15558

This book describes seven phenomena about the outer planets of the solar system and their moons, including the great red spot of Jupiter and the underground sea of Europa. Index. "Grades five to eight." (Sci Books Films)

This "celebrates the most unique features of Jupiter, Saturn, Uranus and Neptune, including companion moons and Saturn's mysterious rings. . . . [This] volume makes basic concepts clear in lively, energetic language that, along with the mesmerizing color photos and artists' renderings of space, will easily captivate a young audience, while up-to-date examples, including discoveries made in the last five years, will only increase the sense of immediacy and excitement." Booklist

Includes glossary and bibliographical references

Seven wonders of the rocky planets and their moons. Twenty-First Century Books 2011 80p il (Seven wonders) lib bdg $33.26
Grades: 4 5 6   **523.4**
1. Planets
ISBN 978-0-7613-5448-2 lib bdg; 0-7613-5448-4 lib bdg; 9780761372837
LC 2010-15553

This book shows "views of features on Mercury, Venus, Earth (and its moon), and Mars. [Glossary. Index.] Grades five to eight." (Sci Books Films)

This "compares the fascinating diversity of Earth's land masses with those on Mars, Venus and Mercury. . . . [This] volume makes basic concepts clear in lively, energetic language that, along with the mesmerizing color photos and artists' renderings of space, will easily captivate a young audience, while up-to-date examples, including discoveries made in the last five years, will only increase the sense of immediacy and excitement." Booklist

Includes glossary and bibliographical references

Poynter, Margaret

Doomsday rocks from space. Enslow Publishers 2011 48p il (Bizarre science) lib bdg $23.93
Grades: 5 6 7 8   **523.4**
1. Comets 2. Asteroids 3. Meteorites
ISBN 978-0-7660-3673-4; 0-7660-3673-1
LC 2009053601

First published 1996 with title: Killer asteroids

"Aimed at reluctant readers, [this title is] sure to disgust and delight in equal measure. . . . [The title] will pique interest and get kids lining up at the reference desk looking for more. The text is complemented by illustrations and magnified photos of things that you would hope never to see." SLJ

Includes glossary and bibliographical references

Scott, Elaine

★ **When** is a planet not a planet? the story of Pluto. Clarion Books 2007 43p il $17

Grades: 3 4 5 6   **523.4**
1. Planets
ISBN 978-0-618-89832-9; 0-618-89832-8

"Scott takes the 2006 downgrading of Pluto from planet to dwarf planet as a teachable moment for discussing questions such as how the number of planets has changed through the centuries, what can be called a planet, and how scientists come to conclusions—and occasionally change their minds. . . . Beautifully designed, the book includes many well-captioned, color illustrations, from period portraits to NASA images to artist's conceptions." Booklist

Sherman, Josepha

Asteroids, meteors, and comets. Marshall Cavendish Benchmark 2009 64p il (Space!) lib bdg $22.95
Grades: 4 5 6 7   **523.4**
1. Comets 2. Meteors 3. Asteroids
ISBN 978-0-7614-4252-3 lib bdg; 0-7614-4252-9 lib bdg
LC 2008037281

This stands out for its "clear, accurate [presentation] of basic facts punctuated by lively turns of phrase and, sometimes, details not commonly found in the plethora of similar tours of the solar system and beyond." SLJ

Includes glossary and bibliographical references

Neptune. Marshall Cavendish Benchmark 2009 63p il (Space!) lib bdg $22.95
Grades: 4 5 6 7   **523.4**
1. Neptune (Planet)
ISBN 978-0-7614-4246-2 lib bdg; 0-7614-4246-4 lib bdg; 9780761445562
LC 2008037279

"Describes Neptune, including its history, its composition, and its role in the solar system." Publisher's note

Includes glossary and bibliographical references

Uranus. Marshall Cavendish Benchmark 2010 63p il (Space!) lib bdg $22.95
Grades: 4 5 6 7   **523.4**
1. Astronomers 2. Uranus (Planet)
ISBN 978-0-7614-4248-6 lib bdg; 0-7614-4248-0 lib bdg; 9780761445586
LC 2008037274

"Describes Uranus, including its history, its composition, and its role in the solar system." Publisher's note

Includes glossary and bibliographical references

Sparrow, Giles

Destination Uranus, Neptune, and Pluto. PowerKids Press 2010 32p il (Destination solar system) lib bdg $23.95; pa $10
Grades: 3 4 5 6   **523.4**
1. Uranus (Planet) 2. Neptune (Planet) 3. Pluto (Dwarf planet) 4. Pluto (Planet)
ISBN 978-1-4358-3446-0 lib bdg; 978-1-4358-3463-7 pa
LC 2009-2985

Examines the outer planets, and discusses their moons, interiors, atmospheres, locations, and exploration.

Includes glossary

523.43 Mars

Aldrin, Buzz, 1930-
Welcome to Mars; making a home on the Red Planet. Buzz Aldrin, with Marianne J. Dyson. National Geographic 2015 96 p. color illustrations (hardcover : alk. paper) $18.99
Grades: 4 5 6 7 8   **523.43**
1. Space flight to Mars 2. Mars (Planet) -- Exploration 3. Space colonies
ISBN 9781426322068; 9781426322075
LC 2014038088
This children's book, by Buzz Aldrin, with Marianne J. Dyson, "challenges curious kids to think about Mars as not just a faraway red planet but as a possible future home for Earthlings! What will your new home be like? How will you get there? What will you eat for breakfast? Find out what life might be like far, far from Earth." (Publisher's note)
"Colorful images, a time line, and a map of Mars enhance the text. . . . A solid option for readers doing school reports or those curious about exploring a new frontier." SLJ
Includes bibliographical references and index

Rusch, Elizabeth
★ The **mighty** Mars rovers; the incredible adventures of Spirit and Opportunity. by Elizabeth Rusch. Houghton Mifflin Books for Children 2012 79 p. ill. (chiefly col.) (hardcover) $18.99; (hardcover) $18.99
Grades: 4 5 6   **523.43**
1. Mars probes 2. Mars (Planet) -- Exploration 3. Astronautics 4. Roving vehicles (Astronautics)
ISBN 054747881X; 9780547478814
LC 2011012159
In this book, "[Elizabeth] Rusch covers not only the scientific aspects of Mars exploration but also the personalities of the people who made it happen, and profiles the rovers themselves, Spirit and Opportunity." She looks at "the behind-the-scenes efforts of launching a scientific mission." Also included are "[f]ull-color photographs," a glossary, and a list of further resources. (School Library Journal)
Includes bibliographical references (p. 76), discography (p. 78), filmograophy (p. 78), and index.

Simon, Seymour
Destination: Mars; Seymour Simon. 3rd edition HarperCollins 2016 32 p. color illustrations hbk $17.99; pbk $6.99
Grades: 3 4 5   **523.43**
1. Mars (Planet)
ISBN 9780062344977; 0062344978; 9780062345042; 0062345044
"Award-winning science writer Seymour Simon explores the Red Planet through fascinating facts and amazing full-color photographs. Readers will learn about the recent discovery of water, the Valles Marineris--the biggest valley on Mars--the ice caps, recent expeditions, and more." (Publisher's note)

523.45 Jupiter

Mist, Rosalind
Jupiter and Saturn; by Rosalind Mist. QEB Pub. 2012 24 p. col. ill. (Up in space) (hardcover) $25.65
Grades: K 1 2   **523.45**
1. Saturn (Planet) 2. Jupiter (Planet)
ISBN 1609923219; 9781609923211
LC 2012007023
This book by Rosalind Mist, part of the Up in Space series, looks at Jupiter and Saturn. "Each planet is discussed individually, while a

separate page on the solar system shows the relative size of the planets." Photographs from the Hubble Space Telescope and other space missions are included. (Booklist)

523.46 Saturn

Miller, Ron
Saturn; Ron Miller. Twenty-First Century Books 2003 80p ill. (library) $27.93
Grades: 5 6 7 8   **523.46**
1. Saturn (Planet)
ISBN 9780761323600; 0761323600
Chronicles the discovery and exploration of the planet Saturn and discusses its rings and moons, its place in the solar system, and more.
"Concepts are explained clearly, and helpful diagrams and carefully chosen illustrations assist understanding." SLJ
Includes bibliographical references

523.49 Trans-Neptunian objects

Devorkin, David
Pluto's secret; an icy world's tale of discovery. by Margaret Weitekamp with David DeVorkin; illustrated by Diane Kidd. Abrams Books for Young Readers 2013 40 p. (reinforced) $16.95
Grades: 2 3 4   **523.49**
1. Picture books for children 2. Pluto (Dwarf planet)
ISBN 1419704230; 9781419704239
LC 2012033546
This children's picture book looks at Pluto. "The ninth planet from its discovery in 1930 to its demotion in 2006, Pluto has been revealing more of its 'secrets' as technology improved, and is now considered a 'dwarf planet' in the Kuiper belt. . . . The book provides a factual history of our faraway 'dwarf,' and on its companion icy worlds, and on the discovery of Kuiper-like bands around other stars." (School Library Journal)
Includes bibliographical references.

523.5 Meteors, solar wind, zodiacal light

Hartland, Jessie
★ **How** the meteorite got to the museum; by Jessie Hartland. Blue Apple Books 2013 40 p. (hardcover) $17.99
Grades: 1 2 3 4   **523.5**
1. Meteorites 2. Museums and schools 3. American Museum of Natural History 4. Meteorites -- New York (State) -- Peekskill
ISBN 1609052528; 9781609052522
LC 2013007801
This children's picture book looks at "the travels of the Peekskill meteorite to the American Museum of Natural History." Here, "a science teacher chronicles for her students the travels of a meteoroid from outer space to the atmosphere over the United States, across several states, into a parked car in Peekskill, N.Y., and on to the museum." (Kirkus Reviews)

523.6 Comets

Simon, Seymour
★ **Comets,** meteors, and asteroids. Morrow Junior Bks. 1994 un il. hardcover o.p. pa $6.95

Grades: 3 4 5 6   **523.6**
1. Comets 2. Meteors 3. Asteroids
ISBN 0-688-15843-9 pa

LC 93-51251

"Simon presents basic information about comets, meteors, and asteroids in an attractive oversize book. . . . Blocks of text appear in fairly large type, usually facing a full-page illustration. . . . Simon writes in plain language, without talking down to his audience. The intriguing photographs include shots of comets and meteor showers in the sky, a meteorite in Antarctica, and an enormous impact crater in Arizona." Booklist

523.7   Sun

Branley, Franklyn Mansfield

★ The **sun**, our nearest star; by Franklyn M. Branley; illustrated by Edward Miller. HarperCollins Pubs. 2002 25p il (Let's-read-and-find-out science) hardcover o.p. pa $4.95
Grades: K 1 2   **523.7**
1. Sun
ISBN 0-06-028534-6; 0-06-028535-4 lib bdg; 0-06-445202-6 pa

LC 2001-24951

A revised and newly illustrated edition of the title first published 1961

Describes the sun and how it provides the light and energy which allow plant and animal life to exist on the earth

"This edition marks the third incarnation of an old standby. . . . The gently edited text reads better than the old one. The new design features a larger format, bolder typography, and eye-catching artwork." Booklist

Capaccio, George

The **sun**. Marshall Cavendish Benchmark 2009 64p il (Space!) lib bdg $22.95
Grades: 4 5 6 7   **523.7**
1. Sun
ISBN 978-0-7614-4242-4 lib bdg; 0-7614-4242-1 lib bdg

LC 2008037275

"Describes the Sun, including its history, its composition, and its role in the solar system." Publisher's note

Includes glossary and bibliographical references

Carson, Mary Kay

Far-out guide to the sun. Enslow Publishers 2010 48p il (Far-out guide to the solar system) lib bdg $23.93; pa $7.95
Grades: 3 4 5   **523.7**
1. Sun 2. Solar system
ISBN 978-0-7660-3179-1 lib bdg; 0-7660-3179-9 lib bdg; 978-1-59845-180-1 pa; 1-59845-180-4 pa

LC 2008050039

"Presents information about the sun, including fast facts, history, and technology used to study it." Publisher's note

Includes glossary and bibliographical references

Gibbons, Gail

Sun up, sun down; written and illustrated by Gail Gibbons. Harcourt Brace Jovanovich 1983 un il hardcover o.p. pa $7
Grades: K 1 2 3   **523.7**
1. Sun
ISBN 0-15-282781-1; 0-15-282782-X pa

LC 82-23420

This book provides a look at the sun's effect on the daily life of a little girl, told in first person. From the sun's first beam through her window in the morning to the dark night, the little girl focuses on the sun. She sees patterns (from the sun's beams through the window) on

her floor; shades her eyes from looking at the sun and eats cereal made of wheat ('My dad tells me the sun made the wheat grow'). . . . Grades one to three. (SLJ)

The author explains "the sun and its effect on the earth. Narrated by a little girl who notices the sun shining when she wakes up one morning, this . . . [book covers] what the sun does, what makes shadows, how the sun helps form rain clouds, and how it keeps the planet warm." Booklist

Wells, Robert E.

★ **Why** do elephants need the sun? Albert Whitman & Co. 2010 un il $16.99
Grades: 2 3 4   **523.7**
1. Sun 2. Water 3. Photosynthesis
ISBN 0-8075-9081-9; 978-0-8075-9081-2

This "book, on the sun, provides an approachable introduction to the subject while laying the groundwork for understanding topics (gravity, nuclear fusion) that students will tackle in later years. Beginning with the sun itself, the presentation quickly comes down to earth in a child-friendly way, with an elephant who needs our closest star. . . . The discussion of gravity starts with the elephant, then shifts to the solar system and the sun's core. Wells also shows how people have used the sun. . . . The book's naive ink-and-watercolor illustrations are often playful in approach. Simple diagrams are often used to clarify more abstract concepts. . . . This title offers an appealing introduction to the sun, as well as a solid stepping-stone toward scientific literacy." Booklist

523.8   Stars

Abramson, Andra Serlin

Inside stars; by Andra Serlin Abramson and Mordecai-Mark Mac Low. Sterling Children's Books 2011 48p il (Inside . . .) $16.95; pa $9.95
Grades: 5 6 7 8   **523.8**
1. Stars
ISBN 978-1-4027-7709-7; 1-4027-7709-4; 978-1-4027-8162-9 pa; 1-4027-8162-8 pa

LC 2011283564

Presents an illustrated overview of stars, including information on how they affect the Earth, how scientists study them, how they are classified, how they form and die, and specific information about our star, the Sun.

"On full but not crowded-looking pages, the captions, vocabulary words and digestible blocks of text are set into and around an engagingly diverse mix of cutaway views, digital paintings and eye-widening deep-space photographs. . . . There's plenty here to stimulate both random browsers and confirmed young sky watchers." Kirkus

Includes bibliographical references

Aguilar, David A.

Super stars; the biggest, hottest, brightest, and most explosive stars in the Milky Way. National Geographic 2010 48p il $16.95; lib bdg $27.90
Grades: 4 5 6 7   **523.8**
1. Stars
ISBN 978-1-4263-0601-3; 1-4263-0601-6; 978-1-4263-0602-0 lib bdg; 1-4263-0602-4 lib bdg

LC 2009-37124

"Pairing dramatic space art with souped-up prose, Aguilar introduces more than a dozen types of stars and stellar phenomena. . . . Aside from the occasional alien or interstellar spacecraft set against glowing star fields, the information in both pictures and texts sticks to the facts, accurately reflecting current knowledge without ever coming close to turning into a dry recitation of data. . . . [This is an] unusually exuberant ticket to ride for young sky watchers and armchair space travelers." SLJ

Includes glossary and bibliographical references

Asimov, Isaac

The **life** and death of stars; by Isaac Asimov. rev and updated ed; Gareth Stevens Pub. 2005 32p il lib bdg $24.67

Grades: 4 5 6   **523.8**

1. Stars

ISBN 0-8368-3967-6

LC 2004-57842

This "begins with the birth of stars in dust cloud nurseries; goes on to profile the different types of stars; describes supernovas, neutron stars, and other late-stage developments; then closes with an account of our Sun's probable fate. . . . [This is an] excellent collection [enhancer]." SLJ

Includes bibliographical references

Branley, Franklyn Mansfield

The **Big** Dipper; by Franklyn M. Branley; illustrated by Molly Coxe. rev ed; HarperCollins Pubs. 1991 32p il (Let's-read-and-find-out science book) hardcover o.p. pa $4.95

Grades: K 1   **523.8**

1. Ursa Major

ISBN 0-06-445100-3 pa

LC 90-31199

A revised and newly illustrated edition of the title first published 1962

Explains basic facts about the Big Dipper, including which stars make up the constellation, how its position changes in the sky, and how it points to the North Star

Croswell, Ken

★ The **lives** of stars. Boyds Mills Press 2009 72p il $19.95

Grades: 5 6 7 8   **523.8**

1. Stars 2. Astronomy

ISBN 978-1-59078-582-9; 1-59078-582-7

LC 2008033913

"Extensive, detailed information about stars is coupled with amazing colorful photographs, many from the Hubble Space Telescope, in this stunning book. Packed with facts about the stars and their life cycle, the text often relates them to situations or objects familiar to readers." SLJ

Includes glossary

DeCristofano, Carolyn Cinami

★ A **black** hole is not a hole; Carolyn Cinami DeCristofano; Illustrated by Michael Carroll. Charlesbridge 2012 v, 74 p.p col ill. (reinforced for library use) $18.95

Grades: 4 5 6 7   **523.8**

1. Stars 2. Universe 3. Black holes (Astronomy)

ISBN 9781570917837; 9781570917844

LC 2010022764

In this non-fiction children's book, Carolyn Cinami DeCristofano discusses black holes. "Covering the life cycles of stars; the formation of black holes and weird optical and physical effects associated with them; more recent revelations of super-sized black holes at the centers of galaxies; and the general effects of mass on space, light, and matter, she presents a . . . picture of the strange structure and stranger physics of black holes." (Booklist)

Gifford, Clive

Stars, galaxies, and the Milky Way; Clive Gifford. Crabtree Publishing Company 2016 32 p. color illustrations (reinforced library binding : alk. paper) $27.60; (ebook) $41.40

Grades: 4 5 6   **523.8**

1. Stars 2. Galaxies 3. Milky Way

ISBN 9780778720225; 9780778720263; 9781427116857

LC 2015015360

Readers of this children's book by Clive Gifford, part of the Watch This Space! series, will "learn all about the sparkling world of stars from their beautiful births to their dramatic deaths. This . . . book describes our very own star, the Sun, as well as best-friend binary star pairs and dense neutron stars. [Readers will] gaze at gorgeous galaxies and marvel at the Milky Way." (Publisher's note)

"Together, these books cover all aspects of space, combining pertinent facts with a cool factor." Booklist

Includes index

Jackson, Ellen B.

★ The **mysterious** universe; supernovae, dark energy, and black holes. text by Ellen Jackson; photographs and illustrations by Nic Bishop. Houghton Mifflin 2008 60p il (Scientists in the field) $18

Grades: 5 6 7 8 9   **523.8**

1. Supernovas 2. Black holes (Astronomy)

ISBN 978-0-618-56325-8; 0-618-56325-3

LC 2007-41165

"Splitting its attention evenly between the scientist and his field, this handsomely designed volume displays the joys of being fascinated by one's work in a way that will encourage students to seek similar professional satisfaction for themselves." Booklist

Includes glossary and bibliographical references

Kim, F. S.

★ **Constellations**. Children's Press 2009 48p il (True book) lib bdg $26; pa $6.95

Grades: 3 4 5   **523.8**

1. Constellations

ISBN 978-0-531-16895-0 lib bdg; 0-531-16895-6 lib bdg; 978-0-531-22802-9 pa; 0-531-22802-9 pa

LC 2008050629

Though this title "dabbles in the science of planetary orbits and early stargazing gear, . . . it mostly focuses on the rich myths surrounding the constellations, in one illustration transforming the night sky into a draped tapestry of monsters and gods. . . . Short but solid back matter closes out [this] impressive [offering]." Booklist

Mack, Gail

The **stars**. Marshall Cavendish Benchmark 2009 64p il (Space!) lib bdg $32.79

Grades: 4 5 6 7   **523.8**

1. Stars 2. Galaxies

ISBN 978-0-7614-4250-9 lib bdg; 0-7614-4250-2 lib bdg

LC 2009014655

This stands out for its "clear, accurate [presentation] of basic facts punctuated by lively turns of phrase and, sometimes, details not commonly found in the plethora of similar tours of the solar system and beyond." SLJ

Includes glossary and bibliographical references

Miller, Ron

Seven wonders beyond the solar system. Twenty-First Century Books 2011 80p il (Seven wonders) lib bdg $33.26

Grades: 5 6 7 8   **523.8**

1. Extrasolar planets 2. Solar system

ISBN 978-0-7613-5454-3; 0-7613-5454-9

LC 2010028446

This "discusses how stars and galaxies form and how scientists search for 'the most Earthlike planet,' as well as the noteworthy nebulae, pulsars, and superclusters. . . . [This] volume makes basic concepts clear in lively, energetic language that, along with the mesmerizing color photos and artists' renderings of space, will easily captivate a young audience, while up-to-date examples, including discoveries made in the last five years, will only increase the sense of immediacy and excitement." Booklist

Includes glossary and bibliographical references

Mitton, Jacqueline

★ **Once** upon a starry night; a book of constellations. [illustrated by] Christina Balit. National Geographic 2004 un il $16.95

Grades: K 1 2 3   **523.8**

1. Constellations 2. Classical mythology

ISBN 0-7922-6332-4

LC 2003-10993

Companion volume to Zoo in the sky (1998)

First published 2003 in the United Kingdom

Presents facts about stars, nebulas, galaxies, and constellations and recounts the Greek myths that provided widely-known names for ten constellations, from Andromeda to Pegasus.

"Although the stories are quite short, Mitton's vivid word choices make the text as dynamic as Balit's striking pictures. Partly abstract and partly representational, the artwork features bold figures of mythological characters with silver-foil stars highlighting the points of light that make up the constellations." Booklist

Rey, H. A.

★ **Find** the constellations; 2nd ed.; Houghton Mifflin Harcourt 2008 72p il $20; pa $9.99

Grades: 3 4 5 6   **523.8**

1. Stars 2. Constellations

ISBN 978-0-547-13140-5; 0-547-13140-2; 978-0-547-13178-8 pa; 0-547-13178-X pa

First published 1954

"This much-needed update of Rey's classic work . . . features a cleaner typeface but retains the layout and most of the graphics of the previous edition. . . . The primary update . . . involves the change in Pluto's status; a great touch is the inclusion of definitions for 'planet' and 'dwarf planet.' . . . Statistical data . . . are updated; the planet finder now covers the years 2007 through 2016; and there is a new list of books for further reading. With its enduring appeal, current information, and exceptional sky charts . . . this revision should be an essential purchase for all libraries." SLJ

Rockwell, Anne F.

Our stars; written and illustrated by Anne Rockwell. Silver Whistle Bks. 1999 un il hardcover o.p. pa $6.99

Grades: K 1 2   **523.8**

1. Stars 2. Planets 3. Outer space

ISBN 0-15-201868-9; 0-15-216360-0 pa

LC 97-49518

A simple introduction to the stars, planets, and outer space

"This book clearly explains many science facts without 'talking down' to youngsters. The storybook-style illustrations, . . . invite children to look at the night sky and think about the information presented in the text." Sci Books Films

Than, Ker

★ **Stars**. Children's Press 2009 48p il (True book) lib bdg $26; pa $6.95

Grades: 3 4 5   **523.8**

1. Stars

ISBN 978-0-531-16899-8 lib bdg; 0-531-16899-9 lib bdg; 978-0-531-22806-7 pa; 0-531-22806-1 pa

LC 2008051630

This introduction to stars "is simply gorgeous. The ghostly veils of the Cat's Eye Nebula, the ominous gas pillars of the Eagle Nebula, the coral-reef depths of the Crab Nebula—the only complaint will be that the photos aren't bigger. The diagrams (including the cradle-to-grave 'A Star's Life') are remarkably educational. Short but solid back matter closes out [this] impressive [offering]." Booklist

Waxman, Laura Hamilton

Exploring black holes. Lerner Publications Company 2011 40p il (What's amazing about space?) lib bdg $27.93

Grades: 4 5 6   **523.8**

1. Black holes (Astronomy)

ISBN 978-0-7613-5442-0; 0-7613-5442-5

LC 2010035378

This book about black holes in space is "written in simple language, [and] illustrated nicely. . . . The information presented is factually correct. . . . Every page includes a well-chosen illustration or photograph." Sci Books Films

525   Earth (Astronomical geography)

Bailey, Jacqui

Sun up, sun down; the story of day and night. written by Jacqui Bailey; illustrated by Matthew Lilly. Picture Window Books 2004 31p il (Science works) lib bdg $23.93

Grades: 2 3 4   **525**

1. Day 2. Night 3. Sun 4. Moon 5. Earth

ISBN 1-4048-0567-2

LC 2003-20119

Follows the sun from dawn to dusk to explain how light rays travel, how shadows are formed, how the moon lights up the night sky, and more

This "excellent science [book explains its subject] lucidly and sometimes amusingly. . . . Children will be illuminated and engaged." SLJ

Includes bibliographical references

Carson, Mary Kay

Far-out guide to Earth. Enslow Publishers 2010 48p il (Far-out guide to the solar system) lib bdg $23.93; pa $7.95

Grades: 3 4 5   **525**

1. Earth 2. Solar system

ISBN 978-0-7660-3182-1 lib bdg; 0-7660-3182-9 lib bdg; 978-1-59845-183-2 pa; 1-59845-183-9 pa

LC 2008049781

"Lively writing with specific facts systematically presented and plenty of dramatic space art and photography add up to a winning formula." SLJ

Includes glossary and bibliographical references

Gibbons, Gail

The **reasons** for seasons. Holiday House 1995 un il $16.95; pa $6.95

Grades: K 1 2 3   **525**

1. Seasons 2. Earth

ISBN 0-8234-1174-5; 0-590-90735-2 pa

LC 94-32904

"Gibbons uses simple words and clear, colorful pictures to explain the seasons, the solstices, and the equinoxes. Besides discussing the earth's tilt and orbit, she also comments on what people and animals do in each season of the year." Booklist

Hicks, Terry Allan

Earth and the moon. Marshall Cavendish Benchmark 2009 64p il (Space!) lib bdg $22.95

Grades: 4 5 6 7

1. Moon 2. Earth

ISBN 978-0-7614-4254-7 lib bdg; 0-7614-4254-5 lib bdg

LC 2009014663

"Describes Earth and its Moon, including their history, their composition, and their roles in the solar system." Publisher's note

Includes glossary and bibliographical references

Karas, G. Brian

★ On Earth; written and illustrated by G. Brian Karas. Putnam 2005 un il $16.99

Grades: K 1 2

1. Earth

ISBN 0-399-24025-X

LC 2004-18204

This book describes the Earth's cycles of rotation and revolution, plus how they affect our lives through the days and seasons. "Ages five to eight." (Bull Cent Child Books)

"Karas covers the earth's rotation and revolution, space and time, hemispheres, and gravity. The spare text alternates between technical descriptions and personal experiences. Artistic renderings of the earth and its cycles introduce diagrams and offer concrete images showing what happens as day turns to night, seasons change, and the earth rotates on its axis." Horn Book Guide

Landau, Elaine

Earth; [by] Elaine Landau. Children's Press 2007 48p il (True book) lib bdg $26; pa $6.95

Grades: 2 3 4

1. Earth

ISBN 978-0-531-12558-8 lib bdg; 0-531-12558-0 lib bdg; 978-0-531-14788-7 pa; 0-531-14788-6 pa

LC 2007012278

Describes the planet Earth, exploring its composition, the conditions which support life, theories about how it formed, and its relationship with the moon

This "matches a clearly reasoned, matter-of-fact text to plenty of small but sharply reproduced color photos." SLJ

Includes glossary and bibliographical references

Miller, Ron

Earth and the moon. 21st Cent. Bks. (Brookfield) 2003 96p il (Worlds beyond) lib bdg $25.90

Grades: 5 6 7 8

1. Moon 2. Earth

ISBN 0-7613-2358-9

LC 2001-8479

This book chronicles the origin, evolution, and exploration of the Earth and the Moon, and discusses their composition, their place in the solar system, along with other topics. Glossary. Index. "Grades five to eight." (Sci Books Films)

This is illustrated "with a mix of NASA photos and wide-angle, computer-generated art. . . . Students with a serious interest in the physical history of the Earth and its moon will be engrossed by his account of our planet's first few billion years, the Moon's probable origin, and the rise of life." SLJ

Includes glossary and bibliographical references

Nardo, Don

The Blue marble; how a photograph revealed Earth's fragile beauty. by Don Nardo. Compass Point Books 2014 64 p. (Compass point books. Captured history) (library binding) $33.99

Grades: 5 6 7 8 9

1. Earth 2. Photographs 3. Apollo project 4. Apollo 17 (Spacecraft) 5. Photographs -- History

ISBN 0756547326; 9780756547325; 9780756547882

LC 2013031184

"The astronauts headed to the moon in December 1972 thought they knew what to expect. . . . But what they didn't expect came as a huge bonus. The astronauts of Apollo 17 would produce an amazing photograph of planet Earth--a lonely globe floating in inky black space. Their stunning Blue Marble image was destined to become one of the most reproduced and recognizable photos in history." (Publisher's note)

"This outstanding follow-up to Capstone's 'Captured History' series continues the same format, focusing on a single, emblematic photograph that defines an era or event. . . . This set will show students how a single image can 'capture' history and influence the perceptions and actions of those who see it. The books will certainly draw a large readership and are must-buys for all middle-level and secondary collections." SLJ

Includes bibliographical references (page 63) and index

Ride, Sally K.

Mission: planet Earth; our world and its climate--and how humans are changing them. [by] Sally Ride & Tam O'Shaughnessy. Roaring Brook Press 2009 80p il map (Sally Ride science) $19.95

Grades: 5 6 7 8

1. Earth 2. Climate -- Environmental aspects

ISBN 978-1-59643-310-6; 1-59643-310-8

LC 2009-29253

"This environmental-science primer introduces a range of important concepts necessary to understand climate change and global warming. Topics include the carbon cycle, water cycle, long-range carbon emissions data, biological evidence of climate change, and much more. The authors have an extensive background in science education, and their text exhibits an excellent balance of concept thoroughness with ease of comprehension. Attractive photographs and colorful graphics, including many charts and diagrams, are incorporated throughout." SLJ

Simon, Seymour

★ Earth: our planet in space; rev ed; Simon & Schuster Bks. for Young Readers 2003 un il $17.95

Grades: 4 5 6 7

1. Earth

ISBN 0-689-83562-0

LC 2001-31304

First published 1984 by Four Winds Press

This describes the relationship between the Earth, the sun, and the moon and explains the seasons, day and night, the atmosphere, and changes in the planet's surface. Illustrated with photographs taken from space

Wells, Robert E.

What's so special about planet Earth? Albert Whitman & Co. 2009 un il $16.99

Grades: K 1 2 3

1. Earth

ISBN 978-0-8075-8815-4; 0-8075-8815-6

LC 2008056045

"Wells elaborates on the idea that our planet is 'a pretty good place for people to live' by, first, giving each of the other seven planets a quick flyby, then explaining how Earth's water and atmosphere create conditions suitable for life. His lively cartoon illustrations feature a pair of overall-clad young explorers (and a spaniel) boarding a jalopy-like spaceship for their spin around the solar system, then landing back on their home planet to demonstrate recycling, energy conservation, and other environmentally friendly activities." Booklist

526   Mathematical geography

Boothroyd, Jennifer

   Map my home; by Jennifer Boothroyd. Lerner Publications Company 2014 24 p. (First step nonfiction - map it out) (lib. bdg. : alk. paper) $22.60

Grades: PreK K 1 2   **526**

   1. Maps 2. Cartography

   ISBN 1467711101; 9781467711104

                                   LC 2012042554

In this children's book, by by Jennifer Boothroyd, "see how a boy makes a map of his home showing fire escape routes. Simple text takes early readers step by step through the types of features a fire safety map needs to have." (Publisher's note)

   "These easy-to-read titles are for youngsters just learning about maps. Color photographs intermingle with hand-drawn diagrams to help readers understand the vocabulary . . . Good examples of beginning narrative nonfiction that includes well-explained hands-on activities." SLJ

   Other titles in the series include:

Map my Continent (2014)

Map my Country (2014)

Map my Room (2014)

Map my State (2014)

May my Neighborhood (2014)

   Map my neighborhood; by Jennifer Boothroyd. Lerner Publications Co. 2014 24 p. $6.95

Grades: PreK K 1 2   **526**

   1. Maps

   ISBN 146771111X; 146771531X; 9781467711111; 9781467715317

                                     LC 2012037533

In this children's book, by Jennifer Boothroyd, "a child narrator shown in a photograph sets up a situation, such as a grandma coming to visit, and creates a map to fit that situation. The maps, drawn with colored markers in a childlike style, follow the same steps in each volume: planning the map and then drawing it. 'Map My Neighborhood' features a girl helping her visiting grandma by drawing a map to various local spots." (Booklist)

Borden, Louise

   Sea clocks; the story of longitude. illustrated by Erik Blegvad. Margaret K. McElderry Bks. 2003 un il $18.95

Grades: 3 4 5 6   **526**

   1. Longitude 2. Navigation 3. Clocks and watches 4. Mechanical engineers 5. Clock and watch makers

   ISBN 0-689-84216-3

                                     LC 00-45599

This "picture book introduces John Harrison, the 18th-century English carpenter turned clockmaker who spent more than 40 years perfecting a device that solved the centuries-old problem of determining longitude. . . . The writing has a measured pace that helps readers to keep the details straight and the scientific concepts are clearly explained and smoothly incorporated into the text. Blegvad's precise illustrations create a strong sense of time and place." SLJ

Galat, Joan Marie

   The **discovery** of longitude; by Joan Marie Galat; illustrated by Wes Lowe. Pelican Pub. Co. 2012 32 p. (hardcover : alk. paper) $16.99

Grades: 3 4 5   **526**

   1. Inventors 2. Longitude 3. Clocks and watches 4. Measuring instruments 5. Picture books for children 6. Chronometers -- History 7. Longitude -- Measurement -- History 8. Clock and watch makers -- Great Britain -- Biography

   ISBN 1455616370; 9781455616374; 9781455616381

                                     LC 2011052911

This children's book tells "the story of inventing a watch to compute longitude aboard the great sailing ships." Joan Galat explains that 300 years ago, the British government sought a way to measure longitude that was better than the current two clock system. "Enter John Harrison, carpenter and clockmaker, who toiled for over 40 years to make just such a clock." (Kirkus)

Lasky, Kathryn

   ★ The **man** who made time travel; pictures by Kevin Hawkes. Farrar, Straus & Giroux 2003 un il $17

Grades: 3 4 5   **526**

   1. Longitude 2. Navigation 3. Clocks and watches 4. Mechanical engineers 5. Clock and watch makers

   ISBN 0-374-34788-3

                                     LC 2001-33266

Describes the need for sailors to be able to determine their position at sea and the efforts of John Harrison, an eighteenth century man who spent his life refining instruments to enable them to do this

   "With Hawkes's luminous full-color paintings on every page, its clear science, and its compelling social commentary, this title is not to be missed." SLJ

   Includes bibliographical references

526.9   Surveying

Petersen, Christine

   The **surveyor**. Marshall Cavendish Benchmark 2010 48p il (Colonial people) lib bdg $29.93

Grades: 3 4 5 6   **526.9**

   1. Surveying 2. United States -- History -- 1600-1775, Colonial period

   ISBN 978-0-7614-4805-1; 0-7614-4805-5

This describes the life of a colonial surveyor and his importance to the community, as well as everyday life, responsibilities, and social practices during that time.

   "The type font, just slightly larger than usual, makes the text very visually appealing. . . . [The] book is liberally illustrated with artwork dating from the colonial period . . . [and] information boxes offer supplemental material." Libr Media Connect

   Includes glossary and bibliographical references

529   Chronology

Adamson, Thomas K.

   How do you measure time? by Thomas K. and Heather Adamson. Capstone Press 2011 32p il (Measure it!) lib bdg $25.99

Grades: PreK K 1 2   **529**

   1. Time 2. Calendars 3. Measurement

   ISBN 978-1-4296-4459-4; 1-4296-4459-1

                                     LC 2010002787

Simple text and color photographs describe the units and tools used to measure time.

"The large picture-book format and inviting color photographs make [this] clearly written [title a] welcome [addition]. . . . The [author uses] common objects, giving readers recognizable points of reference. . . . Solid." SLJ

Includes glossary and bibliographical references

Formichelli, Linda

Timekeeping; Explore the History and Science of Telling Time With 15 Projects. by Linda Formichelli, W. Eric Martin; illustrated by Sam Carbaugh. Independent Pub Group 2012 128 p. (hardcover) $21.95

Grades: 4 5 6 7 8   **529**
1. Time 2. Science -- Experiments
ISBN 1619301369; 9781619301368

This juvenile activity book, by Linda Formichelli, W. Eric Martin, with illustrations by Sam Carbaugh, is part of the "Build It Yourself" series. It teaches "the cultural history of time" through providing several activities and projects such as "making a shadow clock, tracking time like an ancient Egyptian, using a protractor to create a sundial, measuring time with water, and making a candle clock." (Publisher's note)

Gleick, Beth

Time is when; [by] Beth Gleick; illustrated by Marthe Jocelyn. Tundra Books 2008 un il $15.95

Grades: PreK K 1   **529**
1. Time
ISBN 978-0-88776-870-5; 0-88776-870-9

A newly illustrated edition of the title first published 1960 by Rand McNally

"Gleick successfully answers the age-old question, 'What is time?.'. . . Breaking down time into all of its components, the author explains each one, using events that children face daily. . . . The story then builds upon each part of time as it is woven back together to make up the four seasons, explaining that a year is the time between one birthday and the next—a concept readers are sure to grasp. Jocelyn's illustrations give this account a fresh look with multicultural characters and digital clocks while still keeping an old-fashioned, nostalgic feel in the paper and fabric collages, which have bright colors and fun, busy patterns. The simple, lyrical text has a timeless quality that works well as a read-aloud and is still easy enough for beginning readers to work out on their own." SLJ

Jenkins, Steve

★ **Just** a second. Houghton Mifflin Books for Children 2011 un il $16.99

Grades: PreK K 1 2   **529**
1. Time 2. Nature
ISBN 978-0-618-70896-3; 0-618-70896-0

LC 2011002104

This non-fiction picture book explores time and how we think about it in a different way—as a series of events in the natural world (some of them directly observable, others not) that take place in a given unit of time.

"Jenkins brings fresh perspective to the passage of time in a thought-provoking picture book that features his typically elegant cut-paper collages. . . . Back matter offers information about life spans, population growth, and Earth's history. This subtly philosophical examination of time, scale, and the mechanics of life is all but certain to leave readers reconsidering the world and their place in it." Publ Wkly

Koscielniak, Bruce

★ **About** time; a first look at time and clocks. by Bruce Koscielniak. Houghton Mifflin 2004 un il map $16

Grades: 3 4 5   **529**
1. Time 2. Calendars 3. Clocks and watches
ISBN 0-618-39668-3

LC 2003-17469

Describes the concept of time and how it has been measured throughout history, using water clocks, sundials, calendars, and atomic vibrations.

"Koscielniak gives an instructive yet entertaining march through the ages. . . . Attractive watercolor illustrations in green and tan tones enhance the text." SLJ

Maestro, Betsy

The **story** of clocks and calendars; marking a millennium. illustrated by Giulio Maestro. Lothrop, Lee & Shepard Bks. 1999 48p il hardcover o.p. pa $9.99

Grades: 3 4 5 6   **529**
1. Time 2. Calendars 3. Clocks and watches
ISBN 0-688-14548-5; 0-688-14549-3 lib bdg; 0-06-058945-0 pa

LC 98-21305

"This overview of timekeeping begins with prehistoric 'calendar sticks' and stone structures, and continues through today's ultra-precise atomic clocks. The text takes a broad multicultural approach, showing how science, history, and societal differences have influenced the calendar; the color illustrations are executed in styles that match the eras and cultures discussed in the volume." Horn Book Guide

Murphy, Stuart J.

★ **It's** about time! illustrated by John Speirs. HarperCollins Publishers 2005 33p il (MathStart) $15.99; pa $4.99

Grades: K 1 2   **529**
1. Day 2. Time 3. Night
ISBN 0-06-055768-0; 0-06-055769-9 pa

LC 2003-27524

"Each page shows an analog clock and a digital clock displaying the time, from seven o'clock one morning through the day and night to seven the next morning. The illustrations show the child's activities and, in the night, his dreams. . . . Soft pencil drawings deliniate the rounded forms of children engaged in their daily activities. The rich colors of the washes glow against the white backgrounds." Booklist

Nagda, Ann Whitehead

Chimp math; learning about time from a baby chimpanzee. by Ann Whitehead Nagda and Cindy Bickel. Holt & Co. 2002 29p il $16.95

Grades: 2 3 4   **529**
1. Time 2. Chimpanzees
ISBN 0-8050-6674-8

LC 00-57529

"The details of the chimp's young life will fascinate readers. . . . The time lines, in particular, illuminate the narrative and can lead to classroom projects." SLJ

Older, Jules

Telling time; how to tell time on digital and analog clocks! written by Jules Older; illustrated by Megan Halsey. Charlesbridge Pub. 2000 un il $16.95; pa $6.95

Grades: K 1 2 3   **529**
1. Time 2. Clocks and watches
ISBN 0-88106-396-7; 0-88106-397-5 pa

LC 99-18764

Humorous text explains the concept of time, from seconds to hours on both analog and digital clocks, from years to millennia on the calendar

"The cartoon illustrations, showing children and many, many types of clocks are colorful, plentiful, and inviting. . . . This jovial look at time and time telling is as handy as they come." SLJ

Perrin, Clotilde

At the same moment, around the world; by Clotilde Perrin. Chronicle Books 2014 36 p. chiefly color illustrations (alk. paper) $17.99
Grades: K 1 2 3   **529**

  1. Time   2. Space and time
ISBN 1452122083; 9781452122083
                  LC 2013028005

In this children's book, by Clotilde Perrin, "discover Benedict drinking hot chocolate in Paris, France; Mitko chasing the school bus in Sofia, Bulgaria; and Khanh having a little nap in Hanoi, Vietnam! . . . Perrin takes readers eastward from the Greenwich meridian, from day to night, with each page portraying one of (the original) 24 time zones." (Publisher's note)

The pictures, in pencil and digital color, fill the tall oblong shape of the book dramatically. . . . A brief but excellent description of time zones and timekeeping closes the volume. . . . A very fine working of story, information, art and culture. Kirkus

Raum, Elizabeth

The story behind time. Heinemann Library 2009 32p il (True stories) lib bdg $28.21
Grades: 3 4 5   **529**

  1. Time   2. Calendars   3. Clocks and watches
ISBN 978-1-4329-2343-3 lib bdg; 1-4329-2343-9 lib bdg
                  LC 2008037393

This offers information about time, including a history of time measurement

  Includes bibliographical references

Skurzynski, Gloria

On time; from seasons to split seconds. National Geographic Soc. 2000 41p il $17.95
Grades: 4 5 6 7   **529**

  1. Time
ISBN 0-7922-7503-9
                  LC 99-33927

Examines the ways humans have measured time throughout history and discusses the various units that are used to keep track of it

"This attractive offering is brimming with information. . . . The conversational tone helps readers get through the more difficult concepts. . . . The book is heavily illustrated with full-color drawings, photographs, and diagrams." SLJ

530   Physics

Adams, Tom

Feel the force! full of pop-up physics fun! illustrated by Thomas Flintham. Candlewick 2011 20p il (Super science)
Grades: 2 3 4   **530**

  1. Physics   2. Pop-up books
ISBN 0-7636-5566-X; 978-0-7636-5566-2

"This high-energy pop-up takes a hands-on approach to physics. The text explains such concepts as force, gravity, friction, sound waves, light, and magnetism. . . . Cartoons, pop-ups, mini-books, flaps, tabs, and sidebars further elaborate on the various topics, and numerous experiments encourage further exploration and scrutiny."

"This high-energy pop-up takes a hands-on approach to physics. The text explains such concepts as force, gravity, friction, sound waves, light, and magnetism. . . . Cartoons, pop-ups, mini-books, flaps, tabs, and sidebars further elaborate on the various topics, and numerous experiments encourage further exploration and scrutiny." Publ Wkly

Baxter, Roberta

The particle model of matter. Raintree 2009 48p il (Sci-hi: physical science) lib bdg $31.43; pa $8.99
Grades: 4 5 6 7   **530**

  1. Atoms   2. Matter
ISBN 978-1-4109-3244-0 lib bdg; 978-1-4109-3259-4 pa
                  LC 2008030582

This takes a look at atoms, the building blocks of matter. It describes the different kinds of atoms, the particles that make up an atom, and the different states that matter can take

  Includes bibliographical references

Bonnet, Robert L.

Home run! science projects with baseball and softball. [by] Robert L. Bonnet and Dan Keen. Enslow Publishers 2009 104p il (Score! Sports science projects) lib bdg $31.93
Grades: 5 6 7 8   **530**

  1. Motion   2. Baseball   3. Force and energy   4. Science projects   5. Science -- Experiments
ISBN 978-0-7660-3365-8 lib bdg; 0-7660-3365-1 lib bdg
                  LC 2008-3005

"In addition to colorful, digital drawings illustrating the projects, a few photos and period prints also brighten the pages. . . . [This] will appeal to those looking for fresh science-project ideas." Booklist

  Includes glossary and bibliographical references

Gaff, Jackie

Looking at solids, liquids, and gases; how does matter change? [by] Jackie Gaff. Enslow Publishers 2008 32p il (Looking at science: how things change) lib bdg $22.60
Grades: 1 2 3   **530**

  1. Matter
ISBN 978-0-7660-3092-3 lib bdg; 0-7660-3092-X lib bdg
                  LC 2007-24514

"Fills a huge void in elementary science collections. . . . Text is arranged in succinct 'chunks,' giving important facts without overwhelming readers. . . . [This] is an essential addition." Libr Media Connect

  Includes glossary and bibliographical references

Gardner, Robert

Ace your physical science project; great science fair ideas. [by] Robert Gardner, Madeline Goodstein, and Thomas R. Rybolt. Enslow Publishers 2009 128p il (Ace your physics science project) lib bdg $31.93
Grades: 5 6 7 8   **530**

  1. Physics   2. Science projects   3. Science -- Experiments
ISBN 978-0-7660-3225-5 lib bdg; 0-7660-3225-6 lib bdg
                  LC 2008-29637

"Dozens of . . . science activities are presented with background information, step-by-step instructions, and suggestions for extending to the science fair level. . . . Color illustrations and important safety information are included." Horn Book Guide

  Includes bibliographical references

Slam dunk! science projects with basketball; [by] Robert Gardner and Dennis Shortelle. Enslow Publishers 2009 104p il (Score! sports science projects) lib bdg $31.93
Grades: 5 6 7 8   **530**

  1. Physics   2. Basketball   3. Science projects   4. Science -- Experiments
ISBN 978-0-7660-3366-5 lib bdg; 0-7660-3366-X lib bdg
                  LC 2008-24879

"Introductions include information about the history of the sport, safety steps to follow, and the scientific method. . . . Detailed diagrams help clarify many of the directions." SLJ

Includes glossary and bibliographical references

Goodstein, Madeline

Wheels! science projects with bicycles, skateboards, and skates. Enslow Publishers 2009 104p il (Score! sports science projects) lib bdg $31.93

Grades: 5 6 7 8 9 10   **530**

1. Wheels 2. Physics 3. Science projects 4. Science -- Experiments
ISBN 978-0-7660-3107-4 lib bdg; 0-7660-3107-1 lib bdg

LC 2008-24880

"Introductions include information about the history of the sport, safety steps to follow, and the scientific method. . . . Detailed diagrams help clarify many of the directions." SLJ

Includes glossary and bibliographical references

Green, Dan

Physics; why matter matters! [by] Dan Green; Simon Basher, illustrator. Kingfisher 2008 128p il pa $8.95

Grades: 5 6 7 8   **530**

1. Physics
ISBN 978-0-7534-6214-0 pa; 0-7534-6214-1 pa

LC 2007-31805

This "introduces the elements of physics as anthropomorphic, cartoon-style characters. . . . Each of the groupings begins with an introduction and each concept is given its own spread that shows the cartoon figure and describes its 'personality.' The information is presented in a chatty and conversational tone. . . . Along with the narrative, which is written in the first person from the concept's point of view, other key facts are presented. This book would be handy as a supplement to a physics curriculum." SLJ

Includes glossary

Hartman, Eve

Light and sound; [by] Eve Hartman and Wendy Meshbesher. Raintree 2008 48p il (Sci-hi: physical science) lib bdg $22; pa $8.99

Grades: 5 6 7 8   **530**

1. Light 2. Sound
ISBN 978-1-4109-3378-2 lib bdg; 1-4109-3378-4 lib bdg; 978-1-4109-3383-6 pa; 1-4109-3383-0 pa

LC 2009-3506

A "compelling read for both browsers and science buffs. . . . Information is clearly presented and flows smoothly. . . . A treasure trove of information." SLJ

Includes glossary and bibliographical references

Lee, Cora

The **great** motion mission; a surprising story of physics in everyday life. illustrated by Steve Rolston. Annick Press 2009 114p il $24.95; pa $14.95

Grades: 4 5 6   **530**

1. Physics
ISBN 978-1-55451-185-3; 1-55451-185-2; 978-1-55451-184-6 pa; 1-55451-184-4 pa

"This book is a combination of narrative and concepts about physics. . . . Jeremy and his friends are distraught when the local summer fair is canceled in order to host a physics conference. While Jeremy helps his uncle campaign to save the fair, his new neighbor, Aubrey, sets out to prove that physics isn't only necessary, but also fun. The text is chatty and accessible to students. Topics include 'Physics and Sight,' 'Physics and Sound,' and 'Physics in Motion.' Each chapter profiles a featured physicist, from Albert Einstein to Richard Feynman. . . . Cartoon illus-

trations help to explain concepts such as the water cycle and wave patterns. Photographs are scattered throughout, and boxed areas highlight specific topics. This title would be especially useful for students wanting a good introduction to physics." SLJ

Includes glossary and bibliographical references

Mason, Adrienne

Change it! solids, liquids, gases and you. written by Adrienne Mason; illustrated by Claudia Davila. Kids Can Press 2006 32p il (Primary physical science) $12.95; pa $5.95

Grades: K 1 2   **530**

1. Matter 2. Science -- Experiments
ISBN 978-1-55337-837-2; 1-55337-837-7; 978-1-55337-838-9 pa; 1-55337-838-5 pa

This describes the three states of matter and includes experiments
This uses "colorful eye-catching graphics." Sci Books Films
Includes glossary

Motion, magnets and more; the big book of primary physical science. written by Adrienne Mason; illustrated by Claudia Dávila. Kids Can Press 2011 127p il $18.95

Grades: PreK K 1 2   **530**

1. Physical sciences
ISBN 978-1-55453-707-5; 1-55453-707-X

This book "is divided into four chapters that start readers off with the easy and familiar and work up to some larger science concepts, introducing and defining proper vocabulary along the way. . . . Short sentences, simple vocabulary and only a few paragraphs per page make this accessible for even the youngest of science explorers, while the 19 activities scattered throughout will deepen their understanding and hold their focus. . . . Dávila's charming digital illustrations depict rosy, round-faced multiethnic children in a variety of settings exploring the world around them." Kirkus

Mercer, Bobby

Junk drawer physics; 50 awesome experiments that don't cost a thing. Bobby Mercer. First edition Chicago Review Press, Inc. 2014 208 p. (trade paper) $14.95

Grades: 5 6 7 8   **530**

1. Physics 2. Science -- Experiments 3. Physics -- Experiments
ISBN 1613749201; 9781613749203

LC 2013046726

In this book, Bobby Mercer "provides readers with more than 50 . . . hands-on experiments. . . . Turn a plastic cup into a pinhole camera using waxed paper, a rubber band, and a thumbtack. Build a swinging wave machine using a series of washers suspended on strings from a yardstick. . . . Each project has a materials list, detailed step-by-step instructions with illustrations, and a brief explanation of the scientific principle being demonstrated." (Publisher's note)

"This book is filled with practical and easy experiments that demonstrate many different principles of physics. Though it joins a crowded market of similar at-home science books, this title offers experiments that are fresh and different." SLJ

Silverstein, Alvin

Matter; by Alvin Silverstein, Virginia Silverstein, Laura Silverstein Nunn. Twenty-First Century Books 2009 112p il (Science concepts) lib bdg $31.93

Grades: 5 6 7 8   **530**

1. Matter
ISBN 978-0-8225-7515-3 lib bdg; 0-8225-7515-9 lib bdg

LC 2007049493

This is a "simple and straightforward [discussion] of the [subject]. The layout . . . is attractive and inviting, with full-color photographs and/

or diagrams on almost every spread. In addition, the authors make good use of fact boxes. . . . [This] discusses the states of matter, the elements, chemical reactions, and more. [This title] will interest browsers and provide ample information for reports." SLJ

Includes glossary and bibliographical references

Sullivan, Navin

Weight. Marshall Cavendish Benchmark 2007 48p il (Measure up!) lib bdg $20.90

Grades: 4 5 6 7 **530**

1. Gravity 2. Weights and measures

ISBN 978-0-7614-2324-9 lib bdg; 0-7614-2324-9 lib bdg

"Examples using familiar objects and excellent full-color graphics help to bring concepts to life." SLJ

Includes glossary and bibliographical references

Taylor-Butler, Christine

Think like a scientist in the gym. Cherry Lake 2011 32p il (Science explorer junior) $27.07

Grades: 3 4 5 **530**

1. Sports 2. Physics 3. Science -- Experiments

ISBN 978-1-61080-163-8; 1-61080-163-6

"This is a kid-friendly approach to physics in particular and the scientific method in general, arranging much of the information around places and ideas kids can relate to: the gym, the track, and sports. . . . Five short chapters highlight how scientists and kids can find out how things work through experiments. . . . Photos of kids playing sports and simple but bright cartoon illustrations make this a lively read." Booklist

Weir, Jane

Matter. Compass Point Books 2009 40p il (Mission: science) lib bdg $26.60

Grades: 4 5 6 **530**

1. Matter

ISBN 978-0-7565-4069-2 lib bdg; 0-7565-4069-0 lib bdg

LC 2008-37624

An introduction to the scientific concept of matter, including elements, atoms, and molecules

Includes glossary

530.078 Physics experiments

Brown, Jordan D.

Science stunts; fun feats of physics. by Jordan D. Brown. Charlesbridge Publishing, an Imagine Book 2016 80 p. illustrations (some color) (reinforced for library use) $16.95

Grades: 4 5 6 7 **530.078**

1. Physics 2. Science -- Experiments 3. Physics -- Experiments

ISBN 9781607349419; 9781607349426; 9781623540647

LC 2014045661

In this book, by Jordan D. Brown, "readers will be amazed and delighted as they try magic tricks that are based in important physics concepts such as gravity, inertia, magnetism, sound vibrations, and more. Narrated by a humorous science showman, Dr. Dazzleberry . . . , readers go on a journey through many amazing scientific discoveries. Amusing, edifying commentary from cartoon versions of Newton, Galileo, and Einstein inspire student scientist to experiment with glee." (Publisher's note)

"Magical science that's amazing, astounding, and sure to appeal to middle-grade and middle school readers." Kirkus

530.1 Theories and mathematical physics

Rand, Casey

Time. Heinemann Library 2011 32p il map (Measure it!) lib bdg $29; pa $7.99

Grades: 3 4 5 **530.1**

1. Space and time

ISBN 978-1-4329-3766-9 lib bdg; 1-4329-3766-9 lib bdg; 978-1-4329-3772-0 pa; 1-4329-3772-3 pa

LC 2009-35210

"This book teaches the concept of time (including seasons, daylight savings, time zones)." Publisher's note

Includes glossary and bibliographical references

530.11 Relativity theory

Whiting, Jim

Space and time; Jim Whiting; photographs by Getty Images; folio illustration, Alex Ryan. 1st ed. Creative Education 2013 48 p. col. ill., col. maps (library) $35.65

Grades: 4 5 6 7 **530.11**

1. Physics 2. Space and time 3. Relativity (Physics)

ISBN 1608181928; 9781608181926

LC 2011040146

This book, by Jim Whiting, explores the concepts of space and time as part of the "Mysteries of the Universe" series. It appeals "to report writers and serious astronomy students. Each book carefully examines the history behind attempts to unravel explanations for the subjects, going back to Anaxagoras's work on energy in 450 B.C. all the way up to the contemporary findings of Stephen Hawking." (School Library Journal)

Includes bibliographical references (p. 46-47) and index.

530.4 States of matter

Boothroyd, Jennifer

What is a gas? by Jennifer Boothroyd. Lerner Publications Co. 2007 23p il (First step nonfiction: states of matter) lib bdg $21.27

Grades: K 1 2 **530.4**

1. Gases

ISBN 978-0-8225-6837-7 lib bdg; 0-8225-6837-3 lib bdg

LC 2006006303

"This small book introduces a single state of matter: a gas. Each page in the main section offers one or more colorful photographs and a brief line or two of large-print text. After a brief introduction to matter, the discussion moves on to the characteristics of gases and a few examples." Booklist

What is a liquid? by Jennifer Boothroyd. Lerner Publications Co. 2007 23p il (First step nonfiction: states of matter) lib bdg $21.27; pa $5.95

Grades: K 1 2 **530.4**

1. Liquids

ISBN 978-0-8225-6838-4 lib bdg; 0-8225-6838-1 lib bdg; 978-0-8225-6817-9 pa; 0-8225-6817-9 pa

LC 2006006304

This explains liquids "along with basic vocabulary. The layout is bright with many color photographs featuring children of different ethnicities. The text is spare; each spread includes, on average, three sentences." SLJ

What is a solid? by Jennifer Boothroyd. Lerner Publications Co. 2007 23p il (First step nonfiction: states of matter) lib bdg $21.27; pa $5.95

Grades: K 1 2   **530.4**

1. Solids

ISBN 978-0-8225-6836-0 lib bdg; 0-8225-6836-5 lib bdg; 978-0-8225-6816-2 pa; 0-8225-6816-0 pa

LC 2006006307

This explains solids "along with basic vocabulary. The layout is bright with many color photographs featuring children of different ethnicities. The text is spare; each spread includes, on average, three sentences." SLJ

Claybourne, Anna

The **nature** of matter; [by] Anna Claybourne. Gareth Stevens Pub. 2007 48p il (Gareth Stevens vital science: physical science) lib bdg $26.60; pa $11.95

Grades: 4 5 6 7   **530.4**

1. Matter

ISBN 978-0-8368-8088-5 lib bdg; 978-0-8368-8097-7 pa

LC 2006033732

This describes uses for matter and what happens when it changes from one form to another, the basic physical laws and properties of matter, and the various ways in which we control how matter behaves.

This is "straightforward and clear. . . . The layout is bright and colorful, with photographs and illustrations on almost every page." SLJ

Includes glossary and bibliographical references

Gardner, Robert

Melting, freezing, and boiling science projects with matter; [by] Robert Gardner. Enslow Elementary 2006 48p il (Fantastic physical science experiments) lib bdg $23.93

Grades: 4 5 6   **530.4**

1. Matter 2. Temperature 3. Science -- Experiments

ISBN 0-7660-2589-6

LC 2005033753

This offers experiments on the nature of solids, liquids, and gases and temperature.

"The ink-and-wash pictures illustrate the scientific principles as well as the equipment used in various activities. . . . Gardner's explanations are clear and his discussions lead readers to think about causes as well as what is happening to matter . . . as it changes form." Booklist

Includes glossary and bibliographical references

Hurd, Will

Changing states; solids, liquids, and gases. Heinemann Library 2009 48p il (Do it yourself) lib bdg $31.43; pa $8.99

Grades: 3 4 5 6   **530.4**

1. Gas 2. Matter 3. Solids 4. Liquids

ISBN 978-1-4329-2312-9 lib bdg; 1-4329-2312-9 lib bdg; 978-1-4329-2319-8 pa; 1-4329-2319-6 pa

LC 2008034939

The describes the fluctuating states of matter and includes experiments

This "would make an ideal supplement to science classes. A modular layout and dynamic photos keep things moving, while the experiments . . . feature lists of readily available materials, steps required to pull off the magic, and warnings as the when adult supervision is required." Booklist

Includes bibliographical references

Lawrence, Ellen

Water; by Ellen Lawrence. Bearport Publishing 2013 24 p. (Science Slam: Fundamental experiments) (library binding) $23.93

Grades: 1 2 3   **530.4**

1. Water 2. Science -- Experiments 3. Change of state (Physics)

ISBN 1617727369; 9781617727368

LC 2012046342

In this book by Ellen Lawrence, readers "will get the opportunity to conduct experiments that show how water can be a liquid, a gas, or a solid. Kids will also investigate questions such as 'What floats in water?' and 'What dissolves in water?' Using everyday items that kids can easily find around the house, students will turn into scientists as they carry out step-by-step experiments to answer interesting questions." (Publisher's note)

Includes bibliographical references (page 24) and index

Mason, Adrienne

Touch it! materials, matter and you. written by Adrienne Mason; illustrated by Claudia Dávila. Kids Can Press 2005 32p il (Primary physical science) $12.95; pa $5.95

Grades: K 1 2   **530.4**

1. Matter 2. Materials

ISBN 1-55337-760-5; 1-55337-761-3 pa

"Large-scale digital illustrations show children, animals, and adults commenting on and exploring the properties of matter. Some sections discuss ideas such as mass, buoyancy, or magnetism, while others suggest informal activities, for example describing different foods. Five double-page spreads present very simple science projects, beginning with a question-and-answer section followed by a short list of materials, a few steps to follow, and a brief concluding paragraph. . . . This colorful beginning science series is suitable for primary-grade students in groups and even younger children one-on-one." Booklist

Includes glossary

Oxlade, Chris

★ **Changing** materials; [by] Chris Oxlade. Crabtree Publishing Company 2008 32p il (Working with materials) lib bdg $26.60; pa $7.95

Grades: 2 3 4   **530.4**

1. Matter 2. Chemical reactions 3. Strength of materials

ISBN 978-0-7787-3638-7 lib bdg; 0-7787-3638-5 lib bdg; 978-0-7787-3648-6 pa; 0-7787-3648-2 pa

LC 2007027419

This describes how materials change by such processes as bending, breaking, melting, boiling, evaporating, dissolving, and burning

This "title has numerous captioned color photographs. . . . The [book offers] three simple, easy, and safe reproducible experiments. . . . Students will appreciate the pleasing design, easy-to-read font, and direct, clear writing style." Libr Media Connect

Includes glossary and bibliographical references

Cooling. Heinemann Library 2009 32p il (Changing materials) lib bdg $25.36; pa $7.99

Grades: K 1 2   **530.4**

1. Cold

ISBN 978-1-4329-3273-2 lib bdg; 1-4329-3273-X lib bdg; 978-1-4329-3278-7 pa; 1-4329-3278-0 pa

Introduces the concept of freezing points.

"A few simple activities provide opportunities to experiment. The color photographs are engaging." SLJ

Includes glossary and bibliographical references

Heating. Heinemann Library 2009 32p il (Changing materials) lib bdg $25.36; pa $7.99

Grades: K 1 2　　　　　　　　　　　　530.4
　1. Heat
　ISBN 978-1-4329-3272-5 lib bdg; 1-4329-3272-1 lib bdg; 978-1-4329-3277-0 pa; 1-4329-3277-2 pa
　Introduces the concept of boiling points.
　"A few simple activities provide opportunities to experiment. The color photographs are engaging." SLJ
　Includes glossary and bibliographical references

Shores, Lori
　How to make bubbles. Capstone Press 2011 24p il (Hands-on science fun) lib bdg $23.99; pa $6.95
Grades: PreK K 1　　　　　　　　　　530.4
　1. Bubbles 2. Science -- Experiments
　ISBN 978-1-4296-5293-3 lib bdg; 1-4296-5293-4 lib bdg; 978-1-4296-6215-4 pa; 1-4296-6215-8 pa
　Simple text and full-color photos instruct readers on how to make bubbles.
　"Bright, glossy photos and irresistible ideas make these science lessons effortless fun." Booklist

Spilsbury, Richard
　What are solids, liquids, and gases? exploring science with hands-on activities. [by] Richard and Louise Spilsbury. Enslow Elementary 2008 32p il (In touch with basic science) lib bdg $22.60
Grades: 3 4 5　　　　　　　　　　　　530.4
　1. Matter 2. Science -- Experiments
　ISBN 978-0-7660-3094-7 lib bdg; 0-7660-3094-6 lib bdg
　　　　　　　　　　　　　　　LC 2007024516
　This book "covers the three phases of matter described in its title. . . . Properties of each are explored. . . . The activities are all doable with simple household items, and they definitely reinforce the concepts being explored. This volume would a plus for budding scientists." Sci Books Films
　Includes glossary and bibliographical references

Weakland, Mark
　Bubbles float, bubbles pop. Capstone Press 2011 32p il (Science starts) lib bdg $25.99; pa $7.95
Grades: 1 2 3　　　　　　　　　　　　530.4
　1. Bubbles
　ISBN 978-1-4296-5250-6 lib bdg; 1-4296-5250-0 lib bdg; 978-1-4296-6141-6 pa; 1-4296-6141-0 pa
　　　　　　　　　　　　　　　LC 2010038874
　Simple text and photographs explain the basic science behind bubbles.
　"The text is simple and easily understood. . . . The large, up-close photographs are informative, . . . funny, . . . and intriguing." Booklist
　Includes bibliographical references

Zoehfeld, Kathleen Weidner
　What is the world made of? all about solids, liquids, and gases. illustrated by Paul Meisel. HarperCollins Pubs. 1998 32p il (Let's-read-and-find-out science) hardcover o.p. pa $4.95
Grades: K 1 2 3　　　　　　　　　　　530.4
　1. Matter
　ISBN 0-06-027143-4; 0-06-027144-2 lib bdg; 0-06-445163-1 pa
　　　　　　　　　　　　　　　LC 97-30658
　In simple text, presents the three states of matter, solid, liquid, and gas, and describes their attributes
　"The explanations are clear with a simple, informal text for the new reader, and the lively line-and-water-color pictures bring in humor and common-sense." Booklist

530.8　Measurement

Adamson, Thomas K.
　How do you measure length and distance? by Thomas K. and Heather Adamson. Capstone Press 2011 32p il (Measure it!) lib bdg $25.99
Grades: PreK K 1 2　　　　　　　　　530.8
　1. Measurement
　ISBN 978-1-4296-4456-3; 1-4296-4456-7
　　　　　　　　　　　　　　　LC 2010002811
　Simple text and color photographs describe the units and tools used to measure length and distance.
　"The large picture-book format and inviting color photographs make [this] clearly written [title a] welcome [addition]. . . . The [author uses] common objects, giving readers recognizable points of reference. . . . Solid." SLJ
　Includes glossary and bibliographical references

　How do you measure liquids? by Thomas K. and Heather Adamson. Capstone Press 2011 32p il (Measure it!) lib bdg $25.99
Grades: PreK K 1 2　　　　　　　　　530.8
　1. Liquids 2. Measurement
　ISBN 978-1-4296-4457-0; 1-4296-4457-5
　　　　　　　　　　　　　　　LC 2010002812
　Simple text and color photographs describe the units and tools used to measure liquids.
　"The large picture-book format and inviting color photographs make [this] clearly written [title a] welcome [addition]. . . . The [author uses] common objects, giving readers recognizable points of reference. . . . Solid." SLJ
　Includes glossary and bibliographical references

　How do you measure weight? by Thomas K. and Heather Adamson. Capstone Press 2011 32p il (Measure it!) lib bdg $25.99
Grades: PreK K 1 2　　　　　　　　　530.8
　1. Weights and measures
　ISBN 978-1-4296-4458-7; 1-4296-4458-3
　　　　　　　　　　　　　　　LC 2010002784
　Simple text and color photographs describe the units and tools used to measure weight.
　"The large picture-book format and inviting color photographs make [this] clearly written [title a] welcome [addition]. . . . The [author uses] common objects, giving readers recognizable points of reference. . . . Solid." SLJ
　Includes glossary and bibliographical references

Adler, David A.
　★ How tall, how short, how faraway; illustrated by Nancy Tobin. Holiday House 1999 un il $16.95; pa $6.95
Grades: K 1 2 3　　　　　　　　　　　530.8
　1. Measurement
　ISBN 0-8234-1375-6; 0-8234-1632-1 pa
　　　　　　　　　　　　　　　LC 98-18802
　Introduces several measuring systems such as the Egyptian system, the inch-pound system, and the metric system
　"In this wonderful hands-on concept book, easy technological measuring tools are superbly introduced and explained. . . . The informative text and colorful illustrations clearly explain the difference between customary and metric systems." Sci Child

Ball, Johnny
　Why pi; how math applies to everyday life. DK Pub. 2009 93p il map $16.99

Grades: 4 5 6 7   **530.8**
1. Pi 2. Mathematics 3. Measurement
ISBN 978-0-7566-5164-0; 0-7566-5164-6

"Author Johnny Ball focuses on how people have used numbers to measure things through the ages, from the ways the ancient Egyptians measured the pyramids to how modern scientists measure time and space." Publisher's note

Cleary, Brian P.
On the scale; a weighty tale. by Brian P. Cleary; illustrated by Brian Gable. Millbrook Press 2008 31p il (Math is categorical) lib bdg $15.95
Grades: 2 3 4 5   **530.8**
1. Weights and measures
ISBN 978-0-8225-7851-2 lib bdg; 0-8225-7851-4 lib bdg
LC 2007033670

"In bubbly verse, Cleary presents a basic introduction to weights and measures. . . . Cheery, child-friendly examples are used for both English and metric measurements, progressing from smaller to larger weights in this approachable explanation of the topic. . . . Gable's watercolor cartoons depict rainbow-hued cats engaged in all manner of activities. This humorous title should prove useful in both classroom and family discussions." SLJ

Gardner, Robert
Ace your math and measuring science project; great science fair ideas. Enslow Publishers 2009 128p il (Ace your physics science project) lib bdg $31.93
Grades: 5 6 7 8   **530.8**
1. Measurement 2. Science projects 3. Weights and measures 4. Science -- Experiments
ISBN 978-0-7660-3224-8 lib bdg; 0-7660-3224-8 lib bdg
LC 2008-23926

"Dozens of . . . science activities are presented with background information, step-by-step instructions, and suggestions for extending to the science fair level. . . . Color illustrations and important safety information are included." Horn Book Guide
Includes bibliographical references

Super-sized science projects with volume; how much space does it take up? Enslow Pubs. 2003 48p il (Sensational science experiments) lib bdg $18.95
Grades: 3 4 5 6   **530.8**
1. Measurement 2. Science projects 3. Volume (Cubic content) 4. Science -- Experiments
ISBN 0-7660-2014-2
LC 2002-153850

This "explores topics ranging from determining the volume of a quart and a liter to the amount of air in a container of sand. Gardner's clear, informal explanations are echoed in LaBaff's colorful illustrations." Booklist
Includes bibliographical references and index

Higgins, Nadia
Weigh it! by Nadia Higgins. Jump!, Inc. 2017 24 p. color illustrations (ebook) $25.65; (hardcover : alk. paper) $17.95
Grades: 2 3 4   **530.8**
1. Weights and measures 2. Measurement 3. Weight (Physics) -- Measurement
ISBN 9781624964589; 9781620314111
LC 2016011648

In this book, by Nadia Higgins, "early fluent readers learn about weighing in both the imperial and metric systems by exploring a variety of real-world examples. Vibrant, full-color photos and carefully leveled

text encourage young readers to look around them for opportunities to practice weighing." (Publisher's note)

"A fun concluding activity involves making a balance from paper plates. Readers will likely enjoy this practical yet lighthearted approach to a weighty subject." Booklist
Includes bibliographical references and index

How Big Is Big? How Far Is Far? Measurements for Children. illustrated by Jan Van Der Veken, translated by Jen Metcalf. Prestel Pub 2015 48 p. color illustrations (hardcover) $24.95
Grades: K 1 2 3   **530.8**
1. Size 2. Measurement
ISBN 9783899557329; 3899557328

This children's book, illustrated by Jan Van Der Veken and translated by Jen Metcalf, presents "comparisons that make units of length, distance, weight, speed, volume, and time easier to grasp. The Queen of England's crown, for example, weighs more than 100 portions of cotton candy. Some babies can cry as loud as a jet fighter sounds when it takes off. When the world's oldest living tortoise was born, there were no electric lights, telephones, cars, or airplanes." (Publisher's note)

"This metacognitive approach to understanding units of measurement is sure to captivate young readers." Booklist

Murphy, Stuart J.
★ **Room** for Ripley; illustrated by Sylvie Wickstrom. HarperCollins Pubs. 1999 33p il (MathStart) hardcover o.p. pa $4.95
Grades: 1 2 3   **530.8**
1. Aquariums 2. Measurement
ISBN 0-06-027621-5 lib bdg; 0-06-446724-4 pa
LC 98-26109

Uses a story about a young boy who is getting a fish bowl ready for his new pet to introduce various units of liquid measure

"The writing is breezy and reads like a story about a boy who wants a pet, but the text constantly reinforces the mathematical concepts (how many cups in a pint, a quart, etc.). The illustrations are painted in muted primary colors against a lot of white space. . . . A fun, painless math lesson." SLJ

Parker, Victoria
How big is big? comparing plants. [by] Vic Parker. Heinemann Library 2011 32p il (Measuring and comparing) lib bdg $26; pa $7.99
Grades: 2 3 4   **530.8**
1. Plants 2. Weights and measures
ISBN 978-1-4329-3959-5 lib bdg; 1-4329-3959-9 lib bdg; 978-1-4329-3967-0 pa; 1-4329-3967-X pa
LC 2010000932

This "contains vivid photographs, charts, and diagrams with captions, explanations, and examples. Questions are posed throughout . . . to entice young learners to 'stop and think' or continue reading for more information. . . . [This] would make an excellent addition to any classroom library." Libr Media Connect
Includes glossary and bibliographical references

How full is full? comparing bodies of water. [by] Vic Parker. Heinemann Library 2011 32p il map (Measuring and comparing) lib bdg $26; pa $7.99
Grades: 2 3 4   **530.8**
1. Volume (Cubic content)
ISBN 978-1-4329-3957-1 lib bdg; 1-4329-3957-2 lib bdg; 978-1-4329-3965-6 pa; 1-4329-3965-3 pa
LC 2010000927

This "contains vivid photographs, charts, and diagrams with captions, explanations, and examples. Questions are posed throughout . . . to entice young learners to 'stop and think' or continue reading for more information. . . . [This] would make an excellent addition to any classroom library." Libr Media Connect

Includes glossary and bibliographical references

How heavy is heavy? comparing vehicles. [by] Vic Parker. Heinemann Library 2011 32p il (Measuring and comparing) lib bdg $26; pa $7.99

Grades: 2 3 4   **530.8**
1. Vehicles 2. Weights and measures
ISBN 978-1-4329-3954-0 lib bdg; 1-4329-3954-8 lib bdg; 978-1-4329-3962-5 pa; 1-4329-3962-9 pa
LC 2010000923

This "contains vivid photographs, charts, and diagrams with captions, explanations, and examples. Questions are posed throughout . . . to entice young learners to 'stop and think' or continue reading for more information. . . . [This] would make an excellent addition to any classroom library." Libr Media Connect

Includes glossary and bibliographical references

How long is long? comparing animals. [by] Vic Parker. Heinemann Library 2011 32p il (Measuring and comparing) lib bdg $26; pa $7.99

Grades: 2 3 4   **530.8**
1. Size 2. Measurement
ISBN 978-1-4329-3958-8 lib bdg; 1-4329-3958-0 lib bdg; 978-1-4329-3966-3 pa; 1-4329-3966-1 pa
LC 2010000930

This "contains vivid photographs, charts, and diagrams with captions, explanations, and examples. Questions are posed throughout . . . to entice young learners to 'stop and think' or continue reading for more information. . . . [This] would make an excellent addition to any classroom library." Libr Media Connect

Includes glossary and bibliographical references

Robbins, Ken
★ **For** good measure; the ways we say how much, how far, how heavy, how big, how old. Roaring Brook Press 2010 un il $17.99

Grades: 3 4 5 6   **530.8**
1. Measurement
ISBN 978-1-59643-344-1; 1-59643-344-2

"By tossing in tidbits of history, word origins and meanings, Robbins takes the everyday subject of measurement and makes it accessible, interesting and memorable. Beginning with the units for lengths and distances, readers will not only learn about feet and inches, but also hands . . . and cubits. . . . From distances, the author moves on to area—measured in acres, hectares and sections—and then on to weigh—pound, ounce, ton, stone, dram and carat. . . . Liquid measures, dry capacity and time round out the volume. The photographs are a good complement, clearly illustrating the concepts without distracting from the text." Kirkus

Schwartz, David M.
★ **Millions** to measure; pictures by Steven Kellogg. HarperCollins Pubs. 2003 un il $16.99; lib bdg $17.89

Grades: 2 3 4   **530.8**
1. Measurement 2. Metric system 3. Weights and measures
ISBN 0-688-12916-1; 0-06-623784-X lib bdg
LC 2001-39683

Marvelosissimo the Magician explains the development of standard units of measure, and shows the simplicity of calculating length, height, weight, and volume using the metric system

"Schwartz not only manages to impart a good deal of basic information . . . but also entertains the reader. He receives ample support from illustrator Kellogg, who contributes enough merry madness to make

learning fun. Bright with shining colors, the large, detailed pictures brim with action and humor as well as history and math." Booklist

Somervill, Barbara A.
Mass and weight. Heinemann Library 2011 32p il (Measure it!) lib bdg $29; pa $7.99

Grades: 3 4 5   **530.8**
1. Measurement 2. Weights and measures
ISBN 978-1-4329-3765-2 lib bdg; 1-4329-3765-0 lib bdg; 978-1-4329-3771-3 pa; 1-4329-3771-5 pa
LC 2009-35208

"Size of text and font is suitable for this age group with uncluttered pages designed so that text is set off with the illustrations, graphs, or drawings placed vertically. Key words appear in bold." Libr Media Connect

Includes glossary and bibliographical references

Vogel, Julia
Measuring volume; by Julia Vogel; illustrated by Luanne Marten. The Child's World 2013 24 p. col. ill. (library) $27.07

Grades: 2 3 4   **530.8**
1. Picture books for children 2. Volume (Cubic content)
ISBN 1614732833; 9781614732839
LC 2012933675

In this book, part of the Simple Measurement series, Julia Vogel "addresses the topic of measuring volume with a number of . . . examples. Pouring milk? Taking medicine? Filling the backyard pool? Well, then you're participating in figuring out volume." It includes a "What Equals What?" page with equivalency charts. (Booklist)

Includes bibliographical references (p. 24) and index.

531   Classical mechanics

Bradley, Kimberly Brubaker
Forces make things move; illustrated by Paul Meisel. HarperCollins 2005 33p il (Let's-read-and-find-out science) $15.99; lib bdg $16.89; pa $4.99

Grades: K 1 2 3   **531**
1. Gravity 2. Force and energy
ISBN 0-06-028906-6; 0-06-028907-4 lib bdg; 0-06-445214-X pa
LC 2002-14763

Simple language and humorous illustrations show how forces make things move, prevent them from starting to move, and stop them from moving

"Colorful line-and-watercolor-wash illustrations brighten the pages. . . . A practical starting place for understanding forces." Booklist

Claybourne, Anna
Forms of energy. Raintree 2008 48p il (Sci-hi: physical science) lib bdg $22; pa $8.99

Grades: 5 6 7 8   **531**
1. Force and energy
ISBN 978-1-4109-3377-5 lib bdg; 1-4109-3377-6 lib bdg; 978-1-4109-3382-9 pa; 1-4109-3382-2 pa
LC 2009-3504

A "compelling read for both browsers and science buffs. . . . Information is clearly presented and flows smoothly. . . . A treasure trove of information." SLJ

Includes glossary and bibliographical references

Gut-wrenching gravity and other fatal forces; Anna Claybourne. Crabtree Publishing Company 2013 32 p. (Disgusting & dreadful science) (pbk. : alk. paper) $9.95

Grades: 4 5 6   **531**

1. Gravity 2. Physics 3. Force and energy
ISBN 0778709574; 9780778709503; 9780778709572

LC 2012043529

This book by Anna Claybourne is part of the Disgusting & Dreadful Science series and focuses on gravity and other physical forces. It shares facts including that "a mouse can survive a 328-foot fall, black holes have superstrong gravity that causes 'spaghettification,' and" more. Illustrations are included. (Booklist)

Includes bibliographical references and index

Pushes and pulls. QEB Pub. 2008 24p il (Why it works) $24.25
Grades: 2 3 4 5   **531**

1. Force and energy 2. Power (Mechanics)
ISBN 978-1-59566-558-4; 1-59566-558-7

LC 2008-11713

This is "colorfully illustrated and should help young students relate better to the concepts being presented. A glossary of key words and a page of suggestions for parents and teachers to extend the learning experience round out the text." Sci Books & Films

Includes glossary and bibliographical references

Conrad, David

Gravity all around. Capstone Press 2011 24p il (Pebble plus: physical science) lib bdg $23.99
Grades: PreK K 1 2   **531**

1. Gravity
ISBN 978-1-4296-6606-0; 1-4296-6606-4

LC 2010034310

This describes the science of gravity.

This book "addresses its topic in a direct and simple manner. . . . [The] title includes a hands-on experiment with both textual and visual directions." SLJ

Includes glossary and bibliographical references

Gardner, Robert

Ace your forces and motion science project; great science fair ideas. [by] Robert Gardner and Madeline Goodstein. Enslow Publishers 2009 128p il (Ace your physics science project) lib bdg $31.93
Grades: 5 6 7 8   **531**

1. Force and energy 2. Science projects 3. Science -- Experiments
ISBN 978-0-7660-3222-4 lib bdg; 0-7660-3222-1 lib bdg

LC 2008-49778

"Presents several science experiments and project ideas about forces and motion." Publisher's note

Includes bibliographical references

Gray, Susan Heinrichs

Experiments with motion; [by] Susan H. Gray. Children's Press 2011 48p il (True books: experiments) lib bdg $28; pa $6.95
Grades: 4 5 6   **531**

1. Motion 2. Science -- Experiments
ISBN 978-0-531-26346-4 lib bdg; 0-531-26346-0 lib bdg; 978-0-531-26646-5 pa; 0-531-26646-X pa

LC 2011011971

"In just four short chapters with glossy pages and plentiful color photographs, the author breaks down some fairly complicated concepts and takes readers through laws governing motion and scientific investigation. . . . Multiethnic upper elementary children demonstrate experiments using readily available everyday materials, while the text gives clear explanations." Booklist

Includes glossary and bibliographical references

Hillman, Ben

How fast is it? a zippy book all about speed. Scholastic 2008 47p il $14.99
Grades: 3 4 5   **531**

1. Speed
ISBN 978-0-439-91867-1; 0-439-91867-7

LC 2007039983

"Twenty-two full-color, full-page spreads convey the quickness (or lack) of the most ordinary things in a unique and amazing way. Examples: * How fast is a bullet-bike? * Which one is faster? A coyote or a roadrunner? * Can a sneeze be faster than a tennis serve? * How fast is the population growing? * What is the fastest-growing plant?" Publisher's note

Hopwood, James

Cool gravity activities; fun science projects about balance. [by] James Hopwood. ABDO Pub. 2008 32p il (Cool science) lib bdg $16.95
Grades: 4 5 6   **531**

1. Gravity 2. Science projects 3. Science -- Experiments
ISBN 978-1-59928-908-3 lib bdg; 1-59928-908-3 lib bdg

LC 2007010204

This offers science projects about gravity, including "The Old Cane Trick"

The projects "will attract boys and girls. [The] book begins with [an] upbeat introduction and three chapters about the scientific method, keeping a journal, and safety. . . . Background on the science concepts involved is presented along with a complete list of supplies. . . . The numbered instructions are easy to follow and are accompanied by small, closeup photos." SLJ

Lawrence, Ellen

Motion; by Ellen Lawrence. Bearport Publishing 2013 22 p. (Science Slam: Fundamental experiments) (library binding) $23.93
Grades: K 1 2 3   **531**

1. Motion
ISBN 1617727393; 9781617727399

LC 2012049188

This book by Ellen Lawrence presents information on motion, including friction, force, and gravity, through the use of toy cars and milk cartons. It "contains seven experiments about motion with detailed, age -- appropriate instructions, background information, facts about motion, and a glossary of science words relating to motion. The book is written for students in kindergarten to grade three." (NSTA Recommends)

Includes bibliographical references and index

Macdonald, Wendy

Galileo's leaning tower experiment; a science adventure. illustrated by Paolo Rui. Charlesbridge 2009 32p il $16.95; pa $7.95
Grades: 3 4 5   **531**

1. Gravity 2. Physics 3. Astronomers 4. Writers on science
ISBN 978-1-57091-869-8; 1-57091-869-4; 978-1-57091-870-4 pa; 1-57091-870-8 pa

LC 2008010652

"In this fictionalized account of Galileo's legendary experiments on the speed of falling objects, the young professor meets a poor farm boy, Massimo, who drops bread and cheese to his uncle passing under a bridge in a boat. Stunned that the bread and cheese hit the boat at the same time, contradicting Aristotle's teachings, Galileo begins experimenting with other pairs of falling objects. . . . The story excels at teaching the concept involved and is admirably enhanced by Rui's attractive, colorful, and informative acrylics." SLJ

O'Leary, Denyse

What are Newton's laws of motion? Crabtree Pub. Co. 2011 64p il (Shaping modern science) lib bdg $30.60; pa $10.95

Grades: 5 6 7 8   **531**

1. Motion 2. Physicists 3. Mathematicians 4. Writers on science
ISBN 978-0-7787-7200-2 lib bdg; 0-7787-7200-4 lib bdg; 978-0-7787-7207-1 pa; 0-7787-7207-1 pa

LC 2010-52629

This book examines how Sir Isaac Newton developed three basic laws that govern the way in which objects move. It explains how Newton expanded on the work of other scientists, including Galileo and Copernicus, to make his discovery. The book also explains how Newton's laws have influenced modern science and technology in areas such as sports and transportation.

This title is "not only written and organized well, but [it is] also gorgeous in design. Full-color photographs and illustrations are set over colorful backgrounds that add depth but not distraction. [The title] includes thought-provoking quotes from famous authors and scientists and some eyebrow-raising 'Quick Facts' throughout." SLJ

Includes glossary and bibliographical references

Riley, Peter D.

Forces; [by] Peter Riley. Sea-to-Sea Publications 2011 32p il (The real scientist investigates) lib bdg $28.50

Grades: 3 4 5   **531**

1. Force and energy 2. Science -- Methodology
ISBN 978-1-59771-280-4 lib bdg; 1-59771-280-9 lib bdg

LC 2010-05371

In this book about forces "solid scientific material is presented in accessible language and a visually engaging, boldly colored layout. Budding scientists are encouraged to hone their skills by recording observations, making predictions, and analyzing results. Hands-on activities are included on almost every spread. . . . The many color photos feature diverse children demonstrating the activities." SLJ

Includes glossary and bibliographical references

Royston, Angela

Looking at forces and motion; how do things move? [by] Angela Royston. Enslow Publishers 2008 32p il (Looking at science: how things change) lib bdg $22.60

Grades: 1 2 3   **531**

1. Motion 2. Force and energy
ISBN 978-0-7660-3089-3 lib bdg; 0-7660-3089-X lib bdg

LC 2007-24508

"Fills a huge void in elementary science collections. . . . Text is arranged in succinct 'chunks,' giving important facts without overwhelming readers. . . . [This] is an essential addition." Libr Media Connect

Includes glossary and bibliographical references

Silverstein, Alvin

Forces and motion; [by Alvin & Virginia Silverstein & Laura Silverstein Nunn] Twenty-First Century Books 2008 112p il (Science concepts) lib bdg $31.93

Grades: 5 6 7 8   **531**

1. Motion 2. Force and energy
ISBN 978-0-8225-7514-6 lib bdg; 0-8225-7514-0 lib bdg

LC 2007-48826

"The breadth of material the authors cover in this volume is impressive. They discuss energy (kenetic and potential), forces (friction, gravity, electricity, and magnetism), simple machines (lever, wheel, pulley, ramp, and wedge), motion in fluids, and Newton's laws of motion. . . . [This offers] simple writing, many colorful pictures, and lots of examples." Sci Books Films

Includes glossary and bibliographical references

Somervill, Barbara A.

Speed and acceleration. Heinemann Library 2011 32p il (Measure it!) lib bdg $29; pa $7.99

Grades: 3 4 5   **531**

1. Speed 2. Measurement
ISBN 978-1-4329-3764-5 lib bdg; 1-4329-3764-2 lib bdg; 978-1-4329-3770-6 pa; 1-4329-3770-7 pa

LC 2009-35204

"Size of text and font is suitable for this age group with uncluttered pages designed so that text is set off with the illustrations, graphs, or drawings placed vertically. Key words appear in bold." Libr Media Connect

Includes glossary and bibliographical references

Spilsbury, Richard

What are forces and motion? exploring science with hands-on activities. [by] Richard and Louise Spilsbury. Enslow Publishers 2008 32p il (In touch with basic science) lib bdg $22.60

Grades: 3 4 5   **531**

1. Motion 2. Force and energy 3. Science -- Experiments
ISBN 978-0-7660-3095-4 lib bdg; 0-7660-3095-4 lib bdg

LC 2007024517

This book "introduces children to forces through a simple introduction to Newton's three laws, simple machines, the relationship of energy and motion through potential and kinetic energy, buoyant forces, and structural forces. . . . This volume is an excellent resource for any child who is interested in science." Sci Books Films

Includes glossary and bibliographical references

VanCleave, Janice Pratt, 1942-

Step-by-step science experiments in energy; by Janice VanCleave. Rosen Pub. 2013 80 p. col. ill. (Janice VanCleeve's first-place science fair projects) (library) $33.25; (paperback) $14.15

Grades: 5 6 7 8   **531**

1. Energy 2. Science -- Experiments 3. Science projects 4. Force and energy -- Experiments
ISBN 144886979X; 9781448869794; 9781448884711

LC 2012006835

This book by Janice VanCleave is part of the First-Place Science Fair Projects series. The books have an introduction to the subject—here, energy, followed by 22 simple . . . experiments. Van Cleave states the basic goal of the experiments, followed by a list of necessary materials, most of which can be found around the house or easily acquired with minimal cost. Step-by-step instructions are clearly detailed and accompanied by diagrams where needed." (School Library Journal)

Includes bibliographical references and index.

Waters, Jennifer

All kinds of motion. Capstone Press 2011 24p il (Pebble plus: physical science) lib bdg $23.99

Grades: PreK K 1 2   **531**

1. Motion 2. Kinematics
ISBN 978-1-4296-6607-7; 1-4296-6607-2

LC 2010034309

This decribes the science of motion.

This book "addresses its topic in a direct and simple manner. . . . [The] title includes a hands-on experiment with both textual and visual directions." SLJ

Includes glossary and bibliographical references

531.14 Mass and gravity

Chin, Jason

★ **Gravity**; Jason Chin. Roaring Brook Press 2014 32 p. (hardcover) $16.99

Grades: PreK K 1 2   **531.14**

1. Gravity

ISBN 1596437170; 9781596437173

LC 2013001634

This children's book, by Jason Chin, focus on gravity. The book will answer children's questions such as: "What keeps objects from floating out of your hand? What if your feet drifted away from the ground? What stops everything from floating into space?" It is aimed at children from age 5 to 8. (Publisher's note)

"This book's images of space and objects floating or falling therein are hypnotically arresting. However, the science here is oversimplified to the point of inaccuracy. Objects do not "have gravity"; they have mass. To say "without gravity, everything would float away" misses the essential point--without gravity there would be no anything to float anywhere. Appended "More About Gravity" provides fuller explanations. Bib." (Horn Book)

Rooney, Anne

You wouldn't want to live without gravity! written by Anne Rooney; illustrated by Mark Bergin; series created by David Salariya. Franklin Watts, an imprint of Scholastic Inc. 2016 32 p. color illustrations (library binding : alkaline paper) $29.00

Grades: 3 4 5 6   **531.14**

1. Gravity 2. Weightlessness

ISBN 9780531214879; 9780531224373

LC 2015036599

In this book, by Anne Rooney, illustrated by Mark Bergin, "you don't really get a choice about gravity. If you live on Earth, you're going to have to live with it. . . . But gravity does a lot of useful things - such as keeping us on the Earth and holding the entire universe together! Learn how gravity was discovered and why it helps us to understand everything from how toothpaste comes out of the tube to the movements of the planets." (Publisher's note)

"The books feature a time line and numerous ancillaries, but the myriad entertaining facts are the real hit. Who wouldn't want to read them?" Booklist

Includes bibliographical references and index

532 Fluid mechanics

Adler, David A., 1947-

Things that float and things that don't; by David A. Adler; illustrated by Anna Raff. Holiday House 2013 32 p. (hardcover) $16.95

Grades: PreK K 1 2   **532**

1. Density 2. Science -- Experiments 3. Hydrostatics 4. Floating bodies 5. Buoyant ascent (Hydrodynamics)

ISBN 0823428621; 9780823428625

LC 2012045827

This book by David A. Adler is an "introduction to density." The "examples provide extension activities that can be done at home or in the classroom. . . . Readers meet a boy, a girl, and their dog as they embark on an adventure to discover what will float and what won't. For example, a spread . . . shows the dog looking over a kitchen sink full of water as a piece of aluminum foil floats as a loose ball and sinks as a tight one." (School Library Journal)

Cobb, Vicki

I get wet; illustrated by Julia Gorton. HarperCollins Pubs. 2002 un il $15.99; lib bdg $17.89

Grades: K 1 2   **532**

1. Water 2. Science -- Experiments

ISBN 0-688-17838-3; 0-688-17839-1 lib bdg

LC 00-49882

"The simple yet well-conceived activities engage children in more than just observations—the questions and explanations are constructed to help young kids draw conclusions from their observations. Remarkably, all this is accomplished in a child-friendly, straightforward text. The illustrations are bright and energetic." Horn Book

Parker, Steve, 1952-

The **science** of water; projects with experiments with water and power. [by] Steve Parker. Heinemann Library 2005 32p il (Tabletop scientist) lib bdg $29.29; pa $7.85

Grades: 4 5 6 7   **532**

1. Water 2. Science -- Experiments

ISBN 1-4034-7282-3 lib bdg; 1-4034-7289-0 pa

LC 2005007027

This "has experiments on the water cycle, water density, water as a solvent, surface tension, capillary action, buoyancy, water power, and water propulsion. . . . The colorful illustrations, organization, and ease of use of [this title makes it an] excellent [addition]." SLJ

Includes glossary

534 Specific forms of energy

Gardner, Robert

Jazzy science projects with sound and music; [by] Robert Gardner. Enslow Publishers 2006 48p il (Fantastic physical science experiments) lib bdg $23.93

Grades: 4 5 6   **534**

1. Sound 2. Science -- Experiments

ISBN 0-7660-2588-8

LC 2005018729

This offers science experiments illustrating such concepts as pitch, vibration, how sound travels and how it is perceived

Includes glossary and bibliographical references

Guillain, Charlotte

Different sounds. Heinemann Library 2009 24p il (Sounds all around us) lib bdg $20.71; pa $5.99

Grades: PreK K 1   **534**

1. Sound 2. Sound waves

ISBN 978-1-4329-3202-2 lib bdg; 1-4329-3202-0 lib bdg; 978-1-4329-3208-4 pa; 1-4329-3208-X pa

LC 2008-51740

This book "introduces the basics of sound through vibrant photographs, large text, and simple sentences. . . . [A] great introduction[s] and worthy addition[s]." SLJ

Includes glossary and bibliographical references

Making sounds. Heinemann Library 2008 24p il (Sounds all around us) lib bdg $20.71; pa $5.99

Grades: PreK K 1   **534**

1. Sound

ISBN 978-1-4329-3200-8 lib bdg; 1-4329-3200-4 lib bdg; 978-1-4329-3206-0 pa; 1-4329-3206-3 pa

LC 2008-51682

This book "introduces the basics of sound through vibrant photographs, large text, and simple sentences. . . . [A] great introduction[s] and worthy addition[s]." SLJ

Includes glossary and bibliographical references

What is sound? Heinemann Library 2009 24p il (Sounds all around us) lib bdg $20.71; pa $5.99

Grades: PreK K 1 **534**

1. Sounds 2. Sound waves

ISBN 978-1-4329-3199-5 lib bdg; 1-4329-3199-7 lib bdg; 978-1-4329-3205-3 pa; 1-4329-3205-5 pa

LC 2008-51681

This describes vibrations, sound waves, and echoes.

This book "introduces the basics of sound through vibrant photographs, large text, and simple sentences. . . . [A] great introduction[s] and worthy addition[s]." SLJ

Inlcudes glossary

Oxlade, Chris

Experiments with sound; explaining sound. Heinemann Library 2009 48p il (Do it yourself) $22; pa $8.99

Grades: 3 4 5 6 **534**

1. Sound 2. Science -- Experiments

ISBN 978-1-4329-2311-2; 978-1-4329-2318-1 pa

LC 2008034938

This explains the science of sound and includes such experiments as making a pan flute from straws and a homemade record player

This "would make an ideal supplement to science classes. A modular layout and dynamic photos keep things moving, while the experiments . . . feature lists of readily available materials, the steps required to pull off the magic, and warnings when adult supervision is required." Booklist

Includes bibliographical references

Riley, Peter D.

Sound; [by] Peter Riley. Sea-to-Sea Publications 2011 32p il (The real scientist investigates) lib bdg $28.50

Grades: 3 4 5 **534**

1. Sound

ISBN 978-1-59771-283-5; 1-59771-283-3

LC 2010005374

In this book about sound "solid scientific material is presented in accessible language and a visually engaging, boldly colored layout. Budding scientists are encouraged to hone their skills by recording observations, making predictions, and analyzing results. Hands-on activities are included on almost every spread. . . . The many color photos feature diverse children demonstrating the activities." SLJ

Includes glossary and bibliographical references

535 Light and related radiation

Branley, Franklyn Mansfield

★ **Day** light, night light; where light comes from. by Franklyn M. Branley; illustrated by Stacey Schuett. newly il ed; HarperCollins Pubs. 1998 32p col il (Let's-read-and-find-out science) hardcover o.p. pa $4.95

Grades: K 1 2 3 **535**

1. Light

ISBN 0-06-027294-5; 0-06-027295-3 lib bdg; 0-06-445171-2 pa

LC 96-33316

First published 1975 with title: Light and darkness

Discusses the properties of light, particularly its source in heat

"This is a beautifully illustrated children's book about a basic concept in science. The pictures add to the clearly written text." Sci Books Films

Bulla, Clyde Robert

What makes a shadow? illustrated by June Otani. rev ed; HarperCollins Pubs. 1994 32p il (Let's-read-and-find-out science) lib bdg $15.89

Grades: K 1 **535**

1. Shades and shadows

ISBN 0-06-022916-0

LC 92-36350

A revised and newly illustrated edition of the title first published 1962 by Crowell

"Using short sentences and developmentally appropriate language, the author explains how shadows are formed, gives numerous examples of shadows, and describes how to make shadow pictures on the wall. Each page is illustrated with bright, colorful drawings, and the gender and cultural representation is excellent." Sci Books Films

Caes, Charles J.

★ **Discovering** the speed of light; by Charles J. Caes. 1st ed. Rosen Pub. 2012 112 p. ill. (chiefly col.) (Scientist's guide to physics) (library) $34.60

Grades: 5 6 7 8 **535**

1. Light -- Speed 2. Light -- Study and teaching -- History 3. Light -- Speed -- Measurement

ISBN 1448846994; 9781448846993

LC 2010048426

This book by Charles J. Caes is part of the "Scientist's Guide to Physics" series. It "uncovers the earliest study of the speed of light, around 550 BCE in classical Greece. From classical Greece to Galileo and later Albert Einstein, this title also details the history of the discovery of light speed measurement and theories." (VOYA)

Includes bibliographical references (p. 107-108) and index.

Claybourne, Anna

Light and dark. QEB Pub. 2008 24p il (Why it works) $24.25

Grades: 2 3 4 5 **535**

1. Light 2. Shades and shadows

ISBN 978-1-59566-556-0; 1-59566-556-0

LC 2008-11709

This is "colorfully illustrated and should help young students relate better to the concepts being presented. A glossary of key words and a page of suggestions for parents and teachers to extend the learning experience round out the text." Sci Books & Films

Includes glossary and bibliographical references

Cobb, Vicki

I see myself; illustrated by Julia Gorton. HarperCollins Pubs. 2002 un il (Science play) $15.99; lib bdg $17.89

Grades: K 1 2 **535**

1. Light 2. Optics

ISBN 0-688-17836-7; 0-688-17837-5 lib bdg

LC 00-57220

"The simple yet well-conceived activities engage children in more than just observations—the questions and explanations are constructed to help young kids draw conclusions from their observations. Remarkably, all this is accomplished in a child-friendly, straightforward text. The illustrations are bright and energetic." Horn Book

Gardner, Robert

Dazzling science projects with light and color. Enslow Elementary 2006 48p il (Fantasic physical science experiments) lib bdg $23.93

Grades: 4 5 6 **535**

1. Color 2. Light 3. Science -- Experiments

ISBN 0-7660-2587-X

LC 2005-09498

This "title is devoted to light and seeing, mixing colors, and more. Each of 10 chapters includes an experiment, followed by an explanation of why it works, and offers ideas for devising projects to present at a science fair. . . . Large colorful, cartoonlike drawings complement the [text]. . . . [This offers] solid information." SLJ

Includes glossary and bibliographical references

Lauw, Darlene

Light; [by Darlene Lauw & Lim Cheng Puay; series illustrator, Roy Chan Yoon Loy] Crabtree 2002 31p il (Science alive!) $25.27; pa $7.95

Grades: 3 4 5 6 **535**

1. Light 2. Optics 3. Science -- Experiments

ISBN 0-7787-0560-9; 0-7787-0606-0 pa

LC 2001-42423

Presents activities that demonstrate how light works in our everyday lives. History boxes feature the scientists who made significant discoveries in the field of light

This book explains its subject matter "in a colorful and easy to understand format. . . . All experiments use easily obtainable parts and in some cases actual household items." Sci Books Films

Includes glossary

Meiani, Antonella

Light. Lerner Publs. 2003 40p il (Experimenting with science) lib bdg $23.93

Grades: 4 5 6 7 **535**

1. Light 2. Science -- Experiments

ISBN 0-8225-0084-1

LC 2001-38947

Experiments with light explain shadows and colors, and demonstrate such concepts as reflection and refraction

This offers "straightforward, well-designed experiments. . . . Numerous clear diagrams, some photos, and occasional historical sidebars extend this material, which is notable for its substance." Horn Book Guide

Includes glossary and bibliographical references

Riley, Peter D.

Light; [by] Peter Riley. Sea-to-Sea Publications 2011 32p il (The real scientist investigates ...) lib bdg $28.50

Grades: 3 4 5 **535**

1. Light 2. Science -- Experiments 3. Light 4. Science -- Experiments

ISBN 9781597712811; 1597712817

LC 2010005372

"The design of, and concepts presented . . . are exciting and appropriate for third-and-fourth grade students. Each page is filled with colorful descriptions that are appropriate for exploring light. The scientific method is outlined for each exploration, and simple techniques are offered for how to conduct exciting experiments. . . . The safety aspects of doing science experiments are covered in clear details. Any science class or children's library would be an appropriate place for this beautifully designed book." Sci Books & Films

Includes bibliographical references

Spilsbury, Louise

What is light? exploring science with hands-on activities. [by] Richard and Louise Spilsbury. Enslow Publishers 2008 32p il (In touch with basic science) lib bdg $22.60

Grades: 3 4 5 **535**

1. Light 2. Optics 3. Science -- Experiments

ISBN 978-0-7660-3097-8 lib bdg; 0-7660-3097-0 lib bdg

LC 2007024550

This book "introduces the reader to concepts such as reflection, refraction, taking pictures, using lenses, and light waves—specifically as manifested in rainbows and spectrometers. . . . What makes this volume so useful is that children are learning while they are doing the experiments. The graphics are excellent." Sci Books Films

Includes glossary and bibliographical references

Winterberg, Jenna

★ **Light** and its effects; Jenna Winterberg. Teacher Created Materials 2016 32 p. (pbk.) $8.99

Grades: 4 5 6 **535**

1. Light 2. Wave theory of light

ISBN 9781480746855

LC 2014045208

This children's book, by Jenna Winterberg, part of the "Content and Literacy in Science Grade 4" series, describes the characteristics and effects of light for elementary school students. It includes "high-interest text and vibrant images and photographs . . . [and a] lab activity that supports STEM instruction. . . . A helpful glossary, table of contents, and index are also included for additional support." (Publisher's note)

"Smartly written, these innovative and imaginative volumes make learning fun... First-rate nonfiction." SLJ

535.6 Color

Barton, Chris

★ The **Day**-Glo brothers; the true story of Bob and Joe Switzer's bright ideas and brand-new colors. illustrated by Tony Persiani. Charlesbridge 2009 un il $18.95

Grades: K 1 2 3 **535.6**

1. Color 2. Paint 3. Inventors 4. Fluorescence 5. Chemical industry executives

ISBN 1-57091-673-X; 978-1-57091-673-1

LC 2008-26959

ALA ALSC Siebert Medal Honor Book (2010)

This biography of Bob and Joe Switzer "tells the little-known story of the inventors of Day-Glo colors, who developed the fluorescent colors after much trial and error. Their creation has gone on to be featured on many different products to enhance visibility for safety reasons or just to get attention. The brothers have different ways of going about their making--one plans things out, while the other just tries things as he goes--but they work together to create these new colors." (Booklist)

"Still in their teens in 1933, brothers Bob and Joe Switzer began experimenting with fluorescent colors and trying to create paints that would glow in the dark. . . . After years of experimentation, they succeeded in creating paints that glowed in daylight as well as ultraviolet light. . . . In stylized, digital artwork with a retro feel, Persiani illustrates early scenes of the Switzers' life in black, white, and shades of gray, then gradually introduces colors. . . . Organizing his material well and writing with a sure sense of what will interest children, Barton creates a picture book that celebrates ingenuity and invention." Booklist

Brocket, Jane

Ruby, violet, lime; looking for color. [text and photographs by Jane Brocket] Millbrook Press 2012 30p il (Jane Brocket's clever concepts) lib bdg $25.26

Grades: PreK K **535.6**

1. Color

ISBN 978-0-7613-4612-8; 0-7613-4612-0

LC 2010051757

Presents brightly colored photograph illustrations that demonstrate the three primary colors and three secondary colors, as well as brown, pink, black, white, gray, silver, and gold.

"Isolating each featured color in snapshots (often close-ups) of everyday objects, the spreads are completely filled with a grid of three to five photos that prove to readers that colors can be found anywhere and everywhere. . . . Worthy of even the most overflowing of colorful collections, this is sure to be the beginning of many a color adventure, both in school and out." Kirkus

Carle, Eric

What's your favorite color? Eric Carle and friends. Henry Holt and Co. 2017 40 p. color illustrations (hardcover) $17.99

Grades: PreK K 1 2   **535.6**
1. Art 2. Color
ISBN 9780805096149

LC 2016953950

In this book, by Eric Carle "fifteen beloved children's book artists draw their favorite colors and explain why they love them. This personal collection will undoubtedly inspire readers to create favorite color drawings and stories of their own! Contributors includes . . . Lauren Castillo, Bryan Collier, Mike Curato, Etienne Delessert, Anna Dewdney, Rafael Lopez, William Low, Marc Martin, Jill McElmurry, Yuyi Morales, Frann Preston-Gannon, . . . [and] Melissa Sweet." (Publisher's note)

Color; illustrations and photos by Ella Doran, David Goodman & Zoe Miller. Abrams 2006 un il $19.95

Grades: K 1 2 3   **535.6**
1. Color
ISBN 978-1-85437-697-8; 1-85437-697-7

"This riotous and bold concept book presents the basic ideas about color with simple text and clear, inviting images. . . . Arty photo collages [introduce] each of the three primary colors. . . . [The book introduces] the idea of color mixing, followed by spreads for each of the secondary colors. . . . Black and white provide an introduction to the concepts of shading and tinting. The language of color, including word associations (e.g., blue: cool, calm, sad), and different shades printed in their appropriate hues are included as are some craft activities and a few trompe l'oeils." SLJ

Gifford, Peggy

The great big green; Peggy Gifford. Boyds Mills Press 2014 32 p. color illustrations $15.95

Grades: PreK K 1 2 3   **535.6**
1. Earth 2. Ecology
ISBN 1620916290; 9781620916292

LC 2013947714

This children's book, written by Peggy Gifford and illustrated by Lisa Desimini, is "both a riddle and an ode to the earth. . . . Perfect for budding environmentalists and lovers of poetry alike, . . . [it] is illustrated with . . . [a] mix of collage and painting." (Publisher's note) The text and illustrations highlight the green plants, animals, and objects which populate the earth. "There are green socks, a green light for 'go' and an old green door." (Kirkus Reviews)

Hoban, Tana

★ Colors everywhere. Greenwillow Bks. 1995 un il $18.99; lib bdg $17.89

Grades: PreK K   **535.6**
1. Color
ISBN 0-688-12762-2; 0-688-12763-0 lib bdg

LC 93-24847

"Very young children will enjoy naming the pictured objects, while older readers will be drawn into exploring the colors' varying tones. A book children will come back to over and over." Horn Book

★ Of colors and things. Greenwillow Bks. 1989 un il hardcover o.p. pa $7.99

Grades: PreK K   **535.6**
1. Color
ISBN 0-688-04585-5 pa

LC 88-11101

Photographs of toys, food, and other common objects are grouped on each page according to color

"Hoban hits on a simple device to heighten a child's awareness, but what lifts this above the average concept book is the quality of its design and illustration." Booklist

Houblon, Marie

A world of colors; seeing colors in a new way. National Geographic 2009 43p il $16.95; lib bdg $25.90

Grades: K 1 2 3   **535.6**
1. Color
ISBN 978-1-4263-0556-6; 1-4263-0556-7; 978-1-4263-0559-7 lib bdg; 1-4263-0559-1 lib bdg
Original French edition, 2004

"This sophisticated book shows the uses of color and encourages children to find examples in their own environments. Most hues are allotted two spreads. The first one features a solid, saturated page with the color's name in a contrasting shade, facing a closeup photograph framed in black. The second includes two or three additional photos with engaging commentary or questions. . . . The images are unexpected and captivating." SLJ

Lawrence, Ellen

Color; by Ellen Lawrence; consultants: Suzy Gazlay, MA, Recipient, Presidential Award for Excellence in Science Teaching, Kimberly Brenneman, PhD, National Institute for Early Education Research, Rutgers University, New Brunswick, New Jersey. Bearport Publishing 2013 24 p. col. ill. (Science Slam: Fundamental experiments) (library) $23.93

Grades: K 1 2 3   **535.6**
1. Color
ISBN 1617727385; 9781617727382

LC 2012050812

In this book by Ellen Lawrence "students will have the opportunity to conduct experiments that help them investigate what color is, as well as why things in our world are different colors. Using everyday items that kids can easily find around their homes, young students will turn into scientists as they carry out step-by-step experiments to answer intriguing questions." (Publisher's note)

Includes bibliographical references (page 24) and index

536   Heat

Auch, Alison

All about temperature. Capstone Press 2011 24p il (Pebble plus: physical science) lib bdg $23.99

Grades: PreK K 1 2   **536**
1. Temperature
ISBN 978-1-4296-6608-4; 1-4296-6608-0

LC 2010034308

This explains the science of temperature.

This book "addresses its topic in a direct and simple manner. . . . [The] title includes a hands-on experiment with both textual and visual directions." SLJ

Includes glossary and bibliographical references

Gardner, Robert

Easy genius science projects with temperature and heat; great experiments and ideas. by Robert Gardner and Eric Kemer. Enslow Publishers 2009 128p il (Easy genius science projects) lib bdg $31.93

Grades: 5 6 7 8   **536**

1. Heat 2. Temperature 3. Science projects 4. Science -- Experiments

ISBN 978-0-7660-2939-2 lib bdg; 0-7660-2939-5 lib bdg

LC 2008-4675

"Presents several science experiments and science project ideas dealing with temperature and heat." Publisher's note

Includes glossary and bibliographical references

Sizzling science projects with heat and energy; [by] Robert Gardner. Enslow Elementary 2006 48p il (Fantastic physical science experiments) $23.93

Grades: 4 5 6   **536**

1. Heat 2. Force and energy 3. Science -- Experiments

ISBN 0-7660-2586-1

LC 2005033755

This offers science experiments concerning heat and temperature, kinetic energy, elastic potential energy, light and electric energy, insulation, and ice.

Includes glossary and bibliographical references

Rand, Casey

Temperature. Heinemann Library 2011 32p il (Measure it!) lib bdg $29; pa $7.99

Grades: 3 4 5   **536**

1. Measurement 2. Temperature

ISBN 978-1-4329-3767-6 lib bdg; 1-4329-3767-7 lib bdg; 978-1-4329-3773-7 pa; 1-4329-3773-1 pa

LC 2009-35275

"Size of text and font is suitable for this age group with uncluttered pages designed so that text is set off with the illustrations, graphs, or drawings placed vertically. Key words appear in bold." Libr Media Connect

Includes glossary and bibliographical references

Sullivan, Navin

Temperature; [by] Navin Sullivan. Marshall Cavendish Benchmark 2007 48p il (Measure up!) lib bdg $20.90

Grades: 4 5 6 7   **536**

1. Heat 2. Temperature 3. Thermometers

ISBN 978-0-7614-2322-5 lib bdg; 0-7614-2322-2 lib bdg

LC 2006011981

This is "engaging and informative.... The excellent blend of photographs, charts, and diagrams complements the [text]." SLJ

Includes glossary and bibliographical references

537   Electricity and electronics

Berger, Melvin

Switch on, switch off; illustrated by Carolyn Croll. Crowell 1989 32p il (Let's-read-and-find-out science book) hardcover o.p. pa $4.95

Grades: K 1 2 3   **537**

1. Electricity

ISBN 0-690-04786-X lib bdg; 0-06-445097-X pa

LC 88-17638

"This book presents rudimentary exploration of electricity and how electrical current flows to the light switch in a child's room. Follow the current from the generator to a power plant to the switch on the wall.

Includes instructions for a simple generator. A good, first look at a topic that mystifies young scientists." Sci Child

Farndon, John

Electricity. Benchmark Bks. 2001 32p il (Science experiments) lib bdg $16.95

Grades: 3 4 5 6   **537**

1. Electricity 2. Science -- Experiments

ISBN 0-7614-1086-4

LC 00-39752

A collection of activities that explore electricity "discussing charges, circuits, conductors, and insulators. Activities include creating a Xerox effect and making an electroscope." SLJ

Includes glossary

Gardner, Robert

Easy genius science projects with electricity and magnetism; great experiments and ideas. Enslow Publishers 2009 128p il (Easy genius science projects) lib bdg $31.93

Grades: 5 6 7 8   **537**

1. Magnetism 2. Electricity 3. Science projects 4. Science -- Experiments

ISBN 978-0-7660-2923-1 lib bdg; 0-7660-2923-9 lib bdg

LC 2007-38470

"Science projects and experiments about electricity and magnetism." Publisher's note

Includes glossary and bibliographical references

Energizing science projects with electricity and magnetism; [by] Robert Gardner. Enslow Elementary 2006 48p il (Fantastic physical science experiments) lib bdg $23.93

Grades: 4 5 6   **537**

1. Magnetism 2. Electricity 3. Science -- Experiments

ISBN 0-7660-2584-5

LC 2005018730

This offers science experiments concerning electric charges, magnetism and compasses, batteries, electric bulbs, and wires, and electromagnets

Includes glossary and bibliographical references

Riley, Peter D.

Electricity; [by] Peter Riley. Sea-to-Sea Publications 2011 32p il (The real scientist investigates) lib bdg $28.50

Grades: 3 4 5   **537**

1. Electricity

ISBN 978-1-59771-279-8; 1-59771-279-5

LC 2010005370

In this book about electricity "solid scientific material is presented in accessible language and a visually engaging, boldly colored layout. Budding scientists are encouraged to hone their skills by recording observations, making predictions, and analyzing results. Hands-on activities are included on almost every spread.... The many color photos feature diverse children demonstrating the activities." SLJ

Includes glossary and bibliographical references

Van Vleet, Carmella

Explore Electricity! With 25 Great Projects. Nomad Press 2013 96 p. $13.95

Grades: 2 3 4   **537**

1. Magnetism 2. Electricity

ISBN 1619301806; 9781619301801

This activity book, by Carmella Van Vleet, "explains the workings of batteries, simple circuits, conductors and insulators, motors and generators, electricity and magnetism, and the steps being taken toward more

Earth-friendly electricity. The 25 simple projects . . . will reinforce the lessons through fun and experience, and young readers will advance their understanding of electricity further with the fun bits of trivia, side-bars, and jokes found throughout the book." (Publisher's note)

VanCleave, Janice Pratt

Janice VanCleave's electricity; mind-boggling experiments you can turn into science fair projects. [by] Janice VanCleave. Wiley 1994 89p il $10.95

Grades: 4 5 6 7   **537**

1. Electricity 2. Science projects 3. Science -- Experiments
ISBN 0-471-31010-7

LC 93-40913

"The experiments move from the simple, which do not require the use of batteries, to those that require small batteries, sizes AA, AAA, C, or D. An appendix shows how to make strips of aluminum foil that can be used to form the electrical circuits that are part of some of the ex-periments. By encouraging students to move beyond the basic problems (with adult supervision), the author encourages them to be creative in designing science fair projects." Booklist

Includes glossary

Woodford, Chris

Experiments with electricity and magnetism. Gareth Stevens Pub. 2010 32p il (Cool science) lib bdg $28; pa $10.50

Grades: 4 5 6 7   **537**

1. Magnetism 2. Electricity 3. Science -- Experiments
ISBN 9781433934445 lib bdg; 1433934442 lib bdg;
9781433934452 pa; 1433934450 pa

LC 2009037141

"The book [is] written in an easy-to-understand, straightforward style with helpful real-life photographs... Students who need simple ex-periments or those who need more advanced projects will find [it] help-ful." Library Media Connection

Includes bibliographical references

538   Magnetism

Branley, Franklyn Mansfield

What makes a magnet? by Franklyn M. Branley; illustrated by True Kelley. HarperCollins Pubs. 1996 31p il (Let's-read-and-find-out science) hardcover o.p. pa $4.95

Grades: K 1 2 3   **538**

1. Magnets
ISBN 0-06-026441-1; 0-06-445148-8 pa

LC 95-32181

Describes how magnets work and includes instructions for making a magnet and a compass

"Kelley's happy line drawings incorporate a humorous mouse to add safety warnings and goofy side comments. The clear diagrams and lucid explanations are both informative and engaging." Horn Book

539.7   Atomic and nuclear physics

Campbell, Margaret Christine

★ **Discovering** atoms; Margaret Christine Campbell, Natalie Goldstein. 1st ed. Rosen Pub. 2012 112 p. ill. (The scientist's guide to physics) (library) $34.60

Grades: 5 6 7 8 9   **539.7**

1. Atoms 2. Atomic theory -- History 3. Atomic structure 4.

Matter -- Constitution
ISBN 1448847001; 9781448847006

LC 2010048416

This book by Margaret Christine Campbell is part of the "Scientist's Guide to Physics" series. It "presents the . . . story of the atom's discov-ery, which is full of bizarre theories, false starts, dead ends, and . . . intel-lectual insight." (Publisher's note) "Campbell includes a . . . chronologi-cal foundation upon which the discovery of elements and the creation of the periodic table build up to the discovery of the atom, atomic rays, particles, models . . . and subatomic particles." (VOYA)

Includes bibliographical references and index.

Cregan, Elizabeth R.

The **atom**. Compass Point Books 2009 40p il (Mission: science) lib bdg $26.60

Grades: 4 5 6   **539.7**

1. Atoms 2. Atomic theory 3. Nuclear energy
ISBN 978-0-7565-3953-5 lib bdg; 0-7565-3953-6 lib bdg

LC 2008007724

"Cregan discusses the structure of the atom, key scientists, cathode rays and electrons, radioactivity, and atom smashers.... The [book has an] open [layout] and large, easy-to-read type. . . . Large eye-catching and colorful photographs and illustrations appear on every page. The [book] includes a simple activity." SLJ

Includes glossary and bibliographical references

Jerome, Kate Boehm

Atomic universe; the quest to discover radioactivity. by Kate Boehm Jerome. National Geographic 2006 59p il (Science quest) $17.95; lib bdg $25.90

Grades: 5 6 7 8   **539.7**

1. Radioactivity 2. Nuclear physics
ISBN 0-7922-5543-7; 0-7922-5544-5 lib bdg

LC 2006001316

The text offers "key concepts in a pleasing and readable format that would appeal to reluctant readers." SLJ

Includes glossary and bibliographical references

Lepora, Nathan

Atoms and molecules. Marshall Cavendish Benchmark 2010 48p il (Invisible worlds) lib bdg $28.50

Grades: 4 5 6 7   **539.7**

1. Atoms 2. Molecules 3. Nanotechnology
ISBN 978-0-7614-4192-2 lib bdg; 0-7614-4192-1 lib bdg

LC 2008037237

This describes the details and characteristics of atoms and molecules that are too small for the unaided eye to see.

The narrative is "clear, well written, broken down into manageable pieces, and peppered with eye-opening facts. The numerous photo-graphs are so phenomenal that they will inspire kids to read the text . . . so that they can wrap their minds around what they see." SLJ

Includes glossary and bibliographical references

McLean, Adam

What is atomic theory? Crabtree Pub. Co. 2011 64p il (Shaping modern science) lib bdg $30.60; pa $10.95

Grades: 5 6 7 8   **539.7**

1. Atoms 2. Chemists 3. Physicists 4. Atomic theory 5. Nuclear energy 6. Writers on science
ISBN 978-0-7787-7197-5 lib bdg; 0-7787-7197-0 lib bdg; 978-0-7787-7204-0 pa; 0-7787-7204-7 pa

This title is "not only written and organized well, but [it is] also gorgeous in design. Full-color photographs and illustrations are set over colorful backgrounds that add depth but not distraction. [The title] includes thought-provoking quotes from famous authors and scientists and some eyebrow-raising 'Quick Facts' throughout." SLJ

Includes glossary and bibliographical references

Paris, Morgaine

Composition of matter; Morgaine Paris. Teacher Created Materials 2016 32 p. chiefly color illustrations (ebook) $8.99; (pbk.) $8.99
Grades: 4 5 6   **539.7**
1. Matter   2. Atomic theory   3. Matter -- Properties   4. Matter -- Constitution
ISBN 9781480751187; 1480747203; 9781480747203
     LC 2015002695
In this book, by Morgaine Paris, "join nuclear physicists in exploring how matter acts to make predictions about the world. . . . Fifth-grade readers will examine subatomic particles and electron shells, elements and compounds, covalent and ionic bonds, the periodic table of elements, and more through this high-interest informational text filled with vibrant photographs." (Publisher's note)

540   Chemistry and allied sciences

Coelho, Alexa

Why Is Milk White? & 200 Other Curious Chemistry Questions. Alexa Coelho and Simon Quellen Field. Independent Pub Group 2013 288 p. ill. (paperback) $14.95
Grades: 4 5 6 7 8   **540**
1. Chemistry -- Miscellanea
ISBN 1613744528; 9781613744529
     LC 2012040205
This juvenile chemistry book, by Alexa Coelho and Simon Quellen Field, is a "question-and-answer primer [that] provides straightforward, easy-to-understand explanations for inquisitive young scientists' questions. . . . From lifting latent fingerprints from a 'crime scene' using super glue (for smooth surfaces) or iodine (for paper) to hollowing out the zinc interior of a penny using muriatic acid . . . , this handy guide is [a] . . . resource for the budding chemist." (Publisher's note)

Green, Dan

Chemistry; getting a big reaction. created by Basher; written by Dan Green. Kingfisher 2010 128p il $14.99; pa $8.99
Grades: 4 5 6 7   **540**
1. Chemistry
ISBN 978-0-7534-6615-5; 0-7534-6615-5; 978-0-7534-6413-7 pa; 0-7534-6413-6 pa
This "begins with a short overview of [chemistry] and information on Antoine Lavoisier's 18th-century scientific findings. Concepts are grouped by associations: 'Basic States' (solid, liquid, etc.), 'Nuts and Bolts' (atom, ion, etc.), 'Nasty Boys' (acid, base, etc.), and more. The individual concepts are each introduced over a spread that features a computer-generated cartoon of a character representing the idea and a brief introduction to its characteristics and personality. . . . The information is presented in a chatty, first-person voice." SLJ

Newmark, Ann

Chemistry; written by Ann Newmark. rev ed; DK Pub. 2005 72p il (DK eyewitness books) $15.99
Grades: 4 5 6 7   **540**
1. Chemistry
ISBN 0-7566-1385-X
First published 1993
Explores the world of chemical reactions and shows the role that chemistry plays in our world.

Van Gorp, Lynn

Elements. Compass Point Books 2009 40p il (Mission: science) lib bdg $26.60
Grades: 4 5 6   **540**
1. Chemical elements
ISBN 978-0-7565-3951-1 lib bdg; 0-7565-3951-X lib bdg
     LC 2008007284
"Van Gorp provides an overview of matter and the elements and how the latter combine to form compounds; ionic and covalent bonds; the periodic table of the elements; reactions; and mixtures and solutions. The [book has an] open [layout] and large, easy-to-read type. . . . Large eye-catching and colorful photographs and illustrations appear on every page. . . . The [book] includes a simple activity." SLJ

Includes glossary and bibliographical references

540.7   Education, research, related topics

Gardner, Robert

Ace your chemistry science project; great science fair ideas. [by] Robert Gardner, Salvatore Tocci, and Kenneth G. Rainis. Enslow Publishers 2009 112p il (Ace your science project) lib bdg $31.93
Grades: 5 6 7 8   **540.7**
1. Chemistry 2. Science projects 3. Science -- Experiments
ISBN 978-0-7660-3227-9 lib bdg; 0-7660-3227-2 lib bdg
     LC 2008-30800
"Presents several science projects and science project ideas about chemistry." Publisher's note

Includes bibliographical references

Ace your science project using chemistry magic and toys; great science fair ideas. Enslow Publishers 2009 128p il (Ace your science project) lib bdg $31.93
Grades: 5 6 7 8   **540.7**
1. Toys 2. Chemistry 3. Science projects 4. Science -- Experiments
ISBN 978-0-7660-3226-2 lib bdg; 0-7660-3226-4 lib bdg
     LC 2008-4685
"Dozens of . . . science activities are presented with background information, step-by-step instructions, and suggestions for extending to the science fair level. . . . Color illustrations and important safety information are included." Horn Book Guide

Includes bibliographical references

Easy genius science projects with chemistry; great experiments and ideas. Enslow Publishers 2009 112p il (Easy genius science projects) lib bdg $31.93
Grades: 5 6 7 8   **540.7**
1. Chemistry 2. Science projects 3. Science -- Experiments
ISBN 978-0-7660-2925-5 lib bdg; 0-7660-2925-5 lib bdg
     LC 2007-38469
This book offers science projects and experiments about chemistry divided into the following chapters: atoms, molecules, elements, and compounds; chemical reactions; oxygen and oxidation; separating and testing substances

"Illustrations are bright and useful in explaining the techniques presented. . . . An excellent resource." Sci Books Films

Includes glossary and bibliographical references

541   Chemistry

Ballard, Carol

   Mixtures and solutions. Raintree 2010 48p il (Sci-hi: physical science) lib bdg $22; pa $8.99

Grades: 5 6 7 8   **541**

   1. Chemistry 2. Molecules

   ISBN 978-1-4109-3376-8 lib bdg; 1-4109-3376-8 lib bdg; 978-1-4109-3381-2 pa; 1-4109-3381-4 pa

                             LC 2009-13452

   A "compelling read for both browsers and science buffs. . . . Information is clearly presented and flows smoothly. . . . A treasure trove of information." SLJ

   Includes glossary and bibliographical references

Kyi, Tanya Lloyd, 1973-

   50 burning questions; a sizzling history of fire. illustrated by Ross Kinnaird. Annick Press 2010 104p il (50 questions series) $21.95; pa $12.95

Grades: 3 4 5 6   **541**

   1. Fire

   ISBN 978-1-55451-221-8; 1-55451-221-2; 978-1-55451-220-1 pa; 1-55451-220-4 pa

   The author answers "questions in engagingly written vignettes that reveal how important fire has been and continues to be in nearly every aspect of human life. . . . Interspersed throughout the text are simple fire-related activities readers can perform utilizing a few common household items. . . . Kinnaird's colorful cartoon illustrations complement the text's humorous tone. . . . Accessibly written and appealingly designed." Kirkus

   Includes bibliographical references

Oxlade, Chris

   Mixing and separating. Heinemann Library 2009 32p il (Changing materials) lib bdg $25.36; pa $7.99

Grades: K 1 2   **541**

   1. Materials

   ISBN 978-1-4329-3274-9 lib bdg; 1-4329-3274-8 lib bdg; 978-1-4329-3279-4 pa; 1-4329-3279-9 pa

                             LC 2008-55124

   "Discusses the ideas of mixtures, materials that combine to form a new marterial, and materials that cannot be combined. A few simple activities provide opportunities to experiment. The color photographs are engaging." SLJ

   Includes glossary and bibliographical references

546   Inorganic chemistry

Angliss, Sarah

   Gold; [by] Sarah Angliss. Benchmark Bks. 2000 32p il (The elements) lib bdg $28.50

Grades: 5 6 7 8   **546**

   1. Gold

   ISBN 978-0-7614-0887-1; 0-7614-0887-8

                             LC 98-46800

   Explores the history of the precious metal gold and explains its chemistry, how it reacts, its uses, and its importance in our lives.

   Includes glossary

Beatty, Richard

   Phosphorus; by Richard Beatty. Benchmark Books 2001 32p il (The elements) lib bdg $28.50

Grades: 5 6 7 8   **546**

   1. Phosphorus

   ISBN 978-0-7614-0946-5; 0-7614-0946-7

                             LC 99-88821

   Explores the history of the nonmetallic element phosphorus and explains its chemistry, its reactions with other substances, its uses, and its importance in our lives

   Offers "clear, basic information, without oversimplification, in an appealing format." SLJ

   Includes glossary

   Sulfur; [by] Richard Beatty. Benchmark Books 2000 32p il (The elements) lib bdg $28.50

Grades: 5 6 7 8   **546**

   1. Sulphur

   ISBN 978-0-7614-0948-9; 0-7614-0948-3

                             LC 99-86992

   Explores the history of the element sulfur and explains its chemistry, its reactions with other substances, its uses, and its importance in our lives

   Offers "clear, basic information, without oversimplification, in an appealing format." SLJ

   Includes glossary

Dingle, Adrian

   The **periodic** table; elements with style! [created by Simon Basher; written by Adrian Dingle] Kingfisher 2007 128p il pa $8.95

Grades: 4 5 6 7   **546**

   1. Chemical elements

   ISBN 978-0-7534-6085-6 pa; 0-7534-6085-8 pa

                           LC 2006022515

   "After a brief introduction to Mendeleev's famous table and a spread on the chart-topping loner, hydrogen, Dingle presents the elements by group. . . . Data on featured elements includes symbol, atomic number and weight, color, standard state, classification, density, boiling and melting points, . . . a diagram of the position in the periodic table, a full-page original anime-styled icon, . . . and descriptive paragraphs that rise from informative all the way to entertaining." Bull Cent Child Books

Gray, Leon

   Iodine; [by] Leon Gray. Benchmark Books 2005 32p il (The elements) lib bdg $28.50

Grades: 5 6 7 8   **546**

   1. Iodine

   ISBN 978-0-7614-1812-2; 0-7614-1812-1

                             LC 2004-47644

   "After discussing the structure of the iodine atom and its place on the periodic table, Gray considers its special characteristics, the history of its discovery, and its production and uses, particularly in the medical field. . . . The color illustrations include well-designed, clearly labeled diagrams and many excellent photographs. A solid choice for science collections." Booklist

   Includes glossary

   Zinc; [by] Leon Gray. Marshall Cavendish Benchmark 2006 32p il (The elements) lib bdg $28.50

Grades: 5 6 7 8   **546**

   1. Zinc

   ISBN 978-0-7614-1922-8; 0-7614-1922-5

                             LC 2005-42163

   Discusses zinc and where it can be found, how it was discovered, its special characteristics, and their importance.

"Numerous captioned photos and sidebars augment the accurate and well-organized text." Horn Book Guide

Includes glossary

Higgins, Nadia

Splash! Learn about water; illustrated by Jane Yamada. Child's World 2010 24p il (Science definitions) lib bdg $22.79

Grades: PreK K 1 2   546

1. Water

ISBN 978-1-60253-514-5 lib bdg; 1-60253-514-0 lib bdg

LC 2010010982

This book about water is "attractive and succinct. . . . Large, eye-catching photos cover the recto of each spread. . . . Varying, jewel-toned accents are used in headings, highlighted glossary terms, and in a sidebar on each spread." SLJ

Includes glossary

Just add water; science projects you can sink, squirt, splash & sail. Children's Press 2008 32p il (Experiment with science) lib bdg $25; pa $7.95

Grades: 5 6 7 8   546

1. Water 2. Science -- Experiments

ISBN 978-0-531-18545-2 lib bdg; 0-531-18545-1 lib bdg; 978-0-531-18762-3 pa; 0-531-18762-4 pa

LC 2007-21682

"The book consists of nine hands-on activities that target physical science concepts inherent in water (e.g. density, buoyancy, and hardness.) . . . Students . . . will likely find the age-appropriate activities engaging and purposeful. . . . The colorful photos augment the narrative and the science is sound." Sci Books Films

Includes glossary and bibliographical references

Lepora, Nathan

Molybdenum; [by] Nathan Lepora. Marshall Cavendish Benchmark 2007 32p il (The elements) lib bdg $28.50

Grades: 5 6 7 8   546

1. Molybdenum

ISBN 978-0-7614-2201-3; 0-7614-2201-3

LC 2005-57096

Introduces the element of molybdenum, discussing its physical and chemical properties, where it is found, and what processes or objects it is used in.

"Provides a comprehensive, yet easy-to-read overview in large, bold print. Explanations are concise and clear without being oversimplified, and the arrangement is attractive." SLJ

Includes glossary

O'Daly, Anne

Sodium; [by] Anne O'Daly. Benchmark Books 2001 32p il (The elements) lib bdg $28.50

Grades: 5 6 7 8   546

1. Sodium

ISBN 978-0-7614-1271-7; 0-7614-1271-9

LC 2001-25253

Discusses the characteristics, sources, and uses of sodium.

Includes glossary

Oxlade, Chris

★ Mixing and separating; [by] Chris Oxlade. Crabtree Pub. 2008 32p il (Working with materials) lib bdg $26.60; pa $7.95

Grades: 2 3 4   546

1. Matter 2. Materials

ISBN 978-0-7787-3640-0 lib bdg; 0-7787-3640-7 lib bdg; 978-0-7787-3650-9 pa; 0-7787-3650-4 pa

LC 2007027421

This defines and gives examples of mixtures and describes how materials are mixed or separated by such processes as sieving, dissolving, straining, using magnets, settling and skimming, filtering, and evaporating.

This "title has numerous captioned color photographs. . . . The [book offers] three simple, easy, safe reproducible experiments. . . . Students will appreciate the pleasing design, easy-to-read font, and direct, clear writing." Libr Media Connect

Includes glossary and bibliographical references

Sparrow, Giles

Iron; [by] Giles Sparrow. Benchmark Bks. 1999 32p il (The elements) lib bdg $28.50

Grades: 5 6 7 8   546

1. Iron

ISBN 978-0-7614-0880-2; 0-7614-0880-0

LC 97-48524

Discusses the origin, discovery, special characteristics, and uses of iron.

Includes glossary

Uttley, Colin

Magnesium; [by] Colin Uttley. Benchmark Bks. 2000 32p il (The elements) lib bdg $28.50

Grades: 5 6 7 8   546

1. Magnesium

ISBN 978-0-7614-0889-5; 0-7614-0889-4

LC 98-53200

Explores the history of the bright-colored metal magnesium and explains its chemistry, how it reacts, its uses, and its importance in our lives.

Includes glossary

Watt, Susan

Mercury; [by] Susan Watt. Benchmark Books 2005 32p il (The elements) lib bdg $28.50

Grades: 5 6 7 8 9 10 11 12   546

1. Mercury

ISBN 978-0-7614-1814-6; 0-7614-1814-8

LC 2004-47633

This book is part "of the 28-title The Elements series. Mercury tells the history of mercury, where it is found in nature, its place in mythology, how it is mined and refined, how it forms compounds, its uses, and its position in the periodic table." Sci Books Films

Includes glossary

West, Krista

Bromine; [by] Krista West. Marshall Cavendish Benchmark 2008 32p il (The elements) lib bdg $28.50

Grades: 5 6 7 8   546

1. Bromine

ISBN 978-0-7614-2685-1; 0-7614-2685-X

LC 2006-51812

Introduces the element of bromine and its compounds, discussing its physical and chemical properties, where it is found, and how it is used.

"Provides a comprehensive, yet easy-to-read overview. . . . The explanations are succinct and clear, without being oversimplified, and the layout is attractive. Diagrams and photographs complement the text on every page." SLJ

Includes glossary

Yasuda, Anita

Explore water! 25 Great Projects, Activities, Experiments. Nomad Press 2011 92 p.

Grades: 2 3 4   **546**

1. Water 2. Aqueducts 3. Water pollution 4. Water conservation 5. Water resources development

ISBN 1936313421; 9781936313426

This book for children looks at the "world of water," offering a "guide that features hands-on activities, . . . illustrations, and . . . projects about this . . . natural resource. A deluge of . . . facts and . . . information about the history and science of water teach children about topics such as the water cycle, pollution and conservation, water folklore and festivals, and the latest in water technology. With projects ranging from a rain harvester made out of plastic containers to an edible aqueduct, this . . . guide brings the world of water straight into kids' hands." (Amazon. com)

549   Mineralogy

Spilsbury, Richard

Crystals; [by] Richard and Louise Spilsbury. Heinemann Library 2011 32p il (Let's rock) $29; pa $7.99

Grades: 4 5 6   **549**

1. Crystals

ISBN 978-1-4329-4684-5; 1-4329-4684-6; 978-1-4329-4692-0 pa; 1-4329-4692-7 pa

LC 2010022241

"Enhanced by plenty of photos, digital paintings, and diagrams, [this examination] of [crystals treats its topic] in unusual detail. [It] describes distinguishing characteristics, creation, history, . . . and human uses in [a] central [narrative] with additional notes, suggestions for activities during walks outside, and occasional thumbnail biographies of scientists in side boxes. [The] volume ends with a simple activity." SLJ

Includes bibliographical references

Minerals; [by] Richard and Louise Spilsbury. Heinemann Library 2011 32p il (Let's rock) $29; pa $7.99

Grades: 4 5 6   **549**

1. Minerals

ISBN 978-1-4329-4683-8; 1-4329-4683-8; 978-1-4329-4691-3 pa; 1-4329-4691-9 pa

LC 2010022235

"Enhanced by plenty of photos, digital paintings, and diagrams, [this examination] of [minerals treats its topic] in unusual detail. [It] describes distinguishing characteristics, creation, history, . . . and human uses in [a] central [narrative] with additional notes, suggestions for activities during walks outside, and occasional thumbnail biographies of scientists in side boxes. [The] volume ends with a simple activity." SLJ

Includes bibliographical references

550   Earth sciences

Bow, James

Earth's secrets. Marshall Cavendish Benchmark 2010 48p il (Invisible worlds) lib bdg $28.50

Grades: 4 5 6 7   **550**

1. Earth sciences

ISBN 978-0-7614-4196-0 lib bdg; 0-7614-4196-4 lib bdg

The narrative is "clear, well written, broken down into manageable pieces, and peppered with eye-opening facts. The numerous photographs are so phenomenal that they will inspire kids to read the text . . . so that they can wrap their minds around what they see." SLJ

Includes glossary and bibliographical references

Dorion, Christiane

How the world works; a hands-on guide to our amazing planet. written by Christiane Dorion; illustrated by Beverley Young. Templar Books 2010 un il $17.99

Grades: 3 4 5   **550**

1. Earth sciences 2. Pop-up books

ISBN 978-0-7636-4801-5; 0-7636-4801-9

"This pop-up survey devotes pages or spreads to Earth's history and structure, the origins of life, plate tectonics, the water cycle, weather, ocean currents, the carbon cycle, greenhouse effect, plants, and food chains. In snippets of text tucked into every available nook, Dorion provides commentary ranging from basic information on seasons and other cycles to abbreviated catalogs of cloud types and kinds of boundaries between tectonic plates." SLJ

Gaff, Jackie

Looking at earth; how does it change? [by] Jackie Gaff. Enslow Publishers 2008 32p il (Looking at science: how things change) lib bdg $22.60

Grades: 1 2 3   **550**

1. Earth

ISBN 978-0-7660-3088-6 lib bdg; 0-7660-3088-1 lib bdg

LC 2007-24507

"Fills a huge void in elementary science collections. . . . Text is arranged in succinct 'chunks,' giving important facts without overwhelming readers. . . . [This] is an essential addition." Libr Media Connect

Includes glossary and bibliographical references

Gilpin, Daniel

Planet Earth; what planet are you on? created by Basher; written by Dan Gilpin. Kingfisher 2010 128p il $14.99; pa $8.99

Grades: 5 6 7 8   **550**

1. Earth sciences

ISBN 978-0-7534-6616-2; 0-7534-6616-3; 978-0-7534-6412-0 pa; 0-7534-6412-8 pa

LC 2010015976

Presents concepts in earth sciences using lively descriptions and cartoon illustrations personifying each concept.

"The authors blend a surprising wealth of facts into the chatty, humorous text, which is filled with analogies kids can relate to. . . . The highly approachable language, animated cast of characters, awe-inspiring facts, and conservation messages make this an appealing starting point for students seeking basic earth-science information." Booklist

Simon, Seymour

Seymour Simon's extreme earth records; by Seymour Simon. San Francisco 2012 57 p. (hbk. : alk. paper) $17.99

Grades: 2 3 4   **550**

1. Earth 2. Earth sciences 3. Natural disasters

ISBN 1452107858; 9781452107851

LC 2011045937

This book, by Seymour Simon, "explor[es] the most extreme parts of our amazing planet--trekking though the driest desert, climbing the snowiest mountaintops, and diving to the deepest regions of the ocean floor. Seymour Simon . . . investigates Earth's biggest, smallest, deepest, and coldest environments, animals, plants, and most severe weather." (Publisher's note)

Includes bibliographical references (p. 57) and index

Solway, Andrew

Understanding cycles and systems. Raintree 2008 48p il map (Sci-hi: Earth and space science) lib bdg $31.43; pa $8.99

Grades: 4 5 6 7   **550**

1. Earth sciences 2. Earth

ISBN 978-1-4109-3348-5 lib bdg; 1-4109-3348-2 lib bdg; 978-1-4109-3358-4 pa; 1-4109-3358-X pa

LC 2009-3531

"Multiple colorful sidebars and large and small diagrams and photographs will help students to grasp the fundamentals being discussed, and the easy but interesting science experiments will act as further reinforcements." SLJ

Includes glossary and bibliographical references

Strother, Ruth

B is for blue planet; an earth science alphabet. written by Ruth Strother and illustrated by Bob Marstall. Sleeping Bear Press 2011 40 p.

Grades: 1 2   **550**

1. Earth 2. Geology 3. Earth sciences 4. Picture books for children 5. English language -- Alphabet 6. Geology

ISBN 9781585364541

LC 2010030635

In this picture book, "[t]he . . . poetic text and . . . illustrations provide an . . . entree into . . . Earth science topics . . . while sidebars provide . . . information on each topic." (Science & Children) "Planet Earth has been home to mankind for hundreds of thousands of years and while scientists have learned a lot about it, they're still unraveling many of its mysteries. "B is for Blue Planet: An Earth Science Alphabet" explains what we do know about our planet and what more we have to learn. [It e]xamine[s] Earth's diverse ecosystems (deserts), . . . geological wonders (karst caves), . . . weather phenomena (hurricanes), and much more." (Publisher's note)

VanCleave, Janice Pratt

Janice VanCleave's earth science for every kid; 101 easy experiments that really work. Wiley 1991 231p il hardcover o.p. pa $12.95

Grades: 4 5 6 7   **550**

1. Earth sciences 2. Science -- Experiments

ISBN 0-471-53010-7 pa

LC 90-42724

Instructions for experiments, each introducing a different earth science concept

"An entertaining, educational, and nonthreatening aid to understanding earth science. The easy experiments are carefully organized." SLJ

Woodward, John

Planet Earth; written by John Woodward; consultant Kim Bryan. DK Pub. 2009 123p il (One million things) $18.99

Grades: 5 6 7 8   **550**

1. Earth

ISBN 978-0-7566-5235-7; 0-7566-5235-9

This book features "photographic spreads that . . . showcase the rocks, minerals, streams, oceans, layers, clouds, ancient sediments, and brand-new islands that make up our planet." Publisher's note

550.78 Earth sciences -- experiments

Gardner, Robert

Planet Earth science fair projects; revised and expanded using the scientific method. Robert Gardner. Enslow Publishers 2010 160 p. il (Earth science projects using the scientific method) $35.94

Grades: 5 6 7 8   **550.78**

1. Science projects 2. Geology 3. Astronomy 4. Earth sciences 5. Science -- Experiments

ISBN 0766034232; 9780766034235

LC 2009026546

A revised edition of Planet Earth Science Fair Projects Using the Moon, Stars, Beach Balls, Frisbees, and Other Far-out Stuff, published 2005

This book, by Robert Gardner, presents "simple projects . . . [that] will help young scientists begin to understand Earth, including its place in the solar system, its atmosphere, its only natural satellite—the Moon, and its resources and geology. For students interested in competing in science fairs, the book contains lots of great suggestions and ideas for further experiments." (Publisher's note)

Includes bibliographical references and index

VanCleave, Janice Pratt, 1942-

Step-by-step science experiments in earth science; by Janice VanCleave. Rosen Pub. 2013 80 p. col. ill. (library) $33.25; (paperback) $14.15

Grades: 5 6 7 8   **550.78**

1. Earth sciences 2. Science -- Experiments 3. Earth sciences -- Experiments

ISBN 1448869838; 9781448869831; 9781448884674

LC 2012007944

This book by Janice VanCleave is part of the First-Place Science Fair Projects series. The books have an introduction to the subject—here, earth science, followed by 22 simple . . . experiments. Van Cleave states the basic goal of the experiments, followed by a list of necessary materials, most of which can be found around the house or easily acquired with minimal cost. Step-by-step instructions are clearly detailed and accompanied by diagrams where needed." (School Library Journal)

Includes bibliographical references (p. 78) and index.

551 Geology, hydrology, meteorology

Blobaum, Cindy

Geology rocks! 50 hands-on activities to explore the earth. illustrations by Michael Kline. Williamson 1999 96p il pa $10.95

Grades: 4 5 6   **551**

1. Geology 2. Science -- Experiments

ISBN 1-885593-29-5

LC 98-53299

Presents fifty hands-on activities to introduce the science of geology and explain the formation and history of the earth

"The text is witty but conveys much factual material. The experiments can be done easily with household items and include safety precautions. . . . The book is illustrated with red-and-purple tinted cartoons and photographs." SLJ

Includes bibliographical references

Gray, Susan H.

Geology the study of rocks; Susan H. Gray. Children's Press 2012 48 p. (pbk.) $6.95

Grades: 2 3 4 5   **551**

1. Rocks 2. Geology 3. Drilling and boring (Earth and rocks) 4.

Geology

ISBN 0531282708; 9780531246764; 9780531282700

LC 2011031091

Author Susan Heinrichs Gray presents a book on geography, the history of the earth, and the study of rocks.

Includes bibliographical references and index.

Kelly, Erica

★ **Evolving** planet; [by] Erica Kelly & Richard Kissel. Harry N. Abrams 2008 136p il map $19.95

Grades: 5 6 7 8   **551**

1. Evolution 2. Earth 3. Field Museum of Natural History

ISBN 978-0-8109-9486-7; 0-8109-9486-0

LC 2007-36342

"Based on a exhibit at Chicago's Field Museum, this big spacious volume packs in a wealth of information about evolution over four billion years. . . . There are detailed, beautiful photographs and glorious paintings on every double-page spread and the chatty text is accessible for grade-schoolers." Booklist

Includes glossary and bibliographical references

551.1   Gross structure and properties of the earth

Larson, Paul

The **four** spheres of Earth; Paul Larson. Teacher Created Materials 2016 32 p. color illustrations (ebook) $8.99; (pbk.) $8.99

Grades: 4 5 6   **551.1**

1. Earth 2. Science 3. Earth (Planet) 4. Earth sciences

ISBN 9781480751231; 9781480747258

LC 2015003016

In this book, by Paul Larson, "geosphere, hydrosphere, atmosphere, and biosphere—each of these spheres make up planet Earth. From deep below Earth's surface where metals are made to the thermosphere that protects our planet from harmful sunrays, travel through each layer of these spheres to see how every living thing is connected. In this engaging science book." (Publisher's note)

Saunders, Craig

What is the theory of plate tectonics? Crabtree Pub. Co. 2011 64p il (Shaping modern science) lib bdg $30.60; pa $10.95

Grades: 5 6 7 8   **551.1**

1. Plate tectonics 2. Geophysicists 3. Meteorologists 4. College teachers

ISBN 978-0-7787-7202-6 lib bdg; 0-7787-7202-0 lib bdg; 978-0-7787-7209-5 pa; 0-7787-7209-8 pa

LC 2010-52622

This title is "not only written and organized well, but [it is] also gorgeous in design. Full-color photographs and illustrations are set over colorful backgrounds that add depth but not distraction. [The title] includes thought-provoking quotes from famous authors and scientists and some eyebrow-raising 'Quick Facts' throughout." SLJ

Includes glossary and bibliographical references

Snedden, Robert

Earth's shifting surface. Raintree 2010 48p il (Sci-hi: Earth and space science) lib bdg $31.43; pa $8.99

Grades: 4 5 6 7   **551.1**

1. Plate tectonics 2. Earth -- Surface

ISBN 978-1-4109-3349-2 lib bdg; 1-4109-3349-0 lib bdg; 978-1-4109-3359-1 pa; 1-4109-3359-8 pa

LC 2009-3532

"Multiple colorful sidebars and large and small diagrams and photographs will help students to grasp the fundamentals being discussed,

and the easy but interesting science experiments will act as further reinforcements." SLJ

Includes glossary and bibliographical references

Storad, Conrad J.

Uncovering Earth's crust; Conrad J. Storad. Lerner Publications 2013 40 p. color illustrations (Searchlight books. Do you dig earth science?) (lib. bdg. : alk. paper) $27.93

Grades: 3 4 5 6   **551.1**

1. Earth -- Surface 2. Geology 3. Earth -- Crust 4. Earth -- Surface

ISBN 1467700207; 9781467700207

LC 2012017604

This children's book by Conrad J. Storad explores how "the outside layer of our planet is an active place. Earth's crust is always growing and changing. But do you know how Earth's crust forms? And what happens when its plates shift suddenly? Find out more about the moves that make mountains and ocean ridges in this interesting book!" (Publisher's note)

"Diagrams, maps, and other visuals are very clear." Horn Book

Includes bibliographical references (page 39) and index

551.136   Plate tectonics

Reilly, Kathleen M.

Fault lines & tectonic plates; discover what happens when the Earth's crust moves. by Kathleen M. Reilly, illustrated by Chad Thompson. Nomad Press 2017 122 p. color ill., color maps $22.95; (ebook) $12.99

Grades: 4 5 6 7   **551.136**

1. Earth -- Surface 2. Volcanoes 3. Earthquakes

ISBN 1619304619; 9781619304611; 9781619304628

LC 2017000861

In this book, by Kathleen M. Reilly, illustrated by Chad Thompson, "readers ages 9 through 12 learn what exactly is going on under the dirt. When slowly drifting continents bump up against each other along fault lines we experience earthquakes, volcanoes, and tidal waves! Mountains and trenches are visible results of the slow movement of the earth's crust, as tectonic plates create the landscape of our world over time." (Publisher's note)

Includes bibliographical references (pages 118-119) and index.

551.2   Volcanoes, earthquakes, thermal waters and gases

Benoit, Peter

The **Krakatau** eruption. Children's Press 2011 48p il (True book) lib bdg $28; pa $6.99

Grades: 3 4 5   **551.2**

1. Volcanoes 2. Indonesia

ISBN 978-0-531-20628-7 lib bdg; 978-0-531-29027-9 pa

LC 2010045930

This describes the 1883 volcanic eruption on the island of Krakatau. "Benoit provides unbiased information that is on target for the intended audience. . . . The photographs and reproductions enhance the [text]. . . . [This book is] well-conceived." SLJ

Includes bibliographical references

Branley, Franklyn Mansfield

Earthquakes; by Franklyn M. Branley; illustrated by Megan Lloyd. newly il ed.; HarperCollinsPublishers 2005 33p il (Let's-read-and-find-out science) hardcover o.p. pa $4.99

Grades: K 1 2 3 **551.2**
1. Earthquakes
ISBN 0-06-028008-5; 0-06-028009-3 lib bdg; 0-06-445188-7 pa
LC 2003-25458
A newly illustrated edition of the title first published 1990
"The most effective pictures are those that show the unseen and un-seeable, such as cross-sections of mountains, volcanoes, and faults in the earth's moving crust." Booklist

Volcanoes; by Franklyn M. Branley; illustrated by Megan Lloyd. newly illustrated ed.; Collins 2008 30p il map (Let's-read-and-find-out science) $16.99; pa $5.99
Grades: 2 3 4 **551.2**
1. Volcanoes
ISBN 978-0-06-028011-6; 0-06-028011-5; 978-0-06-445189-5 pa; 0-06-445189-5 pa
LC 2006000465
A newly illustrated edition of the title first published 1985
Discusses volcanoes, what causes an eruption, and the warning signs
"The new illustrations excel at depicting ideas presented in the text and include scenes of destruction. . . . This work remains a sound, basic introduction to the topic." SLJ

Fradin, Judith Bloom
★ **Earthquakes**; witness to disaster. by Judy and Dennis Fradin. National Geographic 2008 48p map (Witness to disaster) $16.95; lib bdg $26.90
Grades: 4 5 6 7 **551.2**
1. Earthquakes
ISBN 978-1-4263-0211-4; 1-4263-0211-8; 978-1-4263-0212-1 lib bdg; 1-4263-0212-6 lib bdg
LC 2007044164
"The combination of good writing and excellent graphics paired with archival and personal perspectives makes this book a valuable addition." SLJ
Includes glossary and bibliographical references

Volcano! the Icelandic eruption of 2010 and other hot, smoky, fierce, and fiery mountains. [by] Judy & Dennis Fradin. National Geographic 2010 48p il map (National Geographic kids) pa $6.95
Grades: 4 5 6 7 **551.2**
1. Volcanoes
ISBN 978-1-4263-0815-4 pa; 1-4263-0815-9 pa
"The format includes text, quotes, and facts in sidebars, as well as photographs on each page, with a colorful layout. The photographs and maps that are shown are of good quality." Sci Books & Films
Includes glossary and bibliographical references

★ **Volcanoes**; by Judy and Dennis Fradin. National Geographic 2007 48p il map (Witness to disaster) $16.95; lib bdg $26.90
Grades: 4 5 6 7 **551.2**
1. Volcanoes
ISBN 978-0-7922-5376-1; 0-7922-5376-0; 978-0-7922-5377-8 lib bdg; 0-7922-5377-9 lib bdg
LC 2006-102817
This "introduces readers to these violent eruptions, using eyewitness accounts to explain the history and science involved. They begin with a report of the 1943 birth of a volcano in Paricutín, Mexico. . . . Subsequent chapters describe other celebrated volcanoes, explain their causes and types, note the benefits of these eruptions, and clarify how they are currently predicted. . . . Numerous clear, well-chosen photographs and diagrams help to convey the great power of volcanic activity and the

consequences to humans. . . . This will be useful for report writers, and a fascinating pick for browsers." Booklist
Includes bibliographical references

Hague, Bradley
Alien deep; Revealing the Mysterious Living World at the Bottom of the Ocean. by Bradley Hague. National Geographic 2012 48 p. col. ill. (hardcover : alk. paper) $17.95
Grades: 5 6 7 8 **551.2**
1. Oceanography -- Research 2. Hydrothermal vent ecology 3. Natural history -- Galapagos Islands 4. Hydrothermal vents 5. Hydrothermal vent animals
ISBN 1426310676; 9781426310676; 9781426310683
LC 2012012939
This book by Bradley Hague "depicts adventurous and thrilling elements in oceanographic fieldwork in conjunction with a National Geographic television show." (Publisher's note) "The book takes readers along on the 2011 exploration of vents in the Galapagos Reef area of the Pacific Ocean. . . . Future scientists will be hooked by the excitement of finding newly developing vents and the disappointment of finding older vents that once disappeared under layers of magma." (Booklist)
Includes bibliographical references and index.

Jennings, Terry
Earthquakes and tsunamis. Smart Apple Media 2010 32p il map (Amazing planet earth) lib bdg $28.50
Grades: 4 5 6 **551.2**
1. Tsunamis 2. Earthquakes
ISBN 978-1-59920-372-0 lib bdg; 1-59920-372-3 lib bdg
LC 2008-55496
This book shows readers how the shifting plates far below the earth's surface can result in violent earthquakes and tsunamis
"Chapters are labeled as 'Case Study' or 'Science Report,' making the presentation lively. The concise explanations include just the right number of examples and clear diagrams, and have perfect color photo accompaniments." SLJ
Includes glossary

Violent volcanoes. Smart Apple Media 2010 32p il map (Amazing planet earth) lib bdg $28.50
Grades: 4 5 6 **551.2**
1. Volcanoes
ISBN 978-1-59920-374-4 lib bdg; 1-59920-374-X lib bdg
LC 2008-55499
This explains how powerful forces beneath the Earth's crust cause volcanoes to erupt
"Chapters are labeled as 'Case Study' or 'Science Report,' making the presentation lively. The concise explanations include just the right number of examples and clear diagrams, and have perfect color photo accompaniments." SLJ
Includes glossary

Levy, Matthys
Earthquakes, volcanoes, and tsunamis; projects and principles for beginning geologists. [by] Matthys Levy and Mario Salvadori. Chicago Review Press 2009 136p il pa $14.95
Grades: 5 6 7 8 **551.2**
1. Tsunamis 2. Volcanoes 3. Earthquakes
ISBN 978-1-55652-801-9 pa; 1-55652-801-9 pa
LC 2008040143
This "is an excellent introduction for young minds to the subject of earthquakes, volcanoes, and related phenomena. . . . The book is filled with projects to help young people understand the occurrence and consequences of earthquakes, volcanoes, and tsunamis." Sci Books Films

Person, Stephen

Devastated by a volcano! Bearport Pub. 2010 32p il map (Disaster survivors) lib bdg $25.27

Grades: 4 5 6 7   **551.2**

1. Volcanoes

ISBN 978-1-936087-50-1 lib bdg; 1-936087-50-2 lib bdg

"Captivating photos and illustrations and sidebars present interesting facts or brief anecdotes. . . . [This] should be purchased for all school and public libraries as . . . [it gives] a new perspective on the topic." Libr Media Connect

Includes glossary and bibliographical references

Silverstein, Alvin

Earthquakes; the science behind seismic shocks and tsunamis. [by] Alvin Silverstein, Virginia Silverstein, and Laura Silverstein Nunn. Enslow Publishers 2010 48p il map (The science behind natural disasters) lib bdg $23.93

Grades: 4 5 6   **551.2**

1. Tsunamis 2. Earthquakes

ISBN 978-0-7660-2975-0 lib bdg; 0-7660-2975-1 lib bdg

LC 2008-38589

"Scientific explanations are accompanied by plentiful color diagrams that will help students to grasp causes and effects. . . . Photos . . . are effective, and are sometimes turned into helpful, lively diagrams by the addition of such features as wind-direction arrows." SLJ

Includes glossary and bibliographical references

Volcanoes; the science behind fiery eruptions. [by] Alvin Silverstein, Virginia Silverstein, and Laura Silverstein Nunn. Enslow Publishers 2010 48p il map (The science behind natural disasters) lib bdg $23.93

Grades: 4 5 6   **551.2**

1. Volcanoes

ISBN 978-0-7660-2972-9 lib bdg; 0-7660-2972-7 lib bdg

LC 2008-42866

"Scientific explanations are accompanied by plentiful color diagrams that will help students to grasp causes and effects. . . . Photos . . . are effective, and are sometimes turned into helpful, lively diagrams by the addition of such features as wind-direction arrows." SLJ

Includes glossary and bibliographical references

Simon, Seymour

★ **Earthquakes**; rev ed.; Collins 2006 30p il map pa $6.99

Grades: 3 4 5 6   **551.2**

1. Earthquakes

ISBN 978-0-06-087715-6 pa; 0-06-087715-4 pa

LC 2006279219

First published 1991 by Morrow Junior Books

Examines the phenomenon of earthquakes, describing how and where they occur, how they can be predicted, and how much damage they can inflict

Spilsbury, Louise

Shattering earthquakes; [by] Louise and Richard Spilsbury. rev and updated.; Heinemann Library 2010 32p il map (Awesome forces of nature) lib bdg $29; pa $7.99

Grades: 3 4 5 6   **551.2**

1. Earthquakes

ISBN 978-1-4329-3784-3 lib bdg; 1-4329-3784-7 lib bdg; 978-1-4329-3791-1 pa; 1-4329-3791-X pa

LC 2009037565

First published 2004

This book about earthquakes discusses "causes, characteristics, and relevant science, including progress in predicting the events. Case stud-

ies illustrate the human response. Numerous color photographs and sidebars are interwoven into the well-organized and absorbing [narrative]." SLJ

Includes glossary and bibliographical references

Violent volcanoes; [by] Louise and Richard Spilsbury. rev and updated; Heinemann Library 2010 32p il map (Awesome forces of nature) lib bdg $29; pa $7.99

Grades: 3 4 5 6   **551.2**

1. Volcanoes

ISBN 978-1-4329-3783-6 lib bdg; 1-4329-3783-9 lib bdg; 978-1-4329-3790-4 pa; 1-4329-3790-1 pa

LC 2009-37564

First published 2004

This book about volcanoes "is sure to catch the eyes of students and educators. . . . The interesting and accurate facts are presented in an easily understood vocabulary. . . . Incredible eye-catching photographs, diagrams, or maps are tastefully positioned on every page." Libr Media Connect

Includes glossary and bibliographical references

Stewart, Melissa

Inside Earthquakes. Sterling Publishing Co., Inc. 2011 48p il map (Inside . . .) $16.95; pa $9.95

Grades: 5 6 7 8   **551.2**

1. Earthquakes

ISBN 978-1-4027-5877-5; 978-1-4027-8163-6 pa

LC 2010046452

This book about earthquakes "explores its topic in an engaging way, and the many illustrations work well with adjacent text and captions. . . . The [book's] varied page layouts and attractive and the quality of photos, computer-generated images, original illustrations, and charts is . . . excellent. . . . [The book] looks at the geology of the earth's crust as well as the effects of quakes on people and cities, landforms and coastlines." Booklist

Includes bibliographical references

Inside Volcanoes. Sterling Publishing Co. 2011 48p il map (Inside) $16.95; pa $9.95

Grades: 5 6 7 8   **551.2**

1. Volcanoes

ISBN 978-1-4027-5876-8; 1-4027-5876-6; 978-1-4027-8164-3 pa; 1-4027-8164-4 pa

LC 2010046451

Examines the nature of volcanoes, how they are formed, what they look like, and how they are measured, in a text with ten foldout pages.

"With pages that fold out or flip up, well-reproduced photographs of volcanoes at rest and in action, diagrams, maps, charts, timelines and short explanations, there is much to look at and to learn. . . . Appropriately for a book that is clearly designed to stimulate interest, there are solid suggestions for both books and websites for further exploration. A good starting-place for volcano explorations." Kirkus

Stille, Darlene R.

Great shakes; the science of earthquakes. Compass Point Books 2009 43p il map (Headline science) lib bdg $27.93; pa $7.95

Grades: 5 6 7 8   **551.2**

1. Earthquakes

ISBN 978-0-7565-3947-4 lib bdg; 0-7565-3947-1 lib bdg; 978-0-7565-3368-7 pa; 0-7565-3368-6 pa

LC 2008-05739

This "is an accessible, technically accurate introduction to [earthquakes]. . . . In addition to the ludic writing, this slim volume offers . . . readers comprehensive coverage of the fundamentals of earthquakes, including the effects, plate tectonics, fault systems, seismic waves, forecasting, and safer building designs. . . . The many charts and graphs enrich the volume and clarify technical issues." Sci Books Films

Includes glossary and bibliographical references

Tagliaferro, Linda

How does a volcano become an island? Raintree 2010 32p il (How does it happen?) lib bdg $27.50; pa $7.99
Grades: 3 4 5   **551.2**
1. Islands 2. Volcanoes
ISBN 978-1-4109-3447-5 lib bdg; 1-4109-3447-0 lib bdg; 978-1-4109-3455-0 pa; 1-4109-3455-1 pa

LC 2008-52652

"Information is clearly presented using a large font, diagrams, and photographs formatted to resemble Polaroid pictures. . . . A first-rate job answering some important scientific questions." SLJ

Includes glossary and bibliographical references

551.21 Volcanoes

Rusch, Elizabeth

Volcano rising; Elizabeth Rusch; illustrated by Susan Swan. Charlesbridge 2013 32 p. (reinforced for library use) $17.95
Grades: 2 3 4   **551.21**
1. Picture books for children 2. Volcanoes
ISBN 1580894089; 9781580894081; 9781580894098; 9781607346166

LC 2012000793

This children's picture book by Elizabeth Rousch explores volcanoes. "Blowing their tops off, growing taller and wider, and forming new mountains and islands, volcanoes can be both destructive and creative. . . . A dual-level narrative provides both a simple explanation of how volcanoes work and longer paragraphs that go into greater depth." Examples of eight volcanoes from around the world are discussed. (Kirkus Reviews)

Smith, Kelly

★ How hot is lava? and other questions about volcanoes. text by Kelly Smith; illustrations by Sterling Publishing Co., Inc. Sterling Pub Co Inc 2016 40 p. color ill., color map $12.95
Grades: 3 4 5 6   **551.21**
1. Volcanoes
ISBN 1454916001; 9781454916000

LC 2016427912

This book in the Good Question! series, by Kelly Smith, answers children's questions such as "What exactly is a volcano? Can it really destroy an entire city? And how hot is lava? Kids will learn all about this force of nature, from where to find the ring of fire to whether volcanoes exist on other planets." (Publisher's note)

"In a question-and-answer format, the book presents basic facts about volcanoes under subtopics including the mechanics of volcanoes and plate tectonics; volcano locations; types of eruptions and lava; and historical volcanic events." Horn Book

Includes bibliographical references (page 31) and index.

551.22 Earthquakes

Winchester, Simon

When the earth shakes; earthquakes, volcanoes, and tsunamis. Simon Winchester. Viking 2015 71 p. color ill., color maps (hardcover) $18.99

Grades: 5 6 7 8   **551.22**
1. Earthquakes 2. Earthquakes -- Psychological aspects
ISBN 9780670785360

LC 2014039743

In this book, by Simon Winchester,"Earthquakes, volcanoes, tsunamis making natural disasters with devastating consequences for millions of people. The author who's been shaken by earthquakes in New Zealand . . .looks at the science, technology, and societal impact of these interconnected natural phenomena. . . .And the earthquake that flattened San Francisco, to the 21st-century tsunamis that devastated Indonesia and Japan." (Publisher's note)

"A must-buy for libraries serving middle school, this title works both as a basic overview of earth science and as a fine example of how to incorporate personal narrative into nonfiction" SLJ

Includes bibliographical references (page 66) and index.

551.3 Surface and exogenous processes and their agents

Harrison, David Lee

Glaciers; nature's icy caps. [by] David L. Harrison; illustrated by Cheryl Nathan. Boyds Mills Press 2006 un il (Earthworks) $15.95
Grades: K 1 2 3   **551.3**
1. Glaciers
ISBN 1-59078-372-7

LC 2005-24988

The author "provides a straightforward introduction to glaciers. Opening with the sinking of the Titanic, he explains how they form, move, and drop icebergs into the sea, going on to discuss where glaciers can be found and how their range shifts as Earth cycles in and out of ice ages. . . . The text reads like clear, informational prose. Nathan's digital illustrations vary in quality, but the best double-page spreads . . . are exceptionally fine." Booklist

Sepehri, Sandy

Glaciers; [by] Sandy Sepehri. Rourke Pub. 2008 32p il (Landforms) lib bdg $28.50; pa $7.95
Grades: 1 2 3 4   **551.3**
1. Glaciers
ISBN 978-1-60044-544-6 lib bdg; 1-60044-544-6 lib bdg; 978-1-60044-705-1 pa; 1-60044-705-8 pa

LC 2007012143

"The illustrations and photographs are plentiful and colorful. . . . The [volume is] well written and successfully [conveys] the basics of the topic." Sci Books Films

Includes glossary and bibliographical references

Silverman, Buffy

Exploring dangers in space; asteroids, space junk, and more. Lerner Publications 2011 40p il (What's amazing about space?) $27.93
Grades: 4 5 6   **551.3**
1. Comets 2. Meteors 3. Asteroids 4. Space debris
ISBN 978-0-7613-5446-8

LC 2010046078

This discusses meteoroids, space junk, comets and asteroids that fall to Earth, how scientists watch out for large collisions, and what they might do if Earth is in danger.

This book is "written in simple language, [and] illustrated nicely. . . . The information presented is factually correct. . . . Every page includes a well-chosen illustration or photograph." Sci Books Films

Includes bibliographical references

551.4 Geomorphology and hydrosphere

Henzel, Cynthia Kennedy

Great Barrier Reef. ABDO Pub. Co. 2011 32p il (Troubled treasures: world heritage sites) $25.65

Grades: 3 4 5 **551.4**

1. Coral reefs and islands 2. Great Barrier Reef (Australia)

ISBN 978-1-61613-564-5; 1-61613-564-6

LC 2010021310

This "book describes in general terms [the Great Barrier Reef's] . . . creation, distinctive features, and history, as well as threats to its continued existence and both current and past restoration intitiatives. Revealing color photos taken from different heights and angles are supplemented by maps and by graphic reconstructions. . . . Henzel's distinctive approach gives this [book] unusual value for both assignment and general reading." SLJ

Includes glossary

Hughes, Catherine D.

First big book of the ocean; by Catherine D. Hughes. National Geographic Children's Books 2013 128 p. $14.95

Grades: K 1 2 3 **551.4**

1. Marine animals 2. Marine biology

ISBN 9781426313684; 1426313683

This book, by Catherine D. Hughes, presents an "animal reference that includes the sea's high-interest animals, such as dolphins, sharks, sea otters, and penguins, and introduces kids to some of its lesser-known creatures. More than 100 . . . animal photos illustrate the profiles, with facts about the creatures' sizes, diets, homes, and more." (Publisher's note)

Jennings, Terry

Massive mountains. Smart Apple Media 2010 32p il map (Amazing planet earth) lib bdg $28.50

Grades: 4 5 6 **551.4**

1. Mountains

ISBN 978-1-59920-370-6 lib bdg; 1-59920-370-7 lib bdg

LC 2008-55497

This book explains how mountains form and change over time

"Chapters are labeled as 'Case Study' or 'Science Report,' making the presentation lively. The concise explanations include just the right number of examples and clear diagrams, and have perfect color photo accompaniments." SLJ

Includes glossary

Lindeen, Mary

At the beach; by Mary Lindeen. Norwood House Press 2016 32 p. color illustrations (library edition : alk. paper) $22.60

Grades: PreK K 1 **551.4**

1. Easy reading materials 2. Beaches

ISBN 1599536986; 9781599536989

LC 2014047631

In this children's book, by Mary Lindeen, part of the publisher's "Beginning-to-Read" series, "take a trip to the beach. See water, sand, seashells, a tide pool, and other interesting things you can find there. This informational text . . . contains high-frequency words and content vocabulary." (Publisher's note)

"These slight books use high-frequency words to encourage early readers to read independently." Horn Book

Sheehan, Thomas F.

Islands; [by] Thomas F. Sheehan. Rourke Pub. 2008 32p il map (Landforms) lib bdg $28.50; pa $7.95

Grades: 1 2 3 4 **551.4**

1. Islands

ISBN 978-1-60044-545-3 lib bdg; 1-60044-545-4 lib bdg; 978-1-60044-706-8 pa; 1-60044-706-6 pa

LC 2007012183

"The illustrations and photographs are plentiful and colorful. . . . The [volume is] well written and successfully [conveys] the basics of the topic." Sci Books Films

Includes glossary and bibliographical references

Mountains; [by] Thomas Sheehan. Rourke Pub. 2008 32p il map (Landforms) lib bdg $28.50; pa $7.95

Grades: 1 2 3 4 **551.4**

1. Mountains

ISBN 978-1-60044-547-7 lib bdg; 1-60044-547-0 lib bdg; 978-1-60044-708-2 pa; 1-60044-708-2 pa

LC 2007012290

"The illustrations and photographs are plentiful and colorful. . . . The [volume is] well written and successfully [conveys] the basics of the topic." Sci Books Films

Includes glossary and bibliographical references

Wilson, Hannah

Seashore; illustrated by Simon Mendez. Kingfisher 2010 18p il (Flip the flaps) $9.99

Grades: PreK K 1 **551.4**

1. Seashore

ISBN 978-0-7534-6445-8; 0-7534-6445-4

This "features beautiful spreads by Mendez, who paints his coastal scenes with a soft realism so accurate they are occasionally indistinguishable from photographs. Wilson, meanwhile, introduces readers to the plants and wildlife present at shorelines everywhere—not just the classic sandy beach but also salt marsh, arctic region, and mangrove swamp. Each top flap presents three questions . . . which are answered underneath. . . . Perfect for light, educational browsing." Booklist

551.46 Oceanography and submarine geology

Aronin, Miriam

Slammed by a tsunami! Bearport Pub. 2010 32p il map (Disaster survivors) lib bdg $25.27

Grades: 4 5 6 7 **551.46**

1. Tsunamis

ISBN 978-1-936087-48-8 lib bdg; 1-936087-48-0 lib bdg

LC 2009-34574

"Introduces tsunamis, discussing how they form and when they tend to occur, and describing the devastating effects of the 2004 tsunami in Sumatra and of some of the other well-known tsunamis of the past." Publisher's note

Includes glossary and bibliographical references

Basher, Simon

Oceans; [making waves!] designed and created by Simon Basher; text written by Dan Green. Kingfisher 2012 128 p. ill. (paperback) $8.99; (hardcover) $14.99

Grades: 5 6 7 8 **551.46**

1. Oceanography 2. Marine ecology 3. Aquatic animals

ISBN 0753468220; 9780753468227; 9780753468210

"Following a brief introduction to oceans, the text employs an easy-to-navigate field guide like format, where facts and figures about ocean habitats, processes, and animals that live in various areas (e.g., shore, reef, deep water) face illustrations in manga style" Horn Book

"A rewarding wade, particularly for readers who think oceanography is a dry study." Booklist

Bodden, Valerie

To the ocean deep; by Valerie Bodden. Creative Education 2011 48 p. col. ill. (Great expeditions) (library) $34.25

Grades: 5 6 7 8   **551.46**

1. Ocean 2. Underwater exploration 3. Explorers -- Biography 4. Trieste (Bathyscaphe) -- History 5. Bathyscaphe -- History -- 20th century 6. Underwater exploration -- History -- 20th century

ISBN 1608180670; 9781608180677

LC 2010033416

This book by Valerie Bodden is part of the Great Expeditions series and looks at oceanic exploration expeditions. "Bodden includes brief biographies of major people involved in each expedition, interspersed with the text. There are also numerous photographs or reproductions of paintings and woodcuts from the time of the expeditions." (Library Media Connection)

Includes bibliographical references (p. 46-47) and index.

Burns, Loree Griffin

★ **Tracking** trash; flotsam, jetsam, and the science of ocean motion. Houghton Mifflin 2007 56p il map (Scientists in the field) $18

Grades: 5 6 7 8   **551.46**

1. Pollution 2. Ocean currents 3. Oceanographers 4. Marine debris

ISBN 0-618-58131-6; 978-0-618-58131-3

LC 2006-11534

Boston Globe-Horn Book Honor: Nonfiction (2007)

This book describes "Curt Ebbesmeyer's ongoing work. . . . The oceanographer has been tracing the surface currents of the seas via the movement of plastic rubbish that has escaped from broken cargo containers. [Index.] Grades five to nine." (Bull Cent Child Books)

"The book profiles two oceanographers who devised experiments using computer-modeling programs of ocean surface current movement to predict the landfall of . . . drifting objects. . . . Spacious layout, exceptionally fine color photos, and handsome maps give this book an inviting look. . . . A unique and often fascinating book." Booklist

Includes glossary and bibliographical references

Dwyer, Helen

Tsunamis! Marshall Cavendish Benchmark 2010 32p il map (Eyewitness disaster) lib bdg $28.50

Grades: 4 5 6   **551.46**

1. Tsunamis

ISBN 978-1-60870-005-9; 1-60870-005-4

LC 2010001801

Provides information about tsunamis through eyewitness accounts from survivors and rescue workers.

"Bold subheadings and color captions break information into readable chunks for the younger learner. Important vocabulary is in bold print. . . . An excellent addition to your science collection." Libr Media Connect

Includes glossary and bibliographical references

Earle, Sylvia A.

Dive! my adventures in the deep frontier. National Geographic Soc. 1999 64p il map $18.95

Grades: 4 5 6   **551.46**

1. Underwater exploration 2. Submarine diving

ISBN 0-7922-7144-0

LC 98-11480

The author relates some of her adventures studying and exploring the world's oceans, including tracking whales, living in an underwater laboratory, and helping to design a deep water submarine

"In this extraordinary photo-essay, an eminent marine biologist and ocean explorer combines personal adventure and scientific fact with glorious color action pictures." Booklist

Includes glossary

Fradin, Judith Bloom

★ **Tsunamis**; witness to disaster. [by] Judy & Dennis Fradin. National Geographic 2008 48p il map (Witness to disaster) $16.95; lib bdg $20.90

Grades: 4 5 6 7   **551.46**

1. Tsunamis

ISBN 978-0-7922-5380-8; 0-7922-5380-9; 978-0-7922-5381-5 lib bdg; 0-7922-5381-7 lib bdg

LC 2008010536

This "explores the science, history, and personal experience of tsunamis and shows kids what scientists are doing to develop early warning systems so we can survive such disasters in the future." Publisher's note

Includes glossary and bibliographical references

Gray, Susan H.

Oceanography the study of oceans; Susan H. Gray. Children's Press 2012 48 p.

Grades: 2 3 4 5   **551.46**

1. Oceanography

ISBN 0531246795; 0531282732; 9780531246795; 9780531282731

LC 2011031074

This book by Susan Heinrichs Gray is an introduction to oceanography for young readers. "Earth's oceans are almost like a foreign world, filled with millions of strange, fascinating animals and plants. Oceanographers dive into the watery depths to learn more about the incredible ocean ecosystems that make up the majority of our planet. Readers will discover how the ocean changes as it goes deeper, how deep sea animals survive in harsh environments, and more." (Google Books)

Includes bibliographical references (p. 44-45) and index

Green, Jen

The **world's** oceans. Smart Apple Media 2010 32p il map (Amazing planet earth) lib bdg $28.50

Grades: 4 5 6   **551.46**

1. Ocean

ISBN 978-1-59920-373-7 lib bdg; 1-59920-373-1 lib bdg

LC 2008-55500

This covers how ocean waves shape the seashore, the makeup of the ocean bed, underwater hazards, storm surges, and the effects of global warming. Interspersed with these are six "Case Study" chapters, which take an in-depth look at various oceanic events throughout history such as the creation of Iceland or the deadly tsunami that hit Indonesia in December, 2004

"Chapters are labeled as 'Case Study' or 'Science Report,' making the presentation lively. The concise explanations include just the right number of examples and clear diagrams, and have perfect color photo accompaniments." SLJ

Includes glossary

MacQuitty, Miranda

Eyewitness ocean; written by Miranda MacQuitty; photographed by Frank Greenaway. DK Publishing 2008 72 p. illustrations (chiefly color) $9.99

Grades: 4 5 6 7   **551.46**
1. Ocean 2. Marine animals 3. Marine biology 4. Marine ecology
ISBN 1465420541; 1465420967; 9780756637767;
9781465420541
LC 2008276032
In this book, by Miranda MacQuitty, "dive in and discover the watery world covering most of our earth and the amazing wildlife in its
depths. . . . Through images, maps and informative text learn about life
on the shore to the darkest depths of the ocean floor, including predators
and prey, gas and oil exploration, products of the ocean, brave explorers
and what the human race can do to help preserve one of the earth's most
valuable resources." (Publisher's note)

Mallory, Kenneth
   Adventure beneath the sea; living in an underwater science station. [photographs by Brian Skerry] Boyds Mills Press 2010 48p il
map $18.95
Grades: 4 5 6 7   **551.46**
   1. Underwater exploration
   ISBN 978-1-59078-607-9; 1-59078-607-6
The author "invites readers to squeeze into Aquarius, a venerable
science-station habitat resting on the sea floor at a depth of 60 feet in
the Florida Keys. The readable text explains the complexities of training
for a weeklong stay, the aims of the scientists on the team, and what it is
like to spend 24/7 in squashed companionship in a 43' × 9' cylinder as
part of a crew of seven. . . . Sidebars contain interesting information. . .
. Full-color photos abound." SLJ
   Includes glossary and bibliographical references

   ★ **Diving** to a deep-sea volcano. Houghton Mifflin Company 2006
60p il map (Scientists in the field) $17
Grades: 5 6 7 8   **551.46**
   1. Ocean bottom 2. Marine biology 3. Underwater exploration
   ISBN 978-0-618-33205-2; 0-618-33205-7
LC 2005-25449
   This describes the exploration by marine biologist Rich Lutz and his
crew of deep sea hydrothermal vents and the creatures that survive there.
   "The profile of an enthusiastic scientist injects excitement into even
unassuming facts." Booklist
   Includes glossary and bibliographical references

Marsico, Katie
   ★ **Puget** Sound; by Katie Marsico. Cherry Lake Pub. 2013 32
p. (It's cool to learn about America's waterways) (lib. bdg.) $28.50
Grades: 3 4 5   **551.46**
   1. Puget Sound region (Wash.) 2. Puget Sound (Wash.)
   ISBN 162431015X; 9781624310157; 9781624310393;
9781624310638
LC 2012034741
   This book by Katie Marsico is part of a series that "provide[s] a
wealth of information regarding each waterway's history, geographical characteristics, wildlife, and influence on the development of nearby towns and cities. Conservation is emphasized in all the titles. The
importance of each waterway commercially and recreationally is also
discussed." (Publisher's note) "In 'Puget Sound,' they graph local wildlife." (Booklist)
   Includes bibliographical references and index

Nivola, Claire A.
   ★ **Life** in the ocean; Claire A. Nivola. Frances Foster Books, Far-
rar Straus Giroux 2012 1 v. (unpaged) col. ill.
Grades: K 1 2 3 4   **551.46**
   1. Biography 2. Explorers 3. Oceanography 4. Marine biologists
-- United States 5. Women marine biologists -- United States 6.

Women explorers -- United States -- Biography
ISBN 9780374380687
LC 2011016645
This picture book presents a "biography of oceanographer Sylvia
Earle, a pioneer and entrepreneur in her field who also set an example for
women of the mid-20th century." It covers life on her "childhood farm,"
her "relocat[ion] to the Gulf Coast, and her interest [in]ocean explora-
tion. . . . The . . . narrative highlights Earle's career and also provides a
few . . . closeups from specific dives." (Publishers Weekly)
   Includes bibliographical references and index

Rizzo, Johnna
   Oceans; dolphins, sharks, penguins, and more!: meet 60 cool sea
creatures and explore their amazing watery world. introduction by Sylvia A. Earle. National Geographic 2010 64p il $14.95; lib bdg $24.90
Grades: 4 5 6   **551.46**
   1. Ocean 2. Marine animals
   ISBN 978-1-4263-0686-0; 1-4263-0686-5; 978-1-4263-0724-9
lib bdg; 1-4263-0724-1 lib bdg
"A colorful olio of marine animals in eye-catching photos accompanies a cheerful conversational text. . . . Information boxes pop up all
over the place as well, but it is the bright photos that steal the show. . . .
This splashy volume is a nice introduction to a salty water-world." SLJ
   Includes glossary

Schuh, Mari C.
   Tsunamis. Capstone Press 2010 24p il (Earth in action) lib bdg
$21.32
Grades: K 1 2   **551.46**
   1. Tsunamis
   ISBN 978-1-4296-3438-0 lib bdg; 1-4296-3438-3 lib bdg
LC 2009-2175
This book "boasts a full-page color photograph. . . . [It shows] the
aftermath of a disaster . . . but there are also some diagrams showing
physical mechanisms and maps highlighting commonly affected places.
The left side of each spread provides a few sentences of large-print text,
with short, clear explanations." SLJ
   Includes glossary and bibliographical references

Simon, Seymour
   Seymour Simon's extreme oceans; Seymour Simon. Chronicle
Books 2013 60 p. col. ill. (reinforced) $17.99
Grades: 4 5 6   **551.46**
   1. Ocean
   ISBN 1452108331; 9781452108339
LC 2012012590
   In this work of children's nonfiction, author "[Seymour] Simon
examines the things that are 'most,' pertaining to oceans: the tallest
sea mounts, the largest waves, the highest tides in the world, the most
dangerous and largest animals, the coldest and warmest waters, the biggest storms and tsunamis, and the longest journeys, as well as a closing chapter predicting scenarios if sea levels continue to rise." (School
Library Journal)

Spilsbury, Louise
   Sweeping tsunamis; [by] Louise and Richard Spilsbury. rev ed.;
Heinemann Library 2010 32p il map (Awesome forces of nature) lib
bdg $29; pa $7.99
Grades: 3 4 5 6   **551.46**
   1. Tsunamis
   ISBN 978-1-4329-3785-0 lib bdg; 1-4329-3785-5 lib bdg; 978-1-
4329-3792-8 pa; 1-4329-3792-8 pa
LC 2009037567
First published 2004

This book about tsunamis "causes, characteristics, and relevant science, including progress in predicting the events. Case studies illustrate the human response. Numerous color photographs and sidebars are interwoven into the well-organized and absorbing [narrative]." SLJ

Includes glossary and bibliographical references

Stille, Darlene R.

Oceans. Children's Press 1999 47p il maps (True book) $22; pa $6.95

Grades: 2 3 4   **551.46**

1. Ocean

ISBN 0-516-21510-8; 0-516-26768-X pa

LC 98-53857

An introduction to the ocean describing its physical characteristics, the plants and animals that live in or near it, and its importance to life on Earth

Includes bibliographical references

Tagliaferro, Linda

How does an earthquake become a tsunami? Raintree 2008 32p il map (How does it happen?) lib bdg $27.50; pa $7.99

Grades: 3 4 5   **551.46**

1. Waves 2. Tsunamis 3. Earthquakes 4. Plate tectonics

ISBN 978-1-4109-3446-8 lib bdg; 1-4109-3446-2 lib bdg; 978-1-4109-3454-3 pa; 1-4109-3454-3 pa

LC 2008-52643

"Information is clearly presented using a large font, diagrams, and photographs formatted to resemble Polaroid pictures.... A first-rate job answering some important scientific questions." SLJ

Includes glossary and bibliographical references

VanCleave, Janice Pratt

Janice VanCleave's oceans for every kid; easy activities that make learning science fun. Wiley 1996 245p il map (Science for every kid series) hardcover o.p. pa $12.95

Grades: 4 5 6 7   **551.46**

1. Oceanography

ISBN 0-471-12453-2 pa

LC 95-9201

Includes information on techniques and technologies of oceanography, the topology of the ocean floor, movement of the sea, properties of sea water, and life in the sea

"An engaging overview of marine sciences. Each chapter explores a topic in two to four pages, then poses questions accompanied by lucid explanations." SLJ

Includes glossary

Woodward, John

The **deep,** deep ocean. Brown Bear Books 2009 32p il map (Oceans alive!) lib bdg $28.50

Grades: 2 3 4 5   **551.46**

1. Oceanography

ISBN 978-1-933834-63-4 lib bdg; 1-933834-63-3 lib bdg

This describes "deep parts of the ocean. Colored drawings, photos, and themed factual sidebars all enhance the story, navigated by a variety of submarines.... Differences in temperatures from the surface to the midnight zone are elegantly explained." Sci Books Films

Includes glossary and bibliographical references

On the seabed. Brown Bear Books 2009 32p il map (Oceans alive!) lib bdg $28.50

Grades: 2 3 4 5   **551.46**

1. Oceanography

ISBN 978-1-933834-64-1 lib bdg; 1-933834-64-1 lib bdg

Describes plants, animals, and different habitats that are found on the ocean's floor, and offers information on kelp forests, sunken treasure, and hydrothermal vents.

"From deep hot areas to cold places, strange, but wonderful, events and organisms are discussed. . . . Through the various photos and the text, the reader should develop an appreciation for the diversity found on the sea floor." Sci Books Films

Includes glossary and bibliographical references

Under the waves. Brown Bear Books 2009 32p il map (Oceans alive!) lib bdg $28.50

Grades: 2 3 4 5   **551.46**

1. Oceanography 2. Marine animals

ISBN 978-1-933834-62-7 lib bdg; 1-933834-62-5 lib bdg

Explores and describes both different oceans and different parts of the ocean.

"Explanations on notebook-style illustrations offer asides, a delightful extra along with appropriate maps and impressive photos. . . . Accurate details are given for such wonders as the Portuguese man-of-war, red tides, manta rays, and lion-fish." Sci Books Films

Includes glossary and bibliographical references

Zoehfeld, Kathleen Weidner

How deep is the ocean? by Kathleen Weidner Zoehfeld; illustrated by Eric Puybaret. Harper, an imprint of HarperCollins Publishers 2016 40 p. color illustrations (hardcover) $17.99; (ebook) $6.99

Grades: K 1 2 3   **551.46**

1. Oceanography 2. Underwater exploration 3. Ocean 4. Children's questions and answers

ISBN 9780062328199; 9780062328205; 9780062446961

LC 2015018471

This book, in the Let's-Read-and-Find-Out Science 2 series, by Kathleen Weidner Zoehfeld, illustrated by Eric Puybaret, "will guide young readers into the deepest parts of the ocean. Featuring a find-out-more section with a water-pressure experiment, a lesson in making a sounding line to learn how scientists measure the depth of the ocean, a glossary of new terms, and web research prompts, this book will begin children's explorations of the deep sea." (Publisher's note)

"Readers will surface with not only a better understanding of the diversity of ocean life, but a firmer grasp of how little we really know about vasty deeps that have seen fewer human visitors than has space." Kirkus

551.48   Hydrology

Bang, Molly

★ **Rivers** of sunlight; How the Sun Moves Water Around the Earth. Molly Bang and Penny Chisholm. The Blue Sky Press 2016 48 p. (hardcover : alk. paper) $18.99

Grades: 2 3 4 5 6   **551.48**

1. Sun 2. Sunshine 3. Hydrologic cycle

ISBN 9780545805414

LC 2015031582

In this children's book, by Molly Bang and Penny Chisholm, "readers will learn about the constant movement of water as it flows around the Earth and the sun's important role as water changes between liquid, vapor, and ice. From sea to sky, the sun both heats and cools water, ensuring that life can exist on Earth. How does the sun keep ocean currents moving, and lift fresh water from the seas? And what can we do to conserve one of our planet's most precious resources?" (Publisher's note)

"An outstanding choice for introducing young children to the water cycle. This is a book to return to many times." SLJ

Dorros, Arthur

Follow the water from brook to ocean; written and illustrated by Arthur Dorros. HarperCollins Pubs. 1991 32p il (Let's-read-and-find-out science book) $13.95; lib bdg $13.89

Grades: K 1 2 3   **551.48**
   1. Water
   ISBN 0-06-021598-4; 0-06-021599-2 lib bdg
                                              LC 90-1438

Explains how water flows from brooks, to streams, to rivers, over waterfalls, through canyons and dams, to eventually reach the ocean

"An excellent presentation of introductory material about water. ... The illustrations are simple, almost childlike, in soft colors." SLJ

Dwyer, Helen

Floods! Marshall Cavendish Benchmark 2010 32p il map (Eyewitness Disaster) lib bdg $28.50

Grades: 4 5 6   **551.48**
   1. Floods
   ISBN 978-1-60870-002-8; 1-60870-002-X

Provides information about floods through eyewitness accounts from survivors and rescue workers.

"Bold subheadings and color captions break information into readable chunks for the younger learner. Important vocabulary is in bold print. .... An excellent addition to your science collection." Libr Media Connect

Includes glossary and bibliographical references

Gallant, Roy A.

Water. Benchmark Bks. 2001 48p il (Kaleidoscope) lib bdg $15.95

Grades: 3 4 5   **551.48**
   1. Water
   ISBN 0-7614-1040-6
                                              LC 99-49627

Explains why water, although common, has characteristics which make it an unusual substance

"The large-print [text is] easy to read, and the explanations are clear and concise. Outstanding full-page, full-color photographs appear throughout." SLJ

Includes glossary and bibliographical references

Green, Jen

Mighty rivers. Smart Apple Media 2010 32p il map (Amazing planet earth) lib bdg $28.50

Grades: 4 5 6   **551.48**
   1. Rivers
   ISBN 978-1-59920-371-3 lib bdg; 1-59920-371-5 lib bdg
                                              LC 2008-55498

Starting with a quick introduction to the water cycle, this book shows readers how rivers are formed, and how they, in turn, form waterfalls, carve out canyons, create fertile deltas, cause flooding, and have a great impact on the daily lives of people all over the world

"Chapters are labeled as 'Case Study' or 'Science Report,' making the presentation lively. The concise explanations include just the right number of examples and clear diagrams, and have perfect color photo accompaniments." SLJ

Includes glossary

Kenah, Katharine

Flood warning; Katharine Kenah, Amy Schimler-Safford; [edited by] Tamar Mays. HarperCollins 2016 36 p. color illustrations (hardcover) $17.99

Grades: K 1 2 3   **551.48**
   1. Floods 2. Natural disasters 3. Flood forecasting 4. Flood

damage prevention
   ISBN 006238662X; 9780062386618; 9780062386625
                                              LC 2016936036

This juvenile book on floods, by Katharine Kenah, illustrated by Amy Schimler-Safford, "is a fascinating look into a dangerous natural disaster. Featuring rich vocabulary bolded throughout the text, this book also includes a Find-Out-More section with instructions on how to make a rain gauge and an infographic about saving water at home." (Publisher's note)

"A sidebar offers a short, illustrated list of emergency supplies. A good starting place for learning about floods." Booklist

Lawrence, Ellen

The water beneath your feet; by Ellen Lawrence. Bearport Publishing 2016 24 p. color illustrations (library binding) $23.93

Grades: 1 2 3   **551.48**
   1. Water 2. Aquifers 3. Groundwater 4. Hydrologic cycle
   ISBN 9781943553242; 9781943553587
                                              LC 2015040334

With this book, by by Ellen Lawrence, "readers will learn all about groundwater, including: How does water get into the ground? How does underground water end up in rivers, lakes, and oceans? How do people build wells to access groundwater? And how does groundwater bubble up to the surface to create an oasis in a hot, dry desert?" (Publisher's note)

"The book's unusual focus on a single aspect of the water cycle makes this a useful resource for the classroom." Booklist

Includes bibliographical references (page 24) and index

Lyon, George Ella

★ All the water in the world. Atheneum Books for Young Readers 2011 un il $15.99

Grades: K 1 2 3   **551.48**
   1. Water 2. Hydrologic cycle
   ISBN 978-1-4169-7130-6; 1-4169-7130-0
                                              LC 2010-29530

"Lyrical text compactly describes the hydrological cycle and global contrast between plenty and dearth of the key life-giving substance. ... The text ... [is] lucid yet imaginative, turning scientific and geographical explanation into sonorous sound play. ... Visuals are strong and supple: the text is creatively laid out with pattern-poem precision, and the digital art effortlessly balances crisp collage-style composite ... and splashy, fluid splatters of pigment, providing impeccable rhythm and flow." Bull Cent Child Books

Paul, Miranda

Water is water; a book about the water cycle. Miranda Paul; illustrated by Jason Chin. Roaring Brook Press 2015 40 p. (hardback) $17.99

Grades: PreK K 1 2   **551.48**
   1. Water 2. Cycles 3. Hydrologic cycle
   ISBN 159643984X; 9781596439849
                                              LC 2014031493

This picture book, by Miranda Paul and illustrated by Jason Chin, "highlights various forms water takes as it follows a brother and sister through the year. It includes autumn fog and rain, frozen ponds and falling snow, steam from cups of cocoa, and snowmelt turning dirt to mud." (School Library Journal)

Peters, Marilee

10 rivers that shaped the world; by Marilee Peters; illustrated by Kim Rosen. Firefly Books Ltd 2015 135 p. $24.95

Grades: 4 5 6 7   **551.48**
   1. Rivers 2. Nile River 3. Rhine River 4. Amazon River 5. Tigris

River 6. Yangtze River 7. Euphrates River 8. Mississippi River 9. Thames River (England) 10. Ganges River (India and Bangladesh) 11. Rivers -- History 12. Rivers -- Social aspects -- History
ISBN 1554517397; 9781554517398

This book, by Marilee Peters, illustrated by Kim Rosen, presents "10 surprising stories about the power of rivers through the ages, [including] the Nile's unique flooding patterns, . . . [h]ow medieval robber barons seized -- then lost -- control of the Rhine, [w]hy the Amazon helped scientists discover how species evolve, . . . [and how] the massive Three Gorges Dam displaced over one million Chinese in the Yangtze River Valley." (Publisher's note)

"Each of the 10 rivers detailed in this book has its own chapter, which includes chronological narratives about the groups of people who have called the river home. Full-color maps show each river's headwaters and terminus, and photographs detail major cultural attractions, wildlife, and artifacts. . . . The book is intent on helping young readers make the connection between physical and human geography and on understanding the myriad of forces that shape a people's culture. With a colorful, engaging layout and a unique approach to its topic, this title is a solid entry point to both geography and world history." Booklist

Rauzon, Mark J.
Water, water everywhere; [by] Mark J. Rauzon and Cynthia Overbeck Bix. Sierra Club Bks. for Children 1994 32p il $14.95; pa $6.95
Grades: K 1 2 3   **551.48**
1. Water
ISBN 0-87156-598-6; 0-87156-383-5 pa
                                         LC 92-34521
Describes the forms water takes, how it has shaped Earth, and its importance to life

"Water's vital role in the life of our planet is vividly portrayed in a crisp, economical text that cultivates respect for the environment. . . . Striking, often full-page, color photographs will engage the imagination of young readers." Horn Book Guide

Sayre, April Pulley
★ **Raindrops** roll; April Pulley Sayre. Beach Lane Books 2015 40 p. color illustrations (hardcover) $17.99; (ebook) $15.99
Grades: PreK K 1 2   **551.48**
1. Rain 2. Water 3. Hydrologic cycle 4. Rain and rainfall
ISBN 9781481420648; 9781481420655
                                         LC 2014018995
This book, by April Pulley Sayre, presents a "refreshingly fun and fascinating exploration of rain, raindrops, and the water cycle. . . . Raindrops drop. They plop. They patter. They spatter. And in the process, they make the whole world feel fresh and new and clean." (Publisher's note)

"Not only do the photos beautifully capture water in action but they zoom in on things most kids could see in their own backyards or neighborhoods—an especially useful approach for visual or hands-on learners." Booklist

Spilsbury, Louise
Raging floods; [by] Louise and Richard Spilsbury. Heinemann Library 2010 32p il (Awesome forces of nature) lib bdg $29; pa $7.99
Grades: 3 4 5 6   **551.48**
1. Floods
ISBN 978-1-4329-3782-9 lib bdg; 1-4329-3782-0 lib bdg; 978-1-4329-3789-8 pa; 1-4329-3789-8 pa
                                         LC 2009-37562
First published 2004

This book about floods "is sure to catch the eyes of students and educators. . . . The interesting and accurate facts are presented in an easily understood vocabulary. . . . Incredible eye-catching photographs,

diagrams, or maps are tastefully positioned on every page." Libr Media Connect

Includes glossary and bibliographical references

Waldman, Neil
The **snowflake**; a water cycle story. [by] Neil Waldman. Millbrook Press 2003 un il $14.95
Grades: K 1 2 3   **551.48**
1. Snow 2. Water
ISBN 0-7613-2347-3
                                         LC 2003-4806
Follows the journey of a water droplet through the various stages of the water cycle, from precipitation to evaporation and condensation

"The clear text is undeniably lyrical. . . . The real stunners here, though, are the dazzling, cool-toned paintings that convey the wonders of nature with delicate precision." SLJ

Wells, Robert E.
Did a dinosaur drink this water? A. Whitman 2006 un il $15.95; pa $6.95
Grades: K 1 2 3   **551.48**
1. Water
ISBN 978-0-8075-8839-0; 978-0-8075-8840-6 pa
                                         LC 2006-01039
This describes "the water cycle, explaining that the earth's water has been constantly recycled not just since dinosaur days but for billions of years. The simple text asks good questions and offers clearly worded answers, enhanced by lively, colorful ink-and-watercolor illustrations." Booklist

551.5   Meteorology

Bodden, Valerie
Hurricanes; Valerie Bodden. Creative Education 2012 24 p. color illustrations library $29.95
Grades: 1 2 3 4   **551.5**
1. Hurricanes
ISBN 9781608181476
                                         LC 2010052762
Provides a simple exploration of hurricanes, examining how these massive sea storms develop, how scientists watch for them and measure their strength, and the damage hurricanes can cause.

Includes bibliographical references and index

Branley, Franklyn Mansfield
Air is all around you; by Franklyn M. Branley; illustrated by John O'Brien. newly illustrated ed.; HarperCollinsPublishers 2006 36p il (Let's-read-and-find-out science) hardcover o.p. pa $4.99
Grades: K 1 2   **551.5**
1. Air
ISBN 0-06-059413-6; 0-06-059414-4 lib bdg; 0-06-059415-2 pa
                                         LC 2004005043
A revised and newly illustrated edition of the title first published 1962

This "title introduces the concept of air, its presence in our world, and its importance to the environment. The text describes several interesting facts, clearly explaining ideas and incorporating experiments that are easy to reproduce at home or in the classroom. The appealing artwork supports the narrative. . . . Produced in pen and warm, earthy watercolors, the pictures are filled with amusing details." SLJ

Cosgrove, Brian
Weather; written by Brian Cosgrove. rev ed; DK Publishing 2007 72p il map (DK eyewitness books) $15.99; lib bdg $19.99

Grades: 4 5 6 7 **551.5**
1. Climate 2. Weather 3. Atmosphere
ISBN 978-0-7566-3006-5; 0-7566-3006-1; 978-0-7566-0737-1
lib bdg; 0-7566-0737-X lib bdg
LC 2007-281112
First published 1991 by Knopf
"Discover the world's weather—from heat waves and droughts to blizzards and floods"—Cover. Includes discussion of why the climate may change in the future.

"Accompanying the book are a poster, additional images on CD-ROM, and a useful glossary. Altogether, this book and its supplements are well crafted to motivate young learners about the importance of weather, to deepen their conceptual understanding of it, and to pique their interest in participating in its study." Sci Books Films
Includes glossary

DeLallo, Laura
    Hammered by a heat wave! consultants, Daphne Thompson, Keith C. Heidorn. Bearport Pub. 2010 32p il map (Disaster survivors) lib bdg $25.27
Grades: 4 5 6 7 **551.5**
1. Meteorology
ISBN 978-1-936087-51-8 lib bdg; 1-936087-51-0 lib bdg
"Captivating photos and illustrations and sidebars present interesting facts or brief anecdotes. . . . [This] should be purchased for all school and public libraries as . . . [it gives] a new perspective on the topic." Libr Media Connect
Includes glossary and bibliographical references

Gardner, Robert
    Easy genius science projects with weather; great experiments and ideas. Enslow Publishers 2009 128p il (Easy genius science projects) lib bdg $31.93
Grades: 5 6 7 8 **551.5**
1. Weather 2. Science projects 3. Science -- Experiments
ISBN 978-0-7660-2924-8 lib bdg; 0-7660-2924-7 lib bdg
LC 2008-23972
"Science experiments and science project ideas about weather." Publisher's note
Includes glossary and bibliographical references

    Stellar science projects about Earth's sky; [by] Robert Gardner; illustrations by Tom Labaff. Enslow Elementary 2007 48p il (Rockin' earth science experiments) lib bdg $23.93
Grades: 3 4 5 **551.5**
1. Sky 2. Science projects 3. Science -- Experiments
ISBN 978-0-7660-2732-9 lib bdg; 0-7660-2732-5 lib bdg
LC 2006-13790
This offers experiments on topics such as the weight of air, air pressure, why the sky is blue, why sunsets are red, clouds, stars, and balloons in sky and water
This is "just right for students with limited experience looking for projects that are fairly interesting and manageable." SLJ
Includes glossary and bibliographical references

VanCleave, Janice Pratt
    Janice VanCleave's weather; mind-boggling experiments you can turn into science fair projects. [by] Janice VanCleave. Wiley 1995 89p il (Spectacular science projects series) pa $10.95
Grades: 4 5 6 7 **551.5**
1. Weather 2. Science projects 3. Science -- Experiments
ISBN 0-471-03231-X
LC 94-25646

"Using everyday household items, the reading audience can demonstrate to itself such phenomena as differences in climate at different points on the Earth, lightning, wind direction and intensity, clouds, rain, fronts, etc. Through excellent directions and adequate illustrations, the reader can do 20 simple experiments at little or no cost that demonstrate many aspects of the weather." Sci Books Films
Includes glossary

Whitt, Kelly Kizer
    Solar system forecast; by Kelly Kizer Whitt; illustrated by Laurie Allen Klein. Sylvan Dell Publishing 2012 1 v. (unpaged) col. ill. (hardcover) $17.95; (paperback) $9.95; (English ebook) $9.95
Grades: 1 2 3 **551.5**
1. Weather forecasting 2. Pluto (Dwarf planet) 3. Planets -- Exploration 4. Solar system 5. Planetary meteorology
ISBN 9781607185239; 9781607185321; 9781607185413
LC 2012007599
Author Kelly Kizer Whitt's book is narrated by "a friendly, green-skinned TV weatheralien . . . [who] begins with the Sun . . . and moves on to each planet in turn. There are additional reports for the moon Titan . . . and the dwarf planet Pluto. . . . [The story features] space-suited commuters, melted or frozen science gear and views of prominent storms, from a hurricane on Earth to Jupiter's Great Red Spot. . . . Charts, tables, diagrams, quizzes and other . . . material" provide information on "meteorological data." (Kirkus Reviews)

551.51 Composition, regions, dynamics of atmosphere

Cobb, Vicki
    I face the wind; illustrated by Julia Gorton. HarperCollins Pubs. 2003 un il (Science play) $16.99
Grades: K 1 2 **551.51**
1. Winds 2. Science -- Experiments
ISBN 0-688-17840-5; 0-688-17841-3 lib bdg
LC 2001-26480
Introduces the characteristics and actions of the wind through simple hands-on activities
"All demonstrations . . . are conducted with readily available materials. . . . Streamlined and jargon-fee though the text may be, it gets the basics across in kid-friendly terms. . . . Gorton's strong, angular graphics feature a redheaded little gal with wide-set eyes and a powerful curiosity who alternately serves as wind-tousled subject of forces real but unseen and as demonstrator for each experiment." Bull Cent Child Books

Kaner, Etta
    Who likes the wind? written by Etta Kaner; illustrated by Marie Lafrance. Kids Can Press 2006 un il (Exploring the elements) $14.95
Grades: PreK K 1 2 **551.51**
1. Winds
ISBN 1-55337-839-3
"On each double-page spread, a child expresses why he or she likes the wind ('because it pushes my boat'). The child then wonders how the event happens ('I wonder why the wind blows') and lifts a flap for a scientific explanation. The narrative sections are illustrated in child-friendly acrylics, with the explantions set off in white. Clear diagrams supplement the scientific details." Horn Book Guide

Sayre, April Pulley
    ★ **Stars** beneath your bed; the surprising story of dust. pictures by Ann Jonas. Greenwillow Books 2005 un il $15.99; lib bdg $16.89

Grades: K 1 2 3   **551.51**
    1. Dust
    ISBN 0-06-057188-8; 0-06-057189-6 lib bdg
                                        LC 2004-2108
"Dust gets a poetic treatment in a picture book that tells all about dust's what and where, and sometimes its why. Using free verse, Sayre explains how dust is made everywhere. . . . The watercolors in the well-composed two-page spreads sometimes soar . . . but there are also smaller images . . . that are equally effective." Booklist

551.55   Atmospheric disturbances and formations

Aronin, Miriam
    Mangled by a hurricane! consultant, James L. Franklin. Bearport Pub. 2010 32p il map (Disaster survivors) lib bdg $25.27
Grades: 4 5 6 7   **551.55**
    1. Hurricanes 2. Hurricane Katrina, 2005
    ISBN 978-1-936087-49-5 lib bdg; 1-936087-49-9 lib bdg
"Captivating photos and illustrations and sidebars present interesting facts or brief anecdotes. . . . [This] should be purchased for all school and public libraries as . . . [it gives] a new perspective on the topic." Libr Media Connect
Includes glossary and bibliographical references

Bailer, Darice
    Why does it thunder and lightning? Marshall Cavendish Benchmark 2011 32p il (Tell me why, tell me how) lib bdg $29.93
Grades: 2 3 4 5   **551.55**
    1. Lightning 2. Thunderstorms
    ISBN 978-0-7614-4825-9; 0-7614-4825-X
This offers information about thunder and lightning.
    This title has "clear explanations of natural phenomena, beautiful full-color illustrations, and an uncluttered design. [The] book approaches its topic in a methodical, logical fashion, using examples from a child's world." SLJ

Bodden, Valerie
    Tornadoes; by Valerie Bodden. Creative Education 2012 24 p. color illustrations library $29.95
Grades: 1 2 3 4   **551.55**
    1. Tornadoes
    ISBN 9781608181506
                                        LC 2010053671
Provides a simple exploration of tornadoes, examining how these spinning storms develop, how scientists watch for them and measure their strength, and the damage 'twisters' can cause.
    Includes bibliographical references (p. 24) and index

Carson, Mary Kay
    ★ **Inside** hurricanes. Sterling 2010 48p il map (Inside) $16.95; pa $9.95
Grades: 5 6 7 8   **551.55**
    1. Hurricanes
    ISBN 978-1-4027-5880-5; 1-4027-5880-4; 978-1-4027-7780-6 pa; 1-4027-7780-9 pa
"This trip into the eye of the storm is enveloping in more ways than one. . . . The pages fold up, or down, or left, or right, with every turn guided by an icon familiar to anyone who lives in a storm zone: a circular blue 'Hurricane Evacuation Route' road sign. This constant motion can't help but engage. . . . The design and layout is well above par, featuring excellent cutaways of storm systems, meteorological maps, thrilling photography, and a spectacular foldout Saffir-Simpson Hurricane Scale. The text is packed with info, data, and case studies broken

into digestible chunks, and boxes and sidebars . . . make this . . . very appealing." Booklist

Fleisher, Paul
    Lightning, hurricanes, and blizzards; the science of storms. Lerner Publications 2011 48p il (Weatherwise) lib bdg $29.27
Grades: 4 5 6 7   **551.55**
    1. Blizzards 2. Lightning 3. Hurricanes
    ISBN 978-0-8225-7536-8; 0-8225-7536-1
                                        LC 2009044918
This describes how storms form, where they strike, and what makes them so powerful.
    "Chapters are well-organized and contain clear explanations. The crisp layout contains plenty of captioned photos and diagrams, as well as sidebars that feature interesting facts and suggestions for observations readers can record in their backyards." Horn Book Guide
    Includes glossary and bibliographical references

Fradin, Judith Bloom
    ★ **Hurricanes**; by Judy and Dennis Fradin. National Geographic 2007 48p il (Witness to disaster) $16.95; lib bdg $26.90
Grades: 4 5 6 7   **551.55**
    1. Hurricanes
    ISBN 978-1-4262-0111-0; 1-4262-0111-7; 978-1-4262-0112-7 lib bdg; 1-4262-0112-5 lib bdg
                                        LC 2006-103003
This describes Hurricane Katrina, the science of hurricanes, some hurricanes of the past, and the prediction of hurricanes.
    This offers "dramatic first-person quotes and an array of impressive photographs." Horn Book Guide
    Includes glossary and bibliographical references

    Tornado! the story behind these twisting, turning, spinning, and spiraling storms. by Judith Bloom Fradin & Dennis Brindell Fradin. National Geographic 2011 63p il map (National Geographic kids) $16.95; lib bdg $26.90
Grades: 4 5 6 7   **551.55**
    1. Tornadoes
    ISBN 978-1-4263-0779-9; 1-4263-0779-9; 978-1-4263-0780-5 lib bdg; 1-4263-0780-2 lib bdg
                                        LC 2010042813
"Two of the four chapters describe deadly twisters in the U.S., while the others discuss the science and predictability of tornadoes. Throughout, there are first-person accounts. . . . Excellent color photos make this book a magnet for browsers, while the informative text and diagrams bring meaning to the images and provide content that students will find helpful for reports." Booklist
    Includes glossary and bibliographical references

Gibbons, Gail
    Hurricanes! Holiday House 2009 32p il $17.95
Grades: K 1 2   **551.55**
    1. Hurricanes
    ISBN 978-0-8234-2233-3; 0-8234-2233-X
                                        LC 2009-8761
"Gibbons uses a picture-book format to detail [hurricanes'] destructive power without the information ever becoming too frightening. . . . Gentle watercolors are Gibbons' main weapons here, and the painted panoramas . . . are engagingly tumultuous. . . . Famous hurricanes, from Andrew to Katrina, are among the multitude of . . . topics broached in this intriguing introduction." Booklist

    Tornadoes! Holiday House 2009 32p il $16.95

Grades: K 1 2 3   **551.55**
1. Tornadoes
ISBN 978-0-8234-2216-6; 0-8234-2216-X
LC 2008035828

"Gibbons uses her trademark watercolor cartoon images and simple text to introduce readers to scientific information.... Gibbons's style is appealing and accessible." SLJ

Goin, Miriam Busch
Storms. National Geographic 2009 32p il (National Geographic kids) lib bdg $11.90; pa $3.99
Grades: K 1 2   **551.55**
1. Storms
ISBN 978-1-4263-0395-1 lib bdg; 978-1-4263-0394-4 pa
LC 2008-51883

"Blizzards, monsoons, hurricanes: the excitement of wild, stormy weather will draw beginning readers to this dramatic title with color photos and an interactive text." Booklist

Markovics, Joyce L.
Blitzed by a blizzard! by Joyce Markovics; consultant, Daphne Thompson. Bearport Pub. 2010 32p il map (Disaster survivors) lib bdg $25.27
Grades: 4 5 6 7   **551.55**
1. Blizzards
ISBN 978-1-936087-54-9 lib bdg; 1-936087-54-5 lib bdg
LC 2009-36960

"Captivating photos and illustrations and sidebars present interesting facts or brief anecdotes.... [This] should be purchased for all school and public libraries as ... [it gives] a new perspective on the topic." Libr Media Connect
Includes glossary and bibliographical references

Royston, Angela
Hurricanes! Marshall Cavendish Benchmark 2010 32p il map (Eyewitness disaster) lib bdg $28.50
Grades: 4 5 6   **551.55**
1. Hurricanes
ISBN 978-1-60870-003-5; 1-60870-003-8
LC 2010001800

Provides information about hurricanes through eyewitness accounts from survivors and rescue workers.

"Bold subheadings and color captions break information into readable chunks for the younger learner. Important vocabulary is in bold print.... An excellent addition to your science collection." Libr Media Connect
Includes glossary and bibliographical references

Storms! Marshall Cavendish Benchmark 2010 32p il map (Eyewitness disaster) lib bdg $28.50
Grades: 4 5 6   **551.55**
1. Storms
ISBN 978-1-60870-004-2; 1-60870-004-6
LC 2009041697

Provides information about storms through eyewitness accounts from survivors and rescue workers.

"Bold subheadings and color captions break information into readable chunks for the younger learner. Important vocabulary is in bold print.... An excellent addition to your science collection." Libr Media Connect
Includes glossary and bibliographical references

Rudolph, Jessica
Erased by a tornado! Bearport Pub. 2010 32p il map (Disaster survivors) lib bdg $25.27
Grades: 4 5 6 7   **551.55**
1. Tornadoes
ISBN 978-1-936087-52-5 lib bdg; 1-936087-52-9 lib bdg
LC 2009-34363

"Captivating photos and illustrations and sidebars present interesting facts or brief anecdotes.... [This] should be purchased for all school and public libraries as ... [it gives] a new perspective on the topic." Libr Media Connect
Includes glossary and bibliographical references

Schuh, Mari C.
Tornadoes. Pebble Plus 2010 24p il map (Earth in action) lib bdg $21.32
Grades: K 1 2   **551.55**
1. Tornadoes
ISBN 978-1-4296-3434-2 lib bdg; 1-4296-3434-0 lib bdg
LC 2009-2174

This book "boasts a full-page color photograph.... [It shows] the aftermath of a disaster ... but there are also some diagrams showing physical mechanisms and maps highlighting commonly affected places. The left side of each spread provides a few sentences of large-print text, with short, clear explanations." SLJ
Includes glossary and bibliographical references

Shores, Lori
How to build a tornado in a bottle. Capstone Press 2011 24p il (Hands-on science fun) lib bdg $17.99; pa $6.95
Grades: PreK K 1   **551.55**
1. Tornadoes 2. Science -- Experiments
ISBN 978-1-4296-4493-8 lib bdg; 1-4296-4493-1 lib bdg; 978-1-4296-5577-4 pa; 1-4296-5577-1 pa
LC 2010013585

Simple text and full-color photos instruct readers how to build a tornado in a bottle and explain the science behind the activity.

"Bright, glossy photos and irresistible ideas make these science lessons effortless fun." Booklist
Includes bibliographical references

Silverstein, Alvin
Hurricanes; the science behind killer storms. [by] Alvin Silverstein, Virginia Silverstein, and Laura Silverstein Nunn. Enslow Publishers 2009 48p il map (The science behind natural disasters) lib bdg $23.93
Grades: 4 5 6   **551.55**
1. Hurricanes
ISBN 978-0-7660-2971-2 lib bdg; 0-7660-2971-9 lib bdg
LC 2008-26264

"Examines the science behind hurricanes, including how and where tropical storms form, the various types of tropical storms, how scientists track hurricanes, and provides hurricane safety tips." Publisher's note
Includes glossary and bibliographical references

Tornadoes; the science behind terrible twisters. [by] Alvin Silverstein, Virginia Silverstein, and Laura Silverstein Nunn. Enslow Publishers 2009 48p il map (The science behind natural disasters) lib bdg $23.93
Grades: 4 5 6   **551.55**
1. Tornadoes
ISBN 978-0-7660-2976-7 lib bdg; 0-7660-2976-X lib bdg
LC 2008-29635

"Scientific explanations are accompanied by plentiful color diagrams that will help students to grasp causes and effects. . . . Photos . . . are effective, and are sometimes turned into helpful, lively diagrams by the addition of such features as wind-direction arrows." SLJ

Includes glossary and bibliographical references

Simon, Seymour

★ **Hurricanes**; updated ed; Collins 2007 31p il map $16.99; pa $6.99

Grades: 3 4 5 6   551.55

1. Hurricanes

ISBN 978-0-06-117072-0; 0-06-117072-0; 978-0-06-117071-3 pa; 0-06-117071-2 pa

LC 2007-280766

First published 2003

Discusses where and how hurricanes are formed, the destruction caused by legendary storms, and the precautions to take when a hurricane strikes

This is written "in a simple and precise manner. . . . The photos include computer-enhanced radar images and shots of storm damage from recent (Katrina in 2005) and historical (Glaveston in 1900) times." Sci Books Films

Includes bibliographical references

Spilsbury, Louise

Howling hurricanes; [by] Louise and Richard Spilsbury. rev ed.; Heinemann Library 2010 32p il map (Awesome forces of nature) lib bdg $29; pa $7.99

Grades: 3 4 5 6   551.55

1. Hurricanes

ISBN 978-1-4329-3781-2 lib bdg; 1-4329-3781-2 lib bdg; 978-1-4329-3788-1 pa; 1-4329-3788-X pa

LC 2009037483

First published 2004

This book about hurricanes discusses "causes, characteristics, and relevant science, including progress in predicting the events. Case studies illustrate the human response. Numerous color photographs and sidebars are interwoven into the well-organized and absorbing [narrative]." SLJ

Includes glossary and bibliographical references

Terrifying tornadoes; [by] Louise and Richard Spilsbury. Heinemann Library 2010 32p il map (Awesome forces of nature) lib bdg $29; pa $7.99

Grades: 3 4 5 6   551.55

1. Tornadoes

ISBN 978-1-4329-3786-7 lib bdg; 1-4329-3786-3 lib bdg; 978-1-4329-3793-5 pa; 1-4329-3793-6 pa

LC 2009-37459

First published 2004

This book about tornadoes "is sure to catch the eyes of students and educators. . . . The interesting and accurate facts are presented in an easily understood vocabulary. . . . Incredible eye-catching photographs, diagrams, or maps are tastefully positioned on every page." Libr Media Connect

Includes glossary and bibliographical references

Stewart, Mark

Blizzards and winter storms. Gareth Stevens Pub. 2009 48p il map (The ultimate 10. Natural disasters) lib bdg $31

Grades: 5 6 7 8   551.55

1. Storms 2. Blizzards

ISBN 978-0-8368-9150-8 lib bdg; 0-8368-9150-3 lib bdg

LC 2008-28230

Blizzards and winter storms "are described, while color photos illustrate the resulting damage, conveying a significant part of the information through their captions. . . . An especially useful book." SLJ

Includes glossary and bibliographical references

551.56   Atmospheric electricity and optics

Person, Stephen

Struck by lightning! Bearport Pub. 2010 32p il map (Disaster survivors) lib bdg $25.27

Grades: 4 5 6 7   551.56

1. Lightning

ISBN 978-1-936087-47-1 lib bdg; 1-936087-47-2 lib bdg

"Captivating photos and illustrations and sidebars present interesting facts or brief anecdotes. . . . [This] should be purchased for all school and public libraries as . . . [it gives] a new perspective on the topic." Libr Media Connect

Includes glossary and bibliographical references

Stewart, Melissa

★ **Inside** lightning; illustrations by Cynthia Shaw. Sterling 2011 48p il (Inside . . .) $16.95

Grades: 5 6 7 8   551.56

1. Lightning

ISBN 978-1-4027-5878-2; 1-4027-5878-2

This book about lightning "explores its topic in an engaging way, and the many illustrations work well with adjacent text and captions. . . . The [book's] varied page layouts and attractive and the quality of photos, computer-generated images, original illustrations, and charts is . . . excellent. . . . Featuring a step-by-step, illustrated explanation of lightning formation as well as comments from people who have had close encounters with the phenomenon, Inside Lightning provides a vivid and unusually informative introduction to the subject." Booklist

Includes bibliographical references

551.57   Hydrometeorology

Branley, Franklyn Mansfield

Down comes the rain; by Franklyn M. Branley; illustrated by James Graham Hale. HarperCollins Pubs. 1997 31p il (Let's-read-and-find-out science) hardcover o.p. pa $4.95

Grades: K 1 2 3   551.57

1. Rain 2. Clouds

ISBN 0-06-025338-X; 0-06-445166-6 pa

LC 96-3519

A revised and newly illustrated edition of Rain & hail published 1983 by Crowell

The author explains "how water is recycled, how clouds are formed, and why rain and hail occur. A few easy science activities are included. . . . The pen-and-ink with watercolor wash paintings clearly interpret the concepts presented on each page." SLJ

Snow is falling; by Franklyn M. Branley; illustrated by Holly Keller. HarperCollins Pubs. 2000 33p il (Let's-read-and-find-out science) hardcover o.p. pa $4.95

Grades: K 1   551.57

1. Snow

ISBN 0-06-027990-7; 0-06-027991-5 lib bdg; 0-06-445186-0 pa

LC 98-23106

A revised and newly illustrated edition of the title first published 1963 by Crowell

Describes snow's physical qualities and how quantities of it can be fun as well as dangerous

"Keller's new illustrations are a good match for the spare, informative text. A few easy activities explore snow's different properties, and a list of websites is appended." Horn Book Guide

Cassino, Mark

★ The **story** of snow; the science of winter's wonder. by Mark Cassino, with Jon Nelson; illustrations by Nora Aoyagi. Chronicle Books 2009 33p il $16.99

Grades: 2 3 4 5   551.57

1. Snow

ISBN 978-0-8118-6866-2; 0-8118-6866-4

LC 2009-04368

"Aoyagi's clean ink-and-watercolor diagrams and backgrounds allow the spectacular photographs to take center stage and provide supplemental information. Sure to get young scientists outside in the cold, particularly as it helpfully includes crystal-catching instructions." Kirkus

DePaola, Tomie, 1934-

The **cloud** book; words and pictures by Tomie de Paola. Holiday House 1975 30p il lib bdg $16.95; pa $6.95

Grades: K 1 2 3   551.57

1. Clouds

ISBN 0-8234-0259-2 lib bdg; 0-8234-0531-1 pa

The author instructs "young readers about the ten most common types of clouds, how they were named, and what they mean in terms of changing weather. Actually a very good text to use for early science instruction. Includes a scattering of traditional myths that have clouds as a basis." Adventuring with Books

Ehlert, Lois

★ **Snowballs**. Harcourt Brace & Co. 1995 un il $17; pa $7; bd bk $6.95

Grades: PreK K 1   551.57

1. Snow -- Fiction

ISBN 0-15-200074-7; 0-15-202095-0 pa; 0-15-216275-5 bd bk

LC 94-47183

"Using 'good stuff' like seeds, nuts, corn kernels, and colorful yarn kids create a wonderful snow family. Placed on vertical page spreads, the snow characters extend the full length of the book, a perspective that enhances the drama of their inevitable demise when the sun comes out. Large, well-designed illustrations effectively blend open space, colorful paper cutouts, and real objects." Horn Book Guide

Gibbons, Gail

It's snowing! Holiday House 2011 32p il $17.95

Grades: K 1 2 3   551.57

1. Snow

ISBN 978-0-8234-2237-1

LC 2010029570

Introduces snow, discussing how snowflakes are formed, what causes it to snow, where snow occurs around the world, different types of snowstorms, and what to do during a heavy winter storm.

"This is a crystal-clear introduction that illustrates how snow can be dangerous, but plenty of fun, too." Booklist

Kaner, Etta

Who likes the rain? written by Etta Kaner; llustrated by Marie Lafrance. Kids Can Press 2007 un il (Exploring the elements) $14.95

Grades: PreK K 1 2   551.57

1. Rain

ISBN 978-1-55337-841-9; 1-55337-841-5

On each double-page spread, a child expresses why he or she likes the rain ("because I can jump in puddles"). The child then wonders how the event happens ("I wonder where puddles come from") and lifts a flap for a scientific explanation

"An attractive, straight-forward presentation of concepts related to rain." Booklist

Who likes the snow? written by Etta Kaner; illustrated by Marie Lafrance. Kids Can Press 2006 un il (Exploring the elements) $14.95

Grades: PreK K 1 2   551.57

1. Snow

ISBN 978-1-55337-842-6; 1-55337-842-3

"This slim book is packed with fascinating information about snow. Each spread is divided into three parts: a statement, a query, and, with the turn of a flap, a simply stated scientific explanation. . . . Lafrance's naive acrylic paintings have a flat appearance, as if they were carved of wood, and clearly depict the topics being discussed." SLJ

Libbrecht, Kenneth G.

The **secret** life of a snowflake; an up-close look at the art & science of snowflakes. [by] Kenneth Libbrecht. Voyageur Press 2010 48p il $17

Grades: 3 4 5 6   551.57

1. Snow

ISBN 978-0-7603-3676-2; 0-7603-3676-8

LC 2009-07892

"Extraordinary photographs of individual snowflakes are the true highlight of this informational book. With crisp detail and lit up with colored light, the crystals are mesmerizing in their clarity and brilliance. Libbrecht uses a first-person narration to describe the microphotography process that he uses to create the images and then goes on to outline the life cycle of a snowflake. . . . A solid addition to any science collection, this book will draw in young enthusiasts, and the beautiful photographs will engage casual browsers." SLJ

Martin, Jacqueline Briggs

★ **Snowflake** Bentley; illustrated by Mary Azarian. Houghton Mifflin 1998 un il $16; pa $7.99

Grades: K 1 2 3   551.57

1. Snow 2. Farmers 3. Scientists 4. Photographers 5. Meteorologists

ISBN 0-395-86162-4; 0-547-24829-6 pa

LC 97-12458

Awarded the Caldecott Medal, 1999

A biography of a self-taught scientist who photographed thousands of individual snowflakes in order to study their unique formations

"Azarian's woodblock illustrations, hand tinted with watercolors, blend perfectly with the text and recall the rural Vermont of Bentley's time. . . . The story of this man's life is written with graceful simplicity." SLJ

Rockwell, Anne F.

Clouds; by Anne Rockwell; illustrated by Frané Lessac. Collins 2008 33p il (Let's-read-and-find-out-science) $16.99; pa $5.99

Grades: 1 2 3   551.57

1. Clouds

ISBN 978-0-06-029101-3; 0-06-029101-X; 978-0-06-445220-5 pa; 0-06-445220-4 pa

"Rockwell introduces 11 different types of clouds according to their positions in the atmosphere. . . . The author describes each type of cloud formation, explains where it is found in the sky, and tells what kind of weather is associated with it. Attractive folk-art-style paintings show the clouds and children playing or working outside. The information is solid." SLJ

Schuh, Mari C.

Avalanches. Pebble Plus 2010 24p il (Earth in action) lib bdg $21.32

Grades: K 1 2 **551.57**

1. Avalanches

ISBN 978-1-4296-3437-3 lib bdg; 1-4296-3437-5 lib bdg

LC 2009-2163

Describes avalanches, how they occur, and the damage they cause

This book "boasts a full-page color photograph. . . . [It shows] the aftermath of a disaster . . . but there are also some diagrams showing physical mechanisms and maps highlighting commonly affected places. The left side of each spread provides a few sentences of large-print text, with short, clear explanations." SLJ

Includes glossary and bibliographical references

551.6 Climatology and weather

Aitken, Stephen

Ecosystems at risk; Stephen Aitken. Marshall Cavendish Benchmark 2013 63 p. (Climate crisis) (print) $31.36

Grades: 4 5 6 7 **551.6**

1. Ecology 2. Climate change 3. Biodiversity conservation 4. Climatic changes -- Environmental aspects

ISBN 1608704637; 9781608704637; 9781608706341

LC 2011025243

In this book, by Stephen Aitken, "readers are introduced to topics relating to climatology, thermal expansion, and biodiversity. . . . The case studies . . . provide a global perspective on the ecological concepts being presented. In addition, teachers may find the book helpful in meeting several Common Core literacy standards. . . .The book concludes with . . . ways that individuals can take action to prevent species extinctions, followed by a glossary of conservation-related terms." (Science & Children)

"These sobering overviews present current observable results of climate change and offer scientific predictions about its future effects on the Earth's ecosystems and inhabitants...Suggested websites from educational and action-oriented organizations offer more options. These books should be considered to update collections on this important topic." SLJ

Includes bibliographical references and index

Other titles include:

Animal Life

People

Ocean Life

Plants and Insects

Bailey, Gerry

Changing climate. Gareth Stevens Pub. 2011 48p il map (Planet SOS) lib bdg $31.95; pa $14.05

Grades: 4 5 6 **551.6**

1. Climate -- Environmental aspects

ISBN 978-1-4339-4962-3 lib bdg; 1-4339-4962-8 lib bdg; 978-1-4339-4963-0 pa; 1-4339-4963-6 pa

LC 2010032885

This "well-designed [book presents changing climate] . . . and how [it affects] human beings. With information about water supplies and melting ice and their impact on ecosystems, the discussion . . . of global water levels is especially enlightening. . . . The many large, colorful photos will engage readers and assist them in understanding the important concepts introduced." SLJ

Includes glossary

Baker, Stuart

In temperate zones. Marshall Cavendish Benchmark 2009 32p il map (Climate change) lib bdg $19.95

Grades: 5 6 7 8 **551.6**

1. Forest ecology 2. Greenhouse effect

ISBN 978-0-7614-4441-1 lib bdg; 0-7614-4441-6 lib bdg

LC 2009-5769

The book about climate change in the temperate zones "is perfectly organized for students. . . . Unique layout features serve as signposts and will help focus readers' attention. . . . [The book] features an outstanding chart of possible effects of global warming on the area in question, listing 'Possible Event', 'Predicted Result', and 'Impact' in short, bulleted statements." SLJ

Includes glossary

Evans, Bill

It's raining fish and spiders; by Bill Evans. Forge 2012 xiv, 223 p.p col. ill. (paperback) $18.99

Grades: 5 6 7 8 **551.6**

1. Extreme weather 2. Weather forecasting 3. Weather 4. Severe storms

ISBN 0765321327; 9780765321329

LC 2011278417

This book offers "information, lists, and accounts of personal experiences involving extreme weather by meteorologist and TV personality [Bill] Evans. Included are sections on tornadoes, hurricanes, and blizzards, with a good amount of information on each and . . . photos and diagrams sprinkled throughout." (Booklist)

Includes bibliographical references (p.221-222)

Gibbons, Gail

Weather words and what they mean. Holiday House 1990 un il $16.95; pa $6.95

Grades: K 1 2 3 **551.6**

1. Weather

ISBN 0-8234-0805-1; 0-8234-0952-X pa

LC 89-39515

The author discusses the meaning of meteorological terms such as temperature, air pressure, thunderstorm and moisture

"Gibbons' easily identifiable artistic style works well with her explanations of sometimes misunderstood weather-related terms. Drawings are appealing, attractively arranged, and closely matched to the textual information. . . . An attractive introduction for weather units in the primary grades." SLJ

Hartman, Eve

Climate change; [by] Eve Hartman and Wendy Meshbesher. Raintree 2010 48p il map (Sci-hi: Earth and space science) lib bdg $31.43; pa $8.99

Grades: 4 5 6 7 **551.6**

1. Greenhouse effect 2. Climate -- Environmental aspects

ISBN 978-1-4109-3352-2 lib bdg; 1-4109-3352-0 lib bdg; 978-1-4109-3362-1 pa; 1-4109-3362-8 pa

LC 2009-3538

Examine the causes of climate change, and how scientists gather data about global warming. Learn about the different ways people and nations are combating climate change, and how people and animals adapt to a new climate.

"Multiple colorful sidebars and large and small diagrams and photographs will help students to grasp the fundamentals being discussed, and the easy but interesting science experiments will act as further reinforcements." SLJ

Includes glossary and bibliographical references

Kallio, Jamie

    12 things to know about climate change; by Jamie Kallio. 12-Story Library 2015 32 p color illustrations paperback $9.95; hardcover $31.35

    Grades: 4 5 6   **551.6**

    1. Climate change 2. Global warming

    ISBN 1632350882; 9781632350886; 1632350289; 9781632350282

    Describes twelve factors involved in climate change, including that the world is warming up, that farming and deforestation play a role in the process, and that it could change ecosystems.

    Includes bibliographic references and index

Parker, Steve, 1952-

    Climate. QEB Pub. 2010 32p il (QEB changes in . . .) lib bdg $28.50

    Grades: 3 4 5 6   **551.6**

    1. Climate

    ISBN 978-1-59566-776-2 lib bdg; 1-59566-776-8 lib bdg

                    LC 2008-56068

    "The information is presented in brief paragraphs and sidebars. Suggestions for kids to help improve the planet are sprinkled throughout. . . . Students will enjoy this appealing layout and the information can spark further research on the topic[s]. . . . Either digitally or on paper, students could make fantastic presentations using a similar design." Libr Media Connect

    Includes glossary

Royston, Angela

    Looking at weather and seasons; how do they change? [by] Angela Royston. Enslow Publishers 2008 32p il (Looking at science: how things change) lib bdg $22.60

    Grades: 1 2 3   **551.6**

    1. Seasons 2. Weather

    ISBN 978-0-7660-3093-0 lib bdg; 0-7660-3093-8 lib bdg

                    LC 2007-24515

    "Fills a huge void in elementary science collections. . . . Text is arranged in succinct 'chunks,' giving important facts without overwhelming readers. . . . [This] is an essential addition." Libr Media Connect

    Includes glossary and bibliographical references

Simpson, Kathleen

    ★ **Extreme** weather; science tackles global warming and climate change. by Kathleen Simpson; Jonathan D.W. Kahl, consultant. National Geographic 2008 64p il map (National Geographic investigates) $17.95; lib bdg $27.90

    Grades: 4 5 6 7   **551.6**

    1. Greenhouse effect 2. Climate -- Environmental aspects

    ISBN 978-1-4263-0359-3; 1-4263-0359-9; 978-1-4263-0281-7 lib bdg; 1-4263-0281-9 lib bdg

    This "is a well-written and engaging book. . . . Excellent descriptions of how and why these various weather patterns occur are presented. The book includes dramatic photographs and clear diagrams." Sci Books Films

    Includes glossary and bibliographical references

551.609   History, geographic treatment, biography

Christie, Peter

    50 climate questions; a blizzard of blistering facts. Peter Christie; illustrated by Ross Kinnaird. Annick Press 2012 117 p. ill. (50 Questions) (paperback) $14.95; (hardcover) $22.95; (ebook) $10.99

    Grades: 4 5 6 7   **551.609**

    1. Climate 2. Climate change 3. Climate -- History

    ISBN 155451374X; 9781554513741; 9781554513758; 9781554515165

    This book by Peter Christie presents a "survey of the effects of climate through history and prehistory." (Kirkus Reviews) "Topics include global warming's effect on the Arctic . . . and how a cooling climate 2.5 million years ago forced early humans to diversify their diets. Christie also provides insight into weather events throughout history -- for example, how weather change contributed to civil unrest that spawned the French Revolution." (Publishers Weekly)

551.63   Weather forecasting and forecasts, reporting and reports

Breen, Mark

    ★ The **kids'** book of weather forecasting; build a weather station, read the sky & make predictions. with meteorologist Mark Breen and Kathleen Friestad; illustrations by Michael Kline. Williamson 2000 140p il maps music pa $12.95

    Grades: 4 5 6 7   **551.63**

    1. Weather forecasting 2. Science -- Experiments

    ISBN 1-88559-339-2

                    LC 99-89954

    A hands-on introduction to the science of meteorology, explaining how to make equipment to measure rainfall, wind direction, and humidity, record measurements and observations in a weather log, make weather predictions, and perform other related activities

    "A useful, accessible book illustrated with black-and-white diagrams and cartoons." SLJ

    Includes bibliographical references

Fleisher, Paul

    Doppler radar, satellites, and computer models; the science of weather forecasting. Lerner Publications 2010 48p il map (Weatherwise) lib bdg $29.27

    Grades: 4 5 6   **551.63**

    1. Weather forecasting

    ISBN 978-0-8225-7535-1; 0-8225-7535-3

                    LC 2009-44919

    This describes how scientists predict the weather, the tools and instruments that help them make forecasts, and how far in advance can they make good predictions.

    "Chapters are well-organized and contain clear explanations. The crisp layout contains plenty of captioned photos and diagrams, as well as sidebars that feature interesting facts and suggestions for observations readers can record in their backyards." Horn Book Guide

    Includes glossary and bibliographical references

Gibbons, Gail

    Weather forecasting. Four Winds Press 1987 un il hardcover o.p. pa $5.99

    Grades: K 1 2 3   **551.63**

    1. Weather forecasting

    ISBN 0-689-71683-4 pa

                    LC 86-7602

    "Any child can learn the basic concepts from the text at the bottom of each page, while the precocious can garner an impressive weather vocabulary by absorbing the terms labeled and defined within the artwork. Brightly illustrated with the artist's usual bold, flat colors, this book will serve as an appealing introduction to weather forecasting for young children." Booklist

552   Petrology

Aston, Dianna Hutts

A **rock** is lively; Dianna Hutts Aston, Sylvia Long. Chronicle Books 2012 40 p. (alk. paper) $16.99

Grades: 3 4 5 6   552

1. Rocks 2. Minerals 3. Rocks 4. Minerals
ISBN 1452106452; 9781452106458

LC 2011048375

This book by Dianna Hutts Aston explores "seemingly sedentary world of rocks and minerals, showing them to be anything but (when you know your geology). Boiling underground, freezing in space, colorful or drab, enormous or minuscule, health food (grits for gizzards), tools for prehistoric man and modern chimps, canvas for paleolithic art or construction material for the Taj Mahal -- rocks get around." (School Library Journal)

Calver, Paul

Rocks, crystals, and gems. Barron's Educational Series, Inc. 2016 32 p. color illustrations $6.99

Grades: 4 5 6 7   552

1. Gems 2. Rocks 3. Crystals
ISBN 1438008287; 9781438008288

LC 2015956071

In this children's book by Toby Reynolds and illustrated by Paul Calver, part of the Visual Explorers series, "engaging text, detailed facts, and impressive statistics give children exciting scientific insight into the rocks, crystals, and gems...and the world around them. A glossary at the end of the book helps reinforce the information. Parents, teachers, and librarians will want to collect all of the books in this series to create a very cool first encyclopedia to build early research skills." (Publisher's note)

"Inexpensive and relatively sturdy, these large-format paperbacks make for a visually enticing series." Booklist

Faulkner, Rebecca

Igneous rock; [by] Rebecca Faulkner. Raintree 2007 48p il (Geology rocks!) lib bdg $31.43; pa $8.99

Grades: 4 5 6   552

1. Rocks
ISBN 978-1-4109-2747-7 lib bdg; 1-4109-2747-4 lib bdg; 978-1-4109-2755-2 pa; 1-4109-2755-5 pa

LC 2006037174

This "describes all three categories of rocks and what distinguishes them from each other, minerals, identification of igneous rocks, and their formation through volcanic activity. . . . [The book] includes quality color photographs and diagrams that do an exemplary job of expanding on the topics covered." SLJ

Includes glossary and bibliographical references

Metamorphic rock. Raintree 2007 48p il (Geology rocks!) lib bdg $31.43; pa $8.99

Grades: 4 5 6   552

1. Rocks
ISBN 978-1-4109-2749-1 lib bdg; 1-4109-2749-0 lib bdg; 978-1-4109-2757-6 pa; 1-4109-2757-1 pa

LC 2006037063

"This title covers the following: Squeeze and heat; Crust, mantle, and core; The world's rocks; Marvelous Metamorphism; Metamorphic rock types; Hard beauty; Metamorphic landforms." Publisher's note

Includes glossary and bibliographical references

Sedimentary rock; [by] Rebecca Faulkner. Raintree 2007 48p il (Geology rocks!) lib bdg $31.43; pa $8.99

Grades: 4 5 6   552

1. Rocks
ISBN 978-1-4109-2748-4 lib bdg; 1-4109-2748-2 lib bdg; 978-1-4109-2756-9 pa; 1-4109-2756-3 pa

LC 2006037173

This "covers the Earth's structure, how these rocks are formed, fossils, and the various types. [The] book includes quality color photographs and diagrams that do an exemplary job of expanding on the topics covered." SLJ

Includes glossary and bibliographical references

Gans, Roma

Let's go rock collecting; illustrated by Holly Keller. newly il ed; HarperCollins Pubs. 1997 31p il (Let's-read-and-find-out science) hardcover o.p. pa $5.99

Grades: K 1 2   552

1. Rocks -- Collectors and collecting
ISBN 0-06-027282-1; 0-06-027283-X lib bdg; 0-06-027283-X pa

LC 95-44999

A revised and newly illustrated edition of Rock collecting, published 1984 by Crowell

Describes the formation and characteristics of igneous, metamorphic, and sedimentary rocks and how to recognize and collect them

"The excellent diagrams, full-color photographs of specimens, and minor textual changes clarify the concepts (for example, Mohs' scale of hardness) and extend the presentation. . . . The pair of youngsters featured in Keller's brightly colored illustrations . . . convey the joys of being a rock hound." SLJ

Green, Dan

Rocks and minerals; a gem of a read! by Dan Green and Simon Basher; illustrated by Simon Basher. Kingfisher 2009 128p il pa $8.99

Grades: 5 6 7 8   552

1. Rocks 2. Minerals
ISBN 978-0-7534-6314-7 pa; 0-7534-6314-8 pa

This "presents a portrait gallery of 56 rocks and minerals (plus four kinds of fossils) composed of smiling, round-headed, usually peanut-shaped cartoon figures wearing or bearing distinctive identifiers. . . . The entries make lighthearted but unexpectedly meaty reading." Booklist

Honovich, Nancy

Rocks & minerals; Nancy Honovich. National Geographic 2016 160 p. color illustrations $22.90

Grades: 4 5 6 7 8   552

1. Rocks 2. Minerals
ISBN 1426323018; 1426323026; 9781426323010; 9781426323027

LC 2016304812

This book, by Nancy Honovich, is a "fact-packed guide to rocks and minerals. . . . Created for the ultimate explorer, this book gives kids the knowledge and skills they need to identify just about anything they dig up and become true rock hounds. With tons of info and interactivity prompts, it's the perfect companion for backyard or field trip, camping and vacation. Durable and portable, it's just right for pocket or backpack." (Publisher's note)

"A useful supplement for elementary and middle-school science curricula, the book includes a well-considered glossary and further resources." booklist

Includes bibliographical references (page 157) and index
Rocks and minerals

Rocks and minerals; facts at your fingertips. DK Pub. 2012 156 p. col. ill., map (Pocket genius) (hardcover) $7.99

Grades: 5 6 7 8   552
1. Rocks 2. Minerals
ISBN 0756692857; 9780756692858

LC 2011277725

This book, part of the "Pocket Genius" encyclopedia series, "profiles nearly 200 types of rocks and minerals from volcanic rocks and granite to sparkling diamonds and explosive sulfur, and tells what they are made of, how they are formed and what they are used for." It "offers a . . . catalog-style presentation, which clearly lays out individual subcategories." (Publisher's note)

Salas, Laura Purdie

A **rock** can be . . . by Laura Purdie Salas; illustrated by Violeta Dabija. Millbrook Press 2015 32 p. color illustrations (lib. bdg) $17.99

Grades: PreK K 1 2 3   552
1. Rocks 2. Stories in rhyme
ISBN 1467721107; 9781467721103

LC 2014009377

"Laura Purdie Salas's lyrical rhyming text and Violeta Dabija's . . . illustrations show how rocks decorate and strengthen the world around them. Rocks may seem like boring, static objects--until you discover that a rock can spark a fire, glow in the dark, and provide shelters of all shapes and sizes." (Publisher's note)

"The ideas expressed in this picture book's pithy text are varied and wide-ranging. Each two-word phrase appears on its own page, accompanied by a luminous illustration. . . . The sometimes cryptic phrases create a natural guessing game, and an appended section offers a paragraph of text explaining each one." Booklist

Smithsonian Institution

Extreme **rocks** & minerals! Q & A. Collins 2007 47p il $17.99; pa $6.99

Grades: 4 5 6   552
1. Rocks 2. Minerals
ISBN 978-0-06-089982-0; 0-06-089982-4; 978-0-06-089981-3 pa; 0-06-089981-6 pa

LC 2007001760

This describes types of rocks and minerals, how they are formed, and how people use them.

"It's hard to beat this title for a clear, accurate, and appealing survey. Illustrations are key to this subject, and the range of crisp photos is excellent." SLJ

Includes bibliographical references

Tomecek, Steve

Everything **rocks** and minerals. National Geographic 2011 64p il (National Geographic kids) lib bdg $25.90; pa $12.95

Grades: 3 4 5 6   552
1. Rocks 2. Minerals
ISBN 978-1-4263-0801-7 lib bdg; 1-4263-0801-9 lib bdg; 978-1-4263-0768-3 pa; 1-4263-0768-3 pa

LC 2010038112

A book about rocks and minerals.

"Exploding with astounding full-color photographs and written in an appealing conversational tone, [this book is] for every kid. . . . The [text] will keep kids interested and turning pages to discover more and more facts. . . . [This] compelling, browseable, and completely engrossing [title] will delight readers." SLJ

Includes glossary and bibliographical references

Rocks & minerals; illustrated by Kyle Poling. National Geographic 2010 32p il (Jump into science) $16.95; lib bdg $25.90

Grades: 1 2 3   552
1. Rocks 2. Minerals
ISBN 978-1-4263-0538-2; 1-4263-0538-9; 978-1-4263-0539-9 lib bdg; 1-4263-0539-7 lib bdg

LC 2010-07145

"Playful and interactive, this picture-book title . . . makes geology accessible with colorful diagrams, photos, and computer graphics. The spreads discuss how the three main types of rock are formed, as well as facts about fossils and the more than 2,500 different minerals on the planet. The visuals will capture kids." Booklist

VanCleave, Janice Pratt

Janice VanCleave's **rocks** and minerals; mind-boggling experiments you can turn into science fair projects. Wiley 1996 90p il (Spectacular science projects series) pa $10.95

Grades: 4 5 6 7   552
1. Rocks 2. Minerals 3. Science projects 4. Science -- Experiments
ISBN 0-471-10269-5

LC 95-10324

"VanCleave presents stunningly clear, direct, and informative projects. They are generally simple enough for self-directed students to do on their own, but a teacher's guidance would be helpful." SLJ

Includes glossary

552.5   Sedimentary rocks

Otfinoski, Steven

Quicksand; by Steven Otfinoski. Children's Press, an imprint of Scholastic Inc. 2016 48 p. illustrations (some color) (pbk.) $6.95

Grades: 3 4 5   552.5
1. Quicksand
ISBN 0531225119; 9780531222959; 9780531225110

LC 2015020987

In this book, by Steven Otfinoski, part of the True Book Extreme Earth series, "learn all about quicksand, from how it is formed to what you should do if you encounter it." (Publisher's note)

"The authors discuss scientific advances in prediction, efforts to mitigate deaths and injury, and locations where the phenomena occur most frequently. They also offer survival tips." SLJ

Includes bibliographical references and index

553.2   Carbonaceous materials

Green, Robert

Coal. Cherry Lake Pub. 2010 32p il (21st century skills library. Power up!) lib bdg $27.07

Grades: 4 5 6   553.2
1. Coal
ISBN 978-1-60279-508-2 lib bdg; 1-60279-508-8 lib bdg

LC 2008-44184

This "provides a basic introduction to [coal]. . . . The writing is clear and succinct, and the information is accurate, timely and unbiased. The plentiful photographs are outstanding and reinforce the text. . . . Certain to appeal to young readers and their teachers." Libr Media Connect

Includes glossary and bibliographical references

Tagliaferro, Linda

How does a plant become oil? Raintree 2010 32p il (How does it happen?) lib bdg $27.50; pa $7.99

Grades: 3 4 5 **553.2**
1. Gasoline 2. Petroleum
ISBN 978-1-4109-3443-7 lib bdg; 1-4109-3443-8 lib bdg; 978-1-4109-3451-2 pa; 1-4109-3451-9 pa
LC 2008-52290
"Information is clearly presented using a large font, diagrams, and photographs formatted to resemble Polaroid pictures. . . . A first-rate job answering some important scientific questions." SLJ
Includes glossary and bibliographical references

553.4 Metals and semimetals

Raum, Elizabeth
The **story** behind gold. Heinemann Library 2009 32p il map (True stories) lib bdg $28.21
Grades: 3 4 5 **553.4**
1. Gold 2. Gold mines and mining
ISBN 978-1-4329-2340-2 lib bdg; 1-4329-2340-4 lib bdg
LC 2008037525
This offers history, ephemera, and basic facts about gold, gold mining, and the uses of gold
Includes bibliographical references

553.6 Other economic materials

Kurlansky, Mark
★ The **story** of salt; [illustrated by] S. D. Schindler. G.P. Putnam's Sons 2006 48p il map $16.99
Grades: 3 4 5 6 **553.6**
1. Salt
ISBN 0-399-23998-7
LC 2005-032629
An adaptation of the author's title for adults: Salt: a world history (2002)
"The informal narrative and the exquisitely detailed, sometimes playful ink-and-watercolor illustrations dramatize the sweeping world history of salt's essential role in human life—from prehistoric times and the early voyages of discovery through the breakthrough of refrigeration and the latest drilling technology." Booklist
Includes bibliographical references

Moore, Heidi
The **story** behind salt. Heinemann Library 2009 32p il map (True stories) lib bdg $28.21
Grades: 3 4 5 **553.6**
1. Salt
ISBN 978-1-4329-2348-8 lib bdg; 1-4329-2348-X lib bdg
LC 2008037390
This describes the properties of salt and how it is used, including its history and miscellaneous facts, answering such questions as: Why is the sea salty? Why is it so easy to float in the Dead Sea? Why do people put salt on icy roads?
Includes bibliographical references

553.7 Water

Banyard, Antonia
Water wow! a visual exploration. by Paula Ayer, Antonia Banyard, Belle Wuthrich. Annick Press 2016 64 p. (hardcover) $22.95

Grades: 3 4 5 6 **553.7**
1. Water
ISBN 1554518229; 9781554518227
In this children's book, by Paula Ayer, Antonia Banyard, and Belle Wuthrich, is "a colorful infographic look at the many surprising and fascinating facts about water. Where did water come from before it got to Earth? Why is the water you drink the same stuff that was around when dinosaurs were alive? If water can't be created or destroyed, how can we run out? Find out the answers to these and many more intriguing questions." (Publisher's note)
"Ayer's simple narrative, set largely within text and callout boxes, tastefully surrounds Wuthrich's colorful display of photographs, diagrams, clear illustrations, charts, and maps. Unique to the book's design is providing young readers with a diverse worldview in an effort to help them better understand how water affects people on the earth." Booklist
Includes bibliographical references and index.

Lauw, Darlene
Water; {by Darlene Lauw and Lim Cheng Puay} Crabtree 2003 31p il (Science alive!) lib bdg $21.28; pa $7.95
Grades: 3 4 5 6 **553.7**
1. Water 2. Science -- Experiments
ISBN 0-7787-0567-6 lib bdg; 0-7787-0613-3 pa
LC 2002-11640
Uses simple experiments to demonstrate the properties of water
"The directions are kid friendly, and the graphics that support them are very helpful. . . . The science content is within the range of understanding of an upper elementary school student." Sci Books Films
Includes glossary

Strauss, Rochelle
★ **One** well; the story of water on Earth. written by Rochelle Strauss; illustrated by Rosemary Woods. Kids Can Press 2007 32p il $17.95
Grades: 4 5 6 **553.7**
1. Water
ISBN 978-1-55337-954-6; 1-55337-954-3
"Looking at all the water on Earth . . . as 'One Well' into which all life dips to survive, Strauss presents a timely discussion of the use and abuse of a not-so-limitless resource. Liberally sprinkled with interesting facts, . . . [the book has a] readable text. . . . Woods's delicate paintings keep perfect step and provide a gentle framework for the plentiful statistical snippets." SLJ

Wick, Walter
★ A **drop** of water; a book of science and wonder. written and photographed by Walter Wick. Scholastic 1997 40p il $16.95
Grades: 4 5 6 **553.7**
1. Water
ISBN 0-590-22197-3
LC 95-30068
"This title is an elegant synthesis of science and art. . . . The close-up photographs are breathtakingly distinct; and the clarity provided by the combination of concept, text, and photography of this quality is noteworthy." Bull Cent Child Books

553.8 Gems

Moore, Heidi
The **story** behind diamonds. Heinemann Library 2009 32p il (True stories) lib bdg $28.21

Grades: 3 4 5   **553.8**
1. Diamonds
ISBN 978-1-4329-2345-7 lib bdg; 1-4329-2345-5 lib bdg
LC 2008043374
This describes the history, ephemera, basic facts, and uses of diamonds
Includes bibliographical references

557   Earth sciences of North America

Chin, Jason
Grand Canyon; Jason Chin. Roaring Brook Press 2017 56 p. color illustrations (hardcover) $19.99
Grades: 1 2 3 4 5 6   **557**
1. Grand Canyon (Ariz.) 2. Geology 3. Natural history
ISBN 1596439505; 9781596439504
LC 2016025024
This book, by Jason Chin, focuses on "the Grand Canyon. Home to an astonishing variety of plants and animals that have lived and evolved within its walls for millennia, the Grand Canyon is much more than just a hole in the ground. Follow a father and daughter as they make their way through the cavernous wonder, discovering life both present and past." (Publisher's note)
"With vivid imagination, a crystal-clear grasp of the facts, and brilliant artwork, this illuminating look at one of the planet's most fascinating features will entrance young readers." Booklist
Includes bibliographical references

560   Paleontology

Aliki
Fossils tell of long ago; rev ed; Crowell 1990 32p il (Let's-read-and-find-out science book) hardcover o.p. pa $4.95
Grades: K 1 2 3   **560**
1. Fossils
ISBN 0-06-445093-7 pa
LC 89-17247
First published 1972
"Information about how fossils are formed and discovered is presented in simple text and an appealing variety of colorful illustrations. Includes directions for creating a fossil." Sci Child

Barner, Bob
Dinosaurs roar, butterflies soar! Chronicle Books 2009 un il $16.99
Grades: K 1 2 3   **560**
1. Fossils 2. Dinosaurs 3. Butterflies
ISBN 978-0-8118-5663-8; 0-8118-5663-1
LC 2008016783
"This gently informative book describes the role butterflies played in helping dinosaurs and their environment flourish. The main text offers a simpler narrative than the supplementary and more detailed one in small type that appears below or next to it. . . . A few of the predominant theories about the dinosaurs' extinction and explanations of the continuing survival of butterflies are put forth. . . . Barner's illustrations are, as always, fantastically bright, eye-catching cut-paper collages. A useful, engaging, and illuminating book." SLJ

Bonner, Hannah
★ When fish got feet, sharks got teeth, and bugs began to swarm; a cartoon prehistory of life long before dinosaurs. written and illustrated by Hannah Bonner. National Geographic 2007 45p il $16.95; lib bdg $25.90
Grades: 2 3 4 5   **560**
1. Prehistoric animals
ISBN 978-1-4263-0078-3; 1-4263-0078-6; 978-1-4263-0079-0 lib bdg; 1-4263-0079-4 lib bdg
LC 2006-20768
"Bonner explores life on Earth during the Silurian and Devonian periods. . . . Bonner's clear, engaging writing conveys plenty of information without overwhelming readers, and her illustrations offer fascinating visual representations of unusual creatures and landscapes." SLJ

Bradley, Timothy J.
★ Paleo bugs; survival of the creepiest. written and illustrated by Timothy J. Bradley. Chronicle Books 2008 44p il $15.99
Grades: 4 5 6 7   **560**
1. Fossils 2. Insects 3. Prehistoric animals
ISBN 978-0-8118-6022-2; 0-8118-6022-1
LC 2007-18174
This offers an "eye-widening gallery of extinct arthropods, from the mayfly-like heptagenia to a seven-foot-long arthropleura. . . . Bradley decks out each of his painted figures in bright hues, poses them in natural settings . . . and sets them aside a human hand or body in silhouette to suggest scale. . . . Readers will . . . pore over the pictures and come away knowing more about both these extinct animals and their modern descendants." Booklist
Includes glossary and bibliographical references

Brown, Charlotte Lewis
Beyond the dinosaurs; monsters of the air and sea. by Charlotte Lewis Brown; pictures by Phil Wilson. HarperCollinsPublishers 2007 30p il (I can read!) $15.99; lib bdg $16.89
Grades: K 1 2 3   **560**
1. Fossils 2. Prehistoric animals
ISBN 978-0-06-053056-3; 0-06-053056-1; 978-0-06-053057-0 lib bdg; 0-06-053057-X lib bdg
LC 2007014462
"This introduction to creatures 'just as strange and wonderful as any dinosaur' pairs a straightforward text with action-packed, life-like illustrations. . . . [It has] a spread devoted to each of 11 prehistoric animals, including the Elasmosaurus, Hainosaurus , and Archaeopteryx. Helpful pronunciation guides are included. Readers of this book will get a close-up feel for life millions of years ago." SLJ

Brown, Don
★ Rare treasure: Mary Anning and her remarkable discoveries. Houghton Mifflin 1999 un il hardcover o.p. pa $5.95
Grades: K 1 2 3   **560**
1. Fossils 2. Paleontologists
ISBN 0-395-92286-0; 0-618-31081-9 pa
LC 98-32372
Describes the life of the English girl whose discovery of an Ichthyosaurus fossil led to a lasting interest in other prehistoric animals
"Brown dwells on Mary's self-determination, focusing on her adventurous spirit . . . and lifelong quest for knowledge in her chosen field of study. . . . The understated watercolors suit the mood. Their subdued palette (ocean blues, sand browns) and simple compositions are undistracting." Bull Cent Child Books

Brown, Grace
Explore Fossils! With 25 Great Projects. Cynthia Light Brown and Grace Brown; illustrated by Bryan Stone. Nomad Press 2016 96 p. color illustrations $14.95; (ebook) $9.99

Grades: 2 3 4 5 **560**
1. Fossils 2. Prehistoric animals
ISBN 1619303310; 9781619303317; 9781619303355; 9781619303324

LC 2016001262

This book in the Explore Your World series, by Cynthia Light Brown and Grace Brown, illustrated by Bryan Stone, "introduces young readers to the history of life on Earth as revealed by fossils. Kids learn how fossils form and about the different types of fossils and the world of long ago—its landscape and the plants and animals that lived then. . . . Activities include creating plaster fossils . . . and exploring what might have caused mass extinctions." (Publisher's note)

"Clear, straightforward writing helps introduce sometimes complex topics like radiometric dating, as well as how human understanding of dinosaurs has changed through research and discovery." Pub Wkly

Includes bibliographical references (pages 89-90) and index.

Camper, Cathy
★ **Bugs** before time; prehistoric insects and their relatives. illustrated by Steve Kirk. Simon & Schuster Bks. for Young Readers 2002 un il $16.95
Grades: 4 5 6 7 **560**
1. Fossils 2. Insects
ISBN 0-689-82092-5

LC 98-22872

Describes the physical characteristics, habits, and natural environment of various prehistoric insects some of which, including cockroaches, centipedes, and dragonflies, have survived into the present day

"A handsome introduction to prehistoric insects and other arthropods. . . . [Includes] up-to-date, conversational text and informative captions and date boxes. . . . Kirk's eye-catching, realistic watercolors portray a fascinating array of creatures." SLJ

Includes glossary and bibliographical references

Forbes, Scott
How to be a dinosaur hunter; your globe-trotting, time-travelling guide. Lonely Planet 2013 159 p. ill., maps. $17.99
Grades: 3 4 5 6 **560**
1. Fossils 2. Dinosaurs
ISBN 1743219083; 9781743219089

". . . Assuming that readers are embarking on a journey through both time and space to learn about and find dinosaurs, this guide supplies tips for budding paleontologists on everything from what to pack to how to outrun an enormous meat eater. Children are invited to explore three periods of time . . . Triassic, Jurassic, and Cretaceous. Scientific data is made easily accessible, including new discoveries. . . . The full-color, cartoon illustrations offer numerous sidebars with supplemental facts and asides filled with puns, jokes, and other humorous elements that will appeal to children. Though the volume is best suited for casual browsing, a thorough index makes it a useful tool for research projects as well. Recommended for most collections." SLJ.

Gray, Susan H.
Paleontology the study of prehistoric life; Susan H. Gray. Children's Press 2012 48 p.
Grades: 2 3 4 5 **560**
1. Paleontology
ISBN 0329917145; 0531246809; 0531282740; 9780329917142; 9780531246801; 9780531282748

LC 2011030965

This book by Susan H. Gray provides an introduction to paleontology for young readers. It "presents general information about paleontolo-

gists . . . [and] what they learn about prehistoric animals and vegetation by studying them." (Open Library)

Includes bibliographical references (p. 44) and index

Holmes, Thom
★ **Dinosaur** scientist; careers digging up the past. Enslow Publishers 2009 128p il (Wild science careers) lib bdg $31.93
Grades: 5 6 7 8 **560**
1. Fossils 2. Vocational guidance
ISBN 978-0-7660-3053-4 lib bdg; 0-7660-3053-9 lib bdg

LC 2008-19634

"A great read for middle school students, the book provides vocational guidance while introducing the reader to a challenging, but very exciting, career as a paleontologist." Sci Books Films

Includes glossary and bibliographical references

Jenkins, Steve
★ **Prehistoric** actual size. Houghton Mifflin Co. 2005 un il $16
Grades: K 1 2 3 **560**
1. Prehistoric animals 2. Dinosaurs
ISBN 0-618-53578-0

LC 2004-25124

Jenkins "provides portraits of animals that flourished long, long ago. . . . [Each animal] receives a caption including common name or scientific name (pronunciation provided), general era of its flourishing, and its overall body size. . . . Grades three to seven." (Bull Cent Child Books)

Illustrated with cut-paper artwork, "the animals pictured here include the minuscule protozoa; . . . the eight-foot-tall 'terror bird'; and the Giganotosaurus. . . . The most arresting spreads are those in which the animal is too large to picture in its entirety. . . . Information about and an illustration of the entire creature (not to scale) completes this colorful volume." Booklist

Leedy, Loreen
My teacher is a dinosaur; and other prehistoric poems, jokes, riddles, and amazing facts. written and illustrated by Loreen Leedy. Marshall Cavendish Childrens 2010 47p il $17.99
Grades: 3 4 5 6 **560**
1. Geology 2. Earth sciences 3. Prehistoric animals
ISBN 978-0-7614-5708-4; 0-7614-5708-9

LC 2009052901

This "introduces readers to the history of the Earth and its plants and animals. Children will have no problem following the succession of life through the pages. . . . Each spread presents one topic with a poem conveying the primary information; surrounding that poem are goofy riddles, factlets and question-limericks that expand on it. The pages are unapologetically jam-packed with information, but they never overwhelm." Kirkus

Spilsbury, Richard
Fossils; [by] Richard and Louise Spilsbury. Heinemann Library 2011 32p il (Let's rock) $29; pa $7.99
Grades: 4 5 6 **560**
1. Fossils
ISBN 978-1-4329-4682-1; 1-4329-4682-X; 978-1-4329-4690-6 pa; 1-4329-4690-0 pa

LC 2010022233

"Enhanced by plenty of photos, digital paintings, and diagrams, [this examination] of [fossils treats its topic] in unusual detail. [It] describes distinguishing characteristics, creation, history, . . . and human uses in [a] central [narrative] with additional notes, suggestions for activities during walks outside, and occasional thumbnail biographies of scientists in side boxes. [The] volume ends with a simple activity." SLJ

Includes bibliographical references

Stewart, Melissa

How does a bone become a fossil? Raintree 2010 32p il (How does it happen?) lib bdg $27.50; pa $7.99

Grades: 3 4 5   560

1. Fossils

ISBN 978-1-4109-3445-1 lib bdg; 1-4109-3445-4 lib bdg; 978-1-4109-3453-6 pa; 1-4109-3453-5 pa

LC 2008-52596

"Information is clearly presented using a large font, diagrams, and photographs formatted to resemble Polaroid pictures. . . . A first-rate job answering some important scientific questions." SLJ

Includes glossary and bibliographical references

Taylor, Paul D.

Fossil; written by Paul D. Taylor. rev ed; DK Pub. 2004 72p il map (DK eyewitness books) $15.99; lib bdg $19.99

Grades: 4 5 6 7   560

1. Fossils

ISBN 0-7566-0682-9; 0-7566-0681-0 lib bdg

First published 1990 by Knopf

This book describes different types of fossils, from algae to birds and mammals

560.9   History, geographic treatment, biography

Fern, Tracey

★ Barnum's bones; how Barnum Brown discovered the most famous dinosaur in the world. Tracey Fern; pictures by Boris Kulikov. Farrar Straus Giroux 2012 40 p. $17.99

Grades: 2 3 4 5   560.9

1. Fossils 2. Picture books for children 3. Paleontologists -- United States -- Biography

ISBN 9780374305161

LC 2010048846

This book tells the story of "Barnum Brown," who "had a nose for fossils, trudging along behind his father as he plowed his Kansas fields, picking up ancient clams and corals. And that nose, according to [Tracey] Fern, . . . led to a lifetime of work for the American Museum of Natural History in New York. . . . A brief glimpse at Brown's early years leads to his expeditions to Patagonia and the American West, and the discovery . . . [of the] Tyrannosaurus rex." (School Library Journal)

Includes bibliographical references.

Johnson, Rebecca L.

Battle of the dinosaur bones; Othniel Charles Marsh vs. Edward Drinker Cope. by Rebecca L. Johnson. Twenty-First Century Books 2013 64 p. ill., plates, charts (Scientific rivalries and scandals) (library) $33.27

Grades: 5 6 7 8   560.9

1. Paleontology -- History 2. Paleontologists -- United States -- Biography 3. Paleontology -- United States -- History -- 19th century

ISBN 0761354883; 9780761354888

LC 2011045648

"This entry in the Scientific Rivalries and Scandals series focuses on the bitter antagonism between two pioneering nineteenth-century paleontologists. Marsh and Cope. Their contentious rivalry to discover the largest and most unusual dinosaur fossils of the American West became know as the Bone Wars and was at the forefront of American science for decades. The moral of the story is clear, revealing how rivalry can be positive and detrimental." (Booklist)

Includes bibliographical references (p. 58 - 60) and index.

566   Fossil chordates

Lach, William

I Am Not a Dinosaur! Sterling Pub Co Inc 2016 40 p. color illustrations $14.95

Grades: PreK K 1 2 3   566

1. Prehistoric animals

ISBN 1454914912; 9781454914914

In this juvenile book, by Will Lach, illustrated by Jonny Lambert, "you'll meet some . . . amazing prehistoric creatures, from a very big fish with 7-inch teeth to a flying reptile. Based on specimens in the collections of the American Museum of Natural History, . . . [this book] uses riddle-like rhymes and bright illustrations to reveal 16 creatures." (Publisher's note)

"An author's note on dinosaurs helps put when they lived, respectively, into perspective—T. rex would have never met Stegosaurus, for instance. A succinct, illustrated time line concludes, placing all the prehistoric creatures into their respective geological periods or epochs. Lovely and informative." Booklist

567.9   Reptiles

Abramson, Andra Serlin

Inside dinosaurs; by Andra Serlin Abramson, Jason Brougham, and Carl Mehling; illustrated by Jason Brougham. Sterling Innovation 2010 48p il (Inside) $16.95; pa $9.95

Grades: 5 6 7 8   567.9

1. Birds 2. Fossils 3. Dinosaurs

ISBN 978-1-4027-7074-6; 1-4027-7074-X; 978-1-4027-7778-3 pa; 1-4027-7778-7 pa

LC 2010010122

"This pleasantly specific overview covers not only the dinosaurs' distinctive physical characteristics (the authors include modern birds in the group), but the work of paleontologists in both field and lab, the types and typical life cycles of what are carefully dubbed 'non-avian' dinos within each 'clade,' the mass extinction of 65,000,000 years ago . . . and how new discoveries have refined theories about wings and feathers. . . . The art mixes small color photos with soft-edged paint-and-pencil reconstructions of bones, individual live portraits and prehistoric herds in natural settings. . . . [This is an] above average series entry." Kirkus

Includes glossary and bibliographical references

Bacchin, Matteo

Giant vs. giant; Argentinosaurus and Giganotosaurus. drawings and story, Matteo Bacchin; essays, Marco Signore; translated from the Italian by Marguerite Shore. Abbeville Kids 2010 61p il (Dinosaurs) $15.95

Grades: 4 5 6 7   567.9

1. Fossils 2. Dinosaurs

ISBN 978-0-7892-1013-5; 0-7892-1013-4

LC 2010-21120

This "book is split into two sections: the first contains parts . . . of a serial graphic novel about dinosaur survival, complete with dramatic narrative and grisly, to-the-death battles. The second half is a higher-level traditional nonfiction text with color photographs and diagrams, focusing on the science behind the comics. The unique format is generally engaging and effective." Horn Book Guide

T. rex and the great extinction; drawings and story, Matteo Bacchin; essays, Marco Signore; translated from the Italian by Marguerite Shore. Abbeville Kids 2010 il (Dinosaurs) $15.95

Grades: 4 5 6 7   **567.9**
1. Fossils 2. Dinosaurs
ISBN 9780789210142; 0789210142

LC 2010021123

This "book is split into two sections: the first contains parts . . . of a serial graphic novel about dinosaur survival, complete with dramatic narrative and grisly, to-the-death battles. The second half is a higher-level traditional nonfiction text with color photographs and diagrams, focusing on the science behind the comics. The unique format is generally engaging and effective." Horn Book Guide

Barton, Byron
★ **Bones,** bones, dinosaur bones. Crowell 1990 un il $16.99
Grades: PreK K   **567.9**
1. Fossils -- Fiction 2. Dinosaurs -- Fiction
ISBN 0-690-04825-4

LC 89-71306

"From the field search for dinosaur bones to reconstructed skeletons for museum display, paleontology as process is revealed in simple text, bold print, and flat illustrations with heavy, black outlines. Includes labeled illustrations of eight dinosaurs." Sci Child

Basher, Simon
Dinosaurs; the bare bones. written by Dan Green; illustrations by Simon Basher. Kingfisher 2012 64 p. (paperback) $7.99; (hardcover) $12.99; (prebind) $16.99
Grades: 2 3 4   **567.9**
1. Dinosaurs 2. Picture books for children
ISBN 0753468247; 9780753468241; 9780753468234;
9781451766288

This children's picture book by Dan Green presents a "one-stop guide to the world of dinosaurs. . . . Join the primeval party and meet terrifying Tyrannosaurus rex, huge Giganotosaurus and tiny Compsognathus. Also includes lots of information from the Triassic, Jurassic, and Cretaceous Periods, including dinosaur dinners, habitats, and fossil discoveries." (Publisher's note)

Benton, Mike
The **Kingfisher** dinosaur encyclopedia. Kingfisher 2010 159p il $19.99
Grades: 3 4 5 6   **567.9**
1. Fossils 2. Dinosaurs
ISBN 978-0-7534-6440-3; 0-7534-6440-3

"This thorough, fact-filled dinosaur encyclopedia contains full-color digital images of dinosaurs, in order of their appearance through geological time. . . . Profiles offer descriptions of various species' anatomy and speculations on issues like mobility, diet, and predation. Easy-to-read time lines and charts discuss the origins of and extinctions of species, while abundant photographs of skeletans, dig sites, and paleontogists at work integrate relevance and texture." Publ Wkly

Berkowitz, Jacob
★ **Jurassic** poop; what dinosaurs (and others) left behind. written by Jacob Berkowitz; illustrated by Steve Mack. Kids Can Press 2006 40p il $14.95; pa $7.95
Grades: 4 5 6 7   **567.9**
1. Feces 2. Fossils 3. Dinosaurs
ISBN 978-1-55337-860-0; 1-55337-860-1; 978-1-55337-867-9 pa; 1-55337-867-9 pa

This describes fossilized feces, or coprolites, and what we can learn from them

"Berkowitz' style is goofy and lighthearted, but there's plenty of real information. . . . The browsable format combines cartoony digital art,

photographs . . . and design elements such a spiky borders and background shading." Bull Cent Child Books
Includes glossary

Bishop, Nic
★ **Digging** for bird-dinosaurs; an expedition to Madagascar. Houghton Mifflin 2000 48p il $16; pa $4.95
Grades: 4 5 6 7   **567.9**
1. Birds 2. Fossils 3. Dinosaurs 4. Madagascar
ISBN 0-395-96056-8; 0-618-1982-X pa

LC 99-36145

The story of Cathy Forster's experiences as a member of a team of paleontologists who went on an expedition to the island of Madagascar in 1998 to search for fossil birds

"Throughout the engaging, personal story, Bishop presents a great deal of information in highly readable, age-appropriate language, well matched by exceptional full-color images of scientists at work and the Malagasy landscape and people." Booklist
Includes bibliographical references

Bonner, Hannah
Dining with dinosaurs; a tasty guide to mesozoic munching. By Hannah Bonner. National Geographic Kids 2016 48 p. color illustrations (hardcover : alk. paper) $18.99
Grades: 3 4 5 6   **567.9**
1. Dinosaurs -- Food 2. Dinosaurs -- Behavior 3. Food chains (Ecology)
ISBN 1426323395; 9781426323393; 9781426323409

LC 2016030993

This children's book by Hannah Bonner answers the question of what "was on the dino dining menu during the Mesozoic era? Meet the 'vores: carnivores, piscivores, herbivores, insectivores, 'trashivores,' 'sunivores,' and omnivores like us. Readers will be surprised and inspired to learn about dino diets and they'll get to explore how scientists can tell which dinosaurs ate what just from looking at fossils!" (Publisher's note)

"Although this volume will not completely satisfy students hungry for dinosaur information, it is an excellent appetizer to encourage further reading on the topic." SLJ
Includes bibliographical references and index

When dinos dawned, mammals got munched, and Pterosaurs took flight; a cartoon pre-history of life in the Triassic. Hannah Bonner. National Geographic Children's Books 2012 44 p. col. ill., col. maps (hardback) $25.90
Grades: 3 4 5 6 7   **567.9**
1. Dinosaurs 2. Triassic Period 3. Graphic novels 4. Paleontology -- Triassic -- Comic books, strips, etc.
ISBN 9781426308628; 9781426308635

LC 2011029212

In this book Hannah Bonner "chronicles developments in the Triassic Period, during which life got a fresh lease on the planet in the wake of the massive Permian extinction. She tracks an explosion of biological diversity as the oceans were repopulated, lush forests grew and the dominant kinds of land animals went from clumsy-looking therapsids to sleek archosaurian dinosaurs and proto-crocodiles. Early mammals are already waiting in the wings." (Kirkus Reviews)
Includes bibliographical references and index

Brewster, Hugh
Dinosaurs in your backyard; illustrated by Alan Barnard. Abrams Books for Young Readers 2009 32p il $15.95

Grades: 3 4 5   **567.9**
1. Dinosaurs
ISBN 978-0-8109-7099-1; 0-8109-7099-6

LC 2008030406

First published 2008 in Canada with title: Breakout dinosaurs

"This informative book . . . transports readers back to a time when North America was defined by substantially different coastlines and divided by a broad inland seaway. Introducing some of the dinosaurs living there . . . the book uses double-page spreads that typically describe one animal in a paragraph of descriptive or dramatic text as well as a section of fast facts relating its size, weight, era, diet, and range. Large, painterly illustrations set the tone, supported by smaller maps and photos of fossils. The occasional dramatic tooth-and-claw scene is more than balanced by the weight of accessible, interesting information." Booklist

Includes bibliographical references

Brown, Charlotte Lewis

The **day** the dinosaurs died; written by Charlotte Lewis Brown; illustrated by Phil Wilson. HarperCollins Publishers 2006 48p il (I can read book) $15.99; lib bdg $16.89

Grades: K 1 2 3   **567.9**
1. Dinosaurs
ISBN 978-0-06-000528-3; 0-06-000528-9; 978-0-06-000529-0 lib bdg; 0-06-000529-7 lib bdg

LC 2005-15135

"Beginning with a pronunciation guide for the names of various dinosaurs, this book describes what probably happened to those reptiles 65 million years ago, when a comet or an asteroid most likely slammed into the Earth in the area of the Yucatán Peninsula. . . . Second graders will be able to read this book independently, and with its expressive, fairly naturalistic illustrations, younger children will find that it answers the question of how the dinosaurs became extinct." SLJ

Dixon, Dougal

Meat-eating dinosaurs; by Dougal Dixon. North American ed. New Forest Press 2010 47 p. col. ill., col. maps (Dinosaur files) (library) $28.50

Grades: 4 5 6 7   **567.9**
1. Fossils 2. Dinosaurs 3. Carnivorous animals
ISBN 9781848983342; 1848983344

LC 2010925204

This volume "contains detailed information about dinosaurs and other prehistoric life, covering species development in chronological order. Careful links to the fossil finds that helped scientists with their explanations are found throughout. Additional text boxes cover topics from structure-function to footprints, and interpretive color illustrations and photographs further enhance the [text]." Horn Book Guide

Includes bibliographical references (p. 44-45) and index.

Plant-eating dinosaurs; by Dougal Dixon. North American ed. New Forest Press 2010 48 p. col. ill., col. maps (library) $28.50

Grades: 4 5 6 7   **567.9**
1. Fossils 2. Dinosaurs 3. Herbivores
ISBN 1848983336; 9781848983335

LC 2010925201

This volume "contains detailed information about dinosaurs and other prehistoric life, covering species development in chronological order. Careful links to the fossil finds that helped scientists with their explanations are found throughout. Additional text boxes cover topics from structure-function to footprints, and interpretive color illustrations and photographs further enhance the [text]." Horn Book Guide

Includes bibliographical references (p. 44-45) and index.

Prehistoric oceans. New Forest Press 2010 48p il map (Dinosaur files) lib bdg $28.50

Grades: 4 5 6 7   **567.9**
1. Fossils 2. Dinosaurs 3. Marine animals
ISBN 978-1-8489-8332-8; 1-8489-8332-8

This volume "contains detailed information about dinosaurs and other prehistoric life, covering species development in chronological order. Careful links to the fossil finds that helped scientists with their explanations are found throughout. Additional text boxes cover topics from structure-function to footprints, and interpretive color illustrations and photographs further enhance the [text]." Horn Book Guide

Includes glossary

Prehistoric skies. New Forest Press 2010 48p il map (Dinosaur files) lib bdg $28.50

Grades: 4 5 6 7   **567.9**
1. Fossils 2. Dinosaurs 3. Prehistoric animals
ISBN 978-1-8489-8331-1; 1-8489-8331-X

Discusses the physical characteristics, behavior, diet, and fossil evidence of prehistoric animals that lived in the sky.

This volume "contains detailed information about dinosaurs and other prehistoric life, covering species development in chronological order. Careful links to the fossil finds that helped scientists with their explanations are found throughout. Additional text boxes cover topics from structure-function to footprints, and interpretive color illustrations and photographs further enhance the [text]." Horn Book Guide

Includes glossary

DK first dinosaur encyclopedia. DK Pub. 2007 127p il $15.99

Grades: 2 3 4 5   **567.9**
1. Reference books 2. Dinosaurs -- Encyclopedias
ISBN 978-0-7566-2539-9

LC 2006016039

"Solid introductory information and strong visual appeal make this a fine choice for dinosaur fans. Crystal-clear photographs of models and artifacts fill every spread. . . . The text is clear, with enough intriguing facts to fascinate without overwhelming." SLJ

Farlow, James Orville

★ **Bringing** dinosaur bones to life; how do we know what dinosaurs were really like? [by] James O. Farlow; with illustrations by James E. Whitcraft. Watts 2001 63p il lib bdg $25

Grades: 5 6 7 8   **567.9**
1. Fossils 2. Dinosaurs
ISBN 0-531-11403-1

LC 00-38150

"Clearly written and well organized, this book will interest children intrigued by the process of scientific thinking as well as its results." Booklist

Includes glossary and bibliographical references

Forss, Sarah

Alphasaurs and other prehistoric types; by Sharon Werner and Sarah Forss. Blue Apple Books 2012 56 p. (hardback) $22.99

Grades: 1 2 3 4   **567.9**
1. Alphabet 2. Picture books for children 3. Animals 4. Dinosaurs 5. Alphabet books 6. English language -- Alphabet
ISBN 1609051939; 9781609051938

LC 2012023718

Author Sharon Werner presents a picture book for children. "Like the creatures so artfully rendered in the best-selling Alphabeasties, the dinosaurs in this stylish book are ingeniously engineered out of letters. A different typeface comprises each animal. Factual information about each dinosaur appears in multiple entries and fonts, making for an eye-catching and witty way to look at the ABC-DINO's." (Publisher's note)

French, Vivian
T. Rex; illustrated by Alison Bartlett. Candlewick Press 2004 29p il $15.99; pa $6.99; pa with audio CD $8.99
Grades: K 1 2 3   **567.9**
1. Dinosaurs
ISBN 978-0-7636-2184-1; 0-7636-2184-6; 978-0-7636-3177-2 pa; 0-7636-3177-9 pa; 978-0-7636-3999-0 pa with audio CD; 0-7636-3999-0 pa with audio CD
LC 2003-69563
In a "dialogue with his grandfather, a boy discovers the thrill of the intellectual hunt while touring a T. Rex exhibition. . . . Bartlett . . . working in saturated acrylics and bold shapes, travels back to the era when T. Rex was indeed king. . . . The author eloquently makes the case that a willingness to seek answers, rather than merely receive them, has its own rewards." Publ Wkly

Funston, Sylvia
Dino-why? the dinosaur question and answer book. updated and rev.; Maple Tree Press 2008 64p il $22.95; pa $10.95
Grades: 4 5 6 7   **567.9**
1. Dinosaurs
ISBN 978-1-897349-24-3; 1-897349-24-6; 978-1-897349-25-0 pa; 1-897349-25-4 pa
LC 2007-939082
First published 1992 by Joy Street Books with title: The dinosaur question and answer book
"This book is an excellent and highly readable introduction to dinosaurs. . . . The questions are well conceived, and the answers . . . are scientifically sound and up to date. . . . The illustrations, a few of them cartoon-like, are nicely drawn and useful." Sci Books Films

Gibbons, Gail
Dinosaurs! by Gail Gibbons. Holiday House 2008 32p il $16.95
Grades: K 1 2 3   **567.9**
1. Dinosaurs
ISBN 978-0-8234-2143-5; 0-8234-2143-0
LC 2007034425
Simple text and illustrations introduce young readers to dinosaurs
"The combination of clear writing and lively artwork makes this an accessible choice for young dinosaur enthusiasts." Booklist

Greenwood, Marie
Amazing giant dinosaurs; [written by Marie Greenwood; illustrated by Peter Minister] DK 2012 15 p. $19.99
Grades: 2 3 4   **567.9**
1. Dinosaurs 2. Paleontology 3. Picture books for children
ISBN 075669308X; 9780756693084
LC 2011279215
This book features "large foldout flaps" that create pop-up illustrations of dinosaurs. "Each dinosaur appears in a . . . graphic along with a bulletin board collection of facts about its diet, habitat, behavior, and other characteristics. . . . Profiles of 'Dinosaur hunters' provide insight into the paleontology profession." (Publishers Weekly)

Guiberson, Brenda Z., 1946-
Feathered dinosaurs; Brenda Z. Guiberson; illustrated by William Low. Henry Holt & Co. 2016 40 p. color illustrations (hardcover) $17.99

Grades: 2 3 4 5   **567.9**
1. Feathers 2. Dinosaurs 3. Birds -- Origin
ISBN 9780805098280
LC 2015003535
This juvenile book, by Brenda Z. Guiberson and illustrated by William Low, describes how "millions of years ago, before there were red-breasted robins and busy blue jays . . . there were feathered dinosaurs. Scientists have found evidence that Anchiornis, Caudipteryx, Confuciusornis, and many more dinosaurs all had feathers." (Publisher's note)
"An intriguing introduction to the evolutionary connection between dinosaurs and birds, as well as the process of ongoing scientific discovery." Booklist

★ The **greatest** dinosaur ever; by Brenda Guiberson and illustrated by Gennady Spirin. Henry Holt and Company 2013 32 p. (hardcover) $17.99
Grades: PreK K 1 2 3   **567.9**
1. Dinosaurs 2. Dinosaurs -- Pictorial works
ISBN 0805096256; 9780805096255
LC 2013001725
This book, by Brenda Z. Guiberson and illustrated by Gennady Spirin, features "facts and . . . illustrations [designed to] inspire young readers to choose their own favorite dinosaurs! Which dinosaur was the greatest? Was it the tallest, the biggest, the strongest, the smartest, the weirdest, the fastest, or the smallest? Or was it the oldest bird, the best parent, the one with the best night vision, the best armor, or the longest tail spikes?" (Publisher's note)
"Here a dozen dinosaurs compete for the title of "greatest dinosaur that ever lived" by giving their credentials, from the Sauroposeidon as the tallest and biggest herbivore to the Microraptor as the smallest of all. The compact, information-light text is dwarfed by Spirin's lavish, detailed paintings--a double-spread for each candidate. The package includes pronunciation keys and concludes with a fact page." (Horn Book)
Includes bibliographical references

Hartland, Jessie
★ **How** the dinosaur got to the museum. Blue Apple Books 2011 un il $17.99
Grades: 1 2 3 4   **567.9**
1. Fossils 2. Museums 3. Dinosaurs 4. National Museum of Natural History (U.S.)
ISBN 978-1-60905-090-0; 1-60905-090-8
LC 2011018921
"This cumulative narrative follows the journey of a set of dinosaur bones belonging to a Diplodocus longus that lived 145 million years ago to its present home in the display halls of the Smithsonian National Museum of Natural History in Washington, DC. . . . It . . . describes the work of many hands involved, . . . starting with the dinosaur hunter who discovered the bones and the paleontologist who went to Utah to identify them and culminating with the museum director who opened the exhibit. . . . [The author's] verbs are interestingly varied, as are the many things these people do. The text is printed on double-page illustrations, painted in a childlike manner but detailed enough to show all the people and activities." Kirkus

Henry, Michel
Raptor; the life of a young deinonychus. illustrations by Rich Penney. Abrams Books for Young Readers 2007 un il map $15.95
Grades: 2 3 4   **567.9**
1. Dinosaurs
ISBN 978-0-8109-5775-6; 0-8109-5775-2
LC 2004-12588
This "is a beautifully illustrated book that brings a dinosaur and his environment to life. Based on informed speculation . . . this book fol-

lows the life experiences of several raptors that are part of a pack that lived in the western part of North America 100 million years ago." Sci Books Films

Includes glossary and bibliographical references

Hughes, Catherine D.

First big book of dinosaurs. National Geographic 2011 127p (National Geographic little kids) $14.95; lib bdg $21.90

Grades: PreK K 1 2   **567.9**

1. Dinosaurs

ISBN 978-1-4263-0846-8; 1-4263-0846-9; 978-1-4263-0847-5 lib ed; 1-4263-0847-7 lib bdg

LC 2011015051

"A bright, eye-catching format, naturalistic illustrations, and concise prose introduce readers to 52 dinosaur species, organized by size—small, big, giant, or gigantic. Distinguishing characteristics of each dinosaur . . . appear in a large font like a headline on each spread; informative sidebars, charts that compare each dino's size to a human, phonetic pronunciations, and lively interactive prompts . . . make this an especially engaging primer." Publ Wkly

Judge, Lita

★ Born to be giants; how baby dinosaurs grew to rule the world. Flash Point 2010 un il $17.99

Grades: 2 3 4   **567.9**

1. Dinosaurs

ISBN 978-1-59643-443-1; 1-59643-443-0

"Expanding on the idea that the hugest dinosaurs hatched from (relatively speaking) small eggs, Judge depicts cute hatchlings with outsized heads and feet wobbling about as their gargantuan parents look on indulgently. Along with a full measure of visual appeal, she also delivers a terse but clear explanation of how scientists gain insight into dino parenting from both fossil evidence." Booklist

Includes glossary and bibliographical references

How big were dinosaurs? Lita Judge. Roaring Brook Press 2013 40 p. (hardback) $17.99

Grades: 1 2 3 4   **567.9**

1. Picture books for children 2. Dinosaurs 3. Dinosaurs -- Size

ISBN 1596437197; 9781596437197

LC 2013001327

This children's picture book by Lita Judge looks at dinosaur size. "Moving from smallest to largest, [Judge's] illustrations juxtapose 12 dinos with modern-day objects and animals for comparison. A close-up of a fierce microraptor is followed by a scene showing the same microraptor cowering in the presence of a crowing rooster," for example. (Publishers Weekly)

Kerley, Barbara

★ The dinosaurs of Waterhouse Hawkins; an illuminating history of Mr. Waterhouse Hawkins, artist and lecturer. with drawings by Brian Selznick, many of which are based on the original sketches of Mr. Hawkins. Scholastic 2001 un il

Grades: 3 4 5   **567.9**

1. Artists 2. Dinosaurs 3. Sculptors 4. Modelmakers -- Great Britain

ISBN 0-439-11494-2

LC 00058376

A Caldecott Medal honor book, 2002

This is the true story of Victorian artist Benjamin Waterhouse Hawkins, who built life-sized models of dinosaurs in the hope of educating the world about these ancient animals and what they were like. "Ages five to eight." (Bull Cent Child Books)

"Kerley suffuses her text with a sense of wonder and amazement, a tone well-matched by Selznick's lush, dramatic illustrations." Publ Wkly

Kudlinski, Kathleen V., 1950-

★ Boy, were we wrong about dinosaurs! illustrated by S. D. Schindler. Dutton Children's Books 2005 un il $15.99

Grades: K 1 2 3   **567.9**

1. Dinosaurs

ISBN 0-525-46978-8

LC 2003-53140

This book examines what is known about dinosaur bones, behavior, and other characteristics and how different the facts often are from what scientists, from ancient China to the recent past, believed to be true. "Ages six to ten." (Bull Cent Child Books)

"Intelligently designed and imaginatively conceived, the artwork makes the text more understandable and the whole book more beautiful. . . . Best of all, the closing paragraph acknowledges that the search is not over yet." Booklist

Includes bibliographical references

Lessem, Don

The fastest dinosaurs; by Don Lessem; illustrations by John Bindon. Lerner Publications 2005 32p il (Meet the dinosaurs) lib bdg $23.93; pa $6.95

Grades: 2 3 4   **567.9**

1. Dinosaurs

ISBN 0-8225-1422-2 lib bdg; 0-8225-2620-4 pa

LC 2004-7055

This "looks at how paleontologists determine living speed when only the fossil record remains, and cites some prime examples of dinosprinters, such a Gallimimus and Troodon. The realistic, soft illustrations . . . are lively enough to please budding paleontologists. Simple, eye-catching, and informative." SLJ

Flying giants of dinosaur time. Lerner Publications Co. 2005 32p il map (Meet the dinosaurs) lib bdg $23.93; pa $6.95

Grades: 2 3 4   **567.9**

1. Pterosaurs 2. Pterodactyls

ISBN 0-8225-1424-9 lib bdg; 0-8225-2622-0 pa

LC 2004-17918

This "covers the pterosaurs and pterodactyls, extrapolating some behaviors using modern birds as models, and speculates on beak shapes and sizes in the food-gathering process. . . . The realistic, soft illustrations . . . are lively enough to please budding paleontologists. Simple, eye-catching, and informative." SLJ

Sea giants of dinosaur time. Lerner Publications Co. 2005 32p il map (Meet the dinosaurs) lib bdg $23.93; pa $6.95

Grades: 2 3 4   **567.9**

1. Dinosaurs

ISBN 0-8225-1425-7 lib bdg; 0-8225-2623-9 pa

LC 2004-17916

"A quick glimpse at eight of the larger prehistoric marine reptiles, ranging in eras from 220 million to 65 million years ago. The simple text presents a time line for these creatures, a global map of fossil finds, and some details of their physiology and distribution. The colorful double-page illustrations on blue backgrounds are accompanied by a paragraph or two of particulars." SLJ

The smartest dinosaurs; by Don Lessem; illustrations by John Bindon. Lerner Publications 2005 32p il (Meet the dinosaurs) lib bdg $23.93; pa $6.95

Grades: 2 3 4   567.9
1. Dinosaurs
ISBN 0-8225-1373-0 lib bdg; 0-8225-2618-2 pa

LC 2004-11152

"After a discussion of brain/body-size ratios, Lessem goes on to describe the importance of fossil finds in determining intelligence possibilities, leading to brief descriptions of seven dinosaurs that scientists feel may have been brighter than their contemporaries. . . . This is a clear look at a facet of dinosaur makeup not often touched on in other works." SLJ

The **ultimate** dinopedia; the most complete dinosaur reference ever. illustrated by Franco Tempesta; with a foreword by Rodolfo Coria. National Geographic 2010 272p il map $24.95; lib bdg $34.90
Grades: 3 4 5 6   567.9
1. Dinosaurs
ISBN 978-1-4263-0164-3; 1-4263-0164-2; 978-1-4263-0165-0 lib bdg; 1-4263-0165-0 lib bdg

LC 2010-07146

In the opening chapter, Lessem "presents broad basics on [dinosaur] behavior and habitats as well as a look at major discoveries in paleontology. However, it's the later chapters, which devote two pages each to specific dinosaurs, that will hook hard-core dino lovers. . . . Tempesta's full-page illustrations appear on every spread and jump off the page, and the dynamic layout . . . is immensely appealing. . . . Lessem's comprehensive overview will satisfy the interested browser as much as the ardent dinosaur enthusiast." Booklist
Includes bibliographical references

Long, John A.
★ **Dinosaurs**; [by] John Long. Simon & Schuster Books for Young Readers 2007 64p il (Insiders) lib bdg $16.99
Grades: 4 5 6 7   567.9
1. Dinosaurs
ISBN 978-1-4169-3857-6 lib bdg; 1-4169-3857-5 lib bdg

LC 2007-61735

"Richly hued, crisp computer-generated art and 3D model imagery serve as a stunning and sophisticated graphic counterpoint to the educational text." Publ Wkly
Includes glossary

Macken, JoAnn Early
The **dinosaur** museum. Amicus 2010 24p il (My community) lib bdg $14.95
Grades: K 1 2   567.9
1. Fossils 2. Museums 3. Dinosaurs
ISBN 978-1-6075-3023-7 lib bdg; 1-6075-3023-6 lib bdg

LC 2010010554

The design offers "clear font, colorful layout, and glossy photos. . . . What's most delightful about the museum images are the juxtapositions of the fantastic (a giant dinosaur skeleton) paired with the mundane (a guy on a step-ladder using a vacuum to clean the bones. . . . A solid effort." Booklist

MacLeod, Elizabeth
Monster fliers; from the time of the dinosaurs. written by Elizabeth MacLeod; illustrated by John Bindon. Kids Can Press 2010 31p il $16.95
Grades: K 1 2 3   567.9
1. Birds 2. Dinosaurs 3. Pterosaurs
ISBN 978-1-55453-199-8; 1-55453-199-3

"This attractive picture book [is] sure to appeal to dinophiles eager to learn more about dinosaurs' flying cousins. Nineteen pterosaurs, a few early birds, and a dromaeosaur (a dinosaur that both walked and flew) are briefly described and illustrated in their presumed native habitats. . . . The realistic illustrations [are] painted with remarkable detail." Booklist

Markle, Sandra
★ **Outside** and inside dinosaurs. Atheneum Bks. for Young Readers 2000 40p il hardcover o.p. pa $7.99
Grades: 2 3 4   567.9
1. Fossils 2. Dinosaurs
ISBN 0-689-82300-2; 0-689-85778-0 pa

LC 99-45808

Describes the inner and outer workings of dinosaurs, discussing what has been learned about their anatomy, diet, and behavior from fossils
"Excellent, large color photos march hand in hand with Markle's readable, informative text." SLJ
Includes glossary

McGowan, Chris
Dinosaur discovery; everything you need to be a paleontologist. illustrated by Erica Lyn Schmidt. Simon & Schuster Books for Young Readers 2011 48p il $17.99
Grades: 4 5 6 7   567.9
1. Fossils 2. Dinosaurs
ISBN 978-1-4169-4764-6; 1-4169-4764-7; 1416947647; 9781416947646

LC 2009044604

"In-depth facts about 13 dinosaurs are interspersed with activities that teach readers about anatomy and how paleontologists understand body structure. . . . The 27 activities and experiments illustrate the concepts presented and focus on the featured dinosaurs. By following the well-written directions as well as the picture steps, budding paleontologists will explore how a tail affects balance, discover binocular vision and learn how the two parts of a bone make them both stiff and elastic. . . . Schmidt's acrylic illustrations give life to the dinosaurs, and her scientific renderings of bones could have come straight out of an anatomy textbook. . . . A thinking, active alternative for readers who fall between adult nonfiction and all the rhyming dino fare meant for the younger set." Kirkus

Munro, Roxie
Inside-outside dinosaurs. Marshall Cavendish Children 2009 un il $17.99
Grades: PreK K   567.9
1. Dinosaurs
ISBN 978-0-7614-5624-7; 0-7614-5624-4

LC 2008055322

"This large-format book offers paired double-page spreads showing each featured dinosaur twice. In the first spread, a black-and-gray skeleton in a dramatic pose stands out clearly against a white background. . . . The second spread portrays the living dinosaur within its habitat. Typically these pictures, india-ink drawings washed with colors, depict action in the background or foreground. . . . An appended section offers a bit of information about each species and identifies all the dinosaurs in the action scenes. . . . Eye-catching illustrations and minimal text make this a good choice for young dino fans." Booklist
Includes bibliographical references

Myers, Tim
If you give a T-rex a bone; illustrated by Anisa Claire Hovemann. Dawn Publications 2007 un il (A sharing nature with children book) $16.95; pa $8.95

Grades: PreK K 1 2   567.9
   1. Dinosaurs
   ISBN 978-1-58469-097-9; 1-58469-097-6; 978-1-58469-098-6
   pa; 1-58469-098-4 pa
                                LC 2007-08332
"The book is illustrated throughout with bright, and quite beautiful, watercolors. . . . This is a fine first introduction to prehistoric reptiles for the very young." Sci Books Films
   Includes bibliographical references

Parker, Steve
   Age of the Dinosaur; by Steve Parker. Trafalgar Square 2014 48 p. $7.99
Grades: 1 2 3   567.9
   1. Dinosaurs 2. Paleontology
   ISBN 0565093290; 9780565093297
   This book, by Steve Parker, "explains what the world looked like when dinosaurs existed and how it changed; which . . . creatures, plants, and animals lived then; who survived to live another day; and how scientists know all this. Each colorful double-page spread explores a different dinosaur subject, from a particular period of time or group of animals to dinosaur diets and the study of fossils." (Publisher's note)
   "Learn about dinosaur diets, fossils, and—hooray!—poop in this introduction to dinosaurs and the time in which they lived. This UK import provides an overview of the Mesozoic era by giving snapshots of the climate, landscape, and dinosaurs common to each of the era's periods: the Triassic, Jurassic, and Cretaceous. Information is distilled and simply explained, ensuring that readers will not be overwhelmed by a page's content." (Booklist)

Peterson, Sheryl
   Pterodactyl. Creative Education 2010 48p il (Age of dinosaurs) lib bdg $34.25
Grades: 5 6 7 8   567.9
   1. Dinosaurs
   ISBN 978-1-58341-975-5 lib bdg; 1-58341-975-6 lib bdg
                                  LC 2009025175
"Peterson nicely balances the known with conjecture. . . . The inviting design, on glossy pages, elegantly detours from the main text into details tantalizing . . . ; informative . . . and incredible. . . . The illustrations, from sharp diagrams to dramatic paintings to B-movie-worthy recreation scenes, add some nice flair to this solid entry." Booklist

Podesto, Martine
   Dinosaurs; by Martine Podesto. Gareth Stevens 2009 102p il (My science notebook) lib bdg $31
Grades: 4 5 6   567.9
   1. Dinosaurs
   ISBN 978-0-8368-9213-0 lib bdg; 0-8368-9213-5 lib bdg
                                  LC 2008-12427
"Designed to resemble a notebook with illustrated paper clips, pasting, and tape appearing on most pages, this [book] . . . offers comprehensive information. . . . supplemented by colorful drawings, diagrams, and photographs." SLJ
   Includes glossary and bibliographical references

Prap, Lila
   Dinosaurs?! North South Books 2010 un il $16.95
Grades: K 1 2 3   567.9
   1. Birds 2. Dinosaurs 3. Evolution
   ISBN 978-0-7358-2284-9; 0-7358-2284-0
   "In this humorous look at evolution, Prap makes the case that all modern-day birds, including chickens, are descended from dinosaurs. The book's illustrations are fun and well-laid-out, and the witty text is

chock-full of information. A group of chickens makes snarky comments about their disparate relatives . . . and side notes provide interesting details about the 'terrible lizards.' Dino lovers will clamor for this title." SLJ

Ray, Deborah Kogan
   ★ **Dinosaur** mountain; digging into the Jurassic Age. Frances Foster Books 2010 un il map $16.99
Grades: 3 4 5 6   567.9
   1. Fossils 2. Dinosaurs 3. Paleontologists 4. Dinosaur National Monument (Colo. and Utah)
   ISBN 978-0-374-31789-8; 0-374-31789-5
                                  LC 2008027877
   This describes how, beginning in 1908, Earl Douglass set out to discover "a mountain in Utah that would reveal some of the grandest dinosaur skeletons anyone had ever seen. . . . Ray's expressive art . . . excels in capturing the grandeur and wonder of key moments. . . . Excited journal entries from Douglass enliven the informative text, and small sketch book-style drawings of fossils and tools add a scholarly touch." Booklist
   Includes glossary and bibliographical references

Reed, M. K.
   Dinosaurs; fossils and feathers. by MK Reed, illustrated by Joe Flood. First Second 2016 117 p. chiefly color illustrations $9.99; (ebook) $60; $19.99
Grades: 4 5 6 7 8   567.9
   1. Dinosaurs 2. Paleontology
   ISBN 1626721432; 9781626721432; 9781626727281; 9781626721449; 1626721440
                                  LC 2016012765
   In this graphic novel by MK Reed, illustrated by Joe Flood, published as part of the Science Comics series, "learn all about the history of paleontology! This fascinating look at dinosaur science covers the last 150 years of dinosaur hunting, and illuminates how our ideas about dinosaurs have changed--and continue to change." (Publisher's note)
   "There's some humor along with a solid presentation of facts, and the clean design helps makes the information accessible; the somewhat advanced content makes the book most appropriate for upper-elementary-age readers." Horn Book
   Includes bibliographical references.

Sloan, Christopher
   Bizarre dinosaurs; some very strange creatures and why we think they got that way. [by] Christopher Sloan; with a foreword by James Clark and Cathy Forster. National Geographic 2008 31p il $16.95; lib bdg $25.90
Grades: 4 5 6 7   567.9
   1. Dinosaurs
   ISBN 978-1-4263-0330-2; 1-4263-0330-0; 978-1-4263-0331-9 lib bdg; 1-4263-0331-9 lib bdg
   This "book should engage children of all ages who are fascinated by dinosaurs. . . . The illustrations are of uniformly high quality. . . . Each species gets two pages of text, including a full-page illustration; an inset with basic facts such as range, diet, and geological period in which it lived; a silhouette comparing their size with that of humans; and a paragraph of text." Sci Books Films

Snow, Alan
   How Dinosaurs Really Work! written and illustrated by Alan Snow. Atheneum Books 2013 32 p. $17.99
Grades: K 1 2 3   567.9
   1. Dinosaurs
   ISBN 144248294X; 9781442482944

This book, written and illustrated by Alan Snow, examines dinosaurs and attempts to answer questions such as "what color were the dinosaurs? Where did they all go? And just how sharp were their teeth?" (Publisher's note)

Thimmesh, Catherine

★ **Scaly** spotted feathered frilled; how do we know what dinosaurs really looked like? by Catherine Thimmesh. Houghton Mifflin Books for Children, Houghton Mifflin Harcourt 2013 64 p. $17.99

Grades: 4 5 6 7 **567.9**

1. Dinosaurs 2. Paleontology 3. Paleoart

ISBN 0547991347; 9780547991344

LC 2012048466

Author Catherine Thimmesh "explores the border between science and speculation in this [book about] how paleontologists . . . reconstruct prehistoric creatures from fossil evidence. . . . [She] explains how surviving evidence—including fossilized bone fragments, plant matter, bits of skin and, recently, feathers, prehistoric 'trackways' (preserved pathways of dino footprints) and similar physical features in modern animals—is assembled and interpreted by scientists." (Kirkus Reviews)

Includes bibliographical references (page 55) and index

Williams, Judith

The **discovery** and mystery of a dinosaur named Jane. Enslow Publishers 2007 48p il map

Grades: 3 4 5 6 **567.9**

1. Fossils 2. Dinosaurs 3. Tyrannosaurus rex

ISBN 0766027090 pa; 0766027309 lib bdg; 9780766027091 pa; 9780766027305 lib bdg

LC 2006010475

This book deals with how paleontologists and researchers discovered, excavated and put on display a Tyrannosaurus skeleton found in Montana's Hell Creek formation. Glossary. Index. "Grades three to eight." (Sci Books Films)

This describes "the 2001 discovery of a fossilized dinosaur skeleton in Montana's Hell Creek Formation. . . . Williams carefully reports the entire event, from discovery through excavation and preparation to exhibition at the Burpee Museum of Natural History in Rockford, IL. Small color photos and artwork, simple diagrams, and a map help readers to visualize the complex process." SLJ

Includes bibliographical references

Woodward, John

Dinosaurs eye to eye; zoom in on the world's most incredible dinosaur. digital sculptor Peter Minister. Dorling Kindersley 2010 96p il map $19.99

Grades: 3 4 5 6 **567.9**

1. Fossils 2. Dinosaurs

ISBN 978-0-7566-5760-4; 0-7566-5760-1

"This oversize reference book features striking digital images of dinosaurs, along with abundant information about them and the Triassic, Jurassic, and Cretaceous periods in which they thrived. . . . Action scenes . . . offer visual excitement, while diagrams, sidebars with dino-stats, and photographs of fossils emphasize the educational." Publ Wkly

Zoehfeld, Kathleen Weidner

Dinosaur tracks; by Kathleen Weidner Zoehfeld; illustrated by Lucia Washburn. HarperCollinsPublishers 2007 33p il (Let's-read-and-find-out science) $15.99; lib bdg $16.89; pa $5.99

Grades: K 1 2 3 **567.9**

1. Fossils 2. Dinosaurs

ISBN 0-06-029024-2; 978-0-06-02904-5; 0-06-029025-0 lib bdg; 978-0-06-029025-2 lib bdg; 0-06-445217-4 pa; 978-0-06-445217-5 pa

LC 2004-06242

Describes how footprints made by the dinosaurs have been preserved and what these impressions tell scientists about the animals which made them.

"The clear text is illustrated with informal, colorful spreads of kids at play on the beach where millions of years earlier dinosaurs may have 'splooshed through gloppy mud . . . [leaving] footprints behind them.'" Booklist

Where did dinosaurs come from? illustrated by Lucia Washburn. HarperCollinsPublishers 2010 40p il (Let's-read-and-find-out science book) **567.9**

1. Fossils 2. Dinosaurs

ISBN 978-0-06-029022-1; 978-0-06-445216-8 pa

LC 2009020543

Presents information about the evolution of the dinosuars, from the earliest four-limbed tetrapos of the Paleozoic age, to the meat-eating eoraptors of early Triassic, to the fully-developed dinosaurs of the Jurassic and Cretaceous periods.

"Zoehfeld is remarkably precise with language, no easy feat when writing on this topic for beginning readers, providing outstanding explanations of key evolution concepts in the finest tradition of the series. The color illustrations include anatomical details, a helpful phylognetic timeline, and imagined portrayals of dinosaurs active in verdant habitats." Horn Book

Includes glossary

567.91   Specific dinosaurs and other archosaurs

Sloan, Christopher

Tracking Tyrannosaurs; meet T. rex's fascinating family, from tiny terrors to feathered giants. by Christopher Sloan. National Geographic 2013 48 p. (trade hard cover) $18.95

Grades: 5 6 7 8 **567.91**

1. Tyrannosaurus rex 2. Dinosaurs

ISBN 1426313748; 9781426313745; 9781426313752

LC 2013004988

This book, by Christopher Sloan, "highlights a newly discovered T. rex relative in China with a coat of downy feathers! This one-ton predator is the largest known animal to ever have walked the Earth. [Readers] meet 19 kinds of tyrannosaurs--including seven new species discovered in the last two years--that came before T. rex." (Publisher's note)

568   Fossil birds

Zoehfeld, Kathleen Weidner

Did dinosaurs have feathers? illustrated by Lucia Washburn. HarperCollins Publishers 2004 33p il (Let's-read-and-find-out science) $15.99; lib bdg $16.89; pa $4.99

Grades: K 1 2 3 **568**

1. Birds 2. Fossils 3. Dinosaurs 4. Archaeopteryx

ISBN 0-06-029026-9; 0-06-029027-7 lib bdg; 0-06-029027-7 pa

LC 2002-10585

Discusses the discovery and analysis of Archaeopteryx, a feathered dinosaur which may have been an ancestor of modern birds

"Using short sentences and simple words, Zoehfeld clearly explains what we know about dinosaurs with feathers. . . . Iridescent shades of blue and orange give the theropods and their settings an appealing glow." Horn Book Guide

569   Fossil mammals

Arnold, Caroline
★ **When** mammoths walked the earth; illustrated by Laurie Caple. Clarion Bks. 2002 40p il $16
Grades: 3 4 5 6   569
1. Mammoths
ISBN 0-618-09633-7
                                              LC 2001-47192
Describes the physical characteristics, known habits, and fossil sites of mammoths, prehistoric animals closely related to the elephant

"The information is brief but thorough, with realistic watercolor illustrations depicting the giant animals and their surroundings." Booklist

Bardoe, Cheryl
Mammoths and mastodons; titans of the Ice Age. Abras Books for Young Readers 2010 43p il map
Grades: 4 5 6 7   569
1. Fossils 2. Mammoths 3. Mastodon
ISBN 0-8109-8413-X lib bdg; 978-0-8109-8413-4 lib bdg
                                              LC 2009-22006
The author presents a "case study in how paleontologists examine both ancient and modern clues for insights into the diets, physical development and behavior of extinct animals. Cousins to modern elephants, mammoths and mastodons once roamed large portions of the Earth, but for reasons that are not completely understood . . . vanished relatively suddenly. Focusing particularly on . . . remnants like the 55 fossilized skeletons found near one sinkhole in South Dakota and 'Lyuba,' the well preserved 'prehistoric popsicle' discovered in 2007 in Siberia, the author presents both facts and educated guesses--while leaving it clear that there is much still to be learned." (Kirkus)

"This well-designed book opens with two boys finding a strange animal dead on the arctic tundra. Their father hikes four days to a village where the news can be spread; then scientists take away the frozen baby mammoth, the first example found intact, and study it intensively. The book intersperses accounts of the scientists' research and deductions with general information about mammoths and mastodons as well as imagined scenes taking place when they walked the earth. . . . A handsome introduction." Booklist

Includes glossary and bibliographical references

Lister, Adrian
The **Ice** Age tracker's guide; illustrated by Martin Ursell. Frances Lincoln Children's Books 2010 31p il map $17.95
Grades: 4 5 6 7   569
1. Ice Age 2. Fossil mammals
ISBN 978-1-84507-718-1; 1-84507-718-0

"'Hunters' of Ice Age fauna will find the tawny pages in this 'guide' a trove of pointers for identifying a round dozen of predators and prey. What does a giant ground sloth's poop look like? Just how big is a dwarf elephant? . . . Size, shape, food, fur (if any), locations, and other tidbits are scattered about the watercolor and ink illustrations, and are reinforced by two pages of solid paragraphs of text on each creature. Lister . . . writes with authority in this lighthearted, informational work." SLJ

Manning, Mick
Woolly mammoth; [by] Mick Manning [and] Brita Granström. Frances Lincoln 2009 un il $16.95

Grades: K 1 2 3   569
1. Mammoths
ISBN 978-1-84507-860-7; 1-84507-860-8

"Manning and Granström pair rhyming couplets, in this case describing the life of a mammoth, alongside columns of information. Simple pencil drawings fill sidebars with specific details about these huge beasts, including their habitat and natural enemies, their physical characteristics and behavior. . . . Bright watercolor-over-pencil paintings dominate the pages, which feature simple stanzas that deliver the mammoth's side of the story." SLJ

Markle, Sandra
★ **Outside** and inside woolly mammoths. Walker & Co. 2007 40p il $17.95; lib bdg $18.85
Grades: 4 5 6   569
1. Mammoths
ISBN 978-0-8027-9589-2; 0-8027-9589-7; 978-0-8027-9590-8 lib bdg; 0-8027-9590-0 lib bdg
                                              LC 2006027621
"Markle explains what scientists have discovered from the preserved remains of mammoths: their food, and the structure of their hair, their soft tissues, and even their DNA. Asking readers leading questions and systematically noting similarities to and differences from modern elephants, she speculates about why mammoths became extinct. . . . Except for the cover picture, the illustrations are all big, sharp color photos and digital tomography images rather than artistic re-creations. A closing multimedia resource list that is accurately pitched to the level of her intended audience makes this as valuable for student use as for pleasure reading." Booklist

Parker, Steve, 1952-
Ice age giants. QEB Pub. 2011 32p il (Wild age) lib bdg $28.50
Grades: 2 3 4   569
1. Fossils 2. Ice Age 3. Fossil mammals
ISBN 978-1-59566-911-7; 1-59566-911-6
                                              LC 2010001152
This describes prehistoric mammals of the ice age, including giant sloths, mammoths, giant deer, giant cats, Neanderthals and modern humans.

"Vivid writing . . . lifts [this] otherwise ordinary [survey] a bit above average. . . . The art combines photos of fossils, distribution maps, illustrations of prehistoric monsters . . . and, on each spread, a human silhouette to indicate scale." SLJ

Includes glossary

Sloan, Christopher
Baby mammoth mummy; frozen in time: a prehistoric animal's journey into the 21st century. National Geographic 2011 il map $17.95; lib bdg 26.90
Grades: 4 5 6 7   569
1. Fossils 2. Mammoths
ISBN 978-1-4263-0865-9; 1-4263-0865-5; 978-1-4263-0866-6 lib bdg; 1-4263-0866-3 lib bdg
                                              LC 2010044003
"From CAT scans to the use of surgical cameras, the mummy of a baby mammoth found dislodged from Siberian ice undergoes veritable CSI treatment in the Netherlands, Japan, the U.S., and in her Russian homeland as scientists scramble to discover her historic age (42,000 years), her chronological age (32 days), her diet (mother's milk), and the cause of her demise (suffocation in mud). Sloan's clear, readable text follows this journey in nicely defined stages, with explanations along the way for possibly unfamiliar processes. Plentiful photos, a pair of maps, some diagrams, and colorful artwork accompany the information." SLJ

Includes glossary and bibliographical references

Turner, Alan

★ **National** Geographic prehistoric mammals; illustrated by Mauricio Antón. National Geographic 2004 192p il map $29.95; lib bdg $49.90

Grades: 5 6 7 8   **569**

1. Fossil mammals

ISBN 0-7922-7134-3; 0-7922-6997-7 lib bdg

LC 2004-1189

This describes the Age of Mammals and profiles over 100 prehistoric mammals, including time lines, fact boxes, distribution maps, photos of fossils, and illustrations

"Dramatic full-color pictures . . . and captions enhance the brief, informative text." SLJ

Wheeler, Lisa

Mammoths on the move. Harcourt, Inc. 2006 un il $16

Grades: K 1 2   **569**

1. Mammoths

ISBN 0-15-204700-X

LC 2004-19112

"The text describes a group of female mammoths and their young traveling south for the winter, reaching their destination only to turn around and begin their long trek back. Wheeler uses wordplay skillfully, her verse shows originality. . . . The beautifully composed scratchboard illustrations offer strong line work, subtle use of color, and a fine sense of what migrating mammoths may have looked like." Booklist

569.9 Humans and related genera

Aronson, Marc

★ The **skull** in the rock; how a scientist, a boy, and Google Earth opened a new window on human origins. by Marc Aronson and Lee Berger. National Geographic 2012 64 p. (hardcover : alk. paper) $18.95

Grades: 5 6 7 8 9 10   **569.9**

1. Human origins 2. Fossil hominids 3. Paleoanthropology 4. Excavations (Archeology) 5. Human beings -- Origin 6. Fossil hominids -- South Africa -- Witwatersrand Region 7. Human evolution -- South Africa -- Witwatersrand Region 8. Excavations (Archaeology) -- South Africa -- Witwatersrand Region

ISBN 1426310102; 9781426310102; 9781426310539

LC 2012012943

This book by Marc Aronson and Lee R. Berger tells the story of how "in 2008 [Berger]--with the help of his curious 9-year-old son--discovered two remarkably well preserved, two-million-year-old fossils . . . known as 'Australopithecus sediba'; a previously unknown species of ape-like creatures that may have been a direct ancestor of modern humans." (Publisher's note)

Includes bibliographical references and index.

Deem, James M.

★ **Bodies** from the bog. Houghton Mifflin 1998 42p il hardcover o.p. pa $5.95

Grades: 4 5 6 7   **569.9**

1. Mummies 2. Archeology 3. Prehistoric peoples

ISBN 0-395-85784-8; 0-618-35402-6 pa

LC 97-12010

Describes the discovery of bog bodies in northern Europe and the evidence which their remains reveal about themselves and the civilizations in which they lived

"The text is engaging and accessible, and the starkly dramatic photos are given dignity by the spacious and understated page design." Horn Book Guide

Includes bibliographical references

570 Biology

Green, Dan

Extreme biology; from superbugs to clones... get to the edge of science. written and illustrated by Simon Basher. Kingfisher 2013 64 p. col. ill. (hardcover) $12.99

Grades: 4 5 6 7   **570**

1. Biology

ISBN 0753470519; 9780753470510

This book written and illustrated by Simon Basher is designed to help readers "learn about the amazing research that is revolutionizing biology, from advances in medicine to genetic engineering. [Readers will] meet the world's toughest bacterium and a biologically immortal flatworm whilst learning about epigenetics, superbugs, nanomedicine and cloning. 'Extreme Biology' is a compelling guide to developments at the very forefront of science." (Publisher's note)

Kalman, Bobbie

What is symmetry in nature? Crabtree Pub. Co. 2010 24p il (Looking at nature) lib bdg $21.27; pa $6.95

Grades: K 1 2   **570**

1. Nature 2. Symmetry

ISBN 978-0-7787-3327-0 lib bdg; 0-7787-3327-0 lib bdg; 978-0-7787-3347-8 pa; 0-7787-3347-5 pa

LC 2010016400

Reveals examples of symmertry found in nature.

"Bright, colorful photographs were selected with young readers in mind, and the type is large—perfect for reading together. . . Throughout the book are questions that challenge the reader to identify the opposites shown on the pages. . . . Parents and teachers will find . . . [this book] a great addition to a child's library." Sci Books & Films

Includes glossary

Latham, Donna

★ **Backyard** Biology; Investigate Habitats Outside Your Door With 25 Projects. by Donna Latham; illustrated by Beth Hetland. Nomad Press 2013 128 p. ill. (Build it yourself) (paperback) $15.95

Grades: 4 5 6 7   **570**

1. Biology 2. Front yards and backyards

ISBN 1619301512; 9781619301511

This book, part of the Built It Yourself series, "incorporates 25 projects for kids to try as they explore the 'ecosystems that are outside your door.' The book's eight chapters cover biology (and microbiology), cells, and the life cycles of both plants and animals, among other topics; definitions of key terms appear throughout, as do [illustrator Beth] Hetland's cartoons and diagrams." (Publishers Weekly)

McManus, Lori

Cell systems. Heinemann Library 2011 48p il (Investigating cells) lib bdg $32

Grades: 5 6 7 8   **570**

1. Cells 2. Life (Biology)

ISBN 978-1-4329-3879-6; 1-4329-3879-7

LC 2009049974

This book looks at cell systems, including the cell, tissues, organ, and organ system hierarchy.

"The abundant graphic matter—photographs, diagrams, charts and graphs—work together with the text to create visually appealing pages. .

. . . [This] would be very useful in any kind of formal investigation of the topic and yet attractive enough to encourage browsing. . . . [This] . . . is exceptionally well done." Libr Media Connect

Includes glossary and bibliographical references

VanCleave, Janice Pratt, 1942-

Step-by-step science experiments in biology; by Janice VanCleave. Rosen 2013 80 p. col. ill. (Janice Vancleave's first-place science fair projects) (library) $33.25; (paperback) $14.15

Grades: 5 6 7 8   **570**

1. Biology 2. Science -- Experiments 3. Biology -- Experiments

ISBN 144886982X; 9781448869824; 9781448884636

LC 2012007943

This book by Janice VanCleave presents 22 science experiments in biology for children. "Van Cleave states the basic goal of the experiments, followed by a list of necessary materials. . . . Step-by-step instructions are . . . accompanied by diagrams where needed. The results section states exactly what is expected to happen and the 'Why?' section explains in accessible terms why those specific results were achieved." (School Library Journal)

Includes bibliographical references and index.

Winston, Robert

Life as we know it; Robert Winston. 1st American ed. DK Publishing 2012 96 p. col. ill. (hardcover) $16.99

Grades: 4 5 6   **570**

1. Ecology 2. Zoology 3. Food chains (Ecology) 4. Life (Biology)

ISBN 0756691699; 9780756691691

LC 2011277462

Author Robert Winston "begins with Earth's formation billions of years ago and continues to the present day, exploring cells, the animal kingdom, ecosystems, food chains, and creatures that tolerate extreme conditions (including bacteria that thrive in volcanic pools and coffinfish that live under high pressure on the sea floor). The book's . . . design incorporates numerous photographs, sidebars, . . . digital art, and light humor, usually in the form of speech-bubble captions for the animals." (Publishers Weekly)

571   Internal biological processes and structures

Green, Jen

Inside animals. Marshall Cavendish Benchmark 2010 48p il (Invisible worlds) $28.50

Grades: 4 5 6 7   **571**

1. Cells 2. Anatomy 3. Physiology 4. Microorganisms

ISBN 978-0-7614-4195-3; 0-7614-4195-6

LC 2008037241

This describes the animal details that are too small for the unaided eye to see, and how these microscopic systems work to keep the animal alive and healthy.

The narrative is "clear, well written, broken down into manageable pieces, and peppered with eye-opening facts. The numerous photographs are so phenomenal that they will inspire kids to read the text . . . so that they can wrap their minds around what they see." SLJ

Includes glossary and bibliographical references

571.1   Animals

Singer, Marilyn

A strange place to call home; the world's most dangerous habitats & the animals that call them home. Marilyn Singer & Ed Young. Chronicle Books 2012 44 p. ill.

Grades: 3 4 5   **571.1**

1. Habitat (Ecology) 2. Exotic animals 3. Animals -- Habitations

ISBN 1452101205; 9781452101200

LC 2011046379

This book, describes how "[u]nder the desert's cracked and barren skin, spadefoot toads are waiting for rain. In the endless black of the deepest caves, blind fish find their way. Even in the frozen hearts of glaciers, ice worms by the billion flourish. In this . . . look at fourteen animals who defy the odds by thriving in Earth's most dangerous places, . . . poet Marilyn Singer and . . . artist Ed Young show that of all the miracles of life, it is life's persistence that astounds the most." (Publisher's note)

571.4   Biophysics

Amstutz, Lisa J.

Discover cryobiology; Lisa J. Amstutz. Lerner Publications 2017 40 p. color illustrations (ebook) $30.65; (ebook) $30.65; (lb : alk. paper) $30.65

Grades: 3 4 5   **571.4**

1. Cryobiology 2. Cold -- Physiological effect 3. Cryopreservation of organs, tissues, etc

ISBN 9781512423082; 9781512410631; 9781512408072; 9781512412840

LC 2015047375

This book, by Lisa J. Amstutz, part of the Searchlight Books What's Cool about Science? series, explores the theories behind cryobiology. "Cryobiologists study how cold affects living things. This research has many amazing uses, but what do icy temperatures have to do with organ transplants? And how can researchers use a freezer to save endangered species? Learn about the work cryobiologists are doing today and the breakthroughs they hope to achieve in the future." (Publisher's note)

"In four clear, concise chapters, accompanied by glossy close-up photos of technological gear and frozen organs, this explains the effects, both preservative and damaging, of cold on bodies and examines the natural reactions of animals (i.e., hibernation), before more thoroughly discussing the potential for freezing—and perhaps one day reanimating—human bodies." Booklist

Includes bibliographical references and index

Chisholm, Sallie W., 1947-

★ Ocean sunlight; how tiny plants feed the seas. by Molly Bang and Penny Chisholm; illustrated by Molly Bang. Blue Sky Press 2012 48 p. (hardcover : alk. paper) $18.99

Grades: K 1 2 3 4   **571.4**

1. Oceanography 2. Marine biology 3. Photosynthesis 4. Sunshine 5. Photobiology 6. Plants -- Effect of light on 7. Marine life -- Effect of light on

ISBN 0545273226; 9780545273220

LC 2011024823

AAAS/Subaru SB&F Prize for Excellence in Science Books: Children's Science Picture Book (2013)

In this book, the authors "turn their attention to the ocean and its vast population of phytoplankton. . . . The . . . text follows the food chain from the tiniest of green plants (powered into life by the sun) to the biggest predators dependent on plankton-gobblers for food. The authors explain photosynthesis and the ocean layer exchange wrought by sunlight-driven currents, and even touch on the life below, where the strongest sunbeam cannot reach." (School Library Journal)

571.6   Cell biology

Cohen, Marina

What is cell theory? Crabtree Pub. Co. 2011 64p il (Shaping modern science) lib bdg $30.60; pa $10.95

Grades: 5 6 7 8

1. Cells   **571.6**

ISBN 978-0-7787-7199-9 lib bdg; 0-7787-7199-9 lib bdg; 978-0-7787-7206-4 pa; 0-7787-7206-3 pa

LC 2010052633

This title is "not only written and organized well, but [it is] also gorgeous in design. Full-color photographs and illustrations are set over colorful backgrounds that add depth but not distraction. [The title] includes thought-provoking quotes from famous authors and scientists and some eyebrow-raising 'Quick Facts' throughout." SLJ

Includes glossary and bibliographical references

Johnson, Rebecca L.

Mighty animal cells; [by] Rebecca L. Johnson; illustrations by Jack Desrocher; diagrams by Jennifer E. Fairman. Millbrook Press 2007 48p il (Microquests) lib bdg $29.27

Grades: 4 5 6

1. Cells   **571.6**

ISBN 978-0-8225-7137-7 lib bdg; 0-8225-7137-4 lib bdg

LC 2006-36394

In this introduction to animal cells, "Johnson builds one scientific concept at a time using authentic terminology and connecting new information to familiar things. . . . Full-color microscope images, drawings, and cartoons appear in a clean, uncluttered format, combining solid science with humor." Horn Book Guide

Includes glossary and bibliographical references

Lee, Kimberly Fekany

Cells. Compass Point Books 2009 40p il (Mission: science) lib bdg $26.60

Grades: 4 5 6

1. Cells   **571.6**

ISBN 978-0-7565-3954-2 lib bdg; 0-7565-3954-4 lib bdg

LC 2008007719

"Lee describes the difference between plant and animal cells, and their contents; diffusion; and cell storage, movement, and reproduction. . . . Large eye-catching and colorful photographs and illustrations appear on every page. . . . The [book] includes a simple activity." SLJ

Includes glossary and bibliographical references

571.8   Reproduction, development, growth

Mitchell, Susan K.

Animal body-part regenerators; growing new heads, tails, and legs. by Susan K. Mitchell. Enslow Publishers 2009 48p il (Amazing animal defenses) lib bdg $23.93

Grades: 4 5 6

1. Regeneration (Biology)   **571.8**

ISBN 978-0-7660-3295-8 lib bdg; 0-7660-3295-7 lib bdg

LC 2008-11453

"The closeup photos are frequent and well chosen, and accompanied by clear, simply phrased [text], which [is] more detailed than average and [takes] up most or all of the space on each page." SLJ

Includes glossary and bibliographical references

Royston, Angela

Looking at life cycles; how do plants and animals change? [by] Angela Royston. Enslow Publishers 2008 32p il (Looking at science: how things change) lib bdg $22.60

Grades: 1 2 3

1. Life cycles (Biology)   **571.8**

ISBN 978-0-7660-3091-6 lib bdg; 0-7660-3091-1 lib bdg

LC 2007-24513

"Fills a huge void in elementary science collections. . . . Text is arranged in succinct 'chunks,' giving important facts without overwhelming readers. . . . [This] is an essential addition." Libr Media Connect

Includes glossary and bibliographical references

Silverstein, Virginia B.

★ **Growth** and development; by Alvin Silverstein, Virginia Silverstein, and Laura Silverstein Nunn. Twenty-First Century Books 2008 112p il (Science concepts) lib bdg $31.93

Grades: 4 5 6 7

1. Growth 2. Biology   **571.8**

ISBN 978-0-8225-6057-9 lib bdg; 0-8225-6057-7 lib bdg

LC 2006030299

This "considers the growth process, animals with and without skeletons, human and plant growth, and future trends as a result of medical technology. Clear organization, engaging anecdotes, and generally good photos and diagrams are strengths of the [volume]." Horn Book Guide

Includes glossary and bibliographical references

Wade, Mary Dodson

Plants grow! Enslow Elementary 2009 24p il (I like plants!) lib bdg $21.26; pa $6.95

Grades: K 1 2

1. Growth 2. Plants   **571.8**

ISBN 978-0-7660-3152-4 lib bdg; 0-7660-3152-7 lib bdg; 978-0-7660-3612-3 pa; 0-7660-3612-X pa

LC 2007039453

"The life cycle and parts of a plant are discussed in a clear, concise manner. Beautifully detailed professional photographs of plants, animals, and people complement the subject matter. [The] book includes a simple activity." SLJ

Includes glossary and bibliographical references

571.9   Diseases

Stewart, Melissa

Germ wars! the secrets of keeping healthy. illustrated by Janet Hamlin. Marshall Cavendish Benchmark 2010 48p il (The gross and goofy body) $29.95

Grades: 2 3 4

1. Bacteria 2. Immune system   **571.9**

ISBN 978-0-7614-4165-6; 0-7614-4165-4

LC 2008033562

This offers information on the role the immune system plays in the body science of humans and animals.

572 Biochemistry

Bang, Molly
★ **Living** sunlight; how plants bring the Earth to life. by Molly Bang & Penny Chisholm; illustrated by Molly Bang. Blue Sky Press 2009 un il $16.99

Grades: PreK K 1 2 3   **572**

1. Photosynthesis 2. Sun
ISBN 978-0-545-04422-6; 0-545-04422-7

LC 2008-14238

This book "talks to young children about photosynthesis . . . in a way that tells what is actually happening on a molecular level. It also tells children why this process matters and leads them into a broad understanding of their personal connection with plant life and energy from the sun. . . . The amiable, well-informed narrator is the sun. Alight with unusual intensity, the artwork fills the pages with vibrant images. . . . Each double-page spread illustrates its lines of text with intelligence and originality." Booklist

Includes bibliographical references

Haelle, Tara
Edible Sunlight; by Tara Haelle. Rosen Publishing 2016 48 p. color illustrations $10.95; (ebook) $24.95

Grades: 5 6 7 8   **572**

1. Sun 2. Food 3. Agriculture
ISBN 1681913992; 1681914417; 9781681913995; 9781681914411; 9781681914800

LC 2015951566

This children's nonfiction book, by Tara Haelle, part of the "Let's Explore Science" series, presents "a taste of sunshine! [It] discusses the fascinating ways the Sun is involved in food production." (Publisher's note)

Includes bibliographical references (page 47) and index.

Lunis, Natalie
Glow-in-the-dark animals. Bearport Pub. 2011 24p il (Animals with super powers) lib bdg $22.61

Grades: 3 4 5   **572**

1. Bioluminescence
ISBN 978-1-61772-119-9; 1-61772-119-0

LC 2010038281

This describes animals which glow in the dark including fireflies, glowworms, fireworms, deep-sea jellyfish, anglerfish, cucujos, and dinoflagellates.

"Large color photos of animals in natural settings and clear, cogent presentations of information combine to boost this [book] well above the average for both assignments and casual browsing." SLJ

Includes glossary and bibliographical references

Sitarski, Anita
★ **Cold** light; creatures, discoveries, and inventions that glow. Boyds Mills Press 2007 48p il $16.95

Grades: 5 6 7 8   **572**

1. Light 2. Bioluminescence
ISBN 1-59078-468-5; 978-1-59078-468-6

"A clearly written, chatty text not only discusses the expected bioluminescent critters (think fireflies), but delves into the realms of chemiluminescence, photoluminescence, and LEDs (light-emitting diodes) as well. . . . The text lays out the historical hows and whys of cold light, its success in the natural world, and its application in medicine and domestic/industrial illumination. Clear color photos and information boxes abound." SLJ

572.8 Biochemical genetics

Johnson, Rebecca L.
Amazing DNA; [by] Rebecca L. Johnson; illustrations by Jack Desrocher; diagrams by Jennifer E. Fairman. Millbrook Press 2008 48p il (Microquests) lib bdg $29.27

Grades: 4 5 6   **572.8**

1. DNA 2. Genetics
ISBN 978-0-8225-7139-1 lib bdg; 0-8225-7139-0 lib bdg

LC 2006-102324

This describes DNA structure, cell replication and genetic transmission.

"Johnson builds one scientific concept at a time using authentic terminology and connecting new information to familiar things. . . . Full-color microscope images, drawings, and cartoons appear in a clean, uncluttered format, combining solid science with humor." Horn Book Guide

Includes glossary and bibliographical references

Rand, Casey
DNA and heredity. Heinemann Library 2011 48p il (Investigating cells) lib bdg $32

Grades: 5 6 7 8   **572.8**

1. DNA 2. Cells 3. Heredity
ISBN 978-1-4329-3880-2; 1-4329-3880-0

LC 2009049978

Learn about cells, DNA and scientists who made an impact in cell research.

"The abundant graphic matter—photographs, diagrams, charts and graphs—work together with the text to create visually appealing pages. . . [This] would be very useful in any kind of formal investigation of the topic and yet attractive enough to encourage browsing. . . . [This] . . . is exceptionally well done." Libr Media Connect

Includes glossary and bibliographical references

572.86 DNA

Conklin, Wendy
DNA; Wendy Conklin, M.A. Teacher Created Materials 2016 32 p. color illustrations (ebook) $8.99; (pbk.) $8.99

Grades: 4 5 6   **572.86**

1. DNA 2. Heredity 3. Genes
ISBN 9781480751170; 148074719X; 9781480747197

LC 2015002692

In this book, by Wendy Conklin, "climb the double helix ladder and crack the DNA code. . . . Fifth-grade readers will learn about DNA structure and replication, proteins and genes, chromosomes, inherited traits and alleles, cloning, and more through this high-interest informational text filled with vibrant photographs." (Publisher's note)

573.8 Nervous and sensory systems

Buchanan, Shelly C.
★ **Animal** senses; by Shelly C. Buchanan. Teacher Created Materials 2016 32 p. (pbk. : alk. paper) $8.99

Grades: 4 5 6   **573.8**

1. Animals 2. Senses and sensation in animals 3. Physiology
ISBN 9781480746787

LC 2014045243

This book, by Shelly C. Buchanan, focuses on "the unique ways in which animals use their senses. . . . High-interest text paired with colorful images and graphics fill the pages of this book to engage students from cover to cover. Encourage students to apply what they've learned in the text by completing the Think Like a Scientist activity, that supports STEM instruction, included at the end of the book." (Publisher's note)

"First-rate nonfiction." SLJ

Jenkins, Steve

★ **What** do you do with a tail like this? [by] Steve Jenkins & Robin Page. Houghton Mifflin 2003 un il $15

Grades: K 1 2 3   **573.8**

1. Senses and sensation

ISBN 0-618-25628-8

LC 2002-11673

A Caldecott Medal honor book, 2004

"Jenkins' handsome paper-cut collages are both lovely and anatomically informative. . . . This is a striking, thoughtfully created book with intriguing facts made more memorable through dynamic art." Booklist

573.88   Eyes

Jenkins, Steve

★ **Eye** to eye; how animals see the world. Steve Jenkins. Houghton Mifflin Books for Children, Houghton Mifflin Harcourt 2014 32 p. $17.99

Grades: K 1 2 3 4 5   **573.88**

1. Vision in animals 2. Eye

ISBN 0547959079; 9780547959078

LC 2013024004

In this picture book, author Steve Jenkins "explains how for most animals, eyes are the most important source of information about the world in a biological sense. The simplest eyes—clusters of light-sensitive cells—appeared more than one billion years ago, and provided a big survival advantage to the first creatures that had them. Since then, animals have evolved an amazing variety of eyes, along with often surprising ways to use them." (Publisher's note)

"...Toward the end of the book, Jenkins devotes a page to describing the "evolution of the eye," enabling readers to easily follow the changes. Jenkins's outstanding torn- and cut-paper illustrations offer a fascinating look at these important organs, which range in size from the tiniest holes (starfish) to basketballs (colossal squid)...Animal facts, a bibliography, and a glossary round out this slim volume that will captivate readers of all ages." SLJ

Includes bibliographical references

575   Specific parts of and physiological systems in plants

Farndon, John

Leaves. Blackbirch Press 2006 24p il (World of plants) lib bdg $24.90

Grades: 2 3 4 5   **575**

1. Leaves

ISBN 978-1-4103-0422-3 lib bdg; 1-4103-0422-1 lib bdg

LC 2005047048

This book examines leaf shapes, the process of photosynthesis, the turning of leaves in the fall season, and unusual leaves that can trap insects

This uses "clear language and short sentences..... Helpful diagrams and sharp, colorful photographs supplement the [text]. . . . [This book offers] solid information in an attractive format." SLJ

Includes bibliographical references

Hicks, Terry Allan

Why do leaves change color? Marshall Cavendish Benchmark 2011 32p il (Tell me why, tell me how) lib bdg $29.93

Grades: 2 3 4 5   **575**

1. Leaves

ISBN 978-0-7614-4827-3; 0-7614-4827-6

This offers information about why leaves change color.

This title has "clear explanations of natural phenomena, beautiful full-color illustrations, and an uncluttered design. [The] book approaches its topic in a methodical, logical fashion, using examples from a child's world." SLJ

Includes glossary

575.6   Reproductive organs

Buchanan, Shelly C.

★ **Plant** reproduction; Shelly C. Buchanan, M.S. Teacher Created Materials 2016 32 p. (pbk.) $8.99

Grades: 4 5 6   **575.6**

1. Plants 2. Seeds 3. Pollination 4. Plants -- Reproduction

ISBN 1480746762; 9781480746763

LC 2014045201

In this juvenile reference book, by Shelly C. Buchanan, part of the publisher's "Content and Literacy in Science Grade 4" series, "filled with engaging diagrams and interesting facts, students will get an in-depth look at how plant reproduction works and why each plant is quite different. High-interest text and vibrant images and photographs fill the pages of this book to make learning about plant reproduction fun and interesting." (Publisher's note)

"The latest additions to this ongoing series deliver the same authoritative, comprehensive, and relevant information that educators have come to expect from the publisher. The high-interest subjects support inquiry-based learning and encourage readers to think critically about science, and they do so in an engaging way that holds students' attention. . . . First-rate nonfiction." SLJ

575.9   Animal-like physiological processes

Lawrence, Ellen

Meat-eating plants; toothless wonders. by Ellen Lawrence. Bearport Pub. 2013 24 p. (library binding) $23.93

Grades: 1 2 3   **575.9**

1. Carnivorous plants

ISBN 1617725897; 9781617725890

LC 2012014335

This juvenile reference book, by Ellen Lawrence, "explores the world of carnivorous plants that obtain nutrients by 'eating' animals. From plants that act like sticky flypaper to trap their prey, to other plants that lure their victims into deep pitchers of liquid from which the animals will never escape, children will learn about a variety of plants that employ interesting techniques to capture food." (Publisher's note)

Includes bibliographical references and index

576.5   Genetics

Duke, Shirley Smith

You can't wear these genes. Rourke Pub. LLC 2010 48p il (Let's explore science) $32.79

Grades: 4 5 6 7   **576.5**
1. Genetics
ISBN 978-1-61590-324-5; 1-61590-324-0
                                            LC 2010009911
This "offers a clear introduction to the complexities of genetics
while inviting students to think about how their own DNA shaped who
they are. In [this] title, well chosen boxed examples, abundant color photos, diagrams, and an appended glossary add interest and support the
engaging [text]." Booklist
Includes glossary and bibliographical references

Simpson, Kathleen
★ **Genetics**; from DNA to designer dogs. Sarah Tishkoff, consultant. National Geographic 2008 64p il map (National Geographic
investigates) $27.90
Grades: 4 5 6 7   **576.5**
1. Genetics
ISBN 978-1-4263-0361-6; 1-4263-0361-0; 978-1-4263-0327-2
lib bdg; 1-4263-0327-0 lib bdg
This discusses topics in genetics such as the identification of an
Egyptian mummy by DNA testing, the genetics of pea plants studied
by Gregor Mendel, cloning, the Human Genome Project, and stem
cell research.
"The content is fairly exciting and should grab the attention of its
target audience. . . . The photographs throughout are of high quality. . . .
An engaging look at a complex topic." Booklist

576.8   Evolution

Berkowitz, Jacob
Out of this world; the amazing search for an alien earth. Kids Can
Press 2009 48p il $16.95; pa $8.95
Grades: 4 5 6 7   **576.8**
1. Life on other planets 2. Outer space -- Exploration
ISBN 978-1-55453-197-4; 1-55453-197-7; 978-1-55453-198-1
pa; 1-55453-198-5 pa
The author "has written a miniencyclopedic, profusely illustrated,
picture book that describes, in much detail, what we all know about the
universe in which we live and about the conditions that must be present
on any planet in our solar system, or on an exoplanet . . . for life as we
know it to exist." Sci Books Films

Bortz, Alfred B.
Astrobiology. Lerner Publications 2008 48p il map (Cool science) lib bdg $26.60
Grades: 4 5 6   **576.8**
1. Space biology 2. Life on other planets
ISBN 978-0-8225-6771-4 lib bdg; 0-8225-6771-7 lib bdg
                                            LC 2006033268
This describes "the search for life in the universe. Astrobiologists
compare life on Earth to signs of life on other planets. They test meteorites for evidence of alien bacteria. They collect soil and atmospheric
samples from other planets. They study photographs taken on space missions. And they listen for signals from alien civilizations on enormous
radio dishes." Publisher's note
Includes bibliographical references

Brake, Mark
Alien Hunter's Handbook; How to Look for Extra-terrestrial Life.
by Mark Brake; illustrated by Colin Jack and Geriant Ford. Kingfisher
2012 111 p. (paperback) $10.99

Grades: 4 5 6 7   **576.8**
1. Extraterrestrial beings
ISBN 0753468859; 9780753468852
This book on extra-terrestrial life by Mark Brake "opens with an
overview of the defining characteristics of life and some of Earth's remarkable creatures, such as the microscopic tardigrade, which can exist
in the vacuum of space. Topics like the development of solar systems,
the speed of evolution, and the formation of language also get attention,
laying factual groundwork for suppositions about what alien life could
look like." (Publishers Weekly)

Gamlin, Linda
Evolution; written by Linda Gamlin. rev ed.; DK Pub. 2009 72p
il (DK eyewitness books) $16.99
Grades: 4 5 6 7   **576.8**
1. Evolution
ISBN 978-0-7566-5028-5; 0-7566-5028-3
First published 1993
Text about and photography of experiments, animals, plants, bones,
and fossils reveal the ideas and discoveries that have changed our understanding of the natural world and how life began. Includes a CD and
wall chart.

Hartman, Eve
Changing life on Earth; [by] Eve Hartman and Wendy Meshbesher.
Raintree 2009 48p il (Sci-hi: life science) lib bdg $31.43; pa $8.99
Grades: 5 6 7 8   **576.8**
1. Evolution
ISBN 978-1-4109-3324-9 lib bdg; 1-4109-3324-5 lib bdg; 978-1-
4109-3332-4 pa; 1-4109-3332-6 pa
                                            LC 2009003459
In this introduction to evolution "clear language, embedded definitions, and interesting examples illustrate abstract concepts through both
text and well-chosen photographs. . . . [The book] provides a clear and
useful explanation of the theory of evolution, with multiple sources of
evidence and a discussion of how it helps scientists to predict the implications of changes to the environment. . . . [The] book also includes
suggested activities to test ideas as well as a thorough glossary and a
Webliography." SLJ
Includes glossary and bibliographical references

Mehling, Randi
Great extinctions of the past; by Randi Mehling. Chelsea House
2007 72p il (Scientific American) lib bdg $30
Grades: 5 6 7 8   **576.8**
1. Dinosaurs 2. Mass extinctions 3. Prehistoric animals 4. Mass
extinction of species
ISBN 978-0-7910-9049-7 lib bdg; 0-7910-9049-3 lib bdg
                                            LC 2006014851
Examines extinctions of prehistoric species including the dinosaurs,
looks at the five largest extinctions ever, and explores the idea of a future
mass extinction.
"The ideas in this book are . . . clearly explained. . . . [The book has]
captioned color photos thoughout." SLJ
Includes glossary and bibliographical references

Newland, Sonya
Extinction! by Jim Pipe. Crabtree Publishing Company 2013 48
p. col. ill. (Crabtree chrome) (library) $30.60; (paperback) $9.95
Grades: 4 5 6   **576.8**
1. Extinct animals 2. End of the world 3. Mass extinctions 4.
Extinction (Biology)
ISBN 0778779254; 9780778779254; 9780778779346
                                            LC 2012032046

This book by Sonya Newland "explores both the history of extinction--dating back to the mass extinction of the Ordovician period 450 million years ago and the extinction of the dinosaurs 65 million years ago--as well as the possibility of the extinction of species in existence today. . . . In addition . . . Newland considers possible scenarios that might end life on Earth: an asteroid colliding with our planet . . . or an exploding nuclear bomb that blocks out the sun." (School Library Journal)

Includes bibliographical references and index

Pringle, Laurence, 1935-

★ **Billions** of years, amazing changes; the story of evolution. Boyds Mills Press 2011 102p il $17.95

Grades: 4 5 6 7   **576.8**

1. Evolution

ISBN 978-1-59078-723-6; 1-59078-723-4

"Pringle provides an accessible introduction to complex concepts such as natural selection and genetics, paired with Jenkins's characteristically elegant collages. . . . Compelling photographs of fossils and living creatures, as well as Jenkins's paper collages, augment the substantial text. The presentation should help children gain a confident grasp on the fundamentals of evolution." Publ Wkly

Skurzynski, Gloria

★ **Are** we alone? scientists search for life in space. National Geographic Society 2004 92p il $18.95

Grades: 5 6 7 8   **576.8**

1. Life on other planets

ISBN 0-7922-6567-X

LC 2003-17732

The author begins with a "history of how the idea of flying saucers and extraterrestrials became part of the American consciousness. Later chapters trace specific quests . . . for signs of life beyond earth. . . . The text remains readable even while explaining intricate scientific concepts and complex . . . ideas. The vibrant full-color photos enhance the work impressively." Booklist

Includes glossary and bibliographical references

Solway, Andrew

Why is there life on Earth? Raintree 2012 48p il (Earth, space, and beyond) $32; pa $8.99

Grades: 5 6 7 8   **576.8**

1. Life on other planets 2. Earth 3. Life -- Origin

ISBN 978-1-4109-4160-2; 978-1-4109-4166-4 pa

LC 2010040160

"Delivering compact but broad summations about...life on Earth, [this] survey [is] well suited for review or reinforcement reading." SLJ

Includes glossary and bibliographical references

Turner, Pamela S.

★ **Life** on earth--and beyond; an astrobiologist's quest. Charlesbridge 2008 109p il map lib bdg $19.95; pa $11.95

Grades: 5 6 7 8   **576.8**

1. Space biology 2. Life on other planets 3. Astrophysicists

ISBN 978-1-58089-133-2 lib bdg; 1-58089-133-0 lib bdg; 978-1-58089-134-9 pa; 1-58089-134-9 pa

LC 2007-01475

"Astrobiologists look outward from the Earth seeking evidence of life elsewhere in the universe. But, as this fascinating book shows, they also travel to places on Earth where extreme conditions may be similar to those on distant worlds. Turner follows astrobiologist Chris McKay as he looks for life in apparently hostile environments. . . . Illustrated with many excellent color photos and other images." Booklist

Includes bibliographical references

Walker, Robert

What is the theory of evolution? Crabtree Pub. Co. 2011 64p il (Shaping modern science) lib bdg $30.60; pa $10.95

Grades: 5 6 7 8   **576.8**

1. Evolution 2. Naturalists 3. Travel writers 4. Writers on science

ISBN 978-0-7787-7198-2 lib bdg; 0-7787-7198-9 lib bdg; 978-0-7787-7205-7 pa; 0-7787-7205-5 pa

LC 2010052628

This title is "not only written and organized well, but [it is] also gorgeous in design. Full-color photographs and illustrations are set over colorful backgrounds that add depth but not distraction. [The title] includes thought-provoking quotes from famous authors and scientists and some eyebrow-raising 'Quick Facts' throughout." SLJ

Includes glossary and bibliographical references

Weaver, Anne H.

The **voyage** of the beetle; a journey around the world with Charles Darwin and the search for the solution to the mystery of mysteries, as narrated by Rosie, an articulate beetle. [by] Anne H. Weaver; illustrated by George Lawrence. University of New Mexico Press 2007 80p il map $16.95

Grades: 4 5 6   **576.8**

1. Evolution 2. Naturalists 3. Travel writers 4. Writers on science 5. Beagle Expedition (1831-1836)

ISBN 978-0-8263-4304-8; 0-8263-4304-X

LC 2007008924

This book "is playful, creative, and beautifully conceived and executed, in terms of both the writing and the wonderful illustrations. . . . Through the eyes and narration of Darwin's fictional beetle friend Rosie, the reader is taken on the outer journey of Darwin's voyage (1831-1836) on the H.M.S. Beagle and the inner intellectual journey of Darwin's formulation of the theory of natural selection and the origin of the species." Sci Books Films

Includes bibliographical references

Winston, Robert M. L.

★ **Evolution** revolution; [by] Robert Wilson. DK Pub. 2009 96p il $16.99

Grades: 5 6 7 8   **576.8**

1. Evolution

ISBN 978-0-7566-45243-; 0-7566-4524-7

"The first two thirds of the book are devoted to the history of thought and research on evolution, from stories of Creation, through Darwin, to genetics. The last third looks at 'Evolution in Action.' Information on the fetuses of related species rubs shoulders with variations within species and a time line of the Earth. Visually, the book snaps with colored backgrounds, cool graphics, topflight photos, and clever word balloons coming from vintage black-and-white reproductions." SLJ

577 Ecology

Ecology; the delicate balance of life on earth. edited by Sherman Hollar. Rosen Educational Services, LLC 2012 87 p. col. ill. (library) $31.70

Grades: 5 6 7 8   **577**

1. Ecology 2. Environmentalism

ISBN 1615305076; 9781615305070

LC 2010052490

This book on ecology, edited by Sherman Hollar, "explores the formation of ecological communities and examines the biological diversity that forms the backbone of life on the planet. . . . By parsing the natural world into various ecosystems and biomes" it looks at "interaction among species and between organisms and their natural habitats". (Publisher's note)

Includes bibliographical references (p. 84) and index.

Gardner, Robert

Ace your ecology and environmental science project; great science fair ideas. [by] Robert Gardner, Phyllis J. Perry, and Salvatore Tocci. Enslow Publishers 2009 128p il (Ace your science project) lib bdg $31.93

Grades: 5 6 7 8   577

1. Ecology 2. Science projects 3. Environmental sciences 4. Science -- Experiments

ISBN 978-0-7660-3216-3 lib bdg; 0-7660-3216-7 lib bdg
LC 2008-4683

"Dozens of . . . science activities are presented with background information, step-by-step instructions, and suggestions for extending to the science fair level. . . . Color illustrations and important safety information are included." Horn Book Guide

Includes bibliographical references

Godkin, Celia

Wolf island. Fitzhenry & Whiteside 2007 un il $17.95; pa $9.95

Grades: K 1 2 3   577

1. Ecology 2. Food chains (Ecology)

ISBN 1-55455-007-6; 1-55455-008-4 pa

A newly formatted edition of the title first published 1989 in Canada; first U.S. edition 1993 by Scientific American Books for Young Readers

When a family of wolves is removed from the food chain on a small island, the impact on the island's ecology is felt by the other animals living there.

"The food chain, especially its harsher aspects, can be difficult to explain to young children, but this gentle narrative conveys the realism without mawkish sentimentality. . . . With a large format, arresting cover, and beautiful soft-edged illustrations, this presentation offers an effective balance between a documentary and a nature story." Booklist

Gray, Susan H.

Ecology the study of ecosystems; Susan H. Gray. Children's Press 2012 48 p. (pbk.) $6.95

Grades: 2 3 4 5   577

1. Environment 2. Biodiversity 3. Environmental sciences 4. Ecology

ISBN 0531282694; 9780531246757; 9780531282694
LC 2011030963

Author Susan Heinrichs Gray presents a children's book on ecology and ecosystems. She provides a history of ecology and discusses how ecosystems impact human beings. Gray also looks at the research being done by ecologists on the environment today and compares different ecosystems to one another, focusing on the importance of the rain forest to our environment.

Includes bibliographical references and index.

Housel, Debra J.

Ecosystems. Compass Point Books 2009 40p il map (Mission: science) lib bdg $26.60

Grades: 4 5 6   577

1. Ecology

ISBN 978-0-7565-4068-5 lib bdg; 0-7565-4068-2 lib bdg
LC 2008-35730

An introduction to the ways in which plants and animals interact with each other

Includes glossary

Larsen, Laurel

One night in the Everglades; Laurel Larsen; illustrated by Joyce Mihran Turley. Moonlight Pub./Taylor Trade Pub. 2012 30 p. (cloth : alk. paper) $15.95

Grades: 4 5 6   577

1. Nature study 2. Wetland ecology 3. Natural history -- Florida 4. Everglades (Fla.) 5. Ecologists -- Florida -- Everglades 6. Long-Term Ecological Research Program

ISBN 0981770045; 9780981770048; 9780981770062
LC 2012007375

This children's book, by Laurel Larsen, illustrated by Joyce Mihran Turley, "follow[s] two scientists as they spend a night in the Everglades collecting water samples, photographing wildlife, and sloshing through marshes in an attempt to understand this mysterious ecosystem. Part of a long-term effort to return the Everglades to a natural state after a century of development, the scientists try to figure out what the 'river of grass' was like prior to human settlement." (Publisher's note)

Latham, Donna

Amazing biome projects you can build yourself; illustrated by Farah Rizvi. Nomad Press 2009 122p il map (Build it yourself) pa $15.95

Grades: 4 5 6 7   577

1. Ecology 2. Handicraft 3. Earth sciences 4. Science -- Experiments

ISBN 978-1-934670-40-8; 1-934670-40-5

"Although the text addresses young 'eco explorers' directly, this book will likely be used as much by teachers, parents, and organization leaders in planning group activities. Offering an overview of eight terrestrial biomes as well as the ocean, Latham crams a lot of information about climate, plants, animals, soil, and other characteristics onto every page. . . . Instructions for hands-on activities related to different biomes include craft projects such as pictographs and a cornhusk doll. Students can learn how to make a glacier, an erupting volcano, and a tornado in a bottle." SLJ

Includes glossary and bibliographical references

Ecology. Raintree 2009 48p il (Sci-hi: life science) lib bdg $31.43; pa $8.99

Grades: 5 6 7 8   577

1. Ecology

ISBN 978-1-4109-3328-7 lib bdg; 1-4109-3328-8 lib bdg; 978-1-4109-3336-2 pa; 1-4109-3336-9 pa
LC 2009003465

In this introduction to ecology "clear language, embedded definitions, and interesting examples illustrate abstract concepts through both text and well-chosen photographs. . . . [It] includes suggested activities to test ideas as well as a thorough glossary and a Webliography." SLJ

Includes glossary and bibliographical references

Lauber, Patricia

Who eats what? food chains and food webs. illustrated by Holly Keller. HarperCollins Pubs. 1995 32p il (Let's-read-and-find-out science) hardcover o.p. pa $4.95

Grades: K 1 2 3   577

1. Food chains (Ecology)

ISBN 0-06-022981-0; 0-06-022982-9 lib bdg; 0-06-445130-5 pa
LC 93-10609

"Clear, simple ink-and-watercolor drawings illustrate the clear, simple text. Informative and intriguing, this basic science book leads children to think about the complex and interdependent web of life on Earth." Booklist

Schwartz, David M.

Rotten pumpkin; A Rotten Tale in 15 Voices. David Schwarz; photographs by Dwight Kuhn. Creston Books 2013 32 p. $16.99

Grades: 1 2 3 4 5   **577**

1. Compost 2. Pumpkin

ISBN 1939547032; 9781939547033

In this book, by David Schwarz, with photographs by Dwight Kuhn, "Compost won't mean the same thing after readers have seen the . . . transformation of Jack from grinning pumpkin to mold-mottled wreckage. . . . The story of decomposition is . . . told so that science comes to life (and death)." The book "features a teacher guide in the back of the book, and additional material." (Publisher's note)

"What's scarier than a grinning jack-o'-lantern? How about what happens to it after Halloween? Kuhn's upbeat prose poems are written from the perspectives of 15 scavengers, insects, and molds that aid in a gourd's decomposition, which Kuhn captures in gruesomely vivid photographs. As the pumpkin transforms from a crisp orange specimen to a blackened, sunken puddle of mush, the speakers include a mouse, "black rot" mold, and a fly ("You're gonna love hearing how I eat. I vomit on the pumpkin flesh. My vomit dissolves pumpkin nutrients so I can lap them up"). The inventive concept combines a Halloween theme with science that readers can easily replicate—if they have the stomach for it." (Publishers Weekly)

Stille, Darlene R.

Nature interrupted; the science of environmental chain reactions. Compass Point Books 2009 48p il map (Headline science) lib bdg $27.93

Grades: 5 6 7 8   **577**

1. Ecology 2. Food chains (Ecology) 3. Environmental degradation

ISBN 978-0-7565-3949-8 lib bdg; 0-7565-3949-8 lib bdg

LC 2008007282

This "reviews the importance of subtle links in the environmental chain and the far-reaching consequences of its disruption. The possible harm to the food chain caused by the use of antibacterial soap is one case study. The flow of energy from one organism to the next in the food web and the unexpected results when this relationship is disrupted are shown in examinations of monarch butterflies, zebra mussels, and algal blooms. The color illustrations and charts . . . are clear and helpful, and the text, although information rich, is not overly difficult." SLJ

Includes glossary and bibliographical references

Suzuki, David T.

★ **You** are the Earth; know your world so you can make it better. [by] David Suzuki and Kathy Vanderlinden; art by Wallace Edwards; diagrams by Talent Pun. rev ed; Greystone Books 2010 159p il $16.95

Grades: 4 5 6 7   **577**

1. Ecology 2. Human ecology

ISBN 978-1-55365-476-6; 1-55365-476-5

First published 1999 with title: You are the Earth: from dinosaur breath to pizza from dirt

"After devoting a chapter to each of life's necessities—air, water, soil (earth), energy (fire), love, and a spiritual connection with the universe—the authors close with a look at three social and environmental initiatives by young people; a set of review questions (with answers); and 10 consciousness-raising activities, from science projects to storytelling. Sourced, briefly told versions of folktales from several traditions are interspersed throughout, and the plentiful illustrations include color diagrams, comics, and crisply reproduced photos. . . . [The authors'] eloquent plea to see ourselves and the Earth as interdependent will inspire readers to sit up, look around, and take a little less for granted." SLJ

Includes glossary

VanCleave, Janice Pratt

Janice Vancleave's ecology for every kid; easy activities that make learning science fun. Wiley 1996 219p il maps (Science for every kid series) hardcover o.p. pa $10.95

Grades: 4 5 6 7   **577**

1. Ecology 2. Habitat (Ecology) 3. Science -- Experiments

ISBN 0-471-10100-1; 0-471-10086-2 pa

LC 95-6112

This book of science activities covers "25 topics, ranging from plant and animal food chains to the effect of plastics on the environment. Subjects are introduced in a 'What You Need to Know' section that gives explanation of the scientific principles, plus plenty of everyday examples. A brief preparatory exercise follows, usually in the form of an imaginative game. . . . Simple black-line drawings are crisp, uncluttered, and well placed. . . . Solid information and a generous portion of fun are combined to elevate this selection above the standard collection of experiments." SLJ

Includes glossary

Step-by-step science experiments in ecology; by Janice VanCleave. Rosen Pub. 2013 80 p. col. ill. (Janice VanCleave's first-place science fair projects) (library) $33.25; (paperback) $14.15

Grades: 5 6 7 8   **577**

1. Ecology 2. Science -- Experiments 3. Ecology -- Experiments

ISBN 1448869803; 9781448869800; 9781448884698

This book by Janice VanCleave is part of the First-Place Science Fair Projects series. The books have an introduction to the subject—here, ecology, followed by 22 simple . . . experiments. Van Cleave states the basic goal of the experiments, followed by a list of necessary materials, most of which can be found around the house or easily acquired with minimal cost. Step-by-step instructions are clearly detailed and accompanied by diagrams where needed." (School Library Journal)

Includes bibliographical references (p. 76-78) and index.

Woodford, Chris

Arctic tundra and polar deserts; Revised ed. Raintree 2011 64p il map $34

Grades: 5 6 7 8 9   **577**

1. Tundra ecology 2. Polar regions

ISBN 978-1-4329-4172-7; 1-4329-4172-0

LC 2010012428

"...Provides detailed information suitable for middle school research projects, and browsing potential is high due to the colorful, graphic nature." Library Media Connection

577.09 History, geographic treatment, biography

Pelletier, Mia

Avati; discovering Arctic ecology. Inhabit Media 2013 32 p. $14.95

Grades: 3 4 5   **577.09**

1. Arctic regions 2. Tundra ecology

ISBN 1927095131; 9781927095133

This book on arctic ecology by Mia Pelletier describes "a complex ecosystem that contains many thriving habitats, each supported by dozens of ecological relationships between plants and animals. From the many animals that live and hunt at the floe edge to the hundreds of insects that abound on the summer tundra, this book gives a . . . bird's-eye view of the . . . ways that animals, plants, and insects coexist in the Arctic ecosystem." (Publisher's note)

577.2   Specific factors affecting ecology

Godkin, Celia

Fire! Fitzhenry & Whiteside 2006 un il $17.95

Grades: 2 3 4   **577.2**

1. Forest fires 2. Forest ecology

ISBN 1-55041-889-0

"Focusing on events in one location, this handsome volume presents the cycle of forest fires in words and pictures.... Clear, concise writing and vivid artwork make this a fine presentation on the subject." Booklist

Peluso, Beth A.

The **charcoal** forest; how fire helps animals and plants. written and illustrated by Beth A. Peluso. Mountain Press Pub. Co. 2007 56p il pa $12

Grades: 3 4 5 6   **577.2**

1. Forest fires 2. Forest plants 3. Forest animals 4. Forest ecology 5. Rocky Mountains

ISBN 978-0-87842-532-7 pa; 0-87842-532-2 pa

LC 2007003358

This "explores the new habitat created by [a forest] fire. Focusing on the Northern Rocky Mountains of the United States and Canada, the book describes twenty species of animals and plants that contribute to the reclamation and renewal of the charcoal forest." Publisher's note

Simon, Seymour

Wildfires. Morrow Junior Bks. 1996 un il hardcover o.p. pa $6.99

Grades: 4 5 6 7   **577.2**

1. Forest fires 2. Forest ecology

ISBN 0-688-17530-9 pa

LC 95-12653

"Exploring the place of fire in nature, Simon explains that ... forest fires have important functions in the ecosystem. With a brilliantly clear and colorful photograph facing each page of text, the book describes the causes and the progression of the wildfires that burned areas of Yellowstone National Park in 1988, explains how the fires were beneficial in many ways.... Lucid writing and excellent book design." Booklist

577.3   Ecology of specific environments

Brenner, Barbara

One small place in a tree; illustrated by Tom Leonard. HarperCollins Publishers 2004 un il $15.99; lib bdg $16.89

Grades: 2 3 4   **577.3**

1. Forest ecology

ISBN 0-688-17180-X; 0-688-17181-8 lib bdg

LC 2002-1181

A child visitor observes as one tiny scratch in a tree develops into a home for a variety of woodland animals over many years, even after the tree has fallen.

"Brenner makes the science enjoyable and understandable, and Leonard's highly detailed, realistic illustrations provide great visual aid." Booklist

Collard, Sneed B.

Forest in the clouds; by Sneed Collard III; illustrated by Michael Rothman. Charlesbridge Pub. 2000 un il map $16.95; pa $7.95

Grades: 2 3 4   **577.3**

1. Cloud forests 2. Forest ecology 3. Natural history -- Costa Rica

ISBN 0-88106-985-X; 0-88106-986-8 pa

LC 98-6150

Describes some of the exotic plants and animals that live in the cloud forest of Costa Rica, and discusses some environmental threats faced by this region

"Rothman's detailed acrylic paintings, dominated by rich greens and browns, cover the better part of each spread.... Although valuable for reports, Collard's book will interest browsers as well." SLJ

Fusco Castaldo, Nancy

Rainforests; an activity guide for ages 6-9. {by} Nancy F. Castaldo. Chicago Review Press 2003 133p il $14.95

Grades: 2 3 4 5   **577.3**

1. Rain forest ecology

ISBN 1-55652-476-5

LC 2002-152661

Provides facts and activities that explore tropical and temperate ancient forests, discusses how individuals can help preserve them, and describes well-known and unfamiliar creatures of the rain forest

"The activities are varied and interesting, ranging from science projects to crafts to recipes. . . . The book would serve as a valuable resource." SLJ

Includes bibliographical references

Gibbons, Gail

Nature's green umbrella; tropical rain forests. Morrow Junior Bks. 1994 un il maps hardcover o.p. pa $5.95

Grades: K 1 2 3   **577.3**

1. Rain forest ecology

ISBN 0-688-12353-8; 0-688-12354-6 lib bdg; 0-688-15411-5 pa

LC 93-17569

Describes the climatic conditions of the rain forest as well as the different layers of plants and animals that comprise the ecosystem

The language is "simple, yet poetic and evocative. . . . Colorful maps pinpoint the locations of these global resources. Green vines entwine around the borders of each page and enclose the text and bright illustrations." Sci Books Films

Johnson, Rebecca L.

A **walk** in the boreal forest; with illustrations by Phyllis V. Saroff. Carolrhoda Bks. 2001 48p il map (Biomes of North America) lib bdg $23.93

Grades: 3 4 5 6   **577.3**

1. Forest ecology

ISBN 1-57505-156-7

LC 00-8240

Describes the climate, seasons, plants, animals, and soil of the boreal forest, a biome or land zone, which stretches across the northern parts of North America, Europe, and Asia

"A fine overview of the plant and animal life of the boreal forest. . . . Excellent full-color photographs." SLJ

Includes glossary and bibliographical references

A **walk** in the deciduous forest; with illustrations by Phyllis V. Saroff. Carolrhoda Bks. 2001 48p il map (Biomes of North America) lib bdg $23.93

Grades: 3 4 5 6   **577.3**

1. Forest ecology

ISBN 1-57505-155-9

LC 00-8243

Takes readers on a walk through a forest of trees that lose their leaves in the fall, showing examples of how the animals and plants depend on each other and their environment to survive

"The simple design and clearly written, informative text will appeal to readers who enjoy nature." Horn Book Guide

Includes glossary and bibliographical references

Lasky, Kathryn

The **most** beautiful roof in the world; exploring the rainforest canopy. photographs by Christopher G. Knight. Harcourt Brace & Co. 1997 un il hardcover o.p. pa $9

Grades: 4 5 6 7   **577.3**

  1. Botanists 2. Rain forest ecology

  ISBN 0-15-200893-4; 0-15-200897-7 pa

LC 95-48193

Describes the work of Meg Lowman in the rainforest canopy, an area unexplored until the last ten years and home to previously unknown species of plants and animals

  "Fresh in out-look and intriguing in details, this memorable book features colorful photographs that reflect the you-are-there quality of the text." Booklist

  Includes glossary

Levy, Janey

Discovering rain forests; [by] Janey Levy. PowerKids Press 2007 32p il map (World habitats) lib bdg $23.95

Grades: 3 4 5   **577.3**

  1. Rain forests 2. Rain forest ecology

  ISBN 978-1-4042-3782-7 lib bdg; 1-4042-3782-8 lib bdg

LC 2006036867

This book about rain forest ecology "includes 10 chapters with information on climate, location, plants, animals, people, conservation, and page of relevant facts and figures. Clear, colorful photographs show the landscape and the varied plants and wildlife." SLJ

  Includes glossary

Lundgren, Julie K.

Forest fare; studying food webs in the forest. [by] Julie K. Lundgren. Rourke Pub. 2009 32p il map (Studying food webs) lib bdg $28.50

Grades: 3 4 5   **577.3**

  1. Forest ecology 2. Food chains (Ecology)

  ISBN 978-1-60472-316-8 lib bdg; 1-60472-316-5 lib bdg

LC 2008-24858

This book has "stunning photos, fascinating facts, and intriguing examples. . . . Herbivores, omnivores, and carnivores specific to . . . [the forest] ecosystem are presented. . . . 'Chew on this' insets add further interest and information. . . . [This] will appeal to readers." SLJ

  Includes glossary and bibliographical references

Pfeffer, Wendy

A **log's** life; illustrations by Robin Brickman. Simon & Schuster Bks. for Young Readers 1997 un il $16

Grades: K 1 2 3   **577.3**

  1. Oak 2. Forest ecology 3. Animals -- Food 4. Animals -- Habitations

  ISBN 0-689-80636-1

LC 95-30020

This is an "introduction to the life, death, and decay of an oak tree. The simple, informative text presents the complex cast of characters residing in or on the living tree as well as the decomposing log. . . . The verbal descriptions of this rich ecosystem are enhanced by striking illustrations of three-dimensional paper sculptures, often so realistic as to seem to be preserved natural specimens." SLJ

Pyers, Greg

The **biodiversity** of rain forests. Marshall Cavendish 2010 32p il (Biodiversity) lib bdg $28.50

Grades: 4 5 6   **577.3**

  1. Rain forest ecology

  ISBN 978-1-60870-073-8 lib bdg; 1-60870-073-9 lib bdg

"Page format is attractive, filled with easy-to-understand fact boxes, charts, graphs, maps and diagrams, and interesting captioned color photographs, all well-balanced within the main text." Libr Media Connect

  Includes glossary

The **biodiversity** of woodlands. Marshall Cavendish 2010 32p il (Biodiversity) lib bdg $28.50

Grades: 4 5 6   **577.3**

  1. Forest ecology

  ISBN 978-1-60870-074-5 lib bdg; 1-60870-074-7 lib bdg

"Page format is attractive, filled with easy-to-understand fact boxes, charts, graphs, maps and diagrams, and interesting captioned color photographs, all well-balanced within the main text." Libr Media Connect

  Includes glossary

Simon, Seymour

Tropical rainforests. Collins 2010 30p il $16.99; lib bdg $17.89

Grades: 3 4 5 6   **577.3**

  1. Rain forests 2. Rain forest ecology

  ISBN 978-0-06-114253-6; 0-06-114253-0; 978-0-06-114254-3 lib bdg; 0-06-114254-9 lib bdg

"Simon's short overview has a familiar format: large pages of oversize text facing sharp color photos of trees, animals, and plants provide an inviting overview of the biome that is populated by the largest variety of plant and animal species on the planet, with many of them yet to be discovered. . . . Simon's careful descriptions hold a great deal of appeal for young people." SLJ

  Includes glossary

Slade, Suzanne

What if there were no gray wolves? a book about the temperate forest ecosystem. illustrated by Carol Schwartz. Picture Window Books 2011 24p il map (Food chain reactions) lib bdg $25.99; pa $8.95

Grades: 2 3 4   **577.3**

  1. Wolves 2. Forest ecology

  ISBN 978-1-4048-6020-9 lib bdg; 1-4048-6020-7 lib bdg; 978-1-4048-6395-8 pa; 1-4048-6395-8 pa

LC 2010009877

Discusses the temperate forest ecosystem and the role of the gray wolf in helping to maintain it, describing the wolf's place on the food chain and what would happen to the temperate forest if the gray wolf were to become extinct.

  "Radiant illustrations are paired with simple, perceptive sentences to underscore the impact of the loss of [gray wolves]. . . . In a very effective convention extinct plants and animals are placed in silhouettes within many illustrations—the black void left by the loss of each species increases with each page. This . . . will engage readers on many levels." SLJ

  Includes glossary and bibliographical references

Tagliaferro, Linda

Explore the tropical rain forest; by Linda Tagliaferro. Capstone Press 2007 32p il map (Explore the biomes) $16.95; pa $6.95

Grades: PreK K 1 2   **577.3**

  1. Rain forest ecology

  ISBN 978-0-7368-6407-7; 0-7368-6407-5; 978-0-7368-9630-6 pa; 0-7368-9630-9 pa

LC 2006004107

This is an introduction to the tropical rain forest habitat and some of its plants and animals.

  This book "uses vivid, sense-appealing language. . . . An attractive . . . format displays the captions to colorful photographs." Sci Books Films

  Includes bibliographical references

Vogt, Richard Carl

★ **Rain** forests. Simon & Schuster Books for Young Readers 2009 64p il (Insiders) $16.99

Grades: 4 5 6 7   **577.3**

1. Rain forests

ISBN 978-1-4169-3866-8; 1-4169-3866-4

LC 2008061111

"The layers of a rain forest are drawn with exacting detail in every imaginable shade of green, while circular inserts zoom in on flora with accompanying stats. Running down the length of the spread are markers delineating the cutoff points for each layer—emergent, canopy, and so on. The rest of the book is similarly fine, bringing animals, reptiles, and insects into the mix. . . . Some photographs join the mostly hand-illustrated affair. . . . What will grab browsers are the 3D cover and vivid drawings on thick, oversize pages, but what will keep them reading is a cumulative sense of the rain forest as a verdant universe nearly festering with life." Booklist

577.34   Rain forest ecology

Clarke, Ginjer L.

What's Up in the Amazon Rainforest; Ginjer L. Clarke. Penguin Group USA 2015 144 p. color ill., color maps $8.99

Grades: 4 5 6   **577.34**

1. Amazon River valley   2. Rain forest animals

ISBN 0448481030; 9780448481036

LC 2015020924

In this book by Ginjer L. Clarke readers can get "lost in the largest rainforest in the world to climb trees that are 500 years old, swim with a pink dolphin, avoid the deadly poison dart frogs, and sleep with a troop of twenty howler monkeys. In What's Up in the Amazon Rainforest, you'll learn all about the plants and animals, as well as the people that live there and the habitat itself." (Publisher's note)

"The Amazon itself is enormous ... and Clarke capably covers substantial terrain in this book, too, making it an asset for readers looking to learn about one of the world's most vibrant and important regions." Pub Wkly

Includes bibliographical references and index.

Duke, Kate

In the rainforest; written and illustrated by Kate Duke. HarperCollins Publishers 2014 40 p. color illustrations (hardcover) $17.99

Grades: K 1 2 3   **577.34**

1. Rain forests -- Pictorial works

ISBN 0060282592; 9780060282592; 9780064451970

LC 2013047947

"The rainforest is home to millions of plant and animal species. Some animals live high up in the trees, some crawl across the forest floor, and some tunnel underground, but they all depend on one another and the rain to survive." (Publisher's note)

"This informative volume from the dependable Let's-Read-and-Find-Out science series offers an uncommonly readable introduction to rain forests. Instructions for making a terrarium are appended." Booklist

Messner, Kate

Tree of wonder; The Many Marvelous Lives of a Rainforest Tree. by Kate Messner; illustrated by Simona Mulazzani. Chronicle Books LLC 2014 36 p. color illustrations (alk. paper) $16.99

Grades: PreK K 1 2   **577.34**

1. Rain forest animals   2. Rain forest ecology   3. Dipteryx oleifera   4. Habitat (Ecology)

ISBN 9781452112480

LC 2013032910

In this children's book, by Kate Messner, illustrated by Simona Mulazzani, "[d]eep in the forest, in the warm-wet green, [an] almendro tree grows, stretching its branches toward the sun. Who makes their homes here? . . . Count each and every one as life multiplies again and again in this lush and fascinating book about the rainforest." (Publisher's note)

"The main text is descriptive and poetic, complementing the more straightforward, factual writing of the sidebars." SLJ

Pettiford, Rebecca

Rain forest food chains; by Rebecca Pettiford. Jump!, Inc. 2016 24 p. (hardcover : alk. paper) $17.95

Grades: K 1 2 3   **577.34**

1. Rain forest animals   2. Rain forest ecology   3. Food chains (Ecology)

ISBN 9781620313046

LC 2015028824

In this book, by Rebecca Pettiford, "early fluent readers explore the rain forest biome and the food chains it supports. Vibrant, full-color photos and carefully leveled text engage young readers as they explore how energy flows through plants and animals in a wet and wooded environment." (Publisher's note)

"Well-chosen photos depict hunting and eating without too much gore and feature helpful labels of the animal's food chain role plus a simple food chain diagram." SLJ

Welsbacher, Anne

Protecting Earth's rain forests; by Anne Welsbacher. Lerner Publications 2009 72p il map (Saving our living Earth) lib bdg $30.60

Grades: 5 6 7 8   **577.34**

1. Rain forests   2. Environmental protection

ISBN 978-0-8225-7562-7 lib bdg; 0-8225-7562-0 lib bdg

LC 2007-38859

"Provides a thorough, interesting discussion of multiple aspects of [rain forest protection], including historical origins, the current situation, and potential solutions. . . . Photos from around the world accompany discussions. . . . Solid choice to replace outdated books." SLJ

Includes glossary and bibliographical references

577.4   Grassland ecology

Bateman, Donna M.

Out on the prairie; Donna M. Bateman; illustrated by Susan Swan. Charlesbridge 2012 32 p. (reinforced for library use) $15.95

Grades: PreK K 1 2   **577.4**

1. Counting 2. Prairie animals 3. Picture books for children 4. Badlands National Park (S.D.) 5. Prairie animals -- South Dakota -- Badlands National Park 6. Prairie ecology -- South Dakota -- Badlands National Park

ISBN 1580893775; 9781580893770; 9781580893787

LC 2011025782

For this counting book, "[Donna M.] Bateman Bateman has chosen representative features and creatures" of the mixed-grass prairie of Badlands National Park in South Dakota "to introduce a remarkable ecosystem. Counting from one to 10, she goes on to include pronghorns, meadowlarks, prairie dogs, grasshoppers, grouse, owls, rattlesnakes, coyotes and toads in a series of verses that also span the day from dawn to night." (Kirkus)

Collard, Sneed B.

The **prairie** builders; reconstructing America's lost grasslands. written and photographed by Sneed B. Collard III. Houghton Mifflin Co. 2005 66p il (Scientists in the field) $17; pa $8.95

Grades: 4 5 6 7 **577.4**

1. Prairies 2. Nature conservation

ISBN 978-0-618-39687-0; 0-618-39687-X; 978-0-547-01441-8 pa; 0-547-01441-4 pa

LC 2004-13201

This describes an effort to restore part of the native tallgrass prairie in the the 8,000-acre Neal Smith National Wildlife Refuge in Iowa

"The engaging text is accompanied by large, inviting color photographs. . . . An essential purchase for libraries in prairie regions and a worthwhile choice for others." SLJ

Includes bibliographical references

Jackson, Kay

Explore the grasslands; by Kay Jackson. Capstone Press 2007 32p il map (Explore the biomes) $16.95; pa $6.95

Grades: PreK K 1 2 **577.4**

1. Grassland ecology

ISBN 978-0-7368-6405-3; 0-7368-6405-9; 978-0-7368-9628-3 pa; 0-7368-9628-7 pa

LC 2006005641

This is a introduction to grassland ecology and some of its plants and animals

This book "uses vivid, sense-appealing language. . . . An attractive . . . format displays the captions to colorful photographs." Sci Books Films

Includes bibliographical references

Johnson, Rebecca L.

A **walk** in the prairie; with illustrations by Phyllis V. Saroff. Carolrhoda Bks. 2001 48p il map (Biomes of North America) lib bdg $23.93

Grades: 3 4 5 6 **577.4**

1. Prairie ecology

ISBN 1-57505-153-2

LC 00-8252

Describes the climate, soil, seasons, plants, and animals of the North American prairie and the ways in which the plants and animals depend on each other and their environment to survive

Includes glossary and bibliographical references

Levy, Janey

Discovering the tropical savanna; [by] Janey Levy. PowerKids Press 2008 32p il map (World habitats) lib bdg $23.95

Grades: 3 4 5 **577.4**

1. Grassland ecology

ISBN 978-1-4042-3783-4 lib bdg; 1-4042-3783-6 lib bdg

LC 2006103368

This book about the ecology of the tropical savanna "includes 10 chapters with information on climate, location, plants, animals, people, conservation, and page of relevant facts and figures. The [text is] concise and accessible. Clear, colorful photographs show the landscape and the varied plants and wildlife." SLJ

Includes glossary

Pattison, Darcy

Prairie storms; by Darcy Pattison; illustrated by Kathleen Rietz. Sylvan Dell Pub. 2011 un il map $16.95; pa $8.95

Grades: K 1 2 3 **577.4**

1. Storms 2. Prairie animals 3. Prairie ecology

ISBN 978-1-60718-129-3; 1-60718-129-0; 978-1-60718-139-2 pa; 1-60718-139-8 pa; 978-1-60718-149-1 e-book; 1-60718-149-5 english e-book; 978-1-60718-159-0 spanish e-book; 1-60718-159-2 spanish e-book

LC 2011016339

This describes the prairie ecosystem through its ever-changing weather. Each month features a storm typical of that season and a prairie animal who must shelter, hide, escape, or endure those storms.

"Beautiful two-page framed spreads do a good job of showing an animal or bird of the plains and the weather conditions that might be currently affecting. The book gives a unique look at the differing plains habitats." Sci Books Films

Root, Phyllis

Plant a pocket of prairie; Phyllis Root; illustrations by Betsy Bowen. University of Minnesota Press 2014 40 p. chiefly color illustrations (hc : alk. paper) $14.95

Grades: 1 2 3 4 **577.4**

1. Gardening 2. Prairie ecology 3. Prairie plants

ISBN 0816679800; 9780816679805

LC 2013040345

AAAS/Subaru SB & F Prize in Excellence in Science Books Finalists, Hands-on Science (2014)

In this book, "free verse poems invite readers to plant flowers and reconstruct pockets of lost prairie in backyards and on balconies to entice insects and birds to return, such as butterfly weed to attract monarch butterflies or rough blazing star for great spangled fritillaries. A map shows the once extensive prairie in Minnesota and the less than one percent now remaining, while the plant list will inspire the planting of at least some of the 14 recommended flowers and grasses." (School Library Journal)

"There isn't much prairie left in the U.S., thanks to human farming and development. Readers are encouraged to reverse this trend by planting native plants in their own backyards and watching what animals are attracted by each plant species. Mixed-media illustrations are placed on white backgrounds, their chunky outlines a modern twist on botanical illustration. The conservation and restoration message is universal." Horn Book

Sill, Cathryn P.

Grasslands; written by Cathryn Sill; illustrated by John Sill. Peachtree Publishers 2011 un il (About habitats) $16.95

Grades: K 1 2 3 4 **577.4**

1. Grasslands 2. Grassland ecology

ISBN 978-1-56145-559-1; 1-56145-559-8

LC 2010026690

"With simple, informative sentences paired with beautifully detailed watercolor paintings, this title . . . will introduce young grade-schoolers to grassland ecology across the world: the climate, plants that grow there, and the wildlife that have adapted to survive in the large open spaces. . . . Great for classroom sharing." Booklist

Slade, Suzanne

What if there were no bees? a book about the grassland ecosystem. illustrated by Carol Schwartz. Picture Window Books 2010 24p il map (Food chain reactions) lib bdg $25.99; pa $8.95

Grades: 2 3 4 **577.4**

1. Bees 2. Grassland ecology 3. Fertilization of plants

ISBN 978-1-4048-6019-3 lib bdg; 1-4048-6019-3 lib bdg; 978-1-4048-6394-1 pa; 1-4048-6394-X pa

LC 2010006035

"Radiant illustrations are paired with simple, perceptive sentences to underscore the impact of the loss of [bees]. . . . In a very effective convention extinct plants and animals are placed in silhouettes within many illustrations—the black void left by the loss of each species increases with each page. This . . . will engage readers on many levels." SLJ

Includes glossary and bibliographical references

577.5 Ecology of miscellaneous environments

Banting, Erinn

Caves; Erinn Banting. AV2 by Weigl 2012 32 p. col. ill., col. map (Ecosystems) (hardcover) $28.55; (paperback) $13.95

Grades: 4 5 6 **577.5**

1. Caves 2. Cave ecology 3. Ecology 4. Cave ecology
ISBN 1616906391; 1616906456; 9781616906399; 9781616906450

LC 2010050985

This book by Erinn Banting is part of the "Biomes" series. "Caves are unique ecosystems that are found on all seven continents. This book explores the plants and animals that have adapted to life in this unique environment." (Publisher's note) "Explanations of climate and physical characteristics are accompanied by appropriate diagrams and illustrations." (School Library Journal)

Callery, Sean

Polar lands. Kingfisher 2011 il (Life cycles) $12.99

Grades: 2 3 4 **577.5**

1. Food chains (Ecology) 2. Antarctica 3. Arctic regions
ISBN 978-0-7534-6691-9; 0-7534-6691-0

"This focuses on 11 Arctic and Antarctic animals, exploring their life cycles and the ways in which they are interconnected by a food chain. The first food chain Callery presents is hermit crab, Arctic tern, Arctic fox, polar bear. Each spread is devoted to a single animal. . . . Beautiful closeup photographs show the animals in their natural habitats eating, playing and interacting with one another. . . . A great beginning look at the lifecycles of some fascinating animals and a solid tool for learning about food chains." Kirkus

Johansson, Philip

The dry desert; a web of life. Enslow Publishers 2004 48p il (World of biomes) lib bdg $18.95

Grades: 3 4 5 **577.5**

1. Desert ecology
ISBN 0-7660-2200-5

LC 2003-20443

This describes the plants, animals, and ecology of deserts of the world
Includes glossary and bibliographical references

Johnson, Rebecca L.

A walk in the tundra; with illustrations by Phyllis V. Saroff. Carolrhoda Bks. 2001 48p il map (Biomes of North America) lib bdg $23.93; pa $8.95

Grades: 3 4 5 6 **577.5**

1. Tundra ecology
ISBN 1-57505-157-5 lib bdg; 1-57505-526-0 pa

LC 00-8245

Takes readers on a walk in the tundra, showing examples of how the animals and plants of the tundra are connected and dependent on each other and the tundra's soil and climate

"A visually pleasing title with plenty of clear, colorful photographs of the biome's flora and fauna throughout the year." SLJ

Includes glossary and bibliographical references

Kopp, Megan

Islands; inside out. Megan Kopp. Crabtree Publishing Co. 2015 32 p. color illustrations (Ecosystems inside out) (reinforced library binding : alk. paper) $27.60

Grades: 4 5 6 **577.5**

1. Ecology 2. Islands 3. Island ecology
ISBN 0778714977; 9780778714972; 9780778715016

LC 2014046708

In this juvenile book, by Megan Kopp, part of the "Ecosystems inside out" series, "Step onto an island . . . , a habitat for land-living organisms as well as creatures that visit from their ocean homes. Peel back the corners of the island to discover the incredible organisms that live in this ecosystem, from lizards and birds to possums and bats. Discover how each organism functions within its island home." (Publisher's note)

"Using full-page color photographs and concise, informative writing, the Ecosystems Inside Out series offers readers an overview of biomes around the globe. Each volume begins with an introduction to the concept of ecosystems before moving on to examine specific examples within the featured biome. . . . Each book ends with an activity, usually requiring adult supervision; a glossary; and additional resources. A solid primer with great visual appeal." Booklist

Includes index

Levy, Janey

Discovering mountains; [by] Janey Levy. PowerKids Press 2008 32p il map (World habitats) lib bdg $23.95

Grades: 3 4 5 **577.5**

1. Mountains 2. Mountain ecology
ISBN 978-1-4042-3785-8 lib bdg; 1-4042-3785-2 lib bdg

LC 2006103369

This book about mountain ecology "includes 10 chapters with information about climate, location, plants, animals, people, conservation, and a page of relevant facts and figures. The [text is] concise and accessible. Clear, colorful photographs show the landscape and the varied plants and wildlife." Booklist

Includes glossary

Discovering the Arctic tundra; [by] Janey Levy. PowerKids Press 2008 32p il map (World habitats) lib bdg $23.95

Grades: 3 4 5 **577.5**

1. Tundra ecology 2. Arctic regions
ISBN 978-1-4042-3787-2 lib bdg; 1-4042-3787-9 lib bdg

LC 2006103405

This book about the ecology of the Arctic tundra "includes 10 chapters with information on climate, location, plants, animals, people, conservation, and a page of relevant facts and figures. The [text is] concise and accessible. Clear, colorful photographs show the landscape and the varied plants and wildlife." Booklist

Includes glossary

Lynch, Wayne

Sonoran Desert; text and photographs by Wayne Lynch; assisted by Aubrey Lang. NorthWord Books 2009 64p il (Our wild world ecosystems) $16.95

Grades: 5 6 7 8 **577.5**

1. Desert ecology 2. Sonoran Desert 3. Natural history -- Sonoran Desert
ISBN 978-1-58979-389-7; 1-58979-389-7

LC 2008036635

"An in-depth look at a vibrant ecosystem. Spilling over the Mexican border into Arizona and New Mexico, the Sonoran Desert is especially rich in varied plants, animals, insects, and other critters that call it home. Lynch shares his expertise and experiences in a clearly written, conversational text, lavishly illustrated with his own crisp color photos." SLJ

Marsico, Katie

A home on the tundra; by Katie Marsico. Children's Press 2007 24p il (Scholastic news nonfiction readers) $20

Grades: 1 2 3 **577.5**

1. Tundra ecology
ISBN 0-516-25345-X; 978-0-516-25345-9

LC 2006002306

An introduction to tundra ecology

"Simple, easy-to-read. . . . Everything students need for reports is beautifully depicted with scenic full-color photographs of the land, the plants, and the animals that live there." SLJ

Includes bibliographical references

Moss, Miriam

This is the mountain; illustrated by Adrienne Kennaway. Frances Lincoln 2011 un il $17.95

Grades: K 1 2 3   **577.5**

1. Mountain ecology 2. Natural history -- Africa 3. Mount Kilimanjaro (Tanzania)

ISBN 978-1-84507-984-0; 1-84507-984-1

"Illustrated with attractive accessible watercolors, this picture book introduces Mount Kilimanjaro, from the people and animals living on the plains around it to the mountainside and the glaciers at its peak. . . . The book has real value for children. Not only does it show life on and around Mount Kilimanjaro, it shows how the landforms and ecosystems change as one moves up the mountain." Booklist

Pyers, Greg

The **biodiversity** of coasts. Marshall Cavendish 2010 32p il map (Biodiversity) lib bdg $28.50

Grades: 4 5 6   **577.5**

1. Coasts 2. Seashore ecology

ISBN 978-1-60870-069-1 lib bdg; 1-60870-069-0 lib bdg

"Page format is attractive, filled with easy-to-understand fact boxes, charts, graphs, maps and diagrams, and interesting captioned color photographs, all well-balanced within the main text." Libr Media Connect

Includes glossary

The **biodiversity** of deserts. Marshall Cavendish 2010 32p il (Biodiversity) lib bdg $28.50

Grades: 4 5 6   **577.5**

1. Desert ecology

ISBN 978-1-60870-071-4 lib bdg; 1-60870-071-2 lib bdg

"Page format is attractive, filled with easy-to-understand fact boxes, charts, graphs, maps and diagrams, and interesting captioned color photographs, all well-balanced within the main text." Libr Media Connect

Includes glossary

The **biodiversity** of polar regions. Marshall Cavendish 2010 32p il (Biodiversity) lib bdg $28.50

Grades: 4 5 6   **577.5**

1. Polar regions

ISBN 978-1-60870-072-1 lib bdg; 1-60870-072-0 lib bdg

"Page format is attractive, filled with easy-to-understand fact boxes, charts, graphs, maps and diagrams, and interesting captioned color photographs, all well-balanced within the main text." Libr Media Connect

Includes glossary

Slade, Suzanne

What if there were no lemmings? a book about the tundra ecosystem. illustrated by Carol Schwartz. Picture Window Books 2011 24p il map (Food chain reactions) lib bdg $25.99; pa $8.95

Grades: 2 3 4   **577.5**

1. Lemmings 2. Tundra ecology 3. Animals -- Arctic regions

ISBN 978-1-4048-6021-6 lib bdg; 1-4048-6021-5 lib bdg; 978-1-4048-6396-5 pa; 1-4048-6396-6 pa

LC 2010009878

Discusses the tundra ecosystem and the role of lemmings as a keystone species in helping to maintain it, describing the lemmings' place on the food chain and what would happen to the tundra if they were to become extinct.

"Radiant illustrations are paired with simple, perceptive sentences to underscore the impact of the loss of [lemmings]. . . . In a very effective convention extinct plants and animals are placed in silhouettes within many illustrations—the black void left by the loss of each species increases with each page. This . . . will engage readers on many levels." SLJ

Includes glossary and bibliographical references

Tagliaferro, Linda

Explore the tundra; by Linda Tagliaferro. Capstone Press 2007 32p il map (Explore the biomes) $16.95; pa $6.95

Grades: PreK K 1 2   **577.5**

1. Tundra ecology

ISBN 978-0-7368-6408-4; 0-7368-6408-3; 978-0-7368-9631-3 pa; 0-7368-9631-7 pa

LC 2006004108

This is an introduction to the tundra and some of its plants and animals.

This book "uses vivid, sense-appealing language. . . . An attractive . . . format displays the captions to colorful photographs." Sci Books Films

Includes bibliographical references

Wojahn, Rebecca Hogue

A **tundra** food chain; a who-eats-what adventure in the Arctic. [by] Rebecca Hogue Wojahn, Donald Wojahn. Lerner Publications 2009 64p il map (Follow that food chain) lib bdg $30.60

Grades: 3 4 5 6   **577.5**

1. Tundra ecology 2. Food chains (Ecology) 3. Animals -- Arctic regions

ISBN 978-0-8225-7500-9 lib bdg; 0-8225-7500-0 lib bdg

LC 2008027092

"Numerous photos of plants and animals in their habitats appear on these pages, accompanied by an explanation of the basic elements of a food chain and definitions of terms such as predators, consumers, producers, and decomposers. What sets [this book] apart . . . is [its] 'choose your own adventure' style. . . . The authors instruct [readers] to choose one of the region's carnivores and explore its food chain. Six animals (grizzly bear, snowy owl, Arctic wolf, polar bear, wolverine, and peregrine falcon) are presented. . . . Choices result in returning to some pages more than once and sometimes discovering a 'dead end,' a critically endangered or extinct animal. . . . The interconnections created by the choices effectively illustrate the complexity of food webs while providing information about the plants and animals that form the components. Lively, engaging writing helps sustain interest." SLJ

Includes glossary and bibliographical references

577.54 Desert ecology

Johnson, Rebecca L.

A **walk** in the desert; with illustrations by Phyllis V. Saroff. Carolrhoda Bks. 2001 48p il map (Biomes of North America) lib bdg $23.93; pa $8.95

Grades: 3 4 5 6   **577.54**

1. Desert ecology

ISBN 1-57505-152-4 lib bdg; 1-57505-529-5 pa

LC 00-8251

Describes the climate, soil, plants, and animals of North American deserts and the ways in which the plants and animals depend on each other and their environment to survive

"The many full-color, close-up photographs and black-and-white drawings are sure to engage readers' interest." SLJ

Includes glossary and bibliographical references

Pettiford, Rebecca

Desert food chains; by Rebecca Pettiford. Jump!, Inc. 2016 24 p. color illustrations (hardcover : alk. paper) $25.65

Grades: K 1 2 3   **577.54**

1. Desert ecology 2. Food chains (Ecology) 3. Desert animals

ISBN 1620313014; 9781620313015

LC 2015022982

In this children's book, by Rebecca Pettiford, part of the "Who Eats What?" series, "early fluent readers explore the desert biome and the food chains it supports. Vibrant, full-color photos and carefully leveled text engage young readers as they explore how energy flows through plants and animals in a desert environment." (Publisher's note)

"Well-chosen photos depict hunting and eating without too much gore and feature helpful labels of the animal's food chain role plus a simple food chain diagram." SLJ

577.6 Aquatic ecology

Hooks, Gwendolyn

Freshwater feeders; studying food webs in freshwater. Rourke Pub. 2009 32p il map (Studying food webs) lib bdg $28.50

Grades: 3 4 5   **577.6**

1. Freshwater ecology 2. Food chains (Ecology)

ISBN 978-1-60472-317-5 lib bdg; 1-60472-317-3 lib bdg

LC 2008-24857

This book has "stunning photos, fascinating facts, and intriguing examples. . . . Herbivores, omnivores, and carnivores specific to . . . [the freshwater] ecosystem are presented. . . . 'Chew on this' insets add further interest and information. . . . [This] will appeal to readers." SLJ

Includes glossary

Johansson, Philip

Lakes and rivers; a freshwater web of life. [by] Philip Johansson. Enslow Elementary 2007 48p il (Wonderful water biomes) lib bdg $23.93

Grades: 3 4 5   **577.6**

1. Lakes 2. Rivers 3. Freshwater ecology

ISBN 978-0-7660-2812-8 lib bdg; 0-7660-2812-7 lib bdg

LC 2006100470

This describes the plants, animals, and ecology of lakes and rivers.

Includes glossary and bibliographical references

Marshes and swamps; a wetland web of life. [by] Philip Johansson. Enslow Elementary 2007 48p il (Wonderful water biomes) lib bdg $23.93

Grades: 3 4 5   **577.6**

1. Wetlands 2. Marsh ecology

ISBN 978-0-7660-2814-2 lib bdg; 0-7660-2814-3 lib bdg

LC 2006039769

This describes the plants, animals, and ecology of marshes and swamps.

This has "good-quality color photos. . . . Well written and engaging." SLJ

Includes glossary and bibliographical references

Lynette, Rachel

River food chains. Heinemann Library 2011 48p il map (Protecting food chains) lib bdg $32; pa $8.99

Grades: 4 5 6 7   **577.6**

1. River ecology 2. Food chains (Ecology)

ISBN 978-1-4329-3861-1 lib bdg; 1-4329-3861-4 lib bdg; 978-1-4329-3868-0 pa; 1-4329-3868-1 pa

LC 2009049552

This book explores the species found in river food chains and webs, and discusses why these food chains and webs need to be protected.

"Featuring colorful, glossy images and accessible prose, this . . . . offers a good introduction to the web of life in rivers. . . . Conservation issues are highlighted throughout, with specific suggestions for youth to get involved. . . . An informative, thought-provoking resource that conveys the fragile, interconnected web that holds ecosystems together." Booklist

Includes glossary and bibliographical references

Marx, Trish

★ **Everglades** forever; restoring America's great wetland. photographs by Cindy Karp. Lee & Low Books 2004 40p il map $17.95; pa $8.95

Grades: 3 4 5 6   **577.6**

1. Wetlands 2. Everglades (Fla.)

ISBN 978-1-58430-164-6; 1-58430-164-3; 978-1-60060-339-6 pa; 1-60060-339-4 pa

LC 2004-2934

The author offers an "introduction to the natural history and environment of the Everglades by documenting the studies of a fifth-grade class. . . . Complementing the excellent, informative text are high-quality color photographs and maps." Booklist

Root, Phyllis

Big belching bog; illustrations by Betsy Bowen. University of Minnesota Press 2010 un il $15.95

Grades: 2 3 4   **577.6**

1. Marshes 2. Minnesota

ISBN 978-0-8166-3359-3; 0-8166-3359-2

LC 2010018733

"Couching the adaptations of plants, insects, and animals that live in the Big Bog in Minnesota as secrets of survival, this oversize picture book becomes a real page-turner. . . . The stunning full-color woodblocks, many full spread, are beautiful enough to frame. The deep purples, browns, and teals are highlighted with stark white circles." SLJ

Sill, Cathryn P.

Wetlands; written by Cathryn Sill; illustrated by John Sill. Peachtree 2008 un il (About habitats) $16.95

Grades: K 1 2 3 4   **577.6**

1. Wetlands

ISBN 978-1-56145-432-7; 1-56145-432-X

LC 2007031280

This introduction to wetland ecology "features full-page watercolor paintings that strikingly illustrate the factual information conveyed by a sentence or two on the facing pages. . . . The artwork is stunning, filled with realistic details and a beautiful balance of colors. The format would work well as a read-aloud choice. . . . Independent readers or browsers could enjoy perusing the book themselves." SLJ

Toupin, Laurie

Freshwater habitats; life in freshwater ecosystems. F. Watts 2005 63p il map (Biomes and habitats) lib bdg $25.50; pa $8.95

Grades: 4 5 6 7   **577.6**

1. Freshwater ecology

ISBN 0-531-12305-7 lib bdg; 0-531-16675-9 pa

LC 2003-16572

A look at the plants, animals, locations, and various habitats that make up the freshwater ecosystems of the world

Trumbore, Cindy

★ The **mangrove** tree; planting trees to feed families. Lee & Low Books 2011 40p il $19.95

Grades: 2 3 4   **577.6**
  1. Mangrove ecology 2. Eritrea
ISBN 978-1-60060-459-1; 1-60060-459-5

LC 2010034501

"Roth's artwork is a treat, cut-paper and fabric collages of intense, shimmering color on a ground of paper that is electric with thick veins of fiber (photos join glossary in backmatter). . . . Hitting home hard is the project's simple practicality: no high-tech, no great infusions of capital or energy—in a word, motivating, in the best possible way." Kirkus

Wechsler, Doug
  Frog heaven; ecology of a vernal pool. [by] Doug Wechsler; photographs by the author. Boyds Mills Press 2006 48p il $17.95
Grades: 3 4 5 6   **577.6**
  1. Frogs 2. Vernal pool ecology 3. Natural history -- Delaware
ISBN 978-1-59078-253-8; 1-59078-253-4

LC 2005037562

"Wechsler offers a close-up view of a vernal pool in Delaware as it cycles through the year. . . . Wechsler's clear, color photos provide an excellent visual counterpoint to the text. This well-focused book will open readers' eyes." Booklist

Includes glossary and bibliographical references

577.63   Lake and pond ecology

Lindeen, Mary
  At the pond; by Mary Lindeen. Norwood House Press 2015 32 p. color illustrations (library edition : alk. paper) $22.6
Grades: PreK K 1   **577.63**
  1. Ponds 2. Pond ecology
ISBN 1599536951; 9781599536958

LC 2014047630

This children's book, by Mary Lindeen, part of the publisher's "Beginning-To-Read" series, describes ponds. "Take a trip to a pond. See fish, cattails, dragonflies, turtles, and other interesting plants and animals that live there. Take a ride in the water on a canoe. You never know what you'll find." (Publisher's note)

"These books are clearly intended for instructional use or supplementary skills practice, with back matter sections for parents and teachers corresponding closely to Common Core reading standards on vocabulary, craft and structure, foundational skills, close reading, and fluency." Booklist

Ridley, Kimberly
  The secret pool; by Kimberly Ridley; illustrated by Rebekah Raye. Tilbury House 2013 32 p. (hardcover : alk. paper) $16.95
Grades: K 1 2 3   **577.63**
  1. Forest ecology 2. Vernal pool ecology 3. Pond animals 4. Vernal pools
ISBN 0884483398; 9780884483397

LC 2013006032

This book, by Kimberly Ridley and illustrated by Rebekah Raye, "introduces young readers to the wonders right underfoot as the voice of a vernal pool shares its secrets through the seasons, and sidebars provide fun facts on its inhabitants and the crucial role these small, often overlooked wetlands play in maintaining a healthy environment." (Publisher's note)

577.636   Pond ecology

Messner, Kate
  Over and under the pond; by Kate Messner; illustrated by Christopher Silas Neal. Chronicle Books LLC 2017 48 p. color illustrations (alk. paper) $16.99
Grades: K 1 2 3   **577.636**
  1. Ponds 2. Pond ecology
ISBN 9781452145426

LC 2016010976

In this book, by Kate Messner, illustrated by Christopher Silas Neal, "readers will discover the plants and animals that make up the rich, interconnected ecosystem of a mountain pond. Over the pond, the water is a mirror, reflecting the sky. But under the pond is a hidden world of minnows darting, beavers diving, tadpoles growing. These and many other secrets are waiting to be discovered...over and under the pond." (Publisher's note)

Includes bibliographical references

577.68   Wetland ecology

Gibbons, Gail
  Marshes & swamps. Holiday House 1998 un il $16.95; pa $6.95
Grades: K 1 2 3   **577.68**
  1. Ecology 2. Wetlands
ISBN 0-8234-1347-0; 0-8234-1515-5 pa

LC 97-17995

Defines marshes and swamps, discusses how conditions in them may change, and examines the life found in and around them

"Gibbons balances a succinct, informative text with well-labeled watercolors." Horn Book Guide

577.69   Saltwater wetland and seashore ecology

Yezerski, Thomas
  Meadowlands; a wetlands survival story. Thomas F. Yezerski. Farrar, Straus, Giroux 2011 40 p. il
Grades: 2 3   **577.69**
  1. Wetland ecology 2. Meadowlands (N.J.) 3. New Jersey -- History 4. Natural history -- New Jersey 5. Ecology 6. Hackensack Meadowlands (N.J.)
ISBN 0374349134; 9780374349134

LC 2010005503

This is an "ecological history of the Meadowlands of New Jersey, an estuary trapped in a dense industrial, commercial, and residential area. . . . Primary." (Horn Book)

"Yezerski adroitly captures the tensions and hope in the sometimes adversarial, sometimes beneficial relationship between humans and the environment in this marvelous ecological history of the Meadowlands of New Jersey, an estuary trapped in a dense industrial, commercial, and residential area. . . . Despite humans' best efforts, the relationship is still fragile, and here captured beautifully in the expansive watercolor illustrations. . . . Each main double-page-spread illustration is bordered by tiny images with a wealth of additional taxonomical information (and sly humor) about the diverse flora and fauna (and mobsters and sports enthusiasts) of northern New Jersey." Horn Book

Includes bibliographical references

577.7   Marine ecology

Becker, Helaine

The **big** green book of the big blue sea; written by Helaine Becker; illustrated by Willow Dawson. Kids Can Press 2012 80 p. $15.95

Grades: 3 4 5   **577.7**

1. Science -- Experiments 2. Marine biology 3. Marine ecology 4. Environmental protection

ISBN 1554537460; 9781554537464

This book, by Helaine Becker, "shows how the ocean works and why this immense ecosystem needs our protection. Experiments using everyday materials help explain scientific concepts. . . . A focus on pollution and other ecological hazards raises awareness. Young scientists will gain a hands-on understanding of how 'booms' clean oil spills and how a garbage patch roughly twice the size of Texas came to exist in the middle of the Pacific Ocean." (Publisher's note)

Callery, Sean

Ocean. Kingfisher 2011 32p il (Life cycles)

Grades: 2 3 4   **577.7**

1. Marine animals 2. Marine ecology 3. Food chains (Ecology)

ISBN 0-7534-6577-9; 978-0-7534-6577-6

After a brief introduction to the ocean ecosystem "examples of three actual food chains within that ecosystem are presented. . . . Well-designed double-page spreads . . . provide brief information about each creature and its place in the chain. Vivid photos and vibrantly colored pages are eye-catching. Useful food web charts summarizing content are appended." Horn Book Guide

Chin, Jason

Coral reefs. Roaring Brook Press 2011 un il $16.99

Grades: K 1 2 3   **577.7**

1. Coral reefs and islands

ISBN 978-1-5964-3563-6; 1-5964-3563-1

LC 2010045189

"Chin, who pioneered this hybrid form of straightforward nonfiction text and fanciful pictures with Redwoods (2009), offers another a statement about the power of reading for an imaginative child with this appealing introduction to a complex world. He opens and closes his narrative with accurate and clearly labeled pencil sketches of a large variety of reef-dwellers. Inside, realistic watercolor images, some in panels, some in full-bleed pages and even double-page spreads, complement the text." Kirkus

Cousteau, Philippe, 1980-

Make a splash! a kid's guide to protecting our oceans, lakes, rivers & wetlands. by Cathryn Berger Kaye; with Philippe Cousteau and EarthEcho International. Free Spirit Pub. Inc. 2013 125 p. ill. (chiefly col.) (paperback) $13.99

Grades: 3 4 5 6   **577.7**

1. Environmentalists 2. Water conservation 3. Marine ecology 4. Environmentalism 5. Marine pollution -- Prevention

ISBN 1575424177; 9781575424170

LC 2012032120

This book for elementary-age readers has "colorful photos and digital drawings [that] illustrate many aspects of water on Earth, while the text provides information and tells stories of children in elementary schools around the world who have translated their own environmental concerns into action." (Booklist)

Crenson, Victoria

★ **Horseshoe** crabs and shorebirds; the story of a food web. illustrated by Annie Cannon. Marshall Cavendish 2003 un il lib bdg $16.95

Grades: 2 3 4   **577.7**

1. Crabs 2. Food chains (Ecology) 3. Delaware Bay (Del. and N.J.)

ISBN 0-7614-5115-3

LC 2002-156473

Presents a portrait of the Delaware Bay in the spring when a wide variety of animals, including minnows, mice, turtles, raccoons, and especially migrating shorebirds, come to feed on the billions of eggs laid by horseshoe crabs

"Crenson's text is highly descriptive and reads like an adventure story, conveying the action and excitement of nature. Cannon's watercolors fill the pages with atmosphere and motion." SLJ

Hooks, Gwendolyn

Makers and takers; studying food webs in the ocean. [by] Gwendolyn Hooks. Rourke Pub. 2009 32p il map (Studying food webs) lib bdg $28.50

Grades: 3 4 5   **577.7**

1. Marine ecology 2. Food chains (Ecology)

ISBN 978-1-60472-319-9 lib bdg; 1-60472-319-X lib bdg

LC 2008-24860

This book has "stunning photos, fascinating facts, and intriguing examples. . . . Herbivores, omnivores, and carnivores specific to . . . [The ocean] ecosystem are presented. . . . 'Chew on this' insets add further interest and information. . . . [This] will appeal to readers." SLJ

Includes glossary and bibliographical references

Jackson, Kay

Explore the ocean; by Kay Jackson. Capstone Press 2007 32p il (Explore the biomes) $16.95; pa $6.95

Grades: PreK K 1 2   **577.7**

1. Marine ecology

ISBN 978-0-7368-6406-0; 0-7368-6406-7; 978-0-7368-9629-0 pa; 0-7368-9629-5 pa

LC 2006004110

This an introduction to the ocean habitat and some of its plants and animals.

This book "uses vivid, sense-appealing language. . . . An attractive . . . format displays the captions to colorful photographs." Sci Books Films

Includes bibliographical references

Parker, Steve, 1952-

Seashore; written by Steve Parker. rev ed; DK Pub. 2004 72p il (DK eyewitness books) $15.99

Grades: 4 5 6 7   **577.7**

1. Seashore 2. Marine plants 3. Marine animals

ISBN 0-7566-0721-3; 0-7566-0720-5 lib bdg

First published 1989 by Knopf

Brief text and photos introduce the animal inhabitants of the seashore, including fish, crustaceans, snails, and shorebirds

Pfeffer, Wendy

★ **Life** in a coral reef; illustrated by Steve Jenkins. Collins 2009 32p il (Let's-read-and-find-out science) $16; pa $5.99

Grades: K 1 2 3   **577.7**

1. Coral reefs and islands

ISBN 978-0-06-029553-0; 0-06-029553-8; 978-0-06-445222-9 pa; 0-06-445222-0 pa

LC 2008000498

"Jenkins' striking paper-collage illustrations nicely complement Pfeffer's clear and engaging text in this successful explanation of what lies beneath the surface of the ocean in and around a coral reef." Booklist

Pyers, Greg

The **biodiversity** of coral reefs. Marshall Cavendish 2010 32p il map (Biodiversity) lib bdg $28.50

Grades: 4 5 6 7   **577.7**

1. Coral reefs and islands

ISBN 978-1-60870-070-7 lib bdg; 1-60870-070-4 lib bdg

"Discusses the variety of living things in a coral reef's ecosystem." Publisher's note

Includes glossary

Ridley, Kimberly

The **secret** bay; Kimberly Ridley; Illustrated by Rebekah Raye. Tilbury House Publishers 2015 40 p. (hardcover) $17.95

Grades: 1 2 3 4 5   **577.7**

1. Estuaries 2. Estuaries 3. Estuarine ecology

ISBN 9780884484332

LC 2015019734

This book, by Kimberly Ridley, Illustrated by Rebekah Raye, is about estuaries. "Teeming with life, these places of salt marshes, mud-flats, and tidal backwaters serve as nursery areas for oceangoing fish, migratory stopovers for shorebirds, and homes for an amazing diversity of snails, bivalves, fish, mammals, horseshoe crabs, fiddler and blue crabs, terrapin turtles, plankton, and many others, all of whom we meet in the pages of this delightful book." (Publisher's note)

"The importance of preserving all players in the estuary ecosystem does come out clearly, and there are interesting tidbits of word derivation, as well as a lively section about how various animals avoid/escape predators." Kirkus

Slade, Suzanne

What if there were no sea otters? a book about the ocean ecosystem. illustrated by Carol Schwartz. Picture Window Books 2011 24p il map (Food chain reactions) lib bdg $25.99; pa $8.95

Grades: 2 3 4   **577.7**

1. Otters 2. Marine ecology

ISBN 978-1-4048-6018-6 lib bdg; 1-4048-6018-5 lib bdg; 978-1-4048-6397-2 pa; 1-4048-6397-4 pa

LC 2010009879

Discusses the ocean ecosystem and the role of the sea otter as a keystone species in helping to maintain it, describing the otter's place on the food chain and what would happen if the sea otter were to become extinct.

"Radiant illustrations are paired with simple, perceptive sentences to underscore the impact of the loss of [sea otters]. . . . In a very effective convention extinct plants and animals are placed in silhouettes within many illustrations—the black void left by the loss of each species increases with each page. This . . . will engage readers on many levels." SLJ

Includes glossary and bibliographical references

Wicks, Maris

Coral reefs; Coral Reefs: Cities of the Ocean. by Maris Wicks. First Second 2016 119 p. color illustrations $9.99; $19.99

Grades: 4 5 6 7 8   **577.7**

1. Marine biology 2. Ocean 3. Marine ecology 4. Coral reef ecology

ISBN 9781626727250; 1626721459; 1626721467; 9781626721456; 9781626721463

In this graphic novel by Maris Wicks, published as part of the Science Comics series, "learn all about these tiny, adorable sea animals! This absorbing look at ocean science covers the biology of coral reefs as well as their ecological importance. . . . Wicks brings to bear her signature combination of hardcore cuteness and in-depth science." (Publisher's note)

"The jokes, puns, and humorous commentary will draw sea-life fans to this informative, tropical-hued introduction to coral reefs." Booklist

Includes bibliographical references (page 118).

577.789   Reef ecology

Schuetz, Kari

Life in a coral reef; by Kari Schuetz. Bellwether Media 2016 24 p. color ill., color maps (ebook) $22.95; (hardcover : alk. paper) $24.95

Grades: 1 2 3   **577.789**

1. Coral reef ecology 2. Coral reefs and islands

ISBN 9781681031408; 9781626173156

LC 2015033093

This children's book in the Biomes Alive! series, by Kari Schuetz, examines how "coral reefs are home to thousands of living species, including some of the most vibrant plants and animals on the planet. Many reef inhabitants help each other survive. Sea anemones, for example, provide shelter for clownfish. In return, the striped fish bring tasty treats to the anemones and help lure prey into their tentacles!" (Publisher's note)

"First-rate choices to update or supplement resources about biomes for beginning researchers." SLJ

Includes bibliographical references and index

578   Natural history of organisms and related subjects

Kelsey, Elin

Strange new species; astonishing discoveries of life on earth. Maple Tree Press 2005 96p il $24.95; pa $16.95

Grades: 5 6 7 8   **578**

1. Biology 2. Scientists 3. Natural history

ISBN 1-897066-31-7; 1-897066-32-5 pa

"This large-format book showcases new species . . . and the scientists who have discovered them. . . . The discussion ends with information on cloning, genetically modified food, and the future of life. . . . With many excellent photos, this introductory book on new species will be an intriguing addition to classroom units on classification or biology." Booklist

Strauss, Rochelle

Tree of life; the incredible biodiversity of life on Earth. Kids Can Press 2004 40p il $16.95

Grades: 5 6 7 8   **578**

1. Biological diversity 2. Biology -- Classification

ISBN 1-55337-669-2

The "text first introduces the concept of a family tree for all living things, then goes on to name the five kingdoms of scientific classification. . . . The author describes the life-forms included in each species, with specific examples shown in the softly colorful illustrations accompanied by informative captions. . . . Striking, lucid, and deceptively simple." SLJ

578.4   Adaptation

Davies, Monika

★ **Adaptations**; Monika Davies. Teacher Created Materials 2016 32 p. (pbk.) $8.99

Grades: 4 5 6   **578.4**

1. Adaptation (Biology) 2. Animals -- Adaptation 3. Competition

(Biology)
ISBN 1480746797; 9781480746794

LC 2014045202

This children's book by Monika Davies explains "how adaptation has helped animals survive and change over time. High-interest, age appropriate text paired with colorful images and graphics fill the pages of this book to make learning about adaptation fun and interesting! A Think Like a Scientist activity that supports STEM instruction is included at the end of the book for students to apply what they've learned." (Publisher's note)

Rustad, Martha E. H.

Animals in fall; preparing for winter. illustrated by Amanda Enright. Millbrook Press 2011 24p il (Fall's here!) lib bdg $23.93
Grades: K 1 2 3   **578.4**
1. Autumn 2. Winter 3. Animal behavior
ISBN 978-0-7613-5066-8; 0-7613-5066-7

LC 2010053468

This "relates the animals preparation for winter through pictures and text. . . . At the end of the book an activity that children can do to understand how extra fat can keep you warm is featured. . . . Children will enjoy the colorful, expressive illustrations." Sci Books Films

Includes glossary and bibliographical references

Silverstein, Alvin

★ **Adaptation**; by Alvin Silverstein, Virginia Silverstein, and Laura Silverstein Nunn. Twenty-First Century Books 2008 112p il (Science concepts) lib bdg $31.93
Grades: 4 5 6 7   **578.4**
1. Adaptation (Biology)
ISBN 978-0-8225-3434-1 lib bdg; 0-8225-3434-7 lib bdg

LC 2007-02862

This "provides an accessible introduction to how living beings adapt to survive in diverse habitats. . . . The narrative gains clarity from abundant examples, colorful photos and diagrams, and fascinating sidebars." Booklist

Includes bibliographical references

578.6 Miscellaneous nontaxonomic kinds of organisms

Drake, Jane

Alien invaders; species that threaten our world. [by] Jane Drake & Ann Love; illustrated by Mark Thurman. Tundra Books 2008 56p il map $19.95
Grades: 3 4 5 6   **578.6**
1. Nonindigenous pests 2. Biological invasions
ISBN 0-88776-798-2; 978-0-88776-798-2

The authors examine invasive species and their effects on ecosystems. Index. "Ages nine to twelve." (Quill Quire)

"This book discusses non-native flora and fauna that endanger native species. The authors present historical cases (Irish potato blight, toad invasion in Australia), the most notorious invasive species, and threatened communities. Each double-page spread features a detailed gouache illustration, a conversational overview of problems, and some species-specific facts." Horn Book Guide

Jackson, Cari

Alien invasion; invasive species become major menaces. Gareth Stevens Pub. 2010 48p il (Current science) lib bdg $31
Grades: 4 5 6   **578.6**
1. Nonindigenous pests 2. Biological invasions
ISBN 978-1-4339-2057-8 lib bdg; 1-4339-2057-3 lib bdg
LC 2009002279

This "lively, well-organized [text profiles] dozens of organisms that threaten our health and well-being. Jackson succinctly describes the characteristics of more than three dozen invasive species of plants and animals. . . . One or more illustrations accompany the text on every page—a mix of sharp, color photographs and some color drawings, maps, life cycle diagrams, etc." SLJ

Includes glossary and bibliographical references

Johnson, Rebecca L.

★ **Zombie** makers; true stories of nature's undead. Rebecca L. Johnson. Millbrook Press 2013 48 p.
Grades: 4 5 6   **578.6**
1. Zombies 2. Invertebrates 3. Parasites 4. Host-parasite relationships
ISBN 0761386335; 9780761386339

LC 2011046181

In this book, by Rebecca L. Johnson, real biological examples of "zombies" in nature are profiled. "[D]ead people do not come back to live and start walking around, looking for trouble. But there are things that can take over the bodies and brains of innocent creatures, turning them into senseless slaves. Meet nature's zombie makers--including a fly-enslaving fungus, a suicide worm, and a cockroach-taming wasp--and their victims." (Publisher's note)

Includes bibliographical references (p. 46-47) and index

Metz, Lorijo

What can we do about invasive species? PowerKids Press 2010 24p il (Protecting our planet) lib bdg $21.25; pa $8
Grades: 2 3 4   **578.6**
1. Nonindigenous pests 2. Biological invasions
ISBN 978-1-4042-8084-7 lib bdg; 1-4042-8084-7 lib bdg; 978-1-4358-2487-4 pa; 1-4358-2487-3 pa

LC 2008-55828

This book provides "straightforward information . . . complemented by full-page, color photographs. . . . Links for further information . . . are housed at the publisher's Web site (which allows feedback so that readers can suggest more sites)." SLJ

Includes glossary

Owen, Ruth

Gross body invaders. Bearport Pub. 2011 24p il (Up close and gross) lib bdg $22.61
Grades: 3 4 5   **578.6**
1. Parasites
ISBN 978-1-61772-127-4; 1-61772-127-1

LC 2010044416

This describes small creatures which can invade the body, including head lice, eyelash mites, mosquitoes, ticks, fleas, hookworms, tapeworms, and horseflies.

"Never have the wonders of electron microscopy been more thrillingly displayed. . . . These knife-sharp, all-too-explicit photos are riveting. The [text doesn't] trail far behind in appeal either." SLJ

Includes glossary and bibliographical references

Icky house invaders. Bearport Pub. 2011 24p il (Up close and gross) lib bdg $22.61
Grades: 3 4 5   **578.6**
1. Microbiology 2. Household pests
ISBN 978-1-61772-124-3; 1-61772-124-7

LC 2010041241

This describes insects and other small creatures which can inhabit a home, including houseflies, fleas, dust mites, bedbugs, moths, cockroaches, woodworms, and silverfish.

"Never have the wonders of electron microscopy been more thrillingly displayed. . . . These knife-sharp, all-too-explicit photos are riveting. The [text doesn't] trail far behind in appeal either." SLJ

Includes glossary and bibliographical references

578.68   Rare and endangered species

Pobst, Sandy
★ **Animals** on the edge; science races to save species threatened with extinction. by Sandra Pobst; Todd K. Fuller, consultant. National Geographic 2008 64p il (National Geographic investigates) $17.95; lib bdg $27.90
Grades: 4 5 6 7   **578.68**
1. Endangered species 2. Wildlife conservation
ISBN 978-1-4263-0358-6; 1-4263-0358-0; 978-1-4263-0265-7 lib bdg; 1-4263-0265-7 lib bdg

This "eye-catching [title features] full-color photographs. . . . The approach is to understand the challenges to protecting endangered animals, including global warming, destruction of habitat, tagging and tracking, poaching, captive breeding, and cloning." Voice Youth Advocates

Includes glossary and bibliographical references

578.7   Organisms characteristic of specific kinds of environments

Arnosky, Jim
★ **Beachcombing**; exploring the seashore. Dutton Children's Bks. 2004 un il $15.99
Grades: K 1 2 3   **578.7**
1. Seashore
ISBN 0-525-47104-9

Illustrations and text describe some of the many things that can be found on a walk along a beach, including coconuts, shark teeth, jellyfish, crabs and different kinds of shells.

"Young beachcombers will discover old and new ideas about collecting or just identifying their finds, and the book will appeal to those children who are looking for relaxing fun." SLJ

Conlan, Kathy
Under the ice. Kids Can Press 2002 55p il $16.95; pa $8.95
Grades: 4 5 6 7   **578.7**
1. Marine biology 2. Marine pollution 3. Polar regions
ISBN 1-55337-001-5; 1-55337-060-0 pa

"The first-person text creates a feeling of immediacy. . . . Well-captioned, color photos appear throughout the book. . . . Conlan . . . offers readers an engaging account of her adventurous career in scientific field research." Booklist

Ernst, Lisa Campbell
How things work in the yard. Blue Apple Books 2011 un il $14.99
Grades: K 1 2 3   **578.7**
1. Urban ecology
ISBN 978-1-60905-009-2; 1-60905-009-6
LC 2010046821

"Graph paper style backgrounds emphasize the schematic approach to nature that Campbell-Ernst uses to explain how different items and creatures—such as birds, butterflies, rocks, and dirt—that can be found in a typical backyard 'work.' There's a playful aesthetic in evidence, from the bright palette and friendly cut-paper artwork to the innate humor in some of the questions themselves. . . . The various parts of the animals, plants, and objects are labeled, and brief facts about each sub-

ject dot the spreads. . . . It's an elegantly designed primer to the natural world." Publ Wkly

Guiberson, Brenda Z.
★ **Life** in the boreal forest; paintings by Gennady Spirin. Henry Holt and Co. 2009 un il $16.99
Grades: 2 3 4 5   **578.7**
1. Forest ecology
ISBN 978-0-8050-7718-6; 0-8050-7718-9
LC 2008-18329

"Gorgeously intricate illustrations perfectly complement equally evocative text in this introduction to the great northern, or boreal, forest, which sprawls across the entire northern hemisphere. . . . Any child interested in animals or the outdoors will be fascinated by the array portrayed here in a series of vignettes, each of which intersperses factual information information with lively action scenes." Booklist

Kirby, Richard R.
Ocean drifters; a secret world beneath the waves. Firefly Books 2011 192p il $29.95
Grades: 5 6 7 8 9 10 11 12 Adult   **578.7**
1. Marine plankton
ISBN 978-1-55407-982-7; 1-55407-982-9
LC 2011284690

"Kirby (Marine Inst. Research Fellow, Plymouth Univ., UK), who has published widely in scientific journals, combines in this book his area of expertise-plankton-with magnificent color photography of each species. He details the importance of the ocean's plankton layer to the health of the globe and its effects on sea and human life in the photos' descriptions...Recommended for readers interested in the smaller denizens of the natural world, the ocean, or microphotography." (Library Journal)

Includes bibliographical references

Lawrence, Ellen
Dirt; by Ellen Lawrence; consultants, Suzy Gazlay, MA, recipient of the Presidential Award for Excellence in Science Teaching and Kimberly Brenneman, PhD, National Institute for Early Education Research, Rutgers University, New Brunswick, New Jersey. Bearport Pub. Co. 2013 24 p. col. ill. (library) $23.93
Grades: K 1 2 3   **578.7**
1. Soils 2. Soil biology
ISBN 1617727377; 9781617727375
LC 2012046349

This book on dirt by Ellen Lawrence "includes in the materials list a notebook for children to keep records of predictions, observations, and conclusions. There are seven experiments with detailed, age -- appropriate instructions complete with pictures to support the experiments. There are also graphics that provide students with additional instructions. The author answers the questions in an appendix." (NSTA Recommends)

Includes bibliographical references and index.

Montgomery, Sy
The **Great** White shark scientist; written by Sy Montgomery. Houghton Mifflin Harcourt 2016 80 p. color illustrations (hardcover) $18.99
Grades: 5 6 7 8 9   **578.7**
1. Marine biologists 2. White shark 3. Wildlife conservation 4. Marine resources conservation 5. Marine biologists -- United States -- Biography
ISBN 9780544352988
LC 2015003494

This juvenile book, by Sy Montgomery with photographs by Keith Ellenbogen, part of the "Scientists in the Field" series, follows "Dr. Greg Skomal, biologist and head of the Massachusetts Shark Research

Program, [who] is investigating a controversial possibility: Might Cape Cod's waters serve as a breeding ground for the great white shark, the largest and most feared predatory fish on Earth?" (Publisher's note)

"This appreciative introduction to a much-maligned species will thrill readers while it encourages them to see great white sharks in a new way." Kirkus

Includes bibliographical references

O'Neill, Michael Patrick

Ocean magic. Batfish 2008 45p il $19.95

Grades: 1 2 3 4   **578.7**

1. Ocean 2. Marine animals

ISBN 978-0-9728653-5-7; 0-9728653-5-7

LC 2007-904079

"O'Neill introduces readers to coral reefs, kelp forests, and the ocean bottom. Especially stunning are the photos of the Hairy Frogfish, an incredibly camouflaged member of the Anglerfish family that prowls off the coast of Florida. Nevertheless, the colorful creatures of the coral reef are the stars of this book. The author's strong support of conservation comes through loud and clear in his narrative, and photographs amplify this message by showing the amazing life-forms that could be lost." SLJ

Owen, Ruth

Creepy backyard invaders. Bearport Pub. 2011 24p il (Up close and gross) lib bdg $22.61

Grades: 3 4 5   **578.7**

1. Insects 2. Agricultural pests

ISBN 978-1-61772-125-0; 1-61772-125-5

LC 2010041212

This describes organisms which can inhabit a backyard, including earwigs, honeybees, aphids, ants, lacewings, jumping spiders, woodlice, and stinging nettles.

"Never have the wonders of electron microscopy been more thrillingly displayed. . . . These knife-sharp, all-too-explicit photos are riveting. The [text doesn't] trail far behind in appeal either." SLJ

Includes glossary and bibliographical references

Person, Stephen

The coral reef; a giant city under the sea. consultant, Rod Salm. Bearport Pub. 2009 32p il map (Spectacular animal towns) lib bdg $25.27

Grades: 2 3 4   **578.7**

1. Coral reefs and islands

ISBN 978-1-59716-869-4 lib bdg; 1-59716-869-6 lib bdg

LC 2009-12952

"Through excellent photographs, high-interest texts, sidebars, maps, and other material, children learn about both the animals and their habitats. The . . . book also provides brief profiles of animals with similar habitats. . . . [This book is] much better than average 'report' titles." SLJ

Includes glossary and bibliographical references

Santoro, Lucio

Wild oceans; [by] Lucio and Meera Santoro. Little Simon 2010 un il $27.99

Grades: 2 3 4 5   **578.7**

1. Marine biology 2. Pop-up books

ISBN 978-1-4169-8467-2; 1-4169-8467-4

"Using the ocean as their milieu, the Santoros . . . provide solid information along with amazing visuals. Beginning with a 3-D re-creation of a tide pool, the book then moves to the open sea, where a whale rises out of the pages. An explanation of light zones underwater is illustrated by an anglerfish that lives 3,000 feet below the water's surface. Views of a coral reef and life in the frozen sea complete the treatment. Fact-filled fun." Booklist

Serafini, Frank

Looking closely across the desert. Kids Can Press 2008 un il (Looking closely) $16.95

Grades: K 1 2 3   **578.7**

1. Deserts

ISBN 978-1-55453-211-7; 1-55453-211-6

"An extreme closeup color photo of a section of a plant, animal, or other natural object set in a circle on a black background challenges readers to guess its identity. Turning the page reveals a large photo of the item in its natural setting, accompanied by two paragraphs of descriptive and informative text." SLJ

Looking closely along the shore; [by] Frank Serafini. Kids Can Press 2008 un il (Looking closely) $16.95

Grades: K 1 2 3   **578.7**

1. Seashore

ISBN 978-1-55453-141-7; 1-55453-141-1

This title about plants and animals of the seashore "will pique the interest of children and encourage them to seek out more information. . . . [It is] set up like a guessing game, allowing for interaction. . . . Each entry opens with a white page with large black type that asks viewers to 'Look very closely. What do you see?' The facing page is black with what seems like a hole to peep through to the next spread. . . . Readers are given a couple of possibilities to start them guessing on what image might be depicted, and, when the page is turned, an enlarged closeup is in full view, along with a few interesting facts about the plant or animal." SLJ

Looking closely around the pond. Kids Can Press 2010 un il (Looking closely) $16.95

Grades: K 1 2 3   **578.7**

1. Ponds

ISBN 978-1-55337-395-7; 1-55337-395-2

"Close-ups of a portion of a pond animal, insect, or plant on a spread invite children to guess the featured subject. . . . The animal, insect, or plant is then described in a couple of jaunty paragraphs on a page facing a full-color photograph." SLJ

Looking closely in the rain forest. Kids Can Press 2010 un il (Looking closely) $16.95

Grades: K 1 2 3   **578.7**

1. Rain forests

ISBN 978-1-55337-543-2; 1-55337-543-2

This "spotlights life in the tropical rain forest, including a squirrel monkey, a banana plant, a moth orchid, and a scarlet macaw. The crisp, beautiful photos and the interactive text will draw kids into both the interactive fun and scientific facts." Booklist

Looking closely inside the garden. Kids Can Press 2008 un il (Looking closely) $16.95

Grades: K 1 2 3   **578.7**

1. Gardens

ISBN 978-1-55453-210-0; 1-55453-210-8

"An extreme closeup color photo of a section of a plant, animal, or other natural object set in a circle on a black background challenges readers to guess its identity. Turning the page reveals a large photo of the item in its natural setting, accompanied by two paragraphs of descriptive and informative text." SLJ

Looking closely through the forest. Kids Can Press 2008 un il (Looking closely) $16.95

Grades: K 1 2 3   **578.7**

1. Forest plants 2. Forest animals

ISBN 978-1-55453-212-4; 1-55453-212-4

This book about forest plants and animals "will pique the interest of children and encourage them to seek out more information. . . . [It is] set up like a guessing game, allowing for interaction. . . . Each entry opens with a white page with large black type that asks viewers to 'Look very closely. What do you see?' The facing page is black with what seems like a hole to peep through to the next spread. . . . Readers are given a couple of possibilities to start them guessing on what image might be depicted, and, when the page is turned, an enlarged closeup is in full view, along with a few interesting facts about the plant or animal." SLJ

Somervill, Barbara A.

Marine biologist. Cherry Lake Pub. 2009 32p il (Cool science careers) lib bdg $27.07

Grades: 3 4 5 6   **578.7**

1. Marine biology 2. Vocational guidance

ISBN 978-1-60279-504-4 lib bdg; 1-60279-504-5 lib bdg

LC 2008045234

This describes the career of marine biologist, including ways to become involved in the profession, the interests and skills required, and activities for learning more

This is "highly readable. . . . Colorful photographs illustrate [the] book." SLJ

Includes glossary and bibliographical references

Thomas, William David

Marine biologist. Gareth Stevens Pub. 2010 32p il (Cool careers: cutting edge) lib bdg $26; pa $8.95

Grades: 4 5 6   **578.7**

1. Marine biology 2. Vocational guidance

ISBN 978-1-4339-1957-2 lib bdg; 1-4339-1957-5 lib bdg; 978-1-4339-2156-8 pa; 1-4339-2156-1 pa

LC 2009000239

Describes the work of a marine biologist.

This title offers "clear, solid information in a large font. . . . [This] short [book is] packed with relevant, current material." SLJ

Includes glossary and bibliographical references

Wallace, Marianne D.

America's forests; guide to plants and animals. Fulcrum Pub. 2009 47p il (America's ecosystems) pa $11.95

Grades: 5 6 7 8   **578.7**

1. Forest plants 2. Forest animals 3. Forest ecology 4. Forests and forestry

ISBN 978-1-55591-595-7 pa; 1-55591-595-7 pa

LC 2008041005

This "is a guide to plants and animals within the context of forest communities. Marianne Wallace . . . expertly crafts this introduction to forests. . . . The book contains abundant illustrations." Sci Books Films

Includes glossary

Wechsler, Doug

Marvels in the muck; life in the salt marshes. Boyds Mills Press 2008 48p il $17.95

Grades: 4 5 6 7   **578.7**

1. Salt marshes 2. Marsh ecology

ISBN 978-1-59078-588-1

LC 2007052583

"A season-by-season look at the ecology of an oft-overlooked habitat. Wechsler's lucid text introduces the insects, birds, reptiles, crustaceans, and other critters that claim this salty expanse as home. . . . Clear color photos present species mentioned in the text." SLJ

Includes glossary and bibliographical references

Winner, Cherie

Life on the edge. Lerner Publications Co. 2006 48p il (Cool science) lib bdg $26.60

Grades: 4 5 6   **578.7**

1. Adaptation (Biology)

ISBN 978-0-8225-2499-1 lib bdg; 0-8225-2499-6 lib bdg

LC 2005011071

This book "introduces creatures in extreme conditions such as thermal pools, Antarctica, and the deep sea. [The book provides] clear explanations of the science and [covers] possible benefits to humans. A variety of photos and information boxes provide an eye-catching . . . layout." Horn Book Guide

Includes glossary and bibliographical references

579 Natural history of microorganisms, fungi, algae

Arato, Rona

Protists; algae, amoebas, plankton, and other protists. Crabtree Pub. Co. 2010 48p il (A class of their own) lib bdg $29.27; pa $9.95

Grades: 5 6 7 8   **579**

1. Algae 2. Protists 3. Protozoa

ISBN 978-0-7787-5377-3 lib bdg; 0-7787-5377-8 lib bdg; 978-0-7787-5391-9 pa; 0-7787-5391-3 pa

LC 2009-51386

Looks at the protist kingdom, providing information and examples of species from the major phyla, as well as information about the role of protists in the food chain and in various diseases.

"Lively section headings . . . and notes on uncommon achievements, . . . lighten the substantial load of biological terminology. Illustrated with a plethora of closeup color photos and microphotos, and closing with annotated lists of recommended Web sites, . . . [this captures] the remarkable diversity of life." SLJ

Includes glossary and bibliographical references

Brown, Jordan

Micro mania; a really close-up look at bacteria, bedbugs & the zillions of other gross little creatures that live in, on & all around you! [by] Jordan D. Brown. Imagine! 2010 80p il $19.95

Grades: 4 5 6   **579**

1. Microorganisms

ISBN 978-0-9823064-2-0; 0-9823064-2-3

"This engrossing book goes into squirm-inducing detail about the bacteria, microbes, and other assorted mini-organisms that dwell in our bodies and our homes. Each spread is well laid out with plenty of white space, large text, and colorful photos of these little critters . . . and the havoc they wreak. The writing is vivid without being breathless." SLJ

Burillo-Kirch, Christine

Microbes; Discover an Unseen World with 25 Projects. Christine Burillo-Kirch; illustrated by Tom Casteel. Nomad Press 2015 128 p. color illustrations $22.95

Grades: 1 2 3   **579**

1. Viruses 2. Bacteria 3. Microorganisms

ISBN 161930306X; 9781619303065

In this children's book, by Christine Burillo-Kirch and illustrated by Tom Casteel, "readers journey through microscopic worlds that collide with our own on a daily basis to encounter bacteria, viruses, fungi, protists, and archaea. [It] looks at some of the ways the body protects itself from diseases and infections through critical thinking exercises that explore the differences between harmful and beneficial microbes." (Publisher's note)

"As a series of fun experiments in a dynamic layout that also remains faithful to the basic tenets of scientific inquiry, this is sure to engage young biologists." Booklist

Includes bibliographical references (page 119) and index.

Davies, Nicola, 1958-

★ **Tiny** creatures; the world of microbes. Nicola Davies, illustrated by Emily Sutton. Candlewick Press 2014 40 p. $15.99
Grades: PreK K 1 2 3   **579**
1. Microorganisms 2. Science
ISBN 0763673153; 9780763673154
           LC 2013953401
Written by Nicola Davies and illustrated by Emily Sutton, this children's book describes how "All around the world--in the sea, in the soil, in the air, and in your body--there are living things so tiny that millions could fit on an ant's antenna. They're busy doing all sorts of things, from giving you a cold and making yogurt to eroding mountains and helping to make the air we breathe." (Publisher's note)

"A pleasant, picture book-style look at a rather icky topic: microbes, the teeny tiny critters that live on us and in us and everywhere around us, with an impact that belies their minute size...This really is an enjoyable beginner's look at these miniscule organisms and the effect they can have on everything from our bodies to the soil to the clouds in the sky." SLJ

Eamer, Claire

Inside your insides; A Guide to the Microbes That Call You Home. by Claire Eamer; illustrated by Marie-Eve Tremblay. Kids Can Press 2016 36 p. color illustrations $17.95
Grades: 3 4 5 6   **579**
1. Bacteria 2. Microorganisms 3. Human body
ISBN 1771383321; 9781771383325
In this book, by Claire Eamer, illustrated by Marie-Eve Tremblay, "six of the most common critters that live in and on our bodies are introduced: . . . bacteria, archaea, viruses, fungi, protists and mites. Each one has its own preferred environment, and readers will be startled (and likely a little grossed out!) by the many places they live, including the hair follicles on our faces, the folds of our tongues and the lengths of our guts." (Publisher's note)

"The jazzy design and plentiful, brightly colored illustrations add appeal. Solid information presented in a sprightly manner that's sure to appeal." Kirkus

Wearing, Judy

Fungi; mushrooms, toadstools, molds, yeasts, and other fungi. Crabtree 2010 48p il (A class of their own) lib bdg $29.27; pa $9.95
Grades: 5 6 7 8   **579**
1. Fungi
ISBN 978-0-7787-5375-9 lib bdg; 0-7787-5375-1 lib bdg; 978-0-7787-5389-6 pa; 0-7787-5389-1 pa
Features an examination of the four major groups of fungi: yeasts, toadstools, chytrids, and bread molds.

"Lively section headings . . . and notes on uncommon achievements, . . . lighten the substantial load of biological terminology. Illustrated with a plethora of closeup color photos and microphotos, and closing with annotated lists of recommended Web sites, . . . [thi scaptures] the remarkable diversity of life." SLJ

Includes glossary and bibliographical references

Zabludoff, Marc

The **protoctist** kingdom. Benchmark Books 2006 95p il (Family trees) lib bdg $29.92

Grades: 5 6 7 8   **579**
1. Protoctista
ISBN 0-7614-1818-0
           LC 2004-21821
This examines the physical traits, adaptations, diets, habitats, and life cycles of such life forms as bacteria, amoebas, slime nets, molds, algae, coccoliths, forams, and diatoms.

"Fact-filled, yet surprisingly readable. . . . [This] title contains a wide variety of excellent-quality, full-color photographs; interesting sidebars; and diagrams." SLJ

Zamosky, Lisa

Simple organisms. Compass Point Books 2009 40p il (Mission: science) lib bdg $26.60
Grades: 4 5 6   **579**
1. Microorganisms
ISBN 978-0-7565-3955-9 lib bdg; 0-7565-3955-2 lib bdg
           LC 2008-7723
An introduction to microscopic organisms, including germs
Includes glossary and bibliographical references

579.3   Prokaryotes (Bacteria)

Barker, David M.

Archaea; salt-lovers, methane-makers, thermophiles, and other archaeans. by David Barker. Crabtree Pub. 2010 48p il (A class of their own) lib bdg $29.27; pa $9.95
Grades: 5 6 7 8   **579.3**
1. Bacteria
ISBN 978-0-7787-5373-5 lib bdg; 0-7787-5373-5 lib bdg; 978-0-7787-5387-2 pa; 0-7787-5387-5 pa
           LC 2009-51393
Looks at the archaea domain, providing information and examples of species from the three major phyla, as well as information about why so little is known about this diverse domain.

"Lively section headings . . . and notes on uncommon achievements, . . . lighten the substantial load of biological terminology. Illustrated with a plethora of closeup color photos and microphotos, and closing with annotated lists of recommended Web sites, . . . [this captures] the remarkable diversity of life." SLJ

Includes glossary and bibliographical references

Wearing, Judy

Bacteria; staph, strep, clostridium, and other bacteria. Crabtree 2010 48p il (A class of their own) lib bdg $29.27; pa $9.95
Grades: 5 6 7 8   **579.3**
1. Bacteria
ISBN 978-0-7787-5374-2 lib bdg; 0-7787-5374-3 lib bdg; 978-0-7787-5388-9 pa; 0-7787-5388-3 pa
Examines bacteria that are found in virtually every environment-including those that are characterized by extreme heat, cold, and depth-and, of course, bacteria that are found inside our bodies.

"Lively section headings . . . and notes on uncommon achievements, . . . lighten the substantial load of biological terminology. Illustrated with a plethora of closeup color photos and microphotos, and closing with annotated lists of recommended Web sites, . . . [this captures] the remarkable diversity of life." SLJ

Includes glossary and bibliographical references

579.6   Mushrooms

Royston, Angela
Life cycle of a mushroom; rev and updated ed.; Heinemann Library 2009 32p il (Life cycle of a) $25.36; pa $7.99
Grades: 2 3 4   **579.6**
   1. Mushrooms
ISBN 978-1-4329-2530-7; 1-4329-2530-X; 978-1-4329-2547-5 pa; 1-4329-2547-4 pa
                                     LC 2009517694
Introduces the life cycle of a mushroom, from formation of spores through underground growth of the mycelia to formation of mature mushrooms
This offers "easily accessible information in [an] attractive [package]." SLJ
Includes glossary and bibliographical references

580   Natural history of plants and animals

Goodman, Emily
Plant secrets; illustrated by Phyllis Limbacher Tildes. Charlesbridge 2009 un il $16.95; pa $7.95
Grades: PreK K 1 2   **580**
   1. Plants
ISBN 978-1-58089-204-9; 1-58089-204-3; 978-1-58089-205-6 pa; 1-58089-205-1 pa
                                     LC 2008-07256
"Children will look at plants with new eyes after reading this fresh introduction. The plant cycle is introduced, beginning and ending with seeds. . . . The text will draw readers into the wonder of the topic. Bold color-coded headings introduce each of the four stages. Realistic spot illustrations, beginning with the endpapers, present the variety described in the text." SLJ

Gould, Margee
Giant plants. The Rosen Pub. Group 2011 24p il (The strangest plants on Earth) lib bdg $21.25
Grades: 3 4 5   **580**
   1. Size 2. Plants
ISBN 978-1-4488-4990-1; 1-4488-4990-X
                                     LC 2010052217
This "colorful [introduction has] bright, full-color photographs that are detailed enough to enable identification in the field. . . . [The book] includes not only the tallest and most massive plants, but also those with giant odors. One of the illustrations for the corpse flower shows kids at a greenhouse holding their noses as they observe the huge flower that smells like rotting meat. . . . Useful for reports and fun to browse, read, and learn." SLJ
Includes glossary

Hirsch, Rebecca E.
Plants can't sit still; by Rebecca E. Hirsch; illustrated by Mia Posada. Millbrook Press 2016 32 p. color illustrations (lb : alk. paper) $19.99
Grades: PreK K 1 2 3   **580**
   1. Plants 2. Growth (Plants)
ISBN 9781467780315
                                     LC 2015036957
In this picture book by Rebecca E. Hirsch, illustrated by Mia Posada, published as part of the Millbrook Picture Books series, "you might be surprised by all ways plants can move. Plants might not pick up their roots and walk away, but they definitely don't sit still! Discover the many ways plants . . . move. Whether it's a sunflower, a Venus flytrap,

or an exotic plant like an exploding cucumber, this . . . book shows just how excitingly active plants really are." (Publisher's note)
"Excellent collaboration produced a winner: graceful, informative, and entertaining." Kirkus

Levine, Shar
Plants; flowering plants, ferns, mosses, and other plants. by Shar Levine and Leslie Johnstone. Crabtree Pub. 2010 48p il (A class of their own) lib bdg $29.27; pa $9.95
Grades: 5 6 7 8   **580**
   1. Plants
ISBN 978-0-7787-5376-6 lib bdg; 0-7787-5376-X lib bdg; 978-0-7787-5390-2 pa; 0-7787-5390-5 pa
                                     LC 2009-51342
Describes the main groups of plants, including mosses, ferns, conifers, and flowering plants.
"Lively section headings . . . and notes on uncommon achievements, . . . lighten the substantial load of biological terminology. Illustrated with a plethora of closeup color photos and microphotos, and closing with annotated lists of recommended Web sites, . . . [this captures] the remarkable diversity of life." SLJ
Includes glossary and bibliographical references

Taylor, Barbara
Inside plants. Marshall Cavendish Benchmark 2010 48p il (Invisible worlds) lib bdg $28.50
Grades: 4 5 6 7   **580**
   1. Plants
ISBN 978-0-7614-4189-2 lib bdg; 0-7614-4189-1 lib bdg
                                     LC 2008037247
This describes the plant details that are too small for the unaided eye to see, and how these microscopic systems work to keep the plant alive and healthy.
The narrative is "clear, well written, broken down into manageable pieces, and peppered with eye-opening facts. The numerous photographs are so phenomenal that they will inspire kids to read the text . . . so that they can wrap their minds around what they see." SLJ
Includes glossary and bibliographical references

Wade, Mary Dodson
Trees, weeds, and vegetables--so many kinds of plants! Enslow Elementary 2009 24p il (I like plants!) lib bdg $21.26; pa $6.95
Grades: K 1 2   **580**
   1. Plants
ISBN 978-0-7660-3156-2 lib bdg; 0-7660-3156-X lib bdg; 978-0-7660-3616-1 pa; 0-7660-3616-2 pa
                                     LC 2007039460
This does "an excellent job of introducing basic concepts about seeds and plants. Large text on colored pages explains terms and covers a lot of ground in the simplest manner imaginable. The full-color illustrations amplify the narrative." SLJ
Includes glossary and bibliographical references

580.7   Education, research, related topics

Benbow, Ann
Lively plant science projects; [by] Ann Benbow and Colin Mably; illustrations by Tom Labaff. Enslow Publishers 2009 48p il (Real life science experiments) lib bdg $23.93
Grades: 3 4 5   **580.7**
   1. Botany 2. Plants 3. Science projects
ISBN 978-0-7660-3146-3 lib bdg; 0-7660-3146-2 lib bdg
                                     LC 2008-01745

"Color drawings, photographs, a glossary, and suggestions for further research enliven . . . [this] title . . . [and provide] solid curricular support." Booklist

Includes glossary and bibliographical references

Sprouting seed science projects; [by] Ann Benbow and Colin Mably; illustrations by Tom Labaff. Enslow Publishers 2009 48p il (Real life science experiments) lib bdg $23.93

Grades: 3 4 5   **580.7**
  1. Seeds 2. Germination 3. Science projects
  ISBN 978-0-7660-3147-0 lib bdg; 0-7660-3147-0 lib bdg
                                          LC 2008-1731
"Color drawings, photographs, a glossary, and suggestions for further research enliven . . . [this] title . . . [and provide] solid curricular support." Booklist

Includes glossary and bibliographical references

Gardner, Robert
  Ace your plant science project; great science fair ideas. [by] Robert Gardner and Phyllis J. Perry. Enslow Publishers 2009 104p il (Ace your biology science project) lib bdg $31.93

Grades: 5 6 7 8   **580.7**
  1. Plants 2. Science projects 3. Science -- Experiments
  ISBN 978-0-7660-3221-7 lib bdg; 0-7660-3221-3 lib bdg
                                          LC 2008-4687
"Presents several science experiments and project ideas using plants." Publisher's note

Includes bibliographical references

581 Specific topics in natural history of plants

Wade, Mary Dodson
  Plants live everywhere! Enslow Elementary 2009 24p il (I like plants!) lib bdg $21.26; pa $6.95

Grades: K 1 2   **581**
  1. Plants
  ISBN 978-0-7660-3155-5 lib bdg; 0-7660-3155-1 lib bdg; 978-0-7660-3615-4 pa; 0-7660-3615-4 pa
                                          LC 2007039457
This book does "an excellent job of introducing basic concepts about seeds and plants. Large text on colored pages explains terms and covers a lot of ground in the simplest manner imaginable. The full-color illustrations amplify the narrative." SLJ

Includes glossary and bibliographical references

581.4 Adaptation

Aston, Dianna Hutts
  ★ A **seed** is sleepy; by Dianna Hutts Aston; illustrated by Sylvia Long. Chronicle Books 2007 un il $16.95

Grades: K 1 2 3   **581.4**
  1. Seeds
  ISBN 0-8118-5520-1; 978-0-8118-5520-4
                                          LC 2006-13302
"Following the format of their previous title An Egg is Quiet, Aston and Long turn their attention to the structure, function, and diversity of seeds. . . . Grades two to four."

"The topic is seeds, and . . . Long's masterful watercolors dominate each spread, which includes text on two levels. Short poetic phrases in large print, airmed at younger children, give seeds accessible, anthropomorphic qualities. . . . Paragraphs in smaller print, which tackle sci-

ence concepts and expand on the phrases, are geared to older readers." Booklist

Farndon, John
  Seeds. Blackbirch Press 2006 24p il (World of plants) lib bdg $27.44

Grades: 2 3 4 5   **581.4**
  1. Seeds
  ISBN 978-1-4103-0419-3 lib bdg; 1-4103-0419-1 lib bdg
                                          LC 2005047047
This book examines germination, the ways seeds are spread, types and sizes of seeds, and the role of seeds in the diets of both humans and animals

This uses "clear language and short sentences. . . . Helpful diagrams and sharp, colorful photographs supplement the [text]. . . . [This book offers] solid information in an attractive format." SLJ

Includes bibliographical references

  Stems. Blackbirch Press 2006 24p il (World of plants) lib bdg $27.44

Grades: 2 3 4 5   **581.4**
  1. Stems (Plants)
  ISBN 978-1-4103-0420-9 lib bdg; 1-4103-0420-5 lib bdg
                                          LC 2005047049
This book examines how stems grow, the sizes of various types of stems, underground stems, and the ways people and animals use stems for food and shelter

This uses "clear language and short sentences. . . . Helpful diagrams and sharp, colorful photographs supplement the [text]. . . . [This book offers] solid information in an attractive format." SLJ

Includes bibliographical references

Galbraith, Kathryn O.
  Planting the wild garden; written by Kathryn O. Galbraith; illustrated by Wendy Anderson Halperin. Peachtree 2011 32 p. il

Grades: K 1   **581.4**
  1. Seeds 2. Wild plants 3. Picture books for children 4. Plants
  ISBN 1561455636; 9781561455638
                                          LC 2010026898
This picture book answers the question "how do wild plants grow and spread? In . . . prose punctuated with sound effects ("Per-chik-o-ree! Per-chiko-ree!" cries a goldfinch) . . . [Kathryn O.] Galbraith . . . explains that seeds from wild plants float in the wind, snap off plants, fall in the rain, and get carried--intentionally or unintentionally--by animals to new places where they sprout and thrive. "A family of raccoons feasts on blackberries. . . . When they amble home again, bits of berries and seeds go with them. Next spring, new prickly canes will pop up everywhere." [Wendy Anderson] Halperin's . . . spreads are divided into contiguous panels tinted in the lightest of watercolors, with delicate pencil shading that conveys the force of wind and rain alike." (Publishers Weekly)

"Seeds grow in wild meadows because they are carried by wind and water, birds and animals, plants and people. This title celebrates the power of these tiny wonders—so delicate, so hardy—with simple, poetic words. . . . The soft, pencil-and-watercolor images alternate expansive landscapes with small, framed details that show tiny, dramatic stories. . . . A natural choice for curriculum connections." Booklist

Gould, Margee
  Prickly plants. PowerKids Press 2011 24p il (The strangest plants on Earth) lib bdg $21.25

Grades: 3 4 5   **581.4**
  1. Cactus 2. Plants
  ISBN 978-1-4488-4991-8; 1-4488-4991-8
                                          LC 2010053141

This describes prickly plants including cacti, stinging nettles, the silk floss tree and the honey locust tree.

This "colorful [introduction has] bright, full-color photographs that are detailed enough to enable identification in the field. . . . Useful for reports and fun to browse, read, and learn." SLJ

Includes glossary

Heneghan, Judith

Once there was a seed; written by Judith Anderson; illustrated by Mike Gordon. Barron's 2010 32p il (Nature's miracles) pa $5.99
Grades: K 1 2   **581.4**
1. Seeds 2. Plants
ISBN 978-0-7641-4493-6 pa; 0-7641-4493-6 pa
First published 2009 in the United Kingdom
Introduces the life cycle of plants, describing how a plant is grown from a seed, sprouts roots and leaves, and eventually forms a mature plant or flower which contains new seeds.

"This proves that science for even the very youngest readers can retain the same nonfiction qualities as that for older students and still be captivating as well as educational." Libr Media Connect

Includes bibliographical references

Kim, Sue

How does a seed grow? a book with fold-out pages. photos by Tilde. Little Simon 2010 un il bd bk $7.99
Grades: PreK   **581.4**
1. Seeds 2. Board books for children 3. Plants -- Growth
ISBN 978-1-4169-9435-0; 1-4169-9435-1
"From seed to sprout to finished fruit, plants spring to life in this inventive picture book that folds out into four scenes on every spread. In a question-and-answer format, the smooth, rhyming text introduces botany basics. . . . Right-hand pages fold out to show the emerging plant in bright color photos, finally reaching an oversize scene of a child enjoying the mature fruit. . . . Both entertaining and informative." Booklist

Macken, Joann Early

Flip, float, fly; seeds on the move. by JoAnn Early Macken; illustrated by Pam Paparone. Holiday House 2008 un il $16.95
Grades: K 1 2 3   **581.4**
1. Seeds 2. Seeds -- Dispersal
ISBN 0-8234-2043-4; 978-0-8234-2043-8
LC 2006-37278
This book describes how seeds are dispersed. "Grades one to four." (Sci Books Films)

This book introduces "methods of seed distribution. Each is introduced on a double-page spread, in which a few lines of poetic text provide information succinctly. . . . Pleasing in their colors, compositions, and decorative elements, the pictures clearly show points made in the text. . . . Satisfying and well designed for both classroom sharing and individual reading." Booklist

Includes glossary and bibliographical references

Richards, Jean

A **fruit** is a suitcase for seeds; illustrated by Anca Hariton. Millbrook Press 2002 un il lib bdg $21.90
Grades: K 1 2   **581.4**
1. Fruit 2. Seeds -- Dispersal
ISBN 0-7613-1622-1
LC 2001-32959
Provides an illustrated description of seed dispersal by which plants, most specifically fruits, travel from one place to another

"Richard's carefully worded information provides an excellent introduction to seeds, their purpose, and growth that should be easy for young

children to grasp. . . . Hariton's use of bright watercolors adds sensual appeal to her illustrations." SLJ

Robbins, Ken

★ **Seeds**; text and pictures by Ken Robbins. Atheneum Books for Young Readers 2005 un il $15.95
Grades: K 1 2 3   **581.4**
1. Seeds
ISBN 0-689-85041-7
This "book focuses on seed basics: differences in shapes and sizes, and links between structure and function. . . . Seeds are show alongside the whole plants and fruits they come from. . . . The superb photographs lend themselves to scientific scrutiny: the details are sharp and clear." Horn Book

Rustad, Martha E. H.

Fall leaves; colorful and crunchy. illustrated by Amanda Enright. Millbrook Press 2011 24p il (Fall's here!) lib bdg $23.93
Grades: K 1 2 3   **581.4**
1. Autumn 2. Leaves
ISBN 978-0-7613-5062-0; 0-7613-5062-4
LC 2010053301
In this book "a young girl spies leaves changing color in the fall. She explores how different weather and amounts of sunlight allow the leaves to grow, get food and water, change color, and then fall as the seasons change. . . . In the back of the book, instructions are given for making a leaf print. . . . Children will enjoy the colorful, expressive illustrations." Sci Books Films

Includes glossary and bibliographical references

Wade, Mary Dodson

Seeds sprout! Enslow Elementary 2009 24p il (I like plants!) lib bdg $21.26; pa $6.95
Grades: K 1 2   **581.4**
1. Seeds 2. Plants
ISBN 978-0-7660-3154-8 lib bdg; 0-7660-3154-3 lib bdg; 978-0-7660-3614-7 pa; 0-7660-3614-6 pa
LC 2007039461
This book does "an excellent job of introducing basic concepts about seeds and plants. Large text on colored pages explains terms and covers a lot of ground in the simplest manner imaginable. The full-color illustrations amplify the narrative." SLJ

Includes glossary and bibliographical references

581.6   Miscellaneous nontaxonomic kinds of plants

Farrell, Courtney

Plants out of place. Rourke Pub. 2010 48p il (Let's explore science) $32.79
Grades: 4 5 6 7   **581.6**
1. Plants 2. Biological invasions 3. Food chains (Ecology)
ISBN 978-1-61590-322-1; 1-61590-322-4
LC 2010009909
This "takes a lively look at invasive plants . . . and shows both the destruction that non-native plants cause and what can be done about it. . . . In [this] title, well-chosen boxed examples, abundant color photos, diagrams, and an appended glossary add interest and support the engaging [text]." Booklist

Includes glossary and bibliographical references

Gould, Margee

Poisonous plants. PowerKids Press 2011 24p il (The strangest plants on Earth) lib bdg $21.25

Grades: 3 4 5   **581.6**
1. Poisonous plants
ISBN 978-1-4488-4989-5; 1-4488-4989-6

LC 2010050512

This "colorful [introduction has] bright, full-color photographs that are detailed enough to enable identification in the field, especially of such common poisonous plants as poison ivy, oak, and sumac.... Useful for reports and fun to browse, read, and learn." SLJ

Includes glossary

Rockwell, Lizzy
Plants feed me; by Lizzy Rockwell. Holiday House 2014 32 p. col. ill. (hardcover) $16.95
Grades: PreK K 1   **581.6**
1. Plants
ISBN 0823425266; 9780823425266

LC 2012007674

This children's book, by Lizzy Rockwell, features "illustrations [that] show plants and the parts we harvest for food—leaves from lettuce and chard plants; roots and tubers from carrot and potato plants; fruits from apple trees, tomato plants, blueberry bushes, and pumpkin vines; seeds from wheat grass and walnut trees; and all kinds of beans from pods of many shapes." (Booklist)

"It's easy to forget where everyday food comes from, but this gentle, colorful picture book explains, simply and accurately, how food gets from the garden and farm onto dining-room tables." Booklist

Wade, Mary Dodson
People need plants! Enslow Elementary 2009 24p il (I like plants!) lib bdg $21.26; pa $6.95
Grades: K 1 2   **581.6**
1. Plants
ISBN 978-0-7660-3153-1 lib bdg; 0-7660-3153-5 lib bdg; 978-0-7660-3613-0 pa; 0-7660-3613-8 pa

LC 2007039458

"Beautifully detailed professional photographs of plants, animals, and people complement the subject matter. [The] book includes a simple activity." SLJ

Includes glossary and bibliographical references

582   Plants noted for specific vegetative characteristics and flowers

Schaefer, Lola M.
★ **Pick,** pull, snap! where once a flower bloomed. illustrated by Lindsay Barrett George. Greenwillow Bks. 2003 un il $15.99
Grades: K 1 2 3   **582**
1. Fruit 2. Seeds 3. Plants 4. Flowers
ISBN 0-688-17834-0

LC 2002-66818

Describes how raspberries, peanuts, corn, and other foods are produced as various plants flower, create seeds, and finally bear fruit

"On each spread, rhythmic, poetic text describes a plant's flower or husk and shows a cross section that reveals the seeds inside. A few lines of text explain a plant's growth, and then the page folds out to reveal the mature plant.... George's inviting, realistic color art brings youngsters up close to plants that produce familiar foods." Booklist

Includes glossary

582.13   Plants noted for their flowers

Souza, D. M.
Freaky flowers. Watts 2002 63p il (Watts library) lib bdg $24.50; pa $8.95
Grades: 5 6 7 8   **582.13**
1. Flowers
ISBN 0-531-11981-5 lib bdg; 0-531-16221-4 pa

LC 2001-17573

"The book begins with a short course in botany that stresses vocabulary and processes. Subsequent chapters discuss different ways plants attract pollinators through colors, odors, and habitats. The last chapter acts as a warning that many plants are endangered because their pollinators are threatened, emphasizing the balance of nature. The outstanding full-color photos feature some of the most spectacular flowers found anywhere. Small sidebars offer interesting bits of trivia about similar plants. The text is packed with biological information and pertinent vocabulary." SLJ

Includes bibliographical references

Wade, Mary Dodson
Flowers bloom! Enslow Elementary 2009 24p il (I like plants!) lib bdg $21.26; pa $6.95
Grades: K 1 2   **582.13**
1. Flowers
ISBN 978-0-7660-3157-9 lib bdg; 0-7660-3157-8 lib bdg; 978-0-7660-3617-8 pa; 0-7660-3617-0 pa

LC 2007039462

"Beautifully detailed professional photographs of plants, animals, and people complement the subject matter. [The] book includes a simple activity." SLJ

Includes glossary and bibliographical references

582.16   Trees

Bernhard, Durga Yael
Just like me, climbing a tree; exploring trees around the world. written & illustrated by Durga Yael Bernhard. Wisdom Tales 2015 32 p. color illustrations, maps (hardcover ; alk. paper) $16.95
Grades: K 1 2   **582.16**
1. Trees 2. Forest ecology 3. Ecology 4. Tree climbing
ISBN 9781937786342

LC 2014040810

This children's book, written and illustrated by Durga Yael Bernhard, presents " a trip around the world to climb its weirdest and most wonderful trees. No matter if you are in Africa, Asia, Europe, or America, there is a grand adventure waiting for you—provided you have a tree to climb in your neighborhood!" (Publisher's note)

"A great addition, particularly for those doing lesson plans on trees." SLJ

Ehlert, Lois
★ **Red** leaf, yellow leaf. Harcourt Brace Jovanovich 1991 un il $16
Grades: K 1 2 3   **582.16**
1. Trees
ISBN 0-15-266197-2

LC 90-21195

"In a quiet, first-person narrative, a young child details the life cycle of a sugar maple tree.... The story is quite brief, and the choice of a very large typeface makes the main portion of the book accessible to beginning readers. The concluding section offers more detailed and concrete botanical information and provides hints on selecting and planting one's own tree. . . . Ehlert has combined many media to create the book's dazzling illustrations." Horn Book

Galat, Joan Marie

Branching out; How Trees Are Part of Our World. Joan Marie Galat. Owlkids Books, Inc. 2014 64 p. color illustrations (hardcover) $18.95

Grades: 4 5 6 7   **582.16**

1. Trees

ISBN 1771470496; 9781771470490; 9781771470827

LC 2014932714

This book, by Joan Marie Galat, " takes an in-depth look at [trees], introducing the basics of tree biology and profiling 11 different trees from around the world, including familiar ones such as the Red Maple and lesser-known trees like the Tall-Stilted Mangrove. Showcasing the inextricable ways in which trees are part of our society, culture, and economy, this illustrated volume also outlines how animals need trees and how, sometimes, they even help trees survive through symbiosis." (Publisher's note)

"This short, lively introduction to the subject focuses on 11 trees from all over the world...This title is truly worldwide in its coverage; only one tree, the Red Maple, is a native of North America. Appended glossary and index are extensive and complete. A solid overview." SLJ

Gerber, Carole

Winter trees; illustrated by Leslie Evans. Charlesbridge 2008 un il $15.95

Grades: PreK K 1 2   **582.16**

1. Trees 2. Winter

ISBN 978-1-58089-168-4; 1-58089-168-3

LC 2007-26197

"Alone in the snowy woods with his dog, a boy discovers the wonder of winter trees. . . . On every double-page spread, four lines of simple verse and bright linoleum block prints decorated with watercolor and collage capture the stark outlines and the details of what he sees, hears, and touches. . . . The blend of play, science, poetry, and art is beautiful; and notes at the back provide more facts about each tree." Booklist

Gibbons, Gail

Tell me, tree; all about trees for kids. Little, Brown 2002 un il $15.95

Grades: K 1 2 3   **582.16**

1. Trees

ISBN 0-316-30903-6

LC 00-64967

"The bright, watercolor illustrations show cheerful children and adults observing, planting, using, and enjoying many kinds of trees. In this simple, informative book, Gibbons provides a basic guide that is sure to please parents and teachers as well as children." Booklist

Howse, Jennifer

Trees. Weigl Publishers 2010 24p il (World of wonder: watch them grow) lib bdg $25.70; pa $9.95

Grades: 1 2   **582.16**

1. Trees

ISBN 978-1-60596-916-9 lib bdg; 1-60596-916-8 lib bdg; 978-1-60596-917-6 pa; 1-60596-917-6 pa

LC 2009-52098

Learn about the parts of a tree, how it matures from a tiny sprout, and how to learn its age.

The text "is simple without being simplistic; it is thoughtful and comprehensive without being overwhelming. The real appeal for teachers, students, and independent young readers, however, will be the photographs that fill the facing pages. Bold, bright, and colorful, the photo-

graphs bring you marvelously close to the subject. . . . On many different levels, this is a very appealing [book]." Libr Media Connect

Includes glossary

Maestro, Betsy

Why do leaves change color? illustrated by Loretta Krupinski. HarperCollins Pubs. 1994 32p il (Let's-read-and-find-out science) hardcover o.p. pa $4.95

Grades: K 1 2 3   **582.16**

1. Autumn 2. Leaves

ISBN 0-06-022874-1 lib bdg; 0-06-445126-7 pa

LC 93-9611

Explains how leaves change their colors in autumn and then separate from the tree as the tree prepares for winter

"This is an informative concept book. . . . Krupinski's bright gouache-and-colored pencil illustrations show a boy and a girl playing in a country landscape that changes with weather and light. There are also detailed pictures of leaves in different sizes, shapes, and colors. Maestro includes simple instructions for making a leaf rubbing and for pressing leaves, as well as suggestions for places to visit where the fall foliage is special." Booklist

Pallotta, Jerry

Who will plant a tree? written by Jerry Pallotta; illustrated by Tom Leonard. Sleeping Bear Press 2010 un il $15.95

Grades: PreK K 1 2   **582.16**

1. Seeds 2. Trees

ISBN 1-58536-502-5; 978-1-58536-502-9

LC 2009037411

"Each spread features an animal in a different habitat that, by simply going about its everyday activities, unknowingly plants a tree. . . . The range of habitats and animals shown is impressive, from monkeys throwing figs in the jungle to Amazon River fish excreting seeds from their fruit dinners. . . . With simple, rhythmic language and engaging illustrations, this book encourages readers to see how the actions of each creature impact the Earth. An excellent accompaniment to science lessons." SLJ

Preus, Margi

Celebritrees; historic & famous trees of the world. illustrated by Rebecca Gibbon. Henry Holt & Co. 2011 un il $16.99

Grades: 2 3 4   **582.16**

1. Trees

ISBN 978-0-8050-7829-9; 0-8050-7829-0

"Preus introduces 14 trees famous in history or legend. Some are renowned for their age, height, girth, or other physical characteristics. For example, Methuselah, a bristlecone pine in California, is more than 4000 years old, while the Tule Tree in Mexico measures 177 feet around. Others are associated with historic events. . . . Each featured specimen receives a spread with several paragraphs of text plus Gibbon's charming colored pencil and watercolor illustrations. Readers who want to learn more about one or more of the tree varieties can find additional information at the book's end." SLJ

Includes bibliographical references

Rene, Ellen

Investigating why leaves change their color. Rosen/PowerKids 2008 24p il (Science detectives) lib bdg $15.95

Grades: 3 4 5   **582.16**

1. Trees 2. Leaves

ISBN 978-1-4042-4485-6 lib bdg; 1-4042-4485-9 lib bdg

"With a chatty text, oversize font, and beautiful, full-page color photos, the open design of this . . . book . . . will invite young readers to look at the astonishing science happening around them. The page headings are appealing . . . leading into text that details the process of photosynthesis and chlorophyll's role in trapping sunlight; the botany is quite technical and will encourage kids to talk about it in the classroom and at home. . . . [This is a] fine account of one of nature's most vibrant transformations, leading kids to an elementary understanding of how the sun and sky affect each and every leaf." Booklist

Russo, Monica

Treecology; 30 activities and observations for exploring the world of trees and forests. Monica Russo; photographs by Kevin Byron. Chicago Review Press Incorporated 2016 144 p. (trade paper) $15.99; (ebook) $15.99

Grades: 3 4 5 6 7 8 9   **582.16**

1. Trees   2. Trees -- Study and teaching (Elementary) -- Activity programs   3. Forest ecology -- Study and teaching (Elementary) -- Activity programs

ISBN 1613733968; 9781613733967; 9781613733998

LC 2015050678

In this book in the Young Naturalists series by Monica Russo with photographs by Kevin Byron, "young nature enthusiasts will learn . . . fascinating facts about the wonderful world of trees. . . . [This] resource includes plentiful full-color photos and drawings and clear, kid-friendly discussions of tree structures, families, and foods; the interaction between trees and the wildlife that depend on them; tree and forest—related jobs and preservation, and much more." (Publisher's note)

"A labor of love reflecting years of experience in the field as well as in writing for young readers, this offers a path to interesting explorations of the natural world." Kirkus

Includes bibliographical references and index

Tate, Nikki

Deep Roots; How Trees Sustain Our Planet. Orca Book Publishers 2016 48 p. color illustrations (ebook) $19.99; $19.95

Grades: 4 5 6 7   **582.16**

1. Trees   2. Ecology   3. Forest ecology

ISBN 9781459805835; 1459805828; 9781459805828

LC 2015944487

Written by Nikki Tate, "'Deep Roots' celebrates the central role trees play in our lives, no matter where we live. Each chapter in 'Deep Roots' focuses on a basic element--water, air, fire and earth--and explores the many ways in which we need trees to keep our planet healthy and livable. From making rain to producing fruit to feeding fish, trees play an integral role in maintaining vibrant ecosystems all over the world." (Publisher's note)

"Color photographs, activity suggestions, trivia bursts, sidebars, and Tate's own arboreal anecdotes create an accessible and involving layout, while supplying a broad take on the global diversity and varying roles of trees." Pub Wkly

Includes bibliographical references (page 43-44) and index.

583   Dicotyledons

Aaseng, Nathan

Weird meat-eating plants. Enslow Publishers 2011 48p il (Bizarre science) lib bdg $23.93

Grades: 5 6 7 8   **583**

1. Carnivorous plants

ISBN 978-0-7660-3672-7; 0-7660-3672-3

LC 2010016602

First published 1996 with title: Meat-eating plants

This describes meat-eating plants such as butterworts, sundews, byblis, pitcher plants, cobra lilies, venus flytraps, and bladderworts.

"Aimed at reluctant readers, [this title is] sure to disgust and delight in equal measure. . . . [The title] will pique interest and get kids lining up at the reference desk looking for more. The text is complemented by illustrations and magnified photos of things that you would hope never to see." SLJ

Includes glossary and bibliographical references

Bash, Barbara

Desert giant; the world of the saguaro cactus. Sierra Club Bks. 1989 un il hardcover o.p. pa $6.95

Grades: 3 4 5   **583**

1. Cactus   2. Desert ecology

ISBN 1-57805-085-5 pa

LC 88-4706

"Animals find food and shelter in the towering plant of the Sonoran desert, and the local Tohono O'odom Indians have multiple uses for it. The cactus's 200-year life cycle is depicted as part of the ecosystem with colorful illustrations and clear text." Sci Child

Dickmann, Nancy

A bean's life. Heinemann Library 2010 24p il (Watch it grow) lib bdg $21.50; pa $5.99

Grades: PreK K 1   **583**

1. Beans

ISBN 978-1-4329-4142-0 lib bdg; 1-4329-4142-9 lib bdg; 978-1-4329-4151-2 pa; 1-4329-4151-8 pa

LC 2009-49158

"Practically unique among early introductions to life cycles because death is mentioned . . . this . . . follows [a bean] . . . from . . . seed to maturity with a set of close-up color photographs, one per page, paired to large-type, one or two-sentence captions. . . . Offers nourishing fare for young naturalists." SLJ

Includes glossary

An oak tree's life. Heinemann Library 2010 24p il (Watch it grow) lib bdg $21.50; pa $5.99

Grades: PreK K 1   **583**

1. Oak

ISBN 978-1-4329-4143-7 lib bdg; 1-4329-4143-7 lib bdg; 978-1-4329-4152-9 pa; 1-4329-4152-6 pa

LC 2009-49159

"Practically unique among early introductions to life cycles because death is mentioned . . . this . . . follows [an oak tree] . . . from . . . seed to maturity with a set of close-up color photographs, one per page, paired to large-type, one or two-sentence captions. . . . Offers nourishing fare for young naturalists." SLJ

Includes glossary and bibliographical references

A sunflower's life. Heinemann Library 2010 24p il (Watch it grow) lib bdg $21.50; pa $5.99

Grades: PreK K 1   **583**

1. Sunflowers

ISBN 978-1-4329-4144-4 lib bdg; 1-4329-4144-5 lib bdg; 978-1-4329-4153-6 pa; 1-4329-4153-4 pa

LC 2009-49161

"Practically unique among early introductions to life cycles because death is mentioned . . . this . . . follows [a sunflower] . . . from . . . seed to maturity with a set of close-up color photographs, one per page, paired to large-type, one or two-sentence captions. . . . Offers nourishing fare for young naturalists." SLJ

Includes glossary and bibliographical references

Gould, Margee

Meat-eating plants. PowerKids Press 2011 24p il (The strangest plants on Earth) lib bdg $21.25

Grades: 3 4 5   583

1. Carnivorous plants

ISBN 978-1-4488-4988-8; 1-4488-4988-8

LC 2010047870

This describes meat-eating plants including the venus flytrap, the bladderwort, the pitcher plant, and the sundew.

This "colorful [introduction has] bright, full-color photographs that are detailed enough to enable identification in the field. . . . Useful for reports and fun to browse, read, and learn." SLJ

Includes glossary

Guiberson, Brenda Z.

Cactus hotel; illustrated by Megan Lloyd. Holt & Co. 1991 un il $16.95; pa $6.95

Grades: K 1 2 3   583

1. Cactus 2. Desert ecology

ISBN 0-8050-1333-4; 0-8050-2960-5 pa

LC 90-41748

Describes the life cycle of the giant saguaro cactus, with an emphasis on its role as a home for other desert dwellers

"Guiberson's simple, understandable text gives an enjoyable lesson in desert ecology. Crisply attractive illustrations in color pencil and watercolor show the beauty of the desert landscape and its variety of wildlife." Booklist

Hall, Zoe

The apple pie tree; illustrated by Shari Halpern. Blue Sky Press (NY) 1996 un il $15.95

Grades: K 1   583

1. Apples

ISBN 0-590-62382-6

LC 95-31134

"From bud to fruit, two children follow the cycle of an apple tree as it is nurtured through the seasons. . . . The story ends with a nice, warm apple pie being taken from the oven. The large pictures and text are suitable for young children. The colorful, clear-cut illustrations use a paint and paper collage technique. An end note shows how bees pollinate the tree's flowers and offers a recipe for apple pie." SLJ

Johnson, Jinny

Dandelion; illustrations by Graham Rosewarne. Smart Apple Media 2010 32p il (How does it grow?) lib bdg $28.50

Grades: 1 2 3   583

1. Dandelions

ISBN 978-1-59920-351-5 lib bdg; 1-59920-351-0 lib bdg

LC 2009-5693

Explains the life cycle of a dandelion

"Each stage is described on a spread that features clearly written, oversized text and a caption opposite a full-page, realistic watercolor, or, occasionally, a photograph. . . . A worthwhile purchase." SLJ

Includes glossary

Oak tree; illustrations by Graham Rosewarne. Smart Apple Media 2010 32p il (How does it grow?) lib bdg $28.50

Grades: 1 2 3   583

1. Oak

ISBN 978-1-59920-356-0 lib bdg; 1-59920-356-1 lib bdg

LC 2009-3399

Presents a basic overview of how an acorn grows into an oak tree and explains each stage in its development

"Each stage is described on a spread that features clearly written, oversized text and a caption opposite a full-page, realistic watercolor, or, occasionally, a photograph. . . . A worthwhile purchase." SLJ

Includes glossary and bibliographical references

Markovics, Joyce

Oak tree; Joyce Markovics. Bearport Publishing Company, Inc. 2016 24 p. color illustrations (library binding : alk. paper) $23.93

Grades: PreK K 1   583

1. Oak 2. Trees

ISBN 1627248447; 9781627248440

LC 2015007548

This children's book on oak trees, by Joyce L. Markovics, is part of a series offering " introductions to familiar plants. Starting with the plant's most recognizable feature-whether seed, fruit, or flower-each volume answers the question 'How did it get that way?' As readers follow the life cycle, they learn how seeds develop into shoots, grow stems and leaves, and flower and produce fruits." (School Library Journal)

"Focused on particular plants and colorfully illustrated, the series offers useful, attractive books for library collections serving younger students." Booklist

Includes bibliographical references and index

Sunflower; by Joyce Markovics. Bearport Publishing 2016 24 p. color illustrations (library binding : alk. paper) $23.93

Grades: PreK K 1   583

1. Plants 2. Sunflowers

ISBN 1627248439; 9781627248433

LC 2015007543

This juvenile book, by Joyce L. Markovics, part of the publisher's "See It Grow" series, explores sunflowers. "Starting with the plant's most recognizable feature-whether seed, fruit, or flower-each volume answers the question 'How did it get that way?' As readers follow the life cycle, they learn how seeds develop into shoots, grow stems and leaves, and flower and produce fruits." (School Library Journal)

"Focused on particular plants and colorfully illustrated, the series offers useful, attractive books for library collections serving younger students." Booklist

Includes bibliographical references and index

Pfeffer, Wendy

From seed to pumpkin; illustrated by James Graham Hale. HarperCollins 2004 33p il (Let's-read-and-find-out science) hardcover o.p. lib bdg $16.89; pa $4.99

Grades: K 1   583

1. Pumpkin

ISBN 0-06-028038-7; 0-06-028039-5 lib bdg; 0-06-445190-9 pa

LC 00-54039

This explains the stages in the development of a seed into a pumpkin

Written "in simple, clear language. . . . A couple of easy recipes and experiments are appended. Appealing watercolor-and-pencil illustrations show children involved in planting and tending the pumpkins, and help make the process and the passage of time understandable to this audience." SLJ

Royston, Angela

Life cycle of an oak tree; rev and updated ed.; Heinemann Library 2009 32p il (Life cycle of a) $25.36; pa $7.99

Grades: 2 3 4   583

1. Oak

ISBN 978-1-4329-2531-4; 1-4329-2531-8; 978-1-4329-2548-2 pa; 1-4329-2548-2 pa

LC 2009517688

First published 2000

Introduces the life cycle of an oak tree, from the sprouting of an acorn through its more than 100 years of growth

This offers "easily accessible information in [an] attractive [package]." SLJ

Includes glossary and bibliographical references

585   Gymnosperms

Chin, Jason

★ **Redwoods**. Roaring Brook Press 2009 un il $16.95

Grades: PreK K 1 2   **585**

1. Redwood

ISBN 978-1-59643-430-1; 1-59643-430-9

"The framing story opens with a boy finding a copy of Redwoods on a subway station bench (he's even on the cover). He delves in, and facts about the ancient trees spring to life around him. . . . Emerging from the station to find himself in the middle of a redwood forest, his adventures mirror what he's learning. . . . The straightforward narrative is given enormous energy by the inventive format and realistic watercolor illustrations. . . . Chin adeptly captures the singular and spectacular nature of redwoods in this smartly layered book." Publ Wkly

586   Seedless plants

Pascoe, Elaine

Plants without seeds; photography by Dwight Kuhn. PowerKids Press 2003 32p il (Kid's guide to the classification of living things) $20.65

Grades: 2 3 4 5   **586**

1. Ferns 2. Mosses

ISBN 0-8239-6315-2

LC 2001-7794

An introduction to the life cycles and characteristics of bryophytes, or plants without seeds, such as mosses and ferns

This "slim, well-organized . . . {introduction is} a must for schools in which plant studies are a part of the curriculum. . . . Useful for reports, with browsing appeal as well." SLJ

Includes glossary and bibliographical references

590   Animals

125 true stories of amazing animals; [inspiring tales of animal friendship & four-legged heroes, plus crazy animal antics] National Geographic Publishers Group 2012 112 p. (pbk.) $12.95

Grades: 4 5 6   **590**

1. Animals 2. Rescue work 3. Animal behavior 4. Animals -- Anecdotes

ISBN 142630918X; 9781426309182

LC 2012471745

This book is a "collection of favorite animal antics from 'National Geographic Kids' 'Amazing Animals' column [and] has a little of everything: dramatic rescues, incredible adventures, mistaken identities, strange bedfellows, odd couples, and much more." Among those featured are a "hippo that opens doors with his lips, a bison that rides in cars, an owl that goes on bike rides, and a group of elephants that play in an orchestra." (School Library Journal)

Ablow, Gail

A **horse** in the house, and other strange but true animal stories; illustrated by Kathy Osborn. Candlewick Press 2007 un il $17.99

Grades: 2 3 4 5   **590**

1. Animals

ISBN 978-0-7636-2838-3; 0-7636-2838-7

LC 2006051855

"Some of these 16 short tales would be very hard to believe, had Ablow, a journalist, not provided specific source notes for each at the end. It wouldn't be too hard to buy the moose that does laps in a Spokane swimming pool . . . —but a man successfully giving mouth-to-mouth to a distressed ornamental fish? . . . Osborn's stylized paintings capture the humor in each report. . . . Even skeptical young readers will come back for more." Booklist

Includes bibliographical references

Animals alive; the fight for survival in the wild. DK Pub. 2011 80p il map $15.99

Grades: 3 4 5 6   **590**

1. Animals

ISBN 978-0-7566-7213-3; 0-7566-7213-9

Explains biodiversity, discusses the role animals play in ecosystems, describes the threats affecting the lives of animals, and profiles various animals, including jaguars, black rhinoceros, and bluefin tuna.

This is an "excellently crafted book. . . . The layout invites readers in through the use of different fonts and bolded words, small paragraphs, circular quotes, and fact blurbs. Each spread has stunning photos of the animals and simple illustrations. A good choice for reports, and a great read for anyone interested in endangered species." SLJ

Arnosky, Jim

★ **Wild** tracks! a guide to nature's footprints. [by] Jim Arnosky. Sterling Pub. Co. 2008 32p il $14.95

Grades: 1 2 3   **590**

1. Animal tracks

ISBN 978-1-4027-3985-9; 1-4027-3985-0

LC 2007033972

"Tracks are separated into categories (bear, deer, cat, and so on), each presented in a two-page spread. On the left, a full-color painting displays an animal, and its tracks, in its natural habitat. On the right, information about the tracks, and how to read them, appears as pencil-sketch reproductions from Arnosky's own notebook. . . . Arnosky supplements the track identification information with fascinating related material in notebook-style entries. . . . The uniformly lovely illustrations and the compelling concept make this a book that young naturalists will enjoy year-round." Booklist

Baby animal pop! with 5 incredible, life-size foldouts. National Geographic 2011 il (National Geographic little kids) $14.95

Grades: PreK K 1 2   **590**

1. Animal babies

ISBN 978-1-4263-0765-2; 1-4263-0765-9

"This well-written book has exquisite life-size photos. Between the appealing pictures, an educational text for older children details the environment, anatomy, food, and homes of bunnies, ducklings, piglets, lambs, and ponies. The diagrams and photos give youngsters insight into the first year of the animals' lives." SLJ

Bayrock, Fiona

Bubble homes and fish farts; illustrated by Carolyn Conahan. Charlesbridge 2009 45p il $16.95; pa $7.95

Grades: 2 3 4   **590**

1. Animals 2. Bubbles

ISBN 978-1-57091-669-4; 1-57091-669-1; 978-1-57091-670-0 pa; 1-57091-670-5 pa

LC 2008-06151

"Fast Repetitive Tick (FaRT) is the term scientists use to describe the flatulencelike noise that herring make as they communicate their locations to one another other. That might be the most amusing description of the uses of bubbles in the natural world, but this entire book is enjoyable and engaging. . . . The illustrations are pale and less-detailed versions of scientifically accurate drawings overlaid with entertaining comments. . . . Creative, accessible, and fact-filled." SLJ

Berger, Gilda

101 animal records. Scholastic Inc. 2013 112 p. ill. (paperback) $8.99; (prebind) $19.65

Grades: 2 3 4 5   590

1. Picture books for children 2. Animals

ISBN 0545427967; 0606315055; 9780545427968; 9780606315050

In this book, "readers will find a list of 101 animal superlatives. . . . There are such accolades as 'Loudest Insect' (the cicada) and 'Strongest Tongue' (the anteater) and 'Most Useful Insect' (the honeybee). The authors [Melvin Berger and Gilda Berger] skip an introduction, diving straight in with #1, then present a new superlative on each page accompanied by a paragraph of explanatory text." (Booklist)

Berkes, Marianne Collins

Animalogy; animal analogies. by Marianne Berkes; illustrated by Cathy Morrison. Sylvan Dell 2011 un il $16.95; pa $8.95; English ebook $9.95; Spanish ebook $9.95

Grades: PreK K 1 2 3 4   590

1. Animals 2. Analogy

ISBN 978-1-60718-127-9; 1-60718-127-4; 978-1-60718-137-8 pa; 1-60718-137-1 pa; 978-1-60718-147-7 English ebook; 978-1-60718-157-6 Spanish ebook

LC 2011006510

"Use this rhyming book about animals with students to explain the concept of analogies. 'Robin is to wing, as goldfish is to fin. Beaver is to build, as spider is to spin.' Body parts, size, sounds, actions, and animal classification are all included in the examples. Detailed and realistic illustrations give moose, bears, and frogs a ready-to-jump-off-the-page appearance. . . . This book makes learning about analogies, new vocabulary, and animals easy to understand and fun." SLJ

BishopRoby, Joshua

Animal kingdom. Compass Point Books 2009 40p il (Mission: science) lib bdg $26.60

Grades: 4 5 6   590

1. Animals -- Classification

ISBN 978-0-7565-4057-9 lib bdg; 0-7565-4057-7 lib bdg

LC 2008-37574

An introduction to the animal kingdom, which is made up of a variety of animals that are organized into categories based on physical attributes or ancestors

Includes glossary

Broom, Jenny

Animalium; Jenny Broom, illustrated by Katie Scott. Candlewick Press 2014 112 p. color illustrations (reinforced) $35

Grades: 3 4 5 6 7   590

1. Animals 2. Museums

ISBN 9780763675080; 0763675083

LC 2013952848

"Open 365 days a year and unrestricted by the constraints of physical space, each title in this series is organized into galleries that display more than 200 full-color specimens accompanied by lively, informative text. Offering hours of learning, this first title within the series--[Jenny

Broom's book] Animalium--presents the animal kingdom in glorious detail with illustrations from Katie Scott." (Publisher's note)

"Each basic group includes several spreads offering examples from subgroups within the class as well as a spread with a connected habitat: coastal waters, coral reefs, rain forest, deserts, woodlands and tundra. No information sources are given, but there are good suggestions for general websites for further learning." Kirkus

★ The **wonder** garden; Jenny Broom; illustrated by Kristjana S. Williams. Wide Eyed Editions 2015 48 p. $30

Grades: 2 3 4 5   590

1. Animals 2. Habitat (Ecology)

ISBN 1847807038; 9781847807038

In this book by Jenny Broom, readers "open the gates of the Wonder Garden to explore five of Earth's most extraordinary habitats, each filled with incredible creatures and epic scenery. Trek through the Amazon Rainforest, travel to the Chihuahuan Desert, dive in the Great Barrier Reef, delve deep into the Black Forest and stand on the roof of the world - the Himalayan Mountains - to see nature at its wildest." (Publisher's note)

"Once open, the volume reveals glorious engraved illustrations that reflect great skill with line and color. The text offers a wealth of brief bits of information about life in five biomes: the Amazon Rainforest, the Great Barrier Reef, the Himalayas, the Chihuahuan Desert, and the Black Forest. With the world as their canvas and oversize pages to fill, the author and illustrator offer a tremendous breadth of material. Each page is densely packed with a detailed mix of flora and fauna. . . ," SLJ

Brown, Martin

Lesser Spotted Animals; by Martin Brown. Scholastic Inc. 2016 56 p. color illustrations, maps $18.99; (ebook) $18.99

Grades: 2 3 4 5   590

1. Animals 2. Zoology

ISBN 133808934X; 9781338089349; 9781338128093

In this guide book, by Martin Brown, readers will learn about unusual animals like numbat, zorilla, onager, gaur and hirola. "Each of the subjects receives approximately two pages of treatment. Page layout is consistent and well organized. . . . Brown offers vivid analogies rather than precise measurements when describing animal sizes. . . . Among other details are diet and conservation status, derived from the International Union for Conservation of Nature Red List." (School Library Journal)

"With a compulsively engaging tone, lighthearted artwork, and a meaningful kernel of education at its heart, this excellent book will entrance a wide variety of readers, who will surely be eager for more." Booklist

Buckley, James

Animals; a visual encylopedia. James Buckley, Beth Landis Hester, Catherine Nichols, Carl Jackson, Anita Ganeri, and Lori Stein. Time Home Entertainment Inc 2015 303 p. color illustrations (hardcover) $24.95

Grades: 3 4 5 6 7   590

1. Animals 2. Encyclopedias and dictionaries

ISBN 1618931539; 9781618931535

LC 2015940344

This book, by James Buckley, Beth Landis Hester, Catherine Nichols, Carl Jackson, Anita Ganeri, and Lori Stein, "profiles the seven major animal classes--mammals, birds, reptiles, amphibians, fish, arthropods, and other invertebrates--and features more than 1,000 stunning color photographs of animals in action." (Publisher's note)

"Gorgeous photographs of a panoply of animals are surrounded with various interesting factoids." Booklist

Cusick, Dawn

Get the scoop on animal poop; from lions to tapeworms, 251 cool facts about scat, frass, dung & more. Dawn Cusick. Imagine Pub. 2012 80 p.

Grades: 3 4 5   **590**

1. Feces 2. Wildlife 3. Excretion 4. Digestive system 5. Animal droppings

ISBN 9781936140428

LC 2011025982

This book is a "guide to coprology, the study of feces. . . . Every page is packed with colorful photographs, and the text is an accumulation of snippets, a few sentences about each of the hundreds of topics." (Kirkus) "Topics covered include digestive systems of various animals, parasites, animals that eat feces, and bathroom habits. Back matter includes a guide to identify types of animal feces, a "poo interview" with a veterinarian, activity ideas, a glossary and reading list . . . , a subject index, and an index by organism." (School Libr J)

Davies, Nicola, 1958-

Everything you need to know about animals. Kingfisher 2010 160p il $16.99

Grades: 1 2 3   **590**

1. Animals

ISBN 978-0-7534-6433-5; 0-7534-6433-0

Presents a brief overview of animal life, including types of animals and the ways their bodies are different, their means of locomotion, their food and how they find it, their senses, and how they reproduce themselves.

"As a beginner's encyclopedia of animals, this book is outstanding. The text is divided into five color-coded sections which range from the variety of animals in the world to how animals get around and get their food. . . . The text is full of colorful illustrations and the language is very readable. This is the type of book that the reader will come to again and again." Libr Media Connect

★ Extreme animals; the toughest creatures on Earth. illustrated by Neal Layton. Candlewick Press 2006 61p il $12.99; pa $7.99

Grades: 3 4 5 6   **590**

1. Animals 2. Adaptation (Biology)

ISBN 978-0-7636-3067-6; 0-7636-3067-5; 978-0-7636-4127-6 pa; 0-7636-4127-8 pa

LC 2005-43544

"There is life everywhere on Earth . . . and much of that life thrives in conditions that humans could not endure for five minutes or less. This funny and appealing little book describes who these amazing life-forms are and how they manage to survive. Simple and inviting cartoon drawings enliven the text and convey the types of extremes in an easy-to-understand manner." SLJ

Includes glossary

Who's like me? by Nicola Davies and illustrated by Marc Boutavant. Candlewick Press 2012 24 p. (alk. paper) $9.99

Grades: PreK K   **590**

1. Animals -- Classification 2. Animals 3. Anatomy

ISBN 0763658022; 9780763658021

LC 2011047180

This book, by Nicola Davies and illustrated by Marc Boutavant, examines how "some animals have fins to swim with, some have feathers and a beak, some have skin that is scaly, or smooth and wet. But whatever features a creature has, someone else has them, too. Can [readers] guess who? Big flaps and a matching spread at the end [are designed to] make animal classification fun." (Publisher's note)

Faulkner, Mark

★ A zeal of zebras; an alphabet of collective nouns. by Woop Studios. Chronicle Books 2011 un il

Grades: PreK K   **590**

1. Animals 2. Alphabet

ISBN 1452104921; 9781452104928

LC 2011008011

"From the graphic designers of the Harry Potter franchise, this ABC book of collective nouns couples informative text with digitally created tableaus reminiscent of vintage posters that wryly play on the terms. . . . The thoughtful and provocative portraits will leave readers teasing out their subtleties." Publ Wkly

Gervais, Bernadette

★ Out of sight; [by] Pittau & Gervais. Chronicle Books 2010 16p il $19.99

Grades: PreK K 1   **590**

1. Animals

ISBN 0811877124; 9780811877121

LC 2010016150

This work presents animal facts, "hidden beneath flaps of black-and-white animal silhouettes, . . paw prints [and] cutouts." (SLJ) "Ages three to ten." (Sci Books Films)

"In this sophisticated guess-the-animal book, oversize pages feature large flaps offering visual clues about the animals concealed underneath. . . . The unexpected details about each animal . . . should fascinate even adults, but the core appeal is in the abstract elements that challenge readers' way of seeing." Publ Wkly

Gibbs, Edward

★ I spy with my little eye. Candlewick Press 2011 un il $14.95

Grades: PreK K 1   **590**

1. Animals -- Color

ISBN 978-0-7636-5284-5; 0-7636-5284-9

LC 2010039167

"A classic childhood guessing game gets an elegant treatment from newcomer Gibbs in this introduction to colors and animals. . . . Defined by joyful scribbled outlines, the exuberant, friendly animal portraits dazzle." Publ Wkly

Green, Jen

Barron's totally wild fact-packed fold-out animal atlas; Jen Green. Barrons Educational Series, Inc. 2015 56 p. color ill., color maps (hardcover) $18.99

Grades: 4 5 6 7   **590**

1. Atlases 2. Animals

ISBN 9780764168086

LC 2015932861

In this children's book, by Jen Green and illustrated by Christiane Engel, "all of the weird and wonderful animals that inhabit our extraordinary earth are here to delight and enchant young readers (Mom and Dad, too!). . . . Youngsters love learning about animals, natural history and world geography, and this book teaches them all about each topic in fun, engaging ways." (Publisher's note)

"Green and Engel follow their 2014 atlas with an animal-themed tour of the world, and a large foldout map greets readers when they open the book." Pub Wkly

Hearst, Michael

Unusual creatures; a mostly accurate account of some of the Earth's strangest animals. by Michael Hearst; illustrations by Jelmer Noordeman. Chronicle Books 2012 109 p. (alk. paper) $16.99

Grades: 3 4 5   **590**
  1. Animals -- Miscellanea
  ISBN 1452104670; 9781452104676

LC 2011048646

In "this guide to 'unusual creatures' . . . [Michael] Hearst introduces species like the echidna, flying snake, and narwhal, describing their physical characteristics, habitats, and behaviors, with tidbits, quizzes, and even poems. . . . Each animal appears in a matte illustration that combines naturalistic features with subtle hints of personality." (Publishers Weekly)

Hestermann, Josh
  Zoology for kids; understanding and working with animals : with 21 activities. Josh and Bethanie Hestermann. Chicago Review Press, Incorporated 2015 144 p. color illustrations $18.95
Grades: 5 6 7 8 9   **590**
  1. Zoology 2. Zoology -- Vocational guidance 3. Zoology -- Study and teaching -- Activity programs
  ISBN 1613749619; 9781613749616

LC 2014042745

This book, by Josh and Bethanie Hestermann, "invites the next generation of zoologists to discover the animal kingdom through clear, entertaining information and anecdotes, lush color photos, hands-on activities, and peer-reviewed research. Young minds are introduced to zoology as a science by discussing animals' forms, functions, and behaviors as well as the history behind zoos and aquariums." (Publisher's note)

"Studded with fun activities and attractive animal photos, this comprehensive resource will excite those not already smitten with the animal world to enthusiastically join in the delightful exploration of what it means to study and care for animals in today's world. . . . Charming photos, hand-drawn graphics, highlighted words, and a correlative glossary enhance the clear-cut writing style." SLJ

  Includes bibliographical references and index

Hughes, Catherine D.
  Little kids first big book of animals. National Geographic 2010 128p il map $14.95
Grades: K 1 2 3   **590**
  1. Animals
  ISBN 9781426307041; 1426307047; 9781426307218 lib bdg; 1426307217 lib bdg

"This book, well organized by type of habitat . . . introduces animals from all over the world. The easy-to-follow text consists of somewhat random facts about the creatures; the real stars of the show are the many vivid nature photographs." Horn Book Guide

Hynes, Margaret
  Picture This! Animals; Amazing Information-right Before Your Eyes. by Margaret Hynes. Kingfisher 2014 64 p. color illustrations $12.99
Grades: 3 4 5 6   **590**
  1. Animals
  ISBN 0753468875; 9780753468876

This book, by Margaret Hynes, is a "reference book all about the animal world. Designed for . . . middle schoolers, fascinating facts and important information alike about all types of animals is presented both visually and in text form. . . . Topics covered include animal characteristics, defense, habitats, migration patterns, food webs, adaptation, birth and growth, and conservation." (Publisher's note)

"This eclectic but organized book presents comparative data about animals, such as depth distribution of deep-sea life and flying abilities of bird species, through minimal text and busy, colorful infographics (tables, graphs, maps, callout labels, etc.). The volume requires careful

study instead of light browsing, but occasional humor heightens the appeal. Though generally correct, there are few inaccuracies." Horn Book

Jenkins, Steve
  ★ The **Animal** Book; A Collection of the Fastest, Fiercest, Toughest, Cleverest, Shyest--and Most Surprising--animals on Earth. by Steve Jenkins. Houghton Mifflin Harcourt 2013 208 p. col. ill. (hardcover) $21.99
Grades: K 1 2 3 4 5   **590**
  1. Picture books for children 2. Animals
  ISBN 054755799X; 9780547557991
  Boston Globe-Horn Book Honor: Nonfiction (2014)

This children's picture book by Steve Jenkins provides an "introduction to the vast animal kingdom. After a chapter of definition, information is presented in sections on animal families, senses, predators, defenses, extremes and the story of life. More facts appear in the final chapter, which serves both as index (with page numbers and thumbnails) and quick reference." (Kirkus Reviews)

  ★ **Biggest**, strongest, fastest. Ticknor & Fields Bks. for Young Readers 1995 un il $16; pa $5.95
Grades: K 1 2   **590**
  1. Animals 2. Animals -- Miscellanea
  ISBN 0-395-69701-8; 0-395-86136-5 pa

LC 94-21804

Jenkins uses "cut-paper collages to explore extremes—including longest lived, smallest, and slowest—in the animal world. These 'record holders' include the largest kind of spider, the bird-spider; the strongest for its size, the ant; and the biggest animal that has ever lived, the blue whale. . . . The book closes with a chart that includes brief facts about the animals' diet, range, and size." (Horn Book) "Ages four to nine." (Booklist)

"A helpful chart at the end contains further information about each creature, such as diet and habitat. An all-round superlative effort." SLJ

Johnson, Jinny
  ★ **Animal** tracks & signs. National Geographic Society 2008 192p il $24.95; lib bdg $32.90
Grades: 5 6 7 8   **590**
  1. Animals 2. Animal tracks 3. Tracking and trailing
  ISBN 978-1-4263-0253-4; 1-4263-0253-3; 978-1-4263-0254-1 lib bdg; 1-4263-0254-1 lib bdg

"This attractive book describes the tracks (paw prints, bird claw prints, slimy trails) and signs (molted skin, food remains, scat, tree markings) that animals leave in their wake. . . . A typical two-page layout includes a photo and short paragraph about the animal category, three or four colored boxes containing a photo or drawing of a specific animal (serval, bobcat), and a description of its size, geographic range, habitat, food, tracks and signs, and comments. . . . The beautiful photos vary from action . . . to informational. . . . The language is simple and readable." Voice Youth Advocates

  Includes glossary and bibliographical references

Komiya, Teruyuki
  Life-size zoo; from tiny rodents to gigantic elephants, an actual-size animal encyclopedia. editorial supervisor of Japanese edition, Teruyuki Komiya; photographer, Toyofumi Fukuda; Japanese translation by Makiko Oku; English language adaptation by Kristin Earhart. Seven Footer Kids 2009 43p il $17.95
Grades: PreK K 1 2   **590**
  1. Size 2. Zoos 3. Animals
  ISBN 978-1-934734-20-9; 1-934734-20-9

"The claim to fame for this oversize collection of animal portraits is that each animal is shown at 'actual size.' The striking photographs, taken at Japanese zoos, provide a rare opportunity to see animal faces up close. . . . Animal facts are provided in side panels that feature stick figures who engage readers. . . . The stellar photographs, playful format and informative content create a highly appealing package." Publ Wkly

More life-size zoo: lion, hippopotamus, polar bear and more: an all-new actual-size animal encyclopedia. photographer, Toshimitsu Matsuhashi; Japanese translation by Junko Miyakoshi; English language adaptation by Kristin Earhart. Seven Footer Press 2010 47p il $18.95
Grades: PreK K 1 2 **590**
1. Size 2. Zoos 3. Animals
ISBN 978-1-934734-19-3; 1-934734-19-5

This volume highlights "a second batch of zoo animals . . . in crisp, full-color photos. Some like . . . a large fruit bat, can be shown in entirety, but many others, like a fully maned African lion . . . require foldout pages for even a partial view. The eye-catching photos are the main thrust, while extra data flows along the edges of the page. . . . This is a great introduction to animals." SLJ

Lewin, Ted
★ **Look!** by Ted Lewin. Holiday House 2013 32 p. col. ill.
Grades: PreK K 1 **590**
1. Animals -- Africa 2. Animal ecology -- Africa
ISBN 9780823426072
LC 2011049607

" A satisfying challenge and a fun animal adventure made thrilling by Lewin's characteristically spectacular use of light." Kirkus

What am I? where am I? written and illustrated by Ted Lewin. Holiday House 2013 32 p. (I like to read) (hardcover) $14.95
Grades: PreK K 1 **590**
1. Biomes 2. Animals 3. Habitat (Ecology)
ISBN 0823428567; 9780823428564
LC 2012039289

This book, by Ted Lewin, uses drawings to "illustrate a guessing game that fosters an appreciation of both art and science, while introducing animals in the five major biomes: Grassland, desert, forest, tundra, and water. Inspired by his many travels, classically inspired compositions communicate the regal magnificence of five stunning animals: lion, camel, tiger, reindeer, and sea otter." (Publisher's note)

Limentani, Alison
How Much Does a Ladybug Weigh? by Alison Limentani. Sterling Pub Co Inc 2016 32 p. color illustrations $14.95
Grades: PreK K 1 2 **590**
1. Weights and measures 2. Animals
ISBN 1910716111; 9781910716113

In this book, author Alison Limentani "introduces children to a fascinating world of wildlife, weight, numbers, and comparisons. Did you know that five starlings weigh the same as one squirrel—or that three rabbits weigh the same as one fox cub?" (Publisher's note)

"Relative size and counting are combined in this elegant picture-book exploration of math that truly speaks to the intended audience." Booklist

Loh-Hagan, Virginia
Top 10; oddities. by Virginia Loh-Hagan. Cherry Lake Publishing 2016 32 p. color illustrations (pbk.) $14.21
Grades: 1 2 3 4 **590**
1. Animals
ISBN 9781634705042; 9781634706247
LC 2015026856

With this book, by Virginia Loh-Hagan, "dive into the Wild Wicked Wonderful world of the animal kingdom with the Top 10: Oddities. Writ-

ten with a high interest level to appeal to a more mature audience and a lower level of complexity with clear visuals to help struggling readers along. Considerate text includes tons of fascinating information and wild facts that will hold the readers' interest, allowing for successful mastery and comprehension." (Publisher's note)

"An inviting introduction to the world of weird critters." Booklist
Top ten
Oddities

McGuinness, Lisa
The **dictionary** of ordinary extraordinary animals; by Lisa McGuinness and Leslie Jonath; illustrated by Lisa Congdon. Running Press 2011 un il $18.95
Grades: K 1 2 3 **590**
1. Animals -- Encyclopedias
ISBN 978-0-7624-4063-4; 0-7624-4063-5
LC 2010935841

"An alphabetically organized discussion of 150 animals, this informative guidebook combines casual descriptions of the animals with grainy illustrations reminiscent of vintage flashcards. . . . Congdon's paintings are characterized by naturalistic details and touches of surprising whimsy . . . communicating a palpable sense of wonder." Publ Wkly

Montgomery, Heather L.
★ **Wild** discoveries; wacky new animals. by Heather L. Montgomery. Scholastic, Inc. 2013 62 p. (pbk.) $6.99
Grades: 3 4 5 6 7 **590**
1. Discoveries in science 2. Animals
ISBN 0545477670; 9780545477673
LC 2012285070

This book by Heather Montgomery features "newly discovered species from around the world--such as the Shocking Pink Dragon and the Green Bomber. These . . . species are organized by region with . . . facts about each one's . . . abilities and traits. The book . . . has a special section featuring new species discovered by kids." (Publisher's note)

Myers, Jack
The **puzzle** of the platypus; and other explorations of science in action. [by] Jack Myers; illustrated by John Rice. Boyds Mills Press 2008 64p il map (Scientists probe 11 animal mysteries) $17.95
Grades: 3 4 5 6 **590**
1. Animals
ISBN 978-1-59078-556-0; 1-59078-556-8
LC 2007023741

"This collection of 11 articles originally appeared in Highlights magazine during the 1990s and early 2000s. Each article tells how a scientist was able to unravel a mystery about some kind of animal. Myers's stories about dolphins, polar bears, elephants, and other animals contain many interesting scientific facts and are written in accessible and engaging prose. . . . Most of the pages have attractive watercolor illustrations." SLJ

Roop, Connie
Tales of Famous Animals; Peter Roop and Connie Roop. Scholastic 2012 112 p. (reinforced) $17.99
Grades: 4 5 6 7 8 **590**
1. Pets 2. Animals
ISBN 0545430291; 9780545430296

This children's book, by Peter and Connie Roop, illustrated by Zachary Pullen, offers an "illustrated introduction to some of the most fascinating and admirable animals we've ever known! Everyone knows about President Obama's first dog Bo, but would you believe President Adams had a pet alligator . . . ? . . . Readers will also learn about heroic animals like Balto the sled dog and unique animals like Koko the gorilla." (Publisher's note)

Selsam, Millicent Ellis

Big tracks, little tracks; following animal prints. illustrated by Marlene Hill Donnelly. rev ed; HarperCollins Pubs. 1999 31p il (Let's-read-and-find-out science) hardcover o.p. pa $4.95

Grades: K 1 2 3   **590**

1. Animal tracks 2. Tracking and trailing

ISBN 0-06-028209-6; 0-06-445194-1 pa

LC 98-18315

First published with this title 1995; originally published with title How to be a nature detective

This book "teaches young readers how to track animals by finding footprints and other clues. . . . Included is a new Find Out More page with lots of hands-on activites." Publisher's note

Seuling, Barbara

Cows sweat through their noses; and other freaky facts about animal habits, characteristics, and homes. by Barbara Seuling; illustrated by Matthew Skeens. Picture Window Books 2008 40p il (Freaky facts) lib bdg $16.95

Grades: 2 3 4 5   **590**

1. Animals

ISBN 978-1-4048-3749-2 lib bdg; 1-4048-3749-3 lib bdg

LC 2007004028

"This delightful little book contains a potpourri of facts about many members of the animal kingdom, large and small, from insects to elephants. . . . The information presented . . . is . . . fascinating." Sci Books Films

Includes glossary and bibliographical references

Silverman, Buffy

Can an old dog learn new tricks? and other questions about animals. illustrations by Colin W. Thompson. Lerner 2010 40p il (Is it a fact?) lib bdg $26.60

Grades: 4 5 6   **590**

1. Questions and answers 2. Animals -- Miscellanea

ISBN 978-0-8225-9083-5; 0-8225-9083-2

LC 2009-20587

Includes glossary and bibliographical references

Silverstein, Alvin

Dung beetles, slugs, leeches, and more; the yucky animal book. by Alvin and Virginia Silverstein, and Laura Silverstein Nunn; illustrated by Gerald Kelley. Enslow Publishers 2010 48p il (Yucky science) lib bdg $23.93

Grades: 4 5 6 7   **590**

1. Insects 2. Invertebrates 3. Animal behavior

ISBN 978-0-7660-3317-7 lib bdg; 0-7660-3317-1 lib bdg

LC 2009012281

"Written in an engaging and conversational style and full of revolting descriptions and entertaining cartoon illustrations . . . [this is] sure to turn even the strongest stomach. An introduction . . . puts 'yucky' in perspective, reminding kids that our world is diverse and that everyone has a different definition of repulsive." SLJ

Includes glossary and bibliographical references

Siwanowicz, Igor

Animals up close; zoom in on the world's most incredible creatures. DK Pub. 2009 96p il $19.99

Grades: 4 5 6   **590**

1. Animals

ISBN 978-0-7566-4513-7; 0-7566-4513-1

"An eye-catching cover will attract readers to this amazing look at some of the world's insects, fish, mammals, reptiles, amphibians, and birds. The focus is on animals small enough to fit in a child's hand. Siwanowicz showcases each creature with a spread containing a full-color, high-quality, close-up photo surrounded by multiple factual asides. . . . The book is packed with interesting material that captures the author's fascination for small creatures." SLJ

Includes glossary

Spelman, Lucy

Animal encyclopedia; 2,500 animals with photos, maps, and more! National Geographic 2012 303 p. col. ill., col. maps (hardcover) $24.95; (library) $33.90

Grades: 5 6 7   **590**

1. Animals -- Encyclopedias

ISBN 1426310226; 9781426310225; 9781426310232

LC 2012023783

This encyclopedia about animals "is separated into vertebrate and invertebrate animals and then further subdivided by phylum. Each species gets its own page with dynamic color photos of creatures in their natural habitat, while . . . information on variations within the species celebrates the diversity of animals across the globe." (Booklist)

Includes bibliographical references (p. 295) and index.

Swanson, Diane

Animal aha! thrilling discoveries in wildlife science. Annick Press 2009 48p il $19.95; pa $9.95

Grades: 4 5 6   **590**

1. Animals

ISBN 978-1-55451-165-5; 1-55451-165-8; 978-1-55451-164-8 pa; 1-55451-164-X pa

"An olio of 'AHA!' moments in natural science. Who knew that a Burmese python's heart enlarges to aid in digestion? Or that a parrot might comprehend human language and be able to use it creatively? Such are the tidbits in this browsable book. 'Fun Facts' and 'Fast Facts' boxes abound, and a color photo pops up on almost every page. With a lively text, this interesting pastiche will be enjoyed by kids pawing through the classroom library seeking an engaging nonfiction read." SLJ

Thomas, Keltie

Animals that changed the world. Annick Press 2010 112p il map $21.95; pa $12.95

Grades: 4 5 6   **590**

1. Animals

ISBN 978-1-55451-243-0; 1-55451-243-3; 978-1-55451-242-3 pa; 1-55451-242-5 pa

"Thomas takes a breezy, conversational look at more than 20 species—from microbes to codfish—that have impacted the Earth in extreme ways. . . . Animals profiled include the cat, dog, beaver, pigeon, and horse. . . . The busy format features narrow columns of text layered on color backgrounds alongside visually stimulating photographs, an occasional drawing, and 'Fact Track' and 'Speak of the Beast' sections, which explain the etymology of animal idioms." SLJ

Twist, Clint

A **little** book of slime; Clint Twist. Firefly Books 2012 80 p. $9.95

Grades: 3 4 5 6 7   **590**

1. Algae 2. Mucus 3. Molds (Fungi)

ISBN 1770850066; 9781770850064

Contents: What is slime? -- Slimy stuff in water -- Pond slime -- Slime tube -- Red tide -- Lungfish -- Horrible hagfish -- Jellyfish -- Sea cucumber -- Sea slug -- Sea hare -- Frogspawn -- Slimy stuff on land -- Poison arrow frog -- Foam-nest frog -- California newt -- Water-holding frog -- Cane toad -- Velvet worm -- Slime light -- Snail -- Banana slug -- Slime mold beetle -- Froghopper -- Starfish stinkhorn -- Other slimy stuff -- Saliva -- Phlegm -- Sundew plant -- Slime flux -- Decomposing vegetables -- Jelly fungus -- Lattice stinkhorn -- Creeping slime -- Living snot mold.

This book "provides a[n] . . . introduction to slime in the natural world. From pond slime and red tide to phlegm and living snot mold, the author surveys the slick, sticky substance produced by living organisms for protection, digestion, defense and more. In some cases the organism itself is the slime. This disparate material has been organized into three sections: 'Slimy Stuff in Water,' 'Slimy Stuff on Land' and 'Other Slimy Stuff.' . . . A . . . glossary defines terms bolded in the text. There's an index but no sources or suggestions for further research for those who want more." (Kirkus Reviews)

Wright, Anna

A **tower** of giraffes; animals in groups. by Anna Wright. Charlesbridge 2015 32 p. color illustrations (reinforced for library use) $17.95

Grades: 1 2 3 **590**

1. Animals 2. English language -- Collective nouns 3. Animals -- Nomenclature (Popular)

ISBN 9781580897075

LC 2014029098

This children's book, by Anna Wright, "introduces young readers to some of the words we use to refer to animals in a group. The ink, watercolor, and fabric collage art is brightly colored and uniquely sets this fun book apart from the crowd. Each page presents information about an animal and its group behavior, such as how geese fly in a V-shape and honk to encourage the leaders, and that sometimes tens of thousand of flamingos meet up in one location." (Publisher's note)

"A visually expressive take on collective nouns." Pub Wkly.

Young, Judy

Sleepy snoozy cozy coozy; a book of animal beds. written by Judy Young; illustrated by Michael Glenn Monroe. Sleeping Bear Press 2015 32 p. illustrations (hbk.) $15.99

Grades: PreK K 1 2 3 **590**

1. Animals -- Habitations 2. Nursery rhymes 3. Animals -- Habitations -- North America

ISBN 158536908X; 9781585369089

LC 2014026952

This children's book, by Judy Young, illustrated by Michael Glenn Monroe, "explains the bedtime habits of some common North American animals, including moles, moose, and beavers. Young readers will learn not only where certain animals make their beds but also how and why they sleep as they do." (Publisher's note)

"The soft, lifelike illustrations of slumbering beasts enhance the text. The final page depicts a child in bed with stuffed toys, making this offering a soothing bedtime story." SLJ

590.7   Education, research, related topics

Benbow, Ann

Awesome animal science projects; [by] Ann Benbow and Colin Mably; illustrations by Tom Labaff. Enslow Publishers 2010 48p il (Real life science experiments) lib bdg $23.93

Grades: 3 4 5 **590.7**

1. Animal behavior 2. Science projects

ISBN 978-0-7660-3148-7 lib bdg; 0-7660-3148-9 lib bdg

LC 2008-23932

"Color drawings, photographs, a glossary, and suggestions for further research enliven . . . [this] title . . . [and provide] solid curricular support." Booklist

Includes glossary and bibliographical references

Gardner, Robert

Ace your animal science project; great science fair ideas. [by] Robert Gardner . . . [et al.] Enslow Publishers 2009 128p il (Ace your biology science project) lib bdg $31.93

Grades: 5 6 7 8 **590.7**

1. Animal behavior 2. Science projects 3. Science -- Experiments

ISBN 978-0-7660-3220-0 lib bdg; 0-7660-3220-5 lib bdg

LC 2008-4234

"Dozens of . . . science activities are presented with background information, step-by-step instructions, and suggestions for extending to the science fair level. . . . Color illustrations and important safety information are included." Horn Book Guide

Includes bibliographical references

590.72   Research

Burns, Loree Griffin

Citizen scientists; be a part of scientific discovery from your own backyard. Loree Griffin Burns; photographs by Ellen Harasimowicz. H. Holt 2012 80 p. col. ill., col. maps

Grades: 3 4 5 6 7 8 **590.72**

1. Suburbs 2. Animals -- Classification 3. Research -- Citizen participation 4. Wildlife -- Geographical distribution 5. Suburban animals -- Research -- Citizen participation 6. Suburban animals -- Monitoring -- Citizen participation

ISBN 0805090622; 9780805090628; 9780805095173

LC 2011021673

AAAS/Subaru SB&F Prize for Excellence in Science Books: Hands On Science Book (2013)

In this children's book, Loree Griffin Burns "brings . . . attention to four . . . scientific projects that enlist regular people in data collection. . . . The projects include . . . the Monarch Watch butterfly tagging project, . . . the Audubon Christmas Bird Count," and a "project documenting ladybug species . . . . For each project, Burns gives detailed accounts of the procedures employed by citizen scientists." (Horn Book Magazine)

Includes bibliographical references and index

Jenkins, Steve

★ **Animals** by the Numbers; A Book of Infographics. Steve Jenkins. Houghton Mifflin Harcourt 2016 48 p. color illustrations (ebook) $16.99; $17.99

Grades: 3 4 5 6 **590.72**

1. Animals -- Miscellanea 2. Animals 3. Graphic methods 4. Charts, diagrams, etc.

ISBN 9781328664129; 0544630920; 9780544630925

LC 2016288289

In this children's book, Steve Jenkins answers various questions about animals "with numbers, images, innovation, and authoritative science. . . . Jenkins layers his signature cut-paper illustrations alongside computer graphics and a text that is teeming with fresh, unexpected, and accurate zoological information ready for readers to easily devour." (Publisher's note)

"A brilliantly executed take on a perennially high-interest topic." Booklist

Includes bibliographical references (page 48).

590.73 Collections and exhibits of living mammals

Alexander, Richard

Zoo workers; Richard Alexander. PowerKids Press 2016 24 p. color illustrations (library bound) $23.60

Grades: 3 4 5 **590.73**

1. Zoos 2. Zoo keepers

ISBN 9781508143758; 9781508143765; 9781508143772

LC 2015035950

In this book, by Richard Alexander, "readers discover what zoo workers do and how a person can prepare for a career in this field. Additional information is provided in a clear graphic organizer. Colorful photographs of zoo animals and the workers who care for them keep readers entertained with each turn of the page. It takes special skills to be a successful zoo worker, and readers discover what those skills are as they learn about this exciting career." (Publisher's note)

"Animal health and training, the contributions zoos make to science, and the education required to work in a zoo are touched upon, and glossy photographs featuring a variety of animals—and those who work with them—will draw plenty of eyes." Booklist

Includes bibliographical references and index.

Krull, Kathleen

★ What's new? the zoo! a zippy history of zoos. by Kathleen Krull; illustrated by Marcellus Hall. Arthur A. Levine Books, an imprint of Scholastic, Inc. 2014 40 p. (alk. paper) $17.99

Grades: K 1 2 3 4 **590.73**

1. Zoos 2. Human-animal relationships 3. Zoos -- History

ISBN 0545135710; 9780545135719; 9780545135726

LC 2013021189

This illustrated children's book, by Kathleen Krull, illustrated by Marcellus Hall, presents a history of zoos and provides several entertaining trivia facts surrounding them. The book brings "jazzy style and a globe-trotting eye to our millennia-long history of keeping animals -- and the ways animals have changed us in turn." (Publisher's note)

" whirlwind, episodic tour of zoos around the world through the ages. Krull takes readers back 4000 years to zoos in Sumeria and ancient China, India, Greece, and Ethiopia, as well as to the menageries of Kublai Khan, Charlemagne, Pope Leo, and Aztec emperor Moctezuma II straight through to modern times...This thoroughly researched title cites sources that include books and websites, making it ideal for browsing purposes or for school reports." SLJ

Includes bibliographical references

590.911 Frigid zones -- Zoology

Kainen, Dan

Polar; a photicular book. Dan Kainen and Carol Kaufmann. Workman Publishing 2015 24 p. color illustrations (alk. paper) $25.95

Grades: 4 5 6 7 8 **590.911**

1. Animals 2. Polar regions 3. Photicular books 4. Animals -- Polar regions 5. Polar regions -- Pictorial works 6. Animals -- Polar regions -- Pictorial works

ISBN 9780761185697; 0761185690

LC 2015026789

This book by Dan Kainen and Carol Kaufmann "brings the reader along on a voyage to the North and South Poles, and writes a lively and informative essay for each image, including vital statistics for each animal, such as their size, range, habitat, and more. Photicular technology uses sliding lenses and video imagery to display realistic living motion in the pages of a book." (Publisher's note)

"Perhaps no place on earth is more extreme than the poles, and the environmental changes occurring there take center stage in the future of all of the animals included in this intriguing," Booklist

591 Specific topics in natural history of animals

Arnold, Caroline

Living fossils; clues to the past. Caroline Arnold; Illustrated by Andrew Plant. Charlesbridge 2015 32 p. color illustrations (reinforced for library use) $16.95

Grades: 2 3 4 5 **591**

1. Fossils 2. Living fossils 3. Animals, Fossil

ISBN 9781580896917

LC 2014049180

This book, by author Caroline Arnold and illustrator Andrew Plant, focuses on "Living fossils, or modern-day animals that very closely resemble their ancient relatives. Meet the coelacanth, horseshoe crab, dragonfly, tuatara, nautilus, and Hula painted frog. All are living fossils. Why have they changed so little over time, while other animals evolved or went extinct?" (Publisher's note)

"An intriguing look at animals, past and present, and a fine addition to the science shelves." Booklist

George, Lindsay Barrett

In the woods: who's been here? Greenwillow Bks. 1995 un il hardcover o.p. pa $7.99

Grades: PreK K 1 2 **591**

1. Forest animals

ISBN 0-688-12318-X; 0-688-16163-4 pa

LC 93-16244

A boy and girl in the autumn woods find an empty nest, a cocoon, gnawed bark, and other signs of unseen animals and their activities

"Children will be drawn to George's vivid gouache paintings, especially those depicting the animals in their natural surroundings.... For most childen this will be an excellent introduction to classroom nature units and the perfect prelude to a walk in the woods." Booklist

Other titles in this series are:

Around the pond: who's been here? (1996)

Around the world: who's been here? (1999)

In the garden: who's been here? (2006)

In the snow: who's been here? (1995)

Thurlby, Paul

Paul Thurlby's wildlife; Paul Thurlby. Candlewick Press 2013 32 p. $17.99

Grades: PreK K 1 **591**

1. Picture books for children 2. Animals

ISBN 0763665630; 9780763665630

LC 2012943660

This children's picture book looks at wildlife. "A menagerie of animals is introduced," with "snippets of information [that] provide unique facts about 24 individual species; for example, 'monkeys split bananas from the bottom up—it's easier that way!' Blocky digital cartoon characters saturated in rich colors against faded backgrounds vibrantly exemplify each unique trait." (School Library Journal)

Wildlife of the world; contributors Jamie Ambrose [and nine others] DK Publishing 2015 480 p. illustrations, color maps $50

Grades: K 1 2 3 4 5 6 7 8 9 10 11 12 Adult **591**

1. Animals 2. Animals -- Pictorial works

ISBN 1465438041; 9781465438041

LC 2015458474

This book, by DK Publishing, foreword by Don E. Wilson and produced in association with the Smithsonian Institution,"takes you on a journey through some of the most scenic and rich animal habitats--from the Amazon rain forests to the Himalayas, the Sahara to the South Pole--meeting the most important animals in each ecosystem along the way. . . . An additional eighty-page illustrated reference section on the animal kingdom explains the animal groups and profiles additional species." (Publisher's note)

"A chart at the beginning of each section indicates the number of species in each order, class, or phylum. . . . [T]his is an important, gorgeous, accessible introduction to hundreds of species and their habitats throughout the world at a very small price." Booklist

591.3   Genetics, evolution, age characteristics

Bleiman, Andrew
ZooBorns; zoo babies from around the world. [written by] Andrew Bleiman and [photographed by] Chris Eastland. Beach Lane Books 2010 un il $12.99
Grades: PreK K 1   591.3
1. Animal babies
ISBN 978-1-4424-1272-9; 1-4424-1272-0
LC 2010009590

"If a picture is worth 1,000 words, then these stunning photographs starring precious animal tykes may be priceless. The range of real-life infants featured is extraordinary in its breadth, covering such unusual zoo or aquarium residents as the crowned sifaka and the tawny frogmouth. The captivating, clear photographs pose every cub, kit and so on at its most adorable." Kirkus

Carle, Eric
★ Does a kangaroo have a mother, too? HarperCollins Pubs. 2000 un il $16.99; lib bdg $18.89; pa $6.99; bd bk $7.99
Grades: PreK K 1   591.3
1. Animals
ISBN 0-06-028768-3; 0-06-028767-5 lib bdg; 0-06-443642-X pa; 0-694-01456-7 bd bk
LC 99-36147

"The repetitious text is perfect for the toddler set. 'Does a lion have a mother, too? Yes! A lion has a mother. Just like me and you.' The text is repeated on every spread as the author showcases a dozen different animal mothers and their babies. . . . The vibrant artwork is classic Carle and should delight its audience." SLJ

Jenkins, Steve
My first day; written by Steve Jenkins and Robin Page; illustrated by Steve Jenkins. Houghton Mifflin 2013 32 p. $16.99
Grades: PreK K 1   591.3
1. Picture books for children 2. Animal babies 3. Animal behavior
ISBN 054773851X; 9780547738512
LC 2011048210

Authors Steve Jenkins and Robin Page present a picture book on animals. "The first day of life is different for every animal. Human newborns don't do much at all, but some animals hit the ground running." Their book reveals "how twenty two different species, from the emperor penguin to the Siberian tiger, adapt to that traumatic first few hours of life, with or without parental help." (Publisher's note)

Judge, Lita
★ Born in the wild; Lita Judge. Roaring Brook Press 2014 48 p. (hardcover) $18.99
Grades: PreK K 1 2 3   591.3
1. Animal babies 2. Mammals -- Infancy 3. Familial behavior

in animals
ISBN 1596439254; 9781596439252
LC 2013044934

This children's book by Lita Judge describes how "Every baby mammal, from a tiny harvest mouse 'pinky' to a fierce lion cub, needs food, shelter, love, and a family. Filled with illustrations of some of the most adorable babies in the kingdom, this awww-inspiring book looks at the traits that all baby mammals share and proves that, even though they're born in the wild, they're not so very different from us, after all!" (Publisher's note)

"This charming picture book presents more than 20 baby animals and their parents...This title will surely be popular in the library as a beginning research tool, but some may find it quite appropriate as bedtime reading, too." SLJ

Kajikawa, Kimiko
Close to you; how animals bond. [by] Kimiko Kajikawa. Henry Holt 2008 un il $16.95
Grades: PreK K 1   591.3
1. Animal babies
ISBN 978-0-8050-8123-7; 0-8050-8123-2
LC 2007002959

"This tender title about the bonding between baby and adult animals gets some punch from additional facts appended at the end. The body of the book has a brief rhyming text, notable for its precise and engaging verbs. . . . Large, heartwarming stock photos of animal families clearly illustrate each verse. . . . The information seems carefully selected to be understandable and interesting to young children." SLJ

Kalman, Bobbie
Baby mammals; by Bobbie Kalman. Crabtree Publishing Company 2013 24 p. col. ill. (library) $22.60; (paperback) $6.95
Grades: 1 2 3 4   591.3
1. Mammals 2. Animals -- Infancy
ISBN 0778710084; 9780778710080; 9780778710134
LC 2012043723

In this book by Bobbie Kalman "close-up images of baby animals highlight the basic facts about different kinds of mammals, such as hoofed mammals, elephants, rodents, rabbits, marsupials, and primates. Children will learn about the bodies of mammals, the kinds of foods they eat, and how they are raised by their mothers after they are born. The books also show how mammals survive in different habitats." (Publisher's note)

Includes bibliographical references and index.

Patkau, Karen
Creatures yesterday and today; [by] Karen Patkau. Tundra Books 2008 un il $18.95
Grades: K 1 2 3   591.3
1. Animals 2. Fossils 3. Evolution 4. Prehistoric animals
ISBN 978-0-88776-833-0; 0-88776-833-4

"On the first page of this oversize book a huge diplodocus speaks. . . . Turn the page, and his descendant, a little skylark high in a tree, speaks. . . . Then there are the mollusks. . . . With large computer-created graphics in dramatic colors and a few lines of text, each double-page spread makes a similar connection for reptiles, fish, arachnids, birds, amphibians, mammals, crustaceans, and insects. . . . The amazing science will engage dinosaur fans with the wonder of evolution and the evidence of fossils." Booklist

Includes glossary

Rose, Deborah Lee
Ocean babies; illustrations by Hiroe Nakata. National Geographic 2005 un il $16.95; lib bdg $25.90

Grades: K 1 2   **591.3**
1. Animal babies 2. Marine animals
ISBN 0-7922-6669-2; 0-7922-8312-0 lib bdg

LC 2003-14075

Describes baby animals that live in the ocean, pointing out their many differences as well as the most important similarity.

"Nakata's cheerful watercolor paintings clearly illustrate the book's ideas while creating a beautiful undersea setting, bright with colors, teeming with varied creatures, and studded with intriguing details. Many books present information in this format, but few manage to stay as focused on the topic and sensitive to the intended audience as this one." Booklist

591.4   Physical adaptation

Aston, Dianna Hutts
★ An **egg** is quiet; illustrated by Sylvia Long. Chronicle Books 2006 un il $16.95
Grades: K 1 2 3   **591.4**
1. Eggs 2. Animals 3. Embryology
ISBN 0-8118-4428-5; 978-0-8118-4428-4

LC 2005-12090

This book introduces some 60 types of eggs and various egg facts. "Kindergarten to grade four." (Sci Books Films)

"An exceptionally handsome book on eggs, from the delicate ova of the green lacewing to the rosy roe of the Atlantic salmon to the mammoth bulk of an ostrich egg. Aston's simple, readable text celebrates their marvelous diversity, commenting on size, shape, coloration, and where they might be found." SLJ

Baines, Rebecca
What's in that egg? a book about life cycles. by Becky Baines. National Geographic 2009 27p il $16.95; lib bdg $25.90
Grades: PreK K 1   **591.4**
1. Eggs 2. Animals
ISBN 978-1-4263-0408-8; 1-4263-0408-0; 978-1-4263-0409-5 lib bdg; 1-4263-0409-9 lib bdg

LC 2008-47895

This describes the eggs of various animals, including turtles, frogs, fish, butterflies, and swans

This title engages "children through humor, clear language, interesting facts, and abundant photos. . . . [An] excellent [introduction] for young science students." SLJ

Burnie, David
How animals work. Dorling Kindersley 2010 132p il $24.99
Grades: 5 6 7 8   **591.4**
1. Animals 2. Animal behavior
ISBN 978-0-7566-5897-7; 0-7566-5897-7

Describes the anatomy of many animal species and explains how their bodies work to help them survive. Covers such animals as birds, butterflies, elephants, crocodiles, and wolves, and includes color photos, illustrations, and diagrams.

"This beautifully photographed encyclopedia of animals is divided into categories that include movement, diet, senses, and animal families. . . . Diagrams showing internal organs and intimate closeups of eyes, skin, fur, and wings, should engage budding biologists." Publ Wkly

Cusick, Dawn
Animal eggs; an amazing clutch of mysteries & marvels! [by] Dawn Cusick & Joanne O'Sullivan. Charlesbridge 2011 48p il $14.95

Grades: K 1 2 3   **591.4**
1. Eggs 2. Animals -- Infancy
ISBN 978-0-9797455-3-9; 0-9797455-3-5

"Cusick and O'Sullivan compare the egg-laying and -hatching habits of a broad spectrum of animals. . . . Each tidily composed double-page spread offers color photographs of three or four examples of the topic under discussion, with brief descriptive paragraphs that will do double duty as quick captions for casual browsers. Although the emphasis is on protective adaptations and strategies that maximize chances for survival, the predator's point of view is not neglected. . . . [This is an] inviting offering." Bull Cent Child Books

Davies, Nicola, 1958-
Just the right size; why big animals are big and little animals are little. illustrated by Neal Layton. Candlewick Press 2009 61p il $14.99
Grades: 3 4 5 6   **591.4**
1. Size 2. Animals
ISBN 978-0-7636-3924-2; 0-7636-3924-9

This "book uses the 'Big Thing, Little Thing' rule (which explains how the length, surface area and cross section of an object or creature are relative to its volume and weight) . . . to explore how size affects living things. Davies's often humorous text and Layton's energetic illustrations demonstrate why humans don't have superpowers . . . and later spreads discuss the advantages and limitations of being very small or very big. . . The spot-on comic delivery and readily comprehensible explanations make this a prime pick for readers curious about physical science in the natural world." Publ Wkly

Eamer, Claire
Lizards in the sky; animals where you least expect them. Annick 2010 97p il $21.95; pa $12.95
Grades: 3 4 5   **591.4**
1. Animals -- Habitations
ISBN 978-1-55451-265-2; 1-55451-265-4; 978-1-55451-264-5 pa; 1-55451-264-6 pa

"Eamer looks at animals living unexpected lives in unanticipated habitats. Birds and spiders underwater, snakes far out in the open ocean, fish on land, burrowing owls, and shrimp in the desert are just a few of the creatures introduced. The physiological adaptations they have made to survive are described. . . . Text boxes with factual tidbits add to the narrative. The drawings and photographs on every page are in full color. . . . Overall, an enjoyable and fascinating title." SLJ

Fielding, Beth
Animal eyes. EarlyLight Books 2011 36p il $14.95
Grades: 1 2 3 4   **591.4**
1. Eye 2. Animals
ISBN 0979745551; 9780979745553; 978-0-9797455-5-3; 0-9797455-5-1

This book explores the morphology and behavior of animal eyes. Included are mammals, insects, birds, reptiles, amphibians, and mollusks. Glossary. Index. "Grades one to four." (Sci Books Films)

"Children who pick up this appealing book will instantly have their curiosity piqued. Each spread features a different animal and includes a full-color photo of it, close-ups of its eyes, and a few photographs of text. 'Test It Out' experiments using easily accessible materials such as colored pencils add a participatory element to the book. . . . An attractive, informative title." SLJ

★ **Animal** tails. EarlyLight Books 2011 36p il
Grades: 1 2 3   **591.4**
1. Tails 2. Animals
ISBN 0-9797455-8-6; 978-0-9797455-8-4

"Fielding describes how tails work for elephants, kangaroos, primates, cats, squirrels, chameleons, lizards, snakes, birds, whales, stingrays, and caterpillars. More than 13 styles of tails, such as scaly, stinging, and spraying, are paired with various functions performed by these animals. . . . The full-color photography is quite bright, clear, and eye-catching. . . . A visually appeal and interesting introduction." SLJ

Hodgkins, Fran

Amazing eggs; with illustrations by Wendy Smith. Treasure Bay 2011 41p il (We both read)

Grades: K 1 2　　　　　　　　　　**591.4**

1. Eggs

ISBN 1-60115-251-5; 1-60115-252-3 pa; 978-1-60115-251-0; 978-1-60115-252-7 pa

"A colorful and scientific explanation of eggs and the development of insects, reptiles, birds, and fish. The well-written, easy-to-understand text and the inviting format will encourage emerging readers to pick up the book on their own. Intended as a shared reading experience for adult and child, the dual differentiated text appears on each page, accompanied by clear, informative, full-color photos. An attractive addition that covers an important science-curriculum subject." SLJ

Hulbert, Laura

Who has these feet? illustrated by Erik Brooks. Henry Holt 2011 un il $16.99

Grades: PreK K 1 2　　　　　　　　**591.4**

1. Foot 2. Animals

ISBN 978-0-8050-8907-3; 0-8050-8907-1

LC 2010033429

"This guess-the-animal book asks readers to identify species by looking at their feet. Hulbert describes how each animal's treads are acclimated to its particular environment: a tree frog's toes are sticky; a squirrel uses the claws on its toes to scamper along trees; and a sea turtle has flippers for swimming. A gatefold features all of the animals together. . . . Brooks's naturalistic yet affable animals will likely inspire readers to take a closer look at their own feet." Publ Wkly

Jenkins, Steve

★ **Actual** size. Houghton Mifflin 2004 un il $16

Grades: K 1 2 3　　　　　　　　　**591.4**

1. Size 2. Animals

ISBN 0-618-37594-5

LC 2003-17462

In "torn-and-cut paper collages, Jenkins depicts 18 animals and insects—or a part of their body—in actual size. . . . The end matter offers full pictures of the creatures and more details about their habitats and habits. Mixing deceptive simplicity with absolute clarity, this beautiful book is an enticing way to introduce children to the glorious diversity of our natural world, or to illustrate to budding scientists the importance of comparison, measurement, observation, and record keeping. A thoroughly engaging read-aloud and a must-have for any collection." SLJ

Big & little. Houghton Mifflin 1996 un il $16

Grades: K 1 2　　　　　　　　　　**591.4**

1. Size 2. Animals

ISBN 0-395-72664-6

LC 95-41162

Jenkins "points out the differences in size between animals who are similar in other ways. The artwork combines cuttings of colored, textured papers to form animals that stand out strikingly against white backgrounds. . . . One line of text comments on the two animals' sizes, habits, or habitats. The final pages include a presentation of the compar-

ative sizes of all the animals, [and] a paragraph of additional information about each species." Booklist

Includes bibliographical references

Johnson, Jinny

Animal Planet atlas of animals; by Jinny Johnson. Millbrook Press 2013 128 p. (lib. bdg. : alk. paper) $35.93

Grades: 1 2 3 4 5　　　　　　　　**591.4**

1. Atlases 2. Animals 3. Zoogeography

ISBN 1467713279; 9781467713276

LC 2013001746

This children's book is an atlas of animals. "Grouped by continent and then by habitat type, the selected animals share space on full but not congested spreads with maps, labels and . . . notes on size, diet, memorable physical features or behavior. Though generally trimmed or cut out, the photos all seem to have been taken in natural settings, and they show each creature at revealing angles or in action poses." (Kirkus Reviews)

Kaner, Etta

Have you ever seen a hippo with sunscreen? written by Etta Kaner; illustrated by Jeff Szuc. Kids Can Press 2010 il $14.95

Grades: K 1 2 3　　　　　　　　　**591.4**

1. Animals

ISBN 978-1-55453-337-4; 1-55453-337-6

"People may wear sunscreen, sunglasses, and snowshoes, but the seven featured animals have their own physical adaptations to their environments. Large type, very brief question-and-answer text . . . and humorous illustrations make the volume accessible and entertaining for young readers." Horn Book Guide

Lunis, Natalie

Electric animals. Bearport Pub. 2011 24p il (Animals with super powers) lib bdg $22.61

Grades: 3 4 5　　　　　　　　　　**591.4**

1. Platypus 2. Electric fishes

ISBN 978-1-61772-121-2; 1-61772-121-2

LC 2010034521

This describes electric animals including eels, rays, platypuses, and great white sharks.

"Large color photos of animals in natural settings and clear, cogent presentations of information combine to boost this [book] well above the average for both assignments and casual browsing." SLJ

Includes glossary and bibliographical references

Messner, Kate

★ **Over** and under the snow. Chronicle Books 2011 un il $16.99

Grades: PreK K 1 2　　　　　　　　**591.4**

1. Winter 2. Animals -- Habitations

ISBN 978-0-8118-6784-9; 0-8118-6784-6

LC 2009028984

"The lyrical descriptions of the text and the gray/brown/ice-blue palette of the illustrations leave readers with a retro feel that harkens back to earlier days of children's books and bygone times when life seemed simpler. Utterly charming, and informative, to boot; readers brought up on a diet of rhymes, bright colors and adorable fluffy animals will find its simple beauty a balm." Kirkus

Miller, Debbie S.

Arctic lights, arctic nights; illustrations by Jon Van Zyle. Walker & Co. 2003 un il map $16.95; pa $7.95

Grades: 2 3 4　　　　　　　　　　**591.4**

1. Animals -- Arctic regions 2. Natural history -- Alaska

ISBN 0-8027-8856-4; 0-8027-9636-2 pa

LC 2002-191047

Describes the unique light phenomena of the Alaskan Arctic and the way animals adapt to the temperature and daylight changes each month of the year

The "brief text includes not only lyrical messages about light and its partner, darkness, but also references to the reaction of wildlife to the waxing and waning. . . . Wrapped about this unfamiliar (to many of us) swirl of seasons of light are Van Zyle's superb and quietly beautiful acrylic paintings, which capture both light and dark in perfect harmony with the text." SLJ

Includes glossary

Miller, Sara Swan

★ **All** kinds of ears. Marshall Cavendish Benchmark 2007 48p il (All kinds of . . .) lib bdg $29.93

Grades: 3 4 5 6   **591.4**

1. Ear 2. Animals

ISBN 978-0-7614-2518-2 lib bdg; 0-7614-2518-7 lib bdg

This describes the various forms and functions of animal ears

Includes glossary and bibliographical references

★ **All** kinds of eyes. Marshall Cavendish Benchmark 2007 48p il (All kinds of . . .) lib bdg $29.93

Grades: 3 4 5 6   **591.4**

1. Eye 2. Animals

ISBN 978-0-7614-2519-9 lib bdg; 0-7614-2519-5 lib bdg

This describes the various forms and functions of eyes in animals

"The excellent content and rare photographs will appeal to children, whether for research or leisure reading." SLJ

Includes glossary and bibliographical references

★ **All** kinds of feet. Marshall Cavendish Benchmark 2007 48p il (All kinds of . . .) lib bdg $29.93

Grades: 3 4 5 6   **591.4**

1. Foot 2. Animals

ISBN 978-0-7614-2520-5 lib bdg; 0-7614-2520-9 lib bdg

This describes the various forms and functions of animal feet

"The excellent content and rare photographs will appeal to children, whether for research of leisure reading." SLJ

Includes glossary and bibliographical references

★ **All** kinds of mouths. Marshall Cavendish Benchmark 2007 48p il (All kinds of . . .) lib bdg $29.93

Grades: 3 4 5 6   **591.4**

1. Mouth 2. Animals

ISBN 978-0-7614-2521-2 lib bdg; 0-7614-2521-7 lib bdg

This describes the various forms and functions of animal mouths

"The excellent content and rare photographs will appeal to children, whether for research or leisure reading." SLJ

Includes glossary and bibliographical references

★ **All** kinds of noses. Marshall Cavendish Benchmark 2007 48p il (All kinds of . . .) lib bdg $29.93

Grades: 3 4 5 6   **591.4**

1. Nose 2. Animals

ISBN 978-0-7614-2522-9 lib bdg; 0-7614-2522-5 lib bdg

This describes the various forms and functions of animal noses

"The excellent content and rare photographs will appeal to children, whether for research or leisure reading." SLJ

Includes glossary and bibliographical references

★ **All** kinds of skin. Marshall Cavendish Benchmark 2007 48p il (All kinds of . . .) lib bdg $29.93

Grades: 3 4 5 6   **591.4**

1. Skin 2. Animals

ISBN 978-0-7614-2713-1 lib bdg; 0-7614-2713-9 lib bdg

This describes the shapes and functions of animal exteriors found in nature, including skin, feathers, fur, and scales

Includes glossary and bibliographical references

Patkau, Karen

Creatures great and small. Tundra Books 2006 un il $17.95

Grades: K 1 2 3   **591.4**

1. Size 2. Animals

ISBN 978-0-88776-754-8; 0-88776-754-0

"Each spread in this informational picture book shows a large animal filling a page-and-a-half scene and a small one from a similar classification on the right edge. . . . Sharp lines, bold colors, and careful composition of the computer-generated art successfully convey the rich variety of creatures and environments, accentuating similarities and differences. . . . Labeled illustrations at the back of the book introduce concepts of scale in a clear and inviting way." SLJ

Includes glossary

Posada, Mia

Guess what is growing inside this egg. Millbrook Press 2007 un il lib bdg $15.95

Grades: K 1 2 3   **591.4**

1. Eggs 2. Animals

ISBN 978-0-8225-6192-7 lib bdg; 0-8225-6192-1 lib bdg

LC 2006-16250

"This attractive picture book presents six animals that hatch from eggs: penguins, alligators, ducklings, sea turtles, spiders, and octopuses. . . . The first spread is a guessing game, telling a little about the animal in two rhymed couplets, showing a closeup of an egg in its natural setting, and asking 'Can you guess what is growing inside this egg?' The next spread reveals the answer to the riddle and offers information about the featured animal's physical attributes and behaviors. Distinctive collage-and-watercolor artwork offers eye-catching views of the animals within their habitats." Booklist

Schaefer, Lola M.

★ **Just** one bite; 11 animals and their bites at life size! by Lola Schaefer; illustrated by Geoff Waring. Chronicle Books 2010 un il $17.99

Grades: K 1 2 3   **591.4**

1. Animals -- Food

ISBN 978-0-8118-6473-2; 0-8118-6473-1

"In this bold, oversized picture book, readers will see—at actual size—how much tasty giant squid a sperm whale can eat in one gulp . . . and how much dirt a worm can eat at once. . . . Nine other animals and their eating habits are illustrated. . . . The terrific, artfully composed brush, crayon and computer-aided artwork is lavish, the perspectives dramatically up-close. The text is lively, minimal and perfect for reading aloud." Kirkus

Schwartz, David M.

Where else in the wild? more camouflaged creatures concealed and revealed. by David M. Schwartz and Yael Schy; eye-tricking photographs by Dwight Kuhn. Tricycle Press 2009 un il $16.99

Grades: 2 3 4   **591.4**

1. Animals 2. Camouflage (Biology) 3. Poetry -- By individual authors

ISBN 978-1-58246-283-7; 1-58246-283-6

Presents poems and brief facts about eleven animals that rely on the ability to camouflage within nature to survive in the wilderness

"Poetry and photography work well together in this beautifully illustrated book. . . . Notable for its finesse and variety, the poetry includes rhymed verse, as well as haiku and concrete poems. A playful, informative introduction to camouflage in nature." Booklist

Where in the wild? camouflaged creatures concealed--and revealed. ear-tickling poems by David M. Schwartz and Yael Schy; eye-tricking photos by Dwight Kuhn. Tricycle Press 2007 un il $15.95

Grades: 2 3 4   **591.4**

1. Animals 2. Camouflage (Biology) 3. Poetry -- By individual authors

ISBN 978-1-58246-207-3; 1-58246-207-0

LC 2006-101406

"The well-crafted, short poems . . . offer clues to the hidden animals' identities. Beautifully photographed and designed with great attention to detail, this book will intrigue and challenge children." Booklist

Zoehfeld, Kathleen Weidner

What lives in a shell? illustrated by Helen K. Davie. HarperCollins Pubs. 1994 32p il (Let's-read-and-find-out science) hardcover o.p. pa $5.99

Grades: K 1   **591.4**

1. Shells 2. Animal defenses

ISBN 0-06-445124-0 pa

LC 93-12428

Describes such animals as snails, turtles, and crabs, which live in shells and use these coverings as protection

This book uses "interesting and accurate illustrations and just the right words. . . . The science here is good, and the explanations should cause young readers to want to learn more." Sci Books Films

591.47 Protective and locomotor adaptations, color

Beck, W. H.

Glow; Animals With Their Own Night-lights. by W. H. Beck. Houghton Mifflin Harcourt 2016 32 p. color illustrations $17.99

Grades: K 1 2 3 4   **591.47**

1. Biologists 2. Marine biology 3. Bioluminescence 4. Marine animals

ISBN 054441666X; 9780544416666

LC 2016304819

In this book, by W. H. Beck, "Why be afraid of the dark when there is so much to see? Whether it's used to hunt, hide, find a friend, or escape an enemy, bioluminescence --the ability to glow--is a unique adaptation in nature. In this [book] . . . join world-renowned photographers and biologists on their close encounters with the curious creatures that make their own light." (Publisher's note)

"Aspiring scientists and casual observers alike will be attracted to the layout of this volume: photographs of the various glowing creatures are suspended on a black background, creating a stark, eerie effect that will entrance readers as much as the content itself." Booklist

Includes bibliographical references.

Collard, Sneed B.

Teeth; illustrated by Phyllis Saroff. Charlesbridge 2008 32p il lib bdg $16.95; pa $7.95

Grades: 1 2 3   **591.47**

1. Teeth 2. Animals

ISBN 978-1-58089-120-2 lib bdg; 1-58089-120-9 lib bdg; 978-1-58089-121-9 pa; 1-58089-121-7 pa

LC 2007-02266

This describes types of animal teeth, how they are used, how they grow, and the differences between teeth and horns or antlers

"Packed with exciting information, this large-size picture book combines chatty prose . . . and clear, full-color illustrations to tell amazing facts." Booklist

Wings; illustrated by Robin Brickman. Charlesbridge 2008 31p il lib bdg $16.95; pa $7.95

Grades: 1 2 3   **591.47**

1. Wings 2. Flight 3. Animals

ISBN 978-1-57091-611-3 lib bdg; 1-57091-611-X lib bdg; 978-1-57091-612-0 pa; 1-57091-612-8 pa

LC 2007-02265

This "looks at wing design and the shapes of birds, insects, and mammals, as well as at prehistoric flyers and birds that no longer fly. Human fascination with flying rounds out the discussion. Brickman's paper collages of winged animals are . . . impressive in texture and color." SLJ

Includes glossary and bibliographical references

Halpern, Monica

Underground towns, treetops, and other animal hiding places; by Monica Halpern. National Geographic 2007 40p (National Geographic science chapters) lib bdg $17.90

Grades: 3 4 5 6   **591.47**

1. Animal defenses 2. Animals -- Habitations

ISBN 978-1-4263-0183-4 lib bdg; 1-4263-0183-9 lib bdg

LC 2007007894

This is an introduction to hidden animal habitats, such as underground burrows, underwater, or treetops

This "book provides a clear, engaging introduction to the topic. . . . The [book's] clear design features many well-captioned photographs . . . charts, and diagrams." Horn Book Guide

Helman, Andrea

Hide and seek; nature's best vanishing acts. photographs by Gavriel Jecan. Walker Pub. Co. 2008 un il $16.95; lib bdg $17.85

Grades: 2 3 4   **591.47**

1. Animal defenses 2. Camouflage (Biology)

ISBN 978-0-8027-9690-5; 0-8027-9690-7; 978-0-8027-9691-2 lib bdg; 0-8027-9691-5 lib bdg

LC 2007024242

"Animals' camouflage is equally effective at hiding prey from predators and predators from prey. This large-format book offers plenty of excellent photographs of animals in each category, arranged by type of habitat. . . . Throughout the book, the words seem to elaborate on the pictures." Booklist

Jenkins, Steve

★ **Living** color. Houghton Mifflin 2007 un il $17

Grades: 3 4 5 6   **591.47**

1. Animals -- Color

ISBN 0-618-70897-9; 978-0-618-70897-0

LC 2007-12751

"Each of seven colors gets a spread or two featuring animals in that color. . . . Grades three to five." (Bull Cent Child Books)

This "offers a pageant of the most stunning, vividly hued creatures on the planet. . . . This book opens by explaining that bright coloration goes beyond mere decoration. . . . Arranged by color, subsequent spreads feature a rainbow of animals rendered in Jenkins' celebrated cut-paper style. Each picture is accompanied by a paragraph of nicely distilled information." Booklist

★ **What** do you do when something wants to eat you? Houghton Mifflin 1997 un il $16

Grades: K 1 2 3   **591.47**
   1. Animal defenses
   ISBN 0-395-82514-8

LC 96-44993

Describes how various animals, including an octopus, a bombadier beetle, a puff adder, and a gliding frog, escape danger

"Jenkins achieves remarkable anatomical detail in his boldly textured cut-paper collages; simple backgrounds keep attention tightly focused on the animals and their survival strategies." Bull Cent Child Books

Johnson, Rebecca L.
   ★ **When** lunch fights back; wickedly clever animal defenses. by Rebecca L. Johnson. Millbrook Press 2015 48 p. (lib. bdg. : alk. paper) $29.27
Grades: 4 5 6 7   **591.47**
   1. Animal defenses 2. Animals
   ISBN 1467721093; 9781467721097

LC 2013046646

This book, by Rebecca L. Johnson, explains that "in nature, good defenses can mean the difference between surviving a predator's attack and becoming its lunch. Some animals rely on sharp teeth and claws or camouflage. But that's only the beginning. Meet creatures with some of the strangest defenses known to science." (Publisher's note)

"Along with the ever popular hagfish (aka "snot eel") and the horned lizard—which can indeed squirt blood from one or both eyes—Johnson... profiles 10 animals with particularly noxious defense mechanisms... This is an outstanding way for readers to meet scientists at work in both field and lab, as well as to learn that, for instance, fulmar chicks can project vomit up to 6 feet and, creepily, that a school of the Amazonian two-spot astyanax will attack and eject one of its own to distract an approaching predator. Thrilling reading for budding biologists." Kirkus

   Includes bibliographical references and index

Lunis, Natalie
   See-through animals. Bearport Pub. 2011 24p il (Animals with super powers) lib bdg $22.61
Grades: 3 4 5   **591.47**
   1. Camouflage (Biology)
   ISBN 9781617721205; 1617721204

LC 2010045408

This describes see-through animals including the clearwing butterfly, the glass frog, transparent anemone shrimp, jellyfish, the transparent sea butterfly, glass squid, transparent octopus and zebrafish and frog.

"Large color photos of animals in natural settings and clear, cogent presentations of information combine to boost this [book] well above the average for both assignments and casual browsing." SLJ

   Includes bibliographical references and index.

Mitchell, Susan K.
   Animal chemical combat; poisons, smells, and slime. [by] Susan K. Mitchell. Enslow Publishers 2009 48p il (Amazing animal defenses) lib bdg $23.93
Grades: 4 5 6   **591.47**
   1. Animal defenses
   ISBN 978-0-7660-3294-1 lib bdg; 0-7660-3294-9 lib bdg

LC 2008-11075

"The closeup photos are frequent and well chosen, and accompanied by clear, simply phrased [text], which [is] more detailed than average and [takes] up most or all of the space on each page." SLJ

   Includes glossary and bibliographical references

   Animal mimics; look-alikes and copycats. [by] Susan K. Mitchell. Enslow Publishers 2009 48p il (Amazing animal defenses) lib bdg $23.93

Grades: 4 5 6   **591.47**
   1. Animal defenses
   ISBN 978-0-7660-3293-4 lib bdg; 0-7660-3293-0 lib bdg

LC 2008-11449

"The closeup photos are frequent and well chosen, and accompanied by clear, simply phrased [text], which [is] more detailed than average and [takes] up most or all of the space on each page." SLJ

   Includes glossary and bibliographical references

   Animals with awesome armor; shells, scales, and exoskeletons. [by] Susan K. Mitchell. Enslow Publishers 2009 48p il (Amazing animal defenses) lib bdg $23.93
Grades: 4 5 6   **591.47**
   1. Animal defenses
   ISBN 978-0-7660-3296-5 lib bdg; 0-7660-3296-5 lib bdg

LC 2008-11456

"The closeup photos are frequent and well chosen, and accompanied by clear, simply phrased [text], which [is] more detailed than average and [takes] up most or all of the space on each page." SLJ

   Includes glossary and bibliographical references

   Animals with crafty camouflage; hiding in plain sight. [by] Susan K. Mitchell. Enslow Publishers 2009 48p il (Amazing animal defenses) lib bdg $23.93
Grades: 4 5 6   **591.47**
   1. Animal defenses 2. Camouflage (Biology)
   ISBN 978-0-7660-3291-0 lib bdg; 0-7660-3291-4 lib bdg

LC 2008-11073

"The closeup photos are frequent and well chosen, and accompanied by clear, simply phrased [text], which [is] more detailed than average and [takes] up most or all of the space on each page." SLJ

   Includes glossary and bibliographical references

   Animals with wicked weapons; stingers, barbs, and quills. [by] Susan K. Mitchell. Enslow Publishers 2009 48p il (Amazing animal defenses) lib bdg $23.93
Grades: 4 5 6   **591.47**
   1. Animal defenses
   ISBN 978-0-7660-3292-7 lib bdg; 0-7660-3292-2 lib bdg

LC 2008-11075

"The closeup photos are frequent and well chosen, and accompanied by clear, simply phrased [text], which [is] more detailed than average and [takes] up most or all of the space on each page." SLJ

   Includes glossary and bibliographical references

Morlock, Lisa
   Track that scat! written by Lisa Morlock; illustrated by Carrie Anne Bradshaw. Sleeping Bear Press 2012 32 p. col. ill $15.95
Grades: K 1 2   **591.47**
   1. Feces 2. Animal tracks 3. Animal behavior 4. Animal droppings
   ISBN 158536536X; 9781585365364

LC 2011028148

In this book, "for young Finn and her hound, . . . exploring the outdoors becomes . . . a vehicle to introduce readers to identifying commonly known animals through their tracks and, particularly, droppings. From the onset, the pair encounters -- and sometimes steps in -- a progression of animal excrement, . . . includ[ing] goose, raccoon, and bird poop." (Booklist)

"The large spreads are inviting, and the dog, a basset hound, is cute, cute, cute, and the gross factor is likely to draw kids in." SLJ

Pryor, Kimberley Jane
   Amazing armor. Marshall Cavendish Benchmark 2009 32p il (Animal attack and defense) $19.95

Grades: 2 3 4   **591.47**
  1. Animal defenses
  ISBN 978-0-7614-4424-4; 0-7614-4424-6
                                LC 2009-4996
  "Students will enjoy the large vivid photographs that allow for a closeup look at the animal, along with the excellent descriptions of the different survival methods. . . . Pryor does a good job of bringing the information down to a level that an elementary student would understand without losing any of the important details. . . . [This] would be a great addition to any nonfiction collection." Libr Media Connect
  Includes glossary

  Clever camouflage. Marshall Cavendish Benchmark 2009 32p il (Animal attack and defense) $19.95
Grades: 2 3 4   **591.47**
  1. Animal defenses 2. Camouflage (Biology)
  ISBN 978-0-7614-4420-6; 0-7614-4420-3
                                LC 2009-4997
  "Students will enjoy the large vivid photographs that allow for a closeup look at the animal, along with the excellent descriptions of the different survival methods. . . . Pryor does a good job of bringing the information down to a level that an elementary student would understand without losing any of the important details. . . . [This] would be a great addition to any nonfiction collection." Libr Media Connect
  Includes glossary

  Mimicry and relationships. Marshall Cavendish Benchmark 2009 32p il (Animal attack and defense) $19.95
Grades: 2 3 4   **591.47**
  1. Animal defenses
  ISBN 978-0-7614-4421-3; 0-7614-4421-1
                                LC 2009-4995
  "Students will enjoy the large vivid photographs that allow for a closeup look at the animal, along with the excellent descriptions of the different survival methods. . . . Pryor does a good job of bringing the information down to a level that an elementary student would understand without losing any of the important details. . . . [This] would be a great addition to any nonfiction collection." Libr Media Connect
  Includes glossary

  Tricky behavior. Marshall Cavendish Benchmark 2009 32p il (Animal attack and defense) $19.95
Grades: 2 3 4   **591.47**
  1. Animal defenses
  ISBN 978-0-7614-4425-1; 0-7614-4425-4
                                LC 2009-4993
  "Students will enjoy the large vivid photographs that allow for a closeup look at the animal, along with the excellent descriptions of the different survival methods. . . . Pryor does a good job of bringing the information down to a level that an elementary student would understand without losing any of the important details. . . . [This] would be a great addition to any nonfiction collection." Libr Media Connect
  Inlcudes glossary

  Warning colors. Marshall Cavendish Benchmark 2009 32p il (Animal attack and defense) $19.95
Grades: 2 3 4   **591.47**
  1. Animal defenses
  ISBN 978-0-7614-4419-0; 0-7614-4419-X
                                LC 2009-4992
  "Students will enjoy the large vivid photographs that allow for a closeup look at the animal, along with the excellent descriptions of the different survival methods. . . . Pryor does a good job of bringing the information down to a level that an elementary student would understand

without losing any of the important details. . . . [This] would be a great addition to any nonfiction collection." Libr Media Connect
  Includes glossary

Racanelli, Marie
  Animals with armor. PowerKids Press 2010 24p il (Crazy nature) lib bdg $21.25; pa $8.25
Grades: 2 3 4 5   **591.47**
  1. Animal defenses
  ISBN 978-1-4358-9386-3 lib bdg; 1-4358-9386-7 lib bdg; 978-1-4358-9864-6 pa; 1-4358-9864-8 pa
                                LC 2009036527
  This describes the different animals that have adapted defensive coverings, from turtles and snakes to armadillos, snails, and bugs
  This book "combines attention-grabbing information with a well-organized format. . . . [The book has] spectacular color photography and eye-popping facts." SLJ

  Camouflaged creatures. PowerKids 2010 24p il (Crazy nature) lib bdg $21.25; pa $8.25
Grades: 2 3 4 5   **591.47**
  1. Animals 2. Camouflage (Biology)
  ISBN 978-1-4358-9383-2 lib bdg; 1-4358-9383-2 lib bdg; 978-1-4358-9858-5 pa; 1-4358-9858-3 pa
  This explains how color, texture, and body shape allow animals to blend in seamlessly with their surroundings, with examples of camouflage in lizards, moths, beetles and other creatures
  This book "combines attention-grabbing information with a well-organized format. . . . [The book has] spectacular color photography and eye-popping facts. . . . Excellent for reports." SLJ

Stewart, Melissa
  The **skin** you're in; the secrets of skin. illustrated by Janet Hamlin. Marshall Cavendish Benchmark 2010 48p il (The gross and goofy body) lib bdg $29.93
Grades: 2 3 4   **591.47**
  1. Skin
  ISBN 978-0-7614-4169-4; 0-7614-4169-7
                                LC 2008033620
  This provides information on the role skin plays in the body science of humans and animals.
  This "offers detailed science facts in a fashion approachable enough to make it a welcome supplement to school textbooks. . . . The layout is fresh, clean, and colorful, sidebars keep things conversational, and the back matter is solid." Booklist
  Includes glossary and bibliographical references

  World's fastest animals; Melissa Stewart. Sterling Children's 2014 32 p. $9.95
Grades: 1 2 3   **591.47**
  1. Speed 2. Animals 3. Animal locomotion
  ISBN 1454906332; 9781402777936; 9781454906339
                                LC 2013028735
  This book asks, "Which creature moves so rapidly it can even run on water? Which bird's heart beats 1,200 times a minute?" It invites readers to "Come learn about the world's fastest animals, from speedy cheetahs and swiftly swinging tree gibbons to colorful chameleons whose tongues grab an insect quicker than you can blink an eye." (Publisher's note)
  Other titles in the series include:
  Penguins Are Cool! (2012)
  Deadly and Dangerous (2013)
  Extreme Survivors (2014)
  Snakes up Close! (2012)
  Strangest Animals (2013)

Stockdale, Susan

 Spectacular spots; written and illustrated by Susan Stockdale. Peachtree Publishers 2015 32 p. color illustrations $15.95

Grades: PreK K 1 **591.47**

 1. Animals -- Color 2. Camouflage (Biology)

ISBN 1561458171; 9781561458172

LC 2014006503

This children's book, written and illustrated by Susan Stockdale, "introduces young readers to the many ways in which animals benefit from their spots. An afterword tells a little bit more about each animal and where it lives, and readers can test their knowledge of animal spots with a fun matching game at the end!" (Publisher's note)

"A simple, rhyming text graced with large, colorful acrylics provides a wide window into the physical characteristic of spots in the natural world. Relying on minimalist text . . . and a painterly hand, Stockdale introduces a variety of creatures." SLJ

 Stripes of all types; written and illustrated by Susan Stockdale. Peachtree Publishers 2013 32 p. $15.95

Grades: PreK K 1 **591.47**

 1. Stripes 2. Animals -- Color 3. Camouflage (Biology)

ISBN 1561456950; 9781561456956

LC 2012025541

In this children's picture book "[Susan] Stockdale pairs . . . acrylic illustrations with . . . verse to depict 19 striped animals. . . . The accompanying images show purple-striped jellyfish, an eastern garter snake, ring-tailed lemurs, and an American bittern. Elsewhere . . . a poison frog in shocking orange, yellow, and red stripes is 'propped on a log.' Closer to home, two children cuddle with striped cats." (Publishers Weekly)

591.472 Camouflage and color

Harrison, David L.

 Now you see them, now you don't; poems about creatures that hide. David L. Harrison; illustrated by Giles Laroche. Charlesbridge 2016 32 p. color illustrations (reinforced for library use) $17.95

Grades: K 1 2 3 4 5 **591.472**

 1. Animals -- Poetry 2. Camouflage (Biology) 3. Adaptation (Biology) 4. Protective coloration (Biology)

ISBN 1580896103; 9781580896108

LC 2014049184

In this poetry collection, by David Harrison and illustrated by Giles Laroche, readers "meet animals such as the polar bear and the octopus; the ghost crab and the copperhead snake; and many more that use camouflage to hunt or to hide. Back matter offers additional information about each of the nineteen animals." (Publisher's note)

"An attractive, informative blend of science and the arts." Kirkus

Includes bibliographical references.

Keating, Jess

 Pink is for blobfish; discovering the world's perfectly pink animals. Jess Keating; illustrations by David DeGrand. Alfred A. Knopf 2016 48 p. color illustrations (trade) $16.99

Grades: K 1 2 3 **591.472**

 1. Pink 2. Animals -- Color

ISBN 9780553512274; 9780553512281

LC 2015013906

Author Jess Keating presents this "nonfiction picture book introducing the weirdest, wildest, pinkest critters in the animal kingdom! Some people think pink is a pretty color. A fluffy, sparkly, princess-y color. But it's so much more. Sure, pink is the color of princesses and bubblegum, but it's also the color of monster slugs and poisonous insects. Not to mention ultra-intelligent dolphins, naked mole rats and bizarre, bloated blobfish." (Publisher's note)

"The comical tone makes this particularly inviting, and DeGrand's cartoonish illustrations only add to the fun. A playful introduction to the kookier corners of the animal kingdom." Booklist

591.473 Mimicry

Johnson, Rebecca L.

 Masters of disguise; amazing animal tricksters. Rebecca L. Johnson. Millbrook Press 2016 48 p. color illustrations (lb : alk. paper) $31.99

Grades: 5 6 7 8 **591.473**

 1. Animal behavior 2. Camouflage (Biology) 3. Mimicry (Biology)

ISBN 9781512400878

LC 2015031648

In this book, by Rebecca L. Johnson, "A number of animals rely on particularly clever tricks to fool predators or prey. A baby bird mimics a poisonous caterpillar. A moth escapes bats by making sounds that interfere with the bats' echolocation. A tiny rainforest spider builds a big spider 'puppet' out of bits of dead leaves, insect parts, and other items." (Publisher's note)

"With an almost equal number of men and women scientists featured, this work makes it easy for today's students to picture themselves in similar scientific shoes... This exciting and easy-to-digest title will make for an excellent purchase and addition to booktalk lists." SLJ

Includes bibliographical references and index

591.5 Behavior

Barner, Bob

 Animal baths. Chronicle Books 2011 un il $15.99

Grades: PreK K 1 **591.5**

 1. Baths 2. Animal behavior

ISBN 978-1-4521-0056-2; 1-4521-0056-X

LC 2011008001

"Eleven colorful two-page spreads (illustrated in cut paper, ribbon and pastel) show a variety of animals bathing, with accompanying two-line verses. . . . Finally, there's a little boy in a tub rub-a-dubbing and covered in bubbles. Then, a fitting encore: A longer poem against a background of bubbles and a child's bathtime accessories goes through the child's whole bath routine with shoutouts to some of the animals. . . . Barner's text is crisp and age-appropriate, but his well-composed, clever pictures really carry the story. . . . Well-conceived in its simplicity from beginning to end; even pre-readers can follow along." Kirkus

Cusick, Dawn

 Get the Scoop on Animal Snot, Spit & Slime! From Snake Venom to Fish Slime, 251 Cool Facts About Mucus, Saliva & More! Dawn Cusick. Quarto Pub Group USA 2016 80 p. color illustrations $14.95; (ebook) $14.95

Grades: 3 4 5 **591.5**

 1. Mucus 2. Animal behavior 3. Animal chemical defenses

ISBN 1633221156; 9781633221154; 9781633222755

LC 2016039181

In this book, by Dawn Cusick, "you'll learn that snot, spit, and slime may seem gross, but there's a lot of amazing science in these icky fluids. Animals use them for communication, defense, to find food, to travel fast, and more. Jellyfish and corals produce 'mucus nets' to capture prey.

... Many mammals use saliva to help them recognize offspring and others spit saliva at predators and prey." (Publisher's note)

"All of this is presented in easily digestible observations placed among, and often referring to, color photos of slime-covered goby fish, a giraffe with its tongue up its nose, various drooling animals, including a white infant, and like photogenic subjects." Kirkus

Fielding, Beth

Animal baths; wild & wonderful ways animals get clean! illustrations by Susan Greenelsh. EarlyLight Books 2009 47p il $14.95
Grades: 3 4 5   **591.5**
    1. Baths 2. Cleanliness 3. Animal behavior
    ISBN 978-0-9797455-2-2; 0-9797455-2-7

"Written in a conversational tone, this book is divided into three parts based on how animals clean themselves. . . . Each section begins with a brief description of how and why they engage in specific activities, followed by a spread about which ones utilize this method. A full-page, softly colored drawing of the animals 'bathing' faces each page of text. This fascinating book provides some unusual details about the unique behavior of the featured creatures." SLJ

Jenkins, Steve

★ **How** many ways can you catch a fly? [by] Steve Jenkins & Robin Page. Houghton Mifflin Company 2008 un il $16
Grades: PreK K 1 2 3   **591.5**
    1. Animal behavior 2. Food chains (Ecology)
    ISBN 978-0-618-96634-9; 0-618-96634-X

                         LC 2008-01864

"This picture book is about the food chain. . . . The facts about how particular animals escape danger and evade predators to stay alive are just as exciting as the facts about hunting. With clear, gorgeous, free-standing images in cut- and torn-paper collage, each double-page spread shows detailed species close up, as well as the connections between animals." Booklist

Includes bibliographical references

★ **Time** to eat; written and illustrated by Steve Jenkins and Robin Page. Houghton Mifflin 2011 un il $12.99
Grades: PreK K 1 2 3   **591.5**
    1. Animals -- Food
    ISBN 978-0-547-25032-8; 0-547-25032-0

                         LC 2010025127

"This small, square picture book presents an exciting introduction to what animals eat and how they collect, store, and digest their food. . . . The beautiful cut- and torn-paper collage illustrations are . . . expertly colored, detailed, and expressive . . . and the layout, featuring plenty of white space, nicely spotlights each animal in action." Booklist

Time to sleep; written and illustrated by Steve Jenkins and Robin Page. Houghton Mifflin 2011 un il $12.99
Grades: K 1 2 3   **591.5**
    1. Sleep 2. Animal behavior
    ISBN 978-0-547-25040-3; 0-547-25040-1

                         LC 2010025128

"Jenkins and Page introduce an array of creatures, showcasing how they . . . sleep. [The title concludes] with an appendix detailing further information about the featured animals. The illustrations are rendered in torn- and cut-paper collage, with each animal against a white background. . . . [The book] introduces animals from the familiar red fox to the lesser-known basilisk. Fascinating behaviors are detailed with explanations. . . . Readers will be captivated." SLJ

Knapp, Ron

Bloodsucking creatures. Enslow Publishers 2011 48p il (Bizarre science) lib bdg $23.93
Grades: 5 6 7 8   **591.5**
    1. Bloodsucking animals
    ISBN 978-0-7660-3671-0; 0-7660-3671-5

                         LC 2010009761

First published 1996 with title: Bloodsuckers

This describes bloodsucking animals such as mosquitoes, vampire bats, and fleas.

"Aimed at reluctant readers, [this title is] sure to disgust and delight in equal measure. . . . [The title] will pique interest and get kids lining up at the reference desk looking for more. The text is complemented by illustrations and magnified photos of things that you would hope never to see." SLJ

Includes glossary and bibliographical references

Lunde, Darrin

★ **After** the kill; [by] Darrin Lunde; illustrated by Catherine Stock. Charlesbridge 2011 un il lib bdg $16.95; pa $7.95
Grades: 2 3 4 5   **591.5**
    1. Food chains (Ecology) 2. Animals -- Food 3. Animals -- Africa 4. Predatory animals
    ISBN 978-1-57091-743-1 lib bdg; 1-57091-743-4 lib bdg; 978-1-57091-744-8 pa; 1-57091-744-2 pa

                         LC 2010007524

This is a "blunt portrayal of animal life in the Seregeti. A lioness stalks and faltering zebra, kills it, and eats it with her family; meanwhile, white-backed vultures arrive. . . . Then come hyenas, jackals, two other types of vultures, and ultimately meat-eating beetles, until all that remains of the zebra is bones. . . . Given the inherent grisliness of the topic, the text is notably reined in and matter-of-fact, and the pictures, expansive horizontal spreads, are almost impressionistic, focusing more on the ferocity of the predators than on the details of their prey." Horn Book

Page, Robin

Animals upside down; A Pull, Pop, Lift & Learn Book! Steve Jenkins and Robin Page. Houghton Mifflin Harcourt 2013 24 p. $24.99
Grades: K 1 2 3   **591.5**
    1. Picture books for children 2. Animal behavior
    ISBN 054734127X; 9780547341279

This children's picture book looks at animals that spend time upside down. The "three-toed sloth is topsy-turvy most of the time. The upside-down jellyfish rests on its back to feed. Skunks do stink-warning headstands and mallards upend in this colorful, interactive exploration of the hows and whys of upside-down animal behavior." (Publisher's note)

How to swallow a pig; step-by-step advice from the animal kingdom. by Steve Jenkins and Robin Page. Houghton Mifflin Harcourt 2015 32 p. color illustrations $17.99
Grades: K 1 2 3 4   **591.5**
    1. Animal behavior 2. Children's questions and answers 3. Animals -- Miscellanea
    ISBN 0544313658; 9780544313651

                         LC 2015000243

In this book, authors Steve Jenkins and Robin Page "reveal the skills animals use to survive in the wild in an imaginative and humorous how-to format. With step-by-step instructions, readers learn about specific behaviors; how to catch thousands of fish like a humpback whale or how to sew up a nest like a tailorbird. This fascinating and fun illustrated nonfiction melds science, art, biology, and the environment together." (Publisher's note)

"Beneath the irreverent tone, there's ample information about the animals' traits and behavior (and even more in an appendix), adding up to a highly enjoyable mix of science and humor." Pub Wkly

Pipe, Jim

Swarms; written by Jim Pipe; created and designed by David Salariya. Franklin Watts 2009 32p il (Scary creatures) lib bdg $26; pa $8.95

Grades: 3 4 5   **591.5**

1. Animal behavior

ISBN 978-0-531-21674-3 lib bdg; 0-531-21674-8 lib bdg; 978-0-531-21045-1 pa; 0-531-21045-6 pa

LC 2009010800

This describes the behavior of large groups of similar animals such as insects, birds, or fish, all moving in the same direction

This title has "two-page chapters of accessible, large-type text and bright color photos and illustrations. . . . The series distinguishes itself with 'X-Ray Vision.' When readers hold the page with this prompt up to the light, an image emerges. The X-rays mostly show the skeletal structures of the animals. Text boxes throughout add to the visual appeal. . . . [This is an] excellent [resource] for school assignments and browsing." SLJ

Includes glossary

Racanelli, Marie

Animal mimics. PowerKids Press 2010 24p il (Crazy nature) lib bdg $21.25; pa $8.25

Grades: 2 3 4 5   **591.5**

1. Animal behavior

ISBN 978-1-4358-9382-5 lib bdg; 1-4358-9382-4 lib bdg; 978-1-4358-9856-1 pa; 1-4358-9856-7 pa

Mimicry is an animal adaptation used both by prey and predators to disguise them in their habitats. The different kinds of mimicry are explored, along with specific examples of each type

This book "combines attention-grabbing information with a well-organized format. . . . [The book has] spectacular color photography and eye-popping facts. . . . Excellent for reports." SLJ

Underground animals. PowerKids 2010 24p il (Crazy nature) lib bdg $21.25; pa $8.25

Grades: 2 3 4 5   **591.5**

1. Animals

ISBN 978-1-4358-9384-9 lib bdg; 1-4358-9384-0 lib bdg; 978-1-4358-9860-8 pa; 1-4358-9860-5 pa

This describes animals that live underground from burrowers to cave-dwellers, such as earthworms, moles, ants, badgers, desert tortoises

This book "combines attention-grabbing information with a well-organized format. . . . [The book has] spectacular color photography and eye-popping facts. . . . Excellent for reports." SLJ

Ruurs, Margriet, 1952-

Amazing animals; the remarkable things creatures do. illustrated by W. Allan Hancock. Tundra Books 2011 32p il $17.95

Grades: 2 3 4 5   **591.5**

1. Animal behavior

ISBN 978-0-88776-973-3; 0-88776-973-X

Detailed illustrations and short descriptions present facts about animals from around the world, including their homebuilding, diet, and hunting.

"Though only a few lines are devoted to each animal, the detailed paintings and surprising details should captivate readers." Publ Wkly

Stewart, Melissa

Beneath the sun; by Melissa Stewart; illustrated by Constance Bergum. Peachtree Publishers 2014 32 p. illustrations $16.95

Grades: PreK K 1 2 3   **591.5**

1. Heat 2. Sun 3. Animal behavior 4. Animals -- Adaptation

ISBN 1561457337; 9781561457335

LC 2013026214

This children's book, written by Melissa Stewart and illustrated by Constance Bergum, asks "how do wild animals react to . . . heat? Journey from your neighborhood to a field where an earthworm loops its long body into a ball underground, to a desert where a jackrabbit loses heat through its oversized ears, to a wetland where a siren salamander burrows into the mud to stay cool, and to a seashore where a sea star hides in the shade of a seaweed mat." (Publisher's note)

"The framing of illustrations within the double-page spreads gives readers a sense of spatiality within the environment depicted. A well-designed, well-written book that offers readers a greater awareness of and sense of relationship to the other inhabitants in their environments." Kirkus

591.56   Behavior relating to life cycle

Aston, Dianna Hutts

A **nest** is noisy; by Dianna Aston; illustrated by Sylvia Long. Chronicle Books 2015 40 p. color illustrations (alk. paper) $16.99

Grades: K 1 2 3   **591.56**

1. Nest building 2. Nests 3. Animal behavior 4. Animals -- Habitations

ISBN 1452127131; 9781452127132

LC 2013047998

This children's book, by Dianna Aston and illustrated by Sylvia Long, "look[s] at the fascinating world of nests. From tiny bee hummingbird nests to orangutan nests high in the rainforest canopy, an incredible variety of nests are showcased here in all their splendor. . . . This carefully researched book introduces children to a captivating array of nest facts and will spark the imaginations of children." (Publisher's note)

"Coming full circle from An Egg Is Quiet (2006), the first entry in Aston and Long's beautifully designed series of nature books, this volume presents close-up views of nests as well as information about them. . . . The concise, precisely worded text is illustrated with impressive, large-scale watercolor paintings that are gracefully composed and sometimes intricately detailed. While there is no back matter, this beautiful picture book will be an asset to science collections." Booklist

Other titles in the series are:

An egg is quiet (2006)

A seed is sleepy (2007)

A butterfly is quiet (2011)

A rock is lively (2012)

Bancroft, Henrietta

Animals in winter; by Henrietta Bancroft and Richard G. Van Gelder; illustrated by Helen K. Davie. rev ed; HarperCollins Pubs. 1997 32p il (Let's-read-and-find-out science) hardcover o.p. pa $4.95

Grades: K 1   **591.56**

1. Winter 2. Animal behavior

ISBN 0-06-027158-2; 0-06-445165-8 pa

LC 95-36246

First published 1963

Describes the many different ways animals cope with winter, including migration, hibernation, and food storage

"The words are immediate . . . and the clear, active illustrations will draw new readers to a popular subject." Booklist

Berkes, Marianne

Going home; the mystery of animal migration. illustrated by Jennifer DiRubbio. Dawn 2010 un il map $16.95; pa $8.95

Grades: 2 3 4   591.56

1. Children's poetry 2. Animals -- Migration

ISBN 1-58469-126-3; 1-58469-127-1 pa; 978-1-58469-126-6; 978-1-58469-127-3 pa

LC 2009-38568

In illustrations and text, including poems, this book examines "the migration of 10 animals ranging from monarch butterflies to California gray whales.. . . . Kindergarten to grade four." (Sci Books Films)

"The illustrations enhance the text with softly colored two-page spreads. This book is perfect for a read-aloud to introduce the topic of migration. The rhyming verse flows smoothly, enhanced by the informational text." Libr Media Connect

Includes bibliographical references

Carney, Elizabeth

Great migrations; whales, wildebeests, butterflies, elephants, and other amazing animals on the move. National Geographic 2010 45p il map (National Geographic kids) $17.95; lib bdg $27

Grades: 3 4 5   591.56

1. Animals -- Migration

ISBN 9781426307003; 1426307004; 9781426307010 lib bdg; 1426307012 lib bdg

LC 2010008501

"This colorful book offers excellent photos of eight migrating animals: Mali elephants, red crabs, monarch butterflies, golden jellyfish, zebras, army ants, wildebeests, and sperm whales. . . . The writing style is often lively, tha maps are excellent, and the photos are exceptionally clear and vibrant." Booklist

Collard, Sneed B.

Animal dads; [by] Sneed B. Collard III; illustrated by Steve Jenkins. Houghton Mifflin 1997 un il $15.95; pa $5.95

Grades: K 1 2 3   591.56

1. Animal behavior

ISBN 0-395-83621-2; 0-618-03299-1 pa

LC 96-22171

"Each father and his offspring are presented on a single or double-page spread, illustrated with striking, cut-paper collage figures. The large, lifelike creatures are set against backgrounds that are true to each animal's natural habitat." SLJ

Dowson, Nick

North; the amazing story of Arctic migration. illustrated by Patrick Benson. Candlewick Press 2011 56p il $16.99

Grades: 1 2 3   591.56

1. Arctic regions 2. Animals -- Migration

ISBN 978-0-7636-5271-5; 0-7636-5271-7

LC 2010048131

"In the dark Arctic winters, few species can survive, but in short, lush summers, millions of animals return to reproduce. This combination of lyrical prose and striking illustrations conveys the mystery and magic of the far North and the cycle of darkness and rebirth that includes some astonishing migratory journeys. . . . Simple but effective, this is a beautiful introduction to a remarkable region that should encourage any child's sense of wonder." Kirkus

Fraser, Mary Ann

How animal babies stay safe. HarperCollins Pubs. 2002 33p il (Let's-read-and-find-out science) hardcover o.p. pa $4.95

Grades: K 1   591.56

1. Animal babies

ISBN 0-06-028803-5; 0-06-445211-5 pa

LC 00-57267

The author "describes how animal babies are cared for by their parents, including alligator babies who are carried about in their mother's mouth and young elephants who are placed in the middle of the herd for protection. Watercolor illustrations in muted colors help expand the simple text." Horn Book Guide

Jenkins, Steve

★ Sisters & brothers; sibling relationships in the animal world. [by] Steve Jenkins & Robin Page. Houghton Mifflin 2008 un il $16

Grades: 2 3 4   591.56

1. Siblings 2. Animal behavior

ISBN 978-0-618-37596-7; 0-618-37596-1

LC 2007-34305

"This riveting picture book . . . is packed with amazing facts. . . . [The subjects are] depicted in crisp, gorgeous, cut-and-torn paper collages set against lots of white space. . . . The sibling focus is a way to include a wealth of fascinating facts." Booklist

Time for a bath; written and illustrated by Steve Jenkins and Robin Page. Houghton Mifflin 2011 un il $12.99

Grades: K 1 2 3   591.56

1. Baths 2. Animal behavior

ISBN 978-0-547-25037-3; 0-547-25037-1

LC 2010025126

"Jenkins and Page introduce an array of creatures, showcasing how they bathe. . . . [The title concludes] with an appendix detailing further information about the featured animals. The illustrations are rendered in torn- and cut-paper collage, with each animal . . . set against a white background. . . . Readers are informed that animals bathe for different reasons: to clean themselves, to cool off, to warm up, to dissuade parasites. . . . Readers will be captivated." SLJ

Marsh, Laura

Amazing animal journeys. National Geographic 2010 48p il (Great migrations) $11.90; pa $3.99

Grades: 1 2 3   591.56

1. Crabs 2. Zebras 3. Walruses 4. Animals -- Migration

ISBN 978-1-4263-0742-3; 1-4263-0742-X; 978-1-4263-0741-6 pa; 1-4263-0741-1 pa

LC 2010017958

This describes the migration patterns of zebras, red crabs, and walruses.

"Dynamic full-color photographs, informative writing, and consistent organization work well together in [this volume]. . . . Along with the many photographs, the fascinating details are supported by boxes of related information, helpful definitions of new terms, and a sprinkling of entertaining jokes/riddles." SLJ

Includes glossary

O'Sullivan, Joanne

Migration Nation; Animals on the Go from Coast to Coast. Joanne O'Sullivan. Imagine Publishing Incorporated 2015 96 p. col. illustrations, col. maps $15.95

Grades: 4 5 6 7 8   591.56

1. Animals 2. Animals -- Migration

ISBN 162354050X; 9781623540500

This children's book, by Joanne O'Sullivan, part of the "Ranger Rick" series, "introduces the migratory habits of a dozen (mostly) North American animals. O'Sullivan explores migration by land (examining snakes, pronghorns, bison, and polar bears), by sea (salmon, manatees, and gray whales), and by sky (cranes and monarch butterflies)." (School Library Journal)

Roemer, Heidi B.
Whose nest is this? by Heidi Bee Roemer; illustrated by Connie McLennan. NorthWord Books for Young Readers 2009 un il $16.95
Grades: PreK K 1 2 **591.56**
1. Birds -- Nests 2. Animals -- Habitations
ISBN 978-1-58979-386-6; 1-58979-386-2
LC 2007021870
"This picture book describes the nests of various birds, insects, mammals, fish, and reptiles. Whether it's an elf owl's cavity in a giant Saguaro, a Caribbean flamingo's mound of mud in shallow water, or a sea turtle's sandy pit, these shelters are described in brief rhymed texts. . . . The creatures are brought to life in the engaging rhymes and vivid art." SLJ

Stockdale, Susan
Carry me! animal babies on the move. written and illustrated by Susan Stockdale. Peachtree Publishers 2005 un il $15.95
Grades: PreK K 1 **591.56**
1. Animal behavior
ISBN 1-56145-328-5
LC 2004-16585
"The facts of zoology are both exciting and cuddly in this science picture book with clear, bright acrylic illustrations that show how various animals carry their babies. The settings give the big picture—from the African savannah and Antarctica to South America. Then children can look closely and find animal babies tucked into pouches, clinging to bellies, propped on shoulders, perched on feet, gripped between teeth." Booklist

Includes bibliographical references

591.57 Locomotion

Page, Robin
Flying frogs and walking fish; leaping lemurs, tumbling toads, jet-propelled jellyfish, and more surprising ways that animals move. by Steve Jenkins and Robin Page. Houghton Mifflin Harcourt 2015 40 p. color illustrations (hbk) $17.99
Grades: PreK K 1 2 3 **591.57**
1. Animal locomotion 2. Marine animals -- Locomotion
ISBN 9780544630901
LC 2015011620
This juvenile book, by Steve Jenkins and Robin Page, "show[s] how animals roll, fly, walk, leap, climb, swim and even flip! This . . . illustrated nonfiction melds science, art, biology, and the environment together in a detailed and well-researched book about how animals move in our world today." (Publisher's note)
"With a collection of more than 40 species, this spectacular arrangement of creatures is delicately rendered in Jenkins' signature, eye-catching collage style. Closing with a list of categories and its accompanying critters, this is highly educational and a treat to behold." Booklist
Includes bibliographical references

591.59 Communication

Davies, Nicola, 1958-
Talk talk squawk; How and Why Animals Communicate. illustrated by Neal Layton. Walker & Company 2011 64 p.

Grades: 3 4 5 **591.59**
1. Animal communication
ISBN 0763650889 (Candlewick); 1406321184 (Walker & Co.); 9780763650889 (Candlewick); 9781406321180 (Walker & Co.)
LC 2010040794
"Davies and Layton turn to animal communication, describing how animals send and receive messages by sound, sight, smell and touch, for a variety of purposes. . . . Cartoonlike illustrations, almost doodles, done in ink and colored digitally, add humor to every page, even in the back-matter. They often include speech balloons demonstrating the animals' messages. . . . Something to crow about." Kirkus

Weill, Cynthia
Animal talk; Mexican folk art animal sounds in English and Spanish. Cynthia Weill. Cinco Puntos Press 2016 32 p. color illustrations (hardback) $14.95
Grades: PreK K **591.59**
1. Folk art 2. Animal sounds 3. Animals in art 4. Folk art -- Mexico -- Oaxaca (State)
ISBN 194102632X; 9781941026328
LC 2015024954
This children's book, by Cynthia Weill, asks "dd you know that animals that live in one country don't always talk the same language as animals from somewhere else? Take a rooster, for instance. In English-speaking countries, he says cock-a-doodle-doo when he has a notion to announce himself or to greet the dawn. But in Spanish-speaking countries, he says ki-kiri-ki. The bilingual text invites parent and child into an interactive and playful reading experience." (Publisher's note)
"This interactive picture book is sure to be a young crowd-pleaser and storytime favorite." SLJ
Mexican folk art animal sounds in English and Spanish

591.594 Acoustical communication

Stewart, Melissa
Can an aardvark bark? Melissa Stewart; illustrated by Steve Jenkins. Beach Lane Books 2017 32 p. color illustrations (hardcover : alk. paper) $17.99
Grades: PreK K 1 2 **591.594**
1. Animal sounds 2. Animal communication
ISBN 9781481458528
LC 2016036557
In this book, by Melissa Stewart, illustrated by Steve Jenkins, "animals make all kinds of sounds to communicate and express themselves. With a growling salamander and a whining porcupine, bellowing giraffes and laughing gorillas, this boisterous book is chock-full of fun and interesting facts and is sure to be a favorite of even the youngest animal enthusiasts." (Publisher's note)
Includes bibliographical references and index

591.6 Miscellaneous nontaxonomic kinds of animals

Claybourne, Anna
100 deadliest things on the planet. Scholastic 2012 112 p. $7.99
Grades: 4 5 6 **591.6**
1. Tsunamis 2. Volcanoes 3. Animal attacks 4. Animal behavior 5. Natural disasters
ISBN 0545434378; 9780545434379
This book by Anna Claybourne looks at Earth's deadliest animals and natural disasters. "There are animals that can use an arsenal of deadly weapons--teeth, claws, stinging spines, powerful pincers, or scary

suckers--to fight, hunt, or defend themselves. There are natural disasters--from towering tsunamis to massive volcanic eruptions--that can destroy whole cities in the blink of an eye." The book "includes side panels, a 'deadly factor' rating, and photos throughout." (Publisher's note)

Davies, Nicola, 1958-
What's eating you? parasites--the inside story. [by] Nicola Davies; illustrated by Neal Layton. Candlewick Press 2007 60p il $12.99
Grades: 3 4 5 6   **591.6**
1. Parasites
ISBN 978-0-7636-3460-5; 0-7636-3460-3
LC 2007-25634
"Davies uses a conversational approach to introduce readers to those weird critters that consider their host to be 'just a pantry.' . . . The subject is inherently fascinating for kids and those who settle into read will find a good deal of information about some of the more familiar parasites. . . . The artwork adds a welcome comic veneer." Booklist

Graham, Ian
Microscopic scary creatures; written by Ian Graham; created and designed by David Salariya. Franklin Watts 2009 32p il (Scary creatures) lib bdg $26; pa $8.95
Grades: 3 4 5   **591.6**
1. Protozoa 2. Parasites 3. Microorganisms
ISBN 978-0-531-21673-6 lib bdg; 0-531-21673-X lib bdg; 978-0-531-21044-4 pa; 0-531-21044-8 pa
LC 2009-11224
This defines microscopic creatures and describes their habitats and life cycles, and their relationships to humans.
This title has "two-page chapters of accessible, large-type text and bright color photos and illustrations. . . . The series distinguishes itself with 'X-Ray Vision.' When readers hold the page with this prompt up to the light, an image emerges. The X-rays mostly show the skeletal structures of the animals. Text boxes throughout add to the visual appeal. . . . [This title is an] excellent [resource] for school assignments and browsing." SLJ
Includes glossary

Jenkins, Steve
★ **Never** smile at a monkey; and 17 other important things to remember. Houghton Mifflin Books for Children 2009 un il $16
Grades: 1 2 3 4   **591.6**
1. Dangerous animals
ISBN 978-0-618-96620-2; 0-618-96620-X
LC 2009-32964
"A visually stunning book illustrated with cut paper and torn collages. . . . This superlative illustrator has given children yet another work that educates and amazes." SLJ

Racanelli, Marie
Albino animals. PowerKids Press 2010 24p il (Crazy nature) lib bdg $21.25; pa $8.25
Grades: 2 3 4 5   **591.6**
1. Albinos and albinism 2. Animals -- Color
ISBN 978-1-4358-9381-8 lib bdg; 1-4358-9381-6 lib bdg; 978-1-4358-9854-7 pa; 1-4358-9854-0 pa
This explains why different types of animals are born without skin pigmentation and about the challenges they must face in their natural environments
This book "combines attention-grabbing information with a well-organized format. . . . [The book has] spectacular color photography and eye-popping facts. . . . Excellent for reports." SLJ

Stewart, Melissa
Deadliest animals. National Geographic 2011 48p il (National Geographic readers) lib bdg $11.90; pa $3.99
Grades: K 1 2 3   **591.6**
1. Dangerous animals
ISBN 978-1-4263-0758-4 lib bdg; 1-4263-0758-6 lib ed; 978-1-4263-0757-7 pa; 1-4263-0757-8 pa
LC 2011284182
This describes 12 dangerous species including sharks, snakes, jellyfish, bears, tigers and mosquitoes.
"Vivid nature photos show the deadly creatures in action. Silly jokes . . . and . . . sidebars maintain readers' attention." Horn Book Guide

591.68 Rare and endangered animals

Allgor, Marie
Endangered desert animals; by Marie Allgor; edited by Jennifer Way. PowerKids Press 2013 24 p. col. ill. (Save Earth's animals!) (library) $22.60; (paperback) $8.25
Grades: 1 2 3   **591.68**
1. Desert animals 2. Desert ecology 3. Endangered species 4. Wildlife conservation
ISBN 9781448874231; 9781448874965
LC 2011051875
This book on endangered desert animals by Marie Allgor is part of the "Save the Earth's Animals!" series. "Before launching into the individual creatures, the title explores the region's climate and the various habitats: shrubs, cacti, and so on. The five featured animals are the slender-horned gazelle, the Egyptian vulture. Nelson's antelope squirrel, the Bactrian camel, and the desert tortoise." (Booklist)
Includes bibliographical references (p. 24) and index

Barry, Frances
Let's save the animals; a flip-the-flap book. Candlewick Press 2010 un il $12.99
Grades: PreK K   **591.68**
1. Endangered species 2. Wildlife conservation
ISBN 978-0-7636-4501-4; 0-7636-4501-X
LC 2009-22117
"Barry's engaging entry brings young children into the conversation [about wildlife conservation] without sacrificing an ounce of kid appeal. Sporting a rounded cover, sturdy pages, and inventive die-cut flaps, this primer presents 10 endangered species in their natural habitats. . . . Barry's superb, colorful paper-collage illustrations feature close-ups of friendly looking animals." Booklist

Jenkins, Martin
★ **Can** we save the tiger? illustrated by Vicky White. Candlewick Press 2011 50p il $16.99
Grades: 1 2 3   **591.68**
1. Tigers 2. Extinct animals 3. Wildlife conservation 4. Extinction (Biology)
ISBN 0763649090; 9780763649098; 978-0-7636-4909-8; 0-7636-4909-0
LC 2010008899
Boston Globe-Horn Book Honor: Nonfiction (2011)
"Magnificent artwork and a careful balance of good and bad news are the strengths of this examination of endangered species. . . . Conversational text . . . explains difficult nuances of politics and sociology with verve. White's animals—meticulously drafted and shaded with the subtlest of earth tones—could almost walk off the page. The book's large trim size allows the inclusion of many sketches of creatures in a variety

of positions, while intelligent design and typography decisions make each page worth lingering over. An excellent resource." Publ Wkly

McKenna, Virginia

★ **Counting** lions; Portraits from the Wild. by Virginia McKenna, illustrated by Steven Walton. Candlewick Press 2015 40 p. illustrations $22

Grades: 5 6 7 8   **591.68**

    1. Animals 2. Counting

    ISBN 9780763682071

LC 2014957760

This book, by Virginia McKenna, illustrated by Steven Walton, is a "spectacular, visually stunning celebration of wildlife—and gentle counting book—that can be enjoyed by the entire family. Exquisite charcoal drawings of ten endangered creatures—lions, elephants, giraffes, pandas, tigers, chimpanzees, penguins, turtles, macaws, and zebras—startle the viewer with their size and astonishing detail." (Publisher's note)

"It's beautifully executed, but it will be a devil to shelve, and it's hard to see many families adopting it for the coffee table." Kirkus

591.7 Animal ecology, animals characteristic of specific environments

Barnhill, Kelly Regan

    Monsters of the deep; deep sea adaptation. by Kelly Regan Barnhill. Capstone Press 2008 32p il (Fact finders. Extreme life) lib bdg $22.60

Grades: 2 3 4   **591.7**

    1. Ocean bottom 2. Marine animals

    ISBN 978-1-4296-1264-7 lib bdg; 1-4296-1264-9 lib bdg

LC 2007-20897

This reveals "the world of deep-sea creatures. A conversational text explains how the animals have adapted to the incredible depth and darkness of the ocean's 'midnight zone.' Readers will be fascinated—or terrified—by the unusual-looking fish." Horn Book Guide

Includes glossary and bibliographical references

Bateman, Donna M.

    Deep in the swamp; [by] Donna M. Bateman; illustrated by Brian Lies. Charlesbridge 2007 un il lib bdg $15.95; pa $6.95

Grades: K 1 2 3   **591.7**

    1. Counting 2. Swamp animals

    ISBN 978-1-57091-596-3 lib bdg; 978-1-57091-597-0 pa

LC 2006009026

"This stunning book spotlights the flora and fauna of Florida's Okefenokee Swamp. . . . The text is a version of the familiar poem 'Over in the Meadow,' with impeccable meter. . . . Lie's meticulous and glowing acrylic illustrations feature myriad shades of green, yellow, and blue." SLJ

Carlson-Voiles, Polly

    Someone walks by; the wonders of winter wildlife. story and illustrations by Polly Carlson-Voiles. Raven Productions 2008 un il $18.95; pa $12.95

Grades: K 1 2 3   **591.7**

    1. Winter 2. Forest animals

    ISBN 978-0-9801045-5-4; 0-9801045-5-6; 978-0-9801045-6-1 pa; 0-9801045-6-4 pa

LC 2008036871

"Set in the northern woodland in winter, this picture book shows how a variety of animals adapt to the frigid, snowy environment. . . . Poetic metaphors, internal rhymes, and repeated sounds give a lyrical

tone to the prose. A typical double-page spread introduces several animals . . . in a few lines of text and two collage illustrations that combine cut papers into effective compositions enhanced with ink drawings and watercolors for details and patterns." Booklist

Downer, Ann

    Wild animal neighbors; sharing our urban world. Ann Downer. Twenty-First Century Books 2014 64 p. (library binding : alkaline paper) $33.27

Grades: 5 6 7 8   **591.7**

    1. Wildlife 2. Urban ecology 3. Suburban life 4. Urban animals 5. City and town life 6. Human-animal relationships 7. Nature -- Effect of human beings on

    ISBN 0761390219; 9780761390213

LC 2012043817

This book, by Ann Downer, explains that "as the human population tops seven billion, animals are running out of space. Their natural habitats are surrounded and sometimes even replaced by highways, shopping centers, office parks, and subdivisions. The result? A wildlife invasion of our urban neighborhoods. What kinds of animals are making cities their new home? How can they survive in our ecosystem of concrete, steel, and glass? And what does their presence there mean for their future and ours?" (Publisher's note)

"Although this book's editorial stance advocates for wild animals in city habitats, it's candid about problems such animals cause humans--from messy raccoons that may carry rabies to potentially dangerous mountain lions in Los Angeles. Accurate information unhampered by a rigid template and supported by good documentation is presented in readable, balanced prose; compelling photographs illustrate the text." (Horn Book)

Includes bibliographical references (page 62) and index

Himmelman, John

    Who's at the seashore? written and illustrated by John Himmelman. NorthWord Books 2009 un il $15.95

Grades: K 1   **591.7**

    1. Animal behavior 2. Seashore ecology

    ISBN 978-1-58979-387-3; 1-58979-387-0

LC 2008038264

"This quiet little book introduces some seaside creatures via a simple rhyming text and realistic illustrations. A ruddy turnstone uncovers a sand hopper, a watchful gull hits on the hopper, while a moon snail creates a sand collar to hold her eggs, and so on in a soft litany of beach denizens and their activities. Himmelman's larger-than-life watercolors spread across the facing pages, revealing not only the action described in the text, but also the participants in the next sequence." SLJ

Hodge, Deborah

    Desert animals; written by Deborah Hodge; illustrated by Pat Stephens. Kids Can Press 2008 24p il (Who lives here?) $14.95; pa $5.95

Grades: K 1 2 3   **591.7**

    1. Desert animals

    ISBN 978-1-55453-047-2; 1-55453-047-4; 978-1-55453-048-9 pa; 1-55453-048-2 pa

This introduces animals that are built for living in the extremes of deserts, including Elf owls, sand cats, and scorpions.

    Forest animals; written by Deborah Hodge; illustrated by Pat Stephens. Kids Can Press 2009 24p il (Who lives here?) $14.95; pa $5.95

Grades: K 1 2 3   **591.7**
1. Forest animals
ISBN 978-1-55453-070-0; 1-55453-070-9; 978-1-55453-071-7
pa; 1-55453-071-7 pa

"This mini-guide to creatures of the northern forest features one animal per spread. A brief introduction . . . includes facts about the animal's home, diet, young, unique features and abilities, and/or survival techniques. The text provides enough detail to engage readers without overwhelming them. Uncluttered design and finely crafted realistic illustrations are strengths." Horn Book Guide

Polar animals; written by Deborah Hodge; illustrated by Pat Stephens. Kids Can Press 2008 24p il (Who lives here?) $14.95; pa $5.95

Grades: K 1 2 3   **591.7**
1. Animals -- Arctic regions
ISBN 978-1-55453-043-4; 1-55453-043-1; 978-1-55453-044-1
pa; 1-55453-044-X pa

This book describes "the animal inhabitants of [the arctic region]. . . . Each double-page spread highlights a specific animal [and] . . . muted illustrations . . . effectively supplement and help explain the text." Horn Book Guide

Rain forest animals; written by Deborah Hodge; illustrated by Pat Stephens. Kids Can Press 2008 24p il (Who lives here?) $14.95; pa $5.95

Grades: K 1 2 3   **591.7**
1. Rain forest animals
ISBN 978-1-55453-041-0; 1-55453-041-5; 978-1-55453-042-7
pa; 1-55453-042-3 pa

This book describes "the animal inhabitants of [the rain forest]. . . . Each double-page spread highlights a specific animal [and] . . . muted illustrations . . . effectively supplement and help explain the text." Horn Book Guide

Savanna animals; written by Deborah Hodge; illustrated by Pat Stephens. Kids Can Press 2009 24p il (Who lives here?) $14.95; pa $5.95

Grades: K 1 2 3   **591.7**
1. Grassland ecology 2. Animals -- Africa
ISBN 978-1-55453-072-4; 1-55453-072-5; 978-1-55453-073-1
pa; 1-55453-073-3 pa

"This well-illustrated book introduces . . . readers to . . . animals that live in the African savanna. . . . Basic information about the elephant, wildebeest (aka, the gnu), giraffe, meerkat, zebra, black mamba (a snake), lion, and ostrich is presented to two-page spreads. . . . The highlight of the book is the excellent illustrations that complement the brief text." Sci Books Films

Wetland animals; written by Deborah Hodge; illustrated by Pat Stephens. Kids Can Press 2008 24p il (Who lives here?) $14.95; pa $5.95

Grades: K 1 2 3   **591.7**
1. Wetlands 2. Freshwater animals
ISBN 978-1-55453-045-8; 1-55453-045-8; 978-1-55453-046-5
pa; 1-55453-046-6 pa

Introduces the animals that are built for living in or on the water of swamps, ponds, bogs, and marshes, including hippos, moose, capybaras, and bullfrogs.

Jenkins, Steve
★ **Down**, down, down; a journey to the bottom of the sea. Houghton Mifflin Harcourt 2009 un il $17

Grades: 2 3 4 5   **591.7**
1. Ocean bottom 2. Marine animals
ISBN 978-0-618-96636-3; 0-618-96636-6
LC 2008-36082

"Starting at the surface of the Pacific Ocean, Jenkins introduces some of the animals that inhabit descending layers of water all the way down to the Marianas Trench. At nearly 36,000 feet, this zone has been visited only once, by human passengers of a research vessel. Depicted in Jenkins's signature handsome collages, the denizens of each level swim against ever-darkening backgrounds ranging from sunny blue to deepest black. . . . The repeated message that humans have much to explore and learn in the deeper ocean is intriguing and inviting. " SLJ

★ **How** to clean a hippopotamus; a look at unusual animal partnerships. [by] Steve Jenkins & Robin Page. Houghton Mifflin Books for Children 2010 un il lib bdg $16

Grades: K 1 2 3   **591.7**
1. Symbiosis
ISBN 978-0-547-24515-7 lib bdg; 0-547-24515-7 lib bdg
LC 2009-45452

This picture book "explores unexpected animal partnerships. . . . The spreads have an exciting, comics-inspired feel. Each page combines panels of multiple images, rendered in Jenkins' superbly crafted paper-collage style, with brief lines of concise, clear text and attention-grabbing headlines. . . . These fascinating stories from the natural world will easily interest young people." Booklist

★ **I** see a kookaburra! discovering animal habitats around the world. [by] Steve Jenkins & Robin Page. Houghton Mifflin Co. 2005 un il map $16

Grades: K 1 2 3   **591.7**
1. Animals 2. Habitat (Ecology)
ISBN 0-618-50764-7
LC 2004-13188

A pictorial introduction to desert, tide pool, jungle, savana, forest, and pond habitats, with examples of the animals that live in each

"Filled with vibrant colors and palpable textures, the illustrations are breathtaking and give a real sense of the vitality, diversity, and beauty of nature. A first-rate foray into ecology that will encourage readers to explore the world around them." SLJ

Includes bibliographical references

Johnson, Rebecca L.
★ **Journey** into the deep; discovering new ocean creatures. with a foreword by Sylvia A. Earle. Millbrook Press 2010 64p il lib bdg $31.93

Grades: 4 5 6 7   **591.7**
1. Ocean bottom 2. Marine animals 3. Scientific expeditions
ISBN 978-0-7613-4148-2 lib bdg; 0-7613-4148-X lib bdg
LC 2009049603

"This strikingly illustrated book takes its readers on a series of research voyages exploring the ocean from its shallow edges to unfathomable depths during the recently completed ten-year International Census of Marine Life. Clearly organized text and pictures combine to introduce newly discovered marine creatures of all kinds. . . . The excitement and challenge of discovery in tangible. Scientific photographs printed on blue-to-black background . . . illustrate animals mentioned in a nicely legible text. . . . Rich, revealing and rewarding." Kirkus

Includes glossary and bibliographical references

Lynette, Rachel
Who lives in a colorful coral reef? PowerKids Press 2011 24p il map (Exploring habitats) lib bdg $21.25; pa $8.25

Grades: 2 3   591.7
1. Animals 2. Coral reefs and islands
ISBN 978-1-4488-0677-5 lib bdg; 1-4488-0677-1 lib bdg; 978-1-4488-1281-3 pa; 1-4488-1281-X pa

LC 2009-54350

Presents the various types of animals that live in a coral reef, including sea anemones, sea stars, cleaner shrimp, clown fish, and sponges.
"Sharp color photographs provide visual interest. Text is arranged in photo caption boxes or is well divided into frames spaced between the photographs in a visually pleasing array. Loads of information is packed into fairly short sentences, containing vocabulary that can be easily read by second or third graders." Libr Media Connect
Includes glossary

Who lives in a deep, dark cave? PowerKids Press, 2011 24p il map (Exploring habitats) lib bdg $21.25; pa $8.25
Grades: 2 3   591.7
1. Caves 2. Animals 3. Cave dwellers
ISBN 978-1-4488-0676-8 lib bdg; 1-4488-0676-3 lib bdg; 978-1-4488-1277-6 pa; 1-4488-1277-1 pa
Introduces several types of animals that live in caves.
"Sharp color photographs provide visual interest. Text is arranged in photo caption boxes or is well divided into frames spaced between the photographs in a visually pleasing array. Loads of information is packed into fairly short sentences, containing vocabulary that can be easily read by second or third graders." Libr Media Connect
Includes glossary

Who lives in a wet, wild rain forest? PowerKids Press 2011 24p il map (Exploring habitats) lib bdg $21.25; pa $8.25
Grades: 2 3   591.7
1. Rain forest animals 2. Rain forest ecology
ISBN 978-1-4488-0678-2 lib bdg; 1-4488-0678-X lib bdg; 978-1-4488-1283-7 pa; 1-4488-1283-6 pa

LC 2010000423

Introduces some of the animals of rain forests and how they live.
"Sharp color photographs provide visual interest. Text is arranged in photo caption boxes or is well divided into frames spaced between the photographs in a visually pleasing array. Loads of information is packed into fairly short sentences, containing vocabulary that can be easily read by second or third graders." Libr Media Connect
Includes glossary

Who lives on a towering mountain? PowerKids Press 2010 24p il map (Exploring habitats) lib bdg $21.25; pa $8.25
Grades: 2 3   591.7
1. Mountain animals
ISBN 978-1-4488-0680-5 lib bdg; 1-4488-0680-1 lib bdg; 978-1-4488-1287-5 pa; 1-4488-1287-9 pa

LC 2010003466

Presents the various types of animals that live in the mountains, including snow leopards, bighorn sheep, elk, marmots, and mountain lions
"Sharp color photographs provide visual interest. Text is arranged in photo caption boxes or is well divided into frames spaced between the photographs in a visually pleasing array. Loads of information is packed into fairly short sentences, containing vocabulary that can be easily read by second or third graders." Libr Media Connect
Includes glossary

Who lives on the icy, cold tundra. PowerKids Press 2011 24p il map (Exploring habitats) lib bdg $21.25; pa $8.25

Grades: 2 3   591.7
1. Animals 2. Tundra ecology
ISBN 978-1-4488-0675-1 lib bdg; 1-4488-0675-5 lib bdg; 978-1-4488-1279-0 pa; 1-4488-1279-8 pa

LC 2009-54351

Presents the various types of animals that live on the tundra, including polar bears, the arctic fox, the giant petrel, the emperor penguin, and musk oxen.
"Sharp color photographs provide visual interest. Text is arranged in photo caption boxes or is well divided into frames spaced between the photographs in a visually pleasing array. Loads of information is packed into fairly short sentences, containing vocabulary that can be easily read by second or third graders." Libr Media Connect
Includes glossary

Miller, Debbie S.
Survival at 120 above; by Debbie S. Miller; illustrations by Job Van Zyle. Walker & Co. 2012 40 p. col. ill. (hardback) $17.99; (reinforced) $18.89
Grades: 3 4 5   591.7
1. Animals 2. Climate 3. Desert animals 4. Adaptation (Biology) 5. Desert animals -- Australia -- Simpson Desert 6. Desert ecology -- Australia -- Simpson Desert 7. Heat adaptation -- Australia -- Simpson Desert
ISBN 0802798136; 9780802798138; 9780802798145

LC 2011021943

Author Deborah S. Miller "records a day in the life of . . . Australia's Simpson Desert . . . as birds, mammals, reptiles, amphibians, insects and plants revel in the glory of water and relative coolness of the world's longest parallel sand dunes. . . . The book introduces young readers to many animals children have likely never seen nor heard of and helps them understand the . . . ways in which animals and other life-forms have adapted to this extreme climate. . . . [P]ronunciation guides are incorporated within the text." (Kirkus Reviews)
Includes bibliographical references.

Survival at 40 below; illustrations by Jon Van Zyle. Walker & Co. 2010 un il $17.99; lib bdg $18.89
Grades: 2 3 4   591.7
1. Animals -- Arctic regions 2. Natural history -- Alaska
ISBN 978-0-8027-9815-2; 0-8027-9815-2; 978-0-8027-9816-9 lib bdg; 0-8027-9816-0 lib bdg

LC 2009013328

"Miller describes the terrain of Alaska's Gates of the Arctic National Park and explains how the seasonal changes affect a diverse array of animals . . . that live in the area year-round. . . . The text moves smoothly and quickly, offering interesting glimpses of varied hibernation patterns and the physical characteristics enabling some animals to survive winter's deep chill aboveground. . . . Van Zyle's acrylic paintings span the spreads, offering good impressionistic views of varied landscapes and fauna." SLJ

Miller, Sara Swan
Secret lives of burrowing beasts. Marshall Cavendish Benchmark 2010 48p il (Secret lives) lib bdg $29.93
Grades: 3 4 5 6   591.7
1. Burrowing animals
ISBN 978-0-7614-4221-9 lib bdg; 0-7614-4221-9 lib bdg
"The bright, sharp color photos . . . enhance, but take second fiddle to Miller's lively, well-knit [narrative]. . . . [This] volume closes with a generous selection of print and web resources." SLJ
Includes glossary

Secret lives of cave creatures. Marshall Cavendish Benchmark 2010 48p il (Secret lives) lib bdg $29.93

Grades: 3 4 5 6   **591.7**

1. Animals 2. Cave dwellers

ISBN 978-0-7614-4224-0 lib bdg; 0-7614-4224-3 lib bdg

"The bright, sharp color photos . . . enhance, but take second fiddle to Miller's lively, well-knit [narrative]. . . . [This] volume closes with a generous selection of print and web resources." SLJ

Includes glossary

Secret lives of deep-sea creatures. Marshall Cavendish Benchmark 2010 48p il (Secret lives) lib bdg $29.93

Grades: 3 4 5 6   **591.7**

1. Marine animals

ISBN 978-0-7614-4226-4 lib bdg; 0-7614-4226-X lib bdg

LC 2010000376

"The bright, sharp color photos . . . enhance, but take second fiddle to Miller's lively, well-knit [narrative]. . . . [This] volume closes with a generous selection of print and web resources." SLJ

Includes glossary

Secret lives of soil creatures. Marshall Cavendish Benchmark 2010 48p il (Secret lives) lib bdg $29.93

Grades: 3 4 5 6   **591.7**

1. Animals 2. Soil ecology

ISBN 978-0-7614-4229-5 lib bdg; 0-7614-4229-4 lib bdg

"The bright, sharp color photos . . . enhance, but take second fiddle to Miller's lively, well-knit [narrative]. . . . [This] volume closes with a generous selection of print and web resources." SLJ

Includes glossary

Mitton, Tony

Ocean odyssey; [illustrated by] Ant Parker. Kingfisher 2010 un il (Amazing animals) $9.99

Grades: K 1 2 3   **591.7**

1. Marine animals

ISBN 978-0-7534-3006-4; 0-7534-3006-1

"Three animal friends in human garb . . . explore the undersea world to introduce young readers to various animals in [that habitat]. The bouncy rhymed [text] and colorful cartoonlike illustrations, along with being entertaining, offer some surprisingly substantive facts about the creatures." Horn Book Guide

Rainforest romp; [by] Tony Mitton and [illustrated by] Ant Parker. Kingfisher 2009 un il (Amazing animals) $9.99 **591.7**

1. Rain forest animals

ISBN 978-0-7534-6298-0; 0-7534-6298-2

"In bouncy rhymes, Mitton describes animals that live in the rainforest. . . . Parker's vibrant cartoon illustrations show three animal friends, dressed in safari gear, exploring in the rainforest, along with the smiling creatures they encounter." Horn Book Guide

Parker, Steve, 1952-

Animal habitats. QEB Pub. 2010 32p il (QEB changes in . . .) lib bdg $28.50

Grades: 3 4 5 6   **591.7**

1. Habitat (Ecology)

ISBN 978-1-59566-773-1 lib bdg; 1-59566-773-3 lib bdg

LC 2008-56067

"Outstanding photography and informative summaries uniquely combine to make this text a must have for any elementary school library. . . . Short, succinct paragraphs and marginalia combine to appeal to readers of all ages and literary abilities. The author guides the juvenile reader through a series of environmental concerns such as the preservation of rare and endangered species, sustainability, overpopulation, biodiversity hot spots, conservation techniques, and introduced and invasive species." Sci Books Films

Includes glossary

Stewart, Melissa

Under the snow; written by Melissa Stewart; illustrated by Constance R. Bergum. Peachtree 2009 un il $16.95

Grades: K 1 2 3   **591.7**

1. Snow 2. Winter 3. Animal behavior

ISBN 978-1-56145-493-8; 1-56145-493-1

This describes how animals live under the snow in fields, forests, ponds, and wetlands

This is a "lyrical portrait. . . . Bergum's watercolor illustrations painted in panels suggest the passage of time and include close-up insets of wildlife in various habitats. . . . Many of the facts will wow children . . . and pique interest to read more." Booklist

When rain falls; written by Melissa Stewart; illustrated by Constance R. Bergum. Peachtree 2008 un il $16.95

Grades: PreK K 1 2   **591.7**

1. Rain 2. Animal behavior

ISBN 978-1-56145-438-9; 1-56145-438-9

LC 2007-31395

"After two children hurry inside to escape the rain, they gaze outdoors and wait for the end of the storm. Stewart elaborates on how various animals react to rain in different habitats: a forest, a field, a wetland, and a desert. The examples are clearly presented and interesting. . . . Bergum's well-rendered watercolors will facilitate group sharing." SLJ

Swinburne, Stephen R.

Ocean soup; tide pool poems. illustrated by Mary Peterson. Charlesbridge 2010 un il lib bdg $16.95

Grades: 1 2 3   **591.7**

1. Marine animals 2. Tide pool ecology 3. Animals -- Poetry

ISBN 978-1-58089-200-1 lib bdg; 1-58089-200-0 lib bdg

LC 2008026960

"This brightly illustrated, large-format book offers a collection of poems in the voices of tide-pool animals. . . . Each species is presented through first-person verse and a paragraph of information. . . . Clean, curving pencil lines with digitally added colors portray the animals in child-friendly, cartoon-style pictures." Booklist

Includes glossary and bibliographical references

Turner, Pamela S.

Prowling the seas; exploring the hidden world of ocean predators. Walker & Co. 2009 39p il map $17.99; lib bdg $18.89

Grades: 4 5 6   **591.7**

1. Ocean 2. Marine animals 3. Predatory animals

ISBN 978-0-8027-9748-3; 0-8027-9748-2; 978-0-8027-9749-0 lib bdg; 0-8027-9749-0 lib bdg

"In each chapter, a clearly delineated map makes it easy to follow the animals' routes, and many clear color photos show the animals and the scientists who study them. . . . A clearly written presentation of an unusual topic." Booklist

Webb, Sophie

Far from shore; a naturalist explores the deep ocean. written and illustrated by Sophie Webb. Houghton Mifflin Books for Children 2011 80p il $17.99

Grades: 4 5 6 7   **591.7**

1. Dolphins 2. Water birds 3. Marine animals

ISBN 978-0-618-59729-1; 0-618-59729-8

LC 2010025121

Webb "returns with another richly detailed journal of her travels as a naturalist, combining scientific information, field guide-like illustrations, and a thorough account of the day-to-day experiments of a field scientist. The setting is a four-month-long research cruise on a National Ocean and Atmospheric Administration ship to study the impact of fishing on two dolphin populations that reside in the Eastern Tropical Pacific." Horn Book

Includes glossary

591.734   Rain forest animals

Lawler, Janet

Rain Forest Colors; Janet Lawler; photographs by Tim Laman. Natl Geographic Soc Childrens books 2014 32 p. color illustrations, color map $16.99

Grades: PreK K 1 2 3   591.734

1. Color 2. Animals -- Color 3. Rain forest animals

ISBN 1426317336; 9781426317330

Janet Lawler presents "a color concept book [for children]. It features their favorite animals that illustrate 10 basic colors. Lyrical text is sprinkled with 'Did You Know?' animal facts. The photography is by National Geographic field biologist and wildlife photojournalist Tim Laman." (Publisher's note)

"Stunning animal photos introduce children to 10 basic colors in this latest from National Geographic Kids. From the brilliant blue Ulysses butterfly and yellow orb weaver spider to the scarlet ibis and purple honeycreeper, the colors of these animals are never in doubt, and the photos get readers so close that the scales on the iguana are visible, as are the hairs and bumps on the fiddler crab...Readers will not only practice their colors, they'll get an inkling of what a colorful and wonderful world we live in." Kirkus

Part of the National Geographic Kids series of informational picture books.

591.754   Desert animals

Pattison, Darcy

Desert baths; by Darcy Pattison; illustrated by Kathleen Rietz. Sylvan Dell Pub. 2012 32 p. (hardcover) $17.95

Grades: K 1 2 3 4   591.754

1. Baths 2. Animal behavior 3. Desert animals 4. Desert animals -- Habitat

ISBN 1607185253; 9781607185253; 9781607185345; 9781607185437; 9781607185529

LC 2012004377

In author Darcy Pattison's book, "all animals bathe to keep their bodies clean and healthy. Humans might use soap and water, but what do animals, especially those living in dry climates, do to keep clean?" This book explores "the desert to find out how snakes, spiders, and birds bathe. This . . . book teaches children about hygiene and how some exciting desert creatures manage to stay clean without the help of soap and water." (Publisher's note)

591.77   Marine animals

Arnosky, Jim

Shimmer & splash; the sparkling world of sea life. Jim Arnosky. Sterling Children's Books 2013 41 p. col. ill. (hardcover) $14.95

Grades: 2 3 4 5   591.77

1. Picture books for children 2. Marine biology 3. Marine animals

ISBN 1402786239; 9781402786235

LC 2012012863

In this book, author and illustrator Jim Arnosky explores life in the sea. With foldout pages and many life-size illustrations, this overview" touches "on sea life from coral reefs to sailfish, from sea jellies to fiddler crabs, all depicted in a . . . blues and greens with splashes of yellow." The text features "personal experiences as Arnosky wades, kayaks, boats, and fishes in the 'sparkling' world of water." (School Library Journal)

Includes bibliographical references (p. 41).

Fitzsimmons, David

Curious Critters; Marine. David FitzSimmons. Wild Iris Publishing 2015 32 p. color illustrations $16.95

Grades: K 1 2 3   591.77

1. Marine biology 2. Nature photography 3. Marine animals

ISBN 1936607727; 9781936607723

This book "features some of North America's most incredible marine animals captured through the award-winning photography of David FitzSimmons. The amazing photographs depict 20 common and fascinating animals of the Atlantic and Pacific Oceans, as well as the Gulf of Mexico." (Publisher's note)

"In his third Curious Critters book, FitzSimmons pairs breathtakingly detailed photographs of 20 aquatic creatures with offbeat accounts of the animals' lives, which take the form of poems, songs, and first-person monologues. . . . From a wisecracking sea cucumber to a frogfish trying to hide its predatory nature, FitzSimmons offers a cheeky guide to the sea's odder denizens." PW

Other titles in the series are:

Curious Critters (2011)

Curious Critters, Volume two (2014)

Curious Critters Michigan (2015)

Curious Critters Ohio (2015)

Greenwood, Marie

Amazing giant sea creatures; swim with the whales, dolphins, and sharks. written by Marie Greenwood; illustrated by Peter Minister. DK Publishing 2014 15 p. color illustrations $19.99

Grades: PreK K 1 2   591.77

1. Marine animals 2. Toy and movable books 3. Lift-the-flap books

ISBN 1465419012; 9781465419019

LC 2014395931

NSTA Outstanding Science Trade Books for Students K-12 (2015)

This preschool reference book "provides an introduction to the biggest creatures found in the ocean, including the lion's mane jellyfish, the great white shark, the sperm whale, and the giant squid." (Publisher's note)

Guiberson, Brenda Z., 1946-

The **most** amazing creature in the sea; Brenda Z. Guiberson; illustrated by Gennady Spirin. Henry Holt & Co. 2015 32 p. color illustrations (hardcover) $17.99

Grades: K 1 2 3 4   591.77

1. Marine animals 2. Marine biology

ISBN 0805099611; 9780805099614

LC 2014041224

This children's book by Brenda Z. Guiberson, illustrated by Gennady Spirin, asks "which sea creature is the greatest? Is it the one with the most venom, the greatest diver, the one with blue blood, or the best rotating eyes? Or is it the master of disguise, the one with the best light, the most slime, or the most eggs? Fascinating facts and spectacular illustrations will inspire young readers to choose their own favorite sea creatures!" (Publisher's note)

"Handsome, softly realistic illustrations depict an assortment of ocean dwellers, each accompanied by a brief paragraph full of interesting factoids as each creature proclaims itself "the most amazing creature in the sea." . . . An eye-catching jumping-off point for further investigation." SLJ

Hoyt, Erich

★ **Weird** sea creatures; Erich Hoyt. Firefly Books 2013 63 p. (pbk.) $9.95; (bound) $19.95

Grades: 5 6 7 8 9 10　　　　　　　　　　**591.77**

1. Marine biology 2. Abyssal zone 3. Deep-sea animals -- Pictorial works

ISBN 9781770851917; 1770851917; 1770851976; 9781770851979

LC 2012554415

This book celebrates "odd and recently discovered [undersea] species. Through 50 . . . photos, readers are introduced to a yeti crab; a spined pigmy shark; Dumbo, the octopod; and many other deep-sea dwellers." The introduction "presents the physical characteristics of the abyssal ocean—its cold darkness, its cruel pressure—and of the difficulties in finding, collecting, and photographing the creatures that call it home." (School Library Journal)

"Eerie, riveting eye candy for budding biologists and casual browsers alike." Kirkus

Rake, Matthew

Creatures of the deep; Matthew Rake; illustrated by Simon Mendez. Hungry Tomato 2016 32 p. color illustrations (pb : alk. paper) $7.99

Grades: 3 4 5 6　　　　　　　　　　　**591.77**

1. Marine biology 2. Aquatic animals 3. Marine animals 4. Dangerous marine animals

ISBN 1467776432; 9781467763608; 9781467776431

LC 2015014282

In this children's book by Matthew Rake, illustrated by Simon Mendez, readers will "encounter the ten strangest creatures living in the oceans, seas, and rivers. You'll discover a fish with an angling light, a snail that harpoons its prey, a squid with eyes bigger than a human head, and more. Come face to face with these extreme animals and learn their secrets!" (Publisher's note)

Roderick, Stacey

Ocean animals from head to tail; Stacey Roderick, illustrated by Kwanchai Moriya. Kids Can Press 2016 36 p. color illustrations $16.95

Grades: K 1 2 3　　　　　　　　　　　**591.77**

1. Fishes 2. Marine animals

ISBN 1771383453; 9781771383455

In this book about ocean animals in the Head to Tail series, by Stacey Roderick, illustrated by Kwanchai Moriya, "each subject is given two spreads: the question spread (for example, 'What ocean animal has a head like this?') is accompanied by a close-up illustration (for this example, the head of a hammerhead shark), with the next spread showing the reveal ('A hammerhead shark!') along with a paragraph explaining a bit about the particular creature." (School Library Journal)

"Enjoyable and interactive, this title is ideal for read-alouds, especially in the summer." SLJ

Woodward, John

Ocean; an amazing window on our world. written by John Woodward; illustrations by Gary Hanna. DK Pub. 2012 59 p. col. ill. (Look closer) (hardcover) $10.99

Grades: 4 5 6　　　　　　　　　　　**591.77**

1. Picture books for children 2. Ocean 3. Marine biology 4. Marine animals

ISBN 0756692377; 9780756692377

LC 2011277622

This book is part of DK Publishing's Look Closer series and allows readers to "explore different perspectives of . . . underwater scenes as they zoom in, zoom out, and go sideways, forward, and backward. . . . Specially commissioned computer-generated imagery" is included. (Publisher's note)

Shark wars; John Woodward, illustrated by Simon Mendez. Ticktock Books 2015 79 p. color illustrations (hardcover) $12.99

Grades: 3 4 5　　　　　　　　　　　**591.77**

1. Marine animals

ISBN 9781783251483; 1783251484

This juvenile book, by John Woodward, illustrated by Simon Mendez, part of the publisher's "Animal Wars" series, explores conflicts between marine creatures. "Would a giant squid stand a chance against a whopping whale? Which is the deadliest shark in the world? We all know the ocean can be dangerous but what kind of creatures are really lurking in the deep and who would come out on top in a battle of tentacles, teeth and traps?" (Publisher's note)

592　Specific taxonomic groups of animals

Dixon, Norma

Lowdown on earthworms. Fitzhenry & Whiteside 2005 32p il $16.95

Grades: 3 4 5　　　　　　　　　　　**592**

1. Worms

ISBN 1-55041-114-8

"This project-oriented study combines basic facts about worm anatomy and behavior with general instructions for building, maintaining, and performing simple experiments with both a 'plastic-bottle wormery'; and a more ambitious compost bin. A mix of color photos and simple paintings offer cutaways views of worms and their burrows, representations of several types of earthworms, and pictures of finished projects." Booklist

Includes bibliographical references

Pfeffer, Wendy

Wiggling worms at work; illustrated by Steve Jenkins. HarperCollins Publishers 2004 33p il (Let's-read-and-find-out science) $15.99; lib bdg $16.89; pa $4.99

Grades: K 1 2 3　　　　　　　　　　　**592**

1. Worms

ISBN 0-06-028448-X; 0-06-028449-8 lib bdg; 0-06-445199-2 pa

"This book is filled with clear explanations. . . . The concluding activities . . . are important because Jenkins's cut-paper illustrations, while lovely, include only a few anatomical details." Horn Book Guide

592.3　Worms

Murray, Laura K.

Worms; Laura Murray. Creative Education 2015 32 p. chiefly color illustrations (hardcover : alk. paper) $28.50

Grades: PreK K 1　　　　　　　　　　**592.3**

1. Worms

ISBN 1608185850; 9781608185856

LC 2014034724

This juvenile book, by Laura Murray, part of the "Seedlings" series, offers "a kindergarten-level introduction to worms, covering their growth process, behaviors, the ground they call home, and such defining features as their bands." (Publisher's note)

"On a double-page spread, the content might be as minimal as a single photo with a two-word sentence or as lengthy as three sentences, but children will learn from the clearly reproduced pictures as well as the limited texts." Booklist

Includes bibliographical references and index

592.66   Leeches

Marsico, Katie
  Leeches; by Katie Marsico. Children's Press, an imprint of Scholastic Inc. 2016 48 p. color illustrations (library binding : alk. paper) $28
  Grades: 3 4 5 6   **592.66**
    1. Leeches
    ISBN 0531213943; 0531214974; 9780531213940;
  9780531214978
                                                        LC 2014046960
  This children's book, by Katie Marsico, part of the "Nature's Children" series, profiles leeches. "These additions to this ongoing series follow a tried-and-true format: text on one page facing a full-page photo. An opening 'Fact File' breaks down info such as taxonomy, habits, habitats, and diets and provides a preview for the information that will be covered.... [And] the first chapter depicts an encounter with the animal and describes a typical behavior." (School Library Journal)

"With more than 700 species, readers will learn about blood-sucking and nonparasitic varieties and their role in human medicine." Booklist

Includes bibliographical references (page 46) and index

593.4   Sponges

Coldiron, Deborah
  Sea sponges; by Deborah Coldiron. ABDO Pub. 2008 32p il (Underwater world) lib bdg $24.21
  Grades: 2 3 4   **593.4**
    1. Sponges
    ISBN 978-1-59928-812-3 lib bdg; 1-59928-812-5 lib bdg
                                                        LC 2007-17851
  "Present[s] basic information about [sea sponges].... Vibrant captioned photos enhance the accessible text." Horn Book Guide
  Includes glossary

593.5   Coelenterates

Gish, Melissa
  Jellyfish; Melissa Gish. Creative Education 2015 46 p. color ill., color map (hardcover : alk. paper) $39.95
  Grades: 4 5 6   **593.5**
    1. Jellyfishes
  ISBN 1608185680; 9781608185689
                                                        LC 2014028017
  This book, by Melissa Gish, presents "a look at jellyfish, including their habitats, physical characteristics such as their bells, behaviors, relationships with humans, and their overabundance in the world today." (Publisher's note)

"Stunning photographs, sidebars with intriguing facts, and engaging prose are hallmarks of this set, and the chapters describing each creature's role in folklore or pop culture add to the fun." SLJ

Includes bibliographical references and index

Metz, Lorijo
  Discovering jellyfish. PowerKids Press 2011 24p il (Along the shore) lib bdg $21.25
  Grades: 3 4 5   **593.5**
    1. Jellyfishes
    ISBN 978-1-4488-4997-0; 1-4488-4997-7
                                                        LC 2011000159
  This book about jellyfish "briefly describes the major physical and behavioral characteristics common to all [jellyfish] and one or two distinctive characteristics of about a half dozen species.... One or two sharp color photographs of representative species, most of which are close-ups, accompany the text on every page.... [This is] well organized and smoothly written in an engaging style." SLJ

Includes glossary

Spilsbury, Louise
  Jellyfish. Heinemann Library 2010 24p il (A day in the life. sea animals) lib bdg $22; pa $6.49
  Grades: 1 2   **593.5**
    1. Jellyfishes
    ISBN 978-1-4329-4000-3 lib bdg; 1-4329-4000-7 lib bdg; 978-1-4329-4007-2 pa; 1-4329-4007-4 pa
                                                        LC 2010000624
  Introduces jellyfish, describing their physical characteristics, feeding habits, senses, and defense mechanisms.

This pairs "well-chosen color photos . . . with one or two sentences of simple commentary for each.... [Though this title] includes references to several varieties of the chosen creature, one species in particular is highlighted.... [Good choice] for pleasure or purpose reading." SLJ

Includes glossary and bibliographical references

593.6   Anthozoa

Collard, Sneed B.
  ★ One night in the Coral Sea; [by] Sneed B. Collard III; illustrated by Robin Brickmann. Charlesbridge 2005 32p il $15.95; pa $6.95
  Grades: 3 4 5   **593.6**
    1. Corals 2. Coral reefs and islands
    ISBN 1-57091-389-7; 1-57091-390-0 pa
                                                        LC 2004-3307
  "On a single spring night . . . the coral in the Great Barrier Reef releases millions of eggs into the ocean.... Collard explains the unique spawning event and provides some background about coral and the sea creatures that share the reef.... Whether or not children understand the specifics of fertilization, they will be captivated by Brickman's realistic, astonishingly detailed colored-paper collages of the brilliant underwater world." Booklist

Includes glossary and bibliographical references

593.9   Echinoderms and hemichordates

Halfmann, Janet
  Star of the sea; a day in the life of a starfish. illustrated by Joan Paley. H. Holt 2011 un il $16.99

Grades: K 1 2 3   **593.9**
1. Starfishes
ISBN 978-0-8050-9073-4; 0-8050-9073-8
LC 2010024952

"Simple, elegant text allows readers to follow a female ochre sea star as she comes ashore during high tide, finds and eats mussels, and is herself seized by a gull, escaping with only one ray lost. Accurate information is nicely embedded in the lyrical narration, while rich-hued watercolor collages . . . give both large-scale and close-up views." Horn Book Guide

Includes bibliographical references

Meister, Cari
Sea stars; by Cari Meister. Bullfrog Books 2012 24 p. (hardcover) $25.65

Grades: K 1 2 3   **593.9**
1. Starfishes
ISBN 1620310120; 9781620310120
LC 2012008430

This book, by author Cari Meister, presents a "photo-illustrated nonfiction story for young readers [that] describes the body parts of sea stars and how they are adapted to find food in the ocean. Picture glossaries introduce new vocabulary and simple quizzes and activities [to] help solidify comprehension." (Publisher's note)

Includes bibliographical references (p. 24) and index

Metz, Lorijo
Discovering starfish. PowerKids Press 2011 24p il (Along the shore) lib bdg $21.25

Grades: 3 4 5   **593.9**
1. Starfishes
ISBN 978-1-4488-4996-3; 1-4488-4996-9
LC 2011000152

This book about starfish "briefly describes the major physical and behavioral characteristics common to all [starfish] and one or two distinctive characteristics of about a half dozen species. . . . One or two sharp color photographs of representative species, most of which are closeups, accompany the text on every page. . . . [This is] well organized and smoothly written in an engaging style." SLJ

594   Mollusks and molluscoids

Bodden, Valerie
Slugs; Valerie Bodden. Creative Education 2013 24 p. col. ill. (library) $25.65

Grades: 1 2 3 4   **594**
1. Picture books for children 2. Slugs (Mollusks)
ISBN 1608182339; 9781608182336
LC 2011050283

This book is part of the Creepy Creatures series by Valerie Bodden. The series uses "clear white backgrounds to showcase . . . magnified photos, while the simple, educational text is . . . arranged around the page." This entry looks at slugs, discussing "the slimy textures and spotted patterns of this mollusk, which are hermaphroditic and can produce from 20 to 100 eggs each." (Booklist)

Includes bibliographical references and index

Campbell, Sarah C.
★ Wolfsnail; a backyard predator. photographs by Sarah C. Campbell and Richard P. Campbell. Boyds Mills Press 2008 32p il $16.95

Grades: PreK K 1 2   **594**
1. Snails
ISBN 978-1-59078-554-6; 1-59078-554-1
LC 2007-30838

A Geisel Award honor book, 2009

"The tiny wolfsnail eats garden snails and slugs. This dramatic photo-essay . . . shows the predator stalking its prey, . . . eating it, and leaving the empty shell behind. The back matter includes a small photo of the tiny wolfsnail at its true size and lots of fascinating facts about where snails live, how they mate, and more." Booklist

Cerullo, Mary M.
Giant squid; searching for a sea monster. by Mary M. Cerullo with Clyde F.E. Roper. Capstone Press 2012 48 p. ill. (chiefly col.) (Smithsonian) (library) $26.86; (paperback) $8.95

Grades: 4 5 6   **594**
1. Giant squids
ISBN 1429680237; 9781429675413; 9781429680233
LC 2011029181

This book "recounts some of the legends and historical clues that led to the giant squid's identification in the 19th century before focusing on Dr. Clyde Roper, a renowned specialist on cephalopods. . . . The text describes how Roper gathered facts by autopsying the carcasses of giant squids and sperm whales (its chief predator), examining other squid species, etc.; it also outlines several expeditions he led in search of a live specimen." (School Library Journal)

Gilpin, Daniel
★ Snails, shellfish & other mollusks; by Daniel Gilpin. Compass Point Books 2006 48 p. (Animal kingdom classification)

Grades: 4 5 6   **594**
1. Snails. 2. Mollusks. 3. Shellfish.
ISBN 0-7565-1613-7 (hard cover)
LC 2005029182

"...Smoothly written, well-organized...With succinct texts and colorful formats, [this] will appeal to students and browsers alike." SLJ

Includes bibliographical references

Gray, Susan Heinrichs
Giant African snail. Cherry Lake Pub. 2009 32p il map (Animal invaders) lib bdg $27.07

Grades: 3 4 5   **594**
1. Snails 2. Biological invasions
ISBN 978-1-60279-241-8 lib bdg; 1-60279-241-0 lib bdg
LC 2008000803

Looks at the qualities of giant African snails and examines how they became an invasive species in many of the world's tropical and subtropical regions, how they cause problems in their new environments, and the ways that people have attempted to deal with them

"Clear color photographs, most of which are closeups, accompany the [text] on about every other page. . . . [This title provides] report writers with in-depth and up-to-date information on these invaders and the serious problems they cause." SLJ

Includes glossary and bibliographical references

Metz, Lorijo
Discovering clams. PowerKids Press 2011 24p il (Along the shore) lib bdg $21.25

Grades: 3 4 5   **594**
1. Clams
ISBN 978-1-4488-4994-9; 1-4488-4994-2
LC 2011000158

This book about clams "briefly describes the major physical and behavioral characteristics common to all [clams] and one or two distinctive characteristics of about a half dozen species. . . . One or two sharp color photographs of representative species, most of which are closeups, accompany the text on every page. . . . [This is] well organized and smoothly written in an engaging style." SLJ

Miller, Sara Swan

Secret lives of seashell dwellers. Marshall Cavendish Benchmark 2010 48p il (Secret lives) lib bdg $29.93

Grades: 3 4 5 6   **594**

1. Mollusks

ISBN 978-0-7614-4228-8 lib bdg; 0-7614-4228-6 lib bdg

LC 2010000377

"The bright, sharp color photos . . . enhance, but take second fiddle to Miller's lively, well-knit [narrative]. . . . [This] volume closes with a generous selection of print and web resources." SLJ

Includes glossary

Montgomery, Sy

The **Octopus** Scientists; exploring the mind of a mollusk. written by Sy Montgomery; photographs by Keith Ellenbogen. Houghton Mifflin Harcourt 2015 80 p. illustrations (chiefly color) $18.99

Grades: 5 6 7 8 9   **594**

1. Octopuses 2. Marine biology 3. Octopuses -- Research -- French Polynesia -- Morea

ISBN 0544232704; 9780544232709

This book by Sy Montogomery and illustrated by Keith Ellenborgen, "an inquiry into the mind of an intelligent invertebrate, is also a foray into our own unexplored planet. With three hearts and blue blood, its gelatinous body unconstrained by jointed limbs or gravity, the octopus seems to be an alien, an inhabitant of another world. But most intriguing of all, octopuses--classed as mollusks, like clams--are remarkably intelligent with quirky personalities." (Publisher's note)

"Amazing photographs reveal the octopuses' remarkable shape-changing abilities and help readers visualize this experience. Science in the field at its best." Kirkus

Newquist, H. P.

Here there be monsters; the legendary kraken and the giant squid. Houghton Mifflin Harcourt 2010 73p il map $18

Grades: 4 5 6 7   **594**

1. Squids

ISBN 978-0-547-07678-2; 0-547-07678-9

"This intriguing book offers a chronological account of giant squids, beginning with sailors' tales about krakens and leading up to the ground-breaking discoveries of the past few decades. . . . The many illustrations, in color when available, include photos, engravings, and maps. . . . An attractive, informative book on an underrepresented topic." Booklist

Owens, L. L.

The **life** cycle of a snail. Child's World 2011 il (Life cycles) $27.07

Grades: K 1 2 3   **594**

1. Snails

ISBN 978-1-60973-191-5; 1-60973-191-3

"The life cycle of a snail is divided as follows: egg, hatchling, and adult. With big, clear full-page photos . . . as well as straightforward text, readers can follow along on the slimy journey from egg to snail. . . . This title features beautiful photos and text simple enough for very young gastropod lovers." Booklist

Rand, Casey

Glass squid and other spectacular squid. Raintree 2011 32p il (Creatures of the deep) lib bdg $29; pa $7.99

Grades: 3 4 5 6   **594**

1. Squids

ISBN 978-1-4109-4194-7 lib bdg; 978-1-4109-4201-2 pa

LC 2010038186

"This informative and colorful series will engage younger children to learn more about the sea and its creatures." Library Media Connection

Includes glossary and bibliographical references

Redmond, Shirley-Raye

Tentacles! tales of the giant squid. illustrated by Bryn Barnard. Random House 2003 44p il (Step into reading) $11.99; pa $3.99

Grades: 1 2 3   **594**

1. Squids

ISBN 0-375-91307-6; 0-375-81307-1 pa

LC 2002-10238

Describes some of the exaggerated stories that have been told about giant squids and also what scientists have learned about their real physical characteristics and behavior

"An excellent choice to introduce early elementary students to nonfiction titles." Booklist

Spilsbury, Louise

Octopus. Heinemann Library 2011 24p il (A day in the life. sea animals) lib bdg $22; pa $6.49

Grades: 1 2   **594**

1. Octopuses

ISBN 978-1-4329-4004-1 lib bdg; 1-4329-4004-X lib bdg; 978-1-4329-4011-9 pa; 1-4329-4011-2 pa

LC 2010000922

This explores how an octopus swims, defends itself, hunts, and sleeps.

This pairs "well-chosen color photos . . . with one or two sentences of simple commentary for each. . . . [Though this title] includes references to several varieties of the chosen creature, one species in particular is highlighted. . . . [Good choice] for pleasure or purpose reading." SLJ

Includes glossary and bibliographical references

Waxman, Laura Hamilton

Let's look at snails. Lerner Publications Company 2010 32p il (Lightning bolt books: Animal close-ups) lib bdg $25.26

Grades: PreK K 1 2   **594**

1. Snails

ISBN 978-0-8225-7899-4 lib bdg; 0-8225-7899-9 lib bdg

LC 2007-29226

Introduces snails, describing their physical characteristics, life cycle, habitat, and predators

"Fresh photography, a creative use of graphics, and a collagelike layout make[s] . . . [this book] eye-catching. . . . [The] book ends with a labeled diagram of the animal, a range map, and a further-reading list that includes print and online resources in a single list, a nice way of validating both types of materials." SLJ

Includes glossary

594.56   Octopuses

Jackson, Ellen

Octopuses one to ten; Ellen Jackson; illustrated by Robin Page. Beach Lane Books 2016 32 p. color illustrations (hardcover : alk. paper) $17.99

Grades: PreK K 1 2   **594.56**

1. Counting 2. Octopuses

ISBN 148143182X; 9781481431828

LC 2015043351

In this counting book, by Ellen Jackson, illustrated by Robin Page, "everyone knows octopuses have eight arms. But did you know that they have three hearts and nine brains? This intriguing exploration of octopuses goes through numbers one to ten, with a snappy rhyme and fascinating octopus facts for each number. The book also includes octopus crafts and activities for more learning fun!" (Publisher's note)

"An appealing introduction for preschool and storytime." Kirkus

Includes bibliographical references and index

594.58　Decapoda

Fleming, Candace

★ Giant squid; written by Candace Fleming, illustrated by Eric Rohmann. Roaring Brook Press 2016 40 p. color illustrations (hardcover) $18.99

Grades: 1 2 3 4　　　　　　　　　　　　　　　**594.58**

1. Giant squids

ISBN 1596435992; 9781596435995

LC 2015038610

Sibert Honor Book (2017)

"The giant squid is one of the most elusive creatures in the world. As large as whales, they hide beyond reach deep within the sea, forcing scientists to piece together their story from those clues they leave behind, . . . until a giant squid was finally filmed in its natural habitat only two years ago." (Publisher's note)

"The artwork is marvelous; the murky blues and blacks of the ocean make it easy to appreciate how hard it has been for scientists and sailors to see the elusive squid. . . . A diagram of the squid's anatomy, a bibliography, and an explanation of the ways scientists literally piece together information about squids from body parts that wash ashore follow the main text." Horn Book

Includes bibliographic references

595　Arthropods

Frost, Helen, 1896-1986

Among a Thousand Fireflies; Helen Frost; illustrated by Rick Lieder. Candlewick Press 2016 32 p. color illustrations $15.99

Grades: PreK K 1 2 3　　　　　　　　　　　　　　**595**

1. Summer 2. Fireflies

ISBN 076367642X; 9780763676421

LC 2015937121

In this book, by Helen Frost and illustrated by Rick Lieder, "on a summer evening, just as the stars blink on, a firefly lands on a flower. Lights start to flash all around her -- first one, then three, seven. Hundreds. Thousands. How will she find just one flash among them? And will he see her flash in return?" (Publisher's note)

"The blend of science, gentle poetry, and spectacular photography will make children long for a warm summer night perfect for firefly gazing." Horn Book

Reynolds, Toby

Insects and spiders. Barron's Educational Series 2016 32 p. color illustrations (paperback) $6.99

Grades: 4 5 6 7　　　　　　　　　　　　　　　**595**

1. Insects 2. Spiders

ISBN 1438008279; 9781438008271

LC 2015956068

In this children's book by Toby Reynolds and illustrated by Paul Calver, part of the Visual Explorers series, "engaging text, detailed facts, and impressive statistics give children exciting scientific insight into the world of insects and spiders. A glossary at the end of the book helps reinforce the information. Parents, teachers, and librarians will want to collect all of the books in this series to create a very cool first encyclopedia to build early research skills." *(Publisher's note)

"Inexpensive and relatively sturdy, these large-format paperbacks make for a visually enticing series." Booklist

595.3　Crustaceans

Gilpin, Daniel

Lobsters, crabs & other crustaceans; by Daniel Gilpin. Compass Point Books 2006 48 p. (Animal kingdom classification)

Grades: 4 5 6　　　　　　　　　　　　　　　　**595.3**

1. Crabs . 2. Lobsters . 3. Crustacea .

ISBN 0-7565-1612-9 (hard cover)

LC 2005029180

Introduces the physical characteristics and habitats of crustaceans, from lobsters and shrimps to sow bugs and barnacles.

Includes bibliographical references

Metz, Lorijo

Discovering crabs. PowerKids Press 2011 24p il (Along the shore) lib bdg $21.25

Grades: 3 4 5　　　　　　　　　　　　　　　　**595.3**

1. Crabs

ISBN 978-1-4488-4993-2; 1-4488-4993-4

LC 2011000153

This book about crabs "briefly describes the major physical and behavioral characteristics common to all [crabs] and one or two distinctive characteristics of about a half dozen species. . . . One or two sharp color photographs of representative species, most of which are closeups, accompany the text on every page. . . . [This is] well organized and smoothly written in an engaging style." SLJ

Includes glossary

Sill, Cathryn P.

About crustaceans; a guide for children. written by Cathryn Sill; illustrated by John Sill. Peachtree Publishers 2004 un il $15.95

Grades: K 1 2 3　　　　　　　　　　　　　　　**595.3**

1. Crustaceans

ISBN 1-56145-301-3

LC 2003-16838

Describes the anatomy, behavior, and habitat of various crustaceans, including the lobster, crab, and shrimp

"Done in bright watercolors, the illustrations give a sense of these creatures' different habitats. . . . This is an excellent example of easy nonfiction, perfect for beginning readers or for sharing aloud with budding naturalists." SLJ

595.386　Crabs

Gish, Melissa

★ Crabs; Melissa Gish. Creative Education/Creative Paperbacks 2016 46 p. color ill., color map (Living Wild) (hardcover : alk. paper) $39.95

Grades: 4 5 6　　　　　　　　　　　　　　　**595.386**

1. Crabs

ISBN 1608185656; 9781608185658

LC 2014028008

This illustrated children's book by Melissa Gish, which is a part of the Living Wild children's book series, offers "a look at crabs, including their habitats, physical characteristics such as their chelipeds, behaviors, relationships with humans, and their threatened status in the world today." (Publisher's note)

"Stunning photographs, sidebars with intriguing facts, and engaging prose are hallmarks of this set, and the chapters describing each creature's role in folklore or pop culture add to the fun." SLJ

Includes bibliographical references and index.

595.4 Chelicerates

Barton, Bethany

I'm trying to love spiders; (it isn't easy) written and illustrated by Bethany Barton. Viking 2015 40 p. color illustrations (hardcover) $16.99

Grades: PreK K 1 2 3 4   **595.4**
   1. Fear 2. Spiders 3. Spiders
   ISBN 0670016934; 9780670016938

                        LC 2014031680

This children's book on spiders by Bethany Barton "will help you see these amazing arachnids in a whole new light, from their awesomely excessive eight eyes, to the seventy-five pounds of bugs a spider can eat in a single year! There's heaps more information in here to help you forget your fears." (Publisher's note)

"This informational picture book takes an amusing and novel approach. An unseen arachnophobe relates a series of fascinating facts about spiders (their appearance and anatomy, their eating habits, venomous spiders, and more) as she attempts to talk herself out of her fear after she encounters one. . . . A creative addition to animal collections. Pair with Elise Gravel's "Disgusting Creatures" (Tundra) books for a fun lesson plan." SLJ

I am trying to love spiders

Berger, Melvin

Spinning spiders; illustrated by S.D. Schindler. HarperCollins Pubs. 2003 33p il (Let's-read-and-find-out science) hardcover o.p. pa $4.99

Grades: K 1 2 3   **595.4**
   1. Spiders
   ISBN 0-06-445207-7 pa; 0-06-028696-2

                        LC 2001-39507

Describes the characteristics of spiders and the methods they use to trap their prey in webs

Written "in a clear, easy-to-read style. . . . Detailed, full-color illustrations, often on spreads, highlight the well-organized text." SLJ

Bishop, Nic, 1955-

Spiders; written and photographed by Nic Bishop. Scholastic 2012 32 p. $3.99

Grades: K 1 2   **595.4**
   1. Spiders
   ISBN 0545237572; 9780545237574

This book by Nic Bishop adapts his 2007 book of the same title for younger readers. "Designed for independent readers in first and second grades, the current book offers a completely new text that is shorter, simpler, and printed in larger type. Like its predecessor, the book discusses spiders' physical features, behaviors, and life cycles, and it provides illustrations of different species, which are clearly identified." (Booklist)

Bodden, Valerie

Ticks; Valerie Bodden. Creative Education 2013 24 p. col. ill. (Creepy creatures) (library) $25.65

Grades: 1 2 3 4   **595.4**
   1. Ticks 2. Picture books for children 3. Ticks
   ISBN 1608182347; 9781608182343

                        LC 2011050287

This book is part of the Creepy Creatures series. The series uses "clear white backgrounds to showcase . . . magnified photos, while the simple, educational text is . . . arranged around the page." This book "features shots of the parasites feeding, and describes how some ticks balloon to 600 times their weight when bloated with blood." (Booklist)

Includes bibliographical references (p. 24) and index

Bredeson, Carmen

Tarantulas up close; [by] Carmen Bredeson. Enslow Elementary 2008 24p il (Zoom in on animals!) lib bdg $21.26

Grades: 1 2 3   **595.4**
   1. Tarantulas
   ISBN 978-0-7660-3076-3 lib bdg; 0-7660-3076-8 lib bdg

                        LC 2007025609

In this introduction to tarantulas, "short, large-print paragraphs describe key body parts . . . and how they function; . . . [the book outlines] hunting techniques, defense mechanisms, diet, and life cycle. Complementing the text is a large, usually full-page, sharp, color close-up of a representative species. . . . The text is well-organized and clearly written. . . . Bredeson's excellent illustrations and lucid text provide valuable insights into the nature of these hairy, and unjustly feared, spiders." SLJ

Camisa, Kathryn

Hairy tarantulas; by Kathryn Camisa. Bearport Pub. 2009 24p il (No backbone!: The world of invertebrates) lib bdg $21.28

Grades: 1 2 3   **595.4**
   1. Tarantulas
   ISBN 978-1-59716-704-8 lib bdg; 1-59716-704-5 lib bdg

                        LC 2008-12106

"Spreads include four or five simple sentences, each neatly spaced by a carriage return, facing a vivid, close-up view of the spider in action. Word balloon captions highlight details when needed and smaller photographs on the text pages provide further visual reference." SLJ

Includes glossary and bibliographical references

Ganeri, Anita

Scorpion. Heinemann Library 2011 24p il map (A day in the life: desert animals) $22; pa $6.49

Grades: K 1 2   **595.4**
   1. Scorpions
   ISBN 978-1-4329-4776-7; 1-4329-4776-1; 978-1-4329-4785-9 pa; 1-4329-4785-0 pa

                        LC 2010022827

"The engaging full-color photographs are key to [this] well-organized [book]. . . . Basic global maps show where the animal is found, and a diagram called a 'body map' labels its parts. The [text is] appropriate for the age group, and the pictures will draw in youngsters. [An] excellent [purchase] if material is needed on these animals." SLJ

Includes glossary and bibliographical references

Tarantula. Heinemann Library 2011 24p il map (A day in the life: Rain forest animals) lib bdg $22; pa $6.49

Grades: 1 2   **595.4**
   1. Tarantulas
   ISBN 978-1-4329-4109-3 lib bdg; 1-4329-4109-7 lib bdg; 978-1-4329-4120-8 pa; 1-4329-4120-8 pa

                        LC 2010000970

This book follows a tarantula through its day as it sleeps, eats, and moves.

"Ganeri presents information clearly and simply in large type, two-sentence comments placed below a bright, sharply reproduced color photograph of the animal in a natural setting. . . . [This is] sufficiently specific to support assignment as well as pleasure reading." SLJ

Includes glossary and bibliographical references

Gonzales, Doreen

Scorpions in the dark. PowerKids Press 2010 24p il (Creatures of the night) lib bdg $21.25; pa $8.05

Grades: 2 3 4   **595.4**

1. Scorpions

ISBN 978-1-4042-8100-4 lib bdg; 1-4042-8100-2 lib bdg; 978-1-4358-3257-2 pa; 1-4358-3257-4 pa

LC 2009-2076

A look at scorpions and their world in the dark.

"Basic details are complemented by eclectic trivia, . . . [and] each volume concludes with a defense of the animal . . . and why it is vital to humans. The layout is attractive, with easy-to-read text and eye-catching photography. Good for reports." SLJ

Includes glossary

Heos, Bridget

Stronger Than Steel; Spider Silk DNA and the Quest for Better Bulletproof Vests, Sutures, and Parachute Rope. Bridget Heos; [illustrated by] Andy Comins. Houghton Mifflin Books for Children 2013 79 p. col. ill. (hardcover) $18.99

Grades: 5 6 7 8   **595.4**

1. Silk 2. Spiders 3. Inventions 4. Scientists 5. Spider webs 6. Nephila maculata 7. Spider webs -- Therapeutic use

ISBN 0547681267; 9780547681269

LC 2012010992

This children's book, by Bridget Heos, illustrated by Andy Comis, is part of the "Scientists in the Field" series. In it "readers enter Randy Lewis' lab where they come face to face with golden orb weaver spiders, and transgenic alfalfa, silkworm silk, and goats, whose milk contains the proteins to spin spider silk--and to weave a nearly indestructible fiber." (Publisher's note)

Lasky, Kathryn

Silk & venom; searching for a dangerous spider. photographs by Christopher G. Knight. Candlewick Press 2011 57p il map

Grades: 4 5 6 7   **595.4**

1. Spiders 2. Biologists 3. Arachnologists 4. College teachers

ISBN 0-7636-4222-3; 978-0-7636-4222-8

LC 2010-41888

This book focuses on the the field work of arachnologist Greta Binford. "Binford's effort to trace the migration of Loxosceles from South American to North America . . . [led] her to field exploration in the Dominican Republic. [Glossary. Index.] Grades four to seven." (Bull Cent Child Books)

"Biology professor Greta Binford studies spiders in an Oregon lab and in the field in the Dominican Republic, where she searches for L. Taino, a Caribbean relative of the venomous brown recluse that might provide clues to how and when the recluse genus arrived in North America. . . . In leisurely, literary prose, Lasky presents the ancient class of arachnids before introducing the scientist and explaining her quest. . . . On most spreads, a full-bleed photograph is opposed by substantial text and one or two smaller pictures." Kirkus

Lunis, Natalie

Deadly black widows; by Natalie Lunis. Bearport Pub. 2009 24p il (No backbone!: The world of invertebrates) lib bdg $21.28

Grades: 1 2 3   **595.4**

1. Spiders

ISBN 978-1-59716-667-6 lib bdg; 1-59716-667-7 lib bdg

LC 2008-1997

A discussion of the black widow spider, the most dangerous kind of spider in the United States

"Spreads include four or five simple sentences, each neatly spaced by a carriage return, facing a vivid, close-up view of the spider in action. Word balloon captions highlight details when needed and smaller photographs on the text pages provide further visual reference." SLJ

Includes glossary and bibliographical references

Markle, Sandra

Black widows; deadly biters. Lerner Publications 2011 48p il (Arachnid world) lib bdg $29.27

Grades: 5 6 7 8   **595.4**

1. Spiders

ISBN 978-0-7613-5038-5; 0-7613-5038-1

This describes how black widows are similar to and different from other arachnids. Close-up photographs and diagrams reveal details about the black widow's body both inside and out. A hands-on activity compares the black widow's web to a human hair.

Markle "presents a mix of common and less-common facts . . . and her commentary accompanies a particularly strong suite of illustrations featuring large, clear, labeled outside and inside views that display body parts. Photos go beyond the standard portraits. . . . First rate." SLJ

Includes glossary and bibliographical references

Crab spiders; phantom hunters. Sandra Markle. Lerner Pub. Company 2012 48 p. col. ill. (Arachnid world)

Grades: 4 5 6 7   **595.4**

1. Spiders 2. Zoology 3. Predatory animals 4. Arachnids 5. Crab spiders

ISBN 0761350454; 9780761350453

LC 2011020443

This book is part of Sandra Markle's "Arachnid World" series. "In this book, you will learn how crab spiders are similar to and different from other arachnids. Close-up photographs and diagrams reveal extraordinary details about the crab spider's body both inside and out. A hands-on activity illustrates how a crab spider can quickly ambush a flying insect. . . . Enter the . . . world of the arachnid family with award-winning science author Sandra Markle! Too often lumped together with insects, these fascinating animals have distinctive characteristics and habits that are all their own." (Publisher's note)

Includes bibliographical references (p. 44-45) and index

Fishing spiders; water ninjas. Sandra Markle. Lerner Publications Company 2012 48 p. col. ill. (Arachnid world)

Grades: 4 5 6 7   **595.4**

1. Spiders 2. Aquatic animals 3. Predatory animals 4. Zoology -- Encyclopedias 5. Arachnids 6. Dolomedes

ISBN 9780761350446

LC 2011020442

This book is part of Sandra Markle's "Arachnid World" series. "In this book, you will learn how fishing spiders are similar to and different from other arachnids. Close-up photographs and diagrams reveal extraordinary details about the fishing spider's body both inside and out. A hands-on activity shows how the fishing spider's hairy coat helps it walk on water. . . . Enter the . . . world of the arachnid family with award-winning science author Sandra Markle! Too often lumped together with insects, these fascinating animals have distinctive characteristics and habits that are all their own." (Publisher's note)

Includes bibliographical references and index

Harvestmen; secret operatives. Lerner Publications 2011 48p il (Arachnid world) lib bdg $29.27

Grades: 5 6 7 8   **595.4**

1. Spiders

ISBN 978-0-7613-5042-2; 0-7613-5042-X

LC 2010023491

This describes how harvestmen are similar to and different from other arachnids. Close-up photographs and diagrams reveal details about the harvestmen's bodies, both inside and out. A hands-on activity reveals how harvestmen walk on long legs using only their sense of touch to get around.

Markle "presents a mix of common and less-common facts . . . and her commentary accompanies a particularly strong suite of illustrations featuring large, clear, labeled outside and inside views that display body parts. Photos go beyond the standard portraits. . . . First rate." SLJ

Includes glossary and bibliographical references

Jumping spiders; gold-medal stalkers. by Sandra Markle. Lerner Publications 2012 48 p. col. ill.

Grades: 4 5 6 7   **595.4**

1. Spiders 2. Animal behavior 3. Zoology -- Encyclopedias 4. Arachnids 5. Jumping spiders

ISBN 0761350470; 9780761350477

LC 2011021598

This book is part of Sandra Markle's "Arachnid World" series. "In this book, you will learn how jumping spiders are similar to and different from other arachnids. Close-up photographs and diagrams reveal extraordinary details about the jumping spider's body both inside and out. A hands-on activity compares the reader's jumping ability with that of a jumping spider. . . . Enter the . . . world of the arachnid family with award-winning science author Sandra Markle! Too often lumped together with insects, these fascinating animals have distinctive characteristics and habits that are all their own." (Publisher's note)

Includes bibliographical references (p. 44-45) and index

Mites; master sneaks. by Sandra Markle. Lerner Publications 2012 48 p. (Arachnid world)

Grades: 4 5 6 7   **595.4**

1. Mites 2. Animals -- Anatomy 3. Arachnids 4. Mites

ISBN 9780761350460

LC 2011021462

In this book, a volume of the Arachnid World series, readers "will learn how mites are similar to and different from other arachnids. Close-up photographs, micrographs, and diagrams reveal . . . details about a mite's body both inside and out. A hands-on activity shows how quickly a few mites can multiply into hundreds." (Publisher's note) The book "discuss[es] . . . [their] physical structure, life cycle, and characteristic behaviors. . . . In "Mites," [author Sandra] Markle discusses a variety of these . . . creatures." (Booklist)

Includes bibliographical references and index

Orb weavers; hungry spinners. Lerner Publications 2011 48p il (Arachnid world) lib bdg $29.27

Grades: 5 6 7 8   **595.4**

1. Spiders

ISBN 978-0-7613-5039-2; 0-7613-5039-X

LC 2010023490

This describes how orb weavers are similar to and different from other arachnids. Close-up photographs and diagrams reveal details about the spider's body both inside and out. And a hands-on activity will give you an idea of how the orb weaver can detect prey caught in its web.

Markle "presents a mix of common and less-common facts . . . and her commentary accompanies a particularly strong suite of illustrations

featuring large, clear, labeled outside and inside views that display body parts. Photos go beyond the standard portraits. . . . First rate." SLJ

Includes glossary and bibliographical references

Scorpions; armed stingers. Lerner Publications 2011 48p il (Arachnid world) lib bdg $29.27

Grades: 5 6 7 8   **595.4**

1. Scorpions

ISBN 978-0-7613-5037-8; 0-7613-5037-3

LC 2010004275

This describes how scorpions are similar to and different from other arachnids. Close-up photographs and diagrams reveal details about the scorpion's body both inside and out. And a hands-on activity reveals how a scorpion's senses help it find its prey.

Markle "presents a mix of common and less-common facts . . . and her commentary accompanies a particularly strong suite of illustrations featuring large, clear, labeled outside and inside views that display body parts. Photos go beyond the standard portraits. . . . First rate." SLJ

Includes glossary and bibliographical references

Sneaky, spinning, baby spiders; [by] Sandra Markle. Walker & Company 2008 32p il $16.99; lib bdg $17.89

Grades: 3 4 5   **595.4**

1. Spiders 2. Animal babies

ISBN 978-0-8027-9697-4; 0-8027-9697-4; 978-0-8027-9698-1 lib bdg; 0-8027-9698-2 lib bdg

LC 2007-49139

"Markle's intimate style beckons readers into her text and immediately immerses them in the world of spiderlings. . . . The full-color photographs are the work of many photographers and are filled with energy. . . . [Markle] introduces about 14 species (of the 30,000 spiders worldwide), but she does it in such vivid detail and with such respect and appreciation that youngsters will feel connected to these spider moms and their babies." SLJ

Tarantulas; supersized predators. by Sandra Markle. Lerner Publications Company 2012 48 p. (Arachnid world)

Grades: 4 5 6 7   **595.4**

1. Tarantulas 2. Predatory animals 3. Arachnids 4. Tarantulas

ISBN 9780761350439

LC 2011020437

In this book, a volume of the Arachnid World series, readers "will learn how tarantulas are similar to and different from other arachnids. Close-up photographs and diagrams reveal extraordinary details about the tarantula's body both inside and out. A hands-on activity illustrates how a tarantula grows bigger and bigger by molting." (Publisher's note) The book "discuss[es] . . . [their] physical structure, life cycle, and characteristic behaviors. . . . "Tarantulas" looks at the lives of these large, hairy spiders and points out that they help control insect populations." (Booklist)

Includes bibliographical references and index

Ticks; dangerous hitchhikers. Lerner Publications 2011 48p il (Arachnid world) lib bdg $29.27

Grades: 4 5 6 7   **595.4**

1. Ticks

ISBN 978-0-7613-5041-5; 0-7613-5041-1

LC 2010023484

This book about ticks offers "a clear, conversational text that will draw young people into the zoological facts with gripping, even gruesome examples that are well matched with unsparingly detailed photos. . . . The handsome design, featuring crisply magnified photos, and the approachable text from an experienced writer combine into a strong offering for both personal and classroom reading." Booklist

Includes bibliographical references

Wind scorpions; killer jaws. Sandra Markle. Lerner Publications 2012 48 p. (Arachnid world) (lib. bdg. : alk. paper) $30.60

Grades: 4 5 6 7   **595.4**

1. Scorpions 2. Animals -- Anatomy 3. Arachnids 4. Solpugida 5. Solpugida

ISBN 0761350489; 9780761350484

LC 2011021599

In this book, a volume of the Arachnid World series, readers "will learn how wind scorpions are similar to and very different from other arachnids. Close-up photographs and diagrams reveal extraordinary details about the wind scorpion's body both inside and out. A hands-on activity demonstrates how wind scorpions are able to pick up prey to eat it." (Publisher's note)

The book "discuss[es] . . . [their] physical structure, life cycle, and characteristic behaviors. . . . 'Wind Scorpions' introduces a group of arachnids that use supersize jaws to defend themselves and to attack their prey." (Booklist)

Includes bibliographical references and index

Wolf spiders; mothers on guard. Lerner Publications 2010 48p il (Arachnid world) lib bdg $29.27

Grades: 5 6 7 8   **595.4**

1. Spiders

ISBN 978-0-7613-5040-8; 0-7613-5040-3

LC 2010004273

This describes how wolf spider mothers carry their young on their backs and how wolf spiders are similar to and different from other arachnids. Close-up photographs and diagrams reveal details about the spider's body both inside and out. And hands-on activities will let you experience how a wolf spider female keeps her eggs and young safe.

Markle "presents a mix of common and less-common facts . . . and her commentary accompanies a particularly strong suite of illustrations featuring large, clear, labeled outside and inside views that display body parts. Photos go beyond the standard portraits. . . . First rate." SLJ

Includes glossary and bibliographical references

Montgomery, Sy

★ The **tarantula** scientist. Houghton Mifflin Co. 2004 80p il map (Scientists in the field) $18; pa $7.95

Grades: 4 5 6 7   **595.4**

1. Tarantulas

ISBN 0-618-14799-3; 0-618-91577-X pa

LC 2003-20125

Describes the research that Samuel Marshall and his students are doing on tarantulas, including the largest spider on earth, the Goliath birdeating tarantula

"Enthusiasm for the subject and respect for both Marshall and his eight-legged subjects come through on every page of the clear, informative, and even occasionally humorous text. Bishop's full-color photos . . . are amazing." Booklist

Includes glossary and bibliographical references

Murawski, Darlyne

Spiders and their webs; [by] Darlyne A. Murawski. National Geographic 2004 31p il $16.95

Grades: 2 3 4 5   **595.4**

1. Spiders

ISBN 0-7922-6979-9

LC 2004-397

This describes nine species of spiders and how they make and use webs

"Even fainthearted arachnophobes will appreciate this gallery of spider profiles featuring full-color, telephoto views. . . . Murawski writes about her subjects with an awe and a reverence that will encourage reluctant children to move beyond spiders' creepy reputation to their fascinating features." Booklist

Includes bibliographical references

Otfinoski, Steven

Scorpions. Marshall Cavendish Benchmark 2011 il (Animals, animals) lib bdg $20.95

Grades: 3 4 5   **595.4**

1. Scorpions

ISBN 978-0-7614-4878-5; 0-7614-4878-0

LC 2010016035

Provides information on the anatomy, special skills, habitats, and diet of scorpions

This offers "comprehensive text and striking, well-chosen photos. . . . [This is] packed with engaging facts and trivia, as well as an upbeat tone." Booklist

Includes glossary and bibliographical references

Schnell, Lisa Kahn

High tide for horseshoe crabs; Lisa Kahn Schnell; illustrated by Alan Marks. Charlesbridge 2015 40 p. (reinforced for library use) $16.95

Grades: PreK K 1 2   **595.4**

1. Crabs 2. Coastal ecology 3. Horseshoe crabs 4. Animal migration 5. Limulus polyphemus

ISBN 1580896049; 9781580896047

LC 2013049024

This children's picture book, by Lisa Kahn Schnell and illustrated by Alan Marks, "describes the annual spawning of horseshoe crabs at Delaware Bay. . . . The crabs gathering on the beach to mate and lay their eggs in the sand, migratory birds arriving to feast on the eggs that haven't been buried deeply enough, scientists and volunteers coming to watch, and the baby crabs eventually hatching and making their way to the sea." (School Library Journal)

Simon, Seymour

★ **Spiders**; [by] Seymour Simon. updated ed.; Smithsonian 2008 31p il $16.99; pa $6.99

Grades: 3 4 5 6   **595.4**

1. Spiders

ISBN 978-0-06-089104-6; 0-06-089104-1; 978-0-06-089103-9 pa; 0-06-089103-3 pa

First published 2003 by HarperCollins

An introduction to the physical characteristics, behavior, and life cycle of different kinds of spiders.

"The fantastic color photos of the original edition are all here, as is Simon's crisp, informative text. . . . An attention grabber." SLJ

Wadsworth, Ginger

Up, up, and away; illustrated by Patricia J. Wynne. Charlesbridge 2009 un il lib bdg $16.95

Grades: PreK K 1 2   **595.4**

1. Spiders

ISBN 1-58089-221-3 lib bdg; 978-1-58089-221-6 lib bdg

LC 2008040752

This traces the life cycle of a garden spider

"Simply told with well-chosen words and phrases, the story reads aloud well. . . . Wynne uses watercolor, gouache, and colored pencil to add hue and shading to the precise ink drawings that define the spiders and their surroundings." Booklist

595.46 Scorpions

Pringle, Laurence, 1935-
  Scorpions! strange and wonderful. by Laurence Pringle and illustrated by Meryl Henderson. Boyds Mills Press 2013 32 p. (Strange and wonderful) $16.95
Grades: 3 4 5   **595.46**
  1. Scorpions
  ISBN 1590784731; 9781590784730
       LC 2013931088
  This book, by Laurence Pringle and illustrated by Meryl Henderson, describes scorpions' "life cycle, body structure, habits, and habitat [through] realistic illustrations." (Publisher's note) "Besides briefly discussing the fossil evidence of early scorpions and the place of scorpions in ancient Greek, Mayan, and Egyptian cultures, Pringle introduces a wide variety of scorpions living around the world today." (Booklist)

595.6 Myriapods

Elkin, Matthew
  20 fun facts about centipedes; by Matthew Elkin. Gareth Stevens Pub. 2013 32 p. col. ill. (Fun fact file: bugs!) (library) $25.25; (paperback) $10.50
Grades: 3 4 5   **595.6**
  1. Centipedes 2. Centipedes -- Miscellanea
  ISBN 1433982307; 9781433982309; 9781433982316
       LC 2012021903
  This book by Matthew Elkin is part of a series " that presents a basic bulleted list of facts [with] a few sentences of information, engaging captions, and bright photographs. The basics are covered, including anatomy, eating habits, and offspring. 'Centipedes' uncovers info on the arthropods (and uncovers is the right word, as they commonly hide in cool, dark places like under rocks and, yes, in your bathroom)." (Publisher's note)
  Includes bibliographical references and index.

595.7 Insects

Albee, Sarah
  Bugged; How Insects Changed History. by Sarah Albee. Bloomsbury/Walker 2014 176 p. illustrations (some color) (pbk.) $17.99; (library edition) $23.89
Grades: 4 5 6 7   **595.7**
  1. Insects 2. Human-animal relationship
  ISBN 0802734227; 0802734235; 9780802734228; 9780802734235
       LC 2013025968
  This book, by Sarah Albee, illustrated by Robert Leighton, focuses on the impact of insects on the world throughout history. According to the book, "beneficial bugs have built empires. Bad bugs have toppled them." The book is a "combination of world history, social history, natural science, epidemiology, public health, conservation, and microbiology." (Publisher's note)
  "Overall, this title is astonishing, disgusting, revolting, and ultimately fascinating, making it perfect for emerging entomologists, budding historians, reluctant readers, and gross-out junkies alike." SLJ
  How insects have changed human history

Anderson, Margaret Jean
  Bugged-out insects; [by] Margaret J. Anderson. Enslow Publishers 2011 48p il (Bizarre science) lib bdg $23.93
Grades: 4 5 6 7   **595.7**
  1. Insects
  ISBN 978-0-7660-3674-1; 0-7660-3674-X
       LC 2010006474
  First published 1996 with title: Bizarre insects
  This describes insects such as cicadas, butterflies, praying mantises, walkingsticks, beetles, stinkbugs, botflies, mayflies, mosquitoes, bees, ants, and locusts.
  "Aimed at reluctant readers, [this title is] sure to disgust and delight in equal measure. . . . [The title] will pique interest and get kids lining up at the reference desk looking for more. The text is complemented by illustrations and magnified photos of things that you would hope never to see." SLJ
  Includes glossary and bibliographical references

Arnold, Tedd
  Fly guy presents; insects. Tedd Arnold. Scholastic 2015 32 p. color illustrations $3.99
Grades: K 1 2   **595.7**
  1. Insects
  ISBN 0545757142; 9780545757140
  In this illustrated children's book by Tedd Arnold "Fly Guy and Buzz are ready for their next field trip! They go outside to learn all about other insects like Fly Guy! With straightforward text, humorous asides, and kid-friendly full-bleed photographs throughout, young readers will learn lots of fun facts about all sorts of bugs." (Publisher's note)
  "Teachers and series fans alike will be satisfied by this latest installment." SLJ

Aronin, Miriam
  ★ The ant's nest; a huge, underground city. Bearport Pub. 2009 32p il (Spectacular animal towns) lib bdg $18.95
Grades: 2 3 4   **595.7**
  1. Ants
  ISBN 978-1-59716-868-7 lib bdg; 1-59716-868-8 lib bdg
       LC 2009-03065
  "Through excellent photographs, high-interest texts, sidebars, maps, and other material, children learn about both the animals and their habitats. The . . . book also provides brief profiles of animals with similar habitats. . . . [This book is] much better than average 'report' titles." SLJ
  Includes glossary and bibliographical references

Baker, Nick
  Bug zoo. DK 2010 64p il $12.99
Grades: 2 3 4   **595.7**
  1. Insects 2. Collectors and collecting
  ISBN 978-0-7566-6166-3; 0-7566-6166-8
       LC 2010-279437
  Naturalist Nick Baker shows the reader how to make miniature habitats for insects, snails and worms, some interesting aspects of their lives and how to feed the contained creatures
  "This is a colorful, informative, and engaging book about keeping insects-if not as pets, then as creatures worthy of intense study. . . . Baker's enthusiasm for the subject is evident throughout. Because it provides interesting facts about insects as well as how-to tips, this title will find an audience with curious readers and would-be zookeepers alike. It may even intrigue avowed entomophobes." SLJ

Beccaloni, George
  Biggest bugs life-size. Firefly Books 2010 84p il $19.95

Grades: 4 5 6 7   **595.7**
1. Insects
ISBN 978-1-55407-699-4; 1-55407-699-4

"This book presents 35 of the world's biggest, longest, and heaviest bugs. . . . Double-page spreads feature each bug's statistics, a map with its area of distribution, and straightforward text that explains its living conditions, eating habits, and life cycle. . . . The highlights, of course, are the numerous life-size and up-close full-color photographs of the bugs. . . . The visual appeal alone will entice even the most reluctant readers." Booklist

Berger, Melvin
Chirping crickets; illustrated by Megan Lloyd. HarperCollins Pubs. 1998 32p il (Let's-read-and-find-out science) lib bdg $15.89; pa $4.95
Grades: K 1 2 3   **595.7**
1. Crickets
ISBN 0-06-024962-5 lib bdg; 0-06-445180-1 pa
LC 96-51661

Describes the physical characteristics, behavior, and life cycle of crickets while giving particular emphasis to how they chirp

"Clear and detailed, the ink-and-watercolor artwork is often visually striking as well as educationally sound. . . . A well-rounded introduction." Booklist

Bishop, Nic
Butterflies; written and photographed by Nic Bishop. Scholastic Inc. 2011 31p il (Scholastic reader) pa $3.99
Grades: 1 2   **595.7**
1. Butterflies
ISBN 978-0-545-28434-9 pa; 0-545-28434-1 pa

★ **Nic** Bishop butterflies and moths. Scholastic Nonfiction 2009 48p il $17.99
Grades: 2 3 4   **595.7**
1. Butterflies
ISBN 978-0-439-87757-2; 0-439-87757-1
LC 2008-15290

"The text covers the all-important topic of metamorphosis, of course, but also discusses feeding and predation, migration, and reproduction. . . . The real draw here, though, is the art; even for Bishop, the photographs are breathtaking. . . . Kids will be drawn to this like Bishop's subject to flame." Bull Cent Child Books

Blobaum, Cindy
Insectigation! 40 hands-on activities to explore the insect world. [by] Cindy Blobaum. Chicago Review Press 2005 133p il pa $12.95
Grades: 3 4 5 6   **595.7**
1. Insects
ISBN 1-55652-568-0

"Raising mealworms, testing the visual acuity of bees, setting up a watering hole for butterflies—these are just a few of the 40 activities included in this earnest introduction to entomology. Each of eight chapters focuses on a different topic, such as physical and behavioral characteristics; metamorphosis; communication; methods to attract, collect and keep insects, etc. . . . Clear line drawings, diagrams of body parts and project materials, plus the occasional black-and-white photograph are found on almost every page. . . . The text is clearly written and well organized." SLJ

Includes bibliographical references

Bodden, Valerie
Cockroaches; Valerie Bodden. 1st ed. Creative Education 2013 24 p. col. ill. (Creepy creatures) (library) $25.65

Grades: 1 2 3 4   **595.7**
1. Cockroaches 2. Picture books for children
ISBN 1608182320; 9781608182329
LC 2011050277

This book is part of the Creepy Creatures series. The series uses "clear white backgrounds to showcase . . . magnified photos, while the simple, educational text is . . . arranged around the page." This book looks at "the 4,000 varieties of roach and [details] how they can hold their breath to crawl up drains into bathtubs." (Booklist)

Includes bibliographical references and index

Termites; Valerie Bodden. 1st ed. Creative Education 2013 24 p. col. ill. (Creepy creatures) (library) $25.65
Grades: 1 2 3 4   **595.7**
1. Picture books for children 2. Termites
ISBN 1608182355; 9781608182350
LC 2011050279

This children's picture book, part of the Creepy Creatures Series by Valerie Bodden, looks at termites. "Throughout most of each title, a page of large-print text, set on a plain white background, alternates with a full-page, extreme close-up photo of one or more of the featured animals. . . . Each book succinctly outlines the animals' basic structure, key body parts, distinctive characteristics of particular species, behavior, habitats, diet, natural enemies, and life cycle." (School Library Journal)

Includes bibliographical references and index

Bulion, Leslie
Hey there, stink bug! illustrated by Leslie Evans. Charlesbridge 2006 45p il lib bdg $12.95
Grades: 3 4 5 6   **595.7**
1. Insects
ISBN 9781580893046 lib bdg; 1-58089-304-X lib bdg
LC 2005-19627

This book "describes various types of insects using different poetic forms." (Publisher's note) "Grades four to seven." (Bull Cent Child Books)

"Bulion uses gory, visceral facts to pull children into both the science and the various poetic forms. . . . Striking, watercolor-washed linoleum prints and notes about poetic forms round out this title." Booklist

Catt, Thessaly
Migrating with the monarch butterfly. PowerKids Press 2011 24p il (Animal journeys) lib bdg $21.25; pa $8.25
Grades: 2 3 4   **595.7**
1. Butterflies -- Migration
ISBN 978-1-4488-2546-2 lib bdg; 978-1-4488-2676-6 pa
LC 2010030647

This describes the yearly migration of the monarch butterfly, which can travel between 50 to 100 miles a day.

Dickmann, Nancy
A **bee's** life. Heinemann Library 2010 24p il (Watch it grow) lib bdg $21.50; pa $5.99
Grades: PreK K 1   **595.7**
1. Bees
ISBN 978-1-4329-4137-6 lib bdg; 1-4329-4137-2 lib bdg; 978-1-4329-4146-8 pa; 1-4329-4146-1 pa
LC 2009-49151

"Practically unique among early introductions to life cycles because death is mentioned . . . this . . . follows [a bee] . . . from egg . . . to maturity with a set of close-up color photographs, one per page, paired to large-type, one or two-sentence captions. . . . Offers nourishing fare for young naturalists." SLJ

Includes glossary

A **butterfly's** life. Heinemann Library 2010 24p il (Watch it grow) lib bdg $21.50; pa $5.99

Grades: PreK K 1   **595.7**

1. Butterflies

ISBN 978-1-4329-4138-3 lib bdg; 1-4329-4138-0 lib bdg; 978-1-4329-4147-5 pa; 1-4329-4147-X pa

LC 2009-49152

"Practically unique among early introductions to life cycles because death is mentioned . . . this . . . follows [a butterfly] . . . from egg . . . to maturity with a set of close-up color photographs, one per page, paired to large-type, one or two-sentence captions. . . . Offers nourishing fare for young naturalists." SLJ

Dixon, Norma

Focus on flies. Fitzhenry & Whiteside 2008 32p il $18.95

Grades: 4 5 6 7   **595.7**

1. Flies

ISBN 978-1-55005-128-5; 1-55005-128-8

This "chatty, informative title, illustrated with many clear color photos and diagrams, will hook readers with its fascinating view of a fly's 'creepy cool world.' . . . The gross details will appeal to middle-grade readers, who will then go on to learn about anatomy, metamorphosis, adaptation, diversity, classification, and flies' roles in plant pollination." Booklist

Includes bibliographical references

Dorros, Arthur

Ant cities; written and illustrated by Arthur Dorros. Crowell 1987 28p il (Let's-read-and-find-out science book) hardcover o.p. lib bdg $11.89; pa $5.99

Grades: K 1 2 3   **595.7**

1. Ants

ISBN 0-690-04568-9; 0-690-04570-0 lib bdg; 0-06-445079-1 pa

LC 85-48244

"Using harvester ants as a basic example, Dorros shows how the insects build tunnels with rooms for different functions and how workers, queens, and males have distinct roles in the ant hill. Along the way, she works in details of food and reproduction, ending with descriptions of other kinds of ants and suggestions for ways to observe them (including instructions for making an ant farm). The text is simple without becoming choppy, the full-color illustrations are inviting as well as informative." Bull Cent Child Books

Glaser, Linda

Dazzling dragonflies; a life cycle story. illustrated by Mia Posada. Millbrook Press 2008 un il (Linda Glaser's classic creatures) lib bdg $22.60

Grades: K 1 2 3   **595.7**

1. Dragonflies

ISBN 0-8225-6753-9 lib bdg; 978-0-8225-6753-0 lib bdg

LC 2007-21886

This book shows how a dragonfly nymph grows, sheds its skin and then flies. "Ages five to nine." (Publisher's note)

"Clearly written text and bright-hued watercolor collage illustrations introduce the life cycle of that zip-a-dipping aerialist, the dragonfly, from newly laid eggs, through months of aquatic life as a nymph, to the final metamorphosis into a glitter-winged creature. . . . [This] is basic, attractive, and easy to read." SLJ

Not a buzz to be found; insects in winter. illustrations by Jaime Zollars. Millbrook Press 2011 31p il lib bdg $25.26

Grades: K 1 2 3   **595.7**

1. Winter 2. Insects

ISBN 978-0-7613-5644-8; 0-7613-5644-4

LC 2011001148

"This look at how insects survive the cold may have young naturalists scouring the winter landscape to find them for themselves. From those who migrate or hibernate to ones that hide or are still eggs, Glaser has assembled a wide variety of 12 of the more common insects, including ants, ladybugs, dragonflies, honeybees, monarchs, praying mantises and black swallowtail butterflies. Short verses present readers with how each gets through the winter. . . . Gorgeous full-bleed illustrations filled with color and detail depict the insects in winter." Kirkus

Gonzales, Doreen

Crickets in the dark. PowerKids Press 2010 24p il (Creatures of the night) lib bdg $21.25; pa $8.05

Grades: 2 3 4   **595.7**

1. Crickets

ISBN 978-1-4042-8098-4 lib bdg; 1-4042-8098-7 lib bdg; 978-1-4358-3253-4 pa; 1-4358-3253-1 pa

LC 2009-483

A look at crickets and their world in the dark.

"Basic details are complemented by eclectic trivia, . . . [and] each volume concludes with a defense of the animal . . . and why it is vital to humans. The layout is attractive, with easy-to-read text and eye-catching photography. Good for reports." SLJ

Includes glossary

Gray, Susan Heinrichs

The **life** cycle of insects; [by] Susan H. Gray. Heinemann Library 2011 48p il (Life cycles) lib bdg $35; pa $8.95

Grades: 3 4 5   **595.7**

1. Insects

ISBN 978-1-4329-4983-9 lib bdg; 978-1-4329-4990-7 pa

LC 2010038508

This describes what an incsect is, types of insects, their life cycles, habitats, foods, defenses, and relationships to humans.

Includes glossary and bibliographical references

Hamilton, Sue L.

Swarmed by bees; [by] Sue Hamilton. ABDO Pub. Co. 2010 32p il (Close encounters of the wild kind) lib bdg $27.07

Grades: 4 5 6 7   **595.7**

1. Bees 2. Animal attacks

ISBN 978-1-60453-933-2 lib bdg; 1-60453-933-X lib bdg

LC 2009-45598

Readers learn of actual human-bee encounters, information about bees, survival strategies, and attack statistics.

"Students will be drawn to the realistic full-color photographs, the realistic diagrams of the creatures' bodies, the real-life stories told by victims, and the interesting, attractive formatting that includes text, diagrams, photographs, and graphics on each page. . . . [This is] exciting and attractive in a 'gross' sort of way and will appeal particularly to boys for both leisure reading and research." Libr Media Connect

Includes glossary

Hansen, Amy S.

Bugs and bugsicles; insects in the winter. [by] Amy S. Hansen; illustrations by Robert C. Kray. Boyds Mills Press 2010 32p il

Grades: 3 4 5   **595.7**

1. Winter 2. Insects

ISBN 1590782690; 9781590782699

"This colorful book describes what happens in winter to seven different insects: a praying mantis, a field cricket, a ladybug, a honeybee, a pavement ant, a monarch butterfly, and an Arctic woolly bear caterpillar. . . . The title concludes with an author's note and two science activities related to freezing water. A typical double-page spread includes a few paragraphs of text accompanied by large-scale illustrations." Booklist

Includes glossary and bibliographical references

Himmelman, John, 1959-
  Noisy bug sing-along; by John Himmelman. 1st ed. Dawn Publications 2013 32 p. (hardcover) $16.95; (paperback) $8.95
  Grades: 2 3 4   595.7
    1. Picture books for children 2. Insects 3. Insect sounds
    ISBN 1584691913; 9781584691914; 9781584691921
                                                        LC 2012024253
  This children's picture book looks at the noises made by bugs. "The opening page tells readers that bugs sing day and night, loudly and softly, and that they should sing along. . . . Each double-page spread is devoted to one insect and its sound, a sentence telling the name of the creature and what it does, followed by the sound the bug makes—in a huge display type that spreads across and fills the pages." (Kirkus)

  There's a bug on my book! written and illustrated by John Himmelman. Dawn Publications 2017 32 p. color illustrations (hard) $16.95
  Grades: PreK K 1   595.7
    1. Insects
    ISBN 9781584695875; 9781584695882
                                                        LC 2016024977
  "Beetles fly, frogs hop, and slugs slide over the pages of this book, made to be read by a child while lying on the grass. . . . [Author] John Himmelman brings together his expertise as both a naturalist and an artist to encourage children to explore nature in their own backyard." (Publisher's note)

Johnson, Jinny
  Butterfly; illustrations by Michael Woods. Smart Apple Media 2010 32p il (How does it grow?) lib bdg $28.50
  Grades: 1 2 3   595.7
    1. Butterflies
    ISBN 978-1-59920-352-2 lib bdg; 1-59920-352-9 lib bdg
                                                        LC 2009-3397
  Introduces children to the lifecycle of a butterfly
  "Each stage is described on a spread that features clearly written, oversized text and a caption opposite a full-page, realistic watercolor, or, occasionally, a photograph. . . . A worthwhile purchase." SLJ
  Includes glossary

  Insects and creepy-crawlies; Jinny Johnson. Kingfisher 2011 32 p.
  Grades: 3 4 5   595.7
    1. Animal behavior 2. Insects -- Pictorial works 3. Insects
    ISBN 0753465922; 9780753465929
  In this book, "readers get an up-close view of life in a wide variety of insect colonies through six—illustrated story scenes that each examine a key aspect of entomological study-from insect homes, to reproduction, life in the water, hunting and gathering, and insects that fly. Once readers absorb the key elements of the story, they explore the science through photos and fact boxes on the following page." (Publisher's note)
  This book is "[p]art of [Kingfisher/Macmillan Children's Books]'s 'Explorer' series." (Children's Lit)

  Simon & Schuster children's guide to insects and spiders. Simon & Schuster Bks. for Young Readers 1996 80p il $19.95

Grades: 4 5 6 7   595.7
    1. Insects 2. Spiders
    ISBN 0-689-81163-2
                                                        LC 96-27600
  Provides an introduction to more than 100 insects and arachnids, giving general information about family characteristics and habits, and more specific facts about some species
  "Crisp and well-designed, this is an inviting visual introduction to insects and arachnids." Booklist
  Includes glossary

Knudsen, Shannon
  From egg to butterfly. Lerner Publs. 2003 24p il (Start to finish) lib bdg $18.60
  Grades: K 1 2   595.7
    1. Butterflies
    ISBN 0-8225-0713-7
                                                        LC 2001-4652
  Follows the development of a butterfly from the egg its mother lays on a plant to the fully developed insect that flies away
  "Readers will be transfixed by the incredibly crisp and clear photographs accompanying the text. This up-close and intimate look at the life stages of a monarch butterfly will be an asset to any young entomologist's library." Sci Teach

Koontz, Robin Michal
  What's the difference between a butterfly and a moth? by Robin Koontz; illustrated by Bandelin-Dacey. Picture Window Books 2010 24p il (What's the difference) lib bdg $25.32
  Grades: K 1 2   595.7
    1. Moths 2. Butterflies
    ISBN 978-1-4048-5543-4 lib bdg; 1-4048-5543-2 lib bdg
                                                        LC 2009-6884
  "Compares and contrasts the habitats, physical characteristics, location, and lifestyles of [butterflies and moths]. The picture-book format is used to great effect as it allows the two animals to be compared side by side on each spread. The bold, expressive watercolors provide the same visual impact as photographs. . . . Short sentences and highlighted fun facts make this a . . . [book] with broad appeal for both researchers and browsers." SLJ
  Includes glossary

Latimer, Jonathan P.
  Caterpillars; [by] Jonathan P. Latimer, Karen Stray Nolting; illustrations by Amy Bartlett Wright; foreword by Virginia Marie Peterson. Houghton Mifflin 2000 48p il (Peterson field guides for young naturalists) pbk. $5.95
  Grades: 4 5 6 7   595.7
    1. Caterpillars
    ISBN 9780395979457
                                                        LC 99-38944
  Describes the physical characteristics, behavior, and habitat of a variety of caterpillars, arranged by the categories "Smooth," "Bumpy," "Sluglike," "Horned," "Hairy," "Bristly," and "Spiny"

Lawrence, Ellen
  A dragonfly's life; by Ellen Lawrence. Bearport Pub. 2013 24 p. (Animal diaries: life cycles) (library binding) $23.93
  Grades: 1 2 3 4   595.7
    1. Insects 2. Dragonflies 3. Dragonflies -- Life cycles
    ISBN 1617725943; 9781617725944
                                                        LC 2012019344
  This book seeks to "help children understand the amazing life cycle of dragonflies. Each page showcases stunning photographs of dragon-

flies from egg to adult. . . . The primary text of the book is presented as a child's diary. The diary entries are presented as though they were constructed by a young boy, Joseph, over the course of a summer when he and his grandfather observed and learned about dragonflies." (SB&F: Your Guide to Science Resources for All Ages)

"Through the eyes of a child who shares observations of animal life in ongoing journal entries, Lawrence keeps readers thoroughly engaged as they process a generous amount of information pertaining to the natural world...Memorable photos and a thoughtful narrative are perfectly organized to maximize comprehension in these outstanding titles." (School Library Journal)

Includes bibliographical references (p. 24) and index

Lockwood, Sophie

Ants; by Sophie Lockwood. Child's World 2008 40p il map (World of insects) lib bdg $29.93

Grades: 4 5 6   **595.7**

1. Ants

ISBN 978-1-59296-817-6 lib bdg; 1-59296-817-1 lib bdg

LC 2006103452

This describes ants' "basic anatomy, outstanding physical and behavioral characteristics, [diet, life cycle], roles in myths and legends, and effects on humans. . . . With [its] well-organized, succinct [text] and excellent photography, [this] solid [introduction] will be [a] valuable [resource]." SLJ

Includes glossary and bibliographical references

Dragonflies; by Sophie Lockwood. Child's World 2008 40p il map (World of insects) lib bdg $29.93

Grades: 4 5 6   **595.7**

1. Dragonflies

ISBN 978-1-59296-821-3 lib bdg; 1-59296-821-X lib bdg

LC 2006103454

This describes dragonflies' "basic anatomy, outstanding physical and behavioral characteristics, [diet, life cycle], roles in myths and legends, and effects on humans. . . . With [its] well-organized, succinct [text] and excellent photography, [this] solid [introduction] will be [a] valuable [resource]." SLJ

Includes glossary and bibliographical references

Flies; by Sophie Lockwood. Child's World 2008 40p il (World of insects) lib bdg $29.93

Grades: 4 5 6   **595.7**

1. Flies

ISBN 978-1-59296-822-0 lib bdg; 1-59296-822-8 lib bdg

LC 2007000182

This describes flies' "basic anatomy, outstanding physical and behavioral characteristics, [diet, life cycle], roles in myths and legends, and effects on humans. . . . With [its] well-organized, succinct [text] and excellent photography, [this] solid [introduction] will [a] be valuable [resource]." SLJ

Includes glossary and bibliographical references

Maley, Adrienne Houk

20 fun facts about praying mantises; by Adrienne Houk Maley. 1st ed. Gareth Stevens Pub. 2013 32 p. col. ill. (library) $25.25; (paperback) $10.50

Grades: 3 4 5   **595.7**

1. Praying mantis 2. Mantodea

ISBN 1433982404; 9781433982408; 9781433982415

LC 2012031287

This book by Adrienne Houk Maley focuses on praying mantises and states that "female praying mantises sometimes eat the head of their mate, and then offers possible reasons for this behavior. Other entries

briefly describe: key body parts, senses, defense mechanisms, hunting and/or feeding methods, diets, life cycles, etc. Captions, mounted on yellow backgrounds mimicking sticky notes, provide additional information." (Publisher's note)

Includes bibliographical references (page 31) and index.

Markle, Sandra

Hornets; incredible insect architects. by Sandra Markle. Lerner Publications Company 2008 48p il (Insect world) lib bdg $27.93

Grades: 2 3 4 5   **595.7**

1. Hornets and yellowjackets

ISBN 978-0-8225-7297-8 lib bdg; 0-8225-7297-4 lib bdg

LC 2007022290

This describes the anatomy, life cycle, and behavior of hornets

This "will please report writers, budding entomologists, and anyone who expects children's nonfiction to be as carefully documented as adult nonfiction. . . . The [book is] notable for the sharp photos placed precisely to enhance understanding. . . . The main [text is] clear and [flows] well." SLJ

Includes glossary and bibliographical references

Insects; biggest! littlest! photographs by Simon Pollard. Boyds Mills Press 2009 32p il $16.95

Grades: 2 3 4 5   **595.7**

1. Size 2. Insects

ISBN 978-1-59078-512-6; 1-59078-512-6

LC 2008-33524

"This simply written introduction examines insects from the perspective of size. Employing over a dozen kinds as examples, Markle explains why those that are unusually large, small, or equipped with extraordinary body parts have an edge over predators or competing species. . . . An amazingly detailed, closeup color photograph of one or more of the insects discussed complements the text on almost every page. . . . Well organized and clearly written in an engaging style." SLJ

Includes glossary and bibliographical references

Luna moths; masters of change. by Sandra Markle. Lerner Publications Co. 2008 48p il (Insect world) lib bdg $27.93

Grades: 2 3 4 5   **595.7**

1. Moths

ISBN 978-0-8225-7302-9 lib bdg; 0-8225-7302-4 lib bdg

LC 2007025260

This describes the anatomy, life cycle, and behavior of luna moths

This "will please report writers, budding entomologists, and anyone who expects children's nonfiction to be as carefully documented as adult nonfiction. . . . The [book is] notable for the sharp photos placed precisely to enhance understanding. . . . The main [text is] clear and [flows] well." SLJ

Includes glossary and bibliographical references

★ **Praying** mantises; hungry insect heroes. Lerner Publications Company 2008 48p il (Insect world) lib bdg $27.93

Grades: 2 3 4 5   **595.7**

1. Praying mantis

ISBN 978-0-8225-7300-5 lib bdg; 0-8225-7300-8 lib bdg

LC 2007-25961

This describes the anatomy, life cycle, and behavior of praying mantises.

This "will please report writers, budding entomologists, and anyone who expects children's nonfiction to be as carefully documented as adult nonfiction. . . . The [book is] notable for the sharp photos placed precisely to enhance understanding. . . . The main [text is] clear and [flows] well." SLJ

Includes glossary and bibliographical references

Termites; hard-working insect families. by Sandra Markle. Lerner Publications Co. 2008 48p il (Insect world) lib bdg $27.93
Grades: 2 3 4 5   595.7
1. Termites
ISBN 978-0-8225-7301-2 lib bdg; 0-8225-7301-6 lib bdg
LC 2007025963
This describes the anatomy, life cycle, and behavior of termites

This "will please report writers, budding entomologists, and anyone who expects children's nonfiction to be as carefully documented as adult nonfiction. . . . The [book is] notable for the sharp photos placed precisely to enhance understanding. . . . The main [text is] clear and [flows] well." SLJ

Includes glossary and bibliographical references

Markovics, Joyce L.
The **honey** bee's hive; a thriving city. by Joyce Markovics; consultant, Brian V. Brown. Bearport Pub. 2009 32p il map (Spectacular animal towns) lib bdg $25.27
Grades: 2 3 4   595.7
1. Bees
ISBN 978-1-59716-867-0 lib bdg; 1-59716-867-X lib bdg
LC 2009-11295
Describes the activities within a honey bee hive

"Through excellent photographs, high-interest texts, sidebars, maps, and other material, children learn about both the animals and their habitats. The . . . book also provides brief profiles of animals with similar habitats. . . . [This book is] much better than average 'report' titles." SLJ
Includes glossary and bibliographical references

Marsh, Laura
Butterflies. National Geographic 2010 48p il map (Great migrations) $11.90; pa $3.99
Grades: 1 2 3   595.7
1. Butterflies
ISBN 978-1-4263-0740-9; 1-4263-0740-3; 978-1-4263-0739-3 pa; 1-4263-0739-X pa
This offers facts about monarch butterflies and their migration from Northern United States and Canada to the Oyamel forest of Mexico.

"Dynamic full-color photographs, informative writing, and consistent organization work well together in [this volume]. . . . Along with the many photographs, the fascinating details are supported by boxes of related information, helpful definitions of new terms, and a sprinkling of entertaining jokes/riddles." SLJ
Includes glossary

Marshall, Stephen A.
Insects A to Z. Firefly 2009 32p il lib bdg $19.95; pa $7.95
Grades: 4 5 6   595.7
1. Insects
ISBN 978-1-55407-555-3 lib bdg; 1-55407-555-6 lib bdg; 978-1-55407-503-4 pa; 1-55407-503-3 pa
This is an illustrated dictionary of 26 insects which includes the Latin and common names of the order, family, genus and species, as well as information on geographic distribution. Fact boxes for each entry provide information detailing each insect's scientific name, diet, average size and the location at which each was photographed.

"The photography . . . is well composed and sharply focused, with a nicely varied layout from page to page. . . . The [text is] clearly written." SLJ

Miller, Heather
This is your life cycle; by Heather Lynn Miller; illustrated by Michael Chesworth. Clarion Books 2008 32p il $16
Grades: K 1 2 3   595.7
1. Dragonflies 2. Life cycles (Biology)
ISBN 978-0-618-72485-7; 0-618-72485-0
LC 2007-7245
Told in the form of a TV show, this describes the different stages of the life of Dahlia the dragonfly, including the various predators she faced, what she ate, and other facts.

"Lively, vibrant watercolor illustrations supplement the ambitious text. . . . Children will find this playful science book memorable." Libr Media Connect

Mortensen, Lori
In the trees, honeybees! illustrated by Cris Arbo. Dawn Publications 2009 un il $16.95; pa $8.95
Grades: PreK K 1 2 3   595.7
1. Bees
ISBN 978-1-58469-114-3; 1-58469-114-X; 978-1-58469-115-0 pa; 1-58469-115-8 pa
LC 2008038513
"Short, simple rhyming words and phrases, printed in large type on realistic illustrations, describe the amazing life cycle of the honeybee. The vibrantly colored scenes center on a beehive hidden in a tree trunk and the grass and gardens surrounding it. Brief paragraphs in a smaller font provide more information about the insect's depicted activities. . . . A wonderful choice for sharing aloud, Mortensen's finely crafted book makes a solid addition." SLJ

Mound, L. A.
Insect; written by Laurence Mound. rev ed; DK Pub. 2007 72p il (Eyewitness books) $15.99; lib bdg $19.99
Grades: 4 5 6 7   595.7
1. Insects
ISBN 978-0-7566-3004-1; 0-7566-3004-5; 978-0-7566-0691-6 lib bdg; 0-7566-0691-8 lib bdg
LC 2007-281241

First published 1990 by Knopf
Includes glossary and bibliographical references

Munro, Roxie
Busy builders; written and illustrated by Roxie Munro. Marshall Cavendish Children 2012 40 p. (hardcover) $17.99
Grades: 3 4 5   595.7
1. Picture books for children 2. Insects 3. Arachnids 4. Insects -- Habitations
ISBN 0761461051; 9780761461050; 9780761461067
LC 2011017391
This children's book, by Roxie Munro, describes "eight insects, one spider, and [offers] an inside look at the unique structures they each build. Roxie Munro's . . . art, drawn in India ink and colored ink, brings these remarkable feats of engineering into full focus. A glossary and resources to learn more are included." (Publisher's note)

Murawski, Darlyne
Face to face with butterflies; by Darlyne A. Murawski. National Geographic 2010 31p il map (Face to face) $16.95
Grades: 3 4 5 6   595.7
1. Butterflies
ISBN 978-1-4263-0618-1; 1-4263-0618-0
The author describes the life cycle and behavior of butterflies.
Includes glossary and bibliographical references

★ **Face** to face with caterpillars; by Darlyne A. Murawski. National Geographic 2007 32p il (Face to face) $16.95; lib bdg $25.90
Grades: 3 4 5 6   **595.7**
1. Caterpillars
ISBN 978-1-4263-0052-3; 1-4263-0052-2; 978-1-4263-0053-0 lib bdg; 1-4263-0053-0 lib bdg

LC 2006-20499

"Murawski tells how to find caterpillars and discusses their developmental stages, body parts, diet problems, and self-defense mechanisms. . . . Attractive, well written, and fascinating." SLJ

Includes bibliographical references

Nelson, Maria
20 fun facts about dragonflies; by Maria Nelson. 1st ed. Gareth Stevens Pub. 2013 32 p. col. ill. (Fun fact file: bugs!) (library) $25.25; (paperback) $10.50
Grades: 3 4 5   **595.7**
1. Dragonflies
ISBN 1433982358; 9781433982354; 9781433982361

LC 2012021207

This book by Maria Nelson provides information on dragonflies and presents "one or two sentences per page, in large, eye-catching red print [and] offer[s] salient facts about the featured insects, usually involving an unusual physical or behavioral characteristic. Each numbered statement is followed by a short paragraph with more detail." (Publisher's note)

Niver, Heather Moore
20 fun facts about stick bugs; by Heather Moore Niver. 1st ed. Gareth Stevens Publishing 2013 32 p. col. ill. (library) $25.25; (paperback) $10.50
Grades: 3 4 5   **595.7**
1. Stick insects 2. Insects
ISBN 143398251X; 9781433982514; 9781433982521

LC 2012031356

In this book by Heather Moore Niver "readers get the . . . opportunity to [see stick bugs] blending in with their natural habitat while learning many fun facts about stick bugs—including which is the longest, which resembles a lobster, and the many devious ways they avoid being caught by predators." (Publisher's note)

Includes bibliographical references (page 31) and index.

Pringle, Laurence P.
Cicadas! strange and wonderful. [by] Laurence Pringle; illustrated by Meryl Henderson. Boyd Mills Press 2010 32p il map $16.95
Grades: 3 4 5   **595.7**
1. Cicadas
ISBN 978-1-59078-673-4; 1-59078-673-4

LC 2010-925563

This "provides an attractive introduction to cicadas, which typically spend 1, 13, or 17 years below ground before emerging for only a few weeks. . . . Pringle describes cicadas' physical features, behaviors, life cycle, and loss of habitat. . . . Henderson's watercolor paintings are precisely delineated, informative, and sometimes lovely as well. . . . This [is a] clearly written, informative introduction." Booklist

Includes bibliographical references

Prischmann, Deirdre A.
Poop-eaters; dung beetles in the food chain. by Deirdre A. Prischmann. Capstone Press 2008 32p il (Fact finders. Extreme life) lib bdg $23.93

Grades: 2 3 4   **595.7**
1. Beetles
ISBN 978-1-4296-1265-4 lib bdg; 1-4296-1265-7 lib bdg

LC 2007-20440

"The beetles' features, traits, and development are explained in breezy text, accompanied by vivid photographs and additional 'Gross!' fact boxes. . . . The volume provides an informative introduction to an underappreciated insect." Horn Book Guide

Includes glossary and bibliographical references

Rockwell, Anne F.
Bugs are insects; by Anne Rockwell; illustrated by Steve Jenkins. HarperCollins Pubs. 2001 29p il (Let's-read-and-find-out science) hardcover o.p. lib bdg $15.89; pa $4.95
Grades: K 1 2 3   **595.7**
1. Insects
ISBN 0-06-028568-0; 0-06-028569-9 lib bdg; 0-06-445203-4 pa

LC 99-39846

Introduces common backyard insects and explains the basic characteristics of these creatures

This is a "well-written and informative book. . . . The collage illustrations are beautifully rendered with layered colored papers of a variety of textures that add both depth and details to the creatures." SLJ

Honey in a hive; by Anne Rockwell; illustrated by S. D. Schindler. HarperCollinsPublishers 2005 33p il (Let's-read-and-find-out science) $15.99; lib bdg $16.89; pa $4.99
Grades: K 1 2 3   **595.7**
1. Bees 2. Honey
ISBN 0-06-028566-4; 0-06-028567-2 lib bdg; 0-06-445204-2 pa

LC 2003-10357

An introduction to the behavior and life cycle of honeybees, with particular emphasis on the production of honey

"Schindler's realistic artwork is both colorful and nicely matched to the text. . . . This attractive introduction to honey production will serve students well." Booklist

Rodriguez, Ana Maria
Secret of the plant-killing ants . . . and more! Enslow Publishers 2008 48p il (Animal secrets revealed!) lib bdg $23.93
Grades: 5 6 7 8   **595.7**
1. Ants 2. Insects
ISBN 978-0-7660-2953-8 lib bdg; 0-7660-2953-0 lib bdg

LC 2007039494

"Explains why ants in the Amazon rainforest kill all but one species of plant and details other strange abilities of different types of animals." Publisher's note

Includes glossary and bibliographical references

Rustad, Martha E. H.
Ants and aphids work together. Capstone Press 2011 24p il (Pebble Plus: animals working together) lib bdg $23.99; pa $6.95
Grades: K 1 2   **595.7**
1. Ants 2. Aphids 3. Symbiosis
ISBN 978-1-4296-5298-8 lib bdg; 1-4296-5298-5 lib bdg; 978-1-4296-6197-3 pa; 1-4296-6197-6 pa

LC 2010025460

Simple text and full-color photographs introduce the symbiotic relationship of ants and aphids.

In this series "the easy-to-understand examples are well selected to show of range of relationships in a variety of environments, and children will come away with some exposure to the concepts of 'parasite' and 'predator' as well." SLJ

Includes glossary and bibliographical references

Senior, Kathryn

Bugs; Kathryn Senior. Smart Apple Media 2016 32 p. color illustrations (hbk.) $31.35

Grades: 1 2 3 4   **595.7**

1. Insects

ISBN 1625883374; 9781625883377

This book, by Kathryn Senior, "offers a high-interest introduction to insects for reluctant readers and will hold special appeal for visual learners. It's filled with a dynamic mix of labeled illustrations, cutaway views, maps, graphs, and process diagrams that reveal an insider look at the world of insects. Accessible text accompanies the images, and all elements combine to provide compare-and-contrast strategies that support CCSS learning." (Publisher's note)

"Gross, beautiful, engaging, and straightforward, this book, like the others of the series, manages to convey significant depth of knowledge for emergent readers." Booklist

Simon, Seymour

★ Butterflies. Collins 2011 30p il $17.99

Grades: 1 2 3 4   **595.7**

1. Butterflies

ISBN 978-0-06-191493-5; 0-06-191493-2

LC 2010032203

"Science writer Simon vividly explores the life cycles of butterflies and moths around the globe. . . . Simon's often breathtaking photographs offer closeup views of the insects, demonstrating color variations and their incredible transformations from pupa to adult moth or butterfly. Readers will be armed for the field with juicy vocabulary . . . and tantalizing anatomical descriptions to share." Publ Wkly

Singer, Marilyn, 1948-

Caterpillars. EarlyLight Books 2011 40p il $14.95

Grades: PreK K 1 2 3 4   **595.7**

1. Caterpillars

ISBN 978-0-9797455-7-7; 0-9797455-7-8

"This basic introduction to caterpillar reproduction, development, diet, survival, habitat, and anatomy is combined with powerfully clear photography that will captivate a wide audience. The book has two levels of text: simple capitalized red letters that swirl across the pages for the youngest readers to more complicated paragraphs easy enough for third or fourth graders to enjoy." SLJ

Siy, Alexandra

Bug shots; the good, the bad, and the bugly. text and photographys by Alexandra Siy; photomicrographs by Dennis Kunkel. Holiday House 2011 il $16.95

Grades: 3 4 5 6   **595.7**

1. Insects

ISBN 978-0-8234-2286-9; 0-8234-2286-0

LC 2010024063

"Insects are virtually on trial in this unusual introduction. The book begins by suggesting that readers 'Join the FBI-become a Fellow Bug Investigator' study the insects' 'mug shots,' read their 'rap sheets,' and decide if they are good or bad. After offering general information on classification, anatomy, numbers of species, etc., successive chapters focus on the 'suspects,' comprised of five large insect groups: true bugs; beetles; butterflies and moths; bees, ants, and wasps; and true flies. Each chapter describes the group's outstanding characteristics, as well as the distinctive physical and/or behavioral characteristics of representative species, their diet, harmful or beneficial effects on humans, and so on. . . . Photomicrographs of the insects or body parts illustrate the text on every page; all are brightly colored to highlight anatomical features. . .

. The text is clearly written, and the photomicrographs are remarkably detailed." SLJ

★ Mosquito bite; [by] Alexandra Siy & Dennis Kunkel. Charlesbridge 2005 32p il $16.95; pa $6.95

Grades: 3 4 5   **595.7**

1. Mosquitoes

ISBN 1-57091-591-1; 1-57091-592-X pa

LC 2004-18959

"Black-and-white photographs of an evening game of hide-and-seek are interspersed with stunning color-enhanced microphotographs that record the life cycle of another seeker: a female Culex pipiens mosquito looking for a meal. . . . This title is fascinating for its photography and the informative text and captions." SLJ

Stewart, Melissa

Ants. National Geographic 2010 32p il (National Geographic readers) $13.90; pa $3.99

Grades: 1 2 3   **595.7**

1. Ants

ISBN 978-1-4263-0609-9; 1-4263-0609-1; 978-1-4263-0608-2 pa; 1-4263-0608-3 pa

Describes different types of ants and their behavior.

Butterfly or moth? how do you know? Enslow Publishers 2011 24p il (Which animal is which?) lib bdg $21.26; pa $6.95

Grades: 1 2 3   **595.7**

1. Moths 2. Butterflies

ISBN 978-0-7660-3678-9 lib bdg; 0-7660-3678-2 lib bdg; 978-1-59845-235-8 pa; 1-59845-235-5 pa

LC 2010003276

"This clearly written volume lays out the differences between butterflies and moths in double-page spreads that allow readers to compare the characteristics of the two animals. . . . The precisely worded, informative text is brief but does not simplify the facts. . . . Captions identify each species shown in the highly magnified, color photos." Booklist

Includes bibliographical references

Insect or spider? how do you know? Enslow Publishers 2011 24p il (Which animal is which?) lib bdg $21.26; pa $6.95

Grades: 1 2 3   **595.7**

1. Insects 2. Spiders

ISBN 978-0-7660-3681-9 lib bdg; 0-7660-3681-2 lib bdg; 978-1-59845-237-2 pa; 1-59845-237-1 pa

LC 2010003278

This describes the differences between insects and spiders.

This "should give budding naturalists an increased understanding of how scientists use appearance and behavior of classify sometimes-similar living things. . . . Spreads feature sharply detailed paired photographs of identified specimens seen from the same angle and at roughly equal size." SLJ

Includes bibliographical references

Tait, Noel

Insects & spiders. Simon & Schuster Books for Young Readers 2008 64p il map (Insiders) $16.99

Grades: 5 6 7 8   **595.7**

1. Insects 2. Spiders

ISBN 978-1-4169-3868-2; 1-4169-3868-0

LC 2008-61110

Provides an overview of insects and spiders in a book that includes detailed three-dimensional illustrations.

"Sharp, hyper-realistic, larger-than-life drawings . . . are . . . set against a plain colored background or within a natural setting. . . . [This] title succinctly describes basic anatomy; physical and behavioral characteristics common to all [insects and spiders]." SLJ

Includes glossary

Trueit, Donna

Grasshoppers. Marshall Cavendish Benchmark 2009 23p il (Benchmark rebus. Creepy critters) lib bdg $22.79

Grades: PreK K 1   595.7

1. Grasshoppers

ISBN 978-0-7614-3964-6 lib bdg; 0-7614-3964-1 lib bdg

LC 2008-24210

This book on grasshoppers is part of the "Backyard Safari series," which provides "a hands-on, practical point of view on discovering local insects. . . . The first part of each book offers information on the life cycle and anatomy of the title creatures." The book also includes "three hands-on sections" offering "practical instructions and tips for finding and observing the title creatures . . . characteristics and about a dozen pictures . . . and a final section suggest[ing] additional projects." (Booklist)

"Brilliant closeup photos will help beginning readers make meaning and appeal to students who like these creatures. . . . Glossary, print and media resources for further learning, and an about the author section conclude . . . [the] book. Reading specialists will want to be advised about [this book] . . . as will teachers. . . . This . . . is an excellent resource for beginning research projects." Publisher's note

Includes glossary and bibliographical references

Trueit, Trudi Strain

Ants; reading consultant, Nanci R. Vargus. Marshall Cavendish Benchmark 2009 23p il (Benchmark rebus. Creepy critters) lib bdg $22.79

Grades: PreK K 1   595.7

1. Ants

ISBN 978-0-7614-3961-5; 0-7614-3961-7

LC 2008-12152

"Brilliant close-up photos will help beginning readers make meaning and appeal to students who like these creatures. . . . Glossary, print and media resources for further learning, and an about the author section conclude . . . [the] book. Reading specialists will want to be advised about [this book] . . . as will teachers. . . . This . . . is an excellent resource for beginning research projects." Libr Media Connect

Includes glossary and bibliographical references

Beetles. Marshall Cavendish Benchmark 2010 23p il (Benchmark rebus. Creepy critters) lib bdg $22.79

Grades: PreK K 1   595.7

1. Beetles

ISBN 978-0-7614-3962-2; 0-7614-3962-5

LC 2008-23153

This book on beetles is part of the "Backyard Safari series," which provides "a hands-on, practical point of view on discovering local insects. . . . The first part of each book offers information on the life cycle and anatomy of the title creatures." The book also includes "three hands-on sections" offering "practical instructions and tips for finding and observing the title creatures . . . characteristics and about a dozen pictures . . . and a final section suggest[ing] additional projects." (Booklist)

"Brilliant closeup photos will help beginning readers make meaning and appeal to students who like these creatures. . . . Glossary, print and media resources for further learning, and an about the author section conclude . . . [the] book. Reading specialists will want to be advised about [this book] . . . as will teachers. . . . This . . . is an excellent resource for beginning research projects." Libr Media Connect

Includes glossary and bibliographical references

Caterpillars. Marshall Cavendish Benchmark 2009 23p il (Benchmark rebus. Creepy critters) lib bdg $22.79

Grades: PreK K 1   595.7

1. Caterpillars

ISBN 978-0-7614-3963-9 lib bdg; 0-7614-3963-3 lib bdg

LC 2008-17108

"Brilliant closeup photos will help beginning readers make meaning and appeal to students who like these creatures. . . . Glossary, print and media resources for further learning, and an about the author section conclude . . . [the] book. Reading specialists will want to be advised about [this book] . . . as will teachers. . . . This . . . is an excellent resource for beginning research projects." Libr Media Connect

Includes glossary and bibliographical references

Voake, Steve

★ Insect detective; illustrated by Charlotte Voake. Candlewick Press 2010 28p il $16.99; pa $6.99

Grades: K 1 2 3   595.7

1. Insects

ISBN 978-0-7636-4447-5; 1-4063-1051-4; 978-0-7636-5816-8 pa

LC 2009-11152

"This charming collaboration . . . gently encourages young readers to explore their natural surroundings and observe some of the more commonly found insects in it. In spare prose, brief facts about a variety of creatures, such as leaf-miner caterpillars, ground beetles, ants, earwigs, and dragonflies, are shared, as are hints on where and how to find them. . . . Simple but elegant pen and watercolor illustrations show the creatures in their habitats." SLJ

Webster, Christine

Mosquitoes. Weigl 2010 24p il (Backyard animals) $24.45; pa $8.95

Grades: 1 2 3   595.7

1. Mosquitoes

ISBN 978-1-60596-086-9; 1-60596-086-1; 978-1-60596-087-6 pa; 1-60596-087-X pa

LC 2009004447

This is "packed with information and [includes] fine close-up photos." Booklist

Includes glossary

Werner, Sharon

Bugs by the numbers; facts and figures for multiple types of bugbeasties. by Sharon Werner and Sarah Forss. Blue Apple Books 2011 un il $19.99

Grades: 2 3 4   595.7

1. Insects 2. Counting

ISBN 978-1-60905-061-0; 1-60905-061-4

LC 2010046644

Provides readers with facts about bugs and other creepy-crawlers while introducing the concept of numbers and counting.

"Werner and Forss use 1s, 2s, and 3s, to distinguish between an ant's head, thorax, and abdomen; a mosquito consists of 75s . . . and a group of ladybugs are made up of numerals that correspond to the number of spots on their wings. Add in several liftable flaps and a wealth of facts about the featured species, and this duo has another winner on their hands." Publ Wkly

Wilson, J. V.

Bumblebee. Frances Lincoln 2011 il $16.95

Grades: K 1 2 3   595.7

1. Bees

ISBN 1847800084; 1-84780-008-4

"The pastoral life of a bumblebee queen. Her yearly cycle begins on the first day of spring, when she sleepily flies in search of food and a nest. . . . On the last day of summer, 'the old bumblebee queen flies out of her wonderful nest for the last time.' And in the autumn, all the new queens fly out to find drones to mate with before settling into another winter of sleep. Wilson's narrative is crisp and concise. . . . Kennaway's watercolors are straightforward and mostly realistic in their particulars. A valuable page about 'Helping bumblebees' and a glossary conclude the book. Informative and, in its way, lovely." Kirkus

Includes glossary

Winnick, Nick

Butterflies. Weigl Publishers 2010 24p il (World of wonder: watch them grow) lib bdg $25.70; pa $9.95

Grades: 1 2   **595.7**

1. Butterflies

ISBN 978-1-60596-928-2 lib bdg; 1-60596-928-1 lib bdg; 978-1-60596-929-9 pa; 1-60596-929-X pa

LC 2009052102

Learn about the fascinating transition these insects make from egg to caterpillar, pupa, and finally, colorful butterfly.

The text "is simple without being simplistic; it is thoughtful and comprehensive without being overwhelming. The real appeal for teachers, students, and independent young readers, however, will be the photographs that fill the facing pages. Bold, bright, and colorful, the photographs bring you marvelously close to the subject. . . . On many different levels, this is a very appealing [book]." Libr Media Connect

Includes glossary

Woodward, John

Super bug encyclopedia; DK Publishing. DK Publishing 2016 207 p. color illustrations (ebook) $65; $24.99

Grades: 4 5 6 7 8   **595.7**

1. Insects

ISBN 9781465455000; 1465446001; 9781465446008

LC 2016427602

This book takes "a look at the 100 most amazing insects on the planet! . . . With incredible facts and stats for every bug, [it] showcases the superstars of the insect world. Find out which insect can snap a pencil in half, how a tiny moth can fly up to 70 miles an hour, and meet a dung beetle that can pull over 1,100 times its own body weight." (Publisher's note)

"This selection has high appeal for browsers and will be useful for report writers." SLJ

595.76   Beetles

Aston, Dianna Hutts

A **beetle** is shy; by Dianna Aston; illustrated by Sylvia Long. Chronicle Books Llc 2016 40 p. color illustrations (alk. paper) $16.99

Grades: K 1 2 3   **595.76**

1. Beetles

ISBN 9781452127125

LC 2015002300

This book, by Dianna Aston, illustrated by Sylvia Long, is a "look at the fascinating world of beetles. From flea beetles to bombardier beetles, an incredible variety of these beloved bugs are showcased here in all their splendor." (Publisher's note)

"Long's watercolors capture the vibrant details of the rainbow stag beetle, dead-nettle leaf beetle, and other striking specimens in a sparkling homage to a diverse category of insect." Pub Wkly

Burns, Loree Griffin

★ **Beetle** busters; a rogue insect and the people who track it. Loree Griffin Burns; photographs by Ellen Harasimowicz. Houghton Mifflin Harcourt 2014 64 p. color illustrations, color map (Scientists in the field) $18.99

Grades: 5 6 7 8   **595.76**

1. Beetles 2. Insects 3. Nonindigenous pests 4. Asian longhorned beetle

ISBN 0547792670; 9780547792675

LC 2013050160

This book, by Loree Griffin Burns, focuses on the "Asian longhorned beetle (ALB). . . . These beetles came to America from China, living in wood turned into shipping material. At first the beetles invaded urban areas, where hardwood trees were in limited supply. . . . But . . . now . . . infestations have erupted in . . . hardwood forests, and these beetles, while bad at flying, are very good at killing trees. Clint McFarland's job? Stop the ALB at any cost." (Publisher's note)

"The author lives within the quarantined area in Massachusetts and has seen firsthand areas where swatches of infested (and other) trees have been cut down. Her questions about the method employed will leave readers asking some of their own--as they should. A timely, well-told story and a call to action." SLJ

Gibbons, Gail

Ladybugs; by Gail Gibbons. Holiday House 2012 32 p. col. ill., col. map (hardcover) $17.95

Grades: K 1 2   **595.76**

1. Ladybugs 2. Beneficial insects 3. Picture books for children

ISBN 0823423689; 9780823423682

LC 2011014700

This book is about ladybugs. It features illustrations done in "watercolors, enhanced with black ink outline and detail and some crayon highlighting . . . Half of the illustrations include one or more brief notes and/or labels in addition to the oversize text. [Gail] Gibbons identifies the small beetle's body parts; shows some species of ladybugs from around the world; details the four stages of its life cycle; and discusses its usefulness to farmers and how it protects itself from predators and cold weather. Appended are some additional facts (e.g., "Ladybugs can swim") and the National Geographic websites for the U.S. and Canada." (School Library Journal)

Jenkins, Steve

The **beetle** book; Steve Jenkins. Houghton Mifflin Books for Children 2011 31 p. $16.99

Grades: 4 5 6 7   **595.76**

1. Beetles 2. Ecology -- Encyclopedias 3. Insects -- Encyclopedias

ISBN 9780547680842

LC 2011027129

This nonfiction natural history book presents pictures and information about an "array of beetles." Author/illustrator Steve Jenkins describes "the colors and patterns of this ubiquitous insect . . . [and] the details about the various adaptations that beetles have made over millennia in response to their environment, diet, and predators." Jenkins claims that "one out of four creatures on the planet is a beetle." (Kirkus Reviews)

Smith, Siàn

Ladybugs; Siàn Smith. Raintree 2013 24 p. (paperback) $8.95

Grades: PreK K   **595.76**

1. Ladybugs 2. Picture books for children

ISBN 1410948226; 9781410948090; 9781410948229

LC 2011041230

This children's picture book by Siàn Smith "introduces readers to ladybugs. The text is presented in . . . rhyming patterns" and includes photographs. It is part of the Creepy Critters series, which "gives readers an up close and personal view of some of their favorite creepy critters." (Publisher's note)

Includes bibliographical references and index

595.77 Flies (Diptera) and fleas

Gravel, Élise, 1977-
The **fly**; Elise Gravel. Tundra Books of Northern New York 2014 32 p. color illustrations (Disgusting critters) (hardcover) $10.99
Grades: K 1 2 3   **595.77**
   1. Flies 2. Insects
   ISBN 177049636X; 9781770496361; 9781770496385
           LC 2013940756
This children's book, part of Elise Gravel's "Disgusting Critters" series, is an "illustrated non-fiction book about the house fly. . . . It covers such topics as the hair on the fly's body (requires a lot of shaving), its ability to walk on the ceiling (it's pretty cool, but it's hard to play soccer up there), and its really disgusting food tastes (garbage juice soup followed by dirty diaper with rotten tomato sauce, for example)." (Publisher's note)

"This humorous, informative volume gives basic facts about the title creature. Cartoon illustrations and speech-bubble text play up the kid-friendly silliness: 'The housefly is a member of the Muscidae family. Mom Muscidae, Dad Muscidae . . . Teenager Muscidae: 'Yo!'" The familiar subject and friendly presentation give this book broad appeal." Horn Book

Heos, Bridget
I, **fly**; the buzz about flies and how awesome they are. Bridget Heos; illustrated by Jennifer Plecas. Henry Holt & Co. 2015 48 p. color illustrations (hardcover) $17.99
Grades: 2 3 4   **595.77**
   1. Flies 2. Housefly
   ISBN 0805094695; 9780805094695
           LC 2014023463
In this book, written by Bridget Heos and illustrated by Jennifer Plecas, "Fly is fed up with everyone studying butterflies. Flies are so much cooler! They flap their wings 200 times a second, compared to a butterfly's measly five to twelve times. Their babies--maggots--are much cuter than caterpillars (obviously). And when they eat solid food, they even throw up on it to turn it into a liquid. Who wouldn't want to study an insect like that?" (Publisher's note)

"The pictures incorporate chalkboard notes and charts to back up the fly's overview of muscid physiology, habits and life cycle. A breezy bucketful of buggy braggadocio, with tasty nuggets of well-digested natural history stirred in." Kirkus
   Includes bibliographical references

595.78 Moths and butterflies

Aston, Dianna Hutts
A **butterfly** is patient; by Dianna Aston; illustrated by Sylvia Long. Chronicle Books 2011 40 p. col. ill., col. maps $16.99
Grades: 1 2   **595.78**
   1. Butterflies 2. Insects -- Metamorphosis 3. Picture books for children 4. Insects
   ISBN 0811864790; 9780811864794
           LC 2010008548

"Aston explains the life cycle of a butterfly through a series of themed spreads on the insect's various attributes. . . . Ages five to eight." (Bull Cent Child Books)

This picture book "offers specific and accurate descriptions of metamorphosis, pollination, camouflage, migration and other butterfly features and functions, along with the differences between butterflies and moths. Imagination-stretching comparisons--monarchs weigh only as much as a few rose petals, the wingspan of the Arian Small Blue is "about the length of a grain of rice"--lend wings to the body of facts, and though the author avoids direct mention of reproduction or death, a quick closing recapitulation that harks back to the opening page's hatching egg provides [a] . . . hint of life's cyclical pattern. . . . [Illustrator Sylvia] Long depicts dozens of caterpillars and butterflies, each one posed to best advantage, unobtrusively labeled." (Kirkus)

"Aston explores the development, habits, migration, and attributes of one of nature's flashier, yet familiar creations. Long's watercolors are precise but enchanting as ever. . . . A lovely mix of science and wonder." Publ Wkly

Burns, Loree Griffin
Handle with care; an unusual butterfly journey. Loree Griffin Burns; Photographs by Ellen Harasimowicz. Millbrook Press 2014 33 p. (lib. bdg. : alk. paper) $26.60
Grades: 1 2 3 4   **595.78**
   1. Butterflies 2. Butterfly farming -- Costa Rica
   ISBN 0761393420; 9780761393429
           LC 2013018086
In this book, author Loree Griffin Burns "focuses first on the life of the blue morpho butterfly at the El Bosque Nuevo butterfly farm in Costa Rica and concludes with its a final destination, the Museum of Science in Boston. . . . Factual back matter further supports the story. Additional information appears in the section 'Insects and Their Life Cycles,' which discusses the process of metamorphosis." (School Library Journal)

"An explanation of the life cycle of butterflies gets an intriguing twist in this account of the work of a Costa Rican butterfly farm, where blue morpho butterflies are raised and the pupae eventually shipped to museums for display and observation. Detailed discussion of each life stage is accompanied by wonderfully sharp, close-up photographs that show intricate structural details." Horn Book
   Includes bibliographical references (page 33) and index

Ehlert, Lois
★ **Waiting** for wings. Harcourt 2001 un il $17
Grades: PreK K 1 2   **595.78**
   1. Butterflies 2. Stories in rhyme
   ISBN 0-15-202608-8
           LC 00-9765
Eggs clinging to leaves become caterpillars which become butterflies which lay their eggs

"A brief rhyming text and cheery tone invite readers to explore the full and half pages that form this brilliantly designed book-within-a book." Publ Wkly

Gibbons, Gail
Monarch butterfly. Holiday House 1989 un il $16.95; pa $6.95
Grades: K 1 2 3   **595.78**
   1. Butterflies
   ISBN 0-8234-0773-X; 0-8234-0909-0 pa
           LC 89-1880
"Large-scale paintings, clearly detailed, and a simply written, sequential text describe the life cycle of the monarch butterfly and its migratory patterns. This is Gibbons at her best, providing information in a text that is cohesive and comprehensible." Bull Cent Child Books

Heiligman, Deborah

From caterpillar to butterfly; illustrated by Bari Weissman. HarperCollins Pubs. 1996 31p il (Let's-read-and-find-out science) $15.95; pa $4.95

Grades: K 1   **595.78**

1. Butterflies 2. Caterpillars

ISBN 0-06-024264-7; 0-06-024268-X lib bdg; 0-06-445129-1 pa

LC 93-39055

Young children observe the metamorphosis of a caterpillar into a butterfly in a jar in their classroom

"Pen-and-ink and watercolor illustrations create a cheerful setting. . . . A small collection of butterflies commonly found in most parts of the U.S. and a list of addresses of butterfly centers are appended. An inviting book that young children can relate to and one that teachers will find valuable to support nature-study projects." SLJ

Marsh, Laura

Caterpillar to butterfly; Laura Marsh. National Geographic 2012 32 p.

Grades: K 1 2   **595.78**

1. Butterflies 2. Caterpillars 3. Insects -- Metamorphosis

ISBN 1426309201; 142630921X; 9781426309205; 9781426309212

LC 2011277485

Author Laura March describes the transformation from caterpillars to butterflies, focusing on the wingspan, colors, and wing patterns of butterflies. "This level 1 Reader gives kids an up-close look at exactly how a caterpillar becomes a butterfly. . . . [The book also includes] bonus information including different types of butterflies and poisonous caterpillars." (Publisher's note)

Pasternak, Carol

How to raise monarch butterflies; a step-by-step guide for kids. Carol Pasternak. Firefly Books 2012 48 p. col. ill. (bound) $19.95

Grades: 3 4 5 6 7   **595.78**

1. Caterpillars 2. Insects -- Care 3. Monarch butterflies 4. Monarch butterfly 5. Monarch butterfly -- Life cycles

ISBN 1770850015; 1770850023; 9781770850019; 9781770850026

LC 2012419489

This book by Carol Pasternak presents a "detailed guide to locating and hatching. . . Monarch butterflies. . . . [R]eaders will learn about the life cycle of the Monarch and how to encourage populations in their own backyards, with tips on which plants to grow, as well as the care and feeding of their pet caterpillars. 'How to Raise Monarch Butterflies' explains what threats face Monarchs and how readers can help conserve the Monarch's feeding grounds from encroachment." (Publisher's note)

Includes bibliographical references and index.

Whalley, Paul

Butterfly & moth; written by Paul Whalley. Revised ed. DK Pub. 2012 72 p. ill. (chiefly col.), col. map (Eyewitness books) (hardcover) $16.99; (library) $19.99

Grades: 4 5 6 7   **595.78**

1. Moths 2. Butterflies

ISBN 0756692989; 0756692997; 9780756692988; 9780756692995

LC 2012418030

This book is part of the DK Eyewitness Books series and focuses on butterflies and moths. The titles in this series "focus on subjects that complement students' personal interests and areas of study to make learning simple and fun." Wall charts, clip art CDs, and photographs and illustrations are included. (Publisher's note)

595.79 Hymenoptera

Blobaum, Cindy

Explore Honey Bees! With 25 Great Projects. by Cindy Blobaum; illustrated by Bryan Stone. Nomad Press 2015 96 p. color illustrations $19.95

Grades: 3 4 5 6   **595.79**

1. Bees

ISBN 1619302861; 9781619302860

In this book, by Cindy Blobaum, illustrated by Bryan Stone, "young readers learn about honey bee colonies, why honey bees live in hives, how honey bees communicate with each other, and why they are so important to human lives. . . . Activities include designing a hive and making a model of a flower's reproductive system, reinforcing the math and science skills readers gain from the text." (Publisher's note)

"A solid text that lends itself well to classroom use as well as to individual research." SLJ

Huber, Raymond

★ **Flight** of the honey bee; by Raymond Huber and illustrated by Brian Lovelock. Candlewick Press 2013 32 p. $16.99

Grades: PreK K 1 2   **595.79**

1. Bees -- Fiction 2. Fertilization of plants 3. Picture books for children 4. Honeybee

ISBN 0763667609; 9780763667603

LC 2013931462

Author Raymond Huber presents an illustrated children's book. "A tiny honey bee emerges from the hive for the first time. Using sunlight, landmarks, and scents to remember the path, she goes in search of pollen and nectar to share with the thousands of other bees in her hive. She uses her powerful sense of smell to locate the flowers that sustain her, avoids birds that might eat her, and returns home to share her finds with her many sisters." (Publisher's note)

"As the hive prepares for winter, worker bee Scout embarks on a food-foraging expedition, searching for enough nectar and pollen to survive. Huber's simple but dynamic language hums with an avian vibrancy. In Lovelock's watercolor, acrylic ink, and colored-pencil illustrations, splattered dots represent pollen and hailstones; textured brushstrokes convey flight patterns, vibrating wings, and pelting rain. A satisfying early science book." (Horn Book)

Markle, Sandra, 1946-

The **case** of the vanishing honey bees; a scientific mystery. by Sandra Markle. Lerner Pub Group 2013 48 p. (lib. bdg. : alk. paper) $29.27

Grades: 4 5 6 7 8   **595.79**

1. Bees 2. Honey 3. Insects -- Behavior 4. Honeybee 5. Honeybee -- Health

ISBN 1467705926; 9781467705929

LC 2012046913

This book, by Sandra Markle, "explores the world of honeybees and the mysterious malady that threatens them. After an opening in which a beekeeper discovers that most of the bees in his 400 hives are gone due to colony collapse disorder (CCD), the book describes how healthy honeybees pollinate flowering plants, gather nectar, and raise their young." (Booklist)

Micucci, Charles

★ The **life** and times of the ant. Houghton Mifflin 2003 32p hardcover o.p. pa $6.95

Grades: 2 3 4   **595.79**

1. Ants

ISBN 0-618-00559-5; 0-618-68949-4 pa

LC 2002-478

Describes the evolution, physical characteristics, behavior, and social nature of ants

This "offers succinct text and an impressive amount of information presented in an attractive, picture-book format." Booklist

Includes bibliographical references

Rissman, Rebecca

Ants; Rebecca Rissman. Raintree 2013 24 p. (lib. bdg.) $24.50
Grades: PreK K   **595.79**
1. Ants 2. Animal behavior 3. Insects -- Behavior
ISBN 1410948013; 1410948145; 9781410948014;
9781410948144

LC 2011038864

This "book uses . . . rhymes and . . . images to teach readers about ants." (Publisher's note) "'Ants' begins with counting exercises that use both body segments and legs, before showing off cool photos of differently colored ants, ants marching in rows, and . . . a nest of larvae." It "concludes with a two-page exercise involving finding the titular insects within a cartoon landscape." (Booklist)

Includes bibliographical references and index.

Bees; Rebecca Rissman. Raintree 2013 24 p. (lib. bdg.) $24.50
Grades: PreK K   **595.79**
1. Bees 2. Picture books for children
ISBN 1410948021; 1410948153; 9781410948021;
9781410948151

LC 2011038869

This book is part of the Creepy Critters series, which offers "readers an up close and personal view of some of their favorite creepy critters! This book introduces readers to bees. The text is presented in . . . rhyming patterns." A "cartoon-like design combined with . . . photos" is meant to be "visually appealing for young readers." (Publishers Weekly)

Includes bibliographical references and index.

595.799 Bees

Barton, Bethany

Give Bees a Chance; words & pictures by Bethany Barton. Penguin Group USA 2017 40 p. color illustrations $16.99
Grades: PreK K 1 2 3 4   **595.799**
1. Bees
ISBN 0670016942; 9780670016945

This book, by Bethany Barton, "is for anyone who doesn't quite appreciate how extra special and important bees are to the world, and even to humankind! Besides making yummy honey, they help plants grow fruits and vegetables. And most bees wouldn't hurt a fly (unless it was in self-defense!)." (Publisher's note)

596 Chordates

Lord, Michelle

Animal school; what class are you? by Michelle Lord; illustrated by Michael Garland. Holiday House 2014 32 p. color illustrations (hardcover) $16.95
Grades: 1 2 3 4   **596**
1. Animals -- Classification 2. Vertebrates 3. Vertebrates -- Classification
ISBN 0823430456; 9780823430451

LC 2013019680

This children's book, written by Michelle Lord and illustrated by Michael Garland, is an "exploration of the five vertebrate classifica-

tions—mammals, birds, reptiles, amphibians, and fish. . . . With a focus on trademark characteristics, such as birds' beaks or the scales of fish, the book explains the differences between the five classes. Back matter includes an index and a glossary of scientific terms." (Publisher's note)

"The verse flows quickly throughout the book, though young children may need to stop and ask about terms such as fingerlings, temp, or brood pouch. An appended chart lists each class' characteristics, a few familiar species, and an 'exception,' an animal that might not seem to fit within the category but does. In an intriguing departure from his usual colorful, glossy children's book illustrations, Garland's dynamic digital pictures resemble linocut prints." Booklist

Includes bibliographical references

597 Cold-blooded vertebrates

Bodden, Valerie

Sharks. Creative Education 2010 24p il (Amazing animals) lib bdg $24.25
Grades: K 1 2   **597**
1. Sharks
ISBN 978-1-58341-812-3 lib bdg; 1-58341-812-1 lib bdg

LC 2009002715

A basic exploration of the appearance, behavior, and habitat of sharks, the feared fishes of the sea. Also included is a story from folklore explaining why sharks have a bump on their heads.

This is illustrated with "dynamically colored photographs." Booklist

Includes bibliographical references

Butterworth, Christine

★ **Sea** horse; the shyest fish in the sea. [by] Chris Butterworth; illustrated by John Lawrence. Candlewick Press 2006 27p il $16.99; pa $6.99
Grades: K 1 2   **597**
1. Sea horses
ISBN 978-0-7636-2989-2; 0-7636-2989-8; 978-0-7636-4140-5 pa; 0-7636-4140-5 pa

LC 2005-50755

"Pairing a central narrative about a male Barbour's sea horse with facts in smaller type, Butterworth first pinpoints the creatures' most immediately appealing attributes . . . then goes on to discuss the males' gestational role in reproduction and survival tactics of newly independent offspring. . . . Butterworth has a flair for dynamic writing. . . . Lawrence has created vinyl engravings that masterfully capture the delicate textures of sea horses' graceful, spiny bodies and of their undersea habitats." Booklist

Catt, Thessaly

Migrating with the salmon. PowerKids Press 2011 24p il map (Animal journeys) lib bdg $21.25; pa $8.25
Grades: 2 3 4   **597**
1. Salmon 2. Animals -- Migration
ISBN 978-1-4488-2545-5 lib bdg; 1-4488-2545-8 lib bdg; 978-1-4488-2674-2 pa; 1-4488-2674-8 pa

LC 2010029655

Learn about the life cycle and migration patterns of the salmon.

"Keywords are bolded throughout and can be found in the glossary. The format is attractive with inset captioned photographs and page heading that seem to move across the page." Libr Media Connect

Includes glossary

Coldiron, Deborah

Eels; by Deborah Coldiron. ABDO Pub. 2008 32p il (Underwater world) lib bdg $24.21

Grades: 2 3 4   597
1. Eels
ISBN 978-1-59928-818-5 lib bdg; 1-59928-818-4 lib bdg
LC 2007-14850

"The captioned photographs are engaging. . . . 'Fast Facts' appear on some pages. . . . Provide[s] solid information for elementary school reports." Horn Book Guide

Includes glossary

Stingrays; by Deborah Coldiron. ABDO Pub. 2008 32p il (Underwater world) lib bdg $24.21
Grades: 2 3 4   597
1. Rays (Fishes)
ISBN 978-1-59928-817-8 lib bdg; 1-59928-817-6 lib bdg
LC 2007-14856

"The captioned photographs are engaging. . . . 'Fast Facts' appear on some pages. . . . Provide[s] solid information for elementary school reports." Horn Book Guide

Includes glossary

Curtis, Jennifer Keats
Seahorses; Jennifer Keats Curtis; illustrated by Chad Wallace. Henry Holt 2012 32 p.
Grades: 1 2 3   597
1. Sea horses
ISBN 0805092390; 9780805092394
LC 2011034059

In this children's book by Jennifer Keats Curtis, illustrated by Chad Wallace, "a baby seahorse is born, turning and tumbling as he floats through ocean currents alongside his three hundred brothers and sisters. . . . [H]e changes color to fit in with the surroundings of his spectacular coral reef and sea grass surroundings; his lizard-like eyes can look in two directions at once; and when he has grown, he -- not the female -- will give birth to the next batch of whirling seahorses." (Publisher's note)

Includes bibliographical references

Doubilet, David
★ **Face** to face with sharks; by David Doubilet and Jennifer Hayes. National Geographic 2009 31p il (Face to face) $16.95; lib bdg $25.90
Grades: 3 4 5 6   597
1. Sharks
ISBN 978-1-4263-0404-0; 1-4263-0404-8; 978-1-4263-0405-7 lib bdg; 1-4263-0405-6 lib bdg
LC 2008038244

The authors describe the life cycle and behavior of sharks and their own experiences with sharks in the wild

Includes glossary and bibliographical references

Ganeri, Anita
Piranha. Heinemann Library 2011 24p il map (A day in the life: Rain forest animals) lib bdg $22; pa $6.49
Grades: 1 2   597
1. Piranhas
ISBN 978-1-4329-4108-6 lib bdg; 1-4329-4108-9 lib bdg; 978-1-4329-4119-2 pa; 1-4329-4119-4 pa
LC 2010000969

This book follows a piranha through its day as it sleeps, eats, and moves.

"Ganeri presents information clearly and simply in large type, two-sentence comments placed below a bright, sharply reproduced color photograph of the animal in a natural setting. . . . [This is] sufficiently specific to support assignment as well as pleasure reading." SLJ

Includes glossary and bibliographical references

Gibbons, Gail
Sharks. Holiday House 1992 un il $16.95; pa $6.95
Grades: K 1 2 3   597
1. Sharks
ISBN 0-8234-0960-0; 0-8234-1068-4 pa
LC 91-31524

Describes shark behavior and different kinds of sharks

The author's "bold, appealing illustrations (many of them labeled and explained) are the strength of the presentation. An excellent choice for even the youngest shark fan, this will be useful for simple reports as well." Booklist

Gray, Susan Heinrichs
Walking catfish; by Susan H. Gray. Cherry Lake Pub. 2009 32p il map (Animal invaders) lib bdg $27.07
Grades: 3 4 5   597
1. Catfish 2. Biological invasions
ISBN 978-1-60279-242-5 lib bdg; 1-60279-242-9 lib bdg
LC 2008000804

"Clear color photographs, most of which are closeups, accompany the [text] on about every other page. . . . [This title provides] report writers with in-depth and up-to-date information on these invaders and the serious problems they cause." SLJ

Includes glossary and bibliographical references

Hall, Katharine
Amphibians and reptiles; a compare and contrast book. Katharine Hall. Arbordale Publishing 2015 32 p. (english hardcover) $17.95
Grades: PreK K 1 2   597
1. Reptiles 2. Amphibians 3. Reptiles
ISBN 1628555513; 9781628555516; 9781628555608
LC 2015009084

In this children's book Katharine Hall " introduces these coldblooded vertebrates and points out some essential differences in egg-laying, early development, breathing, skin, and poison or venom. Close-up stock pictures that accompany each statement . . . help visual learners retain these important facts." (Kirkus Reviews)

Includes bibliographical references

Hamilton, Sue L.
Eaten by a shark; [by] Sue Hamilton. ABDO Pub. 2010 32p il (Close encounters of the wild kind) lib bdg $22.61
Grades: 4 5 6 7   597
1. Sharks 2. Animal attacks
ISBN 978-1-60453-931-8 lib bdg; 1-60453-931-3 lib bdg
LC 2009-37230

In this volume, readers learn of actual human-wildlife encounters, creature information, survival strategies, and attack statistics.

"Students will be drawn to the realistic full-color photographs, the realistic diagrams of the creatures' bodies, the real-life stories told by victims, and the interesting, attractive formatting that includes text, diagrams, photographs, and graphics on each page. . . . [This is] exciting and attractive in a 'gross' sort of way and will appeal particularly to boys for both leisure reading and research." Libr Media Connect

Includes glossary

Markle, Sandra
Great white sharks; by Sandra Markle. Carolrhoda Books 2004 40p il (Animal predators) lib bdg $25.26; pa $7.95
Grades: 3 4 5 6   597
1. Sharks
ISBN 1-57505-731-X lib bdg; 1-57505-747-6 pa
LC 2003-23180

"The role of camouflage is aptly explained in flowing text and illustrated in clear photography. . . . The full-color photography bedazzles on almost every page." SLJ

Includes bibliographical references

Miller, Sara Swan

Seahorses, pipefishes, and their kin; Sara Swan Miller. Franklin Watts 2002 47 p. col. ill. (Animals in order) (library) $26.50; (paperback) $6.95

Grades: 4 5 6   597

1. Picture books for children 2. Marine biology 3. Marine animals 4. Gasterosteiformes

ISBN 9780531121719; 0531163792; 9780531163795

LC 2001003034

This book by Sara Swan Miller is part of the Animals in Order series and looks at seahorses, pipefishes, and related animals. "These colorful series entries present a wide variety of creatures that have been sorted by scientific classification into similar groupings called orders . . . . Family names, common names, genus, species, size, and/or location are given, and paragraphs describe various behaviors (food gathering, courtship, etc.)." (School Library Journal)

Includes bibliographical references (p. 46) and index.

Musgrave, Ruth

Everything sharks; all the shark facts, photos, and fun that you can sink your teeth into. National Geographic 2011 64p il (National Geographic kids) lib bdg $25.90; pa $12.95

Grades: 3 4 5 6   597

1. Sharks

ISBN 978-1-4263-0802-4 lib bdg; 1-4263-0802-7 lib bdg; 978-1-4263-0769-0 pa; 1-4263-0769-1 pa

LC 2010049108

This offers facts and photos of sharks, and scientists' tales about encounters with sharks.

"Exploding with astounding full-color photographs and written in an appealing conversational tone, [this book is] for every kid. . . . The [text] will keep kids interested and turning pages to discover more and more facts. . . . [This] compelling, browseable, and completely engrossing [title] will delight readers." SLJ

Includes glossary and bibliographical references

Pfeffer, Wendy

What's it like to be a fish? illustrated by Holly Keller. HarperCollins Pubs. 1996 32p il (Let's-read-and-find-out science) hardcover o.p. pa $4.95

Grades: K 1   597

1. Fishes 2. Goldfish

ISBN 0-06-024429-1 lib bdg; 0-06-445151-8 pa

LC 94-6543

"By comparing goldfish to wild fish and human beings, this book describes the basic physiology of fish. The colorful illustrations are done in watercolors and pastels. . . . In a very accessible narrative that flows from point to point, the basic external anatomy of fish and such behaviors as movement, breathing, eating, and maintenance of temperature are defined in terms of caring for a goldfish in a bowl." Sci Books Films

Pringle, Laurence P.

Sharks!: strange and wonderful; by Laurence Pringle; illustrated by Meryl Henderson. Boyds Mills Press 2001 32p il $15.95

Grades: 3 4 5   597

1. Sharks

ISBN 1-56397-863-6

"Basic information about sharks—including physical characteristics, feeding habits, and their role in the chain of ocean life—is presented in clear, accessible prose. The acrylic paintings serve as a veritable catalog showcasing the variety of known sharks." Horn Book Guide

Rodriguez, Ana Maria

Secret of the suffocating slime trap . . . and more! Enslow Publishers 2008 48p il (Animal secrets revealed!) lib bdg $23.93

Grades: 5 6 7 8   597

1. Fishes

ISBN 978-0-7660-2954-5 lib bdg; 0-7660-2954-9 lib bdg

LC 2007039493

This book offers "fascinating accounts of how scientists systematically analyzed, tested, and proved their theories or how their findings led to other, serendipitous discoveries. . . . Science experiments are thoughtfully placed to inspire exploration, and captioned, full-color photos appear throughout." SLJ

Includes glossary and bibliographical references

Roth, Susan L.

★ **Parrots** over Puerto Rico; by Susan L. Roth and Cindy Trumbore. Lee & Low Books 2013 48 p. color illustrations (hardcover) $19.95

Grades: 2 3 4 5   597

1. Parrots 2. Puerto Rico -- History 3. Natural history -- Puerto Rico 4. Endangered species -- Puerto Rico 5. Puerto Rican parrot -- Conservation 6. Puerto Rico -- Environmental conditions

ISBN 9781620140048; 1620140047

LC 2012048195

Robert F. Sibert Informational Book Award (2014)

Orbis Pictus Awards Honor Book (2014)

Authors Susan L. Roth and Cindy Trumbore present "a picture book telling the intertwined histories of the Puerto Rican parrot and the island of Puerto Rico, culminating with current efforts to save the parrots from extinction. Roth and Trumbore recount the efforts of the scientists of the Puerto Rican Parrot Recovery Program to save the parrots and ensure their future. Woven into the parrots' story is a brief history of Puerto Rico itself." (Publisher's note)

"Every paper-and-fabric collage is frame-worthy, from depictions of waterfalls and rain forest to sailing ships, hazards and, of course, parrots. From the commanding cover illustration to the playful image on the back, simply spectacular." Kirkus

Includes bibliographical references

Rustad, Martha E. H.

Clown fish and sea anemones work together. Capstone Press 2011 24p il (Pebble Plus: animals working together) lib bdg $23.99; pa $6.95

Grades: K 1 2   597

1. Anemones 2. Clownfish 3. Symbiosis

ISBN 978-1-4296-5297-1 lib bdg; 1-4296-5297-7 lib bdg; 978-1-4296-6198-0 pa; 1-4296-6198-4 pa

LC 2010025462

Simple text and full-color photographs introduce the symbiotic relationship of clown fish and sea anemones.

In this series "the easy-to-understand examples are well selected to show of range of relationships in a variety of environments, and children will come away with some exposure to the concepts of 'parasite' and 'predator' as well." SLJ

Includes glossary and bibliographical references

Moray eels and cleaner shrimp work together. Capstone Press 2011 24p il (Pebble Plus: animals working together) lib bdg $23.99; pa $6.95

Grades: K 1 2 **597**
1. Eels 2. Shrimps 3. Symbiosis
ISBN 978-1-4296-5299-5 lib bdg; 1-4296-5299-3 lib bdg; 978-1-4296-6199-7 pa; 1-4296-6199-2 pa

This describes the lives of moray eels and cleaner shrimp and how they work together to survive.

In this series "the easy-to-understand examples are well selected to show of range of relationships in a variety of environments, and children will come away with some exposure to the concepts of 'parasite' and 'predator' as well." SLJ

Simon, Seymour
★ **Sharks**. HarperCollins Pubs. 1995 un il $16.95; pa $6.95
Grades: 2 3 4 **597**
1. Sharks
ISBN 0-06-023029-0; 0-06-446187-4 pa
LC 95-1593

The author "explores the fascinating undersea life of sharks, examining the truths and myths about these amazing creatures. Astounding close-up photographs enhance the informative and exciting text." Sci Child

Stewart, Melissa
A **place** for fish; written by Melissa Stewart; illustrated by Higgins Bond. Peachtree 2011 un il map $16.95
Grades: K 1 2 3 **597**
1. Fishes 2. Wildlife conservation
ISBN 978-1-56145-562-1; 1-56145-562-8

"Environmental threats facing fish in various habitats around the world are introduced in a picture-book, read-aloud format. . . . Sidebars briefly describe a species affected by the threat and actions that can be taken to resolve it. Each entry repeats the same phrase, 'fish can live and grow.' The information is presented in a simple and idealistic way for young readers. The full-color illustrations on every page are very detailed, but some of the fish have humanlike eyes." SLJ

Shark or dolphin? how do you know? Enslow Publishers 2011 24p il (Which animal is which?) lib bdg $21.26; pa $6.95
Grades: 1 2 3 **597**
1. Sharks 2. Dolphins
ISBN 978-0-7660-3680-2 lib bdg; 0-7660-3680-4 lib bdg; 978-1-59845-239-6 pa; 1-59845-239-8 pa
LC 2010003280

This describes the differences between sharks and dolphin.

This "should give budding naturalists an increased understanding of how scientists use appearance and behavior of classify sometimes-similar living things. . . . Spreads feature sharply detailed paired photographs of identified specimens seen from the same angle and at roughly equal size." SLJ

Includes bibliographical references

Stille, Darlene R.
The **life** cycle of fish. Heinemann Library 2011 48p il (Life cycles) lib bdg $35; pa $8.95
Grades: 3 4 5 **597**
1. Fishes
ISBN 978-1-4329-4980-8 lib bdg; 978-1-4329-4987-7 pa
LC 2010038278

This describes what a fish is, types of fishes, their life cycles, habitats, foods, defenses, and relationships to humans.

Includes glossary and bibliographical references

Stockdale, Susan
★ **Fabulous** fishes; written and illustrated by Susan Stockdale. Peachtree 2008 un il $15.95
Grades: PreK K 1 2 3 **597**
1. Fishes
ISBN 978-1-56145-429-7; 1-56145-429-X
LC 2007-29749

"With simple, rhyming text and full-page illustrations in acrylic and collage, this picture book introduces dramatic facts about more than 20 different fishes. . . . Young children will enjoy pointing out the various fish in the illustrations, while older children will switch back and forth from the pictures to the fascinating biological facts about fish behavior, habitat, and camouflage gathered in notes at the back." Booklist

Swinney, Geoff
Fish facts; illustrated by Janeen Mason. Pelican Pub. Co. 2011 48p il $17.99
Grades: 5 6 7 8 **597**
1. Fishes
ISBN 978-1-58980-908-6; 1-58980-908-4
LC 2010046220

"This comprehensive collection of facts about fish is sure to educate as well as fascinate. . . . From fish that produce light and fish that are capable of powered flight, to fish that can change sex and fish that carry their offspring in their mouths, this is chock full of both the amazing and the weird. . . . While the rather advanced vocabulary and biology that Swinney delves into mark this as a book for older readers, younger ones can certainly enjoy both the illustrations and the occasional factoid. Mason's artwork is both painstakingly detailed and realistically colored, even down to the muting effect that water has on colors. Few books come close to this one's inclusiveness." Kirkus

Turner, Pamela S.
★ **Project** Seahorse; [photographs by Scott Tuason] Houghton Mifflin Harcourt 2010 56p il (Scientists in the field) $18
Grades: 4 5 6 7 **597**
1. Sea horses
ISBN 978-0-547-20713-1; 0-547-20713-1
LC 2009-49707

"With striking images of coral-reef inhabitants, this photo-essay introduces Project Seahorse, an international effort to protect and rehabilitate the Danajon Bank, a double reef off a Philippine Island where seahorses once flourished . . . Tuason, a noted Asian marine photographer whose specialty is the Philippines, seems equally adept at photographing the land and people and the underwater world. This is another splendid demonstration of the work of Scientists in the Field." Kirkus

Wallace, Karen
Think of an eel; illustrated by Mike Bostock. Candlewick Press 1993 un il hardcover o.p. pa $6.99; pa with audio CD $8.99
Grades: K 1 2 3 **597**
1. Eels
ISBN 1-56402-180-7; 978-0-7636-1522-2 pa; 0-7636-1522-6 pa; 978-0-7636-3994-5 pa with audio CD; 0-7636-3994-X pa with audio CD
LC 92-53131

Text and illustrations discuss the characteristics and life cycle of the eel

"Bostock's watercolor paintings illustrate the places and creatures in the text without diminishing the mystery of the eel's journey. . . . The short phrases of the prose create a rhythm almost like unrhymed verse that will please readers." Booklist

Wearing, Judy

Manta rays. Weigl Publishers 2010 24p il (World of wonder: underwater life) lib bdg $24.45; pa $8.95

Grades: K 1 2   **597**

1. Rays (Fishes)

ISBN 978-1-60596-104-0 lib bdg; 1-60596-104-3 lib bdg; 978-1-60596-105-7 pa; 1-60596-105-1 pa

LC 2009-25988

This book about mantra rays begins "with introductory information and progress[es] to more unique details of the featured creatures. Bold photographs juxtaposed on colorful background graphic will hold the attention of even the most novice readers. . . . [This book is] sure to make a splash with budding marine biologists everywhere." SLJ

Includes glossary

Seahorses. Weigl 2010 24p il (World of wonder: underwater life) lib bdg $24.45; pa $8.95

Grades: K 1 2   **597**

1. Sea horses

ISBN 978-1-60596-102-6 lib bdg; 1-60596-102-7 lib bdg; 978-1-60596-103-3 pa; 1-60596-103-5 pa

LC 2009-4986

This book about seahorses begins "with introductory information and progress[es] to more unique details of the featured creatures. Bold photographs juxtaposed on colorful background graphic will hold the attention of even the most novice readers. . . . [This book is] sure to make a splash with budding marine biologists everywhere." SLJ

Includes glossary

597.3 Selachii, Holocephali, fleshy-finned fishes

Davey, Owen

Smart About Sharks; by Owen Davey. Flying Eye Books 2016 40 p. color illustrations $19.95

Grades: 1 2 3 4   **597.3**

1. Sharks

ISBN 1909263915; 9781909263918

In this book, "Owen Davey returns to nonfiction to explain the mysteries of those denizens of the deep. Some deadly, some not-so-deadly, and almost all just generally misunderstood. Exciting and detailed illustrations fill the page and educate young readers about these thrilling residents of the sea!" (Publisher's note)

"Witty parlance characterizes the section headings, and detailed scientific facts are presented alongside beautifully immersive illustrations." Booklist

Green, Jen

Great white shark; By Jen Green. Bearport Publishing 2013 24 p. (library binding) $23.93

Grades: 1 2   **597.3**

1. Sharks 2. Marine biology 3. White shark

ISBN 1617729183; 9781617729188

LC 2013010869

In this book, by Jen Green, "readers will explore the underwater world of [the great white shark] through clear text, full-color photos, and diagrams. Age-appropriate activities, such as describing the differences between an adult and a pup, give readers a chance to make observations and to develop animal-science skills." (Publisher's note)

Includes bibliographical references and index

MacQuitty, Miranda

Shark; written by Miranda MacQuitty. DK Pub. 2008 72 p. col. ill (Eyewitness books) (hardcover) $16.99

Grades: 4 5 6 7   **597.3**

1. Sharks 2. Marine biology

ISBN 0756637783; 9780756637781

LC 2008276031

This book is part of the DK Eyewitness Books series and focuses on sharks. The titles in this series "focus on subjects that complement students' personal interests and areas of study to make learning simple and fun." Wall charts, clip art CDs, and photographs and illustrations are included. (Publisher's note)

Mallory, Kenneth

Swimming with hammerhead sharks. Houghton Mifflin 2001 48p il (Scientists in the field) pbk. $7.99

Grades: 4 5 6 7   **597.3**

1. Sharks

ISBN 9780618250790

LC 00-61401

"Mallory, editor-in-chief of publishing programs at the New England Aquarium, uses the context of an IMAX film production on hammerhead sharks to explain how scientists—in particular, marine biologist Pete Klimley—are studying these {animals. Index.} Intermediate." (Horn Book)

This book follows "marine biologist Pete Klimley and an IMAX film team to seamounts off Cocos Island in the Pacific Ocean to observe and film schooling hammerhead sharks. . . . A fascinating record of research and investigation, this inviting book is larded with numerous dramatic color photos." SLJ

Includes bibliographical references

Roy, Katherine

★ Neighborhood sharks; hunting with the great whites of California's Farallon Islands. Katherine Roy. David Macaulay Studio, Roaring Brook Press 2014 48 p. color illustrations, color map (hardcover) $17.99

Grades: 2 3 4 5   **597.3**

1. Sharks 2. Marine biology

ISBN 1596438746; 9781596438743

LC 2014008940

Robert F. Sibert Honor Book (2015)

In this book, author Katherine Roy presents a "portrait of the life cycle, biology, and habitat of the great white shark, based on the latest research and an up-close visit with these amazing animals. In the fall of 2012 . . . Roy visited the Farallons with the scientists who study the islands' shark population. She witnessed seal attacks, observed sharks being tagged in the wild, and got an up close look at the dramatic Farallons--a wildlife refuge." (Publisher's note)

"Scientific facts and concepts mesh smoothly with sequential action scenes, making the content accessible and logical. It is difficult to talk about sharks and their feeding habits without a bit of gore, and the illustrations, though not overly sensational, do not disappoint." Booklist

Includes bibliographical references

Sharks; facts at your fingertips. DK Pub. 2012 156 p. col. ill., map (Pocket genius) (hc) $7.99

Grades: 5 6 7 8   **597.3**

1. Sharks 2. Rays (Fishes) 3. Sharks

ISBN 0756692865; 9780756692865

LC 2011277726

This book, part of the "Pocket Genius" encyclopedia series, "profiles more that 150 sharks and rays -- from the great white to the tiny dwarf lantern -- and tells what they eat, where they live and how fast they swim." It "offers a . . . catalog-style presentation, which clearly lays out individual subcategories." (Publisher's note)

Shingu, Susumu

Wandering whale sharks; Susumu Shingu. Owlkids Books, Inc. 2015 40 p. color illustrations $18.95

Grades: PreK K 1 2   **597.3**

1. Sharks 2. Marine biology

ISBN 1771471301; 9781771471305

LC 2014947493

In this children's book by Susumu Shingu, readers "meet the world's largest living fish: the whale shark. This informational picture book introduces readers to these stunning creatures in spare, poetic text. It's a lyrical meditation that gives a sense of the whale shark's slow, grand journey through the Earth's oceans while creating an opportunity for inquiry and awe." (Publisher's note)

"A counterpoint to the jam-packed, lively layout of current popular nonfiction, this book celebrates the beauty of the world's biggest fish with simple prose and uncluttered illustrations." Booklist

Walker, Sally M.

Fossil fish found alive; discovering the coelacanth. Carolrhoda Bks. 2002 72p il map lib bdg $17.95

Grades: 5 6 7 8   **597.3**

1. Coelacanth

ISBN 1-57505-536-8

LC 2001-3815

Describes the 1938 discovery of the coelacanth, a fish previously believed to be extinct, and subsequent research about it

"Walker writes well, making this relatively unknown area of science history an exciting story of exploration and discovery. Excellent, full-color photos illustrate the text." Booklist

Includes bibliographical references

Waters, John F.

Sharks have six senses; by John F. Waters; illustrated by Bob Barner. Harper, an imprint of HarperCollins Publishers 2015 40 p. illustrations (hardcover) $17.99

Grades: 1 2 3   **597.3**

1. Sharks 2. Marine biology 3. Senses and sensation in animals 4. Sharks -- Sense organs

ISBN 0060281405; 9780060281403; 9780064451918

LC 2014022687

In this children's book, author John F. Waters explains that "[s]harks have the same five senses as humans do, but they have an extra sixth sense that makes them especially deadly hunters. ... Featuring rich marine-biology vocabulary bolded throughout the text, this book also includes a Find Out More section with additional shark facts and web research prompts about shark conservation efforts." (Publisher's note)

"Paper-collage portraits with only an occasional flash of jagged dentifrice illustrate this appreciative description of how sharks use their extraordinarily sharp senses to find prey. ... A distinct and refreshing change of pace from the usual melodramatic shark fare." Kirkus

597.43 Elopomorpha

Green, Jen

Moray eel; by Jen Green. Bearport Publishing 2013 24 p. (library binding) $23.93

Grades: 1 2   **597.43**

1. Eels 2. Morays 3. Morays

ISBN 1617729213; 9781617729218

LC 2013010804

In this book, by Jen Green, "young readers will explore the underwater world of [moray eels] through clear text, full-color photos, and diagrams. Age-appropriate activities, such as matching descriptions of various moray eels to pictures of the fish, give readers a chance to make observations and develop key animal-science skills." (Publisher's note)

Includes bibliographical references and index

597.8 Amphibians

Allen, Kathy

Deformed frogs; a cause and effect investigation. Capstone Press 2010 32p il map (Fact finders. Animals on the edge) lib bdg $25.99

Grades: 3 4 5 6   **597.8**

1. Frogs

ISBN 978-1-4296-4533-1 lib bdg; 1-4296-4533-4 lib bdg

LC 2010004412

"Excellent discussions address those who doubt the severity of the issue and those who wonder why people should care what happens to animals. The captioned photographs are timely and poignant. ... [This] makes serious subject matter interesting and accessible." SLJ

Includes glossary and bibliographical references

Bekkering, Annalise

Frogs. Weigl 2011 24p il (World of wonder: watch them grow) lib bdg $25.70; pa $9.95

Grades: 1 2   **597.8**

1. Frogs

ISBN 978-1-60596-925-1 lib bdg; 1-60596-925-7 lib bdg; 978-1-60596-926-8 pa; 1-60596-926-5 pa

LC 2009050954

Readers will discover the world of frogs and their transition from swimming tadpoles to amphibious adults.

The text "is simple without being simplistic; it is thoughtful and comprehensive without being overwhelming. The real appeal for teachers, students, and independent young readers, however, will be the photographs that fill the facing pages. Bold, bright, and colorful, the photographs bring you marvelously close to the subject. ... On many different levels, this is a very appealing [book]." Libr Media Connect

Includes glossary and bibliographical references

Bishop, Nic

★ **Nic** Bishop frogs. Scholastic Nonfiction 2008 48p il $17.99

Grades: 2 3 4   **597.8**

1. Frogs

ISBN 978-0-439-87755-8; 0-439-87755-5

LC 2007-08699

Boston Globe-Horn Book Award honor book: Nonfiction (2008)

Bishop "presents a number of large, striking photos illustrating a clearly written discussion of the physical characteristics and habits of frogs. Dominating the book are Bishop's remarkably fine color photographs of frogs from around the world." Booklist

Includes glossary

Bluemel Oldfield, Dawn

Leaping ground frogs. Bearport 2010 24p il map (Amphibiana) lib bdg $22.61

Grades: 3 4 5 6   **597.8**

1. Frogs

ISBN 978-1-936087-35-8 lib bdg; 1-936087-35-9 lib bdg

This book about ground frogs "is informative, eye-catching, well organized, and useful for reports. ... Large, clear color photos depict the animals in their natural habitats." SLJ

Includes glossary and bibliographical references

Bredeson, Carmen

Poison dart frogs up close; [by] Carmen Bredeson. Enslow Elementary 2008 24p il (Zoom in on animals!) lib bdg $21.26

Grades: 1 2 3   **597.8**

1. Frogs

ISBN 978-0-7660-3077-0 lib bdg; 0-7660-3077-6 lib bdg

LC 2007039467

"Short paragraphs of simply written text describe [poison dart frogs'] key body parts and how they function. . . . Behavior, diet, and care and development of the young are briefly addressed. Facing the text on each spread is a full-page, sharp, color close-up of one or more of the . . . animals in their natural habitat. . . . Bredeson's simply written and colorful [title] will provide younger readers with [a] satisfying first [introduction] to these fascinating creatures." SLJ

Includes glossary and bibliographical references

Carney, Elizabeth

Frogs! National Geographic 2009 32p il (National Geographic kids) $11.90; pa $3.99

Grades: K 1 2   **597.8**

1. Frogs

ISBN 978-1-4263-0393-7; 1-4263-0393-9; 978-1-4263-0392-0 pa; 1-4263-0392-0 pa

LC 2008014028

This "volume employs simple sentence structures to convey basic facts about frogs . . . including life cycles, habitats, and feeding information. The excellent photographs showcase a variety of species in vivid detail. Vocabulary-word text boxes and goofy jokes . . . increase accessibility." Horn Book Guide

Cowley, Joy

★ **Red**-eyed tree frog; story by Joy Cowley; illustrated with photographs by Nic Bishop. Scholastic Press 1999 un il $16.95

Grades: PreK K 1 2   **597.8**

1. Frogs 2. Rain forests

ISBN 0-590-87175-7

LC 98-15674

This frog found in the rain forest of Central America spends the night searching for food while also being careful not to become dinner for some other animal

"Stunning color photographs and a gripping interactive text." Booklist

Crump, Marty

The **mystery** of Darwin's frog; by Marty Crump; illustrated by Steve Jenkins and Edel Rodriquez. Boyds Mills Press 2013 40 p. ill. (reinforced) $16.95

Grades: 3 4 5 6 7   **597.8**

1. Picture books for children 2. Frogs

ISBN 1590788648; 9781590788646

LC 2012947844

In this book, Marty Crump, a researcher who has investigated the Rhinoderma darwinii, an inch-long frog discovered by Charles Darwin in Chile in 1834, "describes the earlier investigations of this intriguing frog and records her own efforts to document how it lives in the wild. She discusses her findings and goes on to present the problems facing not only Darwin's frogs, but also frogs in general-loss of habitat, pollution, and the assault of the lethal Bd fungus." (School Library Journal)

Dickmann, Nancy

A **frog's** life. Heinemann Library 2010 24p il (Watch it grow) lib bdg $21.50; pa $5.99

Grades: PreK K 1   **597.8**

1. Frogs

ISBN 978-1-4329-4140-6 lib bdg; 1-4329-4140-2 lib bdg; 978-1-4329-4149-9 pa; 1-4329-4149-6 pa

LC 2009-49156

"Practically unique among early introductions to life cycles because death is mentioned . . . this . . . follows [a frog] . . . from egg . . . to maturity with a set of close-up color photographs, one per page, paired to large-type, one or two-sentence captions. . . . Offers nourishing fare for young naturalists." SLJ

Includes glossary and bibliographical references

Firestone, Mary

What's the difference between a frog and a toad? illustrated by Bandelin-Dacey. Picture Window Books 2010 24p il (What's the difference) lib bdg $25.32

Grades: K 1 2   **597.8**

1. Frogs 2. Toads

ISBN 978-1-4048-5544-1 lib bdg; 1-4048-5544-0 lib bdg

LC 2009-6885

"Compares and contrasts the habitats, physical characteristics, location, and lifestyles of [frogs and toads]. The picture-book format is used to great effect as it allows the two animals to be compared side by side on each spread.The bold, expressive watercolors provide the same visual impact as photographs. . . . Short sentences and highlighted fun facts make this . . . [a book] with broad appeal for both researchers and browsers." SLJ

Includes glossary

Ganeri, Anita

Poison dart frog. Heinemann Library 2011 24p il map (A day in the life. Rain forest animals) lib bdg $22; pa $6.49

Grades: 1 2   **597.8**

1. Frogs

ISBN 978-1-4329-4104-8 lib bdg; 1-4329-4104-6 lib bdg; 978-1-4329-4115-4 pa; 1-4329-4115-1 pa

LC 2010000959

This book follows a poison dart frog through its day as it sleeps, eats, and moves.

"Ganeri presents information clearly and simply in large type, two-sentence comments placed below a bright, sharply reproduced color photograph of the animal in a natural setting. . . . [This is] sufficiently specific to support assignment as well as pleasure reading." SLJ

Includes glossary and bibliographical references

Goldish, Meish

Amazing water frogs. Bearport 2010 24p il map (Amphibiana) lib bdg $22.61

Grades: 3 4 5 6   **597.8**

1. Frogs

ISBN 978-1-936087-34-1 lib bdg; 1-936087-34-0 lib bdg

This book about water frogs "is informative, eye-catching, well organized, and useful for reports. . . . Large, clear color photos depict the animals in their natural habitats." SLJ

Includes glossary and bibliographical references

Little newts. Bearport 2010 24p il map (Amphibiana) lib bdg $22.61

Grades: 3 4 5 6   **597.8**

1. Newts

ISBN 978-1-936087-38-9 lib bdg; 1-936087-38-3 lib bdg

This book about newts "is informative, eye-catching, well organized, and useful for reports. . . . Large, clear color photos depict the animals in their natural habitats." SLJ

Includes glossary and bibliographical references

Slimy salamanders. Bearport 2010 24p il map (Amphibiana) lib bdg $22.61
Grades: 3 4 5 6   **597.8**
1. Salamanders
ISBN 978-1-936087-37-2 lib bdg; 1-936087-37-5 lib bdg
This book about salamanders "is informative, eye-catching, well organized, and useful for reports. . . . Large, clear color photos depict the animals in their natural habitats." SLJ

Includes glossary and bibliographical references

Warty toads. Bearport 2010 24p il (Amphibiana) lib bdg $22.61
Grades: 3 4 5 6   **597.8**
1. Toads
ISBN 978-1-936087-36-5 lib bdg; 1-936087-36-7 lib bdg
This book about toads "is informative, eye-catching, well organized, and useful for reports. . . . Large, clear color photos depict the animals in their natural habitats." SLJ

Includes glossary and bibliographical references

Guiberson, Brenda Z., 1946-
Frog song; by Brenda Guiberson; illustrations by Gennady Spirin. Henry Holt and Company 2012 40 p. (hc) $17.99
Grades: K 1 2 3   **597.8**
1. Frogs -- Vocalization 2. Frogs -- Behavior
ISBN 0805092544; 9780805092547
    LC 2011041940
This children's book, by Brenda Z. Guiberson, illustrated by Gennady Spirin, profiles exotic frogs and their sounds. "Since the time of the dinosaurs, frogs have added their birrups and bellows to the music of the earth. . . . Onomatopoeic text and . . . illustrations introduce young readers to these fascinating and important creatures, from Chile to Nepal to Australia." (Publisher's note)

Kolpin, Molly
Salamanders; consulting editor, Gail Saunders-Smith. Capstone Press 2010 24p il map (Pebble plus. Amphibians) lib bdg $22.65
Grades: K 1 2   **597.8**
1. Salamanders
ISBN 978-1-4296-3990-3 lib bdg; 1-4296-3990-3 lib bdg
This "is well suited to emerging readers. Dynamic, full-page color photographs complement controlled, repetitive vocabulary, printed in a large font against solid backgrounds. . . . The information and its presentation are solid." SLJ

Includes glossary and bibliographical references

Lunis, Natalie
Tricky tree frogs. Bearport 2010 24p il map (Amphibiana) lib bdg $22.61
Grades: 3 4 5 6   **597.8**
1. Frogs
ISBN 978-1-936087-33-4 lib bdg; 1-936087-33-2 lib bdg
This book about tree frogs "is informative, eye-catching, well organized, and useful for reports. . . . Large, clear color photos depict the animals in their natural habitats." SLJ

Includes glossary and bibliographical references

Markle, Sandra, 1946-
★ The **case** of the vanishing golden frogs. Milbrook Press 2011 48p il

Grades: 4 5 6   **597.8**
1. Frogs 2. Endangered species 3. Wildlife conservation
ISBN 0761351086; 9780761351085
    LC 2010042642
"Notable for clarity, directness, and simplicity of writing and design alike, this volume [is] both handsome and fascinating. . . . Excellent photos, microscopic views, and maps illustrate the book." Booklist

Includes glossary and bibliographical references

★ **Hip-**pocket papa; illustrated by Alan Marks. Charlesbridge 2010 un il lib bdg $15.95
Grades: K 1 2 3   **597.8**
1. Frogs 2. Natural history -- Australia
ISBN 978-1-57091-708-0 lib bdg; 1-57091-708-6 lib bdg
    LC 2008025334
"Markle writes with clarity and precision, while Marks' evocative watercolor, ink, and pencil artwork brings the frogs' world to life." Booklist

Toad weather; by Sandra Markle; illustrations by Thomas Gonzalez. Peachtree Publishers 2015 32 p. color illustrations $16.95
Grades: PreK 1 2 3   **597.8**
1. Toads 2. Weather 3. Toads -- Climatic factors
ISBN 156145818X; 9781561458189
    LC 2014006505
In this book, by Sandra Markle, "[t]here's nothing to do on a rainy day or so Ally thinks. But Mama says she's seen something amazing, so despite Ally's misgivings, she sets out on an adventure with her mother and grandmother. On her journey, she sees all sorts of things: dripping awnings, wet cardboard, splashing cars...but also earthworms, storm drain geysers, and oil slick patterns. And then they turn the corner, just in time to see a big crowd. What's happening?" (Publisher's note)
"At the end of a walk in the rain on a gloomy March evening, Ally and her grandmother find the surprise Mama promised: a street full of migrating toads that need their help. Based on an actual annual occurrence in Philadelphia and other places around the world where toads have been cut off from their preferred egg-laying ponds by human roads, this appealing story celebrates a human-natural world connection." Kirkus

Moffett, Mark W.
Face to face with frogs. National Geographic 2008 31p il map (Face to face) $16.95; lib bdg $25.90
Grades: 3 4 5 6   **597.8**
1. Frogs
ISBN 978-1-4263-0205-3; 1-4263-0205-3; 978-1-4263-0206-0 lib bdg; 1-4263-0206-1 lib bdg
    LC 2007-12445
This book has "personal accounts of [Moffett's] own explorations providing entertaining specifics to go with the arresting visuals, as casual sidebars offer information on random hoppy topics." Bull Cent Child Books

Includes glossary and bibliographical references

Pfeffer, Wendy
From tadpole to frog; illustrated by Holly Keller. HarperCollins Pubs. 1994 32p il (Let's-read-and-find-out science) $15.95; pa $4.95
Grades: K 1   **597.8**
1. Frogs
ISBN 0-06-023044-4; 0-06-445123-2 pa
    LC 93-3135
"The illustrations are simple, interesting, and just right for young children. The science is accurate and presented in a way to excite

young readers to get outside and look for some frogs and tadpoles." Sci Books Films

Pringle, Laurence, 1935-

Frogs! strange and wonderful. Laurence Pringle; illustrated by Meryl Henderson. Boyds Mills Press 2012 30 p. col. ill (reinf. trade ed.) $16.95

Grades: 3 4 5   **597.8**

1. Frogs 2. Poisonous animals 3. Camouflage (Biology) 4. Picture books for children 5. Amphibians

ISBN 1590783719; 9781590783719

LC 2011928834

In this book, author Laurence P. Pringle offers a "look at the similarities and differences among the many and varied species of frogs . . . The Reinwardt's flying frog glides between trees, the mantella and poison frogs come in all the colors of the rainbow and one can guess what makes the marsupial frog stand out. Camouflage, mating, development, coloring, size, locomotion, how and what they eat and how and why they make sounds are just some of the topics." (Kirkus)

Includes bibliographical references

Salas, Laura Purdie

Amphibians; water-to-land animals. illustrated by Kristin Kest. Picture Window Books 2010 24p il (Amazing science. Animal classification) lib bdg $25.32

Grades: K 1 2   **597.8**

1. Amphibians

ISBN 978-1-4048-5521-2 lib bdg; 1-4048-5521-1 lib bdg

LC 2009-3290

"This is the way to introduce kids to science as well as lead them to a deeper level of understanding how the animal kingdom is divided into phylum, class, order, family, genus, and species. Excellent picture book-quality illustrations fill each page with a few well chosen words to extend visual understanding. . . . The writing is clear, age-appropriate science writing. Every school should purchase this book." Libr Media Connect

Includes glossary

Simon, Seymour

Frogs; Seymour Simon. Harper, an imprint of HarperCollinsPublishers 2015 40 p. color illustrations (pbk.) $6.99; (hardcover) $17.99

Grades: 1 2 3 4   **597.8**

1. Frogs

ISBN 006228911X; 9780062289117; 9780062289124

LC 2014027411

This children's book, by Seymour Simon, "takes readers on a journey through a frog's life cycle, from egg to tadpole to grown frog, with fascinating facts, stunning full-color photographs, and an underlying message of ecological preservation. Readers will learn about the different types of frogs and toads that are found all over the world!" (Publisher's note)

"Among the plethora of books about frogs currently in print, Simon's stands out as one of the best...A smart choice for reports and recreational reading for all libraries." SLJ

Stewart, Melissa

Frog or toad? how do you know? Enslow Publishers 2011 24p il (Which animal is which?) lib bdg $21.26; pa $6.95

Grades: 1 2 3   **597.8**

1. Frogs 2. Toads

ISBN 978-0-7660-3682-6 lib bdg; 0-7660-3682-0 lib bdg; 978-1-59845-236-5 pa; 1-59845-236-3 pa

LC 2010003277

This describes the differences between frogs and toads.

Includes bibliographical references

A place for frogs; written by Melissa Stewart; illustrated by Higgins Bond. Peachtree Publishers 2010 un il map $16.95

Grades: K 1 2 3   **597.8**

1. Frogs 2. Wildlife conservation

ISBN 978-1-5614-5521-8; 1-5614-5521-0

LC 2009-24515

"This wide-format book shows how people's actions have endangered frogs and what has been done to reverse those environmental threats. A typical double-page spread includes a large, detailed acrylic painting showing various frogs in their habitats. . . . Written and illustrated with young children in mind, this book is a good starting place for environmental studies." Booklist

Salamander or lizard? how do you know? Enslow Publishers 2011 24p il (Which animal is which?) lib bdg $21.26; pa $6.95

Grades: 1 2 3   **597.8**

1. Lizards 2. Salamanders

ISBN 978-0-7660-3679-6 lib bdg; 0-7660-3679-0 lib bdg; 978-1-59845-238-9 pa; 1-59845-238-X pa

LC 2010003279

This describes the differences between salamanders and lizards.

This "should give budding naturalists an increased understanding of how scientists use appearance and behavior of classify sometimes-similar living things. . . . Spreads feature sharply detailed paired photographs of identified specimens seen from the same angle and at roughly equal size." SLJ

Includes bibliographical references

Stille, Darlene R.

The **life** cycle of amphibians. Heinemann Library 2011 48p il (Life cycles) lib bdg $32; pa $8.99

Grades: 3 4 5   **597.8**

1. Amphibians

ISBN 978-1-4329-4978-5 lib bdg; 978-1-4329-4985-3 pa

LC 2010038276

This describes how amphibians "are born or hatched, where they live, and how they grow, move, protect themselves, spend their time, and reproduce. Focusing on frogs, toads, salamanders, and caecilians, [this book] is informative."

Includes glossary and bibliographical references

Sweeney, Alyse

Toads. Capstone Press 2010 24p il map (Pebble plus. Amphibians) lib bdg $22.65

Grades: K 1 2   **597.8**

1. Toads

ISBN 978-1-4296-3991-0 lib bdg; 1-4296-3991-1 lib bdg

This "is well suited to emerging readers. Dynamic, full-page color photographs complement controlled, repetitive vocabulary, printed in a large font against solid backgrounds. . . . While the information and its presentation are solid." SLJ

Includes glossary and bibliographical references

Turner, Pamela S.

★ The **frog** scientist; photographs by Andy Comins. Houghton Mifflin Books for Children 2009 58p il (Scientists in the field) lib bdg $18

Grades: 5 6 7 8   **597.8**

1. Frogs 2. Biologists 3. College teachers

ISBN 978-0-618-71716-3 lib bdg; 0-618-71716-1 lib bdg

LC 2008-39770

This volume "opens with biologist Tyrone Hayes and his team collecting frogs at a pond in Wyoming. After a short chapter on Hayes' background, the discussion returns to his work: he addresses the general question of why amphibian populations world-wide are declining by studying the effects of atrizine, an agricultural pesticide, on the reproductive organs of leopard frogs from a particular pond. Well organized and clearly written. . . . Excellent color photos offer clear pictures of frogs and of this scientific team at work in the field and in the lab. . . . A vivid, realistic view of one scientist at work." Booklist

Includes glossary and bibliographical references

Wechsler, Doug

The **hidden** life of the toad; Doug Wechsler. Charlesbridge 2017 48 p. color illustrations, color map (reinforced for library use) $17.99

Grades: K 1 2 3　　　　　　　　　　　　　**597.8**

1. Toads 2. Frogs 3. American toad -- Behavior 4. American toad -- Life cycles

ISBN 9781580897389

LC 2015043918

This book, by Doug Wechsler, "captures the life cycle of the American toad from egg to tadpole to adult. To get these images, Wechsler sat in a pond wearing waders, went out night after night in search of toads, and cut his own glass to make a home aquarium. The resulting photos reveal metamorphosis in extreme close-up as readers have never seen it before. Budding naturalists will be transfixed by this unprecedented peek into the secrets of tadpole transformation." (Publisher's note)

Winnick, Nick

Salamanders. Weigl 2010 24p il (Backyard animals) lib bdg $24.45; pa $8.95

Grades: 1 2 3　　　　　　　　　　　　　　**597.8**

1. Salamanders

ISBN 978-1-60596-084-5 lib bdg; 1-60596-084-5 lib bdg; 978-1-60596-085-2 pa; 1-60596-085-3 pa

LC 2008052060

This describes the physical characteristics, natural habitats, history, and folklore of salamanders.

This is "packed with information and [includes] fine close-up photos." Booklist

Includes glossary

597.9　Reptiles

Arnosky, Jim

★ **Slither** and crawl; eye to eye with reptiles. Sterling Pub. 2009 31p il $14.95

Grades: 2 3 4 5　　　　　　　　　　　　　**597.9**

1. Reptiles

ISBN 978-1-4027-3986-6; 1-4027-3986-9

LC 2008022493

"Arnosky's painterly eye and personal observations match handsomely in this face-to-face experience. The slim volume presents head-on-life-size depictions of a plethora of scaly or otherwise armored critters, along with a nice selection of data included in the conversational text. Neat foldouts of a passel of snakes, an American crocodile, . . . a skitter of lizards, and the heads of a variety of sea turtles add an interactive touch to the artist's outstanding acrylics." SLJ

Includes bibliographical references

Herrington, Lisa M.

Remarkable reptiles; by Lisa M. Herrington. Children's Press, an imprint of Scholastic Inc. 2016 32 p. color illustrations (library binding) $23

Grades: K 1 2　　　　　　　　　　　　　**597.9**

1. Reptiles

ISBN 0531226034; 9780531226032; 9780531227497

LC 2015021146

This book, by Lisa M. Herrington, "Introduces the reader to remarkable reptiles." (Publisher's note)

"This series finds the right balance between scientific information and accessibility for young readers enthralled by nature's novelties." Booklist

Hutchinson, Mark

Reptiles. Simon & Schuster Books for Young Readers 2011 64p il (Insiders) $16.99

Grades: 4 5 6 7　　　　　　　　　　　　　**597.9**

1. Reptiles

ISBN 978-1-4424-3276-5; 1-4424-3276-4

"Arranged around the digitally rendered, sharply focused central images . . . smaller inset pictures and blocks of text systematically present distinctive physical features, typical behaviors, habitats, ranges, diets, and other information about each type of reptile. . . . This book will wow casual browsers and budding herpetologists alike." Booklist

McCarthy, Colin

Reptile; written by Colin McCarthy. Revised edition DK Publishing 2012 72 p color illustrations (DK Eyewitness) library $19.99

Grades: 4 5 6 7　　　　　　　　　　　　　**597.9**

1. Reptiles

ISBN 0756693055; 9780756693053

Photographs and text depict the many different kinds of reptiles, their similarities and differences, habitats, and behavior.

Stille, Darlene R., 1942-

The **life** cycle of reptiles. Heinemann Library 2011 48p il map (Life cycles)

Grades: 3 4 5　　　　　　　　　　　　　　**597.9**

1. Reptiles

ISBN 9781432949822 lib bdg; 9781432949891

LC 2010038507

This describes what a reptile is, types of reptiles, their life cycles, habitats, foods, and defenses.

"The book offers a good sense of the variety of reptiles in the world. The books' colorful illustrations include many fine photos from a variety of sources as well as some clearly delineated digital drawings." Booklist

Includes glossary and bibliographical references

Wilson, Hannah

Life-size reptiles; written by Hannah Wilson. Sterling 2007 48p il $9.95

Grades: 3 4 5 6　　　　　　　　　　　　　**597.9**

1. Reptiles

ISBN 1-4027-4542-7

This "covers lizards, crocodilians, and others of their cold-blooded kin. Colorful, realistic illustrations fill the pages, depicting reptiles in all their scaly/shelled splendor, many—as promised in the title—life-sized." SLJ

597.92　Turtles

Allen, Kathy

★ **Sea** turtles' race to the sea; a cause and effect investigation. Capstone Press 2011 32p il map (Animals on the edge) lib bdg $25.99

Grades: K 1 2 3 **597.92**
1. Sea turtles 2. Endangered species
ISBN 978-1-4296-5402-9; 1-4296-5402-3

LC 2010033003

Describes the sea turtle and its disappearing habitat.

"The thoughtfulness with which this . . . book is arranged shows through on each page. Photos truly complement the text without overwhelming it. . . . The book merits praise for its content and its compound contribution to the environment." Sci Books Films

Includes glossary and bibliographical references

Berger, Melvin
Look out for turtles! illustrated by Megan Lloyd. HarperCollins Pubs. 1992 32p il (Let's-read-and-find-out science book) hardcover o.p. pa $4.95
Grades: K 1 2 3 **597.92**
1. Turtles
ISBN 0-06-022540-8 lib bdg; 0-06-445156-9 pa

LC 90-36894

"This simple introductory resource provides an overview of the different types of turtles and their characteristics and habits. It is a good resource for young children to use independently." Sci Child

Gibbons, Gail
Sea turtles. Holiday House 1995 un il $16.95; pa $6.95
Grades: K 1 2 3 **597.92**
1. Sea turtles
ISBN 0-8234-1191-5; 0-8234-1373-X pa

LC 94-48579

This is "a very appealing book. . . . The illustrations are lovely paintings, highlighted with black outlines and clear labels. Children should find the diagram that shows differences between sea turtles and other turtles fascinating because they are often familiar only with the latter." Sci Books Films

Guiberson, Brenda Z.
Into the sea; illustrated by Alix Berenzy. Holt & Co. 1996 un il $16.95; pa $6.95
Grades: K 1 2 3 **597.92**
1. Sea turtles
ISBN 0-8050-2263-5; 0-8050-6481-8 pa

LC 95-46757

"Guiberson uses italicized sound words such as tap, tap, and scritch to draw readers into the story. Berenzy captures the essence of the text with her colored-pencil and gouache illustrations that alternate from dark to light, reflecting the various habitats." SLJ

Jackson, Tom
Green sea turtle; by Tom Jackson. Bearport Publishing 2013 24 p. (library binding) $23.93
Grades: 1 2 **597.92**
1. Sea turtles 2. Marine biology 3. Green turtle
ISBN 1617729205; 9781617729201

LC 2013011548

In this book, by Tom Jackson, "readers will explore the underwater world of [the green sea turtle] through clear text, full-color photos, and diagrams. Age-appropriate activities, such as using tape on the floor to show how big green sea turtles can grow, give readers a chance to make observations and to develop animal-science skills." (Publisher's note)

Includes bibliographical references and index

Spilsbury, Louise
Sea turtle. Heinemann Library 2011 24p il (A day in the life. sea animals) lib bdg $22; pa $6.49

Grades: 1 2 **597.92**
1. Sea turtles
ISBN 978-1-4329-4001-0 lib bdg; 1-4329-4001-5 lib bdg; 978-1-4329-4008-9 pa; 1-4329-4008-2 pa

LC 2010000626

This pairs "well-chosen color photos . . . with one or two sentences of simple commentary for each. . . . [Though this title] includes references to several varieties of the chosen creature, one species in particular is highlighted. . . . [Good choice] for pleasure or purpose reading." SLJ

Includes glossary and bibliographical references

Swinburne, Stephen R.
Sea turtle scientist; by Stephen R. Swinburne. Houghton Mifflin Harcourt 2013 65 p. ill. (chiefly col.), col. map (Scientists in the field) $18.99
Grades: 5 6 7 8 9 **597.92**
1. Biologists 2. Sea turtles
ISBN 0547367554; 9780547367552

LC 2012034045

"Dr. Kimberly Stewart, also known as the Turtle Lady of St. Kitts, is already waiting at midnight when an 800-pound leatherback sea turtle crawls out of the Caribbean surf and onto the sandy beach. The mother turtle has a vital job to do: dig a nest in which she will lay eggs that will hatch into part of the next generation of leatherbacks." (Publisher's note)

"This refreshing journey with a dedicated woman hard at work in her chosen field will resonate with readers." SLJ

Includes bibliographical references and index

Turtle tide; the ways of sea turtles. illustrated by Bruce Hiscock. Boyds Mills Press 2005 un il $15.95
Grades: 2 3 4 **597.92**
1. Sea turtles
ISBN 1-59078-081-7

LC 2004-16856

"Simple, lyrical prose accompanies brilliant watercolors in this account." SLJ

Wearing, Judy
Sea turtle. Weigl 2010 24p il (World of wonder: underwater life) lib bdg $24.45; pa $8.95
Grades: K 1 2 **597.92**
1. Sea turtles
ISBN 978-1-60596-106-4 lib bdg; 1-60596-106-X lib bdg; 978-1-60596-107-1 pa; 1-60596-107-8 pa

LC 2009-4987

This book about sea turtles begins "with introductory information and progress[es] to more unique details of the featured creatures. Bold photographs juxtaposed on colorful background graphic will hold the attention of even the most novice readers. . . . [This book is] sure to make a splash with budding marine biologists everywhere." SLJ

Includes glossary

597.95 Lizards

Bishop, Nic
★ **Lizards**. Scholastic Nonfiction 2010 48p il $17.99
Grades: 2 3 4 **597.95**
1. Lizards
ISBN 978-0-545-20634-1; 0-545-20634-0

"Bishop introduces lizards from around the world: their habitats, egg-laying and lack of child-rearing, their specialized bodies and behaviors, their feeding and courtship. His astonishing photographs are beautifully composed and clearly reproduced. . . . The well-organized two-level text is . . . inviting." Kirkus

Includes glossary and bibliographical references

Bodden, Valerie

Komodo dragons; by Valerie Bodden. 1st ed. Creative Education 2013 24 p. col. ill. (library) $25.65

Grades: 1 2 3 4   **597.95**

1. Animals 2. Komodo dragon

ISBN 1608180875; 9781608180875

LC 2011050275

This book, part of the Amazing Animals series from author Valerie Bodden, is a "basic exploration of the appearance, behavior, and habitat of Komodo dragons, Earth's heaviest lizards. Also included is a story from folklore explaining why Indonesians respect Komodo dragons." (Publisher's note)

Includes bibliographical references and index

Collard, Sneed B. III

Sneed B. Collard III's most fun book ever about lizards; Sneed B. Collard III. Charlesbridge 2012 47 p. (reinforced for library use) $16.95

Grades: 3 4 5 6 7   **597.95**

1. Lizards 2. Lizards as pets 3. Wildlife photography 4. Lizards -- Miscellanea

ISBN 9781580893244; 9781580893251

LC 2011000809

This book offers an "introduction to the world of lizards [which] describes their . . . variety and life in the wild and offers cautions from a long-time reptile fan for those who want to keep lizards as pets. [Author Sneed B.] Collard . . . turns his attention . . . to modern-day lizards. After presenting an exemplar, 'Joe Lizard,' a western fence lizard, he goes on to describe other well-known species, including Komodo dragons, Gila monsters, chameleons and iguanas, as well as some with unusual talents, including 'religious lizards' that can walk on water. He covers eating and being eaten, the ways saurians keep warm and reproduce, and threats to their survival. . . . [Photographs] show lizard characteristics. . . . Captions and sidebars add further information." (Kirkus)

Cowley, Joy

★ Chameleon chameleon; story by Joy Cowley; illustrated with photographs by Nic Bishop. Scholastic Press 2005 un il $16.95

Grades: K 1 2   **597.95**

1. Chameleons

ISBN 0-439-66653-8

LC 2004-7291

A chameleon creeps through the rain forest avoiding danger and searching for food

This is a "stunning photo-essay. . . . Crisp, clear, full-color photos portray this reptile and its habitat. . . . An informative, thoughtfully produced science book that will be popular with a wide range of animal lovers. Excellent for browsing as well as learning." Booklist

Crump, Marty

Mysteries of the Komodo dragon; the biggest, deadliest lizard gives up its secrets. Boyd Mills Press 2010 40p il map $18.95

Grades: 3 4 5 6   **597.95**

1. Komodo dragon

ISBN 978-1-59078-757-1; 1-59078-757-9

"While Crump's lively text does not supply a stage-by-stage description of the animal's life cycle and physiology, it does give enough data to satisfy many readers and researchers. More importantly, it follows a long-term research project into the chemical makeup of 'dragon drool' and the possible practical applications of the chemicals in this deadly

substance to human pharmacology. Clear, color photos depict dragons from hatchlings to adults, scientists hiding in blinds and weighing catches, and zookeepers cuddling dragons with 'gentle' dispositions. . . . A surefire selection in terms of appeal and information." SLJ

Includes glossary and bibliographical references

Gish, Melissa

Iguanas; Melissa Gish. Creative Education 2015 46 p. color ill., color map (hardcover : alk. paper) $39.95

Grades: 4 5 6   **597.95**

1. Iguanas 2. Rare reptiles

ISBN 1608185672; 9781608185672

LC 2014028010

This book, by Melissa Gish, presents "a look at iguanas, including their habitats, physical characteristics such as their dewlaps, behaviors, relationships with humans, and their protected status in the world today." (Publisher's note)

"Stunning photographs, sidebars with intriguing facts, and engaging prose are hallmarks of this set, and the chapters describing each creature's role in folklore or pop culture add to the fun." SLJ

Includes bibliographical references and index

Komodo dragons. Creative Education 2011 48p il (Living wild) lib bdg $23.95; pa $8.99

Grades: 5 6 7 8   **597.95**

1. Komodo dragon

ISBN 978-1-60818-080-6 lib bdg; 1-60818-080-8 lib bdg; 978-0-89812-672-3 pa; 0-89812-672-X pa

LC 2010028307

A look at Komodo dragons, including their habitats, physical characteristics such as their sawlike teeth, behaviors, relationships with humans, and threatened status in the world today.

"Stunning, full-page photographs create immediate visual interest. A brief narrative introduction sets the scene for the richer, more scientific information in the rest of the text." Booklist

Includes glossary and bibliographical references

Jango-Cohen, Judith

Let's look at iguanas. Lerner Publications Co. 2010 32p il map (Lightning bolt books: Animal close-ups) lib bdg $25.26; pa $7.95

Grades: PreK K 1 2   **597.95**

1. Iguanas

ISBN 978-0-7613-3888-8 lib bdg; 0-7613-3888-8 lib bdg; 978-0-7613-5005-7 pa; 0-7613-5005-5 pa

LC 2008-51857

Introduces desert iguanas, describing their physical characteristics, habitat, and predators.

"Fresh photography, a creative use of graphics, and a collagelike layout make[s] . . . [this book] eye-catching. . . . [The] book ends with a labeled diagram of the animal, a range map, and a further-reading list that includes print and online resources in a single list, a nice way of validating both types of materials." SLJ

Includes glossary

Lunis, Natalie

Black spiny-tailed iguana; lizard lightning! Bearport Pub. 2010 24p il map (Blink of an eye. Superfast animals!) lib bdg $22.61

Grades: 1 2 3   **597.95**

1. Iguanas 2. Lizards

ISBN 978-1-936087-91-4; 1-936087-91-X

LC 2010019671

This describes the black spiny-tailed iguana, including where it lives, what it eats, and the ways its body helps it reach its record-breaking speeds.

This "is sure to appeal to a wide variety of readers. Vibrant photos illustrate each animal from multiple perspectives, providing opportunity for readers to closely examine the animal. Information is organized by subject heading and branches into the animal's physical features and how they contribute to its speed, the animal's natural predators, and how the animal makes use of speed as a means of survival. . . . This . . . will be a worthwhile addition to your nonfiction collection." Libr Media Connect

Includes glossary and bibliographical references

Somervill, Barbara A.

Monitor lizard. Cherry Lake 2010 32p il (Animal invaders) lib bdg $27.07

Grades: 5 6 7 8   **597.95**

1. Lizards 2. Biological invasions

ISBN 978-1-60279-627-0 lib bdg; 1-60279-627-0 lib bdg

This offers "an introduction to the problems caused by [the monitor lizard], a discussion of its physical characteristics and habits, a history of how it arrived in its new habitat, and an analysis of challenges encountered by those trying to limit its spread. . . . [It] describes the threat posed by these aggressive 7-foot reptiles, sold as babies by pet vendors and now loose in Florida. . . . [This] well-focused [book is] clearly written. The uncluttered page design features at least one color photo on each page." Booklist

Includes glossary and bibliographical references

597.96 Snakes

Bishop, Nic, 1955-

★ **Nic** Bishop snakes; Nic Bishop. Scholastic Nonfiction 2012 48 p. ill. (jacketed hardcover) $17.99

Grades: 3 4 5   **597.96**

1. Snakes

ISBN 0545206383; 9780545206389

LC 2011039316

In this juvenile zoology book, "Sibert Medal-winning photographer Nic Bishop introduces the terrifying and beautiful world of snakes. The . . . text presents both basic information and . . . details about the appearance, habits, and remarkable abilities of these amazing reptiles. An index and glossary are included, along with an author's note detailing his research and the . . . stories behind the photographs." (Publisher's note)

Blobaum, Cindy

Awesome snake science; 40 activities for learning about snakes. Cindy Blobaum. 1st ed. Chicago Review Press 2012 x, 118 p.p ill. (ebook) $11.99; (prebind) $23.95; (paperback) $14.95

Grades: 4 5 6   **597.96**

1. Science projects 2. Educational games 3. Science -- Experiments 4. Snakes -- Experiments 5. Snakes -- Study and teaching (Elementary) -- Activity programs

ISBN 9781613743188; 9781451775303; 9781569768075

LC 2011050257

Author Cindy Blobaum's book includes "40 science experiments, art projects, and games . . . [about snakes] from cobras and copperheads to pythons and boas . . . Activities include making foldable fangs to learn how snakes' teeth and jaws work together . . . [and] simulating cytotoxic snake venom . . . Engaging, simple, and safe experiments teach kids about the biology of snakes, such as how they use their tongues and nostrils to detect smells, how they are cold-blooded and sensitive to subtle changes in temperature, and how they can detect the slightest vibrations or tremors." (Amazon)

Includes bibliographical references (p. 115-116) and index.

Bodden, Valerie

Snakes. Creative Education 2010 24p il (Amazing animals) lib bdg $24.25

Grades: K 1 2   **597.96**

1. Snakes

ISBN 978-1-58341-813-0 lib bdg; 1-58341-813-X lib bdg

LC 2009002717

A basic exploration of the appearance, behavior, and habitat of snakes, a family of scaly reptiles. Also included is a story from folklore explaining why snakes do not have legs.

Includes bibliographical references

Franchino, Vicky

Black mambas; by Vicky Franchino. Children's Press, an imprint of Scholastic Inc. 2015 48 p. color ill., color map (pbk. : alk. paper) $6.95

Grades: 3 4 5 6   **597.96**

1. Snakes 2. Black mamba

ISBN 9780531213926; 9780531214954

LC 2014043960

This children's book, by Vicky Franchino, part of the "Nature's Children" series, profiles Black Mamba snakes. "An opening 'Fact File' breaks down info such as taxonomy, habits, habitats, and diets. . . . Five chapters are broken down into several single-page sections. The first chapter depicts an encounter with the animal and describes a typical behavior. The rest of the book delves further into the topics brought up in the 'Fact File.'" (School Library Journal)

"Sophisticated scientific terms such as bilateral symmetry or anticoagulant are often defined in-text. 'Fun Fact' boxes are scattered throughout." SLJ

Includes bibliographical references and index

Ganeri, Anita

Anaconda. Heinemann Library 2011 24p il map (A day in the life. Rain forest animals) lib bdg $22; pa $6.49

Grades: 1 2   **597.96**

1. Anacondas

ISBN 978-1-4329-4112-3 lib bdg; 1-4329-4112-7 lib bdg; 978-1-4329-4123-9 pa; 1-4329-4123-2 pa

LC 2010001135

This book follows an anaconda through its day as it sleeps, eats, and moves.

"Ganeri presents information clearly and simply in large type, two-sentence comments placed below a bright, sharply reproduced color photograph of the animal in a natural setting. . . . [This is] sufficiently specific to support assignment as well as pleasure reading." SLJ

Includes glossary and bibliographical references

Gibbons, Gail

Snakes. Holiday House 2007 32p il map $16.95

Grades: K 1 2 3   **597.96**

1. Snakes

ISBN 978-0-8234-2122-0; 0-8234-2122-8

LC 2007-24585

"Gibbons injects a healthy dose of snake basics, delivered in her customary matter-of-fact style and illustrated with watercolor portraits of dozens of different species, pictured mostly in natural settings." Booklist

Hamilton, Sue L.

Bitten by a rattlesnake; [by] Sue Hamilton. ABDO Pub. 2010 32p il (Close encounters of the wild kind) lib bdg $27.07

Grades: 4 5 6 7   **597.96**
1. Rattlesnakes 2. Animal attacks
ISBN 978-1-60453-930-1 lib bdg; 1-60453-930-5 lib bdg
LC 2009-45423
Readers learn of actual human-rattlesnake encounters, information about rattlesnakes, survival strategies, and attack statistics.

"Students will be drawn to the realistic full-color photographs, the realistic diagrams of the creatures' bodies, the real-life stories told by victims, and the interesting, attractive formatting that includes text, diagrams, photographs, and graphics on each page. . . . [This is] exciting and attractive in a 'gross' sort of way and will appeal particularly to boys for both leisure reading and research." Libr Media Connect

Includes glossary

Markle, Sandra
Rattlesnakes. Lerner Publications 2009 39p il (Animal predators) lib bdg $26.60
Grades: 4 5 6   **597.96**
1. Rattlesnakes
ISBN 978-1-58013-539-9 lib bdg; 1-58013-539-0 lib bdg
LC 2008-38038
Introduces the physical characteristics, habitat, and predatory behavior of rattlesnakes.

"Vivid close-up photographs accompany a narrative." Horn Book Guide

Includes glossary and bibliographical references

Montgomery, Sy
★ The **snake** scientist; photographs by Nic Bishop. Houghton Mifflin 1999 48p il map $16; pa $5.95
Grades: 4 5 6 7   **597.96**
1. Snakes
ISBN 0-395-87169-7; 0-618-11119-0 pa
LC 98-6124
Discusses the work of Bob Mason and his efforts to study and protect snakes, particularly red-sided garter snakes

"The lively text communicates both the meticulous measurements required in this kind of work and the thrill of new discoveries. Large, full-color photos of the zoologist and young students at work, and lots of wriggly snakes, pull readers into the presentation." SLJ

Includes bibliographical references

Simon, Seymour
Giant snakes; [by] Seymour Simon. Chronicle Books 2006 un il (See more readers) lib bdg $14.95; pa $3.95
Grades: K 1 2 3   **597.96**
1. Snakes
ISBN 978-0-8118-5410-8 lib bdg; 0-8118-5410-8 lib bdg; 978-0-8118-5411-5 pa; 0-8118-5411-6 pa
LC 2005-25360
An easy-to-read illustrated introduction to large snakes.

"The text is lively, well organized, and clear, with the many facts it presents cleverly woven into the story. The illustrations, which are beautiful, show distinctly the intricate patterns of the snakes' skin." Sci Books Films

Stewart, Melissa
Snakes! National Geographic 2009 31p il (National Geographic kids) lib bdg $11.90; pa $3.99
Grades: K 1 2   **597.96**
1. Snakes
ISBN 978-1-4263-0429-3 lib bdg; 978-1-4263-0428-6 pa
LC 2008-47001

An introduction to the types, physical features, behavior, and pet potential of snakes.

"The excellent photographs showcase a variety of species in vivid detail. Vocabulary-word text boxes and goofy jokes . . . increase accessibility." Horn Book Guide

597.98   Crocodilians

Bodden, Valerie
Crocodiles. Creative Education 2010 24p il (Amazing animals) lib bdg $24.25; pa $5.99
Grades: K 1 2   **597.98**
1. Crocodiles
ISBN 978-1-58341-806-2 lib bdg; 1-58341-806-7 lib bdg; 978-1-926722-21-4 pa; 1-926722-21-3 pa
LC 2009002706
A basic exploration of the appearance, behavior, and habitat of crocodiles, a family of sharp-toothed reptiles. Also included is a story from folklore explaining why crocodiles have rough skin.

This is illustrated with "dynamically colored photographs . . . showcasing the animal's intricately textured scales, craggy ridges, and of course, hide-rending teeth." Booklist

Includes bibliographical references

Feigenbaum, Aaron
American alligators; freshwater survivors. Bearport Pub. Company, Inc. 2008 32p il map (America's animal comebacks) lib bdg $25.27
Grades: 2 3 4   **597.98**
1. Alligators
ISBN 978-1-59716-503-7 lib bdg; 1-59716-503-4 lib bdg
LC 2007-13160
Explains why American alligators became an endangered species, and describes the efforts of scientists to bring them back from the brink of extinction

"Closeup photos, maps, and an accessible text provide solid information for readers and report writers. Statistics and information about other endangered alligators are appended." Horn Book Guide

Includes glossary and bibliographical references

Gibbons, Gail
Alligators and crocodiles. Holiday House 2010 32p il map $17.95
Grades: K 1 2 3   **597.98**
1. Alligators 2. Crocodiles
ISBN 0-8234-2234-8; 978-0-8234-2234-0
Gibbons "draws young readers into the world of alligators and crocodiles by first asking readers to distinguish between them. She describes the physical similarities and differences between the two most common species of the world's largest reptiles, as well as their habitats, habits, prey, locomotion, senses, communication, mating and nesting behavior, and status as endangered species. The author has chosen facts that will engage her readers, organized the information logically, and presented it in straightforward exposition. Pen-and-ink and watercolor illustrations show both species in their likely environment." Booklist

Gish, Melissa
Alligators. Creative Education 2010 46p il (Living wild) $23.95; pa $9.95
Grades: 5 6 7 8   **597.98**
1. Alligators
ISBN 978-1-58341-967-0; 1-58341-967-5; 978-0-89812-550-4 pa; 0-89812-550-2 pa
LC 2010017372

The "book lucidly discusses conservation and the animals' often tenuous relationships with humans. The layout is uniformly simple but effective, constructed with a nice balance of main text for the report writers, smaller chunks of esoterica for browsers, and . . . killer photos." Booklist

Hamilton, Sue L.

Attacked by a crocodile; [by] Sue Hamilton. ABDO Pub. 2010 32p il (Close encounters of the wild kind) lib bdg $27.07
Grades: 4 5 6 7   **597.98**
1. Crocodiles 2. Animal attacks
ISBN 978-1-60453-929-5; 1-60453-929-1

LC 2009-45514

Readers learn of actual human-crocodile encounters, information about crocodiles, survival strategies, and attack statistics.

"Students will be drawn to the realistic full-color photographs, the realistic diagrams of the creatures' bodies, the real-life stories told by victims, and the interesting, attractive formatting that includes text, diagrams, photographs, and graphics on each page. . . . [This is] exciting and attractive in a 'gross' sort of way and will appeal particularly to boys for both leisure reading and research." Libr Media Connect

Includes glossary

Jackson, Tom

Saltwater crocodile; by Tom Jackson. Bearport Publishing 2013 24 p. (library binding) $23.93
Grades: 1 2   **597.98**
1. Crocodiles 2. Crocodylus porosus
ISBN 161772923X; 9781617729232

LC 2013011638

In this book, by Tom Jackson, "readers will explore the underwater world of [saltwater crocodiles] through clear text, full-color photos, and diagrams. Age-appropriate activities, such as describing the advantages of ambushing prey, give readers a chance to make observations and develop animal-science skills." (Publisher's note)

Includes bibliographical references and index

Markle, Sandra

★ **Crocodiles**; by Sandra Markle. Carolrhoda Books 2004 39p il (Animal predators) lib bdg $25.26; pa $7.95
Grades: 3 4 5 6   **597.98**
1. Crocodiles
ISBN 1-57505-726-3 lib bdg; 1-57505-742-5 pa

LC 2003-15402

"The straightforward, descriptive text and superb photos give [this title] surefire appeal to middle readers." Booklist

Includes glossary and bibliographical references

Meinking, Mary

Crocodile vs. wildebeest. Raintree 2011 32p il (Predator vs. prey) $29; pa $7.99
Grades: 1 2 3   **597.98**
1. Gnus 2. Crocodiles 3. Predatory animals
ISBN 978-1-4109-3935-7; 1-4109-3935-9; 978-1-4109-3944-9 pa; 1-4109-3944-8 pa

Explores the features of crocodiles and gnu that make them particularly suited to catch or evade.

"The struggle between predator crocodile and its wildebeest prey is described in clear language and illustrated with engaging color photographs." Horn Book Guide

Otfinoski, Steven

★ **Alligators**; by Steven Otfinoski. Marshall Cavendish Benchmark 2009 47p il (Animals animals) lib bdg $20.95

Grades: 3 4 5 6   **597.98**
1. Alligators
ISBN 978-0-7614-2930-2 lib bdg; 0-7614-2930-1 lib bdg

LC 2007-25448

"Provides comprehensive information on the anatomy, special skills, habitats, and diet of alligators." Publisher's note

Includes glossary

Pringle, Laurence P.

Alligators and crocodiles! strange and wonderful. [by] Laurence Pringle; illustrated by Meryl Henderson. Boyds Mills Press 2009 32p il $16.95
Grades: 3 4 5   **597.98**
1. Alligators 2. Crocodiles
ISBN 978-1-59078-256-9; 1-59078-256-9

LC 2008-30018

This describes alligators' and crocodiles' "habitats and nesting behavior, and explains their common anatomical features and distinguishing characteristics. . . . Henderson presents a gallery of full-body portraits of 21 crocodilian species, as well as a series of close-ups. These illustrations are drawn and colored in . . . clear, precise detail." Booklist

Riggs, Kate

Alligators; by Kate Riggs. Creative Education 2012 24 p. (Amazing animals)
Grades: K 1 2   **597.98**
1. Aquatic animals 2. Alligators -- Folklore
ISBN 1608181049; 9781608181049

LC 2010049122

This book, a volume of the Amazing Animals series, offers an "exploration of the appearance, behavior, and habitat of alligators. . . . Also included is a story from folklore explaining why alligators and dogs don't get along." (Publisher's note) "This book also shows alligator hatchlings breaking free from an egg, open-jawed waiting to feed, and clinging as it rides on its mother's back. This book also addresses the question: How do you tell the difference between an alligator and a crocodile? . . . This book shares with readers how the alligator lives in the swamplands, how it hunts, raises young, and lives mostly alone." (Children's Literature)

Includes bibliographical references (p. 24) and index

Rockwell, Anne F.

Who lives in an alligator hole? by Anne Rockwell; illustrated by Lizzy Rockwell. HarperCollins 2006 33p il (Let's-read-and-find-out science) $15.99; pa $4.99
Grades: K 1 2 3   **597.98**
1. Ecology 2. Alligators
ISBN 0-06-028530-3; 0-06-445200-X pa

Describes the habitats of these reptiles which scientists call a "keystone species" because they change the environment for their own use in a way that helps many other plants and animals.

"Information and illustration work well together in this picture book presentation. . . . Simplified yet not anthropomorphized, the clearly delineated paintings feature alligators and other animals as the focal points of well-composed scenes." Booklist

Stewart, Melissa

Alligator or crocodile? how do you know? Enslow Publishers 2011 24p il (Which animal is which?) lib bdg $21.26
Grades: 1 2 3   **597.98**
1. Alligators 2. Crocodiles
ISBN 978-0-7660-3677-2; 0-7660-3677-4

LC 2010003275

This explains the differences between alligators and crocodiles.

This "should give budding naturalists an increased understanding of how scientists use appearance and behavior of classify sometimes-similar living things. . . . Spreads feature sharply detailed paired photographs of identified specimens seen from the same angle and at roughly equal size." SLJ

Includes bibliographical references

598 Birds

Alderfer, Jonathan

National Geographic kids bird guide of North America; the best birding book for kids from National Geographic's bird experts. by Jonathan Alderfer. National Geographic 2013 176 p. (paperback) $15.95; (library) $23.90

Grades: 4 5 6 7 8   **598**

1. Birds -- North America 2. Birds -- Identification 3. Birds -- North America -- Identification

ISBN 1426310943; 9781426310942; 9781426310959

LC 2012028615

Author "[Jonathan] Alderfer offers in-depth studies of 60 birds native to North America (plus 'mini-profiles' of another 60 specimens) in a guide for nascent birders. . . . The book is organized by region, and each bird's spread offers . . . color photographs, 'vital statistics' (including its call, diet, and habitat), maps of where it can be found, and other background." (Publishers Weekly)

Includes bibliographical references and index

Arnold, Caroline

A **bald** eagle's world; written and illustrated by Caroline Arnold. Picture Window Books 2010 24p il (Caroline Arnold's animals) lib bdg $25.32

Grades: PreK K 1 2   **598**

1. Bald eagle

ISBN 978-1-4048-5741-4 lib bdg; 1-4048-5741-9 lib bdg

LC 2009033358

This narrative describes the life of a bald eagle from the time it hatches until it can fly on its own.

The story "related in the present tense, [feels] immediate and engaging. . . . The plainness of the fact boxes [contrast] with Arnold's beautiful but simple artwork, which cleanly captures the essence of [the] animal. . . . [This book's] perfectly balanced mix of facts, story, and pictures will hold young readers' attention and help then learn." Booklist

Birds; nature's magnificent flying machines. illustrated by Patricia J. Wynne. Charlesbridge Pub. 2003 32p il $16.95; pa $6.95

Grades: 3 4 5 6   **598**

1. Birds -- Flight

ISBN 1-57091-516-4; 1-57091-572-5 pa

LC 2002-10441

An introduction to the science that explains how birds fly

"A clear, interesting book. . . . Each spread contains one or two paragraphs with a large, full-color illustration as well as smaller, captioned pictures that cover such topics as bone structure and preening. The colorful artwork consistently clarifies the concepts being discussed." SLJ

Includes glossary and bibliographical references

A **penguin's** world; written and illustrated by Caroline Arnold. Picture Window Books 2005 24p il $23.93

Grades: K 1 2 3   **598**

1. Penguins

ISBN 1-4048-1323-3

LC 2005023159

"This title follows an Adelie penguin family from scenes in which the parents build a nest and warm their eggs to final pages showcasing the four-month-old, newly independent chicks. The simple, well-paced text weaves basic concepts into the captivating narrative, and the artwork's strong colors and bold, uncluttered compositions capture the expression and movement of the birds." Booklist

Includes glossary and bibliographical references

Arnosky, Jim

★ **Thunder** birds; nature's flying predators. Sterling 2011 32p il $14.95

Grades: 3 4 5 6   **598**

1. Birds of prey

ISBN 978-1-4027-5661-0; 1-4027-5661-5

LC 2010019680

"Foldout pages group birds according to species and common characteristics. Lifelike owls peer at readers with deep, glassy eyes; in a section featuring birds of prey, an osprey's spectacular wing spans three panels, and journallike passages vividly document Arnosky's observations of each bird. . . . Arnosky's enthusiasm is evident in his deftly crafted images and in the immediacy of his 'field-note' style." Publ Wkly

Bailer, Darice

Geese. Marshall Cavendish Benchmark 2010 47p il (Animals animals) lib bdg $29.93

Grades: 3 4 5   **598**

1. Geese

ISBN 978-0-7614-4840-2 lib bdg; 0-7614-4840-3 lib bdg

LC 2009019482

This offers information on the anatomy, special skills, habitats, and diet of geese.

Includes glossary and bibliographical references

Barner, Bob

Penguins, penguins, everywhere! Chronicle Books 2007 un il $14.95

Grades: PreK K 1   **598**

1. Penguins

ISBN 978-0-8118-5664-5; 0-8118-5664-X

LC 2006-20960

"Colorful collages depict plump penguins performing a plethora of penguiny pastimes. . . . Barner's simply rhyming text presents a variety of the birds. . . . A final spread proffers a parade of all 17 species, including data on global location, size, and weight." SLJ

Bash, Barbara

★ **Urban** roosts; where birds nest in the city. Sierra Club Bks. 1990 un il hardcover o.p. pa $6.95

Grades: 1 2 3 4   **598**

1. Birds -- Nests

ISBN 0-316-08312-7 pa

LC 89-70187

"Excellent treatment of an unusual subject reveals that human-made places of steel, stone, and concrete are home to a variety of birds. Includes information on sparrows, finches, barn and snowy owls, swallows, swifts, nighthawks, killdeers, pigeons, wrens, crows, starlings, and falcons that have successfully adapted to city life." Sci Child

Berendt, John

My baby blue jays. Viking 2011 un il $16.99

Grades: K 1 2 3   **598**

1. Blue jays

ISBN 978-0-670-01290-9; 0-670-01290-4

LC 2010033296

The author "delivers a warm photo-essay about a pair of blue jays that make their home on his apartment balcony in New York City. While the arc of the story—nestbuilding, laying eggs, the first flight of a fledgling—is an old one, Berendt's telling is welcoming and personal, as if he were relating the story to a child in his lap while paging through a family photo album. . . . Set within scalloped borders against a cream backdrop, the photographs provide a remarkably intimate view of the birds' lives." Publ Wkly

Bodden, Valerie

Parrots. Creative Education 2010 24p il (Amazing animals) lib bdg $24.25

Grades: K 1 2 **598**

1. Parrots

ISBN 978-1-58341-809-3 lib bdg; 1-58341-809-1 lib bdg

LC 2009002711

A basic exploration of the appearance, behavior, and habitat of parrots, a family of colorful birds. Also included is a story from folklore explaining why parrots can imitate speech.

Includes bibliographical references

Penguins. Creative Education 2010 24p il (Amazing animals) lib bdg $24.25

Grades: K 1 2 **598**

1. Penguins

ISBN 978-1-58341-810-9 lib bdg; 1-58341-810-5 lib bdg

LC 2009002712

A basic exploration of the appearance, behavior, and habitat of penguins, a family of flightless birds. Also included is a story from folklore explaining why emperor penguins are so big.

This is illustrated with "dynamically colored photographs." Booklist

Includes bibliographical references

Bouler, Olivia

★ **Olivia's** birds; saving the Gulf. Sterling Pub. 2011 32p il $14.95

Grades: 4 5 6 **598**

1. Birds 2. Nature conservation

ISBN 978-1-4027-8665-5; 1-4027-8665-4

LC 2010046002

"Eleven-year-old Bouler, who raised more than $150,000 for the Audubon Society's Gulf Coast oil spill recovery efforts through the sale of her bird paintings, pairs her artwork with casual, informative passages to create an upbeat lesson on bird identification, habitat, and nature preservation. . . . Bouler's depictions of familiar birds like the Canada goose, bald eagle, and hummingbird are carefully observed and spirited; her vivacious attitude may inspire ecologically minded readers to get involved." Publ Wkly

Burnie, David

Bird; written by David Burnie. rev ed.; DK Pub. 2008 72p il (DK eyewitness books) $15.99

Grades: 4 5 6 7 **598**

1. Birds

ISBN 978-0-7566-3768-2; 0-7566-3768-6

First published 1988 by Knopf

A photo essay on the world of birds examining such topics as body construction, feathers and flight, the adaptation of beaks and feet, feeding habits, courtship, nests and eggs, and bird watching.

Includes glossary

Cate, Annette LeBlanc

★ **Look** up! bird-watching in your own backyard. Annette LeBlanc Cate. Candlewick Press 2013 64 p. $15.99

Grades: 2 3 4 5 **598**

1. Birds

ISBN 0763645613; 9780763645618

LC 2012942416

Robert F. Sibert Honor Book (2014)

This children's picture book puts an "emphasis on looking at the birds near home-from suburbs to inner cities." It groups "birds by colors, shapes, behaviors, feathers, calls, habitat, migration, and more" and "emphasizes the importance of observation and includes sketching instructions as a way to hone those skills on the individual aspects of a bird along with its species' characteristics." (School Library Journal)

"...Jam-packed with accurate information likely to increase any potential birder's enthusiasm and knowledge." Kirkus

Catt, Thessaly

Migrating with the Arctic tern. PowerKids Press 2011 24p il map (Animal journeys) lib bdg $21.25; pa $8.25

Grades: 2 3 4 **598**

1. Terns 2. Birds -- Migration

ISBN 978-1-4488-2542-4 lib bdg; 1-4488-2542-3 lib bdg; 978-1-4488-2668-1 pa; 1-4488-2668-3 pa

LC 2010025389

This book follows "the yearly migratory patterns of the [arctic tern] and [covers] anatomy, diet, mating, parenting, climate change as caused by people, pollution, and more. . . . [It is illustrated] with clear color photographs. . . . Go-to nonfiction for animal enthusiasts." SLJ

Includes glossary

Dunning, Joan

★ **Seabird** in the forest; the mystery of the marbled murrelet. Boyds Mills Press 2011 un il $17.95

Grades: K 1 2 3 **598**

1. Murrelets

ISBN 978-1-59078-715-1; 1-59078-715-3

"A marbled murrelet chick's early life is surprising. Most seabirds lay their eggs on the sand or high cliffs at the water's edge, but the marbled murrelet usually lays a single egg high on a branch of an old-growth tree, far from the ocean. . . . The hatched chick spends a month hunkered down on the branch, camouflaged by its own down, waiting for a parent to arrive with fish. This large-format picture book describes the life of one such chick. . . . The text runs beneath expressive illustrations, with close-ups of adult birds and their chick as well as landscapes suggesting their contrasting worlds; they support the mood of mystery and show well at a distance. Text boxes set on the illustrations add further detail. A beautiful addition." Kirkus

Evert, Laura

Birds of prey; explore the fascinating worlds of eagles, falcons, owls, vultures. by Laura Evert and Wayne Lynch; illustrations by Sherry Neidigh and John F. McGee. NorthWord 2005 191p il (Our wild world) $16.95

Grades: 3 4 5 6 **598**

1. Birds of prey

ISBN 1-55971-925-7

LC 2005000189

This "volume is divided into four sections, each addressing one of the major groups of raptors: eagles, falcons, owls, and vultures. The chapters, which have color-coded pages for quick reference, are similarly organized, making for easier reading, and deal with all aspects of the birds' life cycles and habits. Plentiful, high-quality photographs . . . and clear illustrations elucidate the narrative." SLJ

Everything You Need to Know About Birds. DK Publishing 2016 80 p. color ill., color map $15.99; (ebook) $47.97

Grades: 3 4 5 6   **598**

1. Birds

ISBN 1465443886; 9781465443885; 9781465452924

LC 2015510900

"A fact-filled, highly visual guide to different types of birds all across the world, 'Everything You Need to Know About Birds' is packed with information on habitats, breeding habits, oddities, shocking trivia, and anatomy. Read about the different types of birds that hunt, dive, swim, run, and dig, including vultures, crows, parrots, chickens, and more." (Publisher's note)

"Each double-page spread is packed with photos, maps, diagrams, and even some infographic-style layouts, which nicely encapsulate concepts. There is plenty of information in the text, helped along by the accessible, descriptive style." Booklist

Ganeri, Anita

Macaw. Heinemann Library 2011 24p il map (A day in the life. Rain forest animals) lib bdg $22; pa $6.49

Grades: 1 2   **598**

1. Birds 2. Cage birds

ISBN 978-1-4329-4105-5 lib bdg; 1-4329-4105-4 lib bdg; 978-1-4329-4116-1 pa; 1-4329-4116-X pa

LC 2010000960

This book follows a macaw through its day as it sleeps, eats, and moves.

"Ganeri presents information clearly and simply in large type, two-sentence comments placed below a bright, sharply reproduced color photograph of the animal in a natural setting. . . . [This is] sufficiently specific to support assignment as well as pleasure reading." SLJ

Includes glossary and bibliographical references

Gibbons, Gail

Owls; [by] Gail Gibbons. Holiday House 2005 32p il $16.95; pa $6.95

Grades: K 1 2 3   **598**

1. Owls

ISBN 0-8234-1880-4; 0-8234-2014-0 pa

LC 2004-48225

A "factual look at raptors of the night, full of information tied specifically to the owls of North America. General facts on physiology, hunting tactics, digestion, habitats, and communication are offered, as is a section on mating, egg laying and incubation, and owlet development. . . . Gibbons's trademark watercolors provide lively renditions of a variety of these silent hunters. . . . This is a bright addition to owl lore for younger readers." SLJ

Gish, Melissa

★ **Eagles.** Creative Education 2010 46p il (Living wild) lib bdg $23.95; pa $9.95

Grades: 5 6 7 8   **598**

1. Eagles

ISBN 978-1-58341-968-7 lib bdg; 1-58341-968-3 lib bdg; 978-0-89812-551-1 pa; 0-89812-551-0 pa

LC 2010-17373

This "book lucidly discusses conservation and the animals' often tenuous relationship with humans. The layout is uniformly simple but effective, constructed with a nice balance of main text for the report writers, smaller chunks of esoterica for browsers, and . . . killer photos." Booklist

Hummingbirds. Creative Education 2011 46p il map (Living wild) lib bdg $23.95; pa $8.95

Grades: 5 6 7 8   **598**

1. Hummingbirds

ISBN 978-1-60818-078-3; 1-60818-078-6; 978-0-89812-670-9 pa; 0-89812-670-3 pa

LC 2010028314

A look at hummingbirds, including their habitats, physical characteristics such as their ability to hover, behaviors, relationships with humans, and admired status in the world today.

"Stunning, full-page photographs create immediate visual interest. A brief narrative introduction sets the scene for the richer, more scientific information in the rest of the text." Booklist

Includes glossary and bibliographical references

Owls. Creative Education 2011 46p il map (Living wild) lib bdg $23.95

Grades: 5 6 7 8   **598**

1. Owls

ISBN 978-1-60818-081-3; 1-60818-081-6

LC 2010028308

A look at owls, including their habitats, physical characteristics such as their large and observant eyes, behaviors, relationships with humans, and protected status in the world today.

"Stunning, full-page photographs create immediate visual interest. A brief narrative introduction sets the scene for the richer, more scientific information in the rest of the text." Booklist

Includes glossary and bibliographical references

Goldin, Augusta R.

Ducks don't get wet; by Augusta Goldin; illustrated by Helen K. Davie. newly il ed; HarperCollins Pubs. 1999 32p il (Let's-read-and-find-out science) hardcover o.p. pa $4.95

Grades: K 1 2 3   **598**

1. Ducks

ISBN 0-06-027881-1; 0-06-027882-X lib bdg; 0-06-445187-9 pa

LC 97-43597

A newly illustrated edition of the title first published 1965 by Crowell

Describes the behavior of different kinds of ducks and, in particular, discusses how all ducks use preening to keep their feathers dry

"The text is well focused throughout. . . . Notable for its clarity, subtlety, and beauty, the artwork illustrates the text with precision and imagination." Booklist

Gonzales, Doreen

Owls in the dark. PowerKids Press 2010 24p il (Creatures of the night) lib bdg $21.25; pa $8.05

Grades: 2 3 4   **598**

1. Owls

ISBN 978-1-4042-8097-7 lib bdg; 1-4042-8097-9 lib bdg; 978-1-4358-3251-0 pa; 1-4358-3251-5 pa

A look at owls and their world in the dark.

"Basic details are complemented by eclectic trivia, . . . [and the] volume concludes with a defense of the animal . . . and why it is vital to humans. The layout is attractive, with easy-to-read text and eye-catching photography. Good for reports." SLJ

Includes glossary

Gray, Susan H.

The **life** cycle of birds; [by] Susan H. Gray. Heinemann Library 2011 48p il (Life cycles)

Grades: 3 4 5   **598**

1. Birds

ISBN 9781432949792 lib bdg; 9781432949860

LC 2010038277

This describes how birds are "hatched, where they live, and how they grow, move, protect themselves, spend their time, and reproduce. . . . [This book] provides a well-organized account of avian creatures, including topics such as preening, digestion, and adaptations to different habitats." Booklist

Includes glossary and bibliographical references

Hanel, Rachael

Penguins. Smart Apple Media 2009 46p il (Living wild) lib bdg $32.80

Grades: 4 5 6 7   **598**
1. Penguins
ISBN 978-1-58341-658-7 lib bdg; 1-58341-658-7 lib bdg
LC 2007008503

"The 17 species of penguins . . . fill [this] slim, informative [volume]. [The] overview is divided into several chapters . . . describing the shared and distinct physical characteristics of the various species, the location of their particular habitats, life cycle, social behavior, and the history of human awareness of and impact on these animals. Fine color photographs face pages of text with smaller views placed in colored sidebars or insets. The [book concludes] with current environmental threats and conservation efforts. . . . Handsome and appealing." SLJ

Helget, Nicole Lea

Swans; by Nicole Helget. Smart Apple Media 2009 46p il (Living wild) lib bdg $32.80

Grades: 4 5 6 7   **598**
1. Swans
ISBN 978-1-58341-659-4 lib bdg; 1-58341-659-5 lib bdg
LC 2007015242

The "7 [species] of swans fill [this] slim, informative [volume]. [The] overview is divided into several chapters . . . describing the shared and distinct physical characteristics of the various species, the location of their particular habitats, life cycle, social behavior, and the history of human awareness of and impact on these animals. Fine color photographs face pages of text with smaller views placed in colored sidebars or insets. The [book concludes] with current environmental threats and conservation efforts. . . . Handsome and appealing." SLJ

Includes bibliographical references

Hiscock, Bruce

Ookpik; the travels of a snowy owl. Boyds Mills Press 2008 un il map $16.99

Grades: 2 3 4   **598**
1. Owls 2. Birds -- Migration
ISBN 978-1-59078-461-7; 1-59078-461-8
LC 2007-17327

A snowy owl hatches on Baffin Island and migrates over the taiga, past Ottawa, spends the winter in northern New York, and returns to his arctic home.

"An informative author's note comments on the range, size, food, courtship, nesting, growth, and survival of snowy owls. Varied in composition, well focused, and often panoramic in effect, the watercolor paintings depict the snowy owl's world as well as the bird himself. . . . The owl's journey becomes an involving story for children." Booklist

Holub, Joan

★ **Why** do birds sing? illustrations by Anna DiVito. Dial Books for Young Readers 2004 47p il (Dial easy-to-read) hardcover o.p. pa $3.99

Grades: K 1 2   **598**
1. Birds
ISBN 0-8037-2999-5; 0-14-240106-4 pa
LC 2003-64945

Questions and answers present information about the behavior and characteristics of birds

"The photos and attractive ink drawings with color washes that come two to three to a page result in a colorful presentation with illustrations in different styles from many sources." Booklist

Hoose, Phillip

★ **Moonbird;** a year on the wind with the great survivor B95. Phillip Hoose. Farrar Straus Giroux 2012 148 p. col. ill. (hardcover) $21.99

Grades: 5 6 7 8   **598**
1. Endangered species 2. Birds -- Protection 3. Wildlife conservation 4. Red knot 5. Bird watching 6. Red knot -- Migration
ISBN 0374304688; 9780374304683
LC 2011035612

Robert F. Sibert Honor Book (2013)

YALSA Award for Excellence in Nonfiction for Young Adults Finalist (2013)

In this book, Phillip Hoose "explores the tragedy of extinction through a single bird species, but there is hope for survival in this story, and that hope is pinned on understanding the remarkable longevity of a single bird. . . . Hoose takes readers around the hemisphere, showing them the obstacles rufa red knots face, introducing a global team of scientists and conservationists, and offering insights about what can be done to save them before it's too late." (Kirkus Reviews)

Hudak, Heather C., 1975-

Robins; [by] Heather Hudak. Weigl Publishers Inc. 2011 24p il (World of wonder: watch them grow) lib bdg $25.70; pa $9.95

Grades: 1 2   **598**
1. Robins
ISBN 978-1-60596-922-0 lib bdg; 1-60596-922-2 lib bdg; 978-1-60596-923-7 pa; 1-60596-923-0 pa
LC 2010037947

Explore the life of a robin from egg to adult, as well as learn about the special ways robins communicate with each other.

The text is "well-written, providing examples that put a human face to each problem. Quotes and facts are clearly attributed, and their sources are noted in the extensive back matter. . . . Sidebars provide further information, or, more compellingly, offer stories about those touched by the topic. . . . [This] will be of great assistance to students writing reports." Libr Media Connect

Includes glossary

Jacquet, Luc

March of the penguins; [by] Luc Jacquet; including narration written by Jordan Roberts; photographs by Jérôme Maison; translated and adapted by Donnali Fifield. National Geographic 2006 160p il $30

Grades: K 1 2 3   **598**
1. Penguins 2. Antarctica
ISBN 0-7922-6190-9

"From summer's end in Antarctica, the book takes the reader on a journey through a year's cycle in the life of emperor penguins. . . . The quality of the photographs makes this simple story accessible to a wide audience." Sci Books Films

Johnson, Jinny

Duck; illustrations by Michael Woods. Smart Apple Media 2010 32p il (How does it grow?) lib bdg $28.50

Grades: 1 2 3   **598**
1. Ducks
ISBN 978-1-59920-353-9 lib bdg; 1-59920-353-7 lib bdg
LC 2008-53338

Introduces the life cycle of a duck and explains each stage in its development

"Each stage is described on a spread that features clearly written, oversized text and a caption opposite a full-page, realistic watercolor, or, occasionally, a photograph. . . . A worthwhile purchase." SLJ

Includes glossary

Johnson, Sylvia A.

Crows; by Sylvia A. Johnson. Carolrhoda Books 2005 48p il (Carolrhoda nature watch book) lib bdg $25.26

Grades: 3 4 5 6   **598**

1. Crows

ISBN 1-57505-628-3

            LC 2004-564

This "book introduces the American crow, its broader family of corvids, and its range, habitats, cooperative breeding system, life cycle, winter migration, roosting behavior, language, and relations with people. . . . Though the clear, color photographs take up most of the space on the pages, the text offers a well-organized, informative discussion of the species." Booklist

Judge, Lita

Bird talk; what birds are saying and why. Lita Judge. Roaring Brook Press 2011 48 p.

Grades: 1 2 3 4 5   **598**

1. Birdsongs 2. Birds -- Behavior 3. Animal communication 4. Picture books for children 5. Birdsongs 6. Birds -- Behavior 7. Animal communication

ISBN 1596436468; 9781596436466

            LC 2010030353

In this picture book, "[a] simple ornithological discourse for very young readers offers several examples of feathered non-verbal communication. Over two dozen bird species--most, but not all, with North American ranges, and many fairly familiar--are shown communicating essential messages via calls, displays of plumage and other, less well-known behaviors. Birds from distant parts of the world may appear in the same opening describing behaviors that accomplish similar aims: wooing mates, camouflage, encouragement to fledglings, protection. . . . Further information about each of the species, including their habitats and ranges, appears on several pages at the back, along with a brief glossary and list of sources." (Kirkus)

Kelly, Irene

★ Even an ostrich needs a nest; where birds begin. Holiday House 2009 un il map $16.95

Grades: K 1 2 3   **598**

1. Birds -- Nests

ISBN 978-0-8234-2102-2; 0-8234-2102-3

            LC 2007-51059

"This nonfiction picture book describes materials used by 40 species of birds from all parts of the world to build their unique nests and how they go about building them. . . . The diversity of materials and designs . . . make this a topic that will appeal to many. The pleasant format features text, creatively placed with the softly colored illustrations, and makes the engaging subject matter even more accessible." Booklist

Kirby, Pamela F.

What bluebirds do. Boyds Mills Press 2009 48p il $18.95

Grades: K 1 2 3   **598**

1. Bluebirds

ISBN 978-1-59078-614-7; 1-59078-614-9

            LC 2008-34057

"Big, full-color photos provide the drama in this personal, picture-book introduction to a common North American bird. . . . The captions

include some brief commentary, and kids will feel the call for conservation as they marvel, along with Kirby, at the bird behavior she sees in her yard." Booklist

Includes glossary and bibliographical references

Landau, Elaine

Emperor penguins. Enslow Elementary 2010 31p il (Animals of the snow and ice) lib bdg $22.60

Grades: 2 3 4   **598**

1. Penguins

ISBN 978-0-7660-3462-4 lib bdg; 0-7660-3462-3 lib bdg

            LC 2009006479

This describes emperor penguins, including habitat, eating habits, mating, babies, and conservation

"Throughout most of [this] title, a full-page, or page and a quarter, sharp, color photograph . . . alternates with a page of text. An addendum of miscellaneous facts, a short list for further reading, and some websites are appended. Landau's smoothly written, well-illustrated [title is] right on target for the intended audience." SLJ

Includes glossary and bibliographical references

Larson, Jeanette C.

Hummingbirds; facts and folklore from the Americas. written by Jeanette Larson and Adrienne Yorinks; illustrated by Adrienne Yorinks. Charlesbridge 2011 64p il $16.95; pa $8.95

Grades: 5 6 7 8   **598**

1. Hummingbirds 2. Birds -- Folklore 3. Native Americans -- Folklore

ISBN 978-1-58089-332-9; 1-58089-332-5; 978-1-58089-333-6 pa; 1-58089-333-3 pa

            LC 2010-07578

"In a narrative that flows easily between fact and lore, hummingbird behavior is thoroughly described and interwoven with the folktales it generated among Native American peoples. . . . All the stories show how ancient people answered the 'how and why' questions of the behaviors they observed, and these stories beautifully echo modern-day scientific observations. The full-color photos of quilts and embroidery by Yorinks invite readers to stop and savor each one." SLJ

Includes glossary and bibliographical references

Lunis, Natalie

Peregrine falcon; dive, dive, dive! Bearport 2010 24p il (Blink of an eye: superfast animals) lib bdg $22.61

Grades: 1 2 3   **598**

1. Falcons

ISBN 978-1-936087-93-8 lib bdg; 1-936087-93-6 lib bdg

            LC 2010008023

"In terms of pure velocity, no animal can touch a diving peregrine falcon, which this [book] . . . points out right off the bat. Subsequent spreads cover such topics as where peregrine falcons live and their nesting habits, aerial abilities, and, best of all, hunting techniques. . . . Dynamic, sometimes exhilarating photos . . . accompany the straightforward text." Booklist

Includes glossary and bibliographical references

Lynch, Wayne

Penguins! text and photographs by Wayne Lynch. Firefly Bks. (Willowdale) 1999 64p il map $19.95; pa $9.95

Grades: 4 5 6 7   **598**

1. Penguins

ISBN 1-55209-421-9; 1-55209-424-3 pa

This "is a delightful book. . . . The beautiful color photographs and the text tell a fascinating, exciting, and revealing story." Sci Books Films

Mara, Wil

★ **Ducks**; by Wil Mara. Marshall Cavendish Benchmark 2009 47p il (Animals animals) $20.95

Grades: 3 4 5 6   **598**

1. Ducks

ISBN 978-0-7614-2927-2; 0-7614-2927-1

LC 2007-26004

"The material is well researched and would be an excellent source for reports, and the [book has] a narrative flow that makes [it] easy and enjoyable to read. [The] title includes expert full-color photography." SLJ

Includes glossary and bibliographical references

Markle, Sandra

Eagles. Lerner Publications Company 2009 39p il (Animal predators) lib bdg $26.60

Grades: 4 5 6   **598**

1. Eagles

ISBN 978-1-58013-519-1; 1-58013-519-6

LC 2008038119

Introduces the physical characteristics, habitat, and predatory behavior of different types of eagles.

"Crisp photographs illustrate the hunting activities of eagles. . . . Facts are presented in a dramatic and informational manner." Horn Book Guide

Includes glossary and bibliographical references

★ A **mother's** journey; illustrated by Alan Marks. Charlesbridge 2005 32p il $15.95; pa $6.95

Grades: K 1 2 3   **598**

1. Penguins

ISBN 1-57091-621-7; 1-57091-622-5 pa

LC 2004-18954

Boston Globe-Horn Book Honor: Nonfiction (2006)

"A simple, lyrical text follows the fortunes of an Emperor penguin from laying her first egg through her epic journey to open sea seeking food and culminating in her timely return with a belly full to regurgitate for her newly hatched chick. The whole is perfectly accompanied by Marks's luminous blue-toned watercolors." SLJ

Marzollo, Jean

Pierre the penguin; a true story. written by Jean Marzollo; illustrated by Laura Regan. Sleeping Bear Press 2010 un il $15.95

Grades: PreK K 1 2   **598**

1. Penguins

ISBN 978-1-58536-485-5; 1-58536-485-1

LC 2009040871

Rhyming text and colorful illustrations describe the efforts of aquatic biologist Pam to help Pierre, an African penguin living at the California Academy of Sciences, when he begins to go bald.

"Stories don't come any sweeter than this. . . . Regan's realistic paintings work well with the text and enhance the drama and appeal of the storytelling." SLJ

Metz, Lorijo

Discovering seagulls. PowerKids Press 2011 24p il (Along the shore) lib bdg $21.25

Grades: 3 4 5   **598**

1. Gulls

ISBN 978-1-4488-4995-6; 1-4488-4995-0

LC 2011000154

This book about seagulls "briefly describes the major physical and behavioral characteristics common to all [seagulls] and one or two distinctive characteristics of about a half dozen species. . . . One or two

sharp color photographs of representative species, most of which are closeups, accompany the text on every page. . . . [This is] well organized and smoothly written in an engaging style." SLJ

Includes glossary

Momatiuk, Yva

★ **Face** to face with penguins; by Yva Momatiuk and John Eastcott. National Geographic 2009 31p il (Face to face) $16.99; lib bdg $25.90

Grades: 3 4 5 6   **598**

1. Penguins

ISBN 978-1-4263-0561-0; 1-4263-0561-3; 978-1-4263-0562-7 lib bdg; 1-4263-0562-1 lib bdg

LC 2009011439

The authors describe the life cycle and behavior of penguins and their own experiences with penguins in the wild.

"The exquisite photos and firsthand information provide an in-depth and personal look into the lives of these animals." SLJ

Includes glossary and bibliographical references

Munro, Roxie

Hatch! Marshall Cavendish Children's 2011 un il $17.99

Grades: 1 2 3 4   **598**

1. Eggs 2. Birds

ISBN 0761458824; 9780761458821; 978-0-7614-5882-1; 0-7614-5882-4

LC 2010021297

This picture book describes and helps readers learn to identify nine birds and their eggs and nests. "For each bird, we start with a two-page spread: on one side, a close-up of eggs; . . . and on the other side, a series of clues about the producers of those eggs. . . . Primary." (Horn Book)

"Munro uses a guessing game format to deliver an impressive amount of trivia about nine types of birds. 'Can you guess whose eggs these are?' is the repeated refrain that appears above clusters of eggs against a cream-colored backdrop; opposite, a silhouette of the eggs' shape contains several sentences to aid in the guessing. . . . Straightforward, but packed with information." Publ Wkly

Peterson, Roger Tory

Peterson field guide to birds of Eastern and Central North America; [by] Roger Tory Peterson, with contributions from Michael DiGiorgio [et al.]. 6th ed. Houghton Mifflin Harcourt 2010 445p il map (Peterson field guide series) $19.95

Grades: 5 6 7 8 9 10 11 12 Adult   **598**

1. Birds -- North America

ISBN 978-0-547-15246-2; 0-547-15246-9

LC 2009-37681

First published 1934 with title: A field guide to the birds

This guide to birds found east of the Rocky Mountains contains colored illustrations painted by the author, with a description of each species on the facing page. Views of young birds and seasonal variations in plumage are included.

★ **Peterson** field guide to birds of North America; with contributions from Michael DiGiorgio . . . [et al.] Houghton Mifflin Co. 2008 527p il map (Peterson field guide series) $26

Grades: 5 6 7 8 9 10 11 12 Adult   **598**

1. Birds -- North America

ISBN 0-618-96614-5; 978-0-618-96614-1

LC 2007-39803

First published 1934 with title: A field guide to the birds. Previously published in two separate parts as A field guide to western birds (1990) and A field guide to the birds of eastern and central North America (2002)

This guide to birds found in North America contains colored illustrations painted by the author, with a description of each species on the facing page. Views of young birds and seasonal variations in plumage are included. The book also includes a URL to video podcasts.

"This field guide is of high quality and should be in millions of birders' and other nature lovers' backpacks." Sci Books Films

Peterson field guide to birds of Western North America; with contributions from Michael DiGiorgio [et al.] 4th ed; Houghton Mifflin Harcourt 2010 493p il map (Peterson field guide series) pa $19.95
Grades: 5 6 7 8 9 10 11 12 Adult   **598**
  1. Birds -- North America
  ISBN 978-0-547-15270-7; 0-547-15270-1
                         LC 2009-39158
First published 1941 with title: A field guide to western birds

This guide illustrates over 600 species of birds on 176 color plates. In addition, over 588 range maps are included.

Piehl, Janet
  Let's look at pigeons. Lerner Publications Co. 2010 32p il (Lightning bolt books: Animal close-ups) lib bdg $25.26; pa $7.95
Grades: PreK K 1 2   **598**
  1. Pigeons
  ISBN 978-0-8225-7897-0 lib bdg; 0-8225-7897-2 lib bdg; 978-1-58013-863-5 pa; 1-58013-863-2 pa
                         LC 2007-29224
Introduces pigeons, describing their physical characteristics, habitat, and predators

"Fresh photography, a creative use of graphics, and a collagelike layout make[s] . . . [this book] eye-catching. . . . [The] book ends with a labeled diagram of the animal, a range map, and a further-reading list that includes print and online resources in a single list, a nice way of validating both types of materials." SLJ

Includes glossary

Post, Hans
  Sparrows; [by Hans Post & Kees Heij; illustrated by Irene Goede] Lemniscaat 2008 un il $16.95
Grades: PreK K 1 2   **598**
  1. Sparrows
  ISBN 978-1-59078-570-6; 1-59078-570-3
                         LC 2008-02563
Original Dutch edition 2006

"A year in the life of the European House Sparrow is conveyed to young readers through a friendly text and beguiling illustrations. . . . The tone of the text is both playful and informative. . . . The realistic illustrations intersperse views from the birds' prespective . . . with field guide-like pages that help illustrate bird anatomy and behavior and introduce other animals in the sparrow habitat." Horn Book

Pringle, Laurence P.
  Penguins! strange and wonderful; illustrated by Meryl Henderson. Boyds Mills Press 2007 un il $16.95
Grades: 3 4 5   **598**
  1. Penguins
  ISBN 978-1-59078-090-9; 1-59078-090-6
                         LC 2006000521
This "highlights the diversity among the habitats, physical traits, and behaviors of the 17 amazingly adaptable species. Pringle's succinct text provides an engaging overview of penguin life. . . . Henderson's realistic paintings vary between double-page spreads of penguins in their diverse Southern Hemisphere environments and finely detailed insets that echo the text." Booklist

Includes bibliographical references

Read, Tracy C.
  Exploring the world of eagles. Firefly 2010 24p il (Exploring the world of . . .) $16.95; pa $6.95
Grades: 3 4 5   **598**
  1. Eagles
  ISBN 978-1-55407-647-5; 1-55407-647-1; 978-1-55407-656-7 pa; 1-55407-656-0 pa
This describes the American bald eagle and the golden eagle, including their anatomy and behavior and the ways they have been affected by the human environmental footprint.

This offers "an abundance of in-depth, intriguing information and [is] appropriate for research or pleasure reading. . . . Two- to four-page chapters mix smaller photos with full-page color photos, and the attractive format will help less-able readers navigate the sometimes dense, detailed paragraphs." Booklist

Rebman, Renee C.
  Vultures. Marshall Cavendish Benchmark 2011 il (Animals, animals) lib bdg $20.95
Grades: 3 4 5   **598**
  1. Vultures
  ISBN 978-0-7614-4880-8; 0-7614-4880-2
                         LC 2010016037
Provides information on the anatomy, special skills, habitats, and diet of vultures.

This offers "comprehensive text and striking, well-chosen photos. . . . [This is] packed with engaging facts and trivia, as well as an upbeat tone." Booklist

Includes glossary and bibliographical references

Rockwell, Lizzy
  A **bird** is a bird; by Lizzy Rockwell. Holiday House 2015 32 p. (hardcover) $16.95
Grades: PreK K 1   **598**
  1. Birds
  ISBN 0823430421; 9780823430420
                         LC 2013018289
This children's book, written and illustrated by Lizzy Rockwell, explains how "some birds are huge and some are tiny. Some birds are fantastically colorful and some are plain. What do all birds share? . . . [It] explains that birds have beaks, wings, and feathers, and hatch from eggs. Other animals might have some of these features in common, but only a bird has them all. Only a bird is a bird!" (Publisher's note)

"Rockwell walks readers through the characteristics that make birds, well, birds, accompanied by vivid, mixed-media portraits of dozens of avian specimens. . . . Direct writing and handsome labeled images of birds in their native environments (egrets and spoonbills hunt in shallow water, an owl and whip-poor-will appear camouflaged against tree bark) clearly demonstrate their breadth and diversity." Pub Wkly

Sayre, April Pulley
  ★ **Honk,** honk, goose! Canada geese start a family. illustrated by Huy Voun Lee. Henry Holt and Company 2009 un il $16.95
Grades: K 1 2 3   **598**
  1. Geese
  ISBN 978-0-8050-7103-0; 0-8050-7103-2
                         LC 2008013423
"A fun read-aloud grounded by informational back matter. . . . Lee's cut-paper collage illustrations wonderfully complement the text—they're simple yet expressive." Booklist

  ★ **Vulture** view; illustrated by Steve Jenkins. Henry Holt 2007 un il $16.95

Grades: K 1 2   **598**
1. Vultures
ISBN 978-0-8050-7557-1; 0-8050-7557-7
LC 2006-30766

"Sayre's poetic text begins with the sun rising. . . . The words, almost startling in their brevity, describe a group of turkey vultures as they soar in the sky, seeking food that reeks. . . . Jenkins . . . places the birds against strong, vivid colors—brilliant sky blues, hot desert reds—and gives them wide wingspans that make them seem to soar across the pages. . . . A final two-page spread . . . does a solid job of explaining how turkey vultures live." Booklist

Sill, Cathryn
   About hummingbirds; a guide for children. [by] Cathryn Sill; illustrated by John Sill. Peachtree Publishers 2011 un il $16.95
Grades: K 1 2 3   **598**
1. Hummingbirds
ISBN 1561455881; 9781561455881; 978-1-56145-588-1; 1-56145-588-1
LC 2010051999

"The Sills cover the [hummingbird's] diet, size, migratory habits, anatomical features, reproduction, predators, and habitats. Of special interest are their hovering skills and aerobatic displays. Each spread consists of one large-type sentence and a large watercolor depiction with just enough information for youngsters to gain an introduction to hummingbirds. The text and art combine to make this title a useful and engaging read."

"The Sills cover the [hummingbird's] diet, size, migratory habits, anatomical features, reproduction, predators, and habitats. Of special interest are their hovering skills and aerobatic displays. Each spread consists of one large-type sentence and a large watercolor depiction with just enough information for youngsters to gain an introduction to hummingbirds. The text and art combine to make this title a useful and engaging read." SLJ

   ★ **About** raptors; a guide for children. [by] Cathryn Sill; illustrated by John Sill. Peachtree 2010 un il $16.95
Grades: K 1 2 3   **598**
1. Birds of prey
ISBN 978-1-56145-536-2; 1-56145-536-9

"One short, clearly written sentence or phrase per page communicates the basics about raptors: who they are, where they live, what they eat, and how they hunt. Their similarities, such as strong feet with sharp claws, and their differences, such as locations and kinds of nests, communicate diversity in raptors throughout the world. Eighteen quality watercolors focus on the birds in their natural habitats. . . . This book is a must-buy for all libraries interested in building a strong natural-science collection for their young patrons." SLJ

Simon, Seymour
   Penguins. HarperCollins Publishers 2007 31p il (Smithsonian) $16.99; lib bdg $17.89
Grades: 2 3 4   **598**
1. Penguins
ISBN 978-0-06-028395-7; 0-06-028395-5; 978-0-06-028396-4 lib bdg; 0-06-028396-3 lib bdg
LC 2006-24116

This describes penguin behavior, reproduction, and feeding

This is written "in a voice perfectly attuned to the conceptual level of elementary-age readers. . . . The full-page color photographs competently capture . . . penguin appeal and are skillfully discussed in the narrative." Horn Book

Stearns, Precious McKenzie
   Whooping cranes; [by] Precious McKenzie. Rourke Pub. 2010 24p il map (Eye to eye with endangered species) lib bdg $27.07
Grades: 2 3 4   **598**
1. Cranes (Birds)
ISBN 978-1-60694-401-1 lib bdg; 1-60694-401-0 lib bdg
LC 2009-5992

Examines the issues endangered whooping cranes face and how they can be saved

"Sets out to introduce readers to [whooping cranes] . . . explain the dangers they face, and detail the efforts of biologists and conservationists to save them. . . . Serviceable and informative." SLJ

Includes glossary

Stewart, Melissa
   ★ **Feathers;** not just for flying. Melissa Stewart; illustrated by Sarah S. Brannen. Charlesbridge 2014 32 p. (softcover) $7.95
Grades: K 1 2 3 4   **598**
1. Feathers 2. Birds -- Anatomy 3. Birds -- Behavior
ISBN 1580894313; 9781580894302; 9781580894319
LC 2012038694

In this book by Melissa Stewart, readers "meet sixteen birds in this elegant introduction to the many uses of feathers. A concise main text highlights how feathers are not just for flying. Informative sidebars, which underscore specific ways each bird uses its feathers for a variety of practical purposes [are included]. A scrapbook design showcases life-size feather illustrations." (Publisher's note)

"Depicting birds from around the United States as well as South America, India, Africa, and Antarctica, Stewart illuminates the various functions of feathers. Presented in a scrapbook format with images and text that appear to be taped, stapled, or pinned to the pages, the book explains that feathers can provide sun protection, assist in carrying nest materials, or attract a mate with sound or color... With its simple text and captivating art, this title could be featured in a group storytime or in a unit on birds." (SLJ)

Includes bibliographical references and index

   A **place** for birds; written by Melissa Stewart; illustrated by Higgins Bond. Peachtree 2009 un il $16.95
Grades: K 1 2 3   **598**
1. Birds
ISBN 1-56145-474-5; 978-1-56145-474-7
LC 2008036744

"In simple yet informative language, 'A Place for Birds' introduces young readers to the ways human action or inaction can affect bird populations and opens kids' minds to a wide range of environmental issues. Describing various examples, the text provides an intriguing look at birds, at the ecosystems that support their survival, and at the efforts of some people to save them." (Publisher's note)

"This title focuses on the effects, good and bad, that human behavior has on birds, highlighting the progress that we've made toward living in harmony with our winged friends and acknowledging problems still not solved. The rhythmic main text highlights birds' needs and what people can do to see that they are met. Insets on each page then provide specific examples to drive the point home. . . . This format . . . is effective and engaging, and Bond's acrylic illustrations depict realistic scenes with a crisp vibrancy." Kirkus

Stockdale, Susan
   Bring on the birds; written and illustrated by Susan Stockdale. Peachtree 2011 un il $15.95

Grades: PreK K 1 2   **598**
   1. Birds
   ISBN 1-56145-560-1; 978-1-56145-560-7
               LC 2010-26893
This book celebrates the different types of birds found around the world, from dancing birds, to swimming birds, to birds with bills. Bibliography. "Ages two to six." (Publisher's note)
"This cheerful survey introduces 21 species [of birds] from varied parts of the world in spare, rhyming text and attractive acrylic paintings. . . . Picture placement follows the nice rhythm of the text with each two sets of facing framed paintings followed by a double-page view for each of the longer phrases of verse. Simple, flat stylized settings . . . showcase the lively, colorful birds. . . . Carefully crafted in charm and simplicity, the book offers many possibilities for use and enjoyment in reading aloud, browsing, and teaching." SLJ

Thomson, Ruth
   The **life** cycle of an owl. PowerKids Press 2009 24p il lib bdg $21.23; pa $8.25
Grades: K 1 2   **598**
   1. Owls
   ISBN 978-1-4358-2833-9 lib bdg; 1-4358-2833-X lib bdg; 978-1-4358-2883-4 pa; 1-4358-2883-6 pa
               LC 2008026176
This introduction to the life cycle of the owl is "arranged in a series of spreads, each of which covers a subtopic. Pages feature one to three simple sentences of large-print text and a clear, color photograph of one or more animals in various stages of growth. . . . With [its] easily accessible format, and clear [text] and photographs, [this book] will appeal to both browsers and report writers." SLJ

Thornhill, Jan
   ★ The **tragic** tale of the great auk; Jan Thornhill. Groundwood Books 2016 44 p. color ill., color map (hardcover) $18.95; (ebook) $14.95
Grades: 2 3 4 5   **598**
   1. Auks 2. Extinct animals
   ISBN 9781554988655; 1554988659; 9781554988662
               LC 2016043874
In this illustrated book, author "Jan Thornhill tells the tragic story of [auk birds.] . . . Their demise came about in part because of their anatomy. They could swim swiftly underwater, but their small wings meant they couldn't fly and their feet were so far back on their bodies, they couldn't walk very well. Still the birds managed to escape their predators much of the time . . . until humans became seafarers." (Publisher's note)
"A sobering, beautifully presented extinction story." Kirkus
Includes bibliographical references.

Underwood, Deborah
   Colorful peacocks; by Deborah Underwood. Lerner Publications Co. 2007 32p il (Pull ahead books) lib bdg $22.60; pa $5.95
Grades: K 1 2 3   **598**
   1. Peacocks
   ISBN 978-0-8225-5930-6 lib bdg; 0-8225-5930-7 lib bdg; 978-0-8225-6507-9 pa; 0-8225-6507-2 pa
               LC 2005017977
"This charming introduction to the peafowl family presents facts and color photographs in an easy-to-read format. Underwood covers what they eat, where they sleep, and how they care for their young. An outline drawing of a peafowl with the parts labeled and a map showing countries native to the species are included. An informative and enjoyable book." SLJ
Includes bibliographical references

Vande Griek, Susan
   Loon; pictures by Karen Reczuch. Groundwood Books 2011 il $18.95
Grades: K 1 2   **598**
   1. Loons
   ISBN 978-1-55498-077-2; 1-55498-077-1
"This book follows two loon chicks from birth to maturity and has a lyrical text and lush, full-color illustrations. The acrylic-on-canvas paintings are presented from different perspectives to engage viewers—straight on, closeup, and far away." SLJ

Vanderwater, Amy Ludwig
   Every day birds; by Amy Ludwig VanDerwater; paper cuttings by Dylan Metrano. Orchard Books, an imprint of Scholastic Inc. 2016 32 p. color illustrations $17.99
Grades: PreK K   **598**
   1. Birds 2. Birds -- Identification
   ISBN 9780545699808
               LC 2015025444
This picture book, by Amy Ludwig VanDerwater, with paper cuttings by Dylan Metrano, "helps children identify and learn about common birds. . . . [It] focuses on twenty North American birds, with a poem and descriptions. . . . Interesting facts about each bird are featured in the back of the book." (Publisher's note)
"The big, bold illustrations and lyrical lines make this a great choice for a read-aloud, while further information in the closing pages will satisfy burgeoning birders." Booklist

Vogel, Carole Garbuny
   The **man** who flies with birds; [by] Carole G. Vogel and Yossi Leshem. Kar-Ben Pub. 2009 64p il map lib bdg $18.95
Grades: 5 6 7 8   **598**
   1. Aircraft accidents 2. Birds -- Migration
   ISBN 978-0-8225-7643-3 lib bdg; 0-8225-7643-0 lib bdg
               LC 2008-31198
Discusses the work of the bird expert whose lifelong study of the patterns of bird migration in Israel has led to a significant reduction in the number of collisions between aircraft and bird flocks.
"The book is heavily illustrated with good-quality color photos, maps, and diagrams, many of them captioned with incredible facts about wildlife and migration. This inspiring title on a most timely topic will appeal to those who are fascinated with wildlife, Earth science, and technology." SLJ
Includes bibliographical references

Webster, Christine
   Ravens. Weigl Publishers 2010 24p il (Backyard animals) lib bdg $24.45; pa $8.95
Grades: 1 2 3   **598**
   1. Ravens
   ISBN 978-1-60596-082-1 lib bdg; 1-60596-082-9 lib bdg; 978-1-60596-083-8 pa; 1-60596-083-7 pa
               LC 2009004175
This describes the physical characteristics, natural habitats, history, and folklore of ravens
This is "packed with information and [includes] fine close-up photos." Booklist
Includes glossary

Willis, Nancy Carol
   Red knot; a shorebird's incredible journey. Birdsong Books 2006 un il map $15.95; pa $6.95

Grades: 2 3 4   **598**
1. Sandpipers 2. Birds -- Migration
ISBN 0-9662761-4-0; 0-9662761-5-9 pa

"This title introduces an endangered sandpiper and chronologically documents her journey from Tierra del Fuego along a 20,000-mile route to the Arctic where she has her young and then makes her way back down south for the winter. . . . The smooth, simple text is complemented with well-composed, colored-pencil drawings." SLJ

Wolf, Sallie
★ The **robin** makes a laughing sound; a birder's journal. designed by Micah Bornstein. Charlesbridge 2010 43p il $11.95
Grades: 5 6 7 8   **598**
1. Birds 2. Bird watching
ISBN 978-1-58089-318-3; 1-58089-318-X

LC 2008-7248
Presents observations made through every season of the year of different birds and their behavior, from robins taking a bath, to cardinals searching for food in the snow, to an owl perched on a tree at night.

"The charming, eye-catching format includes short dated nature notes written in script, some of them on glued or taped-in torn paper pieces; other paper scraps contain short typeset poems and small, labeled watercolors. . . . Pen-and-ink sketches capture a baby house sparrow, a V-formation of geese, a downy woodpecker at a suet feeder, and more. . . . This small, instructional guide may provide the inspiration for young authors with even a bit of artistic talent to begin keeping nature journals of their own." SLJ

598.3   Water birds

Gish, Melissa
Flamingos; Melissa Gish. Creative Education 2014 46 p. color illustrations (hardcover : alk. paper) $37.10
Grades: 5 6 7 8   **598.3**
1. Animals 2. Flamingos
ISBN 1608184161; 9781608184163

LC 2013031813
This book, by Melissa Gish, is a "scientific look at flamingos, including their habitats, physical characteristics such as their coloration, behaviors, relationships with humans, and numbers of the tropical birds in the world today." (Publisher's note)

"Stewart continues with a topic near and dear to devotees of the 590s, once more providing both fascinating and well-written facts and some truly arresting images. Scientific material on each species is offered, along with pop cultural and historical information. . . . Thorough in scope and elegant in design, these stellar titles will attract the browser and the report writer alike." SLJ

Includes bibliographical references and index
Part of recommended series "Living Wild," which includes 62 titles, each with details on different animals.

Lawrence, Ellen
Roseate spoonbill; by Ellen Lawrence. Bearport Publishing 2017 24 p. color ill., color map (library binding) $23.93
Grades: 1 2 3   **598.3**
1. Swamp animals 2. Swamp ecology 3. Roseate spoonbill
ISBN 9781944997212; 1944102531; 9781944102531

LC 2016012271
In this book, by Ellen Lawrence, "it's early morning in a swamp. A roseate spoonbill is wading through a shallow pond. Slowly, the bird sweeps its long, spoon-shaped bill back and forth through the water. The colorful bird is feeling for small fish and shrimp. When its super-

sensitive bill detects movement in the murky waters, the bird grabs its prey and gobbles it down." (Publisher's note)

"Text boxes caption the eye-catching photographs, point out details, and pose questions that are answered on the following page. End materials include a science activity, glossary, and index." Booklist
Includes bibliographical references and index

Markle, Sandra, 1946-
The **long,** long journey; the godwit's amazing migration. by Sandra Markle; illustrated by Mia Posada. Millbrook Press 2013 32 p. col. ill., col. map (library) $26.60
Grades: 1 2 3   **598.3**
1. Picture books for children 2. Bar-tailed godwit 3. Bar-tailed godwit -- Migration
ISBN 0761356231; 9780761356233

LC 2012020915
This children's picture book by Sandra Markle follows the migration journey of the bar-tailed godwit chick. "Migrating 7,000 miles south from their breeding grounds, bar-tailed godwits flee the Arctic winter for the Southern-Hemisphere summer, making the longest known nonstop flight of any bird." (Kirkus Reviews)
Includes bibliographical references

Riggs, Kate
Flamingos; by Kate Riggs. Creative Education/Creative Paperbacks 2015 24 p. color illustrations (hardcover : alk. paper) $28.50
Grades: K 1 2 3   **598.3**
1. Birds 2. Flamingos
ISBN 1608184889; 9781608184880

LC 2013051248
This book offers "a basic exploration of the appearance, behavior, and habitat of flamingos, the long-legged wading birds. Also included is a story from folklore explaining how flamingos came to live at salt lakes." (Publisher's note)

"Vivid photographs providing up-close views of the daily lives and habits of the title birds are the highlights of these slim volumes. Minimal text touches on habitat, appearance, food, and offspring, and supplies a folk-story answer to a question about each creature." Horn Book
Includes bibliographical references (page 24) and index

598.34   Storks

Gish, Melissa
Storks; Melissa Gish. Creative Education 2015 46 p. color ill., color map (hardcover : alk. paper) $39.95
Grades: 4 5 6   **598.34**
1. Storks 2. Storks 3. Rare birds
ISBN 1608185710; 9781608185719

LC 2014028013
This book, by Melissa Gish, part of the Living Wild series, presents "a look at storks, including their habitats, physical characteristics such as their long legs, behaviors, relationships with humans, and their threatened status in the world today." (Publisher's note)
Includes bibliographical references and index

598.4   Miscellaneous orders of water birds

Bodden, Valerie
Swans; by Valerie Bodden. Creative Education 2009 24 p. (hardcover : alk. paper) $24.25

Grades: K 1 2 3   **598.4**
1. Swans 2. Animals 3. Swans
ISBN 1583417192; 9781583417195

LC 2007051589

In this book, by Valerie Bodden, "photos are paired with accessible text to examine the [swan's] appearance, behaviors, and life cycle. [The] book also presents a folk story that helps explain a defining feature [of the animal]." (Publisher's note)

Includes bibliographical references and index

598.47   Penguins

Gibbons, Gail
Penguins! Holiday House 1998 un il maps $16.95; pa $6.95
Grades: K 1 2 3   **598.47**
1. Penguins
ISBN 0-8234-1388-8; 0-8234-1516-3 pa

LC 98-5194

Describes the habitat, physical characteristics, and behavior of different kinds of penguins

This book has "simply written, clear text. . . . The oversized format, brightly colored illustrations, and large type font result in an eye-catching appearance that will attract young researchers and the curious minded alike." SLJ

Guiberson, Brenda Z.
★ **The emperor** lays an egg; illustrated by Joan Paley. Holt & Co. 2001 un il $16.95; pa $7.99
Grades: K 1 2 3   **598.47**
1. Penguins
ISBN 0-8050-6204-1; 0-8050-7636-3 pa

LC 00-40980

"Guiberson's vivid prose fleshes out the bare bones of the penguin's life cycle. . . . Paley's collages of painted and cut papers provide exceptionally beautiful scenes of the birds." Booklist

Tatham, Betty
Penguin chick; illustrated by Helen K. Davie. HarperCollins Pubs. 2002 33p il (Let's-read-and-find-out science) $15.95; pa $4.95
Grades: K 1 2 3   **598.47**
1. Penguins
ISBN 0-06-028594-X; 0-06-445206-9 pa

LC 00-59696

This book "follows the growth of one penguin chick from egg to adulthood. The story has been told before, but the clear, simple text provides intriguing details and inherent drama that will keep young children involved straight through till the end." Booklist

598.53   Cassowaries and emus

Saxby, Claire
Emu; Claire Saxby, illustrated by Graham Byrne. Candlewick Press 2015 28 p. color illustrations $16.99
Grades: K 1 2 3 4   **598.53**
1. Animals -- Australia 2. Emus
ISBN 0763674796; 9780763674793

LC 2013957348

In this book, by Claire Saxby, illustrated by Graham Byrne, "[f]ollow a doting dad as he keeps his brood safe. . . . In the open eucalyptus forest of Australia, an emu . . . settles down on his nest to warm and protect the eggs left by his mate. When they hatch, the chicks will be ten

times bigger than domestic chicken hatchlings and covered in chocolate-and-cream stripes to provide camouflage in the grasslands. This unusual family sticks together until the hatchlings grow up." (Publisher's note)

"A short index and a page of additional emu-related information are appended. A bit darker and edgier than standard picture-book illustrations of animals, the digital artwork is distinctive and handsome in its own way." Booklist

598.7   Miscellaneous orders of land birds

Evans, Marilyn Grohoske
Spit and sticks; a chimney swift story. Marilyn Grohoske Evans; illustrated by Nicole Gsell. Charlesbridge 2015 32 p. color illustrations (reinforced for library use) $16.95
Grades: PreK K 1   **598.7**
1. Chimneys 2. Country life 3. Birds 4. Farm life 5. Chimney swift
ISBN 9781580895880; 9781580895897

LC 2014010500

This book, by Marilyn Grohoske Evans, illustrated by Nicole Gsell, "follows chimney swifts as they arrive on a Texas farm, build their nest, lay eggs, ready for fledglings to take flight, and eventually prepare to migrate back to South America. In a parallel, wordless story, a mom, dad, and young girl on the farm watch the chimney swifts. . . . As they enjoy their baby's first months, they also celebrate the fledglings' first flight and bid the birds good-bye until next year." (Publisher's note)

"An engaging, informational picture book." Booklist

Riggs, Kate
Woodpeckers; by Kate Riggs. Creative Education 2014 24 p. col ill. $7.99
Grades: K 1 2   **598.7**
1. Woodpeckers 2. Birds in literature
ISBN 0898129311; 9780898129311; 9781608183524

LC 2013005401

This children's book by Kate Riggs, part of the Amazing Animals series, provides "A basic exploration of the appearance, behavior, and habitat of woodpeckers, nature's drummers. Also included is a story from folklore explaining how woodpeckers take good care of their young." (Publisher's note)

"Across from the photos, the text is laid out cleanly in a large, clear font, and the sentences are simple and easy to read. Photo captions, meanwhile, add interesting facts, while occasional vocabulary words are defined at the bottoms of pages. At the end of each book, the author retells a myth or story about that kind of animal." Booklist

Includes bibliographical references (p. 24) and index

Sayre, April Pulley
Woodpecker wham! April Pulley Sayre; illustrated by Steve Jenkins. Henry Holt & Co. 2015 40 p. color illustrations (hardcover) $17.99
Grades: PreK K 1 2 3   **598.7**
1. Woodpeckers 2. Birds -- Behavior 3. Woodpeckers -- Behavior
ISBN 0805088423; 9780805088427

LC 2014038047

In this children's book, by April Pulley Sayre, illustrated by Steve Jenkins, "enter woodpecker world and get a bird's eye view of everyday life: hiding from hawks, feeding hungry chicks, and drilling holes to build homes. Woodpeckers are nature's home builders, creating holes that many other animals live in when the woopeckers move on." (Publisher's note)

Includes bibliographical references

598.864 Corvids

Turner, Pamela S.

Crow smarts; Inside the Brain of the World's Brightest Bird. by Pamela S. Turner with photographs by Andy Comins. Houghton Mifflin Harcourt 2016 80 p. color illustrations (ebook) $18.99; $18.99

Grades: 4 5 6 7 8 **598.864**

1. Crows 2. Animal behavior 3. Animal intelligence 4. Crows -- Behavior

ISBN 9780544829336; 9780544416192

LC 2015013903

This book by Pamela S. Turner with photographs by Andy Comins, part of the "Scientists in the Field Series" takes a journey to New Caledonia to see local species of crow in action. "There, Dr. Gavin R. Hunt takes them into the forest for field observations and into aviaries and testing areas where captive crows demonstrate their capabilities with unfamiliar materials. Only five animal species are known to make multiple kinds of tools; only crows and humans make hooked tools." (Kirkus Reviews)

"With an approachable writing style and photos of crows festooning almost every page, this engaging volume will attract budding scientists, and the lively descriptions not only of the crows but of the scientists at work will give students plenty to ponder." Booklist

Includes bibliographical references (page 71) and index.

598.9 Falconiformes, Caprimulgiformes, owls

Bodden, Valerie

Owls; by Valerie Bodden. 1st ed. Creative Education 2013 24 p. (Amazing animals) (paperback) $25.65

Grades: 1 2 3 4 **598.9**

1. Owls

ISBN 1608180883; 9781608180882

LC 2011050280

This book, by Valerie Bodden, as part of the publisher's "Amazing Animals" series, presents an introduction to various species of owls. It presents "a basic exploration of the appearance, behavior, and habitat of owls, the winged nighttime hunters. Also included is a story from folklore explaining why some owls have big eyes and ears." (Publisher's note)

Includes bibliographical references and index

Harasymiw, N. D.

Condors in danger. Gareth Stevens Publishing 2013 24 p. $22.60

Grades: 2 3 4 **598.9**

1. Condors 2. Vultures 3. Endangered species

ISBN 1433991543; 9781433991547

This book, by N. D. Harasymiw, offers "information and . . . photographs . . . for kids beginning to learn about endangered species. [The book] explains that although vultures (a kind of condor) might sound like "scary birds," they perform important tasks in the food chain. Condor captivity-and-release programs have been successful, but the birds still face dangers from poisoning and hitting power lines." (Booklist)

Hoena, Blake

Everything birds of prey; Blake Hoena; with National Geographic explorer Hillary S. Young. National Geographic 2015 64 p. color ill., color maps (pbk.) $12.99

Grades: 2 3 4 5 **598.9**

1. Birds of prey

ISBN 1426318898; 1426318901; 9781426318894; 9781426318900

LC 2015304787

This book, by Blake Hoena, "introduces readers to the world's most ferocious fliers. With stunning visuals and energetic, impactful design, readers won't stop until they've learned everything there is to know about birds of prey." (Publisher's note)

"The bold and brassy, factoid-filled text is broken into chapters that flow logically from the birds' characteristics and behavior to geography and interactions with humans." Booklist

Includes bibliographical references (page 62) and index

Pringle, Laurence, 1935-

Owls! Laurence Pringle, illustrated by Meryl Henderson. Boyds Mills Press 2016 32 p. color illustrations (hardcover) $16.95

Grades: 3 4 5 6 **598.9**

1. Owls

ISBN 9781620916513; 1620916517

LC 2015946893

This children's book, by Laurence Pringle, illustrated by Meryl Henderson, "is an easy-to-read and comprehensive introduction to owl species from all over the world. Stuffed with scintillating science facts and large, colored illustrations from Meryl Henderson, this great educational book is sure to resonate with young animal lovers seeking to learn more about these elusive ghost birds." (Publisher's note)

"Complete with a glossary of terms, index, and suggested-reading list, this book—true to its swooping subject matter—is swift, exacting, and sure to hook any reader." Booklist

Includes bibliographical references (pages 31-32) and index.

Riggs, Kate

Eagles; by Kate Riggs. Creative Paperbacks 2012 24p. col. ill.

Grades: K 1 2 **598.9**

1. Eagles

ISBN 9780898126914

LC 2012008602

"A basic exploration of the appearance, behavior, and habitat of eagles, Earth's most widespread birds of prey. Also included is a story from folklore explaining why people respect eagles." (Publisher's note)

Includes bibliographical references (p. 24) and index.

Sattler, Helen Roney

The book of North American owls; illustrated by Jean Day Zallinger. Clarion Bks. 1995 64p il maps hardcover o.p. pa $7.95

Grades: 4 5 6 7 **598.9**

1. Owls

ISBN 0-395-60524-5; 0-395-90017-4 pa

LC 91-43626

This "is a superb ornithological primer. . . . The book is lavishly illustrated." Appraisal

Includes bibliographical references

598.96 Falcons

Gish, Melissa

Falcons; Melissa Gish. Creative Education 2015 46 p. color ill., color map (hardcover : alk. paper) $39.95

Grades: 4 5 6 **598.96**

1. Falcons 2. Rare birds

ISBN 9781608185665

LC 2014028009

Written by Melissa Gish, "the . . . large-format Living Wild series introduces middle-grade readers to a range of wildlife through creature-specific volumes. . . . In 'Falcons,' this keen-eyed raptor is revealed to be the fastest animal on earth and to inhabit every continent but Antarctica." (Booklist)

"Stunning photographs, sidebars with intriguing facts, and engaging prose are hallmarks of this set, and the chapters describing each creature's role in folklore or pop culture add to the fun." SLJ

Includes bibliographical references and index

599   Mammals

★ **Exploring** the world of mammals; [edited by Nancy Simmons, Richard Beatty, Amy Jane Beer] Chelsea House 2008 6v il map set $210

Grades: 5 6 7 8   **599**
1. Reference books 2. Mammals -- Encyclopedias
ISBN 978-0-7910-9651-2 set; 0-7910-9651-3 set
                                                          LC 2007028223

"This colorful and appealing set offers an introduction to the world of mammals. Most of entries are 2 to 4 pages in length. Sidebars offer extra details, and bright photographs and illustrations appear on every 2-page spread." Booklist

Gray, Susan Heinrichs
The **life** cycle of mammals; [by] Susan H. Gray. Heinemann Library 2011 48p il (Life cycles) lib bdg $32; pa $8.95

Grades: 3 4 5   **599**
1. Mammals
ISBN 978-1-4329-4981-5 lib bdg; 978-1-4329-4988-4 pa
                                                          LC 2010038498

This describes what a mammal is, types of mammals, their life cycles, habitats, foods, defenses, and relationships to humans.

Includes glossary and bibliographical references

Hall, Katharine
Mammals; by Katharine Hall. Arbordale Publishing 2016 32 p. (english hardcover) $17.95

Grades: PreK K 1 2   **599**
1. Mammals
ISBN 162855729X; 9781628557299; 9781628557367
                                                          LC 2015034843

In this book, by Katharine Hall, "All mammals share certain characteristics that set them apart from animal classes. But some mammals live on land and other mammals spend their lives in water each is adapted to its environment. Land mammals breathe oxygen through nostrils but some marine mammals breathe through blowholes. Compare and contrast mammals that live on land to those that live in the water." (Publisher's note)

"Together with its companion, strong additions to a series sure to find its way to classroom and school libraries." Kirkus

Includes bibliographical references

599.2   Marsupials and monotremes

Arnold, Caroline
A **wombat's** world; written and illustrated by Caroline Arnold. Picture Window Books 2008 24p il (Caroline Arnold's animals) lib bdg $26.60

Grades: PreK K 1 2   **599.2**
1. Wombats
ISBN 978-1-4048-3986-1
                                                          LC 2007032891

"This introduction to wombats combines a narrative story with boxed facts about the animals. The uncluttered cut-paper collages and simple, straightforward text show and tell events in a wombat's life over

a year's time. . . . Arnold gives a mostly clear, compelling sense of the lives and characteristics of these unique animals." Booklist

Bishop, Nic
★ **Nic** Bishop marsupials. Scholastic 2009 48p il $17.99

Grades: 3 4 5 6   **599.2**
1. Marsupials
ISBN 978-0-439-87758-9; 0-439-87758-X
                                                          LC 2008-53379

"This broad-ranging discussion includes the Virginia opossum and related animals in the Americas before turning to the main topic, the varied marsupials of Australia. Large in scale and often exceptionally clear, the many color photos will attract animal lovers to the book. . . . This inviting title pairs some remarkable photos with a wealth of intriguing facts." Booklist

Bredeson, Carmen
Kangaroos up close; [by] Carmen Bredeson. Enslow Elementary 2008 24p il (Zoom in on animals!) lib bdg $21.26

Grades: 1 2 3   **599.2**
1. Kangaroos
ISBN 978-0-7660-3079-4 lib bdg; 0-7660-3079-2 lib bdg

"Short paragraphs of simply written text describe [kangaroos'] key body parts and how they function. . . . Behavior, diet, and care and development of the young are briefly addressed. Facing the text on each spread is a full-page, sharp, color closeup. . . . Bredeson's simply written and colorful [title] will provide younger readers with [a] satisfying first [introduction] to these fascinating creatures." SLJ

Includes glossary and bibliographical references

Doudna, Kelly
It's a baby kangaroo! ABDO Pub. Co. 2009 24p il (Baby Australian animals) $13.95

Grades: K 1 2 3   **599.2**
1. Kangaroos
ISBN 978-1-60453-576-1; 1-60453-576-8
                                                          LC 2008055075

The "book opens with a page of vital statistics: the 'baby name,' number in litter, 'weight at birth,' 'age of independence,' 'adult weight,' and 'life expectancy.' The [book] then [goes] on to describe where the animals live and their predators and conclude with a 'Fun Fact.' The photography is excellent. Sidebars on some pages include more facts or reinforce the text." SLJ

Eszterhas, Suzi
Koala Hospital; Suzi Eszterhas. Owlkids Books 2015 48 p. color ill., color portraits (hardcover) $17.95

Grades: 2 3 4 5   **599.2**
1. Koalas 2. Animal rescue
ISBN 9781771471404; 1771471409

This children's book, by Suzi Eszterhas, part of the "Wildlife Rescue" series, "features a koala rescue center in Australia. It shows why koalas are in danger, how they come to be in the sanctuary, and the process of healing and rehabilitating koalas for return to the wild. . . . [The book] also focuses on the people who work at the rescue center and how they aid the animals." (Publisher's note)

"The moments captured in Eszterhas's crisp photographs are as adorable as one would expect, and facts about koala characteristics and behavior provide a sense of the marsupials' behavior once they are released into the wild, and end sections discuss conservation efforts." Pub Wkly

Includes bibliographical references and index.

Gish, Melissa

Kangaroos. Creative Education 2010 46p il (Living wild) $23.95; pa $9.95

Grades: 5 6 7 8   **599.2**

1. Kangaroos

ISBN 978-1-58341-970-0; 1-58341-970-5; 978-0-89812-553-5 pa; 0-89812-553-7 pa

LC 2010017375

"A look at kangaroos, including their habitats, physical characteristics such as the females' pouches, behaviors, relationships with humans, and valued status in the world today." Publisher's note

Heos, Bridget

What to expect when you're expecting joeys; a guide for marsupial parents (and curious kids) illustrated by Stephane Jorisch. Millbrook Press 2011 il (Expecting animal babies)

Grades: 2 3 4 5   **599.2**

1. Marsupials

ISBN 0761358595; 9780761358596

LC 2010051506

"Directed at marsupial parents of all kinds, from kangaroos and koalas to possums and bandicoots, this tongue-in-cheek guide to joey development takes it step by step, from the birth of your pinkie to where your baby goes after it leaves the pouch. Never once dropping the pretense that this is written for pouched mammals, this manages to be both entertaining and informative. . . . [The author] uses appropriate vocabulary, making meanings clear in context and also providing a glossary. Jorisch's painted pen-and-ink sketches show lively, lightly anthropomorphized animals and add considerably to the humor." Kirkus

Includes glossary and bibliographical references

Markle, Sandra

★ **Finding** home; [by] Sandra Markle; illustrated by Alan Marks. Charlesbridge 2008 un il lib bdg $15.95

Grades: K 1 2 3   **599.2**

1. Koalas

ISBN 978-1-58089-122-6

LC 2007-01473

"Based on the true story of a koala that survived multiple bushfires and wandered into a residential area, this picture book, narrated in dramatic free verse, tells a gripping story of animal survival. . . . Markle's smooth, elegant poetry and Marks' expressive, realistic mixed-media images give a strong sense of the animals' terror and the mother's intense bond with her child." Booklist

Includes bibliographical references

Markovics, Joyce L.

Tasmanian devil; nighttime scavenger. by Joyce L. Markovics. Bearport Pub. 2009 32p il map (Uncommon animals) lib bdg $25.27

Grades: 1 2 3   **599.2**

1. Tasmanian devils

ISBN 978-1-59716-733-8 lib bdg; 1-59716-733-9 lib bdg

LC 2008-9307

"The explanatory text works spendidly, with large photographs that bring readers as close as they'll ever get to such beasts." Booklist

Includes glossary and bibliographical references

Montgomery, Sy

★ **Quest** for the tree kangaroo; an expedition to the cloud forest of New Guinea. text by Sy Montgomery; photographs by Nic Bishop. Houghton Mifflin 2006 79p il map (Scientists in the field) $18

Grades: 5 6 7 8   **599.2**

1. Zoologists 2. Tree kangaroos 3. New Guinea

ISBN 0-618-49641-6

LC 2005-34849

"The writer and photographer of this exemplary description of science field work accompanied researcher Lisa Dabek on an expedition high in New Guinea's mountains to study tree kangaroos and promote the conservation of this elusive and endangered species. . . . Montgomery . . . paces her narrative well . . . keeping the reader engaged and concerned. . . . Bishop's photographs . . . are beautifully reproduced." Publ Wkly

Racanelli, Marie

Animals with pockets. PowerKids Press 2010 24p il (Crazy nature) lib bdg $21.25; pa $8.25

Grades: 2 3 4 5   **599.2**

1. Marsupials

ISBN 978-1-4358-9385-6 lib bdg; 1-4358-9385-9 lib bdg; 978-1-4358-9862-2 pa; 1-4358-9862-1 pa

LC 2009036517

This book takes a look at different kinds of marsupials, and what makes them unique from other mammals.

This book "combines attention-grabbing information with a well-organized format. . . . [The book has] spectacular color photography and eye-popping facts. . . . Excellent for reports." SLJ

Includes glossary

Riggs, Kate

Kangaroos; by Kate Riggs. Creative Education 2012 24 p. col. ill.

Grades: K 1 2   **599.2**

1. Kangaroos 2. Animal behavior 3. Animals -- Folklore 4. Wildlife photography 5. Zoology -- Encyclopedias

ISBN 1608181081; 9781608181087

LC 2010049210

This children's book, part of Kate Riggs' "Amazing Animals" series, focuses on kangaroos. "This . . . popular series continues traveling the planet to study alligators, bats, and other fascinating animals. . . . [P]hotos are paired with . . . text to examine the featured creature's appearance, habitat, behaviors, and life cycle. . . . A basic exploration of the appearance, behavior, and habitat of kangaroos, Australia's iconic marsupials. Also included is a story from folklore explaining why kangaroos jump instead of run." (Publisher's note)

Includes bibliographical references (p. 24) and index

Saxby, Claire

Big red kangaroo; Claire Saxby, illustrated by Graham Byrne. Candlewick Press 2015 32 p. color illustrations $16.99

Grades: K 1 2 3 4   **599.2**

1. Kangaroos 2. Red kangaroo

ISBN 0763670758; 9780763670757

LC 2013955949

This juvenile book, by Claire Saxby, illustrated by Graham Byrne, follows "a dominant male kangaroo. . . . In the center of Australia, the sun is setting over the baked earth, and Red Kangaroo stirs from his rest. It's breakfast time, and Red must lead his mob of kangaroos off to find grasses for grazing. But Red is also on the watch for young male kangaroos who are ready to challenge him and try to take his place as leader." (Publisher's note)

"First-time illustrator Bryne's digitally enhanced charcoals offer haunting depictions of a male kangaroo and his mob in the Australian outback. . . . Italicized paragraphs provide further information about kangaroo behavior." Pub Wkly

Sill, Cathryn P.

About marsupials; a guide for children. [by] Cathryn Sill; illustrated by John Sill. Peachtree 2006 un il $15.95

Grades: K 1 2 3　　　　　　　　　　　　　　　　　**599.2**

1. Marsupials

ISBN 1-56145-358-7

LC 2005-20582

This introduces the characteristics and behavior of 17 marsupials, such as the marsupial mole, the red kangaroo, the numbat, the spotted cuscus, the koala and tasmanian devil.

"Written with simplicity and dignity. . . . Well-suited to classroom sharing, the paintings are attractively composed and clearly delineated." Booklist

Includes glossary and bibliographical references

Webster, Christine

Opossums; [by] Christine Webster. Weigl Publishers Inc. 2008 24p il map (Backyard animals) lib bdg $24.45; pa $6.95

Grades: 2 3 4　　　　　　　　　　　　　　　　　**599.2**

1. Opossums

ISBN 978-1-59036-677-6 lib bdg; 978-1-59036-678-3 pa

LC 2006-102107

This describes the physical characteristics, behavior, and life cycle of the opossum.

"Large, full-color photos appear thoughout, and the [text is] clearly written and well organized." SLJ

Includes glossary and bibliographical references

599.3　Miscellaneous orders of placental mammals

Aronin, Miriam

The **prairie** dog's town; a perfect hideaway. Bearport Pub. 2009 32p il map (Spectacular animal towns) lib bdg $25.27

Grades: 2 3 4　　　　　　　　　　　　　　　　　**599.3**

1. Prairie dogs

ISBN 978-1-59716-870-0 lib bdg; 1-59716-870-X lib bdg

LC 2009-4064

"Introduces prairie dogs and how they live, covering the building of burrows and towns for families, different types of communication skills, and conservation efforts to protect them." Publisher's note

Includes glossary and bibliographical references

Bailer, Darice

Prairie dogs. Marshall Cavendish Benchmark 2011 il (Animals, animals) lib bdg $20.95

Grades: 3 4 5　　　　　　　　　　　　　　　　　**599.3**

1. Prairie dogs

ISBN 978-0-7614-4876-1; 0-7614-4876-4

LC 2010016033

Provides information on the anatomy, special skills, habitats, and diet of prairie dogs.

Includes glossary and bibliographical references

Cooke, Lucy

★ A **little** book of sloth; by Lucy Cooke. Margaret K. McElderry Books 2013 64 p. col. ill. (hardcover) $16.99

Grades: PreK K 1 2 3　　　　　　　　　　　　　**599.3**

1. Sloths 2. Picture books for children 3. Sloths -- Costa Rica

ISBN 1442445572; 9781442445574

LC 2012018737

In this children's picture book, author Lucy Cooke "offers an encyclopedic look at" sloths "by way of a photo-tour of their . . . sanctuary in Costa Rica. There are sloths in pajamas (which are actually necessary because they can't control their body temperature), sloths in a 'cuddle puddle,' sloths hugging stuffed animals, [and] sloths gazing into the camera with small but trusting eyes." (Publishers Weekly)

George, Lynn

Prairie dogs; tunnel diggers. PowerKids Press 2011 24p il (Animal architects) lib bdg $21.25; pa $8.25

Grades: 1 2 3　　　　　　　　　　　　　　　　　**599.3**

1. Prairie dogs 2. Animals -- Habitations

ISBN 978-1-4488-0695-9 lib bdg; 1-4488-0695-X lib bdg; 978-1-4488-1351-3 pa; 1-4488-1351-4 pa

LC 2010008867

Includes glossary

Gibbons, Gail

Rabbits, rabbits, & more rabbits! Holiday House 2000 un il $16.95; pa $6.95

Grades: K 1 2 3　　　　　　　　　　　　　　　　**599.3**

1. Rabbits

ISBN 0-8234-1486-8; 0-8234-1660-7 pa

LC 99-16765

Describes different kinds of rabbits, their physical characteristics, behavior, where they live, and how to care for them

"Colored washes and crayon shading enliven the clearly delineated ink drawings." Booklist

Glaser, Linda

Hello, squirrels! scampering through the seasons. by Linda Glaser; illustrated by Gay W. Holland. Millbrook Press 2006 32p il lib bdg $22.60

Grades: K 1 2　　　　　　　　　　　　　　　　　**599.3**

1. Squirrels

ISBN 978-0-7613-2887-2 lib bdg; 0-7613-2887-4 lib bdg

LC 2005003692

"The book documents a year in a squirrel's life in a first-person narration that imitates a child's voice and cadences. . . . The text is filled with the kind of natural details that a child would observe. Holland's realistic colored-pencil drawings . . . are complemented by generous white space and easy-to-read print. More scientific information is provided in the answers to four questions at the end of the book." Booklist

Gregory, Josh

Hedgehogs; by Josh Gregory. Children's Press, an imprint of Scholastic Inc. 2016 48 p. color illustrations, map (library binding : alk. paper) $28

Grades: 3 4 5 6　　　　　　　　　　　　　　　　**599.3**

1. Hedgehogs

ISBN 0531213900; 0531214931; 9780531213902; 9780531214930

LC 2014043978

This children's book, by Josh Gregory, part of the "Nature's children" series, profiles hedgehogs. "An opening 'Fact File' breaks down info such as taxonomy, habits, habitats, and diets and provides a preview for the information that will be covered. . . . The first chapter depicts an encounter with the animal and describes a typical behavior. The rest of the book delves further into the topics brought up in the 'Fact File.'" (Publisher's note)

"Sophisticated scientific terms such as bilateral symmetry or anticoagulant are often defined in-text." SLJ

Includes bibliographical references (page 46) and index

Sloths; by Josh Gregory. Children's Press, an imprint of Scholastic Inc. 2016 48 p. color illustrations (library binding : alk. paper) $28

Grades: 3 4 5 6   **599.3**

1. Sloths

ISBN 0531213919; 053121494X; 9780531213919; 9780531214947

LC 2014044037

This children's book, by Josh Gregory, part of the "Nature's Children" series, explores sloths. "These additions to this ongoing series follow a tried-and-true format: text on one page facing a full-page photo. An opening 'Fact File' breaks down info such as taxonomy, habits, habitats, and diets and provides a preview for the information that will be covered. . . . [And] the first chapter depicts an encounter with the animal and describes a typical behavior." (School Library Journal)

"Sophisticated scientific terms such as bilateral symmetry or anticoagulant are often defined in-text. "Fun Fact" boxes are scattered throughout." SLJ

Includes bibliographical references (page 46) and index

Kalman, Bobbie

The **life** cycle of a beaver; [by] Bobbie Kalman. Crabtree 2007 32p il lib bdg $25.27; pa $6.95

Grades: 2 3 4   **599.3**

1. Beavers

ISBN 978-0-7787-0628-1 lib bdg; 0-7787-0628-1 lib bdg; 978-0-7787-0702-8 pa; 0-7787-0702-4 pa

LC 2006023330

The beaver "is described as a mammal (a term that is explained) belonging to the rodent family. Its habitat is outlined, along with information on how it builds lodges, dams, and burrows. Diet, growth, and facts about the young are included. The information is presented in a flowing narrative accompanied by color photographs and drawings that perfectly illustrate the [text]." SLJ

Markle, Sandra

Prairie dogs. Lerner Publications Company 2007 39p il map (Animal prey) lib bdg $25.26; pa $7.95

Grades: 4 5 6   **599.3**

1. Prairie dogs

ISBN 978-0-8225-6438-6 lib bdg; 0-8225-6438-6 lib bdg; 978-0-8225-6441-6 pa; 0-8225-6441-6 pa

LC 2006-598

Describes the behavior of prairie dogs in their native habitat, where they are the prey of larger animals and birds and where they must work together as a colony to create burrows and warning systems to protect themselves and their young

Includes glossary and bibliographical references

Markovics, Joyce L.

My body is tough and gray; by Joyce Markovics. Bearport Publishing 2017 24 p. color illustrations (ebook) $23.93; (library binding) $23.93

Grades: K 1 2 3   **599.3**

1. Armadillos   2. Zoo animals   3. Nine-banded armadillo

ISBN 9781944102845; 9781944102630

LC 2016006804

In this children's book, by Joyce Markovics, "what has a sticky tongue, curved claws, and a tough gray body? If you guessed a nine-banded armadillo, you're right! This book introduces early readers to a mystery animal by describing its features, one by one, using short simple sentences and eye-popping full-color photos. At the end of the book, the secret animal is revealed across a colorful, two-page spread." (Publisher's note)

"A well-executed concept useful for new readers and curious animal lovers." SLJ

Includes bibliographical references and index

Otfinoski, Steven

Squirrels. Marshall Cavendish Benchmark 2010 47p il (Animals, animals) lib bdg $29.93

Grades: 3 4 5   **599.3**

1. Squirrels

ISBN 978-0-7614-4843-3; 0-7614-4843-8

LC 2009022628

This offers information on the anatomy, special skills, habitats, and diet of squirrels.

Includes glossary and bibliographical references

Reingold, Adam

The **beaver's** lodge; building with leftovers. Bearport Pub. 2009 32p il map (Spectacular animal towns) lib bdg $25.27

Grades: 2 3 4   **599.3**

1. Beavers

ISBN 978-1-59716-872-4 lib bdg; 1-59716-872-6 lib bdg

LC 2009-11723

Explores the remarkable homes built by beavers.

"Through excellent photographs, high-interest texts, sidebars, maps, and other material, children learn about both the animals and their habitats. The . . . book also provides brief profiles of animals with similar habitats. . . . [This book is] much better than average 'report' titles." SLJ

Includes glossary and bibliographical references

Swinburne, Stephen R.

Armadillo trail; the northward journey of the armadillo. illustrated by Bruce Hiscock. Boyds Mills Press 2009 un il $16.95

Grades: K 1 2 3   **599.3**

1. Armadillos

ISBN 978-1-59078-463-1

LC 2008028774

"In a burrow beneath a Texas field, an armadillo gives birth to four pups. As the little ones grow, they venture outside with her to hunt for food. . . . This handsome picture book offers enough detail to engage them in understanding armadillos, and a refreshing lack of sensationalism and sentimentality about events in the animals' lives." Booklist

Zuchora-Walske, Christine

Let's look at prairie dogs. Lerner Publications Co. 2010 32p il map (Lightning bolt books: Animal close-ups) lib bdg $25.26

Grades: PreK K 1 2   **599.3**

1. Prairie dogs

ISBN 978-0-7613-3891-8 lib bdg; 0-7613-3891-8 lib bdg

LC 2008-51856

Introduces prairie dogs, describing their physical characteristics, habitat, and predators

"Fresh photography, a creative use of graphics, and a collagelike layout make[s] . . . [this book] eye-catching. . . . [The] book ends with a labeled diagram of the animal, a range map, and a further-reading list that includes print and online resources in a single list, a nice way of validating both types of materials." SLJ

Includes glossary

599.35   Rodents

Bill, Tannis

★ **Pika**; life in the rocks. photographs by Jim Jacobson. Boyds Mills Press 2010 32p il $18.95

Grades: K 1 2 3   **599.35**

1. Pikas

ISBN 978-1-59078-803-5; 1-59078-803-6

"The pika is a cousin to the rabbit. . . . Using short, declarative sentences, Tannis follows the laborious life of a pika living in the Rocky Mountains. It is a daily grind of gathering leaves and branches for his hay pile, a massive thatch that can grow as large as a bathtub and that serves as a food reserve, particularly during winter months. . . . The photos capture the pika at his cutest. . . . Loaded with rich back matter on the pika and its predators, this is a cycle-of-life book that satisfies to the end." Booklist

Includes glossary and bibliographical references

Ganeri, Anita
Capybara. Heinemann Library 2011 24p il map (Day in the life. rain forest animals) lib bdg $22; pa $6.49
Grades: 1 2　　　　　　　　　　　　　　　　　　**599.35**
　1. Capybara
　ISBN 978-1-4329-4110-9 lib bdg; 1-4329-4110-0 lib bdg; 978-1-4329-4121-5 pa; 1-4329-4121-6 pa
　　　　　　　　　　　　　　　　　　LC 2010001132
This book follows a capybara through its day as it sleeps, eats, and moves.

"Ganeri presents information clearly and simply in large type, two-sentence comments placed below a bright, sharply reproduced color photograph of the animal in a natural setting. . . . [This is] sufficiently specific to support assignment as well as pleasure reading." SLJ

Includes glossary and bibliographical references

Hansen, Grace
Capybaras; Grace Hansen. Abdo Kids 2016 24 p. color illustrations (ebook) $28.50; (hard cover) $28.50
Grades: PreK K 1 2　　　　　　　　　　　　　　**599.35**
　1. Rodents 2. Capybara
　ISBN 9781680807110; 9781680805437; 9781680805994; 9781680806557
　　　　　　　　　　　　　　　　　　LC 2015959226
In this children's book in the Super Species series by Grace Hansen, "meet the biggest rodent in the world--the capybara...Readers will learn all that is super-size about this cute mammal." (Publisher's note)

"Youngsters will love poring over the crisp, oversize photos that occupy each long, horizontal two-page spread, and the simple, large-type sentences are ideal for emergent readers. An attractive introduction to the nonfiction format, as well as to a subject guaranteed to fascinate." Booklist

Kalman, Bobbie
Baby rodents; by Bobbie Kalman. Crabtree Publishing Company 2013 24 p. col. ill. (library) $22.60; (paperback) $6.95
Grades: 1 2 3 4　　　　　　　　　　　　　　　**599.35**
　1. Rodents 2. Animal babies 3. Rodents -- Infancy
　ISBN 9780778710097; 9780778710141
　　　　　　　　　　　　　　　　　　LC 2012043742
This book by Bobbie Kalman presents "photographs of different kinds of rodents from cute baby chipmunks to chubby capybaras. Easy-to-understand text explains in which habitats rodents live and how their babies are born and raised. Young readers will also learn about rodent teeth, rodent diets, how different rodents move, build their homes, and which rodents are popular pets." (Publisher's note)

Includes bibliographical references and index.

Lunde, Darrin
Dirty rats? Darrin Lunde; illustrated by Adam Gustavson. Charlesbridge 2015 32 p. color illustrations (reinforced for library use) $16.95

Grades: K 1 2 3　　　　　　　　　　　　　　　**599.35**
　1. Rats
　ISBN 1580895662; 9781580895668
　　　　　　　　　　　　　　　　　　LC 2013049022
This children's book, by Darrin Lunde, illustrated by Adam Gustavson, discusses rats. "Nobody likes a rat. . . . But, hold on . . . are rats really so bad? There are hundreds of rat species all around the world that defy common stereotypes. Rats help predators survive, allow plants to spread their seeds, and even contribute to medical research that helps humans stay healthy." (Publisher's note)

"Few animals are as maligned as rats, something mammal specialist Lunde knows well. 'Dirty rats. Their beady eyes and naked tails make us scream. Eek! Aargh! Yikes!' he writes as a frightened woman in hair curlers tries to sweep rats off her apartment's fire escape . . . Gustavson's typically lush oil paintings do their part to help sway opinions—his sewer rats come across as intelligent, curious, and even adorable." PW

Markle, Sandra
Outside and inside rats and mice. Atheneum Bks. for Young Readers 2001 39p il hardcover o.p. pa $10.99
Grades: 2 3 4　　　　　　　　　　　　　　　**599.35**
　1. Mice 2. Rats
　ISBN 0-689-82301-0; 1-4169-7571-3 pa
　　　　　　　　　　　　　　　　　　LC 00-29290
Describes the external and internal physical characteristics of mice and rats and their behavior

"Markle skillfully draws readers into careful observation of outstanding close-up photographs of mice and rats. . . . The friendly text maintains its scientific rigor." Horn Book

Includes glossary

★ **Porcupines**; [by] Sandra Markle. Lerner Publications Company 2007 39p il (Animal prey) lib bdg $25.26
Grades: 3 4 5　　　　　　　　　　　　　　　**599.35**
　1. Porcupines
　ISBN 978-0-8225-6439-3 lib bdg; 0-8225-6439-4 lib bdg
　　　　　　　　　　　　　　　　　　LC 2006000601
This describes the physical characteristics, habits, and life cycle of porcupines

"An outstanding combination of fascinating [text] and informative, appealing photos." SLJ

Includes glossary and bibliographical references

Marrin, Albert
★ **Oh,** rats! the story of rats and people. illustrated by C.B. Mordan. Dutton Children's Books 2006 48p il $16.99
Grades: 3 4 5 6　　　　　　　　　　　　　　**599.35**
　1. Rats
　ISBN 0-525-47762-4
　　　　　　　　　　　　　　　　　　LC 2004-24512
This is "lively and informative. . . . The nine short chapters are set in a handsome slim book with striking black-and-white scratchboard illustrations and muted red framing on many pages." SLJ

Includes bibliographical references

Savage, Stephen
Mouse. PowerKids Press 2009 32p il (Animal neighbors) lib bdg $23.95
Grades: 3 4 5 6　　　　　　　　　　　　　　**599.35**
　1. Mice
　ISBN 978-1-4358-4990-7 lib bdg; 1-4358-4990-6 lib bdg
　　　　　　　　　　　　　　　　　　LC 2008-5414
This describes the life cycle, habitat, and behavior of mice

Rat. PowerKids Press 2009 32p il (Animal neighbors) lib bdg $23.95

Grades: 3 4 5   **599.35**

1. Rats

ISBN 978-1-4358-4991-4 lib bdg; 1-4358-4991-4 lib bdg

LC 2008-5451

This describes the life cycle, habitat, and behavior of rats

This title features "beautiful, detailed, close-up photos of animals displayed on child-friendly page layouts. The information is well organized for reports." SLJ

Sill, Cathryn P.

About rodents; [by] Cathryn Sill; illustrated by John Sill. Peachtree 2008 un il $15.95

Grades: K 1 2 3   **599.35**

1. Rodents

ISBN 978-1-56145-454-9; 1-56145-454-0

Explains what rodents are, how they live, and what they do.

"Beautifully illustrated with clear, well-composed paintings of animals, this book shows respect for its audience as well as its subject." Booklist

Includes glossary and bibliographical references

Tait, Leia

Mice. Weigl 2010 24p il (Backyard animals) lib bdg $24.45; pa $8.95

Grades: 1 2 3   **599.35**

1. Mice

ISBN 978-1-60596-080-7 lib bdg; 1-60596-080-2 lib bdg; 978-1-60596-081-4 pa; 1-60596-081-0 pa

LC 2008052059

This is "packed with information and [includes] fine close-up photos. . . . [It] does a solid job of introducing the tiny animal's habits and habitats." Booklist

Includes glossary

Webster, Christine

Porcupines. Weigl 2010 24p il (Backyard animals) lib bdg $24.45; pa $8.95

Grades: 1 2 3   **599.35**

1. Porcupines

ISBN 978-1-60596-078-4 lib bdg; 1-60596-078-0 lib bdg; 978-1-60596-079-1 pa; 1-60596-079-9 pa

LC 2009004446

This describes the physical characteristics, natural habitats, history, and folklore of porcupines.

Includes glossary

599.36   Squirrel family

Roth, Susan L.

Prairie dog song; the key to saving North America's grasslands. by Susan L. Roth and Cindy Trumbore; collages by Susan L. Roth. Lee & Low Books Inc. 2016 40 p. (hardcover : alk. paper) $18.95

Grades: K 1 2 3 4 5 6   **599.36**

1. Prairie dogs 2. Prairie animals 3. Grassland ecology 4. Children's songs -- Texts 5. Grassland animals

ISBN 9781620142455

LC 2015025915

In this book, by Susan L. Roth and Cindy Trumbore, "The prairie and desert grasslands were home to a variety of animals, from small prairie dogs to huge bison. But in the nineteenth century, ranching and farming took hold in the grasslands, and over time, many of the animals

and plants vanished. Then, in the late 1980s, scientists discovered a region in Mexico where green and gold grasses still waved and prairie dogs still barked." (Publisher's note)

"The supplemental materials, which include music for the song, prairie dog facts, a time line, and an extensive list of sources, are illustrated with color photos. A combination of simple verse and detailed context makes this well suited for children of various reading levels." Booklist

Sayre, April Pulley

Squirrels Leap, Squirrels sleep; April Pulley Sayre; illustrated by Steve Jenkins. Henry Holt & Co. 2016 40 p. color illustrations (hardcover) $17.99

Grades: PreK K 1 2   **599.36**

1. Squirrels

ISBN 9780805092516

LC 2015036529

In this book, by April Pulley Sayre, illustrated by Steve Jenkins, "Squirrels wrestle. Squirrels leap. Squirrels climb. Squirrels sleep. If you followed a squirrel for a day, what would you see? Climbing branches, storing seeds, making homes in tree holes, and maybe even flying!" (Publisher's note)

"A fine introductory and informational book that would be equally at home in picture book and nonfiction collections." SLJ

Includes bibliographical references

599.37   Beavers

Gibbons, Gail

Beavers; by Gail Gibbons. Holiday House 2013 32 p. (hardcover) $17.95

Grades: K 1 2 3   **599.37**

1. Beavers 2. Picture books for children 3. Beavers

ISBN 082342412X; 9780823424122

LC 2011049420

Author and illustrator Gail Gibbons features a children's picture book on beavers. "Beavers are fascinating animals. They build their own homes and live in family groups. They keep busy with their sharp teeth, powerful tails, and big webbed feet. Their work helps to preserve wetlands. Gibbons explores where they live, what they eat, how they raise their young, and much more." (Publisher's note)

599.4   Bats

Bekkering, Annalise

Bats. Weigl 2010 24p il (Backyard animals) lib bdg $24.45; pa $8.95

Grades: 1 2 3   **599.4**

1. Bats

ISBN 978-1-60596-076-0 lib bdg; 1-60596-076-4 lib bdg; 978-1-60596-077-7 pa; 1-60596-077-2 pa

LC 2008052056

This describes the "outstanding physical and behavioral characteristics [of bats]; some historical background; natural habitats and life cycle; role in the mythology of various cultures (a short myth is recounted); and tips on how to respond to (or avoid) encounters with the creatures. . . . A large, clear color photograph of one or more of the . . . animals . . . appears on about every other page." SLJ

Includes glossary

Berman, Ruth

Let's look at bats. Lerner Publications Co. 2010 32p il (Lightning bolt books: Animal close-ups) lib bdg $25.26
Grades: PreK K 1 2　　　　　　　　　　　　　　**599.4**
　1. Bats
ISBN 978-0-7613-3885-7 lib bdg; 0-7613-3885-3 lib bdg

　　　　　　　　　　　　　　　　　　　LC 2008-51858

Introduces bats, describing their physical characteristics, habitat, nocturnal behavior, and feeding habits

"Fresh photography, a creative use of graphics, and a collagelike layout make[s] . . . [this book] eye-catching. . . . [The] book ends with a labeled diagram of the animal, a range map, and a further-reading list that includes print and online resources in a single list, a nice way of validating both types of materials." SLJ

Includes glossary

Carney, Elizabeth

Bats. National Geographic 2010 31p il (National Geographic readers) pa $3.99; $11.90
Grades: 1 2 3　　　　　　　　　　　　　　　**599.4**
　1. Bats
ISBN 978-1-4263-0710-2 pa; 1-4263-0710-1 pa; 978-1-4263-0711-9; 1-4263-0711-X

　　　　　　　　　　　　　　　　　　　LC 2010011636

"This leveled reader offers very basic information about bats. Topics range from types of bats to bat diet to behaviors such as echolocation and hanging upside down. . . . 'Bat Myths,' such as consuming human blood, are debunked. Simple sentence structures, along with corny jokes and excellent well-captioned photos, increase accessibility." Horn Book Guide

Includes glossary

Carson, Mary Kay

★ The **bat** scientists; with photographs by Tom Uhlman. Houghton Mifflin Books for Children 2010 79p il (Scientists in the field) $18
Grades: 4 5 6 7　　　　　　　　　　　　　　**599.4**
　1. Bats 2. Bat Conservation International　3. Conservation biology -- Research
ISBN 0-547-19956-2; 978-0-547-19956-6

　　　　　　　　　　　　　　　　　　　LC 2010006767

This title in the Scientists in the Field series looks at the work of Dr. Merlin Tuttle and his colleagues at Bat Conservation International. It explores the bat's role in the natural world while seeking to "raise awareness about the problems threatening bat populations, including white-nose syndrome." (Publisher's note) Glossary. Index. "Intermediate, middle school." (Horn Book)

This describes "patient field work, rescue and conservation efforts to save bats. . . . Woven into particular researchers' stories is an enormous amount of information about bat biology and behavior. Uhlman's photographs are clearly identified in context and the backmatter supports further research." Kirkus

Includes glossary and bibliographical references

Davies, Nicola, 1958-

★ **Bat** loves the night; illustrated by Sarah Fox-Davies. Candlewick Press 2001 28p il hardcover o.p. pa $6.99
Grades: PreK K 1 2　　　　　　　　　　　　**599.4**
　1. Bats 2. Bats -- Fiction
ISBN 0-7636-1202-2; 0-7636-2438-1 pa

　　　　　　　　　　　　　　　　　　　LC 00-66681

Bat wakes up, flies into the night, uses the echoes of her voice to navigate, hunts for her supper, and returns to her roost to feed her baby. "Ages five to seven." (Bull Cent Child Books)

"An enticing picture book . . . that blends story with fact. . . . Lovely, atmospheric watercolor-and-pencil illustrations show surprising detail and succeed in making an oft-maligned animal appear realistically fuzzy and appealing." Booklist

Earle, Ann

Zipping, zapping, zooming bats; illustrated by Henry Cole. HarperCollins Pubs. 1995 32p il (Let's-read-and-find-out science) hardcover o.p. pa $4.95
Grades: K 1 2 3　　　　　　　　　　　　　　**599.4**
　1. Bats
ISBN 0-06-023480-6; 0-06-445133-X pa

　　　　　　　　　　　　　　　　　　　LC 93-11052

"Brown bats are introduced as fliers, hunters, and contributors to good ecology in this simple discussion of the flying mammals' physical characteristics and behavior. The illustrations include realistic close-ups, informative diagrams, and scenes incorporating children. Instructions for building a bat house are included." Horn Book Guide

Gibbons, Gail

Bats. Holiday House 1999 un il $16.95; pa $6.95
Grades: K 1 2 3　　　　　　　　　　　　　　**599.4**
　1. Bats
ISBN 0-8234-1457-4; 0-8234-1637-2 pa

　　　　　　　　　　　　　　　　　　　LC 99-12051

Describes different kinds of bats, their physical characteristics, habits and behavior, and efforts to protect them

"The occasional splashes of color light up brilliantly against the dark backgrounds. Well suited for classroom use, this book makes a good case for bats as an admirable part of the natural world." Booklist

Gish, Melissa

Bats. Creative Paperbacks 2010 46p il (Living wild) $23.95; pa $9.95
Grades: 5 6 7 8　　　　　　　　　　　　　　**599.4**
　1. Bats
ISBN 978-1-58341-966-3; 1-58341-966-7; 978-0-89812-549-8 pa; 0-89812-549-9 pa

　　　　　　　　　　　　　　　　　　　LC 2010017371

The "book lucidly discusses conservation and the animals' often tenuous relationship with humans. The layout is uniformly simple but effective, constructed with a nice balance of main text for the report writers, smaller chunks of esoterica for browsers, and . . . killer photos." Booklist

Gonzales, Doreen

Bats in the dark. PowerKids Press 2010 24p il (Creatures of the night) lib bdg $21.25; pa $8.05
Grades: 2 3 4　　　　　　　　　　　　　　　**599.4**
　1. Bats
ISBN 978-1-4042-8096-0 lib bdg; 1-4042-8096-0 lib bdg; 978-1-4358-3249-7 pa; 1-4358-3249-3 pa

　　　　　　　　　　　　　　　　　　　LC 2008-53802

A look at bats and their world in the dark

"Basic details are complemented by eclectic trivia, . . . [and] each volume concludes with a defense of the animal . . . and why it is vital to humans. The layout is attractive, with easy-to-read text and eye-catching photography. Good for reports." SLJ

Includes glossary

Koch, Falynn

Science comics; bats: learning to fly. Falynn Koch. First Second 2017 128 p. color illustrations (hardcover) $19.99

Grades: 3 4 5 6 **599.4**

1. Bats 2. Animal flight 3. Animal rescue
ISBN 9781626724082; 9781626724099

LC 2016938728

This graphic novel in the Science Comics series, by Falynn Koch, follows "a little brown bat whose wing is injured by humans on a nature hike. He is taken to a bat rehabilitation center where he meets many different species of bats. They teach him how they fly, what they eat, and where they like to live." (Publisher's note)

"With plenty of informative back matter, this inviting, engaging nonfiction comic is perfect for kids hungry for science." Booklist

Lunde, Darrin P.

Hello, bumblebee bat; [by] Darrin Lunde; illustrated by Patricia J. Wynne. Charlesbridge 2007 un il lib bdg $15.95

Grades: PreK K 1 2 **599.4**

1. Bats

ISBN 978-1-57091-374-7 lib bdg; 1-57091-374-9 lib bdg

LC 2006-20952

A Geisel Award honor book, 2008

"Meet the inch-long bumblebee bat, the smallest bat species in the world. Each left-hand page poses a question to a little bat. . . . Beginning each question with the bat's memorable name heightens the pleasing sense of pattern in the text, which offers information that children can understand, but avoids overwhelming them with too many facts. Wynne . . . contributes an appealing set of pictures that complement the text." Booklist

Markle, Sandra, 1946-

The **case** of the vanishing little brown bats; a scientific mystery. Sandra Markle. Millbrook Press 2014 48 p. illustrations, maps (lib. bdg. : alk. paper) $29.27

Grades: 4 5 6 **599.4**

1. Bats 2. Animals -- Diseases 3. Little brown bat
ISBN 1467714631; 9781467714631

LC 2013030953

"This informative title sheds light on a mystery of nature: how little brown bats, nature's insect eaters, are mysteriously dying in their caves during hibernation. Each chapter takes readers into the problems that plague this endangered member of our ecosystem, describing how teams of scientists examined how 'white-nose syndrome,' caused by a fungus called Pd, is infecting the brown bat population." (School Library Journal)

"With plentiful details about the scientific work, photographs showing scientists and their tiny subjects, clear explanations, and an organization that is both topical and chronological, this title brings science to life." Kirkus

Includes bibliographical references and index

Markovics, Joyce L.

The **bat's** cave; a dark city. by Joyce Markovics. Bearport Pub. 2009 32p il map (Spectacular animal towns) lib bdg $25.27

Grades: 2 3 4 **599.4**

1. Bats

ISBN 978-1-59716-871-7 lib bdg; 1-59716-871-8 lib bdg

LC 2009-8146

A look inside a bat's dark world, how bats hunt, sleep, and raise their young, and more

"Through excellent photographs, high-interest texts, sidebars, maps, and other material, children learn about both the animals and their habitats. The . . . book also provides brief profiles of animals with similar habitats. . . . [This book is] much better than average 'report' titles." SLJ

Includes glossary and bibliographical references

Riggs, Kate

Bats; by Kate Riggs. Creative Education 2012 24 p. col. ill.

Grades: K 1 2 **599.4**

1. Bats 2. Animals -- Food 3. Bats -- Folklore 4. Wildlife photography 5. Zoology -- Encyclopedias 6. Bats
ISBN 1608181057; 9781608181056

LC 2010049117

This children's book is part of Kate Riggs' "Amazing Animals" series, which presents photographs and "general facts about physiology, behaviors, eating habits, habitats, and life spans" of various animals. (Booklist)

"A basic exploration of the appearance, behavior, and habitat of bats, Earth's only flying mammals. Also included is a story from folklore explaining how bats helped shape the earth." (Publisher's note)

Includes bibliographical references (p. 24) and index

Rodriguez, Cindy

Bats. Rourke Pub. 2010 24p il map (Eye to eye with endangered species) lib bdg $27.07

Grades: 2 3 4 **599.4**

1. Bats

ISBN 978-1-60694-406-6 lib bdg; 1-60694-406-1 lib bdg

LC 2009-5997

Text examines the issues endangered bats face and how they can be saved

"Sets out to introduce readers to [bats] . . . explain the dangers they face, and detail the efforts of biologists and conservationists to save them. . . . Serviceable and informative." SLJ

Includes glossary

Stewart, Melissa

How do bats fly in the dark? Marshall Cavendish Benchmark 2009 32p il (Tell me why, tell me how) lib bdg $20.95

Grades: 3 4 5 **599.4**

1. Bats

ISBN 978-0-7614-2924-1 lib bdg; 0-7614-2924-7 lib bdg

LC 2007023821

"Provides comprehensive information on bats and the process of how they use their sensory system to find their way in the dark" Publisher's note

Includes glossary and bibliographical references

A **place** for bats; written by Melissa Stewart; illustrated by Higgins Bond. 1st ed. Peachtree Publishers 2012 32 p. col. ill. (reinforced) $16.95

Grades: K 1 2 **599.4**

1. Bats 2. Habitat (Ecology) 3. Human influence on nature 4. Bats

ISBN 1561456241; 9781561456246

LC 2011020468

"This book introduces 12 varieties of bats and their habitats around Canada, the United States, and Mexico, and brings to life their challenges to survive." (School Library Journal) "[Melissa] Stewart points out problems faced by bats and what specific steps people have taken . . . to help the bats, such as . . . putting up 'bat boxes' to house bats that can no longer find dead trees for shelter. The text clearly conveys the idea that people can make a difference in animal survival." (Booklist)

Includes bibliographical references.

599.5   Cetaceans and sea cows

Arnosky, Jim

Jim Arnosky's All about manatees. Scholastic Nonfiction 2008 un pa $5.99

Grades: K 1 2 3   **599.5**

1. Manatees

ISBN 0-439-90361-0 pa; 978-0-439-90361-5 pa

LC 2007061717

This is an "introductory guide to manatees. . . . Artwork, captions, and paragraphs of information work together seamlessly to present the physical characteristics, behaviors, and habitats of manatees living in Florida waters, as well as the threats to their survival. Fluid paintings illustrate points in the text and depict the animals' lumbering grace." Booklist

Baker, Molly

The **secret** world of whales; illustrated by Molly Baker. Chronicle Books 2011 108p il $16.99

Grades: 4 5 6 7   **599.5**

1. Whales

ISBN 978-0-8118-7641-4; 0-8118-7641-1

LC 2010-27355

"In this small-format volume, Siebert creates a concise introduction to whales, addressing myths and stories, the history of the whaling industry, communication and intelligence, and encounters between whales and humans. With playful, anthropomorphic cartoons, striking photographs, and a discussion of the dangers facing whales—noise pollution from boats, potentially lethal sonar—readers should gain a vivid impression of their behavior in the wild, as well as an appreciation for their majesty." Publ Wkly

Catt, Thessaly

Migrating with the humpback whale. PowerKids Press 2011 24p il (Animal journeys) lib bdg $21.25; pa $8.25

Grades: 2 3 4   **599.5**

1. Whales 2. Animals -- Migration

ISBN 978-1-4488-2543-1 lib bdg; 1-4488-2543-1 lib bdg; 978-1-4488-2670-4 pa; 1-4488-2670-5 pa

LC 2010027076

This book follows "the yearly migratory patterns of the [humpback whale] and [covers] anatomy, diet, mating, parenting, climate change as caused by people, pollution, and more. . . . [It is illustrated] with clear color photographs. . . . Go-to nonfiction for animal enthusiasts." SLJ

Christopherson, Sara Cohen

Top 50 reasons to care about whales and dolphins; animals in peril. Enslow Publishers 2010 103p il (Top 50 reasons to care about endangered animals) lib bdg $31.93

Grades: 4 5 6 7   **599.5**

1. Whales 2. Dolphins 3. Endangered species

ISBN 978-0-7660-3453-2 lib bdg; 0-7660-3453-4 lib bdg

LC 2008-48695

This describes whales and dolphins—their life cycles, diets, young, habitats, and reasons why they are endangered animals

"The illustrations, mostly color photographs, represent a wonderful selection of the animals and their habitats. Reluctant readers may be enticed by this . . . simply because of the great images. This . . . would make a substantial supplement to the science curriculum when studying endangered animals." Libr Media Connect

Includes glossary and bibliographical references

Davies, Nicola, 1958-

Big blue whale; illustrated by Nick Maland. Candlewick Press 1997 27p il hardcover o.p. pa $6.99

Grades: K 1 2 3   **599.5**

1. Whales

ISBN 1-56402-895-X; 0-7636-1080-1 pa

LC 96-42327

Examines the physical characteristics, habits, and habitats of the blue whale

"Davies's brief overview offers young readers exactly what they want to know about this magnificent animal, and her judicious use of comparison makes the abstract more understandable. . . . Maland's cross-hatched pen-and-ink drawings rest on blue watercolor wash backgrounds." Horn Book Guide

Esbensen, Barbara Juster

Baby whales drink milk; illustrated by Lambert Davis. HarperCollins Pubs. 1994 32p il (Let's-read-and-find-out science) hardcover o.p. pa $4.95

Grades: K 1   **599.5**

1. Whales 2. Mammals

ISBN 0-06-445119-4 pa

LC 92-30375

Describes the behavior of the humpback whale, with an emphasis on the fact that it is a mammal and shares the characteristics of other mammals

"Full-color paintings, mainly in watery greens and blues, show the animals in their habitat, along with a scene of a whale model in a museum and a map of migration. The book's strong point, though, is Esbensen's simple, informative text, which keeps its young audience clearly in view." Booklist

Gish, Melissa

Killer whales. Creative Paperbacks 2010 46p il map (Living wild) $23.95; pa $9.95

Grades: 5 6 7 8   **599.5**

1. Whales

ISBN 978-1-58341-971-7; 1-58341-971-3; 978-0-89812-554-2 pa; 0-89812-554-5 pa

LC 2010017376

"A look at killer whales, including their habitats, physical characteristics such as their unique coloration, behaviors, relationships with humans, and protected status in the world today." Publisher's note

Whales. Creative Education 2011 46p il map (Living wild) lib bdg $23.95

Grades: 5 6 7 8   **599.5**

1. Whales

ISBN 978-1-60818-084-4

LC 2010028414

A look at whales, including their habitats, physical characteristics such as their streamlined bodies, behaviors, relationships with humans, and threatened status in the world today.

Includes glossary and bibliographical references

Goldish, Meish

Florida manatees; warm water miracles. by Meish Goldish. Bearport Pub. 2007 32p il map (America's animal comebacks) lib bdg $18.95

Grades: 2 3 4   **599.5**

1. Manatees 2. Wildlife conservation

ISBN 978-1-59716-507-5 lib bdg; 1-59716-507-7 lib bdg

LC 2007010311

"This accessible title discusses the environmental threats facing the Florida manatee and the efforts that saved this appealing sea creature from extinction. . . . Double-page spread feature attention-grabbing fact boxes and large, full-color photos." Booklist

Includes glossary and bibliographical references

Greenberg, Daniel A.

Whales; [by] Dan Greenberg, with Nina Hess. Cavendish Square Publishing 2010 24p il map (Benchmark rockets. Animals) lib bdg $16.95

Grades: 3 4 5 6   **599.5**
    1. Whales
    ISBN 978-0-7614-4346-9; 0-7614-4346-0
                                        LC 2008-52110

"Describes the physical characteristics, habitat, behavior, diet, life cycle, and conservation status of whales." Publisher's note

Includes glossary

Harris, Caroline

Whales and dolphins. Kingfisher 2010 56p il (Discover science) $9.99

Grades: 1 2 3   **599.5**
    1. Whales 2. Dolphins
    ISBN 978-0-7534-6448-9; 0-7534-6448-9

First published in the series Kingfisher young knowledge in 2005

Introduces readers to some of the largest and most acrobatic mammals in oceans and seas. Young students will discover the many types of whales and dolphins and learn about their behavior and how they survive in their watery world

"There is enough information for basic reports, but . . . [this] will also be popular with browsers. . . . [Features] large, colorful images as well as smaller, more detailed close-up." Libr Media Connect

Includes glossary and bibliographical references

Hodgkins, Fran

★ The **whale** scientists; solving the mystery of whale strandings. Houghton Mifflin Co. 2007 63p il map (Scientists in the field) $18

Grades: 5 6 7 8   **599.5**
    1. Whales
    ISBN 978-0-618-55673-1; 0-618-55673-7
                                        LC 2006-34634

This describes the evolution of whales and their relationship to humans and offers various scientific theories about their strandings.

"Hodgkins packs her text with an impressive amount of information. . . . Well-chosen color photographs amply illustrate the well-organized discussion." SLJ

Includes glossary and bibliographical references

Landau, Elaine

Beluga whales. Enslow Elementary 2010 31p il map (Animals of the snow and ice) lib bdg $22.60

Grades: 2 3 4   **599.5**
    1. Whales
    ISBN 978-0-7660-3459-4 lib bdg; 0-7660-3459-3 lib bdg
                                        LC 2009006478

This describes beluga whales, including habitat, eating habits, mating, babies, and conservation

"Throughout most of [this] title, a full-page, or page and a quarter, sharp, color photograph . . . alternates with a page of text. An addendum of miscellaneous facts, a short list for further reading, and some websites are appended. Landau's smoothly written, well-illustrated titles are right on target for the intended audience." SLJ

Includes glossary and bibliographical references

Lourie, Peter

★ The **manatee** scientists; saving vulnerable species. Houghton Mifflin Books for Children 2011 80p il map (Scientists in the field) $18.99

Grades: 4 5 6 7   **599.5**
    1. Manatees 2. Scientists 3. Marine biology 4. Endangered species 5. Wildlife conservation
    ISBN 978-0-547-15254-7; 0-547-15254-X

This book highlights the work scientists are doing to protect the manatee, including John Reynolds, who does an aerial count of manatees from the Florida sky; Lucy Keith who spends a weekend rescuing manatees trapped in a dam in Senegal; and Fernando Rosas who takes the author on an Amazonian boat trip, looking for a young manatee he released back into the wild.

"The manatees photographed by Lourie and others add plenty of visual appeal. . . . A sturdy addition to a standard-setting nonfiction series." Booklist

★ **Whaling** season; a year in the life of an arctic whale scientist. Houghton Mifflin Books for Children 2009 80p il map (Scientists in the field) $18

Grades: 4 5 6 7   **599.5**
    1. Inuit 2. Whales 3. Biologists 4. Alaska
    ISBN 978-0-618-77709-9; 0-618-77709-1
                                        LC 2009-18596

Profiles the work of John Craighead George, an Arctic whale scientist, as he studies the bowhead whale and works with the indigenous people of Alaska to better understand the history of the animal.

"Combining exemplary color photos and simple, vivid language, the chapters detail not only George's day-today methodology but also his motivation." Booklist

Includes glossary and bibliographical references

Lunde, Darrin P.

Hello, baby beluga; [by] Darrin Lunde; illustrated by Patricia J. Wynne. Charlesbridge 2011 un il $15.95; pa $6.95

Grades: PreK K 1   **599.5**
    1. Whales 2. Animal babies
    ISBN 978-1-57091-739-4; 1-57091-739-6; 978-1-57091-740-0 pa; 1-57091-740-X pa
                                        LC 2010007550

"Lunde delivers facts about baby belunga whales in a simple direct-address question-and-answer format, almost as if a child is conducting a casual interview with a candid young whale. . . . Cool blues, whites, and grays dominate the illustrations, which showcase the happy calf in its arctic surroundings." Horn Book Guide

Markle, Sandra

Killer whales; [by] Sandra Markle. Carolrhoda Books 2004 39p il (Animal predators) lib bdg $25.26; pa $7.95

Grades: 3 4 5 6   **599.5**
    1. Whales
    ISBN 1-57505-728-X lib bdg; 1-57505-743-3 pa
                                        LC 2003-25944

"Dramatic, large color photos keep step with informative, readable [text]." SLJ

Includes glossary and bibliographical references

Marsh, Laura

Whales. National Geographic 2010 48p il map (Great migrations) $11.90; pa $3.99

Grades: 1 2 3   **599.5**
  1. Whales
  ISBN 978-1-4263-0746-1; 1-4263-0746-2; 978-1-4263-0745-4
  pa; 1-4263-0745-4 pa

LC 2010017959

This offers facts about sperm whales in an easy reader format.

"Dynamic full-color photographs, informative writing, and consistent organization work well together in [this volume]. . . . Along with the many photographs, the fascinating details are supported by boxes of related information, helpful definitions of new terms, and a sprinkling of entertaining jokes/riddles." SLJ

Includes glossary

Nicklin, Flip

★ **Face** to face with dolphins; by Flip and Linda Nicklin. National Geographic 2007 32p il (Face to face) $16.95; lib bdg $25.90
Grades: 3 4 5 6   **599.5**
  1. Dolphins
  ISBN 978-1-4263-0141-4; 1-4263-0141-3; 978-1-4263-0142-1
  lib bdg; 1-4263-0142-1 lib bdg

LC 2006-36273

"The Nicklins outline the special abilities and physical features of dolphins, such as echolocation, as well as diet, reproduction, swimming habits, and threats to their existence. . . . [This] attractive, smoothly written [book], topped off with advice about self-directed research, will catch the attention of enthusiasts and motivate them toward personal investigation." SLJ

Includes glossary and bibliographical references

★ **Face** to face with whales; by Flip & Linda Nicklin. National Geographic 2008 31p il map (Face to face) $16.95; lib bdg $25.95
Grades: 3 4 5 6   **599.5**
  1. Whales
  ISBN 978-1-4263-0244-2; 1-4263-0244-4; 978-1-4263-0245-9
  lib bdg; 1-4263-0245-2 lib bdg

LC 2007-34249

The authors describe the life cycle and behavior of whales and their own experiences with whales in the wild.

Includes glossary and bibliographical references

O'Connell, Jennifer

The **eye** of the whale; a rescue story. Jennifer O'Connell. 1st hardcover ed. Tilbury House, Publishers 2012 32 p. col. ill. (hardcover) $16.95
Grades: 5 6 7 8   **599.5**
  1. Whales 2. Animal rescue 3. Humpback whale -- California -- San Francisco 4. Wildlife rescue -- California -- San Francisco
  ISBN 0884483355; 9780884483359

LC 2012031165

This true children's story, by Jennifer O'Connell, begins when, "near San Francisco, a distress call was radioed to shore by a local fisherman. He had discovered a humpback whale tangled in hundreds of yards of crab-trap lines. . . . A team of volunteers answered the call, and four divers risked their lives to rescue the enormous animal." (Publisher's note)

Rake, Jody Sullivan

Blue whales up close. Capstone Press 2010 24p il (First facts. Whales and dolphins up close) lib bdg $21.32
Grades: K 1 2 3   **599.5**
  1. Whales
  ISBN 978-1-4296-3336-9 lib bdg; 1-4296-3336-0 lib bdg

LC 2009-6005

This "title has colorful pages and chapter heading to capture the interest of young readers as well as short, straightforward sentence struc-

ture to keep them reading. Captivating photographs of whales in the wild are present on each spread and feature up close images of body parts such as blow holes and baleen. . . . This . . . will be a fabulous addition to any elementary school library collection." Libr Media Connect

Includes glossary and bibliographical references

Humpback whales up close. Capstone Press 2010 24p il (First facts. Whales and dolphins up close) lib bdg $21.32
Grades: K 1 2   **599.5**
  1. Whales
  ISBN 978-1-4296-3337-6 lib bdg; 1-4296-3337-9 lib bdg

LC 2009-6004

This "title has colorful pages and chapter heading to capture the interest of young readers as well as short, straightforward sentence structure to keep them reading. Captivating photographs of whales in the wild are present on each spread and feature up close images of body parts such as blow holes and baleen. . . . This . . . will be a fabulous addition to any elementary school library collection." Libr Media Connect

Includes glossary and bibliographical references

The **mystery** of whale strandings; a cause and effect investigation. Capstone Press 2010 32p il map (Fact finders. Animals on the edge) lib bdg $25.99
Grades: 3 4 5 6   **599.5**
  1. Whales
  ISBN 978-1-4296-4531-7 lib bdg; 1-4296-4531-8 lib bdg

LC 2010008561

"Excellent discussions address those who doubt the severity of the issue and those who wonder why people should care what happens to animals. The captioned photographs are timely and piognant. . . . [This] makes serious subject matter interesting and accessible." SLJ

Includes glossary and bibliographical references

Riggs, Kate

Dolphins. Creative Education 2011 24p il (Amazing animals) $24.25; pa $5.99
Grades: K 1 2   **599.5**
  1. Dolphins
  ISBN 978-1-58341-989-2; 1-58341-989-6; 978-0-89812-562-7
  pa; 0-89812-562-6 pa

LC 2010019053

"The large, beautiful photos on each spread include vivid shots of animals in action as well as close-ups of their faces. Photo captions consistently add interesting animal facts. . . . The text is laid out in a large, easy-to-read font. The text, although made up of simple sentences, conveys plenty of interesting information." Booklist

Whales; Kate Riggs. Creative Education 2015 24 p. $7.99
Grades: K 1 2   **599.5**
  1. Whales 2. Animals -- Folklore
  ISBN 0898129303; 9780898129304; 9781608185177

LC 2014000189

This children's book by Kate Riggs, part of the Amazing Animals series, provides "(a) basic exploration of the appearance, behavior, and habitat of whales, the large ocean animals. Also included is a story from folklore explaining why New Zealanders traditionally rode whales. " (Publisher's note)

"Across from the photos, the text is laid out cleanly in a large, clear font, and the sentences are simple and easy to read. Photo captions, meanwhile, add interesting facts, while occasional vocabulary words are defined at the bottoms of pages." Booklist

Rockwood, Leigh

Dolphins are smart! PowerKids Press 2010 24p il (Super smart animals) lib bdg $21.25; pa $8.25

Grades: 2 3 4 5   **599.5**

1. Dolphins

ISBN 978-1-4358-9398-6 lib bdg; 1-4358-9398-0 lib bdg; 978-1-4358-9842-4 pa; 1-4358-9842-7 pa

Examines the intelligence of dolphins.

"Readers get an overview of the . . . [dolphin's] life cycle, its domestic history (where relevant), and natural habitat, and examples of how it is smart in the wild as well as when helped by human tutelage. . . . Interesting color photographs and large, easy-to-read print will attract browsers and report writers alike." SLJ

Includes glossary

Sayre, April Pulley

Here come the humpbacks! April Pulley Sayre; illustrated by Jamie Hogan. Charlesbridge 2013 40 p. (reinforced for library use) $17.95

Grades: 2 3 4   **599.5**

1. Whales 2. Whale watching 3. Humpback whale

ISBN 1580894054; 9781580894050; 9781580894067

LC 2012000785

This children's picture book by April Pulley Sayre looks at humpback whales. The male whales' singing is described. "As mother and calf move from the shallows into the open ocean, they encounter other creatures and objects, which Sayre introduces in offset text about whale-watching tours, barnacles, suckerfish, chemical pollution, and more." (Publishers Weekly)

Sill, Cathryn

About marine mammals; A Guide for Children. Cathryn Sill; illustrated by John Sill. Peachtree Publishers 2016 48 p. color illustrations (alk. paper) $16.95

Grades: PreK K 1 2   **599.5**

1. Marine mammals

ISBN 9781561459063

LC 2015041866

This book by former teacher Cathryn Sill and illustrated by John Sill "explains to children what marine mammals are, what they do, and how they live. . . . [It] tells children what is essential for understanding and appreciating these fascinating creatures. An afterword--which includes a glossary and recommended books and websites--provides further detail for children and their parents about a wide variety of marine mammals." (Publisher's note)

"A glossary, suggestions for further reading, and a list of bibliographic resources used by the creators round off this solid nonfiction treat for budding naturalists." Booklist

Includes bibliographical references and index

Simon, Seymour

Dolphins. Smithsonian/Collins 2009 32p il $17.99; lib bdg $18.89

Grades: 1 2 3 4   **599.5**

1. Dolphins

ISBN 978-0-06-028393-3; 0-06-028393-9; 978-0-06-028394-0 lib bdg; 0-06-028394-7 lib bdg

LC 2008010654

"Simon presents fascinating facts about these playful mammals and describes the difference between dolphins, porpoises, and whales in terms that children can understand. Without being didactic, he discusses the physiology and habits of dolphins, as well as the greatest threat to the species—humans. Accompanied by full-page color photographs of dolphins, the text is presented with considerable white space in the margins." Booklist

Skerry, Brian

Face to face with manatees. National Geographic 2010 31p il map (Face to face) $16.95; lib bdg $25.90

Grades: 3 4 5 6   **599.5**

1. Manatees

ISBN 978-1-4263-0616-7; 1-4263-0616-4; 978-1-4263-0617-4 lib bdg; 1-4263-0617-2 lib bdg

LC 2009-40783

The author describes the life cycle and behavior of the manatee and his own experiences with manatees in the wild.

"The amazing, literally face-to-face photographs dominate the book. . . . Although written for children, this colorful, informative book will appeal to adults as well." Sci Books Films

Includes glossary and bibliographical references

Spilsbury, Louise

Dolphin. Heinemann Library 2010 24p il (A day in the life: sea animals) lib bdg $22; pa $6.49

Grades: 1 2   **599.5**

1. Dolphins

ISBN 978-1-4329-3999-1 lib bdg; 1-4329-3999-8 lib bdg; 978-1-4329-4006-5 pa; 1-4329-4006-6 pa

LC 2010000485

This pairs "well-chosen color photos . . . with one or two sentences of simple commentary for each. . . . [Though this title] includes references to several varieties of the chosen creature, one species in particular is highlighted. . . . [Good choice] for pleasure or purpose reading." SLJ

Includes glossary and bibliographical references

Stearns, Precious McKenzie

Manatees; [by] Precious McKenzie. Rourke 2010 24p il map (Eye to eye with endangered species) lib bdg $27.07

Grades: 2 3 4   **599.5**

1. Manatees

ISBN 978-1-60694-403-5 lib bdg; 1-60694-403-7 lib bdg

LC 2009-6011

This describes manatees and why they are threatened with extinction

"Sets out to introduce readers to [manatees] . . . explain the dangers they face, and detail the efforts of biologists and conservationists to save them. . . . Serviceable and informative." SLJ

Includes glossary and bibliographical references

Thomson, Sarah L.

★ **Amazing** whales! written by Sarah L. Thomson; photographs provided by the Wildlife Conservation Society. HarperCollins 2004 27p il (I can read book) $15.99; lib bdg $16.89

Grades: 1 2 3   **599.5**

1. Whales

ISBN 0-06-054465-1; 0-06-054466-X lib bdg

LC 2004-2473

"Thomson's superior text sustains readers' attention with interesting facts and apt comparisons. . . . Spectacular color photographs add detail and drama." SLJ

599.53 Dolphins and porpoises

Coleman, Janet Wyman

Eight Dolphins of Katrina; A True Tale of Survival. written by Janet W. Coleman; illustrated by Yan Nascimbene. Houghton Mifflin Harcourt 2013 40 p. $16.99

Grades: 2 3 4 5   **599.53**
  1. Dolphins 2. Hurricane Katrina, 2005
  ISBN 054771923X; 9780547719238

LC 2012024419

"This story of the rescue of eight dolphins off the coast of Mississippi after Hurricane Katrina underscores the bonds between dolphins and their trainers. . . . After a 40-foot tidal wave destroys the dolphin pool at the Marine Life Oceanarium in Gulfport, eight dolphins disappear. . . . Via helicopter and boat, the trainers set out to search for the dolphins, who were raised in captivity and thus unaccustomed to feeding or protecting themselves." (Publishers Weekly)

Riggs, Kate
  Killer whales; by Kate Riggs. Creative Education 2012 24 p. (Amazing animals)
Grades: K 1 2   **599.53**
  1. Killer whales 2. Marine animals 3. Marine biology
  ISBN 9781608181094

LC 2010049129

This book offers a "look at killer whales, including their habitats, physical characteristics such as their unique coloration, behaviors, relationships with humans, and protected status." (Publisher's note) "This book shares with readers how the whale waits above water for food, how there is only one killer whale and it is found in the coldest oceans. The reader is then informed about the whale's ability to maintain its warmth thanks to blubber before attention turns toward how the whale moves and swims with the help of its strong tail and flukes." (Children's Literature)

Includes bibliographical references and index

Turner, Pamela S.
  The **dolphins** of Shark Bay; by Pamela S. Turner. Houghton Mifflin Harcourt 2013 76 p. $18.99
Grades: 5 6 7 8   **599.53**
  1. Dolphins 2. Bottlenose dolphin -- Behavior -- Australia -- Shark Bay (W.A.) 3. Bottlenose dolphin -- Research -- Australia -- Shark Bay (W.A.)
  ISBN 0547716389; 9780547716381

LC 2012048463

In this book, "ride alongside the author Pamela S. Turner and her scientific team . . . as they seek to answer the question: just why are dolphins so smart? And what does their behavior tell us about human intelligence, captive animals, and the future of the ocean?" (Publisher's note)

599.6   Ungulates

Lunis, Natalie
  Pronghorn; long-distance runner! Bearport Pub. 2011 24p il map (Blink of an eye. Superfast animals!) lib bdg $21.26
Grades: 1 2 3   **599.6**
  1. Pronghorn antelopes
  ISBN 978-1-936087-94-5; 1-936087-94-4

LC 2010011127

This decribes the pronghorn antelope, including where it lives, what it eats, and the ways its body helps it reach its record-breaking speeds.

This "is sure to appeal to a wide variety of readers. Vibrant photos illustrate each animal from multiple perspectives, providing opportunity for readers to closely examine the animal. Information is organized by subject heading and branches into the animal's physical features and how they contribute to its speed, the animal's natural predators, and how the animal makes use of speed as a means of survival. . . . This

. . . will be a worthwhile addition to your nonfiction collection." Libr Media Connect

Includes glossary and bibliographical references

599.63   Even-toed ungulates

Anderson, Jill
  Giraffes; by Jill Anderson. NorthWord 2005 un il (Wild ones) $12.95; pa $8.95
Grades: K 1 2   **599.63**
  1. Giraffes
  ISBN 978-1-55971-928-5; 1-55971-928-1; 978-1-55971-929-2 pa; 1-55971-929-X pa

LC 2004031117

This describes the physiology, habitat, and life cycle of giraffes

"With simple, direct words and clear, closeup color photo images, this . . . does an excellent job of introducing preschoolers to basic facts about giraffe physiology and habitat, and, especially, how the animals get their food and digest it, and how they care for their young." Booklist

Clarke, Penny
  ★ **Hippos**; written by Penny Clarke. F. Watts 2009 32p il (Scary creatures) lib bdg $26; pa $8.95
Grades: 3 4 5   **599.63**
  1. Hippopotamus
  ISBN 978-0-531-21671-2 lib bdg; 0-531-21671-3 lib bdg; 978-0-531-21042-0 pa; 0-531-21042-1 pa

LC 2009010798

This describes the hippo's life cycle, habitat, behavior, and relationship to humans

This title has "two-page chapters of accessible, large-type text and bright color photos and illustrations. . . . The series distinguishes itself with 'X-Ray Vision.' When readers hold the page with this prompt up to the light, an image emerges. The X-rays mostly show the skeletal structures of the animals. Text boxes throughout add to the visual appeal. . . . [This title is an] excellent [resource for school assignments and browsing." SLJ

Includes glossary

Hatkoff, Isabella
  ★ **Owen** & Mzee; the true story of a remarkable friendship. told by Isabella Hatkoff, Craig Hatkoff, and Paula Kahumbu; with photographs by Peter Greste. Scholastic Press 2006 un il map $16.99
Grades: K 1 2 3   **599.63**
  1. Turtles 2. Hippopotamus 3. Indian Ocean earthquake and tsunami, 2004 4. Kenya
  ISBN 0-439-82973-9

LC 2005-21341

"The text and the back matter are brimming with information about the animals, their caregivers, and the locale. This touching story of the power of a surprising friendship to mitigate the experience of loss is full of heart and hope." SLJ

  ★ **Owen** & Mzee; the language of friendship; told by Isabella Hatkoff, Craig Hatkoff, and Paula Kuhumbu; with photographs by Peter Greste. Scholastic Press 2007 un il $16.99
Grades: K 1 2 3   **599.63**
  1. Turtles 2. Hippopotamus 3. Kenya
  ISBN 978-0-439-89959-8; 0-439-89959-1

LC 2006015612

"Owen & Mzee: The True Story of a Remarkable Friendship (Scholastic, 2006) chronicled the fascinating story of a baby hippo who was orphaned by the December 2004 tsunami and the bond he formed with

Mzee, a 130-year-old Alhambra tortoise at a wildlife sanctuary in Kenya. This sequel updates readers on the status of that friendship a year and a half later, particularly with regard to the way this unusual duo has learned to communicate with one another. . . . The text is clearly written and accompanied by numerous high-quality, full-color photos of this unique pair." SLJ

Includes bibliographical references

London, Jonathan, 1947-

Hippos are huge! Jonathan London; illustrated by Matthew Trueman. Candlewick Press 2015 32 p. color illustrations $16.99

Grades: PreK K 1 2   **599.63**

  1. Animals 2. Hippopotamus

ISBN 0763665924; 9780763665920

                  LC 2014944797

This children's book by Jonathan London, illustrated by Matthew Trueman, is designed to "spur interest in the world of hippos. Trueman's vivid images take advantage of every inch of available space to convey the size of these creatures. Two types of text appear on each page: larger print encompasses the main narrative full of fascinating facts (ideal for reading aloud), while smaller print presents drier statistics and additional facts of interest." (School Library Journal)

Tourville, Amanda Doering

A **giraffe** grows up; by Amanda Doering Tourville; illustrated by Michael Denman and William J. Huiett. Picture Window Books 2007 24p il map hardcover o.p. lib bdg $25.26

Grades: PreK K 1 2   **599.63**

  1. Giraffes

ISBN 978-1-4048-3158-2 lib bdg; 1-4048-3158-4 lib bdg; 978-1-4048-3565-8 pa; 1-4048-3565-2 pa

                  LC 2006027307

"Each spread has an acrylic painting with a paragraph or two of text and a box of facts. . . . Easy-to-read . . . with enough information for basic reports." SLJ

Includes glossary and bibliographical references

Walden, Katherine

Warthogs. PowerKiDS Press 2009 24p il (Safari animals) lib bdg $21.25

Grades: PreK K 1 2   **599.63**

  1. Warthogs

ISBN 978-1-4358-2688-5 lib bdg; 1-4358-2688-4 lib bdg

                  LC 2008019531

This book provides "succinctly written introductory information about [warthogs'] range, habitat, social groups, and diet. Spreads consist of one to three short, simply constructed sentences opposite crisp, color photographs, most of which represent the subject perfectly." SLJ

599.638   Giraffe and okapi

Dagg, Anne Innis

5 Giraffes; Anne Innis Dagg; introduction by Rob Laidlaw. Midpoint Trade Books Inc 2016 88 p. ill. (some color), color map $22.95

Grades: 4 5 6   **599.638**

  1. Giraffe

ISBN 1554553563; 9781554553563

This children's book in the 5 Animals series, by Anne Innis Dagg, with an introduction by Rob Laidlaw, "profiles five unique giraffes from both captivity and the wild. Accompanying the five giraffe profiles is information on their diet, social life, and chapters on some of their more unique aspects, like the giraffe's unusual body. Includes full color photo-

graphs throughout, glossary, bibliography, table of contents and index." (Publisher's note)

"Written by a heroic living scientist, this is a worthy purchase for animal collections." SLJ

Includes bibliographical references (page 62) and index.

599.64   Bovids

Caper, William

American bison; a scary prediction. by William Caper. Bearport 2007 32p il map (America's animal comebacks) lib bdg $25.27

Grades: 2 3 4   **599.64**

  1. Bison 2. Zoologists 3. Wildlife conservation 4. Bronx Zoo 5. Zoo directors 6. Writers on nature 7. Writers on science

ISBN 978-1-59716-504-4 lib bdg; 1-59716-504-2 lib bdg

                  LC 2007010863

This describes how the American bison was saved from extinction by William Temple Hornaday, the American Bison Society, and the The Bronx Zoo.

This book is "well organized and [has] an easy style and an accessible vocabulary and text size . . . [and] color photographs." SLJ

Includes glossary and bibliographical references

Catt, Thessaly

Migrating with the wildebeest. PowerKids Press 2011 24p il map (Animal journeys) lib bdg $21.25; pa $8.25

Grades: 2 3 4   **599.64**

  1. Gnus 2. Animals -- Migration

ISBN 978-1-4488-2544-8 lib bdg; 1-4488-2544-X lib bdg; 978-1-4488-2795-4 pa; 1-4488-2795-7 pa

                  LC 2010028194

Learn about the wildebeest and its migration patterns.

"Keywords are bolded throughout and can be found in the glossary. The format is attractive with inset captioned photographs and page heading that seem to move across the page." Libr Media Connect

Includes glossary

Ganeri, Anita

Arabian oryx. Heinemann Library 2011 24p il map (A day in the life: desert animals) $22; pa $6.49

Grades: K 1 2   **599.64**

  1. Oryx

ISBN 978-1-4329-4769-9; 1-4329-4769-9; 978-1-4329-4778-1 pa; 1-4329-4778-8 pa

                  LC 2010022817

"The engaging full-color photographs are key to [this] well-organized [book]. . . . Basic global maps show where the animal is found, and a diagram called a 'body map' labels its parts. The [text is] appropriate for the age group, and the pictures will draw in youngsters. [An] excellent [purchase] if material is needed on these animals." SLJ

Includes glossary and bibliographical references

George, Jean Craighead

The **buffalo** are back; paintings by Wendell Minor. Dutton Children's Books 2010 un il $16.99

Grades: 3 4 5   **599.64**

  1. Bison 2. West (U.S.) -- History

ISBN 978-0-525-42215-0; 0-525-42215-3

"This handsome book discusses the history of the buffalo on the American plains. Succinctly and gracefully written, it envisions the centuries when Indians carefully managed the land, using the buffalo for food, shelter, and clothing. . . . Illustrated with beautiful landscape paintings and striking close-ups of people and animals, this book offers a very effective presentation of the buffalo's story." Booklist

Gish, Melissa

Bison. Creative Education 2011 46p il map (Living wild) $23.95
Grades: 5 6 7 8   **599.64**
1. Bison
ISBN 978-1-60818-077-6; 1-60818-077-8
LC 2010028305

A look at bison, including their habitats, physical characteristics such as their shaggy coats, behaviors, relationships with humans, and threatened status in the world today.

This offers "an array of interesting facts. Photography is large and beautiful—a real draw." SLJ
Includes bibliographical references

Martin, Jacqueline Briggs

★ The chiru of high Tibet; a true story. written by Jacqueline Briggs Martin; illustrated by Linda Wingerter. Houghton Mifflin Harcourt 2010 un il $17.99
Grades: 1 2 3   **599.64**
1. Chirus 2. Zoologists 3. Wildlife conservation 4. Tibet (China) 5. Nonfiction writers
ISBN 978-0-618-58130-6; 0-618-58130-8

"The antelope-like chiru of the Chang Tang in northern Tibet were a million strong before they were hunted nearly to extinction for their marvelously soft wool. . . . Wildlife champion George Schaller . . . hoped to save the chiru by protecting the remote valley where females give birth each spring. . . . The birthing ground is now protected from poachers. Martin's account of all this is brief, dramatic, and supplemented with boxed facts, and nicely amplified in Wingerter's art." Horn Book
Includes bibliographical references

Walden, Katherine

Wildebeests. Rosen Pub. Group's PowerKids Press 2009 24p il (Safari animals) lib bdg $21.25; pa $8.25
Grades: PreK K 1 2   **599.64**
1. Gnus
ISBN 978-1-4358-2692-2 lib bdg; 1-4358-2692-2 lib bdg; 978-1-4358-3066-0 pa; 1-4358-3066-0 pa
LC 2008021587

This book provides "succinctly written introductory information about [wildebeests'] range, habitat, social groups, and diet. Spreads consist of one to three short, simply constructed sentences opposite crisp, color photographs, most of which represent the subject perfectly." SLJ
Includes glossary

599.65 Deer

Arnold, Caroline

A moose's world; written and illustrated by Caroline Arnold. Picture Window Books 2010 24p il (Caroline Arnold's animals) lib bdg $25.32
Grades: PreK K 1 2   **599.65**
1. Moose
ISBN 978-1-4048-5742-1 lib bdg; 1-4048-5742-7 lib bdg
LC 2009033360

This narrative tells the story of a moose from birth until it can live on its own.

Catt, Thessaly

Migrating with the caribou. PowerKids Press 2011 24p il map (Animal journeys) lib bdg $21.25; pa $8.25

Grades: 2 3 4   **599.65**
1. Caribou 2. Animals -- Migration
ISBN 978-1-4488-2541-7 lib bdg; 1-4488-2541-5 lib bdg; 978-1-4488-2666-7 pa; 1-4488-2666-7 pa
LC 2010024146

Learn about the life cycle of the caribou and its migration patterns.

"Keywords are bolded throughout and can be found in the glossary. The format is attractive with inset captioned photographs and page heading that seem to move across the page." Libr Media Connect
Inlcudes glossary

Gish, Melissa

Moose. Creative Education 2010 46p il map (Living wild) $23.95; pa $9.95
Grades: 5 6 7 8   **599.65**
1. Moose
ISBN 978-1-58341-973-1; 1-58341-973-X; 978-0-89812-556-6 pa; 0-89812-556-1 pa
LC 2010017378

"A look at moose, including their habitats, physical characteristics such as their imposing antlers, behaviors, relationships with humans, and secure status in the world today." Publisher's note

Heuer, Karsten

★ Being caribou; five months on foot with a caribou herd. Walker & Co. 2007 48p il map $17.95; lib bdg $18.95
Grades: 4 5 6 7   **599.65**
1. Caribou 2. Arctic regions
ISBN 978-0-8027-9565-6; 0-8027-9565-X; 978-0-8027-9566-3 lib bdg; 0-8027-9566-8 lib bdg
LC 2006-27651

This is an adaptation of an adult title by the same name, published 2005 by Mountaineers Books

"The caribou calving grounds in the Arctic National Wildlife Refuge are being threatened by oil exploration. [This title] will help make kids aware of what is at stake and give them a glimpse of an extraordinary part of the world and the lengths the caribou go to traverse it. It is an important book." Quill Quire
Includes bibliographical references

Riggs, Kate

Moose; by Kate Riggs. Creative Education 2012 24 p. col. ill.
Grades: K 1 2   **599.65**
1. Moose 2. Animal behavior 3. Habitat (Ecology) 4. Animals -- Folklore 5. Zoology -- Encyclopedias
ISBN 9781608181117
LC 2010049131

This children's book, part of Kate Riggs' "Amazing Animals" series, focuses on moose. "This . . . popular series continues traveling the planet to study alligators, bats, and other fascinating animals. . . . [P]hotos are paired with . . . text to examine the featured creature's appearance, habitat, behaviors, and life cycle. . . . "A basic exploration of the appearance, behavior, and habitat of moose, Earth's largest deer. Also included is a story from folklore explaining how moose interact with other animals." (Publisher's note)
Includes bibliographical references (p. 24) and index

Urbigkit, Cat

★ Path of the pronghorn; photographs by Mark Gocke. Boyds Mills Press 2010 32p il map $17.95
Grades: 3 4 5 6   **599.65**
1. Pronghorn antelopes
ISBN 978-1-59078-756-4; 1-59078-756-0

"Large, eye-catching color photos accompany a quiet, informative text in this elegant book that celebrates an equally elegant North American mammal: Antilocapra americana—'the antelope-goat of America.' Urbigkit provides enough quality information to satisfy many young researchers, and Gocke's outstanding photos record the migratory year of Wyoming's Sublette herd." SLJ

Includes bibliographical references

599.66   Odd-toed ungulates

Carson, Mary Kay

★ **Emi** and the rhino scientist; [by] Mary Kay Carson; with photographs by Tom Uhlman. Houghton Mifflin Company 2007 57p il (Scientists in the field) $18

Grades: 5 6 7 8   **599.66**

1. Rhinoceros 2. Zoo employees 3. Animal scientists

ISBN 978-0-618-64639-5; 0-618-64639-6

LC 2006-34517

This describes "how Terri Roth, an expert in endangered-species reproduction at the Cincinnati Zoo, helped Emi to give birth to the first Sumatran rhino born in captivity in more than 100 years. . . . The text is full of important details, and the photographs are unfailingly crisp, bright, and full of variety." SLJ

Firestone, Mary

Top 50 reasons to care about rhinos; animals in peril. Enslow Publishers 2010 103p il (Top 50 reasons to care about endangered animals) lib bdg $31.93

Grades: 4 5 6 7   **599.66**

1. Rhinoceros 2. Endangered species

ISBN 978-0-7660-3457-0 lib bdg; 0-7660-3457-7 lib bdg

LC 2008048692

This describes the different types of rhino, their life cycle, diet, young, habitat, and reasons why they are endangered animals

"The illustrations, mostly color photographs, represent a wonderful selection of the animals and their habitats. Reluctant readers may be enticed by this . . . simply because of the great images. This . . . would make a substantial supplement to the science curriculum when studying endangered animals." Libr Media Connect

Includes glossary and bibliographical references

Gish, Melissa

Rhinoceroses. Creative Education 2011 46p il map (Living wild) lib bdg $23.95

Grades: 5 6 7 8   **599.66**

1. Rhinoceros

ISBN 978-1-60818-083-7; 1-60818-083-2

LC 2010028316

A look at rhinoceroses, including their habitats, physical characteristics such as their horned noses, behaviors, relationships with humans, and protected status in the world today.

Includes glossary and bibliographical references

Holmes, Mary Tavener

My travels with Clara; illustrated by Jon Cannell. J. Paul Getty Museum 2007 un il $17.95

Grades: 2 3 4   **599.66**

1. Rhinoceros

ISBN 978-0-89236-880-8

LC 2006-35719

"In the mid-eighteenth century, a Dutch sea captain bought an orphaned baby rhinoceros in India, named her Clara, and toured with her around western Europe. . . . His first-person, fictionalized narrative af-

fectionately tells of his kindness, his bond with his extraordinary companion, and the public excitement she caused. . . . Illustrations include costumed period figures and reproductions of the art Clara inspired. . . . The facts about Clara . . . are as fascinating as the art and pet story." Booklist

Meeker, Clare Hodgson

Rhino rescue! Clare Hudgson Meeker. National Geographic 2016 111 p. color illustrations (ebook) $15.99; (pbk. : alk. paper) $5.99

Grades: 2 3 4 5   **599.66**

1. Rhinoceros 2. Animal rescue 3. Joubert, Beverly 4. White rhinoceros -- Conservation -- South Africa

ISBN 9781426323133; 9781426323119; 9781426323126

LC 2015027914

"What happens when conservationists meet rhinos in trouble? They arrange to airlift them to safety! Follow National Geographic Explorers-in-Residence Dereck and Beverly Joubert as they move rhinos out of harm's way, meet a courageous little Hawaiian monk seal, and a pair of Siberian tiger cubs fighting for survival. Readers will cheer as they read these completely true stories of animal rescues. Filled with engaging photos, fast facts, and fascinating sidebars." (Publisher's note)

"Animal-loving independent readers will be drawn in to the true accounts, which focus on the collaborative efforts necessary to rescue animals and reintroduce them into the wild." Horn Book

Includes bibliographical references and index

Momatiuk, Yva

★ **Face** to face with wild horses; by Yva Momatiuk and John Eastcott. National Geographic 2009 31p il (Face to face) $16.95; lib bdg $25.90

Grades: 3 4 5 6   **599.66**

1. Horses

ISBN 978-1-4263-0466-8; 1-4263-0466-8; 978-1-4263-0467-5 lib bdg; 1-4263-0467-6 lib bdg

LC 2008-38247

The authors describe the behavior of wild horses and their personal encounters with them.

Includes bibliographical references

Montgomery, Sy

★ The **tapir** scientist; written by Sy Montgomery; photographed by Nic Bishop. Houghton Mifflin Harcourt 2013 80 p. $18.99

Grades: 5 6 7 8   **599.66**

1. Brazil 2. Tapirs 3. Tapirs -- Brazil 4. Tapirs -- Research -- Brazil

ISBN 0547815484; 9780547815480

LC 2012018678

In this book, author Sy Montgomery and photographer Nic Bishop "experience long, hot days, cramped conditions, nervous waiting and itchy tick bites while searching for [tapirs]. . . . In less than a week, they see tapirs in the wild, find their tracks, take photographs, locate them through radio telemetry, collect 'samples of tapir poop, skin, fur, and blood,' and capture and collar two new tapirs, with more to come. This research matters, and the author . . . explains why." (Kirkus Reviews)

Rustad, Martha E. H.

Zebras and oxpeckers work together. Capstone Press 2011 24p il (Pebble Plus: animals working together) lib bdg $23.99; pa $6.95

Grades: K 1 2   **599.66**

1. Zebras 2. Symbiosis 3. Oxpeckers (Birds)

ISBN 978-1-4296-5300-8 lib bdg; 1-4296-5300-0 lib bdg; 978-1-4296-6200-0 pa; 1-4296-6200-X pa

LC 2010025465

Simple text and full-color photographs introduce the symbiotic relationship of zebras and oxpeckers.

In this series "the easy-to-understand examples are well selected to show of range of relationships in a variety of environments, and children will come away with some exposure to the concepts of 'parasite' and 'predator' as well." SLJ

Includes glossary and bibliographical references

Walden, Katherine

Rhinoceroses. PowerKids Press 2009 24p il (Safari animals) lib bdg $21.25

Grades: PreK K 1 2   **599.66**

1. Rhinoceros

ISBN 978-1-4358-2687-8 lib bdg; 1-4358-2687-6 lib bdg

LC 2008019534

This book provides "succinctly written introductory information about [rhinoceroses'] range, habitat, social groups, and diet. Spreads consist of one to three short, simply constructed sentences opposite crisp, color photographs, most of which represent the subject perfectly." SLJ

Includes glossary and bibliographical references

599.665 Horse family

Riggs, Kate

Wild horses; by Kate Riggs. Creative Education/Creative Paperbacks 2015 24 p. color illustrations (Amazing animals) (hardcover : alk. paper) $28.50

Grades: K 1 2 3   **599.665**

1. Horses -- Folklore 2. Wild horses 3. Przewalski's horse

ISBN 1608184935; 9781608184934

LC 2013051255

In this children's book, author Kate Riggs presents " basic exploration of the appearance, behavior, and habitat of wild horses, animals that roam in bands. Also included is a story from folklore explaining how people began riding horses." (Publisher's note)

"What sets these offerings apart are the sumptuous, full-page photographs, featuring these breathtaking beasts in their natural habitats. A quick and effective way to beef up any 590 section." SLJ

Includes bibliographical references (page 24) and index

599.67 Elephants

Allen, Kathy

Elephants under pressure; a cause and effect investigation. Capstone Press 2010 32p il map (Fact finders. Animals on the edge) lib bdg $25.99

Grades: 3 4 5 6   **599.67**

1. Elephants

ISBN 978-1-4296-4534-8; 1-4296-4534-2

LC 2010008562

"Excellent discussions address those who doubt the severity of the issue and those who wonder why people should care what happens to animals. The captioned photographs are timely and poignant. . . . [This] makes serious subject matter interesting and accessible." SLJ

Includes glossary and bibliographical references

Arnold, Katya

★ Elephants can paint, too! pictures and text by Katya Arnold. Atheneum Books for Young Readers 2005 un il $16.95

Grades: K 1 2 3   **599.67**

1. Painting 2. Elephants

ISBN 0-689-86985-1

LC 2004-17387

The author "tells how she trains elephants to paint and compares the work of her human and elephant pupils. The spare narrative is easy to understand and reads like a picture book. . . . Arnold's amusing and colorful photographs—of elephants and children at work—will have readers laughing as they view them side-by-side." SLJ

Buckley, Carol

Tarra & Bella; the elephant and dog who became best friends. text and photography by Carol Buckley. G.P. Putnam's Sons 2009 un il $16.99

Grades: K 1 2 3 4   **599.67**

1. Dogs 2. Elephants 3. Animal behavior

ISBN 978-0-399-25443-7; 0-399-25443-9

LC 2009-18888

Spotlights the true-life friendship between Tarra, a retired circus elephant, and one of the Tennessee Elephant Sanctuary's stray dogs, Bella

"Shots of Tarra petting Bella with her trunk are among the book's most endearing pictures, which range from snapshotlike to skillfully framed images; also notable are photographs that underscore the dramatic difference in the animals' sizes. . . . The animals' friendship will inspire young readers." Publ Wkly

Buzzeo, Toni

★ A passion for elephants; the real life adventure of field scientist Cynthia Moss. by Toni Buzzeo; illustrated by Holly Berry. Dial Books for Young Readers, a division of Penguin Young Readers Group 2015 32 p. color illustrations (hardcover : acid-free paper) $16.99

Grades: K 1 2 3   **599.67**

1. Elephants 2. Amboseli National Park (Kenya) 3. African elephant -- Kenya -- Amboseli National Park

ISBN 0399187251; 9780399187254

LC 2013025476

This book, by Toni Buzzeo, illustrated by Holly Berry, is a "biography of Cynthia Moss, the elephant expert. . . . Cynthia has spent years learning everything she can about elephants and sharing these fascinating creatures with the world. She is a scientist, nature photographer, and animal-rights activist, fighting against the ivory poachers who kill so many elephants for their tusks." (Publisher's note)

"This well-executed narrative biography will pique the curiosity of animal lovers and young scientists alike." SLJ

Cowcher, Helen

Desert elephants. Farrar Straus Giroux 2011 un il $16.99

Grades: K 1 2 3   **599.67**

1. Elephants 2. Desert ecology 3. Mali

ISBN 978-0-374-31774-4; 0-374-31774-7

LC 2010019817

"In Mali, West Africa, the last remaining desert elephants migrate 300 miles in search of water in a circular route just south of the Sahara Desert. In this picture book introduction, Cowcher's beautiful watercolor-and-mixed media illustrations chart the animals' route. . . . The present-day interaction with people is a crucial part of the well-told story." Booklist

Downer, Ann

Elephant talk; the surprising science of elephant communication. Twenty-First Century Books 2011 112p il map lib bdg $33.26

Grades: 4 5 6 7 8   **599.67**
1. Elephants 2. Animal communication
ISBN 978-0-7613-5766-7 lib bdg; 0-7613-5766-1 lib bdg
LC 2010-24880
"The complex behavior of wild elephants is introduced in a flowing narrative accompanied by full-color photographs, diagrams and maps. Downer provides an overview of elephant evolution, places the creatures in their African and Asian contexts, and describes the lives of these intelligent social animals. Her narrative then focuses on the elephants' inticate verbal and nonverbal communication techniques. . . . The illustrations and clearly labeled diagrams and maps are well placed to amplify the text. . . . Throughout this highly readable, informative title are profiles of individuals . . . who work with these animals." SLJ

Includes glossary and bibliographical references

Ellis, Gerry
   Natumi Takes the Lead; The True Story of an Orphan Elephant Who Finds Family. Gerry Ellis with Amy Novesky. Natl Geographic Soc Childrens books 2016 32 p. color ill., color map $16.99
Grades: K 1 2   **599.67**
   1. Elephants 2. African elephant 3. Orphaned animals -- Africa
ISBN 1426325614; 9781426325618
LC 2016029018
   In this book, by Gerry Ellis with Amy Novesky, "after losing her mother, shy Natumi is rescued by a team from the David Sheldrick Wildlife Trust, an orphanage for baby elephants. At the shelter, Natumi . . . meets several other orphans, and the eight of them play together in the surrounding bush. As the babies become closer and more like a real family, they need a leader, someone they can trust. Can Natumi grow into this role?" (Publisher's note)
   "Thoughtful design sets legible, large white text on a dark-color background graced by images of local flora in a lighter color and often bordered by a Samburu-inspired pattern." Kirkus
   Includes bibliographical references.

Gibbons, Gail
   Elephants of Africa. Holiday House 2008 32p il
Grades: K 1 2 3   **599.67**
   1. Elephants
ISBN 0-8234-2168-6; 978-0-8234-2168-8
LC 2007051619
   This book describes the habitats, physical characteristics, diet, offspring development, and behavior of the African elephant. "Grades one to four." (Sci Books Films)
   "Gibbons introduces young readers to [African elephants]. Each page is filled with illustrations and a succinct but informative text that details the habitats, physical characteristics, diet, offspring development, and behavior of these dwellers of Africa's savannas and forests. . . . The text is well organized and simple to understand, enhanced by the pen-and-ink and watercolor artwork." SLJ

Jackson, Donna M.
   ★ The **elephant** scientist; by Caitlin O'Connell and Donna M. Jackson; photographs by Caitlin O'Connell and Timothy Rodwell. Houghton Mifflin Books for Children 2011 70p il map $17.99
Grades: 4 5 6 7   **599.67**
   1. Elephants 2. Biologists 3. Ecologists
ISBN 9780547053448; 0547053444
LC 2010014134
   Boston Globe-Horn Book Honor: Nonfiction (2012)
   In this book, "O'Connell traveled to Africa in 1992 to observe wild animals; the trip turned into a job offer to study elephants at Etosha National Park; the text focuses on the scientists' work, findings, and problems encountered. The authors offer [a] . . . look at new discoveries

about elephant communication and how this knowledge can be used to slow the animal's slump into extinction. Combined with . . . full-color photographs by the scientists, the elephants' world is brought to the forefront. Readers enter the researchers' camp to see their setup, fieldwork, and takedown in action. They will learn how elephant anatomy and hierarchy work together to aid in communication." (School Library Journal)
   O'Connell "worked with other scientists to [identify] the vibration-sensitive cells in elephants' feet and trunks that enabled to them to 'hear' sounds transmitted through the ground. Illustrated with many well-captioned, color photos, this eye-catching book provides a sometimes fascinating look at O'Connell's work with elephants in America and in Namibia." Booklist

Joubert, Beverly
   ★ **Face** to face with elephants; by Beverly and Dereck Joubert. National Geographic 2008 31p il map (Face to face) $16.95; lib bdg $25.90
Grades: 3 4 5 6   **599.67**
   1. Elephants
ISBN 978-1-4263-0325-8; 1-4263-0325-4; 978-1-4263-0326-5 lib bdg; 1-4263-0326-2 lib bdg
LC 2007-41229
   The authors describe the life cycle and behavior of elephants and their own experiences with elephants in the wild
   "The photographs are stunning, sometimes intimate, sometimes epic. . . . [This book] conveys [elephants'] magnificence and fascination." Bull Cent Child Books
   Includes glossary and bibliographical references

Marsh, Laura
   Elephants. National Geographic 2010 48p il map (Great migrations) $11.90; pa $3.99
Grades: 1 2 3   **599.67**
   1. Elephants
ISBN 978-1-4263-0744-7; 1-4263-0744-6; 978-1-4263-0743-0 pa; 1-4263-0743-8 pa
LC 2010017961
   This offers facts about elephants in an easy reader format.
   "Dynamic full-color photographs, informative writing, and consistent organization work well together in [this volume]. . . . Along with the many photographs, the fascinating details are supported by boxes of related information, helpful definitions of new terms, and a sprinkling of entertaining jokes/riddles." SLJ
   Includes glossary

Morgan, Jody
   Elephant rescue; changing the future for endangered wildlife. Firefly Books 2004 64p il $19.95; pa $9.95
Grades: 5 6 7 8   **599.67**
   1. Elephants 2. Wildlife conservation
ISBN 1-55297-595-9; 1-55297-594-0 pa
   This is "well-written. . . . Stunning, full-color photographs bring [these animals] to life." SLJ

O'Connell, Caitlin
   ★ A **baby** elephant in the wild; by Caitlin O'Connell; with photographs by Timothy Rodwell. 1st ed. Houghton Mifflin Harcourt 2014 40 p. $16.99
Grades: K 1 2 3   **599.67**
   1. Animal babies 2. Elephants 3. African elephant -- Pictorial works 4. African elephant -- Infancy -- Namibia
ISBN 0544149440; 9780544149441
LC 2013017880

"In this account of a journey into the scrub desert of Namibia, readers meet a newborn elephant and her family. Children learn about Liza's early accomplishments: walking within hours, keeping up with the herd as they travel, and learning how to use her trunk and what is safe to eat. The animals walk 10 to 20 miles a day to find food, with the babies hidden behind their mothers or under them between their legs." (School Library Journal)

Riggs, Kate

    Elephants. Creative Education 2011 24p il (Amazing animals) $24.25; pa $5.99

    Grades: K 1 2   **599.67**

       1. Elephants

    ISBN 978-1-58341-990-8; 1-58341-990-X; 978-0-89812-563-4 pa; 0-89812-563-4 pa

                      LC 2010019054

    "A basic exploration of the appearance, behavior, and habitat of elephants, Earth's biggest land animals. Also included is a story from folklore explaining why elephants' trunks are so long." Publisher's note

Schwabacher, Martin

    Elephants; by Martin Schwabacher, with Lori Mortensen. Marshall Cavendish Benchmark 2010 24p il map (Animals) lib bdg $16.95

    Grades: 3 4 5   **599.67**

       1. Elephants

    ISBN 978-0-7614-4343-8 lib bdg; 0-7614-4343-6 lib bdg

                      LC 2008-52103

    "The straightforward presentation of the information and the uncluttered and attractive layout make [this] . . . good . . . for reports. Color photographs . . . are well utilized and complete a solid package." SLJ

    Includes glossary and bibliographical references

599.674   African elephants

Markle, Sandra

    Thirsty, thirsty elephants; Sandra Markle; illustrated by Fabricio Vanden Broeck. Charlesbridge 2017 32 p. color illustrations, color map (reinforced for library use) $16.99

    Grades: PreK K 1 2   **599.674**

       1. Droughts   2. Elephants   3. African elephant   4. Droughts -- Tanzania

    ISBN 9781580896344

                      LC 2015017345

    In this book, by Sandra Markle, illustrated by Fabricio Vanden Broeck, "during a drought in Tanzania, Grandma Elephant is in search of water for her herd. Little Calf follows along and mimics her grandmother at each stop on their journey. When Grandma leads them to a watering hole . . . , the elephants are overjoyed and Little Calf splashes about with her tender leader. Grandma's persistence and powerful memory is something Little Calf will never forget." (Publisher's note)

    Includes bibliographical references (page [32])

599.7   Carnivores

Gonzales, Doreen

    Raccoons in the dark. PowerKids Press 2010 24p il (Creatures of the night) lib bdg $21.25; pa $8.05

    Grades: 2 3 4   **599.7**

       1. Raccoons

    ISBN 978-1-4042-8101-1 lib bdg; 1-4042-8101-0 lib bdg; 978-1-4358-3259-6 pa; 1-4358-3259-0 pa

                      LC 2009-2758

    A look at raccoons and their world in the dark.

    "Basic details are complemented by eclectic trivia, . . . [and] each volume concludes with a defense of the animal . . . and why it is vital to humans. The layout is attractive, with easy-to-read text and eye-catching photography. Good for reports." SLJ

    Includes glossary

    Skunks in the dark. PowerKids Press 2010 24p il (Creatures of the night) lib bdg $21.25; pa $8.05

    Grades: 2 3 4   **599.7**

       1. Skunks

    ISBN 978-1-4042-8099-1 lib bdg; 1-4042-8099-5 lib bdg; 978-1-4358-3255-8 pa; 1-4358-3255-8 pa

                      LC 2009-718

    A look at skunks and their world in the dark.

    "Basic details are complemented by eclectic trivia, . . . [and] each volume concludes with a defense of the animal . . . and why it is vital to humans. The layout is attractive, with easy-to-read text and eye-catching photography. Good for reports." SLJ

    Includes glossary

Kalman, Bobbie

    Baby carnivores; by Bobbie Kalman. Crabtree Publishing Company 2013 24 p. ill. (library) $22.60; (paperback) $6.95

    Grades: 1 2 3 4   **599.7**

       1. Carnivorous animals   2. Food chains (Ecology)   3. Carnivorous animals -- Infancy

    ISBN 0778710106; 9780778710103; 9780778710158

                      LC 2012043739

    This book by Bobbie Kalman presents "images of many kinds of baby carnivores that belong to a group of mammals with sharp teeth and claws. Fascinating text explains how baby carnivores are cared for by their mothers and how they learn to hunt. Young readers will learn about the food chain and where dogs, cats, bears, seals, weasels, meerkats, and other animals live." (Publisher's note)

    Includes bibliographical references and index.

Leardi, Jeanette

    Southern sea otters; fur-tastrophe avoided. by Jeanette Leardi. Bearport Pub. 2008 32p il map (America's animal comebacks) lib bdg $25.27

    Grades: 2 3 4   **599.7**

       1. Otters   2. Wildlife conservation

    ISBN 978-1-59716-534-1 lib bdg; 1-59716-534-4 lib bdg

                      LC 2007012593

    This describes efforts by scientists and environmentalists to protect southern sea otters from hunting, pollution, and other dangers

    This book is "well organized and [has] an easy style and an accessible vocabulary and text size . . . [and] color photographs." SLJ

    Includes glossary and bibliographical references

Lunis, Natalie

    California sea lion; fast and smart. Bearport Pub. 2011 24p il map (Blink of an eye. Superfast animals!) lib bdg $22.61

    Grades: 1 2 3   **599.7**

       1. Seals (Animals)

    ISBN 978-1-936088-08-9; 1-936088-08-8

                      LC 2010017683

This describes the California sea lion, where it lives, how it hunts, and the ways its body helps it reach its record-breaking speeds.

This "is sure to appeal to a wide variety of readers. Vibrant photos illustrate each animal from multiple perspectives, providing opportunity for readers to closely examine the animal. Information is organized by subject heading and branches into the animal's physical features and how they contribute to its speed, the animal's natural predators, and how the animal makes use of speed as a means of survival. . . . This . . . will be a worthwhile addition to your nonfiction collection." Libr Media Connect

Includes glossary and bibliographical references

Otfinoski, Steven

★ **Skunks**; by Steven Otfinoski. Marshall Cavendish Benchmark 2009 47p il (Animals animals) lib bdg $20.95

Grades: 3 4 5 6   **599.7**

1. Skunks

ISBN 978-0-7614-2929-6 lib bdg; 0-7614-2929-8 lib bdg

LC 2007-24117

"The material is well researched and would be an excellent source for reports, and the [book has] a narrative flow that makes [it] easy and enjoyable to read. [The] title includes expert full-color photography." SLJ

Includes glossary

599.74   Land carnivores

Ganeri, Anita

Meerkat. Heinemann Library 2011 24p il map (A day in the life: desert animals) $22; pa $6.49

Grades: K 1 2   **599.74**

1. Meerkats

ISBN 978-1-4329-4773-6; 1-4329-4773-7; 978-1-4329-4782-8 pa; 1-4329-4782-6 pa

LC 2010022821

"The engaging full-color photographs are key to [this] well-organized [book]. . . . Basic global maps show where the animal is found, and a diagram called a 'body map' labels its parts. The [text is] appropriate for the age group, and the pictures will draw in youngsters. [An] excellent [purchase] if material is needed on these animals." SLJ

Includes glossary and bibliographical references

Gibbons, Gail

Wolves. Holiday House 1994 un il $16.95; pa $6.95

Grades: K 1 2 3   **599.74**

1. Wolves

ISBN 0-8234-1127-3; 0-8234-1202-4 pa

LC 94-2108

"A simply written introduction that focuses on the gray, or timber, wolf. . . . Material covered includes physical characteristics, behavior within a pack, and communication by howling and body language. . . . The format is open and spacious, the print is large, and the realistic, watercolor illustrations are set against backgrounds of white and deep blues." SLJ

Goldish, Meish

Fossa; a fearsome predator. by Meish Goldish. Bearport Pub. 2009 32p il map (Uncommon animals) lib bdg $25.27

Grades: 1 2 3   **599.74**

1. Fossa (Mammals)

ISBN 978-1-59716-732-1 lib bdg; 1-59716-732-0 lib bdg

LC 2008-4817

"The explanatory text works spendidly, with large photographs that bring readers as close as they'll ever get to such beasts." Booklist

Includes glossary and bibliographical references

Lunde, Darrin

Meet the Meerkat; by Darrin Lunde and illustrated by Patricia J. Wynne. Charlesbridge Publishing 2007 28 p. il $7.95

Grades: PreK K 1 2   **599.74**

1. Meerkats

ISBN 1580891101; 1580891543; 9781580891103; 9781580891547

LC 200621252

In this book, by Darrin Lunde and illustrated by Patricia J. Wynne, "a series of questions and answers introduce children to the life and habitat of Little Meerkat. Scientifically accurate illustrations make these exotic animals accessible to young readers. Back matter includes additional child-friendly facts." (Publisher's note)

"Addressing Little Meerkat, the author receives responses from the animal about its habitat, family structure, food, enemies, and so on. Watercolor, ink, and colored-pencil illustrations capture the activities of the meerkat family and are large enough to share with a small group." SLJ

Ryder, Joanne

Little panda; the world welcomes Hua Mei at the San Diego Zoo. Simon & Schuster 2001 un il $16.95; pa $7.99

Grades: K 1 2 3   **599.74**

1. Giant panda

ISBN 0-689-84310-0; 0-689-86616-X pa

"Ryder's photo-essay chronicles the life of Hua Mei, born at the World Famous San Diego Zoo in 1999. . . . Ryder's brief, almost haiku-like text is bolstered by informative paragraphs set in smaller type. The crisp, engaging photos were provided by the zoo." Booklist

Somervill, Barbara A.

Small Indian Mongoose. Cherry Lake Pub. 2010 32p il map (Animal invaders) lib bdg $27.07

Grades: 5 6 7 8   **599.74**

1. Mongooses 2. Biological invasions

ISBN 978-1-60279-630-0 lib bdg; 1-60279-630-0 lib bdg

LC 2009028179

This offers "an introduction to the problems caused by [the Small Indian Mongoose], a discussion of its physical characteristics and habits, a history of how it arrived in its new habitat, and an analysis of challenges encountered by those trying to limit its spread. . . . [This] considers the destructive effects of these mammals on islands (including several in Hawaii), where they were initially introduced to prey on rats. . . . [This] well-focused [book is] clearly written. The uncluttered page design features at least one color photo on each spread." Booklist

Includes glossary and bibliographical references

Walden, Katherine

Meerkats. PowerKids Press 2009 24p il (Safari animals) lib bdg $21.25

Grades: PreK K 1 2   **599.74**

1. Meerkats

ISBN 978-1-4358-2691-5 lib bdg; 1-4358-2691-4 lib bdg

LC 2008020793

This book provides "succinctly written introductory information about [meerkats'] range, habitat, social groups, and diet. Spreads consist of one to three short, simply constructed sentences opposite crisp, color photographs, most of which represent the subject perfectly." SLJ

599.742   Viverrids

Gish, Melissa

Meerkats; Melissa Gish. Creative Education/Creative Paperbacks 2016 46 p. color ill., color map (Living Wild) (hardcover : alk. paper) $39.95

Grades: 4 5 6   **599.742**

1. Meerkats   2. Rare mammals

ISBN 1608185699; 9781608185696

LC 2014028011

This children's book, by Melissa Gish, a part of the Living Wild illustrated children's book series, offers "a look at meerkats, including their habitats, physical characteristics such as their tails, behaviors, relationships with humans, and their stable status in the world today." (Publisher's note)

"Appearance, habitat, diet, behavior, conservation efforts, and presence in human culture are all addressed in great detail, while sidebars provide additional information." Horn Book

Includes bibliographical references and index.

599.75   Cat family

Becker, John E.

★ **Wild** cats: past & present; illustrations by Mark Hallett. Darby Creek 2008 80p il $18.95

Grades: 5 6 7 8   **599.75**

1. Wild cats

ISBN 978-1-58196-052-5; 1-58196-052-2

"Becker provides an informative introduction to wild cats, including an account of their ancient ancestors, an overview of the family Felidae and its subdivisions, accounts of wild cats alive in the world today, and woven throughout, discussions of the endangered status of many species. . . . Clearly written and well organized, the text is enhanced by many side-bars, maps, photos, and paintings." Booklist

Bodden, Valerie

Jaguars; by Valerie Bodden. 1st ed. Creative Education 2013 24 p. col. ill. (library) $25.65

Grades: 1 2 3 4   **599.75**

1. Jaguars

ISBN 1608180867; 9781608180868

LC 2011050284

This book, part of the Amazing Animals series, focuses on jaguars. "Jaguars, the third largest member of the cat family, are found in Mexico, Central and South America. They can spring as far as 6 meters to catch prey. Families, which include one to four cubs, live together, but by age two the cubs live alone and stalk their own territory. Like other books in the series, glossary words are explained on pages where they first are mentioned." (NSTA Recommends)

Includes bibliographical references and index.

Lions. Creative Education 2010 24p il map (Amazing animals) lib bdg $24.25

Grades: K 1 2   **599.75**

1. Lions

ISBN 978-1-58341-807-9 lib bdg; 1-58341-807-5 lib bdg

LC 2009002709

A basic exploration of the appearance, behavior, and habitat of lions, the majestic big cats of Africa and India. Also included is a story from folklore explaining why lions roar

Includes bibliographical references

Bredeson, Carmen

Lions up close; [by] Carmen Bredeson. Enslow Elementary 2008 24p il (Zoom in on animals!) $21.26

Grades: 1 2 3   **599.75**

1. Lions

ISBN 978-0-7660-3080-0; 0-7660-3080-6

LC 2007025610

This describes the anatomy, behavior, and life cycle of lions. Includes glossary and bibliographical references

Carney, Elizabeth

Everything big cats. National Geographic 2011 64p il map (National Geographic kids) lib bdg $25.90; pa $12.95

Grades: 3 4 5 6   **599.75**

1. Wild cats

ISBN 978-1-4263-0806-2 lib bdg; 1-4263-0806-X lib bdg; 978-1-4263-0805-5 pa; 1-4263-0805-1 pa

LC 2010026963

This describes four big predators, the lion, leopard, jaguar, and tiger. "Exploding with astounding full-color photographs and written in an appealing conversational tone, [this book is] for every kid. . . . The [text] will keep kids interested and turning pages to discover more and more facts. . . . [This] compelling, browseable, and completely engrossing [title] will delight readers." SLJ

Includes glossary and bibliographical references

Clutton-Brock, Juliet

Cat; by Juliet Clutton-Brock. DK Publishing 2014 72 p color illustrations (DK Eyewitness) library $19.99

Grades: 4 5 6 7   **599.75**

1. Cats   2. Wild cats

ISBN 1465420924; 9781465420923

First published 1991

Text and photographs present the anatomy, behavior, habitats, and other aspects of wild and domestic cats.

Firestone, Mary

Top 50 reasons to care about tigers; animals in peril. Enslow Publishers 2010 103p il (Top 50 reasons to care about endangered animals) lib bdg $31.93

Grades: 4 5 6 7   **599.75**

1. Tigers   2. Endangered species

ISBN 978-0-7660-3452-5 lib bdg; 0-7660-3452-6 lib bdg

LC 2008-48689

This describes a tiger's life, how they hunt, the purpose of its stripes, caring for young, competing with people for space, and that these animals are very close to extinction

"The illustrations, mostly color photographs, represent a wonderful selection of the animals and their habitats. Reluctant readers may be enticed by this . . . simply because of the great images. This . . . would make a substantial supplement to the science curriculum when studying endangered animals." Libr Media Connect

Includes glossary and bibliographical references

Ganeri, Anita

Jaguar. Heinemann Library 2011 24p il map (A day in the life. Rain forest animals) lib bdg $22; pa $6.49

Grades: 1 2   **599.75**

1. Jaguars

ISBN 978-1-4329-4106-2 lib bdg; 1-4329-4106-2 lib bdg; 978-1-4329-4117-8 pa; 1-4329-4117-8 pa

LC 2010000962

This book follows a day in the life of a jaguar.

"Ganeri presents information clearly and simply in large type, two-sentence comments placed below a bright, sharply reproduced color photograph of the animal in a natural setting. . . . [This is] sufficiently specific to support assignment as well as pleasure reading." SLJ

Includes glossary and bibliographical references

Gish, Melissa

Jaguars. Creative Education 2011 46p il map (Living wild) lib bdg $23.95

Grades: 5 6 7 **599.75**

1. Jaguars

ISBN 978-1-60818-079-0; 1-60818-079-4

LC 2010028315

A look at jaguars, including their habitats, physical characteristics such as their powerful jaws, behaviors, relationships with humans, and threatened status in the world today.

This offers "an array of interesting facts. Photography is large and beautiful–a real draw." SLJ

Includes glossary and bibliographical references

Leopards. Creative Education 2010 46p il (Living wild) lib bdg $34.25; pa $8.99

Grades: 5 6 7 8 **599.75**

1. Leopards

ISBN 978-1-58341-972-4 lib bdg; 1-58341-972-1 lib bdg; 978-0-89812-555-9 pa; 0-89812-555-3 pa

LC 2010017377

"A look at leopards, including their habitats, physical characteristics such as their spotted fur, behaviors, relationships with humans, and threatened status in the world today." Publisher's note

Hamilton, Sue L.

Ambushed by a cougar; [by] Sue Hamilton. ABDO Pub. Co. 2010 32p il (Close encounters of the wild kind) lib bdg $27.07

Grades: 4 5 6 7 **599.75**

1. Pumas 2. Animal attacks

ISBN 978-1-60453-928-8 lib bdg; 1-60453-928-3 lib bdg

LC 2009-45521

Readers learn of actual human-cougar encounters, information about cougars, survival strategies, and attack statistics.

"Students will be drawn to the realistic full-color photographs, the realistic diagrams of the creatures' bodies, the real-life stories told by victims, and the interesting, attractive formatting that includes text, diagrams, photographs, and graphics on each page. . . . [This is] exciting and attractive in a 'gross' sort of way and will appeal particularly to boys for both leisure reading and research." Libr Media Connect

Includes glossary

Hanel, Rachael

Tigers. Creative Education 2008 46p il map (Living wild) lib bdg $22.95

Grades: 3 4 5 **599.75**

1. Tigers

ISBN 978-1-58341-660-0 lib bdg; 1-58341-660-9 lib bdg

LC 2007-08504

This describes the behavior, life cycle, and physical characteristics of tigers and their relationships to humans.

"Children will turn first to the excellent, informatively captioned photos. . . . But this . . . also has solid, informative content to accompany the captivating visuals." Booklist

Hatkoff, Juliana

★ **Leo** the snow leopard; the true story of an amazing rescue. told by Juliana Hatkoff, Isabella Hatkoff, and Craig Hatkoff. Scholastic Press 2010 un il $17.99

Grades: 3 4 5 6 **599.75**

1. Snow leopard 2. Wildlife conservation 3. New York Zoological Society

ISBN 978-0-545-22927-2; 0-545-22927-8

"This inspirational picture book conveys the importance of caring and protecting the world's wildlife. The story recounts the rescue of an orphaned snow leopard cub from Pakistan, and how the goodwill between people and nations can make a difference in the survival of endangered species. Excellent photographic detail recreates Leo's discovery by a goat herder, who in turn contacted the authorities when he got too large, and his cross-country adventure before being relocated to the Bronx Zoo in New York." SLJ

Johns, Chris

★ **Face** to face with cheetahs; by Chris Johns with Elizabeth Carney. National Geographic 2008 32p il map (Face to face) $16.95; lib bdg $25.90

Grades: 3 4 5 6 **599.75**

1. Cheetahs

ISBN 978-1-4263-0323-4; 1-4263-0323-8; 978-1-4263-0324-1 lib bdg; 1-4263-0324-6 lib bdg

LC 2007041220

Chris Johns describes the life cycle and behavior of cheetahs and his own experiences with cheetahs in the wild.

Includes glossary and bibliographical references

Joubert, Beverly

★ **Face** to face with leopards; by Beverly and Dereck Joubert. National Geographic 2009 31p il (Face to face) $16.95; lib bdg $25.90

Grades: 3 4 5 6 **599.75**

1. Leopards

ISBN 978-1-4263-0636-5; 1-4263-0636-9; 978-1-4263-0637-2 lib bdg; 1-4263-0637-7 lib bdg

LC 2009011441

The authors describe the life cycle and behavior of leopard and their own experiences with leopards in the wild.

"The exquisite photos and firsthand information provide an in-depth and personal look into the lives of these animals." SLJ

Includes glossary and bibliographical references

★ **Face** to face with lions; by Beverly and Dereck Joubert. National Geographic 2008 31p il (Face to face) $16.95; lib bdg $25.90

Grades: 3 4 5 6 **599.75**

1. Lions

ISBN 978-1-4263-0207-7; 1-4263-0207-X; 978-1-4263-0208-4 lib bdg; 1-4263-0208-8 lib bdg

LC 2007-11118

The authors describe the life cycle and behavior of lions and their own experiences with lions in the wild.

This is "well written and complete. . . . [It contains] many beautiful color photographs." Sci Books Films

Includes glossary and bibliographical references

Landau, Elaine

Big cats; hunters of the night. Enslow Publishers 2007 32p il (Animals after dark) $16.95

Grades: 1 2 3 4 **599.75**

1. Wild cats

ISBN 978-0-7660-2770-1; 0-7660-2770-8

LC 2006-16805

This "book presents basic information on the night-hunting big cats—lions, tigers, leopards, and jaguars—in an entertaining and informative format. . . . The photographs and clear text on mostly black pages add to a rewarding reading experience." Sci Books Films

Includes bibliographical references

Lunis, Natalie

Cheetah; speed demon! Bearport Pub. 2011 24p il map (Blink of an eye. Superfast animals!) lib bdg $22.61

Grades: 1 2 3   **599.75**

1. Cheetahs

ISBN 978-1-936087-89-1; 1-936087-89-8

LC 2009-53573

This describes the cheetah, including where it lives, how it hunts, and the ways its body helps it reach its record-breaking speeds.

This "is sure to appeal to a wide variety of readers. Vibrant photos illustrate each animal from multiple perspectives, providing opportunity for readers to closely examine the animal. Information is organized by subject heading and branches into the animal's physical features and how they contribute to its speed, the animal's natural predators, and how the animal makes use of speed as a means of survival. . . . This . . . will be a worthwhile addition to your nonfiction collection." Libr Media Connect

Includes glossary and bibliographical references

Markle, Sandra, 1946-

The **great** leopard rescue; Saving the Amur Leopards. Sandra Markle. Millbrook Press 2017 48 p. color ill., color maps (ebook) $30.65; (ebook) $30.65; (lb : alk. paper) $30.65

Grades: 3 4 5 6   **599.75**

1. Leopard -- Amur River Valley (China and Russia) 2. Animal rescue -- Amur River Valley (China and Russia) 3. Wildlife conservation -- Amur River Valley (China and Russia) 4. Wildlife rescue -- Amur River Valley (China and Russia)

ISBN 9781512420494; 9781467797559; 9781467792479

LC 2015044387

This book, by Sandra Markle, focuses on saving Amur leopards. " In 2007 only thirty Amur leopards remained in the wild. . . . With the help of new technology and the cooperation of scientists and governments around the world, people have learned more than ever before about these rare cats. An innovative plan is under way to give Amur leopards a more secure future. Can these cats rebound from the brink before it's too late?" (Publisher's note)

"An informative presentation showing what is being done to save this beautiful but critically endangered species." Booklist

Includes bibliographical references and index

Marks, Jennifer L.

Bobcats. Capstone Press 2011 24p il map (Pebble plus. Wildcats) lib bdg $23.99

Grades: K 1 2   **599.75**

1. Bobcats

ISBN 978-1-4296-4480-8 lib bdg; 1-4296-4480-X lib bdg

LC 2010002795

"Plenty of full-page, close-up photos of . . . [bobcats] . . . in natural (or seemingly natural) settings will attract a broad audience. . . . [The book] covers geographical range (with a small map), average size, physical adaptations for the cat's habitat, typical prey, life cycle, threats, and average life span in the wild." SLJ

Includes glossary and bibliographical references

Clouded leopards. Capstone Press 2011 24p il map (Pebble plus. Wildcats) lib bdg $23.99

Grades: K 1 2   **599.75**

1. Leopards

ISBN 978-1-4296-4482-2 lib bdg; 1-4296-4482-6 lib bdg

LC 2010002797

"Plenty of full-page, close-up photos of . . . [clouded leopards] . . . in natural (or seemingly natural) settings will attract a broad audience. . . . [The book] covers geographical range (with a small map), average size, physical adaptations for the cat's habitat, typical prey, life cycle, threats, and average life span in the wild." SLJ

Includes glossary and bibliographical references

Jaguars. Capstone Press 2011 24p il map (Pebble plus. Wildcats) lib bdg $23.99

Grades: K 1 2   **599.75**

1. Jaguars

ISBN 978-1-4296-4481-5 lib bdg; 1-4296-4481-8 lib bdg

LC 2010002798

"Plenty of full-page, close-up photos of . . . [jaguars] . . . in natural (or seemingly natural) settings will attract a broad audience. . . . [The book] covers geographical range (with a small map), average size, physical adaptations for the cat's habitat, typical prey, life cycle, threats, and average life span in the wild." SLJ

Includes glossary and bibliographical references

Meinking, Mary

Polar bear vs. seal. Raintree 2011 32p il (Predator vs. prey) $29; pa $7.99

Grades: 1 2 3   **599.75**

1. Polar bear 2. Seals (Animals) 3. Predatory animals

ISBN 978-1-4109-3939-5; 978-1-4109-3948-7 pa

Explores the features of the polar bear and the seal that make them particularly suited to catch or evade the other.

"The struggle between polar bear and seal is described in clear language and illustrated with engaging color photographs." Horn Book Guide

Includes glossary and bibliographical references

Montgomery, Sy

★ **Chasing** cheetahs; the race to save Africa's fastest cats. written by Sy Montgomery; photographs by Nic Bishop. Houghton Mifflin Harcourt 2014 80 p. illustrations $18.99

Grades: 5 6 7 8   **599.75**

1. Cheetahs 2. Cheetah -- Africa 3. Cheetah Conservation Fund

ISBN 0547815492; 9780547815497

LC 2013017611

Scientists in the field

This book, by Sy Montgomery, focuses on cheetahs. "At the Cheetah Conservation Fund's (CCF) African headquarters in Namibia, Laurie Marker and her team save these . . . creatures from extinction. Since the organization's start in 1990, they've rescued more than 900 cheetahs. . . . But this arduous challenge continues. For most African livestock farmers, cheetahs are the last thing they want to see on their properties. In the 1980s, as many as 19 cheetahs per farmer died each year." (Publisher's note)

"Montgomery introduces readers to Laurie Marker and her team at the Cheetah Conservation Fund's site in Namibia. Scientific information about the cheetahs and profiles of the people who study them are interspersed with in-the-moment, journal-style accounts of activities at the site. Striking photographs capture the dedication of the scientists and the awesome power of the cheetahs." Horn Book

Includes bibliographical references and index.

Saving the ghost of the mountain; an expedition among snow leopards in Mongolia. text by Sy Montgomery; photographs by Nic Bishop.

Houghton Mifflin Books for Children 2009 48p il map (Scientists in the field) $18

Grades: 5 6 7 8   599.75

1. Biologists 2. Snow leopard 3. Conservationists 4. Mongolia

ISBN 978-0-618-91645-0; 0-618-91645-8

LC 2008-36762

Author Sy Montgomery and photographer Nic Bishop accompany conservationist Tom McCarthy and his team as they travel to Mongolia's Altai Mountains to gather data about snow leopard populations in an attempt to save this endangered species

"Montgomery's enthusiasm translates well to the page and will have readers cheering for the entourage as they attempt to spot a snow leopard. This slender book abounds with information. Bishop's trademark stunning photography fills out the book with breathtaking views of the extreme environs of Central Asia and warm portraits of the charming people who live there." SLJ

Person, Stephen

Cougar; a cat with many names. by Stephen Person. Bearport Pub. 2013 32 p. (America's hidden animal treasures) (library binding) $26.60

Grades: 1 2 3 4   599.75

1. Pumas 2. Animals -- North America

ISBN 1617725692; 9781617725692

LC 2012003342

This book by Stephen Person "opens with an intriguing introduction that shows the cougar and a housecat appearing to recognize each other. This is followed by a discussion of how the cougar adapts to a variety of habitats and its ability to swim, climb trees and jump unusual heights. . . . In their quest for survival, readers will learn how they hunt for a variety of animals and are excellent predators." (SB&F: Your Guide to Science Resources for All Ages)

Includes bibliographical references and index.

Riggs, Kate

Leopards; by Kate Riggs. Creative Education 2012 24 p. col. ill.

Grades: K 1 2   599.75

1. Leopards 2. Animal behavior 3. Habitat (Ecology) 4. Animals -- Folklore 5. Zoology -- Encyclopedias

ISBN 1608181103; 9781608181100

LC 2010049130

This children's book, part of Kate Riggs' "Amazing Animals" series, focuses on leopards. "This . . . popular series continues traveling the planet to study alligators, bats, and other fascinating animals. . . . [P]hotos are paired with . . . text to examine the featured creature's appearance, habitat, behaviors, and life cycle. . . . "A basic exploration of the appearance, behavior, and habitat of leopards, Earth's fourth-largest cats. Also included is a story from folklore explaining why leopards and baboons don't get along." (Publisher's note)

Includes bibliographical references and index

Rodriguez, Cindy

Cougars. Rourke Pub. 2009 24p il map (Eye to eye with endangered species) lib bdg $27.07

Grades: 2 3 4   599.75

1. Pumas

ISBN 978-1-60694-404-2 lib bdg; 1-60694-404-5 lib bdg

LC 2009-5995

Text examines the issues endangered cougars face and how they can be saved

"Sets out to introduce readers to [cougars] . . . explain the dangers they face, and detail the efforts of biologists and conservationists to save them. . . . Serviceable and informative." SLJ

Includes glossary

Schafer, Susan

Lions; by Susan Schafer, with Susan Markowitz Meredith. Marshall Cavendish Benchmark 2010 24p il map (Animals) lib bdg $16.95

Grades: 3 4 5   599.75

1. Lions

ISBN 978-0-7614-4344-5 lib bdg; 0-7614-4344-4 lib bdg

LC 2008-52104

"The straightforward presentation of the information and the uncluttered and attractive layout make [this] . . . good . . . for reports. Color photographs . . . are well utilized and complete a solid package." SLJ

Includes glossary and bibliographical references

Tigers; by Susan Schafer, with Fay Robinson. Marshall Cavendish Benchmark 2010 24p il map (Animals) lib bdg $16.95

Grades: 3 4 5   599.75

1. Tigers

ISBN 978-0-7614-4345-2 lib bdg; 0-7614-4345-2 lib bdg

LC 2008-52109

"The straightforward presentation of the information and the uncluttered and attractive layout make [this] . . . good . . . for reports. Color photographs . . . are well utilized and complete a solid package." SLJ

Includes glossary and bibliographical references

Shores, Erika L.

Canada lynx. Capstone Press 2011 24p il map (Pebble plus. Wildcats) lib bdg $23.99

Grades: K 1 2   599.75

1. Lynx

ISBN 978-1-4296-4484-6 lib bdg; 1-4296-4484-2 lib bdg

LC 2010002796

"Plenty of full-page, close-up photos of . . . [the Canada Lynx] . . . in natural (or seemingly natural) settings will attract a broad audience. . . . [The book] covers geographical range (with a small map), average size, physical adaptations for the cat's habitat, typical prey, life cycle, threats, and average life span in the wild." SLJ

Includes glossary and bibliographical references

Mountain lions. Capstone Press 2011 24p il map (Pebble plus. Wildcats) lib bdg $23.99

Grades: K 1 2   599.75

1. Pumas

ISBN 978-1-4296-4485-3 lib bdg; 1-4296-4485-0 lib bdg

LC 2010002799

"Plenty of full-page, close-up photos of . . . [mountain lions] . . . in natural (or seemingly natural) settings will attract a broad audience. . . . [The book] covers geographical range (with a small map), average size, physical adaptations for the cat's habitat, typical prey, life cycle, threats, and average life span in the wild." SLJ

Includes glossary and bibliographical references

Snow leopards. Capstone Press 2011 24p il map (Pebble plus. Wildcats) lib bdg $23.99

Grades: K 1 2   599.75

1. Snow leopard

ISBN 978-1-4296-4483-9 lib bdg; 1-4296-4483-4 lib bdg

LC 2010002800

"Plenty of full-page, close-up photos of . . . [snow leopards] . . . in natural (or seemingly natural) settings will attract a broad audience. . . . [The book] covers geographical range (with a small map), average size, physical adaptations for the cat's habitat, typical prey, life cycle, threats, and average life span in the wild." SLJ

Includes glossary and bibliographical references

Seymour, Simon

★ **Big** cats; all about the different species, their strength, hunting skills, and more! Seymour Simon. Revised edition Harpercollins Childrens Books 2017 40 p color illustrations reinforced $17.99

Grades: 3 4 5 6　　　　　　　　　　**599.75**
1. Wild cats
ISBN 0062470361; 9780062470362
First published 1991

"In this completely updated edition of Big Cats, award-winning writer Seymour Simon celebrates the grace and power of lions, tigers, leopards, jaguars, cheetahs, pumas, and snow leopards. Readers will learn all about how they hunt, care for their young, and rest in their varied natural habitats." (Publisher's note)

Squire, Ann

Cheetahs; by Ann O. Squire. Children's Press 2005 47p il (True book) lib bdg $25; pa $6.95

Grades: 2 3 4　　　　　　　　　　**599.75**
1. Cheetahs
ISBN 0-516-22792-0 lib bdg; 0-516-27932-7 pa
LC 2003-5174

"Beginning with cheetahs' best-known quality, their speed, this very readable volume goes on to discuss their prowess and limitations as hunters as well as their prey, social habits, life cycle, and use of camouflage. . . . Remarkably clear, often-dramatic color photos of cheetahs in the wild offer unusually good views of the animals." Booklist

Includes bibliographical references

Wells, Robert E.

Can we share the world with tigers? by Robert E. Wells. Albert Whitman & Company 2012 32 p. (hardcover) $16.99

Grades: 3 4 5　　　　　　　　　　**599.75**
1. Ecology 2. Biodiversity conservation 3. Picture books for children 4. Bengal tiger -- India 5. Endangered species -- India 6. Wildlife conservation -- India 7. Bengal tiger -- Conservation -- India
ISBN 0807510556; 9780807510551
LC 2011038269

In this children's picture book, "using threats to endangered Bengal tigers' survival as a springboard, [Robert E.] Wells teaches young readers about the many ways humans interfere with the natural world and its biodiversity." A tigress, her cubs, and a monkey "travel through the book together, teaching readers about habitat destruction, pollution, overharvesting, invasive species, biodiversity and extinction." (Kirkus)

599.752　Wildcats

Esterhas, Suzi

Moto and me; my year as a wildcat's foster mom. By Suzi Eszterhas; [edited by] Sarah Howden. Owlkids Books, Inc. 2017 40 p. color illustrations, color map $17.95

Grades: K 1 2 3 4　　　　　　　　　　**599.752**
1. Wild cats
ISBN 9781771472425
LC 2016952800

This book "tells the remarkable firsthand story of wildlife photographer Suzi Eszterhas's care for an orphaned baby serval—a small, spotted wildcat—in Kenya. When a grass fire separates the serval from his family, a ranger asks Suzi, who is living in a bush camp and is skilled with animals, to be the serval's foster mom." (Publisher's note)

599.757　Lion

Hague, Bradley

Rise of the lioness; Restoring a Habitat and its Pride on the Liuwa Plains. by Bradley Hague. National Geographic 2016 56 p. hardcover $18.99

Grades: 4 5 6 7　　　　　　　　　　**599.757**
1. Lions 2. Wildlife refuges -- Zambia 3. Wildlife conservation -- Zambia 4. Lion -- Zambia
ISBN 9781426325335; 9781426325328
LC 2015024883

In this children's book by Bradley Hague, "poaching and war damaged an isolated wilderness in West Zambia, reducing its lion population to just one: Lady, the last lioness. Witness Lady's fight for survival in this evocative narrative on the decline, fall, and rebirth of the Liuwa Plains. Follow Lady as she grapples with a landscape altered by human hands and discover how both Lady and humankind restore balance to the environment." (Publisher's note)

"Full color photographs document the journey of Lady and her pride. This enlightening work offers in-depth information on the diverse needs of an ecosystem and offers hope for its restoration." SLJ

Includes bibliographical references and index

599.76　Canoidea

Gish, Melissa

Raccoons; Melissa Gish. Creative Education 2015 46 p. color ill., color map (hardcover : alk. paper) $39.95

Grades: 4 5 6　　　　　　　　　　**599.76**
1. Raccoons
ISBN 1608185702; 9781608185702
LC 2014028012

This book, by Melissa Gish, part of the Living Wild series, presents "a look at raccoons, including their habitats, physical characteristics such as their facial masks, behaviors, relationships with humans, and their hunted status in the world today." (Publisher's note)

"Stunning photographs, sidebars with intriguing facts, and engaging prose are hallmarks of this set, and the chapters describing each creature's role in folklore or pop culture add to the fun." SLJ

Includes bibliographical references and index

599.763　Procyonids

Markle, Sandra

The **search** for Olinguito; discovering a new species. Sandra Markle. Millbrook Press 2017 40 p. color ill., color map (ebook) $30.65; (lb : alk. paper) $30.65

Grades: 3 4 5 6　　　　　　　　　　**599.763**
1. Procyonidae 2. Cloud forest animals 3. Rare mammals -- South America
ISBN 9781512428421; 9781512410150
LC 2016010446

This book, by Sandra Markle, focuses on "the olinguito, an adorable relative of raccoons living among treetops in cloud forests of Central and South America. It was the first new mammal species in the Carnivora order to be discovered in 35 years. Learn how scientists solved the mystery piece by piece over more than ten years, traveling to museums all over the world to look at similar species and eventually scouting cloud forests at night." (Publisher's note)

"This quick but wondrous look at the scientific search for the olinguito is an excellent addition to science collections." SLJ

Includes bibliographical references

599.769 Otters

Green, Jen

Sea otter; by Jen Green. Bearport Publishing 2013 24 p. (library binding) $23.93

Grades: 1 2   **599.769**

1. Sea otter 2. Marine biology

ISBN 1617729221; 9781617729225

LC 2013011520

In this book, by Jen Green, "readers will explore the underwater world of this marine mammal [,the sea otter,] through clear text, full-color photos, and diagrams. Age-appropriate activities give readers a chance to make observations and develop animal-science skills." (Publisher's note)

Includes bibliographical references and index

London, Jonathan, 1947-

Otters Love to Play; Jonathan London; illustrated by Meilo So. Candlewick Press 2016 32 p. chiefly color illustrations $16.99

Grades: PreK K 1 2   **599.769**

1. Play -- fiction 2. Otters -- fiction

ISBN 076366913X; 9780763669133

In this children's book, by Jonathan London and illustrated by Meilo So, "tt's spring, and a litter of baby river otters emerges from a den . . . to play! Follow the otters through the seasons as they chase one another, slide down a mudbank, jump in a pile of leaves, and learn to swim. Even while catching fish for their dinner or grooming themselves in the snow, otters love to play." (Publisher's note)

"Fun and informative, this beautifully illustrated, strong narrative belongs in every collection." SLJ

599.77 Dog family

Brandenburg, Jim

★ Face to face with wolves; by Jim and Judy Brandenburg. National Geographic 2008 31p il map (Face to face) $16.95; lib bdg $25.90

Grades: 3 4 5 6   **599.77**

1. Wolves

ISBN 978-1-4263-0242-8; 1-4263-0242-8; 978-1-4263-0243-5 lib bdg; 1-4263-0243-6 lib bdg

LC 2007-41217

The authors describe the life cycle and behavior of wolves and their own experiences with wolves in the wild.

This is "well written and complete. . . . [It contains] many beautiful color photographs." Sci Books Films

Includes glossary and bibliographical references

Cohn, Scotti

One wolf howls; by Scotti Cohn; illustrated by Susan Detwiler. Sylvan Dell Pub. 2009 un il $16.95; pa $8.95

Grades: PreK K 1   **599.77**

1. Months 2. Wolves 3. Counting 4. Stories in rhyme

ISBN 978-1-934359-92-1; 1-934359-92-0; 978-1-607180-37-1 pa; 1-607180-37-5 pa

The months of the year and the numbers 1 through 12 are used in rhyming text to introduce children to the behavior of wolves in natural settings

"Readers should be captivated by the animals' resilient joie de vivre as well as by their habitats' seasonal glories. The educational guide offers wolf facts, activities and details about their life cycle." Publ Wkly

Ganeri, Anita

Fennec fox. Heinemann Library 2011 24p il map (A day in the life: desert animals) lib bdg $22; pa $6.49

Grades: K 1 2   **599.77**

1. Foxes

ISBN 978-1-4329-4771-2 lib bdg; 1-4329-4771-0 lib bdg; 978-1-4329-4780-4 pa; 1-4329-4780-X pa

LC 2010022819

"The engaging full-color photographs are key to [this] well-organized [book]. . . . Basic global maps show where the animal is found, and a diagram called a 'body map' labels its parts. The [text is] appropriate for the age group, and the pictures will draw in youngsters. [An] excellent [purchase] if material is needed on these animals." SLJ

Includes glossary and bibliographical references

George, Jean Craighead

★ The wolves are back; paintings by Wendell Minor. Dutton Children's Books 2008 un il lib bdg $16.99

Grades: 2 3 4 5   **599.77**

1. Wolves 2. Yellowstone National Park

ISBN 978-0-525-47947-5

LC 2007017064

"In 1995, wolves were reintroduced to Yellowstone Park. . . . The emphasis here is not as much on the wolves and their habits, but on how their presence has changed the ecosystem and returned its natural balance. . . . George writes . . . in simple, rhythmic, informative prose. Adding to the book's appeal are Minor's finely detailed illustrations, featuring spectacularly rendered animals in the foreground of the bold, western landscapes." Booklist

Gianferrari, Maria

Coyote moon; Maria Gianferrari; pictures by Bagram Ibatoulline. Roaring Brook Press 2016 32 p. color illustrations (hardcover) $17.99

Grades: PreK K 1 2   **599.77**

1. Coyotes 2. Animals 3. Urban animals

ISBN 9781626720411

LC 2015012694

In this book, by Maria Gianferrari, with pictures by Bagram Ibatoulline, "a mother coyote stalks prey to feed her hungry pups. Her hunt takes her through a suburban town, where she encounters a mouse, a rabbit, a flock of angry geese, and finally an unsuspecting turkey on the library lawn. . . . Perhaps Coyote's family won't go hungry today." (Publisher's note)

"Simple text and remarkable artwork make this a great selection for read-alouds and parent-child bonding." SLJ

Includes bibliographical references.

Goldish, Meish

Red wolves; and then there were (almost) none. Bearport Pub. 2009 32p il map (America's animal comebacks) lib bdg $25.27

Grades: 2 3 4   **599.77**

1. Wolves 2. Wildlife conservation

ISBN 978-1-59716-742-0 lib bdg; 1-59716-742-8 lib bdg

LC 2008-30831

Through this true tale of wildlife survival, young readers discover the bold and creative ideas that Americans and their government have used to protect and care for the countrys endangered red wolves

"Crisp photos and maps on every page work well with the text and give faces to the scientists and animals. The back matter includes a facts page, information on related species, and an up-to-date reading list." SLJ

Includes glossary and bibliographical references

Mara, Wil

★ **Coyotes**. Marshall Cavendish Benchmark 2009 48p il (Animals animals) $20.95

Grades: 3 4 5 6   **599.77**
1. Coyotes

ISBN 978-0-7614-2928-9; 0-7614-2928-X

LC 2007023411

"The material is well researched and would be an excellent source for reports, and the [book has] a narrative flow that makes [it] easy and enjoyable to read. [The] title includes expert full-color photography." SLJ

Includes glossary and bibliographical references

Markle, Sandra

★ **Wolves**; by Sandra Markle. Lerner Publications 2004 40p il (Animal predators) hardcover o.p. pa $7.95

Grades: 3 4 5 6   **599.77**
1. Wolves

ISBN 1-57505-732-8; 1-57505-748-4 pa

LC 2003-11197

"The text works well with the often striking full-color photos that illustrate the book." Booklist

Includes glossary and bibliographical references

McAllister, Ian

The **sea** wolves; living wild in the Great Bear Rainforest. written by Ian McAllister and Nicholas Read; photographs by Ian McAllister. Orca Book Publishers 2010 121p il $19.95

Grades: 5 6 7 8   **599.77**
1. Wolves 2. Rain forest ecology

ISBN 978-1-55469-206-4; 1-55469-206-7

The coastal wolf, a genetically distinct strain that swims and fishes, inhabits the Great Bear Rainforest on British Columbia's rugged west coast.

"This extensive, informative text is illustrated with remarkable photographs taken by McAllister, who has lived in and studied the area for years. They show the lush, old-growth forest and rocky shoreline and a variety of animals that share this habitat, but the wolves are the stars: at rest, at play, on the prowl and catching fish. . . . Fascinating and useful." Kirkus

Nobleman, Marc Tyler

★ **Foxes**; by Marc Tyler Nobleman. Marshall Cavendish Benchmark 2007 47p il (Animals, animals) lib bdg $19.95

Grades: 3 4 5 6   **599.77**
1. Foxes

ISBN 978-0-7614-2237-2 lib bdg; 0-7614-2237-4 lib bdg

LC 2005025608

"Describes the physical characteristics, behavior, habitat, and endangered status of foxes." Publisher's note

Includes glossary and bibliographical references

Patent, Dorothy Hinshaw

When the wolves returned; restoring nature's balance in Yellowstone. photographs by Dan Hartman and Cassie Hartman. Walker 2008 39p il $17.95; lib bdg $18.85

Grades: 3 4 5   **599.77**
1. Wolves 2. Yellowstone National Park

ISBN 978-0-8027-9686-8; 0-8027-9686-9; 978-0-8027-9687-5 lib bdg; 0-8027-9687-7 lib bdg

LC 2007-37141

NCTE Orbis Pictus Award honor book (2009)

When wolves were eliminated from Yellowstone National Park the natural system was out of balance. Shows the return of the wolves to the park and the natural balance being restored.

"Outstanding historical and present-day photographs of Yellowstone, its inhabitants, and its visitors capture the rugged natural beauty of the park." Horn Book

Includes bibliographical references

Person, Stephen

Arctic fox; very cool! by Stephen Person. Bearport Pub. 2009 32p il map (Uncommon animals) lib bdg $25.27

Grades: 1 2 3   **599.77**
1. Foxes

ISBN 978-1-59716-730-7 lib bdg; 1-59716-730-4 lib bdg

LC 2008-10637

"Easily readable sections detail the bitter natural habitat of the arctic fox and highlight the ways in which the animal is uniquely outfitted to survive such harsh conditions. The text works splendidly with the large, clear photographs on each page that will delight readers." Booklist

Includes glossary and bibliographical references

Read, Tracy C.

Exploring the world of coyotes. Firefly 2011 24p il (Exploring the world of) $16.95; pa $6.95

Grades: 4 5 6   **599.77**
1. Coyotes

ISBN 978-1-55407-795-3; 1-55407-795-8; 978-1-55407-796-0 pa; 1-55407-796-6 pa

This describes the physical features, habitat, diet, and behavior of coyotes.

A "well-organized [text] and good-quality pictures taken from photo archives provide the basics. [This book] reveals how North America's 'super dog' has had to adapt to survive humankind's continuous assault. . . . Insets of information in colorful circles add to the attractive configuration. [The book offers] simple language and good use of space." SLJ

Exploring the world of wolves. Firefly 2010 24p il (Exploring the world of . . .) $16.95; pa $6.95

Grades: 3 4 5   **599.77**
1. Wolves

ISBN 978-1-55407-646-8; 1-55407-646-3; 978-1-55407-655-0 pa; 1-55407-655-2 pa

This describes the anatomy and behavior of wolves.

This offers "an abundance of in-depth, intriguing information and [is] appropriate for research or pleasure reading. . . . Two- to four-page chapters mix smaller photos with full-page color photos, and the attractive format will help less-able readers navigate the sometimes dense, detailed paragraphs." Booklist

Riggs, Kate

Wolves. Creative Education 2011 24p il (Amazing animals) $24.25; pa $5.99

Grades: K 1 2   **599.77**
1. Wolves

ISBN 978-1-58341-991-5; 1-58341-991-8; 978-0-89812-564-1 pa; 0-89812-564-2 pa

LC 2010019055

"A basic exploration of the appearance, behavior, and habitat of wolves, a family of wild dogs. Also included is a story from folklore explaining why wolves are different from domestic dogs." Publisher's note

Swinburne, Stephen R.

Coyote; North America's dog. Boyds Mills Press 1999 32p il $16.95; pa $8.95

Grades: 4 5 6   **599.77**

1. Coyotes

ISBN 1-56397-765-6; 1-59078-485-5 pa

This book "packs a lot of information about North American coyotes into a small space. The author, a veteran park ranger, knows his subject well and succeeds in making it interesting to his audience. . . . The full-color photographs are clean and clear and enliven the text." Booklist

599.775 Foxes

Holland, Mary

Ferdinand Fox's first summer; by Mary Holland. Sylvan Dell Publishing 2013 32 p. ill. (reinforced) $17.95; (paperback) $9.95

Grades: K 1 2 3   **599.775**

1. Foxes

ISBN 1607186144; 9781607186144; 9781607186267

LC 2012030121

In this children's picture book, author "[Mary] Holland presents the first part of the red fox's life cycle with the story of Ferdinand, one fox kit she photographed throughout his first summer. Short, bland paragraphs of information describe how the five fox kits grow and learn, their mother nursing and grooming them and, when they are ready, bringing back food for them to eat." (Kirkus Reviews)

Pringle, Laurence

The secret life of the red fox; Laurence Pringle; Illustrated by Kate Garchinsky. Boyds Mills Press 2017 32 p. color illustrations $16.95

Grades: 1 2 3 4   **599.775**

1. Picture books for children 2. Foxes

ISBN 9781629792606

LC 2016942352

This "picture book from renowned science author Laurence Pringle and debut illustrator Kate Garchinsky follows a year in the life of a red fox named Vixen as she finds food, hunts, escapes threats, finds a mate, and raises her kits--all the way to the day that she and her mate watch their kits head off to lead their own secret lives." (Publisher's note)

Includes bibliographical references

599.78 Bears

Arnold, Caroline

A polar bear's world; written and illustrated by Caroline Arnold. Picture Window Books 2010 24p il (Caroline Arnold's animals) lib bdg $25.32

Grades: PreK K 1 2   **599.78**

1. Polar bear

ISBN 978-1-4048-5743-8 lib bdg; 1-4048-5743-5 lib bdg

LC 2009033366

This narrative tells the story of a polar bear from birth until it is on its own.

The story, "related in the present tense, [feels] immediate and engaging. . . . The plainness of the fact boxes contrasts with Arnold's beautiful but simple artwork, which cleanly captures the essence of [the] animal. .

. . [This book's] perfectly balanced mix of facts, story, and pictures will hold young readers' attention and help them learn." Booklist

Baines, Rebecca

A den is a bed for a bear; a book about bears. by Becky Baines. National Geographic 2008 29p il (Zig zag) $14.95; lib bdg $19.90

Grades: PreK K 1   **599.78**

1. Bears 2. Hibernation

ISBN 978-1-4263-0309-8; 1-4263-0309-2; 978-1-4263-0310-4 lib bdg; 1-4263-0310-6 lib bdg

LC 2008-07221

"Readers curiosity will be piqued by the vibrant color photographs, accommodating illustrations, large font size, and helpful captions. Special features include drawings superimposed over photographs, and a zigzag path at the end of . . . [the] book prompting readers to further explore the topic in new and fun ways." SLJ

Barner, Bob

Bears! bears! bears! Chronicle Books 2010 un il $14.99

Grades: PreK K 1   **599.78**

1. Bears -- Fiction

ISBN 978-0-8118-7057-3; 0-8118-7057-X

"Collages rendered in vibrant hues lead youngsters through a fanciful expedition. The colorful spreads and rhyming text will entertain children as they discover the variety of bears found around the world. . . . Two concluding spreads contain facts about bears and ursine habitats. . . . Beginning readers might like to attempt this one on their own." SLJ

Bekoff, Marc

Jasper's story; saving moon bears. by Jill Robinson & Marc Bekoff; illustrated by Gijsbert van Frankenhuyzen. Sleeping Bear Press 2013 40 p. (reinforced) $16.99

Grades: 1 2 3 4 5   **599.78**

1. Bears 2. Animal welfare 3. Wildlife rescue 4. Asiatic black bear

ISBN 1585367982; 9781585367986

LC 2012033687

This book by Jill Robinson was written after she encountered the practice of bear farming in China. The book "tells of one moon bear [Jasper] and how he came to symbolize the forgiveness and trust that come with love. . . . At the time of his rescue, he was both physically and emotionally battered, but through the gentle care of Robinson and her helpers, he can play and interact with other bears and humans, and seems to have forgiven the cruelties that were once inflicted upon him." (School Library Journal)

Berman, Ruth

Let's look at brown bears. Lerner Publications Co. 2010 32p il map (Lightning Bolt Books: Animal close-ups) lib bdg $25.26

Grades: PreK K 1 2   **599.78**

1. Bears

ISBN 978-0-7613-3890-1 lib bdg; 0-7613-3890-X lib bdg

LC 2008-51855

Introduces the Alaskan brown bear, describing its physical characteristics, hibernation behavior, and feeding habits

"Fresh photography, a creative use of graphics, and a collagelike layout make[s] . . . [this book] eye-catching. . . . [The] book ends with a labeled diagram of the animal, a range map, and a further-reading list that includes print and online resources in a single list, a nice way of validating both types of materials." SLJ

Includes glossary

Bodden, Valerie

Polar bears. Creative Education 2010 24p il (Amazing animals) lib bdg $24.25

Grades: K 1 2   **599.78**

1. Polar bear

ISBN 978-1-58341-811-6 lib bdg; 1-58341-811-3 lib bdg

LC 2009002714

A basic exploration of the appearance, behavior, and habitat of polar bears, Earth's biggest land predators. Also included is a story from folklore explaining why polar bears have short tails.

This is illustrated with "dynamically colored photographs." Booklist

Includes bibliographical references

Brett, Jeannie

Wild about bears; Jeannie Brett. Charlesbridge 2013 32 p. col. ill., col. map (softcover) $7.95

Grades: K 1 2 3   **599.78**

1. Bears

ISBN 1580894194; 9781580894180; 9781580894197; 9781607346364

LC 2012038700

This children's book, written and illustrated by Jeannie Brett, offers a "comprehensive look at the world's eight bear species focuses first on common physical traits and behaviors before profiling each bear. [Topics include] the habits and habitats of the polar bear, brown bear, American black bear, spectacled bear, Asiatic black bear, sloth bear, sun bear, and giant panda." (Publisher's note)

"This fact-filled guide provides an overview of each species, focusing on their physical and behavioral characteristics in relationship to their environments. After initial introductory paragraphs, Brett scatters brief, captionlike sentences throughout her warm, naturalistic watercolor scenes." Pub Wkly

Includes bibliographical references and index

Davies, Nicola, 1958-

★ Ice bear; in the steps of the polar bear. illustrated by Gary Blythe. Candlewick Press 2005 un il $16.99

Grades: K 1 2 3   **599.78**

1. Polar bear

ISBN 0-7636-2759-3

Describes how the polar bear, also called Nanuk, thrives in the Arctic and explains the lessons that the Inuit people have learned from watching the creature.

"This inviting picture book delivers facts about polar bears and conveys respect for their adaptive success. . . . Children will be fascinated by the impressionistic oil paintings of stunning polar settings and bears at play, tenderly nursing young, and, yes, hunting seals, an activity represented by a stark image of a bear's crimson-stained muzzle that may startle the youngest readers." Booklist

De Vries, Maggie

Fraser bear; a cub's life. illustrated by Renné Benoit. Greystone Books 2010 il $16.95

Grades: 2 3 4   **599.78**

1. Bears 2. Salmon

ISBN 978-1-55365-521-3; 1-55365-521-4

"Set along British Columbia's Fraser River and arranged chronologically by months of the year, this story follows a cub from his birth through his first season of independence. With each phase of his growth, the life cycle of the chinook salmon is also explained as they migrate out to the ocean then back up the river to spawn and die, providing an abundance of rich food for Fraser and other animals. . . . A good resource for any study of the life cycle of bears or salmon." SLJ

Firestone, Mary

Top 50 reasons to care about giant pandas; animals in peril. Enslow Publishers 2010 103p il (Top 50 reasons to care about endangered animals) lib bdg $31.93

Grades: 4 5 6 7   **599.78**

1. Giant panda 2. Endangered species

ISBN 978-0-7660-3451-8 lib bdg; 0-7660-3451-8 lib bdg

LC 2008-48953

This describes the giant panda's life cycle, habitat, young, diet, living in the wild and in captivity, and why it is endangered

"The illustrations, mostly color photographs, represent a wonderful selection of the animals and their habitats. Reluctant readers may be enticed by this . . . simply because of the great images. This . . . would make a substantial supplement to the science curriculum when studying endangered animals." Libr Media Connect

Includes glossary and bibliographical references

Gish, Melissa

Pandas. Creative Education 2011 48p il (Living wild) lib bdg $23.95; pa $8.95

Grades: 5 6 7 8   **599.78**

1. Giant panda

ISBN 978-1-60818-082-0 lib bdg; 1-60818-082-4 lib bdg; 978-1-60818-082-0 pa; 1-60818-082-4 pa

LC 2010028311

A look at pandas, including their habitats, physical characteristics such as their black-and-white fur, behaviors, relationships with humans, and threatened status in the world today.

Includes glossary and bibliographical references

Greene, Jacqueline Dembar

Grizzly bears; saving the silvertip. by Jacqueline Dembar Greene. Bearport Pub. 2008 32p il map (America's animal comebacks) lib bdg $25.27

Grades: 2 3 4   **599.78**

1. Grizzly bear 2. Wildlife conservation

ISBN 978-1-59716-533-4 lib bdg; 1-59716-533-6 lib bdg

LC 2007012606

This describes efforts by environmentals to save the silvertip grizzly bear from extinction in the American West

This book is "well organized and [has] an easy style and an accessible vocabulary and text size . . . [and] color photographs." SLJ

Includes glossary and bibliographical references

Guiberson, Brenda Z.

Ice bears; [by] Brenda Z. Guiberson; illustrated by Ilya Spirin. Henry Holt & Co. 2008 un il $16.95

Grades: 1 2 3 4   **599.78**

1. Polar bear 2. Arctic regions

ISBN 978-0-8050-7607-3; 0-8050-7607-7

LC 2007040895

"This story of the struggle of a polar bear mother and her two cubs to survive introduces both the harsh conditions of the Arctic and the challenges of global warming for polar bears in general. Guiberson uses precise verbs and onomatopoeia to paint a picture of the daily activities of the bears while gracefully weaving in facts about their weight, diet, and climate. Spirin's detailed watercolors are surprisingly varied in depicting an essentially frozen world, using interesting perspectives." SLJ

★ Moon bear; illustrated by Ed Young. Henry Holt & Co. 2010 un il $16.99

Grades: PreK K 1 2 3 **599.78**
1. Bears
ISBN 978-0-8050-8977-6; 0-8050-8977-2
LC 2009017931
"This picture book both celebrates the endangered black moon bear in Southeast Asia and warns about the urgent threats against the species. Filled with physical details, the spare, question-and-answer text . . . is illustrated with Young's stark, large silhouette images of a beautiful, dark bear throughout the seasons." Booklist

Hamilton, Sue L.
Mauled by a bear; [by] Sue Hamilton. ABDO Pub. Co. 2010 32p il (Close encounters of the wild kind) lib bdg $27.07
Grades: 4 5 6 7 **599.78**
1. Bears 2. Animal attacks
ISBN 978-1-60453-932-5 lib bdg; 1-60453-932-1 lib bdg
LC 2009-35078
Readers learn of actual human-bear encounters, information about bears, survival strategies, and attack statistics.
"Students will be drawn to the realistic full-color photographs, the realistic diagrams of the creatures' bodies, the real-life stories told by victims, and the interesting, attractive formatting that includes text, diagrams, photographs, and graphics on each page. . . . [This is] exciting and attractive in a 'gross' sort of way and will appeal particularly to boys for both leisure reading and research." Libr Media Connect
Includes glossary

Hirsch, Rebecca E.
Top 50 reasons to care about polar bears; animals in peril. Enslow Publishers 2010 103p il (Top 50 reasons to care about endangered animals) lib bdg $31.93
Grades: 4 5 6 7 **599.78**
1. Polar bear 2. Endangered species
ISBN 978-0-7660-3458-7 lib bdg; 0-7660-3458-5 lib bdg
LC 2008-48693
This describes polar bears--their life cycle, diet, young, habitat, and reasons why they are endangered animals
"The illustrations, mostly color photographs, represent a wonderful selection of the animals and their habitats. Reluctant readers may be enticed by this . . . simply because of the great images. This . . . would make a substantial supplement to the science curriculum when studying endangered animals." Libr Media Connect
Includes glossary and bibliographical references

Hirschi, Ron
Our three bears; [by] Ron Hirschi; photographs by Thomas D. Mangelsen. Boyds Mills Press 2008 32p il $16.95
Grades: 2 3 4 5 **599.78**
1. Bears
ISBN 978-1-59078-015-2
LC 2007049380
"North America's bears—black, grizzly, and polar—are introduced in this attractive presentation made compelling by Mangelsen's full-color photographic delights. . . . Hirschi reveals the differences in each bear's hibernation patterns, habitats, diets, size, and population estimates. These short paragraphs are chock-full of information. Beginning researchers as well as young wildlife enthusiasts will find Our Three Bears well suited to their interests." SLJ
Includes bibliographical references

Kvatum, Lia
Saving Yasha; The Incredible True Story of an Adopted Moon Bear. by Lia Kvatum; photographs by Liya Pokrovskaya. National

Geographic 2012 32 p. col. ill., col. maps (hardcover) $16.95; (lib. bdg.) $25.90
Grades: 1 2 3 **599.78**
1. Bears 2. Wildlife 3. Animal behavior
ISBN 142631051X; 9781426310515; 1426310765; 9781426310768
LC 2012288404
In this book, Lia Kvatum tells the story of "Yasha, joined later by Shum and Shiksha, [who] are nurtured by" scientists after being "orphaned by poachers . . . [in] the Siberian wild. . . . Kvatum chronicles the cubs' development as they learn to forage on their own while playing together and learning to climb trees. She also notes how important it is for human observers to remain aloof . . . to prevent the animals from becoming dependent or domesticated." (Kirkus Reviews)

Leathers, Dan
Polar bears on the Hudson Bay; by Dan Leathers. Mitchell Lane Publishers 2008 32p il map (On the verge of extinction: crisis in the environment) lib bdg $17.95
Grades: 3 4 5 **599.78**
1. Polar bear
ISBN 978-1-58415-586-7
LC 2007000797
This describes the life cycle of polar bears on the Hudson Bay and how they are threatened by climate change and other environmental dangers.
"Short chapters, large font, and pronunciation guides to key words engage children doing research, but the depth of information is not compromised. . . . Colorful, up-close photographs are accompanied by satisfying explanatory captions." SLJ
Includes glossary and bibliographical references

Markle, Sandra
Grizzly bears. Lerner Publications Company 2010 39p il (Animal predators) $26.60
Grades: 4 5 6 **599.78**
1. Grizzly bear
ISBN 978-1-58013-537-5; 1-58013-537-4
LC 2008-38120
Introduces the physical characteristics, habitat, and predatory behavior of grizzly bears.
"Vivid photographs alongside Markle's narrative, which provides factual information about grizzly bears' physical characteristics and hunting behaviors, introduce readers to these majestic and dangerous creatures." Horn Book Guide
Includes glossary and bibliographical references

★ **How** many baby pandas? Walker 2009 23p il map $15.99; lib bdg $16.89
Grades: K 1 2 3 **599.78**
1. Giant panda 2. Animal babies
ISBN 978-0-8027-9783-4; 0-8027-9783-0; 978-0-8027-9784-1 lib bdg; 0-8027-9784-9 lib bdg
"Clear accessible text . . . and sharp photos provide an engaging, informative introduction to baby pandas, highlighting those born at China's Wolong Giant Panda Breeding Center in 2005. . . . Scientific concepts are well explained, and pages are filled with panda facts." Booklist
Includes glossary and bibliographical references

Marsh, Laura
Polar bears; by Laura Marsh. National Geographic Children's Books 2013 32 p. (pbk. : alk. paper) $13.90

Grades: K 1 2   **599.78**
1. Polar bear
ISBN 1426311052; 9781426311048; 9781426311055
LC 2012039727

In this book, by Laura Marsh, readers will "learn all . . . about polar bears. With their beautiful white fur and powerful presence, polar bears rule the Arctic. These majestic giants swim from iceberg to iceberg in chilling waters, care for their adorable cubs, and are threatened by global warming. [It is] complete with fascinating facts, beautiful images." (Publisher's note)

McAllister, Ian
★ **Salmon** bears; giants of the Great Bear Rainforest. [by] Ian McAllister & Nicholas Read; photographs by Ian McAllister. Orca Book Publishers 2010 89p il map pa $18.95
Grades: 5 6 7 8   **599.78**
1. Bears 2. Salmon 3. Rain forest ecology
ISBN 978-1-55469-205-7 pa; 1-55469-205-9 pa

"Read's conversational text and McAllister's excellent photos provide a perfect framework for this evocative look at the big bears of the Great Bear Rainforest of British Columbia, and an intriguing investigation of its ecological pattern of dependency. The authors present a round of seasons from one winter to the next, touching upon such topics as the effects of fish farms on wild salmon populations, what happens during a salmon run, and what the future may hold for the fish, the bears, and the Great Bear Rainforest itself. . . . Superbly readable, informative, and attractive." SLJ
Includes bibliographical references

Newman, Mark
Moon bears; Mark Newman. Henry Holt & Co. 2015 32 p. color illustrations (hardcover) $18.99
Grades: K 1 2 3   **599.78**
1. Asiatic black bear
ISBN 9780805093445
LC 2014048392

This children's book, by Mark Newman, presents information on the Asiatic black bear, also known as the moon bear. "With their big round ears, moon-shaped crescents, and irresistible personalities, there is plenty to love about moon bears. Full of fascinating facts, this book is brought to life with stunning photographs by [a] renowned wildlife photographer." (Publisher's note)
"Variations in format and arrangement of text and images provide enough visual pop to keep readers engaged." Kirkus

Polar bears. Henry Holt & Co. 2011 un il map $16.99
Grades: K 1 2 3   **599.78**
1. Polar bear
ISBN 978-0-8050-8999-8; 0-8050-8999-3
"Irresistibly endearing polar bear photographs are the highlight of this picture book, although each spread also includes a factual statement about polar bears . . . , accompanied by smaller additional text that goes into deeper detail." Horn Book
Includes bibliographical references

Olson, Gillia M.
Polar bears' search for ice; a cause and effect investigation. Capstone Press 2010 32p il map (Fact finders. Animals on the edge) lib bdg $25.99
Grades: 3 4 5 6   **599.78**
1. Polar bear 2. Greenhouse effect
ISBN 978-1-4296-4532-4 lib bdg; 1-4296-4532-6 lib bdg
LC 2010007719

"Excellent discussions address those who doubt the severity of the issue and those who wonder why people should care what happens to animals. The captioned photographs are timely and poignant. . . . [This] makes serious subject matter interesting and accessible." SLJ
Includes glossary and bibliographical references

Rosing, Norbert
Face to face with polar bears; by Norbert Rosing with Elizabeth Carney. National Geographic 2007 32p il (Face to face) $16.95; lib bdg $25.90
Grades: 3 4 5 6   **599.78**
1. Polar bear
ISBN 978-1-4263-0139-1; 978-1-4263-0140-7 lib bdg
LC 2006032847

"Rosing tells how he and his wife tried to fend off a polar bear 'with a toothache' and a yen for their spaghetti dinner while they waited for a helicopter rescue. The book describes the animal's diet, physical features, and habitat, and the dangers of global warming. . . . [This] attractive, smoothly written [book], topped off with advice about self-directed research, will catch the attention of enthusiasts and motivate them toward personal investigation." SLJ
Includes glossary and bibliographical references

Polar bears. Firefly Books 2010 55p il map $19.95; pa $9.95
Grades: 3 4 5   **599.78**
1. Polar bear
ISBN 978-1-55407-599-7; 1-55407-599-8; 978-1-55407-623-9 pa; 1-55407-623-4 pa
LC 2010294457

Photographs and captions present the life of polar bears across the four seasons of the year. Topics covered include habitat activities, diet, anatomy, and survival.
"The high quality of the photos and their reproduction will draw many readers to this visually appealing book, which provides plenty of worthwhile information in the captions and back matter." Booklist

Ryder, Joanne
A **pair** of polar bears; twin cubs find a home at the San Diego Zoo. photos by the world-famous San Diego Zoo. Simon & Schuster Books for Young Readers 2006 un il $16.95
Grades: K 1 2   **599.78**
1. Polar bear
ISBN 0-689-85871-X
LC 2005014013

"This photo-essay introduces children to an engaging, true story from the San Diego Zoo. . . . The stars are rescued polar bear twins Tatqiq and Kalluk, who progress through the photo-rich pages from needy, quarantined cubs to fully acclimated adults with mastery over their outdoor habitat. The images, all provided by the zoo and most sharply focused and closeup, will elicit coos from readers." Booklist

Sartore, Joel
★ **Face** to face with grizzlies. National Geographic 2007 32p il (Face to face) $16.95; lib bdg $25.90
Grades: 3 4 5 6   **599.78**
1. Grizzly bear
ISBN 978-1-4263-0050-9; 1-4263-0050-6; 978-1-4263-0051-6 lib bdg; 1-4263-0051-4 lib bdg
LC 2006-20500

"In accessible, exciting language, Sartore . . . describes his close encounters with bears while on assignment. . . . He matches stunning photographs of bears playing, fighting, eating, and chasing prey . . . with basic information about bears' bodies, habitats, and behavior." Booklist
Includes bibliographical references

Schreiber, Anne

Pandas. National Geographic 2010 32p il (National Geographic readers) pa $3.99

Grades: 1 2 3   599.78

1. Giant panda

ISBN 978-1-4263-0610-5; 1-4263-0610-5

This describes pandas and their behavior.

Schwabacher, Martin

Bears; by Martin Schwabacher with Terry Miller Shannon. Marshall Cavendish Benchmark 2010 24p il map (Animals) lib bdg $16.95

Grades: 3 4 5   599.78

1. Bears

ISBN 978-0-7614-3820-5 lib bdg; 0-7614-3820-3 lib bdg

"The straightforward presentation of the information and the uncluttered and attractive layout make [this] . . . good . . . for reports. Color photographs . . . are well utilized and complete a solid package." SLJ

Includes glossary and bibliographical references

Sirota, Lyn A.

Giant pandas. Capstone Press 2010 24p il map (Pebble plus. Asian animals) lib bdg $22.65

Grades: PreK K 1   599.78

1. Giant panda

ISBN 978-1-4296-4028-2; 1-4296-4028-6

"This . . . is an excellent resource for great pictures and information to share with students in storytimes or to support other content areas. This will be an excellent addition to nonfiction collections, especially for very young readers." Libr Media Connect

Includes bibliographical references

Swinburne, Stephen R.

★ Black bear; North America's bear. Boyds Mills 2003 32p il map $15.95

Grades: 3 4 5   599.78

1. Bears

ISBN 1-59078-023-X

An examination of black bears, their behavior and habitat.

"Stunning, full-color photos and a lively text make for an intriguing introduction to these fascinating animals." SLJ

Thomson, Sarah L.

Where do polar bears live? illustrated by Jason Chin. Collins 2010 37p il (Let's-read-and-find-out science) $16.99; pa $5.99

Grades: K 1 2 3   599.78

1. Polar bear 2. Arctic regions

ISBN 978-0-06-157518-1; 0-06-157518-6; 978-0-06-157517-4 pa; 0-06-157517-8 pa

LC 2008056030

"This title explores a year in the life of a polar bear, focusing on facts about the animal's diet, hunting techniques, and habitat. Thomson also covers the impact of global warming on polar bears' food sources. . . . This is an affecting introduction to polar bears and their threatened existence for young children." Booklist

Walker, Sally M.

Winnie; the remarkable tale of a real bear. Sally M. Walker; illustrated by Jonathan D. Voss. Henry Holt & Co. 2015 40 p. color illustrations, portraits (hardcover) $17.99 599.78

1. Bears 2. World War, 1914-1918 3. Black bear 4. Winnipeg (Bear) 5. Canada. Canadian Armed Forces -- Mascots 6. Winnie-

the-Pooh (Fictitious character) -- History

ISBN 9780805097153; 0805097155

LC 2014028434

In this children's book, by Sally M. Walker, illustrated by Jonathan D. Voss, "Harry Colebourn saw a baby bear for sale at the train station [and] he knew he could care for it. Harry was a veterinarian. But he was also a soldier in training for World War I. Harry named the bear Winnie, short for Winnipeg, his company's home town, and he brought her along to the training camp in England. . . . But who could care for the bear when Harry had to go to the battleground in France?" (Publisher's note)

Includes bibliographical references

599.786 Polar bear

Markle, Sandra, 1946-

Waiting for ice; by Sandra Markle; illustrated by Alan Marks. Charlesbridge 2012 32 p.

Grades: 1 2 3   599.786

1. Polar bear 2. Arctic region 3. Global warming 4. Polar bear -- Effect of global warming on

ISBN 1580892558; 9781580892551; 9781580892568

LC 2011002113

This children's book by Sandra Markle, illustrated by Alan Marks, "provides a . . . look at polar bears, the largest hunters on land, in this narrative that follows an orphaned cub barely old enough to survive on her own. Trapped on Wrangel Island in the Arctic Sea, waiting late into the fall for the annual floating pack ice to form, she and other polar bears subsist on the few animals they can find—typically only birds and walruses, as a note on global warming explains. . . . [The story offers a] look at how polar bears survive during so much of the year, when there's no ice to help them in their hunt for seals in the Arctic waters." (Kirkus)

599.79 Marine carnivores

Arnold, Caroline

A walrus' world; written and illustrated by Caroline Arnold. Picture Window Books 2010 24p il (Caroline Arnold's animals) lib bdg $25.32

Grades: PreK K 1 2   599.79

1. Walruses

ISBN 978-1-4048-5744-5 lib bdg; 1-4048-5744-3 lib bdg

LC 2009033380

This narrative tells the story of a walrus from birth until it can live on its own.

The story, "related in the present tense, [feels] immediate and engaging. . . . The plainness of the fact boxes contrasts with Arnold's beautiful but simple artwork, which cleanly captures the essence of [the] animal. . . . [This book's] perfectly balanced mix of facts, story, and pictures will hold young readers' attention and help them learn." Booklist

Butterworth, Chris

See what a seal can do! by Chris Butterworth and illustrated by Kate Nelms. Candlewick Press 2013 32 p. $14.99

Grades: K 1 2   599.79

1. Marine animals 2. Seals (Animals)

ISBN 0763665746; 9780763665746

LC 2012947729

This book, by Chris Butterworth and illustrated by Kate Nelms, features illustrations that "portray the seal's transformation from awkward land dweller to sinuous and powerful denizen of the deep. The below-water scenes . . . evoke the murky ocean habitat and the singular seal's steep descent to the bottom." (School Library Journal)

Green, Jen

California sea lion; by Jen Green. Bearport Publishing 2013 24 p. (library binding) $23.93

Grades: 1 2   **599.79**

1. Sea lions 2. California sea lion

ISBN 1617729191; 9781617729195

LC 2013011505

In this book, by Jen Green, "readers will explore the underwater world of the marine mammal [the California sea lion] through clear text, full-color photos, and diagrams. Age-appropriate activities, such as researching how California sea lions compare to other pinnipeds, [are designed to] give readers a chance to make observations and to develop animal-science skills." (Publisher's note)

Includes bibliographical references and index

Harvey, Jeanne

Astro the Steller sea lion; illustrated by Shennen Bersani. Sylvan Dell Pub. 2010 un il $16.95; pa $8.95

Grades: 1 2 3   **599.79**

1. Seals (Animals) -- Fiction

ISBN 978-1-60718-076-0; 1-60718-076-6; 978-1-60718-087-6 pa; 1-60718-087-1 pa

LC 2010-921908

"Harvey tells a gentle tale of an orphaned Steller sea lion pup whose early imprinting on his human nurturers at the Marine Mammal Center in Sausalito, CA, leaves him determinedly reluctant to live in the wild on any terms. Bersani's nearly photographic illustrations keep perfect time with the simple text." SLJ

Hengel, Katherine

It's a baby Australian fur seal! ABDO 2010 24p il (Baby Australian animals) lib bdg $19.93

Grades: K 1 2 3   **599.79**

1. Animal babies 2. Seals (Animals)

ISBN 978-1-60453-574-7 lib bdg; 1-60453-574-1 lib bdg

LC 2008-55073

This book about fur seals "is a great choice. Though the focus of . . . [the] book is the animal baby, the reader will learn a great many facts. Information includes how they are born, how they are fed, age of independence, food, habitat, predators, and features that help them find food and protect themselves. . . . This . . . is a sound addition for any school library." Libr Media Connect

Includes glossary

Malam, John

Pinnipeds; written by John Malam; created and designed by David Salariya. Franklin Watts 2009 32p il (Scary creatures) lib bdg $26; pa $8.95

Grades: 3 4 5   **599.79**

1. Walruses 2. Marine mammals 3. Seals (Animals)

ISBN 978-0-531-21672-9 lib bdg; 0-531-21672-1 lib bdg; 978-0-531-21043-7 pa; 0-531-21043-X pa

LC 2009010799

This defines pinnipeds and describes their life cycles, habitats, behavior, and relationship to humans

This title has "two-page chapters of accessible, large-type text and bright color photos and illustrations. . . . The series distinguishes itself with 'X-Ray Vision.' When readers hold the page with this prompt up to the light, an image emerges. The X-rays mostly show the skeletal structures of the animals. Text boxes throughout add to the visual ap-

peal. . . . [This title is an] excellent [resource] for school assignments and browsing." SLJ

Includes glossary

Markovics, Joyce L.

Weddell seal; fat and happy. by Joyce L. Markovics. Bearport Pub. 2009 32p il map (Uncommon animals) lib bdg $25.27

Grades: 1 2 3   **599.79**

1. Seals (Animals)

ISBN 978-1-59716-734-5 lib bdg; 1-59716-734-7 lib bdg

LC 2008-14391

"The explanatory text works spendidly, with large photographs that bring readers as close as they'll ever get to such beasts." Booklist

Includes glossary and bibliographical references

Metz, Lorijo

Discovering sea lions. PowerKids Press 2011 24p il (Along the shore) lib bdg $21.25

Grades: 3 4 5   **599.79**

1. Seals (Animals)

ISBN 978-1-4488-4992-5; 1-4488-4992-6

LC 2010047570

This book about sea lions "briefly describes the major physical and behavioral characteristics common to all [sea lions] and one or two distinctive characteristics of about a half dozen species. . . . [The book] outlines the major physical differences between [sea lions] and seals. . . . One or two sharp color photographs of representative species, most of which are closeups, accompany the text on every page. . . . [This is] well organized and smoothly written in an engaging style." SLJ

Includes glossary

Peterson, Brenda

★ **Leopard** & Silkie; one boy's quest to save the seal pups. by Brenda Peterson; photographs by Robin Lindsey. 1st ed. Henry Holt and Co. (BYR) 2012 32 p. col. ill. (hardback) $16.99

Grades: 1 2 3   **599.79**

1. Compassion 2. Animal welfare 3. Seals (Animals) 4. Wildlife rescue 5. Seals (Animals) -- Conservation

ISBN 080509167X; 9780805091670

LC 2011029041

Author Brenda Peterson tells the story of "concerned volunteers [who] become seal sitters [in the Pacific Northwest], keeping vigil over the vulnerable baby seals that are left on the shore while their mothers hunt for food. . . . With its emphasis on human compassion, this true account teaches children to appreciate the natural world by helping in any way they can. The star of the book is six year old Miles, who organizes his own rescue mission to help the seals survive." (Publisher's note)

Includes bibliographical references.

Read, Tracy C.

Exploring the world of seals and walruses. Firefly 2011 24p il (Exploring the world of) $16.95; pa $6.95

Grades: 4 5 6   **599.79**

1. Walruses 2. Seals (Animals)

ISBN 978-1-55407-784-7; 1-55407-784-2; 978-1-55407-797-7 pa; 1-55407-797-4 pa

This describes the physical features, habitats, diets, and behavior of seals and walruses.

A "well-organized [text] and good-quality pictures taken from photo archives provide the basics. . . . [This focuses] on the different habitats and challenges faced by three pinniped subgroups: eared and earless seals and the walrus. Insets of information in colorful circles add to the attractive configuration. [The book offers] simple language and good use of space." SLJ

Rebman, Renee C.

Walruses. Marshall Cavendish Benchmark 2011 il (Animals, animals) lib bdg $20.95

Grades: 3 4 5   **599.79**

1. Walruses

ISBN 978-0-7614-4881-5; 0-7614-4881-0

LC 2010016036

This offers information on the anatomy, special skills, habitats, and diet of walruses.

This offers "comprehensive text and striking, well-chosen photos. . . . [This is] packed with engaging facts and trivia, as well as an upbeat tone." Booklist

Includes glossary and bibliographical references

Riggs, Kate

Sea lions; Kate Riggs. Creative Education 2015 24 p. (Amazing Animals) $7.99

Grades: K 1 2   **599.79**

1. Animals -- Folklore 2. Sea lions

ISBN 0898129281; 9780898129281; 9781608185160

LC 2013051259

"A basic exploration of the appearance, behavior, and habitat of sea lions, oceanic mammals related to seals. Also included is a story from folklore explaining why Japanese fishers respected sea lions. . . . Photos are paired with accessible text to examine the [sea lion's] appearance, habitat, behaviors, and life cycle." (Publisher's note)

"Large, appealing photos on each spread include more vivid close-ups, showing both animals' faces as well as the creatures in action. Across from the photos, the text is laid out cleanly in a large, clear font, and the sentences are simple and easy to read. Photo captions, meanwhile, add interesting facts, while occasional vocabulary words are defined at the bottoms of pages." Booklist

Snyder, Eleanor

Alarming leopard seals; Eleanor Snyder. Gareth Stevens Publishing 2017 24 p. color ill., color map (ebook) $22.60; (library bound) $22.60

Grades: 3 4 5   **599.79**

1. Leopard seal 2. Marine animals

ISBN 9781482449037; 9781482448979; 9781482449099; 9781482449150

LC 2015046971

In this children's book in the Cutest Animals...That Could Kill You! series by Eleanor Snyder, "leopard seals look so cute, but even their name gives us a clue about their true nature: they're carnivores with a taste for penguin meat. The marine mammals' size, sometimes exceeding 12 feet (3.7 m), makes them dangerous, even to people. This absorbing volume combines attention-grabbing text with exciting photographs of leopard seals in their native habitats." (Publisher's note)

"An informative, highly readable, and high-interest series." Booklist

Includes bibliographical references and index

Spilsbury, Louise

Seal. Heinemann Library 2011 24p il (A day in the life. sea animals) lib bdg $22; pa $6.49

Grades: 1 2   **599.79**

1. Seals (Animals)

ISBN 978-1-4329-4002-7 lib bdg; 1-4329-4002-3 lib bdg; 978-1-4329-4009-6 pa; 1-4329-4009-0 pa

LC 2010000628

This book follows a seal through its day as it sleeps, eats, and moves.

This pairs "well-chosen color photos . . . with one or two sentences of simple commentary for each. . . . [Though this title] includes refer-ences to several varieties of the chosen creature, one species in particular is highlighted. . . . [Good choice] for pleasure or purpose reading." SLJ

Includes glossary and bibliographical references

599.8   Primates

Aronin, Miriam

Aye-aye; an evil omen. by Miriam Aronin. Bearport Pub. 2009 32p il map (Uncommon animals) lib bdg $25.27

Grades: 1 2 3   **599.8**

1. Lemurs 2. Aye-aye (Animal)

ISBN 978-1-59716-731-4 lib bdg; 1-59716-731-2 lib bdg

LC 2008-15387

This describes the aye-aye, a lemur from Madagascar, believed, according to legend, to be an evil omen

"The explanatory text works splendidly, with large photographs that bring readers as close as they'll ever get to such beasts." Booklist

Includes glossary and bibliographical references

Barker, David

Top 50 reasons to care about great apes; animals in peril. Enslow Publishers 2010 103p il (Top 50 reasons to care about endangered animals) lib bdg $31.93

Grades: 4 5 6 7   **599.8**

1. Apes 2. Endangered species

ISBN 978-0-7660-3456-3 lib bdg; 0-7660-3456-9 lib bdg

LC 2008048691

This describes the great apes—their life cycle, habitats, young, and why these animals are endangered

"The illustrations, mostly color photographs, represent a wonderful selection of the animals and their habitats. Reluctant readers may be enticed by this . . . simply because of the great images." Libr Media Connect

Includes glossary and bibliographical references

Bodden, Valerie

Monkeys. Creative Education 2010 24p il (Amazing animals) lib bdg $24.25

Grades: K 1 2   **599.8**

1. Monkeys

ISBN 978-1-58341-808-6 lib bdg; 1-58341-808-3 lib bdg

LC 2009002710

A basic exploration of the appearance, behavior, and habitat of monkeys, a family of tree-climbing mammals. Also included is a story from folklore explaining why monkeys look like people.

Includes bibliographical references

Bredeson, Carmen

Orangutans up close; [by] Carmen Bredeson. Enslow Elementary 2008 24p il (Zoom in on animals!) lib bdg $21.26

Grades: 1 2 3   **599.8**

1. Orangutan

ISBN 978-0-7660-3078-7 lib bdg; 0-7660-3078-4 lib bdg

LC 2007039466

"Short paragraphs of simply written text describe [orangutans'] key body parts and how they function. . . . Behavior, diet, and care and development of the young are briefly addressed. Facing the text on each spread is a full-page, sharp, color closeup. . . . Bredeson's simply written and colorful [title] will provide younger readers with [a] satisfying first [introduction] to these fascinating creatures." SLJ

Includes glossary and bibliographical references

Burnham, Cathleen

Doyli to the Rescue; Saving Baby Monkeys in the Amazon. by Cathleen Burnham. Itasca Books 2015 32 p. color ill. and photos $18.95

Grades: K 1 2　　　**599.8**

1. Animal rescue

ISBN 1933987227; 9781933987224

In this book, by Cathleen Burnham, "10-year-old Doyli, with the help of her family, rescues endangered, orphaned monkeys from the perils of native hunters and the black market. She carries the rescued animals home to her island home in the Peruvian Amazon, where she nurtures them with her strong medicine of love and nourishing food. When the little monkey orphans are old enough and strong enough, she releases them back to their natural habitat: the Amazon rainforest." (Publisher's note)

"A fluid narrative makes this informational text a fun read-aloud, in addition to a research resource." Booklist

Bustos, Eduardo

Going ape! Eduardo Bustos. Tundra Books of Northern New York 2012 24 p. col. ill. (hardcover) $9.95

Grades: K 1 2　　　**599.8**

1. Apes 2. Monkeys 3. Gorillas 4. Primates

ISBN 1770492828; 9781770492820

LC 2011923289

In this book, "[Eduardo] Bustos offers simple facts about a variety of primates, from the well-known gorilla to the lesser-known De Brazza's monkey." The illustrations offer "large close-ups of face of the different apes on the recto, and one or two sentences and a smaller illustration of each one on the verso." (School Library Journal)

Coxon, Michele

Termites on a stick; a chimp learns to use a tool. by Michèle Coxon. Star Bright Books 2008 un il $17.95; pa $7.95

Grades: PreK K 1 2　　　**599.8**

1. Termites 2. Chimpanzees

ISBN 978-1-59572-121-1; 1-59572-121-5; 978-1-59572-183-9 pa; 1-59572-183-5 pa

"A young chimpanzee is rewarded with a tasty treat once he figures out how to fish termites out of their nest. Simple text and realistic paintings follow Little Chimp and his mother through a day in which the youngster emulates his mother's use of a handy tool.... Carefully crafted, this picture-book introduction to tool-using chimps could work as a read-aloud story or as independent reading." SLJ

Ganeri, Anita

Howler monkey. Heinemann Library 2011 24p il map (A day in the life. Rain forest animals) lib bdg $22; pa $6.49

Grades: 1 2　　　**599.8**

1. Monkeys

ISBN 978-1-4329-4113-0 lib bdg; 1-4329-4113-5 lib bdg; 978-1-4329-4124-6 pa; 1-4329-4124-0 pa

LC 2010001137

This book follows a day in the life of a howler monkey.

"Ganeri presents information clearly and simply in large type, two-sentence comments placed below a bright, sharply reproduced color photograph of the animal in a natural setting.... [This is] sufficiently specific to support assignment as well as pleasure reading." SLJ

Includes glossary and bibliographical references

Lemur. Heinemann Library 2011 24p il map (A day in the life. Rain forest animals) lib bdg $22; pa $6.49

Grades: 1 2　　　**599.8**

1. Lemurs

ISBN 978-1-4329-4111-6 lib bdg; 1-4329-4111-9 lib bdg; 978-1-4329-4122-2 pa; 1-4329-4122-4 pa

LC 2010001134

This book follows a lemur through its day as it sleeps, eats, and moves.

"Ganeri presents information clearly and simply in large type, two-sentence comments placed below a bright, sharply reproduced color photograph of the animal in a natural setting.... [This is] sufficiently specific to support assignment as well as pleasure reading." SLJ

Includes glossary and bibliographical references

Orangutan. Heinemann Library 2011 24p il map (A day in the life. Rain forest animals) lib bdg $22; pa $6.49

Grades: 1 2　　　**599.8**

1. Orangutan

ISBN 978-1-4329-4107-9 lib bdg; 1-4329-4107-0 lib bdg; 978-1-4329-4118-5 pa; 1-4329-4118-6 pa

LC 2010000966

This book follows an orangutan through its day as it sleeps, eats, and moves.

"Ganeri presents information clearly and simply in large type, two-sentence comments placed below a bright, sharply reproduced color photograph of the animal in a natural setting.... [This is] sufficiently specific to support assignment as well as pleasure reading." SLJ

Includes glossary and bibliographical references

Gibbons, Gail

Gorillas. Holiday House 2010 32p il map $17.95

Grades: K 1 2 3　　　**599.8**

1. Gorillas

ISBN 978-0-8234-2236-4; 0-8234-2236-4

LC 2010012418

"In her familiar, winning style, Gibbons introduces wild gorillas. Through detailed watercolor illustrations, she takes readers to Africa to explore the habitat and diet of the western lowland, eastern lowland, and mountain gorillas.... Readers will enjoy examining the many inset diagrams and maps that accompany the informational text, and they're sure to find Gibbons's 'extras,' like the skeletal view of a gorilla's jaw, fascinating." SLJ

Gish, Melissa

Gorillas. Creative Education 2010 46p il (Living wild) $23.95; pa $9.95

Grades: 5 6 7 8　　　**599.8**

1. Gorillas

ISBN 978-1-58341-969-4; 1-58341-969-1; 978-0-89812-552-8 pa; 0-89812-552-9 pa

LC 2010017374

This "book lucidly discusses conservation and the animals' often tenuous relationship with humans. The layout is uniformly simple but effective, constructed with a nice balance of main text for the report writers, smaller chunks of esoterica for browsers, and ... killer photos." Booklist

Goodall, Jane, 1934-

Chimpanzee Children of Gombe; by Jane Goodall; photography by Michael Neugebauer. minedition 2014 64 p. color illustrations $19.99

Grades: K 1 2 3　　　**599.8**

1. Chimpanzees 2. Endangered species 3. Chimpanzees -- Behavior

ISBN 9789888240838; 9888240838

This book, by Jane Goodall, with photography by Michael Neugebauer, shares "stories and photos of chimpanzee children living in the Gombe National Park. . . . Dr. Goodall has campaigned unceasingly for the protection of the chimpanzee—now an endangered species—and this moving, personal account will educate readers about the many threats to the animals in the wild and inspire readers of all ages to join in her vital work." (Publisher's note)

"Absorbing photographs from publisher Neugebauer provide intimate glimpses of baby chimps playing with family members, as well as of the other animals that populate the Gombe. A lovely look at Goodall's service to the welfare of the great apes." Pub Wkly

Greenberg, Daniel A.
Chimpanzees; by Dan Greenberg, with Christina Wilsdon. Marshall Cavendish Benchmark 2010 24p il map (Benchmark rockets. Animals) lib bdg $16.95
Grades: 3 4 5   **599.8**
1. Chimpanzees
ISBN 978-0-7614-4341-4; 0-7614-4341-X
LC 2008-52102

"The straightforward presentation of the information and the uncluttered and attractive layout make [this title] . . . good . . . for reports. Color photographs . . . are well utilized and complete a solid package." SLJ

Includes glossary and bibliographical references

Jenkins, Martin
★ **Ape**; illustrated by Vicky White. Candlewick Press 2007 45p il $16.99
Grades: K 1 2 3   **599.8**
1. Apes
ISBN 978-0-7636-3471-1; 0-7636-3471-9
LC 2007023456

Close-up illustrations and facts about five great apes: chimps, orangutans, bonobos, gorillas, and humans.

"Working in oil and pencil, White portrays [the apes] . . . as having psychologically complex, fully realized personalities. The pictures are consistently stunning. . . . Jenkins's . . . economical, conservation-oriented text ably sets each scene . . . . while occasional captions add information about the apes' habitat or behavior." Publ Wkly

Kalman, Bobbie
Baby primates; by Bobbie Kalman. Crabtree Publishing Company 2013 24 p. (library) $22.60; (paperback) $6.95
Grades: 1 2 3 4   **599.8**
1. Primates 2. Habitat (Ecology) 3. Primates -- Infancy
ISBN 0778710076; 9780778710073; 9780778710110
LC 2012043728

In this book by Bobbie Kalman "simple text and captivating photos inform young readers about [primates] and the different groups to which they belong, including monkeys, apes, humans, lemurs, and more. Children will also learn about the habitats of baby primates and why some are endangered." (Publisher's note)

Includes bibliographical references and index.

Laman, Tim
★ **Face** to face with orangutans; by Tim Laman & Cheryl Knott. National Geographic 2009 31p il (Face to face) $16.95; lib bdg $25.90
Grades: 3 4 5 6   **599.8**
1. Orangutan
ISBN 978-1-4263-0464-4; 1-4263-0464-1; 978-1-4263-0465-1 lib bdg; 1-4263-0465-X lib bdg
LC 2009-00170

The authors describe orangutan behavior and their personal encounters with orangutans in Borneo.

Includes glossary and bibliographical references

Mad about monkeys; illustrated by Owen Davey. Flying Eye Books 2015 40 p. color illustrations (hardcover) $19.95
Grades: K 1 2 3 4 5   **599.8**
1. Monkeys
ISBN 9781909263574; 1909263575

This children's book, illustrated by Owen Davey, "explores the many different types of monkeys from the smallest Pygmy Marmoset to the largest Mandrill, and provides all the facts you wanted to know and more. Discover where monkeys come from, how they swing from tree to tree, and why they fight and play with each other." (Publisher's note)

"The design of the book is stellar, interweaving text and stylized-but-accurate illustrations into a vibrant, cohesive whole that stands out for its appeal and clarity. A vast amount of information on monkeys is expertly delivered in both text and image without patronizing either readers or monkeys—a delight." Kirkus

Mattern, Joanne
Orangutans. Capstone Press 2010 24p il map (Pebble plus. Asian animals) lib bdg $22.65
Grades: PreK K 1   **599.8**
1. Orangutan
ISBN 978-1-4296-4030-5; 1-4296-4030-8

"This . . . is an excellent resource for great pictures and information to share with students in storytimes or to support other content areas. This will be an excellent addition to nonfiction collections, especially for young readers." Libr Media Connect

Includes bibliographical references (p. 23)

Nichols, Michael
★ **Face** to face with gorillas; by Michael Nick Nichols with Elizabeth Carney. National Geographic 2009 31p il map (Face to face) $16.95; lib bdg $25.90
Grades: 3 4 5 6   **599.8**
1. Gorillas
ISBN 978-1-4263-0406-4; 1-4263-0406-4; 978-1-4263-0407-1 lib bdg; 1-4263-0407-2 lib bdg
LC 2008023002

"Nichols has spent much of his life raising awareness about the plight of gorillas, and through brief text and accompanying photographs he shares some of his experiences as well as information about their family structure, habits, habitats, and connections to humans. . . . The attractive format will appeal to the intended audience." Booklist

Includes glossary and bibliographical references

Rockwood, Leigh
Chimpanzees are smart! PowerKids Press 2010 24p il (Super smart animals) lib bdg $21.25; pa $8.25
Grades: 2 3 4 5   **599.8**
1. Chimpanzees
ISBN 978-1-4358-9375-7 lib bdg; 1-4358-9375-1 lib bdg; 978-1-4358-9840-0 pa; 1-4358-9840-0 pa

This book examines the intelligence of chimpanzees.

"Readers get an overview of the . . . [chimpanzee's] life cycle, its domestic history (where relevant), and natural habitat, and examples of how it is smart in the wild as well as when helped by human tutelage. . . . Interesting color photographs and large, easy-to-read print will attract browsers and report writers alike." SLJ

Includes glossary

Sayre, April Pulley

Meet the howlers; illustrated by Woody Miller. Charlesbridge 2010 un il lib bdg $16.95

Grades: K 1 2   **599.8**

1. Monkeys

ISBN 978-1-57091-733-2 lib bdg; 1-57091-733-7 lib bdg

LC 2009-3953

"Sayre's . . . latest is a rhyming introduction to the howler monkeys of Central and South America. Verses appear in a jaunty typeface atop . . . Miller's full-bleed spreads; prose paragraphs in smaller type provide additional information. . . . A solid read-aloud for young animal enthusiasts." Publ Wkly

Schindel, John

Busy gorillas; [by] John Schindel, Andy Rouse. Tricycle Press 2010 un il (A busy book) bd bk $6.99

Grades: PreK   **599.8**

1. Gorillas 2. Board books for children

ISBN 978-1-58246-352-0 bd bk; 1-58246-352-2 bd bk

Simple text and color photographs describe gorillas participating in various activities.

"Intimate close-ups of winsome baby faces and blurred, movement-filled action photos combine with more standard longshots of our primate cousins. Playfully active text . . . and vivid color-block backgrounds help to keep the necessarily limited palette . . . sparkling. Another standout." Kirkus

599.86   Old World monkeys

Daly, Ruth

Mandrills; Ruth Daly. AV2 by Weigl 2014 24 p. color illustrations (hard cover : alk. paper) $27.13

Grades: 3 4 5   **599.86**

1. Mandrill 2. Primates

ISBN 9781489628824; 9781489628831

LC 2014038984

This book in the Amazing Primates series, by Ruth Daly, "introduces young readers to some of the most fascinating primates on Earth. Readers will explore the history, natural habitats, physical features, diets, myths and legends, and life cycles of the world's most fascinating primates. Did you know that mandrills have large cheek pouches? They can store almost a stomach-load of food inside these pouches." (Publisher's note)

"Readers and report writers will not be disappointed." SLJ

599.865   Baboons

Roumanis, Alexis

Baboons; Alexis Roumanis. AV2 by Weigl 2014 24 p. color illustrations hbk $27.13

Grades: 3 4 5   **599.865**

1. Baboons

ISBN 9781489628664; 9781489628671; 1489628665

LC 2014038981

This book, by Alexis Roumanis, "offer[s] a comprehensive look at [baboons]. Standard information is covered, along with charts and diagrams that introduce additional material. A chart called 'Comparing Primates,' for example, describes each of the six superfamilies. Physical features and life cycle are described as well. 'History' and 'Myths and Legends' pages add further context, while an 'Activity' page and re-

view questions help readers to consider what they've learned." (School Library Journal)

Includes bibliographical references and index

599.88   Great apes and gibbons

Antle, Bhagavan

The tiger cubs and the chimp; the true story of how Anjana the chimp helped raise two baby tigers. written and illustrated by Bhagavan Antle. Henry Holt and Co. 2013 32 p. (hardcover) $16.99

Grades: K 1 2   **599.88**

1. Tigers 2. Chimpanzees 3. Animal sanctuaries 4. Tiger cubs 5. Chimpanzees -- Behavior

ISBN 0805093192; 9780805093193

LC 2012047320

In this book by Bhagavan, "when two baby white tigers on an animal preserve get into trouble during a storm, they are taken in by a human animal worker named China and her helper, a chimpanzee named Anjana. China and Anjana soon become the tigers' mothers. Set on a preserve for endangered animals, The Institute of Greatly Endangered and Rare Species (T.I.G.E.R.S.), Anjana's amazing true story showcases her surprising love for two adorable tiger cubs." (Publisher's note)

599.882   Gibbons

Yasuda, Anita

Gibbons; Anita Yasuda. AV2 by Weigl 2014 24 p. color illustrations (hard cover : alk. paper) $27.13

Grades: 3 4 5   **599.882**

1. Primates 2. Gibbons

ISBN 1489628746; 9781489628749; 9781489628756

LC 2014038982

This book, by Anita Yasuda, "offer[s] a comprehensive look at [gibbons]. . . . Standard information is covered, along with charts and diagrams that introduce additional material. A chart called 'Comparing Primates,' for example, describes each of the six superfamilies. Physical features and life cycle are described as well. 'History' and 'Myths and Legends' pages add further context, while an 'Activity' page and review questions help readers to consider what they've learned." (Publisher's note)

Includes bibliographical references and index

599.883   Orangutans

Eszterhas, Suzi

Orangutan Orphanage; Suzi Eszterhas. Owlkids Books 2016 44 p. chiefly color illustrations (hardcover) $17.95

Grades: 2 3 4 5 6   **599.883**

1. Wildlife rehabilitation 2. Orangutan

ISBN 1771471417; 9781771471411

This book "invites readers inside the Orangutan Care Center and Quarantine, operated by Orangutan Foundation International, in the South Pacific jungles of Borneo. It explores why baby orangutans become orphaned and the process of healing and rehabilitating them for return to the wild. It also highlights the people who work at the rescue center and how they aid the animals." (Publisher's note)

Includes bibliographical references and index.

Marshall, Deb

Orangutans; Deb Marshall. AV2 by Weigl 2014 24 p. color illustrations (hard cover : alk. paper) $27.13

Grades: 3 4 5   **599.883**

1. Orangutan

ISBN 148962886X; 9781489628862; 9781489628879

LC 2014038999

In this book, by Deb Marshall, "readers will explore the history, natural habitats, physical features, diets, myths and legends, and life cycles of the worlds most fascinating primates. Did you know that orangutans spend about 90 percent of their time in trees? This is where they eat, sleep, and raise their young." (Publisher's note)

"A conservation page explains what is being done to help save threatened and endangered animals and their habitats. The large, clear photos are carefully chosen." SLJ

Includes bibliographical references and index

599.884 Gorillas

Applegate, Katherine

Ivan; the remarkable true story of the shopping mall gorilla. written by Katherine Applegate; illustrated by G. Brian Karas. Clarion Books, Houghton Mifflin Harcourt 2014 40 p. illustrations (chiefly color) (hardcover) $17.99

Grades: K 1 2 3   **599.884**

1. Gorillas 2. Animal welfare 3. Animal rescue 4. Shopping centers and malls 5. Tacoma (Wash.) 6. Gorilla -- Washington (State) -- Tacoma 7. Shopping malls -- Washington (State) -- Tacoma

ISBN 0544252306; 9780544252301

LC 2013043952

This children's book, by Katherine Applegate and illustrated by G. Brian Karas, is the "real story of a special gorilla. Captured as a baby, Ivan was brought to a Tacoma, Washington, mall to attract shoppers. Gradually, public pressure built until a better way of life for Ivan was found at Zoo Atlanta." (Publisher's note)

"Applegate introduces picture-book readers to the true story that inspired her Newbery-winning The One and Only Ivan. In poetic prose she describes gorilla Ivan's early life in Africa; his dramatic capture; his time on display in a shopping mall; and his transition to the Atlanta Zoo. Karas's mixed-media illustrations--in his warm and unaffected style--are at once straightforward and provocative." Horn Book

Eszterhas, Suzi

Gorilla. Frances Lincoln Children's Books 2012 32 p. col. ill. (hbk.) $15.99; (hbk.) $15.99

Grades: K 1 2   **599.884**

1. Gorillas 2. Wildlife photography

ISBN 1847802990; 9781847802996

This book, the first in the "Eye on the Wild series . . . follows a newborn gorilla from birth to age 6, the age of maturity, although the majority focuses on her first two years of life. From nestling in her mother's arms and napping to sucking her thumb and drinking her mother's milk . . . [Suzi] Esterhas . . . slightly anthropomorphiz[es] the actions, feelings and intentions of her subjects . . . Backmatter offers children more facts about gorillas, along with a website for more information." (Kirkus Reviews)

McDowell, Pamela

Gorillas; Pamela McDowell. AV2 by Weigl 2014 24 p. color illustrations (hard cover : alk. paper) $27.13

Grades: 3 4 5   **599.884**

1. Gorillas

ISBN 1489628789; 9781489628787; 9781489628794

LC 2014038983

This book, by Pamela McDowell, "introduces young readers to some of the most fascinating primates on Earth. Readers will explore the history, natural habitats, physical features, diets, myths and legends, and life cycles of the worlds most fascinating primates. Did you know that in nature, gorillas rarely drink water? They get enough water from the lush plants they eat." (Publisher's note)

"The large, clear photos are carefully chosen. In addition, a trove of pass-coded online resources specific to each title is promised. VERDICT Readers and report writers will not be disappointed." SLJ

Includes bibliographical references and index

Riggs, Kate

Gorillas; by Kate Riggs. Creative Education 2012 24 p. col. ill.

Grades: K 1 2   **599.884**

1. Gorillas 2. Animal behavior 3. Habitat (Ecology) 4. Animals -- Folklore 5. Zoology -- Encyclopedias

ISBN 1608181073; 9781608181070

LC 2010049121

This children's book is part of Kate Riggs' illustrated "Amazing Animals" series, which presents "general facts about physiology, behaviors, eating habits, habitats, and life spans. . . . In "Gorillas," an African story answers the arguably accurate question, "Why do gorillas do nothing but eat and sleep all day long?" Legend has it that they tried to help after a flood but goofed up so badly that they quit doing just about everything ever since." (Booklist)

"A basic exploration of the appearance, behavior, and habitat of gorillas, Earth's largest apes." (Publisher's note)

"The books' easy-reading text will be a boon to both beginning and struggling readers, and the beautiful photos are inviting enough to linger over." Booklist

Includes bibliographical references (p. 24) and index

Wilson, Rachel M.

Social lives of gorillas; Rachel M. Wilson; [edited by] Keli Sipperley. Rourke Educational Media 2016 24 p. color illustrations, map (ebook) $20.95; $29.93

Grades: K 1 2 3   **599.884**

1. Gorillas

ISBN 9781681919003; 9781681917023

LC 2016932580

This book, by Rachel M. Wilson, presents "a look at the social and emotional lives, as well as communication methods, of gorillas." (Publisher's note)

"Perfect for school reports, a great choice for a read-aloud, and irresistible to animal-lovers, this appealing offering on a perennially popular subject should be in great demand." Booklist

599.885 Chimpanzees

Friesen, Helen Lepp

Chimpanzees; Helen Lepp Friesen. AV2 by Weigl 2016 24 p. color ill., color map (hard cover : alk. paper) $27.13

Grades: 3 4 5   **599.885**

1. Chimpanzees 2. Primates

ISBN 1489628703; 9781489628701; 9781489628718

LC 2014039003

This book, by Helen Lepp Friesen, "introduces young readers to some of the most fascinating primates on Earth. Readers will explore the history, natural habitats, physical features, diets, myths and legends, and life cycles of the worlds most fascinating primates. Did you know that chimpanzees went into space before humans? In 1961, a chimpanzee named Ham was sent into space in a rocket." (Publisher's note)

"All the books in the series are colorful, compact, and chock-full of interesting tidbits and clear color photos. A short knowledge-retention quiz concludes, along with other back matter." Booklist

Includes bibliographical references and index

599.9   Humans

Szpirglas, Jeff

You just can't help it! your guide to the wild and wacky world of human behavior. Josh Holinaty, illustrator. Owlkids Books 2011 64p il $22.95; pa $10.95

Grades: 4 5 6 7   **599.9**

1. Human behavior 2. Human biology

ISBN 1-926818-07-5; 1-926818-08-3 pa; 978-1-926818-07-8; 978-1-926818-08-5 pa

"How many times have you been frightened and felt the hairs on the back of your neck stand up? Or been unable to hold back a laugh? Or flinched when an object whizzed by, too close for comfort? . . . [This] book provides a cultural, historical, and sociobiological perspective on human behavior. . . . [It is an] exploration of the basic human biology that determines our reactions, social interactions, and the ways we communicate with one another." (Publisher's note) Index. "Ages nine to twelve." (Quill Quire)

This is a "collection of curious facts and intriguing studies about human behavior. With a breezy text supported by a lively design, the author . . . presents science in a way certain to attract middle-grade and middle-school readers. Chapters on the senses, emotions, communication, and interactions with other human beings cover a variety of topics. . . . The digital art includes bits of photographs, line drawings, the use of color and shapes to help organize the print and plenty of symbols." Kirkus

Includes index

599.93   Genetics, sex and age characteristics, evolution

Goldenberg, Linda

★ **Little** people and a lost world; an anthropological mystery. Twenty-First Century Books 2007 112p il (Discovery!) lib bdg $31.93

Grades: 5 6 7 8   **599.93**

1. Pygmies 2. Fossil hominids 3. Excavations (Archeology) -- Indonesia

ISBN 978-0-8225-5983-2 lib bdg; 0-8225-5983-8 lib bdg

LC 2005-33431

This is an account of the 2003 discovery of small fossil hominids on Flores Island, Indonesia

"This will add important insights to the study of early humans as well as, more broadly, how science and politics interact." Booklist

Includes bibliographical references

Tattersall, Ian

★ **Bones,** brains and DNA; the human genome and human evolution. by Ian Tattersall & Rob DeSalle; illustrated by Patricia J. Wynne. Bunker Hill Pub., Inc. 2007 47p il $16.95

Grades: 5 6 7 8   **599.93**

1. Genetics 2. Evolution 3. Human origins

ISBN 978-1-59373-056-7; 1-59373-056-X

LC 2006931578

The "text follows the trail of human evolution, basing its factual content on current data exhibited in the New Hall of Human Origins in New York City's American Museum of Natural History. Using the skills of anthropologists, archaeologists, and paleontologists, the authors track clues laid down in the fossil record, and, more importantly, in our DNA. . . . The very unsimple concepts are presented clearly, in an attractive format, with splashings of small photos, colorful artwork, diagrams, and maps to attract the eye and elucidate the text." SLJ

Thimmesh, Catherine

★ **Lucy** long ago; uncovering the mystery of where we came from. Houghton Mifflin Harcourt 2009 63p il $18

Grades: 4 5 6 7   **599.93**

1. Human origins 2. Fossil hominids

ISBN 978-0-547-05199-4; 0-547-05199-9

LC 2008-36761

"The 1974 discovery of the fossilized partial skeleton of a small-brained primate who apparently walked upright 3.2 million years ago in what is now Ethiopia significantly changed accepted theories about human origins. Step by step, Thimmesh presents the questions the newly discovered bones raised and how they were answered. . . . Extensive research, clear organization and writing, appropriate pacing for new ideas and intriguing graphics all contribute to this exceptionally accessible introduction to the mystery of human origins." Kirkus

599.943   Teeth

Levine, Sara

Tooth by tooth; comparing fangs, tusks, and chompers. Sara Levine; illustrations by T.S Spookytooth. Millbrook Press 2016 32 p. color illustrations (lb : alk. paper) $26.65

Grades: K 1 2 3   **599.943**

1. Teeth 2. Comparative anatomy 3. Mammals 4. Anatomy, Comparative

ISBN 9781467752152; 9781467797276

LC 2015001021

This children's book, by Sara Levine, with illustrations by T. S. Spookytooth, "adopting an interactive, question-and-answer approach, . . . introduces children to common characteristics and variations in the teeth of mammals. . . . Next, Levine asks readers to guess which kind of mammal they'd be if they sported particular types of teeth." (Kirkus Reviews)

Includes bibliographical references.

600   TECHNOLOGY

600   Technology (Applied sciences)

Enz, Tammy

Batman science; the real-world science behind Batman's gear. by Agnieszka Biskup and Tammy Enz; Batman created by Bob Kane. Capstone Press Inc. 2014 144 p. color illustrations (pbk.) $9.95

Grades: 4 5 6 7   **600**

1. Technology -- Comic books, strips, etc. 2. Inventions 3. Technology 4. Batman (Comic strip) 5. Crime prevention -- Technological innovations

ISBN 1623700647; 9781623700645

LC 2013028330

This book, by Agnieszka Biskup and Tammy Enz, presents "the real-world science behind Batman's gear. . . .When it comes to fighting crime, technology is Batman's greatest weapon. From his gadget-packed Utility Belt to his high-tech Batmobile, the Dark Knight tackles

Gotham's criminal underworld. But does any of his gear have a basis in reality? Or is it merely the stuff of fiction?" (Publisher's note)

Repurpose it; invent new uses for old stuff. by Tammy Enz. Capstone Press 2012 32 p. col. ill. (Fact finders. Invent it) (library) $26.65
Grades: 3 4 5   **600**
1. Recycling 2. Art 3. Recycling (Waste, etc.) 4. Refuse and refuse disposal 5. Conservation of natural resources 6. Conservation projects (Natural resources)
ISBN 1429676361; 9781429676366
LC 2011028738
This book by Tammy Enz is part of the Invent It series "focuses on using basic engineering skills—and your own imagination—to repurpose garbage. After leading readers through the 'Six Steps of Inventing,' the book offers step-by-step numbered instructions for seven do-it-yourself projects." Examples of projects include plastic bag rain ponchos and out-of-date textbooks as hollowed-out hiding places. (Booklist)
Includes bibliographical references and index

Macaulay, David
The **Way** Things Work Now; From Levers to Lasers, Windmills to Wi-fi, a Visual Guide to the World of Machines. [by] David Macaulay with Neil Ardley. Houghton Mifflin Harcourt 2016 400 p. illustrations hbk $35
Grades: 4 5 6 7 8 9 10 11 12 Adult   **600**
1. Machinery 2. Inventions 3. Technology
ISBN 9780544824386; 0544824385
Originally published 1988 and 1998 as The Way Things Work and The New Way Things Work
"Famously packed with information on the inner workings of everything from windmills to Wi-Fi, this extraordinary and humorous book both guides readers through the fundamental principles of machines, and shows how the developments of the past are building the world of tomorrow. This sweepingly revised edition embraces all of the latest developments, from touchscreens to 3D printer." (Publisher's note)
"Macaulay's brilliantly designed, engagingly informal diagrams and cutaways bring within the grasp of even casual viewers a greater understanding of the technological wonders of both past and present." Kirkus

Solway, Andrew
Inventions and investigations. Raintree 2008 48p il (Sci-hi: physical science) lib bdg $22; pa $8.99
Grades: 5 6 7 8   **600**
1. Inventors 2. Inventions
ISBN 978-1-4109-3379-9 lib bdg; 1-4109-3379-2 lib bdg; 978-1-4109-3384-3 pa; 1-4109-3384-9 pa
LC 2009-3508
This explores the scientific processes used by inventors throughout history.
A "compelling read for both browsers and science buffs. . . . Information is clearly presented and flows smoothly. . . . A treasure trove of information." SLJ
Includes glossary and bibliographical references

Zuckerman, Amy
2030; a day in the life of tomorrow's kids. [by] Amy Zuckerman and James Daly; illustrated by John Manders. Dutton Children's Books 2009 un il $16.99
Grades: K 1 2 3   **600**
1. Technology 2. Forecasting
ISBN 978-0-525-47860-7; 0-525-47860-4
LC 2008-14606
"A talking dog, a housecleaning robot, and a three-dimensional data orb" are among the many cool features that kids might enjoy in the fu-

ture, according to this lighthearted look at 2030. The breezy narrative follows one boy through a typical day, highlighting many interesting aspects of his world. Fanciful cartoon drawings show a lively and appealing world full of new and intriguing activities that correspond neatly to modern equivalents." SLJ

608   Patents

Lee, Dora
Biomimicry; Inventions inspired by nature. written by Dora Lee; illustrated by Margot Thompson. Kids Can Press 2011 40 p. $18.95
Grades: 4 5 6   **608**
1. Inventions 2. Nature study 3. Human ecology 4. Technological innovations
ISBN 9781554534678
This book explores "modern innovations [that] have sprung from observation and imitation of the natural world. In topically organized double-page spreads, [Dora] Lee describes shapes and structures, materials and designs, as well as systems for exploration, communication, rescue and delivery. . . . Three or four specific examples, each with illustrative vignettes, follow or sometimes precede the general explanation. These topics range widely and include medical marvels, new power sources, [and] biological computers and robots. . . . [The book] includes a strong ecological message: The most important natural model is the sustainable ecosystem. Through biomimicry, humans can learn to live in balance on the Earth as well." (Kirkus)

St. George, Judith
★ **So** you want to be an inventor? illustrated by David Small. Philomel Bks. 2002 53p il $16.99; pa $7.99
Grades: 3 4 5 6   **608**
1. Inventors 2. Inventions
ISBN 0-399-23593-0; 0-14-240460-8 pa
LC 2001-55447
Presents some of the characteristics of inventors by describing the inventions of people such as Alexander Graham Bell, Thomas Edison, and Eli Whitney
"St. George and Small take a skewed, funny, and informative look at the history of inventions and their inventors and what it takes to become one. . . . Small's lively, fluid caricatures make for a winning collaboration." SLJ
Includes bibliographical references

609   History, geographic treatment, biography

Barretta, Gene
Neo Leo; the ageless ideas of Leonardo da Vinci. Henry Holt & Co. 2009 un il
Grades: 2 3 4 5   **609**
1. Artists 2. Painters 3. Inventors 4. Scientists 5. Writers on science 6. Inventions -- History
ISBN 0805087036; 9780805087031
LC 2008038220
"This book focuses on sketches found in Leonardo's writings that reveal an understanding of inventions that would not come into being until hundreds of years after the death of this quintessential Renaissance man. Vivid watercolor illustrations depict more than a dozen, including the hang glider, contact lenses, the tank, and robots. . . . Barretta provides clear information without veering into scientific explanations." SLJ
Includes bibliographical references

Now & Ben; the modern inventions of Benjamin Franklin. by Gene Barretta. Henry Holt & Co. 2006 un il $16.95

Grades: 2 3 4 5 **609**

1. Authors 2. Diplomats 3. Inventors 4. Statesmen 5. Inventions 6. Scientists 7. Writers on science 8. Members of Congress
ISBN 978-0-8050-7917-3; 0-8050-7917-3

LC 2005012491

"This humorous book covers twenty-two inventions, first by showing their use in today's world . . . and a second by explaining Franklin's role in their development. . . . Read this one aloud; the busy cartoon illustrations offer plenty for listeners to contemplate." Horn Book Guide

Includes bibliographical references

Becker, Helaine

What's the big idea? inventions that changed life on Earth forever. illustrated by Steve Attoe. Maple Tree Press 2010 96p il $27.95; pa $17.95

Grades: 3 4 5 6 **609**

1. Inventions -- History
ISBN 978-1-897349-60-1; 1-897349-60-2; 978-1-897349-61-8 pa; 1-897349-61-0 pa

This book shares the big ideas behind more than thirty of the world's greatest innovations

"Identifying significant inventions in a historic timeline, this book has wonderful kid appeal. It begins with prehistory to the Middle Ages, advancing to the 1900s, finishing with not so long ago. . . . Information is displayed in short paragraphs making it easier to read than many invention books. . . . Author Helaine Becker does an excellent job of crediting diverse cultural and female contributions known or presumed." Libr Media Connect

Bender, Lionel

Invention; by Lionel Bender. 3rd edition DK Publishing 2013 72 p ill. (chiefly col.) (DK Eyewitness) library $16.99; hardcover $16.99

Grades: 4 5 6 7 **609**

1. Inventions 2. Technology
ISBN 9781465409027; 9781465409010

"A fascinating look at the world's earliest simple machines--wheels, gears, pulleys, and levers--to today's complicated telephones and plastics." (Publisher's note)

Crowther, Robert

Robert Crowther's pop-up house of inventions; hundreds of fabulous facts about your home. Candlewick Press 2009 un il $17.99

Grades: 4 5 6 7 **609**

1. Inventions 2. Pop-up books
ISBN 978-0-7636-4253-2; 0-7636-4253-3

First published 2000 with title: Robert Crowther's amazing pop-up house of inventions

"As a beautifully engineered pop-up book, it is complex, highly visual, and inviting. . . . It is also durably manufactured. . . . The book is essentially an encyclopedic assortment of facts and anecdotes about the earliest forms of household appliances, furnishings, novelties, . . . games, clothing, and consumables such as soap, soda and candles. The author integrates history and science in a chatty, colorful, and humorous way that quickly draws readers into his subject." Sci Books Films

Gifford, Clive

50 Things You Should Know About Inventions; by Clive Gifford; consultant, Dr. Mike Goldsmith. Motorbooks Intl 2016 80 p. illustrations (chiefly color) $15.95

Grades: 4 5 6 7 **609**

1. Inventors 2. Inventions
ISBN 1682970205; 9781682970201

In this book in the 50 Things You Should Know About series, by Clive Gifford, readers will discover the stories behind the world's most important inventions, from everyday essentials to major scientific discoveries. Scientists featured include Archimedes, Leonardo da Vinci, James Watt, and Thomas Edison. "Step inside the world of invention and see where it might take us next." (Publisher's note)

"Fact-packed and visual, these overviews provide plenty of intriguing factoids for would-be researchers to pursue." Booklist

Harper, Charise Mericle

Imaginative inventions; the who, what, where, when, and why of roller skates, potato chips, marbles, and pie and more! Little, Brown 2001 32p il $14.95

Grades: K 1 2 3 **609**

1. Inventions
ISBN 0-316-34725-6

LC 00-62443

This "volume explains how such everyday items as gum, roller skates and potato chips came to be, describing each item in doggerel verse. With its crazy-quilt visual patterns, bouncy stanzas and fun facts, this collection of miscellany zigzags between informational and whimsical." Publ Wkly

Jedicke, Peter

Great inventions of the 20th century; by Peter Jedicke. Chelsea House 2007 72p il (Scientific American) $30

Grades: 5 6 7 8 **609**

1. Inventions -- History 2. Technology -- History
ISBN 978-0-7910-9048-0; 0-7910-9048-5

LC 2006014773

"The text is simple, clear, and concise. . . . [The book has] captioned color photos throughout." SLJ

Includes glossary and bibliographical references

Landau, Elaine

The history of everyday life. 21st Century Bks. 2005 56p il (Major inventions through history) $26.60

Grades: 5 6 7 8 **609**

1. Inventions -- History
ISBN 0-8225-3808-3

This "explores fireplaces and central heating, indoor plumbing, the washing machine, food and clothing production, and microwave ovens. . . . [It] presents information about daily living from ancient times to the present. . . . The text . . . is breezy but informative. . . . Illustrations are a mixture of period black-and-white and color photos." SLJ

Includes bibliographical references

Lee, Richard B.

Africans thought of it! amazing innovations. [by] Bathseba Opini [and] Richard B. Lee. Annick Press 2011 48p il (We thought of it) $21.95; pa $11.95

Grades: 3 4 5 6 **609**

1. Inventions 2. Africa -- Civilization
ISBN 978-1-55451-277-5; 1-55451-277-8; 978-1-55451-276-8 pa; 1-55451-276-X pa

Describes the inventions created by the peoples of Africa in hunting, agriculture, architecture, metalwork, medicine, the arts, and other fields, and how they have spread through the world and continue to fit into modern African civilization.

"Vivid photographs feature authentic objects used . . . while people engaged in activities capture an enthusiastic look at the reliance on community. Colored backgrounds and borders present a busy, though uncluttered, dynamic portrayal of nuanced cultures. . . . Succinct definitions and compact descriptions provide a brief and interesting blend of the contemporary with the traditional." SLJ

Rossi, Ann

★ **Bright** ideas; the age of invention in America, 1870-1910. [by] Ann Rossi. National Geographic 2005 40p il (Crossroads America) $12.95

Grades: 4 5 6   **609**

1. Inventions -- History

ISBN 0-7922-8276-0

LC 2003-19834

This describes the history of late 19th and early 20th century inventions such as the light bulb, the telegraph, the telephone, and the automobile.

This "solid [title] for report writers may even pull in a few curious browsers because of [its] plentiful, full-color photos and reproductions. The [layout is] inviting, and the [text is] clear, informative, and readable." SLJ

Includes glossary

Ye, Ting-xing

The **Chinese** thought of it; amazing inventions and innovations. Annick Press 2009 48p il map (We thought of it) $19.95; pa $9.95

Grades: 5 6 7 8   **609**

1. China -- Civilization 2. Inventions -- History 3. Technology -- History

ISBN 978-1-55451-196-9; 1-55451-196-8; 978-1-55451-195-2 pa; 1-55451-195-X pa

In this survey of Chinese inventions "at least one double-page spread is devoted to each of the eleven topics: farming, working with metal, transportation and exploration, canals and bridges, weapons and warfare, paper and printing, silk, and everyday innovations. . . . The layout of the book is appealing and just right for quick reading or browsing. . . . The author's personal story about her childhood in Shanghai effectively draws the reader in." Voice Youth Advocates

Includes bibliographical references

610 Medicine and health

Auden, Scott

Medical mysteries; science researches conditions from bizarre to deadly. by Scott Auden; Elizabeth Brownell, consultant. National Geographic 2008 64p il (National Geographic investigates) $17.95; lib bdg $27.90

Grades: 4 5 6 7   **610**

1. Diseases 2. Medicine -- Research

ISBN 978-1-4263-0356-2; 1-4263-0356-4; 978-1-4263-0261-9 lib bdg; 1-4263-0261-4 lib bdg

This title features "full-color photographs that readers have come to expect from this publisher. . . . [It] focuses on diseases that are regarded as bizarre and are often deadly, including Creutzfeldt-Jakob, Progeria, and Morgellons. The approach is to examine the way in which these mysterious diseases were discovered and how they are being studied to find a cure. . . . [This book offers] explanations simple enough for middle school students but with enough content to make them a useful resource for high school students as well." Voice Youth Advocates

Includes glossary and bibliographical references

Bredeson, Carmen

Don't let the barber pull your teeth; could you survive medieval medicine? illustrated by Gerald Kelley. Enslow Publishers 2011 48p il (Ye yucky Middle Ages) lib bdg $23.93

Grades: 3 4 5 6   **610**

1. Medieval civilization 2. Medicine -- History

ISBN 978-0-7660-3693-2

LC 2010011898

This describes medieval medicine.

Includes glossary and bibliographical references

★ **Encyclopedia** of health; 4th ed.; Marshall Cavendish 2009 18v il set $514.21

Grades: 5 6 7 8 9 10   **610**

1. Reference books 2. Medicine -- Encyclopedias

ISBN 978-0-7614-7845-4; 0-7614-7845-0

LC 2008033014

First published 1995 with title: The Marshall Cavendish encyclopedia of health

This reference features alphabetically arranged entries on body function; diet and nutrition; human behavior; illness, injury and disorders; and prevention and care

"Easy-to-understand language, an attractive design, and content that supports student research and interest lend value to the set." Booklist

Includes bibliographical references

Lew, Kristi

Bat spit, maggots, and other amazing medical wonders. Capstone Press 2010 32p il (Fact finders. Nasty (but useful!) science) lib bdg $25.99

Grades: 3 4 5   **610**

1. Medicine

ISBN 978-1-4296-4537-9 lib bdg; 1-4296-4537-7 lib bdg

This informative guide also explains "relevant chemical processes, medical rationales, and ecological functions in reasonably specific detail. . . . A list of relevant web resources is maintained on the publisher's page." SLJ

Includes glossary and bibliographical references

Murphy, Liz

ABC doctor. Blue Apple 2007 un il $15.95

Grades: PreK K 1   **610**

1. Medicine 2. Medical care

ISBN 978-1-593545-93-2; 1-593545-93-2

"The basics of seeing a doctor and/or nurse are . . . explained with clever, colorful collage illustrations setting the scene and clarifying the explanation. . . . Some medical tools are included. Physical conditions such as fever and vomit appear, and procedures such as a urine sample and X-ray take readers through the alphabet. Murphy has compiled an interesting array of terms to help children realize that medical professionals are there to help them." SLJ

Newquist, H. P.

The **human** body; HP Newquist. Viking, published by the Penguin Group 2015 112 p. illustrations (some color) (ebook) $56.97; (hardcover) $18.99

Grades: 4 5 6 7   **610**

1. Human body 2. Medicine -- History 3. Human physiology 4. Medical technology 5. Medical innovations

ISBN 9781101997147; 9780451476432

LC 2015011670

A book written by H. P. Newquist and part of the Invention and Impact series, "From artificial eyeballs to aspirin to 3-D printed body parts, 'The Human Body' profiles the objects that scientists and tinkerers throughout history have invented (or cobbled together) to protect, repair, or improve our physical selves." (Publisher's note)

"The open page design and ample full-color photos and historical diagrams will easily draw in middle-grade readers, especially those looking for a more macabre look at history and science. A list of resources, including abundant websites, closes out this handsome volume." Booklist

Includes bibliographical references and index.

Singer, Marilyn

I'm getting a checkup; illustrated by David Milgrim. Clarion Books 2009 32p il $16

Grades: PreK K   **610**

1. Medicine 2. Medical care 3. Stories in rhyme

ISBN 978-0-618-99000-9; 0-618-99000-3

LC 2007034977

"Informative and fun, this rhyming picture book will help prepare preschoolers for a visit to the doctor's office. The digitally rendered oil-and-pastel pictures show three kids, each with a parent or caregiver, getting a checkup from three different doctors. . . . Each quick rhyme is followed by a long explanatory note. . . . The bright, cartoon-style pictures keep the visit playful." Booklist

Woolf, Alex, 1964-

Death and disease; [by] Alex Woolf. Lucent Books 2004 48p il map (Medieval realms) $29.95

Grades: 5 6 7 8   **610**

1. Medieval civilization 2. Medicine -- History

ISBN 1-59018-533-1

LC 2003-61797

"Clear, well-organized [text] along with full-color reproductions of art and artifacts and photos of period structures immerse readers in . . . medieval life and offer sufficient information for reports." SLJ

Includes glossary and bibliographical references

610.69   Medical personnel and relationships

Marsico, Katie

The doctor. Marshall Cavendish Benchmark 2011 il (Colonial people) $29.93

Grades: 3 4 5 6   **610.69**

1. Physicians 2. Medicine -- History 3. United States -- History -- 1600-1775, Colonial period

ISBN 978-1-60870-412-5; 1-60870-412-2

LC 2010033895

This descibes the life of a colonial doctor and his importance to the community, as well as everyday life, responsibilities, and social practices during that time.

This "lively [text] and colorful reproductions and photos will engage casual readers and researchers alike. . . . Large illustrations and thoughtful captions explain complicated scientific ideas. . . . [The] volume also includes step-by-step instructions for a related craft project. . . . [This is a] must-have." SLJ

Includes glossary and bibliographical references

610.73   Nursing and services of allied health personnel

Glasscock, Sarah

How nurses use math; math curriculum consultant: Rhea A. Stewart. Chelsea Clubhouse 2010 32p il (Math in the real world) lib bdg $28

Grades: 4 5 6   **610.73**

1. Nurses 2. Mathematics 3. Vocational guidance

ISBN 978-1-60413-607-4 lib bdg; 1-60413-607-3 lib bdg

LC 2009-20199

This describes how nurses use math in such tasks as giving eye tests, keeping records, taking the pulse, and measuring medicine and includes relevant math problems and information about how to become a nurse

Includes glossary and bibliographical references

Kenney, Karen Latchana

Nurses at work; by Karen L. Kenney; illustrated by Brian Caleb Dumm; content consultant, Judith Stepan-Norris. Magic Wagon 2010 32p il (Meet your community workers!) lib bdg $18.95

Grades: K 1 2 3   **610.73**

1. Nurses 2. Vocational guidance

ISBN 978-1-60270-651-4 lib bdg; 1-60270-651-4 lib bdg

LC 2009-2393

This book about nurses has "an uncluttered layout and consistent organization. . . . Chapter headings such as 'Problems on the Job' and 'Technology at Work,' and 'Special Skills and Training' make it easy to pinpoint specific information." SLJ

Includes glossary

611   Human anatomy, cytology, histology

Allen, Kathy

The human head. Capstone Press 2010 32p il (Fact finders. Anatomy class) lib bdg $23.99; pa $7.95

Grades: 3 4 5   **611**

1. Head

ISBN 978-1-4296-3338-3 lib bdg; 1-4296-3338-7 lib bdg; 978-1-4296-3882-1 pa; 1-4296-3882-6 pa

LC 2009-2793

"The vivid scientific photographs . . . and micrographs . . . are a plus. . . . On-page definitions, current further-reading lists, and a webliography maintained at the publisher's FactHound Web site all add value." SLJ

Includes glossary and bibliographical references

Delafosse, Claude

Inside the body; created by Claude Delafosse and Gallimard Jeunesse; illustrated by Pierre-Marie Valat. Reprint Moonlight Pub. 2012 36 p. col. ill. (hardcover: spiral) $12.99

Grades: K 1 2   **611**

1. Picture books for children 2. Human body

ISBN 1851034129; 9781851034123

This children's picture book explores the human body. "This is a beginner's guide . . . with short sentences providing basic groundwork: 'You have a skeleton! This frame of bones helps you stay upright and move around.'" Some step-by-step diagrams are included that show "the process of digestion, the growth of a fetus, or the passing down of physical traits from parents and grandparents." (Booklist)

Gold, Susan Dudley

Learning about the respiratory system; Susan Dudley Gold. Enslow Publishers 2013 48 p. (library) $23.93

Grades: 5 6 7 8   **611**

1. Picture books for children 2. Respiratory system 3. Respiratory organs

ISBN 0766041611; 9780766041615

LC 2012011104

This book by Susan Dudley Gold is part of the Learning About the Human Body Systems series and looks at the respiratory system. She "discusses what this body system is and what organs are involved in its various processes. She discusses the potential health problems that can affect the respiratory system, such as cancer, pneumonia, and emphysema, as well as ways to keep healthy and problem-free." (Publisher's note)

Includes bibliographical references and index.

Lew, Kristi

Human organs. Capstone Press 2010 32p il (Fact finders. Anatomy class) lib bdg $23.99; pa $7.99

Grades: 3 4 5   **611**

1. Human body

ISBN 978-1-4296-3339-0 lib bdg; 1-4296-3339-5 lib bdg; 978-1-4296-3886-9 pa; 1-4296-3886-9 pa

LC 2009-2775

"The vivid scientific photographs . . . and micrographs . . . are a plus. . . . On-page definitions, current further-reading lists, and a webliography maintained at the publisher's FactHound Web site all add value." SLJ

Includes glossary and bibliographical references

Rake, Jody Sullivan

The **human** skeleton. Capstone Press 2010 32p il (Fact finders. Anatomy class) lib bdg $23.99; pa $7.95

Grades: 3 4 5   **611**

1. Bones 2. Skeleton

ISBN 978-1-4296-3340-6 lib bdg; 1-4296-3340-9 lib bdg; 978-1-4296-3888-3 pa; 1-4296-3888-5 pa

LC 2009-2771

"The vivid scientific photographs . . . and micrographs . . . are a plus. . . . On-page definitions, current further-reading lists, and a webliography maintained at the publisher's FactHound Web site all add value." SLJ

Includes glossary and bibliographical references

Wheeler-Toppen, Jodi

Human muscles. Capstone Press 2010 32p il (Fact finders. Anatomy class) lib bdg $23.99; pa $7.95

Grades: 3 4 5   **611**

1. Muscles

ISBN 978-1-4296-3341-3 lib bdg; 1-4296-3341-7 lib bdg; 978-1-4296-3884-5 pa; 1-4296-3884-2 pa

LC 2009-2766

"The vivid scientific photographs . . . and micrographs . . . are a plus. . . . On-page definitions, current further-reading lists, and a webliography maintained at the publisher's FactHound Web site all add value." SLJ

Includes glossary and bibliographical references

612   Human physiology

Aliki

My feet. Crowell 1990 31p il (Let's-read-and-find-out science book) hardcover o.p. pa $5.99

Grades: PreK K 1   **612**

1. Foot

ISBN 0-690-04815-7 lib bdg; 0-06-445106-2 pa

LC 89-49357

"An extensive discussion of feet, through simple text and playful illustration, demonstrates their parts, relative sizes, what they do, and what they wear in different seasons. Includes a handicapped child whose crutches supplement feet." Sci Child

My hands; rev ed; Crowell 1990 32p il (Let's-read-and-find-out science book) hardcover o.p. pa $5.99

Grades: PreK K 1   **612**

1. Hand

ISBN 0-690-04880-7 lib bdg; 0-06-445096-1 pa

LC 89-49158

First published 1962

The author "calls attention to hand structure—fingers, nails, an opposable thumb—and the special ways we use our hands to carry on everyday activities. . . . The jaunty illustrations and simple but efficient text combine for a fresh take on some very basic information." Booklist

Arnold, Caroline

Too hot? too cold? keeping body temperature just right. Caroline Arnold; Illustrated by Annie Patterson. Charlesbridge 2013 32 p. (reinforced) $17.95; (paperback) $7.95

Grades: 1 2 3 4 5   **612**

1. Body temperature 2. Biology 3. Body temperature -- Regulation

ISBN 1580892760; 9781580892766; 9781580892773

LC 2012000792

"Have you ever wondered why you shiver when you're cold, or sweat when you're hot?' This book explores "the many different ways humans and animals adapt to heat and cold. The book includes [an] . . . explanation of cold-blooded and warm-blooded animals." (Publisher's note)

Bailey, Gerry

Body and health; discover science through facts and fun. by Gerry Bailey & Steve Way. Gareth Stevens Pub. 2009 32p il (Simply science) lib bdg $26

Grades: 3 4 5   **612**

1. Human body

ISBN 978-1-4339-0030-3 lib bdg; 1-4339-0030-0 lib bdg

LC 2008-27573

Along with facts that explore concepts across a wide range of topics, comic-strip illustrations present historical background information and foster modern-day science connections.

"The brightly colored cover with its montage of people and cartoon characters is a real eye-catcher. This is a wonderful little book that is packed with lots of information." Sci Books Films

Includes glossary and bibliographical references

Basher, Simon

Human body; a book with guts! by Simon Basher and Dan Green; illustrated by Simon Basher. Kingfisher 2011 128p il $14.95; pa $8.99

Grades: 5 6 7 8   **612**

1. Human body

ISBN 978-0-7534-6628-5; 0-7534-6628-7; 978-0-7534-6501-1 pa; 0-7534-6501-9 pa

"Basher brings his signature informative irreverence and smiley little cartoon icons to the world of human biology. Not a comprehensive resource, but supplemental science reading doesn't come much more fun." Booklist

Bruhn, Aron

Inside the human body; illustrations by Joel Ito and Kathleen Kemly. Sterling 2010 48p il (Inside) $19.95; pa $9.95

Grades: 4 5 6   **612**

1. Human body

ISBN 978-1-4027-7091-3; 1-4027-7091-X; 978-1-4027-7779-0 pa; 1-4027-7779-5 pa

LC 2010002503

"The illustrations in [this] cool . . . [title is] enhanced by 10 large gatefolds that allow kids to dig deeper into the topics and enjoy amazing illustrations. [The] title clearly defines fact and theory, leaving puzzles for the next generation of scientists to solve. . . . [The book] touches on each of the body systems and provides a highly detailed look at a human cell." SLJ

Includes glossary and bibliographical references

Calabresi, Linda

Human body. Simon & Schuster Books for Young Readers 2008 un il (Insiders) $16.99

Grades: 4 5 6 7   612

1. Human body

ISBN 978-1-4169-3861-3; 1-4169-3861-3

LC 2007-61744

This volume "offers excellent pictures of systems, organs, and even individual cells in the human body. . . . A visually dynamic introduction to the human package." Booklist

Cole, Joanna, 1944-

The **magic** school bus inside the human body; illustrated by Bruce Degen. Scholastic 1989 un il hardcover o.p.

Grades: 2 3 4   612

1. Human body 2. Physiology 3. Human anatomy 4. Metabolism

ISBN 0-590-41426-7; 0-590-41427-5 pa

LC 8803070

"Ms. Frizzle's class leaves on a trip to the science museum, but stops for a snack along the way. Arnold is left behind when his classmates reboard the bus. Meanwhile, Ms. Frizzle has miniaturized the bus and its riders. Unwittingly, Arnold swallows it. Traveling through Arnold's insides, the class visits his digestive system, arteries, lungs, heart, brain, and muscles, finally departing through his nostrils when he sneezes. . . . Grades two to five." (Booklist)

"This is an enjoyable look at factual material painlessly packaged with the ribbons and balloons of jokes and asides meant to appeal to kids. Degen's zany, busy, full-color drawings fill the pages with action and information far beyond the text." SLJ

Cunti, Loredana

To **Burp** or Not to Burp; A Guide to Your Body in Space. Dave Williams and Loredana Cunti. Annick Press 2016 56 p. color illustrations $22.95

Grades: 2 3 4 5 6   612

1. Astronauts 2. Human body

ISBN 1554518547; 9781554518548

This book, by Dave Williams and Loredana Cunti, "uses age-appropriate language to explain the different phenomena that astronauts encounter during a mission. The bright, colorful pages, short blocks of text accompanied by photos and humorous illustrations make this a very attractive choice for young readers." (Publisher's note)

"The implications for future space colonies are exciting, and learning about the challenges to the human body present interesting opportunities for STEM-related problem-solving opportunities." Booklist

Includes bibliographical references (page 48) and index.

Fromer, Liza

My achy body. Tundra Books 2011 un il (Body works) $14.99

Grades: 2 3 4 5   612

1. Pain 2. Human body 3. Wounds and injuries

ISBN 978-1-77049-204-2; 1-77049-204-6

This describes bruises, scrapes, scabs, broken bones, sprains, stomach aches, earaches, and sore throats.

Includes glossary

My messy body; [by] Liza Fromer and Francine Gerstein; illustrated by Joe Weissmann. Tundra Books 2011 un il (Body works) $12.95

Grades: 2 3 4 5   612

1. Human body

ISBN 978-1-77049-202-8; 1-77049-202-X

This describes the purpose of the body's secretions, including tears, sweat, snot, urine, excrement, earwax, vomit, pus, and mucus.

Includes glossary

My noisy body; [by] Liza Fromer and Francine Gerstein; illustrated by Joe Weissmann. Tundra Books 2011 un il (Body works) $12.95

Grades: 2 3 4 5   612

1. Human body

ISBN 978-1-77049-201-1; 1-77049-201-1

This describes the meaning of sounds the body creates, including the voice, burps, hiccups, stomach growls, farts, sneezes and coughs.

The authors explain noisy body functions "with a playful attitude and with that buffet a solid body of factual information. . . . Weissmann's squiggly paintings are amusing. . . . This . . . offers a fun, frank look at sometimes taboo topics." Booklist

Gardner, Robert

Ace your human biology science project; great science fair ideas. [by] Robert Gardner and Barbara Gardner Conklin. Enslow Publishers 2009 128p il (Ace your biology science project) lib bdg $31.93

Grades: 5 6 7 8   612

1. Biology 2. Science projects 3. Science -- Experiments

ISBN 978-0-7660-3219-4 lib bdg; 0-7660-3219-1 lib bdg

LC 2008-30799

"Dozens of . . . science activities are presented with background information, step-by-step instructions, and suggestions for extending to the science fair level. . . . Color illustrations and important safety information are included." Horn Book Guide

Includes bibliographical references

Goddard, Jolyon

Inside the human body. Marshall Cavendish Benchmark 2010 48p il (Invisible worlds) lib bdg $28.50

Grades: 4 5 6 7   612

1. Human body 2. Physiology

ISBN 978-0-7614-4190-8 lib bdg; 0-7614-4190-5 lib bdg

LC 2008037254

This describes the details of the human body that are too small for the unaided eye to see, and how these microscopic systems work to keep the body alive and healthy.

The narrative is "clear, well written, broken down into manageable pieces, and peppered with eye-opening facts. The numerous photographs are so phenomenal that they will inspire kids to read the text . . . so that they can wrap their minds around what they see." SLJ

Includes glossary and bibliographical references

Green, Dan

Human body factory; the nuts and bolts of your insides. Kingfisher 2012 48 p. $16.99

Grades: 1 2 3 4   612

1. Biology 2. Human body 3. Picture books for children

ISBN 0753468085; 9780753468081

This children's book describes human anatomy by comparing the body to a factory. From "the CEO sending out orders in the brain to 'waste' being sorted and delivered out of the body at the other end, the busy workers who keep everything running smoothly introduce each 'department.' All the major systems are covered, and the . . . illustrations are packed with. . . details . . . . All of this . . . artwork is backed up with. . . facts and . . . explanations of the body's essential processes." Images include "toxic signs and workers wearing biohazard suits in the large intestine, lab workers in dinghies mixing gastric juices in the stomach with a giant whisk, or park keepers on the skin keeping things clean among glades of gently swaying hairs and sweat-gland sprinklers." (Publisher's note)

Greenwood, Marie

Animals and me; [written by Marie Greenwood] DK Pub. 2010 48p il $12.99

Grades: 2 3 4 5   **612**

1. Human body 2. Physiology

ISBN 978-0-7566-6886-0; 0-7566-6886-7

Photographs and text examine different parts of the human body, explaining what they are for, and comparing them to the similar body parts of animals.

"The full-color photography is fantastic and clearly illustrates each point. Because of the wealth of information presented, this book would be enjoyed by browsers as well as students looking for report topics." SLJ

Griffiths, Andy

What Body Part Is That? A Wacky Guide to the Funniest, Weirdest, and Most Disgustingest Parts of Your Body. by Andy Griffiths; illustrated by Terry Denton. 1st U.S. ed. Feiwel & Friends 2012 ix, 180 p.p ill. (hardcover) $12.99

Grades: 3 4 5   **612**

1. Human anatomy 2. Wit and humor, Juvenile 3. Human body -- Juvenile humor

ISBN 0312367902; 9780312367909

LC 2012288587

"This humorous book is about every body part and then some -- from your head to your toes and everything in-between that you can and can't see." (Library Media Connection) Author "[Andy] Griffiths' anatomical tour in general steers clear of anything that would be marked as correct on a test. From 'Ears can be big or small, depending on their size' to 'Capillaries are the larval form of butterflies,' he offers . . . inanities about 68 mostly real body features." (Kirkus Reviews)

Hoffman, Mary

The **great** big body book; Mary Hoffman, illustrated by Ros Asquith. Motorbooks Intl 2016 40 p. color illustrations $18.99

Grades: PreK K 1 2   **612**

1. Human body 2. Physiology

ISBN 1847808727; 9781847808721

In this children's book in the Great Big Book series, by Mary Hoffman, illustrated by Ros Asquith, "find out all about your body and how it works. . . . Bodies come in all shapes and sizes and they change throughout our lives as we grow from babies to children to teenagers to adults. Find out about growing and learning, keeping fit, breaks and bruises, the five senses, using our minds, how we are the same and how we are different—and lots more." (Publisher's note)

"Cheerful and informative, this is a splendid introduction for humans of all shapes and sizes to share." Kirkus

Lew, Kristi

Farts, vomit, and other functions that help your body. Capstone Press 2010 32p il (Fact finders. Nasty (but useful!) science) lib bdg $25.99

Grades: 3 4 5   **612**

1. Physiology

ISBN 978-1-4296-4539-3 lib bdg; 1-4296-4539-3 lib bdg

This informative guide also explains "relevant chemical processes, medical rationales, and ecological functions in reasonably specific detail. . . . A list of relevant web resources is maintained on the publisher's page." SLJ

Includes glossary and bibliographical references

Li, Maggie

The **Amazing** Human Body Detectives; Facts, Myths and Quirks of the Body. by Maggie Li. Trafalgar Square Books 2016 32 p. color illustrations $14.99

Grades: K 1 2 3   **612**

1. Human body

ISBN 1843652978; 9781843652977

This book, by Maggie Li, "leaves no nook or cranny undiscovered, no goosebump unexplored. We know that we all have unique fingerprints, but did you know we also have a unique tongue print? Did you know that when you are awake, the human brain has enough electricity to power a light bulb? Our eyelashes have little creatures living on them—come and take a look at them!" (Publisher's note)

"An inviting introduction for curious children from pre-K through early elementary school, but unfamiliar terms may require a little extra interpretation." Kirkus

Manning, Mick

Under your skin; your amazing body. [by] Mick Manning and Brita Granström. Albert Whitman 2007 23p il $16.95

Grades: 1 2 3   **612**

1. Human body

ISBN 978-0-8075-8313-5; 0-8075-8313-8

LC 2007-02350

"This well-designed introduction to human body parts and their functions features eight half-page flaps that lift up to reveal simple views of internal organs. The terminology allows for different levels of comprehension . . . and the cartoon illustrations in bright colors help make the science aproachable." Horn Book Guide

Nicolson, Cynthia Pratt

Totally human; why we look and act the way we do. illustrated by Dianne Eastman. Kids Can Press 2011 40p il $16.95

Grades: 3 4 5   **612**

1. Human body 2. Psychology

ISBN 978-1-55453-569-9; 1-55453-569-7

"This playful science book introduces the biology of human evolution and behavior with an accessible, interactive text packed with information and wry, bright computer graphics on each spread. . . . The wild images . . . and the detailed text reveal astonishing answers to questions readers might never have thought to ask." Booklist

Parker, Nancy Winslow

★ **Organs!** how they work, fall apart, and can be replaced (gasp!) Greenwillow Books 2009 48p il $17.99; lib bdg $18.89

Grades: 1 2 3 4   **612**

1. Human body

ISBN 978-0-688-15105-8; 0-688-15105-1; 978-0-688-15106-5 lib bdg; 0-688-15106-X lib bdg

LC 2008-20718

"This is an engaging children's textbook on human anatomy and functioning. . . . Spot illustrations, charmingly rendered in colored pencil, show people with their organs in action. . . . Author Nancy Winslow Parker admirably tackles the challenge of visualizing objects that are typically masked from everyday view. . . . This fun and lighthearted book is . . . recommend[ed] for every child's library and one that will easily become a go-to reference for many years." Sci Books Films

Podesto, Martine

The **body;** by Martine Podesto. Gareth Stevens Pub. 2009 104p il (My science notebook) lib bdg $31

Grades: 4 5 6   **612**
1. Human body
ISBN 978-0-8368-9212-3 lib bdg; 0-8368-9212-7 lib bdg
LC 2008-12428
This book answers questions about the human body
"Designed to resemble a notebook with illustrated paper clips, pasting, and tape appearing on most pages, this [book] . . . offers comprehensive information. . . . supplemented by colorful drawings, diagrams, and photographs." SLJ
Includes glossary and bibliographical references

Reilly, Kathleen M.
The **human** body; 25 fantastic projects illuminate how the body works. illustrated by Shawn Braley. Nomad Press 2008 120p il $21.95; pa $15.95
Grades: 5 6 7 8   **612**
1. Human body
ISBN 978-1-934670-25-5; 1-934670-25-1; 978-1-934670-24-8 pa; 1-934670-24-3 pa
"The workings of the human body are expertly summarized in 11 tidy chapters, which include experiments that explain how the body works by creating models that either imitate or test its functions. . . . Many of the activities require adult supervision due to the materials required. . . . Simple drawings and cartoons enliven and illuminate the text. . . . The scientific explanations are superb." SLJ

Rockwell, Lizzy
The **busy** body book; a kid's guide to fitness. Crown 2004 un il $15.95
Grades: K 1   **612**
1. Exercise 2. Physiology
ISBN 0-375-82203-8; 0-375-92203-2 lib bdg
An introduction to the human body, how it functions, and its need for exercise.
"The text is purposely motivating, yet easy to understand and informative. The age-appropriate artwork is colorful and lively, and provides just the right amount of detail." SLJ

Rotner, Shelley
Body actions; Shelley Rotner and David A. White. Holiday House 2012 32 p. (hardcover) $16.95
Grades: 1 2 3   **612**
1. Human body 2. Nervous system 3. Digestive system 4. Musculoskeletal system 5. Picture books for children
ISBN 0823423662; 9780823423668
LC 2011007268
This children's picture book is a "brief overview of the entire human body. The nervous, skeletal, muscular, respiratory, circulatory and digestive systems; the five senses; skin, and hair are all touched on. The full-color photographs . . . feature racially diverse children, and some of the photographs include an illustration of the body system superimposed on the child." (School Library Journal)

Seuling, Barbara
Your skin weighs more than your brain; and other freaky facts about your skin, skeleton, and other body parts. by Barbara Seuling; illustrated by Matthew Skeens. Picture Window Books 2008 40p il (Freaky facts) lib bdg $23.93; pa $4.95
Grades: 2 3 4 5   **612**
1. Human body
ISBN 978-1-4048-3751-5 lib bdg; 1-4048-3751-5 lib bdg; 978-1-4048-3756-0 pa; 1-4048-3756-6 pa
LC 2007004030
A collection of amazing facts and statistics about the human body

"This quick read is a light, fun, and at times fascinating collection of various facts about the human body. . . . The book is eye-catching—a convenient and kid-friendly small size, with illustrations on every couple of pages." Sci Books Films
Includes glossary and bibliographical references

Silverstein, Alvin
Snot, poop, vomit, and more; the yucky body book. [by] Alvin Silverstein, Virginia Silverstein, and Laura Silverstein Nunn; illustrated by Gerald Kelley. Enslow Publishers 2010 48p il (Yucky science) lib bdg $23.93
Grades: 3 4 5 6   **612**
1. Human body 2. Physiology
ISBN 978-0-7660-3318-4 lib bdg; 0-7660-3318-X lib bdg
LC 2009012280
"Explores 'Yucky' things about the human body, including earwax, gas, bodily wastes, and more" Publisher's note
Includes bibliographical references

Somervill, Barbara A.
★ The **human** body. Gareth Stevens Pub. 2008 48p il (Gareth Stevens vital science: life science) lib bdg $26.60; pa $11.95
Grades: 5 6 7 8   **612**
1. Human body
ISBN 978-0-8368-8441-8 lib bdg; 978-0-8368-8450-0 pa
LC 2007-16175
First published 2006 in the United Kingdom
This describes "human anatomy and physiology. . . . Factoids are scattered throughout the text in a fashion that captures the reader's attention and interest. . . . [The book offers] excellent graphics, namely photos and diagrams. The artwork complements and enhances the written content." Sci Books Films
Includes glossary and bibliographical references

Stewart, David Evelyn
How your body works; a good look inside your insides. written by David Stewart; illustrated by Carolyn Franklin. Children's Press 2008 32p il (Amaze) $26; pa $8.95
Grades: K 1 2   **612**
1. Human body
ISBN 978-0-531-20444-3; 0-531-20444-8; 978-0-531-20455-9 pa; 0-531-20455-3 pa
This "is a bright, colorful, vivid, and easy-to-digest children's book about the basics of physiology. The book includes simple, well-illustrated chapters on the eyes, ears, intestines, cardiovascular system, liver and kidneys. . . . Organs are represented with big, colorful blocks, with very little distracting detail." Sci Books Films

Swanson, Diane
You are weird; your body's peculiar parts and funny functions. written by Diane Swanson; illustrated by Kathy Boake. Kids Can Press 2009 40p il $16.95; pa $7.95
Grades: 2 3 4 5   **612**
1. Human body
ISBN 978-1-55453-282-7; 1-55453-282-5; 978-1-55453-283-4 pa; 1-55453-283-3 pa
"This chatty, interactive humorous science book make[s] human physiology accessible and interesting, with lots of wild facts about hair, bacteria, sweat, skin, joints, muscles, and more. . . . The irreverence is right on . . . and the sound of words extend the fun without jargon." Booklist

Walker, Richard, 1951-

Dr. Frankenstein's human body book; the monstrous truth about how your body works. [author, Richard Walker; artist, Nick Abadzis] DK Pub. 2008 93p il $24.99

Grades: 4 5 6 7   **612**

1. Human body
ISBN 978-0-7566-4091-0; 0-7566-4091-1

"This anatomy book is as engrossing as any science fiction. Dr. Frankenstein, shown in a sepia photograph standing in a laboratory, gazing at a skull he holds in one hand, invites readers to join him as he creates a human being.... The story line is sustained with brief, pun-happy journal entries.... Gothic fonts and engraved illustrations and vignettes (in red and black and also hand-colored) blend with state-of-the-art images from MEG scans, gamma scans and other advanced technology. Clear explanations broken into easily assimilable captions and text blocks encourage the reader." Publ Wkly

Includes glossary

Human body; written by Richard Walker. DK Pub. 2009 72 p. ill. (chiefly col.) (DK eyewitness books) (hardcover) $16.99

Grades: 4 5 6 7   **612**

1. Human body
ISBN 9780756645458; 075664545X

LC 2009419529

In this book, text and illustrations present information on the parts of the body and how they work

Includes glossary and bibliographical references

Ouch! how your body makes it through a very bad day. written by Richard Walker. DK Pub. 2007 71p il $16.99

Grades: 4 5 6 7   **612**

1. Human body
ISBN 978-0-7566-2536-8; 0-7566-2536-X

"Tag along on a rotten day as a body copes with sneezing, getting cut, being stung by a bee, and vomiting, as well as performing more mundane actions such as urinating, tapping into its melanin supply, acting reflexively, and sweating.... Dramatic color graphics, both large and small, are accompanied by a multitude of informative captions. Researchers who find the information on the busy pages hard to grasp can pop in the accompanying CD-ROM and catch a ride up the esophagus on a wave of vomit.... Eye-catching, highly pictorial, informative, and with a megadose of ick! factor." SLJ

Includes glossary

Wicks, Maris

★ **Human** Body Theater; a nonfiction revue. Maris Wicks. First Second 2015 240 p. chiefly color illustrations (hardcover) $19.99

Grades: 4 5 6 7 8   **612**

1. Human anatomy
ISBN 1626722773; 9781626722774; 9781596439290

This book by Maris Wicks explores human anatomy on a performing stage. In it, "your master of ceremonies is going to lead you through a theatrical revue of each and every biological system of the human body! Starting out as a skeleton, the MC puts on a new layer of her costume (her body) with each 'act.'" (Publisher's note)

"Wicks' playful cartoon artwork in saturated colors makes the potentially daunting and embarrassing subject of anatomy approachable and fun, but never at the expense of accuracy or clarity. This informative, frank exploration of the body perfectly balances science and silliness." Booklist

Includes bibliographical references

Zoehfeld, Kathleen Weidner

Human body. Scholastic Inc. 2010 32p il (Scholastic reader) pa $3.99

Grades: K 1   **612**

1. Human body
ISBN 978-0-545-23752-9 pa; 0-545-23752-1 pa

A simple explanation of how the human body works, discussing the five senses, muscles, bones, digestion, the heart, and the brain.

"With simple chatty sentences and clearly labeled images of kids in action, this ... title packs in fascinating facts about body parts, how they work individually and together." Booklist

Includes glossary

612.1   Specific functions, systems, organs

Bassington, Cyril

Your heart; Cyril Bassington. Gareth Stevens Publishing 2017 24 p. (library bound) $22.60

Grades: 1 2 3   **612.1**

1. Heart 2. Physiology 3. Cardiovascular system 4. Human physiology
ISBN 9781482443998; 9781482444384; 9781482444551

LC 2015021477

With this book, by Cyril Bassington, "readers will learn about the different chambers of the heart, the path of blood through it, and how it works with blood vessels. Supportive illustrations, vivid photographs, and essential vocabulary make this a must-read introduction to the circulatory system."(Publisher's note)

"The relatable text lives up to the series title, as they truly help young readers know their bodies." Booklist

Includes bibliographical references and index

Corcoran, Mary K.

The **circulatory** story; illustrated by Jef Czekaj. Charlesbridge 2010 41p il lib bdg $17.95

Grades: 2 3 4   **612.1**

1. Cardiovascular system 2. Blood -- Circulation
ISBN 978-1-58089-208-7 lib bdg; 1-58089-208-6 lib bdg

LC 2008025332

"The author and illustrator of The Quest to Digest (2006) take young readers on an equally engaging ride through the heart, lungs, arteries, veins, capillaries, and back again. In the big, labeled cartoon illustrations a small, green Smoo-like creature rides a red blood cell down a river of plasma.... Corcoran's breezy commentary lays out the whole 60,000-mile system in easy-to-understand terms.... An irresistable invitation to go with the flow." Booklist

Gold, John Coopersmith

Learning about the circulatory and lymphatic systems; by John C. Gold. Enslow Publishers 2013 48 p. (library) $23.93

Grades: 5 6 7 8   **612.1**

1. Picture books for children 2. Lymphatic system 3. Lymphatics 4. Cardiovascular system
ISBN 0766041565; 9780766041561

LC 2012011099

This book by John Coopersmith Gold is part of the Learning About the Human Body Systems series and looks at the circulatory and lymphatic systems. "The circulatory system runs through the body carrying oxygen and nutrients to our cells and removes waste. It's driven by the never-resting heart, which pumps blood through more than 60,000 miles of arteries and veins. The lymphatic system regulates the amount of liquid in the body among other tasks." (Publisher's note)

Includes bibliographical references and index.

Guillain, Charlotte

Our hearts. Heinemann Library 2010 24p il (Our bodies) lib bdg $20.71; pa $5.99

Grades: K 1 2 3   **612.1**

1. Heart

ISBN 978-1-4329-3590-0 lib bdg; 1-4329-3590-9 lib bdg; 978-1-4329-3599-3 pa; 1-4329-3599-2 pa

LC 2009-22294

This describes what the heart is, how it pumps blood through the body, and how to keep it healthy.

This explains "visually and verbally complicated medical information in a clear, understandable way. . . . Large, vivid photographs are placed alongside one or two sentences per page." Booklist

Includes bibliographical references

Halvorson, Karin

Inside the heart; Karin Halvorson, M.D.; consulting editor, Diane Craig, M.A./Reading Specialist. ABDO Publishing Company, a division of ABDO 2013 32 p. (Super simple body) $27.07

Grades: 2 3 4 5   **612.1**

1. Heart -- Anatomy 2. Heart -- Physiology

ISBN 1617836125; 9781617836121

LC 2012030978

Author Karin Halvorson's book "offers children an exciting voyage through the heart. Detailed illustrations, color photos, and simple text combine to make a fun and easy introduction to how the heart works. This book also includes simple activities and crafts like We've Got a Beat, Valuable Valves and how to make a Heart with how-to photos to further engage young learners." (Publisher's note)

Kyi, Tanya Lloyd, 1973-

Seeing red; the true story of blood. Annick Press 2012 121 p. (hardcover) $22.95

Grades: 4 5 6   **612.1**

1. Blood

ISBN 1554513855; 9781554513857

This book by Tanya Lloyd Kyi, illustrated by Steve Rolston, discusses "the symbolism and reality of blood, from its role in ancient sacrifices to its uses in modern medicine and forensics. . . . Around the world, blood has always been a symbol of both life and death: blood rites, blood oaths, and blood-soaked legends. Today, we have scientific facts about blood types, transfusions, blood-borne illnesses, and crime-scene blood spatter. Yet the fluid still holds mystery." (Publisher's note)

Includes bibliographical references (p. 112-115), Internet addresses and index.

Markle, Sandra

Faulty hearts; true survival stories. Lerner Pub. 2010 48p il (Powerful medicine) lib bdg $27.93

Grades: 5 6 7 8   **612.1**

1. Heart 2. Heart diseases 3. Cardiovascular system

ISBN 978-0-8225-8699-9 lib bdg; 0-8225-8699-1 lib bdg

LC 2009-33980

This book "is extremely well done, with a number of great examples of survival stories. The examples exemplify different and important heart diseases, symptoms, and treatments. . . . That the author is a former science teacher enables her to write clearly for the intended audience. The illustrations and photographs are perfect, adding to a full understanding of the diseases described." Sci Books & Films

Includes glossary and bibliographical references

Newquist, Hp

The **book** of blood; from legends and leeches to vampires and veins. HP Newquist. Houghton Mifflin Books for Children 2012 160 p. ill. (chiefly col.) (hardback) $17.99

Grades: 4 5 6   **612.1**

1. Blood

ISBN 0547315848; 9780547315843

LC 2011025134

In this book, "[H.P.] Newquist . . . demystifies one of the most elemental and (literally) vital components of life as we know it. After an overview of the complex makeup of blood, Newquist dives into humankind's history with, beliefs about, and study of blood, including missteps and misconceptions along the way . . . . Newquist goes into detail to explain how blood moves through the human body and the critical role it plays in keeping us alive." (Publishers Weekly)

Showers, Paul

A **drop** of blood; illustrated by Edward Miller. HarperCollins Pub. 2004 32p il (Let's-read-and-find-out science) hardcover o.p. pa $4.99

Grades: K 1 2 3   **612.1**

1. Blood

ISBN 0-06-009108-8; 0-06-009109-6 lib bdg; 0-06-009110-X pa

A newly illustrated edition of the title first published 1967 and revised in 1989

A simple introduction to the composition and functions of blood

"Showers's classic introduction to this vital fluid is cleverly updated by Miller's amusing illustrations featuring a Dracula-like vampire and his Igorish friend. . . . High-quality, closeup photographs of blood cells, platelets, and fibrin under the microscope are well placed within the illustrations, and science concepts are presented with just the right amount of detail for the intended audience." SLJ

Hear your heart; illustrated by Holly Keller. HarperCollins Pubs. 2001 33p il (Let's-read-and-find-out science) hardcover o.p. pa $4.95

Grades: K 1 2 3   **612.1**

1. Heart

ISBN 0-06-025410-6; 0-06-025411-4 lib bdg; 0-06-445139-9 pa

LC 99-41336

A revised and newly illustrated edition of the title first published 1968

A simple explanation of the structure of the heart and how it works

"This is an excellent introduction to the heart and how it works. . . . The open, informal design brings the physiology right into daily life. Factual, accurate, and fun." Booklist

Simon, Seymour

★ The **heart**; our circulatory system. [by] Seymour Simon. rev ed.; Collins 2006 30p il hardcover o.p. pa $6.99

Grades: 4 5 6 7   **612.1**

1. Heart 2. Cardiovascular system

ISBN 978-0-06-087720-0; 0-06-087720-0; 978-0-06-087721-7 pa; 0-06-087721-9 pa

LC 2006-279215

First published 1996

Describes the heart, blood, and other parts of the body's circulatory system and explains how each component functions

"The text is succinct and direct, making the details understandable without losing the sense that the whole process of circulation is 'strange and wonderful.' . . . The often striking pictures include many computer-enhanced photographs as well as diagrams and highly enlarged images made possible by electron microscopes. Handsome and well-conceived in every way." Booklist [review of 1996 edition]

Tieck, Sarah

Circulatory system. ABDO Pub. 2011 32p il (Body systems) lib bdg $27.07; e-book $27.07

Grades: 2 3 4   **612.1**

1. Cardiovascular system

ISBN 978-1-61613-497-6 lib bdg; 1-61613-497-6 lib bdg; 978-1-61613-987-4 e-book

LC 2010019665

"Double-page spreads describe the workings of the [circulatory system] . . . with simple text on left-hand pages and large, colorful photographs or diagrams on the right. The [text touches] on common disorders (e.g., high blood pressure . . .) and healthy practices. 'Brain Food' spreads pose three questions and provide answers. Ample white space, engaging images, and 'Word of Mouth' sidebars are reader-friendly." Horn Book Guide

Includes glossary

612.2   Respiratory system

Guillain, Charlotte

Our lungs. Heinemann Library 2010 24p il (Our bodies) lib bdg $20.71; pa $5.99

Grades: K 1 2 3   **612.2**

1. Lungs

ISBN 978-1-4329-3594-8 lib bdg; 1-4329-3594-1 lib bdg; 978-1-4329-3603-7 pa; 1-4329-3603-4 pa

LC 2009-22298

This describes what lungs are, why we need lungs, and how to keep them healthy.

This explains "visually and verbally complicated medical information in a clear, understandable way. . . . Large, vivid photographs are placed alongside one or two sentences per page." Booklist

Includes bibliographical references

Korb, Rena

My nose; illustrated by Remy Simard; content consultant, Anthony J. Weinhaus. Magic Wagon 2010 32p il (My body) lib bdg $27.07

Grades: 1 2 3   **612.2**

1. Nose

ISBN 978-1-60270-808-2; 1-60270-808-8

This "volume stars a child narrator who straightforwardly describes [the nose] and how it works. A round-faced, lab-coat-wearing man appears at the bottom of every spread to provide additional details and tidbits of anatomical information. . . . Black-outlined digital-looking cartoon illustrations enliven the [text]." Horn Book Guide

Includes glossary

Simon, Seymour

Lungs; your respiratory system. [by] Seymour Simon. Smithsonian/Collins 2007 30p il hardcover o.p. $16.77; lib bdg $17.89

Grades: 3 4 5 6   **612.2**

1. Respiratory system

ISBN 978-0-06-054654-0; 978-0-06-054655-7 lib bdg; 0-06-054655-7 lib bdg; 0-06-054656-5 pa

LC 2006003768

"This straightforward overview of the respiratory system follows the journey of a breath through the body. Color diagrams, X-rays, and photos provide visual support. . . . The writing is concise and full of clear examples meaningful to kids." SLJ

Includes glossary and bibliographical references

Siy, Alexandra

★ **Sneeze!** [by] Alexandra Siy and Dennis Kunkel. Charlesbridge 2007 45p il lib bdg $16.95; pa $6.95

Grades: 4 5 6 7   **612.2**

1. Allergy 2. Sneezing

ISBN 978-1-57091-653-3 lib bdg; 978-1-57091-654-0 pa

LC 2005-27567

"Kunkel's big, clear, beautiful color electron micrographs on every double-page spread show everything from dust mites, mildew, and pollen to the influenza A virus." Booklist

Includes glossary and bibliographical references

Tieck, Sarah

Respiratory system. ABDO Pub. 2011 32p il (Body systems) lib bdg $27.07; e-book $27.07

Grades: 2 3 4   **612.2**

1. Respiratory system

ISBN 978-1-61613-501-0 lib bdg; 1-61613-501-8 lib bdg; 978-1-61613-991-1 e-book

LC 2010019652

"Double-page spreads describe the workings of the [respiratory system] . . . with simple text on lefthand pages and large, colorful photographs or diagrams on the right. The [text touches] on common disorders . . . and healthy practices. 'Brain Food' spreads pose three questions and provide answers. Ample white space, engaging images, and 'Word of Mouth' sidebars are reader-friendly." Horn Book Guide

Includes glossary

612.3   Digestive system

Corcoran, Mary K.

The **quest** to digest; illustrated by Jef Czekaj. Charlesbridge 2006 32p il lib bdg $16.95; pa $6.95

Grades: 2 3 4   **612.3**

1. Digestion

ISBN 978-1-57091-664-9 lib bdg; 978-1-57091-665-6 pa

LC 2005-19622

"This graphically appealing, colorful, and fact-rich story describes the importance of food to the body by following an apple as it goes through the human digestion system. . . . Abundant, humorous cartoons and clever text handle explanations of belching, passing gas, and diarrhea." SLJ

Includes glossary

Donovan, Sandra, 1967-

Hawk & Drool; gross stuff in your mouth. by Sandy Donovan; illustrated by Michael Slack. Millbrook Press 2010 48p il (Gross body science) lib bdg $29.27

Grades: 4 5 6   **612.3**

1. Saliva 2. Mouth -- Diseases

ISBN 978-0-8225-8966-2 lib bdg; 0-8225-8966-4 lib bdg

LC 2008-50699

Presents disgusting facts about the human mouth, how it works to aid in digestion, the organisms that live there, and ways to keep it clean and healthy

"Solid information layered between sarcastic comments and kid-friendly terminology like fart, poop, barf, and puke will keep readers engaged. . . . Labeled, captioned (and graphic) photographs, cartoon-style illustrations, and micrographs add information." SLJ

Includes glossary and bibliographical references

Rumble & spew; gross stuff in your stomach and intestines. by Sandy Donovan; illustrated by Michael Slack. Millbrook Press 2010 48p il (Gross body science) lib bdg $29.27

Grades: 4 5 6   **612.3**

1. Intestines

ISBN 978-0-8225-8899-3 lib bdg; 0-8225-8899-4 lib bdg

LC 2008-37713

Presents disgusting facts about the human digestive system and its functions

"Solid information layered between sarcastic comments and kid-friendly terminology like fart, poop, barf, and puke will keep readers engaged. . . . Labeled, captioned (and graphic) photographs, cartoon-style illustrations, and micrographs add information." SLJ

Includes glossary and bibliographical references

Gold, Susan Dudley

Learning about the digestive and excretory systems; by Susan Dudley Gold. Enslow Publishers 2013 48 p. (Learning about the human body systems) (library) $23.93

Grades: 5 6 7 8   **612.3**

1. Picture books for children 2. Digestive system 3. Urinary organs 4. Digestive organs

ISBN 0766041573; 9780766041578

LC 2012011100

This book by Susan Dudley Gold is part of the Learning About the Human Body Systems series and looks at the digestive and excretory systems. She "explains why these systems are discussed together, how they work, and ways to keep healthy." Illustrations and color photographs are included. (Publisher's note)

Includes bibliographical references and index.

Guillain, Charlotte

Our stomachs. Heinemann Library 2010 24p il (Our bodies) lib bdg $20.71; pa $5.99

Grades: K 1 2 3   **612.3**

1. Stomach 2. Digestion

ISBN 978-1-4329-3591-7 lib bdg; 1-4329-3591-7 lib bdg; 978-1-4329-3600-6 pa; 1-4329-3600-X pa

LC 2009-22295

This describes what the stomach is, what it does to food, and how to keep it healthy.

This explains "visually and verbally complicated medical information in a clear, understandable way. . . . Large, vivid photographs are placed alongside one or two sentences per page." Booklist

Includes bibliographical references

Korb, Rena

My mouth. Magic Wagon 2011 32p il (My body) lib bdg $27.07

Grades: 1 2 3   **612.3**

1. Mouth

ISBN 978-1-60270-806-8; 1-60270-806-1

This "volume stars a child narrator who straightforwardly describes [the mouth] and how it works. A round-faced, lab-coat-wearing man appears at the bottom of every spread to provide additional details and tidbits of anatomical information. . . . Black-outlined digital-looking cartoon illustrations enliven the [text]." Horn Book Guide

Includes glossary

My stomach; illustrated by Remy Simard; content consultant, Anthony J. Weinhaus. Magic Wagon 2010 32p il (My body) lib bdg $27.07

Grades: 1 2 3   **612.3**

1. Stomach

ISBN 978-1-60270-810-5; 1-60270-810-X

This "volume stars a child narrator who straightforwardly describes [the stomach] and how it works. A round-faced, lab-coat-wearing man appears at the bottom of every spread to provide additional details and tidbits of anatomical information. . . . Black-outlined digital-looking cartoon illustrations enliven the [text]." Horn Book Guide

Includes glossary

Showers, Paul

What happens to a hamburger? illustrated by Edward Miller. HarperCollins Pubs. 2001 33p il (Let's-read-and-find-out science) hardcover o.p. pa $5.99

Grades: K 1 2 3   **612.3**

ISBN 0-06-027947-8; 0-06-027948-6 lib bdg; 0-06-445183-6 pa

LC 97-39007

A newly illustrated edition of the title first published 1970

Explains the processes by which a hamburger and other foods are used to make energy, strong bones, and solid muscles as they pass through the digestive system

This edition offers "attractive new illustrations, enhanced in a few places with photos that show body parts such as the epiglottis and the stomach lining. . . . Miller's digital artwork has a jaunty, retro look." Booklist

Simon, Seymour

★ **Guts**; our digestive system. [by] Seymour Simon. HarperCollins 2005 un il $16.99; lib bdg $17.89

Grades: 4 5 6 7   **612.3**

1. Digestion

ISBN 0-06-054651-4; 0-06-054652-2 lib bdg

LC 2004-14508

"Simon's specialty of drawing in readers through large, detailed, breathtaking photos and then entertaining them with facts is again in evidence. . . . The text is enhanced with detailed colored X rays, computer-generated pictures, and microscopic photos." SLJ

Thomas, Isabel

Why do I burp? digestion and diet. Raintree 2011 32p il (Inside my body) lib bdg $29; pa $7.99

Grades: 3 4 5 6   **612.3**

1. Digestion

ISBN 978-1-4109-4014-8 lib bdg; 1-4109-4014-4 lib bdg; 978-1-4109-4025-4 pa; 1-4109-4025-X pa

LC 2010024679

"Double-page spreads begin with questions related to the . . . digestive system. The answers, in the form of short paragraphs, bulleted lists, labeled diagrams and schematics, charts, and captioned photos, pack a surprising amount of information into relatively uncluttered pages. . . . Sidebars debunk common misconceptions, give practical advice, and add quirky facts." Horn Book Guide

Includes glossary and bibliographical references

Tieck, Sarah

Digestive system. ABDO Pub. 2011 32p il (Body systems) lib bdg $27.07; e-book $27.07

Grades: 2 3 4   **612.3**

1. Digestion

ISBN 978-1-61613-498-3 lib bdg; 1-61613-498-4 lib bdg; 978-1-61758-988-1 e-book

LC 2010019663

"Double-page spreads describe the workings of the [digestive system] . . . with simple text on lefthand pages and large, colorful photographs or diagrams on the right. The [text touches] on common disorders . . . and healthy practices. 'Brain Food' spreads pose three questions and provide answers. Ample white space, engaging images, and 'Word of Mouth' sidebars are reader-friendly." Horn Book Guide

Includes glossary

612.36 Large intestine

Goodman, Susan E.

The **truth** about poop and pee; all the facts on the ins and outs of bodily functions. by Susan E. Goodman; illustrated by Elwood Smith. Penguin Group USA 2014 133 p. col. ill. $6.99

Grades: 2 3 4 5 **612.36**

1. Human body

ISBN 0147510376; 9780147510372

This children's book, by Susan E. Goodman, illustrated by Elwood Smith, presents "All the Facts on the Ins and Outs of Bodily Functions! . . . Did you know the chemicals in pee can be used to reduce city smog? Or that poop can fuel a trip to Mars? While we politely avoid the subject, amazing things are happening in digestive tracts all over the world, and you won't believe some of the gross-but-true details!" (Publisher's note)

"This volume briefly describes the biological function of human elimination, recounts the history of toilets and toilet paper, and explains what happens to waste after it's flushed away. A breezy tone and comical illustrations keep things fairly tasteful, even when exploring such topics as the amount and frequency of animal elimination and the souvenirs one can buy at Alaska's Moose Dropping Festival." Horn Book

Woolf, Alex

You wouldn't want to live without poop! written by Alex Woolf; illustrated by David Antram; series created by David Salariya. Franklin Watts, an imprint of Scholastic Inc. 2016 32 p. color illustrations (library binding) $29.00

Grades: 3 4 5 6 **612.36**

1. Feces 2. Digestion 3. Defecation 4. Animal droppings

ISBN 9780531214893; 9780531224397

LC 2015031490

This book, by Alex Woolf, illustrated by David Antram, explains that "going to the toilet is a natural and necessary part of our lives. We couldn't live without poop because there are some parts of our food that contain no nutrients that can be used by our bodies . . . and those parts have to be ejected. But poop can also be used to power our cars, heat our homes and help grow our crops. Learn why and how animals and people produce poop, and about [its] many marvelous uses." (Publisher's note)

"The books feature a time line and numerous ancillaries, but the myriad entertaining facts are the real hit. Who wouldn't want to read them?" Booklist

612.4 Hematopoietic, lymphatic, glandular, urinary systems

Kim, Melissa

Learning about the endocrine and reproductive systems; by Melissa L. Kim. Enslow Publishers 2013 48 p. (Learning about the human body systems) (library) $23.93

Grades: 5 6 7 8 **612.4**

1. Picture books for children 2. Endocrine glands 3. Reproductive system 4. Generative organs

ISBN 0766041581; 9780766041585

LC 2012011101

This book by Melissa L. Kim is part of the Learning About the Human Body Systems series and looks at the endocrine and reproductive systems. "The endocrine system is essential to human life. It enables a

person to grow, respond to change and stress, and helps turn food into energy. The reproductive system has one crucial task: that of making the next generation of people." (Publisher's note)

Includes bibliographical references and index.

612.6 Reproduction, development, maturation

Brown, Laurene Krasny

What's the big secret? talking about sex with girls and boys. [by] Laurie Krasny Brown and Marc Brown. Little, Brown 1997 31p il hardcover o.p. pa $5.95

Grades: K 1 2 3 **612.6**

1. Sex education

ISBN 0-316-10915-0; 0-316-10183-4 pa

LC 96-15521

This "picture book's subject is sex and sexuality: not simply physical differences but also gender roles, the issue of privacy, and reproduction. . . . The Browns do an outstanding and very responsible job of introducing a wide variety of terms (everything from the expected, umbilical cord, to the unexpected, masturbation, which is handled with honesty but restraint), synthesizing a great deal of information kids want to know at this age, and presenting facts in a nonthreatening but forthright context. They even manage a good deal of humor along the way. . . . The words and illustrations work extremely well together, with the busy, bright cartoon art and balloon dialogue conveying as much of the information as the text." Booklist

Butler, Dori Hillestad

★ My mom's having a baby! illustrated by Carol Thompson. Albert Whitman & Co. 2005 un il $15.95

Grades: 2 3 4 **612.6**

1. Pregnancy 2. Childbirth 3. Sex education

ISBN 0-8075-5344-1

LC 2004-18585

"Elizabeth describes the month-by-month development of the baby as well as the changes in Mom's body. . . . Through very direct language and clear illustrations, children will learn about a man's testicles where sperm are made and the fallopian tube where an egg is fertilized. . . . Mom answers Elizabeth's big question, 'how do Dad's sperm and your egg get together?' . . . Details are not spared when the birth is described. The playful and colorful illustrations add exuberance to the text, combining full-page paintings, cartoon panels, word balloons, and free-floating images. The joy and love felt by all of the family members is palpable. This volume is an excellent choice for those readers who are ready to ask and be told some of life's basic facts." SLJ

Cocovini, Abby

★ What's inside your tummy, Mommy? [by] Abby Cocovini. Henry Holt & Co. 2008 un il pa $8.95

Grades: PreK K **612.6**

1. Pregnancy

ISBN 978-0-8050-8760-4 pa; 0-8050-8760-5 pa

"Cocovini has designed this oversize guide so that 'if the mommy holds the book up to her belly, you will see what the baby looks like (actual size) inside her every month!' . . . This book is warm and nonthreatening to the max, its crayoned and watercolor spot illustrations and hand-drawn timeline lending it a homey, scrapbook/journal feel. The five or so factoids on each page are shaped around easy-to-grasp, domestic concepts." Publ Wkly

Cole, Joanna

★ How you were born; photographs by Margaret Miller. rev & expanded ed; Morrow Junior Bks. 1993 48p il $15.95; pa $6.99

Grades: K 1 2   **612.6**
1. Infants 2. Pregnancy 3. Childbirth
ISBN 0-688-12059-8; 0-688-12061-X pa

LC 92-23970

A revised and newly illustrated edition of the title first published 1984
"Illustrated with photographs of culturally diverse families, Cole's text explains conception, the development of the fetus, and the birth process. A note to parents and a suggested reading list are included." J Youth Serv Libr

When you were inside Mommy; illustrated by Maxie Chambliss. HarperCollins Pubs. 2001 un il $7.99
Grades: PreK K 1   **612.6**
1. Infants 2. Pregnancy 3. Childbirth
ISBN 0-688-17043-9

LC 00-40890

This "begins with a simple explanation of a baby's development in the mother's uterus. It goes on to show the baby's birth, followed by his growth to a child of perhaps three or four years old. An appended 'Note to Parents' offers a sound approach to talking with children. . . . The simplicity and sensitivity of the writing is well matched by Chambliss' line and watercolor wash illustrations." Booklist

Fromer, Liza
My stretchy body; [by] Liza Fromer and Francine Gerstein; illustrated by Joe Weissmann. Tundra Books 2011 un il (Body works) $12.95
Grades: 2 3 4 5   **612.6**
1. Growth
ISBN 978-1-77049-203-5; 1-77049-203-8

This describes how we grow, including hair, skin, nails, teeth, muscles, and bones, as well as growth spurts and growing pains.
Includes glossary

Gaff, Jackie
Looking at growing up; how do people change? [by] Jackie Gaff. Enslow Publishers 2008 32p il (Looking at science: how things change) lib bdg $22.60
Grades: 1 2 3   **612.6**
1. Growth
ISBN 978-0-7660-3090-9 lib bdg; 0-7660-3090-3 lib bdg

LC 2007-24509

"Fills a huge void in elementary science collections. . . . Text is arranged in succinct 'chunks,' giving important facts without overwhelming readers. . . . [This] is an essential addition." Libr Media Connect
Includes glossary and bibliographical references

Gravelle, Karen
The **period** book; a girl's guide to growing up. Karen Gravelle; illustrated by Debbie Palen. 3rd edition Bloomsbury USA 2017 136 p illustrations paperback $13.99
Grades: 4 5 6 7   **612.6**
1. Menstruation
ISBN 9781619636620; 161963662X
First published 1996

"Written in consultation with preteen girls, this guide offers a supportive, practical approach, providing clear and sensitive answers to common questions on periods, as well as advice dealing with pimples and mood swings." (Publisher's note)

Harris, Robie H.
★ **It's** not the stork! a book about girls, boys, babies, bodies, families, and friends. illustrated by Michael Emberley. Candlewick Press 2006 59p il $16.99

Grades: K 1 3   **612.6**
1. Pregnancy 2. Childbirth 3. Sex education
ISBN 0-7636-0047-4

LC 2005-54280

"Harris opens by introducing two cartoon characters—a green-feathered bird clad in a purple shirt and blue hightop sneakers and his spike-haired friend, a bee. They wonder, 'So where DO babies come from?' Their conversational commentary, given in word balloons, is a lighthearted supplement to a more focused narrative. Told in the second person, the text is straightforward, informative, and personable. Facts are presented step-by-step, starting from the similarities and differences between boys' and girls' bodies, moving to a baby's conception, growth in the womb, and birth, ending with an exploration of different configurations of families as well as a section on 'okay' versus 'not okay' touches." SLJ

★ **Who** has what? all about girls' bodies and boys' bodies. Candlewick Press 2011 un il $15.99
Grades: PreK K 1   **612.6**
1. Human body 2. Sex education
ISBN 978-0-7636-2931-1; 0-7636-2931-6

LC 2010040464

"A family outing to the beach provides the opportunity for a discussion of the similarities and differences between boys and girls. Nellie's play on the words 'everybody' and 'every body' leads Gus to wondering about body parts. Their beach visit provides an opportunity to see a variety of people and puppies, to itemize all the parts that boys and girls and dogs have in common. . . . Harris . . . matter-of-factly combines common childhood language . . . and anatomically correct terms. . . . Westcott's digital cartoonlike illustrations show different compositions of families representing a wide range of ages, races and nationalities." Kirkus

Harris, Robie H., 1940-
★ **It's** so amazing! a book about eggs, sperm, birth, babies, and families. Robie H. Harris; illustrated by Michael Emberley. 15th anniversary edition Candlewick Press 2014 82 p color illustrations hardcover $22.99; paperback $12.99
Grades: 2 3 4   **612.6**
1. Pregnancy 2. Childbirth 3. Sex education
ISBN 9780763668730; 0763668737; 0763668745; 9780763668747
Uses bird and bee cartoon characters to present straightforward explanations of topics related to sexual development, love, reproduction, adoption, and sexually transmitted diseases.
Features "updated text and art, a broader definition of the term gender, and expanded information about using the internet." Horn Book

★ **What's** in there? all about you before you were born. by Robie H. Harris and illustrated by Nadine Bernard Westcott. Candlewick Press 2013 40 p. (All about us!) (hardback : alk. paper) $15.99
Grades: PreK K 1   **612.6**
1. Pregnancy 2. Childbirth 3. Human reproduction 4. Sex instruction for children
ISBN 0763636304; 9780763636302

LC 2008025455

This book, by Robie H. Harris and illustrated by Nadine Bernand Westcott, "follows the stages of pregnancy and childbirth in a matter-of-fact and comfortable way. Gus and Nellie have some exciting news: there's going to be a baby in their family! Join them through the seasons as they watch their mother's pregnancy with fascination and curiosity while awaiting the birth of their new baby sibling." (Publisher's note)

Jukes, Mavis

★ **Growing** up: it's a girl thing; straight talk about first bras, first periods, and your changing body. illustrations by Debbie Tilley. Knopf 1998 72p il hardcover o.p. pa $10

Grades: 4 5 6 7　　　**612.6**

1. Girls 2. Adolescence 3. Menstruation

ISBN 0-679-89027-0 pa

LC 98-18113

This "covers body hair and shaving, perspiration and deodorant, and how to buy your first bra. The second half of the book is devoted to what to expect and how to plan for your first period. . . . The narration has an easy, comfortable voice and imparts accurate and important information." SLJ

Katz, Anne

Girl in the know; your inside-and-out guide to growing up. written by Anne Katz; illustrated by Monika Melnychuk. Kids Can Press 2010 111p il $18.95

Grades: 4 5 6 7　　　**612.6**

1. Puberty 2. Girls -- Health and hygiene 3. Life skills guides 4. Girls -- Psychology

ISBN 978-1-55453-303-9; 1-55453-303-1

"This reassuring title is aimed at girls who want clear facts about puberty but who may not be ready to read in-depth specifics of sex and birth-control. The author . . . offers a holistic guide that covers the body changes puberty brings as well as tips about maintaining physical and emotional health. . . . The warm, straightforward, useful advice on a broad range of topics . . . will captivate both middle graders and middle-schoolers, and the frequent color drawings of stylish, diverse girls . . . . reinforce the book's appeal to a wide age group." Booklist

Madaras, Lynda

★ **On** your mark, get set, grow! a what's happening to my body? book for younger boys. [by] Lynda Madaras; illustrations by Paul Gilligan. Newmarket Press 2008 123p il $22; pa $12

Grades: 3 4 5 6　　　**612.6**

1. Puberty 2. Boys -- Health and hygiene

ISBN 978-1-55704-780-9; 1-55704-780-4; 978-1-55704-781-6 pa; 1-55704-781-2 pa

LC 2007043095

"Madaras draws on her experience teaching sex education (called puberty classes here) to inform boys about the physical changes they will experience as they start to mature. . . . The age-appropriate presentation includes cartoon art on almost every page and a sprinkling of humor. Along with covering sex-organ growth, height, weight, and muscle gain, Madaras also discusses health and nutrition, hygiene, and 'becoming your own self.' A reassuring tone pervades the text. . . . This is an excellent resource for both children and parents." SLJ

★ **Ready,** set, grow! a what's happening to my body? book for younger girls. illustrations by Linda Davick. Newmarket Press 2003 127p il $22; pa $12

Grades: 3 4 5 6　　　**612.6**

1. Puberty 2. Girls -- Health and hygiene

ISBN 1-55704-587-9; 1-55704-565-8 pa

LC 2003-9489

This "is a timely and important book. In a consistently sensitive and encouraging tone, Madaras reassures preadolescents that the changes they know are approaching or they are beginning to experience are normal, natural, and cause for celebration. Humorous sketches illustrate the emotions and stages of puberty, and keep the tone light." SLJ

★ The **what's** happening to my body? book for boys; [by] Lynda Madaras with Area Madaras; drawings by Simon Sullivan. 3rd rev ed.; Newmarket Press 2007 xx, 233p il $24.95; pa $12.95

Grades: 4 5 6 7　　　**612.6**

1. Puberty 2. Adolescence 3. Sex education 4. Boys -- Health and hygiene

ISBN 978-1-55704-769-4; 1-55704-769-3; 978-1-55704-765-6 pa; 1-55704-765-0 pa

LC 2007009874

First published 1984

Discusses the changes that take place in a boy's body during puberty, including information on the body's changing size and shape, the growth spurt, reproductive organs, pubic hair, beards, pimples, voice changes, wet dreams, and puberty in girls

Includes bibliographical references

★ The **what's** happening to my body? book for girls; [by] Lynda Madaras with Area Madaras; drawings by Simon Sullivan. 3rd rev ed.; Newmarket Press 2007 xxvi, 259p il $24.95; pa $12.95

Grades: 4 5 6 7　　　**612.6**

1. Puberty 2. Adolescence 3. Sex education 4. Girls -- Health and hygiene

ISBN 978-1-55704-768-7; 1-55704-768-5; 978-1-55704-764-9 pa; 1-55704-764-2 pa

LC 2007009862

Discusses the changes that take place in a girl's body during puberty, including information on the body's changing size and shape, pubic hair, breasts, reproductive organs, the menstrual cycle, and puberty in boys

Includes bibliographical references

Mar, Jonathan

The **body** book for boys; by Jonathan Mar and Grace Norwich. Scholastic 2010 128p il pa $8.99

Grades: 4 5 6　　　**612.6**

1. Boys 2. Puberty 3. Adolescence

ISBN 978-0-545-23751-2 pa; 0-545-23751-3 pa

"In this reassuring title aimed at boys just entering adolescence, the authors present frank information on such topics as hygiene, the changes brought on by puberty, exercise, and dealing with girls. The tone is kept light, and the many bright illustrations also have a fun, jokey quality." Booklist

Plaisted, Caroline

Boy talk; a survival guide to growing up. illustrated by Chris Dickason. QEB Pub. 2011 il (Growing up)

Grades: 4 5 6 7　　　**612.6**

1. Boys 2. Puberty

ISBN 1-60992-085-6; 978-1-60992-085-2

LC 2011009206

Discusses body changes that happen to boys during puberty, such as acne, body hair, body odor, mood swings, crushes, and more, and gives suggestions to teen boys for taking care of their hygiene and keeping good relationships.

"Using a colorful design featuring Dickason's wacky, mugging cartoon characters, this is about as appealing as a book on these topics can get, and it maintains a mildly funny, usually frank, and always healthy tone." Booklist

Girl talk; a survival guide to growing up. illustrated by Chris Dickason. QEB Pub. 2011 il (Growing up) lib bdg $23.95

Grades: 4 5 6 7　　　**612.6**

1. Girls 2. Puberty

ISBN 978-1-60992-084-5; 1-60992-084-8

LC 2011009125

Discusses body changes that happen to girls during puberty, such as acne, periods, cramps, body hair, mood swings, and more, and gives suggestions to teen girls for taking care of their health.

Pringle, Laurence P.

Everybody has a bellybutton; your life before you were born. by Laurence Pringle; illustrated by Clare Wood. Boyds Mills Press 1997 un il $14.95

Grades: PreK K 1 2 3   **612.6**

1. Fetus 2. Pregnancy 3. Childbirth

ISBN 1-56397-009-0

LC 95-83168

Pringle "offers a gently phrased, solidly scientific look at the growth of a baby.... The narrative gives specific, sensorial details that will keep even young children engaged, and the description of childbirth is matter-of-fact and undisturbing.... Illustrations are softly realistic pencil drawings on pink and blue backgrounds." Booklist

Includes bibliographical references

Rand, Casey

Human reproduction. Raintree 2009 48p il (Sci-hi: life science) lib bdg $31.43; pa $8.99

Grades: 5 6 7 8   **612.6**

1. Reproduction 2. Sex education

ISBN 978-1-4109-3327-0 lib bdg; 1-4109-3327-X lib bdg; 978-1-4109-3335-5 pa; 1-4109-3335-0 pa

LC 2009003464

In this introduction to human reproduction "clear language, embedded definitions, and interesting examples illustrate abstract concepts through both text and well-chosen photographs.... [It] includes suggested activities to test ideas as well as a thorough glossary and a Webliography." SLJ

Includes glossary and bibliographical references

Saltz, Gail

★ **Amazing** you; getting smart about your private parts. illustrated by Lynne Avril Cravath. Dutton Children's Books 2005 un il $15.99

Grades: PreK K 1   **612.6**

1. Growth 2. Reproduction 3. Sex education

ISBN 0-525-47389-0

LC 2004-22014

"This upbeat picture book, illustrated with sunny cartoon drawings, introduces kids to basic reproductive physiology. Saltz offers simple, accessible definitions of terms, accompanied by pictures of unclothed kids and labeled diagrams of internal organs. Subsequent drawings show three stages of body development from baby to young adult, followed by an abbreviated explanation, illustrated with a heart-shaped drawing of a smiling egg and sperm, of reproduction.... Saltz presents the information clearly in a cheerful, positive tone." Booklist

Changing you! a guide to body changes and sexuality. [by] Gail Saltz; illustrated by Lynne Avril Cravath. Dutton Children's Books 2007 un il $16.99

Grades: 3 4 5   **612.6**

1. Puberty 2. Sex education

ISBN 978-0-525-47817-1; 0-525-47817-5

LC 2006035593

"This is an introduction to puberty and sexual intercourse in the context of a loving relationship between a man and woman. The book covers topics that kids often inquire about, such as bodily changes and how babies are born. Bright, cartoon illustrations of the human body at different stages and ages and labeled diagrams fill the pages. The clear, straightforward text uses language that young children can easily grasp

while the running commentary that accompanies the art takes a lighter, more conversational approach." SLJ

Schwartz, John

Short; walking tall when you're not tall at all. Roaring Brook Press 2010 132p il $16.99

Grades: 4 5 6 7 8   **612.6**

1. Size 2. Growth 3. Body image 4. Prejudices

ISBN 978-1-59643-323-6; 1-59643-323-X

"In a humorous, personal voice, ... Schwartz combines his own memories of growing up short with related discussions about physiology, statistics, popular culture, and societal prejudice, always returning to his own self-image.... Short kids will want every word.... and many readers will move on to the resource list of articles, Web sites, and scientific papers in the detailed, informal back matter." Booklist

Includes bibliographical references

Silverberg, Cory

★ **Sex** is a funny word; a book about bodies, feelings, and YOU. by Cory Silverberg & Fiona Smyth. Seven Stories Press 2015 160 p. illustrations (hardcover) $23.95

Grades: 2 3 4 5   **612.6**

1. Sex 2. Sex education 3. Sex instruction for children 4. Sex (Biology) 5. Sex differences

ISBN 1609806069; 9781609806064

LC 2014043859

Stonewall Book Awards Honor Book, Youth (2016)

This book, by Cory Silverberg and illustrated by Fiona Smyth, is "a comic book for kids that includes children and families of all make-ups, orientations, and gender identities, ... [The book] is an essential resource about bodies, gender, and sexuality for children ages 8 to 10 as well as their parents and caregivers." (Publisher's note)

"Silverberg and Smyth follow What Makes a Baby with a highly visual introduction to sex education for older readers, featuring four characters between the ages of eight and 10 with skin in a rainbow of crayon-box colors. Full-page artwork and comics sequences follow the students as they react to discussions of gender, bodies (including what Silverberg calls "middle parts"), touching, and the emotions that lead to sexual contact; the book stops short of getting into the mechanics of intercourse.... mphasizing the importance of trust, respect, justice, and joy—as well as open communication—it's a thoughtful and affirming exploration of relationships, gender identity, and growing sexual awareness." PW

612.7 Musculoskeletal system, integument

Baines, Rebecca

The **bones** you own; a book about the human body. by Becky Baines. National Geographic 2009 27p il (Zigzag) $16.95; lib bdg $25.90

Grades: PreK K 1   **612.7**

1. Bones 2. Skeleton

ISBN 978-1-4263-0410-1; 1-4263-0410-2; 978-1-4263-0411-8 lib bdg; 1-4263-0411-0 lib bdg

LC 2008-47900

This describes functions that bones perform in a human body.

This title engages "children through humor, clear language, interesting facts, and abundant photos.... [An] excellent [introduction] for young science students." SLJ

Your skin holds you in; a book about your skin. by Becky Baines. National Geographic 2008 29p il (Zigzag) $14.95; lib bdg $19.90

Grades: PreK K 1   **612.7**
1. Skin
ISBN 978-1-4263-0311-1; 1-4263-0311-4; 978-1-4263-0312-8 lib bdg; 1-4263-0312-2 lib bdg
LC 2007-44156

"Thirteen short sentences describe skin . . . in all its glory. Additional facts appear in smaller print . . . on the same pages with the main idea sentences. Photographs of people, outlined in white and reproduced on brightly colored pages, serve as diagrams for important elements. . . . Exuberant double-page spreads encourage looking and talking." Horn Book

Barner, Bob
Dem bones; [illustrations and informational bone text by] Bob Barner. Chronicle Bks. 1996 un il $16.99
Grades: K 1 2 3   **612.7**
1. Bones 2. Skeleton
ISBN 0-8118-0827-0
LC 95-29

"A rollicking read-aloud, sing-along treat for children as they learn anatomy, rhyme, and language.... Scientific facts and names combined with lyrics make this a fascinating book." Exploring Sci in the Libr

Bassington, Cyril
Your bones; Cyril Bassington. Gareth Stevens Publishing 2017 24 p. color illustrations (library bound) $22.60; (ebook) $22.60
Grades: 1 2 3   **612.7**
1. Bones 2. Skeleton 3. Physiology 4. Human physiology
ISBN 9781482443974; 9781482444353; 9781482444537; 9781482444155
LC 2015021475

This book, by Cyril Bassington, is a "helpful guide to the human skeleton [and] presents readers with a key body system. They will be acquainted with groups of bones such as the spine and skull and learn what they need to do to keep their bones healthy. Carefully chosen photographs and illustrations support the accessible text, which is a valuable introduction to several key biology concepts." (Publisher's note)

"The relatable text lives up to the series title, as they truly help young readers know their bodies." Booklist
Includes bibliographical references and index

Berger, Melvin
Why I sneeze, shiver, hiccup, and yawn; illustrated by Paul Meisel. HarperCollins Pubs. 2000 un il (Let's-read-and-find-out science) hardcover o.p. pa $4.99
Grades: K 1 2 3   **612.7**
1. Reflexes 2. Nervous system
ISBN 0-06-028144-8; 0-06-445193-3 pa
LC 98-55542

A revised and newly illustrated edition of Why I cough, sneeze, shiver, hiccup & yawn, published 1983 by Crowell

An introduction to reflex acts that explains why we sneeze, shiver, hiccup, and yawn

"The writing is simple but effective, and the charming, colorful pen-and-ink and watercolors are [detailed]. . . . Attractive introductory nonfiction." SLJ

Fittleworth, George
Your muscles; George Fittleworth. Gareth Stevens Publishing 2017 24 p. (library bound) $22.60
Grades: 1 2 3   **612.7**
1. Muscles 2. Physiology 3. Human physiology
ISBN 9781482444018; 9781482444216; 9781482444575
LC 2015021479

In this book, by George Fittleworth, "readers will discover how the three kinds of muscles, skeletal, cardiac, and smooth, work in collaboration with their other body parts to keep them moving. They'll learn what extraordinary machines the human body's more than 600 muscles are as well as how to keep them healthy and toned. Accessible text and supporting diagrams and photographs make this book a valuable tool in addressing an important topic of the elementary science curriculum." (Publisher's note)

"The relatable text lives up to the series title, as they truly help young readers know their bodies." Booklist
Includes bibliographical references and index

Gold, Susan Dudley
Learning about the musculoskeletal system and the skin; Susan Dudley Gold. Enslow Publishers 2013 48 p. (Learning about the human body systems) (library) $23.93
Grades: 5 6 7 8   **612.7**
1. Picture books for children 2. Musculoskeletal system 3. Skin
ISBN 076604159X; 9780766041592
LC 2012011102

This book by Susan Dudley Gold is part of the Learning About the Human Body Systems series and looks at the musculoskeletal system. "Bone and muscles join forces to move us from one place to another. The musculoskeletal system controls our breathing, allows our eyes to focus, and shapes our smiles. It enables us to talk and to eat. Our strong bones support our weight. Skin wraps our body in a tough layer of tissue that keeps moisture in and germs out." (Publisher's note)

Includes bibliographical references and index..

Guillain, Charlotte
Our bones. Heinemann Library 2010 24p il (Our bodies) lib bdg $20.71; pa $5.99
Grades: K 1 2 3   **612.7**
1. Bones
ISBN 978-1-4329-3596-2 lib bdg; 1-4329-3596-8 lib bdg; 978-1-4329-3605-1 pa; 1-4329-3605-0 pa
LC 2009-22300

This describes what bones are, how they support the body, and how to keep them healthy.

This explains "visually and verbally complicated medical information in a clear, understandable way. . . . Large, vivid photographs are placed alongside one or two sentences per page." Booklist
Includes bibliographical references

Our muscles. Heinemann Library 2010 24p il (Our bodies) lib bdg $20.71; pa $5.99
Grades: K 1 2 3   **612.7**
1. Muscles
ISBN 978-1-4329-3593-1 lib bdg; 1-4329-3593-3 lib bdg; 978-1-4329-3602-0 pa; 1-4329-3602-6 pa
LC 2009-22297

This describes what muscles are, how they help us move, and how to keep them healthy.

This explains "visually and verbally complicated medical information in a clear, understandable way. . . . Large, vivid photographs are placed alongside one or two sentences per page." Booklist
Includes bibliographical references

Our skin. Heinemann Library 2010 24p il (Our bodies) lib bdg $20.71; pa $5.99

Grades: K 1 2 3   **612.7**
    1. Skin
    ISBN 978-1-4329-3597-9 lib bdg; 1-4329-3597-6 lib bdg; 978-1-4329-3606-8 pa; 1-4329-3606-9 pa

                                                        LC 2009-22301

This describes what skin is, how it protects the body, and how to keep it healthy.

This explains "visually and verbally complicated medical information in a clear, understandable way. . . . Large, vivid photographs are placed alongside one or two sentences per page." Booklist

Includes bibliographical references

Jenkins, Steve
    ★ **Bones**; skeletons and how they work. Scholastic Press 2010 un il $16.99
Grades: 3 4 5 6   **612.7**
    1. Bones 2. Skeleton
    ISBN 978-0-545-04651-0; 0-545-04651-3

Jenkins "begins with a single human finger bone, then shows where it fits in the hand, then attaches the arm bones and sets it aside the forelimbs of a mole, spider monkey, gray whale, turtle, and fruit bat to illustrate how they all share the same basic structure. Similar comparisons take a look at feet, legs, rib cages, necks, and heads, almost always using a consistent scale to display the relative size of elephant and stork legs or a giraffe and human neck. Jenkins provides concise chunks of text alongside his always impressive cut-paper collages. . . . The clean design of the intricate skeletons set against solid background colors is striking and provides a wonderful visual introduction to what keeps us all upright." Booklist

Kaner, Etta
    And the Winner Is ... Amazing Animal Athletes. by Etta Kaner; illustrated by David Anderson. Kids Can Press 2013 32 p. ill. (hardcover) $16.95
Grades: PreK K 1 2 3   **612.7**
    1. Animals 2. Athletics
    ISBN 1554539048; 9781554539048

This book "presents the World Animal Games, with quartets of different of critters competing in a variety of Olympic-type events. A walrus and a cockatoo provide facts and color as the contestants vie for the gold in the high jump, sprinting, weight lifting, swimming, and other trials . . . . A data box for each entrant is provided, as is information on just why the winner came out on top, and how the record stands up to human athletes." (School Library Journal)

Korb, Rena
    My muscles; illustrated by Remy Simard; Content Consultant; Anthony J. Weinhaus. Magic Wagon 2010 32p il (My body) lib bdg $27.07
Grades: 1 2 3   **612.7**
    1. Muscles
    ISBN 978-1-60270-807-5; 1-60270-807-X

This "volume stars a child narrator who straightforwardly describes [muscles] and how [they work]. A round-faced, lab-coat-wearing man appears at the bottom of every spread to provide additional details and tidbits of anatomical information. . . . Black-outlined digital-looking cartoon illustrations enliven the [text]." Horn Book Guide

Includes glossary

My spine; illustrated by Remy Simard; content consultant, Anthony J. Weinhaus. Magic Wagon 2010 32p il (My body) lib bdg $27.07
Grades: 1 2 3   **612.7**
    1. Spine
    ISBN 978-1-6027-0809-9; 1-60270-809-6

This "volume stars a child narrator who straightforwardly describes [the spine] and how it works. A round-faced, lab-coat-wearing man appears at the bottom of every spread to provide additional details and tidbits of anatomical information. . . . Black-outlined digital-looking cartoon illustrations enliven the [text]." Horn Book Guide

Includes glossary

Parker, Steve, 1952-
    How do my muscles get strong? Raintree 2011 32p il (Inside my body) lib bdg $29; pa $7.99
Grades: 3 4 5 6   **612.7**
    1. Muscles 2. Exercise
    ISBN 978-1-4109-4017-9 lib bdg; 1-4109-4017-9 lib bdg; 978-1-4109-4028-5 pa; 1-4109-4028-4 pa

                                                        LC 2010024800

"Double-page spreads begin with questions related to the human muscular . . . system. The answers, in the form of short paragraphs, bulleted lists, labeled diagrams and schematics, charts, and captioned photos, pack a surprising amount of information into relatively uncluttered pages. . . . Sidebars debunk common misconceptions, give practical advice, and add quirky facts." Horn Book Guide

Includes glossary and bibliographical references

The **skeleton** and muscles; [by] Steve Parker. Raintree 2004 48p il (Our bodies) lib bdg $29.93
Grades: 5 6 7 8   **612.7**
    1. Musculoskeletal system
    ISBN 0-7398-6622-2

                                                        LC 2003-6594

This "takes a look at bones, muscles, and joints; how they are connected and function; and how to keep them healthy. The anatomy is accurate, and the format, with plenty of pictures, diagrams, and magnified photos, is very accessible. There are also lots of lively boxed facts." Booklist

Includes bibliographical references

Simon, Seymour
    Bones; our skeletal system. Morrow Junior Bks. 1998 un il hardcover o.p. pa $6.99
Grades: 4 5 6 7   **612.7**
    1. Bones 2. Skeleton
    ISBN 0-688-14645-7 lib bdg; 0-688-17721-2 pa

                                                        LC 97-44751

Describes the skeletal system and outlines the many important roles that bones play in the healthy functioning of the human body

"Simon once again proves his remarkable facility for making complicated science clear and understandable." Booklist

Muscles; our muscular system. Morrow Junior Bks. 1998 un il hardcover o.p. pa $6.99
Grades: 4 5 6 7   **612.7**
    1. Muscles
    ISBN 0-688-14642-2; 0-688-14643-0 lib bdg; 0-688-17720-4 pa

                                                        LC 97-44758

Describes the nature and work of muscles, the different kinds, and the effects of exercise and other activities on them

"The full-paged illustrations are great and include full-color photographs, MRI scans, X rays, and excellent drawings." SLJ

Stewart, Melissa
    Here we grow; the secrets of hair and nails. illustrated by Janet Hamlin. Marshall Cavendish Benchmark 2010 48p il (The gross and goofy body) lib bdg $20.95

Grades: 2 3 4   **612.7**
1. Hair
ISBN 978-0-7614-4172-4 lib bdg; 0-7614-4172-7 lib bdg
LC 2008033563
This provides information on the role hair and nails play in the body science of humans and animals.

This "offers detailed science facts in a fashion approachable enough to make it a welcome supplement to school textbooks. . . . The layout is fresh, clean, and colorful, sidebars keep things conversational, and the back matter is solid." Booklist
Includes glossary and bibliographical references

Moving and grooving; the secrets of muscles and bones. illustrated by Janet Hamlin. Marshall Cavendish Benchmark 2010 48p il (The gross and goofy body) lib bdg $20.95
Grades: 2 3 4   **612.7**
1. Musculoskeletal system
ISBN 978-0-7614-4166-3 lib bdg; 0-7614-4166-2 lib bdg
LC 2008033557
This offers information on the role bones and muscles play in the body science of humans and animals
Includes glossary and bibliographical references

Tieck, Sarah
Muscular system. ABDO Pub. Co. 2011 32p il (Body systems) lib bdg $27.07; ebook $27.07
Grades: 2 3 4   **612.7**
1. Muscles 2. Musculoskeletal system
ISBN 978-1-61613-499-0; 1-61613-499-2 lib bdg; 978-1-61613-989-8 ebook
LC 2010019664
"Double-page spreads describe the workings of the [muscular system] . . . with simple text on left-hand pages and large, colorful photographs or diagrams on the right. The [text touches] on common disorders . . . and healthy practices. 'Brain Food' spreads pose three questions and provide answers. Ample white space, engaging images, and 'Word of Mouth' sidebars are reader-friendly." Horn Book Guide
Includes glossary

Skeletal system. ABDO Pub. 2011 32p il (Body systems) lib bdg $27.07; e-book $27.07
Grades: 2 3 4   **612.7**
1. Bones 2. Skeleton
ISBN 978-1-61613-502-7 lib bdg; 1-61613-502-6 lib bdg; 978-1-61613-992-8 e-book
LC 2010019651
"Double-page spreads describe the workings of the [skeletal system] . . . with simple text on left-hand pages and large, colorful photographs or diagrams on the right. The [text touches] on common disorders . . . and healthy practices. 'Brain Food' spreads pose three questions and provide answers. Ample white space, engaging images, and 'Word of Mouth' sidebars are reader-friendly." Horn Book Guide
Includes glossary

612.8   Nervous system

Aliki
My five senses; Aliki. Revised edition Harper 2015 31 p color illustrations (Let's read and find out) hardcover $17.99; paperback $6.99

Grades: PreK K 1   **612.8**
1. Senses and sensation
ISBN 9780062381910; 9780062381927; 0062381911; 006238192X
LC 2015458670
First published 1962
"Sight, smell, taste, hearing, and touch--our five senses teach us about our world. Beloved author-illustrator Aliki's simple, engaging text and colorful artwork show young readers how they use their senses to smell a rose or play with a puppy." (Publisher's note)

Bassington, Cyril
Your brain; Cyril Bassington. Gareth Stevens Publishing 2017 24 p. (library bound) $22.60
Grades: 1 2 3   **612.8**
1. Brain 2. Physiology 3. Brain 4. Human physiology
ISBN 9781482443981; 9781482444360; 9781482444544
LC 2015021476
With this book, by Cyril Bassington, "readers will appreciate the mysterious, fascinating organ in their skull known as the brain as they learn about the five main parts of the brain and their special functions. They'll also find out what they can do to keep their brain working well. Simple illustrations and bright photographs make this volume a fun and informative introduction to the nervous system." (Publisher's note)
"The relatable text lives up to the series title, as they truly help young readers know their bodies." Booklist
Includes bibliographical references and index

Boothroyd, Jennifer
What is hearing? Lerner Publications Co. 2010 32p il (Lightning Bolt Books TM-Your amazing senses) lib bdg $25.26
Grades: K 1 2   **612.8**
1. Sound 2. Hearing
ISBN 978-0-7613-4250-2 lib bdg; 0-7613-4250-8 lib bdg
LC 2008-51848
Describes the properties of sound and hearing, including everyday examples and information on how an ear functions
"Given [its] . . . simple sentences, colorful layout, full-page photos, and well-chosen diagrams, [this title] . . . will be useful for reports." SLJ
Includes glossary and bibliographical references

What is sight? Lerner Publications Co. 2010 32p il (Lightning Bolt Books TM-Your amazing senses) lib bdg $25.26
Grades: K 1 2   **612.8**
1. Vision
ISBN 978-0-7613-4248-9 lib bdg; 0-7613-4248-6 lib bdg
LC 2008-51849
Describes the importance of the sense of sight and how the human eye works, including information on color, depth perception, and protecting sight
"Given [its] . . . simple sentences, colorful layout, full-page photos, and well-chosen diagrams, [this title] . . . will be useful for reports." SLJ
Includes glossary and bibliographical references

What is smell? Lerner Publications Co. 2010 32p il (Lightning Bolt Books TM-Your amazing senses) lib bdg $25.26
Grades: K 1 2   **612.8**
1. Smell
ISBN 978-0-7613-4253-3 lib bdg; 0-7613-4253-2 lib bdg
LC 2008-51850
Provides information on the sense of smell, including why there are good and bad smells and how noses function

"Given [its] . . . simple sentences, colorful layout, full-page photos, and well-chosen diagrams, [this title] . . . will be useful for reports." SLJ
Includes glossary and bibliographical references

What is taste? Lerner Publications Co. 2010 32p il (Lightning Bolt Books TM-Your amazing senses) lib bdg $25.26
Grades: K 1 2   **612.8**
1. Taste
ISBN 978-0-7613-4251-9 lib bdg; 0-7613-4251-6 lib bdg
LC 2008-51847

Explains how human beings use their sense of taste and illustrates good and bad tastes
"Given [its] . . . simple sentences, colorful layout, full-page photos, and well-chosen diagrams, [this title] . . . will be useful for reports." SLJ
Includes glossary and bibliographical references

What is touch? Lerner Publications Co. 2010 32p il (Lightning Bolt Books TM-Your amazing senses) lib bdg $25.26
Grades: K 1 2   **612.8**
1. Touch
ISBN 978-0-7613-4252-6 lib bdg; 0-7613-4252-4 lib bdg
LC 2008-51587

The book about touch has "simple sentences, colorful layout, full-page photos, and well-chosen diagrams . . , [and] will be useful for reports." SLJ

Brocket, Jane
Spiky, slimy, smooth; what is texture? [text and photographs by Jane Brocket] Millbrook Press 2011 un il (Jane Brocket's clever concepts) lib bdg $25.26
Grades: PreK K 1 2   **612.8**
1. Touch
ISBN 978-0-7613-4614-2; 0-7613-4614-7
LC 2010028933

"Bright, attention-grabbing, and, in some cases, enlarged photographs of hard candies, duck slippers, stone walls, and other common objects give viewers the impression that they can reach out and touch them. That's exactly the point in this . . . book, which introduces texture to young children. It not only lets readers imagine what a woolly blanket or cactus plant might feel like but offers a host of adjectives, highlighted in color, to describe their textures. . . . Clever, indeed." Booklist

Degen, Bruce
The **magic** school bus explores the senses; illustrated by Bruce Degen. Scholastic Press 1999 47p il hardcover o.p. pa $5.99
Grades: 2 3 4   **612.8**
1. Senses and sensation
ISBN 0-590-44697-5; 0-590-44698-3 pa
LC 98-18662

Ms. Frizzle and her science class explore the senses by traveling on the magic school bus. "Grades two to five." (SLJ)
"Along the margins are snippets of information in the form of Frizzle Facts and excerpts from kids' school reports. Degen's clever illustrations are both humorous and informative, acting as excellent visual aids for little learners." Booklist

Ganeri, Anita
Hearing; by Anita Ganeri. Smart Apple Media 2013 24 p. (hardcover, library bound : alk. paper) $25.65
Grades: K 1 2   **612.8**
1. Hearing 2. Senses and sensation 3. Ear 4. Hearing
ISBN 1599208512; 9781599208510
LC 2012004122

This book by Anita Ganeri, part of a series on the senses, "begins with a succinct definition: 'Sounds make the air wobble.' From there, [readers] learn how our ear flaps catch sound with ear hair, why we have two ears, and other relevant stuff like ear wax, balance, and how the sense varies in other animals." (Publisher's note)

Sight; by Anita Ganeri. Smart Apple Media 2013 24 p. (The senses) (hardcover, library bound : alk. paper) $25.65
Grades: K 1 2   **612.8**
1. Picture books for children 2. Vision 3. Eye
ISBN 1599208520; 9781599208527
LC 2012004123

This children's picture book by Anita Ganeri is part of the Senses series and looks at sight. At the beginning, a "diagram orients [readers] to all five senses . . . . The texts "discuss what each particular sense provides and the organs involved and how they work. . . . A final spread shares three or four facts that extend the topic." (School Library Journal)

Smell; Anita Ganeri. A+/Smart Apple Media 2013 24 p. (Senses) (hardcover, library bound) $25.65
Grades: K 1 2   **612.8**
1. Picture books for children 2. Smell 3. Nose
ISBN 1599208539; 9781599208534
LC 2012004124

This children's picture book by Anita Ganeri is part of the Senses series and looks at smell. At the beginning, a "diagram orients [readers] to all five senses . . . . The texts "discuss what each particular sense provides and the organs involved and how they work. . . . A final spread shares three or four facts that extend the topic." (School Library Journal)

Taste; Anita Ganeri. A+/Smart Apple Media 2013 24 p. (Senses) (hardcover, library bound) $25.65
Grades: K 1 2   **612.8**
1. Picture books for children 2. Taste
ISBN 1599208547; 9781599208541
LC 2012008594

This children's picture book by Anita Ganeri is part of the Senses series and looks at smell. At the beginning, a "diagram orients [readers] to all five senses . . . . The texts "discuss what each particular sense provides and the organs involved and how they work. . . . A final spread shares three or four facts that extend the topic." (School Library Journal)

Gardner, Robert
Ace your science project about the senses; great science fair ideas. [by] Robert Gardner . . . [et al.] Enslow Publishers 2009 112p il (Ace your biology science project) lib bdg $31.93
Grades: 5 6 7 8   **612.8**
1. Science projects 2. Senses and sensation 3. Science -- Experiments
ISBN 978-0-7660-3217-0 lib bdg; 0-7660-3217-5 lib bdg
LC 2008-30797

"Presents several science projects and science project ideas about the senses." Publisher's note
Includes glossary and bibliographical references

Gold, Martha V.
Learning about the nervous system; by Martha V. Gold. Enslow Publishers 2013 48 p. (Learning about the human body systems) (library) $23.93
Grades: 5 6 7 8   **612.8**
1. Picture books for children 2. Nervous system
ISBN 0766041603; 9780766041608
LC 2012011103

This book by Martha V. Gold is part of the Learning About the Human Body Systems series and looks at the nervous system. "The nervous system is made up of the brain, the spinal cord and nerves. It is responsible for telling the heart to beat, the lungs to breathe, and the muscles to move. The brain—the central command center—processes everything from understanding a teacher's instructions to enjoying a piece of chocolate cake." (Publisher's note)

Includes bibliographical references and index.

Guillain, Charlotte

How do we hear? Heinemann Library 2008 24p il (Sounds all around us) lib bdg $20.71; pa $5.99

Grades: PreK K 1   **612.8**

1. Sound 2. Hearing 3. Sound waves

ISBN 978-1-4329-3201-5 lib bdg; 1-4329-3201-2 lib bdg; 978-1-4329-3207-7 pa; 1-4329-3207-1 pa

LC 2008-51738

Learn about sound waves, how the human ear works, and how animals can have a special sense of hearing.

This book "introduces the basics of sound through vibrant photographs, large text, and simple sentences. . . . [A] great introduction[s] and worthy addition[s]." SLJ

Includes glossary and bibliographical references

Our brains. Heinemann Library 2010 24p il (Our bodies) lib bdg $20.71; pa $5.99

Grades: K 1 2 3   **612.8**

1. Brain

ISBN 978-1-4329-3592-4 lib bdg; 1-4329-3592-5 lib bdg; 978-1-4329-3601-3 pa; 1-4329-3601-8 pa

LC 2009-22296

This explains what the brain is, how it controls other body parts, and how to keep it healthy.

This explains "visually and verbally complicated medical information in a clear, understandable way. . . . Large, vivid photographs are placed alongside one or two sentences per page." Booklist

Includes bibliographical references

Halvorson, Karin

Inside the brain; Karin Halvorson; consulting editor, Diane Craig. ABDO Pub. Co. 2013 32 p. (Super simple body) $27.07

Grades: 2 3 4 5   **612.8**

1. Brain 2. Brain -- Physiology

ISBN 1617836095; 9781617836091

LC 2012028763

Author Karin Halvorson's book "offers children an exciting voyage through the brain. Detailed illustrations, color photos, and simple text combine to make a fun and easy introduction to how the brain works. This book also includes simple activities and crafts like Reaction Action, Thinking Cap and how to make a Brain with how-to photos to further engage young learners." (Publisher's note)

Inside the ears; by Karin Halvorson. ABDO 2013 32 p. $27.07

Grades: 2 3 4 5   **612.8**

1. Ear 2. Human anatomy 3. Hearing

ISBN 1617836109; 9781617836107

LC 2012028770

In this book, by Karin Halvorson, readers will "find out what goes on every day inside of the human body! This title offers children [a] . . . voyage through the ears. Detailed illustrations, color photos, and simple text combine to make [an] introduction to how ears work. This book also includes simple activities and crafts like Tin Can Telephone, Music to My Ears and how to make an Ear with how-to photos." (Publisher's note)

Hewitt, Sally

Hear this! [by] Sally Hewitt. Crabtree Pub. 2008 24p il (Let's start! science) pa $6.95

Grades: PreK K 1 2   **612.8**

1. Sounds 2. Hearing

ISBN 978-0-7787-4058-2 pa; 0-7787-4058-7 pa

LC 2008-5007

First published 2005 by QEB publications

This book about hearing "will provide a good starting point for younger students to learn more about their senses. . . . Most chapters are accompanied by a related activity, none are too complex for the intended audience." Libr Media Connect

Includes glossary and bibliographical references

Look here! [by] Sally Hewitt. Crabtree 2008 24p il (Let's start! science) pa $6.95

Grades: PreK K 1 2   **612.8**

1. Vision

ISBN 978-0-7787-4059-9 pa; 0-7787-4059-5 pa

LC 2008-5008

First published 2005 by QEB publications with title: Look out!

This book about vision "will provide a good starting point for younger students to learn more about their senses. . . . Most chapters are accompanied by a related activity, none are too complex for the intended audience." Libr Media Connect

Includes glossary and bibliographical references

Smell it! Crabtree Pub. Company 2008 24p il (Let's start! science) pa $6.95

Grades: PreK K 1 2   **612.8**

1. Smell

ISBN 978-0-7787-4060-5 pa; 0-7787-4060-9 pa

LC 2008-5009

First published 2005 by QEB publications with title: Smell that!

This book "will provide a good starting point for younger students to learn more about their senses. . . . Most chapters are accompanied by a related activity, none are too complex for the intended audience." Libr Media Connect

Includes glossary and bibliographical references

Tastes good! [by] Sally Hewitt. Crabtree Pub. Company 2008 24p il (Let's start! science) pa $6.95

Grades: PreK K 1 2   **612.8**

1. Taste

ISBN 978-0-7787-4061-2 pa; 0-7787-4061-7 pa

LC 2008-5010

First published 2005 by QEB publications

This book "will provide a good starting point for younger students to learn more about their senses. . . . Most chapters are accompanied by a related activity, none are too complex for the intended audience." Libr Media Connect

Includes glossary and bibliographical references

Touch that! [by] Sally Hewitt. Crabtree Pub. Co. 2008 24p il (Let's start! science) pa $6.95

Grades: PreK K 1 2   **612.8**

1. Touch

ISBN 978-0-7787-4062-9 pa; 0-7787-4062-5 pa

LC 2008-5011

First published 2005 by QEB publications

This book "will provide a good starting point for younger students to learn more about their senses. . . . Most chapters are accompanied by a related activity, none are too complex for the intended audience." Libr Media Connect

Includes glossary and bibliographical references

Korb, Rena

My brain; illustrated by Remy Simard; content consultant, Anthony J. Weinhaus. Magic Wagon 2011 32p il (My body) lib bdg $27.07

Grades: 1 2 3   **612.8**

1. Brain

ISBN 978-1-60270-805-1; 1-60270-805-3

This "volume stars a child narrator who straightforwardly describes [the brain] and how it works. A round-faced, lab-coat-wearing man appears at the bottom of every spread to provide additional details and tidbits of anatomical information. . . . Black-outlined digital-looking cartoon illustrations enliven the [text]." Horn Book Guide

Includes glossary

Larsen, C. S.

Crust and spray; gross stuff in your eyes, ears, nose, and throat. illustrated by Michael Slack. Millbrook Press 2010 48p il (Gross body science) lib bdg $29.27

Grades: 4 5 6   **612.8**

1. Ear 2. Eye 3. Nose 4. Throat

ISBN 978-0-8225-8964-8 lib bdg; 0-8225-8964-8 lib bdg

LC 2008-33777

"Solid information layered between sarcastic comments and kid-friendly terminology like fart, poop, barf, and puke will keep readers engaged. . . . Labeled, captioned (and graphic) photographs, cartoon-style illustrations, and micrographs add information." SLJ

Includes glossary and bibliographical references

Macaulay, David

★ Eye; how it works. David Macaulay. Roaring Brook Press 2013 28 p. (hardcover) $15.99

Grades: 1 2 3   **612.8**

1. Eye 2. Human anatomy

ISBN 1596437812; 9781596437814; 9781596437821

LC 2012951526

This children's nonfiction book discusses and illustrates the working of the human eye, providing an anatomical perspective for young independent readers. Through both text and drawings, author and illustrator "David Macaulay shows how this extraordinary organ works to capture light and send signals to our brains." (Publisher's note)

Mooney, Carla

The Brain; Journey Through the Universe Inside Your Head. by Carla Mooney; illustrated by Tom Casteel. Nomad Press 2015 119 p. color illustrations $17.95

Grades: 5 6 7 8   **612.8**

1. Brain

ISBN 1619302780; 9781619302785

This book, by Carla Mooney, illustrated by Tom Casteel, "introduces students to the fascinating world of the human brain and its effect on behavior. Readers learn about the main anatomy and functions of the brain while discovering the brain's role in learning, memory, communication, and emotions. Kids also read about new technologies being used to research the brain in its various states of performance while being introduced to the effects of sleep, alcohol, and exercise." (Publisher's note)

"Sidebars offer descriptions of jobs that involve the brain, links to online resources, and questions for discussion; ideas for experiments and activities appear throughout. It's an extensive introduction to the brain's capability and function, with just enough humor and interactivity to keep readers engaged." Pub Wkly

Includes bibliographical references (page 116) and index.

Read, Leon

My senses. Sea-to-Sea Publications 2010 23p il (Tiger talk. All about me) lib bdg $24.25

Grades: PreK K   **612.8**

1. Senses and sensation

ISBN 978-1-59771-188-3 lib bdg; 1-59771-188-8 lib bdg

LC 2008-45010

This book about the senses "makes learning fun. . . . [The] book employs a simplified game of 'Where's Waldo?' by hiding a cartoon tiger on almost every page. This approach, combined with questions . . . will encourage discussion and involvement." SLJ

Royston, Angela

Why do I sleep? QEB Pub. 2010 24p il (QEB my body) lib bdg $28.65

Grades: PreK K 1 2   **612.8**

1. Sleep

ISBN 978-1-59566-974-2 lib bdg; 1-59566-974-4 lib bdg

LC 2009-15226

Introduces the function and importance of sleep, and outlines good sleeping habits

"This . . . is meant to be read to young children because it is written at a higher reading level than its intended audience. The information is straightforward, well presented, and easy to understand. . . . [This] title is well designed, filled with color photographs, and scattered with fact boxes. . . . This . . . will be useful in preschool and primary classrooms where health and hygiene are stressed." Libr Media Connect

Includes glossary and bibliographical references

Showers, Paul

Sleep is for everyone; illustrated by Wendy Watson. HarperCollins Pubs. 1997 32p il (Let's-read-and-find-out science) hardcover o.p. pa $4.99

Grades: K 1 2   **612.8**

1. Sleep

ISBN 0-06-025392-4; 0-06-025393-s lib bdg; 0-06-445141-0 pa

LC 96-49375

A newly illustrated edition of the title first published 1974 by Crowell

This volume examines "how different animals sleep, why we sleep, and what happens while we sleep and when we don't sleep enough. Colorful paper cut-out illustrations are simple and light-hearted with mottled paper as background creating a restful, gentle feeling." Horn Book Guide

Simon, Seymour

★ The brain; our nervous system. [by] Seymour Simon. rev ed.; Collins 2006 30p il $17.99; pa $6.99

Grades: 4 5 6 7   **612.8**

1. Brain 2. Nervous system

ISBN 978-0-06-087718-7; 0-06-087718-9; 978-0-06-087719-4 pa; 0-06-087719-7 pa

LC 2007-272349

First published 1997

Describes the various parts of the brain and the nervous system and how they function to enable us to think, feel, move, and remember.

Simon's "clear, concise writing style is complemented by stunning color images taken with radiological scanners, such as CAT scans, MRIs, and SEMs (scanning electron microscopes.)" SLJ [review of 1997 edition]

Includes bibliographical references

★ Eyes and ears. HarperCollins Pubs. 2003 un il hardcover o.p. pa $6.99

Grades: 4 5 6 7 **612.8**

1. Ear 2. Eye 3. Vision 4. Hearing
ISBN 0-688-15303-8; 978-0-06-073302-5 pa; 0-06-073302-0 pa
LC 2002-19060

Describes the anatomy of the eye and ear, how those organs function and some ways in which they may malfunction, and how the brain is also involved in our seeing and hearing

"Simon is at his very best here. . . . The large, exquisitely reproduced photographs from a number of sources look like fiery planets, galaxies, and monster creatures. . . . The anatomy and physiology are detailed and accurate, with clear diagrams." Booklist

Simpson, Kathleen

The **human** brain; inside your body's control room. National Geographic 2009 64p il (National Geographic investigates) lib bdg $27.90

Grades: 5 6 7 8 **612.8**

1. Brain
ISBN 978-1-4263-0421-7 lib bdg; 1-4263-0421-8 lib bdg

"Readers will learn about . . . new brain research in this title, which includes a basic discussion of the parts of the brain, their functions, and how neurons send messages throughout the body. Information is also included about the role of the brain during sleep, dreaming, and various emotional states, as well as explanations of the various technologies available to measure brain activity. This is a well-organized, compelling introduction, sure to pique the curiosity of many children. Full-color photographs and illustrations enliven the text." SLJ

Includes bibliographical references

Stewart, Melissa

You've got nerve! the secrets of the brain and nerves. illustrated by Janet Hamlin. Marshall Cavendish Benchmark 2010 48p il (The gross and goofy body) lib bdg $20.95

Grades: 2 3 4 **612.8**

1. Nervous system
ISBN 978-0-7614-4157-1 lib bdg; 0-7614-4157-3 lib bdg
LC 2008033560

This includes information on the role the brain and nerves play in the body science of humans and animals

This "offers detailed science facts in a fashion approachable enough to make it a welcome supplement to school textbooks. . . . The layout is fresh, clean, and colorful, sidebars keep things conversational, and the back matter is solid." Booklist

Includes glossary and bibliographical references

Tieck, Sarah

Nervous system. ABDO Pub. 2011 32p il (Body systems) lib bdg $27.07; ebook $27.07

Grades: 2 3 4 **612.8**

1. Nervous system
ISBN 978-1-61613-500-3 lib bdg; 1-61613-500-X lib bdg; 978-1-61613-990-4 ebook
LC 2010019654

"Double-page spreads describe the workings of the [nervous system] . . . with simple text on left-hand pages and large, colorful photographs or diagrams on the right. The [text touches] on common disorders . . . and healthy practices. 'Brain Food' spreads pose three questions and provide answers. Ample white space, engaging images, and 'Word of Mouth' sidebars are reader-friendly." Horn Book Guide

Includes glossary

Veitch, Catherine

Sound and hearing. Heinemann Library 2009 24p il (Sounds all around us) lib bdg $20.71; pa $5.99

Grades: PreK K 1 **612.8**

1. Sound 2. Hearing 3. Sound waves
ISBN 978-1-4329-3224-4 lib bdg; 1-4329-3224-1 lib bdg; 978-1-4329-3225-1 pa; 1-4329-3225-X pa
LC 2008-51741

This book "introduces the basics of sound through vibrant photographs, large text, and simple sentences. . . . [A] great introduction[s] and worthy addition[s]." SLJ

Includes glossary

Winston, Robert M. L., 1940-

What goes on in my head? how your brain works and why you do what you do. [by] Robert Winston. DK Pub. 2010 96p il $16.99

Grades: 4 5 6 7 **612.8**

1. Brain 2. Psychology
ISBN 978-0-7566-6885-3; 0-7566-6885-9

"The author presents a great deal of scientific content and supplements it with examples, anecdotes, and current findings in the field. . . . In addition, interactive brain teasers and exercises make the science come alive. . . . The book combines vibrant colors and illustrations with explanations to keep young readers engaged." Sci Books Films

613   Personal health and safety

Ajmera, Maya

Healthy kids; Maya Ajmera, Victoria Dunning, Cynthia Pon. Charlesbridge 2012 32 p. (reinforced) $17.95

Grades: PreK K 1 2 **613**

1. Everyday life 2. Children -- Health and hygiene 3. Children 4. Multiculturalism
ISBN 1580894364; 9781580894364; 9781580894371
LC 2012000784

This book, by Maya Ajmera, Victoria Dunning, and Cynthia Pon, part of the "Global Fund of Children Book" series, offers photographs of children throughout the world doing about active and healthy daily life. Activities profiled include eating food, playing, and doing chores. Children from several countries are illustrated, including Argentina, Bhutan, Canada, Guatemala, Romania and Kenya.

Gardner, Robert

Ace your exercise and nutrition science project: great science fair ideas; [by] Robert Gardner, Barbara Gardner Conklin, and Salvatore Tocci. Enslow Publishers 2009 128p il (Ace your biology science project) lib bdg $31.93

Grades: 5 6 7 8 **613**

1. Exercise 2. Nutrition 3. Science projects 4. Science -- Experiments
ISBN 978-0-7660-3218-7 lib bdg; 0-7660-3218-3 lib bdg
LC 2008-30798

"Presents several science projects and science project ideas about exercise and nutrition." Publisher's note

Includes bibliographical references

Lehman, Robert

★ **Will** puberty last my whole life? real answers to real questions from preteens about body changes, sex, and other growing-up stuff. Julie Giesy Metzger and Robert Lehman; illustrated by Cerizo. Sasquatch Books 2011 90 p. col. ill. (pbk.) $16.95

Grades: 4 5 6 7 8 **613**

1. Puberty 2. Questions and answers 3. Boys -- Health and hygiene 4. Girls -- Health and hygiene 5. Teenage boys -- Physiology 6.

Teenage girls -- Physiology 8. Interpersonal relations in adolescence
ISBN 1570617392; 9781570617393

LC 2011038401

This book "for boys and girls between the ages of 9 and 12 has questions asked by girls in one half of the book" and "questions asked by boys are on the other side." The book contains "answers to questions pre-adolescents have about puberty, friends, feelings, sex, pimples, babies, body hair, menstruation, bras, and much more." (Amazon.com)

Miller, Edward, 1964-
★ The **monster** health book; a guide to eating healthy, being active, & feeling great for monsters & kids! [by] Edward Miller. Holiday House 2006 40p il $16.95
Grades: 2 3 4   613
1. Health 2. Nutrition
ISBN 978-0-8234-1956-2; 0-8234-1956-8

LC 2005046383

"Featuring a friendly, rotund, green monster determined to make healthy choices, this book presents basic information about food, exercise, and health. . . . Subjects include food nutrients, counting calories and understanding food labels, tips for making healthy lunches and snacks, the benefits of getting enough sleep and exercise, and ways to improve self-esteem. Miller's retro-style illustrations fill the pages with color, shapes, and humorous details, and silly jokes are tucked everywhere. . . . This lively, visually appealing book . . . belongs in children's hands." SLJ

Natterson, Cara
The **care** & keeping of you 2; the body book for older girls. Dr. Cara Natterson; illustrated by Josee Masse. American Girl 2013 96 p. (paperback) $12.99
Grades: 5 6 7 8   613
1. Puberty 2. Life skills -- Handbooks, manuals, etc. 3. Teenage girls -- Health and hygiene 4. Girls -- Life skills guides
ISBN 1609580427; 9781609580421

LC 2012045813

This book, by Cara Natterson, illustrated by Josee Masse, is a body image and physiology guide written for girls going through puberty.

"The friendly illustrations support the overall tone and style. . . . Its neutral, matter-of-fact approach will help show readers . . . that all the changes they may be feeling are perfectly normal." SLJ

Pfeifer, Kate Gruenwald
American Medical Assocation boy's guide to becoming a teen. Jossey-Bass 2006 128p il pa $12.95
Grades: 4 5 6 7   613
1. Puberty 2. Adolescence 3. Boys -- Health and hygiene
ISBN 0-7879-8343-8

"This guide addresses puberty's changes clearly. . . . The text's approach is straightforward, accessible, and nonjudgmental, whether the topic is same-sex attraction or divorcing parents. The volume closes with an extensive resource section, including hotlines." Booklist
Includes bibliographical references

American Medical Association girl's guide to becoming a teen. Jossey-Bass 2006 128p pa $12.95
Grades: 4 5 6 7   613
1. Puberty 2. Adolescence 3. Girls -- Health and hygiene
ISBN 0-7879-8344-6

This "covers the physical and emotional changes that puberty brings, along with solid tips about grooming, diet, exercise, and other health issues, such as eating disorders. . . . The clear text communicates concepts clearly . . . and girls will find plenty of useful information." Booklist
Includes bibliographical references

Read, Leon
Keeping well. Sea-to-Sea Publications 2010 23p il (Tiger talk. All about me) lib bdg $24.25
Grades: PreK K   613
1. Health 2. Hygiene
ISBN 978-1-59771-186-9 lib bdg; 1-59771-186-1 lib bdg

LC 2008-45008

This book about keeping well "makes learning fun. . . . [The] book employs a simplified game of 'Where's Waldo?' by hiding a cartoon tiger on almost every page. This approach, combined with questions . . . will encourage discussion and involvement." SLJ

Royston, Angela
Why do I wash my hands? QEB Pub. 2010 24p il (QEB my body) lib bdg $28.65
Grades: PreK K 1 2   613
1. Hygiene
ISBN 978-1-59566-972-8 lib bdg; 1-59566-972-8 lib bdg

LC 2009-15228

Introduces the effects of germs on the skin and outlines the principles of personal hygiene.

"The information is straightforward, well presented, and easy to understand. . . . [This] title is well designed, filled with color photographs, and scattered with fact boxes." Libr Media Connect
Includes glossary and bibliographical references

Schaefer, Adam
Staying healthy; [by] A. R. Schaefer. Heinemann Library 2010 32p il (Health and fitness) lib bdg $25.36; pa $7.99
Grades: PreK K 1   613
1. Health 2. Hygiene 3. Exercise
ISBN 978-1-4329-2769-1 lib bdg; 1-4329-2769-8 lib bdg; 978-1-4329-2774-5 pa; 1-4329-2774-4 pa

LC 2008-52298

Find out about the importance of a good diet, exercise, staying clean, and what to do if you are injured or sick.

"Spare, declarative sentences coupled with bright, full-color photos . . . [makes this book] appropriate for reading aloud in the classroom or even during a themed story hour. . . . While each spread introduces a new topic . . . [a] solid [introduction] and [conclusion] make for [a] cohesive [package]." SLJ
Includes glossary and bibliographical references

Schaefer, Valorie
The **care** & keeping of you; the body book for younger girls. by Valorie Schaefer; Cara Natterson, MD, medical consultant; illustrated by Josee Masse. American Girl Publishing 2012 102 p. (pbk.) $12.99
Grades: 3 4 5 6   613
1. Puberty 2. Girls -- Health and hygiene 3. Grooming for girls 4. Preteens -- Health and hygiene
ISBN 1609580834; 9781609580834

LC 2012045846

This book by Valorie Schaefer, illustrated by Josee Masse includes "all-new illustrations and updated content for girls ages 8 and up, it features tips, how-tos, and facts from the experts." Readers will "find answers to questions about your changing body, from hair care to healthy eating, bad breath to bras, periods to pimples, and everything in between." (Publisher's note)

"Head-to-toe advice for preteen girls. This cheerful discussion of the changes puberty brings combines friendly, conversational advice from the author with signed comments and questions, perhaps from preteens... Positive and personal, this might be an especially good choice for early bloomers." Kirkus
Companion to:

The Care and Keeping of You 2: The Body Book for Older Girls

613.2 Dietetics

Are you what you eat? Discovery Kids. DK Publishing 2015 94 p. color illustrations $16.99

Grades: 3 4 5 6   **613.2**

1. Nutrition 2. Eating customs 3. Food habits

ISBN 1465429441; 9781465429445

LC 2015295275

This children's book "uses color and fun presentation to communicate nutritional information in a fun and eye-catching way. Kids learn to see their food as more than just taste, learning things like which foods will make you sleepy, how to tell if you're hungry or full, and why our bodies need nutrition." (Publisher's note)

"A solid addition to most collections." SLJ

Carole, Bonnie

Junk food, yes or no; Bonnie Carole. Rourke Pub Group 2015 24 p. color illustrations (ebook) $29.93; $8.95

Grades: 1 2 3   **613.2**

1. Nutrition 2. Authorship 3. Snack foods 4. Convenience foods

ISBN 9781634305495; 9781634304504; 1634303504; 9781634303507

This book in the Seeing Both Sides series, by Bonnie Carole , "offers two opposing sides, and asks readers to choose one. . . . Each page features two to three sentences, which sometimes take the form of questions. . . . Color photos are used heavily, taking up more space than the text. At the end of each volume is a set of 'Writing Tips' . . . to help students write an opinion paper; these prompts stress the importance of using facts rather than feelings." (School Library Journal)

"Despite some weaknesses, these books will likely help young readers and writers find their voices and express opinions on the mildly divisive issues they cover." Booklist

Includes webibliography (page 23) and index.

Currie, Stephen

Junk food. Cherry Lake Pub. 2009 32p il (Health at risk) lib bdg $27.07

Grades: 4 5 6 7 8   **613.2**

1. Nutrition

ISBN 978-1-60279-284-5 lib bdg; 1-60279-284-4 lib bdg

LC 2008017498

This describes what junk food is, why it's not good for your body, and what's being done to help us control our junk food habit.

"Great for reports or reluctant readers." Booklist

Includes bibliographical references

Durrie, Karen

Health. Weigl 2011 il (Community helpers) $27.13

Grades: PreK K 1 2   **613.2**

1. Health 2. Nutrition

ISBN 978-1-61690-950-5; 1-61690-950-1

LC 2011024904

"A diverse group of people represents seven occupations: doctor, nurse, optometrist, fitness teacher, nutritionist, counselor, and dentist. A large, color photo fills each double-page spread, along with a text box carrying a sentence, such as 'I check your teeth and gums to make sure they are healthy.' . . . All the clearly reproduced photos provide clues that will help children guess who is speaking." Booklist

Furgang, Adam

Carbonated beverages; the incredibly disgusting story. Rosen Central 2011 48p il (Incredibly disgusting food) lib bdg $26.50; pa $11.75

Grades: 4 5 6 7   **613.2**

1. Carbonated beverages

ISBN 978-1-4488-1266-0 lib bdg; 1-4488-1266-6 lib bdg; 978-1-4488-2282-9 pa; 1-4488-2282-3 pa

LC 2010023227

This presents "straightforward information about why [carbonated beverages] are unhealthy without resorting to extreme gross-out factors. The [book contains] a breakdown of the foods' components . . . insight into how they are processed, and both short- and long-term effects of consumption. . . . Readers may or may not be disgusted, but they will definitely learn a thing or two about smart eating habits." SLJ

Includes glossary and bibliographical references

Salty and sugary snacks; the incredibly disgusting story. Rosen Central 2011 48p il (Incredibly disgusting food) lib bdg $26.50; pa $11.75

Grades: 4 5 6 7   **613.2**

1. Salt 2. Sugar 3. Nutrition 4. Snack foods

ISBN 978-1-4488-1267-7 lib bdg; 1-4488-1267-4 lib bdg; 978-1-4488-2283-6 pa; 1-4488-2283-1 pa

LC 2010025751

This book describes how salty and sugary snacks put dangerous amounts of sugar and salt into our bodies and how these unnecessary calories can have terrible effects on the body.

"Readers may or may not be disgusted, but they will definitely learn a thing or two about smart eating habits." SLJ

Includes glossary and bibliographical references

Harris, Robie H., 1940-

What's so yummy? all about eating well and feeling good. Robie H. Harris, illustrated by Nadine Bernard Westcott. 1st edition Candlewick Press 2014 40 p. color illustrations (reinforced) $15.99

Grades: PreK K 1   **613.2**

1. Health 2. Nutrition

ISBN 9780763636326; 0763636320

LC 2013955674

In this children's book by Robie H. Harris, illustrated by Nadine Bernard Westcott, "Gus, Nellie, and baby Jake can't wait to go on a picnic! In the morning the family heads to their community garden, then to the farmer's market and the grocery store to gather vegetables, fruit, meat, and other fresh and delicious foods." (Publisher's note)

"[T]he main text discusses topics related to wholesome eating and feeling good. Speech balloons on every double-page spread carry the children's dialogue. . . . Including a wide variety of people in the backgrounds, Westcott's digital line-and-wash illustrations are clearly delineated, cheerful, and appealing." Booklist

Head, Honor

Healthy eating; Honor Head. Sea to Sea Publications 2013 30 p. (alk. paper) $28.50

Grades: 2 3 4   **613.2**

1. Nutrition 2. Food 3. Health 4. Nutrition

ISBN 1597713945; 9781597713948

LC 2011052695

This book, by Honor Head, "asks and answers questions about healthy eating. It explores why fruit and vegetables are good for us, what are the best snacks, why we shouldn't just eat sweet foods and much more. It is part of the 'Let's read and talk about' series which includes ready-to-use questions and discussion points to help young readers gain more from their reading experience, and to give . . . teachers and parents quality extension material." (Publisher's note)

Hunt, Jamie

The **truth** about diets; what's right for you? Mason Crest Publishers 2011 48p il (Kids & obesity) lib bdg $19.95; pa $7.95

Grades: 3 4 5   **613.2**

1. Diet 2. Nutrition 3. Weight loss

ISBN 978-1-4222-1710-8 lib bdg; 1-4222-1710-8 lib bdg; 978-1-4222-1898-3 pa; 1-4222-1898-8 pa

LC 2010010014

Learn about diets and whether or not they are actually a good way to lose weight.

This "presents the expected information about the food pyramid, the need for physical activity, and the influence of the media on our psyches. Where the material shines is in its holistic approach. Readers are encouraged to develop their inner lives as much as their physical selves and to take responsibility for their own health and eating habits. . . . This brightly-colored, ego-boosting, responsibility-championing . . . [book] is a winner." SLJ

Includes bibliographical references

Johanson, Paula

Fake foods; fried, fast, and processed: the incredibly disgusting story. Rosen Central 2011 48p il (Incredibly disgusting food) lib bdg $26.50; pa $11.75

Grades: 4 5 6 7   **613.2**

1. Nutrition 2. Natural foods 3. Convenience foods

ISBN 978-1-4488-1269-1 lib bdg; 1-4488-1269-0 lib bdg; 978-1-4488-2285-0 pa; 1-4488-2285-8 pa

LC 2010020534

This presents "straightforward information about why various junk foods are unhealthy without resorting to extreme gross-out factors. The [book contains] a breakdown of the foods' components . . . insight into how they are processed, and both short- and long-term effects of consumption. . . . Readers may or may not be disgusted, but they will definitely learn a thing or two about smart eating habits." SLJ

Includes glossary and bibliographical references

Rau, Dana Meachen, 1971-

Going vegetarian; a healthy guide to making the switch. by Dana Meachen Rau. Compass Point Books 2012 64 p. (hardcover) $33.99

Grades: 5 6 7 8 9   **613.2**

1. Nutrition 2. Vegetarianism 3. Vegetarian cooking 4. Nutrition 5. Vegetarianism 6. Vegetarian children

ISBN 0756545226; 9780756545222; 9780756545307

LC 2011040836

Author Dana Meachen Rau presents a guide to becoming a vegetarian. "Learn about the benefits and challenges of a diet that does not include red meat, poultry, or fish. Helpful tips, delicious vegetarian recipes, and how tos will make the switch so much easier." The book also offers various organic, meatless, and vegan recipes and meal ideas. (Publisher's note)

"Whether looking to go organic, ovo-lacto vegetarian, or vegan, kids will find the information necessary to make the switch in these titles... Organic focuses on the USDA's National Organic Program (NOP) regulations, making no mention of other certification programs. It does, however, warn kids about trusting organic labels implicitly and recommends that they go straight to the source when possible by researching and even visiting companies. Serve these up to budding health foodies.." (School Library Journal)

Includes bibliographical references (p. 62) and index

Simons, Rae

Bigger isn't always better; choosing your portions. Mason Crest Publishers 2011 48p il (Kids & obesity) lib bdg $19.95; pa $7.95

Grades: 3 4 5   **613.2**

1. Diet 2. Obesity 3. Nutrition 4. Eating customs

ISBN 978-1-4222-1706-1 lib bdg; 1-4222-1706-X lib bdg; 978-1-4222-1894-5 pa; 1-4222-1894-5 pa

LC 2010028159

Explores the contributions of increasingly larger portion sizes to the problem of obesity in America.

This book "presents the expected information about the food pyramid, the need for physical activity, and the influence of the media on our psyches. Where the material shines is in its holistic approach. Readers are encouraged to develop their inner lives as much as their physical selves and to take responsibility for their own health and eating habits. . . . This brightly-colored, ego-boosting, responsibility-championing . . . [book] is a winner." SLJ

Includes bibliographical references

Thompson, Helen

Cookies or carrots? you are what you eat. Mason Crest Publishers 2010 48p il (Kids & obesity) lib bdg $19.95; pa $7.95

Grades: 3 4 5   **613.2**

1. Diet 2. Nutrition

ISBN 978-1-4222-1707-8 lib bdg; 1-4222-1707-8 lib bdg; 978-1-4222-1895-2 pa; 1-4222-1895-3 pa

LC 2010025502

This book about nutrition and diet "presents the expected information about the food pyramid, the need for physical activity, and the influence of the media on our psyches. Where the material shines is in its holistic approach. Readers are encouraged to develop their inner lives as much as their physical selves and to take responsibility for their own health and eating habits. . . . This brightly-colored, ego-boosting, responsibility-championing . . . [book] is a winner." SLJ

Includes bibliographical references

Watson, Stephanie

Mystery meat; hot dogs, sausages, and lunch meats: the incredibly disgusting story. Rosen Pub. Group 2011 48p il (Incredibly disgusting food) lib bdg $26.50; pa $11.75

Grades: 4 5 6 7   **613.2**

1. Meat 2. Sausages 3. Nutrition 4. Frankfurters

ISBN 978-1-4488-1268-4 lib bdg; 1-4488-1268-2 lib bdg; 978-1-4488-2284-3 pa; 1-4488-2284-X pa

LC 2010013649

"The short but substantive chapters begin with a look at typical hot-dog ingredients and manufacturing practices, followed by discussions of how 'mystery meats,' including common, highly processed sandwich fillers, affect the body. A closing chapter about the components of a healthy diet widens the book into an opportunity for adults and kids to discuss general nutrition and includes useful tips on reading food labels. . . . Young readers will find plenty of browsing and report fodder in these pages." Booklist

Includes bibliographical references

613.4 Personal cleanliness

Head, Honor
  Keeping clean; by Honor Head. Sea-to-Sea Publications 2013 30 p. (Let's read and talk about) (hdbk. : alk. paper) $28.50
  Grades: 2 3 4   **613.4**
    1. Children -- Health and hygiene 2. Hygiene
    ISBN 1597713953; 9781597713955
                                                   LC 2011052696
  This book, by Honor Head, "asks and answers questions about keeping clean. It explores why you should wash, how you can stop germs spreading, how to keep hair and teeth clean and much more. It is part of the 'Let's read and talk about' series which includes ready-to-use questions and discussion points to help young readers gain more from their reading experience, and to give busy teachers and parents quality extension material." (Publisher's note)

613.6 Personal safety and special topics of health

Catel, Patrick
  Surviving stunts and other amazing feats. Raintree 2011 56p il (Extreme survival)
  Grades: 4 5 6 7   **613.6**
    1. Stunts
    ISBN 1-4109-3969-3; 978-1-4109-3969-2
                                                   LC 2010028690
  This book is "fun and informative. [This] well-organized title starts with an overview, offers some specific examples, and includes additional facts or tips and resources. Catel defines activities that encompass adventure and amazement and then leads readers through a discussion of sideshows, movies, and daring stunts (some of which include fire). . . . [It features] dramatic archival and full-color photos on nearly every page. . . . [This is a book] that youngsters will enjoy and talk about." SLJ
  Includes glossary and bibliographical references

Champion, Neil
  Finding food and water. Amicus 2010 32p il (Survive alive) lib bdg $28.50
  Grades: 4 5 6 7   **613.6**
    1. Wilderness survival
    ISBN 978-1-60753-037-4 lib bdg; 1-60753-037-6 lib bdg
                                                   LC 2009030889
  This offers survival tips for finding food and water in the wild, including how to know what is safe to eat or drink from land, plant, and animal sources.
  This "colorful [book contains] numerous photos and illustrations that effectively break the [text] into small, readable chunks. There's lots of practical, everyday information here. . . . Brief yet gripping real-life survival stories are interspersed throughout the [book]." SLJ
  Includes glossary

  Finding your way. Amicus 2011 32p il (Survive alive) lib bdg $28.50
  Grades: 4 5 6 7   **613.6**
    1. Orienteering 2. Wilderness survival
    ISBN 978-1-60753-038-1 lib bdg; 1-60753-038-4 lib bdg
                                                   LC 2009030888
  "With eye-catching photographs, clear explanations, a survival skills quiz, a glossary, Web sites, and 'True Survival' stories . . . this engaging text encourages readers to figure out where they are and where they want to go." Booklist
  Includes glossary

  In an emergency. Amicus 2010 32p il (Survive alive) lib bdg $28.50
  Grades: 4 5 6 7   **613.6**
    1. Survival skills
    ISBN 978-1-60753-040-4; 1-60753-040-6
                                                   LC 2010002517
  This offers survival tips on what to do in emergency situations. Includes scenarios about fire, bad weather, accidents, injuries, extreme conditions, and more.'
  This "colorful [book contains] numerous photos and illustrations that effectively break the [text] into small, readable chunks. There's lots of practical, everyday information here. . . . Brief yet gripping real-life survival stories are interspersed throughout the [book]." SLJ
  Includes glossary

  Making shelter. Amicus 2010 32p il (Survive alive) lib bdg $28.50
  Grades: 4 5 6 7   **613.6**
    1. Wilderness survival
    ISBN 978-1-60753-041-1 lib bdg; 1-60753-041-4 lib bdg
                                                   LC 2010001378
  This offers survival tips for building shelter in the wild, including using natural means in different regions such as the desert, forest, jungle, and cold areas. Also includes information on what to bring for aid when building shelters.

Hurley, Michael
  Surviving the wilderness. Raintree 2011 56p il (Extreme survival) lib bdg $33.50
  Grades: 4 5 6 7   **613.6**
    1. Wilderness survival
    ISBN 978-1-4109-3972-2; 1-4109-3972-3
                                                   LC 2010028839
  This book is "fun and informative. [This] well-organized title starts with an overview [of wilderness survival], offers some specific examples, and includes additional facts or tips and resources. . . . [It features] dramatic archival and full-color photos on nearly every page. . . . [This is a book] that youngsters will enjoy and talk about." SLJ
  Includes glossary and bibliographical references

Long, Denise
  Survivor kid; a practical guide to wilderness survival. Chicago Review Press 2011 222p il $12.95
  Grades: 4 5 6 7   **613.6**
    1. Wilderness survival
    ISBN 978-1-56976-708-5; 1-56976-708-4
                                                   LC 2011004952
  "Long offers lessons on how to stay healthy and out of trouble while awaiting rescue. Her matter-of-fact, no-nonsense tone will play well with young readers, and the clear writing style is appropriate to the content. The engaging guide covers everything from building shelters to avoiding pigs and javelinas. . . . The volume invites browsing as much as studying. . . . An excellent bibliography will lead young readers to a host of fascinating websites, and 150 clipart-style line drawings complement the text." Kirkus
  Includes bibliographical references

Miller, Edward, 1964-
  Fireboy to the rescue! a fire safety book. Holiday House 2010 un il $16.95
  Grades: K 1 2   **613.6**
    1. Fire fighting 2. Fire prevention 3. Safety education
    ISBN 978-0-8234-2222-7; 0-8234-2222-4

"Fireboy is a superhero intent on keeping the world's children safe from fire. After heralding all the great things fire can do . . . the cut paper-style artwork bursts into reds and yellows and oranges as all manners of things—including homes—catch aflame. . . . The snazzy presentation is entertaining in its own right. . . . Some of the especially vital details (fire alarms, extinguishers) are incorporated as photos." Booklist

Schaefer, Adam

Staying safe. Heinemann Library 2009 32p il (Health and fitness) lib bdg $25.36; pa $7.99

Grades: PreK K 1   **613.6**

1. Safety education

ISBN 978-1-4329-2770-7 lib bdg; 1-4329-2770-1 lib bdg; 978-1-4329-2775-2 pa; 1-4329-2775-2 pa

LC 2008-52300

Find out what to do in a fire, how to stay safe in the street, and who to call in an emergency.

"Spare, declarative sentences coupled with bright, full-color photos . . . [makes this book] appropriate for reading aloud in the classroom or even during a themed story hour. . . . While each spread introduces a new topic . . . [a] solid [introduction] and [conclusion] make for [a] cohesive [package]." SLJ

Includes glossary and bibliographical references

613.7   Physical fitness

Aikman, Louise

Pilates step-by-step; [by] Louise Aikman and Matthew Harvey. Rosen Central 2011 93p il (Skills in motion) lib bdg $31.95

Grades: 5 6 7 8   **613.7**

1. Pilates method

ISBN 978-1-4488-1549-4; 1-4488-1549-5

LC 2010007510

Presents a general guide to the Pilates exercise system using a sequence of stop-action images and text instructions to illustrate some of the most common movements.

Includes bibliographical references

Atha, Antony

Fitness for young people; step-by-step. [by] Antony Atha and Simon Frost. Rosen Central 2010 93p il (Skills in motion) lib bdg $31.95

Grades: 5 6 7 8   **613.7**

1. Physical fitness

ISBN 978-1-4358-3364-7; 1-4358-3364-3

LC 2009-13245

Describes how to maintain physical fitness for youth, providing exercises that are both effective and fun.

"Colorful photographs show the entire movement of each skill presented, giving new meaning to the term 'step-by-step.' Progression borders at the bottom of the pages highlight the salient points to notice in performing each skill from beginning to end." SLJ

Includes bibliographical references

Birkemoe, Karen

★ Strike a pose; the Planet Girl guide to yoga. written by Karen Birkemoe; illustrated by Heather Collett. Kids Can Press 2007 96p il (Planet girl) spiral $12.95

Grades: 5 6 7 8   **613.7**

1. Yoga 2. Girls -- Health and hygiene

ISBN 978-1-55337-004-8

"This compact book offers a well-rounded overview of Hatha yoga. Using an easy conversational tone, Birkemoe relates the general practice

and specific poses to reader's lives. The simple line drawings and color illustrations partner effectively with text to explain each move." SLJ

Includes glossary

Eason, Sarah

Free running; by Paul Mason and Sarah Eason. Lerner Publications 2011 il (On the radar: sports)

Grades: 5 6 7 8   **613.7**

1. Running 2. Parkour

ISBN 076137759X; 9780761377597

LC 2011000467

"Free running, also known as parkour, is a combination of speed running, gymnastics, and, in some cases, sheer fearlessness. Lovers of the sport launch over walls, clear fences in a single bound, and somersault down stairwells. This . . . captures the adrenaline-fueled energy of runners, using bold graphics, bright colors, and short interviews to showcase professionals, demonstrate moves, and trace the origins of free running." Booklist

Head, Honor

Keeping fit; by Honor Head. Sea to Sea Publications 2013 30 p. (hdbk. : alk. paper) $28.50

Grades: 2 3 4   **613.7**

1. Exercise 2. Physical fitness 3. Exercise -- Physiological aspects

ISBN 1597713961; 9781597713962

LC 2011052697

In this book, by Honor Head, readers can "find out all about keeping fit from how to get started, what exercise does for the body to how exercise can help you at school. Keeping Fit is part of the Let's read and talk about series. Each book has a range of questions to help children with speaking and listening skills, and 'take action' panels which give ideas for activities." (Publisher's note)

Hunt, Jamie

Getting stronger, getting fit; the importance of exercise. Mason Crest Publishers 2011 48p il (Kids & obesity) lib bdg $19.95; pa $7.95

Grades: 3 4 5   **613.7**

1. Exercise 2. Physical fitness

ISBN 978-1-4222-1709-2 lib bdg; 1-4222-1709-4 lib bdg; 978-1-4222-1897-6 pa; 1-4222-1897-X pa

LC 2010017921

This book about nutrition and exercise "presents the expected information about the food pyramid, the need for physical activity, and the influence of the media on our psyches. Where the material shines is in its holistic approach. Readers are encouraged to develop their inner lives as much as their physical selves and to take responsibility for their own health and eating habits. . . . This brightly-colored, ego-boosting, responsibility-championing . . . [book] is a winner." SLJ

Includes bibliographical references

Jennings, Madeleine

Tai chi step-by-step; [by] Madeleine Jennings and James Drewe. Rosen Central 2011 93p il (Skills in motion) lib bdg $31.95

Grades: 5 6 7 8   **613.7**

1. Tai chi

ISBN 978-1-4488-1551-7; 1-4488-1551-7

LC 2010008411

This book introduces both basic and higher level techniques of tai chi, with step-by-step instructions, illustrated by stop-motion sequential photography.

Includes bibliographical references

Kuskowski, Alex

Cool relaxing; healthy & fun ways to chill out! Alex Kuskowski. ABDO Pub. Co. 2012 32 p. col. ill. (Cool health and fitness) (library) $28.50

Grades: 4 5 6   **613.7**

1. Creative activities 2. Rest 3. Relaxation

ISBN 1617834289; 9781617834288

LC 2012010345

This nonfiction children's book by Alex Kuskowski presents a "hodgepodge of activities and techniques to achieve zen calm. The suggestions in this 'Cool Health and Fitness' title are all over the place--cooking, running, reading, baths, even cleaning--but that's the unspoken truth: whatever pleasantly distracts you does the trick. Eight activities are given step-by-step attention, including yoga, stretching, making a lavender pillow, and meditation." (Booklist)

Mason, Paul, 1967-

Improving endurance. PowerKids Press 2011 32p il (Training for sports) lib bdg $25.25

Grades: 5 6 7 8   **613.7**

1. Sports 2. Exercise

ISBN 978-1-4488-3300-9; 1-4488-3300-0

LC 2010024356

This offers "detailed tips on improving . . . endurance. All-around athletes will love this and so will kids who just want to work on getting fit." Booklist

Improving flexibility. PowerKids Press 2011 32p il (Training for sports) lib bdg $25.25

Grades: 5 6 7 8   **613.7**

1. Sports 2. Exercise

ISBN 978-1-4488-3299-6; 1-4488-3299-3

LC 2010024359

This offers tips on improving flexibility for sports.

"All-around athletes will love this and so will kids who just want to work on getting fit." Booklist

Improving speed. PowerKids Press 2011 32p il (Training for sports) lib bdg $25.25

Grades: 5 6 7 8   **613.7**

1. Speed 2. Sports 3. Exercise

ISBN 978-1-4488-3302-3; 1-4488-3302-3

LC 2010024354

This offers "detailed tips on improving speed. . . . All-around athletes will love this and so will kids who just want to work on getting fit." Booklist

Improving strength & power. PowerKids Press 2011 32p il (Training for sports) lib bdg $25.25

Grades: 5 6 7 8   **613.7**

1. Exercise 2. Physical fitness

ISBN 978-1-4488-3301-6; 1-4488-3301-6

LC 2010024425

This offers tips on improving strength and power for sports.

"All-around athletes will love this and so will kids who just want to work on getting fit." Booklist

Royston, Angela

Why do I run? QEB Pub. 2010 24p il (QEB my body) lib bdg $28.65

Grades: PreK K 1 2   **613.7**

1. Running 2. Exercise 3. Physical fitness

ISBN 978-1-59566-971-1 lib bdg; 1-59566-971-X lib bdg

LC 2009-15223

Introduces the effects of running and other exercise on the body, and outlines the principles of physical fitness and healthy, safe exercise

"The information is straightforward, well presented, and easy to understand. . . . [This] title is well designed, filled with color photographs, and scattered with fact boxes." Libr Media Connect

Includes glossary and bibliographical references

Schaefer, Adam

Exercise; [by] A. R. Schaefer. Heinemann Library 2010 32p il (Health and fitness) lib bdg $25.36; pa $7.99

Grades: PreK K 1   **613.7**

1. Exercise

ISBN 978-1-4329-2767-7 lib bdg; 1-4329-2767-1 lib bdg; 978-1-4329-2772-1 pa; 1-4329-2772-8 pa

LC 2008-52297

This book about exercise has "spare, declarative sentences coupled with bright, full-color photos. . . . While each spread introduces a new topic . . . [a] solid [introduction] and [conclusion] make for [a] cohesive [package]." SLJ

Includes glossary and bibliographical references

Spilling, Michael

Yoga step-by-step; [by] Michael Spilling and Liz Lark. Rosen Central 2011 95p il (Skills in motion) lib bdg $31.95

Grades: 5 6 7 8   **613.7**

1. Yoga

ISBN 978-1-4488-1550-0; 1-4488-1550-9

LC 2010008665

Readers are introduced to basic yoga techniques through step-by-step instructions, depicted with numerous photographs.

Includes bibliographical references

Tuminelly, Nancy

Super simple bend & stretch; healthy & fun activities to move your body. ABDO Pub. Company 2012 32p il (Super simple exercise) lib bdg $27.07

Grades: 1 2 3   **613.7**

1. Exercise 2. Physical fitness

ISBN 978-1-61714-959-7; 1-61714-959-4

LC 2011000963

"This volume opens with general pages on the benefits of healthy eating and physical activities as well as instructions for making a chart to track each week's efforts. Some of the book's double-page spreads explain and demonstrate several exercise ideas related to a theme. . . . Other spreads present a single activity. . . . Colorful photos show smiling children demonstrating the moves. A cheerful introduction to some basic exercises." Booklist

Includes glossary

613.9 Birth control, reproductive technology, sex hygiene, sexual techniques

Cole, Joanna

Asking about sex & growing up; a question-and-answer book for kids. illustrated by Bill Thomas. rev ed.; Collins 2009 89p il $15.99; pa $6.99

Grades: 4 5 6   **613.9**

1. Sex education

ISBN 978-0-06-142987-3; 0-06-142987-2; 978-0-06-142986-6 pa; 0-06-142986-4 pa

LC 2008022710

First published 1988 by Morrow Junior Books

This book "offers straightforward information about topics such as physical changes in puberty, masturbation, birth control, pregnancy, homosexuality, and STDs. . . . Libraries . . . should consider adding it as a source of basic information for curious preteens." SLJ

Harris, Robie H., 1940-

★ It's perfectly normal; changing bodies, growing up, sex and sexual health. Robie H. Harris; illustrated by Michael Emberley. 20th anniversary edition Candlewick Press 2014 98 p. color illustrations (reinforced) $22.99; (pbk) $12.99

Grades: 4 5 6 7 **613.9**

1. Puberty 2. Sex education
ISBN 0763668710; 0763668729; 9780763668716; 9780763668723

This provides information about sex, puberty, family relationships and reproduction, sexual decision-making and birth control, abortion laws, sexual abuse, sexual health, sexually transmitted diseases, and internet safety.

"This edition has been revised for a new generation, including updates in scientific and medical information about reproduction, birth control, abortion, sexual abuse, and sexually transmitted diseases." SLJ

614 Forensic medicine; incidence of injuries, wounds, disease; public preventive medicine

Spilsbury, Richard

Bones speak! solving crimes from the past. Enslow Publishers 2009 48p il (Solve that crime!) lib bdg $23.93

Grades: 5 6 7 8 **614**

1. Forensic sciences 2. Forensic anthropology
ISBN 978-0-7660-3377-1 lib bdg; 0-7660-3377-5 lib bdg
LC 2008-33309

This "title boasts in-depth information, sidebars detailing events of true crime, and activities that will increase understanding. . . . Photographs are colorful, well-captioned, and related to the text." SLJ

Includes glossary and bibliographical references

614.4 Incidence of and public measures to prevent disease

Barnard, Bryn

★ Outbreak; plagues that changed history. written and illustrated by Bryn Barnard. Crown Publishers 2005 47p il maps $17.95

Grades: 5 6 7 8 **614.4**

1. Diseases 2. Epidemics 3. Diseases and history 4. Communicable diseases
ISBN 0-375-82986-5
LC 2005-15086

This "assessment of the historical role of diseases examines plague, smallpox, yellow fever, cholera, tuberculosis, and influenza. [Glossary.] Grades six to nine." (Bull Cent Child Books)

This "volume explores specific plagues that have impacted society. Barnard begins with an introduction to microbes and the positive and negative effects that they can have on humans. A history of the study of microorganisms follows. The bulk of the book then focuses on specific plagues with a chapter devoted to each, including the Black Death, smallpox, yellow fever, cholera, tuberculosis, and influenza. The final chapter discusses the modern struggle against disease. . . . The evocative paintings help to clarify the text. Browsers and report writers alike will find this to be a fascinating and informative resource." SLJ

Cunningham, Kevin

Pandemics. Children's Press 2011 48p il (True book: disasters) lib bdg $28; pa $6.99

Grades: 3 4 5 **614.4**

1. Epidemics 2. Communicable diseases
ISBN 978-0-531-25423-3 lib bdg; 0-531-25423-2; 978-0-531-26628-1 pa; 0-531-26628-1 pa
LC 2011007507

This describes epidemics of smallpox, cholera, plague, influenza, and HIV/AIDS.

This is "thoughtfully designed. . . . The information . . . . is right on target: concise, accurate, and thorough. . . . The photographs . . . . are especially effective at putting a human face on large-scale devastation." Booklist

Includes glossary and bibliographical references

Fox, Nancy

Hide and Seek; No Ticks Please. by Nancy Fox and illustrated by Daniel Seward. Morgan James Pub 2014 42 p. $9.95

Grades: 2 3 4 5 **614.4**

1. Lyme disease 2. Tick-borne diseases
ISBN 9781614487050; 1614487057

This children's book by Nancy Fox "teaches strategies for preventing Lyme disease and tick-borne diseases. Through the story of Alex and José, children will learn about José's discovery of a hidden danger (a tick) and how their activities may put them at risk of getting a tick bite." (Publisher's note)

Gleason, Carrie

Feasting bedbugs, mites, and ticks. Crabtree Pub. Co. 2010 32p il (Creepy crawlies) lib bdg $26.60; pa $8.95

Grades: 4 5 6 7 **614.4**

1. Mites 2. Ticks 3. Bedbugs
ISBN 978-0-7787-2500-8 lib bdg; 0-7787-2500-6 lib bdg; 978-0-7787-2507-7 pa; 0-7787-2507-3 pa
LC 2010009552

"The informational yet easy-to-read text in double-page spreads explains the classification, anatomy, life cycles, and ideal feeding and living conditions for mites, ticks, and bedbugs as well as the differences among them. . . . Children will be most interested in the long history, myths, and lore associated with these pests as well as the eye-catching layout, with numerous color photographs. . . . [This is an] equally repulsive and fascinating book." Booklist

Includes glossary and bibliographical references

Platt, Richard

Plagues, pox, and pestilence; written by Richard Platt; illustrated by John Kelly. Kingfisher 2011 48 p. col. ill. (hardcover) $15.99

Grades: 4 5 6 **614.4**

1. Diseases -- Causes 2. Animals -- Diseases 3. Communicable diseases -- History 4. Epidemics -- History 5. Animals as carriers of disease 6. Communicable diseases -- Transmission
ISBN 0753466872; 9780753466872
LC 2011041641

Author Richard Platt provides a "history of disease and pestilence, told from the point of view of the bugs and pests that cause them. The book features case histories of specific epidemics, 'eyewitness' accounts from the rats, flies, ticks and creepy-crawlies who spread diseases, plus plenty of fascinating facts and figures on the biggest and worst afflictions." (Publisher's note)

614.5 Incidence of and public measures to prevent specific diseases and kinds of diseases

Jarrow, Gail

Bubonic panic; when plague invaded America. Gail Jarrow. Calkins Creek 2016 200 p. illustrations (some color) (hardcover) $18.95

Grades: 5 6 7 8 9 **614.5**

1. Plague 2. Public health -- United States

ISBN 9781620917381; 9781629795621

LC 2015953543

This book, by Gail Jarrow, "tells the true story of America's first plague epidemic—the public health doctors who desperately fought to end it, the political leaders who tried to keep it hidden, and the brave scientists who uncovered the plague's secrets. Jarrow brings the history of a medical mystery to life in vivid and exciting detail for young readers. This title includes photographs and drawings, a glossary, a timeline, further resources, an author's note, and source notes." (Publisher's note)

"In her third book in this trilogy (Red Madness; Fatal Fever), Jarrow focuses on the nineteenth century, when the bubonic plague reared its ugly head in places like Hong Kong, Honolulu, and San Francisco. The thorough, fascinating treatment is complemented by a handsome design that includes numerous primary source artifacts. An exemplary contribution to the history of science and medicine." Horn Book

Includes bibliographical references (p. 188-192) and index.

Murphy, Jim

★ An **American** plague; the true and terrifying story of the yellow fever epidemic of 1793. Clarion Bks. 2003 165p il map $18

Grades: 5 6 7 8 **614.5**

1. Yellow fever 2. Philadelphia (Pa.) -- History

ISBN 0-395-77608-2

LC 2002-151355

Boston Globe-Horn Book Award: Nonfiction (2004)

National Book Award Finalist: Young People's Literature (2003)

"Murphy culls from a number of historical records the story of the yellow fever epidemic that swept Philadelphia in 1793, skillfully drawing out from these sources the fear and drama of the time and making them immediate to modern readers. . . . Thoroughly documented, with an annotated source list, the work is both rigorous and inviting." Horn Book

Person, Stephen

Bubonic plague; the Black Death! Bearport Pub. 2010 32p il map (Nightmare plagues) lib bdg $25.27

Grades: 4 5 6 7 **614.5**

1. Plague

ISBN 978-1-936088-03-4; 1-936088-03-7

This describes what causes bubonic plague and how it affects the body.

"The writing is accessible and interspersed with interesting photographs and fact boxes. . . . [The book relies] on an honest discussion of [bubonic plague and is an] . . . effective, easily navigated [introduction]." SLJ

Includes glossary and bibliographical references

Malaria; super killer! Bearport Pub. 2011 32p il map (Nightmare plagues) lib bdg $25.27

Grades: 4 5 6 7 **614.5**

1. Malaria

ISBN 978-1-936088-07-2 lib bdg; 1-936088-07-X lib bdg

LC 2010012018

Discover what causes malaria and how it affects the body.

"The writing is accessible and interspersed with interesting photographs and fact boxes. . . . [The book relies] on an honest discussion of [malaria and is an] . . . effective, easily navigated [introduction]." SLJ

Includes glossary and bibliographical references

Reingold, Adam

Smallpox; is it over? Bearport Pub. 2010 32p il map (Nightmare plagues) lib bdg $25.27

Grades: 4 5 6 7 **614.5**

1. Smallpox

ISBN 978-1-936088-02-7; 1-936088-02-9

LC 2010009371

Discover what causes smallpox and how it affects the body.

"The writing is accessible and interspersed with interesting photographs and fact boxes. . . . [The book relies] on an honest discussion of [smallpox and is an] . . . effective, easily navigated [introduction]." SLJ

Includes glossary and bibliographical references

Rudolph, Jessica

The **flu** of 1918; millions dead worldwide! Bearport Pub. 2011 32p il map (Nightmare plagues) lib bdg $25.27

Grades: 4 5 6 7 **614.5**

1. Influenza

ISBN 978-1-936088-05-8 lib bdg; 1-936088-05-3 lib bdg

LC 2010004684

Discover what caused the Influenza epidemic of 1918 and how it affected the body.

"The writing is accessible and interspersed with interesting photographs and fact boxes. . . . [The book relies] on an honest discussion of [Influenza epidemic of 1918 and is an] . . . effective, easily navigated [introduction]." SLJ

Includes glossary and bibliographical references

615 Pharmacology and therapeutics

Hyde, Natalie

What is germ theory? Crabtree Pub. Co. 2011 64p il (Shaping modern science) lib bdg $30.60; pa $10.95

Grades: 5 6 7 8 **615**

1. Chemists 2. Germ theory of disease 3. Microbiologists 4. Writers on science

ISBN 978-0-7787-7201-9 lib bdg; 0-7787-7201-9 lib bdg; 978-0-7787-7208-8 pa; 0-7787-7208-X pa

LC 2010052631

This title is "not only written and organized well, but [it is] also gorgeous in design. Full-color photographs and illustrations are set over colorful backgrounds that add depth but not distraction. [The title] includes thought-provoking quotes from famous authors and scientists and some eyebrow-raising 'Quick Facts' throughout." SLJ

Includes glossary and bibliographical references

Petersen, Christine

The **apothecary**. Marshall Cavendish Benchmark 2010 48p il (Colonial people) lib bdg $29.93

Grades: 3 4 5 6 **615**

1. Pharmacy 2. United States -- History -- 1600-1775, Colonial period

ISBN 978-0-7614-4795-5; 0-7614-4795-4

LC 2009015274

This describes the life of a colonial apothecary and his importance to the community, as well as everyday life, responsibilities, and social practices during that time.

"The type font, just slightly larger than usual, makes the text very visually appealing. . . . [The] book is liberally illustrated with artwork dating from the colonial period . . . [and] information boxes offer supplemental material." Libr Media Connect

Includes glossary and bibliographical references

615.8   Specific therapies and kinds of therapies

Beccia, Carlyn

I feel better with a frog in my throat: history's strangest cures; written and illustrated by Carlyn Beccia. Houghton Mifflin Books for Children 2010 48p il $17.99

Grades: 2 3 4   **615.8**

1. Therapeutics 2. Medicine -- History
ISBN 978-0-547-22570-8; 0-547-22570-9

                   LC 2010-01138

This discusses some of history's "disgusting and futile medical practices. . . . [Characterized by] dry-witted artwork, conversational text, [and] engaging historical detective work, [this book] asks readers to guess which 'cures' may actually have helped a handful of ailments. . . . The author provides intriguing background information on the cures—where they arose, why they were thougth to be efficacious—and pulls more than one gem out of the nastiness." Kirkus

615.9   Toxicology

Day, Jeff

Don't touch that! the book of gross, poisonous, and downright icky plants and critters. Chicago Review Press 2008 108p il pa $9.95

Grades: 3 4 5 6   **615.9**

1. Poisonous plants 2. Poisonous animals 3. Poisons and poisoning
ISBN 978-1-55652-711-1 pa; 1-556527-11-X pa

                   LC 2007027466

"Packed with potentially lifesaving information, this guide is humorous without sacrificing usefulness. The author, a medical doctor, begins with some basic plants (poison ivy, poison oak, and poison sumac) that might be encountered. Drawings of the leaves are carefully labeled and accompanied by the warning not to touch any part of the plant, and not to burn it as even the smoke can irritate. Poisonous insects, spiders, amphibians, reptiles, and mammals are also included, and every entry explains why the creature's venom causes the bad reaction it does and how to treat it. . . . Genuinely funny, colorful drawings on every page amplify the text and make it memorable." SLJ

Jakubiak, David J.

What can we do about toxins in the environment? PowerKids Press 2011 24p il (Protecting the planet) lib bdg $21.25; pa $8.25

Grades: 2 3 4   **615.9**

1. Pollution 2. Poisons and poisoning
ISBN 978-1-4488-4987-1 lib bdg; 978-1-4488-5121-8 pa

                   LC 2011000151

This explains the harm that toxins do in the environment and what can be done about them.

"Every spread has a full-page, thoughtfully captioned color photograph. . . . School and public libraries will want [this title] to round out collections or as [an update] to replace older books." SLJ

Includes glossary

Owen, Ruth

Disgusting food invaders. Bearport Pub. 2011 24p il (Up close and gross) lib bdg $22.61

Grades: 3 4 5   **615.9**

1. Parasites 2. Food contamination
ISBN 978-1-61772-126-7; 1-61772-126-3

                   LC 2010044417

This describes impurities and parasites which can be found in food, including fruit flies, moths, cheese mites, mold, grubs, rat hairs and insect parts, maggots, and bacteria.

"Never have the wonders of electron microscopy been more thrillingly displayed. . . . These knife-sharp, all-too-explicit photos are riveting. The [text doesn't] trail far behind in appeal either." SLJ

Includes glossary and bibliographical references

616   Diseases

Barber, Nicola

Cloning and genetic engineering; Nicola Barber. Rosen Pub.'s Rosen Central 2013 48 p. (Both sides of the story) (library binding) $29.25

Grades: 5 6 7 8   **616**

1. Cloning 2. Genetic engineering
ISBN 1448871875; 9781448871872

                   LC 2012013797

Author Nicola Barber's book focuses on cloning and genetic engineering. The book "offers arguments for both sides of the cloning and genetic engineering debate. Among the subjects examined are the human genome, transgenics, reproductive cloning, research cloning, stem cell therapy, genetic disease and testing, gene therapy, plant and animal pharming, genetically modified animals and crops, and gene doping." (Publisher's note)

Includes bibliographical references (p. 46) and index

Calamandrei, Camilla

★ Fever. Marshall Cavendish Benchmark 2009 64p il (Health alert) $22.95

Grades: 4 5 6 7   **616**

1. Fever
ISBN 978-0-7614-2915-9; 0-7614-2915-8

                   LC 2007-26002

This "title features a handsome format, with well-chosen illustrations, a substantial amount of information, and some practical insights." Booklist

Includes glossary

Dendy, Leslie A.

★ Guinea pig scientists; bold self-experimenters in science and medicine. [by] Leslie Dendy and Mel Boring; with illustrations by C. B. Mordan. Henry Holt & Co. 2005 213p il $19.95

Grades: 5 6 7 8   **616**

1. Scientists 2. Medicine -- Research
ISBN 9780805073164; 0-8050-7316-7

                   LC 2004-52364

This is a collection of "stories of human 'guinea pigs' who have tested the limits of the human body for the sake of science. Starting with Sir Charles Blagden, M.D., and his heat experiments, the stories are chronologically ordered from the 1770s to 1989. Included are descriptions of experiments dealing with digestion, laughing gas, vaccinations, mosquitoes as vectors of yellow fever, radioactivity, [and] G-forces." (Sci Books Films) Index.

"The accounts are lively, compelling, and not always for the squeamish. . . . The authors cogently discuss each experiment's significance in advancing our understanding of science and medicine. Illustrated with a mix of period black-and-white photos and Mordan's nineteenth-century-style portraits." Booklist

Includes bibliographical references

Evans, Michael

The **adventures** of Medical Man; kids' illnesses and injuries explained. by Michael Evans & David Wichman; illustrated by Gareth Williams. Annick 2010 72p il $21.95; pa $12.95

Grades: 5 6 7 8   616

1. Diseases 2. Wounds and injuries

ISBN 978-1-55451-263-8; 1-55451-263-8; 978-1-55451-262-1 pa; 1-55451-262-X pa

"Using tangible experiences that kids can relate to, this book does a fantastic job of explaining common medical issues in an accessible way. A variety of heroic characters explain otherwise complicated and seemingly scary conditions and occurrences. Through the use of science fiction, adventure, and comics, the book covers nut allergies, concussions, broken bones, strep throat, ear infections, and asthma. . . . The extensive glossary is straightforward and user-friendly. The pumped-up graphic illustrations are extremely engaging and further bring these otherwise abstract concepts to life." SLJ

Murphy, Patricia J.

Illness; [by] Patricia J Murphy. Heinemann Library 2008 32p il (Tough topics) lib bdg $25.36; pa $7.99

Grades: PreK K 1 2 3   616

1. Diseases

ISBN 978-1-4034-9777-2 lib bdg; 978-1-4034-9782-6 pa

LC 2007005345

This "book talks about different kinds of illnesses, coping mechanisms, and varieties of medical treatments available. . . . Murphy gives an overview of the topic in a way that young readers can understand. . . . The two-page chapters include full-color photos and two paragraphs of text that are frank yet sensitive in their approach." SLJ

Includes glossary and bibliographical references

Ollhoff, Jim

What are germs? ABDO Pub. Co. 2010 32p il (A history of germs) $27.07

Grades: 3 4 5 6   616

1. Bacteria 2. Germ theory of disease

ISBN 978-1-60453-502-0; 1-60453-502-4

"What Are Germs? includes kinds of germs and germ-fighting organizations. The short, informative chapters provide plenty of details for reports. The illustrations, many of which are color photos, enhance the information." SLJ

Includes glossary

Rhatigan, Joe

Ouch! the weird & wild ways your body deals with agonizing aches, ferocious fevers, lousy lumps, crummy colds, bothersome bites, breaks, bruises & burns & makes them feel better. Joe Rhatigan; original Illustrations by Anthony Owsley. Imagine! 2013 80 p. $14.95

Grades: 3 4 5 6   616

1. Wounds and injuries 2. Children -- Health and hygiene 3. Pain -- Popular works 4. Psychology, Pathological

ISBN 1623540054; 9781623540050

LC 2012048462

This book by author Joe Rhatigan is a "compendium of low-key medical information for the upper grade school set. Got a headache? A rash? A pulled muscle or a sprained ankle? Disease by disease and injury by injury, this basic medical text takes young readers through various ailments, breaking each one down into a simple explanation of the problem." (Kirkus Reviews)

Silverstein, Alvin

Tapeworms, foot fungus, lice, and more; the yucky disease book. by Alvin Silverstein, Virginia Silverstein, and Laura Silverstein Nunn; illustrated by Gerald Kelley. Enslow Publishers 2010 48p il (Yucky science) lib bdg $23.93

Grades: 3 4 5 6   616

1. Diseases 2. Medicine

ISBN 978-0-7660-3314-6 lib bdg; 0-7660-3314-7 lib bdg

LC 2009012282

"Explores 'yucky' diseases, including leprosy, plague, tapeworms, and more" Publisher's note

Includes glossary and bibliographical references

Stoyles, Pennie

The **A-Z** of health. Black Rabbit/Smart Apple 2010 6v il set $119.70

Grades: 5 6 7 8   616

1. Health 2. Reference books 3. Medicine -- Encyclopedias

ISBN 978-1-59920-654-7; 1-59920-654-4

"This reference set provides a simple, brief, and easy-to-read introduction to key aspects of physical and mental health, including various body processes and diseases as well as information on treatments and preventative measures. . . . The explanations are concise, clear, and easy to understand. In addition to the abundance of images, the large type and white space that is prevalent on every page will make this set accessible to a broad array of young readers." Booklist

616.2   Diseases of respiratory system

Chilman-Blair, Kim

Medikidz explain sleep apnea; [by] Kim Chilman-Blair and Shawn Deloache; medical content reviewed for accuracy by Paul Gringras and David Rapoport. Rosen Central 2011 40p il (Superheroes on a medical mission) lib bdg $29.25; pa $11.75

Grades: 3 4 5 6   616.2

1. Sleep apnea 2. Superheroes 3. Graphic novels

ISBN 978-1-4358-9459-4 lib bdg; 1-4358-9459-6 lib bdg; 978-1-4488-1841-9 pa; 1-4488-1841-9 pa

LC 2010002554

"A team of superheroes rides around on a medi-jet and whisks ill children, or their siblings, off to Mediland, a giant replica of the human body, to teach them about [sleep apnea]. . . . The comic panels are visually exciting with eye-popping colors. Inside Mediland, the science behind various conditions is expertly simplified and explained with a sometimes tongue-in-cheek repartee among the characters as well as with very basic analogies reminiscent of video games. . . . This approach makes the health issues accessible and much less scary for readers wanting to learn more for personal or academic reasons." SLJ

Includes glossary and bibliographical references

Cobb, Vicki

★ **Your** body battles a cold; written by Vicki Cobb; photomicrographs by Dennis Kunkel; illustrated by Andrew N. Harris. Millbrook Press 2009 32p il (Body battles) lib bdg $25.26

Grades: 3 4 5   616.2

1. Immune system 2. Cold (Disease)

ISBN 978-0-8225-6813-1; 0-8225-6813-6

LC 2008002839

Color illustrations and photomicrographs show what happens when a human body is attacked by a cold virus

"The body's immune system has never looked like this before with plasma cells using sling shots to fire antibodies into viruses, platelets riding inner tubes down a stream of blood, and viruses multiplying in a 'Germco' factory. [The] title introduces five or six defense cells, disguised as superheroes protecting the body from adversarial viruses. . . . The oversize text uses metaphors that readers will understand. . . . The micrographs will fascinate and compel young readers to read everything." SLJ

Includes glossary and bibliographical references

Landau, Elaine

★ The **common** cold. Marshall Cavendish Benchmark 2009 32p il (Head-to-toe health) lib bdg $19.95

Grades: 2 3 4   **616.2**

1. Cold (Disease)

ISBN 978-0-7614-2844-2; 0-7614-2844-5

LC 2007-35005

"Photo illustrations are apt and age appropriate. . . . Pervading the [book] . . . is an overall sense of reassurance that even if something hurts, 'all better' is never too far away. Appealing and readable nonfiction." SLJ

Includes glossary and bibliographical references

Moore-Mallinos, Jennifer

I have asthma; illustrated by Rosa M. Cirto. Barron's 2007 35p il (What do I know about?) pa $6.99

Grades: K 1 2 3   **616.2**

1. Asthma

ISBN 0-7641-3785-9

After a young boy has trouble breathing during soccer practice, he is taken to his doctor who says that he has asthma, but he learns that with proper treatment and medical supervision, his asthma can be kept under control.

"The easy text, combined with soft, rounded figures in the colorful illustrations, results in a sensitively told story that offers encouragement to children suffering from this condition, complete with helpful advice." SLJ

Ollhoff, Jim

The **flu**. ABDO Pub. Co. 2010 32p il (A history of germs) $27.07

Grades: 3 4 5 6   **616.2**

1. Viruses 2. Influenza

ISBN 978-1-60453-498-6; 1-60453-498-2

LC 2008055063

"Flu provides a concise look at the illness, pandemics, treatments, and recent strains, including H1N1. . . . The short, informative chapters provide plenty of details for reports. The illustrations, many of which are color photos, enhance the information." SLJ

Includes glossary

Robbins, Lynette

How to deal with asthma. PowerKids Press 2010 24p il (Kids' health) lib bdg $21.25

Grades: 2 3 4   **616.2**

1. Asthma

ISBN 978-1-4042-8141-7 lib bdg; 1-4042-8141-X lib bdg

LC 2009-7653

"Hypothetical situations with fictional characters put readers in the moment and provide a solid foundation for comprehending [asthma]. . . . Robbins maintains a comforting tone, reassuring readers that it is possible to lead active lives with proper attention to diet and guidance from parents and doctors." SLJ

Includes glossary

Royston, Angela

Asthma. Black Rabbit Books 2009 30p il (How's your health) lib bdg $27.10

Grades: 1 2 3   **616.2**

1. Asthma

ISBN 978-1-59920-219-8 lib bdg; 1-59920-219-0 lib bdg

LC 2007-35689

First published 2004 by Heinemann Library

"Encourages further learning with sidebars that help readers think concretely about the subject. . . . Altogether a pitch perfect presentation." SLJ

Includes glossary and bibliographical references

Explaining asthma. Smart Apple Media 2010 45p il (Explaining) lib bdg $34.25

Grades: 5 6 7 8   **616.2**

1. Asthma

ISBN 978-1-59920-315-7 lib bdg; 1-59920-315-4 lib bdg

LC 2008-49284

Describes what living with asthma is like, discussing symptoms, triggers, treatments, and lifestyle changes that may be necessary to prevent asthma attacks

The book provides a "basic [overview] of the health concerns related to the disease; information on diagnosis and treatment; and a discussion of the challenges or complications experienced by the affected person and their family/friends, and how to manage those problems. . . . The incorporation of quotes and personal accounts in 'Case Notes' sidebars adds to the sensitive tone found throughout [the title]." SLJ

Includes glossary

616.3   Diseases of digestive system

Allman, Toney

Obesity. Cherry Lake Pub. 2009 32p il (Health at risk) lib bdg $27.07

Grades: 4 5 6 7   **616.3**

1. Obesity

ISBN 978-1-60279-285-2 lib bdg; 1-60279-285-2 lib bdg

LC 2008017499

This describes the causes and dangers of obesity and the many efforts being made to help people control their weight.

"Great for reports or reluctant readers." Booklist

Includes bibliographical references

Bjorklund, Ruth

★ **Cystic** fibrosis. Marshall Cavendish Benchmark 2009 64p il (Health alert) $22.95

Grades: 4 5 6 7   **616.3**

1. Cystic fibrosis

ISBN 978-0-7614-2912-8; 0-7614-2912-3

LC 2007-46674

This "title features a handsome format, with well-chosen illustrations, a substantial amount of information, and some practical insights." Booklist

Cobb, Vicki

★ **Your** body battles a stomachache; written by Vicki Cobb; with photomicrographs by Dennis Kunkel; illustrations by Andrew N. Harris. Millbrook Press 2009 32p il (Body battles) lib bdg $25.26

Grades: 3 4 5   **616.3**

1. Stomach 2. Intestines 3. Immune system

ISBN 978-0-8225-7166-7 lib bdg; 0-8225-7166-8 lib bdg

LC 2008002852

Color illustrations and photomicrographs show what happens when a human digestive system is attacked by a rotavirus

"The body's immune system has never looked like this before with plasma cells using sling shots to fire antibodies into viruses, platelets riding inner tubes down a stream of blood, and viruses multiplying in a 'Germco' factory. [The] title introduces five or six defense cells, disguised as superheroes protecting the body from adversarial viruses. . . . The oversize text uses metaphors that readers will understand. . . . The micrographs will fascinate and compel young readers to read everything." SLJ

Includes glossary and bibliographical references

Hicks, Terry Allan

★ **Obesity**. Marshall Cavendish Benchmark 2009 63p il (Health alert) $22.95

Grades: 4 5 6 7   **616.3**

1. Obesity

ISBN 978-0-7614-2911-1; 0-7614-2911-5

LC 2007-31246

This "title features a handsome format, with well-chosen illustrations, a substantial amount of information, and some practical insights." Booklist

Includes glossary

Hunt, Jamie

Tired of being teased; obesity and others. Mason Crest Publishers 2010 48p il (Kids & obesity) lib bdg $19.95; pa $7.95

Grades: 3 4 5   **616.3**

1. Obesity

ISBN 978-1-4222-1711-5 lib bdg; 1-4222-1711-6 lib bdg; 978-1-4222-1899-0 pa; 1-4222-1899-6 pa

LC 2010012759

Teaches that a person is more than appearance, and discusses how to deal with being teased about one's appearance.

This book about obesity "presents the expected information about the food pyramid, the need for physical activity, and the influence of the media on our psyches. Where the material shines is in its holistic approach. Readers are encouraged to develop their inner lives as much as their physical selves and to take responsibility for their own health and eating habits. . . . This brightly-colored, ego-boosting, responsibility-championing . . . [book] is a winner." SLJ

Includes bibliographical references

Jarrow, Gail

Red madness; how a medical mystery changed what we eat. Gail Jarrow. Calkins Creek 2014 192 p. $16.95

Grades: 5 6 7 8 9   **616.3**

1. Diseases 2. Malnutrition 3. Pellagra -- History 4. Epidemics -- United States -- History 5. United States. Public Health Service -- History

ISBN 1590787323; 9781590787328

LC 2008049497

In this book, author Gail Jarrow "tracks [a] disease, commonly known as pellagra, and highlights how doctors, scientists, and public health officials finally defeated it. Illustrated with 100 archival photographs, [it] includes stories about real-life pellagra victims and accounts of scientific investigations. It concludes with a glossary, timeline, further resources, author's note, bibliography, and index." (Publisher's note)

"In 1902, a young man in Georgia displayed symptoms of a disease believed to be nonexistent in the U.S.: pellagra, a deficiency disease. Jarrow unfolds the suspenseful search for a cause of the South's epidemic, as corn fungus, insect- and bird-born parasites, and more were all blamed and rejected." Horn Book

Powell, Jillian

Explaining cystic fibrosis. Smart Apple Media 2010 45p il (Explaining) lib bdg $34.25

Grades: 5 6 7 8   **616.3**

1. Cystic fibrosis

ISBN 978-1-59920-312-6 lib bdg; 1-59920-312-X lib bdg

LC 2008-49288

Describes the illness, including its causes, how it is diagnosed, current treatments for the illness, and how those with cystic fibrosis lead everyday lives

The book provides a "basic [overview] of the health concerns related to the disease; information on diagnosis and treatment; and a discussion of the challenges or complications experienced by the affected person and their family/friends, and how to manage those problems. . . . The incorporation of quotes and personal accounts in 'Case Notes' sidebars adds to the sensitive tone found throughout [the title]." SLJ

Includes glossary and bibliographical references

Robbins, Lynette

How to deal with obesity. PowerKids Press 2010 24p il (Kids' health) lib bdg $21.25

Grades: 2 3 4   **616.3**

1. Obesity

ISBN 978-1-4042-8143-1 lib bdg; 1-4042-8143-6 lib bdg

LC 2009-8902

"Hypothetical situations with fictional characters put readers in the moment and provide a solid foundation for comprehending [obesity]. . . . Robbins maintains a comforting tone, reassuring readers that it is possible to lead active lives with proper attention to diet and guidance from parents and doctors." SLJ

Includes glossary

Simons, Rae

Too many Sunday dinners; family and diet. Mason Crest Publishers 2010 48p il (Kids & obesity) lib bdg $19.95; pa $7.95

Grades: 3 4 5   **616.3**

1. Obesity 2. Heredity

ISBN 978-1-4222-1713-9 lib bdg; 1-4222-1713-2 lib bdg; 978-1-4222-1901-0 pa; 1-4222-1901-1 pa

LC 2010019188

Discusses how obesity can be hereditary.

This book "presents the expected information about the food pyramid, the need for physical activity, and the influence of the media on our psyches. Where the material shines is in its holistic approach. Readers are encouraged to develop their inner lives as much as their physical selves and to take responsibility for their own health and eating habits. . . . This brightly-colored, ego-boosting, responsibility-championing . . . [book] is a winner." SLJ

Includes bibliographical references

616.4 Diseases of endocrine, hematopoietic, lymphatic, glandular systems; diseases of male breast

Loughrey, Anita

Explaining diabetes. Smart Apple Media 2010 45p il (Explaining) lib bdg $34.25

Grades: 5 6 7 8   **616.4**

1. Diabetes

ISBN 978-1-59920-314-0 lib bdg; 1-59920-314-6 lib bdg

LC 2008-49290

Provides an overview of Type 1 and Type 2 diabetes, discussing causes and symptoms, recommended and required lifestyle changes, how the disease is managed, and possible complications that may occur

The book provides a "basic [overview] of the health concerns related to the disease; information on diagnosis and treatment; and a discussion of the challenges or complications experienced by the affected person and their family/friends, and how to manage those problems. . . . The incorporation of quotes and personal accounts in 'Case Notes' sidebars adds to the sensitive tone found throughout [the title]." SLJ

Includes glossary and bibliographical references

Pirner, Connie White

Even little kids get diabetes; pictures by Nadine Bernard Westcott. Whitman, A. 1991 un il hardcover o.p. pa $6.95

Grades: K 1   616.4
    1. Diabetes
    ISBN 0-8075-2158-2; 0-8075-2159-0 pa
                                            LC 90-12738

A young girl who has had diabetes since she was two years old describes her adjustments to the disease

"Language is simple, age appropriate, and effectively gets the point across. The ink-and-watercolor drawings are lively and often upbeat. . . . Perhaps the most valuable part of the book is the 'note for parents,' which relates Pirner's personal experience over the last three years in caring for a diabetic child." SLJ

Robbins, Lynette

How to deal with diabetes. PowerKids Press 2010 24p il (Kids' health) lib bdg $21.25

Grades: 2 3 4   616.4
    1. Diabetes
    ISBN 978-1-4042-8144-8 lib bdg; 1-4042-8144-4 lib bdg
                                            LC 2009-10467

"Hypothetical situations with fictional characters put readers in the moment and provide a solid foundation for comprehending [diabetes]. . . . Robbins maintains a comforting tone, reassuring readers that it is possible to lead active lives with proper attention to diet and guidance from parents and doctors." SLJ

Includes glossary

616.5   Diseases of integument

Caffey, Donna

Yikes!-lice! illustrations by Patrick Girouard. Whitman, A. 1998 un il $14.95; pa $5.95

Grades: K 1 2 3   616.5
    1. Lice
    ISBN 0-8075-9374-5; 0-8075-9375-3 pa
                                            LC 97-30679

Rhyming text describes what happens when a family discovers lice in the home and fights against them. Includes factual information about how lice live, spread, and can be eradicated

DerKazarian, Susan

You have head lice! by Susan DerKazarian. Children's Press 2005 31p il (Rookie read-about health) $20.50; pa $5.95

Grades: PreK K 1 2   616.5
    1. Lice
    ISBN 0-516-25879-6; 0-516-27920-3 pa
                                            LC 2004-15308

This "approaches the sometimes-touchy subject of head lice in a straightforward, reassuring manner. . . . Adults wanting to explain head lice to children will find this a helpful source of basic information." Booklist

Faulk, Michelle

The **case** of the flesh-eating bacteria; Annie Biotica solves skin disease crimes. by Michelle Faulk. Lake Book Manufacturing, Inc. 2013 48 p. (Body system disease investigations) (library) $23.93

Grades: 5 6 7 8   616.5
    1. Picture books for children 2. Skin -- Diseases 3. Virus diseases 4. Skin -- Infections
    ISBN 0766039455; 9780766039452
                                            LC 2011023985

This book by Michelle Faulk "from the Body System Disease Investigations series introduces Agent Annie Biotica, a 'Disease Scene Investigator with the Major Health Crimes Unit'. This cartoon-style heroine is called in to solve a series of skin-related medical cases . . . caused by flesh-eating bacteria, pinkeye, ringworm, chicken pox, [and] measles." (Booklist)

Includes bibliographical references (p. 47) and index

Landau, Elaine

★ **Warts**. Marshall Cavendish Benchmark 2010 32p il (Head-to-toe health) lib bdg $28.50

Grades: 2 3 4   616.5
    1. Warts
    ISBN 978-0-7614-4836-5 lib bdg; 0-7614-4836-5 lib bdg
This provides information about warts.

This "manages to pack in surprising amount information, including facts about good hygiene. The text addresses the readers directly, and the photos are real grabbers." Booklist

Includes glossary and bibliographical references

Lew, Kristi

Itch & ooze; gross stuff on your skin. illustrations by Michael Slack. Millbrook Press 2010 48p il (Gross body science) lib bdg $29.27

Grades: 4 5 6   616.5
    1. Skin 2. Skin -- Diseases
    ISBN 978-0-8225-8963-1 lib bdg; 0-8225-8963-X lib bdg
                                            LC 2008-45591

Presents disgusting facts about human skin, the diseases and parasites that can cause problems with it, and how it functions to protect the body and itself.

"Solid information layered between sarcastic comments and kid-friendly terminology like fart, poop, barf, and puke will keep readers engaged. . . . Labeled, captioned (and graphic) photographs, cartoon-style illustrations, and micrographs add information." SLJ

Includes glossary and bibliographical references

Royston, Angela

Head lice. Black Rabbit Books 2009 30p il (How's your health) lib bdg $27.10

Grades: 1 2 3   616.5
    1. Lice
    ISBN 978-1-59920-218-1 lib bdg; 1-59920-218-2 lib bdg
First published 2001 by Heinemann Library

"Encourages further learning with sidebars that help readers think concretely about the subject. . . . Altogether a pitch perfect presentation." SLJ

Includes glossary

616.8 Diseases of nervous system and mental disorders

Ali-Walsh, Rasheda

★ **I'll** hold your hand so you won't fall; a child's guide to Parkinson's disease. [by] Rasheda Ali; foreword for Muhammad Ali. Merit 2005 40p il $19.95

Grades: 2 3 4 **616.8**

1. Parkinson's disease

ISBN 1-873413-13-0

"Ali's father, Muhammad Ali, suffers from Parkinson's disease, and she answers questions children may have about the illness. . . . The text is well written and basic, without being oversimplified. . . . A short CD-ROM of the author introducing the book and its contents is included. An excellent overview written in an approachable style that will be reassuring to young readers." SLJ

Bender, Lionel

Explaining epilepsy. Smart Apple Media 2010 45p il (Explaining) lib bdg $34.25

Grades: 5 6 7 8 **616.8**

1. Epilepsy

ISBN 978-1-59920-309-6 lib bdg; 1-59920-309-X lib bdg

LC 2008-49292

Describes the nature, symptoms, and possible causes of epilepsy, gives a history of its study, and discusses its treatment

The book provides a "basic [overview] of the health concerns related to the disease; information on diagnosis and treatment; and a discussion of the challenges or complications experienced by the affected person and their family/friends, and how to manage those problems. . . . The incorporation of quotes and personal accounts in 'Case Notes' sidebars adds to the sensitive tone found throughout [the title]." SLJ

Includes glossary and bibliographical references

Bjorklund, Ruth

★ **Cerebral** palsy. Marshall Cavendish Benchmark 2007 64p il (Health alert) lib bdg $31.36

Grades: 4 5 6 7 **616.8**

1. Cerebral palsy

ISBN 978-0-7614-2209-9; 0-7614-2209-9

LC 2006-15818

This "title features a handsome format, with well-chosen illustrations, a substantial amount of information, and some practical insights." Booklist

Includes glossary and bibliographical references

★ **Epilepsy**. Marshall Cavendish Benchmark 2007 63p il (Health alert) lib bdg $21.95

Grades: 4 5 6 7 **616.8**

1. Epilepsy

ISBN 978-0-7614-2206-8; 0-7614-2206-4

LC 2006-15816

This "title features a handsome format, with well-chosen illustrations, a substantial amount of information, and some practical insights." Booklist

Includes glossary and bibliographical references

Colligan, L. H.

★ **Sleep** disorders. Marshall Cavendish Benchmark 2009 64p il (Health alert) $22.95

Grades: 4 5 6 7 **616.8**

1. Sleep disorders

ISBN 978-0-7614-2913-5; 0-7614-2913-1

This "title features a handsome format, with well-chosen illustrations, a substantial amount of information, and some practical insights." Booklist

Includes glossary

Klosterman, Lorrie

★ **Meningitis**. Marshall Cavendish Benchmark 2007 64p il (Health alert) lib bdg $31.36

Grades: 4 5 6 7 **616.8**

1. Meningitis

ISBN 978-0-7614-2211-2; 0-7614-2211-0

LC 2006015819

This "title features a handsome format, with well-chosen illustrations, a substantial amount of information, and some practical insights." Booklist

Includes glossary and bibliographical references

Levete, Sarah

Explaining cerebral palsy. Smart Apple Media 2010 45p il (Explaining) lib bdg $34.25

Grades: 5 6 7 8 **616.8**

1. Cerebral palsy

ISBN 978-1-59920-311-9 lib bdg; 1-59920-311-1 lib bdg

LC 2008-49287

Describes the illness, including its causes, how it is diagnosed, current treatment methods, and how those with cerebral palsy live everyday lives

The book provides a "basic [overview] of the health concerns related to the disease; information on diagnosis and treatment; and a discussion of the challenges or complications experienced by the affected person and their family/friends, and how to manage those problems. . . . The incorporation of quotes and personal accounts in 'Case Notes' sidebars adds to the sensitive tone found throughout [the title]." SLJ

Includes glossary and bibliographical references

616.85 Miscellaneous diseases of nervous system and mental disorders

Amenta, Charles A.

Russell's world; a story for kids about autism. illustrated by Monika Pollak. Magination Press 2011 un il $14.95; pa $9.95

Grades: K 1 2 3 **616.85**

1. Autism

ISBN 978-1-4338-0975-0; 1-4338-0975-3; 978-1-4338-0976-7 pa; 1-4338-0976-1 pa

LC 2010048837

First published 1992 with title: Russell is extra special

"Likable young Russell puts a face on autism. Amenta's experience with his own son (now grown) shapes this heartfelt approach. This child craves routine and rituals and struggles to relate to his younger brothers. . . . Focusing on Russell's experiences, the book avoids sweeping generalizations while fairly outlining the condition's complexities. . . . Vivid mixed-media spreads include black-and-white childhood photos and display a hodgepodge of household objects and crayon scribbles. . . . Supportive without sugarcoating, this realistic account of a disorder that affects so many contains at its core a raw emotional heart." Kirkus

Andrews, Beth

Why are you so scared? a child's book about parents with PTSD. illustrated by Katherine Kirkland. Magination Press 2011 un il $14.95; pa $9.95

Grades: 1 2 3 4   **616.85**
1. Post-traumatic stress disorder
ISBN 978-1-4338-1045-9; 1-4338-1045-X; 978-1-4338-1044-2
pa; 1-4338-1044-1 pa
                                              LC 2011011082

"This straightforward, reassuring guide strives to explain some of the causes of Posttraumatic Stress Disorder . . . while not skimping on day-to-day survival tips. . . . Kirkland uses soft, hopeful illustrations that underscore the message that kids are not alone and that their parent's tired, cranky, jumpy emotions are to be expected. . . . The material is far too useful to be ignored." Booklist

Barton, Michael
It's raining cats and dogs; an autism spectrum guide to the confusing world of idioms, metaphors, and everyday expressions. Michael Barton; foreword, Delia Barton; illustrator, Michael Barton. Jessica Kingsley Publishers 2012 95 p. (alk. paper) $15.95
Grades: 3 4 5 6   **616.85**
1. Autism 2. Metaphor 3. Figures of speech 4. English language -- Idioms 5. Autistic people -- Language 6. Autism spectrum disorders -- Patients -- Language
ISBN 1849052832; 9781849052832
                                              LC 2011039514

This book offers "insight into the mind of someone with an ASD [autism spectrum disorder]. It . . . illustrates why people with ASDs have problems understanding common phrases and idioms that others accept unquestioningly as part of everyday speech. The . . . drawings" are meant to "entertain and inspire those on the spectrum, giving them the confidence to recognise figures of speech, feel less alienated and even use idioms themselves. The drawings' are designed to "form instantly memorable references for those with ASDs to recall whenever they need to and" should "be helpful for anyone curious to understand the ASD way of thinking." (Publisher's note)

Bennett, Howard J.
Max Archer, kid detective: the case of the wet bed; illustrated by Spike Gerrell. Magination Press 2011 48p il $14.95; pa $9.95
Grades: K 1 2 3   **616.85**
1. Enuresis
ISBN 978-1-4338-0953-8; 1-4338-0953-2; 978-1-4338-0954-5
pa; 1-4338-0954-0 pa
                                              LC 2010051485

"Max is a detective who like to 'help kids with their problems'—this case takes on bedwetting. . . . Bennett strikes the right balance between story and self-help to provide a title whose tone and careful explanations both parents and kids will appreciate. . . . Even if there were not an alarming dearth of titles on this subject aimed at kids, this would stand out as a most thorough, highly readable resource." Kirkus

Chilman-Blair, Kim
Medikidz explain ADHD; [by] Kim Chilman-Blair and John Taddeo; medical content reviewed for accuracy by Peter D. Hill. Rosen Central 2011 40p il (Superheroes on a medical mission) lib bdg $29.25; pa $11.75
Grades: 3 4 5 6   **616.85**
1. Superheroes 2. Graphic novels 3. Attention deficit disorder
ISBN 978-1-4358-9456-3 lib bdg; 1-4358-9456-1 lib bdg; 978-1-4488-1833-4 pa; 1-4488-1833-8 pa
                                              LC 2010001063

"A team of superheroes rides around on a medi-jet and whisks ill children, or their siblings, off to Mediland, a giant replica of the human body, to teach them about [ADHD]. . . . The comic panels are visually exciting with eye-popping colors. Inside Mediland, the science behind various conditions is expertly simplified and explained with a sometimes

tongue-in-cheek repartee among the characters as well as with very basic analogies reminiscent of video games. . . . This approach makes the health issues accessible and much less scary for readers wanting to learn more for personal or academic reasons." SLJ
Includes glossary and bibliographical references

Medikidz explain autism; [by] Kim Chilman-Blair and John Taddeo. Rosen Central 2011 40p il (Superheroes on a medical mission) lib bdg $29.25; pa $11.75
Grades: 3 4 5 6   **616.85**
1. Autism 2. Superheroes 3. Graphic novels
ISBN 978-1-4358-9460-0 lib bdg; 1-4358-9460-X; 978-1-4488-1835-8 pa; 1-4488-1835-4 pa
                                              LC 2010008830

"A team of superheroes rides around on a medi-jet and whisks ill children, or their siblings, off to Mediland, a giant replica of the human body, to teach them about [autism]. . . . The comic panels are visually exciting with eye-popping colors. Inside Mediland, the science behind various conditions is expertly simplified and explained with a sometimes tongue-in-cheek repartee among the characters as well as with very basic analogies reminiscent of video games. . . . This approach makes the health issues accessible and much less scary for readers wanting to learn more for personal or academic reasons." SLJ
Includes glossary and bibliographical references

Donovan, Sandra, 1967-
Keep your cool! what you should know about stress. illustrations by Jack Desrocher. Lerner Publications Co. 2009 64p il (Health zone) lib bdg $30.60
Grades: 4 5 6 7   **616.85**
1. Stress (Psychology)
ISBN 978-0-8225-7555-9; 0-8225-7555-8
                                              LC 2007038858

This describes what causes stress and what you can do to relieve it.
"The format is beyond lively, with lots of color, cartoons, and an informal writing style, but it manages to present sometimes frightening material in a non-threatening and browsable way." Booklist
Includes glossary and bibliographical references

Jones, Viola
Conquering negative body image; Viola Jones and Edward Willett. Rosen Publishing 2016 64 p. illustrations (chiefly color) (ebook) $34.45; (library bound) $34.45
Grades: 6 7 8 9   **616.85**
1. Body image 2. Self-acceptance 3. Eating disorders -- Psychological aspects 4. Body image in adolescence 5. Self-acceptance in adolescence 6. Body image -- Social aspects -- United States
ISBN 9781499462067; 9781499462050
                                              LC 2015019516

This book in the Conquering eating disorders series, by Viola Jones and Edward Willett, "helps readers determine whether they have a negative body image, understand the roots and potential dangers of such thinking, and learn to overcome the problem and accept and celebrate their bodies." (Publisher's note)
"Young readers will find it a useful and engaging starting point for discussions on a difficult topic." Booklist
Includes bibliographical references and index

Levy, Joel
Phobiapedia; all the things we fear the most! Scholastic 2011 80p il pa $8.99

Grades: 4 5 6 7   **616.85**
  1. Phobias
  ISBN 978-0-545-34929-1; 0-545-34929-X
This briefly describes over 50 phobias.

"With an appealing layout, plenty of color, and enough germs, snakes, and bats to get the heart racing, this title has kid written all over it." Booklist

Quinn, Patricia O.

Attention, girls! a guide to learn all about your AD/HD. illustrated by Carl Pearce. Magination Press 2009 119p il $16.95; pa $12.95
Grades: 4 5 6 7   **616.85**
  1. Attention deficit disorder
  ISBN 978-1-4338-0447-2; 1-4338-0447-6; 978-1-4338-0448-9 pa; 1-4338-0448-4 pa
                                          LC 2008054524
"Quinn has attention deficit hyperactivity disorder and is a medical doctor; she addresses the types of AD/HD; who can help; differences between girls and boys with AD/HD; making friends; talking with adults about the condition; relaxation techniques; and medication. Her aim is to give girls a variety of ways to manage their disorders. . . . The book is attractive and inviting with colorful cartoon illustrations, sidebars, and highlighted reminders." SLJ

Robbins, Lynette

How to deal with ADHD. PowerKids Press 2010 24p il (Kids' health) lib bdg $21.25
Grades: 2 3 4   **616.85**
  1. Attention deficit disorder
  ISBN 978-1-4042-8140-0 lib bdg; 1-4042-8140-1 lib bdg
                                          LC 2009-6412
"Hypothetical situations with fictional characters put readers in the moment and provide a solid foundation for comprehending [ADHD]. . . . Robbins maintains a comforting tone, reassuring readers that it is possible to lead active lives with proper attention to diet and guidance from parents and doctors." SLJ
  Includes glossary

How to deal with autism. PowerKids Press 2010 24p il (Kids' health) lib bdg $21.25
Grades: 2 3 4   **616.85**
  1. Autism
  ISBN 978-1-4042-8142-4 lib bdg; 1-4042-8142-8 lib bdg
                                          LC 2009-7862
"Hypothetical situations with fictional characters put readers in the moment and provide a solid foundation for comprehending [autism]. . . . Robbins maintains a comforting tone, reassuring readers that it is possible to lead active lives with proper attention to diet and guidance from parents and doctors." SLJ
  Includes glossary

Royston, Angela

★ **Explaining** down syndrome. Smart Apple Media 2010 45p il (Explaining) lib bdg $34.25
Grades: 5 6 7 8   **616.85**
  1. Down syndrome
  ISBN 978-1-59920-308-9 lib bdg; 1-59920-308-1 lib bdg
                                          LC 2008-49291
This book about down syndrome provides a "basic [overview] of the health concerns related to the disease; information on diagnosis and treatment; and a discussion of the challenges or complications experienced by the affected person and their family/friends, and how to manage those problems. . . . The incorporation of quotes and per-

sonal accounts in 'Case Notes' sidebars adds to the sensitive tone found throughout [the title]." SLJ
  Includes glossary

Shapiro, Ouisie

Autism and me; sibling stories. photographs by Steven Vote. Albert Whitman 2009 un il $16.99
Grades: 3 4 5 6   **616.85**
  1. Autism 2. Siblings
  ISBN 978-0-8075-0487-1; 0-8075-0487-4
                                          LC 2008-31700
Children tell their stories of what it is like to live with a sibling who has autism.

"The children's emotions ring true, telling what they love about their sibling; the preaching comes from their hearts. This book would be useful in families and in classrooms to help explain both the struggles and the triumphs of living with someone who has this disorder." SLJ

Silverstein, Alvin

The **ADHD** update; understanding attention-deficit/hyperactivity disorder. [by] Alvin and Virginia Silverstein and Laura Silverstein Nunn. Enslow Publishers 2008 112p il (Disease update) lib bdg $31.93
Grades: 5 6 7 8   **616.85**
  1. Attention deficit disorder
  ISBN 978-0-7660-2800-5 lib bdg; 0-7660-2800-3 lib bdg
                                          LC 2007-13853
This describes Attention-deficit hyperactivity disorder (ADHD) and its history, diagnosis and treatment, living with it, and its future

"This book is an excellent primer on AD/HD." Sci Books Films
  Includes glossary and bibliographical references

The **eating** disorders update; understanding anorexia, bulimia, and binge eating. [by] Alvin and Virginia Silverstein and Laura Silverstein Nunn. Enslow Publishers 2008 128p il (Disease update) lib bdg $31.93
Grades: 5 6 7 8   **616.85**
  1. Bulimia 2. Anorexia nervosa 3. Eating disorders
  ISBN 978-0-7660-2802-9 lib bdg; 0-7660-2802-X lib bdg
                                          LC 2007013985
"An introduction to the history and most up-to-date research and treatment of eating disorders." Publisher's note
  Includes glossary and bibliographical references

Simons, Rae

I eat when I'm sad; food and feelings. Mason Crest Publishers 2010 48p il (Kids & obesity) lib bdg $19.95; pa $7.95
Grades: 3 4 5   **616.85**
  1. Obesity 2. Weight loss 3. Eating disorders
  ISBN 978-1-4222-1714-6 lib bdg; 1-4222-1714-0 lib bdg; 978-1-4222-1902-7 pa; 1-4222-1902-X pa
                                          LC 2010007065
This book about childhood obesity makes "a compelling case by plainly stating the consequences of carrying around 'a little extra.' . . . The tone is highly sympathetic, capturing the vicious cycle of emotional eating and giving kids tools to combat weight gain." Booklist
  Includes bibliographical references

Skotko, Brian

Fasten your seatbelt; a crash course on Down syndrome for brothers and sisters. [by] Brian G. Skotko and Susan P. Levine. Woodbine House 2009 191p il pa $18.95

Grades: 4 5 6 7   **616.85**
1. Siblings 2. Down syndrome
ISBN 978-1-890627-86-7 pa; 1-890627-86-0 pa
LC 2008049753

"Skotko and Levine address preteens and teenagers who have a sibling with Down syndrome, answering questions that have been generated through their work with this population. . . . With a wealth of information, numerous resources, and the reassurance that all siblings of people with disabilities sometimes go through periods of contradictory feelings, this is an excellent guide for young people who are trying to figure out how to negotiate an often-confusing relationship." SLJ

Includes bibliographical references

Snedden, Robert
  Explaining autism. Smart Apple Media 2010 45p il (Explaining) lib bdg $34.25
Grades: 5 6 7 8   **616.85**
1. Autism 2. Asperger's syndrome
ISBN 978-1-59920-307-2 lib bdg; 1-59920-307-3 lib bdg
LC 2008-49285

Describes the illness, including its symptoms, how it affects physical and mental health, current treatments, and how people with autism live everyday lives

"The incorporation of quotes and personal accounts in 'Case Notes' sidebars adds to the sensitive tone found throughout [the title]." SLJ

Includes glossary and bibliographical references

Stefanski, Daniel, 1997-
  ★ **How** to talk to an autistic kid; illustrated by Hazel Mitchell. Free Spirit 2011 43p il $12.99
Grades: 3 4 5 6   **616.85**
1. Autism
ISBN 978-1-57542-365-4; 1-57542-365-0

"Stefanski provides clear, sometimes blunt, often humorous advice for readers on how to interact with autistic classmates. An authority on this topic—he is a 14-year-old boy with autism—he begins by describing autism. . . . He describes, using a brief paragraph or two per page, some of the traits many autistic people share. . . . For each trait, he offers down-to-earth suggestions for resolving problems. . . . His insightful, matter-of-fact presentation demystifies behaviors that might confuse or disturb non-autistic classmates. Simple cartoon illustrations in black, gray and two shades of turquoise accompany the text. . . . A thought-provoking introduction to autism . . . and an essential purchase for every primary and middle-school classroom." Kirkus

Stewart, Gail
  Anorexia; [by] Gail B. Stewart. Cherry Lake Pub. 2009 32p il (Health at risk) lib bdg $27.07
Grades: 4 5 6 7   **616.85**
1. Anorexia nervosa
ISBN 978-1-60279-281-4 lib bdg; 1-60279-281-X lib bdg
LC 2008017496

This explains why anorexics feel the need to keep losing weight, what can happen to them as a result of their desperate struggle to be thin, and how they can get help.

"Great for reports or reluctant readers." Booklist
Includes bibliographical references

  Bulimia; [by] Gail B. Stewart. Cherry Lake Pub. 2009 32p il (Health at risk) lib bdg $27.07
Grades: 4 5 6 7   **616.85**
1. Bulimia
ISBN 978-1-60279-282-1 lib bdg; 1-60279-282-8 lib bdg
LC 2008-17497

This describes the health risks of bulimia and what can be done to help people fight this disease.

"Great for reports or reluctant readers." Booklist
Includes bibliographical references

Thomas, Pat
  I see things differently a first look at autism; Pat Thomas. Barrons Educational Series, Inc. 2014 29 p. color illustrations (A first look at) $6.99
Grades: K 1 2   **616.85**
1. Autism 2. Autistic children
ISBN 1438004796; 9781438004792
LC 2013957082

This children's book on autism, by Pat Thomas, is part of the "A First Look At . . . " series. "Aimed at siblings and classmates," the book "comments on how and why kids with autism 'see things differently' and on behaviors that may seem puzzling. . . . The appended section for parents and teachers offers . . . advice as well as suggested books and online resources." (Booklist)

Part of the "First Look At..." series

616.86   Substance abuse (Drug abuse)

Allman, Toney
  Drugs. Cherry Lake Pub. 2009 32p il (Health at risk) lib bdg $27.07
Grades: 4 5 6 7   **616.86**
1. Drug abuse
ISBN 978-1-60279-283-8 lib bdg; 1-60279-283-6 lib bdg
LC 2008017503

This describes the dangers of drug abuse, the programs that help people get off drugs, and how to avoid drug use.

"Great for reports or reluctant readers." Booklist
Includes bibliographical references

Miller, Heather
  Smoking. Cherry Lake Pub. 2009 32p il (Health at risk) lib bdg $27.07
Grades: 4 5 6 7   **616.86**
1. Smoking 2. Tobacco habit
ISBN 978-1-60279-286-9 lib bdg; 1-60279-286-0 lib bdg
LC 2008017501

This describes why smoking is dangerous, how difficult it is to stop once you start, and what efforts are underway to put the brakes on this habit.

"Great for reports or reluctant readers." Booklist
Includes bibliographical references

616.89   Mental disorders

Rashkin, Rachel
  Feeling better; a kid's book about therapy. by Rachel Rashkin; illustrated by Bonnie Adamson. Magination Press 2005 48p il $14.95; pa $8.95
Grades: 4 5 6 7   **616.89**
1. Psychotherapy
ISBN 1-59147-237-7; 1-59147-238-5 pa
LC 2004022727

"Clearly written and well-organized. . . . Animated black-and-white sketches portray the girl's various emotions. This title gently encourages kids who are struggling with issues to seek help." SLJ

616.9 Other diseases

Aronin, Miriam

Tuberculosis; the white plague! Bearport Pub. 2011 32p il map (Nightmare plagues) lib bdg $25.27

Grades: 4 5 6 7   **616.9**

1. Tuberculosis

ISBN 978-1-936088-06-5; 1-936088-06-1

LC 2010010679

Discover what causes tuberculosis and how it affects the body.

"The writing is accessible and interspersed with interesting photographs and fact boxes. . . . [The book relies] on an honest discussion of [tuberculosis and is an] . . . effective, easily navigated [introduction]." SLJ

Includes glossary and bibliographical references

Berger, Melvin

Germs make me sick! illustrated by Marylin Hafner. rev ed; HarperCollins Pubs. 1995 32p il (Let's-read-and-find-out science) hardcover o.p. pa o.p.; paperback $6.99

Grades: K 1 2 3   **616.9**

1. Viruses 2. Bacteria

ISBN 0-06-024250-7 lib bdg; 0-06-445154-2 pa; 0062381873; 9780062381873

LC 93-27059

First published 1985

Explains how bacteria and viruses affect the human body and how the body fights them

This features "Hafner's lively color cartoon illustrations. . . . [It offers a] lively combination of fact and narrative that has made this a great title for easy reading and for sharing aloud." Booklist

Colligan, L. H.

★ **Tick**-borne illnesses. Marshall Cavendish Benchmark 2009 64p il (Health alert) $22.95

Grades: 4 5 6 7   **616.9**

1. Tick-borne diseases

ISBN 978-0-7614-2914-2; 0-7614-2914-X

LC 2007-38517

This "title features a handsome format, with well-chosen illustrations, a substantial amount of information, and some practical insights." Booklist

Includes glossary

Duke, Shirley Smith

Infections, infestations, and disease; [by] Shirley Duke. Rourke Pub. 2010 48p il (Let's explore science) $32.79

Grades: 4 5 6 7   **616.9**

1. Communicable diseases

ISBN 978-1-61590-321-4; 1-61590-321-6

LC 2010009908

This describes communicable diseases.

Includes bibliographical references

Glaser, Jason

Chicken pox; consultant, James R. Hubbard. Capstone Press 2006 24p il (First facts: Health matters) $21.26

Grades: K 1 2 3   **616.9**

1. Chickenpox

ISBN 978-0-7368-4288-4; 0-7368-4288-8

LC 2004028549

This introduction to chicken pox is "general and straightforward. Two or three simple sentences in large font appear on each page and address the causes, symptoms, appearances, and treatments." SLJ

Includes bibliographical references

Strep throat. Capstone Press 2007 il (First facts: health matters) $21.26

Grades: K 1 2 3   **616.9**

1. Strep throat

ISBN 978-0-7368-6393-3; 0-7368-6393-1

LC 2006002821

"Describes strep throat, how people get it, and how to treat and prevent it." Publisher's note

Includes bibliographical references

Hoffmann, Gretchen

★ **Chicken** pox. Marshall Cavendish Benchmark 2009 62p il (Health alert) $22.95

Grades: 4 5 6 7   **616.9**

1. Chickenpox

ISBN 978-0-7614-2916-6; 0-7614-2916-6

This "title features a handsome format, with well-chosen illustrations, a substantial amount of information, and some practical insights." Booklist

Includes glossary

Jarrow, Gail

Chiggers; [by] Gail Jarrow. KidHaven Press 2004 32p il (Parasites) $22.45

Grades: 4 5 6   **616.9**

1. Mites

ISBN 0-7377-1778-5

LC 2003-9614

"Several short chapters briefly describe the distinctive physical and behavioral characteristics of [chiggers] and special characteristics of particular species. [The book] also [highlights] the symptoms, victims' experiences, the organisms' potential threats as disease vectors, current treatments, and prevention methods. . . . Clear, color photographs illustrate the [text]. . . . Well organized and clearly written." SLJ

Kornberg, Arthur

Germ stories; illustrations by Adam Alaniz; photography by Roberto Kolter. University Science Books 2007 70p il $22

Grades: 2 3 4   **616.9**

1. Bacteria 2. Microbiology

ISBN 978-1-891389-51-1; 1-891389-51-3

LC 2007-09960

"This book of poems is a visual and lyrical journey into the wonderful world of . . . germs. . . . Nobel Prize winner Arthur Kornberg gives readers a look at the structures, methods, and cycles of germs. . . . The poetry is easy and flowing. Cartoon germs—fanged slime bacteria and wispy penicillin—are bright additions. After each poem is an electron micrograph, plus a visual comparison to help children understand just how small germs are." Libr Media Connect

Includes glossary

Landau, Elaine

★ **Chickenpox**. Marshall Cavendish Benchmark 2010 32p il (Head-to-toe health) $28.50

Grades: 2 3 4   **616.9**

1. Chickenpox

ISBN 978-0-7614-3498-6; 0-7614-3498-4

LC 2008-10782

"The book will satisfy researchers as well as those with a personal interest in the virus. . . . [This is] well-organized, informative." SLJ

Includes glossary and bibliographical references

★ **Strep** throat. Marshall Cavendish Benchmark 2010 32p il (Head-to-toe health) lib bdg $28.50

Grades: 2 3 4   **616.9**

1. Strep throat

ISBN 978-0-7614-4834-1 lib bdg; 0-7614-4834-9 lib bdg

This provides basic information about strep throat and its prevention. This "manages to pack in a surprising amount of information, including facts about good hygiene. The text addresses the reader directly, and the photos are real grabbers." Booklist

Includes glossary and bibliographical references

Murphy, Jim

Invincible microbe; tuberculosis and the never-ending search for a cure. Jim Murphy, Alison Blank. Clarion Books 2012 149 p. (hardback) $18.99

Grades: 5 6 7 8 9   **616.9**

1. Tuberculosis 2. Lungs -- Diseases 3. Communicable diseases -- Treatment 4. Microorganisms

ISBN 0618535748; 9780618535743

LC 2011025951

This book looks at tuberculosis. It "starts with archeologists finding evidence of tuberculosis in a 500,000 year old skull and continues through to the present day. Various 'cures' such as the medieval 'king's touch' . . . , bloodletting of the 19th century, twentieth century sanatoriums and modern day drug cocktails are all discussed." Also "covered is the socioeconomic side of the disease, with a discussion of how treatment often varied depending on the race and economic status of the patient." (Children's Literature)

Includes bibliographical references

Newman, Patricia

Ebola; fears and facts. by Patricia Newman. Lerner Publishing Group, Inc. 2016 48 p. color illustrations, maps (lb : alk. paper) $31.99

Grades: 4 5 6 7 8   **616.9**

1. Ebola virus 2. Epidemics 3. Hemorrhagic diseases

ISBN 1467792403; 9781467792400

LC 2015001167

This juvenile reference book, by Patricia Newman, "takes you behind the sensational headlines to address questions and concerns about the [Ebola] virus. Learn about the history of the disease, its symptoms, and how it spreads. Find out how the 2014 epidemic compares to past Ebola outbreaks, as well as to outbreaks of other infectious diseases." (Publisher's note)

"Breaking new ground, Newman has written a truly excellent book for middle grade students that tackles the terrifying spector of Ebola. As the title suggests, readers will come away with more facts and less fears." SLJ

Ollhoff, Jim

The **Black** Death. ABDO Pub. Co. 2010 32p il map (A history of germs) lib bdg $27.07

Grades: 3 4 5 6   **616.9**

1. Plague

ISBN 978-1-60453-497-9 lib bdg; 1-60453-497-4 lib bdg

LC 2008-55061

This book "examines the plague's origins, causes, effects, cures, and historical legacy. . . . The short, informative chapters provide plenty of

details for reports. The illustrations, many of which are color photos, enhance the information." SLJ

Includes glossary

The **germ** detectives. ABDO Pub. Co. 2010 32p il (A history of germs) lib bdg $27.07

Grades: 3 4 5 6   **616.9**

1. Bacteria 2. Chemists 3. Surgeons 4. Physicians 5. Scientists 6. Microbiology 7. Microscopists 8. Microbiologists 9. Writers on science 10. Writers on medicine 11. Nobel laureates for physiology or medicine

ISBN 978-1-60453-499-3 lib bdg; 1-60453-499-0 lib bdg

LC 2008-55062

This book "highlights the work of Antoni van Leeuwenhoek, Ignaz Semmelweis, Joseph Lister, Louis Pasteur, and Robert Koch, all of whom contributed to current knowledge about germs. . . . The short, informative chapters provide plenty of details for reports. The illustrations, many of which are color photos, enhance the information." SLJ

Includes glossary

Malaria. ABDO Pub. Co. 2010 32p il (A history of germs) lib bdg $27.07

Grades: 3 4 5 6   **616.9**

1. Malaria

ISBN 978-1-60453-500-6 lib bdg; 1-60453-500-8 lib bdg

"Malaria explains why the disease is so deadly, notes types of treatments, looks at efforts to control it, and suggests the future development of a vaccine. . . . The short, informative chapters provide plenty of details for reports. The illustrations, many of which are color photos, enhance the information." SLJ

Smallpox. ABDO Pub. Co. 2010 32p il (A history of germs) lib bdg $27.07

Grades: 3 4 5 6   **616.9**

1. Smallpox 2. Physicians 3. Writers on medicine

ISBN 978-1-60453-501-3 lib bdg; 1-60453-501-6 lib bdg

"Smallpox discusses the disease's symptoms, highlights Edward Jenner's work in developing a vaccine, and touches upon the potential use of the virus as a biological weapon. . . . The short, informative chapters provide plenty of details for reports. The illustrations, many of which are color photos, enhance the information." SLJ

Includes glossary

616.97   Diseases of immune system

Ballard, Carol

Explaining food allergies. Smart Apple Media 2010 45p il (Explaining) $23.95

Grades: 5 6 7 8   **616.97**

1. Food allergy

ISBN 978-1-59920-316-4; 1-59920-316-2

LC 2008049936

This "does an excellent job of discussing complex clinical science while showing what daily life is like for kids living with food allergies, from the signs and symptoms to the tests and treatments. . . . This blend of the technical and the personal will have wide appeal." Booklist

Landau, Elaine

★ **Food** allergies. Marshall Cavendish Benchmark 2010 32p il (Head-to-toe health) lib bdg $28.50

Grades: 2 3 4 **616.97**
1. Food allergy
ISBN 978-0-7614-3500-6; 0-7614-3500-X

LC 2008-10785

"Color photographs appear throughout. . . . [This is] well-organized, informative." SLJ

Includes glossary and bibliographical references

Marsico, Katie
I can't eat peanuts; Katie Marsico. Cherry Lake Publishing 2015 24 p. color illustrations (Tell me why) (hardcover) $25.64
Grades: 1 2 3 **616.97**
1. Food allergy 2. Curiosities and wonders 3. Peanuts 4. Food allergy in children
ISBN 1631889931; 9781631889936; 9781633620322; 9781633620711

LC 2014031778

This children's book by Katie Mariscio is part of a "series [that] addresses a scientific issue that kids may encounter in their daily lives. The story and situation in 'I Can't Eat Peanuts,' about peanut allergies, is likely the most relatable, for many children attend nut-free schools and activities." (Booklist)

"Addressing the many questions that curious kids ask, this series offers age-appropriate explanations without veering on the didactic. Each book begins with a fictional scene that drives the narrative, setting up a central question and allowing an "expert" (a park ranger, a character's parent), who is also part of the story, to share useful knowledge with both the information-seeker and the audience. . . . A smart and incredibly appealing series." SLJ

Includes bibliographical references and index

Royston, Angela
Allergies. Black Rabbit Books 2009 30p il (How's your health?) lib bdg $27.10
Grades: 1 2 3 **616.97**
1. Allergy
ISBN 978-1-59920-220-4 lib bdg; 1-59920-220-4 lib bdg

LC 2007-35174

First published 2004 by Heinemann Library

"Encourages further learning with sidebars that help readers think concretely about the subject. . . . Altogether a pitch perfect presentation." SLJ

Includes glossary and bibliographical references

Thomas, Pat
I think I am going to sneeze; a first look at allergies. [by] Pat Thomas; illustrated by Lesley Harker. Barron's Educational Series 2008 29p il pa $6.99
Grades: PreK K 1 2 **616.97**
1. Allergy
ISBN 978-0-7641-3900-0 pa; 0-7641-39002 pa
This "title covers the causes and effects of allergies and treatments and reassures youngsters that they don't have to be left out of school activities. Sidebars . . . ask questions about children's personal experiences and thoughts, which can be used as discussion starters. [The] title ends with an extensive note to parents, with practical advice for . . . helping children cope with allergies. [This is a] solid [addition] for most collections." SLJ

616.99 Tumors and miscellaneous communicable diseases

Markle, Sandra
Leukemia; true survival stories. Lerner Publications 2010 48p il (Powerful medicine) lib bdg $27.93
Grades: 5 6 7 8 **616.99**
1. Leukemia
ISBN 978-0-8225-8700-2 lib bdg; 0-8225-8700-9 lib bdg

LC 2009-34441

This book about leukemia "will grab the attention of middle school readers. . . . The illustrations and photos are stunning with medically accurate captions. Real-life patients, whose photos are included in the text, are highlighted, with updates on their progress at the end of . . . [the] book. . . . This . . . fills the need for up-to-date books on medical topics using vocabulary that a young teenager can understand." Voice Youth Advocates

Includes glossary and bibliographical references

Watters, Debbie
Where's Mom's hair? a family's journey through cancer. by Debbie Watters; with Haydn and Emmett Watters; photographs by Sophie Hogan. Second Story Press 2005 31p il pa $10.95
Grades: 2 3 4 **616.99**
1. Hair 2. Cancer
ISBN 1-896764-94-0
"When the author underwent chemotherapy following cancer surgery, she faced the loss of her hair with courage and humor. Family and friends gathered for a 'haircutting party,' where her husband and two young sons . . . joined her in getting buzz cuts. . . . The gentle kindness conveyed in the often-humorous writing will reassure young children facing similar circumstances." SLJ

617 Surgery, regional medicine, dentistry, ophthalmology, otology, audiology

Markle, Sandra
Wounded brains; true survival stories. Lerner Publications 2011 48p il (Powerful medicine) lib bdg $27.93
Grades: 5 6 7 8 **617**
1. Brain -- Wounds and injuries
ISBN 978-0-8225-8704-0 lib bdg; 0-8225-8704-1 lib bdg

LC 2009034440

Describes several true cases of traumatic brain injury and the medical treatment that followed.

This narrative reads "like information from the Discovery Health channel, for kids: part fascinating science, part human interest story, and part 'Eew, gross!'. . . Clear, straightforward prose is supplemented by definitions and explanations of medical techniques and jargon. The numerous color photos and medical images will satisfy readers' curiosity." SLJ

Includes glossary and bibliographical references

Murphy, Jim
★ Breakthrough! how three people saved "blue babies" and changed medicine forever. Jim Murphy. Clarion Books 2015 144 p. illustrations $18.99; (hardback) $18.99
Grades: 4 5 6 7 8 **617**
1. Heart -- Surgery 2. Cardiovascular system -- Surgery 3. Surgeons -- Maryland -- Biography
ISBN 0547821832; 9780547821832

LC 2015013601

In this book, author Jim Murphy details how "in 1944 a groundbreaking operation repaired the congenital heart defect known as blue baby syndrome. The operation's success brought the surgeon Alfred Blalock international fame and paved the way for open-heart surgery. But the technique had been painstakingly developed by Vivien Thomas, Blalock's African American lab assistant, who stood behind Blalock in the operating room to give him step-by-step instructions." (Publisher's note)

"Murphy's dramatic nonfiction narrative recounting of one of the first open heart surgeries ever performed is not to be missed—even reluctant readers will be hooked." SLJ

Woog, Adam

The **bionic** hand. Norwood House Press 2009 48p il (A great idea) lib bdg $25.27

Grades: 3 4 5 6   **617**
1. Bionics 2. Artificial limbs
ISBN 978-1-59953-341-4 lib bdg; 1-59953-341-3 lib bdg
LC 2009-15640

"Explores the development and creation of the i-LIMB which is the first commercially available bionic hand." Publisher's note

Includes glossary and bibliographical references

617.1   Injuries and wounds

Cobb, Vicki

★ **Your** body battles a broken bone; written by Vicki Cobb; photomicrographs by Dennis Kunkel; illustrations by Andrew N. Harris. Millbrook Press 2009 32p il (Body battles) lib bdg $25.26

Grades: 3 4 5   **617.1**
1. Bones 2. Fractures
ISBN 978-0-8225-7468-2; 0-8225-7468-3
LC 2008002837

This book provides comic illustrations and photomicrographs that describe how the body heals a broken bone

"Many of the vibrant illustrations anthropomorphize various cells and other 'battle' participants, making the science explained approachable and easy to understand. Photomicrographs further illuminate the text. These amazing pictures, taken with a scanning electron microscope, are greatly magnified and colored to highlight certain features." SLJ

Includes glossary and bibliographical references

★ **Your** body battles a skinned knee; written by Vicki Cobb; photomicrographs by Dennis Kunkel; illustrations by Andrew N. Harris. Millbrook Press 2009 32p il (Body battles) lib bdg $25.26

Grades: 3 4 5   **617.1**
1. Skin 2. Immune system 3. Wounds and injuries
ISBN 978-0-8225-6814-8; 0-8225-6814-4
LC 2008002826

"By combining simple yet engaging text; comic-like illustrations; and greatly magnified photomicrographs, this book describes the healing process of a bloodied knee in a fashion that is both entertaining and easy to understand." Booklist

Includes glossary and bibliographical references

Landau, Elaine

★ **Bites** and stings. Marshall Cavendish Benchmark 2009 32p il (Head-to-toe health) lib bdg $28.50

Grades: 2 3 4   **617.1**
1. Bites and stings
ISBN 978-0-7614-2850-3; 0-7614-2850-X
LC 2007-43022

"Photo illustrations are apt and age appropriate. . . . Pervading the [book] . . . is an overall sense of reassurance that even if something

hurts, 'all better' is never too far away. Appealing and readable nonfiction." SLJ

Includes glossary and bibliographical references

★ **Broken** bones. Marshall Cavendish Benchmark 2009 32p il (Head-to-toe health) lib bdg $28.50

Grades: 2 3 4   **617.1**
1. Bones 2. Fractures
ISBN 978-0-7614-2847-3; 0-7614-2847-X
LC 2007-26665

"Photo illustrations are apt and age appropriate. . . . Pervading the [book] . . . is an overall sense of reassurance that even if something hurts, 'all better' is never too far away. Appealing and readable nonfiction." SLJ

Includes glossary and bibliographical references

★ **Bumps,** bruises, and scrapes. Marshall Cavendish Benchmark 2009 32p il (Head-to-toe health) lib bdg $28.50

Grades: 2 3 4   **617.1**
1. Wounds and injuries
ISBN 978-0-7614-2849-7; 0-7614-2849-6
LC 2007-26959

"Photo illustrations are apt and age appropriate. . . . Pervading the [book] . . . is an overall sense of reassurance that even if something hurts, 'all better' is never too far away. Appealing and readable nonfiction." SLJ

Includes glossary and bibliographical references

★ **Burns.** Marshall Cavendish Benchmark 2010 32p il (Head-to-toe health) lib bdg $28.50

Grades: 2 3 4   **617.1**
1. Burns and scalds
ISBN 978-0-7614-4832-7 lib bdg; 0-7614-4832-2 lib bdg

This provides basic information about the different types of burns a person can get.

This "manages to pack in a surprising amount of information, including facts about good hygiene. The text addresses the reader directly, and the photos are real grabbers." Booklist

Includes glossary and bibliographical references

★ **Sprains** and strains. Marshall Cavendish Benchmark 2010 32p il (Head-to-toe health) lib bdg $28.50

Grades: 2 3 4   **617.1**
1. Wounds and injuries
ISBN 978-0-7614-4833-4 lib bdg; 0-7614-4833-0 lib bdg

This provides basic information about the different types of sprains and strains the body can get.

This "manages to pack in a surprising amount of information, including facts about good hygiene. The text addresses the reader directly, and the photos are real grabbers." Booklist

Includes glossary and bibliographical references

Lew, Kristi

Clot & scab; gross stuff about your scrapes, bumps, and bruises. illustrations by Michael Slack. Millbrook Press 2010 48p il (Gross body science) lib bdg $29.27

Grades: 4 5 6   **617.1**
1. Wounds and injuries
ISBN 978-0-8225-8965-5 lib bdg; 0-8225-8965-6 lib bdg
LC 2008-45626

"Solid information layered between sarcastic comments and kid-friendly terminology like fart, poop, barf, and puke will keep readers engaged. . . . Labeled, captioned (and graphic) photographs, cartoon-style illustrations, and micrographs add information." SLJ

Includes glossary and bibliographical references

Machajewski, Sarah

What if I break a tooth? Sarah Machajewski. Gareth Stevens Publishing 2017 24 p. color illustrations (ebook) $22.60; (library bound) $22.60

Grades: 2 3 4   **617.1**

1. Wounds and injuries 2. Teeth 3. Athletes -- Wounds and injuries 4. Sports injuries 5. Sports accidents 6. Teeth -- Wounds and injuries

ISBN 9781482448771; 9781482448399; 9781482448863; 9781482448924

LC 2016005383

In this book, author Sarah Machajewski explains that "dental work is never fun, especially after an accident on the soccer field or basketball court. Whether a tooth is chipped or broken, any sort of dental injury requires immediate attention. Dealing with the pain and blood can be hard for young athletes, but this book will help them understand just whats happening in their mouth and what dentists need to do to help them get better." (Publisher's note)

"This informative guide should find a place on most sports shelves." Booklist

Includes bibliographical references and index

Markle, Sandra

Bad burns; true survival stories. Lerner Publications 2010 48p il (Powerful medicine) lib bdg $27.93

Grades: 5 6 7 8   **617.1**

1. Burns and scalds

ISBN 978-0-8225-8702-6 lib bdg; 0-8225-8702-5 lib bdg

LC 2009034439

Explores how advancements in medicine and technology have helped victims of severe skin burns, and includes real-life stories of burn survivors and tips on burn prevention and treatment.

This narrative reads "like information from the Discovery Health channel, for kids: part fascinating science, part human interest story, and part 'Eew, gross!'. . . Clear, straightforward prose is supplemented by definitions and explanations of medical techniques and jargon. The numerous color photos and medical images will satisfy readers' curiosity." SLJ

Includes glossary and bibliographical references

Shattered bones; true survival stories. Lerner Publications 2010 48p il (Powerful medicine) lib bdg $27.93

Grades: 5 6 7 8   **617.1**

1. Bones 2. Fractures

ISBN 978-0-8225-8703-3 lib bdg; 0-8225-8703-3 lib bdg

LC 2009034442

Offers true stories of people who suffered broken bones, along with information on the skeleton, its structure and function, and the treatments doctors use for injuries.

This narrative reads "like information from the Discovery Health channel, for kids: part fascinating science, part human interest story, and part 'Eew, gross!'. . . Clear, straightforward prose is supplemented by definitions and explanations of medical techniques and jargon. The numerous color photos and medical images will satisfy readers' curiosity." SLJ

Includes glossary and bibliographical references

Royston, Angela

Cuts, bruises, and breaks. Black Rabbit Books 2009 30p il (How's your health) lib bdg $27.10

Grades: 1 2 3   **617.1**

1. Wounds and injuries

ISBN 978-1-59920-222-8 lib bdg; 1-59920-222-0 lib bdg

"Encourages further learning with sidebars that help readers think concretely about the subject. . . . Altogether a pitch perfect presentation." SLJ

Includes glossary

617.6 Dentistry

Cobb, Vicki

★ **Your** body battles a cavity; written by Vicki Cobb; photomicrographs by Dennis Kunkel; illustrations by Andrew N. Harris. Millbrook Press 2009 32p il (Body battles) lib bdg $25.26

Grades: 3 4 5   **617.6**

1. Teeth 2. Immune system

ISBN 978-0-8225-7469-9 lib bdg; 0-8225-7469-1 lib bdg

LC 2008002827

With comic illustrations and photomicrographs, this shows what happens when a person gets a cavity, depicting the body's defenses as superheroes

Includes glossary and bibliographical references

Guillain, Charlotte

Visiting the dentist. Heinmann Library 2011 24p il (Growing up) lib bdg $22; pa $6.49

Grades: PreK K 1 2   **617.6**

1. Dentistry

ISBN 978-1-4329-4804-7 lib bdg; 1-4329-4804-0 lib bdg; 978-1-4329-4814-6 pa; 1-4329-4814-8 pa

LC 2010024198

This book examines a "common, often scary [event] in children's lives and [guides] readers through [it] step-by-step. The [author discusses] the who, what, and why of [the] experience . . . By confronting . . . fears head-on, children will feel 'in the know' and be prepared to experience [this first]. The text—two sentences per page in a large font and placed on white space—is accompanied by large color photos of children, families, and adults of a variety of ethnic backgrounds. [The] volume includes boldface vocabulary words, a picture glossary, and dos and don'ts." SLJ

Includes glossary and bibliographical references

Landau, Elaine

★ **Cavities** and toothaches. Marshall Cavendish Benchmark 2008 32p il (Head-to-toe health) lib bdg $28.50

Grades: 2 3 4   **617.6**

1. Teeth 2. Dentistry

ISBN 978-0-7614-2848-0; 0-7614-2848-8

LC 2007-19192

"Photo illustrations are apt and age appropriate. . . . Pervading the [book] . . . is an overall sense of reassurance that even if something hurts, 'all better' is never too far away. Appealing and readable nonfiction." SLJ

Includes glossary and bibliographical references

Miller, Edward, 1964-

★ The **tooth** book; a guide to healthy teeth and gums. [by] Edward Miller. Holiday House 2008 un il $16.95

Grades: K 1 2 3   **617.6**

1. Teeth 2. Dentistry

ISBN 978-0-8234-2092-6; 0-8234-2092-2

LC 2007018302

"In this brightly illustrated picture book, Miller goes well beyond the basics of brushing, flossing, and visiting the dentist. Readers view the inside of a tooth and learn about primary and permanent teeth, decay, losing teeth, and dental first aid. Especially welcome is the emphasis on eating healthy foods and avoiding sugar. . . . The cleanly designed, computer-generated artwork is appealing, lively, and instructive." SLJ

Royston, Angela

    Tooth decay. Black Rabbit Books 2009 30p il (How's your health) lib bdg $27.10

Grades: 1 2 3   **617.6**

  1. Teeth

  ISBN 978-1-59920-221-1 lib bdg; 1-59920-221-2 lib bdg

  First published 2004 by Heinemann Library

"Encourages further learning with sidebars that help readers think concretely about the subject. . . . Altogether a pitch perfect presentation." SLJ

  Includes glossary

    Why do I brush my teeth? QEB Pub. 2010 24p il (QEB my body) lib bdg $28.65

Grades: PreK K 1 2   **617.6**

  1. Teeth 2. Dentistry

  ISBN 978-1-59566-973-5 lib bdg; 1-59566-973-6 lib bdg

                            LC 2009-15219

Introduces the structure and growth of the teeth, and outlines the principles of dental health and hygiene

"The information is straightforward, well presented, and easy to understand. . . . [This] title is well designed, filled with color photographs, and scattered with fact boxes." Libr Media Connect

  Includes glossary and bibliographical references

Schuh, Mari C.

    All about teeth; by Mari Schuh. Capstone Press 2008 24p il (Pebble plus. Healthy teeth) lib bdg $21.26; pa $5.95

Grades: K 1 2 3   **617.6**

  1. Teeth

  ISBN 978-1-4296-1238-8 lib bdg; 1-4296-1238-X lib bdg; 1-4296-1784-5 pa; 978-1-4296-1784-0 pa

                            LC 2007-27115

"Feature[s] bright close-up photographs . . . and simple vocabulary and sentences to engage pre-readers as well as new readers." Horn Book Guide

  Includes glossary and bibliographical references

Thomas, Pat

    Do I have to go to the dentist? a first look at healthy teeth. [by] Pat Thomas; illustrated by Lesley Harker. Barron's Educational Series 2008 29p il pa $6.99

Grades: PreK K 1 2   **617.6**

  1. Teeth 2. Dentistry

  ISBN 978-0-7641-3901-7 pa; 0-7641-3901-0 pa

This "book addresses the purpose of dental visits, what to expect, the dental exam and tooth cleaning, and cavities. . . . Sidebars . . . ask questions about children's personal experiences and thoughts, which can be used as discussion starters. [The] title ends with an extensive note to parents, with practical advice for lessening anxiety about going to the dentist. . . . [This is a] solid [addition] for most collections." SLJ

617.7   Ophthalmology

Bender, Lionel

    Explaining blindness. Smart Apple Media 2010 45p il (Explaining) lib bdg $34.25

Grades: 5 6 7 8   **617.7**

  1. Blind

  ISBN 978-1-59920-310-2 lib bdg; 1-59920-310-3 lib bdg

                            LC 2008-49286

Describes blindness, including its possible causes, the different types of visual impairment, current treatments and cures, and how blind and visually impaired people live everyday lives

"The incorporation of quotes and personal accounts in 'Case Notes' sidebars adds to the sensitive tone found throughout [the title]." SLJ

  Includes glossary

Glaser, Jason

    Pinkeye. Capstone Press 2006 24p il (First facts: health matters) $21.26

Grades: K 1 2 3   **617.7**

  1. Conjunctivitis

  ISBN 978-0-7368-4292-1; 0-7368-4292-6

                           LC 2004031054

"Introduces pinkeye, its causes, symptoms, treatments, and prevention." Publisher's note

  Includes bibliographical references

Markle, Sandra

    Lost sight; true survival stories. Lerner Publications 2010 48p il (Powerful medicine) lib bdg $27.93

Grades: 5 6 7 8   **617.7**

  1. Eye 2. Blind 3. Vision

  ISBN 978-0-8225-8701-9 lib bdg; 0-8225-8701-7 lib bdg

                           LC 2009-34443

This book about vision loss "will grab the attention of middle school readers. . . . The illustrations and photos are stunning with medically accurate captions. Real-life patients, whose photos are included in the text, are highlighted, with updates on their progress at the end of . . . [the] book." Voice Youth Advocates

  Includes glossary and bibliographical references

Parker, Victoria

    Having an eye test; [by] Vic Parker. Heinemann Library 2011 24p il (Growing up) lib bdg $22; pa $6.49

Grades: PreK K 1 2   **617.7**

  1. Eye

  ISBN 978-1-4329-4798-9 lib bdg; 1-4329-4798-2 lib bdg; 978-1-4329-4808-5 pa; 1-4329-4808-3 pa

                           LC 2010024192

This explains what to expect from an eye test.

  Includes bibliographical references

617.8   Otology and audiology

Cobb, Vicki

    ★ **Your** body battles an earache; written by Vicki Cobb; photomicrographs by Dennis Kunkel; illustrated by Andrew N. Harris. Millbrook Press 2009 32p il (Body battles) lib bdg $25.26

Grades: 3 4 5   **617.8**

  1. Immune system 2. Ear infections

  ISBN 978-0-8225-6812-4 lib bdg; 0-8225-6812-8 lib bdg

                           LC 2008002846

Microphotographs and comic illustrations show what happens when a person has an earache

"Many of the vibrant illustrations anthropomorphize various cells and other 'battle' participants, making the science explained approachable and easy to understand. Photomicrographs further illuminate the text." SLJ

Includes glossary and bibliographical references

Glaser, Jason

Ear infections. Capstone Press 2007 24p il (First facts: health matters) $21.26

Grades: K 1 2 3   617.8

1. Ear infections

ISBN 978-0-7368-6390-2; 0-7368-6390-7

LC 2006002809

"Describes ear infections, how and why they occur, and how to treat and prevent them." Publisher's note

Includes bibliographical references

Landau, Elaine

★ **Earaches**. Marshall Cavendish Benchmark 2010 32p il (Head-to-toe health) lib bdg $28.50

Grades: 2 3 4   617.8

1. Ear infections

ISBN 978-0-7614-4831-0 lib bdg; 0-7614-4831-4 lib bdg

This provides basic information about earaches and their prevention. This "manages to pack in a surprising amount of information, including facts about good hygiene. The text addresses the reader directly, and the photos are real grabbers." Booklist

Includes glossary and bibliographical references

Levete, Sarah

Explaining deafness. Smart Apple Media 2010 45p il (Explaining) lib bdg $34.25

Grades: 5 6 7 8   617.8

1. Deafness

ISBN 978-1-59920-313-3 lib bdg; 1-59920-313-8 lib bdg

LC 2008-49289

Discusses the history, diagnosis, and treatment of deafness, including ways to cope with living with the condition

"The incorporation of quotes and personal accounts in 'Case Notes' sidebars adds to the sensitive tone found throughout [the title]." SLJ

Includes glossary, bibliographical references and filmography

Parker, Victoria

Having a hearing test; [by] Vic Parker. Heinmann Library 2011 24p il (Growing up) lib bdg $22; pa $6.49

Grades: PreK K 1 2   617.8

1. Hearing

ISBN 978-1-4329-4799-6 lib bdg; 1-4329-4799-0 lib bdg; 978-1-4329-4809-2 pa; 1-4329-4809-1 pa

LC 2010024193

This explains how a hearing test works and possible next steps for those with hearing problems.

"The text is simple, and the pictures are big and bright." Booklist

Includes bibliographical references

617.9 Operative surgery and special fields of surgery

Fullick, Ann

Rebuilding the body; organ transplantation. Ann Fullick. Rev. and updated Heinemann Library 2009 64 p. col. ill. (library) $34.29; (library) $35

Grades: 5 6 7 8   617.9

1. Medicine 2. Medical ethics 3. Transplantation of organs, tissues, etc.

ISBN 9781588107008 out of print; 1432924524; 9781432924522

LC 2001006082

This book is part of the Science at the Edge series and looks at organ transplantation. It "begins with a survey of the major human body organs.... This is followed by a description of the failure of major organs, infections that occur within them, and gradual damage and deterioration. This leads to a discussion about organ transplants .... The challenges of organ transplantation, pitfalls of rejection, and ethics of transplantation from the dead are all touched upon." (NSTA Recommends)

Includes bibliographical references (p. 63) and index.

Jango-Cohen, Judith

Bionics; [by] Judith Jango-Cohen. Lerner Publications Co. 2007 48p il (Cool science) lib bdg $26.60

Grades: 4 5 6 7   617.9

1. Bionics 2. Artificial organs

ISBN 978-0-8225-5937-5 lib bdg; 0-8225-5937-4 lib bdg

LC 2005032221

This "introduction to the field of bionics is divided into four chapters: 'Replacing Parts,' 'Fixing Malfunctions,' 'Assisting the Senses,' and 'Facing the Future.' Jango-Cohen uses a number of personal stories and references to pop culture to engage readers.... The explanations are clearly written and easily understood. Colorful photographs and illustrations are featured throughout the text." SLJ

Includes bibliographical references

618.92 Pediatrics

Chaloner, Kim

Diabetes and me; an essential guide for kids and parents. written by Kim Chaloner & illustrated by Nick Bertozzi. Hill and Wang, a division of Farrar, Straus, and Giroux 2013 176 p. illustrations (hardcover) $30

Grades: 4 5 6 7 8 9 10 11 12 Adult   618.92

1. Diabetes 2. Diabetes in children

ISBN 0809028190; 9780809028191; 9780809038718; 9781466848481

LC 2012036543

In this book, author Kim Chaloner "gives kids the tools they need to take charge of their health and understand what it means to be diagnosed with diabetes. In this graphic guide, she walks four young people through the basics of diabetes, both Type 1 and Type 2.... Illustrated by the award-winning artist Nick Bertozzi." (Publisher's note)

"Bertozzi ... ably depicts a diverse group of diabetics, detailed accounts of handling monitors during the course of the school day, and some apt metaphorical battles between sugars and insulin. This easy-to-read resource is a standout for its wealth of information and welcoming format." Booklist

Includes bibliographical references

Grossberg, Blythe

★ **Asperger's** rules! how to make sense of school and friends. by Blythe Grossberg. Magination Press 2012 127 p. col. ill. (paperback) $9.95; (hardcover) $14.95

Grades: 5 6 7 8   618.92

1. Life skills 2. Social skills 3. Asperger's syndrome 4. Autism in children 5. Autistic children -- Education 6. Asperger's syndrome -- Social aspects

ISBN 1433811286; 9781433811272; 9781433811289

LC 2011053483

This book by Blythe Grossberg presents a "guide for readers with Asperger's, covering feelings and emotions, teachers, asking for help, and dealing with bullies. Quizzes let readers reflect on their own approaches to situations like interacting with kids at school, and Grossberg also includes tips on how to interpret social situations. . . . Flowcharts illustrate how various conversations might progress, and other sections focus on dressing properly and eating healthful meals." (Publishers Weekly)

Thomas, Pat

Don't call me fat; a first look at being overweight. Pat Thomas. Barrons Educational Series, Inc. 2014 29 p. color illustrations (A first look at) $6.99

Grades: K 1 2   **618.92**

1. Obesity 2. Obesity in children

ISBN 1438004710; 9781438004716

LC 2013957084

This children's book on being overweight by Pat Thomas is part of the "A First Look At . . . " series. It "acknowledges the difficulties faced by children who are overweight but encourages them to work with others toward healthy changes and ask for support along the way. . . . The appended section for parents and teachers offers . . . advice as well as suggested books and online resources." (Booklist)

"Though the picture books in the A First Look at . . . series deal with a wide range of conditions, they all begin with respect for children. Thomas doesn't define individuals by their differences, instead discussing their physical, mental, and emotional challenges in a straightforward, kindly manner... Some unusually positive features include apt discussion questions, illustrations showing children with autism sometimes looking happy, and even girls with autism (often only boys are depicted). A worthwhile series of helpful picture books." Booklist

Verdick, Elizabeth

The **survival** guide for kids with autism spectrum disorders (and their parents) by Elizabeth Verdick & Elizabeth Reeve; illustrated by Nick Kobyluch. Free Spirit Pub. 2012 234 p. col. ill. (pbk.) $16.99

Grades: 5 6 7 8 Adult   **618.92**

1. Autism 2. Autistic children 3. Parents of autistic children 4. Children with autism spectrum disorders 5. Autistic children -- Family relationships

ISBN 1575423855; 9781575423852; 9781575426747

LC 2011046520

This book "offers kids with autism spectrum disorders (ASDs) their own comprehensive resource for both understanding their condition and finding tools to cope with the challenges they face every day . . . with an emphasis on helping children gain new self-understanding and self-acceptance. Meant to be read with a parent, the book addresses questions . . . and provides strategies for communicating, making and keeping friends, and succeeding in school." (Publisher's note)

"This volume could become a treasured resource for families looking for help in successfully working through some of the problems faced by higher-functioning children with ASD." SLJ

620   Engineering and allied operations

Mercer, Bobby

Junk drawer engineering; 25 construction challenges that don't cost a thing. Bobby Mercer. Chicago Review Press Inc. 2017 224 p. (trade paper : alk. paper) $14.99

Grades: 4 5 6 7 8   **620**

1. Engineering 2. Science -- Experiments 3. Engineering -- Experiments

ISBN 9781613737163

LC 2016037089

In this book, by Bobby Mercer, "there's no need for expensive, high-tech materials to test your engineering skills—you probably have all you need in your home junk drawer. Each hands-on project in this book will challenge you to come up with a unique solution to a specific design problem." (Publisher's note)

620.1   Engineering mechanics and materials

Blaxland, Wendy

Plates and mugs. Marshall Cavendish Benchmark 2009 32p il (How are they made?) $19.95

Grades: 3 4 5 6   **620.1**

1. Ceramics 2. Tableware

ISBN 978-0-7614-3809-0; 0-7614-3809-2

LC 2008026210

This describes how plates and mugs are made, including their history, raw materials, design, manufacture, and relationship to the environment.

Claybourne, Anna

Materials. QEB Pub. 2008 24p il (Why it works) $24.25

Grades: 2 3 4 5   **620.1**

1. Materials

ISBN 978-1-59566-557-7; 1-59566-557-9

LC 2008-11711

This is "colorfully illustrated and should help young students relate better to the concepts being presented. A glossary of key words and a page of suggestions for parents and teachers to extend the learning experience round out the text." Sci Books & Films

Includes glossary and bibliographical references

Hillman, Ben

How strong is it? a mighty book all about strength. [by] Ben Hillman. Scholastic Reference 2008 48p il (What's the big idea?) $14.99

Grades: 3 4 5   **620.1**

1. Power (Mechanics)

ISBN 978-0-439-91866-4; 0-439-91866-9

This describes the strength of such things as spiderwebs, bulldozers, wood, elephants, glue, lasers, hair, rope, and volcanoes.

"The conversational, fact-filled text and computer-manipulated illustrations add humor to this random sampling of awesome powers." Horn Book Guide

Morris, Neil

Glass. Amicus 2010 48p il (Materials that matter) lib bdg $28.50

Grades: 4 5 6 7   **620.1**

1. Glass

ISBN 978-1-60753-065-7 lib bdg; 1-60753-065-1 lib bdg

LC 2009029796

"The clean layout includes photographs and occasional charts, graphs, and technical illustrations against a range of pastel backgrounds. Inset boxes provide further detail, interesting extras, and recycling information. . . . [This book offers] easily accessible background information for report writers." SLJ

Includes glossary and bibliographical references

Other titles in this series are:

Metals

Paper

Plastics

Textiles

Wood

Oxlade, Chris

Changing shape. Heinemann Library 2008 32p il (Changing materials) lib bdg $25.36; pa $7.99

Grades: K 1 2   **620.1**

1. Materials

ISBN 978-1-4329-3271-8 lib bdg; 1-4329-3271-3 lib bdg; 978-1-4329-3276-3 pa; 1-4329-3276-4 pa

LC 2008-54586

Discusses "the properties of materials and whether or not they can bend or twist or are brittle, or are in liquid or gas form. . . . A few simple activities provide opportunities to experiment. The color photographs are engaging." SLJ

Includes glossary and bibliographical references

Other titles in this series are:

Joining materials

Shaping materials

Riley, Peter D.

Materials. Sea-to-Sea Publications 2011 32p il (The real scientist investigates) lib bdg $28.50

Grades: 3 4 5   **620.1**

1. Materials

ISBN 978-1-59771-282-8; 1-59771-282-5

LC 2010005373

In this book about materials "solid scientific material is presented in accessible language and a visually engaging, boldly colored layout. Budding scientists are encouraged to hone their skills by recording observations, making predictions, and analyzing results. Hands-on activities are included on almost every spread. . . . The many color photos feature diverse children demonstrating the activities." SLJ

Includes glossary and bibliographical references

Ward, David J.

Materials science; by D. J. Ward. Lerner Publications 2009 47p il (Cool science) lib bdg $26.60

Grades: 4 5 6   **620.1**

1. Materials

ISBN 978-0-8225-7588-7 lib bdg; 0-8225-7588-4 lib bdg

LC 2007042176

This describes how scientists study the microscopic parts of materials such as plastic, glass, or stainless steel, how they learn how each part makes something hard or soft, strong or weak, or good or bad at carrying heat, and how they use that knowledge to create supermaterials to help make better sports equipment, tinier computer chips, and more.

Includes glossary and bibliographical references

621 Applied physics

Spilsbury, Richard

What is energy? exploring science with hands-on activities. [by] Richard and Louise Spilsbury. Enslow Elementary 2008 32p il (In touch with basic science) lib bdg $22.60

Grades: 3 4 5   **621**

1. Energy resources 2. Force and energy 3. Power (Mechanics) 4. Science -- Experiments

ISBN 978-0-7660-3099-2 lib bdg; 0-7660-3099-7 lib bdg

LC 2007024521

This book includes "a discussion about what energy is and then moves on to examine heat energy, chemical energy, energy for life, electrical energy, and finally renewable energy. Energy is such a broad topic, yet this small volume masterfully provides a good basis for understanding the concept." Sci Books Films

Includes glossary and bibliographical references

621.1 Fluid-power technologies

O'Neal, Claire

How to use waste energy to heat and light your home. Mitchell Lane Publishers 2009 47p il (Tell your parents) lib bdg $21.50

Grades: 4 5 6 7   **621.1**

1. Recycling 2. Waste products as fuel

ISBN 978-1-58415-765-6 lib bdg; 1-58415-765-8 lib bdg

LC 2009-4483

Explores how to reduce the amount of trash produced and stored by reusing items and recycling materials, and describes how these efforts can help protect the environment

This title "offers numerous facts and statistics, all of which are cited. . . . Chapters cover present-day issues and . . . are interspersed with full-color photographs and short 'Did You Know' trivia boxes. . . . Back matter includes detailed resource lists and 'Try This!' experiments." SLJ

Includes glossary and bibliographical references

621.3 Electrical, magnetic, optical, communications, computer engineering; electronics, lighting

Price, Sean

The story behind electricity; [by] Sean Stewart Price. Heinemann Library 2009 32p il (True stories) $28.21

Grades: 3 4 5   **621.3**

1. Electricity 2. Electrical engineering

ISBN 978-1-4329-2339-6; 1-4329-2339-0

LC 2008043408

This answers such questions as: How does a lightning rod work? What animals use electricity? Why did Thomas Edison have to build a power station?

Includes bibliographical references

621.31 Generation, modification, storage, transmission of electric power

Benduhn, Tea

Wind power; by Tea Benduhn. Weekly Reader Pub. 2009 24p il (Energy for today) lib bdg $21; pa $5.95

Grades: 2 3 4   **621.31**

1. Wind power 2. Energy resources

ISBN 978-0-8368-9265-9 lib bdg; 0-8368-9265-8 lib bdg; 978-0-8368-9364-9 pa; 0-8368-9364-6 pa

LC 2008012019

This explains how wind forms and the ways we may use it as an energy source in the future.

"New readers will be able to wrap their hands around the small, square size, and their minds around the clear enlightening text. [This book has] crisp photos and strong back matter." Booklist

Includes glossary and bibliographical references

Other titles in this series are:

Nuclear power

Solar power

Water power

Graf, Mike

How does a waterfall become electricity? Raintree 2008 32p il (How does it happen?) lib bdg $27.50; pa $7.99

Grades: 3 4 5   **621.31**
1. Electricity 2. Water power 3. Hydrodynamics
ISBN 978-1-4109-3448-2 lib bdg; 1-4109-3448-9 lib bdg; 978-1-
4109-3456-7 pa; 1-4109-3456-X pa
LC 2008-52653
The explains the cause and effect of waterfalls, and the many ways
they can be used to make electricity.
"Information is clearly presented using a large font, diagrams, and
photographs formatted to resemble Polaroid pictures. . . . A first-rate job
answering some important scientific questions." SLJ
Includes glossary and bibliographical references

Rusch, Elizabeth
The **next** wave; the quest to harness the power of the oceans. by
Elizabeth Rusch. Houghton Mifflin Harcourt 2014 80 p. color illustrations (Scientists in the field) $18.99
Grades: 5 6 7 8 9   **621.31**
1. Ocean 2. Ocean energy resources 3. Renewable energy
resources 4. Tidal power 5. Renewable energy sources
ISBN 0544099990; 9780544099999
LC 2013050150
In this book, by Elizabeth Rusch, part of the Scientists in the Field
series, readers "journey to the wave-battered coast of the Pacific Northwest to meet some of the engineers and scientists working to harness the
punishing force of our oceans. . . . With an array of amazing devices that
cling to the bottom of the sea floor and surf on the crests of waves, these
explorers are using a combination of science, imagination, and innovation to try to capture wave energy." (Publisher's note)
"Rusch captures the determined, entrepreneurial spirit of the profiled
engineers as well as the need for creative problem-solving and ingenuity. Photographs and illustrations feature prototypes in both small-scale
laboratory and full-ocean tests." Horn Book
Includes bibliographical references and index

621.319   Transmission

Cole, Joanna
The **magic** school bus and the electric field trip; illustrated by
Bruce Degen. Scholastic 1997 48p il hardcover o.p. pa $6.99
Grades: 2 3 4   **621.319**
1. Electricity 2. Electric power
ISBN 0-590-44682-7; 0-590-44683-5 pa
LC 97-2080
Ms. Frizzle takes her class on a field trip through the town's electri-
cal wires so they can learn how electricity is generated and how it is used
"Spiced with plenty of puns and jokes, the writing and the colorful
artwork continue the series' unbeatable combination of clearly presented
information and plenty of fun." Booklist

621.385   Telephony

Spilsbury, Richard
The **telephone**; [by] Richard and Louise Spilsbury. Heinemann
Library 2011 32p il (Tales of invention) lib bdg $29; pa $7.99
Grades: 4 5 6 7   **621.385**
1. Telephone 2. Cellular telephones
ISBN 978-1-4329-3826-0 lib bdg; 1-4329-3826-6 lib bdg; 978-1-
4329-3833-8 pa; 1-4329-3833-9 pa
LC 2009049027
"Beginning with the first telegraph, the book discusses how sound
travels, how speech is transmitted by wire, and how Alexander Graham

Bell's first telephones worked. Then the text quickly traces later technological developments, from transatlantic cables to early cell phones
to the small, light, versatile models available today. . . . The many photographs and other illustrations include excellent labeled diagrams."
Booklist
Includes bibliographical references

621.4   Prime movers and heat engineering

Woelfle, Gretchen
The **wind** at work; an activity guide to windmills. Gretchen
Woelfle. 2nd ed. Chicago Review Press 2013 vii, 145 p.p ill. (paperback) $16.95
Grades: 4 5 6   **621.4**
1. Windmills 2. Wind power 3. Science -- Experiments
ISBN 1613741006; 9781613741009
LC 2012046319
This introduction to windmills "discusses their history and function
through modern times. . . . About one-third of the book is devoted to
activities illustrating the properties of wind and the jobs performed by
windmills. . . . The concluding chapters focus on windmills as a source
of energy and suggest how to chart household energy use." (Booklist)
Index. "Grades four to eight." (SLJ)
"The historical information is excellent, and includes Persian windmills of 1000 years ago, Dutch windmills of the 17th century, and modern wind turbines. Amusing anecdotes and intriguing facts are woven
into the text, keeping it lively. . . . Black-and-white historical prints,
photographs, and diagrams appear throughout." SLJ
Includes bibliographical references (pages 133-135) and index

621.43   Internal-combustion engines

Mooney, Carla
Rocketry; investigate the science and technology of rockets and
ballistics. Carla Mooney; illustrations by Caitlin Denham. Nomad
Press 2014 120 p. color illustrations hbk $22.95
Grades: 3 4 5   **621.43**
1. Rocketry 2. Aeronautics
ISBN 1619302322; 9781619302327
This book by Carla Mooney, illustrated by Caitlin Denham, "introduces students to the fascinating world of rocketry and ballistics.
Readers discover the history of rocket development, from the earliest
fire arrows in China to modern-day space shuttles, as well as the main
concepts of rocketry, including how rockets are launched, move through
the atmosphere, and return to earth safely." (Publisher's note)
"The projects, which properly include both systematic safety provisions and suggestions for further experimentation, are illustrated with
diagrammatic cartoons and use materials like paper, string, balloons,
and, occasionally, PVC pipe to make a variety of air- or CO2-driven
models." Booklist
Includes bibliographical references and index

Shores, Lori
How to build a fizzy rocket. Capstone Press 2011 24p il (Hands-
on science fun) lib bdg $17.99; pa $6.95
Grades: PreK K 1   **621.43**
1. Science -- Experiments 2. Rockets (Aeronautics) -- Models
ISBN 978-1-4296-4491-4 lib bdg; 1-4296-4491-5 lib bdg; 978-1-
4296-5573-6 pa; 1-4296-5573-9 pa
LC 2009051419

Simple text and full-color photos instruct readers how to build a fizzy rocket and explain the science behind the activity.

"Bright, glossy photos and irresistible ideas make these science lessons effortless fun." Booklist

Includes bibliographical references

621.47   Solar-energy engineering

Bang, Molly
★ My light. Blue Sky Press 2004 un il $16.95
Grades: 1 2 3   **621.47**
1. Electricity 2. Solar energy
ISBN 0-439-48961-X
"Bang's strong design sense comes through in compositions that gracefully incorporate diagrams and strike a balance between graphic forms and delicate, decorative patterns. A lovely and illuminating book that presents sound science while expressing the wonder of flipping a switch and flooding a room with light." Booklist

Bearce, Stephanie
How to harness solar power for your home. Mitchell Lane Publishers 2009 47p il map (Tell your parents) lib bdg $21.50
Grades: 4 5 6 7   **621.47**
1. Solar energy
ISBN 978-1-58415-761-8 lib bdg; 1-58415-761-5 lib bdg
LC 2009-4529
This title about solar power "offers numerous facts and statistics, all of which are cited. . . . Chapters cover present-day issues and . . . are interspersed with full-color photographs and short 'Did You Know' trivia boxes. . . . Back matter includes detailed resource lists and 'Try This!' experiments." SLJ

Includes glossary and bibliographical references

621.48   Nuclear engineering

Feigenbaum, Aaron
Emergency at Three Mile Island; by Aaron Feigenbaum. Bearport Pub. 2007 32p il map (Code red) lib bdg $23.96
Grades: 3 4 5   **621.48**
1. Nuclear power plants 2. Three Mile Island Nuclear Power Plant (Pa.)
ISBN 978-1-59716-364-4 lib bdg; 1-59716-364-3 lib bdg
LC 2006031635
This "discusses the 1979 malfunction of a nuclear reactor that could have cost thousands of lives and devastated the area but, fortunately, did not. . . . The writing is clear and concise. . . . The facts are allowed to speak for themselves. The [book is] liberally laced with pertinent period photographs and numerous quotes."

Includes glossary and bibliographical references

621.5   Pneumatic, vacuum, low-temperature technologies

Pringle, Laurence, 1935-
Ice! the amazing history of the ice business. Laurence Pringle. Calkins Creek 2012 74 p. $17.95
Grades: 4 5 6 7 8   **621.5**
1. Ice 2. Refrigeration 3. Food -- Preservation
ISBN 159078801X; 9781590788011
LC 2012937320

This book looks at "iceboxes, icehouses, icemen, and . . . more about the history of the harvesting, storage, and delivery of ice." Author Laurence Pringle "briefly covers early food preservation . . . before delving into the rise of the ice industry in the early 1800s, and, in particular, the harvesting of the frozen stuff at pristine Rockland Lake in New York." (School Library Journal)

Includes bibliographical references and index.

621.8   Machine engineering

Bodden, Valerie
Levers. Creative Education 2011 23p il (Simple machines) $24.25; pa $8.99
Grades: K 1 2 3   **621.8**
1. Levers
ISBN 978-1-60818-009-7; 1-60818-009-3; 978-0-89812-580-1 pa; 0-89812-580-4 pa
"The pages are uncluttered and are typeset in a large font, making the words practically pop off the [page]. Also, the author makes the definitions that are presented simple to understand with her selection of photographs. . . . [This is] outstanding and well suited to young elementary school children." Sci Books & Films

Includes glossary

Other titles in this series are:
Pulleys
Screws
Wheels and axles

Caterpillar Inc.
My big book of trucks & diggers. Chronicle Books 2011 il bd bk $7.99
Grades: PreK K   **621.8**
1. Trucks 2. Construction equipment 3. Board books for children
ISBN 978-0-8118-7892-0; 0-8118-7892-9
LC 2010053590
An oversized board book featuring photos of 10 Caterpillar machines-a bulldozer, excavator, dump truck, skid steer loader, paver, motor grader, wheel loader, backhoe loader, material handler, and telehandler.

"This board book uses excellent photographs. . . . The bold colors and clear text enhance the presentation. Even though the terms are a bit challenging, the simplicity of the book and the sharp photographs will have youngsters very excited." SLJ

Coppendale, Jean
The great big book of mighty machines; [by] Jean Coppendale and Ian Graham. Firefly Books 2009 160p il $19.95
Grades: PreK K 1 2 3   **621.8**
1. Vehicles 2. Machinery
ISBN 978-1-55407-521-8; 1-55407-521-1
"A vehicle-lover's dream come true, this meaty volume focuses on cars, bikes, trains, tractors, rescue vehicles, construction trucks and monster trucks. Each section . . . ends with an activity page. . . . The text is easy to read and understand. Brightly colored page edges draw eyes inward to the exciting full-color photos that fill the pages." Kirkus

Includes glossary

De Medeiros, Michael
Screws. Weigl Publishers 2009 24p il (Science matters: simple machines) lib bdg $24.45; pa $8.95

Grades: 2 3 4   **621.8**
1. Screws
ISBN 978-1-60596-039-5 lib bdg; 1-60596-039-X lib bdg; 978-1-60596-040-1 pa; 1-60596-040-3 pa

LC 2009-1941

Discusses what a screw is, where it can be found, and how it is used.

"De Medeiros' description of the object's function is unusually elegant: Screws convert movement in a circle to movement straight ahead. . . . The back matter (including online suggestions, a craft, a quiz, a well-chosen glossary, and more) is strong and features what is likely the only 10-word index in existence to feature the terms nuts, bolts, and King Nebuchadnezzar." Booklist

Includes glossary
Other titles in this series are:
Pulleys
Inclined planes
Levers
Wedges

Gardner, Robert

Sensational science projects with simple machines; [by] Robert Gardner. Enslow Elementary 2006 48p il (Fantastic physical science experiments) $23.93
Grades: 4 5 6   **621.8**
1. Simple machines 2. Science -- Experiments
ISBN 0-7660-2585-3

LC 2005008974

"The first chapter of [this book] explains force, friction, distance, and work. The book then introduces levers, inclined planes, pulleys, etc. . . . Large colorful, cartoonlike drawings complement the [text]. . . . [This offers] solid information." SLJ

Includes glossary and bibliographical references

Kulling, Monica

Going up! Elisha Otis's trip to the top. Monica Kulling. Tundra Books of Northern New York 2012 32 p. (hardcover) $17.95
Grades: 2 3 4   **621.8**
1. Elevators 2. Picture books for children 3. Otis, Elisha Graves, 1811-1861
ISBN 1770492402; 9781770492400

LC 2011938777

This children's book offers a biography of Elisha Otis. Fascinated by farm machines, he notes "the dangerous possibility of the hoisting platform in the factory falling if the cable breaks" and "designs a safety brake. He realizes that with this, people can also be moved up and down safely. When he gives a demonstration at the New York World's Fair, the Otis Elevator Company takes off." (Children's Literature)

Low, William

Machines go to work. Holt & Co. 2009 un il $14.95
Grades: PreK K 1   **621.8**
1. Machinery
ISBN 978-0-8050-8759-8; 0-8050-8759-1

"The realistic digital paintings will delight youngsters; spreads alternate with three-page foldouts that show the machines at work. . . . This well-constructed picture book is a surefire hit." SLJ

Macaulay, David

★ **How** Machines Work; Zoo Break! David Macaulay. DK Publishing 2015 32 p. color illustrations $19.99
Grades: 1 2 3 4   **621.8**
1. Zoos 2. Simple machines
ISBN 1465440127; 9781465440129

Author David Macaulay "uses models and illustrations to demonstrate the technology of six simple machines: levers, pulleys, screws, inclined planes, wedges, and wheels.Follow the mad antics of Sloth and his sidekick Sengi as they try to find their way out of the zoo with the help of machines. Their efforts are brought to life through novelty elements including pop-ups, pull-outs, and lift-the-flaps, allowing readers to explore in greater depth how and why machines work." (Publisher's note)

"An intriguing work that raises troubling questions about the culture of violence in American high school sports." SLJ

Solway, Andrew

Castle under siege! simple machines. [by] Andrew Solway. Raintree 2005 32p il lib bdg $28.21; pa $7.85
Grades: 3 4 5   **621.8**
1. Castles 2. Simple machines
ISBN 1-4109-1918-8 lib bdg; 1-4109-1949-8 pa

LC 2005014549

"The author leads readers through the construction of a castle, the workings of the drawbridge, the execution of a siege and how the inhabitants would protect the castle from attack, methods the invaders might use, and what would happen afterward to repair the damage. While readers are drawn into the action, they are also introduced to the simple machines used during this period of time. . . . Detailed, easily interpreted diagrams are included for added understanding of concepts. Vivid and realistic photos add to the appeal. An excellent choice for research or for general interest." SLJ

Thales, Sharon

Wedges to the rescue; by Sharon Thales. Capstone Press 2007 24p il (Simple machines to the rescue) lib bdg $21.26
Grades: K 1 2 3   **621.8**
1. Wedges 2. Simple machines
ISBN 978-0-7368-6750-4 lib bdg; 0-7368-6750-3 lib bdg

LC 2006021495

"The presentation of the material . . . is impressive." Sci Books Films
Includes glossary and bibliographical references
Other titles in this series are:
Inclined planes to the rescue
Levers to the rescue
Pulleys to the rescue
Screws to the rescue
Wheels and axles to the rescue

Walker, Sally M.

Put screws to the test; by Sally M. Walker and Roseann Feldmann. Lerner Publications Company 2011 40p il (How do simple machines work?) lib bdg $27.93
Grades: 3 4 5   **621.8**
1. Screws
ISBN 978-0-7613-5323-2; 0-7613-5323-2

LC 2010035552

"Written in simple language and sentences, [this title offers a] straightforward [explanation] of how [screws] work. Starting with the basics, the material gradually builds upon readers' growing understanding of the concepts presented. The experiments suggested can be performed with little assistance and with materials found in the home. Clear, distinct, color photos of children demonstrating the activities on each page help reinforce the concepts, as do the many drawings and diagrams." SLJ

Other titles in this series are:
Put inclined planes to the test
Put levers to the test
Put pulleys to the test

Put wedges to the test

Put wheels and axles to the test

Yasuda, Anita

Explore simple machines; 25 great projects, activities, experiments. illustrated by Bryan Stone. Nomad Press 2011 il (Explore your world) pa $12.95

Grades: 2 3 4 **621.8**

1. Simple machines

ISBN 978-1-936313-82-2; 1-936313-82-0

This "introduces the six simple machines in enough detail to include worm gears, all three kinds of levers, compound pulleys, and unusual examples. . . . Yasuda writes in particularly clear simple language and intersperses her explanations with historical notes, jokes . . . and 25 easy projects or demonstrations constructed from common materials." Booklist

621.9 Tools

Blaxland, Wendy

Helmets. Marshall Cavendish Benchmark 2011 32p il map (How are they made?) lib bdg $12.99

Grades: 4 5 6 **621.9**

1. Helmets 2. Plastics

ISBN 978-0-7614-4755-9 lib bdg; 0-7614-4755-5 lib bdg

LC 2009039881

"The opening spread of Helmets, which shows both a football player and an astronaut, illustrates the wide range of protective headgear, which stretches back to the leather war apparel of 3,000 BCE. Shots of gleaming orbs shuttling down assembly lines accompany text on thermoplastics, testing methods, and laws." Booklist

Includes glossary

Tomecek, Steve

Tools and machines; by Stephen M. Tomecek. Chelsea House Publishers 2010 182p il (Experimenting with everyday science) $35

Grades: 5 6 7 8 **621.9**

1. Tools 2. Machinery 3. Science -- Experiments

ISBN 978-1-60413-171-0; 1-60413-171-3

LC 2009-22332

This "offers 25 easy-to-perform activities that illuminate scientific principles. . . . [This] discusses levers, pulleys, and meters and explains how people use them in their daily lives. . . . Following each experiment are additional comments on the science behind the experiment and link to the one that follows. Photographs, simple diagrams and illustrations, and sample data tables appear throughout, and the [layout is] clear and colorful." SLJ

Includes bibliographical references

622 Mining and related operations

Squire, Ann O.

Hydrofracking; the process that has changed America's energy needs. by Ann O. Squire. Children's Press, an imprint of Scholastic Inc. 2013 64 p. (Cornerstones of freedom) (library binding) $30

Grades: 4 5 6 **622**

1. Hydraulic fracturing 2. Shale gas 3. Gas well drilling

ISBN 0531236048; 9780531219621; 9780531236048

LC 2012034322

This book by Ann O. Squire is part of the "Cornerstones of Freedom" series, which provides "overviews of important national and global is-

sues and their effects on current world development, especially in the United States." It "discusses the advantages and disadvantages of this method of extracting petroleum and natural gas, by pumping water and chemicals deep below the Earth's surface. Renewable energy sources are discussed as alternatives to this practice." (School Library Journal)

Includes bibliographical references (page 61) and index

623 Military and nautical engineering

Keenan, Sheila

★ **Castle**; how it works. David Macaulay with Sheila Keenan. Roaring Brook 2012 31 p. col. ill. (My readers) (hardcover) $15.99

Grades: 1 2 3 **623**

1. Picture books for children 2. Castles 3. Fortification

ISBN 1596437448; 9780395329207; 9781596437449

LC 2011962088

In this children's book, author David Macaulay provides "a tour of a medieval castle. . . . Walls keep the enemy out. Towers protect the lord and the soldiers. From the moat and portcullis to the great hall and dungeon . . . [readers can] see how a castle works as an enemy army tries to storm the walls." (Publisher's note)

Mooney, Carla

Becoming invisible; from camouflage to cloaks. Norwood House Press 2010 48p il (A great idea) lib bdg $25.27

Grades: 3 4 5 6 **623**

1. Optics 2. Camouflage (Military science)

ISBN 978-1-59953-378-0 lib bdg; 1-59953-378-2 lib bdg

LC 2010016516

This "traces the history of camouflage; looks at invisibility in stealth aircraft, films, and television today; considers current research into light and light-bending materials; and imagines future uses for invisibility technology. . . . Presenting specific, current information, [this book] will appeal to young people intrigued by inventions." Booklist

Includes glossary and bibliographical references

623.4 Ordnance

Gurstelle, William

The **art** of the catapult; build Greek ballistae, Roman onagers, English trebuchets, and more ancient artillery. Chicago Review Press 2004 172p il map $16.95

Grades: 5 6 7 8 **623.4**

1. Catapult

ISBN 1-55652-526-5

"This collection of 10 working catapult projects offers a fascinating look at world history, military strategy, and physics, related with an engaging yet lighthearted touch. . . . Instructions are clear, with full materials lists, helpful diagrams, and no skipped steps. . . . There's excellent booktalk potential here, and lively reading even for those who never get around to constructing a catapult." SLJ

Includes bibliographical references

Sheinkin, Steve

★ **Bomb**; the race to build and steal the world's most dangerous weapon. Steve Sheinkin. Roaring Brook Press 2012 266 p. ill. (hc) $19.99

Grades: 5 6 7 8 9 10 11 12 Adult **623.4**

1. Nuclear warfare 2. Nuclear weapons 3. World War, 1914-1918 -- Chemical warfare 4. Atomic bomb -- History 5. Operation Freshman, 1942 6. Atomic bomb -- Germany -- History 7. World

War, 1939-1945 -- Secret service -- Soviet Union 8. World War, 1939-1945 -- Secret service -- Great Britain 9. World War, 1939-1945 -- Commando operations -- Norway -- Vemork
ISBN 1596434872; 9781596434875
LC 2011044096

John Newbery Honor Book (2013); National Book Award Finalist: Young People's Literature (2012)

Robert F. Sibert Informational Book Medal (2013)

YALSA Award for Excellence in Nonfiction for Young Adults (2013)

Author Steve Sheinkin's "story unfolds in three parts, covering American attempts to build the [atomic] bomb, how the Soviets tried to steal American designs and how the Americans tried to keep the Germans from building a bomb. It was the eve of World War II, and the fate of the world was at stake . . . all along the way spies in the United States were feeding sensitive information to the KGB." (Kirkus Reviews)

Includes bibliographical references (p. [243]-259) and index

623.74 Vehicles

Abramson, Andra Serlin

Fighter planes up close. Sterling 2008 48p (Up close) lib bdg $9.95

Grades: 2 3 4   **623.74**

1. Fighter planes

ISBN 978-1-4027-4796-0 lib bdg; 1-4027-4796-9 lib bdg
LC 2007008215

An introduction to fighter planes

Other titles in this series are:

Fire engines up close

Heavy equipment up close

Submarines up close

Marsico, Katie

Drones; Katie Marsico. Children's Press, an imprint of Scholastic Inc. 2016 48 p. illustrations (library binding) $29

Grades: 3 4 5   **623.74**

1. Drone aircraft 2. Drone aircraft -- History

ISBN 0531224805; 9780531222706; 9780531224809
LC 2015024703

In this book, by Katie Marsico, "readers will find out how drones work and what it takes to pilot them. They will also learn why the use of drones has become a controversial issue, how unmanned aircraft have been improved over time, and what today's engineering innovators are planning for the future of drone technology." (Publisher's note)

"The book's short chapters feature easy-to-read text in a large font and colored stock photographs. A glossary, resource list, and index conclude this accessible introduction to an intriguing invention." Booklist

Includes bibliographical references (page 45) and index

623.82 Nautical craft

Farndon, John

★ **Stickmen's** guide to watercraft; by John Farndon; illustrated by John Paul de Quay. Lerner Pub Group 2016 32 p. illustrations (chiefly color) (ebook) $26.65; $7.99

Grades: 3 4 5 6   **623.82**

1. Ships 2. Aircraft carriers 3. Boats and boating

ISBN 9781467795944; 1467793620; 9781467793629; 9781467795937
LC 2015032760

This children's book in the Stickmen's Guides to How Everything Works, by John Farndon, illustrated by John Paul de Quay, answers questions such as "How does a giant cruise ship stay upright? Just how big is an aircraft carrier? How are submarines powered? Join the Stickmen for a close look at how watercrafts work, though be careful you may get into deep water!" (Publisher's note)

"Deeply informative and pleasantly approachable, this is sure to make a splash." Booklist

Kirk, Shoshanna

T is for tugboat; navigating the seas from A to Z. [text by Shoshanna Kirk; designed by Sara Gillingham] Chronicle Books 2008 un il $15.99

Grades: 2 3 4   **623.82**

1. Ships 2. Navigation

ISBN 978-0-8118-6094-9; 0-8118-6094-9
LC 2007018333

This is an introduction to sea-related terms such as buoy, figurehead, hornpipe, and sextant

"This attractive title is an eye-pleaser filled with a mix of photographs, illustrations, and graphic images set on textured, woodgrain backgrounds. Images are both vintage and contemporary, and range from black-and-white to full-color reproductions. . . . A spread depicting an array of sailors' knots, a page illustrating Morse code, a spread labeling the parts of a ship, and the endpapers with the international code of maritime flags will be of interest to older children." SLJ

Lindeen, Mary

Ships; by Mary Lindeen. Bellwether Media 2007 24p il (Mighty machines) lib bdg $18.95

Grades: PreK K 1 2 3   **623.82**

1. Ships

ISBN 978-1-60014-060-0 lib bdg; 1-60014-060-2 lib bdg
LC 2006035262

This explains what a ship is, describes its major parts, and what it does

The glossary features "easy-to-read-and-understand definitions. . . . With [its] exciting, full-color photos on every spread [this] colorful [title] will certainly appeal to the mighty curiosity of young readers." SLJ

Includes glossary and bibliographical references

Other titles in this series are:

Trains

Tractors

Trucks

Spilsbury, Richard, 1963-

Robots underwater; Richard and Louise Spilsbury. Gareth Stevens Publishing 2016 48 p. color illustrations $31.95

Grades: 4 5 6 7   **623.82**

1. Robots 2. Underwater exploration

ISBN 1482430223; 9781482430226
LC 2014415766

In this book, by Richard and Louise Spilsbury, part of the Amazing Robots series, "without underwater robots, people never would have been able to explore the shipwreck of the Titanic as much as they have. From mapping the ocean floor to testing water quality, the jobs these robots can do are astounding. Through many examples and full-color photographs, readers dive deep with underwater robots, learning the technology behind these amazing machines and how they help people every day." (Publisher's note)

"The full-color photos of robots in action and the high-interest nature of robotics may catch the interest of science-minded kids." Booklist

Sutherland, Jonathan
Aircraft carriers; [by] Jonathan Sutherland and Diane Canwell. Gareth Stevens Pub. 2008 32p il (Amazing ships) lib bdg $23.93
Grades: 4 5 6   **623.82**
1. Aircraft carriers
ISBN 978-0-8368-8376-3

LC 2007017049

This is an illustrated introduction to aircraft carriers from various parts of the world

"Bright colors and eye-catching photos are an enticing invitation of younger readers.... Vocabulary is appropriate in both text and captions. ... Attractive, accurate, and informative." SLJ

Includes glossary and bibliographical references
Other titles in this series are:
Container ships and oil tankers
Cruise ships
Submarines

623.89 Navigation

Morrison, Taylor
The coast mappers. Houghton Mifflin Co. 2004 45p il map $16
Grades: 5 6 7 8   **623.89**
1. Maps 2. Surveying 3. Astronomers 4. Geographers 5. Cartographers 6. College teachers 7. Pacific Coast (North America)
ISBN 0-618-25408-0

LC 2003-13534

Chronicles the difficulties encountered by George Davidson and others as they attempted to create nautical charts to complete the U.S. Coast Survey of the West Coast in the mid-nineteenth century

"Cartographic methods are clearly explained through both the carefully researched text and the precise illustrations.... The artwork clarifies the text, depicts the breathtaking beauty of the coastline, and adds a sense of adventure." SLJ

Includes glossary and bibliographical references

Young, Karen Romano
Across the wide ocean; the why, how, and where of navigation for humans and animals at sea. Greenwillow Books 2007 78p il $18.99; lib bdg $19.89
Grades: 4 5 6 7   **623.89**
1. Ocean 2. Navigation 3. Marine animals
ISBN 978-0-06-009086-9; 0-06-009086-3; 978-0-06-009087-6 lib bdg; 0-06-009087-1 lib bdg

LC 2005-46146

"Readers follow such disparate entities as a loggerhead sea turtle, a nuclear submarine, and a sailboat crew seeking scientific sightings of North Atlantic right whales as Young explores the concept of navigation. ... Larded with photos, diagrams, and maps.... Deceptively simple in appearance, the informative text can push some intense mental activity." SLJ

624 Civil engineering

Caney, Steven
★ Steven Caney's ultimate building book. Running Press 2006 596p il $29.95
Grades: 4 5 6 7 8   **624**
1. Building 2. Civil engineering
ISBN 0-7624-0409-4

"Caney examines 'building' in its broadest sense, encompassing everything from skyscrapers and bridges to bird feeders and peanut-shell 'bricks.' Opening sections investigate the history and techniques of construction, with clearly written explanations supported by black-and-white photographs and diagrams..... The author reinforces important concepts of design in a way that is fascinating and effective." SLJ

Macaulay, David
★ Underground. Houghton Mifflin 1976 109p il hardcover o.p. pa $9.95
Grades: 5 6 7 8 9   **624**
1. Subways 2. Building 3. Sewerage 4. Electric lines 5. Public utilities 6. Civil engineering
ISBN 0-395-24739-X; 0-395-34065-9 pa

"Introduced by a visual index—a bird's eye view of a busy, hypothetical intersection with colored indicators marking the specific locations analyzed in subsequent pages—detailed illustrations are combined with a clear, precise narrative to make the subject comprehenssible and fascinating." Horn Book

Includes glossary

Roberts, Russell
The Eiffel Tower; by Russell Roberts. Purple Toad Pub Inc 2016 32 p. illustrations (some color) $26.50
Grades: 4 5 6 7 8   **624**
1. Eiffel Tower (Paris, France)
ISBN 1624692036; 9781624692031

LC 2016937176

This book, by Russell Roberts, presents "the story of how the Eiffel Tower was built, and the people who made it happen. Learn how they did it and see what materials they used in this real life building journey that kids who love to build in Lego and Minecraft will be thrilled to read." (Publisher's note)

"An enlightening look at this famous landmark." Booklist
Includes bibliographic references (page 29) and index.

Sullivan, George
Built to last; building America's amazing bridges, dams, tunnels, and skyscrapers. Scholastic Nonfiction 2005 128p il map $18.99
Grades: 5 6 7 8   **624**
1. Civil engineering
ISBN 0-439-51737-0

LC 2004-60996

This is a "survey of American building—from the Erie Canal to Boston's current 'Big Dig.' Chronological chapters describe the historical forces that helped drive each project as well as the specific technological feats linked to each pioneering structure.... The wide selection of captivating illustrations includes archival photos and engravings, architectural drawings, and color photos.... Sullivan's skillful integration of social and economic history distinguishes this clear, well-designed title." Booklist

624.1 Structural engineering and underground construction

Askew, Amanda
Bulldozers. QEB Pub. 2010 24p il (Mighty machines) lib bdg $25.65; pa $5.95
Grades: PreK K 1 2   **624.1**
1. Construction equipment
ISBN 978-1-59566-925-4 lib bdg; 1-59566-925-6 lib bdg; 978-1-55407-703-8 pa; 1-55407-703-6 pa

LC 2010001217

"With huge, clear color photos of machines at work, the Mighty Machines series is an exciting way to connect books with kids' vrooming play and with what they see on the road, construction sites, and farms. . . . In Bulldozers, the parts called 'blades' and 'rippers' say it all, and the pages of full-bleed photographs show the machines building roads and even clearing a path as part of an army convoy." Booklist

Other titles in this series are:

Cranes

Diggers

Loaders

Mason, Adrienne

Build it! structures, systems and you. written by Adrienne Mason; illustrated by Claudia Dávila. Kids Can Press 2006 32p il (Primary physical science) $14.95; pa $5.95

Grades: K 1 2   **624.1**

1. Building 2. Structural engineering

ISBN 978-1-55337-835-8; 1-55337-835-0; 978-1-55337-836-5 pa; 1-55337-836-9 pa

This provides "a first glimpse of how structures and structural systems exist both in nature and in human-made designs. The author makes reading this book an easy and enjoyable reading experience. The book uses carefully worded descriptions, creative and vivid colors with striking graphics representations, and clear fonts." Sci Books Films

Stefoff, Rebecca, 1951-

Building tunnels; Rebecca Stefoff. Cavendish Square 2016 32 p. (library bound) $28.50

Grades: 3 4 5   **624.1**

1. Tunnels 2. Civil engineering 3. Underground construction 4. Tunnels -- Design and construction

ISBN 1502606011; 9781502606006; 9781502606013

LC 2014049189

This juvenile book, by Rebecca Stefoff, part of the publisher's "Great Engineering" series, focuses on the construction of tunnels. "These examinations of large-scale infrastructure elements focus particularly on the role of civil engineers in planning and construction. Each volume opens with a lucid explanation of the chosen structure's function . . . , proceeding to present a historical overview, describing construction methods, and highlighting significant examples." (School Library Journal)

"Budding engineers will find these great introductions indeed." Booklist

Includes bibliographical references (page 30) and index

624.2 Bridges

Cornille, Didier

Bridges; an introduction to ten great bridges and their architects. Didier Cornille; translated by Yolanda Stern Broad. Princeton Architectural Press 2016 93 p. color illustrations (hardback) $17.95

Grades: 1 2 3 4 5 6   **624.2**

1. Bridges 2. Architecture 3. Civil engineers

ISBN 1616895160; 9781616895167

LC 2016001407

This book in the Who Built That? series by Didier Cornille, translated by Yolanda Stern Broad, presents "ten of the most important bridges in the world, from the Brooklyn to the Golden Gate; from the first in cast iron to the longest in concrete; from small footbridges to the tallest in the world. Cornille introduces each engineer or architect and the main concepts of their work through charming step-by-step drawings and accessible text." (Publisher's note)

"A work of beauty and a conveyance into human ingenuity." Kirkus

Graham, Ian

Fabulous bridges. Amicus 2010 32p il (Superstructures) lib bdg $28.50

Grades: 5 6 7 8   **624.2**

1. Bridges

ISBN 978-1-60753-132-6; 1-60753-132-1

LC 2009030864

"The vivid illustrations often help clarify points made in the text. . . . [This] colorful, informative [book offers] intriguing glimpses of notable engineering feats." Booklist

Includes glossary and bibliographical references

Johmann, Carol

Bridges! amazing structures to design, build & test. [by] Carol Johmann & Elizabeth Rieth; illustrations by Michael Kline. Williamson 1999 96p il pa $12.95

Grades: 4 5 6 7   **624.2**

1. Bridges

ISBN 1-88559-330-9

LC 98-53272

Describes different kinds of bridges, their history, design, construction, and effects on populations, environmental dilemmas, safety, and more

"Eye-catching photographs and cartoon illustrations in blue and orange tones abound; clear organization of text and unifying page borders create an attractive graphic package. The volume includes a list of notable bridges by state and country." SLJ

Mattern, Joanne

Bridges; Joanne Mattern. Smart Apple Media 2003 23 p. illustrations $10.95

Grades: 4 5 6   **624.2**

1. Bridges

ISBN 1583401504; 1634305191; 9781634305198

LC 2001049972

This book on bridges, by Joanne Mattern, is part of the "Engineering Wonders" series. "Learn about the different types of bridges, the civilizations and people who engineered and risked their lives to construct them, and the advances in bridge building that have made them safe and effective ways to keep us moving!" (Publisher's note)

"Sidebars throughout relate interesting facts and ideas to consider, while a concluding time line, glossary, list of websites, and comprehension questions reinforce the content. An inspiring blend of history and STEM." Booklist

Includes bibliographical references (p. [24]) and index

Stefoff, Rebecca, 1951-

Building bridges; Rebecca Stefoff. Cavendish Square 2016 32 p. (library binding) $28.50

Grades: 3 4 5   **624.2**

1. Bridges 2. Civil engineering 3. Bridges -- Design and construction

ISBN 1502605988; 9781502605979; 9781502605986

LC 2014046859

This juvenile book, by Rebecca Stefoff, part of the publisher's "Great Engineering" series, focuses on the construction of bridges. "These examinations of large-scale infrastructure elements focus particularly on the role of civil engineers in planning and construction. Each volume opens with a lucid explanation of the chosen structure's function . . . , proceeding to present a historical overview, describing construction methods, and highlighting significant examples." (School Library Journal)

"Budding engineers will find these great introductions indeed."
Booklist

Includes bibliographical references (page 30) and index

625.1 Railroads

Crowther, Robert
Trains : a pop-up railroad book. Candlewick Press 2006 un il $17.99
Grades: 2 3 4 5   625.1
1. Railroads 2. Pop-up books
ISBN 978-0-7636-3082-9; 0-7636-3082-9
"With pop-up effects that, appropriately enough, tend to be long, narrow, and placed in parallel tracks, this history of railroading opens with outside and inside views of a small steam locomotive and closes with a full-spread, double-tiered train station. In between, the book covers methods of propulsion, the development of passenger cars, speed and other records, tunnels, bridges, and other engineering feats. . . . Crowther simplifies technological details in his neat, brightly colored collage illustrations." SLJ

National Railway Museum (Great Britain)
Big book of trains; [by] National Railway Museum, York, England. DK Pub. 1998 32p il $14.99
Grades: 4 5 6   625.1
1. Railroads
ISBN 0-7894-3436-9
                                                    LC 98-18830
Describes the locomotives, cars, tunnels, stations, and functions of such trains as freight trains, channel tunnel trains, bullet trains, mountain trains, and snow trains
Includes glossary

625.26 Locomotives

Zimmermann, Karl
The **Stourbridge** Lion; America's First Locomotive. Karl Zimmermann; illustrated by Steven Walker. 1st ed. Boyds Mills Press 2012 32 p. ill., maps (hardcover) $16.95
Grades: 2 3 4   625.26
1. Steam locomotives 2. Railroads -- History 3. Locomotives 4. Transportation -- United States -- History 5. Stourbridge Lion (Steam locomotive) 6. Steam locomotives -- United States -- History 7. Railroads -- Pennsylvania -- Honesdale -- History 8. Railroads -- United States -- History -- 19th century
ISBN 1590788591; 9781590788592
                                                    LC 2011939995
Includes bibliographical references.
"While the scope of the book is narrow, it will have broad appeal to children interested in railroading. It would also be a good read-aloud to introduce students to informational texts and a worthy choice for incorporation into lessons on transportation history." SLJ

625.4 Local rail transit systems

McKendry, Joe
Beneath the streets of Boston; building America's first subway. written & illustrated by Joe McKendry. David R. Godine 2005 un il maps $19.95

Grades: 4 5 6   625.4
1. Subways 2. Boston (Mass.) -- History
ISBN 1-56792-284-8
                                                    LC 2004-16418
This book covers over twenty years of the early history of the Boston subway system
"The text is clear and well written. . . . The paintings convey the sense of story, while the drawings provide specific details. Both are equally well executed and contribute to the overall understanding of the text." SLJ

Weitzman, David L.
A **subway** for New York; [by] David Weitzman. Farrar, Straus and Giroux 2005 un il map $17
Grades: 4 5 6 7   625.4
1. Subways 2. New York (N.Y.) -- History
ISBN 0-374-37284-5
                                                    LC 2004-56286
"Weitzman recounts the construction of [New York's] first subterranean train system, beginning above ground with descriptions of [the city's] crowded streets in 1904. . . . The text and captivating images convey the awe-inspiring scope of the project and the engineering feats that produced what remains the fastest method of navigating the city." Booklist
Includes bibliographical references

627 Hydraulic engineering

Mann, Elizabeth
Hoover Dam; with illustrations by Alan Witschonke. Mikaya Press 2001 44p il (Wonders of the world) $19.95; pa $9.95
Grades: 4 5 6 7   627
1. Hoover Dam (Ariz. and Nev.)
ISBN 978-1-931414-02-9; 1-931414-02-5; 978-1-931414-13-5 pa; 1-931414-13-0 pa
                                                    LC 2001-34520
Describes the engineering, construction, and social and historical contexts of the Hoover Dam
"A wonderfully readable, well-organized book filled with fascinating detail." SLJ

Zuehlke, Jeffrey
The **Hoover** Dam. Lerner Publications Co. 2010 32p il map (Lightning Bolt Books. Famous places) lib bdg $25.26
Grades: 2 3 4   627
1. Hoover Dam (Ariz. and Nev.)
ISBN 978-0-8225-9408-6 lib bdg; 0-8225-9408-0 lib bdg
                                                    LC 2008-31245
Describes the Hoover Dam and includes information on its design, construction, and environmental issues
This book uses "high-quality photos, illustrations, maps, and diagrams. . . . Readers will enjoy learning about [the Hoover Dam] . . . and the challenges of building and maintaining large structures." SLJ
Includes glossary and bibliographical references

627.42 Flood barriers

Stefoff, Rebecca, 1951-
Building dikes and levees; Rebecca Stefoff. Cavendish Square 2016 32 p. color illustrations (library bound) $28.50

Grades: 3 4 5   **627.42**

1. Levees   2. Civil engineering   3. Levees   4. Dikes (Engineering)
ISBN 1502606100; 9781502606099; 9781502606105

LC 2015006645

This juvenile book, by Rebecca Stefoff, part of the publisher's "Great Engineering" series, focuses on the construction of dikes and levees. "These examinations of large-scale infrastructure elements focus particularly on the role of civil engineers in planning and construction. Each volume opens with a lucid explanation of the chosen structure's function . . . , proceeding to present a historical overview, describing construction methods, and highlighting significant examples." (School Library Journal)

Includes bibliographical references (page 30) and index

Other titles in this series are:

Building bridges

Building dams

Building tunnels

627.8   Dams and reservoirs

Nagelhout, Ryan

How do dams work? Ryan Nagelhout. PowerKids Press 2016 32 p. (pbk.) $11.75

Grades: 4 5 6   **627.8**

1. Dams   2. Hydraulic engineering   3. Dams -- Environmental aspects   4. Dams -- Design and construction
ISBN 9781499419993; 9781499420005; 9781499420012

LC 2016013444

This children's book, in the STEM waterworks series, by Ryan Nagelhout, shows that "all dams rely on science to function properly. People first began damming rivers to stop flooding and provide water for irrigation. These early dams were made with simple techniques and technology. Today, dams are constructed to prevent flooding and to provide water for irrigation, hydroelectric power, and freshwater for large populations." (Publisher's note)

"The book ends with a hopeful outlook as scientists rethink ways to use dams to protect the environment. Colorful diagrams, panoramic views, and photos of dam construction not only relate the roles of these structures but show STEM in action." Booklist

Stefoff, Rebecca, 1951-

Building dams; Rebecca Stefoff. Cavendish Square Publishing 2016 32 p. (Great engineering) (library bound) $28.50

Grades: 3 4 5   **627.8**

1. Dams   2. Civil engineering   3. Dams -- Design and construction
ISBN 1502605953; 9781502605948; 9781502605955

LC 2015004884

This juvenile book, by Rebecca Stefoff, part of the "Great Engineering" series, focuses on the construction of hydrological dams. The author "opens with a lucid explanation of the chosen structure's function . . . , going on to explain why and how [to] build dams--and proceeding to present a historical overview, describing construction methods, and highlighting significant examples." (School Library Journal)

"Budding engineers will find these great introductions indeed." Booklist

Includes bibliographical references (page 30) and index

628   Sanitary engineering

Horn, Geoffrey

Environmental engineer; by Geoffrey M. Horn. Gareth Stevens Pub. 2010 32p il (Cool careers: cutting edge) lib bdg $26; pa $8.95

Grades: 4 5 6   **628**

1. Vocational guidance   2. Sanitary engineering   3. Environmental protection
ISBN 978-1-4339-1956-5 lib bdg; 1-4339-1956-7 lib bdg; 978-1-4339-2155-1 pa; 1-4339-2155-3 pa

LC 2009004746

This introduction to environmental engineering careers offers "clear, solid information in a large font. . . . [This] short [book is] packed with relevant, current material." SLJ

Includes glossary and bibliographical references

628.1   Water supply

Cartlidge, Cherese

Water from air; water-harvesting machines. by Cherese Cartlidge. Norwood House Press 2008 48p il (A great idea) lib bdg $25.27

Grades: 3 4 5 6   **628.1**

1. Humidity   2. Water supply   3. Water resources development
ISBN 978-1-59953-196-0 lib bdg; 1-59953-196-8 lib bdg

LC 2008-10780

"Describes the invention and development of water harvesting machines." Publisher's note

Includes glossary and bibliographical references

Person, Stephen

Saving animals from oil spills. Bearport Pub. 2011 32p il map (Rescuing animals from disasters) lib bdg $25.27

Grades: 3 4 5 6   **628.1**

1. Oil spills   2. Animal rescue
ISBN 978-1-61772-288-2; 1-61772-288-X

LC 2011002430

"Featuring colorful, visually packed pages and readable prose, this title . . . offers an acceessible introduction to the impact of oil spills on a variety of creatures. . . . Throughout, basic concepts are well conveyed, and inset text adds additional, useful commentary on each page." Booklist

Includes glossary and bibliographical references

628.9   Other branches of sanitary and municipal engineering

Allman, Toney

The Jaws of Life. Norwood House Press 2008 48p il (A great idea) lib bdg $25.27

Grades: 3 4 5 6   **628.9**

1. Rescue work
ISBN 978-159953-191-5 lib bdg; 1-59953-191-7 lib bdg

LC 2008007041

"Full-color photographs and copious fun facts help make this . . . enjoyable reading, but it's really the choice of [topic] that is so enthralling." Booklist

Includes glossary and bibliographical references

Bingham, Caroline

Fire truck. DK Pub. 2003 29p il (Machines at work) $8.99

Grades: K 1 2 3   628.9
1. Fire engines 2. Fire fighting
ISBN 0-7894-9221-0

Introduces fire engines and the work that they help firefighters do in all kinds of settings

"Bingham immediately grabs the reader's attention with brilliantly colored pictures. . . . An excellent stimulant for a child's imagination." Sci Books Films

Includes glossary

Butler, Dori Hillestad

F is for firefighting; by Dori Hillestad Butler; illustrated by Joan C. Waites. Pelican 2007 un il $15.95

Grades: PreK K 1   628.9
1. Alphabet 2. Fire fighting
ISBN 978-1-58980-420-3; 1-58980-420-1

LC 2006031113

"From 'A is for Alarm' to 'Z is for Zones,' each page introduces a different aspect of firefighting. Crisp, colorful illustrations depict the topics, and thick borders frame the artwork as well as the text boxes at the bottom of the pages." SLJ

Kenney, Karen Latchana

Firefighters at work; by Karen L. Kenney; illustrated by Brian Caleb Dumm. Magic Wagon 2010 32p il (Meet your community workers!) lib bdg $18.95

Grades: K 1 2 3   628.9
1. Fire fighters 2. Vocational guidance
ISBN 978-1-60270-648-4 lib bdg; 1-60270-648-4 lib bdg

LC 2009-2384

This book about firefighters has "an uncluttered layout and consistent organization. . . . Chapter headings such as 'Problems on the Job,' and 'Technology at Work,' and 'Special Skills and Training' make it easy to pinpoint specific information." SLJ

Includes glossary

Lindeen, Mary

A visit to the firehouse; by Mary Lindeen. Norwood House Press 2016 32 p. color illustrations (library edition : alk. paper) $22.60

Grades: PreK K 1   628.9
1. Fire fighters 2. Fire departments 3. Fire stations 4. Fire extinction
ISBN 1599536935; 9781599536934

LC 2014047628

In this children's book, by Mary Lindeen, "see what firefighters wear, what equipment they use, and what they do when theyre not fighting fires. Tour inside a firehouse and see what happens when the alarm bell rings. . . . Reading reinforcement pages include a word list and activities to strengthen early literacy skills, such as understanding the craft and structure of informational text, key vocabulary words, foundation skills, close reading, and fluency." (Publisher's note)

"These books are clearly intended for instructional use or supplementary skills practice, with back matter sections for parents and teachers corresponding closely to Common Core reading standards on vocabulary, craft and structure, foundational skills, close reading, and fluency." Booklist

See how they work & look inside fire trucks; edited by Johannah Gilman and Ashley Rideout. Flowerpot Press 2015 32 p. color illustrations $7.99

Grades: 2 3 4 5 6   628.9
1. Trucks 2. Fire engines
ISBN 1486708056; 9781486708055

This book, edited by Johannah Gilman and Ashley Rideout, is part of the "World of Wonder" series. "Now dive into Fire Trucks to see all the incredible things machines can do, from spraying hundreds of gallons of water to putting out forest fires, and learn just how cool fire trucks are!" (Publisher's note)

629   Other branches of engineering

The amazing International Space Station; by the editors of YES Mag. Kids Can Press 2003 48p il $15.95; pa $8.95

Grades: 4 5 6   629
1. Space stations
ISBN 1-55337-380-4; 1-55337-523-8 pa

This describes the construction, crew, life, and work aboard the International Space Station.

"This book packs a lot of information into clear, short chapters that are chock-full of facts, action, and cool language." SLJ

Biggs, Brian

Everything goes: On land. Balzer + Bray 2011 un il (Everything goes) $14.99

Grades: PreK K 1   629
1. Vehicles
ISBN 0-06-195809-3; 978-0-06-195809-0

LC 2011019349

A young boy learns about land vehicles from bicycles to subways and trolleys as he and his father travel to the train station.

"Biggs has a cheery cartooning style that's reminiscent of R. Crumb and ideal for populating his oversized pages with a multitude of players and detail. With running visual jokes and mini-narratives adding to the fun, Biggs gives readers lots to take in and enjoy." Publ Wkly

Other titles in this series are:
Everything goes in the air
Everything goes by sea

Ganeri, Anita

Things that go; illustrated by Mark Bergin. Kingfisher 2010 18p il (Flip the flaps) $9.99

Grades: PreK K 1   629
1. Vehicles
ISBN 978-0-7534-6409-0; 0-7534-6409-8

This provides "cutaways of airplanes and trains and [shows] a fire in progress along with a spread about emergency vehicles. Some questions . . . are given suprisingly thorough answers. . . . Perfect for light, educational browsing." Booklist

629.04   Transportation engineering

Arlon, Penelope

Emergency vehicles; by Penelope Arlon and Tory Gordon-Harris. 1st ed. Scholastic 2013 32 p. col. ill. (Scholastic discover more) (reinforced) $7.99

Grades: PreK K 1   629.04
1. Vehicles 2. Fire engines 3. Rescue work 4. Emergency vehicles
ISBN 0545495636; 9780545495639

LC 2012285426

This book, written by Penelope Arlon, presents a "reference book about emergency vehicles for emergent readers. 'Emergency Vehicles' is full of facts and . . . pictures of rescue vehicles. Big, annotated photos reveal . . . details of how fire trucks, ambulances, police cars, motorbikes, and helicopters really work. Alongside are explorations of more unusual vehicles . . . from superscoopers to fireboats. (Publisher's note)

Green, Rod

   Giant vehicles; Rod Green, illustrated by Stephen Biesty. Candlewick Press 2014 16 p. $15.99

Grades: K 1 2 3   **629.04**

   1. Vehicles 2. Ships 3. Dump trucks 4. Flying machines 5. Railroad trains

   ISBN 0763674044; 9780763674045

                                    LC 2013953451

   "[Author Rod] Green and [illustrator Stephen] Biesty explore the biggest of the big in this oversize [children's] book devoted to vehicles. . . . Biesty's detailed colored-pencil illustrations demonstrate how each machine operates, with labels and captions explaining how various components work together." (Publishers Weekly)

   "Known for his exceptionally fine cutaway drawings in books such as Stephen Biesty's Cross-Sections: Man-of-War (1993) and Egypt in Spectacular Cross-Section (2005), Biesty uses this new book's wide format to showcase gargantuan vehicles, such as an exceptionally long train, a double-decker passenger jet, a gigantic dump truck, an enormous container ship, a jumbo Russian submarine, and (turn the book 90 degrees) the Saturn V rocket for NASA's 1969 moonshot..hildren intrigued by the subject will pore over the handsome illustrations—intricately detailed pen-and-ink drawings with colored-pencil shading. An engaging, interactive learning experience." Booklist

Perritano, John

   Revolution in transportation. Marshall Cavendish Benchmark 2010 32p il (It works!) lib bdg $19.95

Grades: 3 4 5   **629.04**

   1. Transportation

   ISBN 978-0-7614-4379-7 lib bdg; 0-7614-4379-7 lib bdg

                                    LC 2008-54366

   "This interesting, information packed [book] . . . motivates students to do their own exploring. . . . The appealing cartoon-like photographs add humor. . . . This . . . just may be that spark needed to create eager budding scientists." Libr Media Connect

   Includes glossary and bibliographical references

   Other titles in this series are:

   Revolution in communications

   Revolution in construction

   Revolution in medicine

   Revolution in space

629.13 Aeronautics

Adler, David A.

   A **picture** book of Amelia Earhart; illustrated by Jeff Fisher. Holiday House 1998 un il $16.95; pa $6.95

Grades: 1 2 3   **629.13**

   1. Air pilots 2. Missing persons 3. Women air pilots 4. Memoirists

   ISBN 0-8234-1315-2; 0-8234-1517-1 pa

                                    LC 96-54854

   Discusses the life of the pilot who was the first woman to cross the Atlantic by herself in a plane

   This offers "a straightforward, informative text full of detail. The illustrations ably reflect both the humorous and more serious moments in the narrative." Horn Book Guide

   Includes bibliographical references

Bailey, Gerry

   Flight. Gareth Stevens Pub. 2009 32p il (Simply science) lib bdg $26

Grades: 3 4 5   **629.13**

   1. Flight 2. Aeronautics

   ISBN 978-1-4339-0032-7 lib bdg; 1-4339-0032-7 lib bdg

                                    LC 2008-27569

   "In this little book, various vehicles associated with human flight are introduced . . . [and] fundamental principles underlying how these various vehicles are able to travel through the air are explained in a straightfoward and understandable manner. . . . This text will provide . . . an entertaining and informative introduction to aircraft and aerodynamic vehicles." Sci Books Films

   Includes glossary and bibliographical references

Borden, Louise

   Touching the sky; the flying adventures of Wilbur and Orville Wright. [by] Louise Borden & Trish Marx; illustrated by Peter Fiore. Margaret K. McElderry Bks. 2003 un il map $18.95

Grades: 3 4 5   **629.13**

   1. Inventors 2. Aeronautics -- History 3. New York (N.Y.) -- History 4. Aircraft industry executives

   ISBN 0-689-84876-5

                                    LC 2002-12041

   A look at how the Wright Brothers became the first celebrities of the twentieth century through their 1909 public flying exhibitions in New York City and Germany

   "Fiore's detailed watercolors dramatically and accurately record the two venues. The narrative, too, is laced with engaging facts that are successfully married to the pictures." SLJ

Brown, Don, 1949-

   Ruth Law thrills a nation; story and pictures by Don Brown. Ticknor & Fields 1993 un il $16; pa $5.95

Grades: K 1 2 3   **629.13**

   1. Air pilots 2. Women air pilots 3. Women -- Biography 4. Aeronautics -- Flights

   ISBN 0-395-66404-7; 0-395-73517-3 pa

                                    LC 92-45701

   The author discusses the flight performed by Ruth Law, who in 1916 "tried to fly from Chicago to New York City in one day. She did not succeed (she landed outside Binghamton, New York), but she broke a nonstop cross-county flying record." (Booklist) "Kindergarten to grade three." (School Library Journal)

   "Using a simple text and effective watercolors, Brown successfully re-creates the remarkable flying feat. He sets Law in her historical context with humor and precision." Booklist

Burleigh, Robert

   Flight : the journey of Charles Lindbergh; illustrated by Mike Wimmer; introduction by Jean Fritz. Philomel Bks. 1991 un il hardcover o.p. pa $6.99

Grades: 2 3 4   **629.13**

   1. Generals 2. Air pilots 3. Memoirists 4. Air force officers 5. Aeronautics -- Flights

   ISBN 0-399-22272-3; 0-698-11425-6 pa

                                    LC 90-35401

   Describes how Charles Lindbergh achieved the remarkable feat of flying nonstop and solo from New York to Paris in 1927

   "Using Charles Lindbergh's autobiography, The Spirit of St. Louis, as the basis for his text, Burleigh vividly creates that first solo flight in words, while Wimmer fashions exhilarating pictures that are, above all else, emotional. . . . This artistic emotion . . . works terrifically with the terseness of the near-poetic text." Booklist

★ **Night** flight; Amelia Earhart crosses the Atlantic. [illustrated by] Wendell Minor. Simon & Schuster Books for Young Readers 2011 un il $16.99

Grades: K 1 2 **629.13**

1. Air pilots 2. Missing persons 3. Women air pilots 4. Memoirists 5. Aeronautics -- Flights 6. Transatlantic flights

ISBN 1-4169-6733-8; 978-1-4169-6733-0

LC 2008-52269

This is an account of Amelia Earhart's 1932 flight across the Atlantic Ocean from Newfoundland to Ireland. Bibliography. "Grades three to six." (Bull Cent Child Books)

"A gripping narrative and dynamic art immediately pull readers into the story of Earhart's historic 1932 solo transatlantic flight. . . . Minor's . . . gouache and watercolor paintings easily convey the journey's intense drama, balancing lifelike closeups of Earhart with images of her imperiled plane. . . . Hearts will be racing. Back matter includes notes on Earhart's life." Publ Wkly

Includes bibliographical references

Carson, Mary Kay

★ The **Wright** Brothers for kids; how they invented the airplane: 21 activities exploring the science and history of flight. illustrations by Laura D'Argo. Chicago Review Press 2003 146p il pa $14.95

Grades: 4 5 6 7 **629.13**

1. Inventors 2. Aeronautics -- History 3. Science -- Experiments 4. Aircraft industry executives

ISBN 1-55652-477-3

LC 2002-155449

This account of the Wright brothers' invention of the airplane, explains the forces of flight-lift, thrust, gravity, and drag and includes such activities as making a Chinese flying top, building a kite, bird watching, making a paper glider and a rubber-band-powered flyer

"A treasure trove of activities awaits readers of this wonderfully executed survey of the Wright brothers and their invention. The narrative flows easily and is complemented by numerous photographs that give a sense of history and this event. . . . This is a valuable resource for student reports and projects, and for classroom units." SLJ

Includes glossary and bibliographical references

Cummins, Julie

Flying solo; how Ruth Elder soared into America's heart. Julie Cummins; illustrated by Malene Laugesen. Roaring Brook Press 2013 32 p.

Grades: K 1 2 **629.13**

1. Air pilots -- United States -- Biography 2. Women air pilots -- United States -- Biography

ISBN 9781596435094

LC 2012029743

Amelia Bloomer Project (2014)

Includes bibliographical references (p.)

Goldish, Meish

Freaky-big airplanes. Bearport Pub. 2010 24p il (World's biggest) lib bdg $22.61

Grades: 2 3 4 **629.13**

1. Airplanes

ISBN 978-1-59716-959-2 lib bdg; 1-59716-959-5 lib bdg

LC 2009-14620

Describes different types of aircraft used around the world, including information on their history, dimensions, weight, and performance

"The simply phrased narrative and captions describe what each vehicle carries, along with top speed, full weight, and other basic facts. . . . . A visual glossary and a look at four other outsize flying machines . . . . cap this awe-inspiring entry in the World's Biggest series." Booklist

Includes glossary and bibliographical references

Hardesty, Von

Epic flights. Kingfisher 2011 il (Epic adventure) $19.99

Grades: 5 6 7 8 **629.13**

1. Aeronautics -- History

ISBN 978-0-7534-6669-8; 0-7534-6669-4

LC 2011041637

This describes Charles Lindbergh's transatlantic flight; the Breitling Orbiter 3 which set a record for non-stop around the world flight by balloon; the Apollo 11 flight to the moon; Amy Johnson's solo flight from England to Australia in a small bi-plane; and the Voyager, which set a record by flying non-stop around the world without refueling.

"The graphics will grab readers in [this] exciting, extra-large-size [title] . . . packed with high-quality color photos on every double-page spread. Just as gripping are the narratives, captions, and technical details of exploration, adventure, and survival." Booklist

Includes glossary

Hense, Mary

How fighter pilots use math; math curriculum consultant: Rhea A. Stewart. Chelsea Clubhouse 2010 32p il (Math in the real world) lib bdg $28

Grades: 4 5 6 **629.13**

1. Air pilots 2. Aeronautics 3. Mathematics 4. Vocational guidance

ISBN 978-1-60413-605-0 lib bdg; 1-60413-605-7 lib bdg

LC 2009-20242

This describes how fighter pilots use math to judge speed, attain altitude, and maintain safety, and includes relevant math problems and information about how to become a fighter pilot

Includes glossary and bibliographical references

Hodgkins, Fran

How people learned to fly; by Fran Hodgkins; illustrated by True Kelley. HarperCollinsPublishers 2007 33p il (Let's-read-and-find-out science) $15.99; pa $5.99

Grades: K 1 2 3 **629.13**

1. Flight 2. Aeronautics

ISBN 978-0-06-029558-5; 0-06-029558-9; 978-0-06-445221-2 pa; 0-06-445221-2 pa

LC 2006000482

"This book explains the development of aircraft and the scientific principles behind them. Complex ideas, such as gravity and lift, are made accessible through concise explanations and excellent illustrations and diagrams, which are always bright, clear, and appealing." SLJ

629.133 Aircraft types

Clark, Willow

Planes on the move. PowerKids Press 2010 24p il (Transportation station) lib bdg $21.25; pa $8.25

Grades: 2 3 **629.133**

1. Airplanes 2. Aeronautics

ISBN 978-1-4358-9332-0 lib bdg; 1-4358-9332-8 lib bdg; 978-1-4358-9752-6 pa; 1-4358-9752-8 pa

Learn about all kinds of planes, including passenger planes, seaplanes, and planes used by the military.

"Clark has done a fine job of including meaningful content in a limited space. . . . [This] title consists of 10 two-page chapters printed in a font of an inviting size. Full-page photos–all color except one vintage photograph–with informative captions face two-paragraph text blocks. . . Will make readers feel they have learned something." SLJ

Includes glossary

Other titles in this series are:

Bikes on the move

Boats on the move

Cars on the move

Motorcycles on the move

Trains on the move

Graham, Ian

Aircraft; [by] Ian Graham. Black Rabbit Books 2009 32p il (How machines work) $18.95

Grades: 3 4 5   629.133

1. Airplanes

ISBN 978-1-59920-292-1; 1-59920-292-1

LC 2008002399

This "uses informational drawings, cutaway diagrams, and photos—including some dazzling shots of cockpit control panels. The layout is sufficiently busy to capture interest." Booklist

Hosking, Wayne

Asian kites. Tuttle 2005 63p il (Asian arts & crafts for creative kids) $12.95

Grades: 3 4 5 6   629.133

1. Kites 2. Handicraft

ISBN 0-8048-3545-4

"This survey offers brief anecdotes and legends along with carefully annotated construction diagrams for 15 simple kites commonly flown in Asia. . . . Closing with notes on running a kite-making workshop for children, lists of associations and sources of supplies, and a relatively extensive bibliography, this title merits, and will find, a wide audience in libraries large or small." SLJ

Macaulay, David

Jet plane; how it works. David Macaulay with Sheila Keenan. 1st ed. David Macaulay Studio 2012 28 p. col. ill. (My readers) (hardcover) $15.99; (paperback) $3.99

Grades: 2 3 4   629.133

1. Jet planes 2. Picture books for children

ISBN 1596437642; 1596437677; 9781596437647; 9781596437678

LC 2012289085

This book is part of David Macaulay's The Way Things Work series. This installment looks at the jet plane. "It weighs as much as 100 elephants, but it can fly for hours. How does a jet do that? From the engine that provides the power and wings that lift the plane off the ground to the cockpit controls and passenger cabin, see how these modern marvels work and what makes them stay in the air." (Publisher's note)

Includes bibliographical references and index

Nahum, Andrew

Flying machine; written by Andrew Nahum. rev ed; DK Pub. 2004 72p il (DK eyewitness books) $15.99; lib bdg $19.99

Grades: 4 5 6 7   629.133

1. Aeronautics -- History

ISBN 0-7566-0680-2; 0-7566-0679-9 lib bdg

First published 1990 by Knopf

A photo essay tracing the history and development of aircraft from hot-air balloons to jetliners. Includes information on the principles of flight and the inner workings of various flying machines.

Rau, Dana Meachen

Hot air balloons. Marshall Cavendish Benchmark 2010 24p il (Surprising science) lib bdg $22.79

Grades: 2 3 4   629.133

1. Balloons 2. Air-cushion vehicles

ISBN 978-0-7614-4873-0; 0-7614-4873-X

"Colorfully illustrated with photographs on each page, this . . . will be well received by elementary students and educators." Libr Media Connect

Includes glossary and bibliographical references

White, Rowland

Cleared for takeoff; The Ultimate Book of Flight. by Rowland White. Chronicle Books 2016 320 p. color ill., color maps (ebook) $22.09; (hardcover) $21.99

Grades: 4 5 6 7 8   629.133

1. Aeronautics -- History 2. Flying-machines -- History

ISBN 9781452143484; 9781452135502

LC 2014044858

This book on flight for young readers, by Rowland White, is "packed with stories of heroic and innovative pioneers, fascinating profiles of remarkable planes from Spitfires to space shuttles, and how-to instructions for making everything from origami helicopters to bottle rockets—all accompanied by sensational photographs, illustrations, and diagrams." (Publisher's note)

"For anybody with an interest in aviation, this will prove a fascinating resource for browsing. Wings up!" Kirkus

629.2   Motor land vehicles, cycles

Cooper, Wade

On the road. Cartwheel Books 2008 30p il (Scholastic reader) pa $3.99

Grades: PreK K 1   629.2

1. Vehicles

ISBN 978-0-545-00720-7 pa; 0-545-00720-8 pa

"Vehicles—from lumbering tractors and cement mixers to sleek sports cars—roll across the pages of this Level One entry in the Scholastic Reader series. Each spread combines a large, crisp color photo of a vehicle, with a banner of smaller photos. The rhyming sentences are well tuned for brand-new readers." Booklist

Includes glossary

Mara, Wil

From locusts to...automobile anti-collision systems; by Wil Mara. Cherry Lake Pub. 2012 32 p. col. ill. (Innovations from nature) (library) $28.50; (e-book) $28.50; (paperback) $14.21

Grades: 4 5 6 7   629.2

1. Biomimicry 2. Automobiles -- Collision avoidance systems 3. Locusts

ISBN 1610805011; 9781610805018; 9781610805889; 9781610806756

LC 2012011856

"This . . . entry in the '21st Century Skills Innovation Library: Innovations from Nature' series explores how automobile manufacturers and scientists are trying to develop . . . collision avoidance systems based on the instincts of the humble locust, which has the ability to avoid oncoming objects while in a swarm. . . . [Wil] Mara describes the science of biomimicry, or 'the practice of copying nature--plants and animals--to build or improve something.'" (Booklist)

Includes bibliographical references (p. 31) and index

Smith, Miranda

Speed machines; and other record-breaking vehicles. Kingfisher 2009 63p il (Kingfisher knowledge) $12.95

Grades: 5 6 7 8 **629.2**

1. Speed 2. Vehicles

ISBN 978-0-7534-6287-4; 0-7534-6287-7

"This well-organized, full-color book is packed with facts, photos, and history. It covers all aspects in history dealing with humankind's quest for speed, including land, water and air. . . . There are short blocks of main text and sidebars or blurbs to add additional information. Besides the usual suspects in books that cover this topic—cars, motorcycles, and planes—this book includes boats, gliders, hot air balloons, trains, and windsurfing among other speed machines. . . . It is an essential purchase, especially where books about racing, cars, planes, trucks, motorcycles, etc. are popular." Voice Youth Advocates

629.222 Gasoline-powered, oil-powered, man-powered vehicles

Juettner, Bonnie

Hybrid cars; by Bonnie Juettner. Norwood House Press 2009 48p il (A great idea) lib bdg $25.27

Grades: 3 4 5 6 **629.222**

1. Electric automobiles

ISBN 978-1-59953-193-9 lib bdg; 1-59953-193-3 lib bdg

LC 2008-22970

"Full-color photographs and copious fun facts help make this . . . enjoyable reading, but it's really the choice of [topic] that is so enthralling." Booklist

Includes glossary and bibliographical references

Niver, Heather Moore

Camaros. Gareth Stevens Pub. 2011 32p il (Wild wheels) lib bdg $26.60; pa $10.50

Grades: 3 4 5 6 **629.222**

1. Automobiles

ISBN 978-1-4339-4735-3 lib bdg; 1-4339-4735-8 lib bdg; 978-1-4339-4736-0 pa; 1-4339-4736-6 pa

LC 2010032883

This book about Camaro automobiles "is sure to be . . . popular. . . . The light, somewhat breezy [text moves] quickly, presenting the history of the cars and just the right amount of information. . . . The bright, colorful illustrations are excellent. . . . A first purchase." SLJ

Includes glossary and bibliographical references

Other titles in this series are:

GTOs

Chargers

Chevelles

Mustangs

Torinos

Steggall, Susan

The **life** of a car. Henry Holt & Co. 2008 un il $16.95

Grades: PreK K 1 2 **629.222**

1. Automobiles

ISBN 0-8050-8747-8

"With torn-paper collages in saturated color and just three words for every spread except the last, Steggall presents the life cycle of a car from its manufacture to its destruction and recycling, when the process begins anew." SLJ

Swanson, Jennifer

★ **How** hybrid cars work; illustrated by Glen Mullaly. Child's World 2011 il (How things work) lib bdg $28.50

Grades: 4 5 6 **629.222**

1. Electric automobiles

ISBN 1-60973-217-0; 978-1-60973-217-2

LC 2011010917

This volume "is bouncy, savvy, and, above all, clear; it is hard to come away without a working knowledge of everything from the mechanics of hybrid engines to why dependence on foreign oil is bad. Hosting the series are two cartoons—a robot and a caveman—especially apt choices for a book couched in the concept of discarding old energy sources for new. . . . This is a model of how to make science appeal to young readers." Booklist

Includes bibliographical references

Warhol, Tom

Aptera. Marshall Cavendish Benchmark 2010 47p il (Green cars) $28.50

Grades: 3 4 5 6 **629.222**

1. Electric automobiles

ISBN 978-1-60870-008-0; 1-60870-008-9

"The futuristic Aptera appeared in a 'Star Trek' film. . . . [The] book opens with [an] . . . introduction explaining how global warming and limited oil availability are among the factors reshaping automobile design and technology. The [book provides a] clear [explanation] of how hybrid and all-electrical vehicles operate. . . . Color photos in various sizes add visual appeal." SLJ

Includes glossary and bibliographical references

Other titles in this series are:

Ebox

Prius

Volt

Wheeler, Jill C.

Alternative cars; [by] Jill C. Wheeler. ABDO 2008 32p il (Eye on energy) $16.95

Grades: 3 4 5 **629.222**

1. Alternative fuel vehicles

ISBN 978-1-59928-803-1; 1-59928-803-6

LC 2007007107

This "begins with an explantion of the internal-combustion engine and its shortcomings. Wheeler then introduces readers to more efficient methods of powering automobiles, including electricity, a combination of gas and electricty, diesel fuel, hydrogen, natural gas, and ethanol. For each alternative she describes advantages, disadvantages, and the current availability of this technology. Captioned, full-color photographs . . . appear on nearly every page, complementing the clearly written text." Booklist

Includes glossary

Williams, Brian

Who invented the automobile? Arcturus Pub. 2010 46p il (Breakthroughs in science and technology) lib bdg $32.80

Grades: 5 6 7 8 **629.222**

1. Engines 2. Automobiles

ISBN 978-1-84837-681-6; 1-84837-681-2

LC 2010011019

Examines the history of the automobile.

This book is "divided into easy to read short chapters with large, colorful photographs and graphics on every page. . . . The added inserts provide additional information to engage readers and help them connect with the scientific details." Libr Media Connect

629.224   Trucks (Lorries)

Farndon, John

  Megafast Trucks; John Farndon; illustrated by Mat Edwards and Jeremy Pyke. Lerner Pub Group 2016 32 p. $7.99

Grades: 3 4 5 6   **629.224**

  1. Speed 2. Trucks

  ISBN 9781467795876; 1467793663; 9781467793667

                            LC 2015031656

  In this children's book, by John Farndon and illustrated by Mat Edwards and Jeremy Pyke, readers can "climb into the cabs of the world's fastest trucks. They may be big, but these machines can really move! Roar off in the three jet engines of the Shockwave powered to 376 mph (605 km/h)! Ride in the Banks Sidewinder Dodge Dakota, which set a world record at 217 mph (349 km/h)! Go off-roading in the fastest off-road terrain conqueror, the Ford F-150 SVT Raptor." (Publisher's note)

  "With considerable panache, Farndon bestows these beasts with their very own brand of beauty." Kirkus

    Another titles in this series is:

    Megafast Motorcycles

Maass, Robert

  Little trucks with big jobs; [by] Robert Maass. Henry Holt & Co. 2007 un il $16.95

Grades: PreK K   **629.224**

  1. Trucks

  ISBN 978-0-8050-7748-3; 0-8050-7748-0

                            LC 2006030617

  "Children are introduced to 15 little rigs and the important work they do. Simple, clear explanations accompany each full-page photograph. . . . Bright, primary colored backgrounds frame the pictures, and the text appears inside road-sign shapes. This high-interest book is sure to be popular with vehicle fans." SLJ

Mara, Wil

  Trucks. National Geographic 2009 32p il (National Geographic readers) $12.99; pa $3.99

Grades: K 1 2   **629.224**

  1. Trucks

  ISBN 978-1-4263-0527-6; 1-4263-0527-3; 978-1-4263-0526-9 pa; 1-4263-0526-5 pa

                            LC 2009-21037

  "Mara describes truck parts and their functions in brief, simple text for early readers. Colorful close-up photographs dominate each spread, often using arrows to point to and clarify labeled parts." Horn Book Guide

Murrell, Deborah Jane

  Mega trucks. Tangerine Press 2008 32p il $6.99

Grades: PreK K 1 2   **629.224**

  1. Trucks

  ISBN 0-439-85056-8

  First published in 2005 by Scholastic

  "Discusses the parts and functions of different kinds of trucks, including tractor-trailers, loaders, and monster trucks." Publisher's note

See how they work & look inside big rigs; edited by Johannah Gilman Paiva and Ashley Rideout; illustrated by Simon Tegg and Graham White. Flowerpot Press 2015 32 p. color illustrations $7.99

Grades: K 1 2 3   **629.224**

  1. Trucks 2. Construction equipment

  ISBN 1486708048; 9781486708048

                            LC 2015052327

  This book in the World of Wonder series, edited by Johannah Gilman Paiva and Ashley Rideout, and illustrated by Simon Tegg and Graham White, invites readers to "take a Look Inside Machines to learn what makes your favorite machines tick! . . . Now dive into Big Rigs to see all the incredible things machines can do, from lifting heavy materials on construction sites to transporting heavy loads on long journeys, and learn just how cool big rigs are!" (Publisher's note)

  "Technical language (suspension, axle seal, fifth wheel skid plate) mixes smoothly with accessible descriptors to engage a broad range of readers." Booklist

Stille, Darlene R.

  Trucks. Children's Press 1997 47p il (True book) lib bdg $22; pa $6.95

Grades: 2 3 4   **629.224**

  1. Trucks

  ISBN 0-516-20343-6 lib bdg; 0-516-26179-7 pa

                            LC 96-25727

  Describes different kinds of trucks, including tractor trailers and tank trucks, pick-ups, tow trucks, fire trucks, garbage trucks, vans, and recreational vehicles

  Includes bibliographical references

629.225   Work vehicles

See How They Work & Look Inside Diggers; Big Rigs, Fire Trucks, Diggers, Farm Equipment. illustrated by Simon Tegg and Ross Watton. Flowerpot Press 2015 32 p. color illustrations $7.99

Grades: 2 3 4 5 6   **629.225**

  1. Construction equipment

  ISBN 1486708064; 9781486708062

  This book, "will teach you a load about your favorite machines that you never knew before. Now dive into Diggers to see all the incredible things machines can do, from digging up rocks on construction sites to boring huge tunnels, and learn just how cool diggers are!" (Publisher's note)

629.227   Cycles

Lakin, Patricia

  Bicycles; Patricia Lakin. Aladdin 2017 32 p. color illustrations (Made by hand) (hardback) $17.99

Grades: 3 4 5 6 7   **629.227**

  1. Bicycles 2. Bicycles -- Design and construction

  ISBN 9781481478960; 9781481478977

                            LC 2016034643

  With this book, by Patricia Lakin, "go behind the scenes and learn how craftsman Aaron Dykstra makes one-of-a-kind bicycles by hand. . . . Aaron Dykstra of Six-Eleven Bicycles in Roanoke, Virginia, got his first job at a small local bike shop when he was fifteen and he spent the majority of his teen years riding and racing bikes. After a stint in the air force, Aaron realized his true passion was on land: making these beautiful machines." (Publisher's note)

  "A must-have for school and public libraries in need of materials to support STEM curricula and maker spaces." School Library Journal.

  Includes bibliographical references.

Gibbons, Gail

  Bicycle book. Holiday House 1995 un il $16.95; pa $6.95

Grades: K 1 2 3 **629.227**
1. Cycling 2. Bicycles
ISBN 0-8234-1199-0; 0-8234-1408-6 pa

LC 95-5911

"The history of bicycles, the science behind their design, descriptions of different types, their care, and safety rules are all clearly and simply presented in Gibbons's typical, inimitable style. Lots of color, accurate explanations, and interesting facts make this a winning choice." SLJ

Haduch, Bill
★ **Go** fly a bike! the ultimate book about bicycle fun, freedom & science. illustrated by Chris Murphy. Dutton Children's Books 2004 83p il $16.99
Grades: 4 5 6 7 **629.227**
1. Cycling 2. Bicycles
ISBN 0-525-47024-7

Gives the history, science, types of cycles, safety and the basics and maintenance of bicycles

"Halftone cartoonlike illustrations are scattered throughout, and a funny fact or joke appears in an inset on most pages. . . . This is a versatile, fact-packed book that can work for both research and recreational reading." Booklist

Smedman, Lisa
From boneshakers to choppers; the rip-roaring history of motorcycles. Annick Press 2007 120p il $24.95; pa $14.95
Grades: 5 6 7 8 **629.227**
1. Motorcycles
ISBN 978-1-55451-016-0; 1-55451-016-3; 978-1-55451-015-3 pa; 1-55451-015-5 pa

"Smedman defines 'motorcycles' broadly enough to include everything from Harleys to Vespas, and even bicycles, in this lively, wide-ranging history. . . . Illustrated with a generous array of action photos, historical shots, and period advertisements." Booklist

Includes bibliographical references

629.228 Racing cars

Bodensteiner, Peter
Formula 1 cars; Peter Bodensteiner. Black Rabbit Books 2017 32 p. (library binding) $31.35
Grades: 3 4 5 **629.228**
1. Automobile racing
ISBN 1680720295; 9781680720297; 9781680720716

LC 2015954673

In this book, by Peter Bodensteiner, "through engaging text and dynamic infographics, charts, timelines, photos and levelling control this high interest title describes the history, features, and future of Formula 1 cars." (Publisher's note)

"Supplementing informational text such as this are sidebars, time lines, and charts that lend visual interest and bite-sized facts, while the use of blues, oranges, and yellows throughout give each volume a comic book vibe. What really stands out are the vibrant photos of the various cars and motorcycles." SLJ

Rex, Michael
My race car. Holt & Co. 2000 un il lib bdg $15.95
Grades: PreK K 1 **629.228**
1. Automobiles 2. Automobile racing
ISBN 0-8050-6101-0

LC 99-31773

"'I have a race car. I drive it all the time,' says a boy sitting on the floor with his toy cars. As the pages turn, the toy world becomes reality: the boy finds himself on the track with his crew, checking his car engine, and then driving his laps. . . . Short, simple sentences create excitement . . . and Rex's bright, thick-lined cartoon drawings are appealingly energetic and clear. A great choice for young race car enthusiasts who are beginning to read on their own." Booklist

Sandler, Michael
Dynamic drag racers. Bearport Pub. 2011 24p il (Fast rides) lib bdg $22.61
Grades: 3 4 5 6 **629.228**
1. Automobiles 2. Automobile racing
ISBN 978-1-61772-138-0; 1-61772-138-7

LC 2010041872

This describes different types of vehicles used in drag races including top fuel dragsters, pro stock motorcycles, funny cars, and exhibition wheelstanders.

"Sharp, colorful photos and [a] succinct [text provides a] brief but informative [introduction] to record-setting vehicles. . . . This [book] deserves first consideration." SLJ

Includes glossary and bibliographical references
Other titles in this series are:
Electrifying eco-race cars
Hot hot rods
Jet-powered speed

629.4 Astronautics

Aldrin, Buzz
Look to the stars. G. P. Putnam's Sons 2009 40p il $17.99
Grades: 2 3 4 **629.4**
1. Astronautics 2. Space flight 3. Outer space
ISBN 978-0-399-24721-7; 0-399-24721-1

LC 2008018575

This is "a quick overview of the past and near future of human space flight. Paired with Minor's clean-lined, realistically detailed scenes of significant aircraft, spacecraft, and high spots, [the] narrative opens with Galileo, [and] closes with the rousing suggestion that the opportunity to venture into space lies just a tantalizing few years down the road for many young readers." SLJ

Bortz, Alfred B.
Seven wonders of space technology; by Fred Bortz. Twenty-First Century Books 2011 80p il (Seven wonders) lib bdg $33.26; ebook $24.95
Grades: 5 6 7 8 **629.4**
1. Astronautics 2. Space vehicles 3. Outer space -- Exploration
ISBN 978-0-7613-5453-6 lib bdg; 0-7613-5453-0 lib bdg; 9780761372806

LC 2010-23996

This book examines the science involved in the Great Observatories, the International Space Station, New Horizons, Moon bases and lunar water, Mars rovers, rocketry, and weather satellites. Glossary. Index. "Grades seven to twelve." (Sci Books Films)

"Highlights some of astronomy's greatest technical advancements, from land observatories to spinning satellites to moon bases. . . . [This] volume makes basic concepts clear in lively, energetic language that, along with the mesmerizing color photos and artists' renderings of space, will easily captivate a young audience, while up-to-date examples, including discoveries made in the last five years, will only increase the sense of immediacy and excitement." Booklist

Includes glossary and bibliographical references

Houran, Lori Haskins

A **trip** into space; An Adventure to the International Space Station. Lori Haskins Houran; illustrated by Francisca Marquez. Albert Whitman & Company 2014 24 p. $15.99

Grades: PreK K 1   **629.4**

1. Astronauts 2. Space flight 3. International Space Station

ISBN 0807580910; 9780807580912

LC 2013033073

This children's book, by Lori Haskins Houran, is a "look at life on the International Space Station. . . . It features . . . full-bleed illustrations," by Francisca Marquez, "of astronauts loading supplies, taking a space walk, eating, sleeping, etc." (School Library Journal)

"Although scientifically slight, this book adeptly captures some of the key personal experiences of astronauts on the International Space Station, from blastoff to zipping themselves into stationary sleeping bags at bedtime. Understated verse is illustrated with approachable illustrations that reinforce such details as straps to hold down food. Additional information on each rhymed heading ("Whipping through space"; "Flipping in space") is appended." Horn Book Guide Review

Jones, Tom

Ask the astronaut; a galaxy of astonishing answers to your questions on spaceflight. Tom Jones. Smithsonian Books 2016 224 p. illustrations $12.95

Grades: 5 6 7 8   **629.4**

1. Astronauts 2. Space flight 3. Children's questions and answers 4. Astronautics 5. Outer space -- Exploration 6 Space flight -- Physiological effect

ISBN 1588345378; 9781588345370

LC 2015037850

In this book author Tom Jones "answers every question you have ever had about space. His . . . blend of wit, personal experience, and technical expertise shines in each answer, and together all the answers illuminate the true space experience from start to finish. His engaging and informative responses remind readers of historic space achievements, acquaint them with exciting new ambitions, [and] make them feel like they have experienced space firsthand." (Publisher's note)

Includes bibliographical references

Skurzynski, Gloria

★ **This** is rocket science; true stories of the risk-taking scientists who figure out ways to explore beyond Earth. National Geographic 2010 80p il $18.95; lib bdg $28.90

Grades: 5 6 7 8   **629.4**

1. Rocketry 2. Aeronautics 3. Aerospace engineers

ISBN 978-1-4263-0597-9; 1-4263-0597-4; 978-1-4263-0598-6 lib bdg; 1-4263-0598-2 lib bdg

LC 2009-20386

"This concise book provides a historical, as well as contemporary, introduction to the field of aeronautical engineering with a decidedly human interest perspective. . . . This text will be a great introduction to many of the significant contributors to the field of rocket science." Sci Books Films

Includes glossary and bibliographical references

Stott, Carole

Space exploration; written by Carole Stott; photographed by Steve Gorton. Dorling Kindersley 2009 71p il (DK eyewitness books) $16.99

Grades: 4 5 6 7   **629.4**

1. Astronautics 2. Outer space -- Exploration

ISBN 978-0-7566-5828-1; 0-7566-5828-4

First published 1997 by Knopf

Describes rockets, exploratory vehicles, and other technological aspects of space exploration, satellites, space stations, and the life and work of astronauts.

629.43   Unmanned space flight

Carson, Mary Kay

Mission to Pluto; The First Visit to an Ice Dwarf and the Kuiper Belt. Mary Kay Carson; with photographs by Tom Uhlman. Houghton Mifflin Harcourt 2016 73 p. illustrations (chiefly color) $18.99; (ebook) $18.99

Grades: 5 6 7 8   **629.43**

1. Pluto (Dwarf planet) 2. Kuiper Belt 3. Space flight 4. Interplanetary voyages 5. New Horizons (Spacecraft) 6. Outer space -- Exploration

ISBN 9780544416710; 9780544868106

LC 2015037656

This book, by Mary Kay Carson, with photos by Tom Uhlman, "goes where no person or spacecraft has ever gone before. Follow along with the team of scientists as they build New Horizons, fly it across the solar system, and make new discoveries about a world three billion miles away." (Publisher's note)

"This enthusiastic, accessible look at both cutting-edge scientific discovery and the dynamic work behind the scenes will be an easy sell to space-mad kids and a valuable addition to any school library." Booklist

Includes bibliographical references (page 72) and index.

Jefferis, David

Space probes; exploring beyond Earth. Crabtree Pub. 2009 32p il (Exploring our solar system) lib bdg $26.60; pa $8.95

Grades: 3 4 5   **629.43**

1. Space probes

ISBN 978-0-7787-3724-7 lib bdg; 0-7787-3724-1 lib bdg; 978-0-7787-3741-4 pa; 0-7787-3741-1 pa

LC 2008-46249

"The author explains what space probes are for, names many that have visited each of the major planets, and then suggests where models and mock-ups (since they can't be observed directly) might be found. . . . [The book is] designed with easily digestible blocks of question-and-answer text sharing page space with large, sharply reproduced space photos and graphic art." SLJ

Includes glossary

Spilsbury, Richard, 1963-

Robots in space; Richard and Louise Spilsbury. Gareth Stevens Publishing 2016 48 p. color illustrations $31.95

Grades: 4 5 6 7   **629.43**

1. Robots 2. Outer space

ISBN 1482430142; 9781482430141

LC 2014415767

In this book, by Richard and Louise Spilsbury, part of the Amazing Robots series, "readers learn all about these incredible robots as well as other space technology including robotnauts, or robot astronauts! Examples of the robots used in space are shown in full-color photographs, complete with explanations of their abilities. The main content and sidebars delve into the technological and scientific side of creating robots and how important theyve become to space exploration." (Publisher's note)

"The full-color photos of robots in action and the high-interest nature of robotics may catch the interest of science-minded kids." Booklist

Siy, Alexandra

★ **Cars** on Mars; roving the red planet. Charlesbridge 2009 57p il $18.95

Grades: 5 6 7 8   **629.43**

1. Space vehicles 2. Mars (Planet) -- Exploration

ISBN 978-1-57091-462-1; 1-57091-462-1

LC 2008-40751

Presents an introduction to the Mars Exploration Rovers (MERS), 'Spirit' and 'Opportunity,' with photographs of the Mars landscape taken over a five-year period as the rovers searched for water on the red planet

"This title will sweep readers up in an exploratory mission that has come closer than any other so far to finding sure signs of extraterrestrial life." SLJ

Includes glossary and bibliographical references

629.44 Auxiliary spacecraft

Holden, Henry M.

The **coolest** job in the universe; working aboard the International Space Station. Henry M. Holden. Enslow 2013 48 p. (American space missions, astronauts, exploration, and discovery) (hbk.) $23.93

Grades: 4 5 6 7 8   **629.44**

1. International Space Station 2. Space flight 3. Manned space flight 4. Space sciences -- Research

ISBN 0766040747; 9780766040748

LC 2012002222

This book, by Henry M. Holden, is part of the "American Space Missions: Astronauts, Exploration, and Discovery" series. In it the daily life of astronauts working on the International Space Station is explored. This book "focuses on the construction of the ISS, what life is like onboard, and the importance of the research projects conducted.... Throughout, the courage, dedication, and sacrifice of the astronauts are emphasized." (School Library Journal)

Includes bibliographical references (p. 43-45, 47) and index

Waxman, Laura Hamilton

Exploring the International Space Station. Lerner Publications 2011 40p il (What's amazing about space?) lib bdg $27.23

Grades: 4 5 6   **629.44**

1. Astronautics 2. Space stations

ISBN 978-0-7613-5443-7; 0-7613-5443-3

LC 2010035394

This describes how the International Space Station was built and how crew members live and work there.

This book is "written in simple language, [and] illustrated nicely.... The information presented is factually correct.... Every page includes a well-chosen illustration or photograph." Sci Books Films

Includes glossary and bibliographical references

629.45 Manned space flight

Bodden, Valerie

To the moon; by Valerie Bodden. Creative Education 2011 48 p. col. ill. (Great expeditions) (paperback) $12.00; (hardcover) $34.25

Grades: 5 6 7 8   **629.45**

1. Apollo project 2. Space flight to the moon -- History 3. Project Apollo (U.S.) -- History

ISBN 1608180689; 9780898126662; 9781608180684

LC 2010033549

This book by Valerie Bodden on the 1969 moon landing is part of the "Great Expeditions" series. "This factual account is ... accompanied

with both black and white and color photographs. Profiles of four of the astronauts, reproductions of some of their significant journal entries, and inset boxes of supplemental information aid in understanding. Includes a table of contents, a timeline, end notes, a bibliography, and an index." (Children's Literature)

Includes bibliographical references (p. 46-47) and index.

Branley, Franklyn Mansfield

Mission to Mars; by Franklyn M. Branley; illustrated by True Kelley; foreword by Neil Armstrong. HarperCollins Pubs. 2002 33p il (Let's-read-and-find-out science) hardcover o.p. lib bdg $17.89; pa $4.99

Grades: K 1 2 3   **629.45**

1. Space flight to Mars 2. Mars (Planet) -- Exploration

ISBN 0-06-029807-3; 0-06-029808-1 lib bdg; 0-06-445233-6 pa

LC 00-54036

The author invites readers to envision "themselves as members of the first Mars Mission's crew.... Along with a sprinkling of black-and-white and full-color photos, the illustrations mix clearly drawn schematics with scenes of crew members working busily inside the Mars Station or outside in heavy protective suits. An informative, inspirational introduction." SLJ

Burleigh, Robert

★ **One** giant leap; paintings by Mike Wimmer. Philomel Books 2009 un il $16.99

Grades: 1 2 3   **629.45**

1. Astronautics 2. Apollo project 3. Space flight to the moon 4. Project Apollo (U.S.) -- History

ISBN 978-0-399-23883-3; 0-399-23883-2

LC 2008-15695

"Distinguished language and compelling imagery make this commemoration of the first Moon landing's 40th anniversary particularly intense.... The sense of immediacy is irresistible." SLJ

Chaikin, Andrew

★ **Mission** control, this is Apollo; the story of the first voyages to the moon. [by] Andrew Chaikin, with Victoria Kohl; [with paintings by] Alan Bean. Penguin Group 2009 114p il $23.99

Grades: 5 6 7 8 9   **629.45**

1. Astronautics 2. Space flight to the moon 3. Project Apollo

ISBN 978-0-670-01156-8; 0-670-01156-8

LC 2009000833

"Based on interviews with 28 astronauts, this history of the Apollo program masterfully describes the missions and personalizes them with astronauts' own words. Chaikin starts with a brief overview of its origins and of the Mercury and Gemini missions. He then highlights the significance of each manned Apollo mission in chronological chapters, with full-page sidebars on such topics as food, TV coverage, space sickness and going to the bathroom in space. The handsome design has many photographs, diagrams of the rockets and modules and more than 30 well-reproduced paintings by Apollo 12 astronaut Bean." Kirkus

Includes bibliographical references

Dyer, Alan

Mission to the moon. Simon & Schuster Books for Young Readers 2009 80p il $19.99

Grades: 5 6 7 8   **629.45**

1. Space flight to the moon 2. Project Apollo 3. Moon -- Exploration

ISBN 978-1-4169-7935-7; 1-4169-7935-2

LC 2008-61118

"Sporting a highly visual encyclopedic format, this informative book features 200 photographs documenting early research into mankind's history with the moon, early space exploration and the space race, and the Apollo missions. Detailed cross-sections of modules, space suits and other equipment offer a sound technological overview, while information on the phases, structure and surface of the moon provides added insight. . . . A DVD and poster are included." Publ Wkly

Dyson, Marianne J.

Home on the moon; living on a space frontier. National Geographic Soc. 2003 64p il $18.95

Grades: 4 5 6 7   **629.45**

1. Moon

ISBN 0-7922-7193-9

LC 2002-5280

Considers the moon as a frontier that has been only partially explored, looking at its history, geography, and weather, as well as what people would require to live and work there. Includes activities

"Clear writing, vivid images, interesting details, and quotes from astronauts and scientists make this a lively, fact-filled introduction." Booklist

Includes glossary and bibliographical references

Floca, Brian

★ Moonshot; the flight of Apollo 11. written and illustrated by Brian Floca. Atheneum Books for Young Readers 2008 un il $17.99

Grades: K 1 2 3   **629.45**

1. Astronautics 2. Space flight to the moon 3. Apollo 11 (Spacecraft) 4. Project Apollo

ISBN 1-4169-5046-X; 978-1-4169-5046-2

LC 2007-52358

ALA ALSC Sibert Medal Honor Book (2010)

This is the story of the 1969 Apollo 11 mission to the Moon. (Bull Cent Child Books)

"Forty years after NASA's Apollo 11 mission first landed astronauts on the moon, this striking nonfiction picture book takes young readers along for the ride. . . . Written with quiet dignity and a minimum of fuss, the main text is beautifully illustrated with line-and-wash artwork that provides human interest, technological details, and some visually stunning scenes." Booklist

Goodman, Susan E.

How do you burp in space? and other tips every space tourist needs to know. by Susan Goodman; illustrated by Michael Slack. Bloomsbury Pub. Distributed by Macmillan Publishers 2013 80 p. (hardback) $16.99

Grades: 4 5 6   **629.45**

1. Space flight 2. Interplanetary voyages 3. Space tourism 4. Manned space flight

ISBN 1599900688; 9781599900681; 9781599909349

LC 2011035303

In this children's book, author Susan E. Goodman "gives readers who will be the first generation of true space tourists general advice about how to prepare for the trip, what to pack, what food and accommodations will be like, and recreational opportunities both in Earth's orbit and on the moon. She also highlights some hazards, such as drinking carbonated drinks: Burping in microgravity brings up more than just CO2." (Kirkus Reviews)

Green, Carl R.

Spacewalk; the astounding Gemini 4 mission. Carl R. Green. Enslow Publishers 2013 48 p. $23.93

Grades: 4 5 6 7 8   **629.45**

1. Gemini project 2. Outer space 3. Space flight 4. Project Gemini (U.S.) -- History

ISBN 0766040755; 9780766040755

LC 2011030869

This children's book, by Carl R. Green, "explores the astounding GEMINI 4 mission. . . . Pilot Ed White could see Hawaii, California, Texas, and Florida . . . while walking in space! . . . The first American spacewalk was a monumental achievement, and it helped push the space program toward its ultimate goal of landing men on the Moon." (Publisher's note)

Includes bibliographical references and index

Hartman, Eve

Mission to Mars; [by] Eve Hartman and Wendy Meshbesher. Raintree 2010 56p il lib bdg $33.50; pa $9.49

Grades: 5 6 7 8   **629.45**

1. Space flight to Mars 2. Mars (Planet)

ISBN 9781-4109-3821-3 lib bdg; 1-4109-3821-2 lib bdg; 978-1-4109-3996-8 pa; 1-4109-3996-0 pa

LC 2009-53209

""Will human beings ever explore Mars? Can it be colonized? Find out in this fascinating book on Martian exploration." (Publisher's note)

"Excellent black-and-white and color photos throughout are matched perfectly to the texts and well captioned. Good choices for reports and debates." SLJ

Hense, Mary

How astronauts use math; math curriculum consultant: Rhea A. Stewart. Chelsea Clubhouse 2010 32p il (Math in the real world) lib bdg $28

Grades: 4 5 6   **629.45**

1. Astronauts 2. Mathematics 3. Astronautics 4. Vocational guidance

ISBN 978-1-60413-610-4 lib bdg; 1-60413-610-3 lib bdg

LC 2009-23926

This describes how astronauts use math for such tasks as calculating distance, speed, and velocity, and includes relevant math problems and information about how to become an astronaut

Includes glossary and bibliographical references

Holden, Henry M.

Danger in space; surviving the Apollo 13 disaster. Henry M. Holden. Enslow Publishers 2013 48 p. $23.93

Grades: 4 5 6 7 8   **629.45**

1. Apollo project 2. Picture books for children 3. Apollo 13 (Spacecraft) 4. Project Apollo (U.S.) 5. Space vehicle accidents -- United States

ISBN 0766040720; 9780766040724

LC 2011037734

This children's picture book tells the story of the U.S. National Aerospace and Space Administration's Apollo 13 mission. "Soaring through space at twenty-five thousand miles per hour, Apollo 13 was on course for the Moon. Suddenly, the three astronauts aboard the spacecraft heard a loud bang. A strong vibration rumbled through the crew cabin. There had been an explosion in the oxygen tank! More than two hundred thousand miles from Earth, Apollo 13 was in grave danger." (Publisher's note)

Includes bibliographical references and index

McCarthy, Meghan

Astronaut handbook. Alfred A. Knopf 2008 un il $16.99; lib bdg $19.99

Grades: K 1 2 3   **629.45**

1. Astronautics

ISBN 978-0-375-84459-1; 0-375-84459-7; 978-0-375-94459-8 lib bdg; 0-375-94459-1 lib bdg

LC 2007-31951

"Readers follow four aspiring astronauts from classroom to cockpit as they focus, study, practice, and ultimately take off. McCarthy applies a light, comic tone to the subject, reflected in her simple, expressive, cartoony acrylic paintings. . . . McCarthy introduces the paraphernalia of rocket travel with direct humor that understands and respects its audience." Booklist

McNulty, Faith

★ **If** you decide to go to the moon; illustrated by Steven Kellogg. Scholastic Press 2005 un il $16.99

Grades: K 1 2 3   **629.45**

1. Space flight to the moon 2. Moon
ISBN 0-590-48359-5

LC 2004-27755

Boston Globe-Horn Book Award: Nonfiction (2006)

In this "picture book, readers accompany a boy on a fascinating excursion to the moon. The lyrical text provides tips on what to pack and describes the distance to be covered. After blastoff, facts about space travel are mingled with descriptions of what the journey might be like. . . . Rich artwork complements the strong text." SLJ

McReynolds, Linda

Eight days gone; Linda McReynolds; illustrated by Ryan O'Rourke. Charlesbridge 2012 44 p. col. ill. (reinforced for library use) $16.95

Grades: 1 2 3   **629.45**

1. Astronauts 2. Outer space -- Exploration 3. Project Apollo (U.S.) 4. Apollo 11 (Spacecraft) 5. Space flight to the moon
ISBN 1580893643; 9781580893640

LC 2011025776

In this book, Linda McReynolds tells the story of Apollo 11. "Eighteen two-page spreads illustrate the story, and McReynolds tells it in tight four-line verses using identical rhyme schemes. . . . The rocket blasts into space, begins its orbit, and, after a uniform check, the lunar module disconnects and lands safely on the moon." McReynolds looks at astronauts Michael Collins, Neil Armstrong, and Buzz Aldrin. (Kirkus Reviews)

"The bold, punchy text and vivid illustrations combine to make this a great candidate for storytime as well as exciting solo enjoyment." SLJ

O'Brien, Patrick

★ **You** are the first kid on Mars. G.P. Putnam's Sons 2009 un il $16.99

Grades: K 1 2 3   **629.45**

1. Life on other planets 2. Mars (Planet) -- Exploration
ISBN 978-0-399-24634-0; 0-399-24634-7

LC 2008-29486

"This intriguing vision of space exploration should set imaginations soaring." Publ Wkly

Ottaviani, Jim

T-Minus: the race to the moon; [illustrated by] Zander Cannon, Kevin Cannon. Aladdin 2009 124p il $21.99; pa $12.99

Grades: 4 5 6 7 8 9 10 11 12 Adult   **629.45**

1. Graphic novels 2. Apollo project -- Graphic novels 3. Gemini project -- Graphic novels 4. Space flight to the moon -- Graphic novels
ISBN 978-1-4169-8682-9; 1-4169-8682-0; 978-1-4169-4960-2 pa; 1-4169-4960-7 pa

LC 2009-920999

Ottaviani, Zander Cannon, and Kevin Cannon show what happened when the U.S. and the U.S.S.R. started the space race in the 1950s, and how it progressed to the NASA Apollo 11 mission which landed two men on the moon in July of 1969.

"Organized as a countdown, making the outcome seem inevitable, the frequent, prominent sidebars list a type of rocket, the duration of its flight, and whether the mission was a success or a failure. There are more than 30 attempts chronicled, and the shift between Soviet and U.S. successes creates an interesting balance in the narrative. . . . Ottaviani is particular with facts and eager to inspire readers with regard to the scientific process." SLJ

Platt, Richard

★ **Moon** landing; a pop-up celebration of Apollo 11. by Richard Platt; paper engineering by David Hawcock. Candlewick Press 2008 un il $29.99

Grades: 4 5 6 7   **629.45**

1. Space flight to the moon 2. Pop-up books 3. Apollo 11 (Spacecraft)
ISBN 978-0-7636-4046-0; 0-7636-4046-8

"This is a handsome, carefully engineered compendium. The text begins with the so-called space race between the United States and the Soviet Union in the 1950s and '60s and then offers brief descriptions of the 17 flights that made up the Apollo program. Here the emphasis is on the famous landing of the Eagle on the Moon in July 1969. The pop-ups and foldout pages on sturdy, shiny paper demonstrate the mechanical aspects of the spacecraft and offer a bold sense of both the rocketry and the trip. Small photographs and drawings surround the larger views." SLJ

Ross, Stewart

Moon : science, history, and mystery. Scholastic 2009 128p il lib bdg $18.99

Grades: 4 5 6   **629.45**

1. Astronautics 2. Space flight to the moon 3. Project Apollo 4. Moon -- Exploration
ISBN 978-0-545-12732-5 lib bdg; 0-545-12732-7 lib bdg

"Jam-packed with information, this colorful oversize volume chronicles the race to land a person on the Moon. Alternating chapters describe Moon mythologies and superstitions, the history of astronomical study, and the efforts involved in launching a lunar expedition. . . . The photographs pop with color and action. . . . The invaluable contribution of Muslim scientists is included. . . . [The book's] multicultural history will expand any collection." SLJ

Includes glossary

Thimmesh, Catherine

★ **Team** moon; how 400,000 people landed Apollo 11 on the moon. Houghton Mifflin Company 2006 80p il $19.95

Grades: 5 6 7 8   **629.45**

1. Space flight to the moon 2. Apollo 11 (Spacecraft)
ISBN 0-618-50757-4

LC 2005-10755

"Thimmesh retraces the course of the space mission that landed an actual man, on the actual Moon. It's an oft-told tale, but the author tells it from the point of view not of astronauts or general observers, but of some of the 17,000 behind-the-scenes workers at Kennedy Space Center, the 7500 Grumman employees who built the lunar module, the 500 designers and seamstresses who actually constructed the space suits, and other low-profile contributors who made the historic flight possible. . . . This dramatic account will mesmerize even readers already familiar with the event. . . . This stirring, authoritative tribute to the collective effort . . . belongs in every collection." SLJ

Includes glossary and bibliographical references

Waxman, Laura Hamilton

Exploring space travel. Lerner Publications Company 2011 40p il (What's amazing about space?) lib bdg $27.93

Grades: 4 5 6   **629.45**
1. Astronautics 2. Space flight
ISBN 978-0-7613-5447-5; 0-7613-5447-6

LC 2010042471

This describes what it's like to be an astronaut in space.

"Readers will come away with new knowledge, such as how scientists observe the behavior of other stars to infer the presence of exoplanets." Booklist

Includes bibliographical references

629.46   Engineering of unmanned spacecraft

Johnson, Rebecca L.
Satellites. Lerner Publications Co. 2006 48p il (Cool science) lib bdg $25.26
Grades: 4 5 6   **629.46**
1. Artificial satellites
ISBN 978-0-8225-2908-8 lib bdg; 0-8225-2908-4 lib bdg

LC 2004-30298

This book has "an attractive, colorful layout that will appeal to readers. Each spread includes captioned, color photographs and/or illustrations; text boxes; and, often, a 'fun fact.' . . . [This] title explains what a satellite is and discusses many aspects of satellites, including how they pertain to television broadcasts, weather forecasting, and locating black holes. Numerous amazing facts are included to pique readers' interest." SLJ

Includes bibliographical references

629.8   Automatic control engineering

Chaffee, Joel
How to build a prize-winning robot. Rosen Central 2011 48p il (Robotics) lib bdg $26.50; pa $11.75
Grades: 5 6 7 8   **629.8**
1. Robots
ISBN 978-1-4488-1238-7 lib bdg; 1-4488-1238-0 lib bdg; 978-1-4488-2252-2 pa; 1-4488-2252-1 pa

LC 2010025748

"Kids who are fascinated with robots will want [this title] available." SLJ

Includes glossary and bibliographical references

Graham, Ian
Robot technology. Smart Apple Media 2012 il (New technology)
Grades: 4 5 6 7   **629.8**
1. Robots
ISBN 1-599-20533-5; 978-1-599-20533-5

LC 2010044240

Describes current robotics technology, including the applications of robots in space, in the military, in industry, and around the house. Discusses the pros and cons of creating fully autonomous robots.

This "offers a fine overview for reports, and its attractive design may also entice middle-grade readers to learn more." Booklist

Mara, Wil
Robotics; from concept to consumer. by Wil Mara. Children's Press, an imprint of Scholastic Inc. 2015 64 p. illustrations (some color) (Calling all innovators: a career for you) (library binding) $30
Grades: 4 5 6   **629.8**
1. Vocational guidance 2. Robots 3. Robotics -- History 4. Robotics -- Vocational guidance 5. Robotics -- Technological

innovations
ISBN 0531205401; 0531212378; 9780531205402; 9780531212370

LC 2014030286

This book, by Wil Mara, part of the "Calling all innovators: a career for you" series, presents an exploration into the history of robotics and offers vocational guidance for youth considering the field. "With this exciting series, readers can get a close look at how people in these careers are helping to build our future. They will also discover how workers have used . . . skills to solve problems and innovate throughout history." (Publisher's note)

Includes bibliographical references and index

Mason, Adrienne
Robots: from everyday to out of this world; written by the editors of Yes mag. Kids Can Press 2008 48p il $16.95; pa $8.95
Grades: 3 4 5 6   **629.8**
1. Robots
ISBN 978-1-55453-203-2; 1-55453-203-5; 978-1-55453-204-9 pa; 1-55453-204-3 pa

This is a history of robots from Leonardo da Vinci's "robot-knight" to those of the present and future. Index. "Ages eight to twelve." (Quill Quire)

This "introduces robots that work (defusing bombs, assembling cars, assisting surgeons, exploring Mars) and play (riding camels, kicking soccer balls). . . . Each section is packed with fascinating information, entertaining cartoon graphics, and numerous full-color photographs. The text is hip and accessible. . . . Well-organized and engaging." Booklist

Includes glossary

Rau, Dana Meachen
Robots. Marshall Cavendish Benchmark 2010 24p il (Surprising science) lib bdg $22.79
Grades: 2 3 4   **629.8**
1. Robots
ISBN 978-0-7614-4871-6; 0-7614-4871-3

LC 2009053764

"Colorfully illustrated with photographs on each page, this . . . will be well received by elementary students and educators." Libr Media Connect

Includes glossary and bibliographical references

Shea, Therese
The **robotics** club; teaming up to build robots. Rosen Central 2011 48p il (Robotics) lib bdg $26.50; pa $11.75
Grades: 5 6 7 8   **629.8**
1. Clubs 2. Robots
ISBN 978-1-4488-1237-0 lib bdg; 1-4488-1237-2 lib bdg; 978-1-4488-2251-5 pa; 1-4488-2251-3 pa

This title "will provide students with the information necessary to form a club and compete at making and using robots. Kids who are fascinated with robots will want [this title] available." SLJ

Spilsbury, Louise
Robots in law enforcement; Richard and Louise Spilsbury. Gareth Stevens Publishing 2016 48 p. color illustrations $31.95
Grades: 4 5 6 7   **629.8**
1. Robotics 2. Industrial robots 3. Police -- Safety measures
ISBN 9781482430066

LC 2014415753

This book in the Amazing Robots series, by Richard and Louise Spilsbury, focuses on how "robotics is already used to protect people in cities all around the United States. . . . Humanoid robots might be rolling around city streets or heading into dangerous situations in place of police officers. From surveillance cameras to bomb disposal, the incredible robots already used in law enforcement will engage and surprise readers." (Publisher's note)

"The full-color photos of robots in action and the high-interest nature of robotics may catch the interest of science-minded kids." Booklist

Includes bibliographical references (page 47) and index.

VanVoorst, Jennifer

Rise of the thinking machines; the science of robots. Compass Point Books 2009 48p il (Headline science) lib bdg $27.93; pa $7.95

Grades: 5 6 7 **629.8**

1. Robots

ISBN 978-0-7565-3377-9 lib bdg; 0-7565-3377-5 lib bdg; 978-0-7565-3518-6 pa; 0-7565-3518-2 pa

LC 2008-05732

"Describes various types of robots and their functions, discusses technological advancements in the field of robotics, and considers the ethical issues surrounding autonomous robots." Publisher's note

Includes glossary and bibliographical references

629.89 Computer control

Gilby, Nancy Benovich

FIRST robotics; by Nancy Benovich Gilby. Cherry Lake Publishing 2016 32 p. color illustrations (lib. bdg.) $29.93

Grades: 4 5 6 7 8 **629.89**

1. Robotics 2. Inventions

ISBN 9781633623781; 9781633624061

LC 2015013323

This juvenile book, by Nancy Benovich Gilby, focuses on robotics. In it "students learn more about this recent innovation through detailed explanations built to foster creativity and critical thinking. Fun, engaging text introduces readers to new ideas and builds on maker-related concepts they may already know." (Publisher's note)

"Though narrowly focused, each title presents enough basic concepts that students shouldn't have much trouble expanding beyond the fundamentals." Booklist

Includes bibliographical references and index

629.892 Robots

Sjonger, Rebecca

Robotics engineering and our automated world; Rebecca Sjonger. Crabtree Publishing Co. 2017 32 p. color illustrations (ebook) $41.40; (reinforced library binding : alk. paper) $27.60

Grades: 5 6 7 8 **629.892**

1. Robotics 2. Technological innovations

ISBN 9781427117861; 0778775372; 9780778775379; 9780778775416

LC 2016027282

In this book, by Rebecca Sjonger, "readers will learn how robotics engineers find new ways for robots to do work that would be dangerous, time-consuming, dull, or impossible for humans to perform. Real-life examples and a design challenge help students understand key concepts related to the engineering design process, and how robotics engineers play a vital role in expanding our knowledge of the universe." (Publisher's note)

"A fascinating and thoughtfully arranged presentation of modern engineering." Booklist

Includes bibliographical references (page 30) and index

Spilsbury, Richard, 1963-

Robots in industry; Richard and Louise Spilsbury. Gareth Stevens Publishing 2016 48 p. color illustrations $31.95

Grades: 4 5 6 7 **629.892**

1. Industrial robots

ISBN 9781482430028

LC 2014415754

In this book in the Amazing Robots series, by Richard and Louise Spilsbury, "readers learn how integral robots have become in many parts of industry, including in production, factories, and in situations dangerous for people. Full-color photographs provide readers with a unique look at a growing branch of science. The main content and sidebars highlight real-life examples of robots at work as well as understandable explanations of their technology." (Publisher's note)

"The full-color photos of robots in action and the high-interest nature of robotics may catch the interest of science-minded kids." Booklist

Robots in medicine; Richard and Louise Spilsbury. Gareth Stevens Publishing 2016 48 p. color illustrations $31.95

Grades: 4 5 6 7 **629.892**

1. Robots

ISBN 148243010X; 9781482430103

LC 2014415763

In this book, by Richard and Louise Spilsbury, part of the Amazing Robots series, "readers are introduced to cutting-edge medical technology with full-color photographs of robots actually used in hospitals and doctors offices today. The main content offers detailed, but understandable, information about the science of these incredible machines. Additionally, readers learn about the integration of these robots into many careers in medicine, technology, and science." (Publisher's note)

"The full-color photos of robots in action and the high-interest nature of robotics may catch the interest of science-minded kids." Booklist

Includes bibliographical references (page 47) and index.

630 Agriculture and related technologies

Apte, Sunita

Eating green. Bearport Pub. 2009 32p il map (Going green) lib bdg $25.27

Grades: 4 5 6 7 **630**

1. Natural foods 2. Sustainable agriculture

ISBN 978-1-59716-965-3 lib bdg; 1-59716-965-X lib bdg

LC 2009-19183

"Color photographs (most full page) and a few diagrams accompany the informative text. . . . Overall, the [book] . . . is user-friendly and covers topics that are not easily found elsewhere." SLJ

Includes glossary and bibliographical references

Bailey, Gerry

Farming for the future. Gareth Stevens Pub. 2011 48p il (Planet SOS) lib bdg $31.95; pa $14.05

Grades: 4 5 6 **630**

1. Agriculture 2. Food supply

ISBN 978-1-4339-4966-1 lib bdg; 1-4339-4966-0 lib bdg; 978-1-4339-4967-8 pa; 1-4339-4967-9 pa

LC 2010032887

This well-designed book presents farming methods "and how they affect human beings. . . . [It] includes a chapter on new types of farms and foods. . . . The many large, colorful photos will engage readers and assist them in understanding the important concepts introduced." SLJ

Includes glossary

Hodge, Deborah

★ **Up** we grow! a year in the life of a small, local farm. written by Deborah Hodge; photographed by Brian Harris. Kids Can Press 2010 32p il $16.95

Grades: PreK K 1 2   630

1. Farm life 2. Agriculture 3. Organic farming

ISBN 978-1-55453-561-3; 1-55453-561-1

This is "a photo-essay about a year on a communal organic farm. Moving chronologically through the seasons, the spreads, illustrated with close-up photographs, follow a small collective of farmers. . . . Filled with sensory descriptions, the rhythmic text gives a strong sense of life on the farm and in the field." Booklist

Watch me grow! a down-to-earth look at growing food in the city. written by Deborah Hodge; photographed by Brian Harris. Kids Can Press 2011 32p il $16.95

Grades: PreK K 1 2   630

1. Gardening 2. Urban agriculture

ISBN 978-1-55453-618-4; 1-55453-618-9

This "explores ways that gardeners are growing food in community gardens, on rooftops, and in backyards. Harris contributes numerous photos of children getting in on the action—watering plants, tilling soil, and enjoying the (literal) fruits of their labor. . . . Direct and informative, this should inspire many kids to test out how green their thumbs are." Publ Wkly

Michelson, Richard

Tuttle's Red Barn; the story of America's oldest family farm. illustrated by Mary Azarian. G.P. Putnam's Sons 2007 un il $17

Grades: K 1 2 3   630

1. Family farms

ISBN 978-0-399-24354-7; 0-399-24354-2

LC 2007-07514

Michelson and Azarian "salute 12 generations of Tuttles from Dover, N.H., operators of the longest continuously running family farm in the country. . . . Each chapter focuses on the male Tuttle who inherits the farm, and that Tuttle, glimpsed in his youth, observes some history. . . . In Azarian's tableau-like woodcuts, styles change while character endures. Her hand-crafted aesthetic enhances the story's warmth and humanity." Publ Wkly

Parker, Steve, 1952-

Food and farming. QEB Pub. 2010 32p il (QEB changes in . . .) lib bdg $28.50

Grades: 3 4 5 6   630

1. Farms 2. Agriculture 3. Food supply

ISBN 978-1-59566-775-5 lib bdg; 1-59566-775-X lib bdg

LC 2008-56069

"The information is presented in brief paragraphs and sidebars. Suggestions for kids to help improve the planet are sprinkled throughout. . . . Students will enjoy this appealing layout and the information can spark further research on the topic. . . . Either digitally or on paper, students could make fantastic presentations using a similar design." Libr Media Connect

Includes glossary

Richardson, Gillian

10 plants that shook the world; Gillian Richardson; illustrated by Kim Rosen. Annick Press 2013 132 p. (hardcover) $24.95

Grades: 4 5 6 7 8   630

1. Plants 2. Agriculture -- History

ISBN 1554514452; 9781554514458

This book, by Gillian Richardson, illustrated by Kim Rosen, profiles ten plants with significant histories. It describes how "countries went to war to control trade centers for pepper . . . , a grass called papyrus became the first effective tool for sharing knowledge through writing . . . , Europeans in the 1600s cut down rainforests to grow sugar, contributing to soil erosion . . . [and] dependence on the potato caused one of the greatest tragedies in history." (Publisher's note)

"With bold, lively caricatures from Rosen throughout, it's an intriguing and well-designed study of the ways plants have helped start wars, cure diseases, and advance technology." Pub Wkly

Rosen, Michael J.

★ **Our** farm; four seasons with five kids on one family's farm. written and photographed by Michael J. Rosen. Darby Creek Pub. 2008 144p il $18.95

Grades: 4 5 6 7 8   630

1. Family life 2. Ohio 3. Farm life -- United States

ISBN 978-1-58196-067-9; 1-58196-067-0

A journal of one year on the Bennett farm in central Ohio. Shows how one family, with the help of relatives and friends, creates a life and livelihood on a 150-acre farm.

"This engaging book is an unsentimental, appreciative look into the world of one farm family." SLJ

Vogel, Julia

Local farms and sustainable foods. Cherry Lake 2010 32p il (Save the planet) lib bdg $27.07

Grades: 3 4 5 6   630

1. Farms 2. Sustainable agriculture

ISBN 978-1-60279-660-7 lib bdg; 1-60279-660-2 lib bdg

LC 2009-38096

Teaches young readers about locally grown fruits and vegetables

"At the beginning of . . . [the] book, readers are given a mission and advised to be alert to the facts provided so that they can successfully answer the questions at the end. . . . Children are made to feel part of the process; suggestions for how they can become involved abound." SLJ

Includes glossary and bibliographical references

Watterson, Carol

The **edible** alphabet; 26 reasons to love the farm. illustrated by Michela Sorrentino. Tricycle Press 2011 un il $16.99; lib bdg $19.99

Grades: K 1 2 3   630

1. Farms 2. Alphabet 3. Farm produce 4. Domestic animals

ISBN 1-58246-421-9; 1-58246-422-7 lib bdg; 978-1-58246-421-3; 978-1-58246-422-0 lib bdg

LC 2010030478

"This informative alphabet book focuses on the importance of agricultural and animal farms. For each letter, Watterson uses bouncy alliteration to introduce her subjects. . . . Sorrentino matches Watterson's friendly prose with lively mixed-media collages that include polka-dotted fowl and cars fashioned from zucchini, while interactive prompts and intriguing facts give readers a lot to much on." Publ Wkly

631.3   Tools, machinery, apparatus, equipment

Peterson, Cris

★ **Fantastic** farm machines; photographs by David R. Lundquist. Boyd Mills Press 2006 un il $17.95

Grades: K 1 2 3   631.3

1. Agricultural machinery

ISBN 1-59078-271-2

LC 2005-33561

"Peterson gives readers an accurate firsthand view of modern, often computerized equipment used on today's farms. Her easy-to-understand text describes both the machines and their functions. . . . The short, informative paragraphs are surrounded by excellent color photographs that extend the text." SLJ

631.37   Power and power machinery

Paiva, Johannah Gilman
  Look Inside Farm Equipment; edited by Johannah Gilman Paiva and Ashley Rideout; illustrated by Simon Tegg and Ross Watton. Flowerpot Press 2015 32 p. color illustrations $7.99
  Grades: K 1 2 3   **631.37**
  1. Tractors 2. Agricultural machinery
  ISBN 148670803X; 9781486708031
                                                                   LC 2015052339
  This book in the World of Wonder series, edited by Johannah Gilman Paiva and Ashley Rideout, and illustrated by Simon Tegg and Ross Watton, invites readers to "take a Look Inside Machines to learn what makes your favorite machines tick! . . . Now dive into Farm Equipment to see all the incredible things machines can do, from plowing the earth to harvesting crops, and learn just how cool farm machines are!" (Publisher's note)
  "Technical language (suspension, axle seal, fifth wheel skid plate) mixes smoothly with accessible descriptors to engage a broad range of readers." Booklist

631.4   Soil science

Bourgeois, Paulette
  The **dirt** on dirt; by Paulette Bourgeois with Kathy Vanderlinden; illustrated by Martha Newbigging. Kids Can Press 2008 48p il $15.95; pa $7.95
  Grades: 3 4 5 6   **631.4**
  1. Soils 2. Soil ecology
  ISBN 978-1-55453-101-1; 1-55453-101-2; 978-1-55453-1028 pa; 1-55453-102-0 pa
  "From dirty toes, fossils, earthworms, and animal burrows to buried treasure, cities, and dog bones, this engaging introduction to soil touches on a wide variety of topics clearly and concisely. 'Fun with Dirt' experiments and activities demonstrate concepts and stimulate imagination. Illustrated with well-captioned photographs and cartoon-style sketches." Booklist

Gardner, Robert
  Super science projects about Earth's soil and water; [by] Robert Gardner; illustrations by Tom Labaff. Enslow Elementary 2007 48p il (Rockin' earth science experiments) $17.95
  Grades: 3 4 5   **631.4**
  1. Soils 2. Water 3. Science projects 4. Science -- Experiments
  ISBN 978-0-7660-2735-0; 0-7660-2735-X
                                                                   LC 2006006680
  This is a "selection of earth-science projects, all focused on soil and water concepts, such as evaporation, the water cycle, and the components of soil. Each experiment is clearly explained in step-by-step instructions, illustrated with Labaff's clean-lined diagrams and formatted on uncluttered pages." Booklist
  Includes glossary and bibliographical references

Graham, Ian
  You wouldn't want to live without dirt; written by Ian Graham; illustrated by Mark Bergin; series created by David Salariya. Franklin Watts, an imprint of Scholastic Inc. 2016 32 p. color ill., color map (library binding) $29.00

Grades: 3 4 5 6   **631.4**
  1. Soils
  ISBN 9780531214886; 9780531224380
                                                                   LC 2015030229
  This book, by Ian Graham, illustrated by Mark Bergin, asks "what if we didn't have any dirt or soil? . . . The ground would look different and many of the plants, trees and animals we know today would disappear. Dirt, and or soil, supplies a surprising variety of raw materials for making things. Learn about the ways dirt and soil have been used by humans over the centuries, from cave paintings to crop farming, and the exciting prospects for dirt and soil we may see in the future." (Publisher's note)
  "The books feature a time line and numerous ancillaries, but the myriad entertaining facts are the real hit. Who wouldn't want to read them?" Booklist

Hall, Pamela
  Dig in! Learn about dirt; illustrated by Jane Yamada. Child's World, Inc. 2010 24p il (Science definitions) lib bdg $22.79
  Grades: PreK K 1 2   **631.4**
  1. Soils
  ISBN 978-1-60253-507-7 lib bdg; 1-60253-507-8 lib bdg
                                                                   LC 2010010974
  This book about soil is "attractive and succinct. . . . Large, eye-catching photos cover the recto of each spread. . . . Varying, jewel-toned accents are used in headings, highlighted glossary terms, and in a sidebar on each spread." SLJ
  Includes glossary

Spilsbury, Richard
  Soil; [by] Richard and Louise Spilsbury. Heinemann Library 2011 32p il (Let's rock) $29; pa $7.99
  Grades: 4 5 6   **631.4**
  1. Soils
  ISBN 978-1-4329-4685-2; 1-4329-4685-4; 978-1-4329-4693-7 pa; 1-4329-4693-5 pa
                                                                   LC 2010022242
  "Enhanced by plenty of photos, digital paintings, and diagrams, [this examination] of [soil treats its topic] in unusual detail. [It] describes distinguishing characteristics, creation, history, . . . and human uses in [a] central [narrative] with additional notes, suggestions for activities during walks outside, and occasional thumbnail biographies of scientists in side boxes. [The] volume ends with a simple activity." SLJ
  Includes bibliographical references

631.5   Cultivation and harvesting

Juettner, Bonnie
  The **seed** vault. Norwood House Press 2009 48p il (A great idea) lib bdg $25.27
  Grades: 3 4 5 6   **631.5**
  1. Seeds 2. Endangered species 3. Biological diversity 4. Plants -- Collection and preservation
  ISBN 978-1-59953-343-8 lib bdg; 1-59953-343-X lib bdg
                                                                   LC 2009-16567
  "With a mix of scientific terminology and accessible sentence structure, the [book] effectively [describes] how the [idea] took shape and were put into practice by the scientists involved. . . . Color photographs are included on every page and provide a visual complement to the [text]." SLJ
  Includes glossary and bibliographical references

Rustad, Martha E. H.

Fall harvests; bringing in food. illustrated by Amanda Enright. Millbrook Press 2011 24p il (Fall's here!) lib bdg $23.95

Grades: K 1 2 3   **631.5**

1. Autumn 2. Agriculture

ISBN 978-0-7613-5067-5; 0-7613-5067-5

LC 2010053467

"This offers . . . information about planting or reaping, and directions for making a cornhusk doll. . . . Colorful illustrations fill the spreads with active, cartoonlike boys and girls surrounded by the green, brown, and orange hues of autumn." SLJ

631.8   Fertilizers, soil conditioners, growth regulators

Barker, David

Compost it. Cherry Lake Pub. 2010 32p il (Save the planet) lib bdg $27.95

Grades: 3 4 5 6   **631.8**

1. Compost

ISBN 978-1-60279-656-0 lib bdg; 1-60279-656-4 lib bdg

LC 2009038092

"Written as dispatches from an imaginary journalist, the pages follow several individuals who explain different types of composting: a soil ecologist, . . . a home owner, . . . an apartment dweller, . . . and, finally, the manager of large-scale, urban operation. The creative, uncrowded format features text printed in an old-fashioned typewriter font on a notebook-paper background, numerous color photos, and facts boxes. . . . This upbeat, lucid overview of compost and its benefits is a strong choice." Booklist

Glaser, Linda

Garbage helps our garden grow; a compost story. story by Linda Glaser; photography by Shelley Rotner. Millbrook 2010 32p il lib bdg $25.26

Grades: K 1 2 3   **631.8**

1. Compost

ISBN 978-0-7613-4911-2 lib bdg; 0-7613-4911-1 lib bdg

"Clear, vivid photos give this simple introduction to composting a realistic look that makes the process look downright doable. . . . Most of Rotner's excellent photos feature one or two children as they scrape their dinner plates into a bucket indoors, add kitchen and yard waste to the compost bin outside, observe the leaves and food rotting over time, add the compost to their vegetable garden, put new plants into the ground, and watch them grow." Booklist

632   Plant injuries, diseases, pests

Mooney, Carla

Sunscreen for plants. Norwood House Press 2009 48p il (A great idea) lib bdg $25.27

Grades: 3 4 5 6   **632**

1. Plants 2. Sun

ISBN 978-1-59953-344-5 lib bdg; 1-59953-344-8 lib bdg

LC 2009-15641

"With a mix of scientific terminology and accessible sentence structure, the [book] effectively [describes] how the [idea] took shape and were put into practice by the scientists involved. . . . Color photographs are included on every page and provide a visual complement to the [text]." SLJ

Includes glossary and bibliographical references

633.1   Cereals

Gibbons, Gail

Corn; by Gail Gibbons. Holiday House 2008 32p il $16.95

Grades: K 1 2 3   **633.1**

1. Corn

ISBN 978-0-8234-2169-5; 0-8234-2169-4

LC 2007051632

"The colorful watercolors are sure to attract even the most reluctant readers. . . . A simple, yet informative and engaging look at an important food source." SLJ

Micucci, Charles

The life and times of corn; written and illustrated by Charles Micucci. Houghton Mifflin Books for Children 2009 32p il $16

Grades: 2 3 4   **633.1**

1. Corn

ISBN 978-0-618-50751-1; 0-618-50751-5

LC 2008040466

This focuses on the science, uses and history of corn

This is an "entertaining and informative mix of bite-size scientific information and historical facts and mouth-watering watercolors." Booklist

Includes bibliographical references

Reynolds, Jan

★ Cycle of rice, cycle of life; a story of sustainable farming. Lee & Low Books 2009 un il map $19.95

Grades: 3 4 5   **633.1**

1. Rice 2. Sustainable agriculture 3. Bali Island (Indonesia)

ISBN 978-1-60060-254-2; 1-60060-254-1

LC 2008-30518

This is "filled with beautiful color images. . . . [It is written] in precise, accessible language. . . . Reynolds offers young readers a broad, deep understanding of the concept, even as she provides a fascinating introduction to a specific culture." Booklist

Includes glossary

Sobol, Richard

The life of rice; from seedling to supper. Candlewick Press 2010 36p il map (Traveling photographer) $17.99

Grades: 3 4 5 6   **633.1**

1. Rice 2. Thailand

ISBN 978-0-7636-3252-6; 0-7636-3252-X

LC 2009-15138

"Turning his lens to the rice fields of Thailand, Sobol begins this affectionate account with a description of the Royal Plowing Ceremony that kicks off the planting season and continues through cultivation and into the harvest. Brief explanations of the growing stages of rice are accompanied by beautiful color photographs of the fields in their various phases. . . . Sobol offers an interesting look at a country and its people, and their relationship to the land. The writing is accessible and lively, providing a unique, specific look at one of the world's most important staples." SLJ

633.3   Legumes, forage crops other than grasses and legumes

Bial, Raymond

The super soybean. Albert Whitman & Co. 2007 40p il $16.95

Grades: 4 5 6   **633.3**
1. Soybean
ISBN 978-0-8075-7549-9; 0-8075-7549-6

LC 2007-14165

"Pairing a densely informational text with color photos, mostly of soybeans being grown and harvested, [the author] traces their cultivation's historical background, catalogs many of the uses to which they are put, and . . . trumpets enthusiastic appreciation for their twin roles as a major U.S. export and a renewable natural resource." Booklist

633.5   Fiber crops

Moore, Heidi
The **story** behind cotton. Heinemann Library 2009 32p il (True stories) $28.21
Grades: 3 4 5   **633.5**
1. Cotton
ISBN 978-1-4329-2341-9; 1-4329-2341-2

LC 2008043334

This offers history, ephemera, and basic facts about cotton and its production and uses.
Includes bibliographical references

633.7   Alkaloidal crops

Stewart, Melissa
No monkeys, no chocolate; Melissa Stewart and Allen Young; illustrated by Nicole Wong. Charlesbridge 2013 32 p.
Grades: K 1 2 3   **633.7**
1. Cocoa 2. Monkeys 3. Fertilization of plants 4. Chocolate 5. Cacao beans
ISBN 9781580892872 (reinforced for library use); 9781580892889 (softcover)

LC 2012000789

This children's picture book explores "the rain forest microhabitat of the cocoa tree. In each spread, the authors take children backward through the life cycle of the tree: pods, flowers, leaves, stems, roots and back to beans. The interdependence of plants and animals is introduced in the process: Midges carry pollen from one flower to another; aphids destroying tender stems are kept in check by an anole." (Kirkus Reviews)

633.8   Other crops grown for industrial processing

Smith, Danna
Balloon trees; by Danna Smith; illustrated by Laurie Allen Klein. Sylvan Dell Publishing 2013 32 p. (English hardcover) $17.95
Grades: PreK K 1 2   **633.8**
1. Rubber 2. Rubber plants
ISBN 1607186128; 9781607186120; 9781607186243

LC 2012030119

In this children's book, by Danna Smith, illustrated by Laurie Allen Klein, "rhyming couplets and effective illustrations describe the general process by which latex is extracted from trees, converted into a colorful mix, shaped into forms, treated and sent to stores to be sold as balloons. Each double-page spread shows a separate step, watched over by what looks like a warbler with an observant eye." (Kirkus)

634   Orchards, fruits, forestry

Dickmann, Nancy
An **apple's** life. Heinemann Library 2010 24p il (Watch it grow) lib bdg $21.50; pa $5.99
Grades: PreK K 1   **634**
1. Apples
ISBN 978-1-4329-4141-3 lib bdg; 1-4329-4141-0 lib bdg; 978-1-4329-4150-5 pa; 1-4329-4150-X pa

LC 2009-49157

This title shows the reader how an apple begins life, grows, and reproduces.
"Practically unique among early introductions to life cycles because death is mentioned . . . this . . . follows [an apple] . . . from . . . seed to maturity with a set of close-up color photographs, one per page, paired to large-type, one or two-sentence captions. . . . Offers nourishing fare for young naturalists." SLJ
Includes glossary

Esbaum, Jill
Apples for everyone. National Geographic 2009 16p il (Picture the seasons) pa $5.95
Grades: K 1 2   **634**
1. Apples
ISBN 978-1-4263-0523-8 pa; 1-4263-0523-0 pa

LC 2009-12719

Discusses how apples develop from blossoms to fruit, how they are harvested, how people use them, the history of apples in the United States, and different varieties of them
This does "a fabulous job of conjuring up the sights, smells, and sensations of a brisk autumn. Using minimal text with National Geographic's typically fine photographs, Esbaum brings out familiar, comforting details of the outdoors. . . . The writing flows with sensory details." Booklist

Farmer, Jacqueline
Apples; illustrated by Phyllis Limbacher Tildes. Charlesbridge 2007 un il map lib bdg $16.95; pa $6.95
Grades: 1 2 3 4   **634**
1. Apples
ISBN 978-1-57091-694-6 lib bdg; 1-57091-694-2 lib bdg; 978-1-57091-695-3 pa; 1-57091-695-0 pa

LC 2006-20942

"Farmer provides a wealth of information here. The process of grafting is clearly explained, as are the differences between apple juice and cider, the nutritional value of the popular fruit, and the apple in history and legend. A handy chart detailing the various kinds of apples and their appropriate uses is included, as is a page of facts and records and a recipe for apple pie. Watercolor illustrations feature a multicultural cast of smiling children. The pictures accurately reflect the text and are attractive." SLJ

Gibbons, Gail
Apples. Holiday House 2000 un il $17.95; pa $6.95
Grades: K 1 2 3   **634**
1. Apples
ISBN 0-8234-1497-3; 0-8234-1669-0 pa

LC 99-54246

Explains how apples were brought to America, how they grow, their traditional uses and cultural significance, and some of the varieties grown
"With its cheerful, bright illustrations and clear, simple presentation, this title will be the perfect pick for the perennial fall apple-book requests." SLJ

The **berry** book. Holiday House 2002 un il $16.95
Grades: K 1 2 3 **634**
1. Berries 2. Cooking
ISBN 0-8234-1697-6

LC 2001-40602

Describes different types of berries and how they grow. Includes recipes with berry ingredients

This is a "brief, informative account. . . . Cheerful illustrations with clear labels enliven the accessible text." Horn Book Guide

Kellogg, Steven
★ **Johnny** Appleseed; a tall tale retold and illustrated by Steven Kellogg. Morrow Junior Bks. 1988 un il $16.95; lib bdg $16.89
Grades: K 1 2 3 **634**
1. Frontier and pioneer life 2. Pioneers 3. Fruit growers
ISBN 0-688-06417-5; 0-688-06418-3 lib bdg

LC 87-27317

"Oversize pages have given Kellogg a fine opportunity for pictures that are on a large scale, colorful and animated if often busy with details. His version of Chapman's life is more substantial than the subtitle (A TallTale) would indicate, since the text makes clear the difference between what Chapman really did and what myths grew up about his work, his life, his personality, and his achievements. There's some exaggeration, but on the whole the biography is factual and written with clarity." Bull Cent Child Books

Maestro, Betsy
How do apples grow? illustrated by Giulio Maestro. HarperCollins Pubs. 1992 32p il (Let's-read-and-find-out science book) hardcover o.p. pa $5.99
Grades: K 1 2 3 **634**
1. Apples
ISBN 0-06-020056-1 lib bdg; 0-06-445117-8 pa

LC 91-9468

Describes the life cycle of an apple from its initial appearance as a spring bud to that point in time when it becomes a fully ripe fruit

"Clear, complete. . . . Inquisitive children will find simple yet scientifically accurate answers to their questions about apple trees and their fruit. Large illustrations and limited text facilitate group-reading. The endearing, soft-toned drawings are clearly labelled, providing an excellent teaching tool or reference point for the science teacher." Sci Child

Malam, John
Grow your own smoothie. Heinemann Library 2011 32p il (Grow it yourself!) lib bdg $26; pa $7.99
Grades: K 1 2 **634**
1. Cooking 2. Strawberries 3. Vegetable gardening
ISBN 978-1-4329-5111-5 lib bdg; 978-1-4329-5118-4 pa

LC 2010049836

This describes how to grow strawberries and how to make a strawberry smoothie.

Includes glossary and bibliographical references

Rustad, Martha E. H.
Fall apples; crisp and juicy. illustrated by Amanda Enright. Millbrook Press 2011 24p il (Fall's here!) lib bdg $23.93
Grades: K 1 2 3 **634**
1. Apples 2. Cooking
ISBN 978-0-7613-5064-4; 0-7613-5064-0

LC 2010051510

"In this book, the reader discovers how fall apples grow and the many things that you can make with them. . . . Colorful illustrations enhance the lively text." Sci Books Films

Includes glossary and bibliographical references

Smucker, Anna Egan
Golden delicious; a Cinderella apple story. by Anna Egan Smucker; illustrated by Kathleen Kemly. Albert Whitman & Company 2008 un il $16.99
Grades: 1 2 3 **634**
1. Apples
ISBN 978-0-8075-2987-4; 0-8075-2987-7

LC 2007052792

This is "the story of the discovery and successful marketing of the Golden Delicious apple. The narrative is simple and direct, with an occasional flair. . . . Kemly's soft pastel illustrations provide interesting historical details, including dress and transportation, and help to move the story along. An author's note gives more background, along with details about the grafting process." SLJ

Ziefert, Harriet
One red apple; paintings by Karla Gudeon. Blue Apple Books 2009 un il $16.99

634
1. Apples
ISBN 978-1-934706-67-1; 1-934706-67-1

LC 2009012663

This follows the life cycle of an apple: from fruit growing on the tree to market, to picnic, to seed, to sapling and tree, and finally to a new apple.

"With lyrical text and folk-style artwork, this handsome picture book celebrates the pleasures of a favorite food while accentuating nature's cycles and Earth's bounty." SLJ

634.11 Apples

Codell, Raji Esme
Seed by seed; the legend and legacy of Johnny "Appleseed" Chapman. by Esme Raji Codell; illustrations by Lynne Rae Perkins. Greenwillow Books 2012 32 p. (trade ed.) $16.99
Grades: K 1 2 3 **634.11**
1. Legendary characters 2. Picture books for children 3. Frontier and pioneer life -- Middle West 4. Apple growers -- United States -- Biography
ISBN 0061455156; 9780061455155; 9780061455162

LC 2011033653

In this children's picture book, the author looks at American folk hero John Chapman, also known as Johnny Appleseed, and answers the question "Why should we remember him today, more than two hundred years later, and call him a hero?" by presenting the "five tenets Chapman lived by: 'Use what you have. Share what you have. Respect nature. Try to make peace where there is war. You can reach your destination by taking small steps.'" (Publishers Weekly)

Oldfield, Dawn Bluemel
Apple; by Dawn Bluemel Oldfield. Bearport Publishing Company, Inc. 2016 24 p. color illustrations (library binding) $23.93
Grades: PreK K 1 **634.11**
1. Apples
ISBN 1627248390; 9781627248396

LC 2015015274

This juvenile book, by Dawn Bluemel Oldfield, part of the publisher's "See It Grow" series, explores apples. "Starting with the plant's most recognizable feature-whether seed, fruit, or flower-each volume answers the question 'How did it get that way?' As readers follow the life cycle, they learn how seeds develop into shoots, grow stems and leaves, and flower and produce fruits." (School Library Journal)

"A clean design, simple sentences, and large, well-labeled photos provide attractive introductions to familiar plants." SLJ

Includes bibliographical references and index

634.76 Cranberries

Lee, Jackie

Cranberry; by Jackie Lee. Bearport Publishing Company, Inc 2016 24 p. color illustrations (library binding) $23.93

Grades: PreK K 1   **634.76**

1. Agriculture 2. Cranberries

ISBN 1627248412; 9781627248419

LC 2015013382

This juvenile book, by Jackie Lee, part of the publisher's "See It Grow" series, explores cranberries. "Starting with the plant's most recognizable feature-whether seed, fruit, or flower-each volume answers the question 'How did it get that way?' As readers follow the life cycle, they learn how seeds develop into shoots, grow stems and leaves, and flower and produce fruits." (School Library Journal)

"A clean design, simple sentences, and large, well-labeled photos provide attractive introductions to familiar plants." SLJ

Includes bibliographical references and index

634.9 Forestry

Collard, Sneed B.

Fire birds; valuing natural wildfires and burned forests. Sneed B. Collard III. Bucking Horse Books 2015 48 p. color illustrations (alk. paper) $17

Grades: 4 5 6 7 8   **634.9**

1. Birds 2. Wildfires

ISBN 9780984446070

LC 2014945653

In this book, author Sneed B. Collard III "explores how a forest devastated by a fire slowly recuperates, focusing on the work of biologist Richard Hutto, who studies the birds that thrive in burned forests. . . . . Individual birds like the hairy woodpecker and mountain bluebird are profiled in sidebars, and a chart lists the birds that most frequently populate new burn areas." (Publishers Weekly)

"A book that will leave readers asking questions and challenging assumptions--and with a keener appreciation of our environment." SLJ

Includes bibliographical references and index.

Jakubiak, David J.

What can we do about deforestation? PowerKids Press 2011 24p il (Protecting our planet) lib bdg $21.25; pa $8.25

Grades: 2 3 4   **634.9**

1. Deforestation

ISBN 978-1-4488-4986-4 lib bdg; 1-4488-4986-1 lib bdg; 978-1-4488-5119-5 pa; 1-4488-5119-X pa

LC 2011000160

This explains the importance of forests and trees in our environment, the reasons for deforestation and the damage caused by the destruction of trees.

"Every spread has a full-page, thoughtfully captioned color photograph. . . . School and public libraries will want [this title] to round out collections or as [an update] to replace older books." SLJ

Includes glossary

Lee, Jackie

Coconut; by Jackie Lee. Bearport Publishing Company, Inc. 2016 24 p. color illustrations (library binding) $23.93

Grades: PreK K 1   **634.9**

1. Plants 2. Coconut

ISBN 1627248420; 9781627248426

LC 2015008706

This children's book, by Jackie Lee, part of the publisher's "See It Grow" series, profiles the coconut. "Starting with the plant's most recognizable feature-whether seed, fruit, or flower-each volume answers the question 'How did it get that way?' As readers follow the life cycle, they learn how seeds develop into shoots, grow stems and leaves, and flower and produce fruits." (School Library Journal)

"Focused on particular plants and colorfully illustrated, the series offers useful, attractive books for library collections serving younger students." Booklist

Includes bibliographical references and index

Silverstein, Alvin

★ Wildfires; the science behind raging infernos. [by] Alvin and Virginia Silverstein and Laura Silverstein Nunn. Enslow Publishers 2010 48p il map (The science behind natural disasters) lib bdg $23.93

Grades: 4 5 6   **634.9**

1. Wildfires

ISBN 978-0-7660-2973-6 lib bdg; 0-7660-2973-5 lib bdg

LC 2008-48025

"Scientific explanations are accompanied by plentiful color diagrams that will help students to grasp causes and effects. . . . Photos . . . are effective, and are sometimes turned into helpful, lively diagrams by the addition of such features as wind-direction arrows." SLJ

Includes glossary and bibliographical references

Trammel, Howard K.

Wildfires; by Howard K. Trammel. Children's Press 2009 48 p. col. ill. (A true book) (library) $29

Grades: 4 5 6   **634.9**

1. Wildfires 2. Natural disasters

ISBN 0531168875; 9780531168875

LC 2008014796

This book by Howard K. Trammel is part of the True Books: Earth Science series and looks at wildfires. The series answers questions such as "what makes the earth quake, rivers flood, and volcanoes blow their tops? How do natural forces become natural disasters?" (Publisher's note)

635 Garden crops (Horticulture)

Berkes, Marianne

What's in the garden? by Marianne Berkes; illustrated by Cris Arbo. 1st ed. Dawn Publications 2013 32 p. ill. (hardcover) $16.95; (paperback) $8.95

Grades: K 1 2   **635**

1. Gardens -- Poetry 2. Picture books for children 3. Gardening 4. Kitchen gardens 5. Vegetable gardening 6. Cooking (Vegetables)

ISBN 1584691891; 9781584691891; 9781584691907

LC 2012024245

This children's gardening book from Marianne Berkes combines "rhyming verses with recipes celebrating the garden's bounty. . . . From the popular ants on a log to the more daring French onion soup, breakfast-y carrot muffins to a dessert of blueberry pie, young chefs are likely to get a wide introduction to both the products of the garden and the culinary arts." (Kirkus Reviews)

Cohen, Whitney

The **book** of gardening projects for kids; 101 ways to get kids outside, dirty, and having fun. Whitney Cohen and John Fisher. 1st ed. Timber Press 2012 264 p. col. ill. $29.95

Grades: Adult　　　　　　　　　　**635**

1. Gardening 2. Gardens -- Guidebooks 3. Gardens -- Activity projects 4. Gardening for children
ISBN 1604693738; 9781604692457

LC 2011036778

In this book, "Whitney Cohen and John Fisher draw on years of experience in the Life Lab Garden Classroom and gardening with their own children to teach parents how to integrate the garden into their family life, no matter its scope or scale. The book features . . . gardening advice, including how to design a play-friendly garden, ideas for fun-filled theme gardens, and how to cook and preserve the garden's bounty. 101 . . . garden activities are also featured." (Publisher's note)

Cornell, Kari

The **nitty**-gritty gardening book; fun projects for all seasons. Kari Cornell; photography by Jennifer Larson. Millbrook Press 2015 48 p. color illustrations lib. bdg $26.65

Grades: 3 4 5 6　　　　　　　　**635**

1. Gardening 2. Gardening for children
ISBN 9781467726474

LC 2014009384

This book, by Kari Cornell, focuses on gardening. "Become a gardener in any season with these fun and easy projects. You don't even need a garden space—many of these activities can be done by planting in containers to set on a porch or a patio or even in a window. Try your hand at growing potatoes and strawberries. Plant bright flowers that attract butterflies, birds, and bees. Learn how to get daffodils to bloom in the winter! You can even make your own compost." (Publisher's note)

"Pleasant photographs by Larson are supplemented with clear diagrams and stock photos." Kirkus

Includes bibliographical references and index.

Creasy, Rosalind

Blue potatoes, orange tomatoes; illustrations by Ruth Heller. Sierra Club Bks. for Children 1994 40p il hardcover o.p. pa $6.95

Grades: 3 4 5　　　　　　　　**635**

1. Vegetables 2. Vegetable gardening
ISBN 0-87156-576-5; 0-87156-919-1 pa

LC 92-38800

Describes how to plant and grow a variety of colorful vegetables, including red corn, yellow watermelons, and multicolored radishes, and includes recipes

"With interesting and authentic information about gardening accompanied by brilliant, life-like illustrations, this book will not only promote the delight in growing plants but enhance the wonder in the natural world right in your own backyard." Appraisal

Ehlert, Lois, 1934-

★ **Growing** vegetable soup; written and illustrated by Lois Ehlert. Harcourt Brace Jovanovich 1987 un il $17; pa $7; bd bk $6.95

Grades: PreK K 1 2　　　　　　**635**

1. Vegetable gardening
ISBN 0-15-232575-1; 0-15-232580-8 pa; 0-15-205055-8 bd bk

LC 86-22812

"Brightly-colored large illustrations and a boldly-worded text show how to plant and grow vegetables for Dad's soup. Shocking pinks, reds and greens give the illustrations an almost three-dimensional quality and will be good for large audiences of preschoolers." Child Book Rev Serv

Esbaum, Jill

Seed, sprout, pumpkin, pie. National Geographic 2009 16p il (Picture the seasons) pa $5.95

Grades: K 1 2　　　　　　　　**635**

1. Pumpkin
ISBN 978-1-4263-0582-5 pa; 1-4263-0582-6 pa

LC 2009-12735

Discusses how pumpkins grow, the different varieties of pumpkins, and the many ways people use them

"Using minimal text with National Geographic's typically fine photographs, Esbaum brings out familiar, comforting details of the outdoors. . . . Perfect for Halloween, [this] is a veritable festival of orange featuring . . . panoramas of pumpkin fields and market stands, . . . the rarely appreciated pumpkin flower, pumpkins so big people make boats out of them, and . . . jack-'o-lanterns. . . . Fun, cozy, evocative stuff." Booklist

Fridell, Ron

Life cycle of a pumpkin; [by] Ron Fridell and Patricia Walsh. rev ed; Heinemann Library 2009 32p il (Life cycle of a) $25.36; pa $7.99

Grades: 2 3 4　　　　　　　　**635**

1. Pumpkin
ISBN 978-1-4329-2527-7; 1-4329-2527-X; 978-1-4329-2544-4 pa; 1-4329-2544-X pa

LC 00011234

First published 2002

"From seed to seedling, vine, and finally full-grown fruit, the life cycle of the pumpkin is clearly and colorfully described. Bright and engaging full-color photographs amplify the text on each page." SLJ

Includes bibliographical references

Gaarder-Juntti, Oona

What in the world is a green garden? ABDO Pub. Co. 2011 24p il (Going green) lib bdg $24.21

Grades: 1 2 3 4　　　　　　　　**635**

1. Sustainable agriculture
ISBN 978-1-61613-188-3; 1-61613-188-8

LC 2010004322

"The lively layout design, featuring colorful headings, short paragraphs, and attractive photographs, has a scrapbook-like quality. . . . [The title explains] how all our choices require energy and resources, and encourage readers to make changes in their lifestyles. . . . [This] . . . will inspire and empower readers to make a difference." SLJ

Includes glossary and bibliographical references

Gibbons, Gail

The **pumpkin** book. Holiday House 1999 un il $16.95; pa $6.95

Grades: K 1 2 3　　　　　　　　**635**

1. Pumpkin
ISBN 0-8234-1465-5; 0-8234-1636-4 pa

LC 98-45267

Describes how pumpkins come in different shapes and sizes, how they grow, and their traditional uses and cultural significance. Includes instructions for carving a pumpkin and drying the seeds

"Bold, clear watercolor illustrations and a concise text work together. . . . Gibbons succeeds once again at covering a topic in a useful way at just the right level for beginning readers." SLJ

The **vegetables** we eat; by Gail Gibbons. Holiday House 2007 32p il $16.95

Grades: K 1 2 3　　　　　　　　**635**

1. Vegetables
ISBN 0-8234-2001-9; 978-0-8234-2001-8

LC 2005052654

"A clear, informative introduction to eight groups of vegetables, categorized by the part of the plant that is eaten. For each group, Gibbons includes an illustration of one representative veggie as it grows in a garden. The rest of the page includes illustrations of related plants. . . . The author offers basic suggestions for starting a garden and shows how produce goes from large farms to processing plants and grocery stores. . . . Familiar paneled illustrations and accessible text combine to present a simple, effective approach to the topic." SLJ

Grow it, cook it. DK Pub. 2008 80p il $15.99
  Grades: 3 4 5 6   **635**
  1. Cooking 2. Vegetable gardening
  ISBN 978-0-7566-3367-7; 0-7566-3367-2

This "title combines instructions for growing edible plants with recipes based on the harvest. . . . The lush photos of ripening vegetables . . . will spark children's curiosity and inspire them to learn more. . . . Most children will need help . . . as they prepare the delicious, often sophisticated culinary treats. . . . An attractive introduction to both gardening and healthy meals." Booklist

Hirsch, Rebecca E.
  Growing your own garden; by Rebecca Hirsch. Cherry Lake Pub. 2010 32p il (Save the planet) lib bdg $27.07
Grades: 3 4 5 6   **635**
  1. Vegetable gardening
  ISBN 978-1-60279-657-7 lib bdg; 1-60279-657-2 lib bdg
                                    LC 2009-38093

"At the beginning of . . . [the] book, readers are given a mission and advised to be alert to the facts provided so that they can successfully answer the questions at the end. . . . Children are made to feel part of the process; suggestions for how they can become involved abound." SLJ

Includes glossary and bibliographical references

Lee, Jackie
  Pumpkin; Jackie Lee. Bearport Publishing Company 2016 24 p. color illustrations (library binding) $23.93
Grades: PreK K 1   **635**
  1. Pumpkin 2. Vegetables
  ISBN 1627248404; 9781627248402
                                   LC 2015008704

This children's book on pumpkins, by Jackie Lee, is part of a series designed to "provide attractive introductions to familiar plants. Starting with the plant's most recognizable feature-whether seed, fruit, or flower-each volume answers the question 'How did it get that way?' As readers follow the life cycle, they learn how seeds develop into shoots, grow stems and leaves, and flower and produce fruits." (Publisher's note)

"Focused on particular plants and colorfully illustrated, the series offers useful, attractive books for library collections serving younger students." Booklist

Includes bibliographical references and index

Malam, John
  Grow your own sandwich. Heinemann Library 2011 32p il (Grow it yourself!) lib bdg $26; pa $7.99
Grades: K 1 2   **635**
  1. Cooking 2. Tomatoes 3. Vegetable gardening
  ISBN 978-1-4329-5108-5 lib bdg; 978-1-4329-5115-3 pa
                                   LC 2010049833

This describes how to grow tomatoes and how to make a cheese and tomato sandwich.

Includes glossary and bibliographical references

  Grow your own soup. Heinemann Library 2011 32p il (Grow it yourself!) lib bdg $26; pa $7.99

Grades: 2 3 4   **635**
  1. Cooking 2. Pumpkin 3. Vegetable gardening
  ISBN 978-1-4329-5106-1 lib bdg; 978-1-4329-5113-9 pa
                                   LC 2010049830

This describes how pumpkins grow, how to plant and raise your own, and how to make pumpkin soup.

Includes glossary and bibliographical references

Messner, Kate
  Up in the garden and down in the dirt; by Kate Messner; with art by Christopher Silas Neal. Chronicle Books 2015 52 p. illustrations (alk. paper) $16.99
Grades: K 1 2 3   **635**
  1. Gardening 2. Gardens 3. Soils -- Composition
  ISBN 9781452119366
                                   LC 2014001786

In this book, by Kate Messner, illustrated by Christopher Silas Neal, "up in the garden, the world is full of green -- leaves and sprouts, growing vegetables, ripening fruit. But down in the dirt exists a busy world -- earthworms dig, snakes hunt, skunks burrow --populated by all the animals that make a garden their home." (Publisher's note)

"Neal's art is stunning, with muted greens and soft browns providing tonal symmetry to illustrations teeming with plant and animal life, and further underscoring the connections among all living organisms in the environment." Horn Book

Ready set grow! quick and easy gardening projects. DK Pub. 2010 79p il $12.99
  Grades: 3 4 5   **635**
  1. Gardening
  ISBN 978-0-7566-5887-8; 0-7566-5887-X

"Sunny and energetic spreads feature more than 30 garden project ideas, aimed at getting kids outdoors and in the dirt. Photographs and illustrations teach the basics about plant cultivation. . . . Recycling is a recurring theme, . . . many of the garden-related projects tend toward the whimsical, . . . and there's a strong emphasis on growing edible plants. . . . The fun, easy, and green concepts should have readers eagerly awaiting spring." Publ Wkly

Rockwell, Anne F.
  One bean; pictures by Megan Halsey. Walker & Co. 1998 un il hardcover o.p. pa $6.95
Grades: K 1 2   **635**
  1. Beans
  ISBN 0-8027-8648-0; 0-8027-7572-1 pa
                                    LC 97-36249

"An easy-to-read text combines with lively illustrations to create the story of what happens to one small bean when it interacts with some soil, just a little water, a lot of sunlight, and a young child's tender care." Sci Child

Rustad, Martha E. H.
  Fall pumpkins; orange and plump. illustrated by Amanda Enright. Millbrook Press 2011 24p il (Fall's here) lib bdg $23.93
Grades: K 1 2 3   **635**
  1. Pumpkin
  ISBN 978-0-7613-5065-1; 0-7613-5065-9
                                   LC 2010048310

The author "takes the young reader on a journey to learn how pumpkins are planted, tended, and grown. . . . The book also shows the reader how to use fully grown pumpkins: carving them for Halloween, making roasted pumpkins seeds, and us the pumpkin meat to make pumpkin pie. . . . The illustrations are very colorful." Sci Books Films

Includes glossary and bibliographical references

Sayre, April Pulley

Touch a butterfly; wildlife gardening with kids. April Pulley Sayre. 1st ed. Roost Books 2013 xiv, 207 p.p (paperback) $19.95

Grades: Adult Professional   **635**

1. Wildlife attracting 2. Gardening 3. Garden animals 4. Gardening to attract wildlife

ISBN 1590309170; 9781590309179

LC 2012021579

This book, by April Pulley Sayre, offers instructions on how to "turn your garden into a hummingbird hotspot, a haven for butterflies, and a thriving ecosystem that will delight and inspire the young and young-at-heart. . . . Begin to see your yard from an animal's perspective; discover plants that attract colorful birds and bugs; embrace sensory experiences that native plants and creatures bring; and understand how your yard fits into the surrounding landscape." (Publisher's note)

Woolf, Alex

You wouldn't want to live without vegetables; written by Alex Woolf; illustrated by David Antram; series created by David Salariya. Franklin Watts, an imprint of Scholastic Inc. 2016 32 p. color illustrations (library binding) $29.00

Grades: 3 4 5 6   **635**

1. Vegetables

ISBN 9780531214909; 9780531224403

LC 2015035314

This book, by Alex Woolf, illustrated by David Antram, explains that "vegetables provide us with essential vitamins and minerals that make our bodies healthier and stop us from getting sick. They're also used to make things like dyes, lotions and adhesives. Learn how vegetables are grown and cultivated, and the often inspired innovations made with such humble foodstuffs as the potato and the carrot." (Publisher's note)

"The books feature a time line and numerous ancillaries, but the myriad entertaining facts are the real hit. Who wouldn't want to read them?" Booklist

635.9   Flowers and ornamental plants

Bearce, Stephanie

A **kid's** guide to container gardening. Mitchell Lane Publishers 2009 48p il (Gardening for kids) lib bdg $29.95

Grades: 3 4 5 6   **635.9**

1. Container gardening

ISBN 978-1-58415-814-1 lib bdg; 1-58415-814-X lib bdg

LC 2009001314

This is a guide to growing plants in tubs, buckets, and other containers This book is "filled with information, which is divided into neat chapters written in a chatty, enthusiastic voice. . . . [The book features] large type, embedded with bolded vocabulary words, . . . as well as sharp color photos on every page." Booklist

Includes bibliographical references

A **kid's** guide to making a terrarium. Mitchell Lane Publishers 2009 48p il (Gardening for kids) lib bdg $29.95

Grades: 3 4 5 6   **635.9**

1. Terrariums

ISBN 978-1-58415-813-4 lib bdg; 1-58415-813-1 lib bdg

LC 2009001319

This book is "filled with information, which is divided into neat chapters written in a chatty, enthusiastic voice. . . . [The book features] large type, embedded with bolded vocabulary words, . . . as well as sharp color photos on every page." Booklist

Includes bibliographical references

Stockdale, Susan

Fantastic flowers; written and illustrated by Susan Stockdale. Peachtree Publishers 2017 32 p. color illustrations $16.95

Grades: PreK K 1   **635.9**

1. Picture books for children 2. Flowers

ISBN 9781561459520

LC 2016017194

This book, by Susan Stockdale, "introduces young readers to 17 flowers that resemble all kinds of things. Budding botanists will be amazed at how much they look like upside-down pants, wild monkeys and even tiny babies! . . . Back matter explains what a flower is and how it is pollinated, and provides photos of each flower along with its common and scientific name, native range and pollinators." (Publisher's note)

"The simple rhyming text paired with the close-up illustrations could make this a good pick for storytime, while the facts would be useful in a science program." Booklist

636   Animal husbandry

Becker, Helaine

Worms for Breakfast; How to Feed a Zoo. by Helaine Becker; illustrated by Kathy Boake. Owlkids Books 2016 40 p. color illustrations $16.95

Grades: 2 3 4 5   **636**

1. Animals -- Food 2. Zoos

ISBN 1771471050; 9781771471053

LC 2015948454

This book, by Helaine Becker, illustrated by Kathy Boake, is "a cookbook-style primer packed with facts from experts at zoos and aquariums. Covering everything from regular animal nutrition to feeding babies to mimicking how animals hunt and eat in the wild, this book explores the eating habits of carnivores, omnivores, herbivores, and insectivores. Inside, you'll also find real-life recipes from zoos around the world." (Publisher's note)

"While the tone is light and Boake's photo-collage illustrations zany, Becker doesn't avoid the tough stuff: though conservation and species protection are important jobs zoos do, animals kept there aren't always happy." Booklist

Gunter, Veronika Alice

Pet science; 50 purr-fectly woof-worthy activities for you & your pets. by Veronika Alice Gunter and Rain Newcomb; illustrated by Tom LaBaff. Lark Books 2006 80p il $14.95

Grades: 3 4 5 6   **636**

1. Pets 2. Science -- Experiments

ISBN 1-57990-786-5

LC 2005-4860

This "book of 50 activities encourages budding ethnologists to investigate, explore, and record their pet's behavior. . . . Delightful four-color illustrations fill the pages. . . . This engaging book is a delightful way to bring science to young children." Sci Books Films

Includes glossary

Jones, Charlotte Foltz

The **king** who barked; real animals who ruled. illustrated by Yayo. Holiday House 2009 40p il $16.95

Grades: 3 4 5   **636**

1. Animals

ISBN 978-0-8234-1925-8; 0-8234-1925-8

LC 2008-25669

"The brief accounts in this whimsical collection of animal anecdotes introduce symbolic leaders such as goat mayors, dog-kings, and a rhinoceros who won a seat on the São Paulo city council in a write-in campaign. The stories, which are arranged by continent of origin, hail from legends and oral histories, though some are more recent and better documented. Yayo's acrylic-on-canvas paintings capture the topsy-turvy spirit of the tales and add playful details." SLJ

Includes bibliographical references

Keenan, Sheila

★ **Animals** in the house; a history of pets and people. Scholastic Nonfiction 2007 112p il $17.99

Grades: 4 5 6   636

1. Pets

ISBN 978-0-439-69286-1; 0-439-69286-5

"Keenan provides an overview of pets and their people. Beginning with statistics about pet ownership, the text goes on to describe how animals and humans came together . . . and discusses how this relationship has changed and deepened. . . . Eye-catchingly designed, the format uses Photoshop to best advantage, providing interesting graphics, popping borders, and plenty of pictures featuring adorable animals." Booklist

Includes bibliographical references

Love, Ann

Talking tails; the incredible connection between people and their pets. [by] Ann Love & Jane Drake; illustrated by Bill Slavin. Tundra Books 2010 80p il $22.95

Grades: 3 4 5 6   636

1. Pets

ISBN 978-0-88776-884-2; 0-88776-884-9

"Focusing mainly on dogs and cats but with some attention to fish, reptiles, rodents, and birds, Love and Drake celebrate the affection that connects people with their pets. Along with providing a historical overview of animal domestication, . . . the authors profile some famous real pets. . . . They run through major cat and dog breeds; discuss characteristic instincts, personalities, behavior, and body language; and explain how to plan for, choose, . . . and care for an animal. . . . Slavin skillfully captures the bountiful warmth here. . . . This will draw animal lovers like a magnet." Booklist

Martin, Claudia

Farming. Marshall Cavendish Benchmark 2010 64p il (Working animals) $28.50

Grades: 4 5 6 7   636

1. Agriculture 2. Domestic animals

ISBN 978-1-60870-162-9; 1-60870-162-X

LC 2010006895

"Attractively designed and packed with information. . . . The composition of each page is attractively set up with well-selected and reproduced stock and historical photos." SLJ

Matzke, Ann

★ **Hedgehog**; Ann Matzke; [edited by] Keli Sipperley. Rourke Educational Media 2015 32 p. color illustrations (hardcover) $32.79

Grades: 3 4 5 6   636

1. Pets 2. Hedgehog

ISBN 9781634305334; 9781634304337

LC 2015931856

This children's book, Ann Matzke, edited by Keli Sipperley, part of the "You Have a Pet What!?" series, explores hedgehogs. "Hedgehogs are not your typical pet. These interesting and unusual nocturnal animals with bright eyes, sweet faces and prickly backs require special care and handling. . . . Learn . . . a lot more facts about these cute, quirky little pets and see if a hedgehog is the right pet for you." (Publisher's note)

"Well written, with a clean design, these titles will be useful for educators and popular with potential pet owners." SLJ

Steele, Christy

Cattle ranching in the American West; by Christy Steele. World Almanac Library 2005 48p il map (America's westward expansion) lib bdg $30; pa $11.95

Grades: 5 6 7 8   636

1. Cattle 2. Ranch life 3. West (U.S.) -- History

ISBN 0-8368-5787-9 lib bdg; 0-8368-5794-1 pa

LC 2004-56769

This volume describing Western cattle ranching is "richly illustrated with historical photographs, illustrations, maps, and quotes from primary sources presented in sidebars." SLJ

Includes bibliographical references

Tafuri, Nancy

★ **Spots,** feathers, and curly tails. Greenwillow Bks. 1988 un il $16.95

Grades: PreK K 1 2   636

1. Domestic animals

ISBN 0-688-07536-3; 0-688-07537-1 lib bdg

LC 87-15638

Questions and answers highlight some outstanding characteristics of farm animals, such as a chicken's feathers and a horse's mane

"In the watercolor illustrations with black pen outline, Nancy Tafuri manages in the simplest style to give energy and personality to the animals through the angle of a head or the set of a snout. The story will provide a successful experience for both child and adult reader and is an ideal book for the beginning reader to entertain a younger sibling in a game they'll both enjoy." Horn Book

636.08 Specific topics in animal husbandry

Curtis, Jennifer Keats

Sanctuaries; by Jennifer Keats Curtis; with Karine Aigner [and nine others] Sylvan Dell Publishing 2013 32 p. (Animal helpers) hbk $17.95

Grades: K 1 2   636.08

1. Animal rescue 2. Animal sanctuaries 3. Wildlife refuges

ISBN 160718611X; 9781607186236; 9781607186113

LC 2012039949

In this book, "using examples from six animal-rescue organizations . . . [Jennifer Keats] Curtis describes what wild-animal sanctuaries do. Short informational paragraphs are set on . . . photographs of animals being cared for. The account begins with a series of portraits of shelter animals: several tigers, a binturong, a declawed Canadian lynx, a pair of blind bobcats and a bear. The author goes on to describe animal medical and dental treatments, training and enrichment." (Kirkus Reviews)

Doner, Kim

On a road in Africa; [by] Kim Doner; afterword by Chryssee Perry Martin. Tricycle Press 2008 un il $15.95

Grades: PreK K 1 2   636.08

1. Stories in rhyme 2. Wildlife conservation 3. Animals -- Africa

ISBN 978-1-58246-230-1; 1-58246-230-5

LC 2007-18199

"This is a lovely picture book to share as a rhyming story, animal book, or cultural introduction." Libr Media Connect

Kehret, Peg

Animals welcome; a life of reading, writing, and rescue. Peg Kehret. W.W. Norton & Co. Inc. 2012 272 p. (hardback) $16.99

Grades: 4 5 6 7   636.08

1. Wildlife 2. Autobiography 3. Animal behavior 4. Animal rescue -- United States -- Anecdotes 5. Animal welfare -- United

States -- Anecdotes 6. Animal shelters -- United States -- Anecdotes
ISBN 0525423990; 9780525423997

LC 2011035440

Author Peg Kehret shares "her life on a small wildlife sanctuary, . . . the tragedy of her husband's sudden death, and the pain of losing Pete, the shelter cat who co-authored three of her books." In addition to stories of animal rescue and facts about birds and animals, the book is "a personal glimpse into the life of an author who loves animals, and the philosophy by which she lives." (Publisher's note)

Larson, Kirby

Two Bobbies; a true story of Hurricane Katrina, friendship, and survival. [by] Kirby Larson and Mary Nethery; illustrations by Jean Cassels. Walker & Co. 2008 un il $16.99

Grades: K 1 2 3   **636.08**

1. Cats 2. Dogs 3. Hurricane Katrina, 2005

ISBN 978-0-8027-9754-4; 0-8027-9754-7

"Abandoned during the [Hurricane] Katrina evacuations, pets Bobbi [the dog] and Bob Cat wander dangerous, debris-strewn streets seeking food and water. Eventually taken to a rescue shelter, the Bobbies show distress when separated but remain calm when together. Workers then discover that Bob Cat is blind and that Bobbi seems to serve as his seeing-eye dog. . . . The descriptive, sometimes folksy prose and realistically rendered gouache illustrations accessibly convey the Bobbies' experiences and mutual devotion. . . . This moving story about the importance of friendship and home highlights the plight of the hurricane's lost and left-behind animals, as well as the value of animal shelters." Booklist

636.088   Animals for specific purposes

Grayson, Robert

Transportation. Marshall Cavendish Benchmark 2010 64p il (Working animals) $28.50

Grades: 4 5 6 7   **636.088**

1. Pack animals (Transportation)

ISBN 978-1-60870-167-4; 1-60870-167-0

LC 2010006899

"Describes animals that people all over the world use to transport people and goods, such as elephants, horses, yaks, water buffalo, and dogs." Publisher's note

Includes glossary and bibliographical references

Halls, Kelly Milner

Saving the Baghdad Zoo; a true story of hope and heroes. by Kelly Milner Halls, with William Sumner. Greenwillow Books 2010 64p il map $17.99

Grades: 4 5 6 7   **636.088**

1. Zoos 2. Wildlife conservation 3. Baghdad (Iraq) 4. Baghdad Zoo (Iraq)

ISBN 978-0-06-177202-3; 0-06-177202-X

LC 2008-52820

"This eye-opening tale of compassion and cooperation chronicles the mission of an international team of military personnel, zoo staffers, veterinarians, and relief workers to rescue neglected animals in Baghdad. . . . Sobering and uplifting photographs—many taken by Sumner—underscore both the direness of the situation and the spirit of hope that drove the project." Publ Wkly

Includes bibliographical references

Laidlaw, Rob

Wild animals in captivity; [by] Rob Laidlaw. Fitzhenry & Whiteside 2008 48p il $19.95

Grades: 4 5 6 7 8   **636.088**

1. Zoos 2. Animal welfare

ISBN 978-1-55455-025-8; 1-55455-025-4

"A passionate, well-written, and well-researched argument against the practices of most zoos around the world. . . . Describes the damage done when animals are unnaturally confined and moved to inhospitable climates, and compares the wild and captive lives of polar bears, orcas, elephants, and great apes—the four species most harmed by captivity. . . . The issues raised in this important and powerful book will resonate with young and old." SLJ

Markle, Sandra

Animal heroes; true rescue stories. by Sandra Markle. Millbrook Press 2009 64p il lib bdg $29.27

Grades: 4 5 6 7   **636.088**

1. Pets 2. Animals 3. Rescue work

ISBN 978-0-8225-7884-0 lib bdg; 0-8225-7884-0 lib bdg

LC 2007-50435

"Nine stories, based on interviews with the grateful survivors, describe how brave animals rescued people in catastrophic circumstances. Each edgy retelling reveals details that only the participants could know, including sounds, smells, sights, and the knowledge that at any moment they could die, deepening the tension. Mixed in are Markle's broad and perfectly attuned insights about animal behavior." SLJ

Includes glossary and bibliographical references

636.089   Veterinary medicine

Jackson, Donna M.

ER vets; life in an animal emergency room. Houghton Mifflin 2005 88p il $17

Grades: 5 6 7 8   **636.089**

1. Veterinary medicine

ISBN 0-618-43663-4

"With plentiful, excellent-quality photographs, this highly visual book offers a behind-the-scenes look at an emergency animal hospital in Colorado. . . . A section on grief counseling for families with critically ill pets and a spread on how to put together a pet first-aid kit are included. Well-researched and well-written, ER Vets is an engaging book on a hot topic." SLJ

636.1   Horses

Barnes, Julia

Horses at work; [by] Julia Barnes. North American ed.; Gareth Stevens 2006 32p il (Animals at work) lib bdg $23.93

Grades: 3 4 5   **636.1**

1. Horses 2. Working animals

ISBN 0-8368-6225-2

LC 2005054066

This describes horses' uses throughout history, their relationship with humans, habitat, diet, and appearance.

This is "well-written, well-organized, . . . visually appealing and fun to read." SLJ

Includes bibliographical references

Bowers, Nathan

4-H guide to training horses. Voyageur Press 2009 176p il $18.99

Grades: 5 6 7 8 **636.1**
1. Horses -- Training
ISBN 978-0-7603-3627-4; 0-7603-3627-X
LC 2009015299

This provides "sound and comprehensive information. [The book] covers basic training techniques and riding skills such as mounting, saddling, reining, stopping and starting, and posture among other topics. The training techniques offer insight into equine behavior based on their history as prey animals. The authors also emphasize that horse owners' success will be determined by how much effort they are willing to expend on their relationship with their animals. The many color photographs clearly depict the methods and activities that are taking place, and the accompanying images further clarify what is happening and its significance." SLJ

Includes glossary

Bozzo, Linda
My first horse; [by] Linda Bozzo. Enslow Elementary 2007 32p il (My first pet library from the American Humane Association) lib bdg $22.60

Grades: 1 2 3 **636.1**
1. Horses
ISBN 978-0-7660-2753-4 lib bdg; 0-7660-2753-8 lib bdg
LC 2006014969

This offers brief basic advice on selecting a horse and caring for it.
Includes glossary and bibliographical references

Crosby, Jeff
Harness horses, bucking broncos & pit ponies; a history of horse breeds. written and illustrated by Jeff Crosby and Shelley Ann Jackson. Tundra Books 2011 69p il map $21.99

Grades: 4 5 6 7 **636.1**
1. Horses
ISBN 978-0-88776-986-3; 0-88776-986-1

"After a brief introduction, the animals are grouped by the roles they have played in relation to people: 'Rapid Transit,' 'Military Advantage,' 'Horsepower,' 'Equine Entertainment,' and 'Feral Horses.' The concise and interesting information on each of the 43 breeds is accompanied by an illustration of the type as well as one of the horse in action and often includes a small map showing its origins. The excellent painterly pictures clearly capture the unique life of each horse." SLJ

Includes bibliographical references

Draper, Judith
★ **My** first horse and pony care book; [by] Judith Draper. Kingfisher 2006 48p il $9.95

Grades: K 1 2 3 **636.1**
1. Horses 2. Horsemanship
ISBN 978-0-7534-5989-8; 0-7534-5989-2
LC 2006005962

"Draper focuses on pony breeds commonly used in the United Kingdom and on English-style riding and tack. The information about feeding, grooming, and riding is detailed, accurate, and accessible. . . . The photographs are beautiful and in sharp focus. . . . This book is a must-have for young horse lovers." SLJ

Includes glossary

Gibbons, Gail
Horses! Holiday House 2003 un il $17.95; pa $6.95

Grades: K 1 2 3 **636.1**
1. Horses 2. Horsemanship
ISBN 0-8234-1703-4; 0-8234-1875-8 pa
LC 2003-41683

Presents information on horses, including their physical characteristics, behavior, and how to ride a horse

"Attractive, full-color labeled illustrations fill every page, with many expanding on a particular point in the main text. . . . The book's accessible format will attract browsers as well as legions of young would-be equestrians." Booklist

Hamilton, Libby
Horse : the essential guide for young equestrians; writer, Libby Hamilton; illustrators: Sophie Allsopp . . . [et al.] Candlewick Press 2008 24p il $15.99

Grades: 2 3 4 5 **636.1**
1. Horses
ISBN 978-0-7636-3547-3; 0-7636-3547-2

"This clever and pleasing guide contains a wealth of information on horses, including history, breeds, care and grooming, equipment, riding, and shows. Facts and tips are presented in an imaginative and lively format. The excellent, realistic illustrations are colorful and accurate and even occasionally humorous." SLJ

Lewin, Ted
★ **Stable.** Roaring Brook Press/Flash Point 2010 un il $17.99

Grades: K 1 2 3 **636.1**
1. Horses 2. Brooklyn (New York, N.Y.) 3. Kensington Stables (New York, N.Y.)
ISBN 978-1-59643-467-7; 1-59643-467-8
LC 2009-44431

"Lewin conveys the spirit of a Brooklyn institution through sumptuously detailed, luminous watercolors. Kensington Stables, a relic from the days when horses provided necessary transportation, shelters 37 animals, large and small. . . . The straightforward, present-tense prose conveys the central point that horses are important to the community, and they should be preserved." Kirkus

Lomberg, Michelle
Horse. Weigl Publishers 2009 32p il (My pet) lib bdg $26; pa $9.95

Grades: 3 4 5 **636.1**
1. Pets 2. Horses
ISBN 978-1-60596-092-0 lib bdg; 1-60596-092-6 lib bdg; 978-1-60596-093-7 pa; 1-60596-093-4 pa
LC 2009-25974

Information about how to house, feed, and care for horses.

"With clear, formal writing, and extensive coverage . . . [this title is] useful for reports. . . . Numerous color photographs, charts . . . and question-and-answer boxes supplement the [text]." SLJ

Includes glossary

Lunis, Natalie
Miniature horses. Bearport 2010 24p il (Peculiar pets) lib bdg $22.61

Grades: 3 4 5 **636.1**
1. Horses
ISBN 978-1-59716-861-8 lib bdg; 1-59716-861-0 lib bdg
LC 2009-10379

Introduces the miniature horse, describing its physical characteristics, history, and behavior, and discussing the care and diet that it needs

"The language . . . is lively . . . [and] the illustrations are vivid, with photos offering some amusing shots. . . . This [book] . . . will hold readers' attention, but also challenge them to consider the responsibilities required of owners of unusual creatures." SLJ

Includes glossary and bibliographical references

Mack, Gail

Horses. Marshall Cavendish Benchmark 2010 48p il (Great pets) lib bdg $29.93

Grades: 2 3 4   **636.1**

1. Horses

ISBN 978-0-7614-4147-2 lib bdg; 0-7614-4147-6 lib bdg

LC 2008037262

"Describes the characteristics and behavior of pet horses, also discussing their physical appearance and place in history." Publisher's note

Includes glossary and bibliographical references

MacLeod, Elizabeth

Why do horses have manes? Kids Can Press 2009 64p $14.95

Grades: 3 4 5 6   **636.1**

1. Horses

ISBN 978-1-55453-312-1; 1-55453-312-0

In a question and answer format "this slim volume covers standard information . . . and branches out to the more esoteric. . . . Freestanding text sections with a light and engaging tone combined with glossy photo vignettes of horses vamping for the camera make the book highly browsable." Horn Book Guide

Matzke, Ann H.

★ Mini horse; Ann Matzke; [edited by] Keli Sipperley. Rourke Educational Media 2015 32 p. color illustrations (hardcover) $32.78

Grades: 3 4 5 6   **636.1**

1. Pets 2. Miniature horses

ISBN 9781634304344

LC 2015931857

This children's book, by Ann Matzke, edited by Keli Sipperley, part of the "You Have a Pet What?!" series, is an entry on miniature horses where the series focuses on "exotic pets . . . , covering history, natural habitat, care, and characteristics both positive and negative. . . . The animals' personalities are described, and information on bonding and communication is provided." (School Library Journal)

"Well written, with a clean design, these titles will be useful for educators and popular with potential pet owners." SLJ

Niven, Felicia Lowenstein

Learning to care for a horse. Enslow Publishers 2010 48p il (Beginning pet care with American Humane) lib bdg $23.93

Grades: 2 3 4   **636.1**

1. Horses

ISBN 978-0-7660-3196-8; 0-7660-3196-9

LC 2008048961

"Readers will learn how to choose a horse and care for a horse, from what kind of horse is best for them and how long they live." Publisher's note

Includes glossary and bibliographical references

Ransford, Sandy

★ The Kingfisher illustrated horse and pony encyclopedia; written by Sandy Ransford; photographed by Bob Langrish. Revised edition Kingfisher 2010 224p il hardcover $24.99

Grades: 4 5 6 7   **636.1**

1. Horses 2. Horsemanship

ISBN 9780753464854; 0753464853

"The first section focuses on the horse itself--breeds, life cycle, domestication, and anatomy. The next section covers many areas of horse management, including feeding, housing, grooming, health care and first aid, and equipment. The third section examines the various aspects of riding, both western and English, although the majority of the photos feature English saddlery." (SLJ)

Rockwood, Leigh

Horses are smart! PowerKids Press 2010 24p il (Super smart animals) lib bdg $21.25; pa $8.25

Grades: 2 3 4 5   **636.1**

1. Horses

ISBN 978-1-4358-9399-3 lib bdg; 1-4358-9399-9 lib bdg; 978-1-4358-9838-7 pa; 1-4358-9838-9 pa

Examines the intelligence of horses.

"Bright, colorful, captioned photographs complement the text. Rockwood does an excellent job of simplifying the information without making it choppy or boring." Libr Media Connect

Includes glossary

Simon, Seymour

★ Horses. HarperCollins Pubs. 2006 un il $15.99; lib bdg $16.89

Grades: 2 3 4   **636.1**

1. Horses

ISBN 0-06-028944-9; 0-06-028945-7 lib bdg

LC 2004-30392

"Simon provides the basic facts, which include the importance of horses to humans throughout history, their evolution, physical traits, interactions among themselves, and the various breeds. The information is clear and accurate. The striking color photos will capture readers attention." SLJ

Wilsdon, Christina

For horse-crazy girls only; everything you want to know about horses. illustrated by Alecia Underhill. Feiwel and Friends 2010 150p il $14.99

Grades: 4 5 6 7   **636.1**

1. Horses

ISBN 978-0-312-60323-6; 0-312-60323-1

LC 2010015677

"Filled with quizzes, trivia, top 10 lists, and information about equine behavior, history, sports, and more, this guidebook aims straight at the hearts of horse-loving tweens. . . . The book runs the gamut from how to pick a horse's name to horses in popular culture, the evolution of the species, and horse-related events nationwide. The many sidebars, tidbits, and anecdotes encourage casual browsing-horse lovers will be in heaven." Publ Wkly

636.2   Cattle and related animals

Barnes, Julia

Camels and llamas at work; [by] Julia Barnes. Gareth Stevens 2006 32p il map (Animals at work) lib bdg $23.93

Grades: 3 4 5   **636.2**

1. Camels 2. Llamas 3. Working animals

ISBN 0-8368-6222-8

LC 2005054065

This is "well-written, well-organized, . . . visually appealing and fun to read." SLJ

Includes bibliographical references

Boynton, Sandra

Amazing cows; udder absurdity for children. Workman Pub. 2010 89p il $15.99; pa $10.95

Grades: K 1 2   **636.2**

1. Cattle

ISBN 978-0-7611-6371-8; 0-7611-6371-9; 978-0-7611-6214-8 pa; 0-7611-6214-3 pa

LC 2010034583

Jokes, humorous stories and poems, a comic book and other misinformation about cows.

"Not since the heyday of Gary Larson has so much adoration been shown to bovines. With her trademark irreverence, Boynton offers an impassioned and hyperbolic ode to cows, replete with jokes, a spread devoted to cow fashion, a cow 'myth' that takes place in ancient Athens . . ., limericks, and puns aplenty. . . . It's pure fun." Publ Wkly

Diemer, Lauren

 Cows. Weigl Publishers 2010 24p il (World of wonder: watch them grow) lib bdg $25.70; pa $9.95

Grades: 1 2   **636.2**

 1. Cattle

 ISBN 978-1-60596-919-0 lib bdg; 1-60596-919-2 lib bdg; 978-1-60596-920-6 pa; 1-60596-920-6 pa

           LC 2009052101

Learn about how cows are born and grow up, as well as their role in the world.

The text "is simple without being simplistic; it is thoughtful and comprehensive without being overwhelming. The real appeal for teachers, students, and independent young readers, however, will be the photographs that fill the facing pages. Bold, bright, and colorful, the photographs bring you marvelously close to the subject. . . . On many different levels, this is a very appealing [book]." Libr Media Connect

 Includes glossary

Freedman, Russell

 ★ **In** the days of the vaqueros; America's first true cowboys. Clarion Bks. 2001 70p il $18; pa $9.99

Grades: 4 5 6 7   **636.2**

 1. Cowhands 2. Ranch life 3. Mexican Americans 4. Southwestern States

 ISBN 0-395-96788-0; 978-0-395-96788-1; 978-0-547-13365-2 pa; 0-547-13365-0 pa

          LC 2001-17357

The author "tells the story with depth, clarity, and a vigor that conveys the thrilling excitement of the work and the macho swagger of the culture. . . . The book's design is beautiful, with spacious type on thick paper, and the dazzling illustrations—prints, paintings, and photos on almost every page." Booklist

 Includes glossary and bibliographical references

Peterson, Cris

 Clarabelle; making milk and so much more. [by] Cris Peterson; photographs by David R. Lundquist. Boyds Mills Press 2007 un il $16.95

Grades: 1 2 3   **636.2**

 1. Cattle 2. Dairying

 ISBN 1-59078-310-7; 978-1-59078-310-8

This focuses on "a dairy farm in northern Wisconsin, introduced through the daily life of a single cow, Clarabelle. In describing the basics of cow physiology and care and the dairy's operations, Peterson illuminates facts with comparisons that will grab kids' attention. . . . Lundquist's sharp, close-up photographs . . . will easily draw curious kids back into the science." Booklist

 Includes glossary

636.3 Sheep and goats

Minden, Cecilia

 Sheep. Cherry Lake Pub. 2010 24p il (21st century junior library: farm animals) lib bdg $22.80

Grades: 1 2 3   **636.3**

 1. Sheep

 ISBN 978-1-60279-544-0 lib bdg; 1-60279-544-4 lib bdg

          LC 2009-3318

This is an introduction to sheep as farm animals

This manages "to parlay [its] low page count into surprisingly deep and wide-ranging discussions on the various aspects of [the sheep's] existence. . . . It's the text that is so impressive, with its use of simple, explanatory language to introduce unusually advanced vocabulary. . . . [The] animal is not only shown in its natural (and often adorable) state but also as meat on a plate. Info boxes called 'Think!' expand the discussion even further." Booklist

 Includes glossary and bibliographical references

Urbigkit, Cat

 The **shepherd's** trail; [by] Cat Urbigkit. Boyds Mills Press 2008 32p il $16.95

Grades: 2 3 4   **636.3**

 1. Sheep 2. Shepherds

 ISBN 978-1-59078-509-6

          LC 2007017475

This "discusses the migration of domestic sheep in the western U.S. . . . Clear color photos offer close-ups of individual animals and long-range views of the flocks and the often striking landscapes. Topics discussed in the text include the roles of sheepherders, camptenders, herding dogs, guardian dogs, and sheepshearers, as well as details of the sheep's lives through the cycle of a year." Booklist

 A **young** shepherd. Boyd Mills Press 2006 un il $15.95

Grades: K 1 2 3   **636.3**

 1. Sheep 2. Shepherds

 ISBN 1-59078-364-6

"This photo-essay features a 12-year-old 4-H member (Urbigkit's son) who tends his own flock of sheep. Urbigkit . . . communicates Cass' commitment to his task in compelling photos that showcase the gamboling baby animals. . . . The close-up look at a fascinating, animal-focused activity will appeal even to readers who rarely rub shoulders with livestock." Booklist

636.4 Swine

Gibbons, Gail

 Pigs. Holiday House 1999 un il $16.95; pa $6.95

Grades: K 1 2 3   **636.4**

 1. Pigs

 ISBN 0-8234-1441-8; 0-8234-1554-6 pa

          LC 98-28807

Examines the basic characteristics, common breeds, intelligence, behavior, life cycle, and uses of pigs

"Bright with spring greens and yellows, this attractive book introduces pigs through simple sentences and many colorful pictures." Booklist

King-Smith, Dick

 ★ **All** pigs are beautiful; illustrated by Anita Jeram. Candlewick Press 1993 un il (Read and wonder) hardcover o.p. pa $6.99; pa with audio CD $9.99

Grades: K 1 2 3   **636.4**

 1. Pigs

 ISBN 978-0-7636-1433-1 pa; 0-7636-1433-5 pa; 978-0-7636-4195-5 pa with audio CD; 0-7636-4195-2 pa with audio CD

          LC 92-53136

The author "interlards fond reminiscences of porkers he has known with interesting facts about them that are sure to keep children absorbed. His tone is affectionate, amusing, and informative. Jeram's pen-and-ink and watercolor illustrations, done in soft, earthy colors, are a warm match for the text." SLJ

Minden, Cecilia

Pigs. Cherry Lake Pub. 2010 24p il (21st century junior library: farm animals) lib bdg $22.80

Grades: 1 2 3   **636.4**

1. Pigs

ISBN 978-1-60279-542-6 lib bdg; 1-60279-542-8 lib bdg

LC 2009-3676

This is an introduction to pigs as farm animals

This manages "to parlay [its] low page count into surprisingly deep and wide-ranging discussions on the various aspects of [the pig's] existence. . . . It's the text that is so impressive, with its use of simple, explanatory language to introduce unusually advanced vocabulary. . . . [The] animal is not only shown in its natural (and often adorable) state but also as meat on a plate. Info boxes called 'Think!' expand the discussion even further ([The book] encourages readers to ask why some of their friends may not eat pork)." Booklist

Includes glossary and bibliographical references

Reed, Cristie

★ **Mini** pig; Cristie Reed; [edited by] Keli Sipperley. Rourke Educational Media 2015 32 p. color illustrations; color map (hardcover) $32.79

Grades: 3 4 5 6   **636.4**

1. Pets 2. Miniature pigs

ISBN 9781634304313

LC 2015931854

This children's book, by Cristie Reed, edited by Keli Sipperley, part of the 'You Have a Pet What?!' series, is an entry on miniature pigs where the series focuses on "exotic pets . . . , covering history, natural habitat, care, and characteristics both positive and negative. . . . The animals' personalities are described, and information on bonding and communication is provided." (School Library Journal)

"Well written, with a clean design, these titles will be useful for educators and popular with potential pet owners." SLJ

Rockwood, Leigh

Pigs are smart! PowerKids Press 2010 24p il (Super smart animals) lib bdg $21.25; pa $8.25

Grades: 2 3 4 5   **636.4**

1. Pigs

ISBN 978-1-4358-9373-3 lib bdg; 1-4358-9373-5 lib bdg; 978-1-4358-9834-9 pa; 1-4358-9834-6 pa

Examines the intelligence of pigs

"Readers get an overview of the . . . [pig's] life cycle, its domestic history (where relevant), and natural habitat, and examples of how it is smart in the wild as well as when helped by human tutelage. . . . Interesting color photographs and large, easy-to-read print will attract browsers and report writers alike." SLJ

Includes glossary

636.5   Chickens and other kinds of domestic birds

Arnold, Caroline

Hatching chicks in room 6; Caroline Arnold. Charlesbridge 2017 40 p. color illustrations (reinforced for library use) $16.99

Grades: PreK K 1 2   **636.5**

1. Eggs 2. Chicks 3. Chickens

ISBN 9781580897358

LC 2015044368

In this children's book, written and photographed by Caroline Arnold, "follow a classroom of kindergartners as they participate in a popular activity: hatching chicks. Readers learn about the life cycle of a chicken, incubating eggs, watching them hatch, and raising the chicks until they are old enough to return to the chicken coop." (Publisher's note)

"Readers will come away with a good understanding of chickens' origins and will likely want to rush off to hatch an egg of their own, but Arnold wisely cautions that chickens do not make good pets. " Booklist

Includes bibliographical references.

Dickmann, Nancy

A **chicken's** life. Heinemann Library 2011 24p il (Watch it grow) lib bdg $21.50; pa $5.99

Grades: PreK K 1   **636.5**

1. Chickens

ISBN 978-1-4329-4139-0 lib bdg; 1-4329-4139-9 lib bdg; 978-1-4329-4148-2 pa; 1-4329-4148-8 pa

LC 2009-49153

"Practically unique among early introductions to life cycles because death is mentioned . . . this . . . follows [a chicken] . . . from egg . . . to maturity with a set of close-up color photographs, one per page, paired to large-type and one or two-sentence captions. . . . Offers nourishing fare for young naturalists." SLJ

Includes glossary and bibliographical references

Gibbons, Gail

Chicks & chickens. Holiday House 2003 un il $17.95; pa $6.95

Grades: K 1 2 3   **636.5**

1. Chickens

ISBN 0-8234-1700-X; 0-8234-1939-8 pa

LC 2002-27472

An introduction to the physical characteristics, behavior, and life cycle of chickens, as well as a discussion of how chickens are raised on farms

The author "offers lots of solid information as well as bits of trivia that will be of interest to this audience. Cartoon illustrations are large, colorful, and plentiful." SLJ

Heppermann, Christine

City chickens; by Christine Heppermann. Houghton Mifflin Books for Children 2012 47 p. ill. (chiefly col.) (hardcover) $16.99; (ebook) $16.99

Grades: 4 5   **636.5**

1. Animal housing 2. Animal behavior 3. Birds -- Protection 4. Chickens 5. Animal welfare 6. Animal shelters

ISBN 0547518307; 9780547518305; 9780547518336

LC 2011009754

In author Christine Hepperman's book, she provides stories of adopted chickens. "Just outside of downtown Minneapolis, follow the sounds of crowing and clucking and you will find Mary Britton Clouse's Chicken Run Rescue. Over the years, Mary and her husband have given hundreds of homeless birds a safe place to rest until they can be adopted by caring families." (Publisher's note)

Includes bibliographical references.

Kindschi, Tara

4-H guide to raising chickens. Voyageur Press 2010 176p il pa $18.99

Grades: 5 6 7 8   **636.5**
1. Chickens
ISBN 978-0-7603-3628-1 pa; 0-7603-3628-8 pa
LC 2009015300
"This title has everything one ever wanted to know about chickens but didn't know enough to ask. Eight chapters divide the text into broad topics such as getting started, choosing a breed, housing equipment, and exhibiting chickens. . . . Line drawings and charts give additional information, and the excellent color photography is profuse." SLJ
Includes glossary and bibliographical references

Minden, Cecilia
   Ducks. Cherry Lake Pub. 2010 24p il (21st century junior library: farm animals) lib bdg $22.80
Grades: 1 2 3   **636.5**
1. Ducks
ISBN 978-1-60279-546-4 lib bdg; 1-60279-546-0 lib bdg
LC 2009-5033
This is an introduction to ducks as farm animals
This manages "to parlay [its] low page count into surprisingly deep and wide-ranging discussions on the various aspects of [the duck's] existence. . . . It's the text that is so impressive, with its use of simple, explanatory language to introduce unusually advanced vocabulary. In [this book] readers learn such terminology as clutch, dabbling, and gland. . . . [The] animal is not only shown in its natural (and often adorable) state but also as meat on a plate. Info boxes called 'Think!' expand the discussion even further." Booklist
Includes glossary and bibliographical references

Page, Robin
   A **chicken** followed me home; questions and answers about a familiar fowl. by Robin Page. Beach Lane Books 2015 40 p. color illustrations (hardcover : alk. paper) $17.99
Grades: PreK K 1 2 3   **636.5**
1. Chickens
ISBN 1481410288; 9781481410281
LC 2013041955
In this nonfiction book for children "author-illustrator Robin Page leads a step-by-step, question-and-answer-style journey through the world of chickens. Along the way you'll explore different breeds, discover different types of coops, and learn everything there is to know about chicken reproduction and hatching." (Publisher's note)
Includes bibliographical references

Sklansky, Amy E.
   Where do chicks come from? illustrated by Pam Paparone. HarperCollins Publishers 2005 un il (Let's-read-and-find-out science) hardcover o.p. pa $4.99
Grades: K 1 2   **636.5**
1. Eggs 2. Chickens
ISBN 0-06-028892-2; 0-06-028893-0 lib bdg; 0-06-445212-3 pa
LC 2003-7711
Describes what happens day-by-day for the three weeks from the time a hen lays an egg until the baby chick hatches
This offers "clear and accurate text. . . . The illustrations are soft and friendly, but retain enough realism for children to understand the subject matter. . . . This is an enjoyable and informative introduction to scientific information." SLJ

Wearing, Judy
   Chickens. Weigl 2011 24p il (World of wonder: watch them grow) lib bdg $25.70; pa $9.95

Grades: 1 2   **636.5**
1. Eggs 2. Chickens
ISBN 978-1-60596-913-8 lib bdg; 1-60596-913-3 lib bdg; 978-1-60596-914-5 pa; 1-60596-914-1 pa
LC 2009050943
Learn about the transition these birds make from egg to chick, and finally, to full-grown chicken.
The text is "well-written, providing examples that put a human face to each problem. Quotes and facts are clearly attributed, and their sources are noted in the extensive back matter. . . . Sidebars provide further information, or, more compellingly, offer stories about those touched by the topic. . . . [This] will be of great assistance to students writing reports." Libr Media Connect
Includes glossary and bibliographical references

636.6   Birds other than poultry

Bozzo, Linda
   My first bird; [by] Linda Bozzo. Enslow Elementary 2007 32p il (My first pet library from the American Humane Association) lib bdg $22.60
Grades: 1 2 3   **636.6**
1. Cage birds
ISBN 978-0-7660-2749-7 lib bdg; 0-7660-2749-X lib bdg
LC 2006008405
"The material is brief, providing a general overview. . . . [Illustrated with] attractive, heartwarming color photographs." SLJ
Includes glossary and bibliographical references

Haney, Johannah
   Small birds. Marshall Cavendish Benchmark 2010 46p il (Great pets) lib bdg $29.93
Grades: 2 3 4   **636.6**
1. Cage birds
ISBN 978-0-7614-4150-2 lib bdg; 0-7614-4150-6 lib bdg
LC 2008037258
"Describes the characteristics and behavior of small pet birds, also discussing their physical appearance and place in history." Publisher's note
Includes glossary and bibliographical references

Mead, Wendy
   Top 10 birds for kids; [by] Wendy Mead. Enslow Publishers 2008 48p il (Top pets for kids with American Humane) lib bdg $23.93
Grades: 2 3 4 5   **636.6**
1. Pets 2. Cage birds
ISBN 978-0-7660-3072-5 lib bdg; 0-7660-3072-5 lib bdg
LC 2007-38479
"Includes beautiful full-color photos showing the animals at their best. Judicious use of text boxes, crisp fonts, and white space will make it easy for readers to follow the flow of information." SLJ
Includes glossary and bibliographical references

Niven, Felicia Lowenstein
   Learning to care for a bird. Enslow Publishers 2010 48p il (Beginning pet care with American Humane) lib bdg $23.93
Grades: 2 3 4   **636.6**
1. Cage birds
ISBN 978-0-7660-3192-0; 0-7660-3192-6
LC 2008048964
"Readers will learn how to choose, train, and care for a bird." Publisher's note
Includes glossary and bibliographical references

Rockwood, Leigh

Parrots are smart! PowerKids Press 2010 24p il (Super smart animals) lib bdg $21.25; pa $8.25

Grades: 2 3 4 5   **636.6**

1. Parrots

ISBN 978-1-4358-9376-4 lib bdg; 1-4358-9376-X lib bdg; 978-1-4358-9844-8 pa; 1-4358-9844-3 pa

Examines the intelligence of parrots.

"Bright, colorful, captioned photographs complement the text. Rockwood does an excellent job of simplifying the information without making the text choppy or boring." Libr Media Connect

Includes glossary and bibliographical references

Spinner, Stephanie

Alex the parrot; no ordinary bird. by Stephanie Spinner; illustrations by Meilo So. Alfred A. Knopf 2012 41 p. $17.99

Grades: 1 2 3 4   **636.6**

1. Birds 2. Parrots 3. Animal intelligence 4. African gray parrot

ISBN 0375868461; 9780375868467; 9780375968464

LC 2011014381

In this picture-book biography, author Stephanie Spinner tells the story of how "Irene Pepperberg's African gray parrot learned to speak and understand English so well [that] he changed both public and scientific beliefs about animal communication and cognition. Named Alex, for Avian Learning Experiment, the parrot was randomly acquired from a pet shop for graduate student Pepperberg's research." (Kirkus Reviews)

636.7 Dogs

Arlon, Penelope

Puppies and kittens; by Penelope Arlon and Tory Gordon-Harris. Scholastic 2013 32 p. (Scholastic discover more) (hardcover) $7.99

Grades: PreK K 1   **636.7**

1. Cats 2. Dogs 3. Animals -- Infancy 4. Cats -- Habits and behavior 5. Dogs -- Habits and behavior 6. Kittens 7. Puppies

ISBN 0545495660; 9780545495660

LC 2012285421

This book by Penelope Arlon and Tory Gordon-Harris "is packed with facts about everyone's favorite pets. Each double-page spread features as aspect of the life of animal babies for children to compare with their own lives. Where to eat and sleep, learning, playing, even fighting with your brothers and sisters! Collection spreads feature many puppy and kitten breeds and there's lots of information about these mammals' wild cousins." (Publisher's note)

Baines, Becky

Everything dogs; All the canine facts, photos, and fun that you can get your paws on! by Becky Baines; with Dr. Gary Weitzman. National Geographic 2012 64 p. col. ill. (paperback) $12.95; (library) $21.90

Grades: 3 4 5   **636.7**

1. Picture books for children 2. Dogs

ISBN 1426310242; 1426310250; 9781426310249; 9781426310256

LC 2012289035

This book by Becky Baines looks at dogs. "Baines starts with the basics ('What is a dog?') and moves on to discuss small and large breeds, answer doggie-related questions ('Why do dogs roll in smelly stuff?'), and imagine your pet's daily schedule. . . . This also presents a chart for decoding canine moods and looks at the dog family, which includes coyotes, dingoes, and jackals, among others." (Booklist)

Includes bibliographical references (page 62) and index.

Barnes, Julia

Pet dogs; [by] Julia Barnes. Gareth Stevens Pub. 2007 un il (Pet pals) lib bdg $23.93

Grades: 2 3 4 5   **636.7**

1. Dogs

ISBN 0-8368-6777-7

LC 2006042378

This places dogs "within the context of [their] wild roots and [their] relationship to humans. . . . Barnes explains what makes the animal an ideal pet, recommends how to be a good caregiver, and reveals how the creature communicates (as well as how to answer). The [book mixes] practical advice with trivia in a way that children will find informative and easy to navigate. Crisp, full-color photos enhance the [text]." SLJ

Includes glossary and bibliographical references

Bial, Raymond

Rescuing Rover; saving America's dogs. Houghton Mifflin 2011 80p il

Grades: 4 5 6 7   **636.7**

1. Dogs 2. Animal welfare

ISBN 0-547-34125-3; 978-0-547-34125-5

LC 2010025123

"This accessible, amply illustrated title offers and informative introduction to canine-rescue endeavors. After recounting his own moving story of adopting a rescue dog, Bial provides a history of human-dog relationships. . . . Bial also explores rescue organizations, such as the ASPCA. . . . Bial frankly discusses the abuse many dogs experience . . . as well as euthanasia. . . . Historical and contemporary photos; extensive book lists . . .; websites; and detailed index complete this well-presented resource." Booklist

Includes bibliographical references

Bidner, Jenni

Is my dog a wolf? how your pet compares to its wild cousin. Lark Books 2006 64p il $9.95

Grades: 3 4 5 6   **636.7**

1. Dogs 2. Wolves

ISBN 978-1-57990-732-7; 1-57990-732-6

LC 2005-34865

"This book identifies instinctual behaviors in wolves, such as pack living, licking and biting at one another, and howling, and describes how they are manifested in the common house dog, even though the species changed thousands of years ago. . . . Clear color photographs beautifully illustrate the text. This informative, entertaining title is suitable for reports and for general reading." SLJ

Biniok, Janice

The **miniature** schnauzer. Eldorado Ink 2010 112p il (Our best friends) lib bdg $34.95

Grades: 4 5 6 7   **636.7**

1. Dogs

ISBN 978-1-932904-61-1 lib bdg; 1-932904-61-1 lib bdg

"The Our Best Friends series continues to be an ideal resource for those kids (or even adults) looking for a cradle-to-grave primer on responsible pet ownership. . . . These [books] offer far more than the customary cursory enticements and warnings usually aimed at first-time animal caregivers, with in-depth information on health issues and extensive explanations of the various types of species. . . . This is required (if sobering) reading for the serious pet owner." Booklist

Includes bibliographical references

The **rottweiler**. Eldorado Ink 2010 112p il (Our best friends) lib bdg $34.95

Grades: 4 5 6 7 **636.7**
1. Dogs
ISBN 978-1-932904-64-2 lib bdg; 1-932904-64-6 lib bdg

"The Our Best Friends series continues to be an ideal resource for those kids (or even adults) looking for a cradle-to-grave primer on responsible pet ownership. . . . These [books] offer far more than the customary cursory enticements and warnings usually aimed at first-time animal caregivers, with in-depth information on health issues and extensive explanations of the various types of species. . . . This is required (if sobering) reading for the serious pet owner." Booklist

Includes bibliographical references

Bozzo, Linda
Fire dog heroes. Enslow Publishers 2010 48p il (Amazing working dogs with American Humane) lib bdg $23.93
Grades: 2 3 4 **636.7**
1. Arson 2. Working dogs 3. Fire fighting
ISBN 978-0-7660-3202-6; 0-7660-3202-7
LC 2008048019

"The text opens with a true story of an arson dog, and then it explains the history of the arson K-9 team and the training methods used to transform an ordinary dog into a canine hero." Publisher's note

Includes glossary and bibliographical references

Search and rescue dog heroes. Enslow Publishers 2010 48p il (Amazing working dogs with American Humane) lib bdg $23.93
Grades: 2 3 4 **636.7**
1. Rescue dogs
ISBN 978-0-7660-3201-9; 0-7660-3201-9
LC 2008048018

"The text opens with a true story of a search and rescue (SAR) dog, and then it explains the history of the SAR K-9 team and the training methods used to transform an ordinary dog into a canine hero." Publisher's note

Includes glossary and bibliographical references

Therapy dog heroes. Enslow Publishers 2010 48p il (Amazing working dogs with American humane) lib bdg $23.93
Grades: 2 3 4 **636.7**
1. Working dogs
ISBN 978-0-7660-3200-2; 0-7660-3200-0
LC 2008048020

"The text opens with a true story of a therapy dog, and then it explains the history of the therapy dog and the training methods used to transform an ordinary dog into a canine hero." Publisher's note

Includes glossary and bibliographical references

Calmenson, Stephanie
May I pet your dog? the how-to guide for kids meeting dogs (and dogs meeting kids) by Stephanie Calmenson; illustrated by Jan Ormerod. Clarion Books 2007 32p il $9.95
Grades: PreK K 1 2 **636.7**
1. Dogs
ISBN 978-0-618-51034-4; 0-618-51034-6
LC 2005-34955

Harry the dog explains how to safely meet him and his friends.

"Straightforward guidelines and a positive, encouraging tone make this book appealing and practical. Young dog lovers will delight in the variety of breeds shown in the bright, clear illustrations." SLJ

Rosie; a visiting dog's story. photographs by Justin Sutcliffe. Clarion Bks. 1994 47p il hardcover o.p. pa $6.95

Grades: K 1 2 3 **636.7**
1. Dogs
ISBN 0-395-65477-7; 0-395-92722-6 pa
LC 93-21243

"Rosie is the true story of an endearing Tibetan terrier who works as a therapy dog with Delta Society's Pet Partners Program of New York City. Rosie's tenderness and enthusiasm come through in Sutcliffe's fantastic photos that chronicle Rosie's training and first visit to a children's hospital and a nursing home." Child Book Rev Serv

Carnesi, Monica
Little dog lost; a true story of a brave dog named Baltic. Nancy Paulsen Books 2012 il $15.99
Grades: PreK K **636.7**
1. Dogs 2. Animal rescue
ISBN 978-0-399-25666-0; 0-399-25666-0

On a cold winter day, a curious dog wandered onto a frozen river, and before he knew it he was traveling fast on a sheet of ice. Many people tried to help, but the dog could not be reached. Finally, after two nights and seventy-five miles, the little dog was saved by a ship out in the Baltic Sea.

"The story is told simply and charmingly. The author's use of the present tense gives the narrative immediacy, and with very brief sentences, some dialogue and questions posed to readers, Carnesi imbues the tale with a strong sense of drama that will captivate young listeners." Kirkus

Castaldo, Nancy F.
Sniffer dogs; how dogs (and their noses) save the world. Nancy F. Castaldo. Houghton Mifflin Harcourt 2014 160 p. color illustrations $16.99
Grades: 4 5 6 7 8 **636.7**
1. Rescue dogs 2. Search dogs 3. Smell 4. Detector dogs 5. Dogs -- Sense organs
ISBN 054408893X; 9780544088931
LC 2013017612

This middle grade book by Nancy F. Castaldo describes how "some dogs work with police officers, soldiers and even scientists to put their 'sniffers' to work. Sniffer dogs make use of the amazing biology behind their noses to protect people from bombs, catch criminals smuggling drugs, or help researchers locate a hard to find snail in a forest." (Publisher's note)

"The attractive color photos that capture many of these canines in action and the accessible tone of the text make this an appealing read. A well-organized, thoughtfully written title that celebrates the achievements of these great dogs." SLJ

Includes bibliographical references and index

Coren, Stanley
Why do dogs have wet noses? Kids Can Press 2006 63p il $14.95; pa $9.95
Grades: 3 4 5 6 **636.7**
1. Dogs
ISBN 1-55337-657-9; 1-55337-658-7 pa

"This interesting, entertaining book has chapters on 'How Humans and Dogs Became Friends,' 'How Dogs See the World,' 'How Dogs Talk,' and 'How Dogs Think.' The question-and-answer format is interspersed with facts and stories in sidebars. . . . Beautiful full-color photos show many breeds." SLJ

Crosby, Jeff
Little lions, bull baiters & hunting hounds; a history of dog breeds. written and illustrated by Jeff Crosby and Shelley Ann Jackson. Tundra Books 2008 72p il $19.95

Grades: 2 3 4 5   **636.7**
1. Dogs
ISBN 978-0-88776-815-6; 0-88776-815-6
     LC 2007927387
"Featuring more than breeds that are categorized as hunting, herding, working, or companion dogs, this attractive volume includes interesting and sometimes unusual facts about canines. . . . The painterly illustrations are often action-packed. . . . There is also a brief history of the origin of dogs and a succinct look at mixed breeds. . . . This is a great browsing book." SLJ
Includes bibliographical references

Dennis, Brian
  ★ **Nubs**; the true story of a mutt, a Marine & a miracle. by Brian Dennis, Kirby Larson, and Mary Nethery. Little, Brown Books for Young Readers 2009 un il $17.99
Grades: K 1 2 3   **636.7**
1. Dogs 2. Iraq War, 2003- -- Personal narratives
ISBN 978-0-316-05318-1; 0-316-05318-X
     LC 2009003808
This is a "hugely inspirational true account. . . . The gritty, low-res shots of the two companions against the bleak Iraqi horizon are married with text so gracefully that many of the compositions could be book jackets." Booklist

Gaines, Ann
Top 10 dogs for kids; [by] Ann Graham Gaines. Enslow Publishers 2008 48p il (Top pets for kids with American Humane) lib bdg $23.93
Grades: 2 3 4 5   **636.7**
1. Dogs
ISBN 978-0-7660-3070-1 lib bdg; 0-7660-3070-9 lib bdg
     LC 2007-24510
"Includes beautiful full-color photos showing the animals at their best. Judicious use of text boxes, crisp fonts, and white space will make it easy for readers to follow the flow of information." SLJ
Includes glossary and bibliographical references

George, Jean Craighead
  ★ **How** to talk to your dog; illustrated by Sue Truesdell. Harper-Collins Pubs. 2000 26p il $9.95
Grades: 2 3 4   **636.7**
1. Dogs
ISBN 0-06-027092-6
     LC 98-41515
Describes how dogs communicate with people through their behavior and sounds and explains how to talk back to them using sounds, behavior, and body language
"The mixed photography (of George, representing the humans) and illustration (an endearingly scruffy yellow mutt is the main canine representative) is . . . effective. . . . This will be an accessible and perhaps paradigm-shifting introduction for young readers." Bull Cent Child Books

Gewirtz, Elaine Waldorf
The **bulldog**. Eldorado Ink 2010 112p il (Our best friends) lib bdg $34.95
Grades: 4 5 6 7   **636.7**
1. Dogs
ISBN 978-1-932904-58-1 lib bdg; 1-932904-58-1 lib bdg
"The Our Best Friends series continues to be an ideal resource for those kids (or even adults) looking for a cradle-to-grave primer on responsible pet ownership. These [books] offer far more than the customary cursory enticements and warnings usually aimed at first-time animal caregivers, with in-depth information on health issues and extensive ex-

planations of the various types of species. . . . This is required (if sobering) reading for the serious pet owner." Booklist
Includes bibliographical references

Fetch this book. Eldorado Ink 2010 112p il (Our best friends) lib bdg $34.95
Grades: 4 5 6 7   **636.7**
1. Dogs -- Training
ISBN 978-1-932904-60-4 lib bdg; 1-932904-60-3 lib bdg
This "is a dog-training manual, with pet-care advice only in reference to training. [This] well-written [book provides] examples to support [its] points and solid online and text resources and feature [a] clean, uncluttered [layout]. . . . There is plenty of practical information that motivated readers can glean from [this title]." SLJ
Includes bibliographical references

Goldish, Meish
Ground zero dogs; by Meish Goldish. Bearport Pub. 2013 32 p. col. ill. (library binding) $25.27
Grades: 2 3 4   **636.7**
1. Search dogs 2. Picture books for children 3. September 11 terrorist attacks, 2001 4. Rescue dogs 5. World Trade Center Site (New York, N.Y.)
ISBN 1617725765; 9781617725760
     LC 2012003341
This children's picture book is part of the Dog Heroes series. The book introduces "readers to a select few of the roughly 300 search-and-rescue dogs that used their agile feet and powerful senses of smell . . . to locate both survivors and bodies among the World Trade Center rubble. . . . Salty helped his blind owner escape alive from the seventy-first floor, and Trakr uncovered a woman who had been buried for 24 hours." (Booklist)
Includes bibliographical references and index

Goodman, Susan E.
It's a dog's life; how man's best friend sees, hears, and smells the world. written by Susan E. Goodman; illustrated by David Slonim. 1st ed. Roaring Brook Press 2012 32 p. col. ill.
Grades: 2 3 4   **636.7**
1. Dogs 2. Dogs -- humor 3. Dogs -- Behavior 4. Dogs -- Evolution
ISBN 9781596434486
     LC 2011022965
This book by Susan E. Goodman and illustrated by David Slonim focuses on dog breeds and dog behavior. "Have you ever wondered what your dog sees when he looks at a sunset? Or what she smells when she has her nose to the ground? And what IS your pooch trying to say when he looks at you with those big puppy eyes? . . . [Goodman] answers those questions and a whole lot more." (Publisher's note)
Includes bibliographical references.

Gorrell, Gena K.
Working like a dog; the story of working dogs through history. Tundra 2003 156p il pa $16.95
Grades: 4 5 6 7   **636.7**
1. Working dogs
ISBN 0-88776-589-0
"Gorrell begins by tracing the evolution of 'household canids' from the wild into the civilized world. Other chapters delve into the many ways in which these animals have been viewed throughout history, what makes particular breeds right for certain jobs, dogs at war, famous pooches, etc. . . . The well-captioned, black-and-white photographs and

reproductions add greatly to a narrative that's packed with intriguing details." SLJ

Includes bibliographical references

Grogan, John

Marley; a dog like no other. Collins 2007 196p il $16.99; lib bdg $17.89

Grades: 4 5 6   **636.7**

1. Dogs

ISBN 978-0-06-124033-1; 978-0-06-124034-8 lib bdg

LC 2007-08600

"Grogan's anecdotal adaptation of his bestselling memoir, Marley & Me: Life and Love with the World's Worst Dog speaks to a middle-grade audience.... The narrative maintains all the energy, humor and poignancy of the adult book.... Grogan leaves young readers with fond memories of this exasperating yet thoroughly endearing creature." Publ Wkly

Hart, Joyce

Big dogs; by Joyce Hart. Marshall Cavendish Benchmark 2008 48p il (Great pets) lib bdg $29.93

Grades: 2 3 4   **636.7**

1. Dogs

ISBN 978-0-7614-2707-0 lib bdg; 0-7614-2707-4 lib bdg

LC 2007013042

This is an "enthusiastic, warm [introduction].... [It is] clearly written and [is] the most thorough, honest [introduction] to owning [big dogs] for this audience." SLJ

Includes glossary and bibliographical references

Small dogs. Marshall Cavendish Benchmark 2008 48p il (Great pets) lib bdg $29.93

Grades: 2 3 4   **636.7**

1. Dogs

ISBN 978-0-7614-2995-1 lib bdg; 0-7614-2995-6 lib bdg

LC 2007-36784

"Describes the characteristics and behavior of small dogs, also discussing their physical appearance and place in history." Publisher's note

Includes glossary and bibliographical references

Hoffman, Mary Ann

Guard dogs. Gareth Stevens Pub. 2011 24p il (Working dogs) lib bdg $22.60; pa $8.15

Grades: 2 3 4   **636.7**

1. Working dogs

ISBN 978-1-4339-4647-9 lib bdg; 1-4339-4647-5 lib bdg; 978-1-4339-4648-6 pa; 1-4339-4648-3 pa

LC 2010035241

This describes guard "dogs and the training they receive. The short chapters, complemented by numerous color photographs, provide examples of particular breeds that do [this] job and show how their characteristics are suited for the tasks. The charts provided are especially helpful, covering commands and more specific tasks. There is enough information to make the [text] feel fresh.... A solid choice for readers looking for more than cute pictures." SLJ

Herding dogs. Gareth Stevens Pub. 2011 24p il (Working dogs) lib bdg $22.60; pa $8.15

Grades: 2 3 4   **636.7**

1. Dogs

ISBN 978-1-4339-4655-4 lib bdg; 1-4339-4655-6 lib bdg; 978-1-4339-4656-1 pa; 1-4339-4656-4 pa

LC 2010035243

This describes herding "dogs and the training they receive. The short chapters, complemented by numerous color photographs, provide ex-

amples of particular breeds that do [this] job and show how their characteristics are suited for the tasks. The charts provided are especially helpful, covering commands and more specific tasks. There is enough information to make the [text] feel fresh.... A solid choice for readers looking for more than cute pictures." SLJ

Houston, Dick

Bulu, African wonder dog. Random House 2010 323p il $15.99; lib bdg $18.99

Grades: 5 6 7 8   **636.7**

1. Dogs 2. Wildlife conservation 3. Zambia

ISBN 978-0-375-84723-3; 0-375-84723-5; 978-0-375-94720-9 lib bdg; 0-375-94720-5 lib bdg

LC 2009015804

"In the Nyanja language, bulu means 'wild dog,' and that's what Steve and Anna Tolan named the beloved little Jack Russell mix they adopted. Disregarding warnings about the dangers of raising a dog in the bush, the Tolans moved from England to rural Zambia to fulfill their lifelong dream of setting up an animal rescue and conservation center... .. Bulu's energy, high spirits, and loyalty to his masters make the book read like a praise song to dogs. Houston's account is an animal-lover's delight, complete with the action-adventure of surviving the bush, fighting poachers, and spreading a message of conservation." Booklist

Huneck, Stephen

Even bad dogs go to heaven; more from the dog chapel. Abrams 2010 un il $19.95

Grades: 2 3 4   **636.7**

1. Dogs 2. Bereavement

ISBN 978-0-8109-9629-8; 0-8109-9629-4

"After recovering from a near-fatal illness, Huneck established a chapel dedicated to the relationship between dogs and their owners on his property in Vermont.... The introduction is lengthy ... but touching. It is illustrated with color photographs of the small chapel.... Following the introduction, the artist presents about 30 short sayings about dogs, one per spread, in large informal print and illustrates each one with his characteristic style. The sayings are clever and celebrate the richness that pets bring to life. They also offer comfort for those who might have lost a beloved canine friend. The illustrations are simple and solid, but brightly colored and have a gentle humor of their own." SLJ

Jackson, Emma

A home for Dixie; the true story of a rescued puppy. by Emma Jackson, with full-color photographs by Bob Carey. Collins 2008 un il $16.99; lib bdg $17.89

Grades: 1 2 3 4   **636.7**

1. Dogs

ISBN 978-0-06-144962-8; 0-06-144962-8; 978-0-06-144963-5 lib bdg; 0-06-144963-6 lib bdg

LC 2008-006049

"In this photo-essay, the author, a high school student, chronicles her quest for a puppy, her family's decision to adopt one, and their trip to Aunt Mary's Doghouse—a nonprofit rescue agency—to find the right animal.... The book's strengths are the large, full-color, often full-page photos of the appealing pup and her new owner. The Web sites recommended for potential pet owners are regularly updated." SLJ

Jeffrey, Laura S.

Dogs; how to choose and care for a dog. Enslow Publishers 2004 48p il (American humane pet care library) lib bdg $23.93

Grades: 3 4 5   **636.7**

1. Dogs

ISBN 0-7660-2520-9

LC 2003-22971

Explains who to consult, where to go to pick the right dog, and how to keep them happy and healthy

Includes glossary and bibliographical references

Jenkins, Steve

★ **Dogs** and cats; written and illustrated by Steve Jenkins. Houghton Mifflin Co. 2007 un il $16

Grades: 1 2 3 4   **636.7**

1. Cats 2. Dogs

ISBN 978-0-618-50767-2; 0-618-50767-1

LC 2006-24654

"The lively narrative provides a copious amount of information, examining each species in human history, describing evolution and domestication, highlighting physical characteristics and behaviors, and finishing up with amazing facts about each animal. The layout is excellent, with images dominating the text. Jenkins's cut and torn-paper collages are stunning." SLJ

Johnson, Jinny

Dogs and puppies; [by] Jinny Johnson. Smart Apple Media 2008 32p il (Get to know your pet) $27.10

Grades: 3 4 5 6   **636.7**

1. Dogs

ISBN 978-1-59920-089-7; 1-59920-089-9

LC 2007-52598

"Spreads include in-depth care instruction, and 'Q & A' sidebars that answer common behavioral questions. . . . The layout is clear, with full color photos and illustrations breaking up the text." SLJ

Includes glossary

Katz, Jon

★ **Meet** the dogs of Bedlam Farm; a true story. Henry Holt and Company 2011 un il $16.99

Grades: K 1 2 3   **636.7**

1. Farm life 2. Working dogs

ISBN 978-0-8050-9219-6; 0-8050-9219-6

LC 2010011698

"Border collies Rose and Izzy; Frieda, a rottweiler/German shepherd mix; and black Lab Lenore are four dogs living on Bedlam Farm in Upstate New York. Katz lives on the farm and has written about it for older audiences. . . . The large, full-color photographs are totally engaging and capture the animals' distinct personalities. . . . The writing is crisp and clear, and the stories (each dog gets its own turn) are sweet and filled with gentle humor." SLJ

Laidlaw, Rob

No shelter here; Making the world a kinder place for dogs. Rob Laidlaw. Pajama Press 2012 63 p.

Grades: 3 4 5 6 7 8   **636.7**

1. Dogs 2. Animal rights 3. Animal welfare

ISBN 0986949558; 9780986949555

This book provides an "informative and visually varied introduction to problems affecting dogs worldwide. In a short, colorful volume with sidebars and photographs on nearly every page, professional dog advocate [Rob] Laidlaw . . . presents facts about how dogs live, provides an overview of the cruelty dogs face at the hands of humans and offers profiles of young activists who are working to better dogs' lives. . . . A list of animal welfare websites points interested readers toward further information." (Kirkus)

Includes bibliographical references and index.

Lunis, Natalie

Greyhound; canine blur! Bearport Pub. 2011 24p il map (Blink of an eye. Superfast animals!) lib bdg $22.61

Grades: 1 2 3   **636.7**

1. Dogs 2. Animal locomotion

ISBN 978-1-936087-90-7; 1-936087-90-1

LC 2010010576

This describes the greyhound dog, including where it was first bred, why it was so helpful to hunters, and the ways its body helps it reach its record-breaking speeds.

This "is sure to appeal to a wide variety of readers. Vibrant photos illustrate each animal from multiple perspectives, providing opportunity for readers to closely examine the animal. Information is organized by subject heading and branches into the animal's physical features and how they contribute to its speed, the animal's natural predators, and how the animal makes use of speed as a means of survival. . . . This . . . will be a worthwhile addition to your nonfiction collection." Libr Media Connect

Includes glossary and bibliographical references

McCarthy, Meghan

The **incredible** life of Balto. Alfred A. Knopf 2011 un il $16.99; lib bdg $19.99

Grades: K 1 2   **636.7**

1. Sled dogs 2. Diphtheria 3. Nome (Alaska) 4. Balto (Dog)

ISBN 978-0-375-84460-7; 0-375-84460-0; 978-0-375-94460-4 lib bdg; 0-375-94460-5 lib bdg

LC 2009-52707

"After making an arduous journey to deliver medicine to combat diphtheria in Nome, Alaska, in 1925, Balto and his owner at first enjoy fame. But after a statue and a starring movie role, Balto's fortunes change when he's sold to a vaudeville act. . . . Straightforward narration keeps this picture-book biography moving toward its happy conclusion. . . . It's an accessible introduction to the story of Balto, and a reminder of the fickle nature of fame." Publ Wkly

Medway, Jim

Big Dogs, Little Dogs; a visual guide to the world's dogs. Jim Medway. Firefly Books Ltd 2016 32 p. color illustrations $19.95

Grades: PreK K 1 2 3   **636.7**

1. Dogs 2. Dog breeds

ISBN 1770858288; 9781770858282

LC 2016047596

This book, by Jim Medway, "features 300 dog breeds, including every breed recognized by the American Kennel Club. Fun double-page spreads show dogs in the seven official groupings -- Working, Toy, Hound, Terrier, Herding, Sporting, Non-Sporting -- as well as 'designer' dogs like the Labradoodle and Chiweenie. There are also some obscure breeds recognized by other kennel clubs in Europe, . . . as well as some dogs not yet officially recognized by the American Kennel Club." (Publisher's note)

"Those seeking facts for school reports should stick to more traditional resources, but dog lovers will spend hours poring over these winsome illustrations." SLJ

Mehus-Roe, Kristin

Dogs for kids! everything you need to know about dogs. by Kristin Mehus-Roe. BowTie Press 2007 384p il pa $14.95

Grades: 4 5 6 7   **636.7**

1. Dogs

ISBN 978-1-931993-83-8 pa; 1-931993-83-1 pa

LC 2006035434

"If you are looking for a book about canines that is entertaining as well as immensely informative, this is it. In a lively, conversational tone, Mehus-Roe offers a vast amount of material, from the history of dogs to vacationing with a pet, and provides practical and upbeat explanations, ideas, offbeat tidbits, and pertinent details." SLJ

Includes bibliographical references

Morn, September B.

The **pug**. Eldorado Ink 2010 112p il (Our best friends) lib bdg $34.95

Grades: 4 5 6 7   **636.7**

1. Dogs

ISBN 978-1-932904-63-5 lib bdg; 1-932904-63-8 lib bdg

"The Our Best Friends series continues to be an ideal resource for those kids (or even adults) looking for a cradle-to-grave primer on responsible pet ownership. . . . These [books] offer far more than the customary cursory enticements and warnings usually aimed at first-time animal caregivers, with in-depth information on health issues and extensive explanations of the various types of species. . . . This is required (if sobering) reading for the serious pet owner." Booklist

Includes bibliographical references

Niven, Felicia Lowenstein

Learning to care for a dog. Enslow Publishers 2010 48p il (Beginning pet care with American Humane) lib bdg $23.93

Grades: 2 3 4   **636.7**

1. Dogs

ISBN 978-0-7660-3190-6; 0-7660-3190-X

LC 2008048962

"Readers will learn how to choose, train, and care for a dog." Publisher's note

Includes glossary and bibliographical references

Patent, Dorothy Hinshaw

★ **Saving** Audie; a pit bull puppy gets a second chance. photographs by William Muñoz. Walker & Company 2011 un il $16.99; lib bdg $17.89

Grades: 2 3 4   **636.7**

1. Dogs 2. Animal welfare 3. Football players

ISBN 978-0-8027-2272-0; 0-8027-2272-5; 978-0-8027-2273-7 lib bdg; 0-8027-2273-3 lib bdg

LC 2010-36547

When Michael Vick's dog fighting ring was discovered, more than forty dogs were rescued. But their struggle was far from over. Most animal advocates believed the former fighting dogs were too damaged to save, but Audie and his kennel mates would prove them wrong when public outcry and the publicity surrounding Michael Vick's punishment won them a chance at a happy life.

"Munoz's photographs range from moody . . . to adorable. . . . Patent wrings emotion from her understated text and remains nonjudgmental about Vick's reemergence." Booklist

Prap, Lila

Doggy whys. North-South Books 2011 un il $16.95

Grades: 2 3 4   **636.7**

1. Dogs

ISBN 0-7358-4014-8; 978-0-7358-4014-0

"Although this book could have coasted by entirely on the strength of the funky, ruff-n-tuff cartoon pooches that are the centerpiece of each spread, Prap goes one better and provides insightful information on why dogs are so, well, darn doggy. . . . A few of her inquiries will enlighten even veteran fact hounds." Booklist

Rajczak, Kristen

Pulling dogs. Gareth Stevens Pub. 2011 24p il (Working dogs) lib bdg $22.60; pa $8.15

Grades: 2 3 4   **636.7**

1. Working dogs 2. Sled dog racing

ISBN 978-1-4339-4663-9 lib bdg; 1-4339-4663-7 lib bdg; 978-1-4339-4664-6 pa; 1-4339-4664-5 pa

LC 2010037168

This describes pulling "dogs and the training they receive. The short chapters, complemented by numerous color photographs, provide examples of particular breeds that do [this] job and show how their characteristics are suited for the tasks. The charts provided are especially helpful, covering commands and more specific tasks. There is enough information to make the [text] feel fresh. . . . A solid choice for readers looking for more than cute pictures." SLJ

Rescue dogs. Gareth Stevens Pub. 2011 24p il (Working dogs) lib bdg $22.60; pa $7

Grades: 2 3 4   **636.7**

1. Rescue dogs

ISBN 978-1-4339-4667-7 lib bdg; 1-4339-4667-X lib bdg; 978-1-4339-4668-4 pa; 1-4339-4668-8 pa

LC 2010037169

This describes rescue "dogs and the training they receive. The short chapters, complemented by numerous color photographs, provide examples of particular breeds that do [this] job and show how their characteristics are suited for the tasks. The charts provided are especially helpful, covering commands and more specific tasks. There is enough information to make the [text] feel fresh. . . . A solid choice for readers looking for more than cute pictures." SLJ

Rockwood, Leigh

Dogs are smart! PowerKids Press 2010 24p il (Super smart animals) lib bdg $21.25; pa $8.25

Grades: 2 3 4 5   **636.7**

1. Dogs

ISBN 978-1-4358-9374-0 lib bdg; 1-4358-9374-3 lib bdg; 978-1-4358-9836-3 pa; 1-4358-9836-2 pa

Examines the intelligence of dogs.

"Bright, colorful, captioned photographs complement the text. Rockwood does an excellent job of simplifying the information without making the text choppy or boring." Libr Media Connect

Includes glossary

Rogers, Tammie

4-H guide to dog training and dog tricks. Voyageur Press 2009 176p il pa $18.99

Grades: 5 6 7 8 9 10   **636.7**

1. Dogs -- Training

ISBN 978-0-7603-3629-8; 0-7603-3629-6

LC 2009-17040

"This is not simply a how-to-train book; it is also a guide to cultivating a respectful relationship with your dog. The excellent information is comprehensive, and it is presented in a clear and detailed style. The author covers different training methods, discussing the tools needed from food to collar selection. Using this manual, dog owners can move through the basics (sit, down, etc.) to obedience competition and fun tricks and activities." SLJ

Includes bibliographical references

Rutherford, Clarice

★ **A dog** is a dog; and that's why he's so special. by Clarice Rutherford. Alpine 2012 xi, 98 p.p col. ill. (paperback : alk. paper) $14.95

Grades: 4 5 6   **636.7**

1. Pets 2. Wolves 3. Animal behavior 4. Dogs -- Behavior 5.

Dogs -- Training
ISBN 1577791037; 9781577791034

LC 2009003029

"The author, Clarice Rutherford, brings her many years of experience with dogs into this book, and explains dogs, how to manage, train, as well as understand them . . . The reader will learn the basic history of dogs and their relationship to the wolf. How the dog's brain develops and the importance of early socialization and basic training is explained, as well as how the genetics and instincts of the wolf play an important role in the behavior of the dog." (Barnes & Noble)

Includes bibliographical references and index.

Schweitzer, Karen

The **beagle**. Eldorado Ink 2010 112p il (Our best friends) lib bdg $34.95

Grades: 4 5 6 7   **636.7**

1. Dogs

ISBN 978-1-932904-57-4 lib bdg; 1-932904-57-3 lib bdg

"The Our Best Friends series continues to be an ideal resource for those kids (or even adults) looking for a cradle-to-grave primer on responsible pet ownership. . . . These [books] offer far more than the customary cursory enticements and warnings usually aimed at first-time animal caregivers, with in-depth information on health issues and extensive explanations of the various types of species. . . . This is required (if sobering) reading for the serious pet owner." Booklist

Includes bibliographical references

The **dachshund**. Eldorado Ink 2010 112p il (Our best friends) lib bdg $34.95

Grades: 4 5 6 7   **636.7**

1. Dogs

ISBN 978-1-932904-59-8 lib bdg; 1-932904-59-X lib bdg

"The Our Best Friends series continues to be an ideal resource for those kids (or even adults) looking for a cradle-to-grave primer on responsible pet ownership. . . . These [books] offer far more than the customary cursory enticements and warnings usually aimed at first-time animal caregivers, with in-depth information on health issues and extensive explanations of the various types of species. . . . This is required (if sobering) reading for the serious pet owner." Booklist

Includes bibliographical references

Simon, Seymour

★ **Dogs**. HarperCollinsPublishers 2004 un il $17.99; lib bdg $18.89; pa $6.99

Grades: 1 2 3 4   **636.7**

1. Dogs

ISBN 0-06-028942-2; 0-06-028943-0 lib bdg; 978-0-06-446255-6 pa; 0-06-446255-2 pa

LC 2003-12484

Provides a basic introduction to the physical characteristics and behavior of dogs

"The striking color photos, including many close-ups, create a feeling of intimacy. . . . Simon succeeds in addressing his topic in clear, easily understood vocabulary without writing down to children." SLJ

Stamper, Judith Bauer

Eco dogs. Bearport Pub. 2011 32p il (Dog heroes) lib bdg $25.27

Grades: 3 4 5   **636.7**

1. Working dogs 2. Endangered species

ISBN 978-1-61772-152-6; 1-61772-152-2

LC 2010041191

"Eco Dogs help scientists by sniffing out scat, which is analyzed for signs of pollutants or changes in the food chain that might have harmful effects on the environment and on indigenous species. [This book is]

engaging not just because the content is so compelling, but also because the [author has] highlighted specific dogs currently working in [this field]. The use of real names and full-color photographs on every page, many contributed by the individuals who work with these dogs, makes reading [this book] a personal experience. . . . [An] excellent [introduction] to [this] new [development] in service-dog training." SLJ

Includes glossary and bibliographical references

Sundance, Kyra

101 dog tricks, kids edition; fun and easy activities, games, and crafts. Kyra Sundance. Quarry Books 2014 191 p. color illustrations $19.99

Grades: 3 4 5 6   **636.7**

1. Dogs -- Training

ISBN 1592538932; 9781592538935

LC 2014014373

This book on dog tricks, by Kyra Sundance, "features full color step-by-step photos of every trick, making it easy to follow along. Real kids are featured in the photos, actually training dogs--you can do it too! Many tricks are simple enough that your dog can learn them in ten minutes." (Publisher's note)

"The tricks only require common household or easily accessible items, and they include helpful tips for preparation, troubleshooting, and what to expect. Many of the tips also differentiate for differently sized and more fearful or shy dogs." Booklist

Urbigkit, Cat

Brave dogs, gentle dogs; how they guard sheep. Boyds Mills Press 2005 32p il $15.95; pa $8.95

Grades: K 1 2 3   **636.7**

1. Sheep dogs

ISBN 1-59078-317-4; 978-1-59078-674-1 pa

LC 2004-16855

A "photo-essay on guardian dogs. Accompanied by clear, full-color photos, the simple, informative text describes the raising of these sheepdogs and their natural proclivity for guarding 'their' flocks." SLJ

The **guardian** team; on the job with Rena and Roo. Boyds Mills Press 2011 32p il

Grades: K 1 2 3   **636.7**

1. Sheep 2. Donkeys 3. Ranch life 4. Working dogs

ISBN 1590787706; 9781590787700

"Orphaned wild burro Roo and litter-runt puppy Rena become livestock guardians and, eventually, friends on the author's ranch. They are initially paired to protect lamb orphans from predators. Youthful, mutual wariness eventually unfolds into friendship between the two. . . . Heartwarming photos and clear, accessible text combine to make this story a winner." SLJ

Includes bibliographical references

Wadsworth, Ginger

Poop detectives; Working Dogs in the Field. by Ginger Wadsworth. Charlesbridge 2016 80 p. color illustrations (reinforced for library use) $17.95; (ebook) $9.99

Grades: 3 4 5 6 7   **636.7**

1. Working dogs -- Training 2. Detector dogs -- Training 3. Working Dogs for Conservation

ISBN 9781580896504; 9781607346500

LC 2015026876

In this book, by Ginger Wadsworth, "scat-detection dogs like Wicket, Tucker, and Orbee are conservation heroes and pioneers in a cutting-edge field of science. Canine detectives use their super sense of smell to locate the scat of target animals. From loose bear dung to gooey whale poop, scat can tell scientists valuable information about an animal's sex, age, diet, and health--all without harming the animal or endangering the researcher." (Publisher's note)

"This book encourages readers to think about unconventional sources of information and the unusual methods of data collection necessary to scientific discovery." Booklist

Includes bibliographical references (pages 77-78) and index.

Weitzman, Gary

How to Speak Dog; A Guide to Decoding Dog Language. by Aline Alexander Newman and Gary Weitzman. Natl Geographic Soc Childrens books 2013 176 p. $12.95

Grades: 4 5 6   636.7

1. Dogs -- Behavior 2. Animal communication

ISBN 142631373X; 1426315597; 9781426313738; 9781426315596

Authors Aline Alexander Newman and Gary Weitzman present an "informative, and photographically driven book that helps kids understand what their dog is trying to tell them through body language and behavior. Quick-hit tip boxes, fun facts about mankind's best friends, and informative sidebars from the experts enliven the text." (Publisher's note)

636.73   Working and herding dogs

Katz, Jon

Lenore finds a friend; a true story from Bedlam Farm. Story and photographs by Jon Katz. Henry Holt and Company 2012 32 p. (hc) $15.99

Grades: K 1 2 3   636.73

1. Friendship 2. Animal behavior 3. Picture books for children 4. Farm life 5. Animals -- Anecdotes 6. Animal communication 7. Bedlam Farm (West Hebron, N.Y.) 8. Emotions in animals -- Anecdotes

ISBN 080509220X; 9780805092202

LC 2011029040

This children's picture book is based on the story of the friendship between puppy Lenore and ram Brutus at Bedlam Farm. Lenore "was lonely because the other animals . . . were not friendly towards her. Rose, the other dog at the farm, was too busy herding the sheep" to play. Lenore starts making friends with Brutus by giving him daily kisses. "Despite Rose's attempts to keep Lenore away from Brutus, Lenore does not give up and the friendship . . . grows." (Children's Literature)

Kimmel, Elizabeth Cody

Balto and the great race; illustrated by Nora Koerber. Random House 1999 99p il map (Stepping stone book) hardcover o.p. pa $3.99

Grades: 3 4 5   636.73

1. Diphtheria 2. Sled dog racing 3. Nome (Alaska)

ISBN 0-679-99198-0 lib bdg; 0-679-89198-6 pa

LC 98-35753

Recounts how the sled dog Balto saved Nome, Alaska, in 1925 from a diphtheria epidemic by delivering medicine through a raging snowstorm

"Kimmel's writing deftly combines geography, sled racing, and historical background with the gripping adventure of Balto's race to save lives. In many ways, the book reads like fast-paced fiction. Koerber's serviceable black-and-white illustrations appear throughout and reflect the action. Sure to appeal to beginning chapter-book readers." SLJ

636.755   Terriers

Gagne, Tammy

West Highlands, Scotties, and other terriers; by Tammy Gagne. Capstone Press 2017 32 p. color illustrations (ebook) $27.99; (library binding) $27.99

Grades: 4 5 6   636.755

1. Dogs 2. Terriers 3. Dog breeds

ISBN 9781515703136; 9781515703044

LC 2015043106

In this book, by Tammy Gagne, "learn all about the characteristics of terrier dog breeds and much more! Packed with amazing photographs and fun facts, dog owners and fans will get an in-depth look at these intelligent canines." (Publisher's note)

"While Gagne points out positive qualities in each breed discussed, readers looking for a new pet will find the carefully phrased comments in the personality, training, and care paragraphs very useful in deciding whether to choose a terrier and, if so, which one. A solid choice for libraries." Booklist

Includes bibliographical references and index

636.8   Cats

Barnes, Julia

Pet cats; [by] Julia Barnes. Gareth Stevens Pub. 2007 32p il (Pet pals) lib bdg $23.93

Grades: 2 3 4 5   636.8

1. Cats

ISBN 0-8368-6776-9

LC 2006042377

"In spreads filled with color photographs, Barnes presents a short explanation of the feline family tree, as well as the history of cat-human relationships, before delving into cat breeds, characteristics, and behavior. Final sections offer ideas for new cat owners." Booklist

Includes glossary and bibliographical references

Bidner, Jenni

Is my cat a tiger? how your cat compares to its wild cousins. Lark Books 2006 64p il $9.95

Grades: 3 4 5 6   636.8

1. Cats 2. Wild cats

ISBN 1-57990-815-2

LC 2006023356

"This book shows how domestic cats compare with their wild cousins. Specifically, it addresses what domestic behavior reveals about wild roots. . . . The color photographs are fantastic. . . . This is a fascinating volume." SLJ

Biniok, Janice

Mixed breed cats. Eldorado Ink 2010 112p il (Our best friends) lib bdg $34.95

Grades: 4 5 6 7   636.8

1. Cats

ISBN 978-1-932904-62-8 lib bdg; 1-932904-62-X lib bdg

This "is a cradle-to-grave overview of a cat's life. . . . [This] well-written [book provides] examples to support [its] points and solid online and text resources and feature [a] clean, uncluttered [layout]. . . . There is plenty of practical information that motivated readers can glean from [this title]. [It] debunks some presumptions about domesticated felines, commenting that the 'finicky eater' tag is unwarranted, and that cats are easier to train than people think." SLJ

Includes bibliographical references

Bozzo, Linda

My first cat; [by] Linda Bozzo. Enslow Elementary 2007 32p il (My first pet library from the American Humane Association) lib bdg $22.60

Grades: 1 2 3   **636.8**

1. Cats

ISBN 978-0-7660-2750-3 lib bdg; 0-7660-2750-3 lib bdg

LC 2006008403

This offers brief basic advice on selecting a cat and caring for it.

Includes glossary and bibliographical references

George, Jean Craighead

How to talk to your cat; illustrated by Paul Meisel. HarperCollins Pubs. 2000 28p il $9.95

Grades: 2 3 4   **636.8**

1. Cats

ISBN 0-06-027968-0

LC 98-41517

Describes how cats communicate with people through their behavior and sounds and explains how to talk back to them using sounds, behavior, and body language

"The writing style is breezy, conversational, and amusing, and is helped along by the many color illustrations. The photographs of the author are cleverly combined with humorous cartoon drawings of cats that display a great deal of intelligence and comedic personality. . . . A useful and readable addition to any pet collection." SLJ

Hart, Joyce

Cats; by Joyce Hart. Marshall Cavendish Benchmark 2008 48p il (Great pets) lib bdg $29.93

Grades: 2 3 4   **636.8**

1. Cats

ISBN 978-0-7614-2710-0 lib bdg; 0-7614-2710-4 lib bdg

LC 2007016462

This is an "enthusiastic, warm [introduction]. . . . [It is] clearly written and [is] the most thorough, honest [introduction] to owning [pet cats] for this audience." SLJ

Johnson, Jinny

Cats and kittens; [by] Jinny Johnson. Black Rabbit Books 2009 32p il (Get to know your pet) $27.10

Grades: 3 4 5 6   **636.8**

1. Cats

ISBN 978-1-59920-088-0; 1-59920-088-0

LC 2007-43435

"Spreads include in-depth care instruction, and 'Q & A' sidebars that answer common behavioral questions. . . . The layout is clear, with full color photos and illustrations breaking up the text." SLJ

Includes glossary

Laidlaw, Rob

★ Cat champions; caring for our feline friends. By Rob Laidlaw. Orca Book Pub 2014 64 p. illustrations (chiefly color) $19.95

Grades: 4 5 6 7 8   **636.8**

1. Cats 2. Animal welfare 3. Voluntarism 4. Cats -- Health 5. Animal shelters

ISBN 1927485312; 9781927485316

In this book, readers "meet kids who are helping at shelters, fostering kittens, volunteering with sterilization programs and caring for abandoned cats. Animal advocate Rob Laidlaw brings readers a hopeful, inspiring look at the issues facing domesticated and feral cats, and the cat champions who are working to help them." (Publisher's note)

"The format is busy, but cat lovers probably won't mind so many photos, and the sidebars are all informative. The list of organizations where kids can learn about ways they can help is extensive and useful." Booklist

MacLeod, Elizabeth

Why do cats have whiskers? Kids Can Press 2008 64p il $14.95

Grades: 3 4 5 6   **636.8**

1. Cats

ISBN 978-1-55453-196-7; 1-55453-196-9

"With its lively text and copious photographs, this title offers readers an accessible introduction to the world of felines. . . . MacLeod's interesting facts and anecdotes are sure to keep young cat owners engaged." Horn Book Guide

Malam, John

Grow your own cat toy. Heinemann Library 2011 32p il (Grow it yourself!) lib bdg $26; pa $7.99

Grades: 2 3 4   **636.8**

1. Gardening 2. Handicraft 3. Catnip

ISBN 978-1-4329-5110-8 lib bdg; 1-4329-5110-6; 978-1-4329-5117-7 pa; 1-4329-5117-3 pa

LC 2010049835

This describes the catnip plant and why cats like it, how to grow it, and how to make a catnip toy.

This book "turns the idea [of growing a catnip toy] into a fun and fascinating project. . . . A big part of the book's appeal is the crisp color photographs. . . . Simple sentences in an easily read typeface . . . are just right for the elementary-school age group. . . . A well-done package in every way." Booklist

Includes glossary and bibliographical references

Myron, Vicki

Dewey the library cat; a true story. [by] Vicki Myron with Bret Witter. Little, Brown 2010 214p $16.99

Grades: 4 5 6 7 8   **636.8**

1. Cats 2. Libraries

ISBN 978-0-316-06871-0; 0-316-06871-3

Adapted from: Dewey: the small town library cat who touched the world, published 2008 by Grand Central Publisher for adults

"From the opening chapter, when librarian Vicki Myron finds a fragile, freezing kitten in the book return, children will be hooked on her heartwarming story about Dewey Readmore Books. . . . Anecdotes such as Dewey's fascination with rubber bands, his bizarre behavior during a bat invasion, and his finicky eating habits are ideal booktalk material. So are descriptions of Dewey's tender, intuitive interactions with people of all ages and backgrounds." Booklist

Niven, Felicia Lowenstein

Learning to care for a cat. Enslow Publishers 2010 48p il (Beginning pet care with American Humane) lib bdg $23.93

Grades: 2 3 4   **636.8**

1. Cats

ISBN 978-0-7660-3191-3; 0-7660-3191-8

LC 2008048963

"Readers will learn how to choose, train, and care for a cat." Publisher's note

Includes glossary and bibliographical references

Rau, Dana Meachen

Top 10 cats for kids; [by] Dana Meachen Rau. Enslow Publishers 2008 48p il (Top pets for kids with American Humane) lib bdg $23.93

Grades: 2 3 4 5   **636.8**

1. Cats

ISBN 978-0-7660-3071-8 lib bdg; 0-7660-3071-7 lib bdg

LC 2007-24440

"Includes beautiful full-color photos showing the animals at their best. Judicious use of text boxes, crisp fonts, and white space will make it easy for readers to follow the flow of information." SLJ

Includes glossary and bibliographical references

Rebman, Renee C.

Cats. Marshall Cavendish Benchmark 2009 47p il (Animals, animals) lib bdg $20.95

Grades: 3 4 5   **636.8**

1. Cats

ISBN 978-0-7614-3975-2

LC 2008020918

Provides comprehensive information on the anatomy, special skills, habitats, and diet of cats.

Includes glossary and bibliographical references

Simon, Seymour

★ Cats. HarperCollins Pub. 2004 un il lib bdg $16.89; pa $6.99

Grades: 1 2 3 4   **636.8**

1. Cats

ISBN 0-06-028940-6; 0-06-028941-4 lib bdg; 0-06-446254-4 pa

LC 2003-8337

Discusses the history, physical characteristics, behavior, and various breeds of cats, and provides basic information on caring for one as a pet.

"The striking color photos, including many closeups, create a feeling of intimacy. . . . Simon succeeds in addressing his topic in clear, easily understood vocabulary without writing down to children." SLJ

Tildes, Phyllis Limbacher

Calico's cousins; cats from around the world. Charlesbridge Pub. 1999 un il lib bdg $15.95; pa $6.95

Grades: K 1 2 3   **636.8**

1. Cats

ISBN 0-88106-648-6 lib bdg; 0-88106-649-4 pa

LC 98-4011

"Calico, a domestic longhair cat, introduces various breeds by describing both their origin and common traits. Each double-page spread features realistic illustrations of several cats in an environment appropriate to their origin, and a map at the end provides geographical reference." Horn Book Guide

Whitehead, Sarah

How to speak cat. Scholastic 2009 96p il pa $6.99

Grades: 4 5 6 7 8   **636.8**

1. Cats

ISBN 978-0-545-02079-4 pa; 0-545-02079-4 pa

"This pet-care book focuses on developing a relationship with a pet. The author states that the communication process is a two-way street, and she describes how readers can translate a cat's body language and vocalizations. . . . the bright color photographs of children with their cats on every page will appeal greatly to readers. This is a fun book that offers a good understanding of its audience and subject." SLJ

636.9 Other mammals

Bjorklund, Ruth

Rabbits; by Ruth Bjorklund. Marshall Cavendish Benchmark 2008 48p il (Great pets) lib bdg $28.50

Grades: 2 3 4   **636.9**

1. Rabbits

ISBN 978-0-7614-2708-7 lib bdg; 0-7614-2708-2 lib bdg

LC 2007013044

The offers an introduction to rabbits as pets and how to choose and care for them

This is an "enthusiastic, warm [introduction]. . . . [This is] clearly written and [is] the most thorough, honest [introduction] to owning a pet [rabbit] for this audience." SLJ

Includes glossary and bibliographical references

Boruchowitz, David E.

Sugar gliders; David E. Boruchowitz; [editor, Thomas Mazorlig] T.F.H. 2012 111 p. (Animal planet. Pet care library) (pbk. : alk. paper) $10.95

Grades: 4 5 6 7   **636.9**

1. Sugar gliders as pets 2. Sugar glider

ISBN 0793837111; 9780793837113

LC 2011049947

This book on sugar gliders by David E. Boruchowitz is part of the "Animal Planet Pet Care Library" series. "According to Boruchowitz, they make excellent house pets due to their affinity for cuddling in tiny places. . . . Every aspect of ownership is covered, from basic dietary requirements to grooming and socialization." (Booklist)

Includes bibliographical references and index

Bozzo, Linda

My first guinea pig and other small pets; [by] Linda Bozzo. Enslow Elementary 2007 32p il (My first pet library from the American Humane Association) lib bdg $22.60

Grades: 1 2 3   **636.9**

1. Mice 2. Pets 3. Rats 4. Ferrets 5. Gerbils 6. Rabbits 7. Hamsters 8. Guinea pigs

ISBN 978-0-7660-2752-7 lib bdg; 0-7660-2752-X lib bdg

LC 2006014970

This offers advice on selecting and caring for small pets including guinea pigs, hamsters, gerbils, rabbits, ferrets, rats, and mice.

Includes glossary and bibliographical references

Ellis, Carol

Hamsters and gerbils. Marshall Cavendish Benchmark 2009 46p il (Great pets) $20.95

Grades: 2 3 4   **636.9**

1. Gerbils 2. Hamsters

ISBN 978-0-7614-2999-9; 0-7614-2999-9

LC 2008-24336

"Describes the characteristics and behavior of pet hamsters and gerbils, also discussing their physical appearance and place in history." Publisher's note

Includes glossary and bibliographical references

Foran, Jill

Guinea pig. Weigl 2010 32p il (My pet) lib bdg $26; pa $9.95

Grades: 3 4 5   **636.9**

1. Pets 2. Guinea pigs

ISBN 978-1-60596-090-6 lib bdg; 1-60596-090-X lib bdg; 978-1-60596-091-3 pa; 1-60596-091-8 pa

LC 2009-5128

Information about how to house, feed, and care for guinea pigs.

"With clear, formal writing, and extensive coverage . . . [this title is] useful for reports. . . . Numerous color photographs, charts . . . and question-and-answer boxes supplement the [text]." SLJ

Includes glossary

Gaines, Ann

Top 10 small mammals for kids; [by] Ann Graham Gaines. Enslow Publishers 2008 48p il (Top pets for kids with American Humane) lib bdg $23.93

Grades: 2 3 4 5   **636.9**
1. Pets 2. Mammals
ISBN 978-0-7660-3075-6 lib bdg; 0-7660-3075-X lib bdg
LC 2007-38480
"Includes beautiful full-color photos showing the animals at their best. Judicious use of text boxes, crisp fonts, and white space will make it easy for readers to follow the flow of information." SLJ
Includes glossary and bibliographical references

Ganeri, Anita
★ **Rabbits**. Heinemann 2009 32p il (A pet's life) $17.75
Grades: 3 4 5   **636.9**
1. Rabbits
ISBN 978-1-4329-3394-4; 1-4329-3394-9
"Pretty much everything a child needs to know about taking care of rabbits in this title. . . . The book is organized in a logical way that will keep kids focused. . . . [The book uses] a good-size typeface and clear, adorable photos. . . . Fact-filled, fun to look at, and a pleasure to read." Booklist

Hamilton, Lynn
Ferret. Weigl 2010 32p il (My pet) lib bdg $26; pa $9.95
Grades: 3 4 5   **636.9**
1. Pets 2. Ferrets
ISBN 978-1-60596-096-8 lib bdg; 1-60596-096-9 lib bdg; 978-1-60596-097-5 pa; 1-60596-097-7 pa
LC 2009-4985
Information about how to house, feed, and care for ferrets.
"With clear, formal writing, and extensive coverage . . . [this title is] useful for reports. . . . Numerous color photographs, charts . . . and question-and-answer boxes supplement the [text]." SLJ
Includes glossary

Haney, Johannah
Ferrets. Marshall Cavendish Benchmark 2010 46p il (Great pets) lib bdg $29.93
Grades: 2 3 4   **636.9**
1. Pets 2. Ferrets
ISBN 978-0-7614-4153-3 lib bdg; 0-7614-4153-0 lib bdg
LC 2009020561
"Describes the characteristics and behavior of pet ferrets, also discussing their physical appearance and place in history." Publisher's note
Includes glossary and bibliographical references

Heos, Bridget
Do you really want a guinea pig? by Bridget Heos; illustrated by Katya Longhi. Amicus 2016 24 p. color illustrations (Do you really want a pet?) (library binding) $28.50
Grades: K 1 2   **636.9**
1. Guinea pigs 2. Pets 3. Guinea pigs as pets
ISBN 9781607537496
LC 2014033270
In this book, by Bridget Heos, illustrated by Katya Longhi, part of the "Do you really want a pet?" series, a "mischievous guinea pig (and the narrator) teach a young boy the responsibility—and the joys—of caring for a pet guinea pig. Includes 'Is this pet right for me?' quiz." (Publisher's note)
Includes bibliographical references

Johnson, Jinny
Guinea pigs; [by] Jinny Johnson. Black Rabbit Books 2009 32p il (Get to know your pet) $27.10

Grades: 3 4 5 6   **636.9**
1. Guinea pigs
ISBN 978-1-59920-211-2; 1-59920-211-5
LC 2007-43437
"Spreads include in-depth care instruction, and 'Q & A' sidebars that answer common behavioral questions. . . . The layout is clear, with full color photos and illustrations breaking up the text." SLJ
Includes glossary

Hamsters and gerbils; [by] Jinny Johnson. Black Rabbit Books 2009 32p il (Get to know your pet) $27.10
Grades: 3 4 5 6   **636.9**
1. Gerbils 2. Hamsters
ISBN 978-1-59920-092-7; 1-59920-092-9
LC 2007-52813
"Spreads include in-depth care instruction, and 'Q & A' sidebars that answer common behavioral questions. . . . The layout is clear, with full color photos and illustrations breaking up the text." SLJ
Includes glossary

Rabbits; [by] Jinny Johnson. Black Rabbit Books 2009 32p il (Get to know your pet) $27.10
Grades: 3 4 5 6   **636.9**
1. Rabbits
ISBN 978-1-59920-090-3; 1-59920-090-2
LC 2007-43436
"Spreads include in-depth care instruction, and 'Q & A' sidebars that answer common behavioral questions. . . . The layout is clear, with full color photos and illustrations breaking up the text." SLJ
Includes glossary

Rats and mice; [by] Jinny Johnson. Black Rabbit Books 2009 32p il (Get to know your pet) $27.10
Grades: 3 4 5 6   **636.9**
1. Mice 2. Rats
ISBN 978-1-59920-091-0; 1-59920-091-0
LC 2007-52815
"Spreads include in-depth care instruction, and 'Q & A' sidebars that answer common behavioral questions. . . . The layout is clear, with full color photos and illustrations breaking up the text." SLJ
Includes glossary

Kenney, Karen Latchana
★ **Sugar** glider; Karen Kenney; edited by Keli Sipperley. Rourke Educational Media 2015 32 p. color illustrations. $32.79
Grades: 3 4 5 6   **636.9**
1. Marsupials 2. Sugar gliders as pets
ISBN 1634304365; 9781634304368
LC 2015931859
Author Karen Kenney presents this children's book on sugar gliders as pets "covering history, natural habitat, care, and characteristics both positive and negative. Restrictions on ownership and any special housing and health care requirements are carefully pointed out. The animals' personalities are described, and information on bonding and communication is provided. A short list of 'Things to Think About...' encapsulates all the issues." (School Library Journal)
"Though most kids will be (thankfully) dissuaded by the amount of specialized care these animals require, the beautifully reproduced photos of oddball pets are undeniably appealing, and there are enough fascinating and informative facts to keep readers enthralled. Highly recommended." Booklist

Lewin, Ted

★ **Balarama**; a royal elephant. [by] Ted and Betsy Lewin. Lee & Low Books 2009 un il $19.95

Grades: 3 4 5 6   **636.9**

1. Elephants 2. India

ISBN 978-1-60060-265-8; 1-60060-265-7

LC 2009-1499

"Ted Lewin's brilliant, realistic watercolors capture the sun-drenched pageantry of Mysore as well as the dusty, filtered light of the forest, while Betsy Lewin's lively cartoons aptly depict the action and personalities involved. The story has pathos and tension." SLJ

Lunis, Natalie

Furry ferrets. Bearport 2010 24p il (Peculiar pets) lib bdg $22.61

Grades: 3 4 5   **636.9**

1. Pets 2. Ferrets

ISBN 978-1-59716-860-1 lib bdg; 1-59716-860-2 lib bdg

LC 2009-10378

Introduces the furry ferret, describing its physical characteristics, habitat, and behavior, and discussing the care and diet that it needs if it is kept as a pet

"The language . . . is lively . . . [and] the illustrations are vivid, with photos offering some amusing shots. . . . This [book] . . . will hold readers' attention, but also challenge them to consider the responsibilities required of owners of unusual creatures." SLJ

Includes glossary and bibliographical references

Newcomb, Rain

Is my hamster wild? the secret lives of hamsters, gerbils & guinea pigs. by Rain Newcomb & Rose McLarney. Lark Books 2008 64p il $9.95

Grades: 2 3 4   **636.9**

1. Gerbils 2. Hamsters 3. Guinea pigs

ISBN 978-1-60059-242-3; 1-60059-242-2

LC 2007-44312

"Crisp photo album-style pictures with humorous captions reinforce the deft main text." Horn Book Guide

Niven, Felicia Lowenstein

Learning to care for small mammals. Enslow Publishers 2010 48p il (Beginning pet care with American Humane) lib bdg $23.93

Grades: 2 3 4   **636.9**

1. Ferrets 2. Rabbits 3. Rodents

ISBN 978-0-7660-3195-1; 0-7660-3195-0

This describes how to care for small mammals such as rabbits, guinea pigs, gerbils, hamsters, rats, mice, or ferrets.

"The pictures are colorful and engaging, with a no-fuss layout. The text is easy to follow, pitched at just the right level for the audience." SLJ

Includes glossary and bibliographical references

Petrylak, Ashley

Guinea pigs. Marshall Cavendish Benchmark 2009 44p il (Great pets) lib bdg $29.93

Grades: 2 3 4   **636.9**

1. Guinea pigs

ISBN 978-0-7614-4148-9 lib bdg; 0-7614-4148-4 lib bdg

LC 2008037238

"Describes the characteristics and behavior of pet guinea pigs, also discussing their physical appearance and place in history." Publisher's note

Includes glossary and bibliographical references

McNichols, June

Rats; June McNicholas. 2nd edition Heinemann Library 2010 48 p illustrations library $32.65

Grades: 4 5 6 7   **636.9**

1. Rats

ISBN 9781432938505; 1432938509

LC 2009035278

Describes how to select a pet rat, what to feed it, and when to take it to the vet, as well as how to keep a pet scrapbook.

Reed, Cristie

Ferret; Cristie Reed. Rourke Educational Media 2015 32 p. color illustrations $32.79

Grades: 2 3 4 5   **636.9**

1. Ferrets 2. Pets

ISBN 1634304322; 9781634304320

LC 2015931855

This children's book by Cristie Reed on ferrets as pets "introduces these animals, covering history, natural habitat, care, and characteristics both positive and negative. Restrictions on ownership and any special housing and health care requirements are carefully pointed out. The animals' personalities are described, and information on bonding and communication is provided." (Publisher's note)

"Well written, with a clean design, these titles will be useful for educators and popular with potential pet owners." SLJ

Sobol, Richard

An **elephant** in the backyard; text and photographs by Richard Sobol. Dutton Children's Books 2004 un il $17.99

Grades: K 1 2 3   **636.9**

1. Elephants 2. Thailand

ISBN 0-525-47288-6

LC 2003-52492

Describes how special elephants are in the village of Tha Kleng in Thailand and looks at the life of one particular young elephant named Wan Pen.

This is an "engaging photo-essay. Large, colorful photographs enhance the text. . . . The text is packed with interesting tidbits about these large mammals." SLJ

636.93   Rodents

Kenney, Karen Latchana

★ **Rat**; Karen Kenney; [edited by] Keli Sipperley. Rourke Educational Media 2015 32 p. color illustrations (hbk.) $32.79; (pbk.) $9.95

Grades: 3 4 5 6   **636.93**

1. Pets 2. Rats

ISBN 1634304357; 9781634304351; 9781634305358; 1634305353

LC 2015931858

Author Karen Kenney presents this children's book on rats as pets "covering history, natural habitat, care, and characteristics both positive and negative. Restrictions on ownership and any special housing and health care requirements are carefully pointed out. The animals' personalities are described, and information on bonding and communication is provided. A short list of 'Things to Think About...' encapsulates all the issues." (School Library Journal)

"Well written, with a clean design, these titles will be useful for educators and popular with potential pet owners." SLJ

637   Processing dairy and related products

Aliki

Milk from cow to carton; rev ed; HarperCollins Pubs. 1992 31p il (Let's-read-and-find-out science book) hardcover o.p. pa $5.95

Grades: K 1 2 3   **637**

1. Milk 2. Cattle 3. Dairying

ISBN 0-06-445111-9 pa

LC 91-23807

First published 1974 by Crowell with title: Green grass and white milk

Briefly describes how a cow produces milk, how the milk is processed in a dairy, and how various other dairy products are made from milk

This features "full-color artwork. . . . An excellent primary-level introduction to dairy science." Booklist

Gibbons, Gail

The **milk** makers. Macmillan 1985 un il hardcover o.p. pa $5.99

Grades: K 1 2 3   **637**

1. Milk 2. Cattle 3. Dairying

ISBN 0-02-736640-5; 0-689-71116-6 pa

LC 84-20081

Explains how cows produce milk and how it is processed before being delivered to stores

"Starting with dairy cows grazing at pasture, nothing is overlooked in the procedure, from the role of the calf to winter feed and shelter, the function of four stomachs, milking, milk handling, and the operation of a dairy. Diagrams of the cow stomachs as well as the machines used at farm and dairy leave no question unanswered, although city children will be unfamiliar with what it means to breed a cow. Finally, there is a pictorial list of the many other dairy products found in most homes." Sci Books Films

Malam, John

Journey of a glass of milk; John Malam. Heinemann Library 2013 32 p. (hb) $26.65

Grades: 1 2 3   **637**

1. Milk supply 2. Picture books for children 3. Milk 4. Milk trade 5. Dairy processing

ISBN 1432966030; 9781432966034; 9781432966102

LC 2011050559

This book is part of the "Journey of a . . . " series that "looks at how common products end up in our homes, starting with the raw materials and ending with the finished goods. This title looks at the journey of a glass of milk, examining how cows are milked, how the milk is treated, how it is packaged, transported and distributed to stores, and how it is sold and eventually drunk!" (Publisher's note)

Includes bibliographical references and index

Peterson, Cris

Extra cheese, please! mozzarella's journey from cow to pizza. photographs by Alvis Upitis. Boyds Mills Press 1994 un il $16.95; pa $9.95

Grades: K 1 2 3   **637**

1. Cheese 2. Dairying

ISBN 1-56397-177-1; 1-59078-246-1 pa; 9781590782460

LC 93-70876

"Nicely balanced pages contain brief blocks of clearly written text and many full-color photographs." SLJ

Includes glossary and bibliographical references

638   Insect culture

Burns, Loree Griffin

★ The **hive** detectives; chronicle of a honey bee catastrophe. by Loree Griffin Burns with photographs by Ellen Harasimowicz. HMH Books for Young Readers 2010 80 p. il (Scientists in the field) $18.99

Grades: 5 6 7 8 9 10   **638**

1. Bees 2. Beekeeping 3. Insects -- Behavior 4. Honeybee 5. Bee culture

ISBN 0547152310; 9780547152318

LC 2009045249

In this book, author Loree Griffin Burns "profiles bee wranglers and bee scientists who have been working to understand colony collapse disorder, or CCD. In this dramatic and enlightening story, readers explore the lives of the fuzzy, buzzy insects and learn what might happen to us if they were gone." (Publisher's note)

"Not long after beekeepers encountered a devastating new problem in their hives in 2006, a team of bee scientists began working to discover the causes of colony collapse disorder (CCD), now attributed to a combination of factors possibly including pesticides, nutrition, mites and viruses. . . . Mock notebook pages break up the narrative with biographies of the individual scientists, information about who and what can be found inside the hive and the features of bee bodies. An appendix adds varied fascinating facts about bees—again using the format of an illustrated research journal. Harasimowicz's clear, beautifully reproduced photographs support and extend the text." Kirkus

Includes bibliographical references (p. 65) and index

Fujiwara, Yumiko

Honey; a gift from nature. written by Yumiko Fujiwara; illustrated by Hideko Ise. Kane/Miller 2006 un il (Nature: a child's eye view) pa $7.95

Grades: PreK K 1   **638**

1. Bees 2. Honey

ISBN 1-929132-94-8 pa; 978-1-929132-94-2 pa

LC 2005-930528

Original Japanese edition 1997

A young Japanese girl spends the day with her beekeeping father in the mountains where he keeps his hives. Explains how bees gather nectar, how it is turned into honey, and how the honey is collected.

Harkins, Susan Sales

Design your own butterfly garden; by Susan Sales Harkins and William H. Harkins. Mitchell Lane Publishers 2008 48p il (Gardening for kids) lib bdg $29.95

Grades: 3 4 5 6   **638**

1. Butterfly gardens

ISBN 978-1-58415-638-3 lib bdg; 1-58415-638-4 lib bdg

LC 2008-2245

Introduces the principles of butterfly gardening, discussing how to plan the garden, what flowers to plant there, and how to maintain it in all seasons

"All the tasks delineated are well within the scope of children's abilities, and the items needed to complete them are not hard to find. . . . [The book has] excellent full-color photography and include[s] charts and diagrams to assist in the completion of the projects." SLJ

Includes bibliographical references

Malam, John

Grow your own butterfly farm. Heinemann Library 2011 32p il (Grow it yourself!) lib bdg $26; pa $7.99

Grades: K 1 2   **638**
1. Gardening 2. Butterflies
ISBN 978-1-4329-5109-2 lib bdg; 978-1-4329-5116-0 pa
    LC 2010049834
This describes how to grow a flower garden which attracts butterflies.
Includes glossary and bibliographical references

639   Hunting, fishing, conservation, related technologies

Lomberg, Michelle
    Spider. Weigl Publishers 2009 32p il (My pets) lib bdg $26; pa $9.95
Grades: 3 4 5   **639**
1. Pets 2. Spiders
ISBN 978-1-60596-094-4 lib bdg; 1-60596-094-2 lib bdg; 978-1-60596-095-1 pa; 1-60596-095-0 pa
    LC 2009-25979
Information about how to house, feed, and care for spiders.
"With clear, formal writing, and extensive coverage . . . [this title is] useful for reports. . . . Numerous color photographs, charts . . . and question-and-answer boxes supplement the [text]." SLJ
Includes glossary

639.2   Commercial fishing, whaling, sealing

Foster, Mark
    ★ **Whale** port; a history of Tuckanucket. written by Mark Foster; illustrated by Gerald Foster. Houghton Mifflin Company 2007 64p il $18
Grades: 4 5 6 7   **639.2**
1. Whaling
ISBN 978-0-618-54722-7; 0-618-54722-3
    LC 2006018772
This describes the history of whaling in New England through the fictional village of Tuckanucket and Zachariah Taber, his family and neighbors.
The village is "depicted in precisely detailed ink and crayon pictures. . . . The Fosters . . . have elegantly synthesized a tremendous amount of information into a beguiling format." Horn Book

Kurlansky, Mark
    ★ The **cod's** tale; illustrated by S.D. Schindler. Putnam 2002 43p il map $16.99
Grades: 3 4 5 6   **639.2**
1. Codfish 2. Commercial fishing
ISBN 0-399-23476-4
    LC 00-68412
"Schindler's line-and-watercolor scenes are rendered with the delicate hatching of fine engraving and suffused with gentle humor. . . . This is a classic example of an unlikely subject made not only likely but fascinating and informative through authorial and illustrative craftsmanship." Bull Cent Child Books
Includes bibliographical references

McKissack, Pat, 1944-2017
    ★ **Black** hands, white sails; the story of African-American whalers. [by] Patricia C. McKissack & Fredrick L. McKissack. Scholastic Press 1999 xxiv, 152p il $17.95

Grades: 5 6 7 8   **639.2**
1. Whaling 2. Abolitionists 3. African Americans
ISBN 0-590-48313-7
    LC 99-11439
A Coretta Scott King honor book for text, 2000
A history of African-American whalers between 1730 and 1880, describing their contributions to the whaling industry and their role in the abolitionist movement
"A well-researched and detailed book." SLJ
Includes bibliographical references

Sandler, Martin W.
    ★ **Trapped** in ice! an amazing true whaling adventure. Scholastic Nonfiction 2006 168p il $16.99
Grades: 5 6 7 8   **639.2**
1. Whaling
ISBN 0-439-74363-X
    LC 2005-42644
"In 1871, people aboard 32 whaling ships discovered just how dangerous Arctic waters could be after they ignored warnings of an early winter. As conditions worsened, the ships were trapped by ice, forcing the 1,219 people to abandon the vessels or die. Sandler's account of this true story is both informative and absorbing. . . . Well-chosen illustrations and side notes on such topics as life aboard ship and women at sea extend readers' understanding." Booklist
Includes glossary and bibliographical references

Somervill, Barbara A.
    Commercial fisher. Cherry Lake Pub. 2011 32p il (Cool careers) lib bdg $27.07
Grades: 4 5 6 7   **639.2**
1. Commercial fishing 2. Vocational guidance
ISBN 978-1-60279-986-8; 1-60279-986-5
    LC 2010029123
This book begins "with a personal story of a teen and then [segues] into the occupation [of commercial fisher]. . . . [It covers] the necessary training and skills for the job (and options for obtaining them), a typical day, salary expectations, and well-known professionals in the field. The [text is] accessible and clearly written. . . . The [volume has] a generous number of clear color photographs that depict people at work." SLJ
Includes glossary and bibliographical references

639.3   Culture of cold-blooded vertebrates

Bjorklund, Ruth
    Lizards. Marshall Cavendish Benchmark 2009 48p il (Great pets) $20.95
Grades: 2 3 4   **639.3**
1. Lizards
ISBN 978-0-7614-2997-5; 0-7614-2997-2
    LC 2008-17560
"Describes the characteristics and behavior of pet lizards, also discussing their physical appearance and place in history." Publisher's note
Includes glossary and bibliographical references

Cone, Molly
    ★ **Come** back, salmon; how a group of dedicated kids adopted Pigeon Creek and brought it back to life. photographs by Sidnee Wheelwright. Sierra Club Bks. for Children 1992 48p il $16.95; pa $7.95
Grades: 3 4 5 6   **639.3**
1. Salmon 2. Wildlife conservation
ISBN 0-87156-572-2; 0-87156-489-0 pa
    LC 91-29023

Describes the efforts of the Jackson Elementary School in Everett, Washington, to clean up a nearby stream, stock it with salmon, and preserve it as an unpolluted place where the salmon could return to spawn

"The photographs are superb. . . . Personal and inspiring, the text alternates between descriptions of the project, background information about pollution and renewal, and dialogue of the students recorded; additional scientific information is displayed in panels set off from the main text." Horn Book

Includes glossary

Craats, Rennay

Gecko. Weigl Publishers 2009 32p il (My pet) lib bdg $26; pa $9.95

Grades: 3 4 5   **639.3**

1. Pets 2. Geckos

ISBN 978-1-60596-098-2 lib bdg; 1-60596-098-5 lib bdg; 978-1-60596-099-9 pa; 1-60596-099-3 pa

LC 2009-25985

Information about how to house, feed, and care for geckos.

"With clear, formal writing, and extensive coverage . . . [this title is] useful for reports. . . . Numerous colorful photographs, charts . . . and question-and-answer boxes supplement the [text]." SLJ

Includes glossary

Gaines, Ann

Top 10 reptiles and amphibians for kids; [by] Ann Graham Gaines. Enslow Publishers 2008 48p il (Top pets for kids with American Humane) lib bdg $23.93

Grades: 2 3 4 5   **639.3**

1. Pets 2. Reptiles 3. Amphibians

ISBN 978-0-7660-3074-9 lib bdg; 0-7660-3074-1 lib bdg

LC 2007047884

"Includes beautiful full-color photos showing the animals at their best. Judicious use of text boxes, crisp fonts, and white space will make it easy for readers to follow the flow of information." SLJ

Includes glossary and bibliographical references

Hamilton, Lynn

Turtle. Weigl Publishers 2009 32p il (My pet) lib bdg $26; pa $9.95

Grades: 3 4 5   **639.3**

1. Pets 2. Turtles

ISBN 978-1-60596-088-3 lib bdg; 1-60596-088-8 lib bdg; 978-1-60596-089-0 pa; 1-60596-089-6 pa

LC 2009-25973

Information about how to house, feed, and care for turtles.

"With clear, formal writing, and extensive coverage . . . [this title is] useful for reports. . . . Numerous color photographs, charts . . . and question-and-answer boxes supplement the [text]." SLJ

Includes glossary

Haney, Johannah

Frogs. Marshall Cavendish Benchmark 2009 48p il (Great pets) lib bdg $29.93

Grades: 2 3 4   **639.3**

1. Pets 2. Frogs

ISBN 978-0-7614-4151-9 lib bdg; 0-7614-4151-4 lib bdg

LC 2008037242

"Describes the characteristics and behavior of pet frogs, also discussing their physical appearance and place in history." Publisher's note

Includes glossary and bibliographical references

Turtles; [by] Johannah Haney. Marshall Cavendish Benchmark 2008 48p il (Great pets) lib bdg $28.50

Grades: 2 3 4   **639.3**

1. Pets 2. Turtles

ISBN 978-0-7614-2709-4 lib bdg; 0-7614-2709-0 lib bdg

LC 2006038157

The offers an introduction to turtles as pets and how to choose and care for them

This is an "enthusiastic, warm [introduction]. . . . [It is] clearly written and [is] the most thorough, honest [introduction] to owning a pet [turtle] for this audience." SLJ

Includes glossary and bibliographical references

Hart, Joyce

Snakes. Marshall Cavendish Benchmark 2008 48p il (Great pets) $20.95

Grades: 2 3 4   **639.3**

1. Pets 2. Snakes

ISBN 978-0-7614-2996-8; 0-7614-2996-4

LC 2008-24333

"Describes the characteristics and behavior of pet snakes, also discussing their physical appearance and place in history." Publisher's note

Includes glossary and bibliographical references

Hernandez-Divers, Sonia

Geckos. Heinemann Lib. 2003 48p il (Keeping unusual pets) lib bdg $24.22

Grades: 3 4 5 6   **639.3**

1. Pets 2. Geckos

ISBN 1-4034-0282-5

LC 2002-3163

This offers information about geckos and advice about keeping them as pets

"Lively and informative, with photos scattered across and around the pages . . . [this offers] a wealth of valuable advice." SLJ

Includes glossary and bibliographical references

Lunis, Natalie

Green iguanas. Bearport Pub. 2010 24p il map (Peculiar pets) lib bdg $25.26

Grades: 3 4 5   **639.3**

1. Pets 2. Iguanas

ISBN 978-1-59716-863-2 lib bdg; 1-59716-863-7 lib bdg

LC 2009-17545

Introduces the green iguana, describing its physical characteristics, habitat, and behavior, and discussing the care and diet that it needs if it is kept as a pet

"The language . . . is lively . . . [and] the illustrations are vivid, with photos offering some amusing shots. . . . This [book] . . . will hold readers' attention, but also challenge them to consider the responsibilities required of owners of unusual creatures." SLJ

Includes glossary and bibliographical references

Niven, Felicia Lowenstein

Learning to care for reptiles and amphibians. Enslow Publishers 2010 48p il (Beginning pet care with American Humane) lib bdg $23.93

Grades: 2 3 4   **639.3**

1. Reptiles 2. Amphibians

ISBN 978-0-7660-3194-4; 0-7660-3194-2

This describes how to care for pet reptiles and amphibians such as frogs, geckos, snakes, salamanders, newts, and turtles.

Includes glossary and bibliographical references

639.34 Fish culture in aquariums

Aliki

★ **My** visit to the aquarium. HarperCollins Pubs. 1993 un il $15.95; pa $6.95

Grades: K 1 2 3   **639.34**

1. Marine animals 2. Marine aquariums 3. Freshwater animals
ISBN 0-06-021458-9; 0-06-446186-6 pa

LC 92-18678

During his visit to an aquarium, a boy finds out about the characteristics and environments of many different marine and freshwater creatures

"Fish facts, selected for their child-appeal and delivered in a brisk, conversational tone, are neatly organized by marine environment. . . . The dominant blues and greens of Aliki's watercolors are not only cool and inviting; they also provide visual continuity amid the riot of brightly colored fish." Booklist

Bozzo, Linda

My first fish; [by] Linda Bozzo. Enslow Publishers 2007 32p il (My first pet library from the American Humane Association) lib bdg $22.60

Grades: 1 2 3   **639.34**

1. Fishes 2. Aquariums
ISBN 978-0-7660-2751-0 lib bdg; 0-7660-2751-1 lib bdg

LC 2006010500

"This book explores how to choose the right fish and how to care for your new pet." Publisher's note

Includes glossary and bibliographical references

Buckmaster, Marjorie L.

Freshwater fishes; [by] Marjorie L. Buckmaster. Marshall Cavendish Benchmark 2007 48p il (Great pets) $19.95

Grades: 2 3 4   **639.34**

1. Fishes 2. Aquariums
ISBN 978-0-7614-2712-4

LC 2007017809

The offers an introduction to freshwater fish as pets and how to choose and care for them.

This is an "enthusiastic, warm [introduction]. . . . [It is] clearly written and [is] the most thorough, honest [introduction] to owning [pet fish] for this audience." SLJ

Niven, Felicia Lowenstein

Learning to care for fish. Enslow Publishers 2010 48p il (Beginning pet care with American Humane) lib bdg $23.93

Grades: 2 3 4   **639.34**

1. Fishes 2. Aquariums
ISBN 978-0-7660-3193-7; 0-7660-3193-4

This describes how to care for pet fish.

"The pictures are colorful and engaging, with a no-fuss layout. The text is easy to follow, pitched at just the right level for the audience." SLJ

Includes glossary and bibliographical references

Rau, Dana Meachen

Top 10 fish for kids; [by] Dana Meachen Rau. Enslow Publishers 2008 48p il (Top pets for kids with American Humane) lib bdg $23.93

Grades: 2 3 4 5   **639.34**

1. Fishes 2. Aquariums
ISBN 978-0-7660-3073-2 lib bdg; 0-7660-3073-3 lib bdg

LC 2007-32319

"Includes beautiful full-color photos showing the animals at their best. Judicious use of text boxes, crisp fonts, and white space will make it easy for readers to follow the flow of information." SLJ

Includes glossary and bibliographical references

Richardson, Adele

Caring for your fish; by Adele Richardson. Capstone Press 2007 24p il (Positively pets) $21.26

Grades: K 1 2 3   **639.34**

1. Fishes 2. Aquariums
ISBN 978-0-7368-6386-5; 0-7368-6386-9

LC 2005035854

This is a "concise, competent [introduction] to the responsibility and fun of being a pet owner. . . . Attractive and well suited for young readers in both tone and content. The clear color photographs display the animals in all their glory." SLJ

Includes bibliographical references

639.39 Reptile culture

Heos, Bridget

Do you really want a lizard? by Bridget Heos; illustrated by Katya Longhi. Amicus 2016 24 p. color illustrations (Do you really want a pet?) (library binding) $28.50

Grades: K 1 2   **639.39**

1. Lizards as pets 2. Pets
ISBN 9781607537502

LC 2014033272

In this book, by Bridget Heos, illustrated by Katya Longhi, part of the "Do you really want a pet?" series, "[s]everal lizards (and the narrator) teach a young boy the responsibility—and the joys—of caring for a pet lizard. Includes 'Is this pet right for me?' quiz." (Publisher's note)

Includes bibliographical references

Do you really want a turtle? Bridget Heos; illustrated by Katya Longhi. Amicus 2016 24 p. color illustrations (Do you really want a pet?) (library binding) $28.50

Grades: K 1 2   **639.39**

1. Pets 2. Turtles 3. Turtles as pets
ISBN 1607537524; 9781607537526

LC 2014033271

This children's book by Bridget Heos, illustrated by Katya Longhi, on turtles as pets is part of a series of "humorous but cautionary tales [that] show kids why they should be careful what they wish for... or at least be prepared for the responsibility." (Publisher's note)

Includes bibliographical references

639.9 Conservation of biological resources

Buckley, Carol

Just for elephants. Tilbury House 2006 un il $16.95

Grades: 3 4 5 6   **639.9**

1. Elephants 2. Wildlife conservation
ISBN 978-0-88448-283-3; 0-88448-283-9

LC 2006-22283

"This is a beautifully written, compelling story of a conscientious drive to care for these animals in a humane way." SLJ

Coey, Julia

Animal Hospital; Rescuing Urban Wildlife. Julia Coey. Firefly Books Ltd 2015 64 p. color illustrations (hardcover) $19.95

Grades: 4 5 6 7   **639.9**

1. Wildlife rehabilitation 2. Animal rescue
ISBN 9781770855724; 1770855726

LC 2015458728

This juvenile book, by Julia Coey, "describes how injured and orphaned wild animals are rehabilitated and cared for after being rescued from perilous situations. It follows the activities of an urban animal rescue facility and the efforts of the trained professionals that rescue, treat, rehabilitate and release the animals." (Publisher's note)

"The author's suggestions for readers' involvement include reminders about appropriate trash disposal as well as names of organizations, and a concluding chapter describes three similar rehab centers around the world. A straightforward introduction to an appealing topic for upper-elementary and middle school readers." Kirkus

Includes bibliographical references and index.

Curtis, Jennifer Keats

Animal helpers; wildlife rehabilitators. Jennifer Keats Curtis. Sylvan Dell Pub. 2012 32 p. (hardcover) $17.95

Grades: K 1 2   **639.9**

1. Animals 2. Veterinarians 3. Wildlife rehabilitation

ISBN 1607186713; 9781607186717; 9781607186724; 9781607186731; 9781607186748

LC 2012937373

This "photographic journal takes readers 'behind the scenes' at four different wildlife rehabilitation centers" that help "wild animals when they are injured, become ill, or are orphaned." It shows "backyard animals as they are nursed back to health and released back to the wild when possible." (Publisher's note)

Fleming, Denise, 1950-

★ **Where** once there was a wood. Holt & Co. 1996 un il $16.95; pa $6.95

Grades: K 1 2   **639.9**

1. Habitat (Ecology) 2. Wildlife conservation

ISBN 0-8050-3761-6; 0-8050-6482-6 pa

LC 95-18906

"Lush, textured collage artwork features a stunning combination and arrangement of colors with brilliant hues juxtaposed against muted earth tones. . . . The gentle, poetic narration is never overpowered by the pictures." SLJ

Includes bibliographical references

George, Jean Craighead

The **tarantula** in my purse; and 172 other wild pets. written and illustrated by Jean Craighead George. HarperCollins Pubs. 1996 134p il hardcover o.p. pa $5.99

Grades: 4 5 6   **639.9**

1. Pets 2. Artists 3. Authors 4. Naturalists 5. Illustrators 6. Women authors 7. Authors, American 8. Children's authors

ISBN 0-06-023626-4; 0-06-446201-3 pa

LC 95-54151

"Brief, engaging stories about the many wild animals that lived in and around the author's home over the years are filled with humor, affection, and just enough drama." Horn Book

"George tells of the many wild pets that lived with her family, particularly while her children were growing up. Each chapter describes a different animal or incident." Booklist

Hatkoff, Juliana

Winter's tail; how one little dolphin learned to swim again. told by Juliana Hatkoff, Isabella Hatkoff, and Craig Hatkoff. Scholastic Press 2009 un il $16.99

Grades: 3 4 5 6   **639.9**

1. Dolphins 2. Artificial limbs

ISBN 978-0-545-12335-8; 0-545-12335-6

"A compassionate look at the true odyssey of an orphaned Atlantic bottlenose dolphin. Rescued from a crab trap, with severe injuries, 'Winter' was brought to the Clearwater (FL) Marine Aquarium and, despite the heroic efforts of the staff, lost her tail. . . . Winter caught the attention of a prosthetic engineer, and the Hatkoffs' clear text follows the efforts of a mixed team from the aquarium and Hanger Prosthetics & Orthotics to design a workable 'tail' to keep her healthy. Full-color photos reveal the cooperative efforts of the human team and Winter in this journey toward a more normal life." SLJ

Lasky, Kathryn

★ **Interrupted** journey; illustrated by Christopher Knight. Candlewick Press 2001 un il hardcover o.p. pa $6.99

Grades: 3 4 5 6   **639.9**

1. Sea turtles 2. Rare animals 3. Wildlife conservation

ISBN 0-7636-0635-9; 0-7636-2883-2 pa

LC 99-57126

Describes efforts to protect sea turtles, particularly Kemp's ridley turtles, and help them reproduce and replenish their once-dwindling numbers

"There's a sense of wonder in the simple words and the huge, thrilling color pictures in this photo-essay." Booklist

Montgomery, Sy

★ **Kakapo** rescue; saving the world's strangest parrot. text by Sy Montgomery; photographs by Nic Bishop. Houghton Mifflin 2010 73p il map (Scientists in the field) $18

Grades: 4 5 6 7   **639.9**

1. Parrots 2. Endangered species 3. Wildlife conservation 4. New Zealand

ISBN 978-0-618-49417-0; 0-618-49417-0

LC 2009-45250

Awarded the Robert F. Sibert Medal, 2011

Montgomery and Bishop head "to a remote island off the southern tip of New Zealand, where they join a local government-sponsored research team that is working to save the Kakapo parrot from extinction. . . . Montgomery's delight in her subject is contagious, and throughout her enthusiastic text, she nimbly blends scientific and historical facts with immediate, sensory descriptions of fieldwork. Young readers will be fascinated. . . . Bishop's photos of the creatures and their habitat are stunning." Booklist

Stetson, Emily

Kids' easy-to-create wildlife habitats; [by] Emily Stetson. Williamson Books 2004 128p il map (Quick starts for kids!) pa $12.95

Grades: 2 3 4   **639.9**

1. Habitat (Ecology) 2. Wildlife conservation

ISBN 0-8249-8665-2

LC 2004-40871

This "book shows children how to observe and support wildlife around their homes, schools, and communities. Packed with useful information. . . . With sound advice and many helpful illustrations, precisely drawn in blue and gray ink, this offers children small ways to support wildlife close to home." Booklist

640   Home and family management

Drummond, Allan

Green city; how one community survived a tornado and rebuilt for a sustainable future. Allan Drummond. Farrar, Straus & Giroux 2016 40 p. color illustrations (hardback) $17.99

Grades: 1 2 3 4 5   **640**

1. Sustainable architecture 2. Buildings -- Maintenance and repair 3. Greensburg (Kan.) 4. Tornadoes -- Kansas -- Greensburg 5.

Green movement -- Kansas -- Greensburg
ISBN 9780374379995

LC 2015018065

This children's book, by Allan Drummond, describes how "in 2007, a tornado destroyed Greensburg, Kansas, and the residents . . . didn't want to rebuild if their small town would just be destroyed in another storm. So they decided they wouldn't just rebuild the same old thing; this time, they would build a town that could not only survive another storm, but one that was built in an environmentally sustainable way." (Publisher's note)

"From the dark, chaotic scenes at the story's beginning to the light, bright, and breezy ones at the end, Drummond's line-and-wash illustrations set just the right tone for this informative picture book." Booklist

Includes bibliographical references.

Ernst, Lisa Campbell, 1957-

How things work in the house; Lisa Campbell Ernst. 1st ed. Blue Apple Books 2012 1 v. (unpaged) col. ill. (hardcover) $16.99

Grades: 1 2 3   **640**

1. Kitchen utensils 2. Questions and answers 3. Household equipment and supplies 4. Home economics -- Equipment and supplies

ISBN 1609051890; 9781609051891

LC 2011038908

In her book, author Lisa Campbell Ernst "explains what can be done with things in our houses" and how things work. "The varied uses of . . . bananas . . . and spoons" are discussed. "Similarly, popcorn, sandwiches, scissors, glue, piggy banks and kazoos are featured." The book offers a "glimpse at how things work in our houses . . . [and] everyday worlds." (Kirkus Reviews)

Gaarder-Juntti, Oona

What in the world is a green home? ABDO Pub. Co. 2010 24p il (Going green) lib bdg $24.21

Grades: 1 2 3 4   **640**

1. Housing -- Environmental aspects

ISBN 978-1-61613-189-0 lib bdg; 1-61613-189-6 lib bdg

LC 2010004340

"The lively layout design, featuring colorful headings, short paragraphs, and attractive photographs, has a scrapbook-like quality. . . . [The title explains] how all our choices require energy and resources, and encourage readers to make changes in their lifestyles. . . . [This] . . . will inspire and empower readers to make a difference." SLJ

Includes glossary and bibliographical references

641.3   Food

Butterworth, Chris

★ **How** Did That Get in My Lunchbox? the story of food. by Chris Butterworth and illustrated by Lucia Gaggiotti. Candlewick 2013 25 p. il $5.99

Grades: K 1 2 3   **641.3**

1. Food 2. Nutrition

ISBN 0763665037; 9780763665036

LC 2010003034

This book, by Chris Butterworth and illustrated by Lucia Gaggiotti, "look[s] at the steps involved in producing some common foods." Topics covered include "planting wheat to mixing dough, climbing trees to machine-squeezing fruit, picking cocoa pods to stirring a vat of melted bliss. Health tips and a peek at basic food groups [are included]." (Publisher's note)

"With reader-directed prose and cheerfully retro artwork, Butterworth and Gaggiotti use a balanced meal—sandwich, fruit, veggies,

juice box, and cookie—to explain how foodstuffs make it from farms, dairies, and factories into kids' lunches." Publ Wkly

Chapman, Garry

Coffee; by Garry Chapman and Gary Hodges. Black Rabbit 2010 32p il (World commodities) lib bdg $28.50

Grades: 5 6 7 8   **641.3**

1. Coffee

ISBN 978-1-59920-584-7 lib bdg; 1-59920-584-X lib bdg

"The first part of the book discusses how coffee beans are grown, treated, prepared, and enjoyed around the world. . . . The second section offers an opportunity to use the commodity of coffee to understand such economics concepts as supply and demand or futures trading. . . . Finally, the book spins through a look at fair trade practices; political, environmental, and social issues surrounding coffee trade; and the sustainability and outlook of the global coffee industry. In all, the book gleans a pretty impressive and diverse array of accessible information from such a small bean." Booklist

Includes glossary

Cleary, Brian P.

Apples, cherries, red raspberries; what is in the fruits group? illustrations by Martin Goneau; consultant, Jennifer K. Nelson. Millbrook Press 2010 31p il (Food is CATegorical) lib bdg $25.26

Grades: K 1 2 3   **641.3**

1. Fruit 2. Nutrition

ISBN 978-1-58013-589-4 lib bdg; 1-58013-589-7 lib bdg

LC 2009049582

"With highly readable bits and pieces about which yummy foods have which nutrients and vitamins [this book is] . . . just right for sharing with young kids, introducing the value of healthy foods and exercise through silly rhymes, puns, zany color cartoons of cats in wild action. The scenarios . . . range from cat characters picking apples in an orchard to a big cat that triumphs in a boxing ring after eating 'cool' bananas." Booklist

Green beans, potatoes, and even tomatoes; what is in the vegetable group? by Brian P. Cleary; illustrations by Martin Goneau; consultant, Jennifer K. Nelson. Millbrook Press 2010 31p il (Food is CATegorical) lib bdg $25.26

Grades: K 1 2 3   **641.3**

1. Nutrition 2. Vegetables

ISBN 978-1-58013-588-7 lib bdg; 1-58013-588-9 lib bdg

LC 2009-49592

"With highly readable bits and pieces about which yummy foods have which nutrients and vitamins [this book is] . . . just right for sharing with young kids, introducing the value of healthy foods and exericse through silly rhymes, puns, and zany color cartoons of cats in wild action. . . . Sweet potatoes, carrots, and more are portrayed as both wholesome and tasty." Booklist

D'Amico, Joan

The **science** chef; 100 fun food experiments and recipes for kids. [by] Joan D'Amico, Karen Eich Drummond; illustrations by Tina Cash-Walsh. Wiley 1995 180p il $12.95

Grades: 4 5 6   **641.3**

1. Food 2. Cooking 3. Science -- Experiments

ISBN 0-471-31045-X

LC 94-9045

This includes facts about food, recipes, and experiments with food

"Attractively illustrated with black-and-white line drawings, easy and interesting to read, and filled with tidbits of information." SLJ

Includes glossary

Eamer, Claire

The **world** in your lunch box; the wacky history and weird science of everyday foods. Claire Eamer; artwork by Sa Boothroyd. Annick Press 2012 121 p.

Grades: 4 5 6   **641.3**

1. Nutrition 2. Food -- History 3. Food -- Composition
ISBN 1554513936; 9781554513932

This book by Claire Eamer presents an "exploration of food history and food science . . . "[E]verything's interesting if you take the time to learn about it," says the cooking teacher, who challenges his students to keep a record of their lunches and research their backgrounds. . . . The lunches described are usually well-balanced. From each, the author has chosen a selection of ingredients, providing examples of their use in history and offering . . . science connections. Most topics are covered in a single page [along with] cartoon-styled drawings . . . [and] jokes . . . Ten favorite food facts conclude the narrative, but there are also suggestions for further reading, an extensive bibliography and even an index". (Kirkus)

Includes bibliographical references and index.

Gaarder-Juntti, Oona

What in the world is green food? ABDO Pub. Co. 2010 24p il (Going green) lib bdg $24.21

Grades: 1 2 3 4   **641.3**

1. Food -- Environmental aspects
ISBN 978-1-61613-192-0 lib bdg; 1-61613-192-6 lib bdg
LC 2010004321

"The lively layout design, featuring colorful headings, short paragraphs, and attractive photographs, has a scrapbook-like quality. . . . [The title explains] how all our choices require energy and resources, and encourage readers to make changes in their lifestyles. . . . [This] . . . will inspire and empower readers to make a difference." SLJ

Includes glossary and bibliographical references

Hewitt, Sally

Your food. Crabtree Pub. Co. 2009 32p il (Green team) $26.60; pa $8.95

Grades: 3 4 5 6   **641.3**

1. Food
ISBN 978-0-7787-4099-5; 0-7787-4099-4; 978-0-7787-4106-0 pa; 0-7787-4106-0 pa
LC 2008023291

"The color graphics and layouts are highly appealing and will definitely be attractive to young readers. . . . This . . . is an excellent resource for school libraries, science teachers, and community sponsors." Libr Media Connect

Includes glossary

Jango-Cohen, Judith

The **history** of food; [by] Judith Jango-Cohen. Twenty-First Century Books 2006 56p il (Major inventions through history) lib bdg $26.60

Grades: 5 6 7 8   **641.3**

1. Food -- History
ISBN 0-8225-2484-8
LC 2004-23022

This history of food "discusses canning, pasteurization, refrigeration, supermarkets, and genetically modified foods. . . . The text . . . is breezy but informative; unfamiliar terms are defined. Illustrations are a mixture of period black-and-white and color photos." SLJ

Includes bibliographical references

Llewellyn, Claire

Cooking with fruits and vegetables; by Claire Llewellyn with recipes by Clare O'Shea. Rosen Central 2011 48p il (Cooking healthy) lib bdg $27.95

Grades: 5 6 7 8   **641.3**

1. Fruit 2. Cooking 3. Vegetables
ISBN 978-1-4488-4844-7; 1-4488-4844-X
LC 2010039333

This book pairs "facts about [fruits and vegetables], including where it is eaten, with eye-catching photos. . . . Each course (section) has an overview of the vegetable group . . . followed by recipes from all over the world. They vary in difficulty. . . . The cooking directions are clear and straightforward. . . . [The book is] profusely illustrated with full-color photos. Students who are learning to cook will appreciate [this] excellently organized [read]." SLJ

Includes bibliographical references

Malam, John

Grow your own snack. Heinemann Library 2011 32p il (Grow it yourself!) lib bdg $26; pa $7.99

Grades: 2 3 4   **641.3**

1. Beans 2. Cooking 3. Vegetable gardening
ISBN 978-1-4329-5107-8 lib bdg; 978-1-4329-5114-6 pa
LC 2010049849

This describes how to grow broad beans, and how to fry them for a snack.

Includes glossary and bibliographical references

Menzel, Peter

★ **What** the world eats; photographed by Peter Menzel; written by Faith D'Aluisio. Tricycle Press 2008 160p il map $22.99

Grades: 4 5 6 7 8   **641.3**

1. Diet 2. Eating customs 3. Food -- Pictorial works
ISBN 978-1-58246-246-2; 1-58246-246-1
LC 2007-41439

An adaptation of Hungry Planet, published 2005 by Ten Speed Press for adults

"Stunning color photographs of mealtimes and daily activities illustrate the warm, informative, anecdotal narratives. . . . This is a fascinating, sobering, and instructive look at daily life around the world." Booklist

Includes bibliographical references

Miller, Jeanne

Food science. Lerner Publications 2009 48p il (Cool science) lib bdg $27.93

Grades: 4 5 6   **641.3**

1. Food
ISBN 978-0-8225-7589-4 lib bdg; 0-8225-7589-2 lib bdg

This describes how food scientists "explore how cooking changes food, create dishes that surprise the senses, and help farmers grow food in healthier ways." Publisher's note

Includes glossary and bibliographical references

Peterson, Cris

★ **Seed** soil sun; earth's recipe for food. photographs by David R. Lundquist. Boyd Mills Press 2010 un il $17.95

Grades: PreK K 1 2   **641.3**

1. Food 2. Seeds 3. Plants
ISBN 978-1-59078-713-7; 1-59078-713-7

The children's book discusses "[p]hotosynthesis . . . [and how] plants take our planet's basic resources (sunlight, water, and air) and generate food and oxygen. . . . Peterson's . . . text is [accompanied by David Lundquist's] . . . photography [that] illustrates her account, which features maize as an example. Lundquist shows . . . worms that till the soil as well as corn plants ranging from seedlings, through knee-highs, to full-grown harvestable stalks." (Science)

"Peterson explains how most food comes from seeds, which—thanks to nutrients from soil and energy from the sun—grow into fruits and vegetables. Lundquist's color photographs . . . may have kids considering an attempt at growing their own food." Publ Wkly

Includes bibliographical references

Price, Sean
The **story** behind chocolate; [by] Sean Stewart Price. Heinemann Library 2009 32p il map lib bdg $28.21
Grades: 3 4 5 **641.3**
1. Chocolate
ISBN 978-1-4329-2347-1 lib bdg; 1-4329-2347-1 lib bdg
LC 2008037524
"Price explains how chocolate was discovered and became popular, its ingredients, the chocolate-making process, and how companies like Hershey and Cadbury became successful. . . . The well-organized [text is] informative and clearly written, and the numerous color photographs and drawings are eye-catching and complement the [narrative] well." SLJ

Includes bibliographical references

Reilly, Kathleen M.
Food; 25 amazing projects investigate the history and science of what we eat. illustrated by Farah Rizvi. Nomad Press 2010 124p il (Build it yourself) pa $15.95
Grades: 4 5 6 **641.3**
1. Food
ISBN 978-1-934670-59-0; 1-934670-59-6
"This broad overview of food touches on its history and future, production and packaging, social and cultural practices, and health and safety concerns. . . . The information presented and questions posed on food packaging, mega-farming, locally grown vs. commercially grown foods, free-range grazing, and healthy food choices make this a particularly up-to-date survey. . . . Every chapter concludes with two to three hands-on activities that range from cooking to science and art projects. . . . This soup-to-nuts look at the business and consumption of food will make a good addition to most collections." SLJ

Includes glossary and bibliographical references

Robbins, Ken
★ **Food** for thought; the stories behind the things we eat. Roaring Brook Press 2009 45p il $17.95
Grades: 2 3 4 **641.3**
1. Food
ISBN 978-1-59643-343-4; 1-59643-343-4
LC 2007-44062
"Robbins focuses on a mouthwatering array of produce: apples, oranges, potatoes, tomatoes, grapes, bananas, mushrooms, and pomegranates. Each spacious spread combines Robbins' vibrantly hued photographs with engaging text filled with information about each food, including its nutritional content, history, current methods of cultivation, and appearance in figures of speech ('couch potato'), as well as mythology and folklore. . . . The enticing images will draw young readers into the captivating assortment of facts." Booklist

Rotner, Shelley
Grow! Raise! Catch! how we get our food. Shelley Rotner. Holiday House 2016 32 p. color illustrations (hardcover) $16.95; (ebook) $16.95

Grades: PreK K 1 **641.3**
1. Food 2. Farmers 3. Fishers
ISBN 0823436438; 9780823436439; 9780823437207
LC 2015040849
This children's book by Shelley Rotner shows where the food we eat each day comes from. "Who grows our juicy fruits and yummy vegetables? Who raises animals for our tasty eggs, milk and meat? Who catches fresh fish for our table? Farmers and fishermen show off their bounty in this lively look at the people who produce the food on which we all rely." (Publisher's note)

"This will prove to be an attractive, useful book for food and nutrition units in the lower grades. This volume may even lure children (and adults) back to the farm." Kirkus

Sayre, April Pulley
★ **Go,** go, grapes! April Pulley Sayre. 1st ed. Simon & Schuster 2012 1v. (unpaged) col. ill. (hardcover) $16.99
Grades: K 1 2 **641.3**
1. Fruit 2. Children's poetry 3. Picture books for children 4. Grapes
ISBN 1442433906; 9781442433908
LC 2011011602
In this book, April Pulley Sayre presents photographs of "the standard apple, orange, banana, grapes and berries, [and] she entices readers with such exotics as tamarillo, kiwano, guava, rambutan, currant, durian and . . . dragon fruit. . . . Sayre shows off the colors and textures. . . . Several fruits are cut to show off their insides, such as the seeds of the kiwi and pomegranate and the intriguing cross sections of a lychee and mangosteen." (Kirkus Reviews)

★ **Rah,** rah, radishes! a vegetable chant. Beach Lane Books 2011 un il $14.99
Grades: PreK K **641.3**
1. Vegetables 2. Food -- Poetry
ISBN 978-1-4424-2141-7; 1-4424-2141-X
LC 2010034360
Photographs of vegetables and rhyming text celebrate vegetables in all their colorful and tasty variety.

"Each page calls out a cheer-worthy vegetable in two short lines of text, accompanied by a large, colorful photograph. . . . With its upbeat, easy-to-digest text and large, clear images, this book will become a go-to choice in spring-themed preschool storytimes and early elementary health or environmental units." SLJ

Sylver, Adrienne
Hot diggity dog; the history of the hot dog. illustrated by Elwood H. Smith. Dutton Children's Books 2010 un il $16.99
Grades: K 1 2 3 **641.3**
1. Frankfurters
ISBN 978-0-525-47897-3; 0-525-47897-3
"How did hot dogs become so popular? asks Sylver in this popular history of the wiener. . . . Accompanied by Smith's handsomely goofy, retro artwork, the narrative offers sidebars with factual tidbits galore." Kirkus

Thornhill, Jan
Who wants pizza? the kids' guide to the history, science & culture of food. Maple Tree Press 2010 64p il $22.95; pa $10.95
Grades: 4 5 6 **641.3**
1. Food 2. Agriculture
ISBN 978-1-897349-96-0; 1-897349-96-3; 978-1-897349-97-7 pa; 1-897349-97-1 pa
This discusses "where food comes from and if there's enough to go around. Amid color photographs and sidebars, Thornhill writes concise-

ly about hunter-gatherers, agriculture, processed foods, globalization, and poverty, among numerous other topics, providing a straightforward and balanced overview of the modern food industry, and the choices readers have when it comes to their own meals." Publ Wkly

641.5 Cooking

Arroyo, Sheri L.

How chefs use math; math curriculum consultant, Rhea A. Stewart. Chelsea Clubhouse 2010 32p il (Math in the real world) lib bdg $28

Grades: 4 5 6   **641.5**
1. Cooks 2. Cooking 3. Mathematics 4. Vocational guidance
ISBN 978-1-60413-608-1 lib bdg; 1-60413-608-1 lib bdg
LC 2009-14180

This describes how chefs use math for such tasks as measuring ingredients, watching temperatures, buying food, setting menu prices, and managing restaurant and catering businesses, and includes relevant math problems and information about how to become a chef

Includes glossary and bibliographical references

Batmanglij, Najmieh

Happy Nowruz; cooking with children to celebrate the Persian New Year. [by] Najmieh Batmanglij. Mage Publishers 2008 119p il $40

Grades: 4 5 6 7 8   **641.5**
1. New Year 2. Eating customs 3. Middle Eastern cooking 4. Iran -- Social life and customs
ISBN 1-933823-16-X; 978-1-933823-16-4
LC 2007-036047

"Combining a cookbook format with straightforward, informational text, this amply illustrated title offers a detailed introduction to the history and customs surrounding Nowruz, the Persian New Year. . . . The covered spiral binding allows pages to remain open while cooking, and the uncluttered, attractive format, featuring color photos of kids in the kitchen and whimsical illustrations, will attract interested browsers." Booklist

Beery, Barbara

Barbara Beery's pink princess party cookbook; photography by Zac Williams. Simon & Schuster Books for Young Readers 2011 55p il spiral $15.99

Grades: 2 3 4 5   **641.5**
1. Cooking 2. Parties 3. Entertaining
ISBN 978-1-4424-1231-6; 1-4424-1231-3
LC 2010017691

"Beery offers ideas for six themed celebrations, such as a mermaid princess party, a garden fairy princess party, and a spa princess party. They all include delicate but easy-to-follow recipes for punch, cookies, cakes, sushi, and decorations, as well as themed crafts such as body lotion and floral headbands. These are well-planned ideas, with plenty of full-color photographs to support the text." SLJ

Berman, Karen

Easy-peasy recipes; snacks and treats to make and eat. Karen Berman; [edited by] Kirsten Hall. Running Press Kids 2012 40 p. $14.95

Grades: 1 2 3   **641.5**
1. Cooking 2. Cookbooks 3. Children -- Nutrition
ISBN 0762444436; 9780762444434
LC 2011937816

This cookbook by Karen Berman is "geared toward independent child chefs. The 13 snack and treat recipes . . . [include] a taco-salad pirate face, a breakfast buffet shaped like a train with individual cars and a berry-and-yogurt-snowcapped mountain. To assemble these cre-

ations, young chefs are directed to use a pair of (washed) safety scissors instead of knives. . . . 'Do It Another Way' sections accompanying each recipe give readers ideas for substituting ingredients or trying new ones." (Kirkus Reviews)

Blaxland, Wendy

American food. Smart Apple Media 2012 32p il map (I can cook!) lib bdg $28.50

Grades: 3 4 5 6   **641.5**
1. Cooking
ISBN 978-1-59920-667-7; 1-59920-667-6
LC 2011005443

Describes historical, cultural, and geographical factors that have influenced the cuisine of the United States. Includes recipes to create American food.

This includes "recipes with kid appeal. . . . Captioned, full-color photographs provide step-by-step directions. . . . [An] ideal [supplement] to culture and country studies." SLJ

Includes glossary

Chinese food. Smart Apple Media 2012 32p il map (I can cook!) lib bdg $28.50

Grades: 3 4 5 6   **641.5**
1. Chinese cooking
ISBN 978-1-59920-671-4; 1-59920-671-4
LC 2011005448

Describes historical, cultural, and geographical factors that have influenced the cuisine of China. Includes recipes to create Chinese food.

This includes "recipes with kid appeal. . . . Captioned, full-color photographs provide step-by-step directions. . . . [An] ideal [supplement] to culture and country studies." SLJ

Includes glossary

French food. Smart Apple Media 2012 32p il map (I can cook!) lib bdg $28.50

Grades: 3 4 5 6   **641.5**
1. French cooking
ISBN 978-1-59920-669-1; 1-59920-669-2
LC 2011005445

Describes historical, cultural, and geographical factors that have influenced the cuisine of France. Includes recipes to create French food.

This includes "recipes with kid appeal. . . . Captioned, full-color photographs provide step-by-step directions. . . . [An] ideal [supplement] to culture and country studies." SLJ

Includes glossary

Italian food. Smart Apple Media 2012 32p il map (I can cook!) lib bdg $28.50

Grades: 3 4 5 6   **641.5**
1. Italian cooking
ISBN 978-1-59920-670-7; 1-59920-670-6
LC 2011005446

Describes historical, cultural, and geographical factors that have influenced the cuisine of Italy. Includes recipes to create Italian food.

Includes glossary

Mexican food. Smart Apple Media 2012 32p il map (I can cook!) lib bdg $28.50

Grades: 3 4 5 6   **641.5**
1. Mexican cooking
ISBN 978-1-59920-668-4; 1-59920-668-4
LC 2011005444

Describes historical, cultural, and geographical factors that have influenced the cuisine of Mexico. Includes recipes to create Mexican food.

This includes "recipes with kid appeal. . . . Captioned, full-color photographs provide step-by-step directions. . . . [An] ideal [supplement] to culture and country studies." SLJ
Includes glossary

Middle Eastern food. Smart Apple Media 2012 32p il map (I can cook!) lib bdg $28.50
Grades: 3 4 5 6   641.5
1. Middle Eastern cooking
ISBN 978-1-59920-672-1
LC 2011005450
Describes historical, cultural, and geographical factors that have influenced the cuisine of the Middle East. Includes recipes to create Middle-Eastern food.
This includes "recipes with kid appeal. . . . Captioned, full-color photographs provide step-by-step directions. . . . [An] ideal [supplement] to culture and country studies." SLJ
Includes glossary

Bloomfield, Jill
Jewish holidays cookbook; by Jill Colella Bloomfield; Janet Ozur Bass, consultant; photography by Angela Coppola. DK Pub. 2008 128p il spiral bdg $19.99
Grades: 4 5 6 7   641.5
1. Jewish cooking 2. Jewish holidays
ISBN 978-0-7566-4089-7 spiral bdg; 0-7566-4089-X spiral bdg
"More than 40 recipes are included for celebrations from Shabbat to Lag B'Omer. Several introductions explain cooking tools, kitchen safety, and the general principles of keeping kosher, and brief background information is given for each holiday. Simple step-by-step instructions make the recipes easy. . . . Beautiful color photographs, both full page and spot, whet the appetite." SLJ

Bowers, Sharon
Ghoulish goodies. Storey Pub. 2009 153p il pa $14.95
Grades: 3 4 5 6   641.5
1. Desserts 2. Halloween 3. Holiday cooking
ISBN 978-1-60342-146-1 pa; 1-60342-146-7 pa
LC 2009007802
This offers recipes for Halloween-themed desserts such as Monster Eyeballs, Chocolate Spider Clusters, Buried Alive Cupcakes, and Screaming Red Punch
"Perfect for Halloween and beyond, this conveniently organized, well-illustrated cookbook is sure to be a crowd-pleaser. . . . Most recipes are complemented by a full-color photograph of the finished product. . . . Hauntingly appetizing." SLJ

D'Amico, Joan
★ The **coming** to America cookbook; delicious recipes and fascinating stories from America's many cultures. [by] Joan D'Amico, Karen Eich Drummond. Wiley 2005 180p il pa $14.95
Grades: 5 6 7 8   641.5
1. Cooking 2. United States -- Immigration and emigration
ISBN 0-471-48335-4
LC 2004-14947
The authors "provide information about American immigrants from 18 nations as well as recipes representing each group. . . . Accompanied by line drawings of ethnic families choosing, preparing, and eating food, . . . chapters discuss each country's climate, history, major waves of emigration, and traditional foods. Typically, three recipes follow. . . . Teachers and students looking for recipes from American immigrant cultures will make good use of this handy resource." Booklist

Dodge, Abigail Johnson
★ **Around** the world cookbook. DK Publishing 2008 124p il map spiral bdg $19.99
Grades: 3 4 5 6   641.5
1. Cooking
ISBN 978-0-7566-3744-6 spiral bdg; 0-7566-3744-9 spiral bdg
"This book presents more than 50 step-by-step recipes for ethnic cuisine. Dodge opens with instructions for basic cooking skills, an illustrated list of kitchen tools, a glossary of terms used in the recipes, and tips for working with different types of ingredients. . . . Possibly tricky steps are clarified with photographs and captions." SLJ

Ejaz, Khadija
Recipe and craft guide to India. Mitchell Lane Publishers 2010 63p il map (World crafts and recipes) lib bdg $33.95
Grades: 4 5 6 7 8   641.5
1. Handicraft 2. Indic cooking
ISBN 978-1-58415-938-4 lib bdg; 1-58415-938-3 lib bdg
LC 2010008950
Provides recipes for several popular Indian dishes and includes instructions on creating colorful and traditional Indian crafts.
This provides "plenty of ideas for adding tasty treats and impressive visual aids to cultural reports or presentations." SLJ
Includes glossary and bibliographical references

Gerasole, Isabella
The **Spatulatta** cookbook; by Isabella and Olivia Gerasole; photographs by John Zich. Scholastic 2007 128p il spiral bdg $16.99
Grades: 3 4 5 6   641.5
1. Cooking
ISBN 978-0-439-02250-7 spiral bdg; 0-439-02250-9 spiral bdg
"This lively, colorful companion book to the Gerasole sisters' Web site . . . contains an enticing array of dishes both sweet and savory, easy and complicated. . . . Beautifully reproduced color photos show the completed dishes and smaller photos show some of the steps. . . . This book strikes a great balance between fun and practical." SLJ
Includes glossary

Gold, Rozanne
Kids cook 1-2-3; recipes for young chefs using only 3 ingredients. illustrated by Sara Pinto. Bloomsbury Children's Books 2006 144p il $17.95
Grades: 3 4 5 6   641.5
1. Cooking
ISBN 978-1-58234-735-6; 1-58234-735-2
LC 2006-00623
"This very basic cookbook offers 125 recipes for breakfast, lunch, dinner, healthy snacks, side dishes, and desserts. The recipes are clearly presented, and are broken into easy-to-follow steps." SLJ

Gregory, Josh
Chef. Cherry Lake Pub. 2011 32p il (Cool careers) lib bdg $27.07
Grades: 4 5 6 7   641.5
1. Cooks 2. Cooking 3. Vocational guidance
ISBN 978-1-60279-985-1; 1-60279-985-7
LC 2010029085
This book begins "with a personal story of a teen and then [segues] into the occupation [of chef]. . . . [It covers] the necessary training and skills for the job (and options for obtaining them), a typical day, salary expectations, and well-known professionals in the field. The [text is] accessible and clearly written. . . . The [volume has] a generous number of clear color photographs that depict people at work." SLJ
Includes glossary and bibliographical references

Ichord, Loretta Frances

Skillet bread, sourdough, and vinegar pie; cooking in pioneer days. illustrated by Jan Davey Ellis. Millbrook Press 2003 64p il map hardcover o.p. pa $8.95

Grades: 3 4 5   **641.5**

1. Cooking 2. Frontier and pioneer life -- West (U.S.)

ISBN 0-7613-1864-X lib bdg; 0-7613-9521-0 pa

LC 2002-8157

Presents a look at what was eaten in the American West by pioneers on the trail, cowboys on cattle drives, and gold miners in California camps, with available ingredients, cooking methods, and equipment. Includes recipes and appendix of classroom cooking directions

"This unique title effectively combines recipes with history, a must for any collection needing information on the old West." Libr Media Connect

Includes bibliographical references

Karmel, Annabel

My favorite recipes. DK Pub. 2011 96p il $14.99

Grades: 3 4 5 6   **641.5**

1. Cooking

ISBN 978-0-7566-7195-2; 0-7566-7195-7

"These recipes . . . look good enough to eat. Each one includes a full-page, full-color picture of the dish, as well as step-by-step instructions, with smaller pictures. . . . All recipes need adult assistance, and some require more than basic cooking skills. The recipes are organized in four sections: light bites, main meals, fruity treats, and cakes and cookies. They include children's favorites like spaghetti and chicken dippers . . . as well as more exotic dishes like paella and lamb tagine. Where this cookbook really shines is in the creative and fun plating. Karmel often creates faces or animals out of a dish. . . . A bright and colorful cookbook that is sure to appeal to children." SLJ

Katzen, Mollie

★ **Salad** people and more real recipes; a new cookbook for preschoolers and up. Tricycle Press 2005 93p il $17.95

Grades: K 1 2 3   **641.5**

1. Cooking

ISBN 1-58246-141-4

"Katzen offers a range of vegetarian, kid-friendly recipes in an artistic, innovative format. Each recipe receives two spreads. The first contains detailed, step-by-step instructions for adults; the second, directed to children, illustrates stages of preparation in a series of clear, boxed drawings. Katzen's whimsical color pictures of dancing produce and animals decorate the pages. . . . These detailed, practical, and inspired ideas may extend far beyond the kitchen, helping adults approach parenting in new ways and helping kids develop a lifelong interest and confidence in healthy food." Booklist

Kozlowski, Bryan

Cook me a story; A treasury of stories and recipes inspired by classic fairy tales. Bryan Kozlowski. Quarto Pub Group USA 2016 80 p. color illustrations $16.95

Grades: K 1 2 3 4   **641.5**

1. Cooking 2. Fairy tales -- Adaptations

ISBN 1633220664; 9781633220669

In this cookbook for children by Bryan Kozlowski, "the most beloved fairy tales are retold with deliciously clever recipes for families to create and enjoy together. From breakfast adventures to evening stories, anytime is a perfect time for fairy tales and food. Join the fun as children learn to cook with familiar kitchen-time tales. . . [It] combines the magic of storytelling with the fun of cooking." (Publisher's note)

"An attractive and well-organized work that would make a solid purchase for libraries where cookbooks circulate well." SLJ

LaPenta, Marilyn

Way cool drinks. Bearport Pub. 2011 24p il (Yummy tummy recipes) lib bdg $22.61

Grades: 3 4 5 6   **641.5**

1. Cooking 2. Beverages

ISBN 978-1-61772-163-2; 1-61772-163-8

LC 2011017444

This offers recipes for fruit drinks such as mango tango, fruit fusion, and blueberry bash smoothie.

"All 14 recipes are easy to follow with little more than four or five listed steps, clearly defined serving sizes, and minimal prep time. A healthy tip and oather facts are included with each recipe." Booklist

Includes glossary and bibliographical references

LaRoche, Amelia

Recipe and craft guide to France. Mitchell Lane Publishers 2010 63p il map (World crafts and recipes) lib bdg $33.95

Grades: 4 5 6 7 8   **641.5**

1. Handicraft 2. French cooking

ISBN 978-1-58415-936-0 lib bdg; 1-58415-936-7 lib bdg

LC 2010008949

Provides recipes for several popular French dishes and includes instructions on creating crafts using household items.

This provides "plenty of ideas for adding tasty treats and impressive visual aids to cultural reports or presentations." SLJ

Includes glossary and bibliographical references

Larson, Jennifer S.

Delicious vegetarian main dishes; by Jennifer S. Larson; photographs by Brie Cohen. Millbrook Press 2013 32 p. col. ill. (library) $26.60

Grades: 1 2 3 4   **641.5**

1. Cooking 2. Vegetarian cooking 3. Entrées (Cooking)

ISBN 0761366350; 9780761366355

LC 2012020923

This book by Jennifer S. Larson presents "easy-to-follow recipes such as baked potato pile up, lemony couscous, crispy tofu sticks, and tasty tortilla towers. [Also included are] simple drawings of important steps as well as photographs of the finished dishes. This book also provides key information, such as an equipment list, a technique list, safety tips, notes on special ingredients, and more." (Publisher's note)

Includes bibliographical references (page 32) and index.

Lee, Frances

Fun with Chinese cooking. PowerKids Press 2009 32p il (Let's get cooking!) lib bdg $18.95; pa $11.75

Grades: 4 5 6 7   **641.5**

1. Chinese cooking

ISBN 978-1-4358-3453-8 lib bdg; 1-4358-3453-4 lib bdg; 978-1-4358-3475-0 pa; 1-4358-3475-5 pa

LC 2009010337

This includes recipes for such Chinese dishes as spring rolls and braised mushrooms, and highlights the history and dishes that surround the Chinese New Year.

"The photography is exceptional, with children engaged in the cooking process. . . . Children, and the adults who assist them, will spend hours together mastering the techniques." SLJ

Locricchio, Matthew

★ The **2nd** international cookbook for kids; photographs by Jack McConnell. Marshall Cavendish 2008 176p il $18.99

Grades: 5 6 7 8 **641.5**
   1. Cooking
   ISBN 978-0-7614-5513-4
                       LC 2008003178
The recipes are "presented in a challenging yet teen-friendly step-by-step sequence. The book is best for patient chefs with kitchen experience and adventurous appetites. Informative sidebars provide facts about the recipes and cultures." Horn Book Guide

★ The **international** cookbook for kids; by Matthew Locricchio; photographs by Jack McConnell. Reprint Marshall Cavendish 2012 175p il $12.99
Grades: 5 6 7 8 **641.5**
   1. Cooking
   ISBN 9780761463139
                       LC 2004-5894
This includes "60 classic recipes from Italy, France, China, and Mexico, . . . chef's tips discussing ingredients, nutrition, and technique, safety section discussing basic kitchen precautions, cooking terms and definitions." Publisher's note

Mattern, Joanne
   Recipe and craft guide to China. Mitchell Lane Publishers 2010 63p il map (World crafts and recipes) lib bdg $33.95
Grades: 4 5 6 7 8 **641.5**
   1. Handicraft 2. Chinese cooking
   ISBN 978-1-58415-937-7 lib bdg; 1-58415-937-5 lib bdg
                       LC 2010009242
Provides recipes for several popular Chinese dishes and includes instructions on creating crafts using household items.
This provides "plenty of ideas for adding tasty treats and impressive visual aids to cultural reports or presentations." SLJ
Includes glossary and bibliographical references

McCallum, Ann
   Eat your math homework; recipes for hungry minds. illustrated by Leeza Hernandez. Charlesbridge 2011 46p il $16.95; pa $7.95
Grades: 2 3 4 **641.5**
   1. Cooking 2. Mathematics
   ISBN 978-1-57091-779-0; 1-57091-779-5; 978-1-57091-780-6 pa; 1-57091-780-9 pa
                       LC 2010033631
"McCallum combines math with cooking in this attractive book. After a brief introduction and a few basic cooking tips, she explains the Fibonacci sequence and shows how to demonstrate it using chunks of fruit on skewers. Fractions are expressed through fried flour tortillas cut into fractional portions; tessellations with two-tone brownies; tangrams with flat cookies; variables and pi with pizza and probability with trail mix. In six-page chapters, the recipe sounds good, the math is clearly explained, and there's a playfulness of presentation that makes each activity look inviting. The mixed-media illustrations feature dressed rabbits, whose zany attitudes broaden their appeal. . . . Witty and smart." Booklist

Mofford, Juliet Haines
   Recipe and craft guide to Japan. Mitchell Lane Publishers 2010 63p il map (World crafts and recipes) lib bdg $33.95
Grades: 4 5 6 7 8 **641.5**
   1. Handicraft 2. Japanese cooking
   ISBN 978-1-58415-933-9 lib bdg; 1-58415-933-2 lib bdg
                       LC 2010008951
Provides recipes for several popular Japanese dishes and includes instructions on creating traditional Japanese crafts using household items.

This provides "plenty of ideas for adding tasty treats and impressive visual aids to cultural reports or presentations." SLJ
Includes glossary and bibliographical references

Recipe and craft guide to the Caribbean. Mitchell Lane Publishers 2010 64p il map (World crafts and recipes) lib bdg $33.95
Grades: 4 5 6 7 8 **641.5**
   1. Handicraft 2. Caribbean cooking
   ISBN 978-1-58415-935-3 lib bdg; 1-58415-935-9 lib bdg
                       LC 2010009240
Provides recipes for several popular Caribbean dishes and includes instructions on creating traditional Caribbean crafts using household items.
This provides "plenty of ideas for adding tasty treats and impressive visual aids to cultural reports or presentations." SLJ
Includes glossary and bibliographical references

Reusser, Kayleen
   Recipe and craft guide to Indonesia. Mitchell Lane Publishers 2010 64p il map (World crafts and recipes) lib bdg $33.95
Grades: 4 5 6 7 8 **641.5**
   1. Handicraft 2. Indonesian cooking
   ISBN 978-1-58415-934-6 lib bdg; 1-58415-934-0 lib bdg
                       LC 2010009243
Provides recipes for several popular Indonesian dishes and includes instructions on creating crafts using household items.
This provides "plenty of ideas for adding tasty treats and impressive visual aids to cultural reports or presentations." SLJ
Includes glossary and bibliographical references

Sheen, Barbara
   Foods of Chile. KidHaven Press 2011 64p il map (A taste of culture) $28.75
Grades: 4 5 6 **641.5**
   1. Chilean cooking 2. Chile -- Social life and customs
   ISBN 978-0-7377-5421-6; 0-7377-5421-4
                       LC 2010035995
"Demonstrating that a nation's cuisine springs from its geography, history, and traditions, [this volume explores Chile's background], the availability of fresh ingredients, and recipes that followed. . . . Culturally specific foods are described alongside some accompanying recipes and photos of people enjoying the dishes." Horn Book Guide
Includes glossary and bibliographical references

   Foods of Cuba. KidHaven Press 2011 64p il map (A taste of culture) $28.75
Grades: 4 5 6 **641.5**
   1. Cuban cooking 2. Cuba -- Social life and customs
   ISBN 978-0-7377-5113-0; 0-7377-5113-4
                       LC 2010030795
"Demonstrating that a nation's cuisine springs from its geography, history, and traditions, [this volume explores Cuba's background], the availability of fresh ingredients, and recipes that followed. . . . Culturally specific foods are described alongside some accompanying recipes and photos of people enjoying the dishes." Horn Book Guide
Includes glossary and bibliographical references

   Foods of Egypt. KidHaven Press 2010 64p il map (A taste of culture) $28.75
Grades: 4 5 6 **641.5**
   1. Egyptian cooking 2. Egypt -- Social life and customs
   ISBN 978-0-7377-4843-7; 0-7377-4843-5
                       LC 2009038461

"Sheen explores how different native dishes and types of local celebrations emerge from [Egypt's] culture and surroundings. [An] introductory [map] with a [key] to areas of food production illuminate the country's cuisine by identifying geographical landforms and climate. Traditions and tastes are described in accessible detail; key recipes are included and unfamiliar foods are pictured." Horn Book Guide

Includes glossary and bibliographical references

Foods of Ireland. KidHaven Press 2011 64p il map (A taste of culture) $28.75
Grades: 4 5 6   **641.5**
  1. Irish cooking 2. Ireland -- Social life and customs
  ISBN 978-0-7377-5114-7; 0-7377-5114-2
                                            LC 2010018791
"Sheen explores how different native dishes and types of local celebrations emerge from [Ireland's] culture and surroundings. [An] introductory [map] with a [key] to areas of food production illuminate the country's cuisine by identifying geographical landforms and climate. Traditions and tastes are described in accessible detail; key recipes are included and unfamiliar foods are pictured." Horn Book Guide

Includes glossary and bibliographical references

Foods of Kenya. KidHaven Press 2010 64p il map (A taste of culture) $28.75
Grades: 4 5 6   **641.5**
  1. African cooking 2. Kenyan cooking 3. Kenya -- Social life and customs
  ISBN 978-0-7377-4813-0; 0-7377-4813-3
                                            LC 2009048378
"Sheen explores how different native dishes and types of local celebrations emerge from [Kenya's] culture and surroundings. [An] introductory [map] with a [key] to areas of food production illuminate the country's cuisine by identifying geographical landforms and climate. Traditions and tastes are described in accessible detail; key recipes are included and unfamiliar foods are pictured." Horn Book Guide

Includes glossary and bibliographical references

Foods of Korea. KidHaven Press 2011 64p il map (A taste of culture) $26.75
Grades: 4 5 6   **641.5**
  1. Korean cooking 2. Korea -- Social life and customs
  ISBN 978-0-7377-5115-4; 0-7377-5115-0
                                            LC 2010018789
"Demonstrating that a nation's cuisine springs from its geography, history, and traditions, [this volume explores Korea's background], the availability of fresh ingredients, and recipes that followed.... Culturally specific foods are described alongside some accompanying recipes and photos of people enjoying the dishes." Horn Book Guide

Includes glossary and bibliographical references

Foods of Peru. KidHaven Press 2011 64p il map (A taste of culture) $28.75
Grades: 4 5 6   **641.5**
  1. Peruvian cooking 2. Peru -- Social life and customs
  ISBN 978-0-7377-5346-2; 0-7377-5346-3
                                            LC 2010032959
"Demonstrating that a nation's cuisine springs from its geography, history, and traditions, [this volume explores Peru's background], the availability of fresh ingredients, and recipes that followed.... Culturally specific foods are described alongside some accompanying recipes and photos of people enjoying the dishes." Horn Book Guide

Includes glossary and bibliographical references

Tuminelly, Nancy
  Cool creepy food art; easy recipes that make food fun to eat! ABDO Pub. Company 2011 32p il (Cool food art) lib bdg $25.65
Grades: 3 4 5   **641.5**
  1. Food 2. Cooking
  ISBN 978-1-61613-363-4; 1-61613-363-5
                                            LC 2010003286
This offers recipes for such dishes as severed finger pizza; floating head cider, to die for dip, eyeball spaghetti, gross-out pita, garbage goop, bloody hand punch, and snot stick pretzels.

"Photographs provide clear step-by-step instructions as well as images of the finished products." Horn Book Guide

Includes glossary

  Cool fruit & veggie food art; easy recipes that make food fun to eat! ABDO Pub. Company 2010 32p il (Cool food art) lib bdg $25.65
Grades: 3 4 5   **641.5**
  1. Food 2. Fruit 3. Cooking -- Vegetables
  ISBN 978-1-61613-364-1; 1-61613-364-3
                                            LC 2010003285
Provides step-by-step instructions for creating fruit and vegetable food art, such as a funny face salad, an apple flutterfly, and a flying cucumber; and includes tips on techniques.

"Photographs provide clear step-by-step instructions as well as images of the finished products." Horn Book Guide

Includes glossary

  Cool holiday food art; easy recipes that make food fun to eat! ABDO Pub. Company 2010 32p il (Cool food art) lib bdg $25.65
Grades: 3 4 5   **641.5**
  1. Food 2. Holiday cooking
  ISBN 978-1-61613-365-8; 1-61613-365-1
                                            LC 2010003476
Provides step-by-step instructions for creating holiday-themed food art, such as reindeer cookies, dreidel pretzels, and creepy popcorn balls; and includes tips on techniques.

"Photographs provide clear step-by-step instructions as well as images of the finished products." Horn Book Guide

Includes glossary

  Cool meat-free recipes; delicious & fun foods without meat. Nancy Tuminelly. ABDO Pub. Co. 2013 32 p. (Checkerboard how-to library. Cool recipes for your health) $28.50
Grades: 3 4 5 6 7 8   **641.5**
  1. Cooking 2. Vegetarian cooking
  ISBN 161783582X; 9781617835827
                                            LC 2012023989
Author Nancy Tuminelly's book "gives young readers the tools to make healthy, tasty--and safe--dishes for anybody, anytime. This book has kid-tested, easy meat-free recipes, perfect for those who follow a vegetarian or vegan diet. Basic baking techniques, tools, and ingredients are illustrated so kids can quickly prepare each recipe, such as Breakfast Bars and Sloppy Joes." (Publisher's note)

Includes bibliographical references and index

  Cool snack food art; easy recipes that make food fun to eat! ABDO Pub. Company 2010 32p il (Cool food art) lib bdg $25.65
Grades: 3 4 5   **641.5**
  1. Food 2. Snack foods
  ISBN 978-1-61613-367-2; 1-61613-367-8
                                            LC 2010003573

Provides step-by-step instructions for creating snack food art, such as chili snake dogs, a peanut butter and candy pizza, and a sweet treat flowerpot; and includes tips on techniques.

Includes glossary

Walker, Barbara Muhs

The **Little** House cookbook; frontier foods from Laura Ingalls Wilder's classic stories. by Barbara M. Walker; illustrated by Garth Williams. Harper & Row 1979 240p il $16.95; pa $9.95

Grades: 5 6 7 8   **641.5**

1. Authors 2. Cooking 3. Novelists 4. Frontier and pioneer life 5. Western writers 6. Children's authors 7. Young adult authors

ISBN 0-06-026418-7; 0-06-446090-8 pa

LC 76-58733

Recipes based on the pioneer food written about in the "Little House" books of Laura Ingalls Wilder, along with quotes from the books and descriptions of the food and cooking of pioneer times

"Illustrated by Williams's familiar warm drawings, the adaptations of menus from pioneer days include paragaphs describing the Wilder and Ingalls families working together, preparing holiday meals, individual foods, special treats and staple fare." Publ Wkly

Includes bibliographical references

Webb, Lois Sinaiko

Holidays of the world cookbook for students; [by] Lois Sinaiko Webb and Lindsay Grace Roten, updated and rev.; Greenwood 2011 442p il map $95; pa $32.95

Grades: 5 6 7 8 9 10   **641.5**

1. Cooking 2. Holidays

ISBN 978-0-313-38393-9; 0-313-38393-6; 978-0-313-39790-5 pa; 0-313-39790-2 pa; 978-0-313-38394-6 ebook

LC 2011-8458

First published 1995 by Oryx Press

"The recipes appear with each country entry, and the countries are arranged in alphabetical order within each region: Africa, Asia and the South Pacific, the Caribbean, Europe, Latin America, the Middle East, and North America." Publisher's note

Yolen, Jane

Fairy tale feasts; a literary cookbook for young readers and eaters. [by] Jane Yolen and Heidi E. Y. Stemple; illustrated by Philippe Beha. Crocodile Books 2006 197p il $24.95

Grades: 2 3 4 5   **641.5**

1. Cooking 2. Folklore

ISBN 1-56656-543-6

This "folds fairy tales into a cookbook of kid-friendly recipes. The stories, with the exception of one original story by Yolen, represent mostly European folktales, and Yolen retells them with her usual verve and ease. . . . Each story is paired with at least one recipe that connects with the story's themes or references. . . . Stemple's recipes require adult supervision, but the resulting dishes, as well as Beha's spare, whimsical spot illustrations, will capture children's fancy." Booklist

Jewish fairy tale feasts; stories retold by Jane Yolen; recipes by Heidi E.Y. Stemple; illustrations by Sima Elizabeth Shefrin. 1st American ed. Crocodile Books, an imprint of Interlink Pub. Group, Inc. 2012 200 p. (hardcover) $25

Grades: 2 3 4 5   **641.5**

1. Fairy tales 2. Jewish cooking 3. Cooking

ISBN 1566569095; 9781566569095

LC 2012016174

This children's book, by Jane Yolen, Heidi E. Y. Stemple, illustrated by Sima Elizabeth Shefrin, offers Jewish cooking recipes and fairy tales to accompany them. "Here you'll find Yolen's . . . retellings of Jew-

ish tales from around the world paired with Stemple's recipes-for everything from challah to matzo brei to pomegranate couscous, tzimmes chicken, and rugelah, in creative versions of classic dishes that any family will delight in cooking together." (Publisher's note)

Includes bibliographical references and index

641.509   History, geographic treatment, biography

Hartland, Jessie

Bon appetit! the delicious life of Julia Child. Jessie Hartland. Schwartz & Wade Books 2012 48 p. (hbk.) $17.99

Grades: 2 3 4 5   **641.509**

1. Women cooks 2. Women -- Biography 3. Picture books for children 4. Women cooks -- United States -- Biography

ISBN 0375869441; 0375969446; 9780375869440; 9780375969447

LC 2011018658

This juvenile biography, by Jessie Hartland, follows "Julia Child--chef, author, and television personality--from her childhood in Pasadena, California, to her life as a spy in WWII, . . . to the publication of 'Mastering the Art of French Cooking,' to the funny moments of being a chef on TV. This is a comprehensive and enchanting picture book biography, told in many panels and jam-packed with lively, humorous, and child-friendly details." (Publisher's note)

Includes bibliographical references.

641.59   Cooking characteristic of specific geographic environments, ethnic cooking

Blaxland, Wendy

Chinese food; by Wendy Blaxland. Smart Apple Media 2012 32 p. (library binding) $28.50

Grades: 4 5 6 7   **641.59**

1. Food 2. Chinese cooking

ISBN 1599206714; 9781599206714

LC 2011005448

Author Wendy Blaxland's book "offers them the tastes of foreign or favorite cuisine. Beginning with a discussion about this area's culinary roots, it shows the growing of favorite foods are grown, its purchase and preparation. Step-by-step illustrated instructions for recipes are included along with nutritional data, safety and hygiene information." (Wheelers)

Mexican food; by Wendy Blaxland. Smart Apple Media 2012 32 p. (I can cook!) (library binding) $28.50

Grades: 4 5 6 7   **641.59**

1. Cookbooks 2. Cooking, Mexican 3. Food -- Mexico -- History

ISBN 1599206684; 9781599206684

LC 2011005444

This book, by Wendy Blaxland, "presents a good amount of information on the geography, food staples, and even culture of [Mexico]. 'Mexican Food' finds a balance of spicy and sweet flavors in dishes from huevos rancheros to pan de muertos. Each recipe features helpful digital step-by-step illustrations and ideas for variations, underlining the fact that cooking is a creative process." (Booklist)

Locricchio, Matthew

The **cooking** of France; by Matthew Locricchio. Benchmark Books 2011 96 p. (Superchef) (print) $35.64

Grades: 4 5 6 7 8   **641.59**
1. Cookbooks 2. French cooking 3. Food habits -- France
ISBN 160870551X; 9781608705511; 9781608707393
    LC 2010052549

Author Matthew Locricchio presents a book on French cooking. "After a shared introduction about safety, [it] introduces . . . regional cuisines, mentioning festivals, traditions, and music to give readers a broader cultural view of [France]. Recipes, divided into categories such as soups and salads, main courses, and so on, make up the bulk of [the] book." (Booklist)
Includes bibliographical references and index

The **cooking** of Greece; Matthew Locricchio. Marshall Cavendish Benchmark 2011 96 p. (print) $35.64
Grades: 4 5 6 7 8   **641.59**
1. Cookbooks 2. Greek cooking 3. Food habits -- Greece 4. Cooking, Mediterranean
ISBN 1608705528; 9781608705528; 9781608707409
    LC 2010052548

In this book, author Matthew Locricchio "begins with a region-by-region overview of Greece, highlighting the natural produce of each area and the resulting cuisine, then groups his recipes by type–'Pies & Pitas,' 'Entrées,' etc. A section on kitchen safety . . . gives particulars on using knives. Fresh, healthful ingredients are emphasized, and suggestions are offered for adapting the recipes for vegetarians." (School Library Journal)
Includes bibliographical references and index

The **cooking** of Italy; by Matthew Locricchio. Marshall Cavendish Benchmark 2011 96 p. (print) $35.64
Grades: 4 5 6 7 8   **641.59**
1. Cookbooks 2. Italian cooking 3. Food habits -- Italy
ISBN 1608705544; 9781608705542; 9781608707423
    LC 2010051849

In this book, by Matthew Locricchio, Italian cooking recipes are presented. It also "discusses general safety rules in the kitchen as well as specific rules for using knives. Regions of Italy . . . are defined along with a description of how geography influences crops, celebrations, and traditions that flourish within each area. Cooking terms are [also] explained." (Publisher's note)
Includes bibliographical references and index

Mendez, Sean
One world kids cookbook; easy, healthy and affordable family meals. by Sean Mendez. Interlink 2011 96 p. $20
Grades: 5 6 7 8   **641.59**
1. Diet 2. Cookbooks 3. Eating habits
ISBN 1566568668; 9781566568661

Author Sean Mendez presents a cookbook "aimed at encouraging young people to think about what they eat through emphasizing the importance of a balanced diet. It contains kitchen tips and suggests vegetarian substitutes to the meat recipes. One World Kids Cookbook aims to instill a passion for good, wholesome, healthy food as well as a passion for life." (Publisher's note)

Sheen, Barbara
Foods of Australia; by Barbara Sheen. KidHaven Press 2010 64 p. (hardcover) $31.95
Grades: 4 5 6   **641.59**
1. Australian cooking 2. Australia -- Social life and customs 3. Cooking -- Australia
ISBN 0737748125; 9780737748123
    LC 2009032643

This book, by Barbara Sheen, "explores the foods, cooking traditions, customs, eating habits, and food sources of [Australia]. [It discusses] ingredients that form the staples of cooking . . ., the favorite dishes, the snacks and sweets, the traditional holiday meals, and the preparations and traditions associated with these foods." (Publisher's note)
Includes bibliographical references and index

641.594   Cooking -- Europe

Bucholz, Dinah
The **unofficial** Narnia cookbook; from Turkish delight to gooseberry fool--over 150 recipes inspired by the Chronicles of Narnia. Dinah Bucholz. Sourcebooks Jabberwocky 2012 233 p. $19.99
Grades: 4 5 6   **641.594**
1. Cookbooks 2. Narnia (Imaginary place)
ISBN 1402266413; 9781402266416

In this cookbook by Dinah Bucholz "each recipe is clearly tied to particular incidents and chapters in the books of Narnia. . . . While striving to stick to the actual meals in the stories (Eel Stew! Boar's Head!), [Bucholz] creates or re-creates Beautiful Breakfasts; Snacks, Teas, and Meals on the Run; Lunch and Dinner Menus; and Fabulous Feasts in four chapters." (Kirkus)

Wagner, Lisa
Cool French cooking; fun and tasty recipes for kids. by Lisa Wagner. Checkerboard Library 2011 32 p. $28.50
Grades: 3 4 5 6   **641.594**
1. French cooking 2. Cooking
ISBN 1617146609; 9781617146602
    LC 2010022192

This book, by Lisa Wagner, "introduces readers to world geography and authentic, easy-to-make recipes [for French cuisine]. Cooking teaches kids about food, math and measuring, and following directions. Each kid-tested recipe includes step-by-step instructions and how-to photos. Tools and ingredients lists are also provided, as well as pronunciation guides when needed." (Publisher's note)

Cool Italian cooking; fun and tasty recipes for kids. by Lisa Wagner. Checkerboard Library 2011 32 p. $28.50
Grades: 3 4 5 6   **641.594**
1. Italian cooking 2. Cooking 3. Cooking, Italian
ISBN 1617146617; 9781617146619
    LC 2010022193

This book, by Lisa Wagner, "introduces readers to world geography and authentic, easy-to-make recipes [for Italian cuisine}. Cooking teaches kids about food, math and measuring, and following directions. Each kid-tested recipe includes step-by-step instructions and how-to photos. Tools and ingredients lists are also provided, as well as pronunciation guides when needed." (Publisher's note)

641.595   Cooking -- Asia

Wagner, Lisa
Cool Chinese and Japanese cooking; fun and tasty recipes for kids. by Lisa Wagner. ABDO Pub. 2011 32 p. (Cool world cooking) $28.50
Grades: 3 4 5 6   **641.595**
1. Chinese cooking 2. Japanese cooking 3. Cooking
ISBN 1617146595; 9781617146596
    LC 2010022191

This book, by Lisa Wagner, "introduces readers to world geography and authentic, easy-to-make recipes [for Chinese and Japanese cuisine].

Cooking teaches kids about food, math and measuring, and following directions. Each kid-tested recipe includes step-by-step instructions and how-to photos. Tools and ingredients lists are also provided, as well as pronunciation guides when needed." (Publisher's note)

641.5972 Cooking – Mexico

Wagner, Lisa

Cool Mexican cooking; fun and tasty recipes for kids. by Lisa Wagner. Checkerboard Library 2011 32 p. (Cool world cooking) $28.50
Grades: 3 4 5 6   **641.5972**
1. Cooking 2. Cooking, Mexican
ISBN 1617146625; 9781617146626

LC 2010022194

This book, by Lisa Wagner, "introduces readers to world geography and authentic, easy-to-make recipes [for Mexican cuisine]. Cooking teaches kids about food, math and measuring, and following directions. Each kid-tested recipe includes step-by-step instructions and how-to photos. Tools and ingredients lists are also provided, as well as pronunciation guides when needed." (Publisher's note)

641.5973 Cooking – United States

McCallum, Ann

Eat your U.S. history homework; recipes for revolutionary minds. by Ann McCallum; illustrated by Leeza Hernandez. Charlesbridge 2015 48 p. colour illustrations (reinforced for library use) $15.95
Grades: 2 3 4   **641.5973**
1. American cooking -- History 2. United States -- History -- 1600-1775, Colonial period 3. United States -- History -- 1775-1783, Revolution
ISBN 9781570919237; 9781570919244

LC 2014010492

This book, by Ann McCallum, illustrated by Leeza Hernandez is a "collection of unique recipes [that] will fill you up with lip-smacking history facts that reveal what cuisine was like for people between the 1600s to the 1800s, during the birth of America. Budding chefs will devour time-period inspired recipes for healthy entrees and snacks, as well as desserts, including Thanksgiving Succotash, Revolutionary Honey-Jumble Cookies, Colonial Cherry-Berry Grunts, and more." (Publisher's note)

"Social studies teachers aren't likely to assign these for homework, but some could easily be made in class to finish off Colonial studies." Kirkus

641.6 Cooking specific materials

Llewellyn, Claire

Cooking with meat and fish; [by] Claire Llewellyn, Clare O'Shea. Rosen Central 2011 48p il map (Cooking healthy) lib bdg $27.95
Grades: 5 6 7 8   **641.6**
1. Meat 2. Cooking 3. Seafood
ISBN 978-1-4488-4845-4; 1-4488-4845-8

LC 2010039337

A description of each type of meat and fish, how to cook them in a healthy manner, and recipe examples of each.

This book pairs "facts about [meat and fish], including where it is eaten, with eye-catching photos. . . . Each course (section) has an overview of the . . . [meat] followed by recipes from all over the world. They vary in difficulty. . . . The cooking directions are clear and straight-

forward. . . . [The book is] profusely illustrated with full-color photos. Students who are learning to cook will appreciate [this] excellently organized [read]." SLJ

Includes glossary and bibliographical references

MacLeod, Elizabeth

Chock full of chocolate; written by Elizabeth MacLeod; illustrated by June Bradford. Kids Can Press 2005 40p il (Kids can do it) hardcover o.p. pa $6.95
Grades: 4 5 6   **641.6**
1. Cooking 2. Chocolate
ISBN 1-55337-762-1; 1-55337-763-X pa

This includes recipes for chocolate cookies, cakes, and other desserts.

641.8 Cooking specific kinds of dishes and preparing beverages

Dunnington, Rose

Sweet eats; mmmore than just desserts. [by] Rose Dunnington. Lark Books 2008 112p $9.95
Grades: 3 4 5 6   **641.8**
1. Baking 2. Desserts
ISBN 978-1-60059-236-2; 1-60059-236-8

LC 2007037094

This "offers mouthwatering recipes, explains how to cook safely and efficiently, and introduces basic skills. In a breezy first-person style, the author covers such useful aspects as how to organize a work space, safety tips, the tools needed, and how and why to do things. The 35 recipes include a pie crust and various frostings/toppings and are accompanied by plenty of full-color visual aids along the way." SLJ

Includes glossary

Gibbons, Gail

Ice cream; the full scoop. by Gail Gibbons. Holiday House 2006 un il $16.95
Grades: K 1 2 3   **641.8**
1. Ice cream, ices, etc.
ISBN 978-0-8234-2000-1; 0-8234-2000-0

LC 2005052575

"Gibbons explains how this favorite food developed from flavored ice to the creamy dessert we know today, describes the invention and workings of the ice-cream maker, follows the journey from cow to factory to grocery-store shelves, and mentions the innovative creation of the cone. . . . The narrative is simple and direct and the cartoon illustrations are colorful and cheerful." SLJ

Goodman, Susan

All in just one cookie; by Susan E. Goodman; illustrated by Timothy Bush. Greenwillow Books 2006 un il $16.99; lib bdg $17.89
Grades: 2 3 4   **641.8**
1. Baking 2. Cookies
ISBN 978-0-06-009092-0; 0-06-009092-8; 978-0-06-009093-7 lib bdg; 0-06-009093-6 lib bdg

LC 2005040308

"As Grandma gathers the ingredients for her chocolate-chip cookies, her cat collects facts about the process of making butter, vanilla, baking soda, and other cookie components. . . . Cartoonlike illustrations show where each ingredient comes from, along with side comments from the cat and dog." Horn Book Guide

Love, Ann

Sweet! the delicious story of candy. [by] Ann Love & Jane Drake; illustrated by Claudia Dávila. Tundra Books 2007 64p il map $19.95

Grades: 4 5 6 7 **641.8**
　1. Candy
　ISBN 978-0-88776-752-4

"This history of things sweet and sugary is a yummy feast. The prose is chatty and inviting. Color cartoon illustrations show multiethnic people in the process of making or enjoying everything from honey to ice cream to cotton candy (called candy floss here) to jelly beans and chocolate." SLJ

MacLeod, Elizabeth
　Bake and make amazing cookies; written by Elizabeth MacLeod; illustrated by June Bradford. Kids Can Press 2004 40p il (Kids can do it) hardcover o.p. pa $6.95
Grades: 4 5 6 **641.8**
　1. Cookies
　ISBN 1-55337-631-5; 1-55337-632-3 pa

This offers "32 recipes under four headings 'Holidays,' 'For Special People,' 'Seasons,' and 'Just for Fun.' This book is sure to please bakers. The step-by-step instructions . . . are easy to follow, and the ingredients/tools listed are readily available or easily obtainable. . . . Each recipe is accompanied by precise, softly colored illustrations." SLJ

Raum, Elizabeth
　The **story** behind bread. Heinemann Library 2009 32p il (True stories) lib bdg $28.21
Grades: 3 4 5 **641.8**
　1. Bread
　ISBN 978-1-4329-2346-4 lib bdg; 1-4329-2346-3 lib bdg
　　　　　　　　　　　　　　　　　　　　LC 2008037394

The story behind "bread covers the history of the staple and its importance, the harvesting of grains, and the equipment used to bring it 'From Fields to Tables.' Readers will learn, for example, that bagels were originally created in the shape of a stirrup to honor the King of Poland. . . . The well-organized [text is] informative and clearly written, and the numerous color photographs and drawings are eye-catching and complement the [narrative] well." SLJ
　Includes bibliographical references

Smart, Denise
　The **children's** baking book; recipes & styling by Denise Smart; photography by Howard Shooter. DK 2009 128p il $17.99
Grades: 3 4 5 **641.8**
　1. Baking
　ISBN 0-7566-5788-1; 978-0-7566-5788-8

Instructions for making bread, pastry, muffins, cakes and cookies. Includes more than 50 easy-to-follow recipes.
　"This accessible baking book features more than 50 sweet and savory recipes . . . with full-color photographs that show both preparations and tasty end results. Divided into sections on cookies and baked goods, dough, cakes, and pastry, the recipes are further labeled with levels of difficulty. . . . The sweet-toothed should find the mouthwatering pictures and straightforward instructions hard to resist." Publ Wkly

Tuminelly, Nancy
　Cool sandwich food art; easy recipes that make food fun to eat! ABDO Pub. Company 2011 32p il (Cool food art) lib bdg $25.65
Grades: 3 4 5 **641.8**
　1. Food 2. Sandwiches
　ISBN 978-1-61613-366-5; 1-61613-366-X
　　　　　　　　　　　　　　　　　　　　LC 2010003475

Provides step-by-step instructions for creating sandwich food art, such as a peanut butter and jelly flower, a happy hippo hoagie, and a caterpillar wrap; and includes tips on techniques.
　Includes glossary

641.81　Side dishes, sauces, garnishes

Larson, Jennifer S.
　Yummy soup and salad recipes; Jennifer S. Larson; photographs by Brie Cohen. Millbrook Press 2013 32 p. (You're the chef) (lib. bdg. : alk. paper) $26.60
Grades: 1 2 3 4 **641.81**
　1. Soups 2. Cookbooks 3. Cooking 4. Salads
　ISBN 0761366334; 9780761366331
　　　　　　　　　　　　　　　　　　　　LC 2012020921

This illustrated kids' cookbook by Jennifer S. Larson is part of the You're the Chef series and offers soup and salad recipes. It "proves that soups can include everything from chili to chowder to fruit. Each title" includes a glossary of technique terms, "notes about special ingredients and a website link." (Booklist)
　Includes bibliographical references and index

641.82　Main dishes

Larson, Jennifer S.
　Meaty main dishes; Jennifer S. Larson; photographs by Brie Cohen. Millbrook Press 2013 32 p. (You're the chef) (lib. bdg. : alk. paper) $26.60
Grades: 1 2 3 4 **641.82**
　1. Cooking -- Meat 2. Entrées (Cooking)
　ISBN 0761366342; 9780761366348
　　　　　　　　　　　　　　　　　　　　LC 2012020922

This cookbook by Jennifer S. Larson presents "easy-to-follow recipes for Asian shrimp stir fry, juicy chicken drumsticks, taco meatballs, and other tasty dishes. You'll find simple drawings of important steps as well as photographs of the finished dishes. This book also provides key information, such as an equipment list, a technique list, safety tips, notes on special ingredients, and more." (Publisher's note)
　Includes bibliographical references (page 32) and index

642　Meals and table service

Duncan, Karen
　The **good** fun! book; 12 months of parties that celebrate service. by Karen Duncan & Kate Hannigan Issa; illustrated by Anthony Alex LeTourneau. Blue Marlin Publications 2010 un il $15.95
Grades: 3 4 5 6 **642**
　1. Cooking 2. Parties 3. Handicraft 4. Social action
　ISBN 978-0-9792918-5-2; 0-9792918-5-2
　　　　　　　　　　　　　　　　　　　　LC 2010025848

"For each month of the year, Duncan and Issa suggest a party with a service theme. For example, they suggest making Valentines for children at a local hospital in February, cleaning up a park for Earth Day in April, or making jacko-lanterns for a nursing home in October. The ideas are realistic, age appropriate, and thoughtful. The authors have done a good job mixing fun with function. . . . Each plan contains two ideas, a treat recipe, a craft, and information about a national charity related to the theme. The book is illustrated with child-friendly color cartoons featuring youngsters doing good deeds." SLJ
　Includes bibliographical references

644.6 Plumbing

Macaulay, David

★ **Toilet**; how it works. David Macaulay, Sheila Keenan. Roaring Brook Press 2013 28 p. (hardcover) $15.99

Grades: K 1 2 **644.6**

1. Toilets 2. Sewage disposal 3. Water purification

ISBN 1596437790; 9781596437791; 9781596437807

LC 2012947300

This book, by David Macaulay and Sheila Keenan, "takes readers on a tour of the bathroom and the sewer system, from the familiar family toilet to the mysterious municipal water treatment plant. Everyone knows what a toilet is for, right? But what exactly happens after you flush? Where does our waste go, and how is it made safe?" (Publisher's note)

"In this beginning reader/nonfiction chapter book, clear step-by-step directions and unobstructed diagrams and cross sections outline how waste is produced by the body, disposed of through a toilet, sent to either a septic tank or sewer system, and purified. Macaulay's humor is evident, as he reminds readers that the language of science can be both precise and lively." (Horn Book)

646 Sewing, clothing, management of personal and family life

Neitzel, Shirley

The **jacket** I wear in the snow; pictures by Nancy Winslow Parker. Greenwillow Bks. 1989 un il $16.99; pa $6.99

Grades: PreK K 1 2 **646**

1. Stories in rhyme 2. Snow -- Fiction 3. Clothing and dress -- Fiction

ISBN 0-688-08028-6; 0-688-04587-1 pa

LC 88-18767

A young girl names all the clothes that she must wear to play in the snow

"Written in cheerful, cumulative verse that recalls the well-known favorite nursery rhyme 'The House That Jack Built,' the text, with its easy-going rhythm, will be simple for children to recite from memory. . . . The artist's drawings are executed in . . . watercolor, pencil, and pen; they combine with the large typeface and a generous amount of white space to create a tremendously appealing book." Horn Book

646.2 Sewing and related operations

Plumley, Amie Petronis

Sewing school; 21 sewing projects kids will love to make. [by] Amie Petronis Plumley & Andria Lisle; photography by Justin Fox Burks. Storey Pub. 2010 143p il $16.95

Grades: 3 4 5 6 **646.2**

1. Sewing

ISBN 978-1-60342-578-0; 1-60342-578-0

LC 2010022154

"This large-format book offers appealing projects illustrated with color photos of step-by-step directions as well as kids engaged in sewing and showing off work. The opening 12 lessons begin with topics such as threading a needle, knotting the thread, and making a basic running stitch. After covering basic knowledge and skills, the presentation moves on to instructions for fun easy projects." Booklist

Sadler, Judy Ann

Simply sewing; written by Judy Ann Sadler; illustrated by Jane Kurisu. Kids Can Press 2004 48p il (Kids can do it) hardcover o.p. pa $6.95

Grades: 4 5 6 **646.2**

1. Sewing

ISBN 1-55337-659-5; 1-55337-660-9 pa

This "book opens with a section on sewing supplies. . . . Subsequent chapters discuss fabric and the basics of hand and machine stitching. . . . Each of the 12 projects is accompanied by a color photo, step-by-step color illustrations, and a list of supplies needed. . . . This attractive book has a wide assortment of ideas to spark interest." SLJ

646.4 Clothing and accessories construction

D'Cruz, Anna-Marie

Make your own masks. PowerKids Press 2009 24p il (Do it yourself projects!) lib bdg $23.95; pa $9.40

Grades: 2 3 4 **646.4**

1. Handicraft 2. Masks (Facial)

ISBN 978-1-4358-2853-7 lib bdg; 1-4358-2853-4 lib bdg; 978-1-4358-2923-7 pa; 1-4358-2923-9 pa

LC 2008033677

This offers "step-by-step instructions and full-color photos to illustrate the crafts. Projects have a broad cultural representation and are not gender specific. Materials are easily obtained. [The projects include] an Aztec skull, a Bwa sun mask, a Greek Medusa, and a Viking mask." SLJ

Includes glossary and bibliographical references

Make your own purses and bags. PowerKids Press 2009 24p il (Do it yourself projects!) lib bdg $23.95; pa $9.40

Grades: 2 3 4 **646.4**

1. Bags 2. Handicraft

ISBN 978-1-4358-2856-8 lib bdg; 1-4358-2856-9 lib bdg; 978-1-4358-2929-9 pa; 1-4358-2929-8 pa

LC 2008033671

This offers "step-by-step instructions and full-color photos to illustrate the crafts. Projects have a broad cultural representation and are not gender specific. Materials are easily obtained. . . . A Didgeridoo pencil case and an MP3-player case are among the projects [included]." SLJ

Includes glossary and bibliographical references

Petersen, Christine

The **tailor**. Marshall Cavendish Benchmark 2011 il (Colonial people) $29.93

Grades: 3 4 5 6 **646.4**

1. Tailoring 2. United States -- History -- 1600-1775, Colonial period

ISBN 978-1-60870-417-0; 1-60870-417-3

LC 2010016864

This describes the life of a colonial tailor and his importance to the community, as well as everyday life, responsibilities, and social practices during that time.

This "lively [text] and colorful reproductions and photos will engage casual readers and researchers alike. . . . Large illustrations and thoughtful captions explain complicated scientific ideas. . . . [The] volume also includes step-by-step instructions for a related craft project. . . . [This is a] must-have." SLJ

Includes glossary and bibliographical references

Schwarz, Renee

Making masks; written and illustrated by Renée Schwarz. Kids Can Press 2002 40p il (Kids can do it) $12.95; pa $5.95

Grades: 4 5 6   **646.4**
1. Handicraft 2. Masks (Facial)
ISBN 1-55074-929-3; 1-55074-931-5 pa

This offers instructions for creating a variety of masks using such materials as cardboard, felt, paper, and pipe cleaners

This includes "appealing projects and easy-to-follow directions. . . . Schwarz does a good job constructing and illustrating a variety of masks." SLJ

Torres, Laura
Rock your wardrobe. QEB Pub. 2010 32p il (Rock your . . .) lib bdg $28.50
Grades: 4 5 6   **646.4**
1. Fashion 2. Handicraft 3. Clothing and dress
ISBN 978-1-59566-937-7; 1-59566-937-X

LC 2010010671

This book "gives kids easy step-by-step ways to . . . fashion clothes with simple, easily found scraps and a little glue and paint. Colorful photographs show youngsters crafting appealing T-shirts . . . etc., some of which are created from recycled found items. All are projects they can complete by themselves." Horn Book Guide

646.7   Management of personal and family life

Buchholz, Rachel
How to survive anything; shark attack, quicksand, embarrassing parents, pop quizzes, and other perilous situations. illustrations by Chris Philpot. National Geographic 2011 176p il (National geographic kids) pa $12.95
Grades: 5 6 7 8   **646.7**
1. Life skills 2. Survival skills
ISBN 978-1-4263-0774-4; 1-4263-0774-8

LC 2010028045

"Buchholz doles out hilarious and handy advice for suffering though both natural and manmade catastrophes. Part survival guide and part self-help book, it provides honest, tongue-in-cheek answers to questions teens may be reluctant to ask out loud, in addition to imparting disaster preparedness strategies. It's a clever, winning combination. Superb full-color digital illustrations and photographs and a lively, conversational tone will catch and keep readers' attention, and the list-heavy layout is fun to read and easy to understand." SLJ

Chancellor, Deborah
Happy and healthy. QEB Pub. 2011 32p il (For girls!) lib bdg $18.95
Grades: 2 3 4 5   **646.7**
1. Life skills 2. Personal grooming 3. Girls -- Health and hygiene
ISBN 978-1-60992-104-0; 1-60992-104-6

LC 2011006913

This guide for girls gives advice on how to keep healthy, including exercise and keeping fit, creative cooking, skin and hair care, healthy foods, and sports.

"Each lively, readable spread is packed with color photos, computer graphics, and lots of boxes filled with facts, lists, and practical suggestions." Booklist

Heinrichs, Ann
The **barber**. Marshall Cavendish Benchmark 2010 48p il (Colonial people) lib bdg $29.93
Grades: 3 4 5 6   **646.7**
1. Barbers and barbershops 2. United States -- History -- 1600-

1775, Colonial period
ISBN 978-0-7614-4800-6; 0-7614-4800-4

LC 2009018626

"The type font, just slightly larger than usual, makes the text very visually appealing. . . . [The] book is liberally illustrated with artwork dating from the colonial period . . . [and] information boxes offer supplemental material." Libr Media Connect

Includes glossary and bibliographical references

Peskowitz, Miriam
The **daring** book for girls; Andrea Buchanan, Miriam Peskowitz; illustrated by Alexis Seabrook. 1st ed. Collins 2007 viii, 279 p.p ill. (some col.), col. map (hardcover) $26.95
Grades: 4 5 6 7 8 9   **646.7**
1. Girls 2. Amusements 3. Recreation 4. Curiosities and wonders
ISBN 0061472573; 9780061472572

LC 2007031986

This book is "filled with interesting activities to try and important facts [girls] may not know, but are sure to keep them busy for hours. The authors cover everything from making a lemon-powered clock to the history of writing and cursive, from how to paddle a canoe to the Periodic Table of the Elements." (School Library Journal)

Includes bibliographical references (p. 274-276).

647.9   Specific kinds of public households and institutions

Mara, Wil
The **innkeeper**. Marshall Cavendish Benchmark 2010 48p il (Colonial people) lib bdg $29.93
Grades: 3 4 5 6   **647.9**
1. Hotels and motels 2. United States -- History -- 1600-1775, Colonial period
ISBN 978-0-7614-4796-2; 0-7614-4796-2

LC 2009011873

This describes the life of a colonial innkeeper and his importance to the community, as well as everyday life, responsibilities, and social practices during that time.

"The type font, just slightly larger than usual, makes the text very visually appealing. . . . [The] book is liberally illustrated with artwork dating from the colonial period . . . [and] information boxes offer supplemental material." Libr Media Connect

Includes glossary and bibliographical references

648   Housekeeping

Barber, Nicola
Moving to a new house. PowerKids Press 2009 24p il (The big day!) lib bdg $21.25; pa $8.25
Grades: PreK K 1   **648**
1. Moving
ISBN 978-1-4358-2841-4 lib bdg; 978-1-4358-2897-1 pa

LC 2008026222

"Children in kindergarten will enjoy [this book] as [a read-aloud] . . . while those at the end of first grade will be able to read [it] independently. The writing is straightforward and reassuring, and the content provides a realistic view of what youngsters might experience in [a new home]. . . . [The book] mentions the possibility of feeling strange in the new environment, but also discusses how quickly the child will adjust and make new friends." SLJ

Includes bibliographical references

Parker, Victoria

Moving; [by] Vic Parker. Heinemann Library 2011 24p il (Growing up) lib bdg $22; pa $6.49

Grades: PreK K 1 2   **648**

1. Moving

ISBN 978-1-4329-4800-9 lib bdg; 1-4329-4800-8 lib bdg; 978-1-4329-4810-8 pa; 1-4329-4810-5 pa

LC 2010024194

This explains what to expect from a move across the street or across the country.

Includes bibliographical references

649   Child rearing; home care of people with disabilities and illnesses

Buckley, Annie

Be a better babysitter; by Annie Buckley. Child's World 2007 32p il (Girls rock!) lib bdg $24.21

Grades: 5 6 7 8   **649**

1. Babysitting

ISBN 1-59296-740-X

LC 2006001639

This "describes what babysitting entails, examines pros and cons, discusses safety issues, offers tips for doing a good job, and suggests saving as much as half of any money earned.... [This] realistic [title is] well written and [provides] excellent information." SLJ

Includes bibliographical references

Chasse, Jill D.

The **babysitter's** survival guide; fun games, cool crafts, and how to be the best babysitter in town. illustrated by Jessica Secheret. Sterling Pub. Co. 2010 107p il $12.95

Grades: 5 6 7 8   **649**

1. Babysitting

ISBN 978-1-4027-4654-3; 1-4027-4654-7

LC 2009-2538

"This useful, up-to-date handbook offers plenty of practical advice with a wise emphasis on safety, which makes it a good choice for new sitters as well as those with experience. Chassé starts with information on starting a business, including references, advertising, and interviewing. Child development is a main focus; suggested activities and tips on interaction with children at different developmental stages will be appreciated by sitters and parents alike.... Occasional two-color cartoons feature diverse children and sitters." SLJ

Includes bibliographical references

Danzig, Dianne

Babies don't eat pizza; the big kids' book about baby brothers and baby sisters. by Dianne Danzig; illustrated by Debbie Tilley. Dutton Children's Books 2009 un il $16.99

Grades: PreK K   **649**

1. Infants 2. Siblings

ISBN 978-0-525-47441-8; 0-525-47441-2

"Focusing on day-to-day living with an infant, the text adopts an unfussy tone that subtly flatters readers as being sensible and mature (relatively speaking).... Tilley's ink and watercolor cartoons are sunny and empathic ... and include plenty of visual jokes to encourage anxious kids—and their parents—to bond. Headings on most spreads make this volume eminently browsable—and therefore a handy family resource." Publ Wkly

Wells, Rosemary

My shining star; raising a child who is ready to learn. [by] Rosemary Wells. Scholastic Press 2006 un il $8.99

Grades: PreK K   **649**

1. Parenting

ISBN 0-439-84701-X

LC 2005010481

"Young children will enjoy the adorable bunny characters and the small size that is just right for their little hands. But this gem of a picture book is directed to adults—and it belongs in the big hands of every teacher and parent. On each colorful spread, Wells expands on 10 principles to help any child succeed. The direct, simple advice is illustrated with Wells' favorite rabbits demonstrating the recommendations." Booklist

650.1   Personal success in business

Orr, Tamra

A **kid's** guide to earning money; by Tamra Orr. Mitchell Lane Publishers 2008 47p il (Money matters: a kid's guide to money) lib bdg $29.95

Grades: 4 5 6   **650.1**

1. Personal finance 2. Money-making projects for children

ISBN 978-1-58415-643-7 lib bdg; 1-58415-643-0 lib bdg

LC 2008-2253

"This chatty, interactive guide offers practical suggestions for finding jobs, from babysitting and dogwalking to delivering newspapers.... Also included is useful advice on setting price points, how to cut costs, and what the labor laws allow for kids under 18, as well as a frank view of the negatives associated with the working world.... Stress is laid on the importance of getting parental permission before setting out on the trail to riches." Booklist

Includes glossary and bibliographical references

652   Processes of written communication

Bell-Rehwoldt, Sheri

Speaking secret codes. Capstone Press 2010 32p il (Edge books: making and breaking codes) lib bdg $26.65

Grades: 4 5 6 7   **652**

1. Ciphers 2. Cryptography

ISBN 978-1-4296-4569-0 lib bdg; 1-4296-4569-5 lib bdg

LC 2010004163

"Spoken codes in history, including the Underground Railroad and POWs during the Vietnam War, are introduced by using various examples of word substitutions. Educators will appreciate the concise information provided by codes that have shaped world history.... Historical photographs, highlighted vocabulary words and definitions, and do-it-yourself suggestions will keep readers interested." SLJ

Includes glossary and bibliographical references

Blackwood, Gary L.

Mysterious messages; a history of codes and ciphers. [by] Gary Blackwood; designed and illustrated by Jason Henry. Dutton Children's Books 2009 170p il $16.99

Grades: 5 6 7 8   **652**

1. Ciphers 2. Cryptography

ISBN 978-0-525-47960-4; 0-525-47960-0

LC 2008-48970

"This well-written history of cryptography begins with a pottery-glaze formula encrypted in cuneiform on a clay tablet (1500 BCE) and traces the uses of secret messages in statecraft, espionage, warfare, crime, literature, and business up to the present. Along the way, Blackwood . . . discusses the historical development of coding and encryption and tells many good stories of messages ciphered and deciphered. . . . The many sidebars and illustrations, including photos, reproductions of artworks and artifacts, and the pictures demonstrating the codes themselves, contribute to the book's approachable look." Booklist

Gilbert, Adrian

    Codes and ciphers. Firefly 2009 32p il (Spy files) pa $6.95
Grades: 3 4 5 6   **652**
    1. Ciphers 2. Espionage 3. Cryptography
    ISBN 978-1-55407-573-7 pa; 1-55407-573-4 pa
    First published 2008 in the United Kingdom
    Discusses the difference between codes and ciphers, common codes and ciphers that have been used during wars, and how to create simple ciphers
    This "gives an excellent overview of the historical and practical use of codes and ciphers in spy work. . . . The [text's] short paragraphs and great pictures are combined in a collage style that will draw readers quickly through the information." SLJ
    Includes glossary

Gregory, Jillian

    Breaking secret codes. Capstone Press 2010 32p il (Edge books: making and breaking codes) lib bdg $26.65
Grades: 4 5 6 7   **652**
    1. Ciphers 2. Cryptography
    ISBN 978-1-4296-4568-3 lib bdg; 1-4296-4568-7 lib bdg
                  LC 2010004162
    "Educators will appreciate the concise information provided by codes that have shaped world history. Sample cryptographs are scattered throughout the pages, along with other noteworthy facts. Historical photographs, highlighted vocabulary words and definitions, and do-it-yourself suggestions will keep readers interested." SLJ
    Includes glossary and bibliographical references

    Making secret codes. Capstone Press 2010 32p il (Edge books: making and breaking codes) lib bdg $26.65
Grades: 4 5 6 7   **652**
    1. Ciphers 2. Cryptography
    ISBN 978-1-4296-4567-6 lib bdg; 1-4296-4567-9 lib bdg
                  LC 2010004161
    "Educators will appreciate the concise information provided by codes that have shaped world history. Sample cryptographs are scattered throughout the pages, along with other noteworthy facts. Historical photographs, highlighted vocabulary words and definitions, and do-it-yourself suggestions will keep readers interested." SLJ
    Includes glossary and bibliographical references

Mitchell, Susan K.

    Spy codes and ciphers. Enslow Publishers 2011 48p il (The secret world of spies) lib bdg $23.93
Grades: 4 5 6   **652**
    1. Spies 2. Ciphers 3. Espionage 4. Cryptography
    ISBN 978-0-7660-3709-0
                  LC 2010006176
    Discusses different methods of secret communications used by spies, such as Morse code, the Enigma machine, the Najavo language, and digital steganography, and includes career information.
    Includes glossary and bibliographical references

658   General management

Bochner, Arthur Berg

    The **new** totally awesome business book for kids (and their parents) with twenty super businesses you can start right now! [by] Arthur Bochner & Rose Bochner; foreword by Andriane G. Berg. rev and updated 3rd ed.; Newmarket Press 2007 188p il pa $9.95
Grades: 4 5 6 7   **658**
    1. Small business 2. Money-making projects for children
    ISBN 978-1-55704-757-1 pa; 1-55704-757-X pa
                  LC 2007002637
    First published 1995 with title: The totally awesome business book for kids
    A comprehensive look at the basic financial and management aspects of moneymaking businesses for children
    "This book can certainly be thought provoking for young people with an entrepreneurial spirit. . . . The illustrations are lively and engaging, and the text non-threatening." Voice Youth Advocates
    Includes bibliographical references

Mooney, Carla

    Starting a business; have fun and make money. Norwood House Press 2010 48p il (Creative adventure guides) lib bdg $25.27
Grades: 3 4 5 6   **658**
    1. Business enterprises 2. Money-making projects for children
    ISBN 978-1-59953-386-5; 1-59953-386-3
    This book "outlines a small business plan for kids, with examples of successful young entrepreneurs." Horn Book Guide
    Includes glossary and bibliographical references

662   Technology of explosives, fuels, related products

Benduhn, Tea

    Ethanol and other new fuels; by Tea Benduhn. Weekly Reader Pub. 2009 24p il (Energy for today) lib bdg $21; pa $5.95
Grades: 2 3 4   **662**
    1. Energy resources 2. Alcohol as fuel
    ISBN 978-0-8368-9260-4 lib bdg; 0-8368-9260-7 lib bdg; 978-0-8368-9359-5 pa; 0-8368-9359-X pa
                  LC 2008014483
    This describes how ethanol and other new fuels work and how they can be used in the future.
    "New readers will be able to wrap their hands around the small, square size, and their minds around the clear, enlightening text. [This book has] crisp photos and strong back matter." Booklist
    Includes glossary and bibliographical references

Cobb, Vicki

    Fireworks; photographs by Michael Gold. Millbrook Press 2005 48p il (Where's the science here?) lib bdg $23.93
Grades: 3 4 5   **662**
    1. Fireworks
    ISBN 0-7613-2771-1
                  LC 2004-29823
    "From pictures of different types of display formations to those of chemicals being loaded into mortar tubes, readers will find interesting illustrations that support the text in Fireworks. They will learn about the science of pyrotechnics and be exposed to words like chemical reaction, combustion, and lift charges. Sections offer a historical overview of the evolution of the study of fire, the mechanics of building fireworks . . . how explosions are timed, and how pyrotechnicians avoid nasty surprises." SLJ

Rau, Dana Meachen

Fireworks. Marshall Cavendish Benchmark 2010 24p il (Surprising science) $22.79

Grades: 2 3 4   **662**

1. Fireworks

ISBN 978-0-7614-4868-6; 0-7614-4868-3

LC 2009053723

This book "opens with the experience of watching fireworks, traces their history from China to Europe to colonial America, and discusses the rocketry and chemistry that make them possible. Although the discussions are relatively short, they provide good, basic knowledge as well as some intriguing details. . . . Rau provides information about the dangers of fireworks as well. . . . The book's paper quality and page layouts are quite good, maximizing the effectiveness of the clear, colorful photos and well-chosen period artworks that illustrate the text." Booklist

Includes glossary and bibliographical references

664   Food technology

Cobb, Vicki

Junk food; photographs by Michael Gold. Millbrook 2005 48p il (Where's the science here?) lib bdg $23.93

Grades: 3 4 5   **664**

1. Food industry 2. Food -- Composition

ISBN 0-7613-2773-8

The author "focuses on food chemistry, not nutrition, in examinations of six seductive snack foods (popcorn, corn chips, chocolate, candy, potato chips, and soda). Well-digested explanations and low-tech projects reinforce Cobb's reputation for snappy hands-on science writing for children. . . . Gold's photos stand well above those in most nonfiction science series and directly support Cobb's intentions." Booklist

Gardner, Robert

Ace your food science project; great science fair ideas. [by] Robert Gardner, Salvatore Tocci, and Thomas R. Rybolt. Enslow Publishers 2009 128p il (Ace your science project) lib bdg $31.93

Grades: 5 6 7 8   **664**

1. Food 2. Science projects 3. Science -- Experiments

ISBN 978-0-7660-3228-6 lib bdg; 0-7660-3228-0 lib bdg

LC 2008-49780

"Presents several science experiments and project ideas using food." Publisher's note

Includes bibliographical references

McCarthy, Meghan

★ **Pop!** the accidental invention of bubble gum. Simon & Schuster Books for Young Readers 2010 un il $15.99

Grades: 1 2 3   **664**

1. Bubble gum

ISBN 978-1-4169-7970-8; 1-4169-7970-0

LC 2008-49272

Traces the 1928 invention of bubble gum by a hardworking accountant at a candy company, describing how in his spare time he experimented with different recipes and ingredients to eventually create the product known today as Double Bubble.

"Kids who enjoy blowing gum bubbles may never have considered how the treat came to be, but here, in easy language and with amusing illustrations, McCarthy changes that. . . . The acrylic paintings portray humor throughout, in part by peopling the book with googly-eyed characters who are often chewing a wad of gum." Booklist

Petersen, Christine

The **miller**. Marshall Cavendish Benchmark 2011 il (Colonial people) $29.93

Grades: 3 4 5 6   **664**

1. Flour mills 2. United States -- History -- 1600-1775, Colonial period

ISBN 978-1-60870-416-3; 1-60870-416-5

LC 2010033890

This describes the life of a colonial miller and his importance to the community, as well as everyday life, responsibilities, and social practices during that time.

This "lively [text] and colorful reproductions and photos will engage casual readers and researchers alike. . . . Large illustrations and thoughtful captions explain complicated scientific ideas. . . . [The] volume also includes step-by-step instructions for a related craft project. . . . [This is a] must-have." SLJ

Includes glossary and bibliographical references

Ridley, Sarah

A **chocolate** bar; [by] Sarah Ridley. Gareth Stevens Pub. 2006 32p il (How it's made) lib bdg $23.93

Grades: 3 4 5   **664**

1. Chocolate

ISBN 0-8368-6293-7

LC 2005054075

First published 2005 in the United Kingdom

This presents "the origins of a chocolate bar, from a Ghana cocoa farm to a factory. The facts are clear and well organized; each spread shows a logical progression in the process, and sharp color photos and maps will help cement the concepts in readers' minds." Booklist

Rotner, Shelley

Where does food come from? by Shelley Rotner and Gary Goss; photographs by Shelley Rotner. Millbrook Press 2006 32p il lib bdg $22.60

Grades: K 1 2   **664**

1. Food 2. Food industry

ISBN 0-7613-2935-8

LC 2005000874

Explains where various foods originate from, how food is grown, and brought to supermarkets and other stores, in simple text with illustrations.

"Large print, a well-spaced text, varied typeface, simple explanations, and appealing color photos of children on every page make this book a pleasant reading experience. . . . This is a book that teachers, librarians, and parents will find useful, informative, and fun to share." SLJ

665   Technology of industrial oils, fats, waxes, gases

Walker, Niki

Hydrogen; running on water. [by] Niki Walker. Crabtree Pub. 2007 32p il (Energy revolution) lib bdg $25.20; pa $8.95

Grades: 5 6 7 8   **665**

1. Hydrogen as fuel

ISBN 978-0-7787-2915-0 lib bdg; 0-7787-2915-X lib bdg; 978-0-7787-2929-7 pa; 0-7787-2929-X pa

LC 2006014369

This describes various sources of hydrogen power, including natural gas, gasified coal, fuel from water, and biomass gas, and how it is stored and distributed, and offers energy conservation tips.

Includes glossary

665.5   Petroleum

Rockwell, Anne F.

What's so bad about gasoline? fossil fuels and what they do. by Anne Rockwell; illustrated by Paul Meisel. Collins 2009 33p il (Let's-read-and-find-out science) $16.99; pa $5.99

Grades: 1 2 3   **665.5**

1. Gasoline 2. Air pollution 3. Energy resources 4. Energy conservation 5. Greenhouse effect

ISBN 978-0-06-157528-0; 0-06-157528-3; 978-0-06-157527-3 pa; 0-06-157527-5 pa

LC 2007-52947

"Rockwell presents the basic facts about how gasoline is produced, how it was first discovered, and its uses. She then discusses how gasoline and other fossil fuels . . . have contributed to polluting the environment. Suggestions are offered on how to cut back our gas consumption, and alternatives such as solar power, wind power, nuclear energy, and alternative fuels are addressed. . . . Detailed pen-and-ink and watercolor drawings in shades of blue and brown appear throughout, and text balloons help provide humor to various scenarios." SLJ

666   Ceramic and allied technologies

Blaxland, Wendy

Bottles and jars. Marshall Cavendish Benchmark 2011 32p il map (How are they made?) lib bdg $28.50

Grades: 3 4 5 6   **666**

1. Plastics 2. Glassware 3. Glass -- History

ISBN 978-0-7614-4752-8 lib bdg; 0-7614-4752-0 lib bdg

LC 2009040080

This discusses how bottles and jars are made, including their history, raw materials, design, manufacture, packaging and distribution, marketing and advertising, and their relationship to the environment.

Includes glossary

Koscielniak, Bruce

Looking at glass through the ages; by Bruce Koscielniak. Houghton Mifflin Co. 2006 un $16

Grades: 3 4 5 6   **666**

1. Glass -- History

ISBN 0-618-50750-7

LC 2005003916

"A handsome book on the history of glassmaking. Starting with faience, developed in Egypt around 2500 B.C., the author's precisely worded, carefully detailed text and watercolor artwork explain the steps for producing various types of glass and glassware. . . . Much information is compacted into the smoothly written narrative. Captioned illustrations are well matched with the text and extend the information value of the book." SLJ

Petersen, Christine

The **glassblower**. Marshall Cavendish Benchmark 2011 il (Colonial people) $29.93

Grades: 3 4 5 6   **666**

1. Glassblowing 2. United States -- History -- 1600-1775, Colonial period

ISBN 978-1-60870-413-2; 1-60870-413-0

LC 2010033901

This describes the life of a colonial glassblower and his importance to the community, as well as everyday life, responsibilities, and social practices during that time.

This "lively [text] and colorful reproductions and photos will engage casual readers and researchers alike. . . . Large illustrations and thoughtful captions explain complicated scientific ideas. . . . [The] volume also includes step-by-step instructions for a related craft project. . . . [This is a] must-have." SLJ

Includes glossary and bibliographical references

Stewart, Melissa

How does sand become glass? Raintree 2010 32p il (How does it happen?) lib bdg $27.50; pa $7.99

Grades: 3 4 5   **666**

1. Sand 2. Glass 3. Erosion

ISBN 978-1-4109-3449-9 lib bdg; 1-4109-3449-7 lib bdg; 978-1-4109-3457-4 pa; 1-4109-3457-8 pa

LC 2008-52654

"Information is clearly presented using a large font, diagrams, and photographs formatted to resemble Polaroid pictures. . . . A first-rate job answering some important scientific questions." SLJ

Includes glossary and bibliographical references

668   Technology of other organic products

Wagner, Lisa, 1958-

Cool melt & pour soap; [by] Lisa Wagner. ABDO Pub. 2005 32p il (Cool crafts) lib bdg $22.78

Grades: 4 5 6   **668**

1. Soap 2. Handicraft

ISBN 1-59197-741-X

LC 2004-46291

This guide to soap crafting "discusses premade bases, coloring and fragrance, layered soaps, treasure-packed soaps, relief soaps, and packaging ideas." SLJ

668.4   Plastics

Langley, Andrew

Plastic; [by] Andrew Langley. Crabtree Pub. Co. 2009 24p il (Everyday materials) lib bdg $21.27; pa $6.95

Grades: K 1 2 3   **668.4**

1. Plastics

ISBN 978-0-7787-4129-9 lib bdg; 0-7787-4129-X lib bdg; 978-0-7787-4136-7 pa; 0-7787-4136-2 pa

LC 2008-25324

This title "introduces [plastics] in an engaging style. The text and photos work together, progressing from a definition of the material to how it is manufactured and what it is used for. . . . [It] concludes with a recycling section, a simple comprehension quiz, and a topic web that offers extension ideas. The large type, bright photos, and uncluttered layout will allow large and small group use." SLJ

Includes glossary

Other titles in this series are:

Glass

Metal

Paper products

Wood

Wool

670   Manufacturing

Slavin, Bill

Transformed; how everyday things are made. written by Bill Slavin with Jim Slavin; illustrated by Bill Slavin. Kids Can Press 2005 160p il $24.95

Grades: 4 5 6 7   **670**

1. Manufactures

ISBN 1-55337-179-8

This describes the manufacture of such items "as baseballs, plastic dinosaurs, toothpaste, cereal, paper, and bricks. Each two-page spread covers the making of one of the 69 items in numbered paragraphs. The pictures are the best part—clear watercolor and ink images, made all the more engaging by folks in overalls directing the action." Booklist

Includes glossary and bibliographical references

671   Manufacture of products from specific materials

Blaxland, Wendy

Cans. Marshall Cavendish Benchmark 2011 32p il map (How are they made?) lib bdg $28.50

Grades: 3 4 5 6   **671**

1. Cans

ISBN 978-0-7614-4753-5 lib bdg; 0-7614-4753-9 lib bdg

LC 2009039876

This discusses how cans are made, including their history, raw materials, design, manufacture, packaging and distribution, marketing and advertising, production, and their relationship to the environment.

674   Lumber processing, wood products, cork

Blaxland, Wendy

Pencils. Marshall Cavendish Benchmark 2009 32p il (How are they made?) $19.95

Grades: 3 4 5 6   **674**

1. Pencils

ISBN 978-0-7614-3807-6; 0-7614-3807-6

LC 2008026215

This describes how pencils are made, including raw materials, design, manufacture, and relationship to the environment.

675   Leather and fur processing

Petersen, Christine

The **tanner.** Marshall Cavendish Benchmark 2011 il (Colonial people) $29.93

Grades: 3 4 5 6   **675**

1. Leather industry   2. United States -- History -- 1600-1775, Colonial period

ISBN 978-1-60870-418-7; 1-60870-418-1

LC 2010033896

This describes the life of a colonial tanner and his importance to the community, as well as everyday life, responsibilities, and social practices during that time.

This "lively [text] and colorful reproductions and photos will engage casual readers and researchers alike. . . . Large illustrations and thoughtful captions explain complicated scientific ideas. . . . [The] volume also includes step-by-step instructions for a related craft project. . . . [This is a] must-have." SLJ

Includes glossary and bibliographical references

677   Textiles

Butterworth, Chris

Where did my clothes come from? Chris Butterworth, Lucia Gaggiotti. Candlewick Press 2015 25 p. color illustrations (hardcover) $12.99

Grades: K 1 2 3   **677**

1. Clothing industry   2. Clothing and dress

ISBN 0763677507; 9780763677503

LC 2014951787

This children's book, by Chris Butterworth and illustrated by Lucia Gaggiotti, asks, "did you know that the cotton for your jeans was picked from a bush? How did the colorful wool in your sweater get from a sheep's back to a ball of yarn? . . . And what does recycling plastic bottles have to do with anything? Visit farms, forests, and factories all over the world to find out how everything you wear has a story behind it." (Publisher's note)

Includes bibliographical references (page 28) and index.

Sobol, Richard

★ The **story** of silk; from worm spit to woven scarves. Richard Sobol. Candlewick Press 2012 36 p. col. ill., col. maps (reinforced) $17.99

Grades: 2 3 4 5   **677**

1. Thailand 2. Silkworms 3. Silk

ISBN 0763641650; 9780763641658

LC 2012942294

This children's educational book answers the question "What does worm spit have to do with the world's most luxurious fabric? . . . Join author and photographer Richard Sobol as he picks up his camera once more and travels to a small village in Thailand for an in-depth exploration of the story of silk and the labor-intensive process of making it." (Publisher's note)

678   Elastomers and elastomer products

Allman, Toney

Recycled tires; by Toney Allman. Norwood House Press 2008 48p il (A great idea) lib bdg $25.27

Grades: 3 4 5 6   **678**

1. Tires 2. Recycling

ISBN 978-1-59953-197-7 lib bdg; 1-59953-197-6 lib bdg

LC 2008-15736

"'Describes the invention and development of recycled rubber tires." Publisher's note

Includes glossary and bibliographical references

680   Manufacture of products for specific uses

Tunis, Edwin

★ **Colonial** craftsmen and the beginnings of American industry; written and illustrated by Edwin Tunis. Johns Hopkins Univ. Press 1999 159p pa $18.95

Grades: 4 5 6 7   **680**

1. Handicraft 2. Decorative arts 3. United States -- Social life and customs -- 1600-1775, Colonial period

ISBN 0-8018-6228-0

LC 99-20398

The author describes the working methods and products, houses and shops, town and country trades, individual and group enterprises by which the early Americans forged the economy of the New World.

He discusses such trades as papermaking, glassmaking, shipbuilding, printing, and metalworking

"An oversize book that is impressively handsome and that should be tremendously useful; well-organized and superbly illustrated, the text is comprehensive, lucid, and detailed. . . . An extensive index is appended." Chicago. Children's Book Center

681   Precision instruments and other devices

Rau, Dana Meachen

Become an explorer; make and use a compass. Norwood House Press 2010 48p il (Creative adventure guides) lib bdg $25.27

Grades: 3 4 5 6   **681**

1. Compass

ISBN 978-1-59953-383-4; 1-59953-383-9

                  LC 2010010359

"Some historical background and scientific or cultural information places the making and use of . . . compasses in context for young readers. [The] book has four chapters that culminate in step-by-step projects." Horn Book Guide

Includes glossary and bibliographical references

682   Small forge work (Blacksmithing)

Petersen, Christine

The blacksmith. Marshall Cavendish Benchmark 2010 48p il (Colonial people) lib bdg $29.93

Grades: 3 4 5 6   **682**

1. Blacksmithing 2. United States -- History -- 1600-1775, Colonial period

ISBN 978-0-7614-4799-3; 0-7614-4799-7

This describes the life of a colonial blacksmith and his importance to the community, as well as everyday life, responsibilities, and social practices during that time.

"The type font, just slightly larger than usual, makes the text very visually appealing. . . . [The] book is liberally illustrated with artwork dating from the colonial period . . . [and] information boxes offer supplemental material." Libr Media Connect

Includes glossary and bibliographical references

683   Hardware and household appliances

Blaxland, Wendy

Knives and forks. Marshall Cavendish Benchmark 2009 32p il (How are they made?) $19.95

Grades: 3 4 5 6   **683**

1. Cutlery 2. Tableware

ISBN 978-0-7614-3805-2; 0-7614-3805-X

                  LC 2008026214

This describes how knives and forks are made, including their history, raw materials, design, manufacture, and relationship to the environment.

683.4   Small firearms

Mara, Wil

The gunsmith; Wil Mara. Marshall Cavendish 2013 48 p.

Grades: 3 4 5 6   **683.4**

1. Guns -- United States -- History 2. United States -- History -- 1600-1775, Colonial period 3. United States -- Social life and

customs -- To 1775 4. Gunsmiths -- United States -- History -- 17th century 5. Gunsmiths -- United States -- History -- 18th century

ISBN 9781608704149; 9781608709854

                  LC 2011028342

This book on gunsmiths in colonial America, by Wil Mara, is part of the Colonial People series. It "traces the increasing use of guns and their manufacture in the colonies from the early 1600s to the late 1700s. . . . The informative text is illustrated with tinted engravings and paintings from earlier eras as well as . . . color photos of artifacts and replicas and reenactments of historical trades in Colonial Williamsburg." (Booklist)

"These excellent titles provide context about when people working during the colonial period would have first come to America and why, how they fit into the community, and the skills and tools required for their jobs...Illustrations include some period engravings and paintings, but primarily use photographs from modern interpreters, such as the Colonial Williamsburg Foundation...Many libraries own Leonard Everett Fisher's "Colonial Craftsmen" titles (Cavendish Square); the intricate pictorial spreads in those titles portray craft procedures in wonderful detail, but the text is difficult for elementary students. This new series is much easier for children to navigate and understand." (School Library Journal)

Includes bibliographical references and indexes

684   Furnishings and home workshops

Robertson, J. Craig

The kids' building workshop; 15 woodworking projects for kids and parents to build together. [by] J. Craig and Barbara Robertson, with their daughters Camille and Allegra. Storey Kids 2004 136p il $22.96; pa $12.95

Grades: 3 4 5 6   **684**

1. Woodwork

ISBN 1-58017-572-4; 1-58017-488-4 pa

                  LC 2004-1521

"The first section, 'Setting Up Shop: Getting to Know Your Tools,' includes a basic introduction to hammering, sawing, drilling, block planing, and measuring. Next, 'Down to Business: Building Your Own Projects' puts these tools and techniques to work in simple, yet cleverly designed, kid-friendly projects that increase in complexity. . . . Clear instructions, black-and-white photos, and cutting diagrams are included for each one. . . . Practical and enjoyable introduction to the subject." SLJ

685   Leather and fur goods, and related products

Blaxland, Wendy

Sneakers. Marshall Cavendish Benchmark 2009 32p il (How are they made?) $19.95

Grades: 4 5 6   **685**

1. Sneakers

ISBN 978-0-7614-3810-6; 0-7614-3810-6

                  LC 2008026211

This is an "introduction to athletic shoes and the global trade involved in their manufacture and marketing. . . . A typical page offers a paragraph or more of informative text as well as a color photo and, perhaps, a small sidebar." Booklist

Cobb, Vicki

Sneakers; photographs by Michael Gold. Millbrook Press 2006 48p il (Where's the science here?) lib bdg $23.93

Grades: 3 4 5 **685**
1. Sneakers
ISBN 0-7613-2772-X

LC 2004-29816

"From photographs of the inside of a sneaker factory to X-rays of the foot to a picture of how rubber is extracted from a rubber tree, readers will find a new angle to spark their interest in Sneakers. They will learn about how sneakers are designed and made, and even how to test their fit. [An] attractive [choice] that [relates] science to [a topic] that fascinate kids." SLJ

D'Cruz, Anna-Marie
  Make your own slippers and shoes. PowerKids Press 2009 24p il (Do it yourself projects!) lib bdg $23.95; pa $9.40
Grades: 2 3 4 **685**
1. Shoes 2. Handicraft
ISBN 978-1-4358-2852-0 lib bdg; 1-4358-2852-6 lib bdg; 978-1-4358-2921-3 pa; 1-4358-2921-2 pa

LC 2008033669

Learn how to make different types of shoes from around the world using easy-to-find materials.
Includes glossary and bibliographical references

Heinrichs, Ann
  The **shoemaker**. Marshall Cavendish Benchmark 2010 48p il (Colonial people) lib bdg $29.93
Grades: 3 4 5 6 **685**
1. Shoemakers 2. United States -- History -- 1600-1775, Colonial period
ISBN 978-0-7614-4798-6; 0-7614-4798-9

LC 2009007938

This describes the life of a colonial shoemaker and his importance to the community, as well as everyday life, responsibilities, and social practices during that time
"The type font, just slightly larger than usual, makes the text very visually appealing. . . . [The] book is liberally illustrated with artwork dating from the colonial period . . . [and] information boxes offer supplemental material." Libr Media Connect
Includes glossary and bibliographical references

686 Printing and related activities

D'Cruz, Anna-Marie
  Make your own books. PowerKids Press 2009 24p il (Do it yourself projects!) lib bdg $23.95; pa $9.40
Grades: 2 3 4 **686**
1. Books 2. Handicraft 3. Bookbinding
ISBN 978-1-4358-2855-1 lib bdg; 1-4358-2855-0 lib bdg; 978-1-4358-2927-5 pa; 1-4358-2927-1 pa

LC 2008033659

Projects for creating many different kinds of books from easy-to-find materials
Includes glossary and bibliographical references

Petersen, Christine
  The **printer**. Marshall Cavendish Benchmark 2010 48p il (Colonial people) lib bdg $29.93
Grades: 3 4 5 6 **686**
1. Printing -- History 2. United States -- History -- 1600-1775, Colonial period
ISBN 978-0-7614-4802-0; 0-7614-4802-0

LC 2009044588

This describes the life of a colonial printer and his importance to the community, as well as everyday life, responsibilities, and social practices during that time.
"The type font, just slightly larger than usual, makes the text very visually appealing. . . . [The] book is liberally illustrated with artwork dating from the colonial period . . . [and] information boxes offer supplemental material." Libr Media Connect
Includes glossary and bibliographical references

686.2 Printing

Adler, David A.
  A **picture** book of Louis Braille; illustrated by John & Alexandra Wallner. Holiday House 1997 un il $16.95; pa $6.95
Grades: 1 2 3 **686.2**
1. Blind 2. Inventors 3. Teachers of the blind 4. Blind -- Books and reading
ISBN 0-8234-1291-1; 0-8234-1413-2 pa

LC 96-38453

Presents the life of the nineteenth-century Frenchman, accidentally blinded as a child, who originated the raised dot system of reading and writing used by the blind throughout the world
"The text is simple yet informative. . . . Adler sprinkles in interesting facts about early 19th-century France that help readers better grasp Braille's world. . . . Softly colored illustrations in line and watercolor add visual clues for younger children." SLJ

Koscielniak, Bruce
  Johann Gutenberg and the amazing printing press. Houghton Mifflin Co. 2003 un il $16
Grades: 2 3 4 **686.2**
1. Inventors 2. Printers 3. Printing -- History
ISBN 0-618-26351-9

LC 2002-151176

A history of the modern printing industry, including how paper and ink are made, looking particularly at the printing press invented by Gutenberg around 1450 but also at its precursors
"The pleasing line drawings and the subtle hues of Boscielniak's watercolors give the illustrations an informal look that makes their informative content all the more accessible." Booklist

687 Clothing and accessories

Kent, Peter
  Peter Kent's big book of armor; from armadillos to armored cars. Kingfisher 2010 64p il $16.99
Grades: 1 2 3 4 **687**
1. Armor
ISBN 978-0-7534-6423-6; 0-7534-6423-3
Describes the history of armor and protective clothing, from prehistoric protection and the armors of ancient Egypt and Assyria to medieval and modern armor, armored transport, and fortified buildings.
"With its broad definition of armor and the plentiful color illustrations, this informative volume will appeal to a large audience for pleasure reading, as well as providing a solid volume for research purposes." Libr Media Connect
Includes glossary

688.7   Recreational equipment

Bedford, Allan

The **unofficial** LEGO builder's guide; by Allan Bedford. No Starch Press 2005 xviii, 319 p.p $24.95

Grades: 4 5 6 7 8   **688.7**

     1. LEGO toys

     ISBN 1593270542; 1593274416; 9781593274412

                        LC 2005013747

This is a handbook about building LEGO structures. "Starting with the basic structure, anatomy, and flexibility of the Lego system, readers are taught different building techniques to add stability and ideas to their creations. Much of the book is devoted to the kinds of scale used in the Lego world and provides mathematical explanations for one's work. Chapters on sculpting and mosaic-making are also" offered. (School Library Journal)

Blaxland, Wendy

Basketballs. Marshall Cavendish Benchmark 2011 32p il map (How are they made?) lib bdg $28.50

Grades: 3 4 5 6   **688.7**

     1. Basketball 2. Sporting goods

     ISBN 978-0-7614-4751-1 lib bdg; 0-7614-4751-2 lib bdg

                        LC 2009039874

This book "starts out with the raw materials used to make [basketballs]. . . . Next, [a] time [line] handily [sums] up basketball from 1891 to 1992, when composite rubber balls were developed. . . . Design and stages of production are then explained. . . . Nicely designed and well executed." SLJ

     Includes glossary

Fridell, Ron

Sports technology. Lerner Publications 2009 48p il (Cool science) lib bdg $27.93

Grades: 4 5 6   **688.7**

     1. Sports 2. Technology

     ISBN 978-0-8225-7587-0 lib bdg; 0-8225-7587-6 lib bdg

                        LC 2007050905

This describes "how science helps athletes stay safer, perform better, and have more fun." Publisher's notes

     Includes glossary and bibliographical references

Hirschmann, Kris

LEGO toys. Norwood House Press 2008 48p il (A great idea) lib bdg $25.27

Grades: 3 4 5 6   **688.7**

     1. Toys 2. LEGO (Firm)

     ISBN 978-1-59953-194-6 lib bdg; 1-59953-194-1 lib bdg

                        LC 2008010712

Describes the invention and development of LEGO toys

"Full-color photographs and copious fun facts help make this . . . enjoyable reading, but it's really the choice of [topic] that is so enthralling." Booklist

     Includes glossary and bibliographical references

Lyles, Brian

The **LEGO** neighborhood book; build your own town! by Brian Lyles and Jason Lyles. No Starch Press 2014 200 p. $19.95

Grades: 4 5 6 7   **688.7**

     1. LEGO toys 2. City planning 4. Neighborhoods -- Models

     ISBN 1593275714; 9781593275716

                        LC 2014022194

With this LEGO book, by Brian Lyles and Jason Lyles, "you'll create buildings with real-world details like cornices and facades, and try your hand at interior design by filling your buildings with furniture and light fixtures. Then add the finishing touches to your models with plants, traffic lights, scaffolding, and park benches. Snap together a few houses, shops, and apartment buildings to create your own neighborhood!" (Publisher's note)

Oxlade, Chris

Gadgets and games; Chris Oxlade. Capstone Heinemann Library 2013 56 p. col. ill. (Design and engineering for STEM) (library) $33.50; (paperback) $9.49

Grades: 5 6 7   **688.7**

     1. Electronics 2. Industrial design 3. Product life cycle 4. Toys -- Design and construction 5. Household appliances -- Design and construction 6. Electronic apparatus and appliances -- Design and construction

     ISBN 1432970364; 9781432970314; 9781432970369

                        LC 2012013468

This book, part of the Design and Engineering for STEM series, looks at electronic devices and mobile games. It looks at the life cycle of these items, or "the stages from their design, manufacture, and sale to their use, maintenance, and disposal." Topics include "prototyping, the sourcing of components, the production process, the decisions made by designers and engineers, and recycling." (Publisher's note)

     Includes bibliographical references (p. 54) and index.

Ross, Stewart

Sports technology. Smart Apple Media 2011 il (New technology)

Grades: 4 5 6 7   **688.7**

     1. Sports

     ISBN 1-599-20534-3; 978-1-599-20534-2

                        LC 2010044241

Describes the technological advances in the sports industry, including the technology used to create better equipment, sports wear, judging tools, and playing surfaces.

This "offers a fine overview for reports, and its attractive design may also entice middle-grade readers to learn more." Booklist

Rothrock, Megan

The **LEGO** adventure book; cars, castles, dinosaurs & more! Megan Rothrock. No Starch Press 2013 199 p. [Vol. 1] color illustrations $24.95

Grades: 4 5 6 7 8 9   **688.7**

     1. LEGO toys 2. Models and modelmaking

     ISBN 1593274424 (v. 1); 9781593274429 (v. 1)

                        LC 2012033902

This book on LEGO building, by Megan Rothrock, "is filled with bright visuals, step-by-step breakdowns of 25 models, and nearly 200 example models from the world's best builders. Learn to build robots, trains, medieval villages, spaceships, airplanes, and much more." (Publisher's note)

"LEGO enthusiast Megs builds an Idea Lab for creating projects and, with its completion, travels by Transport-O-lux to see what others are inspired to make...This one certainly won't sit on shelves. A fun read for LEGO fans of all ages." SLJ

Wulffson, Don L.

Toys! amazing stories behind some great inventions. [by] Don Wulffson; with illustrations by Laurie Keller. Holt & Co. 2000 137p il $16.95

Grades: 4 5 6 7   **688.7**

     1. Toys 2. Inventions

     ISBN 0-8050-6196-7

                        LC 99-58440

Describes the creation of a variety of toys and games, from seesaws to Silly Putty and toy soldiers to Trivial Pursuit

"Each of the 25 chapters is illustrated with small, humorous drawings and discusses a particular toy or game's origin and development. The book ends with a bibliography and a list of Web sites. Good, readable fare for browsing or light research." Booklist

Includes bibliographical references

690 Construction of buildings

Barton, Byron

Building a house. Greenwillow Books 1981 un il lib bdg $17.89; pa $6.99

Grades: PreK K 1   **690**

1. House construction

ISBN 978-0-688-84291-8 lib bdg; 0-688-84291-7 lib bdg; 978-0-688-09356-3 pa; 0-688-09356-6 pa

"In the simplest possible book on building a house, a step-by-step, one-line description is given of the major factors in construction. Such workers as bricklayers, carpenters, plumbers, electricians, and painters do their own jobs until the small, bright red-and-green house is completed and a family moves in. Flat drawings in brilliant primary colors enable the very young to visualize the methods of housebuilding." Horn Book

★ **Machines** at work. Crowell 1987 un il $17.99; bd bk $7.99

Grades: PreK K 1   **690**

1. Building

ISBN 0-694-00190-2; 0-694-01107-X bd bk

LC 86-24221

"The short, punchy narrative reinforces the dynamics of the illustrations. . . . This should be a popular read-aloud for preschoolers and satisfying read-alone for beginners." Publ Wkly

Byers, Ann

Jobs as green builders and planners. Rosen Pub. 2010 80p il (Green careers) lib bdg $30.60

Grades: 5 6 7 8   **690**

1. Building 2. Vocational guidance 3. Environmental science

ISBN 978-1-4358-3566-5 lib bdg; 1-4358-3566-2 lib bdg

LC 2009015517

This "well-conceived [introduction focuses] on various jobs in [building and construction planning], the education and experience required, and expected earnings. The [book is] well organized, making it easy to gain an overview of the major aspects of the work. . . . [This book] will make [a] good [addition] to career collections. Photographs from the field and website and contact information for professional organizations add value." SLJ

Includes glossary and bibliographical references

Dillon, Patrick

The **Story** of buildings; from the pyramids to the Sydney Opera House and beyond. Patrick Dillon, illustrated by Stephen Biesty. Candlewick Press 2014 96 p. $19.99

Grades: 5 6 7 8   **690**

1. Building 2. Architecture -- History

ISBN 0763669903; 9780763669904

LC 2013943096

This book, by Patrick Dillon and illustrated by Stephen Biesty, is a "narrative history of buildings. . . . Why and how did people start making buildings? How did they learn to make them stronger, bigger, and more comfortable? Why did they start to decorate them in different ways? . . . Dillon's stories of remarkable buildings—and the remarkable

people who made them—celebrates the ingenuity of human creation." (Publisher's note)

"This large, handsome volume combines broad discussions of architectural history with exceptional drawings of significant buildings from ancient to modern times...Through his signature cross sections, details of interiors and construction can be seen as well. While the text, illustrations, and captions all provide information, it's the drawings of buildings that make this a valuable resource. " Booklist

Gibbons, Gail

How a house is built. Holiday House 1990 un il $16.95; pa $6.95

Grades: K 1 2 3   **690**

1. Houses 2. Building 3. House construction

ISBN 0-8234-0841-8; 0-8234-1232-6 pa

LC 90-55107

This book describes how the surveyor, heavy machinery operators, carpenter crew, plumbers, and other workers build a house

"With her customary bright illustrations, Gibbons gives a fine introduction to the construction of a wood-frame house. . . . Construction machines and materials as well as parts of the house are identified, and each stage of construction logically follows the others. Workers are drawn in both sexes and several skin tones." Booklist

Hudson, Cheryl Willis

★ **Construction** zone; photographs by Richard Sobol; text by Cheryl Willis Hudson. Candlewick Press 2006 un il $15.99

Grades: 2 3 4   **690**

1. Building

ISBN 0-7636-2684-8

"Large photographs of the construction of the MIT Stata Center in Cambridge, MA, are the core of this book. The simple text explains the process from the design by Frank O. Gehry to the completed building. Construction-zone activity, equipment, and jargon are pictured and explained. . . . Words in bold . . . are defined and explained at the bottom of the page on which they appear. . . . Children will be fascinated by both the picture story and the informative text." SLJ

Newhouse, Maxwell

The **house** that Max built. Tundra Books 2008 un il $18.95

Grades: K 1 2 3   **690**

1. House construction

ISBN 978-0-88776-774-6; 0-88776-774-5

"When Max decides to build a house beside the lake, 'he needs a lot of help.' This simple introduction takes readers through the major steps of the construction, from the architect's drawings to the completed house. In one or two sentences per page, the present-tense narrative neatly applies the personal viewpoint of the homeowner to each construction phase. . . . Warmly rendered folk-art-style oil paintings show the house coming together over time. . . . [This has] strong visual appeal and just enough detail." SLJ

Ritchie, Scot

Look at that building! a first book of structures. written and illustrated by Scot Ritchie. Kids Can Press 2011 32 p. col. ill. (hardcover) $16.95

Grades: PreK K 1 2 3 4   **690**

1. Houses 2. Buildings 3. Picture books for children 4. Building

ISBN 1554536960; 9781554536962

This book introduces young readers to basic construction concepts through the eyes of five friends keen on building a doghouse for their pet pooch, Max. To find out more about the task, Yulee, Martin, Nick, Sally and Pedro head to the library, where they learn about foundations, beams, frames and other building fundamentals.

"Winsome cartoon art shows a mutlicultural group of friends taking steps to tackle their project. . . . Budding architects and anyone researching the process will appreciate this colorful overview." Booklist

Schwarz, Renee

Birdfeeders. Kids Can Press 2005 40p il (Kids can do it) $12.95; pa $6.95

Grades: 4 5 6   **690**

1. Bird feeders

ISBN 1-55337-699-4; 1-55337-700-1 pa

This offers instructions for constructing nine types of bird feeders composed of recycled or common household materials such as flowerpots, juice cans, Frisbees and ketchup bottles.

Birdhouses. Kids Can Press 2005 40p il (Kids can do it) $12.95; pa $6.95

Grades: 4 5 6   **690**

1. Woodwork 2. Birdhouses

ISBN 1-55337-549-1; 1-55337-550-5 pa

This "shows and tells how to build nine birdhouses using inexpensive materials such as wood, plastic drainage pipes, flower pots, and even an old boot. . . . Small, clear pictures illustrate the step-by-step directions." Booklist

Somervill, Barbara A.

Green general contractor. Cherry Lake Pub. 2011 32p il (Cool careers) lib bdg $27.07

Grades: 4 5 6 7   **690**

1. Building 2. Vocational guidance 3. Sustainable architecture

ISBN 978-1-60279-987-5; 1-60279-987-3

LC 2010029535

This book begins "with a personal story of a teen and then [segues] into the occupation [of general contractor]. . . . [It covers] the necessary training and skills for the job (and options for obtaining them), a typical day, salary expectations, and well-known professionals in the field. The [text is] accessible and clearly written. . . . The [volume has] a generous number of clear color photographs that depict people at work." SLJ

Includes glossary and bibliographical references

Stefoff, Rebecca, 1951-

Building skyscrapers; Rebecca Stefoff. Cavendish Square 2016 32 p. (library bound) $28.50

Grades: 3 4 5   **690**

1. Skyscrapers 2. Civil engineering

ISBN 1502606070; 9781502606068; 9781502606075

LC 2015000199

This juvenile book, by Rebecca Stefoff, part of the publisher's "Great Engineering" series, focuses on the construction of skyscrapers. "These examinations of large-scale infrastructure elements focus particularly on the role of civil engineers in planning and construction. Each volume opens with a lucid explanation of the chosen structure's function . . . , proceeding to present a historical overview, describing construction methods, and highlighting significant examples." (School Library Journal)

"Budding engineers will find these great introductions indeed." Booklist

Includes bibliographical references (page 30) and index

696 Utilities

Gregory, Josh

Plumber. Cherry Lake Pub. 2011 32p il (Cool careers) lib bdg $27.07

Grades: 4 5 6 7   **696**

1. Plumbing 2. Vocational guidance

ISBN 978-1-60279-984-4; 1-60279-984-9

LC 2010029538

This book begins "with a personal story of a teen and then [segues] into the occupation [of plumber]. . . . [It covers] the necessary training and skills for the job (and options for obtaining them), a typical day, salary expectations, and wellknown professionals in the field. The [text is] accessible and clearly written. . . . The [volume has] a generous number of clear color photographs that depict people at work." SLJ

Includes glossary and bibliographical references

Raum, Elizabeth

★ The **story** behind toilets. Heinemann Library 2009 32p il (True stories) $19.75

Grades: 2 3 4   **696**

1. Toilets

ISBN 978-1-4329-2350-1; 1-4329-2350-1

LC 2008037392

"Virtually everything related to toilets is covered, from the bodily functions that require such facilities all the way to the technology of the toilets of tomorrow. . . . 'A Short History of Toilets' is the most surprising chapter, with its running time line of toilet innovations. . . . Raum has the arcana down. . . . But there's real educational value here, too, notably in the discussion of sewage plants, the debate over pay toilets, the international scope of health problems related to poor sanitation, and the twisty time line that ends the book." Booklist

Includes bibliographical references

700 ARTS

700 The arts

Ajmera, Maya

★ To be an artist; [by] Maya Ajmera & John D. Ivanko; foreword by Jacques d'Amboise. Charlesbridge 2004 un il $15.95

Grades: K 1 2 3   **700**

1. Arts

ISBN 1-57091-503-2

LC 2003-8154

This includes "photographs of youngsters from many different countries engaged in a variety of art forms, including dancing, singing, writing, and painting. The bold text introduces each discipline and is supported with more extensive descriptions of the individual endeavors and the nature of artistic expression in general. . . . This vibrant book pulsates with the energy and sense of accomplishment that accompanies participation in the arts." SLJ

Apodaca, Blanca

Behind the canvas; an artist's life. by Blanka Apodaca and Michael Serwich. Teacher Created Materials 2012 48 p. (paperback) $8.96; (prebind) $18.99

Grades: 4 5 6   **700**

1. Artists 2. Art -- Technique

ISBN 1433348268; 145177074X; 9781433348266; 9781451770742

This book is part of the TIME for Kids Nonfiction Readers series and looks at the lives of artists. "Most of the books tie the subject to related professions, sharing ways in which students could help solve the dilemmas. . . . Colorful photographs with extensive captioning, 'Dig Deeper' sections that provide added detail and ask probing questions, diagrams, and informative maps all help guide students." (Library Media Connection)

McArthur, Meher

An **ABC** of what art can be; pictures by Esther Pearl Watson. J. Paul Getty Museum 2010 un il $17.95

Grades: 2 3 4 5   **700**

    1. Art 2. Alphabet

    ISBN 978-0-89236-999-7; 0-89236-999-X

                    LC 2009-15387

"This lighthearted artist's alphabet finds inspiration from many forms. . . . Each page is unique in the color and style choices enriching the text and is unified by the collage style used throughout. . . . Watson's fun-loving illustrations are a good match for McArthur's rhyming text. An enjoyable alphabet for young artists." SLJ

Speaking of art; colorful quotes by famous painters. edited by Bob Raczka. Millbrook Press 2010 31 p. col. ill.

Grades: 3 4 5   **700**

    1. Art 2. Artists -- Quotations 3. Art -- Quotations, maxims, etc

    ISBN 9780761350545

                    LC 2009023484

This book presents information about eighteen famous artists and answers questions such as "When did Vincent Van Gogh feel most alive? Why did Juan Gris always pet a dog with his left hand? . . . Art lover [and author] Bob Raczka pairs . . . quotes by famous painters with . . . examples of their best work. The result is a . . . gallery of observations about the joys and the mysteries of art. From Edgar Degas' The Rehearsal (1878-79) to Georgia O'Keeffe's Evening Star, No. III (1917) to Romare Bearden's Family (1986), you'll discover the works - and the wisdom - of eighteen artistic masters." (Publisher's note)

    Includes bibliographical references

700.9   History, geographic treatment, biography of the arts

Flatt, Lizann

    Arts and culture in the early Islamic world; Lizann Flatt. Crabtree Pub. Company 2012 48 p. col. ill., col. map (Life in the early Islamic world) (reinforced library binding : alk. paper) $30.60

Grades: 5 6 7   **700.9**

    1. Islamic art 2. Islamic civilization

    ISBN 0778721671; 9780778721673; 9780778721741; 9781427195609; 9781427198372

                    LC 2012000074

This book by Lizann Flatt is part of the "Life in the Early Islamic World" series. It "introduces the important roles that many of the arts, but especially calligraphy, architecture, and the decorative arts, have had in Islamic culture, in which art is meant to be 'useful as well as beautiful.'" (Booklist) "The main texts are supplemented with blue boxes of information, subsections, and many high-quality reproductions, maps, and paintings." (School Library Journal)

701   Philosophy and theory of fine and decorative arts

Benduhn, Tea

    What is color? Crabtree Pub. Co. 2009 24p il (Get art smart) lib bdg $15.95; pa $6.95

Grades: K 1 2 3   **701**

    1. Color in art

    ISBN 978-0-7787-5123-6 lib bdg; 0-7787-5123-6 lib bdg; 978-0-7787-5137-3 pa; 0-7787-5137-6 pa

                    LC 2009-22914

Isolates the artistic element of color, discusses what thoughts and feelings can be conveyed by different colors, and examines how they contribute to a work of art through various examples

This book has a "first-person plural tone that uses accessible, well-thought-out phrases. Concrete visual examples are in the form of frequent and excellent reproductions of fine art in a variety of mediums. . . . [A] respectable and respectful resource[s]." SLJ

    Includes glossary and bibliographical references

    What is shape? Crabtree Pub. 2009 24p il (Get art smart) lib bdg $15.95; pa $6.95

Grades: K 1 2 3   **701**

    1. Shape

    ISBN 978-0-7787-5139-7 lib bdg; 0-7787-5139-2 lib bdg; 978-0-7787-5125-0 pa; 0-7787-5125-2 pa

This describes how shapes of all kinds, including geometric shapes and the organic shapes found in nature, can be used in art.

This book has a "first-person plural tone that uses accessible, well-thought-out phrases. Concrete visual examples are in the form of frequent and excellent reproductions of fine art in a variety of mediums. . . . [A] respectable and respectful resource[s]." SLJ

    Includes glossary and bibliographical references

Ehlert, Lois

    ★ **Color** zoo. Lippincott 1989 un il $17.99; lib bdg $17.89; bd bk $7.99

Grades: PreK K 1   **701**

    1. Color 2. Shape

    ISBN 0-397-32259-3; 0-397-32260-7 lib bdg; 0-694-01067-7 bd bk

                    LC 87-17065

A Caldecott Medal honor book, 1990

"Not only an effective method for teaching basic concepts, the book is also a means for sharpening visual perception, which encourages children to see these shapes in other contexts." Horn Book

Fitzgerald, Stephanie

    What is texture? Crabtree Pub. Co. 2009 24p il (Get art smart) lib bdg $15.95; pa $6.95 **701**

    1. Handicraft 2. Art -- Technique

    ISBN 978-0-7787-5127-4 lib bdg; 0-7787-5127-9 lib bdg; 978-0-7787-5141-0 pa; 0-7787-5141-4 pa

                    LC 2009-22917

Introduces different kinds of texture and how they are used in art, and includes information on making a rubbing

This book has a "first-person plural tone that uses accessible, well-thought-out phrases. Concrete visual examples are in the form of frequent and excellent reproductions of fine art in a variety of mediums. . . . [A] respectable and respectful resource[s]." SLJ

    Includes glossary and bibliographical references

Gonyea, Mark

    A **book** about color. Henry Holt & Co. 2010 un il $19.99

Grades: 1 2 3 4 5   **701**

    1. Color in art

    ISBN 978-0-8050-9055-0; 0-8050-9055-X

"Topics presented include primary and secondary colors, warm and cool colors, saturation, and the addition of black and white. In the digital illustrations, simple forms in solid colors stand out sharply against white or other solid backgrounds. . . . This attractive volume offers plenty to observe, ponder, and discuss." Booklist

Hensley, Laura

Art for all; what is public art? Raintree 2010 32p il (Culture in action) $29

Grades: 5 6 7 8   **701**

1. Art

ISBN 978-1-4109-3923-4; 1-4109-3923-5

LC 2009051126

This "briefly surveys public art, from murals and graffiti to obelisks and religious statues. . . . A world map shows the locations of 16 public artworks mentioned in the text. . . . The quality of the illustrations is fine. . . . Given the book's broad scope and few pages, it accomplishes a good deal. Three activities, a time line, a glossary, and a brief bibliography round out this attractive presentation." Booklist

Includes glossary and bibliographical references

Kutschbach, Doris

The **art** treasure hunt; I spy with my little eye. Doris Kutschbach. Prestel 2012 48 p. $14.95

Grades: 3 4 5   **701**

1. Art 2. Painters 3. Picture books for children

ISBN 3791370979; 9783791370972

LC 2011942236

In this book, readers "are . . . challenged to find details 'hidden' in some of the world's greatest paintings. On each double-page spread, a large reproduction of a masterpiece such as Kandinsky's 'Heavenly Blue,' Seurat's 'A Sunday Afternoon on the Island of La Grande Jatte,' Rousseau's 'The Dream' or Breugel's 'Children's Games' is paired with a list of items to search for: a dog, an umbrella, or a ball, for instance." (Publisher's note)

Meredith, Susan

What is form? by Susan Markowitz Meredith. Crabtree Pub. Co. 2009 24p il (Get art smart) lib bdg $15.95; pa $6.95

Grades: K 1 2 3   **701**

1. Composition (Art)

ISBN 978-0-7787-5124-3 lib bdg; 0-7787-5124-4 lib bdg; 978-0-7787-5138-0 pa; 0-7787-5138-4 pa

Introduces the concept of form, demonstrates how it is used in art, and includes information on reliefs, sculpture, and identifying forms in everyday life

This book has a "first-person plural tone that uses accessible, well-thought-out phrases. Concrete visual examples are in the form of frequent and excellent reproductions of fine art in a variety of mediums. . . . [A] respectable and respectful resource[s]." SLJ

Includes glossary and bibliographical references

What is line? by Susan Markowitz Meredith. Crabtree Pub. Co. 2009 24p il (Get art smart) lib bdg $15.95; pa $6.95

Grades: K 1 2 3   **701**

1. Line (Art)

ISBN 978-0-7787-5122-9 lib bdg; 0-7787-5122-8 lib bdg; 978-0-7787-5136-6 pa; 0-7787-5136-8 pa

LC 2009-22912

Identifies lines in art and demonstrates how differently shaped lines are used to create texture, movement, patterns, and emotion.

This book has a "first-person plural tone that uses accessible, well-thought-out phrases. Concrete visual examples are in the form of frequent and excellent reproductions of fine art in a variety of mediums. . . . [A] respectable and respectful resource[s]." SLJ

Includes glossary and bibliographical references

What is space? by Susan Markowitz Meredith. Crabtree Pub. Co. 2009 24p il (Get art smart) lib bdg $15.95; pa $6.95

Grades: K 1 2 3   **701**

1. Space and time in art

ISBN 978-0-7787-5126-7 lib bdg; 0-7787-5126-0 lib bdg; 978-0-7787-5140-3 pa; 0-7787-5140-6 pa

Introduces the concept of space; how differences in space are used in art; and includes information on distance, form, and overlap.

This book has a "first-person plural tone that uses accessible, well-thought-out phrases. Concrete visual examples are in the form of frequent and excellent reproductions of fine art in a variety of mediums. . . . [A] respectable and respectful resource[s]." SLJ

Includes glossary and bibliographical references

Museum of Modern Art (New York, N.Y.)

Make art mistakes; an inspired sketchbook for everyone. Chronicle Books 2010 un il $16.99

Grades: 3 4 5 6   **701**

1. Art

ISBN 978-0-8118-7076-4; 0-8118-7076-6

"This lively sketchbook contains decorative graphic spreads and prompts that ask readers to integrate their own words and drawings. Quotations from artists such as O'Keeffe and Picasso invite deeper reflection on making art while loosely introducing themes on line, color, pattern, and texture. Most of the exercises emphasize free expression . . . while others introduce concepts like perspective. Young artists are likely to enjoy the balance between instruction and independent exploration." Publ Wkly

Renshaw, Amanda

★ The **art** book for children; [texts by Amanda Renshaw and Gilda Williams Ruggi] Phaidon Press 2005 79p il $19.95

Grades: 2 3 4 5   **701**

1. Art appreciation

ISBN 978-0-7148-4530-2

Invites the reader to take a closer look at art work while pointing out tiny details hidden in famous works of art, providing information about a work or an artist, or explaining the techniques used to create the pieces

This is "an excellent, accessible introduction to art that speaks directly to children without condescension." Booklist

★ The **art** book for children: book two; text by Amanda Renshaw. Phaidon Press 2007 79p il $19.95

Grades: 2 3 4 5   **701**

1. Art appreciation

ISBN 978-0-7148-4706-1

"Each double-page spread features a top-quality reproduction of an artwork, accompanied by simple text that will engage both young children and mature, independent readers. . . . The brief words . . . encourage viewers to imagine themselves in the scenes, to find objects in the compositions, or to reflect on the moods and activities depicted and in their own lives. This interactive approach creates a wonderful introduction to the history of Western art." Booklist

Tomecek, Steve

Art & architecture; by Stephen M. Tomecek. Chelsea House Publishers 2010 174p il (Experimenting with everyday science) $35

Grades: 4 5 6 7   **701**

1. Architecture 2. Art and science 3. Science -- Experiments 4. Art -- Study and teaching

ISBN 978-1-60413-168-0; 1-60413-168-3

LC 2009030195

"This fun and informative book features 25 simple experiments using common household items and foods such as blueberries, colored cellophane, food coloring, Magic Markers, miniature marshmallows, and wooden toothpicks to demonstrate principles and inspire creative thought about the intersection of science with the visual and mechanical arts. The six chapters include activities that illuminate certain scientific aspects of each respective subject. . . . Accessible for independent reading by children with a scientific bent or curiosity about how the world works, these experiments would also be useful for scout projects or science clubs." SLJ

Includes bibliographical references

702.8 Auxiliary techniques and procedures; apparatus, equipment, materials

Hanson, Anders

Cool collage; the art of creativity for kids! [by] Anders Hanson. ABDO Pub. Co. 2009 32p il (Cool art) lib bdg $24.21

Grades: 2 3 4   702.8

1. Collage

ISBN 978-1-60453-146-6 lib bdg; 1-60453-146-0 lib bdg

LC 2008-8641

This book about collage making is "well organized, with clearly written sections . . . and several clever projects and exercises. . . . [It] should have substantial child appeal." SLJ

Includes glossary

Luxbacher, Irene

1 **2 3 I** can collage! [by] Irene Luxbacher. Kids Can Press 2009 23p il (Starting art) $14.95; pa $6.95

Grades: 2 3 4   702.8

1. Collage

ISBN 978-1-55453-313-8; 1-55453-313-9; 978-1-55453-314-5 pa; 1-55453-314-7 pa

Collage activities with step-by-step instructions will help kids create a whale, a crab, a sea turtle and more.

Schwake, Susan

3-D art lab for kids; 36 hands-on adventures in sculpture and mixed media. Susan Schwake; Phototgraphy by Rainer Schwake. Quarry Books 2013 144 p. color illustrations (pbk.) $24.99

Grades: 4 5 6   702.8

1. Sculpture 2. Handicraft for children 3. Sculpture -- Technique 4. Mixed media (Art) -- Technique

ISBN 1592538150; 9781592538157

LC 2013012624

In this book, author Susan Schwake "combines 32 3-D art projects with interviews with four artists, each of whom is photographed. The first two chapters give general instructions for setting up for each project, providing an exhaustive list of materials needed. The subsequent five chapters each focus on a single medium: paper, clay, textiles, sculpture, and jewelry." (Booklist)

Vry, Silke

13 art illusions children should know; Silke Vry. Prestel Pub. Random House 2012 48 p. (hardcover) $14.95

Grades: 4 5 6   702.8

1. Optical illusions 2. Art

ISBN 379137110X; 9783791371108

LC 2012939037

This book by Silke Vry is part of the "Children Should Know" series. "This collection features artworks that incorporate a variety of methods for tricking our eyes: including trompe l'oeil, clever uses of color and perspective, Surrealism, and Photo-Realism. Arranged thematically,

each work is presented in a two-page spread. . . . [T]exts explain the methods the artists employed to shape their illusions." (Publisher's note)

704 Special topics in fine and decorative arts

Barber, Nicola

★ **Islamic** empires; [by] Nicola Barber. Raintree 2005 48p il map (History in art) $31.43

Grades: 4 5 6 7   704

1. Islam 2. Islamic art

ISBN 1-4109-0522-5

LC 2004-7527

This is an introduction to the art, culture, and history of Islamic empires.

This book has "a depth of content that is unusual in art-history books for this age group. . . . [It] is amply illustrated with full-color photographs and reproductions. . . . Well-written, informative." SLJ

Includes bibliographical references

Brooks, Susie

Get into Art! Enjoy Great Art--then Create Your Own! by Susie Brooks. Kingfisher 2013 31 p. col. ill. (hardcover) $14.99

Grades: 3 4 5 6 7   704

1. Art -- Guidebooks 2. Art 3. Picture books for children

ISBN 0753470586; 9780753470589

For this book, Susie Brooks' "goal is to convince her readers that art is not just something one observes, but rather something that one does. Using a topic beloved by many kids - animals - she presents 13 works by famous artists, each of which incorporates animals into its subject and theme. Each reproduced masterpiece occupies its own two-page spread, and Brooks explores one major art technique for each." (Booklist)

Coyne, Jennifer Tarr

Come look with me: discovering women artists for children; [by] Jennifer Tarr Coyne. Lickle 2005 32p il $15.95

Grades: 3 4 5   704

1. Women artists 2. Art appreciation

ISBN 1-890674-08-7

Introduces twelve women artists, including Faith Ringgold, Mary Cassatt, Frida Kahlo, and Grandma Moses, each with a short biography, a full-page color plate, a description of the image, and a set of discussion questions.

"This offering encourages children to learn biographical facts about artists and to look closely at the images and think about artistic decisions. . . . Each spread features a beautifully reproduced image." Booklist

Raczka, Bob

Before they were famous; how seven artists got their start. Millbrook Press 2010 32p il (Art adventures) $25.26

Grades: 4 5 6 7   704

1. Artists 2. Creative ability

ISBN 978-0-7613-6077-3; 0-7613-6077-8

LC 2009049596

"Short biographies written in conversational, jargon-free text introduce seven great artists, as young beginners and then as creators of famous works. From Dürer and Michelangelo to Picasso and Dali, the featured artists are presented chronologically on uncluttered, open spreads that include beautiful full-page reproductions. . . . Great preparation for a gallery visit, this will appeal to older readers, too, for its exciting, never-condescending talk about the pictures and the artists who created them." Booklist

Rolling, James Haywood

Come look with me: discovering African American art for children;
[by] James Haywood Rolling, Jr. Lickle 2005 32p il $15.95
Grades: 3 4 5   **704**

1. Art appreciation 2. African American art
ISBN 1-890674-07-9

This volume presents 12 works of African American art "reproduced
in full color and accompanied by descriptive information; the facing
page contains several questions designed to engage young viewers and
an adult in conversation as well as a few paragraphs of background. . . .
Artists . . . include . . . Palmer Hayden and Clementine Hunter . . . Henry
Ossawa Tanner, Romare Bearden, and Jacob Lawrence." SLJ

704.9   Iconography

Luxbacher, Irene

★ The jumbo book of outdoor art; written and illustrated by Irene
Luxbacher. Kids Can Press 2006 144p il pa $16.95
Grades: 3 4 5 6   **704.9**

1. Art 2. Nature craft
ISBN 978-1-55337-680-4 pa; 1-55337-680-3 pa

"Four major sections (Digging Deep, Going Green, It's All Elemental, and Fertile Ground) each contain more than a dozen activities and/
or experiments. Good-quality illustrations and photos bring these ideas
to life. . . . Children will polish their creative skills with a wide variety
of artistic experiences, such as a secret garden, silly sprouts, terrific topiaries, beautiful batik, super spider's web, weathervanes, great flowing
fountain, sparkling ice chandeliers, and more." SLJ

Raczka, Bob

Action figures; paintings of fun, daring, and adventure. Millbrook
Press 2010 31p il lib bdg $25.26
Grades: 1 2 3 4   **704.9**

1. Art appreciation
ISBN 978-0-7613-4140-6 lib bdg; 0-7613-4140-4 lib bdg
LC 2008053976

"Eighteen paintings, and not a bowl of fruit in sight. Whether it is
the knockout punch of George Bellows's Dempsey and Firpo or the fiery
blasts of Diego Rivera's The Conquest of Mexico, this art is not about
sitting still. Raczka threads selections together using few words. . . .
The book includes works in various styles, dating from 1450 to 1962.
Rounded out with some fun facts about the selections, this enjoyable
collection presents an array of action-packed art fit for independent perusal or group discussion." SLJ

The art of freedom; how artists see America. by Bob Raczka.
Millbrook Press 2008 32p il lib bdg $25.26
Grades: 1 2 3   **704.9**

1. American art 2. Art appreciation 3. United States in art
ISBN 978-0-8225-7508-5
LC 2007023831

"The 18 beautifully reproduced works of art in this collection cut a
swath across the country—including farms and cities, baseball and jazz,
hard work and sacrifice, native peoples and immigrants. . . . Concise
notes about each picture at the back of the book will help children and
those reading to them find out more about the artists and their work."
Booklist

708   Galleries, museums, private collections of fine and decorative arts

An eye for art; focusing on great artists and their work. National Gallery of Art with Chicago Review Press, Incorporated 2013 180 p.
(pbk.) $19.95
Grades: 4 5 6 7 8 9 10 11 12   **708**

1. Art 2. Art appreciation 3. National Gallery of Art (U.S.)
ISBN 1613748973; 9781613748978
LC 2013009403

This book is an "introduction to the works collected in the National
Gallery of Art. More than 50 great artists are highlighted, from the 13th
to the 21st centuries. The artists and their works and techniques are .
. . arranged stylistically in categories that include 'Studying Nature,'
'Observing Everyday Life,' 'Exploring Places,' and 'Telling Stories.'"
(School Library Journal)

709   History, geographic treatment, biography

Ayres, Charlie

Lives of the great artists. Thames & Hudson 2008 96p il $19.95
Grades: 5 6 7 8   **709**

1. Artists 2. Art -- History
ISBN 978-0-500-23853-0; 0-500-23853-7
LC 2008-91000

Presents illustrated and age-appropriate imaginary tours of the studios of famous artists from Leonardo da Vinci and Michelangelo to
Monet and van Gogh, in an anecdotal reference that is complemented by
reproductions of famous works and introductory portraits

This is "brightly written and augmented with activities, Web resources, and fun facts. . . . The works of art chosen to represent each
artist are heavy on the drama and detail, resulting in high kid appeal and
interesting captions. . . . The layout is clean and clear." SLJ

Children's book of art; an introduction to the world's most amazing
paintings and sculptures. DK Pub. 2009 139p il $24.99
Grades: 4 5 6 7   **709**

1. Art appreciation 2. Art -- History
ISBN 978-0-7566-5511-2; 0-7566-5511-0

"From prehistoric to modern times, this expertly designed survey
delivers a wealth of information. Much more than a mere time line, the
focus shifts from artist to movement to medium with fluidity. Gallery
pages examine how particular subjects are depicted in art from a variety
of cultures and time periods. Hundreds of color reproductions are sure
to hold readers' interest. . . . The vast amount of information presented is
neither overwhelming nor superficial." SLJ

Finger, Brad

13 American artists children should know. Prestel 2010 46p il
$14.95
Grades: 4 5 6   **709**

1. American art 2. Art appreciation 3. Artists -- United States
ISBN 978-3-7913-7036-1; 3-7913-7036-7

"Beginning with Winslow Homer and ending with Andy Warhol
and Jasper Johns, this picture-book overview introduces 13 well-known
American artists. On each double-page spread, short biographies com-
bine with richly reproduced images of the artists' famous works. . . .
Finger . . . writes with clarity and enthusiasm." Booklist
Includes glossary

Guery, Anne

Alphab'art; by Anne Guery, Olivier Dussutour. Frances Lincoln
2009 un il $19.95

Grades: 3 4 5 6 **709**

1. Alphabet 2. Art appreciation

ISBN 978-1-84780-013-8; 1-84780-013-0

One letter of the alphabet is concealed in each of these 26 paintings by some of the masters of Western art, including Picasso, Dalí, Van Gogh, Matisse, Giotto, Chagall, Mondrian, Hopper, Kandinsky, Klee, Magritte, and Bosch.

"Readers are challenged by representational and abstract paintings spanning seven centuries, as the text encourages close inspection of the art. . . . This [is a] rich, well-thought-out book." SLJ

Johnson, Stephen

A is for art; an abstract alphabet. [by] Stephen T. Johnson. Simon & Schuster Books for Young Readers 2008 un il $16.99

Grades: K 1 2 3 **709**

1. Alphabet 2. Abstract art

ISBN 978-0-689-86301-1; 0-689-86301-2

LC 2007-30224

"This exciting alphabetic compendium began with a dictionary. Following years of study and work as a realistic painter, Johnson found himself wanting to explore abstract art. He started by collecting words for each letter of the alphabet. Then, he created a piece based on their meanings. . . . The works vary from paintings and collages to sculptures to installations, and an index reveals the locations of the hidden letters as well as dimensions and materials for the pieces. Children will enjoy seeing everyday objects like candy used in his creations, and will no doubt be inspired to come up with some abstract art of their own." SLJ

Lane, Kimberly

Come look with me: Asian art. Charlesbridge 2008 32p il $15.95

Grades: 3 4 5 **709**

1. Asian art 2. Art appreciation

ISBN 978-1-890674-19-9; 1-890674-19-2

LC 2007037926

"The book is intended to introduce children to fine art in various Asian countries in an accessible manner, and it succeeds. . . . Lane presents a dozen full-color reproductions, done in various mediums and representing different time periods, along with background information and discussion starters." SLJ

Come look with me: Latin American art; [by] Kimberly Lane. Charlesbridge 2007 32p il $15.95

Grades: 3 4 5 **709**

1. Art appreciation 2. Latin American art

ISBN 978-1-890674-20-5

LC 2006034237

This book provides an introduction to Latin American art, pairing reproductions of works of art with questions about the artists lives and work.

"The paintings are reproduced in full color on high-quality paper. The writing is lively and interesting, yet the discussions of artistic ideas and theories are concise and easy to understand." SLJ

Raczka, Bob

★ **Name** that style; all about isms in art. by Bob Raczka. Millbrook Press 2008 32p il (Art adventures) lib bdg $25.26; pa $9.95

Grades: 5 6 7 8 **709**

1. Art -- History

ISBN 978-0-8225-7586-3 lib bdg; 0-8225-7586-8 lib bdg; 978-1-58013-824-6 pa; 1-58013-824-1 pa

LC 2008000312

"Beginning with naturalism and ending with photorealism, with many stops along the way, this compact overview documents the shifts, both in terms of technique as well as subject matter, that differentiate

each style from its predecessors. Each 'ism' gets a two-page spread, with a beautifully reproduced example. . . . . This is . . . . indispensible for any middle-grade classrooms introducing art history." Booklist

Schumann, Bettina

13 women artists children should know; [by] Bettina Schumann; [translated from German by Jane Michael] Prestel 2009 46p il $14.95

Grades: 5 6 7 8 **709**

1. Women artists 2. Art appreciation

ISBN 978-3-7913-4333-4; 3-7913-4333-5

This is profiles women artists such as Sofonisba Anguissola, Maria Sybilla Merian, Mary Cassatt, Georgia O'Keeffe, Frida Kahlo, Louise Bourgeois, and Cindy Sherma

This "large-format, brightly colored [survey proves a] solid, even inspiring [introduction] to the art world. . . . Leading questions encourage budding artists to use the featured subjects and artworks as inspiration." Horn Book Guide

Includes glossary

Shoemaker, Marla K.

Art museum opposites; [by] Katy Friedland, Marla K. Shoemaker. Temple University Press 2010 un il $16.95

Grades: PreK K 1 2 3 **709**

1. Opposites 2. Art appreciation

ISBN 978-1-4399-0523-4; 1-4399-0523-1

LC 2010020731

This is a "collection of fine art in a child-friendly format. Each spread pairs full-color reproductions that suggest opposites. For example, Chagall's A Wheatfield on a Summer's Afternoon is juxtaposed with Miró's Dog Barking at the Moon to suggest 'day' and 'night.' Friedland and Shoemaker have chosen a wide variety of art from ancient to modern times. . . . The layouts are attractively designed. . . . Each paired entry includes a short paragraph that discusses the two pieces exhibited. The authors ask questions and suggest activities. . . . The thoughtfully written text adds interest to the illustrations." SLJ

Wenzel, Angela

13 artists children should know; [translation by Jane Michael] Prestel 2010 46p il $14.95

Grades: 4 5 6 **709**

1. Artists 2. Art appreciation 3. Art -- History

ISBN 978-3-7913-4173-6; 3-7913-4173-1

This profiles 13 artists such as Leondardo da Vinci, Vincent Van Gogh, Vermeer, and Henri Matisse

This "large-format, brightly colored [survey provides a] solid, even inspiring [introduction] to the art world. . . . Leading questions encourage budding artists to use the featured subjects and artworks as inspiration." Horn Book Guide

Includes glossary

709.04   20th century, 1900-1999

Finger, Brad

13 modern artists children should know. Prestel 2010 il $14.95

Grades: 4 5 6 **709.04**

1. Artists 2. Art appreciation 3. Modern art

ISBN 978-3-7913-7015-6; 3-7913-7015-4

This "large-format, brightly colored [survey provides a] well-oranized [introduction] to the [modern] art world. . . . [It provides] short bios and reproductions of one or more works that illustrate the artist's accomplishments. Leading questions encourage budding artists to use the featured subjects and artworks as inspiration." Horn Book Guide

Includes glossary

Laidlaw, Jill

Modern art adventures; 36 creative, hands-on projects inspired by artists from Monet to Banksy. Maja Pitamic and Jill Laidlaw. Chicago Review Press, Inc. 2015 144 p. illustrations (mostly color) (trade paper) $19.95

Grades: 5 6 7 8 9   **709.04**

1. Art   2. Art appreciation   3. Art, Modern -- 19th century   4. Art, Modern -- 20th century   5. Art, Modern -- 21st century

ISBN 1613731779; 9781613731772

LC 2014037521

This book, by Maja Pitamic and Jill Laidlaw, "introduces young artists to groundbreaking masterpieces and fresh techniques, then lets them loose to create their own works of art. . . . Children create two artworks based on the techniques and visual effects of the each featured piece of art and the projects cover a wide range of media, from tissue paper mosaics to stencils to comic cut-outs, with a variety of difficulty levels." (Publisher's note)

"This intriguing title introduces readers to modern art movements, from impressionism to contemporary street art, through child-friendly projects. Each movement includes examples of famous works of art, basic information (title, artist's name and nationality, and year painted) on the piece, and a brief discussion. . . . well-organized introduction to modern art concepts, perfect for classroom use." SLJ

Includes bibliographical references and index

Raimondo, Joyce

★ **Imagine** that! activities and adventures in surrealism. Watson-Guptill Publications 2004 48p il (Art explorers) $13.95

Grades: 2 3 4 5   **709.04**

1. Surrealism   2. Art appreciation

ISBN 0-8230-2502-0

LC 2003-19487

An introduction to Surrealism which includes guidance for related activities as well as brief biographies of six artists: Salvador Dali, Rene Magritte, Max Ernst, Joan Mir, Merit Oppenheim, and Frida Kahlo

"One of the strengths of this book is the inclusion of artwork produced by children. . . . It offers a wealth of intriguing and easy-to-do activities." SLJ

What's the big idea? activities and adventures in abstract art. Watson-Guptill 2008 48p il (Art explorers) $13.95

Grades: 2 3 4 5   **709.04**

1. Abstract art   2. Art appreciation

ISBN 978-0-8230-9998-6; 0-8230-9998-9

"Using the works of famous abstract artists, Raimondo invites readers to discover this genre. Her tone is lively and inquisitive. . . . The activities encourage the investigation of shapes, colors, and patterns, as well as personal creativity. Instructions are clear and thorough. . . . The color photos are reproductions are well chosen and the vivid layout will draw readers to the featured works and projects." SLJ

709.2 Biography

Krull, Kathleen

★ **Lives** of the artists; masterpieces, messes (and what the neighbors thought) written by Kathleen Krull; illustrated by Kathryn Hewitt. Harcourt Brace & Co. 1995 96p il $21

Grades: 4 5 6 7   **709.2**

1. Artists

ISBN 0-15-200103-4

LC 94-35357

"Krull's brief biographies provide basic facts as well as intriguing details. The subjects chosen range from the famous (Michelangelo Buonarroti) to the infamous (Andy Warhol) to the less well known. Hewitt's caricaturelike illustrations reflect and extend the lively text." Horn Book Guide

Includes glossary and bibliographical references

Winter, Jonah

Just behave, Pablo Picasso! by Jonah Winter; pictures by Kevin Hawkes. Arthur A. Levine Books, an imprint of Scholastic 2012 48 p.

Grades: 1 2 3 4   **709.2**

1. Conformity   2. Child artists   3. Creative ability

ISBN 9780545132916; 9780545132923

LC 2011026234

This book offers aspiring children artists encouragement through the story of artist Pablo "Picasso [who] did not always behave. He refused to conform to popular taste or replicate his own successes. . . . In covering his early years (his experimentation with style, perspective, and color were not always appreciated), the author delivers a . . . message to today's young artists: don't be discouraged if your creative efforts are criticized." (School Library Journal)

709.3 Specific continents, countries, localities

Campbell-Hinshaw, Kelly

Ancient Mexico; [by] Kelly Campbell-Hinshaw. Chronicle Books 2007 32p il (Art across the ages) hardcover o.p. pa $4.95

Grades: 2 3 4   **709.3**

1. Mexican art   2. Mexico -- Antiquities

ISBN 0-8118-5670-4; 0-8118-5671-2 pa

"A brief text and striking photos introduce the art of ancient Mexico in this distinctive early reader, which features artifacts such as stone and clay sculptures, a jade mask, a wall painting, and a shield decorated with feathers and inlaid gold. . . . This offers a visually impressive introduction to the arts of Mexico's earliest cultures." Booklist

711 Area planning (Civic art)

Macaulay, David

★ **City** : a story of Roman planning and construction. Houghton Mifflin 1974 112p il $18; pa $10.99

Grades: 4 5 6 7 8 9 10   **711**

1. Civil engineering   2. Roman architecture   3. City planning -- Rome

ISBN 0-395-19492-X; 0-395-34922-2 pa

LC 74-4280

"By following the inception, construction, and development of an imaginary Roman city, the account traces the evolution of Verbonia from the selection of its site under religious auspices in 26 B.C. to its completion in 100 A.D." Horn Book

Includes glossary

Rome antics. Houghton Mifflin 1997 79p il $18

Grades: 4 5 6 7   **711**

1. Rome (Italy) -- Description and travel

ISBN 0-395-82279-3

LC 97-20941

"Modern Rome is seen through the skewed perspective of a homing pigeon's erratic flight through the city streets as she delivers a message to an artist in a garret. . . . Macaulay adds sly touches of humor to the pen-and-ink sketches. . . . The book includes a map of the city 'As the pigeon flies' with each structure numbered, and an addendum shows the

22 featured buildings with a paragraph or two of interesting facts about each one." SLJ

712 Landscape architecture (Landscape design)

Gourley, Robbin

★ **First** garden; the White House garden and how it grew. written and illustrated by Robbin Gourley; foreword by Alice Waters. Clarion Books 2011 36p il $16.99

Grades: 1 2 3 4   **712**

1. Vegetable gardening 2. White House Gardens (Washington, D.C.)

ISBN 978-0-547-48224-8; 0-547-48224-8

LC 2010024643

The White House kitchen garden, part of Michelle Obama's campaign to encourage healthful eating, was established in 2009. This book tells the story of Mrs. Obama's garden, as well as the story of the White House grounds, the other gardens that came before, the White House children who have played there, and the teamwork that led to the garden now flourishing on the South Lawn.

"In the many watercolor illustrations, splashes of color show up brilliantly against the bright, white pages. Although Gourley includes plenty of factoids for kids intrigued by past and present residents of the White House, she also makes gardening look enjoyable and rewarding. . . . Gourley's clear, focused writing and lively illustrations will keep children engaged." Booklist

Includes bibliographical references

720 Architecture

Curlee, Lynn

★ **Skyscraper.** Atheneum Books for Young Readers 2007 40p il $17.99

Grades: 3 4 5 6   **720**

1. Skyscrapers

ISBN 0-689-84489-1

"Dramatic paintings and lucid prose highlight this excellent history of skyscrapers." SLJ

Finger, Brad

13 skyscrapers children should know; by Brad Finger. Prestel Pub 2016 45 p. illustrations (chiefly color) $14.95

Grades: 4 5 6 7 8   **720**

1. Skyscrapers

ISBN 3791372513; 9783791372518

This book, by Brad Finger, "takes young readers around the world to investigate how tall buildings are constructed. . . . There's something irresistible about a skyscraper. It can reshape an entire city skyline, and from the building's top floors, people can see the world from a different perspective. Travelling from New York City to Dubai, from London to Shanghai, and from Kuala Lumpur to Chicago, this colorful book features double-page spreads for each of the skyscrapers it profiles." (Publisher's note)

"Still, fascinating anecdotes about the state of the world during each building's inception make this an interesting read, and it provides plenty of valuable information, both at a glance and for more in-depth study." Booklist

Hale, Christy

★ **Dreaming** up; a celebration of building. Christy Hale. Lee & Low Books, Inc. 2012 40 p. (hardcover) $18.95

Grades: K 1 2 3   **720**

1. Creative ability 2. Building 3. Imagination -- fiction 4. Children's art 5. Architecture

ISBN 1600606512; 9781600606519

LC 2012007376

Boston Globe-Horn Book Honor: Nonfiction (2013).

Author Christy Hale presents a story about architecture and play. "Children building--Concrete poetry--Pair them with notable structures from around the world and see children's constructions taken to the level of architectural treasures. Here is a unique celebration of children's playtime explorations and the surprising ways childhood experiences find expression in the dreams and works of innovative architects. Come be inspired to play--dream--build--discover!" (Publisher's note)

Hosack, Karen

Buildings; [by] Karen Hosack. Raintree 2009 32p il map (What is art?) lib bdg $27.50

Grades: 5 6 7 8   **720**

1. Buildings 2. Architecture

ISBN 978-1-4109-3165-8 lib bdg; 1-4109-3165-X lib bdg

LC 2008-9700

This "features public spaces and private residences created from a variety of materials. Every page includes a paragraph about the structure with glossary terms in bold type. . . . [Title is] consistent in quality of design and content." SLJ

Includes glossary and bibliographical references

Kaner, Etta

Earth-friendly buildings, bridges, and more; the eco-journal of Corry Lapont. written by Etta Kaner; illustrated by Stephen MacEachern. Kids Can Press 2012 64 p. ill. $18.95

Grades: 3 4 5   **720**

1. Urban ecology 2. English Channel Tunnel 3. Sustainable architecture

ISBN 1554535700; 9781554535705

Author Etta Kaner addresses topics including "site selection, planning, designing, the integration of green engineering solutions (like using rainwater for cooling) and nifty details on the how-tos of constructing eco-friendly structures. Across a series of two-page spreads, [protagonist] Corry explores not only new buildings (domes and skyscrapers) but also such diverse projects as the Vizcaya Bridge (Spain), the English Channel Tunnel and the locks of Ottawa's Rideau Canal, as well as dams, dikes and levees." (Kirkus Reviews)

"Though sustainable architecture is becoming more and more a part of school curriculum and family discussions, there are surprisingly few books available on the topic. This handsome, information-rich, yet brief illustrated "eco-journal" fills a gap--and more." Kirkus

Macaulay, David

★ **Building** big. Houghton Mifflin 2000 192p il $30; pa $12.95

Grades: 5 6 7 8 9 10   **720**

1. Dams 2. Bridges 3. Tunnels 4. Engineering 5. Skyscrapers 6. Architecture

ISBN 0-395-96331-1; 0-618-46527-8 pa

LC 00-28116

"Macaulay combines his detailed yet vaguely whimsical illustrations with simple, straightforward prose that breaks down complex architectural and engineering accomplishments into easily digestible tidbits that don't insult the intelligence of the reader of any age." N Y Times Book Rev

Includes glossary

Parker, Victoria

How tall is tall? comparing structures. [by] Vic Parker. Heinemann Library 2011 32p il (Measuring and comparing) lib bdg $26; pa $7.99

Grades: 2 3 4   **720**

1. Skyscrapers 2. Weights and measures

ISBN 978-1-4329-3955-7 lib bdg; 1-4329-3955-6 lib bdg; 978-1-4329-3963-2 pa; 1-4329-3963-7 pa

LC 2010000924

This "contains vivid photographs, charts, and diagrams with captions, explanations, and examples. Questions are posed throughout . . . to entice young learners to 'stop and think' or continue reading for more information. . . . [This] would make an excellent addition to any classroom library." Libr Media Connect

Includes glossary and bibliographical references

Paxmann, Christine

From mud huts to skyscrapers; architecture for children. by Christine Paxmann; illustrated by Anne Ibelings. Prestel Pub. Random House 2012 64 p. ill. (hardcover) $19.95

Grades: 4 5 6   **720**

1. Picture books for children 2. Architecture

ISBN 3791371134; 9783791371139

LC 2012939038

This book "takes readers on a journey through time, exploring well-known structures such as the pyramids, Hagia Sophia, Versailles, and the Guggenheim Museum. Each spread is dedicated to a single building; in addition to a detailed illustration of the structure, it also includes information about the architect, the architectural style, and/or definitions of particular details." (School Library Journal)

Roeder, Annette

13 buildings children should know; [translator, Jane Michael] Prestel 2009 46p il $14.95

Grades: 5 6 7 8   **720**

1. Architecture

ISBN 978-3-7913-4171-2; 3-7913-4171-5

"The famous buildings featured in this pictorial collection include Notre Dame cathedral in Paris, Neuschwanstein Castle in Germany, New York City's Guggenheim Museum and the Beijing National Stadium (built for the 2008 Olympics), each pictured in color photographs, cross-sections and/or ground plans, with time lines tracing the buildings' developments and changes over time. . . . A sound introduction to some impressive structures." Publ Wkly

Stern, Steven L.

Building greenscrapers; consultant, Frank Robbins. Bearport Pub. 2009 32p il (Going green) lib bdg $25.27

Grades: 4 5 6 7   **720**

1. Skyscrapers 2. Sustainable architecture

ISBN 978-1-59716-962-2 lib bdg; 1-59716-962-5 lib bdg

LC 2009-12494

"Color photographs (most full page) and a few diagrams accompany the informative text. . . . Overall, the [book] . . . is user-friendly and covers topics that are not easily found elsewhere." SLJ

Includes glossary and bibliographical references

720.973   Architecture – United States

Wing, Natasha

When Jackie saved Grand Central; the true story of Jacqueline Kennedy's fight for an American icon. Natasha Wing; illustrated by Alexan-

dra Boiger. Houghton Mifflin Harcourt 2017 48 p. color illustrations $17.99

Grades: 2 3 4   **720.973**

1. Historic buildings -- United States 2. Historic buildings -- New York (N.Y.) 3. Architecture -- Conservation and restoration 4. New York (N.Y.) -- Buildings, structures, etc 5. Grand Central Terminal (New York, N.Y.) 6. Railroad stations -- Conservation and restoration -- New York (State) -- New York

ISBN 9780547449210

LC 2016000983

This children's book, by Natasha Wing, illustrated by Alexandra Boiger, tells how Jacqueline Kennedy "helped inspire thousands of people to come together and fight to protect the historic [Grand Cetral] landmark. From letter-writing campaigns all the way to the Supreme Court, this little-known story celebrates winning in the face of immeasurable odds and how one person can make a big difference." (Publisher's note)

724   Architecture from 1400

Alphin, Tom

The LEGO architect; by Tom Alphin. No Starch Press 2015 186 p. illustrations (hardcover) $24.95

Grades: 4 5 6 7 8 9   **724**

1. LEGO toys 2. Architecture -- History 3. Architectural models 4. Architecture, Modern -- Themes, motives

ISBN 9781593276133; 1593276133

LC 2015017603

This book, by Tom Alphin, "travel[s] through the history of architecture [reproduced with LEGO blocks.] . . . You'll learn about styles like Art Deco, Modernism, and High-Tech, and find inspiration in galleries of LEGO models. Then take your turn building 12 models in a variety of styles. Snap together some bricks and learn architecture the fun way!" (Publisher's note)

Includes bibliographical references

725   Specific types of structures

Low, William

Old Penn Station; [by] William Low. Henry Holt and Co. 2007 un il $16.95

Grades: 3 4 5 6   **725**

1. Railroad stations 2. Historic buildings 3. Pennsylvania Station (New York, N.Y.)

ISBN 978-0-8050-7925-8; 0-8050-7925-4

LC 2006015359

"Low contributes both words and pictures in this ode to New York City's Pennsylvania Station. Introductory pages describe why and how the glorious train station was erected. Later spreads focus on how the building was utilized before it fell into disuse and was finally demolished to make way for the smaller, subterranean station used today. . . . The artwork . . . is magnificent. Full-spread, oil-and-digital, mixed-media paintings depicting people moving through the beautiful structure will draw children into Low's underlying message: 'Buildings are not just concrete and steel. They are the heart and soul of all great cities.'" Booklist

Includes bibliographical references

Nardo, Don

Roman amphitheaters. Watts 2002 63p il (Watts library) lib bdg $25.50; pa $8.95

Grades: 5 6 7 8   **725**
    1. Roman architecture 2. Colosseum (Rome, Italy)
    ISBN 0-531-12036-8 lib bdg; 0-531-16224-9 pa

LC 2001-17769

The author discusses the Colosseum in Rome as an example of how amphitheaters were constructed and "provides a brief cultural context; a history of the development of the building type; and a history of the [Colosseum] including how it was built, what it was used for, and what happened after the society that created it lost prominence. . . . The writing is informative and engaging and not oversimplified. The illustrations are mainly clear, high-quality, full-color photographs." SLJ

Includes glossary and bibliographical references

726   Buildings for religious and related purposes

Curlee, Lynn
    ★ **Parthenon**. Atheneum Books for Young Readers 2004 un il $17.95
Grades: 3 4 5 6   **726**
    1. Parthenon (Athens, Greece)
    ISBN 0-689-84490-5

LC 2003-2615

A detailed history of the Parthenon exploring its construction and restoration.

This is a "splendid introduction to Greece's most renowned monument. . . . [The author's] examination of the architectural details is particularly accurate and absorbing. . . . The limpid, forthright prose matches artwork of similar clarity and elegant simplicity. The acrylic paintings balance areas of flat color with finely controlled line." SLJ

Henzel, Cynthia Kennedy
    Taj Mahal. ABDO Pub. Co. 2011 32p il map (Troubled treasures: world heritage sites) $25.65
Grades: 3 4 5   **726**
    1. Taj Mahal (Agra, India)
    ISBN 978-1-61613-568-3; 1-61613-568-9

LC 2010021306

This "book describes in general terms [the Taj Mahal's] construction, . . . distinctive features, and history, as well as threats to its continued existence and both current and past restoration intitiatives. Revealing color photos taken from different heights and angles are supplemented by maps and by graphic reconstructions. . . . Henzel's distinctive approach gives this [book] unusual value for both assignment and general reading." SLJ

Includes glossary

Hyman, Teresa L.
    Pyramids; [by] Teresa Hyman. KidHaven Press 2004 48p il (Wonders of the world) lib bdg $23.70
Grades: 3 4 5 6   **726**
    1. Pyramids
    ISBN 0-7377-2055-7

LC 2004-12063

This "introduces structures in ancient Egypt, Africa, Cambodia, and Mexico and is full of large, colorful photos and illustrations. . . . Attractive, readable." SLJ

Includes bibliographical references

Macaulay, David
    ★ **Mosque**. Houghton Mifflin 2003 96p il $18

Grades: 4 5 6 7 8 9 10   **726**
    1. Mosques -- Design and construction
    ISBN 0-618-24034-9

LC 2003-177

"Once again Macaulay uses clear words and exemplary drawings to explore a majestic structure's design and construction. . . . In his respectful, straightforward explanation of the mosque's design, Macaulay offers an unusual, inspiring perspective into Islamic society." Booklist

Includes glossary

    ★ **Pyramid**. Houghton Mifflin 1975 80p il $20; pa $9.95
Grades: 4 5 6 7 8 9 10   **726**
    1. Pyramids 2. Egypt -- Civilization
    ISBN 0-395-21407-6; 0-395-32121-2 pa

LC 75-9964

The construction of a pyramid in 25th century B.C. Egypt is described. "Information about selection of the site, drawing of the plans, calculating compass directions, clearing and leveling the ground, and quarrying and hauling the tremendous blocks of granite and limestone is conveyed as much by pictures as by text." Horn Book

Includes glossary

Mann, Elizabeth
    The **Parthenon**; illustrations by Yuan Lee. Mikaya Press 2006 47p il (Wonders of the world) $22.95
Grades: 4 5 6 7   **726**
    1. Athens (Greece) -- History 2. Greece -- Civilization 3. Parthenon (Athens, Greece)
    ISBN 1-931414-15-7

This "volume introduces the history of ancient Athens culminating in the building of the Parthenon. . . . [The text is] well-researched and clearly written. . . . The color illustrations include an excellent map of Greece, photos of artifacts and sculptures, and many clearly deliniated, large-scale paintings." Booklist

726.6   Cathedrals

Macaulay, David
    ★ **Building** the book Cathedral. Houghton Mifflin 1999 112p il $29.95
Grades: 4 5 6 7 8 9   **726.6**
    1. Cathedrals 2. Gothic architecture
    ISBN 0-395-92147-3

LC 99-17975

"On its twenty-fifth anniversary, the author recounts the origins of his first book and suggests revisions he'd make in light of what he's learned. . . . Most of the original Cathedral: the story of it's construction is reproduced in this oversized celebratory volume, along with lots of preliminary sketches, new commentary, and revised, or newly deployed, art. . . . Touches of informal humor further enliven a book that's already mesmerizing for both its original content and its insights into this author-illustrator's incisive, ebulliently creative mind." Horn Book

728.8   Large and elaborate private dwellings

Humphrey, Paul
    Building a castle; by Paul Humphrey. Arcturus Pub. 2012 32 p. col. ill. (library) $28.50
Grades: 4 5 6   **728.8**
    1. Castles -- Design and construction   2. Castles -- Europe --

Design and construction
ISBN 1848585594; 9781848585591

LC 2011051450

This book by Paul Humphrey "takes readers on a journey from the very beginnings of castles as fortresses to the lavish tourist destinations of today." The text, along with "contextual photographs, staged reenactments, and detailed diagrams offers . . . [an] overview of how an architectural structure reveals the culture, class system, and daily life of the Middle Ages. Castles from the Czech Republic, Scotland, England, Turkey, and Holland are highlighted." (Children's Literature)

729   Design and decoration of structures and accessories

Hill, Isabel (Isabel T.)
  Urban animals. Star Bright Books 2009 un il $17.95; pa $7.95
Grades: K 1 2 3   **729**
  1. Animals in art 2. Architectural decoration and ornament
  ISBN 978-1-59572-209-6; 1-59572-209-2; 978-1-59572-210-2 pa; 1-59572-210-6 pa

LC 2009028378

"Vivid photographs invite children to look closely at a variety of city buildings to find a column adorned with a dog's face, a bronze frieze featuring flying geese, etc. On each double-page spread, lefthand pages show wide views while right-hand pages zoom in on the highlighted animal. The child-friendly topic and approach and the small trim size make this a winning introduction to architecture." Horn Book Guide

Macaulay, David
  ★ **Built** to last. Houghton Mifflin Harcourt 2010 272p il $24.99
Grades: 4 5 6 7 8 9 10   **729**
  1. Castles 2. Cathedrals 3. Architecture 4. Mosques -- Design and construction
  ISBN 978-0-547-34240-5; 0-547-34240-3

"Significantly updating the Caldecott Honor-winning Castle (1977) and Cathedral (1973) with new text and full-color illustrations, this hefty volume combines them with a very lightly revised Mosque (2003) for a three-in-one architectural spree. No mere colorization of the black-and-white originals of the first two books, . . . the all-new, often breathtaking images have been drawn by hand and then digitally colored to harmonize, beautifully with the look of Mosque. . . . Take a moment to mourn the originals, then celebrate this entirely worthy revision." Kirkus

730   Sculpture and related arts

Raczka, Bob
  ★ **3**-D ABC; a sculptural alphabet. by Bob Raczka. Millbrook Press 2007 32p il lib bdg $23.93
Grades: K 1 2 3   **730**
  1. Alphabet 2. Sculpture
  ISBN 978-0-7613-9456-3 lib bdg; 0-7613-9456-7 lib bdg

LC 2005013472

"This alphabetically arranged primer on 20th-century sculpture includes Marcel Duchamp's Bicycle Wheel, Constantin Brancusi's The Kiss (paired with Robert Indiana's Love), and Claes Oldenburg's Spoonbridge and Cherry. The selections are international in scope, and the media range from scrap metal and found objects to wood and fluorescent lights." SLJ

730.9   History, geographic treatment, biography of sculpture and related arts together, of sculpture alone

Niepold, Mil
  Oooh! Picasso; [by] Mil Niepold & Jeanyves Verdu. Tricycle Press 2009 un il (The Oooh! artist) $14.95
Grades: 2 3 4   **730.9**
  1. Artists 2. Painters 3. Sculpture 4. Art appreciation
  ISBN 978-1-58246-265-3; 1-58246-265-8

LC 2008010646

"Niepold and Verdu introduce five of Picasso's sculptures. For each one, a close-up detail of the artwork is shown first, along with the question, 'What is this?' Two more spreads present zoomed-in images with possible answers, followed by a third spread showing the entire sculpture along with a statement like, 'oooh! i am a guitar.' . . . Bold text floating on bright solid-color pages complements the pictures. A photo of the artist is appended along with reproductions of the artworks and identifying information. . . . This book will ignite readers' imaginations and is both an effective gateway to art appreciation for young children and a fun exercise for elementary students." SLJ

730.92   Biography

Fritz, Jean
  Leonardo's horse; illustrated by Hudson Talbott. Putnam 2001 un il $16.99
Grades: 4 5 6 7   **730.92**
  1. Artists 2. Bronzes 3. Painters 4. Air pilots 5. Scientists 6. Art collectors 7. Airline employees 8. Writers on science 9. Patrons of the arts
  ISBN 0-399-23576-0

LC 00-41550

"Combining biography, history, and art, Fritz's absorbing text is both a lively introduction to Leonardo and a tribute to Dent." Booklist

731   Sculpture

Kenney, Karen Latchana
  Super simple masks; fun and easy-to-make crafts for kids. ABDO Pub. Company 2010 32p il (Super simple crafts) lib bdg $17.95
Grades: K 1 2 3 4   **731**
  1. Handicraft 2. Masks (Sculpture)
  ISBN 978-1-60453-627-0 lib bdg; 1-60453-627-6 lib bdg

LC 2009-357

"Colorful photos; clean layout in a bright, primary palette; and large, abundant step-by-step instructional photos give [this book] great appeal. The . . . crafts . . . are functional and attractive. . . . Readily obtainable household materials and easy-to-follow instructions mean that children can do these crafts independently." SLJ
  Includes glossary

Wenzel, Angela
  13 sculptures children should know. Prestel 2010 il $14.95
Grades: 4 5 6   **731**
  1. Sculpture 2. Art appreciation
  ISBN 978-3-7913-7010-1; 3-7913-7010-3

This "large-format, brightly colored [survey provides a] well-oranized [introduction] to the . . . world [of sculpture]. [It] highlights a variety of works from antiquity to modern times. . . . Leading questions encourage budding artists to use the featured subjects and artworks as inspiration." Horn Book Guide

Includes glossary

731.4   Techniques and procedures

Hanson, Anders

Cool sculpture; the art of creativity for kids. [by] Anders Hanson. ABDO Pub. Co. 2009 32p il (Cool art) lib bdg $24.21

Grades: 2 3 4   **731.4**

1. Sculpture -- Technique

ISBN 978-1-60453-144-2 lib bdg; 1-60453-144-4 lib bdg

LC 2008-22324

This book about sculpture is "well organized, with clearly written sections . . . and several clever projects and exercises. . . . [It] should have substantial child appeal." SLJ

Includes glossary

Luxbacher, Irene

1   2 3 I can build! Kids Can Press 2009 23p il (Starting art) $14.95; pa $6.95

Grades: 2 3 4   **731.4**

1. Sculpture -- Technique

ISBN 978-1-55453-315-2; 978-1-55453-316-9 pa

"Illustrated step-by-step projects show kids how to build small structures out of household materials, encouraging both hands-on creativity and imaginative play. Clear photos of brightly colored materials appear on spacious layouts against white backgrounds. Each project looks sharp and appealing, with sketched cartoon characters adding liveliness and humor." SLJ

1   2 3 I can sculpt! Kids Can Press 2007 23p il (Starting art) $12.95

Grades: 2 3 4   **731.4**

1. Sculpture -- Technique

ISBN 978-1-55453-038-0; 1-55453-038-5

This "introduces the various types of simple materials and techniques that can be used to create animal sculptures. This book is . . . project-oriented, although such concepts as three-dimensionality, texture, and balance are mentioned. Children can make an egg-carton crocodile, an aluminum-foil-and-clay snake, a clay-and-pipe-cleaner giraffe, a paper-bag dinosaur, and more. . . . [The book has] lively pages with color photos and easy-to-follow directions." SLJ

736   Other plastic arts

Alexander, Chris

Difficult origami; by Chris Alexander. Capstone Press 2009 32p il (Snap books) lib bdg $25.26

Grades: 3 4 5 6   **736**

1. Origami

ISBN 978-1-4296-2022-2 lib bdg; 1-4296-2022-6 lib bdg

LC 2007-52196

This book includes "clearly illustrated diagrams and attractive photos of the completed projects using different colors and textures of paper." SLJ

Includes glossary and bibliographical references

Sort-of-difficult origami; by Chris Alexander. Capstone Press 2009 32p il (Snap books) lib bdg $25.26

Grades: 3 4 5 6   **736**

1. Origami

ISBN 978-1-4296-2023-9 lib bdg; 1-4296-2023-4 lib bdg

LC 2007-52208

This book includes "clearly illustrated diagrams and attractive photos of the completed projects using different colors and textures of paper." SLJ

Includes glossary and bibliographical references

Boursin, Didier

Origami for everyone; beginner-intemediate-advanced. Firefly 2011 il pa $29.95; pa $19.95

Grades: 3 4 5 6   **736**

1. Origami

ISBN 978-1-55407-958-2; 1554079586; 978-1-55407-792-2 pa; 1-55407-792-3 pa

"Though most (possibly all) of the photographs and step diagrams for these 68 paper-folding projects are recycled from Boursin's earlier collections, he has both revised the instructions and commentary and grouped the models according to estimated difficulty. After an extensive opening tutorial of folds and bases adorned with savvy general folding tips, he offers a randomly ordered assortment of aircraft, animals, stars, ornaments, and spinners. . . . The author's lighthearted, fanciful outlook gives this extensive sampler a bright and inviting tone." SLJ

Harbo, Christopher L.

Easy animal origami. Capstone Press 2011 24p (First facts: easy origami) lib bdg $23.99

Grades: 1 2 3   **736**

1. Origami 2. Animals in art

ISBN 978-1-4296-5384-8; 1-4296-5384-1

LC 2010024791

Provides instructions and photo-illustrated diagrams for making a variety of easy animal origami models.

"There is one project per brightly colored spread, with the boxed pictures of the steps large enough to see the folding process. . . . Further appeal comes from the fact that many of the origami figures do not have to remain stationary. Some can be manipulated and played with after completion. . . . There may only be seven projects in [the] book, but they are more than enough to hold the interest of young ones smitten by the idea of folding paper into shapes." SLJ

Includes bibliographical references

Easy holiday origami. Capstone Press 2011 24p il (First facts: easy origami) lib bdg $23.99

Grades: 1 2 3   **736**

1. Origami 2. Holiday decorations

ISBN 978-1-4296-5387-9; 1-4296-5387-6

LC 2010024785

Provides instructions and photo-illustrated diagrams for making a variety of easy holiday origami models.

"There is one project per brightly colored spread, with the boxed pictures of the steps large enough to see the folding process. . . . Further appeal comes from the fact that many of the origami figures do not have to remain stationary. Some can be manipulated and played with after completion. . . . There may only be seven projects in [the] book, but they are more than enough to hold the interest of young ones smitten by the idea of folding paper into shapes." SLJ

Includes bibliographical references

Easy ocean origami. Capstone Press 2011 24p il (First facts: easy origami) lib bdg $23.99

Grades: 1 2 3 **736**
1. Origami
ISBN 978-1-4296-5385-5; 1-4296-5385-X
LC 2010024786

Provides instructions and photo-illustrated diagrams for making a variety of easy water-related origami models.

"There is one project per brightly colored spread, with the boxed pictures of the steps large enough to see the folding process. . . . Further appeal comes from the fact that many of the origami figures do not have to remain stationary. Some can be manipulated and played with after completion. . . . There may only be seven projects in [the] book, but they are more than enough to hold the interest of young ones smitten by the idea of folding paper into shapes." SLJ

Includes bibliographical references

Easy origami toys. Capstone Press 2011 24p il (First facts: easy origami) lib bdg $23.99
Grades: 1 2 3 **736**
1. Toys 2. Origami
ISBN 978-1-4296-5386-2; 1-4296-5386-8
LC 2010024788

Provides instructions and photo-illustrated diagrams for making a variety of easy origami toys.

"There is one project per brightly colored spread, with the boxed pictures of the steps large enough to see the folding process. . . . Further appeal comes from the fact that many of the origami figures do not have to remain stationary. Some can be manipulated and played with after completion. . . . There may only be seven projects in [the] book, but they are more than enough to hold the interest of young ones smitten by the idea of folding paper into shapes." SLJ

Includes bibliographical references

Henry, Sally
Paper folding; [by] Sally Henry. PowerKids Press 2009 32p il (Make your own crafts) lib bdg $25.25
Grades: 3 4 5 6 **736**
1. Origami 2. Paper crafts
ISBN 978-1-4358-2507-9 lib bdg; 1-4358-2507-1 lib bdg
LC 2008-4524

"After describing different kinds of paper, Henry explains the difference between a fold, a crease, and a burnished fold, and then lists all the other supplies besides paper (glue, rubber cement) that should be on hand. The rest of the book devotes two-page spreads to each project. . . . The ideas are fantastic. . . . This will keep plenty of hands and minds busy." Booklist

Includes glossary

Jackson, Paul
Origami toys; that tumble fly and spin. Gibbs Smith 2010 127p il $19.99 **736**
1. Toys 2. Origami
ISBN 1-4236-0524-1; 978-1-4236-0524-9

"In this handsomely packaged volume, Jackson offers 29 elegantly simple toys that he has either invented or modified. The models . . . include percussive 'instruments,' a wriggling fish, dogs, . . . a spinning star, two gliders, and even a catapult. . . . The particularly clear step diagrams use standard origami notation, and the directions that accompany them are just as easy to follow. . . . [This is an] above-average offering." SLJ

Meinking, Mary
Easy origami; by Mary Meinking. Capstone Press 2009 32p il (Snap books) lib bdg $25.26

Grades: 3 4 5 6 **736**
1. Origami
ISBN 978-1-4296-2020-8 lib bdg; 1-4296-2020-X lib bdg
LC 2008-1677

This book includes "clearly illustrated diagrams and attractive photos of the completed projects using different colors and textures of paper." SLJ

Includes glossary and bibliographical references

Not-quite-so-easy origami; by Mary Meinking. Capstone Press 2009 32p il (Snap books) lib bdg $25.26
Grades: 3 4 5 6 **736**
1. Origami
ISBN 978-1-4296-2021-5 lib bdg; 1-4296-2021-8 lib bdg
LC 2008-1679

This book includes "clearly illustrated diagrams and attractive photos of the completed projects using different colors and textures of paper." SLJ

Includes glossary and bibliographical references

Nguyen, Duy
Zombigami; paper folding for the living dead. Sterling 2011 il pa $9.95
Grades: 5 6 7 8 **736**
1. Origami 2. Zombies
ISBN 978-1-4027-8646-4; 1-4027-8646-8

"Featuring both a detachable photo gallery of folded ghouls placed in atmospheric settings and a package of origami paper in suitably ominous colors and patterns, this collection of 13 undead figures may not survive intact for long but this offers experienced paper folders hours of creepy fun. Nguyen opens with a tutorial of creases and folding symbology then . . . goes on to show how each figure is folded with plenty of carefully drawn and clearly labeled step diagrams. Nonetheless, most of these models are challenging projects." SLJ

Owen, Ruth
Valentine's Day origami; by Ruth Owen. PowerKids Press 2013 32 p. col. ill. (library) $26.50; (paperback) $11.75
Grades: 4 5 6 **736**
1. Origami 2. Valentine's Day 3. Valentine decorations
ISBN 1448878659; 9781448878659; 9781448879243
LC 2012009647

"This . . . title in the Holiday Origami series encourages young people to create an original I-love-you offering. . . . After a brief history of the origin and traditions of Valentine's Day, the origami instructions start off simply, with pictures and directions on exactly how and when to fold and crease. First, there are two spreads with 9 steps that show how to make an origami heart. Later, 13 steps over four pages show how to make a red rose. Nine steps make a heart box." (Booklist)

Song, Sok
Everyday origami; by Sok Song. Capstone Press 2016 47 p. chiefly color illustrations (Savvy. Fashion origami) (ebook) $31.99; (library binding) $31.99
Grades: 4 5 6 7 8 **736**
1. Origami 2. Fashion 3. Paper work 4. Clothing and dress
ISBN 9781515716471; 1515716309; 9781515716303
LC 2016022942

With this book, by Sok Song, "transform a simple sheet of paper into a fashion-forward outfit with easy-to-follow instructions and illustrated diagrams. Create everyday outfit essentials such as jeans, sweaters, and jackets to amp up your wardrobe. With ten original, one-of-a-kind origami pieces, everyday outfits are sure to be runway-ready. All you have to do is fold it, shape it, and style it." (Publisher's note)

"Upgrade your origami section with these original models and excellent instructions." SLJ

737.4   Coins

Reid, Margarette S.

Lots and lots of coins; illustrations by True Kelley. Dutton Children's Books 2010 un il $16.99

Grades: K 1 2 3   737.4

1. Coins

ISBN 978-0-525-47879-9; 0-525-47879-5

LC 2009053286

"In this cheerful book, a boy tells about an interest he shares with his dad: coin collecting. . . . Throughout the book, text shares the pages with brightly colored, mixed-media artwork, captions, and speech or thought balloons. Photos of common coins appear in boxes along with a little information, and the backs of the state quarters appear on one double-page spread. . . . With an upbeat tone and plenty of interesting facts, this is a fine introduction to coin collecting for young children." Booklist

Includes bibliographical references

738   Ceramic arts

Andrews-Goebel, Nancy

★ The pot that Juan built; pictures by David Diaz. Lee & Low Bks. 2002 un il $16.95

Grades: K 1 2 3   738

1. Artists 2. Pottery 3. Ceramists

ISBN 1-58430-038-8

LC 2001-38139

A cumulative rhyme summarizes the life's work of renowned Mexican potter, Juan Quezada. Additional information describes the process he uses to create his pots after the style of the Casas Grandes people.

"This unusual book is set up to allow for differing levels of reading expertise. . . . One page contains a catchy cumulative rhyme modeled on 'This Is the House That Jack Built,' which outlines the process of making a pot. The facing page offers a clearly written prose presentation. . . . Diaz's arresting illustrations, rendered in Adobe Photoshop, use yellows, oranges, and reds in a layered effect that seems to glow with an inward light." SLJ

738.1   Techniques, procedures, apparatus, equipment, materials

Cuxart, Bernadette

Modeling clay animals; easy-to-follow projects in simple steps. Barron's 2010 95p il pa $9.99

Grades: 1 2 3 4   738.1

1. Clay 2. Handicraft 3. Animals in art

ISBN 978-0-7641-4579-7 pa; 0-7641-4579-7 pa

"In this well-put-together resource, Cuxart shows readers how to make more than 50 different figures using clay and other materials. The book begins with basic tips and instructions and then devotes a page or two to each of the projects. . . . For each one there are illustrated step-by-step instructions and a photo of the final product. The instructions are primarily visual and are accompanied by a sentence or two of text. They are very clear, and even fairly young children should be able to follow the directions without much adult intervention. Some of the final products are more stylized than others, but all are appealing." SLJ

Kenney, Karen Latchana

Super simple clay projects; fun and easy-to-make crafts for kids. ABDO Pub. Company 2010 32p il (Super simple crafts) lib bdg $17.95

Grades: K 1 2 3 4   738.1

1. Clay 2. Pottery 3. Handicraft

ISBN 978-1-60453-623-2 lib bdg; 1-60453-623-3 lib bdg

LC 2009-351

"Colorful photos; clean layout in a bright, primary palette; and large, abundant step-by-step instructional photos give [this book] great appeal. The . . . crafts . . . are functional and attractive. . . . [The book] shows kids how to make a pencil holder out of an empty can, for example. . . . Readily obtainable household materials and easy-to-follow instructions mean that children can do these crafts independently." SLJ

Includes glossary

Llimos, Anna

Easy clay crafts in 5 steps. Enslow Elementary 2008 31p il (Easy crafts in 5 steps) lib bdg $22.60

Grades: 2 3 4   738.1

1. Clay 2. Ceramics

ISBN 978-0-7660-3085-5 lib bdg; 0-7660-3085-7 lib bdg

Original Spanish edition 2005

The offers instructions for 14 clay craft projects, among them a pear-shaped box, a flower vase, and a paperweight

The text is "easy to read, and the results are quirky and pleasing; steps are illustrated with bright photographs." Horn Book Guide

Includes bibliographical references

739.27   Jewelry

Kenney, Karen Latchana

Super simple jewelry; fun and easy-to-make crafts for kids. ABDO Pub. Co. 2010 32p il (Super simple crafts) lib bdg $17.95

Grades: K 1 2 3 4   739.27

1. Jewelry 2. Handicraft

ISBN 978-1-6045-3625-6 lib bdg; 1-6045-3625-X lib bdg

LC 2009000354

"From bright jewelry pendants made from metal washers to necklaces made from scrap-paper beads, the likable projects featured in this slim title create bright baubles from easy-to-find, inexpensive materials. Each spread combines sharp photos both during construction and then in their finished state, and the book's design makes following along easy." Booklist

740   Graphic arts

Kidd, Chip

Go; a Kidd's guide to graphic design. Chip Kidd. Workman Publishing Company, Inc. 2013 160 p. (alk. paper) $17.95

Grades: 5 6 7 8 9 10 11 12 Adult   740

1. Graphic design 2. Children and design 3. Graphic arts -- Technique

ISBN 076117219X; 9780761172192

LC 2013032394

YALSA Award for Excellence in Nonfiction for Young Adults: Finalist (2014)

This book is an introduction to graphic design. It introduces "the aspiring designer to the thought processes behind typography and visual organization. Among the topics are color, juxtaposition, typography, design history, and the use of design to convey concepts such as irony and metaphor." (Library Journal)

Includes bibliographical references and index

741   Drawing and drawings

Artell, Mike

Funny cartooning for kids. Sterling Pub. 2007 128p il $17.95
Grades: 3 4 5 6   **741**
1. Drawing 2. Cartooning -- Technique
ISBN 978-1-4027-2260-8

"This volume approaches the basics of traditional cartooning with what is funny—what creates humor. Pointing out the difference between 'regular' illustrations and cartoons, the author divides the book into chapters that give readers instruction in six areas—exaggeration; simplification; animals and objects doing 'people' things; people in different poses; unusual body types and gestures; and monsters, weird creatures, and aliens. . . . Black-and-white pen-and-ink drawings throughout are designed to encourage readers to add and create their own individual changes to cartoon figures." SLJ

741.2   Techniques, procedures, apparatus, equipment, materials

Emberley, Ed

Ed Emberley's big green drawing book. Little, Brown 1979 91p il hardcover o.p. pa $10.99
Grades: 2 3 4 5   **741.2**
1. Drawing
ISBN 0-316-23596-2 pa

                     LC 79-16247

The author "combines basic shapes (circles, triangles, lines, squiggles) to create a variety of cartoon people and animals. The crisp green-and-black illustrations on a white background are large and well spaced. . . . As in his other drawing books, Emberley's wordless step-by-step method is easy to follow; even very young children can successfully reproduce the simple but appealing figures." SLJ

Ed Emberley's big red drawing book. Little, Brown 1987 un il hardcover o.p. pa $10.99
Grades: 2 3 4 5   **741.2**
1. Drawing
ISBN 0-316-23435-4 pa

                     LC 87-3091

The author explains "how to create objects and figures by building up a series of simple lines and squiggles into a more complicated and complete whole. The color red suggests most of the subjects, among them a U.S. flag, a fire engine, and assorted red-and-green Christmas items." Booklist

Ed Emberley's drawing book: make a world. Little, Brown 1972 un il hardcover o.p. pa $6.99
Grades: 2 3 4 5   **741.2**
1. Drawing
ISBN 0-316-78972-0 pa

"The final three pages, which supply suggestions for making comic strips, posters, mobiles and games, help make the volume particularly appealing. For all developing artists and even plain scribblers." Horn Book

★ **Ed** Emberley's fingerprint drawing book. Little, Brown 2000 un il hardcover o.p. pa $7.99

Grades: 2 3 4 5   **741.2**
1. Drawing
ISBN 0-316-23215-7; 0-316-78969-0 pa

                     LC 00-31026

"A step-by-step approach to drawing for beginners and those who are artistically challenged. Each figure introduced can be made with a basic fingerprint or more, and then lines and dots are placed beneath the form to take budding artists to a complete picture. It is so easy to do that even very young children can enjoy a simple art adventure." SLJ

Ed Emberley's great thumbprint drawing book. Little, Brown 1977 37p il lib bdg $15.95; pa $6.95
Grades: 2 3 4 5   **741.2**
1. Drawing
ISBN 0-316-23613-6 lib bdg; 0-316-23668-3 pa

                     LC 76-57346

"There is little text; most of the book consists of illustrations, step-by-step, of making pictures out of thumbprints. A few Emberley embellishments and a page that suggests other ways of making prints (carrot or potato) are included." Bull Cent Child Books

Hanson, Anders

Cool drawing; the art of creativity for kids! [by] Anders Hanson. ABDO Pub. Co. 2009 32p il (Cool art) lib bdg $24.21
Grades: 2 3 4   **741.2**
1. Drawing
ISBN 978-1-60453-142-8 lib bdg; 1-60453-142-8 lib bdg

                     LC 2008-8642

This book about drawing is "well organized, with clearly written sections . . . and several clever projects and exercises. . . . [It] should have substantial child appeal." SLJ

Includes glossary and bibliographical references

Temple, Kathryn

★ **Drawing**; the only drawing book you'll ever need to be the artist you've always wanted to be. [by] Kathryn Temple. Lark Books 2005 112p il (Art for kids) $17.95
Grades: 5 6 7 8   **741.2**
1. Drawing
ISBN 1-57990-587-0

                     LC 2004-17909

This "introduction to essential drawing techniques builds from the starting points of lines and simple shapes. . . . Eight concise chapters explore seeing with artist's eyes, line drawing, light and shadow, proportion and scale, perspective, drawing faces, drawing bodies, and using imagination. The succinct text reads smoothly and is written in a clear, understandable style. Sample sketches and crisp, color photographs extend the text." SLJ

741.5   Cartoons, graphic novels, caricatures, comics

Abadzis, Nick

★ **Laika**. First Second Books 2007 205p il
Grades: 5 6 7 8 9 10 11 12 Adult   **741.5**
1. Graphic novels 2. Space flight -- Graphic novels 3. Soviet Union -- History -- 1953-1991 -- Graphic novels
ISBN 1-59643-101-6; 978-1-59643-101-0

                     LC 2006-51907

Laika was the abandoned puppy destined to become Earth's first space traveler. This is her journey. Along with Laika, there is Korolev, once a political prisoner and now a driven engineer at the top of the Soviet space program, and Yelena, the lab technician responsible for Laika's health and life. The book depicts the dedication and struggles of the scientists and technicians who worked in the Soviet space program, based on research Abadzis did before writing this book. The book includes a bibliography of books and websites.

"Abadzis's tear-inducing and solidly researched graphic novel treatment of Laika's surpassingly tragic story is a standout." Publ Wkly

Aguirre, Jorge

★ **Giants** beware! written by Jorge Aguirre; illustrated by Rafael Rosado. First Second 2012 202 p.

Grades: 3 4 5   **741.5**

1. Humorous graphic novels 2. Adventure graphic novels 3. Giants -- Graphic novels 4. Fairy tales -- Graphic novels 5. Fairy tales 6. Graphic novels

ISBN 1596435828; 9781596435827

LC 2011030471

In this children's graphic novel, "spunky Claudette is set on becoming a monster slayer like her father. . . . When she hears the story of a giant on the loose, she is determined to leave her home--accompanied by her cowardly brother, Gaston, and best friend Marie--in order to set things right. . . . When Claudette discovers that not all stories are as they seem, she and her friends must fool the adults who have come to bring them home to protect an innocent monster." (Publishers Weekly)

Followed by Dragons beware! (2015)

Arni, Samhita

★ **Sita's** Ramayana; Moyna Chitrakar, illustrator. Groundwood Books 2011 il $24.95

Grades: 5 6 7 8   **741.5**

1. Graphic novels 2. Ramayana 3. Hindu mythology -- Graphic novels

ISBN 978-1-55498-145-8; 1-55498-145-X

"The Ramayana is the story of the exiled prince Rama and his beautiful wife, Sita. When she is kidnapped by a love-struck demon king, her husband's efforts to rescue her result in a war that eventually involves not only demons and mortals, but also gods, monsters, and even animals. . . . Here, a Patua scroll painter has adapted it as a fast-paced, brilliantly bold graphic novel. All of the suspense, treachery, sorcery, and pathos of this epic is depicted in homemade natural dyes layered onto paper in energetic lines, rhythmic patterns, and fields of hot, bright colors. . . . This book would be a must-purchase based on the strength of its dramatic story and arresting art, enhanced by superior design and high-quality production. Brilliant and fresh." SLJ

Baldwin, Christopher

Little Dee and the penguin; by Christopher Baldwin. Dial Books for Young Readers 2016 128 p. color illustrations lib bdg $17.99; (pbk.) $10.99

Grades: 3 4 5 6   **741.5**

1. Animals -- Graphic novels 2. Friendship -- Graphic novels 3. Graphic novels 4. Humorous stories 5. Animals -- Fiction 6. Human-animal relationships -- Fiction

ISBN 9781101994290; 1101994290; 9780803741089

LC 2015010378

In this graphic novel, by Christopher Baldwin, "when Little Dee meets a motley crew of animals deep in the forest, she knows she's found the perfect set of new friends. Between the bossy vulture, the slightly dim dog, the nurturing bear, and the happy-go-lucky penguin, . . . they're a family. And they're on the run. A pair of hungry polar bears are after the penguin, and the rest of the team are determined to protect her." (Publisher's note)

"Baldwin's full-color illustrations appeal to all of the senses and keep the story moving--through travel by plane, raft, boat, and on foot, ahead of a pair of hungry polar bears all the way. A must-read for all would-be adventurers." Kirkus

Baltazar, Art

Billy Batson and the magic of Shazam!: Mr. Mind over matter; Art Baltazar & Franco, writers; Byron Vaughns, artist & covers; David Tanguay, colors; Steve Wands, Travis Lanham, letterers. DC Comics 2011 un il pa $12.99

Grades: 3 4 5   **741.5**

1. Graphic novels 2. Superhero graphic novels 3. Captain Marvel (Fictional character)

ISBN 978-1-4012-2993-1; 1-4012-2993-X

Eleven-year-old Billy Batson has been given an amazing gift: The magic word Shazam!, which transforms him into Captain Marvel and gives him incredible superpowers. In this volume, Billy and his superpowered sister, Mary Marvel, fight side by side (and, occasionally, with each other) in amazing adventures featuring the world's greatest villains.

"Baltazar has hit upon exactly the right note with stories that will appeal solidly to young readers. . . . He also bothers to write up to young readers rather than down, with resonant themes, strong emotional stakes, battles won through wit as well as strength, and a complex narrative that works on many levels." Booklist

Superman Family Adventures; Volume 1 by Art Baltazar and Franco Aureliani, illustrated by Art Baltazar. DC Comics 2013 128 p. chiefly color illustrations (Superman Family Adventures) pbk $12.99

Grades: 1 2 3   **741.5**

1. Superhero graphic novels 2. Graphic novels 3. Superheroes -- Comic books, strips, etc. 4. Superman (Fictitious character) -- Comic books, strips, etc.

ISBN 140124050X; 9781401240509

LC 2013009138

This graphic novel, by Art Baltazar and Franco, features superheroes such as "Superman, Superboy, Supergirl [and] Krypto the Superdog. The entire Superman family is re-imagined here in this energetic all-ages graphic novel. Read on as the heroes of Metropolis fight foes such as Bizarro, Metallo, Lex Luthor and...giant monkeys." (Publisher's note)

"Adult readers will get a kick out of the clever homage to their favorite superhero, and kids will be powerless to resist the silly playfulness; colorful animated characters; and easy-to-follow, superpower-packed stories." Booklist

Followed by: Volume 2 (2014)

Tiny Titans: welcome to the treehouse. DC Comics 2009 144p il $12.99

Grades: K 1 2 3   **741.5**

1. Graphic novels 2. Humorous graphic novels 3. Superhero graphic novels 4. Teen Titans (Fictional characters)

ISBN 978-1-4012-2078-5

Eisner Award: Best Publication for Kids (2009)

Eisner Award: Best Publication for Kids (2011)

Here are the Teen Titans as never seen before: as little kids. They all attend Sidekick City Elementary School, where their principal and teachers are supervillains, and they get into playground showdowns with the Fearsome Five. Baltazar and Franco, who have created such characters as Patrick the Wolf Boy, present a series of short stories, most one or two pages long, featuring little kid versions of Robin, Starfire, Wonder Girl, Cassie, Speedy, Kid Flash, Cyborg, Beast Boy, Raven, and more. While these stories are written for the young readers, the humor may also appeal to teens and adults.

Other titles in this series are:

Tiny Titans: adventures in awesomeness (2009)

Tiny Titans: sidekickin' it (2010)

Tiny Titans: the first rule of pet club (2010)

Tiny Titans: field trippin' (2011)

Tiny Titans: the treehouse and beyond! (2011)

Tiny Titans: growing up tiny! (2012)

Tiny Titans: aw yeah Titans! (2013)

Tiny Titans: return to the treehouse (2015)

Bell, Cece

★ **El** deafo; Cece Bell; color by David Lasky. Abrams Books 2014 233 p. color illustrations $21.95

Grades: 3 4 5 6 7   **741.5**

1. Deaf children 2. Autobiographical graphic novels 3. Schools 4. Friendship 5. Hearing aids for children

ISBN 1419710206; 9781419710209

               LC 2013955590

Newbery Honor Book (2015)

Eisner Award: Best Publication for Kids (2015)

"In this . . . . graphic novel memoir, author/illustrator Cece Bell chronicles her hearing loss at a young age and her subsequent experiences with the Phonic Ear, a very powerful--and very awkward--hearing aid. The Phonic Ear gives Cece the ability to hear--sometimes things she shouldn't--but also isolates her from her classmates." (Publisher's note)

"Bell's bold and blocky full-color cartoons perfectly complement her childhood stories--she often struggles to fit in and sometimes experiences bullying, but the cheerful illustrations promise a sunny future." Booklist

Bendis, Brian Michael

Takio; vol. 2 Brian Michael Bendis, illustrated by Michael Avon Oeming. Marvel Enterprises 2013 96 p. col. ill. hbk $16.99

Grades: 5 6 7 8   **741.5**

1. Graphic novels 2. Sisters -- Fiction

ISBN 0785165533; 9780785165538

"Taki and Olivia are sisters with super-powers! In fact, they are the only ones in the world with super-powers! So obviously, they have to become super heroes! But is the world ready for real-life super heroes? Are the girls ready for the challenge? And will the accident that made them who they are reveal secrets that will change their lives forever?" (Publisher's note)

"Taki and Olivia face down danger in this bright, colorful, action-heavy series, which is unconventionally (and refreshingly) girl-focused." Booklist

Takio, vol. 1. Marvel Icon 2011 un il $9.95

Grades: 5 6 7 8   **741.5**

1. Graphic novels 2. Superhero graphic novels 3. Sisters -- Graphic novels

ISBN 978-0-7851-5326-9; 0-7851-5326-8

"This entertaining graphic novel features a crunchy and kinetic art style, quick pacing, realistic dialogue, and enough action to appeal to most middle-school readers." Booklist

Big fat Little Lit; [edited by] Art Spiegelman and Francoise Mouly. Puffin 2006 144p il pa $14.99

Grades: 2 3 4 5 6 7 8   **741.5**

1. Graphic novels 2. Folklore -- Graphic novels

ISBN 0-14-240706-2

This volume collects all three previously published Little Lit books: Little Lit: Once Upon a Time, Little Lit: Strange Stories for Strange Kids, and Little Lit: It Was a Dark and Silly Night. Many comics creators and children's book writers and illustrators contributed stories, including Ian Falconer, Daniel Clowes, Maurice Sendak, David Sedaris, Chris Ware, Jules Feiffer, Barbara McClintock, Crockett Johnson, J. Otto Siebold, Neil Gaiman, Art Spiegelman, and Lemony Snicket.

Bliss, Harry

★ **Luke** on the loose; a Toon Book. TOON Books 2009 32p il map $12.95

Grades: PreK K 1 2   **741.5**

1. Graphic novels 2. Humorous graphic novels 3. New York (State) -- Graphic novels

ISBN 978-1-935179-00-9; 1-935179-00-4

               LC 2008-35699

A young boy's fascination with pigeons soon erupts into a full-blown chase around Central Park, across the Brooklyn Bridge, through a fancy restaurant, and into the sky

"The cartoon panels are so successful at engaging readers that young children do not have to be able to read the text to enjoy the story. Each drawing is filled with humorous details." SLJ

Bouchard, Hervé

Harvey; how I became invisible. [by] Hervé Bouchard and Janice Nadeau; translated by Helen Mixter. Groundwood Books/House of Anansi Press 2010 un il $19.95

Grades: 5 6 7 8   **741.5**

1. Graphic novels 2. Death -- Fiction 3. Fathers -- Fiction 4. Bereavement -- Fiction 5. Family life -- Fiction

ISBN 978-1-55498-075-8; 1-55498-075-5

Original French edition 2009

"This open-ended book is deserving of discussion, difficult though it may be." Booklist

Brallier, Max

★ The **last** kids on Earth; by Max Brallier; illustrated by Doug Holgate. Viking 2015 240 p. chiefly illustrations (hardback) $13.99

Grades: 3 4 5 6   **741.5**

1. Humorous graphic novels 2. Monsters -- Graphic novels 3. Apocalyptic fiction -- Juvenile fiction 4. Humorous stories 5. Monsters -- Fiction 6. Survival -- Fiction

ISBN 0670016616; 9780670016617

               LC 2015013012

In this graphic novel, by Max Brallier, illustrated by Doug Holgate, "ever since the monster apocalypse hit town, average thirteen year old Jack Sullivan has been living in his tree house. . . . But Jack alone is no match for the . . . eerily intelligent monster known only as Blarg. So Jack builds a team. . . . With their help, Jack is going to slay Blarg, achieve the ultimate Feat of Apocalyptic Success, and be average no longer!" (Publisher's note)

"A gross-out good time with surprisingly nuanced character development." SLJ

Another title in this series is:

The last kids on Earth and the zombie parade (2016)

Brown, Jeffrey

★ **Star** Wars; Jedi Academy. Jeffrey Brown; [edited by] Rex Ogle. Scholastic, Inc 2013 160 p. illustrations (Star Wars: Jedi Academy) (paper over board) $12.99

Grades: 3 4 5 6 7   **741.5**

1. Outer space -- Fiction 2. Middle schools -- Fiction 3. Star Wars -- Comic books, strips, etc.

ISBN 0545505178; 9780545505178; 9780545609999

               LC 2013931939

In this book, by Jeffrey Brown, "Roan Novachez thought he was destined to attend Pilot Academy Middle School, just as his older brother and father did. His dreams are crushed when he is rejected by Pilot Academy and accepted into a sketchy new school called Coruscant Jedi Academy. . . . Confused and struggling to keep up, Roan tries to fly under the radar and passes the time drawing comics of his daily life at his strange boarding school." (Booklist)

"While it might be disappointing for those familiar with this world to see scant representation of beloved characters, it makes the book an easy starting point for new fans. There are plenty of references to other elements (the T-16 Skyhopper and Jedi training remotes, for example) for diehards to get excited about." SLJ

Other titles in this series are:
Return of the Padawan (2014)
The Phantom Bully (2015)

Cammuso, Frank
Knights of the lunch table: the battling bands. Graphix 2011 127p pa $10.99
Grades: 3 4 5 6   **741.5**
1. Graphic novels 2. Humorous graphic novels 3. Schools -- Graphic novels 4. Rock music -- Graphic novels
ISBN 978-0-439-90318-9; 0-439-90318-1
Sequel to: Knights of the lunch table: the dragon players (2009)
Artie, Wayne, and Percy enter the talent show at Camelot Middle School in a rock music band.

Knights of the lunch table: the dodgeball chronicles. Graphix 2008 141p pa $9.99
Grades: 3 4 5 6   **741.5**
1. Graphic novels 2. Humorous graphic novels 3. School stories -- Graphic novels
ISBN 978-0-439-90322-6 pa; 0-439-90322-X pa
Artie King's family has moved and now he has to start at a new school, Camelot Middle School. Dodgeball is the big game at Camelot, and the Horde is a champion team; the Horde members are also the worst bullies in the school. . . . Artie immediately gets into trouble with Joe, the leader of the Horde. . . . However, he manages to open the broken old locker . . . [which] provides mysterious, useful stuff, such as a lunch. Joe challenges Artie to a dodgeball game; Artie has new friends Percy and Wayne who'll help him, and then he meets Gwen. And science teacher Mr. Merlyn is also on his side.
"Arthurian legend gets an update for young readers in this outstanding graphic novel. . . . The funny, fast-paced tale of young Arthur's quest to defeat the bullies stands well on its own. The appealing illustrations are full of color, action, and life." SLJ
Followed by: Knights of the lunch table: the dragon players (2009)

Knights of the lunch table: the dragon players. Scholastic/Graphix 2009 127p pa $9.99
Grades: 3 4 5 6   **741.5**
1. Graphic novels 2. Humorous graphic novels 3. Schools -- Graphic novels 4. Contests -- Graphic novels 5. Conduct of life -- Graphic novels 6. Arthurian romances -- Adaptations -- Graphic novels
ISBN 978-0-439-90323-3 pa; 0-439-90323-8 pa
LC 2008-51463
Sequel to: Knights of the lunch table: the dodgeball chronicles (2008)
Artie King may have won the dodgeball game against the school bullies, but life is not easy. The new challenge comes with the dueling robot tournament at school; it's all part of Dragon Day, and The Horde has won every year by cheating—they force the smartest kid in school to design and build their robot. This year, they've done it to Percy. Circumstances force Artie's hand and willy nilly, he has entered the tournament. Seeking an edge, they go to Evo, a mysterious techno wiz kid who can build any gadget; the problem for Artie is, is he cheating by getting help from Evo? Cammuso's bright, cartoony art and schoolyard version of Arthurian legend provides lots of fun action as well as making readers think about ethics
Followed by: Knights of the lunch table: the battling bands (2011)

Otto's backwards day; a Toon book. by Frank Cammuso with Jay Lynch. Toon Books, is an imprint of Candlewick Press 2013 32 p. (reinforced) $12.95
Grades: K 1 2   **741.5**
1. Cats -- Fiction 2. Humorous fiction 3. Birthdays -- Fiction 4. Graphic novels 5. Humorous stories
ISBN 1935179330; 9781935179337
LC 2012047661
Eisner Nominee: Best Publication for Early Readers (2014)
"Someone stole Otto's birthday! When Otto and his robot sidekick, Toot, follow the crook, they discover a topsy-turvy world where rats chase cats and people wear underpants over their clothes. To get his presents back, Otto needs to solve a slew of backwards puzzles--but his greatest challenge comes at the journey's very end. On this special day, will Otto discover something even better than cake or gifts?" (Publisher's note)

★ **Otto's** orange day; a Toon Book. by Frank Cammuso [art] & Jay Lynch [story] TOON Books 2008 40p il $12.95
Grades: K 1 2   **741.5**
1. Graphic novels 2. Cats -- Graphic novels 3. Color -- Graphic novels 4. Magic -- Graphic novels
ISBN 978-0-9799238-2-1; 0-9799238-2-4
LC 2007040759
"This is a text-book example of how to use page composition, expanding panel size, color, and stylized figures to make sequential art fresh, energetic, and lively." Booklist

Camper, Cathy
Lowriders in space; book 1 by Cathy Camper; illustrated by Raul Gonzalez III. Chronicle Books 2014 112 p. chiefly color illustrations (Lowriders) hc $22.99
Grades: 4 5 6 7 8   **741.5**
1. Space vehicles 2. Mechanics (Persons) 3. Automobiles -- Fiction 4. Graphic novels 5. Lowriders -- Fiction 6. Friendship -- Fiction 7. Mexican Americans -- Fiction 8. Competition (Psychology) -- Fiction 9. Lowriders -- Comic books, strips, etc
ISBN 9781452121550; 1452121559
LC 2013040709
Cathy Camper "introduces readers to Lupe Impala, Flapjack Octopus, and Elirio Malaria, three friends who love working with cars and dream of having their own garage shop. One day they see an opportunity to achieve their goal--a car competition. When they start working on a lowrider to prepare it for the competition, an out-of-this world journey begins." (School Library Journal)
"Raúl's snazzy panels--impressively drawn in only red, blue, and black ballpoint pen on tea-stained paper--resemble an amped-up Mighty Mouse cartoon rendered in anarchic yet skillful doodles. It's a joyfully explosive style, and it perfectly matches the Latino characters and barrio setting." Booklist
Another title in this series is:
Lowriders to the center of the Earth (2016)

Lowriders to the center of the Earth; by Cathy Camper; illustrated by Raul the Third. Chronicle Books 2016 128 p. chiefly color illustrations hbk $22.99
Grades: 4 5 6 7 8   **741.5**
1. Cats -- Graphic novels 2. Automobiles -- Graphic novels 3. Mexican Americans -- Graphic novels 4. Gods and goddesses -- Graphic novels 5. Lowriders -- Juvenile fiction 6. Aztec gods -- Comic books, strips, etc
ISBN 1452138362; 9781452123431; 9781452138367; 1452123438
LC 2015021996

Pura Belpré Illustrator Award (2017)

"Lupe Impala, Elirio Malaria, and El Chavo Octopus are living their dream at last. They're the proud owners of their very own garage. But when their beloved cat Genie goes missing, they need to do everything they can to find him. Little do they know the trail will lead them to the realm of Mictlantecuhtli, the Aztec god of the Underworld, who is keeping Genie prisoner!" (Publisher's note)

"Raúl the Third's ultradetailed crosshatched artwork more than meets the demands of this cast-of-thousands comic opus." Kirkus

Casty

Walt Disney's Mickey Mouse and the world to come. Boom Kids! 2010 un il pa $9.99
Grades: 3 4 5 6   **741.5**
1. Graphic novels 2. Science fiction graphic novels 3. Mickey Mouse (Cartoon character)
ISBN 978-1-60886-562-8; 1-60886-562-2

Mickey Mouse and his friend from the future Eega Beeva take an amazing journey into the future.

"Disney fans, both children and adults, will enjoy [this] graphic [novel]." SLJ

Cavallaro, Michael

L. Frank Baum's The Wizard of Oz; the graphic novel. Puffin Books 2005 176p pa $9.99
Grades: 3 4 5 6 7 8   **741.5**
1. Oz (Imaginary place) 2. Fantasy graphic novels
ISBN 0-14-240471-3

LC 2006-273599

This graphic novel adaptation remains true to the story by Baum: Dorothy and her dog Toto are whisked to Oz, where they meet the Tin Woodsman, the Cowardly Lion, and the Scarecrow and they all journey to find the Wizard to grant their desires.

"The black-and-white illustrations are action packed, and the characters, with their Bazooka Joe eyes, combine classic comic touches with the popular manga style. Reluctant readers will gravitate toward the cartoon cover." SLJ

Chad, Jon

Leo Geo and the cosmic crisis; Matt Data and the cosmic crisis. Jon Chad. Roaring Brook Press 2013 40 p. chiefly color illustrations (hardcover) $16.99
Grades: 2 3 4 5   **741.5**
1. Astronomy 2. Graphic novels 3. Magic -- Fiction 4. Astronauts -- Fiction 5. Space flight -- Fiction 6. Adventure and adventurers -- Fiction
ISBN 1596438223; 9781596438224

LC 2013001296

Sequel to Leo Geo and His Miraculous Journey through the Center of the Earth (2012)

In this 2-in-1 book, "[Leo Geo] and his space-based scientist brother Matt Data trace looping paths through crowded spacescapes toward each other. Before they meet in the middle, both encounter black holes, white holes, wormholes, asteroids, space pirates and some distinctly more unusual 'space sights.'" (Kirkus Reviews)

"The bright, detailed, full-page panels are covered with strange creatures and planetary objects that will catch and hold young readers' attention, and the scientific information is simply presented and well-integrated into the dialogue. The varied layout of the pages, vertical and horizontal, and the 'search engine,' a hunt for specific objects throughout the book, encourage engagement with the story." SLJ

Chantler, Scott

The **iron** hand; Scott Chantler. Kids Can Press 2016 126 p. color illustrations (Three thieves) $16.95
Grades: 3 4 5 6   **741.5**
1. Adventure fiction 2. Orphans -- Graphic novels 3. Knights and knighthood -- Graphic novels
ISBN 1771380527; 9781771380522

LC 2016032329

In this conclusion to the Three Thieves series, by Scott Chantler, "now that Dessa has learned the truth about her past, she agrees to form an alliance with the badly injured Captain Drake against Greyfalcon. The pair travel together to the royal city to rescue Dessa's twin brother, Jared, from Greyfalcon's evil clutches and put Jared in his rightful place on the throne. But their plans go awry when they arrive to find Jared already on the throne!" (Publisher's note)

"A well-wrought, well-timed, and satisfying finale to this well-conceived series." Kirkus

Tower of treasure. Kids Can Press 2010 112p il (Three thieves) $17.99; pa $8.95
Grades: 3 4 5 6   **741.5**
1. Graphic novels 2. Adventure graphic novels 3. Circus -- Fiction 4. Thieves -- Fiction 5. Acrobats and acrobatics -- Fiction
ISBN 978-1-55453-414-2; 1-55453-414-3; 978-1-55453-415-9 pa; 1-55453-415-1 pa

"As an acrobat in a traveling circus, 14-year-old orphan Dessa Redd flies through the air with ease. Still, she is weighed down by troubling memories. But when her ragtag circus troupe pulls into the city of Kingsbridge, Dessa feels a tickle of hope. Maybe here in the royal city she will finally find her twin brother--or the mysterious man who snatched him away when they were just children. Meanwhile, Topper, the circus juggler, recruits Dessa and the circus strongman, Fisk, for the job of robbing the royal treasury." (Publisher's note)

"Young gymnast Dessa, searching for her kidnapped twin brother, joins two fellow circus performers in an attempted heist, a prison escape and a merry chase through and out of the fortress of Kingsbridge. . . . Artfully using exchanged glances and wordless panels to add both humor and emotional depth, Chantler introduces a likable trio of thieves in a medieval-ish setting. . . . The banter among the three is sharp and witty and balances the visual pacing effortlessly. Fast paced, cleanly illustrated, great fun." Kirkus

Other titles in this series are:
The sign of the black rock (2011)
The captive prince (2012)
The king's dragon (2014)
Pirates of the silver coast (2014)
The dark island (2016)
The iron hand (2016)

Chwast, Seymour

The **odyssey**; adapted by Tim Mucci, writer; Ben Caldwell, Rick Lacy, pencils; Emanuel Tenderini, colors. 1st U.S. ed. Sterling 2010 128 p. color illustrations (All-action classics) $7.95
Grades: 5 6 7 8   **741.5**
1. Epic literature 2. Adventure graphic novels 3. Odysseus (Greek mythology) 4. Graphic novels 5. Greek mythology -- Graphic novels
ISBN 1402731558; 9781402731556

LC 2012010047

In this graphic retelling of Homer's "The Odyssey," "Odysseus faces storm and shipwreck, a terrifying man-eating Cyclops, the alluring but deadly Sirens, and the fury of the sea-god Poseidon as he makes his ten-year journey home from the Trojan War. While Odysseus struggles to make it home, his wife, Penelope, fights a different kind of battle as her palace is invaded by forceful, greedy men who tell her that Odysseus is dead and she must choose a new husband." (Publisher's note)

This graphic novel adaptation of Homer's classic epic is "a crackling adventure that also penetrates the recesses of the human heart. . . . Caldwell's art has the force and vibrant life of a Samurai Jack cartoon." Booklist

Clanton, Ben

Narwhal; Unicorn of the Sea. Ben Clanton. McClelland & Stewart Ltd 2016 64 p. color illustrations (Narwhal and Jelly) $12.99
Grades: 1 2 3   741.5
1. Narwhal -- Fiction 2. Friendship 3. Jellyfishes -- Fiction
ISBN 1101918268; 9781101918265
                                                    LC 2016042380
"Narwhal is a happy-go-lucky narwhal. Jelly is a no-nonsense jellyfish. The two might not have a lot in common, but they do they love waffles, parties and adventures. Join Narwhal and Jelly as they discover the whole wide ocean together." (Publisher's note)

"The incessant charm and unabashed joy should make this an easy sell. Swimmingly delightful and a guaranteed smile-maker." Kirkus
Another title in this series is:
Super Narwhal and Jelly Jolt (2017)

Colfer, Eoin

★ Artemis Fowl: the graphic novel; adapted by Eoin Colfer and Andrew Donkin; art by Giovanni Rigano; color by Paolo Lammana. Hyperion Books for Children 2007 un il $18.99; pa $9.99
Grades: 4 5 6 7 8 9   741.5
1. Graphic novels 2. Fantasy graphic novels 3. Adventure graphic novels
ISBN 978-0-7868-4881-2; 0-7868-4881-2; 978-0-7868-4882-9 pa; 0-7868-4882-0 pa
Twelve-year-old genius and criminal mastermind Artemis Fowl runs his missing father's crime empire and gets his hands on a book that will give him access to the underground fairy world. This graphic novel adaptation gives the book a European look and color palette

"Excellent use of color and shading gives the panels a tremendous sense of light with enchanting effect. Characters are expressively brought to life with fun, exaggerated style." SLJ
Other Artemis Fowl graphic novels are:
Artemis Fowl: the Arctic incident (2009)
Artemis Fowl: the eternity code (2013)
Artemis Fowl: the opal deception (2014)

Collar, Orpheus

The red pyramid; the graphic novel. Rick Riordan; adapted by Orpheus Collar; lettered by Jared Fletcher. Disney/Hyperion Books 2012 un chiefly color illustrations (The Kane chronicles) pbk $12.99; hbk $21.99
Grades: 4 5 6 7 8 9   741.5
1. Magic -- Fiction 2. Egyptian mythology -- Fiction 3. Brothers and sisters -- Fiction
ISBN 1423150694; 1423150686; 9781423150695; 9781423150688
                                                    LC 2012007905
"Since their mother's death, Sadie and Carter have become near-strangers. While Sadie has lived with her grandparents in London, Carter has traveled the world with their father, the famed Egyptologist Dr. Julius Kane. One night, Dr. Kane brings the siblings to the British Museum, where he hopes to set things right for his family. Instead, he unleashes the Egyptian god Set, who banishes him to oblivion and forces the children to flee for their lives." (Publisher's note)

"Out of necessity, much of the dialogue is dedicated to explaining actions and events, but a constant stream of humor prevents the reader

from getting bogged down by logistics. The colorful artwork has an almost painting-like quality, . . . and some clever visual jokes and thoughtful use of panels make good use of the format." VOYA

Collicutt, Paul

City in peril! Templar Books/Candlewick Press 2009 un il (Robot City) pa $8.99
Grades: 3 4 5   741.5
1. Graphic novels 2. Mystery graphic novels 3. Science fiction graphic novels 4. Robots -- Graphic novels
ISBN 978-0-7636-4120-7 pa; 0-7636-4120-0 pa
                                                    LC 2009-931660
In Robot City, a metropolis of 15 million humans and 1 million robots, Curtis, the Colossal CoastGuard Robot works as part of a team of robots and humans to keep the Robot City Bay safe. In the middle of the night, the Red Star oil rig sends out a desperate distress call when something attacks it in the middle of a storm. Curtis, who looks like a light house on huge, long legs, helps to save the crew on the oil rig, but there's something out there in the ocean, and it means to attack Robot City. He has suffered damage in one of his legs, but Curtis knows he has to stop the menace. This science fiction adventure is full of action and derring-do with colorful retro-style comic book illustrations. Young readers, as well as adults, will appreciate the twist in the story.

"Curtis is a walking, talking lighthouseheaded robot who protects the coast of Robot City with his trusty human crew, Ali and Steve. When an oil rig out at sea catches fire, Curtis rushes to the rescue and then investigates the fishy mystery of the causes of this near disaster. . . . The illustrations . . . are full of retro-comicbook-style action and classic movieserial banter." Kirkus

Comics Squad; recess! comics by Jarrett J. Krosoczka, Gene Yang, Eric Wight, Jennifer L. Holm and Matthew Holm, Ursula Vernon, Dan Santat, Raina Telgemeier and Dave Roman, Dav Pilkey; edited by Jennifer L. Holm, Matthew Holm, and Jarrett J. Krosoczka. Random House Inc. 2014 144 p. ill. (chiefly col.) (trade paperback) $7.99; (library binding) $12.99
Grades: 2 3 4 5 6   741.5
1. School stories 2. Comic books, strips, etc. 3. Short stories 4. Graphic novels 5. Humorous stories 6. Recess -- Fiction 7. Schools -- Fiction
ISBN 0385370032; 9780385370035; 9780385370042
                                                    LC 2013035223
"An all-star lineup of graphic novel notables contributes original works to this anthology, sharing the common thread of recess." (School Library Journal)

"[T]his lively, upbeat and all-around-awesome offering is consistently convivial and laugh-out-loud funny from cover to cover." Kirkus
Another title in this series is:
Lunch! (2016)

Conway, Gerry

Crawling with zombies; Gerry Conway, writer; Paulo Henrique, artist; based on the series by Franklin W. Dixon. Papercutz 2010 un il (The Hardy Boys: the new case files) $10.99; pa $6.99
Grades: 4 5 6 7   741.5
1. Graphic novels 2. Mystery graphic novels 3. Zombies -- Graphic novels 4. Brothers -- Graphic novels
ISBN 978-1-59707-219-9; 1-59707-219-2; 978-1-59707-220-5 pa; 1-59707-220-6 pa
"This mix of the Hardy Boys with zombies is . . . a fast-paced story that should entice reluctant readers. Frank and Joe race motorcycles, communicate with ATAC (American Teens Against Crime), and try to solve the mystery of why teenagers who've been participating in flash mob stunts called 'zombie crawls' (because they dress and act like zom-

bies) have started losing control of themselves in a decidedly zombielike way. The book is a simple page-turner. . . . Henrique's artwork is colorful, shiny, and bright, a pleasing mix of traditional American cartoon and Japanese manga styles." SLJ

Coudray, Philippe

★ **Benjamin** Bear in "Bright ideas!" a Toon book. by Philippe Coudray. Toon Books 2013 32 p. $12.95

Grades: PreK K 1　　　　　　　　　　　　　　**741.5**

　　1. Animals -- Graphic novels　2. Picture books for children　3. Graphic novels　4. Bears -- Fiction　5. Humorous stories

　　ISBN 1935179225; 9781935179221

　　　　　　　　　　　　　　　　　LC 2012022895

This children's picture book is part of the Benjamin Bear series, where the bear and his animal friends appear in minimalist fables drawn . . . from French cartoonist [Philippe] Coudray's original series. . . . In 'Can I Get a Ride?' [Benjamin] picks up one woodland hitchhiker after another until, in the last panel, tables turn and they have to carry him. In 'See-Saw,' he 'helps' a fox carry a log (and demonstrates a principle of physics) not by lifting the long end, but by hopping onto the short end." (Kirkus)

Benjamin Bear in Fuzzy thinking; a Toon book. Toon Books 2011 32p il $12.99

Grades: PreK K 1 2　　　　　　　　　　　　　**741.5**

　　1. Graphic novels　2. Humorous graphic novels　3. Bears -- Graphic novels

　　ISBN 978-1-935179-12-2; 1-935179-12-8

　　　　　　　　　　　　　　　　　LC 2011000801

"The latest entry in the TOON Books line of emerging-reader comics pushes a whole new sort of envelope: outré humor for the early grade-school set. These single-page strips starring a peculiar bear and his critter pals will feel fresh to young readers not just because the jokes rely on incisive understatement rather than broad-stroke exaggeration but also because the humor requires a bit of work to arrive at the surprising, sometimes sophisticated, and yet rarely out-of-reach punch lines." (Booklist)

"Coudray's droll vignettes in a muted palette will be the perfect enticement for those with a visual sense of humor who are just starting to read." Kirkus

　　Other titles in this series are:
　　Benjamin Bear in Bright Ideas (2013)
　　Benjamin Bear in Brain Storms (2015)

Craddock, Erik

BC mambo. Random House Children's Books 2009 95p il (Stone rabbit) lib bdg $11.99; pa $5.99

Grades: 2 3 4 5　　　　　　　　　　　　　　**741.5**

　　1. Graphic novels　2. Rabbits -- Graphic novels

　　ISBN 9780375939228; 9780375843600

　　　　　　　　　　　　　　　　　LC 2008-00681

After Stone Rabbit is transported back to prehistoric times, his bottle of barbecue sauce becomes the key ingredient in a power-hungry Neanderthal's plan to dominate the world

Craddock "brings a brightly colored, zany cartoon quality to the story and art, with the hero rabbit falling into one peril after another. The proposed fast-food empire is just the kind of plot that young readers can follow; reading this book is just as fun as watching Saturday morning cartoons." Booklist

　　Other titles in this series are:
　　Pirate palooza (2009)
　　Deep-space disco (2009)
　　Superhero stampede (2010)
　　Ninja slice (2010)

Night of the living dust bunnies (2011)
Dragon boogie (2012)
Robot frenzy (2013)

Crane, Jordan

The **clouds** above. Fantagraphics 2005 216p il $18.95

Grades: 3 4 5 6 7 8　　　　　　　　　　　　**741.5**

　　1. Graphic novels　2. Fantasy graphic novels

　　ISBN 1-560976-27-6

Simon and his cat Jack embark on an adventure among the clouds one day when Simon skips school and finds a rickety stairway leading skyward. They find a friendly cloud, flee thunderstorms and trick a flock of belligerent birds, only to find themselves back at school.

"Everything's exciting . . . and the dialogue is witty and bubbly. . . . The book is a joy to look at—Crane's loose, gliding lines burst with character, and his compositional gifts make every panel worth contemplating on its own." Publ Wkly

Dauvillier, Loic

Hidden; a child's story of the Holocaust. written by Loic Dauvillier; illustrated by Marc Lizano; color by Greg Salsedo; translated by Alexis Siegel. First Second 2014 80 p. chiefly color illustrations (hardback) $16.99

Grades: 1 2 3 4 5　　　　　　　　　　　　　**741.5**

　　1. Holocaust, 1939-1945 -- Fiction　2. Graphic novels　3. Grandmothers -- Fiction　4. Jews -- France -- Fiction　5. France -- History -- German occupation, 1940-1945 -- Fiction

　　ISBN 1596438738; 9781596438736

　　　　　　　　　　　　　　　　　LC 2013023168

Mildred L. Batchelder Honor Book (2015)

"Dounia, a grandmother, tells her granddaughter the story even her son has never heard: how, as a young Jewish girl in Paris, she was hidden away from the Nazis by a series of neighbors and friends who risked their lives to keep her alive when her parents had been taken to concentration camps." (Publisher's note)

"Lizano's stylized illustrations depict characters with oversize heads, reminiscent of 'Peanuts' comics, giving this difficult subject an age-appropriate touch." SLJ

Davis, Eleanor

★ The **secret** science alliance and the copycat crook. Bloomsbury 2009 153p il $18.99; pa $10.99

Grades: 3 4 5 6 7 8　　　　　　　　　　　　**741.5**

　　1. Graphic novels　2. School stories　3. Humorous graphic novels　4. Adventure graphic novels　5. Inventors -- Fiction

　　ISBN 978-1-59990-142-8; 1-59990-142-0; 978-1-59990-396-5 pa; 1-59990-396-2 pa

　　　　　　　　　　　　　　　　　LC 2008-45399

Eleven-year-old Julian Calendar thought changing schools would mean leaving his "nerdy" persona behind, but instead he forms an alliance with fellow inventors Greta and Ben and works with them to prevent an adult from using one of their gadgets for nefarious purposes

"With its frenetically eye-catching, full-color panels chock-full of humorous and informative detail, Davis's first (of many, one hopes) graphic adventure of the SSA pumps new life into the kids' secret society formula." Kirkus

★ **Stinky**; a Toon Book. RAW Junior 2008 40p il $12.95

Grades: K 1 2 3　　　　　　　　　　　　　　**741.5**

　　1. Graphic novels　2. Humorous graphic novels　3. Monsters -- Graphic novels　4. Friendship -- Graphic novels

　　ISBN 978-0-9799238-4-5; 0-9799238-4-0

　　　　　　　　　　　　　　　　　LC 2007-94387

A Geisel Award honor book, 2009

Stinky the monster is sort of a young Shrek—a little grumpy, he loves pickles and likes his swamp nicely yucky and mucky, with no kids. Kids are gross, they like to take baths. When a new boy dares to build a treehouse in the middle of his swamp, Stinky takes action with all kinds of crazy plans to scare the boy away. However, every plan backfires, so what's a monster to do?

"The charming cartoon artwork, full of humorous details, complements the text, and the muted color scheme makes Stinky endearing rather than scary. The simple vocabulary and repetition of words make the text accessible for emergent readers." SLJ

Dawson, Willow
Lila & Ecco's do-it-yourself comics club. Kids Can Press 2010 112p il $16.95
Grades: 4 5 6 7   741.5
1. Graphic novels 2. Cartoons and caricatures
ISBN 978-1-55453-438-8; 1-55453-438-0

Twelve-year-olds Lila and Ecco are obsessed with comics. Every summer, they dress up as their favorite characters to attend the local comic book convention. This year, after they stumble into a workshop of comics creators, Lila and Ecco come to an exciting realization they can make their very own comic books!.

"Is it a story of two friends creating a comic, or a step-by-step guide to making comics? Why, it's both, actually. And what's most surprising is not that the guide is so comprehensive and easy to follow but that the framing story not only couches the lessons in comfortable language but is also diverting in its own right. . . . Dawson's savvy, sassy black-and-white art gives the static idea of instructions some pep, and the information is quite complete." Booklist

Deas, Mike
Dalen & Gole; scandal in Port Angus. Orca Book Publishers 2011 123p il pa $9.95
Grades: 4 5 6 7   741.5
1. Graphic novels 2. Science fiction graphic novels 3. Extraterrestrial beings -- Graphic novels
ISBN 978-1-55469-800-4; 1-55469-800-6

Dalen and Gole, refugees on Earth from the distant planet of Budap, must solve the mystery of diminishing fish stocks and save their home planet from an evil plot.

Deas "provides solid graphics, pacing, dialogue, and humor. . . . A fun mystery-adventure that's just right for young space cases." Booklist

Deutsch, Barry
★ Hereville : how Mirka got her sword; colors by Jake Richmond. Amulet Books 2010 137p il $15.95
Grades: 4 5 6 7   741.5
1. Graphic novels 2. Fantasy graphic novels 3. Jews -- Graphic novels 4. Dragons -- Graphic novels
ISBN 978-0-8109-8422-6; 0-8109-8422-9

LC 2010-924236
Mirka and her family live in an Orthodox Jewish village called Hereville. All she really wants to do is fight dragons, but what she has to fight is a troublesome pig that talks. Then Mirka meets the witch who lives nearby, and then confronts a troll, and soon she finds she has much more adventure than she knows how to handle.

"Deutsch creates authentic characters spiced with just enough fantasy to surprise. . . . Details of Orthodox daily life are well blended into the art and given just the right touches of explanation to keep readers on track." Booklist

Other titles in this series are:
How Mirka met a meteorite (2012)
How Mirka caught a fish (2014)

Duffy, Chris
Fairy Tale Comics; Classic Tales Told by Extraordinary Cartoonists. compiled by Chris Duffy. First Second 2013 128 p. chiefly ill. (hardcover) $19.99
Grades: K 1 2 3 4 5   741.5
1. Dogs -- Graphic novels 2. Princesses -- Graphic novels 3. Fairy tales -- Graphic novels
ISBN 1596438231; 9781596438231

In this book, editor Chris Duffy "has assembled a . . . lineup of comics versions of more than a dozen fairy tales in this . . . follow-up to 'Nursery Rhyme Comics.' Favorites like 'The Twelve Dancing Princesses' and 'Rapunzel' (whose heroines gain significant agency) join rarities like 'The Small Tooth Dog' and 'The Boy Who Drew Cats.'" (Publishers Weekly)

"Every artist here knows how to turn in an elegant, flowing story, and every tale is pitch-perfect for young readers and intimate read-alouds. Overall, the book is an ideal choice for a child's first comics experience and a new way to enjoy old favorites." Booklist

★ Nursery rhyme comics; 50 timeless rhymes by 50 celebrated cartoonists. edited by Chris Duffy. First Second 2011 il $18.99
Grades: K 1 2 3 4 5   741.5
1. Graphic novels 2. Nursery rhymes
ISBN 978-1-59643-600-8; 1-59643-600-X

In this anthology, "classic nursery rhymes get a contemporary spin from artists as varied as the New Yorker's Roz Chast and Hellboy creator Mike Mignola. . . . In Dave Roman's 'One, Two, Buckle My Shoe,' the numbers in the title refer to tiny clones created by a wizard inventor." In "Lucy Kinsley's . . . 'There Was an Old Woman Who Lived in a Shoe' . . . the titular woman lives in a funky boot and runs Ruth's Rock & Rock Babysitting." (Publishers Weekly)

"No fewer than 50 cartoonists and comic-book artists provide distinctive visual riffs on as many nursery rhymes in this memorable showcase. . . . Visually far more complicated than the usual toddler-friendly nursery fare, this is best saved for older children. . . . As much as the visual styles may vary, the high levels of wit and invention never falter." Kirkus

DuPrau, Jeanne, 1944-
The city of Ember; the graphic novel. [an abridgment of the novel by] Jeanne DuPrau; adapted by Dallas Middaugh; art by Niklas Asker; color by Niklas Asker and Bo Ashi; lettering by Chris Dickey. 1st ed. Random House 2012 144 p. col. ill. (trade) $18.99
Grades: 4 5 6 7   741.5
1. Graphic novels 2. Science fiction 3. Apocalyptic fiction 4. Friendship -- Fiction 5. Fantasy
ISBN 0375868216; 9780307919100; 9780375867934; 9780375868214; 9780375968211

LC 2011051619
In this graphic novel adaptation, Lina and Doon live in darkness. "A chance encounter on Assignment Day allows the two children to . . . exchange jobs"; Doon can work underground and Lina as a messenger. "They start to unearth an evil plot by the city's . . . mayor to steal precious resources from the people who live there. Using clues left behind by Lina's late grandmother, they travel beneath Ember's tunnels in a desperate attempt to find a way out." (School Library Journal)

Eliopoulos, Chris
Okie Dokie Donuts; open for business! Top Shelf 2011 il $9.95
Grades: 1 2 3   741.5
1. Graphic novels 2. Baking -- Fiction 3. Robots -- Fiction
ISBN 978-1-603090-68-1; 1-603090-68-1

"Big Mama, proprietor of Okie Dokie Donuts, is so beloved and her donuts so coveted that she is regaled in rhyming song by her customers every morning. . . . Mr. Mayweather [is] a kitchen-appliance salesman. His new ware, Mr. Baker, is a doughnut-making robot that will streamline the workload and multiply the profits. . . . Young readers may well see what's coming . . . especially when Mr. Baker's ingredient slot is accidentally loaded with garbage, but that won't detract one iota from the fun. . . . Eliopoulos creates a confection of zaniness, from the breathless slapstick and the wild, blocky art right down to the childlike lettering that fills the speech balloons." Booklist

Espinosa, Rod

The **courageous** princess. Dark Horse Comics 2007 240p il pa $9.95

Grades: 3 4 5 6 7 8 9   741.5

1. Graphic novels 2. Fantasy graphic novels 3. Princesses -- Graphic novels

ISBN 978-1-59307-719-8

Plain Princess Mabelrose doesn't get along with the other, prettier princesses, but her intelligence helps her when a dragon kidnaps her. Instead of waiting for rescue, Mabelrose escapes, taking a friendly hedgehog and a few useful-looking items (a pouch, a length of rope) that she doesn't know are magic.

Explorer; the hidden doors. edited by Kazu Kibuishi. Abrams Books 2014 128 p. chiefly color illustrations (Explorer) (hardcover) $19.95

Grades: 4 5 6 7 8   741.5

1. Doors -- Fiction 2. Comic books, strips, etc. 3. Bullying -- Fiction 4. Monsters -- Fiction

ISBN 1419708821; 9781419708824; 9781419708848

LC 2014938941

In this collection of comics edited by Kazu Kibuishi, "a bullied boy discovers a door guarded by a sly monster . . . A painting of a door opens in a forgotten Egyptian tomb . . . A portal in the park promises to turn you into a much cooler version 2.0 - if you can just get the bugs out." (Publisher's note)

"Readers are once again presented with an array of stories created by a cast of comics authors and illustrators smartly assembled by Kibuishi... The range in this slim volume is expansive. From funny to deep and fantastical to refined, all of the stories have a compelling narrative arc. The colors are just as varied, and are universally dynamic and nuanced. Consider this (and previous series installments) as a necessary addition to any graphic novel collection." SLJ

Other titles in the series are:

The Mystery Boxes (2012)

The Lost Islands (2013)

Farshtey, Greg

Bionicle #1: rise of the Toa Nuva; Greg Farshtey, writer; Carlos D'Anda [and] Randy Elliott, artist. Papercutz 2008 un il $12.95; pa $7.95

Grades: 3 4 5 6   741.5

1. Graphic novels 2. Adventure graphic novels 3. Science fiction graphic novels

ISBN 978-1-59707-110-9; 978-1-59707-109-3 pa

Six mighty heroes the Toa arrive on a tropical island to find a land under siege. The Great Spirit Mata Nui has been cast into an unending sleep by the evil Makuta. Now Makuta is attacking the island's Matoran villagers with vicious Rahi beasts. The Toa must combine their skills and elemental and mask powers to defeat Makuta and restore peace to the island.

"The art is vivid and attention grabbing, and the story line, which weaves in Polynesian mythology, is exciting and action-packed." SLJ

Other titles in this series are:

Challenge of the Rahkshi (2008)

City of legends (2008)

Trial by fire (2008)

The battle of Voya Nui (2009)

The underwater city (2009)

Realm of fear (2009)

Legends of Bara Magna (2010)

The fall of Atero (2010)

Flight explorer; edited by Kazu Kibuiski. Villard 2008 112p il pa $10

Grades: 4 5 6 7   741.5

1. Graphic novels 2. Fantasy graphic novels 3. Humorous graphic novels 4. Adventure graphic novels 5. Science fiction graphic novels

ISBN 978-0-345-50313-8 pa; 0-345-50313-9 pa

This anthology includes stories that Kibuishi kept from Flight Volume 4 because they had all-ages appeal, as well as stories submitted especially for this volume. Kibuishi's own Copper and his talking dog cross a deep canyon by leaping onto mushrooms, only to discover the vegetation is intelligent. Kean Soo's Jellaby and his human friends frolic in the snow. Missile Mouse by Jake Parker defends a village on another planet, only to discover his coming was prophesied (this story includes two uses of the word "crap"). The other stories will appeal to younger readers, while some of the humor will also appeal to older readers. Other than the one bad word in "Missile Mouse" (noted above), there shouldn't be any other content that would keep this book out of most elementary and middle schools.

"Every story has a layout that promotes an acute sense of pacing and showcases the crisp, defined, full-color art." SLJ

Ford, Christopher

Stickman Odyssey; an epic doodle. Philomel Books 2011 200p il $12.99

Grades: 5 6 7 8   741.5

1. Graphic novels 2. Humorous graphic novels 3. Adventure graphic novels 4. Greek mythology -- Graphic novels

ISBN 978-0-399-25426-0; 0-399-25426-9

LC 2010-36900

In this humorous take on the Odyssey, Zozimos, banished from his country by his evil stepmother, has many adventures as he prepares to return home to reclaim the throne that is rightfully his.

"The black-and-white illustrations are occasionally simple to the point of hilarity. . . . There is subtlety and depth here, however, and the contrast between the intentionally plain characters and their seemingly larger-than-life (but ultimately universal) quests . . . makes the final product both the promised Greek epic tale and an examination of the ways in which modern humans are isolated and lost. . . . Ford balances allegory and madcap quest so perfectly that the book inspires reflection even while it is clearly a quick-reading, ridiculous, often gross adventure." Bull Cent Child Books

Friesen, Ray

A **cheese** related mishap and other stories. Don't Eat Any Bugs 92p il (LOOKIT! comedy and mayhem) pa $8.95

Grades: 3 4 5 6   741.5

ISBN 0-9728177-6-X pa

"Held together by dueling narrators, this volume features Mellville the penguin and a cast of several as they struggle to save exploding cheese from a horde of evil chicken ninjas! Interspersed are stories of Captain Cautious, the timid super hero, and Tbyrd Fearlessness, the inept ostrich outlaw." (Publisher's note)

Other titles in this series are:

Yarg! and other stories (2007)

Cupcakes of doom! (2009)

Piranha pancakes (2011)

Fuji, Machiko

The **big** adventures of Majoko, volume 1; illustrated by Tomomi Mizuna. UDON Entertainment 2009 200p il pa $7.99

Grades: 3 4 5 6 7 8   741.5

1. Manga 2. Graphic novels 3. Fantasy graphic novels 4. Witches -- Graphic novels

ISBN 978-1-89737-681-2 pa; 1-89737-681-2 pa

"Young witch Majoko sends her diary to the human world to find an adventuring partner and through it finds shy, quiet Nana. Together the two girls have a rollicking series of escapades. . . . Characters are simply drawn, but the backgrounds are nicely detailed and the plot elements are clearly thought out and easy to follow. . . . The content is very appropriate for the intended audience." Booklist

Volume 1 of a 5-volume series

Gagne, Michel

The **saga** of Rex. Image 2010 200p il $17.99

Grades: 4 5 6 7 8   741.5

1. Graphic novels 2. Foxes -- Graphic novels 3. Science fiction -- Graphic novels

ISBN 978-1-60706-322-3; 1-60706-322-0

The adorable little fox named Rex is plucked from his home world by a mysterious spaceship and transported to the arcane world of Edernia, where he meets Aven, an enigmatic biomorph with a flying saucer.

"While children may enjoy this graphic novel for its gorgeous art—especially the cute characters—its story line will more likely be appreciated by older readers. The almost wordless story isn't meant to be read on a literal level but instead on more a mystical and dreamlike level. . . . Gagné . . . offers a sensitive and intriguing graphic novel for people who like a little enigma in what they read." Publ Wkly

Gaiman, Neil, 1960-

★ The **graveyard** book graphic novel Volume 1; based on the novel by Neil Gaiman; adapted by P. Craig Russell; illustrated by Kevin Nowlan, P. Craig Russell, Tony Harris, Scott Hampton, Galen Showman, Jill Thompson, Stephen B. Scott; colorist, Lovern Kindzierski; letterer, Rick Parker. HarperCollins 2014 188 p. color illustrations $19.99

Grades: 5 6 7 8 9 10   741.5

1. Graphic novels 2. Orphans -- Fiction 3. Cemeteries -- Fiction

ISBN 9780062194817; 006219481X

LC 2013953799

This graphic novel is an adaptation of the "Newbery Medal-winning novel, [where] Bod is an unusual boy . . . , the only living resident of a graveyard. Raised from infancy by the ghosts, werewolves, and other cemetery denizens, Bod has learned the antiquated customs of his guardians' time as well as their ghostly teachings." (Publisher's note)

"Russell brings his decades of comics know-how to this lovely, lyrical adaptation of [Gaiman's] well-loved, Newbery Medal--winning book. Not content to rely exclusively on his own distinctive talents, Russell has enlisted some of the industry's greatest contemporary illustrators as contributors, who fill the panels with appropriately gothic tones. In order to give ample room to the novel's twists and turns, the adaptation has been divided into two parts." Booklist

The **graveyard** book graphic novel Volume 2; based on the novel by Neil Gaiman; adapted by P. Craig Russell; illustrated by David LaFuente, Scott Hampton, P. Craig Russell, Kevin Nowlan, Galen Showman; colorist, Lovern Kindzierski; letterer, Rick Parker. HarperCollins 2014 188 p. color illustrations (hardcover) $19.99

Grades: 5 6 7 8 9 10   741.5

1. Dead -- Fiction 2. Orphans -- Fiction 3. Cemeteries -- Fiction

4. Supernatural graphic novels 5. Graphic novels 6. Supernatural -- Fiction

ISBN 0062194836; 9780062194831

LC 2013497350

"Russell concludes the two-part adaptation of Gaiman's Newbery Medal winner, encompassing the final three chapters of the novel. Bod, raised by the ghostly denizens of a graveyard, is a young adult now, yearning for knowledge of the world of the living. After a showdown with a pair of school bullies . . . Bod finally confronts the ancient order who murdered his family and overcomes them with his supernatural know-how and his innate courage and cleverness." (Booklist)

"Russell and his team of illustrators continue to do this amazing story justice with images that lead readers down a path into Bod's dark and magical graveyard world. Gaiman has the ability to weave beauty and intrigue into a story that has a strong potential to frighten." VOYA

Hansel & Gretel; a Toon graphic. Neil Gaiman, Lorenzo Mattotti. Toon Books 2014 56 p. black and white illustrations hbk $16.95

Grades: 2 3 4 5 6   741.5

1. Folklore -- Germany 2. Fairy tales -- Graphic novels 3. Fairy tales 4. Graphic novels

ISBN 9781935179627; 1935179624

LC 2014000694

This graphic novel offers a retelling of the Germanic folk tale of Hansel and Gretel. "Hansel overhears his mother presenting her logical argument to abandon the children in the forest so that she and her husband might have some hope of surviving the famine caused by the war. He reluctantly agrees, but he is happy when the children outsmart the plan. However, as conditions worsen, their mother persuades their father to abandon them a second time." (Bulletin of the Center for Children's Books)

"Mattotti contributes elegant b&w ink spreads that alternate with spreads of text. His artistry flows from the movement of his brush and the play of light and shadow. . . . Gaiman makes the story's horrors feel very real and very human, and Mattotti's artwork is genuinely chilling." Pub Wkly

Includes bibliographical references

Giarrusso, Chris

G-Man, volume 1: learning to fly. Image Comics 2010 un il pa $9.99

Grades: 3 4 5 6   741.5

1. Graphic novels 2. Humorous graphic novels 3. Superhero graphic novels

ISBN 978-1-60706-270-7 pa; 1-60706-270-4 pa

Mikey G. is G-Man, the newest superhero on the block, in a town full of superheroes (he made his cape from the family's magic blanket). His friends Billy Demon, Tan Man, Sparky, and the Suntrooper are all ready to help, but G-Man also has to deal with his older brother Great Man (aka Dave) and their superhero dad, Mr. G.

This "hits all the right notes, from its friendly cartoon figures to the occasionally hilarious one-liners." Booklist

Other titles in this series are:

Cape crisis (2010)

Coming home (2013)

Gownley, Jimmy

Amelia rules!: the whole world's crazy! Renaissance Press 2003 176p $24.95; pa $14.95

Grades: 3 4 5 6   741.5

1. Graphic novels 2. Humorous graphic novels 3. Friendship -- Graphic novels 4. Family life -- Graphic novels

ISBN 0-9712169-3-2; 0-9712169-2-4 pa

"Amelia . . . is getting used to life with her newly divorced mom and her hip, young aunt Tanner; settling in at a strange new school; and finding a group of friends. Amelia is no sweet innocent, nor are her three G.A.S.P (Gathering of Awesome Superpals) buddies: Reggie, superhero in the making; Rhonda, Amelia's tough bete noire with a fourth-grade 'thing' for Reggie; and quiet, mysterious Pajamaman. Jealousy, meanness, sadness, and confusion, as well as surprising generosity, and love crisscross the pages in energetic, freewheeling, full-color cartoon art that unwraps a kid's-eye view of life honestly, poignantly, and with a hefty dollop of melodrama." Booklist

Other titles in this series are:
Amelia rules!: What makes you happy? (2004)
Amelia rules! Superheroes (2005)
Amelia rules! a very ninja Christmas (2009)
Amelia rules! When the past is a present (2010)
Amelia rules! The tweenage guide to not being unpopular (2010)
Amelia rules! True things (adults don't want kids to know (2010)
Amelia rules! The meaning of life. . . and other stuff (2011)
Amelia rules! Her permanent record (2012)

★ **Graphic** novels and comic books; edited by Kat Kan. The H.W. Wilson Co. 2010 195p il (Reference shelf) pa $35
Grades: Adult Professional   **741.5**
1. Graphic novels -- History and criticism
ISBN 978-0-8242-1100-4; 0-8242-1100-6
LC 2010-34209

"This collection of articles from scholarly journals, newspapers, and blogs gives a well-rounded overview of graphic novels, as well as a strong argument for their place in schools and libraries. The first section chronicles the growing mainstream acceptance of graphic novels in the United States. . . . Susequent sections look at these books as complex works of literature, as education and literacy aids, and as significant additions to library collections, with advice for librarians on how to purchase, catalog, file, and promote them. In the final section, readers hear from writers and artists . . . who clearly convey the joy they get from this medium. This is both an entertaining and highly practical read." SLJ
Includes bibliographical references

Gravel, Elise
A **day** in the office of Doctor Bugspit. Blue Apple 2011 il (Balloon toons) $10.99
Grades: K 1 2 3   **741.5**
1. Graphic novels 2. Physicians -- Fiction 3. Extraterrestrial beings -- Fiction
ISBN 978-1-60905-092-4; 1-60905-092-4

"Looking like a cross between a slug and a sock puppet in Gravel's crudely drawn, garishly colored cartoons, alien Doctor Bugspit plies his trade. He blithely dispenses jars of 'Fix-It-Up Syrup' (made from sock juice, dead flies, moldy meat, pickle juice and ear wax) and other nostrums to extraterrestrial patients complaining of maladies ranging from split brains . . . to an all-body outbreak of toes. . . . Presented in a loose assortment of graphic panels, page-sized or smaller, this . . . will exert a strong draw on budding graphic-novel fans as well as children fascinated by yucky stuff." Kirkus

Guibert, Emmanuel
Ariol; Just a Donkey Like You and Me. Papercutz 2013 124 p. ill. (paperback) $12.99
Grades: 2 3 4 5   **741.5**
1. Animals -- Graphic novels 2. School stories -- Graphic novels
ISBN 1597073997; 9781597073998

This book follows Ariol and his ensemble, a "cast of anthropomorphized animal children," in "10 10-page stories, originally from France, which offer . . . slice-of-life vignettes. Whether Ariol is joining his father

for a trip to the ATM, arguing with a friend about sneakers, accompanying his grandmother to the movies, pursuing his great crush, or emulating his favorite superhero, the author dares to depict the exclusionary, argumentative, self-centered ways children can sometimes behave." (Booklist)

Other titles in this series are:
Thunder horse (2013)
Happy as a pig (2013)
A beautiful cow (2014)

Sardine in outer space; [by] Emmanuel Guibert; illustrated by Joann Sfar; translated by Sasha Watson; colorist, Walter Pezzali. First Second 2006 128p il pa $12.95
Grades: 3 4 5 6   **741.5**
1. Graphic novels 2. Humorous graphic novels 3. Science fiction graphic novels
ISBN 978-1-59643-126-3 pa; 1-59643-126-1 pa
LC 2005-21790

In this volume of twelve interconnected stories, little space pirate Sardine cruises in the spaceship Huckleberry with Uncle Yellow Shoulder and Little Louie. They do battle with Supermuscleman, who runs a tough space orphanage where children are taught "good behavior"

"Sfar's off-kilter, slightly uglified art, reminiscent of a toned-down Beavis and Butthead, gives the simple fun an unusual punch." Booklist
Other titles in this series are:
Sardine in outer space 2 (2006)
Sardine in outer space 3 (2007)
Sardine in outer space 4 (2007)
Sardine in outer space 5 (2008)
Sardine in outer space 6 (2009)

Guojing, 1983-
★ The **only** child; by Guojing. Schwartz & Wade Books 2015 112 p. chiefly ill. (hardcover) $19.99
Grades: K 1 2 3 4 5   **741.5**
1. Adventure fiction 2. Stories without words -- Graphic novels 3. Graphic novels 4. Lost children -- Fiction 5. Adventure and adventurers -- Fiction
ISBN 9780553497045; 9780553497052
LC 2014026977

Eisner Nominee: Best Publication for Early Readers (2016)
In this wordless graphic novel, by Guojing, a "little girl--lost and alone--follows a mysterious stag deep into the woods, and, like Alice down the rabbit hole, she finds herself in a strange and wondrous world. But... home and family are very far away. How will she get back there?" (Publisher's note)

"Each arresting, softly penciled panel is surprisingly luminous in spite of its monochromatic palette, and in those gentle scenes, Guojing evokes a wide range of feeling, especially the lonesomeness of the little girl, who never quite seems at ease alone." Booklist

Hale, Nathan
Nathan Hale's hazardous tales; one dead spy. Nathan Hale. Amulet Books 2012 128 p. (hardcover) $12.95
Grades: 3 4 5 6 7   **741.5**
1. Storytelling -- Graphic novels 2. United States -- History -- Graphic novels
ISBN 141970396X; 9781419703966
LC 2012947189

In this graphic novel, historical figure "[Nathan] Hale, convicted of espionage, forestalls death by telling stories from American history. In this volume, he's helped by the hangman in telling the story of the early days of the revolution. He takes readers from his college days at Yale to the Boston Massacre, the Boston Tea Party, his joining the 7th Connecticut regiment, the Battle of Bunker Hill and other pivotal scenes in New England and New York City." (Kirkus)

Other titles in this series are:
Big bad ironclad! (2012)
Donner dinner party (2013)
Treaties, trenches, mud, and blood (2014)
The underground abductor (2015)
Alamo all-stars (2016)
Raid of no return (2017)

The **underground** abductor; an abolitionist tale. Nathan Hale. Harry N Abrams Inc. 2015 125 p. illustrations (chiefly color) (Nathan Hale's Hazardous Tales) (hardcover) $12.95
Grades: 3 4 5 6 7 **741.5**
1. Biographical graphic novels 2. Underground Railroad -- Comic books, strips, etc. 3. Fugitive slaves -- United States -- Comic books, strips, etc.
ISBN 9781419715365; 1419715364
Eisner Nominee: Best Publication for Kids (2016)
In this graphic novel, "a fictionalized Nathan Hale (a patriot from the American Revolutionary War) tells stories about America's most extraordinary heroes and villains. In this installment, Hale tells his British captors about Harriet Tubman, the spy and nurse who helped hundreds of American slaves run away in the 1800s on the Underground Railroad." (School Library Journal)
Includes bibliographical references

Hale, Shannon
Calamity Jack; [by] Shannon Hale, Dean Hale, and Nathan Hale. Bloomsbury 2010 144p il $19.99; pa $14.99
Grades: 5 6 7 8 **741.5**
1. Graphic novels 2. Fairy tales -- Graphic novels
ISBN 978-1-59990-076-6; 1-59900-076-9; 978-1-59990-373-6 pa; 1-59990-373-3 pa
LC 2008-41332
In this graphic novel interpretation of "Jack and the beanstalk," Jack is a born schemer who climbs a magical beanstalk in the hope of exacting justice from a mean giant and gaining a fortune for his widowed mother, aided by some friends.
"The urban setting suits this retelling of the familiar beanstalk tale; Nathan Hale's art gives it a steampunk twist, and the addition of fairy-tale creatures like giants and pixies is natural and convincing." Booklist

★ **Rapunzel's** revenge; [by] Shannon and Dean Hale; illustrated by Nathan Hale. Bloomsbury 2008 144p il map $18.99; pa $14.99
Grades: 5 6 7 8 **741.5**
1. Graphic novels 2. Fantasy graphic novels 3. Humorous graphic novels 4. Fairy tales -- Graphic novels
ISBN 1-59990-070-X; 1-59990-288-5 pa; 978-1-59990-070-4; 978-1-59990-288-3 pa
LC 2007-37670
In this graphic novel, Rapunzel escapes "from the enchanted tree where Mother Gothel imprisoned her. Rapunzel sets off alone through the ghost towns and Badlands of Gothel's Reach. She is determined to find Gothel's Villa and teach Mother Gothel a long-overdue lesson for her years of treachery and lies, and help her real mother get out of the mine camps where Mother Gothel has kept her enslaved." (Publisher's note)
"The dialogue is witty, the story is an enticing departure from the original, and the illustrations are magically fun and expressive." SLJ
Another title about these characters is:
Calamity Jack (2009)

Hale, Shannon
Real friends; Shannon Hale; illustrated by LeUyen Pham. First Second 2017 224 p. color illustrations (hardcover) $21.99
Grades: 3 4 5 6 **741.5**
1. Bullies 2. Friendship
ISBN 9781626724167; 9781626727854
LC 2016945552
In this graphic memoir, by Shannon Hale, illustrated by LeUyen Pham, "Shannon and Adrienne have been best friends ever since they were little. But one day, Adrienne starts hanging out with Jen, the most popular girl in class and the leader of a circle of friends called The Group. Everyone in The Group wants to be Jen's #1, and some girls would do anything to stay on top . . . even if it means bullying others." (Publisher's note)

Hamilton, Martha
Noodlehead nightmares; by Tedd Arnold, Martha Hamilton and Mitch Weiss; illustrated by Tedd Arnold. Holiday House 2016 48 p. chiefly color illustrations (ebook) $15.95; (hardcover) $15.95
Grades: K 1 2 3 **741.5**
1. Bedtime -- Fiction 2. Brothers -- Fiction 3. Humorous fiction
ISBN 9780823436064; 9780823435661
LC 2015022726
In this book, by Tedd Arnold, Martha Hamilton and Mitch Weiss, "Mac and Mac, who love pie and hate making their beds, are hollow-headed. 'See in here? Nothing! Zippo! Nada!' Mac explains. That's why they get duped by their friend Meatball and fooled out of their fair shares of apple pie." (Publisher's note)
"Endlessly wacky; fast-moving antics and incessant fretting that would make Chicken Little look mellow give this familiar topic a fresh feel." Kirkus
Includes bibliographical references.

Harrell, Rob
Monster on the Hill; by Rob Harrell. Top Shelf Productions 2013 192 p. color illustrations pbk $19.95
Grades: 4 5 6 7 8 **741.5**
1. Monsters -- Graphic novels 2. Friendship -- Graphic novels
ISBN 1603090754; 9781603090759
This graphic novel by Rob Harrell is set in "1860s England [where] every . . . township is terrorized by a . . . monster - much to the townsfolk's delight! Each town's . . . monster is a source of local pride [and] tourism. Unfortunately, for . . . Stoker-on-Avon, their monster isn't quite as impressive. Can the morose Rayburn get a monstrous makeover and become a proper horror? It's up to the eccentric Dr. Charles Wilkie and plucky street urchin Timothy to get him up to snuff." (Publisher's note)

Hart, Christopher
The **cartoonist's** big book of drawing animals; [by] Christopher Hart. Watson-Guptill Publications 2008 224p il pa $21.95
Grades: 3 4 5 6 **741.5**
1. Drawing 2. Animals in art 3. Cartoons and caricatures
ISBN 978-0-8230-1421-7 pa; 0-8230-1421-5 pa
LC 2007-29102
"The simple text that accompanies each drawing explains the artist's choices and focuses readers' attention on important details in each drawing. Children will love this thorough and easy-to-use how-to guide." SLJ

Drawing the new adventure cartoons; cool spies, evil guys and action heroes. Sixth & Spring Books 2008 126p il pa $19.95
Grades: 4 5 6 7 **741.5**
1. Drawing 2. Cartoons and caricatures
ISBN 978-1-933027-60-9 pa; 1-933027-60-6 pa

"This fun guide works best for those with some previous figure-drawing experience. . . . Sections on 'Drawing the Head,' 'Drawing the Teen Action Body,' and 'Using Body Language to Convey Emotion' offer detailed and, for the most part, step-by-step instructions. Subsequent sections . . . provide examples of unique and zany aspects of adventure-style characters. . . . Throughout the book, Hart also includes useful tip boxes, often demonstrating how not to draw a character. These suggestions are invaluable, providing insight into creating kinetic and expressive cartoons." SLJ

You can draw cartoon animals; a simple step-by-step drawing guide. Walter Foster 2009 120p il (Just for kids!) pa $12.99
Grades: 2 3 4 5 6   **741.5**
1. Drawing 2. Cartoons and caricatures
ISBN 978-1-60058-611-8 pa; 1-60058-611-2 pa
"Hart begins by giving some general guidelines for drawing head and body shapes, and line thickness. Then he demonstrates, step by step, how to draw a variety of animals, both wild and domesticated. He includes an informative paragraph at the beginning of each set of instructions and side notes for some of the steps. . . . The projects are simple but yield a pleasing result reminiscent of animated characters the target age group might see on TV. Colored boarders at the top and bottom of each page unify the book and add visual appeal. Sure to be a favorite." SLJ

Hatke, Ben
     Legends of Zita the spacegirl; Ben Hatke. First Second 2012 205 p. col. ill. (pbk.) $12.99; (hardcover) $18.99
Grades: 4 5 6   **741.5**
1. Science fiction 2. Adventure fiction 3. Robots -- Fiction 4. Science fiction graphic novels 5. Graphic novels 6. Fame -- Fiction 7. Heroes -- Fiction
ISBN 1596434473; 9781596434479; 9781596438064
     LC 2012012748
This graphic novel, by Ben Hatke, is a children's science fiction adventure story. "Zita is determined to find her way home to earth, following the events of the first book. . . . Zita's exploits from her first adventure have made her an intergalactic megastar! But she's about to find out that fame doesn't come without a price. And who can you trust when your true self is being eclipsed by your public persona, and you've got a robot doppelganger wreaking havoc . . . while wearing your face?" (Publisher's note)
"Hatke's arrestingly vibrant art commands instant adoration of its reader... Readers would be hard-pressed to not find something to like in these tales; they're a winning formula of eye-catching aesthetics, plot and creativity, adeptly executed. Imaginative and utterly bewitching." Kirkus

★ **Little** Robot; by Ben Hatke. First Second 2015 144 p. chiefly color illustrations $16.99
Grades: K 1 2 3 4 5   **741.5**
1. Robots -- Graphic novels 2. Girls -- Comic books, strips, etc. 3. Robots -- Comic books, strips, etc. 4. Friendship -- Comic books, strips, etc. 5. Good and evil -- Comic books, strips, etc.
ISBN 1626720800; 9781626720800
Eisner Award: Best Publication for Early Readers (2016)
In this graphic novel, by Ben Hatke, "when a little girl finds an adorable robot in the woods, she presses a button and accidentally activates him for the first time. Now, she finally has a friend. But the big, bad robots are coming to collect the little guy for nefarious purposes, and it's all up to a five-year-old armed only with a wrench and a fierce loyalty to her mechanical friend to save the day!" (Publisher's note)
"Unframed panel illustrations lend an expansive quality to this lively, mostly wordless graphic novel for younger readers. The absence of defined frames allows the watercolor to bleed out into the plentiful white

space between panels, giving the girl and the robot space to move and even allowing the characters and dialogue to break the pattern in organic ways." Horn Book

★ **Nobody** likes a goblin; by Ben Hatke. First Second 2016 40 p. color illustrations (hardcover) $17.99
Grades: PreK K 1 2   **741.5**
1. Goblins -- Fiction 2. Friendship -- Fiction
ISBN 1626720819; 9781626720817
     LC 2015944387
In this children's story, by Ben Hatke, "Goblin, a cheerful little homebody, lives in a cosy, rat-infested dungeon, with his only friend, Skeleton. Every day, Goblin and Skeleton play with the treasure in their dungeon. But one day, a gang of 'heroic' adventurers bursts in. These marauders trash the place, steal all the treasure, and make off with Skeleton—leaving Goblin all alone!" (Publisher's note)
"Hatke (Little Robot) renders the characters' antic facial expressions, their fairy tale costumes, and the fantasy landscape with polished skill, and his story gallops along cheerfully with the clear prospect of a happy ending. Especially gratifying is Hatke's casting of reviled characters as heroes; without moralizing, he makes it clear that sometimes it's the most unassuming creatures who have the warmest hearts." Pub Wkly

★ The **Return** of Zita the Spacegirl; by Ben Hatke. First edition First Second 2014 240 p. $18.99
Grades: 3 4 5 6   **741.5**
1. Science fiction 2. Prisoners -- Fiction 3. Outer space -- Fiction 4. Science fiction graphic novels 5. Graphic novels 6. Good and evil -- Fiction
ISBN 1626720584; 9781626720589
"Zita the Spacegirl has saved planets, battled monsters, and wrestled with interplanetary fame. But she faces her biggest challenge yet in the third and final installment of the Zita adventures. Wrongfully imprisoned on a penitentiary planet, Zita has to plot the galaxy's greatest jailbreak before the evil prison warden can execute his plan of interstellar domination!" (Publisher's note)
"The art is colorful, detailed, and child-friendly. Readers of all ages can relate to the themes of friendship and loyalty while enjoying the fantasy of a far-out sci-fi adventure." Horn Book

★ **Zita** the spacegirl. First Second 2011 182p il pa $10.99; $17.99
Grades: 3 4 5 6   **741.5**
1. Graphic novels 2. Science fiction graphic novels
ISBN 1-59643-446-5 pa; 1-59643-695-6; 978-1-59643-446-2 pa; 978-1-59643-695-4
When her best friend is abducted by an alien doomsday cult, Zita leaps to the rescue and finds herself a stranger on a strange planet.
Hatke "doles out an increasingly loony and charming array of aliens, robots, and unclassifiable blobs and hairy things for Zita . . . to encounter. It's fun, plenty funny, and more than a little random. Kids will love it." Booklist

Hayes, Geoffrey
★ **Benny** and Penny in How to say goodbye; Geoffrey Hayes. Toon Books 2016 32 p. color illustrations (Benny and Penny) (hardback) $12.95
Grades: PreK K 1 2   **741.5**
1. Graphic novels 2. Loss (Psychology) -- Fiction 3. Mice -- Fiction 4. Death -- Fiction 5. Brothers and sisters -- Fiction
ISBN 9781935179993; 1935179993
     LC 2016003372
"Penny found a dead salamander, but her brother Benny is refusing to help her bury it. Is it silly to hold a service for Little Sallie, or

could this tiny salamander mean something more to the siblings? . . . Hayes shares this gentle tale of a child's early encounter with death." (Publisher's note)

"With humor, directness, and unfailing honesty, Hayes's sensitive cartooning and sharp dialogue play up the big emotions of these little mice." Pub Wkly

★ **Benny** and Penny in just pretend; a Toon Book. [by] Geoffrey Hayes. Toon Books 2008 32p il $12.95

Grades: PreK K 1 2   **741.5**

1. Graphic novels 2. Mice -- Graphic novels 3. Siblings -- Graphic novels

ISBN 978-0-9799238-0-7; 0-9799238-0-8

"The sweet, delicately colored illustrations have an old-fashioned feel that gives the familiar sibling story a timeless quality. . . . The text uses a limited vocabulary with sufficient repetition to help with word recognition. . . . A charmer that will invite repeated readings." Booklist

Other titles about Benny and Penny are:
Benny and Penny in the big no-no! (2009)
Benny and Penny in the toy breaker (2010)
Benny and Penny in Lights out! (2012)
Benny and Penny in Lost and found! (2014)
Benny and Penny in How to say goodbye (2016)

★ **Benny** and Penny in The big no-no! a Toon Book. RAW Junior 2009 32p il $12.95

Grades: PreK K 1 2   **741.5**

1. Graphic novels 2. Mice -- Graphic novels 3. Siblings -- Graphic novels

ISBN 978-0-9799238-9-0; 0-9799238-9-1

LC 2008-36307

Theodor Seuss Geisel Award (2010)

"Benny and his sister Penny know it's wrong to sneak into someone else's backyard but their mysterious new neighbor – or is it a monster? – may be a thief. They go snooping and discover a lot about themselves and...a new friend." (Publisher's note)

"The simple text uses basic vocabulary and repetition, making it accessible to emerging readers. Young children will love the graphic-novel format and the sweet, charming illustrations will draw them into the narrative." SLJ

★ **Patrick** in A teddy bear's picnic and other stories; a Toon book. Toon Books 2011 32p il $12.95

Grades: PreK K 1 2   **741.5**

1. Graphic novels 2. Bullies -- Fiction 3. Teddy bears -- Fiction 4. Mother-child relationship -- Fiction

ISBN 978-1-935179-09-2; 1-935179-09-8

LC 2010-40209

The adventures of Patrick the little teddy bear as he goes on a picnic with his mother, tries to avoid his nap, goes to the bakery to buy cookies, and contends with the bullying Big Bear.

"The bears have an endearing physicality . . . and Hayes displays a keen awareness of the volatility of a child's moods. . . . The rich vocabulary talks to kids on their own level but will also gently push their reading abilities." Booklist

Helfand, Lewis

Conquering Everest; the lives of Edmund Hillary and Tenzing Norgay. illustrated by Amit Tayal. Kalyani Navyug Media 2011 91p il (Campfire Graphic Novels Series) pa $12.99

Grades: 5 6 7 8   **741.5**

1. Mountaineering 2. Mountaineers 3. Nonfiction writers

ISBN 978-93-80741-24-6; 93-80741-24-3

LC 2011321480

"The exploits of two young men mad for climbing mountains are retold in graphic panels. . . . Tayal captures their likeness in flurries of small but visually varied cartoon scenes, often placing figures in front of reworked photos of forbidding ice fields and peaks. Helfand fills the dialogue-heavy narrative with specific biographical details amd exciting accounts of some of the great triumphs and tragedies of Himalayan mountaineering. . . . A vivid double character portrait, enhanced by equally sharp glimpses of climbing techniques, strategies and hazards." Kirkus

Hergé, 1907-1983

The **adventures** of Tintin, vol. 1; Tintin in America, Cigars of the Pharaoh, The Blue Lotus. Little, Brown 1994 192p il $18.99

Grades: 4 5 6 7 8 9   **741.5**

1. Graphic novels 2. Adventure graphic novels 3. Tintin (Fictional character) -- Graphic novels

ISBN 0-316-35940-8

Tintin, the heroic boy reporter from France, travels to America where he outwits gangsters in Chicago of the 1930s and adventures in the Wild West; sails the Mediterranean Sea with faithful dog Snowy and finds himself in a mystery involving a movie tycoon, drugs, and cigars in an ancient Egyptian tomb; then he travels to India to finally solve the mystery. This Little, Brown edition reprints some of the early Tintin adventures published in the 1930s in a 3-in-1 volume. This is the first in a series that reprints most of the Tintin stories by Herge. Librarians and teachers should note that the books retain some stereotypical depictions of people of other cultures and remember that these were acceptable and expected at the time of original publication.

Herrod, Mike

Doggie dreams. Blue Apple Books 2011 il (Balloon toons) $10.99

Grades: K 1 2 3   **741.5**

1. Graphic novels 2. Dogs -- Fiction 3. Dreams -- Fiction

ISBN 978-1-60905-065-8; 1-60905-065-7

LC 2010046646

Simple text and illustrations in comic book style reveal a dog's dreams, which feature abundant food, singing, and an opportunity to demonstrate courage.

"Unfussy illustrations of the ambitious pup in repose enhance the story's humor." Horn Book Guide

Holm, Jennifer L.

★ **Babymouse**: queen of the world. Random House Books for Young Readers 2005 91p il lib bdg $12.99; pa $5.95

Grades: 3 4 5 6   **741.5**

1. Graphic novels 2. Humorous graphic novels 3. Mice -- Graphic novels 4. Friendship -- Graphic novels 5. Babymouse (Fictional character)

ISBN 0-375-93229-1 lib bdg; 0-375-83229-7 pa

LC 2004-51166

"In this energetic comic . . . Babymouse, a wise-cracking rodent stand-in for your average, adventure-seeking nine-year-old, strives to capture popular Felicia's goodwill, finally achieving her end at the expense of Wilson Weasel, truest of friends. But, wouldn't you know it, Felicia's world has little to offer a smart, fun-loving mouse, after all." Booklist

Other titles in this series are:
Our hero (2005)
Beach babe (2006)
Rock star (2006)
Heartbreaker (2006)
Camp Babymouse (2007)
Skater girl (2007)
Puppy love (2007)

Monster mash (2008)
Babymouse the musical (2009)
Dragonslayer (2009)
Babymouse burns rubber (2010)
Cupcake tycoon (2010)
Mad scientist (2011)
A very Babymouse Christmas (2011)
Babymouse for president (2012)
Extreme Babymouse (2012)
Happy birthday Babymouse (2014)
Bad babysitter (2015)
Babymouse goes for the gold (2016)

Brave new pond; by Jennifer L. Holm and Matthew Holm. Random House Childrens Books 2011 90p il (Squish) lib bdg $12.99; pa $6.99
Grades: 3 4 5   741.5
1. Graphic novels 2. School stories 3. Amebas -- Fiction 4. Popularity -- Fiction 5. Superheroes -- Fiction
ISBN 978-0-375-93784-2 lib bdg; 0-375-93784-6 lib bdg; 978-0-375-84390-7 pa; 0-375-84390-6 pa
LC 2010028084
Starting a new school year, Squish, a meek amoeba who loves the comic book exploits of his favorite hero, "Super Amoeba," is determined to get picked for kickball and hang out with the cool kids.

★ **Squish,** Super Amoeba; by Jennifer L. Holm & Matthew Holm. Random House 2011 90p il (Squish) lib bdg $12.99; pa $6.99
Grades: 3 4 5   741.5
1. Graphic novels 2. School stories 3. Amebas -- Fiction 4. Bullies -- Fiction 5. Superheroes -- Fiction
ISBN 978-0-375-93783-5 lib bdg; 0-375-93783-8 lib bdg; 978-0-375-84389-1 pa; 0-375-84389-2 pa
LC 2010-08004
"The hilarious misadventures of a hapless young everylad who happens to be an amoeba. . . . If ever a new series deserved to go viral, this one does." Kirkus

Other titles in this series are:
Brave new pond (2011)
The power of the parasite (2012)
Captain Disaster (2012)
Game on! (2013)
Fear the amoeba (2014)

★ **Sunny** side up; Jennifer L. Holm & Matthew Holm; with color by Lark Pien. Graphix 2015 224 p. illustrations (jacketed hardcover) $23.99
Grades: 3 4 5 6   741.5
1. Adventure fiction 2. Summer -- Fiction 3. Florida -- Fiction 4. Friendship -- Fiction 5. Grandfathers -- Fiction
ISBN 0545741653; 9780545741651
LC 2014957906
Eisner Nominee: Best Publication for Kids (2016)
In this book, by Jennifer L. Holm, illustrated by Matthew Holm, "Sunny Lewin has been packed off to Florida to live with her grandfather for the summer. At first she thought Florida might be fun. . . . But the place where Gramps lives is no amusement park. It's full of . . . old people. Really old people. Luckily, Sunny isn't the only kid around. She meets Buzz, a boy who is completely obsessed with comic books, and soon they're having adventures of their own." (Publisher's note)
"Woven into the Florida frolic though, through dated flashback images, is the real reason for Sunny's last-minute visit: her older brother is struggling with addiction, and Sunny thinks she got him in trouble. Though Sunny will appeal to all kinds of readers, an authors' note shares

the Holms' hope to let kids in similar situations know that it's OK to feel sad and to talk about it. Clear dialogue bubbles, plenty of wordless spreads, and Matthew's cartoons and beach-umbrella color palette keep Sunny's story an upbeat one that readers will easily stick with." Booklist

Horowitz, Anthony
Stormbreaker : the graphic novel; [by] Anthony Horowitz; adapted Antony Johnston; illustrated by Kanako Damerum & Yusuru Takasaki. Philomel Books 2006 un il (Alex Rider) pa $14.99
Grades: 5 6 7 8   741.5
1. Graphic novels 2. Spies -- Graphic novels
ISBN 0-399-24633-9
In this graphic novel version on Horowitz's novel, fourteen-year-old Alex Rider is coerced into continuing his uncle's dangerous work for Britain's intelligence agency, MI6.
"If it's possible, this is even more rapidly paced than the novel. Alex remains an appealing hero here, and the idea of a heroic teen up against insidious adults continues to be an extremely powerful draw for readers." Booklist
Other graphic novel adaptations in this series are:
Point blank (2007)
Skeleton key (2009)
Eagle strike (2012)

Hotta, Yumi
Hikaru No Go, Volume 1; [by] Yumi Hotta and Takeshi Obata. Viz Media, LLC 2004 192p il pa $7.95
Grades: 5 6 7 8 9 10 11 12   741.5
1. Manga 2. Shonen manga 3. Graphic novels 4. Board games -- Graphic novels
ISBN 1-59116-222-X
Sixth-grade Hikaru Shindo's discovery of a bloodstained game board leads to an encounter with the ghost of Go master Fujiwara-no-Sai and the formation of an unbeatable Go team.
Volume 1 of 23

Ita, Sam
★ The **Odyssey**; a pop-up book. Sterling 2011 il $26.95
Grades: 4 5 6 7   741.5
1. Graphic novels 2. Adventure graphic novels 3. Pop-up books
ISBN 978-1-4027-5867-6; 1-4027-5867-7
"A highlight-reel version of Odysseus' journey home, framed as a graphic novel and plastered with fantastically dramatic pop-ups and other special effects. Opening with Penelope working on a tapestry that transforms into an entirely different scene with the drop of a step-flap, the tale plunges on into the many escapes of Odysseus and his crew. . . . Ita . . . tells the tale in balloons of colloquial dialogue. . . . Even newbies will be riveted by this nonstop, high-energy retelling. Homer himself would be agog." Kirkus

Jamieson, Victoria
The **great** pet escape; Victoria Jamieson. Henry Holt & Co. 2016 64 p. color illustrations (Pets on the Loose!) (hardback) $15.99
Grades: 1 2 3 4   741.5
1. Graphic novels 2. Pets -- Fiction 3. Humorous stories 4. Escapes -- Fiction 5. Schools -- Fiction
ISBN 9781627791052; 1627791051; 9781627791069
LC 2015003257
In this book, by Victoria Jamieson, the "class pets at Daisy P. Flugelhorn Elementary School want OUT . . . and GW (short for George Washington), the deceptively cute hamster in the second-grade classroom, is just the guy to lead the way. But when he finally escapes and goes to find his former partners in crime, Barry and Biter, he finds that they actually LIKE being class pets. Impossible!" (Publisher's note)

"The hilariously expressive rodents guarantee laughs from page one with plenty of slapstick humor and pointed one-liners. Jamieson makes excellent use of a variety of panel sizes to maximize the action." Booklist

Another title in this series is:
The great art caper (2017)

★ **Roller** girl; by Victoria Jamieson. Dial Books 2015 240 p. chiefly color illustrations (paperback) $12.99
Grades: 4 5 6 7 8   **741.5**
1. Graphic novels 2. Friendship -- Fiction 3. Roller derby -- Fiction 4. Roller skating -- Fiction
ISBN 0803740166; 9780803740167
LC 2014011310
Eisner Nominee: Best Publication for Kids (2016)
Newbery Honor Book (2016)
This graphic novel, by Victoria Jamieson, is "about friendship and surviving junior high through the power of roller derby. For most of her twelve years, Astrid has done everything with her best friend Nicole. But after Astrid falls in love with roller derby and signs up for derby camp, Nicole decides to go to dance camp instead. And so begins the most difficult summer of Astrid's life as she struggles to keep up with the older girls at camp." (Publisher's note)
"Jamieson captures this snapshot of preteen angst with a keenly decisive eye, brilliantly juxtaposing the nuances of roller derby with the twists and turns of adolescent girls' friendships." Kirkus

Keenan, Sheila
Dogs of war; by Sheila Keenan and illustrated by Nathan Fox. Graphix 2013 208 p. (hardcover) $22.99
Grades: 4 5 6 7   **741.5**
1. Dogs -- Fiction 2. War -- Graphic novels 3. Graphic novels 4. Dogs -- War use -- Fiction 5. World War, 1914-1918 -- Fiction 6. World War, 1939-1945 -- Fiction 7. Vietnam War, 1961-1975 -- Fiction
ISBN 0545128870; 9780545128872; 9780545128889
LC 2011006735
This graphic novel, by Sheila Keenan, "tells the stories of the canine military heroes of World War I, World War II, and the Vietnam War. This collection of three fictional stories was inspired by historic battles and real military practice. Each story tells the remarkable adventures of a soldier and his service dog . . . bringing to life the faithful dogs who braved bombs, barrages, and battles to save the lives of countless soldiers." (Publisher's note)
Includes bibliographical references

Kibuishi, Kazu
★ **Amulet,** book one: The Stonekeeper. Graphix 2008 185p $21.99; pa $9.99
Grades: 3 4 5 6 7 8   **741.5**
1. Graphic novels 2. Fantasy graphic novels 3. Mystery graphic novels 4. Adventure graphic novels
ISBN 978-0-439-84680-6; 0-439-84680-3; 978-0-439-84681-3 pa; 0-439-84681-1 pa
After a family tragedy, Emily, Navin, and their mother move to an ancestral home to start a new life. When their mother is kidnapped by a tentacled creature, Em and Navin have to figure out how to set things straight and save their mother's life.
"Filled with excitement, monsters, robots, and mysteries, this fantasy adventure will appeal to many readers." SLJ
Other titles in this series are:
The Stonekeeper's curse (2009)
The Cloud Searchers (2010)
The Last Council (2011)

Prince of the elves (2012)
Escape from Lucien (2014)
Firelight (2016)

Copper. Graphix/Scholastic 2010 94p il $21.99; pa $12.99
Grades: 5 6 7 8   **741.5**
1. Graphic novels 2. Adventure graphic novels 3. Science fiction graphic novels 4. Dogs -- Graphic novels
ISBN 978-0-545-09892-2; 0-545-09892-0; 978-0-545-09893-9 pa; 0-545-09893-9 pa
A collection of graphic novel adventures about a boy named Copper and his dog, Fred, including "navigating a dangerous forest of giant mushrooms, [and] surviving a crash landing in a homemade airplane— that run from lyrical to the downright apocalyptic. Illustrated in a deceptively simple style, its solemn tenor and deep strangeness . . . will likely inspire heavy investment from those who prefer a somewhat off-kilter read." Booklist

Klavan, Laurence
★ **City** of spies; [by] Susan Kim [and] Laurence Klavan; illustrated by Pascal Dizin. First Second 2010 172p il pa $17
Grades: 4 5 6 7   **741.5**
1. Graphic novels 2. Adventure graphic novels 3. Spies -- Graphic novels 4. World War, 1939-1945 -- Graphic novels
ISBN 1-59643-262-4 pa; 978-1-59643-262-8 pa
"With her mother gone and a father who has better things to do than be bothered raising a daughter, Evelyn is sent to live with her unconventional Aunt Lia in the bohemian art world of 1942 New York City. . . . Evelyn spends much of her time in the company of imaginary superheroes, fouling up the plans of Nazi spies. Before long she finds an unlikely friend in the building superintendent's son, Tony. Together, they . . . stumble upon an actual Nazi plot. With stupefying precision, Dizin's art channels Hergé's Tintin in tone, palette, and with the remarkable expressiveness of the clean, flexible figures. . . . With villains and danger that just border on the genuinely scary, the tale is filled not only with a thrilling sense of excitement but also with a child's longing for a grownup to believe in." Booklist

Kochalka, James
Dragon Puncher. Top Shelf 2010 36p il $9.95
Grades: PreK K 1 2   **741.5**
1. Graphic novels 2. Cats -- Graphic novels 3. Dragons -- Graphic novels
ISBN 978-1-60309-057-5; 1-60309-057-6
This is the story of The Dragon Puncher, a cute but ruthless kitty in an armored battle suit who is dedicated to defeating dangerous dragons, and his would-be sidekick Spoony-E (a fuzzy little fellow armed with a wooden spoon).
This is illustrated using Kochalka's "signature child-like figures collaged onto photographed backgrounds with the faces of himself, his son, and his cat. . . . Through Kochalka's guerilla, one-man-and-a-pen style of creation, it magically captures the exact sense of zaniness often discovered in . . . playtime. . . . Remarkably, it does this without losing coherence; and with huge panels and spare dialogue that will amuse kids and adults, it's also the rare graphic novel that makes an excellent read-aloud." Booklist

Johnny Boo: the best little ghost in the world! Top Shelf Productions 2008 40p pa $9.95
Grades: K 1 2 3   **741.5**
1. Graphic novels 2. Humorous graphic novels 3. Ghosts -- Graphic novels 4. Friendship -- Graphic novels
ISBN 978-1-60309-013-1

"Johnny Boo may be the best little ghost in the world, with the best little ghost pet, Squiggle, but that doesn't mean he's ready to face down scary Ice Cream Monster. When the monster turns out not to be scary after all, Johnny and Squiggle take it on as a new, if unpredictable, friend. Kochalka's simple line drawings and bright crayon colors stand out in this sweet, silly graphic novel. . . . The dialogue is fairly simple but never simplistic, and the text is printed clearly enough to make the book accessible to children just beginning to pick up chapter books." Booklist

Other titles in this series are:

Johnny Boo: Twinkle power (2009)

Johnny Boo and the happy apples (2009)

Johnny Boo and the mean little boy (2010)

Johnny Boo does something! (2013)

Johnny Boo zooms to the moon! (2014)

Johnny Boo goes like this! (2016)

Kovac, Tommy

Wonderland; written by Tommy Kovac; illustrated by Sonny Liew. Disney Press 2008 159p il $19.99

Grades: 4 5 6 7 8   **741.5**

1. Graphic novels 2. Fantasy graphic novels

ISBN 978-1-4231-0451-3; 1-4231-0451-X

First published as single-issue comics by SLG Publishing

"Ever wonder what happened in Wonderland after Alice left? Follow the quirky tale of Mary Ann, the meticulous and dutiful housekeeper for the White Rabbit, as she continues the tale. Her boss is now wanted for treason by the Queen of Hearts for allowing the Alice Monster to enter the kingdom–off with his head! On the run and fearing for their lives, Mary Ann and White Rabbit encounter the meddlesome Cheshire Cat, the ever-contentious troublemaker, sending the White Rabbit straight into the clutches of the queen and poor Mary Ann tumbling into the Treacle Well. . . . This is a terrific look at a great classic. The energetic, action-packed illustrations complement the story in Disney-cartoon style, making for a great read for all ages" SLJ

Krosoczka, Jarrett J.

Lunch Lady and the League of Librarians. Alfred A. Knopf 2009 un il lib bdg $11.99; pa $5.99

Grades: 3 4 5 6 7 8   **741.5**

1. Graphic novels 2. Humorous graphic novels 3. Games -- Graphic novels 4. Librarians -- Graphic novels 5. School stories -- Graphic novels 6. School children -- Food -- Graphic novels

ISBN 978-0-375-94684-4 lib bdg; 0-375-94684-5 lib bdg; 978-0-375-84684-7 pa; 0-375-84684-0 pa

LC 2008043117

The school lunch lady, a secret crime fighter, sets out to stop a group of librarians bent on destroying a shipment of video games, while a group of students known as the Breakfast Bunch provides back-up

"The black-and-white pen-and-ink illustrations have splashes of yellow in nearly every panel. The clean layout, featuring lots of open space, is well suited for the intended audience. . . . With its appealing mix of action and humor, this clever, entertaining addition to the series should have wide appeal." SLJ

Other titles about the Lunch Lady are:

Lunch lady and the cyborg substitute (2009)

Lunch Lady and the author visit vendetta (2009)

Lunch Lady and the summer camp shakedown (2010)

Lunch Lady and the bake sale bandit (2010)

Lunch Lady and the field trip fiasco (2011)

Lunch Lady and the mutant mathletes (2012)

Lunch Lady and the picture day peril (2012)

Lunch Lady and the video game villain (2013)

Lunch Lady and the schoolwide shuffle (2014)

Larson, Hope

Chiggers; [by] Hope Larson; lettered by Jason Azzopardi. Atheneum Books for Young Readers 2008 170p il $17.99; pa $9.99

Grades: 5 6 7 8 9   **741.5**

1. Graphic novels 2. Camps -- Fiction 3. Friendship -- Graphic novels

ISBN 978-1-4169-3584-1; 978-1-4169-3587-2 pa

LC 2008-09557

When Abby returns to the same summer camp she always goes to, she is dismayed to find that her old friends have changed, and the only person who wants to be her friend is the strange new girl, Shasta.

"Chiggers provides a ticket to summer fun. Larson delicately handles both the usual middle-school angst and the additional pressures that come with being somewhat different. . . . The content is perfect for upper elementary and middle school students." SLJ

Le Gall, Frank

Freedom! Frank Le Gall; illustrated by Flore Balthazar; coloring by Robin Doo. Graphic Universe 2012 40 p. col. ill.

Grades: 2 3 4   **741.5**

1. Animals -- Fiction 2. Freedom -- Fiction 3. Cats -- Graphic novels 4. Mice -- Graphic novels 5. Graphic novels

ISBN 0761378847; 9780761378846

LC 2011021726

"Miss Annie is a kitten, and she does all of the expected kitten activities--playing with pens and yarn, napping on armchairs, and begging for food. But she does the unexpected, too, like befriending a mouse she knows she's supposed to hunt. On her first adventure outside of the house, she meets two older cats, Zeno and Miss Rostropovna, who guide her through the big, new world. Annie has a wide range of expressions, from her perked ears to the tip of her pert tail." (Publishers Weekly)

"A charming balance of cartoon and natural kitty-ness in full-color, eight-panel pages, this cat's-eye view of life will induce purrs in feline fans everywhere." Kirkus

Rooftop cat; by Frank Le Gall; illustrated by Flore Balthazar; coloring by Robin Doo. 1st American ed. Lerner/Graphic Universe 2012 40 p. col. ill. (paperback) $6.95; (lib. bdg. : alk. paper) $29.27

Grades: 2 3 4   **741.5**

1. Graphic novels 2. Cats -- Fiction 3. Children's literature 4. Mice -- Fiction 5. Animals -- Infancy -- Fiction

ISBN 0761385479; 9780761385479; 9780761378853

LC 2011025646

The author, Frank Le Gall, presents another entry in his Miss Annie book series. "Miss Annie is just a kitten, but she loves having adventures on the rooftops outside her home. When a gang of dangerous alley cats invade her street, Miss Annie will have to prove her bravery and determination . . . and her loyalty to her very best friend, a mouse." (Publisher's note)

Liniers, 1973-

★ The **big** wet balloon; a Toon book. by Liniers. Toon Books 2013 32 p. chiefly color illustrations (Easy-to-read comics. Level 2) (alk. paper) $12.95

Grades: PreK K 1 2   **741.5**

1. Graphic novels 2. Sisters -- Fiction 3. Balloons -- Fiction 4. Rain and rainfall -- Fiction

ISBN 1935179322; 9781935179320

LC 2012047662

Eisner Nominee: Best Publication for Early Readers (2014)

This book by Ricardo Liniers "shows several tableaus of two little girls who wake up in the room they share and spend the day together. The older sister suggests fun things to do, like shouting at the top of their lungs while they run through a rain shower. Though they have one small misunderstanding, these siblings are loving and thoughtful--good companions whatever the weather." (New York Times Book Review)

"An uncommonly family-friendly tale, great for parents to share with their kids." Booklist

★ **Written** and Drawn by Henrietta; by Liniers. TOON Books 2015 64 p. chiefly color illustrations (hardback) $12.95
Grades: 1 2 3 4   **741.5**
1. Graphic novels 2. Drawing -- Fiction 3. Authorship -- Fiction
ISBN 9781935179900; 193517990X

LC 2015004010

Mildred L. Batchelder Honor Book (2016)
Eisner Nominee: Best Publication for Early Readers (2016)

"Reading books is fun . . . but what about making them? Armed with new colored pencils, Henrietta's ready to try. Peek over her shoulder as she draws the story of a brave young girl, a three-headed monster, and an impossibly wide world of adventure." (Publisher's note)

"Argentine cartoonist Liniers presents a graphic ode to the pleasures and challenges of composition, starring his recurring character Henrietta, a young bibliophile. The little girl's cat, Fellini, looks on as she writes and illustrates 'The Monster with Three Heads and Two Hats.' Page by page, she narrates her process, her own story appearing in a childlike, colored-pencil scrawl alongside Liniers' polished panels. . . . Henrietta and her creator are kindred spirits, displaying equal knacks for the surreal and the utterly charming." Kirkus

Littlefield, Holly
The **rooftop** adventure of Minnie and Tessa, factory fire survivors; by Holly Littlefield; adaptation by Amanda Doering Tourville; illustrated by Ted Hammond and Richard Carbajal. Graphic Universe 2011 31p il (History's kid heroes) $26.60
Grades: 3 4 5 6   **741.5**
1. Graphic novels 2. Catholics -- Fiction 3. Immigrants -- Fiction 4. New York (N.Y.) -- Fiction 5. Jews -- United States -- Fiction 6. Triangle Shirtwaist Company, Inc. -- Fiction
ISBN 978-0-7613-6179-4; 0-7613-6179-0

LC 2010028952

Adapted from the 1996 novel Fire at the Triangle Factory by Holly Littlefield

Two immigrant friends, Jewish Minnie and Catholic Tessa, work long hours at New York City's Triangle Shirtwaist Factory, and when a fire breaks out on March 25, 1911, trapping dozens of workers inside, they help one another to escape the flames. Includes facts about the factory, the fire, and its aftermath.

"Presented in graphic novel form, the dark intensity of the illustrations engages the reader." Jewish Book World
Includes bibliographical references

Liu, Na
★ **Little** White Duck; a childhood in China. by Andrés Vera Martínez and Na Liu; illustrated by Andrés Vera Martínez. Graphic Universe 2012 96 p. col. ill. (lib. bdg. : alk. paper) $29.27; (pbk.) $9.95
Grades: 4 5 6   **741.5**
1. China -- History -- 1976- 2. Biographical graphic novels 3. Graphic novels
ISBN 0761365877; 9780761365877; 9780761381150; 0761381155

LC 2011005347

This graphic novel provides a "glimpse into Chinese girlhood during the 1970s and '80s." It begins with the 3-year-old narrator trying to understand the death of Chairman Mao. "From there, her life unfolds in short sketches. . . . She explains about the four pests that plague China . . . and her stomach-turning school assignment to catch rats and deliver the

severed tails to her teacher . . . [as well as] the origins of Chinese New Year, her favorite holiday." (Kirkus Reviews)

"This picturesque treasure introduces Chinese culture through a personal perspective that is both delightful and thought-provoking." SLJ

Long, Ethan
Rick & Rack and the great outdoors. Blue Apple 2010 un il (Balloon toons) $10.99
Grades: 1 2 3   **741.5**
1. Graphic novels 2. Deer -- Fiction 3. Nature -- Fiction 4. Raccoons -- Fiction 5. Friendship -- Fiction
ISBN 978-1-60905-034-4; 1-60905-034-7

LC 2010-32388

Rick the raccoon and Rack the deer spend a day fishing, tracking wild animals, and canoeing on a lake.

"This graphic novel takes beginning readers through three very short and humorous stories. . . . This . . . puts the comics medium to good use: tracking the visual elements of the story will help emerging readers decode the text with ease." Booklist

Luciani, Brigitte
Mr. Badger and Mrs. Fox #1: The meeting; illustrated by Eve Tharlet. Graphic Universe 2010 32p il (Mr. Badger and Mrs. Fox) lib bdg $25.26; pa $6.95
Grades: 1 2 3   **741.5**
1. Graphic novels 2. Foxes -- Graphic novels 3. Badgers -- Graphic novels 4. Siblings -- Graphic novels
ISBN 0-7613-5625-8 lib bdg; 0-7613-5631-2 pa; 978-0-7613-5625-7 lib bdg; 978-0-7613-5631-8 pa

LC 2009032617

Having lost their home, a fox and her daughter move in with a badger and his three children, but when the youngsters throw a big party hoping to prove that they are incompatible, their plan backfires.

"Rendered as a beginning graphic novel, the story and characters are presented with plenty of heart and soul: expressive anthropomorphic faces and postures and rich dialogue require and reward engagement. Watercolor panels vary in size on folio pages, and balloons contain an easy-to-read font." Booklist

Other titles in this series are:
A hubbub (2010)
What a team! (2011)
Peace and quiet (2012)
The carnival (2014)

Lynch, Jay
Mo and Jo: fighting together forever; a toon book. by [illustrator] Dean Haspiel & [writer] Jay Lynch. RAW Junior 2008 40p il $12.95
Grades: K 1 2 3   **741.5**
1. Graphic novels 2. Humorous graphic novels 3. Superhero graphic novels 4. Siblings -- Graphic novels
ISBN 978-0-9799238-5-2

Mona and Joey are battling twins, and everything they do turns into a fight. They both love the same superhero, the Mighty Mojo. One day he comes to their house and says he needs to retire and gives them his costume, which has all his powers

"The text is peppered with puns and some clever idiom work, reinforced by repetition as well as what's happening in the clean panels and art." Booklist

Macherot, R.
Sibyl-Anne vs. Ratticus; translated from the French by Kim Thompson. Fantagraphics 2011 64p il $16.99

Grades: 5 6 7 8   **741.5**
1. Graphic novels 2. Mice -- Graphic novels
ISBN 978-1-60699-452-8; 1-60699-452-2

"This collection of comics, originally published in Spirou magazine in 1966 and 1967, contains several stories in which the mouse Sibyl-Anne and her friends fight back the greedy villain Ratticus. This is the first time that American audiences will be able to appreciate this story arc from the golden age of Franco-Belgian comics. . . . [The stories] are lighthearted and sometimes surreal adventures that use an artistic style reminiscent of classic comics such as Blondie or Pogo. The colors are bright and the creatures are adorable. . . . An enjoyable read for kids, teens, and even adults." SLJ

Manning, Matthew K.
Ali Baba and the forty thieves; retold by Matthew K. Manning; illustrated by Ricardo Osnaya. Stone Arch Books 2010 63p il lib bdg $26.65; pa $6.95
Grades: 4 5 6   **741.5**
1. Graphic novels 2. Folklore -- Graphic novels
ISBN 978-1-4342-1988-6 lib bdg; 1-4342-1988-7 lib bdg; 978-1-4342-2776-8 pa; 1-4342-2776-6 pa
       LC 2010020144

"Ali Baba is a poor man who stumbles upon a hidden cave where a band of thieves hides its loot, opening the cave with the phrase open sesame and closing it with close sesame. When he brings some of the treasure home, his greedy brother, Kasim, finds out and forces Ali Baba to tell him everything; but the thieves discover Kasim in their cave and kill him. When they hunt after Ali Baba, it takes the courage and cunning of the servant girl Marjana to save Ali Baba and his family. Osnaya's stylish art and Manning's story combine to make a dynamic comic book." Booklist

Martin, Ann M.
The **Baby**-sitter's Club: Kristy's great idea; a graphic novel. story by Ann M. Martin; adapted by Raina Telgemeier. Scholastic Graphix 2006 192p il $16.99; pa $8.99
Grades: 3 4 5 6   **741.5**
1. Graphic novels 2. Friendship -- Graphic novels 3. Babysitting -- Graphic novels
ISBN 0-439-80241-5; 0-439-73933-0 pa
       LC 2005-37749

Follows the adventures of Kristy and the other members of the Baby-sitters Club as they deal with crank calls, uncontrollable two-year-olds, wild pets, and parents who do not always tell the truth. A graphic novel based on the 1988 book by the same name.

"Comics artist Telgemeier's clean-lined, black-and-white art with stark black details nicely differentiates the four personable seventh-graders who parlay their babysitting experience into a business." Booklist

Other titles about the Baby-sitters Club are:
The truth about Stacey (2006)
Mary Anne saves the day (2007)
Claudia and Mean Janine (2008)

McCann, Jim
★ **Return** of the Dapper Men; written by Jim McCann; art by Janet Lee; lettered by Dave Lanphear; edited by Stephen Christy. Archaia Comics 2010 un il $24.95
Grades: 4 5 6 7 8   **741.5**
1. Graphic novels 2. Science fiction graphic novels 3. Robots -- Graphic novels
ISBN 978-1-932386-90-5; 1-932386-90-4

"In the dreamy land of Anorev, children, all under age 11, live underground among intricate gear-work mechanisms, while elegant robots live in abandoned houses aboveground. . . . All are perpetually stuck in the same day, and time has, essentially, ceased to mean anything—until 314 Dapper Men rain from the sky and set in motion the impetus for change. . . . Where this book truly stands out is how well the story works in concert with Lee's stunning artwork, which employs an art nouveau sheen. . . . A true dazzler that speaks on multiple levels for both child and adult readers and one that gets richer with each read." Booklist

McCranie, Stephen
★ **Mal** and Chad; the biggest, bestest time ever. Philomel Books 2011 218p il pa $9.99
Grades: 2 3 4 5   **741.5**
1. Graphic novels 2. Adventure graphic novels 3. Dogs -- Graphic novels 4. Schools -- Graphic novels 5. Time travel -- Graphic novels
ISBN 978-0-399-25221-1; 0-399-25221-5
       LC 2010036904

Fourth-grade genius Mal and his talking dog Chad shrink themselves to microscopic size and travel through time, but girls and the school bully present bigger challenges.

"McCranie captures both the big-eyed, round-headed cartoon adorableness of his characters and the realistic (though age-appropriate) menace of the dinosaurs with equal aplomb. . . . An unusually satisfying read." Booklist

McGuiness, Dan
Pilot & Huxley: the first adventure. Graphix 2011 62p il pa $7.99
Grades: 3 4 5   **741.5**
1. Graphic novels 2. Adventure graphic novels
ISBN 978-0-545-26504-1 pa; 0-545-26504-5 pa

"After a late video-game rental puts them on the wrong side of some aliens who want to destroy Earth, innocent boys Pilot and Huxley are transported into an alternate dimension where Huxley's name is the ultimate swear word and boats sail on bees instead of water. . . . Our heroes will see a city inside a dragon's nose and a burger made of live rat before the exciting conclusion. It's delightfully surreal and filled with imaginative dialogue. . . . McGuinness's illustrations are colorful and kinetic, fitting the tale's many humorous twists. " Publ Wkly

Pilot & Huxley: the next adventure. Graphix 2011 60p il pa $7.99
Grades: 3 4 5   **741.5**
1. Graphic novels 2. Adventure graphic novels
ISBN 978-0-545-26845-5; 0-545-26845-1

Pilot and Huxley just want to get home, but an unexpected glitch hurtles them into the holiday lands instead. Now they're stuck in a bizarre world where ghouls and zombies in Halloween Land are friendly, and Santa and his elves in Christmas Land are evil.

"The book is full of inspired nonsense." Kirkus

McLeod, Bob
★ **SuperHero** ABC. HarperCollins Pubs. 2006 40p il $15.99; lib bdg $16.89; pa $7.99
Grades: PreK K 1 2   **741.5**
1. Alphabet 2. Graphic novels 3. Superheroes -- Fiction
ISBN 0-06-074514-2; 0-06-074515-0 lib bdg; 0-06-074516-9 pa
       LC 2004-22180

Humorous SuperHeroes such as Goo Girl and The Volcano represent the letters of the alphabet from A to Z.

"There's strong appeal here for the youngest comic-book fans, with many doses of humor along the way. Each figure has special powers, of course, which readers learn about through alliterative captions and action-packed illustrations." SLJ

Medley, Linda

★ **Castle** waiting; the definitive edition Fantagraphics 2006 456p il $29.95

Grades: 5 6 7 8 9 10 11 12   **741.5**

1. Graphic novels 2. Fantasy graphic novels 3. Fairy tales -- Graphic novels

ISBN 1-56097-747-7

All of Medley's previously self-published comics are collected here in one volume for the first time. The titular castle was the home of Sleeping Beauty, whose story is retold from the viewpoint of the flibbertigibbet ladies in waiting. After the flighty princess awakens with the kiss of a handsome but not too bright prince, the castle becomes a sanctuary for various misfits. Readers will find references to many fairy tales, folk tales, and nursery rhymes in Medley's book, and her clean, clear black-and-white art reflects the works of classic illustrators such as Arthur Rackham.

Meister, Cari

Clues in the attic; illustrated by Rémy Simard. Stone Arch Books 2010 25p il (My 1st graphic novel) $21.32; pa $3.95

Grades: K 1 2   **741.5**

1. Graphic novels 2. Mystery graphic novels 3. Siblings -- Graphic novels

ISBN 978-1-4342-1889-6; 1-4342-1889-9; 978-1-4342-2283-1 pa; 1-4342-2283-7 pa

"Siblings Ben and Sofia investigate strange noises that they hear coming from above them. . . . [This title provides an] effective early-reader [equivalent] to comics and graphic novels. [Its] traditional beginning-reader trim size as well as bold and brightly colored illustrations are appealing to novice readers, while the inclusion of a 'How to Read a Graphic Novel' section, a glossary, discussion questions, and writing prompts will appeal to parents and teachers. The texts include simple sentences that closely match the art, while panels are limited to a maximum of four per page. Good fun for early graphic-novel readers." SLJ

Morse, Scott

★ **Magic** Pickle; with color by Jose Garibaldi. Scholastic/Graphix 2008 un il pa $9.99

Grades: 2 3 4 5   **741.5**

1. Graphic novels 2. Humorous graphic novels 3. Superhero graphic novels

ISBN 978-0-439-87995-8 pa; 0-439-87995-7 pa

"Starting with an irresistibly goofy premise, Morse layers on sly humor, astute references, and blazing action, turning in a charming, slam-bang story." Booklist

Other titles in this series are:

Magic Pickle and the Planet of the Grapes (2008)
Magic Pickle vs. the Egg Poacher (2008)
Magic Pickle and the Garden of Evil (2009)
Magic Pickle and the Creature from the Black Legume (2009)

Naujokaitis, Pranas T.

The **totally** awesome epic quest of the brave boy knight. Blue Apple Books 2011 40p il (Balloon toons) $10.99

Grades: K 1 2 3   **741.5**

1. Graphic novels 2. Monsters -- Fiction 3. Buried treasure -- Fiction 4. Knights and knighthood -- Fiction

ISBN 978-1-60905-099-3; 1-60905-099-1

LC 2011019009

A young boy and his furry friend, Butterscotch, as brave knights, battle a green monster that is destroying a princess's kingdom, seek a hidden treasure, and patrol the kingdom.

"The tales are loopily involving, allowing both the boy and the girl to play big parts, with humor that comes in broad strokes that Naujokaitis vividly paints on the faces of the actors." Kirkus

Nordling, Lee

SheHeWe; by Lee Nordling; illustrated by Meritxell Bosch. Graphic Universe 2015 32 p. chiefly color illustrations (lib. bdg) $25.26; pbk $6.95

Grades: 1 2 3 4   **741.5**

1. Games -- Graphic novels 2. Friendship -- Fiction 3. Imagination -- Fiction 4. Stories without words -- Graphic novels 5. Graphic novels 6. Games -- Fiction

ISBN 146774574X; 9781467745741; 9781467745789

LC 2014021929

Eisner Nominee: Best Publication for Early Readers (2016)

In this wordless graphic novel by Lee Nordling, illustrated by Meritxell Bosch, "Alex hosts a tea party and makes new friends. Drew soars through the sky, searching for adventure. Two kids play in a park, imagining they're somewhere else. In one afternoon, the worlds of imagination and reality collide." (Publisher's note)

"Readers can follow each story individually or read all three gradually intertwining tales together and imagine their own dialogue and narration. Bosch uses a different color palette for the highly detailed, cartoonish illustrations, while the clouds reveal clever hints along the way. The book ends with a neat twist on gender expectations that could spark meaningful discussions." Booklist

Nykko, pseud.

The **shadow** door; art by Bannister; story by Nykko; [colors by Jaffre; translation by Carol Klio Burrell] Lerner Publishing Group/Graphic Universe 2009 46p il (The Elsewhere chronicles) lib bdg $27.93; pa $6.95

Grades: 4 5 6 7   **741.5**

1. Graphic novels 2. Horror graphic novels 3. Fantasy graphic novels 4. Adventure graphic novels

ISBN 978-0-7613-4459-9 lib bdg; 0-7613-4459-4 lib bdg; 978-0-7613-3963-2 pa; 0-7613-3963-9 pa

LC 2008-39442

Four friends discover a movie projector that opens a passageway into a world threatened by creatures of shadow, where their only weapon is light

"This is an undeniably attractive offering, as the artwork, with deep darks and effervescent lights splayed across large, glossy pages, is strikingly rendered. . . . [This] should have no problem gaining an appreciative readership." Booklist

Other titles in this series are:

The shadow spies (2009)
The master of shadows (2009)
The calling (2010)
The parting (2011)
The tower of shadows (2013)

Nytra, David

The **secret** of the stone frog; a Toon graphic novel. by David Nytra. Toon Books 2012 80 p. $14.95

Grades: 2 3 4 5   **741.5**

1. Siblings -- Fiction 2. Fantasy graphic novels 3. Fantasy 4. Graphic novels 5. Brothers and sisters -- Fiction

ISBN 1935179187; 9781935179184

LC 2011050431

In this children's book by David Nytra, "Leah and her younger brother, Alan, awake to find their beds relocated to the middle of a lush forest. They soon come across a stone frog that guides them toward their home. . . . Their long, strange trip is full of bees, fanciful lions, and a subway ride . . . After they make a narrow escape when an entire town . . . comes alive, the story ends with our hero and heroine back in their beds as a new day begins." (School Library Journal)

O'Brien, Anne Sibley

★ The **legend** of Hong Kil Dong, the Robin Hood of Korea. Charlesbridge 2006 un il $14.95

Grades: 3 4 5 6 7   **741.5**

  1. Graphic novels 2. Korea -- Graphic novels 3. Hong Kil Dong (Legendary character)

  ISBN 978-1-58089-302-2; 1-58089-302-3

              LC 2005-56941

Hong Kil Dong is the son of a powerful government minister and one of his servants; this means the father will not recognize his son as his own. The boy grows up with great intelligence and wit, and leaves home to find his fortune. He learns martial arts and magic, and when he encounters thieves who rob only because corrupt government officials have ruined them, he turns the thieves into an army to right the wrongs. This story is based on a seventeenth century Korean legend.

  Includes bibliographical references

O'Connor, George

★ **Zeus**; king of the gods. First Second 2010 76p il (Olympians) $16.99; pa $9.99

Grades: 5 6 7 8   **741.5**

  1. Graphic novels 2. Classical mythology 3. Zeus (Greek deity)

  ISBN 978-1-59643-431-8; 1-59643-625-5; 978-1-59643-432-5 pa; 1-59643-431-7 pa

"O'Connor unveils his new Olympians graphic-novel series with this story of the daddy of Greek gods. Most immediately striking about this, aside from the exciting artwork, is the care O'Connor takes to visualize the creation myth that begins with Gaea creating and taking as a husband the sky, Ouranos. Their children the Titans and other proto-Olympian entities are often neglected or at best murkily covered, but here they're vividly portrayed with all the magnificence of their beyond-good-and-evil power. After this breathtaking and lengthy sequence, Zeus enters the scene to grow from a feisty nymph-needling youth to a lightning bolt-wielding avenger." (Booklist)

"It's [the] balance between respect for myth and adherence to comic-book form that works so wonderfully well here." Bull Cent Child Books

  Other titles in this series are:

  Athena: grey-eyed goddess (2010)

  Hera: the goddess and her glory (2011)

  Hades: lord of the dead (2012)

  Poseidon: earth shaker (2013)

  Aphrodite: goddess of love (2013)

  Ares: bringer of war (2015)

  Apollo: the brilliant one (2016)

  Artemis: wild goddess of the hunt (2017)

O'Donnell, Liam

Power play; illustrated by Mike Deas. Orca Book Publishers 2011 64p il (Graphic guide adventure) pa $9.95

Grades: 3 4 5 6 7 8 9   **741.5**

  1. Graphic novels 2. Mystery graphic novels

  ISBN 978-1-55469-069-5; 1-55469-069-2

Siblings Devin and Nadia team up with their friend Marcus, Marcus' stepbrother Bounce, and Bounce's best friend Pema when they all attend the World Leaders Summit, where Marcus' father, Dr. Ashmore is scheduled to speak. The friends find themselves mixed up in a fight between some of the most powerful people in the world and those who want more equitable rights to clean water and other environmental concerns. They investigate when one of Dr. Ashmore's assistants is murdered at the summit, and Dr. Ashmore receives threats.

"An enjoyable story with educational value, this strong mystery is presented along with information about world politics, power, and the benefits of political protest for social good." Booklist

O'Malley, Kevin

Desk stories. Albert Whitman 2011 32p il

Grades: 1 2 3   **741.5**

  1. Graphic novels 2. Schools -- Graphic novels

  ISBN 0-8075-1562-0; 978-0-8075-1562-4

             LC 2010050423

Six separate stories tell, in words and cartoons, the surprising history and activities of the ordinary school desk.

"Presented in a graphic-novel format, six fanciful, silly stories incorporate situations that any child who has endured a tedious class will appreciate. . . . This lighthearted offering will likely produce cheers rather than jeers and makes a great choice for reluctant readers." Booklist

O'Neill, Katie

Princess princess ever after; Katie O'Neill; [edited by] Ari Yarwood. Oni Press 2016 56 p. chiefly color illustrations (hardcover) $12.99

Grades: 4 5 6 7 8   **741.5**

  1. Magic -- Fiction 2. Fantasy graphic novels 3. LGBT people -- Fiction 4. Princesses -- Fiction

  ISBN 1620103400; 9781620103401

             LC 2016931407

In this book, by Katie O'Neill, "when the heroic princess Amira rescues the kind-hearted princess Sadie from her tower prison, neither expects to find a true friend in the bargain. Yet as they adventure across the kingdom, they discover that they bring out the very best in the other person. They'll need to join forces and use all the know-how, kindness, and bravery they have in order to defeat their greatest foe yet: a jealous sorceress." (Publisher's note)

"The princesses' affection for each other deepens with every challenge--and every round of snappy banter--and when wedding bells ring, they're for a couple who truly know and have freely chosen one another. O'Neill delivers an alternative fairy tale that challenges conventions with every twist of the plot but doesn't veer into heavy-handed preachiness that pulls readers out of the story." Kirkus

Ottaviani, Jim

Primates; The Fearless Science of Jane Goodall, Dian Fossey, and Biruté Galdikas. Jim Ottaviani; illustrated by Maris Wicks. First edition First Second 2013 133 p. chiefly color illustrations (hardcover) $19.99

Grades: 5 6 7 8 9 10 Adult   **741.5**

  1. Primates

  ISBN 1596438657; 9781596438651

             LC 2013427678

This book presents an "account of the three greatest primatologists of the last century: Jane Goodall, Dian Fossey, and Biruté Galdikas. These three ground-breaking researchers were all students of the great Louis Leakey, and each made profound contributions to primatology--and to our own understanding of ourselves." (Publisher's note)

"More story than study, the book provides an accessible introduction to Goodall's, Fossey's and Galdikas' lives and work." Kirkus

  Includes bibliographical references, page 138

Parker, Jake

Missile Mouse: rescue on Tankium3. Graphix 2011 146p

Grades: 3 4 5 6   **741.5**

  1. Graphic novels 2. Adventure graphic novels 3. Science fiction graphic novels 4. Mice -- Graphic novels

  ISBN 0545117178; 9780545117173

The daring agent Missile Mouse must help free a planet forced into slavery by evil King Bognarsh. But things get dicey when Bognarsh hires the Blazing Bat to take Missile Mouse out before he can shut the operation down.

"The crisp, vivid illustrations combine with a clear layout to create a graphic novel that works for veterans of the genre as well as newcomers. . . . Brisk and entertaining." SLJ

Missile Mouse: the star crusher. Graphix 2010 172p (Missile Mouse) $21.99; pa $10.99

Grades: 3 4 5 6   **741.5**

1. Graphic novels 2. Adventure graphic novels 3. Science fiction graphic novels 4. Mice -- Graphic novels
ISBN 978-0-545-11714-2; 0-545-11714-3; 978-0-545-11715-9 pa; 0-545-11715-1 pa

"When his mission to recover an ancient star compass goes wrong, intrepid Galactic Security Agent Missile Mouse finds himself saddled with a partner. . . . The two are to retrieve a missing scientist who holds the key to a horrible weapon, the Star Crusher, in his hereditary memory. . . . [This is] a gem in story and art. Bright, action-filled, at times wordless panels keep the pages turning. Intelligent space opera and a realistically rounded hero will have young fans of the future demanding the next volume." Kirkus

Pearson, Luke

★ **Hilda** and the troll; Luke Pearson. Flying Eye Books 2013 40 p. chiefly color illustrations (Hildafolk) $18.95

Grades: 3 4 5 6   **741.5**

1. Adventure fiction 2. Trolls -- Fiction 3. Explorers -- Fiction
ISBN 1909263141; 9781909263147

Originally published 2010 as Hildafolk

This book, by Luke Pearson, is "about an adventurous little girl and her habit of befriending anything, no matter how curious it might seem. While on an expedition to illustrate the magical creatures of the mountains around her home, Hilda spots a mountain troll. As the blue-haired explorer sits and sketches, she slowly starts to nod off. By the time she wakes up, the troll has totally disappeared and, even worse, Hilda is lost in a snowstorm." (Publisher's note)

"The art is as whimsical as the protagonist, and the bright colors enhance this comic book's magical-realistic effect." Horn Book

Other titles about Hilda are:
Hilda and the Midnight Giant (2012)
Hilda and the Bird Parade (2013)
Hilda and the Black Hound (2014)
Hilda and the Stone Forest (2016)

Petersen, David E., 1977-

Mouse guard; volume 1 legends of the guard. Jeremy Bastian, Ted Naifeh, Alex Sheikman, et al. Archaia Entertainment 2010 144 p. col. ill. (hbk.) $19.95

Grades: 5 6 7 8   **741.5**

1. Mice -- Fiction 2. Adventure fiction 3. Short stories -- Collections
ISBN 1932386947 Vol. 1; 9781932386943 Vol. 1
Eisner Award: Best Anthology (2011)

"Petersen turns to the tested and reliable bar story as a framing device to allow other writers and artists to play in his Mouse Guard universe, where heroic mice heroes are set in a world of epic fantasy. . . . One night barkeep June . . . stages a story-telling contest. What follows are thirteen tales of danger and adventure, as protagonists contend against the predators around them and the flaws that divide mouse from mouse." (Publisher's note)

"More than just supplemental material, this book broadens Petersen's magnificently imagined miniature world and is a welcome addition for any collection that values quality, all-ages graphic novels." Booklist

★ **Mouse** Guard: Fall 1152. Archaia Studios Press 2007 un il $24.95

Grades: 5 6 7 8   **741.5**

1. Graphic novels 2. Fantasy graphic novels 3. Mice -- Graphic novels
ISBN 978-1-932386-57-8; 1-932386-57-2
Eisner Award: Best Publication for Kids (2008)

In a medieval world populated by animals, mice have their own civilization but live in constant peril from predators. They live in hidden towns protected by the Guard, who also escort travelers between towns. Three young members of the Guard, Lieam, Saxon, and Kenzie, go in search of a missing grain merchant. They find him dead in the belly of a snake who tried to eat them; but they also find evidence that the dead merchant is a traitor. Now they need to find out to whom he was betraying the Guard and why. While this story features animals and is suitable for most readers who can handle some fighting action, there's nothing cute or Disney-esque in the art. Characters die, this is a serious story, but readers who have read Bone or the Harry Potter series can handle the action in this book. This is the first in a series.

Followed by: Mouse Guard: Winter 1152 (2009)

Mouse Guard: Winter 1152; story & art by David Petersen. Archaia Studios Press 2009 un il $24.95

Grades: 5 6 7 8   **741.5**

1. Graphic novels 2. Fantasy graphic novels 3. Mice -- Graphic novels
ISBN 978-1-932386-74-5; 1-932386-74-2
Sequel to: Mouse Guard: Fall 1152 (2007)

"In the Winter of 1152, the Mouse Guard face a food and supply shortage threatening the lives of many mouse through a cold and icy season. Some of the Guard's finest--Saxon, Kenzie, Lieam, and Sadie, led by Celanawe, the legendary Black Axe--traverse the snow-blanketed territories acting as diplomats to improve relations between the mouse cities and the Guard, and find themselves on a race against time to deliver crucial medicines." (Publisher's note)

"Picking up where Fall 1152 . . . left off, Winter 1152 follows the darkening adventures of the brave troops of the Mouse Guard as they battle the elements, predators, and even other mice in order to secure their way of life. The high-quality artwork found in the first volume carries over into this one. The narrative . . . is fast paced and compelling. . . . Combining a tale of action, romance, comedy, and tragedy with the graphic-novel format results in a topnotch work with wide appeal." SLJ

Followed by: Mouse Guard: The black axe (2013)

Petrucha, Stefan

Mickey Mouse: 300 Mickeys; writers, Stefan Petrucha . . . [et al.]; artists, César Ferioli Pelaez . . . [et al.] Boom! Kids 2011 un il pa $9.99

Grades: 3 4 5   **741.5**

1. Graphic novels 2. Mickey Mouse (Cartoon character)
ISBN 978-1-60886-627-4; 1-60886-627-0

A collection of four Mickey Mouse stories, including tales about a cloning experiment gone wrong that leads to countless copies of Mickey Mouse and an attack by an army of robot presidents during Mickey and Minnie's vacation to Mount Rushmore.

"This book combines classic comics stories with original comics from Italy and the U.S. featuring Mickey Mouse and a few of his friends. . . . The colorful art . . . is right on model with the Disney characters. Anyone who has enjoyed Mickey Mouse cartoons will have fun with these adventures, full of action and humor that is just right for younger readers." Booklist

Peyo

The **purple** smurfs; by Yvan Delporte and Peyo. Papercutz 2010 55p chiefly color illustrations pa $5.99; hbk $10.99

Grades: 1 2 3 4   **741.5**
1. Graphic novels
ISBN 1-59707-206-0; 978-1-59707-206-9; 978-1-59707-207-6; 1-59707-207-9

"[T]his previously untranslated version of the [Smurfs'] first solo collection (1963) offers three tales: A fly's contagious bite turns nearly all of the Smurfs into aggressive purple grunters. . . one Smurf's determination to fly results in multiple crashes and calamities; another's desire to find peace and quiet away from Smurf Village runs afoul of a mosquito and other hazards. Replete with pratfalls, butt-biting and like slapstick, the neatly squared-off comic-strip–style panels look small at first glance, but coated paper and high production values make both the dialogue and the brightly colored art easy to read." (Kirkus Reviews)

Other titles in this series are:

The Smurfs and the magic flute (2010)

The Smurf king (2010)

The Smurfette (2011)

The Smurfs and the egg (2011)

The Smurfs and the howlibird (2011)

Astrosmurf (2011)

The smurf apprentice (2011)

Gargamel and the Smurfs (2011)

The return of the Smurfette (2012)

The Smurf Olympics (2012)

Smurf vs. Smurf (2012)

Smurf soup (2012)

The baby Smurf (2013)

The Smurflings (2013)

The Aerosmurf (2013)

The Smurfs Christmas (2013)

Phelan, Matt

★ **Around** the world. Candlewick Press 2011 240p il $24.99

Grades: 4 5 6 7   **741.5**
1. Graphic novels 2. Voyages and travels
ISBN 978-0-7636-3619-7; 0-7636-3619-3

LC 2010043153

"Phelan presents three true stories of around-the-world adventures inspired by Jules Verne's Around the World in Eighty Days that, even though they were undertaken in the late 1800s, would be hardly less arduous today. Thomas Stevens, Joshua Slocum, and Nellie Bly saw the world from the seat of a bicycle, aboard a 36-foot sloop, and via trains and ships, respectively. The small, specific pleasures of Phelan's work . . . are showcased in panels laid out in horizontal bands, reinforcing the linear, ever-onward nature of each narrative. The use of limited color palettes enhances the artist's characteristic delicate, expressive pen-and-ink drawings without overpowering them, allowing each traveler's character to be the dominant story element. . . . Design elements such as borders and frames lend a jaunty festivity to a graphic novel that will appeal to aficionados of the form and any reader in search of engrossing true journeys." SLJ

★ **Bluffton**; my summers with Buster Keaton. written and illustrated by Matt Phelan. Candlewick Press 2013 240 p. chiefly color illustrations (reinforced) $22.99

Grades: 3 4 5 6   **741.5**
1. Vaudeville -- Fiction
ISBN 076365079X; 9780763650797

LC 2012740260

In this graphic novel by Matt Phelan, set "in the summer of 1908, in Muskegon, Michigan, a visiting troupe of vaudeville performers is about the most exciting thing since baseball. Henry has a few months to ogle . . . a slapstick actor his own age named Buster Keaton. Henry longs to learn to take a fall like Buster . . . but Buster just wants to play ball with Henry and his friends." (Publisher's note)

"Historical detail, a rich sense of place, expert pacing--Phelan . . . keeps all the plates in the air in this fictionalized recreation of the boyhood summers of Buster Keaton. In lightly sketched, gently tinted watercolor panels, Phelan conveys the excitement a troupe of summering vaudeville actors brings to sleepy Bluffton." Pub Wkly

Snow White; A Graphic Novel. by Matt Phelan. Candlewick Press 2016 216 p. chiefly ill. (some color) $19.99

Grades: 4 5 6 7 8   **741.5**
1. New York (N.Y.) -- Fiction 2. Depressions -- 1929 -- Fiction
ISBN 0763672335; 9780763672331

This graphic novel, by Matt Phelan, "delivers a darkly stylized noir Snow White set against the backdrop of Depression-era Manhattan. The scene: New York City. . . . Enter a cast of familiar characters: a young girl, Samantha White, returning after being sent away by her cruel stepmother, the Queen of the Follies, years earlier; her father, the King of Wall Street, who survives the stock market crash only to suffer a strange and sudden death; [and] seven street urchins." (Publisher's note)

"With a keen historical slant, a bit of action and intrigue, high visual interest, and the fairy-tale leaning, this will awe a wide readership. Brilliant." Kirkus

★ The **storm** in the barn. Candlewick Press 2009 201p il $24.99; pa $14.99

Grades: 4 5 6 7 8 9   **741.5**
1. Graphic novels 2. Adventure graphic novels 3. Kansas -- Graphic novels 4. Monsters -- Graphic novels 5. Dust storms -- Graphic novels 6. United States -- History -- 1933-1945 -- Graphic novels
ISBN 978-0-7636-3618-0; 0-7636-3618-5; 978-0-7636-5290-6 pa; 0-7636-5290-3 pa

In Kansas of 1937, the land has been in the grip of the Dust Bowl for four years, and eleven-year-old Jack Carter has seen his family worn down by it. But the day Jack outruns a dust storm all the way home from town, he glimpses something odd in the abandoned Talbot barn, and he tries to find the courage to go into the barn and confront what is there.

"Children can read this as a work of historical fiction, a piece of folklore, a scary story, a graphic novel, or all four. Written with simple, direct language, it's an almost wordless book: the illustrations' shadowy grays and blurry lines eloquently depict the haze of the dust. A complex but accessible and fascinating book." SLJ

Pien, Lark

★ **Long** Tail Kitty; by Lark Pien. Blue Apple Books 2009 51 p. col. ill. (hbk.) $17.99

Grades: 1 2 3 4   **741.5**
1. Humorous graphic novels 2. Cats -- Fiction 3. Neighborhoods -- Fiction
ISBN 9781934706442; 2008042448

"Long Tail Kitty narrates five episodes of his daily life. First he introduces his house and his town, including landmarks from each of his tales. He picks flowers, finds they can talk and plays chase with a bee. In winter he slides on the ice and has cocoa with Good Tail Mouse. He hosts a food fest with friends and refrains from eating all the Choco

Crispy Doggy Discs. Finally, he spends an activity-filled day with buddies from outer space." (Kirkus Reviews)

"The volume's appeal lies in the tidy, thoughtfully shaded panels and the cast's playful banter and witty barbs." Horn Book

Long Tail Kitty, come out and play; Lark Pien. Blue Apple Books 2015 80 p. color illustrations (hardback) $17.99

Grades: 1 2 3 4 **741.5**
1. Graphic novels 2. Humorous graphic novels 3. Cats -- Juvenile fiction 4. Jealousy -- Juvenile fiction 5. Friendship -- Juvenile fiction 6. Cats -- Fiction 7. Animals -- Fiction 8. Friendship -- Fiction

ISBN 9781609053949; 160905394X

LC 2014045909

Author and illustrator "Lark Pien offers a companion book to 'Long Tail Kitty' with five new adventures featuring the eponymous feline and his whimsical gang of animal pals. Inter-friendship rivalries, woes, and jealousies fuel these gently humorous tales of the wise-beyond-his-furry-years Long Tail Kitty." (Publisher's note)

"Unfussy cartoon illustrations in a simple layout make this a good introduction to comics for young readers, and the action is comforting enough for a bedtime read. The watercolor illustrations depict a pastoral, dreamy land of rolling hills and cozy houses, in a primarily pastel palette evocative of cupcake frostings." SLJ

Pilkey, Dav, 1966-
★ **Dog** man; Dav Pilkey. Graphix 2016 240 p. color illustrations (Dog Man) hbk $9.99

Grades: 2 3 4 **741.5**
1. Working dogs -- Fiction 2. Dogs -- Fiction 3. Human-animal relationships -- Fiction

ISBN 9780545581608; 9780545581639

LC 2016932063

"George and Harold have created a new hero who digs into deception, claws after crooks, and rolls over robbers. When Greg the police dog and his cop companion are injured on the job, a life-saving surgery changes the course of history. . . . With the head of a dog and the body of a human, this heroic hound has a real nose for justice. But can he resist the call of the wild to answer the call of duty?" (Publisher's note)

"From the doodle-scratch art and jumbled panel borders to crossed-out words with simulated grammar and spelling lapses to the generous helpings of potty humor, the book feels like a frantic message of delirious imagination from one child to another." Booklist

Dog man unleashed; Dav Pilkey. Graphix 2017 224 p. chiefly color illustrations (hc) $9.99

Grades: 2 3 4 **741.5**
1. Dogs -- Graphic novels 2. Police -- Graphic novels 3. Adventure fiction

ISBN 9780545935203; 9780545935432

LC 2016936340

In this graphic novel in the Dog Man series, by Dav Pilkey, "Dog Man, the newest hero from the creator of Captain Underpants, is still learning a few tricks of the trade. Petey the cat is out of the bag, and his criminal curiosity is taking the city by storm. Something fishy is going on! Can Dog Man unleash justice on this ruffian in time to save the city, or will Petey get away with the purr-fect crime?" (Publisher's note)

"The frenetic plot, full of treasure chests, mountain escapes, jail-breaks, magic ploys, potty humor, and over-the-top reactions, will have magnetic appeal for kids." Booklist

Powell, Martin
The **tall** tale of Paul Bunyan: the graphic novel; retold by Martin Powell; illustrated by Aaron Blecha. Stone Arch Books 2010 35p il (Tall tale) $22.65

Grades: 1 2 3 4 **741.5**
1. Tall tales 2. Graphic novels 3. Folklore -- Graphic novels 4. Bunyan, Paul (Legendary character)

ISBN 978-1-4342-1897-1; 1-4342-1897-X

The legendary woodsman Paul Bunyan was the biggest man who ever lived. One day, Paul finds a big blue ox frozen in the snow. He nurses the behemoth back to health, and names his new companion Babe.

"The book is complemented by excellent design work that mixes advertising tropes with frontier photographic elements to help reinforce the legendary quality of the myth." SLJ

Pyle, Kevin C.
Take what you can carry; Kevin C. Pyle. Henry Holt and Co. 2012 176 p. chiefly ill. (some col.) (hc) $12.99

Grades: 4 5 6 **741.5**
1. Teenagers -- Graphic novels 2. Shoplifting -- Graphic novels 3. Japanese Americans -- Evacuation and relocation, 1942-1945 -- Graphic novels

ISBN 0805082867; 9780805082869

LC 2011924430

In this graphic novel, in "1977 suburban Chicago, Kyle runs wild with his friends and learns to shoplift from the local convenience store. In 1941 Berkeley, the Himitsu family is forced to leave their home for a Japanese-American internment camp, and their teenage son must decide how to deal with his new life. But though these boys are growing up in wildly different places and times, their lives intersect in more ways than one, as they discover compassion, learn loyalty, and find renewal." (Publisher's note)

Ransom, Candice F.
The **lifesaving** adventure of Sam Deal, shipwreck rescuer; adaptation by Amanda Doering Tourville; illustrated by Zachary Trover. Graphic Universe 2011 31p il (History's kid heroes) lib bdg $26.60; pa $8.95

Grades: 2 3 4 **741.5**
1. Graphic novels 2. Horses -- Graphic novels 3. Shipwrecks -- Graphic novels 4. North Carolina -- Graphic novels 5. African Americans -- Graphic novels

ISBN 978-0-7613-6177-0 lib bdg; 0-7613-6177-4 lib bdg; 978-0-7613-6196-1 pa; 0-7613-6196-0 pa

LC 2009051719

In 1896, ten-year-old Sam Deal and Ginger, the wild horse he has tamed, assist an all-Black lifesaving crew as they attempt to rescue survivors of a shipwreck off North Carolina's Outer Banks.

This book provides an "exciting [glimpse] into the past, with just the right amount of tension and intensity to capture readers' attention. . . . [It] will serve as [a] good [introduction] to graphic novels and historical fiction for early readers. Added bonuses are the brief yet informative [introduction] and [afterword] providing more facts about the [setting]." SLJ

Includes bibliographical references

Reinhart, Matthew
DC super heroes: The ultimate pop-up book. Little, Brown 2010 un il $29.99

Grades: PreK K 1 2 **741.5**
1. Pop-up books 2. Superheroes -- Fiction

ISBN 978-0-316-01998-9; 0-316-01998-4

"The illustrations in this detailed and decidedly heroic pop-up compendium of superheroes and supervillains feel ripped from the pages of classic DC comics. Favorites like Superman, Batman, and Wonder Woman get their own majestic spreads . . . while mini-booklets highlight their allies, nemeses, and histories. Each spread is dramatic and dynamic. . . . Expertly crafted and superfun." Publ Wkly

Renier, Aaron

Spiral-bound. Top Shelf Productions 2005 144p il pa $14.95
Grades: 4 5 6 7 8 9   **741.5**
1. Graphic novels 2. Mystery graphic novels
ISBN 1-891830-50-3

"Turnip the elephant is using the summer to find his artistic voice through sculpture, his friend Stucky the dog is building a submarine, and Ana the rabbit is working on the town's underground newspaper. Their stories all wind around the town's deep, dark secret about the monster that lives in the pond. . . . The characters seem like real children, wholesome without being too sweet, and Renier's art is light and fun, a sort of Babar meets underground comix." Booklist

★ The **Unsinkable** Walker Bean; written and illustrated by Aaron Renier; colored by Alec Longstreth. First Second 2010 191p il pa $13.99
Grades: 5 6 7 8   **741.5**
1. Graphic novels 2. Adventure graphic novels
ISBN 978-1-59643-453-0 pa; 1-59643-453-8 pa

The story "centers around a cursed skull stolen from the lair of two deep-sea crustacean witches. Like all who look upon the skull, Walker's beloved grandpa falls deathly ill when he finds it, and the boy sets out to return the skull from whence it came. . . . The generous page size lets [the] reader dive into Renier's quavery and painstakingly detailed cartooning, and he really shows off his stuff with a bounty of full-splash dazzlers. . . . Exciting, deep, funny, and scary, with tremendous villains and valor galore." Booklist

Reynolds, Aaron

Joey Fly, private eye in big hairy drama; written by Aaron Reynolds; illustrated by Neil Numberman. Henry Holt 2010 128p il (Joey Fly, private eye) $16.99
Grades: 3 4 5 6   **741.5**
1. Graphic novels 2. Mystery graphic novels
ISBN 978-0-8050-8243-2; 0-8050-8243-3

When Greta Divawing, butterfly star of the Scarab Beetle Theatre, goes missing a week before the opening performance of "Bugliacci," Joey Fly is called in to investigate her puzzling disappearance.

"Numberman's stripped-down art combines just the right amount of grotesquerie with lively storytelling to propel the story along." Publ Wkly

Joey Fly, private eye in Creepy crawly crime; illustrations by Neil Numberman. Henry Holt & Co. 2009 96p il (Joey Fly, private eye) $16.95; pa $9.95
Grades: 3 4 5 6   **741.5**
1. Graphic novels 2. Mystery graphic novels
ISBN 978-0-8050-8242-5; 0-8050-8242-5; 978-0-8050-8786-4 pa; 0-8050-8786-9 pa

LC 2007-40041

"In a city inhabited by insects, Joey fly is a private eye combating crime for a fee. . . . Young readers will be amused by this noir-type story filled with classic detective dialogue and swarms of insect humor." Booklist

Robbins, Trina

The **drained** brains caper; [by] Trina Robbins and Tyler Page. Graphic Universe 2010 64p il (Chicagoland Detective Agency) lib bdg $27.97; pa $6.95

Grades: 4 5 6 7   **741.5**
1. Graphic novels 2. Mystery graphic novels 3. Humorous graphic novels 4. Brainwashing -- Fiction 5. Schools -- Graphic novels 6. Japanese Americans -- Graphic novels
ISBN 978-0-7613-4601-2 lib bdg; 0-7613-4601-5 lib bdg; 978-0-7613-5635-6 pa; 0-7613-5635-5 pa

LC 2009-32620

Required to attend summer school after moving to Chicagoland, thirteen-year-old manga-love Megan Yamamura needs help from twelve-year-old computer genius Raf Hernandez to escape the maniacal principal's mind control experiment.

This tells "an entertaining story. . . . Page's black-and-white cartooning has a loose manga slant, with peppy goofiness popping out from stippled screen tones." Booklist

Other titles in this series are:
The Maltese mummy (2011)
Night of the living dogs (2012)
The big flush (2012)
The bark in space (2013)
A midterm night's scheme (2014)

Roche, Art

★ **Cartooning**; the only cartooning book you'll ever need to be the artist you've always wanted to be. Lark Books 2005 111p il (Art for kids) $17.95
Grades: 3 4 5 6   **741.5**
1. Drawing 2. Cartooning -- Technique
ISBN 1-57990-623-0

"This how-to guide is a step above the average cartooning instruction book. The glossy, full-color pages are visually attractive. . . . Roche's engaging writing style is informative and fun. . . . His loose, spacious cartooning style is perfect for beginners or kids who might be intimidated by more detail-oriented techniques." SLJ

Roman, Dave

Astronaut Academy: Zero gravity. First Second Books 2011 185p il pa $9.99; $16.99
Grades: 4 5 6 7 8   **741.5**
1. Graphic novels 2. Humorous graphic novels 3. Science fiction graphic novels 4. School life -- Graphic novels
ISBN 9781596436206; 9781596437562

LC 2010-941434

Hakata Soy has been the leader of a futuristic superhero team, but he has given that up and just wants to be a normal student at Astronaut Academy, a school on a space station, where students take such courses as anti-gravity gymnastics and fire-throwing. Other students include Doug Hiro, who always wears his space helmet, rich girl Maribelle Mellonbelly, Miyumi San (Maribelle's rival), and egotistical Billy Lee. Hakata Soy has some trouble adjusting to school life, and things get much worse when the villainous Gotcha Birds steal a robotic twin to Hakata Soy and reprogram it to kill him. The comics originally appeared as web comics, then as mini comics that Roman took to various comic cons; this is the first trade book collection of the stories. Middle grade students, boys and girls, will enjoy this book, which is full of humor and action with little actual violence.

"Students like the introspective Hakata Soy, the space-gymnastics-obsessed Doug Hiro, and the snooty rich girl Mirabelle Mellonbelly meet up at Astronaut Academy, a middle school where the zany mixes with the postmodern. . . . Silliness is high on the agenda, aided by minimal, cartoonish art that plays on manga tropes but also manages to build character into the simple lines of a face. . . . This is one for readers looking for more involved and complex comedy than a cursory glance at the images might lead one to expect." Booklist

Followed by: Astronaut academy: Re-entry (2013)

Roop, Peter

The **stormy** adventure of Abbie Burgess, lighthouse keeper; by Peter Roop and Connie Roop; adapted by Amanda Doering Tourville; illustrated by Zachary Trover. Graphic Universe 2011 31p il (History's kid heroes) lib bdg $26.60; pa $8.95

Grades: 3 4 5 6 **741.5**

1. Graphic novels 2. Lighthouse keepers 3. Maine -- Graphic novels 4. Lighthouses -- Graphic novels

ISBN 978-0-7613-6172-5 lib bdg; 0-7613-6172-3 lib bdg; 978-0-7613-6191-6 pa; 0-7613-6191-X pa

LC 2010006748

Based on Peter & Connie Roop's Keep the lights burning, Abbie, published 1985 by Carolrhoda Books

In Maine in 1856 seventeen-year-old Abbie Burgess lives with her family on a tiny island where her father is the lighthouse keeper. A storm hits when her father is away and Abbie must keep the lights burning until he returns.

This book provides an "exciting [glimpse] into the past, with just the right amount of tension and intensity to capture readers' attention. . . . [It] will serve as [a] good [introduction] to graphic novels and historical fiction for early readers. Added bonuses are the brief yet informative [introduction] and [afterword] providing more facts about the [setting]." SLJ

Includes bibliographical references

Rosenstiehl, Agnès

★ **Silly** Lilly and the four seasons. Toon Books 2008 36p il $12.95

Grades: PreK K 1 **741.5**

1. Graphic novels 2. Humorous graphic novels 3. Seasons -- Graphic novels

ISBN 978-0-9799238-1-4; 0-9799238-1-6

"Rosenstiehl follows Lilly . . . as she undertakes simple, familiar activities through the seasons. . . . Lilly is bold and engaging. . . . The text is very brief, . . . the colors are warm and bright, and the panels are large enough to draw in children new to books and reading." Booklist

Silly Lilly in what will I be today? RAW Junior 2010 32p il $12.95

Grades: PreK K 1 **741.5**

1. Graphic novels 2. Week -- Fiction 3. Occupations -- Fiction

ISBN 978-1-935179-08-5; 1-935179-08-X

LC 2010005308

No job is too tough for Silly Lilly: first she's a cook who paints, then an acrobat who tumbles, then a vampire.

"This concept book meets comic is an excellent addition for beginning readers. . . . Almost all of the text appears in word bubbles written in very basic vocabulary level in simple sentences. The India ink and watercolor cartoon illustrations are clear, with white backgrounds to keep the scenes uncluttered. . . . A fine example of a book that knows its audience." SLJ

Rosinsky, Natalie M.

Graphic content! the culture of comic books. Compass Point Books 2010 64p il (Pop culture revolutions) lib bdg $31.99

Grades: 5 6 7 8 9 10 **741.5**

1. Comic books, strips, etc. -- History and criticism

ISBN 978-0-7565-4241-2 lib bdg; 0-7565-4241-3 lib bdg

Traces the origins of comic books and discusses the emergence of superheroes, censorship issues, their depiction of increased social diversity, and their impact on society

"This slim and splashily designed book . . . does an admirable job of keeping things succinct yet thorough. . . . [The author] maintains a nice international scope throughout. . . . This is a super resource to have on

hand to give a broader context of the medium and its fascinating history." Booklist

Ruiz, Emilio

Waluk; by Emilio Ruiz; illustrated by Ana Miralles; translated and adapted by Dan Oliverio. Graphic Universe 2013 52 p. (lib. bdg. : alk. paper) $26.60; $7.95

Grades: 3 4 5 6 **741.5**

1. Friendship -- Fiction 2. Polar bear -- Fiction 3. Graphic novels 4. Bears -- Fiction 5. Tundras -- Fiction

ISBN 1467715980; 1467716065; 9781467715980; 9781467716062

LC 2012047787

"Young Waluk is all alone. His mother has abandoned him, as is the way of polar bears, and now he must fend for himself. But he doesn't know much about the world--and unfortunately, his Arctic world is changing quickly. The ice is melting, and food is hard to find." (Publisher's note)

"Marrying exemplary sequential storytelling, mythology, and science and enhanced through respectful anthropomorphizing, Waluk takes readers into a realistic world of polar bears endangered by climate change." Booklist

Runton, Andy

Owly : The way home and The bittersweet summer; [by] Andy Runton. Top Shelf 2004 160p il pa $10

Grades: K 1 2 3 4 5 6 7 8 9 10 11 12 **741.5**

1. Graphic novels 2. Owls -- Graphic novels 3. Friendship -- Graphic novels

ISBN 1-891830-62-7

LC 2005298860

Rotund little Owly befriends Wormy despite their differences, and together they help a couple of hummingbirds and learn that friendship doesn't end with separation.

"The whimsical black-and-white art is done with great facility for expressing emotion, and Runton's reliance on icons and pictures in lieu of the usual dialogue makes the story perfect for give-and-take between children and their parents." Booklist

Other titles in this series are:

Owly: Just a little blue (2005)

Owly: Flying lessons (2005)

Owly: A time to be brave (2007)

Owly: Tiny tales (2008)

Russell, P. Craig

★ **Coraline**; based on the novel by Neil Gaiman; adapted and illustrated by P. Craig Russell; colorist, Lovern Kindzierski; letterer, Todd Klein. HarperCollins 2008 186p il $18.99; lib bdg $19.89

Grades: 4 5 6 7 **741.5**

1. Graphic novels 2. Horror graphic novels

ISBN 978-0-06-082543-0; 978-0-06-082544-7 lib bdg

LC 2007-930658

"An adaptation of Gaiman's 2002 novel Coraline, . . . a tale of childhood nightmares. As in the original story, Coraline wanders around her new house and discovers a door leading into a mirror place, where she finds her button-eyed 'other mother,' who is determined to secure Coraline's love one way or another. This version is a virtuoso adaptation. . . . A master of fantastical landscapes, Russell sharpens the realism of his imagery, perserving the humanity of the characters and heightening the horror." Booklist

Salati, Giorgio

Race for the Ultrapods; writers, Giorgio Salati & Alessandro Ferrari; artists, Roberta Migheli & Antonello Dalena. Boom Kids! 2010 un il (Disney's Hero Squad: Ultraheroes) pa $9.99

Grades: 4 5 6 7   **741.5**

1. Graphic novels 2. Superhero graphic novels
   ISBN 978-1-60886-560-4; 1-60886-560-6

It's the year 2734 and the only one standing in the way of earth's utter destruction . . . Mickey Mouse?! In this volume, the battle for the Ultrapods is reaching it's boiling point as The Duck Avenger and the Ultraheroes clash with the villainous Emil Eagle and his Sinister Seven.

"Disney fans, both children and adults, will enjoy [this] graphic [novel]." SLJ

Santat, Dan

Sidekicks. Arthur A. Levine Books 2011 215p il $24.99; pa $12.99

Grades: 3 4 5 6   **741.5**

1. Graphic novels 2. Superhero graphic novels 3. Pets -- Graphic novels
   ISBN 978-0-439-29811-7; 0-439-29811-3; 978-0-439-29819-3 pa; 0-439-29819-9 pa

LC 2010034704

When Captain Amazing feels he is getting too old to be a reliable superhero, he tries to hire a new sidekick, but his pets have different ideas.

"Despite the presence of its charming animal characters, Santat produces much more of a dramatic adventure than a hilarious romp. . . . Realistic relationship dynamics come out. . . . Well-crafted art balances the lighthearted and the rough-and-tumble art works equally well for the character moments and the epic battle at the end." Booklist

Sava, Scott Christian

★ **Hyperactive**; by Scott Christian Sava; artist, Joseph Bergin. IDW Publishing/Worthwhile Children's Books 2009 108p il pa $12.99

Grades: 3 4 5 6 7 8   **741.5**

1. Graphic novels 2. Humorous graphic novels 3. Adventure graphic novels 4. Superhero graphic novels
   ISBN 978-1-60010-313-1; 1-60010-313-8

"Joey Johnson learns he can move at super speed and puts his power to good use doing household chores. But when word gets out, a shady executive sees the opportunity to make big bucks off of Joey's super DNA. . . . With its surprise ending, which suggests more to come, a readership of young boys will ensure that this one flies off the shelf at the speed of light." Booklist

Schwarz, Viviane

The **Sleepwalkers**; Viviane Schwarz. Candlewick Press 2013 96 p. (paperback) $9.99

Grades: 2 3 4 5   **741.5**

1. Nightmares -- Fiction 2. Fantasy fiction
   ISBN 0763662305; 9780763662301

LC 2012947253

This book by Viviane Schwarz offers a "tale of a band of intrepid dream warriors who rescue defenseless sleeping children from nightmares. Bonno (short for Bonifacius), a blanket transformed into a timid bear; Amali, an exuberant sock monkey; and Sophia, a crow made from a writing quill who communicates by writing, are the Sleepwalkers' newest recruits, learning the ropes from a trio of seasoned sheep." (Publishers Weekly)

Sfar, Joann

★ The **little** prince; adapted from the book by Antoine de Saint-Exupéry; translated by Sarah Ardizzone; colour by Brigitte Findakly. Houghton Mifflin Harcourt 2010 110p il $19.99

Grades: 5 6 7 8 9   **741.5**

1. Graphic novels 2. Fantasy graphic novels 3. Extraterrestrial beings -- Graphic novels
   ISBN 978-0-547-33802-6; 0-547-33802-3

"On the surface, this is a straight graphic-novel retelling of the narrator pilot getting stranded in the desert, where he meets a curious little boy who claims to be from a wee planet very far away. . . . The ultimately tricky task is to honor the source but not sound like an adaptation (otherwise, why not just read the original?) and Sfar nails it on both counts. . . . Everything is handled with both reverence and ingenuity." Booklist

Little Vampire; stories and drawings by Joann Sfar; colors by Walter; translated by Alexis Siegel and Edward Gauvin. First Second 2008 92p il pa $13.95

Grades: 3 4 5 6   **741.5**

1. Graphic novels 2. Vampires -- Graphic novels 3. School stories -- Graphic novels
   ISBN 1-59643-233-0 pa; 978-1-59643-233-8 pa

LC 2007-38498

First published in France

An unusual friendship forms between a vampire and a human, when Little Vampire leaves notes on homework Michael has left at school. (Bull Cent Child Books)

"Joann Sfar's art is surreal, with vivid colors, busy panels and fabulous monsters." KLIATT

Shiga, Jason

★ **Meanwhile.** Abrams/Amulet 2010 un il $15.95

Grades: 4 5 6 7 8 9   **741.5**

1. Graphic novels 2. Science fiction graphic novels
   ISBN 0-8109-8423-7; 978-0-8109-8423-3

LC 2009-39844

In this choose-your-own adventure graphic novel, a boy stumbles on the laboratory of a mad scientist who asks him to choose between testing a mind-reading device, a time machine, and a doomsday machine. (Bull Cent Child Books)

"In this graphic novel mind boggler . . . readers play the role of little Jimmy and on the first page make the seemingly innocuous decision of ordering a vanilla or chocolate ice-cream cone. Tubes connect panels in all directions and veer off into tabs to other pages, creating a head-spinningly tangled web of story. . . . The crux is that Jimmy stumbles into the lab of an affable mad scientist and is allowed to tinker with three inventions: a mind reader, a time machine, and the Killitron, which obliterates all life on earth aside from the user's. . . . It's maddening and challenging, all right, but that's precisely what makes it so crazy fun." Booklist

Sias, Ryan

Zoe and Robot: let's pretend. Blue Apple 2011 un il (Balloon Toons) $10.99

Grades: K 1 2 3   **741.5**

1. Graphic novels 2. Humorous graphic novels 3. Robots -- Graphic novels 4. Imagination -- Graphic novels
   ISBN 978-1-60905-063-4; 1-60905-063-0

LC 2010046829

A young girl named Zoe wants Robot to play pretend with her, but she has to teach Robot how to pretend, because "Robots do not know how to pretend." From imagining a pile of pillows is a mountain to feeling the wind from a whirring fan, Zoe tries to help Robot. Finally, she draws mountains on a pair of goggles that she puts on Robot.

"The colorful art and simple panel designs make it easy to follow the story. . . . Beginning readers can easily catch the visual cues that help them interpret the simple dialogue, and they will enjoy the humor. . . . This is a fun, easy-to-read graphic novel for beginning readers." Booklist

Siegel, Mark

The **sand** warrior; Mark Siegel and Alexis Siegel; illustrated by Xanthe Boume, Matt Rockefeller, and Boya Sun. Random House 2017 256 p. chiefly color ill., color maps (5 worlds) (hardcover) $18.99

Grades: 3 4 5 6   **741.5**
1. Fantasy fiction -- Graphic novels 2. Graphic novels 3. Science fiction 4. Heroes -- Fiction 5. Adventure and adventurers -- Fiction
ISBN 1101935863; 9781101935866; 9781101935873; 9781101935880

LC 2016018284

In this book, by Mark Siegel and Alexis Siegel, illustrated by Xanthe Boume, Matt Rockefeller, and Boya Sun, "the Five Worlds are on the brink of extinction unless five ancient and mysterious beacons are lit. When war erupts, three unlikely heroes will discover there's more to themselves—and more to their worlds—than meets the eye." (Publisher's note)

Siegel, Siena Cherson

★ **To** dance; a ballerina's graphic novel. [by] Siena Cherson Siegel; [illustrated by] Mark Siegel. Simon & Schuster 2006 un il pa $9.99

Grades: 4 5 6 7   **741.5**
1. Ballet 2. Ballet dancers 3. Graphic novels 4. Puerto Ricans -- Biography 5. Autobiographical graphic novels
ISBN 1-4169-2687-9 pa

In this memoir of her youth in dance from ages six to eighteen, Siegel tells what it was like to be totally involved in dance, in ballet—all the joys and the physical pain. She worked as a young dancer with George Ballanchine. Her absolute desire to be a dancer took her from her native Puerto Rico to New York City to study. Her simple but heartfelt narration is ably illustrated by her husband Mark Siegel.

Simpson, Dana

Phoebe and Her Unicorn; Dana Simpson. Andrews McMeel 2014 224 p. chiefly col. ill. $9.99

Grades: 3 4 5   **741.5**
1. Unicorns -- Fiction 2. Girls -- Graphic novels
ISBN 1449446205; 9781449446208

LC bl2014039099

In this graphic novel, by Dana Simpson, "Phoebe skipped a rock across a pond and accidentally hit a unicorn in the face. Improbably, this led to Phoebe being granted one wish, and she used it to make the unicorn, Marigold Heavenly Nostrils, her obligational best friend. But can a vain mythical beast and a nine-year-old daydreamer really forge a connection?" (Publisher's note)

"A pink, bubble-gum bonbon of a tale spun of a likable, albeit self-centered, fourth-grader and her magical, self-obsessed, although sometimes-kind, unicorn." Kirkus

Other titles in this series are:
Unicorn on a roll (2015)
Unicorn vs. Goblins (2016)
Razzle Dazzle Unicorn (2016)

Unicorn on a Roll; Another Phoebe and Her Unicorn Adventure, by Dana Simpson. Paw Prints 2015 222 pages color illustrations $9.99

Grades: 3 4 5   **741.5**
1. Unicorns -- Fiction 2. Friendship -- Fiction
ISBN 9781449470760

LC 2014921935

This book, by Dana Simpson, is about the "magical friendship of Phoebe and her best friend, unicorn Marigold Heavenly Nostrils. . . . [The] reader is invited on a journey into the lives of Phoebe and Marigold as they navigate the difficulties of grade school, celebrate the winter

holidays, and explore their super hero/super villain personas together." (Publisher's note)

"Phoebe always has a friend to rely on, and Marigold always has someone to admire her extraordinary beauty, her clever wit, and her exceptional modesty. The character designs for Phoebe and Marigold are charming, and the artwork is admirably consistent." Booklist

Slavin, Bill

Big city Otto: elephants never forget. Kids Can Press 2011 il

Grades: 3 4 5 6   **741.5**
1. Graphic novels 2. Adventure graphic novels 3. Elephants -- Fiction
ISBN 1-55453-476-3; 1-55453-477-1 pa; 978-1-55453-476-0; 978-1-55453-477-7 pa

"Simpleton pachyderm Otto enlists his friend, a clever green parrot named Crackers, to help him find Otto's very best friend, Georgie, a chimpanzee who was stolen from their African jungle home by 'the man with the wooden nose.' The duo must make their way out of the jungle and soon find themselves across the pond in America, in the big city. When the pair falls in with a gang of crooked gators who take advantage of Otto's unfortunate peanut allergy (to help them steal gator-ade, of course), Otto and Crackers need to learn who is trustworthy—and who is out to take advantage of their naivete. Slavin's lush, full-color illustrations have a yesteryear feel with a dash of European influence." Kirkus

Big Top Otto; Big top otto. Bill Slavin. Kids Can Press 2013 88 p. (Elephants never forget) $7.95

Grades: 3 4 5 6   **741.5**
1. Circus -- Fiction 2. Elephants -- Fiction
ISBN 9781554538072; 9781554538065; 1554538068; 1554538076

LC 2013036468

"Otto the elephant continues his search for his childhood friend Georgie, a chimpanzee who was abducted from their forest home in Africa and shipped to the wilds of America by the Man with the Wooden Nose. When Otto sees a circus poster with a chimp that looks just like Georgie, he and his parrot friend, Crackers, follow the trail of the traveling circus." (Publisher's note)

"Silly text and illustrations will make readers laugh, but some jokes will likely go over their heads." Horn Book

Followed by: Big Star Otto (2015)

Smith, Jeff

★ **Bone** : out from Boneville. Scholastic Graphix 2005 144p il paperback $12.99; hardcover $26.99

Grades: 4 5 6 7 8 9 10 11 12   **741.5**
1. Graphic novels 2. Fantasy graphic novels 3. Adventure graphic novels
ISBN 9780439706407; 0439706408; 0439706238; 9780439706230

"After being run out of Boneville, the three Bone cousins -- Fone Bone, Phoney Bone, and Smiley Bone -- are separated and lost in a vast, uncharted desert. One by one, they find their way into a deep, forested valley filled with wonderful and terrifying creatures. Eventually, the cousins are reunited at a farmstead run by tough Gran'ma Ben and her spirited granddaughter, Thorn. But little do the Bones know, there are dark forces conspiring against them and their adventures are only just beginning!" (Publisher's note)

"The nine-volume Bone graphic novel series was the toast of the comics world when it was published by Smith's own Cartoon Books beginning in the early 1990s; in this first volume of Scholastic's new edition, the original b&w art has been beautifully converted into color." Pub Wkly

Other titles in this series are:

Bone: the great cow race (vol. 2)
Bone: eyes of the storm (vol. 3)
Bone: the dragonslayer (vol. 4)
Bone: Rock Jaw: master of the Eastern border (vol. 5)
Bone: old man's cave (vol. 6)
Bone: ghost circles (vol. 7)
Bone: treasure hunters (vol. 8)
Bone: crown of horns (vol. 9)

Bone : Rose; with illustrations by Charles Vess. Scholastic Graphix 2009 138p il $21.99; pa $10.99

Grades: 4 5 6 7 8   **741.5**

1. Graphic novels 2. Fantasy graphic novels 3. Adventure graphic novels

ISBN 978-0-545-13542-9; 0-545-13542-7; 978-0-545-13543-6 pa; 0-545-13543-5 pa

"When a terrifying dragon attacks the small towns of the Northern Valley, a young Princess Rose (known later as Gran'ma Ben) must defeat it. The beast is actually the ancient evil, the Lord of the Locusts, and while Rose faces danger with honor, her elder sister, Princess Briar, follows a more sinister path." (Publisher's note)

Bone : tall tales; by Jeff Smith with Tom Sniegoski; color by Steve Hamaker. Graphix 2010 108p il $21.99; pa $10.99

Grades: 4 5 6 7 8   **741.5**

1. Graphic novels 2. Fantasy graphic novels 3. Adventure graphic novels

ISBN 978-0-545-14095-9; 0-545-14095-1; 978-0-545-14096-6 pa; 0-545-14096-X pa

"Long before the Bone cousins were ever lost in the uncharted desert on the outskirts of the Valley, Big Johnson Bone, the discoverer of the Rolling Bone River, founded Boneville. But little is known of the mighty explorer's adventures before he started his famous trading post. So when Smiley Bone sits down with a group of young campers to retell the legendary stories of Boneville's origin and its tough, no-nonsense founder, what they hear are tall tales in typical BONE fashion." (Publisher's note)

★ **Little** Mouse gets ready. TOON Books 2009 32p il $12.95

Grades: PreK K 1   **741.5**

1. Graphic novels 2. Humorous graphic novels 3. Mice -- Graphic novels 4. Clothing and dress -- Graphic novels

ISBN 978-1-935179-01-6; 1-935179-01-2

LC 2008-55403

ALA ALSC Geisel Award Honor Book (2010)

"Little Mouse is eager to go to the barn with his mother. He slowly and methodically gets dressed, which is quite an accomplishment for the little guy, only to be reminded, in classic noodlehead fashion, that mice don't wear clothes. . . . The cartoon illustrations are large and uncomplicated without being babyish, and the punch line is preceded with places for knowing giggles." SLJ

Sonishi, Kenji

Leave it to PET!: the misadventures of a recycled super robot, vol. 1; story & art by Kenji Sonishi; translation, Katherine Schilling; touch-up art & lettering, John Hunt; editor, Traci N. Todd. Viz Media/VizKids 2009 192p il $7.99

Grades: 3 4 5 6   **741.5**

1. Manga 2. Graphic novels 3. Humorous graphic novels 4. Recycling -- Graphic novels

ISBN 978-1-4215-2649-2

PET (polyethylene terephthalate, a type of recyclable plastic) was a simple plastic bottle until nine-year-old Noboru recycled him. Now PET is a super robot programmed to "repay" Noboru for recycling him by helping him. Unfortunately for Noboru, PET's help usually ends up causing even more trouble; being a super robot doesn't mean PET has a clue about what he is doing. The book includes lots of short stories that follow the formula of Noboru getting into a bit of a fix, calling for PET, then getting into more trouble as PET does the wrong thing. Some of the stories do include some information about recycling plastics and aluminum, which is done somewhat differently in Japan than in the U.S.

Volume 1 of a 4-volume series

Soo, Kean

Jellaby; Volume 1 the lost monster. by Kean Soo. Stone Arch Books 2014 160 p. color illustrations (Jellaby) (pbk.) $12.95; (library binding) $19.99

Grades: 4 5 6 7 8 9   **741.5**

1. Monsters -- Fiction 2. Friendship -- Fiction 3. Extraterrestrial beings -- Fiction 4. Human-alien encounters -- Comic books, strips, etc

ISBN 1434291952; 9781434264206; 9781434291950

LC 2013037026

First published 2008

"Portia has just moved to a new neighborhood with her mom. Adjusting to life without a father is hard enough, but school is boring and her classmates are standoffish. . . . But things start to get better when Portia mounts a midnight excursion into the woods behind her house where she discovers a shy and sweet purple monster. Life with Jellaby is exciting, but Portia's purple friend has secrets of his own." (Publisher's note)

"Soo grounds the story in a fairly gritty contemporary reality, where kids deal with bullies and well-meaning adults try to help. Clear, clean lines and easy-to-follow panel layouts round out the package." Booklist

Jellaby : monster in the city. Hyperion Books 2009 172p il pa $9.99

Grades: 4 5 6 7 8 9   **741.5**

1. Graphic novels 2. Fantasy graphic novels 3. Monsters -- Graphic novels 4. Friendship -- Graphic novels

ISBN 1-4231-0565-6 pa; 978-1-4231-0565-7 pa

Beginning right where the first book ended, Portia, Jason, and Jellaby continue on their way to Toronto, walking after Portia panicked and they got off the train. They're searching for a way home for Jellaby, and they think a door somewhere in Exhibition Place, where the Canadian National Exhibition is taking place, holds a clue. Portia feels torn between wanting to help her friend yet not wanting to say goodbye forever, and her ambivalence causes a rift between her and Jason. When she doesn't want to trust a masked magician who seems to know too much about them and Jellaby, Portia leaves Jason. They all end up in the Automotive Building, where the masked man leads Jason and Jellaby down below the building, while Portia seems to find her long lost father. But is he really her father, and just what is waiting for Jason and Jellaby under the Automotive Building? Soo again uses a mostly purple color palette.

Spires, Ashley

★ **Binky** the space cat. Kids Can Press 2009 64p il $16.95; pa $7.95

Grades: 2 3 4 5   **741.5**

1. Graphic novels 2. Humorous graphic novels 3. Cats -- Graphic novels 4. Space flight -- Graphic novels

ISBN 978-1-55453-309-1; 1-55453-309-0; 978-1-55453-419-7 pa; 1-55453-419-4 pa

Binky the cat lives with two humans (an unnamed mother and son) in what he thinks of as a space station. He's determined to become a space cat and venture into outer space with his stuffed mousie Ted, and to that end he gets his space cat kit through the mail, complete with instructions to build a space ship.

"Spires's mix of sly, dry and slapstick humor in her first graphic novel is perfect. . . . Details in the muted watercolor illustrations, like mousie Ted covering his nose as Binky releases 'space gas,' will keep readers of all ages giggling, whether they're cat lovers or not." Kirkus

Other titles about Binky are:

Binky to the rescue (2010)
Binky under pressure (2011)
Binky takes charge (2012)
License to scratch (2013)

Steinberg, David

★ **Sound** off! by D. J. Steinberg; illustrated by Brian Smith. Grosset & Dunlap 2008 un il (Adventures of Daniel Boom AKA Loud Boy) pa $5.99

Grades: 3 4 5   **741.5**

1. Graphic novels 2. Superhero graphic novels
ISBN 978-0-448-44698-1

LC 2007019009

"Bursting with action, color, and intriguing characters . . . this works in every way. Smith's visual wit, which puts a retro gloss on cartoon art of the 1950s, is on display without sidetracking the story, and pacing and plotting are superb." Booklist

Steinke, Aron Nels

The **Super** Duper Dog Park. Blue Apple Books 2011 il (Balloon toons) $10.99

Grades: K 1 2 3   **741.5**

1. Graphic novels 2. Dogs -- Fiction 3. Amusement parks -- Fiction
ISBN 978-1-60905-093-1; 1-60905-093-2

LC 2011019077

Dog lovers and their canine friends make their way to the Super Duper Dog Park on Dog Island, where dogs ride bicycles, make music, and enjoy a perfect day.

"Steinke's text is geared to be easy reading, but it is not without cleverness: snatches of rhyme or onomatopoeic devices that give a good taste of sound. . . . The artwork follows the text's accessible engagement. . . . Both colorful and high spirited, this title will give new readers a good run for their money." Kirkus

Sturm, James

★ **Adventures** in cartooning; how to turn your doodles into comics. [by] James Sturm, Andrew Arnold, Alexis Frederick-Frost. First Second 2009 109p il pa $12.95

Grades: 2 3 4 5   **741.5**

1. Drawing 2. Graphic novels 3. Graphic novels -- Authorship 4. Comic books, strips, etc. -- Authorship
ISBN 978-1-59643-369-4 pa; 1-59643-369-8 pa

When a princess wants to draw her own comic book, the magic comic book elf shows her how to do it through the course of a story about a knight, his hungry (and easily scared) horse, and the knight's quest to find a dragon. Young aspiring cartoonists will learn about the importance of panels to convey the passage of time, how to use word balloons and different lettering to convey emotion, how to show motion, create sound effects, and lots more, even as they will giggle over the action in the story. As the magic comic book elf says, anyone who can draw simple shapes and objects can be a cartoonist.

"In fairy-tale fashion, the Magic Cartooning Elf helps a young princess with writer's block produce her first comic. A story-within-a-story emerges. . . . Simple cartooning basics offered after the story are quite appealing; even the most reluctant artist may be inspired to pick up a pencil and give it a shot. Entertaining and surprisingly edifying." Kirkus

Other titles in this series are:

Adventures in cartooning activity book (2010)

Christmas special (2012)
Characters in action (2013)
Sleepless knight (2015)
Gryphons aren't so great (2015)

Telgemeier, Raina

★ **Drama**; Raina Telgemeier; with color by Gurihiru. 1st ed. Graphix 2012 233 p. chiefly ill. $23.99

Grades: 5 6 7 8   **741.5**

1. Graphic novels 2. School stories 3. LGBT youth -- Fiction 4. Middle schools -- Fiction 5. Children's plays -- Fiction 6. Schools -- Fiction 7. Theater -- Fiction 8. Interpersonal relations -- Fiction
ISBN 0545326982; 0545326990; 9780545326988; 9780545326995

LC 2011040748

Stonewall Honor Book (2013)

Author Raina Telgemeier's book focuses on a middle school drama production. "Callie loves theater . . . [S]he's the set designer for the stage crew, and this year she's determined to create a set worthy of Broadway on a middle-school budget. But how can she, when she doesn't know much about carpentry, ticket sales are down, and the crew members are having trouble working together?" (Publisher's note)

"In this realistic and sympathetic story, feelings and thoughts leap off the page, revealing Telgemeier's keen eye for young teen life." Booklist

Includes bibliographical references

★ **Ghosts**; Raina Telgemeier; with color by Braden Lamb. Graphix, an imprint of Scholastic 2016 256 p. chiefly color illustrations pbk $10.99; hbk $24.99

Grades: 3 4 5 6 7   **741.5**

1. Moving -- Fiction 2. Ghost stories 3. Graphic novels 4. Ghosts -- Fiction 5. Sisters -- Fiction 6. Cystic fibrosis -- Fiction 7. California, Northern -- Fiction 8. Family life -- California, Northern -- Fiction
ISBN 0545540623; 9780545540629; 9780545540612; 0545540615

LC 2016004672

"Catrina and her family have just moved to Northern California. Bahía de la Luna is different from Cat's hometown—for one thing, everyone is obsessed with ghosts—but the sea air makes it easier for Cat's younger sister, Maya, who has cystic fibrosis (CF), to breathe. Carlos, a new friend and neighbor, introduces the girls to a different perspective on the spiritual world." (School Library Journal)

"In her treatment of illness and death, Telgemeier (Sisters) nudges readers toward the edge of their comfort zone, but she never leaves them alone there. The story is consistently engaging, the plot is tightly built, and--as always--Telgemeier excels at capturing facial expressions." Pub Wkly

★ **Sisters**; Raina Telgemeier; with color by Braden Lamb. First edition Graphix 2014 197 p. chiefly color illustrations hbk $24.99; pbk $10.99

Grades: 5 6 7 8   **741.5**

1. Siblings 2. Family life 3. Autobiographical graphic novels 4. Interpersonal relations
ISBN 9780545540599; 9780545540605

LC 2013008700

"Raina can't wait to be a big sister. But once Amara is born, things aren't quite how she expected them to be. . . . They are sisters, after all. Raina uses her signature humor . . . in both present-day narrative and perfectly placed flashbacks to tell the story of her relationship with her sister, which unfolds during the course of a road trip from their home in San Francisco to a family reunion in Colorado." (Publisher's note)

"The author's narrative style is fresh and sharp, and the combination of well-paced and well-placed flashbacks pull the plot together, moving the story forward and helping readers understand the characters' point of view. The volume captures preadolescence in an effortless and uncanny way and turns tough subjects, such as parental marriage problems, into experiences with which readers can identify." (School Library Journal)

★ **Smile**. Scholastic/Graphix 2010 213p il $21.99; pa $10.99

Grades: 5 6 7 8   **741.5**

1. Graphic novels 2. Autobiographical graphic novels 3. Dentistry -- Graphic novels 4. Friendship -- Graphic novels 5. Personal appearance -- Graphic novels

ISBN 978-0-545-13205-3; 0-545-13205-3; 978-0-545-13206-0 pa; 0-545-13206-1 pa

LC 2008-51782

Eisner Award: Best Publication for Teens (2011)

Boston Globe-Horn Book Honor: Nonfiction (2010)

Sixth grader Raina just wants to be normal, but when she falls down going home from a Girl Scout meeting, she severely injures her two front teeth, and this starts her down a long road with braces, surgery, retainers, embarrassing headgear—all sure to make her stand out from her middle school classmates for all the wrong reasons. There's also a major earthquake, then boy confusion, friends who turn out not to be good friends, sibling jealousy, all the stuff that makes life interesting, if not fun. Telgemeier wrote and drew the autobiographical Smile as a webcomic; this volume collects the story in color.

"The dental case that Telgemeier documents in this graphic memoir was extreme: a random accident led to front tooth loss when she was 12, and over the next several years, she suffered through surgery, implants, headgear, false teeth, and a rearrangement of her remaining incisors. . . . Both adults and kids . . . are vividly and rapidly portrayed. . . . Telgemeier's storytelling and full-color cartoony images form a story that will cheer and inspire any middle-schooler dealing with orthodontia." Booklist

TenNapel, Doug

Cardboard; Doug TenNapel. Graphix / Scholastic 2012 288 p. $24.99

Grades: 5 6 7 8   **741.5**

1. Boxes -- Fiction 2. Gifts -- Graphic novels 3. Magic -- Graphic novels 4. Bullies -- Graphic novels 5. Father-son relationship -- Graphic novels

ISBN 0545418720; 9780545418720; 9780545418737

LC 2011934533

In this graphic novel, "Cam Howerton's out-of-work father is so broke, the best he can do for Cam's birthday is an empty cardboard box purchased from a toy seller with two mysterious rules: return every unused scrap of cardboard and don't ask for any more. . . . [T]he box becomes a project. What should father and son make out of the box? 'A boxer,' Cam suggests. . . . 'Boxer Bill,' created from inanimate material, comes alive. Unfortunately, Marcus, the neighborhood bully . . . steals the scrap materials, and begins turning out a whole evil empire of cardboard monsters. . . . [A]fter losing control of them he must unite with Cam and his father to defeat the massive cardboard army. . . . [Q]uestions are raised about what it means to be a man, what makes a good man, and what forms people's character." (Horn Book)

Thielbar, Melinda

The **ancient** formula; a mystery with fractions. illustrated by Tintin Pantoja. Graphic Universe 2010 46p il (Manga math mysteries) lib bdg $29.27

Grades: 1 2 3 4   **741.5**

1. Graphic novels 2. Mystery graphic novels 3. Kung fu -- Graphic novels 4. Schools -- Graphic novels 5. Mathematics -- Graphic novels

ISBN 978-0-7613-4907-5 lib bdg; 0-7613-4907-3 lib bdg

LC 2010001431

The students of Sifu Faiza's Kung Fu School use their knowledge of fractions as they try to discover what happened to Leung Jan's long-lost healing formula.

"The book is a great read and provides the reader with mathematical instruction, practice solving problems, and entertainment all at once. . . . The images and colors are exciting and vibrant." Sci Books Films

Thompson, Craig, 1975-

Space dumplins; Craig Thompson with color by Dave Stewart. Graphix / Scholastic 2015 320 p. color illustrations $24.99

Grades: 3 4 5 6   **741.5**

1. Missing persons -- Fiction 2. Interplanetary voyages -- Fiction 3. Father-daughter relationship -- Fiction

ISBN 0545565413; 9780545565417; 9780545565431

LC 2014956159

In this graphic novel by Craig Thompson, "for Violet Marlocke, family is the most important thing in the whole galaxy. So when her father goes missing while on a hazardous job, she can't just sit around and do nothing. To get him back, Violet throws caution to the stars and sets out with a group of misfit friends on a quest to find him. But space is vast and dangerous, and she soon discovers that her dad is in big, BIG trouble." (Publisher's note)

"Thompson's art is wild and busy, with overcrowded, unconventional panel structures. The worldbuilding is a strikingly imaginative pastiche that seamlessly blends biblical references, poop jokes, and social satire." Kirkus

Thompson, Jill

Magic Trixie; written and illustrated by Jill Thompson; lettered by Jason Arthur. Harper Trophy 2008 93p il pa $7.99

Grades: 3 4 5   **741.5**

1. Graphic novels 2. Fantasy graphic novels 3. Humorous graphic novels 4. Magic -- Graphic novels

ISBN 978-0-06-117045-4 pa

LC 2007-24298

Magic Trixie is feeling a bit put out; everything in her house seems to revolve around her baby sister, and she doesn't get to do anything fun. If that wasn't bad enough, Show & Tell time is coming up at Monstersorri School, and all her classmates have seen all her tricks too many times. She'll have to come up with a new one that's really special.

"Bright colors and a whimsical style make everything friendly rather than scary. Underneath the supernatural trappings lies a classical story of sibling envy to which every big sister and big brother can relate." Booklist

Other titles in this series are:

Magic Trixie sleeps over (2008)

Magic Trixie and the dragon (2009)

★ **Scary** Godmother; written and illustrated by Jill Thompson. Dark Horse 2010 207p il $24.99

Grades: 3 4 5   **741.5**

1. Graphic novels 2. Supernatural graphic novels 3. Halloween -- Graphic novels

ISBN 978-1-59582-589-6; 1-59582-589-4

It's Halloween night and it's up to Scary Godmother to show one little girl just how much fun spooky can be! Meet Hannah Marie, who, with the help of Scary Godmother, stands up to her mean-spirited cousin Jimmy and her fear of monsters on her first Halloween adventure with the big kids. Later, Hannah joins forces with Orson, the vampire boy, to unravel a mystery near and dear to their hearts.

This is a "collection compiling all four of Thompson's original Scary Godmother stories plus extra goodies. Told in often-rhyming prose and word balloons on vibrant pages that balance a visually lavish picture book aesthetic with sequential-art page composition, the stories burst with complex color tones and creepy cartoon figures." Booklist

★ The TOON treasury of classic children's comics; selected and edited by Art Spiegelman and Francoise Mouly; introduction by Jon Scieszka. Abrams ComicArts 2009 350p il $40
Grades: 3 4 5 6   **741.5**
1. Comic books, strips, etc.
ISBN 978-0-8109-5730-5; 0-8109-5730-2
                         LC 2009009830
"These stories are terrifically funny, joltingly exuberant, bafflingly bizarre, and best of all, compiled into one hearty, hefty, handsome volume." Booklist

Torres, J.
Into the woods; J. Torres; illustrated by Faith Erin Hicks. Kids Can Press 2012 100 p. col. ill. (Bigfoot Boy) (hardcover) $17.95
Grades: 3 4 5 6 7   **741.5**
1. Magic -- Graphic novels 2. Sasquatch -- Graphic novels 3. Totems and totemism -- Graphic novels
ISBN 1554537118; 9781554537112
In this fantasy graphic novel, "city boy Rufus is staying at his grandmother's house on the edge of a forest for a few days without his parents," and he "decides to explore the woods. He meets a girl named Penny. . . . When looking for her in the woods, Rufus finds a glowing necklace in a tree. After reading the word on the back, he turns into Bigfoot! . . . There's danger in the forest as well as magic, and when Penny disappears, Rufus . . . use[s] the totem to effect a rescue." (Kirkus Reviews)
Followed by: The unkindness of ravens (2013)

The **Sound** of Thunder; written by J. Torres; illustrated by Faith Erin Hicks. Kids Can Press 2014 100 p. chiefly color illustrations (Bigfoot boy) hbk $17.95; pbk $9.95
Grades: 3 4 5 6 7   **741.5**
1. Graphic novels 2. Adventure fiction 3. Pacific Northwest -- Fiction
ISBN 9781894786584; 9781894786591
Sequel to: The unkindness of ravens (2013)
"This conclusion to the Bigfoot Boy graphic novel trilogy adds a backdrop of Pacific Northwest mythology to the popular story about an ordinary boy who becomes a hero through the power of magic. As the book begins, Rufus, Penny and their squirrel friend, Sidney, are eager to recapture the magic totem they lost to the ravens in the previous book." (Publisher's note)
"Torres and Hicks conclude their woodsy trilogy with an exciting adventure dotted with humor. Rufus and Penny's attempts to understand Sidney's charades are a hoot. Rufus has worked a bit of his city-boy out, but his bumbles and stumbles continue to round out his character." Kirkus

The **unkindness** of ravens; by J. Torres; illustrated by Faith Erin Hicks. Kids Can Press 2013 100 p. col. ill. (Bigfoot boy) $17.95; pa $9.95
Grades: 3 4 5 6 7   **741.5**
1. Magic 2. Ravens -- Fiction
ISBN 9781554537136; 9781554537143; 1554537134; 1554537142
                         LC 2013040319
Sequel to: Into the woods (2012)
This book, by J. Torres and illustrated by Faith Erin Hicks, tells the story of "another weekend of Rufus using his magic totem to transform himself into Bigfoot Boy! But when you're big, hairy and loud, it's hard to keep your powers a secret, especially when there are trickster ravens that want the magic for themselves." (Publisher's note)
"Hicks's illustrations are done in bold, black lines and rich colors and are sometimes reminiscent of Native Canadian art styles. The story's adventure, magic, and characters will appeal." SLJ
Followed by: The sound of thunder (2014)

Townsend, Michael
Kit Feeny: on the move. Alfred A. Knopf 2009 un il lib bdg $12.99; pa $5.99
Grades: 3 4 5   **741.5**
1. Graphic novels 2. Moving -- Fiction 3. Bullies -- Fiction 4. Friendship -- Fiction
ISBN 978-0-375-95614-0 lib bdg; 0-375-95614-X lib bdg; 978-0-375-85614-3 pa; 0-375-85614-5 pa
                         LC 2008-37443
When plucky Kit Feeny moves to a new town, he immediately makes an enemy of the sadistic school bully and must struggle to find friends who share his interests.
"Kit, a mischievous, silly, ambiguous anthropomorphic animal, . . . is an easy hero to cheer for in this graphic novel, which reluctant readers will find hard to put down." Booklist

Kit Feeny: the ugly necklace. Alfred A. Knopf 2009 un lib bdg $12.99; pa $5.99
Grades: 3 4 5   **741.5**
1. Graphic novels 2. Bears -- Fiction 3. Gifts -- Fiction 4. Family life -- Fiction
ISBN 978-0-375-95615-7 lib bdg; 0-375-95615-8 lib bdg; 978-0-375-85615-0 pa; 0-375-85615-3 pa
                         LC 2008040155
Kit Feeny, a young bear, enters into a competition with his sisters to see who can give their mother the best birthday present

Trondheim, Lewis
Monster Christmas; [Joe Johnson, translation; Lea Hernandez, lettering] Papercutz 2011 32p il (Monster) $9.99
Grades: K 1 2 3   **741.5**
1. Graphic novels 2. Monsters -- Graphic novels 3. Christmas -- Graphic novels 4. Family life -- Graphic novels
ISBN 978-1-59707-288-5; 1-59707-288-5
Orginal French edition, 1999
"A brother, Petey, and a sister, Jean, go on a Christmas vacation to the snowy mountains with their Mom and Dad and pet monster, Kriss. On the way they encounter another monster chasing Santa Claus and have to rely on their creativity, quick thinking, and a monster of their own to save Santa and themselves. Both Trondheim's art and the English-language translation create a story that could come from the mind of a child, despite its bizarre creatures and sudden surprises. Yet it's also the work of a talented artist channeling that childish wonder into a finely crafted tale for young audiences." Publ Wkly

Tiny Tyrant; by Lewis Trondheim; translated from the French by Alexis Siegel; illustrated by Fabrice Parme. First Second Books 2007 124p il $12.95
Grades: 4 5 6 7 8 9 10 11 12 Adult   **741.5**
1. Graphic novels 2. Humorous graphic novels
ISBN 978-1-59643-094-5
                         LC 2006021479
"Tiny child-king Ethelbert is spoiled and difficult, expecting to have his every whim fulfilled-or else. . . . In the end, though, he becomes a hero. The dynamic cartoons are filled with details and riddled with humor; most pages have between six and eight small pictures. . . . This title

will have wide appeal. It's young and accessible enough for elementary-grade kids, but teens will also be charmed by the rascally king." SLJ

Varon, Sara

Bake sale. First Second 2011 157p il $19.99; pa $16.99

Grades: 3 4 5 6 7 8   **741.5**

1. Graphic novels 2. Cupcakes -- Graphic novels 3. Bakers and bakeries -- Graphic novels

ISBN 978-1-59643-740-1; 1-59643-740-5; 978-1-59643-419-6 pa; 1-59643-419-8 pa

LC 2010051587

"The book has a mellow, easygoing feel, using soft colors and showing many yummy foods. As an added bonus, recipes for how to make the various scrumptious meals readers watch Cupcake prepare are provided. . . . Varon's art is simple and cozy, making this sweet tale a confection of its own." Publ Wkly

Venable, Colleen AF

Hamster and cheese; illustrated by Stephanie Yue. Graphic Universe 45p il (Guinea Pig, pet shop private eye) lib bdg $27.93; pa $6.95

Grades: 2 3 4   **741.5**

1. Mystery graphic novels 2. Animals -- Graphic novels 3. Hamsters -- Graphic novels 4. Guinea pigs -- Graphic novels

ISBN 978-0-7613-4598-5 lib bdg; 0-7613-4598-1 lib bdg; 978-0-7613-5479-6 pa; 0-7613-5479-4 pa

"There is skullduggery afoot at Mr. Venezi's Pets & Stuff: Someone keeps stealing his sandwich, which he puts outside the koala cage every day. No, he doesn't sell koalas; they're really hamsters, but Mr. Venezi is both shortsighted and incompetent (though very kind). The only cage that's correctly labeled is the one holding the guinea pig--but someone has stolen the G, so little Hamisher the koala, er, hamster has decided that guinea pig Sasspants must be a P.I. and therefore can crack the case." (Kirkus)

"Who is stealing Mr. Venezi's sandwiches? The befuddled pet-shop owner misidentifies the store's animals, leading the hamsters to think they're koalas. . . . Hamisher the koala-hamster thinks Sasspants the guinea pig is a private investigator because the second G on her cage's sign has fallen off, so he asks her to investigate. . . . Young readers will appreciate the zaniness of the pet shop and the fun mystery, and Yue's colorful art uses a straightforward panel design that's easy to follow." Booklist

Other titles in this series are:

And then there were gnomes (2010)

The ferret's a foot (2011)

Fish you were here (2011)

Raining cats and detectives (2012)

Going, going, dragon! (2013)

Venditti, Robert

★ The **lightning** thief; the graphic novel; by Rick Riordan; adapted by Robert Venditti; art by Attila Futaki; color by Jose Villarrubia; layouts by Orpheus Collar; lettering by Chris Dickey. Disney/Hyperion Books 2010 un il (Percy Jackson and the Olympians) $19.99; pa $9.99

Grades: 5 6 7 8   **741.5**

1. Graphic novels 2. Greek mythology -- Graphic novels

ISBN 978-1-4231-1696-7; 1-4231-1696-8; 978-1-4231-1710-0 pa; 1-4231-1710-7 pa

LC 2010035512

After learning that he is the son of a mortal woman and Poseidon, god of the sea, twelve-year-old Percy is sent to a summer camp for demigods like himself, and joins his new friends on a quest to prevent a war between the gods.

This graphic novel adaptation of Rick Riordan's novel "succeeds in spectacular fashion. . . . The book retains the excellent pacing of the original and gives a face to Riordan's vision of the mythological made modern. Futaki's artwork is exemplary but what leaves such a lasting impression is Villarrubia's coloring, which reveals both subtlety and spectacle when needed." Publ Wkly

Other graphic adaptations in this series are:

The sea of monsters (2013)

The Titan's curse (2013)

Weigel, Jeff

★ **Thunder** from the sea; adventure on board the HMS Defender. G. P. Putnam's Sons 2010 46p il $17.99

Grades: 3 4 5 6   **741.5**

1. Graphic novels 2. Adventure graphic novels 3. Naval art and science -- Graphic novels 4. Great Britain -- Royal Navy -- Graphic novels 5. Europe -- History -- 1789-1815 -- Graphic novels

ISBN 978-0-399-25089-7

LC 2009-32801

In 1805, during the Napoleonic Wars, twelve-year-old Jack Hoyton becomes a member of the crew of HMS Defender, a midsize ship in the British Royal Navy. The Defender patrols along a portion of the French coast to block French ships, but a major gun emplacement in Dumont hampers the ship's efforts. When some of the crew land to fill their barrels with fresh water, French gunmen fire upon them, killing an officer and wounding a crewman. The Captain assigns Jack to be part of the crew that will land and take the guns; when the men arrive, they find that there is no small village, but a major shipbuilding facility, and they're captured.

"Weigel's old-fashioned comics art shows lots of authentic details of eighteenth-century shipboard life, and there is some battle violence. . . . This picture-book-size graphic novel should find a ready audience of young adventure-loving readers." Booklist

Includes bibliographical references

Weing, Drew

The **creepy** case files of Margo Maloo; by Drew Weing. First Second 2016 121 p. chiefly color illustrations $15.99

Grades: 3 4 5 6   **741.5**

1. Mystery graphic novels 2. Moving -- Fiction 3. Monsters -- Fiction

ISBN 1626723397; 9781626723399

"Charles just moved to Echo City, and some of his new neighbors give him the creeps. They sneak into his room, steal his toys, and occasionally, they try to eat him. The place is teeming with monsters! Lucky for Charles, Echo City has Margo Maloo, monster mediator. No matter who's causing trouble, Margo knows exactly what to do." (Publisher's note)

"Weing's colorful drawings reward extended examination; Echo City is rife with monster life, and creepy crawlies turn up in the most unexpected places, but domestic scenes and the city streets also show the artist's keen eye for details." SLJ

Wetterer, Margaret K.

The **snowshoeing** adventure of Milton Daub, blizzard trekker; by Margaret K. Wetterer and Charles M. Wetterer; adaptation by Emma Carlson Berne; illustrated by Zachary Trover. Graphic Universe 2011 31p il (History's kid heroes) lib bdg $26.60; pa $8.95

Grades: 2 3 4   **741.5**

1. Graphic novels 2. Adventure graphic novels 3. Snowshoers 4. Blizzards -- Graphic novels 5. Bronx (New York, N.Y.) -- Graphic

novels

ISBN 978-0-7613-6175-6 lib bdg; 0-7613-6175-8 lib bdg; 978-0-7613-6194-7 pa; 0-7613-6194-4 pa

LC 2009051717

An 1888 blizzard has paralyzed much of the Northeast United States, but twelve-year-old Milton Daub puts on a pair of homemade snowshoes and braves the storm to bring food and medicine to many of his neighbors in the Bronx, New York.

This book provides an "exciting [glimpse] into the past, with just the right amount of tension and intensity to capture readers' attention. . . . [It] will serve as [a] good [introduction] to graphic novels and historical fiction for early readers. Added bonuses are the brief yet informative [introduction] and [afterword] providing more facts about the [setting]." SLJ

Includes bibliographical references

White, Mike

Amity Blamity, book one. SLG 2011 un il pa $10.95

Grades: 4 5 6   741.5

1. Graphic novels 2. Farm life -- Graphic novels

ISBN 978-1-59362-209-1; 1-59362-209-0

"Four-year-old Gretchen doesn't speak. Thankfully, she's got her potbellied pig, Chester, who's not only something of a motormouth but an ambitious one at that. He's the founder of Pig Corp. . . . Their main threat is Gretchen's lazy ex-jailbird uncle, Downey. . . . The resulting humor is enjoyable funny-paper fare. . . . Quirky talking-animal fare with just enough edge to tickle." Booklist

Wight, Eric

★ Frankie Pickle and the closet of doom; written and illustrated by Eric Wight. Simon & Schuster Books for Young Readers 2009 79p il $9.99

Grades: 2 3 4 5   741.5

1. Graphic novels 2. Humorous graphic novels 3. Cleanliness -- Fiction 4. Family life -- Fiction 5. Imagination -- Fiction 6. Family life -- Graphic novels 7. Orderliness -- Graphic novels

ISBN 978-1-4169-6484-1; 1-4169-6484-3

LC 2008-30865

Fourth-grader Frankie Piccolini has a vivid imagination when it comes to cleaning his disastrously messy room, but eventually even he decides that it is just too dirty.

"Wight's hilarious twists of language are matched with a wicked sense of fun in the illustrations and frequent sequential-paneled episodes of pretend play." Kirkus

Other titles about Frankie Pickle are:

Frankie Pickle and the Pine Run 3000 (2010)

Frankie Pickle and the mathematical menace (2011)

Frankie Pickle and the land of the lost recess (2012)

Winick, Judd, 1970-

Hilo; the boy who crashed to Earth. by Judd Winick; with color by Guy Major. Random House Inc 2015 208 p. color illustrations (Hilo) (hardcover) $13.99

Grades: 2 3 4 5   741.5

1. Graphic novels 2. Science fiction 3. Robots -- Fiction 4. Amnesia -- Fiction 5. Identity -- Fiction 6. Friendship -- Fiction 7. Extraterrestrial beings -- Fiction

ISBN 0385386176; 9780385386173; 9780385386180

LC 2014030736

"D.J. and his friend Gina are totally normal kids. But that was before a mysterious boy came crashing down from the sky! Hilo doesn't know where he came from, or what he's doing on Earth. . . . But what if Hilo wasn't the only thing to fall to our planet? Can the trio unlock the secrets

of his past? Can Hilo survive a day at school? And are D.J. and Gina ready to save the world?" (Publisher's note)

"Winick has concocted a universally appealing tale with bright, expressive illustrations that gently reminds readers that in this era of over-scheduling and insistence on perfection, sometimes just being true to yourself is important enough." Kirkus

Other titles about Hilo are:

Saving the whole wide world (2016)

The great big boom (2017)

Yang, Gene Luen, 1973-

Secret coders; Gene Yuen Lang & Mike Holmes. First Second 2015 96 p. color illustrations (Secret coders) (hardcover) $17.99

Grades: 4 5 6 7   741.5

1. School stories -- Graphic novels 2. Computer programming -- Graphic novels

ISBN 9781626722767; 9781626720756; 1626722765

In this graphic novel, by Gene Yuen Lang and Mike Holmes, "Hopper, an enthusiastic 12-year-old girl . . . , has just started school at the creepy Stately Academy. After getting in a fight . . . with Eni . . . , Hopper and Eni become friends while unraveling the secrets of the school. Robotic birds, family troubles, and sinister, child-hating school administrators lead to a story both emotionally rich and rife with learning opportunities." (School Library Journal)

"Holmes' blocky cartoon illustrations, in black, white, and green, clearly depict basic programming concepts with tidy visual cues, such as grids of floor tiles. Yang and Holmes do such a great job explaining the concepts that even programming newbies will be likely to catch on." Booklist

Other titles in this series are:

Path and portals (2016)

Secrets and sequences (2017)

Yoon, Salina

Duck, Duck, Porcupine! Salina Yoon. Bloomsbury Childrens Books 2016 64 p. color illustrations (hardback) $9.99

Grades: PreK K 1 2   741.5

1. Ducks -- Fiction 2. Porcupines 3. Brothers and sisters -- Fiction

ISBN 9781619637238; 1619637235

LC 2015022813

In this book, by Salina Yoon, "Big Duck likes to boss around her younger brother, Little Duck, and she fancies herself the leader of their trio--when joined by their gentle friend Porcupine. Little Duck doesn't speak yet, but through his expressions and his actions, he shows that he has a better grasp on any situation than his older sister." (Publisher's note)

"Fresh and funny; a welcome addition to the easy-reader shelf." Horn Book

Zornow, Jeff

The legend of Sleepy Hollow; adapted and illustrated by Jeff Zornow; based upon the works of Washington Irving. Magic Wagon 2007 un il (Graphic horror) $18.95

Grades: 5 6 7 8 9 10 11 12   741.5

1. New York (State) -- Graphic novels

ISBN 978-1-60270-060-4; 1-60270-060-5

LC 2007-9615

This "is an entertaining and faithful, if much adapted version of Irving's classic story. Zornow's illustrations are the highlight of the work, successfully bringing the characters of the story to life." Booklist

741.6 Graphic design, illustration, commercial art

★ **Artist** to artist; 23 major illustrators talk to children about their art. Philomel Books 2007 105p il $30

Grades: 4 5 6 7   **741.6**
1. Illustrators 2. Illustration of books 3. Picture books for children
ISBN 978-0-399-24600-5

"This anthology celebrates and elucidates contemporary picture-book art. . . . Ashley Bryan, Quentin Blake, Leo Lionni, Alice Provensen, and Gennady Spirin are among the contributors, whose comments are formatted as signed letters illustrated with childhood photographs. . . . Each artist includes glorious self-portraits and a gatefold page that reveals a marvelous array of sketches, color mixes, and studio scenes. All readers will find something that piques curiosity or provides insight." Booklist

Carle, Eric
The **art** of Eric Carle. Philomel Bks. 1996 125p il $35; pa $19.99

Grades: Adult Professional   **741.6**
1. Illustration of books 2. Picture books for children
ISBN 0-399-22937-X; 0-399-24002-0 pa
LC 95-24940

This is "both a textual and visual anthology: in addition to Carle's autobiographical chapter and the text of his 1990 speech at the Library of Congress, chapters include accolades from Ann Beneduce (Carle's U.S. editor) and from Dr. Viktor Christen (Carle's German editor). A photoessay on the artist's collage technique rubs shoulders with a forty-page gallery of his illustrations over the last quarter of a century, which precedes a look at some of his quick sketches and an illustrated bibliography of his oeuvre. The book's inviting layout may appeal to artistic youngsters as well as grown Carle fans, and the information about his working process, particularly the technical details, is absorbing." Bull Cent Child Books

Kushner, Tony
The **art** of Maurice Sendak; 1980 to present. text by Tony Kushner. Abrams 2003 223p il $60

Grades: Adult Professional   **741.6**
1. Artists 2. Authors 3. Illustrators 4. Set designers 5. Children's authors
ISBN 0-8109-4448-0
LC 2003-9293

This "collection presents 350 illustrations, many of which are drawings for set and costume design work, . . . others of which are posters for plays and for events such as the New York is Book Country fair. . . . Sendak's precise, intensely shaded yet welcoming shapes and figures have lost none of their luster. They would ordinarily be enough in themselves in a survey like this, but Kushner's lovely, funny, partisan text . . . lifts the book to another level." Publ Wkly

Includes bibliographical references

Maguire, Gregory
Making mischief; a Maurice Sendak appreciation. William Morrow 2009 200p il $27.50

Grades: Adult Professional   **741.6**
1. Artists 2. Authors 3. Illustrators 4. Set designers 5. Children's authors
ISBN 978-0-06-168916-1; 0-06-168916-5
LC 2009017357

"Maguire constructs a thoughtful and accessible overview of Sendak's works and artistic process, making for a tender homage to the famed artist that only a true fan could produce. . . . He presents a series of five essays, expounding upon the various influences seen in Sendak's work.

. . as well as an analysis of motifs and techniques. Maguire often allows the art to speak for itself, displaying a generous selection of Sendak's illustrations, both famed and lesser known." Bull Cent Child Books

Marcus, Leonard S., 1950-
Randolph Caldecott; the man who could not stop drawing. Leonard S. Marcus. Farrar, Straus & Giroux (BYR) 2013 64 p. (hardcover) $24.99

Grades: 5 6 7 8   **741.6**
1. Picture books for children 2. Illustrators -- England -- Biography
ISBN 0374310254; 9780374310257
LC 2012050406

This book is a biography of Randolph Caldecott, "the illustrator for whom the Caldecott Medal is named." Leonard S. Marcus begins by "describing the changes wrought in 19th-century Great Britain by the steam engine, which eased travel and greatly expanded distribution of media. He details Caldecott's early days clerking in a bank and his search for freelance illustration work, then describes how diligence and charm lead to his first book-illustrating assignment" and then to a career in illustration. (Publishers Weekly)

Nahson, Claudia J.
The **snowy** day and the art of Ezra Jack Keats; Claudia J. Nahson; with an essay by Maurice Berger. Jewish Museum, under the auspices of the Jewish Theological Seminary of America 2011 104p il $27.50

Grades: Adult Professional   **741.6**
1. Artists 2. Authors 3. Illustrators 4. Authors, American 5. Children's authors
ISBN 978-0-300-17022-1; 0-300-17022-X
LC 2011007880

"Keats's Caldecott-winning story about a boy's wintertime exploration of his neighborhood turns 50 in 2012; this fascinating examination of Keats and his oeuvre, complete with 80 full-color reproductions, coincides with the first major U.S. exhibition devoted to his work. . . . Nahson, curator at the Jewish Museum, writes that The Snowy Day reflected Keats's interest in 'rendering visible what has hitherto been invisible to his audience, be that an inner-city child, a message graffitied on a wall, or a dilapidated building.' Her essay joins one from historian/art critic Maurice Berger that makes abundantly clear the book's societal importance." Publ Wkly

Includes bibliographical references

Neuburger, Emily K.
★ A **Caldecott** celebration; seven artists and their paths to the Caldecott medal. rev ed.; Walker & Co. 2008 55p il $19.95; lib bdg $20.85

Grades: Adult Professional   **741.6**
1. Illustrators 2. Caldecott Medal 3. Illustration of books
ISBN 978-0-8027-9703-2; 0-8027-9703-2; 978-0-8027-9704-9 lib bdg; 0-8027-9704-0 lib bdg
LC 2007-23132

First published 1998

Profiles seven Caldecott award winning books and their authors, including Robert McCloskey's "Make Way for Ducklings," Marcia Brown's "Cinderella," Maurice Sendak's "Where the Wild Things Are," William Steig's "Sylvester and the Magic Pebble," Chris Van Allsburg's "Jumanji," David Wiesner's "Tuesday," and Mordicai Gerstein's "The Man Who Walked Between the Towers"

"The value of this volume is that Marcus makes these exceptional author/illustrators, and the processes by which they created their award-winning picture books, accessible to children and to adults who value children's literature." SLJ

Say, Allen

★ **Drawing** from memory; Allen Say. 1st ed. Scholastic Press 2011 63 p. il map $17.99

Grades: 3 4 5 6 **741.6**

1. Artists 2. Authors 3. Illustrators 4. Autobiography -- Graphic novels 5. Children's authors 6. Japanese Americans -- Biography

ISBN 9780545176866; 0545176867

LC 2011016324

Sibert Honor Book, 2012

This book "opens with a . . . watercolor map of Japan on the left, framed in a rectangle, while on the right is a . . . watercolor of Yokohama's seashore and fishing village, with two black-and-white photographs pasted on: Say as a child, and the stone beach wall. The early arc takes readers from [Allen] Say's 1937 birth, through family moves to escape 1941 bombings and then Say's nigh-emancipation at age 12, when his mother supported him in his own Tokyo apartment. The one-room apartment 'was for me to study in, but studying was far from my mind... this was going to be my art studio!' The art table's drawer handle resembles a smile. . . . [A]pprenticing with famous cartoonist Noro Shinpei, Say works dedicatedly on comic panels, still-lifes and life drawing. Nothing—not political unrest, not U.S. occupation, not paternal disapproval—derails his singular goal of becoming a cartoonist." (Kirkus)

"Say's account is complex, poignant, and unfailingly honest. Say's fans—and those who also feel the pull of the artist's life—will be captivated." Publ Wkly

Stevens, Janet

From pictures to words; a book about making a book. written and illustrated by Janet Stevens. Holiday House 1995 un il $16.95

Grades: K 1 2 3 **741.6**

1. Authorship 2. Picture books for children

ISBN 0-8234-1154-0

LC 94-18976

"The straightforward text carefully presents information while maintaining the narrative flow. Dialogue balloons and funny asides from the characters keep the presentation lively." SLJ

Tan, Shaun

★ The **bird** king; an artist's notebook. Shaun Tan. Arthur A. Levine Books 2013 128 p. (hardcover : alk. paper) $19.99

Grades: 3 4 5 6 7 **741.6**

1. Artists' notebooks

ISBN 0545465133; 9780545465137

LC 2012016625

This book by author and illustrator Shaun Tan "is a collection of sketches, random jottings, preliminary designs for book, film and theatre projects, sketchbook pages and drawings from life. Each of these represent some aspect of a working process, whereby stories generally evolve from visual research and free-wheeling doodles. They are also 'unfinished' pieces created in a single sitting, not originally intended for publication." (Publisher's note)

Under the spell of the moon; art for children from the world's great illustrators. [edited by Patricia Aldana; texts translated by Stan Dragland] Groundwood Books 2004 80p il $25

Grades: Adult Professional **741.6**

1. Illustrators 2. Illustration of books 3. Illustrated children's books

ISBN 0888995598

This volume includes the work of thirty-three illustrators of books for children. The illustrators "each have a double page including both their illustration and a short piece of text (written either by them or another author), or a traditional verse or saying. . . . Original texts in a language

other than English are included, followed by a translation by Canadian poet and editor Stan Dragland. . . . Age four and up." (Quill Quire)

This "collection features the artwork of children's book illustrators who, together, represent more than 25 countries. Each double-page spread includes a different artist's image accompanied by a poem, nursery rhyme, song, or bit of nonsense that appears in both English and the illustrator's native language. . . . Katherine Paterson offers a stirring introduction that discusses IBBY (The International Board on Books for Young People)." Booklist

741.9 Collections of drawings

Volavkova, Hana

★ --I never saw another butterfly-- children's drawings and poems from Terezin concentration camp, 1942-1944. edited by Hana Volavková; foreword by Chaim Potok; afterword by Vaclav Havel. expanded 2nd ed; Schocken Bks. 1993 xxii, 106p il hardcover o.p. pa $17.50

Grades: 4 5 6 7 **741.9**

1. Child artists 2. Children's writings 3. Holocaust, 1933-1945 4. Terezin (Czechoslovakia: Concentration camp)

ISBN 0-8052-1015-6 pa

LC 92-50477

Original Czech edition, 1959; first American edition published 1964 by McGraw-Hill

"Of the 15,000 children who passed through Terezin before going to Auschwitz, only 100 lived. This book is a collection of poems and drawings by some of them. . . . This touching book adds another facet to library collections on the Holocaust." SLJ

743 Drawing and drawings by subject

Ames, Lee J.

Draw 50 aliens, UFO's galaxy ghouls, milky way marauders, and other extra terrestrial creatures; [by] Lee J. Ames with Ric Estrada. Doubleday 1998 un il (Draw 50) hardcover o.p. pa $8.95

Grades: 4 5 6 7 **743**

1. Drawing

ISBN 978-0-385-49144-0; 0-385-49144-1; 978-0-385-49145-7 pa; 0-385-49145-X pa

LC 98-20077

A step-by-step guide to drawing outer space creatures

Draw 50 beasties and yugglies and turnover uglies and things that go bump in the night. Doubleday 1988 il (Draw 50) hardcover o.p. pa $8.95

Grades: 4 5 6 7 **743**

1. Drawing 2. Monsters in art

ISBN 978-0-385-24625-5; 0-385-24625-0; 978-0-385-26767-0 pa; 0-385-26767-3 pa

LC 88-16143

Provides step-by-step instructions for drawing monsters, goons, and gruesome beasts

Ames "encourages readers to take plenty of time and suggests very lightly sketching out the step-by-step drawings so that mistakes may be rectified. This one, with its popular subject of imaginative monsters and other nightmare inhabitants, will be a sure-fire circulator." SLJ

Other Draw 50 titles are:

Draw 50 animal 'toons

Draw 50 animals

Draw 50 athletes

Draw 50 buildings and other structures

Draw 50 boats, ships, trucks & trains

Draw 50 cats

Draw 50 dinosaurs and other prehistoric animals

Draw 50 dogs

Draw 50 horses

Draw 50 monsters, creeps, superheroes, demons, dragons, nerds, dirts, ghouls, giants, vampires, zombies, and other curiosa

Draw 50 baby animals

Draw 50 flowers, trees, and other plants

Draw 50 birds; [by] Lee J. Ames with Tony D'Adamo. Doubleday 1996 un il (Draw 50) hardcover o.p. pa $8.95

Grades: 4 5 6 7   743

1. Drawing 2. Birds in art

ISBN 978-0-385-47006-3; 0-385-47006-1; 978-0-385-47163-3 pa; 0-385-47163-7 pa

LC 96-27621

Draw 50 endangered animals; [by] Lee J. Ames with Warren Budd. Doubleday 1992 un il (Draw 50) hardcover o.p. pa $8.95

Grades: 4 5 6 7   743

1. Drawing 2. Animals in art 3. Animal painting and illustration

ISBN 978-0-385-41191-2; 0-385-41191-X; 978-0-385-46985-2 pa; 0-385-46985-3 pa

LC 92-23092

Step-by-step instructions on how to draw a variety of threatened species from all over the world

Draw 50 people; [by] Lee J. Ames with Creig Flessel. Doubleday 1993 un il (Draw 50) hardcover o.p. pa $8.95

Grades: 4 5 6 7   743

1. Portraits 2. Drawing -- Technique

ISBN 978-0-385-41193-6; 0-385-41193-6; 978-0-385-41194-3 pa; 0-385-41194-4 pa

LC 93-20631

[Draw 50 series] Doubleday 1974 21v

Grades: 4 5 6 7   743

1. Drawing

Each volume presents step-by-step instructions for drawing a variety of animals, people, or objects

Bergin, Mark

How to draw pets. PowerKids Press 2011 32p il (How to draw) lib bdg $25.25; pa $11.75

Grades: 4 5 6 7   743

1. Animals in art 2. Drawing -- Technique

ISBN 978-1-4488-4511-8 lib bdg; 978-1-4488-4517-0 pa

LC 2010049184

"The cover features sketches of a cat, dog, and rabbit, allowing children to see both structure as well as finished product. Inside, the book starts by showing pictures of animals drawn with different materials such as pencils, ink, charcoals, and pastels, and explains what each medium accomplishes. Next comes an introduction to perspective and looks at different parts of animals. The familiar circle method then gets kids drawing pets from head to tails. . . . The amount of information throughout is just right: thorough but not overwhelming." Booklist

Includes glossary

Emberley, Ed

Ed Emberley's drawing book of faces. Little, Brown 1975 32p il hardcover o.p. pa $6.95

Grades: 2 3 4 5   743

1. Drawing 2. Face in art

ISBN 0-316-23655-1 pa

Provides step-by-step instructions for drawing a wide variety of faces reflecting various emotions and professions

Farrell, Russell

All about drawing horses & pets. Walter Foster 2010 80p (All about drawing) $34.25; pa $9.95

Grades: K 1 2 3   743

1. Horses in art 2. Animals in art 3. Drawing -- Technique

ISBN 978-1-936309-06-1; 1-936309-06-8; 978-1-600585-80-7 pa; 1-600585-80-9 pa

LC 2010004211

First published 2008 in paperback

"Starting with simple geometric shapes, readers are led step-by-step through stages to draw [horses and pets]; close observation is presented as key to drawing lifelike forms. Photos or illustrations of the real creatures are included with 'Fun Facts' about them for readers' reference." Horn Book Guide

All about drawing sea creatures & animals; illustrated by Russell Farrell and Diana Fisher. Walter Foster 2010 80p il (All about drawing) $34.25; pa $9.95

Grades: K 1 2 3   743

1. Marine animals in art 2. Drawing -- Technique

ISBN 978-1-936309-08-5; 1-936309-08-4; 978-1-600585-81-4 pa; 1-600585-81-7 pa

First published 2008 in paperback

"Starting with simple geometric shapes, readers are led step-by-step through stages to draw [sea creatures and animals]; close observation is presented as key to drawing lifelike forms. Photos or illustrations of the real creatures are included with 'Fun Facts' about them for readers' reference." Horn Book Guide

Fisher, Diana

All about drawing dinosaurs & reptiles. Walter Foster 2011 80p (All about drawing) $34.25

Grades: K 1 2 3   743

1. Reptiles in art 2. Dinosaurs in art 3. Drawing -- Technique

ISBN 978-1-936309-07-8; 1-936309-07-6

LC 2010004210

"Starting with simple geometric shapes, readers are led step-by-step through stages to draw [dinosaurs and reptiles]; close observation is presented as key to drawing lifelike forms. Photos or illustrations of the real creatures are included with 'Fun Facts' about them for readers' reference." Horn Book Guide

Masiello, Ralph

Ralph Masiello's Halloween drawing book; Ralph Masiello. Charlesbridge 2012 48 p. (softcover) $7.95

Grades: 2 3 4   743

1. Halloween 2. Drawing -- Technique 3. Halloween in art

ISBN 1570915415; 9781570915413; 9781570915420

LC 2011036736

In this book, author and illustrator Ralph Masiello "brings a haunting twist to his popular drawing series. Step-by-step diagrams show young artist how to draw ghosts, witches, jack-o'-lanterns, skeletons, a haunted house, and more. Just follow the simple steps to create creepy critters and eerie objects. Bonus challenge steps show you how to add frightfullyfun details to your drawings." (Publisher's note)

Ralph Masiello's robot drawing book. Charlesbridge 2011 un lib bdg $16.95; pa $7.95

Grades: 2 3 4 5 **743**

1. Robots in art 2. Drawing -- Technique

ISBN 978-1-57091-535-2 lib bdg; 1-57091-535-0 lib bdg; 978-1-57091-536-9 pa; 1-57091-536-9 pa

LC 2010033634

"Masiello begins with a discussion of how to use circles, squares, and other basic forms to draw robot parts like switches, plugs, and antennae. He includes a brief discussion of drawing and coloring tools and shows young artists how to draw eight different robots. . . . The instructions are simple enough for primary-grade students to have success without adult assistance. Masiello's creations are humorous, old-fashioned, and two dimensional." SLJ

Peffer, Jessica

DragonArt; how to draw fantastic dragons and fantasy creatures. Impact Books 2005 127p il pa $19.99

Grades: 5 6 7 8 **743**

1. Dragons 2. Drawing 3. Mythical animals

ISBN 1-58180-657-4

LC 2005013013

This is a guide to drawing dragons and other mythical beasts such as griffins, guardian gargoyles, and deadly basilisks.

"This book has great writing and superb illustrations and manages to do everything right from the front cover to the index." SLJ

Roza, Greg

Drawing Dracula. Windmill Books 2011 24p il (Drawing movie monsters step-by-step) lib bdg $25.65; pa $12.85

Grades: 3 4 5 6 **743**

1. Monsters in art 2. Drawing -- Technique 3. Motion pictures -- History and criticism

ISBN 978-1-61533-015-7 lib bdg; 1-61533-015-1 lib bdg; 978-1-61533-021-8 pa; 1-61533-021-6 pa

LC 2010004901

A "surefire [hit] with movie fans and aspiring artists, [this volume traces] the cinematic history of [Dracula] and gives step-by-step instructions on how to bring [him] to life on paper. The instructions and accompanying illustrations explaining how to draw the [monster start] with basic shapes such as circles and rectangles and gradually adding more details. . . . Each pose comes from a notable cinematic depiction of the monster . . . and includes a brief description of the movie with entertaining trivia about its cultural significance, special effects, or popularity over time. The drawing poses are logically organized in chronological order. . . . With text printed in a large, clear font and simply structured sentences, [this book provides] an accessible introduction to film history, and young artists will undoubtedly enjoy trying their hand at depicting [the monster] in a variety of poses." SLJ

Includes glossary and bibliographical references

Other titles in this series are:

Drawing Frankenstein

Drawing Godzilla

Drawing King Kong

Stephens, Jay

Heroes! draw your own superheroes, gadget geeks & other do-gooders. [by] Jay Stephens. Lark Books 2007 64p il $12.95; pa $5.95

Grades: 4 5 6 7 **743**

1. Drawing 2. Superheroes 3. Cartoons and caricatures

ISBN 978-1-57990-934-5; 1-57990-934-5; 978-1-60059-179-2 pa; 1-60059-179-5 pa

LC 2006101661

"Stephens shows just how to draw [superheroes]. . . . Stephens does a good job organizing his material, beginning with a bit of history, then

moving quickly to hero heads, . . . and on to masks, disguises, physical features, power effects, and action moves. The brightly colored illustrations offer plenty of how-to info and lots of great heroes, male and female, to use as models." Booklist

Other titles in this series are:

Monsters!

Robots!

745 Decorative arts

Dhom, Christel

The **Advent** Craft and Activity Book; Stories, Crafts, Recipes and Poems for the Christmas Season. Christel Dhom. Floris Books 2012 144 p. $19.95

Grades: 4 5 6 **745**

1. Advent 2. Baking 3. Children's stories 4. Handicraft for children

ISBN 0863159125; 9780863159121

This book is a "compendium of old-fashioned craft projects, recipes and stories was written by a Waldorf kindergarten teacher in Germany and translated for English-speaking countries. . . . Recipes for holiday cookies and candies are included, with measurements given in both grams and ounces. Craft projects include traditional advent wreaths, beeswax candles and Nativity figures made from unspun sheep's wool." (Kirkus)

Tejubehan (Singer)

★ **Drawing** from the City; Teju Behan. Pgw 2012 28 p. $35.95

Grades: 3 4 5 6 7 8 **745**

1. India 2. Artists 3. Poverty

ISBN 9380340176; 9789380340173

This "autobiographical art book recounts self-taught artist Teju Behan's journey from an impoverished childhood in rural India, through her family's efforts to improve their lot in a tent city in Mumbai, and into her adulthood, when she lived as a singer and artist with her husband. . . . Hand-screen-printed illustrations comprised of intricate linework and patterns of dots underscore elements of the text." (Kirkus)

745.2 Industrial art and design

Arato, Rona

Design it! the ordinary things we use every day and the not-so-ordinary ways they came to be. illustrations by Claudia Newell. Tundra Books 2010 71p il pa $20.95

Grades: 4 5 6 7 **745.2**

1. Industrial design 2. Inventors 3. Inventions 4. Design, Industrial

ISBN 978-0-88776-846-0 pa; 0-88776-846-6 pa

"This book opens with an explanation of what industrial designers do and with whom they work to make better products. Brief chapters then cover such topics as home, communications, lighting, and toy design and include a good-design checklist that takes function, usability, ergonomics, aesthetics, and greenness into consideration. The language is chatty and inviting, and the pages are full of cartoon illustrations and text superimposed on colorful geometric backgrounds. Sidebars offer a wealth of further information." SLJ

Welsbacher, Anne

Earth-friendly design; by Anne Welsbacher. Lerner Publications Company 2009 72p il (Saving our living Earth) lib bdg $30.60

Grades: 5 6 7 8   **745.2**
    1. Industrial design 2. Environmental protection
    ISBN 978-0-8225-7564-1 lib bdg; 0-8225-7564-7 lib bdg
                                                LC 2007-35925
    "Provides a thorough, interesting discussion of multiple aspects of
[Earth-friendly design], including historical origins, the current situation,
and potential solutions. . . . Photos from around the world accompany
discussions. . . . [This is a] solid choice to replace outdated books."
SLJ
    Includes glossary and bibliographical references

745.5   Handicrafts

Alter, Anna
    What can you do with an old red shoe? a green activity book about
re-use. [by] Anna Alter. Henry Holt & Co. 2009 32p il $16.95
Grades: 1 2 3   **745.5**
    1. Salvage 2. Recycling 3. Handicraft
    ISBN 978-0-8050-8290-6; 0-8050-8290-5
                                                LC 2008018341
    "Recycling becomes lots of fun in this sprightly activity book. Alter
offers 13 projects, and . . . the finished products are usually items kids
will want to use. . . . The instructions are clear and simple . . . and what
really makes this a standout is Alter's adorable artwork featuring a coterie of animals at work and play. Short poems introduce each project."
Booklist

Blake, Susannah
    Crafts for pampering yourself; Susannah Blake. Enslow Publish-
ers, Inc. 2013 32 p. color illustrations (Eco chic) $22.60
Grades: 4 5 6 7 8   **745.5**
    1. Cosmetics 2. Handicraft 3. Green products
    ISBN 0766043142; 9780766043145
                                                LC 2012045280
    In this book, author Susannah Blake offers suggestions on how read-
ers can "have an eco-friendly pampering party with these . . . craft ideas.
From lip balm to bath infusion, this book offers easy step-by-step instructions to upcycle, customise and add sparkle to your bathroom routines." (Publisher's note)
    "Numbered step-by-step illustrations; a fresh, tween-friendly de-
sign; explanations of basic craft skills; and instructions for throwing a
'pamper party' round out the beauty-meets-responsibility fun."

Carlson, Laurie
    Knit, hook, and spin; a kid's activity guide to fiber arts and crafts.
Laurie Carlson. Chicago Review Press Inc. 2016 144 p. illustrations
(trade paper) $14.99
Grades: 4 5 6 7   **745.5**
    1. Handicraft for children 2. Textile crafts
    ISBN 9781613734001
                                                LC 2015044783
    This book, by Laurie Carlson, is an "activity book packed with over
70 projects across a variety of fiber arts including knitting, felting, knotting and braiding, spinning, weaving, crocheting, and dyeing. Clear
instructions and illustrations guide you in creating these cute, useful
crafts." (Publisher's note)
    "From slippers to tote bags and from friendship bracelets to comfort
dolls, there is something for almost anyone wanting to learn how to create from these very tactile sources." Kirkus

Enz, Tammy
    Cool plastic bottle and milk jug science; by Tammy Enz. Capstone
Press 2017 31 p. chiefly color illustrations (Edge books. Recycled science) (ebook) $27.99; (library binding) $27.99
Grades: 3 4 5 6   **745.5**
    1. Recycling   2. Handicraft   3. Science -- Experiments   4.
    Plastic bottles   5. Plastic bottle craft   6. Recycling (Waste, etc.)
    7. Science -- Study and teaching
    ISBN 9781515708667; 1515708624; 9781515708629
                                                LC 2015045604
    This book, by Tammy Enz, "why throw used plastic bottles and milk
jugs in the reycling when you can reuse them yourself? These fun and informative science experiments and projects will keep readers entertained
as they learn about scientific principles." (Publisher's note)
    "Great page design and cool projects combine to make this series a
winner." SLJ
    Includes bibliographical references (page 45) and index

Garner, Lynne
    ★ **African** crafts; fun things to make and do from West Africa.
Chicago Review Press 2008 48p il $12.95
Grades: 4 5 6   **745.5**
    1. Handicraft 2. African art 3. Ghana -- Social life and customs
    ISBN 978-1-55652-748-7; 1-55652-748-9
    First published 2004 in the United Kingdom
    Presents an overview of West African culture and provides step-by-
step instructions for using simple household materials to make such traditional items as a mask, a coiled pot, block-printed and woven cloths,
and a drum.
    "Despite the generic title, the focus is on one country, Ghana, and
that is the strength of this hands-on crafts book, illustrated with clear
step-by-step instructions and lots of color photos. . . . Written in chatty
style, the spaciously laid out chapters cover adinkra block printing, pot
coiling, mask making, music makers, and kente strip weaving. . . . An
excellent source for school and home." Booklist

Harvey, Karen
    Face Painting; Over 30 faces to paint, with simple step-by-step
instructions. by Karen Harvey. Motorbooks Intl 2016 64 p. color
illustrations $12.95
Grades: K 1 2 3   **745.5**
    1. Face painting 2. Painting -- Technique 3. Painting
    ISBN 160992925X; 9781609929251
                                                LC 2016022947
    This children's book by Karen Harvey "contains everything you
need to start face painting! . . . Clear, step-by-step photographic instructions mean that all the faces are easy to follow and try, plus there are
tips and suggestions for ways to tweak the designs. All projects use a set
colour palette and are carefully chosen to appeal to girls and boys alike."
(Publisher's note)
    "Whether cute or creepy, the designs are so appealing that readers
will be hard-pressed to wait for a special occasion to replicate them."
Pub Wkly

Henry, Sandi
    Making amazing art; 40 activities using the 7 elements of art de-
sign. by Sandi Henry; illustrated by Sarah Rakitin Cole. Williamson-
books 2007 128p il (Kids can) $16.99; pa $12.99
Grades: 2 3 4 5   **745.5**
    1. Art 2. Design 3. Handicraft
    ISBN 978-0-8249-6794-9; 0-8249-6794-1; 978-0-8249-6795-6
    pa; 0-8249-6795-X pa
                                                LC 2006101173

"Each chapter in this well-organized, heavily illustrated book features one element—line, texture, color, etc.—with five or six projects that cleverly support it. . . . Icons display three challenge levels; step-by-step instructions help to ensure success." SLJ

Jocelyn, Marthe

Sneaky art; crafty surprises to hide in plain sight. Marthe Jocelyn. Candlewick Press 2013 64 p. $12.99

Grades: 3 4 5   745.5

1. Handicraft for children
ISBN 0763656488; 9780763656485

LC 2012942615

This children's craft book, by Marthe Jocelyn, is a "how-to manual for creating removable and shareable art projects from easily found materials. The sneaky part is in the installation! Each work of art is custom-created for display in public places. . . . This utterly unique guide--part craft book, part art-philosophy--offers a stylish and sweet . . . spirit of fun meant to put a smile on the faces of strangers and loved ones alike." (Publisher's note)

Llimos, Anna

Easy cardboard crafts in 5 steps. Enslow Elementary 2008 31p il (Easy crafts in 5 steps) lib bdg $22.60

Grades: 2 3 4   745.5

1. Handicraft
ISBN 978-0-7660-3083-1 lib bdg; 0-7660-3083-0 lib bdg
Original Spanish edition 2005

This "has instructions for 14 projects, among them a folder, drum, and hang-glider. . . . A materials list is provided for each item, with general supplies and recyclables sufficient for most crafts. The simple directions are adequately spaced on the page and accompanied by step-by-step color photos." SLJ

Includes bibliographical references

Other titles in this series are:
Easy cloth crafts in 5 steps
Easy earth-friendly crafts in 5 steps

Haunted house adventure crafts. Enslow Elementary 2010 32p il (Fun adventure crafts) lib bdg $22.60; pa $6.95

Grades: 1 2 3   745.5

1. Halloween 2. Handicraft
ISBN 978-0-7660-3730-4 lib bdg; 0-7660-3730-4 lib bdg; 978-0-7660-3731-1 pa; 0-7660-3731-2 pa

LC 2009041462
Original Spanish edition 2008

"In simple language and bright pictures, 11 crafts are laid out, including the magnum opus: a cardboard haunted house. . . . Small illustrated versions of the final products cavort across the pages, and story ideas conclude." Booklist

Includes bibliographical references

Monaghan, Kimberly

Organic crafts; 75 earth-friendly art activities. [by] Kimberly Monaghan. Chicago Review Press 2007 140p pa $14.95

Grades: 2 3 4 5   745.5

1. Handicraft 2. Nature craft
ISBN 978-1-55652-640-4 pa; 1-55652-640-7 pa

LC 2006031659

"These activities, crafts, and games are arranged by type of material used, such as rocks, pebbles, and shells; soil, clay, and sand, etc. There's a wide range of interesting projects, including clay beads, a glittering sand castle, potpourri, a sea sparkler, a wind sock, a gourd birdhouse, broken-china mosaics, homemade paper, rock sculpture, and garden

chimes. Children will also learn how to make natural glue, cornstarch paint, and salt clay." SLJ

Includes bibliographical references

My art book; amazing art projects inspired by masterpieces. DK Pub. 2011 80p il $15.99

Grades: 3 4 5 6   745.5

1. Art 2. Handicraft
ISBN 978-0-7566-7582-0; 0-7566-7582-0

"Representing a variety of cultures and styles, this book highlights 14 famous artworks and offers a craft project related to each one. The arrangement is roughly chronological, beginning with the cave paintings of Lascaux, France, and ending with the Pop Art of Andy Warhol. Each work is reproduced in a high-quality color photograph and described in a few paragraphs of succinct but interesting text. The projects are varied and appealing, and no two use the same medium or technique. . . . A great resource for teaching art history though hands-on activities." SLJ

Oldham, Todd

★ **Kid** made modern. AMMO 2009 184p il $22.95

Grades: 3 4 5 6   745.5

1. Design 2. Handicraft
ISBN 978-1-934429-36-5; 1-934429-36-8

LC 2009-934393

"This activity book from renowned designer Oldham uses the work of Mid-Century modern visual artists—including Isamu Noguchi, Alexander Calder, and Charles and Ray Eames—as springboards for 52 hands-on creative projects. Brief tutorials introduce skills and techniques, paired with full-color photos of kids and the various processes. . . . There's much here to capture the eye of ambitious, crafty readers." Publ Wkly

Owen, Cheryl

Gifts for kids to make. Hamlyn 2006 128p il pa $14.95

Grades: K 1 2 3 4 5   745.5

1. Gifts 2. Handicraft
ISBN 0-600-61502-2

"This useful volume is divided into six categories—bric-a-brac, stationery, scented gifts, floral garden gifts, accessories, and edible treats—with 7 to 10 projects in each. Examples are magnets, bookmarks, gift wrap, birdfeeder, glasses case, and cookies. . . . The items are appealing to children and age appropriate. Both the written and visual instructions are clear and easy to follow." SLJ

Sirrine, Carol

Cool crafts with old jeans; green projects for resourceful kids. Capstone Press 2010 32p il (Snap books. Green crafts) lib bdg $26.65

Grades: 3 4 5 6   745.5

1. Recycling 2. Handicraft 3. Jeans (Clothing)
ISBN 978-1-4296-4006-0 lib bdg; 1-4296-4006-5 lib bdg

"Steps are easy to follow and well documented, and the projects encourage experimentation and creativity. Materials are generally easy to find. . . . This . . . is original, well-presented, and bound to inspire classroom and individual projects." SLJ

Includes glossary and bibliographical references

Cool crafts with old t-shirts; green projects for resourceful kids. Capstone Press 2010 32p il (Snap Books. Green crafts) lib bg $26.65

Grades: 3 4 5 6   745.5

1. Salvage 2. Handicraft
ISBN 1-4296-4009-X lib bdg; 978-1-4296-4009-1 lib bdg

"Steps are easy to follow and well documented, and the projects encourage experimentation and creativity. Materials are generally easy to find. . . . This . . . is original, well-presented, and bound to inspire classroom and individual projects." SLJ

Includes glossary and bibliographical references

Cool crafts with old wrappers, cans and bottles; green projects for resourceful kids. Capstone Press 2010 32p il (Snap books. Green crafts) lib bdg $26.65

Grades: 3 4 5 6   **745.5**

1. Salvage 2. Handicraft

ISBN 978-1-4296-4008-4 lib bdg; 1-4296-4008-1 lib bdg

"Steps are easy to follow and well documented, and the projects encourage experimentation and creativity. Materials are generally easy to find. . . . This . . . is original, well-presented, and bound to inspire classroom and individual projects." SLJ

Includes glossary and bibliographical references

Torres, Laura

Rock your school stuff. QEB Pub. 2010 32p il (Rock your . . .) lib bdg $28.50

Grades: 4 5 6   **745.5**

1. Handicraft 2. Schools -- Equipment and supplies

ISBN 978-1-59566-936-0; 1-59566-936-1

LC 2010010670

This book "gives kids easy step-by-step ways to . . . personalize school supplies. . . . Colorful photographs show youngsters crafting [such items as beaded pens, recycled paperclip bookmarks, backpack zipper pulls] . . . some of which are created from recycled found items. All are projects they can complete by themselves." Horn Book Guide

Wheeler-Toppen, Jodi Lyn

Amazing cardboard tube science; by Jodi Wheeler-Toppen. Capstone Press 2017 32 p. illustrations (chiefly color) (Edge books. Recycled science) (library binding) $27.99

Grades: 3 4 5 6   **745.5**

1. Recycling 2. Handicraft 3. Science -- Experiments 4. Cardboard tube craft 5. Recycling (Waste, etc.) 6. Science -- Study and teaching

ISBN 1515708608; 9781515708605

LC 2015045734

This book, by Jodi Wheeler-Toppen, asks "why throw old cardboard tubes in the reycling when you can reuse them yourself? These fun and informative science experiments and projects will keep readers entertained as they learn about scientific principles." (Publisher's note)

"Great page design and cool projects combine to make this series a winner." SLJ

Includes bibliographical references and index

Wolf, Laurie Goldrich

Recyclo-gami; 40 crafts to make your friends green with envy! Running Press Teens 2010 112p il $14.95

Grades: 4 5 6 7   **745.5**

1. Recycling 2. Handicraft

ISBN 978-0-7624-4052-8; 0-7624-4052-X

"Wolf's fun, resourceful projects offer straightforward ways to reuse common materials to make accessories, jewelry, household decorations, games, and gifts. Leftover tissue or wrapping paper can be used to create decoupage plates; old crayons are melted and baked into molds to make multicolored crayons; and unused CDs and DVDs are transformed into funky, freeform bowls when melted in the oven. . . . The ease of most of the activities should inspire readers to see the recycling bin as a potential treasure trove." Publ Wkly

Yanish, Brian

Scrapkins; Junk Re-Thunk: Amazing Creations You Can Make from Junk! Brian Yanish. Christy Ottaviano Books/Henry Holt & Company 2016 80 p. (trade pbk.) $12.99

Grades: 2 3 4 5   **745.5**

1. Handicraft for children 2. Recycling 3. Waste products 4. Handicraft 5. Recycling (Waste, etc.)

ISBN 9781627791335

LC 2015003031

This book by Brian Yanish introduces children to "Scrap City, home of an inventive tribe of creatures called ScrapKins. Using materials that people throw away . . . these creatures make new things that are useful. . . . With character profiles of the ScrapKins and instructions to make all kinds of puppets, instruments, and toys out of everyday items, this activity book . . . fosters creativity and encourages eco-friendliness." (Publisher's note)

"A great STEAM-focused craft book for at-home rainy day fun." SLJ

745.54   Papers

Garza, Carmen Lomas

★ **Making** magic windows; creating papel picado/cut-paper art with Carmen Lomas Garza. Children's Bk. Press 1999 61p il pa $9.95

Grades: 3 4 5 6   **745.54**

1. Paper crafts

ISBN 0-89239-159-6

LC 98-38518

Provides instructions for making paper banners and more intricate cut-outs. Includes diagrams for creating specific images

"Based on workshops conducted by the artist, the step-by-step instructions and illustrations have been fine-tuned and are clear and easy to follow. . . . Multiculturally authentic and a guaranteed kid-crowd pleaser, this workbook is enthusiastically recommended for all craft collections." Booklist

Latno, Mark

The **paper** boomerang book; build them, throw them, and get them to return every time. Chicago Review Press 2010 245p il pa $12.95

Grades: 5 6 7 8   **745.54**

1. Boomerangs 2. Paper crafts

ISBN 978-1-56976-282-0 pa; 1-56976-282-1 pa

LC 2010007251

"In a unique . . . guide Latno . . . [explains] how to make, fine-tune, and decorate a type of paper boomerang that can be constructed with commonly available materials and thrown with (relative) safety indoors. The instructions and simply drawn diagrams are embedded in a history of boomerangs and throwing sticks, a challenging technical discussion of the physics of boomerangs and gyroscopes, and very detailed descriptions of the characteristics of railroad board (Latno's preferred paper) and alternatives, plus art-and-craft materials that can be used to dress up finished models." SLJ

Includes glossary and bibliographical references

Llimos, Anna

Easy paper crafts in 5 steps. Enslow Elementary 2008 31p il (Easy crafts in 5 steps) lib bdg $22.60

Grades: 2 3 4   **745.54**

1. Paper crafts

ISBN 978-0-7660-3087-9 lib bdg; 0-7660-3087-3 lib bdg

Original Spanish edition 2005

This offers instructions for 14 paper craft projects, among them a basket, a butterfly, and pop-up card

The text is "easy to read, and the results are quirky and pleasing; steps are illustrated with bright photographs." Horn Book Guide

Includes bibliographical references

Torres, Laura

Rock your party. QEB Pub. 2010 32p il (Rock your . . .) lib bdg $28.50

Grades: 4 5 6   **745.54**

1. Parties 2. Handicraft 3. Paper crafts

ISBN 978-1-59566-935-3; 1-59566-935-3

LC 2010010668

This book "gives kids easy step-by-step ways to make decorations for their . . . parties. . . . Colorful photographs show youngsters crafting appealing . . . party hats, etc. some of which are created from recycled found items. All are projects they can complete by themselves." Horn Book Guide

745.58   Beads, found and other objects

Boonyadhistarn, Thiranut

Beading; bracelets, barrettes, and beyond. by Thiranut Boonyadhistarn. Capstone Press 2007 32p il (Snap books) $25.26

Grades: 4 5 6 7   **745.58**

1. Beadwork

ISBN 978-0-7368-6472-5; 0-7368-6472-5

LC 2006004102

This describes how to create such bead crafts as safety-pin bracelets and bag charms.

"Girls will appreciate these ideas for recreating fashion trends and for achieving the artistic effects that they want. . . . Page layouts are lively and attractive. The projects use easily obtainable materials, and the directions are simple and well numbered." SLJ

Includes bibliographical references

Ross, Kathy

Beautiful beads; illustrated by Nicole in den Bosch. Millbrook Press 2009 48p il lib bdg $26.60

Grades: 2 3 4 5   **745.58**

1. Beadwork

ISBN 978-0-8225-9214-3 lib bdg; 0-8225-9214-2 lib bdg

LC 2008044441

"A diverse collection of 21 fun and unique projects. Young readers will learn how to make different types of beads (fabric, textured, thread, ribbon, sparkle stem), two games, a felt-bead bracelet, a cluster pin, a seed-bead flower magnet, whimsical items (beaded dog, spaghetti doll, and others), a bookmark, a tissue box, and more. The colors are vivid, and the illustrations perfectly complement the text." SLJ

Scheunemann, Pam

★ **Cool** beaded jewelry; [by] Pam Scheunemann. ABDO Pub. 2005 32p il (Cool crafts) $22.78

Grades: 4 5 6   **745.58**

1. Jewelry 2. Beadwork

ISBN 1-59197-739-8

LC 2004-46292

This "has an extensive section on bead history, sizes, shapes, types, and metal findings (clasps, etc.). Projects include a memory wire bracelet, a beaded necklace and bracelet, daisy chain necklace, and beaded rings." SLJ

Sirrine, Carol

Cool crafts with old CDs; green projects for resourceful kids. Capstone Press 2010 32p il (Snap books. Green crafts) lib bdg $26.65

Grades: 3 4 5 6   **745.58**

1. Salvage 2. Compact discs 3. Plastics craft

ISBN 978-1-4296-4007-7 lib bdg; 1-4296-4006-5 lib bdg

"Steps are easy to follow and well documented, and the projects encourage experimentation and creativity. Materials are generally easy to find. . . . This . . . is original, well-presented, and bound to inspire classroom and individual projects." SLJ

Includes glossary and bibliographical references

745.59   Making specific objects

Hufford, Deborah

★ **Greeting** card making; send your personal message. by Deborah Hufford. Capstone Press 2006 32p il (Snap books crafts) lib bdg $25.26

Grades: 3 4 5   **745.59**

1. Handicraft 2. Greeting cards

ISBN 0-7368-4385-X

LC 2005006899

"A pop-up birthday cake, a dried flower-petal design, and a lacey valentine are among the homemade card ideas featured in this simple, easy-to-follow title. . . . Introductory pages cover basic paper folds and materials; later spreads present mostly clear, step-by-step instructions." Booklist

Includes glossary and bibliographical references

Kenney, Karen Latchana

Super simple magnets; fun and easy-to-make crafts for kids. ABDO Pub. Co. 2010 32p il (Super simple crafts) lib bdg $17.95

Grades: K 1 2 3 4   **745.59**

1. Magnets 2. Handicraft

ISBN 978-1-60453-626-3 lib bdg; 1-60453-626-8 lib bdg

LC 2009-355

"Colorful photos; clean layout in a bright, primary palette; and large, abundant step-by-step instructional photos give [this book] great appeal. The . . . crafts . . . are functional and attractive. . . . Readily obtainable household materials and easy-to-follow instructions mean that children can do these crafts independently." SLJ

Includes glossary

745.592   Toys, models, miniatures, related objects

Harbo, Christopher L.

The **kids'** guide to paper airplanes. Capstone Press 2009 32p il (Kids' guides) $23.93

Grades: 4 5 6 7   **745.592**

1. Paper crafts 2. Airplanes -- Models

ISBN 978-1-4296-2274-5; 1-4296-2274-1

LC 2008029688

"Using colorful, vivid, and clear step-by-step illustrations, Harbo demonstrates how to construct everything from the classic Dart to the circular Space Ring to the 18-step Silent Huntress." Booklist

Includes glossary and bibliographical references

Paper airplanes: Flight school, level 1. Capstone Press 2010 32p il (Edge books. Paper airplanes) lib bdg $26.65

Grades: 3 4 5 6   **745.592**

1. Paper crafts 2. Airplanes -- Models

ISBN 978-1-4296-4741-0 lib bdg; 1-4296-4741-8 lib bdg

LC 2010001005

This "includes a list of basic materials and an overview of folding instructions and techniques. . . . Along with hints on how to hold the plane for takeoff to maximize strengths are suggestions on conducting friendly competitions with the finished products. Sure to keep readers busy for hours." SLJ

Includes bibliographical references

Other titles in this series are:

Copilot, level 2

Pilot, level 3

Captain, level 4

Mercer, Bobby

The **flying** machine book; build and launch 35 rockets, gliders, helicopters, boomerangs, and more. Bobby Mercer. Chicago Review Press 2012 ix, 197 p.p ill. (pbk.) $14.95

Grades: 4 5 6   **745.592**

1. Flight 2. Aeronautics 3. Airplanes -- Models 4. Models and modelmaking 5. Paper airplanes 6. Flying-machines -- Models

ISBN 9781613740866

LC 2011041174

This book provides "step-by-step instructions for 35 aerodynamic projects . . . Physics teacher [Bobby] Mercer . . . here provides . . . directions for building a variety of flying machines including rockets, gliders, helicopters, boomerangs and assorted launchers. An opening chapter called 'Flight School' introduces the Bernoulli principle and four forces: lift, thrust, drag and weight. . . . Each subsequent chapter begins with more flight school, repeating the relevant principles and applying them to the different forms of flying machines described. Many of the constructions use similar techniques and most are not difficult. The models are made of common materials: card stock and old folders, drinking straws, rubber bands and duct tape." (Kirkus Reviews)

Rigsby, Mike

★ **Amazing** rubber band cars; easy-to-build wind-up racers, models, and toys. [by] Mike Rigsby. Chicago Review Press 2007 121p il lib bdg $12.95

Grades: 4 5 6 7   **745.592**

1. Toys 2. Handicraft 3. Automobiles -- Models

ISBN 978-1-55652-736-4 lib bdg; 1-55652-736-5 lib bdg

LC 2007013969

This offers instructions for making toy and model cars "using mostly cardboard, glue, pencils, rubber bands, and a few other easily obtainable materials. . . . Readers will learn about corrugated and flat cardboard, and how to use glue and work with templates. Excellent instructions are accompanied by black-and-white photos every step of the way. . . . These projects are fun to construct, and inquisitive minds will be fascinated by the moving cars." SLJ

Schwarz, Renee

Wind chimes and whirligigs. Kids Can Press 2007 40p il (Kids can do it) $12.95; pa $6.95

Grades: 4 5 6   **745.592**

1. Handicraft 2. Whirligigs 3. Wind chimes

ISBN 978-1-55337-868-6; 1-55337-868-7; 978-1-55337-870-9 pa; 1-55337-870-9 pa

"A colorfully designed and artfully arranged photographic cover is the perfect introduction to the 12 unique and creative projects within. An overall neat appearance and precise, vibrant illustrations or sharp photos add to the attractive layout. . . . The techniques, using plastic, nylon fishing line, tape, glue, and screwdrivers, are carefully explained." SLJ

Thomson, Ruth

Toys and models; photography by Neil Thomson. Sea-to-Sea Publications 2010 32p il (World of design) lib bdg $28.50

Grades: 4 5 6 7   **745.592**

1. Toys 2. Handicraft 3. Models and modelmaking

ISBN 978-1-59771-209-5 lib bdg; 1-59771-209-4 lib bdg

LC 2008-43868

This "volume presents examples of crafts made around the world, then offers six simple items inspired by these goods that children can make (mostly using recycled materials). The directions allow for easy replication, while information about the crafts provides a window into world cultures. . . . The colorful close-up photographs provide . . . interesting details." Horn Book Guide

Includes glossary and bibliographical references

745.593   Useful objects

Mooney, Carla

Light your way; make a candle. Norwood House Press 2010 48p il (Creative adventure guides) lib bdg $25.27

Grades: 3 4 5 6   **745.593**

1. Candles

ISBN 978-1-59953-387-2; 1-59953-387-1

LC 2010010399

"Some historical background and scientific or cultural information places the making and use of candles . . . in context for young readers. [The] book has four chapters that culminate in step-by-step projects." Horn Book Guide

Includes glossary and bibliographical references

Price, Pamela S.

★ **Cool** scrapbooks; [by] Pam Price. ABDO Pub. 2005 32p il (Cool crafts) lib bdg $25.65

Grades: 4 5 6   **745.593**

1. Scrapbooks

ISBN 1-59197-744-4

LC 2004-46290

This guide to scrapbooks "addresses the use of photos, embellishments, adding words, computer possibilities, and more. . . . [This book lists] required materials, [has] small color photos, and [includes] clearly explained, numbered steps." SLJ

Ransom, Candice F.

Scrapbooking just for you! how to make fun, personal, save-them-forever keepsakes. [by] Candice Ransom. Sterling Pub. 2010 120p il $14.95

Grades: 4 5 6 7   **745.593**

1. Scrapbooks

ISBN 978-1-4027-4096-1; 1-4027-4096-4

LC 2008038982

"Ransom's well-organized introduction showcases her enthusiasm for scrapbooking and also includes material for more experienced crafters. . . . High-quality color photos that are a good match with the directions make the pages pop, and directions are clear." SLJ

745.594   Decorative objects

Bledsoe, Karen E.

Chinese New Year crafts; [by] Karen E. Bledsoe. Enslow Publishers 2005 32p il (Fun holiday crafts kids can do) lib bdg $22.60

Grades: 2 3 4   **745.594**

1. Handicraft 2. Chinese New Year

ISBN 0-7660-2347-8

LC 2004-9622

This includes directions for ten craft projects related to Chinese New Year including a dragon-streamer puppet, a ribbon lantern, and Chinese zodiac pictures

This is "aesthetically pleasing with . . . bright colorful pages, clear concise instructions on the left side and photographs of various stages of the final product on the right. . . . Use of everyday items such as paper cups, cupcake liners, and construction paper makes these activities practical for both students and teachers." SLJ

Includes bibliographical references

Di Salle, Rachel

Junk drawer jewelry; written by Rachel Di Salle and Ellen Warwick; illustrated by Jane Kurisu. Kids Can Press 2006 40p il (Kids can do it) hardcover o.p. pa $6.95

Grades: 4 5 6   **745.594**

1. Jewelry 2. Handicraft

ISBN 978-1-55337-965-2; 978-1-55337-966-9 pa

This introduces the "world of jewelry crafting. . . . Projects of varying difficulty include bracelets, necklaces, rings, wristbands, chokers, and earrings. Each project is accompanied by a color photo, a You Will Need list, and step-by-step instructions. This book will be a popular addition to libraries." SLJ

Fritsch, P.

Pennsylvania Dutch Halloween scherenschnitte; written and illustrated by Peter V. Fritsch. Pelican 2011 78p il $19.95

Grades: 3 4 5 6   **745.594**

1. Paper crafts 2. Pennsylvania Dutch folk art 3. Halloween -- Poetry

ISBN 978-1-58980-956-7; 1-58980-956-4

LC 2011012276

"In the tradition of Pennsylvania Dutch folk art, Fritsch arranges scherenschnitte (scissor-cut) silhouettes against flaming orange backgrounds. Short poems, which appear both in the Pennsylvania Dutch dialect and in English, mine folklore with rascally and sometimes frightening results, and are set against often symmetrical scenes of angular cats, ghosts, witches, and other devilish creatures. An elegant treat harkens back to early American celebrations of Halloween." Publ Wkly

McGee, Randel

Paper crafts for Chinese New Year; [by] Randel McGee. Enslow Elementary 2008 48p il (Paper craft fun for holidays) lib bdg $23.93

Grades: 2 3 4   **745.594**

1. Paper crafts 2. Chinese New Year

ISBN 978-0-7660-2950-7 lib bdg; 0-7660-2950-6 lib bdg

LC 2007014026

This explains the significance of Chinese New Year and offers instructions for making paper crafts including a dancing dragon puppet, a lion dancer mask, a lai see or red gift envelope, shadow puppets, a tangram, a chinese lantern, firecracker decorations, and Chinese symbols and banners.

"The crafts contain materials lists and color photos of the steps and of the finished product. The directions are easy to follow, and enlargeable patterns are provided." SLJ

Includes bibliographical references

Other titles in this series are:

Paper crafts for Christmas

Paper crafts for Day of the Dead

Paper crafts for Halloween

Paper crafts for Kwanzaa

Paper crafts for Valentine's Day

Rau, Dana Meachen

Get connected; make a friendship bracelet. Norwood House Press 2010 48p il (Creative adventure guides) lib bdg $25.27

Grades: 3 4 5 6   **745.594**

1. Beadwork 2. Bracelets

ISBN 978-1-59953-385-8; 1-59953-385-5

LC 2010010404

"Some historical background and scientific or cultural information places the making and use of . . . jewelry . . . in context for young readers. [The] book has four chapters that culminate in step-by-step projects." Horn Book Guide

Includes glossary and bibliographical references

Trusty, Brad

The kids' guide to balloon twisting; by Brad and Cindy Trusty. Capstone Press 2011 32p il (Kids' guides) lib bdg $26.65

Grades: 4 5 6 7   **745.594**

1. Balloons 2. Handicraft

ISBN 978-1-4296-5444-9; 1-4296-5444-9

LC 2010036470

Gives kids step-by-step instructions about how to twist balloon animals and other shapes.

"Rare is the kid not dazzled by the squeaking, twisting balloon maestros out there, and this brightly illustrated, step-by-step guide makes it easy—well, easy-ish." Booklist

Includes bibliographical references

745.6 Calligraphy, heraldic design, illumination

Hanson, Anders

Cool calligraphy; the art of creativity for kids. [by] Anders Hanson. ABDO Pub. Co. 2009 32p il (Cool art) lib bdg $24.21

Grades: 2 3 4   **745.6**

1. Calligraphy

ISBN 978-1-60453-145-9 lib bdg; 1-60453-145-2 lib bdg

LC 2008-19885

This book about calligraphy is "well organized, with clearly written sections . . . and several clever projects and exercises. . . . [It] should have substantial child appeal." SLJ

Includes glossary

745.7 Decorative coloring

Wagner, Lisa, 1958-

★ **Cool** painted stuff; [by] Lisa Wagner. ABDO Pub. 2005 32p il (Cool crafts) $22.78

Grades: 4 5 6   **745.7**

1. Painting 2. Handicraft

ISBN 1-59197-742-8

LC 2004-53117

This guide to painted crafts "includes four projects (in six or seven steps): a flowered mini-tote, checkered frame, treasure box, and fancy flowerpot. [This book lists] required materials, [has] small color photos, and [includes] clearly explained, numbered steps." SLJ

746.1   Products and processes

Roessel, Monty

Songs from the loom; a Navajo girl learns to weave. text and photographs by Monty Roessel. Lerner Publs. 1995 48p il (We are still here) lib bdg $21.27; pa $6.95

Grades: 3 4 5 6   746.1

1. Weaving 2. Navajo Indians

ISBN 0-8225-2657-3 lib bdg; 0-8225-9712-8 pa

LC 94-48765

"Ten-year-old Jaclyn's grandmother teaches her the art of traditional Navajo rug-weaving. Jaclyn learns the songs and stories that invest the weaving with meaning, as well as the use of the proper tools and techniques. The color photographs of contemporary Navajo life are clear and engrossing, enhancing the solid text." Horn Book Guide

Includes glossary and bibliographical references

746.4   Needlework and handwork

Sadler, Judy Ann

★ The **jumbo** book of needlecrafts; written by Judy Ann Sadler ... [et al.]; illustrated by Esperança Melo . . . [et al.] Kids Can Press 2005 208p il $16.95

Grades: 4 5 6   746.4

1. Needlework

ISBN 1-55337-793-1

A compilation with a new introduction of 5 books previously published: Knitting by Judy Ann Sadler (2002); Crocheting by Gwen Blakely Kinsler (2003); Simply sewing by Judy Ann Sadler (2004); Embroidery by Judy Ann Sadler (2004); Quilting by Biz Storms (2001)

This is a "how-to guide to the basics of knitting, crocheting, embroidery, quilting, and sewing. . . . The volume begins with helpful suggestions on gathering supplies, measuring, selecting fabric, and stitching. The rest of the book presents detailed, step-by-step directions on basic techniques for projects that range from very simple to intricate. . . . Color drawings and photographs are appealing as well as instructive. . . . An excellent addition to needlework collections." SLJ

746.42   Nonloom weaving and related techniques

Sadler, Judy Ann

Hemp jewelry; written by Judy Ann Sadler; illustrated by June Bradford. Kids Can Press 2005 40p il (Kids can do it) hardcover o.p. pa $6.96

Grades: 4 5 6   746.42

1. Jewelry 2. Beadwork 3. Macramé

ISBN 1-55337-774-5; 1-55337-775-3 pa

This "provides instructions for making jewelry from strands of hemp that are woven in various patterns while incorporating beads, clasps, and other findings. . . . Attractive and easy to follow. . . . Detailed, step-by-step instructions, . . . are clearly illustrated with large-scale, colorful ink-and-wash drawings." Booklist

★ **Knotting**; make your own basketball nets, guitar straps, sports bags and more! written by Judy Ann Sadler; illustrated by Céleste Gagnon. Kids Can Press 2006 40p il (Kids can do it) $12.95; pa $6.99

Grades: 4 5 6   746.42

1. Handicraft 2. Knots and splices

ISBN 1-55337-541-6; 1-55337-834-2 pa

This describes how use rope to make various types of knots, lanyards, guitar straps, ladders, hanging holders, swings, dog leashes, and basketball nets.

746.43   Knitting, crocheting, tatting

Bradberry, Sarah

★ **Kids** knit! simple steps to nifty projects. [by] Sarah Bradberry. Sterling Pub. Co. 2004 96p il hardcover o.p. pa $9.95

Grades: 5 6 7 8   746.43

1. Knitting

ISBN 0-8069-7733-7; 978-1-4027-4057-2 pa; 1-4027-4057-3 pa

LC 2004-19375

Presents basic knitting techniques and instructions for making a backpack, pillow, doll, and other simple projects

This "book works equally well for beginners and experienced knitters. . . . Besides the requisite information on knitting and purling, there are invaluable tips about finishing garments, fixing mistakes, and adding embellishments. The projects have been chosen with an eye toward simplicity, yet they have real appeal." Booklist

Junor, Betty

Fun & funky knits; over 20 simple knit stitch projects. by Betty Junor. 1st North American ed. Barron's Educational Series, Inc. 2012 80 p. col. ill. (paperback) $7.99

Grades: 4 5 6   746.43

1. Knitting 2. Sewing -- Technique 3. Needlework -- Patterns 4. Knitting -- Patterns

ISBN 1438001746; 9781438001746

LC 2012932175

Author Betty Junor presents a book on knitting projects, "starting with very basic instructions and recommending the use of brilliantly colored yarns." Junor discusses slipknots, casting off, and finishing and gives directions for making headbands, belts, drawstring bags, and purses. She also shows readers how to make knitted flowers and how to incorporate pompoms into projects. (Publisher's note)

746.44   Embroidery

Sadler, Judy Ann

Embroidery; written by Judy Ann Sadler; illustrated by June Bradford. Kids Can Press 2004 40p il (Kids can do it) $12.95; pa $6.95

Grades: 4 5 6   746.44

1. Embroidery

ISBN 1-55337-616-1; 1-55337-617-X pa

"With an attractively designed cover featuring photos of sample projects, this book is sure to encourage interest in needlework." SLJ

746.46   Patchwork and quilting

Rau, Dana Meachen

Quilting for fun! Compass Point Books 2009 48p il (For fun) lib bdg $25.26

Grades: 3 4 5   746.46

1. Quilting

ISBN 978-0-7565-3860-6 lib bdg; 0-7565-3860-2 lib bdg

LC 2008008274

This covers the basics of quilting, a brief history, and instructions for five quilting projects

"Varied typefaces and colors, large print, good spacing, and lively and creative arrangement make [this book] attractive, and color photos and other illustrations throughout are easy to follow. . . . Materials are easily obtainable from craft stores, and some are readily available at home." SLJ

Includes glossary and bibliographical references

746.9   Other textile products

Bertoletti, John C.

How fashion designers use math; math curriculum consultant: Rhea A. Stewart. Chelsea Clubhouse 2010 32p il (Math in the real world) lib bdg $28

Grades: 4 5 6   746.9

1. Mathematics 2. Fashion design 3. Fashion -- Vocational guidance

ISBN 978-1-60413-606-7 lib bdg; 1-60413-606-5 lib bdg

LC 2009-22683

This describes how designers use math to measure, create, and produce their fashions, and includes problems to solve and information about how to become a fashion designer

"Color photos of designers in action combine with diagrams that further clarify the easily digestible text." Booklist

Includes glossary and bibliographical references

Spilsbury, Richard

Hi-tech clothes; Richard Spilsbury. Capstone Heinemann Library 2013 56 p. (Design and engineering for STEM) (hb) $33.50

Grades: 5 6 7   746.9

1. Fashion 2. Clothing and dress 3. Fashion design 4. Product life cycle 5. Clothing factories -- Technological innovations

ISBN 1432970321; 9781432970321; 9781432970376

LC 2012013469

This book by Richard Spilsbury focuses on clothes, discussing "design, manufacture, and sale to their use, cleaning, and repair, and eventually their disposal. This book explains what happens during these stages, such as prototyping, the sourcing of materials and components, the manufacturing process, the decisions made by designers, and recycling." (Publisher's note)

Includes bibliographical references and index

Wooster, Patricia

So, you want to work in fashion? how to break into the world of fashion and design. Patricia Wooster. Aladdin 2014 192 p. illustrations (Be what you want series) (hardcover) $19.99

Grades: 4 5 6 7 8   746.9

1. Clothing industry 2. Fashion -- Vocational guidance

ISBN 1582704538; 9781582704524; 9781582704531

LC 2014005268

"In addition to tips and interviews from a variety of fashion professionals, 'So, You Want to Work in Fashion?' includes inspiring stories from young people who are in the industry right now, as well as activities, a glossary, and resources to help you on your way to a successful career in fashion." (Publisher's note)

"A wonderfully comprehensive, accessible and realistic entree into the dynamic world of fashion." Kirkus

Includes bibliographical references

747   Interior decoration

Weaver, Janice

★ It's your room; a decorating guide for real kids. [by] Janice Weaver and Frieda Wishinsky; illustrated by Claudia Dávila. Tundra Books 2006 63p il pa $14.95

Grades: 5 6 7 8   747

1. Interior design

ISBN 0-88776-711-7

"Budding interior designers and readers who want to personalize their rooms will appreciate this title. It is filled with step-by-step guidelines for creating a budget, selecting paint colors and fabrics, organizing closets and desks, laying everything out, and adding finishing touches. The illustrations will be a hit with first-time decorators just starting to develop their own color sense." SLJ

748.5   Stained, painted, leaded, mosaic glass

Kenney, Karen Latchana

Super simple glass jar art; fun and easy-to-make crafts for kids. ABDO Pub. Co. 2010 32p il (Super simple crafts) lib bdg $17.95

Grades: K 1 2 3 4   748.5

1. Glass 2. Handicraft

ISBN 978-1-60453-624-9 lib bdg; 1-60453-624-1 lib bdg

LC 2009-352

"Colorful photos; clean layout in a bright, primary palette; and large, abundant step-by-step instructional photos give [this book] great appeal. The . . . crafts . . . are functional and attractive. . . . Readily obtainable household materials and easy-to-follow instructions mean that children can do these crafts independently." SLJ

Includes glossary

750   Painting and paintings

Cressy, Judith

★ Can you find it? Abrams 2002 40p il $15.95

Grades: 2 3 4 5   750

1. Painting 2. Art appreciation 3. Metropolitan Museum of Art (New York, N.Y.)

ISBN 0-8109-3279-2

LC 2002-18358

"Nineteen paintings from New York City's Metropolitan Museum of Art were chosen for careful scrutiny in this book. Next to each striking, full-color reproduction is a list of items to search for: e.g., '2 cats, 6 lotus blossoms, 3 eye amulets,' etc., for a painting from ancient Egypt. The works of art are from around the globe and range from illuminated manuscripts to 20th-century canvases. Designed to encourage discovery, the tiny, sometimes indistinct details will keep children engrossed for hours." SLJ

Other titles in this series are:

Can you find it, too? by Judith Cressey (2004)

Can you find it inside? by by Jessica Schulte (2005)

Can you find it outside? by Jessice Schulte (2005)

Can you find it? America by Linda Falken (2010)

Micklethwait, Lucy

Children; a first art book. Frances Lincoln Children's 2006 un il $14.95

Grades: K 1 2 3   750

1. Painting 2. Children in art 3. Art appreciation

ISBN 1-84507-116-6

"This title uses works by 18 different artists to illustrate its theme. Children are shown in nine activities, from Reading and writing to Sleeping. . . . The artwork represents several cultures and ethnic groups, as well as styles and time periods. Text is minimal—just enough to encourage conversation about the reproductions. An excellent first exposure to fine art, and great preparation for museum visits." SLJ

In the picture; get looking! get thinking! Frances Lincoln 2010 un il $17.95
Grades: K 1 2 3 4   **750**
1. Painting 2. Art appreciation
ISBN 978-1-84507-636-8; 1-84507-636-2

Micklethwait "combines familiar techniques that fold a hunt-and-find game into a survey of such diverse artworks as Marc Chagall's dreamy 1911 painting I and the Village and an amazingly intricate 1590s battle scene from the Mughal Empire text The Akbarnama. Intriguing close-ups pulled from each artwork appear across from a crisp reproduction of the full image. . . . Additional activities . . . are included on each spread and an extensive, appended section." Booklist

Raczka, Bob
    ★ **Artful** reading; [by] Bob Raczka. Millbrook Press 2007 32p il lib bdg $25.26
Grades: 1 2 3 4   **750**
1. Painting 2. Reading in art 3. Art appreciation
ISBN 978-0-8225-6754-7
                                        LC 2006035083

"Through 23 works of art, Raczka shows the timeless appeal of reading. . . . Simple sentences serve as captions to these masterpieces. . . . Each work is clearly labelled, and endnotes provide information about the artists and their paintings, among them Edgar Degas and Dante Gabriel Rossetti." SLJ

    ★ **More** than meets the eye; seeing art with all five senses. by Bob Raczka. Millbrook Press 2003 32p il hardcover o.p. pa $9.95
Grades: K 1 2 3   **750**
1. Painting 2. Art appreciation
ISBN 0-7613-2797-5 lib bdg; 0-7613-1994-8 pa
                                        LC 2003-343

Provides images of paintings and new, sensory ways to experience them, such as tasting the milk in Vermeer's "The Milkmaid," hearing the music in Tanner's "The Banjo Lesson," or feeling the fur in da Vinci's "Lady with an Ermine."

"Raczka's short, rhyming text gives structure to the book, but the color reproductions of well-chosen, vivid paintings steal the show. This art book rests on a simple concept, beautifully executed." Booklist

    ★ **Unlikely** pairs; fun with famous works of art. [by] Bob Raczka. Millbrook Press 2006 31p il lib bdg $23.93; pa $9.95
Grades: 4 5 6 7   **750**
1. Painting 2. Art appreciation
ISBN 0-7613-2936-6 lib bdg; 0-7613-2378-3 pa
                                        LC 2003-14078

Invites the reader to discover fourteen funny stories produced by pairing twenty-eight paintings from different eras and styles

"Raczka deserves an A+ for cleverness. . . . Rodin's The Thinker is juxtaposed with Klee's modernistic painting of a chessboard so that the statue looks as if it is contemplating the next move. Siméon-Chardin's picture of a boy blowing soap bubbles seems to be creating Kandinsky's Several Circles. Each selection takes up a page and is reproduced in crisp color. . . . This book is an amusing way to introduce children to famous works of art." SLJ

Wenzel, Angela
    13 paintings children should know. Prestel 2009 46p il $14.95
Grades: 5 6 7 8   **750**
1. Painting 2. Art appreciation
ISBN 978-3-7913-4323-5; 3-7913-4323-8

This book examines "Mona Lisa's beguiling smile, Van Gogh's hypnotic night sky, and Frida Kahlo's depiction of herself with a monkey. These [paintings] and ten others are featured in the book in large reproductions with accompanying details. The . . . text offers biographical information about each artist and important facts about the painting's technical and historical aspects." Publisher's note

Includes glossary

750.1   Philosophy and theory

Richardson, Joy
    Looking at pictures; an introduction to art for young people. with illustrations by Charlotte Voake. rev ed.; Abrams Books for Young Readers 2009 80p il $21.95
Grades: 4 5 6 7   **750.1**
1. Painting 2. Art appreciation 3. National Gallery (Great Britain)
ISBN 978-0-8109-8288-8; 0-8109-8288-9
                                        LC 2008055684
First published 1997

This "exploration of thirteenth- to twentieth-century European paintings examines the subject matter and techniques used and also delves into how the pieces were restored. Other topics covered are pigments, the use of light and perspective, the depiction of special events and daily life, and painting people and nature. Occasional well-placed illustrations supplement the numerous color reproductions." Horn Book Guide

Includes bibliographical references

Wolfe, Gillian
    Look! Drawing the line in art. Frances Lincoln 2008 44p il $17.95
Grades: 3 4 5   **750.1**
1. Art appreciation
ISBN 978-1-84507-824-9; 1-84507-824-1

"Each spread introduces a different technique, such as 'strong lines' and 'leafy lines' and shows a work of fine art demonstrating it, reproduced with clarity and in full color. Occasionally, the text defines artistic techniques, such as perspective and shading. Each spread has kid-friendly ideas for making one's own creations. . . . There is a wide range of dates for the art featured, beginning in the 1600s and ending in 2003. The text describes how each piece was created and includes some anecdotal stories about the artist and the work. . . . This is an accessible introduction to art history." SLJ

    Look! Seeing the light in art. Frances Lincoln 2007 45p il $16.95
Grades: 3 4 5   **750.1**
1. Art appreciation
ISBN 978-1-84507-467-8; 1-84507-467-X

"Wolfe invites readers to examine how artists have tried to convey qualities of light in works that represent night, day, rainstorms, sunlight, heat, cold, and use light to create the texture and shape of objects. Each spread includes a suggestion for an art activity . . . as well as a page of accessible text, in large print, that presents questions and observations designed to draw viewers back into the well-reproduced artworks. With a few exceptions, the artists represented are well-known, male, European masters, such as Caravaggio and Renoir." Booklist

751.4 Techniques and procedures

Luxbacher, Irene

1 2 3 I can paint! Kids Can Press 2007 23p il (Starting art) $14.95; pa $5.95

Grades: 2 3 4   **751.4**

   1. Painting -- Technique

   ISBN 978-1-55453-037-3; 978-1-55453-150-9 pa; 1-55453-150-0 pa; 1-55453-037-7

This "introduces aspiring artists to some materials and techniques that can be successfully used to create pictures with paint. Luxbacher discusses primary and secondary colors; backgrounds; color tones; cool warm, and complementary colors; perspective and line; and several brush strokes. The brief text offers clear definitions of terms and easy-to-follow instructions for projects. . . . The artwork . . . will be easy for children to replicate." Booklist

Peot, Margaret

★ Inkblot; drip, splat, and squish your way to creativity. Boyds Mills Press 2011 56p il $19.95

Grades: 4 5 6 7   **751.4**

   1. Ink painting 2. Art -- Technique 3. Painting -- Technique

   ISBN 1-59078-720-X; 978-1-59078-720-5

                                 LC 22010-929541

This describes how to make inkblots and use them in art and as inspiration for writing and other forms of creativity.

"Peot's own entrancing inkblots . . . plus a few guest blots, illustrate every step, showing how the pure blot becomes a final artwork. . . . Readers get clear directions and lively encouragement." Kirkus

   Includes bibliographical references

757 Human figures

Raczka, Bob

★ Here's looking at me; how artists see themselves. [by] Bob Raczka. Millbrook Press 2006 32p il lib bdg $23.93

Grades: 3 4 5 6   **757**

   1. Artists 2. Self-portraits

   ISBN 978-0-7613-3404-0 lib bdg; 0-7613-3404-1 lib bdg

                                   LC 2005006144

This is a "top-notch introduction to self-portraiture." SLJ

759 Painting -- History, geographic treatment, biography

D'Harcourt, Claire

Masterpieces up close; Western Painting from the 14th to 20th Centuries. by Claire d'Harcourt. Chronicle Books Llc 2015 64 p. il $29.95

Grades: 4 5 6 7 8   **759**

   1. Art appreciation 2. Painting -- Appreciation

   ISBN 9781616894146; 1616894148

                                   LC 200416341

This book, by Claire d'Harcourt, "will send readers on a journey through the world's most famous paintings from the Middle Ages to the twentieth century. They will see some familiar faces, like Leonardo's Mona Lisa and Warhol's Marilyn, and meet some that may be new to them, like the princess in Velzquez's Las Meninas and the mysterious little girl in Rembrandt's Night Watch. Full-color reproductions of over 20 paintings provide the perfect hunting ground for over a hundred details." (Publisher's note)

"As in earlier entries in this series, readers are invited to find more than one hundred details in twenty-one well-known paintings, ranging from Giotto's frescoes to Warhol's Marilyns. The details are accompanied by statements of their artistic or symbolic significance, and each group of paintings (organized chronologically) is followed by a broader discussion of the works' context and importance." Horn Book

Kelley, True

Claude Monet: sunshine and waterlilies; written and illustrated by True Kelley. Grosset & Dunlap 2001 un il (Smart about art) $14.89; pa $7.50

Grades: 2 3 4   **759**

   1. Artists 2. Painters 3. Artists, French

   ISBN 0-448-42613-7; 0-448-42522-X pa

                                   LC 2001-23147

Written in the format of a school report by a fictitious student named Kristin Cole, this recounts the events in the life of the French artist and offers insight into his work

Illustrated with "charming childlike drawings and reproductions of the artist's paintings in scrapbook-style layouts. . . . [This] is a successful blend of fact and humor that makes sophisticated concepts completely accessible and even entertaining." Booklist

Markel, Michelle

The **fantastic** jungles of Henri Rousseau; by Michelle Markel; illustrated by Amanda Hall. Eerdmans Books for Young Readers 2012 34 p. (alk. paper) $17.00

Grades: PreK K 1 2 3   **759**

   1. Outsider art 2. Painters -- France -- Biography

   ISBN 0802853641; 9780802853646

                                   LC 2011035838

This children's picture book chronicles the life and work of "France's most celebrated naïve painter -- Henri Rousseau. . . . When was in his 40s, Rousseau . . . began to recreate himself as an artist. Though he had no formal training and few financial resources, he persevered. . . . Rousseau was ridiculed repeatedly by critics and artists, yet he continued to create his exotic, seemingly unsophisticated paintings." (Kirkus Reviews)

Serres, Alain

★ **And** Picasso painted Guernica; written and designed by Alain Serres; translated by Rosalind Price. Allen & Unwin Children's 2010 51p il $24.99

Grades: 5 6 7 8   **759**

   1. Artists 2. Painters 3. War in art 4. Spain -- History -- 1936-1939, Civil War

   ISBN 978-1-74175-994-5; 1-74175-994-3

   Original French edition, 2007

"Serres explains the mechanics of cubism . . . , tells the story of the horrifying German bombing of the civilians of Guernica and Picasso's reaction to it . . . , and finishes by tracing the rest of Picasso's career as he paints 'all the beauty of the world and its monstrous face as well.' The oversize pages are packed with period photographs and color reproductions of Picasso's sketches and paintings, each captioned in detail, with a double gatefold of Guernica at the center. . . . A passionate and intelligent tribute to the transformative power of art." Publ Wkly

759.05 Painting 1800-1899

Sabbeth, Carol

★ **Monet** and the impressionists for kids; their lives and ideas, 21 activities. Chicago Review Press 2002 140p il pa $17.95

Grades: 5 6 7 8   **759.05**
1. Art appreciation 2. Impressionism (Art)
ISBN 1-55652-397-1

LC 2001-47191

Discusses the nineteenth-century French art movement known as Impressionism, focusing on the works of Monet, Renoir, Degas, Cassatt, Cezanne, Gauguin, and Seurat

"A beautifully designed introduction to Impressionism. . . . Sabbeth also includes 21 appealing extension activities such as recipes, crafts, games, and writing suggestions. Quality color reproductions on glossy pages, and varied, attractive layouts add to the book." SLJ

Includes glossary and bibliographical references

Van Gogh and the Post-Impressionists for kids; their lives and ideas, 21 activities. Chicago Review Press 2011 160p il pa $17.95
Grades: 4 5 6 7   **759.05**
1. Artists 2. Painters 3. Art appreciation 4. Postimpressionism (Art)
ISBN 1-56976-275-9; 978-1-56976-275-2

LC 2010053908

"The bulk of this wonderfully thorough study of Post-Impressionist artists focuses on van Gogh, with smaller sections devoted to Paul Gauguin, Henri de Toulouse-Lautrec, Paul Signac, and Emile Bernard. The highly engaging text follows the artists' lives with crisp writing and vivid detail, delving into their family backgrounds and relationships, and doesn't sugarcoat dark and gritty incidents such as van Gogh's self-inflicted ear amputation. Information is well organized. . . . Full-color reproductions of paintings discussed in the text add visual interest, and educational sidebars expound on topics mentioned in the main narrative. . . . With its creative, hands-on ideas for teaching art technique and history, this book is an excellent resource for students and teachers." SLJ

Includes glossary and bibliographical references

759.06   Painting 1900-1999

Barsony, Piotr

The **stories** of the Mona Lisa; an imaginary museum tale about the history of modern art. Piotr Barsony; translated from the French by Joanna Oseman. Skyhorse Publishing 2012 55 p. (hardcover : alk. paper) $19.95
Grades: 5 6 7 8   **759.06**
1. Art -- History 2. Mona Lisa (Painting) 3. Art movements 4. Painting, Modern
ISBN 1620872285; 9781620872284

LC 2012015603

"As [this book by Pietr Barsony] begins, a little girl asks: 'Dad, will you tell me a story?' The story her painter father tells is a history of art with the Mona Lisa as its central character. . . . He takes daughter and readers both on a journey of discovery through an imaginary museum. . . . Each painting is of only the Mona Lisa. . . . They are his own responses to and interpretations of Leonardo's masterpiece as filtered through the vision of other artists and movements." (Kirkus Reviews)

759.13   Painting -- United States

Bryant, Jen

★ A **splash** of red; the life and art of Horace Pippin. by Jen Bryant; illustrated by Melissa Sweet. Alfred A. Knopf 2013 40 p. (hard cover) $17.99
Grades: K 1 2   **759.13**
1. Painters -- Biography 2. Veterans -- Biography 3. African

American painters -- Biography   4. Painters -- United States -- Biography
ISBN 0375867120; 9780375867125; 9780375967122

LC 2012003209

Robert F. Sibert Honor Book (2014)
Orbis Pictus Award (2014)
Schneider Family Book Award (2014)

This children's picture book by Jen Bryant presents a "portrait of African-American artist Horace Pippin (1888-1946). . . . From Pippin's young childhood . . . to his Army service in World War I, to the well-deserved fame that arrived only late in his life, he 'couldn't stop drawing.' When a military injury threatens Pippin's painting ability, he tries wood burning--'[u]sing his good arm to move the hurt one'--and works his way back to painting." (Kirkus Reviews)

Close, Chuck, 1940-

Chuck Close; face book. by Chuck Close. Abrams Books for Young Readers 2012 64 p.
Grades: 3 4 5 6 7   **759.13**
1. Face in art 2. Vision disorders 3. Artists -- Interviews 4. Artists -- United States -- Biography
ISBN 9781419701634

LC 2011034557

Boston Globe-Horn Book Award: Nonfiction (2012)

In this book, "[Chuck] Close discloses struggles with childhood ill health and severe dyslexia. He tells how . . . he adjusted for his prosopagnosia (face blindness). . . . He also discloses the many 'hows' of his . . . technique: how he uses gridded photos to build his faces and how he works from his wheelchair and wields his brush with less-abled hands. . . At the book's . . . center is the . . . opportunity to 'mix 'n' match' various eyes, noses and mouths among 14 of the artist's . . . self-portraits." (Kirkus)

Daugherty, James

Lincoln's Gettysburg address; a pictorial interpretation painted by James Daugherty. James Daugherty. Albert Whitman & Co. 2013 48 p. $19.99
Grades: 1 2 3 4   **759.13**
1. Gettysburg (Pa.) 2. Lincoln, Abraham, 1809-1865 3. Gettysburg address
ISBN 0807545503; 9780807545508

LC 2012013288

This children's book, illustrated by Caldecott Honoree and Newbery Medalist James Daugherty, presents the text of U.S. President Abraham Lincoln's Gettysburg Address. "The Gettysburg Address is one of the most influential speeches in our history, written by Abraham Lincoln at a crucial period in his presidency and in United States history." (Publisher's note)

Gherman, Beverly

Norman Rockwell; storyteller with a brush. Atheneum Bks. for Young Readers 2000 57p il $19.95
Grades: 4 5 6 7   **759.13**
1. Artists 2. Painters 3. Illustrators 4. Artists -- United States
ISBN 0-689-82001-1

LC 98-36546

Describes the life and work of the popular American artist who depicted both traditional and contemporary subjects, including children, family scenes, astronauts, and the poor

"The format of the biography is appealing and attractive. The pages are replete with color reproductions of Rockwell's paintings as well as photographs of the man and his family. The text is well researched and authentic; the writing style is free-flowing and the words capture the naturalness of Rockwell's paintings." SLJ

Includes bibliographical references (p. {55}) and index

Honoring our ancestors; stories and pictures by fourteen artists. edited by Harriet Rohmer. Children's Bk. Press 1999 31p il $15.95

Grades: 3 4 5 6   **759.13**

1. Artists -- United States

ISBN 0-89239-158-8

              LC 98-38686

Fourteen artists and picture book illustrators present paintings with descriptions of ancestors or other sources of inspiration that have inspired them

This is "rewarding in its breadth and vivacity. The portraits are thematically rich yet accessible; generally, the texts are cheerful and resist sentimentality." Horn Book Guide

Lawrence, Jacob

The **great** migration; an American story. paintings by Jacob Lawrence; with a poem in appreciation by Walter Dean Myers. HarperCollins Pubs. 1993 un il hardcover o.p. pa $8.99

Grades: 4 5 6 7   **759.13**

1. African Americans in art

ISBN 0-06-023037-1; 0-06-443428-1 pa

              LC 93-16788

"Lawrence is a storyteller with words as well as pictures: his captions and his own 1992 introduction to this book are the best commentary on his work." Booklist

759.2   European painting

Wenzel, Angela

13 art mysteries children should know. Prestel 2011 45p il $14.95

Grades: 4 5 6   **759.2**

1. Art 2. Artists 3. Painting

ISBN 978-3-7913-7044-6; 379-1-37044-8

Presents information about thirteen mysteries from the art world, including questions about the Mona Lisa, van Gogh, and the street artist Banksy.

"Excellent-quality reproductions appear throughout. This is definitely a different approach for introducing young people to various aspects of art history. . . . The illustrations are well chosen to support these succinct inquiries into some perplexing puzzlements from the world of art." SLJ

759.4   French painting

Parker, Marjorie Blain

★ **Colorful** dreamer; the story of artist Henri Matisse. Marjorie Blain Parker; illustrated by Holly Berry. Dial Books For Young Readers 2012 32 p. (hardcover) $16.99

Grades: 3 4 5   **759.4**

1. Painters 2. Picture books for children 3. Artists -- France -- Biography

ISBN 0803737580; 9780803737587

              LC 2011035446

This "picture-book biography covers [Henri] Matisse's entire life but focuses on his career aspirations and achievements." The text includes "details such as young Henri's dream of becoming a magician and his skill with a peashooter. . . . Black-and-white drawings represent the art-

ist's dull youth and colorful paintings are introduced when his career takes off." (School Library Journal)

" Berry's illustrations are the star of the show... The style of the artwork evokes Matisse more and more as the story progresses, ending, as his career did, with paper cut-out collage... A must for art teachers, and a nice addition to history and biography collections." Kirkus

759.9   Other geographic areas

Gogh, Vincent van

★ **Vincent's** colors; words and pictures by Vincent van Gogh. Chronicle Books 2005 un il $14.95

Grades: K 1 2 3   **759.9**

1. Color in art 2. Artists, Dutch

ISBN 0-8118-5099-4

"This text is pulled directly from the letters Van Gogh wrote about his paintings to his brother, Theo. Each line of the rhyming stanzas is accompanied by a rich, full-color reproduction of one of the artist's key works. . . . Van Gogh's poetic descriptions will hold the attention of young readers; even preschoolers will enjoy the simple text and vibrant pictures. The brilliant colors and brush strokes are reproduced faithfully." SLJ

Raczka, Bob

The **Vermeer** interviews; conversations with seven works of art. as imagined by Bob Raczka. Millbrook Press 2009 32p il (Art adventures) lib bdg $25.27

Grades: 3 4 5 6   **759.9**

1. Artists 2. Painters 3. Artists, Dutch 4. Art appreciation

ISBN 978-0-8225-9402-4 lib bdg; 0-8225-9402-1 lib bdg

              LC 2008024969

"Raczka makes Johannes Vermeer's masterpieces accessible by employing an interview format. Clearly stating that these 'conversations' are 'as imagined' by the author, 'Bob' asks the subjects of seven paintings a series of questions about themselves and their surroundings, allowing them to give details about the art techniques, historical context, and cultural elements." SLJ

Includes bibliographical references

Rubin, Susan Goldman

★ **Diego** Rivera; an artist for the people. by Susan Goldman Rubin. Abrams Books for Young Readers 2013 56 p. (reinforced) $21.95

Grades: 5 6 7 8   **759.9**

1. Mural painting and decoration   2. Painters -- Mexico -- Biography

ISBN 0810984113; 9780810984110

              LC 2012010022

This book, by Susan Goldman Rubin, "offers young readers . . . insight into the life and artwork of the famous Mexican painter and muralist [Diego Rivera]. The book follows Rivera's career, looking at his influences and tracing the evolution of his style. His work often called attention to the culture and struggles of the Mexican working class. . . . The book contains a list of museums where you can see Rivera's art, a historical note, a glossary, and a bibliography." (Publisher's note)

Includes bibliographical references and index

Vry, Silke

Paul Klee for children; Silke Vry; [translation, Jane Michael] Prestel 2011 95 p. $14.95

Grades: 4 5 6   **759.9**

1. Art -- Technique 2. Art appreciation

ISBN 3791370774; 9783791370774

              LC 2011937220

This book, by Silke Vry, is about the art work of Paul Klee. "Paul Klee's playful paintings are a natural introduction for children to the world of creativity and art. . . . The German artist was fascinated by children's drawings, and incorporated their energy and simplicity into his own work. This . . . introduction to Klee's paintings focuses on the artist's love of color and symbols, his lighthearted technique, and his belief that music and painting were inextricably linked." (Publisher's note)

760.2   Miscellany

Hanson, Anders
Cool printmaking; the art of creativity for kids. [by] Anders Hanson. ABDO Pub. Co. 2009 32p il (Cool art) lib bdg $24.21
Grades: 2 3 4   **760.2**
1. Prints 2. Printing
ISBN 978-1-60453-147-3 lib bdg; 1-60453-147-9 lib bdg
LC 2008-22323
This book about printmaking is "well organized, with clearly written sections . . . and several clever projects and exercises. . . . [It] should have substantial child appeal." SLJ
Includes glossary

761   Printmaking

Price, Pamela S.
★ Cool rubber stamp art; [by] Pam Price. ABDO Pub. Co. 2005 32p il (Cool crafts) lib bdg $22.78
Grades: 4 5 6   **761**
1. Handicraft 2. Rubber stamp printing
ISBN 1-59197-743-6
LC 2004-53123
This describes five rubber stamp art projects: "a terra-cotta flowerpot, spring greeting card, wrapping paper, canvas beach bag, and homemade stamps (sponge, string, leaf). . . . [This book lists] required materials, [has] small color photos, and [includes] clearly explained, numbered steps. . . . [It will] will appeal to children." SLJ

Ross, Kathy
One-of-a-kind stamps and crafts; illustrated by Nicole in den Bosch. Millbrook Press 2010 48p il (Girl crafts) lib bdg $25.26; pa $7.95
Grades: 3 4 5 6   **761**
1. Handicraft 2. Rubber stamp printing
ISBN 978-0-8225-9216-7 lib bdg; 0-8225-9216-9 lib bdg; 978-1-58013-885-7 pa; 1-58013-885-3 pa
LC 2009020626
"This book describes how to create 20 stamps as well as an ink-pad storage shelf and a stamp storage box. . . . Decorative top borders add to the overall neat, well-spaced pages. The projects include readily available supplies, step-by-step instructions, and clear color illustrations. . . . An enhancement to craft collections." SLJ

770   Photography, computer art, cinematography, videography

Finger, Brad
13 photos children should know. Prestel 2011 45p il lib bdg $14.95
Grades: 4 5 6   **770**
1. Modern history 2. Documentary photography
ISBN 978-3-7913-7047-7; 3-7913-7047-2

Examines the history behind thirteen popular photographs, including the moon landing, the fall of the Berlin Wall, and the wedding of Prince Charles and Princess Diana.

Partridge, Elizabeth
Restless spirit: the life and work of Dorothea Lange. Viking 1998 122p il hardcover o.p. pa $12.99
Grades: 6 7 8 9   **770**
1. Photographers 2. Women photographers
ISBN 0-670-87888-X; 0-14-230024-1 pa
LC 98-9807
A biography of Dorothea Lange, whose photographs of migrant workers, Japanese American internees, and rural poverty helped bring about important social reforms
"Generously placed throughout this accessibly written biography are the photographic images that make Lange a pre-eminent artist of the century. The book is elegantly designed and the photographic reproductions are excellent." Bull Cent Child Books
Includes bibliographical references

Proujansky, Alice
Go photo! An Activity Book for Kids. Alice Proujansky. Aperture 2016 108 p. color illustrations (hardcover : alk. paper) $19.95
Grades: 4 5 6 7   **770**
1. Creative activities 2. Photography
ISBN 9781597113557
LC 2015959630
This children's book by Alice Proujansky "features 25 hands-on and creative activities inspired by photography. Aimed at children between eight and twelve years old, this playful and fun collection of projects encourages young readers to experiment with their imaginations, get messy with materials and engage with the world in new and exciting ways. . . . Each project also features a series of pictures and handy tips to help guide the reader step-by-step." (Publisher's note)
"Proujansky touches on technical aspects of photography, such as composition and lighting... but her emphasis is generally on playful exploration, building readers' confidence behind the camera through an array of creative projects and ideas." Pub Wkly

775   Digital photography

Johnson, Daniel
4-H guide to digital photography. Voyageur Press 2009 176p $18.99
Grades: 5 6 7 8   **775**
1. Digital photography
ISBN 978-0-7603-3652-6; 0-7603-3652-0
LC 2009014679
This guide to digital photography offers "sound and comprehensive information. . . . [It] features numerous excellent photos that support the text. It explores types of digital cameras, how to take good photos, the complexities of lighting, managing images . . . and the importance of just enjoying this activity. Types of photography such as landscape and macro are explained. The author does an excellent job of discussing the importance of both technological details and artistic creativity." SLJ
Includes glossary

Rabbat, Suzy
Using digital images. Cherry Lake Pub. 2010 32p il (Super smart information strategies) lib bdg $27.07

Grades: 3 4 5 6 **775**
1. Digital photography
ISBN 978-1-60279-954-7 lib bdg; 1-60279-954-7 lib bdg
LC 2010018941
"The information on deciding between file formats and resolutions in Using Digital Images will be tremendously helpful, and some beginner techniques on taking and editing effective photos are a nice bonus." Booklist
Includes bibliographical references

778.5 Cinematography and videography

Green, Julie
Shooting video to make learning fun. Cherry Lake Pub. 2010 32p il (Super smart information strategies) lib bdg $27.07
Grades: 3 4 5 6 **778.5**
1. Digital video recording 2. Motion pictures -- Production and direction
ISBN 978-1-60279-955-4 lib bdg; 1-60279-955-5 lib bdg
LC 2010002022
"This books helps students learn how to harness the power of video to inform and entertain. Includes background information and practical hands on activities." Publisher's note
Includes bibliographical references

779 Photographic images

Delannoy, Isabelle
★ **Our** living Earth; a story of people, ecology, and preservation. by Isabelle Delannoy; photographs by Yann Arthus-Bertrand. Harry N. Abrams 2008 157p il $24.95
Grades: 5 6 7 8 **779**
1. Human geography 2. Aerial photography
ISBN 978-0-8109-7132-5; 0-8109-7132-1
LC 2008010324
"Wrapped around Arthus-Bertrand's magnificent aerial photographs from around the world, Delannoy's text is organized thematically, covering fresh water, biodiversity, oceans, land, cities, people, food, and climate. . . . Readers will find surprising information and images to ponder. Almost every page supports the overarching theme that social justice and environmental protection are inextricably related. . . . This volume raises awareness, and the striking images, astonishing statistics, and brief explanations will stimulate readers to investigate further and possibly to take action." SLJ

Haas, Robert B.
★ **I** dreamed of flying like a bird; my adventures photographing wild animals from a helicopter. National Geographic 2010 64p il $17.95; lib bdg $27.90
Grades: 2 3 4 **779**
1. Aerial photography 2. Photography of animals 3. Animals -- Africa
ISBN 978-1-4263-0693-8; 1-4263-0693-8; 978-1-4263-0694-5 lib bdg; 1-4263-0694-6 lib bdg
LC 2009-52955
"Haas, a veteran wildlike photographer, proffers another set of photos from several of his albums for adults. Here he accompanies the pictures . . . with anecdotal commentary on the hazards and pleasures of viewing nature from an aerial perspective. . . . This . . . [provides] young viewers with an unusual perspective on the natural world." Booklist
Includes glossary and bibliographical references

Hoban, Tana
Shadows and reflections. Greenwillow Bks. 1990 un il $16.99
Grades: PreK K **779**
1. Shades and shadows
ISBN 978-0-688-07089-2; 0-688-07089-2
LC 89-30461
Photographs without text feature shadows and reflections of various objects, animals, and people
"This imaginative, wordless book of color photographs is a visual treat, offering witty and subtle sets of images for enriching the eyes of children and adults." SLJ

780 Music

Aliki
★ **Ah,** music! written and illustrated by Aliki. HarperCollins Pubs. 2003 47p il $17.99; pa $6.99
Grades: K 1 2 3 **780**
1. Music
ISBN 0-06-028719-5; 0-06-446236-6 pa
LC 2001-26476
This introduction to music defines such terms as rhythm, melody, pitch, and volume, gives a brief description of written music, instruments of the orchestra, vocal parts, harmony, dynamics, and tempo, cultural diversity in dance and music, and gives a brief outline of musical history
"Terms are explained in an easy, child-friendly manner. . . . Aliki's love of her subject shines through. This enjoyable title is best shared one-on-one and its format makes it ideal for browsing." SLJ

Anderson, M. T., 1968-
★ **Handel,** who knew what he liked; illustrated by Kevin Hawkes. Candlewick Press 2001 un il hardcover o.p. pa $6.99
Grades: 4 5 6 **780**
1. Composers 2. Composers -- Biography
ISBN 0-7636-1046-1; 0-7636-2562-0 pa
LC 00-57210
Boston Globe-Horn Book Award Honor: Nonfiction (2002)
In this biography Handel, who would later compose some of the world's most beautiful music, is shown as a stubborn little boy with a mind of his own
The author "infuses the composer's story with warmth and color, humor and humanity. . . . Relating pithy stories with plain words and short sentences, Anderson never forgets his audience in his enthusiasm for his subject." Booklist

Anniss, Matthew
Recording and promoting your music; Matthew Anniss. Capstone Raintree 2015 48 p. color illustrations (I'm in the band) (hb) $32.65
Grades: 5 6 7 8 9 10 **780**
1. Sound -- Recording and reproducing 2. Music industry -- Vocational guidance 3. Rock music -- Vocational guidance 4. Music trade -- Vocational guidance 5. Sound recordings -- Production and direction
ISBN 1410967263; 9781410967268; 9781410967312
This book, by Matthew Anniss, part of the "I'm in the Band" series, is directed at "aspiring young musicians who want to learn the ins and outs of being in a band. This book looks at recording, releasing, and promoting your music, including how it all works in the digital age." (Publisher's note)
"Teens aiming to get their band out of the garage and onto a stage will find helpful information in this new series. Interspersed with flashy, eye-catching photos of up-to-the-minute music celebrities, the text offers a rough outline of the process from recording to release, as well

as tips on interacting with fans and using interpersonal skills to book gigs." Booklist

Includes bibliographical references and index

Hansen, Dee

The **music** and literacy connection; Dee Hansen, Elaine Bernstorf, and Gayle M. Stuber. Rowman & Littlefield 2014 314 p. illustrations, music (cloth : alk. paper) $80

Grades: Professional   **780**

1. Reading 2. Music and literature 3. Reading (Primary) 4. School music -- Instruction and study 5. Interdisciplinary approach in education

ISBN 1475805985; 9781475805987; 9781475805994

                         LC 2014023926

This book, by Dee Hansen, , Elaine Bernstorf, and Gayle M. Stuber, looks at "the links between reading and music by examining those skills and learning processes that are directly parallel for music learning and language arts literacy in the pre-K, elementary, and secondary levels. This edition includes two new chapters: one dedicated to secondary music education and teacher evaluation, and another that offers a literature review of latest literacy research in education, neuroscience, and neuropsychology." (Publisher's note)

Includes bibliographical references and index

Lach, William

★ **Can** you hear it? Abrams Books for Young Readers 2007 39p il $18.95

Grades: 2 3 4 5   **780**

1. Art and music

ISBN 978-0-8109-5721-3

"This visual and aural feast invites parents, educators, and young listeners to 'listen and look' at 13 examples of pictorial music and visual masterpieces. The introduction prepares readers with an explanation of the connections between composers' notes and art images. A woodblock print by Utagawa Hiroshige, the pointillism of Seurat, and landscapes by Jacob van Ruisdael and Thomas Cole are among those included in the presentation. The paired examples invite listeners to identify solo instruments or orchestral themes that characterize an image found in the visual art." SLJ

780.89   Ethnic and national groups

Igus, Toyomi

★ **I** see the rhythm; paintings by Michele Wood; text by Toyomi Igus. Children's Bk. Press 1998 32p il $18.95; pa $7.95

Grades: 4 5 6 7   **780.89**

1. African American music 2. African Americans -- Music -- History and criticism

ISBN 0892391510; 0892392129; 0-89239-151-0; 0-89239-212-9 pa

                         LC 97-29310

Coretta Scott King Award for illustration

Text and illustrations combine to give an "overview of African American music. . . . {A} time line sets the social context, and brief paragraphs describe the various types of music, from African origins and slave songs through ragtime; the blues; big band, bebop, and cool jazz; gospel; rhythm and blues; and the contemporary sounds of rock, hip-hop, and rap." (Booklist) "Grades four to eight." (Bull Cent Child Books)

"The text, made up of free verse and music lyrics, incorporates different font sizes, shapes, and colors to underline the mood of each genre. . . . The colors of each full-page scenario underline the mood. . . . This book celebrates music with art and words and successfully blends all three." SLJ

780.9   History, geographic treatment, biography

Children's book of music; an introduction to the world's most amazing music and its creators. DK Publishing 2010 142p il $24.99

Grades: 3 4 5 6   **780.9**

1. Music -- History and criticism

ISBN 978-0-7566-6734-4; 0-7566-6734-8

                         LC 2010564872

"Concise summaries and eye-catching photography are combined in this chronological look at music 'from the first hum' to digital recording and reactable electronic instruments. The book explores the nature of music, its origins, and varied sounds. The organization creates a useful resource for research as well as for casual browsing. . . . While the information is succinct, there is enough depth for basic information and unusual facts. . . . Thirty-five musical highlights are included on the CD . . . each tagged by an icon and explanation within the book, provide teaching and listening aids. A solid resource for any library." SLJ

Includes glossary

Solway, Andrew

Africa; [by] Andrew Solway. Heinemann Library 2008 48p il (World of music) lib bdg $22

Grades: 5 6 7 8   **780.9**

1. African music

ISBN 978-1-4034-9891-5 lib bdg; 1-4034-9891-1 lib bdg

                         LC 2006100578

This introduction to African music discusses "instruments, dance, and vocal styles. The photographs presented are wonderfully colorful in quality and narrative. Topics covered include history, famous players, current styles, pop-culture, politics, world-wide connections." Libr Media Connect

Includes glossary and bibliographical references

Latin America and the Caribbean; [by] Andrew Solway. Heinemann Library 2008 48p il (World of music) lib bdg $22

Grades: 5 6 7 8   **780.9**

1. Music -- Latin America 2. Music -- Caribbean region

ISBN 978-1-4034-9889-2 lib bdg; 1-4034-9889-X lib bdg

                         LC 2006100579

This introduction to music of Latin America and the Caribbean discusses "instruments, dance, and vocal styles. The photographs presented are wonderfully colorful in quality and narrative. Topics covered include history, famous players, current styles, pop-culture, politics, and world-wide connections." Libr Media Connect

Includes glossary and bibliographical references

Underwood, Deborah

Australia, Hawaii, and the Pacific; [by] Deborah Underwood. Heinemann Library 2008 48p il (World of music) lib bdg $22

Grades: 5 6 7 8   **780.9**

1. Music -- Hawaii 2. Music -- Oceania 3. Music -- Australia

ISBN 978-1-4034-9894-6 lib bdg; 1-4034-9894-6 lib bdg

                         LC 2006100576

This introduction to the music of Australia, Hawaii, and the Pacific discusses "instruments, dance, and vocal styles. The photographs presented are wonderfully colorful in quality and narrative. Topics covered include history, famous players, current styles, pop-culture, politics, and world-wide connections." Libr Media Connect

Includes glossary and bibliographical references

780.94　Music of Europe

Allen, Patrick

　Europe; [by] Patrick Allen. Heinemann Library 2008 48p il (World of music) lib bdg $22

Grades: 5 6 7 8　　　　　　　　　　　　　　**780.94**

　1. Music -- Europe

　ISBN 978-1-4034-9890-8 lib bdg; 1-4034-9890-3 lib bdg

　　　　　　　　　　　　　　　LC 2006100580

This introduction to European music discusses "instruments, dance, and vocal styles. The photographs presented are wonderfully colorful in quality and narrative. Topics covered include history, famous players, current styles, pop-culture, politics, and world-wide connections." Libr Media Connect

Includes glossary and bibliographical references

781.17　Music – Artistic principles

Ajmera, Maya

　Music everywhere! Maya Ajmera, Elise Hofer Derstine, and Cynthia Pon. Random House Distribution Childrens 2013 32 p. color illustrations and maps (reinforced for library use) $17.95

Grades: PreK K 1 2 3　　　　　　　　　　　**781.17**

　1. Music -- Pictorial works　2. Musical ability in children　3. Music appreciation

　ISBN 1570919364; 9781570919367; 9781570919374; 9781607346708

　　　　　　　　　　　　　　　LC 2012027113

In this book, by Maya Ajmera, Elise Hofer Derstine, and Cynthia Pon, "photographs from around the world celebrate the universal joy that kids get from making music, whether they're playing instruments, clapping their hands, stomping their feet, or singing." According to the book "music can . . . bring a whole community together." (Publisher's note)

"The title conveys this book's straightforward message: music is a universal pleasure, from Canada to Timor-Leste. Proof is demonstrated by a simple yet energetic running text and large photos of children exuberantly making and enjoying music worldwide. Direct captions impart information uncondescendingly: 'Playing a traditional Andean zampoqa. PERU.' A world map and suggestions for homemade musical instruments are included" Horn Book

781.2　Elements of music

Tomecek, Steve

　Music; [by] Stephen M. Tomecek. Chelsea House 2010 165p il (Experimenting with everyday science) $35

Grades: 5 6 7 8　　　　　　　　　　　　　　**781.2**

　1. Musical instruments　2. Science -- Experiments　3. Music -- Acoustics and physics

　ISBN 978-1-60413-169-7; 1-60413-169-1

　　　　　　　　　　　　　　　LC 2009-22333

This "offers 25 easy-to-perform activities that illuminate scientific principles. . . . Topics . . . include the history of music, various instruments, and how scientific principles explain the creation of sounds. . . . Following each experiment are additional comments on the science behind the experiment and link to the one that follows. Photographs, simple diagrams and illustrations, and sample data tables appear throughout, and the [layout is] clear and colorful." SLJ

Includes bibliographical references

781.5　Kinds of music

Stringer, Lauren

　When Stravinsky met Nijinsky; two artists, their ballet, and one extraordinary riot. Lauren Stringer. Houghton Mifflin Harcourt 2013 32 p. $16.99

Grades: K 1 2　　　　　　　　　　　　　　　**781.5**

　1. Picture books for children　2. Rite of spring (Choreographic work)

　ISBN 0547907257; 9780547907253

　　　　　　　　　　　　　　　LC 2012025330

In this children's picture book looks at the dramatic reaction to "The Rite of Spring," a collaboration between Igor Stravinsky and Vaslav Nijinsky. It "introduces the two men and how they worked alone, while noting that they both dreamed of something different. Their collaboration brought the world 'The Rite of Spring' . . . which opened to a riot in Paris during its premier[e]." (Booklist)

781.62　Folk music

Handyside, Chris

　★ **Folk**. Heinemann Library 2006 48p il (A history of American music) lib bdg $31.43

Grades: 5 6 7 8　　　　　　　　　　　　　　**781.62**

　1. Folk music

　ISBN 1-4034-8150-4

This history of folk music is an "excellent, clear [introduction]. . . . [It] starts with the post-Civil War era, when folklorists gathered slave songs. It describes the music's commercial success beginning with early recordings of the Carter family and Jimmie Rodgers in the 1920s and continuing with Leadbelly, Woody Guthrie, Pete Seeger, and the many musicians who became popular during the folk revival of the late 50s and early 60s. . . . It concludes with sections on folk rock, punk rock, and the future of folk music." SLJ

Includes bibliographical references

Orozco, Jose-Luis

　★ **De** colores and other Latin-American folk songs for children; selected, arranged, and translated by José-Luis Orozco; illustrated by Eliza Kleven. Dutton Children's Bks. 1994 56p il hardcover o.p. pa $7.99

Grades: K 1 2 3　　　　　　　　　　　　　　**781.62**

　1. Folk songs　2. Folklore -- Latin America　3. Bilingual books -- English-Spanish

　ISBN 0-525-45260-5; 0-14-056548-5 pa

"Each of the 27 songs is presented with background notes; lyrics in both Spanish and English; simple arrangements for the voice, piano, and guitar; and suggestions for group sing-alongs and musical games. . . . The book is a delight for the eyes as well as the ear. . . . Kleven provides bountiful illustrations—the endpapers are sunshine bright with a crisp quilt of yellow flowers, and playful borders that ripple with colorful patterns and miniature pictures line the edge of every page." Booklist

781.642　Country music

Bertholf, Bret

　★ **Long** gone lonesome history of country music; by Bret Bertholf. Little, Brown 2007 un il $18.99

Grades: 4 5 6   **781.642**
1. Country music
ISBN 978-0-316-52393-6; 0-316-52393-3

LC 2005016036

"This tongue-in-cheek overview features a folksy narrative of how and why country music developed in the barns and back roads of rural America. The text . . . covers instruments, early recordings, yodeling, . . . the Great Depression, gospel, movie cowboys, a 'paper-doll' spoof of singers' costumes, hillbilly jazz, World War II, . . . and much more. While poking fun at itself . . . the book offers a vast amount of historical fact amid a multitude of caricatures of country stars. . . . The ever-changing backgrounds and fonts with colored-pencil and crayon illustrations carry an amazing variation of detail." SLJ

781.643   Blues

Handyside, Chris
★ **Blues**; [by] Christopher Handyside. Heinemann Library 2006 48p il (A history of American music) lib bdg $31.43
Grades: 5 6 7 8   **781.643**
1. Blues music
ISBN 1-4034-8148-2

LC 2005019280

"This book charts the development of this uniquely American Music form from the 1600s through to the present. It also shows how social, economic, and regional factors have all helped to shape the blues over time and, in turn, how this music has gone on to influence other genres." Publisher's note
Includes glossary and bibliographical references

781.644   Soul

Aretha, David
Awesome African-American rock and soul musicians; David Aretha. Enslow Publishers, Inc. 2012 112 p. ill. (African-American Collective Biographies) (library) $31.93
Grades: 6 7 8   **781.644**
1. Rock musicians 2. Soul musicians 3. African American musicians 4. African American rock musicians -- Biography 5. Soul musicians -- United States -- Biography
ISBN 1598451405; 9781598451405

LC 2011019956

"From the African-American Collective Biographies series, this volume introduces nine significant figures in rock and soul music: Chuck Berry, Ray Charles, Little Richard, James Brown, Aretha Franklin, Jimi Hendrix, Diana Ross, Stevie Wonder, and Prince. After a general introduction to rock and soul music, each chapter looks at the individual performer's life, career, musical style, achievements, and contributions to the field." (Booklist)
Includes bibliographical references (p. 108-109) and index.

Handyside, Chris
★ **Soul** and R&B; [by] Christopher Handyside. Heinemann Library 2006 48p il (A history of American music) lib bdg $31.43
Grades: 5 6 7 8   **781.644**
1. Soul music 2. Rhythm and blues music
ISBN 1-4034-8153-9

LC 2005019324

"This book charts the development of this uniquely American music form from the 1800s through to the present. It also shows how social, economic, and regional factors have all helped to shape soul and R&B

over time and, in turn, how this music has gone on to influence other genres." Publisher's note
Includes glossary and bibliographical references

Pinkney, Andrea Davis
★ **Rhythm** ride; a road trip through the Motown sound. Andrea Davis Pinkney. Roaring Brook Press 2015 176 p. illustrations (hardback) $22.99
Grades: 5 6 7 8 9   **781.644**
1. Rhythm and blues music -- Sound recordings 2. Motown Record Corporation 3. Sound recording industry -- United States
ISBN 9781596439733; 1596439734

LC 2014045894

NAACP Image Award Nominee: Outstanding Literary Work- Youth/Teens (2016)

"Berry Gordy began Motown in 1959. . . . He converted the garage of a residential house into a studio and recruited teenagers . . . Smokey Robinson, Mary Wells, Marvin Gaye, Stevie Wonder, and Diana Ross to sing for his new label. Meanwhile, the country was on the brink of a cultural revolution, and one of the most powerful agents of change in the following decade would be this group of young black performers from urban Detroit." (Publisher's note)
"An ebullient, wonderfully told introduction to music that had an indelible influence on a generation and its times." Kirkus

781.65   Jazz

Dillon, Diane
★ **Jazz** on a Saturday night; [by] Leo & Diane Dillon. Blue Sky Press 2007 un il $16.99
Grades: PreK K 1 2   **781.65**
1. Jazz music 2. Jazz musicians 3. Children's poetry
ISBN 0-590-47893-1; 978-0-590-47893-1

LC 2006-34009

In this rhyming picture book, the "imaginary octet of Miles Davis, Max Roach, Charlie Parker, John Coltrane, Thelonious Monk, Stanley Clarke, Ella Fitzgerald, and an unnamed guest guitarist tune up. . . . Primary." (Horn Book)
This takes readers on "an imaginary Saturday night concert featuring seven . . . [jazz] greats, from Thelonius Monk to John Coltrane. Rhythmic text acts as an introduction to the legendary musicians. . . . The sophisticated illustrations . . . recall Harlem Renaissance paintings. . . . Brief biographies of the seven featured artists serve as endnotes, while a bonus CD briefly explores jazz instruments and features an original song that shares the book's title." Publ Wkly

Handyside, Chris
★ **Jazz**; [by] Christopher Handyside. Heinemann Library 2006 48p il (A history of American music) lib bdg $31.43
Grades: 5 6 7 8   **781.65**
1. Jazz music
ISBN 1-4034-8149-0

LC 2005019305

"This book charts the development of this uniquely American Music form from the 1600s through to the present. It also shows how social, economic, and regional factors have all helped to shape Jazz over time and, in turn, how this music has gone on to influence other genres." Publisher's note
Includes glossary and bibliographical references

Marsalis, Wynton, 1961-

★ **Jazz** A-B-Z; [by] Wynton Marsalis and Paul Rogers; with biographical sketches by Phil Schaap. Candlewick Press 2005 un il $24.99

Grades: 5 6 7 8 9 10   781.65

1. Jazz music 2. Jazz musicians

ISBN 978-0-7636-3434-6

LC 2005-48448

This is an illustrated alphabetically arranged introduction to jazz musicians.

This is a "witty, stunningly designed alphabet catalog. . . . The biographical sketches and notes on poetic forms by Phil Schaap are concise and genuinely informative. . . . Rogers's pastiche full-page portraits, his use of expressive typography and the smaller vignettes he sprinkles throughout are bound to heighten any reader's appreciation of both the musicians and the music. . . . [Marsalis offers] clever . . . poems, wordplays, odes and limericks." N Y Times Book Rev

Pinkney, Andrea Davis

★ **Duke** Ellington; the piano prince and his orchestra. illustrated by Brian Pinkney. Hyperion Bks. for Children 1998 un il $15.95; pa $5.99

Grades: 2 3 4   781.65

1. Composers 2. Jazz musicians 3. Band leaders 4. African Americans -- Biography

ISBN 0-7868-0178-6; 0-7868-1420-9 pa

LC 96-46031

A Caldecott Medal honor book, 1999; Coretta Scott King honor book for illustration, 1999

A brief recounting of the career of this jazz musician and composer who, along with his orchestra, created music that was beyond category

This is "written in a folksy, colloquial style. . . . The warmly colored, exquisitely designed scratchboard illustrations have a grand time evoking the sounds of Ellington's music." Horn Book Guide

Includes bibliographical references

Raschka, Chris

The **Cosmobiography** of sun ra; the sound of joy is enlightening. Chris Raschka. Candlewick Press 2014 40 p. $15.99

Grades: 1 2 3 4   781.65

1. Jazz music 2. Jazz musicians -- Biography

ISBN 0763658065; 9780763658069

LC 2013944131

This children's book by Chris Raschka tells how "Jazz musician Sun Ra (1914-1993) always said that he came from Saturn. Being from another planet, he was naturally intrigued by everything earthly--especially music, because music is the one thing on Earth most like the stars. . . . And he traveled with other musicians and singers, calling themselves the Sun Ra Arkestra, playing, singing, and dancing for people all over the planet." (Publisher's note)

"The images themselves are dense and dynamic, painted on a variety of textured papers and musical notation sheets and full of brilliant color and heavy black. Raschka clips and arranges them in irregular, rectilinear space, attempting to capture this individual force of nature. In the end, readers get a bright, impressionistic portrait that follows its subject's refusal to play by the rules. A brief author's note and list of selected recordings are appended." Horn Book

781.66   Rock (Rock 'n' roll)

George-Warren, Holly

Shake, rattle, & roll; the founders of rock & roll. words by Holly George-Warren; pictures by Laura Levine. Houghton Mifflin 2001 un il hardcover o.p. pa $5.95

Grades: 3 4 5 6   781.66

1. Musicians 2. Rock music

ISBN 0-618-05540-1; 0-618-43229-9 pa

LC 00-33480

"A wonderfully entertaining browsing book that will also fill a gap in most music collections." SLJ

Guillain, Charlotte

Punk; music, fashion, attitude! Raintree 2011 32p il (Culture in action) lib bdg $29

Grades: 5 6 7 8   781.66

1. Punk rock music

ISBN 978-1-4109-3916-6; 1-4109-3916-2

LC 2009052585

"Guillain delves into the history of punk and follows its influence on modern art, fashion, and politics. . . . [This volume is] quick, interesting, up-to-date . . . with plenty of supportive, captioned, full-color photographs. [It] also [provides] related project suggestions." SLJ

Includes glossary and bibliographical references

Handyside, Chris

★ **Rock.** Heinemann Library 2006 48p il (A history of American music) lib bdg $31.43

Grades: 5 6 7 8   781.66

1. Rock music

ISBN 1-4034-8150-4

This history of rock music is an "excellent, clear [introduction]. . . . [It] opens with the mid-1950s advent of rock n roll and continues with surf music, girl groups, the British invasion, psychedelic rock, heavy metal, punk, and grunge. Featured musicians range from Elvis Presley to Kurt Cobain." SLJ

Includes bibliographical references

Stamaty, Mark Alan

★ **Shake,** rattle & turn that noise down! how Elvis shook up music, me, and mom. Alfred A. Knopf 2010 un il $17.99; lib bdg $20.99

Grades: 2 3 4   781.66

1. Actors 2. Singers 3. Rock music 4. Rock musicians

ISBN 978-0-375-84685-4; 0-375-84685-9; 978-0-375-94685-1 lib bdg; 0-375-94685-3 lib bdg

LC 2008-02231

"Dividing each page into multiple panels with sizable chunks of text allows Stamaty to cram a lot of information into the picture-book format. . . . [The book] makes a convincing case that that old, dead singer really was cool." Booklist

782.1   Vocal forms

Siberell, Anne

★ **Bravo!** brava! a night at the opera; behind the scenes with composers, cast, and crew. introduction by Frederica von Stade. Oxford Univ. Press 2001 64p il $19.95

Grades: 4 5 6 7   782.1

1. Opera

ISBN 0-19-513966-6

LC 2001-21206

This "book introduces all features of the opera, including stars, stagehands, set designers, conductors, and supernumeraries. . . . Cartoon artwork illustrates the text, and a world map highlighting the settings of well-known operas is also included, as are curtain diagrams, plot summaries of favorite operas, and sample costumes." Horn Book Guide

Includes glossary and bibliographical references

782.25 Small-scale vocal forms

All night, all day; a child's first book of African-American spirituals. selected and illustrated by Ashley Bryan; musical arrangements by David Manning Thomas. Atheneum Pubs. 1991 48p il music hardcover o.p. pa $6.99

Grades: K 1 2 3 4   **782.25**
1. Spirituals (Songs)

ISBN 0-689-31662-3; 0-689-86786-7 pa

LC 90-753145

"An exuberance of warm color and great variety in pattern and design distinguish the illustrations. . . . Excellent piano accompaniments and guitar chords further enrich the beautiful, wholly gratifying book." Horn Book

Igus, Toyomi
★ I see the rhythm of gospel; paintings by Michele Wood; text by Toyomi Igus. Zonderkidz 2010 40p il $16.99

Grades: 4 5 6 7   **782.25**
1. Gospel music 2. African American music

ISBN 978-0-310-71819-2; 0-310-71819-8

LC 2010-08987

"Gospel music—its origins and its effects on the souls and stories of African Americans—gets a strong, loving treatment here. . . . Igus [provides] the stirring text and Wood the inventive folk art. . . . Adding to the book's usefulness is a terrific CD with five songs spanning the history of gospel music." Booklist

★ Let it shine; three favorite spirituals. [illustrated by] Ashley Bryan. Atheneum Books for Young Readers 2007 un il $16.99

Grades: K 1 2 3   **782.25**
1. Spirituals (Songs)

ISBN 0-689-84732-7

"The inspiring words of three well-known spirituals, 'This Little Light of Mine,' 'Oh, When the Saints Go Marching In,' and 'He's Got the Whole World in His Hands,' are matched with powerful construction-paper collage illustrations. Each double-page spread of this over-size picture book is an explosion of shapes and bright colors." Booklist

Nelson, Kadir
★ He's got the whole world in his hands. Dial Books for Young Readers 2005 un il $16.99

Grades: K 1 2   **782.25**
1. Spirituals (Songs)

ISBN 0-8037-2850-6

LC 2004-23075

An illustrated version of the well-known spiritual song

"Nelson uses pencils, oils, and watercolors to create a series of striking, beautifully composed pictures. . . . Nelson envisions the song in a highly personal and involving manner while embodying its strength and spirit." Booklist

★ This little light of mine; illustrated by E. B. Lewis. Simon & Schuster Books for Young Readers 2005 32p il $16.95

Grades: K 1 2 3   **782.25**
1. Spirituals (Songs)

ISBN 0-689-83179-X

"A visual interpretation of an African-American spiritual. It is morning when the book opens, and readers are greeted by a smiling boy. Throughout the day, he spreads his own special brand of joy wherever he goes. . . . Lewis's watercolor illustrations across double pages effectively convey emotions of happiness and the giving and sharing of oneself." SLJ

782.28 Carols

Spirin, Gennady
We three kings; illustrated by Gennady Spirin. Atheneum Books for Young Readers 2007 un il $16.99

Grades: K 1 2 3   **782.28**
1. Carols

ISBN 978-0-689-82114-1; 0-689-82114-X

"This handsome picture book illustrates the verses and repeated choruses of the Christmas carol 'We Three Kings.' . . . Created with watercolors and colored pencils, the formally composed and richly detailed illustrations create a distinctive world, with landscapes reminiscent of Renaissance paintings." Booklist

782.4 Secular forms

Ho, Minfong
★ Hush! a Thai lullaby. pictures by Holly Meade. Orchard Bks. 1996 un il hardcover o.p. pa $6.99

Grades: PreK K 1 2   **782.4**
1. Lullabies 2. Thailand -- Fiction

ISBN 0-531-07166-9 pa

LC 95-23251

A Caldecott Medal honor book, 1997

"A mother goes to each animal, from lizard to water buffalo to elephant, trying to quiet noises that might wake her child. When the animals are silenced and the mother finally falls asleep, the baby lies awake, with wide eyes and a smile. Ho's rhythmic text is fine for reading aloud. . . . The setting, apparently a remote Thai village, is gently evoked in cut paper and ink pictures that are bold enough to be used with groups. . . . The comforting earth tones suit the quiet nature of the story." Booklist

782.42 Songs

Aruego, Jose
Five little ducks; illustrated by Jose Aruego and Ariane Dewey. Crown 1989 un il (Raffi songs to read) hardcover o.p. pa $5.99; bd bk $6.99

Grades: PreK K 1   **782.42**
1. Songs 2. Ducks -- Songs

ISBN 0-517-58360-7; 0-517-56945-0 pa; 0-517-80057-8 bd bk

LC 88-3752

When her five little ducks disappear one by one, Mother Duck sets out to find them

Baum, Maxie
I have a little dreidel; illustrated by Julie Paschkis. Scholastic Press 2006 un il $9.99

Grades: K 1 2   782.42
1. Songs 2. Hanukkah -- Songs
ISBN 0-439-64997-8; 978-0-439-64997-1

LC 2005-31318

An illustrated retelling of the classic Hannukah song, with directions for playing the dreidel game and a recipe for making latkes.

"A favorite Hanukkah song is given new life in this charmingly illustrated variation. . . . Distinctive, folk-art-style illustrations feature a mix of patterns and vibrant solids, thick lines and simple shapes, while the bottom third of each spread frames the text in a bold blue-and-white woodcutlike design." SLJ

Berkes, Marianne Collins

Over in Australia; amazing animals Down Under. by Marianne Berkes; illustrated by Jill Dubin. Dawn Publications 2011 un il $16.95; pa $8.95
Grades: PreK K 1 2   782.42
1. Songs 2. Counting 3. Animals -- Songs 4. Animals -- Australia
ISBN 978-1-58469-135-8; 1-58469-135-2; 978-1-58469-136-5 pa; 1-58469-136-0 pa

LC 2010031038

"Berkes incorporates some of Australia's unique animals in her latest variant of the familiar song, 'Over in the Meadow.' . . . Dubin's charming paper collages deftly use a variety of patterns plus a bonus 'hidden' animal noted on one of the informative pages after the song text. That section also includes more facts about all the mentioned animals, offers suggestions for class activities, explains Dubin's illustration process, and provides the score for those unfamiliar with the tune." SLJ

Boynton, Sandra

Blue Moo; 17 jukebox hits from way back never; deluxe illustrated songbook. lyrics and drawings by Sandra Boynton; music by Sandra Boynton & Michael Ford. Workman Pub. Co. 2007 64p il $16.95
Grades: K 1 2 3   782.42
1. Songs
ISBN 978-0-7611-4775-6; 0-7611-4775-6

A book and audio CD of songs in the style of 1950s pop music.

"Grandparents, parents, and children alike can enjoy this collection. . . . Boynton has combined a roster of celebrity singers, good humor, and lots of creativity for a gift of music and fun for every member of the family." SLJ

Dog train; deluxe illustrated lyrics book of the unpredictable rock-and-roll journey. music by Sandra Boynton & Michael Ford; lyrics and drawings by Sandra Boynton. Workman Pub. 2005 64p il $17.95
Grades: K 1 2 3   782.42
1. Songs 2. Rock music
ISBN 0-7611-3966-4

LC 2005051801

"This collection of songs erupts with energy, humor, and a strong dose of rock n roll. . . . The book has a spread for each song—a colorful, cheerful illustration and excerpts of lyrics—followed by complete lyrics and musical scores at the end. An About the Artists section includes a photo and biographical sketch of each artist who performs on the accompanying CD." SLJ

Philadelphia chickens; a too-illogical zoological musical revue: deluxe illustrated lyrics book of the original cast recording of the unforgettable (though completely imaginary) stage spectacular. music by Sandra Boynton & Michael Ford; lyrics and drawings by Sandra Boynton. Workman Pub. 2002 64p il $16.95

Grades: K 1 2 3   782.42
1. Songs 2. Musicals
ISBN 0-7611-2636-8

LC 2002-27049

This is "a book-and-CD package billed as an 'imaginary musical revue.' The first 32 pages contain lyrics and illustrations, the second half of the book includes musical notation and additional lyrics for each song. An all-star cast, including Meryl Streep, Laura Linney, Eric Stoltz and the Bacon Brothers, headlines the musical recording, which features a variety of original show tunes." Publ Wkly

Sandra Boynton's One shoe blues; starring B.B. King. Workman 2009 59p il $10.95
Grades: PreK K 1 2 3   782.42
1. Songs 2. Singers 3. Guitarists 4. Blues musicians 5. Puppets and puppet plays -- Fiction 6. Lost and found possessions -- Fiction
ISBN 978-0-7611-5138-8; 0-7611-5138-9

LC 2009035847

"Boynton transforms a song from her 2007 book-and-CD title Blue Moo: 17 Jukebox Hits from Way Back Never into a stand-alone book-plus-DVD, starring blues legend B.B. King. Boynton weaves the lyrics of her original song into an extended tale about some colorful sock puppets who watch King perform the song in a cozy country house. . . . Still photographs from Boynton's music video and other complementary shots illustrate the story. . . . In addition to King's humorous and engaging performance (complete with sock puppet accompaniment), the DVD contains other kid-pleasing tidbits." Publ Wkly

Brewer, Paul

The **Beatles** were fab (and they were funny) by Kathleen Krull and Paul Brewer; illustrated by Stacy Innerst. Harcourt Children's Books 2013 40 p. col. ill. (reinforced) $16.99
Grades: 2 3 4   782.42
1. Wit and humor 2. Rock musicians -- England -- Biography 3. Beatles -- humor 4. Rock musicians -- England -- humor
ISBN 054750991X; 9780547509914

LC 2012025483

This book, by Kathleen Krull, Paul Brewer, and illustrated by Stacy Innerst, explores when "the Beatles burst onto the music scene in the early 1960s, . . . their off-the-charts talent and offbeat humor made them the most famous band on both sides of the Atlantic. . . . [This] text and expressive, quirky paintings chronicle the phenomenal rise of Beatlemania, showing how the Fab Four's sense of humor helped the lads weather everything that was thrown their way." (Publisher's note)

Carle, Eric

★ **Today** is Monday; pictures by Eric Carle. Philomel Bks. 1993 un il music hardcover o.p. pa $6.99
Grades: K 1 2 3   782.42
1. Songs 2. Food -- Songs 3. Animals -- Songs
ISBN 0-399-21966-8; 0-698-11563-5 pa

LC 91-45866

Each day of the week brings a new food, until on Sunday all the world's children can come and eat it up

This song "gets new life in a picture book bursting with food, animals, and lots of energy. Beginning with the grinning cat on the cover . . . a zooful of animals act out the lyrics: snakes get tangled in spaghetti, elephants use their trunks to slurp 'Zoooop,' and pelicans catch fish on Friday. With text at a minimum, Carle's always innovative artwork steps center stage in an oversize format that allows gloriously colored collages to spread over two pages." Booklist

Collins, Judy

When you wish upon a star; performed by Judy Collins; paintings by Eric Puybaret; music by Ned Washington; lyrics by Leigh Harline. Charlesbridge 2011 il $17.95

Grades: PreK K 1 2   **782.42**

1. Songs 2. Wishes -- Songs

ISBN 978-1-936140-35-0; 1-936140-35-7

LC 2011004945

"A short introductory verse and the song's lyrics accompany the illustrations, glossy spreads that feature an international group of children—an Eskimo, an Asian child in a bamboo hat, a boy in a turban, and half a dozen others. All of them spot a brilliant star, smiling in the sky; soon after, a woman in a blue cape and fairy wings materializes and leads the children to a country with jaunty toy buildings and candy-cane trees. . . . There, the children's wishes are fulfilled. . . . Puybaret's polished drafting gives the spreads a compelling combination of splendor and restraint." Publ Wkly

Crews, Nina

★ The **neighborhood** sing-along. Greenwillow Books 2011 63p il $17.99

Grades: K 1 2 3   **782.42**

1. Songs 2. Children's songs

ISBN 978-0-06-185063-9; 0-06-185063-2; 978-0-06-185064-6 lib bdg; 0-06-185064-0 lib bdg

LC 2010010340

A collection of songs, both familiar and lesser known, illustrated with photographs in a city setting.

"A valuable collective cultural inheritance resides in these songs, and though there are other, more comprehensive volumes available (some including the music), this bright, attractive package is a good introduction." SLJ

De colores; illustrated by David Diaz. Marshall Cavendish 2008 un il $16.99

Grades: K 1 2 3   **782.42**

1. Songs 2. Bilingual books -- English-Spanish

ISBN 978-0-7614-5431-1; 0-7614-5431-4

LC 2007022133

"This popular folk song, which is also the anthem of the United Farm Workers of America, celebrates the arrival of spring and the connectedness of humankind. Diaz's joyful pictures bring the words to life. Rendered in acrylic, colored pencil, and pencil, the vibrant, fanciful artwork features flying and floating people as well as giant-sized roosters, chickens, and birds. . . . Presented in Spanish and English, each line is illustrated on an expansive spread. Piano music and historical information about the song are included." SLJ

DiPucchio, Kelly S.

Sipping spiders through a straw; campfire songs for monsters. lyrics by Kelly DiPucchio; pictures by Gris Grimly. Scholastic Press 2008 un il $15.99

Grades: 2 3 4   **782.42**

1. Songs 2. Monsters

ISBN 978-0-439-58401-2; 0-439-58401-9

"This book of eighteen clever song parodies captures exactly the type of thing kids might come up with on their own. Grisly watercolor and mixed-media illustrations awash in appropriately putrid shades of brown and gray will definitely appeal to its target readers: those with a ghoulish sense of humor who are not easily grossed out by disgusting monsters or bodily fluids." Horn Book Guide

Dylan, Bob

Man gave names to all the animals; illustrated by Jim Arnosky. Sterling 2010 un il $17.95

Grades: K 1 2 3   **782.42**

1. Songs 2. Animals -- Songs

ISBN 978-1-4027-6858-3; 1-4027-6858-3

"Through vivid paintings of a primeval planet teeming with wildlife, Arnosky translates Dylan's 1979 song about the naming of Earth's animals into a gorgeous picture book. Full lyrics and a CD of the original song are included. In Dylan's narrative, Man takes note of the characteristics of various animals, including a bear, cow, bull, pig, and sheep, and determines a name for each creature. . . . A list of 170 species appears in the back of the book, with hints on locating each creature on Arnosky's website." SLJ

Engels, Christiane

Knick knack paddy whack; illustrated by Christiane Engel; sung by SteveSongs. Barefoot Books 2008 un il $16.99

Grades: PreK K   **782.42**

1. Counting 2. Folk songs

ISBN 978-1-84686-144-4; 1-84686-144-6

LC 2007-25046

An illustrated version of the traditional counting song that tells of the ten things 'this old man' played before he came rolling home.

"This bright, lively, new interpretation of the classic children's song incorporates numbers, musical-instrument families, and a multiethnic group of adorable children who march along with the 'old man' of the song. . . . With its inventive use of numbers, music, and collage illustrations, it's a worthy addition." SLJ

The **Farmer** in the dell; illustrated by Alexandra Wallner. Holiday House 1998 un il music $15.95

Grades: K 1   **782.42**

1. Folk songs -- United States

ISBN 0-8234-1382-9

LC 97-44206

An illustrated version of the traditional game song accompanied by music

"Wallner's primitive folk art sparkles with life, action, and energy. The colored pen-and-ink illustrations are packed with details." SLJ

Fatus, Sophie

Here we go round the mulberry bush; [by] Sophie Fatus and Fred Penner. Barefoot Books 2007 un il $16.99

Grades: PreK K 1 2   **782.42**

1. Songs

ISBN 978-1-84686-035-5; 1-84686-035-0

LC 2006025656

Presents ten verses of the popular song, with illustrations of children from different cultures as they get ready for school.

"The double-page spreads, rendered in bold acrylics, are separated into fours to show the kids side by side. This artfully underscores cultural diversity while uniting the children through their similar routines. Music and a CD of the song are included." Horn Book Guide

Favorite folk songs; The Peter Yarrow songbook. [compiled by Peter Yarrow]; illustrated by Terry Widener. Sterling Pub. 2008 48p il (Peter Yarrow songbook series) $16.95

Grades: PreK K 1 2   **782.42**

1. Folk songs

ISBN 978-1-4027-5961-1; 1-4027-5961-4

LC 2008022435

An illustrated compilation of folk songs with an audio CD of the songs performed by Peter Yarrow and his daughter Bethany.

"Widener's acrylic paintings are expansive and gorgeous, but the [CD is] the real treasure here." SLJ

The **Fox** went out on a chilly night; an old song. illustrated by Peter Spier. Doubleday 1961 un il music hardcover o.p. pa $6.95
Grades: K 1 2 3   **782.42**
1. Foxes -- Songs 2. Folk songs -- United States
ISBN 0-385-07990-7; 0-440-40829-6 pa

Set in New England, this old song tells about the trip the fox father made to town to get some of the farmer's plump geese for his family's dinner, and how he manages to evade the farmer who tries to shoot him
"A true picture book in the Caldecott-Brooke tradition. Fine drawings, lovely colors, and pictures so full of amusing details that young viewers will make fresh discoveries every time they . . . scrutinize these beautiful, action-filled pages." Horn Book

Frazee, Marla
Hush, little baby; a folk song. with pictures by Marla Frazee. Harcourt Brace & Co. 1999 un il hardcover o.p. pa $7
Grades: K 1 2   **782.42**
1. Lullabies 2. Folk songs -- United States
ISBN 0-15-201429-2; 0-15-204761-1 pa
                                                            LC 98-9608
In an old lullaby a baby is promised an assortment of presents from its adoring parent
"True to the song's Appalachian roots, Frazee sets the traditional lullaby in the hills of West Virginia, with big, detailed pictures that add character and exaggerated sibling rivalry to the nonsense story. . . . The music is on the last page, and Frazee's clear narrative pictures in acrylics and pencil capture the rhythm of the words, the historic particulars of the place, the nighttime farce, and the universal family scenarios of jealousy and love." Booklist

Harburg, E. Y.
Over the rainbow; performed by Judy Collins; music by Harold Arlen; lyrics by E.Y. Harburg; paintings by Eric Puybaret. Imagine Pub. 2010 un il $17.95
Grades: K 1 2 3   **782.42**
1. Songs
ISBN 978-1-936140-00-8; 1-936140-00-4
Illustrates the well-known song with paintings of a young girl's search for happiness.
"A musical classic inspires the creation of new images of sweeping horizons and fanciful creatures. The book includes a CD by singer Judy Collins. Her crystal-clear voice floats seamlessly through the lyrics. . . . Two additional songs interpreted by Collins make this brief CD a treasure—'I See the Moon' . . . and 'White Coral Bells.' Readers are treated to deep jewel tones as Puybaret carefully pulls them from one image to another with a succession of dreamlike scenes. . . . The art is unique, delicate, and detailed." SLJ

Henderson, Kathy
Hush, baby, hush! lullabies from around the world. illustrated by Pam Smy. Frances Lincoln Children's Books 2011 43p il $17.95
Grades: PreK K 1   **782.42**
1. Lullabies
ISBN 978-1-84507-967-3; 1-84507-967-1
"This collection includes 29 lullabies from countries including Japan, Nigeria, Malawi and Greenland. . . . Music for about half the lullabies is provided. Most songs are printed in their original languages, but lullabies in languages such as Arabic and Korean are transliterated instead of being rendered in original scripts. Animated oil-and-colored-pencil paintings show adults and children in fully-realized landscapes, city streets, marketplaces and bedrooms. . . . This attractive presentation

is appropriate as a baby gift, for daycare and preschool collections and public libraries." Kirkus

Hillenbrand, Will
★ **Down** by the station. Harcourt Brace & Co. 1999 un il music $17; pa $6.99
Grades: K 1 2   **782.42**
1. Songs 2. Animals -- Songs 3. Railroads -- Songs
ISBN 0-15-201804-2; 0-15-216790-0 pa
                                                           LC 98-41770
In this version of a familiar song, baby animals ride to the children's zoo on the zoo train
"This twist on an old favorite combines sunny illustrations, playful humor, and appealing animals." SLJ

Hinojosa, Tish
Cada nino/Every child; a bilingual songbook for kids. illustrated by Lucia Angela Perez. Cinco Puntos Press 2002 56p il music hardcover o.p. pa $9.95
Grades: K 1 2 3   **782.42**
1. Songs 2. Bilingual books -- English-Spanish
ISBN 0-9383-1760-1; 0-9383-1779-2 pa
"Hinojosa has gathered 11 traditional, original, and adapted songs to celebrate both Hispanic culture and universal experiences and feelings. A brief author's note in English and Spanish prefaces the music, with chords and melody, and verses in both languages. . . . Lovely, bright, folk-art illustrations, brimming with pattern play and whimsical details, create magical worlds of familiar objects and experiences as they incorporate cultural elements. . . . A CD is available for separate purchase." Booklist

Hoberman, Mary Ann
The **eensy**-weensy spider; adapted by Mary Ann Hoberman; illustrated by Nadine Bernard Westcott. Little, Brown 2000 un il hardcover o.p. pa $6.99
Grades: K 1 2 3   **782.42**
1. Songs 2. Finger play 3. Spiders -- Songs
ISBN 0-316-36330-8; 0-316-73412-8 pa
                                                           LC 99-25701
An expanded version of the familiar children's finger-play rhyme describing what the little spider does after being washed out of the water-spout
"Whimsical, watercolor cartoons capture the lighthearted tone of the verse. . . . This sprightly adaptation lends itself to singing aloud and is sure to be a hit." SLJ

Mary had a little lamb; adapted by Mary Ann Hoberman; illustrated by Nadine Bernard Westcott. Little, Brown 2003 un il (Singalong stories) $15.95
Grades: K 1 2   **782.42**
1. Songs 2. Sheep -- Songs
ISBN 0-316-60687-1
                                                          LC 2002-72478
This expanded version of the traditional rhyme shows what happens after the lamb gets to school. Includes music on the last page
"This playful extension of the original nursery rhyme adds to the nonsense with simple words and clear, slapstick watercolor-and-ink illustrations." Booklist

Hort, Lenny
★ The **seals** on the bus; illustrated by G. Brian Karas. Holt & Co. 2000 un il $17.95

Grades: K 1 2   **782.42**
1. Songs 2. Animals -- Songs
ISBN 0-8050-5952-0

LC 99-33612

Different animals—including seals, tigers, geese, rabbits, monkeys, and more—make their own sounds as they ride all around the town on a bus

"Karas' artwork combines cut paper, gouache, acrylic, and pencil to create a series of pleasingly varied scenes of cheerful chaos. A good story hour choice." Booklist

★ **I** hear America singing! folk songs for American families. collected and arranged by Kathleen Krull; illustrated by Allen Garns; introductory note by Arlo Guthrie. Knopf 2003 145p il $24.95

Grades: 3 4 5 6   **782.42**
1. Folk songs -- United States
ISBN 0-375-82527-4

First published 1992 without CD with title: Gonna sing my head off!

"Work songs, love songs, ballads and blues, lullabies, spirituals, protest songs, and sheer nonsense make up this entertaining collection of 62 traditional and contemporary favorites. For each song, Krull provides the simplest piano and guitar arrangements in a clear double-page spread design that includes the words to all the verses. . . . The exuberant illustrations, mostly in bright pastels, manage to be both familiar and dramatic. . . . Informal notes at the head of each song give something about history, origin, performance, and possibilities for variation." Booklist

In the hollow of your hand; slave lullabies. collected by Alice McGill; pictures by Michael Cummings. Houghton Mifflin 2000 un il music $18

Grades: 5 6 7 8   **782.42**
1. Lullabies 2. Slavery -- Poetry 3. African Americans -- Poetry
ISBN 0-395-85755-4

LC 97-20269

A collection of lullabies orally transmitted by African-American slaves revealing their hardships and sorrows as well as soothing notes of well-being and belief in a better time to come

"This moving collection of 13 folk lullabies is a powerful way to communicate what family life was like under slavery. . . . Opposite each song is a handsome full-page quilt collage contributed by Michael Cummings. . . . There's full musical notation at the back, and a CD of the songs, sung by McGill, is included. The people's words are achingly beautiful, and the combination with history and personal experience makes this an enduring collection." Booklist

Jackson, Jill

Let there be peace on earth; and let it begin with me. by Jill Jackson & Sy Miller; [illustrated by David Diaz] Tricycle Press 2009 un il $18.99

Grades: PreK K 1 2   **782.42**
1. Songs 2. Peace -- Songs
ISBN 978-1-58246-285-1; 1-58246-285-2

LC 2008043122

Illustrates the award-winning song about each person's responsibility to help bring about world peace. Includes a history of the song and biographical notes on the husband and wife songwriting team.

"Diaz's luminous artwork brings [the song] to life for picture-book audiences. . . . The CD contains 12 peace-themed, secular songs. The arrangements are airy and fun for children." SLJ

Johnson, James Weldon

★ **Lift** every voice and sing; by James Weldon Johnson; illustrated by Bryan Collier. Amistad 2007 un il $16.99; lib bdg $17.89

Grades: K 1 2 3   **782.42**
1. Songs 2. African American music
ISBN 978-0-06-054147-7; 978-0-06-145897-2 lib bdg

LC 2007008602

An illustrated version of the song that has come to be considered the African American national anthem

"Collier's stirring textured collage-and-watercolor illustrations . . . express his Christian faith and his profound sense of connection with his people's historic struggle." Booklist

Katz, Alan

Mosquitoes are ruining my summer! and other silly dilly camp songs. illustrated by David Catrow. Margaret K. McElderry Books 2011 un il $16.99

Grades: 3 4 5   **782.42**
1. Songs 2. Camps -- Songs
ISBN 978-1-4169-5568-9; 1-4169-5568-2

LC 2009021167

Familiar tunes are given new words relating to summer camp, including "Whose Idea Was This Dumb Hike" sung to the tune of "Twinkle Twinkle Little Star."

"Few elements of the camp-going experience are exempt from the tongue-in-cheek riffing, and the lively cartoon-style illustrations extend the hyperbolic humor through caricature and perspective." Booklist

Langstaff, John M.

Frog went a-courtin' retold by John Langstaff; with pictures by Feodor Rojankovsky. Harcourt Brace Jovanovich 1955 un il music $16; pa $7

Grades: K 1 2 3   **782.42**
1. Folk songs 2. Mice -- Songs 3. Frogs -- Songs
ISBN 0-15-230214-X; 0-15-633900-5 pa

Awarded the Caldecott Medal, 1956

"Retelling of a merry old Scottish ballad with many-colored illustrations about the marriage between Mr. Frog and Miss Mouse. A composite American version set to Appalachian mountain music." Chicago Public Libr

Oh, a-hunting we will go; [by] John Langstaff; pictures by Nancy Winslow Parker. Atheneum Pubs. 1974 un il music hardcover o.p. pa $6.99

Grades: K 1 2   **782.42**
1. Folk songs 2. Animals -- Songs
ISBN 0-689-71503-X pa

The nonsense verses of this folk song trace the hunt for such animals as an armadillo, a fox, and a snake, and describe the imagined treatment of each animal once it is caught

"The 12 stanzas are complemented by Parker's droll crayon illustrations (the fox caught in the box is watching TV), and a score for guitar and piano is appended. An amusing addition to 'song' picture books." SLJ

★ **Over** in the meadow; with pictures by Feodor Rojankovsky. Harcourt Brace & Co. 1957 un il music hardcover o.p. pa $7

Grades: K 1 2   **782.42**
1. Counting 2. Folk songs 3. Animals -- Songs
ISBN 0-15-258854-X; 0-15-670500-1 pa

"This old counting rhyme tells of ten meadow families whose mothers advise them to dig, run, sing, play, hum, build, swim, wink, spin and hop. The illustrations, half in full color, show the combination of realism and imagination which little children like best. The tune, arranged simply, is on the last page, and children will have fun acting the whole thing out." Horn Book

Leodhas, Sorche Nic

Always room for one more; illustrated by Nonny Hogrogian. Holt & Co. 1965 un il music $14.95; pa $5.95

Grades: K 1 2 3   **782.42**

1. Folk songs

ISBN 0-8050-0331-2; 0-8050-0330-4 pa

Awarded the Caldecott Medal, 1966

"A picture book based on an old Scottish folk song about hospitable Lachie MacLachlan, who invited in so many guests that his little house finally burst. Rhymed text . . . a glossary of Scottish words, and music for the tune are combined into an effective whole." Hodges. Books for Elem Sch Libr

Let's sing together; The Peter Yarrow songbook. [selected by Peter Yarrow]; illustrated by Terry Widener. Sterling Pub. 2009 48p il (Peter Yarrow songbook series) $16.95

Grades: PreK K 1 2   **782.42**

1. Folk songs

ISBN 978-1-4027-5963-5; 1-4027-5963-0

"The lyrics of 12 folk songs, rooted in several cultural traditions, are illustrated in Widener's simple yet resonant folk art style, which creatively mingles conventional, earth-toned scenarios . . . with images featuring vividly hued, fanciful flourishes. . . . The author provides guitar chords, historical notes and personal anecdotes for each song. On the included CD, Yarrow sings each song, accompanied by his talented daughter Bethany Yarrow and a quartet of children. An energetic and uplifting package." Publ Wkly

Lightfoot, Gordon

★ **Canadian** railroad trilogy; art by Ian Wallace. Groundwood Books/House of Anansi Press 2010 un il

Grades: 2 3 4 5   **782.42**

1. Children's songs 2. Canada -- History 3. Railroads -- Songs 4. Railroads -- History 5. Canadian Pacific Railway Ltd.

ISBN 0888999534; 9780888999535

This is an illustrated version of Gordon Lightfoot's song written in Canadia's centennial year, 1967, to commemorate the building of the Canadian Pacific Railroad. "Age four and up." (Quill Quire)

"Wallace's . . . sprawling, dreamlike paintings pay homage to the Canadian landscape; they accompany the lyrics of Lightfoot's 1967 song. . . . Mountains, forests, coastline, and plains roll past as on a railway journey—miles of lonely wilderness the Canadian Pacific Railway was built to span. . . . Wallace doesn't avoid showing the realities of the railway workers lives. . . . It's a huge and unusual project, and Wallace has executed it with admirable care." Publ Wkly

Long, Laurel

★ The **twelve** days of Christmas; illustrated by Laurel Long. Dial Books for Young Readers 2011 il $16.99

Grades: PreK K   **782.42**

1. Songs 2. Folk songs 3. Christmas -- Songs

ISBN 978-0-8037-3357-2; 0-8037-3357-7

LC 2008015774

An illustrated version of the traditional song.

"Long's lyrical and lush oil paintings, reminiscent of Russian icon art, combined with a tricky interactive element, make this version of the traditional carol special." SLJ

Lyon, George Ella

Which side are you on? the story of a song. artwork by Christopher Cardinale. Cinco Puntos Press 2011 un il $17.95

Grades: 3 4 5   **782.42**

1. Miners 2. Labor unions 3. Coal mines and mining -- Songs

ISBN 978-1-933693-96-5; 1-933693-96-7

LC 2010037398

This tells the story of a song which was written in 1931 by Florence Reece in a rain of bullets. Florence's husband Sam was a coal miner in Kentucky. Miners went on strike until they could get better pay, safer working conditions, and health care. The company hired thugs to attack the organizers like Sam Reece. George Ella Lyon tells this story through the eyes of one of Florence's daughters.

"Ribbons of song lyrics weave across scenes of the miners' tools of their trade and the guns of hired company toughs. A thorough author's note follows the text, ending with the song's musical notation and one version of the words on the back cover. The use of music as a protest element makes an interesting addendum to resources on union history or the time period." SLJ

Mallett, David

★ **Inch** by inch; the garden song. pictures by Ora Eitan. Harper-Collins Pubs. 1995 un il music hardcover o.p. pa $5.95

Grades: K 1 2   **782.42**

1. Songs 2. Gardens -- Songs

ISBN 0-06-443481-8 pa

LC 93-38352

"In this picture-book version of the song first published in 1975 . . . a young child plants seeds . . . weeds and tends them, and finally, gleans a bountiful harvest. . . . Employing a variety of media including cut paper, Eitan uses color and space to create a striking effect." SLJ

Martin, Steve

Late for school; illustrated by C. F. Payne. Grand Central 2010 un il $17.95

Grades: PreK K 1 2   **782.42**

1. Songs 2. Schools -- Songs

ISBN 978-0-446-55702-3; 0-446-55702-1

An illustrated song about the difficulties of getting to school on time, with an audio CD of the author singing the song with banjo accompaniment.

"In Payne's . . . hands, Martin's goofy verse achieves its comic impact on a cinematic scale. . . . Kids will relish Martin's subversive madness." Publ Wkly

★ **National** anthems of the world; edited by Michael Jamieson Bristow. 11th ed.; Weidenfeld & Nicolson 2006 629p $90

Grades: 5 6 7 8 9 10 11 12 Adult   **782.42**

1. National songs

ISBN 0-304-36826-1

First published 1943 in the United Kingdom with title: National anthems of the United Nations and France

This volume contains national anthems of about 198 nations, including melody and accompaniment. Words are presented in the native language with transliteration provided where necessary. English translations follow. Brief historical notes on the adoption of each anthem are included

"An essential reference resource for all libraries." Libr J

Norworth, Jack

Take me out to the ball game; performed by Carly Simon; written by Jack Norworth; illustrated by Amiko Hirao. Imagine 2011 un il $17.95

Grades: PreK K 1 2   **782.42**

1. Songs 2. Baseball -- Songs

ISBN 978-1-936140-26-8; 1-936140-26-8

LC 2010035438

Text and illustrations present the well-known song about baseball games, with the ball players depicted as animals.

"It's a visual tour de force, with double-page spreads of large, action-packe, brilliantly colored scenes in startlingly off-center perspective. A Carly Simon CD accompanies the book, and youngsters will have a wonderful time reading and singing along." Kirkus

Okee Dokee Brothers

Can you canoe? And Other Adventure Songs. by The Okee Dokee Brothers; Brandon Reese (Illustrator) Sterling Pub Co Inc 2016 40 p. color illustrations, maps $17.95

    Grades: K 1 2 3 4 5   **782.42**
    1. Children's songs 2. Outdoor recreation 3. Adventure and adventurers
    ISBN 1454918039; 9781454918035

This children's book by the Okee Dokee Brothers, illustrated by Brandon Reese, "journeys cross-country in 12 songs, from the rolling hills of Appalachia in the east to the canyons and campfires of the West. Along the way, . . . [the duo's] tunes invite kids to wander through the woods and wilderness, where they'll discover hungry black bears and tall-tale spinners; quiet canoes and cozy camping tents; a jumpin' jamboree and a bullfrog opera." (Publisher's note)

Orozco, Jose-Luis

★ **Diez** deditos. Ten little fingers & other play rhymes and action songs from Latin America; selected, arranged, and translated from José-Luis Orozco; illustrated by Elisa Kleven. Dutton Children's Bks. 1997 56p il music $19.99; pa $7.99

Grades: K 1 2 3   **782.42**
    1. Songs 2. Finger play 3. Folklore -- Latin America 4. Bilingual books -- English-Spanish
    ISBN 0-525-45736-4; 0-14-230087-9 pa

"This collection of fingerplays and action songs in Spanish and English comes with clear instructions for physical movements and simple musical notation. A brief sentence or paragraph introduces each entry. . . . Orozco's selections, some traditional, some written by himself, include versifications on such child-appealing subjects as dancing, singing, animals, weather, and food. . . . Kleven's collage illustrations practically pop off the pages with flashy colors and rich details that make each bustling composition a viewer's delight." Bull Cent Child Books

★ **Fiestas** : a year of Latin American songs of celebration; selected, arranged, and translated by José-Luis Orozco; illustrated by Elisa Kleven. Dutton Children's Bks. 2002 48p il music $17.99

Grades: K 1 2 3   **782.42**
    1. Songs 2. Festivals 3. Bilingual books -- English-Spanish 4. Latin America -- Social life and customs
    ISBN 0-525-45937-5

"Orozco presents 22 songs that center around holidays. . . . Arranged by month, each song is presented with a paragraph of background, the music for the melody (with guitar chords), and the lyrics in both Spanish and English. . . . Kleven's bright borders and busy illustrations . . . make this not only an exemplary songbook, but also a stunning visual experience." SLJ

Paxton, Tom

The **marvelous** toy; words and music by Tom Paxton; illustrated by Steve Cox. Imagine Publishing 2009 un il $17.95

Grades: PreK K 1 2   **782.42**
    1. Songs 2. Toys -- Songs
    ISBN 978-0-9822939-2-8; 0-9822939-2-5

In this picture book adaptation of Paxton's song, a "boy receives [a] toy from his father, they enjoy it together, and the boy passes it on to his own son with similar enthusiasm. . . . Although the spindly, alien-look-

ing toy is never completely visible, the rainbow-colored protrusions that are shown emit airbrushed beams, while sparks zoom and zip behind it, illuminating the night and leaving a trail of magic in its wake. . . . Four Paxton songs are enclosed on a CD." Publ Wkly

Pinkney, Brian

★ **Hush,** little baby; adapted and illustrated by Brian Pinkney. Greenwillow Books 2006 un il $15.99; lib bdg $17.89

Grades: K 1 2   **782.42**
    1. Lullabies 2. Folk songs -- United States
    ISBN 978-0-06-055993-9; 0-06-055993-4; 978-0-06-055994-6 lib bdg; 0-06-055994-2 lib bdg

                                LC 2005-08216

"Pinkney sets his version of the traditional Appalachian folksong in an African American household of the early 1900s. . . . Ink-on-clayboard scenes show a distraught toddler girl comforted by a playful father and older brother, who sing, dance, and, of course, offer a series of whimsical gifts. . . . An appended musical arrangement gives the tune a jazzy beat to match the wheeling, undulating figures in the story." Booklist

Raffi

Baby Beluga; illustrated by Ashley Wolff. Crown 1990 un il music (Raffi songs to read) hardcover o.p. pa $5.99; bd bk $6.99

Grades: K 1 2   **782.42**
    1. Songs 2. Whales -- Songs
    ISBN 0-517-58362-3 pa; 0-517-70977-5 bd bk

                                  LC 89-49367

Presents the illustrated text to the song about the little white whale who swims wild and free

"Wolff's striking double-page spreads show the young whale among its fellow Arctic Sea inhabitants. Diversifying her views, the illustrator eyes Baby Beluga and mother swimming together underwater; takes an aerial angle, looking down on the whales from a puffin's perspective; and observes the icy yet welcoming formations where seals, polar bears, and an Eskimo find shelter. . . . An inviting approach to reading encouragement." Booklist

Down by the bay; illustrated by Nadine Bernard Westcott. Crown 1987 un il music (Raffi songs to read) hardcover o.p. pa $5.99; bd bk $6.99

Grades: K 1 2   **782.42**
    1. Songs
    ISBN 0-517-56645-1 pa; 0-517-80058-6 bd bk

                                  LC 87-750291

This illustrated version of one of Raffi's songs depicts a variety of unusual sights to be seen "down by the bay"

The "cheerful nonsense verses are illustrated with equal cheer. Westcott's scraggly lines and bright, clear colors humorously portray the busy children, jolly animals, and frantic mothers that populate the song." SLJ

Raven, Margot

Happy birthday to you! the mystery behind the most famous song in the world. by Margot Theis Raven; paintings by Chris K. Soentpiet. Sleeping Bear Press 2008 un il $17.95

Grades: 1 2 3 4   **782.42**
    1. Songs 2. Pianists 3. Educators 4. Songwriters
    ISBN 978-1-58536-169-4; 1-58536-169-0

                                LC 2007037438

"A lovely succession of watercolor paintings depicts the latter half of the 19th century in Louisville and illuminates the thoughtful expressions and joyful faces of the Hill family. . . . [This is] an eye-opener for history and trivia lovers in all libraries." SLJ

Ray, Jane

★ The **twelve** days of Christmas. Candlewick Press 2011 un il $16.99

Grades: PreK K 1   **782.42**

1. Songs 2. Folk songs 3. Christmas -- Songs

ISBN 978-0-7636-5735-2; 0-7636-5735-2

LC 2010052222

On each of the twelve days of Christmas, more and more gifts arrive from the recipient's true love.

"Ray's intricate illustrations offer a wealth of details to explore up close. The images are slightly busy for sharing with a large group, but irresistible for a smaller group or one-on-one. A very nice version indeed." SLJ

Reid, Rob

Children's jukebox; the select subject guide to children's musical recordings. 2nd ed; American Library Association 2007 284p a $55

Grades: Adult Professional   **782.42**

1. Reference books 2. Children's libraries 3. Songs -- Indexes

ISBN 0-8389-0940-X pa; 978-0-8389-0940-9 pa

LC 2006103175

First published 1995

This is an index to 548 recordings for children with 147 subject headings, plus subcategories

Includes discography

Roslonek, Steve

The **shape** song swingalong; written and sung by SteveSongs; illustrated by David Sim. Barefoot 2011 il $16.99; pa $9.99

Grades: PreK K 1 2   **782.42**

1. Shape 2. Songs

ISBN 978-1-84686-671-5; 1-84686-671-5; 978-1-84686-679-1 pa; 1-84686-679-0 pa

"Children in primary colored, mixed-media spreads create the very scenes that they inhabit, using large crayons to draw various shapes that form everything from a city of brick skyscrapers to a sunny beach where Sim's naïf figures ride a purple waterslide. A jazzy song by the children's musical group SteveSongs describes the children's drawings and the shapes that they use to create specific images.... The shape-focused chorus, bouncy verses, and whimsical storytelling should have kids singing along with the included CD recording, which also features a video animation of the story." Publ Wkly

Roth, Susan L.

★ **Hanukkah,** oh Hanukkah; [by] Susan L. Roth. Dial Books for Young Readers 2004 un il $10.99; pa $5.99

Grades: K 1 2   **782.42**

1. Songs 2. Hanukkah -- Songs

ISBN 0-8037-2843-3; 0-14-240701-1 pa

LC 2003-13165

A family of mice celebrates the eight days of Hannukah with friends in this illustrated version of the holiday song

"Cloth and paper collages done in many different patterns and textures add interest to the cozy tableaux.... The lovely colors and the appealing tune make this a good holiday choice." SLJ

Sabuda, Robert

★ The **12** days of Christmas; a pop-up celebration by Robert Sabuda. anniversary edition; Little Simon 2006 un il $26.95

Grades: K 1 2 3   **782.42**

1. Folk songs 2. Pop-up books 3. Christmas -- Songs

ISBN 978-1-4169-2792-1; 1-4169-2792-1

A reissue of the edition first published 1996

This pop-up version of the popular Christmas folk song about gift-giving features "a partridge popping, snow scattering, and lords a-leaping off the page.... For this ... anniversary edition .... paper engineer Robert Sabuda encloses ... extra pages with a pop-up Christmas tree with real lights aglow, and a .... pop-up ornament of two turtledoves." Publisher's note

Sedaka, Neil

Waking up is hard to do; illustrated by Daniel Miyares. Imagine 2010 un il $17.95

Grades: PreK K 1 2 3   **782.42**

1. Songs

ISBN 978-1-936140-13-8; 1-936140-13-6

LC 2010001402

"Sedaka has rewritten the lyrics of his 1962 and 1975 chart-topping tune to create this child-pleasing book. The alarm clock is ringing, birds are singing, breakfast is warming, and school is calling. The repeated chorus, 'Wakin' up is hard to do,' will allow children to chime in.... The charming art has fun details and an adorable cast of animal characters. .... A CD includes the title track as well as two new songs: 'Lightnin' Jim' and 'Sing.'" SLJ

Seeger, Ruth Crawford

★ **American** folk songs for children in home, school, and nursery school; a book for children, parents, and teachers. by Ruth Crawford Seeger; illustrated by Barbara Cooney. Oak Publications 2002 190p il pa $24.95

Grades: PreK K 1 2 3 4 Adult Professional   **782.42**

1. Songs 2. Folk music -- United States

ISBN 978-0-8256-0346-4 pa; 0-8256-0346-3 pa

First published 1948 by Doubleday

"This is a unique collection. It will probably be the authoritative source for American folk songs for children for many, many years." Saturday Review of Books

Seskin, Steve

Sing my song; a kid's guide to songwriting. starring Steve Seskin and a chorus of creative kids; illustrated by Eve Aldridge ... [et al.] Tricycle Press 2008 32p il $18.99

Grades: 1 2 3 4 5   **782.42**

1. Songwriters and songwriting

ISBN 978-1-58246-266-0; 1-58246-266-6

LC 2007046966

"Seskin has tapped a mother lode of musical enthusiasm in this book by showing young readers the 'how to' necessary to create songs and set them to music. Following 12 excellent examples and step-by-step instructions, readers discover how to put together the parts of a song. Musical terms are defined, song forms are suggested, and a CD of tunes provides sample accompaniment as Seskin backs up his relaxed vocals on guitar and with choruses from various schools." SLJ

Sleepytime songs; The Peter Yarrow songbook. [compiled by] Peter Yarrow; illustrated by Terry Widener. Sterling Pub. 2008 48p il (Peter Yarrow songbook series) $16.95

Grades: PreK K 1 2   **782.42**

1. Lullabies 2. Folk songs -- United States

ISBN 978-1-4027-5962-8; 1-4027-5962-2

LC 2008022530

"Yarrow, best known as the Peter of Peter, Paul, and Mary, here offers a wonderful compilation of bedtime songs, complete with CD. Beginning with a warm introduction from Yarrow about singing to children, the book continues with two-page spreads containing the lyrics of the songs, set against Widener's imaginative art." Booklist

Spirin, Gennady

★ The **twelve** days of Christmas; illustrated by Gennady Spirin. Marshall Cavendish 2009 un il $16.99

Grades: K 1 2 3   **782.42**

1. Songs 2. Folk songs 3. Christmas -- Songs

ISBN 978-0-7614-5551-6; 0-7614-5551-5

LC 2008-06476

On each of the twelve days of Christmas, unusual and fanciful gifts arrive to celebrate the season.

"This holiday favorite is brought to life through Spirin's gorgeous illustrations. . . . The elaborately detailed and exquisitely executed artwork, rendered in watercolor and colored pencil, has a Renaissance feel. Roman numerals are placed on the tree or the base of the tree planter to indicate which day is being celebrated. As the oval inset fills with calling birds, golden rings, swans-a-swimming, etc., readers will enjoy trying to count all the gifts. A must-have." SLJ

Staines, Bill

★ **All** God's critters; song by Bill Staines; pictures by Kadir Nelson. Simon & Schuster Books for Young Readers 2009 un il $16.99

Grades: PreK K 1   **782.42**

1. Songs 2. Animals -- Songs

ISBN 978-0-689-86959-4; 0-689-86959-2

LC 2008-23624

Celebrates how all the animals in the world make their own music in their own way, some singing low, some singing higher.

The song "is brought to rollicking life by Nelson's artwork. . . . Each delightful spread [is] full-to-bursting with . . . critters' energy. . . . The oversize type of the lyrics nearly shouts off the page." Booklist

Stotts, Stuart

★ **We** shall overcome; a song that changed the world. by Stuart Stotts; foreword by Pete Seeger; with illustrations by Terrance Cummings. Clarion Books 2009 72p il $18

Grades: 5 6 7 8   **782.42**

1. African Americans -- Civil rights -- Songs

ISBN 978-0-547-18210-0; 0-547-18210-4

LC 2009022578

"This smart, effective telling has few missteps. From the informative black-and-white photographs to the solid back matter to the CD sung by Pete Seeger, it is a complete package." Booklist

Taback, Simms

★ **There** was an old lady who swallowed a fly. Viking 1997 un il $16.99

Grades: K 1 2 3   **782.42**

1. Folk songs 2. Animals -- Songs

ISBN 0-670-86939-2

A Caldecott Medal honor book, 1998

Simms Taback's illustrated version of the folk song in which an old lady swallows a variety of progressively larger animals

"Each page is full of details and humorous asides. . . . A die-cut hole allows readers to see inside [the old lady's] belly, first the critters already devoured and, with the turn of the page, the new animal that will join the crowd in her ever-expanding stomach. . . . The text is handwritten on vivid strips of paper that are loosely placed on the patterned page, thus creating a lively interplay between the meaning of the words and their visual power." SLJ

They Might Be Giants (Musical group)

Kids go! [by] They Might Be Giants; illustrations by Pascal Campion. Simon & Schuster 2009 un il $19.99

Grades: K 1 2 3   **782.42**

1. Songs

ISBN 978-0-7432-7275-9; 0-7432-7275-7

LC 2009019668

An illustrated version of the song 'Go, Kid, Go,' exhorting the reader to get up and move around

"With just a hint of retro style about them, Campion's thick and loose black ink lines provide a sense of fluidity in riotous scenes that use a limited but appealing palette of green, gray, and peach, splashed over lots of white space. Befitting the action words in the text, the font size bounces from small to large, adding to the energetic tone. . . . An accompanying DVD features an animated video of the song." Publ Wkly

Vetter, Jennifer Riggs

Down by the station; illustrations by Frank Remkiewicz. Tricycle Press 2009 un il $15.99

Grades: PreK K   **782.42**

1. Songs 2. Vehicles

ISBN 978-1-58246-243-1; 1-58246-243-7

LC 2008011308

This illustrated version of the traditional song expands and describes more vehicles, different locations, and their unique sounds, from pufferbillies to racecars and rockets

"Remkiewicz uses candy-bright colors and a hint of goofy elasticity in his slightly busy watercolor art. With enough repetition to tempt early readers to try the text on their own, the book will also attract the lap-sit crowd." SLJ

Voake, Charlotte

★ **Tweedle** dee dee; [by] Charlotte Voake. Candlewick Press 2008 un il $16.99

Grades: PreK K 1 2   **782.42**

1. Folk songs -- United States

ISBN 978-0-7636-3797-2; 0-7636-3797-1

LC 2007040414

Illustrations of a forest in spring and simple text provide a variation on the traditional folk song, "The green leaves grew around"

The pages are "washed with pale green and covered with squiggly line drawings and watercolors. . . . The minimal text invites a read-aloud—and even before arriving at the musical score on the final spread, readers are likely to find themselves singing." Publ Wkly

Weave little stars into my sleep; Native American lullabies. edited by Neil Philip; photographs by Edward S. Curtis. Clarion Bks. 2001 un il $16

Grades: 2 3 4   **782.42**

1. Lullabies 2. Native American literature

ISBN 0-618-08856-3

LC 00-60324

Published in the United Kingdom with title: Where did you fall from?

This is a "book of 15 lullabies, selected, adapted, and, in some cases, reworked from original Native American material. Striking, carefully chosen photographs, originally published in the early 1900s, portray the spirit of the words." Booklist

Includes bibliographical references

Yolen, Jane

★ **Apple** for the teacher; thirty songs for singing while you work. collected and introduced by Jane Yolen; music arranged by Adam Stemple; art edited by Eileen Michaelis Smiles. Harry N. Abrams 2005 117p il $24.95

Grades: 4 5 6 7   **782.42**
1. Songs 2. Work -- Songs
ISBN 0-8109-4825-7

LC 2004-24404

"Yolen has brought together a collection of 30 work songs . . . which represent a wide variety of occupations. . . . She introduces each job, explaining unusual vocabulary and references in the songs. . . . The artwork . . . is elegant. Ranging from sculpture to paintings to needlework, each selection of Americana has been carefully matched to the occupation, beautifully reproduced on high-quality paper, and meticulously identified." Booklist

Zelinsky, Paul O.
★ Knick-knack paddywhack! a moving parts book. adapted from the counting song and illustrated by Paul O. Zelinsky; paper engineering by Andrew Baron. Dutton 2002 un il $18.99
Grades: K 1 2 3   **782.42**
1. Songs 2. Counting
ISBN 0-525-46908-7

A young boy sets out on a walk—pull the tabs and tiny old men from One to Ten act out the familiar refrain of the traditional counting song on and all around him.

"This glorious title is a paper-engineering and bookmaking marvel as well as a freewheeling romp." SLJ

783 Music for single voices

Fishkin, Rebecca Love
Singing; a practical guide to pursuing the art. Compass Point Books 2010 48p il (Performing arts) lib bdg $28.65
Grades: 5 6 7 8   **783**
1. Singing 2. Vocational guidance
ISBN 978-0-7565-4362-4 lib bdg; 0-7565-4362-2 lib bdg

LC 2010012607

This guide on a singing career includes tips on education, technique, and more.

"Meant for students contemplating a career in the field . . . [this book goes] beyond basic introductions and into more detail about what it takes to make it as a professional. . . . [The author maintains] . . . a frank, realistic tone, stressing the importance of hard work and dedication. Great [resource] . . . for those wanting to make their passions more than just a hobby." SLJ

Includes glossary and bibliographical references

Landau, Elaine
Is singing for you? Lerner Publications 2011 40p il (Ready to make music) lib bdg $27.93
Grades: 4 5 6 7   **783**
1. Singing
ISBN 978-0-7613-5427-7 lib bdg; 0-7613-5427-1 lib bdg

LC 2009052350

Helps readers explore the art of singing. This book covers the basics, including tips for getting started and info on vocal technique.

"Landau covers all the bases so that prospective musicians have the information they need. . . . Kids thinking about taking up an instrument will find . . . [this book] helpful in their decision-making process." SLJ

Includes glossary and bibliographical references

784.19 Instruments

D'Cruz, Anna-Marie
Make your own musical instruments. PowerKids Press 2009 24p il (Do it yourself projects!) lib bdg $23.95; pa $9.40
Grades: 2 3 4   **784.19**
1. Handicraft 2. Musical instruments
ISBN 978-1-4358-2854-4 lib bdg; 1-4358-2854-2 lib bdg; 978-1-4358-2925-1 pa; 1-4358-2925-5 pa

LC 2008033667

This offers "step-by-step instructions and full-color photos to illustrate the crafts. Projects have a broad cultural representation and are not gender specific. Materials are easily obtained. . . . [Projects include] castanets, bongo drums, and a jazz washboard." SLJ

Includes glossary and bibliographical references

Helsby, Genevieve
★ Those amazing musical instruments; [by] Genevieve Helsby; with Marin Alsop as your guide. Sourcebooks Jabberwocky 2007 176p il $19.95
Grades: 4 5 6 7 8 9   **784.19**
1. Musical instruments
ISBN 978-1-4022-0825-6; 1-4022-0825-1

LC 2007013821

This is "a guide to instruments commonly found in an orchestra. . . . Utilizing large print; ample, colorful illustrations; and an open format, the book is logically organized into chapters about each of the musical instrument families, including keyboards, the voice, and modern electronic instruments. Throughout, readers are prompted to listen to the accompanying CD-ROM, which features more than 100 musical samples. Information is clearly presented, and the author's enthusiasm for her subject is contagious." SLJ

VanHecke, Susan
★ Raggin', jazzin', rockin' a history of American musical instrument makers. Boyds Mills Press 2011 136p il $17.95
Grades: 5 6 7 8 9   **784.19**
1. Musical instruments 2. C. G. Conn Ltd. 3. C. F. Martin & Co. 4. Manufacturing executives 5. Musical instrument makers
ISBN 1-59078-574-6; 978-1-59078-574-4

LC 2010-04877

This is a history of American musical instrument making, including the stories of the Zildjian family's cymbals, Steinway's pianos, Charles Gerard Conn's brass instruments, C. F. Martin's guitars, William F. Ludwig's drums, Hammond keyboards, Fender electric guitars, and Moog synthesizers.

"Musicians and music lovers look no further. [This] is a book for everyone. . . . This is an interesting book." Voice Youth Advocates

Includes bibliographical references

Wiseman, Ann Sayre
Making music; [by] Ann Sayre Wiseman and John Langstaff; illustrations by Ann Sayre Wiseman. Storey Bks. 2003 96p il hardcover o.p. pa $9.95
Grades: 3 4 5 6   **784.19**
1. Handicraft 2. Musical instruments
ISBN 1-58017-513-9; 1-58017-512-0 pa

LC 2003-54218

First published 1979 by Scribner with title: Making musical things

Includes instructions for making a variety of simple musical instruments from ordinary household items

Includes glossary and bibliographical references

784.2　Full orchestra (Symphony orchestra)

Celenza, Anna Harwell

Saint-Saens's Danse Macabre; Anna Harwell Celenza; illustrated by JoAnn E. Kitchel. Charlesbridge 2013 32 p. (reinforced for library use) $19.95

Grades: 2 3 4 5　　　　　　　　　　　　　　　**784.2**

1. Music　2. Composition (Music)　3. Saint-Saëns, Camille, 1835-1921. Danse Macabre (Symphonic poem)　4. Composers -- France

ISBN 157091348X; 9781570913488

LC 2012024575

This book is the "eighth in [Anna Harwell] Celenza's series of biographies of famous pieces of music, this account opens with an unsettling scene in which composer Camille Saint-Saëns (1835-1921) and his poet friend Henri Cazalis visit the catacombs of Paris at midnight. . . . Inspired by the visit, Saint-Saëns returns home and writes the famous piece." (Publishers Weekly)

Other biographies by this author include:

Bach's Goldberg Variations (2005)

Duke Ellington's Nutcracker Suite (2011)

The Farewell Symphony (2000)

Gershwin's Rhapsody in Blue (2006)

The Heroic Symphony (2004)

Pictures at an Exhibition (2003)

Vivaldi's Four Seasons (2012)

Ganeri, Anita

★ The **young** person's guide to the orchestra; Benjamin Britten's composition on CD narrated by Ben Kingsley. book written by Anita Ganeri. Harcourt Brace & Co. 1996 56p il $25

Grades: 4 5 6 7　　　　　　　　　　　　　　**784.2**

1. Orchestra　2. Music appreciation　3. Musical instruments

ISBN 0-15-201304-0

LC 95-41478

"Accompanying this book on orchestral music is a CD featuring Britten's A Young Person's Guide to the Orchestra . . . as well as Dukas' The Sorcerer's Apprentice. The book begins with an overview of the orchestra and then centers around groups of instruments, explaining a bit of their history and their sound's distinctive quality. . . . The book also introduces eight famous composers, world music, Benjamin Britten, and the background of The YoungPerson's Guide to the Orchestra. . . . Handsome and useful." Booklist

Includes glossary

Hayes, Ann

Meet the orchestra; written by Ann Hayes; illustrated by Karmen Thompson. Harcourt Brace Jovanovich 1990 un il hardcover o.p. pa $7

Grades: K 1 2 3　　　　　　　　　　　　　　**784.2**

1. Orchestra　2. Musical instruments

ISBN 0-15-200526-9; 0-15-200222-7 pa

LC 89-32959

Describes the features, sounds, and role of each musical instrument in the orchestra

"Spacious watercolors depicting animal musicians in formal evening dress enhance this charming introduction to the orchestra. . . . The descriptive writing has immediacy . . . while the artwork has a subtle sense of color and humor that increases the fun." Booklist

Koscielniak, Bruce

★ The **story** of the incredible orchestra; an introduction to musical instruments and the symphony orchestra. Houghton Mifflin 2000 un il $16; pa $6.95

Grades: 2 3 4　　　　　　　　　　　　　　　**784.2**

1. Orchestra　2. Musical instruments

ISBN 0-395-96052-5; 0-618-31112-2 pa

LC 98-43933

Describes the orchestra, the families of instruments of which it is made, and the individual instruments in each family

"The illustrations are dense with gentle color and filled with scenes of musicians at play and pictures of instruments, with banner labels adding more information. . . . A lot of information about who invented what and how it's played is packed into these engaging pages." Booklist

784.206　Violin

Hood, Susan

Ada's violin; the story of the Recycled Orchestra of Paraguay. Susan Hood; illustrated by Sally Wern Comport. Simon & Schuster Books for Young Readers 2016 40 p. color illustrations (hardcover : alk. paper) $17.99

Grades: K 1 2 3 4　　　　　　　　　　　　　**784.206**

1. Paraguay　2. Orchestra -- Paraguay -- Asunción　3. Orquesta de Instrumentos Reciclados Cateura　4. Orchestral musicians -- Paraguay -- Asunción

ISBN 9781481430951

LC 2015004299

This book, by Susan Hood, illustrated by Sally Wern Comport, is "true tale of the Recycled Orchestra of Paraguay, an orchestra made up of children playing instruments built from recycled trash. Ada Ríos grew up in Cateura, a small town in Paraguay built on a landfill. She dreamed of playing the violin, but with little money for anything but the bare essentials, it was never an option...until a music teacher named Favio Chávez arrived." (Publisher's note)

784.4　Light orchestra

Brown, Monica

Tito Puente, Mambo King; Tito Puente, Rey del Mambo. by Monica Brown; illustrated by Rafael Lopez; translated by Adriana Dominguez. HarperCollins 2013 32 p. col. ill. (hardcover) $17.99

Grades: 2 3 4　　　　　　　　　　　　　　　**784.4**

1. Puente, Tito, 1923-2000　2. Salsa musicians -- United States -- Biography

ISBN 0061227838; 9780061227837

LC 2012025493

Pura Belpre Illustrator Honor Book (2014)

This children's picture-book biography of Tito Puente presents a "bilingual tribute to the salsa drummer and band leader extraordinaire. [Monica] Brown's narrative . . . takes her preschool and primary audience from Tito's toddlerhood . . . through childhood loves: drum lessons, dancing and stickball on the streets of Harlem. Bouncing through the musician's adulthood, Brown highlights early gigs, a Navy stint . . . and regular shows at the Palladium in New York City." (Kirkus Reviews)

786.2　Keyboard instruments

Ganeri, Anita

Pianos and Keyboards. Smart Apple Media 2011 il (How the world makes music)

Grades: 4 5 6   **786.2**
1. Keyboard instruments
ISBN 1-599-20479-7; 978-1-599-20479-6

LC 2010052912

Describes various keyboard instruments from around the world, such as the familiar piano and organ, along with other keyboard instruments such as the accordian, harpsichord, and the hurdy-gurdy.

"The text reads smoothly, the layout is attractive. . . . This will be useful for collections serving schools, especially those assigning instrument reports." Booklist

Includes glossary and bibliographical references

786.8   Percussion instruments

Ganeri, Anita
Drums and percussion instruments. Smart Apple Media 2011 il (How the world makes music) lib bdg $28.50
Grades: 4 5 6   **786.8**
1. Percussion instruments
ISBN 978-1-599-20478-9

LC 2010043356

Describes various percussion instruments from around the world, including current drum kits, orchestral instruments such as the xylophone, and more traditional drums from Africa and Asia.

Includes glossary and bibliographical references

786.9   Drums and devices used for percussive effects

Greenwood, Mark
Drummer boy of John John; by Mark Greenwood; illustrations by Frané Lessac. Lee & Low 2012 40 p. (hardcover : alk. paper) $18.95
Grades: PreK K 1 2 3   **786.9**
1. Music 2. Biography 3. Musical instruments 4. Steel drum (Musical instrument) 5. Musicians -- Trinidad and Tobago -- Biography
ISBN 1600606520; 9781600606526

LC 2011045370

In author Mark Greenwood's book, "Carnival is coming, and the villagers of John John, Trinidad, are getting ready to jump up and celebrate with music, dancing, and a parade. Best of all, the Roti King has promised free rotis--tasty fried pancakes filled with chicken, herbs, and spices--for the best band in the parade. . . . With ingenuity and the help of his friends, Winston takes on the Carnival bands, drumming his way to victory--and to the Roti King's prized treat." (Publisher's note)

Landau, Elaine
Are the drums for you? Lerner Publications 2011 40p il (Ready to make music) lib bdg $27.93
Grades: 4 5 6 7   **786.9**
1. Drums 2. Percussion instruments
ISBN 978-0-7613-5426-0 lib bdg; 0-7613-5426-3 lib bdg

LC 2009-48971

Hear what professional drummers like about their instrument, and learn what skills a good drummer needs.

"Landau covers all the bases so that prospective musicians have the information they need. . . . Kids thinking about taking up an instrument will find . . . [this book] helpful in their decision-making process." SLJ

Includes glossary and bibliographical references

787   Stringed instruments (Chordophones)

Ganeri, Anita
Stringed instruments. Smart Apple Media 2011 32p il (How the world makes music) lib bdg $28.50
Grades: 4 5 6   **787**
1. Stringed instruments
ISBN 978-1-599-20480-2

LC 2010042418

Describes various stringed instruments from around the world including familiar instruments such as the guitar and violin, along with other traditional instruments such as the Japanese Koto and Indian lutes.

787.2   Violins

Landau, Elaine
Is the violin for you? Lerner Publications 2011 40p il (Ready to make music) lib bdg $27.93
Grades: 4 5 6 7   **787.2**
1. Violins
ISBN 978-0-7613-5423-9 lib bdg; 0-7613-5423-9 lib bdg

LC 2009045609

Hear what professional violinists like about their instrument, and learn what skills a good violinist needs.

"Landau covers all the bases so that prospective musicians have the information they need. . . . Kids thinking about taking up an instrument will find . . . [this book] helpful in their decision-making process." SLJ

Includes glossary and bibliographical references

787.87   Guitars

Blaxland, Wendy
Guitars. Marshall Cavendish Benchmark 2011 32p il map (How are they made?) lib bdg $12.99
Grades: 4 5 6   **787.87**
1. Guitars
ISBN 978-0-7614-4754-2 lib bdg; 0-7614-4754-7 lib bdg

LC 2009039880

This describes how guitars are made including their history, parts, materials, design, manufacture, packaging and distribution, marketing and advertising, and affect on the environment

"There is a bounty of color photos, including fascinating contruction shots as well as pics of axe-wielding notables Les Paul, Bruce Springsteen, and Prince." Booklist

Includes glossary

Landau, Elaine
Is the guitar for you? Lerner Publications 2011 40p il (Ready to make music) lib bdg $27.93
Grades: 4 5 6 7   **787.87**
1. Guitars
ISBN 978-0-7613-5424-6 lib bdg; 0-7613-5424-7 lib bdg

LC 2009-48750

Hear what professional guitarists like about their instrument, and learn what skills a good guitarist needs.

"Landau covers all the bases so that prospective musicians have the information they need. . . . Kids thinking about taking up an instrument will find . . . [this book] helpful in their decision-making process." SLJ

Includes glossary and bibliographical references

788   Wind instruments (Aerophones)

Ganeri, Anita

Brass instruments. Smart Apple Media 2011 il (How the world makes music) lib bdg 28.50
Grades: 4 5 6   **788**
  1. Wind instruments
  ISBN 978-1-599-20477-2

                         LC 2010053889

Describes various brass instruments from around the world, such as the familiar trumpet and trombone, along with historical instruments such as the Alphorn, serpent, and traditional instruments still played today, including the didgeridoo and the dung-chen.
Includes glossary and bibliographical references

Wind instruments. Smart Apple Media 2011 il (How the world makes music) lib bdg $28.50
Grades: 4 5 6   **788**
  1. Wind instruments
  ISBN 978-1-599-20482-6

                         LC 2010042423

Describes various wind instruments from around the world, such as the familiar clarinet, saxophone, and flute, along with other traditional instruments such as the Chinese flute, nose flute, and pan pipes.

Landau, Elaine

Is the flute for you? Lerner Publications 2011 40p il (Ready to make music) lib bdg $27.93
Grades: 4 5 6 7   **788**
  1. Flutes
  ISBN 978-0-7613-5420-8 lib bdg; 0-7613-5420-4 lib bdg

                         LC 2009048970

Hear what professional flutists like about their instrument, and learn what skills a good flutist needs.
"Landau covers all the bases so that prospective musicians have the information they need. . . . Kids thinking about taking up an instrument will find . . . [this book] helpful in their decision-making process." SLJ
Includes glossary and bibliographical references

Is the trumpet for you? Lerner Publications 2011 40p il (Ready to make music) lib bdg $27.93
Grades: 4 5 6 7   **788**
  1. Trumpet
  ISBN 978-0-7613-5422-2 lib bdg; 0-7613-5422-0 lib bdg

                         LC 2009048280

Hear what professional trumpeters like about their instrument, and learn what skills a good trumpeter needs.
"Landau covers all the bases so that prospective musicians have the information they need. . . . Kids thinking about taking up an instrument will find . . . [this book] helpful in their decision-making process." SLJ
Includes glossary and bibliographical references

788.7   Saxophones

Golio, Gary

Spirit seeker; John Coltrane's musical journey. by Gary Golio; paintings by Rudy Gutierrez. Clarion Books 2012 48 p. (hardcover) $17.99
Grades: 3 4 5 6 7   **788.7**
  1. Music and religion 2. Creation (Literary, artistic, etc.) 3. Saxophonists -- United States -- Biography 4. Jazz musicians --

United States -- Biography
ISBN 0547239947; 9780547239941

                         LC 2011045948

Includes bibliographical references and discography.
This book, by Gary Golio, illustrated by Rudy Gutierrez, explores the musical career of Jazz saxophonist John Coltrane. "Growing up, John was a seeker. He wondered about spirit, and the meaning of life. And whether music could be a key to unlocking those mysteries. . . . This is the story of a shy, curious boy from a deeply religious family who grew up to find solace and inspiration in his own unique approach to both spirituality and music." (Publisher's note)

788.9   Brass instruments (Lip-reed instruments)

Lynette, Rachel

Miles Davis; legendary jazz musician. by Rachel Lynette. Kid-Haven Press 2010 48 p. ill. (some col.) (hardcover) $29.95
Grades: 5 6 7 8   **788.9**
  1. Jazz music 2. Jazz musicians -- United States -- Biography
  ISBN 0737750340; 9780737750348

                         LC 2009045056

This biography of Miles Davis by Rachel Lynette is part of the Innovators series. Lynette "pinpoints the many works in which Davis pushed musical boundaries." She "refrains from mentioning the album Bitches Brew by name, instead offering . . . 'Davis and his band made an album that sold more than . . . any other jazz record ever.'" (Booklist)
Includes bibliographical references and index.

790   Recreational and performing arts

Glenn, Joshua

Unbored; the essential field guide to serious fun. [compiled by] Joshua Glenn & Elizabeth Foy Larsen; design by Tony Leone. Bloomsbury USA 2012 352 p. (hardback) $25
Grades: 5 6 7   **790**
  1. Amusements 2. Games 3. Handicraft 4. Recreation
  ISBN 1608196410; 9781608196418

                         LC 2012012368

This activity book by Elizabeth Foy Larsen and Joshua Glen, illustrated by Heather Kasunick and Mister Reusch, "provides kids with information to round out their world view and inspire them to learn more. From how-tos on using the library or writing your representative to a graphic history of video games, the book isn't shy about teaching. Yet the bulk of the 350-page mega-resource presents hands-on activities." (Publisher's note)

790.06   Organizations and management of recreation

Rosen, Michael J.

Let's build a playground; Michael J. Rosen. Candlewick Press 2013 32 p. (reinforced) $15.99
Grades: 2 3 4 5   **790.06**
  1. Playgrounds 2. Community development
  ISBN 0763655325; 9780763655327

                         LC 2012943649

This book, by Michael J. Rosen, illustrated by Ellen Kelson and Jennifer Cecil, is part of the "Kaboom! Books" series. It describes how "two hundred kids and grown-ups in an Indianapolis community got together to build the playground in this book--one of over two thousand that Ka-BOOM! has helped create." (Publisher's note)

790.1   General kinds of recreational activities

Ball, Jacqueline A.

Traveling green. Bearport Pub. 2009 32p il (Going green) lib bdg $25.27

Grades: 4 5 6 7   790.1

1. Travel -- Environmental aspects

ISBN 978-1-59716-964-6 lib bdg; 1-59716-964-1 lib bdg

LC 2009-19836

"Color photographs (most full page) and a few diagrams accompany the informative text[s]. . . . Overall, the [book] . . . is user-friendly and covers topics that are not easily found elsewhere." SLJ

Includes glossary and bibliographical references

Bell-Rehwoldt, Sheri

The **kids'** guide to classic games. Capstone Press 2009 32p il (Kids' guides) lib bdg $23.99

Grades: 4 5 6 7   790.1

1. Games

ISBN 978-1-4296-2273-8 lib bdg; 1-4296-2273-3 lib bdg

LC 2008-29686

This provides instructions and rules for indoor and outdoor games such as ping-pong soccer, ringer, paper football, spiderweb, tug-of-war, and pipeline

Includes glossary and bibliographical references

Conner, Bobbi

Unplugged play; no batteries, no plugs, pure fun. illustrations by Amy Patacchiola. Workman Pub. 2007 xxv, 401p il $27.95; pa $16.95

Grades: Adult Professional   790.1

1. Play 2. Games

ISBN 978-0-7611-4114-3; 978-0-7611-4390-1 pa

LC 2007-23999

"Conner has compiled more than 710 games and activities sorted by age level. Good old-fashioned play and fun are the motto here with simple props from around the house or just an imagination. The book is separated into three major parts: 'Toddler Play,' 'Preschool Play,' and 'Grade School Play.' Each has a section on solo play, ideas for parent and child, playing with others, and birthday-party activities. Each chapter and section is loaded with ideas and suggestions for simple crafts. There is such a wealth of information in this book." SLJ

Danks, Fiona

Run wild! outdoor games and adventures. [by] Fiona Danks and [phototgraphy by] Jo Schofield. Frances Lincoln 2011 159p il pa $24.95

Grades: 5 6 7 8   790.1

1. Games 2. Parties 3. Handicraft 4. Nature study 5. Outdoor life 6. Storytelling

ISBN 978-0-7112-3172-6; 0-7112-3172-9

"This large-format book introduces a cornucopia of ideas for outdoor activities, along with mesmerizing color photos of children and teens creatively enjoying themselves in fields, woods, backyards, and at rivers and beaches. . . . From skimming stones to making leaf masks to whittling walking sticks to following treasure trails, here's an enticing array of ideas for outdoor fun and wilderness discovery." Booklist

Davies, Huw

The **games** book; written by Huw Davies; illustrated by Lisa Jackson. Scholastic 2009 118p il pa $9.99

Grades: 1 2 3 4 5 6   790.1

1. Games

ISBN 978-0-545-13403-3 pa; 0-545-13403-X pa

LC 2009004292

"This small book takes a look at the games in simpler times. There are no electronics, batteries, cell phones, or videos involved. They mostly require physical and/or mental action along with the use of an imagination and some sweat, and maybe a little dirt. There are old favorites such as Red Rover and Simon Says as well as Rummy, Hangman, and I Spy. The clear instructions are easy for early readers to follow." SLJ

Ferrer, J. J.

The **art** of stone skipping and other fun old-time games; stoopball, jacks, string games, coin flipping, line baseball, jump rope, and more. by J.J. Ferrer; illustrated by Todd Dakins. Charlesbridge Pub., Inc. 2012 192 p. (paperback) $14.95

Grades: K 1 2 3 4 5 6 7 8 9 10 11 12 Adult   790.1

1. Games

ISBN 1936140748; 9781936140749

LC 2012015052

This book, by J. J. Ferrer, offers a "collection of timeless games that guarantees kids a good time- by themselves, with a group of friends, or with family. Includes ball games . . . , card games . . . , sack races, and old favorites such as Duck, Duck, Goose and Red Rover. There is also a chapter for car games. Simple instructions explain the rules, how many people can play, the object of the game, and what you need." (Publisher's note)

Includes bibliographical references and index.

Gillman, Claire

The **kids'** summer fun book; great games, activities, and adventures for the entire family. [by] Claire Gillman & Sam Martin. Barron's 2011 128p il pa $12.99

Grades: 3 4 5 6   790.1

1. Games 2. Sports 3. Summer 4. Cooking 5. Handicraft 6. Recreation

ISBN 978-0-7641-4581-0; 0-7641-4581-9

This offers ideas for summer activities such as beach parties, sand castle building, hiking and camping trips, kite flying, snorkeling, croquet, fishing, games, water sports, handicrafts, and cooking.

The **kids'** winter fun book; homespun adventures for family fun. [by] Claire Gillman & Sam Martin. Barron's 2011 128p il pa $12.99

Grades: 3 4 5 6   790.1

1. Sports 2. Winter 3. Cooking 4. Amusements 5. Handicraft 6. Recreation 7. Indoor games

ISBN 978-0-7641-4726-5; 0-7641-4726-9

This book "offers a variety of activities, games, crafts, and opportunities for family bonding throughout the winter. Indoor projects include knitting scarves, making a snow globe, and creating an obstacle course. Among the outdoor activities are hiking, winter photography, ice skating, and making a sled; more than a dozen recipes for items like caramel apples and winter stew are also included." Publ Wkly

Goldstone, Bruce

100 ways to celebrate 100 days. Henry Holt and Company 2010 un il $16.99

Grades: K 1 2 3   790.1

1. Amusements 2. Recreation

ISBN 978-0-8050-8997-4; 0-8050-8997-7

"Bright color photographs that pop from white backgrounds invite youngsters to celebrate the first 100 days of school by doing things: 'Recycle 100 cans'; 'Walk 100 steps in any direction.' 'Make a snake with 100 beads'; and even mop. Highlighting the ideas shown on each spread is a number line in 100 hues, which are also backgrounds for saying hello in 100 languages. . . . A more clever collection of 100 ideas is hard to imagine. A must-have for schools." SLJ

Hines-Stephens, Sarah

    Show off; how to do absolutely everything one step at a time. [by] Sarah Hines Stephens and Bethany Mann. Candlewick Press 2009 224p il $18.99

Grades: 5 6 7 8   **790.1**

    1. Amusements 2. Handicraft 3. Recreation

    ISBN 978-0-7636-4599-1; 0-7636-4599-0

                        LC 2009015847

    "This lively illustrated activity book delivers concise instructions for a variety of indoor and outdoor activities. Projects include crafts, pranks and magic tricks; ideas for nature exploration; and other purely entertaining feats. . . . The instructions are heavy on graphics and light on detail, making for an eye-catching but potentially frustrating experience. But readers should enjoy the irreverence and variety." Publ Wkly

Regan, Lisa

    Games on the move! QEB Pub. 2011 32p il (Games handbook) lib bdg $27.10

Grades: 3 4 5   **790.1**

    1. Games

    ISBN 978-1-59566-933-9; 1-59566-933-7

                        LC 2010018098

First published 2010 in the United Kingdom

    These travel games "will keep kids occupied and engaged. . . . The games are formatted by degree of difficulty with easier activities at the beginning; almost all of them take up a single page and can be learned by following the three-step directions. Surrounding these explanations are bright illustrations, suggestions for altering the game if there is a solo player or to make it more challenging, and an occasional fact related to the activity." SLJ

    Outdoor games! QEB Pub. 2011 32p il (Games handbook) lib bdg $27.10

Grades: 3 4 5   **790.1**

    1. Games

    ISBN 978-1-59566-934-6; 1-59566-934-5

                        LC 2010014187

First published 2010 in the United Kingdom

    These games "will keep kids occupied and engaged. . . . The games are formatted by degree of difficulty with easier activities at the beginning; almost all of them take up a single page and can be learned by following the three-step directions. Surrounding these explanations are bright illustrations, suggestions for altering the game if there is a solo player or to make it more challenging, and an occasional fact related to the activity." SLJ

    Party games. QEB Pub. 2011 32p il (Games handbook) lib bdg $27.10

Grades: 3 4 5   **790.1**

    1. Games 2. Parties

    ISBN 978-1-59566-932-2; 1-59566-932-9

                        LC 2010014188

First published 2010 in the United Kingdom

    These party games "will keep kids occupied and engaged. . . . The games are formatted by degree of difficulty with easier activities at the beginning; almost all of them take up a single page and can be learned by following the three-step directions. Surrounding these explanations are bright illustrations, suggestions for altering the game if there is a solo player or to make it more challenging, and an occasional fact related to the activity." SLJ

Rowell, Victoria

    Tag, toss & run; 40 classic lawn games. Paul Tukey & Victoria Rowell. Storey Pub. 2012 207 p. (pbk. : alk. paper) $14.95

Grades: Adult Professional   **790.1**

    1. Games 2. Outdoor recreation

    ISBN 1603425608; 9781603425605

                        LC 2011049410

    This book on "family lawn games" presents a "guide to 40 time-tested favorites -- from classics like capture the flag, croquet, badminton, and bocce to the lesser-known Cherokee marbles, cornhole, and Kubb. The authors offer a quick overview of the basic structure of each game, as well as strategies for playing and tips for creating fun variations." (Publisher's note)

    Includes bibliographical references and index.

791 Public performances

Gerstein, Mordicai, 1935-

    ★ The **man** who walked between the towers. Roaring Brook Press 2003 un il $17.95; lib bdg $24.90

Grades: PreK K 1 2 3   **791**

    1. Tightrope walking 2. Aerialists 3. World Trade Center (New York, N.Y.)

    ISBN 0-7613-1791-0; 0-7613-2868-8 lib bdg

                        LC 2003-9040

Awarded the Caldecott Medal, 2004

Boston Globe-Horn Book Award: Picture Book (2004)

    A lyrical evocation of Philippe Petit's 1974 tightrope walk between the World Trade Center towers

    "The pacing of the narrative is as masterful as the placement and quality of the oil-and-ink paintings. . . . Gerstein captures his subject's incredible determination, profound skill, and sheer joy." SLJ

Lusted, Marcia Amidon

    Entertainment. ABDO Pub. Company 2011 112p il (Inside the industry) $23.95

Grades: 5 6 7 8   **791**

    1. Performing arts -- Vocational guidance

    ISBN 978-1-61714-799-9; 1-61714-799-0

                        LC 2010041255

    This "well-designed [book describes] a variety of careers in [entertainment]. Because [it helps] readers assess if these positions are suitable for their personality types and backgrounds, the [title is a] good [choice] for career exploration and self-discovery. [It is] also useful for research and reports. . . . Sidebars and full-color photos appear throughout." SLJ

    Includes bibliographical references

Rau, Dana Meachen

    Roller coasters. Marshall Cavendish Benchmark 2010 24p il (Surprising science) lib bdg $22.79

Grades: 2 3 4   **791**

    1. Roller coasters

    ISBN 978-0-7614-4872-3; 0-7614-4872-1

                        LC 2009053722

    "Colorfully illustrated with photographs on each page, this . . . will be well received by elementary students and educators." Libr Media Connect

    Includes glossary and bibliographical references

791.06 Organizations and management

Kraft, Betsy Harvey

The **fantastic** Ferris Wheel; the story of inventor George Ferris. Betsy Harvey Kraft; illustrated by Steven Salerno. Christy Ottaviano Books, Henry Holt & Co. 2015 42 p. color illustrations (hardcover) $17.99

Grades: 1 2 3 4 **791.06**

1. Ferris wheels 2. Structural engineering 3. Inventions 4. Inventors -- United States -- Biography

ISBN 1627790721; 9781627790727

LC 2014044914

In this book, by Betsy Harvey Kraft, the "planners of the 1893 Chicago World's Fair were looking for a spectacular, extraordinary, and never-before-seen attraction that would draw in huge crowds. The idea they eventually accepted was George Ferris's huge observation wheel. . . . This book chronicles the story of Ferris's invention, explains how he overcame the initial reluctance of the members of the fair committee, and describes the glorious success of the invention." (School Library Journal)

"A strong addition to book collections dealing with inventors and inventions and useful for discussing how written texts and illustrations work together." SLJ

791.3 Circuses

Helfer, Ralph

The **world's** greatest elephant; illustrated by Ted Lewin. Philomel Books 2006 un il $16.99

Grades: 1 2 3 **791.3**

1. Circus 2. Elephants

ISBN 0-399-24190-6

LC 2005-06490

The true story of the lives and travels of the circus elephant Modoc who travelled widely and experienced dangerous adventures with his owner and trainer Bram Gunterstein.

"The large picture-book format is the typical choice for Lewin's fine watercolors, boldly portraying the dramatic episodes of the elephants life and the story of friendship, separation, and reunion. This bold and heartwarming adventure tale should have wide appeal." SLJ

791.43 Motion pictures

Bliss, John

Art that moves; animation around the world. Raintree 2011 32p il (Culture in action) lib bdg $29

Grades: 5 6 7 8 **791.43**

1. Animated films

ISBN 978-1-4109-3922-7; 1-4109-3922-7

LC 2009051125

This "is a good choice for children interested in animated movies. Bliss looks at techniques from the early beginnings to modern times and mentions recent film releases such as Cars (2006) and Where the Wild Things Are (2010). . . . [This volume is] quick, interesting, up-to-date . . . with plenty of supportive, captioned, full-color photographs. [It] also [provides] related project suggestions." SLJ

Includes bibliographical references

Brown, Don

Mack made movies. Roaring Brook Press 2003 un il $16.95; lib bdg $23.90

Grades: 2 3 4 **791.43**

1. Actors 2. Motion picture producers and directors 3. Motion picture directors 4. Motion picture producers

ISBN 0-7613-1538-1; 0-7613-2504-2 lib bdg

LC 2002-6357

A simple biography of the director whose silent films immortalized such slapstick clowns as the Keystone Kops, Charlie Chaplin, Fatty Arbuckle, Mabel Normand, and Ben Turpin

"sing his inimitable picture-book-biography style, Brown turns a camera's eye on film pioneer Mack Sennett. The opening line sets the stage for this witty, fascinating profile of the King of Comedy: "In 1900, twenty-year-old Mack Sennett was a horse's rear end.""... Especially fine in conveying facial expression, Brown's spare, fluid sketches, softly washed in sepia and butterscotch tones, cunningly capture the look of the times...Ingeniously staged and picture perfect, it's Brown's best book yet." Booklist

Cech, John

Imagination and innovation; the story of Weston Woods. with a foreword by Maurice Sendak. Scholastic Press 2009 175p il $29.99

Grades: Adult Professional **791.43**

1. Animated films 2. Children's literature 3. Motion picture producers and directors 4. Weston Woods, Inc. 5. Motion picture executives

ISBN 978-0-545-08922-7; 0-545-08922-0

LC 2009014207

"This is a fascinating look at Weston Woods and its creator, Morton Schindel. Rich with full-color archival photographs, detailed production notes, animation cels, and first-person accounts, the book gives readers a personal, behind-the-scenes look at the man and the studio that has animated most of the great works of children's literature from the mid-20th century to the present." SLJ

Cohn, Jessica

Animator. Gareth Stevens Pub. 2010 32p il (Cool careers: cutting edge) lib bdg $26; pa $8.95

Grades: 4 5 6 **791.43**

1. Vocational guidance 2. Animation (Cinematography)

ISBN 978-1-4339-1953-4 lib bdg; 1-4339-1953-2 lib bdg; 978-1-4339-2152-0 pa; 1-4339-2152-9 pa

LC 2009002006

Describes the work of an animator.

This title offers "clear, solid information in a large font. . . . [This] short [book is] packed with relevant, current material." SLJ

Includes glossary and bibliographical references

McDonald, Megan

Judy Moody goes to Hollywood; behind the scenes with Judy Moody and friends. by Megan McDonald with Richard Haynes; set photography by Suzanne Tenner. Candlewick Press 2011 144p il map $14.99

Grades: 2 3 4 **791.43**

1. Motion pictures -- Production and direction 2. Judy Moody and the not bummer summer (Motion picture)

ISBN 978-0-7636-5551-8; 0-7636-5551-1

LC 2011283432

"This behind the scenes look to the 2011 movie Judy Moody and the NOT Bummer Summer is filled with facts about the characters and the actors who play them. It also gives a surprisingly detailed yet accessible view of movie-making, explaining key elements of everything from set design to lighting." Horn Book Guide

Reynolds, David West

Star wars: incredible cross sections; illustrated by Hans Jenssen & Richard Chasemore. DK Pub. 1998 32p il $19.95

Grades: 4 5 6 7 **791.43**

1. Star Wars films

ISBN 0-7894-3480-6

LC 98-22878

This book "includes diagrams for the Millennium Falcon, T-65 X-wing, Blockade Runner, Tie Fighters, Sandcrawler, and BLT-A4 Y-wing, among others. An elaborate four-page fold-out analyzes the Death Star in minute detail.... AT-AT Walkers, AT-STs, snowspeeders, and speeder bikes are also included. Diagrams are surrounded by inserts of fascinating trivia, history, and technical notes." Voice Youth Advocates

791.44   Radio

McCarthy, Meghan

★ **Aliens** are coming! the true account of the 1938 War of the worlds radio broadcast. Knopf 2006 un il $16.95; lib bdg $18.99

Grades: 1 2 3 **791.44**

1. War of the worlds (Radio program)

ISBN 0-375-83518-0; 0-375-93518-5 lib bdg

LC 2005-08941

"In an average American living room of 1938, folks gather around the radio for a night's entertainment, when there's a new bulletin: 'Aliens are coming!' Orson Welles' infamous Halloween trick, his October 30 broadcast of H. G. Wells' War of the Worlds, is greatly excerpted and put together with quirky, imaginative artwork that reinforces the fantasy.... Using a 1930's art style, and a palette comprising mostly muted grays and reds, McCarthy evokes an era gone by.... This is packed with age-appropriate thrills and scares." Booklist

791.5   Puppetry and toy theaters

D'Cruz, Anna-Marie

Make your own puppets. PowerKids Press 2009 24p il (Do it yourself projects!) lib bdg $23.95; pa $9.40

Grades: 2 3 4 **791.5**

1. Handicraft 2. Puppets and puppet plays

ISBN 978-1-4358-2851-3 lib bdg; 1-4358-2851-8 lib bdg; 978-1-4358-2919-0 pa; 1-4358-2919-0 pa

LC 2008033661

This offers "step-by-step instructions and full-color photos to illustrate the crafts. Projects have a broad cultural representation and are not gender specific. Materials are easily obtained.... [Projects include] a Venus flytrap and a Chinese dragon." SLJ

Includes glossary and bibliographical references

Exner, Carol R.

Practical puppetry A-Z; a guide for librarians and teachers. [by] Carol R. Exner. McFarland 2005 267p il pa $39.95

Grades: Adult Professional **791.5**

1. Puppets and puppet plays

ISBN 0-7864-1516-9

LC 2005010590

"Exner presents the art of puppetry as a creative and engaging way to snag the interests of both adults and children. Presented in alphabetical order, approximately 135 entries cover everything from starting a puppetry business to puppetry history to creating numerous kinds of pup-

pets: glove, sponge, life-size, even marionettes.... This is an excellent resource for school or public libraries." Booklist

Includes bibliographical references

Kennedy, John E.

★ **Puppet** planet. North Light Books 2006 79p il $16.99

Grades: 4 5 6 7 **791.5**

1. Puppets and puppet plays

ISBN 978-1-58180-794-3; 1-58180-794-5

LC 2005033711

This book offers twelve "puppet projects, each using a variety of techniques, [and] features 'action panels' so readers can see how each puppet comes to life. [It also] Includes staging ideas to play up each project's uniqueness." Publisher's note

Minkel, Walter

★ **How** to do The three bears with two hands; performing with puppets. American Lib. Assn. 2000 154p il pa $28

Grades: Adult Professional **791.5**

1. Children's libraries 2. Puppets and puppet plays

ISBN 0-8389-0756-3

LC 99-28228

This guide to performing puppet plays in libraries offers advice on such topics as voice control and manipulation technique, script writing and adaptation, puppets, stages, scenery and props, and includes five puppet show scripts and stage-building plans

Includes bibliographical references

791.8   Animal performances

Collard III, Sneed B.

The **world** famous Miles City Bucking Horse Sale. Bucking Horse Books 2010 64p il $18

Grades: 5 6 7 8 **791.8**

1. Horses 2. Rodeos 3. Montana

ISBN 0984446001; 9780984446001; 978-0-9844460-0-1; 0-9844460-0-1

"Collard takes readers inside the Miles City [Montana] Bucking Horse Sale, a four-day event that draws visitors from across the country. Started in 1951 as a sale of wild horses, it's evolved into a jamboree of music, rodeo, food, contests, and a parade.... Plenty of action-filled color photographs break up the narrative.... Handsomely designed, ... this is a fascinating look at a fresh topic."

"Collard takes readers inside the Miles City [Montana] Bucking Horse Sale, a four-day event that draws visitors from across the country. Started in 1951 as a sale of wild horses, it's evolved into a jamboree of music, rodeo, food, contests, and a parade.... Plenty of action-filled color photographs break up the narrative.... Handsomely designed, ... this is a fascinating look at a fresh topic." Booklist

Includes glossary

Grayson, Robert

Performers. Marshall Cavendish Benchmark 2010 64p il (Working animals) lib bdg $28.50

Grades: 4 5 6 7 **791.8**

1. Animals in entertainment

ISBN 978-1-60870-165-0 lib bdg; 1-60870-165-4 lib bdg

LC 2010006893

"Describes the role of animals in movies, sporting events, and various competitions." Publisher's note

Includes glossary and bibliographical references

Laidlaw, Rob

On parade; the hidden world of animals in entertainment. Fitzhenry & Whiteside 2010 55p il $19.95

Grades: 4 5 6 **791.8**

1. Zoos 2. Circus 3. Animal welfare 4. Animals in entertainment

ISBN 978-1-55455-143-9; 1-55455-143-9

This book examines animals at the zoo and circus, animals working in movies and television, violence in the world of performing animals and offers ways to improve conditions and prevent animal abuse.

The author's "clearly argued text; crisp, captioned color photos; and appended list of organizations make this an important source for animal advocates." Booklist

Munro, Roxie

Rodeo; by Roxie Munro. Bright Sky Press 2007 un il $15.95

Grades: PreK K 1 2 **791.8**

1. Rodeos

ISBN 978-1-933979-03-8

LC 2007015245

"Clear, concise text and clever lift-the-flap illustrations capture the action and excitement of a rodeo." SLJ

Schubert, Leda

★ Ballet of the elephants; illustrated by Robert Andrew Parker. Roaring Brook Press 2006 un il $17.95

Grades: K 1 2 3 **791.8**

1. Ballet 2. Circus 3. Dancers 4. Composers 5. Elephants 6. Choreographers 7. Circus executives

ISBN 1-59643-075-3

LC 2005-02670

The story of how "Circus polka" a dance of 50 elephants and 50 ballerinas, conceived by John Ringling North, choreographed by George Balanchine to music written by Igor Stravinsky, was created

"Schubert's book tells an astonishing true story. . . . The words are simple and lyrical . . . and the beautiful, freely sketched double-page ink-and-watercolor art celebrates the excitement of the animals' dance." Booklist

792 Stage presentations

Aliki

★ William Shakespeare & the Globe; written & illustrated by Aliki. HarperCollins Pubs. 1999 48p il hardcover o.p. pa $6.99

Grades: 4 5 6 7 8 9 **792**

1. Poets 2. Authors 3. Dramatists 4. Globe Theatre (London, England) 5. Shakespeare's Globe (London, England)

ISBN 0-06-027820-X; 0-06-443722-1 pa

LC 98-7903

"A logically organized and engaging text, plenty of detailed illustrations with informative captions, and a clean design provide a fine introduction to both bard and theater." Horn Book Guide

Chrisp, Peter

Welcome to the Globe; the story of Shakespeare's theater. written by Peter Chrisp. Dorling Kindersley 2000 48p il (Dorling Kindersley readers) $12.95; pa $3.95

Grades: 1 2 3 **792**

1. Poets 2. Authors 3. Dramatists 4. Globe Theatre (London, England)

ISBN 0-7894-6641-4; 0-7894-6640-6 pa

LC 00-21931

Various characters, including a waterman, an actor, a gallant, and an apple seller, from Shakespeare's London describe the Globe Theatre from their own perspective

"Illustrations and photographs are excellent, showing details of the building and the people." SLJ

Includes glossary

Jacobs, Paul DuBois

★ Putting on a play; drama activities for kids. [by] Paul DuBois Jacobs and Jennifer Swender; illustrated by Debra Spina Dixon. Gibbs Smith 2005 64p il pa $9.95

Grades: 2 3 4 **792**

1. Theater -- Production and direction

ISBN 1-58685-767-3

LC 2005011249

"This little book is a powerhouse of information. . . . An excellent beginning resource for any child or group of children interested in theater." SLJ

Kenney, Karen Latchana

Cool costumes; how to stage your very own show. ABDO Pub. Company 2010 32p il (Cool performances) lib bdg $17.95

Grades: 4 5 6 **792**

1. Costume 2. Theater

ISBN 978-1-60453-714-7 lib bdg; 1-60453-714-0 lib bdg

LC 2009-1751

Includes step-by-step instructions on how to create royalty robes, animal ears, baseball T-Shirts and more

"Simple language, colorful page design, and detailed step-by-step photos invite children to gather some easily available household items, apply paint and some imagination, and put on a play—or just play." SLJ

Includes glossary and webliography

Other titles in this series are:

Cool makeup

Cool productions

Cool sets and props

Cool scripts and acting

Cool special effects

Cool productions; how to stage your very own show. ABDO Pub. Co. 2010 32p il (Cool performances) lib bdg $17.95

Grades: 4 5 6 **792**

1. Theater -- Production and direction

ISBN 978-1-60453-716-1 lib bdg; 1-60453-716-7 lib bdg

LC 2009-405

Includes step-by-step instructions on how to make flyers, tickets, programs and more

"Simple language, colorful page design, and detailed step-by-step photos invite children to gather some easily available household items, apply paint and some imagination, and put on a play—or just play." SLJ

Includes glossary

McLean, Dirk

Curtain up! a book for young performers. illustrated by France Brassard. Tundra Books 2010 un il $17.95

Grades: K 1 2 3 **792**

1. Theater -- Fiction

ISBN 978-0-88776-899-6; 0-88776-899-7

"This brief, straightforward depiction of a young girl's theatrical experiences provides a realistic and accurate glimpse into the art. Amaya's dream is to be on the stage, and her mother has been helping her with her memorization and articulation. She auditions for a musical and is chosen to play the lead in a professional play. . . . The realistic illustrations are done in a pastel palette and bring the personalities of the characters to life." SLJ

Schumacher, Thomas L.

How does the show go on? an introduction to the theater. by Thomas Schumacher with Jeff Kurtti. 2nd ed; Disney 2008 128p il $22.95

Grades: 4 5 6 7   **792**

1. Theater

ISBN 978-1-4231-2031-5; 1-4231-2031-0

"Filled with lavish color photos of Disney theater productions, this eye-catching volume has clever chapter titles, beginning with 'Overture,' which tells about 'styles of theaters' and 'kinds of shows.' In 'Act One' and 'Act Two,' aspects of the front and back of the house are discussed, including the marquee, the box office, props, special effects, and so on. Interspersed throughout the facts and photos are 'Stage Notes,' where bits of trivia are doled out." SLJ

Skog, Jason

Acting; a practical guide to pursuing the art. Compass Point Books 2010 48p il (Performing arts) lib bdg $28.65

Grades: 5 6 7 8   **792**

1. Acting 2. Vocational guidance

ISBN 978-0-7565-4364-8 lib bdg; 0-7565-4364-9 lib bdg

LC 2010012604

A guide for those interested in a career in acting, and includes tips on education, technique, and more.

"Meant for students contemplating a career in the field . . . [this book goes] beyond basic introductions and into more detail about what it takes to make it as a professional. . . . [The author maintains] . . . a frank, realistic tone, stressing the importance of hard work and dedication. Great [resource] . . . for those wanting to make their passions more than just a hobby." SLJ

Includes glossary and bibliographical references

Underwood, Deborah

Staging a play. Raintree 2009 32p il (Culture in action) $28.21; pa $7.99

Grades: 5 6 7 8   **792**

1. Theater -- Production and direction

ISBN 978-1-4109-3396-6; 1-4109-3396-2; 978-1-4109-3413-0 pa; 1-4109-3413-6 pa

LC 2009000417

This "discusses the various professionals involved in a production, such as actors, costume designers, prop masters, and stage handlers. Well organized and with bright, colorful photography, [this] introductory [title gives] readers good basic knowledge." SLJ

Includes glossary and bibliographical references

792.6   Musical plays

Amendola, Dana

A day at the New Amsterdam Theatre; photos by Gino Domenico; written by Dana Amendola. Disney Editions 2004 125p il $24.95

Grades: 4 5 6 7   **792.6**

1. Theater 2. New Amsterdam Theatre (New York, N.Y.)

ISBN 0-7868-5438-3

"This title covers a day in the life of Disney's The Lion King, the long-running Broadway musical. . . . A clock in a corner of each spread guides readers through the day as box-office personnel, makeup designers, dancers, actors, cleaning staff, and others do their jobs. Each spread includes several full-color photos that are often gritty, sometimes glamorous. . . . This unique volume provides an honest, realistic, eye-opening

look at the behind-the-scenes work that goes into the running of a Broadway show." SLJ

792.7   Variety shows and theatrical dancing

Dillon, Leo

★ Rap a tap tap; here's Bojangles--think of that! [by] Leo & Diane Dillon. Blue Sky Press (NY) 2002 un il $15.95

Grades: PreK K 1 2 3   **792.7**

1. Actors 2. Tap dancing 3. Stories in rhyme 4. African Americans 5. Tap dancers

ISBN 0-590-47883-4

LC 2001-43896

In illustrations and rhyme describes the dancing of Bill "Bojangles" Robinson, one of the most famous tap dancers of all time

"The spreads feature a bouncy text and eye-catching art. . . . The paintings have the effect of collage and employ strong city shapes, with bridges, buildings, and park benches pressed against feather-white backgrounds." Booklist

792.8   Ballet and modern dance

Augustyn, Frank

★ Footnotes; dancing the world's best-loved ballets. [by] Frank Augustyn and Shelley Tanaka. Millbrook Press 2001 94p il $17.95

Grades: 5 6 7 8   **792.8**

1. Ballet

ISBN 0-7613-1646-9

LC 00-50075

"Footnotes uses seven classical ballets as a jumping-off point to talk about the evolution of this unique art form, partnering, dancer as actor, training, costumes, choreography, and some of the world's most well-known performers." SLJ

Collins, Pat Lowery

I am a dancer; by Pat Lowery Collins; illustrated by Mark Graham. Millbrook Press 2008 un il lib bdg $22.60

Grades: PreK K 1 2 3   **792.8**

1. Dance

ISBN 978-0-8225-6369-3 lib bdg; 0-8225-6369-X lib bdg

LC 2007021885

"This book shows girls and boys in various movements that can be defined as dance steps. . . . Graham's beautiful oil paintings are filled with solidly built children on the move, while some of the backgrounds are almost ethereal. Even the brushstrokes convey action. This book is a lovely merging of art and poetry and gives a delightful sense of joyful motion." SLJ

Friedman, Lise

Becoming a ballerina; a nutcracker story. by Lise Friedman; photographs by Mary Dowdle. Penguin Group 2012 44 p. (hardcover) $18.99

Grades: 4 5 6   **792.8**

1. Ballet 2. Athletes 3. Picture books for children 4. Ballerinas 5. Ballet dancing

ISBN 0670013927; 9780670013920

LC 2012000867

This book follows "13-year-old Fiona, a real-life fledgling ballerina, on her journey from hopeful auditionee to starring performer as Clara in the Boston Ballet's production of 'The Nutcracker.' . . . Fiona talks about her aches and pains ('Sometimes hurt so much that I want to cry'), her sacrifices ('I miss going to birthday parties and the movies, being in school talent shows, sleepovers--normal stuff"), [and] the fierce competition." (Publishers Weekly)

Gladstone, Valerie

A **young** dancer; the life of an Ailey student. photographs by Jose Ivey. Henry Holt and Co. 2009 un il $18.95

Grades: 1 2 3 4   **792.8**

1. Ballet 2. African American dancers 3. Alvin Ailey American Dance Theater

ISBN 978-0-8050-8233-3; 0-8050-8233-6

LC 2008-18343

"This book about a 13-year-old African American dancer . . . combines strong color photos and lively first-person text. Iman Bright is a student at New York City's Ailey School, founded by the late Alvin Ailey. . . . A wide range of readers will find inspiration in Iman's dedication and in her joyful approach to her discipline." Booklist

Goodman, Joan E.

Ballet bunnies; written and illustrated by Joan Elizabeth Goodman. Marshall Cavendish 2008 un il $14.99

Grades: K 1 2   **792.8**

1. Ballet

ISBN 978-0-7614-5392-5; 0-7614-5392-X

LC 2007-11907

This ballet primer demonstrates basic technique in ballet, from warm-ups to the barre to the hop, skip, twirl, and wiggle fun of centerwork.

"The simply drawn acrylic illustrations show the boys and girls demonstrating positions, and the easy-to-understand text gives further guidance. . . . This is a gentle introduction." SLJ

Includes glossary

Greenberg, Jan

★ **Ballet** for Martha; making Appalachian Spring. [by] Jan Greenberg and Sandra Jordan; illustrated by Brian Floca. Flash Point 2010 48p il $17.99

Grades: 2 3 4   **792.8**

1. Ballet 2. Artists 3. Dancers 4. Composers 5. Sculptors 6. American music 7. Choreographers

ISBN 978-1-59643-338-0; 1-59643-338-8

Robert F. Sibert Medal honor book, 2011

Tells the story behind the creation of "Appalachian Spring," describing Aaron Copland's composition and Martha Graham's intense choreography.

"Matching the mood of Graham's moves, the writing is pared down but full of possibilities. Floca's ink-and-watercolor artwork nimbly shifts from the prosaic . . . to the visionary . . . to the several-spread finale of the ballet itself. The book as a whole beautifully captures the process of artistic creation." Booklist

Kupesic, Rajka

The **white** ballets. Tundra Books 2011 40p il $19.95

Grades: 4 5 6 7   **792.8**

1. Ballet -- Stories, plots, etc.

ISBN 978-0-88776-923-8; 0-88776-923-3

This retells the stories of Swan Lake, Giselle, and La Bayadère and includes information and comments on the three ballets.

"The tales are well told, and the author, a former ballerina, provides information on the history of the ballet. Each painting in gold leaf and oil represents a scene from one of the ballets. The richly colored illustrations are very stylized with graceful figures dressed in flowing, romantic costumes, and Kupesic elaborates on the details, symbols, and characters in her artwork. . . . For ballet enthusiasts this is a unique look at these classics." SLJ

Marsico, Katie

Choreographer. Cherry Lake Pub. 2011 32p il (Cool arts careers) lib bdg $18.95

Grades: 4 5 6 7   **792.8**

1. Dance 2. Choreographers 3. Vocational guidance

ISBN 978-1-61080-136-2; 1-61080-136-9

LC 2011001170

"Illustrated with color photos of the famous, the young, and the fabulously festooned, this is a sturdy presentation of facts and case studies that will bring the process of professional choreography home to those students considering such a competitive and demanding career." Booklist

Includes bibliographical references

Mellow, Mary Kate

Ballet for beginners; featuring the School of American Ballet. by Mary Kate Mellow and Stephanie Troeller. Imagine! 2010 80p il $14.95

Grades: 3 4 5 6   **792.8**

1. Ballet

ISBN 978-1-936140-01-5; 1-936140-01-2

"The education of a dancer's body and mind is a long and complicated process, and this book tells that story with a lighthearted grace and brio." SLJ

Miles, Lisa

Ballet spectacular; a young ballet lover's guide and an insight into a magical world. Lisa Miles. Barrons Educational Series, Inc. 2014 80 p. color illustrations $18.99

Grades: 4 5 6 7 8   **792.8**

1. Ballet 2. Ballet dancers 3. Royal Ballet

ISBN 0764167456; 9780764167454

LC 2014940905

Author Lisa Miles presents this "reference volume for children who love ballet. Featuring stunning full-color photos from The Royal Ballet's own collections and informative, fact-filled entries, it covers all things dance. Most intriguing to passionate young lovers of dance will be the exploration of a day in the life of a professional ballet dancer, images of beloved performers such as Margot Fonteyn, Darcey Bussell, and Carlos Acosta, detailed close-ups of costumes, and photos." (Publisher's note)

"Combining aspects of a coffee-table book and an introductory handbook, it provides a hodgepodge of basic information about ballet history, famous ballets, life in a major company, and the elements involved in a performance, such as choreography, music, sets, and costumes, while Britain's Royal Ballet Company and School are referenced throughout the book." Booklist

Nelson, Marilyn

Beautiful ballerina; photographs by Susan Kuklin. Scholastic Press 2009 un il $17.99

Grades: PreK K 1 2   **792.8**

1. Ballet 2. African American dancers

ISBN 978-0-545-08920-3; 0-545-08920-4

LC 2009009135

"The description 'poetry in motion' may be taken quite literally in this paean to the young dancers who train at the Dance Theatre of Harlem. The heartfelt poem's playful words could make a lively read-aloud dance-along, and young balletomanes will be intrigued by the girls in the photographs. The phrase 'Beautiful ballerina, you are the dance' is repeated throughout and invites audience participation." SLJ

Relota, Agatha

Carla and Leo's world of dance; illustrations by Thierry Perez. Thames & Hudson 2011 il $19.95

Grades: 3 4 5 6   **792.8**
1. Dance
ISBN 978-0-500-51560-0; 0-500-51560-3

"Ten-year-old Carla and her friend, Leo, sign up for ballroom-dance classes. As they learn the Viennese waltz, foxtrot, swing, merengue, mambo, cha-cha, rumba, salsa, and tango, their teacher offers information on the history and culture of these dances. The format has a comic-book, poster-art style with the print highlighted in rectangular colored shapes. The bold, linear illustrations of the dancers fill the pages as Carla and Leo demonstrate the steps with grace and zest. . . . This is not a how-to manual but a celebration and introduction to the diverse dances. The enthusiasm of these two characters is infectious, and the slick artwork captures the elegance and drama of these movements and makes them look like lots of fun." SLJ

Thompson, Lauren
★ **Ballerina** dreams; a true story. by Lauren Thompson; photographs by James Estrin. Feiwel & Friends 2007 un il $16.95
Grades: PreK K 1 2   **792.8**
1. Ballet 2. Cerebral palsy
ISBN 978-0-312-37029-6; 0-312-37029-6

LC 2006036338

"Five adorable little girls are given the opportunity to learn to dance like ballerinas and eventually perform on stage. This is no small accomplishment since the girls have cerebral palsy and other muscle disorders and several wear leg braces. . . . This is an inspiring portrayal of determination and love that will foster empathy among young readers. The colorful photographs of this dancing community working toward a common goal accurately and sensitively capture the struggles and joyful enthusiasm of all of the participants." SLJ

Troupe, Thomas Kingsley
If I were a ballerina; illustrated by Heather Heyworth. Picture Window Books 2010 24p il (Dream big) lib bdg $25.32; pa $7.95
Grades: K 1 2 3   **792.8**
1. Ballet
ISBN 978-1-4048-5532-8 lib bdg; 1-4048-5532-7 lib bdg; 978-1-4048-5706-3 pa; 1-4048-5706-0 pa

LC 2009-3295

This "begins with a small girl who imagines herself as a star onstage, dancing to beautiful music played by a glorious orchestra. Then the story tracks back to imagined ballet classes, where she envisions the pointed shoes she would wear and the barre exercises she would do with the other dancers before practicing at home. The simple, first-person narrative and clear, digitally enhanced color drawings partner well together, and even young preschoolers will enjoy the fun blend of the fantasy . . . and facts, including ballet's five basic positions." Booklist

Includes glossary

Vaughan, Carolyn
Invitation to ballet; by Carolyn Vaughan; works of art by Edgar Degas; illustrated by Rachel Isadora. Abrams Books for Young Readers 2012 31 p. col. ill. $16.95
Grades: 2 3 4   **792.8**
1. Dance in art 2. Ballet dancers 3. Artists -- Biography 4. Ballet 5. Ballet in art
ISBN 1419702602; 9781419702600

LC 2011019046

The author Carolyn Vaughan presents provides a book "with a brief history of ballet and a biography of . . . French impressionist Edgar Degas. . . . [Vaughan explains] what happens in ballet class [to young children]. . . . [Illustrations show] modern-day girls and boys practicing ballet positions, [dances,] and steps . . . [and] works of art by . . . Degas." (Publisher's note)

792.9   Stage productions

Cox, Carole
Shakespeare kids; performing his plays, speaking his words. Libraries Unlimited 2010 xx, 126p il pa $30
Grades: Adult Professional   **792.9**
1. Poets 2. Authors 3. Dramatists 4. Theater -- Production and direction
ISBN 978-1-59158-838-2 pa; 1-59158-838-3 pa

LC 2009041731

This is a "practical guide for performing Shakespeare's plays, albeit in condensed form, without changing his poetic dialogue. . . . Cox gears her work to teachers of students in grades 3-8, librarians, or adults leading recreational programs, providing precise, detailed instructions on all facets of youth-oriented Shakespearean play production. . . . The text is clear and concise . . . Black-and-white photos capture specific moments that illustrate the performers' enthusiasm." SLJ

Includes bibliographical references

793   Indoor games and amusements

Gunter, Veronika Alice
★ **The** ultimate indoor games book; the 200 best boredom busters ever! [by] Veronika Alice Gunter. Lark Books 2005 128p il hardcover o.p. pa $7.95
Grades: 3 4 5 6   **793**
1. Indoor games
ISBN 1-57990-625-7; 1-60059-198-1 pa

LC 2005006054

"This compilation of brain games, ball games, pen-and-paper games, etc., provides a good supply of ideas that will appeal to most any player in a variety of circumstances. The activities are suitable for individuals or two or more players. Most of the suggestions require little or no equipment." SLJ

King, Bart
Bart's king-sized book of fun. Gibbs Smith 2010 304p pa $19.99
Grades: 4 5 6   **793**
1. Amusements
ISBN 978-1-4236-0641-3; 1-4236-0641-8

LC 2010011438

"This is a lively and entertaining collection of tricks, jokes, facts, recipes, games, pranks, wordplay, and all-around fun. Inventions include airbag pants, a disco ball made from old CDs, and a remote-control pumpkin. Creative costume ideas include a piñata, an alien, chewed gum, a shooting star, and more. . . . An activity book extraordinaire for cool kids everywhere." SLJ

Includes bibliographical references

Regan, Lisa
Indoor games! QEB Pub. 2011 32p il (Games handbook) lib bdg $27.10
Grades: 3 4 5   **793**
1. Indoor games
ISBN 978-1-59566-931-5; 1-59566-931-0

LC 2010014139

First published 2010 in the United Kingdom

These indoor games "will keep kids occupied and engaged. . . . The games are formatted by degree of difficulty with easier activities at the beginning; almost all of them take up a single page and can be learned by following the three-step directions. Surrounding these explanations are bright illustrations, suggestions for altering the game if there is a solo player or to make it more challenging, and an occasional fact related to the activity." SLJ

793.2   Parties and entertainments

Guillain, Charlotte

My first sleepover. Heinemann Library 2011 24p il (Growing up) lib bdg $22; pa $6.49

Grades: PreK K 1 2   **793.2**

    1. Sleepovers

    ISBN 978-1-4329-4802-3 lib bdg; 1-4329-4802-4 lib bdg; 978-1-4329-4812-2 pa; 1-4329-4812-1 pa

LC 2010024196

This book examines a "common, often scary [event] in children's lives and [guides] readers through [it] step-by-step. The [author discusses] the who, what, and why of [the] experience . . . By confronting . . . fears head-on, children will feel 'in the know' and be prepared to experience [this first]. The text—two sentences per page in a large font and placed on white space—is accompanied by large color photos of children, families, and adults of a variety of ethnic backgrounds. [The] volume includes boldface vocabulary words, a picture glossary, and dos and don'ts." SLJ

Includes glossary and bibliographical references

Kenney, Karen Latchana

Cool family parties; perfect party planning for kids. Abdo Pub. 2011 il (Cool parties) lib bdg $27.07

Grades: 3 4 5 6   **793.2**

    1. Parties

    ISBN 978-1-61714-973-3; 1-61714-973-X

LC 2011003503

This book about family parties "has a lot of child appeal. The vivid photos and well-organized and readable content provide great springboards for party ideas. . . . Step-by-step crafts, sample menus, and easy-to-replicate games and activities add to the fun." SLJ

Cool holiday parties; perfect party planning for kids. Abdo Pub. Co. 2011 il (Cool parties) lib bdg $27.07

Grades: 3 4 5 6   **793.2**

    1. Parties 2. Holidays

    ISBN 978-1-61714-974-0; 1-61714-974-8

LC 2011003504

This book about holiday parties "has a lot of child appeal. The vivid photos and well-organized and readable content provide great springboards for party ideas. . . . Step-by-step crafts, sample menus, and easy-to-replicate games and activities add to the fun." SLJ

Cool international parties; perfect party planning for kids. ABDO Pub. Co. 2011 il (Cool parties) lib bdg $27.07

Grades: 3 4 5 6   **793.2**

    1. Parties

    ISBN 978-1-61714-975-7

LC 2011003498

This book about international parties "has a lot of child appeal. The vivid photos and well-organized and readable content provide great springboards for party ideas. . . . Step-by-step crafts, sample menus, and easy-to-replicate games and activities add to the fun." SLJ

Includes glossary and bibliographical references

Cool slumber parties; perfect party planning for kids. ABDO Pub. Co. 2011 il (Cool parties) lib bdg $27.07

Grades: 3 4 5 6   **793.2**

    1. Parties 2. Sleepovers

    ISBN 978-1-61714-976-4; 1-61714-976-4

LC 2011004213

This book about slumber parties "has a lot of child appeal. The vivid photos and well-organized and readable content provide great springboards for party ideas. . . . Step-by-step crafts, sample menus, and easy-to-replicate games and activities add to the fun." SLJ

Cool sports parties; perfect party planning for kids. Abdo Pub. Co. 2012 il (Cool parties) lib bdg $27.07

Grades: 3 4 5 6   **793.2**

    1. Sports 2. Parties

    ISBN 978-1-61714-977-1; 1-61714-977-2

LC 2011004214

This book about sports parties "has a lot of child appeal. The vivid photos and well-organized and readable content provide great springboards for party ideas. . . . Step-by-step crafts, sample menus, and easy-to-replicate games and activities add to the fun." SLJ

Cool theme parties; perfect party planning for kids. ABDO Pub. Co. 2011 il (Cool parties) lib bdg $27.07

Grades: 3 4 5 6   **793.2**

    1. Parties

    ISBN 978-1-61714-978-8; 1-61714-978-0

LC 2011004215

This book about theme parties "has a lot of child appeal. The vivid photos and well-organized and readable content provide great springboards for party ideas. . . . Step-by-step crafts, sample menus, and easy-to-replicate games and activities add to the fun." SLJ

McGillian, Jamie Kyle

Sleepover party! games and giggles for a fun night. [by] Jamie Kyle McGillian. Sterling Pub. 2007 95p il $14.95

Grades: 3 4 5 6   **793.2**

    1. Parties

    ISBN 978-1-4027-2978-2; 1-4027-2978-2

LC 2006029509

"An attractive, girl-friendly compendium of party-planning ideas. All of the basics are covered, such as house rules, what to make/buy, 'Top 10 Things to Get Straight before the Party,' invitations, menus, music, and more. . . . Dozens of indoor and outdoor games . . . and craft ideas are briefly described. The chapter on food includes snacks, dinners, desserts, breakfasts, and goodie-bag ideas." SLJ

Ross, Kathy

The **best** birthday parties ever! a kid's do-it-yourself guide. art by Sharon Lane Holm. Millbrook Press 1999 78p il lib bdg $24.90; pa $9.95

Grades: 2 3 4   **793.2**

    1. Games 2. Parties 3. Birthdays 4. Handicraft

    ISBN 0-7613-1410-5 lib bdg; 0-7613-0989-6 pa

LC 98-27503

Provides instructions for the invitations, games, crafts, table decorations, and cakes for a dozen birthday parties based on such themes as outer space, puppets, and dinosaurs

"The book is appealing. The illustrations are colorful and plentiful." SLJ

793.3   Social, folk, national dancing

Ancona, George

★ **Capoeira**; game! dance! martial art! [by] George Ancona. Lee & Low Books 2007 un il $18.95

Grades: 3 4 5 6   **793.3**

1. Capoeira (Dance)

ISBN 978-1-58430-268-1

LC 2006028866

This offers "uncomplicated words and engaging, step-by-step photographs of young capoeristas in action. . . . Ancona's . . . enthusiasm and awe for his subject is contagious." Booklist

Includes glossary and bibliographical references

★ **Ole!** Flamenco. Lee & Low 2010 un il map $19.95

Grades: 5 6 7 8   **793.3**

1. Flamenco

ISBN 978-1-60060-361-7; 1-60060-361-0

LC 2010-22272

Ancona tells "the story of flamenco, an art form that's more than dancing and has been around for hundreds of years. He begins with a short introduction that chronicles his visit to Spain. . . . He then returns readers to Santa Fe, New Mexico, where a group of young people are learning flamenco. A helpful map traces the art form's roots, while the text explains both the history of the Gypsies and flamenco. Full-color photographs capture the excitement and dazzle. . . . All aspects of flamenco are explored, including movements, facial expressions, and sound effects." Booklist

Includes glossary and bibliographical references

Fishkin, Rebecca Love

Dance; a practical guide to pursuing the art. content adviser, Hannah Seidel and Chris Ferris and dancers; reading adviser, Alexa L. Sandmann. Compass Point Books 2011 48p il (Performing arts) lib bdg $28.65

Grades: 5 6 7 8   **793.3**

1. Dance 2. Vocational guidance

ISBN 978-0-7565-4363-1 lib bdg; 0-7565-4363-0 lib bdg

LC 2010012605

This guide about a career in dance includes tips on education, technique, and more.

"Meant for students contemplating a career in the field . . . [this book goes] beyond basic introductions and into more detail about what it takes to make it as a professional. . . . [The author maintains] . . . a frank, realistic tone, stressing the importance of hard work and dedication. Great [resource] . . . for those wanting to make their passions more than just a hobby." SLJ

Includes glossary and bibliographical references

Garofoli, Wendy

Hip-hop dancing. Capstone Press 2011 4v il lib bdg ea $30.65

Grades: 4 5 6   **793.3**

1. Dance 2. Hip-hop

ISBN 978-1-4296-5484-5 v1; 1-4296-5484-5 v1; 978-1-4296-5485-2 v2; 1-4296-5485-6 v2; 978-1-4296-5486-9 v3; 1-4296-5486-9 v3; 978-1-4296-5487-6 v4; 1-4296-5487-2 v4

LC 2010030394

Provides instructions for joining or starting a hip-hop dance crew, and includes information about real-life crews.

"These volumes cover the basic moves as well as more detailed movements often seen on television programs. . . . Everything about the set is jazzy and current. Sentences are short and direct, with a small-

sized font detailing step-by-step instructions and fact boxes extending the information." Booklist

Includes bibliographical references

Haney, Johannah

Capoeira. Marshall Cavendish Benchmark 2011 47p il (Martial arts in action) $29.93

Grades: 4 5 6 7   **793.3**

1. Capoeira (Dance)

ISBN 978-0-7614-4932-4; 978-1-6087-0362-3 e-book

LC 2010013829

This describes the history, equipment, and technique of capoeira.

This treats "martial arts with the dignity that serious enthusiasts bring to the sport. . . . Illustrations include not only photos of modern gear and from films but also historical images." Booklist

Keeler, Patricia A.

★ **Drumbeat** in our feet. Lee & Low 2006 un il $16.95

Grades: 3 4 5   **793.3**

1. Dance -- Africa

ISBN 1-58430-264-X

This "book opens with a concise overview of the origins of African dance traditions that highlights the diversity of African peoples, cultures, and landscapes. Other two-page chapters cover how dances are passed on to children, different types of dances, image dances (those that mimic animal movements), costumes and body painting, honoring spirits and ancestors, musical instruments, drums, call-and-response songs, masked dancers, and performance. Keeler's watercolor-and-pencil illustrations impart a sense of vibrancy, movement, and joy. . . . A fresh, uplifting, and captivating offering." SLJ

793.7   Games not characterized by action

Macaulay, David

★ **Black** and white. Houghton Mifflin 1990 un il hardcover o.p. pa $7.99

Grades: 1 2 3   **793.7**

1. Cattle -- Fiction 2. Railroads -- Fiction

ISBN 0-395-52151-3; 0-618-63687-0 pa

LC 89-28888

Awarded the Caldecott Medal, 1990

Four brief "stories" about parents, trains, and cows, or is it really all one story? The author recommends careful inspection of words and pictures to both minimize and enhance confusion

"The magic of Black and White comes not from each story, . . . but from the mysterious interactions between them that creates a fifth story. . . . Eventually, the stories begin to merge into a surrealistic tale spanning several levels of reality. . . . Black and White challenges the reader to use text and pictures in unexpected ways." Publ Wkly

Shortcut. Houghton Mifflin 1995 un il $15.95; pa $7.95

Grades: 1 2 3   **793.7**

ISBN 0-395-52436-9; 0-618-00607-9 pa

LC 95-2542

"This picture book concerns six humans whose paths cross and re-cross in the eight chapters of brief text and distinctive artwork. Albert and his horse, June, take their wagon of melons to market, sell them, and go home. . . . Patty's pet pig, Pearl, wanders onto an abandoned railroad line. . . . Professor Tweet is studying birds when suddenly his hot air balloon breaks free and heads toward a nearby cathedral spire. . . . Seemingly inconsequential details in one story become the moving forces in another." Booklist

793.73   Puzzles and puzzle games

Agee, Jon

Smart feller fart smeller & other Spoonerisms. Hyperion Books 2006 un il $14.95

Grades: 3 4 5 6   **793.73**

1. Spoonerisms

ISBN 0-7868-3692-X

LC 2005-929187

"Using full-page black-and-white cartoons that play with the mixed-up words, Agee captures the fun of spoonerisms. The farce of the verbal puns is extended by pictures that caricature everyone.... A brief introduction explains what a spoonerism is, and the last page summarizes 'what they said' with 'what they meant to say.'" Booklist

Chedru, Delphine

Spot it again! find more hidden creatures. translated from French by Scott Auerbach. Abrams Books for Young Readers 2011 un il $14.95

Grades: PreK K 1   **793.73**

1. Picture puzzles

ISBN 978-0-8109-9736-3; 0-8109-9736-3

LC 2010020924

Original French edition 2009

This "conceals 16 more small creatures within its modish patterns. The simple and lively text prompts readers to poke among the flaps, die cuts, and vibrant lines and shapes to find snails, hungry earthworms, crying crocodiles, and more.... Beautifully designed from its large size to its rounded corners and heavy stock, this interactive adventure concludes with a search for sleepwalking sheep on a nighttime spread. Children will enjoy this striking volume." SLJ

Spot it! find the hidden creatures. Abrams Books for Young Readers 2009 un il $14.95

Grades: PreK K 1   **793.73**

1. Picture puzzles

ISBN 978-0-8109-0632-7; 0-8109-0632-5

LC 2008032549

"This rounded-corner volume employs op-art designs to hide 15 creatures, and a farm girl, for viewers to find. The searches vary in difficulty.... The bright patterns vary from packed geometrics to a gathering of flowers, mushrooms, or trees.... Great for one-on-one lap sharing." SLJ

Cole, Joanna

Why did the chicken cross the road? and other riddles, old and new; compiled by Joanna Cole and Stephanie Calmenson; illustrated by Alan Tiegreen. Morrow Junior Bks. 1994 64p il hardcover o.p. pa $7.95

Grades: 3 4 5   **793.73**

1. Riddles

ISBN 0-688-12204-3

LC 94-2582

The authors "begin with a brief explanation about the origin of riddles and proceed with a collection of over two hundred, classic and new. Though many of the riddles appear in other collections, the book, illustrated with black-and-white line drawings, will be useful for its short bibliography and subject index." Horn Book Guide

Hall, Katy

★ **Creepy** riddles; [by] Katy Hall and Lisa Eisenberg; pictures by S.D. Schindler. Dial Bks. for Young Readers 1998 48p il (Dial easy-to-read) hardcover o.p. pa $3.99

Grades: K 1 2   **793.73**

1. Riddles

ISBN 0-8037-1684-2; 0-14-130988-1 pa

LC 94-37524

"A collection of riddles about vampires, ghosts, ghouls, and assorted monsters.... The illustrations are a scream. Schindler uses a find-nibbed pen to include lots of subtle details before adding vivid watercolor washes.... A superior choice for most joke or beginning-to-read collections." SLJ

★ **Dino** riddles; by Katy Hall and Lisa Eisenberg; pictures by Nicole Rubel. Dial Bks. for Young Readers 2002 40p il (Dial easy-to-read) hardcover o.p. pa $3.99

Grades: K 1 2   **793.73**

1. Riddles

ISBN 0-8037-2239-7; 0-14-250179-4 pa

LC 97-49947

A collection of riddles relating to dinosaurs, such as "What do you get if you cross a dinosaur with a rabbit? Tricerahops!" and "What did dinosaur campers cook over the fire? Dino-s'mores!"

"Rubel's informal ink-and-marker illustrations are suitably silly.... This will be just right for joke-book junkies, beginning readers, and teachers looking to breathe new life into staid dinosaur units." Bull Cent Child Books

Ribbit riddles; by Katy Hall and Lisa Eisenberg; pictures by Robert Bender. Dial Bks. for Young Readers 2001 40p il (Dial easy-to-read) hardcover o.p. pa $3.99

Grades: K 1 2   **793.73**

1. Jokes 2. Riddles

ISBN 0-8037-2525-6; 0-14-240056-4 pa

LC 99-89174

A collection of riddles and jokes about frogs. Example: What do little frogs like to eat on a hot summer day? Hopsicles!

"The distinctive art, cell-vinyl on layers of acetate, has a shimmery, almost fuzzy look that catches the eye—and the jokes." Booklist

★ **Simms** Taback's great big book of spacey, snakey, buggy riddles; riddles by Katy Hall and Lisa Eisenberg; [illustrated by Simms Taback] Viking 2008 un il $17.99

Grades: K 1 2 3   **793.73**

1. Riddles

ISBN 978-0-670-01121-6; 0-670-01121-5

"Taback brings his vibrant trademark exuberance to this picture-book riddle collection, which fairly hums with fun. Rainbow-bright colors pop off black backgrounds, making the riddles bigger than life. As the title suggests, space, snakes, and bugs dominate the subject matter." Booklist

Snakey riddles; by Katy Hall and Lisa Eisenberg; pictures by Simms Taback. Dial Bks. for Young Readers 1990 48p il (Dial easy-to-read) hardcover o.p. pa $3.99

Grades: K 1 2   **793.73**

1. Riddles

ISBN 0-14-037141-9 pa

LC 88-23687

An illustrated collection of riddles about snakes

"Riddle lovers will groan with delight at some of these riddles.... The best thing about the book is the cleverly drawn, lively cartoon illustrations. Long, colorful snakes form borders framing the text and picture for each riddle." SLJ

Turkey riddles; by Katy Hall and Lisa Eisenberg; pictures by Kristin Sorra. Dial Bks. for Young Readers 2002 40p il (Dial easy-to-read) hardcover o.p. pa $3.99

Grades: K 1 2   **793.73**

1. Riddles
ISBN 0-8037-2530-2; 0-14-240369-5 pa

LC 2001-47475

A collection of nearly three dozen riddles featuring turkeys, such as "What happened when Tom Turkey stepped up to the plate? He hit a fowl ball"

"The art, with cross-hatched details, is bright and appealing. . . . Great for a good time alone, with friends, or even in a classroom." Booklist

Kalz, Jill

An **A-MAZE-ing amusement park adventure**; illustrated by Mattia Cerato. Picture Window Books 2010 32p il (A-MAZE-ing adventures) lib bdg $25.99

Grades: K 1 2 3   **793.73**

1. Maps 2. Maze puzzles 3. Amusement parks
ISBN 978-1-4048-6023-0 lib bdg; 1-4048-6023-1 lib bdg

LC 2010009865

"Fantastically illustrated, the adventures take the form of overhead maps, which allow Cerato to give in to her every twisty, turny impulse. . . . The first maze is a view of an entire amusement park, while subsequent mazes zero in on individual areas. . . . It's impressively orchestrated and enjoyable. . . . Navigating maps is an important real-world skill and is rarely—let's face it, never—this much fun." Booklist

Kidslabel (Firm)

Spot 7 animals; by KIDSLABEL. Chronicle Books 2007 un il (Seek & find) $12.95

Grades: K 1 2 3 4   **793.73**

1. Puzzles
ISBN 978-0-8118-5722-2; 0-8118-5722-0

LC 2006018069

"The creative, colorful pictures and the challenge of finding differences and particular items make this book constructive fun." SLJ

Spot 7 Christmas; by KIDSLABEL. Chronicle Books 2006 un il (Seek & find) $12.95

Grades: K 1 2 3 4   **793.73**

1. Puzzles 2. Christmas
ISBN 978-0-8118-5323-1; 0-8118-5323-3

LC 2005028795

"This bright, spot-the-difference book features 13 (if you count the front and back covers) photo spreads of wreaths, Santa-filled dioramas, and Christmas cards, asking readers to find seven oddities and solve a riddle for each one." SLJ

Spot 7 School; by KIDSLABEL. Chronicle Books 2006 un il (Seek & find) $12.95

Grades: K 1 2 3 4   **793.73**

1. Puzzles
ISBN 978-0-8118-5324-8; 0-8118-5324-1

LC 2005026114

Original Japanese edition 2003

"This book has colorful, busy photos of objects and lists of items associated with school for readers to locate. . . . It also offers viewers some additional tasks: the two pages of each spread are identical except for seven differences, and each left-hand page contains a riddle, the answer to which is found on the page. . . . The clear images depict imaginative groupings. . . . It offers entertainment and an opportunity to hone observational skills rolled into one." SLJ

Other titles in this series are:
Spot 7 Christmas (2006)
Spot 7 Animals (2007)
Spot 7 Spooky (2007)
Spot 7 Toys (2008)

Spot 7 spooky. Chronicle Books 2007 un il (Seek & find) $12.95

Grades: K 1 2 3 4   **793.73**

1. Puzzles
ISBN 978-0-8118-5723-9; 0-8118-5723-9

LC 2006032422

Original Japanese edition 2004

"Each spread of this Halloween-themed activity book features two spooky photographs that appear identical. Eagle-eyed readers, however, will spot seven things that have changed from one photo to the other. . . . [There is] a riddle on each spread and [there are] extra things to look for throughout the book." Publisher's note

Spot 7 Toys; by KIDSLABEL. Chronicle Books 2008 un il $12.99

Grades: K 1 2 3 4   **793.73**

1. Puzzles
ISBN 978-0-8118-6563-0; 0-8118-6563-0

"This collection of 12 riddles accompanied by collage-style photos will keep children entertained. Each selection is paired with two full-color photos filled with tiny toys. Upon first glance the paired pictures appear identical. However, close inspection reveals many differences, some of which are more obvious than others. The riddles range in difficulty, and their solutions can be found within the illustrations. . . . The book follows the successful format of other 'Spot 7' titles." SLJ

Lankford, Mary D.

Mazes around the world; by Mary D. Lankford; illustrated by Karen Dugan. Collins 2008 26p il $16.99; lib bdg $17.89

Grades: 3 4 5   **793.73**

1. Maze puzzles
ISBN 978-0-688-16519-2; 0-688-16519-2; 978-0-688-16520-8 lib bdg; 0-688-16520-6 lib bdg

LC 2007008580

"Lankford traces the history of mazes from the ancient Egyptian Labyrinth . . . to today's mazes in North America's corn fields. . . . Each left-hand page offers an engaging account of a particular maze or type of maze, depicted on the facing page in a charming painting by Dugan. . . . Drawing from many cultures and historical periods, this well-researched, accessible book explores a topic with inherent child appeal." Booklist

Includes bibliographical references

Maestro, Giulio

Riddle roundup; a wild bunch to beef up your word power. Clarion Bks. 1989 64p il hardcover o.p. pa $7.95

Grades: 2 3 4   **793.73**

1. Riddles 2. Word games
ISBN 0-89919-537-7 pa

LC 86-33403

A collection of sixty-one riddles based on different kinds of word play such as puns, homonyms, and homographs

Maestro, Marco

What do you hear when cows sing? and other silly riddles. by Marco and Giulio Maestro; pictures by Giulio Maestro. HarperCollins Pubs. 1996 48p il (I can read book) hardcover o.p. pa $3.95

Grades: K 1 2   **793.73**
1. Riddles
ISBN 0-06-444227-6 pa

LC 94-18686

"The subjects of the riddles will be familiar to most readers—trains, bugs, mice, fish, boats. . . . Most of the selections involve plays on words, but some are relatively straightforward. . . . Children will love the silly pictures, laugh at the riddles, enjoy sharing them with others, and expand their vocabularies all at the same time." SLJ

Marzollo, Jean

I spy a Christmas tree; riddles by Jean Marzollo; photographs by Walter Wick. Scholastic 2010 un il $9.99
Grades: PreK K 1 2   **793.73**
1. Christmas 2. Picture puzzles
ISBN 978-0-545-22092-7; 0-545-22092-0

Rhyming verses ask readers to find hidden objects in the photographs of Christmas tree ornaments and toys.

I spy an egg in a nest; riddles by Jean Marzollo; photographs by Walter Wick. Scholastic 2011 un il (Scholastic reader) pa $3.99
Grades: PreK K 1 2   **793.73**
1. Picture puzzles
ISBN 978-0-545-22093-4 pa; 0-545-22093-9 pa

LC 2009051611

This visual game book consists of a series of rhymed riddles listing objects that children must locate in the accompanying photographs of subjects relating to spring.

"Sharpening children's visual discrimination and concentration, this colorful book offers a fun approach to reading skills." Booklist

I spy school days; a book of picture riddles. photographs by Walter Wick; riddles by Jean Marzollo. Scholastic 1995 33p il $18.95
Grades: K 1 2 3 4   **793.73**
1. Puzzles
ISBN 0-590-48135-5

LC 94-43629

"This riddle book in verse follows the . . . format of large, over-sized pages chock-full of objects and realia. This time, the double-page spreads are devoted to unifying activities or themes associated with school, chalkboard, a puppet show, art or science classrooms, a playground, etc. The full-color photographs are sharp, bright, and busy." SLJ

Munro, Roxie

Amazement park; by Roxie Munro. Chronicle Books 2005 37p il $16.95
Grades: K 1 2 3   **793.73**
1. Maze puzzles
ISBN 0-8118-4581-8

LC 2004-8482

This book includes "12 . . . mazes to navigate. . . . All mazes lead from one page to the next and then back again to the first one. . . . The mazes do get tricky and sometimes completely confusing, but an answer key is included for those who get stuck. The cartoon art is eye-catching and colorful." SLJ

Another book of maze puzzles by this author is:
Mazescapes (2001)

Mazeways : A to Z; by Roxie Munro. Sterling Pub. Co., Inc. 2007 un il $12.95
Grades: K 1 2 3   **793.73**
1. Alphabet 2. Maze puzzles
ISBN 978-1-4027-3774-9; 1-4027-3774--2

LC 2007001586

"Each letter is featured on a spread or a page with directions for traveling through the maze and finding different objects along the way. . . . Back pages provide solutions. This engaging title works as an interactive alphabet book, an introduction to mapping skills, or to sharpen visual discrimination skills." SLJ

Nickle, John

Alphabet explosion! search and count from alien to zebra. [by] John Nickle. Schwartz & Wade Books 2006 un il $16.95
Grades: K 1 2 3   **793.73**
1. Puzzles 2. Alphabet
ISBN 0-375-83598-9

LC 2005024372

"Each wordless page features animals and objects whose names begin with a featured letter. A number indicates how many items are buried within the picture. . . . Nickle's finely rendered scenes are imaginative, humorous, and sophisticated, and he incorporates a free-flowing range of artistic styles that adds energy to the pages.." Booklist

Rosenthal, Amy Krouse

Wumbers; it's a word cr8ed with a number! wri10 by Amy Krouse Rosenthal; illustr8ed by Tom Lichtenheld. Chronicle Books 2012 40 p. col. ill. (alk. paper) $16.99
Grades: K 1 2 3   **793.73**
1. Word games
ISBN 1452110220; 9781452110226

LC 2011041591

This children's picture book by Amy Krouse Rosenthal "combines words and numbers ('wumbers') that challenge readers to use their number recognition and phonological skills. . . . From a boy and girl enjoying their '10ts' to the smiling child who is 'el8ed' because he lost his first '2th,' [Tom] Lichenheld's ink and pastel coloring-book-style drawings supply visual clues to decoding the text." (School Library Journal)

Schnur, Steven

Autumn; an alphabet acrostic. illustrated by Leslie Evans. Clarion Bks. 1997 un il $16
Grades: K 1 2 3   **793.73**
1. Autumn 2. Alphabet 3. Acrostics
ISBN 0-395-77043-2

LC 96-50219

"A fall riddle is presented for each letter of the alphabet. The answer is spelled out in the first letter of each line. The riddles are spare with striking images. . . . Evans's stunning hand-colored linoleum block prints are clear, bright, and provide sharp clues for the riddles. . . . This delightful alphabet book with a new twist will provide inspiration and challenges for a wide audience." SLJ

Summer; an alphabet acrostic. illustrated by Leslie Evans. Clarion Books 2001 un il $16
Grades: K 1 2 3   **793.73**
1. Summer 2. Alphabet 3. Acrostics
ISBN 0-618-02372-0

LC 00-31674

"This concept book features a short poem in which the first letter of each line spells out the word it represents. 'Daisy' becomes 'Dragonflies dart/And hover,/Inspecting white flowers with/Sunlike/Yellow centers.' The sheer inventiveness of each poem is impressive. . . . Neatly framed linoleum-block illustrations feature rich colors and bold lines that capture the brightness of the days." SLJ

Sirett, Dawn

Hide and seek first words; [written by Dawn Sirett; photography by Dave King]. DK Publishing 2010 48p il $12.99

Grades: PreK   **793.73**
1. Vocabulary 2. Picture puzzles
ISBN 978-0-7566-6300-1; 0-7566-6300-8

               LC 2010280415

"This seek-and-find, with its colorful collection of photographic puzzles, will capture the attention of young children and draw them into the book. Working with an adult to locate the brightly colored objects hidden throughout loosely themed spreads . . . preschoolers will also be helping build reading readiness and verbal skills through short rhyming text and object labeling." Horn Book Guide

Steig, William
   ★ C D B. Simon & Schuster Bks. for Young Readers 2000 47p
il $16; pa $4.99
Grades: 2 3 4 5   **793.73**
1. Word games
ISBN 0-689-83160-9; 0-671-66689-4 pa

               LC 99-32720

First published 1968 by Windmill Bks.

Letters and numbers are used to create the sounds of words and simple sentences 4 u 2 figure out with the aid of illustrations

Readers "will delight in puzzling out the letter-and-number messages, aided by the simple, thickly outlined drawings and an answer key." Booklist

   C D C? Farrar, Straus & Giroux 2003 57p il $16
Grades: 2 3 4 5   **793.73**
1. Word games
ISBN 0-374-31233-8

               LC 2002-111704

A color illustrated edition of the title first published 1984

Letters, numbers, and symbols are used to create the sounds of words and simple sentences which U R expected to figure out with the aid of illustrations. Includes an answer key

"Flawlessly executed, purely pleasurable, the book is definitely 'D-Q-R' for doldrums at any season." Horn Book

Steiner, Joan
   Look-alikes; photography by Thomas Lindley. Little, Brown 1998
un il $13.95
Grades: K 1 2 3 4   **793.73**
1. Puzzles
ISBN 0-316-81255-2

               LC 97-32795

"Bursting with creativity, this work of visual genius will set imaginations soaring." Publ Wkly

   Look-alikes around the world; concept, constructions & text by Joan Steiner; design by Stephen Blauweiss; photography by Ogden Gigli. Little, Brown and Company 2007 un il $15.99
Grades: K 1 2 3 4   **793.73**
1. Puzzles
ISBN 978-0-316-81172-9; 0-316-81172-6

               LC 2007012332

"Using everyday objects . . . artist Joan Steiner has created three-dimensional scenes of more than 40 famous landmarks and familiar vacation locales. . . . Complete with photographs of the actual sites, . . . facts, and more than 500 look-alikes to search for, this [is in the format of a] postcard album." Publisher's note

Other titles in this series are:
Look-alikes (1998)
Look-alikes Jr (1999)
Look-alikes Christmas (2003)

   Look-alikes Christmas; [by] Joan Steiner; photography by Ogden Gigli. Little, Brown 2003 un il lib bdg $14.95
Grades: K 1 2 3 4   **793.73**
1. Puzzles 2. Christmas
ISBN 0-316-81187-4

               LC 2003-47406

Simple verses challenge readers to identify the everyday objects used to construct nine three-dimensional Christmas scenes, including a cathedral, Nutcracker ballet, and Santa's workshop.

"In both presentation and delivery, this is clever, ingenious, and fun both for readers and nonreaders." SLJ

   Look-alikes, jr. photography by Thomas Lindley. Little, Brown 1999 un il $13.95
Grades: K 1 2 3   **793.73**
1. Puzzles
ISBN 0-316-81307-9

               LC 99-11683

Simple verses challenge readers to identify the everyday objects used to construct eleven three-dimensional scenes, including a house, kitchen, bedroom, school bus, train, farm, and rocket

"The design is both witty and cunning, offering lots of just-hard-enough opportunities for looking and finding." Horn Book

Wick, Walter
   ★ Can you see what I see? picture puzzles to search and solve. Scholastic 2002 35p il $13.95
Grades: PreK K 1 2   **793.73**
1. Puzzles
ISBN 0-439-16391-9

               LC 2001-49032

Presents twelve brain-teasing hidden picture puzzles to solve

"With its range of activities and perspective-shifting challenges, this is sure to appeal to a wide age group of children, who won't be satisfied until they've solved the last puzzle." Booklist

Other titles in this series are:
Can you see what I see?: Cool collections (2004)
Can you see what I see?: Dream machine (2003)
Can you see what I see?: On a scary scary night (2008)
Can you see what I see?: Once upon a time (2006)
Can you see what I see?: Seymour and the juice box boat (2004)
Can you see what I see: Seymour makes new friends (2006)
Can you see what I see?: The night before Christmas (2005)
Can you see what I see?: Treasure ship (2010)

   Can you see what I see? Cool collections; picture puzzles to search and solve. Scholastic 2004 35p il $13.95
Grades: PreK K 1 2   **793.73**
1. Puzzles
ISBN 0-439-61772-3

Readers search for objects hidden in photographs of buttons, dinosaurs, robots, shells, cars, animals, leaves, beads, game pieces, and the contents of a junk drawer.

"Wick offers pleasing rhymes that clearly direct readers to retrieve a requisite number of objects. Once again, his photography engages, even mesmerizes viewers." SLJ

   Can you see what I see? Dream machine; a picture adventure to search and solve. Scholastic 2003 35p il $13.95
Grades: PreK K 1 2   **793.73**
1. Puzzles
ISBN 0-439-39950-5

               LC 2003-3547

A child enters a dream machine and encounters hidden picture puzzles intended for the reader to solve

"Wick uses homonyms and visual tricks, giving children more to see and look for than what may appear at first glance.... A wonderful addition to any collection." SLJ

Can you see what I see? On a scary, scary night; by Walter Wick. Scholastic 2008 35p il $13.99
Grades: PreK K 1 2   **793.73**
1. Puzzles
ISBN 0-439-70870-2; 978-0-439-70870-8
LC 2007029839

Picture puzzles in which the reader is invited to search for hidden objects in scary settings.

Can you see what I see? Seymour and the juice box boat. Scholastic 2004 29p il $8.99
Grades: PreK K 1 2   **793.73**
1. Puzzles
ISBN 0-439-61778-2

The reader is asked to find various animals and objects and a boy named Seymour in the photographs.

"Just right for the youngest seek-and-find aficionados, this engaging offering will sail right off of the shelves." SLJ

Can you see what I see? toyland express. Scholastic 2011 35p il $13.99
Grades: PreK K 1 2   **793.73**
1. Puzzles
ISBN 978-0-545-24483-1; 0-545-24483-8

"Complex seek-and-find images provide an intriguing backdrop for the story of a tenacious toy train. This latest collection of picture puzzles in the Can You See What I See? series provides a nostalgic glimpse into the life, death and resurrection of a wooden train.... Wick plays with similar colors to enhance these expressive camouflaged spreads. Digitally processed photographs capture crisp dimensions with remarkable clarity. No puzzle here—these well-designed scenes are another success from the picture-challenge master." Kirkus

Can you see what I see?: once upon a time; picture puzzles to search and solve. by Walter Wick. Scholastic 2006 35p il $13.99
Grades: K 1 2 3   **793.73**
1. Puzzles
ISBN 0-439-61777-4
LC 2006005853

"Each scene is crammed with delightful details that will be a pleasure to examine while hunting for the specified items." SLJ

Can you see what I see?: Treasure ship; picture puzzles to search and solve. Scholastic Inc. 2010 34p il $13.99
Grades: PreK K 1 2   **793.73**
1. Puzzles
ISBN 978-0-439-02643-7; 0-439-02643-1

Readers are challenged to find objects in photographic scenes related to treasure ships.

★ **I** spy; a book of picture riddles. photographs by Walter Wick; riddles by Jean Marzollo; design by Carol Devine Carson. Scholastic 1992 33p il $13.95
Grades: K 1 2 3 4   **793.73**
1. Puzzles
ISBN 0-590-45087-5
LC 91-28268

This visual game book consists of "a series of rhymed riddles listing objects that children must locate in the accompanying photographs. Each double-page spread features crisp, full-color shots featuring an abundance of familiar items. The objects range from large and easy-to-spot to tiny and partially hidden.... An appealing book for children and adults to share and enjoy together." SLJ

Other titles in this series are:
I spy a Christmas tree (2010)
I spy Christmas (1992)
I spy extreme challenger! (2000)
I spy fantasy (1994)
I spy fun house (1993)
I spy gold challenger! (1998)
I spy mystery (1993)
I spy school days (1995)
I spy spooky night (1996)
I spy super challenger! (1997)
I spy treasure hunt (1999)
I spy ultimate challenger! (2003)
I spy year-round challenger! (2003)

I spy extreme challenger! a book of picture riddles. photographs by Walter Wick; riddles by Jean Marzollo. Scholastic 2000 31p il $13.95
Grades: K 1 2 3 4   **793.73**
1. Puzzles
ISBN 0-439-19900-X
LC 00-27910

This features a collection of favorite I Spy riddles that send readers searching 12 photographs for hidden objects.

I spy fantasy; a book of picture riddles. photographs by Walter Wick; riddles by Jean Marzollo. Scholastic 1994 37p il $13.95
Grades: K 1 2 3 4   **793.73**
1. Puzzles
ISBN 0-590-46295-4
LC 93-44814

"Rhyming riddles direct a hunt for a series of objects in each of 13 sumptuously styled photographs." Publ Wkly

I spy gold challenger! a book of picture riddles. photographs by Walter Wick; riddles by Jean Marzollo. Scholastic 1998 31p il $18.95
Grades: K 1 2 3 4   **793.73**
1. Puzzles
ISBN 0-590-04296-3
LC 98-13982

This "presents photographed setups of carefully arranged objects with riddles underneath each picture that encourage children to find particular objects in the photo. This series entry includes photographs that the author and photographer decided were their favorites from previous books, and substitutes more difficult riddles for the original ones, challenging children who like a truly vigorous search. As in earlier books, a list of riddles at the end gives young seekers the opportunity to work backwards and find the picture that matches the riddle." Booklist

I spy spooky night; a book of picture riddles. photographs by Walter Wick; riddles by Jean Marzollo. Scholastic 1996 31p il $13.99
Grades: K 1 2 3 4   **793.73**
1. Puzzles
ISBN 0-590-48137-1
LC 95-50528

"The puzzles take place in and around a haunted house (an altered Victorian dollhouse). Readers are invited to search for mice, spiders, candles, bats, jacko-lanterns, and bones among other creepy things found in the hallway, library, fireplace, and laboratory of the house, as well as in the graveyard and a garden of ghoulies outside. . . . Wick achieves a definite dramatic effect. Marzollo's clever rhyming puzzles add great flair." SLJ

I spy super challenger! a book of picture riddles. photographs by Walter Wick; riddles by Jean Marzollo. Scholastic 1997 31p il $18.95
Grades: K 1 2 3 4   **793.73**
     1. Puzzles
     ISBN 0-590-34128-6
                 LC 97-6864
"Wick's spectacularly photographed, double-page spreads are taken from favorites such as I Spy Funhouse (1993) and I Spy School Days (1995, both Scholastic). Marzollo's cleverly written new rhyming couplets encourage readers to seek a new batch of items. Playing cards, beads, dominos, blocks, and other trinkets are all arranged attractively and with wit, yet this does not lessen the difficulty of locating the sought-after objects." SLJ

I spy treasure hunt; a book of picture riddles. photographs by Walter Wick; riddles by Jean Marzollo. Scholastic 1999 36p il $13.95
Grades: K 1 2 3 4   **793.73**
     1. Puzzles
     ISBN 0-439-04244-5
                LC 99-30581
"On oversize pages, brightly colored photographs are crammed with small objects; each double-page spread is organized by theme. . . . The rhyming captions at the foot of each page suggest objects to be found. . . . While the pages are very busy, it's the sort of crowding many young children enjoy, and it certainly fosters observation of detail." Bull Cent Child Books

I spy ultimate challenger! a book of picture riddles. photographs by Walter Wick; riddles by Jean Marzollo. Scholastic 2003 31p il $13.99
Grades: K 1 2 3 4   **793.73**
     1. Puzzles
     ISBN 0-439-45401-8
              LC 2002-8196
Rhyming text leads the reader to find objects hidden in the photographs, selected from previously published volumes in the series

793.74   Mathematical games and recreations

Polonsky, Lydia
    Math for the very young; a handbook of activities for parents and teachers. [by] Lydia Plonsky . . . [et al.]; illustrated by Marcia Miller. Wiley 1995 210p il hardcover o.p. pa $14.95
Grades: Adult Professional   **793.74**
     1. Mathematical recreations
     ISBN 0-471-01671-3; 0-471-01647-0 pa
             LC 94-20861
"This guide suggests ways to introduce math to children through everyday activities. Sections include making a record book about the child and the family as well as activities for each month of the year, geometric crafts, math games, counting rhymes and stories, and ways to use math in the home and on the road." Booklist
    Includes bibliographical references

Tang, Greg
    The **grapes** of math; mind-stretching math riddles. illustrated by Harry Briggs. Scholastic Press 2001 un il $16.95

Grades: 2 3 4   **793.74**
     1. Mathematical recreations
     ISBN 0-439-21033-X
              LC 00-30062
Illustrated riddles introduce strategies for solving a variety of math problems in using visual clues
    "This clever collection of puzzles could spark the interest of even the mathematically challenged. . . . The simple, staccato rhymes and crisp lines of the artwork keep attention focused, while those who find themselves stumped can consult the 'Answers' section at the back of the book." Publ Wkly

    Math appeal; mind-stretching math riddles. illustrated by Harry Briggs. Scholastic Press 2003 un il $16.95
Grades: 2 3 4   **793.74**
     1. Mathematical recreations
     ISBN 0-439-21046-1
               LC 2002-5354
Rhyming anecdotes present opportunities for simple math activities and hints for solving
    "Bright, whimsical illustrations and clever rhymes introduce challenging exercises. . . . In a note, Tang states that his goal is 'to encourage clever, creative thinking,' and the questions posed do that." SLJ

    ★ **Math** potatoes; mind-stretching brain food. illustrated by Harry Briggs. Scholastic Press 2005 un il $16.95
Grades: 2 3 4   **793.74**
     1. Mathematical recreations
     ISBN 0-439-44390-3
              LC 2004-16638
"This picture book uses all kinds of visual tricks to demonstrate how to make arithmetic faster and easier. On each double-page spread, a rhyming verse has fun with a variety of subjects. Most rhymes are about foods . . . and the bright, computer-generated pictures are as playful as the words. . . . The games are complex, the visuals are tricky, and although the rhyme seems straightforward . . . readers must think carefully about adding, subtracting, and multiplying." Booklist

793.8   Magic and related activities

Barnhart, Norm
    Amazing magic tricks: a beginner level; by Norm Barnhart. Capstone Press 2009 32p il (Magic Tricks) lib bdg $23.93
Grades: 4 5 6   **793.8**
     1. Magic tricks
     ISBN 978-1-4296-1942-4 lib bdg; 1-4296-1942-2 lib bdg
             LC 2008-2572
"Numbered steps, clearly illustrated by crisp photographs, guide students through the preparation and performance of such classic magician's fare as 'The Magical Sailor's Knot.'. . . The books' design, with the text neatly packaged in boxes, will attract reluctant readers." SLJ
    Includes glossary and bibliographical references

    Amazing magic tricks: apprentice level; by Norm Barnhart. Capstone Press 2009 32p il (Magic Tricks) lib bdg $23.93
Grades: 4 5 6   **793.8**
     1. Magic tricks
     ISBN 978-1-4296-1943-1 lib bdg; 1-4296-1943-0 lib bdg
             LC 2008-2573
"Numbered steps, clearly illustrated by crisp photographs, guide students through the preparation and performance of such classic magi-

cian's fare as 'The Magical Sailor's Knot.'. . . The books' design, with the text neatly packaged in boxes, will attract reluctant readers." SLJ

Includes glossary and bibliographical references

Amazing magic tricks: expert level; by Norm Barnhart. Capstone Press 2009 32p il (Magic Tricks) lib bdg $23.93

Grades: 4 5 6   **793.8**
    1. Magic tricks
    ISBN 978-1-4296-1945-5 lib bdg; 1-4296-1945-7 lib bdg
                  LC 2008-2574

"Numbered steps, clearly illustrated by crisp photographs, guide students through the preparation and performance of such classic magician's fare as 'The Magical Sailor's Knot.'. . . The books' design, with the text neatly packaged in boxes, will attract reluctant readers." SLJ

Includes glossary and bibliographical references

Amazing magic tricks: master level; by Norm Barnhart. Capstone Press 2009 32p il (Magic Tricks) lib bdg $23.93

Grades: 4 5 6   **793.8**
    1. Magic tricks
    ISBN 978-1-4296-1944-8 lib bdg; 1-4296-1944-9 lib bdg
                  LC 2008-2575

"Numbered steps, clearly illustrated by crisp photographs, guide students through the preparation and performance of such classic magician's fare as 'The Magical Sailor's Knot.'. . . The books' design, with the text neatly packaged in boxes, will attract reluctant readers." SLJ

Includes glossary and bibliographical references

Becker, Helaine
  Magic up your sleeve; amazing illusions, tricks, and science facts you'll never believe. illustrated by Claudia Dávila. Maple Tree Press 2010 64p il $22.95; pa $10.95

Grades: 3 4 5 6   **793.8**
    1. Science 2. Magic tricks
    ISBN 978-1-897349-75-5; 1-897349-75-0; 978-1-897349-76-2 pa; 1-8973497-6-9 pa

"Thirty tricks are presented covering optical illusions, mind reading, 'math magic,' chemistry, and physics. All directions are clear and easy to follow. . . . The digital cartoon illustrations are nicely executed and add flashes of humor to the scenarios. . . . A welcome addition that should vanish off library shelves." SLJ

Colgan, Lynda
  Mathemagic! number tricks. written by Lynda Colgan; illustrated by Jane Kurisu. Kids Can Press 2011 40p il $16.95

Grades: 3 4 5   **793.8**
    1. Magic tricks 2. Mathematical recreations
    ISBN 978-1-55453-425-8; 1-55453-425-9

"Colgan introduces 10 magic tricks that are accomplished using mathematical principles. The directions are clear and easy to follow, and each trick is followed by an explanation of how it actually works, as well as suggestions for performing it effectively for an audience. Interesting historical tidbits occasionally appear in sidebars. The simple cartoon illustrations add interest and clarify how the tricks are accomplished." SLJ

Includes glossary

Jennings, Madeleine
  Magic step-by-step; [by] Madeleine Jennings and Colin Francome. Rosen Central 2010 89p il (Skills in motion) lib bdg $31.95

Grades: 5 6 7 8   **793.8**
    1. Magic tricks
    ISBN 978-1-4358-3363-0; 1-4358-3363-5
                  LC 2009-13221

Presents step-by-step instructions on performing magic tricks, including card tricks, rope tricks, and sleight of hand.

"Colorful photographs show the entire movement of each skill presented, giving new meaning to the term 'step-by-step.' Progression borders at the bottom of the pages highlight the salient points to notice in performing each skill from beginning to end." SLJ

Includes bibliographical references

Tremaine, Jon
  Magic with numbers. QEB Pub. 2010 32p il (Magic handbook) lib bdg $28.50

Grades: 4 5 6   **793.8**
    1. Numbers 2. Magic tricks 3. Mathematical recreations
    ISBN 978-1-59566-945-2; 1-59566-945-0
                  LC 2010014138

Provides step-by-step instructions for fifteen magic tricks using numbers, including profiles of famous magicians.

This "is uncommonly good. . . . [The book] uses sharp, comprehensible illustrations set up on old-fashioned marbled backdrops. . . . Best of all, the friendly, crystal-clear [text] makes this one of the most coherent [books] in the genre." Booklist

Magical illusions. QEB Pub. 2010 32p il (Magic handbook) lib bdg $28.50

Grades: 4 5 6   **793.8**
    1. Magic tricks
    ISBN 978-1-59566-944-5; 1-59566-944-2
                  LC 2010008525

This volume explains how to perform magic tricks that involve creating illusions.

This "is uncommonly good. . . . [The book] uses sharp, comprehensible illustrations set up on old-fashioned marbled backdrops. . . . Best of all, the friendly, crystal-clear [text] makes this one of the most coherent [books] in the genre." Booklist

Paper tricks. QEB Pub. 2010 32p il (Magic handbook) lib bdg $28.50

Grades: 4 5 6   **793.8**
    1. Magic tricks 2. Paper crafts
    ISBN 978-1-59566-852-3; 1-59566-852-7
                  LC 2010017910

This offers instructions for magic tricks using paper.

This "is uncommonly good. . . . [The book] uses sharp, comprehensible illustrations set up on old-fashioned marbled backdrops. . . . Best of all, the friendly, crystal-clear [text] makes this one of the most coherent [books] in the genre." Booklist

Pocket tricks. QEB Pub. 2010 32p il (Magic handbook) lib bdg $28.50; pa $13.50

Grades: 4 5 6   **793.8**
    1. Magic tricks
    ISBN 978-1-59566-853-0 lib bdg; 1-59566-853-5 lib bdg; 978-1-84835-443-2 pa; 1-84835-443-6 pa
                  LC 2010008526

This volume explains how to perform simple magic tricks using items that are commonly in a person's pocket.

This "is uncommonly good. . . . [The book] uses sharp, comprehensible illustrations set up on old-fashioned marbled backdrops. . . . Best of all, the friendly, crystal-clear [text] makes this one of the most coherent [books] in the genre." Booklist

Includes bibliographical references

Wyler, Rose

Magic secrets; by Rose Wyler and Gerald Ames; pictures by Arthur Dorros. rev ed.; Harper & Row 1990 63p il (I can read book) hardcover o.p. pa $3.99

Grades: K 1 2   **793.8**

1. Magic tricks

ISBN 0-06-444153-9 pa

LC 89-35841

A revised and newly illustrated edition of the title first published 1967

Easy magic tricks for the aspiring young magician

"Most of the magic tricks presented here are easily understood and appear to be simple to learn and to execute with ample practice." SLJ

794.1 Chess

Basman, Michael

Chess for kids; written by Michael Basman. Dorling Kindersley 2001 45p il $12.99; pa $6.99

Grades: 4 5 6 7   **794.1**

1. Chess

ISBN 0-7894-6540-X; 0-7566-1807-X pa

LC 00-59018

This guide to chess explains the rudiments of the game, techniques and winning strategies

"A solid introduction for novices and good for skilled players wanting to develop their strategies and find out about chess clubs and tournaments." Booklist

King, Daniel

★ **Chess**; from first moves to checkmate. New ed.; Kingfisher 2010 64p il pa $8.99

Grades: 5 6 7 8 9 10 11 12   **794.1**

1. Chess

ISBN 978-0-7534-1930-4

First published 2000

Introduces the rules and strategies of chess, as well as its history and some of the great players and matches.

794.8 Electronic games

Egan, Jill

How video game designers use math; math curriculum consultant: Rhea A. Stewart. Chelsea Clubhouse 2010 32p il (Math in the real world) lib bdg $28

Grades: 4 5 6   **794.8**

1. Mathematics 2. Video games 3. Computer games 4. Computer animation 5. Vocational guidance

ISBN 978-1-60413-603-6 lib bdg; 1-60413-603-0 lib bdg

LC 2009-24173

This describes how video game designers use math to create and produce their games and includes relevant math problems and information about how to become a video game designer

Includes glossary and bibliographical references

Jozefowicz, Chris

Video game developer. Gareth Stevens Pub. 2010 32p il (Cool careers: cutting edge) lib bdg $26; pa $8.95

Grades: 4 5 6   **794.8**

1. Video games 2. Computer games 3. Vocational guidance

ISBN 978-1-4339-1958-9 lib bdg; 1-4339-1958-3 lib bdg; 978-1-4339-2157-5 pa; 1-4339-2157-X pa

LC 2008053549

This introduction to video game developer careers offers "clear, solid information in a large font. . . . [This] short [book is] packed with relevant, current material." SLJ

Includes glossary and bibliographical references

Oxlade, Chris

Gaming technology. Smart Apple Media 2011 46p il (New technology) lib bdg $34.25

Grades: 4 5 6 7   **794.8**

1. Video games 2. Computer games

ISBN 9781599205311

LC 2010044239

Describes the technology used for creating and playing video games. Includes information on how different platforms work and the direction video game technology may be going.

This "offers a fine overview for reports, and its attractive design may also entice middle-grade readers to learn more." Booklist

Includes glossary and bibliographical references

Schrier, Allyson Valentine

Gaming safely; Allyson Valentine Schrier; edited by Jennifer Besel. Capstone Press 2013 32 p. col. ill. (Fact finders. Tech safety smarts) (library binding) $26.65

Grades: 4 5 6 7   **794.8**

1. Internet games 2. Internet and children 3. Internet -- Safety measures

ISBN 1429699469; 9781429699464; 9781476515748; 9781620658000

LC 2012029268

This book by Allyson Valentine Schrier asks "if a strange character offers you a gift in an online game, do you know what to do? Dont worry if you dont. This book is here to help! Learn tech-savvy ways to keep your game sites safe sites without taking away all the fun!" (Publisher's note)

"This pertinent, practical series clearly explains safety protocols students should follow while online. The content includes how to create strong passwords, which information to share, and how to protect yourself from a cyberbully. The authors are respectful of the tween reader's ability to understand difficult realities and to put preventative measures into action." Lib Med Con

Includes bibliographical references and index

796 Athletic and outdoor sports and games

Berman, Len

The **greatest** moments in sports. Sourcebooks 2009 136p il $16.99

Grades: 5 6 7 8   **796**

1. Sports

ISBN 978-1-4022-2099-9; 1-4022-2099-5

LC 2009023686

"Forty years as a sportscaster gives Berman plenty of experience to choose the 25 greatest sports moments. His writing is lively, humorous, and informative—just right to sustain kids' (or adults') interest. Quality photos throughout are another plus. . . . An audio CD that includes many of the moments as they were broadcast live is part of the package." SLJ

Includes bibliographical references

Blumenthal, Karen

Let me play; the story of Title IX, the law that changed the future of girls in America. Atheneum Books for Young Readers 2005 152p il $19.95

Grades: 6 7 8 9 10   796

1. Women athletes 2. Sex discrimination 3. Education Amendments of 1972 -- Title IX

ISBN 0-689-85957-0

LC 2004-1450

Title IX legislation assured "that 'no one could be closed out of any educational program or activity receiving federal money simply because of sex.' After explaining the genesis of the legislation, . . . Blumenthal discusses how evolving guidelines and interpretations brought girls' school athletic programs into its purview. [Bibliography. Index.] Grades nine to twelve." (Bull Cent Child Books)

"The author looks at American women's evolving rights by focusing on the history and future of Title IX, which bans sex discrimination in U.S. education. . . . The images are . . . gripping, and relevant political cartoons and fact boxes add further interest. Few books cover the last few decades of American women's history with such clarity and detail." Booklist

Includes bibliographical references

Bodensteiner, Peter

Indy cars; Peter Bodensteiner. Black Rabbit Books 2017 (library binding) $31.35

Grades: 3 4 5   796

1. Automobile racing

ISBN 1680720317; 9781680720310; 9781680720723

LC 2015954923

This book, by Peter Bodensteiner, focuses on Indy cars. "Rev up your reading engines! Gearhead Garage is ready to take you for a ride. From screaming fast F1 cars to custom choppers, get to know what's 'under the hood' of your favorite vehicles. You're in the driver's seat now. Which book will you start with?" (Publisher's note)

"Supplementing informational text such as this are sidebars, time lines, and charts that lend visual interest and bite-sized facts, while the use of blues, oranges, and yellows throughout give each volume a comic book vibe." SLJ

Colins, Luke

Stock cars; Luke Colins. Black Rabbit Books 2017 31 p. illustrations (chiefly color) (Bolt. gearhead garage) (library binding) $31.35

Grades: 3 4 5   796

1. Automobile racing

ISBN 168072035X; 9781680720358; 9781680720747

LC 2015954680

This book, by Luke Colins, focuses on stock cars. "Rev up your reading engines! Gearhead Garage is ready to take you for a ride. From screaming fast F1 cars to custom choppers, get to know what's 'under the hood' of your favorite vehicles. You're in the driver's seat now. Which book will you start with?" (Publisher's note)

"Close-up looks at shiny chrome and glossy paint jobs are a visual feast and will have intermediate readers oohing and aahing from one page to the next." SLJ

Includes bibliographical references (page 31) and index

Connolly, Sean

The **Book** of Wildly Spectacular Sports Science; 54 All-Star Experiments. by Sean Connolly. Workman Pub Co 2016 256 p. color illustrations (ebook) $14.95; $14.95

Grades: 4 5 6 7 8   796

1. Sports   2. Science -- Experiments

ISBN 9780761189770; 0761189289; 9780761189282

This book, by Sean Connolly, presents "54 all-star experiments that demonstrate the scientific principles powering a wide variety of sports and activities. . . . Using common household objects, each project includes step-by-step instructions, tips, and a detailed explanation of how and why the experiment worked. It's a win-win." (Publisher's note)

"The chatty tone, clear scientific explanations, and broad range of athletics discussed mean there's something here for just about every kind of sports fan." Pub Wkly

Hile, Lori

Surviving extreme sports. Raintree 2011 56p il (Extreme survival) lib bdg $33.50

Grades: 4 5 6 7   796

1. Extreme sports 2. Wilderness survival

ISBN 978-1-4109-3968-5; 1-4109-3968-5

LC 2010028689

This book is "fun and informative. [This] well-organized title starts with an overview [of extreme sports], offers some specific examples, and includes additional facts or tips and resources. . . . [It features] dramatic archival and full-color photos on nearly every page. . . . [This is a book] that youngsters will enjoy and talk about." SLJ

Includes glossary and bibliographical references

Howell, Brian

Sports. ABDO Pub. Co. 2011 112p il (Inside the industry) lib bdg $23.95

Grades: 5 6 7 8   796

1. Sports -- Vocational guidance

ISBN 978-1-61714-804-0; 1-61714-804-0

LC 2010042558

This "well-designed [book describes] a variety of careers in [sports]. Because [it helps] readers assess if these positions are suitable for their personality types and backgrounds, the [title is a] good [choice] for career exploration and self-discovery. [It is] also useful for research and reports. . . . Sidebars and full-color photos appear throughout." SLJ

Includes bibliographical references

Kelley, K. C.

Weird races. Child's World 2011 24p il (Weird sports) lib bdg $25.64

Grades: 3 4 5 6   796

1. Racing

ISBN 978-1-60954-376-1; 1-60954-376-1

LC 2010042898

This describes sports such as lawnmower racing, bed racing, wife carrying, street luge, cheese rolling, and toilet racing.

"Both the writing and the visual style are exuberant-without relying too much on exclamation points." Booklist

Weird sports moments. Child's World 2011 24p il (Weird sports) lib bdg $25.64

Grades: 3 4 5 6   796

1. Sports 2. Curiosities and wonders

ISBN 978-1-60954-377-8; 1-60954-377-7

LC 2010042899

This describes weird moments in sports such as the outfield bonfire, football vs. the band, celebrating too early, and run the other way.

"Both the writing and the visual style are exuberant-without relying too much on exclamation points." Booklist

Krull, Kathleen

★ **Lives** of the athletes; thrills, spills (and what the neighbors thought) written by Kathleen Krull; illustrated by Kathryn Hewitt. Harcourt Brace & Co. 1997 96p il $21

Grades: 4 5 6 7   **796**

1. Actors 2. Athletes 3. Baseball players 4. Football players 5. Golfers 6. Surfers 7. Hurdlers 8. Swimmers 9. Decathletes 10. Ice skaters 11. High jumpers 12. Mountaineers 13. Pentathletes 14. Army officers 15. Hockey players 16. Soccer players 17. Tennis players 18. Martial artists 19. Javelin throwers 20. Olympic athletes 21. Basketball players 22. Nonfiction writers 23. Runners (Athletes) 24. Volleyball players

ISBN 0-15-200806-3

LC 95-50702

"Krull profiles twenty legendary athletes of the twentieth century who broke new ground in their sports and often broke through racial or gender barriers as well. . . . The brief biographies are enhanced by unusual details of personality and Hewitt's lively caricatures of the subjects." Horn Book

Includes bibliographical references

Mattern, Joanne

So, you want to work in sports? the ultimate guide to exploring the sports industry. Joanne Mattern. Aladdin/Beyond Words 2014 224 p. illustrations (Be what you want) (paperback) $9.99; (hardback) $18.99

Grades: 4 5 6 7 8   **796**

1. Sports 2. Vocational guidance

ISBN 1582704481; 158270449X; 9781582704487; 9781582704494

LC 2013025469

This book, by Joanne Mattern, is a "guide that can help you score a career in the sports industry. . . . From the popular careers of professional athlete, coach, sports broadcaster, and photographer, to the lesser-known professions of sports agent, statistician, sports therapist, and scout, [this book] delves into a wide variety of possible futures that are exciting and rewarding." (Publisher's note)

"Information is presented dynamically, with numerous sidebars ("Did you know...") graphs, lists, a career quiz, and hand-drawn illustrations. There are no photos. One of the book's strongest assets is its excellent resource section, including a six-page list of websites for professional organizations . . . and two pages of books and online documents." SLJ

Includes bibliographical references and index

Ralston, Birgitta

Snow play; how to make forts & slides & winter campfires plus the coolest Loch Ness monster and 23 other brrrilliant [i.e. brilliant] project in the snow. Artisan 2010 111p il $14.95

Grades: 4 5 6 7 8 9 10 11 12 Adult   **796**

1. Snow 2. Outdoor recreation

ISBN 978-1-57965-405-4; 1-57965-405-3

"Opening with explanations of different types of snow and the various tools needed to work with it, this how-to book describes more than two dozen projects, most of which will require adult help and supervision. . . . Ratings of difficulty, the number of people and tools needed, the type of snow required, and the time frame are included with each project. Short snow-related facts appear throughout. . . . A brief listing of worldwide snow festivals, snow hotels and igloos, and an ice museum completes the package. While kids can certainly use this book to inspire ideas for winter fun, adults will find it equally useful, especially for generating ideas for family projects." SLJ

Rand, Casey

Graphing sports. Heinemann Library 2009 32p il (Real world data) $28.21; pa $7.99

Grades: 5 6 7 8   **796**

1. Graphic methods 2. Sports -- Statistics

ISBN 978-1-4329-2621-2; 1-4329-2621-7; 978-1-4329-2630-4 pa; 1-4329-2630-6 pa

LC 2009001189

This explains sports related concepts through charts and graphs.

"The writing is spot-on for the audience. Most importantly, the statistics used are well chosen and instantly understandable, and the text clearly explains how each type of graph can be used to best display different types of data." SLJ

Includes glossary and bibliographical references

Rose, Julianna

Go out and play! favorite outdoor games from Kaboom! 1st ed. Candlewick Press 2011 vii, 96 p.p col. ill. (paperback) $11.99

Grades: 3 4 5   **796**

1. Games 2. Recreation

ISBN 0763655309; 9780763655303

LC 2011046634

This resource book is a "collection of 69 group games . . . to encourage children to engage in outdoor play. . . . Organized according to game type, the book focuses on versions of tag, hide-and-seek, ball games, team games, sidewalk games, circle games and races. . . . Sections at the beginning and end tell adults how to best be partners in children's play and how to create safe play spaces that will get kids outdoors." (Kirkus Reviews)

"This lively offering describes and outlines simple games that center on physical activity, including multiple versions of tag, hide-and-seek, ball games, race games, and 'no-rules games.' Each game is introduced in basic language, with a brief sidebar highlighting the number of players, recommended ages, space required, and suggested materials. Enlivened with cartoon spot art and photographs of children at play, the book should give readers plenty of activity options come spring." Publ Wkly

Includes bibliographical references.

Strother, Scott

★ The adventurous book of outdoor games; classic fun for daring boys and girls. [by] Scott Strother. Sourcebooks 2008 293p il pa $14.99

Grades: 4 5 6 7 Adult Professional   **796**

1. Games

ISBN 978-1-4022-1443-1 pa; 1-4022-1443-X pa

This book "outlines more than 100 games, each at different activity levels set by the amount of physical exertion required. . . . Each game discusses the number of players, ages, time allotted, and type of playing field, followed by a brief description of equipment, startup, object of the game, and how to play. . . . The easy-to-read, easy-to-follow format will provide hours of imaginative play for all of those who are willing to try. An excellent resource for parents, teachers, and activity directors and even for children themselves." SLJ

Watson, S. B.

Weird animal sports. Child's World 2011 24p il (Weird sports) lib bdg $25.64

Grades: 3 4 5 6   **796**

1. Sports 2. Animals 3. Curiosities and wonders

ISBN 978-1-60954-3754; 1-60954-375-0

LC 2010042897

This describes sports such as turkey bowling, frog jumping, race car hamsters, camel racing, and elephant soccer.

"Both the writing and the visual style are exuberant—without relying too much on exclamation points." Booklist

Weird sports of the world. Child's World 2011 24p il (Weird sports) lib bdg $25.64

Grades: 3 4 5 6   **796**

    1. Sports 2. Curiosities and wonders

    ISBN 978-1-60954-378-5; 1-60954-378-5

                         LC 2010042901

    This describes sports such as parkour, tough guy, unicycle hockey, mountain boarding, chess boxing, and waterfall kayaking.

    "Both the writing and the visual style are exuberant-without relying too much on exclamation points." Booklist

Weird throwing and kicking sports. Child's World 2011 24p il (Weird sports) lib bdg $25.64

Grades: 3 4 5 6   **796**

    1. Sports 2. Curiosities and wonders

    ISBN 978-1-6095-4379-2; 1-6095-4379-3

                         LC 2010044026

    This describes sports such as fish flinging, toe wrestling, stone tossing, stick kicking, and blanket riding.

    "Both the writing and the visual style are exuberant-without relying too much on exclamation points." Booklist

    Includes bibliographical references

Woods, Mark

    Xtreme! Extreme sports facts and stats; [by] Mark Woods and Ruth Owen. Gareth Stevens Pub. 2011 32p il (Top score math) lib bdg $26.60

Grades: 4 5 6   **796**

    1. Extreme sports

    ISBN 978-1-4339-5020-9; 1-4339-5020-9

                         LC 2010029612

    This book, "chock-full of numbers, presents 'facts and stats' associated with [extreme sports]. Figures include sports records, players' heights, jersey numbers, and surfing speeds. . . . [The book succeeds] at entertaining and instructing fans through engaging text and quiz challenges." Horn Book Guide

796.1   Miscellaneous games

Birmingham, Maria

    Weird zone; sports. Maria Birmingham. Owlkids Books Inc. 2013 128 p. (Weird zone) $22.95

Grades: 4 5 6 7   **796.1**

    1. Sports

    ISBN 1926973607; 9781926973609

                         LC 2012948714

    This book on unusual sports by Maria Birmingham is part of the "Weird Zone" book series. It includes such sports as "rolling down a hill in a plastic ball (aka 'zorbing') . . . professional-grade pillow fighting . . . lawn-mower racing . . . [and] extreme ironing. . . . Each sport gets a two-page spread." (Kirkus Reviews)

★ The **Eentsy**, weentsy spider: fingerplays and action rhymes; compiled by Joanna Cole and Stephanie Calmenson; illustrated by Alan Tiegreen. Morrow Junior Bks. 1991 64p il music hardcover o.p. pa $8.99

Grades: K 1 2 3   **796.1**

    1. Songs 2. Finger play

    ISBN 0-688-10805-9 pa

                         LC 90-44594

    "Tiegreen uses a few simple lines to create a cast of multicultural characters whose enthusiasm is infectious. . . . An attractive, upbeat addition to the finger-play collection." Booklist

    Includes bibliographical references

★ **Miss** Mary Mack and other children's street rhymes; compiled by Joanna Cole and Stephanie Calmenson; illustrated by Alan Tiegreen. Morrow Junior Bks. 1990 64p hardcover o.p. pa $7.95

Grades: K 1 2 3   **796.1**

    1. Games 2. Nursery rhymes

    ISBN 0-688-09749-9 pa

                         LC 89-37266

    This is a collection of over 100 traditional childhood hand-clapping and street rhymes

    "Tiegreen's lighthearted pen-and-ink illustrations are sure to tickle the fancy of young readers. . . . A book that's sure to produce smiles in any story hour or program." SLJ

796.2   Activities and games requiring equipment

Bell-Rehwoldt, Sheri

    The **kids'** guide to jumping rope. Capstone Press 2011 32p il (Kids' guides) lib bdg $26.65

Grades: 4 5 6 7   **796.2**

    1. Rope skipping

    ISBN 978-1-4296-5443-2; 1-4296-5443-0

                         LC 2010035018

    Describes the sport of jumping rope, including how-to information on jumps and tricks.

    This includes "plentiful photos of giddy girls (and a few guys) madly skipping rope. . . . This makes jumping rope look like the best time in the world." Booklist

    Includes bibliographical references

796.22   Skateboarding

Fitzpatrick, Jim

    Skateboarding. Cherry Lake Pub. 2009 32p il (Innovation in sports) lib bdg $27.07

Grades: 4 5 6 7   **796.22**

    1. Skateboarding

    ISBN 978-1-60279-259-3 lib bdg; 1-60279-259-3 lib bdg

                         LC 2008007548

    This describes skateboarding history, equipment, safety, and health benefits

    This "stands out by emphasizing monumental shifts and advances in the events themselves. . . . Concise and occasionally revelatory." Booklist

    Includes glossary and bibliographical references

Lakin, Patricia

    Skateboards; by Patricia Lakin. Aladdin 2017 32 p. color illustrations (Made by hand) (paper over board) $17.99

Grades: 3 4 5 6 7   **796.22**

    1. Board books for children 2. Skateboarding -- History 3. Skateboards -- Design and construction 4. Board books

    ISBN 9781481448338

                         LC 2016016442

    This book in the Made by Hand series, by Patricia Lakin, follows Jake Eshelman's creative process, as he plans and constructs custom skateboards for his company. "Charts, infographics, and bold photographs make this a picture book for anyone who is curious about how a skateboard is made. This book also features a history of skateboarding, a timeline, and resources to inspire kids to make their own objects by hand." (Publisher's note)

Includes bibliographical references

Spencer, Russ

Skateboarding; by Russ Spencer. Child's World 2005 32p il (Kids' guides) lib bdg $24.21

Grades: 4 5 6   **796.22**

1. Skateboarding

ISBN 1-59296-210-6

LC 2003-27370

This "opens with an explanation of the sport and gives reasons why people enjoy it. The four chapters that follow cover background and development, equipment, technique, and stars and competitions. The excellent color photos are clear and exciting." SLJ

Includes bibliographical references

Stock, Charlotte

Skateboarding step-by-step; [by] Charlotte Stock and Ben Powell. Rosen Central 2010 91p il (Skills in motion) lib bdg $31.95

Grades: 5 6 7 8   **796.22**

1. Skateboarding

ISBN 978-1-4358-3365-4; 1-4358-3365-1

LC 2009-11414

Presents instructions on skateboarding from learning to skateboard to executing jumps, flips, and tricks.

"Colorful photographs show the entire movement of each skill presented, giving new meaning to the term 'step-by-step.' Progression borders at the bottom of the pages highlight the salient points to notice in performing each skill from beginning to end." SLJ

Includes bibliographical references

796.3 Ball games

Rosen, Michael J.

Balls! : round 2; illustrations by John Margeson. Darby Creek Pub. 2008 80p il $18.95

Grades: 3 4 5 6   **796.3**

1. Sports 2. Sporting goods

ISBN 978-1-58196-066-2; 1-58196-066-2

"Rosen offers a lighthearted look at a variety of balls, covering their production and history, and how they're used in sports. . . . The author highlights balls used in baseball, softball, bowling, bocce, croquet, shot put, billiards, and lacrosse. Each sport receives a brief introduction . . . complemented by color photographs, cartoons, and graphics. There's an emphasis on fun science, with simple puzzles and experiments. . . . Rosen serves up a feast of whimsical trivia and wordplay, and he rounds out this collection with sections on marbles and extreme goofballs." SLJ

Includes bibliographical references

796.323 Basketball

Bekkering, Annalise

NCAA Basketball. Weigl Publishers 2010 32p il map (Sporting championships) lib bdg $26; pa $9.95

Grades: 3 4 5   **796.323**

1. Basketball 2. Women's National Basketball Association 3.

National Collegiate Athletic Association

ISBN 978-1-60596-634-2 lib bdg; 1-60596-634-7 lib bdg; 978-1-60596-635-9 pa; 1-60596-635-5 pa

LC 2009-8366

This sets the NCAA Basketball championship "within the context of the sport and explains what you need to know when watching the big [event]." Booklist

Includes glossary and bibliographical references

Burns, Brian

Basketball step-by-step; [by] Brian Burns and Mark Dunning. Rosen Central 2010 95p il (Skills in motion) lib bdg $31.95

Grades: 5 6 7 8   **796.323**

1. Basketball

ISBN 978-1-4358-3360-9; 1-4358-3360-0

LC 2009-14417

An introduction to the skills needed to play basketball uses a sequence of stop-action images and text instructions to illustrate such offensive and defensive moves as inside pivot and shoot, blocking out, and overhead pass.

"Colorful photographs show the entire movement of each skill presented, giving new meaning to the term 'step-by-step.' Progression borders at the bottom of the pages highlight the salient points to notice in performing each skill from beginning to end." SLJ

Includes bibliographical references

Coy, John

Game changer; John Mclendon and the secret game. by John Coy; illustrated by Randy DuBurke. Carolrhoda Picture Books 2015 32 p. (lb : alk. paper) $17.99 **796.323**

1. College basketball 2. African Americans -- Segregation 3. North Carolina College for Negroes 4. African American basketball coaches 5. Basketball coaches -- United States 6. Duke University -- Basketball -- History 7. Discrimination in sports -- United States

ISBN 1467726044; 9781467726047

LC 2015000910

Author John Coy and illustrator Randy DuBurke present a picture book that "tells the story of how one spring Sunday afternoon in 1944, two basketball teams came together to change the history of the game. The Duke University Medical School basketball team met secretly in a small gym to play against the North Carolina College of Negros in the first ever intergrated basketball game." (School Library Journal)

Includes bibliographical references and index

Hoop genius; how a desperate teacher and a rowdy gym class invented basketball. by John Coy; illustrated by Joe Morse. Carolrhoda Books 2013 32 p. (reinforced) $16.95

Grades: 2 3 4 5 6   **796.323**

1. Basketball 2. Picture books for children 3. Basketball -- United States -- History

ISBN 0761366172; 9780761366171

LC 2011021235

"In 1891, a teacher named James Naismith invented a game that was destined to become a national sensation. The boys' gym class at his school was particularly rowdy. He needed to find an indoor activity for the energetic lads that was fun, but not too rough. Inspired by a favorite childhood game, he stayed up late one night typing the rules of his new game." The class was captivated and the game's popularity spread. (School Library Journal)

Doeden, Matt

The **greatest** basketball records; by Matt Doeden. Capstone Press 2009 32p il (Sports records) lib bdg $17.95

Grades: 4 5 6 7 8 **796.323**
1. Basketball 2. National Basketball Association
ISBN 978-1-4296-2006-2 lib bdg; 1-4296-2006-4 lib bdg
LC 2008-2033
This "has enough historical insight and trivia to remain appealing over time. . . . Brief, lively sentences sum up individual feats and set them in context. . . . [This] should appeal to a wide audience." SLJ
Includes glossary and bibliographical references

Gibbons, Gail
My basketball book. HarperCollins Pubs. 2000 un il $6.99
Grades: K 1 2 **796.323**
1. Basketball
ISBN 0-688-17140-0
LC 99-87902
Introduces the basics of the game of basketball, describing the players, court, techniques, and rules of play
Includes glossary

Gifford, Clive
Basketball; [by] Clive Gifford. PowerKids Press 2009 32p il (Personal best) lib bdg $25.25
Grades: 4 5 6 7 8 **796.323**
1. Basketball
ISBN 978-1-4042-4444-3 lib bdg; 1-4042-4444-1 lib bdg
LC 2007-42989
This guide to basketball "offers well-organized and easy-to-follow instructions, focusing on rules, clothing, specific skills, and competitions. . . . Informative, readable." SLJ
Includes bibliographical references

Labrecque, Ellen
Basketball; by Ellen Labrecque. Cherry Lake Pub. 2009 32p il (Innovation in sports) lib bdg $27.07
Grades: 4 5 6 7 **796.323**
1. Basketball
ISBN 978-1-60279-256-2 lib bdg; 1-60279-256-9 lib bdg
LC 2008002044
This describes basketball history, rules, equipment, training, and great players
This "stands out by emphasizing monumental shifts and advances in the events themselves. . . . Concise and occasionally revelatory." Booklist
Includes glossary and bibliographical references

Macy, Sue, 1954-
Basketball belles; how two teams and one scrappy player put women's hoops on the map. illustrated by Matt Collins. Holiday House 2010 un il $16.95
Grades: 1 2 3 4 **796.323**
1. Women athletes 2. Basketball players 3. Basketball -- Biography 4. Women basketball players
ISBN 0-8234-2163-5; 978-0-8234-2163-3
LC 2009-42498
This book is told from the perspective of Agnes Morley, who played on Stanford University's women's basketball team. It is a play-by-play account of an 1896 game played between Morley's team and the University of California at Berkeley team. "Ages six to nine." (Bull Cent Child Books)
"In this rousing picture book, Macy and Collins take readers to the (very) early days of women's basketball through the eyes of Agnes Morley, who offers a play-by-play account of an 1896 game between Stanford and Berkeley—the first ever between two women's basketball teams. . . . Whether Agnes is wrangling with a calf on her family's ranch

or diving for a loose ball, her determination shines through in Collins's dynamic, painterly digital spreads." Publ Wkly

McClellan, Ray
Basketball. Bellwether Media 2010 24p il (Blastoff! readers. My first sports) $19.95
Grades: K 1 2 3 **796.323**
1. Basketball
ISBN 978-1-60014-279-6; 1-60014-279-6
LC 2009-8186
Simple text and full color photographs introduce beginning readers to the sport of basketball.
Includes glossary and bibliographical references

Robinson, Tom
Basketball. Norwood House Press 2010 64p il (Girls play to win) lib bdg $26.60
Grades: 4 5 6 7 **796.323**
1. Basketball
ISBN 978-1-59953-388-9; 1-59953-388-X
LC 2010009814
Covers the history, rules, fundamentals and significant personalities of the sport of women's basketball. Topics include: techniques, strategies, competitive events, and equipment.
"With an easy design and format, the [text is] highly accessible to even the most reluctant readers and [provides] great exposure and insight into the world of female professional sports." Horn Book Guide
Includes glossary and bibliographical references

Slade, Suzanne
Basketball; how it works. Capstone Press 2010 48p il (Science of sports) lib bdg $29.32; pa $7.95
Grades: 4 5 6 7 **796.323**
1. Basketball
ISBN 978-1-4296-4021-3 lib bdg; 1-4296-4021-9 lib bdg; 978-1-4296-4873-8 pa; 1-4296-4873-2 pa
The book's "photograph-heavy design works to engage its audience, while the easy-to-read [text explains] the science." Horn Book Guide
Includes glossary

Stewart, Mark
Swish; the quest for basketball's perfect shot. by Mark Stewart and Mike Kennedy. Millbrook Press 2009 64p il lib bdg $25.26
Grades: 5 6 7 8 **796.323**
1. Basketball
ISBN 978-0-8225-8752-1 lib bdg; 0-8225-8752-1 lib bdg
LC 2008-24958
"The wide pages offer plenty of room for well-spaced text, sidebars, and illustrations. Each page has at least one picture, with mostly color photos, and the many action shots make the book more exciting. With information on women's and men's basketball at both collegiate and professional levels, this is a nice addition to sports collections." Booklist
Includes bibliographical references

Thomas, Keltie
★ **How** basketball works. Maple Tree Press 2005 64p il hardcover o.p. $16.95
Grades: 5 6 7 8 **796.323**
1. Basketball
ISBN 1-89706-618-X; 1-89706-619-8 pa
This guide to basketball offers information about the game's origins, history, and equipment as well as positions, training, skills, stats, & rules of the game. It also offers tips and fascinating factoids.

"The writing style is razzle-dazzle energetic. . . . The layout features numerous sidebars and brightly colored photos and digital drawings. Even longtime fans will learn something from this engaging, enthusiastic book." Booklist

Thornley, Stew

Kevin Garnett; champion basketball star. by Stew Thornley. Enslow Publishers 2013 48 p. col. ill. (library) $23.93

Grades: 4 5 6 7   **796.323**

1. Picture books for children 2. Basketball players -- United States -- Biography

ISBN 0766040283; 9780766040281

LC 2011031517

This book by Stew Thornley is a children's picture book biography of professional basketball player Kevin Garnett. In his "career, Garnett has won MVP trophies and other individual awards, but his NBA championship ring is most important to him. The team has always come first for KG." (Publisher's note)

Includes bibliographical references (p. 47) and index.

Kobe Bryant; champion basketball star. by Stew Thornley. Enslow Publishers 2013 48 p. col. ill. (library) $23.93

Grades: 4 5 6 7   **796.323**

1. Picture books for children 2. Bryant, Kobe, 1978- 3. Basketball players -- United States -- Biography

ISBN 0766040291; 9780766040298

LC 2011038174

This picture book by Stew Thornley is a biography of professional basketball player Kobe Bryant. "He can swish shots from long range or drive to the basket for a vicious dunk. Bryant once scored 81 points in a single game! He can also dish it to his teammates and play lockdown defense. . . . The Los Angeles Lakers superstar has won five NBA titles since coming out of high school, and he has earned many individual awards." (Publisher's note)

Tim Duncan; champion basketball star. by Stew Thornley. Enslow Publishers 2013 48 p. col. ill. (Sports Star Champions) (library) $23.93

Grades: 4 5 6 7   **796.323**

1. Basketball players -- United States -- Biography

ISBN 0766040305; 9780766040304

LC 2011050440

This book by Stew Thornley is part of the Sports Star Champions series and looks at basketball player Tim Duncan. The texts "focus on the athletes' professional careers, with very little information about their personal lives. . . . Each book ends with career statistics, the player's address, and a brief list for further reading." (School Library Journal)

Includes bibliographical references (p. 47) and index.

Yancey, Diane

Basketball. Lucent Books 2011 112p il (Science behind sports) lib bdg $33.45

Grades: 5 6 7 8   **796.323**

1. Basketball

ISBN 978-1-4205-0293-0; 1-4205-0293-X

LC 2010035239

This "explores the scientific principles such as momentum, gravity, friction, and aerodynamics, plus many more, behind [basketball]. . . . [The author discusses the sport's] origins, history, and changes, . . . the biomechanics and physiology of playing, related health and medical concerns, and the causes and treatment of sports-related injuries. Additional information tells how exercise, diet and nutrition, warming up, and training relate to peak performance and enjoyment of the sport. . . . [The book] has features on possible side effects of anabolic steroid

use; how MRIs work; and how various improvements to the courts, basketballs, shoes, and uniforms have affected the game. The action photography . . . is fantastic. . . . [A must-have] for sports fans, athletes, science students, and even anyone considering a career in sports-related medicine, coaching, or other connected fields." SLJ

Includes glossary and bibliographical references

796.325   Volleyball

Crossingham, John

Spike it volleyball; [by] John Crossingham. Crabtree Pub. Co. 2008 32p il (Sports starters) lib bdg $18.95; pa $6.95

Grades: 2 3 4   **796.325**

1. Volleyball

ISBN 978-0-7787-3143-6 lib bdg; 0-7787-3143-X lib bdg; 978-0-7787-3175-7 pa; 0-7787-3175-8 pa

LC 2008004853

This "offers a sturdy overview of volleyball, from rules and scoring to basic moves. The accessible text lays out clear explanations of terms and concepts. . . . The eye-catching design combines large color photos of athletes in action with smaller inset pictures." Booklist

McDougall, Chros

Volleyball. Norwood House Press 2010 64p il (Girls play to win) lib bdg $26.60

Grades: 4 5 6 7   **796.325**

1. Volleyball

ISBN 978-1-59953-392-6; 1-59953-392-8

LC 2010009810

Covers the history, rules, fundamentals and significant personalities of the sport of women's volleyball. Topics include: techniques, strategies, competitive events, and equipment.

"With an easy design and format, the [text is] highly accessible to even the most reluctant readers and [provides] great exposure and insight into the world of female professional sports." Horn Book Guide

Includes glossary and bibliographical references

796.332   American football

Buckley, James

The **Child's** World encyclopedia of the NFL; by James Buckley, Jr. . . . [et al.] Child's World 2007 4v il

Grades: 3 4 5 6 7   **796.332**

1. Reference books 2. National Football League 3. Football -- Encyclopedias

ISBN 978-1-59296-922-7 v1; 978-1-59296-923-4 v2; 978-1-59296-924-1 v3; 978-1-59296-925-8 v4

LC 2007005662

This encyclopedia of the National Football League is "full of color photos; significant names, terms, and events; and plenty of popular football figures. The authors are all experienced sportswriters and editors." Booklist

Ultimate guide to football; by James Buckley, Jr. Franklin Watts 2010 160p il $30; pa $7.99

Grades: 4 5 6 7   **796.332**

1. Football

ISBN 978-0-531-20752-9; 0-531-20752-8; 978-0-531-21023-9 pa; 0-531-21023-5 pa

LC 2009011003

This guide to football covers "historical highlights and delectable ephemera . . . with spreads covering each NFL team interspersed among chatty tales. . . . The highlighter-green color scheme matches the loud, vibrant layout and heightens the contrasting black-and-white player photos, while sporadic cartoons add some pep to the presentation." Booklist

Includes bibliographical references

Diemer, Lauren

Rose Bowl. Weigl Publishers 2010 32p il map (Sporting championships) lib bdg $26; pa $9.95

Grades: 3 4 5   796.332

1. Football 2. Rose Bowl (Pasadena, Calif.)

ISBN 978-1-60596-638-0 lib bdg; 1-60596-638-X lib bdg; 978-1-60596-639-7 pa; 1-60596-639-8 pa

LC 2009-8362

This sets the Rose Bowl "within the context of the sport and explains what you need to know when watching the [event]." Booklist

Includes glossary and bibliographical references

Doeden, Matt

Play football like a pro; key skills and tips. Capstone Press 2011 32p il (Play like the pros) lib bdg $25.32; pa $6.95

Grades: 3 4 5   796.332

1. Football

ISBN 978-1-4296-4825-7 lib bdg; 1-4296-4825-2 lib bdg; 978-1-4296-5646-7 pa; 1-4296-5646-8 pa

LC 2010007243

"Provides instructional tips on how to improve one's football skills, including quotes and advice from professional coaches and athletes." Publisher's note

Includes glossary and bibliographical references

Dougherty, Terri

The **greatest** football records; by Terri Dougherty. Capstone Press 2009 32p il (Sports records) lib bdg $17.95

Grades: 4 5 6 7 8   796.332

1. Football 2. National Football League

ISBN 978-1-4296-2007-9 lib bdg; 1-4296-2007-2 lib bdg

LC 2008-2035

This "has enough historical insight and trivia to remain appealing over time. . . . Brief, lively sentences sum up individual feats and set them in context. . . . [This] should appeal to a wide audience." SLJ

Includes glossary and bibliographical references

Gibbons, Gail

My football book. HarperCollins Pubs. 2000 un il $6.99

Grades: K 1 2   796.332

1. Football

ISBN 0-688-17139-7

LC 99-87202

Introduces the basics of the game of football, describing the players, field, and how the game is played

"What shines through [in this book] is Gibbons's dedication to presenting the game as fun. . . . The illustrations, especially those of the players, clearly reflect the action." SLJ

Includes glossary

Gifford, Clive

Football. Marshall Cavendish Benchmark 2009 30p il (Tell me about sports) $19.95

Grades: 3 4 5   796.332

1. Football

ISBN 978-0-7614-4456-5; 0-7614-4456-4

LC 2009-4828

"An introduction to football, including techniques, rules, and the training regimen of professional athletes in the sport." Publisher's note

Includes glossary and bibliographical references

Gigliotti, Jim

Defensive backs. Gareth Stevens Pub. 2010 48p il (Game day. Football) lib bdg $31

Grades: 3 4 5   796.332

1. Football

ISBN 978-1-4339-1964-0 lib bdg; 1-4339-1964-8 lib bdg

LC 2009-6801

"The attractive page design showcases a mix of colorful photographs along with some vintage black-and-white shots, all within an attractive green border that shows yardage marks on a field. . . . This [book] . . . will generate discussion and sharing of opinions about favorite players and record book statistics." SLJ

Includes glossary and bibliographical references

Football. Cherry Lake Pub. 2009 32p il (Innovation in sports) lib bdg $27.07

Grades: 4 5 6 7   796.332

1. Football

ISBN 978-1-60279-257-9 lib bdg; 1-60279-257-7 lib bdg

LC 2008002305

This describes football history, rules, equipment, training and strategy, and innovators

This "stands out by emphasizing monumental shifts and advances in the events themselves. . . . Concise and occasionally revelatory." Booklist

Includes glossary and bibliographical references

Linebackers. Gareth Stevens Pub. 2010 48p il (Game day. Football) lib bdg $31

Grades: 3 4 5   796.332

1. Football

ISBN 978-1-4339-1959-6 lib bdg; 1-4339-1959-1 lib bdg

LC 2009-6802

"The attractive page design showcases a mix of colorful photographs along with some vintage black-and-white shots, all within an attractive green border that shows yardage marks on a field. . . . This [book] . . . will generate discussion and sharing of opinions about favorite players and record book statistics." SLJ

Includes glossary and bibliographical references

Linemen. Gareth Stevens Pub. 2010 48p il (Game day. Football) lib bdg $31

Grades: 3 4 5   796.332

1. Football

ISBN 978-1-4339-1960-2 lib bdg; 1-4339-1960-5 lib bdg

LC 2009-2272

"The attractive page design showcases a mix of colorful photographs along with some vintage black-and-white shots, all within an attractive green border that shows yardage marks on a field. . . . This [book] . . . will generate discussion and sharing of opinions about favorite players and record book statistics." SLJ

Includes glossary and bibliographical references

Receivers. Gareth Stevens Pub. 2010 48p il (Game day. Football) lib bdg $31

Grades: 3 4 5   796.332

1. Football

ISBN 978-1-4339-1962-6 lib bdg; 1-4339-1962-1 lib bdg

LC 2008-55595

"The attractive page design showcases a mix of colorful photographs along with some vintage black-and-white shots, all within an attractive green border that shows yardage marks on a field. . . . This [book] . . . will generate discussion and sharing of opinions about favorite players and record book statistics." SLJ

Includes glossary and bibliographical references

Kelley, K. C.

Quarterbacks. Gareth Stevens Pub. 2010 48p il (Game day. Football) lib bdg $31

Grades: 3 4 5   **796.332**

1. Football

ISBN 978-1-4339-1961-9 lib bdg; 1-4339-1961-3 lib bdg

LC 2008-55596

"The attractive page design showcases a mix of colorful photographs along with some vintage black-and-white shots, all within an attractive green border that shows yardage marks on a field. . . . This [book] . . . will generate discussion and sharing of opinions about favorite players and record book statistics." SLJ

Includes glossary and bibliographical references

Running backs. Gareth Stevens Pub. 2010 48p il (Game day. Football) lib bdg $31

Grades: 3 4 5   **796.332**

1. Football

ISBN 978-1-4339-1963-3 lib bdg; 1-4339-1963-X lib bdg

LC 2009-2277

"The attractive page design showcases a mix of colorful photographs along with some vintage black-and-white shots, all within an attractive green border that shows yardage marks on a field. . . . This [book] . . . will generate discussion and sharing of opinions about favorite players and record book statistics." SLJ

Includes glossary and bibliographical references

Marsico, Katie

Football; by Katie Marsico and Cecilia Minden. Cherry Lake Pub. 2009 32p il (Real world math: Sports) lib bdg $27.07

Grades: 4 5 6   **796.332**

1. Football 2. Arithmetic

ISBN 978-1-60279-247-0 lib bdg; 1-60279-247-X lib bdg

LC 2008-1165

This book "starts with a short story on the history of [football], fundamental rules, and a math challenge in every chapter. . . . [This book] will pique your imagination." Sci Books Films

Includes glossary and bibliographical references

McClellan, Ray

Football. Bellwether Media 2010 24p il (Blastoff! readers. My first sports) $19.95

Grades: K 1 2 3   **796.332**

1. Football

ISBN 978-1-60014-194-2; 1-60014-194-3

LC 2009-8187

"Simple text and full color photographs introduce beginning readers to the sport of football." Publisher's note

Includes glossary and bibliographical references

Rappoport, Ken

Peyton Manning; champion football star. by Ken Rappoport. Enslow Publishers 2013 48 p. col. ill. (Sports Star Champions) (library) $23.93

Grades: 4 5 6 7   **796.332**

1. Quarterbacks (Football) 2. Football players -- United States --

Biography 3. Quarterbacks (Football) -- United States -- Biography

ISBN 0766040275; 9780766040274

LC 2011052759

This book is part of the Sports Star Champion series and looks at quarterback Peyton Manning. The "texts focus on the athletes' professional careers, with very little information about their personal lives. Occasional sidebars add additional interest, and each book ends with career statistics, the player's address, and a brief list for further reading." (School Library Journal)

Includes bibliographical references (p. 47) and index.

Stewart, Mark

Touchdown; the power and precision of football's perfect play. by Mark Stewart and Mike Kennedy. Millbrook Press 2009 64p il lib bdg $27.93

Grades: 5 6 7 8   **796.332**

1. Football

ISBN 978-0-8225-8751-4 lib bdg; 0-8225-8751-3 lib bdg

LC 2008044295

"This attractive book opens with an intriguing history of American football. . . . Next, 10 double-page spreads feature 'Ten Unforgettable Touchdowns' in both professional and collegiate games from 1913 to 2006. After a chapter on 'touchdown makers,' spotlighting outstanding players . . . comes a short section on notable touchdown bloopers and another on trick plays and the element of surprise. . . . Photos, period prints, and reproductions of trading cards illustrate the text while adding color to the pages. . . . This nicely designed book provides plenty of on-the-field drama as well as pertinent information in a smoothly written overview of the touchdown." Booklist

Thomas, Keltie

How football works; illustrated by Stephen MacEachern. Owlkids 2010 64p il (How sports work) $22.95; pa $12.95

Grades: 3 4 5   **796.332**

1. Football

ISBN 978-1-897349-87-8; 1-897349-87-4; 978-1-897349-88-5 pa; 1-897349-88-2 pa

"A wide range of football facts are packed into every double-page spread of this picture-book overview of the sport. The covered topics include the history of the game, the changing turf of the NFL, equipment, and some of the most memorable clashes and players. Each short chapter is laid out with boxes containing a few paragraphs of information, along with color photos and illustrations. Young readers are bound to enjoy this browser-friendly approach, which presents an array of facts that can be absorbed quickly." Booklist

796.334   Soccer (Association football)

Bazemore, Suzanne

Soccer : how it works. Capstone Press 2010 48p il (Science of sports) lib bdg $29.32; pa $7.95

Grades: 4 5 6 7   **796.334**

1. Soccer

ISBN 978-1-4296-4025-1 lib bdg; 1-4296-4025-1 lib bdg; 978-1-4296-4876-9 pa; 1-4296-4876-7 pa

"Describes the science behind the sport of soccer, including kicking, ball control, and goalkeeping." Publisher's note

Includes glossary

Forest, Christopher

Play soccer like a pro; key skills and tips. Capstone Press 2011 32p il (Play like the pros) lib bdg $25.32; pa $6.95

Grades: 3 4 5   **796.334**
1. Soccer
ISBN 978-1-4296-4827-1 lib bdg; 1-4296-4827-9 lib bdg; 978-1-4296-5647-4 pa; 1-4296-5647-6 pa

LC 2010007244

"Provides instructional tips on how to improve one's soccer skills, including quotes and advice from professional coaches and athletes." Publisher's note

Includes glossary and bibliographical references

Gibbons, Gail
My soccer book. HarperCollins Pubs. 2000 un il $6.99
Grades: K 1 2   **796.334**
1. Soccer
ISBN 0-688-17138-9

LC 99-34514

Briefly describes the equipment, terminology, rules, positions, and plays of one of the world's most popular games

This "small, snappily designed book [is] attractive, accessible. . . . Diverse groups of children, drawn in Gibbons' typically bright colors and cheery style, demonstrate sports equipment and game plays." Booklist

Includes glossary

Gifford, Clive
The **Kingfisher** soccer encyclopedia. Kingfisher 2010 144p il $19.99
Grades: 5 6 7 8   **796.334**
1. Reference books 2. Soccer -- Encyclopedias
ISBN 978-0-7534-6397-0; 0-7534-6397-0
First published 2006

"Gifford does an excellent job of covering most aspects of the game from its history of a hundred-plus years to its current rules and tactics, teams, competitions, and famous players. Each section is clearly identified and provides additional information about the game. . . . Students involved in the sport or interested in specific teams or players will appreciate this book." Voice Youth Advocates

Includes glossary and bibliographical references

My first soccer book; Clive Gifford. Kingfisher 2012 48 p. col. ill. (hardcover) $12.99
Grades: 2 3 4   **796.334**
1. Soccer 2. Soccer -- Training
ISBN 0753467836; 9780753467831

LC 2012036444

In this children's picture book about soccer, "[Clive] Gifford discusses the field, positions, gear, and basic rules, then moves on to warm-ups and stretching. The book's main section offers double-page spreads on topics such as ball control, passing, shooting, goalkeeping, tackling, and paying attention to the referee." (Booklist)

Soccer; Clive Gifford. 1st ed. PowerKids Press 2009 32 p. col. ill. (Personal best) (library) $26.50
Grades: 4 5 6 7 8   **796.334**
1. Soccer
ISBN 9781404244412; 1404244417

LC 2007042997

This guide to soccer "offers well-organized and easy-to-follow instructions, focusing on rules, clothing, specific skills, and competitions. . . . Informative, readable." SLJ

Soccer skills; Clive Gifford. Kingfisher 2005 48 p. col. ill. (paperback) $6.99

Grades: 4 5 6   **796.334**
1. Soccer -- Training
ISBN 0753459329; 9780753459324

LC 2005006232

This book presents an "overview of tactics and moves for beginning soccer players by a well-known expert in the field. After an initial chapter on referees and rules, [Clive] Gifford goes on to ball control, various passing techniques, and shooting and tacking skills. Four pages are devoted to goaltending. The text consists of brief paragraphs of information placed around the illustrations rather than a flowing narrative." (School Library Journal)

Includes bibliographical references (p. 47) and index.

Guillain, Charlotte
Soccer. Heinemann Library 2009 24p il (Sports and my body) lib bdg $21.36; pa $6.49
Grades: 1 2   **796.334**
1. Soccer
ISBN 978-1-4329-3456-9 lib bdg; 1-4329-3456-2 lib bdg; 978-1-4329-3461-3 pa; 1-4329-3461-9 pa

LC 2009-7082

Learn what soccer is, how it can help them stay healthy, and how they can play soccer safely.

This book relates "activity to health . . . [and] explains that in order to stay healthy, children should get plenty of rest, eat healthy food, and drink plenty of water." SLJ

Includes glossary

Hornby, Hugh
Soccer; written by Hugh Hornby; photographed by Andy Crawford. DK Pub. 2008 70p il (DK eyewitness books) $15.99
Grades: 4 5 6 7   **796.334**
1. Soccer
ISBN 978-0-7566-3779-8; 0-7566-3779-1

LC 2008276290

First published 2000

Examines all aspects of the game of soccer: its history, rules, techniques, tactics, equipment, playing fields, competitive play, and more.

Hyde, Natalie
Soccer science. Crabtree Pub. Co. 2009 32p il (Sports science) lib bdg $26.60; pa $8.95
Grades: 3 4 5 6   **796.334**
1. Soccer
ISBN 978-0-7787-4537-2 lib bdg; 0-7787-4537-6 lib bdg; 978-0-7787-4554-9 pa; 0-7787-4554-6 pa

LC 2008-46276

This book approachs soccer "from a scientific angle, describing some of the physics behind [the] pursuit and how athletes can use this knowledge to improve performance. . . . Fascinating facts . . . [such as] information about the soccer robots in the RoboCup, are presented in a captivating, lively manner. . . . The layout features colorful text boxes interspersed among photographs." SLJ

Includes glossary

Jennings, Madeleine
Soccer step-by-step; [by] Madeleine Jennings and Ian Howe. Rosen Central 2010 95p il (Skills in motion) lib bdg $31.95
Grades: 5 6 7 8   **796.334**
1. Soccer
ISBN 978-1-4358-3362-3; 1-4358-3362-7

LC 2009-12538

Presents instructions on the basic movements of soccer, including passing, shooting, and goalkeeping.

"Colorful photographs show the entire movement of each skill presented, giving new meaning to the term 'step-by-step.' Progression borders at the bottom of the pages highlight the salient points to notice in performing each skill from beginning to end." SLJ

Includes bibliographical references

Kassouf, Jeff
    Soccer. Norwood House Press 2011 64p il (Girls play to win) lib bdg $26.60
Grades: 4 5 6 7   **796.334**
    1. Soccer
    ISBN 978-1-59953-464-0; 1-59953-464-9

LC 2011011037

Covers the history, rules, fundamentals, and significant personalities of the sport of women's soccer. Topics include: techniques, strategies, competitive events, and equipment.

Includes glossary and bibliographical references

Kelley, K. C.
    Soccer. Cherry Lake Pub. 2008 32p il (Innovation in sports) lib bdg $27.07
Grades: 4 5 6 7   **796.334**
    1. Soccer
    ISBN 978-1-60279-261-6 lib bdg; 1-60279-261-5 lib bdg

LC 2008006749

This describes soccer history, rules, styles of play, equipment, and innovators

This "stands out by emphasizing monumental shifts and advances in the events themselves. . . . Concise and occasionally revelatory." Booklist

Includes glossary and bibliographical references

Stewart, Mark
    ★ **Goal!** : the fire and fury of soccer's greatest moment; [by] Mark Stewart and Mike Kennedy. Millbrook Press 2010 64p il lib bdg $27.93
Grades: 5 6 7 8   **796.334**
    1. Soccer
    ISBN 978-0-8225-8754-5 lib bdg; 0-8225-8754-8 lib bdg

LC 2009014098

"This well-written book explores the nuances of scoring in the world's most popular sport. A quick history of the game lays the groundwork with details that may be new to even hard-core fans. The second chapter jumps right into the good stuff with descriptions of 10 of the most famous goals. . . . Also included is a rundown of the best male and female scorers from the early twentieth century to the present and weird anomalies and amusing anecdotes from soccer lore." Booklist

Wendorff, Anne
    Soccer. Bellwether Media 2010 24p il (Blastoff! readers. My first sports) $19.95
Grades: K 1 2 3   **796.334**
    1. Soccer
    ISBN 978-1-60014-329-8; 1-60014-329-6

LC 2009-8183

"Simple text and full color photographs introduce beginning readers to the sport of soccer." Publisher's note

Includes glossary and bibliographical references

Woods, Mark
    Goal! soccer facts and stats. [by] Mark Woods and Ruth Owen. Gareth Stevens Pub. 2011 32p il (Top score math) lib bdg $26.60

Grades: 4 5 6   **796.334**
    1. Soccer
    ISBN 978-1-4339-5015-5; 1-4339-501505

LC 2010029686

This book, "chock-full of numbers, presents 'facts and stats' associated with [soccer]. Figures include sports records, players' heights, jersey numbers, and surfing speeds. . . . [The book succeeds] at entertaining and instructing fans through engaging text and quiz challenges." Horn Book Guide

Includes glossary

796.34   Racket games

Smolka, Bo
    Lacrosse. Norwood House Press 2011 64p il (Girls play to win) lib bdg $26.60
Grades: 4 5 6 7   **796.34**
    1. Lacrosse
    ISBN 978-1-59953-463-3; 1-59953-463-0

LC 2011011050

Covers the history, rules, fundamentals, and significant personalities of the sport of women's lacrosse. Topics include: techniques, strategies, competitive events, and equipment.

Includes glossary and bibliographical references

796.342   Tennis (Lawn tennis)

Bildner, Phil
    Martina & Chrissie; the greatest rivalry in the history of sports. Phil Bildner; illustrated by Brett Helquist. Candlewick Press 2017 40 p. color illustrations $16.99
Grades: 1 2 3 4   **796.342**
    1. Tennis players -- Biography
    ISBN 0763673080; 9780763673086

LC 2017009508

In this dual biography, by Phil Bildner, illustrated by Brett Helquist, "Martina Navratilova and Chris Evert come from completely different places and play tennis in completely different ways. Chrissie is the all-American girl: practiced, poised, with perfect technique. Martina hails from Czechoslovakia, a Communist country, and her game is ruled by emotion. Everything about them is different, except one thing: they both want to be the best." (Publisher's note)

"The dramatic cover and well-designed pages will draw readers in and make them feel they have courtside seats. A fine sports story." Kirkus

Includes bibliographical references.

Bow, Patricia
    Tennis science. Crabtree Pub. Co. 2009 32p il (Sports science) lib bdg $26.60; pa $8.95
Grades: 3 4 5 6   **796.342**
    1. Tennis
    ISBN 978-0-7787-4539-6 lib bdg; 0-7787-4539-2 lib bdg; 978-0-7787-4556-3 pa; 0-7787-4556-2 pa

LC 2008-48874

This book approachs tennis "from a scientific angle, describing some of the physics behind [the] pursuit and how athletes can use this knowledge to improve performance. . . . Fascinating facts . . . are presented in a captivating, lively manner. . . . The layout features colorful text boxes interspersed among photographs." SLJ

Includes glossary and bibliographical references

Gifford, Clive

Tennis; [by] Clive Gifford. Sea-to-Sea Publications 2009 30p il (Know your sport) lib bdg $27.10

Grades: 5 6 7 8   796.342

1. Tennis

ISBN 978-1-59771-153-1 lib bdg; 1-59771-153-5 lib bdg

LC 2008-7322

"Describes the equipment, courts, training, moves, and competitions of tennis. Includes step-by-step descriptions of moves." Publisher's note

Includes glossary

Marsico, Katie

Tennis; [by] Katie Marsico and Cecilia Minden. Cherry Lake Pub. 2009 32p il (Real world math: Sports) lib bdg $27.07

Grades: 4 5 6   796.342

1. Tennis 2. Arithmetic

ISBN 978-1-60279-248-7 lib bdg; 1-60279-248-8 lib bdg

LC 2008-1179

This book "starts with a short story on the history of [tennis], fundamental rules, and a math challenge in every chapter. . . . [This book] will pique your imagination." Sci Books Films

Includes glossary and bibliographical references

Wendorff, Anne

Tennis. Bellwether Media 2010 24p il (Blastoff! readers. My first sports) $19.95

Grades: K 1 2 3   796.342

1. Tennis

ISBN 978-1-60014-328-1; 1-60014-328-8

LC 2009-8188

"Simple text and full color photographs introduce beginning readers to the sport of tennis." Publisher's note

Includes glossary and bibliographical references

Woods, Mark

Ace! tennis facts and stats. [by] Mark Woods and Ruth Owen. Gareth Stevens Pub. 2011 32p il (Top score math) lib bdg $26.60

Grades: 4 5 6   796.342

1. Tennis

ISBN 978-1-4339-4986-9; 1-4339-4986-9

LC 2010025704

This book, "chock-full of numbers, presents 'facts and stats' associated with [tennis]. Figures include sports records, players' heights, jersey numbers, and surfing speeds. . . . [The book succeeds] at entertaining and instructing fans through engaging text and quiz challenges." Horn Book Guide

796.352 Golf

Gifford, Clive

Golf : from tee to green; the essential guide for young golfers. Sea-to-Sea Publications 2010 64p il (Know your sport) $16.99

Grades: 5 6 7 8   796.352

1. Golf

ISBN 978-1-59771-217-0; 1-59771-217-5

LC 2008045861

Presents an instructional guide to the sport of golf, with information on different aspects of play and the equipment used.

"This book will be welcomed by young golf enthusiasts, whether they're beginners or experienced players. . . . A useful and attractive guide." Horn Book Guide

Includes bibliographical references

Kelley, K. C.

Golf. Cherry Lake Pub. 2009 32p il (Innovation in sports) lib bdg $27.07

Grades: 4 5 6 7   796.352

1. Golf

ISBN 978-1-60279-262-3 lib bdg; 1-60279-262-3 lib bdg

LC 2008002045

This describes golf history, rules, balls, and club technology, and innovators

This "stands out by emphasizing monumental shifts and advances in the events themselves. . . . Concise and occasionally revelatory." Booklist

Includes bibliographical references

Michelson, Richard

Twice as good; the story of William Powell and clearview, the only golf course designed, built and owned by an African-American. written by Richard Michelson; illlustrated by Eric Velasquez. Sleeping Bear Press 2011 32 p. col. ill. $16.95

Grades: 2 3 4   796.352

1. African American businesspeople 2. Golfers -- United States -- Biography 3. Discrimination in sports 4. Golf course architects -- United States -- Biography 5. Golf courses -- United States -- Design and construction -- History

ISBN 1585364665; 9781585364664

LC 2011029114

This children's picture book tells the story of "Willie Powell . . . [who] dreamed of becoming a professional golfer, but his accomplishments went far beyond playing the game of golf. Willie was often denied the opportunity to play golf because he was African American. Determined, he decided to build his own course, and welcome people of all color to play golf." (Publisher's note)

"An inspirational story, suitable for Black History Month and for children interested in the game of golf." LJ

Webster, Christine

Masters Golf Tournament. Weigl Publishers 2009 32p il map (Sporting championships) lib bdg $26; pa $9.95

Grades: 3 4 5   796.352

1. Golf

ISBN 978-1-60596-640-3 lib bdg; 1-60596-640-1 lib bdg; 978-1-60596-641-0 pa; 1-60596-641-X pa

LC 2009-12346

This sets the Masters Golf Tournament "within the context of the sport and explains what you need to know when watching the big [event]." Booklist

Includes glossary and bibliographical references

796.357 Baseball

Adler, David A.

A picture book of Jackie Robinson; illustrated by Robert Casilla. Holiday House 1994 un il $17.95; pa $6.95

Grades: 1 2 3   796.357

1. Baseball players 2. African American athletes 3. Army officers 4. Baseball -- Biography

ISBN 0-8234-1122-2; 0-8234-1304-7 pa

LC 93-27224

"A brief look at the life of baseball great Jackie Robinson. The subject's childhood, sporting accomplishments, and later endeavors are touched upon, as are the bigotry and prejudice he faced as the first African American to play in the major leagues. . . . Casilla's full-and double-page watercolors provide attractive backgrounds for the text. A sound introduction to a significant figure." SLJ

Bertoletti, John C.

How baseball managers use math; math curriculum consultant: Rhea A. Stewart. Chelsea Clubhouse 2010 32p il (Math in the real world) lib bdg $28

Grades: 4 5 6   **796.357**

1. Baseball 2. Mathematics 3. Vocational guidance

ISBN 978-1-60413-604-3 lib bdg; 1-60413-604-9 lib bdg

LC 2009-16265

"The layout for [this] slim [title] is bright and colorful with a photograph and a 'You Do the Math' problem to solve and large, easy-to-read text on every spread. An answer key is included in the back matter, along with a page detailing the career choices and the educational requirements. . . . [It] includes such topics as how managers rely on player statistics to make decisions and why the pitch count is important to monitor. [This title] would be useful to supplement lessons on mathematics. [It] will also appeal to students wanting to learn more about math as it relates to specific careers." SLJ

Includes glossary and bibliographical references

Bildner, Phil

★ The unforgettable season; the story of Joe DiMaggio, Ted Williams and the record-setting summer of '41. illustrated by S. D. Schindler. G. P. Putnam's Sons 2011 un il $16.99

Grades: 1 2 3   **796.357**

1. Baseball 2. Baseball players 3. Baseball managers 4. Baseball -- History

ISBN 978-0-399-25501-4; 0-399-25501-X

LC 2010007382

"In a narrative that's conversational yet informative, Bildner dives into the baseball season of 1941, alternately focusing on Yankee slugger DiMaggio, who had a 56-game hitting streak, and Red Sox star Williams, who ended the season with a batting average of .406. Bildner builds suspense with taut descriptions of critical on-field moments . . . while Schindler's paintings capture the ballpark energy." Publ Wkly

Bow, James

Baseball science. Crabtree Pub. 2009 32p il (Sports science) lib bdg $26.60; pa $8.95

Grades: 3 4 5 6   **796.357**

1. Baseball

ISBN 978-0-7787-4534-1 lib bdg; 0-7787-4534-1 lib bdg; 978-0-7787-4551-8 pa; 0-7787-4551-1 pa

LC 2008-46274

This describes baseball skills and techniques from a scientific point of view.

Includes glossary and bibliographical references

Buckley, James

Ultimate guide to baseball. Shoreline Pub. 2010 160p il $30; pa $7.99

Grades: 4 5 6 7   **796.357**

1. Baseball

ISBN 978-0-531-20750-5; 0-531-20750-1; 978-0-531-21021-5 pa; 0-531-21021-9 pa

LC 2009043684

"This is a wide-ranging, brisk overview of the game. Sections briefly skim baseball history, hitting, pitching, defense and baserunning, and the World Series. Each major league team is introduced in a thumbnail sketch. . . . Other topics include baseball slang and nicknames, the 11 ways to get on base, and the author's choices for the best defensive play-

ers of all time. . . . Buckley writes with a lightly humorous touch that should appeal to fans and browsers." SLJ

Includes bibliographical references

Bugler, Beth,

My first book of baseball; The Editors of Sports Illustrated Kids. Time Home Entertainment Inc 2016 48 p. color illustrations (SI Kids rookie books.) $11.95

Grades: PreK K 1   **796.357**

1. Baseball

ISBN 1618931679; 9781618931672

This book in the Sports Illustrated Kids series by the Editors of Sports Illustrated Kids "coaches young kids through the game of baseball with a visual retelling of an actual MLB game--from the first pitch to the game winning hit! Strikes, outs, steals, foul balls, home runs and more are all explained using a fun mix of Sports Illustrated action photography, simple text with engaging graphics, and a full glossary of essential baseball terms and phrases." (Publisher's note)

"While there are other suitable introductory books on baseball for youngsters, readers will find the presentation of information enjoyable. Libraries would do well to add this option to their collections." SLJ

Child's World (Firm)

The Child's World encyclopedia of baseball; by James Buckley, Jr. . . . [et al.] Child's World 2009 5v il set $247.75

Grades: 4 5 6 7 8   **796.357**

1. Baseball -- Encyclopedias

ISBN 978-1-60253-175-8 set; 1-60253-175-7 set

LC 2008039461

In this baseball encyclopedia, the authors "definitely convey an enthusiasm for their subject." Booklist

Coleman, Janet Wyman

Baseball for everyone; stories from the great game. by Janet Wyman Coleman with Elizabeth V. Warren. Abrams 2003 48p il $16.95

Grades: 4 5 6   **796.357**

1. Baseball

ISBN 0-8109-4580-0

LC 2002-155971

An illustrated history of baseball, covering the origins of the game, some of its best-known players, and significant changes in rules and practices throughout the nineteenth and twentieth centuries

"Drawing on The Perfect Game, Warren's adult book and exhibit of the same name at New York's American Folk Art Museum, . . . this elegant volume may well be irresistible to fans of America's favorite pastime. . . . [This offers] lively, informative text . . . enticingly packaged with a plethora of photographs, memorabilia and often astonishing folk art." Publ Wkly

Cook, Sally

Hey batta batta swing! the wild old days of baseball. [by] Sally Cook & James Charlton; illustrated by Ross MacDonald. Margaret K. McElderry Books 2007 48p il $17.99

Grades: 3 4 5 6   **796.357**

1. Baseball

ISBN 978-1-4169-1207-1; 1-4169-1207-X

LC 2006-08132

"The authors present a lively, puckish history of baseball's earliest years, relating what young readers actually want to know. . . . Boldface words in the text identify jargon, most of which is still used today, and definitions stud the page borders. The jaunty tone is flawlessly matched by MacDonald's illustrations, with their wriggling lines and Katzenjammer Kids colors." Booklist

Curlee, Lynn

★ **Ballpark**; the story of America's baseball fields. Atheneum Books for Young Readers 2005 41p il $17.95

Grades: 3 4 5 6   796.357

1. Baseball 2. Stadiums

ISBN 0-689-86742-5

LC 2003-23144

This is a "succinct and thoughtful overview. . . . Stylized, full-page acrylic paintings add to the nostalgic tone of the book." SLJ

Doeden, Matt

The **World** Series; baseball's biggest stage. by Matt Doeden. Millbrook Press, A division of Lerner Publishing Group, Inc. 2014 64 p. (lib. bdg. : alk. paper) $33.27

Grades: 4 5 6 7   796.357

1. Baseball 2. World Series (Baseball) -- History

ISBN 1467718963; 9781467718967

LC 2013018082

This book describes how "when the top teams face off in the World Series each season, team legacies and fans' hearts are on the line. Author Matt Doeden covers the century-long history of the World Series, from its humble beginnings to becoming a worldwide sensation. Discover the drama behind the statistics and record books that keeps the crowd enthralled!" (Publisher's note)

"This valentine to the Fall Classic opens with a quick history--though only through the 2012 series--then goes on in separate chapters to highlight renowned games, awesome individual performances, and memorable plays or incidents. . . . The color photos on every spread are almost all action shots and capture the excitement of each feat or moment." Booklist

Includes bibliographical references (p. 62) and index

Dreier, David

Baseball; how it works. Capstone Press 2010 48p il (Science of sports) lib bdg $29.32; pa $7.95

Grades: 4 5 6 7   796.357

1. Baseball

ISBN 978-1-4296-4020-6 lib bdg; 1-4296-4020-0 lib bdg; 978-1-4296-4872-1 pa; 1-4296-4872-4 pa

"The well-designed layout, featuring glossy color visuals, is stimulating, and the concepts are further reinforced in brief definitions that appear at the bottom of many pages and in an appended glossary. . . . The clever approach will help draw interest and build understanding." Booklist

Includes glossary

Gibbons, Gail

My baseball book. HarperCollins Pubs. 2000 un il $6.99

Grades: K 1 2   796.357

1. Baseball

ISBN 0-688-17137-0

LC 99-32945

An introduction to baseball, describing the equipment, playing field, rules, players, and process of the game

"The information is well augmented by clearly labeled, colorful drawings." SLJ

Includes glossary

Gitlin, Marty

Softball. Norwood House Press 2011 64p il (Girls play to win) lib bdg $26.60

Grades: 4 5 6 7   796.357

1. Softball

ISBN 978-1-59953-465-7; 1-59953-465-7

LC 2011011051

Covers the history, rules, fundamentals, and significant personalities of the sport of women's softball. Topics include: techniques, strategies, competitive events, and equipment.

Includes glossary and bibliographical references

Glaser, Jason

Batter. Gareth Stevens 2011 48p il (Play ball: baseball) lib bdg $31.95; pa $14.05; ebook $31.95

Grades: K 1 2 3   796.357

1. Baseball

ISBN 978-1-4339-4619-6 lib bdg; 1-4339-4619-X lib bdg; 978-1-4339-4620-2 pa; 1-4339-4620-2 pa; 978-1-4339-4622-6 ebook

LC 2010039132

"A well-conceived, up-to-date look at the particular skills needed to play [batter] in baseball. [This] volume discusses the [batter's] evolution through baseball history, describes the player's responsibilities during games, and highlights famous players. Clearly written and amply illustrated with photos of recent and current stars, [this book offers] solid information for young baseballers and casual fans alike." Horn Book Guide

Includes glossary and bibliographical references

Catcher. Gareth Stevens Pub. 2011 48p il (Play ball: baseball) lib bdg $31.95

Grades: K 1 2 3   796.357

1. Baseball

ISBN 9781433944840 pa; 9781433944833 lib bdg

LC 2010035720

"A well-conceived, up-to-date look at the particular skills needed to play [catcher] in baseball. [This] volume discusses the [catcher's] evolution through baseball history, describes the player's responsibilities during games, and highlights famous players. Clearly written and amply illustrated with photos of recent and current stars, [this book offers] solid information for young baseballers and casual fans alike." Horn Book Guide

Infielders. Gareth Stevens 2011 48p il (Play ball: baseball) lib bdg $31.95; pa $14.05; e-book $31.95

Grades: K 1 2 3   796.357

1. Baseball

ISBN 978-1-4339-4487-1 lib bdg; 1-4339-4487-1 lib bdg; 978-1-4339-4488-8 pa; 1-4339-4488-X pa; 987-1-4339-4490-1 e-book

LC 2010026667

"A well-conceived, up-to-date look at the particular skills needed to play [infield] in baseball. [This] volume discusses the [infielder's] evolution through baseball history, describes the player's responsibilities during games, and highlights famous players. Clearly written and amply illustrated with photos of recent and current stars, [this book offers] solid information for young baseballers and casual fans alike." Horn Book Guide

Outfielders. Gareth Stevens 2011 48p il (Play ball: baseball) lib bdg $31.95; pa $14.05; e-book $31.95

Grades: K 1 2 3   796.357

1. Baseball

ISBN 978-1-4339-4491-8 lib bdg; 1-4339-4491-8 lib bdg; 978-1-4339-4492-5 pa; 1-4339-4492-5 pa; 978-1-4339-4494-9 e-book

LC 2010030690

"A well-conceived, up-to-date look at the particular skills needed to play [outfield] in baseball. [This] volume discusses the [outfielder's]

evolution through baseball history, describes the player's responsibilities during games, and highlights famous players. Clearly written and amply illustrated with photos of recent and current stars, [this book offers] solid information for young baseballers and casual fans alike." Horn Book Guide

Includes glossary and bibliographical references

Pitcher. Gareth Stevens 2011 48p il (Play ball: baseball) lib bdg $31.95; pa $14.05; ebook $31.95

Grades: K 1 2 3   **796.357**
1. Baseball
ISBN 978-1-4339-4495-6 lib bdg; 1-4339-4495-2 lib bdg; 978-1-4339-4496-3 pa; 1-4339-4496-3 pa; 978-1-4339-4498-7 ebook

       LC 2010039136

"A well-conceived, up-to-date look at the particular skills needed to play [pitcher] in baseball. [This] volume discusses the [pitcher's] evolution through baseball history, describes the player's responsibilities during games, and highlights famous players. Clearly written and amply illustrated with photos of recent and current stars, [this book offers] solid information for young baseballers and casual fans alike." Horn Book Guide

Includes glossary and bibliographical references

Golenbock, Peter
★ **Hank** Aaron; brave in every way. illustrated by Paul Lee. Harcourt 2001 un il $16

Grades: 1 2 3   **796.357**
1. Baseball players 2. African American athletes 3. Baseball -- Biography
ISBN 0-15-202093-4

       LC 00-8855

A biography of the Hall of Fame baseball player who broke Babe Ruth's career home run record

"This richly illustrated biography . . . deftly tells the athlete's story. . . . Lee's strong, full-page acrylic illustrations in rich tones and textures work well and give the story depth and intensity." SLJ

Teammates; written by Peter Golenbock; designed and illustrated by Paul Bacon. Harcourt Brace Jovanovich 1990 un il $16; pa $7

Grades: 1 2 3 4   **796.357**
1. Baseball players 2. African American athletes 3. Army officers 4. Baseball -- Biography 5. Brooklyn Dodgers (Baseball team)
ISBN 0-15-200603-6; 0-15-284286-1 pa

       LC 89-38166

Describes the racial prejudice experienced by Jackie Robinson when he joined the Brooklyn Dodgers and became the first black player in Major League baseball and depicts the acceptance and support he received from his white teammate Pee Wee Reese

"Golenbock's bold and lucid style distills this difficult issue, and brings a dramatic tale vividly to life. Bacon's spare, nostalgic watercolors, in addition to providing fond glimpses of baseball lore, present a haunting portrait of one man's isolation. Historic photographs of the major characters add interest and a touch of stark reality to an unusual story, beautifully rendered." Publ Wkly

Hetrick, Hans
Play baseball like a pro; key skills and tips. Capstone Press 2011 32p il (Play like the pros) lib bdg $25.32; pa $6.95

Grades: 3 4 5   **796.357**
1. Baseball
ISBN 978-1-4296-4824-0 lib bdg; 1-4296-4824-4 lib bdg; 978-1-4296-5644-3 pa; 1-4296-5644-1 pa

       LC 2010007241

"Provides instructional tips on how to improve one's baseball skills, including quotes and advice from professional coaches and athletes." Publisher's note

Includes glossary and bibliographical references

Jennings, Madeleine
Baseball step-by-step; [by] Madeleine Jennings, Alan Smith, and Alan Bloomfield. Rosen Central 2009 95p il (Skills in motion) lib bdg $31.95

Grades: 5 6 7 8   **796.357**
1. Baseball
ISBN 978-1-4358-3361-6; 1-4358-3361-9

       LC 2009-13246

An introduction to the skills needed to play baseball uses a sequence of stop-action images and text instructions to illustrate the moves needed to pitch, catch, field, hit, and run bases.

"Colorful photographs show the entire movement of each skill presented, giving new meaning to the term 'step-by-step.' Progression borders at the bottom of the pages highlight the salient points to notice in performing each skill from beginning to end." SLJ

Includes bibliographical references

Kelly, David A.
Miracle mud; Lena Blackburne and the secret mud that changed baseball. by David A. Kelly; illustrated by Oliver Dominguez. Millbrook Press 2013 32 p. (lib. bdg. : alk. paper) $16.95

Grades: 3 4 5   **796.357**
1. Baseball -- History 2. Picture books for children 3. Sports -- United States -- Marketing 4. Inventors -- United States -- Biography 5. Baseball players -- United States -- Biography 6. Baseball -- United States -- Equipment and supplies
ISBN 0761380922; 9780761380924

       LC 2012020917

This children's picture book is a biography of baseball player Lena Blackburne. "Blackburne was never an outstanding player, but he will go down in history for developing a solution to the wet, soggy baseballs that could be difficult to throw during a game. One day after fishing, he stepped in some soft, gooey mud and an idea was born. Because the mud took the shine off any new white baseball, he began to sell it." (School Library Journal)

Kisseloff, Jeff
Who is baseball's greatest pitcher? Cricket Bks. 2003 181p il $15.95

Grades: 5 6 7 8   **796.357**
1. Baseball
ISBN 0-8126-2685-0

       LC 2003-1245

Asks the reader to compare the statistics for thirty-three of baseball's greatest starting pitchers and decide who is the best

"Accomplishments and anecdotes are related in an informative and entertaining manner. . . . Anyone who enjoys baseball will be delighted with this information-packed, informal book." SLJ

Includes bibliographical references

Lipsyte, Robert
★ **Heroes** of baseball; the men who made it America's favorite game. [by] Robert Lipsyte. Atheneum Books for Young Readers 2006 92p il $19.95

Grades: 4 5 6 7   **796.357**
1. Baseball -- Biography
ISBN 0-689-86741-7; 978-0-689-86741-5

       LC 2005010841

"Using as a focus some of baseball's greats—Big Al Spalding, Babe Ruth, Mickey Mantle, Jackie Robinson, Curt Flood . . . —Lipsyte offers a strong history of the game and its place in American culture. . . . Although much of this material, including the pictures, might be familiar to young readers already absorbed in the game, it is nicely laid out and colorfully formatted. Lipsyte has a clear, vivid style." Booklist

Includes glossary and bibliographical references

McClellan, Ray

Baseball. Bellwether media 2010 24p il (Blastoff! readers. My first sports) $19.95

Grades: K 1 2 3   **796.357**

1. Baseball

ISBN 978-1-60014-277-2; 1-60014-277-X

LC 2009-8157

"Simple text and full color photographs introduce beginning readers to the sport of baseball." Publisher's note

Includes glossary and bibliographical references

Moss, Marissa

Barbed wire baseball; by Marissa Moss; illustrated by Yuko Shimizu. Abrams Books for Young Readers 2013 48 p. (reinforced) $18.95

Grades: 3 4 5   **796.357**

1. Baseball -- History 2. Japanese Americans -- Evacuation and relocation, 1942-1945 3. World War, 1939-1945 4. Baseball -- United States -- History -- 20th century

ISBN 1419705210; 9781419705212

LC 2012010021

Asian/Pacific American Awards for Literature: Picture Book Honor (2014)

This children's book, by Marissa Moss, illustrated by Yuko Shimizu, profiles a 1940s Japanese American baseball player. "Kenichi 'Zeni' Zenimura dreams of playing professional baseball, . . . [and] he grows up to be a successful player, playing with Babe Ruth and Lou Gehrig! When the Japanese attack Pearl Harbor in 1941, Zeni and his family are sent to one of ten internment camps. . . . Zeni brings the game of baseball to the camp, along with a sense of hope." (Publisher's note)

Nelson, Kadir

★ **We** are the ship; the story of Negro League baseball. words and paintings by Kadir Nelson; forward by Hank Aaron. Jump at the Sun 2008 88p il $18.99

Grades: 2 3 4   **796.357**

1. Baseball 2. Negro leagues 3. African American athletes 4. Negro leagues -- History 5. African American baseball players

ISBN 978-0-7868-0832-8; 0-7868-0832-2

Awarded the Sibert Medal, 2009

The author "delivers a history of the Negro Leagues in a sumptuous volume that no baseball fan should be without. Using a folksy vernacular, a fictional player gives an insider account of segregated baseball. . . . As illuminating as the text is, Nelson's muscular paintings serve as the true draw. His larger-than-life players have oversized hands, elongated bodies and near-impossible athleticism." Publ Wkly

Nevius, Carol

Baseball hour; illustrated by Bill Thomson. Marshall Cavendish 2008 un il $16.99

Grades: 1 2 3   **796.357**

1. Baseball

ISBN 978-0-7614-5380-2; 0-7614-5380-6

LC 2007014254

This "picture book follows a multicultural group of boys and girls through their team's baseball practice. . . . The rhyming, rhythmic text

works well enough, but . . . the photorealistic artwork, which a note describes as 'rendered in mixed media,' steal the show. Technically impressive, the black, white, and sepia illustrations capture form, details, action, and gesture well." Booklist

Rappaport, Doreen

Dirt on their skirts; the story of the young women who won the world championship. [by] Doreen Rappaport, Lyndall Callan; pictures by E.B. Lewis. Dial Bks. for Young Readers 1999 un il $16.99

Grades: K 1 2 3   **796.357**

1. Baseball -- Fiction 2. All-American Girls Professional Baseball League -- Fiction

ISBN 0-8037-2042-4

LC 98-47080

Margaret experiences the excitement of watching the 1946 championship game of the All-American Girls Professional Baseball League as it goes into extra innings.

"With its economy of language and telling period details, this book provides an exciting slice of sports history and an appealing bit of Americana. . . . Lewis's finely wrought watercolor paintings deftly capture the crowd and the action on the field." SLJ

Robinson, Sharon, 1950-

Jackie Robinson; American hero. by Sharon Robinson. Scholastic, Inc. 2013 48 p. $16.99

Grades: 3 4 5   **796.357**

1. Picture books for children 2. African American baseball players -- Biography 3. Baseball players -- United States -- Biography

ISBN 054556915X; 9780545569156

LC 2012046058

This book by Jackie Robinson's daughter Sharon Robinson is a biography of "the famous African American baseball player" that looks at "the significance of how a young black ballplayer broke the racial barrier and helped desegregate Major League Baseball. . . . The author gives a brief overview from childhood, to marriage, to death while showcasing myriad black-and-white family photos." (School Library Journal)

Rosenstock, Barb

The Streak; how Joe Dimaggio became America's hero. Barb Rosenstock; illustrated by Terry Widener. Calkins Creek 2014 32 p. $16.95

Grades: 2 3 4 5   **796.357**

1. Baseball 2. New York Yankees (Baseball team) 3. Baseball bats 4. Baseball players

ISBN 159078992X; 9781590789926

LC 2013947717

"In the summer of 1941, Yankee center fielder Joe DiMaggio and his favorite bat, Betsy Ann, begin the longest hitting streak in baseball history. But when Betsy Ann goes missing, will DiMaggio keep hitting? Set on the brink of World War II," this book, by Barb Rosenstock and illustrated by Terry Widener, is a "sports story that united the country and made DiMaggio a hero." (Publisher's note)

"Placed within the historical context of the last perfect baseball summer before America's involvement in World War II, Joe DiMaggio's 56-game hitting streak of 1941 becomes even more impressive. Rosenstock also captures the drama surrounding the feat: how a player from humble beginnings with hands that were used to hard work now held a bat, how DiMaggio named his bat "Betsy Ann" and only used it for games, and how the bat was stolen on the very day he was to break the previously held record...Detailed source notes, a lengthy bibliography, and lots of stats round out the presentation." SLJ

Skead, Robert

Something to prove; the great Satchel Paige vs. rookie Joe DiMaggio. by Robert Skead; illustrated by Floyd Cooper. Carolrhoda Books 2013 32 p. ill. (library) $16.95

Grades: 2 3 4 5   **796.357**

1. Baseball 2. Baseball players -- United States -- Social conditions 3. Discrimination in baseball -- United States -- History

ISBN 0761366199; 9780761366195

LC 2012019709

This children's book, by Robert Skead, tells how "in 1936, the New York Yankees wanted to test a hot prospect named Joe DiMaggio to see if he was ready for the big leagues. They knew just the ballplayer to call: Satchel Paige, the best pitcher anywhere, black or white. For the game, Paige joined a group of amateur African American players, and they faced off against a team of white major leaguers plus young DiMaggio." (Publisher's note)

Smith, Charles R., 1969-

Diamond life; baseball sights, sounds, and swings. Orchard Bks. 2004 28p il $15.95

Grades: 2 3 4   **796.357**

1. Baseball

ISBN 0-439-43180-8

"Smith captures the colorful language and vivid images of the game. . . . The energetic, playful language begs to be read aloud. Combined with bright colors, bold print in a variety of fonts, and exceptional photography, this book is a winner." SLJ

Stars in the shadows; the Negro league all-star game of 1934. Charles R. Smith Jr.; illustrated by Frank Morrison. Atheneum 2012 106 p. ill. (hardcover) $14.99

Grades: 2 3 4   **796.357**

1. Negro leagues 2. African American athletes 3. Radio broadcasting of sports 4. Baseball -- History

ISBN 0689866380; 9780689866388

LC 2011017469

In this chapter book, "[Charles R.] Smith uses a fictional radio sports announcer to introduce the players on both Negro League East-West Classic teams. . . . The story takes place during a time when baseball was segregated and fans voted for their favorite players to make the All-Star roster. Within a basic organization plan of nine innings, or chapters, the author writes in a poetic narrative style." (School Library Journal)

"Some of the best-ever baseball players face off in 1934 at the second annual Negro League All-Star game in Chicago. . . . Cool Papa Bell, Josh Gibson, Willie Wells, Satchel Paige and Oscar Charleston are legendary names despite the segregation that kept them from competing in one integrated league for their entire careers. The concept behind this slim volume is excellent—a story in poems told in nine innings, each inning properly divided into the top of the inning and bottom. Graphite illustrations lend an old-timey feel to the text, and various advertisements, fan comments and even a performance by the Jubilee Singers complete the event." Kirkus

Includes bibliographical references.

Stewart, Mark

Long ball; the legend and lore of the home run. [by] Mark Stewart and Mike Kennedy. Millbrook Press 2006 64p il lib bdg $22.60

Grades: 4 5 6 7   **796.357**

1. Baseball

ISBN 978-0-7613-2779-0 lib bdg; 0-7613-2779-7 lib bdg

LC 2005015041

"The highly readable text is extended by excellent graphics, photographs, and reproductions of baseball cards and magazine covers." Booklist

Includes bibliographical references

Stout, Glenn

Baseball heroes. Houghton Mifflin Harcourt 2011 121p il (Good sports) pa $5.99

Grades: 3 4 5 6   **796.357**

1. Baseball players 2. Army officers 3. Baseball -- Biography

ISBN 978-0-547-41708-0 pa; 0-547-41708-X pa

LC 2010006760

"This strong title . . . focuses on the careers of four trailblazing ballplayers: Hank Aaron, Jackie Robinson, Fernando Valenzuela, and Ila Borders. . . . Stout writes with conviction and does not sugar-coat the hateful, sometimes racially motivated comments these players endured. . . . Stout's action-packed, suspenseful descriptions of milestone games will easily draw young people's interest." Booklist

Tavares, Matt

Becoming Babe Ruth; Matt Tavares. Candlewick Pr 2013 40 p. $16.99

Grades: K 1 2 3   **796.357**

1. Baseball players -- Biography

ISBN 0763656461; 9780763656461

LC 2012942357

Author Matt Tavares presents a biography of George Herman Ruth, more commonly known as Babe Ruth. At "Saint Mary's Industrial School for Boys," George is "expected to study hard and follow a lot of rules. But there is one good thing about Saint Mary's: almost every day, George gets to play baseball. Here, under the watchful eye of Brother Matthias, George evolves as a player and as a man." (Publisher's note)

Teitelbaum, Michael

Baseball; by Michael Teitelbaum. Cherry Lake Pub. 2009 32p il (Innovation in sports) lib bdg $18.95

Grades: 5 6 7 8   **796.357**

1. Baseball

ISBN 978-1-60279-255-5 lib bdg; 1-60279-255-0 lib bdg

LC 2008-2310

This title "traces the many leaps forward in the history of baseball. [It] chronicles innovations that changed the game. . . . Nice-sized color photographs and sidebars . . . accompany the concise and easy-to-follow text." Booklist

Includes glossary and bibliographical references

Thorn, John

First pitch; how baseball began. Beach Ball Books 2011 40p il pa $14.99

Grades: 4 5 6 7   **796.357**

1. Baseball -- History

ISBN 978-1-936310-04-3; 1-936310-04-X

"Packed with vintage images and photographs, this history of baseball takes readers from the origins of the sport to the present day. . . . Thorn . . . writes clearly and eloquently. . . . Fans who think they know baseball may discover they have much to learn." Publ Wkly

Tocher, Timothy

Odd ball; hilarious, unusual, and bizarre baseball moments. illustrated by Stacy Curtis. Marshall Cavendish 2011 64p il $15.99

Grades: 3 4 5   **796.357**

1. Baseball

ISBN 978-0-7614-5813-5; 0-7614-5813-1

LC 2010013847

"Tocher and Curtis serve up an enjoyable, offbeat collection of trivia. . . . Tocher's deftly limned accounts are broadly humorous and supplemented by Curtis's giggle-inducing cartoons. . . . Ranging from baseball's early days to the present, this collection offers an appealing selection of entertaining baseball facts." SLJ

Vernick, Audrey

★ **Brothers** at bat; the true story of an amazing all-brother baseball team. by Audrey Vernick; Illustrated by Steven Salerno. Clarion Books 2012 39 p.
Grades: 3 4 5   **796.357**
1. Brothers 2. Baseball -- History 3. Picture books for children 4. Baseball players -- Biography 5. Baseball teams -- New Jersey -- History 6. Acerras (Baseball team) 7. Baseball teams -- United States -- History 8. Brothers -- New Jersey -- Biography 9. Brothers -- United States -- Biography
ISBN 9780547385570
LC 2011025645

This biographical picture book depicts "a time when local baseball was part of the American landscape, one family fielded its own team. The Acerra family numbered 16 children, 12 of whom were brothers who all loved to play baseball. The boys played in high school and later formed their own semi-pro team. They played wherever they could get a good game and were known as highly skilled players and crowd pleasers. They shared a special closeness and loyalty. . . . That loyalty extended to a love of country as six of them fought in World War II. . . . After the war they continued to play in local leagues, with younger brothers taking over when big brothers aged out. In 1997 they were recognized by the Baseball Hall of Fame as the all-time longest playing all-brother team." (Kirkus)

Weatherford, Carole Boston

★ A **Negro** league scrapbook; foreword by Buck O'Neil. Boyds Mills Press 2005 48p il $19.95
Grades: 4 5 6 7   **796.357**
1. Baseball 2. Negro leagues 3. African American athletes
ISBN 1-59078-091-4
LC 2004-19324

"Weatherford's text covers . . . a summation of the history of the Negro Leagues and sections on the pitchers, hitters, utility men, various teams, and so forth. Each topic is briefly covered on a spread of text with black-and-white photos and full-color realia designed to look like a scrapbook. Topics are introduced with a few lines of verse. . . . The book is especially successful in conveying the significance of the Negro Leagues to the black community, and in detailing the realities of segregation. . . . This title succeeds as a thoughtful introduction." SLJ

Wise, Bill

Silent star; the story of deaf major leaguer William Hoy. by Bill Wise; illustrated by Adam Gustavson. Lee & Low Books 2012 40 p. col. ill. (hardcover : alk. paper) $18.95; (ebook) $18.95
Grades: 3 4 5   **796.357**
1. Deaf athletes -- Biography 2. Baseball players -- Biography 3. Deaf athletes -- United States -- Biography 4. Baseball players -- United States -- Biography
ISBN 1600604110; 9781600604119; 9781600609763
LC 2011036827

This "picture-book biography of William Ellsworth Hoy (1862-1961), one of the first deaf players in major league baseball . . . follows Hoy from his childhood . . . through his chance discovery by in amateur league coach and his ascent into the minor leagues and beyond. [Bill] Wise outlines the hardships and prejudices Hoy encountered at every turn . . . but Hoy's determination cuts through all the doubt he faced, and some of the records he set stand to this day." (Publishers Weekly)

Wong, Stephen

Baseball treasures; by Stephen Wong; photographs by Susan Einstein. Collins 2007 58p il $16.99; lib bdg $17.89
Grades: 5 6 7 8   **796.357**
1. Baseball -- History 2. Baseball -- Collectibles
ISBN 978-0-06-114464-6; 0-06-114464-9; 978-0-06-114473-8 lib bdg; 0-06-114473-8 lib bdg
LC 2006036069

This describes collectibles connected with the history of baseball, including balls, gloves and bats, jerseys, baseball cards, World Series memorabilia, and trophies.

This is "a well-designed, well-illustrated book for kids. . . . The text manages to impart the essential information without becoming bogged down in too much detail." Booklist

796.4   Weight lifting, track and field, gymnastics

Bobrick, Benson

A **passion** for victory: the story of the Olympics in ancient and early modern times; the story of the Olympics in ancient and early modern times. Benson Bobrick. Alfred A. Knopf 2012 xvi, 143 p.p ill. (hardback) $19.99
Grades: 4 5 6 7   **796.4**
1. Olympic games 2. Sports tournaments 3. Olympics
ISBN 9780375868696; 9780375968693
LC 2011016036

The book offers an "account of the Olympic Games and their place in history. . . . [Athletes] Milo of Croton, Jim Thorpe, Johnny Weissmuller and Jesse Owens are given their due here. The photo-essay format conveys their stories . . . as well as the glory, shenanigans and pettiness of the Olympics throughout history. Almost every full-page spread includes at least one photograph, and the text . . . addresses the cultural context of the games." (Kirkus Reviews)

Includes bibliographical references.

796.42   Track and field

Adler, David A.

A **picture** book of Jesse Owens; [by] David Adler; illustrated by Robert Casilla. Holiday House 1992 un il lib bdg $16.95; pa $6.95
Grades: 1 2 3   **796.42**
1. Track athletics 2. African American athletes 3. Olympic athletes 4. Runners (Athletes)
ISBN 0-8234-0966-X lib bdg; 0-8234-1066-8 pa
LC 91-44735

A simple biography of the noted black track star who competed in the 1936 Berlin Olympics

"The portrait presented, although brief, is accurate and touches on the major events of the track-and-field champion's life. . . . Casilla contributes full-page watercolor paintings that nicely complement and expand the writing." SLJ

Gifford, Clive

Track and field; [by] Clive Gifford. PowerKids Press 2009 32p il (Personal best) lib bdg $25.25
Grades: 4 5 6 7 8   **796.42**
1. Track athletics
ISBN 978-1-4042-4442-9 lib bdg; 1-4042-4442-5 lib bdg
LC 2007-42984

This guide to track and field "offers well-organized and easy-to-follow instructions, focusing on rules, clothing, specific skills, and competitions. . . . Informative, readable." SLJ

Includes bibliographical references

Track athletics; [by] Clive Gifford. Sea-to-Sea Publications 2009 30p il (Know your sport) lib bdg $27.10

Grades: 5 6 7 8   **796.42**

1. Track athletics

ISBN 978-1-59771-154-8 lib bdg; 1-59771-154-3 lib bdg

LC 2008-7323

"Describes the equipment, training, moves, and running events of track competitions. Includes step-by-step descriptions of moves." Publisher's note

Includes glossary

Lang, Heather

Queen of the track; Alice Coach, olympic high-jump champion. Heather Lang; illustrated by Floyd Cooper. 1st ed. Boyds Mills Press 2012 40 p. col. ill. (reinforced trade ed.) $16.95

Grades: 3 4 5   **796.42**

1. Olympic games 2. Black athletes 3. Olympic athletes

ISBN 1590788508; 9781590788509

LC 2011939994

Author Heather Lang tells the story of "the 1948 Olympics in London, [where] members of the U.S. Women's Track and Field team went down to defeat one by one. Any hope of winning rested on Alice Coachman. . . . She became the first African American woman to win an Olympic gold medal. . . . This book follows Coachman on her journey from rural Georgia, where she overcame adversity both as a woman and as a black athlete, to her triumph in Wembly Stadium." (Publisher's note)

Includes bibliographical references.

Marsico, Katie

Running; [by] Katie Marsico and Cecilia Minden. Cherry Lake Pub. 2009 32p il (Real world math: Sports) lib bdg $27.07

Grades: 4 5 6   **796.42**

1. Running 2. Arithmetic 3. Track athletics

ISBN 978-1-60279-249-4 lib bdg; 1-60279-249-6 lib bdg

LC 2008-1167

This book "starts with a short story on the history of [running], fundamental rules, and a math challenge in every chapter. . . . [This book] will pique your imagination." Sci Books Films

Includes glossary and bibliographical references

McDougall, Chros

Track & field. Norwood House Press 2011 64p il (Girls play to win) lib bdg $26.60

Grades: 4 5 6 7   **796.42**

1. Track athletics

ISBN 978-1-59953-467-1; 1-59953-467-3

LC 2011011053

Covers the history, rules, fundamentals, and significant personalities of the sport of women's track and field. Topics include: techniques, strategies, competitive events, and equipment.

Includes glossary and bibliographical references

Wiseman, Blaine

Boston Marathon. Weigl Publishing 2011 32p il (Sporting championships) lib bdg $26; pa $10.95

Grades: 3 4 5   **796.42**

1. Boston Marathon 2. Marathon running

ISBN 978-1-61690-124-0 lib bdg; 1-61690-124-1 lib bdg; 978-1-61690-125-7 pa; 1-61690-125-X pa

This sets the Boston Marathon "within the context of the sport and explains what you need to know when watching the [event]." Booklist

Includes bibliographical references

796.44   Gymnastics

Schwartz, Heather E.

Gymnastics. Lucent Books 2011 96p il (Science behind sports) lib bdg $33.45

Grades: 5 6 7 8   **796.44**

1. Gymnastics

ISBN 978-1-4205-0277-0; 1-4205-0277-8

LC 2010033544

This "explores the scientific principles such as momentum, gravity, friction, and aerodynamics, plus many more, behind [gymnastics]. . . . [The author discusses the sport's] origins, history, and changes, . . . the biomechanics and physiology of playing, related health and medical concerns, and the causes and treatment of sports-related injuries. Additional information tells how exercise, diet and nutrition, warming up, and training relate to peak performance and enjoyment of the sport. . . . One of the most interesting chapters . . . is 'The Psychology of Gymnastics,' which discusses fears, force of will, honing the competitive edge, and the pressure to succeed. . . . [This volume is] jam-packed full of information. [A must-have] for sports fans, athletes, science students, and even anyone considering a career in sports-related medicine, coaching, or other connected fields." SLJ

Includes glossary and bibliographical references

Veitch, Catherine

Gymnastics. Heinemann Library 2009 24p il (Sports and my body) lib bdg $21.36; pa $6.49

Grades: 1 2   **796.44**

1. Gymnastics

ISBN 978-1-4329-3454-5 lib bdg; 1-4329-3454-6 lib bdg; 978-1-4329-3459-0 pa; 1-4329-3459-7 pa

LC 2009-7084

Readers learn what gymnastics is, how it can help them stay healthy, and how they can do gymnastics safely.

This book relates "activity to health . . . [and] explains that in order to stay healthy, children should get plenty of rest, eat healthy food, and drink plenty of water." SLJ

Includes glossary

Wendorff, Anne

Gymnastics. Bellwether Media 2010 24p il (Blastoff! readers. My first sports) $19.95

Grades: K 1 2 3   **796.44**

1. Gymnastics

ISBN 9781600143274; 160014327X

LC 2009-8181

Simple text and full color photographs introduce beginning readers to the sport of gymnastics.

Includes glossary and bibliographical references

796.48   Olympic games

Butterfield, Moira

Events. Sea-to-Sea Publications 2011 32p il (The Olympics) lib bdg $19.95

Grades: 4 5 6 7 **796.48**
1. Olympic games
ISBN 978-1-5977-1321-4; 1-5977-1321-X

LC 2011006465

This describes events of the Olympics.
Includes glossary and bibliographical references

History. Sea-to-Sea Publications 2011 32p il (The Olympics) lib bdg $28.50
Grades: 4 5 6 7 **796.48**
1. Olympic games
ISBN 978-1-5977-1319-1; 1-5977-1319-8

LC 2011006470

This is a history of the Olympics.
Includes glossary and bibliographical references

Scandals. Sea-to-Sea Publications 2011 32p il (The Olympics) lib bdg $28.50
Grades: 4 5 6 7 **796.48**
1. Olympic games 2. Sports -- Corrupt practices
ISBN 978-1-5977-1320-7; 1-5977-1320-1

LC 2011006473

"The book is divided into chapters that cover such topics as bribes, doping, and political problems. Along with famous events, such as the tragedy at the Munich Olympics, in which Israeli athletes were murdered, and the Marion Jones running scandal, in which she was stripped of her medals, there are other shocking and suprising moments. . . . This . . . volume, full of historical and contemporary photos, gives readers a lot to think about." Booklist

Macy, Sue
★ **Swifter**, higher, stronger; a photographic history of the Summer Olympics. by Sue Macy; foreword by Bob Costas. updated for the 2008 Summer Olympics; National Geographic 2008 96p il $18.95; lib bdg $27.90
Grades: 4 5 6 7 **796.48**
1. Olympic games
ISBN 978-1-4263-0290-9; 1-4263-0290-8; 978-1-4263-0302-9 lib bdg; 1-4263-0302-5 lib bdg
First published 2004
A detailed look at the history of the Olympic Games, from their origins in Ancient Greece, through their rebirth in nineteenth century France, to the present, highlighting the contributions of individuals to the Games' success and popularity.
"While other books on the topic go into more depth on specific sports, athletes, or historical events, none are as enthusiastically broad or as enjoyable to read as this one. And, it's superbly illustrated with colorful, well-chosen, and enticing photographs." SLJ [review of 2004 ed.]
Includes bibliographical references

796.5 Outdoor life

George, Jean Craighead
★ **Pocket** guide to the outdoors; [by] Jean Craighead George; with Twig C. George . . . [et al.] Dutton Children's Books 2009 138p il pa $9.99
Grades: 5 6 7 8 **796.5**
1. Camping 2. Outdoor life 3. Wilderness survival
ISBN 978-0-525-42163-4 pa; 0-525-42163-7 pa
"This survival guide is the book to read before a wilderness adventure. In short, clearly written chapters, it provides practical tips about ways to enjoy nature and includes information about building shelters, starting fires, making a fishing line and cleaning a fish, outdoor cooking,

identifying animal tracks and edible and poisonous plants, and the basics of orienteering. Safety is always considered. Drawings and clearly labeled sketches help with identification." SLJ
Includes bibliographical references

Schofield, Jo
Make it wild; 101 things to make and do outdoors. [by] Jo Schofield and Fiona Danks. Frances Lincoln 2010 159p il pa $24.95
Grades: 4 5 6 7 8 **796.5**
1. Nature craft 2. Outdoor life
ISBN 978-0-7112-2885-6; 0-7112-2885-X
"Using the raw materials nature has to offer, the authors offer clear, concise instructions on how to create ephemeral art, outdoor toys, jewelry, sculptures, and dozens of other things using materials like clay, ice, leaves, sand, and wood. The instructions offer good guidance but also encourage children to use their own creativity and imagination to craft the final product. The projects range in level of difficulty and, depending on the age of the child, can be done individually or in collaboration with siblings, peers, or parents. The authors include safety instructions and recommendations for further resources on outdoor creative exercises. The activities will teach problem solving and commonsense, useful skills; instill a deeper appreciation of nature; and encourage creativity and ingenuity. An excellent choice for any library collection." Booklist

796.52 Walking and exploring by kind of terrain

Athans, Sandra K.
Tales from the top of the world; climbing Mount Everest with Pete Athans. by Sandra K. Athans. Millbrook Press 2013 64 p. ill. (lib. bdg. : alk. paper) $31.93
Grades: 4 5 6 **796.52**
1. Mount Everest (China and Nepal) 2. Mountaineers -- Biography 3. Mountaineering -- Everest, Mount (China and Nepal)
ISBN 0761365060; 9780761365068

LC 2011045834

In this book by Sandra K. Athans and Pete Athans, "readers are invited to accompany Pete Athans (who has climbed Everest some 14 times and stood on top of the world on 7 different occasions) on the arduous journey from below base camp to the summit. The matter-of-fact text is broken by tales of Athans's personal adventures . . . and all are decorated with a plethora of color photos." (School Library Journal)
Includes bibliographical references (p. 61) and index

Bodden, Valerie
To the top of Mount Everest; by Valerie Bodden. 1st ed. Creative Education 2012 48 p. ill. (some col.) (Great Expeditions) (paperback) $12.00; (library) $34.25
Grades: 5 6 7 8 **796.52**
1. Exploration   2. Mount Everest (China and Nepal)   3. Mountaineering -- Everest, Mount (China and Nepal) -- History 4. Mountaineers -- Everest, Mount (China and Nepal) -- Biography
ISBN 1608180700; 9780898126686; 9781608180707

LC 2010033553

This book by Valerie Bodden is part of the Great Expeditions series and looks at expeditions to the top of Mount Everest. "Bodden includes brief biographies of major people involved in each expedition, interspersed with the text. There are also numerous photographs or reproductions of paintings and woodcuts from the time of the expeditions." (Library Media Connection)
Includes bibliographical references and index.

Cleare, John
Epic climbs. Kingfisher 2011 64p il (Epic adventure) $19.95

Grades: 5 6 7 8   **796.52**
1. Mountaineering
ISBN 978-0-7534-6573-8; 0-7534-6573-6

"Cleare gives the history of five of the most famous and dangerous mountains to climb: Eiger, K2, Everest, McKinley, and Matterhorn.
Each section has a short, easy-to-read summary that gives the history
of climbers who have conquered these peaks. Full-color photos include
the view from the top and historical and contemporary climbing equipment." SLJ

Jenkins, Steve
★ The **top** of the world; climbing Mount Everest. Houghton Mif-
flin 1999 un il $16; pa $6.95
Grades: 2 3 4   **796.52**
1. Mountaineering 2. Mount Everest (China and Nepal)
ISBN 0-395-94218-7; 0-618-19676-5 pa
LC 98-42748

"Jenkins' papercut illustrations are extraordinary—feathery light to
catch the effect of fog radiating off the mountains, mottled and striated
to replicate rocky plateaus, pebbled to look like ice flowers. . . . A very
attractive book, with plenty of substance for curious children." Booklist
Includes bibliographical references

Skreslet, Laurie
To the top of Everest; [by] Laurie Skreslet with Elizabeth MacLeod.
Kids Can Press 2001 56p il hardcover o.p. pa $9.95
Grades: 4 5 6 7   **796.52**
1. Mountaineering 2. Mount Everest (China and Nepal)
ISBN 1-55074-721-5; 1-55074-814-9 pa

This is an account of Skreslet's "1982 trek up Everest when he became one of the first Canadians to make it to the top. Skreslet takes readers through every exciting, excruciating element of the climb. Beautiful
color photographs abound." Booklist
Includes glossary

796.522   Mountains, hills, rocks

Athans, Sandra K.
Secrets of the sky caves; danger and discovery on Nepal's Mustang
Cliffs. Sandra K. Athans. Millbrook Press 2014 64 p. color illustra-
tions (lib. bdg. : alk. paper) $33.27
Grades: 4 5 6 7   **796.522**
1. Mountaineering 2. Nepal -- Description and travel 3. Caves
-- Nepal -- Mustang (District) 4. Mustang (Nepal : District) --
Antiquities 5. Mountaineering -- Nepal -- Mustang (District) 6.
Mustang (Nepal : District) -- Discovery and exploration
ISBN 1467700169; 9781467700160
LC 2013017736

"What's more dangerous than scaling Mount Everest? For mountaineer Pete Athans, the answer lies in the ancient kingdom of Mustang,
a remote part of the Asian nation of Nepal. . . From 2007 to 2012, Pete
explored Mustang's sky caves with a team that included scientists,
mountain climbers, and even two children. They found mummies, murals, manuscripts, and other priceless artifacts." (Publisher's note)

"The author, sister of expedition leader Pete Athans, offers a wealth
of information about this little-known archaeological wonder. Color
photographs provide stunning visuals." Horn Book
Includes bibliographical references (pages 61-62) and index

Berne, Emma Carlson
Summiting Everest; how a photograph celebrates teamwork at the
top of the world. by Emma Carlson Berne. Capstone Compass Point

Books 2014 64 p. (Compass point books. Captured history.) (library
binding) $33.99
Grades: 5 6 7 8 9   **796.522**
1. Mountaineering 2. Mount Everest (China and Nepal) 3.
Portrait photography -- Everest, Mount (China and Nepal) 4.
Mountaineering expeditions -- Everest, Mount (China and Nepal)
-- Pictorial works
ISBN 0756547342; 9780756547349; 9780756547905
LC 2013027843

"Not far from the top, before their final hours of climbing, team pho-
tographer Alfred Gregory snapped a picture of [Edmund] Hillary and
[Tenzing] Norgay, with the imposing Himalayas spread out behind them.
It was the highest photograph anyone in human history had ever taken.
With a click of his camera shutter in May 1953, Gregory opened up a
hidden world for the rest of humanity to share." (Publisher's note)
Includes bibliographical references and index

796.54   Camping

Champion, Neil
Fire and cooking. Amicus 2010 32p il (Survive alive) lib bdg
$19.95
Grades: 4 5 6 7   **796.54**
1. Fires 2. Camping 3. Wilderness survival
ISBN 978-1-60753-039-8 lib bdg; 1-60753-039-2 lib bdg
LC 2010001626

This offers survival tips for building a fire and cooking in the wild,
including information on different kinds of fires. Also discusses how to
know what to cook and utensils to use.

This "colorful [book contains] numerous photos and illustrations
that effectively break the [text] into small, readable chucks. There's lots
of practical, everyday information here. . . . Brief yet gripping real-life
survival stories are interspersed throughout the [book]." SLJ

796.6   Cycling and related activities

Bow, James
Cycling science. Crabtree Pub. Co. 2009 32p il (Sports science)
lib bdg $26.60; pa $8.95
Grades: 4 5 6   **796.6**
1. Cycling
ISBN 978-0-7787-4535-8 lib bdg; 0-77874535-X lib bdg; 978-0-
7787-4552-5 pa; 0-7787-4552-X pa
LC 2008-46275

This book approachs cycling "from a scientific angle, describing
some of the physics behind [the] pursuit and how athletes can use this
knowledge to improve performance. . . . Fascinating facts . . . are presented in a captivating, lively manner. . . . The layout features colorful
text boxes interspersed among photographs." SLJ
Includes glossary and bibliographical references

Guillain, Charlotte
Cycling. Heinemann Library 2009 24p il (Sports and my body)
lib bdg $21.36; pa $6.49
Grades: 1 2   **796.6**
1. Cycling
ISBN 978-1-4329-3457-6 lib bdg; 1-4329-3457-0 lib bdg; 978-1-
4329-3462-0 pa; 1-4329-3462-7 pa
LC 2009-7085

Readers learn what cycling is, how it can help them stay healthy, and
how they can cycle safely.

This book relates "activity to health . . . [and] explains that in order to stay healthy, children should get plenty of rest, eat healthy food, and drink plenty of water." SLJ

Includes glossary

Macy, Sue, 1954-

★ **Wheels** of change; how women rode the bicycle to freedom (with a few flat tires along the way) National Geographic 2011 96p il map $18.95; lib bdg $27.90

Grades: 4 5 6 7 8   **796.6**

1. Cycling 2. Bicycles 3. Gender role 4. Women athletes 5. Sex role 6. Feminism

ISBN 978-1-4263-0761-4; 1-4263-0761-6; 978-1-4263-0762-1 lib bdg; 1-4263-0762-4 lib bdg

LC 2010-27141

This is an "engaging look at the emancipating impact that bikes had on late-nineteenth-century U.S. women. The eye-catching chapters, filled with archival images . . . zero in on the profound ways that bicycles subverted traditional notions of femininity. . . . Macy seamlessly weaves together research, direct quotes . . . and historical overviews that put the facts into context, while sidebars expand on related topics. . . . A strong, high-interest choice for both classroom and personal reading." Booklist

Robinson, Laura

★ **Cyclist** bikelist; a book for every rider. illustrated by Ramón K. Pérez. Tundra Books 2010 55p il pa $17.95

Grades: 4 5 6 7   **796.6**

1. Cycling 2. Bicycles

ISBN 978-0-88776-784-5; 0-88776-784-2

The author "covers a broad range of topics, from choosing and caring for a bike to differences in tires, how gear ratios work, and even proper dress and nutrition. She also provides a quick overview of the bicycle's history and inspiring sketches of several renowned racers. . . . Supplemented by photos of different types of bikes, Pérez's bright, cartoon-style pictures add both humor and . . . sharply drawn details. A first-rate guide." Booklist

Schoenherr, Alicia

Mountain biking; by Alicia and Rusty Schoenherr. Child's World 2005 32p il (Kids' guides) lib bdg $24.21

Grades: 4 5 6   **796.6**

1. Mountain biking

ISBN 1-59296-209-2

LC 2003-27371

This "opens with an explanation of the sport and gives reasons why people enjoy it. The four chapters that follow cover background and development, equipment, technique, and stars and competitions. The excellent color photos are clear and exciting." SLJ

Includes bibliographical references

796.622   BMX (Bicycle motocross)

Adamson, Thomas K.

BMX racing; Thomas K. Adamson. Bellwether Media, Inc. 2016 24 p. color illustrations (hardcover : alk. paper) $24.95

Grades: 3 4 5 6 7   **796.622**

1. Bicycle racing 2. Extreme sports 3. Bicycle motocross

ISBN 9781626172746; 1626172749

LC 2015007777

This children's book by Thomas K. Adamson is part of a series "on extreme sports, covering history, gear, events, and famous athletes. Each book begins with an account of a gold-winning performance. Graphics and color photos help convey each sport's difficulty and appeal. 'BMX

Racing' notes that Olympic races usually finish in 40 seconds or less." (School Library Journal)

"The books' exciting tone and dynamic illustrations will draw kids into the world of extreme sports." Booklist

Includes bibliographical references (page 23) and index

796.7   Driving motor vehicles

Nelson, Kristin L.

Monster trucks on the move. Lerner Publications 2011 32p il (Lightning bolt books. Vroom-vroom) lib bdg $25.26

Grades: K 1 2   **796.7**

1. Trucks

ISBN 978-0-7613-6022-3 lib bdg; 0-7613-6022-0 lib bdg

LC 2009038530

This book about monster trucks has "big, high-energy color photos. . . . [The text provides] lively commentary in a mix of declarative statements and non-rhetorical questions. . . . [The] volume closes with a labeled diagram, a page of 'fun facts,' and a short list of print and web resources. . . . [This] will make a worthwhile and popular addition." SLJ

Includes glossary and bibliographical references

796.72   Automobile racing

Arroyo, Sheri L.

How race car drivers use math; math curriculum consultant: Rhea A. Stewart. Chelsea Clubhouse 2010 32p il (Math in the real world) lib bdg $28

Grades: 4 5 6   **796.72**

1. Mathematics 2. Automobile racing 3. Vocational guidance

ISBN 978-1-60413-609-8 lib bdg; 1-60413-609-X lib bdg

LC 2009-21476

"The layout for [this slim [title] is bright and colorful with a photograph and a 'You Do the Math' problem to solve and large, easy-to-read text on every spread. An answer key is included in the back matter, along with a page detailing the career choices and the educational requirements. . . . In [this title], readers learn about qualifying times, track designs, and tracking fuel. . . . [This title] would be useful to supplement lessons on mathematics. [It] will also appeal to students wanting to learn more about math as it relates to specific careers." SLJ

Includes glossary and bibliographical references

Howse, Jennifer

NASCAR Sprint Cup. Weigl Publishers 2009 32p il map (Sporting championships) lib bdg $26; pa $9.95

Grades: 3 4 5   **796.72**

1. Automobile racing 2. National Association for Stock Car Auto Racing

ISBN 978-1-60596-636-6 lib bdg; 1-60596-636-3 lib bdg; 978-1-60596-637-3 pa; 1-60596-637-1 pa

LC 2009-12344

This sets the NASCAR Sprint Cup "within the context of the sport and explains what you need to know when watching the big [event]." Booklist

Includes glossary and bibliographical references

Kelley, K. C.

Hottest NASCAR machines; by K. C. Kelley. Enslow Publishers 2008 48p il (Wild wheels!) lib bdg $23.93

Grades: 4 5 6 7   **796.72**

1. Automobile racing 2. National Association for Stock Car Auto

Racing

ISBN 978-0-7660-2869-2 lib bdg; 0-7660-2869-0 lib bdg

LC 2007007426

"Experience the thrill of a NASCAR race, and learn about the cars, personalities, and races associated with this sport." Publisher's note

Includes glossary and bibliographical references

Other titles in this series are:

Hottest muscle cars

Hottest sports cars

Piehl, Janet

Formula one race cars on the move. Lerner Publications 2010 32p il (Lightning bolt books. Vroom-vroom) lib bdg $25.26

Grades: K 1 2   **796.72**

1. Automobile racing

ISBN 978-0-7613-3920-5 lib bdg; 0-7613-3920-5 lib bdg

LC 2009039745

This book about race cars has "big, high-energy color photos. . . . [The text provides] lively commentary in a mix of declarative statements and non-rhetorical questions. . . . [The] volume closes with a labeled diagram, a page of 'fun facts,' and a short list of print and web resources. . . . [This] will make a worthwhile and popular addition." SLJ

Includes glossary and bibliographical references

Other titles in this series are:

Big rigs on the move

Earthmovers on the move

Fire trucks on the move

Pimm, Nancy Roe

The **Daytona** 500; the thrill and thunder of the great American race. Milbrook Press 2011 64p il (Spectacular sports) lib bdg $29.27

Grades: 5 6 7 8   **796.72**

1. Automobile racing

ISBN 978-0-7613-6677-5; 0-7613-6677-6

LC 2010027263

"Pimm, who worked in the pit box during her husband Ed Pimm's NASCAR racing days, offers an informative introduction to the Daytona 500. Beginning in 1903 . . . this traces the event's history and discusses the cars, drivers, strategies, and memorable moments. Colorful photos illustrate the clear text, while the many sidebars spotlight related facts." Booklist

Includes bibliographical references

796.8   Combat sports

Bjorklund, Ruth

Aikido. Marshall Cavendish Benchmark 2011 47p il (Martial arts in action) $29.93

Grades: 4 5 6 7   **796.8**

1. Aikido

ISBN 978-0-7614-4931-7; 978-1-6087-0361-6 e-book

LC 2010013820

This describes the history, equipment, and technique of aikido.

This treats "martial arts with the dignity that serious enthusiasts bring to the sport. . . . Illustrations include not only photos of modern gear and from films but also historical images." Booklist

Ditchfield, Christin

Wrestling. Children's Press 2000 47p il (True book) hardcover o.p. lib bdg $25

Grades: 2 3 4   **796.8**

1. Wrestling

ISBN 0-516-21611-2 lib bdg; 0-516-27033-8 pa

LC 99-28191

Describes the history, rules, and styles of wrestling

Includes bibliographical references

Ellis, Carol

Judo and jujitsu. Marshall Cavendish Benchmark 2011 47p il (Martial arts in action) $29.93

Grades: 4 5 6 7   **796.8**

1. Judo 2. Jiu-jitsu

ISBN 978-0-7614-4933-1; 978-1-6087-0363-0 e-book

LC 2010013821

This describes the history, equipment, and technique of judo and jujitsu.

This treats "martial arts with the dignity that serious enthusiasts bring to the sport. . . . Illustrations include not only photos of modern gear and from films but also historical images." Booklist

Kendo. Marshall Cavendish Benchmark 2010 47p il (Martial arts in action) $29.93

Grades: 4 5 6 7   **796.8**

1. Kendo

ISBN 978-0-7614-4935-5; 0-7614-4935-3

LC 2010013827

This book about kendo offers "an introduction, a brief history, and expectations for students who begin taking classes. . . . [This title is] outstanding, using an approachable voice without fictionalizing and presenting the history of [kendo] in a way that makes it feel relevant." SLJ

Includes glossary and bibliographical references

Wrestling. Marshall Cavendish Benchmark 2010 47p il (Martial arts in action) $29.93

Grades: 4 5 6 7   **796.8**

1. Wrestling

ISBN 978-0-7614-4941-6; 0-7614-4941-8

LC 2010013819

This book about wrestling offers "an introduction, a brief history, and expectations for students who begin taking classes. . . . [This title is] outstanding, using an approachable voice without fictionalizing and presenting the history of [wrestling] in a way that makes it feel relevant." SLJ

Includes glossary and bibliographical references

Gifford, Clive

Martial arts. Marshall Cavendish Benchmark 2009 30p il (Tell me about sports) $19.95

Grades: 3 4 5   **796.8**

1. Martial arts

ISBN 978-0-7614-4457-2; 0-7614-4457-2

LC 2008-55993

"An introduction to martial arts, including techniques, rules, and the training regimen of professional athletes in the sport." Publisher's note

Includes glossary and bibliographical references

Haney-Withrow, Anna

Tae kwon do. Marshall Cavendish Benchmark 2011 47p il (Martial arts in action) $29.93

Grades: 4 5 6 7   **796.8**

1. Tae kwon do

ISBN 978-0-7614-4940-9; 978-1-6087-0368-5 e-book

LC 2010013828

This describes the history, equipment, and technique of tae kwon do.

This treats "martial arts with the dignity that serious enthusiasts bring to the sport. . . . Illustrations include not only photos of modern gear and from films but also historical images." Booklist

Hicks, Terry Allan

Karate. Marshall Cavendish Benchmark 2010 47p il (Martial arts in action) $29.93

Grades: 4 5 6   **796.8**

1. Karate

ISBN 978-0-7614-4934-8; 0-7614-4934-5

LC 2010013818

This books looks at karate including its history, fighting techniques, training methods, and the values of respect and discipline.

This treats "martial arts with the dignity that serious enthusiasts bring to the sport. . . . Illustrations include not only photos of modern gear and from films but also historical images." Booklist

Includes glossary

Lewin, Ted

★ **At Gleason's gym**. Roaring Brook Press 2007 un il $17.95

Grades: 2 3 4 5   **796.8**

1. Boxing 2. Gleason's Gyms

ISBN 978-1-59643-231-4; 1-59643-231-4

LC 2006-32176

"Gleason's gym in Brooklyn is where 'the world works out.' . . . Nine-year-old Sugar Boy Younan, National Silver Gloves Champion, 110-pound division, goes there to shadow box and spar with partners. This glorious tribute to Gleason's . . . packs a punch of its own, with a text that is both moving and informative and with vibrant artwork so realistic that readers can practically smell the sweat." Booklist

Mack, Gail

Kickboxing. Marshall Cavendish Benchmark 2011 47p il lib bdg $29.93

Grades: 4 5 6 7   **796.8**

1. Kickboxing

ISBN 978-0-7614-4936-2; 978-1-6087-0366-1 e-book

LC 2010014798

This describes the history, equipment, and technique of kickboxing.

This treats "martial arts with the dignity that serious enthusiasts bring to the sport. . . . Illustrations include not only photos of modern gear and from films but also historical images." Booklist

Mason, Paul, 1967-

Boxing. Sea-to-Sea Publications 2011 32p il (Combat sports) lib bdg $28.50

Grades: 4 5 6   **796.8**

1. Boxing

ISBN 978-1-59771-273-6; 1-59771-273-6

"...[Provides] an inviting look for students who are learning about techniques and for examining records and statistics... Use to refresh an older collection." SLJ

Includes glossary and bibliographical references

Watkins, Richard Ross

Gladiator; by Richard Watkins. Houghton Mifflin 1997 80p il map hardcover o.p. pa $8.95

Grades: 4 5 6 7   **796.8**

1. Gladiators 2. Rome -- Social life and customs

ISBN 0-395-82656-X; 0-618-07032-X pa

LC 96-21107

Describes the history of gladiators, including types of armor, use of animals, amphitheaters, and how the practice fit into Roman society for almost 700 years

"In a balanced treatment of a potentially sensational topic, Watkins provides colorfully written, detailed accounts of the fights as well as pithy discussions of what gladiators meant to the Romans and what they tell us about Roman society. . . . The solid gray-and-white drawings illustrate the text effectively." Booklist

Includes glossary and bibliographical references

Wiseman, Blaine

Ultimate fighting. Weigl Publishers 2011 il (Sporting championships) lib bdg $26; pa 10.95

Grades: 3 4 5   **796.8**

1. Martial arts 2. Ultimate Fighting Championship (Organization) .

ISBN 978-1-61690-130-1 lib bdg; 1-61690-130-6 lib bdg; 978-1-61690-131-8 pa; 1-61690-131-4 pa

LC 2010038886

This sets the ultimate fighting championship "within the context of the sport and explains what you need to know when watching the [event]." Booklist

Wouk, Henry

Kung fu. Marshall Cavendish Benchmark 2010 47p il (Martial arts in action) $29.93

Grades: 4 5 6   **796.8**

1. Kung fu

ISBN 978-0-7614-4937-9; 0-7614-4937-X

LC 2010013842

Centuries ago a small band of warrior monks living in the remote forests of ancient China created a mysterious and unique style of fighting that used no weapons. It is known today as kung fu. This is the story of how that once secret martial art has become one of the most famous in the world

This treats "martial arts with the dignity that serious enthusiasts bring to the sport. . . . Illustrations include not only photos of modern gear and from films but also historical images." Booklist

Includes glossary

796.812   Wrestling

Jones, Patrick

The **main** event; the moves and muscle of pro wrestling. Patrick Jones. Millbrook Press 2013 64 p. (lib. bdg. : alk. paper) $31.93

Grades: 4 5 6   **796.812**

1. Wrestling 2. Wrestling -- History

ISBN 0761386351; 9780761386353

LC 2011046180

This book is a "history of wrestling as 'sports entertainment'—read that as meaning staged—from [Patrick] Jones. This is . . . the art of making the blows and throws look like the real thing while the outcome has been predetermined." He tracks "the evolution of the various professional circuits and the shenanigans of the promoter Vince McMahon" and tells stories of wrestlers like "Gorgeous George, Strangler Lewis, Andre the Giant, Hulk Hogan, The Undertaker, [and] The Rock." (Kirkus)

796.815   Oriental martial arts forms

Mason, Paul, 1967-

Judo; [by] Paul Mason. Sea-to-Sea Publications 2009 30 p. col. ill. (Know your sport) (library) $27.10

Grades: 5 6 7 8   **796.815**
1. Judo
ISBN 978-1-59771-151-7; 1-59771-151-9

LC 2008007318

"Describes the equipment, training, moves, and competitions of judo. Includes step-by-step descriptions of moves." Publisher's note
Includes index.

796.9   Ice and snow sports

Woods, Bob
  Snowboarding; by Bob Woods. Child's World 2005 32p il (Kids' guides) lib bdg $24.21
Grades: 4 5 6   **796.9**
1. Snowboarding
ISBN 1-59296-211-4

LC 2003-27365

This "opens with an explanation of the sport and gives reasons why people enjoy it. The four chapters that follow cover background and development, equipment, technique, and stars and competitions. The excellent color photos are clear and exciting." SLJ
Includes bibliographical references

796.91   Ice skating

Marsico, Katie
  Speed skating; [by] Katie Marsico and Cecilia Minden. Cherry Lake Pub. 2009 32p il (Real world math: Sports) lib bdg $27.07
Grades: 4 5 6   **796.91**
1. Arithmetic 2. Ice skating
ISBN 978-1-60279-250-0 lib bdg; 1-60279-250-X lib bdg

LC 2008-806

This book "starts with a short story on the history of [speed skating], fundamental rules, and a math challenge in every chapter. . . . [This book] will pique your imagination." Sci Books Films

McDougall, Chros
  Figure skating. Norwood House Press 2010 64p il (Girls play to win) lib bdg $26.60
Grades: 4 5 6 7   **796.91**
1. Ice skating
ISBN 978-1-59953-389-6; 1-59953-389-8

LC 2010009809

"This begins with a look back at the origin of [figure skating] and the traces the young women who played a role in skating from the olden days to today. The first of six chapters describes skating basics . . . and then the progression of stars begins. . . . Color photos, sidebars, and boxed explanations break up the text. . . . A nicely compact history." Booklist
Includes glossary and bibliographical references

Thomas, Keltie
  How figure skating works; illustrated by Stephen MacEachern. OwlKids 2009 64p il $22.95; pa $10.95
Grades: 3 4 5 6   **796.91**
1. Ice skating
ISBN 978-1-897349-58-8; 1-897349-58-0; 978-1-897349-59-5 pa; 1-897349-59-9 pa
"This lively overview features clear, well-written explanations of the technical elements of figure skating and anecdotes from skating history.

The readable text is supplemented with eye-catching photos, cartoon illustrations, and simple diagrams and charts." SLJ
Includes glossary

796.93   Skiing and snowboarding

Kenney, Karen Latchana
  Skiing & snowboarding. Norwood House Press 2010 64p il (Girls play to win) lib bdg $26.60
Grades: 4 5 6 7   **796.93**
1. Skiing 2. Snowboarding
ISBN 978-1-59953-391-9; 1-59953-391-X

LC 2010009808

Covers the history, rules, fundamentals and significant personalities of the sports of women's skiing and snowboarding. Topics include: techniques, strategies, competitive events, and equipment.
"With an easy design and format, the [text is] highly accessible to even the most reluctant readers and [provides] great exposure and insight into the world of female professional sports." Horn Book Guide
Includes glossary and bibliographical references

Schwartz, Heather E.
  Snowboarding. Lucent Books 2011 104p il (Science behind sports) $33.45
Grades: 5 6 7 8   **796.93**
1. Snowboarding
ISBN 978-1-4205-0322-7; 1-4205-0322-7

LC 2010033274

This "explores the scientific principles such as momentum, gravity, friction, and aerodynamics, plus many more, behind [snowbarding]. . . . [The author discusses the sport's] origins, history, and changes, . . . the biomechanics and physiology of playing, related health and medical concerns, and the causes and treatment of sports-related injuries. Additional information tells how exercise, diet and nutrition, warming up, and training relate to peak performance and enjoyment of the sport. . . . The action photography . . . is fantastic. . . . [This volume is] jam-packed full of information. [A must-have] for sports fans, athletes, science students, and even anyone considering a career in sports-related medicine, coaching, or other connected fields." SLJ
Includes glossary and bibliographical references

796.94   Snowmobiling

Woods, Bob
  Snowmobile racers. Enslow Publishers 2010 48p il (Kid racers) lib bdg $23.93
Grades: 5 6 7 8   **796.94**
1. Snowmobiles
ISBN 978-0-7660-3487-7 lib bdg; 0-7660-3487-9 lib bdg

LC 2009020784

This describes snowmobiles and races for kids, discussing which snowmobiles qualify, how they are built and raced, who the best drivers are, what to look for in a snowmobile, safety, good sportsmanship, and how racing activities can be a good part of family life.
"The easily digestible text gets more visual weight on the page, but there are plenty of captioned color photos depicting different sorts of races as well as recreational snowmobiling." Booklist
Includes glossary and bibliographical references

796.96   Ice games

Wiseman, Blaine

Stanley Cup. Weigl Publishers 2011 32p il map (Sporting championships) lib bdg $26; pa $10.95

Grades: 3 4 5   **796.96**

1. Hockey

ISBN 978-1-61690-127-1 lib bdg; 1-61690-127-6 lib bdg; 978-1-61690-128-8 pa; 1-61690-128-4 pa

LC 2010006164

This sets the Stanley Cup "within the context of the sport and explains what you need to know when watching the [event]." Booklist

796.962   Ice hockey

Adams, Carly

Queens of the ice; they were fast, they were fierce, they were teen-age girls. Lorimer 2011 131p il (Record books) $16.95; pa $9.95

Grades: 5 6 7 8   **796.962**

1. Hockey 2. Women athletes

ISBN 978-1-55277-721-3; 1-55277-721-9; 978-1-55277-720-6 pa; 1-55277-720-0 pa

"Filled with exciting action, this . . . title . . . showcases the history of the Preston Rivulettes, a Canadian hockey team of teenage girls who played together for 10 seasons, from 1931 until 1940, without losing a game and at a time when many believed that girls could not play the sport and needed chaperones. . . . Adams deepens the story with the historical background of the Great Depression and the team's struggle to find money. Occasional achival photos and boxed inserts add to the clear, readable account." Booklist

Johnstone, Robb

Hockey; rev ed.; Weigl Publishers 2009 24p il (In the zone) $24.45; pa $8.95

Grades: 4 5 6 7   **796.962**

1. Hockey

ISBN 978-1-6059-6130-9; 1-6059-6130-2; 978-1-6059-6131-6 pa; 1-6059-6131-0 pa

LC 2009005607

First published 2001

"Colorful, informative. . . . For those just showing an interest in the bone-crushing sport, [this is] an excellent place to get their bearings. Using short, mostly two-page chapters, Johnstone explains the genesis of the sport, the gear needed, the rules, the positions, and the leagues, before concluding with biographies of eight legendary NHL players." Booklist

McClellan, Ray

Hockey. Bellwether Media 2010 24p il (Blastoff! readers. My first sports) $19.95

Grades: K 1 2 3   **796.962**

1. Hockey

ISBN 978-1-60014-330-4; 1-60014-330-X

LC 2009-8180

"Simple text and full color photographs introduce beginning readers to the sport of hockey." Publisher's note

Includes bibliographical references

McKinley, Michael

Ice time; the story of hockey. Tundra Books 2006 80p il $18.95

Grades: 5 6 7 8   **796.962**

1. Hockey

ISBN 978-0-88776-762-3; 0-88776-762-1

"This straightforward history of hockey emphasizes the professional game and Canadian players. . . . Hockey enthusiasts will find this a welcome arrival." Booklist

McMahon, Dave

Hockey. Norwood House Press 2010 64p il (Girls play to win) lib bdg $26.60

Grades: 4 5 6 7   **796.962**

1. Hockey

ISBN 978-1-59953-390-2; 1-59953-390-1

LC 2010009811

Covers the history, rules, fundamentals and significant personalities of the sport of women's hockey. Topics include: techniques, strategies, competitive events, and equipment.

"With an easy design and format, the [text is] highly accessible to even the most reluctant readers and [provides] great exposure and insight into the world of female professional sports." Horn Book Guide

Includes glossary and bibliographical references

Sharp, Anne Wallace

Ice hockey. Lucent Books 2011 112p il map (Science behind sports) lib bdg $33.45

Grades: 5 6 7 8   **796.962**

1. Hockey

ISBN 978-1-4205-0281-7; 1-4205-0281-6

LC 2010025670

This book about ice hockey highlights "performance; chapter headings include topics such as 'Training and Nutrition,' 'High-Tech Equipment,' and 'Injuries and Treatments.' Physics, biology, and psychology concepts related to the [sport] are . . . wrapped into technical discussions of moves and techniques. Many photographs of pros and novices in action add interest." Horn Book Guide

Includes glossary and bibliographical references

Stewart, Mark

Score! the action and artistry of hockey's magnificent moment. Millbrook Press 2010 64p il $29.27

Grades: 5 6 7 8   **796.962**

1. Hockey

ISBN 978-0-8225-8753-8; 0-8225-8753-X

"Stewart and Kennedy take readers on a chatty, photo-studded tour of the art of scoring in the rink. This intermediate-level hockey book definitely isn't for beginners. . . . What savvy readers will get, however, is a bounty of information on the game's defining goals, goal scorers, and goal-scoring techniques. . . . This makes a worthy addition to any sports shelf." Booklist

796.98   Winter Olympic games

Macy, Sue

★ **Freeze** frame; a photographic history of the Winter Olympics. National Geographic 2006 96p il map $18.95

Grades: 5 6 7 8 9 10   **796.98**

1. Olympic games 2. Winter sports

ISBN 0-7922-7887-9; 978-0-7922-7887-0

Highlights in the history of the Winter Olympics from their inception in 1924 to today, including profiles of the Olympic athletes and information on the lesser-known winter sports. Also includes an Olympic almanac with information about each Olympiad.

This book "has spectacular photographs and clear, captivating prose." SLJ

Includes bibliographical references

797 Aquatic and air sports

Kelley, K. C.

Weird water sports. Child's World 2011 24p il (Weird sports) lib bdg $25.64

Grades: 3 4 5 6 **797**

1. Water sports

ISBN 978-1-60954-380-8; 1-60954-380-8

LC 2010044028

This describes sports such as noodling, bog bike racing, concrete canoeing, underwater hockey, and river surfing.

"Both the writing and the visual style are exuberant-without relying too much on exclamation points." Booklist

797.1 Aquatic sports

Bass, Scott

Kayaking; by Scott Bass. Child's World 2005 32p il (Kids' guides) lib bdg $24.21

Grades: 4 5 6 **797.1**

1. Kayaks and kayaking

ISBN 1-59296-208-4

LC 2003-27372

This "opens with an explanation of the sport and gives reasons why people enjoy it. The four chapters that follow cover background and development, equipment, technique, and stars and competitions. The excellent color photos are clear and exciting." SLJ

Includes bibliographical references

Storey, Rita

Sailing. Sea-to-Sea Publications 2011 30p il (Know your sport) lib bdg $28.50

Grades: 4 5 6 **797.1**

1. Sailing

ISBN 978-1-59771-286-6

LC 2010003439

This "volume provides an introduction to the equipment, techniques, and safety measures for [sailing]. . . . Instructive photographs help illustrate such concepts as [tacking a sailboat], . . . while engaging stock images capture the excitement on the water. The [volume concludes] with racing information, profiling top racers, rules, and tactics." Horn Book Guide

Includes glossary

Thorpe, Yvonne

Canoeing and kayaking. Sea-to-Sea Publications 2011 30p il (Know your sport) $28.50

Grades: 4 5 6 **797.1**

1. Canoes and canoeing 2. Kayaks and kayaking

ISBN 9781597712859

LC 2010003438

This "volume provides an introduction to the equipment, techniques, and safety measures for [canoeing and kayaking]. . . . Instructive photographs help illustrate such concepts as . . . paddling a kayak, while engaging stock images capture the excitement on the water. The [volume concludes] with racing information, profiling top racers, rules, and tactics." Horn Book Guide

Includes glossary

797.12 Types of vessels

Brown, Daniel James

The boys in the boat; the true story of an American team's epic journey to win gold at the 1936 olympics. Daniel James Brown; adapted for young readers by Gregory Mone. Viking Childrens Books 2015 240 p. (hardcover) $17.99

Grades: 5 6 7 8 **797.12**

1. Olympic games, 1936 (Berlin, Ger.) 2. Rowing -- United States -- History 3. Rowers -- United States -- Biography

ISBN 0451475925; 9780451475923

LC 2015006199

This juvenile book, by Daniel James Brown, tells "the astonishing tale of nine working-class boys from the American West who at the 1936 Olympics showed the world what true grit really meant. With rowers who were the sons of loggers, shipyard workers, and farmers, the University of Washington's eight-oar crew was never expected to defeat the elite East Coast teams, yet they did, going on to shock the world by challenging the German boat rowing for Adolf Hitler." (Publisher's note)

"Overcoming a difficult childhood, Joe Rantz made the freshman crew team at the University of Washington. There, he met equally determined boys and a coach driven to take the gold at the Olympics in Hitler's Germany. Each team member is profiled; the sport of rowing becomes comprehensible and compelling. This adaptation of the adult bestseller is liberally illustrated with black-and-white photographs." Horn Book

797.2 Swimming and diving

Arroyo, Sheri L.

How deep sea divers use math; math curriculum consultant: Rhea A. Stewart. Chelsea Clubhouse 2010 32p il (Math in the real world) lib bdg $28

Grades: 4 5 6 **797.2**

1. Mathematics 2. Scuba diving 3. Vocational guidance

ISBN 978-1-60413-611-1 lib bdg; 1-60413-611-1 lib bdg

LC 2009-18413

"The layout for [this] slim [title] is bright and colorful with a photograph and a 'You Do the Math' problem to solve and large, easy-to-read text on every spread. An answer key is included in the back matter, along with a page detailing the career choices and the educational requirements. . . . [It] discusses how divers use math to determine how much air they will need in their tanks and use grids to map underwater shipwrecks. The mathematical topics covered include measurement, estimation, data analysis, and problem solving. . . . [This title] would be useful to supplement lessons on mathematics. [It] will also appeal to students wanting to learn more about math as it relates to specific careers." SLJ

Includes glossary and bibliographical references

Boudreau, Helene

Swimming science. Crabtree Pub. Co. 2009 32p il (Sports science) lib bdg $26.60; pa $8.95

Grades: 3 4 5 6 **797.2**

1. Swimming

ISBN 978-0-7787-4538-9 lib bdg; 0-7787-4538-4 lib bdg; 978-0-7787-4555-6 pa; 0-7787-4555-4 pa

LC 2008-48870

This book approachs swimming "from a scientific angle, describing some of the physics behind [the] pursuit and how athletes can use this knowledge to improve performance. . . . Fascinating facts . . . [such as] a discussion of the swimmer who covered 3,270 miles down the Amazon

River . . . are presented in a captivating, lively manner. . . . The layout features colorful text boxes interspersed among photographs." SLJ

Includes glossary and bibliographical references

Gifford, Clive

Swimming; [by] Clive Gifford. PowerKids Press 2009 32p il (Personal best) lib bdg $25.25

Grades: 4 5 6 7 8   797.2

1. Swimming

ISBN 978-1-4042-4443-6 lib bdg; 1-4042-4443-3 lib bdg

LC 2007-43003

This guide to swimming "offers well-organized and easy-to-follow instructions, focusing on rules, clothing, specific skills, and competitions. . . . Informative, readable." SLJ

Guillain, Charlotte

Swimming. Heinemann Library 2009 24p il (Sports and my body) lib bdg $21.36; pa $6.49

Grades: 1 2   797.2

1. Swimming

ISBN 978-1-4329-3455-2 lib bdg; 1-4329-3455-4 lib bdg; 978-1-4329-3460-6 pa; 1-4329-3460-0 pa

LC 2009-7083

Learn what swimming is, how it can help them stay healthy, and how they can swim safely.

This book relates "activity to health . . . [and] explains that in order to stay healthy, children should get plenty of rest, eat healthy food, and drink plenty of water." SLJ

Includes glossary and bibliographical references

Hoblin, Paul

Swimming & diving. Norwood House Press 2011 64p il (Girls play to win) lib bdg $26.60

Grades: 4 5 6 7   797.2

1. Diving 2. Swimming

ISBN 978-1-59953-466-4; 1-59953-466-5

LC 2011011038

Covers the history, rules, fundamentals, and significant personalities of the sport of women's swimming and diving. Topics include: techniques, strategies, competitive events, and equipment.

Includes glossary and bibliographical references

Lourie, Peter

First dive to shark dive. Boyds Mills Press 2006 48p il $17.95 **797.2**

1. Scuba diving 2. Bahamas

ISBN 1-59078-068-X

LC 2005-24987

"In this photo-essay, a father and his 12-year-old daughter, Suzanna, fly to Andros, in the Bahamas, so Suzanna can learn to scuba dive. During an intense seven days, she becomes certified and makes four dives. The narrative . . . also covers information about the island . . . the ocean and its inhabitants . . . and the old Andros traditions. . . . Stunning color photographs . . . reveal why Suzanna wanted to be certified to dive." Booklist

Minden, Cecilia

Swimming; [by] Cecilia Minden and Katie Marsico. Cherry Lake Pub. 2009 32p il (Real world math: Sports) lib bdg $27.07

Grades: 4 5 6   797.2

1. Swimming 2. Arithmetic

ISBN 978-1-60279-246-3 lib bdg; 1-60279-246-1 lib bdg

LC 2008-1198

This book "starts with a short story on the history of [swimming], fundamental rules, and a math challenge in every chapter. . . . [This book] will pique your imagination." Sci Books Films

Includes glossary and bibliographical references

Timblin, Stephen

Swimming. Cherry Lake Pub. 2009 32p il (Innovation in sports) lib bdg $27.07

Grades: 4 5 6 7   797.2

1. Swimming

ISBN 978-1-60279-258-6 lib bdg; 1-60279-258-5 lib bdg

LC 2008002046

This describes swimming history, rules, equipment, training, and swimming stars

This "stands out by emphasizing monumental shifts and advances in the events themselves. . . . Concise and occasionally revelatory." Booklist

Includes glossary and bibliographical references

Wendorff, Anne

Swimming. Bellwether Media 2010 24p il (Blastoff! readers. My first sports) $19.95

Grades: K 1 2 3   797.2

1. Swimming

ISBN 978-1-60014-326-7; 1-60014-326-1

LC 2009-8182

Simple text and full color photographs introduce beginning readers to the sport of swimming.

Includes glossary and bibliographical references

798.4   Horse racing

Joyce, Gare

Northern Dancer; king of the racetrack. Gare Joyce. Fitzhenry & Whiteside 2011 72 p.

Grades: 4 5 6   798.4

1. Northern Dancer (Race horse)

ISBN 1554551633; 9781554551637

This book by Gare Joyce focuses on the racing horse Northern Dancer. "As a colt, he was unimpressive. . . . Eventually, the colt that nobody wanted took the racing world by storm. Northern Dancer won the Kentucky Derby, and went on to win the Preakness Stakes of Baltimore, and nearly won the Belmont of New York. On retirement, Northern Dancer became the greatest horse stud in history, worth over $40 million by 1981." (Publisher's note)

McCarthy, Meghan

★ Seabiscuit; the wonder horse. Simon & Schuster Books for Young Readers 2008 un il $15.99

Grades: K 1 2 3   798.4

1. Horse racing 2. Seabiscuit (Race horse)

ISBN 978-1-4169-3360-1; 1-4169-3360-3

LC 2008-06729

"The book covers Seabiscuit's transformation from scruffy loser to—well, scruffy winner, his loyal team of owner, trainer, and jockey, and his appeal to the economically pinched crowds; the saga here culminates in Seabiscuit's famous match with War Admiral. . . . The account is simplified for the youngest audiences, and they'll get the high points of the story . . . without getting lost in detail. . . . The cartooning is genuinely comic at times; the acrylic paintings are subtly toned, though, with gray touches muting the colors slightly." Bull Cent Child Books

Scanlan, Lawrence

The **big** red horse; the story of Secretariat and the loyal groom who loved him. with photos by Raymond Woolfe. Harper Trophy 2011 166p il pa $7.99

Grades: 4 5 6 7   **798.4**

1. Horse racing 2. Stablehands

ISBN 978-0-06-202669-9; 0-06-202669-0

"This biography of the legendary racehorse provides many intimate details about his daily life and incredible prowess. . . . His good looks and tremendous athletic ability enabled him to win the Triple Crown at a record-breaking pace and the hearts of the American people. Scanlan focuses on the special relationship between Secretariat and his groom, Eddie Sweat. . . . Black-and-white photos are scattered throughout. . . . This solid book will have special appeal for horse lovers." SLJ

Tate, Nikki

Behind the scenes: the racehorse. Fitzhenry & Whiteside 2008 72p il $22.95; pa $18.95

Grades: 5 6 7 8   **798.4**

1. Horse racing

ISBN 978-1-55455-018-0; 1-55455-018-1; 978-1-55455-032-6 pa; 1-55455-032-7 pa

"A short history of horse racing opens this attractive and informative book. Tate discusses the breeding, training, and care of the horses but devotes plenty of space to the people who are involved in the sport. . . . The many color photos . . . are quite clear and well matched to the text." Booklist

Wiseman, Blaine

Kentucky Derby. Weigl Publishers 2010 32p il (Sporting championships) lib bdg $26; pa $10.95

Grades: 3 4 5   **798.4**

1. Horse racing 2. Kentucky Derby

ISBN 978-1-61690-121-9 lib bdg; 1-61690-121-7 lib bdg; 978-1-61690-122-6 pa; 1-61690-122-5 pa

This sets the Kentucky Derby "within the context of the sport and explains what you need to know when watching the [event]." Booklist

Includes bibliographical references

798.8   Dog racing

Miller, Debbie S.

The **great** serum race; blazing the Iditarod Trail. illustrations by Jon van Zyle. Walker & Co. 2002 un il map hardcover o.p. pa $8.95

Grades: 3 4 5   **798.8**

1. Dogs 2. Iditarod Trail Sled Dog Race, Alaska 3. Alaska

ISBN 0-8027-8811-4; 0-8027-8812-2 lib bdg; 0-8027-7723-2 pa

LC 2001-56777

The story of the heroic role played by sled dogs, including the Siberian husky Togo, in the delivery of antitoxin serum to those stricken with diphtheria in 1925 Nome. Includes historical notes about the event as well as about the Iditarod Sled Dog Race which commemorates it

"Zyle, official artist of the Iditarod and a musher himself, has created vivid, full-spread paintings to bring the story to life. . . . This is an excellent account told with lots of detail and drama." SLJ

Includes bibliographical references

799.1   Fishing

Lindeen, Carol

Freshwater fishing; by Carol K. Lindeen. Capstone Press 2011 32p il (Blazers. Wild outdoors) lib bdg $25.32

Grades: 2 3 4   **799.1**

1. Fishing

ISBN 978-1-4296-4810-3 lib bdg; 1-4296-4810-4 lib bdg

LC 2010001015

This "will fill a gap in many rural communities. . . . Blocks of text or 'Wild Facts' are scattered among the pages providing humorous or memorable trivia. . . . Close-up photography fills the pages and shows safe hunting attire." SLJ

Includes glossary and bibliographical references

799.2   Hunting

Adamson, Thomas K.

Bowhunting. Capstone Press 2011 32p il (Blazers. Wild outdoors) lib bdg $25.32

Grades: 2 3 4   **799.2**

1. Hunting 2. Bow and arrow

ISBN 978-1-4296-4808-0 lib bdg; 1-4296-4808-2 lib bdg

LC 2009053410

This "will fill a gap in many rural communities. . . . Blocks of text or 'Wild Facts' are scattered among the pages providing humorous or memorable trivia. . . . Close-up photography fills the pages and shows safe hunting attire." SLJ

Includes glossary and bibliographical references

Deer hunting. Capstone Press 2011 32p il (Blazers. Wild outdoors) lib bdg $25.32

Grades: 2 3 4   **799.2**

1. Deer hunting

ISBN 978-1-4296-4807-3 lib bdg; 1-4296-4807-4 lib bdg

LC 2009053412

Describes how to hunt deer, including the skills and patience required for the hunt, the proper guns and ammunition needed, and the safety skills every hunter should follow.

This "will fill a gap in many rural communities. . . . Blocks of text or 'Wild Facts' are scattered among the pages providing humorous or memorable trivia. . . . Close-up photography fills the pages and shows safe hunting attire." SLJ

Includes glossary and bibliographical references

Duck hunting. Capstone Press 2011 32p il (Blazers. Wild outdoors) lib bdg $25.32

Grades: 2 3 4   **799.2**

1. Ducks 2. Hunting

ISBN 978-1-4296-4809-7 lib bdg; 1-4296-4809-0 lib bdg

LC 2010001097

This "will fill a gap in many rural communities. . . . Blocks of text or 'Wild Facts' are scattered among the pages providing humorous or memorable trivia. . . . Close-up photography fills the pages and shows safe hunting attire." SLJ

Includes glossary and bibliographical references

Peterson, Judy Monroe

Big game hunting. Rosen Central 2011 64p il map (Hunting: pursuing wild game!)) lib bdg $29.25; pa $12.95

Grades: 5 6 7 8 **799.2**
1. Hunting
ISBN 978-1-4488-1240-0 lib bdg; 1-4488-1240-2 lib bdg; 978-1-4488-2270-6 pa; 1-4488-2270-X pa

LC 2010006859

In this introduction to big game hunting "Peterson displays an impressive grasp of the pastime by throwing in almost everything: types of guns and bows, safety laws, licenses, land access, animal behavior, clothing, methods of hunting, and preparing harvested meat. . . . [The book] is jam-packed with info. . . . A green-heavy design, bright photoss of hunters . . . and prey, and above average back matter close out this solid entry." Booklist

Includes bibliographical references

Wolny, Philip
Waterfowl. Rosen Central 2011 64p il (Hunting: pursuing wild game!) lib bdg $29.25; pa $12.95
Grades: 4 5 6 7 **799.2**
1. Hunting 2. Water birds
ISBN 978-1-4488-1243-1 lib bdg; 1-4488-1243-7 lib bdg; 978-1-4488-2273-7 pa; 1-4488-2273-4 pa

LC 2010017396

This guide to waterfowl hunting covers what to wear and pack, shooting strategies, the construction of duck blinds, gun safety, hunting permits and licenses, and other laws relating to hunting limits, seasons, and private and public property.

Includes bibliographical references

800 LITERATURE, RHETORIC & CRITICISM

808 Rhetoric and collections of literary texts from more than two literatures

Children's writer's & illustrator's market; edited by Alice Pope. Writer's Digest Books il
Grades: Adult Professional **808**
1. Publishers and publishing 2. Authorship -- Handbooks, manuals, etc.
Annual. First published 1998

This reference includes listings of children's book publishers, magazines, agents, art reps, contests, clubs, conferences, awards, and grants with contact information, along with articles and interviews on a variety of subjects relating to children's writing, illustrating, and publishing

Includes bibliographical references

Christelow, Eileen
★ **What** do authors do? Clarion Bks. 1995 32p il hardcover o.p. pa $5.95
Grades: 1 2 3 **808**
1. Authors 2. Authorship 3. Illustrators 4. Publishers and publishing
ISBN 0-395-71124-X; 0-395-86621-9 pa

LC 94-19725

"Christelow packs a great deal of humor as well as information into her attractive pages. Best of all, she infuses the whole with a sense of the zest and love that writers feel for their work." Booklist

Cleary, Brian P.
Skin like milk, hair of silk; what are similes and metaphors? illustrated by Brian Gable. Millbrook Press 2009 il (Words are categorical) lib bdg $15.95
Grades: 2 3 4 **808**
1. Simile 2. Metaphor
ISBN 978-0-8225-9151-1; 0-8225-9151-0

LC 2008049643

"Cleary provides brief definitions of similes and metaphors, offers roughly 15 examples of each one, and explains how they are used. Large pen-and-ink illustrations feature cartoon cats rendered in bold, vibrant colors. The style is fun and inviting." SLJ

Cornwall, Phyllis
Put it all together. Cherry Lake Pub. 2010 32p il (Super smart information strategies) lib bdg $27.97
Grades: 3 4 5 6 **808**
1. Report writing
ISBN 978-1-60279-643-0 lib bdg; 1-60279-643-2 lib bdg

LC 2009027806

"The appealing layout includes manageable paragraphs, a variety of engaging illustrations, and examples that clearly guide readers through each topic. In [this book], strategies include gathering resources, organizing information, and ways of presenting discoveries." SLJ

Includes glossary and bibliographical references

Fox, Kathleen
Plagiarism! Plagiarism! 25 fun games and activities to teach documenting and sourcing skills to students. Upstart Books 2011 56p il pa $14.95
Grades: Adult Professional **808**
1. Authorship 2. Plagiarism
ISBN 978-1-60213-050-0; 1-60213-050-7

"This handy book is aimed at teaching a tricky concept to primary and elementary grade children. The author provides a discussion of sources, rewording, when to use quotation marks, etc. Each activity is written in the style of a lesson plan." SLJ

Greenwood, Cathleen
So, you wanna be a writer? how to write, get published, and maybe even make it big! Vicki Hambleton, Cathleen Greenwood. Aladdin/Beyond Words 2012 186 p. ill. (So, you wanna be ..) (pbk.) $9.99
Grades: 4 5 6 **808**
1. Vocational guidance 2. Authorship -- Handbooks, manuals, etc. 3. Authorship
ISBN 9781582700434 2001 edition.; 1582700435 2001 edition; 9781582703534 2012 edition; 1582703590 2012 edition; 9781582703596 2012 edition; 9781442452916 2012 edition

LC 2011046252

This book presents a "[s]oup-to-nuts overview on all aspects of developing a writing career, from picking a genre to publicizing a finished work." It includes "myriad interviews, not only of established professionals such as Wendelin Van Draanen and Todd Strasser, but of young writers who may not be as familiar. Additionally, the authors sample some of these young wordsmiths' work . . . It includes quizzes, writing exercises to loosen up the brain and a handy section on further resources as well as a . . . short glossary of terms that all professional writers should know." (Kirkus Reviews)

Gutman, Dan
My weird writing tips; by Dan Gutman and illustrated by Jim Paillot. HarperCollins Publishers 2013 160 p. $5.99

Grades: 3 4 5 6 7   **808**
1. Language arts 2. English language -- Composition and exercises
ISBN 0062091069; 9780062091062; 9780062091079
LC 2012029985

This book by Dan Gutman "offers tricks for spelling hard words, understanding the difference between similar words like "its" and "it's," and conquering grammar stumbling blocks like commas and apostrophes. He also teaches readers how to write an engaging story, in line with the grades 2-5 Common Core goals for writing a narrative." (Publisher's note)

It rained all day that night; autographs, rhymes & inscriptions. compiled by Lillian Morrison; illustrated by Christy Hale. August House 2003 80p il $16.95; pa $9.95
Grades: 3 4 5 6   **808**
1. American poetry -- Collections
ISBN 0-87483-735-9; 0-87483-726-X pa
LC 2003-51987

An illustrated compilation of short poems and other inscriptions from autograph albums, arranged by such themes as friendship, school, and nonsense.

"Morrison has created a stunning collection of autograph verses. . . . Hale's ink-and-watercolor paintings dance across each page, extending the sentiment . . . implicit in each verse." SLJ

Leedy, Loreen
★ **Look** at my book; how kids can write & illustrate terrific books. written and illustrated by Loreen Leedy. Holiday House 2004 32p il $16.95
Grades: K 1 2 3   **808**
1. Authorship 2. Bookbinding 3. Illustration of books
ISBN 0-8234-1590-2
LC 2003-41713

Provides ideas and simple directions for writing, illustrating, designing, and binding books.

"Following the writing process fairly closely . . . [the author] takes readers through a step-by-step formula that almost guarantees a successful product. . . . Lively, colorful illustrations expand and interpret the text." SLJ

Mack, James
Journals and blogging; [by] Jim Mack. Raintree 2009 32p il (Culture in action) $28.21; pa $7.99
Grades: 5 6 7 8   **808**
1. Diaries 2. Weblogs
ISBN 978-1-4109-3406-2; 1-4109-3406-3; 978-1-4109-3423-9 pa; 1-4109-3423-3 pa
LC 2009000490

This "encourages readers to write as a way to express their feelings. It describes different types of journals and blogs. A page on Internet safety and the danger of downloading material encourages adult supervision. . . . Well organized and with bright, colorful photography, [this] introductory [title gives] readers good basic knowledge." SLJ
Includes glossary and bibliographical references

Miles, Liz
Writing a screenplay. Raintree 2009 32p il (Culture in action) $28.21; pa $7.99
Grades: 5 6 7 8   **808**
1. Drama -- Technique
ISBN 978-1-4109-3407-9; 1-4109-3407-1; 978-1-4109-3424-6 pa; 1-4109-3424-1 pa
This covers writing for "film and television. Plot, location, characters, dialogue, and mood are a few of the components discussed. . . .

Well organized and with bright, colorful photography, [this] introductory [title gives] readers good basic knowledge." SLJ
Includes glossary and bibliographical references

Rau, Dana Meachen
Ace your creative writing project. Enslow Elementary 2009 48p il (Ace it! information literacy) lib bdg $23.93
Grades: 3 4 5   **808**
1. Creative writing
ISBN 978-0-7660-3395-5 lib bdg; 0-7660-3395-3 lib bdg
LC 2008024888

This describes where writers get their ideas, your story's characters and setting, writing, revising, and presenting your writing
Includes bibliographical references

Ace your writing assignment. Enslow Elementary 2009 48p il (Ace it! information literacy) lib bdg $23.93
Grades: 3 4 5   **808**
1. English language -- Composition and exercises
ISBN 978-0-7660-3394-8 lib bdg; 0-7660-3394-5 lib bdg
LC 2008024887

This describes how to make writing better and more interesting
Includes bibliographical references

Rosinsky, Natalie M.
Write your own biography; by Natalie M. Rosinsky. Compass Point Books 2008 64p il (Write your own) lib bdg $31.93
Grades: 5 6 7 8   **808**
1. Biography -- Authorship
ISBN 978-0-7565-3366-3 lib bdg; 0-7565-3366-X lib bdg
LC 2007011471

"Rosinsky adroitly leads readers through the challenging process of researching and writing a biography. Chapters include helpful suggestions, excerpts from published works, and writing exercises. Full-color photos, charts, and graphics break up the text." SLJ
Includes glossary and bibliographical references

Writing and publishing; the librarian's handbook. edited by Carol Smallwood. American Library Association 2010 189p (ALA guides for the busy librarian) pa $65
Grades: Adult Professional   **808**
1. Authorship 2. Library science
ISBN 978-0-8389-0996-6; 0-8389-0996-5
LC 2009-25047

"This important writer's guide is readable from cover to cover or by bits and pieces and is a helpful and handy read for every librarian." Libr Media Connect
Includes bibliographical references

808.02   Authorship techniques, plagiarism, editorial techniques

Levine, Gail Carson, 1947-
Writer to writer; from think to ink. Gail Carson Levine. HarperCollins 2014 304 p. (hardback) $16.99
Grades: 5 6 7 8   **808.02**
1. Authorship 2. Creative writing
ISBN 0062275305; 9780062275301
LC 2014005858

In this book, author Gail Carson Levine "offers a behind-the-scenes take on writing and teaches you how to become a world-class author. Drawing from her popular blog, Gail answers readers' fiction- and poetry-writing questions and dives into how to make a story come alive. If you're interested in writing prose and poetry or just want to be a better and more rounded writer, this book will help you on your creative journey." (Publisher's note)

"Ella Enchanted author Levine offers writing advice and prompts, primarily for fiction writers. The chapters, mostly expanded from her blog, look in-depth at aspects of writing including large-scale character and plot concerns and more specific matters of style. A lengthy section focuses on poetry and its role in fiction. Levine's second book on writing (Writing Magic) takes budding authors' craft questions seriously." Horn Book

808.06 Rhetoric of specific kinds of writing

Fletcher, Ralph
Guy-write; what every guy writer needs to know. by Ralph Fletcher. 1st ed. Christy Ottaviano Books/Henry Holt and Co. 2012 166 p. ill. (hardcover) $15.99
Grades: 4 5 6 **808.06**
1. Writing 2. Boys -- Books and reading 3. Authors 4. Authorship 5. Illustrators 6. Children's literature -- Authorship
ISBN 0805094040; 9780805094046
LC 2011033487
Author Ralph "Fletcher offers a new writing guide with advice aimed squarely at boys. . . . He lets guy writers know it's OK to write what they love: humor, grossness, battles, fantasy and horror. And he counsels guy writers on how to talk with their teachers about writing what they love to satisfy assignments. Along the way Fletcher peppers the text with general writing tips and suggestions for ways to make all types of writing stronger and more enjoyable." (Kirkus Reviews)

808.1 Rhetoric in specific literary forms

Alexander, Kwame
Out of wonder; poems celebrating poets. Kwame Alexander with Chris Colderley and Marjory Wentworth; illustrated by Ekua Holmes. Candlewick Press 2017 56 p. color illustrations $16.99
Grades: 3 4 5 6 7 8 **808.1**
1. Poetry -- Collections
ISBN 076368094X; 9780763680947
LC 2017931505
"Out of gratitude for the poet's art form, . . . author and poet Kwame Alexander, along with Chris Colderley and Marjory Wentworth, present original poems that pay homage to twenty famed poets who have made the authors' hearts sing and their minds wonder. . . . Mixed-media images by Ekua Holmes . . . complete the celebration and invite the reader to listen, wonder, and perhaps even pick up a pen." (Publisher's note)

"Each illustration captures not just the feeling of the poem but wakes readers up to life's excitements and small joys. Exemplary words and pictures make this a multicultural masterwork." Booklist

Prelutsky, Jack
★ **Pizza,** pigs, and poetry; how to write a poem. Greenwillow Books 2008 191p il $16.99; pa $5.99
Grades: 4 5 6 **808.1**
1. Poetics
ISBN 978-0-06-143449-5; 0-06-143449-3; 978-0-06-143448-8 pa; 0-06-143448-5 pa
LC 2007-36738
"Along with easy-to-follow tips for creating verse, haiku, and concrete poetry, the reigning Children's Poet Laureate offers insights into his own thought processes, . . . glimpses of his childhood, and personal

anecdotes. . . . Prelutsky tucks in more than a dozen examples of his own work, plus 10 two-and-part-of-a-third line 'poem starts.'" Booklist

808.3 Rhetoric of fiction

Anderson, Jennifer Joline
Writing fantastic fiction; by Jennifer Joline Anderson. Lerner Publications 2015 56 p. illustrations (chiefly color) (lb : alk. paper) $33.32
Grades: 4 5 6 7 **808.3**
1. Creative writing 2. Authorship 3. Fiction -- Authorship
ISBN 9781467779081; 9781467782906
LC 2014044105
This book, by Jennifer Joline Anderson, "takes you through the steps of writing a story from beginning to end. Learn how to gather inspiration and develop a story's characters. Then visualize and organize your story's plot with a writing map. And after you've written a really rough draft, check out tips for revising your work. You'll also be inspired by unique writing exercises and storytelling insights from popular authors." (Publisher's note)

"Clearly presented and with a colorful design, this will work very well for middle-graders, but the advice is so good, older kids will find it extremely helpful as well. An especially inviting way to step into writing." Booklist
Includes bibliographical references and index

Bullard, Lisa
You can write a story! a story-writing recipe for kids. by Lisa Bullard; illustrated by Deborah Haley Melmon. Two-Can 2007 47p il $16.95
Grades: 2 3 4 **808.3**
1. Authorship 2. Creative writing 3. Fiction -- Technique
ISBN 978-1-58728-587-5; 1-58728-587-8
LC 2006016771
"Bullard takes a clever approach to teaching children the basic steps in story composition by treating the process as a cooking exercise. She begins with the basic ingredients of character, setting, and action, and then takes readers through the various ways they can add flavorings to their stories, including spicy settings, tempting titles, and the all-important taste test (revising). . . . The clear, engaging text speaks directly to a child. . . . Melmon's cartoon illustrations are bright, amusing, and strategically placed to add interest." Booklist
Includes bibliographical references

Giff, Patricia Reilly, 1935-
Writing with Rosie; you can write a story too. Patricia Reilly Giff. Holiday House 2016 73 p. (hardcover) $15.95; (ebook) $15.95
Grades: 3 4 5 6 7 8 **808.3**
1. Creative writing 2. Fiction -- Technique
ISBN 082343656X; 9780823436569; 9780823437504
LC 2015041844
In this book, author Patricia Reilly Giff "breaks down the process of writing fiction into steps, all while trying to cope with the constant distractions from her exuberant seventy-pound golden retriever puppy, Rosie. Citing examples from her award-winning novels she explains how to proceed with each step in chapter sections titled Can You See What I Did? Young writers can find the inspiration and tips they need to try their hand in sections called Your Turn." (Publisher's note)

"An excellent choice for writing classes or for individual inspiration." Booklist

Hershenhorn, Esther

S is for story; a writer's alphabet. written by Esther Hershenhorn; illustrated by Zachary Pullen. Sleeping Bear Press 2009 un il $17.95; lib bdg $7.95

Grades: 3 4 5 6   **808.3**

1. Alphabet 2. Authorship 3. Fiction -- Technique

ISBN 978-1-58536-439-8; 1-58536-439-8; 978-1-58536-511-1 lib bdg; 1-58536-511-4 lib bdg

LC 2009005433

"This engaging, instructive introduction to writing stands out. The concepts paired with each letter cover elements of story (plot, characters); technique (revision, journaling); and basic practices for fostering creativity (observe). Short poems; clear, enthusiastic explanations; tips; and quotes from well-known children's authors appear on each page." Booklist

Levine, Gail Carson

★ Writing magic; creating stories that fly. Collins 2006 167p $16.99; pa $5.99

Grades: 5 6 7 8   **808.3**

1. Authorship 2. Creative writing 3. Fiction -- Technique

ISBN 978-0-06-051961-2; 0-06-051969-4; 978-0-06-051960-5 pa; 0-06-051960-6 pa

LC 2006-00481

"Levine, best known for Ella Enchanted (1997), offers middle-graders ideas about making their own writing take flight. . . . Among the topics she covers are shaping character, beginnings and endings, revising, and finding ideas. . . . Each chapter concludes with writing exercises. . . . A terrific item to have on hand for writing groups or for individual young writers who want to improve." Booklist

Litwin, Laura Baskes

Write horror fiction in 5 simple steps; Laura Baskes Litwin. Enslow Publishers 2013 48 p. (Creative Writing in 5 Simple Steps) $23.93

Grades: 4 5 6   **808.3**

1. Horror fiction -- Authorship 2. Horror tales -- Technique

ISBN 076603836X; 9780766038363

LC 2010038776

This book by Laura Baskes Litwin, part of the Creative Writing in 5 Simple Steps series, "shows aspiring writers how to write a terrifying tale of horror. . . . A good horror story is like a good ride at an amusement park. Feeling scared without having to face real danger is exhilarating. The story builds with tantalizing ideas. The reader inches out on the coaster track, knowing the precarious drop is seconds away." (Publisher's note)

Includes bibliographical references, filmography and index

Mazer, Anne

★ Spilling ink; a young writer's handbook. by Anne Mazer and Ellen Potter; illustrated by Matt Phelan. Flash Point 2010 275p il $17.99; pa $9.99

Grades: 5 6 7 8   **808.3**

1. Authorship 2. Creative writing 3. Fiction -- Technique

ISBN 978-1-59643-514-8; 1-59643-514-3; 978-1-59643-628-2 pa; 1-59643-628-X pa

"Two fine writers put their heads together and come up with an equally fine guide to their craft for beginners. . . . Mazer speaks to beginnings . . . while Potter tackles endings; and both have diverting things to say about everything that happens in between, whether it's the narrative voice or (eek) writer's block. [They are] always agreeable, practical, and commonsensical in their approach. . . . Their text is enlivened with sidebar features, personal anecdotes, and suggestions to readers for exercising their new skills. . . . Such devices, along with the authors' unfailing good humor, will go a long way to convincing their audience that writing

can actually be fun! A notion that is nicely underscored by Phelan's engaging and always appealing illustrations." Booklist

808.5   Rhetoric of speech

Bullard, Lisa

Ace your oral or multimedia presentation. Enslow Elementary 2009 48p il (Ace it! information literacy) lib bdg $23.93

Grades: 3 4 5   **808.5**

1. Multimedia 2. Public speaking

ISBN 978-0-7660-3391-7 lib bdg; 0-7660-3391-0 lib bdg

LC 2008024885

"Learn how to research, write, practice, and present an oral or multimedia presentation with confidence" Publisher's note

Includes bibliographical references

808.8   Collections of literary texts from more than two literatures

The big book for toddlers; edited by Alice Wong & Lena Tabori. Welcome Books 2009 219p il $24.95

Grades: PreK K   **808.8**

1. Games 2. Handicraft 3. Fairy tales 4. Nursery rhymes

ISBN 978-1-59962-071-8; 1-59962-071-5

"Full-bleed vintage illustrations by Jessie Willcox Smith, Maxfield Parrish, Margaret Evans Price and others grace the pages of this cheerful . . . hardcover book, divided into five sections: arts and crafts activities, condensed fairy tales, songs, games and nursery rhymes. The projects are simple and have buoyant instructions, . . . songs such as 'Old MacDonald' and 'Ants Go Marching' include musical notation; and familiar stories and rhymes appear as well. The lively assemblage will appeal to toddlers, and the heirloom images should captivate them as well as nostalgic adults." Publ Wkly

Classic horse stories; compiled by Christina Rossetti Darling and Blue Lantern Studio. Chronicle Books 2010 144p $19.99

Grades: 4 5 6   **808.8**

1. Horses 2. Literature -- Collections

ISBN 978-0-8118-6569-2; 0-8118-6569-X

LC 2010008550

"This compilation of stories, poems, and artwork celebrates the relationship between horses and their devotees. Darling pulls from a wide range of familiar, beloved material: excerpts from Steinbeck's The Red Pony, Farley's The Black Stallion, and Lewis's The Horse and His Boy join poetry from Shakespeare, Farjeon, and Stevenson. Varied paintings and illustrations from throughout the 20th century underscore the point that the book offers something for all tastes." Publ Wkly

DePaola, Tomie, 1934-

Joy to the world; Christmas stories and songs. G.P. Putnam's Sons 2010 111p il lib bdg $24.99

Grades: K 1 2 3   **808.8**

1. Carols 2. Christmas 3. Literature -- Collections

ISBN 978-0-399-25536-6; 0-399-25536-2

LC 2010284499

"This handsome omnibus includes three of dePaola's adaptations of traditional Christmas legends—The Night of Las Posadas, The Story of the Three Wise Kings, and The Legend of the Poinsettia—in addition to five selections from Tomie dePaola's Book of Christmas Carols. The distinctions of tone and style reveal a versitility with which this illustrator is not always credited." Horn Book Guide

Everything I need to know I learned from a children's book. Roaring Brook 2009 233p $29.99

 Grades: Adult Professional **808.8**

 1. Children's literature -- History and criticism

 ISBN 978-1-59643-395-3; 1-59643-395-7

"Over 100 noteworthy figures, from Ursula K. Le Guin to Jay Leno, convey lessons learned from specific children's books in this affirming collaboration, which is divided into six thematic sections and features full-color images. For each selection, a contributor provides a brief essay about how the book influenced him or her, accompanied by an excerpt. . . . A moving patchwork message about the transformative powers of reading." Publ Wkly

Griffiths, Andy

 Killer koalas from outer space; and lots of other very bad stuff that will make your brain explode! illustrations by Terry Denton. Feiwel and Friends 2011 172p il $12.99

 Grades: 3 4 5 6 **808.8**

 1. Literature -- Collections

 ISBN 978-0-312-36789-3; 0-312-36789-9

Portions of this book were originally published in Australia as The Bad Book and The Very Bad Book copyright page

"Sometimes bad can be very, very good indeed. Griffiths proves this time and again in this hilarious collection of rude, lewd and crude poems, jokes and cautionary tales. Deliciously revolting characters in stories . . . are sure to leave young, potty-humor-loving readers in stitches. Denton's edgy, stick-figure illustrations only add to the fun, upping the gross-out ante and giving the collection a frenetic energy that makes the book nearly impossible to put down. . . . The genius of this subversive little tome lies in its perfect combination of zany subject matter that will appeal to a broad spectrum of readers and a format that make it easily accessible to beginning and struggling readers." Kirkus

Julie Andrews' collection of poems, songs, and lullabies; edited by Julie Andrews and Emma Walton Hamilton; paintings by James McMullan. Little, Brown Books for Young Readers 2009 192p il $24.99

 Grades: K 1 2 3 **808.8**

 1. Songs 2. Lullabies 3. Poetry -- Collections

 ISBN 978-0-316-04049-5; 0-316-04049-5

            LC 2009-5121

"Julie Andrews and her daughter's selection of material for children contains works by figures as diverse as Emily Dickinson, Langston Hughes, Rodgers and Hammerstein, A.A. Milne and Shel Silverstein, as well as offerings by Andrews and Hamilton. McMullan's paintings express the sometimes silly, sometimes melancholic temperaments of the pieces, which together form a tapestry of human emotions and experiences, grand and small. The broad potpourri of voices, given a modern yet comforting flair by the artwork, is bound to become a favorite. An audio CD with poems read by Andrews and Hamilton is included." Publ Wkly

The **Norton** anthology of children's literature; the traditions in English. Jack Zipes, general editor . . . [et al.] W.W. Norton 2005 xxxviii, 2471p il pa $65

 Grades: Adult Professional **808.8**

 1. Literature -- Collections 2. Children's literature -- History and criticism

 ISBN 0-393-97538-X

            LC 2004-54172

A collection of fairy tales, picture books, nursery rhymes, fantasy, alphabets, chapbooks, and comics published in English since 1659, representing 170 authors and illustrators, and including more than ninety complete works and excerpts from others

"The delights are abundant. . . . A mile wide and very deep, this is an invaluable resource for professionals, but fun for casual perusing, too." Publ Wkly

Includes bibliographical references

808.81 Collections in specific forms

All the wild wonders; poems of our Earth. edited by Wendy Cooling; illustrated by Piet Grobler. Frances Lincoln 2010 42p il $19.95

 Grades: 2 3 4 5 **808.81**

 1. Nature poetry 2. Poetry -- Collections

 ISBN 978-1-84780-073-2; 1-84780-073-4

"The selections from more than 30 poets in this anthology celebrate the beauty of the wild and warn of the danger that threatens the environment. . . . With a multiracial cast, Grobler's moving, pencil-and-watercolor illustrations extend the global, environmental connections. . . . Great for sharing, this will grab conservationists with both the warnings and the hope." Booklist

Beastly Verse; [illustrated by] JooHee Yoon. Enchanted Lion Books 2015 48 p. color illustrations (hardback) $18.95

 Grades: PreK K 1 2 3 4 **808.81**

 1. Children's poetry 2. Animals -- Juvenile poetry

 ISBN 1592701663; 9781592701667

            LC 2015006011

This book, illustrated by JooHee Yoon, "aims to help return the wonder of poetry to children's lives through sixteen . . . illustrated poems, four of which" include foldouts. The book "transports the reader into a richly worded world of tigers, hummingbirds, owls, elephants, pelicans, yaks, snails, and even telephones!" (Publisher's note)

"Yoon's bold imagination is evidenced by her illustrations of these 16 animal-related poems by an eclectic group of writers including Lewis Carroll, D.H. Lawrence, and surrealist Robert Desnos. . . . An excellent, innovative approach to poetry." SLJ

Carle, Eric

 Eric Carle's animals, animals; Poems compiled by Laura Whipple. Philomel Bks. 1989 87p $21.99; pa $7.99

 Grades: 2 3 4 5 **808.81**

 1. Animals -- Poetry 2. Poetry -- Collections

 ISBN 0-399-21744-4; 0-698-11855-3 pa

            LC 88-31646

"Illustrations take center stage in Eric Carle's Animals Animals . . . compiled by Laura Whipple. The well-chosen poems are from a variety of sources—the Bible, Shakespeare, Japanese Haiku, Pawnee Indian, weather sayings and contemporary poets like Judith Viorst, Ogden Nash, and Jack Prelutsky. On many pages the poem may be only two or three lines but the pictures are full-page spreads in Mr. Carle's familiar vividly colored, collage style." Kobrin Letter

 Eric Carle's dragons dragons and other creatures that never were; compiled by Laura Whipple. Philomel Bks. 1991 69p il $21.99; pa $12.99

 Grades: 2 3 4 5 **808.81**

 1. Poetry -- Collections 2. Mythical animals -- Poetry

 ISBN 0-399-22105-0; 0-399-22837-3 pa

            LC 91-11986

An illustrated collection of poems about dragons and other fantastic creatures by a variety of authors

"The collection offers a sumptuous viewing of Carle's rich blend of tissue-paper and paint collages and a grand introduction to the imaginary beasts. Laura Whipple concludes this adroit compilation with a brief commentary on the fabulous animals as 'a magical part of our human heritage.'" Horn Book

Includes glossary

A **children's** treasury of poems; illustrations by Linda Bleck. Sterling 2008 un il $12.95

Grades: PreK K 1 2   **808.81**

1. Poetry -- Collections

ISBN 978-1-4027-4498-3; 1-4027-4498-6

"This collection of 19 humorous poems includes Robert Louis Stevenson's 'Bed in Summer,' Vachel Lindsay's 'The Little Turtle,' Edward Lear's 'The Owl and the Pussycat,' and Gelett Burgess's 'The Purple Cow,' among other familiar verses. Playful, cartoonlike illustrations with cutout characters and details superimposed on sturdy pages give the book texture and help create a novel effect. Different ethnicities are represented in the illustrations, although most are of fanciful animals and fairies. Young children should find the childlike format appealing." SLJ

Collins-Philippe, Jane

Sail away with me; old and new poems. selected and written by Jane Collins-Philippe; illustrated by Laura Beingessner. Tundra Books 2010 un il $15.95

Grades: K 1 2 3   **808.81**

1. Sea poetry 2. Poetry -- Collections

ISBN 978-0-88776-842-2; 0-88776-842-3

"Starting off with 'My Bonnie Lies Over the Ocean' and other folksong favorites, this picture-book poetry collection celebrates the sea and sailing traditions. . . . The lively watercolor illustrations extend the images i the words. . . . Ranging in theme from adventure to nonsense, these poems will be fun for reading aloud." Booklist

Driscoll, Michael

★ A **child's** introduction to poetry; listen while you learn about the magic words that have moved mountains, won battles and made us laugh and cry. illustrated by Meredith Hamilton. Black Dog & Leventhal 2003 90p il $19.95

Grades: 4 5 6 7   **808.81**

1. Poetry -- Collections 2. Poetry -- History and criticism

ISBN 1-57912-282-5

"The first section discusses the different forms the genre takes: nursery rhyme, narrative verse, ballad, free verse, pastoral, etc. Driscoll offers a clear explanation of each type and defines any difficult, associated vocabulary. Commentary on each example and a note on where to find the recording on the accompanying CD is provided for each selection. The second section covers individual poets from Homer to Maya Angelou and offers at least one example or excerpt from each writer's work. The brief introductions to the forms and poets are lively and often amusing. Readers will find the varied layouts and warm cartoon watercolors inviting." SLJ

Includes glossary and bibliographical references

A **family** of poems; my favorite poetry for children. [selected by] Caroline Kennedy; paintings by Jon J. Muth. Hyperion Books for Children 2005 143p il $19.95

Grades: 3 4 5 6   **808.81**

1. Poetry -- Collections

ISBN 0-7868-5111-2

An anthology of over 100 poems divided into categories such as "About Me," "Animals," "Adventure" and "Bedtime," including works by such poets as A.A. Milne, Robert Louis Stevenson, Jack Prelutsky, Edward Lear, Robert Frost, William Wordsworth, T.S. Eliot, Carl Sandberg, William Shakespeare.

"From the cover photograph of Kennedy as a toddler reading to her teddy to the red linen-textured endpapers; from her thoughtful introduc-

tion and words of encouragement to children at the beginning of each section of carefully chosen poems to Muth's beautifully executed watercolors, this volume is a treasure." SLJ

★ A **foot** in the mouth; poems to speak, sing, and shout. [edited by Paul B. Janeczko; illustrated by Chris Raschka] Candlewick Press 2009 64p il $17.99

Grades: 4 5 6 7   **808.81**

1. Poetry -- Collections

ISBN 978-0-7636-0663-3; 0-7636-0663-4

LC 2008-935581

"The poems in Janeczko and Raschka's collection . . . are not complacent, although plenty are funny and some are familiar. . . . Punchy collages flutter across airy white pages in loose visual arrangements; torn scraps of origami paper layer with fluid lines in tart color. Janeczko introduces the collection with the idea that 'Poetry is sound,' a pleasure to vocalize and memorize. . . . Readers will be emboldened to join in the 'song.'" Publ Wkly

Janeczko, Paul B., 1945-

★ The **Death** of the Hat; A Brief History of Poetry in 50 Objects. selected by Paul B. Janeczko; illustrated by Chris Raschka. Candlewick Press 2015 80 p. color illustrations $17.99

Grades: 3 4 5 6 7   **808.81**

1. Poetry -- Collections 2. Creation (Literary, artistic, etc.)

ISBN 0763669636; 9780763669638

LC 2013957308

This children's book, by Paul B. Janeczko, illustrated by Chris Raschka, focuses on "poems through history inspired by objects. . . . A book-eating moth in the early Middle Ages. A peach blossom during the Renaissance. A haunted palace in the Victorian era. A lament for the hat in contemporary times. Poetry has been a living form of artistic expression for thousands of years, and throughout that time poets have found inspiration in everything." (Publisher's note)

"Janeczko and Raschka's stellar fourth poetry collaboration, following A Poke in the I and other acclaimed titles, presents a chronological 'history' of the development of poetry, from the Middle Ages to the present. The highlighted poems are, ostensibly, about objects, but a cigar is rarely just a cigar. . . . Janeczko's substantial introduction gives an overview of poetry's evolution over the centuries, yet works like Lord Byron's 'A Riddle, on the Letter E' resonate powerfully on their own." Pub Wkly

Julie Andrews' treasury for all seasons; poems and songs to celebrate the year. selected by Julie Andrews & Emma Walton Hamilton; paintings by Marjorie Priceman. Little, Brown and Company 2012 192 p. $19.99

Grades: K 1 2 3   **808.81**

1. Songbooks 2. Children's poetry 3. Seasons -- Poetry

ISBN 0316040517; 9780316040518

LC 2011053202

This book is a "compilation of poems and songs (including some of [Julie] Andrews and [Emma Walton] Hamilton's own) from more than 75 writers, organized by month. Summer sees . . . poems about discovery and outdoor activity, with works by Billy Collins, Joy Harjo, and E.B. White; fall poems include nature, back-to-school, and Thanksgiving themes, with pieces by Emily Dickinson, Sandra Cisneros, and others. Caldecott Honor artist [Marjorie] Priceman" illustrates. (Publishers Weekly)

Leave your sleep; selected by Natalie Merchant; pictures by Barbara McClintock. Frances Foster Books 2012 48 p. (hardcover) $24.99

Grades: K 1 2 3   **808.81**

1. Songbooks 2. Children's poetry 3. Poetry -- Collections

ISBN 0374343683; 9780374343682

LC 2011047064

This book is a children's poetry collection. "For her 2010 hit album with the same title, [Natalie] Merchant composed music for 30 19th- and 20th-century British and American poems, some written for children and some written about childhood. For this volume, she's selected 19 of those poems (18 from the CD set and one other), describing them as 'representing the long conversation I had with my daughter during the first six years of her life.'" (Kirkus Reviews)

My village; rhymes from around the world. collected by by Danielle Wright; illustrated by Mique Moriuchi; introduction by Michael Rosen. Frances Lincoln Children's 2010 53p il $19.95

Grades: PreK K 1 2   **808.81**

1. Nursery rhymes 2. Poetry -- Collections

ISBN 1-84780-086-6; 978-1-84780-086-2

"A sunny cover invites readers into this collection of nursery rhymes from around the world. Selections from 22 countries presented in both English and the original language are included as well as the original script/alphabet when appropriate. . . . The rhymes are well chosen and range from funny and bouncy to quiet and thoughtful. The brightly colored collage illustrations complement them well." SLJ

★ **National** Geographic book of animal poetry; 200 poems that squeak, soar, and roar. [edited by] J. Patrick Lewis. National Geographic 2012 183 p.

Grades: 2 3 4 5   **808.81**

1. Animals -- Poetry -- Collections

ISBN 1426310099; 9781426310096; 9781426310546

LC 2012010404

This collection of poetry about animals, edited by J. Patrick Lewis, features "lighthearted poems from the likes of Basho and Ben Franklin, Leadbelly, Jack Prelutsky and Joyce Sidman . . . [and] animal photographs. Lewis adds advice for budding animal poets to the . . . bibliography and multiple indexes at the end." (Kirkus)

Includes bibliographical references and index

National Geographic book of nature poetry; more than 200 poems with photographs that float, zoom, and bloom! edited by J. Patrick Lewis. National Geographic 2015 192 p. color illustrations (hardback) $24.99

Grades: 2 3 4 5   **808.81**

1. Nature poetry 2. Nature

ISBN 1426320957; 9781426320941; 9781426320958

LC 2015013167

In this book, editor Laureate J. Patrick Lewis "curates an exuberant poetic celebration of the natural world in this stellar collection of nature poems. From trickling streams to deafening thunderstorms to soaring mountains, discover majestic photography perfectly paired with contemporary (such as Billy Collins), classics (such as Robert Frost), and never-before-published works." (Publisher's note)

"This is a full package; a duet of wonder. A beautifully produced collection that will easily snag the attention of young readers." Booklist

The **Oxford** book of story poems; [compiled by] Michael Harrison and Christopher Stuart-Clark. Oxford University Press 2006 175p il pa $18.95

Grades: 5 6 7 8   **808.81**

1. Poetry -- Collections

ISBN 978-0-19-276344-0 pa; 0-19-276344-X pa

LC 2007282711

First published 1990

This anthology contains "narrative verse by British and American poets, from traditional ballads such as 'Sir Patrick Spens' to contemporary poems such as Judith Nicholls' 'Storytime.' . . . The poets include Carroll, Keats, de la Mare, Kennedy, Lear, Lindsay, Longfellow, Noyes, Poe, Southey, and Tolkien. . . . A handy collection of story poems for reading aloud or alone." Booklist [review of 1990 edition]

★ **Poetry** speaks: who I am; poems of discovery, inspiration, independence, and everything else. Sourcebooks Jabberwocky 2010 136p $19.99

Grades: 5 6 7 8 9 10   **808.81**

1. Poetry -- Collections

ISBN 978-1-4022-1074-7; 1-4022-1074-4

This collection "aims at middle-grade readers with more than 100 strikingly diverse poems by writers including Poe, Frost, Nikki Giovanni, and Sandra Cisneros. The works are slotted together in mindful thematic order, beside occasional spot art. . . . Pairing a contemporary poem like Toi Derricotte's 'Fears of the Eighth Grade' alongside Keats's 'When I Have Fears That I May Cease to Be,' results in a refreshing lack of literary hierarchy that enables disparate works to build and reflect upon one another. An accompanying CD features recordings of 44 of the poems. . . . A sound and rewarding introduction to the joys of poetry." Publ Wkly

Rhymes round the world; [compiled by] Kay Chorao. Dutton Children's Books 2009 40p il $17.99

Grades: PreK K 1   **808.81**

1. Poetry -- Collections

ISBN 978-0-525-47875-1; 0-525-47875-2

LC 2008013887

"These 40 poems and songs offer children a taste of many different cultures. Most are anonymous or traditional nursery rhymes; a few are by English or American poets. The tone is light and joyous. Sweet illustrations of babies and toddlers engaged in playful activities depict the universality of children everywhere." SLJ

★ **River** of words; young poets and artists on the nature of things. edited by Pamela Michael; introduced by Robert Hass. Milkweed Editions 2008 298p il hardcover o.p. pa $18

Grades: 4 5 6 7 8 9   **808.81**

1. Nature poetry 2. Children's art 3. Children's writings 4. Teenagers' writings 5. Poetry -- Collections

ISBN 978-1-57131-685-1; 1-57131-685-X; 978-1-57131-680-6 pa; 1-57131-680-9 pa

"In 1995 Michael and Hass . . . cofounded the River of Words project, designed to connect students' art and poetry education to the natural world immediately around them. . . . The poems and pictures in this handsomely designed volume have been culled from yearly contests. . . . The works are startling, many of them dislocating and highly complex." Publ Wkly

The **tree** that time built; a celebration of nature, science, and imagination. selected by Mary Ann Hoberman and Linda Winston; [illustrations by Barbara Fortin] Sourcebooks Jabberwocky 2009 209p il $19.99

Grades: 5 6 7 8   **808.81**

1. Nature poetry 2. Science -- Poetry 3. Poetry -- Collections

ISBN 978-1-4022-2517-8; 1-4022-2517-2

LC 2009032608

An anthology of more than 100 poems celebrating the wonders of the natural world and encouraging environmental awareness. Includes an audio CD that comprises readings of 44 of the poems, many performed by the poets themselves.

"Classic works by Walt Whitman, Emily Dickinson, Christina Rossetti, and the like, and selections from contemporary poets are included. . . . This handsome collection is especially appropriate for classroom use and instruction. . . . From the playful to the profound, the poems invite reflection and inspire further investigation." SLJ

Includes glossary and bibliographical references

808.88   Collections of miscellaneous writings

Alcorn, Stephen

A **gift** of days; the greatest words to live by. Atheneum Books for Young Readers 2009 115p il $21.99

Grades: 5 6 7 8   **808.88**

1. Quotations 2. Celebrities

ISBN 978-1-4169-6776-7; 1-4169-6776-1

LC 2007-48766

"Beautifully designed and imaginatively conceptualized, this volume presents 366 days and 366 quotations from famous people, tagged to the days they were born. Alcorn lays this out on each double-page spread with a stunning polychrome-relief block-print bordered with pattern on one leaf and, facing, a week of birthdays and quotes. These images are often brilliantly inventive. . . . Librarians, educators and historically minded kids will take much pleasure from looking up birthdays to see the associated wisdom from women and men across the ages." Kirkus

809   History, description, critical appraisal of more than two literatures

Carpenter, Humphrey

The **Oxford** companion to children's literature; [by] Humphrey Carpenter and Mari Prichard. Oxford Univ. Press 1984 586p il hardcover o.p. pa $70

Grades: Adult Professional   **809**

1. Reference books 2. Children's literature -- Dictionaries

ISBN 0-19-211582-0; 0-19-860228-6 pa

LC 83-15130

"One volume work with brief critiques of authors, illustrators, books, characters, and radio and television programs. Largely British in coverage of materials but does include most Newbery winners as well as well-known American, Australian and Canadian authors. Contemporary and historical subjects related to children's literature are examined." N Y Public Libr. Ref Books for Child Collect. 2d edition

Krull, Kathleen

★ **Lives** of the writers; comedies, tragedies (and what the neighbors thought) written by Kathleen Krull; illustrated by Kathryn Hewitt. 1st ed. Harcourt Brace & Co. 1994 96 p. col. ill. (reinforced) $21

Grades: 4 5 6 7   **809**

1. Poets 2. Authors 3. Humorists 4. Novelists 5. Dramatists 6.

Historians 7. Journalists

ISBN 0152480099; 9780152480097

LC 93032436

This volume presents biographical sketches of writers. Arranged "in chronological order by date of birth, the selection of writers begins with Murasaki Shikibu, the first-century Japanese author of 'The Tale of Genji' . . . and concludes with Isaac Bashevis Singer, the Jewish American storyteller who died in 1991." (Horn Book Magazine)

This offers "views of twenty writers . . . from various countries and historical periods. Included are William Shakespeare, Edgar Allan Poe, Mark Twain, Zora Neale Hurston, Isaac Bashevis Singer, and many others." Publisher's note

Includes bibliographical references (p. 96) and index.

The **Oxford** encyclopedia of children's literature; Jack Zipes, editor in chief. Oxford University Press 2006 4v il set $495

Grades: Adult Professional   **809**

1. Reference books 2. Children's literature -- Encyclopedias

ISBN 978-0-19-514656-1; 0-19-514656-5

LC 2005-34390

"The 3200 signed articles in this set include brief discussions of the work of major writers, important trends, genres, characters, organizations, and noteworthy publications and people in the field. All of the alphabetical articles are clearly written and most include cross-references. . . . There is no comparable single work that brings together all aspects of the topic, making this a valuable resource." SLJ

Includes bibliographical references

Sutton, Roger

A **family** of readers; the book lover's guide to children's and young adult literature. [by] Roger Sutton and Martha V. Parravano; foreword by Gregory Maguire. Candlewick Press 2010 350p il $22; pa $14.99

Grades: Adult Professional   **809**

1. Children -- Books and reading 2. Teenagers -- Books and reading 3. Children's literature -- History and criticism

ISBN 978-0-7636-3280-9; 0-7636-3280-5; 978-0-7636-5755-0 pa; 0-7636-5755-7 pa

"This collection of essays from editors, reviewers, and authors emanates enthusiasm for books and reading. . . . Each section begins with an overview, followed by a selection of essays. The first chapter addresses the very smallest book lovers, and the last tackles the needs of young adults. Each chapter is followed by an annotated list of books. A complete bibliography and biographical sketches of the contributors are included in the end. . . . It should be required reading for every youth services librarian." Voice Youth Advocates

809.1   Literature in specific forms other than miscellaneous writings

Bodden, Valerie

Concrete poetry. Creative Education 2010 32p il (Poetry basics) $28.50

Grades: 5 6 7 8   **809.1**

1. Poetry -- History and criticism

ISBN 978-1-58341-775-1; 1-58341-775-3

LC 2008009156

This book describes concrete poetry's "history, characteristics, and variations. Many examples are provided as well as ideas for how children can write their own pieces. The information is accessible, and the writing is sufficiently lively to engage readers. The well-designed pages feature a variety of art reproductions from different literary eras and some photographs." Horn Book Guide

Includes glossary and bibliographical references

Haiku. Creative Education 2010 32p il (Poetry basics) $19.95
Grades: 5 6 7 8   **809.1**
1. Haiku
ISBN 978-1-58341-776-8; 1-58341-776-1
                                                        LC 2008-9158
Presents history and examples of the Japanese form of poetry called haiku.

"The information is accessible, and the writing is sufficiently lively to engage readers. The well-designed pages feature a variety of art reproductions from different literary eras and some photographs." Horn Book Guide

Includes glossary and bibliographical references

Limericks. Creative Education 2010 32p il (Poetry basics) $19.95
Grades: 5 6 7 8   **809.1**
1. Limericks
ISBN 978-1-58341-777-5; 1-58341-777-X
                                                        LC 2008-9159
This describes limericks' "history, characteristics, and variations. Many examples are provided as well as ideas for how children can write their own pieces. The information is accessible, and the writing is sufficiently lively to engage readers. The well-designed pages feature a variety of art reproductions from different literary eras and some photographs." Horn Book Guide

Includes glossary and bibliographical references

810   Literatures of specific languages and language families

Wilkin, Binnie Tate
   African and African American images in Newbery Award winning titles; progress in portrayals. Scarecrow Press 2009 195p pa $40
Grades: Adult Professional   **810**
1. Newbery Medal 2. African Americans in literature 3. Children's literature -- History and criticism
ISBN 978-0-8108-6959-2 pa; 0-8108-6959-4 pa
                                                        LC 2009017726
"The author has exhaustively examined all books that have won the Newbery Medal and been cited as honor books since the award's creation in 1922. Her purpose is to evaluate the representation of Africans and African Americans, and to describe how these groups are portrayed in each title's historical context. . . . Books with the most positive images are awarded three pluses, while books with marginal African-American characters are indicated with an 'M.'. . . . An essential volume for scholars, teachers, and librarians." SLJ

Includes bibliographical references

811   American poetry

★ The **20th** century children's poetry treasury; selected by Jack Prelutsky; illustrated by Meilo So. Knopf 1999 87p il $19.95
Grades: 3 4 5 6   **811**
1. American poetry -- Collections
ISBN 0-679-89314-8; 0-679-99314-2 lib bdg
                                                        LC 99-23988

A collection of more than 200 poems by such modern poets as Nikki Grimes, John Ciardi, Karla Kuskin, Ted Hughes, e.e. cummings, Eve Merriam, Deborah Chandra, Arnold Adoff, and more than 100 others

"While all of these selections have been published elsewhere, the format and illustrations in this collection give them new life. . . . So's watercolor illustrations are, by turn, impressionistic, childlike, silly, and serious, as called for by the tone of the poems featured. . . . A splendid collection." SLJ

Ada, Alma Flor
   ★ **Gathering** the sun; an alphabet in Spanish and English. English translation by Rosa Zubizarreta; illustrated by Simón Silva. Lothrop, Lee & Shepard Bks. 1997 un il $16.95; pa $6.99
Grades: 2 3 4   **811**
1. Alphabet 2. Mexican Americans -- Poetry 3. Poetry -- By individual authors 4. Bilingual books -- English-Spanish
ISBN 0-688-13903-5; 0-688-17067-7 pa
"Using the Spanish alphabet as a template, Ada has written 27 poems that celebrate both the bounty of the harvest and the Mexican heritage of the farmworkers and their families. The poems, presented in both Spanish and English, are short and simple bursts of flavor. . . . Silva's sun-drenched gouache paintings are robust, with images sculpted in paint." Booklist

Adoff, Arnold
   ★ **Roots** and blues; a celebration. paintings by R. Gregory Christie. Clarion Books 2011 88p il
Grades: 4 5 6   **811**
1. Children's poetry 2. Blues music -- Poetry 3. African Americans -- Poetry 4. Poetry -- By individual authors 5. Blues (Music) -- History and criticism
ISBN 0547235542; 9780547235547
                                                        LC 2009-26625
Adoff tells the story of the blues in this collection of sixty poems and prose pieces. "Grades eight to twelve." (Bull Cent Child Books)

"In this visceral collaboration, Adoff and Christie honor the enduring legacy of blues music. Vibrant, haunting acrylic paintings portray crowded slave ships, chain gang labor, and the crackling energy of juke joints. . . . Several poems titled 'Listening' capture the sounds of the decades in which they're set . . . and mimic the rhythms and repetitions of the blues. . . . This is a challenging, openhearted collection with images and poems that bleed into one another, but also stand powerfully alone." Publ Wkly

African American Poetry; edited by Arnold Rampersad and Marcellus Blount; illustrated by Karen Barbour. Sterling Pub Co Inc. 2013 48 p. ill. (hardcover) $14.95
Grades: 3 4 5 6 7   **811**
1. American poetry -- Asian American authors
ISBN 1402716893; 9781402716898
This book of poetry by African American authors "introduces 27 poets from the days of Phillis Wheatley to well-established poets writing in the 21st century. A four-page introduction outlines historical periods and influences. Presented chronologically, the entries begin with a paragraph describing the poet's life and work. Paul Laurence Dunbar, Countee Cullen, Langston Hughes, Lucille Clifton, Maya Angelou, and others are joined by George Moses Horton . . . and others." (School Library Journal)

Ahlberg, Allan
   Everybody was a baby once, and other poems; illustrator Bruce Ingman. Candlewick Press 2010 63p il $15.99
Grades: PreK K 1   **811**
1. Infants -- Poetry 2. Poetry -- By individual authors
ISBN 978-0-7636-4682-0; 0-7636-4682-2

"From the creators of The Pencil, these 19 poems cover whimsical territory and feature kids, angels, sausages, and monsters, rendered in kinetic, childlike sketches. A few poems strike nostalgic, melancholy notes . . . but most are upbeat, with gently jazzy rhythms. . . . The Lilliputian cast and memorable verse could make this a dog-eared favorite." Publ Wkly

Alarcon, Francisco X.

Iguanas in the snow and other winter poems; poems, Francisco X. Alarcón; illustrations, Maya Christina Gonzalez. Children's Bk. Press 2001 31p il hardcover o.p. pa $7.95

Grades: 2 3 4   **811**
1. Winter -- Poetry 2. Poetry -- By individual authors 3. Bilingual books -- English-Spanish
ISBN 0-89239-168-5; 0-89239-202-9 pa
                                          LC 00-65667
"Brief, zippy verses express delight in such simple things as a family frolic in the snow and the wonder of giant redwoods. . . . The selections are short of line and long on meter, with a rhythmic roll that begs reading aloud. . . . Gonzalez's illustrations are bright and busy, catching the playful cadence of the words." SLJ

Amazing faces; edited by Lee Bennett Hopkins; illustrated by Chris Soentpiet. Lee & Low 2010 un il $18.95

Grades: 2 3 4 5   **811**
1. American poetry -- Collections
ISBN 978-1-60060-334-1; 1-60060-334-3
"Illustrated with large, handsome watercolor portraits, the 16 poems in this anthology celebrate the rich diversity of American kids—what makes each one special and the connections between them. . . . A great collection for sharing at home and in the classroom." Booklist

★ **America** at war; poems. selected by Lee Bennett Hopkins; illustrated by Stephen Alcorn. Margaret K. McElderry Books 2008 84p il $21.99

Grades: 5 6 7 8   **811**
1. War poetry 2. American poetry -- Collections 3. United States -- History -- Poetry
ISBN 978-1-4169-1832-5; 1-4169-1832-9
                                          LC 2006-08723
"This handsome anthology, expressing Americans' varied experience during wartime, is a fine selection of poems accessible to children. . . . The poems will touch readers with their sharp poignancy and undeniable power. Throughout the well-designed book, the expressive watercolor artwork enhances the poetry." Booklist

Angelou, Maya

Amazing peace; a Christmas poem. by Maya Angelou; paintings by Steve Johnson and Lou Fancher. Schwartz & Wade Books 2008 un il $17.99; lib bdg $20.99

Grades: 3 4 5   **811**
1. Christmas -- Poetry 2. Poetry -- By individual authors
ISBN 978-0-375-84150-7; 0-375-84150-4; 978-0-375-94327-0 lib bdg; 0-375-94327-7 lib bdg
"This poem was largely inspired by the terrible natural disasters occurring throughout the world when Angelou was invited to read at the 2005 White House tree-lighting ceremony. Thus, the opening lines rumble and roil almost menacingly to illustrate the climate of doubt and anxiety into which the spirit of Christmas arrives. Hope enters as a whisper and grows until it is 'louder than the explosion of bombs.' . . . Johnson and Fancher's paintings, rendered in oil, acrylic, and fabric on canvas, elegantly depict a calm, snow-blanketed village where children play, families shop, and artisans ply their crafts. . . . This is a comforting

book that gets to the heart of what Christmas should mean. As an added treat, Angelou reads the poem on the accompanying CD." SLJ

Argueta, Jorge

Talking with Mother Earth; poems. illustrated by Lucia Angela Perez. Groundwood Books 2006 un il $15.95

Grades: 3 4 5 6   **811**
1. Nature poetry 2. Racism -- Poetry 3. Pipil Indians -- Poetry 4. Poetry -- By individual authors 5. Bilingual books -- English-Spanish
ISBN 0-88899-626-8
This presents poems which explore a Pipil Nahua Indian boy's connection to Mother Earth and how it heals the wounds of racism.
"This literary offering stands out for its beauty and depth of expression. . . . Pérez's illustrations are colorful, detailed, and appealing, incorporating many indigenous icons." SLJ

Aronica-Buck, Barbara

Over the moon; the Broadway lullaby project. Easton Studio Press 2012 46 p.

Grades: 3 4 5   **811**
1. Lullabies
ISBN 1935212702; 9781935212706
This book compiled by Kate Dawson and Jodi Glucksman presents a "collection of original lullabies and illustrations featuring music by some of Broadway's biggest stars and brightest composers with illustrations by acclaimed Children's artists and Broadway set designers. . . . each offering a . . . visual interpretation of a song from the CD bound in the book." (Publisher's note)

The **arrow** finds its mark; a book of found poems. edited by Georgia Heard; illustrated by Antoine Guilloppé. Roaring Brook Press 2012 38 p.

Grades: 3 4 5   **811**
1. American poetry 2. Children's poetry 3. Poetry -- Collections 4. Children's poetry, American
ISBN 1596436654; 9781596436657
                                          LC 2011017180
This poetry collection, edited by Georgia Heard with illustrations by Antoine Guillope, features material from "Twitter feeds, school notes, advertisements, street signs. . . .poetry in . . . unlikely places [by] thirty contemporary poets. Imagine picking up a scrap of paper off the floor or reading a sign at a gas station or looking at graffiti on the subway and finding poetry in these words. The literary equivalent of a collage, found poems take existing text, reorder and refashion it, and present it as a poem. (Publisher's note)

★ **Ashley** Bryan's ABC of African-American poetry. Atheneum Bks. for Young Readers 1997 un il hardcover o.p. pa $7.99

Grades: K 1 2 3   **811**
1. Alphabet 2. African Americans -- Poetry 3. American poetry -- African American authors -- Collections
ISBN 0-689-81209-4; 0-689-84045-4 pa
                                          LC 96-25148
Each letter of the alphabet is represented by a line from a poem by a different African American poet, describing an aspect of the black experience
This book is illustrated "by Bryan's vivid tempera and gouache paintings. . . . The selections . . . display a loving acquaintance with poets from James Weldon Johnson to Rita Dove. While there is a full range of emotions, joy and pride predominate." SLJ

Bates, Katharine Lee

★ **America** the beautiful; illustrated by Chris Gall. Little, Brown 2004 un il $16.95

Grades: K 1 2 3   **811**

1. Songs -- United States 2. United States -- Poetry

ISBN 0-316-73743-7

LC 2003-54552

Four verses of the nineteenth-century poem later set to music, illustrated by the author's great-great-grandnephew

"Children will be stirred by Gall's pictures. Using hand engraving on clay-covered board and enhancing elements such as color with a computer, he offers a series of pictures resembling woodcuts in form and WPA paintings in style." Booklist

★ **Behind** the museum door; poems to celebrate the wonders of museums. selected by Lee Bennett Hopkins; illustrated by Stacey Dressen-McQueen. Abrams Books for Young Readers 2007 un il $16.95

Grades: 3 4 5   **811**

1. Art -- Poetry 2. Museums -- Poetry 3. American poetry -- Collections

ISBN 978-0-8109-1204-5; 0-8109-1204-X

LC 2006013576

"This collection of poems touches on the sights and sensations a group of children experience on a field trip. . . . Selections are by such poets as Lilian Moore, Jane Yolen, Alice Schertle, and Myra Cohn Livingston. . . . Each of Dressen-McQueen's folk-art-style 'exhibits,' carefully crafted in acrylic paint, oil pastel, and colored pencil, successfully captures and reinforces the mood of its accompanying poem." SLJ

Bernier-Grand, Carmen T.

Cesar; si, se puede! yes, we can! illustrated by David Diaz. Marshall Cavendish 2004 48p il $16.95

Grades: 3 4 5 6   **811**

1. Agricultural laborers 2. Labor leaders 3. Mexican Americans -- Poetry 4. Poetry -- By individual authors

ISBN 0-7614-5172-2

LC 2003-26866

"The lyrical language describes events and paints evocative pictures to which children will relate. Diaz's stylized, computer-drawn, folk-art illustrations capture the subject's private and public life." SLJ

Inlcudes glossary and bibliographical references

★ The **Bill** Martin Jr. Big book of poetry; edited by Bill Martin Jr., with Michael Sampson; foreword by Eric Carle; afterword Steven Kellogg. Simon & Schuster Books for Young Readers 2008 175p $21

Grades: PreK K 1 2 3   **811**

1. American poetry -- Collections

ISBN 978-1-4169-3971-9; 1-4169-3971-7

"The almost 200 selections in this big handsome anthology . . . have a singing beat. . . . The collection brings together poems from Robert Frost, Christina Rossetti, Langston Hughes, Nikki Grimes, Aliki, Jack Prelutsky, and many other well-known poets. Accompanying the poems are pictures from many of the best picture-book illustrators whose work . . . extends the words' lyrical rhythms and playfulness." Booklist

Blackall, Sophie

★ **Spinster** Goose; twisted rhymes for naughty children. [by] Lisa Wheeler & Sophie Blackall. Atheneum Books for Young Readers 2011 41p il $16.99

Grades: 3 4 5   **811**

1. Parodies 2. Nursery rhymes 3. Children's poetry 4. Poetry -- By individual authors

ISBN 978-1-4169-2541-5; 1-4169-2541-4

"This collection of Mother Goose parodies . . . is as elegant as it is, like Mary, 'quite contrary.' The no-nonsense Spinster Goose oversees a reform school. . . . Blackall's pallid vignettes balance chilly poise and mordant humor. . . . Wheeler adds some intellectual depth to the original nursery rhymes while grossifying them. . . . Though some may shrink from its clever ghastliness, kids with twisted senses of humor will feel right at home." Publ Wkly

Blanco, Richard, 1968-

One Today; Richard Blanco; illustrated by Dav Pilkey. Little, Brown & Co. 2015 40 p. color illustrations (hardcover) $18

Grades: PreK K 1 2   **811**

1. American poetry 2. United States -- poetry

ISBN 0316371440; 9780316371445

LC 2014040294

This book presents a poem by Richard Blanco, "a lush and lyrical, patriotic commemoration of America from dawn to dusk and from coast to coast. President Barak Obama invited . . . Blanco to write a poem to share at his second presidential inauguration. Brought to life here by . . . artist Dav Pilkey, 'One Today' is a tribute to a nation where the extraordinary happens every single day." (Publisher's note)

"A special historic moment, caught in lyrical words and joyous illustration, and an excellent choice for educators seeking options to explore diversity." SLJ

Brooks, Gwendolyn

★ **Bronzeville** boys and girls; illustrated by Faith Ringgold. newly illustrated ed.; Amistad/HarperCollins Publishers 2007 41p il $16.99; lib bdg $18.89

Grades: K 1 2 3   **811**

1. African Americans -- Poetry 2. Poetry -- By individual authors

ISBN 978-0-06-029505-9; 0-06-029505-8; 978-0-06-029506-6 lib bdg; 0-06-029506-6 lib bdg

LC 2006-01947

A newly illustrated edition of the title first published 1956

"Brooks's deceptively simple poems for children combined with Ringgold's vibrant illustrations help to rejuvenate this collection first published in 1956. . . . Each poem is tightly constructed, rhythmic and distinctive. . . . Ringgold's bold illustrations, outlined with her signature thick black lines, are among some of her best and most narrative works since Tar Beach." Publ Wkly

Brown, Calef

★ **Hallowilloween**; nefarious silliness. Houghton Mifflin Books for Children 2010 un il $16.99

Grades: 2 3 4 5   **811**

1. Humorous poetry 2. Monsters -- Poetry 3. Poetry -- By individual authors

ISBN 978-0-547-21540-2; 0-547-21540-1

"Brown's playful collection of poems and paintings is likely to inspire as many giggles as it does shivers. Readers meet a werewolf named Jack, Duncan the shrunken head, and an unhappy mummy. . . . Brown's acrylic illustrations add to the creepy silliness: an artful mix of naive and stylized, whimsical details and vibrant color. Young readers will relish the wordplay and find themselves torn to choose a favorite among this wacky menagerie." SLJ

Soup for breakfast; poems and pictures. Houghton Mifflin Co. 2008 un il $16

Grades: K 1 2 3   **811**

1. Humorous poetry 2. Poetry -- By individual authors

ISBN 978-0-618-91641-2; 0-618-91641-5

LC 2007047734

Brown's "fun-filled poems feature an unpredictable range of topics and imagery. . . . He offsets each poem with one of his flat, idiosyncratic paintings; with their oddball beasts and improbable color combinations, his pictures are somewhere between surreal and folk art." Publ Wkly

Brown, Margaret Wise

Nibble nibble; [by] Margaret Wise Brown; paintings by Wendell Minor. HarperCollins 2007 un il $16.99; lib bdg $17.89

Grades: PreK K 1   **811**

1. Rabbits -- Poetry 2. Poetry -- By individual authors
ISBN 978-0-06-059208-0; 0-06-059208-7; 978-0-06-059209-7 lib bdg; 0-06-059209-5 lib bdg

LC 2006029869

A collection of poetry about rabbits

"Large, almost tactile paintings of birds, butterflies, and bunnies combine well with the flow of Brown's charming poems, originally published in 1959. . . . Onomatopoeic and motion words are reflected in the pictures with their ground-level perspective. These five beautifully and newly illustrated poems will enchant another generation of children." SLJ

Bryan, Ashley

★ Ashley Bryan's Puppets; Making Something from Everything. Ashley Bryan. Simon & Schuster 2014 80 p. $19.99

Grades: PreK K 1 2 3 4 5 6   **811**

1. Poetry 2. Waste products 3. Puppets and puppet plays 4. Children's poetry 5. Puppets -- Poetry 6. Found objects -- Poetry
ISBN 1442487283; 9781442487284

In this book, "storyteller and creator Ashley Bryan reveals the vibrant spirit of found objects in this . . . treasury of poetry and puppets. . . . For decades, Ashley has walked up and down the beach, stopping to pick up sea glass, weathered bones, a tangle of fishing net, an empty bottle, a doorknob. Treasure. And then, with glue and thread and paint and a sprinkling of African folklore, Ashley breathes new life into these materials." (Publisher's note)

"Award-winning author and illustrator Bryan has combined his love of art and poetry in this captivating and beautifully designed book...Traditional African themes abound as the characters introduce themselves through their poems, and readers are invited into the world of puppets and poetry. Bryan has truly created a book for all to treasure." SLJ

Bulion, Leslie

At the sea floor cafe; odd ocean critter poems. written by Leslie Bulion; illustrated by Leslie Evans. Peachtree Publishers 2011 45p il $14.95

Grades: 5 6 7 8   **811**

1. Marine animals -- Poetry 2. Poetry -- By individual authors
ISBN 978-1-56145-565-2; 1-56145-565-2

LC 2010026691

"Using complex poetry forms and cleverly constructed lines, Bulion plays tribute to sea creatures. . . . Evans's spare, well-placed hand-colored linoleum block prints hold their own without overwhelming the text." Horn Book Guide

Burleigh, Robert

★ Home run; the story of Babe Ruth. illustrated by Mike Wimmer. Harcourt Brace & Co. 1998 un il hardcover o.p. pa $7

Grades: K 1 2 3   **811**

1. Baseball players 2. Baseball -- Fiction
ISBN 0-15-200970-1; 0-15-204599-6 pa

LC 95-10038

A poetic account of the legendary Babe Ruth as he prepares to make a home run

"With a flowing minimal text, Burleigh brings the Babe to life through the moment of one at bat. . . . Wimmer's sprawling, photorealistic oil paintings depict the larger-than-life figure and his surroundings with folksy Norman Rockwell-like charm." SLJ

★ Hoops; illustrated by Stephen T. Johnson. Harcourt Brace & Co. 1997 un il hardcover o.p. pa $6

Grades: 6 7 8 9   **811**

1. Basketball -- Poetry 2. Poetry -- By individual authors
ISBN 0-15-201450-0; 0-15-216380-8 pa

LC 96-18440

Illustrations and poetic text describe the movement and feel of the game of basketball

"Burleigh's staccato text is well matched by Johnson's dynamic pastels. Muted colors and a strong sense of motion as bodies leap and lift, pounce and poke, aptly complement the words." SLJ

Child, Lydia Maria Francis

Over the river and through the wood; the New England boy's song about Thanksgiving day. [by] L. Maria Child; illustrated by Matt Tavares. Candlewick Press 2011 un il $16.99

Grades: 2 3 4   **811**

1. Thanksgiving Day -- Poetry 2. Poetry -- By individual authors
ISBN 978-0-7636-2790-4; 0-7636-2790-9

LC 2010038878

"A charming and dynamic rendition of the song about Thanksgiving Day, originally published in 1844. All 12 original verses are included, each old-fashioned scene appropriately matching the text. Tavares's watercolor, ink, and pencil illustrations are crisp and bright, expertly capturing the wind-whipped outdoor scenes of the sleigh moving from page to page and ultimately to grandfather's house for a feast." SLJ

Ciardi, John

★ You read to me, I'll read to you; drawings by Edward Gorey. Lippincott 1962 64p il hardcover o.p. pa $7.95

Grades: 1 2 3 4   **811**

1. Humorous poetry 2. Poetry -- By individual authors
ISBN 0-06-446060-6 pa

Thirty-five "imaginative and humorous poems for an adult and a child to read aloud together. Written in a basic first-grade vocabulary, the poems to be read by the child alternate with poems to be read by the adult." Booklist

Clayton, Dallas

Make magic! do good! Dallas Clayton. Candlewick Press 2012 112 p. $17.99

Grades: 3 4 5   **811**

1. Children's poetry 2. Friendship -- Poetry
ISBN 0763657468; 9780763657468

LC 2012942305

This is a poetry collection for children by Dallas Clayton. "Recurring themes in the nearly 50 poems include seizing the day, making friends of enemies, being kind, and blazing one's own trail. 'You won't be fast forever/ so the clever thing to do/ is to stop and help the others keep up/ because someday/ they'll be you,' writes Clayton in 'Running!'" (Publishers Weekly)

Cleary, Brian P.

Bow tie pasta; acrostic poems. Brian P. Cleary; illustrations by Andy Rowland. Millbrook Press 2016 32 p. color illustrations (lb : alk. paper) $26.65

Grades: 2 3 4 **811**

1. Acrostics 2. Children's poetry 3. Acrostics -- Juvenile poetry

ISBN 146778107X; 9781467720465; 9781467781077

LC 2014041280

In this collection of children's poems, author "Brian P. Cleary shows how even the wackiest words can make an acrostic poem. Acrostic poems are created from a word or phrase written vertically down the page. Each letter becomes part of a line in the poem, revealing a thought or a clue about the poem's topic." (Publisher's note)

"An extremely useful tool for teachers or librarians looking to breathe life into a poetry unit." SLJ

Something sure smells around here; Limericks. by Brian P. Cleary; illustrated by Andy Rowland. Millbrook Press 2015 32 p. color illustrations (Poetry Adventures) (lib. bdg. : alk. paper) $26.60

Grades: 3 4 5 **811**

1. Limericks 2. Children's poetry 3. Limericks, Juvenile 4. Poetry -- Authorship

ISBN 1467720445; 9781467720441; 9781467760355

LC 2014009380

This book, by Brian P. Cleary, illustrated by Andy Rowland, describes and presents several limericks for children. It includes several "five-line rhyming poems [that] are funny, silly, and sly. Award-winning author Brian P. Cleary explains how limericks work--and shows how these little poems can trigger big laughs." (Publisher's note)

"This delightful collection of limericks starts with a useful definition and a few rules for composition, as well as some information on how these humorous poems function rhetorically. Cleary offers some basic advice for readers looking to pen their own poems. Limericks are meant to be funny and concise, and there are plenty of witty verses here and several that end with puns. . . . Educators looking for options for a unit on poetry or limericks will appreciate this one, as will fans of the format and those who enjoy silly humor." SLJ

Clements, Andrew

Dogku; [by] Andrew Clements; illustrations by Tim Bowers. Simon & Schuster Books for Young Readers 2007 un il $16.99

Grades: 1 2 3 4 **811**

1. Haiku 2. Dogs -- Poetry 3. Poetry -- By individual authors

ISBN 978-0-689-85823-9; 0-689-85823-X

LC 2006003691

"A stray dog's first day in a family's home is more or less a test of whether he'll get to stay. . . . [The author] tells the entire tale in haiku, a remarkably effective vehicle for delivering such a sweet and simple story. . . . While each haiku is typically spare, Bowers's vibrant illustrations are busy and bright, filling the pages with the same unbounded energy as the lovable pooch." SLJ

Coombs, Kate

Water sings blue; ocean poems. by Kate Coombs; illustrated by Meilo So. Chronicle Books 2012 36 p.

Grades: PreK K 1 2 3 **811**

1. Sea poetry 2. Ocean -- Poetry 3. Children's poetry 4. Poetry -- Collections 5. Picture books for children

ISBN 9780811872843

LC 2010030163

This picture book presents "twenty-three poems and . . . watercolor paintings [that] pay tribute to the wonders of the ocean world. . . . [Kate Coombs] invites young readers into her celebration with an opening 'Song of the Boat' and ends with the message of the 'Tideline'. . . . [In another poem] Gulper Eel's 'astronomical maw' is compared to a black hole." (Kirkus Reviews)

Crawley, Dave

Reading, rhyming, and 'rithmetic; poems by Dave Crawley; illustrations by Liz Callen. Wordsong 2010 31p il $17.95

Grades: 3 4 5 **811**

1. Schools -- Poetry 2. Poetry -- By individual authors

ISBN 978-1-59078-565-2; 1-59078-565-7

LC 2009019917

This anthology focuses on school-themed poems.

"The verses flow easily and the rhymes are engaging and well done. Each one lends itself to being read aloud. Kids will love this collection. The illustrations are pleasant, humorous, and just enough to complement the verses." Libr Media Connect

Dakos, Kalli

A **funeral** in the bathroom; and other school bathroom poems. illustrated by Mark Beech. Albert Whitman & Co. 2011 47p il

Grades: 3 4 5 **811**

1. Schools -- Poetry 2. Bathrooms -- Poetry 3. Poetry -- By individual authors

ISBN 0-8075-2675-4; 978-0-8075-2675-0

LC 2010045591

"Dakos's humorous, bittersweet poems and Beech's mischievous illustrations center on the school bathroom as a place of refuge, camaraderie, and, of course, necessity. . . . A heartfelt collage of relatable moments." Publ Wkly

Dant, Traci

Some kind of love; a family reunion in poems. illustrated by Eric Velasquez. Marshall Cavendish Children 2010 un il $17.99

Grades: K 1 2 3 **811**

1. Family reunions -- Poetry 2. African Americans -- Poetry 3. Poetry -- By individual authors

ISBN 978-0-7614-5559-2; 0-7614-5559-0

LC 2008-20878

"'Must be some kind of love.' That is the refrain that starts off each moving poem in this picture book about an annual African American family reunion, told in free verse from the viewpoint of a nine-year-old boy. Handsome oil paintings show the 'giant sleepover,' with group pictures of multiple generations, as well as closeups of cousins sharing bikes, eating fried chicken, and sleeping four boys to a bed." Booklist

Dizzy dinosaurs; silly dino poems. edited by Lee Bennett Hopkins; illustrated by Barry Gott. Harper 2011 44p il (I can read!) $16.99; pa $3.99

Grades: K 1 2 3 **811**

1. Dinosaurs -- Poetry 2. American poetry -- Collections

ISBN 978-0-06-135839-5; 0-06-135839-8; 978-0-06-135841-8 pa; 0-06-135841-X pa

"Nineteen dinosaur poems plus a pronunciation guide to dinosaur names make up this easy reader collection. . . . The poets do surprisingly well at writing poems using the short words and easy vocabulary of an I Can Read book. . . . Gott's paintings exaggeate the dinosaurs comically, giving the prehistoric critters a variety of bright colors and showing their disparate sizes by including other animals. . . . Even non-dino-fans will enjoy the humor of these dinosaurs set amidst ordinary modern life." Horn Book

Durango, Julia

★ **Under** the mambo moon; illustrated by Fabricio Vanden Broeck. Charlesbridge Pub. 2011 un il lib bdg $12.95

Grades: 3 4 5 **811**

1. Music -- Poetry 2. Latin Americans -- Poetry 3. Poetry -- By

individual authors
ISBN 157091723X; 9781570917233; 1-57091-723-X; 978-1-57091-723-3

LC 2008007255

"In understated verse, a girl named Marisol explores the role that music plays in her Latino community, introducing the people who visit her father's music store. . . . Grainy grayscale scenes inside the store alternate with kinetic acrylic and colored-pencil tableaus, placed opposite the visitors' monologues. . . . A vivid mingling of poetry, narrative, and art."

"In understated verse, a girl named Marisol explores the role that music plays in her Latino community, introducing the people who visit her father's music store. . . . Grainy grayscale scenes inside the store alternate with kinetic acrylic and colored-pencil tableaus, placed opposite the visitors' monologues. . . . A vivid mingling of poetry, narrative, and art." Publ Wkly

Eliot, T. S. (Thomas Stearns), 1888-1965
★ **Old** Possum's book of practical cats; illustrated by Axel Scheffler. Harcourt Children's Books 2009 64p il $16
Grades: 3 4 5 6   **811**
1. Cats -- Poetry 2. Children's poetry 3. Poetry -- By individual authors
ISBN 0-547-24827-X; 978-0-547-24827-1

This is a newly illustrated version of T.S. Eliot's 1939 poetic celebration of felines. "Primary, intermediate." (Horn Book)

"Scheffler brings his considerable illustrative talents to this new edition of Eliot's much-loved collection of cat whimsy, first published in 1939. Scheffler's cartoon felines, with their expressive eyes, are a deliciously animated cast. . . . These cats by turns baffle and delight the humans around them." SLJ

Elliott, David
In the sea; David Elliott; illustrated by Holly Meade. 1st U.S. ed. Candlewick Press 2012 32 p. col. ill.
Grades: 1 2 3   **811**
1. Children's poetry 2. American poetry -- Collections 3. Marine animals -- Poetry 4. Poetry -- By individual authors
ISBN 9780763644987; 0763644986

LC 2010047666

This book of poems for children by David Elliot and illustrated by Holly Meade presents an "exploration of life in the sea. From the tiny sea horse 'dainty as a wish,' to the clown fish, which is 'not an enemy / of anemone,' to the blue whale who sings 'of shipwrecked sailors down below,' 20 creatures are celebrated with rhymes that accentuate their quirks and charm." (Booklist)

★ **In** the wild; illustrated by Holly Meade. Candlewick Press 2010 un il
Grades: 1 2 3   **811**
1. Animals -- Poetry 2. Children's poetry 3. Poetry -- By individual authors
ISBN 0-7636-4497-8; 978-0-7636-4497-0

LC 2009008244

A woodcut-illustrated collection of poems that celebrates wild animals. "Preschool, primary." (Horn Book)

"A lion standing alone on a grassy plain leads off the assortment of 14 mammals introduced in short, reflective poems and bold, energetic woodblock scenes. . . . Mead's woodblock prints . . . have just a hint of humor and capture the powerful wild nature of the creatures. . . . The poems are read-aloud gems." SLJ

Esbensen, Barbara Juster
★ **Swing** around the sun; poems. art by Cheng-Khee Chee . . . [et al.] Carolrhoda Bks. 2003 un il lib bdg $16.95
Grades: 2 3 4   **811**
1. Seasons -- Poetry 2. Poetry -- By individual authors
ISBN 0-87614-143-2

LC 2002-7980

A newly illustrated edition of the title first published 1965 by Lerner

A collection of poems that celebrates the seasons, with illustrations for each season by a different Minnesota artist

"A rich, vibrant reading and viewing experience. . . . The poetry's impact is heightened by masterful new illustrations from four distinguished artists. . . . Cheng-Khee Chee's textured watercolors sprout and bloom across the pages of 'Spring.' Janice Lee Porter's 'Summer' oil pastels hum with energetic color and sinuous shapes. Mary GrandPré ushers in fall with a warmer palette of pastels. . . . Finally, Stephen Gammell's snowscapes, spattered in icy grays and blue capture winter's wild spirit." SLJ

An eyeball in my garden; and other spine-tingling poems. selected and edited by Jennifer Cole Judd and Laura Wynkoop; with illustrations by Johan Olander. Marshall Cavendish Childrens 2010 64p il $15.99
Grades: 3 4 5 6   **811**
1. Monsters -- Poetry 2. Supernatural -- Poetry 3. American poetry -- Collections
ISBN 978-0-7614-5655-1; 0-7614-5655-4

LC 2010008081

"This compilation of new poems covers scary as well as silly Halloween territory. For every truly chilling ghost train, there's a witch's shopping list or a monster that turns out to be the speaker's own reflection. Easily flowing meter in most of the pieces makes for smooth read-alouds. Black-and-white ink illustratiions are appropriately spooky." Horn Book Guide

Falling down the page; [compiled] by Georgia Heard. Roaring Brook Press 2009 47p il $16.95
Grades: 3 4 5 6   **811**
1. American poetry -- Collections
ISBN 978-1-59643-220-8; 1-59643-220-9

LC 2007-38870

"Thirty-two 'list' poems are presented in a dynamic design and trim size. . . . The accessible yet thought-provoking selections are from mostly well-known poets such as Marilyn Singer, Lee Bennett Hopkins and Rebecca Kai Dotlich, and include a couple from Heard. . . . The poems will spark imagination." Kirkus

Farrar, Sid
The **year** comes round; haiku through the seasons. Sid Farrar; illustrated by Ilse Plume. Albert Whitman & Co. 2012 32 p. $16.99
Grades: K 1 2 3   **811**
1. Haiku 2. Nature poetry 3. Children's poetry 4. Seasons -- Poetry 5. Haiku, American 6. Months -- Juvenile poetry 7. Nature -- Juvenile poetry
ISBN 0807581291; 9780807581292

LC 2011015478

This book, by Sid Farrar, illustrated by Ilse Plume, offers "[t]welve nature-themed haiku accompanied by lush illustrations [that] take the reader from January to December." Describing natural elements such as fireflies and frost on windowpanes, this collection seeks "to introduce children to the traditional Japanese poetry form." (Publisher's note)

Field, Eugene

Wynken, Blynken, and Nod; written by Eugene Field; illustrated by Giselle Potter. Schwartz & Wade Books 2008 un il $16.99; lib bdg $19.99

Grades: PreK K 1 2   **811**

1. Sleep -- Poetry 2. Poetry -- By individual authors

ISBN 978-0-375-84196-5; 0-375-84196-2; 978-0-375-94596-0 lib bdg; 0-375-94596-2 lib bdg

LC 2007-09568

"Field's soothing lullaby of a poem (1889) is handsomely visualized via the classic device of translating the contents of a child's own room into the stuff of dreams. Potter's appealing dreamlike art features a moon-faced child and the three eponymous figures who are as like him . . . as peas in a pod. . . . An idyllic and imaginative new look at an old favorite." Horn Book

Fitch, Sheree

★ **Night** Sky Wheel Ride; Sheree Fitch; illustrated by Yayo. Tradewind 2012 32 p. $16.95

Grades: PreK K 1 2   **811**

1. Fairs -- Poetry 2. Stories in rhyme

ISBN 189658067X; 9781896580678

This illustrated narrative children's poem, by Sheree Fitch and illustrated by the artist Yayo, "take[s] . . . a spectacular ride through the imagination. We fly past illustrations displaying a [kaleidoscope] of colors. Magical, fun fair creatures appear and disappear in a jungle of cotton-candy trees." (Publisher's note)

Fleischman, Paul

★ **Big** talk; poems for four voices. illustrated by Beppe Giacobbe. Candlewick Press 2000 44p il $17.99; pa $7.99

Grades: 4 5 6 7   **811**

1. Poetry -- By individual authors

ISBN 0-7636-0636-7; 0-7636-3805-6 pa

LC 99-46882

A collection of poems to be read aloud by four people, with color-coded text to indicate which lines are read by which readers

"Each poem is more demanding, and more rewarding, than the last. Giacobbe highlights the humor in strips of vignettes that run along the bottom of the page. This is 'toe-tapping, tongue-flapping fun.'" Horn Book Guide

★ **I** am phoenix: poems for two voices; illustrated by Ken Nutt. Harper & Row 1985 51p il hardcover o.p. pa $5.99

Grades: 4 5 6 7   **811**

1. Birds -- Poetry 2. Poetry -- By individual authors

ISBN 0-06-446092-4 pa

LC 85-42615

A collection of poems about birds to be read aloud by two voices

"Devotés of the almost lost art of choral reading should be among the first to appreciate this collection. . . . Printed in script form, the selections . . . have a cadenced pace and dignified flow; their combination of imaginative imagery and realistic detail is echoed by the combination of stylized fantasy and representational drawings in the black and white pictures, all soft line and strong nuance." Bull Cent Child Books

★ **Joyful** noise: poems for two voices; illustrated by Eric Beddows. Harper & Row 1988 44p il $15.99; lib bdg $16.89; pa $5.99

Grades: 4 5 6 7   **811**

1. Insects -- Poetry 2. Poetry -- By individual authors

ISBN 0-06-021852-5; 0-06-021853-3 lib bdg; 0-06-446093-2 pa

LC 87-45280

Awarded the Newbery Medal, 1989

"There are fourteen poems in the handsomely designed volume, with stylish endpapers and wonderfully interpretive black-and-white illustrations. Each selection is a gem, polished perfection." Horn Book

Fletcher, Ralph

A **writing** kind of day; poems for young poets. illustrations by April Ward. Wordsong/Boyds Mills Press 2005 32p il $17.95; pa $9.95

Grades: 3 4 5   **811**

ISBN 1-59078-276-3; 1-59078-353-0 pa

"A young writer's daily experiences and concerns are folded into poems to which many readers can relate. . . . Varied in mood and tone, the offerings entertain as they celebrate words and language. . . . Ward's black-and-white illustrations use a variety of mediums, including pencil, photography, computer-generated images, and ink. " SLJ

Florian, Douglas, 1950-

★ **Autumnblings;** poems and paintings by Douglas Florian. Greenwillow Bks. 2003 48p il $15.99; lib bdg $16.89

Grades: 2 3 4 5   **811**

1. Autumn -- Poetry 2. Poetry -- By individual authors

ISBN 0-06-009278-5; 0-06-009279-3 lib bdg

LC 2002-29780

A collection of poems that portray the essence of the season between summer and winter

"Short verse lines make the entries particularly suitable for reading aloud or reciting. . . . The illustrations, luminous watercolors touched with colored pencils, often move beyond the decorative to witty visual commentary or elegant, streamlined scenes." Bull Cent Child Books

★ **Bing** bang boing; poems and drawings by Douglas Florian. Harcourt Brace & Co. 1994 144p il hardcover o.p. pa $8

Grades: 2 3 4 5   **811**

1. Nonsense verses 2. Poetry -- By individual authors

ISBN 0-15-233770-9; 0-15-205860-9 pa

LC 94-3894

An illustrated collection of more than 150 nonsense verses

"The author's spare, pen-and-ink drawings, like the poems themselves, deftly explore the comic potential in each combination of words. With a few clean lines, he creates an original, funny vision." SLJ

★ **Comets,** stars, the Moon, and Mars; space poems and paintings. Harcourt 2007 45p il $16

Grades: 2 3 4 5   **811**

1. Children's poetry 2. Astronomy -- Poetry 3. Poetry -- By individual authors

ISBN 0-15-205372-7; 978-0-15-205372-7

LC 2006-08274

The subjects of these twenty poems include the planets as well as "other heavenly bodies and phenomena. . . . Grades three to seven." (Bull Cent Child Books)

This "book looks at astronomy through the magnifying, clarifying lens of poetry. Each double-page spread features a short, accessible poem about a subject such as the sun, each of its planets, a comet, a constellation, or the universe, set with an impressive painting." Booklist

★ **Dinothesaurus;** prehistoric poems and paintings. by Douglas Florian. Atheneum 2009 43p il $17.99

Grades: 2 3 4 5   **811**

1. Dinosaurs -- Poetry 2. Poetry -- By individual authors

ISBN 978-1-4169-7978-4; 1-4169-7978-6

"Florian's freeflowing, witty collection of poems and collages about dinosaurs is a giganotosaurus delight. . . . The poems marry facts with a poet's eye for detail. . . . The heart of the book is in its humor, the spontaneity of both illustrations and poems, and Florian's slightly askew view of the Mesozoic creatures." Publ Wkly

Includes glossary and bibliographical references

★ **Laugh**-eteria; poems and drawings by Douglas Florian. Harcourt Brace & Co. 1999 157p $17; pa $8

Grades: 2 3 4 5   811
1. Humorous poetry 2. Poetry -- By individual authors
ISBN 0-15-202084-5; 0-15-206148-7 pa

LC 98-20047

A collection of more than 100 humorous poems on such topics as ogres, pizza, fear, school, dragons, trees, and hair

"Florian's pithy poems echo playground chants (and sometimes, better yet, jeers) in their rhythmic recitability . . . and his focus on orality and absurdity makes them thematically irresistible. The line drawings have a sophisticated quirkiness." Bull Cent Child Books

Poem-mobiles; crazy car poems. by J. Patrick Lewis and Douglas Florian; illustrated by Jeremy Holmes. 1st ed. Schwartz & Wade Books 2014 40 p. $17.99

Grades: K 1 2 3 4   811
1. Automobiles 2. Children's poetry 3. Automobiles -- Poetry 4. Children's poetry, American
ISBN 0375866906; 9780375866906; 9780375966903

LC 2011011023

In this book, authors J. Patrick Lewis and Douglas Florian present "poems packed with wordplay, puns, and double entendre. An impish array of people, monsters, and animals inhabit a loony, on-the-go world with such exotic vehicular mashups as the Fish Car, High-Heel Car, Balloon Car, and Caterpillar Cab." (Publishers Weekly)

★ **Poetrees**. Beach Lane Books 2010 45p il $16.99

Grades: 3 4 5 6   811
1. Trees -- Poetry 2. Poetry -- By individual authors
ISBN 978-1-4169-8672-0; 1-4169-8672-3

LC 2009-03025

"Florian focuses on trees (seeds, bark, leaves, roots, and tree rings) and introduces readers to 13 species from around the world. An oversize, double-page illustration accompanies each poem. . . . The selections are accessible and concise, with child-friendly wordplay and artful design. . . . The primitive illustrations—crafted on 'primed paper bags' using mixed media including gouache watercolor paints, colored pencils, rubber stamps, oil pastels, and collage—range in nuance from whimsy to mystery and reverence." SLJ

★ **UnBEElievables**; honeybee poems and paintings. Douglas Florian. Beach Lane Books 2012 32 p. col. ill. (hardcover) $16.99

Grades: 1 2 3 4 5   811
1. Beehives 2. Children's poetry 3. Bees
ISBN 1442426527; 9781442426528

LC 2011005613

This children's picture book presents a collection of poetry about bees. "The 14 poems introduce the roles of the queen, drones and workers and touch on such matters as anatomy, development from egg to bee, and even Colony Collapse Disorder." (Kirkus Reviews)

"Florian bestows yet another pleasing mix of punny poems and colorful collages that blend whimsy and fact... Spreads like "Swarm" epitomize Florian's skill at combining pithy rhymes, well-chosen facts and playfully tongue-in-cheek pictures." Kirkus

Includes bibliographical references

★ **Winter** eyes; poems & paintings by Douglas Florian. Greenwillow Bks. 1999 48p il $16

Grades: 2 3 4 5   811
1. Winter -- Poetry 2. Poetry -- By individual authors
ISBN 0-688-16458-7

LC 98-19483

A collection of poems about winter, including "Sled," "Icicles," and "Ice Fishing"

"The short rhyming lines are clear and will be easy to read aloud, and the softly toned watercolor-and-colored-pencil pictures show snowy winter scenes, some realistic, some playful." Booklist

★ **Zoo's** who; poems and paintings by Douglas Florian. Harcourt 2005 47p il $17

Grades: K 1 2 3   811
1. Animals -- Poetry 2. Poetry -- By individual authors
ISBN 0-15-204639-9

LC 2004-4576

A collection of short poems about animals

"There's plenty of humor throughout. . . . The artwork . . . always has unexpected bits. . . . The more astute the reader, the better the time he or she will have with this." Booklist

★ **For** laughing out loud; poems to tickle your funnybone. selected by Jack Prelutsky; illustrated by Marjorie Priceman. Knopf 1991 84p il $17

Grades: 3 4 5 6   811
1. Humorous poetry 2. American poetry -- Collections
ISBN 0-394-82144-0

LC 90-33010

A collection of humorous poems by writers including Ellen Raskin, Karla Kuskin, Ogden Nash, and Arnold Lobel

"These nonsense verses by a wide variety of poets combine the domestic and the gross, deadpan and slapstick, with a lilting rhythm and satisfying rhyme. . . . The design is ebullient, often with several poems appearing on a double-page spread surrounded by wildly energetic wash-and-line illustrations." Booklist

Forbes, Robert L.
Beast Friends Forever; by Robert L. Forbes; illustrated by Ronald Searle. Penguin Group USA 2013 80 p. (hardcover) $19.95

Grades: 4 5 6 7   811
1. Animal courtship 2. Animals -- Poetry 3. Animals
ISBN 1590208080; 9781590208083

In this book of children's poetry by Robert Forbes, "animal courtship is infused with quirky human characteristics and some sneaky social commentary. Readers meet Lancelot the Ocelot, doing time for 'his romance turned to tragedy, ending in a crime.' And Babette the Skunk, having studied with 'Parisian perfumers,' has fashioned a new scent, 'packaged in black and called "In-d-scent,"/It's sure to enflame any white-striped gent.'" (School Library Journal)

Forler, Nan
Winterberries and apple blossoms; reflections and flavors of a Mennonite year. paintings by Peter Etril Snyder. Tundra Books 2011 39p il $22.95

Grades: 4 5 6 7   811
1. Cooking 2. Months -- Poetry 3. Mennonites -- Poetry 4. Poetry -- By individual authors
ISBN 978-1-77049-254-7; 1-77049-254-2

With a poem for every month of the year, young Naomi introduces us to her family and hosts a journey through the seasonal rhythms of her rural Mennonite community. Includes a recipe for each month of the year.

This includes "12 evocative poems. . . . Snyder . . . contributes smudgy, sunlit acrylic scenes that convey a close-knit family that works, plays, and prays together. Along with Forler's graceful verse, and recipes for every season, it all adds up to a warm portrait of a community seldom found in the spotlight." Publ Wkly

Franco, Betsy

★ **Bees,** snails, and peacock tails shapes--naturally; [by] Betsy Franco; illustrated by Steve Jenkins. Margaret K. McElderry Books 2008 un il $16.99

Grades: PreK K 1 2   **811**

1. Nature poetry 2. Shape -- Poetry 3. Poetry -- By individual authors

ISBN 978-1-4169-0386-4; 1-4169-0386-0

LC 2006-12094

"The pair behind Birdsongs tackles another science topic—geometry in the animal world. Whether addressing hexagonal beehive cells or a snail's spiral shell, brisk rhymes draw attention to nature's math. . . . Striking color combinations make the illustrations pop. This inviting book is bound to spark more careful observation of the shapes and colors in the reader's natural world." Publ Wkly

A **curious** collection of cats; concrete poems. illustrations by Michael Wertz. Tricycle Press 2009 un il $16.99

Grades: PreK K 1 2 3   **811**

1. Cats -- Poetry 2. Poetry -- By individual authors

ISBN 978-1-58246-248-6; 1-58246-248-8

LC 2008-11359

"Thirty-two unusual, concrete poems, one per page with a single exception, are matched by Wertz's monoprints. The words move in several directions and sometimes inhabit multiple objects. The poems are so embedded within the illustrations that it is hard to imagine them without the artwork. . . . Cat lovers will recognize their felines stretching, purring, and napping." SLJ

Frost, Helen

Wake up! poem by Helen Frost; photographs by Rick Lieder. Candlewick Press 2017 32 p. color illustrations $15.99

Grades: PreK K 1 2   **811**

1. American poetry 2. Stories in rhyme 3. Animals -- Poetry 4. Children's poetry

ISBN 0763681490; 9780763681494

In this book of poetry for children, "poet Helen Frost and photographer Rick Lieder, the creators of 'Step Gently Out, Sweep Up the Sun,' and 'Among a Thousand Fireflies,' invite readers to wake up, open their eyes, and see the awe-inspiring array of new life just outside their door." (Publisher's note)

Frost, Robert

Birches; illustrated by Ed Young. Holt & Co. 1988 un il hardcover o.p. pa $8.95

Grades: 3 4 5   **811**

1. Trees -- Poetry 2. Poetry -- By individual authors

ISBN 0-8050-7230-6 pa

LC 86-4787

An illustrated version of the well-known poem written in 1916, about birch trees and the pleasures of climbing them

"The freedom called for in the sweep and depth of Frost's words should not be hemmed in by rigidly defined illustrations, and Young allows this license, giving the viewer ample opportunity to absorb and be absorbed by the imagery. The text is set two to three lines to a page, with the poem repeated in its entirety at the end." Booklist

George, Kristine O'Connell

★ **Emma** Dilemma: big sister poems. Clarion Books 2011 47p il $16.99

Grades: K 1 2 3   **811**

1. Children's poetry 2. Sisters -- Poetry 3. Poetry -- By individual authors

ISBN 0618428429; 9780618428427; 978-0-618-42842-7; 0-618-42842-9

LC 2008-50647

"A likable fourth-grader shares her frustrations about her preschool-age sister, Emma, in candid narrative poems. . . . There are tender moments, genuinely conveyed in Carpenter's expressive pen-and-ink illustrations. . . . The vignettes form such a vivid portrait of Emma and Jessica that readers may feel as if they personally know them." Publ Wkly

★ The **great** frog race and other poems; pictures by Kate Kiesler; with an introduction by Myra Cohn Livingston. Clarion Bks. 1997 40p il $15; pa $5.95

Grades: 3 4 5   **811**

1. Poetry -- By individual authors

ISBN 0-395-77607-4; 0-618-60478-2 pa

LC 95-51090

A collection of poems about frogs and dragonflies, wind and rain, a visit to the tree farm, the garden hose, and other aspects of country life

"George's astute imagery pairs beautifully with Kiesler's rich, warm-toned oil paintings to impart a strong sense of the pleasures of rural landscape." Booklist

★ **Old** Elm speaks; tree poems. illustrated by Kate Kiesler. Clarion Bks. 1998 48p il $15; pa $5.95

Grades: 2 3 4   **811**

1. Trees -- Poetry 2. Poetry -- By individual authors

ISBN 0-395-87611-7; 0-618-75242-0 pa

LC 97-49333

A collection of short, simple poems which present images relating to trees in various circumstances and throughout the seasons

"George conveys a deep understanding of nature, here particularly of trees, in a way that is readily accessible to children. Kiesler's warm oil paintings beautifully complement the poems." Booklist

Toasting marshmallows; camping poems. illustrated by Kate Kiesler. Clarion Bks. 2001 48p il $15

Grades: 3 4 5   **811**

1. Camping -- Poetry 2. Poetry -- By individual authors

ISBN 0-618-04597-X

LC 00-56984

"All of the selections convey a child-focused sense of wonder. . . . The poems are varied and inventive, replete with marvelous images and universal truths. . . . Each one is accompanied by a well-executed and evocative acrylic painting." SLJ

Gerstein, Mordicai, 1935-

Dear hot dog; poems about everyday stuff. Abrams 2011 un il

Grades: PreK K 1 2   **811**

1. Poetry -- By individual authors

ISBN 0810997320; 9780810997325

This collection of poems follows three friends from the time they wake up and brush their teeth to when they snuggle up for bed with their favorite stuffed animal.

This is "lyrical yet accessible. . . . Gerstein infuses humanity into a toothbrush, shoes, a bowl, a kite, leaves and an ice-cream cone. His acrylic illustrations are in harmony with his verses; sharp black lines and rich colors that spread outside their outlines, giving a dreamy yet vivid effect." Kirkus

Gibson, Amy

Around the world on eighty legs; illustrated by Daniel Salmieri. Scholastic Press 2010 un il $18.99

Grades: K 1 2   **811**

1. Children's poetry 2. Animals -- Poetry 3. Animals 4. Poetry -- By individual authors

ISBN 978-0-439-58755-6; 0-439-58755-7

LC 2009007160

"Gibson's collection of poems cleverly presents creatures from all across the globe in witty, rhythmic, and well-crafted verse. Instructional and entertaining, the poems nicely balance information with humor and wordplay. . . . Emphasizing humor over naturalism, Salmieri's . . . illustrations match the playfulness of Gibson's verse point for point." Publ Wkly

Giovanni, Nikki

★ **Spin** a soft black song: poems for children; illustrated by George Martins. rev ed; Hill & Wang 1985 57p il hardcover o.p. pa $4.95

Grades: 3 4 5 6   **811**

1. African Americans -- Poetry 2. Poetry -- By individual authors

ISBN 0-374-46469-3 pa

LC 84-19287

First published 1971

A poetry collection which recounts the feelings of black children about their neighborhoods, American society, and themselves

"A beautifully illustrated book of poems about black children for children of all ages. . . . Simple in theme but a very moving collection nonetheless." Read Ladders for Hum Relat. 5th edition

★ **The sun** is so quiet; poems. illustrations by Ashley Bryan. Holt & Co. 1996 31p il $14.95

Grades: K 1 2 3   **811**

1. Nature poetry 2. Poetry -- By individual authors

ISBN 0-8050-4119-2

LC 95-39357

A collection of poems primarily about nature and the seasons but also concerned with chocolate and scary movies

"Of the 13 poems presented here, 12 appeared in books published between 1973 and 1993. The new poem, entitled 'Connie,' represents the best of Giovanni: a series of quicksilver images that capture a mood to perfection. Painted in Bryan's signature style, the illustrations fill the pages with sunny colors and bold patterns." Booklist

Got geography! poems. selected by Lee Bennett Hopkins; pictures by Philip Stanton. Greenwillow Books 2006 32p il $15.99; lib bdg $16.89

Grades: 3 4 5   **811**

1. Geography -- Poetry 2. American poetry -- Collections

ISBN 0-06-055601-3; 0-06-055602-1 lib bdg

LC 2004-59662

"Sixteen selections from a variety of poets explore the curiosity piqued by maps, globes, the land we live on, and places far away. The gentle, often-moving verses cover a wide spectrum of ways to explore the Earth from mapping the world to examining its surface to finding one's place within it. . . . The bright acrylic-and-watercolor illustrations bring energy to the pages and set the mood for each poem." SLJ

Gottfried, Maya

★ **Our** farm; by the animals of Farm Sanctuary. [by] Maya Gottfried [and] Robert Rahway Zakanitch. Alfred A. Knopf 2010 un il $17.99; lib bdg $20.99

Grades: PreK K 1 2 3   **811**

1. Animals -- Poetry 2. Farm Sanctuary Inc. 3. Farm life -- Poetry

4. Poetry -- By individual authors

ISBN 978-0-375-86118-5; 0-375-86118-1; 978-0-375-96118-2 lib bdg; 0-375-96118-6 lib bdg

LC 2009-14885

"This homage to the shelter for neglected and abused farm animals where Gottfried served as a volunteer is a book of poems and accompanying paintings that will raise awareness both of the Sanctuary and the sad reasons for which such a place exists. But it has more to recommend it. The poems are 'narrated' by some of the shelter's inhabitants. . . . There's a disarming innocence throughout, and the best of the selections are enchanting. Zakanitch's illustrations are superb. Each one is a collectible work of art, exhibiting a masterful technique, tenderness, subtlety, and humor." SLJ

Graham, Joan Bransfield

★ **Flicker** flash; poems by Joan Bransfield Graham; illustrated by Nancy Davis. Houghton Mifflin 1999 un il $15; pa $6.95

Grades: K 1 2 3   **811**

1. Light -- Poetry 2. Poetry -- By individual authors

ISBN 0-395-90501-X; 0-618-31102-5 pa

LC 98-12956

A collection of poems celebrating light in its various forms, from candles and lamps to lightning and fireflies

"A vivid fusion of ingenious concrete poetry and boldly colored graphics." SLJ

Grandits, John

★ **Blue** lipstick; concrete poems. Clarion Books 2007 un il $15; pa $5.95

Grades: 5 6 7 8 9 10   **811**

1. Poetry -- By individual authors

ISBN 978-0-618-56860-4; 0-618-56860-3; 978-0-618-85132-4 pa; 0-618-85132-1 pa

LC 2006-23332

"This selection introduces readers to Jessie, who impulsively purchases blue lipstick, but later, regretfully decides to give it 'the kiss-off.' Jessie is big sister to Robert, who was featured in Grandits's Technically, It's Not My Fault (Clarion, 2004). As he did in that terrific collection, the author uses artful arrangements of text on the page, along with 54 different typefaces, to bring his images and ideas to life. . . . This irreverent, witty collection should resonate with a wide audience." SLJ

★ **Technically,** it's not my fault; concrete poems. by John Grandits. Clarion Books 2004 un il $15; pa $5.95

Grades: 5 6 7 8   **811**

1. Poetry -- By individual authors

ISBN 0-618-42833-X; 0-618-50361-7 pa

LC 2004-231

A collection of concrete poems on such topics as roller coasters, linguini, basketball, and sisters

"Grandits combines technical brilliance and goofy good humor to provide an accessible, fun-filled collection of poems, dramatically brought to life through a brilliant book design." SLJ

Greenfield, Eloise

Brothers & sisters; family poems. illustrated by Jan Spivey Gilchrist. Amistad 2009 32p il $17.99; lib bdg $18.89

Grades: K 1 2 3   **811**

1. Siblings -- Poetry 2. African Americans -- Poetry 3. Poetry -- By individual authors

ISBN 978-0-06-056284-7; 0-06-056284-6; 978-0-06-056285-4 lib bdg; 0-06-056285-4 lib bdg

LC 2008020209

"Greenfield's poetic observations and commentaries succinctly capture siblings at various ages and stages. . . . With only a few lines, the author grasps the love and admiration, the frustration and hurt, the fun and aggravation that they can engender. . . . The illustrator is equally as skillful in depicting the wide range of emotions and ages in the faces of the individual African Americans peopling the paintings. The realistic watercolors fit around and beside the poems, using the white space to highlight the art and give balance to the pages." SLJ

★ The **Great** Migration; journey to the North. HarperCollins Children's Books 2010 un il $16.99
Grades: K 1 2 3 **811**
   1. African Americans -- Poetry 2. Poetry -- By individual authors 3. United States -- History -- Poetry
   ISBN 978-0-06-125921-0; 0-06-125921-7
                    LC 2008-43821
"Collaborators Greenfield and Gilchrist . . . shape an evocative portrait of African-Americans who moved North during the Great Migration between 1915 and 1930 to escape Ku Klux Klan fueled racism and to secure better lives. . . . Chronicling the journey by train, lilting poetry and pictures capture a sense of both apprehension and hope. . . . Making intriguing use of photographs of people, news headlines, maps, and painted elements, each of Gilchrist's collages has a distinctive look and lighting, ranging from conventional portraits of the travelers to more abstract images." Publ Wkly

★ **Honey,** I love, and other love poems; pictures by Diane and Leo Dillon. Crowell 1978 un il $14.95; pa $5.95
Grades: 2 3 4 **811**
   1. Love poetry 2. African Americans -- Poetry 3. Poetry -- By individual authors
   ISBN 0-690-01334-5; 0-06-443097-9 pa
                    LC 77-2845
"These 16 poems explore facets of warm, loving relationships with family, friends and schoolmates as experienced by a young Black girl. Central to the theme of the book is the idea that the child loves herself and is very confident in expressing that love." Interracial Books Child Bull

When the horses ride by; children in the times of war. poems by Eloise Greenfield; illustrations by Jan Spivey Gilchrist. Lee & Low Books 2006 un il $17.95
Grades: 2 3 4 **811**
   1. War poetry 2. Poetry -- By individual authors
   ISBN 978-1-58430-249-0; 1-58430-249-6
                    LC 2005015393
Collection of poems about children around the world, focusing on the children's perceptions of war and how the turmoil of war affects their lives.
"Combining 17 rhythmic poems with dramatic illustrations, this title addresses a complex topic. Greenfield's deceptively simple verses express universal truths about both conflict and childhood." SLJ

Grimes, Nikki

At Jerusalem's gate; poems of Easter. with woodcuts by David Frampton. Eerdmans Books for Young Readers 2005 un il $20
Grades: 5 6 7 8 **811**
   1. American poetry 2. Easter -- Poetry 3. Children's poetry, American 4. Poetry -- By individual authors
   ISBN 0-8028-5183-5
                    LC 2003-1089
"Twenty-two poems trace the events celebrated by Christians at Easter Week, from Jesus' entry into Jerusalem through his appearance

to disciples after the Resurrection. . . . Grades five to eight." (Bull Cent Child Books)
"Each poem is preceded by a brief synopsis of the event, often accompanied by the author's own musings and queries, which prompt readers to think and ask questions of their own. . . . Bold, handsome woodcuts reinforce the powerful drama depicted in poetry. An outstanding effort." SLJ

★ **Meet** Danitra Brown; illustrated by Floyd Cooper. Lothrop, Lee & Shepard Bks. 1994 un il hardcover o.p. pa $6.99
Grades: 2 3 4 **811**
   1. Friendship -- Poetry 2. African Americans -- Poetry 3. Poetry -- By individual authors
   ISBN 0-688-15471-9 pa
                    LC 92-43707
"A collection of 13 original poems that stand individually and also blend together to tell a story of feelings and friendship between two African-American girls. . . . Cooper's distinguished illustrations in warm dusty tones convey the feeling of closeness. The poignant text and lovely pictures are an excellent collaboration." SLJ
   Other titles about Danitra Brown are:
   Danitra Brown, class clown (2005)
   Danitra Brown leaves town (2002)

Thanks a million; poems by Nikki Grimes; pictures by Cozbi A. Cabrera. Greenwillow Books 2006 31p il $15.99; lib bdg $16.89
Grades: K 1 2 3 **811**
   1. Poetry -- By individual authors
   ISBN 0-688-17292-X; 0-688-17293-8 lib bdg
                    LC 2004-54158
"Sixteen thoughtful poems about being thankful for everyday things. Grimes uses a variety of forms that include haiku, a riddle, and a rebus in selections that speak directly to the experiences of young children. . . . Cabreras acrylic illustrations are distinctive, folksy, and effective." SLJ

★ **When** Gorilla goes walking; by Nikki Grimes; illustrated by Shane Evans. Orchard Books 2007 un il $16.99
Grades: PreK K 1 2 **811**
   1. Cats -- Poetry 2. African Americans -- Poetry 3. Poetry -- By individual authors
   ISBN 978-0-439-31770-2
                    LC 2006017194
"In interlinked poems, Cecilia, a young African American girl, introduces her 'cool cat'—a fierce, tailless, gray shorthair named Gorilla. . . . In spare, expressive lines and bold colors, Evans' dynamic paintings capture the messy intimacy of the cat and human bond." Booklist

Gutman, Dan

★ **Casey** back at bat; paintings by Steve Johnson and Lou Fancher. HarperCollins 2007 un il $16.99; lib bdg $17.89
Grades: K 1 2 3 4 **811**
   1. Baseball -- Poetry 2. Poetry -- By individual authors
   ISBN 978-0-06-056025-6; 0-06-056025-8; 978-0-06-056026-3 lib bdg; 0-06-056026-6 lib bdg
                    LC 2006029468
Sequel to Ernest Lawrence Thayer's Casey at the bat
"Gutman revisits and updates Thayer's classic baseball poem. This time around . . . Casey hits a fly ball that soars out of the park and keeps on going. It crosses the Atlantic Ocean and has an unfortunate encounter with a tower in Pisa before continuing on to the Sphinx in Egypt. . . . It passes dinosaurs . . . and astronauts before heading back to Earth. The ride is uproarious from start to finish, and Gutman's broadly humorous verse hits all the right notes. . . . Johnson and Fancher's paintings have

a playfully nostalgic look, with a mix of textured papers and newsprint splashed across the surfaces of uniforms." SLJ

Hale, Sarah Josepha

Mary had a little lamb; by Sarah Josepha Hale; illustrated by Laura Beith. Marshall Cavendish 2011 il $12.99
Grades: PreK K 1 2   **811**
1. Nursery rhymes 2. Sheep -- Poetry 3. Poetry -- By individual authors
ISBN 978-0-7614-5824-1; 0-7614-5824-7
LC 2010012807

"Though Mary Had a Little Lamb was published in 1830, it seems anything but old-fashioned in this jaunty picture book. . . . The characters clothing and the many touches of fantasy and humor lift the poem out of its historical period and into some timeless, lighthearted landscape of the imagination. All six verses appear, from the very familiar to the nearly forgotten, and each illustrated with one or more double-page pictures that magnify the hilarity. . . . Even the potentially unctuous-sounding ending verse is lightened by the joyous spirit and amusing details in the accompanying illustrations, digital collages combining fabric elements with acrylic and gouache painting. A child-pleasing version of the well-known poem." Booklist

Hamsters, shells, and spelling bees; school poems. edited by Lee Bennett Hopkins; pictures by Sachiko Yoshikawa. HarperCollins 2008 46p il (I can read!) $16.99; lib bdg $17.89
Grades: PreK K 1 2   **811**
1. Schools -- Poetry 2. American poetry -- Collections
ISBN 978-0-06-074112-9; 0-06-074112-0; 978-0-06-074113-6 lib bdg; 0-06-074113-9 lib bdg
LC 2007020881

"Contributed by well-known poets for young people (Jane Yolen, J. Patrick Lewis, Alice Schertle, among others), the poems in this bright compilation . . . describe a wide range of school experiences. . . . The selections range in style from haikus to free verse, although many poems follow a bouncy, rhyming structure. All are written in accessible words targeted straight to emerging readers. . . . [Illustrated with] jellybean-bright cartoon-style illustrations." Booklist

★ **Hanukkah** lights; holiday poetry. selected by Lee Bennett Hopkins; pictures by Melanie Hall. HarperCollins 2004 28p il (I can read book) $15.99; lib bdg $16.89
Grades: K 1 2 3   **811**
1. Hanukkah -- Poetry 2. American poetry -- Collections
ISBN 0-06-008051-5; 0-06-008052-3 lib bdg
LC 2003-18901

A collection of poems that celebrate the activities and experiences of Hanukkah

"The poems are simple, evocative, and rhythmic without lapsing into a singsong cadence. Hall's expressive artwork creates an appealing contemporary tone with vivid pastels and a smattering of collage." SLJ

Harley, Avis

★ **African** acrostics; a word in edgeways. poems by Avis Harley; photographs by Deborah Noyes. Candlewick Press 2009 un il $17.99; pa $6.99
Grades: 4 5 6 7   **811**
1. Acrostics 2. Children's poetry 3. Animals -- Africa 4. Animals -- Poetry 5. Animals
ISBN 978-0-7636-3621-0; 0-7636-3621-5; 978-0-7636-5818-2 pa
LC 2008017916

This volume depicts "such wild animals as giraffes, zebras, and lions, in poems written to contain acrostics, in which beginning or ending

letters from the poetry lines can be used to spell other words." (Publisher's note) "Grades four to six." (Bull Cent Child Books)

"Harley has written 18 poems, each one featuring a different animal. All are written as acrostics, with most of them based on the first letter of each line, but several with more unusual patterns. . . . Much of Harley's poetry consists of carefully crafted descriptive word imagery that is right on target. . . . Most of the full-page, full-color photos of the animals are perfect companions to the facing selections." SLJ

The **monarch's** progress; poems with wings. written and illustrated by Avis Harley. Wordsong 2008 32p il $16.95
Grades: 3 4 5   **811**
1. Butterflies -- Poetry 2. Poetry -- By individual authors
ISBN 978-1-59078-558-4

"This collection of 18 illustrated poems celebrates butterflies in general and monarchs in particular. Cleverly written with obvious attention to craft, the poetry varies in form from rhymed couplets to acrostic verse to haiku and explores topics such as the physical differences between the larval and adult stages, the way monarch wings look when magnified, and the usefulness of having taste sensors in one's feet. Accompanying each poem is a color-pencil drawing, often featuring precise lines and intense hues." Booklist

★ **Sea** stars; saltwater poems. [by] Avis Harley; photographs by Margaret Butschler. Wordsong 2006 35p il $16.95
Grades: 3 4 5   **811**
1. Marine animals -- Poetry 2. Poetry -- By individual authors
ISBN 978-1-59078-429-7; 1-59078-429-4
LC 2006000931

"Butschler's beautiful color photographs came first, and her visual images of creatures on the seashore and in the aquarium inspired Harley's brief, concrete poems—from haiku and tanka to rhyming couplets and nursery rhyme parody. The wordplay will grab readers . . . and so will the exquisite images in both words and pictures." Booklist

Hauth, Katherine B.

What's for dinner? quirky, squirmy poems from the animal world. illustrated by David Clark. Charlesbridge 2011 48p il lib bdg $16.95; pa $7.95
Grades: 3 4 5   **811**
1. Children's poetry 2. Animals -- Poetry 3. Poetry -- By individual authors 4. Animals -- Food
ISBN 978-1-57091-471-3 lib bdg; 1-5709-1471-0 lib bdg; 978-1-57091-472-0 pa; 1-57091-472-9 pa
LC 2010-07588

"Hauth's funny, eloquent poems celebrate the often-grisly realities of the food chain, depicted in Clark's scraggly ink and watercolor illustrations. A mole gags on a banana slug, a rat 'gets a hug' from a boa constrictor, and a flattened toad becomes a roadkill restaurant. . . . Appended notes provide additional animal facts. A satisfying mix of tutelage and repartee." Publ Wkly

★ **Heart** to heart; new poems inspired by twentieth-century American art. edited by Jan Greenberg. Abrams 2001 80p il map $19.95
Grades: 5 6 7 8 9 10   **811**
1. American art 2. Art -- 20th century 3. American poetry -- Collections
ISBN 0-8109-4386-7
LC 99-462335

Michael L. Printz Award honor book, 2002

A compilation of poems by Americans writing about American art in the twentieth century, including such writers as Nancy Willard, Jane Yolen, and X. J. Kennedy.

"From a tight diamante and pantoum to lyrical free verse, the range of poetic styles will speak to a wide age group. . . . Concluding with biographical notes on each poet and artist, this rich resource is an obvious choice for teachers, and the exciting interplay between art and the written word will encourage many readers to return again and again to the book." Booklist

Heidbreder, Robert

Noisy poems for a busy day. Kids Can Press 2012 40 p. col. ill. (hardcover) $16.95

Grades: K 1 2   **811**

1. Day 2. Children 3. Poetry -- Collections

ISBN 1554537061; 9781554537068

This children's picture book by Robert Heibreder presents "a collection of (mostly) five-line poems that recreate the sounds and actions of a prechooler's day. . . . The collection is structured in the shape of a day, and Lori Joy Smith's child-like illustrations introduce us to five children whose lives involve toast and jam, goofing around, playing tag, kissing dogs, turning somersaults, going down the slide, and watching clouds." (Quill and Quire)

★ **Here's** a little poem; a very first book of poetry. collected by Jane Yolen and Andrew Fusek Peters; illustrated by Polly Dunbar. Candlewick Press 2007 104p il $21.99

Grades: PreK   **811**

1. American poetry -- Collections

ISBN 978-0-7636-3141-3; 0-7636-3141-8

LC 2006-40621

"This big, spacious anthology of more than 60 poems is a wonderful first book to read with babies and toddlers over and over again. . . . The clear, active, mixed-media illustrations show very young children outdoors and in; morning to bedtime; loving, teary, absurd, furious." Booklist

Herrera, Juan Felipe

★ **Laughing** out loud, I fly; poems in English and Spanish. drawings by Karen Barbour. HarperCollins Pubs. 1998 un il $15.99

Grades: 6 7 8 9   **811**

1. Mexican Americans -- Poetry 2. Poetry -- By individual authors 3. Bilingual books -- English-Spanish

ISBN 0-06-027604-5

LC 96-45476

A collection of poems in Spanish and English about childhood, place, and identity

"Barbour's black-and-white drawings accompany each poem, delicately underlining its images but allowing the strong sensuality of the words to seep into readers' minds." SLJ

Hines, Anna Grossnickle

Pieces; a year in poems & quilts. Greenwillow Bks. 2001 un il $15.95; lib bdg $15.89

Grades: K 1 2 3   **811**

1. Quilts 2. Nature poetry 3. Poetry -- By individual authors

ISBN 0-688-16963-5; 0-688-16964-3 lib bdg

LC 99-86463

Poems about the four seasons, as reflected in the natural world, are accompanied by photographs of quilts made by the author

"An appendix explains Hines's meticulous quilting process. . . . Hines takes her quilter's stash of fabric swatches and her wordsmith's metaphors for memories of the seasons, and pieces together a unified, artistic whole. An outstanding book for aspiring quilters or anyone at all." Publ Wkly

Includes bibliographical references

★ **Peaceful** pieces; poems and quilts about peace. Henry Holt 2011 32p il

Grades: PreK K 1 2   **811**

1. Peace -- Poetry 2. Poetry -- By individual authors

ISBN 0805089969; 9780805089967

LC 2010011697

"Hines pairs poems with images of her handmade quilts to reflect on the theme of peace. Several works focus on individual relationships: when two sisters fight, their mother makes them face each other at close range, which diffuses their anger into laughter. . . . Poems like 'Soldier Daddy' are socially resonant. . . . Often Hines needs just a few words to convey oceans of meaning. . . . The beauty and painstaking detail evident in each quilt brings the book's vision a stitch closer." Publ Wkly

★ **Winter** lights; a season in poems & quilts. Greenwillow Bks. 2005 un il $16.99; lib bdg $17.89

Grades: K 1 2 3   **811**

1. Quilts 2. Winter -- Poetry 3. Holidays -- Poetry 4. Poetry -- By individual authors

ISBN 0-06-000817-2; 0-06-000818-0 lib bdg

"Winter is the time of lights, and Hines celebrates the season in thoughtful poems and pictures of gorgeous quilts full of bright, beautiful colors. Christmas is only one of the light-producing celebrations that Hines illuminates. The feast of Santa Lucia, Hanukkah, Kwanzaa, and the Chinese New Year are spectacularly introduced with short bursts of poetry and quilts that capture the spirit of the day." Booklist

★ **Hip** hop speaks to children; a celebration of poetry with a beat. editor, Nikki Giovanni; advisory editors, Tony Medina, Willie Perdomo, Michele Scott; series editor, Dominique Raccah; illustrators, Kristen Balouch, Michele Noiset, Jeremy Tugeau, Alicia Vergel de Dios, and Damian Ward. Sourcebooks Jabberwocky 2008 72p il $19.99

Grades: 3 4 5 6   **811**

1. American poetry -- Collections 2. American poetry -- African American authors -- Collections

ISBN 978-1-4022-1048-8; 1-4022-1048-5

LC 2008004627

"Editor Giovanni states, 'Poetry with a beat. That's hip hop in a flash,' and she goes on to link hip-hop to grand opera and present a capsule history of African American vernacular music. This features a wide-ranging selection of 51 entries, plus a CD with new or previously released recorded versions of 29, some with music. The poets range from Langston Hughes and W.E.B. DuBois to Kanye West, Mos Def, and Queen Latifah. . . . Although created by five illustrators, the art shares both vibrant colors and a dancing free-spirited look that matches the general tone of the poetry." Booklist

Hoberman, Mary Ann

Forget-me-nots; poems to learn by heart. selected by Mary Ann Hoberman; illustrated by Michael Emberley. Megan Tingley Books 2012 143 p.

Grades: PreK K   **811**

1. Children's poetry 2. Poetry -- Memorizing 3. Poetry -- Collections 4. Children's poetry, American

ISBN 031612947X; 9780316129473

LC 2011025119

This poetry collection is a "compendium of verse . . . chosen with children in mind. The Children's Poet Laureate from 2008 to 2010, [Mary Ann] Hoberman chose 123 poems that are memorable in both senses of the word. They're 'easy to remember' (though she concedes that the longer ones will take more time) and 'worth remembering.' In an appended section, she discusses an approach to learning poems by heart, making the process a game with a specific prize." (Booklist)

★ **You** read to me, I'll read to you; very short stories to read together. illustrated by Michael Emberley. Little, Brown 2001 un il $15.95
Grades: K 1 2 3   **811**
1. American poetry 2. Books and reading 3. Children's poetry, American 4. Poetry -- By individual authors
ISBN 0-316-36350-2
LC 00-35230

"These rhyming short stories are written in three columns: a left and right-hand column for each of the two readers meant to alternate in the reading of most of the text, and a middle italicized column indicating that the two readers should read those lines together.... Each short story covers a two-page spread and features ... two characters, one for each reader; story subjects range from animals to friendship.... Grades two to three." (Bull Cent Child Books)

"Hoberman offers 13 rhymed variations on the theme of getting together to read. The short poems are designed to be read aloud by two voices, with occasional parts to share.... The energy never flags, neither in Hoberman's trademark bouncy rhythms nor in Emberley's exuberant illustrations, which picture a wonderful array of children and animals tumbling across the pages." Booklist

★ **You** read to me, I'll read to you: very short scary tales to read together; illustrated by Michael Emberley. Little, Brown 2007 32p il $16.99
Grades: K 1 2 3   **811**
1. Monsters -- Poetry 2. Poetry -- By individual authors
ISBN 978-0-316-01733-6

"The fourth uproarious poetry picture book in Hoberman and Emberley's popular You Read to Me, I'll Read to You series continues the pattern of simple, rhyming, illustrated stories for two voices.... The clear words with gorgeously gruesome, comic-style pictures tell of wild action and monster characters as lurid as they come." Booklist

Holbrook, Sara
Zombies! evacuate the school! illustrations by Karen Sandstrom. Wongsong 2010 56p il $16.95
Grades: 2 3 4 5   **811**
1. Schools -- Poetry 2. Poetry -- By individual authors
ISBN 978-1-59078-820-2; 1-59078-820-6

"With a breezy and comedic touch, Holbrook shines a light on school experiences, from academic pursuits to classroom rivalries to gym-class exploits. Humor reigns, and readers will identify with themes and emotions.... Many of the poems utilize an inner voice and encourage self-reflection. They are brief and accessible.... Sandstrom's pen-and-ink illustrations provide additional humor." SLJ

Hopkins, Lee Bennett
★ **City** I love; by Lee Bennett Hopkins; illustrated by Marcellus Hall. Abrams Books for Young Readers 2009 un il $16.95
Grades: K 1 2 3 4   **811**
1. City and town life -- Poetry 2. Poetry -- By individual authors
ISBN 978-0-8109-8327-4; 0-8109-8327-3
LC 2008008226

"A backpack-toting, humble hound with wanderlust and a winged companion tour several of the world's cities. Hopkins's 18 poems observe skyscrapers, hot-dog vendors, subways, taxis, bridges, bright lights, and the diversity of people and pigeons.... These polished poems are equally matched by Hall's graphic-style cartoons, which offer many added layers of narrative delight as well as beautiful colors and an eye-catching sense of design." SLJ

I am the book; poems selected by Lee Bennett Hopkins; illustrated by Yayo. Holiday House 2010 un il $16.95
Grades: K 1 2   **811**
1. Books and reading -- Poetry 2. American poetry -- Collections
ISBN 0823421198; 9780823421190
LC 2009014743

"This collection of poems by contemporary writers celebrates the joys of reading.... In Yayo's acrylic spreads, an open book becomes a whale's tail, a treasure box, and a drifting raft, emphasizing the transformative potential of words." Publ Wly

Hughes, Langston, 1902-1967
★ The **dream** keeper and other poems; including seven additional poems. [by] Langston Hughes; illustrated by Brian Pinkney. 75th anniversary ed.; Alfred A. Knopf 2007 83p il $16.99
Grades: 4 5 6 7   **811**
1. African Americans -- Poetry 2. Poetry -- By individual authors
ISBN 978-0-679-84421-1

First published 1932; this is a reissue of the 1994 edition

A collection of sixty-six poems, selected by the author for young readers, including lyrical poems, songs, and blues, many exploring the black experience

"Black-and-white scratchboard illustrations in Pinkney's signature style express the emotion and beat of the poetry.... The poems are ... colloquial and direct yet mysterious and complex." Booklist

★ **I,** too, am America; Langston Hughes; illustrated by Bryan Collier. Simon & Schuster Books for Young Readers 2012 40 p.
Grades: K 1 2 3   **811**
1. Railroads -- Fiction 2. Picture books for children 3. African Americans -- Poetry 4. United States -- History -- Poetry
ISBN 1442420081; 9781442420083
LC 2011002879

Coretta Scott King Illustrator Book Award (2013)

In this picture book, a "celebration of Pullman porters is the focus of this ... edition of Langston Hughes' classic poem. ... [It] begin[s] with ... a speeding train before moving on to large portraits of African American porters serving white passengers aboard a luxury train.... [T]he porters gather left-behind items--newspapers, blues and jazz albums--and toss them from the train.... [T]he words and music fall into the hands of African Americans across the country." (Booklist)

★ **Langston** Hughes; edited by Arnold Rampersad & David Roessel; illustrations by Benny Andrews. Sterling Pub. 2006 48p il (Poetry for young people) $14.95
Grades: 5 6 7 8   **811**
1. African Americans -- Poetry 2. Poetry -- By individual authors
ISBN 1-4027-1845-4; 978-1-4027-1845-8
LC 2005025369

A brief profile of African American poet Langston Hughes accompanies some of his better known poems for children.

"This charming collection of 26 poems is vibrantly illustrated with depictions of African Americans in varied settings.... This will be a welcome introduction to Hughes's poetry for elementary students, and it includes sufficient detail to make it useful and enjoyable for older students." SLJ

Lullaby (for a Black mother) a poem. Langston Hughes; illustrated by Sean Qualls. Houghton Mifflin Harcourt 2012 32 p. $16.99
Grades: PreK K   **811**
1. Lullabies 2. Children's poetry 3. Mother-child relationship 4. American poetry -- African American authors 5. Infants 6. Mother and child 7. African Americans 8. Lullabies, English 9. Children's

poetry, American
ISBN 054736265X; 9780547362656

LC 2012025484

This book, written by poet Langston Hughes and illustrated by Sean Qualls, "celebrates the love between an African American mother and her baby. . . . In the end, readers will find a rare photo of baby Hughes and his mother, a biographical note, further reading, and the complete lullaby." (Publisher's note)

"The poem's images of night and innocence are well suited for a picture book, too. Qualls (Freedom Song) keeps his artwork simple, painting a series of spreads that hew closely to the words. He renders "A necklace of stars" with a bird flying around mother and child, leaving a trail of stars around the woman's neck. "Moon,/ Moon,/ Great diamond moon" shows the white-gowned, long-haired mother floating among the clouds, holding her son up so he can see the shining disk in a dark, gray-blue sky. Swirls of grass and celestial orbs embellish daytime scenes, while the lights of tall buildings join with the stars above to form a backdrop for several nocturnal spreads." Kirkus

Includes bibliographical references (p.   )

★ **My** people; photographs by Charles R. Smith Jr. Atheneum Books for Young Readers 2009 un il $17.99

Grades: K 1 2 3 **811**

1. African Americans -- Poetry 2. Poetry -- By individual authors
ISBN 978-1-4169-3540-7; 1-4169-3540-1

LC 2008025604

ALA EMIERT Coretta Scott King Illustrator Award (2010)

"Introducing the poem two or three words at a time, Smith pairs each phrase with a portrait of one or more African Americans; printed in sepia, the faces of his subjects materialize on black pages. . . . Smith's faces emerge into the light, displaying the best that humanity has to offer—intelligence, wisdom, curiosity, love and joy." Publ Wkly

Sail Away; Langston Hughes; illustrated by Ashley Bryan. Atheneum Books for Young Readers 2015 40 p. color illustrations (hardcover) $17.99

Grades: K 1 2 3 4 5 **811**

1. Ocean 2. American poetry -- African American authors 3. Sea poetry, American
ISBN 1481430858; 9781481430852

LC 2014035769

This children's book is a "celebration of mermaids, wildernesses of waves, and the creatures of the deep through poems by Langston Hughes and cut-paper collage illustrations by multiple Coretta Scott King Award-winner Ashley Bryan." (Publisher's note)

"An impressive picture book of poetry to be read, reread, and cherished for generations to come." SLJ

★ **I** am the darker brother; an anthology of modern poems by African Americans. edited and with an afterword by Arnold Adoff; drawings by Benny Andrews; introduction by Rudine Sims Bishop; foreword by Nikki Giovanni. rev ed; Simon & Schuster Bks. for Young Readers 1997 208p il hardcover o.p. pa $5.99

Grades: 6 7 8 9 10 **811**

1. American poetry -- African American authors -- Collections
ISBN 0-689-81241-8; 0-689-80869-0 pa

LC 97-144181

First published 1968

This anthology presents "the African-American experience through poetry that speaks for itself. . . . Because of the historical context of many of the poems, the book will be much in demand during Black History Month, but it should be used and treasured as part of the larger canon of literature to be enjoyed by all Americans at all times of the year. An indispensable addition to library collections." SLJ

★ **I,** too, sing America; three centuries of African American poetry. [selected and annotated by] Catherine Clinton; illustrated by Stephen Alcorn. Houghton Mifflin 1998 128p il $21

Grades: 6 7 8 9 **811**

1. African Americans -- Poetry 2. American poetry -- African American authors -- Collections
ISBN 0-395-89599-5

LC 97-46137

"For each poet, Clinton provides a biography and a brief, insightful commentary on the poem(s) she has chosen, including a discussion of political as well as literary connections. Alcorn's dramatic, full-page, full-color illustrations opposite each poem evoke the quiltlike patterns and rhythmic figures of folk art." Booklist

★ **In** daddy's arms I am tall; African Americans celebrating fathers. illustrated by Javaka Steptoe. Lee & Low Bks. 1997 un il pa $6.95; $15.95

Grades: K 1 2 3 **811**

1. Children's poetry 2. Fathers -- Poetry 3. African Americans -- Poetry 4. American poetry -- Collections 5. Fathers
ISBN 1-58430-016-7 pa; 1-880000-31-8

LC 97-7311

Coretta Scott King Award for illustration

This "picture book celebrates the role of fathers in the African-American experience. The artist illustrates 13 poems with collages. . . . {The poems were} written by Angela Johnson, Davida Adedjouma, Carole Boston Weatherford, and others. . . . Grade three and up." (SLJ)

"Certain poems . . . elevate this collection above the mundane, but it is the illustrations that set this volume apart. Steptoe uses a variety of materials and techniques and art forms to enhance the language of the poems, including torn paper, collages, realia, paintings, and drawings." Horn Book

Incredible inventions; poems selected by Lee Bennett Hopkins; illustrations by Julia Sarcone-Roach. Greenwillow Books 2009 27p il $17.99; lib bdg $18.89

Grades: 1 2 3 4 **811**

1. Inventions -- Poetry 2. American poetry -- Collections
ISBN 978-0-06-087245-8; 0-06-087245-4; 978-0-06-087246-5 lib bdg; 0-06-087246-2 lib bdg

LC 2008003830

"Ingenious inventions are the focus of this lively picture-book poetry collection. Contributed by both well-known and emerging poets, the selections represent a wide range of styles. . . . The subjects, drawn from a young person's everyday world, add to the poems' accessiblity. . . . The mixed-media artwork's well-designed compositions add energy without overwhelming the words." Booklist

Iyengar, Malathi Michelle

Tan to tamarind; poems about the color brown. poems by Malathi Michelle Iyengar; illustrations by Jamel Akib. Children's Book Press 2009 30p il $16.95

Grades: K 1 2 3 **811**

1. Color -- Poetry 2. Poetry -- By individual authors
ISBN 978-0-89239-227-8; 0-89239-227-4

LC 2008022225

"Illustrated with pastel pictures in warm autumn colors, both dark and light, the simple poems celebrate the diversity and the connections in nature, culture, place, and language among blacks, Latinos, Indians, Native Americans, and many mixed-race kids. All the names for brown—from tan to honey, beige, and ocher—show the wonder of the senses." Booklist

Janeczko, Paul B., 1945-

★ **Firefly** July and other very short poems; Paul B. Janeczko, illustrated by Melissa Sweet. First edition Candlewick Press 2014 48 p. $16.99

Grades: K 1 2 3 4   **811**

1. Children's poetry 2. Seasons -- Poetry 3. American Poetry

ISBN 0763648426; 9780763648428

LC 2013943087

This collection of poems, by Paul B. Janeczko, is "organized by the seasons, beginning with spring. . . . The poems range from work by William Carlos Williams, Emily Dickinson, and Langston Hughes to that of James Stevenson, Joyce Sidman, and Ralph Fletcher. The first verse opens the book with daybreak, and after exploring the whole year, the final selection sends readers off to sleep." (School Library Journal)

"Sweet's child-friendly mixed-media illustrations--loosely rendered, collage-like assemblages in seasonal palettes--enhance the thirty-six excellent poems showcased on the book's ample spreads. As brief as three lines or a dozen words, most of the verses are by familiar poets (Carl Sandburg, Langston Hughes), including those known for their children s verse (Alice Schertle, Charlotte Zolotow). A fine addition to the seasonal poetry shelf." Horn Book

Katz, Alan

Oops! poems by Alan Katz; drawings by Edward Koren. Margaret K. McElderry Books 2008 132p il $17.99

Grades: 3 4 5 6   **811**

1. Humorous poetry 2. Poetry -- By individual authors

ISBN 978-1-4169-0204-1; 1-4169-0204-X

LC 2005-32439

"This collection of more than 100 short, funny, rhyming poems never lags. It includes occasional (rather funny) potty humor. . . . Puns and other groaners abound and are sure to delight young readers, especially boys. . . . Koren's pen-and-ink cartoons resemble the art in Shel Silverstein's collections. The illustrations match the tone of the book and sometimes add extra interpretations of the poems. This is a great choice for reluctant poetry readers and aspiring class clowns." SLJ

Poems I wrote when no one was looking; drawings by Edward Koren. Margaret K. McElderry Books 2011 153p il $17.99

Grades: 3 4 5   **811**

1. Humorous poetry 2. Poetry -- By individual authors

ISBN 978-1-4169-3518-6; 1-4169-3518-5

LC 2007052523

"Accompanied by Koren's impish, characteristically furry caricatures, Katz's comedic poems take aim at familiar experiences like family squabbling and avoiding homework, while offering child-centric observations about the world. . . . Kids will revel in the gently wicked jokes . . . and mild gross-out gags . . . that run throughout the collection." Publ Wkly

Kennedy, X. J.

City kids; street and skyscraper rhymes. illustrated by Philippe Béha. Tradewind Books 2010 104p il $17.95

Grades: 3 4 5   **811**

1. City and town life -- Poetry 2. Poetry -- By individual authors

ISBN 978-1-896580-44-9; 1-896580-44-0

"The urban world is examined from every angle in this lively collection of verse about city life. Most can apply to cities generally, though there are specific poems about Toronto, San Francisco, London, and others. . . . Béha's illustrations have a naïf, crayon-scrawled exuberance, and most match the upbeat tone of Kennedy's verse." Publ Wkly

★ **A kick** in the head; selected by Paul B. Janeczko; illustrated by Chris Raschka. Candlewick Press 2005 61p il $17.99; pa $9.99

Grades: 4 5 6 7   **811**

1. American poetry -- Collections

ISBN 978-0-7636-0662-6; 0-7636-0662-6; 978-0-7636-4132-0 pa; 0-7636-4132-4 pa

LC 2004-48508

"Raschka's high-spirited, spare torn-paper-and-paint collages ingeniously broaden the poems' wide-ranging emotional tones. . . . Clear, very brief explanations of poetic forms . . . accompany each entry; a fine introduction and appended notes offer further information. . . . This is the introduction that will ignite enthusiasm." Booklist

Kinerk, Robert

Oh, how Sylvester can pester! and other poems more or less about manners. pictures by Drazen Kozjan. Simon & Schuster Books for Young Readers 2011 28p il $16.99

Grades: K 1 2 3   **811**

1. Children's poetry 2. Etiquette -- Poetry 3. Poetry -- By individual authors 4. Etiquette for children and teenagers

ISBN 1-4169-3362-X; 978-1-4169-3362-5

LC 2010000771

In these illustrated poems "Kinerk pokes fun at what can happen when good manners are neglected." (Publisher's note)

"The rhymes in this picture book about manners have fun with names and with nonsense. . . . The clear, bright digital pictures extend the farce." Booklist

Knock at a star; a child's introduction to poetry. [compiled by] X. J. Kennedy and Dorothy M. Kennedy; illustrated by Karen Lee Baker. rev ed; Little, Brown 1999 180p il hardcover o.p. pa $12.99

Grades: 3 4 5 6   **811**

1. English poetry -- Collections 2. American poetry -- Collections

ISBN 0-316-48436-9; 0-316-48800-3 pa

LC 98-21572

A revised and newly illustrated edition of the title first published 1982

An anthology of mostly very short poems by standard, contemporary, and anonymous poets, intended to stimulate interest in reading and writing poetry

"Karen Lee Baker's small, shaded-pencil drawings capture the many moods of the verse." Booklist

Lang, Diane

Vulture verses; love poems for the unloved. written by Diane Lang; illustrated by Lauren Gallegos. Prospect Park Media 2012 32 p.

Grades: 2 3 4   **811**

1. Didactic poetry 2. Animals -- Poetry 3. Children's poetry 4. Children's poetry, American

ISBN 0983459452; 9780983459453

LC 2012002823

Larios, Julie Hofstrand

Yellow elephant; a bright bestiary. poems by Julie Larios; paintings by Julie Paschkis. Harcourt 2006 31p il $16

Grades: K 1 2 3   **811**

1. Color -- Poetry 2. Animals -- Poetry 3. Poetry -- By individual authors

ISBN 0-15-205422-7

LC 2004-25163

Boston Globe-Horn Book Honor: Fiction and Poetry (2006)

"The animals featured in these well-crafted poems flash with color and emotion. Each spread features a picture of a brightly hued animal, and Larios' rhythms and sounds skillfully reinforce the memorable, evocative images. . . . Together with Paschkis' vibrant, patterned, gouache paintings, the poems beautifully show how color and sound create mood and imagery." Booklist

Latham, Irene

★ **Dear** Wandering Wildebeest; And Other Poems from the Water Hole. By Irene Latham; Illustrated by Anna Wadham. Millbrook Press 2014 33 p. (lib. bdg. : alk. paper) $17.95
Grades: 2 3 4 5   **811**
  1. Animals -- Africa 2. Children's poetry 3. Poems. Selections.
ISBN 1467712329; 9781467712323
                LC 2013030195
In this children's poetry book, written by Irene Latham and illustrated by Anna Wadham, readers will "Spend a day at a water hole on the African grasslands. From dawn to nightfall, animals come and go. Giraffes gulp, wildebeest graze, impalas leap, vultures squabble, and elephants wallow." (Publisher's note)
"This will be a much-sought-after book for teaching reading and inquiry skills...Charming illustrations in dusty colors convey the habitat of the African grasslands while portraying the passing of a day. A strong choice." SLJ

Lawrence, Jacob

★ **Harriet** and the Promised Land. Simon & Schuster Bks. for Young Readers 1993 un il $18; pa $6.99
Grades: 2 3 4 5   **811**
  1. Abolitionists 2. Underground railroad -- Poetry 3. Poetry -- By individual authors
ISBN 0-671-86673-7; 0-689-80965-4 pa
                LC 92-33740
A newly illustrated edition of the title first published 1968 by Windmill Books
"The strength of this volume is in the forceful, stylized paintings by the famous black artist, which capture the degradation of slavery." Brooklyn. Art Books for Child

Lesynski, Loris

Crazy about soccer. Annick Press 2012 47 p. $22.95
Grades: 3 4 5   **811**
  1. Soccer -- Poetry 2. Children's poetry 3. Picture books for children
ISBN 1554514223; 9781554514229
This poetry collection "celebrates the sport of soccer. . . . From the commiseration offered to players who must persevere through squalls in 'Rain Game' to . . . 'Turf Burn,' which . . . describes the perils of artificial grass, [Loris] Lesynski's verse explores the gamut of soccer experiences. The format varies, with verses that range from brief . . . , such as the sole line comprising 'The Concussion Discussion,' to the lengthier 'How to Be a Referee,' which pays homage to . . . game officials." (Kirkus)

Levy, Debbie

Maybe I'll sleep in the bathtub tonight; and other funny bedtime poems. illustrated by Stephanie Buscema. Sterling Pub. 2010 24p il $14.95
Grades: PreK K 1 2   **811**
  1. Humorous poetry 2. Bedtime -- Poetry 3. Poetry -- By individual authors
ISBN 978-1-4027-4944-5; 1-4027-4944-9
                LC 2008-48826
"These cozy rhymes for sharing at bedtime have a lot of fun with wordplay, from the literal interpretations of sleepover, showing kids on a roof, and sleep tight (I unkinked myself and vowed: / Tonight I will sleep loose!), to a familiar nursery lullaby. . . . Young children with their caregivers will giggle at the humorous scenes, illustrated with colorful

gouache pictures, which could make a good prelude to the usual soothing lullabies." Booklist

★ The **year** of goodbyes; a true story of friendship, family and farewells. Disney-Hyperion Books 2010 136p il $16.99
Grades: 5 6 7 8   **811**
  1. Jews -- Poetry 2. Holocaust, 1933-1945 -- Poetry 3. Poetry -- By individual authors
ISBN 1-4231-2901-6; 978-1-4231-2901-1
                LC 2009-18671
"In 1930s Germany, it was common for young girls to keep poesiealbums, or autograph books, in which friends could write poems, draw pictures, or offer wishes to the owner. Levy has based this novel in verse on the actual poesiealbum kept by her mother, Jutta Salzberg, when she was twelve years old. . . . Grades four to seven." (Bull Cent Child Books)
"Artfully weaving together her mother's poesiealbum (autograph/poetry album), diary, and her own verse, Levy crafts a poignant portrait of her Jewish mother's life in 1938 Nazi Germany that crackles with adolescent vitality." Publ Wkly

Lewis, J. Patrick

★ **Blackbeard,** the pirate king; several yarns detailing the legends, myths, and real-life adventures of history's most notorious seaman. told in verse by J. Patrick Lewis. National Geographic Society 2006 un il map $16.95; lib bdg $25.90
Grades: 3 4 5   **811**
  1. Pirates 2. Pirates -- Poetry 3. Poetry -- By individual authors
ISBN 0-7922-5585-2; 0-7922-5586-0 lib bdg
                LC 2005-29514
"Lewis crafts around the few facts and many fictions told of Edward Teach, otherwise known as Blackbeard, the seventeenth century pirate king. In antique type, the poems are either set against parchment-style backgrounds or against one of the book's diverse images, which include paintings by N. C. Wyeth, and Caspar David Friedrich, as well as archival prints and striking modern paintings. Despite the broad range of art styles, the story flows cohesively throughout, vividly evoking the buccaneer's adventures in swashbuckling lines that read aloud well." Booklist

Countdown to summer; a poems for every day of the school year. illustrations by Ethan Long. Little, Brown and Co. 2009 un il $15.99
Grades: 4 5 6   **811**
  1. Schools -- Poetry 2. Poetry -- By individual authors
ISBN 978-0-316-02089-3; 0-316-02089-3
                LC 2008016772
"180 poems are here gathered to be enjoyed on a vitamin-like one-a-day basis. . . . Some verses are long, some short, some thought-provoking, some laugh-provoking. Long's penciled spot art provides an agreeable visual accompaniment." Kirkus

★ **Doodle** dandies; poems that take shape. J. Patrick Lewis, words; Lisa Desimini, images; with design and typography by Ann Bobco and Lisa Desimini. Atheneum Bks. for Young Readers 1998 un il hardcover o.p. pa $7.99
Grades: 1 2 3 4   **811**
  1. American poetry 2. Visual poetry 3. Visual poetry, American 4. Children's poetry, American 5. Poetry -- By individual authors
ISBN 0-689-81075-X; 0-689-84889-7 pa
                LC 9601920
This is a collection of poems each of which appears on the page in the shape of its subject so that the poem looks like whatever it's about. "Grades three to six." (SLJ)

"Every page of this book is well designed, creating words and images that work together in harmony. . . . Doodle Dandies captures the joy that wordplay can bring." SLJ

Edgar Allan Poe's apple pie; math puzzlers in classic poems. written by J. Patrick Lewis; illustrated by Michael H. Slack. Harcourt 2012 37 p.

Grades: 4 5 6   **811**
1. Children's poetry 2. Mathematics -- Poetry 3. Mathematical recreations 4. Word problems (Mathematics) 5. Poetry -- Parodies, imitations, etc. 6. Children's poetry, American 7. English poetry -- Adaptations 8. American poetry -- Adaptations
ISBN 9780547513386

LC 2011025735

The author J. Patrick Lewis "combines math and language arts with this collection of humorous poetry parodies that present readers with math word problems to solve. Fourteen famous poets and some of their more prominent works are the basis for Lewis' parodies, which . . . retain the structure, rhyme and rhythm of the originals." The book presents challenges based on works by poets including Walt Whitman, Emily Dickinson, and Shel Silverstein on mathematics concepts such as fractions, decimals, and perimeter. (Kirkus)

★ The **house**; illustrated by Roberto Innocenti. Creative Editions 2009 un il $19.95

Grades: 4 5 6 7   **811**
1. Houses -- Poetry 2. Poetry -- By individual authors
ISBN 978-1-56846-201-1; 1-56846-201-8

"The walls in a stone farmhouse literally talk in this first-person narrative that deals with the ravages of time and their effects on the structure and its inhabitants. After a brief history, the house (constructed in 1656, 'a plague year') fast forwards to the dawn of the 20th century, when children discover its ruins. The quatrains, one to a spread, alternate between an AABB and ABBA rhyme scheme, thus avoiding singsong predictability. . . . Children will pore over Innocenti's marvelously detailed spreads, composed in an oversize, vertical format and set in an Italian hill town. . . . In the subset of books dealing intelligently with the effects of time on a single location, this is a provocative choice." SLJ

If you were a chocolate mustache; J. Patrick Lewis. WordSong 2012 159 p. $18.95

Grades: 3 4 5   **811**
1. Children's poetry 2. Dragons -- Poetry 3. Turtles -- Poetry
ISBN 159078927X; 9781590789278

LC 2012939794

For this book, "in offbeat poems that include haikus, limericks, riddles, and wordplay of every kind, current children's poet laureate [J. Patrick] Lewis offers quirky contemplations, silly vignettes, and improbable events." Here, "a dragon serves as a clothes dryer, Bigfoot laments that he can't find stylish shoes in his size, and an old turtle complains to the sky that there is 'nothing new under the sun,' only to have his claim challenged by a snowflake." (Publishers Weekly)

★ **Monumental** verses. National Geographic 2005 31p il $16.95; lib bdg $25.90

Grades: 5 6 7 8   **811**
1. Monuments -- Poetry 2. Poetry -- By individual authors
ISBN 0-7922-7135-1; 0-7922-7139-4 lib bdg

"Lewis offers 14 poems celebrating monumental structures. From the remnants of civilizations at Stonehenge, Easter Island, and Machu Picchu to the more modern achievements of the Taj Mahal, the Eiffel Tower, and the Statue of Liberty, the subjects are varied and the accompanying photos are striking." Booklist

★ **Self**-portrait with seven fingers; the life of Marc Chagall in verse. [by] J. Patrick Lewis &Jane Yolen. Creative Editions 2011 38p il $18.99

Grades: 5 6 7 8   **811**
1. Artists 2. Painters 3. Jews -- Poetry 4. Artists -- Poetry 5. Jews -- Biography
ISBN 978-1-56846-211-0; 1-56846-211-5

LC 2009034767

"Lewis and Yolen pair 14 poems about Marc Chagall (1887–1985) with reproductions of more than a dozen of his paintings (as well as vintage photographs) in this moving account of the artist's Jewish upbringing in what is now Belarus, . . . his ascent in the art world, and his loves and losses, including arrest by the Nazis while living in Paris. . . . The duo's emphatic and empathetic verse is put into context by informative biographical sidebars that appear beneath each poem. A study in resilience, dedication, and wide-ranging talent." Publ Wkly

Includes bibliographical references

Skywriting; poems to fly. illustrated by Laszlo Kubinyi. Creative Editions 2010 32p il $25.65

Grades: 3 4 5 6   **811**
1. Flight -- Poetry 2. Poetry -- By individual authors
ISBN 978-1-56846-203-5; 1-56846-203-4

LC 2008014229

"Tracing the history of flight, this collection of poems celebrates the daring dreams of humans, from Icarus's doomed journey . . . to modern space shuttles. . . . Kubinyi's precise linework and sense of movement are well-matched to the mechanical subject matter and capture the spirit of flight across the ages." Publ Wkly

Spot the plot; a riddle book of book riddles. illustrated by Lynn Munsinger. Chronicle Books 2009 un il $15.99

Grades: K 1 2 3   **811**
1. Riddles 2. Books and reading -- Poetry 3. Poetry -- By individual authors
ISBN 978-0-8118-4668-4; 0-8118-4668-7

LC 2008-03206

"Short poetic riddles are presented on spreads, each providing the clues in both text and illustrations of the plot of a well-known children's story. Two young detectives and their dog are looking at such activities as farm animals typing letters in a field (Click, Clack, Moo), a train running along snowy railway tracks (The Polar Express), or a pumpkin coach careening along as it's drawn by a bunch of rats (Cinderella). . . . This book is perfect for an interactive read-aloud." SLJ

★ **When** thunder comes; poems for civil rights leaders. by J. Patrick Lewis, 2011-2013 Children's Poet Laureate; illustrated by R. Gregory Christie. Chronicle Books 2012 44 p. (alk. paper) $16.99

Grades: 4 5 6   **811**
1. Children's poetry 2. Civil rights 3. Children's poetry, American
ISBN 1452101191; 9781452101194

LC 2011045938

In this collection, "Children's Poet Laureate J. Patrick Lewis gives . . . voice to seventeen heroes of civil rights. . . . Illustrated by five . . . artists, this . . . collection of poems invites the reader to hear in each verse the thunder that lies in every voice, no matter how small." Civil rights figures profiled include "Coretta Scott King, Harvey Milk, Mohandas Gandhi, Nelson Mandela, Sylvia Mendez, Aung San Suu Kyi, . . . Andrew Goodman, and Michael Schwerner." (Publisher's note)

The **World's** Greatest; poems. [written by] J. Patrick Lewis; [illustrated by Keith Graves] Chronicle Books 2008 33p il $16.99

Grades: K 1 2 3   **811**
  1. World records -- Poetry 2. Poetry -- By individual authors
  ISBN 978-0-8118-5130-5; 0-8118-5130-3
                                                          LC 2007-14717
"This sprightly, clever collection centers on facts found in various editions of the 'Guinness Book of Records.' . . . The droll, distinct illustrations created using acrylic paint and colored pencils capture perfectly the humor and vigor of the text. This attractive book is saturated with color and will charm children who understand its adroit wordplay." SLJ

★ **Lives:** poems about famous Americans; selected by Lee Bennett Hopkins; illustrated by Leslie Staub. HarperCollins Pubs. 1999 31p il $15.99
Grades: 4 5 6 7   **811**
  1. American poetry -- Collections 2. United States -- Biography -- Poetry
  ISBN 0-06-027767-X; 0-06-027768-8 lib bdg
                                                          LC 98-29851
A collection of poetic portraits of sixteen famous Americans from Paul Revere to Neil Armstrong, by such authors as Jane Yolen, Nikki Grimes, and X. J. Kennedy
"Hopkins's eloquent introduction praises the power of poetry. Concluding 'Notes on the Lives' give readers useful biographical information. Full-page portraits feature Staub's distinctive, flat, primitive style, and their backgrounds have details particular to the subject. . . . A winning combination of poems and illustrations." SLJ

Lobel, Arnold
  ★ The **frogs** and toads all sang; color by Adrianne Lobel. HarperCollinsPublishers 2009 29p il $16.99; lib bdg $17.89
Grades: PreK K 1 2   **811**
  1. Frogs -- Poetry 2. Toads -- Poetry 3. Poetry -- By individual authors
  ISBN 978-0-06-180022-1; 978-0-06-180023-8 lib bdg
                                                          LC 2008051768
A collection of poems featuring frogs, toads, and polliwogs
"Originally created by the late Lobel as a handmade book for a fellow author, these poems and pencil sketches (skillfully given washes of color by his daughter, Adrianne) are the progenitors of Lobel's classic Frog and Toad series. But even kids who haven't spent much time with those amphibious friends will find plenty to enjoy. . . . The drawings of genteelly domesticated amphibians large and small bring to mind the spontaneity, intimacy and exuberance of the sketchpad." Publ Wkly

Odd owls & stout pigs; a book of nonsense. color by Adrianne Lobel. Harper 2009 31p il $15.99; lib bdg $16.89
Grades: PreK K 1 2   **811**
  1. Humorous poetry 2. Owls -- Poetry 3. Pigs -- Poetry 4. Poetry -- By individual authors
  ISBN 978-0-06-180054-2; 0-06-180054-6; 978-0-06-180055-9 lib bdg; 0-06-180055-4 lib bdg
                                                          LC 2009001406
Presents a linked collection of brief rhymes featuring owls and pigs
"This collection of nonsense rhymes and poems explodes with fun and frivolity. . . . The verses cover a wide variety of topics, and the words create sound patterns that will engage listeners. . . . Original illustrations were scanned and enhanced with oil pastels and colored pencils. They play buoyantly off Mr. Lobel's clever text and provide a breezy feel." SLJ

Longfellow, Henry Wadsworth
  Hiawatha; pictures by Susan Jeffers. Dial Bks. for Young Readers 1983 un il hardcover o.p. pa $6.99 **811**
  1. Native Americans -- Poetry 2. Native Americans -- Folklore 3. Poetry -- By individual authors
  ISBN 0-14-055882-9 pa
                                                          LC 83-7225
Verses excerpted from the poem first published 1855 with title: Song of Hiawatha
"Jeffers has captured the essence of this brief section from the classic poem. . . . The pale tints of the pictures are in complete harmony with nature and with the text and show in detail how Hiawatha might have seen his world. A fine first exposure to the poem for children and a beautiful artistic experience." SLJ

Lujan, Jorge
  Doggy slippers; poems by Jorge Luján (with the contribution of Latin American children); translated by Elisa Amado; pictures by Isol. Groundwood Books/House of Anansi Press 2010 un il $18.95
Grades: PreK K 1   **811**
  1. Pets -- Poetry 2. Poetry -- By individual authors
  ISBN 978-0-88899-983-2; 0-88899-983-6
"Using suggestions from kids in Mexico and Argentina, Luján crafts this refreshing collection of 12 free-verse poems about children's pets. . . . Abstract, whimsical illustrations in a retro palette of brown, gold, olive and aqua rely on squiggly pencil outlines to economically define details and highlight sublime and ridiculous aspects from each poem. . . . Poetic pet snapshots packaged with panache and translated with aplomb." Kirkus

MacLachlan, Patricia
  I didn't do it; [by] Patricia MacLachlan and Emily MacLachlan Charest; illustrated by Katy Schneider. Katherine Tegan Books 2010 un il $16.99
Grades: PreK K 1 2   **811**
  1. Dogs -- Poetry 2. Poetry -- By individual authors
  ISBN 978-0-06-135833-3; 0-06-135833-9
                                                          LC 2009-27541
This is a "charming volume of verses showing the thoughts of puppies of many breeds. . . . The verses are short, and the authors seem to understand canines and their likes, dislikes and self discipline (or lack thereof). Humor abounds, as do the activities, and illustrated in lively, textured oil paintings that make breeds clearly recognizable." Kirkus

★ **Once** I ate a pie; by Patricia MacLachlan and Emily MacLachlan Charest; illustrated by Katy Schneider. Joanna Cotler Books 2006 un il $15.99; lib bdg $16.89; pa $6.99
Grades: K 1 2 3   **811**
  1. Dogs -- Poetry 2. Poetry -- By individual authors
  ISBN 978-0-06-073531-9; 0-06-073531-7; 978-0-06-073532-6 lib bdg; 0-06-073532-5 lib bdg; 978-0-06-073533-3 pa; 0-06-073533-3 pa
                                                          LC 2004-22225
"Free-verse poems about 14 individual dogs sprawl across oversize spreads accompanied by large oil illustrations. The poems and paintings together delightfully capture each distinct personality in few words and with broad strokes of the brush." SLJ

★ **Marvelous** math; a book of poems. selected by Lee Bennett Hopkins; illustrated by Karen Barbour. Simon & Schuster Bks. for Young Readers 1997 31p il hardcover o.p. pa $6.99
Grades: 3 4 5   **811**
  1. Mathematics -- Poetry 2. American poetry -- Collections
  ISBN 0-689-80658-2; 0-689-84442-5 pa
                                                          LC 96-21597
Presents such poems as "Math Makes Me Feel Safe," "Fractions," "Pythagoras," and "Time Passes," by such writers as Janet S. Wong, Lee Bennett Hopkins, and Ilo Orleans

"Rhymed and open verse styles are represented, as are a variety of tones. . . . Barbour's lively illustrations dance and play around the poems. Her boldly outlined watercolor figures, often wearing ill-fitting hats, fill the pages with childlike whimsy." SLJ

Moore, Clement C.

★ The **night** before Christmas; by Clement C. Moore and illustrated by Holly Hobbie. Little, Brown & Co. 2013 40 p. $18
Grades: PreK K 1 2   **811**
1. Watercolor painting 2. Christmas -- Fiction 3. Christmas poetry 4. Children's poetry, American 5. Santa Claus -- Juvenile poetry
ISBN 0316070181; 9780316070188
LC 2012049185

In this book, by Clement C. Moore and illustrated by Holly Hobbie, "a toddler awakens, looks out the window, and sees a flying sleigh. He makes his way downstairs, where he peeks around a chair to watch St. Nicholas at work. . . . An appended section offers some historical background on Moore and the poem, first published in 1823, while an artist's note comments on Hobbie's technique and her approach to the work." (Booklist)

The **night** before Christmas; retold and illustrated by Rachel Isadora. G. P. Putnam's Sons 2009 un il $16.99
Grades: PreK K 1 2   **811**
1. Christmas -- Poetry 2. Santa Claus -- Poetry 3. Poetry -- By individual authors
ISBN 978-0-399-25408-6; 0-399-25408-0
LC 2008053359

"Santa's Christmas Eve journey takes him to Africa in this charming version of the poem. Isadora uses collaged papers and oil paints to create a vibrant African village, dusted by snow. . . . Full of details, rich color, and an exuberant spirit, this book will provide opportunities for discussion as well as a new cultural landscape for the 'right jolly old elf.'" SLJ

'Twas the **night** before Christmas; illustrated by Christopher Wormell. Running Press Kids 2010 un il $16.95
Grades: PreK K 1   **811**
1. Christmas -- Poetry 2. Santa Claus -- Poetry 3. Poetry -- By individual authors
ISBN 978-0-7624-2717-8; 0-7624-2717-5

The well-known poem about an important Christmas visitor.

"With their strong black lines and deep colors, Wormell's signature block prints are a fittingly iconic pairing for Moore's holiday classic. . . . This is an enchanting and elegant adaptation." Publ Wkly

Moore, Lilian

★ **Beware**, take care; fun and spooky poems. by Lilian Moore; illustrated by Howard Fine. Henry Holt and Co. 2006 un il $16.95
Grades: PreK K 1 2   **811**
1. Fear -- Poetry 2. Monsters -- Poetry 3. Supernatural -- Poetry 4. Poetry -- By individual authors
ISBN 978-0-8050-6917-4; 0-8050-6917-8
LC 2005020257

Poems first published in the author's Spooky Rhymes and Riddles (1973) and See My Lovely Poison Ivy (1975)

"The ghosts, monsters, and dragons are amusing and not the least bit scary in this congenial picture-book gathering of short verses. . . . Illustrated with humor and warmth, these poems are simple enough for independent readers and silly enough to evoke chuckles and giggles during read-aloud sharing." SLJ

Mural on Second Avenue, and other city poems; illustrated by Roma Karas. Candlewick Press 2005 un il $16.99

Grades: K 1 2 3   **811**
1. City and town life -- Poetry 2. Poetry -- By individual authors
ISBN 0-7636-1987-6
LC 2002-73702

"These 17 poems, all but one of which were chosen from Moore's previous collections, celebrate life in the city. . . . The poems appear on pages covered in bright oil paintings. . . . These poems speak loudly to children." SLJ

Mora, Pat

★ **Yum!** mmmm! que rico! Americas' sproutings: haiku. illustrated by Rafael López. Lee & Low 2007 un il map lib bdg $16.95
Grades: 1 2 3 4   **811**
1. Fruit 2. Haiku 3. Vegetables 4. Food -- Poetry 5. Children's poetry 6. Food
ISBN 1-58430-271-2 lib bdg; 978-1-58430-271-1 lib bdg
LC 2006-38199

"From blueberries to vanilla, indigenous foods of the Americas are celebrated in this collection of haiku, which also includes information about each food's origins." (Publisher's note) "Grades three to five." (Bull Cent Child Books)

"This inventive stew of food haiku celebrates indigenous foods of the Americas. Each of the 13 poems appears on a gloriously colorful double-page spread, accompanied by a sidebar that presents information about the origin of the food. . . . The acrylic-on-wood-panel illustrations burst with vivid colors and stylized Mexican flair." Booklist

Includes bibliographical references

Muth, Jon J., 1960-

★ **Hi, Koo!** a year of seasons. presented by Koo and Jon J. Muth. Scholastic Press 2013 32 p. color illustrations (hardcover) $17.99
Grades: PreK K 1 2 3   **811**
1. Children's poetry 2. Seasons -- Poetry 3. Pandas
ISBN 0545166683; 9780545166683
LC 2012040378

In this book of children's poems, author "Jon J. Muth--and his delightful little panda bear, Koo--challenge readers to stretch their minds and imaginations with twenty-six haikus about the four seasons." This book uses the haiku form to take children through the seasons with watercolored images. (Publisher's note)

"Twenty-six haiku are presented by young panda Koo, eventually joined by two human children. The story told through the haiku follows the cycle of the seasons (a note explains Muth's choice to forgo the traditional five-seven-five syllable pattern). Each haiku contains just one capital letter, in order from A to Z. Muth's watercolors are as clear and translucent as the child-friendly, easily understood haiku." (Horn Book)

★ **My** America; a poetry atlas of the United States. selected by Lee Bennett Hopkins; illustrated by Stephen Alcorn. Simon & Schuster Bks. for Young Readers 2000 83p il $21.95
Grades: 4 5 6 7   **811**
1. United States -- Poetry 2. American poetry -- Collections
ISBN 0-689-81247-7
LC 98-47402

A collection of poems evocative of seven geographical regions of the United States, including the Northeast, Southeast, Great Lakes, Plains, Mountain, Southwest, and Pacific Coast States.

"Some poems are purposive, but the best . . . capture places and people in all their diversity. Stephen Alcorn's handsome, multi-textured pictures . . . avoid literal interpretation and capture the sweep of the land and the rhythm of the words." Booklist

Myers, Christopher

★ **We** are America; a tribute from the heart. Walter Dean Myers, Christopher Myers. HarperCollins Children's Books 2011 1 v. (unpaged) $16.99; lib bdg $17.89

Grades: 3 4 5 6 **811**

1. United States -- poetry 2. Children's poetry, American

ISBN 978-0-06-052308-4; 0-06-052308-5; 978-0-06-052309-1 lib bdg; 0-06-052309-3 lib bdg; 0060523085; 0060523093; 9780060523084; 9780060523091

LC 2007011852

Walter Dean and Christopher Myers pay "homage to the entire United States in a soul-searching, free-verse poem examining the people, ideals, and promise of America. The verse journeys along a rough historical chronology. . . . Christopher Myers's evocative paintings often juxtapose different eras. . . . Closing notes explicate quotations that lace the pages and identify figures shown in the artwork. . . . Few will be unmoved by this stirring and provocative collaboration." Publ Wkly

Myers, Walter Dean, 1937-2014

★ **Blues** journey; illustrated by Christopher Myers. Holiday House 2003 un il $18.95; pa $8.95

Grades: 4 5 6 **811**

1. Blues music -- Poetry 2. African Americans -- Poetry 3. Poetry -- By individual authors

ISBN 978-0-8234-1613-4; 0-8234-1613-5; 978-0-8234-2079-7 pa; 0-8234-2079-5 pa

LC 2001-16645

Boston Globe-Horn Book Award Honor: Picture Book (2003)

"In this picture book for older readers, Myers offers blues-inspired verse that touches on the black-and-blue moments of individual lives. . . . Much of Myers' poetry here is terrific, by turn, sweet, sharp, ironic, but it's the memorable collage artwork, executed in the bluest of blue ink and brown paper, that will draw readers first." Booklist

★ **Harlem**; a poem. pictures by Christopher Myers. Scholastic 1997 un il $16.95

Grades: 5 6 7 8 9 10 **811**

1. African Americans -- Poetry 2. Poetry -- By individual authors 3. Harlem (New York, N.Y.) -- Poetry

ISBN 0-590-54340-7

LC 96-8108

A Caldecott Medal honor book, 1998

A poem celebrating the people, sights, and sounds of Harlem

"Myers's paean to Harlem sings, dances, and swaggers across the pages, conveying the myriad sounds on the streets. . . . Christopher Myers's collages add an edge to his father's words, vividly bringing to life the sights and scenes of Lenox Avenue." Horn Book Guide

★ **Jazz**; illustrated by Christopher Myers. Holiday House 2006 un il $18.95; pa $8.95

Grades: 4 5 6 7 **811**

1. Children's poetry 2. Jazz music -- Poetry 3. Jazz

ISBN 0-8234-1545-7; 0-8234-2173-2 pa; 978-0-8234-1545-8; 978-0-8234-2134-2 pa

LC 2005-52639

In poems amd illustrations, this volume depicts "a variety of jazz forms, from New Orleans funerals to bebop, from stride piano to blues. . . . Grades five to eight." (Bull Cent Child Books)

"Walter Dean Myers infuses his lines . . . with so much savvy syncopation that readers can't help but be swept up in the rhythms. . . . Christopher Myers lays black-inked acetate over brilliant, saturated acrylics. The resulting chiaroscuro conjures the deep shadows and lurid reflections of low-lit after-dark jazz clubs." Publ Wkly

Nash, Ogden

★ **Lineup** for yesterday; illustrated by C. F. Payne. Creative Editions 2011 55p il $19.99

Grades: 3 4 5 6 **811**

1. Alphabet 2. Baseball -- Poetry 3. Poetry -- By individual authors

ISBN 978-1-56846-212-7; 1-56846-212-3

LC 2010040121

"Baseball legends of yesteryear come alive more or less alphabetically in Nash's pithy verses. Twenty-four players of the first half of the 20th century are profiled in playful, humorous short poems with an ABCB rhyme scheme. . . . The verses are accompanied by statistical information and delightful, large-scale, closeup depictions of the players in action, rendered by Payne in layers of colored pencil, acrylics, water colors and a variety of other media. . . . Following each group of three or four verses, and headed by a diminutive version of the appropriate illustration, Nash's daughter Linell Nash Smith provides more detailed information about each player. She also contributes a charming introduction." Kirkus

Nelson, Marilyn, 1946-

★ **Sweethearts** of rhythm; the story of the greatest all-girl swing band in the world. written by Marilyn Nelson; illustrated by Jerry Pinkney. Dial Books 2009 un il $21.99

Grades: 4 5 6 7 **811**

1. Women musicians 2. Jazz music -- Poetry 3. Jazz 4. International Sweethearts of Rhythm

ISBN 0-8037-3187-6; 978-0-8037-3187-5

LC 2008-46255

This is a study of the racially mixed group the International Sweethearts of Rhythm. Bibliography. "Grades six to nine." (Bull Cent Child Books)

"On all fronts, a resonant performance." Publ Wkly

Nye, Naomi Shihab

Come with me; poems for a journey. images by Dan Yaccarino. Greenwillow Bks. 2000 32p il $15.95; lib bdg $15.89

Grades: 3 4 5 6 **811**

1. Poetry -- By individual authors

ISBN 0-688-15946-X; 0-688-15947-8 lib bdg

LC 99-34164

"Sixteen poems depict different aspects of going places: subjects include imaginary voyages, the pace of travel, arrival in new places, the trajectory of words, and personal journeys of growth. . . . Nye uses sophisticated metaphor and oblique evocations of emotion in simple and concrete phraseology, making the poems conceptually challenging yet literarily accessible. The visuals are bold and dramatic, making excellent use of collage and mixed media." Bull Cent Child Books

O'Neill, Mary Le Duc

Hailstones and halibut bones; adventures in color. newly illustrated by John Wallner. Doubleday 1989 un il $15.95; pa $9.95

Grades: K 1 2 3 **811**

1. Color -- Poetry 2. Poetry -- By individual authors

ISBN 978-0-385-24484-8; 0-385-24484-3; 978-0-385-41078-6 pa; 0-385-41078-6 pa

LC 88-484

A newly illustrated edition of the title first published 1961

Twelve poems reflect the author's feelings about various colors

"Wallner has created montages of each poem's images and colored them with various hues of the featured color. The results do complement the moods of the poems." SLJ

Ode, Eric

When you're a pirate dog and other pirate poems; Eric Ode, Jim Harris. Pelican Pub. 2012 40 p.

Grades: 1 2 3   **811**

1. Humorous poetry 2. Children's poetry 3. Pirates -- Poetry 4. Children's poetry, American

ISBN 1455614939; 9781455614936; 9781455614943

LC 2011036785

This children's poetry collection by Eric Ode, illustrated by Jim Harris, is centered on pirates. "Pirates find their literary voices in this rollicking romp on the salty seas. Hilarity ensues as they go about their tasks narrated in poetry and song. The jolly illustrations bring their adventures, above and below decks, to life. See all their silly exploits in this swashbuckling adventure!" (Publisher's note)

Paolilli, Paul

Silver seeds; a book of nature poems. by Paul Paolilli and Dan Brewer; paintings by Steve Johnson and Lou Fancher. Viking 2001 un il $15.99; pa $6.99

Grades: K 1 2 3   **811**

1. Nature poetry 2. Poetry -- By individual authors

ISBN 0-670-88941-5; 0-14-250010-0 pa

LC 00-9469

"Paolilli and Brewer have selected 15 . . . words on which to build nature poems. The first letter of the first word in each line of a poem is part of another word that is the title (or subject) of the poem." Booklist

Park, Linda Sue

★ **Tap** dancing on the roof; sijo (poems) illustrated by Istvan Banyai. Clarion Books 2007 un il $16

Grades: 4 5 6   **811**

1. Sijo 2. Poetry -- By individual authors

ISBN 978-0-618-23483-7; 0-618-23483-7

LC 2006-24901

Park's "sijo skip lightly from breakfast . . . to bedtime . . . with excursions to the backyard, the classroom, and the beach. . . . The sijo's contours are clean and spare, qualities echoed in the blue-gray, black and white architecture and crisp shadows of Banyai's . . . digital illustrations." Publ Wkly

Peters, Lisa Westberg

★ **Earthshake**; poems from the ground up. pictures by Cathie Felstead. Greenwillow Bks. 2003 32p il $16.99; lib bdg $17.89

Grades: 3 4 5   **811**

1. Geology -- Poetry 2. Poetry -- By individual authors

ISBN 0-06-029265-2; 0-06-029266-0 lib bdg

LC 2002-32177

Presents twenty-two poems about geology. End notes provide information about the earth's surface and interior, types of rocks, and how volcanoes, glaciers, and erosion modify the landscape

"Exuberant, silly, and serious by turns, the selections engage imagination with often-humorous wordplay. The simple yet clever collages, many of which incorporate clip-art elements, deepen the intellectual and emotional content, yet keep a light tone." SLJ

Volcano wakes up! illustrated by Steve Jenkins. Henry Holt and Company 2010 un il $16.99

Grades: 2 3 4   **811**

1. Hawaii -- Poetry 2. Volcanoes -- Poetry 3. Poetry -- By individual authors

ISBN 0805082875; 9780805082876; 978-0-8050-8287-6; 0-8050-8287-5

LC 2008-38225

"Personified features of a Hawaiian landscape speak in verse during a day in the life of a waking volcano, rendered in Jenkins's atmospheric trademark cut-paper collages. . . . A humorous, imaginative, and artful concept."

"Personified features of a Hawaiian landscape speak in verse during a day in the life of a waking volcano, rendered in Jenkins's atmospheric trademark cut-paper collages. . . . A humorous, imaginative, and artful concept." Publ Wkly

★ The **Place** my words are looking for; what poets say about and through their work. selected by Paul B. Janeczko. Bradbury Press 1990 150p il $17.95

Grades: 4 5 6 7   **811**

1. Poetics 2. American poetry -- Collections

ISBN 0-02-747671-5

LC 89-39331

"More than forty contemporary poets are included: Eve Merriam, X. J. Kennedy, Felice Holman, Gary Soto, Mark Vinz, Karla Kuskin, and John Updike, among others. Their contributions vary widely in theme and mood and style, though the preponderance of the pieces are written in modern idiom and unrhymed meter. The accompanying comments frequently are as insightful and eloquent as the poems themselves." Horn Book

Poetry speaks to children; editor, Elise Paschen; illustrators, Judy Love, Wendy Rasmussen, Paula Zinngrabe Wendland. Sourcebooks 2005 104p il $19.95

Grades: 3 4 5 6   **811**

1. American poetry -- Collections

ISBN 1-4022-0329-2; 978-1-4022-0329-9

"A fine, basic collection. Approximately half of the 97 selections are read or performed on the accompanying CD. The book provides a mix of adult writers (Rita Dove, Seamus Heaney, and Billy Collins, among others) and those whose work is specifically for children, such as X. J. Kennedy and Mary Ann Hoberman. Topics include childhood, animals, nonsense poems, and humor. . . . The three illustrators have captured the different tones of the selections." SLJ

★ A **Poke** in the I; [selected by] Paul Janeczko; illustrated by Chris Raschka. Candlewick Press 2001 35p il hardcover o.p. pa $7.99

Grades: 4 5 6 7 8 9 10   **811**

1. American poetry -- Collections

ISBN 0-7636-0661-8; 0-7636-2376-8 pa

LC 00-33675

"Thirty concrete poems of all shapes and sizes are carefully laid on large white spreads, extended by Raschka's quirky watercolor and paper-collage illustrations. . . . Beautiful and playful, this title should find use in storytimes, in the classroom, and just for pleasure anywhere." SLJ

Prelutsky, Jack

Be glad your nose is on your face and other poems; some of the best of Jack Prelutsky. illustrated by Brandon Dorman. Greenwillow Books 2008 194p il $22.99

Grades: PreK K 1 2 3   **811**

1. Poetry -- By individual authors

ISBN 978-0-06-157653-9; 0-06-157653-0

LC 2008013371

"This fat, sunny volume brings together 112 of Prelutsky's poems. Most are old favorites from the past four decades, but 15 of them have never been published before. Kicking off with a letter from the poet, the book contains five sections, each concluding with a page of activities such as word games and drawing prompts. Digital illustrations with lavish details and colors stand out nicely from the ample white space. .

. . A CD features the author reading 30 of the poems to a . . . musical accompaniment." SLJ

★ **Behold** the bold umbrellaphant; and other poems. illustrations by Carin Berger. Greenwillow Books 2006 31p il $16.99; lib bdg $17.89

Grades: 3 4 5 6   **811**
   1. Humorous poetry 2. Poetry -- By individual authors
   ISBN 978-0-06-054317-4; 0-06-054317-5; 978-0-06-054318-1 lib bdg; 0-06-054318-3 lib bdg
          LC 2005-22185

Each poem in this collection "is about a creature that is part animal and part inanimate object. For instance, the Alarmadillos have alarm clocks for bodies, and the Ballpoint Penguins can write with their beaks. The poems are full of fun and wit, with wordplay and meter that never miss a beat. The whimsical illustrations use cut-print media, old-fashioned print images, and a variety of paper textures to create a rich visual treat well suited to the poetry." SLJ

★ The **carnival** of the animals; music by Camille Saint-Saëns; new verses by Jack Prelutsky; illustrated by Mary GrandPré; with a fully orchestrated CD of the Camille Saint-Saëns music. Alfred A. Knopf 2010 un $19.99; lib bdg $22.99

Grades: 2 3 4 5   **811**
   1. Animals -- Poetry 2. Poetry -- By individual authors
   ISBN 978-0-375-86458-2; 0-375-86458-X; 978-0-375-96458-9 lib bdg; 0-375-96458-4 lib bdg
          LC 2009008734

This is an illustrated collection of verses inspired by Camille Saint-Saens' musical suite The carnival of the animals.

"This delightful collection of new poems . . . serves as both helpful libretto and stand-alone treasure. The poems correlate to the animal-themed movements and neatly capture each creature's essence. . . . GrandPré's . . . vibrant acrylic and paper collage scenes exude the same imaginative insight. . . . An accompanying CD contains music performed by the Württemberg Chamber Orchestra and poems read by Prelutsky." Publ Wkly

★ The **dragons** are singing tonight; pictures by Peter Sís. Greenwillow Bks. 1993 39p il $16; pa $6.95

Grades: 2 3 4 5   **811**
   1. Dragons -- Poetry 2. Poetry -- By individual authors
   ISBN 0-688-09645-X; 0-688-12511-5 lib bdg; 0-688-16162-6 pa
          LC 92-29013

"Dragons are verbally and visually portrayed in this collection with wonder, whimsy, and a touch of wistfulness. . . . The oil and gouache paintings on a gesso background have marvelous details and unexpected bursts of humor." SLJ

★ The **frogs** wore red suspenders; rhymes by Jack Prelutsky; pictures by Petra Mathers. Greenwillow Bks. 2002 63p il $16.95; lib bdg $16.89; pa $6.99

Grades: K 1 2 3   **811**
   1. Nursery rhymes 2. Nonsense verses 3. Poetry -- By individual authors
   ISBN 0-688-16719-5; 0-688-16720-9 lib bdg; 0-06-073776-X pa
          LC 00-68128

A collection of 28 "lighthearted poems, many of which invoke place names in the United States. . . . The mild humor lies not in the action but in Prelutsky's deft use of language, particularly effective shared aloud. The result is enjoyable, but it is Petra Mathers's illustrations that make the book memorable. Demurely naive, her cheerful, delicately delineat-

ed human and animal characters focus on their activities with becoming modesty and grace." Horn Book

★ **Good** sports; illustrated by Chris Raschka. Alfred A. Knopf 2007 un il $16.99; lib bdg $19.99

Grades: 2 3 4 5   **811**
   1. Sports -- Poetry 2. Poetry -- By individual authors
   ISBN 978-0-375-83700-5; 978-0-375-93700-2 lib bdg
          LC 2006-05092

"This picture book uses poetry to express the physical sensations and wide-ranging emotions of participating in sports. Prelutsky's smoothly rhyming quatrains, ideal for recitation, cover team sports . . . as well as several individual ones and celebrate disciplined efforts as exuberantly as noncompetitive play. . . . Raschka's watercolors extend the high-energy verses without overwhelming them." Booklist

Includes bibliographical references

★ The **Headless** Horseman rides tonight; more poems to trouble your sleep. illustrated by Arnold Lobel. Greenwillow Bks. 1980 38p il hardcover o.p. pa $6.99

Grades: 2 3 4 5   **811**
   1. Monsters -- Poetry 2. Poetry -- By individual authors
   ISBN 0-688-11705-8 pa
          LC 80-10372

The author's "rhymes are as lethal, lithe, and literate as ever and Lobel wrings every atmospheric ounce out of them." SLJ

★ **I've** lost my hippopotamus; Jack Prelutsky; illustrations by Jackie Urbanovic. 1st ed. Greenwillow Books 2012 143 p. ill. (trade bdg.) $18.99; (lib. bdg.) $19.89

Grades: K 1 2 3 4 5   **811**
   1. Humorous poetry 2. Animals -- Poetry 3. Children's poetry 4. Humorous poetry, American 5. Children's poetry, American
   ISBN 0062014579; 9780062014573; 9780062014580
          LC 2011002636

This children's book by Jack Prelutsky, illustrated by Jackie Urbanovic, offers "more than 100 . . . poems that poke holes in the serious facade of the adult world. A snake performs arithmetic, a boy is puzzled by the rainstorm in his bedroom, . . . and a thirsty centipede drinks too much water." (Publishers Weekly)

If not for the cat; haiku by Jack Prelutsky; paintings by Ted Rand. Greenwillow Books 2004 40p il $16.99; lib bdg $17.89

Grades: 1 2 3 4   **811**
   1. Haiku 2. Animals -- Poetry 3. Poetry -- By individual authors
   ISBN 0-06-059677-5; 0-06-059678-3 lib bdg
          LC 2003-17064

"Each of the 17 haiku in this collection explores the essence of an animal, the words forming a sort of riddle answered in Rand's accompanying double-page illustration. . . . Prelutsky shows his command of word choice through a minimalist form that is perfectly matched by Rand's control of his mixed-media artwork to create a wonderful celebration of the art of haiku." SLJ

★ **It's** Christmas! by Jack Prelutsky; pictures by Marylin Hafner. HarperCollins Publishers 2008 46p il (I can read!) $16.99

Grades: K 1 2 3   **811**
   1. Christmas -- Poetry 2. Poetry -- By individual authors
   ISBN 978-0-06-053706-7; 0-06-053706-X
          LC 2007040112

A newly illustrated edition of the title first published 1981 by Greenwillow Books

This collection of Christmas poems covers such topics as Christmas trees, mistletoe, Santa Claus, a Christmas play, and gifts.

"Hafner's line-and-watercolor pictures illustrate the bouncing, rhyming words in clear, playful holiday scenes." Booklist

★ **It's** snowing! it's snowing! winter poems. illustrated by Yossi Abolafia. HarperCollins Pubs. 2006 48p il (I can read book) $15.99; lib bdg $16.89

Grades: 1 2 3   **811**

1. Winter -- Poetry 2. Poetry -- By individual authors

ISBN 0-06-053715-9; 0-06-053716-7 lib bdg

A newly illustrated edition of the title first published 1984 by Greenwillow Bks.

A collection of short poems about winter

"The sounds of the rhyming words are as much fun as the snow action in these 16 poems . . . accompanied by exuberant line-and-watercolor illustrations that capture all the play in the cold." Booklist

★ **It's** Thanksgiving! by Jack Prelutsky; pictures by Marylin Hafner. HarperCollins 2007 44p il (I can read!) $15.99; lib bdg $16.89

Grades: 1 2 3   **811**

1. Thanksgiving Day -- Poetry 2. Poetry -- By individual authors

ISBN 978-0-06-053710-4; 978-0-06-053709-8 lib bdg

LC 2007014465

First published 1982 by Greenwillow Books

A collection of twelve Thanksgiving Day poems

★ **It's** Valentine's Day; pictures by Yossi Abolafia. Greenwillow Bks. 1983 47p il (Greenwillow read-alone books) hardcover o.p. pa $5.95

Grades: 1 2 3   **811**

1. Valentine's Day -- Poetry 2. Poetry -- By individual authors

ISBN 0-688-14652-X pa

LC 83-1449

"The 14 poems here range from the genuine joy of 'It's Valentine's Day' . . . to the giddy goofiness of 'I love you more than applesauce' or 'Jelly Jill loves Weasel Will'. . . . The rhymes are generally simple but clever and the line drawings in red and blue, with their expressive faces and explanatory vignettes, add tremendously to the enjoyment of the poetry." SLJ

★ **My** dog may be a genius; poems. [drawings by James Stevenson] Greenwillow Books 2008 159p il $18.99; lib bdg $19.89

Grades: 2 3 4 5   **811**

1. Children's poetry, American. 2. Poetry -- By individual authors

ISBN 978-0-06-623862-3; 978-0-06-623863-0 lib bdg

LC 2007-19462

"Prelutsky has created yet another volume of short poems with guaranteed child appeal. Again he has assembled a zany cast of imaginary creatures and machines. . . . Prelutsky plays with language and does not shy away from challenging vocabulary. . . . Stevenson's simple signature drawings capture the spirit of each poem with just the right amount of illustration." SLJ

★ **The new** kid on the block: poems; drawings by James Stevenson. Greenwillow Bks. 1984 159p il $17.95; lib bdg $17.93

Grades: 3 4 5 6   **811**

1. Humorous poetry 2. Poetry -- By individual authors

ISBN 0-688-02271-5; 0-688-02272-3 lib bdg

LC 83-20621

"The author's rollicking, silly poems bounce and romp with fun; Stevenson's cartoon-like sketches capture the hilarity with equal skill. A book everyone will enjoy dipping into." Child Book Rev Serv

★ **Nightmares** : poems to trouble your sleep; illustrated by Arnold Lobel. Greenwillow Bks. 1976 38p il lib bdg $17.89

Grades: 2 3 4 5   **811**

1. Monsters -- Poetry 2. Poetry -- By individual authors

ISBN 0-688-84053-1

LC 76-4820

This "collection of poems is calculated to evoke icy apprehension, and the poems about wizards, bogeymen, ghouls, ogres (well, one poem apiece to each or to others of their ilk) are exaggerated just enough to bring simultaneous grins and shudders. Prelutsky uses words with relish and his rhyme and rhythm are, as usual, deft. Lobel's illustrations are equally adroit, macabre yet elegant." Bull Cent Child Books

★ **A pizza** the size of the sun; poems by Jack Prelutsky; drawings by James Stevenson. Greenwillow Bks. 1996 159p il $18; lib bdg $17.93

Grades: 3 4 5 6   **811**

1. Humorous poetry 2. Poetry -- By individual authors

ISBN 0-688-13235-9; 0-688-13236-7 lib bdg

LC 95-35930

This collection of humorous poems is "filled with zany people, improbable creatures, and rhythm and rhyme galore, all combining to celebrate the unusual, the mundane, and the slightly gruesome. . . . Each page is brimming with Stevenson's complementary, droll watercolors, reproduced here in black and white." SLJ

★ **Ride** a purple pelican; pictures by Garth Williams. Greenwillow Bks. 1986 64p il $17.95; pa $7.95

Grades: K 1 2 3   **811**

1. Nursery rhymes 2. Nonsense verses 3. Poetry -- By individual authors

ISBN 0-688-04031-4; 0-688-15625-8 pa

LC 84-6024

A collection of short nonsense verses and nursery rhymes

"Prelutsky has caught the rhythm and spirit of nursery rhymes in 29 short poems about drum-beating bunnies, bullfrogs on parade, Chicago winds, giant sequoias and other wondrous things. Many of these easy-to-remember poems are filled with delicious sounding American and Canadian place names. Garth Williams' full-color, full-page illustrations are good complements to the poems. Highly recommended." Child Book Rev Serv

Scranimals; poems by Jack Prelutsky; pictures by Peter Sís. Greenwillow Bks. 2002 40p il $16.99; lib bdg $18.89

Grades: 2 3 4 5   **811**

1. Nonsense verses 2. Poetry -- By individual authors

ISBN 0-688-17819-7; 0-688-17820-0 lib bdg

LC 2001-23620

"The verse sparkles with wit and mad invention. . . . Sís' art picks up on the strange and otherworldly aspects of the poems, evincing a surreal and haunting edge to its intricately lined visions." Bull Cent Child Books

★ **Something** big has been here; drawings by James Stevenson. Greenwillow Bks. 1990 160p il $17.95

Grades: 3 4 5   **811**

1. Humorous poetry 2. Poetry -- By individual authors

ISBN 0-688-06434-5

LC 89-34773

An illustrated collection of humorous poems on a variety of topics

"Puns and verbal surprises abound. Clever use of alliteration and abundant variety in the sound and texture of words add to the pleasure. . . . Stevenson's small cartoons of snaggle-toothed animals and deadpan children extend and expand the mad humor of the poems, supporting but never overwhelming their good-natured fun. A fine prescription against the blues at any time of year." Horn Book

★ **Stardines** swim high across the sky and other poems; by Jack Prelutsky; illustrations by Carin Berger. Greenwillow Books 2012 40 p.

Grades: K 1 2 3   **811**

1. Children's poetry, American 2. Imaginary creatures -- poetry
ISBN 9780062014641; 9780062014658

LC 2011025993

This children's poetry collection, by Jack Prelutsky, illustrated by Carin Berger, presents lyric descriptions of two dozen imaginary "creatures of animal and inanimate origin. . . . Procrastinating pandas, self-adhering geese and cacophonous magpies are a few of the carefully selected creatures on display . . . ," embellished by multi-media dioramas by Berger. (Kirkus Reviews)

The **swamps** of Sleethe; poems from beyond the solar system. illustrated by Jimmy Pickering. Alfred A. Knopf 2009 un il $16.99; lib bdg $19.99

Grades: 3 4 5 6   **811**

1. Extrasolar planets -- Poetry 2. Poetry -- By individual authors 3. Extraterrestrial beings -- Poetry
ISBN 978-0-375-84674-8; 0-375-84674-3; 978-0-375-94674-5 lib bdg; 0-375-94674-8 lib bdg

LC 2008006530

"Nineteen poems with jaunty rhythms lure readers to some very menacing planets. Almost all tell of the horrors to be found in worlds beyond our solar system. . . . Dark colors with sharp contrasts help define these worlds in mixed-media illustrations. Some of the unusual planet names are anagrams to solve with answers in the back of the book. Science-fiction and poetry lovers should unite over this slim and entertaining volume." SLJ

★ **Tyrannosaurus** was a beast; illustrated by Arnold Lobel. Greenwillow Bks. 1988 31p il hardcover o.p. pa $6.99

Grades: 2 3 4 5   **811**

1. Dinosaurs -- Poetry 2. Poetry -- By individual authors
ISBN 0-688-06443-4 lib bdg; 0-688-11569-1 pa

LC 87-25131

A collection of humorous poems about dinosaurs

"Fourteen dinosaurs meet their match in this outstanding author/illustrator team. While Prelutsky's short, pithy, often witty verses sum up their essential characters, Lobel's line and watercolor portraits bring the beasts to life, enormous yet endearingly vulnerable." Booklist

★ **What** a day it was at school! poems by Jack Prelutsky; pictures by Doug Cushman. Greenwillow Books 2006 39p il $15.99; lib bdg $16.89

Grades: K 1 2 3   **811**

1. Schools -- Poetry 2. Poetry -- By individual authors
ISBN 978-0-06-082336-8; 0-06-082336-4; 978-0-06-082335-1 lib bdg; 0-06-082335-6 lib bdg

LC 2005-48968

"Cushman has interpreted Prelutsky's school-aged protagonist as a cat. The feline's journal contains 17 poems about everyday joys and predicaments. . . . Lively and fun, with perfect meter and an abundance of interesting word choices, these poems beg to be read aloud. And they will be. Cushman has created an appealing school environment with a variety of colorful cartoon animal characters that are happily compatible with Prelutsky's silly and energetic verse." SLJ

Raczka, Bob

★ **Guyku**; a year of haiku for boys. illustrated by Peter H. Reynolds. Houghton 2010 un il

Grades: 1 2 3   **811**

1. Haiku 2. Children's poetry 3. Boys -- Poetry 4. Seasons

-- Poetry
ISBN 0547240031; 9780547240039
Claudia Lewis Award for Poetry, 2011

This is a collection of seventeen-syllable poems about a boy's life. "Primary." (Horn Book)

"The poems in this picture-book collection capture natural moments that boys, and many girls, have while playing outdoors. Each season is addressed, and moments like riding bikes in the spring with baseball cards attached to the wheels to mimic the sound of a motorcycle almost define spring. . . . The artwork and the text dovetail beautifully and help set the inquisitive and playful intent of the poems. . . . This wonderful collection will resonate with all children. . . . The pen, ink, and watercolor illustrations mirror the simplicity of each entry and capture the expressions of the boys and their adventures honestly." SLJ

★ **Lemonade,** and other poems squeezed from a single word; illustrations by Nancy Doniger. Roaring Brook Press 2011 43p il

Grades: 2 3 4 5   **811**

1. Children's poetry
ISBN 1596435410; 9781596435414

LC 2010-24807

"Each poem is displayed in two formats, first a patterned visual that . . . aligns the letters in each word under the relevant titular letter, . . . and then a simple one-word-per-line arrangement. . . . Grades three to seven." (Bull Cent Child Books)

"Raczka offers an accessible, playful poetry collection. . . . Doniger's spare illustrations add quirky appeal without distracting from the inventive formations of type." Booklist

★ The Random House book of poetry for children; selected and introduced by Jack Prelutsky; illustrated by Arnold Lobel. Random House 1983 248p il $19.95; lib bdg $21.99

Grades: 3 4 5 6   **811**

1. English poetry -- Collections 2. American poetry -- Collections
ISBN 0-394-85010-6; 0-394-95010-0 lib bdg

LC 83-2990

In this anthology emphasis "is placed on humor and light verse; but serious and thoughtful poems are also included. . . . Approximately two thirds of the selections were written within the past forty years—the splendid contributions of such writers as John Ciardi, Aileen Fisher, Dennis Lee, Myra Cohn Livingston, David McCord, Eve Merriam, and Lilian Moore. [There are] . . . samplings of earlier poets from Shakespeare and Blake to Emily Dickinson and Walter de la Mare." Horn Book

Raschka, Christopher, 1959-

A **song** about myself; Chris Raschka. Candlewick Press 2017 40 p. color illustrations $17.99

Grades: 1 2 3 4   **811**

1. Children's poetry
ISBN 0763650900; 9780763650902

LC 2017009239

In this book, author Chris Raschka "brings English poet John Keats's words to whimsical life in the poet's only work written for children. . . . Keats is remembered for his great odes and sonnets--making this lighthearted, little-known poem a special treat. As written in a letter to his young sister when he was feeling homesick on a visit to Scotland, Keats runs his rhymes up and down and all around, leading the reader on a playful chase in and out of language." (Publisher's note)

"Lively, bright watercolors bring a poem by English Romantic poet Keats into the realm of a contemporary child's experience." Booklist

★ **Read** a rhyme, write a rhyme; poems selected by Jack Prelutsky; illustrated by Meilo So. Alfred A. Knopf 2005 23p il $16.95
Grades: 2 3 4   **811**
1. Poetics 2. American poetry -- Collections
ISBN 0-375-82286-0

LC 2004-26501

"Prelutsky designed this collection to jumpstart children's creative juices. Three short poems were chosen for each theme: dogs, food, birthdays, bugs, cows, friends, snow, turtles, rain, and self. He also includes a poemstart: an unfinished verse, along with advice and lists of rhyming words, so that readers can complete the poem on their own. The compiler displays a fine sense for lighthearted, kid-friendly poetry. . . . So's watercolor-and-ink illustrations add playfully jumbled perspectives." SLJ

★ **Read**-aloud rhymes for the very young; selected by Jack Prelutsky; illustrated by Marc Brown; with an introduction by Jim Trelease. Knopf 1986 98p il $19.95; lib bdg $21.99
Grades: K 1 2   **811**
1. Nursery rhymes 2. English poetry -- Collections 3. American poetry -- Collections
ISBN 0-394-87218-5; 0-394-97218-X lib bdg

LC 86-7147

"Prelutsky has selected and combined joyous, sensitive poems . . . by such traditional poets as Dorothy Aldis and A. A. Milne, as well as by more contemporary poets such as Karla Kuskin, Dennis Lee, and Prelutsky himself. All are lively, rhythmic poems that young children will enjoy. . . . Brown's bright pastel illustrations effectively use framing, action, and cheerful creatures to echo the light tone of the book. The poems are arranged with others of the same topic and include popular concerns of small children such as animals, bath time, dragons, and play. Teachers and librarians will appreciate poems about seasons, months, holidays, and special events that can be easily incorporated into story hours and classroom life." SLJ

Rex, Adam
★ **Frankenstein** makes a sandwich. Harcourt 2006 40p il $16
Grades: 2 3 4 5   **811**
1. Monsters -- Poetry 2. Poetry -- By individual authors
ISBN 0-15-205766-8

LC 2005-13678

A collection of humorous poems about monsters such as Frankenstein, The Creature from the Black Lagoon, Count Dracula, The Invisible Man, Godzilla, and The Phantom of the Opera

"Told with smooth, unstrained rhymes, each selection captures its subject's voice. Rex uses an impressive variety of techniques and media in the artwork while paying homage to famed illustrators. . . . The book is fresh, creative, and funny, with just enough gory detail to cause a few gasps." SLJ

★ **Frankenstein** takes the cake. Harcourt 2008 39p il lib bdg $16
Grades: 2 3 4 5   **811**
1. Monsters -- Poetry 2. Poetry -- By individual authors
ISBN 978-0-15-206235-4 lib bdg; 0-15-206235-1 lib bdg

LC 2007-44634

Frankenstein wants to marry his undead bride in peace, but his best man, Dracula, is freaking out about the garlic bread, and the Headless Horseman wishes everyone would stop drooling over his pumpkin head.

"With maniacal glee, Rex . . . delivers spot-on rhymes about B-movie monsters, loosely organized around the nuptials of Frankenstein and his bride. . . . Rex's eclectic imagery and freewheeling verse will have readers going back for seconds." Publ Wkly

Rockwell, Thomas
Emily Stew; with some side dishes. illustrated by David McPhail. Roaring Brook Press 2010 43p il $16.99
Grades: 2 3 4 5   **811**
1. Poetry -- By individual authors
ISBN 978-1-59643-336-6; 1-59643-336-1

This is "a wildly inventive poetic portrait of a riveting character who's made up—rather literally—of a stew of contradictions. Moody and prone to the most erratic behavior, Emily is depicted in these playful rhymed vignettes as an eccentric yet eminently recognizable and likable young creature. . . . McPhail's pen-and-ink spot art helps capture the defiant Emily as she asserts her individuality in scenes ranging from dancing with a fish to being eaten by a tiger." Kirkus

Rosen, Michael J.
★ The **cuckoo's** haiku; and other birding poems. illustrated by Stan Fellows. Candlewick Press 2009 un il $17.99
Grades: 2 3 4   **811**
1. Haiku 2. Birds -- Poetry 3. Poetry -- By individual authors
ISBN 978-0-7636-3049-2; 0-7636-3049-7

LC 2008-21417

"A rare gift for young and old alike, this exquisite book about birds combines delicate verses and stunning watercolors that celebrate the natural world. Designed as if it were a birder's notebook, the book provides an intriguing haiku for each bird, dazzling paintings of the species in their habitats, as well as notes about their behaviors and traits." Publ Wkly

★ The **Hound** dog's haiku; and other poems for dog lovers. [illustrated by] Mary Azarian. Candlewick Press 2011 56p il
Grades: 2 3 4   **811**
1. Haiku 2. Dogs -- Poetry 3. Poetry -- By individual authors
ISBN 0-7636-4499-4; 978-0-7636-4499-4

"These delightful selections will engage haiku composers and dog lovers. . . . Twenty canines are represented, with each dog given a fully illustrated spread; the breed's name is in large letters and the haiku on the opposing page is in a smaller font. Endnotes take the form of visual avatars culled from the illustrations, with a short paragraph about the breed. Fetch this title full of wordplay, creative romps, and pet prompts for a fun read." SLJ

Ruddell, Deborah
★ A **whiff** of pine, a hint of skunk; a forest of poems. illustrated by Joan Rankin. Margaret K. McElderry Books 2009 un il $16.99
Grades: 3 4 5   **811**
1. Nature poetry 2. Forest animals -- Poetry 3. Poetry -- By individual authors
ISBN 978-1-4169-4211-5; 1-4169-4211-4

LC 2007-38023

"Twenty-three evocative poems about forest animals, beautifully illustrated. Literary variety serves this collection well, with many different lengths, rhyme schemes and moods. The common elements in Ruddell's verse are economy and an observer's respect for her subjects. . . . Similarly, Rankin's watercolors show respect via their accuracy and detail, while still capturing the various flavors of the poems." Kirkus

Salas, Laura Purdie
Bookspeak! poems about books. written by Laura Purdie Salas; illustrated by Josée Bisaillon. Clarion Books 2011 un il $16.99
Grades: PreK K 1 2   **811**
1. Books and reading -- Poetry 2. Poetry -- By individual authors
ISBN 978-0-547-22300-1; 0-547-22300-5

LC 2010043173

"This collection of poems makes its message clear: books are where it's at. Sala's polished verse demonstrates a deep love for all aspects of books. . . . Bisaillon's mixed media illustrations are dizzyingly inventive, their bright colors, sampling of typography, and whimsical details underscoring the idea of the potential that awaits between the covers." Publ Wkly

Scanlon, Liz Garton

★ **All** the world; illustrated by Marla Frazee. Beach Lane Books 2009 un il $17.99

Grades: PreK K 1 **811**

1. Beaches -- Poetry 2. Family life -- Poetry 3. Poetry -- By individual authors

ISBN 978-1-4169-8580-8; 1-4169-8580-8

LC 2008-51057

ALA ALSC Caldecott Medal Honor Book (2010)

"Charming illustrations and lyrical rhyming couplets speak volumes in celebration of the world and humankind, combining to create a lovely book that will be appreciated by a wide audience. The pictures, made with black Prismacolor pencil and watercolors, primarily follow a multicultural family from a summer morning on the beach through a busy day and night." SLJ

Schertle, Alice

★ **Button** up! [illustrations by] Petra Mathers. Harcourt 2009 33p il $16

Grades: PreK K 1 2 **811**

1. Animals -- Poetry 2. Clothing and dress -- Poetry 3. Poetry -- By individual authors

ISBN 978-0-15-205050-4; 0-15-205050-7

LC 2007-42839

An illustrated collection of poetry features animals wearing an array of shoes, jackets, hats, and other fun attire to demonstrate their unique personalities.

"Mathers' charming watercolors show a variety of decked out animals in vignettes and double-page spreads that add to the humor. . . . The whimsical illustrations pair perfectly with the wittiness of the text, and the whole is a clever and original poetic treat." Booklist

Scieszka, Jon

Truckery rhymes; written by Jon Scieszka; characters and environments developed by the Design Garage David Shannon, Loren Long, David Gordon. Simon & Schuster Books for Young Readers 2009 57p il $17.99

Grades: PreK K 1 2 3 **811**

1. Nursery rhymes 2. Trucks -- Poetry 3. Poetry -- By individual authors

ISBN 978-1-4169-4135-4; 1-4169-4135-5

LC 2007037439

"This collection of lively truck-themed 'Mother Goose' rhymes is filled with humor. . . . The digital illustrations are colorful, energetic, and playful: the vehicles have personality plus. . . . This effervescent picture book will zoom off your shelves." SLJ

Sendak, Maurice, 1928-2012

★ **My** brother's book; Maurice Sendak; [edited by] Michael di Capua. HarperCollins 2013 32 p. (hardcover bdg.) $18.95

Grades: 4 5 6 7 8 **811**

1. Poetry 2. Poetry -- Collections

ISBN 0062234897; 9780062234896

LC 2012942549

In this book, "with influences from Shakespeare and William Blake, [Maurice] Sendak pays homage to his late brother, Jack, whom he credited for his passion for writing and drawing. Pairing Sendak's . . . poetry

with his . . . . artwork, . . . Sendak's tribute to his brother is an expression of both grief and love. . . . Pulitzer Prize--winning literary critic and Shakespearean scholar Stephen Greenblatt contributes a[n] . . . introduction." (Publisher's note)

Service, Robert W.

★ The **cremation** of Sam McGee; by Robert W. Service; paintings by Ted Harrison; introduction by Pierre Berton. 20th anniversary ed.; Kids Can Press 2006 un il $17.95

Grades: 4 5 6 7 **811**

1. Yukon Territory -- Poetry 2. Poetry -- By individual authors

ISBN 978-1-55453-092-2; 1-55453-092-X

Text first published 1907. This is a reissue of the edition first published 1986 in Canada and 1987 in the United States by Greenwillow Bks.

This poem "has gripped readers and listeners for decades. . . . [The illustrator] obviously appreciates the humor inherent in the text. . . . As Pierre Berton observes in his introduction, [Harrison's] 'style is unique: part Oriental, part native American, part Ted Harrison.'" Horn Book

Shange, Ntozake

★ **Freedom's** a-callin' me; poems by Ntozake Shange; paintings by Rod Brown. Amisatd/Collins 2012 il $16.99

Grades: 4 5 6 7 **811**

1. Slavery -- Poetry 2. African Americans -- Poetry 3. Underground railroad -- Poetry

ISBN 978-0-06-133741-3; 0-06-133741-2

LC 2010050515

The author and illustrator present "a series of poems and paintings that express the hope and frustration of enslaved people trying to navigate the Underground Railroad. Using dialect to convey a Southern cadence, Shange's poems communicate powerful emotions. . . . These poems are a cry from the heart. . . . The expressive, impressionistic paintings capture attention with their bold strokes and vivid coloring." SLJ

★ **We** troubled the waters; poems by Ntozake Shange; paintings by Rod Brown. Amistad/Collins 2009 un il $16.99; lib bdg $17.89

Grades: 4 5 6 7 8 9 10 **811**

1. Poetry -- By individual authors 2. African Americans -- Civil rights -- Poetry

ISBN 978-0-06-133735-2; 0-06-133735-8; 978-0-06-133737-6 lib bdg; 0-06-133737-4 lib bdg

LC 2008025360

"Each spread pairs a poem with blurred, expressive acrylic paintings, and the pages feature both well-known civil rights leaders and ordinary people who endured oppression. . . . The messages are haunting. . . . The colloquial lines, indelible images, and comparisons between then and now will keep readers talking." Booklist

Shannon, George

Chicken scratches; Grade A poultry poetry and rooster rhymes. by George Shannon & Lynn Brunelle; illustrated by Scott Menchin. Chronicle Books 2010 un il $14.99

Grades: K 1 2 3 **811**

1. Chickens -- Poetry

ISBN 978-0-8118-6648-4; 0-8118-6648-3

"This attractive volume features 16 wacky rhyming verses. The somewhat irreverent poems include odes to imagined daily lives of opera-singing and sumo-wrestling chickens to complex egg laying and eating. . . . Rendered in pen and colored digitally, the simple yet expressive cartoon illustrations really bring out the fun of the poetry." SLJ

★ **Sharing** the seasons; a book of poems. selected by Lee Bennett Hopkins; illustrated by David Diaz. Margaret K. McElderry Books 2010 83p il $21.99

Grades: 3 4 5   **811**

1. Seasons -- Poetry 2. American poetry -- Collections

ISBN 978-1-4169-0210-2; 1-4169-0210-4

LC 2009-19297

"This dynamic collection features 48 poems—12 for each of the seasons—mingling previously published poems by Carl Sandburg, Karla Kuskin, and others, with new works by several poets, including Hopkins. The diverse, accessible selections create a mosaic that stirs the senses. Diaz's ethereal silhouettes of animals and people, which resemble layered, cut-paper shadows, are ornately inlaid with nature motifs." Publ Wkly

Shields, Carol Diggory

★ **English,** fresh squeezed! 40 thirst-for-knowledge-quenching poems. by Carol Diggory Shields; illustrations by Tony Ross. Handprint Books 2004 80p il $14.95

Grades: 4 5 6 7   **811**

1. English language -- Poetry 2. Poetry -- By individual authors

ISBN 1-59354-053-1

LC 2004-53905

"Shields presents humorous poems both celebrating and bemoaning parts of speech, grammatical rules, and other annoyances of English class. Her rhyming verse is generally snappy and pointed. . . . Ross's spot illustrations in black and white with a blue tone add visual amusement without overwhelming." SLJ

Shore, Diane ZuHone

★ **This** is the dream; by Diane Z. Shore and Jessica Alexander; illustrated by James Ransome. HarperCollinsPublishers 2006 un il $15.99; lib bdg $16.89

Grades: 2 3 4   **811**

1. Poetry -- By individual authors 2. African Americans -- Civil rights -- Poetry

ISBN 0-06-055519-X; 0-06-055520-3 lib bdg

LC 2003-26554

"A chronicle of the Civil Rights movement presented through lyrical verses and distinguished illustrations. Ransome juxtaposes collaged archival photographs and newspaper clippings with his paintings. . . . Each succinct and evocative verse is accompanied by a double-page image." SLJ

This is the game; by Diane Z. Shore; illustrated by Owen Smith. HarperCollinsPublishers 2011 32p il $16.99

Grades: K 1 2 3   **811**

1. Baseball -- Poetry 2. Poetry -- By individual authors

ISBN 978-0-06-055522-1; 0-06-055522-X

LC 2008047700

"In this picture-book celebration of baseball, aspects of the game are described in verse and illustrated with, bold double-page spreads." Booklist

Sidman, Joyce

Butterfly eyes and other secrets of the meadow; written by Joyce Sidman; illustrated by Beth Krommes. Houghton Mifflin Co. 2006 un il $16

Grades: 3 4 5 6   **811**

1. Animals -- Poetry 2. Meadows -- Poetry 3. Poetry -- By individual authors

ISBN 0-618-56313-X

LC 2005-03921

"Eight pairs of 'poetry riddles' present such related elements as the spittlebug . . . and the xylem sap it sucks from its host plant. A spread giving answers to the riddle and adding specific details . . . follows each pair of poems. . . . Kromme's scratchboard illustrations are splendid. . . . An elegantly conceived, beautifully integrated volume." Horn Book

★ **Dark** Emperor and other poems of the night; written by Joyce Sidman; illustrated by Rick Allen. Houghton Mifflin Harcount 2010 29p il $16.99

Grades: 3 4 5 6   **811**

1. Children's poetry 2. Night -- Poetry 3. Forest animals -- Poetry 4. Night

ISBN 978-0-547-15228-8; 0-547-15228-0

A Newbery Medal honor book, 2011; Boston Globe-Horn Book Honor: Picture Book (2011)

"This picture book combines lyrical poetry and compelling art with science concepts. . . . Poems about the woods at night reveal exciting biology facts that are explained in long notes on each double-page spread. . . . In an opening note, Allen explains his elaborate, linoleum-block printmaking technique, and each atmospheric image shows the creatures and the dense, dark forest with astonishing clarity." Booklist

★ **Meow** ruff; a story in concrete poetry. written by Joyce Sidman; illustrated by Michelle Berg. Houghton Mifflin 2006 un il $16

Grades: 1 2 3   **811**

1. Cats -- Poetry 2. Dogs -- Poetry 3. Rain -- Poetry 4. Poetry

ISBN 0-618-44894-2

This is a story in concrete poetry in which a dog slips out of his house and meets a white cat left alone on the street. "Grades two to four." (Bull Cent Child Books)

"Sidman develops a simple tale about a cat and dog trapped in a rainstorm, coding much of the substance right into the physical landscape. . . . Berg, who created the pictures digitally and is also the book's graphic designer, intelligently showcases the concept of words as building blocks in a stylized landscape of flat colors, two-dimensional forms, and wildly mutating typefaces." Booklist

★ **Song** of the water boatman; & other pond poems. written by Joyce Sidman; illustrated by Beckie Prange. Houghton Mifflin 2005 un il $16

Grades: 3 4 5   **811**

1. Ponds -- Poetry 2. Poetry -- By individual authors

ISBN 0-618-13547-2

A Caldecott Medal honor book, 2006

A collection of poems that provide a look at some of the animals, insects, and plants that are found in ponds, with accompanying information about each.

"In this strikingly illustrated collection, science facts combine with vivid poems about pond life through the seasons, . . . Throughout, plants and animals come alive in the bold woodcut prints." Booklist

★ **Swirl** by swirl; spirals in nature. Houghton Mifflin Harcourt 2011 40p il $16.99

Grades: PreK K 1 2   **811**

1. Nature poetry 2. Shape -- Poetry 3. Poetry -- By individual authors

ISBN 978-0-547-31583-6; 0-547-31583-X

LC 2010040724

"Krommes's scratchboard illustrations suffuse every spread with color, shape, and movement, vividly depicting spirals in nature. . . . Sidman's very simple text provides the perfect backdrop: powerful, poetic, good for reading aloud and reading again. . . . This book is elegantly constructed, and as poetry, picture book, or nonfiction, a success in every way." Horn Book

This is just to say; poems of apology and forgiveness. by Joyce Sidman; illustrated by Pamela Zagarenski. Houghton Mifflin Co. 2007 47p il $16

Grades: 4 5 6   **811**

1. Children's poetry, American. 2. Apologizing -- Juvenile poetry. 3. Poetry -- By individual authors

ISBN 978-0-618-61680-0; 0-618-61680-2

LC 2006009820

"Mrs. Merz assigns her sixth-grade students to write poems of apology, and what emerges is a surprising array of emotions, poetic forms, and subjects. . . . Sidman's ear is keen, capturing many voices. Her skill as a poet accessible to young people is unmatched. Zagarenski's delicately outlined collage drawings and paintings are created on mixed backgrounds—notebook paper, paper bags, newspaper, graph paper, school supplies." SLJ

★ **Ubiquitous**; celebrating nature's survivors. poetry by Joyce Sidman; illustrated by Beckie Prange. Houghton Mifflin 2010 un il $17

Grades: 2 3 4 5   **811**

1. Children's poetry 2. Animals -- Poetry 3. Poetry -- By individual authors 4. Young adult literature -- Works

ISBN 978-0-618-71719-4; 0-618-71719-6

Sidman and Prange "offer another winning blend of poetry, science, and art in this picture-book collection that celebrates the earth's most resilient and long-lived species. . . . Each dynamic spread features a poem, a prose paragraph, and a captivating illustration that work together to reinforce both the science concepts and the awe they inspire. Prange's watercolor-tinted linocut illustrations beautifully expand both the information and imagery in the words." Booklist

Sierra, Judy

★ **Monster** Goose; illustrated by Jack E. Davis. Harcourt 2001 un il $17; pa $7

Grades: 2 3 4 5   **811**

1. Monsters -- Poetry 2. Poetry -- By individual authors

ISBN 0-15-202034-9; 0-15-205417-0 pa

LC 00-8808

A collection of parodies of Mother Goose rhymes featuring monsters

"Davis, working in acrylics and colored pencil, crowds his illustrations with monsters, vermin and gross gags. . . . This volume strikes a nice balance between goofy and ghastly." Publ Wkly

Silverstein, Shel

★ **Don't** bump the glump and other fantasies; [by] Shel Silverstein. HarperCollins Publishers 2008 un il $17.99; lib bdg $18.89

Grades: 3 4 5 6   **811**

1. Humorous poetry 2. Poetry -- By individual authors

ISBN 978-0-06-149338-6; 978-0-06-149619-6 lib bdg

LC 2007036737

First published 1964 by Simon & Schuster with title: Uncle Shelby's zoo: don't bump the glump!

"This collection of 45 poems tours readers past imaginary creatures. . . . There's no question that the intensity of Silverstein's watercolor palette adds to the fun." Publ Wkly

★ **Every** thing on it; poems and drawings by Shel Silverstein. Harper 2011 194p il $19.99; lib bdg $20.89

Grades: 3 4 5 6   **811**

1. Humorous poetry 2. Nonsense verses 3. Poetry -- By individual

authors

ISBN 978-0-06-199816-4; 0-06-199816-8; 978-0-06-199817-1 lib bdg; 0-06-199817-6 lib bdg

The second original book to be published since Silverstein's passing in 1999, this poetry collection includes more than one hundred and thirty never-before-seen poems and drawings completed by the cherished American artist and selected by his family from his archives.

"Silverstein's inspired word play and impish sense of humor are in abundant evidence. His signature line drawings accompany many of the poems and complete the jokes of some. . . . Adults who grew up with Uncle Shelby will find themselves wiping their eyes by the time they get to the end of this collection; children new to the master will find themselves hooked." Kirkus

★ **Falling** up; poems and drawings by Shel Silverstein. HarperCollins Pubs. 1996 171p il $17.99; lib bdg $18.89

Grades: 3 4 5 6   **811**

1. Humorous poetry 2. Nonsense verses 3. Poetry -- By individual authors

ISBN 0-06-024802-5; 0-06-024803-3 lib bdg

LC 96-75736

This "collection includes more than 150 poems. . . . As always, Silverstein has a direct line to what kids like, and he gives them poems celebrating the gross, the scary, the absurd, and the comical. The drawings are much more than decoration. They often extend a poem's meaning and, in many cases, add some great comedy." Booklist

★ **A light** in the attic; Special edition; Harper 2009 185p il $18.99

Grades: 3 4 5 6   **811**

1. Humorous poetry 2. Nonsense verses 3. Poetry -- By individual authors

ISBN 978-0-06-190585-8; 0-06-190585-2

First published 1981

This collection of more than one hundred poems "will delight lovers of Silverstein's raucous, rollicking verse and his often tender, whimsical, philosophical advice. . . . The poems are tuned in to kids' most hidden feelings, dark wishes and enjoyment of the silly. . . . The witty line drawings are a full half of the treat of this wholly satisfying anthology by the modern successor to Edward Lear and Hilaire Belloc." SLJ [review of 1981 edition]

★ **Runny** Babbit; a billy sook. HarperCollins Pub. 2005 89p il $17.99; lib bdg $18.89

Grades: 3 4 5 6   **811**

1. Humorous poetry 2. Poetry -- By individual authors

ISBN 0-06-025653-2; 0-06-028404-8 lib bdg

In this book "readers are introduced to Runny Babbit and his friends . . . and are encouraged to plunge headlong into this phonemic flipflop world of funny poems. . . . Complete with signature comical bold line drawings that provide visual clues, the poems require concentration to translate the silly phrases. . . . Children will love these clever poems and without prompting will probably create their own." SLJ

★ **Where** the sidewalk ends; the poems & drawings of Shel Silverstein. 30th anniversary special ed; HarperCollins 2004 183p il $17.99; lib bdg $18.89

Grades: 3 4 5 6 7 8 9 10   **811**

1. Humorous poetry 2. Nonsense verses 3. Poetry -- By individual authors

ISBN 0-06-057234-5; 0-06-058653-2 lib bdg

LC 2004-269335

First published 1974

"There are skillful, sometimes grotesque line drawings with each of the 127 poems, which run in length from a few lines to a couple of pages. The poems are tender, funny, sentimental, philosophical, and ridiculous in turn, and they're for all ages." Sat Rev

Singer, Marilyn

★ **Follow** follow; a book of reverso poems. by Marilyn Singer; illustrated by Josée Masse. Dial Books for Young Readers 2013 32 p. (hardcover : acid-free paper) $16.99

Grades: 1 2 3 4   **811**
  1. Children's poetry 2. Fairy tales -- Poetry 3. Children's poetry, American 4. Characters and characteristics in literature -- Juvenile poetry
  ISBN 0803737696; 9780803737693
                                                   LC 2012014359

This children's book, by Marilyn Singer, illustrated by Josee Masse, offers several fairy tales in the form of "reversos--a poetic form in which the poem is presented forward and then backward. . . . Read these . . . poems from top to bottom and they mean one thing. Then reverse the lines and read from bottom to top and they mean something else--it is almost like magic!" (Publisher's note)

A **full** moon is rising; poems. pictures by Julia Cairns. Lee & Low Books 2011 48p il $19.95

Grades: 1 2 3 4   **811**
  1. Moon -- Poetry 2. Poetry -- By individual authors
  ISBN 978-1-60060-364-8; 1-60060-364-5
                                                   LC 2010034693

"Singer's sparkling verses celebrate the majesty of the moon as experienced in settings around the world, each distinctly conveyed in Cairns's perceptive watercolors. . . . The lunar celebration even extends beyond Earth, with a scientist in the International Space Station contemplating both Earth's moon and the Martian moon, Phobos. The breadth of perspectives creates a stirring portrait of a familiar but no less marvelous sight." Publ Wkly

★ **Mirror** mirror; illustrated by Josée Masse. Dutton Children's Books 2010 un il $16.99

Grades: 3 4 5 6   **811**
  1. Children's poetry 2. Fairy tales -- Poetry 3. Poetry -- By individual authors 4. Children's literature -- Works -- Grades two through six
  ISBN 978-0-525-47901-7; 0-525-47901-5; 0525479015; 9780525479017
                                                   LC 2009017917

A collection of short poems which, when reversed, provide new perspectives on the fairy tale characters they feature.

"This appealing collection . . . is a marvel to read. . . . The vibrant artwork is painterly yet unfussy and offers hints to the characters who are narrating the poems. An endnote shows children how to create a 'reverse' poem. This is a remarkably clever and versatile book." SLJ

★ A **stick** is an excellent thing; poems celebrating outdoor play. illustrated by LeUyen Pham. Clarion Books 2012 il $16.99

Grades: PreK K 1 2   **811**
  1. Imagination -- Poetry 2. Outdoor recreation -- Poetry 3. Poetry -- By individual authors
  ISBN 978-0-547-12493-3; 0-547-12493-7
                                                   LC 2011009848

"Singer presents the full spectrum of outdoor activities in rhymed poems consummately animated by Pham's vibrant drawings. . . . While many of the snappy lyrics show off the pleasures of moving . . . a real strength of the collection is its engagement of the imagination. . . . Pham's evocative artwork heightens the imagination's importance

in play, with her digitally colored pencil-and-ink renderings so finely textured that they radiate a warmth as arresting as Ezra Jack Keats'. A thrilling integration of verse and image." Kirkus

The **superheroes'** employment agency; by Marilyn Singer; illustrated by Noah Z. Jones. Clarion Books 2012 39 p. col. ill. (hardcover) $16.99

Grades: 1 2 3   **811**
  1. Superheroes -- poetry
  ISBN 0547435592; 9780547435596
                                                   LC 2011025722

Author Marilyn Singer's book features "underemployed B-list superheroes. . . . Got rats and mice? Call on the . . . Verminator! Supernatural foes will flee from the garlic foam wielded by Muffy the Vampire Sprayer. . . . Along with having distinct individual powers and abilities, several of these eager job seekers combine to offer enhanced services. Armored Sir Knightly and The Masked Man, both aging veterans, can team up to entertain at children's parties, for instance." (Kirkus Reviews)

Sklansky, Amy E.

Out of this world; poems and facts about space. by Amy E. Sklansky; illustrated by Stacey Schuett. Alfred A. Knopf 2012 40 p.

Grades: 3 4 5   **811**
  1. Outer space -- Poetry
  ISBN 0375857915; 0375864598; 0375964592; 0375987339; 9780375857911; 9780375864599; 9780375964596; 9780375987335
                                                   LC 2011032506

This children's book combines astronomy and other space science facts, space-themed poetry by Amy Sklansky, and illustrations and supplemental educational diagrams by Stacey Schuett. "The mysteries of the universe and the science of space exploration are perennially popular subjects, . . . Amy Sklansky has written . . . poems about planets and stars and rockets and moon landings and satellites. Each poem is supported by additional facts and explanations in the margins." Schuett's illustrations depict various subjects such as the Earth's atmospheric layers, star systems and other planets. (Publisher's note)

Smith, Hope Anita

★ **Mother** poems; words and pictures by Hope Anita Smith. Henry Holt and Co. 2009 72p il $16.95

Grades: 4 5 6 7   **811**
  1. Death -- Poetry 2. Mothers -- Poetry 3. Bereavement -- Poetry 4. African Americans -- Poetry 5. Poetry -- By individual authors
  ISBN 978-0-8050-8231-9; 0-8050-8231-X
                                                   LC 2008-18342

"Smith writes about an African American child's grief at the sudden death of her mother. . . . Like the poetry, Smith's simple, torn-paper collages in a folk-art style show the close embraces and vignettes without overwhelming the words." Booklist

Snyder, Betsy

I haiku you; Betsy Snyder. Random House Childrens Books 2012 32 p. (trade) $9.99

Grades: PreK K 1   **811**
  1. Haiku 2. American poetry 3. Children's poetry 4. Haiku, American 5. Children's poetry, American
  ISBN 0375867503; 9780375867507; 9780375967504; 9780375981265
                                                   LC 2012008884

Author Betsy Snyder presents a "collection of haiku [that] captures special moments of friendship and appreciation from a child's point of view. Love is explored in its broadest sense as a cast of winsome, ethnically diverse children are featured in everyday activities such as making snow angels, riding a bicycle and sharing a purple Popsicle." (Kirkus Reviews)

Soto, Gary

Canto familiar; [illustrated by Annika Nelson] Harcourt Brace & Co. 1995 79p il $18; pa $5.95

Grades: 4 5 6 **811**

1. Mexican Americans -- Poetry 2. Poetry -- By individual authors
ISBN 978-0-15-200067-7; 0-15-200067-4; 978-0-15-205885-2 pa; 0-15-205885-0 pa

LC 94-24218

"This collection of simple free verse captures common childhood moments at home, at school, and in the street. Many of the experiences are Mexican American . . . and occasional Spanish words are part of the easy, colloquial, short lines. . . . The occasional full-page, richly colored woodcuts by Annika Nelson capture the child's imaginative take on ordinary things." Booklist

★ **Neighborhood** odes; illustrated by David Diaz. Harcourt Brace Jovanovich 1992 68p il hardcover o.p. pa $5.95

Grades: 4 5 6 **811**

1. Hispanic Americans -- Poetry 2. Poetry -- By individual authors
ISBN 0-15-256879-4; 0-15-205364-6 pa

LC 91-20710

"Twenty-one poems, all odes, celebrate life in a Hispanic neighborhood. Other than the small details of daily life—peoples' names or the foods they eat—these poems could be about any neighborhood. With humor, sensitivity, and insight, Soto explores the lives of children. . . . David Diaz's contemporary black-and-white illustrations, which often resemble cut paper, effortlessly capture the varied moods—happiness, fear, longing, shame, and greed—of this remarkable collection. With a glossary of thirty Spanish words and phrases." Horn Book

★ **Soul** looks back in wonder; [illustrated by] Tom Feelings. Dial Bks. 1993 un il hardcover o.p. pa $7.99

Grades: 4 5 6 7 **811**

1. African Americans -- Poetry 2. American poetry -- African American authors -- Collections
ISBN 0-8037-1001-1; 0-14-056501-9 pa

LC 93-824

Coretta Scott King Award for illustration

Artwork and poems by such writers as Maya Angelou, Langston Hughes, and Askia Toure portray the creativity, strength, and beauty of their African American heritage

"This thoughtful collection of poetry is unique. . . . Feelings selected sketches done while he was in West Africa, South America, and at home in America. The original drawings were enhanced with colored pencils, colored papers, stencil cut-outs, and other techniques to give a collage effect. Marbled textures bring vibrancy to the work." Horn Book

Swaim, Jessica

Scarum fair; poems by Jessica Swaim; illustrations by Carol Ashley. Wordsong 2010 31p il $17.95

Grades: 3 4 5 **811**

1. Monsters -- Poetry 2. Poetry -- By individual authors
ISBN 978-1-59078-590-4; 1-59078-590-4

LC 2008040336

"Clever writing pulls children into a creepy carnival of 29 humorous poems. . . . Dark background colors add a sense of foreboding as the cartoon children meet the ghouls illustrated in acrylics, graphite, and pen and ink." SLJ

★ **Switching** on the moon; a very first book of bedtime poems. collected by Jane Yolen and Andrew Fusek Peters; illustrated by G. Brian Karas. Candlewick Press 2010 95p il $21.99

Grades: PreK K **811**

1. Lullabies 2. Children's poetry 3. Night -- Poetry 4. Sleep -- Poetry 5. Bedtime -- Poetry 6. American poetry -- Collections
ISBN 0763642495; 9780763642495; 978-0-7636-4249-5; 0-7636-4249-5

LC 2008025442

This is an anthology of sixty poems for bedtime reading by authors from Britain, Canada and the United States. Subjects include "the moon, dreams, lullabies, stars, bathtime, bedtime, the dark, night sounds, toothbrushes. [Indexes.] Preschool." (Horn Book)

"Yolen and Peters's 60-poem anthology reveals the many faces of nighttime through the words of these collaborators as well as poets that include Tennyson, Plath, Lee Bennett Hopkins, and Mary Ann Hoberman. . . . With Kara's mixed-media illustrations creating a chalky, dreamlike atmosphere, this book is made for bedtime." Publ Wkly

Thayer, Ernest Lawrence

★ **Casey** at the bat; a ballad of the republic sung in the year 1888. [by] Ernest L. Thayer; illlustrated by C.F. Payne. Simon & Schuster Bks. for Young Readers 2003 un il lib bdg $16.95

Grades: K 1 2 3 **811**

1. Baseball -- Poetry 2. Poetry -- By individual authors
ISBN 0-689-85494-3

LC 2002-3472

Poem first published 1888

A narrative poem about the celebrated baseball player who strikes out at the crucial moment of the game

"Payne's caricatures, rendered in a mix of acrylics, watercolor ink, oils, and colored pencils, are a marvel of texture and personality." SLJ

Ernest L. Thayer's Casey at the bat; a ballad of the Republic sung in the year 1888. reported by Ernest L. Thayer; illustrated by Christopher Bing. Handprint Books 2000 un il $17.95

Grades: 3 4 5 6 **811**

1. Baseball -- Poetry 2. Poetry -- By individual authors
ISBN 1-929766-00-9

LC 00-37010

A Caldecott Medal honor book, 2001

"Thayer's classic poem of the 19th-century baseball legend has been revived for a new generation in this creatively designed package. . . . Bing has orchestrated every detail to great effect. Each double spread, rendered in ink and brush on scratchboard, is a scene from the poem. The multitude of lines adds energy; the multiple perspectives create interest." SLJ

There's no place like school; classroom poems. selected by Jack Prelutsky; illustrations by Jane Manning. Greenwillow Books 2010 32p il $16.99; lib bdg $17.89

Grades: K 1 2 3 **811**

1. Schools -- Poetry 2. American poetry -- Collections
ISBN 978-0-06-082338-2; 0-06-082338-0; 978-0-06-082339-9 lib bdg; 0-06-082339-9 lib bdg

LC 2009020373

This is a "picture-book collection of poems that range from the classroom to the cafeteria to the playground. Contributed by well-known poets, including Carol Diggory Shields and Lee Bennett Hopkins, the mostly rhyming, lighthearted selections hit familiar targets. . . . The energetic, fruit-juice-hued watercolor scenes hum with cheerful energy and subversive humor and, like the poems, capture the chaotic intensity and fun of a typical school day." Booklist

Thomas, Joyce Carol

★ The **blacker** the berry; poems. illustrated by Floyd Cooper. HarperCollins 2008 un il $16.99; lib bdg $17.89
Grades: PreK K 1 2 **811**
1. African Americans -- Poetry 2. Poetry -- By individual authors
ISBN 978-0-06-025375-2; 0-06-025375-4; 978-0-06-025376-9 lib bdg; 0-06-025376-2 lib bdg
Coretta Scott King Award for illustration, 2009
Coretta Scott King honor book for text, 2009
"Black comes in all shades from dark to light, and each is rich and beautiful in this collection of simple, joyful poems and glowing portraits that show African American diversity and connections." Booklist

★ **Brown** honey in broomwheat tea; poems by Joyce Carol Thomas; illustrated by Floyd Cooper. HarperCollins Pubs. 1993 un il $16.95; pa $6.99
Grades: K 1 2 3 **811**
1. African Americans -- Poetry 2. Poetry -- By individual authors
ISBN 0-06-021087-7; 0-06-443439-7 pa
LC 91-46043
"A dozen poems rooted in home, family, and the African American experience combine with a series of warm and evocative watercolors in this highly readable and attractive picture book." Booklist

Thomas, Patricia

Nature's paintbox; a seasonal gallery of art and verse. [by] Patricia Thomas; illustrated by Craig Orback. Millbrook Press, Inc. 2007 un il lib bdg $16.95
Grades: 2 3 4 **811**
1. Seasons -- Poetry 2. Poetry -- By individual authors
ISBN 978-0-8225-6807-0
LC 2006035079
"The verse connects each season with the artist's medium, beginning with pen and ink for winter, then cycling through pastel chalk for springs, watercolor for summer, and oils for fall. . . . This picture book is both intriguing to look at and excellent for reading aloud." Booklist

Updike, John, 1932-2009

★ A **child's** calendar; illustrations by Trina Schart Hyman. Holiday House 1999 un il $16.95
Grades: K 1 2 3 **811**
1. American poetry 2. Months -- Poetry 3. Children's poetry, American 4. Poetry -- By individual authors
ISBN 0-8234-1445-0
LC 98-46166
A newly illustrated edition of the title first published 1965 by Knopf
A Caldecott Medal honor book, 2000
A collection of twelve poems describing the activities in a child's life and the changes in the weather as the year moves from January to December. "Grades three to five." (Booklist)
"Hyman's colorful illustrations portray a multiracial family living in rural New Hampshire. . . . Each evocative illustration has its own story to tell, celebrating the small moments in children's lives with clarity and sensitivity, with empathy and joy." Booklist

Vardell, Sylvia M.

Poetry people; a practical guide to children's poets. Libraries Unlimited 2007 170p $50
Grades: Adult Professional **811**
1. Poets 2. Reference books 3. Children's poetry 4. Poetry -- By individual authors 5. Children's literature -- Bio-bibliography
ISBN 978-1-59158-443-8; 1-59158-443-4
LC 2007003329

This is "a comprehensive survey of 62 contemporary children's poets. Each of the one- to two-page entries begins with a brief biography and includes Web sites, bibliographies, suggestions for use and reading of specific poems, plus connections to other children's literature. . . . This book will be welcomed by all adults interested in connecting children with poetry." SLJ
Includes bibliographical references

Viorst, Judith

If I were in charge of the world and other worries; poems for children and their parents. illustrated by Lynne Cherry. Atheneum Pubs. 1981 56p il lib bdg $16.95; pa $4.95
Grades: 3 4 5 6 **811**
1. Humorous poetry 2. Poetry -- By individual authors
ISBN 0-689-30863-9 lib bdg; 0-689-70770-3 pa
LC 81-2342
"Forty-one lively, funny poems written from a wry, self-deprecating point of view. Some poems verge on adult feelings—such as a broken heart or a lyrical appreciation of spring—but most of them deal with children's worries, to which the author seems to be specially attuned." Horn Book

Walker, Alice

There is a flower at the tip of my nose smelling me; by Alice Walker; illustrated by Stefano Vitale. HarperCollinsPublishers 2006 un il $16.99; lib bdg $17.89
Grades: 2 3 4 **811**
1. Senses and sensation -- Poetry 2. Poetry -- By individual authors
ISBN 978-0-06-057080-4; 0-06-057080-6; 978-0-06-057081-1 lib bdg; 0-06-057081-4 lib bdg
LC 2005014517
"Walker celebrates the beauty of the world and our connection to it through a series of short verses that praise the senses. . . . Vitale's vibrant, jewel-toned illustrations embolden the folk-art simplicity of each verse." SLJ

Why war is never a good idea; illustrations by Stefano Vitale. HarperCollins Publishers 2007 un il $16.99; lib bdg $17.89
Grades: 3 4 5 **811**
1. War poetry 2. Poetry -- By individual authors
ISBN 978-0-06-075385-6; 0-06-075385-4; 978-0-06-075386-3 lib bdg; 0-06-075386-2 lib bdg
LC 2006036255
Simple, rhythmic text explores the wanton destructiveness of War, which has grown old but not wise, as it demolishes nice people and beautiful things with no consideration for the consequences
"A thought-provoking, eloquent poem and brilliant art combine to bring the abstract concept of war to a personal, immediate level." SLJ

Weatherford, Carole Boston

★ **Birmingham,** 1963. Wordsong 2007 39p il $17.95
Grades: 3 4 5 6 **811**
1. Bombings -- Poetry 2. Poetry -- By individual authors 3. African Americans -- Civil rights -- Poetry 4. Birmingham (Ala.) -- Race relations -- Poetry
ISBN 978-1-59078-440-2; 1-59078-440-5
LC 2006038105
"In free verse, a fictional 10-year-old tells of actual events leading up to the Ku Klux Klan bombing of the Sixteenth Street Baptist Church on September 15, 1963, and of the four young girls who died in the explosion. On each double-page spread, a few lines of spare poetry . . . are placed opposite a stirring, unframed archival photograph. . . . The quiet yet arresting book design will inspire readers." Booklist

Remember the bridge; poems of a people. designed by Semador Megged. Philomel Bks. 2002 53p il $17.99

Grades: 5 6 7 8 **811**

1. African Americans -- Poetry 2. Poetry -- By individual authors
ISBN 0-399-23726-7

LC 2001-36161

"The author evokes imagined and actual individual experiences of the people . . . in the historical black-and-white photos, drawings, and etchings. . . . This celebratory, visually striking book will be appreciated in most collections." SLJ

Wilbur, Richard

The **disappearing** alphabet; illustrated by David Diaz. Harcourt Brace & Co. 1998 un il hardcover o.p. pa $7

Grades: 3 4 5 **811**

1. Alphabet 2. Poetry -- By individual authors
ISBN 0-15-201470-5; 0-15-216362-X pa

LC 97-24617

A collection of twenty-six short poems pondering what the world would be like if any letters of the alphabet should disappear

"The poems presented here were first printed in The Atlantic Monthly magazine. A series of rhyming couplets of varying lengths, they range from the innocently whimsical to the cleverly sophisticated. Diaz uses computer-generated illustrations to add just the right touches to the verses; the images are lush and playful at the same time." SLJ

Willard, Nancy

★ A **visit** to William Blake's inn; poems for innocent and experienced travelers. illustrated by Alice and Martin Provensen. Harcourt Brace Jovanovich 1981 44p il $16; pa $7

Grades: 2 3 4 5 **811**

1. Nonsense verses 2. Poetry -- By individual authors
ISBN 0-15-293822-2; 0-15-293823-0 pa

LC 80-27403

Awarded the Newbery Medal, 1982; A Caldecott Medal honor book, 1982

"Nancy Willard's fantasy is pure pleasure, and her joy is expressed in the juxtaposition of sense and nonsense. . . . Done chiefly in glowing tawny colors, the pictures are highly decorative, and the whole book, printed on buff paper speckled to simulate an antique look, presents an elegant appearance." Horn Book

Williams, Vera B.

Amber was brave, Essie was smart; the story of Amber and Essie told here in poems and pictures by Vera B. Williams. Greenwillow Bks. 2001 un il $15.95; lib bdg $15.89; pa $7.99

Grades: 3 4 5 **811**

1. Sisters -- Poetry 2. Poetry -- By individual authors
ISBN 0-06-029460-4; 0-06-029461-2 lib bdg; 0-06-057182-9 pa

LC 00-48438

Boston Globe-Horn Book Award Honor: Fiction (2002)

Two sisters help each other deal with life while their mother is working and their father has been sent to jail

"An engaging, affecting view of the bonds between sisters, this balances reality with hope and love as it shows how small moments tell a big story." Booklist

Wong, Janet S.

Knock on wood; poems about superstitions. written by Janet S. Wong; illustrated by Julie Paschkis. Margaret K. McElderry Bks. 2003 33p il $17.95

Grades: 3 4 5 **811**

1. Superstition -- Poetry 2. Poetry -- By individual authors
ISBN 0-689-85512-5

LC 2002-8319

A collection of seventeen original poems about superstitions, including walking under a ladder, breaking a mirror, and knocking on wood. Includes notes about the superstitions

"Some selections are haunting, and some humorous. . . . Paschkis creates an exquisite backdrop for the verses. Presented on a panoramic spread, each poem and facing watercolor scene have matching frames, anchoring them as reflections of one another. . . . There is much to ponder in both words and pictures." SLJ

Twist; yoga poems. written by Janet S. Wong; illustrated by Julie Paschkis. Margaret K. McElderry Books 2007 39p il $17.99

Grades: 2 3 4 5 **811**

1. Yoga -- Poetry 2. Poetry -- By individual authors
ISBN 0-689-87394-8; 978-0-689-87394-2

LC 2005-15888

"This collection of 16 poems touches on the uplifting and emotional aspects of yoga, putting words to the spirit of the poses and evoking the energy and feelings of the practice. . . . Paschkis's watercolor paintings frame both the poem and a child performing the pose with colorful fauna, flora, and people that suggest India as well as that particular exercise." SLJ

★ **Words** with wings; a treasury of African-American poetry and art. selected by Belinda Rochelle. HarperCollins Pubs. 2001 un il lib bdg $18.99

Grades: 4 5 6 7 **811**

1. African Americans in art 2. African Americans -- Poetry 3. American poetry -- African American authors -- Collections
ISBN 0-688-16415-3

LC 00-26864

Pairs twenty works of art by African-American artists such as Horace Pippin and Jacob Lawrence with twenty poems by African-American poets such as Langston Hughes, Countee Cullen, and Lucille Clifton

"Most of the combinations are stunning. . . . Short biographical paragraphs on each poet and artist round out this moving presentation." SLJ

Worth, Valerie

★ **All** the small poems and fourteen more; pictures by Natalie Babbitt. Farrar, Straus & Giroux 1994 194p il hardcover o.p. pa $6.95

Grades: 2 3 4 5 **811**

1. Poetry -- By individual authors
ISBN 0-374-40345-7 pa

LC 94-8810

"As the title implies, all the original collaborations between this poet and artist are collected in this volume, which includes ninety-nine poems and an additional fourteen new ones. The earlier works have been widely praised, for good reason, and the new verses are every bit as worthy as their predecessors." Horn Book

★ **Animal** poems; pictures by Steve Jenkins. Farrar, Straus & Giroux 2007 un il $17

Grades: 4 5 6 **811**

1. Animals -- Poetry 2. Poetry -- By individual authors
ISBN 0-374-38057-0; 978-0-374-38057-1

LC 2005-56812

A collection of twenty-three illustrated poems about animals

"This pairing of . . . Worth's exquisite poems with Jenkins's . . . extraordinary, cut-paper illustrations make this a volume to treasure. . . .

. Each poem in this handsome volume is a gem—full of crisp language, vivid images and thoughtful ideas." Publ Wkly

Pug and other animal poems; Valerie Worth; pictures by Steve Jenkins. Margaret Ferguson Books, Farrar Straus Giroux 2012 40 p. $16.99

Grades: 2 3 4 5   **811**
    1. Animals -- Poetry 2. Children's poetry 3. Children's poetry, American
    ISBN 0374350248; 9780374350246

LC 2010034300

This juvenile poetry collection, by Valerie Worth, illustrated by Steve Jenkins, "examines a wide range of animal behavior, from the fleetingness of a fly sipping spilled milk to the constant steely presence of a powerful bull; the greedy meal of a street rat to a cat's quiet gift of a dead mouse on the doorstep." (Publisher's note)

Yolen, Jane
    ★ **Birds** of a feather; poems by Jane Yolen; photographs by Jason Stemple; foreword by Donald Kroodsma. Wordsong 2011 32p il $17.95

Grades: 3 4 5   **811**
    1. Birds -- Poetry 2. Poetry -- By individual authors
    ISBN 978-1-59078-830-1; 1-59078-830-3

"Striking photographs of birds that might be seen in the eastern United States illustrate this . . . collection of 14 poems in varied forms. . . . Semple's splendid photographs show birds in the wild. . . . The colors are true, and the details sharp; careful focus and composition make the birds the center of attention. . . . Short sidebars add interesting, informative details about each species." Kirkus

Bug off! creepy, crawly poems. by Jane Yolen; photographs by Jason Stemple. 1st ed. Wordsong 2012 30 p. col. ill. (reinforced) $16.95

Grades: 3 4 5   **811**
    1. Children's poetry 2. Insects -- Poetry 3. Spiders -- Poetry
    ISBN 1590788621; 9781590788622

LC 2011939947

Author Jane Yolen presents a book of poetry for children. In the collection, "[f]ly, praying mantis, butterfly, ants, honey bee, lovebug, daddy longlegs, spider, dragonfly, tick, ladybug and grasshopper each take a spread, the photo opposite a page of text that includes the poem and a paragraph of facts. Most of Yolen's poems rhyme, and an author's note encourages readers to create their own poems." (Kirkus)

The **Emily** sonnets; the life of Emily Dickinson. by Jane Yolen; illustrations by Gary Kelley. 1st ed. Creative Editions 2012 40 p. col. ill. (reinforced) $19.99

Grades: 5 6 7   **811**
    1. Dickinson, Emily, 1830-1886 -- Poetry
    ISBN 1568462158; 9781568462158

LC 2011040841

This book by Jane Yolen presents 15 sonnets about poet Emily Dickinson. "The selections are constructed in various voices. . . . In the first five pieces, Emily speaks of the family's brick house, her close relationship with her sister Vinnie, her schooling, her variance with her family's religious beliefs, and the companionship of her dog. . . . The other speakers . . . tell of her always dressing in white, her life as a recluse, and her work." (School Library Journal)

A **mirror** to nature; poems about reflection. [by] Jane Yolen; photographs by Jason Stemple. Wordsong 2009 31p il $17.95

Grades: 3 4 5   **811**
    1. Nature poetry 2. Poetry -- By individual authors
    ISBN 978-1-59078-624-6

LC 2008031760

"Water acts as a mirror in this picture book that combines short poems with full-page color photographs of animals in the wild. . . . The poetic forms are well matched to the mood in the pictures. . . . Drawn by the rich play in words and pictures, kids will see reflections, strange and beautiful, in the the natural world." Booklist

Zimmer, Tracie Vaughn
    Cousins of clouds; elephant poems. illustrated by Megan Halsey and Sean Addy. Clarion Books 2011 31p il $16.99

Grades: 3 4 5   **811**
    1. Children's poetry 2. Elephants -- Poetry 3. Poetry -- By individual authors 4. Elephants
    ISBN 978-0-618-90349-8; 0-618-90349-6

This "collection of poems and factoids celebrates the 'wonders of elephants,' from glorious winged creatures of myth to the realities of their precarious modern existence. With a wide-ranging stock of lore and fact, Vaughn limns the complex relationship between humans and the largest land animals. In 'Inspiration,' she observes that their image is 'etched in the imagination/of all mankind,/a behemoth of hope.' Poems like 'Ivory' and 'Grace,' however, remind readers that elephants have been hunted and used for hard labor and public performance. . . . 'Fortress' graphically depicts the protective instincts of female elephants, while 'Elephant Blues' places cartoon drawings and verses atop colored sheets of music." (School Library Journal)

"Against fanciful collage backdrops portraying pachyderms in an array of styles and arrangements, Zimmer pairs prose and mostly free-verse tributes to elephants and those who care for them. . . . She writes with passion and sympathy. . . . Along with giving each spread a different look and palette, the illustrators inject dashes of visual wit. . . . Both informative and heartfelt." Kirkus

★ **Steady** hands; poems about work. by Tracie Vaughn Zimmer; illustrated by Megan Halsey and Sean Addy. Clarion Books 2009 48p il $16

Grades: 4 5 6   **811**
    1. Work -- Poetry 2. Occupations -- Poetry 3. Poetry -- By individual authors
    ISBN 978-0-618-90351-1; 0-618-90351-8

LC 2007038848

"Inventive, complicated collages and well-crafted poems focus on the activities of working people in this eye-catching book. With an observant eye, Zimmer . . . captures different individuals performing work with 'steady hands.' . . . Halsey and Addy's . . . hip collages combine individual cut-outs of people along with drawings, photos, textured backgrounds and designs." Publ Wkly

811.008   American poetry -- Collections

Amazing places; poems. selected by Lee Bennett Hopkins; ilustrations by Chris Soentpiet and Christy Hale. Lee & Low Books 2015 40 p. (hardcover : alk. paper) $18.95

Grades: 2 3 4 5 6   **811.008**
    1. Historic sites 2. American poetry -- Collections 3. Children's poetry, American 4. Geography
    ISBN 9781600606533

LC 2015009199

This collection of poems, selected by Lee Bennett Hopkins with illustrations by Chris Soentpiet and Christy Hale, "brings together fourteen selections that celebrate through poetic imagery some of the amazingly diverse places in our nation. These include Denali National Park, the Oneida Nation Museum, San Francisco's Chinatown, the Grand Canyon, the Ringling Circus Museum, Harlem, the Liberty Bell, Fenway Park, and more." (Publisher's note)

"Hopkins has gathered together an impressively diverse and talented group of poets for this polished and inspiring collection, which concludes with additional information about the places in the poems and source notes." Horn

811.54   American poetry -- 1945-1999

Cleary, Brian P., 1959-

If It Rains Pancakes; Haiku and Lantern Poems. Brian P. Cleary; illustrations by Andy Rowland. Millbrook Press 2014 32 p. (Poetry Adventures) (lib. bdg. : alk. paper) $26.60

Grades: 2 3 4   **811.54**
1. Haiku 2. Poetry -- Authorship 3. Poetry
ISBN 146771609X; 9781467716093

LC 2013018079

This children's book, written by Brian P. Cleary and illustrated by Andy Rowland, is about ancient Japanese poetry known as haiku and lanterns. "Cleary explains how each form works--and shows how these little poems can contain big surprises[.] . . . When you've finished reading, you can try your hand at writing your own haiku and lanterns[.]" (Publisher's note)

"Cleary introduces two traditional Japanese poetic forms, the well-known haiku and the less-familiar lantern. The thirty-five verses and accompanying illustrations feature good-natured, kid-pleasing fun (e.g., "Yummy": "When something's so good / you want to taste it again, / that's what burps are for"; and "Sneeze": "Sneeze-- / ah-CHOOOO-- / hurricane / out of my nose / blows"). This amusing collection can't miss with kids or teachers. Reading list, websites." Horn Book

Other titles include:

Ode to a comode: concrete poems (2015)

Underneath my bed; Brian P. Cleary; illustrations by Richard Watson. Millbrook Press 2017 32 p. color illustrations (hardcover : acid-free paper) $26.65; (ebook) $26.65

Grades: 2 3 4   **811.54**
1. Children's poetry
ISBN 9781467793438; 9781512412109; 9781512411126

LC 2015043883

This book in the Poetry Adventures series, by Brian P. Cleary, with illustrations by Richard Watson, "is packed with goofy poems on subjects ranging from summer camp to dinosaurs to messy bedrooms. And when you've finished reading, you can try writing your very own list poem!" (Publisher's note)

"The combination of the poems and illustrations will provoke a laugh in even the most devout of poem dislikers." Booklist

Grimes, Nikki

One last word; Wisdom from the Harlem Renaissance. Nikki Grimes; Illustrated by Cozbi Cabrera [and 12 others] Bloomsbury USA Childrens 2017 128 p. color illustrations (hardback) $18.99; (ebook) $42

Grades: 5 6 7 8   **811.54**
1. American poetry -- African American authors -- Collections 2. African Americans -- Poetry
ISBN 9781619635548; 9781619635555

LC 2016016215

"In this collection of poetry, Nikki Grimes looks afresh at the poets of the Harlem Renaissance -- including voices like Langston Hughes, Georgia Douglas Johnson, and many more writers of importance and

resonance from this era -- by combining their work with her own original poetry. Using 'The Golden Shovel' poetic method, Grimes has written a collection of poetry that is as gorgeous as it is thought-provoking." (Publisher's note)

"This anthology has plenty to offer, including effective introductions to Harlem Renaissance poets, well-expressed ideas and images, and, for young writers, a challenging way to turn admiration into inspiration." Booklist

Paschkis, Julie

★ **Flutter** & Hum/Aleteo y zumba; Animal Poems/Poemas de animales. Written and illustrated by Julie Paschkis. Henry Holt & Co. 2015 32 p. color illustrations hardcover $17.99

Grades: K 1 2 3 4 5   **811.54**
1. Animals 2. Children's poetry
ISBN 1627791035; 9781627791038

"All sorts of animals flutter and hum, dance and stretch, and slither and leap their way through this joyful collection of poems in English and Spanish. Julie Paschkis's poems and art sing in both languages, bringing out the beauty and playfulness of the animal world." (Publisher's Note)

"Written first in Spanish then translated into English by the (non-native Spanish speaker) author, each of these animal poems is intricately connected to its corresponding gouache painting, with additional, thematic words found throughout the pictures. For example, in "Fish / El pez," a boy sleeps on a boat that floats above fish swimming in a sea of lulling words: linger, flow; luna, burbuja." Horn Book

Rogers, Stan

Northwest Passage. Groundwood Books 2013 56 p. $24.95

Grades: 3 4 5   **811.54**
1. Picture books for children 2. Northwest Passage
ISBN 1554981530; 9781554981533

This book is an illustrated version of Canadian folk musician Stan Rogers' song "Northwest Passage." The song "describes Stan's own journey overland as he contemplates the arduous journeys of some of the explorers, including Kelsey, Mackenzie, Thompson and Franklin." Along with the illustrations, the book "contains the music for the song, a note on the Northwest Passage, maps, information about Stan Rogers . . . and notes on the illustrations." (Publisher's note)

Rosen, Michael J.

★ The **Maine** coon's haiku; and other poems for cat lovers. Michael J. Rosen, illustrated by Lee White. Candlewick Press 2015 56 p. color illustrations $17.99

Grades: 2 3 4   **811.54**
1. Haiku 2. Cats -- Poetry
ISBN 0763664928; 9780763664923

LC 2013957344

This book by Michael J. Rosen presents a "haiku-focused collection of poems" about cats. "The book is divided into sections by where certain types of cats are typically found--inside or outside--and highlights cats from around the world. Each cat is featured on a two-page spread that highlights the name of the cat, a haiku or poem about the cat, and an illustration depicting the cat." (Children's Literature)

"The brevity and poignancy of the haiku format perfectly capture the feline essence in this book of verse. Each spread defines an individual breed, some familiar and others less so, with a deft haiku and an inviting illustration about a brief moment." SLJ

Sidman, Joyce

★ **Winter** Bees & Other Poems of the Cold; Written by Joyce Sidman and illustrated by Rick Allen. Houghton Mifflin Books for Children, Houghton Mifflin Harcourt 2014 32 p. colored illustrations $17.99

811.54

1. Children's poetry 2. Winter -- Poetry 3. Animals -- Poetry
ISBN 0547906501; 9780547906508

LC 2013039007

This book by Joyce Sidman, with illustrations by Rick Allen, offers "a new poetic treatment of natural history. Twelve poems treat subjects ranging from moose and snakes to snowflakes and skunk cabbage, each entry partnered with a prose paragraph giving more factual detail behind the subject of the verse." (Bulletin of the Center for Children's Books)

"Sidman exemplifies winter survival strategies of a well-chosen sample of species. Her poems are precise, evocative, lyrical, varied in tone; facts in succinct (separate) prose illuminate the imagery of each. It's as beautiful visually as it is verbally: winter's browns, blues, and whites are warmed with glowing honey tones; a note describes Allen's "unlikely marriage" of hand-colored linoleum blocks with computer techniques. Glos." Horn Book

Winter Bees and Other Poems of the Cold

Singer, Marilyn, 1948-
Echo echo; reverso poems about the Greek myths. Marilyn Singer; illlustrated by Josee Masse. Dial Books for Young Readers 2015 32 p. illustrations (hardcover) $16.99
Grades: 3 4 5 6   **811.54**
1. Greek mythology 2. Poetry -- Collections
ISBN 9780803739925

LC 2014048809

This book, by Marilyn Singer, illlustrated by Josee Masse, presents "reversible poems based on Greek myths. . . . Read one way, each poem tells the story of a familiar myth; but when read in reverse, the poems reveal a new point of view! . . . [It includes] the stories of Pandora's box, King Midas and his golden touch, Perseus and Medusa, Pygmalion, Icarus and Daedalus, Demeter and Persephone, and Echo and Narcissus." (Publisher's note)

"A wonderful addition to poetry collections and accompaniment for the myths." Booklist

Rutherford B., who was he? poems about our presidents. Marilyn Singer; John Hendrix. 1st ed. Disney-Hyperion Books 2013 56 p. $17.99
Grades: 3 4 5 6 7   **811.54**
1. Children's poetry 2. Presidents -- United States 3. Children's poetry, American 4. Historical poetry, American 5. Presidents -- United States -- Biography
ISBN 1423171004; 9781423171003

LC 2013010690

In this collection of children's poetry, author Marilyn Singer and illustrator John Hendrix bring "the presidents of the United States to life--from [George] Washington to [Barack] Obama and contextualizes them in their time. Backmatter enriches the experience with short biographies, quotes by each president, and more." (Publisher's note)

VanHecke, Susan
Under the freedom tree; Susan Vanhecke; Illustrated by London Ladd. Charlesbridge 2013 32 p. (reinforced for library use) $16.95
Grades: 1 2 3 4   **811.54**
1. Poetry 2. Fugitive slaves 3. United States -- History -- 1861-1865, Civil War -- Poetry 4. Fugitive slaves -- Poetry
ISBN 1580895506; 9781580895507; 9781607346340

LC 2012038698

This book, by Susan Vanhecke and illustrated by London Ladd, "illuminates . . . [a] slice of Civil War history: runaway slaves' establishment of a settlement in newly seceded Virginia. In 1861, three slaves--Frank Baker, James Townsend, and Shepard Mallory--escape by boat from a Confederate camp. . . . The three men land at a Union camp whose commander declares them 'contraband of war' and refuses to return them to the Confederates." (Publishers Weekly)

"In 1861, when a Union general refused to return three escaped slaves to their owners, he set off a little-known episode in American history in which more than nine hundred slaves ended up in Hampton, Virginia, working for the Union army. The brief, spare verse is accompanied by realistic acrylic paintings depicting everyday life as the growing community builds a new town." Horn Book

Includes bibliographical references and index

811.6   American poetry -- 2000-

Caswell, Deanna
Boo, haiku; words by Deanna Caswell; pictures by Bob Shea. Abrams Appleseed 2016 24 p. color illustrations (ebook) $12.95; (hardback) $12.95
Grades: PreK K   **811.6**
1. Haiku, American 2. Halloween -- poetry
ISBN 9781613129623; 9781419721182

LC 2015040406

"Bestselling illustrator Bob Shea and poet Deanna Caswell are back, this time with a haiku book filled with frights that delight. . . . A witch, a bat, a skeleton, a jack-o'-lantern, a ghost, a black cat, a spider, an owl, and a scarecrow are all hiding in the pages of this clever Halloween-themed book. . . . [Caswell's] haiku cleverly hint at the creatures revealed after each turn of the page while . . . Shea's bright illustrations capture the scary silliness." (Publisher's note)

"As with the first, this just begs to be read aloud to a group of preschoolers, who won't be able to help shouting out their answers. More please." Kirkus

Fogliano, Julie
★ When green becomes tomatoes; by Julie Fogliano; illustrated by Julie Morstad. Roaring Brook Press 2016 56 p. color illustrations (hardcover) $18.99
Grades: K 1 2 3 4 5   **811.6**
1. Children's poetry 2. Seasons -- Poetry
ISBN 9781596438521

LC 2015004126

In this juvenile poetry collection, by Julie Fogliano and illustrated by Julie Morstad, "flowers blooming in sheets of snow make way for happy frogs dancing in the rain. Summer swims move over for autumn sweaters until the snow comes back again. In Julie Fogliano's skilled hand . . . , the seasons come to life in this gorgeous and comprehensive book of poetry." (Publisher's note)

"This combination of poetry and art in praise of the familiar, natural world is sweetly, successfully dazzling." Kirkus

Orgill, Roxane
★ Jazz Day; The Making of a Famous Photograph. Roxane Orgill; illustrated by Francis Vallejo. Candlewick Press 2016 66 p. color illustrations $18.99
Grades: 4 5 6 7 8   **811.6**
1. Jazz musicians 2. Poetry -- Collections 3. Harlem (New York, N.Y.) 4. Jazz music
ISBN 0763669547; 9780763669546

LC 2015933243

Boston Globe-Horn Book Award: Picture Book (2016)

"When Esquire magazine planned an issue to salute the American jazz scene in 1958, graphic designer Art Kane pitched a crazy idea: how about gathering a group of beloved jazz musicians and photographing them? He didn't own a good camera, didn't know if any musicians would show up, and insisted on setting up the shoot in front of a Harlem brownstone. Could he pull it off?" (Publisher's note)

"In 21 poems, Orgill introduces Art Kane's iconic 1958 Harlem photograph to young readers, spotlighting many of the 57 jazz musicians pictured. . . . Vallejo's acrylic-and-pastel paintings vividly capture the shoot's vignettes and the skittish excitement of neighborhood kids." Kirkus

Includes bibliographical references (pages 54-55)

Raczka, Bob

★ **Santa** Clauses; short poems from the North Pole. By Bob Raczka; Illustrated by Chuck Groenink. Carolrhoda Books 2014 32 p. (lib. bdg. : alk. paper) $16.95

Grades: K 1 2 3 4 5   **811.6**

1. Poetry 2. Christmas -- Poetry 3. Santa Claus -- Fiction 4. Christmas poetry
ISBN 146771805X; 9781467718059

LC 2013030819

In this children's book, by Bob Raczka, "you know that Santa can fly a sleigh, squeeze down chimneys, and circle the globe in a night. But did you know that another of his talents is writing haiku? These twenty-five short poems--composed by Santa himself--give you a peek into life at the North Pole as the December days tick down to Christmas." (Publisher's note)

"Readers are offered a day-by-day "glimpse of life at the North Pole" in twenty-five festive haiku "penned" by Santa himself. The poems are rich with tender emotions and crisp imagery, all reflected affectionately and vividly in Groenink's art. A warm seasonal collection notable for its clever, gently comical visual details (note St. Nick's adult beverage as he relaxes on December 26th)." Horn Book

Wet cement; a mix of concrete poems. Bob Raczka. Roaring Brook Press 2016 48 p. (hardcover) $17.99

Grades: 3 4 5 6   **811.6**

1. Concrete poetry 2. Children's poetry
ISBN 9781626722361

LC 2015027142

This poetry collection, by Bob Raczka, "shapes poems in surprising and delightful ways. Concrete poetry is a perennially popular poetic form because they are fun to look at. But by using the arrangement of the words on the page to convey the meaning of the poem, concrete or shape poems are also easy to write!" (Publisher's note)

"Whether they are watching words about dominoes cascade across a two-page spread, or reading a recipe for icicles that drips down along the top edge, aspiring wordsmiths should find plenty of inspiration here." Booklist

Ruddell, Deborah

The **popcorn** astronauts; and other biteable rhymes. Deborah Ruddell; illustrated by Joan Rankin. Margaret K. McElderry Books 2015 40 p. (hardcover) $17.99

Grades: PreK K 1 2 3 4   **811.6**

1. Food -- Poetry 2. Children's poetry
ISBN 1442465557; 9781442465558

LC 2013037332

In this children's book, author Deborah Ruddell presents a "collection of . . . seasonal poems, each one an ode to a favorite food! . . . In spring, bow to the 'Strawberry Queen' and eat 'Only Guacamole.' In summer you'll meet Bob the Ogre, who only eats corn on the cob, and in fall, you can learn '21 Things to Do with an Apple.' And then in winter, retreat from the cold at 'The Cocoa Cabana!'" (Publisher's note)

Weatherford, Carole Boston, 1956-

You can fly; the Tuskegee Airmen. Carole Boston Weatherford; art by Jeffery Boston Weatherford. Atheneum Books for Young Readers 2015 96 p. illustrations (hardcover : alk. paper) $16.99

Grades: 4 5 6 7 8   **811.6**

1. African American soldiers 2. World War, 1939-1945 -- Aerial operations 3. Tuskegee Army Air Field (Ala.) -- poetry 4. African American air pilots -- History -- poetry 5. World War, 1939-1945 -- Campaigns -- Western Front -- poetry 6. World War, 1939-1945 -- Aerial operations, American -- poetry 7. World War, 1939-1945 -- Participation, African American -- poetry 8. United States. Army Air Forces. Fighter Squadron, 99th -- History -- poetry
ISBN 9781481449380; 9781481449397

LC 2015012393

This book, by Carole Boston Weatherford and Jeffery Boston Weatherford, "celebrates the story of the Tuskegee Airmen. . . . From training days in Alabama to combat on the front lines in Europe, this is the story of the Tuskegee Airmen, the groundbreaking African-American pilots of World War II." (Publisher's note)

" This excellent treatment is enhanced with useful backmatter: author's note, timeline, and list of additional resources. Jeffery Boston Weatherford's scratchboard illustrations complement the text. A masterful, inspiring evocation of an era." Kirkus

Includes filmograpgy (pages 79-80).

Wilson, Karma

Outside the box; Karma Wilson; illustrated by Diane Goode. Margaret K. McElderry Books 2013 176 p. $17.99

Grades: 3 4 5 6   **811.6**

1. American poetry -- Collections 2. Poetry
ISBN 1416980059; 9781416980056

LC 2011049239

This book, by Karma Wilson and illustrated by Diane Goode, is a "collection of more than 100 poems that touch on everything from creativity and luck to animals, siblings, and holidays. The narrator of 'My Pet Robot' stares glumly at her creation. . . . Elsewhere, a boy reflects on the duality of oatmeal . . . and a girl shouts her head off as she's about to be devoured by a monster." (Publishers Weekly)

"Wilson's mostly humorous poems cover the usual ground, touching on imagination, family relationships, and food preferences. The rhyme and meter are often forced, and the poems with messages are heavy-handed. In most cases, the concrete poems are stronger than those in rhyming verse. The calligraphic feel of Goode's line drawings distinguishes them from illustrations in similar collections. Ind." Horn Book

812 American drama in English

Black, Ann N.

Readers theatre for middle school boys; investigating the strange and mysterious. illustrated by Cody Rust. Teachers Idea Press 2008 190p il (Readers theatre) pa $30

Grades: Adult Professional   **812**

1. Readers' theater 2. Drama -- Collections
ISBN 978-1-59158-535-0 pa; 1-59158-535-X pa

LC 2007034923

"This book provides solid offerings of Readers Theater scripts for educators working with middle school boys. Selections include adaptations of such creepy classics as 'The Legend of Sleepy Hollow,' 'The Masque of the Red Death,' . . . and 'The Monkey's Paw.' The scripts have a new, fresh feel, and contain plenty of elements to capture and maintain adolescent males' attention." Libr Media Connect

Includes bibliographical references

Bruchac, Joseph

Pushing up the sky: seven Native American plays for children; illustrated by Teresa Flavin. Dial Bks. for Young Readers 2000 94p il hardcover o.p. $21.99

Grades: 3 4 5   812

1. Native American drama 2. Drama -- Collections

ISBN 0-8037-2168-4; 0-8037-2535-3 pa

LC 98-20483

Uses drama to tell seven different stories from Native American traditions including the Abenaki, Ojibway, Cherokee, Cheyenne, Snohomish, Tlingit, and Zuni

"The short, simple scripts are accessible to young, inexperienced actors. . . . Suggestions are given for easy-to-make costumes, props, and scenery. A variety of pen-and-ink drawings illustrate the plays, as well as one lively gouache illustration per selection." SLJ

Includes bibliographical references

Dabrowski, Kristen

My first monologue book; 100 monologues for young children. by Kristen Dabrowski. Smith and Kraus 2006 112p (Young actors series) pa $11.95

Grades: 2 3 4 5 6   812

1. Acting 2. Monologues

ISBN 1-57525-533-2 pa; 978-1-57525-533-0 pa

LC 2006938162

"Dabrowski offers short, accessible selections on common topics such as games, families, food, friends, school, and wishes. The true-to-life experiences and emotions are delivered in a child's voice and run the gamut from funny to serious." SLJ

My second monologue book; famous and historical people: 101 monologues for young children. Smith and Kraus 2008 115p il (My first acting series) pa $11.95

Grades: 2 3 4 5 6   812

1. Acting 2. Monologues

ISBN 978-1-57525-601-6 pa; 1-57525-601-0 pa

LC 2008927862

Presents over a hundred monologues focusing on ordinary and famous people designed for use by children who are just starting with acting

"The monologues and activities will fire the imaginations of young students." SLJ

My third monologue book; places near and far: 102 monologues for young children. Smith and Kraus Publishers 2008 116p il (My first acting series) pa $11.95

Grades: 2 3 4 5 6   812

1. Acting 2. Monologues

ISBN 978-1-57525-602-3

LC 2008927864

This collection of monologues is "divided into four parts: places you know (the woods, grandma's house), places in the United States (Laredo, TX; Flagstaff, AZ), foreign countries (Italy, Morocco), and imaginary and far-out places (Hogwarts, an alien world). . . . Concluding activities range from figuring out where the character is, to circling or underlining grammar clues, to completing a travel journal. [This is a] good [addition] as [it suggests] well-rounded activities for students to practice reading, writing, speaking, and both critical and imaginative thinking." SLJ

Fredericks, Anthony D.

African legends, myths, and folktales for readers theatre; illustrated by Bongaman. Teachers Ideas Press 2008 xxiii, 166p il map (Readers theatre) pa $25

Grades: Adult Professional   812

1. Readers' theater 2. Folklore -- Africa 3. Drama -- Collections

ISBN 978-1-59158-633-3 pa; 1-59158-633-X pa

LC 2007-44594

Author Tony Fredericks and illustrator, Bongaman, present readers theatre scripts based on traditional African folklore. Includes background information for teachers on each African country, as well as instruction and presentation suggestions, and additional resources for studies of African folklore

"For the most part, the stories . . . are short, lively, and often humorous. . . . A valuable volume." SLJ

Includes bibliographical references

Levine, Karen

★ **Hana's** suitcase on stage; original story by Karen Levine; play by Emil Sher. Second Story 2007 171p il (Holocaust remembrance book for young readers) pa $18.95

Grades: 5 6 7 8   812

1. Holocaust victims 2. Holocaust, 1933-1945 -- Drama

ISBN 978-1-89718-705-0 pa; 1-89718-705-X pa

"Set in the Tokyo Holocaust Center, the two-act play opens with the woman and two of her student helpers questioning and searching for answers to the suitcase's history. . . . Act II blends characters of Ishioka and her students with Hana and her family, each group individually recounting their stories in alternating voices. As with the original book, this title succeeds in recreating a striking representation of one child's tragic and beautiful life in a terrifying world of hate and prejudice. This volume will serve as one of the most effective teaching models for Holocaust curriculums available. Photographs and facsimiles of Nazi documents are included." SLJ

Shepard, Aaron

Stories on stage; children's plays for reader's theater (or readers theatre), with 15 Play scripts from 15 authors. 2nd ed; Shepard 2005 160p pa $15

Grades: Adult Professional   812

1. Readers' theater 2. Drama -- Collections

ISBN 0-938497-22-7

First published 1993 in H. W. Wilson Co.

A collection of twenty-two plays adapted from folk tales, short stories, myths, and novels and intended for use in reader's theater programs

"With its mix of humor, fantasy, and multicultural tales . . . this book gives teachers both a fun and useful tool for bringing reading and literature to their students." SLJ

813   American fiction in English

Hamilton, Virginia

★ **Virginia** Hamilton: speeches, essays, and conversations; edited by Arnold Adoff & Kacy Cook. Blue Sky Press 2010 368p $29.99

Grades: 8 9 10 11 12 Adult Professional   813

1. Authorship 2. Children's literature -- History and criticism

ISBN 978-0-439-27193-6; 0-439-27193-2

LC 2009031676

"A groundbreaking writer of children's fiction, folktales, biography, and picture books, Hamilton won every major award, and much of this book is made up of her acceptance speeches, including those for the Newbery, Hans Christian Andersen, and Coretta Scott King awards, as well as her Arbuthnot and Zena Sutherland lectures. Aimed at a general audience, the book employs a tone both scholarly and informal, as Hamilton talks about her career as a woman and a black writer in America and about the form and content of her work in general and with particular titles. . . . Many speeches include introductions by children's literature scholars and editors, who add perspective on Hamilton's lasting influence, while family members fill in biographical details. A must for YAs who love her books, this will also appeal to librarians, teachers, and children's literature students." Booklist

Includes bibliographical references

Juster, Norton

The **annotated** Phantom tollbooth; by Norton Juster; illustrations by Jules Feiffer; introduction and notes by Leonard Marcus. Alfred A. Knopf 2011 284p il $29.99; lib bdg $32.22

Grades: Adult Professional 813

1. Authors 2. Architects 3. Children's authors
ISBN 978-0-375-85715-7; 0-375-85715-X; 978-0-375-95715-4 lib bdg; 0-375-95715-4 lib bdg

LC 2011013174

"Still ferrying dazzled readers to Dictionopolis and beyond 50 years after his first appearance, young Milo is accompanied this time through by encyclopedic commentary from our generation's leading (and most readable) expert on the history of children's literature and publishing. . . . Leonard opens with typically lucid and well-organized pictures of both Juster's and Feiffer's formative years and later careers, interwoven with accounts of the book's conception, publication and critical response. In notes running alongside the ensuing facsimile, he puts on an intellectual show. . . . he delivers notes on topics as diverse as the etymological origins of "BALDERDASH!" and mimetic architecture to textual parallels with the Wizard of Oz and echoes of Winsor McKay and George Grosz in the art. Family photos, scrawled notes and images of handwritten and typescript manuscript pages further gloss a work that never ages nor fails to astonish." Kirkus

Larsen, Andrew

See you next year; Written by Andrew Larsen, Illustrated by Todd Stewart. Owlkids Books, Inc. 2015 32 p. colour illustrations $16.95

Grades: PreK K 1 813

1. Seasons -- Juvenile fiction 2. Friendship -- Juvenile fiction
ISBN 1926973992; 9781926973999

LC 2014945471

In this children's book, by Andrew Larsen and illustrated by Todd Stewart, "every summer, a girl's family . . . spends a week at the same beachside motel. . . . But this year, something is different: the girl, our narrator, meets a new friend. . . . When it's time to go, she's sad to part ways. But she knows she can look forward to seeing him next year." (Publisher's note)

"Often the colorings are beachy—watery blues and sandy tans—but the night art is dramatic, especially the roaring bonfire, all blazing reds and oranges. A lovely, thoughtful piece of bookmaking." Booklist

Lester, Helen

Author; a true story. Houghton Mifflin 1997 32p il $11

Grades: K 1 2 3 813

1. Authors 2. Authorship 3. Women authors 4. Children's authors 5. Elementary school teachers
ISBN 0-395-82744-2

LC 96-9645

An "autobiographical look at the evolution of a writer describes Lester's experiences—including her earliest three-year-old scribbles and the acceptance of her first manuscript (on the seventh try). Illustrated with Lester's own rather childlike illustrations, this lighthearted but realistic (and helpful) guide for the writer has lots of fresh tips for young authors-in-the-making." Horn Book Guide

Paulsen, Gary

★ **How** Angel Peterson got his name; and other outrageous tales about extreme sports. Wendy Lamb Bks. 2003 111p hardcover o.p. pa $5.99

Grades: 5 6 7 8 813

1. Authors 2. Sled dog racers 3. Authors, American 4. Children's authors 5. Short story writers 6. Young adult authors
ISBN 0-385-72949-9; 0-385-90090-2 lib bdg; 978-0-440-22935-3 pa; 0-440-22935-9 pa

LC 2002-7668

Author Gary Paulsen relates tales from his youth in a small town in northwestern Minnesota in the late 1940s and early 1950s, such as skiing behind a souped-up car and imitating daredevil Evel Knievel

"Writing with humor and sensitivity, Paulsen shows boys moving into adolescence believing they can do anything. . . . None of them dies (amazingly), and even if Paulsen exaggerates the teensiest bit, his tales are side-splittingly funny and more than a little frightening." Booklist

★ **My** life in dog years; with drawings by Ruth Wright Paulsen. Delacorte Press 1998 137p il $15.95; pa $6.50

Grades: 4 5 6 7 813

1. Dogs 2. Authors 3. Sled dog racers 4. Authors, American 5. Children's authors 6. Short story writers 7. Young adult authors
ISBN 0-385-32570-3; 0-440-41471-7 pa

LC 97-40254

The author describes some of the dogs that have had special places in his life, including his first dog, Snowball, in the Philippines; Dirk, who protected him from bullies; and Cookie, who saved his life

"Paulsen differentiates his canine friends beautifully, as only a keen observer and lover of dogs can. At the same time, he presents an intimate glimpse of himself, a lonely child of alcoholic parents, who drew strength and solace from his four-legged companions and a love of the great outdoors. Poignant but never saccharine, honest, and open." Booklist

Scieszka, Jon, 1954-

★ The **Stinky** Cheese Man and other fairly stupid tales; [by Jon Scieszka & Lane Smith] Viking 1992 un il $17.99

Grades: 2 3 4 5 813

1. Fairy tales 2. Short stories
ISBN 0-670-84487-X

LC 91-48194

A Caldecott Medal honor book, 1993

This book presents satirical revisions of ten familiar fairy tales. "Grade two and up." (Booklist)

"The picture-book set will probably recognize the stories enough to know that what's going on isn't what's 'supposed' to happen. But The Stinky Cheese Man isn't a book for little ones. It will take older children (that's teens along with 10s) to follow the disordered story lines and appreciate the narrative's dry wit, wordplay, and wacky, sophomoric jokes. . . . Smith's New Wave art is an intricate part of the whole, extending as well as reinforcing the narrative; the pictures are every bit as comically insolent and deliberately clever as the words." Booklist

Villeneuve, Anne

Loula is leaving for Africa; by Anne Villeneuve. Kids Can Press 2013 32 p. illustrations (color) $16.95

Grades: PreK K 1 2 813

1. Africa -- Fiction 2. Brothers and sisters -- Fiction 3. Adventure and adventurers
ISBN 1554539412; 9781554539413

In this book, by Anne Villeneuve, "Loula has had enough of her terrible triplet brothers and decides to run away to Africa. Luckily, her mother's chauffeur, Gilbert, knows just how to get there. Together, Loula and Gilbert ride camels, cross a desert and, most important, use heaps of imagination in this . . . adventure." (Publisher's note)

"Villeneuve has created a sensitive tale about running away from home. Feeling neglected and ignored, Loula is sitting in a tree with her three favorite possessions and is happy to be away from her "mean, horrible, stinky" brothers. When Gilbert, the family's chauffeur, sees her, he looks up and asks, "What are you doing up in a tree?" She replies, "This is not a tree. This is AFRICA!" What follows is an afternoon of imaginary travel across oceans, jungles, deserts, and restaurants that serve grasshopper sandwiches and ostrich egg soufflé...The ink and watercolor illustrations have the classic look of Ludwig Bemelmans's "Madeline" series (Viking)..." (Library Journal)

817 American humor and satire in English

Freymann, Saxton
Knock, knock! [by] Saxton Freymann . . . [et al.] Dial Books for Young Readers 2007 un il $16.99
Grades: K 1 2   **817**
1. Jokes
ISBN 978-0-8037-3152-3; 0-8037-3152-3
LC 2006-39463
"14 children's book artists . . . illustrate a different groan-inducing knock-knock joke in signature style. Saxton Freymann uses photos of lettuce ('Lettuce who?' 'Lettuce in!') made to look like pigs. Tomie de Paola creates two love-struck gorillas to illustrate 'Gorilla who?' 'Gorilla my dreams, I love you!' and so on. . . . The artwork is . . . just great and varied enough to keep children turning the pages." Booklist

Rosenthal, Amy Krouse
The **wonder** book; drawings by Paul Schmid. Harper 2010 79p il $17.99
Grades: 2 3 4   **817**
1. Wit and humor
ISBN 978-0-06-142974-3; 0-06-142974-0
LC 2008-939052
"Here is a joyous, totally original potpourri of stories, poems, lists, palindromes, visual jokes, and random observations about the universal delights and conundrums of childhood. Set squarely in the world of the 21st-century child . . . these varied musings nonetheless speak to everyone's inner child, young or old. . . . Simple, evocative, and childlike black-and-white line drawings, in concert with judicious and varied use of white space, perfectly capture the happy/sad/serious/silly moods of the selections." SLJ

818 American miscellaneous writings in English

Cooper, Floyd
★ **Coming** home; from the life of Langston Hughes. Philomel Bks. 1994 un il lib bdg $16.95; pa $6.99
Grades: K 1 2 3   **818**
1. Poets 2. Authors 3. Novelists 4. Dramatists 5. African American authors 6. Poets, American 7. Short story writers 8. Young adult authors
ISBN 0-399-22682-6 lib bdg; 0-698-11612-7 pa
LC 93-36332
This "biography highlights pivotal events in Hughes's life, emphasizing his loneliness as a child and his development as a poet. . . . Cooper's hazy illustrations in gold, brown, and sepia tones reveal keen

observations of people and neighborhood. The text and art combine to create a fine tribute and introduction to the writer's life." Horn Book
Includes bibliographical references

★ **Guys** read; true stories. edited and with an introduction by Jon Scieszka; stories by Candace Fleming, Douglas Florian, Nathan Hale, Thanhha Lai, Sy Montgomery, Jim Murphy, T. Edward Nickens, Elizabeth Partridge, Steve Sheinkin, and James Sturm; with illustrations by Brian Floca. Walden Pond Press 2014 272 p. (Guys read) (hardback) $16.99
Grades: 4 5 6 7 8   **818**
1. Essays 2. Short stories 3. American prose literature 4. American prose literature -- 21st century
ISBN 0061963828; 9780061963810; 9780061963827
LC 2014010024
Part of the Guys Read series, edited by Jon Scieszka, this book "features ten stories that are 100% amazing, 100% adventurous, 100% unbelievable--and 100% true. A star-studded group of award-winning nonfiction authors and journalists provides something for every reader, all aligned with the Common Core State Standards." (Publisher's note)
"Ten terrifically told true stories demonstrate the wide range of subjects and formats available for young readers of nonfiction. This fifth anthology in the Guys Read series stars some of the best-known names in informational writing today. . . . Selected, edited, and neatly introduced by Scieszka, National Ambassador for Young People's Literature emeritus, these appetite-whetting accounts are accompanied by occasional illustrations by Floca (not seen). You certainly don't have to be a guy to appreciate these morsels of fact-based storytelling and then beg for more." Booklist

Lewis, J. Patrick
Last laughs; animal epitaphs. J. Patrick Lewis and Jane Yolen; illustrated by Jeffrey Stewart Timmins. Charlesbridge 2012 48 p. ill. (reinforced for library use) $16.95
Grades: 3 4 5 6   **818**
1. Obituaries 2. Death in literature 3. Animals in literature 4. Animals -- humor 5. Animals -- poetry
ISBN 1580892604; 9781580892605
LC 2011025702
Author J. Patrick Lewis provides "30 tombstone remembrances [for a variety of animals]. . . . Sometimes they are gruesome, as with the newt, 'so small, / so fine, / so squashed / beneath / the crossing / sign.' There are the macabre and the simply passing: 'In his pond, / he peacefully soaked, / then, ever so quietly / croaked.' [Other animals include] . . . the eel . . . [and] the piranha." (Kirkus Reviews)

McCurdy, Michael
Walden then & now; an alphabetical tour of Henry Thoreau's pond. Charlesbridge 2010 un il lib bdg $16.95
Grades: 4 5 6 7   **818**
1. Authors 2. Alphabet 3. Naturalists 4. Essayists 5. Pacifists 6. Writers on nature 7. Nonfiction writers 8. Natural history -- Massachusetts
ISBN 978-1-58089-253-7 lib bdg; 1-58089-253-1 lib bdg
LC 2009-26645
"Elegiac woodcarvings evoke the setting of Henry Thoreau's Walden Pond as the text weaves past and present in this lengthy alphabet poem. On each spread, consecutive letters face one another, making a couplet of the lines. A dark, but not somber, woodcarving illustrates each letter, and an explanatory paragraph expands upon the information in the verse. . . . The book ends with entries from Thoreau's diary and McCurdy's inspiration and starting point for this book. Purchase as an introduction to Thoreau and for poetry shelves." SLJ

Paulsen, Gary

★ **Caught** by the sea; my life on boats. Delacorte Press 2001 103p maps $15.95; pa $5.50

Grades: 5 6 7 8 **818**

1. Authors 2. Ocean travel 3. Boats and boating 4. Sled dog racers 5. Authors, American 6. Children's authors 7. Short story writers 8. Young adult authors

ISBN 0-385-32645-9; 0-440-40716-8 pa

LC 2001-17336

"Paulsen traces his life at sea, from buying his first sailboat to getting lost in the Pacific to encountering sharks. . . . His sometimes comic, sometimes near-fatal sea-going errors make for absorbing, captivating reading." Booklist

Sandburg, Carl

The **Sandburg** treasury; prose and poetry for young people. introduction by Paula Sandburg; illustrated by Paul Bacon. Harcourt Brace Jovanovich 1970 480p il hardcover o.p. pa $24

Grades: 5 6 7 8 **818**

1. American literature

ISBN 0-15-202678-9 pa

This volume brings together all of Sandburg's books for young people; his whimsical stories, two books of poetry, a version of his biography of Abraham Lincoln, and portions of his autobiography specially edited for children

821 English poetry

Cohen, Barbara

★ **Canterbury** tales; [by] Geoffrey Chaucer; selected, translated, and adapted by Barbara Cohen; illustrated by Trina Schart Hyman. Lothrop, Lee & Shepard Bks. 1988 87p il $24.99

Grades: 4 5 6 7 **821**

1. Poets 2. Authors 3. Middle Ages 4. Poetry -- By individual authors

ISBN 0-688-06201-6

LC 86-21045

"Cohen's evident love and respect for Chaucer's writing keep her close to the text. Her writing retains the flavor of the times and the spirit of Chaucer's words while her prose retelling, enriched by Hyman's lively full-color paintings, enhances the book's appeal to young people. . . . An excellent introduction to The Canterbury Tales for young readers." Booklist

Howitt, Mary Botham

The **spider** and the fly; based on the poem by Mary Howitt; with illustrations by Tony DiTerlizzi. Simon & Schuster Bks. for Young Readers 2002 un il $16.95

Grades: K 1 2 3 **821**

1. Flies -- Poetry 2. Spiders -- Poetry 3. Poetry -- By individual authors

ISBN 0-689-85289-4

LC 2002-5760

An illustrated version of the well-known poem about a wily spider who preys on the vanity and innocence of a little fly

"Rendered in black-and-white gouache and pencil, then reproduced in silver-and-black duotone, the paintings have a spooky quality perfectly suited to retelling this melancholy tale. Ms. Fly, with her whimsical flower umbrella and Roaring '20s attire, captures the flavor of an old-time Hollywood heroine." SLJ

Hughes, Ted, 1930-1998

Collected poems for children; pictures by Raymond Briggs. Farrar, Straus and Giroux 2007 259p il $18

Grades: 3 4 5 6 **821**

1. Poetry. 2. Children's poetry, English. 3. Poetry -- By individual authors

ISBN 978-0-374-31429-3; 0-374-31429-2

LC 2006-37437

First published 2005 in the United Kingdom

This is a "collection of 250 poems by the late English poet laureate Ted Hughes. . . . Children will love the sounds of the rhythmic lines, and Briggs' scattering of small black-and-white drawings perfectly captures the tiny details in the words." Booklist

Includes bibliographical references

Kipling, Rudyard, 1865-1936

If; a father's advice to his son. [by] Rudyard Kipling; photographs by Charles R. Smith. Atheneum Books for Young Readers 2007 un il $14.99

Grades: 4 5 6 **821**

1. Poetry -- By individual authors

ISBN 978-0-689-87799-5; 0-689-87799-4

LC 2006005312

"Kipling's powerful poem comes to life for a contemporary audience in atmospheric photographs that use the metaphor of sports. A lovely shot of a boy heading a soccer ball accompanies the opening couplet: 'If you can keep your head/when all about you/are losing theirs/and blaming it on you.' The mood and actions in most of the illustrations clearly invoke the verse." SLJ

Lear, Edward

The **complete** verse and other nonsense; compiled and edited with an introduction and notes by Vivien Noakes. Penguin Bks. 2002 566p il pa $18

Grades: 4 5 6 7 8 9 10 11 12 Adult **821**

1. Nonsense verses 2. Poetry -- By individual authors

ISBN 0-14-200227-5

LC 2002-28998

This volume "presents all of Lear's verse and other nonsense writings, including stories, letters, and illustrated alphabets, as well as previously unpublished material, line drawings, and . . . [an] introduction by scholar Vivien Noakes." Publisher's note

Includes bibliographical references

★ **Edward** Lear; edited by Edward Mendelson; illustrated by Laura Huliska-Beith. Sterling 2002 48p il (Poetry for young people) $14.95; pa $6.95

Grades: 4 5 6 7 **821**

1. Limericks 2. Nonsense verses 3. Poetry -- By individual authors

ISBN 0-8069-3077-2; 1-4027-7294-7 pa

LC 2001-20112

"In an analytical introduction, Mendelson looks at Lear's serious and silly sides before selecting 15 limericks and 18 longer poems, all of which feature odd creatures adapting to, or reveling in, their differences. Sporting conical noses or other physical peculiarities, Huliska-Beit's smiling, rubber-limbed figures dance through vertiginously tilted, brightly colored minimalist settings. . . . Thought- and laugh-provoking." Booklist

★ **Edward** Lear's The duck & the kangaroo; illustrated by Jane Wattenberg. Greenwillow Books 2009 un il $17.99

Grades: PreK K 1 2 **821**

1. Nonsense verses 2. Ducks -- Poetry 3. Kangaroos -- Poetry 4.

Poetry -- By individual authors
ISBN 0-06-136683-8; 978-0-06-136683-3

LC 2008024126

"Duck, envious of Kangaroo's hop . . . asks to ride upon the larger animal's back. Upon reflection, Kangaroo expresses his concern that Duck's wet and cold feet will give him rheumitism. Duck solves the problem by wearing beautifully knitted socks. . . . Wattenberg's quirky photo collages . . . are perfectly suited for Lear's nonsensical text." Booklist

His shoes were far too tight; poems. by Edward Lear; selected and introduced by Daniel Pinkwater and illustrated by Calef Brown. Chronicle Books 2010 un il $16.99
Grades: K 1 2 3   **821**
1. Nonsense verses 2. Poetry -- By individual authors
ISBN 978-0-8118-6792-4; 0-8118-6792-7; 0811867927; 9780811867924

LC 2010008549

"Pinkwater and Brown honor a fellow champion of absurdity, Edward Lear, in this frisky collection. Even before readers get to the poems, a cartoon self-portrait of Lear in the introduction . . . hints at the revelry that's to follow. Brown's elegantly quirky collages convey the gentle lunacy of the Owl and the Pussycat . . . and lesser-known characters. . . . These seasoned collaborators provide an assuring nudge for readers to embrace Lear's sumptuously silly verse." Publ Wkly

★ The **owl** and the pussycat; by Edward Lear; illustrated by Anne Mortimer. Katherine Tegen Books 2006 un il $15.99; lib bdg $16.89
Grades: K 1 2 3   **821**
1. Nonsense verses 2. Cats -- Poetry 3. Owls -- Poetry 4. Poetry -- By individual authors
ISBN 0-06-027228-7; 0-06-027229-5 lib bdg

LC 2003015476

After a courtship voyage of a year and a day, Owl and Pussy finally buy a ring from Piggy and are blissfully married
"Lear's poem is beautifully illustrated with a mixture of elaborate, stylized borders and sumptuous portrayals of natural elements like verdant plant and tree leaves and colorful tropical flowers." SLJ

Milne, A. A.
★ **Now** we are six; with decorations by Ernest H. Shepard. Dutton 1961 104p il $22.99; pa $4.99
Grades: K 1 2 3   **821**
1. Poetry -- By individual authors
ISBN 0-525-44960-4; 0-14-0361234-3 pa
First published 1927. Reprinted September 1961 in this completely new format designed by Warren Chappell. Verso of title page
"The boy or girl who has liked 'When were very young' and 'Winnie-the-Pooh' will enjoy reading about Alexander Beetle who was mistaken for a match, the knight whose armor didn't squeak, and the old sailor who had so many things which he wanted to do. There are other entertaining poems, also, and many pictures as delightful as the verses." Pittsburgh

★ **When** we were very young; with decorations by Ernest H. Shepard. Dutton 1961 102p il $11.99; pa $6.99
Grades: K 1 2 3   **821**
1. Poetry -- By individual authors
ISBN 0-525-44445-9; 0-14-036123-5 pa
First published 1924. Reprinted September 1961 in this completely new format designed by Warren Chappell. Verso of title page
"Mr. Milne's gay jingles have found a worthy accompaniment in the charming illustrations of Mr. Shepard." Saturday Rev

Stevenson, Robert Louis, 1850-1894
A **child's** garden of verses; by Robert Louis Stevenson; illustrated by Brian Wildsmith. Star Bright Books 2008 80p il $19.95
Grades: K 1 2 3   **821**
1. Poetry -- By individual authors
ISBN 978-1-59572-057-3; 1-59572-057-X

LC 2007010085

A reissue of the edition published 1966 by Watts
Robert Louis Stevenson's classic poetry collection for children.

★ A **child's** garden of verses; pictures by Barbara McClintock. Harper 2011 80p il $17.99
Grades: K 1 2 3   **821**
1. Children's poetry 2. Poetry -- By individual authors
ISBN 0-06-028228-2; 978-0-06-028228-8

LC 2010007031

This is a newly illustrated edition of Stevenson's celebration of childhood first published in 1885. "Preschool, primary." (Horn Book)
"McClintock offers a complete edition of these old favorites in a format generous with white space and spot art as well as illustrative fantasies. . . . McClintock's blend of old and new should attract a new generation." Horn Book

821.008   English poetry -- Collections

★ **One** minute till bedtime; 60-second poems to send you off to sleep. (edited) by Kenn Nesbitt; illustrator: Christoph Niemann. Little, Brown & Co. 2016 168 p. color illustrations (ebook) $60; (hardcover) $19.99
Grades: PreK K 1 2 3 4   **821.008**
1. Children's poetry
ISBN 9780316318785; 0316341215; 9780316341219

LC 2015040416

In this collection of children's poetry, edited by Kenn Nesbitt and illustrated by Christoph Niemann, "it's time for tuck-in, and your little one wants just one more moment with you--so fill it with something that will feed the imagination, fuel a love of reading, and send them off to sleep in a snap. Reach for a one-minute poem!" (Publisher's note)
"These pithy poetic observations and Niemann's engaging illustrations prove at once antidote and anodyne for the sleep-averse child demanding just one more.... A dreamy collection of bedtime poems and witty illustrations that's anything but sleepy." Kirkus

★ **Poems** to learn by heart; [selected by] Caroline Kennedy; paintings by Jon J Muth. Disney-Hyperion 2012 192 p. (hardcover) $19.99
Grades: 2 3 4 5 6 7 8   **821.008**
1. Poetry -- Collections 2. English poetry 3. American poetry
ISBN 1423108051; 9781423108054

LC 2011022651

This anthology, by Caroline Kennedy, illustrated by John J. Muth, offers "more than a hundred poems that speak to all of us: the young and young at heart, readers new to poetry and devoted fans. These poems explore deep emotions, as well as ordinary experiences. They cover the range of human experience and imagination. Divided into sections about nature, sports, monsters and fairies, friendship and family." (Publisher's note)

822.3 Drama of Elizabethan period, 1558-1625

Coville, Bruce

William Shakespeare's A midsummer night's dream. Dial Bks. 1996 un $17.95; pa $7.99

Grades: 5 6 7 8 9   **822.3**

1. Poets 2. Authors 3. Audiobooks 4. Dramatists
ISBN 0-8037-1784-9; 0-14-250168-9 pa

LC 94-12600

A simplified prose retelling of Shakespeare's play about the strange events that take place in a forest inhabited by fairies who magically transform the romantic fate of two young couples.

"Coville introduces the story and also conveys something of the poetry and drama. Nolan's framed graphite and watercolor paintings express the dreaminess and absurdity of the play, and the pictures have a theatrical flair." Booklist

William Shakespeare's Twelfth night; retold by Bruce Coville; illustrated by Tim Raglin. Dial Bks. 2003 un il $16.99

Grades: 5 6 7 8 9   **822.3**

1. Poets 2. Authors 3. Dramatists
ISBN 0-8037-2318-0

LC 2001-28252

This "provides a short, prose version of Shakespeare's Twelfth Night. . . . Though simplified, the story is intact and bits of the original language are preserved. Large-scale ink drawings, warmed with tints of color and shaded with cross-hatching, clearly depict the action." Booklist

Nettleton, Pamela Hill

William Shakespeare; playwright and poet. by Pamela Hill Nettleton. Compass Point Books 2005 112p il map (Signature lives) lib bdg $30.60

Grades: 5 6 7 8   **822.3**

1. Poets 2. Authors 3. Dramatists
ISBN 0-7565-0816-9

LC 2004-23081

Profiles the life and work of William Shakespeare

"This biography is one of the best available for younger students. Nettleton supplements what little is actually known about the bard's life with detailed and accurate information about everyday life in England during the period, the theater, and publishing practices of the time. The text is enhanced by full-color illustrations and black-and-white reproductions." SLJ

Includes bibliographical references

Raum, Elizabeth

Twenty-first-century Shakespeare. Raintree 2011 32p il (Culture in action) lib bdg $29

Grades: 5 6 7 8   **822.3**

1. Poets 2. Authors 3. Dramatists 4. Dramatists, English 5. Authors, English
ISBN 978-1-4109-3920-3; 1-4109-3920-0

LC 2009050693

This "discusses modern adaptations of the Bard's classic works; teachers may find this a useful resource to help students see how Shakespeare remains a part of today's culture. [This volume is] quick, interesting, up-to-date . . . with plenty of supportive, captioned, full-color photographs. [It] also [provides] related project suggestions." SLJ

Includes glossary and bibliographical references

Stanley, Diane

★ **Bard** of Avon: the story of William Shakespeare; by Diane Stanley and Peter Vennema; illustrated by Diane Stanley. Morrow Junior Bks. 1992 un il hardcover o.p. pa $6.99

Grades: 4 5 6 7   **822.3**

1. Poets 2. Authors 3. Dramatists
ISBN 0-688-09108-3; 0-688-09109-1 lib bdg; 0-688-16294-0 pa

LC 90-46564

A brief biography of the world's most famous playwright, using only historically correct information

"A remarkably rounded picture of Shakespeare's life and the period in which he lived is presented . . . together with a thoughtful attempt to relate circumstances in his personal life to the content of his plays. . . . The text is splendidly supported by the illustrations, which are stylized, yet recognizable, and present a clear view of life in the late sixteenth century. A discerning, knowledgeable biography, rising far above the ordinary." Horn Book

Includes bibliographical references

Weiner, Miriam

Shakespeare's Seasons; created by Miriam Weiner; illustrations by Shannon Whitt; edited by Miriam Weiner & Shannon Whitt. Downtown Bookworks 2012 1 v. (unpaged) col. ill. (hardcover) $16.99

Grades: K 1 2 3   **822.3**

1. Seasons
ISBN 1935703579; 9781935703570

In this book by author Miriam Weiner, "tiny snippets of Shakespeare form the text for an illustrated almanac. . . . Readers see children on the beach flying kites and building sandcastles, watched by a woman with a book. The beachscape is visually anchored by the head of a woman with long hair, hinting that this may be a memory. . . . The longest quote is eight lines but most are four or less. . . . [Weiner incorporates] The Winter's Tale, The Tempest . . . [and] As You Like It." (Kirkus Reviews)

823 English fiction

Colbert, David

The **magical** worlds of Harry Potter; David Colbert. Updated and complete ed. Berkley Books 2008 xi, 209 p.p ill. (paperback) $14.00

Grades: 5 6 7 8   **823**

1. Authors 2. Novelists 3. Fantasy writers 4. Children's authors 5. Young adult authors 6. Fantasy fiction -- History and criticism
ISBN 0425223183; 9780425223185

LC 2008274096

First published 2001 in the United Kingdom; first United States edition 2002

Explores the sources and meanings of aspects of the literary world of Harry Potter within myths, legends, and history.

"Long after the enthusiasm for Harry and friends has abated, this small volume will serve as a resource to answer questions that may result from reading other stories in the genre." SLJ [review of 2002 edition]

Includes bibliographical references (p. 317-318) and index.

Wells-Cole, Catherine

Charles Dickens; England's most captivating storyteller. written by Catherine Wells-Cole; including extracts from the works of Charles Dickens. 1st U.S. ed. Candlewick/Templar Books 2011 28 p. ill., maps (some col.) (Historical notebook) (hardcover) $19.99

Grades: 7 8 9 10 11 12   **823**

1. Authors 2. Novelists 3. Authors, English 4. London (England) -- Social life and customs -- 19th century
ISBN 0763655678; 9780763655679

LC 2011013677

This book by Catherine Wells-Cole "provides a . . . glimpse into the life" of author Charles Dickens. "Like a scrapbook, the book includes excerpts from Dickens' personal letters, illustrations from his original books, family photos, and other images from the Victorian age.

. . . Double-page spreads focus on Dickens' childhood, family life, and fame. Other spreads focus on topics that influenced his writing, including schools, prisons, and workhouses." (Library Media Connection)

"In this scrapbook homage to Dickens, each page teems with images and reproductions, from letters to book excerpts to maps, all pertaining to a different area of Dickens's life and work. The topics range widely, skimming the surface of both the esteemed author's life and the subjects that interested him most. . . . The gorgeous, high-quality reproductions make a strong visual impact, and while the flaps, folds, and envelopes make readers work to uncover information, most will be quickly drawn into the hunt for more treasured tidbits about Dickens and his time." SLJ

828   English miscellaneous writings

Thomas, Dylan

★ A **child's** Christmas in Wales; illustrated by Chris Raschka. Candlewick Press 2004 un il $17.99
Grades: 2 3 4 5 6 7 8 9   **828**
    1. Christmas -- Wales
    ISBN 0-7636-2161-7

                         LC 2003-65274
The Welsh poet Dylan Thomas recalls the celebration of Christmas with his family and the feelings it evoked in him as a child.

"Applied to torn paper, the ink and watercolors spread through the fibers, freely forming soft outlines and shadows. The result is an intriguing contemporary take on a story that is by now part of the rather staid canon of Christmas classics." N Y Times Book Rev

831   German poetry

Rasmussen, Halfdan

★ A **little** bitty man and other poems for the very young; Halfdan Rasmussen; translated by Marilyn Nelson and Pamela Espeland; illustrated by Kevin Hawkes. Candlewick Press 2011 29 p.
Grades: PreK K 1   **831**
    1. Children's poetry, Danish -- Translations into English
    ISBN 9780763623791

                         LC 2009007515
"A charming collection of poems finds an American audience in a splendid translation. . . . Rasmussen (1915-2002) was a beloved Danish poet, known both for his human-rights writings as well as nonsense verse for children. A sweet compendium of the latter is translated here . . . and animated by Hawkes' dynamic, colorful acrylic-and-pencil renderings, effectively capturing the playfulness of Rasmussen's verse in both sound and image." Kirkus

839.31   Dutch literature

Schmidt, Annie M. G., 1911-1995

A **pond** full of ink; By Annie M. G. Schmidt; Illustrated by Sieb Posthuma; translated by David Colmer. Eerdmans Books for Young Readers 2014 34 p. $16
Grades: 1 2 3 4 5 6   **839.31**
    1. Children's poetry 2. Children's poetry, Dutch -- Translations into English
    ISBN 0802854338; 9780802854339

                         LC 2013030888
Originally published in Dutch with the title Een vijver vol inkt
This collection of children's poems, by Annie M. G. Schmidt, "tell the stories of such intriguing characters as three elderly otters who long

to go boating but find themselves biking instead, animated furniture that comes to life when no one is home, and Aunt Sue and Uncle Steve who nest up in a tree!" (Publisher's note)

"Fans of Shel Silverstein will love this collection of light, humorous poems that is full of fantastical characters. The titular pond features in the first selection about a prolific fairy-tale writer who refills his pen at the giant inkwell...The drawings and collage images are colorful and quirky, full of patterns and details that add depth. Illustrated spreads follow some of the poems, providing a closer look at the situation or characters introduced in the preceding poem. This book is a kid-pleasing must-have for any poetry collection." SLJ

841   French poetry

Cendrars, Blaise

★ **Shadow**; translated and illustrated by Marcia Brown from the French of Blaise Cendrars. Scribner 1982 un il $17; pa $6.99
Grades: 1 2 3   **841**
    1. French poetry 2. Africa -- Poetry 3. Shades and shadows -- Poetry 4. Poetry -- By individual authors
    ISBN 0-684-17226-7; 0-689-71875-6 pa

                         LC 81-9424
Original text first published in France
Awarded the Caldecott Medal, 1983

"Inspired by the exotic atmosphere and the dramatic possibilities of the text, Brown has choreographed a sequence of almost theatrical illustrations, placing human and animal figures—and their shadows—against brilliant, contrasting, always changing settings. Resplendent—yet controlled—in color, texture, and form, the work is an impressive, sophisticated example of the art of the picture book." Horn Book

843   French fiction

Gay, Marie-Louise

Princess Pistachio and the Pest; Marie-Louise Gay; translated by Jacob Homel. Pajama Press 2015 48 p. colour illustrations $10.95
Grades: K 1 2 3   **843**
    1. Adventure fiction 2. Sisters -- Juvenile fiction
    ISBN 1927485738; 9781927485736
In this children's book by Marie-Louise Gay "it's the first day of the summer holidays and Pistachio Shoelace has big plans. Plans that involve a compass, a cave, and a buried treasure. Plans that do not involve a troublemaking little sister wearing bunny ears and a Superman cape. Forced to take baby Penny to the park, Pistachio prepares for a dull day. But between fruit thefts, a witch's garden, and an angry park warden with a rulebook, a day with Penny is anything but boring." (Publisher's note)

"This early reader book continues the broad theme of sibling relationships that runs through Gay's work from the Stella and Sam picture books to the Travels with My Family middle-grade series." Booklist

861   Spanish poetry

Argueta, Jorge

★ A **movie** in my pillow; story by Jorge Argueta; illustrations by Elizabeth Gómez. Children's Bk. Press 2001 31p il $15.95
Grades: 3 4 5 6   **861**
    1. Immigrants -- Poetry 2. Hispanic Americans -- Poetry 3. Poetry

-- By individual authors 4. Bilingual books -- English-Spanish
ISBN 0-89239-165-0

LC 00-55582

"Gómez's rich and bright paintings fill every spread with . . . . joy and literal humor. . . . . An excellent addition to any poetry collection." SLJ

Lujan, Jorge

Colors! Colores! by Jorge Luján; illustrated by Piet Grobler; translated by John Oliver Simon and Rebecca Parfitt. Groundwood Books 2008 36p il $17.95

Grades: K 1 2   861

1. Color -- Poetry 2. Poetry -- By individual authors 3. Bilingual books -- English-Spanish
ISBN 978-0-88899-863-7; 0-88899-863-5

This is "a fully illustrated collection of 11 brief, free-verse poems linked by a common theme: colors. Each poem appears in English and then in Spanish on a double-page spread surrounded by white space and accompanied by an eye-catching watercolor painting. . . . . Gobler . . . interprets the verse through watercolor paintings that are as spare and fanciful as the writing." Booklist

Messengers of rain and other poems from Latin America; edited by Claudia M. Lee; illustrated by Rafael Yockteng; translations by Andrew C. Leone . . . [et al.] Douglas & McIntyre 2002 80p il $18.95

Grades: 3 4 5 6   861

1. Spanish poetry -- Collections
ISBN 0-88899-470-2

"The 64 poems from 19 countries include 20th-century classics and more recent selections, and represent women, indigenous writers, and widely published names such as Octavio Paz and Rafael Pombo. . . . Yockteng's fanciful watercolors head each section with a full-page spread, and spots brighten the pages between, here and there, without distracting from the poems." SLJ

861.64   Spanish poetry—1945-1999

Argueta, Jorge

Somos Como Las Nubes / We Are Like the Clouds; by Jorge Argueta, illustrated by Alfonso Ruano. Groundwood Books 2016 36 p. color illustrations $18.95

Grades: 4 5 6 7 8   861.64

1. Refugees 2. Central America
ISBN 1554988497; 9781554988495

This book, by Jorge Argueta, illustrated by Alfonso Ruano, asks "why are young people leaving their country to walk to the United States to seek a new, safe home? Over 100,000 such children have left Central America. . . . A refugee from El Salvador's war in the eighties, Argueta was born to explain the tragic choice confronting young Central Americans today who are saying goodbye to everything they know because they fear for their lives. This book brings home their situation." (Publisher's note)

"The scarcity of Latino children's and young-adult books that center on Central American experiences makes this poignant poetry collection extremely vital." Booklist

883   Classical Greek epic poetry and fiction

Landmann, Bimba

★ The **fate** of Achilles. Getty 2011 36p il $19.95

Grades: 4 5 6 7   883

1. Poets 2. Authors
ISBN 978-1-60606-085-8; 1-60606-085-6

"Landmann (The Incredible Voyage of Ulysses) continues her retelling of Homer's epics with this haunting version of the Iliad. Ghostly, Giacometti-style figures accompany the story of Achilles's life, from his baptism in the river Styx . . . to his departure for Troy, . . . the death of his dearest friend, . . . and his reconciliation with the father of the enemy he has slain. . . . Readers with the patience to sit through saga-length narratives will be fascinated by her prose, which moves easily through the sprawling epic without feeling ponderous or hurried. These kinds of retellings are few and far between, and hers are magic." Publ Wkly

★ The **incredible** voyage of Ulysses; text and illustrations by Bimba Landmann. Getty Publications 2010 un il $19.95

Grades: 4 5 6 7   883

1. Poets 2. Authors
ISBN 978-1-60606-012-4; 1-60606-012-0

"With narrative restraint and illustrative power, Landmann's . . . retelling of Homer's Odyssey follows Ulysses as he battles frightening creatures and endures the treachery of the gods while sailing home to Ithaca. . . . The paintings, worked with swift, bold strokes, combine the solemn stiffness of Greek statuary with the prophetic sweep of William Blake's imaginings." Publ Wkly

891   East Indo-European and Celtic literatures

Laird, Elizabeth

Shahnameh; the Persian book of kings. Retold by Elizabeth Laird; illustrated by Shirin Adl. Frances Lincoln Children's Books 2012 129 p.

Grades: 2 3 4 5   891

1. Epic poetry 2. Persian legends 3. Persian mythology
ISBN 1847802532; 9781847802538

This children's book, by Elizabeth Laird, illustrated by Shirin Adl, is a "collection of stories and myths from ancient Persia, written into an epic poem by . . . Firdousi in the 10th century. . . . The tales describe the beginning of the world, and include amazing birds who bring up orphaned Kings, . . . a feisty princess who goes to war incognito, and above all the great hero Rostam, who tragically kills his own son Sohrab, not knowing his identity." (Publisher's note)

895.6   Japanese literature

Kobayashi, Issa

★ **Today** and today; by Kobayashi Issa; pictures by G. Brian Karas. Scholastic Press 2007 un il $16.99

Grades: K 1 2 3   895.6

1. Haiku
ISBN 0-4395-9078-7

LC 2003-26684

"Karas uses the haiku of the eighteenth-century Japanese poet Issa to limn a gentle, understated tale of one family over a year. . . . The translations . . . are simply and clearly crafted. . . . Kara's art, using rice paper, paint, and pencil, is precise, enticing, and evocative." Booklist

897 Literatures of North American native languages

★ **Dancing** teepees: poems of American Indian youth; selected by Virginia Driving Hawk Sneve, with art by Stephen Gammell. Holiday House 1989 32p il $17.95; pa $8.95

Grades: 4 5 6   **897**

1. Native Americans -- Poetry

ISBN 0-8234-0724-1; 0-8234-0879-5 pa

LC 88-11075

An illustrated collection of poems from the oral tradition of Native Americans

This is an "eclectic collection, drawn from a variety of tribal traditions. Printed on heavy paper, the book is illustrated with a catalogue of marvelously rendered designs and motifs, ranging from those of the Northwest Coast to the intricate beadwork patterns of the Great Lakes and the zigzag geometric borders of Southwestern pottery." N Y Times Book Rev

900   HISTORY

904   Collected accounts of events

Blackwood, Gary L.

Enigmatic events. Marshall Cavendish Benchmark 2005 72p il (Unsolved history) lib bdg $29.93

Grades: 4 5 6 7   **904**

1. Disasters 2. Curiosities and wonders 3. History -- Miscellanea

ISBN 0-7614-1889-X

LC 2004-23755

Explores several events that have baffled scientists and historians for years, such as the demise of the dinosaurs, the "lost colony" of Roanoke, the sinking of the Main, and the Hindenberg disaster

This collection of "tidbits about lingering mysteries of the past . . . [offers] more substance than most. . . . [This offers] a full-page illustration opening each chapter; reproductions, many in color; and a generously spaced format." SLJ

Includes glossary and bibliographical references

Guiberson, Brenda Z.

★ **Disasters**; natural and man-made catastrophes through the centuries. Henry Holt and Company 2010 228p il $18.99

Grades: 5 6 7 8 9   **904**

1. Disasters 2. Natural disasters

ISBN 978-0-8050-8170-1; 0-8050-8170-4

LC 2009018908

"The subtitle provides an accurate outline of the contents of this lively treatment of disasters from smallpox to Hurricane Katrina. In each chapter, Guiberson outlines the sources of the disaster, the results, and means of obviating the problems that caused these tragedies. For example, the chapter on the Great Chicago Fire begins with the construction of the city over unstable marshland. . . . This kind of exhaustive background serves to create an understanding of the contributory issues and demonstrates possible preventive steps. Guiberson's compellingly written exegesis is equally good in the other nine chapters. Well-placed, black-and-white reproductions and photos extend the text. A perfect example of solid historical research coupled with engaging writing." SLJ

Includes bibliographical references

909   World history

Adams, Simon

★ The **Kingfisher** atlas of world history; a pictorial guide to the world's people and events, 10,000 BCE-present. Kingfisher 2010 181p il map $24.99

Grades: 4 5 6 7   **909**

1. World history 2. Historical geography

ISBN 978-0-7534-6388-8; 0-7534-6388-1

"This colorful and fact-packed book is not only informative but well organized. Sections cover 'The Ancient World,' 'The Medieval World,' 'Exploration and Empire,' and 'The Modern World,' and each section contains 15 or 16 thematic maps presented in chronological order. . . . It is very useful and entertaining as well as data-filled." Booklist

Kennedy, Susan

History year by year; written by Peter Chrisp, Joe Fullman, and Susan Kennedy; consultant, Philip Parker. DK Publishing 2013 320 p. col. ill., col. maps $24.99

Grades: 4 5 6 7 8 9   **909**

1. Anthropology 2. World history 3. Chronology, Historical

ISBN 1465414185; 9781465414182

LC 2012286068

Learning Magazine Teacher's Choice Awards for the Classroom (2015)

This book "presents the world through a detailed timeline, letting children follow the influences, patterns, and connections between historical events.Beginning with prehistory and running up to the Arab Spring, budding historians will learn about the history of humans across the world. Spreads highlight major historical eras . . . while quotations from primary and secondary sources alongside insight from experts give proper historical context." (Publisher's note)

"...Every few pages, a particular subtopic gets extra attention. For instance, in the "700 BCE-500 CE" section, there is a two-page discussion, replete with a color picture of Chinese emperor Qin Shi Huangdi's terra-cotta army. Features such as these make this an excellent browsing book, but students can still pull information from the text. A brief history of both the United States and Canada is appended. A good addition to most collections, both for the information it offers and for its appealing format." SLJ

Smithsonian history year by year

Knight, Margy Burns

Talking walls; discover your world. Margy Burns Knight; illustrated by Anne Sibley O'Brien. 2 edition Tilbury House 2014 color illustrations

Grades: 3 4 5   **909**

1. Walls 2. Human geography 3. World history

ISBN 9780884485766; 9780884483564

LC 2013025936

"[This book] introduces young readers to different cultures by exploring the stories of walls around the world and how they can separate or hold communities together." Publisher's Note

"Knight has found a powerful theme for introducing children to the world and its diverse cultures." Booklist

910   Geography and travel

Goodman, Joan E.

A **long** and uncertain journey: the 27,000 mile voyage of Vasco da Gama; by Joan Elizabeth Goodman; illustrated by Tom McNeely. Mikaya Press 2001 47p il map (Great explorers book) $22.95

Grades: 4 5 6 7   **910**
  1. Explorers
ISBN 0-9650493-7-X

LC 00-63795

"McNeely's full-page illustrations, which vibrate with life and action, lighten the format, and quotations from the diary of an anonymous sailor on the voyage add fascinating detail and vivid description. . . . A good resource for reports, but the book is also intelligently written and exciting," Booklist

Jenkins, Steve
  ★ **Hottest,** coldest, highest, deepest. Houghton Mifflin 1998 un il $16
Grades: K 1 2   **910**
  1. Geography
ISBN 0-395-89999-0

LC 97-53080

Describes some of the remarkable places on earth, including the hottest, coldest, windiest, snowiest, highest, and deepest

This book "uses striking colorful paper collage illustrations. . . . This eye-catching introduction to geography will find a lot of use in libraries and classrooms." SLJ

Includes bibliographical references

Jennings, Ken
  Maps and geography; by Ken Jennings; illustrated by TK. Little Simon, an imprint of Simon & Schuster Children's Pub. Division 2014 160 p. (The junior genius guide) $18.99
Grades: 3 4 5 6   **910**
  1. Maps 2. Geography
ISBN 144249848X; 9781442473287; 9781442498488

LC 2012050862

This book, by Ken Jennings and illustrated by Mike Lowery, is part of the "Junior Genius Guides" series. "With this . . . guide to maps and geography, you'll become an expert and wow your friends and teachers with clever facts. . . . With great illustrations, cool trivia, and fun quizzes to test your knowledge, this guide will have you on your way to whiz-kid status in no time!" (Publisher's note)

"The new line of Junior Genius Guide books kicks off with a stellar collection of facts about climate, national flags, maps, and more, all in an engaging, arch tone. Jeopardy! champ and author Jennings, making his first foray into books for children, arranges the trivia in chapters that lightly satirize a school-day schedule, including a lunch period offering an ingenious and easy recipe for an edible map, a craft project in art class, and an official certification exam before the dismissal bell... Lowery's black-and-white spot illustrations help explain concepts, such as cartographic projections, and add the overall levity, making this a successful nonfiction package as well as pure reading fun. Published simultaneously with the second in the series, Greek Mythology." Booklist

  Includes bibliographical references and index

  Other titles include:
  Greek Mythology
  Outer Space
  U.S. Presidents

Kerley, Barbara
  ★ The **world** is waiting for you; by Barbara Kerley. National Geographic 2013 48 p. (hardcover : alk. paper) $17.95
Grades: 1 2 3 4 5 6   **910**
  1. Vocational guidance 2. Discoveries in geography
ISBN 1426311141; 9781426311147; 9781426311154

LC 2012026526

This book, by Barbara Kerley, "shows kids a pathway from their current interests and talents to a future career or interest. And in so do-

ing, it also encourages adventure, exploration, and discovery, three core principles of National Geographic's mission. Selected photos make the connections compelling and the future real for kids, then rich back matter brings the message home with inspirational quotes from the real-life adventurers pictured in the images." (Publisher's note)

Richards, Jon
  Planet Earth; by Jon Richards and illustrated by Ed Simkins. Owl Kids 2013 32 p. $15.95
Grades: 3 4 5 6   **910**
  1. Graphic design 2. Signs and symbols
ISBN 1926973755; 9781926973753

In this book by Jon Richards "explores planet Earth using a wide variety of icons, graphics, and pictograms." Readers can "compare the tallest mountains from each continent, see the entire volume of water on the Earth poured into one glass, stack up Eiffel Towers and compare the height of the world's tallest waterfall." (Publisher's note)

Rockwell, Anne F.
  ★ **Our** earth; written and illustrated by Anne Rockwell. Harcourt Brace & Co. 1998 un il hardcover o.p. pa $6
Grades: K 1 2   **910**
  1. Geography
ISBN 0-15-201679-1; 0-15-202383-6 pa

LC 97-1247

A simple introduction to geography which explains such things as how the earth was shaped, how islands are born from volcanoes, and how gushing springs affect rivers

"The watercolor-and-gouache illustrations are very accessible. The pictures should provoke questions; parents and teachers can use the answers to provide kids with more information." Booklist

Rumford, James
  Traveling man: the journey of Ibn Battuta, 1325-1354; written, illustrated, and illuminated by James Rumford. Houghton Mifflin 2001 un il map hardcover o.p. pa $7.99
Grades: 3 4 5 6   **910**
  1. Travelers 2. Voyages and travels 3. Travel writers 4. Asia -- Description
ISBN 0-618-08366-9; 0-618-43233-7 pa

LC 00-57257

"Rumford's presentation is lavish and undeniably impressive. Ibn Battuta's route snakes across the spreads to create an extended map, with text boxes serving as stopping points along the way. Lush watercolor scenes, awash in gold highlights, are frequently borded by equally lush calligraphy quotes, rendered in Arabic, Persian, or Chinese." Bull Cent Child Books

  Includes glossary

Wojtanik, Andrew, 1989-
  The **National** Geographic Bee ultimate fact book; countries A to Z. Andrew Wojtanik. National Geographic 2012 384 p. maps (pbk.) $21.90; (reinforced library binding) $21.90
Grades: 5 6 7 8 9 10   **910**
  1. Atlases 2. Nations 3. Geography -- Encyclopedias
ISBN 1426309473; 1426309635; 9781426309472; 9781426309632

LC 2011282873

This book "provides statistical information for the world's 195 countries at a glance. The book starts off with a world map and full-page continental maps. Individual entries for countries are listed alphabetically... . A glossary explains terms that may be unfamiliar to students . . . . Each country entry includes a map with longitude and latitude and basic facts: continent, size, population, and capital." (Voice of Youth Advocates)

Includes bibliographical references (p. 382)

910.2   Geography--Miscellany; world travel guides

Ching, Jacqueline

Jobs in green travel and tourism. Rosen Pub. 2010 80p il (Green careers) lib bdg $30.60

Grades: 5 6 7 8   **910.2**

1. Tourist trade 2. Vocational guidance 3. Environmental movement 4. Environmental protection 5. Travel -- Environmental aspects

ISBN 978-1-4358-3571-9 lib bdg; 1-4358-3571-9 lib bdg

LC 2009016587

This "well-conceived [introduction focuses] on various jobs in [travel and tourism], the education and experience required, and expected earnings. The [book is] well organized, making it easy to gain an overview of the major aspects of the work. . . . [This book] will make [a] good [addition] to career collections. Photographs from the field and website and contact information for professional organizations add value." SLJ

Includes glossary and bibliographical references

910.3   Geography--Dictionaries, encyclopedias, concordances, gazetteers

Gifford, Clive

The **Kingfisher** geography encyclopedia; 2nd ed., rev. and updated ed.; Kingfisher 2011 487p il map $34.99

Grades: 4 5 6 7   **910.3**

1. Reference books 2. Geography -- Encyclopedias

ISBN 978-0-7534-6575-2; 0-7534-6575-2

Statistics, text, and color maps reveal the physical geography, peoples, politics, governments, languages, religions, and currencies of each nation of the world.

"The geographical descriptions are well written and include striking photos. The text is large and easy to read. . . . It is a great book to keep around the library for students to browse and dream about their next journey." Voice Youth Advocates

★ **Junior** worldmark encyclopedia of the nations; Timothy L. Gall, Susan Bevan Gall, and Derek M. Gleason, editors. 6th ed; Gale, Cengage Learning 2012 3200 p. 10v col. ill. (set : alk. paper) $677

Grades: 5 6 7 8   **910.3**

1. Geography -- Encyclopedias 2. World history -- Encyclopedias 3. Political science -- Encyclopedias 4. United Nations -- Encyclopedias 5. Political science -- Encyclopedias

ISBN 1414463138; 9781414463131; 9781414463148; 9781414463155; 9781414463162; 9781414463179; 9781414463186; 9781414463193; 9781414463209; 9781414463216; 9781414463223; 9781414463230; 9781414490861

LC 2011050016

First published 1996

This book series, edited by Timothy L. Gall, Susan Bevan Gall, and Derek M. Gleason, is a juvenile national encyclopedia. "Each volume . . . starts with a table of contents for the specific volume and a guide to country articles. Each country profile, organized alphabetically, begins with . . . capital, flag, anthem, monetary unit, weights and measures. . . . Thirty-five color-coded subheadings and their corresponding numbers, as well as geographical profiles, complete each section." (Booklist)

"This new edition contains 196 countries of the world and the Palestinian Territories. Color maps... photos, and charts enhance the overall attractiveness of this updated set... This well-written encyclopedia would be a valuable resource for elementary, middle-school, and public libraries." Booklist

Includes bibliographical references and index

910.4   Accounts of travel and facilities for travelers

Adams, Simon

Titanic; by Simon Adams. Updated edition DK 2014 72 p. color illustrations (DK Eyewitness) hbk $19.99; pbk $9.99

Grades: 4 5 6 7   **910.4**

1. Shipwrecks 2. Titanic (Steamship)

ISBN 1465420576; 1465420991; 9781465420992; 9781465420572

LC 2015302651

First published 1999

In this book about the Titanic, readers "discover the triumphs and tragedies of this 'unsinkable' luxury liner. Detailed images and text highlight all aspects of this fateful journey including how the ship was built and equipped, what kind of passengers and crew she carried, what facilities she offered onboard, how she struck an iceberg, why she sank so quickly, how many people were saved, and how many lives were lost." (Publisher's note)

Aronson, Marc

★ The **world** made new; why the Age of Exploration happened & how it changed the world. [by] Marc Aronson & John W. Glenn. National Geographic 2007 64p il map $17.95; lib bdg $27.90

Grades: 4 5 6 7   **910.4**

1. Explorers 2. Exploration

ISBN 978-0-7922-6454-5; 978-0-7922-6978-6 lib bdg

LC 2006022091

"This highly pictorial, readable overview provides significant depth of coverage. . . . The illustrations, most in full color, make ample and appropriate use of period prints as well as contemporary illustrations and photographs. The result is a visual feast that fleshes out the . . . remarkably evenhanded narrative." SLJ

Includes glossary and bibliographical references

Benoit, Peter

The **Titanic** disaster. Children's Press 2011 il (True book: disasters) lib bdg $26; pa $6.95

Grades: 3 4 5   **910.4**

1. Shipwrecks 2. Titanic (Steamship)

ISBN 978-0-531-20627-0 lib bdg; 0-531-20627-0 lib lib; 978-0-531-29026-2 pa; 0-531-29026-3 pa

LC 2010045932

This describes the sinking of the Titanic in 1912.

"Benoit provides unbiased information that is on target for the intended audience. . . . The photographs and reproductions enhance the [text]. . . . [This book is] well-conceived." SLJ

Includes bibliographical references

Bristow, David

★ **Sky** sailors; true stories of the balloon era. [by] David L. Bristow. Farrar Straus Giroux 2010 134p il $18.99

Grades: 4 5 6 7   **910.4**

1. Balloons

ISBN 978-0-374-37014-5; 0-374-37014-1

LC 2009037285

"This lively look at escapades of daring men—and a surprising number of women—who risked their lives flying in balloons will appeal to adventure, history and science buffs—and perhaps steampunk fans as well. Each of the nine chapters, which are chronologically arranged, focuses on an exciting story, starting with the first confirmed human balloon flight in 1783 . . . and ending with Dolly Shepherd, a young British woman in the early 1900s who parachuted out of balloons, hanging onto a trapeze. . . . Useful captions accompany many full-color illustrations of artwork and photographs." Kirkus

Includes bibliographical references

Brown, Don
★ **All** stations! distress! April 15, 1912, the day the Titanic sank. Roaring Brook Press 2008 un il (Actual times) $17.95
Grades: 2 3 4   **910.4**
1. Shipwrecks 2. Titanic (Steamship)
ISBN 978-1-59643-222-2; 1-59643-222-5

LC 2008-08934
"Don Brown recounts the complicated, compact last moments of the [Titanic's] only voyage. . . . The tale ends with something of the later lives of the survivors. . . . The glory of All Stations! Distress! is in Brown's moody watercolors done with a brush dipped in stardust and frozen mist." Horn Book

Cerullo, Mary M.
★ **Shipwrecks**; exploring sunken cities beneath the sea. [by] Mary M. Cerullo. Dutton Children's Books 2009 64p il $18.99
Grades: 5 6 7 8   **910.4**
1. Shipwrecks 2. Portland (Steamer) 3. Henrietta Marie (Ship)
ISBN 978-0-525-47968-0; 0-525-47968-6

LC 2008-48967
This focuses "on two wrecks: the Henrietta Marie, sunk in 1700 near the Florida Keys, and the Portland, sunk in 1898 off the coast of Massachusetts. The book makes the convincing case that these wrecks are important not only for historical reasons but also for the underwater ecosystems their structures now host. . . . This delivers both education and shivers." Booklist

Clifford, Barry
Real pirates; the untold story of the Whydah from slave ship to pirate ship. by Barry Clifford and Kenneth J. Kinkor with Sharon Simpson; photography by Kenneth Garrett. National Geographic 2008 175p il map $16.95
Grades: 4 5 6 7   **910.4**
1. Pirates 2. Archeology 3. Shipwrecks 4. Slave trade 5. Whidah (Ship) 6. Cape Cod (Mass.)
ISBN 978-1-4263-0279-4; 1-4263-0279-7

LC 2008299778
"Clifford, an underwater archaeological explorer, used research and the artifacts recovered from the Whydah to tell the story of its life as a slave galley and pirate ship. In the process, he dispels many myths about buccaneers. . . . Photographs of artifacts . . . and the recovery crew at work combine with large visually appealing paintings of dramatic battle, storm, and courtroom scenes. . . . The book is a fascinating blend of history, ocean-diving recovery, and archaeology, and demonstrates archaeology in action and the role artifacts play in informing us about the past." SLJ

Includes bibliographical references

Denenberg, Barry
★ **Titanic** sinks! Viking 2011 72p il $19.99
Grades: 5 6 7 8   **910.4**
1. Shipwrecks 2. Titanic (Steamship)
ISBN 0670012432; 9780670012435

LC 2011012040
This is a "gripping recounting of the Titanic's doomed maiden voyage, chronicled in the tabloid-style pages of a fictional magazine. . . . Melding fact and fiction, the book compiles dramatic headlines, articles that range from news bulletins about the building of the ship to a chatty tour of its lavish interior, and an array of stunning period photographs." Publ Wkly

Emery, William
Kodoku; William Emery; illustrations by Hanae Rivera. Heyday 2012 32 p. col. ill. (hardcover : alk. paper) $16.95
Grades: 4 5 6   **910.4**
1. Ocean travel -- Fiction 2. Voyages around the world -- Fiction 3. Mermaid (Boat) 4. Voyages around the world
ISBN 1597141739; 9781597141734

LC 2011032355
This children's picture book by William Emery presents a "recreation of the voyage of Kenichi Horie, the first (recorded) sailor to cross the Pacific solo. . . . Emery places the young mariner aboard a custom-built sailboat and sends him out for intense mid-ocean encounters with a typhoon, whales, sharks, jellyfish and a towering passenger ship before journey's end beneath the Golden Gate Bridge." (Kirkus Reviews)

Gibbons, Gail
★ **Sunken** treasure. Crowell 1988 32p il hardcover o.p. pa $6.95
Grades: K 1 2 3   **910.4**
1. Shipwrecks 2. Buried treasure 3. Nuestra Señora de Atocha (Ship)
ISBN 0-690-04736-3 lib bdg; 0-06-446097-5 pa

LC 87-30114
"Gibbons concentrates on the ancient Spanish galleon, the Atocha, which sank off the coast of Florida in 1662, describing under labeled headings the sinking, the search, the find, recording, salvage, restoration and preservation, cataloguing, and eventual distribution of the treasure. . . . A handsomely designed book, well organized, and easily accessible to younger readers." Horn Book

Grove, Tim
First flight around the world; the adventures of the American fliers who won the race. by Tim Grove. Abrams Books for Young Readers, in assoc. w/Smithsonian Ntl. Air & Space Museum 2015 96 p. col. ill.; maps (hardcover) $21.95
Grades: 5 6 7 8   **910.4**
1. Aeronautics -- Flights 2. Voyages around the world 3. World records 4. Flights around the world 5. United States. Army. Air Corps
ISBN 1419714821; 9781419714825

LC 2014024665
YALSA Award for Excellence in Nonfiction for Young Adults: Shortlist (2016)
This children's book, by Tim Grove, "documents the exciting journey of four American planes--the Chicago, Boston, New Orleans, and Seattle--and their crews on a race around the world. The trip held many challenges: extreme weather, tricky navigation, unfamiliar cultures, fragile planes, and few airfields. The world fliers risked their lives for the sake of national pride." (Publisher's note)
"This gripping, well-designed title details the United States' 1924 successful attempt to become the first nation to circumnavigate the globe by flight. . . . Offering a look at a lesser-known historical event, this

beautiful, well-written book is an essential addition for all collections."
SLJ

Includes bibliographical references

Hagglund, Betty

Epic treks. Kingfisher 2011 64p il (Epic adventure) $19.99

Grades: 5 6 7 8 **910.4**

1. Explorers 2. Voyages and travels

ISBN 978-0-7534-6668-1; 0-7534-6668-6

LC 2011041638

"The graphics will grab readers in [this] exciting, extra-large-size [title] . . . packed with high-quality color photos on every double-page spread. Just as gripping are the narratives, captions, and technical details of exploration, adventure, and survival. . . . Epic Treks covers Lewis and Clark, Livingston and Stanley, Burk and Wells, and Amundsen and Scott, each journey an exciting adventure filled with details about what they endured and what they found, as well as their failures and short-comings." Booklist

Includes glossary

Hopkinson, Deborah

★ Titanic; voices from the disaster. by Deborah Hopkinson. Scholastic Press 2012 289 p. (hardcover) $17.99

Grades: 5 6 7 8 **910.4**

1. Titanic (Steamship) 2. Shipwrecks

ISBN 0545116740; 9780545116749

LC 2011006695

YALSA Award for Excellence in Nonfiction for Young Adults Finalist (2013)

Robert F. Sibert Honor Book (2013)

In this book about the sinking of the Titanic, author Deborah "Hopkinson begins with a description of the ship . . . and introduces some of the passengers who embarked on its maiden voyage. The narrative shifts . . . to the disaster itself with a litany of things gone wrong. . . . [M]emoirs . . . are interlaced throughout the text, as survivors testified . . . on the relative chaos or calm, heroism or cowardice, of passengers and crew." (Bulletin of the Center for Children's Books)

Includes bibliographical references

Hunter, Nick

Pirate treasure; by Nick Hunter. Raintree 2013 48 p. (hb) $29.33

Grades: 5 6 7 8 **910.4**

1. Pirates 2. Buried treasure 3. Treasure troves

ISBN 1410949532; 9781410949530; 9781410949608

LC 2012012890

This book, by Nick Hunter, "examines the hunt for treasures lost or hidden by pirates, and examines whether any of the legends of buried treasure could really be true. Part of the Treasure Hunters series, 'Pirate Treasure' offers a crosscurricular mix of science & technology and history & civilizations. Pirate treasures covered in the book include those of the famous Blackbeard and Captain Kidd, the pirate shipwreck the Whydah, and the mysterious Oak Island Money Pit." (Publisher's note)

Includes bibliographical references and index

Jenson-Elliott, Cindy

Life under the pirate code; by Cindy Jenson-Elliott. Capstone Press 2013 32 p. (Blazers. Pirates) (library binding) $25.99

Grades: 2 3 4 **910.4**

1. Pirates

ISBN 1429686111; 1620652013; 9781429686112; 9781620652015

LC 2011048907

In this book, by Cindy Jenson-Elliott, readers will "look inside to learn about the pirate code and how it guided everyday life on a pirate

ship. Pirates were thieves and murderers. But even these criminals had to follow certain rules. And if they broke the rules, they faced severe punishments." (Publisher's note)

Includes bibliographical references (p. 31) and index

The **most** famous pirates; by Cindy Jenson-Elliott. Capstone Press 2012 32 p. (library binding) $25.99

Grades: 2 3 4 **910.4**

1. Pirates

ISBN; 142968609X; 9781429686099

LC 2011048910

This book, by Cindy Jenson-Elliott, provides an introduction to pirate life for young readers. Pages contain "information about tools, weaponry, the pirate code, life on a ship, and famous buccaneers. The books are . . . organized into short chapters, and some paragraphs have their own simple subtitles." Well-known pirates discussed include Frances Drake, William Kidd, and Blackbeard. (School Library Journa)

Includes bibliographical references (p. 31) and index

Pirate ships ahoy! by Cindy Jenson-Elliott. Capstone Press 2013 32 p. (library binding) $25.99

Grades: 2 3 4 **910.4**

1. Ships 2. Pirates

ISBN 1429686103; 9781429686105

LC 2011048909

This book, by Cindy Jenson-Elliott, examines "how pirates lived, worked, and fought on their ships, [noting that] a ship was more to a pirate than just a place to make a living. Ships often provided more freedom than pirates could get in most places." (Publisher's note)

Includes bibliographical references and index

Pirates' tools for life at sea; by Cindy Jenson-Elliott. Capstone Press 2012 32 p. (library binding) $25.99

Grades: 2 3 4 **910.4**

1. Pirates 2. Weapons

ISBN 142968612X; 9781429686129; 9781620652046

LC 2011048906

This book, by Cindy Jenson-Elliott, looks at "pirates most important gear. From swords and cannons to maps and carpentry tools . . . weapons and tools were as important to pirates as the ships they sailed on. [It examines how] to succeed at sea, pirates kept their gear clean and ready for action." (Publisher's note)

Includes bibliographical references (p. 31) and index

Lewin, Ted

How to babysit a leopard; and other true stories from our travels across six continents. Ted Lewin and Betsy Lewin. Roaring Brook Press 2015 144 p. color illustrations (A Neal Porter book) (hardback) $22.99

Grades: 4 5 6 7 8 9 **910.4**

1. Illustrators 2. Human-animal relationship 3. Travel 4. Voyages and travels

ISBN 1596436166; 9781596436169

LC 2014038732

This book by Ted Lewin and Betsy Lewin, "a husband-and-wife team, seasoned travelers, artists, and children's-book creators, offer[s] readers a selection of highlights from 40 years of careful observation of the natural and human worlds in places near and far. There are scary encounters with lions, elephants, snakes, leeches, and a sharp-billed macaw-not to mention soldiers." (Kirkus)

"This thrilling collection of travel adventures from this celebrated husband-and-wife, author-illustrator team will appeal to a variety of readers, from aspiring biologists and globe-trotters to those who prefer traipsing the face of the planet from a comfortable chair. Featuring short, conversational pieces, and spectacular photos and vibrant artwork laid out like a journal, this enticing title describes the duo's experiences all over the world. . . . A captivating tribute to this glorious orb we call home." SLJ

Marschall, Ken

★ **Inside** the Titanic; illustrated by Ken Marschall; text by Hugh Brewster. Little, Brown 1997 32p il $19.95

Grades: 4 5 6 7 **910.4**

1. Shipwrecks 2. Titanic (Steamship)

ISBN 0-316-55716-1

LC 97-382

"Color cutaway paintings of the Titanic in this oversize book allow readers to view every deck as they follow two 12-year-old boys exploring the vessel, and to see how the liner struck the iceberg and sank." Booklist

Includes glossary and bibliographical references

McPherson, Stephanie Sammartino

★ **Iceberg** right ahead! the tragedy of the Titanic. Twenty-First Century Books 2011 112p il lib bdg $33.26

Grades: 4 5 6 7 8 **910.4**

1. Shipwrecks 2. Titanic (Steamship)

ISBN 9780761367567

LC 2011002352

"With innumerable books, movies, documentaries, novels, and biographies all telling versions of the Titanic story, it would seem that there is little more to learn, yet by providing more details and some of the most up-to-date research, McPherson's compelling, thoughtful narrative proves otherwise. . . . The layout includes plenty of period photographs, diagrams, artwork, and sidebars with interesting tangential tidbits, making for a thorough resource. . . . A comprehensive, well-written, thoroughly researched title." SLJ

Includes bibliographical references

Mundy, Robyn

Epic voyages. Kingfisher 2011 64p il (Epic adventure) $19.99

Grades: 5 6 7 8 **910.4**

1. Explorers

ISBN 978-0-7534-6574-5; 0-7534-6574-4

"The graphics will grab readers in [this] exciting, extra-large-size [title] . . . packed with high-quality color photos on every double-page spread. Just as gripping are the narratives, captions, and technical details of exploration, adventure, and survival. . . . [This] book covers Magellan, Cook, Shackleton, Heyedahl and also Chichester, who, in 1966, sailed alone around the world." Booklist

Riggs, Kate

Pirates. Creative Education 2010 24p il (Great warriors) $24.25; pa $8.99

Grades: K 1 2 **910.4**

1. Pirates

ISBN 978-1-60818-002-8; 1-60818-002-6; 978-0-89812-573-3 pa; 0-89812-573-1 pa

LC 2010019611

A introduction to the roving warriors known as pirates, including their history, lifestyle, weapons, and how they remain a part of today's culture by their continued existence.

This title makes pirates "accessible to students just beginning to read on their own. The text and design of the [book is] spare, and vocabulary words are introduced unobtrusively. . . . The concepts are simple, but introduced without oversimplification that might lead to misunderstandings. [This is an] excellent [introduction] and fun to read aloud." SLJ

Includes glossary and bibliographical references

Ross, Stewart

★ **Into** the unknown; how great explorers found their way by land, sea, and air. illustrated by Stephen Biesty. Candlewick Press 2011 un il map $19.99

Grades: 4 5 6 7 **910.4**

1. Explorers 2. Discoveries in geography

ISBN 978-0-7636-4948-7; 0-7636-4948-1

LC 2010038720

Boston Globe-Horn Book Honor: Nonfiction (2011)

"Biesty's trademark amusing, informatively detailed illustrations are a highlight of this entertaining examination of several voyages of exploration. . . . Chapters cover an impressive range of exploration. In addition to the usual suspects, they include a 340 B.C.E. Greek voyage to the Arctic Circle; Chinese Admiral Zheng He to India; [and] David Livingston and Mary Kingsley into the African interior. . . . Each chapter includes a fold-out section of illustrations with a map of the journey and a cross-section of the method of transportation. . . . An altogether agreeable package for armchair explorers." Kirkus

Sherman, Casey

The **finest** hours; the true story of a heroic sea rescue. Michael J. Tougias and Casey Sherman. Christy Ottaviano Books 2014 176 p. illustrations (hardback) $17.99

Grades: 4 5 6 7 8 **910.4**

1. Shipwrecks 2. Survival after airplane accidents, shipwrecks, etc. 3. CG36500 (Lifeboat) 4. Pendleton (Tanker) 5. Shipwrecks -- Massachusetts 6. Shipwreck survival -- History

ISBN 0805097643; 9780805097641; 9781250044235

LC 2013030661

This book by Michael J. Tougias and Casey Sherman "tells the story of a harrowing Coast Guard rescue when four men in a tiny lifeboat overcame insurmountable odds and saved more than 30 stranded sailors." In this book, the events of the February 18, 1952 wreck of two oil tankers near Cape Cod are adapted for middle-grade readers. (Publisher's note)

"The accounts of each rescue's logistics--for example, sailors trying to time their leaps from their destroyed tanker to the rescue boat amid rocking waves--are nail-biting, and they are relayed by the authors with an effectively sober, just-the-facts terseness." Booklist

Includes bibliographical references

910.92 Geographers, travelers, explorers regardless of country of origin

Fritz, Jean

Around the world in a hundred years; from Henry the Navigator to Magellan. illustrated by Anthony Bacon Venti. Putnam 1994 128p il map hardcover o.p. pa $8.99

Grades: 4 5 6 7 **910.92**

1. Princes 2. Explorers 3. Colonial administrators

ISBN 0-399-22527-7; 0-698-11638-0 pa

LC 92-27042

"Fritz examines the voyages of ten explorers, acknowledging that their contributions, though deserving of recognition, were dearly bought. Opening and closing chapters summarize the fourteenth-century world view and indicate later expansion of geographic understanding. As always, Fritz tempers scholarship with humor in this brief volume—illustrated with drawings in pencil—which reads like an adventure story." Horn Book Guide

Includes bibliographical references

911   Historical geography

Chrisp, Peter

    Atlas of ancient worlds; author, Peter Chrisp; consultant, Philip Parker. DK Pub. 2009 96p il map $21.99

Grades: 4 5 6 7 8   **911**

    1. Reference books 2. Historical atlases 3. Ancient civilization

    ISBN 978-0-7566-4512-0; 0-7566-4512-3

    This atlas consists "of maps and illustrations accompanied by extensive captions outlining the cultures of many civilizations. Each section begins with a map of a continent and a table of contents detailing which peoples will be discussed in it. Each civilization is covered in a chapter spread that includes a small map of the extent of each empire and many photos, pictures, and captioned drawings. . . . The accompanying clip art CD contains images of many of the artifacts as well as of the maps found in the book. . . . This atlas offers a wonderful introduction to [ancient civilizations] as well as solid geography basics." SLJ

    Includes glossary

Leacock, Elspeth

    ★ **Places** in time; a new atlas of American history. [by] Elspeth Leacock and Susan Buckley; illustrations by Randy Jones. Houghton Mifflin 2001 48p il $15; pa $6.95

Grades: 4 5 6 7   **911**

    1. Reference books 2. United States -- Historical geography

    ISBN 0-395-97958-7; 0-618-3113-0 pa

                             LC 00-59741

    This book presents "20 sites in American history at the moment of their historical significance, beginning in 1200 (Cahokia) and ending in 1953. Places and times include New Plymouth—1627, Charlestown—1739, Saratoga—1777, Philadelphia—1787, Abilene—1871, and Chicago—1893. The detailed cutaway views of homes, forts, and mills are impressive enough to keep readers looking again and again. These fascinating slices of life stir the imagination and lead to questions and further research." SLJ

    Includes bibliographical references

Todras, Ellen H.

    Explorers, trappers, and pioneers; by Ellen H. Todras. Kingfisher 2012 32 p. ill. (All About America) (paperback) $9.99

Grades: 4 5 6   **911**

    1. America -- Exploration 2. Frontier and pioneer life -- United States

    ISBN 0753465159; 9780753465158

    This book by Ellen H. Todras is part of the "All About America" series. It "begins with the Vikings landing in Newfoundland 1,000 years ago and concludes with the Oklahoma Land Rush in 1889." It "offers 13 highly illustrated double-page spreads that present topics using a few paragraphs of information, related text boxes, and several color illustrations and five or more captioned illustrations." (Booklist)

912   Graphic representations of surface of earth and of extraterrestrial worlds

    ★ **Atlas** of the World; [prepared by National Geographic Maps for the Book Division] Random House Inc 2014 448 p. 1 atlas; color maps; color ils $195

Grades: 4 5 6 7 8 9 10 11 12 Adult   **912**

    1. Atlases

    ISBN 1426213549; 9781426213540

                        LC 200445002

    This book presents "illustrated maps and informational graphics [that] chart rapidly changing global themes such as population trends, urbanization, health and longevity, human migration, climate change, communications, and the world economy. The core of any atlas is the reference mapping section and the 10th Edition boasts the largest and most comprehensive collection of political maps ever published by National Geographic." (Publisher's note)

    ★ **Beginner's** United States atlas; it's your country, be a part of it! National Geographic 2009 128p il map $18.95

Grades: 1 2 3 4   **912**

    1. Atlases 2. Reference books 3. United States -- Maps

    ISBN 978-1-4263-0512-2; 1-4263-0512-5

    Provides information about the United States, including state flags, birds, flowers, and capitals, as well as key points about the water, people, and physical features of each state

Boyer, Crispin

    National Geographic kids ultimate U.S. road trip atlas; maps, games, activities, and more for hours of backseat fun. by Crispin Boyer. 1st ed. National Geographic 2012 128 p. col. ill., col. maps (pbk. : alk. paper) $5.99; (lib. bdg. : alk. paper) $14.90

Grades: 4 5 6   **912**

    1. Atlases 2. Road maps 3. United States -- Historical geography -- Maps 4. United States -- Maps 5. United States -- Description and travel 6. Recreation areas -- United States -- Maps 7. Outdoor recreation -- United States -- Maps

    ISBN 1426309333; 1426309341; 9781426309335; 9781426309342

                    LC 2011034647

    This book, by author Crispin Boyer, "includes . . . road maps of each state and Washington, D.C., and a map of the United States. State symbols, cool things to do, boredom busters, fun facts, wacky roadside attractions, and games accompany the maps. . . . In the back matter [there is] a comprehensive index . . . for kids to look up names and places." (Publisher's note)

    Includes bibliographical references and index.

Crane, Nick

    Barefoot Books world atlas. Barefoot Books 2011 56p

Grades: 3 4 5   **912**

    1. Maps 2. Atlases 3. Geography

    ISBN 1-84686-333-3; 978-1-84686-333-2

    "This fresh and informative atlas offers engaging, fact-filled overviews of Earth's oceans and continents. Mini-books, flaps, and sidebars address topics ranging from 'People and Places' to 'Transport.' Dean's maps are crowded with warmly illustrated people, animals, places, and objects that represent particular areas of the world. . . . With its emphasis on sustainability, interconnectedness, and diversity, the book offers young armchair travelers and globe-trotters much to discover. Includes a removable world map. An app is also available." Publ Wkly

Leedy, Loreen

    ★ **Mapping** Penny's world. Holt & Co. 2000 un il map $17; pa $7.95

Grades: 1 2 3   **912**

    1. Maps

    ISBN 0-8050-6178-9; 0-8050-7262-4 pa

                    LC 99-48327

    After learning about maps in school, Lisa maps all the favorite places of her dog Penny

    "The concepts are clear, and the digital-painting and photo-collage illustrations are uncluttered and ably clarify the text." SLJ

★ **National** Geographic Kids beginner's world atlas; 3rd ed.; National Geographic 2011 il map $27.90

    Grades: K 1 2 3   **912**

    1. Atlases 2. Reference books

    ISBN 978-1-4263-0839-0; 1-4263-0839-6

First published 1999 with title: National Geographic beginner's world atlas

This is an "eye-catching atlas for the child who is ready to learn about the world beyond his or her own community. Enticing panoramic photographs introduce each continent, and easy-to-decipher maps make this oversize volume one that will fascinate inquisitive young children given to browsing." Booklist

★ **National** Geographic United States atlas for young explorers; 3rd ed.; National Geographic 2008 175p il map $24.95

    Grades: 4 5 6 7   **912**

    1. Atlases 2. Reference books 3. United States -- Maps

    ISBN 978-1-4263-0255-8; 1-4263-0255-X

First published 1999

This atlas offers maps of each of the states in the United States, divided into five geographical regions, plus U.S. territories. Each state map indicates physical features such as mountains and rivers, national forests, cities, major interstate roads, and industries, and is accompanied by color photos and facts about the state. An introductory section describes how to use the companion web site for more information, maps of the United States biomes, climates, natural hazards, political states, population, ethnic diversity, and energy use.

★ **National** Geographic world atlas for young explorers; 3rd ed.; National Geographic 2007 191p il map $24.95

    Grades: 3 4 5 6   **912**

    1. Atlases 2. Reference books

    ISBN 978-1-4263-0088-2

First published 1998

This atlas includes photographs taken from space, political and physical maps, flags and statistics, and links to additional images and information on a companion website.

Parker, Victoria

    How far is far? comparing geographical distances. [by] Vic Parker. Heinemann Library 2011 32p il (Measuring and comparing) lib bdg $26; pa $7.99

    Grades: 2 3 4   **912**

    1. Maps 2. Measurement

    ISBN 978-1-4329-3956-4 lib bdg; 1-4329-3956-4 lib bdg; 978-1-4329-3964-9 pa; 1-4329-3964-5 pa

                              LC 2010000926

This "contains vivid photographs, charts, and diagrams with captions, explanations, and examples. Questions are posed throughout . . . to entice young learners to 'stop and think' or continue reading for more information. . . . [This] would make an excellent addition to any classroom library." Libr Media Connect

    Includes glossary and bibliographical references

Rand McNally Goodes World Atlas; edited by Howard Veregin. Rand McNally 2009 400 p. $45

    Grades: 4 5 6 7 8 9 10 11 12 Adult   **912**

    1. Maps 2. Atlases

    ISBN 0528877542; 9780528877544

This book, edited by Howard Veregin, "features over 250 pages of maps, from definitive physical and political maps to important thematic maps that illustrate the spatial aspects of many important topics. [It] includes 160 pages of new, digitally produced reference maps, as well as new thematic maps on global climate change, sea level rise, CO2 emissions, polar ice fluctuations, deforestation, extreme weather events, infectious diseases, water resources, and energy production." (Publisher's note)

Student atlas; Dorling Kindersley, Inc. 6th ed. DK Pub. 2013 176 p. ill. (hardcover) $14.99

    Grades: 5 6 7 8   **912**

    1. Atlases 2. Geography

    ISBN 0756663199; 9780756663193

This book from DK Publishing is part of the Student Atlas series. It is a "single-volume guide to the nations of the world. [It's] fully revised and updated, and packed with clear, detailed maps highlighting landscape, industry, land use, population, climate and environmental issues." (Publisher's note)

912.01 Philosophy and theory

Waldron, Melanie

    How to read a map; Melanie Waldron. Capstone Raintree 2013 32 p. (Let's get mapping!) (pb) $7.99

    Grades: 2 3 4 5   **912.01**

    1. Maps 2. Atlases 3. Map reading

    ISBN 1410949060; 9781410948991; 9781410949066

                              LC 2012008416

Author Melanie Waldron's book offers a guide to map-reading. "Maps are essential tools for understanding the world around us. Learning to read maps - both printed and online - is a core skill that forms the basis of social studies. This book explores the different types of features used on maps, explaining what they can show us and how to make sense of them." (Publisher's note)

    Includes bibliographical references and index

915 Geography of and travel in Asia

Rockett, Paul

    Mapping Europe; Paul Rockett. Crabtree Publishing Co. 2017 32 p. (reinforced library binding) $27.60; (pbk.) $8.95

    Grades: 3 4 5 6   **915**

    1. Europe 2. Europe -- Geography 3. Cartography -- Europe 4. Europe -- Description and travel

    ISBN 9780778726159; 9780778726210

                              LC 2016016675

"These illustrated atlases use a variety of map types to depict each continent's physical, natural, cultural, and economic geography. Books open with detailed location information, followed by a selection of physical, political, historical, climate, and other informational maps that feature human and animal populations, resources, land uses, and recreational and economic activity. Maps are supplemented with trivia about animals, places, and history." (School Library Journal)

916 Geography of and travel in Africa

Bodden, Valerie

    To the heart of Africa; by Valerie Bodden. Creative Education 2011 48 p. col. ill. (Great Expeditions) (library) $34.25

    Grades: 5 6 7 8   **916**

    1. Exploration 2. Africa -- Exploration 3. Explorers -- Scotland -- Biography 4. Explorers -- Africa, Southern -- Biography 5. Africa, Sub-Saharan -- Discovery and exploration 6. Missionaries,

Medical -- Africa, Southern -- Biography
ISBN 1608180662; 9781608180660

LC 2010033414

This book by Valerie Bodden is part of the Great Expeditions series and looks at expeditions into Africa. "Bodden includes brief biographies of major people involved in each expedition, interspersed with the text. There are also numerous photographs or reproductions of paintings and woodcuts from the time of the expeditions." (Library Media Connection)

Includes bibliographical references (p. 46-47) and index.

917   Geography of and travel in North America

Butts, Edward

Shipwrecks, monsters, and mysteries of the Great Lakes; [by] Ed Butts. Tundra Books 2010 80p il pa $14.95

Grades: 4 5 6 7   917

1. Shipwrecks 2. Great Lakes

ISBN 978-1-77049-206-6 pa; 1-77049-206-2 pa

"In 1679, a French ship called the Griffon left Green Bay on Lake Michigan, bound for Niagara with a cargo of furs. Neither the Griffon nor the five-man crew was ever seen again. . . . Its disappearance was probably the result of the first shipwreck on a Great Lake. Since then, more than six thousand vessels, large and small, have met tragic ends. . . . Shoals and reefs, uncharted rocks, and sandbars could snare a ship or rip open a hull. Unpredictable winds could capsize a vessel at any moment. . . . The wreckage of ships and the bones of the people who sail them litter the bottoms of the five lakes: Ontario, Erie, Huron, Michigan, and Superior. Ed Butts has gathered stories and lake lore in this [volume]." (Publisher's note) "Ages nine to twelve." (Quill Quire)

Clark, Diane C.

★ A **kid's** guide to Washington, D.C. [written by Diane C. Clark; illustrations and maps by Richard E. Brown] rev and updated ed.; Harcourt, Inc. 2008 154p il map pa $14

Grades: 3 4 5 6   917

1. Puzzles 2. Washington (D.C.) 3. Children -- Travel

ISBN 978-0-15-206125-8 pa; 0-15-206125-8 pa

LC 2007-015509

First published 1989

"Brimming with useful information in both text and sidebars, this sturdy, large-format guidebook covers a broad array of topics, everything from a brief history of Washington, D.C., to practical advice on how to get around the city. . . . The extensive appendix now lists 128 places to see and gives their locations in the city and online. Shades of blue and red add color to the pages, which usually include graphic elements such as photos and line drawings. An attractive, practical guide for young visitors to Washington." Booklist

Koehler-Pentacoff, Elizabeth

Jackson and Bud's bumpy ride; America's first cross-country automobile trip. by Elizabeth Koehler-Pentacoff; illustrated by Wes Hargis. Millbrook Press 2009 un il

Grades: 1 2 3   917

1. Physicians 2. Automobile travel 3. United States -- Description and travel

ISBN 0822578859; 9780822578857

LC 2008012752

An account of the first cross-country automobile trip in the United States made in 1903 by Dr. Horatio Jackson, mechanic Sewall J. Crocker, and bulldog Bud

"Short sentences and readable prose capture much of the triumph and challenge of the 63-day trip. . . . The animated, cartoon illustrations are lighthearted and detailed, and add much to the narrative." SLJ

Includes bibliographical references

Rubbino, Salvatore

★ A **walk** in New York. Candlewick Press 2009 37p il map $16.99

Grades: PreK K 1 2 3 4   917

1. New York (N.Y.) -- Description and travel

ISBN 978-0-7636-3855-9; 0-7636-3855-2

LC 2008-20787

This follows a wide-eyed boy and his dad on their walk around Manhattan, from Grand Central Terminal to the top of the Empire State Building, from Greenwich Village to the Statute of Liberty. Includes lots of facts and trivia and a gatefold of the Empire State Building.

"The book's large trim size and the illustrator's perspective provide an entertaining and palpable sense of scale as the small boy marvels at skyscrapers and landmarks. . . . Neophytes and jaded residents alike will embrace this vibrant and enticing slice of the Big Apple." Pub Wkly

Schanzer, Rosalyn

★ **How** we crossed the West; the adventures of Lewis & Clark. National Geographic Soc. 1997 un il hardcover o.p. pa $7.95

Grades: 3 4 5   917

1. Explorers 2. Lewis and Clark Expedition (1804-1806) 3. Territorial governors 4. West (U.S.) -- Exploration

ISBN 0-7922-3738-2; 0-7922-6726-5 pa

LC 96-6585

"Pithy and sometimes humorous, the text tells of contacts with Native Americans, encounters with wildlife . . . and the hardships of the trail. Warm in color and accessible in style, the acrylic paintings have a folk-art inspiration." Booklist

917.3   Geography of and travel in United States

National Geographic kids national parks guide U.S.A. the most amazing sights, scenes, and cool activities from coast to coast. National Geographic. National Geographic Society 2012 160 p.

Grades: 4 5 6   917.3

1. National parks and reserves -- United States -- Guidebooks 2. United States -- Description and travel -- Guidebooks

ISBN 9781426309311; 9781426309328

LC 2011034235

This children's guidebook of America's National Parks, by Sarah Wassner Flynn, features "tips on exploration, information about animals, sidebars, checklists, fun facts, maps, cool things to do, and much more. Conservation information, a 'find out more' section, glossary, and index add ample back matter to round out this book." (Publisher's note)

Includes bibliographical references and index

919   Geography of and travel in Australasia, Pacific Ocean islands, Atlantic Ocean islands, Arctic islands, Antarctica and on extraterrestrial worlds

Martin, Jacqueline Briggs

★ The **lamp,** the ice, and the boat called Fish; based on a true story. pictures by Beth Krommes. Houghton Mifflin 2001 un il $15

Grades: 3 4 5 6   919

1. Inuit 2. Karluk (Ship) 3. Arctic regions 4. Canadian Arctic

Expedition (1913-1918)
ISBN 0-618-00341-X

LC 99-35303

"The quiet, intriguing language, with a poet's attention to sound, will lull young ones into the story's drama, as will Beth Krommes' captivating scratchboard illustrations." Booklist

919.89 Antarctica -- Geography

Bodden, Valerie

To the South Pole; by Valerie Bodden. Creative Education 2011 48 p. col. ill. (Great Expeditions) (library) $34.25

Grades: 5 6 7 8 **919.89**
1. South Pole -- Exploration 2. Amundsen, Roald, 1872-1928 3. Explorers -- Norway -- Biography 4. South Pole -- Discovery and exploration
ISBN 1608180697; 9781608180691

LC 2010033552

This book by Valerie Bodden, part of the "Great Expeditions" series, presents "a history of Roald Amundsen's . . . 1911 trip to the South Pole, detailing the challenges encountered, the individuals involved, the discoveries made, and how the expedition left its mark upon the world." (Publisher's note) . Major historical milestones and details about the search for the southernmost tip of the world are related in" addition to "profiles of four of the major explorers". (Children's Literature)

Includes bibliographical references (p. 46-47) and index.

Dowdeswell, Evelyn

Scott of the Antarctic; Evelyn Dowdeswell, Julian Dowdeswell, and Angela Seddon. Heinemann Library 2013 32 p. (hb) $26.65

Grades: 2 3 4 **919.89**
1. Explorers 2. South Pole 3. Antarctica -- Discovery and exploration -- British
ISBN 1432968904; 9781432968908; 9781432968915

LC 2011037936

This book "[e]xamines Antarctica and [explorer] Robert Scott's epic expedition to the South Pole." (WorldCat) To "commemorate the 100th anniversary of Scott['s] Antarctic trek, and his tragic death before returning home, this book charts the epic race to the South Pole." (Google Books)

Includes bibliographical references and index

92 Individual biography

Aaron, Hank, 1934-

★ Tavares, Matt. **Henry** Aaron's dream. Candlewick Press 2010 un il $16.99; pa $6.99

Grades: 3 4 5 **92**
1. Baseball players 2. African American athletes 3. Baseball -- Biography
ISBN 978-0-7636-3224-3; 0-7636-3224-4; 978-07636-6129-8 pa

LC 2008037417

"Well-written text and brilliantly composed art highlight the poignancy and triumph in Aaron's story. This rousing tribute should resonate with a wide audience." SLJ

Ada, Alma Flor, 1938-

Ada, Alma Flor, 1938- **Under** the royal palms; a childhood in Cuba. Atheneum Bks. for Young Readers 1998 85p il $15

Grades: 4 5 6 7 **92**
1. Authors 2. Educators 3. Dramatists 4. Women authors 5.

Authors, American 6. Children's authors 7. Cuba -- Social life and customs 8. Cuba -- Intellectual life
ISBN 0-689-80631-0

LC 97-48887

Companion volume to Where the flame trees bloom (1994)

This is a "companion volume to Ada's 'Where the Flame Trees Bloom.'. . . {It} is divided into 10 chapters, each a self-contained story about Ada's childhood half a century ago in Camagüey, a city in the province of the same name in the center of Cuba." (N Y Times Book Rev) "Grades three to six." (Booklist)

"The attention paid to small daily things as well as the occasional awareness of historical events will encourage readers to look for their own family stories." Booklist

Parker-Rock, Michelle. Alma Flor Ada; an author kids love. Enslow Publishers 2008 48p bibl il por (Authors kids love) lib bdg $23.93

Grades: 3 4 5 **92**
1. Authors 2. Educators 3. Dramatists 4. Women authors 5. Cuban Americans 6. Authors, American 7. Children's authors
ISBN 978-0-7660-2760-2 lib bdg; 0-7660-2760-0 lib bdg

LC 2008004641

"The frequent use of direct quotes makes the [text] particularly enjoyable. . . . Kids will be fascinated with Ada's childhood home in Cuba. . . . Well written, interesting, and useful for reports." SLJ

Includes bibliographical references

Adams, Abigail, 1744-1818

Adler, David A. A **picture** book of John and Abigail Adams; by David A. Adler and Michael S. Adler; illustrated by Ronald Himler. Holiday House 2010 un il $17.95

Grades: 1 2 3 **92**
1. Presidents 2. Vice-presidents 3. Parents of presidents 4. Spouses of presidents 5. Presidents -- United States 6. Presidents' spouses -- United States
ISBN 978-0-8234-2007-0; 0-8234-2007-8

LC 2006050069

"This excellent picture-book biography introduces the childhoods, courtship, and family life of John and Abigail Adams as well as their years in public service. . . . Himler's graceful and well-composed drawings are brightened with luminous washes." Booklist

Includes bibliographical references

Adams, John, 1735-1826

Adler, David A. A **picture** book of John and Abigail Adams; by David A. Adler and Michael S. Adler; illustrated by Ronald Himler. Holiday House 2010 un il $17.95

Grades: 1 2 3 **92**
1. Presidents 2. Vice-presidents 3. Parents of presidents 4. Spouses of presidents 5. Presidents -- United States 6. Presidents' spouses -- United States
ISBN 978-0-8234-2007-0; 0-8234-2007-8

LC 2006050069

"This excellent picture-book biography introduces the childhoods, courtship, and family life of John and Abigail Adams as well as their years in public service. . . . Himler's graceful and well-composed drawings are brightened with luminous washes." Booklist

Includes bibliographical references

Adams, Samuel, 1722-1803

★ Fritz, Jean. **Why** don't you get a horse, Sam Adams? illustrated by Trina Schart Hyman. 1974 47p il $15.99; pa $5.99

Grades: 2 3 4 **92**
1. Statesmen 2. Members of Congress 3. Writers on politics 4.

United States -- History -- 1775-1783, Revolution
ISBN 0-399-23401-2; 0-698-11416-7 pa

"A piece of history far more entertaining and readable than most fiction. . . . The author has humanized a figure of the Revolution: Adams emerges a marvelously funny and believable man. The illustrations play upon his foibles; they are, in fact, even more outrageously mocking than the text. A tour de force, for both author and illustrator." Horn Book

Addams, Jane, 1860-1935

Stone, Tanya Lee. The **house** that Jane built; a story about Jane Addams. Tanya Lee Stone; illustrated by Kathryn Brown. Henry Holt & Co. 2015 32 p. color illustrations (hardcover) $17.99

Grades: 1 2 3 4 5   92

1. Hull House (Chicago, Ill.) 2. Social workers 3. Women social workers -- United States -- Biography 4. Chicago (Ill.) -- Social conditions -- 20th century 5. Women social reformers -- United States -- Biography
ISBN 0805090495; 9780805090499

LC 2014036098

In this children's nonfiction book, by Tanya Lee Stone and illustrated by Kathryn Brown, "the story of Jane Addams, the first American woman to receive the Nobel Peace Prize, who transformed a poor neighborhood in Chicago[, Illinois] by opening up her house as a community center" is told. (Publisher's note)

"Vowing from an early age to improve the lives of the impoverished, Addams established a settlement home, Hull House, in Chicago in 1889, creating a community refuge. The desperation of the poor is evident in their anguished grimaces as they vie for spoiled food, while children's joy as they play in Chicago's first playground (thanks to Addams) is just as clear. In a moving portrayal of empathy and innovation in action, Stone and Brown convey both the significance of Addams's contributions ("Today, every community center in America, in large part, has Jane Addams to thank"), as well as the physical transformations of those she helped." PW

Includes bibliographical references

Albers, Josef, 1888-1976

★ Wing, Natasha. An **eye** for color: the story of Josef Albers; illustrated by Julia Breckenreid. Holt & Co. 2009 un il $16.99

Grades: 3 4 5 6   92

1. Artists 2. Painters 3. Color in art 4. Artists, German 5. Printmakers 6. Art teachers
ISBN 978-0-8050-8072-8; 0-8050-8072-4

LC 2008038214

"This creative biography explores how Albers, perhaps best known for his paintings of squares in different color combinations, 'saw art in the simplest things.' . . . After visiting Mexico—Albers is shown climbing an abstract templelike structure of colorful rectangles—he reflects on the effects of combining different colors. . . . An accessible and lively introduction to this artist and to color theory." Publ Wkly

Includes glossary and bibliographical references

Alcott, Louisa May, 1832-1888

McDonough, Yona Zeldis. **Louisa**; the life of Louisa May Alcott. illustrated by Bethanne Andersen. Henry Holt and Co. 2009 un il $17.99

Grades: 2 3 4   92

1. Authors 2. Novelists 3. Women authors 4. Authors, American 5. Young adult authors
ISBN 978-0-8050-8192-3; 0-8050-8192-5

LC 2008-38222

"McDonough clearly lays out the essentials of Alcott's life story. Often striking and occasionally memorable, Andersen's gouache-and-

pastel illustrations use strong shapes and rich colors to create iconic images." Booklist

Includes bibliographical references

Aldrin, Buzz

★ Aldrin, Buzz, 1930- **Reaching** for the moon; paintings by Wendell Minor. HarperCollins Children's Books 2005 un il $16.99; pa $6.99; lib bdg $17.89

Grades: 2 3 4   92

1. Astronauts 2. Air force officers 3. Nonfiction writers
ISBN 9780060554453; 9780060554477 pa; 9780060554460 lib bdg

LC 2004-6247

Aldrin "discusses his childhood interest in flight, his military training and academic preparation for a career as an astronaut, and . . . his pride and excitement in both his Gemini 12 extravehicular activity and his moon walk. . . . Ages five to nine." (Bull Cent Child Books)

"In this picture book, Aldrin, the second man to step foot on the moon, relates the life events that led him to the space program and his assignment on Apollo 11. . . . Minor's colorful and precisely rendered illustrations help this effort really take off, especially in the images of Aldrin's space journeys." Booklist

Alexander, the Great, 356-323 B.C.

Adams, Simon. **Alexander**; the boy soldier who conquered the world. National Geographic 2005 64p il map (World history biographies) $17.95; lib bdg $27.90

Grades: 4 5 6 7   92

1. Ancient civilization 2. Kings
ISBN 0-7922-3660-2; 0-7922-3661-0 lib bdg
This describes the life and times of Alexander the Great.

This is a "handsomely designed [book]. . . . illustrated with maps and many color photographs of art and sculpture that give substance to [the era]. . . . Adams does not downplay Alexander's brutality or all-consuming ambition and includes examples of both." SLJ

Includes bibliographical references

Demi. **Alexander** the Great; written and illustrated by Demi. Marshall Cavendish 2010 59p il $19.99

Grades: 4 5 6 7   92

1. Kings and rulers 2. Kings 3. Greece -- History -- 323-1453
ISBN 978-0-7614-5700-8; 0-7614-5700-3

"Demi's meticulous, expansive story highlights the achievements of Alexander the Great, who conquered much of the known world (to the Greeks) in only 12 years. . . . Illustrated with Demi's customary skill, . . . Alexander's conflicts and victories will delight young history lovers with their daring." Publ Wkly

Ali, Muhammad, 1942-2016

Myers, Walter Dean, 1937-2014. **Muhammad** Ali; the people's champion. illustrated by Alix Delinois. Collins Amistad 2010 un il $16.99; lib bdg $17.89

Grades: 1 2 3   92

1. African American athletes 2. Boxers (Persons) 3. Boxing -- Biography
ISBN 978-0-06-029131-0; 0-06-029131-1; 978-0-06-029132-7 lib bdg; 0-06-029132-X lib bdg

LC 2009-05326

"The curious mix of bravado and humility constituting the life of Muhammad Ali receives a sensitive exploration in this vibrantly illustrated biography. . . . Delinois is with Myers every step, using wild splotches of paint and scribbles of chalk not only to capture the velocity of a punch but also fill in contexual blanks. . . . Unexpectedly far reaching, this is a Muhammed Ali for the thinking child." Booklist

★ Smith, Charles R., 1969- **Twelve** rounds to glory: the story of Muhammad Ali; illustrated by Bryan Collier. Candlewick Press 2007 80p il $19.99
Grades: 5 6 7 8   92
1. African American athletes 2. Boxers (Persons) 3. Boxing -- Biography
ISBN 978-0-7636-1692-2; 0-7636-1692-3
LC 2007-25998
"Rap-style cadences perfectly capture the drama that has always surrounded the boxer's life. . . . Collier's compelling watercolor collages with their brown overtones beautifully portray Ali's determination and strength." SLJ

Ali, Rubina
Ali, Rubina. **Slumgirl** dreaming; Rubina's journey to the stars. [by] Rubina Ali in collaboration with Anne Berthod and Divya Dugar. Delacorte Press 2009 187p il pa $9.99
Grades: 5 6 7 8   92
1. Actors 2. Children 3. India 4. Slumdog millionaire (Motion picture)
ISBN 978-0-385-73908-5 pa; 0-385-73908-7 pa
LC 2009029305
The young actress describes her life growing up in the slums of Mumbai, her experiences on the set of the film "Slumdog Millionaire," and how her life has changed as a result of her role in the film
"The writing here has a journalistic feel. It is not poetic or especially nuanced. But in a sea of cookie-cutter biography series, this book stands out. It has heart, and is aimed at an age group that will identify with Ali in essential ways." SLJ

Allen, Will, 1949-
★ Martin, Jacqueline Briggs, 1945- **Farmer** Will Allen and the growing table; Jacqueline Briggs Martin, Eric Larkin. Readers to Eaters 2013 32 p. $17.95
Grades: K 1 2 3 4 5   92
1. Urban agriculture 2. Picture books for children
ISBN 0983661537; 9780983661535
LC 2013937817
In this book, Jacqueline Briggs Martin "shares the real-life story of Will Allen, innovative farmer and founder of Growing Power, an urban farm in Milwaukee. 'Will Allen can see / what others can't see. / When he sees kids, he sees farmers.' Martin begins and ends with this positive premise. In between, she sketches salient events that stoked Allen's commitment to empowering people to grow their own food." (Kirkus Reviews)

Alonso, Alicia
★ Bernier-Grand, Carmen T. **Alicia** Alonso; prima ballerina. illustrated by Raúl Colón. Marshall Cavendish Children's 2011 64p il $19.99
Grades: 4 5 6 7   92
1. Cubans 2. Ballet dancers 3. Choreographers 4. Dance directors
ISBN 978-0-7614-5562-2; 0-7614-5562-0
LC 2010018269
"An informative, beautifully illustrated introduction to the world-renowned dancer. Alonso's focused life and illustrious career are made even more remarkable by the fact that she lost her peripheral vision at age 19 and had to learn to visualize both the stage set and the dance itself in order to execute spins and lifts, and to choreograph ballets. Each one is presented as a titled one-page piece in abbreviated poetic prose; many

face full-page textured paintings rendered in Colón's distinctive mix of watercolor, colored, and lithograph pencils." SLJ
Includes bibliographical references

Alvarez, Luis W., 1911-1988
Venezia, Mike. **Luis** Alvarez; wild idea man. written and illustrated by Mike Venezia. Children's Press 2010 32p il (Getting to know the world's greatest inventors & scientists) lib bdg $28; pa $6.95
Grades: 2 3 4   92
1. Physicists 2. Nobel laureates for physics
ISBN 978-0-531-23703-8 lib bdg; 0-531-23703-6 lib bdg; 978-0-531-20777-2 pa; 0-531-20777-3 pa
LC 2009-356
"Employing oversized font, judicious use of white space, and appealing illustrations . . . readers learn about physicist Luis Alvarez and his numerous contributions to early 20th-century science. . . . Student researchers will appreciate the glossary and index, since there are no chapter headings or subheadings. This title, . . . serves equally well for research assignments, biography units, or as engaging leisure reading for aspiring scientists." Libr Media Connect
Includes glossary

Andersen, Hans Christian, 1805-1875
★ Varmer, Hjordis. **Hans** Christian Andersen; his fairy tale life. illustrated by Lilian Brogger; translated by Tiina Nunnally. Groundwood Books 2005 111p il $19.95
Grades: 5 6 7 8   92
1. Authors 2. Novelists 3. Dramatists 4. Authors, Danish 5. Children's authors 6. Short story writers
ISBN 0-88899-690-X
"Most of this book describes Andersen's childhood and belated schooling, showing his poverty and the grief he experienced over the death of his beloved father, as well as several horrifying events such as being forced by a teacher to witness the beheading of three young people. . . . The biography is divided into 11 chapters, set up as if they were stories. . . . The writing flows smoothly, with many details provided to help students picture the places and events. Brøgger's haunting, mixed-media illustrations add to the somber and at times surreal feeling of the text." SLJ

Anderson, Marian, 1897-1993
★ Freedman, Russell. The **voice** that challenged a nation; Marian Anderson and the struggle for equal rights. Clarion Books 2004 114p il $18
Grades: 5 6 7 8   92
1. African American singers 2. Opera singers 3. African Americans -- Civil rights 4. African American women -- Biography
ISBN 0-618-15976-2
LC 2003-19558
A Newbery Medal honor book, 2005
In the mid-1930s, Marian Anderson was a famed vocalist who had been applauded by European royalty and welcomed at the White House. But, because of her race, she was denied the right to sing at Constitution Hall in Washington, D.C. This is the story of her resulting involvement in the civil rights movement of the time.
"In his signature prose, plain yet eloquent, Freedman tells Anderson's triumphant story, with numerous black-and-white photos and prints that convey her personal struggle, professional artistry, and landmark civil rights role." Booklist
Includes bibliographical references

★ Ryan, Pam Munoz. **When** Marian sang: the true recital of Marian Anderson, the voice of a century; libretto by Pam Muñoz Ryan; staging by Brian Selznick. Scholastic Press 2002 un il $16.95

Grades: 2 3 4   **92**
1. African American singers 2. Opera singers 3. African American women -- Biography
ISBN 0-439-26967-9

LC 2001-49508

An introduction to the life of Marian Anderson, extraordinary singer and civil rights activist, who was the first African American to perform at the Metropolitan Opera, whose life and career encouraged social change

"This book masterfully distills the events in the life of an extraordinary musician. . . . Working with a sepia-toned palette, Selznick's paintings shimmer with emotion." Publ Wkly

Anderson, Tillie
★ Stauffacher, Sue. **Tillie** the terrible Swede; how one woman, a sewing needle, and a bicycle changed history. Alfred A. Knopf 2011 un il $17.99; lib bdg $20.99
Grades: K 1 2   **92**
1. Cycling 2. Women athletes
ISBN 978-0-375-84442-3; 0-375-84442-2; 978-0-375-94442-0 lib bdg; 0-375-94442-7 lib bdg

LC 2010-07083

"Reaching back more than a century, Stauffacher and McMenemy resurrect the story of pioneering woman cyclist Tillie Anderson. . . . Racing in a self-created aerodynamic outfit . . . Anderson both scandalized and thrilled 1890s America as she shattered records for speed and endurance, leaving competitors and conventional wisdom in the dust. . . . Stauffacher's . . . writing is as sprightly and heartfelt as ever, and to her credit, she connects Tillie's accomplishments to the building women's rights movement. An excellent afterword, tucked on the inside back cover, provides fascinating historical context for Anderson's story." Publ Wkly

Anderson, Walter Inglis, 1903-1965
★ Bass, Hester. The **secret** world of Walter Anderson; illustrated by E.B. Lewis. Candlewick Press 2009 un il $17.99
Grades: 2 3 4 5   **92**
1. Artists 2. Artists -- United States
ISBN 978-0-7636-3583-1; 0-7636-3583-9

LC 2008029674

"This sensitive portrait of Anderson—'the most famous American artist you've never heard of'—paints him as a solitary man who kept a private room hidden from his wife and children and often took his rowboat to the Mississippi Gulf Coast's isolated Horn Island to glean inspiration. Subdued watercolors evoke the artist's love of the natural world. . . . A powerful tribute to the lengths artists will go for their passions." Publ Wkly

Andrews, Benny, 1930-2006
Benson, Kathleen, 1947- **Draw** what you see; the life and art of Benny Andrews. by Kathleen Benson; illustrated with paintings by Benny Andrews. Clarion Books 2015 32 p. color illustrations (hardcover) $16.99
Grades: K 1 2 3   **92**
1. African American artists 2. Andrews, Benny, 1930-2006 3. African American artists -- Biography 4. Artists -- United States -- Biography
ISBN 0544104870; 9780544104877

LC 2013046203

This biography, by Kathleen Benson, focuses on artist Benny Andrews. "Benny Andrews loved to draw. . . . And he dreamed of a better life - something beyond the segregation, the backbreaking labor, and the limited opportunities of his world. Benny's dreams took him far from the rural Georgia of his childhood. He became one of the most important

African American painters of the twentieth century, and he opened doors for other artists of color." (Publisher's note)

"Benny Andrews began drawing when he was able to hold pencil in his hands and "once he started, he never stopped...Whether two or three dimensional, existing on a shallow stage or in an expansive landscape, Andrews's often elongated, stylized figures carry weight and their postures tell stories of oppression, of joy, of curiosity, and of pride...A powerful work about an influential artist and activist." SLJ

Andrews, Roy Chapman, 1884-1960
★ Bausum, Ann. **Dragon** bones and dinosaur eggs: a photobiography of Roy Chapman Andrews. National Geographic Soc. 2000 64p il map $17.95
Grades: 5 6 7 8   **92**
1. Fossils 2. Dinosaurs 3. Explorers 4. Zoologists 5. Naturalists 6. Travel writers 7. Writers on nature 8. Writers on science 9. Museum administrators
ISBN 0-7922-7123-8

LC 99-38363

A biography of the great explorer-adventurer, who discovered huge finds of dinosaur bones in Mongolia, pioneered modern paleontology field research, and became the director of the American Museum of Natural History

"Bausum's account reads smoothly, and a layout dense with captioned sepia photographs and quotes from Andrews provides plenty of oases for readers as they follow him through the desert." Bull Cent Child Books

Includes bibliographical references

Andrews, Troy
★ Taylor, Bill. **Trombone** Shorty; by Troy Andrews and Bill Taylor; illustrated by Bryan Collier. Abrams Books for Young Readers 2015 40 p. (hardcover) $17.95
Grades: PreK K 1 2 3   **92**
1. Jazz musicians -- Biography 2. Trombonists -- United States 3. Jazz musicians -- United States
ISBN 1419714651; 9781419714658

LC 2014016106

Caldecott Honor Book (2016)
Coretta Scott King Illustrator Award (2016)
This book, written by Troy "Trombone Shorty" Andrews and Bill Taylor, and illustrated by Bryan Collier, is a "picture book autobiography about how Andrews followed his dream of becoming a musician, despite the odds, until he reached international stardom." (Publisher's note) "He carried his trombone along to the New Orleans Jazz & Heritage Festival, where his playing earned him an invitation from Bo Diddley himself to join him on stage." (Bulletin of the Center for Children's Books)

Appleseed, Johnny, 1774-1845
Worth, Richard. **Johnny** Appleseed; select good seeds and plant them in good ground. Enslow Publishers 2010 128p il map (Americans: the spirit of a nation) $23.95
Grades: 4 5 6 7   **92**
1. Apples 2. Frontier and pioneer life 3. Pioneers 4. Fruit growers
ISBN 978-0-7660-3352-8; 0-7660-3352-X

LC 2008048701

"This nicely illustrated and sourced [biography] . . . includes full-page sidebars." Booklist
Includes glossary and bibliographical references

Yolen, Jane. **Johnny** Appleseed; the legend and the truth. by Jane Yolen; illustrated by Jim Burke. HarperCollinsPublishers 2008 un il $16.99; lib bdg $17.89

Grades: K 1 2 3 **92**

1. Apples 2. Frontier and pioneer life 3. Pioneers 4. Fruit growers

ISBN 978-0-06-059135-9; 0-06-059135-8; 978-0-06-059136-6 lib bdg; 0-06-059136-6 lib bdg

LC 2005017789

"In this comely, homespun picture-book biography, Yolen assembles the fact and fiction surrounding America's favorite orchardist into a tale both substantive and lyrical.... Burke's striking paintings conform to a natural, yarn-dyed palette of apple reds, forest greens, meadow golds, and midnight blues." Booklist

Archimedes, ca. 287-212 B.C.

Hightower, Paul. The **greatest** mathematician; Archimedes and his eureka! moment. Enslow Publishers 2010 128p il (Great minds of ancient science and math) lib bdg $31.93

Grades: 5 6 7 8 **92**

1. Mathematicians 2. Greece -- History 3. Writers on science

ISBN 978-0-7660-3408-2 lib bdg; 0-7660-3408-9 lib bdg

LC 2008051818

This biography is a "solid [choice], as . . . [it provides] a good overview of the cultural and political landscape of the times, as well as pictures." SLJ

Includes glossary and bibliographical references

Armstrong, John Barclay, 1850-1913

Alter, Judy. **John** Barclay Armstrong; Texas Ranger. by Judy Alter. Bright Sky Press 2007 59p il $14.95

Grades: 4 5 6 7 **92**

1. Sheriffs 2. Texas Rangers 3. West (U.S.) -- History

ISBN 978-1-931721-86-8

"Born in 1850 and raised in Tennessee, Armstrong went west to seek his fortune. At 25, he joined the Texas Rangers and soon came to embody the legendary qualities of these remarkable lawmen. He is an interesting character, and the author aptly tells his tale. The archival black-and-white photos add authenticity and help bring the man to life." SLJ

Armstrong, Louis, 1900-1971

★ Kimmel, Eric A. A **horn** for Louis; by Eric A. Kimmel; illustrated by James Bernardin. Random House 2005 86p il $11.95; lib bdg $13.99; pa $3.99

Grades: 2 3 4 **92**

1. Singers 2. Jazz musicians 3. African American musicians 4. Band leaders 5. Trumpet players

ISBN 0-375-83252-1; 0-375-93252-6 lib bdg; 978-0-375-84005-0 pa

LC 2005004151

"Adapted from an unpublished memoir, this beginning chapter book is an account of [Louis] Armstrong's youthful acquisition of his first true horn.... Kimmel's skilled narrative accentuates the diversity of the boys surroundings and the early influence of local music upon his innate gift. Bernardins dynamic black-and-white artwork captures the vivacious subject well and includes many period and cultural details." SLJ

Weinstein, Muriel Harris. **Play,** Louis, play! the true story of a boy and his horn. illustrated by Frank Morrison. Bloomsbury Books for Young Readers 2010 99p il $15.99

Grades: 3 4 5 **92**

1. Singers 2. Jazz musicians 3. African American musicians 4. Band leaders 5. Trumpet players

ISBN 978-1-59990-375-0; 1-59990-375-X

LC 2010025974

"With a bouncy, freewheeling tone that would make her subject proud, Weinstein tells the story of Louis Armstrong's childhood from the point of view of his first cornet.... Morrison's sketchy black-and-

white spot art livens up an already ebullient chapter-book biography of a true artistic pioneer." Booklist

Arn Chorn-Pond

Lord, Michelle. A **song** for Cambodia; by Michelle Lord; illustrated by Shino Arihara. Lee & Low 2008 un il $16.95

Grades: 3 4 5 **92**

1. Musicians 2. Cambodia 3. Flutists 4. Human rights activists

ISBN 978-1-60060-139-2; 1-60060-139-1

LC 2007026248

A biography of Arn Chorn-Pond who, as a young boy in 1970s Cambodia, survived the Khmer Rouge killing fields because of his skill on the khim, a traditional instrument, and later went on to help heal others and revive Cambodian music and culture.

"Filled with drama and tragedy, this picture-book biography skillfully telescopes Arn's tumultuous boyhood. Realistic gouache illustrations depict the terrors of war but refrain from showing graphic violence. Amazing and inspiring." Booklist

Ashe, Arthur, 1943-1993

Hubbard, Crystal. **Game,** set, match, champion Arthur Ashe; illustrated by Kevin Belford. Lee & Low Books 2010 un il $19.95

Grades: 3 4 5 6 **92**

1. African American athletes 2. Tennis players 3. Nonfiction writers 4. Tennis -- Biography

ISBN 978-1-60060-366-2; 1-60060-366-1

LC 2010013304

"Tennis legend Ashe's life, on and off the court, is the focus of this stirring picture-book biography . . . which combines a detailed narrative with powerful acrylic paintings." Booklist

Astaire, Adele, 1896-1981

Orgill, Roxane. **Footwork**; the story of Fred and Adele Astaire. illustrated by Stephane Jorisch. Candlewick Press 2007 un il $17.99

Grades: 2 3 4 5 **92**

1. Actors 2. Dancers 3. Singers

ISBN 978-0-7636-2121-6; 0-7636-2121-8

LC 2006-40068

The biography of Fred and Adele Astaire, from their humble beginnings to Broadway stars.

Orgill's text "brims with well-chosen biographical and period details, and . . . Jorisch's whisper-weight, line-and-watercolor drawings convey the fizz of the footwork and the gritty backdrop of steam trains and stage doors." Booklist

Includes bibliographical references

Astaire, Fred

Orgill, Roxane. **Footwork**; the story of Fred and Adele Astaire. illustrated by Stephane Jorisch. Candlewick Press 2007 un il $17.99

Grades: 2 3 4 5 **92**

1. Actors 2. Dancers 3. Singers

ISBN 978-0-7636-2121-6; 0-7636-2121-8

LC 2006-40068

The biography of Fred and Adele Astaire, from their humble beginnings to Broadway stars.

Orgill's text "brims with well-chosen biographical and period details, and . . . Jorisch's whisper-weight, line-and-watercolor drawings convey the fizz of the footwork and the gritty backdrop of steam trains and stage doors." Booklist

Includes bibliographical references

Audubon, John James, 1785-1851

★ Davies, Jacqueline. The **boy** who drew birds: a story of John James Audubon; illustrated by Melissa Sweet. Houghton Mifflin Co. 2004 un il map $15

Grades: 2 3 4   **92**

1. Birds 2. Artists 3. Painters 4. Naturalists 5. Ornithologists 6. Writers on science 7. Artists -- United States

ISBN 0-618-24343-7

LC 2004-971

This describes how John James Audubon studied and painted birds

"Sweet's mixed-media collage artwork includes sensitive pencil sketches and ink drawings washed with watercolors and gouache, as well as elements such as photos of bird nests and bones. . . . This handsome book makes a beguiling introduction to the painter." Booklist

Includes bibliographical references

Plain, Nancy. **This** strange wilderness; the life and art of John James Audubon. Nancy Plain. University of Nebraska Press 2015 136 p. illustrations (chiefly color) (pbk. : alk. paper) $19.95

Grades: 5 6 7 8 9 10   **92**

1. Bird watching 2. Naturalists -- Biography 3. Naturalists -- United States -- Biography 4. Ornithologists -- United States -- Biography

ISBN 0803248849; 9780803248847; 9780803284012; 9780803284029; 9780803284036

LC 2014020552

YALSA Award for Excellence in Nonfiction for Young Adults: Shortlist (2016)

This book, by Nancy Plain, focuses on the founder of modern ornithology John James Audubon. "His masterpiece, 'The Birds of America' depicts almost five hundred North American bird species, each image - lifelike and life size - rendered in vibrant color. . . . Plain brings together the amazing story of this American icon's career and the beautiful images that are his legacy." (Publisher's note)

"This narrative of the life of a dedicated and hard-working figure is the story of an amazing individual and a glimpse into the natural history of the early United States." SLJ

Includes bibliographical references and index

Babbage, Charles, 1791-1871

Stanley, Diane. **Ada** Lovelace, poet of science; the first computer programmer. Diane Stanley; illustrated by Jessie Hartland. Simon & Schuster Books for Young Readers 2016 40 p. color illustrations (hardcover) $17.99

Grades: K 1 2 3 4   **92**

1. Women mathematicians -- Great Britain -- Biography   2. Women computer programmers -- Great Britain -- Biography   3. Computers -- History -- 19th century   4. Mathematicians -- Great Britain -- Biography

ISBN 9781481452496

LC 2015010872

In this biography of Ada Lovelace, by Diane Stanley, illustrated by Jessie Hartland, "like her father, Ada had a vivid imagination and a creative gift for connecting ideas in original ways. Like her mother, she had a passion for science, math, and machines. . . . A hundred years before the dawn of the digital age, Ada Lovelace envisioned the computer-driven world we know today. And in demonstrating how the machine would be coded, she wrote the first computer program." (Publisher's note)

"This is a solid addition to STEM studies, yes, but also a great choice for any biography lovers." Booklist

Includes bibliographical references

Bach, Johann Sebastian, 1685-1750

Leonard, Tom. **Becoming** Bach; Tom Leonard. Roaring Brook Press 2017 40 p. color illustrations (hardcover) $17.99; (ebook) $60

Grades: K 1 2 3   **92**

1. Composers -- Germany -- Biography

ISBN 9781626722866; 9781250154439

LC 2016025023

In this children's book, by Tom Leonard, "for Johann Sebastian there was always music. His family had been musicians, or bachs as they were called in Germany, for 200 years. He always wanted to be a bach. As he grew, he saw patterns in everything. Patterns he would turn into melodies and song, eventually growing into one of the most important and celebrated musical composers of all time." (Publisher's note)

"This beautifully illustrated picture-book biography inspires further exploration into the life of this superlative composer." Booklist

Includes bibliographical references and discography.

Baker, Alia Muhammad

Bacher, Lindsay. **Alia** Muhammad Baker; saving a library from war. Lindsay Bacher. Childs World 2016 24 p. color illustrations (library bound : alk. paper) $27.07

Grades: 2 3 4 5   **92**

1. Librarians 2. Iraq War, 2003-2011

ISBN 9781634074711

LC 2015946300

In this book, by Lindsay Bacher, "readers learn the amazing story of Alia Muhammad Baker, a librarian who preserved Iraq's history by saving thousands of books from being destroyed during the Iraq War. Additional features to aid comprehension include a table of contents, fact-filled captions, callouts, and sidebars, a glossary, sources for further research, a listing of source notes, and an introduction to the author." (Publisher's note)

"Source notes, glossary, and index make this fine for study, but the story itself requires no assignment to bring in readers." Booklist

Includes bibliographical references (pages 23-24) and index.

★ Winter, Jeanette. The **librarian** of Basra; a true story from Iraq. Harcourt, Inc. 2004 32p il $16

Grades: PreK K 1 2 3   **92**

1. Books 2. Libraries 3. Librarians 4. Iraq War, 2003

ISBN 0-15-205445-6

LC 2004-12969

The story of Alia Muhammad Baker, a librarian in Basra, Iraq, who managed to rescue seventy percent of the library's collection before the library burned in the Iraq War in 2003

"Winter's bright, folk-art style does much to mute the horrific realties of war. . . . The librarian's quiet bravery serves as a point of entry into a freighted topic." Booklist

Baker, Josephine, 1906-1975

★ Powell, Patricia Hruby. **Josephine**; the dazzling life of Josephine Baker. By Patricia Hruby Powell and illustrated by Christian Robinson. Chronicle Books Llc 2014 104 p. color illustrations (alk. paper) $17.99

Grades: 2 3 4 5   **92**

1. Dancers 2. African Americans 3. Dancers -- France -- Biography 4. African American entertainers -- France -- Biography

ISBN 1452103143; 9781452103143

LC 2012030440

Coretta Scott King (Illustrator) Honor Book (2015)

Boston Globe-Horn Book Nonfiction Award (2014)

Robert F. Sibert Honor Book (2015)

In this picture book, author Patricia Hruby Powell presents a biography of Josephine Baker, who "rose from a childhood of poverty and race riots in St. Louis, Mo., to dance in New York and Paris, the city where she finally achieved fame and escaped American segregation and racism. Grateful to the French, she worked as a spy during World War II and later adopted 12 children from around the world." (Kirkus Reviews)

"This incomparable biography conveys dancer Josephine Baker's passion, exuberance, dignity, and eccentricity through words and pictures that nearly jump off the page. Powell doesn't shy away from the challenges (including racism) Baker faced but emphasizes that Baker never let them overwhelm her joy from performing. Robinson's highly stylized, boldly colored illustrations are at once sophisticated and inviting to young readers." Horn Book

★ Winter, Jonah. **Jazz** age Josephine; illustrated by Marjorie Priceman. Atheneum 2012 il $16.99

Grades: K 1 2 3   **92**
1. Actors 2. Dancers 3. Singers 4. Jazz music 5. African American singers 6. African American women -- Biography
ISBN 978-1-4169-6123-9; 1-4169-6123-2

"Even though the ranks of picture-book biographies of significant artists (many of whom kids have likely never heard of) have swollen considerably in recent years, this one about the singer, dancer, and all-around entertainer Josephine Baker still manages to dazzle. . . . The biographical details . . . are covered in broad strokes, with more attention given to recreating the style and swagger of her onstage performances. . . . Winter's syncopated language dances nearly as much as the energized, loose-limbed figures in Priceman's kinetic artwork to convey the spirit, as much as the life, of the subject." Booklist

Banneker, Benjamin, 1731-1806

Maupin, Melissa. **Benjamin** Banneker. Child's World 2010 39p il map (Journey to freedom) lib bdg $20.92

Grades: 3 4 5 6   **92**
1. Astronomers 2. Mathematicians 3. Nonfiction writers 4. Clock and watch makers 5. African Americans -- Biography
ISBN 978-1-60253-117-8 lib bdg; 1-60253-117-X lib bdg
LC 2009003639

A biography of the African American scientist and mathematician

"Maupin has created an accessible account of Banneker's like and accomplishments. Short, uncomplicated text is interspersed with sepia-tone primary source photographs and documents." Booklist

Includes bibliographical references

Barichievich, Antonio, 1925-2003

Gravel, Élise, 1977- The **great** Antonio; by Elise Gravel. TOON Books, an imprint of RAW Junior, LLC 2017 64 p. color illustrations (hardcover) $12.95

Grades: K 1 2 3   **92**
1. Actors -- Canada -- Biography 2. Weight lifters -- Canada -- Biography 3. Strong men -- Canada -- Biography
ISBN 9781943145089
LC 2016003371

This children's book asks, "what made the Great Antonio so great? He weighed as much as a horse! He once wrestled a bear. He could devour twenty-five roasted chickens at one sitting. In this whimsical book [in the Toon Books series], beloved author and illustrator Elise Gravel tells the true story of Antonio Barichievich, the larger-than-life Montreal strongman who had muscles as big as his heart." (Publisher's note)

"The text is spare and engaging, and the type is set to integrate neatly with the playful art. A tribute as heartfelt as it is joyous and a fitting way to remember this larger-than-life performer." Kirkus

Barnum, P. T. (Phineas Taylor), 1810-1891

★ Fleming, Candace. The **great** and only Barnum; the tremendous, stupendous life of showman P.T. Barnum. illustrated by Ray Fenwick. Schwartz & Wade Books 2009 151p il $18.99; lib bdg $21.99

Grades: 5 6 7 8   **92**
1. Circus 2. Circus executives
ISBN 978-0-375-84197-2; 0-375-84197-0; 978-0-375-94597-7 lib bdg; 0-375-94597-0 lib bdg
LC 2008-45847

"In this sweeping yet cohesive biography, Fleming so finely tunes Barnum's legendary ballyhoo that you can practically hear the hucksterism and smell the sawdust. . . . The material is inherently juicy, but credit Fleming's vivacious prose, bountiful period illustrations, and copious source notes for fashioning a full picture on one of the forebearers of modern celebrity." Booklist

Includes bibliographical references

Barrie, J. M. (James Matthew), 1860-1937

★ Yolen, Jane. **Lost** boy; the story of the man who created Peter Pan. illustrated by Steve Adams. Dutton Children's Books 2010 un il $17.99

Grades: 2 3 4   **92**
1. Authors 2. Novelists 3. Dramatists 4. Authors, Scottish 5. Essayists 6. Satirists
ISBN 978-0-525-47886-7; 0-525-47886-8
LC 2009-24697

"This handsome picture-book biography presents the life of James Barrie, the creator of Peter Pan. . . . Adams' paintings provide evocative views of Barrie and his world. Yolen smoothly relates intriguing incidents from Barrie's childhood and adult life without making comments or drawing conclusions." Booklist

Includes bibliographical references

Barton, Clara, 1821-1912

Krensky, Stephen. **Clara** Barton. DK Pub. 2011 128p il (DK biography) $14.99; pa $5.99

Grades: 5 6 7 8   **92**
1. Nurses 2. American Red Cross 3. Red Cross officials 4. Social welfare leaders
ISBN 978-0-7566-7279-9; 0-7566-7279-1; 978-0-7566-7278-2 pa; 0-7566-7278-3 pa

Describes the life and accomplishments of Clara Barton, a teacher who organized efforts to bring nursing care to wounded soldiers during the Civil War and who went on to become the founder of the American Red Cross.

"Barton is placed in historical context, and key concepts, such as the causes of the Civil War, the struggle for women's suffrage, and the importance of the Geneva Convention, are explained. Compact in form, the text is complemented by full-color and archival photographs and reproductions on every spread. . . . An excellent resource for reports that will also appeal to fans of biography." SLJ

Includes bibliographical references

Somervill, Barbara A. **Clara** Barton; founder of the American Red Cross. Compass Point Books 2007 112p bibl il por lib bdg $23.95

Grades: 5 6 7 8   **92**
1. Nurses 2. American Red Cross 3. Red Cross officials 4. Social welfare leaders
ISBN 978-0-7565-1888-2 lib bdg; 0-7565-1888-1 lib bdg
LC 2006027071

"With an open design, clear type, and period prints and photos on every double-page spread, this highly readable biography . . . does a great job of setting Barton's personal story within the history of her time." Booklist

Includes bibliographical references

Wade, Mary Dodson. **Amazing** civil war nurse Clara Barton. Enslow Publishers 2009 24p il (Amazing Americans) lib bdg $21.26
Grades: 1 2 3   92
1. Nurses 2. American Red Cross 3. Red Cross officials 4. Social welfare leaders
ISBN 978-0-7660-3281-1 lib bdg; 0-7660-3281-7 lib bdg
LC 2008-24889
"Colorful photos are found throughout, with a timeline, dictionary, websites concerning the topic, as well as an index making . . . [this] book a wonderful introduction to nonfiction features." Libr Media Connect
Includes glossary

Basquiat, Jean-Michel, 1960-1988
★ Steptoe, Javaka. **Radiant** child; by Javaka Steptoe. Little, Brown & Co. 2016 40 p. (hardcover) $17.99
Grades: 1 2 3 4 5   92
1. Artists
ISBN 0316213888; 9780316213882
LC 2013018520
Coretta Scott King (Illustrator) Book Award (2017)
Caldecott Medal (2017)
This book, by Javaka Steptoe, is a "picture book biography about modern art phenomenon Jean-Michel Basquiat. . . . Basquiat and his unique, collage-style paintings rocked to fame in the 1980s as a cultural phenomenon unlike anything the art work had ever seen. But before that, he was a little boy who saw art everywhere: in poetry books and museums, in games and in the words that we speak, and in the pulsing energy of New York City." (Publisher's note)
"Pairing simple text with expressive, encompassing illustrations, this excellent title offers a new generation a fittingly powerful introduction to an artistic luminary." SLJ

Bates, Peg Leg
★ Barasch, Lynne. **Knockin'** on wood; starring Peg Leg Bates. by Lynne Barasch. Lee & Low Books 2004 un il $16.95
Grades: 2 3 4   92
1. Dancers 2. Tap dancing 3. African American dancers 4. People with disabilities 5. Hotel executives 6. Dancers with disabilities 7. Tap dancers -- United States -- Biography
ISBN 1-58430-170-8
LC 2003-22905
A picture book biography of Clayton "Peg Leg" Bates, an African American who lost his leg in a factory accident at the age of twelve and went on to become a world-famous tap dancer
"Sprightly ink-and-watercolor art ably depicts both the poverty of Bates' early life and the colorful world of entertainment. . . . Barasch subtly sets the story against American racism." Booklist

Baum, L. Frank, 1856-1919
Krull, Kathleen. The **road** to Oz; twists, turns, bumps, and triumphs in the life of L. Frank Baum. illustrated by Kevin Hawkes. Alfred A. Knopf 2008 un il $17.99; lib bdg $20.99
Grades: 2 3 4 5   92
1. Authors 2. Dramatists 3. Journalists 4. Authors, American 5. Children's authors
ISBN 978-0-375-83216-1; 0-375-83216-5; 978-0-375-93216-8 lib bdg; 0-375-93216-X lib bdg
LC 2007-41526
This picture-book biography of the author of The Wonderful Wizard of Oz "displays Krull's usual stylistic strengths: a conversational tone,

well-integrated facts, vivid anecdotes, and sly asides. . . . Hawkes' ink-and-acrylic illustrations . . . support the sense of Baum as a multifaceted, fascinating individual." Booklist

Beatles
Manning, Mick. The **Beatles**; Mick Manning, Brita Granström. Pgw 2014 48 p. $18.99
Grades: 4 5 6   92
1. Beatles 2. Rock musicians -- England -- Biography
ISBN 1847804519; 9781847804518
Mick Manning and Brita Granström "tell the story of the Beatles. . . . This illustrated story covers John Lennon's Liverpool childhood, . . . the friendship between Paul McCartney and George Harrison, . . . the arrival of Brian Epstein as manager, . . . record label boss George Martin's influence, Ringo Starr joining the group, fame and screaming fans, the famous tour to the USA, the making of the albums, . . . and finally the breakup of the band and the beginning of solo careers." (Publisher's note)
"This slim, cheeky book is a delightful introduction to the Beatles, and the fresh, lively art will draw kids right in. The book is arranged chronologically, beginning in 1940...This is clearly an import (references to the Just William stories and jelly babies aren't really explained), but readers will make connections through context. A bouncy way to meet the Beatles. " Booklist

Beebe, William, 1877-1962
Sheldon, David. **Into** the deep; the life of naturalist and explorer William Beebe. Charlesbridge 2009 un il lib bdg $16.95
Grades: 2 3 4   92
1. Authors 2. Explorers 3. Zoologists 4. Naturalists 5. Memoirists 6. Writers on nature 7. Writers on science 8. Deep diving
ISBN 1-58089-341-4 lib bdg; 978-1-58089-341-1 lib bdg
LC 2008-25341
This is a biography of the American "naturalist from his childhood studying animals in New Jersey through his later years studying birds at the research station he started in Trinidad. [Glossary.] Ages five to eight." (Publisher's note)
"This colorful introduction to Beebe's life for younger readers opens with his parents' encouragement of his interests in the natural world and his early work as a curator and collector of birds before he developed the idea of observing animals in their native habitat and began to focus on undersea life. . . . Sheldon's lush double-page paintings, in acrylic, gouache and India ink, show young Will surrounded by animals, alive and stuffed, and the older man at work in a variety of settings. . . . A fine offering for would-be explorers." Kirkus
Includes bibliographical references

Beecher family
Fritz, Jean. **Harriet** Beecher Stowe and the Beecher preachers. Putnam 1994 144p il $15.99; pa $5.99
Grades: 5 6 7 8   92
1. Authors 2. Novelists 3. Abolitionists 4. Women authors 5. Authors, American 6. Children's authors 7. Nonfiction writers 8. Short story writers
ISBN 0-399-22666-4; 0-698-11660-7 pa
LC 93-6408
This is a biography of the abolitionist author of "Uncle Tom's Cabin" with an emphasis on the influence of her preacher father and her family on her life and work.
"Written with vivacity and insight, this readable and engrossing biography is an important contribution to women's history as well as to the history of American letters." Horn Book
Includes bibliographical references

Beethoven, Ludwig van, 1770-1827

Bauer, Helen. **Beethoven** for kids; his life and music with 21 activities. Chicago Review Press 2011 129p il pa $16.95

Grades: 4 5 6 7   **92**

1. Composers 2. Composers, Austrian

ISBN 1-56976-711-4; 978-1-56976-711-5

LC 2011018131

"This introduction to the towering classical composer sets the story of his life and work in the context of the revolutionary events of early-19th-century Europe. . . . The author's own extensive musical experience contributes to the breadth of this title. Sidebars and historical prints add further information about musical forms and instruments, historical events and people mentioned. . . . This will be particularly useful for parents and classroom teachers hoping to make the study of great music more interesting." Kirkus

Includes bibliographical references

Martin, Russell. The **mysteries** of Beethoven's hair; [by Russell Martin and Lydia Nibley] Charlesbridge 2009 120p il lib bdg $15.95

Grades: 5 6 7 8   **92**

1. Composers

ISBN 978-1-57091-714-1 lib bdg; 1-57091-714-0 lib bdg

LC 2008-07257

"Based on Martin's adult book Beethoven's Hair: An Extraordinary Historical Odyssey and Scientific Mystery Solved (Broadway, 2000), this reworking for a young audience presents an intriguing interdisciplinary story. Martin and Nibley trace the labyrinthine journey of a lock of Beethoven's hair encased in a glass and wooden locket from the 18th century to the present. . . . This is a most unusual, thoroughly researched detective story written in a clearly accessible and lively tone. Black-and-white photos and reproductions appear throughout. . . . It is . . . an incredibly readable and absorbing selection that demonstrates the multidimensional nature of true scholarship." SLJ

Viegas, Jennifer. **Beethoven's** world; [by] Jennifer Viegas. Rosen Pub. Group 2008 64p il (Music throughout history) lib bdg $29.25

Grades: 5 6 7 8   **92**

1. Composers

ISBN 1-4042-0724-4 lib bdg; 978-1-4042-0724-0 lib bdg

LC 2005028917

This "book begins with an introduction briefly addressing social issues of the day, historical background, or other significant information. . . . Successive chapters discuss the [man's] early [life], family background, social status, personality characteristics, musical training and education, obstacles or challenges, and influences. A chapter . . . focuses on the musician's well-known compositions, describing through lively and colorful language some of the musical elements employed . . . The format and layout are appealing and uncluttered." SLJ

Includes glossary and bibliographical references

Bell, Alexander Graham, 1847-1922

Garmon, Anita. **Alexander** Graham Bell invents; by Anita Garmon. National Geographic 2007 40p il (National Geographic history chapters) lib bdg $17.90

Grades: 2 3 4   **92**

1. Inventors 2. Teachers of the deaf 3. Telecommunications executives

ISBN 978-1-4263-0189-6

LC 2007007828

This biography of the inventor is "nicely illustrated with photos, paintings, engravings, and facsimiles. [It is] just right for emerging chapter-book readers. . . . Useful for reports . . . and interesting pleasure reading." SLJ

Includes glossary and bibliographical references

Bernstein, Leonard, 1918-1990

★ Rubin, Susan Goldman. **Music** was IT: young Leonard Bernstein. Charlesbridge 2011 178p il lib bdg $19.95

Grades: 5 6 7 8   **92**

1. Composers 2. Conductors (Music) 3. Jews -- Biography

ISBN 1-58089-344-9 lib bdg; 978-1-58089-344-2 lib bdg; 978-1-60734-276-2 e-book

LC 2010-07584

This is a biography of composer and conductor Leonard Bernstein. Bibliography. Index. "Grades five to nine." (Bull Cent Child Books)

"An impeccably researched and told biography of Leonard Bernstein's musical apprenticeship, from toddlerhood to his conducting debut with the New York Philharmonic at age 25. . . . Drawn from interviews, family memoirs and other print resources, quotations are well-integrated and assiduously attributed. Photos, concert programs, early doodles and letters, excerpts from musical scores and other primary documentation enhance the text. Excellent bookmaking—from type to trim size—complements a remarkable celebration of a uniquely American musical genius." Kirkus

Bhutto, Benazir

Naden, Corinne J. **Benazir** Bhutto. Marshall Cavendish Benchmark 2010 96p il (Leading women) $39.93

Grades: 5 6 7 8   **92**

1. Prime ministers 2. Women politicians 3. Political leaders 4. Pakistan -- Politics and government

ISBN 978-0-7614-4952-2; 0-7614-4952-3

In this biography "readers learn about Bhutto's student years at Radcliffe College and her rise to prime minister of Pakistan, the first woman to lead a Muslim state. . . . The [woman's life is] revealed within the political and historical context of [her] times and [includes] quotes from autobiographical material. . . . Color and black-and-white photos are included. . . . The compact size, chronological organization, and accessible writing [style makes this biography a] good [resource] for reports." SLJ

Includes bibliographical references

Bieber, Justin, 1994-

Bieber, Justin. **Justin** Bieber: first step 2 forever; my story. HarperCollins Children's Books 2010 236p il $21.99

Grades: 4 5 6 7   **92**

1. Singers 2. Pop musicians

ISBN 978-0-06-203974-3; 0-06-203974-1

"Bieber, the platinum-selling singer/songwriter . . . debuts with an account of his 16-year-old life that's cheeky yet entirely in line with his safe and wholesome image. . . . The book covers his upbringing in Ontario, his early introduction to music, YouTube stardom, his love of pranks, and the stratospheric success he now enjoys—all interspersed with lyrics, tweets, and numerous full-bleed photographs of Bieber." Publ Wkly

Bishop, Stephen, 1821?-1857

Henson, Heather. **Lift** your light a little higher; the story of Stephen Bishop: slave explorer. Heather Henson, illustrated by Bryan Collier. Simon & Schuster 2016 32 p. color illustrations $17.99

Grades: K 1 2 3   **92**

1. Mammoth Cave (Ky.)

ISBN 148142095X; 9781481420952

This picture book by Heather Henson, illustrated by Bryan Collier, tells the story of "Stephen Bishop, born circa 1821, [who] had intimate knowledge of Mammoth Cave in Kentucky, where he served as [a] guide for visitors who traveled far to tour the underground passageways. Despite the ban against teaching slaves to read, Stephen acquired literacy and wrote his name on the ceiling of Mammoth Cave by using smoke from a lighted candle." (Kirkus Reviews)

"Collier's (Trombone Shorty) collages strongly evoke the dark, claustrophobic confines of the cave system, as well as haunting moments of both strength and injustice." Pub Wkly

Includes bibliographical references.

Black Elk, 1863-1950

★ Nelson, S. D. **Black** Elk's vision; a Lakota story. Abrams Books for Young Readers 2010 47p il $19.95

Grades: 5 6 7 8　　　　92

1. Shamans　2. Oglala Indians　3. Indian leaders　4. Native Americans -- Biography

ISBN 978-0-8109-8399-1; 0-8109-8399-0

LC 2009-9392

"This handsomely designed, large-format book tells the story of Black Elk (1863-1950), a Lakota man who saw many changes come to his people. . . . Often quoting from Black Elk Speaks (1932), Nelson makes vivid the painful ways life changed for the Lakotain in the 1800s. . . . Colorful, imaginative artwork, created using pencils and acrylic paints, is interspersed with nineteenth-century photos, underscoring that this dramatic account reflects the experiences of a man who witnessed history." Booklist

Blanchard, Marie-Madeleine-Sophie Armand, 1778-1819

Smith, Matthew Clark. **Lighter** than air; Sophie Blanchard, the first woman pilot. Matthew Clark Smith; illustrated by Matt Tavares. Candlewick Press 2017 32 p. color illustrations $16.99

Grades: 1 2 3 4　　　　92

1. Women balloonists -- France -- Biography

ISBN 0763677329; 9780763677329

LC 2017009349

This children's book, by Matthew Clark Smith, illustrated by Matt Tavares, presents "the story of Sophie Blanchard, an extraordinary woman who is largely forgotten despite her claim to being the very first female pilot in history. . . . Sophie is not the first woman to ascend in a balloon, nor the first woman to accompany an aeronaut on a trip, but she will become the first woman to climb to the clouds and steer her own course." (Publisher's note)

"A beautifully told story of a young woman with lofty aspirations." Kirkus

Includes bibliographical references.

Bly, Nellie, 1864-1922

★ Macy, Sue. **Bylines** : a photobiography of Nellie Bly; foreword by Linda Ellerbee. National Geographic 2009 64p il map $19.95; lib bdg $28.90

Grades: 5 6 7 8　　　　92

1. Authors　2. Journalists　3. Women journalists　4. Nonfiction writers

ISBN 978-1-4263-0513-9; 1-4263-0513-3; 978-1-4263-0514-6 lib bdg; 1-4263-0514-1 lib bdg

LC 2008-52329

This is a biography of the American reporter. Index. "Grades five to nine." (Bull Cent Child Books)

"This detailed biography of the trailblazing 19th-century journalist incorporates photographs of Bly and her subjects. The extensive text explores the details of a life spent seeking justice. . . . A thorough introduction to the life of a fascinating figure." Publ Wkly

Blériot, Louis, 1872-1936

★ Provensen, Alice. The **glorious** flight: across the Channel with Louis Bleriot, July 25, 1909; [by] Alice and Martin Provensen. Viking 1983 39p il $17.99; pa $6.99

Grades: 1 2 3 4　　　　92

1. Air pilots　2. Aeronautical engineers　3. Airplanes -- Design and construction

ISBN 978-0-670-34259-4; 0-670-34259-9; 978-0-14-050729-4; 0-14-050729-9 pa

LC 82-7034

Awarded the Caldecott Medal, 1984

"A pleasing text recounts Bleriot's adventures with gentle humor and admiration for his earnest, if accident-prone, determination. Best of all, the pictures shine with the illustrator's delight in the wondrous flying machines themselves." Horn Book

Boone, Daniel, 1734-1820

Spradlin, Michael P. **Daniel** Boone's great escape; [by] Michael P. Spradlin; illustrated by Ard Hoyt. Walker & Co. 2008 un il $16.95; lib bdg $17.85

Grades: K 1 2 3　　　　92

1. Escapes　2. Explorers　3. Shawnee Indians　4. Frontier and pioneer life　5. Scouts　6. Pioneers

ISBN 978-0-8027-9581-6; 0-8027-9581-1; 978-0-8027-9582-3 lib bdg; 0-8027-9582-X lib bdg

LC 2007-50382

"Spradlin . . . and Hoyt . . . deliver a thrilling adventure about famed 18th-century frontiersman Daniel Boone. The storytelling is immediate and swift. . . . Gripping prose relates Boone's experiences as the Shawnee hold him captive from February to June in 1778, until he makes a daring escape to warn fellow settlers of an impending attack. Hoyt's skillful blend of closeups and eye-level perspectives pulls readers right into the action. Maintaining the tight-as-a drum tension, the watercolor-and-ink scenes show the escapee hightailing it through thick forests." Publ Wkly

Brady, Tom

Wilner, Barry. **Tom** Brady; a football star who cares. Enslow Publsihers, Inc. 2011 48p il (Sport stars who care) lib bdg $23.93; pa $7.95

Grades: 3 4 5　　　　92

1. Football players　2. Football -- Biography

ISBN 978-0-7660-3773-1 lib bdg; 0-7660-3773-8 lib bdg; 978-1-59845-233-4 pa; 1-59845-233-9 pa

LC 2010041784

A biography of the quarterback for the New England Patriots who also works for charities.

This is "especially good for book reports." Booklist

Includes glossary and bibliographical references

Braille, Louis, 1809-1852

★ Bryant, Jen. **Six** dots; A Story of Young Louis Braille. by Jen Bryant; illustrations by Boris Kulikov. Alfred A. Knopf 2015 40 p. color illustrations (hardcover) $17.99

Grades: 1 2 3 4　　　　92

1. Braille　2. Blind teachers -- France -- Biography

ISBN 044981338X; 0449813371; 9780449813379; 9780449813386

LC 2015007824

Schneider Family Book Award: Children (2017)

This book, by Jen Bryant, with illustrations by Boris Kulikov, is a "picture-book biography of Louis Braille--a blind boy so determined to read that he invented his own alphabet. Louis Braille was just five years old when he lost his sight. He was a clever boy, determined to live like everyone else, and what he wanted more than anything was to be able to read. . . . And so he invented his own alphabet." (Publisher's note)

"Kulikov's engrossing mixed-media illustrations interpose soft pastels with spreads of chalky blue line on ink-black pages, dramatically conveying Louis' isolation and single-minded intensity." Kirkus

Includes bibliographical references.

★ Freedman, Russell. **Out** of darkness: the story of Louis Braille; illustrated by Kate Kiesler. Clarion Bks. 1997 81p il $16.95; pa $7.95
Grades: 4 5 6 7   92
1. Blind 2. Inventors 3. Teachers of the blind 4. Blind -- Books and reading
ISBN 0-395-77516-7; 0-395-96888-7 pa

LC 95-52353

"Without melodrama, Freedman tells the momentous story in quiet chapters in his best plain style, making the facts immediate and personal. . . . A diagram explains how the Braille alphabet works, and Kate Kessler's full-page shaded pencil illustrations are part of the understated poignant drama." Booklist

Branson, Richard
Goldsworthy, Steve. **Richard** Branson. 2011 il (Remarkable people) $27.13; pa $12.95
Grades: 4 5 6 7   92
1. Businessmen 2. Financiers 3. Virgin Group plc 4. Retail executives 5. Airline executives 6. Telecommunications executives
ISBN 978-1-61690-671-9; 978-1-61690-676-4 pa

LC 2010051145

A biography of British financier Richard Branson.

Breckinridge, Mary, 1881-1965
★ Wells, Rosemary. **Mary** on horseback; three mountain stories. pictures by Peter McCarty. Dial Bks. for Young Readers 1998 53p il $16.99; pa $4.99
Grades: 4 5 6 7   92
1. Nurses 2. Midwives
ISBN 0-670-88923-7; 0-14-130815-X pa

LC 97-43409

Tells the stories of three families who were helped by the work of Mary Breckinridge, the first nurse to go into the Appalachian Mountains and give medical care to the isolated inhabitants. Includes an afterword with facts about Breckinridge and the Frontier Nursing Service she founded

"These beautifully written stories will remain with the reader long after the book is closed." Booklist

Breitbart, Siegmund, 1883-1925
Rubinstein, Robert E. **Zishe** the strongman; by Robert Rubinstein; illustrations by Woody Miller. Kar-Ben Pub. 2010 un il lib bdg $17.95; pa $7.95
Grades: K 1 2 3   92
1. Strong men 2. Bodybuilders 3. Jews -- Poland 4. Circus performers 5. Jews -- Biography 6. New York (N.Y.) -- History
ISBN 978-0-7613-3958-8 lib bdg; 0-7613-3958-2 lib bdg; 978-0-7613-3960-1 pa; 0-7613-3960-4 pa

LC 2009001875

"This picture book in warm sepia tones tells of a Polish Jew who emigrated to the U.S. in the early twentieth century and became a famous circus strongman. . . . This title makes a lively addition to other stories of Yiddish immigration." Booklist

Bridges, Ruby
★ Bridges, Ruby. **Through** my eyes: the autobiography of Ruby Bridges; articles and interviews compiled and edited by Margo Lundell. Scholastic Press 1999 63p il $16.95

Grades: 4 5 6   92
1. Travel agents 2. Civil rights activists 3. African Americans -- Civil rights 4. New Orleans (La.) -- Race relations
ISBN 0-590-18923-9

LC 98-49242

Ruby Bridges recounts the story of her involvement, as a six-year-old, in the integration of her school in New Orleans in 1960

"Profusely illustrated with sepia photos—including many gritty journalistic reproductions—this memoir brings some of the raw emotions of a tumultuous period into sharp focus. . . . A powerful personal narrative that every collection will want to own." SLJ

Donaldson, Madeline. **Ruby** Bridges. Lerner Publications 2009 48p il (History maker bios) $27.93
Grades: 3 4 5   92
1. School integration 2. Travel agents 3. Civil rights activists 4. African Americans -- Civil rights 5. New Orleans (La.) -- Race relations
ISBN 978-0-7613-4220-5; 0-7613-4220-6

LC 2008046526

"Donaldson recounts the story of this young African American girl who, in 1960 at the age of six, integrated New Orleans' William Franz Elementary School. . . . Donaldson's book is illustrated will fill-color drawings and carefully chosen period photos. . . . The book . . . makes a good introduction for report writers too young for Bridges' own memoir, Through My Eyes (1999)." Booklist

Includes bibliographical references

Bridgman, Laura Dewey, 1829-1889
Alexander, Sally Hobart. **She** touched the world: Laura Bridgman, deaf-blind pioneer; by Sally Hobart Alexander and Robert Alexander. Clarion Books 2008 100p il $18
Grades: 5 6 7 8   92
1. Deaf 2. Blind 3. Students 4. Physicians 5. Philanthropists 6. Humanitarians 7. Teachers of the blind
ISBN 978-0-618-85299-4; 0-618-85299-9

"At the age of three, in 1832, Laura Bridgman contracted scarlet fever and lost her sight, her hearing, her sense of smell, and much of her sense of taste. Her family sent her to Dr. Samuel [Gridley] Howe at the New England Institute for the Education of the Blind, and by the age of 10, Laura was world-famous for her accomplishments. . . . Alexander . . . presents a well-written and thoroughly researched biography of this remarkable woman, with numerous black-and-white photos." Booklist

Includes bibliographical references

Brown, John, 1800-1859
★ Hendrix, John. **John** Brown; his fight for freedom. written and illustrated by John Hendrix. Abrams Books for Young Readers 2009 39p il $18.95
Grades: 4 5 6 7   92
1. Abolitionists 2. Slavery -- United States
ISBN 978-0-8109-3798-7; 0-8109-3798-0

LC 2008-45969

The author "traces how John Brown went from conducting slaves along the Underground Railroad to espousing violent insurrection as a means to end slavery. . . . Reinforcing Brown as a larger-than-life folk hero, the pictures are exhilarating. . . . By embracing Brown's complexity, especially in the well-argued afterword, Hendrix sows acres of fertile ground for discussion." Booklist

Bruchac, Joseph, 1942-
Parker-Rock, Michelle. **Joseph** Bruchac; an author kids love. Enslow Publishers, Inc. 2009 48p il (Authors kids love) lib bdg $23.93

Grades: 3 4 5   92
1. Poets 2. Authors 3. Storytellers 4. College teachers 5. Magazine editors 6. Authors, American 7. Children's authors 8. Nonfiction writers
ISBN 978-0-7660-3160-9 lib bdg; 0-7660-3160-8 lib bdg
LC 2008-33051
"Clearly written, [this] outstanding [biography provides] many interesting details about the [subject's] personal [life] and [includes] photos that enhance the [text]." SLJ
Includes glossary and bibliographical references

Bryan, Ashley, 1923-
★ Bryan, Ashley. **Ashley** Bryan; words to my life's song. with photographs by Bill McGuinness. Atheneum Books for Young Readers 2009 58p il $18.99
Grades: 3 4 5 6   92
1. Artists 2. Authors 3. Illustrators 4. African American artists 5. African American authors 6. College teachers 7. Authors, American 8. Children's authors
ISBN 978-1-4169-0541-7; 1-4169-0541-3
LC 2008-14369
"In rich collages of words and pictures, this highly visual autobiography introduces artist Ashley Bryan's life and his vision of the world around him. . . . Photos of Bryan's world and reproductions of his often bright-hued and inherently vibrant artworks appear on every page. . . . They infuse the entire presentation with energy, color, and joy. . . . Beautifully designed, the book creates an original, stimulating, and inspiring portrait of the artist . . . as well as a celebration of his vision." Booklist

Buchanan, James, 1791-1868
Burgan, Michael. **James** Buchanan. Marshall Cavendish Benchmark 2011 112p il (Presidents and their times) lib bdg $23.95
Grades: 5 6 7 8   92
1. Presidents 2. Senators 3. Members of Congress 4. Secretaries of state 5. Presidents -- United States
ISBN 978-0-7614-4810-5; 0-7614-4810-1
LC 2009025933
This offers information on President James Buchanan and places him within his historical and cultural context. Also explored are the formative events of his times and how he responded.
"The abundant sidebars provide a good deal of background information that will be helpful to students. . . . Attractive . . . as well as useful." Booklist
Includes glossary and bibliographical references

Buffalo Bill, 1846-1917
Green, Carl R. **Buffalo** Bill Cody; courageous wild west showman. by William R. Sanford and Carl R. Green. Enslow Publishers 2013 48 p. ill., map (library) $21.26; (paperback) $7.95
Grades: 5 6 7 8   92
1. Buffalo Bill's Wild West Show 2. Frontier and pioneer life -- West (U.S.) 3. West (U.S.) -- Biography 4. Pioneers -- West (U.S.) -- Biography 5. Buffalo Bill's Wild West Show -- History 6. Entertainers -- United States -- Biography
ISBN 0766040070; 9780766040076; 9781464400902
LC 2011031052
This book by William Sanford and Carl R. Green is part of the "Courageious Heroes of the American West" series. It presents a biography of Buffalo Bill Cody, who "had many jobs--Pony Express rider, scout, soldier, buffalo hunter. But he was most famous for entertaining audiences with his Wild West show. Many Americans and others around the world could not travel to see the real Wild West, so Buffalo Bill Brought it to them." (Publisher's note)
Includes bibliographical references (p. 47) and index.

Burningham, John, 1936-
Burningham, John. **John** Burningham; preface by Maurice Sendak; commentary by Brian Alderson. Candlewick Press 2009 223p il $70
Grades: Adult Professional   92
1. Artists 2. Authors 3. Illustrators 4. Authors, English 5. Children's authors
ISBN 978-0-7636-4434-5; 0-7636-4434-X
"The British author and illustrator has garnered an international reputation for combining imaginative, offbeat illustrations with highly funny, original stories for children. In this oversize, lavishly illustrated volume, Burningham relates his life story from his nonconformist schooling and his early meanderings around the world to his various artistic ventures, picture books being only one of his endeavors. . . . Students of children's literature will be intrigued by Maurice Sendak's short preface and by the six-page opening commentary by children's literature scholar Brian Alderson. A fascinating and insightful treat for Burningham aficionados." SLJ

Caesar, Julius, 100-44 B.C.
Galford, Ellen. **Julius** Caesar; the boy who conquered an empire. [by] Ellen Galford. National Geographic 2007 64p il map (World history biographies) $17.95; lib bdg $27.90
Grades: 5 6 7 8   92
1. Statesmen 2. Historians 3. Rome -- History 4. Emperors -- Rome
ISBN 978-1-4263-0064-6; 978-1-4263-0065-3 lib bdg
LC 2006020777
A biography of the Roman emperor
This "visually appealing [title is] packed with excellent photographs and reproductions, interesting sidebars, and [has] a time line running along the bottom of every page. . . . [This book is] useful, well-written." SLJ
Includes glossary and bibliographical references

Calamity Jane, 1852-1903
Green, Carl R. **Calamity** Jane; courageous wild west woman. by William R. Sanford and Carl R. Green. Enslow Publishers 2013 48 p. ill., map (library) $21.26; (paperback) $7.95
Grades: 5 6 7 8   92
1. Cowgirls 2. West (U.S.) -- Biography 3. Pioneers -- West (U.S.) -- Biography 4. Women pioneers -- West (U.S.) -- Biography
ISBN 0766040100; 9780766040106; 9781464400933
LC 2011033840
This book by William Sanford is part of the Courageous Heroes of the American West series and focuses on Calamity Jane. "The truth and myth are difficult to separate in the wild life of Calamity Jane. An independent spirit, she never stayed in one place for long. She worked as a gold prospector, bullwhacker, nurse, and had many other jobs, Calamity Jane refused to conform to the typical roles of a nineteenth-century woman." (Publisher's note)
Includes bibliographical references (p. 47) and index.

Calder, Alexander, 1898-1976
★ Stone, Tanya Lee. **Sandy's** circus; a story about Alexander Calder. illustrated by Boris Kulikov. Viking 2008 un il $16.99
Grades: 1 2 3   92
1. Artists 2. Sculptors 3. Circus in art 4. Artists -- United States
ISBN 978-0-670-06268-3; 0-670-06268-5
LC 2008-08380
"This beautifully illustrated picture-book biography . . . [offers a] spare, direct story that focuses on Calder's youth and what are, perhaps, his most kid-accessible artworks: his wire sculptures of circus perform-

ers. . . . Kulikov's elegant, fanciful, multimedia collages extend the story." Booklist

Includes bibliographical references

Campanella, Roy, 1921-1993

Adler, David A. **Campy**; the Roy Campanella story. by David A. Adler; illustrated by Gordon C. James. Viking Penguin 2007 un il $15.99

Grades: 2 3 4   92

1. Baseball players 2. African American athletes 3. Baseball -- Biography

ISBN 0-670-06041-0

LC 2005023314

"Roy Campanella . . . was the second African American signed by Branch Rickey to play for the Brooklyn Dodgers. . . . Adler . . . capably reprises Campy's on-field triumphs . . . and off-field tragedy (he was paralyzed in a car accident in 1958), while James delivers evocative illustrations in the soft-focus, pastel-heavy style that has become standard for baseball." nostalgia. Booklist

Includes bibliographical references

Cannon, Annie Jump, 1863-1941

Gerber, Carole. **Annie** Jump Cannon, astronomer; illustrated by Christina Wald. Pelican Pub. 2011 un il $16.99

Grades: 2 3 4 5   92

1. Deaf 2. Astronomers 3. Women astronomers 4. Curators

ISBN 9781589809116; 1589809114

LC 2011012147

"This inspiring picture-book biography of a trailblazer in the field presents insight into the challenges of women interested in science during the late 19th and early 20th centuries. Cannon was born in 1863 and as a young girl her mother nurtured her interest in the night sky. . . . When her father learned that Wellesley College was the only women's college offering physics classes, he enrolled her. She graduated with a degree in physics and had a successful career in astronomy. . . . The realistic illustrations capture the time period and complement the text. They're scientifically accurate. . . . A solid resource." SLJ

Carson, Rachel, 1907-1964

★ Ehrlich, Amy. **Rachel**; the story of Rachel Carson. illustrated by Wendell Minor. Silver Whistle/Harcourt 2003 un il $16

Grades: 2 3 4   92

1. Authors 2. Conservationists 3. Women scientists 4. College teachers 5. Marine biologists 6. Writers on nature 7. Writers on science

ISBN 0-15-216227-5

LC 00-13115

This "anecdotal biography of nature writer and environmentalist Carson focuses on incidents that influenced Carson's thinking and career aspirations. . . . Minor's . . . impressively realistic watercolor and gouache paintings lend a pleasing cohesiveness to the volume." Publ Wkly

Scherer, Glenn. **Who** on earth is Rachel Carson? mother of the environmental movement. [by] Glenn Scherer and Marty Fletcher. Enslow Publishers 2009 112p il (Scientists saving the earth) lib bdg $31.93

Grades: 5 6 7 8   92

1. Authors 2. Biologists 3. Conservationists 4. Women scientists 5. Environmentalists 6. College teachers 7. Marine biologists 8. Writers on nature 9. Writers on science

ISBN 978-1-59845-116-0 lib bdg; 1-59845-116-2 lib bdg

LC 2008028498

"The writing is clear and informative. . . . Color photographs are relevant and of good quality." SLJ

Includes bibliographical references

Carver, George Washington, 1864?-1943

★ Bolden, Tonya. **George** Washington Carver. Abrams Books for Young Readers 2008 41p il $18.95

Grades: 3 4 5 6   92

1. Botanists 2. Scientists 3. African Americans -- Biography

ISBN 978-0-8109-9366-2; 0-8109-9366-X

LC 2007-28069

NCTE Orbis Pictus Award honor book (2009)

This is a biography of "the slave-born black scientist. . . . Offering sourced quotations throughout, Bolden covers subtleties that simpler treatments tend to bypass. . . . Photos and reproductions, many of Carver's own paintings, are exceptional, and their arrangement in the style of an old-fashioned album lends the book a suitable gravitas. . . . [The book is] absorbing." Booklist

Includes bibliographical references

Harness, Cheryl. The **groundbreaking,** chance-taking life of George Washington Carver and science & invention in America; by Cheryl Harness. National Geographic 2008 143p il map (Cherly Harness histories) $16.95; lib bdg $25.90

Grades: 4 5 6 7   92

1. Botanists 2. Scientists 3. African Americans -- Biography

ISBN 978-1-4263-0196-4; 1-4263-0196-0; 978-1-4263-0197-1 lib bdg; 1-4263-0197-9 lib bdg

LC 2007029316

"Harness presents Carver as a man who, regardless of constant hardship and racial prejudice, persevered to become a beloved teacher and devoted scientist. . . . The author raises challenging questions throughout. . . . The lively prose style conveys his sense of passion and adventure about the man and his intellectual pursuits, and the simple black-and-white drawings add a further sense of drama." SLJ

Includes bibliographical references

Cassatt, Mary, 1844-1926

Harris, Lois V. **Mary** Cassatt; impressionist painter. [by] Lois V. Harris. Pelican 2007 32p il $15.95

Grades: 2 3 4   92

1. Artists 2. Painters 3. Women artists 4. Artists -- United States

ISBN 978-1-58980-452-4

LC 2007011755

"With large, crisply reproduced, color artwork on nearly every page, this picture-book biography of American Impressionist Mary Cassatt will appeal to a broad age-range of readers." Booklist

Cezanne, Paul, 1839-1906

Burleigh, Robert. **Paul** Cezanne; a painter's journey. H.N. Abrams 2006 31p il $17.95

Grades: 4 5 6 7   92

1. Artists 2. Painters 3. Artists, French

ISBN 0-8109-5784-1

LC 2005011779

"Burleigh offers brief insights into Cézanne's personal life, such as his relationship with his father, who did not support his sons interest in art. However, the emphasis is on interpreting some individual paintings and understanding the artist's various styles, including the impact of the Impressionists and his evolution to a freer and simpler manner of expression in his later years. . . . The high-quality reproductions demonstrate Burleigh's points. . . . A solid, lively introduction." SLJ

Champlain, Samuel de, 1567-1635

MacLeod, Elizabeth. **Samuel** de Champlain; written by Elizabeth MacLeod; illustrated by John Mantha. Kids Can Press 2008 32p il (Kids Can Read) $14.95; pa $3.95

Grades: 1 2 3   92

1. Explorers 2. America -- Exploration
ISBN 978-1-55453-049-6; 1-55453-049-0; 978-1-55453-050-2 pa; 1-55453-050-4 pa

A biography of the French explorer of Canada

This is a "fresh, short [biography] for newly independent readers. . . . The writing is clear if sedate, and the type is large. Abundant pen-and-ink illustrations are finely rendered and enhance [the] text." SLJ

Champollion, Jean François, 1790-1832

Rumford, James. **Seeker** of knowledge; the man who deciphered Egyptian hieroglyphs. Houghton Mifflin 2000 un il $15; pa $6.95

Grades: 3 4 5   92

1. Hieroglyphics 2. Archaeologists
ISBN 0-395-97934-X; 0-618-33345-2 pa

LC 99-37254

A biography of the French scholar whose decipherment of the Egyptian hieroglyphic language made the study of ancient Egypt possible

"Despite the book's traditional picture-book appearance, with a short text and nicely rendered watercolor art, the topic requires and gets sturdy treatment. . . . Those intrigued by hieroglyphs . . . will find this a useful introduction." Booklist

Chanel, Coco, 1883-1971

★ Matthews, Elizabeth. **Different** like Coco. Candlewick Press 2007 un il $16.99

Grades: 2 3 4   92

1. Fashion designers 2. Perfumers 3. Cosmetics industry executives
ISBN 978-0-7636-2548-1; 0-7636-2548-5

LC 2006-40622

"A celebration of the life of a major fashion designer and independent spirit. . . . The story is accompanied, appropriately, by elegant pen-and-ink and watercolor cartoons that capture her struggles as a young woman, as well as her innate sense of style." SLJ

Chaplin, Charlie, 1889-1977

★ Fleischman, Sid. **Sir** Charlie; Chaplin, the funniest man in the world. Greenwillow Books 2010 268p il $19.99; lib bdg $20.89

Grades: 5 6 7 8 9   92

1. Actors 2. Comedians 3. Motion pictures 4. Motion picture directors 5. Motion picture producers
ISBN 0-06-189640-3; 0-06-189641-1 lib bdg; 978-0-06-189640-8; 978-0-06-189641-5 lib bdg

LC 2009019689

This is a biography of the actor and director who starred in such films as City Lights (1931), Modern Times (1940), The Great Dictator (1947) and Limelight (1952). Chronology. Bibliography. Index. "Grades six to ten." (Bull Cent Child Books)

"This lively and engaging account of a poor Cockney boy who became the world's greatest silent-movie comedian is a must for biography collections. . . . Brief, easily digestible chapters, an extensive time line, and plenty of photos make the book's well-researched content accessible and appealing." SLJ

Chapman, Oscar L., 1896-1978

★ Hopkinson, Deborah. **Sweet** land of liberty; written by Deborah Hopkinson; illustrated by Leonard Jenkins. Peachtree 2007 un il $16.95

Grades: K 1 2 3 4   92

1. Lawyers 2. African Americans -- Biography 3. United States

-- Race relations 4. African Americans -- Civil rights
ISBN 1-56145-395-1; 978-1-56145-395-5

LC 2006024331

"Jenkins' powerful, bright, mixed-media collages show and tell the connections, past, present, and future." SLJ

Chavez, Cesar, 1927-1993

Adler, David A. A **picture** book of Cesar Chavez; by David A. Adler and Michael S. Adler; illustrated by Marie Olofsdotter. Holiday House 2010 un il $17.95

Grades: 1 2 3 4   92

1. Migrant labor 2. Agricultural laborers 3. Labor leaders 4. Mexican Americans -- Biography
ISBN 978-0-8234-2202-9; 0-8234-2202-X

LC 2009039319

"The selfless struggles of labor leader Chávez are given a tempered and lucid treatment in this educational overview. . . . Olofsdotter keeps her illustrations gentle and ennobling. The characters are drawn in the intentionally stiff style that fits with the depth-challenged folk art backgrounds, most of which are dominated by the color of sand. . . . An elegant introduction to a man who inspired thousands." Booklist

Includes bibliographical references

★ Krull, Kathleen. **Harvesting** hope; the story of Cesar Chavez. illustrated by Yuyi Morales. Harcourt 2003 un il $17

Grades: 2 3 4   92

1. Migrant labor 2. Agricultural laborers 3. Labor leaders 4. Mexican Americans -- Biography
ISBN 0-15-201437-3

LC 2002-5096

A biography of Cesar Chavez, from age ten when he and his family lived happily on their Arizona ranch, to age thirty-eight when he led a peaceful protest against California migrant workers' miserable working conditions

"The brief text creates a remarkably complex view of Chavez—his experiences and feelings. Krull's empathetic words are well paired with artist Yuyi Morales's mixed-media acrylic paintings, which are suffused with a variety of emotions. . . . The pictures glow with intense shades of gold, green, pink, and orange." Horn Book

Chisholm, Shirley, 1924-2005

Raatma, Lucia. **Shirley** Chisholm. Marshall Cavendish Benchmark 2010 96p il (Leading women) $39.93

Grades: 4 5 6 7   92

1. Women politicians 2. Members of Congress 3. Presidential candidates 4. African American women -- Biography
ISBN 978-0-7614-4953-9; 0-7614-4953-1

"The arresting portrait on the cover will guide readers right into this well-written [biography of] . . . . the first African American woman to enter Congress. . . . Raatma vividly explains what was happening in the country at the time and uses those events effectively as a backdrop. The many photos, both black and white and color, are good choices for the well-designed book." Booklist

Includes bibliographical references

Clemens, Susy, 1872-1894

★ Kerley, Barbara. The **extraordinary** Mark Twain (according to Susy) illustrated by Edwin Fotheringam. Scholastic Press 2010 un il $17.99

Grades: 2 3 4 5   92

1. Authors 2. Biography 3. Humorists 4. Novelists 5. Authorship 6. Essayists 7. Satirists 8. Memoirists 9. Travel writers 10.

Authors, American 11. Short story writers
ISBN 978-0-545-12508-6; 0-545-12508-1

LC 2009-04752

"Wanting to present a portrait of her papa beyond that of just humorist and author, Mark Twain's 13-year-old daughter Susy spent a year chronicling her observations and reflections. . . . Kerley contextualizes the teenager's admiring musings with vivid familial backdrops. . . . Minibooklets titled 'Journal' appear in the fold of many spreads, containing excerpts from Susy's notebook. . . . Adding dynamic flair to the limited palettes of each digitally created scene are curlicues representing words, which emanate wildly from pen tips, pages, and mouths. Author notes about Susy and her father, a time line of Twain's life, and tips for writing an 'extraordinary biography' complete this accessible and inventive vision of a American legend." Publ Wkly

Clemente, Roberto, 1934-1972

★ Perdomo, Willie. **Clemente!** illustrated by Bryan Collier. Henry Holt & Co. 2010 un il $16.99
Grades: 1 2 3   **92**
1. Baseball players 2. Baseball -- Biography
ISBN 978-0-8050-8224-1; 0-8050-8224-7

"Perdomo's witty, passionate account of the beloved Puerto Rican baseball pioneer takes an unusual approach. The child narrator, whose father is president of the Roberto Clemente fan club, was named in honor of the great player, and little Clemente can tell you just about everything there is to know about the man. . . . Collier's kinetic artwork uses collage to explosive effect. . . . More than just a biography, this book warmly illustrates the parent-child bond that is one of the finer byproducts of sports fandom." Booklist

★ Winter, Jonah. **Roberto** Clemente; pride of the Pittsburgh Pirates. illustrated by Raul Colón. Atheneum Books for Young Readers 2005 un il $16.95
Grades: 2 3 4   **92**
1. Baseball players 2. Baseball -- Biography 3. Puerto Ricans -- Biography
ISBN 0-689-85643-1

LC 2003-25546

This picture-book biography by Jonah Winter "shows how [Roberto] Clemente went from a boy with a guava tree bat, coffee-bean sack glove and soup can baseballs to a man who lifted the down-trodden Pittsburgh Pirates to victory, brought respect to Hispanic peoples, and fought to relieve his country's poverty until his death." (Children's Literature)

"Winter tells the . . . story of how Clemente's passionate love of the game and unrivaled work ethic took him from poverty in Puerto Rico . . . to World Series triumph with the Pittsburgh Pirates and, later . . . to near-mythic status as a role model for young Latino ballplayers. Soaked in pastoral greens and browns, Colon's evocatively grainy, soft-focus illustrations, rendered with a mix of watercolors, colored pencils, and litho pencils, capture perfectly the worlds in which Clemente was most at home. . . . Baseball history brought vividly to life for a younger audience." Booklist

Cleopatra, Queen of Egypt, d. 30 B.C.

Blackaby, Susan. **Cleopatra**; Egypt's last and greatest queen. Sterling Pub. 2009 124p il (Sterling biographies) $12.95; pa $5.95
Grades: 5 6 7 8   **92**
1. Queens 2. Egypt -- History
ISBN 978-1-4027-6540-7; 1-4027-6540-1; 978-1-4027-5710-5 pa; 1-4027-5710-7 pa

LC 2008030146

"Villainess or goddess, a great queen or a selfish and overly ambitious woman—readers get to decide. They will be drawn into this biography by a description of a legendary magnificent banquet given by Mark Antony for Cleopatra. The lively narrative maintains interest from her birth in 69 BCE to her death in 31 BCE. . . . Sidebars, color photographs, and reproductions appear throughout. . . . This book leaves readers fascinated and eager to learn more about her time in history." SLJ

Includes glossary and bibliographical references

Shecter, Vicky Alvear. **Cleopatra** rules! the amazing life of the original teen queen. Boyds Mills Press 2010 128p il map $17.95
Grades: 5 6 7 8   **92**
1. Queens 2. Egypt -- History
ISBN 1590787188; 9781590787182

LC 2009-26737

This is a biography of "Cleopatra VII, the last pharaoh of Egypt." (Publisher's note) Bibliography. Index. "Grades six to ten." (Bull Cent Child Books)

"This attractive book presents Cleopatra's story through an unusual text, informative sidebars, and excellent color illustrations. . . . Calling attention to the writing as much as its story, the text includes puns, informal language, and contemporary metaphors. . . . Shecter's solid research is evident." Booklist

Includes glossary and bibliographical references

Cleveland, Grover, 1837-1908

Otfinoski, Steven. **Grover** Cleveland. Marshall Cavendish Benchmark 2011 112p il (Presidents and their times) lib bdg $23.95
Grades: 5 6 7 8   **92**
1. Mayors 2. Governors 3. Presidents 4. District attorneys 5. Presidents -- United States
ISBN 978-0-7614-4811-2; 0-7614-4811-X

LC 2009029689

This offers information on President Grover Cleveland and places him within his historical and cultural context. Also explored are the formative events of his times and how he responded.

"The abundant sidebars provide a good deal of background information that will be helpful to students. . . . Attractive . . . as well as useful." Booklist

Includes glossary and bibliographical references

Clinton, Hillary Rodham

Levinson, Cynthia. **Hillary** Rodham Clinton; Do All the Good You Can. Cynthia Levinson. Balzer + Bray 2016 352 p. 8 leaves of plates; ill. $16.99
Grades: 5 6 7 8   **92**
1. Women politicians
ISBN 0062387308; 9780062387301

LC 2015940617

Author Cynthia Levinson presents this "meticulously researched middle grade biography of Hillary Rodham Clinton--First Lady, senator, secretary of state, and Democratic candidate for president in 2016. Levinson creates a compelling and personal portrait of Hillary's historic journey from her childhood to her service as secretary of state and beyond. Includes a timeline of Hillary Rodham Clinton's life and an eight-page photo insert." (Publisher's note)

"A respectful, insightful, and inspiring portrait of a fiercely ambitious, remarkably successful woman who has changed the face of American politics." Kirkus

Includes bibliographical references (pages 293-322) and index.

Coachman, Alice

Malaspina, Ann. **Touch** the sky; Alice Coachman, Olympic high jumper. by Ann Malaspina; illustrated by Eric Velasquez. Albert Whitman 2012 32 p.
Grades: 2 3 4   **92**
1. Picture books for children 2. Women athletes 3. Track athletics

4. African American athletes   5. Jumping -- United States   6. Track and field athletes -- United States   7. African American women athletes -- United States
ISBN 080758035X; 9780807580356

LC 2011008564

This children's picture book by Ann Malaspina tells the story of the African American Olympic high jumper Alice Coachman. "In Alice's Georgia hometown, there was no track where an African-American girl could practice, so she made her own crossbar with sticks and rags. . . . Her dream to compete at the Olympics came true in 1948. This is a . . . free-verse story of the first African-American woman to win an Olympic gold medal. Photos . . . are also included." (Publisher's note)

Includes bibliographical references.

Cogswell, Alice

★ McCully, Emily Arnold. **My** heart glow: Alice Cogswell, Thomas Gallaudet and the birth of American sign language. Hyperion Books for Children 2008 un il $15.99

Grades: 2 3 4   **92**

1. Deaf 2. Sign language 3. Teachers of the deaf
ISBN 978-1-4231-0028-7; 1-4231-0028-X

This is the story of Thomas Gallaudet and his deaf neighbor, Alice Cogswell, and how Gallaudet established a school for the deaf in the United States and developed American Sign Language.

"Emily Arnold McCully's watercolor illustrations are beautifully rendered. . . . Not only does this book accurately present the engrossing story of Alice and Gallaudet, it is also an excellent resource for teaching diversity and encouraging empathy for others." Libr Media Connect

Coleman, Bessie, 1896?-1926

★ Grimes, Nikki. **Talkin'** about Bessie: the story of aviator Elizabeth Coleman; illustrated by E. B. Lewis. Orchard Bks. 2002 un il $16.95

Grades: 3 4 5   **92**

1. Air pilots 2. Women air pilots 3. African American pilots
ISBN 0-439-35243-6

Coretta Scott King Award for illustration, 2003

"Following a brief introduction to Coleman's life, the story, couched in a fictional framework, opens in the parlor of a house in Chicago, where friends and relatives gather to mourn Bessie's death. Each spread features one person speaking about Bessie. . . . Lewis' paintings, subdued in tone and color, reflect the spirit of the verse through telling details and sensitive, impressionistic portrayals." Booklist

Includes bibliographical references

Colt, Samuel, 1814-1862

Wyckoff, Edwin Brit. The **man** behind the gun: Samuel Colt and his revolver. Enslow Publishers 2010 32p il (Genius at work! Great inventor biographies) lib bdg $22.60

Grades: 4 5 6   **92**

1. Inventors 2. Firearms industry 3. Gunsmiths 4. Manufacturing executives
ISBN 978-0-7660-3446-4 lib bdg; 0-7660-3446-1 lib bdg

LC 2009-28129

"Readers will learn about Samuel Colt, the revolver, and mass production." Publisher's note

Includes glossary and bibliographical references

Coltrane, John, 1926-1967

Weatherford, Carole Boston, 1956- **Before** John was a jazz giant: a song of John Coltrane; [illustrated by] Sean Qualls. Henry Holt & Co. 2008 un il $16.95

Grades: K 1 2 3   **92**

1. Jazz musicians 2. African American musicians 3. Saxophonists
ISBN 0-8050-7994-7; 978-0-8050-7994-4

LC 2007-07196

Coretta Scott King honor book for illustration, 2009

This is an account of John Coltrane's childhood in the 1930s. "Ages five to eight." (Bull Cent Child Books)

"The beat of lyrical words and the rhythm of the beautiful illustrations express how, as a child, jazz-musician Coltrane heard music in the world around him. Vibrant with color and movement, double-page spreads in acrylic, collage, and pencil extend the images about the magical sounds of everyday things." Booklist

Columbus, Christopher

Fritz, Jean. **Where** do you think you're going, Christopher Columbus? pictures by Margot Tomes. Putnam 1980 80p il maps $15.99; pa $5.99

Grades: 2 3 4   **92**

1. Explorers 2. America -- Exploration
ISBN 0-399-20723-6; 0-698-11580-5 pa

LC 80-11377

Discusses the voyages of Christopher Columbus who was determined to beat everyone in the race to the Indies

"Reducing a life as well-documented as Columbus's to 80 pages must result in some simplifications of fact or context, but in this case they are not readily apparent. Mrs. Fritz's breezy narrative gives us a highly individual Columbus. . . . Margot Tomes's three-color illustrations are attractive, amusing and informative." N Y Times Book Rev

Comstock, Anna Botsford, 1854-1930

Slade, Suzanne. **Out** of school and into nature; written by Suzanne Slade; illustrated by Jessica Lanan. Sleeping Bear Press 2017 32 p. color illustrations $16.99

Grades: K 1 2 3   **92**

1. Natural history   2. Women naturalists -- United States -- Biography   3. Naturalists -- United States -- Biography
ISBN 9781585369867

LC 2016026786

This picture book biography, by Suzanne Slade, illustrated by Jessica Lanan, "examines the life and career of naturalist and artist Anna Comstock (1854-1930), who defied social conventions and pursued the study of science. From the time she was a young girl, Anna Comstock was fascinated by the natural world. . . . Eventually Anna became known as a nature expert, pioneering a movement to encourage schools to conduct science and nature classes for children outdoors." (Publisher's note)

Cone, Claribel, 1864-1929

★ Fillion, Susan. **Miss** Etta and Dr. Claribel; Bringing Matisse to America. David R. Godine 2011 83p il $18.95

Grades: 4 5 6 7   **92**

1. Artists 2. Painters 3. Physicians 4. Art collectors 5. Art -- Collectors and collecting
ISBN 978-1-56792-434-3; 1-56792-434-4

LC 2010048937

"An affectionate, lively examination of the reciprocal relationship between a great artist and two great art lovers. Etta and Claribel Cone, unmarried sisters from a wealthy Baltimore family . . . [were] discerning collectors of modern art, particularly that of Henri Matisse. . . . Their account is lavishly illustrated in full color by reproductions from the Cone Collection at the Baltimore Museum of Art and Matisse-inflected paintings by the author, who drew extensively on the Cone archive that is also housed at the museum. . . . This appealing work stands as both a portrait of two unconventional women and a celebration of the possibilities of arts patronage." Kirkus

Cone, Etta, 1870-1949

★ Fillion, Susan. **Miss** Etta and Dr. Claribel; Bringing Matisse to America. David R. Godine 2011 83p il $18.95

Grades: 4 5 6 7   **92**

1. Artists 2. Painters 3. Physicians 4. Art collectors 5. Art -- Collectors and collecting

ISBN 978-1-56792-434-3; 1-56792-434-4

LC 2010048937

"An affectionate, lively examination of the reciprocal relationship between a great artist and two great art lovers. Etta and Claribel Cone, unmarried sisters from a wealthy Baltimore family . . . [were] discerning collectors of modern art, particularly that of Henri Matisse. . . . Their account is lavishly illustrated in full color by reproductions from the Cone Collection at the Baltimore Museum of Art and Matisse-inflected paintings by the author, who drew extensively on the Cone archive that is also housed at the museum. . . . This appealing work stands as both a portrait of two unconventional women and a celebration of the possibilties of arts patronage." Kirkus

Copernicus, Nicolaus, 1473-1543

Andronik, Catherine M. **Copernicus**; founder of modern astronomy. rev ed; Enslow Publishers 2009 128p bibl il (Great minds of science) lib bdg $31.93

Grades: 5 6 7 8   **92**

1. Astronomers

ISBN 978-0-7660-3013-8 lib bdg; 0-7660-3013-X lib bdg

LC 2008-23940

First published 2002

"A highly readable book that presents a good balance between the biographical information needed to understand Copernicus as a man and the scientific explanations necessary to understand his work. . . . Good-quality, black-and-white reproductions, illustrations, and photographs add interest to the clearly written text." SLJ [review of 2002 edition]

Includes glossary and bibliographical references

Cosgrove, Miranda, 1993-

Yasuda, Anita. **Miranda** Cosgrove. Weigl 2011 24p il (Remarkable people) $27.13; pa $12.95

Grades: 4 5 6 7   **92**

1. Actors 2. Singers

ISBN 978-1-6169-0668-9; 1-6169-0668-5; 978-1-6169-0673-3 pa; 1-6169-0673-1 pa

LC 2010051144

A biography of actress and singer Miranda Cosgrove

Coup, W. C., 1857-1895

Covert, Ralph. **Sawdust** and spangles: the amazing life of W.C. Coup; [by] Ralph Covert, G. Riley Mills; illustrated by Giselle Potter. Abrams Books for Young Readers 2007 un il $16.95

Grades: K 1 2 3   **92**

1. Circus 2. Circus executives

ISBN 978-0-8109-9351-8; 0-8109-9351-1

LC 2006031981

"As a boy, William Cameron Coup left home to run away with the circus. . . . He eventually became one of the industry's most successful and inventive entrepeneurs. This picture book biography relates Coup's story in an accessible . . . way. Potter's illustrations are beautifully rendered, interpreting Coup's life and world with quirky energy and imaginative color." Horn Book Guide

Cousteau, Jacques Yves, 1910-1997

Berne, Jennifer. **Manfish** : a story of Jacques Cousteau; illustrated by Eric Puybaret. Chronicle Books 2008 un il $16.99

Grades: K 1 2 3   **92**

1. Ocean 2. Authors 3. Scientists 4. Skin diving 5. Divers 6. Naval officers 7. Oceanographers 8. Nonfiction writers 9. Biography, Individual 10. Underwater exploration

ISBN 0-8118-6063-9; 978-0-8118-6063-5

LC 2007-30513

This is a biography of the underwater explorer and marine naturalist. "Ages six to nine." (Bull Cent Child Books)

"Writing in simple poetic language, both lyrical and concise . . . Berne offers a luminous picture-book biography of about Jacques Cousteau. . . . Puybaret's smooth-looking acrylic paintings extend the words' elegant simplicity and beautifully convey the sense of infinite, underwater space." Booklist

★ Yaccarino, Dan. The **fantastic** undersea life of Jacques Cousteau. Knopf 2009 un il $16.99; lib bdg $19.99

Grades: K 1 2 3   **92**

1. Ocean 2. Authors 3. Scientists 4. Skin diving 5. Divers 6. Naval officers 7. Oceanographers 8. Nonfiction writers

ISBN 978-0-375-85573-3; 978-0-375-95573-0 lib bdg

LC 2008-04581

This is a picture-book biography of the oceanographer and environmentalist. Chronology. "Grades two to four." (Bull Cent Child Books)

"Yaccarino deftly provides information about important events in Cousteau's life while conveying the excitement and wonder that the ocean explorer experienced. . . . Effective layout and page design plus colorful gouache illustrations result in a striking visual presentation." SLJ

Coville, Bruce

Parker-Rock, Michelle. **Bruce** Coville; by Michelle Parker-Rock. Enslow Publishers 2008 48p bibl il por (Authors kids love) lib bdg $23.93

Grades: 3 4 5   **92**

1. Authors 2. Authors, American 3. Children's authors

ISBN 978-0-7660-2755-8 lib bdg; 0-7660-2755-4 lib bdg

LC 2006015873

A biography of the popular children's author, Bruce Coville, based on a interview.

The text is "interesting and conversational throughout. . . . [A] colorful [cover], family photos, and a font size that's not too intimidating all contribute to the [book's] appeal. . . . Suitable for reports or for pleasure reading." SLJ

Includes glossary and bibliographical references

Crandall, Prudence, 1803-1890

★ Jurmain, Suzanne. The **forbidden** schoolhouse; the true and dramatic story of Prudence Crandall and her students. Houghton Mifflin 2005 150p il $18

Grades: 5 6 7 8   **92**

1. Teachers 2. Educators 3. Abolitionists 4. African Americans -- Education

ISBN 0-618-47302-5

This is the story of Prudence Crandall, who, in 1831, opened a school for African American girls in Canterbury, Connecticut.

"A compelling, highly readable book. . . . Writing with a sense of drama that propels readers forward . . . Jurmain makes painfully clear what Crandall and her students faced. . . . Including a number of sepia-toned and color photographs as well as historical engravings, the book's look will draw in readers." Booklist

Includes bibliographical references

Crazy Horse, Sioux Chief, ca. 1842-1877

Brimner, Larry Dane. **Chief** Crazy Horse; following a vision. Marshall Cavendish Benchmark 2009 41p il (American heroes) lib bdg $20.95

Grades: 2 3 4   92

1. Indian chiefs 2. Native Americans -- Biography

ISBN 978-0-7614-3061-2

LC 2008002868

A biography of Crazy Horse, warrior chief of the Oglala tribe of the Sioux nation

This "concise and well-written [title covers] key biographical facts without overwhelming young readers, and [includes] captioned illustrations and reproductions, most of which are in color. Text is large, and the layout is age-appropriate and attractive, with wide margins." SLJ

Includes glossary and bibliographical references

Creesy, Eleanor, 1814-1900

Fern, Tracey. **Dare** the wind; Tracey Fern; pictures by Emily Arnold McCully. Farrar, Straus and Giroux 2014 40 p. color illustrations, map (hard) $17.99

Grades: K 1 2 3 4   92

1. Sailing 2. Navigation 3. Women sailors -- Biography 4. Flying Cloud (Clipper-ship)

ISBN 0374316996; 9780374316990

LC 2013007868

Author Tracey Fern presents a biography of Ellen Prentiss. "As soon as she met a man who loved sailing like she did, she married him. When her husband was given command of a clipper ship custom-made to travel quickly, she knew that they would need every bit of its speed for their maiden voyage: out of New York City, down around the tip of Cape Horn, and into San Francisco, where the Gold Rush was well under way." (Publisher's note)

"McCully's expertly rendered watercolor illustrations evoke, in double-page spreads, the rich atmosphere of the sea in all its moods, while many events are shown as round vignettes--as though seen through a spyglass." Kirkus

Crews, Donald

Crews, Donald. **Bigmama's**. Greenwillow Bks. 1991 un il $16; lib bdg $15.93; pa $5.95

Grades: K 1 2 3   92

1. Artists 2. Authors 3. Country life 4. Illustrators 5. Photographers 6. Authors, American 7. Children's authors 8. African Americans -- Biography

ISBN 0-688-09950-5; 0-688-09951-3 lib bdg; 0-688-15842-0 pa

LC 90-33142

Visiting Bigmama's house in the country, young Donald Crews finds his relatives full of news and the old place and its surroundings just the same as the year before

"This is an evocative celebration of the joy and wonder of childhood; would that every child had such a summer. The last page is a hauntingly lovely remembrance. The illustrations are perfect and make this a truly beautiful book." Child Book Rev Serv

Cristofori, Bartolomeo, 1655-1732

Rusch, Elizabeth. The **music** of life; Bartolomeo Cristofori and the invention of the piano. Elizabeth Rusch; illustrated by Marjorie Priceman. Atheneum Books for Young Readers 2017 48 p. color illustrations (hardcover) $17.99

Grades: 2 3 4 5   92

1. Pianos 2. Piano -- History -- 18th century 3. Piano makers -- Italy -- Biography 4. Harpsichord makers -- Italy -- Biography

ISBN 9781481444842; 9781481444859

LC 2015017472

This book, by Elizabeth Rusch, illustrated by Marjorie Priceman, tells "the inspiring story of the invention of the world's most popular instrument: the piano. Bartolomeo Cristofori coaxes just the right sounds from the musical instruments he makes. Some of his keyboards can play piano, light and soft; others make forte notes ring out, strong and loud, but Cristofori longs to create an instrument that can be played both soft and loud." (Publisher's note)

Includes bibliographical references (page 47)

Crum, George, fl. 1853

Taylor, Gaylia. **George** Crum and the Saratoga chip; illustrated by Frank Morrison. Lee & Low Books 2006 32p il $16.95

Grades: 2 3 4   92

1. Cooks 2. Cooking 3. Racially mixed people 4. United States -- Race relations

ISBN 978-1-58430-255-1; 1-58430-255-0

LC 2005015313

"Part Native American, part African American, George Crum coped with prejudice as a boy in New York State during the 1830s. As a young man, he became an excellent cook and was hired as a chef at a renowned restaurant in Saratoga Springs. . . . Once . . . Crum retrieved [a] dish of French fries, whittled them into very thin slices, and cooked them in hot oil, creating the forerunner of the potato chip. . . . This picture-book biography describes dramatic moments that reveal Crum's creativity, artistic temperament, and relentless pursuit of perfection. Buoyant acrylic illustrations accentuate the absurdity of situations, depicting the jaunty chef, all angles and energy." Booklist

Includes bibliographical references

Cummings, E. E. (Edward Estlin), 1894-1962

Burgess, Matthew. **Enormous** smallness; the story of E. E. Cummings. Matthew Burgess; illustrations by Kris DiGiacomo. Enchanted Lion Books 2015 64 p. (alk. paper) $17.95

Grades: 1 2 3 4   92

1. Biography 2. American poets 3. American authors -- Biography

ISBN 159270171X; 9781592701711

LC 2015005781

This juvenile book, by Matthew Burgess with illustrations by Kris DiGiacomo, "is a nonfiction picture book about the poet E.E. cummings. Here E.E.'s life is presented in a way that will make children curious about him and will lead them to play with words and ask plenty of questions as well." (Publisher's note)

Curie, Marie, 1867-1934

Cregan, Elizabeth R. **Marie** Curie; pioneering physicist. Compass Point Books 2009 40p il map (Mission: Science) lib bdg $26.60

Grades: 4 5 6   92

1. Chemists 2. Physicists 3. Women scientists 4. Nobel laureates for physics

ISBN 978-0-7565-3960-3

This biography of the discoverer of radium "does a good job of connecting the scientist's work to our lives today. . . . [The] book has a variety of graphics including diagrams, photos, and reproductions of paintings and sketches. [This volume is] a definite plus for a school library or the juvenile collection in a public library." Libr Media Connect

★ Krull, Kathleen. **Marie** Curie; [illustrations by] Boris Kulikov. Viking 2007 128p il (Giants of science) $15.99

Grades: 5 6 7 8   92

1. Chemists 2. Physicists 3. Women scientists 4. Nobel laureates for physics

ISBN 978-0-670-05894-5; 0-670-05894-7

LC 2007-24251

"The compelling and conversational narrative (ably assisted by Kulikov's black-and-white drawings) portrays a brilliant . . . woman with plenty of idiosyncrasies, and the story of her discovery of radium . . . is as engaging as any of her personal dramas and challenges." Horn Book

Curtis, Christopher Paul

Parker-Rock, Michelle. **Christopher** Paul Curtis; an author kids love. Enslow Publishers 2009 48p il (Authors kids love) lib bdg $23.93

Grades: 1 2 3   92

1. Authors 2. African American authors 3. Authors, American 4. Children's authors 5. Government employees

ISBN 978-0-7660-3161-6 lib bdg; 0-7660-3161-6 lib bdg

LC 2009022379

A biography of the author of the Newbery honor book The Watsons Go to Birmingham—1963 and the Newbery winner Bud, not Buddy

Includes glossary and bibliographical references

Custer, George Armstrong, 1839-1876

Anderson, Paul Christopher. **George** Armstrong Custer; the Indian Wars and the Battle of the Little Bighorn. [by] Paul Christopher Anderson. PowerPlus Books 2004 112p il (Library of American lives and times) lib bdg $31.95

Grades: 4 5 6 7   92

1. Generals 2. Little Bighorn, Battle of the, 1876 3. Army officers 4. Native Americans -- Wars

ISBN 0-8239-6631-3

LC 2002-153404

A biography of the Civil War general who died at the Battle of the Little Bighorn

This "is not an apologia but a carefully measured analysis. . . . Stunning reproductions and photos provide a clear sense of the times and settings." SLJ

Includes bibliographical references

DJ Kool Herc

Hill, Laban Carrick. **When** the beat was born; DJ Kool Herc and the creation of hip hop. Laban Carrick Hill; illustrated by Theodore Taylor III. Roaring Brook Press 2013 32 p. (hardcover) $17.99

Grades: 1 2 3 4 5   92

1. Picture books for children 2. Hip-hop culture 3. Disc jockeys -- United States -- Biography 4. Rap musicians -- United States -- Biography

ISBN 1596435402; 9781596435407

LC 2012029746

Coretta Scott King/John Steptoe New Talent Award (2014)

This children's picture book discusses the origin of hip-hop through the story of DJ Kool Herc. "Young Clive fell in love with music as a child in Jamaica. . . . When he moved to the Bronx, Clive became Kool Herc, and when he had the opportunity to throw his own dance parties, he became DJ Kool Herc. Herc's innovative style as a DJ, stretching the breaks in songs from seconds into minutes, allowed the creativity of others to erupt, such as break dancers, rappers and MCs. Hip-hop was born." (Kirkus Reviews)

Dahl, Roald

Dahl, Roald. The **missing** golden ticket and other splendiferous secrets; illustrated by Quentin Blake. Puffin Books 2010 115p il pa $4.99

Grades: 3 4 5 6   92

1. Authors 2. Authors, English 3. Children's authors 4. Short story writers

ISBN 978-0-14-241742-3 pa; 0-14-241742-4 pa

LC 2010021712

"Containing excerpts from earlier tributes to Dahl's work and wit, this is an eclectic and funny collection of tidbits by and about the late author. The kernel of the book is 'Spotty Powder,' a characteristically droll chapter from an early draft of Charlie and the Chocolate Factory. . . . Highly entertaining, it's a sparkling window into Dahl's vivid personality and oeuvre." Publ Wkly

Dahl, Roald. **More** about Boy; Roald Dahl's tales from childhood. Farrar, Straus, and Giroux 2009 229p il $16.99

Grades: 5 6 7 8   92

1. Authors 2. Authors, English 3. Children's authors 4. Short story writers

ISBN 978-0-374-35055-0; 0-374-35055-8

LC 2009016118

First published 2008 in the United Kingdom

"Containing the entire text and artwork from Dahl's 1984 autobiography Boy, this reworked and expanded version also incorporates previously unpublished materials from the Roald Dahl Museum and Story Centre in England, as well as excerpts that have appeared in earlier books. . . . Dahl's revealing writing, open and full of wicked humor, is certain to endear the beloved writer . . . to a new generation." Publ Wkly

Dalai Lama XIV, 1935-

Kimmel, Elizabeth Cody. **Boy** on the lion throne; the childhood of the 14th Dalai Lama. with a foreword by His Holiness the Dalai Lama. Roaring Brook Press 2009 146p il map $18.95

Grades: 4 5 6 7   92

1. Buddhism 2. Tibet (China) 3. Buddhist leaders 4. Political leaders 5. Nobel laureates for peace

ISBN 978-1-59643-394-6; 1-59643-394-9

Follows the childhood of Lhamo Thondup, who was identified at the age of two as the fourteenth reincarnation of the Dalai Lama, describing the humble life he was born into and how his life changed after he was recognized

"Kimmel is reverent without being adulatory, and her explanation of the Dalai Lama's relationship with Maoist China is presented in simple, clear language. This is a strange and fascinating story told in an engaging style, and young readers will find lots to keep them turning the pages." Bull Cent Child Books

Includes bibliographical references

Darwin, Charles, 1809-1882

Ashby, Ruth. **Young** Charles Darwin and the voyage of the Beagle; written by Ruth Ashby. Peachtree 2009 116p il map $12.95

Grades: 4 5 6   92

1. Evolution 2. Naturalists 3. Travel writers 4. Writers on science 5. Beagle Expedition (1831-1836)

ISBN 978-1-56145-478-5; 1-56145-478-8

LC 2008-36747

"Beginning with the letter inviting him to sail aboard the Beagle, this traditional biography relates Darwin's life with an emphasis on the trip that led him to forge his theory about natural selection. Ashby makes good use of Darwin's own writing, sprinkling quotes throughout the text, which allow his adventures and opinions to come to life. . . . This biography will work well for book reports . . . providing accurate and readable information about the scientist and his journey." Booklist

Includes bibliographical references

★ Krull, Kathleen. **Charles** Darwin; illustrated by Boris Kulikov. Viking 2010 144p il (Giants of science) $15.99

Grades: 5 6 7 8   92

1. Evolution 2. Naturalists 3. Travel writers 4. Writers on science

ISBN 978-0-670-06335-2; 0-670-06335-5

LC 2010-07315

"Krull once again offers an illuminating, humanizing portrait of a famous scientist. . . . Krull . . . writes in easily paced, lively, conversational prose, knitting together interesting facts, anecdotes, and historical overviews into a fascinating whole. She offers clear definitions of not only Darwin's theories but also how his discoveries built on previous scientists' work. . . . Kulikov's whimsical ink drawings and well-culled list of resources round out this strong entry in the series." Booklist

Lasky, Kathryn. **One** beetle too many: the extraordinary adventures of Charles Darwin. Candlewick Press 2009 un il $17.99; pa $6.99
Grades: 3 4 5 6   92
1. Evolution 2. Naturalists 3. Travel writers 4. Writers on science 5. Beagle Expedition (1831-1836)
ISBN 0-7636-1436-X; 978-0-7636-1436-2; 978-0-7636-5821-2 pa
                                                LC 2002-71254
Describes the life and work of the renowned nineteenth-century biologist who transformed conventional Western thought with his theory of natural evolution.
"Distilling tough concepts into light, conversational prose, Lasky . . . gives middle-graders a just-right introduction to Charles Darwin. . . . Trueman . . . up-ends perspective with multilayed mixed-media illustrations; mostly paint, these also incorporate bits of flowers and weeds as well as string, paper, and fabric. . . . Highly accessible." Publ Wkly

Markle, Sandra. **Animals** Charles Darwin saw; an around-the-world adventure. illustrated by Zina Saunders. Chronicle Books 2009 45p il $16.99
Grades: 2 3 4 5   92
1. Animals 2. Evolution 3. Naturalists 4. Travel writers 5. Writers on science 6. Beagle Expedition (1831-1836)
ISBN 978-0-8118-5049-0; 0-8118-5049-8
                                                LC 2007-53058
Looks at the animals that Charles Darwin saw throughout his life, from his early explorations in local woods and fields to his travels on the HMS Beagle, and how they influenced his later thought.
"Sandra Markle tells Darwin's story in clear prose spiced with interesting vignettes, . . . and Zina Saunders brings the scenes alive with colorful woodcut illustrations." NY Times Book Rev

McGinty, Alice B. **Darwin**; illustrated by Mary Azarian. Houghton Mifflin Books for Children 2009 un il $18
Grades: 1 2 3 4   92
1. Evolution 2. Naturalists 3. Travel writers 4. Writers on science 5. Beagle Expedition (1831-1836)
ISBN 978-0-618-99531-8; 0-618-99531-5
                                                LC 2008-33930
"After tracing Charles Darwin's youth and education, this fully illustrated biography focuses on his five-year voyage about the HMS Beagle. . . . Azarian . . . illustrates the book using handsome woodcut prints painted with watercolors. . . . The interplay of the clearly written third-person text with Darwin's own words and occasional quotes from his contemporaries creates a multifaceted view that leads to a broader understanding." Booklist

★ Schanzer, Rosalyn. **What** Darwin saw; the journey that changed the world. National Geographic 2009 47p il map $17.95; lib bdg $26.90
Grades: 3 4 5 6   92
1. Evolution 2. Naturalists 3. Travel writers 4. Writers on science 5. Beagle Expedition (1831-1836)
ISBN 978-1-4263-0396-8; 1-4263-0396-3; 978-1-4263-0397-5 lib bdg; 1-4263-0397-1 lib bdg
                                                LC 2008-39809

"Schanzer uses Darwin's own words, taken from his journals, books, and letters, in the speech balloons of her graphic depiction of the voyage of the Beagle. This is not a full biography, but begins with Darwin's acceptance of the offer to sail on the expedition and ends with the presentation of his theory of evolution in 1860. Bright, watercolor cartoons accurately portray landscapes and specimens while also creating a vivid sense of adventure." SLJ
Includes bibligraphical references

Sis, Peter. The **tree** of life: a book depicting the life of Charles Darwin, naturalist, geologist & thinker. Frances Foster Bks./Farrar, Straus & Giroux 2003 un il map $18
Grades: 4 5 6 7   92
1. Naturalists 2. Travel writers 3. Writers on science
ISBN 0-374-45628-3
                                                LC 2002-40706
Presents the life of the famous nineteenth-century naturalist using text from Darwin's writings and detailed drawings by Sis
"Muted tones of blue, green, and tan, and finely hatched drawings in the manner of old prints lend a period look to the pages. Beautifully conceived and executed, the presentation is a humorous and informative tour de force that will absorb and challenge readers." SLJ

Dave, ca. 1800-ca. 1870
Cheng, Andrea. **Etched** in clay; the life of Dave, enslaved potter and poet. Andrea Cheng; with woodcuts by the author. Lee & Low Books 2012 144 p. (hardcover : alk. paper) $17.95
Grades: 4 5 6   92
1. Slaves 2. Potters 3. African American poèts 4. African American potters 5. Slaves -- South Carolina
ISBN 160060451X; 9781600604515; 9781600608933
                                                LC 2012027280
In this children's biography in verse, Caldecott Honor-winner Andrea Cheng looks at the "life of the enslaved potter Dave," who wrote poetry. "Records indicate Dave, who was born in the United States in 1801, was most likely purchased at a slave auction at age 17 by Harvey Drake, who, with his uncles, held the Pottersville Stoneware Manufactory in South Carolina. Dave took to the wheel within weeks and went on to become one of the most accomplished potters in the region." (Kirkus Reviews)

★ Hill, Laban Carrick. **Dave,** the potter; artist, poet, slave. illustrated by Bryan Collier. Little, Brown Books for Young Readers 2010 un il $16.99
Grades: K 1 2 3 4   92
1. Slaves 2. Artists 3. American pottery 4. African American artists 5. African American authors 6. Ceramists 7. Poets, American 8. Slavery -- United States
ISBN 0-316-10731-X; 978-0-316-10731-0
                                                LC 2010-06382
A Caldecott Medal honor book, 2011
This is a biography of the artist known as Dave, who "spent most of his life in a rural South Carolina district famed for its stoneware. . . . [Dave's] creations included mammoth storage pots. . . . Sometimes he signed his name and put the date. Other times he wrote verse [on the pot], usually a short rhyme. . . . Ages three to six." (N Y Times Book Rev)
"The life of an astonishingly prolific and skilled potter who lived and died a slave in 19th-century South Carolina is related in simple, powerful sentences that outline the making of a pot. The movements of Dave's hands are described using familiar, solid verbs: pulling, pinching, squeezing, pounding. . . . The pithy lines themselves recall the short poems that Dave inscribed on his pots. Collier's earth-toned watercolor and collage art extends the story, showing the landscape, materials, and architecture of a South Carolina farm. . . . A lengthy author's note fleshes

out what is known of the man's life story and reproduces several of his two-line poems." SLJ

David-Neel, Alexandra, 1868-1969

★ Brown, Don. **Far** beyond the garden gate: Alexandra David-Neel's journey to Lhasa. Houghton Mifflin 2002 un il $16
Grades: 3 4 5   92
1. Authors 2. Buddhism 3. Explorers 4. Travelers 5. Centenarians 6. Tibet (China) 7. Travel writers 8. Religious scholars 9. Asian studies specialists
ISBN 0-618-08364-2
LC 2002-222

Describes the life and travels of Alexandra David-Neel, who became a scholar of Buddhism and Tibet in the early twentieth century and trekked thousands of miles to reach Llasa, the Tibetan capital.

This "tells a fascinating tale. . . . David-Neel's vivid quotes are interspersed throughout the story. . . . The beiges, grays, and whites of Brown's palette capture the feeling of the unfamiliar world into which the woman and her companion ventured." SLJ

Includes bibliographical references

Dawes, Dominique, 1976-
Washburn, Kim. **Heart** of a champion; the Dominique Dawes story. Kim Washburn. Zonderkidz 2012 123 p. ill. (softcover) $6.99
Grades: 4 5 6   92
1. Olympic games 2. African American women 3. African American athletes 4. Christian biography 5. Gymnasts -- United States -- Biography
ISBN 0310722683; 9780310722687
LC 2012008588

Author Kim Washburn tells the story of gymnast Dominique Dawes, who "competed in three Olympic games and was one of two women to be the first African American to medal in gymnastics. She was also a member of the celebrated Magnificent Seven, the team that won the gold medal in Atlanta in 1996 over the dominant Russian and Romanian squads. . . . Washburn offers up many of Dawes' less illustrious moments, . . . including disappointing performances at World Championships, a brief stint on Broadway, and her search for a lasting and fulfilling career." (Booklist)

De Paola, Tomie, 1934-

★ DePaola, Tomie, 1934- **26** Fairmount Avenue; written and illustrated by Tomie dePaola. Putnam 1999 56p il $14.99; pa $6.99
Grades: 2 3 4   92
1. Artists 2. Authors 3. Painters 4. Illustrators 5. Authors, American 6. Children's authors
ISBN 0-399-23246-X; 0-698-11864-2 pa
LC 98-12918

A Newbery Medal honor book, 2000

Children's author-illustrator Tomie De Paola describes his experiences at home and in school when he was a boy. "Age four and up." (Commonweal)

"A disarmingly unselfconscious reminiscence. . . . The immediacy of detail resists nostalgia, and dePaola is wise to what recent graduates of his picture books will find interesting. Neat sketches and silhouettes will draw browsers in to this satisfying easy chapter book." Horn Book Guide

Followed by Here we all are

DePaola, Tomie, 1934- **Christmas** remembered; [by] Tomie de-Paola. G. P. Putnam's Sons 2006 86p il $19.99; pa $9.99
Grades: 5 6 7 8   92
1. Artists 2. Authors 3. Painters 4. Christmas 5. Illustrators 6.

Authors, American 7. Children's authors
ISBN 0-399-24622-3; 0-14-241481-6 pa
LC 2005032658

The children's author and artist shares his love of Christmas in 15 memories, which span six decades

"Brightening the pages are illustrations in varied styles and media, from an intriguing portrait of dePaola's Italian grandmother to decorative paper collages to iconic paintings of great stillness and beauty. . . . Written with dialogue and humor as well as reflection." Booklist

DePaola, Tomie, 1934- **For** the duration; a 26 Fairmount Avenue book; the war years. written and illustrated by Tomie dePaola. Putnam's Sons 2009 99p il $15.99
Grades: 2 3 4   92
1. Artists 2. Authors 3. Painters 4. Illustrators 5. World War, 1939-1945 6. Authors, American 7. Children's authors
ISBN 978-0-399-25209-9; 0-399-25209-6

From gas rationing to air-raid drills, as long as the war lasts, life is going to be different for Tomie. And sometimes different is hard. Fortunately, Tomie still has school, his family, and the things he's good at to carry him through.

"DePaola's style and word choices are just right for his audience, and the point of view is consistently that of a second grader. Full-page and spot art black-and-white pencil drawings and silhouette art by the author illustrate this must-read title for fans of the series." SLJ

DePaola, Tomie, 1934- **I'm** still scared; a 26 Fairmount Avenue book, book 6. written and illustrated by Tomie dePaola. G. P. Putnam's Sons 2006 83p il $13.99; pa $5.99
Grades: 2 3 4   92
1. Artists 2. Authors 3. Painters 4. Illustrators 5. Authors, American 6. Children's authors 7. World War, 1939-1945 -- United States
ISBN 0-399-24502-2; 0-14-240826-3 pa
LC 2005-13500

"DePaola picks up his autobiographical series right where his last title, Things Will Never Be the Same (2003), left off: December, 7, 1941. Now in second grade, little Tomie describes the reactions to the Pearl Harbor bombings, first at home, then at church, and finally at school. . . . Once again, the warm, childlike narration captures both the specifics of the time and universal experiences that will connect with most children. The shaded, black-and-white sketches on each page extend the story's small, revealing moments." Booklist

Followed by Why?

DePaola, Tomie, 1934- **On** my way; a 26 Fairmount Avenue book. written and illustrated by Tomie dePaola. Putnam 2001 73p il $13.99; pa $6.99
Grades: 2 3 4   92
1. Artists 2. Authors 3. Painters 4. Illustrators 5. Authors, American 6. Children's authors
ISBN 0-399-23583-3; 0-698-11948-7 pa
LC 00-38229

This is the third installment of De Paola's memoirs of childhood. It "culminates with the artist entering first grade and finally . . . getting to learn to read. . . . The memoir begins in the previous spring, with the crisis of baby sister Maureen's pneumonia. . . . There are happier times as well. . . . Primary." (Horn Book)

"The saga of dePaola's early life related in 26 Fairmount Avenue . . . and Here We All Are . . . continues with this reminiscence of kindergarten and first grade. dePaola describes his baby sister Maureen's recovery from pneumonia, a family trip to the 1939 World's Fair, and his theatrical debut as the blushing bride in a 'Tiny Tot Bridal Party.' . . . The humor is clear and the selection of incidents indicates the author has a comfortable familiarity with the concerns of his audience." Bull Cent Child Books

Followed by What a year!

DePaola, Tomie, 1934- **Why?** a 26 Fairmount Avenue book. written and illustrated by Tomie dePaola. G. P. Putnam's Sons 2007 85p il $14.99

Grades: 2 3 4   92
1. Artists 2. Authors 3. Painters 4. Illustrators 5. Authors, American 6. Children's authors
ISBN 978-0-399-24692-0

LC 2006011911

"This seventh installment in dePaola's autobiography covers New Year's Day through April 20, 1942. . . . Tomie overhears talk of rationing and hoarding, peeks out from behind blackout curtains, and notes that, due to the war, Fleer bubblegum will no longer be available. As ever, the author fills the story with authentically childlike details. . . . The black-and-white full-page and spot pictures convey emotions effectively." SLJ

Followed by For the duration

DePrince, Michaela

Deprince, Michaela, 1995- **Ballerina** dreams; from orphan to ballerina. by Michaela DePrince; illustrated by James Bernardin. Random House Inc 2014 48 p. color illustrations (lib. bdg.) $12.99

Grades: 1 2 3   92
1. Ballet dancers 2. Orphans -- Sierra Leone -- Biography 3. Ballet dancers -- United States -- Biography
ISBN 0385755163; 9780385755153; 9780385755160

LC 2014013111

This children's book, by Michaela and Elaine DePrince, illustrated by James Bernardin, tells the "true story of Michaela DePrince, one of America's top ballerinas. At the age of three, Michaela DePrince found a photo of a ballerina that changed her life. . . . Michaela never forgot the photo of the dancer she once saw, and quickly decided to make her dream of becoming a ballerina come true. She has been dancing ever since and is now a principal dancer in New York City." (Publisher's note)

"This autobiographical title for newly independent readers will reward efforts with an inspiring story about ballerina Michaela DePrince's life and passion for dance. Orphaned as a young child in Sierra Leone, Michaela is a shy girl whose vitiligo causes a loss of pigmentation on parts of her body...At its heart is the core message that hard work and determination are the keys to making any dream come true. A title sure to attract ballet aficionados, with added appeal for its depiction of an adoptive family and a ballerina who just happens to be black." Kirkus

Degas, Edgar, 1834-1917

Cocca-Leffler, Maryann. **Edgar** Degas: paintings that dance; written and illustrated by Maryann Cocca-Leffler. Grosset & Dunlap 2001 un il (Smart about art) hardcover o.p. pa $5.99

Grades: 2 3 4   92
1. Artists 2. Painters 3. Artists, French
ISBN 0-448-42520-3; 0-448-42520-3 pa

LC 2001-23149

Written in the format of a school report by a fictitious student named Kristin Cole, this recounts events in the life of the French artist Degas and offers insight into his work

Illustrated with "charming childlike drawings and reproductions of the artist's paintings in scrapbook-style layouts. . . . [This] is a successful blend of fact and humor that makes sophisticated concepts completely accessible and even entertaining." Booklist

Desmond, Viola Irene

Warner, Jody. **Viola** Desmond won't be budged! pictures by Richard Rudnicki. Groundwood Books/House of Anansi Press 2010 un il $18.95

Grades: K 1 2 3   92
1. Hairstylists 2. Race discrimination 3. Blacks -- Canada 4. Civil rights activists 5. Canada -- Race relations
ISBN 978-0-88899-779-1; 0-88899-779-5

"Using a cadenced style that echoes the oral tradition of African-Canadians, Warner recounts the story simply, allowing children to see raw discrimination for what it was. Rudnicki uses bold acrylics in vivid colors to tell the story. He captures the style, dress and look of the period." Kirkus

Devi, Dulari

Devi, Dulari. **Following** my paint brush; text by Gita Wolf. Tara Books 2011 un il $17.50

Grades: 3 4 5 6   92
1. Artists 2. Painters 3. Women artists 4. Artists, Indian
ISBN 978-93-80340-11-1; 93-80340-11-7

This is the story of Dulari Devi, a domestic helper who went on to become an artist in the Mithila style of folk painting from Bihar, eastern India.

"Set against plain white backgrounds, Devi's artwork . . . vibrates with bold reds, yellows, and greens. The focus of Devi's artwork is her immediate environment—religious imagery, trees, pottery, fish, and children at play—her delicate linework adding complexity and texture to the mural-like tableaus." Publ Wkly

Diakite, Baba Wague

Diakite, Baba Wague. A **gift** from childhood; memories of an African boyhood. Groundwood Books 2010 134p il $18.95

Grades: 5 6 7 8   92
1. Artists 2. Authors 3. Illustrators 4. Mali 5. Children's authors 6. Africa
ISBN 0-88899-931-3; 978-0-88899-931-3

This is a memoir about growing up in a small village in Mali. "Age ten and up." (N Y Times Book Rev)

"Diakite's . . . illustrated memoir focuses on his childhood in a small Malian village. . . . Interspersed with Diakite's recounting of his youth . . . are stories about his grandfather's brokering peaceful relations with the French, a blacksmith who stymies Death, and others. . . . Diakite's precise language and vibrant illustrations, created on earthenware tiles, form an engrossing story of community life. Studded with Malian proverbs, metaphors, and morals . . . it's a memoir alive with far more voices than just that of the author." Publ Wkly

DiMaggio, Joe, 1914-1999

Winter, Jonah. **Joltin'** Joe DiMaggio; Jonah Winter; illustrated by James E. Ransome. Atheneum Books for Young Readers 2014 48 p. (hardback) $17.99

Grades: 1 2 3 4   92
1. Baseball 2. Baseball players -- Biography 3. Baseball players -- United States -- Biography
ISBN 1416940804; 9781416940807

LC 2014009584

This children's book by Jonah Winter, illustrated by James E. Ransome, tells how "In the golden age of baseball, sports announcers ruled the radio, winning and losing was front-page news, and just about every young boy wanted to grow up to wear Yankee pinstripes, including Giuseppe Paolo DiMaggio, Jr., a first generation Italian from San Francisco. 'Baseball is not a job,' said young Joe's dad, but . . . Joe grew up to make headlines as a top centerfielder and ace hitter." (Publisher's note)

""'Joltin' Joe" made headlines wherever he played, especially during his amazing fifty-six-game hitting streak. With a near tall-tale tone, Winter paints baseball as the bright spot in the Depression and DiMaggio as one of the biggest stars of the day. Ransome's warm watercolors capture the emotions of DiMaggio but also life's small moments. An author's note fills in blanks. Bib." Horn Book

Includes bibliographical references and index

Dickens, Charles, 1812-1870

Manning, Mick. **Charles** Dickens; scenes from an extraordinary life. [illustrated by] Brita Granström. Frances Lincoln 2011 un il $18.95

Grades: 2 3 4 5   92

1. Authors 2. Novelists 3. Authors, English

ISBN 978-1-84780-187-6; 1-84780-187-0

"Dickens narrates his own life story in this biography. . . . Loosely rendered pencil-and-watercolor scenes with speech-bubble interjections from characters take center stage, while small illustrated sidebars provide additional context. . . . A bonus: tidy comic strip panels provide quick summaries of several Dickens novels, which may whet readers' appetite to further explore his writing." Publ Wkly

Rosen, Michael, 1946- **Dickens**; his work and his world. illustrated by Robert Ingpen. Candlewick Press 2005 95p il $19.99

Grades: 5 6 7 8   92

1. Authors 2. Novelists 3. Authors, English

ISBN 0-7636-2752-6

LC 2004-61847

"The art adds to the richness of a volume designed and written with care." Booklist

Douglass, Frederick, 1818-1895

Rappaport, Doreen, 1939- **Frederick's** journey; the life of Frederick Douglass. by Doreen Rappaport; illustrated by London Ladd. Disney-Hyperion 2016 48 p. color illustrations $17.99

Grades: 2 3 4 5   92

1. African Americans 2. Abolitionists -- United States -- Biography 3. Antislavery movements -- United States 4. African American abolitionists -- Biography

ISBN 1423114388; 9781423114383

LC 2014034335

This biography of Frederick Douglass, by Doreen Rappaport, illustrated by London Ladd, "focuses on Douglass's oratory and writing accomplishments but tells almost nothing of the man's personal life. In a rare specific example, . . . readers learn that Douglass's friends bought his freedom for $710.96. He went on to lecture in Great Britain and Ireland, started a newspaper, became friendly with Abraham Lincoln, and was involved with the Underground Railroad." (School Library Journal)

"There are many longer books that detail the events of Douglass's life... but this one, in picture-book form, manages to synthesize those details just as well as a much longer work might, and all without losing the essence of the great man." Horn Book

Drew, Charles Richard, 1904-1950

Venezia, Mike. **Charles** Drew; doctor who got the world pumped up to donate blood. written and illustrated by Mike Venezia. Children's Press 2009 32p il (Getting to know the world's greatest inventors & scientists) $28

Grades: 2 3 4   92

1. Blood 2. Surgeons 3. Inventors 4. Physicians 5. College teachers 6. African Americans -- Biography

ISBN 978-0-531-23725-0; 0-531-23725-7

LC 2008-27648

Charles Drew "is the individual credited with discovering how to extract plasma from whole blood and store it for long periods. . . . The book . . . is written in simple terms for children and focuses on the barriers [Drew] faced as an African-American in a pre-civil-rights-era United States. . . . There are interesting pictures of Drew's life, as well as other pictures of blood plasma being used to save the lives of soldiers on the battlefield. . . . [This] is a biography that is outside of the ordinary." Sci Books Films

Du Bois, W. E. B. (William Edward Burghardt), 1868-1963

Whiting, Jim. **W.E.B.** Du Bois; civil rights activist, author, historian. Mason Crest Publishers 2010 64p il (Transcending race in America: biographies of biracial achievers) $22.95; pa $9.95

Grades: 5 6 7 8   92

1. Authors 2. Novelists 3. Historians 4. Editors 5. Essayists 6. Sociologists 7. Nonfiction writers 8. Civil rights activists 9. African Americans -- Biography 10. African Americans -- Civil rights

ISBN 978-1-4222-1618-7; 1-4222-1618-7; 978-1-4222-1632-3 pa; 1-4222-1632-2 pa

LC 2009022049

"The author openly discusses Du Bois' political and ideological struggles, which concluded with his move to Ghana and admittance into the Communist Party. . . . The book . . . provides solid information about Du Bois." Booklist

Includes glossary and bibliographical references

Dylan, Bob, 1941-

Burckhardt, Marc. **When** Bob met Woody; the story of the young Bob Dylan. illustrated by Marc Burckhardt. Little, Brown 2011 40p il $17.99

Grades: 3 4 5   92

1. Rock musicians

ISBN 978-0-316-11299-4; 0-316-11299-2

LC 2010-43030

This picture book biography follows Bob Zimmerman as he renames himself after his favorite poet, Dylan Thomas, and leaves his mining town to pursue his love of music in New York City. There, he meets his folk music hero and future mentor, Woody Guthrie.

"Golio excels at portraying Zimmerman's angst as he flounders for meaning and even invents for himself a more colorful backstory. Burckhardt's acrylics have the fractured look of damaged paintings, and . . . [convey] gravity and emotion. Back matter, including quotation sources, is superb. A stirring introduction to two musical legends." Booklist

Includes bibliographical references

Earhart, Amelia, 1898-1937

★ Fleming, Candace. **Amelia** lost; the life and disappearance of Amelia Earhart. Schwartz & Wade Books 2011 118p il map

Grades: 4 5 6 7   92

1. Air pilots 2. Missing persons 3. Women air pilots 4. Memoirists

ISBN 0-375-84198-9; 0-375-94598-9 lib bdg; 978-0-375-84198-9; 978-0-375-94598-4 lib bdg

LC 2010-05279

Fleming "offers a fresh look at this famous aviatrix. Employing dual narratives—straightforward biographical chapters alternating with a chilling recounting of Earhart's final flight and the search that followed—Fleming seeks to uncover the 'history of the hype,' pointing out numerous examples in which Earhart took an active role in mythologizing her own life. . . . Frequent sidebars, well-chosen maps, archival documents, and photos further clarify textual references without disturbing the overall narrative flow." Booklist

Tanaka, Shelley. **Amelia** Earhart; the legend of the lost aviator. by Shelley Tanaka; illustrated by David Craig. Abrams Books for Young Readers 2008 48p il map $18.95

Grades: 3 4 5 6　　　　　　　　　　　　　　　　　　　**92**

1. Air pilots 2. Missing persons 3. Women air pilots 4. Memoirists

ISBN 978-0-8109-7095-3; 0-8109-7095-3

LC 2007-39749

NCTE Orbis Pictus Award (2009)

This is an account of the life of aviator Amelia Earhart from her childhood up to the time she disappeared on a flight in 1937.

"This title is notable . . . for its smooth, powerful storytelling, ample gallery of well-chosen photographs, and nicely placed sidebar information on such topics as flight delays, navigation, and around-the-world flight records." Bull Cent Child Books

Includes bibliographical references

Earle, Sylvia A., 1935-

Reichard, Susan E. **Who** on earth is Sylvia Earle? undersea explorer of the ocean. Enslow Publishers 2009 112p il (Scientists saving the earth) lib bdg $31.93

Grades: 5 6 7 8　　　　　　　　　　　　　　　　　　　**92**

1. Botanists 2. Marine biology 3. Women scientists 4. Underwater exploration 5. Divers 6. Marine biologists

ISBN 978-1-59845-118-4 lib bdg; 1-59845-118-9 lib bdg

LC 2008032014

"The writing is clear and informative. . . . Color photographs are relevant and of good quality." SLJ

Includes glossary and bibliographical references

Earnhardt, Dale, Jr.

Rappoport, Ken. **Dale** Earnhardt, Jr. a car racer who cares. Enslow Publishers, Inc. 2011 48p il (Sports stars who care) lib bdg $23.93; pa $7.95

Grades: 3 4 5　　　　　　　　　　　　　　　　　　　　**92**

1. Automobile racing 2. Automobile racing drivers

ISBN 978-0-7660-3777-9 lib bdg; 0-7660-3777-0 lib bdg; 978-1-59845-228-0 pa; 1-59845-228-2 pa

LC 2010014947

This is a biography of race car driver Dale Earnhardt Jr. and founder of the Dale Jr. Foundation.

This is "especially good for book reports." Booklist

Includes glossary and bibliographical references

Eastman, George, 1854-1932

Kulling, Monica. **It's** a snap! George Eastman's first photograph. illustrated by Bill Slavin. Tundra Books 2009 un il (Great idea) $17.95

Grades: 2 3 4　　　　　　　　　　　　　　　　　　　　**92**

1. Inventors 2. Philanthropists 3. Photography -- History 4. Manufacturing executives

ISBN 978-0-88776-881-1; 0-88776-881-4

"This picture-book biography begins in 1877, in Rochester, NY, with Eastman buying his first camera. . . . The picture-taking process took too long and the bored townspeople headed home before he could develop the wet plate. Eastman was determined to make photography easier and more affordable for everyone. During the next eight years, he invented the dry plate, the first roll of film, and the Kodak camera, and started the Eastman Kodak Company. The book will entertain and inform readers. . . . Slavin's pen-and-ink and watercolor illustrations . . . complement the text." SLJ

Ederle, Gertrude, 1905-2003

Adler, David A. **America's** champion swimmer: Gertrude Ederle; written by David A. Adler; illustrated by Terry Widener. Harcourt 2000 un il $16; pa $7

Grades: 2 3 4　　　　　　　　　　　　　　　　　　　　**92**

1. Swimming 2. Women athletes 3. Swimmers 4. Olympic athletes

ISBN 0-15-201969-3; 0-15-205251-8 pa

LC 98-54954

Describes the life and accomplishments of Gertrude Ederle, the first woman to swim the English Channel and a figure in the early women's rights movement

This book "illustrated with richly colored acrylic paintings . . . captures the highlights of Ederle's life in evocative images and telling details that will appeal to children." N Y Times Book Rev

Macy, Sue. **Trudy's** big swim; Sue Macy; illustrated by Matt Collins. Holiday House 2017 40 p. illustrations (chiefly color) (hardcover) $16.95

Grades: 1 2 3 4　　　　　　　　　　　　　　　　　　　**92**

1. Swimming 2. Women swimmers -- United States -- Biography

ISBN 9780823436651

LC 2016003168

This book, by Sue Macy, illustrated by Matt Collins, features Gertrude Ederle as she stood "on the beach at Cape Gris-Nez, France, and faced the churning waves of the English Channel. Twenty-one miles across the perilous waterway, the English coastline beckoned. Lyrical text [and illustrations] . . . put the reader right alongside Ederle in her bid to be the first woman to swim the Channel-and contextualizes her record-smashing victory as a defining moment in sports history." (Publisher's note)

Includes bibliographical references (pages 34-35)

Edison, Thomas A. (Thomas Alva), 1847-1931

★ Brown, Don. A **wizard** from the start: the incredible boyhood & amazing inventions of Thomas Edison. Houghton Mifflin Books for Children 2010 un il $16

Grades: 2 3 4　　　　　　　　　　　　　　　　　　　　**92**

1. Inventors

ISBN 978-0-547-19487-5; 0-547-19487-0

"Focusing on the great inventor's youth, roughly from age eight to mid-20s, this anecdotal picture-book biography is both engaging and accessible. . . . Youngsters will find much to relate to. . . . Brown's signature sketches combine digital imagery and watercolors and reflect the period costume and key moments in Edison's early life." SLJ

★ Carlson, Laurie M. **Thomas** Edison for kids; his life and ideas: 21 activities. [by] Laurie Carlson. Chicago Review Press 2006 147p il $14.95

Grades: 5 6 7 8　　　　　　　　　　　　　　　　　　　**92**

1. Inventors 2. Science -- Experiments

ISBN 1-55652-584-2

LC 2005025659

"Part biography, part science activity book, this resource will appeal to casual researchers and novice inventors. It contains a wealth of full-page primary source archival photographs, sidebars, and short biographical profiles of Edison's contemporaries, in addition to short and straightforward experiments." Voice Youth Advocates

Includes bibliographical references

Kesselring, Susan. **Thomas** Edison. Child's World 2010 24p il (Basic biographies) lib bdg $22.79

Grades: PreK K 1   **92**
1. Inventors
ISBN 978-1-60253-345-5; 1-60253-345-8
LC 2009029374
This biography of Thomas Edison "pairs intelligent, brief text with abundant photos. Simple but never basic." Booklist

Venezia, Mike. **Thomas** Edison; inventor with a lot of bright ideas. written and illustrated by Mike Venezia. Children's Press 2008 32p il (Getting to know the world's greatest inventors & scientists) lib bdg $28; pa $6.95
Grades: 2 3 4   **92**
1. Inventors
ISBN 0-531-14978-1 lib bdg; 978-0-531-14978-2 lib bdg; 0-531-22209-8 pa; 978-0-531-22209-6 pa
LC 2008002306
In this biography of inventor Thomas Edison "the humor and silly scenarios depicted in the cartoon drawings will draw readers back into the smooth, straightforward language." Booklist

Edmonds, S. Emma E. (Sarah Emma Evelyn), 1841-1898
Hendrix, John. **Nurse,** soldier, spy: the story of Sarah Edmonds, a Civil War hero; [illustrated by] John Hendrix. Abrams Books for Young Readers 2011 47p il $18.95
Grades: 2 3 4   **92**
1. Spies 2. Nurses 3. Women soldiers 4. Soldiers -- United States 5. United States -- History -- 1861-1865, Civil War -- Women
ISBN 978-0-8109-9735-6; 0-8109-9735-5
LC 2010-23171
A story of a nineteen-year-old woman who disguised herself as a man to avoid an unwanted marriage and who distinguished herself as a male nurse during the Civil War, and later as a spy for the Union Army.
"In ink-and-wash illustrations Hendrix . . . displays his knack for visual narrative. . . . This large-format picture book illustrates Edmonds' courage and determination while conveying a good deal of information in a highly readable way." Booklist

Jones, Carrie. **Sarah** Emma Edmonds was a great pretender; the true story of a Civil War spy. illustrations by Mark Oldroyd. Carolrhoda Books 2011 un il $17.95
Grades: 2 3 4   **92**
1. Spies 2. Nurses 3. Women soldiers 4. Soldiers -- United States 5. United States -- History -- 1861-1865, Civil War -- Women
ISBN 978-0-7613-5399-7; 0-7613-5399-2
This is "an entertaining and powerful Civil War era story about living by one's own rules. Realizing she would never satisfy her father's desire for a son, teenage Sarah Emma Edmonds fled from Canada to America where she assumed the identity of Frank Thompson. Edwards then joined the Union Army, first as a male nurse, then as a spy, passing herself off as a slave and, later, as an Irish peddler. . . . In Oldroyd's full-bleed spreads, characterized by strong cross-hatching and angular shapes, Edmonds's eyes twinkle with her secret knowledge, while Jones delivers her story with the assuredness of a natural storyteller." Publ Wkly

Einstein, Albert, 1879-1955
★ Berne, Jennifer. **On** a beam of light; a story of Albert Einstein. by Jennifer Berne; illustrated by Vladimir Radunsky. Chronicle Books 2013 56 p. ill. (alk. paper) $17.99
Grades: 2 3 4 5   **92**
1. Physicists -- Biography
ISBN 0811872351; 9780811872355
LC 2011004026

In this children's biographical story, by Jennifer Berne, illustrated by Vladimir Radunsky, "a boy rides a bicycle down a dusty road. But in his mind, he envisions himself traveling at a speed beyond imagining, on a beam of light. . . . From a boy endlessly fascinated by the wonders around him, Albert Einstein ultimately grows into a man of genius recognized the world over for profoundly illuminating our understanding of the universe." (Publisher's note)
"Radunsky's humorous, childlike drawings convey Einstein's personality as well as the important ideas in the text... provide[s] a splendid introduction to a man who never stopped questioning." Kirkus

★ Brown, Don. **Odd** boy out: young Albert Einstein. Houghton Mifflin 2004 un il $16
Grades: 2 3 4   **92**
1. Physicists 2. Nobel laureates for physics
ISBN 0-618-49298-4
LC 2003-17701
An introduction to the work and early life of the twentieth-century physicist whose theory of relativity revolutionized scientific thinking.
"Brown's pen-and-ink and watercolor illustrations [are] rendered in a palette of dusky mauve and earthy brown. . . . Through eloquent narrative and illustration, Brown offers a thoughtful introduction to an enigmatic man." SLJ

★ Delano, Marfe Ferguson. **Genius**; a photobiography of Albert Einstein. National Geographic 2005 64p il $17.95; lib bdg $27.90; pa $7.95
Grades: 5 6 7 8   **92**
1. Physicists 2. Nobel laureates for physics
ISBN 0-7922-9544-7; 0-7922-9545-5 lib bdg; 1-4263-0294-0 pa
LC 2004-15001
A biography of the German American physicist.
This "combines a solid text with a particularly attractive format. . . . Delano offers just enough information about Einstein's theories to give a sense of his work. . . . Oversize and filled with well-selected photographs, the book is very handsome." Booklist

Kesselring, Susan. **Albert** Einstein. Child's World 2010 24p il (Basic biographies) lib bdg $22.79
Grades: PreK K 1   **92**
1. Physicists 2. Nobel laureates for physics
ISBN 978-1-60253-338-7; 1-60253-338-5
LC 2009029363
This "pairs intelligent, brief text with abundant photos. Simple but never basic." Booklist

★ Krull, Kathleen. **Albert** Einstein; illustrated by Boris Kulikov. Viking 2009 141p il (Giants of science) $15.99
Grades: 5 6 7 8   **92**
1. Physicists 2. Nobel laureates for physics
ISBN 978-0-670-06332-1; 0-670-06332-0
LC 2009-16037
"Krull delivers a splendidly humane biography of that gold standard of brilliance, Albert Einstein. . . . Drawing extensively on Einstein's writings, she presents a fully rounded portrait of a man whose genius combined with a bad temper and arrogance, to the detriment of his own professional advancement, not to mention his relationships with women and his children. Using concrete examples, the author brings such mind-bending notions as his General Theory of Relativity within the grasp of child readers." Kirkus

Meltzer, Milton. **Albert** Einstein. Holiday House 2008 32p il $16.95

Grades: 3 4 5   92
1. Physicists 2. Scientists 3. Nobel laureates for physics
ISBN 978-0-8234-1966-1; 0-8234-1966-5

LC 2006-43676

"Meltzer offers a sound, cogent introduction to Einstein in this attractive volume, which discusses the scientist's work and its significance within a lively account of his life.... Well-chosen black-and-white photos and a few documents illustrate the narrative that takes both its subject and its audience seriously." Booklist

Includes bibliographical references

Eisenhower, Dwight D. (Dwight David), 1890-1969

Mara, Wil. **Dwight** Eisenhower. Marshall Cavendish Benchmark 2011 112p il (Presidents and their times) lib bdg $34.21
Grades: 5 6 7 8   92
1. Generals 2. Presidents 3. College presidents 4. Presidents -- United States
ISBN 978-0-7614-4812-9; 0-7614-4812-8

LC 2009033042

"The size makes it ideal for that one-hundred page biography assignment; the readability makes the titles accessible to reluctant readers in high school; the succinct, well-presented information makes the volumes fitting for initial research at both the middle and high school level." Voice Youth Advocates

Includes glossary and bibliographical references

Elder, Ruth, 1902-1977

Cummins, Julie. **Flying** solo; how Ruth Elder soared into America's heart. Julie Cummins; illustrated by Malene Laugesen. Roaring Brook Press 2013 32 p. ill. (chiefly col.) (hardcover) $17.99
Grades: K 1 2   92
1. Women air pilots 2. Air pilots -- United States -- Biography 3. Women air pilots -- United States -- Biography
ISBN 1596435097; 9781596435094

LC 2012029743

Amelia Bloomer Project (2014)

Written by Julie Cummins and illustrated by Malene R. Laugesen, this book describes how "Ruth Elder, a contemporary of Amelia Earhart, set her sights on becoming the first woman to fly across the Atlantic. At age 23, and after only a few flying lessons, she and her copilot set forth. Two-thirds of the way into their flight, the gas line sprung a leak, and they were forced to abandon the plane. Fortunately, they were rescued by a nearby ship." (Booklist)

"The clever, anecdotal text and vibrant spreads of the colorful planes and period costumes transport readers to another era, glamorous, yet restrictive toward the 'fairer sex.'" SLJ

Includes bibliographical references

Eleanor, of Aquitaine, Queen, consort of Henry II, King of England, 1122?-1204

Kramer, Ann. **Eleanor** of Aquitaine; the queen who rode off to battle. National Geographic 2006 64p il map (World history biographies) $17.95; lib bdg $27.90
Grades: 5 6 7 8   92
1. Queens 2. France -- History -- 0-1328 3. Great Britain -- History -- 1154-1399, Plantagenets
ISBN 0-7922-5895-9; 0-7922-5896-7 lib bdg

An illustrated biography of the medieval queen who traveled to the Crusades with her first husband King Louis VII of France and later married King Henry II of England.

Includes glossary and bibliographical references

Elizabeth I, Queen of England, 1533-1603

★ Adams, Simon. **Elizabeth** I; the outcast who became England's queen. [by] Simon Adams. National Geographic 2005 64p il map (World history biographies) $17.95; lib bdg $27.90
Grades: 4 5 6 7   92
1. Queens 2. Great Britain -- Kings and rulers 3. Great Britain -- History -- 1485-1603, Tudors
ISBN 0-7922-3649-1; 0-7922-3654-8 lib bdg

LC 2005001359

An illustrated introduction to the life and times of the 16th century queen of England

"Accomplishments and hardships are clearly explained with supporting quotes and facts.... Beautifully illustrated and visually appealing." SLJ

Includes glossary and bibliographical references

Stanley, Diane. **Good** Queen Bess: the story of Elizabeth I of England; by Diane Stanley and Peter Vennema; illustrated by Diane Stanley. HarperCollins Pubs. 2001 un il $16.99
Grades: 4 5 6 7   92
1. Queens 2. Great Britain -- Kings and rulers 3. Great Britain -- History -- 1485-1603, Tudors
ISBN 0-688-17961-4

LC 00-47267

A reissue of the title first published 1990 by Four Winds Press

Follows the life of the strong-willed queen who ruled England in the time of Shakespeare and the defeat of the Spanish Armada

"The handsome illustrations . . . are worthy of their subject. Although the format suggests a picture-book audience, this biography needs to be introduced to older readers who have the background to appreciate and understand this woman who dominated and named an age." SLJ

Includes bibliographical references

Ellington, Duke, 1899-1974

Stein, Stephanie. **Duke** Ellington; his life in jazz with 21 activities. [by] Stephanie Stein Crease. Chicago Review Press 2009 148p il (For kids) pa $16.95
Grades: 5 6 7 8   92
1. Composers 2. Jazz musicians 3. Band leaders
ISBN 978-1-55652-724-1; 1-55652-724-1

LC 2008-23742

"This large-format book combines an illustrated biography of Duke Ellington with activities designed to offer insights into Ellington s era and his music. An informative account in an attractive...format." Booklist

Includes bibliographical references, discography, and filmography

Emerson, Ralph Waldo, 1803-1882

Kerley, Barbara. A **Home** for Mr. Emerson; by Barbara Kerley; illustrated by Edwin Fotheringham. Scholastic Press 2013 48 p. $18.99
Grades: 3 4 5   92
1. American authors 2. Authors, American -- 19th century -- Biography
ISBN 0545350883; 9780545350884

LC 2013007482

This children's book presents an "introduction to the life of Ralph Waldo Emerson.... Emerson grows up in Boston, but yearns to make a life closer to nature where he can surround himself with books and friends. He finds a perfect home in Concord, Massachusetts, where he and his wife raise a family.... A house fire later in his life devastates Emerson, but allows the town to demonstrate their affection for him as they rebuild his home." (School Library Journal)

Erdős, Paul, 1913-1996

★ Heiligman, Deborah. The **boy** who loved math; the improbable life of Paul Erdos. Deborah Heiligman; illustrated by LeUyen Pham. Roaring Brook Press 2013 48 p. (hardcover) $17.99

Grades: 1 2 3 4   92

1. Mathematics 2. Mathematicians -- Hungary -- Biography
ISBN 1596433078; 9781596433076

LC 2012029744

Orbis Pictus Awards Honor Book (2014)

This book is a biography of mathematician Paul Erdős. He was a child prodigy who had to be homeschooled due to his inability to sit still and follow rules. "High school was a better fit, and he made friends with students who shared his love of math. His skills became famous, but Erdős didn't know how to do laundry, cook, or even butter his own bread. He 'didn't fit into the world in a regular way.' So, he created a life that fit him instead." (School Library Journal)

"Heiligman's joyful, warm account invites young listeners and readers to imagine a much-loved boy completely charmed by numbers... The polished, disarming text offers Pham free rein for lively illustration that captures Erdos' childlike spirit." Kirkus

Esquivel, Juan García

Wood, Susan. **Esquivel!** space-age sound artist. Susan Wood; illustrated by Duncan Tonatiuh. Charlesbridge 2016 32 p. color illustrations (reinforced for library use) $17.95

Grades: 1 2 3 4   92

1. Composers -- Mexico
ISBN 1580896731; 9781580896733; 9781607348252; 9781607348269

LC 2015026827

Pura Belpre Illustrator Honor Book (2017)

"Juan Garcia Esquivel was born in Mexico and grew up to the sounds of mariachi bands. He loved music and became a musical explorer. Defying convention, he created music that made people laugh and planted images in their minds. Juan's space-age lounge music--popular in the fifties and sixties--has found a new generation of listeners." (Publisher's note)

"Tonatiuh employs his signature style of Mixtec codex-influenced design, combines it with playful tributes to the fashion and style of the 1960s, sprinkles in text blocks of onomatopoeia that seem to vibrate on the page, and fills in the empty areas with a watery mix of purples and blues that perfectly complements the spacey style expressed in the music. A lively introduction to a somewhat obscure and profoundly innovative musical figure." Kirkus

Includes bibliographical references.

Fabre, Jean-Henri, 1823-1915

Smith, Matthew Clark. **Small** wonders; Jean-henri Fabre and His World of Insects. by Matthew Clark Smith, illustrated by Giuliano Ferri. Two Lions 2015 48 p. color illustrations (hardcover) $17.99

Grades: 2 3 4 5 6   92

1. Entomologists 2. Insects 3. Naturalists -- Biography
ISBN 9781477826324; 1477826327

This children's book, by Matthew Clark Smith and illustrated by Giuliano Ferri, is a "picture book biography [that] examines the life and work of 19th-century French entomologist Jean-Henri Fabre. . . . Readers are then taken back in time to learn about Fabre's childhood, education, and ever-present interest in the natural world, as well as his unconventional teaching and writings on insect behavior." (School Library Journal)

"Little-known outside his native France, nineteenth-century entomologist Jean-Henri Fabre made important discoveries by observing living insects: he learned about metamorphosis and instinctual behaviors hard-wired into wasps and termites, and he proved that insects com-

municate via pheromones. Ferri's watercolor and pencil illustrations in earthy tones help to draw us into Fabre's fascinating world of curious intimacy with nature. " Horn Book

Farnsworth, Philo T.

★ Krull, Kathleen. The **boy** who invented TV; the story of Philo Farnsworth. illustrated by Greg Couch. Alfred A. Knopf 2009 40 p. il $16.99

Grades: 3 4 5   92

1. Inventors 2. Television
ISBN 0375845615; 037594561X; 9780375845611; 9780375945618

LC 2008035500

"Plowing a potato field in 1920, a 14-year-old farm boy from Idaho [named Philo Farnsworth] saw in the parallel rows of overturned earth a way to 'make pictures fly through the air.' This boy was not a magician; he was a scientific genius and just eight years later he made his brainstorm in the potato field a reality by transmitting the world's first television image." (Publisher's note)

"This entertaining book explores the life of inventor Philo Farnsworth, who discovered how to transmit images electronically, leading to the first television. . . . Krull's substantial, captivating text is balanced by Couch's warm, mixed-media illustrations." Publ Wkly

Includes bibliographical references

Farris, Christine King

★ Farris, Christine King. **March** on! the day my brother Martin changed the world. [by] Christine King Farris; illustrated by London Ladd. Scholastic Press 2008 un il $17.99

Grades: 2 3 4   92

1. Clergy 2. Civil rights demonstrations 3. College teachers 4. Nonfiction writers 5. Civil rights activists 6. Nobel laureates for peace 7. African Americans -- Civil rights
ISBN 0-545-03537-6; 978-0-545-03537-8

LC 2007038620

"Describing the 1963 March on Washington, Farris, the older sister of Martin Luther King Jr., maintains the deft touch that made My Brother Martin so moving. . . . Farris . . . effectively uses plain language and well-chosen facts to explain her brother's extraordinary achievements. . . . Ladd . . . demonstrates a rare talent for portraiture. . . . His King looks human—in other words, capable of inspiring the reader." Publ Wkly

Ferris, George Washington Gale, 1859-1896

Davis, Kathryn Gibbs. **Mr.** Ferris and his wheel; by Kathryn G. Davis. Houghton Mifflin Harcourt 2014 40 p. $17.99

Grades: K 1 2 3   92

1. Inventors 2. Inventors -- United States -- Biography 3. Ferris wheels -- History 4. Civil engineers -- United States -- Biography 5. Structural engineers -- United States -- Biography
ISBN 0547959222; 9780547959221

LC 2013050147

Written by Kathryn Gibbs Davis and illustrated by Gilbert Ford, "Capturing an engineer's creative vision and mind for detail, this fully illustrated picture book biography sheds light on how the American inventor George Ferris defied gravity and seemingly impossible odds to invent the world's most iconic amusement park attraction, the Ferris wheel." (Publisher's note)

"It's almost time for the 1893 Chicago World's Fair, and American architects are hoping to design a star attraction to rival the French Eiffel Tower. Mechanical engineer George Washington Gale Ferris Jr. has a daring idea: a huge, round, moving structure made from steel, a new metal unrivaled in both lightness and strength . . . Overall, the modernist look, inherently interesting topic, and strong documentation (including quotations from primary sources) make this title a positive addition, especially those looking to enhance their nonfiction offerings in view of new Common Core standards." SLJ

Fibonacci, Leonardo, ca. 1170-ca. 1240

★ D'Agnese, Joseph. **Blockhead**; the life of Fibonacci. illustrated by John O'Brien. Henry Holt and Company 2010 40p il $16.99

Grades: 2 3 4 5   92

1. Numbers 2. Mathematicians 3. Fibonacci numbers
ISBN 0-8050-6305-6; 978-0-8050-6305-9

LC 2009005264

This is a biography of Leonardo Fibonacci, the twelfth-century mathematician who discovered the numerical sequence named for him. "Intermediate." (Horn Book)

"D'Agnese's introduction to medieval Europe's greatest mathematician offers both a coherent biographical account—spun, with some invented details, from very sketchy historical records—and the clearest explanation to date for younger readers of the numerical sequence that is found throughout nature and still bears his name. O'Brien's illustrations place the prosperously dressed, woolly headed savant in his native Pisa and other settings." Booklist

Fillmore, Millard, 1800-1874

Gottfried, Ted. **Millard** Fillmore; by Ted Gottfried. Marshall Cavendish Benchmark 2007 96p il (Presidents and their times) lib bdg $22.95

Grades: 5 6 7 8   92

1. Presidents 2. Vice-presidents 3. Members of Congress 4. Presidents -- United States
ISBN 978-0-7614-2431-4

LC 2006019707

"Primary-source materials and quotes, helpful insets, and carefully selected . . . reproductions bring history to life and help make [this] clearly written [biography] highly readable." SLJ

Includes glossary and bibliographical references

Fitzgerald, Ella

★ Orgill, Roxane. **Skit**-scat raggedy cat: Ella Fitzgerald; written by Roxane Orgill; illustrated by Sean Qualls. Candlewick Press 2010 un il $17.99

Grades: 2 3 4   92

1. Singers 2. African American singers 3. Pop musicians 4. African American women -- Biography
ISBN 0-7636-1733-4; 978-0-7636-1733-2

LC 2009-47407

This is a biography of the American jazz singer Ella Fitzgerald. "Grades three to six." (Bull Cent Child Books)

This is "a stylish portrayal of Ella Fitzgerald. . . . There's no question that Orgill and Qualls know what makes [jazz] so catchy: it's slinky, rhythmic, and joyful and on full display in both the lively text and swinging artwork." Booklist

★ Pinkney, Andrea Davis. **Ella** Fitzgerald; the tale of a vocal virtuosa. by Andrea Davis Pinkney with Scat Cat Monroe; illustrated by Brian Pinkney. Hyperion 2002 un il $16.99

Grades: 2 3 4   92

1. Singers 2. African American singers 3. Pop musicians 4. African American women -- Biography
ISBN 0-7868-0568-4; 0-7868-2493-X lib bdg

"Scat Cat Monroe, a jazzy feline in a zoot suit, tells Fitzgerald's life story. . . . The general details of an extraordinary life—when, what, where, and how—are related in rhythmic, vivid language that matches the verve of the hand-colored scratchboard illustrations." Bull Cent Child Books

Fleischman, Sid, 1920-2010

★ Fleischman, Sid. The **abracadabra** kid; a writer's life. Greenwillow Bks. 1996 198p il hardcover o.p. $16.99

Grades: 5 6 7 8   92

1. Authors 2. Magicians 3. Magazine editors 4. Authors, American 5. Children's authors 6. Young adult authors
ISBN 0-688-14859-X; 0-688-15855-2 pa

LC 95-47382

This autobiography, "turns real life into a story complete with cliffhangers. And it's a classic boy's story, from card tricks and traveling magic shows to World War II naval experiences and screen-writing gigs for John Wayne movies. En route, we learn how Fleischman learned the craft of writing." Bull Cent Child Books

Includes bibliographical references

Ford, Henry, 1863-1947

★ Mitchell, Don. **Driven**; a photobiography of Henry Ford. foreword by Lee Iacocca. National Geographic 2010 64p il map $18.95; lib bdg $27.90

Grades: 5 6 7 8   92

1. Businessmen 2. Philanthropists 3. Automobile industry 4. Automobile executives
ISBN 978-1-4263-0155-1; 1-4263-0155-3; 978-1-4263-0156-8 lib bdg; 1-4263-0156-1 lib bdg

LC 2009-07136

"Mitchell introduces readers to the founder of the auto company. . . . Thoughts, feelings, and quotes abound, and they are well sourced. . . . The writing is clear, and the organization is chronological. . . . Driven combines fine photography and an inviting text to depict Ford's life and his impact on the world." SLJ

Includes bibliographical references

Foreman, Michael, 1938-

Foreman, Michael, 1938- The **tortoise** and the soldier; a story of courage and friendship in World War I. Michael Foreman. Henry Holt & Co. 2015 128 p. (hardback) $16.99

Grades: 3 4 5 6   92

1. English authors -- Biography 2. World War, 1914-1918 -- Biography 3. Illustrators -- Great Britain -- Biography 4. Authors, English -- 20th century -- Biography 5. World War, 1914-1918 -- Great Britain -- Biography
ISBN 9781627791731

LC 2014047282

In this book, by Michael Foreman, "Henry Friston dreamed of traveling the world. He thought he was signing up for a lifetime of adventure when he joined the Royal Navy. But when World War I begins, it launches the world, and Henry, into turmoil. While facing enemy fire at Gallipoli, Henry discovers the strength he needs to survive in an unexpected source: a tortoise. And so begins the friendship of a lifetime." (Publisher's note)

"An enticing and well-written tale that will be relished by those who enjoyed Michael Morpurgo's War Horse (Scholastic, 2007)." SLJ

Forten, James, 1766-1842

Figley, Marty Rhodes. **Prisoner** for liberty; by Marty Rhodes Figley; illustrations by Craig Orback. Millbrook Press 2008 48p il (On my own history) lib bdg $25.26

Grades: 2 3 4   92

1. Abolitionists 2. Philanthropists 3. Sailmakers 4. African Americans -- Biography 5. United States -- History -- 1775-1783, Revolution
ISBN 978-0-8225-7280-0 lib bdg; 0-8225-7280-X lib bdg

LC 2006028582

"In dramatic words and vivid paintings, this [book] . . . celebrates the heroism of an African American teen in the Revolutionary War. Born free, 15-year-old James Forten joined the crew of the Royal Louis as a sailor. When the British captured the ship, he refused the chance to escape to help a sickly white friend. . . . This inspiring, personal story will help draw early readers into U.S. history." Booklist

Includes bibliographical references

Fossey, Dian

Kushner, Jill Menkes. **Who** on earth is Dian Fossey? defender of the mountain gorillas. Enslow Publishers 2009 112p il (Scientists saving the earth) lib bdg $31.93

Grades: 5 6 7 8   92

1. Authors 2. Gorillas 3. Women scientists 4. Murder victims 5. Primatologists 6. Writers on science

ISBN 1-59845-117-0 lib bdg; 978-1-59845-117-7 lib bdg

            LC 2008029376

"The book is filled with factual information, yet is written in a manner that makes both Fossey and her gorillas come to life for the reader." Sci Books Films

Includes glossary and bibliographical references

Foucault, Jean Bernard Léon, 1819-1868

Mortensen, Lori. **Come** see the Earth turn: the story of Leon Foucault; illustrations by Raúl Allén. Tricycle Press 2010 un il $17.99

Grades: 3 4 5   92

1. Physicists 2. Scientists

ISBN 978-1-58246-284-4; 1-58246-284-4

A biography of the scientist who proved that the Earth spins on its axis.

"Mortensen's prose infuses this small scientific drama with remarkable tension, while Allén's dramatically lit paintings, often organized into elegant panels, have a cinematic quality and amplify the action even further." Publ Wkly

Frank, Anne, 1929-1945

★ Frank, Anne. The **diary** of a young girl: the definitive edition; edited by Otto H. Frank and Mirjam Pressler; translated by Susan Massotty. Bantam 1997 340p $29.95; pa $7.99

Grades: 5 6 7 8 9 10 11 12 Adult   92

1. Children 2. Diarists 3. Holocaust victims 4. Jews -- Netherlands 5. Holocaust, 1933-1945 6. World War, 1939-1945 -- Jews 7. Netherlands -- History -- 1940-1945, German occupation

ISBN 0-385-47378-8; 9780553577129

            LC 94-41379

"This new translation of Frank's famous diary includes material about her emerging sexuality and her relationship with her mother that was originally excised by Frank's father, the only family member to survive the Holocaust." Libr J

★ Metselaar, Menno. **Anne** Frank: her life in words and pictures; from the archives of The Anne Frank House. [by] Menno Metselaar and Ruud van der Rol; translated by Arnold J. Pomerans. Roaring Brook Press 2009 215p il map pa $12.99

Grades: 5 6 7 8   92

1. Children 2. Diarists 3. Holocaust victims 4. Jews -- Netherlands 5. Holocaust, 1933-1945 6. World War, 1939-1945 -- Jews 7. Netherlands -- History -- 1940-1945, German occupation

ISBN 978-1-59643-546-9; 1-59643-546-1; 978-1-59643-547-6 pa; 1-59643-547-X pa

First published 2004 in the Netherlands with title: The story of Anne Frank

Boston Globe-Horn Book Award honor book: Nonfiction (2010)

"Beginning with a single photograph of the cover of Anne Frank's diary and the quote, 'One of my nicest presents,' this small, beautifully formatted book is accessible, compelling, and richly pictorial. . . . The book immediately immerses readers in the girl's life via a series of family photographs, many previously unpublished. Divided chronologically, the accompanying text is enhanced by diary entries, resulting in a historically succinct yet descriptive presentation. . . . Even for those collections where Anne Frank is well represented, this is a moving and valuable book." SLJ

Franklin, Benjamin, 1706-1790

★ Adler, David A. **B.** Franklin, printer. Holiday House 2001 126p il lib bdg $19.95

Grades: 4 5 6 7   92

1. Authors 2. Diplomats 3. Inventors 4. Statesmen 5. Scientists 6. Writers on science 7. Members of Congress 8. Statesmen -- United States

ISBN 0-8234-1675-5

            LC 2001-24535

This "surveys Benjamin Franklin's life as a printer, a scientist, an inventor, a writer, and a statesman. . . . Throughout the book, details, anecdotes, and quotations bring the man's portrait into clearer focus, while period illustrations . . . help readers envision the background of his times." Booklist

Includes bibliographical references

★ Byrd, Robert, 1942- **Electric** Ben; the amazing life and times of Benjamin Franklin. by Robert Byrd. Penguin Group 2012 40 p. (hardcover) $17.99

Grades: 3 4 5   92

1. Biography 2. Inventions -- History 3. United States -- History 4. Printers -- United States -- Biography 5. Inventors -- United States -- Biography 6. Statesmen -- United States -- Biography 7. Scientists -- United States -- Biography

ISBN 0803737491; 9780803737495

            LC 2011050493

Boston Globe-Horn Book Award: Nonfiction (2013).

Robert F. Sibert Honor Book (2013)

This book by Robert Byrd presents a biography of Benjamin Franklin. "A true Renaissance man, Benjamin Franklin was the first American celebrity. In pictures and text, master artist Robert Byrd documents Franklin's numerous and diverse accomplishments, from framing the Constitution to creating bifocals." The book contains "facts, quotes, and captions, while the . . . illustrations make a . . . tribute to the brilliant American." (Publisher's note)

Fleming, Candace. **Ben** Franklin's almanac; being a true account of the good gentleman's life. Atheneum Bks. for Young Readers 2003 120p il $19.95

Grades: 5 6 7 8   92

1. Authors 2. Diplomats 3. Inventors 4. Statesmen 5. Scientists 6. Writers on science 7. Members of Congress 8. Statesmen -- United States

ISBN 0-689-83549-3

            LC 2002-6136

Brings together eighteenth century etchings, artifacts, and quotations to create the effect of a scrapbook of the life of Benjamin Franklin

"An authoritative work of depth, humor, and interest, presenting Franklin in all his complexity, ranging from the heroic to the vulgar, the saintly to the callous." SLJ

★ Freedman, Russell, 1929- **Becoming** Ben Franklin; how a candle-maker's son helped light the flame of liberty. Russell Freedman. 1st ed. Holiday House 2013 86 p. col. ill. (hardcover) $24.95

Grades: 5 6 7 8   **92**
1. Franklin, Benjamin, 1706-1790   2. Founding Fathers of the
United States   3. Printers -- United States -- Biography   4.
Inventors -- United States -- Biography   5. Statesmen -- United
States -- Biography   6. Scientists -- United States -- Biography
ISBN 0823423743; 9780823423743
LC 2012002971
This book is a biography of Ben Franklin. Russell Freedman "chose
episodes that reflect how the young man, disgruntled with being his
brother's apprentice, made a life for himself . . . . By describing the
obstacles Franklin overcame in establishing his print shop in Philadel-
phia, Freedman delineates a . . . path between his subject's early ambition and his ease with people to his success in business and then to
his later roles as a diplomat, revolutionary, and public servant." (School
Library Journal)
Includes bibliographical references (p. 78-82) and index.

★ Fritz, Jean. **What's** the big idea, Ben Franklin? illustrated by
Margot Tomes. Putnam Pub. Group 1976 46p il $15.99; pa $5.99
Grades: 2 3 4   **92**
1. Authors 2. Diplomats 3. Inventors 4. Statesmen 5. Scientists
6. Writers on science 7. Members of Congress 8. Statesmen --
United States
ISBN 0-399-23487-X; 0-698-11372-1 pa
The text "focuses on Franklin's multifaceted career but also gives
personal details and quotes some of his pithy sayings. Enough background information about colonial affairs is given to enable readers to
understand the importance of Franklin's contributions to the public good
but not so much that it obtrudes on his life story. Although the text is not
punctuated by references or footnotes, a page of notes (with numbers for
pages referred to) is appended." Bull Cent Child Books

★ Harness, Cheryl. The **remarkable** Benjamin Franklin; written
& illustrated by Cheryl Harness. National Geographic Society 2005
47p il $17.95
Grades: 2 3 4   **92**
1. Authors 2. Diplomats 3. Inventors 4. Statesmen 5. Scientists
6. Writers on science 7. Members of Congress 8. Statesmen --
United States
ISBN 0-7922-7882-8
LC 2004-20504
"Beginning with Franklin's birth, Harness explores the activities that
filled his days from his quest to open his own print shop to his role in
the American Revolution to his personal intrigues and inventions. Her
conversational writing style and vivid illustrations will appeal to readers
just becoming acquainted with this important figure." SLJ
Includes bibliographical references

Krull, Kathleen. **Benjamin** Franklin; by Kathleen Krull; illustrated
by Boris Kulikov. Viking 2013 121 p. (Giants of science) (hardcover)
$15.99
Grades: 5 6 7 8   **92**
1. Inventors   2. Scientists   3. Franklin, Benjamin, 1706-1790
4. Inventors -- United States -- Biography   5. Scientists -- United
States -- Biography
ISBN 0670012874; 9780670012879
LC 2013018404
This book, by Kathleen Krull, part of the Giants of Science series,
"explains the many ways that Franklin was the American manifestation
of the European Enlightenment, putting his discoveries in clear historical context. Known as 'natural philosophers' in the eighteenth century,
scientists like Franklin specialized in the kind of theoretical thinking
that could result in inventions to make life better, from lightning rods to
efficient heating stoves." (Booklist)

"The majority of this helpful book deals with Franklin's innovative scientific processes and his reasoning behind such inventions as
the Franklin stove and the lightning rod; he coined words (still in use
today) with definitions specific to the field, such as positive, negative,
and charge. Kulikov's occasional black-and-white illustrations add sly
humor to the account." (Horn Book)
Includes bibliographical references and index

Miller, Brandon Marie. **Benjamin** Franklin, American genius; his
life and ideas, with 21 activities. Chicago Review Press 2009 125p il
pa $16.95
Grades: 4 5 6 7   **92**
1. Authors 2. Diplomats 3. Inventors 4. Statesmen 5. Scientists
6. Writers on science 7. Members of Congress
ISBN 978-1-55652-757-9 pa; 1-55652-757-8 pa
LC 2009012456
"Miller does an excellent job of presenting a synopsis of Franklin's
life in a highly readable manner. . . . Imbedded in each chapter are asides
that further elaborate on Franklin's life and times and activities that coordinate with the text or the historical facts presented. The directions are
easy to follow and enhance the overall presentation, especially in terms
of classroom connections. Illustrations accompany each project and reproductions of primary documents, renderings, and paintings provide
added value." SLJ
Includes glossary and bibliographical references

Rosenstock, Barb. **Ben** Franklin's big splash; the mostly true story
of his first invention. Barb Rosenstock. Calkins Creek 2014 32 p.
$16.95
Grades: K 1 2 3 4   **92**
1. Inventors -- Fiction 2. Swimming -- Fiction
ISBN 1620914468; 9781620914465
LC 2014931339
"Ben Franklin loved to swim and, at the age of eleven, he was determined to swim like a fish--fins and all! This . . . account of young Ben's
earliest invention follows the budding scientist's journey as he tests and
retests his swim fins. That first big splash led Ben to even more innovations and inventions." (Publisher's note)
"Schindler's ink-and-watercolor illustrations pick up the comical
nuances of the text (especially Rosenstock's penchant for vivid alliterative verbs) and convey the imagination required for invention. Appended with a list of Franklin's inventions, source notes, and time line."
Booklist

Rushby, Pamela. **Ben** Franklin; printer, author, inventor, politician.
by Pamela Rushby. National Geographic 2007 40p il (National Geographic history chapters) lib bdg $17.90
Grades: 2 3 4   **92**
1. Authors 2. Diplomats 3. Inventors 4. Statesmen 5. Scientists
6. Writers on science 7. Members of Congress 8. Statesmen --
United States
ISBN 978-1-4263-0191-9
LC 2007007896
This biography of Benjamin Franklin is "nicely illustrated with . .
. paintings, engravings, and facsimiles. . . . [It is] just right for emerging chapter-book readers. . . . Useful . . . for reports . . . and interesting
pleasure reading." SLJ
Includes glossary and bibliographical references

★ Schroeder, Alan. **Ben** Franklin; his wit and wisdom from A to
Z. illustrated by John O'Brien. Holiday House 2011 un il $16.95
Grades: 2 3 4   **92**
1. Authors 2. Alphabet 3. Diplomats 4. Inventors 5. Statesmen
6. Scientists 7. Writers on science 8. Members of Congress 9.

Statesmen -- United States

ISBN 978-0-8234-1950-0; 0-8234-1950-9

LC 2010024062

"Alphabetically arranged, but far more than just an alphabet book, this guide to the life of Ben Franklin covers his upbringing, his prominence in early America, his many inventions, and his beliefs and writings. Given the breadth of Franklin's accomplishments, it shouldn't be surprising that each letter gets more than one word..... O'Brien's ink and watercolor images contribute ample humor, and Schroeder creates a well-rounded, fascinating portrait of an iconic American." Publ Wkly

Freeman, Elizabeth, 1744?-1829

Woelfle, Gretchen. **Mumbet's** Declaration of Independence; by Gretchen Woelfle; Illustrated by Alix Delinois. Carolrhoda Books 2014 32 p. color illustrations (lib. bdg. : alk. paper) $17.95

Grades: 1 2 3 4   92

1. Slaves -- Emancipation 2. United States -- History -- 1775-1783, Revolution 3. Slavery -- Massachusetts -- History 4. Slaves -- Massachusetts -- Biography 5. African American women -- Massachusetts -- Biography

ISBN 0761365893; 9780761365891

LC 2013018620

This book, written by Gretchen Woelfle and illustrated by Alix Delinois, describes how "the founders weren't the only ones who believed that everyone had a right to freedom. Mumbet, a Massachusetts slave, believed it too. She longed to be free, but how? Would anyone help her in her fight for freedom? Could she win against her owner, the richest man in town?" (Publisher's note)

"Delinois's thick layers of paint and vibrant palette infuse even the story's upsetting moments with hopefulness, and Mumbet herself glows with determination and integrity. An author's note addresses how many details of Mumbet's life were lost to history, yet her story stands as a potent reminder that the freedoms that accompanied the American Revolution left many behind." Pub Wkly

Fritz, Jean

★ Fritz, Jean. **Homesick** : my own story; illustrated with drawings by Margot Tomes and photographs. Putnam 1982 163p il $16.99; pa $5.99

Grades: 5 6 7 8   92

1. Authors 2. Women authors 3. China 4. Children's authors

ISBN 0-399-20933-6; 0-698-11782-4 pa

LC 82-7646

Companion volume to China homecoming

A Newbery Medal honor book, 1983

"The descriptions of places and the times are vivid in a book that brings to the reader, with sharp clarity and candor, the yearnings and fears and ambivalent loyalties of a young girl." Bull Cent Child Books

Fulton, Robert, 1765-1815

Herweck, Don. **Robert** Fulton; engineer of the steamboat. Compass Point Books 2009 40p il (Mission: Science) lib bdg $26.60

Grades: 4 5 6 7   92

1. Engineers 2. Inventors 3. Steamboats

ISBN 978-0-7565-3961-0 lib bdg; 0-7565-3961-7 lib bdg

LC 2008007728

Covers the life and accomplishments of American inventor and mechanic, Robert Fulton, who is best known for building the first successful steamboat

Galilei, Galileo, 1564-1642

Christensen, Bonnie. **I,** Galileo; Bonnie Christensen. Alfred A. Knopf 2012 40 p.

Grades: 3 4 5   92

1. Inventors -- Biography 2. Physicists -- Biography 3. Astronomers -- Biography 4. Picture books for children 5. Galilei, Galileo, 1564-1642 6. Physicists -- Italy -- Biography 7. Astronomers -- Italy -- Biography

ISBN 0375867538; 9780307974402; 9780375867538; 9780375967535

LC 2011025100

"In this . . . picture book, blind, elderly Galileo sits . . . tells the story of his life. After speaking of his childhood and education, he recalls his scientific work, including developing an improved telescope that enabled him . . . to conclude that Copernicus' 'sun-centered theory' was correct. The church reacted . . . by placing him under house arrest and banning his books. The narrative . . . touches on many of Galileo's accomplishments." (Booklist)

★ Panchyk, Richard. **Galileo** for kids; his life and ideas; 25 activities. foreword by Buzz Aldrin. Chicago Review Press 2005 166p il map pa $16.95

Grades: 5 6 7 8   92

1. Astronomers 2. Writers on science

ISBN 1-55652-566-4

LC 2004-22936

A biography of the Renaissance scientist and his times with related activities

"Clear . . . writing places Galileo squarely within the historical context of the turbulent Italian Renaissance. . . . Panchyk's title is a good choice for those interested in integrating history and science curriculums." SLJ

Includes bibliographical references

★ Steele, Philip. **Galileo**; the genius who faced the Inquisition. National Geographic 2005 64p il (World history biographies) $17.95; lib bdg $27.90

Grades: 4 5 6 7   92

1. Astronomers 2. Writers on science

ISBN 0-7922-3656-4; 0-7922-3657-2 lib bdg

LC 2005-01357

An illustrated introduction to the 16th century astronomer and his times

"Accompliments and hardships are clearly explained with supporting quotes and facts. . . . Beautifully illustrated and visually appealing." SLJ

Gallaudet, T. H. (Thomas Hopkins), 1787-1851

★ McCully, Emily Arnold. **My** heart glow: Alice Cogswell, Thomas Gallaudet and the birth of American sign language. Hyperion Books for Children 2008 un il $15.99

Grades: 2 3 4   92

1. Deaf 2. Sign language 3. Teachers of the deaf

ISBN 978-1-4231-0028-7; 1-4231-0028-X

This is the story of Thomas Gallaudet and his deaf neighbor, Alice Cogswell, and how Gallaudet established a school for the deaf in the United States and developed American Sign Language.

"Emily Arnold McCully's watercolor illustrations are beautifully rendered. . . . Not only does this book accurately present the engrossing story of Alice and Gallaudet, it is also an excellent resource for teaching diversity and encouraging empathy for others." Libr Media Connect

Wyckoff, Edwin Brit. **Sign** language man: Thomas H. Gallaudet and his incredible work. Enslow Elementary 2010 32p il (Genius at work! Great inventor biographies) lib bdg $22.60

Grades: 4 5 6   92

1. Sign language 2. Deaf -- Education 3. Teachers of the deaf 4.

Deaf -- Means of communication
ISBN 978-0-7660-3447-1 lib bdg; 0-7660-3447-X lib bdg

LC 2010005359

"Read about Thomas H. Gallaudet, who helped develop and teach American Sign Language." Publisher's note

Includes glossary and bibliographical references

Gama, Vasco da, 1469-1524

★ Calvert, Patricia. **Vasco** da Gama; so strong a spirit. [by] Patricia Calvert. Benchmark Books 2005 96p il map (Great explorations) lib bdg $29.93

Grades: 5 6 7 8   92

1. Explorers
ISBN 0-7614-1611-0

LC 2003-22946

Recounts the voyages undertaken by fifteenth-century Portuguese explorer Vasco da Gama to strengthen his nation's power by establishing a sea trade route to India.

Includes bibliographical references

Gandhi, Arun

★ Gandhi, Arun. **Grandfather** Gandhi; Arun Gandhi and Bethany Hegedus; illustrated by Evan Turk. Atheneum Books for Young Readers 2012 48 p. (hardcover) $17.99

Grades: K 1 2 3   92

1. Grandfathers 2. Pacifists -- India -- Biography 3. Statesmen -- India -- Biography
ISBN 144242365X; 9781442423657

LC 2011033058

In this book, by Arun Gandhi and Bethany Hegedus, illustrated by Evan Turk, "Mahatma Gandhi's grandson tells the story of how his grandfather taught him to turn darkness into light. . . . When an older boy pushes him on the soccer field, his anger fills him in a way that surely a true Gandhi could never imagine. Can Arun ever live up to the Mahatma? Will he ever make his grandfather proud?" (Publisher's note)

"Mahatma Gandhi's grandson, Arun, who angers easily, feels he will never live up to the Gandhi name. Gandhi explains that he, too, feels anger but has learned to channel it for good. Unusual for its child-centered portrait of Gandhi, the graceful narrative is matched by vivid mixed-media illustrations, rendered in watercolor, paper collage, cotton fabric, yarn, gouache, pencil, tea, and tinfoil." (Horn Book)

Gandhi, Mahatma, 1869-1948

★ Demi. **Gandhi**. Margaret K. McElderry Bks. 2001 un il $19.95

Grades: 3 4 5 6   92

1. Authors 2. Journalists 3. Passive resistance 4. Essayists 5. Pacifists 6. Memoirists 7. Political leaders 8. Writers on politics 9. India -- Politics and government
ISBN 0-689-84149-3

LC 00-32911

"Beginning with Gandhi's failure as a student in India, this . . . biography traces Gandhi's life, from his first rallies against prejudice in South Africa to his remarkable victory over colonialism in India. . . . With extraordinarily detailed illustrations, decorated with gold leaf . . . and accessible, flowing text, veteran artist-author Demi reveals how a simple man who spun his own cloth became one of history's most important political and spiritual leaders." Booklist

★ Gandhi, Arun. **Grandfather** Gandhi; Arun Gandhi and Bethany Hegedus; illustrated by Evan Turk. Atheneum Books for Young Readers 2012 48 p. (hardcover) $17.99

Grades: K 1 2 3   92

1. Grandfathers 2. Pacifists -- India -- Biography 3. Statesmen

-- India -- Biography
ISBN 144242365X; 9781442423657

LC 2011033058

In this book, by Arun Gandhi and Bethany Hegedus, illustrated by Evan Turk, "Mahatma Gandhi's grandson tells the story of how his grandfather taught him to turn darkness into light. . . . When an older boy pushes him on the soccer field, his anger fills him in a way that surely a true Gandhi could never imagine. Can Arun ever live up to the Mahatma? Will he ever make his grandfather proud?" (Publisher's note)

"Mahatma Gandhi's grandson, Arun, who angers easily, feels he will never live up to the Gandhi name. Gandhi explains that he, too, feels anger but has learned to channel it for good. Unusual for its child-centered portrait of Gandhi, the graceful narrative is matched by vivid mixed-media illustrations, rendered in watercolor, paper collage, cotton fabric, yarn, gouache, pencil, tea, and tinfoil." (Horn Book)

★ Wilkinson, Philip. **Gandhi**; the young protester who founded a nation. National Geographic 2005 64p il (World history biographies) $17.95; lib bdg $27.90

Grades: 4 5 6 7   92

1. Authors 2. Journalists 3. Passive resistance 4. Essayists 5. Pacifists 6. Memoirists 7. Political leaders 8. Writers on politics 9. India -- Politics and government
ISBN 0-7922-3647-5; 0-7922-3648-3 lib bdg

"Double-page spreads describe phases in Gandhi's life, from childhood to his tragic death, detailed in Wilkinson's straightforward, succinct language and in anecdotes, which will capture young people's attention and also humanize the great leader." Booklist

Includes glossary and bibliographical references

Garber, Mary, 1916-2008

Macy, Sue, 1954- **Miss** Mary Reporting; The True Story of Sportswriter Mary Garber. Sue Macy; illustrated by C. F. Payne. Simon & Schuster Books for Young Readers 2014 40 p. color illustrations (hardcover) $17.99

Grades: K 1 2 3 4   92

1. Sports journalism 2. Women sportswriters -- United States -- Biography
ISBN 9781481401203

LC 2014000871

This children's book, by Sue Macy and illustrated by C.F. Payne, is a "biography of Mary Garber, one of the first female sports journalists in American history. In a time when African-American sports were not routinely covered, Mary went to the games and wrote about them. Garber was a sportswriter for fifty-six years and was the first woman to receive the Associated Press Sports Editors' Red Smith Award, presented for major contributions in sports journalism." (Publisher's note)

"The narrative is swiftly paced, smoothly written, and filled with interesting details and quotes. Payne's soft-focus mixed-media illustrations feature beautifully delineated period settings and a masterful use of composition for dramatic effect." Booklist

Garnett, Kevin, 1976-

Wilner, Barry. **Kevin** Garnett; a basketball star who cares. Enslow 2011 48p il (Sports stars who care) $23.93

Grades: 3 4 5   92

1. Basketball players 2. Basketball -- Biography
ISBN 978-0-7660-3772-4; 0-7660-3772-X

This is a biography of the forward for the Boston Celtics who, through his 4XL Foundation, helps teens prepare for careers in business and who donated more than $1 million to help rebuild areas devastated by Hurricane Katrina.

This is "especially good for book reports." Booklist

Gaudí, Antoni, 1852-1926

★ Rodriguez, Rachel. **Building** on nature; the life of Antoni Gaudi. illustrated by Julie Paschkis. Henry Holt & Co. 2009 un il $16.99
Grades: 1 2 3   **92**
1. Architects
ISBN 978-0-8050-8745-1; 0-8050-8745-1

LC 2008-38213

This is a biography of "the Catalonian architect Antoni Gaudi. The immediacy of the present-tense narrative is simple, direct, and at times piercingly poetic. . . . Paschkis doesn't try to reproduce the delicate exoticism of Gaudi's buildings in a line-for-line manner but rather soaks up the wondrous strange oozing from his designs and renders their dreamlike qualities in pointed details and large-scale impressions." Booklist

Gee, Maggie

★ Moss, Marissa. **Sky** high: the true story of Maggie Gee; illustrated by Carl Angel. Tricycle Press 2009 un il $16.99
Grades: 3 4 5   **92**
1. Authors 2. Novelists 3. Women air pilots 4. World War, 1939-1945 -- Aerial operations
ISBN 978-1-58246-280-6; 1-58246-280-1

LC 2008042387

This is a biography of the Asian American World War II air pilot, Maggie Gee

"Based on interviews with Gee, this has a lovely, personal feel to it. And while some of the faces in the acrylic and colored-pencil illustrations are a bit stiff, the scenes themselves exude a panoramic joy." Booklist

Gehrig, Lou, 1903-1941

Adler, David A. **Lou** Gehrig; the luckiest man. illustrated by Terry Widener. Harcourt Brace & Co. 1997 un il $17
Grades: 2 3 4   **92**
1. Baseball players 2. Baseball -- Biography
ISBN 0-15-200523-4

LC 95-7997

Traces the life of the Yankees' star ballplayer, focusing on his character and his struggle with the terminal disease amyotrophic lateral sclerosis

"Adler's restrained tone makes his description of Gehrig's stoic and uncomplaining struggle all the more moving. The illustrations, meticulously detailed . . . also pack an emotional wallop." Horn Book Guide

Gehry, Frank

Bodden, Valerie. **Frank** Gehry. Creative Education 2009 48p il (Xtraordinary artists) lib bdg $32.80
Grades: 4 5 6 7   **92**
1. Architects
ISBN 978-1-58341-662-4 lib bdg; 1-58341-662-5 lib bdg

LC 2007004201

This is a biography of architect Frank Gehry

This offers an "interesting [layout]; big, high-quality reproductions and photographs on heavy paper; insightful quotes from diverse sources; and . . . an excerpt from an essay about [Gehry] at the end of the book. Readers get a strong sense of [the] artist's personality along with an excellent survey of his work." SLJ

Includes bibliographical references

Genghis Khan, 1162-1227

★ Demi. **Genghis** Khan. Marshall Cavendish Children 2009 un il $19.99

Grades: 4 5 6 7   **92**
1. Mongols 2. Kings and rulers 3. Kings
ISBN 978-0-7614-5547-9; 0-7614-5547-7

LC 2008006001

A reissue of Chingis Khan, published 1991 by Henry Holt & Co.

A biography of the Mongol leader and military-strategist who, at the height of his power, was supreme master of the largest empire ever created in the lifetime of one man.

"Demi has managed to portray a fierce conqueror as a sympathetic character who follows a strict code that places loyalty, obedience, and discipline above all else. . . . The artist achieves a clever grandeur with the liberal use of iridescent gold and detailed scenes that spill out of their gilded borders and nearly off the pages. . . . This handsome biography is a feast for the eyes from cover to cover." Booklist

George III, King of Great Britain, 1738-1820

★ Fritz, Jean. **Can't** you make them behave, King George? pictures by Tomie de Paola. Putnam 1977 45p il $16.99; pa $6.99
Grades: 2 3 4   **92**
1. Kings 2. Great Britain -- Kings and rulers
ISBN 0-399-23304-0; 0-698-11402-7 pa

LC 75-33722

"As a boy, George is seen to have had struggles in deportment; as King George III, he is mystified that the colonists refuse to be taught. Bits of history, a sense of George's personality, and the loneliness of being king are all conveyed with good humor. The artist's drawings evoke more chuckles." LC. Child Books, 1977

Gershwin, George, 1898-1937

Slade, Suzanne. The **music** in George's head; George Gershwin Creates Rhapsody in Blue. Suzanne Slade, Illustrated by Stacy Innerst. Calkins Creek 2016 48 p. color illustrations $17.95
Grades: 1 2 3 4   **92**
ISBN 9781629790992

LC 2015958417

In this book, "George Gershwin heard music all the time—at home, at school, even on New York City's busy streets. Classical, ragtime, blues, and jazz—George's head was filled with a whole lot of razzmatazz! With rhythmic swirls of words and pictures, author Suzanne Slade and illustrator Stacy Innerst beautifully reveal just how brilliantly Gershwin combined various kinds of music to create his masterpiece." (Publisher's note)

"Readers will get a glimpse into Gershwin's mind and find the music within. Highly recommended for purchase." SLJ

Includes bibliographical references.

Gibson, Althea, 1927-2003

Deans, Karen. **Playing** to win: the story of Althea Gibson; by Karen Deans; illustrated by Elbrite Brown. Holiday House 2007 un il $16.95
Grades: 1 2 3 4   **92**
1. Women athletes 2. African American athletes 3. Tennis players 4. Tennis -- Biography
ISBN 0-8234-1926-6

LC 2004052275

"Not only was Gibson a record-breaking tennis player, but she also played an important role in breaking down racial barriers. . . . The multimedia illustrations are well matched to the power and fluidity of the text, particularly in capturing the champion in action. . . . This well-written and attractive biography will be a popular addition to most collections." SLJ

Includes bibliographical references

★ Stauffacher, Sue. **Nothing** but trouble; the story of Althea Gibson. illustrated by Greg Couch. Alfred A. Knopf 2007 un il $16.99; lib bdg $19.99

Grades: 2 3 4 5   **92**

1. Women athletes 2. African American athletes 3. Tennis players 4. Tennis -- Biography

ISBN 978-0-375-83408-0; 978-0-375-93408-7 lib bdg

LC 2006-12605

A biography of the first African American tennis player to win at Wimbleton and Forest Hills in 1957 and 1958

"Couch's kinetic illustrations done in acrylic with digital imaging wonderfully enhance the text. Althea stands out in a blur of color against somber sepia, blue, and olive-drab backgrounds. The prose is rhythmic and has the cadence of the street, and it's a treat to read aloud." SLJ

Giff, Patricia Reilly

Giff, Patricia Reilly. **Don't** tell the girls; a family memoir. by Patricia Reilly Giff. Holiday House 2005 131p il $16.95

Grades: 4 5 6 7   **92**

1. Authors 2. Teachers 3. Women authors 4. Authors, American 5. Children's authors

ISBN 0-8234-1813-8

LC 2004-47452

"Giff reflects on her childhood and her family, going back through several generations. Spotlighting her two grandmothers, she lovingly relates remembered conversations and incidents involving the one she knew well before turning to the other grandmother, whom she never met. . . . This little book has much to offer thoughtful children. . . . With . . . sharply reproduced family photos and documents, this handsome book's small format reflects its intimate, conversational style." Booklist

Gilbreth, Lillian Moller, 1878-1972

Kulling, Monica. **Spic-and-span!** Lillian Gilbreth's wonder kitchen. Monica Kulling. Tundra Books of Northern New York 2014 32 p. color illustrations

Grades: K 1 2 3   **92**

1. Women engineers 2. Women inventors

ISBN 9781770493803; 9781770493810

LC 2013943889

This book, by Monica Kulling, focuses on Lillian Moller Gilbreth. "She and her husband, Frank, became efficiency experts by studying the actions of factory workers. . . . When Frank suddenly died, Lillian was left to her own devices to raise their eleven children. Eventually, she was hired by the Brooklyn Borough Gas Company to improve kitchen design, which was only the beginning. . . . [She] the first woman elected to the National Academy of Engineering." (Publisher's note)

"This engaging picture-book biography details the many accomplishments of Lillian Gilbreth, the first woman elected to the National Academy of Engineering...Parkins' rich, cartoon-like illustrations provide clear period detail, and his characters' faces portray an extensive range of emotions, adding interest and emphasizing Gilbreth's primary commitment to her family. Student researchers might also enjoy other titles in the Great Idea series, such as Kulling's In the Bag!: Margaret Knight Wraps It Up (2011)." Booklist

Gilmore, P. S. (Patrick Sarsfield), 1829-1892

Potter, Alicia. **Jubilee!** Patrick S. Gilmore's very, very loud idea. Alicia Potter, illustrated by Matt Tavares. Candlewick Press 2014 40 p. $16.99

Grades: 2 3 4 5   **92**

1. Concerts 2. Music -- United States -- History 3. United States -- History -- 1861-1865, Civil War -- Peace 4. Bands (Music) 5. Music festivals -- Massachusetts -- Boston 6. National Peace Jubilee and Musical Festival (1869 : Boston, Mass.)

ISBN 0763658561; 9780763658564

LC 2013943992

This book, by Alicia Potter, focuses on the "man behind the 1869 National Peace Jubilee. . . . As a young boy growing up in Ireland, Patrick Sarsfield Gilmore loved music. . . . This love of music followed him to Boston in 1849, where he became a bandleader. During the brutal Civil War, it was music that kept up his spirits and those of his fellow soldiers. So when the war ended, . . . [he] create the biggest, boldest, loudest concert the world had ever known to celebrate." (Publisher's note)

"After experiencing the horrors of the Civil War firsthand, one man was determined to celebrate the beauty of life through music...his is both a tribute to one man's talent and an insightful look at a different period of history." SLJ

Ginsburg, Ruth Bader

Levy, Debbie. **I** dissent; Ruth Bader Ginsburg Makes Her Mark. Debbie Levy; illustrated by Elizabeth Baddeley. Simon & Schuster Books for Young Readers 2016 40 p. color illustrations (hardcover) $17.99

Grades: 2 3 4 5   **92**

1. Judges -- Biography 2. Women judges 3. Judges -- United States -- Biography

ISBN 9781481465595

LC 2015034756

This children's book by Debbie Levy, illustrated by Elizabeth Baddeley, focuses on "Supreme Court justice Ruth Bader Ginsburg . . . as she proves that disagreeing does not make you disagreeable! . . . Ginsburg has spent a lifetime disagreeing: disagreeing with inequality, arguing against unfair treatment, and standing up for what's right for people everywhere. This . . . book . . . tells the justice's story through the lens of her many famous dissents, or disagreements." (Publisher's note)

"This lively, inviting, and informative biography of a historic woman will empower young ones to bravely voice their opinions." Booklist

Includes bibliographical references.

Glenn, John, 1921-2016

Mitchell, Don. **Liftoff;** a photobiography of John Glenn. National Geographic Society 2006 64p il $17.95; lib bdg $27.90

Grades: 5 6 7 8   **92**

1. Astronauts 2. Senators 3. Statesmen -- United States

ISBN 0-7922-5899-1; 0-7922-5900-9 lib bdg

LC 2005-30916

This is a biography of the American astronaut, pilot, and U.S. Senator from Ohio.

This is "well-written and well-illustrated." Sci Books Films

Includes bibliographical references

Gogh, Vincent van, 1853-1890

Bodden, Valerie. **Vincent** van Gogh. Creative Education 2009 48p il (Xtraordinary artists) lib bdg $32.80

Grades: 4 5 6 7   **92**

1. Artists 2. Painters 3. Artists, Dutch

ISBN 978-1-58341-663-1 lib bdg; 1-58341-663-3 lib bdg

LC 2007002118

This biography of the artist offers an "interesting [layout]; big, high-quality reproductions and photographs on heavy paper; insightful quotes from diverse sources; and meaty selections of the artist's own writing . . . at the end of the book. Readers get a strong sense of [the] artist's personality along with an excellent survey of his work." SLJ

Includes bibliographical references

Goodall, Jane, 1934-

★ McDonnell, Patrick. **Me** . . . Jane. Little, Brown 2011 $15.99

Grades: PreK K 1 2   **92**

1. Chimpanzees 2. Women scientists 3. Primatologists 4. Writers on nature 5. Nonfiction writers
ISBN 978-0-316-04546-9; 0-316-04546-2; 0316045462; 9780316045469

LC 2010019756

This book is "inspirational. . . . McDonnell's homey, earth-toned pen and watercolor pictures give way to that most famous of all Goodall photographs, where the young scientist and an even younger chimp reach across their worlds to touch hands. The simple and intimate paintings are accented with casually arrayed stamped motifs and some of Goodall's childhood drawings." Horn Book

Silvey, Anita. **Untamed**; the wild life of Jane Goodall. Anita Silvey; foreword by Jane Goodall. National Geographic Books 2015 96 p. col. illustrations, col. maps (library binding : alk. paper) $28.90
Grades: 4 5 6 7 8   **92**

1. Primates -- Behavior 2. Primatology 3. Chimpanzees -- Behavior 4. Primatologists -- England -- Biography 5. Women primatologists -- England -- Biography
ISBN 1426315198; 9781426315183; 9781426315190

LC 2014017715

This children's book by Anita Silvey profiles "Jane Goodall, one of the most recognized scientists in the Western world, [who] became internationally famous because of her ability to observe and connect with another species. She began tirelessly fighting to protect the environment so that chimpanzees and other animals will continue have a place and a future on our planet." (Publisher's note)

"Silvey (The Plant Hunters) adeptly chronicles the life of Goodall from her childhood fascination with animal behavior to her groundbreaking field research of chimpanzees in Africa and her work to preserve endangered animals' habitats." Publishers Weekly

★ Winter, Jeanette. The **watcher** : Jane Goodall's life with the chimps. Schwartz & Wade Books 2011 un il $17.99; lib bdg $20.99
Grades: PreK K 1 2   **92**

1. Chimpanzees 2. Women scientists 3. Primatologists 4. Writers on nature 5. Nonfiction writers
ISBN 978-0-375-86774-3; 0-375-86774-0; 978-0-375-96774-0 lib bdg; 0-375-96774-5 lib bdg

LC 2010005280

"This tranquil picture-book biography establishes from the beginning that Jane Goodall has always had the right temperment for the work that made her famous. . . . The theme of persistence, particularly in relation to observing animals, shapes the spare, inviting text, which takes Goodall from backyard observations to scientific study of chimpanzees in Tanzania. In Winter's signature stylized paintings, the jungle is rendered in cool blues and greens." Horn Book

Goodman, Benny, 1909-1986

Cline-Ransome, Lesa. **Benny** Goodman & Teddy Wilson; taking the stage as the first black and white jazz band in history. by Lesa Cline-Ransome; illustrated by James E. Ransome. Holiday House 2014 32 p. (hardcover) $16.95
Grades: 2 3 4 5   **92**

1. Jazz musicians -- Biography 2. Race relations -- History -- 20th century 3. Jazz musicians -- United States -- Biography
ISBN 082342362X; 9780823423620

LC 2010048154

"In 1936, the Benny Goodman Trio became the first interracial band to perform in public, with Benny Goodman (the son of Jewish immigrants) on clarinet and African-American Teddy Wilson on piano (Gene Krupa, on drums, completed the trio). Writing in punchy free verse that echoes the bounce of both men's music," author Lesa Cline-Ransome,

"traces Goodman and Wilson's parallel--but separate--paths to jazz fame, before eventually meeting in 1935." (Publishers Weekly)

"Goodman grew up in Chicago, a working-class Jewish boy; Wilson lived in Tuskegee, Alabama, a middle-class African American boy. The story of how the two jazz musicians met and formed the Benny Goodman Trio (the "first interracial band to perform publicly") is recounted in short bursts of text, almost like jazz riffs, accompanied by pencil and watercolor illustrations that capture distinctive moments. Timeline." Horn Book

Grandin, Temple

Montgomery, Sy. **Temple** Grandin; how the girl who loved cows embraced autism and changed the world. by Sy Montgomery. Houghton Mifflin Harcourt 2012 147 p. col. ill. $17.99
Grades: 4 5 6 7 8   **92**

1. Autism 2. Cattle 3. Biography 4. Women scientists -- Biography 5. Animal welfare -- United States 6. Livestock -- Housing -- United States 7. Livestock -- Handling -- United States 8. Autistic people -- United States -- Biography 9. Animal scientists -- United States -- Biography 10. Animal specialists -- United States -- Biography 11. Women animal specialists -- United States -- Biography
ISBN 0547443153; 9780547443157

LC 2011039911

AAAS/Subaru SB&F Prize for Excellence in Science Books: Middle Grade Science Book (2013)

This book by Sy Montgomery presents a biography of autistic animal scientist Temple Grandin. Sy Montgomery argues that "though one never outgrows autism, it doesn't condemn those who have it to unproductive lives, and an appendix, 'Temple's Advice for Kids on the Spectrum,' provides first-hand wisdom. Photos and diagrams depict Grandin's work as well as documenting her early life and career." (Kirkus Reviews)

Includes bibliographical references and index.

Greenberg, Hank, 1911-1986

Sommer, Shelley. **Hammerin'** Hank Greenberg; baseball pioneer. Calkins Creek 2011 135p il $17.95
Grades: 5 6 7 8   **92**

1. Baseball players 2. Jews -- Biography 3. Baseball -- Biography
ISBN 1-59078-452-9; 978-1-59078-452-5

"Greenberg grew up in an Orthodox Jewish family in New York and went on to be a Hall-of-Fame first baseman and left fielder, playing most of his career with the Detroit Tigers in the 1930s and 1940s. . . . Sommer presents a fast-moving, straightforward biography. . . . Numerous black-and-white photos enhance the text. . . . An excellent choice for kids who enjoy delving into baseball history." Booklist

Greene, Nathanael, 1742-1786

Mierka, Gregg A. **Nathanael** Greene; the general who saved the Revolution. [by] Gregg A. Mierka. OTTN Pub. 2007 88p il map (Forgotten heroes of the American Revolution) $23.95; pa $12.95
Grades: 5 6 7 8   **92**

1. Generals 2. Society of Friends 3. United States -- History -- 1775-1783, Revolution
ISBN 978-1-59556-012-4; 1-59556-012-2; 978-1-59556-017-9 pa; 1-59556-017-3 pa

LC 2006021044

"This lively profile combines an engrossing account of the Revolutionary War with healthy measures of images and passages drawn from primary—and sometimes previously unpublished—sources." Booklist

Includes bibliographical references

Greenwood, Chester, 1858-1937

★ McCarthy, Meghan. **Earmuffs** for everyone! how Chester Greenwood became known as the inventor of earmuffs. Meghan McCarthy. Simon & Schuster Books for Young Readers 2015 48 p. illustrations (chiefly color) (hardback) $17.99

Grades: K 1 2 3 4   92

1. Patents 2. Inventors 3. Earmuffs

ISBN 148140637X; 9781481406376

LC 2014020159

In this picture book, by Meghan McCarthy, "Chester Greenwood went from having cold ears to becoming a great inventor. . . . When your ears are cold, you can wear earmuffs, but that wasn't true for Chester Greenwood back in 1873. Earmuffs didn't exist yet! But during yet another long and cold Maine winter, Chester decided to do something about his freezing ears, and he designed the first pair of ear protectors (a.k.a. earmuffs) out of wire, beaver fur, and cloth." (Publisher's note)

".This unusual book also offers insight into the process of invention and how the muddling of fact, memory, and legend can result in popular history." Booklist

Gross, Elly Berkovits, 1929-

Gross, Elly Berkovits. **Elly**; my true story of the Holocaust. [by] Elly Berkovits Gross. Scholastic Press 2009 125p il $14.99

Grades: 4 5 6 7   92

1. Poets 2. Authors 3. Holocaust survivors 4. Memoirists 5. Jews -- Romania 6. Holocaust, 1933-1945 -- Personal narratives

ISBN 978-0-545-07494-0; 0-545-07494-0

Relates how the author was torn from her happy home and sent to Birkenau by the Nazis, describing how she worked long hours and fought for survival before being set free at the end of the war and beginning a new life in America.

"As a powerful reminder of man's capacity for inhumanity, this memoir is essential reading." Booklist

Guthrie, Woody, 1912-1967

Burckhardt, Marc. **When** Bob met Woody; the story of the young Bob Dylan. illustrated by Marc Burckhardt. Little, Brown 2011 40p il $17.99

Grades: 3 4 5   92

1. Rock musicians

ISBN 978-0-316-11299-4; 0-316-11299-2

LC 2010-43030

This picture book biography follows Bob Zimmerman as he renames himself after his favorite poet, Dylan Thomas, and leaves his mining town to pursue his love of music in New York City. There, he meets his folk music hero and future mentor, Woody Guthrie.

"Golio excels at portraying Zimmerman's angst as he flounders for meaning and even invents for himself a more colorful backstory. Burckhardt's acrylics have the fractured look of damaged paintings, and . . . [convey] gravity and emotion. Back matter, including quotation sources, is superb. A stirring introduction to two musical legends." Booklist

Includes bibliographical references

★ Christensen, Bonnie. **Woody** Guthrie, poet of the people. Knopf 2001 un il hardcover o.p. pa $7.99

Grades: 3 4 5 6   92

1. Singers 2. Folk musicians 3. Memoirists 4. Songwriters 5. Folk singers -- United States -- Biography

ISBN 0-553-11203-1; 0375811133; 0375911138 lib bdg

LC 00-65504

Boston Globe-Horn Book Award Honor: Nonfiction (2002)

This book tells "the life story of American songwriter Woody Guthrie. . . . Grades three to six." (Bull Cent Child Books)

"Christensen makes a fine union of a spirited, vibrant text and hand-colored woodcuts that are sinewy and emotionally compelling." Booklist

Guyton, Tyree

Shapiro, J. H. **Magic** trash; a story of Tyree Guyton and his art. [by] J.H. Shapiro; illustrated by Vanessa Newton. Charlesbridge 2011 32p il

Grades: K 1 3 4   92

1. Artists

ISBN 1580893856 lib bdg; 9781580893855 1

LC 2010023524

"Multicolored, multilayered, multimedia illustrations trace the life of Tyree Guyton and his visionary artwork, which used reclaimed trash to turn a derelict Detroit street into community-activist art. . . . . Readers whiz through Tyree's story, propelled by his energy and zinging, trippy triplets that cap each significant event in his life. . . . An inspiring, exciting introduction to avant-garde art and social commentary, this biography convinces young readers that art can exist, thrive and effect change outside in the real world." Kirkus

Gág, Wanda, 1893-1946

Ray, Deborah Kogan. **Wanda** Gag; the girl who lived to draw. [by] Deborah Kogan Ray. Viking Childrens Books 2008 un il $16.99

Grades: 2 3 4   92

1. Artists 2. Authors 3. Illustrators 4. Women authors 5. Authors, American 6. Children's authors

ISBN 978-0-670-06292-8; 0-670-06292-8

LC 2008-13132

"This charming biography of the creator of Millions of Cats . . . shows how Gág's family and childhood inspired her lifelong pursuit of art. . . . Each page of text is introduced with a quote from the subject's diaries and letters, and faces a white-framed illustration reflecting the Old World charm of her childhood, which comes to life with Ray's evocative paintings." SLJ

Hale, Bruce, 1957-

Parker-Rock, Michelle. **Bruce** Hale; an author kids love. Enslow Publishers 2008 48p bibl il por (Authors kids love) lib bdg $23.93

Grades: 3 4 5   92

1. Artists 2. Authors 3. Illustrators 4. Storytellers 5. Authors, American 6. Children's authors

ISBN 978-0-7660-2758-9 lib bdg; 0-7660-2758-9 lib bdg

LC 2007029319

A biography of the author of the Chet Gecko mystery series for children, based on an interview

"The frequent use of direct quotes makes the [text] particularly enjoyable. . . . Kids will be fascinated with . . . Hale's hat collection and love of surfing. . . . Well written, interesting, and useful for reports." SLJ

Halvorsen, Gail

★ Tunnell, Michael. **Candy** bomber; the story of the Berlin airlift's chocolate pilot. Charlesbridge 2010 110p il $18.95; pa $9.95

Grades: 4 5 6 7   92

1. Air pilots 2. Air force officers 3. Berlin (Germany) -- History -- Blockade, 1948-1949

ISBN 1-58089-336-8; 1-58089-337-6 pa; 978-1-58089-336-7; 978-1-58089-337-4 pa

This book takes place "[i]n 1948, after World War II, [in] Berlin, . . . [where Michael] Tunnell tells us that pilot Gail Halvorsen spent a night in the city, noticing kids behind a fence watching the planes land. He offered sticks of Doublemint gum to two of the kids, who passed them around so their pals could get a whiff. . . . Soon people all over began sending candy-and-handkerchief parachutes to Halvorsen and other pilots to drop over Berlin." (School Library Journal)

"Curious about the city into which he ferried goods during the Berlin Airlift in 1948, pilot Gail Halvorsen stayed over to visit, met some children, and offered to drop candy and gum when he next flew over. This simple idea grew into a massive project with reverberations today. Tunnell tell this appealing story . . . clearly and chronologically, weaving just enough background for twenty-first century readers and illustrating almost every page with black-and-white photographs, many from Halvorsen's own collection." Booklist

Includes bibliographical references

Hamer, Fannie Lou, 1917-1977

★ Weatherford, Carole Boston, 1956- **Voice** of freedom; Fannie Lou Hamer, Spirit of the Civil Rights Movement. Carole Boston Weatherford, illustrated by Ekua Holmes. Candlewick Press 2015 56 p. color illustrations $17.99

Grades: 4 5 6 7 8   92

1. African American women -- Biography 2. Civil rights -- United States

ISBN 9780763665319

LC 2013957319

Boston Globe-Horn Book Nonfiction Honor Book (2016)

Robert F. Sibert Honor Book (2016)

Caldecott Honor Book (2016)

Coretta Scott King/John Steptoe New Talent Illustrator Award (2016)

This book, by Carole Boston Weatherford, illustrated by Ekua Holmes, focuses on "Fannie Lou Hamer . . . a champion of civil rights from the 1950s until her death in 1977. Integral to the Freedom Summer of 1964, Ms. Hamer gave a speech at the Democratic National Convention that, despite President Johnson's interference, aired on national TV news and spurred the nation to support the Freedom Democrats." (Publisher's note)

"This majestic biography offers a detailed, intelligible overview of Hamer's life while never losing the thread of her motivations, fears, and heroic triumphs; and places the civil rights movement in personal, local, national, and international contexts. An extensively detailed timeline, an author's note, source notes, and a bibliography are appended." Horn Book

Hamilton, Alexander, 1757-1804

★ Fritz, Jean. **Alexander** Hamilton; the outsider. illustrations by Ian Schoenherr. G.P. Putnam's Sons 2011 144p il $16.99

Grades: 5 6 7 8   92

1. Statesmen 2. Statesmen -- United States 3. Secretaries of the treasury 4. United States -- History -- 1775-1783, Revolution 5. United States -- Politics and government -- 1783-1809

ISBN 039925546X; 9780399255465

LC 2010006008

Fritz "provides a brisk, well-written account introducing Founding Father Alexander Hamilton as an outsider to America. . . . Fast moving and engaging, this straightforward biography acknowledges Hamilton's flaws while portraying him as an intelligent, energetic man who rose to the challenge of his times. . . . In addition to the black-and-white reproductions of period paintings and prints that illustrate the text, Schoenherr's striking, engraving-like images of Hamilton as scholar, soldier, aide-decamp, statesman, and duelist introduce each section." Booklist

Includes bibliographical references

Kanefield, Teri. Alexander Hamilton; the making of America. by Teri Kanefield. Abrams Books for Young Readers 2017 208 p. illustrations (hardback) $16.95

Grades: 5 6 7 8   92

1. Statesmen -- United States 2. Statesmen -- United States --

Biography 3. United States -- Politics and government -- 1783-1809

ISBN 9781419725784

LC 2016046103

This book on Alexander Hamilton, by Teri Kanefield, "is the story that epitomizes the American dream—a poor immigrant who made good in America. In the end, Hamilton rose from poverty through his intelligence and ability, and did more to shape our country than any of his contemporaries." (Publisher's note)

"A great addition to upper elementary and middle school libraries." Kirkus.

Includes bibliographical references and index.

Hancock, John, 1737-1793

Adler, David A. A **picture** book of John Hancock; by David A. Adler and Michael S. Adler; illustrated by Ronald Himler. Holiday House 2007 un il $16.95

Grades: 1 2 3   92

1. Governors 2. Statesmen 3. Colonial leaders 4. Members of Congress 5. United States -- History -- 1775-1783, Revolution

ISBN 978-0-8234-2005-6; 0-8234-2005-1

LC 2005052649

"This biography begins with what is probably Hancock's most famous act, the signing of the Declaration of Independence. It then takes readers back to the beginning of his life to tell how he became such an important and influential part of America's Revolutionary War. . . . Himler's watercolors in muted tones offer visual guides to historical events. This title . . . is a solid addition to biography collections." SLJ

Includes bibliographical references

★ Fritz, Jean. **Will** you sign here, John Hancock? pictures by Trina Schart Hyman. Putnam Pub. Group 1976 47p il hardcover o.p. pa $5.99

Grades: 2 3 4   92

1. Governors 2. Statesmen 3. Colonial leaders 4. Members of Congress 5. United States -- History -- 1775-1783, Revolution

ISBN 0-399-23306-7; 0-698-11440-X pa

"An affectionate look at a flamboyant, egocentric, but kindly, patriot, the book is a most enjoyable view of history. . . . The delightful illustrations exactly suit the times and the extraordinary character of John Hancock." Horn Book

Harvey, William, 1578-1657

Yount, Lisa. **William** Harvey; discoverer of how blood circulates. [by] Lisa Yount. rev ed.; Enslow Publishers 2008 128p il map (Great minds of science) lib bdg $31.93

Grades: 5 6 7 8   92

1. Biologists 2. Physicians 3. Physiologists 4. Writers on science 5. Writers on medicine 6. Blood -- Circulation

ISBN 978-0-7660-3010-7 lib bdg; 0-7660-3010-5 lib bdg

LC 2007020301

First published 1994

"A biography of the seventeenth-century English physician William Harvey and includes related activities for readers." Publisher's note

Includes glossary and bibliographical references

Hatshepsut, Queen of Egypt

★ Galford, Ellen. **Hatshepsut**; the princess who became king. National Geographic 2005 64p il map (World history biographies) $17.95; lib bdg $27.90

Grades: 4 5 6 7   92

1. Queens 2. Kings and rulers 3. Egypt -- History 4. Egypt -- Civilization

ISBN 0-7922-3645-9; 0-7922-3646-7 lib bdg

This "presents the life of Queen Hatshepsut, who ruled Egypt as pharaoh during the New Kingdom, around 3500 years ago. Illustrated with clear, color photos of artifacts and sites as well as colorful maps, the text discusses aspects of Egyptian life such as education and religion in Hatshepsut's life. . . . With a clearly written text and many handsome photos, this provides an accessible introduction to Hatshepsut and her times." Booklist

Hawking, Stephen W., 1942-

Venezia, Mike. **Stephen** Hawking; cosmologist who gets a big bang out of the universe. written and illustrated by Mike Venezia. Children's Press 2009 32p il (Getting to know the world's greatest inventors & scientists) $28

Grades: 2 3 4   92

1. Cosmology 2. Physicists 3. Black holes (Astronomy) 4. People with disabilities 5. College teachers 6. Writers on science

ISBN 978-0-531-23728-1; 0-531-23728-1

LC 2008-27650

"This exemplary . . . biography will inform and motivate young readers. It introduces Stephen Hawking as a physicist and cosmologist. . . . [The author] introduces a few of Hawking's cosmological ideas in clear, but simple, ways that communicate the nature of the ideas and how scientific understanding is developed by a community of scientists. There are colorful telescopic photographs, entertaining cartoons, and numerous photographs of Hawking's professional and personal life." Sci Books Films

Henry, John William, 1847?-ca. 1875

★ Nelson, Scott Reynolds. **Ain't** nothing but a man; my quest to find the real John Henry. [by] Scott Reynolds Nelson with Marc Aronson. National Geographic 2008 64p il $18.95; lib bdg $27.90

Grades: 4 5 6 7 8   92

1. Railroad workers 2. Railroads -- History 3. African Americans -- Biography 4. John Henry (Legendary character)

ISBN 978-1-4263-0000-4; 1-4263-0000-X; 978-1-4263-0001-1 lib bdg; 1-4263-0001-8 lib bdg

LC 2007-12446

This describes the author's research to find the real man who inspired the songs and legends about the African American steel-driving hero.

"The layout is attractive, with a sepia and beige background for the text and sepia-toned photographs. . . . This is an excellent example of how much detective work is needed for original research." SLJ

Includes bibliographical references

Henry, Patrick, 1736-1799

★ Fritz, Jean. **Where** was Patrick Henry on the 29th of May? illustrated by Margot Tomes. Putnam Pub. Group 1975 47p il $16.99; pa $6.99

Grades: 2 3 4   92

1. Statesmen 2. Colonial leaders 3. United States -- History -- 1600-1775, Colonial period

ISBN 0-399-23305-9; 0-698-11439-6 pa

"The color pictures are artful evocations of the [18th] century in America and the text presents Patrick Henry as a human being—not a sterilized historic 'figure.'" Publ Wkly

Henson, Jim

Krull, Kathleen. **Jim** Henson; the guy who played with puppets. paintings by Steve Johnson and Lou Fancher. Random House 2011 35p il $16.99; lib bdg $19.99

Grades: K 1 2 3   92

1. Television programs 2. Puppets and puppet plays 3. Puppeteers

4. Muppet show (Television program)

ISBN 978-0-375-85721-8; 0-375-85721-4; 978-0-375-95721-5 lib bdg; 0-375-95721-9 lib bdg

LC 2010043837

"Krull, Johnson, and Fancher offer an inspiring and timely portrait of the late Henson. The book covers Henson's upbringing, experimentation with and study of puppetry, and the creation and success of his beloved Muppets on TV and on the big screen. . . . Johnson and Fancher's paintings exude a warm, nostalgic glow as they show the early roots of Henson's creativity and behind-the-scenes images of him at work." Publ Wkly

Includes bibliographical references

Henson, Matthew Alexander, 1866-1955

Hopkinson, Deborah. **Keep** on! the story of Matthew Henson, co-discoverer of the North Pole. written by Deborah Hopkinson; illustrated by Stephen Alcorn. Peachtree Publishers 2009 un il $17.95

Grades: 2 3 4   92

1. Explorers 2. North Pole 3. African Americans -- Biography

ISBN 978-1-56145-473-0; 1-56145-473-7

LC 2008031118

"Written in articulate and straightforward prose, and accompanied by quotes from Henson, Keep On! tells the story of an inspiring and courageous figure and is enhanced by Alcorn's dramatic, sweeping scenes." SLJ

★ Johnson, Dolores. **Onward**; a photobiography of African-American polar explorer Matthew Henson. National Geographic 2006 64p il $17.95

Grades: 5 6 7 8   92

1. Explorers 2. North Pole 3. African Americans -- Biography

ISBN 0-7922-7914-X

LC 2005-05837

"The quest to be the first to reach the North Pole is an exciting adventure story, and Henson got there first, as part of the ninth expedition led by Robert Peary in 1909. But Henson was African American, labeled as Peary's 'Negro manservant,' and he did not get full recognition until 2001. This . . . focuses on the physical details of the dangerous Arctic journeys . . . the repeated failures and the teamwork, as well as Henson's skills, stamina, and essential role in forging relationships with the Inuit. . . . The book design is beautiful: thick paper, spacious type, and stirring photos that capture the icy storms as well as the people involved in the history." Booklist

Hepburn, Audrey, 1929-1993

Cardillo, Margaret. **Just** being Audrey; illustrated By Julia Denos. Balzer + Bray 2011 un il

Grades: 1 2 3   92

1. Actors

ISBN 006185283X; 9780061852831

LC 2010003982

"Growing up in WW II–era Europe, Audrey wanted only to be a dancer, but the other girls made fun of her physical hurdles. . . . She was spotted by entertainment heavyweights . . . and quickly catapulted to fame. Denos' soft pastel illustrations cut just the right Audrey outline . . . and fans will especially enjoy picking out the movie roles depicted in a two-page spread of costumes. Her later humanitarian deeds are given their due, but it is Audrey's simple kindness that is emphasized throughout." Booklist

Includes bibliographical references

Herrera, Juan Felipe, 1948-

Herrera, Juan Felipe. The **upside** down boy; story by Juan Felipe Herrera; illustrations by Elizabeth Gómez. Children's Bk. Press 2000 31p il $15.95

Grades: K 1 2 3 **92**

1. Poets 2. Authors 3. Children's authors 4. Young adult authors 5. Mexican Americans -- Biography 6. Bilingual books -- English-Spanish

ISBN 0-89239-162-6

LC 99-49113

The author recalls the year when his farm worker parents settled down in the city so that he could go to school for the first time

"Herrera's poetic prose sings with a unique voice in both languages, and Gómez's illustrations are colorful and ethereal." Horn book guide

Herrmann, Adelaide, 1853-1932

★ Rockliff, Mara. **Anything** but Ordinary Addie; The True Story of Adelaide Herrmann, Queen of Magic. Mara Rockliff; illustrated by Iacopo Bruno. Candlewick Press 2016 48 p. color illustrations $17.99

Grades: 2 3 4 5 **92**

1. Magicians 2. Women entertainers -- Biography

ISBN 0763668419; 9780763668419

"Adelaide Herrmann (1853-1932) never wanted to be like other girls: she was determined to stand out and dazzle the world. She secretly joined a dancing troupe, scandalizing family and friends. [It] led to her meeting and marrying Alexander Herrmann, aka Herrmann the Great, a famous magician. Addie began working as Alexander's assistant and took over the act when he died. Life was never ordinary again." (School Library Journal)

"Lavish illustrations frame the story, often literally, creating a three-dimensional effect that puts the reader in every scene. Velvet stage curtains, ship's rigging, fellow audience members--all overlap the featured artwork, lending excitement and immediacy to this little-known tale. The rich colors and embellished fonts, meanwhile, create a grandiose effect fitting for Adelaide's life in the spotlight." Booklist

Heschel, Abraham Joshua, 1907-1972

★ Michelson, Richard. **As** good as anybody; Martin Luther King Jr. and Abraham Joshua Heschel's amazing march toward freedom; by Richard Michelson; illustrated by Raul Colón. Knopf 2008 un il $16.99; lib bdg $19.99

Grades: 2 3 4 **92**

1. Clergy 2. Rabbis 3. Theologians 4. Jews -- Biography 5. Nonfiction writers 6. Civil rights activists 7. Nobel laureates for peace 8. African Americans -- Biography 9. African Americans -- Civil rights

ISBN 978-0-375-83335-9; 0-375-83335-8; 978-0-375-93335-6 lib bdg; 0-375-93335-2 lib bdg

This is the story of how Abraham Joshua Heschel, a Polish rabbi who escaped the Holocaust, and Martin Luther King worked together for African American civil rights.

"Michelson writes in poetic language. . . . Also admirable is Michelson's ability to convey complex historical concepts . . . in clear, potent terms that will speak directly to readers. . . . In both palette and style, Colón's colored-pencil and watercolor art . . . suggests the past, but his themes carry into today's headlines." Booklist

Hillary, Edmund Sir

Coburn, Broughton. **Triumph** on Everest; a photobiography of Sir Edmund Hillary. National Geographic Soc. 2000 64p il map $17.95; pa $7.95

Grades: 4 5 6 7 **92**

1. Mountaineering 2. Mountaineers 3. Nonfiction writers 4.

Mount Everest (China and Nepal)

ISBN 0-7922-7114-9; 0-7922-7932-8 pa

LC 00-27009

A biography of Edmund Hillary, whose love of snow, mountains, and the outdoor life culminated in his conquering the highest peak in the world

"Threaded with quotes from Hillary's own writings, and full of fine, blue-toned photographs, the engrossing text presents the life of a reticent but world-renowned mountaineer, adventurer, and philanthropist." SLJ

Includes bibliographical references

Hodgman, Ann

Hodgman, Ann. The **house** of a million pets; with illustrations by Eugene Yelchin. Henry Holt & Co. 2007 263p il $16.95

Grades: 3 4 5 6 **92**

1. Pets 2. Authors 3. Cookbook writers 4. Children's authors

ISBN 978-0-8050-7974-6; 0-8050-7974-2

LC 2006-36447

This is a "witty and personable narrative. . . . Yelchin's inky animal vignettes are inviting, with a cheerful impudence in their scrawled lines that perfectly matches the text." Bull Cent Child Books

Hodgman, Ann. **How** to die of embarrassment every day. Henry Holt and Co. 2011 208p il $16.99

Grades: 5 6 7 8 **92**

1. Authors 2. Women authors 3. Cookbook writers 4. Authors, American 5. Children's authors

ISBN 978-0-8050-8705-5; 0-8050-8705-2

LC 2010-49004

Hodgman offers a "chatty personal narrative . . . focusing on her childhood years and her tendency to land herself into humiliating situations. . . . The generous supply of spot art and relevant images from Hodgman's childhood adds to the browsibility. . . . There's . . . plenty of humor . . . but more importantly there's a tacit message about the survivability of embarrassment and the fact that we all, even seemingly perfect and polished adults, spend our lives goofing up." Bull Cent Child Books

Hokusai (Katsushika Hokusai), 1760-1849

Ray, Deborah Kogan. **Hokusai**; the man who painted a mountain. Foster Bks. 2001 un il $18

Grades: 3 4 5 6 **92**

1. Artists 2. Artists, Japanese

ISBN 0-374-33263-0

LC 00-50395

"The text and evocative artwork provide details and scenes of everyday Japanese life in the 19th century. The illustrations include accomplished soft watercolor and colored-pencil paintings, labeled Chinese characters, drawings from the artist's sketchbooks, and a reproduction of Hokusai's 'The Great Wave off Kanagawa.'" SLJ

Includes bibliographical references

Honda, Sōichirō, 1906-1991

Weston, Mark. **Honda**; the boy who dreamed of cars. illustrated by Katie Yamasaki. Lee & Low Books 2008 un il $17.95

Grades: 3 4 5 **92**

1. Executives 2. Businesspeople 3. Automobile industry 4. Automobile executives

ISBN 978-1-60060-246-7; 1-60060-246-0

LC 2007049040

"Weston's writing is clear and accessible. . . . The book reads like a story, with fictionalization of Honda's thoughts and dialogue. . . . Yamasaki's acrylic illustrations dominate each page. At first glance they seem representational, but on closer inspection readers will find little men climbing on the engine parts, . . . [and] miniature cars going around a globe and down Honda's arm. . . . Yamasaki's creative composition makes the pictures interesting and dynamic." SLJ

Hopkins, Sarah Winnemucca, 1844?-1891

Ray, Deborah Kogan. **Paiute** princess; the story of Sarah Winnemucca. Deborah Kogan Ray. Frances Foster Books, Farrar Straus Giroux 2011 48 p. col. ill., col. map $17.99
Grades: 3 4 5   **92**

1. Paiute Indians 2. Native American women 3. Paiute Indians -- Biography 4. Women political activists -- West (U.S.) -- Biography 5. Indians of North America -- Civil rights -- History -- 19th century 6. American literature -- Indian authors -- Biography
ISBN 0374398976; 9780374398972

LC 2009046090

This book is a biography of Sarah Winnemucca, who was "[b]orn into the Northern Paiute tribe of Nevada in 1844" and who "straddled two cultures: the traditional life of her people, and the modern ways of her grandfather's white friends." Her skill with languages "made her a great leader." The book includes "illustrations and . . . backmatter, including hand-drawn maps, a chronology, archival photographs, an author's notes, and additional resource information." (Publisher's note)

Includes bibliographical references

Hopper, Edward, 1882-1967

Burleigh, Robert. **Edward** Hopper paints his world; Robert Burleigh; paintings by Wendell Minor. Henry Holt & Co. 2014 40 p. color illustrations (hardback) $17.99
Grades: K 1 2 3 4   **92**

1. Artists -- United States -- Biography 2. Painters
ISBN 0805087524; 9780805087529

LC 2013037068

This children's book by Robert Burleigh, illustrated by Wendell Minor, describes how "as a boy, Edward Hopper knew exactly what he wanted to be when he grew up. . . . And even though no one wanted to buy his paintings for a long time, he never stopped believing in his dream to be an artist. He was fascinated with painting light and shadow and his works explore this challenge." (Publisher's note)

Burleigh and Minor "help readers comprehend Hopper from the inside out: from the actual motifs, to the edited and combined studies, to the familiar, finished and admired paintings on the museum walls. Backmatter is particularly well-organized and inclusive." Kirkus

Includes bibliographical references

★ Rubin, Susan Goldman. **Edward** Hopper; painter of light and shadow. Abrams Books for Young Readers 2007 47p il $18.95
Grades: 5 6 7 8   **92**

1. Artists 2. Painters 3. Artists -- United States
ISBN 978-0-8109-9347-1; 0-8109-9347-3

LC 2006-31978

"On every page of this beautifully designed biography, readers will find a reproduction of Hopper's work, matched to clear, eloquent commentary. . . . Readers . . . will come back to read about the man and look at his art again and again." Booklist

Includes bibliographical references

Hopper, Grace, 1906-1992

Wallmark, Laurie. **Grace** Hopper; Queen of Computer Code. by Laurie Wallmark; illustrated by Katy Wu. Sterling Children's Books 2017 48 p. illustrations (some color) $16.95
Grades: 3 4 5 6   **92**

1. Admirals 2. Computer scientists 3. Admirals -- United States -- Biography 4. Women admirals -- United States -- Biography 5. Computer engineers -- United States -- Biography 6. Women

computer engineers -- United States -- Biography
ISBN 9781454920007

LC 2016035342

This book, by Laurie Wallmark, illustrated by Katy Wu, is the "story of Grace Hopper—the boundary-breaking woman who revolutionized computer science. . . . Grace Hopper coined the term 'computer bug' and taught computers to 'speak English.' Throughout her life, Hopper succeeded in doing what no one had ever done before." (Publisher's note)

Includes bibliographical references

Horne, Lena

Weatherford, Carole Boston, 1956- The **legendary** Miss Lena Horne; Carole Boston Weatherford; illustrated by Elizabeth Zunon. Atheneum Books for Young Readers 2017 48 p. illustrations (chiefly color) (hardcover : alk. paper) $17.99
Grades: 2 3 4 5   **92**

1. African American women -- Biography 2. Singers -- United States -- Biography 3. Singers -- United States -- Biography
ISBN 9781481468244; 9781481468251

LC 2016016139

In this biography of African American actress and civil rights activist Lena Horne, by Carole Boston Weatherford, illustrated by Elizabeth Zunon, "Horne was born into the freedom struggle, to a family of teachers and activists. Her mother dreamed of being an actress, so Lena followed in her footsteps as she chased small parts in vaudeville, living out of a suitcase until MGM offered Lena something more—the first ever studio contract for a black actress." (Publisher's note)

"A memorable life dedicated to music and civil rights, presented with commensurate style." Kirkus

Includes bibliographical references and index

Horton, George Moses, 1798-1884

★ Tate, Don. **Poet**; The Remarkable Story of George Moses Horton. Don Tate. Peachtree Pub Ltd 2015 36 p. color illustrations $16.95
Grades: K 1 2 3 4 5   **92**

1. Slaves 2. American literature -- African American authors 3. African American poets -- Biography 4. Freedmen -- United States -- Biography 5. Poets, American -- 19th century -- Biography
ISBN 1561458252; 9781561458257

LC 2015002407

This children's book by Don Tate tells of how "in the nineteenth century, North Carolina slave George Moses Horton taught himself to read and earned money to purchase his time though not his freedom. Horton became the first African American to be published in the South, protesting slavery in the form of verse." (Publisher's note)

"This picture book biography of poet George Moses Horton (1798-1884), a slave and the first African American poet to be published in the South, recounts his fascinating long life and masterly way with words. Tate's distinctive illustrations feature gently curving horizons, bucolic washes of color, and figures with oversize heads and stylized, expressive faces. . . . A lovely introduction to an inspirational American poet." SLJ

Includes bibliographical references

Houdini, Harry, 1874-1926

Biskup, Agnieszka. **Houdini**; the life of the great escape artist. illustrated by Pat Kinsella. Capstone Press 2011 32p il (Graphic library: American graphic) lib bdg $29.32; pa $7.95
Grades: 4 5 6 7   **92**

1. Magicians 2. Biographical graphic novels 3. Nonfiction writers
ISBN 978-1-4296-5474-6 lib bdg; 1-4296-5474-0 lib bdg; 978-1-4296-6268-0 pa; 1-4296-6268-9 pa

LC 2010024848

In graphic novel format, explores the life of Harry Houdini and describes some of his most daring escapes.

"The illustrations are eye-catching and the narration is presented simply, yet compellingly. . . . Fact-filled, entertaining, and accessible." SLJ

Includes bibliographical references

Carlson, Laurie M. **Harry** Houdini for kids; his life and adventures with 21 magic tricks and illusions. Chicago Review Press 2009 136p il pa $16.95

Grades: 4 5 6 7   **92**

1. Magicians 2. Magic tricks 3. Nonfiction writers
ISBN 978-1-55652-782-1 pa; 1-55652-782-9 pa

LC 2008021404

"Reluctant readers (as well as budding troublemakers) will flock to this biography/handbook hybrid about one of the most famous magicians who ever lived. Even for those familiar with Houdini's fascinating story, Carlson's snappy writing gives it new life. . . . Nearly every page is enlivened with period photographs, boxed sections containing biographies and definitions, and, most important, 21 magic tricks that will have readers breaking out their deck of cards and practicing their sleight of hand." Booklist

★ Fleischman, Sid. **Escape!** the story of the great Houdini. Greenwillow Books 2006 210p il $18.99; lib bdg $19.89

Grades: 5 6 7 8   **92**

1. Magicians 2. Nonfiction writers
ISBN 978-0-06-085094-4; 0-06-085094-9; 978-0-06-085095-1 lib bdg; 0-06-0850957-1 lib bdg

LC 2005052631

"Fleischman looks at Houdini's life through his own eyes, as a fellow magician. . . . Fleischman's tone is lively and he develops a relationship with readers by revealing just enough truth behind Houdini's razzle-dazzle to keep the legend alive. . . . Engaging and fascinating." SLJ

Includes bibliographical references

Krull, Kathleen. **Houdini**; the world's greatest mystery man and escape king. in a production written by Kathleen Krull; and illustrated by Eric Velasquez. Walker & Co. 2005 un il hardcover o.p. pa $6.95

Grades: 2 3 4   **92**

1. Magicians 2. Nonfiction writers
ISBN 0-8027-8953-6; 0-8027-8954-4 lib bdg; 0-8027-9646-X pa

LC 2004-49493

"Framed descriptions of some of Houdini's most famous stunts are interspersed within the overview of his life. The author's crisp narrative style and careful choice of detail are evident here. . . . Velasquez's impressive framed, posed oil paintings portray the magician's intensity and sense of showmanship." SLJ

Includes bibliographical references

Houston, Sam, 1793-1883

★ Fritz, Jean. **Make** way for Sam Houston; illustrations by Elise Primavera. Putnam 1986 109p il map hardcover o.p. pa $5.99

Grades: 4 5 6   **92**

1. Governors 2. Statesmen 3. Senators 4. Army officers
ISBN 0-399-21303-1; 0-698-11646-1 pa

LC 85-25601

"Artfully weaving the threads of fact, Fritz creates a biography that is both interesting and informative. Developing Houston as a human character that readers can identify with as well as admire, and drawing him against the scene of America's own political turmoil, Fritz gives us a book to be read and to be felt." Voice Youth Advocates

Includes bibliographical references

Howe, Samuel Gridley, 1801-1876

Alexander, Sally Hobart. **She** touched the world: Laura Bridgman, deaf-blind pioneer; by Sally Hobart Alexander and Robert Alexander. Clarion Books 2008 100p il $18

Grades: 5 6 7 8   **92**

1. Deaf 2. Blind 3. Students 4. Physicians 5. Philanthropists 6. Humanitarians 7. Teachers of the blind
ISBN 978-0-618-85299-4; 0-618-85299-9

"At the age of three, in 1832, Laura Bridgman contracted scarlet fever and lost her sight, her hearing, her sense of smell, and much of her sense of taste. Her family sent her to Dr. Samuel [Gridley] Howe at the New England Institute for the Education of the Blind, and by the age of 10, Laura was world-famous for her accomplishments. . . . Alexander . . . presents a well-written and thoroughly researched biography of this remarkable woman, with numerous black-and-white photos." Booklist

Includes bibliographical references

Hudson, Henry, d. 1611

★ Weaver, Janice. **Hudson**; written by Janice Weaver; illustrated by David Craig. Tundra Books 2010 47p il map $22.95

Grades: 3 4 5 6   **92**

1. Explorers 2. America -- Exploration 3. Canada -- Discovery and exploration -- British 4. America -- Discovery and exploration
ISBN 978-0-88776-814-9; 0-88776-814-8

This is a biography of the explorer. "The grandson of a trader, Hudson sailed under both British and Dutch flags, looking for a northern route to China. Although none of his voyages led to the discovery of a northwest passage, he did explore what is now Hudson's Bay and what is now New York City." (Publisher's note) Index. "Ages eight to twelve." (Quill Quire)

"This dramatic picture-book biography about Henry Hudson, who discovered neither the new land nor the passage to Asia he sought, makes the explorer's lack of success a gripping read. . . . Weaver is clear about what is fact and what is supposition, and the tumultuous early-seventeenth-century history is meticulously documented. . . . Craig's glowing period portraits, landscapes, and watercolors of the ship in dangerous seas intensify the drama, and archival prints and maps add interest." Booklist

Includes bibliographical references

Hunter, Clementine, 1886?-1988

★ Whitehead, Kathy. **Art** from her heart: folk artist Clementine Hunter; [illustrated by] Shane Evans. G.P. Putnam's Sons 2008 un il $16.99

Grades: 4 5 6 7   **92**

1. Artists 2. Folk art 3. Painters 4. Women artists 5. African American artists 6. Centenarians
ISBN 0-399-24219-8; 978-0-399-24219-9

LC 2006-34458

This is a biography of Louisiana artist Clementine Hunter, who depicted life on a plantation. Bibliography. "Ages five to eight." (Bull Cent Child Books) "In the 1950s, segregation laws

denied artist Clementine Hunter admission to the gallery that exhibited her work. . . . Hunter was not stopped by self-pity, and she did not wait for 'the perfect time to paint.' She had no canvas, so she made art with whatever she could find--window shades, glass bottles, old boards." (Booklist)

"Whitehead's lyrical text speaks of Hunter's perseverance and talent as well as of the simplicity, love of nature, and caring of friends and family that informed her work. Evans bolsters Whitehead's words with bold mixed-media illustrations that portray Hunter in hard times and in good." SLJ

Hurston, Zora Neale, 1891-1960

Fradin, Dennis Brindell. **Zora!** the life of Zora Neal Hurston. Judith Bloom Fradin and Dennis Brindell Fradin. Clarion Books 2012 xi, 180 p.p ill. $17.99

Grades: 5 6 7 8   92

1. African American authors -- Biography 2. African American women -- Biography   3. Folklorists -- United States -- Biography
ISBN 0547006950; 9780547006956

LC 2011025949

This book by Dennis Brindell Fradin and Judith Bloom Fradin presents a "biography of . . . African-American author . . . [Zora Neale] Hurston. . . . Beginning with a . . . scene of the 59-year-old Hurston, already a well-known author, working as a white family's domestic helper because she needed a paycheck, the Fradins . . . establish the complexities of Zora's inner and external worlds, before offering highlights of her life in chronological order." (Publishers Weekly)

Includes bibliographical references and index.

Van Wright, Cornelius. **Zora** Hurston and the chinaberry tree; illustrated by Cornelius Van Wright and Ying-hwa Hu. Lee & Low Bks. 1994 un il $15.95; pa $6.95

Grades: K 1 2 3   92

1. Authors 2. Novelists 3. Dramatists 4. Women authors 5. African American authors 6. Memoirists 7. Folklorists 8. Short story writers
ISBN 1-880000-14-8; 1-880000-33-4 pa

LC 94-1291

"Conveying the changing expressions on the face of the young Hurston as easily as they show the grandeur of the sky at nightfall, the versatile artists neatly capture the emotions in this lucidly told story." Publ Wkly

Hutchinson, Anne Marbury, 1591-1643

Atkins, Jeannine. **Anne** Hutchinson's way; [by] Jeannine Atkins; pictures by Michael Dooling. Farrar, Straus and Giroux 2007 un il $17

Grades: 2 3 4   92

1. Colonists 2. Dissenters 3. Religious leaders 4. Massachusetts -- History -- 1600-1775, Colonial period
ISBN 0-374-30365-7

"Anne Hutchinson arrives with her family in Massachusetts colony in 1634 and begins preaching scripture from her home after finding herself in disagreement with the minister's beliefs. . . . Atkins is able to take the issue of religious freedom and make it personal by telling the story through the eyes of Hutchinson's young daughter, Susanna. . . . A sense of sturdiness is everywhere here: in the story . . . and in Dooling's impressive artwork, plain in color but rugged in its portrayal of the demands of colony life. Illustrated in a photo-realistic style that makes the long-ago events seem close." Booklist

Hypatia, ca. 370-415

★ Love, D. Anne. **Of** numbers and stars; the story of Hypatia. by D. Anne Love; illustrated by Pam Paparone. Holiday House 2006 un il $16.95

Grades: 2 3 4   92

1. Philosophers 2. Mathematicians 3. Women mathematicians
ISBN 0-8234-1621-6

LC 2003064725

"In fourth-century C.E. Egypt, women had few opportunities. How Hypatia, daughter of mathematician Theon, became one of the greatest philosophers of her day makes fascinating reading. . . . Attractive paintings add life to a clear and captivating text that offers a unique contribution to units about Egypt, philosophers, or women in history." SLJ

Includes bibliographical references

Irving, Washington, 1783-1859

★ Harness, Cheryl. The **literary** adventures of Washington Irving; American storyteller. by Cheryl Harness. National Geographic Society 2008 43p il $17.95; lib bdg $27.90

Grades: 2 3 4 5   92

1. Authors 2. Historians 3. Essayists 4. Biographers 5. Authors, American 6. Children's authors
ISBN 978-1-4263-0438-5; 1-4263-0438-2; 978-1-4263-0439-2 lib bdg; 1-4263-0439-0 lib bdg

LC 2008024975

A biography of the American author of The adventures of Rip Van Winkle and The Legend of Sleepy Hollow.

"Pairing insightful text with paintings organized into comic-book-style frames, Harness captures with exuberance everything that made Irving's life so exciting." Booklist

Includes bibliographical references

Jackson, Mahalia, 1911-1972

Pinkney, Andrea Davis. **Martin** and Mahalia; his words, her song. by Andrea Davis Pinkney; illustrated by Brian Pinkney. 1st ed. Little, Brown and Co. 2013 40 p. ill. (reinforced) $17.99

Grades: 1 2 3 4   92

1. Picture books for children 2. African Americans -- Civil rights -- History -- 20th century   3. Civil rights movements -- United States -- History -- 20th century
ISBN 0316070130; 9780316070133

LC 2012005499

This children's picture book weaves together "the stories of two giants of the American civil rights movement," Martin Luther King, Jr. and Mahalia Jackson. "At first the stories are distinct, with alternating, dedicated spreads tracing the individuals' paths as gospel preacher and singer until they meet and combine forces at the Montgomery bus boycott in 1955 and forge a collaboration that takes them through Martin's most famous speech, at the Lincoln Memorial." (Booklist)

Jalāl al-Dīn Rūmī, Maulana, 1207-1273

★ Demi. **Rumi**; whirling dervish. written and illustrated by Demi. Marshall Cavendish Children 2009 31p il $19.99

Grades: 4 5 6 7   92

1. Poets 2. Persian poetry
ISBN 978-0-7614-5527-1; 0-7614-5527-2

LC 2008012920

"Demi presents this picture-book introduction to the thirteenth-century mystical poet. . . . Demi condenses her famous subject's life into a brief but substantive text. . . . She adds frequent excerpts from Rumi's poems and writings. . . . In an introductory note, Demi cites Turkish miniatures as her inspiration for the small-scale, elaborately patterned pictures, rendered in Turkish and Chinese inks with gold overlay. . . . The gilded, celebratory pictures create shimmering beauty from the smallest details." Booklist

James, LeBron

Gatto, Kimberly. **Lebron** James; a basketball star who cares. [by] Kimberly A. Gatto. Enslow Publishers, Inc. 2011 48p il (Sport stars who care) lib bdg $23.93; pa $7.95

Grades: 3 4 5   92

1. Basketball players 2. Basketball -- Biography
ISBN 978-0-7660-3776-2 lib bdg; 0-7660-3776-2 lib bdg; 978-1-59845-231-0 pa; 1-59845-231-2 pa

LC 2010014921

A biography of basketball star Lebron James, who helps those in need through several charities, from the Boys and Girls Clubs of America to his own LeBron James Family Foundation.

This is "especially good for book reports." Booklist
Includes glossary and bibliographical references

Yasuda, Anita. **Lebron** James. 2011 24p il (Remarkable people)
$27.13; pa $12.95

Grades: 4 5 6 7 **92**

1. Basketball players 2. Basketball -- Biography
ISBN 978-1-6169-0669-6; 1-6169-0669-3; 978-1-6169-0674-0
pa; 1-6169-0674-X pa

LC 2010051003

This looks at Lebron James' "life, accomplishments, and challenges
while including a page of quotes, an annotated list of contemporaries
and influences, starter suggestions for writing a paper, and a time line
and glossary.... [This book] follows basketball's 'King James' from his
early life with a single teen mother to his splashy entry into the NBA at
age 19." Booklist

Jay-Z, 1969-
Spilsbury, Richard. **Jay-Z**; Richard Spilsbury. Heinemann Library
2013 48 p. (Titans of business) (pbk.) $8.99

Grades: 4 5 6 7 **92**

1. Businessmen 2. Rap musicians 3. Success in business 4. Rap
musicians -- United States -- Biography
ISBN 1432964305; 1432964372; 9781432964306;
9781432964375

LC 2011050758

This book, part of the Titans of Business series, looks at rapper and
entrepreneur Jay-Z. "Starting with Jay-Z's early life as Shawn Corey
Carter in a poor Brooklyn neighborhood, the biography recounts how he
overcame his difficult adolescence as a drug dealer with his desire to be
a musician." (Booklist)
Includes bibliographical references and index

Jefferson, Thomas, 1743-1826
Adler, David A. A **picture** book of Thomas Jefferson; illustrated
by John & Alexandra Wallner. Holiday House 1990 un il lib bdg
$17.95; pa $6.95

Grades: 1 2 3 **92**

1. Architects 2. Presidents 3. Vice-presidents 4. Essayists 5.
Presidents -- United States
ISBN 0-8234-0791-8 lib bdg; 0-8234-0881-7 pa

LC 89-20076

Traces the life and achievements of the architect, bibliophile, president, and author of the Declaration of Independence
"The book includes an amazing amount of material. An appealing
package with simple language and detailed drawings." Horn Book

Kalman, Maira. **Thomas** Jefferson; life, liberty and the pursuit of
everything. Maira Kalman. 1st ed. Nancy Paulsen Books 2014 40 p.
(hardback) $17.99

Grades: 3 4 5 **92**

1. Presidents -- United States 2. Presidents -- United States --
Biography
ISBN 0399240403; 9780399240409

LC 2013034625

In this biography of Thomas Jefferson, author "Maira Kalman sheds
light on the fascinating life and interests of the Renaissance man who
was [the United States'] third president. He played violin, spoke seven
languages and was a scientist, naturalist, botanist, mathematician and
architect. He doubled the size of the United States and sent Lewis and
Clark to explore it." (Publisher's note)

Miller, Brandon Marie. **Thomas** Jefferson for kids; his life and
times, with 21 activities. Chicago Review Press 2011 ix, 132p il
$16.95

Grades: 4 5 6 7 **92**

1. Architects 2. Presidents 3. Vice-presidents 4. Essayists 5.
Presidents -- United States
ISBN 978-1-56976-348-3; 1-56976-348-8

LC 2011019318

"Miller offers a thorough and methodical overview of Jefferson's life
and political career. . . . The presentation is expecially forthright about
Jefferson's ownership of slaves and his fathering of children with Sally
Hemmings. . . . The volume offers the chance to delve into Jefferson's
life and be inspired by the range of his interests." Kirkus
Includes bibliographical references

Thomas, Peggy. **Thomas** Jefferson grows a nation; Peggy Thomas,
Illustrations by Stacy Innerst. Calkins Creek 2015 48 p. color ill., color
maps $16.95

Grades: 3 4 5 6 **92**

1. United States -- Biography
ISBN 1620916282; 9781620916285

LC 2014958527

This juvenile book, by Peggy Thomas and Illustrations by Stacy
Innerst, profiles the U.S. Founding Father Thomas Jefferson. "Jefferson was more than a president and patriot. He was also a planter and
gardener who loved to watch things grow—everything from plants and
crops to even his brand-new nation, . . . Even in his retirement, Jefferson
continued to nurture the nation, laying the groundwork for the University of Virginia." (Publisher's note)
"Hand-lettered quotes from Jefferson and line-drawing caricatures
are incorporated into the paintings, which look simultaneously naive and
sophisticated. An informative supplement to more standard picture-book
biographies of Jefferson." Booklist
Includes bibliographical references.

Jemison, Mae C.
Jemison, Mae C. **Find** where the wind goes; moments from my
life. [by] Mae Jemison. Scholastic Press 2001 196p il hardcover
o.p. $16.95

Grades: 5 6 7 8 **92**

1. Astronauts 2. Physicians 3. African American women --
Biography
ISBN 0-439-13195-2; 0-439-13196-0 pa

LC 00-41008

"Mae Jemsion, doctor, scientist, astronaut, and professor, here tells
of the formative incidents of her life. . . . The author discusses her
youth—her days in the South, her family's move to Chicago's South
Side, school experiences, and growing up—as well as her later life and
her place in the space program. . . . Grades five to eight." (Bull Cent
Child Books)
"Dr. Jemison, the first woman of color to travel in space, shares her
life story in this autobiographical selection." Book Rep

Joan, of Arc, Saint, 1412-1431
Demi, 1942- **Joan** of Arc. Marshall Cavendish Children 2011 un
il $19.99

Grades: 3 4 5 **92**

1. Saints 2. Christian saints 3. France -- History -- 1328-1589,
House of Valois
ISBN 978-0-7614-5953-8; 0-7614-5953-7

LC 2011001123

"Joan of Arc's story told in the ravishing line and color of Demi's
art. . . . The text unequivocally treats the 15th-century Joan as a saint,
casting the craven King Charles VII as the villain he was. Joan's life is

recounted with a strong emphasis on prayer and the will of God, from her beginnings as a devout peasant girl who heeded angelic and saintly voices through her victories and defeats to her imprisonment, trial and martyrdom at the stake.... A young female hero par excellence." Kirkus

Johnson, Jack, 1878-1946

★ Smith, Charles R., 1969- **Black** Jack: the ballad of Jack Johnson; [by] Charles R. Smith Jr.; illustrated by Shane W. Evans. Roaring Brook Press 2010 un il $16.99

Grades: K 1 2 3   **92**

1. African American athletes 2. Boxers (Persons) 3. Boxing -- Biography

ISBN 978-1-59643-473-8; 1-59643-473-2

A picture book biography in verse of boxer Jack Jackson, the first African American heavyweight champion of the world

"The elegant simplicity and rat-a-tat rhythms land some stunners. . . . [The book is] enhanced by Evans' lithe and swaggering artwork, which lends a tremendous visual charisma, grace, and grandeur to the man." Booklist

Includes bibliographical references

Johnson, Lonnie, 1949-

Barton, Chris. **Whoosh!** Lonnie Johnson's super stream of ideas. Chris Barton; illustrated by Don Tate. Charlesbridge 2016 32 p. color illustrations (reinforced for library use) $16.95

Grades: 1 2 3 4   **92**

1. Toys 2. Inventors -- United States -- Biography 3. African Americans -- Alabama -- Biography 4. African American inventors -- Alabama -- Biography

ISBN 9781580892971

                                                                                LC 2015017342

This juvenile book, by Chris Barton and illustrated by Don Tate, profiles the life of the inventor of the Super Soaker squirt gun. "A . . . mind for creativity began early in Lonnie Johnson's life. Growing up in a house full of brothers and sisters, persistence and a passion for problem solving became the cornerstone for a career as an engineer. . . . But it is his invention of the Super Soaker water gun that has made his most memorable splash with kids and adults." (Publisher's note)

"This upbeat tribute makes an engaging and inspiring addition to STEM collections." Booklsit

Johnson, Lyndon B. (Lyndon Baines), 1908-1973

Gold, Susan Dudley. **Lyndon** B. Johnson. Marshall Cavendish Benchmark 2009 112p il (Presidents and their times) lib bdg $34.21

Grades: 5 6 7 8   **92**

1. Presidents 2. Vice-presidents 3. Senators 4. Members of Congress 5. Presidents -- United States

ISBN 978-0-7614-2837-4 lib bdg; 0-7614-2837-2 lib bdg

                                                                                LC 2007038518

A biography of the thirty-sixth president of the United States discusses his personal life, education, and political career and covers the formative events of his time

Includes glossary and bibliographical references

Johnson, Mamie, 1935-

★ Green, Michelle Y. A **strong** right arm: the story of Mamie Peanut Johnson; introduction by Mamie Johnson. Dial Bks. for Young Readers 2002 111p il $15.99; pa $5.99

Grades: 4 5 6 7   **92**

1. Women athletes 2. Baseball players 3. African American athletes 4. Collectibles dealers 5. Baseball -- Biography

ISBN 0-8037-2661-9; 0-14-240072-6 pa

                                                                                LC 2001-28616

"Johnson was a pitcher with the Negro Leagues' Indianapolis Clowns from 1953 to 1955. In the introduction, Johnson speaks directly and movingly to the reader about her meeting with author Green, who then lets the famous ballplayer tell her own story in a lively first-person narrative. Johnson's ebullient personality and determination fairly leap off the page." Booklist

Includes bibliographical references

Jones, John Paul, 1747-1792

Cooper, Michael L. **Hero** of the high seas; John Paul Jones and the American Revolution. National Geographic 2006 128p il map $21.95; lib bdg $32.90

Grades: 5 6 7 8   **92**

1. Admirals 2. Naval officers 3. United States -- History -- 1775-1783, Revolution

ISBN 0-7922-5547-X; 0-7922-5548-8 lib bdg

                                                                                LC 2005-36256

"Cooper charts his subject's life from a scandal-ridden Scottish captain on a trading ship to a man of self-invention who came to the American colonies to start a new life and became a naval hero. Jones is presented as a loyal captain, an arrogant leader, a determined sailor, and a flagrant social climber. The narrative style will appeal to reluctant readers, for it reads like a chronicle of thrilling naval adventures. . . . The text is clear and understandable." SLJ

Includes bibliographical references

Jordan, Michael, 1963-

Cooper, Floyd. **Jump!** from the life of Michael Jordan. Philomel Books 2004 un il $15.99

Grades: K 1 2 3   **92**

1. Basketball 2. Baseball players 3. African American athletes 4. Olympic athletes 5. Basketball players

ISBN 0-399-24230-9

                                                                                LC 2003-25071

This is a "childhood profile of basketball legend Michael Jordan. Each double-page spread features powerful portraits of Jordan. . . . Children who view Jordan as a deity on the court will take comfort in Cooper's stories, written in casual, colloquial language." Booklist

Includes bibliographical references

Joseph, Nez Percé Chief, 1840-1904

Biskup, Agnieszka. **Thunder** rolling down the mountain; the story of Chief Joseph and the Nez Perce. illustrated by Rusty Zimmerman. Capstone Press 2011 32p il (Graphic library: American graphic) lib bdg $29.32; pa $7.95

Grades: 4 5 6 7   **92**

1. Biographical graphic novels 2. Indian chiefs 3. Nez Percé Indians

ISBN 978-1-4296-5472-2 lib bdg; 1-4296-5472-4 lib bdg; 978-1-4296-6270-3 pa; 1-4296-6270-0 pa

                                                                                LC 2010027914

In graphic novel format, explores the battles and hardships faced by Chief Joseph and the Nez Perce when they were forced to leave their homelands.

"The illustrations are eye-catching and the narration is presented simply, yet compellingly. . . . Fact-filled, entertaining, and accessible." SLJ

Includes bibliographical references

Englar, Mary. **Chief** Joseph, 1840-1904. Blue Earth Books 2004 32p (American Indian biographies) lib bdg $23.93

Grades: 3 4 5   **92**

1. Indian chiefs 2. Nez Percé Indians 3. Native Americans --

Biography
ISBN 0-7368-2444-8

LC 2003-11071

A biography of the peace chief who ended the Nez Percé War by surrendering to United States soldiers in 1877, believing that he would be permitted lead his people back to their ancestral lands in Idaho. Includes a recipe for berry fritters and directions for "the stick game."

This "very accessible [title is] well illustrated with maps, photographs, and paintings, and [it offers] an introduction to American Indian history as well as specific information for reports." Booklist

Jumper, Betty Mae, 1923-2011

★ Annino, Jan Godown. **She** sang promise: the story of Betty Mae Jumper, Seminole tribal leader; illustrated by Lisa Desimini; afterword by Moses Jumper, Jr. National Geographic 2010 33p il map lib bdg $26.90

Grades: 1 2 3   92
1. Nurses 2. Seminole Indians 3. Storytellers 4. Indian leaders
ISBN 978-1-4263-0592-4 lib bdg; 1-4263-0592-3 lib bdg

LC 2009-16066

"Elected in 1967 as one of the first women tribal leaders in modern times, Seminole Betty Mae Tiger Jumper overcame oppression and prejudice, starting in her childhood. This picture-book biography tells her story in a dramatic present-tense narrative that blends details of her life with the historical struggle of her people.... The large collage paintings in bright colors blend old and new traditions, the natural world, and Seminole artwork." Booklist

Includes glossary and bibliographical references

Kahanamoku, Duke, 1890-1968

Crowe, Ellie. **Surfer** of the century; the life of Duke Kahanamoku. illustrations by Richard Waldrep. Lee & Low Books 2007 un il map $18.95

Grades: 3 4 5 6   92
1. Actors 2. Surfing 3. Swimming 4. Surfers 5. Swimmers 6. Olympic athletes
ISBN 978-1-58430-276-6

LC 2006036562

"The text is concise and readable, ably supported by Waldrep's full-page color art on every spread. These vibrant, action-filled illustrations . . . add much to the book's overall appeal. Well researched and fact-filled." SLJ

Kahlo, Frida, 1907-1954

★ Frith, Margaret. **Frida** Kahlo; the artist who painted herself. written by Margaret Frith; illustrated by Tomie DePaola. Grosset & Dunlap 2003 un il (Smart about art) hardcover o.p. pa $5.99

Grades: 2 3 4   92
1. Artists 2. Painters 3. Women artists 4. Artists, Mexican
ISBN 0-448-43239-0; 0-448-42677-3 pa

LC 2003-5221

Biography of Mexican artist Frida Kahlo, written as a child's school report

"Kahlo's story is clear, concise, and accessible. All of the basic facts are here, along with many personal details that enliven the narrative. . . . The well-written prose is beautifully complemented both by photos of Kahlo and of some of her best-known paintings and by dePaola's splendid trademark illustrations, all set against vividly colored backgrounds." SLJ

★ Winter, Jonah. **Frida**; illustrated by Ana Juan. Levine Bks. 2002 un il $16.95; pa $5.99

Grades: K 1 2 3   92
1. Artists 2. Painters 3. Women artists 4. Artists, Mexican
ISBN 0-590-20320-7; 0-590-20321-5 pa

LC 00-51421

This "illustrated short biography argues that the seeds of iconic painter Frida Kahlo's genius were planted during her childhood. . . . Winter consistently manages to convey much with a few well-chosen words, and the illustrations are appropriately awash with traditional Mexican folk art motifs and characters. Especially pleasing are Juan's surreal, Kahlo like touches." Horn Book

Kamkwamba, William, 1987-

Mealer, Bryan. The **boy** who harnessed the wind; William Kamkwamba and Bryan Mealer; illustrated by Anna Hymas. Young Readers' Edition Dial Books for Young Readers 2015 293 p. col. ill., col. map $8.99; $16.99

Grades: 4 5 6 7   92
1. Windmills 2. Irrigation 3. Inventors
ISBN 9780147510426; 0803740808; 0147510422; 9780803740808

"When a terrible drought struck William Kamkwamba's tiny village in Malawi, his family lost all of the season's crops, leaving them with nothing to eat and nothing to sell. William began to explore science books in his village library, looking for a solution. There, he came up with the idea that would change his family's life forever: he could build a windmill. Made out of scrap metal and old bicycle parts, William's windmill brought electricity to his home and helped his family pump the water they needed to farm the land." (Publisher's note)

"This youth edition of the original adult book of the same title has been skillfully adapted for middle grade readers." SLJ

★ Mealer, Bryan. The **boy** who harnessed the wind; William Kamkwamba and Bryan Mealer; pictures by Elizabeth Zunon. Picture book edition Dial Books for Young Readers 2012 32 p. illustrations (chiefly color) $17.99

Grades: K 1 2 3   92
1. Malawi 2. Windmills 3. Irrigation 4. Electric power 5. Mechanical engineering 6. Irrigation -- Malawi 7. Windmills -- Malawi 8. Electric power production -- Malawi 9. Mechanical engineers -- Malawi -- Biography
ISBN 0803735111; 9780803735118

LC 2011021536

"When 14-year-old William Kamkwamba's Malawi village was hit by a drought in 2001, everyone's crops began to fail. His family didn't have enough money for food, let alone school, so William spent his days in the library. He came across a book on windmills and figured out how to build a windmill that could bring electricity to his village. Everyone thought he was crazy but William persevered and managed to create a functioning windmill out of junkyard scraps. Several years later he figured out how to use the windmill for irrigation purposes." (Publisher's note)

Kandinsky, Wassily, 1866-1944

★ Rosenstock, Barb. The **noisy** paint box; the colors and sounds of Kandinsky's abstract art. by Barb Rosenstock; illustrated by Mary GrandPre. 1st ed. Alfred A. Knopf 2014 40 p. (hard cover) $17.99

Grades: K 1 2 3 4   92
1. Artists, Russian 2. Artists -- Russia (Federation) -- Biography
ISBN 0307978486; 9780307978486; 9780307978493

LC 2012032800

Caldecott Honor Book (2015)

In this book, author Barb Rosenstock and illustrator Mary Grand-Pré "tell the fascinating story of Vasily Kandinsky, one of the very first painters of abstract art. Throughout his life, Kandinsky experienced colors as sounds, and sounds as colors. Backmatter includes four paintings by Kandinsky, an author's note, sources, links to websites on synesthesia and abstract art." (Publisher's note)

Kearton, Cherry

Bond, Rebecca. **In** the belly of an ox: the unexpected photographic adventures of Richard and Cherry Kearton; written and illustrated by Rebecca Bond. Houghton Mifflin Books for Children 2009 un il $16
Grades: K 1 2 3   **92**
  1. Naturalists 2. Photographers 3. Photography of birds 4. Birds -- Nests
ISBN 978-0-547-07675-1; 0-547-07675-4
"In the late 19th century, these nature-loving brothers spent their youth navigating the British countryside. . . . When they were older, the boys devised a method to photograph wild birds in their nests. . . . Bond's graceful watercolors depict the brothers as they piece together their disguises and gain recognition for their innovative approach to photography. The brothers' dedication and ingenuity are especially resonant, and their elaborate costumes will amuse but also inspire." Publ Wkly

Kearton, Richard, 1862-1928

Bond, Rebecca. **In** the belly of an ox: the unexpected photographic adventures of Richard and Cherry Kearton; written and illustrated by Rebecca Bond. Houghton Mifflin Books for Children 2009 un il $16
Grades: K 1 2 3   **92**
  1. Naturalists 2. Photographers 3. Photography of birds 4. Birds -- Nests
ISBN 978-0-547-07675-1; 0-547-07675-4
"In the late 19th century, these nature-loving brothers spent their youth navigating the British countryside. . . . When they were older, the boys devised a method to photograph wild birds in their nests. . . . Bond's graceful watercolors depict the brothers as they piece together their disguises and gain recognition for their innovative approach to photography. The brothers' dedication and ingenuity are especially resonant, and their elaborate costumes will amuse but also inspire." Publ Wkly

Keaton, Buster, 1895-1966

★ Brighton, Catherine. **Keep** your eye on the kid; the early years of Buster Keaton. Roaring Brook Press 2008 un il $16.95
Grades: 3 4 5   **92**
  1. Actors 2. Motion picture producers and directors 3. Motion picture directors
ISBN 978-1-59643-158-4; 1-59643-158-X
                                           LC 2007-16534
This is a first-person account of the early years of Buster Keaton, who started performing as a child with his parents in vaudeville and "grew up to become a famous movie producer and performer. . . . Brighton's cartoon drawings shaded in umber and gray tones have a graphic look quite appropriate to the comic subject. The account ends with a brief look at the elaborate stage falls typical of Keaton's movie humor, and a full-page author's note gives added information on his career." SLJ
Includes bibliographical references.

Keats, Ezra Jack

Pinkney, Andrea Davis. A **poem** for Peter; The Story of Ezra Jack Keats and the Creation of The Snowy Day. by Andrea Davis Pinkney; illustrated by Steve Johnson and Lou Fancher. Viking Books for Young Readers 2016 60 p. color illustrations (hardback) $18.99
Grades: 1 2 3 4   **92**
  1. Illustrators -- United States 2. Authors, American -- Biography 3. Children's literature -- Authorship 4. Illustrators -- United States -- Biography
ISBN 9780425287705; 9780425287682
                                           LC 2016011990

This children's book by Andrea Davis Pinkney, illustrated by Steve Johnson and Lou Fancher, "dives into the life and work of Ezra Jack Keats, specifically focusing on 'The Snowy Day' and his creation of the main character, Peter. Using poetry . . . , Pinkney pieces together Keats's biography, tracing spots where early versions or hints of Peter can be found, and reflects on what a monumental event the publication of the picture book was and still is." (School Library Journal)
" With rich back matter on Keats' legacy and his art, including a list of sources, this is an important book that belongs in any library where Peter is loved." Booklist
Includes bibliographical references.

Keckley, Elizabeth, ca. 1818-1907

★ Jones, Lynda. **Mrs.** Lincoln's dressmaker: the unlikely friendship of Elizabeth Keckley and Mary Todd Lincoln; by Lynda D. Jones. National Geographic 2009 80p il $18.95; lib bdg $27.90
Grades: 5 6 7 8   **92**
  1. Memoirists 2. Dressmakers 3. Spouses of presidents 4. Slavery -- United States 5. United States -- Race relations 6. African American women -- Biography 7. Presidents' spouses -- United States 8. Washington (D.C.) -- Social life and customs
ISBN 978-1-4263-0377-7; 1-4263-0377-7; 978-1-4263-0378-4 lib bdg; 1-4263-0378-5 lib bdg
                                         LC 2008-29314
"Readers may be familiar with the ups and downs of Lincoln's life, but details of Keckley's story . . . will give them new insights into the life of a slave, in this case, one who was educated and had a profession." Booklist
Includes bibliographical references

Kehret, Peg, 1936-

Kehret, Peg. **Small** steps; the year I got polio. Anniversary ed; Albert Whitman 2006 205p il $15.95; pa $6.99
Grades: 4 5 6   **92**
  1. Authors 2. Poliomyelitis 3. Women authors 4. Authors, American 5. Children's authors
ISBN 978-0-8075-7459-1; 0-8075-7459-7; 978-0-8075-7458-4 pa; 0-8075-7458-9 pa
                                         LC 2006005136
First published 1996
Kehret "writes in an approachable, familiar way, and readers will be hooked from the first page on." SLJ
Includes bibliographical references

Kellar, Harry, 1849-1922

★ Jarrow, Gail. The **amazing** Harry Kellar; great American magician. Gail G. Jarrow. Calkins Creek 2012 96 p. col. ill. $17.95
Grades: 3 4 5 6 7 8   **92**
  1. Magicians 2. Optical illusions
ISBN 1590788656; 9781590788653
                                           LC 2011940465
This book is a biography of Harry Keller (later Kellar), "the first dean of the Society of American Magicians, a man [magician Harry] Houdini regarded as a mentor. . . . Few secrets of the illusions are revealed here, but [Gail] Jarrow makes it clear that it was Kellar's art that made them seem like real magic." The book also includes "[d]ozens of . . . Kellar posters' and a "timeline, bibliography, [and] annotated sources." (Kirkus)

Keller, Helen, 1880-1968

Amoroso, Cynthia. **Helen** Keller; by Cynthia Amoroso and Robert B. Noyed. Child's World 2010 24p il (Basic biographies) lib bdg $22.79

Grades: PreK K 1   92

1. Deaf 2. Blind 3. Authors 4. Memoirists 5. Humanitarians 6. Teachers of the deaf 7. Inspirational writers 8. Teachers of the blind 9. Social welfare leaders

ISBN 978-1-60253-341-7; 1-60253-341-5

LC 2009029369

This biography of Helen Keller "pairs intelligent, brief text with abundant photos. Simple but never basic." Booklist

Includes bibliographical references

Delano, Marfe Ferguson. **Helen's** eyes; a photobiography of Annie Sullivan, Helen Keller's teacher. [foreword by Keller Johnson Thompson] National Geographic 2008 63p il map $17.95; lib bdg $27.90

Grades: 4 5 6 7   92

1. Deaf 2. Blind 3. Authors 4. Teachers 5. Memoirists 6. Humanitarians 7. Teachers of the deaf 8. Inspirational writers 9. Teachers of the blind 10. Social welfare leaders

ISBN 978-1-4263-02-9-1; 1-4263-0209-6; 978-1-4263-0210-7 lib bdg; 1-4263-0210-X lib bdg

"There are many biographies of Helen Keller and Annie Sullivan, but this one is very nicely done. . . . The book is honest in its portrayals, especially of Sullivan. . . . What makes this oversize book so appealing is the clean design, with large typeface. The many fascinating photographs are sometimes placed over historical documents." Booklist

Includes bibliographical references

Lawlor, Laurie. **Helen** Keller: rebellious spirit. Holiday House 2001 168p il $22.95

Grades: 5 6 7 8   92

1. Deaf 2. Blind 3. Authors 4. Memoirists 5. Humanitarians 6. Inspirational writers 7. Social welfare leaders

ISBN 0-8234-1588-0

LC 00-36950

A "biography of the most famous deaf and blind person in history. Drawing on social and scientific studies of deafness and blindness as well as on American history texts, Lawlor puts Keller's experiences in context. . . . At the same time, readers get a strong feel for Keller's personality and for the personalities of Annie Sullivan, Alexander Graham Bell, and other major figures in her life. Aided by numerous well-chosen photographs and excerpts from Keller's writings." Horn Book

Includes bibliographical references

Sullivan, George. **Helen** Keller; her life in pictures. foreword by Keller Johnson Thompson. Scholastic Nonfiction 2007 80p il $17.99

Grades: 4 5 6 7   92

1. Deaf 2. Blind 3. Authors 4. Memoirists 5. Humanitarians 6. Inspirational writers 7. Social welfare leaders

ISBN 0-439-91815-4; 978-0-439-91815-2

LC 2006-51401

"Accompanied by brief, simply phrased commentary from Sullivan, this suite of photos portrays Keller from early childhood into her 80s. . . . This profile will serve equally well as an introduction, or as supplementary reading for confirmed admirers." Booklist

Includes bibliographical references

Kellerman, Annette, 1888-1975

Corey, Shana. **Mermaid** Queen; the spectacular true story of Annette Kellerman, who swam her way to fame, fortune, & swimsuit history! illustrated by Edwin Fotheringham. Scholastic Press 2008 un il $17.99

Grades: K 1 2 3   92

1. Actors 2. Swimming 3. Women athletes 4. Swimmers

ISBN 978-0-439-69835-1; 0-439-69835-9

LC 2007-52664

"Fotheringham's glorious artwork is filled with period details and dress, high-dives and stunts, and priceless expressions on the faces of amazed audiences. . . . This well-written and brightly illustrated account is a perfect pearl." SLJ

Kennedy, John F. (John Fitzgerald), 1917-1963

★ Cooper, Ilene. **Jack**; the early years of John F. Kennedy. by Ilene Cooper. 1st ed. Penguin Group USA 2013 168 p. ill. (paperback) $12.99

Grades: 5 6 7 8 9 10 11 12   92

1. Catholics 2. Presidents 3. Presidents -- United States

ISBN 0147510317; 9780147510310

LC 2002075912

This book by Ilene Cooper offers a "portrait of [John F.] Kennedy's "youth and the forces that shaped it. . . . Readers discover what it was like for Jack to grow up under the paradoxical influences of privilege and prejudice. His father's wealth . . . couldn't remove the perceived taint of the family's Irish Catholic heritage . . . . To compensate, Joseph and Rose Kennedy pushed their children to excel at everything they did," leading to rivalry between Jack and his brother Joe. (Horn Book Magazine)

"Intelligent design and numerous fabulous, well-placed, and well-captioned black-and-white photographs enrich Cooper's clear prose. . . . This sensitive, well-researched biography will enhance any collection." Voice Youth Advocates

Includes bibliographical references and index.

★ Heiligman, Deborah. **High** hopes; a photobiography of John F. Kennedy. National Geographic 2003 63p il map $17.95

Grades: 4 5 6 7   92

1. Presidents 2. Senators 3. Members of Congress 4. Presidents -- United States

ISBN 0-7922-6141-0

LC 2003-7819

Photographs and text trace the life of President John F. Kennedy.

The text "successfully captures the spirit that makes Kennedy an enduring figure in our history. . . . This well-designed book features large, well-chosen, black-and-white photographs." SLJ

Includes bibliographical references

Rappaport, Doreen. **Jack's** path of courage; the life of John F. Kennedy. written by Doreen Rappaport; illustrated by Matt Tavares. Hyperion Books for Children 2010 un il $17.99

Grades: 2 3 4 5   92

1. Presidents 2. Senators 3. Members of Congress 4. Presidents -- United States

ISBN 978-1-4231-2272-2; 1-4231-2272-0

"In her signature succinct style, Rappaport fuses facts about Kennedy's personal and public lives with quotations from his writings and speeches. . . . Tavares's light and shadow-infused paintings balance lifelike portrayals of Kennedy with renderings of dramatic events. . . . An evenhanded, graphically stirring biography." Publ Wkly

Includes bibliographical references

Key, Bill, 1833-1909

Bowman, Donna Janell. **Step** right up; How Doc and Jim Key Taught the World about Kindness. by Donna Janell Bowman; illustrated by Daniel Minter. Lee & Low Books Inc. 2016 48 p. color illustrations (hardcover : alk. paper) $19.95

Grades: 3 4 5 6   92

1. Human-animal communication 2. Beautiful Jim Key (Horse) 3. Human-animal communication -- United States 4. Horse trainers -- United States -- Biography 5. Humane education -- United States -- History 6. Horses -- Training -- United States

-- History

ISBN 9781620141489

LC 2015030604

In this children's book, by Donna Janell Bowman, illustrated by Daniel Minter, "William 'Doc' Key had a special way with animals. . . . When the Civil War ended and Doc was freed, he began to dream of breeding a winning racehorse. But those dreams were dashed when his colt was born weak and sickly. Although many people would have euthanized the colt, Doc nursed him back to health and named him Jim." (Publisher's note)

"An incredible story that ought to be widely known—a must-read." Kirkus

Includes bibliographical references.

King, Coretta Scott, 1927-2006

★ Shange, Ntozake, 1948- **Coretta** Scott; poetry by Ntozake Shange; paintings by Kadir Nelson. Amistad/Katherine Tegen Books 2009 un il $17.99; lib bdg $18.89

Grades: K 1 2 3   **92**

1. Clergy 2. Singers 3. Civil rights activists 4. Nobel laureates for peace 5. African Americans -- Civil rights 6. African American women -- Biography

ISBN 0-06-125364-2; 0-06-125365-0 lib bdg; 978-0-06-125364-5; 978-0-06-125365-2 lib bdg

LC 2008-10486

This introduction to Coretta Scott King looks at her civil rights work within the context of 1950s and 1960s activism. (Bull Cent Child Books)

Nelson's "jacket portrait of Coretta Scott, monumental and tender at the same time, sets the tone for this intimate picture biography. The artist's full-bleed paintings, powerfully molded and saturated with color, depict crucial moments in Scott's life. . . . Shange's . . . rhythmic lines and format syntax roll like waves . . . carrying readers on a soul-stirring ride." Publ Wkly

King, Martin Luther, Jr., 1929-1968

★ Farris, Christine. **My** brother Martin; a sister remembers growing up with the Rev. Dr. Martin Luther King Jr. by Christine King Farris; illustrated by Chris Soentpiet. Simon & Schuster Bks. for Young Readers 2003 35p il $17.95

Grades: K 1 2 3   **92**

1. Clergy 2. Nonfiction writers 3. Civil rights activists 4. Nobel laureates for peace 5. African Americans -- Biography 6. African Americans -- Civil rights

ISBN 0-689-84387-9

LC 2001-44681

Looks at the early life of Martin Luther King, Jr., as seen through the eyes of his older sister.

"The warmth of the text is exquisitely echoed in Soentpiet's realistic, light-filled watercolor portraits. . . . This outstanding book belongs in every collection." SLJ

★ Farris, Christine King. **March** on! the day my brother Martin changed the world. [by] Christine King Farris; illustrated by London Ladd. Scholastic Press 2008 un il $17.99

Grades: 2 3 4   **92**

1. Clergy 2. Civil rights demonstrations 3. College teachers 4. Nonfiction writers 5. Civil rights activists 6. Nobel laureates for peace 7. African Americans -- Civil rights

ISBN 0-545-03537-6; 978-0-545-03537-8

LC 2007038620

"Describing the 1963 March on Washington, Farris, the older sister of Martin Luther King Jr., maintains the deft touch that made My Brother Martin so moving. . . . Farris . . . effectively uses plain language and well-chosen facts to explain her brother's extraordinary achievements. .

. . Ladd . . . demonstrates a rare talent for portraiture. . . . His King looks human—in other words, capable of inspiring the reader." Publ Wkly

King, Martin Luther, III, 1957- **My** daddy, Dr. Martin Luther King, Jr. by Martin Luther King III; illustrated by AG Ford. Amistad 2013 32 p. (hardcover bdg) $17.99

Grades: K 1 2   **92**

1. African Americans -- Civil rights 2. African Americans -- Civil rights -- History -- 20th century

ISBN 0060280751; 9780060280758; 9780060280765

LC 2012030586

This book presents a picture-book biography of Martin Luther King, Jr., written by his eldest son. "Martin Luther King III spent his childhood learning difficult lessons about segregation, jail and protest marches. . . . When he and his brother received toy guns for Christmas, they were told that guns are destructive weapons and watched as their parents burnt them in a bonfire. In the third grade, the author reluctantly integrated a school." (Kirkus Reviews)

★ Michelson, Richard. **As** good as anybody: Martin Luther King Jr. and Abraham Joshua Heschel's amazing march toward freedom; by Richard Michelson; illustrated by Raul Colón. Knopf 2008 un il $16.99; lib bdg $19.99

Grades: 2 3 4   **92**

1. Clergy 2. Rabbis 3. Theologians 4. Jews -- Biography 5. Nonfiction writers 6. Civil rights activists 7. Nobel laureates for peace 8. African Americans -- Biography 9. African Americans -- Civil rights

ISBN 978-0-375-83335-9; 0-375-83335-8; 978-0-375-93335-6 lib bdg; 0-375-93335-2 lib bdg

This is the story of how Abraham Joshua Heschel, a Polish rabbi who escaped the Holocaust, and Martin Luther King worked together for African American civil rights.

"Michelson writes in poetic language. . . . Also admirable is Michelson's ability to convey complex historical concepts . . . in clear, potent terms that will speak directly to readers. . . . In both palette and style, Colón's colored-pencil and watercolor art . . . suggests the past, but his themes carry into today's headlines." Booklist

★ Myers, Walter Dean, 1937-2014. **I've** seen the promised land; the life of Dr. Martin Luther King, Jr. illustrated by Leonard Jenkins. HarperCollins Publishers 2004 un il $15.99; lib bdg $16.89

Grades: K 1 2 3   **92**

1. Clergy 2. Nonfiction writers 3. Civil rights activists 4. Nobel laureates for peace 5. African Americans -- Biography 6. African Americans -- Civil rights

ISBN 0-06-027703-3; 0-06-027704-1 lib bdg

LC 2003-4098

Pictures and easy-to-read text introduce the life of civil rights leader Dr. Martin Luther King, Jr.

"This eloquent picture book presents a brief overview of King's life and accomplishments. . . . Jenkins's stunning collage artwork dramatically reflects the events described in the narrative." SLJ

Pinkney, Andrea Davis. **Martin** and Mahalia; his words, her song. by Andrea Davis Pinkney; illustrated by Brian Pinkney. 1st ed. Little, Brown and Co. 2013 40 p. ill. (reinforced) $17.99

Grades: 1 2 3 4   **92**

1. Picture books for children 2. African Americans -- Civil rights -- History -- 20th century 3. Civil rights movements -- United States -- History -- 20th century -- Juvenile literture

ISBN 0316070130; 9780316070133

LC 2012005499

This children's picture book weaves together "the stories of two giants of the American civil rights movement," Martin Luther King, Jr. and Mahalia Jackson. "At first the stories are distinct, with alternating, dedicated spreads tracing the individuals' paths as gospel preacher and singer until they meet and combine forces at the Montgomery bus boycott in 1955 and forge a collaboration that takes them through Martin's most famous speech, at the Lincoln Memorial." (Booklist)

★ Rappaport, Doreen. **Martin's** big words: the life of Dr. Martin Luther King, Jr. illustrated by Bryan Collier. Hyperion Bks. for Children 2001 un il $15.99; pa $6.99

Grades: K 1 2 3   **92**
1. Clergy 2. Nonfiction writers 3. Civil rights activists 4. Nobel laureates for peace 5. African Americans -- Biography 6. African Americans -- Civil rights
ISBN 0-7868-0714-8; 1-4231-0635-0 pa

LC 00-40957

A Caldecott Medal honor book, 2002; A Coretta Scott King honor book for illustration, 2002

"Rappaport's spare narrative captures the essentials of the man, the movement he led, and his policy of nonviolence. . . . Collier's collage art is glorious. Combining cut-paper, photographs, and watercolor he expresses his own Christian faith and King's power 'to make many different things one.'" Booklist

Watkins, Angela Farris. **My** Uncle Martin's big heart; illustrated by Eric Velasquez. Abrams 2010 un il $18.95

Grades: PreK K 1 2   **92**
1. Clergy 2. Nonfiction writers 3. Civil rights activists 4. Nobel laureates for peace 5. African Americans -- Civil rights
ISBN 978-0-8109-8975-7; 0-8109-8975-1

"In this warm, handsome picture book, Watkins celebrates her loving relationship as a small preschooler with 'Uncle M. L.' . . . The girl speaks about taking pride in her uncle's political role as a civil rights leader and national hero. Even more, though, she focuses on personal moments. . . . Velasquez is at his best here. . . . He shows the affection that the child and her uncle share." Booklist

Knight, Margaret, 1838-1914
McCully, Emily Arnold. **Marvelous** Mattie; how Margaret E. Knight became an inventor. Farrar, Straus & Giroux 2006 un il $16

Grades: K 1 2 3   **92**
1. Inventors 2. Women inventors
ISBN 0-374-34810-3

LC 2004-56415

Margaret (or Mattie) "Knight's design for a safer loom saved textile workers from injuries and death. . . . She fought in court and won the right to patent her most famous invention, a machine that would make paper bags. Mattie's story is told in a style that is not only easy to understand, but that is also a good read-aloud. The watercolor-and-ink illustrations capture the spirited inventor and support the text in style and design." SLJ

Knox, Henry, 1750-1806
★ Silvey, Anita. **Henry** Knox; bookseller, soldier, patriot. pictures by Wendell Minor. Clarion Books 2010 40p il $17.99

Grades: 2 3 4 5   **92**
1. Generals 2. Boston (Mass.) -- History 3. United States -- History -- 1775-1783, Revolution
ISBN 978-0-618-27485-7; 0-618-27485-5

LC 2009045353

"When the first shots were fired at Lexington and Concord, Henry Knox was a portly young bookseller who avidly read books on military science and discussed them with the British officers who frequented his

Boston shop. He would soon put his theoretical knowledge to practical use, for he was placed in charge of the Continental Army's artillery. . . . The first half of this fully illustrated book deftly portrays Knox as a likable, optimistic youth, while the second half shows him as a determined 25-year-old officer leading the expedition that freed Boston in 1776. . . . Painted on wooden panels, Minor's acrylic art creates a vivid sense of the period in varied scenes crafted with a fine grasp of composition, texture, and color." Booklist

Kobayashi, Issa, 1763-1827
★ Gollub, Matthew. **Cool** melons--turn to frogs!: the life and poems of Issa; story and Haiku translations by Matthew Gollub; illustrations by Kazuko G. Stone; calligraphy by Keiko Smith. Lee & Low Bks. 1998 un il $16.95; pa $9.95

Grades: 3 4 5 6   **92**
1. Haiku 2. Poets 3. Authors 4. Japanese poetry
ISBN 1-880000-71-7; 1-58430-241-0 pa

LC 98-13087

A biography and introduction to the work of the Japanese haiku poet whose love for nature finds expression in the more than thirty poems included in this book

This contains the life of the poet "told in simple language; lots of his exquisite and accessible haiku; limpid watercolor and colored pencil illustrations reminiscent of Japanese prints and drawings; and beautiful Japanese calligraphy." Booklist

Korczak, Janusz, 1878-1942
Bogacki, Tomek. The **champion** of children; the story of Janusz Korczak. Farrar Straus Giroux 2009 un il $17.99

Grades: 1 2 3 4   **92**
1. Authors 2. Pediatricians 3. Jews -- Poland 4. Holocaust victims 5. Children's authors 6. Holocaust, 1933-1945
ISBN 978-0-374-34136-7; 0-374-34136-2

LC 2008-16188

This is a "picture-book biography of the Holocaust-era children's advocate and doctor. Early Polish childhood life and interests quickly move into the doctor's student days and expand to his renowned, democratically run orphanage. . . . He steadfastly stayed with his children during the Nazi invasion and deportation and ultimately perished with them at Treblinka. . . . Though this is a story that ends in dark despair, the author succeeds in creating a positive, upbeat atmosphere with his palette of muted reds, blues and greens." Kirkus

Korematsu, Fred, 1919-2005
Adkins, Laura. **Fred** Korematsu speaks up; by Laura Atkins and Stan Yogi; illustrations by Yutaka Houlette. Heyday 2016 112 p. illustrations (hardcover) $18

Grades: 4 5 6 7 8   **92**
1. Japanese Americans 2. Japanese Americans -- Evacuation and relocation, 1942-1945 3. Japanese Americans -- Civil rights -- History -- 20th century
ISBN 9781597143684

LC 2016008098

"When Fred Korematsu, a young Japanese-American man, defied U.S. governmental orders by refusing to report to prison camps during World War II, he and his allies set in motion a landmark civil liberties case." (Kirkus)

Includes bibliographical references and index

Kouanchao, Malichansouk, 1971-
Youme. **Mali** under the night sky; a Lao story of home. written and illustrated by Youme. Cinco Puntos Press 2010 un il $17.95

Grades: K 1 2 **92**

1. Artists 2. Women artists 3. Laos
ISBN 978-1-933693-68-2; 1-933693-68-1

Relates the true story of Laotian American artist Malichansouk Kouanchao, who enjoyed her early childhood playing in the wilderness until civil war forced her family to leave for another country, allowing her to bring only her memories of her homeland.

This story "is told in a simple, straightforward manner, from a child's point of view.... The focus remains tightly on Mali's experiences and feelings, keeping it accessible to young readers.... The watercolor illustrations, while naive in style, convey a real sense of place." SLJ

Koufax, Sandy, 1935-

★ Winter, Jonah. **You** never heard of Sandy Koufax!? illustrations by Andre Carrilho. Schwartz & Wade Books 2009 un il $17.99; lib bdg $20.99 **92**

1. Baseball players 2. Jews -- Biography 3. Baseball -- Biography 4. Los Angeles Dodgers (Baseball team)
ISBN 978-0-375-83738-8; 0-375-83738-8; 978-0-375-93738-5 lib bdg; 0-375-93738-2 lib bdg

LC 2007-41860

The author relates "the story of arguably the greatest left-handed pitcher in baseball history as if he were an unnamed teammate along for the ride.... Winter makes a point to emphasize that at the time, ... Koufax was one of very few Jewish players, and he encountered his share of prejudice.... Carrilho's digitally enhanced graphite artwork, which resembles highly expressionistic cartoons, emphasizes movement, ... with touches of deep gold and swift strokes of red against Dodger blue." Booklist

Includes glossary

Kublai Khan, 1216-1294

★ Krull, Kathleen. **Kubla** Khan; the emperor of everything. illustrated by Robert Byrd. Viking Children's Books 2010 un il $17.99
Grades: 2 3 4 **92**

1. Mongols 2. Kings 3. China -- History
ISBN 978-0-670-01114-8; 0-670-01114-2

LC 2010007322

"Krull assembles a convincingly grand impression of Kubla Khan and his vast accomplishments.... The grandiosity of his reign is well depicted in Bryd's Eastern-style artwork, which provides a subtle buttress to the narrative arc.... A solid choice for reports that is also scintillating enough for pleasure reading." Booklist

Includes bibliographical references

La Salle, Robert Cavelier, sieur de, 1643-1687

Goodman, Joan E. **Despite** all obstacles: La Salle and the conquest of the Mississippi; by Joan Elizabeth Goodman; illustrated by Tom McNeely. Mikaya Press 2001 47p il map (Great explorers book) $19.95
Grades: 4 5 6 7 **92**

1. Explorers 2. Mississippi River valley
ISBN 1-931414-01-7

LC 2001-31732

A biography of the man who explored the St. Lawrence, Ohio, Illinois, and Mississippi rivers, and who claimed America's heartland for King Louis XIV and France

"Vivid color illustrations and Goodman's exciting writing style will attract both researchers and pleasure readers." Voice Youth Advocates

Lafayette, Marie Joseph Paul Yves Roch Gilbert du Motier, marquis de, 1757-1834

Fritz, Jean. **Why** not, Lafayette? illustrated by Ronald Himler. Putnam 1999 87p il $16.99; pa $5.99

Grades: 5 6 7 8 **92**

1. Generals 2. Statesmen 3. United States -- History -- 1775-1783, Revolution
ISBN 0-399-23411-X; 0-698-11882-0 pa

LC 98-31417

Traces the life of the French nobleman who fought for democracy in revolutions in both the United States and France

This biography is "chock-full of quotes, anecdotes, and wry humor." Booklist

Includes bibliographical references

Law, Westley Wallace, 1923-2002

Haskins, James. **Delivering** justice; W.W. Law and the fight for civil rights. [by] Jim Haskins; illustrated by Benny Andrews. Candlewick Press 2005 un il $16.99
Grades: 2 3 4 **92**

1. Postal employees 2. Civil rights activists 3. African Americans -- Civil rights
ISBN 0-7636-2592-2

LC 2005-47114

A biography of Westley (W. W.) Law, a mail carrier who played a leading role in the civil rights movement

"With handsome, full-page illustrations in oil and collage, this picture-book biography tells the stirring story of a quiet hero." Booklist

Lawrence, Jacob, 1917-2000

★ Duggleby, John. **Story** painter: the life of Jacob Lawrence. Chronicle Bks. 1998 55p il $16.95
Grades: 4 5 6 7 **92**

1. Artists 2. Painters 3. Illustrators 4. African American artists 5. African American painters -- Biography 6. African Americans in art
ISBN 0-8118-2082-3

LC 98-4513

This is a biography of the twentieth-century African American painter. Bibliography. "Grades four to eight." (SLJ)

"Lawrence's expressionistic, stark paintings, in excellent full-page color reproduction... nicely complement Duggleby's measured account of a materially poor but culturally rich childhood and Lawrence's subsequent struggles and successes." Publ Wkly

Includes bibliographical references

Rhodes-Pitts, Sharifa. **Jake** makes a world; Jacob Lawrence, an artist in Harlem. Sharifa Rhodes-Pitts; illustrated by Christopher Myers. Museum of Modern Art 2015 44 p. chiefly illustrations $18.95
Grades: PreK K 1 2 3 **92**

1. African American artists
ISBN 9780870709654; 0870709658

LC 2015934888

This children's book by Sharifa Rhodes-Pitts, illustrated by Christopher Myers, "follows the creative adventures of the young Jacob Lawrence as he finds inspiration in the vibrant colors and characters of his community in Harlem. From his mother's apartment, ... to the streets full of familiar and not-so-familiar faces, sounds, rhythms, and smells; to the art studio where he goes each day after school to transform his everyday world on an epic scale." (Publisher's note)

"This is a dynamic and creative introduction to a groundbreaking artist and an iconic collection." Kirkus

Lazarus, Emma, 1849-1887

★ Silverman, Erica. **Liberty's** voice: the story of Emma Lazarus; illustrated by Stacey Schuett. Dutton Children's Books 2011 un il $17.99
Grades: 2 3 4 5 **92**

1. Poets 2. Authors 3. Novelists 4. Women poets 5. Philanthropists

6. Poets, American 7. Social reformers 8. Jews -- Biography
ISBN 0-525-47859-0; 978-0-525-47859-1

LC 2010-13186

This is a biography of the American poet whose lines are inscribed on the Statue of Liberty. "Grades three to five." (Bull Cent Child Books)

"A well-known poet in her day, Emma Lazarus was initially hesitant to pen the poem that would make her famous, 'The New Colossus,' which is engraved on the base of the Statue of Liberty. . . . But her dedication to the plight of immigrant Russian Jews . . . ultimately inspired her message to the 'huddled masses yearning to breathe free.' In a straightforward and smooth narrative style, Silverman . . . tells the story of Lazarus' life and work. The accompanying ink-and-watercolor illustrations serve the historical setting, characters, and plot well." Booklist

Includes bibliographical references

Lee, Bruce, 1940-1973

Mochizuki, Ken. **Be** water, my friend; the early years of Bruce Lee. illustrated by Dom Lee. Lee & Low Books 2006 un il $16.95
Grades: K 1 2 3   92
1. Actors 2. Martial arts 3. Martial artists
ISBN 1-58430-265-0

"This distinctive-looking book offers a smoothly written text and many handsome, textured acrylic paintings done in tones of brown and cream." Booklist

Lee, Sammy, 1920-2016

★ Yoo, Paula. **Sixteen** years in sixteen seconds; the Sammy Lee story. illustrations by Dom Lee. Lee & Low Books 2005 un il $16.95
Grades: 2 3 4   92
1. Diving 2. Physicians 3. Korean Americans 4. Divers 5. Olympic athletes
ISBN 1-58430-247-X

LC 2004-20962

"Yoo introduces Sammy Lee, the son of Korean immigrants who overcame formidable odds to become an Olympic diving champion as well as a doctor. . . . Washed in nostalgic sepia tones, Dom Lee's acrylic-and-wax textured illustrations are reminiscent of his fine work in Ken Mochizuki's watershed Baseball Saved Us (1993) and like Yoo's understated words, the uncluttered images leave a deep impression." Booklist

Lennon, John, 1940-1980

Behnke, Alison Marie. **Death** of a dreamer; the assassination of John Lennon. Alison Marie Behnke. Twenty-First Century Books 2012 96 p.
Grades: 5 6 7 8   92
1. Assassination 2. Rock musicians -- Political activity 3. Rock musicians -- England -- Biography 4. Rock musicians 5. Murder -- New York (State) -- New York 6. Rock musicians -- England -- Biography 7. Murderers -- New York (State) -- Biography
ISBN 0822590360; 9780822590361

LC 2010005550

"Twin narratives converge in New York City on December 8, 1980, when John Lennon was murdered by Mark David Chapman. [Alison Marie] Behnke calls the murder an assassination, and by the general definition of the word--'to murder (a usually prominent person) by sudden or secret attack, often for political reasons'--the murder of John Lennon might qualify. Lennon was political by the end of his life, writing 'Give Peace a Chance,' which became the anthem of the peace movement, but he was hardly a revolutionary, as Behnke terms him. Chapman was not especially political, and he didn't really seem to know why he attacked Lennon; it was certainly not from any well-thought-out political motives, as the author herself describes." (Kirkus)

Includes bibliographical references (p. 92), discography (p. 93), filmography (p. 93), and index

Rappaport, Doreen. **John's** secret dreams; the life of John Lennon. written by Doreen Rappaport; illustrated by Bryan Collier. Hyperion Books for Children 2004 un il $16.99
Grades: 4 5 6 7   92
1. Singers 2. Rock musicians 3. Beatles 4. Songwriters
ISBN 0-7868-0817-9

LC 2003-57116

"Using a combination of simple prose, song lyrics, and illustration, this heartfelt picture-book biography traces Lennon's life from his childhood to his death. Striking in both its simplicity and complexity, it captures this enigmatic singer, artist, songwriter, and folk hero in a way that will move and fascinate those too young to remember the man but are surrounded by his music and myth." SLJ

Leonardo, da Vinci, 1452-1519

★ Krull, Kathleen. **Leonardo** da Vinci; illustrated by Boris Kulikov. Viking 2005 128p il (Giants of science) $15.99
Grades: 5 6 7 8   92
1. Artists 2. Painters 3. Scientists 4. Renaissance 5. Artists, Italian 6. Writers on science
ISBN 0-670-05920-X

This is a "biography of Leonardo da Vinci that highlights his scientific approach to understanding the physical world. The first half of the book describes Leonardo's apprenticeship and his work as an artist in Milan. The second half relates events in his later life, emphasizing his observation and investigation of the human body and nature. . . . Six excellent ink drawings illustrate this attractive volume. A very readable, vivid portrait set against the backdrop of remarkable times." Booklist

Includes bibliographical references

Phillips, John. **Leonardo** da Vinci; the genius who defined the Renaissance. National Geographic 2006 64p bibl il (World history biographies) $17.95; lib bdg $27.90; pa $6.95
Grades: 5 6 7 8   92
1. Artists 2. Painters 3. Scientists 4. Renaissance 5. Artists, Italian 6. Writers on science
ISBN 978-0-7922-5385-3; 0-7922-5385-X; 978-0-7922-5386-0 lib bdg; 0-7922-5386-8 lib bdg; 978-1-4263-0248-0 pa; 1-4263-0249-7 pa

Examines the life of Renaissance genius Leonardo da Vinci, discussing his inquiries and accomplishments in art and various fields of science

Includes bibliographical references

★ Stanley, Diane. **Leonardo** da Vinci. Morrow Junior Bks. 1996 un il $16.95; lib bdg $15.93; pa $6.95
Grades: 4 5 6 7   92
1. Artists 2. Painters 3. Scientists 4. Artists, Italian 5. Writers on science
ISBN 0-688-10437-1; 0-688-10438-X lib bdg; 0-688-16155-3 pa

LC 95-35227

"Stanley begins with a brief introduction to the Italian Renaissance and then looks at the life of the artist. The text pages feature a series of sketches from Leonardo's notebooks. These vivid drawings, chosen to reflect ideas and events in the story, juxtapose well with the large illustrations created with colored pencil, gouache, and watercolors on the facing pages. . . . The craftsmanship that makes this biography so solid in concept, appealing in design, and accessible in presentation extends to the scholarship behind it, as glimpsed in the appended postscript and bibliographies." Booklist

Lewis, Ida, 1842-1911

Moss, Marissa. The **bravest** woman in America; illustrations by Andrea U'Ren. Tricycle Press 2011 un il $16.99

Grades: K 1 2 3   **92**

1. Lighthouses 2. Rhode Island 3. Lighthouse keepers
ISBN 1-58246-369-7; 978-1-58246-369-8

LC 2010008917

This picture book tells the story of Ida Lewis. "In 1857, when she was fifteen, the family moved to the lighthouse at Lime Rock (which guards Rhode Island's Newport Harbor), where Mr. Lewis was lighthouse keeper. Soon after, illness disabled him; Ida took over his duties and, at sixteen, . . . rescued four boys whose boat had capsized. . . . It was the first of many rescues during a lifelong career for which she received a Congressional Lifesaving Medal. . . . Preschool, primary." (Horn Book)

"Moss's . . . short, stirring biography of 19th-century lighthouse keeper Ida Lewis centers on Lewis's first rescue, at age 16, off the coast of Rhode Island. . . . U'Ren's . . . bold, mixed-media illustrations capture the power and many moods of the sea, from calm ultramarine to the foam-topped dark slate and deep green of stormy waters. Heavy brushstrokes and black outlines . . . suggest the deliberate strength with which Ida carried out her vocation." Publ Wkly

Lewis, John, 1940 February 21-

Asim, Jabari. **Preaching** to the chickens; Jabari Asim; illustrated by E. B. Lewis. Nancy Paulsen Books 2016 32 p. color illustrations (hardback) $17.99

Grades: K 1 2 3   **92**

1. Clergy 2. Chickens 3. Preaching 4. African American legislators -- Biography 5. African American civil rights workers -- Religious life 6. Rural children -- Alabama 7. Christian biography -- United States 8. Legislators -- United States -- Biography 9. Alabama -- Rural conditions -- 20th century 10. African American boys -- Alabama -- Biography
ISBN 0399168567; 9780399168567

LC 2015048281

This children's book by Jabari Asim, illustrated by E. B. Lewis, offers a "glimpse into the boyhood of Civil Rights leader John Lewis. John wants to be a preacher when he grows up. . . . But why wait? When John is put in charge of the family farm's flock of chickens, he discovers that they make a wonderful congregation! So he preaches to his flock, and they listen, content under his watchful care, riveted by the rhythm of his voice." (Publisher's note)

"A quietly powerful and joyful look at the childhood of a living legend and a superb introduction to studying heroes of the civil rights era." SLJ

★ Haskins, James. **John** Lewis in the lead; a story of the civil rights movement. [by] Jim Haskins and Kathleen Benson; illustrations by Benny Andrews. Lee & Low 2006 un il $17.95

Grades: 3 4 5   **92**

1. Members of Congress 2. Civil rights activists 3. African Americans -- Civil rights
ISBN 1-58430-250-X

LC 2005-35472

"Born in a sharecropper family in the segregated South in 1940, John Lewis grew up to lead many protests for civil rights, and he has served in Congress for the last 20 years. In this handsome picture book for older readers, the authors blend information on Lewis' political contributions with the history of the civil rights struggle. . . . Andrews' dramatic, folk-art-style, color-saturated illustrations combine handsome individual portraits of Lewis with overviews of the horrific street violence by mobs, police, and troopers." Booklist

Li Cunxin

Li Cunxin. **Dancing** to freedom; the true story of Mao's last dancer. illustrated by Anne Spudvilas. Walker & Co. 2008 un il $16.95; lib bdg $17.85

Grades: K 1 2 3   **92**

1. Ballet 2. Ballet dancers 3. China 4. Securities brokers
ISBN 978-0-8027-9777-3; 0-8027-9777-6; 978-0-8027-9778-0 lib bdg; 0-8027-9778-4 lib bdg

LC 2007-37150

"A poignant memoir of a boy caught in the difficulties of life in Maoist China, this is the author's own story of how he was given a chance to break the bonds of his bleak life and become an international star. . . . [Li] was offered the chance to dance with the Houston Ballet, and his greatest dream was realized when his parents were finally able to come to the U.S. to see him perform. This fascinating, heartfelt story is perfectly matched by Spudvilas's masterful paintings." SLJ

Lichtenstein, Roy, 1923-1997

★ Rubin, Susan Goldman. **Whaam!** : the art & life of Roy Lichtenstein. Abrams 2008 47p il $18.95

Grades: 4 5 6 7   **92**

1. Artists 2. Pop art 3. Painters 4. Sculptors 5. Printmakers 6. Artists -- United States
ISBN 978-0-8109-9492-8; 0-8109-9492-5

LC 2007-42048

"Rubin presents an overview of a modern master with clear writing and an abundance of his eye-popping works, all framed on pages that mirror the artist's signature use of primary colors and Benday dots." Booklist

Lincoln family

★ Rabin, Staton. **Mr.** Lincoln's boys; being the mostly true adventures of Abraham Lincoln's trouble-making sons, Tad and Willie. by Staton Rabin; illustrated by Bagram Ibatoulline. Penguin Group 2008 un il $16.99

Grades: 1 2 3   **92**

1. Lawyers 2. Presidents 3. Pioneers 4. State legislators 5. Members of Congress 6. Children of presidents 7. Presidents -- United States
ISBN 978-0-670-06169-3; 0-670-06169-7

LC 2008-1774

"Tad and Willie, the mischievous sons of President Abraham Lincoln, scampered around the White House surprising and irritating almost everyone. Their pranks, however, delighted their father, who was faced with the grim realities of the Civil War. . . . Fictionalized dialogue throughout is believable. A large part of the appeal of this book can be credited to Ibatoulline's masterful illustrations. Evocative and detailed, they fill the pages with visual information and emotion. Readers will be intrigued by the antics of these famous children." SLJ

Includes bibliographical references

Lincoln, Abraham, 1809-1865

Aylesworth, Jim. **Our** Abe Lincoln; an old tune with new lyrics. adapted by Jim Aylesworth; illustrated by Barbara McClintock. Scholastic Press 2009 un il $16.99

Grades: PreK K 1 2   **92**

1. Songs 2. Lawyers 3. Presidents 4. State legislators 5. Members of Congress 6. Presidents -- United States
ISBN 978-0-439-92548-8; 0-439-92548-7

LC 2007-31060

"With a fresh approach to Lincoln that is both delightful and accurate, Aylesworth sets history to the tune of 'The Old Gray Mare' and the derivative song 'Our Abe Lincoln Came Out of the Wilderness,' which was popular during the 16th president's campaign. . . . McClintock captures the exuberance with charming visuals that outline significant aspects of the leader's life and lore. Scenes rendered in watercolor and pen and ink feature a multicultural cast." SLJ

★ Brewer, Paul. **Lincoln** tells a joke; how laughter saved the President (and the country) [by] Kathleen Krull & Paul Brewer; illustrated by Stacy Innerst. Harcourt 2010 un il $16
Grades: 2 3 4   **92**
  1. Lawyers 2. Presidents 3. Wit and humor 4. State legislators 5. Members of Congress 6. Presidents -- United States
  ISBN 0-15-206639-X; 978-0-15-206639-0
                                                           LC 2009-24197
This biography of the American president focuses on his use of wit and humor, and his love of language. "Ages seven to ten." (Bull Cent Child Books)
  "Moving through the sixteenth president's many challenges, from family deaths to lost elections to fighting slavery, the text emphasizes how Lincoln coped with a joke on his tongue and a smile on his lips. . . . Innerst's acrylic artwork feels homey and humorous." Booklist

Burleigh, Robert. **Abraham** Lincoln comes home; [by] Robert Burleigh; paintings by Wendell Minor. Henry Holt and Co. 2008 un il $16.95
Grades: 2 3 4   **92**
  1. Lawyers 2. Presidents 3. State legislators 4. Members of Congress 5. Presidents -- United States
  ISBN 978-0-8050-7529-8; 0-8050-7529-1
                                                           LC 2007040030
"Following Lincoln's death, his body was taken back to Illinois for burial. Burleigh focuses on one boy's perceptions as he and his father travel through the night by horse-drawn carriage to see the funeral train pass. . . . Minor's gouache watercolors capture the prairie as well as multiple perspectives of the train, while Burleigh's prose is almost poetic." SLJ

Denenberg, Barry. **Lincoln** shot! a president's life remembered. chief writer, Barry Denenberg; artist, Christopher Bing. Feiwel and Friends 2008 40p il $24.95
Grades: 5 6 7 8   **92**
  1. Lawyers 2. Presidents 3. State legislators 4. Members of Congress 5. Presidents -- United States 6. United States -- History -- 1861-1865, Civil War
  ISBN 978-0-312-37013-8; 0-312-37013-X
                                                           LC 2007-48851
"The concept is that this is a commemorative edition of 'The National News' published one year after Lincoln's death . . . Also included is an engaging, readable yet detailed account of Lincoln's life. . . . [This book] is an example of how high-quality bookmaking can turn a history lesson into an authentic experience." Booklist

★ Freedman, Russell. **Abraham** Lincoln and Frederick Douglass; the story behind an American friendship. by Russell Freedman. Houghton Mifflin Harcourt 2012 119 p. $18.99
Grades: 4 5 6 7 8   **92**
  1. Friendship 2. Abolitionists -- United States 3. United States -- History -- 1861-1865, Civil War -- Biography 4. Friendship -- United States 5. Presidents -- United States -- Biography 6. African American abolitionists -- Biography
  ISBN 9780547385624
                                                           LC 2011025953
This book tells the story of Abraham Lincoln, "the 16th president, . . . [along] with his friend and ally, abolitionist Frederick Douglass. The story opens with Douglass anxiously waiting to meet Lincoln for the first time to air grievances about the treatment of African-American soldiers

during the Civil War. . . . Subsequent chapters detail the leaders' often parallel biographies. Both were self-made and shared a passion for reading, rising from poverty to prominence." (Publishers Weekly)
  Includes bibliographical references (p. [108]-109) and index

★ Freedman, Russell. **Lincoln** : a photobiography. Clarion Bks. 1987 149p il $18; pa $7.95
Grades: 5 6 7 8 9 10   **92**
  1. Lawyers 2. Presidents 3. State legislators 4. Members of Congress 5. Presidents -- United States 6. United States -- History -- 1861-1865, Civil War
  ISBN 0-89919-380-3; 0-395-51848-2 pa
                                                           LC 86-33379
Awarded the Newbery Medal, 1988
This is "a balanced work, elegantly designed and enhanced by dozens of period photographs and drawings, some familiar, some refreshingly unfamiliar." Publ Wkly
  Includes bibliographical references

Giblin, James. **Good** brother, bad brother; the story of Edwin Booth and John Wilkes Booth. Clarion Books 2005 244p il $22
Grades: 5 6 7 8   **92**
  1. United States -- History -- 1861-1865, Civil War
  ISBN 0-618-09642-6
                                                           LC 2004-21260
Boston Globe-Horn Book Honor: Nonfiction (2005)
This is a dual biography of John Wilkes Booth, who assassinated Abraham Lincoln, and his brother, Edwin, an actor. (Horn Book)
  Giblin "frames the intertwined tale of two brothers with accounts of their families, friends, the Civil War, and nineteenth-century theater. . . . Alcoholism and depression afflicted the family, but Giblin is brilliant at showing that darkness was only one part of a life. . . . Giblin's book will engross readers until the very last footnote." Booklist
  Includes bibliographical references

Gilpin, Caroline Crosson. **Abraham** Lincoln; by Caroline Gilpin. National Geographic 2013 31 p. (paperback) $3.99; (library) $13.90
Grades: 1 2 3   **92**
  1. Slaves -- Emancipation 2. Presidents -- United States -- Biography 3. United States -- History -- Civil War, 1861-1865
  ISBN 1426310854; 9781426310850; 9781426310867
                                                           LC 2012031885
In this book, "readers will learn about the . . . life and legacy of our 16th President of the United States, Abraham Lincoln and his historic decision to abolish slavery. Readers will also learn why this decision impacted the United States, as well as the extent of Lincoln's impact as a fearless leader of the Civil War." (Publisher's note)

Harness, Cheryl. **Abe** Lincoln goes to Washington, 1837-1865; written and illustrated by Cheryl Harness. National Geographic Soc. 1997 un il maps $18
Grades: 2 3 4   **92**
  1. Lawyers 2. Presidents 3. State legislators 4. Members of Congress 5. Presidents -- United States
  ISBN 0-7922-3736-6
                                                           LC 96-9587
Companion volume to Young Abe Lincoln: the frontier days, 1809-1837 (1996)
Portrays Lincoln's life as a lawyer in Springfield, a devoted husband and father, and president during the Civil War years
  "The text gallops through years of history, with sudden stops for surprisingly vivid little scenes. . . . Filled with color and action, Harness'

paintings and maps dominate the pages and provide a wealth of historical detail as well as a humanizing view of the Lincolns." Booklist

Includes bibliographical references

Herbert, Janis. **Abraham** Lincoln for kids; his life and times with 21 activities. [by] Janis Herbert. Chicago Review Press 2007 149p il pa $14.95

Grades: 4 5 6 7   **92**

1. Lawyers 2. Presidents 3. State legislators 4. Members of Congress 5. Presidents -- United States

ISBN 978-1-55652-656-5 pa; 1-55652-656-3 pa

LC 2007009052

"This attractive biographical guide offers a good mixture of information, anecdotes, and activities, balancing facts about Lincoln's personal and family life with the record of his accomplishments as president and a broader view of his times." Booklist

Includes glossary and bibliographical references

Kalman, Maira. **Looking** at Lincoln; Maira Kalman. Nancy Paulsen Books 2012 1 v.

Grades: K 1 2 3 4 5   **92**

1. Picture books for children 2. Presidents -- United States -- Biography 3. Presidents -- United States -- Biography 4. United States -- History -- Civil War, 1861-1865

ISBN 9780399240393

LC 2011046953

'This children's book offers an account of former U.S. President "Abraham Lincoln [who] is one of the first giants of history children are introduced to. . . . Lincoln's legacy is everywhere - there he is on your penny and five-dollar bill. And we are still the United States because Lincoln helped hold them together. But who was he, really? The little girl in this book wants to find out. Among the many other things, she discovers our sixteenth president was a man who believed in freedom for all, had a dog named Fido, loved Mozart, apples, and his wife's vanilla cake, and kept his notes in his hat. From his boyhood in a log cabin to his famous presidency and untimely death, Kalman shares Lincoln's . . . life with young readers." (Publisher's note)

Includes bibliographical references

★ Rabin, Staton. **Mr.** Lincoln's boys; being the mostly true adventures of Abraham Lincoln's trouble-making sons, Tad and Willie. by Staton Rabin; illustrated by Bagram Ibatoulline. Penguin Group 2008 un il $16.99

Grades: 1 2 3   **92**

1. Lawyers 2. Presidents 3. Pioneers 4. State legislators 5. Members of Congress 6. Children of presidents 7. Presidents -- United States

ISBN 978-0-670-06169-3; 0-670-06169-7

LC 2008-1774

"Tad and Willie, the mischievous sons of President Abraham Lincoln, scampered around the White House surprising and irritating almost everyone. Their pranks, however, delighted their father, who was faced with the grim realities of the Civil War. . . . Fictionalized dialogue throughout is believable. A large part of the appeal of this book can be credited to Ibatoulline's masterful illustrations. Evocative and detailed, they fill the pages with visual information and emotion. Readers will be intrigued by the antics of these famous children." SLJ

Includes bibliographical references

★ Rappaport, Doreen, 1939- **Abe's** honest words; the life of Abraham Lincoln. [illustrated by] Kadir Nelson. Hyperion Books for Children 2008 44p il $16.99

Grades: 2 3 4   **92**

1. Lawyers 2. Presidents 3. State legislators 4. Members of Congress 5. Presidents -- United States

ISBN 1-4231-0408-0; 978-1-4231-0408-7

LC 2006-43608

This is a biography of the 16th president of the United States. Chronology. Bibliography. "Ages six to nine." (Bull Cent Child Books)

"This collaboration between Rappaport and Nelson provides a sweeping arc of Lincoln's life. . . . Rappaport writes in the very free verse and on each page echoes her narrative with prescient samplings of Lincoln's words. In generously sized artwork . . . Nelson makes the familiar face . . . exciting again. . . . The exceptional art, along with Rappaport's and Lincoln's words, makes this a fine celebration of a man who needs little introduction." Booklist

Includes bibliographical references

Schroeder, Alan, 1961- **Abe** Lincoln; his wit and wisdom from A to Z. by Alan Schroeder; illustrated by John O'Brien. Holiday House 2015 32 p. color illustrations (hardcover) $17.95

Grades: K 1 2 3 4   **92**

1. Quotations 2. Alphabet 3. Presidents -- United States -- Biography

ISBN 0823424200; 9780823424207

LC 2013038989

This children's book, by Alan Schroeder, illustrated by John O'Brien, presents a collection of sayings from U.S. President Abraham Lincoln. This "nontraditional tribute to the president who brought the homespun humor of his humble beginnings to the White House uses the alphabet to organize a wealth of information about his life and accomplishments." (Publisher's note)

"Schroeder provides an overview of the 16th president's legacy, his predilections, and some significant events of his era. Each letter introduces several ideas. . . . O'Brien's ink-and-watercolor art has a farcical sensibility that plays on the mythology surrounding Lincoln." Pub Wkly

St. George, Judith. **Stand** tall, Abe Lincoln; [by] Judith St. George; illustrated by Matt Faulkner. Philomel Books 2007 un il $16.99

Grades: 2 3 4   **92**

1. Lawyers 2. Presidents 3. State legislators 4. Members of Congress 5. Presidents -- United States

ISBN 978-0-399-24174-1

LC 2006024877

"This account of Lincoln's childhood is written in fast-paced short sentences. St. George . . . uses a folksy, conversational style. . . . Faulkner's humorous illustrations are a perfect match for the text. . . . The expressive images are done in a caricature style, with slightly exaggerated hands, feet, and heads." SLJ

Includes bibliographical references

Thomson, Sarah L. **What** Lincoln said; by Sarah L. Thomson; art by James Ransome. Collins 2009 un il $17.99; lib bdg $18.89

Grades: K 1 2 3   **92**

1. Lawyers 2. Presidents 3. State legislators 4. Members of Congress 5. Presidents -- United States

ISBN 978-0-06-084819-4; 0-06-084819-7; 978-0-06-084820-0 lib bdg; 0-06-084820-0 lib bdg

LC 2008020095

"By using Lincoln's own words, Thomson builds a portrait that relates his statements to significant events in his life. . . . Short descriptions of the circumstances and a related quote are set on bold, colorful spreads. Ransome delivers a larger-than-life portrait of this homely president with acrylic, almost cartoonlike paintings. . . . An engaging overview, this is a worthy introduction to this famous president." SLJ

Lincoln, Mary Todd, 1818-1882

★ Jones, Lynda. **Mrs.** Lincoln's dressmaker: the unlikely friendship of Elizabeth Keckley and Mary Todd Lincoln; by Lynda D. Jones. National Geographic 2009 80p il $18.95; lib bdg $27.90

Grades: 5 6 7 8   92

1. Memoirists 2. Dressmakers 3. Spouses of presidents 4. Slavery -- United States 5. United States -- Race relations 6. African American women -- Biography 7. Presidents' spouses -- United States 8. Washington (D.C.) -- Social life and customs

ISBN 978-1-4263-0377-7; 1-4263-0377-7; 978-1-4263-0378-4 lib bdg; 1-4263-0378-5 lib bdg

LC 2008-29314

"Readers may be familiar with the ups and downs of Lincoln's life, but details of Keckley's story . . . will give them new insights into the life of a slave, in this case, one who was educated and had a profession." Booklist

Includes bibliographical references

Linné, Carl von, 1707-1778

Sanchez, Anita. **Karl**, get out of the garden! Carolus Linnaeus and the naming of everything. Anita Sanchez; illustrated by Catherine Stock. Charlesbridge 2017 48 p. color illustrations (reinforced for library use) $17.99

Grades: 2 3 4 5   92

1. Classification 2. Natural history 3. Naturalists -- Biography 4. Natural history -- Classification 5. Naturalists -- Sweden -- Biography

ISBN 9781580896061

LC 2015017344

In this book, by Anita Sanchez, illustrated by Catherine Stock, "Carolus (Karl) Linnaeus started off as a curious child who loved exploring the garden. Despite his intelligence—and his mother's scoldings—he was a poor student, preferring to be outdoors with his beloved plants and bugs. As he grew up, Karl's love of nature led him to take on a seemingly impossible task: to give a scientific name to every living thing on earth. The result was the Linnaean system." (Publisher's note)

Includes bibliographical references (pages 46-47)

Anderson, Margaret Jean. **Carl** Linnaeus; father of classification. [by] Margaret J. Anderson. rev ed; Enslow Publishers 2009 128p il (Great minds of science) lib bdg $31.93

Grades: 5 6 7 8 9   92

1. Botanists 2. Naturalists 3. Writers on science

ISBN 978-0-7660-3009-1 lib bdg; 0-7660-3009-1 lib bdg

LC 2008-23941

First published 1997

"Budding scientists will surely draw inspiration from this biography of Linnaeus. . . . Anderson creates a dramatic narrative fully capable of keeping readers enthralled." Kirkus

Includes glossary and bibliographical references

Liston, Melba

★ Russell-Brown, Katheryn. **Little** Melba and her big trombone; by Katheryn Russell-Brown; illustrations by Frank Morrison. First edition Lee & Low Books, Inc. 2014 40 p. (hardcover : alk. paper) $18.95

Grades: K 1 2 3 4   92

1. Jazz musicians -- Biography 2. Jazz music 3. Jazz musicians 4. African American jazz musicians

ISBN 1600608981; 9781600608988

LC 2013033662

Coretta Scott King (Illustrator) Honor Book (2015)

This children's book by Katheryn Russell-Brown, illustrated by Frank Morrison, tells how "Melba Doretta Liston loved the sounds of music. . . . As a child, she daydreamed about beats and lyrics, and hummed along with the music from her family's Majestic radio. . . . Overcoming obstacles of race and gender, Melba went on to become a famed trombone player and arranger, spinning rhythms, harmonies, and melodies into gorgeous songs for all the jazz greats of the twentieth century." (Publisher's note)

"Russell-Brown's account of her subject's early life is as smooth and stimulating as a Liston trombone solo, and will leave readers wanting to know more about the woman and her music. Morrison's oil paintings, in his trademark elongated, angular style, perfectly convey the jazz scene and, of course, Melba's amazing horn." Horn Book

Lockwood, Belva Ann, 1830-1917

Bardhan-Quallen, Sudipta. **Ballots** for Belva; the true story of a woman's race for the presidency. by Sudipta Bardhan-Quallen; illustrated by Courtney A. Martin. Abrams Books for Young Readers 2008 un il $16.95

Grades: 2 3 4 5   92

1. Lawyers 2. Feminism 3. Suffragists 4. Women lawyers 5. Women politicians 6. Lecturers 7. Presidential candidates

ISBN 978-0-8109-7110-3; 0-8109-7110-0

LC 2007049842

"This picture-book biography introduces [Belva Ann Lockwood], the woman who ran for president more than a century ago. . . . She obtained a law degree, fought for equal rights, and ultimately became the first woman to receive certified votes during her 1884 presidential campaign. . . . Quotes from Lockwood and others enliven the text. . . . Handsome illustrations clearly set the time and place, and Lockwood's fortitude comes through in her posture and facial expressions." SLJ

Lomax, John Avery, 1867-1948

Hopkinson, Deborah. **Home** on the range; John A. Lomax and his cowboy songs. illustrated by S. D. Schindler. G. P. Putnam's Sons 2009 un il $16.99

Grades: 2 3 4   92

1. Ethnomusicologists 2. Folklorists 3. Musicologists 4. Folk songs -- United States

ISBN 978-0-399-23996-0; 0-399-23996-0

LC 2008-16802

This traces the early career of John A Lomax, the collector and recorder of American folk songs.

This a "colorful narrative. . . . Glimpses of his thoughts and emotions . . . as well as dialogue help personalize the story. . . . Schindler's . . . realistic illustrations, painted with a light touch in muted hues, ably capture the expressions of skeptical cowboys . . . or the eagerness with which Lomax goes about his work." Publ Wkly

Longworth, Alice Roosevelt, 1884-1980

★ Kerley, Barbara. **What** to do about Alice? how Alice Roosevelt broke the rules, charmed the world, and drove her father Teddy crazy! illustrated by Edwin Fotheringham. Scholastic Press 2008 un il $16.99

Grades: K 1 2 3   92

1. Presidents -- United States -- Family 2. White House (Washington, D.C.)

ISBN 978-0-439-92231-9; 0-439-92231-3

LC 2006-38372

Boston Globe-Horn Book Award honor book: Nonfiction (2008)

"The daughter of Theodore Roosevelt, . . . Alice had a joie de vivre that she called 'eating up the world.' . . . Kerley's text has the same rambunctious spirit as its subject. . . . The large format gives Fotheringhame . . . plenty of room for spectacular art, which includes use of digital media." Booklist

Lorenz, Konrad

Greenstein, Elaine. The **goose** man; the story of Konrad Lorenz. Clarion Books 2009 32p il $16

Grades: K 1 2 3   **92**

1. Geese 2. Scientists 3. Ethologists 4. Writers on nature 5. Writers on science 6. Nobel laureates for physiology or medicine

ISBN 978-0-547-08459-6; 0-547-08459-5

LC 2008-44618

"From childhood, Konrad Lorenz was fascinated by ducks and geese, growing up to become a prizewinning scientist who offered new insights into animal behavior. This picture-book biography . . . summarizes his life's work with geese. . . . The pastel illustrations, in gouache, ink and colored pencil, use a technique that includes scratchboard effects and is childlike in style. . . . These pictures tell the story as clearly as the simple text, whose language and frequent repetition make this scientific biography easily accessible to beginning readers." Kirkus

Includes bibliographical references

Louis, Joe, 1914-1981

Adler, David A. **Joe** Louis; America's fighter. written by David A. Adler; illustrated by Terry Widener. Harcourt 2005 un il $16

Grades: 2 3 4   **92**

1. Soldiers 2. African American athletes 3. Boxers (Persons) 4. Boxing -- Biography

ISBN 0-15-216480-4

LC 2003-12817

The life story of Joe Louis, heavyweight champion boxer, with the complete history of his career in the ring.

"This creative team's collaboration packs a powerful punch. . . . The action-packed acrylics capture the setting and emotions—Widener's signature muscular figures are particularly apt here." SLJ

Includes bibliographical references

★ De la Peña, Matt. A **nation's** hope; the story of boxing legend Joe Louis. illustrated by Kadir Nelson. Dial Books for Young Readers 2011 un il $17.99

Grades: 1 2 3   **92**

1. Soldiers 2. African American athletes 3. Boxers (Persons) 4. Boxing -- Biography 5. Boxing

ISBN 0-8037-3167-1; 978-0-8037-3167-7

LC 2010-13477

This biography focuses on the "1938 rematch between African-American Joe Louis and German Max Schmeling. . . . Ages five to eight." (Bull Cent Child Books)

"Nelson's . . . photographically realistic, luminescent oil paintings bring to life this lyrical tribute to boxing legend Joe Louis. Focusing on Louis's 1938 rematch against German Max Schmeling . . . de la Peña . . . in his first picture book, shows how the event unified a racially divided country for one evening. . . . Spare, evocative verse melds with the eloquent illustrations to create palpable energy around the fight and Louis's struggle to the top. . . . A dramatic introduction to a pugilist who symbolized many things for an entire country." Publ Wkly

Lovelace, Ada King, Countess of, 1815-1852

Stanley, Diane. **Ada** Lovelace, poet of science; the first computer programmer. Diane Stanley; illustrated by Jessie Hartland. Simon & Schuster Books for Young Readers 2016 40 p. color illustrations (hardcover) $17.99

Grades: K 1 2 3 4   **92**

1. Women mathematicians -- Great Britain -- Biography 2. Women computer programmers -- Great Britain -- Biography 3. Computers -- History -- 19th century 4. Mathematicians -- Great

Britain -- Biography

ISBN 9781481452496

LC 2015010872

In this biography of Ada Lovelace, by Diane Stanley, illustrated by Jessie Hartland, "like her father, Ada had a vivid imagination and a creative gift for connecting ideas in original ways. Like her mother, she had a passion for science, math, and machines. . . . A hundred years before the dawn of the digital age, Ada Lovelace envisioned the computer-driven world we know today. And in demonstrating how the machine would be coded, she wrote the first computer program." (Publisher's note)

"This is a solid addition to STEM studies, yes, but also a great choice for any biography lovers." Booklist

Includes bibliographical references.

★ Wallmark, Laurie. **Ada** Byron Lovelace and the thinking machine; by Laurie Wallmark; illustrated by April Chu. Creston Books, LLC. 2015 40 p. color illustrations $17.99

Grades: K 1 2 3   **92**

1. Computers -- History 2. Women mathematicians 3. Computers -- History -- 19th century 4. Mathematicians -- Great Britain -- Biography 5. Women mathematicians -- Great Britain -- Biography 6. Women computer programmers -- Great Britain -- Biography

ISBN 9781939547200

LC 2015017771

In this book, by Laurie Wallmark, illustrated by April Chu, "Ada Lovelace, the daughter of the famous romantic poet, Lord Byron, develops her creativity through science and math. When she meets Charles Babbage, the inventor of the first mechanical computer, Ada understands the machine better than anyone else and writes the world's first computer program in order to demonstrate its capabilities." (Publisher's note)

A picture book biography about the woman considered to be the creator of computer programming.

Includes bibliographical references

Low, Juliette Gordon, 1860-1927

★ Wadsworth, Ginger. **First** Girl Scout; Ginger Wadsworth. Clarion Books 2012 xiii, 210p ill. $17.99

Grades: 7 8 9 10 11 12   **92**

1. Biography 2. Girl Scouts 3. Philanthropists 4. Scout leaders 5. Girl Scouts of the United States of America

ISBN 978-0-547-24394-8; 0-547-24394-4

LC 2011009642

This book offers a biography of the founder of the Girl Scouts organization. "Juliette (Daisy) Gordon Low [who] was a . . . woman with ideas that were ahead of her time. She witnessed important eras in U.S. history, from the Civil War and Reconstruction to westward expansion to post-World War I. And she made history by founding the first national organization to bring girls from all backgrounds into the out-of-doors. Daisy created controversy by encouraging them to prepare not only for traditional homemaking but also for roles as professional women—in the arts, sciences, and business—and for active citizenship outside the home. Her group also welcomed girls with disabilities at a time when they were usually excluded." (Publisher's note)

"Low's personality really comes to life through the details in the narrative. Wadsworth shows readers that this remarkable woman was a skilled leader and hostess in spite of having suffered severe hearing loss that made conversation difficult. . . . The attractive book design features chapter headings that look like Girl Scout badges, and most spreads include period photos or reproductions of primary-source documents." SLJ

Includes bibliographical references (p. 201-204) and index.

Lowry, Lois, 1937-

Lowry. Lois. **Looking** back; a book of memories. Lois Lowry. 2nd edition Houghton Mifflin Harcourt 2016 259 p illustrations hbk $18.99

Grades: 4 5 6 7 8   **92**

1. Women authors -- 20th century -- Biography

ISBN 0544807960; 9780544807969

Originally published 1998

"In an updated edition of her photographic memoir originally published in 1998, Lowry offers reflections on life, work, and literature." (Kirkus)

Ludwick, Christopher, 1720-1801

Rockliff, Mara. **Gingerbread** for liberty! how a German baker helped win the American Revolution. Mara Rockliff; illustrated by Vincent X. Kirsch. HMH Books for Young Readers 2014 32 p. color illustrations (hardback) $17.99

Grades: 1 2 3 4   **92**

1. Bakers and bakeries 2. United States -- History -- 1775-1783, Revolution 3. United States -- History -- Revolution, 1775-1783 -- Biography 4. United States -- History -- Revolution, 1775-1783 -- Participation, German American

ISBN 0544130014; 9780544130012

LC 2013036934

This children's book by Mara Rockliff tells "the story of an unsung hero of the Revolutionary War who changed the course of history one loaf at a time. Christopher Ludwick was a German-born American patriot with a big heart and a talent for baking. When cries of 'Revolution!' began, Christopher was determined to help General George Washington and his hungry troops. Not with muskets or cannons, but with gingerbread!" (Publisher's note)

"A little-known figure from the American Revolution era is given a fresh look for another generation of history lovers. This book relates the tale of a generous, beloved, and industrious member of the Philadelphia community, originally from Germany, referred to as 'the baker.'. . . The simple recipe on the end pages offers options for different skill levels. Back matter, including a list of sources, provides fuller detail and context as well as the baker's name: Christopher Ludwick. A sweet addition to Revolutionary War units where a more behind-the-scenes look is desired and a nonfiction twist on gingerbread-themed storytimes." SLJ

Lustig, Victor, 1890-1947

Pizzoli, Greg. **Tricky** Vic; Greg Pizzoli. Viking 2015 48 p. (hardcover) $17.99

Grades: 2 3 4 5   **92**

1. Paris (France) -- Description and travel 2. Criminals -- Biography 3. Swindlers and swindling -- Biography

ISBN 0670016527; 9780670016525

LC 2014020580

This picture book by Greg Pizzoli "takes a look at Robert Miller, a successful con man who managed to dupe many and by posing as a government official was even able to 'sell' the Eiffel Tower to scrap metal dealers, before being caught and imprisoned. Miller used more than 45 aliases during his life but was known to many as Tricky Vic. This is a fascinating story, with quirky, retro-style, mixed-media art that will appeal to readers." (School Library Journal)

"Amidst the current plethora of picture-book biography role models, it's nice to see a book about a con artist. . . . here's no moral here, except perhaps for the one that closes the excellent author's note: 'Stay sharp.' Sidebars throughout provide historical context, and a glossary and thorough source list will give young crooks cover for school reports." Horn Book

Lynch, John Roy, 1847-1939

Barton, Chris. The **amazing** age of John Roy Lynch; written by Chris Barton; illustrated by Don Tate. Eerdmans Books for Young Readers 2015 50 p. (hardcover) $17

Grades: 2 3 4 5   **92**

1. African Americans -- Biography 2. Reconstruction (U.S. history, 1865-1877) 3. African American legislators -- Biography 4. Legislators -- United States -- Biography 5. United States. Congress. House -- Biography 6. Mississippi -- Politics and government -- 1865-1950 7. United States -- Politics and government -- 1865-1900 8. African American politicians -- Mississippi -- Biography

ISBN 080285379X; 9780802853790

LC 2014018586

This picture book, by Chris Barton, illustrated by Don Tate, tells the story of how "John Roy Lynch spent most of his childhood as a slave in Mississippi, but all of that changed with the Emancipation Proclamation. . . . While many people in the South were unhappy with the social change, John Roy thrived in the new era. He was appointed to serve as justice of the peace and was eventually elected into the United States Congress." (Publisher's note)

Includes bibliographical references

Lyons, Maritcha Rémond, 1848-1929

★ Bolden, Tonya. **Maritcha**; a nineteenth-century American girl. Abrams 2005 47p il $17.95

Grades: 4 5 6 7 8 9 10   **92**

1. Teachers 2. Civic leaders 3. New York (N.Y.) -- Race relations 4. African American women -- Biography 5. African Americans -- New York (N.Y.)

ISBN 0-8109-5045-6

LC 2004-05849

"The high quality of writing and the excellent documentation make this a first choice for all collections." SLJ

Maathai, Wangari, 1940-2001

★ Johnson, Jen Cullerton. **Seeds** of change; planting a path to peace. illustrated by Sonia Lynn Sadler. Lee & Low 2010 un il $18.95

Grades: 2 3 4   **92**

1. Biologists 2. Conservationists 3. Environmentalists 4. Kenya 5. Nobel laureates for peace 6. Green Belt Movement (Kenya)

ISBN 978-1-60060-367-9; 1-60060-367-X

Coretta Scott King/John Steptoe New Talent Award (Illustrator), 2011

This picture biography "draws on Wangari Maathai's autobiographical writing to present an overview of the activist's life from childhood to the present. . . . Richer than other treatments of Maathai for children and more grounded in her work's implicit feminism, this details her education in Nairobi and the United States, her imprisonment for activism and her scientific and environmental work, resulting in the planting of 30,000,000 trees and economic empowerment for Kenyan women. Sadler's beautiful scratchboard illustrations incise white contoured line into saturated landscapes of lush green leaf patterns, brilliant-hued textiles and undulating, stylized hills. . . . Vibrant and accomplished." Kirkus

★ Napoli, Donna Jo. **Mama** Miti: Wangari Maathai and the trees of Kenya; illustrated by Kadir Nelson. Simon & Schuster Books for Young Readers 2010 un il $16.99

Grades: K 1 2 3   **92**

1. Biologists 2. Conservationists 3. Environmentalists 4. Kenya 5. Nobel laureates for peace 6. Green Belt Movement (Kenya)

ISBN 978-1-4169-3505-6; 1-4169-3505-3

LC 2008-23604

"Napoli adopts a folkloric narrative technique to showcase the life work of Wangari Maathai, whose seminal role in Kenya's reforestation earned her the Nobel Peace Prize in 2004. When, one after the other, women journey to Maathai to seek counsel about scarce food, disappearing firewood and ailing animals, she tells them, 'Plant a tree.'. . . . Nelson's pictures, a jaw-dropping union of African textiles collaged with oil paintings, brilliantly capture the villagers' clothing and the greening landscape. The richly modulated oils portray the dignified, intent gazes of Maathai and other Kenyans. . . . This is, in a word, stunning." Kirkus

Includes bibliographical references

Winter, Jeanette. **Wangari's** trees of peace; a true story from Africa. Harcourt 2008 un il $17

Grades: K 1 2 3   92
   1. Biologists 2. Conservationists 3. Environmentalists 4. Kenya 5. Nobel laureates for peace 6. Green Belt Movement (Kenya)
   ISBN 978-0-15-206545-4; 0-15-206545-8
                                              LC 2007-34810
"Wangari Maathai, the 2004 Nobel Peace Prize winner whose Green Belt Movement has planted 30 million trees in Kenya, is the subject of Winter's . . . eloquent picture biography. . . . The tightly focused text moves quickly without sacrificing impact. . . . Winter's images appear in framed, same-size squares on each page, creating a flat, frieze-like effect." Publ Wkly

Madison, Dolley, 1768-1849
   Adler, David A. A **picture** book of Dolley and James Madison; by David A. Adler and Michael S. Adler; illustrated by Ronald Himler. Holiday House 2009 un il $17.95

Grades: 1 2 3   92
   1. Presidents 2. Members of Congress 3. Secretaries of state 4. Spouses of presidents 5. Presidents -- United States 6. Presidents' spouses -- United States
   ISBN 978-0-8234-2009-4; 0-8234-2009-4
                                              LC 2007041178
"Adler's picture-book biography focuses mainly on the War of 1812, but also mentions Madison's contributions to the Constitution and the creation of the three branches of government. Although this is a biography of the couple, there is more specific information on James Madison than on Dolley. Still, readers do learn some interesting facts about her. . . . Adler's writing is clear yet not oversimplified, and is without fictionalization." SLJ

Includes bibliographical references

★ Brown, Don. **Dolley** Madison saves George Washington; written and illustrated by Don Brown. Houghton Mifflin Co. 2007 un il $16

Grades: 1 2 3   92
   1. War of 1812 2. Washington (D.C.) 3. Spouses of presidents 4. Presidents' spouses -- United States
   ISBN 978-0-618-41199-3; 0-618-41199-2
                                              LC 2006-09813
"While First Lady, [Dolley Madison] redecorated the President's Mansion, ensuring that Gilbert Stuart's portrait of George Washington was prominently displayed. However, it was during the War of 1812 that she earned the gratitude of her nation when, despite the fact that the 100 soldiers assigned to protect the mansion ran off, she bravely remained behind to make sure that the painting as well as important government documents were saved from otherwise certain destruction by British forces. Pen and ink and watercolors effectively depict the simplicity and roughness of Colonial life and convey with humor the spirit of the time and characters." SLJ

Madison, James, 1751-1836
   Adler, David A. A **picture** book of Dolley and James Madison; by David A. Adler and Michael S. Adler; illustrated by Ronald Himler. Holiday House 2009 un il $17.95

Grades: 1 2 3   92
   1. Presidents 2. Members of Congress 3. Secretaries of state 4. Spouses of presidents 5. Presidents -- United States 6. Presidents' spouses -- United States
   ISBN 978-0-8234-2009-4; 0-8234-2009-4
                                              LC 2007041178
"Adler's picture-book biography focuses mainly on the War of 1812, but also mentions Madison's contributions to the Constitution and the creation of the three branches of government. Although this is a biography of the couple, there is more specific information on James Madison than on Dolley. Still, readers do learn some interesting facts about her. . . . Adler's writing is clear yet not oversimplified, and is without fictionalization." SLJ

Includes bibliographical references

Elish, Dan. **James** Madison; [by] Dan Elish. Marshall Cavendish Benchmark 2007 96p il (Presidents and their times) lib bdg $22.95

Grades: 5 6 7 8   92
   1. Presidents 2. Members of Congress 3. Secretaries of state 4. Presidents -- United States
   ISBN 978-0-7614-2432-1
                                              LC 2006036856
A biography of the fourth president of the United States.
"Primary-source materials and quotes, helpful insets, and carefully selected . . . reproductions bring history to life and help make [this] clearly written [biography] highly readable." SLJ

Includes glossary and bibliographical references

Fritz, Jean. The **great** little Madison. Putnam 1989 159p il hardcover o.p. pa $6.99

Grades: 5 6 7 8   92
   1. Presidents 2. Members of Congress 3. Secretaries of state 4. Presidents -- United States
   ISBN 0-399-21768-1; 0-698-11621-6 pa
                                              LC 88-31584
"Small, soft-spoken, and by nature diffident, James Madison found it difficult to speak in the midst of controversy, but his zeal and his convictions in the struggle between Republicans and Federalists gave him confidence, and his successes brought him to the presidency. Fritz has given a vivid picture of the man and an equally vivid picture of the problems—especially the internal dissension—that faced the leaders of the new nation. . . . Notes by the author and a bibliography are appended." Bull Cent Child Books

Maiman, Theodore Harold, 1927-2007
   Wyckoff, Edwin Brit. **Laser** man; Theodore H. Maiman and his brilliant invention. [by] Edwin Brit Wyckoff. Enslow Elementary 2008 32p il (Genius at work!: great inventor biographies) lib bdg $20.60

Grades: 4 5 6   92
   1. Lasers 2. Engineers 3. Physicists
   ISBN 978-0-7660-2848-7 lib bdg; 0-7660-2848-8 lib bdg
                                              LC 2006034680
A biography of Theodore H. Maiman, the engineer who invented the laser

Includes glossary and bibliographical references

Wyckoff, Edwin Brit. The **man** who invented the laser; the genius of Theodore H. Maiman. Edwin Brit Wyckoff. Enslow Elementary 2013 48 p. ill. (some col.) (Genius inventors and their great ideas) (alk. paper) $23.93

Grades: 2 3 4   **92**
1. Lasers 2. Physicists
ISBN 0766041387; 9780766041387

LC 2012013979

This book, by Edwin Brit Wyckoff, focuses on physicist Theodore H. Maiman, "Maiman . . . found that the accepted calculations of the fluorescence quantum efficiency of ruby were wrong and that the material could be used for his research. His persistence with ruby eventually paid off, for on May 16, 1960, the device he built using it became the world's first operable laser (acronym for light amplification by stimulated emission of radiation)." (Publisher's note)

Includes bibliographical references and index

Malcolm X, 1925-1965
Gunderson, Jessica. **X** : the biography of Malcolm X; illustrated by Seitu Hayden. Graphic Library 2011 32p il (Graphic library: American graphic) lib bdg $29.32; pa $7.95
Grades: 4 5 6 7   **92**
1. Black Muslims 2. Biographical graphic novels 3. Black Muslim leaders 4. Civil rights activists 5. African Americans -- Biography
ISBN 978-1-4296-5471-5 lib bdg; 1-4296-5471-6 lib bdg; 978-1-4296-6267-3 pa; 1-4296-6267-0 pa

LC 2010037029

In graphic novel format, explores the life and death of Malcolm X.

"The illustrations are eye-catching and the narration is presented simply, yet compellingly. . . . Fact-filled, entertaining, and accessible." SLJ

Includes glossary and bibliographical references

★ Myers, Walter Dean, 1937-2014. **Malcolm** X; a fire burning brightly. illustrated by Leonard Jenkins. HarperCollins Pubs. 2000 un il $15.95
Grades: 3 4 5 6   **92**
1. Black Muslim leaders 2. Civil rights activists 3. African Americans -- Biography
ISBN 0-06-027707-6

LC 99-21527

"Myers's spare and eloquent narrative makes the complexities of Malcolm X's story accessible without compromising its integrity. The book has appeal for reluctant teen readers as well as younger readers. The sophisticated paintings blend realism with abstraction to heighten the underlying emotional drama of scenes." Horn Book Guide

Mandela, Nelson, 1918-2013
Gormley, Beatrice. **Nelson** Mandela; South African revolutionary. by Beatrice Gormley. Aladdin 2014 256 p. illustrations (Real-life story) (hardback) $17.99
Grades: 5 6 7 8   **92**
1. Presidents -- South Africa -- Biography
ISBN 1481420593; 9781481420594; 9781481420600

LC 2014019020

This book, by Beatrice Gormley, is a "comprehensive biography that tells the complete life story of internationally renowned peacemaker Nelson Mandela. . . . Born in 1918 in South Africa, he grew up in a culture of government-enforced racism and became involved in the anti-apartheid movement at a young age. Deeply committed to nonviolent activism, Mandela directed a peaceful campaign against the racist policies of his South African government, and spent 27 years in prison as a result." (Publisher's note)

"More than a year after his death, the influence of Nelson Mandela is still felt keenly by people around the world. This timely biography provides a complete picture of a complex man...This book is an under-standable and multifaceted tribute to an icon of defiance and optimism in the face of tribulation." Booklist

Includes bibliographical references and index

★ Kramer, Ann. **Mandela**; the rebel who led his nation to freedom. National Geographic 2005 63p il (World history biographies) $17.95; lib bdg $27.90
Grades: 4 5 6 7   **92**
1. Presidents 2. Political prisoners 3. Political leaders 4. Human rights activists 5. Nobel laureates for peace 6. South Africa -- Race relations 7. South Africa -- Politics and government
ISBN 0-7922-3658-0; 0-7922-3659-9 lib bdg

"This biography introduces readers not only to Mandela, but also to the political turmoil that affected South Africa for over a century. It begins with his birth, and covers his school years, his political ventures, imprisonment, release, presidency, Nobel Peace Prize, and retirement. Full-color photographs appear throughout and a time line runs along the bottom of each spread. . . . the book is well worth purchasing." SLJ

Includes glossary and bibliographical references

★ Mandela, Nelson. **Nelson** Mandela: long walk to freedom; abridged by Chris van Wyk; illustrated by Paddy Bouma. Roaring Book Press 2009 un il $16
Grades: 2 3 4 5   **92**
1. Presidents 2. Political prisoners 3. Political leaders 4. Human rights activists 5. Nobel laureates for peace 6. South Africa -- Race relations 7. South Africa -- Politics and government
ISBN 978-1-59643-566-7; 1-59643-566-6

"Abridged from Mandela's 1994 autobiography, this picture book distills the basic facts of his childhood, his education, and the influences that led him to become one of the world's most renowned political activists. In a simple, yet effective manner, he describes the growing system of apartheid, and the unjust treatment of blacks in South Africa is made clear without horrifying details. . . . The writing is clear, providing chronological detail for even young students new to the concept and history of apartheid. Full-page, color paintings accompany the text on every spread and depict crucial moments from the narrative in a way that both complements and enhances the story." SLJ

Mankiller, Wilma
Sonneborn, Liz. **Wilma** Mankiller. Marshall Cavendish Benchmark 2010 112p il (Leading women) $39.93
Grades: 5 6 7 8   **92**
1. Cherokee Indians 2. Indian chiefs
ISBN 978-0-7614-4959-1; 0-7614-4959-0

LC 2009029399

"The story of Mankiller's lifelong work for the Cherokee Nation and her role as its first female principal chief will absorb readers. The [woman's life is] revealed within the political and historical context of [her] times and [includes] quotes from autobiographical material. . . . Color and black-and-white photos are included. . . . The compact size, chronological organization, and accessible writing [style makes this biography a] good [resource] for reports." SLJ

Manley, Effa, 1900-1981
★ Vernick, Audrey. **She** loved baseball: the Effa Manley story; written by Audrey Vernick; illustrated by Don Tate. Collins 2010 un il
Grades: 1 2 3   **92**
1. African American athletes 2. Baseball executives 3. Baseball -- Biography 4. African American women -- Biography
ISBN 0061349208; 9780061349201

This is a picture book biography of Effa Manley, the African American baseball team owner and first and only woman ever inducted into the Baseball Hall of Fame.

"Tate's energetic illustrations harmonize well with Vernick's fresh and engaging text. History favors the individuals in the spotlight: here's an entertaining portrait of a woman who made significant strides behind the scenes." Publ Wkly

Manning, Peyton, 1976-

Wilner, Barry. **Peyton** Manning; a football star who cares. Enslow Publishers, Inc. 2011 48p il (Sport stars who care) lib bdg $23.93; pa $7.95

Grades: 3 4 5   **92**

1. Football players 2. Football -- Biography

ISBN 978-0-7660-3774-8 lib bdg; 0-7660-3774-6 lib bdg; 978-1-59845-232-7 pa; 1059845-232-0 pa

LC 2010014946

"The text traces Manning's athletic prowess from his playing days in elementary and high school, his successful college career, and, of course, his outstanding professional play, with Manning winning MVP four times.... A large typeface, a striking design, and plenty of color photographs will entice readers, even reluctant ones. Stats, a glossary, and suggested resources for learning more complete this attractive package." Booklist

Includes glossary and bibliographical references

Mantle, Mickey, 1931-1995

Payne, C. F. **Mickey** Mantle; The Commerce Comet. Jonah Winter, illustrated by C.F. Payne. schwartz & Wade books 2017 40 p. color illustrations $17.99

Grades: 2 3 4 5   **92**

1. Baseball players -- United States -- Biography

ISBN 9781101933527; 9781101933534

LC 2016000763

This children's book, by Jonah Winter, illustrated by C.F. Payne, presents a "biography that traces Mickey Mantle's unparalleled baseball career. He could run from home plate to first base in 2.9 seconds. He could hit a ball 540 feet—the longest home run in major league history. He was the greatest switch hitter ever to play the game. And he did it all despite broken bones, pulled muscles, strains, and sprains, from his shoulders to his feet." (Publisher's note)

"Payne's artwork, created with acrylic and pencil, transports readers to that setting as well as several ballparks, while portraying characters with energy and personality. A worthwhile addition to sports collections." Booklist

Marceau, Marcel

★ Schubert, Leda. **Monsieur** Marceau; Leda Schubert; illustrated by Gérard DuBois. Roaring Brook Press 2012 p. cm. (reinforced) $17.99

Grades: 2 3 4   **92**

1. Marceau, Marcel, 1923-2007 2. Mimes -- France

ISBN 1596435291; 9781596435292

LC 2011033798

This book by Leda Schubert, illustrated by Gérard DuBois, provides a "picture book biography [of] . . . Marcel Marceau, the world's most famous mime. . . . [Marceau] enthralled audiences around the world for more than fifty years. When he waved his hand or lifted his eyebrow he was able to speak volumes without ever saying a word. But few know the story of the man behind those gestures" (Publisher's note)

Includes bibliographical references and index

Spielman, Gloria. **Marcel** Marceau; master of mime. illustrated by Manon Gauthier. Kar-Ben Pub. 2011 un il lib bdg $17.95

Grades: 3 4 5   **92**

1. Mime 2. Actors 3. Mimes 4. Jews -- Biography 5. World War,

1939-1945 -- France

ISBN 978-0-7613-3961-8; 0-7613-3961-2

LC 2010027787

"Readers are introduced to the world-famous reviver of the lost art of mime in this attractive and accessible picture-book biography. Melding Marceau's childhood and evolution as an artist with world events, Spielman reveals how the young son of a kosher butcher in Strasbourg, France, pursued his dream, despite the Nazi invasion in 1939.... Gauthier's childlike mixed-media illustrations feature myriad rosy-cheeked characters and capture both the whimsy of Marceau's performances and the more somber conditions of war-torn France." SLJ

Marley, Bob

★ Medina, Tony. **I** and I; Bob Marley. illustrated by Jesse Joshua Watson. Lee & Low Books 2009 un il $19.95

Grades: 4 5 6   **92**

1. Singers 2. Jamaica 3. Reggae musicians

ISBN 978-1-60060-257-3; 1-60060-257-6

LC 2008-33485

"In the words and rhythms of Jamaican patois, Medina's lyrical, direct lines make the most sense when read in tandem with the extensive appended notes. . . . Like the words, Watson's beautifully expressive acrylic paintings evoke a strong sense of Marley's remarkable life and his Caribbean homeland." Booklist

Includes bibliographical references

Martín, de Porres, Saint, 1579-1639

Schmidt, Gary D. **Martin** de Porres; the rose in the desert. written by Gary D. Schmidt; illustrated by David Diaz. Clarion Books 2012 32 p. col. ill. (reinforced) $16.99

Grades: 1 2 3   **92**

1. Picture books for children 2. Christian saints -- Biography 3. Christian saints -- Peru -- Biography

ISBN 0547612184; 9780547612188

LC 2011025721

Pura Belpré Illustrator Award (2013)

This children's picture book offers a biography of the Catholic saint Martin de Porres. The "illegitimate son of a former slave and a Spanish conquistador in 1579 in Lima, Peru," he "was the first black saint of the Americas." Author Gary Schmidt focuses on the saint's "extreme humility . . . emphasizing his humble servitude and great empathy." (School Library Journal)

Martini, Helen

Lyon, George Ella. **Mother** to tigers; illustrations by Peter Catalanotto. Atheneum Bks. for Young Readers 2003 un il $16.95

Grades: K 1 2 3   **92**

1. Zoos 2. Zoo directors

ISBN 0-689-84221-X

LC 00-45375

"Lyon's succinct, yet elegant, prose emphasizes Martini's dedication to the animals in her care. . . . Catalanotto's watercolor, charcoal, and torn-paper art is particularly effective here." Booklist

Martínez, Pedro, 1971-

Tavares, Matt. **Growing** up Pedro; Matt Tavares. Candlewick Press 2015 40 p. illustrations reinforced $16.99

Grades: 2 3 4 5   **92**

1. Baseball players

ISBN 0763668249; 9780763668242

LC 2014944675

This book, written and illustrated by Matt Tavares, offers the "tale of Dominican pitcher Pedro Martínez, from his days of throwing rocks at mangoes to his years as a major-league star. . . . Pedro loved baseball more than anything, and his older brother Ramon was the best pitcher he'd ever seen. He'd dream of the day he and his brother could play together in the major leagues--and here, Matt Tavares tells the story of how that dream came true." (Publisher's note)

"Tavares traces the career of Pedro Martínez, beginning with his childhood in the Dominican Republic, where he idolized his older brother, Ramón. After Ramón was drafted to play with the Dodgers, Pedro joined the team soon after. Tavares emphasizes how the brothers' careers often ran in concert—both eventually played for the Red Sox and found time to celebrate their team's success back on their childhood turf." Pub Wkly

Includes bibliographical references

Matisse, Henri

Anholt, Laurence. **Matisse**; the king of color. Barron's 2007 un il $14.99

Grades: 2 3 4 5   **92**
1. Artists 2. Painters 3. Artists, French
ISBN 0-7641-6047-8

"Anholt tells the story behind Matisse's final masterpiece—Chapelle du Rosaire. During a serious illness, the artist becomes friends with his nurse, Monique, and he draws and paints several pictures of her. When his health improves, she leaves the man who has been like a grandfather to her and joins a strict religious order. Years later, the two friends are reunited when Matisse moves into a villa close to the nunnery. As a final gift for Monique, now Sister Jacques-Marie, he designs a simple chapel for the nuns. . . . The bright and cheerful illustrations draw heavily on Matisse's drawings, paintings, and collages. Facts about the artist's life and style are also skillfully woven into the story and illustrations." SLJ

★ Fillion, Susan. **Miss** Etta and Dr. Claribel; Bringing Matisse to America. David R. Godine 2011 83p il $18.95

Grades: 4 5 6 7   **92**
1. Artists 2. Painters 3. Physicians 4. Art collectors 5. Art -- Collectors and collecting
ISBN 978-1-56792-434-3; 1-56792-434-4

LC 2010048937

"An affectionate, lively examination of the reciprocal relationship between a great artist and two great art lovers. Etta and Claribel Cone, unmarried sisters from a wealthy Baltimore family . . . [were] discerning collectors of modern art, particularly that of Henri Matisse. . . . Their account is lavishly illustrated in full color by reproductions from the Cone Collection at the Baltimore Museum of Art and Matisse-inflected paintings by the author, who drew extensively on the Cone archive that is also housed at the museum. . . . This appealing work stands as both a portrait of two unconventional women and a celebration of the possibilties of arts patronage." Kirkus

MacLachlan, Patricia, 1938- The **iridescence** of birds; a book about Henri Matisse. Patricia MacLachlan; illustrated by Hadley Hooper. Roaring Brook Press 2014 40 p. color illustrations (hardcover) $17.99

Grades: K 1 2 3 4   **92**
1. Painters -- France -- Biography
ISBN 1596439483; 9781596439481

LC 2013044238

"In two long, lyrical sentences, MacLachlan wonders about the early years of Henri Matisse, who grew up in a cold, gray city in northern France and was warmed by the colors of the paints, fabrics, and birds that surrounded him. Posing her thoughts as questions, MacLachlan distills Matisse's first experiences, assembling them in rough detail to communicate their emotional impact." (Booklist)

"Using relief prints and digital techniques with a decisive and economical rough-edged black line and colors that echo Matisse's evolving

palette, Hooper sets the happily involved small boy amongst images that become bolder and brighter as the book progresses while fluidly incorporating the painter's own imagery. It's a spacious and beautiful book." Horn Book

Welton, Jude. **Henri** Matisse. Watts 2002 46p il (Artists in their time) $22; pa $6.95

Grades: 5 6 7 8   **92**
1. Artists 2. Painters 3. Artists, French
ISBN 0-531-12228-X; 0-531-16621-X pa

LC 2002-69106

Discusses the life and career of this French artist, describing and giving examples of his work

This offers a "clear and lively [text]. . . . Captioned, full-color and black-and-white photographs and art reproductions are liberally scattered throughout." SLJ

★ Winter, Jeanette. **Henri's** scissors; by Jeanette Winter. Beach Lane Books 2013 40 p. (hardcover) $16.99

Grades: K 1 2 3   **92**
1. Picture books for children 2. Art -- Technique 3. Matisse, Henri, 1869-1954 4. Artists -- France -- Biography
ISBN 1442464844; 9781442464841; 9781442464858

LC 2012033171

In this children's picture book, after "quickly tracing French painter [Henri] Matisse's journey to becoming an artist ('He was happy, and his paintings made people happy') and explaining how illness left him unable to paint at the end of his life, [Jeanette] Winter . . . describes his discovery of a medium less physically demanding than painting but just as expressive: painted paper and scissors. 'Why didn't I think of it earlier?' he asks delightedly." (Publishers Weekly)

Matzeliger, Jan, 1852-1889

Mitchell, Barbara. **Shoes** for everyone: a story about Jan Matzeliger; illustrations by Hetty Mitchell. Carolrhoda Bks. 1986 63p il (Carolrhoda creative minds book) hardcover o.p. pa $8.95

Grades: 3 4 5   **92**
1. Inventors 2. Shoe industry 3. African American inventors 4. Clothing industry executives
ISBN 0-87614-290-0; 0-87614-473-3 pa

LC 86-4157

A biography of the half-Dutch half-black Surinamese man who, despite the hardships and prejudice he found in his new Massachusetts home, invented a shoe-lasting machine that revolutionized the shoe industry in the late nineteenth century

This is "a compelling story of human endeavor. A clear text blessedly allows the extraordinary individual in focus, Jan Matzeliger, . . . to emerge without undue exclamatory adulation." Bull Cent Child Books

Mays, Willie, 1931-

★ Winter, Jonah. **You** never heard of Willie Mays?! by Jonah Winter; illustrations by Terry Widener. Schwartz & Wade Books 2013 40 p. (trade) $17.99

Grades: K 1 2 3   **92**
1. Baseball -- History 2. Baseball players -- United States -- Biography
ISBN 0375868445; 9780375868443; 9780375968440

LC 2011047347

This children's book, by Jonah Winter, profiles the baseball star Willy Mays. "Many believe him to be the best baseball player that ever lived. . . . In . . . [this] picture book biography, young readers can follow Mays's unparalleled career from growing up in Birmingham, Alabama, to playing awe-inspiring ball in the Negro Leagues and then the Majors, where he was center fielder for the New York (later San Francisco) Giants." (Publisher's note)

McCloskey, Robert, 1914-2003

McCloskey, Jane. **Robert** McCloskey; a private life in words and pictures. Seapoint Books 2011 il $24.95

Grades: Adult Professional   92

1. Artists 2. Authors 3. Illustrators 4. Authors, American 5. Children's authors

ISBN 978-0-9786899-6-4; 0-9786899-6-8

In this "biography of the great author/illustrator, his younger daughter reconstructs his life, her recollections nicely complemented by scores of beautifully reproduced illustrations from her father's books as well as photos and never-before-published sketches and paintings. The text is artless in the best sense, not a formal biography but a sequence of significant circumstances and events as Jane observed them." Horn Book

McCoy, Elijah, 1844-1929

Kulling, Monica. **All** aboard!: Elijah McCoy's steam engine; illustrated by Bill Slavin. Tundra Books 2010 un il (Great idea) $17.95

Grades: K 1 2 3   92

1. Inventors 2. Railroads 3. African American inventors

ISBN 978-0-88776-945-0; 0-88776-945-4

A picture book biography of the African American inventor of the oil cup, patented in 1872, which continuously greased the engines of steam locomotives.

This is "an engaging biography. . . . Expressive watercolors . . . capture the time period, allowing readers to imagine what life was like in this era, and add energy and touches of humor." SLJ

Meir, Golda, 1898-1978

Blashfield, Jean F. **Golda** Meir. Marshall Cavendish Benchmark 2010 112p il (Leading women) $39.93

Grades: 5 6 7 8   92

1. Diplomats 2. Prime ministers 3. Women politicians 4. Cabinet members 5. Israel -- History 6. Jews -- Biography

ISBN 978-0-7614-4960-7; 0-7614-4960-4

"Meir survived pogroms in Russia as a child and became prime minister of Israel. . . . The [woman's life is] revealed within the political and historical context of [her] times and [includes] quotes from autobiographical material. . . . Color and black-and-white photos are included. . . . The compact size, chronological organization, and accessible writing [style makes this biography a] good [resource] for reports." SLJ

Includes bibliographical references

Menchú, Rigoberta

Menchu, Rigoberta. The **girl** from Chimel; [by] Rigoberta Menchú with Dante Liano; pictures by Domi; translated by David Unger. House of Anansi Press 2005 54p il $16.95

Grades: 4 5 6 7   92

1. Mayas 2. Guatemala 3. Memoirists 4. Indian leaders 5. Human rights activists 6. Nobel laureates for peace

ISBN 0-88899-666-7

This is "Menchú's account of her childhood in the small village of Chimel, Guatamala. . . . Short sketches provide glimpses of Menchú's early years; lyrical language and repeated phrases such as 'when I was a girl in Chimel' link the text to oral storytelling. . . . Each chapter sports a vivid oil painting by Domi, featuring thick strokes of bright oranges, purples, greens, and reds and a naive approach that lends a folk-art feel, effectively capturing the action and emotion of the stories." Bull Cent Child Books

Mendel, Gregor, 1822-1884

Bardoe, Cheryl. **Gregor** Mendel; the friar who grew peas. illustrated by Jos. A. Smith. Abrams Books for Young Readers 2006 un il $18.95

Grades: 2 3 4   92

1. Genetics 2. Scientists 3. Geneticists

ISBN 0-8109-5475-3

LC 2005-22957

A picture book biography of the scientist who became known as the father of genetics

"This slim, oversize volume is as much a treat for the eye as it is for the curious mind. Smith's crisp, realistic paintings, often flooded with the bright green of pea plants, accompany Bardoe's readable text." SLJ

Includes bibliographical references

Van Gorp, Lynn. **Gregor** Mendel; genetics pioneer. science contributor, Sally Ride Science. Compass Point Books 2008 40p il (Mission: Science) lib bdg $26.60

Grades: 4 5 6   92

1. Genetics 2. Scientists 3. Geneticists

ISBN 978-0-7565-3963-4 lib bdg; 0-7565-3963-3 lib bdg

LC 2008-07725

A biography of scientist Gregor Mendel, with an introduction to the principles of genetics

This "will entice students to become excited about an assignment or just satisfy their own curiosity. . . . The text . . . does a good job of connecting the scientist's work to our lives today. . . . [The] book has a variety of graphics including diagrams, [and] photos." Libr Media Connect

Merian, Maria Sibylla, 1647-1717

★ Engle, Margarita. **Summer** birds: the butterflies of Maria Merian; pictures by Julie Paschkis. Henry Holt & Co. 2010 un il $16.99

Grades: K 1 2 3   92

1. Artists 2. Painters 3. Zoologists 4. Butterflies 5. Naturalists 6. Caterpillars 7. Illustrators 8. Women artists 9. Women scientists 10. Caterpillars 11. Butterflies -- Metamorphosis

ISBN 0-8050-8937-3; 978-0-8050-8937-0

LC 2009-05267

This is the story of Maria Merian, a young girl living in the Middle Ages who observed the life cycle of butterflies and challenged the status quo account of their genesis. "Ages five to eight." (Bull Cent Child Books)

"Born in Frankfurt in 1647, Maria Sibylla Merian disagreed with the conventional wisdom . . . that 'summer birds,' or butterflies, were 'beasts of the devil' that sprang alive from the mud . . . . Engle writes in the voice of Maria as a young teen, who carefully watches the slow transformation of caterpillars to winged adults, painting everything that she sees. . . . In expertly pared-down language, the poetic lines deftly fold in basic science concepts about life cycles, along with biographical details that are further developed in an appended historical note. Paschkis' brilliantly colored and patterned paintings are an exuberant counterpoint to the minimal words." Booklist

Michelangelo Buonarroti, 1475-1564

★ Stanley, Diane. **Michelangelo.** HarperCollins Pubs. 2000 un il $18.99; pa $6.99

Grades: 4 5 6 7   92

1. Artists 2. Painters 3. Sculptors 4. Architects 5. Renaissance 6. Artists, Italian

ISBN 0-688-15085-3; 0-06-052113-9 pa

A biography of the Renaissance sculptor, painter, architect, and poet, well known for his work on the Sistine Chapel in Rome's St. Peter's Cathedral

This is "as readable as it is useful. . . . Integrating Michelangelo's art with Stanley's watercolor, gouache, and colored-pencil figures and settings has the desired effect: readers will be dazzled with the master's ability, while at the same time pulled into his daily life and struggles." SLJ

Includes bibliographical references

Miller, Norma, 1919-
Govenar, Alan. **Stompin'** at the Savoy; the story of Norma Miller. collected and edited by Alan Govenar; illustrated by Martin French. Candlewick Press 2006 54p il $15.99

Grades: 3 4 5 6 **92**

1. Dancers 2. African American dancers 3. African American women
ISBN 0-7636-2244-3

LC 2004-57916

This is an autobiography of the African American jazz dancer of the Harlem Renaissance

This "sizzles with spirit and swings with vitality. . . . Miller tells her story with humor and candor. . . . Stylized black-and-white illustrations, produced digitally and in mixed media, nearly swing right off the pages." SLJ

Mills, Florence, 1896-1927
Schroeder, Alan, 1961- **Baby** Flo; Florence Mills lights up the stage. by Alan Schroeder; illustrated by Cornelius Van Wright & Ying-Hwa Hu. Lee & Low Books 2012 40 p. (hardcover : alk. paper) $18.95

Grades: 1 2 3 **92**

1. Biography 2. African American singers -- Biography
ISBN 1600604102; 9781600604102

LC 2011036553

This book, by Alan Schroeder, tells the story of "'Baby Florence' Mills [who] was singing and dancing just about as soon as she could talk and walk. . . . Baby Flo went on to become an international superstar during the Harlem Renaissance—but first she had to overcome a case of stage fright and discover that winning wasn't everything. Here is the spirited story of that spunky young girl learning to chase her dreams with confidence." (Publisher's note)

★ Watson, Renée. **Harlem's** little blackbird; Renee Watson; illustrated by Christian Robinson. 1st ed. Random House Children's Books 2012 1 v. (unpaged) (trade) $17.99

Grades: 2 3 4 **92**

1. African American singers 2. Picture books for children 3. Singers -- New York (State) -- New York -- Biography 4. African American singers -- New York (State) -- New York -- Biography
ISBN 0375869735; 9780375869730; 9780375969737; 9780375985379

LC 2011043314

Author Renée Watson tells the story of "Florence Mills, [who] knew that she was blessed with a gift--a sweet, birdlike singing voice that everyone loved. But she also knew firsthand the profound ache of racism. When she moved to New York City, the stages got bigger, the lights grew brighter, and offers that could make her an international star were hers for the taking. Instead, Florence chose shows that helped promote other black performers. And she sang songs that heralded the call for civil rights." (reneewatson.net)

Mohapatra, Jyotirmayee, 1978-
Woog, Adam. **Jyotirmayee** Mohapatra; by Adam Woog. Kid-Haven Press 2006 48p il $24.95

Grades: 4 5 6 7 **92**

1. Social action 2. Feminists 3. Women -- India 4. Children's rights advocates
ISBN 0-7377-3611-9

LC 2006009121

"Mohapatra grew up in a rural village in India and became a leader in the fight for the rights of girls and women. . . . The power of one individual to inspire others to action is clearly expressed in this well-written profile. Full-color photos and a map enhance the presentation." SLJ

Includes bibliographical references

Monet, Claude, 1840-1926
Maltbie, P. I. **Claude** Monet; the painter who stopped the trains. illustrated by Jos. A. Smith. Abrams Books for Young Readers 2010 32p il $18.95

Grades: K 1 2 3 **92**

1. Artists 2. Painters 3. Artists, French 4. Railroads in art
ISBN 978-0-8109-8961-0; 0-8109-8961-1

LC 2009039459

"Inspired by his son's love of trains, Monet decided to show art critics that impressionism could be more than just seascapes. For three months in 1877, he painted on the platform of the Saint-Lazare train station in Paris. . . . Smith expertly illuminates the changing landscape of an evolving world, as Maltbie's thoughtful story of inspiration and imagination highlights a less remembered portion of Monet's work." Publ Wkly

Includes bibliographical references

Monroe, James, 1758-1831
Naden, Corinne J. **James** Monroe; [by] Corinne J. Naden and Rose Blue. Marshall Cavendish Benchmark 2009 96p il map (Presidents and their times) lib bdg $34.21

Grades: 5 6 7 8 **92**

1. Presidents 2. Secretaries of state 3. Presidents -- United States
ISBN 978-0-7614-2838-1 lib bdg; 0-7614-2838-0 lib bdg

LC 2007-29480

"Provides comprehensive information on President James Monroe and places him within his historical and cultural context. Also explored are the formative events of his times and how he responded." Publisher's note

Includes glossary and bibliographical references

Montezuma, Carlos, 1866?-1923
Capaldi, Gina. A **boy** named Beckoning: the true story of Dr. Carlos Montezuma, Native American hero; adapted and illustrated by Gina Capaldi. Carolrhoda Books 2008 32p il lib bdg $16.95

Grades: 2 3 4 **92**

1. Physicians 2. Physicists 3. Indian leaders 4. Native Americans -- Biography
ISBN 978-0-8225-7644-0

LC 2007021745

"Capaldi uses Montezuma's own words to tell this gripping story of a Yavapai boy who was captured by the Pima in 1871 and grew up to become a prominent doctor and Native American spokesperson. Solidly researched, the well-written text follows Wassaja (later renamed Carlos Montezuma) as he was sold into slavery and purchased by a kind Italian photographer. . . . The illustrations are stunning, with multiple perspectives and rich gold and brown tones." SLJ

Includes bibliographical references

Moran, Thomas, 1837-1926
Judge, Lita. **Yellowstone** Moran; painting the American West. Viking 2009 un il $16.99

Grades: K 1 2 3 **92**

1. Artists 2. Painters 3. Engravers 4. West (U.S.) in art 5. Artists

-- United States 6. Yellowstone National Park
ISBN 978-0-670-01132-2; 0-670-01132-0

LC 2008049879

"In 1871, American artist Thomas Moran journeyed with a team of geologists through the Rocky Mountains to 'the land called the Yellowstone,' observing and sketching the landscape around him. Judge's watercolor illustrations capture the movement and pristine energy of the wilderness along with the team's arduous journey over rocks, ravines and woods." Publ Wkly

Includes bibliographical references

Morgan, Garrett A., 1877-1963

Kulling, Monica. **To** the rescue! Garrett Morgan underground. Monica Kulling. Tundra Books of Northern New York 2015 32 p. color illustrations (hardcover) $17.99

Grades: K 1 2 3   92
1. African American inventors
ISBN 9781770495203; 9781770495210

LC 2014951822

This children's book, by Monica Kulling, illustrated by David Parkins, tells the story of the African American inventor Garrett Morgan. "He began by sweeping floors in a clothing factory in Cleveland, Ohio, where he decided to invent a stronger belt for sewing machines. . . . In 1911, . . . Garrett decided to invent a safety hood for firefighters. Little did he know that most people wouldn't be interested in buying his safety hood when they discovered its inventor was black." (Publisher's note)

"Wonderful nonfiction narratives that can be used to highlight diverse innovators whom history texts may have overlooked." SLJ

Includes bibliographical references (title page verso).

Morgan, Julia

★ Mannis, Celeste Davidson. **Julia** Morgan built a castle; by Celeste Mannis; illustrated by Miles Hyman. Viking 2006 un il $17.99

Grades: 1 2 3 4   92
1. Architects 2. Women architects
ISBN 0-670-05964-1

LC 2004-17401

A picture book biography of "a groundbreaking female architect. Luminescent illustrations, created using soft pastels and pencils in a golden-peach palette, appear to glow with the light of California and France, both seminal locations in Morgan's life. . . . Filled with rich vocabulary, the narrative employs scrumptious architectural terms such as Baroque, flying buttresses, and teakwood cornice." SLJ

Morris, Esther Hobart, 1814-1902

White, Linda. **I** could do that! Esther Morris gets women the vote. [by] Linda Arms White; pictures by Nancy Carpenter. 1st ed; Farrar, Straus and Giroux 2005 32p il

Grades: 2 3 4   92
1. Suffragists 2. Women -- Suffrage 3. Justices of the peace
ISBN 0-374-33527-3

LC 2003-51417

In 1869, a woman whose "can-do" attitude had shaped her life was instrumental in making Wyoming the first state to allow women to vote, then became the first woman to hold public office in the United States.

"White's carefully shaped text is amplified by Carpenter's folksy oils, which combine prim, period details and witty exaggerations." Booklist

Includes bibliographical references

Mozart, Maria Anna, 1751-1829

★ Fancher, Lou. **For** the love of music; the remarkable story of Maria Anna Mozart. paintings by Steve Johnson and Lou Fancher. Tricycle Press 2011 un il $16.99; lib bdg $19.99

Grades: 1 2 3   92
1. Composers 2. Musicians 3. Music
ISBN 978-1-58246-326-1; 1-58246-326-3; 978-1-58246-391-9 lib bdg; 1-58246-391-3 lib bdg

"In an intimate tribute to musical prodigy Maria Anna Mozart (sister of Wolfgang Amadeus), Rusch organizes biographical passages into sonata movements, with musical terms used to mark events in Maria's life. . . . Rusch's rich prose and Johnson and Fancher's lavishly detailed collages—melding paint, paper, fabrics, and weathered musical notation—seamlessly blend to form a moving portrait of an unsung musician." Publ Wkly

Includes bibliographical references

Mozart, Wolfgang Amadeus, 1756-1791

★ Fancher, Lou. **For** the love of music; the remarkable story of Maria Anna Mozart. paintings by Steve Johnson and Lou Fancher. Tricycle Press 2011 un il $16.99; lib bdg $19.99

Grades: 1 2 3   92
1. Composers 2. Musicians 3. Music
ISBN 978-1-58246-326-1; 1-58246-326-3; 978-1-58246-391-9 lib bdg; 1-58246-391-3 lib bdg

"In an intimate tribute to musical prodigy Maria Anna Mozart (sister of Wolfgang Amadeus), Rusch organizes biographical passages into sonata movements, with musical terms used to mark events in Maria's life. . . . Rusch's rich prose and Johnson and Fancher's lavishly detailed collages—melding paint, paper, fabrics, and weathered musical notation—seamlessly blend to form a moving portrait of an unsung musician." Publ Wkly

Includes bibliographical references

Riggs, Kate. **Wolfgang** Amadeus Mozart. Creative Education 2009 48p il (Xtraordinary artists) lib bdg $32.80

Grades: 4 5 6 7   92
1. Composers
ISBN 978-1-58341-664-8 lib bdg; 1-58341-664-1 lib bdg

LC 2007008963

This biography of the composer offers an "interesting [layout]; big, high-quality reproductions and photographs on heavy paper; insightful quotes from diverse sources; and meaty selections of the artist's own writing . . . at the end of the book. Readers get a strong sense of [Mozart's] personality along with an excellent survey of his work." SLJ

Includes bibliographical references

Stanley, Diane. **Mozart,** the wonder child; a puppet play in three acts. Collins 2009 un il $17.99; lib bdg $18.89

Grades: 3 4 5   92
1. Composers 2. Puppets and puppet plays
ISBN 978-0-06-072674-4; 0-06-072674-1; 978-0-06-072676-8 lib bdg; 0-06-072676-8 lib bdg

LC 2008-10487

"Stanley takes a look at one of the Western world's most celebrated prodigies, wee Wolfgang Mozart. . . . [Stanley] manages a neat overview of her subject's life in surprisingly few pages. . . . The illustrations treat the proceedings as a marionette show performed by the famous Salzberg Marionettes." Bull Cent Child Books

Includes bibliographical references

Weeks, Marcus. **Mozart;** the boy who changed the world with his music. [by] Marcus Weeks. National Geographic 2007 64p il map (World history biographies) $17.95; lib bdg $27.90

Grades: 5 6 7 8   **92**
1. Composers
ISBN 978-1-4263-0002-8; 1-4263-0002-6; 978-1-4263-0003-5
lib bdg; 1-4263-0003-4 lib bdg

LC 2006020783

An introduction to the life and music of the composer and musician Mozart.

This "visually appealing [title is] packed with excellent photographs and reproductions, interesting sidebars, and have a time line running along the bottom of every page. . . . [The book is] useful, well-written." SLJ

Includes bibliographical references

Muir, John, 1838-1914

Lasky, Kathryn. **John** Muir; America's first environmentalist. illustrated by Stan Fellows. Candlewick Press 2006 41p il $16.99
Grades: 3 4 5   **92**
1. Authors 2. Naturalists 3. Writers on nature
ISBN 0-7636-1957-4

This is a biography of the naturalist and author of Stickeen (1909), My First Summer in the Sierra (1911), and The Yosemite (1912). Bibliography. "Intermediate." (Horn Book)

"Lasky's clear prose quotes liberally from diary entries Muir recorded. . . . True to Muir's vision, Fellows' spacious double-page watercolors show the beauty of the wide landscapes in storm and sunshine as well as the tiny details in a single meadow." Booklist

Includes bibliographical references

Wadsworth, Ginger. **Camping** with the president; illustrated by Karen Dugan. Calkins Creek 2009 32p il $16.95
Grades: 3 4 5   **92**
1. Authors 2. Governors 3. Presidents 4. Naturalists 5. Vice-presidents 6. Environmental movement 7. National parks and reserves 8. Writers on nature 9. Nobel laureates for peace 10. Presidents -- United States 11. Yosemite National Park (Calif.)
ISBN 978-1-59078-497-6; 1-59078-497-9

LC 2008024155

"Inspired by conservationist John Muir's nature essays, President Theodore Roosevelt traveled west, visiting national parks and learing more about their resources. Wadsworth's well written, lively account highlights the pair's 1903 exploration of the Yosemite wilderness, as well as America's early conservation movement, in an accessible and engaging picture book for older readers. Dugan's abundant, intricately rendered watercolors portray the stunning vistas and wildlife and are set against white backgrounds." Booklist

Includes bibliographical references

Murphy, Lizzie, 1894-1964

McCully, Emily Arnold, 1939- **Queen** of the diamond; the Lizzie Murphy story. Emily Arnold McCully. Farrar, Straus & Giroux 2015 32 p. color illustrations (hardback) $17.99
Grades: K 1 2 3 4   **92**
1. Baseball players 2. Women baseball players -- United States 3. Baseball players -- United States -- Biography
ISBN 0374300070; 9780374300074

LC 2014010987

This book by Emily Arnold McCully focuses on the early life of semi-professional baseball player Lizzie Murphy. "Lizzie Murphy was good at baseball. In fact, she was better than most of the boys. But she was born in 1900, and back then baseball was not a game for girls. Lizzie practiced with her brother anyway, and then she talked her way onto the local boys' team, first as a batboy, then as a player." (Publisher's note)

"Realistic drawings in acrylic ink reflect the attire of the times, particularly Murphy in her feminine dresses. The scenes that show her be-

ing shunned and then gradually accepted by the boys are particularly well done. The dialogue-heavy narrative and subject matter will easily appeal to readers." SLJ

Includes bibliographical references

Naismith, James, 1861-1939

Wyckoff, Edwin Brit. The **man** who invented basketball; the genius of James Naismith. Edwin Brit Wyckoff. Enslow Elementary 2014 48 p. ill. (some col.), col. map (alk. paper) $23.93
Grades: 2 3 4   **92**
1. Basketball -- History
ISBN 0766041425; 9780766041424

Genius inventors and their great ideas

This book, by Edwin Brit Wyckoff, focuses on James Naismith, a "Canadian-American sports coach and innovator. He invented the sport of basketball in 1891 and is often credited with introducing the first football helmet. He wrote the original basketball rulebook, founded the University of Kansas basketball program, and lived to see basketball adopted as an Olympic . . . sport." (Publisher's note)

Includes bibliographical references and index

Nakahama, Manjirō, 1827-1898

★ Blumberg, Rhoda. **Shipwrecked!**: the true adventures of a Japanese boy. HarperCollins Pubs. 2000 80p il map hardcover o.p. pa $7.99
Grades: 5 6 7 8   **92**
1. Survival after airplane accidents, shipwrecks, etc. 2. Interpreters 3. Japan -- History 4. Japan -- Foreign relations -- United States 5. United States -- Foreign relations -- Japan
ISBN 0-688-17484-1; 0-688-17485-X pa

LC 99-86664

In 1841, rescued by an American whaler after a terrible shipwreck leaves him and his four companions castaways on a remote island, fourteen-year-old Manjiro learns new laws and customs as he becomes the first Japanese person to set foot in the United States

"Exemplary in both her research and writing, Blumberg hooks readers with anecdotes that astonish without sensationalizing, and she uses language that's elegant and challenging, yet always clear. Particularly notable is the well-chosen reproductions of original artwork." Booklist

Includes bibliographical references

Napoleon I, Emperor of the French, 1769-1821

Burleigh, Robert. **Napoleon**; the story of the little corporal. Abrams Books for Young Readers 2007 43p il map $18.95
Grades: 4 5 6 7   **92**
1. Emperors 2. France -- Kings and rulers 3. France -- History -- 1799-1815
ISBN 978-0-8109-1378-3; 0-8109-1378-X

LC 2006-23610

"Burleigh's straightforward style and clear focus make accessible this account of the rapid rise and fall of the skilled military leader and emperor of France. The period artwork, accompanied by helpful captions, enhances the cleanly designed presentation." Horn Book Guide

Neruda, Pablo, 1904-1973

★ Brown, Monica. **Pablo** Neruda; poet of the people. illustrations by Julie Paschkis. Henry Holt and Co. 2011 un il
Grades: PreK   **92**
1. Poets 2. Authors 3. Diplomats 4. Novelists 5. Poets, Chilean 6. Nobel laureates for peace 7. Nobel laureates for literature
ISBN 080509198X; 9780805091984

LC 2010025320

This is a picture-book introduction to the Chilean poet. "Primary, intermediate." (Horn Book)

"This gentle tribute to Chilean poet Neruda explores his formative experiences, from searching for 'beetles and birds' eggs' in the forest to discovering his love for books. . . . Brown and Paschkis paint a compelling portrait of a man who saw the world as a joyful, complex, and beautiful poem waiting to be unveiled." Publ Wkly

Includes bibliographical references

Newton, Isaac Sir, 1642-1727

Hollihan, Kerrie Logan. **Isaac** Newton and physics for kids; his life and ideas with 21 activities. Chicago Review Press 2009 131p il map pa $16.95

Grades: 4 5 6 7   92

1. Physicists 2. Scientists 3. Mathematicians 4. Writers on science

ISBN 978-1-55652-778-4 pa; 1-55652-778-0 pa

LC 2008048635

"Hollihan introduces readers to the scientific brilliance, as well as the social isolation, of this giant figure, blending a readable narrative with an attractive format that incorporates maps, diagrams, historical photographs, and physics activities." Booklist

Includes bibliographical references

★ Krull, Kathleen. **Isaac** Newton; illustrated by Boris Kulikov. Viking 2006 126p il (Giants of science) $15.99

Grades: 5 6 7 8   92

1. Physicists 2. Scientists 3. Mathematicians 4. Writers on science

ISBN 0-670-05921-8

LC 2005017741

This "profiles Sir Isaac Newton, the secretive, obsessive, and brilliant English scientist who invented calculus, built the first reflecting telescope, developed the modern scientific method, and discerned many of our laws of physics and optics. . . . The lively, conversational style will appeal to readers. . . . Kulikov's humorous pen-and-ink drawings complement the lighthearted text of this fascinating introduction." Booklist

Steele, Philip. **Isaac** Newton; the scientist who changed everything. [by] Philip Steele. National Geographic Society 2007 64p il map (World history biographies) $17.95; lib bdg $27.90

Grades: 4 5 6 7   92

1. Physicists 2. Scientists 3. Mathematicians 4. Writers on science

ISBN 978-1-4263-0114-8; 978-1-4263-0115-5 lib bdg

LC 2006020772

"The cradle-to-grave text includes vivid descriptions of Newton's youth. . . . The dynamic format is a draw; numerous mostly archival images . . . and a time-line border add interest and cultural context on each spacious page." Booklist

Includes bibliographical references

Nezahualcóyotl, King of Texcoco, 1402-1472

★ Serrano, Francisco. The **poet** king of Tezcoco; a great leader of Ancient Mexico. illustrated by Pablo Serrano; biography translated and adapted by Trudy Balch; poetry translated by Jo Anne Engelbert. Groundwood Books/House of Anansi Press 2007 35p il $18.95

Grades: 4 5 6 7   92

1. Aztecs 2. Kings 3. Mexico -- History

ISBN 978-0-88899-787-6; 0-88899-787-6

"In the fifteenth century, the land where Mexico City now sprawls was a vast, green kingdom called Tezcoco. This . . . introduces one of Tezcoco's greatest rulers, a Toltec royal named Nezahualcoyotl. . . . The folk-art inspired illustrations echo the area's artistic traditions with beautiful patterning and symbolic imagery and flat , simplified characters reminiscent of hieroglyphics. Groundbreaking in its coverage of exciting history, this book offers details that are rarely presented to young people." Booklist

Nightingale, Florence, 1820-1910

Demi, 1942- **Florence** Nightingale; Demi. Henry Holt and Co 2014 40 p. color illustrations (hardback) $17.99

Grades: 2 3 4 5   92

1. Nurses 2. Nurses -- England -- Biography

ISBN 0805097295; 9780805097290

LC 2013030801

Author Demi presents a "picture book biography of Florence Nightingale [which] portrays the story of Florence's life and explores the long-lasting effects of her career. Nightingale revolutionized the world of medicine by emphasizing cleanliness, food that was hot and nutritious, and organization in hospitals. What began as an attempt to make army hospitals safer and more effective became a lifelong mission, and remains relevant today." (Publisher's note)

"This biography offers a clear, concise telling of Nightingale's story, illustrated with Demi's spare, appealing artwork. Graceful fine-line drawings are warmed with tints of color and graced with patterns where appropriate." Booklist

Includes bibliographical references

Gorrell, Gena K. **Heart** and soul: the story of Florence Nightingale. Tundra Bks. 2000 146p il map hardcover o.p. pa $11.95

Grades: 5 6 7 8   92

1. Nurses 2. Nonfiction writers

ISBN 0-88776-494-0; 0-88776-703-6 pa

A biography of the 19th century English woman known as the founder of modern nursing

"This highly readable and well-researched biography does an excellent job of integrating the social and medical conditions of Nightingale's time. . . . Enlivening the narrative are black-and-white reproductions of drawings . . . and period photographs." SLJ

Includes bibliographical references

Nimoy, Leonard

Michelson, Richard. **Fascinating**; the life of Leonard Nimoy. by Richard Michelson; illustrated by Edel Rodriguez. Alfred A. Knopf 2016 40 p. color illustrations $17.99; (ebook) $53.97

Grades: 1 2 3 4   92

1. Actors -- United States -- Biography 2. Actors -- United States -- Biography

ISBN 9781101933305; 9781101933312; 9781101933329

LC 2015029967

Sydney Taylor Honor Book for Young Readers (2017)

This children's biography, by Richard Michelson, illustrated by Edel Rodriguez, tells how "Leonard [Nimoy] reached for the stars . . . and caught them. He moved to Hollywood, where he took acting lessons, and drove a taxi and took every role he could get. He worked hard, learned his lines, showed up on time, and studied his craft. Until one day he was offered the role of an alien science officer on a new TV show called 'Star Trek.'" (Publisher's note)

"Michelson's text is warm and anecdotal. Rodriguez's unfussy illustrations, in sepia browns and out-of-this-world blues, reflect both the time period and the Trekkie universe." Horn Book

Nixon, Richard M. (Richard Milhous), 1913-1994

★ Aronson, Billy. **Richard** M. Nixon; [by] Billy Aronson. Marshall Cavendish Benchmark 2007 96p il (Presidents and their times) lib bdg $22.95

Grades: 5 6 7 8   92

1. Presidents 2. Vice-presidents 3. Senators 4. Nonfiction writers 5. Members of Congress 6. Presidents -- United States

ISBN 978-0-7614-2428-4

LC 2006013839

Aronson "is able to paint a picture so full that readers will come away feeling that they know the man and understand at least some of the forces that shaped him. . . . The narrative moves chronologically, marching through the war years, Nixon's tenure in Congress and as vice-president, his presidential loss to JFK, his successful efforts to remake himself as a politician, and his years as president. . . . The typeface is clear, the photographs are well chosen." Booklist

Includes glossary and bibliographical references

Noguchi, Isamu, 1904-1988

Hale, Christy. The **East**-West house; Noguchi's childhood in Japan. Lee & Low Books 2009 un il $17.95

Grades: 3 4 5 6   **92**

1. Artists 2. Sculptors 3. Japanese Americans 4. Industrial designers

ISBN 978-1-60060-363-1; 1-60060-363-7

LC 2008053728

"The mixed-media collage illustrations reflect the blend of East and West. . . . Thoroughly documented and heavily reliant on primary sources. . . . An original and thought-provoking addition to biography or art collections." SLJ

Nuñez Cabeza de Vaca, Alvar, 16th cent.

Lourie, Peter. **On** the Texas trail of Cabeza de Vaca; 1st ed.; Boyds Mills Press 2008 48p il map $17.95

Grades: 4 5 6 7   **92**

1. Explorers 2. Historians 3. Travel writers 4. Texas -- History 5. Mexico -- History 6. Government officials 7. America -- Exploration 8. Colonial administrators

ISBN 978-1-59078-492-1; 1-59078-492-8

LC 2007049180

"In 1527, Governor Pánfilo de Narváez sailed westward from Spain to explore the land that stretched between present-day Florida and Mexico, colonizing and conquering. With him, as his treasurer and sheriff, was Cabeza de Vaca. . . . He [returned] with a wealth of information, codified in La Relación , his account of his experience. Then, 475 years later, Lourie set out to follow Cabeza de Vaca's trail through Texas. . . . This well-researched, beautifully composed book is the result. Using primary sources and period reproductions as well as the author's experiences and contemporary pictures, it highlights historical information within the context of current circumstances. Beautifully placed photos, reproductions, maps, and sidebars enhance the fluid text." SLJ

Includes bibliographical references

O'Keeffe, Georgia, 1887-1986

Bryant, Jennifer. **Georgia's** bones; [illustrated by] Bethanne Anderson. Eerdmans Books for Young Readers 2005 32p il $16

Grades: K 1 2 3   **92**

1. Artists 2. Painters 3. Women artists 4. Artists -- United States

ISBN 0-8028-5217-3

LC 2004-6800

Artist Georgia O'Keeffe was interested in the shapes she saw around her, from her childhood on a Wisconsin farm to her adult life in New York City and New Mexico

"Bryant writes in spare, lyrical verse, honoring her subject's idiosyncratic impressions and precise observation of the natural world. . . . Cow skulls, southwestern landscapes, and oversize flowers are present and accounted for, but the swooping brushstrokes and earthy textures are unmistakably Andersen's own." Booklist

Rodriguez, Rachel. **Through** Georgia's eyes; illustrated by Julie Paschkis. Henry Holt and Co. 2006 un il $16.95

Grades: K 1 2 3   **92**

1. Artists 2. Painters 3. Women artists 4. Artists -- United States

ISBN 978-0-8050-7740-7; 0-8050-7740-5

LC 2005012479

"Rodríguez gently tells this inspirational artist's story . . . with quiet simplicity. . . . Using short, strong sentences and phrases, the author emphasizes the artist's creative force. Paschkis extends the words with the visual simplicity of colorful, cut-paper collages." SLJ

Winter, Jeanette. **My** name is Georgia; a portrait. Harcourt Brace & Co. 1998 un il $16; pa $7

Grades: K 1 2 3   **92**

1. Artists 2. Painters 3. Women artists 4. Artists -- United States

ISBN 0-15-201649-X; 0-15-204597-X pa

LC 97-7087

This book on Georgia O'Keeffe "follows the artist's journey from home to school in Chicago, to New York, to Texas, and back to New York, . . . and finally to New Mexico. . . . Ages nine to twelve." (Horn Book)

"Winter mirrors the artist's stark imagery and strong personality in spare, poetic text and folk art—inspired illustrations." Publ Wkly

Includes bibliographical references

Oakley, Annie, 1860-1926

Wills, Charles A. **Annie** Oakley: a photographic story of a life; [by] Chuck Wills. DK Pub. 2007 128p il (DK biography) $14.99

Grades: 4 5 6 7   **92**

1. Entertainers 2. Marksmen

ISBN 978-0-7566-2986-1

A biography of the sharp-shooter in Buffalo Bill's Wild West Show, from her humble Quaker heritage, her childhood filled with poverty and abuse, to her rise to international fame.

"This highly readable book has a rich layout of photographs and illustrations on every spread." SLJ

Includes bibliographical references

Obama, Barack, 1961-

Abramson, Jill. **Obama**; the historic journey. Young reader's ed.; Callaway 2009 94p il map $24.95

Grades: 5 6 7 8   **92**

1. Lawyers 2. Presidents 3. Racially mixed people 4. Senators 5. State legislators 6. Nobel laureates for peace 7. Presidents -- United States 8. African Americans -- Biography

ISBN 978-0-670-01208-4; 0-670-01208-4

LC 2009-5051

"This scaled down, teen-friendly version of The New York Times's adult biography is geared for middle school students. Containing many of the same photos, it provides a brief overview of the President's life, information that has been revealed over the election year and during his administration. . . . Its allure is in the many photographs with captions, sidebars, speech quotes, and charts. The book is nicely organized. The writing is direct and simple, explaining things such as convention delegates. . . . The book should entice young readers to explore his life further." Voice Youth Advocates

Feinstein, Stephen. **Barack** Obama. Enslow Publishers 2008 24p il map por (African-American heroes) lib bdg $21.26

Grades: K 1 2 3   **92**

1. Lawyers 2. Presidents 3. Racially mixed people 4. Senators 5. State legislators 6. Nobel laureates for peace 7. Presidents -- United States 8. African Americans -- Biography

ISBN 978-0-7660-2893-7 lib bdg; 0-7660-2893-3 lib bdg

LC 2007036363

This is a "slim introduction to the [president] that begins with his childhood in Hawaii and Indonesia. Feinstein's upbeat text, divided into very short chapters, focuses on details that will capture kids' interest." Booklist

Includes bibliographical references

Grimes, Nikki. **Barack** Obama; son of promise, child of hope. illustrated by Bryan Collier. Simon & Schuster Books for Young Readers 2008 un il $16.99

Grades: 1 2 3 4   **92**

1. Lawyers 2. Presidents 3. Racially mixed people 4. Senators 5. State legislators 6. Nobel laureates for peace 7. Presidents -- United States 8. African Americans -- Biography

ISBN 1-4169-7144-0; 978-1-4169-7144-3

LC 2008-06245

This is a biography of the Illinois senator and Democratic Party 2008 presidential candidate. "Ages five to ten." (N Y Times Book Rev)

Who Obama "is and where he comes from is conveyed in beautifully poetic language [and] . . . the illustrator's impressive interpretation of the author's text takes the story to a more meaningful visual level for younger readers." Libr Media Connect

Includes bibliographical references

Kesselring, Susan. **Barack** Obama. Child's World 2010 24p il (Basic biographies) lib bdg $22.79

Grades: K 1 2   **92**

1. Lawyers 2. Presidents 3. Racially mixed people 4. Senators 5. State legislators 6. Nobel laureates for peace 7. Presidents -- United States 8. African Americans -- Biography

ISBN 978-1-60253-339-4; 1-60253-339-3

LC 2009029365

This "provides a clear description of the man's life before and during his presidency and outlines some of his duties, without delving into politics. The books' clear and relevant black-and-white and color photographs sport captions that aid understanding of the subject matter." SLJ

Includes bibliographical references

Weatherford, Carole Boston. **Obama**; only in America. illustrated by Robert Barrett. Marshall Cavendish Children 2010 un il $17.99

Grades: 2 3 4 5   **92**

1. Lawyers 2. Presidents 3. Racially mixed people 4. Senators 5. State legislators 6. Nobel laureates for peace 7. Presidents -- United States 8. African Americans -- Biography

ISBN 978-0-7614-5641-4; 0-7614-5641-4

LC 2009006338

"Weatherford puts an amazing amount of information about Barack Obama into a rhythmic text that is also wonderfully concise. Most of the major moments of Obama's life are here, both personal and professional. . . . The book makes Obama seem both larger than life yet also someone beset with struggles with which readers can identify. . . . Barrett's illustrations, oils on canvas, add a soft focus to the events." Booklist

Zeiger, Jennifer. **Barack** Obama; by Jennifer Zeiger. Children's Press 2012 64 p. ill. (chiefly col.), col. map (library binding) $30.00; (paperback) $8.95

Grades: 4 5 6   **92**

1. Presidents -- United States -- Biography 2. Racially mixed people -- United States -- Biography 3. Presidents -- United States -- Biography 4. Racially mixed people -- United States -- Biography

ISBN 0531230503; 0531281507; 9780531230503; 9780531281505

LC 2011031124

This book presents a "nonfiction account of President [Barack] Obama's life for middle school students. . . . The book includes many color photographs of the President as a young boy and young adult. It gives the details of his life in Indonesia and Hawaii and traces his ca-

reer up to the 2012 re-election campaign. His education is a focus of the biography and there is ample discussion of his educational career and how it has helped to shape him into the man he is today." (Children's Literature)

Includes bibliographical references (p. 61) and index.

Obama, Michelle

Brophy, David. **Michelle** Obama; meet the First Lady. by David Bergen Brophy. HarperCollins 2009 114p il $16.99; pa $6.99

Grades: 5 6 7 8   **92**

1. Lawyers 2. Spouses of presidents 3. Hospital administrators 4. African American women -- Biography 5. Presidents' spouses -- United States

ISBN 978-0-06-177991-6; 0-06-177991-1; 978-0-06-177990-9 pa; 0-06-177990-3 pa

A brief biography of Michelle Obama, wife of President Barack Obama

"The author . . . mixes personal data with information about the political process that brought the Obamas to the White House. . . . This biography is a must-have for all school libraries." Voice Youth Advocates

Includes glossary

Colbert, David. **Michelle** Obama; an American story. Houghton Mifflin Harcourt 2009 151p il $16

Grades: 5 6 7 8   **92**

1. Lawyers 2. Spouses of presidents 3. Hospital administrators 4. African American women -- Biography 5. Presidents' spouses -- United States

ISBN 978-0-547-24941-4; 0-547-24941-1

This biography delves into "the subject of The First Lady's family roots. . . . It offers a strong sense of who Obama was as a child, her solid upbringing, and her adult choices, all bolstered with numerous quotes from Obama and those who know her best. . . . Two sections of color photos and appended source notes for direct quotes complete this timely, highly readable biography." Booklist

Hopkinson, Deborah. **Michelle**; illustrated by A.G. Ford. Katherine Tegen Books 2009 un il $17.99; lib bdg $18.89

Grades: K 1 2 3   **92**

1. Lawyers 2. Spouses of presidents 3. Hospital administrators 4. African American women -- Biography 5. Presidents' spouses -- United States

ISBN 978-0-06-182739-6; 0-06-182739-8; 978-0-06-182743-3 lib bdg; 0-06-182743-6 lib bdg

LC 2009014551

This biography of the First Lady "touches on Michelle's childhood years in a loving working-class family, her academic accomplishments, courtship, marriage, careers and role as devoted mother and active supporter of her husband's presidential campaign. The straightforward, accessible text at times assumes dramatic overtones. . . . Ford's paintings offer likenesses of Michelle and her family, often capturing facial expressions and nuances of posture and gesture with uncanny realism. This warm, respectful portrait succeeds in presenting its subject as both inspirational and relatable." Publ Wkly

Kesselring, Susan. **Michelle** Obama. Child's World 2010 24p il (Basic biographies) lib bdg $22.79

Grades: PreK K 1   **92**

1. Lawyers 2. Spouses of presidents 3. Hospital administrators 4. African American women -- Biography 5. Presidents' spouses -- United States

ISBN 978-1-60253-343-1; 1-60253-343-1

LC 2009029597

This biography of the First Lady "pairs intelligent, brief text with abundant photos. Simple but never basic." Booklist

Includes bibliographical references

Odetta, 1930-2008

Alcorn, Stephen. **Odetta,** the queen of folk; poem by Samantha Thornhill; conceived and illustrated by Stephen Alcorn. Scholastic Press 2010 un il

Grades: K 1 2 3   92

1. Singers 2. Folk music 3. Folk musicians 4. African American women -- Biography

ISBN 0-439-92818-4; 978-0-439-92818-2

LC 2009-5104

"Thornhill's poem pays powerful tribute to the folk-singing legend, beginning with early experiences that shaped her music . . . and her first exposure to segregation when her family moved to Los Angeles. . . . Filled with stars, candles, lightning bolts, music notes, and angels, Alcorn's rousing compositions borrow from folk art traditions, religious imagery, graphic design, and 1960s album cover art, creating a rich tapestry that trumpets the power of this singular figure." Publ Wkly

Ohr, George E., 1857-1918

Greenberg, Jan. The **mad** potter; George E. Ohr, eccentric genius. Jan Greenberg and Sandra Jordan. Roaring Brook Press 2013 56 p. (hardcover : alk. paper) $17.99

Grades: 4 5 6 7 8   92

1. American pottery 2. Potters -- United States -- Biography 3. Art pottery, American -- Mississippi -- Biloxi

ISBN 159643810X; 9781596438101

LC 2012047601

Robert F. Sibert Honor Book (2014)

This children's book is a biography of American potter George E. Ohr. "Ohr's eccentricities and his penchant for self-promotion are clearly presented. . . . What makes a George E. Ohr vase sell at auction nowadays for $84,000, and is he really America's greatest art potter? Certainly his work is whimsical . . . vases tilting like leaning towers, a teapot with a spout like an open-mouthed serpent, and all manner of wrinkled, twisted and squashed vessels." (Kirkus Reviews)

Includes bibliographical references and index

Paganini, Nicolò, 1782-1840

Frisch, Aaron. **Dark** fiddler: the life and legend of Nicolo Paganini; [by] Aaron Frisch; illustrated by Gary Kelley. Creative Editions 2008 un il lib bdg $17.95

Grades: 3 4 5 6   92

1. Composers 2. Violinists

ISBN 978-1-56846-200-4 lib bdg; 1-56846-200-X lib bdg

"Readers may not be familiar with the name Paganini, but after one look at the dramatic cover, with the spectral violinist staring back, a slight smile on his lips, they will want to find out more. . . . The folksy tone of the narrative will draw kids close as the story of Paganini's life unfolds. All this is set against breathtaking, chalklike art." Booklist

Paige, Satchel, 1906-1982

★ Adler, David A. **Satchel** Paige; don't look back. written by David A. Adler; illustrated by Terry Widener. Harcourt 2006 un il $16

Grades: K 1 2 3   92

1. Baseball players 2. African American athletes 3. Baseball -- Biography

ISBN 978-0-15-205585-1; 0-15-205585-1

LC 2005026354

A brief illustrated biography of the baseball player who, after a long career in the Negro Leagues, joined the Cleveland Indians and became the first African American to pitch in the World Series.

"Widener's acrylic paintings elongate and exaggerate the figures, using a rubbery perspective and old-fashioned hues to great effect." Booklist

Includes bibliographical references

Palmer, Joseph, 1791-1875

Hyatt, Patricia Rusch. The **quite** contrary man; a true American tale. illustrated by Kathryn Brown. Abrams Books for Young Readers 2010 un il $16.95

Grades: K 1 2 3   92

1. Beards 2. Social reformers 3. New England -- History

ISBN 978-0-8109-4065-9; 0-8109-4065-5

LC 2009052211

In nineteenth century New England, Joseph Palmer flouts the law against wearing a beard and is accused by his fellow citizens of being unpatriotic and sinful, stubbornly refusing to shave even when he is sent to jail.

"Although these are serious themes, this picture book offers a positive story with a happy ending, and much of the tone is due to Brown's pleasant and well-designed illustrations in pen and ink and watercolor, which set the scenes helpfully and support the folksy language." Booklist

Park, Linda Sue, 1960-

Parker-Rock, Michelle. **Linda** Sue Park; an author kids love. Enslow Publishers 2009 48p il (Authors kids love) lib bdg $23.93

Grades: 3 4 5   92

1. Authors 2. Authors, American 3. Children's authors

ISBN 978-0-7660-3158-6 lib bdg; 0-7660-3158-6 lib bdg

LC 2008-44549

"Clearly written, [this] outstanding [biography provides] many interesting details about the [subject's] personal [life] and [includes] photos that enhance the [text]." SLJ

Includes glossary and bibliographical references

Parkhurst, Charley, 1812-1879

Kay, Verla. **Rough,** tough Charley; by Verla Kay; illustrated by Adam Gustavson. Tricycle Press 2007 un il $15.95

Grades: K 1 2 3   92

1. Male impersonators 2. Coach drivers 3. Women -- West (U.S.) 4. Frontier and pioneer life -- California

ISBN 978-1-58246-184-7; 1-58246-184-8

LC 2006026611

"Many folks thought they knew the real Charley Parkhurst (1812-1879): a scrappy orphan . . . who became one of the bravest, fastest, saltiest and most respected stagecoach drivers in Gold Country. . . . But everybody had Charley wrong, for . . . Charley had successfully disguised the fact that he was actually a woman. . . . Gustavson's . . . lush, realistic oil illustrations are a lavish counterpoint to Kay's spare verse, [and] are suffused with the romance and roughness of a bygone era." Publ Wkly

Parks, Gordon, 1912-2006

★ Weatherford, Carole Boston, 1956- **Gordon** Parks; how the photographer captured black and white America. Carole Boston Weatherford; illustrations by Jamey Christoph. Albert Whitman & Co. 2015 32 p. color illustrations $16.99

Grades: 1 2 3 4   92

1. Photography 2. African Americans -- Civil rights 3. African American photographers -- Biography 4. Photographers -- United States -- Biography

ISBN 0807530174; 9780807530177

LC 2014034300

NAACP Image Award: Outstanding Literary Work- Children (2016)

This book by Carole Boston Weatherford, illustrated by Jamey Christoph, profiles "Gordon Parks . . ., most famous for being the first black director in Hollywood. But before he made movies and wrote books, he was a poor African American looking for work. When he bought a camera, his life changed forever. . . . Gordon wanted to take a stand against the racism he observed. With his camera in hand, he found a way." (Publisher's note)

"Weatherford writes in the present tense with intensity, carefully choosing words that concisely evoke the man. Christoph's digitally rendered illustrations brilliantly present Parks' world thr ough strong linear images and montages of his photographs." Kirkus

Parks, Rosa, 1913-2005

Amoroso, Cynthia. **Rosa** Parks; by Cynthia Amoroso and Robert B. Noyed. Child's World 2010 24p il (Basic biographies) lib bdg $22.79

Grades: PreK K 1   **92**

1. Civil rights activists 2. African Americans -- Civil rights 3. African American women -- Biography 4. Montgomery (Ala.) -- Race relations

ISBN 978-1-60253-344-8; 1-60253-344-X

LC 2009029372

This biography of Rosa Parks "pairs intelligent, brief text with adundant photos. Simple but never basic." Booklist

Includes bibliographical references

★ Giovanni, Nikki, 1943- **Rosa**; illustrated by Bryan Collier. Henry Holt 2005 32p il $16.95

Grades: 3 4 5   **92**

1. African American women 2. Civil rights activists 3. African Americans -- Civil rights 4. African American women -- Biography

ISBN 0-8050-7106-7

A Caldecott Medal honor book, 2006

This book tells the story of Rosa Parks's "refusal to yield her seat to a white bus rider and that act's direct connection with the Montgomery bus boycott. . . . Ages six to nine." (Bull Cent Child Books)

"Paired very effectively with Giovanni's passionate, direct words, Collier's large watercolor-and-collage illustrations depict Parks as an inspiring force that radiates golden light, and also as part of a dynamic activist community." Booklist

★ Parks, Rosa. **Rosa** Parks: my story; by Rosa Parks with Jim Haskins. Dial Bks. 1992 192p il $17.99; pa $6.99

Grades: 5 6 7 8   **92**

1. Civil rights activists 2. African Americans -- Civil rights 3. African American women -- Biography 4. Montgomery (Ala.) -- Race relations

ISBN 0-8037-0673-1; 0-14-130120-1 pa

LC 89-1124

Rosa Parks describes her early life and experiences with race discrimination, and her participation in the Montgomery bus boycott and the civil rights movement

"A remarkable story, a record of quiet bravery and modesty, a document of social significance, a taut drama told with candor." Bull Cent Child Books

Pasteur, Louis, 1822-1895

Zamosky, Lisa. **Louis** Pasteur; founder of microbiology. Compass Point Books 2009 40p il map (Mission: Science) lib bdg $26.60

Grades: 4 5 6   **92**

1. Chemists 2. Scientists 3. Microbiologists 4. Writers on science

ISBN 978-0-7565-3962-7

LC 2008007726

This biography of the father of microbiology "does a good job of connecting the scientist's work to our lives today. . . . [The] book has a variety of graphics including diagrams, photos, and reproductions of paintings and sketches. [This volume is] a definite plus for a school library or the juvenile collection in a public library." Libr Media Connect

Includes glossary and bibliographical references

Patch, Sam, 1807-1829

Cummins, Julie. **Sam** Patch; daredevil jumper. [illustrated by Michael Allen Austin] Holiday House 2009 un il $16.95

Grades: PreK K 1 2   **92**

1. Stunt performers 2. Factory workers

ISBN 978-0-8234-1741-4; 0-8234-1741-7

LC 2007-34624

This "chronicles the short life of early-19th-century stuntman Sam Patch. . . . The conversational style briskly moves the tale from Sam's childhood jumping exploits to the showstopping stunts of his brief but world-famous career. . . . Austin's . . . sepia-infused acrylics set a tone alternating between whimsical and haunting. The dynamic illustrations make exaggerated use of light and perspective." Publ Wkly

Patrick, Saint, 373?-463?

DePaola, Tomie, 1934- **Patrick** : patron saint of Ireland. Holiday House 1992 un il lib bdg $16.95; pa $6.95

Grades: K 1 2 3   **92**

1. Saints 2. Christian saints 3. Missionaries

ISBN 0-8234-0924-4 lib bdg; 0-8234-1077-3 pa

LC 91-19417

Relates the life and legends of Patrick, the patron saint of Ireland

"The combination of book design, text, and illustration is suitably reverent but never saccharine; the whole is a well-executed treatment of an appealing subject." Horn Book

Paul, Les, 1915-2009

Wyckoff, Edwin Brit. **Electric** guitar man: the genius of Les Paul; [by] Edwin Brit Wyckoff. Enslow Elementary 2008 32p il (Genius at work!: great inventor biographies) lib bdg $22.60

Grades: 4 5 6   **92**

1. Inventors 2. Guitarists

ISBN 978-0-7660-2847-0 lib bdg; 0-7660-2847-X lib bdg

LC 2006034681

"Without the electronic guitar invented by Les Paul, music would never have been the same. In this biography of Paul's life and career, Edwin Brit Wyckoff shares how the rambunctious boy from Waukesha, Wisconsin, was propelled to stardom by his unrivaled playing ability and technological prowess." Publisher's note

Includes glossary and bibliographical references

Paulsen, Gary

Paulsen, Gary, 1939- **This** side of wild; mutts, mares, and laughing dinosaurs. Gary Paulsen. Simon & Schuster Books for Young Readers 2015 120 p. illustrations (hardcover) $16.99

Grades: 4 5 6 7 8   **92**

1. Human-animal relationships -- History 2. Human-animal relationships 3. Authors, American -- 20th century -- Biography

ISBN 1481451502; 9781481451505; 9781481451512

LC 2015004132

In this children's book, author Gary Paulsen shares "true stories about his relationship with animals, highlighting their compassion, intellect, intuition, and sense of adventure." (Publisher's note)

"For anyone who loves the natural world and excellent writing, this is a must-read." Booklist

Pavlov, Ivan Petrovich, 1849-1936

Saunders, Barbara R. **Ivan** Pavlov; exploring the mysteries of behavior. Enslow Publishers 2006 112p il por (Great minds of science) lib bdg $31.93

Grades: 5 6 7 8   **92**

1. Scientists 2. Behaviorism 3. Physiologists 4. Writers on medicine 5. Nobel laureates for physiology or medicine
ISBN 0-7660-2506-3

LC 2005031648

This is a biography of Russian scientist Ivan Pavlov, best known for his experiments with dogs, which were key to the development of behaviorism, and who won the 1904 Nobel Prize for his research on digestion

"The accessible [text has] an inviting, open format and [offers] many anecdotes. . . . Good-quality photos and illustrations complement the [narrative]." SLJ

Includes glossary and bibliographical references

Pavlova, Anna, 1881-1931

Snyder, Laurel. **Swan**; the life and dance of Anna Pavlova. by Laurel Snyder. Chronicle Books LLC 2014 52 p. color illustrations (alk. paper) $17.99

Grades: 1 2 3 4   **92**

1. Ballerinas 2. Ballerinas -- Russia (Federation) -- Biography
ISBN 1452118906; 9781452118901

LC 2013013706

In this book, by Laurel Snyder, illustrated by Julie Morstad, "young Anna's mother takes her to the ballet, and everything is changed. So begins the journey of a girl who will one day grow up to be the most famous prima ballerina of all time, inspiring legions of dancers after her: the brave, the generous, the transcendently gifted Anna Pavlova." (Publisher's note)

"An enchanting glimpse of a dancer whose name has come to be synonymous with her most famous role." SLJ

Peary, Marie Ahnighito, 1893-1978

Kirkpatrick, Katherine. **Snow** baby; the Arctic childhood of Admiral Robert E. Peary's daring daughter. [by] Katherine Kirkpatrick. Holiday House 2007 50p il map $16.95

Grades: 5 6 7 8   **92**

1. Admirals 2. Explorers 3. Arctic regions 4. Children of prominent persons
ISBN 0-8234-1973-8; 978-0-8234-1973-9

LC 2006-02016

This is a biography of Marie Peary, the daughter of the discoverer of the North Pole. Chronology. Bibliography. Index. "Grades four to seven." (Bull Cent Child Books)

"Born north of the Arctic Circle in 1893, Marie Ahnighito Peary published her own version of her youth in 1934 (The Snowbaby's Own Story), on which this book is based. Kirkpatrick's engaging text captures the girl's adventurous spirit and the opportunities that her father's life as an explorer presented, as well as her love of the North and her Inuit friends." SLJ

Peary, Robert Edwin, 1856-1920

Kirkpatrick, Katherine. **Snow** baby; the Arctic childhood of Admiral Robert E. Peary's daring daughter. [by] Katherine Kirkpatrick. Holiday House 2007 50p il map $16.95

Grades: 5 6 7 8   **92**

1. Admirals 2. Explorers 3. Arctic regions 4. Children of prominent persons
ISBN 0-8234-1973-8; 978-0-8234-1973-9

LC 2006-02016

This is a biography of Marie Peary, the daughter of the discoverer of the North Pole. Chronology. Bibliography. Index. "Grades four to seven." (Bull Cent Child Books)

"Born north of the Arctic Circle in 1893, Marie Ahnighito Peary published her own version of her youth in 1934 (The Snowbaby's Own Story), on which this book is based. Kirkpatrick's engaging text captures the girl's adventurous spirit and the opportunities that her father's life as an explorer presented, as well as her love of the North and her Inuit friends." SLJ

Peet, Bill

★ Peet, Bill. **Bill** Peet: an autobiography. Houghton Mifflin 1989 190p il hardcover o.p. pa $15

Grades: 4 5 6 7   **92**

1. Artists 2. Authors 3. Illustrators 4. Authors, American 5. Children's authors 6. Walt Disney Productions
ISBN 0-395-50932-7; 0-395-68982-1 pa

LC 88-37067

A Caldecott Medal honor book, 1990

"Every page of this oversized book is illustrated with Peet's unmistakable black-and-white drawings of himself and the people, places, and events described in the text. Familiar characters from his books and movies appear often." SLJ

Pelé, 1940-

★ Cline-Ransome, Lesa. **Young** Pele; soccer's first star. illustrated by James E. Ransome. Schwartz & Wade Bks. 2007 un il

Grades: K 1 2 3   **92**

1. Soccer players 2. Soccer -- Biography 3. Soccer
ISBN 0-375-83599-7; 0-375-93599-1 lib bdg; 978-0-375-83599-5; 978-0-375-93599-2 lib bdg

This is a biography of the soccer player and author of My Life and the Beautiful Game (1977). "Primary." (Horn Book)

"With handsome oil paintings and a stirring story, this picture-book biography will first grab children with its action. Just as exciting, though, is the account of Brazilian-born Pelé's personal struggle—his amazing rise from poverty to international soccer stardom." Booklist

Pele. **For** the love of soccer! illustrated by Frank Morrison. Disney-Hyperion Books 2010 un il $16.99

Grades: K 1 2 3   **92**

1. Soccer 2. Athletes 3. Soccer players
ISBN 978-1-4231-1538-0; 1-4231-1538-4

LC 2009-15890

"In a spare narrative enlivened by typography of various sizes and colors, soccer legend Pele underscores his lifelong passion for soccer. . . . Following two time lines simultaneously, Morrison's . . . energetic, fluid paintings spotlight Pele's soccer moves beside those of a young player today. . . . Though the narrative links the two players throughout, a warmhearted ending ties their stories together visually, as Pele signs a ball for the boy." Publ Wkly

Penrose, Antony

Penrose, Antony. The **boy** who bit Picasso. Abrams Books for Young Readers 2011 47p il $16.95

Grades: 3 4 5   **92**

1. Artists 2. Painters 3. Artists, French 4. Archivists 5. Children of prominent persons
ISBN 978-0-8109-9728-8; 0-8109-9728-2

LC 2010009444

Presents a story of Tony, the son of photographer Lee Miller and painter-writer Sir Roland Penrose, who shares his childhood memories of his special friend—a world-famous artist by the name of Pablo Picasso.

"Numerous b&w photographs appear, along with original drawings by contemporary children. Reproductions of Picasso's works demonstrate the influence Penrose's family had on Picasso's art. . . . It's a fascinating and highly personal vision of the artist." Publ Wkly

Perón, Eva, 1919-1952

Favor, Lesli J. **Eva** Peron. Marshall Cavendish Benchmark 2010 112p il (Leading women) $39.93

Grades: 5 6 7 8   92

1. Women politicians 2. Argentina -- History 3. Spouses of presidents

ISBN 978-0-7614-4962-1; 0-7614-4962-0

A biography of the influential and admired First Lady of Argentina. Includes bibliographical references

Peterson, Adrian

Sandler, Michael. **Adrian** Peterson. Bearport Pub. 2010 24p il map (Football heroes making a difference) lib bdg $22.61

Grades: 2 3 4   92

1. Football players 2. Football -- Biography

ISBN 978-1-936087-59-4 lib bdg; 1-936087-59-6 lib bdg

LC 2009033352

Looks at the life and accomplishments of the star running back of the Minnesota Vikings.

Includes glossary and bibliographical references

Peterson, Roger Tory, 1908-1996

Thomas, Peggy. **For** the birds: the life of Roger Tory Peterson; illustrated by Laura Jacques. Calkins Creek 2011 il $16.95

Grades: 2 3 4 5   92

1. Birds 2. Artists 3. Naturalists 4. Illustrators 5. Ornithologists 6. Writers on nature 7. Artists -- United States

ISBN 978-1-59078-764-9; 1-59078-764-1

"Intrigued from childhood by the wildlife around him, Roger Tory Peterson grew up to publish, in 1934, the first pocket-sized bird guide. . . . Using language and imagery relevant to her topic, Thomas . . . provides a lively chronological narrative. . . . Jacques' hyper-realistic mixed-media paintings have sharp edges and blended shadows, giving the appearance of acylics and collage digitally combined. . . . An excellent addition to the 'sense of wonder' shelf." Kirkus

Picasso, Pablo, 1881-1973

Jacobson, Rick. **Picasso**; soul on fire. [by] Rick Jacobson; illustrated by Laura Fernandez & Rick Jacobson. Tundra Books 2004 un il $15.95; pa $8.95

Grades: 3 4 5   92

1. Artists 2. Painters 3. Artists, French

ISBN 978-0-88776-599-5; 0-88776-599-8; 978-1-77049-263-9 pa; 1-77049-263-1 pa

This is an introduction the life of the artist, exploring his influences, selected works, and his creative processes.

"Written in simple, clear language. . . . The softly radiant oil paintings are mostly full page and enhance the enjoyment of the book. . . . This eloquent tribute will serve as an introduction to Picasso and to an artist's inspirations." SLJ

Penrose, Antony. The **boy** who bit Picasso. Abrams Books for Young Readers 2011 47p il $16.95

Grades: 3 4 5   92

1. Artists 2. Painters 3. Artists, French 4. Archivists 5. Children of prominent persons

ISBN 978-0-8109-9728-8; 0-8109-9728-2

LC 2010009444

Presents a story of Tony, the son of photographer Lee Miller and painter-writer Sir Roland Penrose, who shares his childhood memories of his special friend—a world-famous artist by the name of Pablo Picasso.

"Numerous b&w photographs appear, along with original drawings by contemporary children. Reproductions of Picasso's works demonstrate the influence Penrose's family had on Picasso's art. . . . It's a fascinating and highly personal vision of the artist." Publ Wkly

Pickett, Bill, ca. 1860-1932

★ Pinkney, Andrea Davis. **Bill** Pickett, rodeo-ridin' cowboy; written by Andrea D. Pinkney; illustrated by Brian Pinkney. Harcourt Brace & Co. 1996 un il hardcover o.p. pa $7

Grades: K 1 2 3   92

1. Rodeos 2. Cowhands 3. Cowboys 4. African Americans -- Biography

ISBN 0-15-200100-X; 0-15-202103-5 pa

LC 95-35920

Describes the life and accomplishments of the son of a former slave whose unusual bulldogging style made him a rodeo star

"The story is told with verve, relish, and just enough of a cowboy twang, with Pinkney giving an excellent overview of the history of rodeos and black cowboys in a closing note. Husband Brian Pinkney's pictures, in his typical scratchboard technique, are well suited to the story, their lines and colors swirling with movement and excitement on the deep black surface." Booklist

Includes bibliographical references

Pike, Lip, 1845-1893

Michelson, Richard. **Lipman** Pike; America's first home run king. written by Richard Michelson; illustrated by Zachary Pullen. Sleeping Bear Press 2011 un il $16.95

Grades: 2 3 4   92

1. Baseball players 2. Jews -- Biography 3. Baseball -- Biography

ISBN 978-1-58536-465-7; 1-58536-465-7

LC 2010032367

This is a picture book biography of Lipman Pike, the son of Jewish immigrants from Holland, who became, in the 1850s, one of America's first professional baseball players.

"Michelson effortlessly hurtles the story through Lip's career . . . and baseball fans will be fascinated by the details. . . . Pullen's unmistakable, big-headed caricatures make this an ideal companion to Jonah Winter's You Never Heard of Sandy Koufax?! (2009)." Booklist

Pike, Zebulon Montgomery, 1779-1813

Green, Carl R. **Zebulon** Pike; courageous Rocky Mountain explorer. by William R. Sanford and Carl R. Green. Enslow Publishers 2013 48 p. ill. (library) $21.26; (paperback) $7.95

Grades: 5 6 7 8   92

1. Exploration 2. West (U.S.) -- Biography 3. West (U.S.) -- History -- To 1848 4. Explorers -- West (U.S.) -- Biography 5. West (U.S.) -- Discovery and exploration

ISBN 1464400954; 9780766040120; 9781464400957

LC 2011051629

This book by William R. Sanford is part of the Courageous Heroes of the American West series and looks at Zebulon Pike. "After the United States purchased the Louisiana Territory in 1803, the young nation needed brave pioneers to explore this vast uncharted land. Zebulon Pike . . . led an expedition across rolling prairies before arriving at the towering mountains" and being the first to explore the southern Rocky Mountains. (Publisher's note)

Includes bibliographical references (p. 47) and index.

Pinchot, Gifford, 1865-1946

Hines, Gary. **Midnight** forests; a story of Gifford Pinchot and our national forests. illustrated by Robert Casilla. Boyds Mills Press 2005 un il $16.95

Grades: 3 4 5   **92**

1. Governors 2. Conservationists 3. Forests and forestry 4. Foresters

ISBN 1-56397-148-8

LC 2003-26876

"This picture-book biography introduces Gifford Pinchot, a wealthy young American who studied forestry in France and returned home to put his knowledge to good use in his own country. Appointed Secretary of Agriculture in 1898, he later joined forces with Theodore Roosevelt to turn 16 million acres into national forests. . . . Mirroring the quiet prose, the dignified pencil-and-watercolor illustrations depict Pinchot at work and in quiet contemplation." Booklist

Includes bibliographical references

Pippin, Horace, 1888-1946

Venezia, Mike. **Horace** Pippin; written and illustrated by Mike Venezia. Children's Press 2008 32p il (Getting to know the world's greatest artists) lib bdg $28

Grades: 3 4 5   **92**

1. Artists 2. Painters 3. African American artists 4. Artists -- United States

ISBN 978-0-531-18527-8 lib bdg; 0-531-18527-3 lib bdg

LC 2007016127

A biography of the African American artist best known for his paintings of life in America during slavery and the years of segregation.

"Though the [text is] simply written, [this title contains] a wealth of information. . . . [The book has] many reproductions of the [artist's] works as well as those of the masters who influenced [him]. To help illustrate his points, Venezia has incorporated his own cartoon-style illustrations." SLJ

Planck, Max, 1858-1947

Weir, Jane. **Max** Planck; revolutionary physicist. Compass Point Books 2009 40p il (Mission: science) lib bdg $26.60

Grades: 4 5 6   **92**

1. Physicists 2. Nobel laureates for physics

ISBN 978-0-7565-4073-9 lib bdg; 0-7565-4073-9 lib bdg

LC 2008-37622

Biography of the physicist Max Planck

Includes glossary and bibliographical references

Pocahontas, d. 1617

Brimner, Larry Dane. **Pocahontas**; bridging two worlds. Marshall Cavendish Benchmark 2009 41p il (American heroes) lib bdg $20.95

Grades: 2 3 4   **92**

1. Princesses 2. Powhatan Indians 3. Indian leaders 4. Virginia -- History 5. United States -- History -- 1600-1775, Colonial period

ISBN 978-0-7614-3065-0

This traces the life of Pocahontas from her birth in about 1595 to her death and considers the impact her life had on American history

This "concise and well-written [title covers] key biographical facts without overwhelming young readers, and [includes] captioned illustrations and reproductions, most of which are in color. Text is large, and the layout is age-appropriate and attractive, with wide margins." SLJ

Krull, Kathleen. **Pocahontas**; princess of the New World. [by] Kathleen Krull; pictures by David Diaz. Walker 2007 un il $16.95; lib bdg $17.85

Grades: K 1 2 3   **92**

1. Princesses 2. Powhatan Indians 3. Indian leaders 4. Virginia

-- History 5. United States -- History -- 1600-1775, Colonial period

ISBN 978-0-8027-9554-0; 0-8027-9554-4; 978-0-8027-9555-7 lib bdg; 0-8027-9555-2 lib bdg

LC 2006025723

This focuses on "the mischievous girl Matoaka, affectionately nicknamed Pocahontas. Primary sources provide the basic facts. . . . Diaz's cut-paper collage illustrations literally glow with vibrancy. He uses a palette of tropical colors—lemon yellow, lime green, ocean blue, and orange." SLJ

Pokiak-Fenton, Margaret

Jordan-Fenton, Christy. **Fatty** legs; a true story. [by] Christy Jordan-Fenton and Margaret Pokiak-Fenton; artwork by Liz Amini-Holmes. Annick Press 2010 104p il $21.95; pa $12.95

Grades: 3 4 5 6   **92**

1. Inuit 2. Authors 3. Artisans 4. Children's authors 5. Native Americans -- Canada 6. Inuit -- Canada

ISBN 978-1-55451-247-8; 1-55451-247-6; 978-1-55451-246-1 pa; 1-55451-246-8 pa

This book chronicles the unbreakable spirit of an Inuit girl while attending an Arctic residential school.

"Dark, expressive original paintings are dotted throughout the story and complement the serious tone of the narrative. . . . An excellent addition to any biography collection, the book is fascinating and unique, and yet universal in its message." SLJ

Followed by: A stranger at home (2011)

Jordan-Fenton, Christy. A **stranger** at home; a true story. [by] Christy Jordan-Fenton and Margaret Pokiak-Fenton; artwork by Liz Amini-Holmes. Annick Press 2011 124p il $21.95; pa $12.95

Grades: 3 4 5 6   **92**

1. Inuit 2. Authors 3. Artisans 4. Children's authors 5. Native Americans -- Canada

ISBN 978-1-55451-362-8; 1-55451-362-6; 978-1-55451-361-1 pa; 1-55451-361-8 pa

Sequel to: Fatty legs (2010)

"After two years in Catholic residential school, 10-year-old Olemaun returns to Tuktoyaktuk on Canada's Arctic coast, a stranger to her friends and family, unaccustomed to the food and clothing and unable to speak or understand her native language. Margaret Pokiak's story continues after the events of Fatty Legs (2010), which described her boarding-school experience. In this stand-alone sequel, she describes a year of reintegration into her Inuvialuit world. . . . Olemaun's spirit and determination shine through this moving memoir." Kirkus

Pollock, Jackson, 1912-1956

★ Greenberg, Jan. **Action** Jackson; [by] Jan Greenberg and Sandra Jordan; illustrated by Robert Andrew Parker. Roaring Brook Press 2002 32p il hardcover o.p. pa $6.95

Grades: 3 4 5 6   **92**

1. Artists 2. Painters 3. Artists -- United States

ISBN 0-7613-1682-5; 0-7613-2770-3 lib bdg; 0-312-36751-1 pa

LC 2002-6211

Imagines Jackson Pollock at work during the creation of one of his paint-swirled and splattered canvasses

"Using spare, lyrical words, the authors layer the exciting story with deep observations about what art is and how it is made. . . . Parker's scribbly pen-and-watercolor illustrations get the mood just right; the loose lines have an improvised, energetic quality that echoes Pollock's painting." Booklist

Includes bibliographical references

Polo, Marco, 1254-1323?

Demi. **Marco** Polo; written and illustrated by Demi. Marshall Cavendish 2008 un il map $19.99
Grades: 4 5 6 7   **92**
1. Explorers 2. Travelers 3. Voyages and travels 4. Travel writers
ISBN 978-0-7614-5433-5; 0-7614-5433-0
"This elegant, scholarly picture-book biography brings the explorer's fantastic journey to life. . . . Demi weaves her subject's own accounts into a seamless tale of wonder. . . . The delicately rendered illustrations, painted with Chinese inks and gold overlays . . . capture the exotic beauty of 13th-century China." SLJ

Markle, Sandra. **Animals** Marco Polo saw; an adventure on the Silk Road. illustrated by Daniela Jaglenka Terrazzini. Chronicle Books 2009 45p il $16.99
Grades: 3 4 5 6   **92**
1. Explorers 2. Travelers 3. Voyages and travels 4. Travel writers 5. Animals -- Asia 6. Asia -- Description and travel
ISBN 978-0-8118-5051-3; 0-8118-5051-X
         LC 2007053057
"This intriguing book discusses generally agreed-upon details of Marco Polo's explorations in Mongolia and the Far East, and speculates about the moths, jackals, van cats, zebu, oxen, Persian lions, snow cats, and camels he may have met along the way. . . . The text is enhanced by color, mixed-media illustrations that occupy one page or the top half of each spread. . . . A useful introduction to 13th-century history." SLJ

McCarty, Nick. **Marco** Polo; the boy who traveled the medieval world. National Geographic 2006 64p il map (World history biographies) $17.95; lib bdg $27.90
Grades: 5 6 7 8   **92**
1. Explorers 2. Travelers 3. Voyages and travels 4. Travel writers
ISBN 0-7922-5893-2; 0-7922-5894-0 lib bdg
A biography of the Italian explorer who became famous for his travels in Asia
Includes glossary and bibliographical references

Twist, Clint. **Marco** Polo; history's great adventurer. Candlewick Press 2011 un il (Historical notebooks) $19.99
Grades: 5 6 7 8   **92**
1. Explorers 2. Travelers 3. Voyages and travels 4. Travel writers
ISBN 978-0-7636-5286-9; 0-7636-5286-5
         LC 2010040131
First published 2010 in the United Kingdom with title: Marco Polo; geographer of distant lands
"In this sumptuous scrapbook, excerpts from Marco Polo's own account of his travels are paired with beautiful maps, drawings, and illustrations. . . . This volume is well suited to browsing, and many readers will want to spend time poring over the many details." SLJ

Posada, Jose Guadalupe, 1852-1913

★ Tonatiuh, Duncan. **Funny** bones; Posada and his Day of the Dead calaveras. by Duncan Tonatiuh. Abrams Books for Young Readers 2015 40 p. colored illustrations (hbk.) $18.95
Grades: 2 3 4 5 6   **92**
1. Engravers 2. Mexican art 3. Day of the Dead 4. Human skeleton in art 5. Engravers -- Mexico -- Biography
ISBN 1419716476; 9781419716478
         LC 2014042319
Robert F. Sibert Informational Book Award (2016)
Pura Belpre Illustrator Honor Book (2016)
This book, by Duncan Tonatiuh, "tells the story of how the amusing calaveras—skeletons performing various everyday or festive activities—came to be. They are the creation of Mexican artist José Guada-

lupe (Lupe) Posada (1852-1913). In a country that was not known for freedom of speech, he first drew political cartoons. . . . [B]ut he is best known today for his calavera drawings. They have become synonymous with Mexico's Día de los Muertos (Day of the Dead) festival." (Publisher's note)
"This exceptional picture-book biography profiles Mexican artist José Guadalupe Posada (1852-1913), who is remembered primarily for his portrayal of calaveras, the droll skeletons prominent in Día de Muertos (Day of the Dead) celebrations. Posada, who loved to draw as a child, later discovered printmaking, the art form that would shape his career. . . . The final scene, a witty, updated version of grinning calaveras, depicts them as young people today. Playful but informative, this picture book offers a fascinating introduction to the artist and his work." Booklist

Potter, Beatrix, 1866-1943

Hopkinson, Deborah. **Beatrix** Potter and the unfortunate tale of a borrowed guinea pig; by Deborah Hopkinson; illustrated by Charlotte Voake. Schwartz & Wade Books 2015 44 p. color illustrations $17.99
Grades: PreK K 1 2 3   **92**
1. English authors -- Biography 2. Authors, English -- 20th century -- Biography
ISBN 9780385373258; 9780385373265
         LC 2014010931
This book, by Deborah Hopkinson, illustrated by Charlotte Voake, "takes readers back to Victorian England and the home of budding young artist and animal lover Beatrix Potter. When Beatrix brings home her neighbor's pet guinea pig so that she can practice painting it, well . . . it dies! Now what?" (Publisher's note)
"Hopkinson's jesting tone combines false grandeur with a note of regret, and Voake's (Ginger) breezy watercolors suggest Beatrix's combination of curiosity and nonchalance. Sensitive souls will feel for Beatrix's victims, even as this diverting narrative sheds light on her childhood fascinations." Pub Wkly

Powell, Barbara Johns, 1935-1991

Kanefield, Teri, 1960- The **girl** from the tar paper school; Barbara Rose Johns and the advent of the civil rights movement. by Teri Kanefield. Abrams Books for Young Readers 2013 56 p. (alk. paper) $19.95
Grades: 5 6 7 8   **92**
1. Segregation in education 2. African Americans -- Civil rights 3. Civil rights -- United States -- History 4. Civil rights workers -- United States -- Biography 5. Virginia -- Race relations -- History -- 20th century 6. Women civil rights workers -- United States -- Biography 7. Segregation in education -- Virginia -- History -- 20th century 8. Civil rights movements -- United States -- History -- 20th century
ISBN 1419707965; 9781419707964
         LC 2012040990
This book, by Teri Kanefield, focuses on "Barbara Rose Johns. . . . In 1951, witnessing the unfair conditions in her racially segregated high school, Barbara Johns led a walkout . . . jumpstarting the American civil rights movement. Ridiculed by the white superintendent and school board . . . Barbara and her classmates held firm and did not give up. Her school's case went all the way to the Supreme Court and helped end segregation as part of Brown v. Board of Education." (Publisher's note)
"A heartfelt tribute to Barbara Rose Johns, a lesser-known heroine of the early civil rights movement. In 1951 Virginia, black Robert R. Moton High School and white Farmville High were separate but definitely not equal, and quiet Barbara and her classmates decided to strike. Profuse details, some extraneous, threaten to overtake the inspiring story of bravery." (Horn Book)
Includes bibliographical references and index

Powell, John Wesley, 1834-1902

★ Ray, Deborah Kogan. **Down** the Colorado; John Wesley Powell, the one-armed explorer. Frances Foster Books/Farrar, Straus & Giroux 2007 un il $17

Grades: 3 4 5   92

    1. Explorers 2. Geologists 3. West (U.S.) -- Exploration 4. Colorado River (Colo.-Mexico)

    ISBN 0-374-31838-7; 978-0-374-31838-3

LC 2006-43994

"This picture-book biography traces the life of explorer John Wesley Powell, whose landmark journey in 1869 down the Colorado River made him a national hero. Each double-page spread combines text on one side describing an episode from Powell's life with a stunning, full-page illustration on the opposite side. . . . An exciting adventure story and an instructive account of the exploration of the West." Booklist

Presley, Elvis, 1935-1977

Christensen, Bonnie. **Elvis**; the story of the rock and roll King. Bonnie Christensen. Christy Ottaviano Books 2015 32 p. color illustrations (hardcover) $17.99

Grades: 1 2 3   92

    1. Singers -- Biography 2. Rock musicians -- United States -- Biography

    ISBN 0805094474; 9780805094473

LC 2014024990

"Elvis [Presley] was a shy kid who struggled to make friends and found comfort singing in church and learning guitar. While in high school, he continued his music but was often ridiculed by students. On a whim, he recorded a song for his mom's birthday at Sun Record Studios as part of a customer promotion. The studio loved it so much that they sent it to local record stations . . . and the rest is history." (Publisher's note)

"The inspired choice to use photocollage for the backgrounds imbues the singer's hardscrabble early years with tenderness, suggesting the nostalgia-tinged look of a 1940s postcard. Written in verse, the text is stripped down; refreshingly free of artifice, it's as soulful as one of the many songs the singer performed." SLJ

Includes bibliographical references

Collins, Terry. **Elvis**; a graphic novel. illustrated by Michele Melcher. Capstone Press 2011 32p il (Graphic library: American graphic) lib bdg $29.32; pa $7.95

Grades: 4 5 6 7   92

    1. Actors 2. Singers 3. Rock musicians 4. Biographical graphic novels

    ISBN 978-1-4296-5476-0 lib bdg; 1-4296-5476-7 lib bdg; 978-1-4296-6266-6 pa; 1-4296-6266-2 pa

LC 2010024847

In graphic novel format, explores the life of Elvis Presley and describes his return to stardom through his '68 Comeback Special.

"The illustrations are eye-catching and the narration is presented simply, yet compellingly. . . . Fact-filled, entertaining, and accessible." SLJ

Includes glossary and bibliographical references

Price, Leontyne

Weatherford, Carole Boston, 1956- **Leontyne** Price; voice of a century. by Carole Boston Weatherford; illustrated by Raul Colon. Alfred A. Knopf 2014 40 p. color illustrations (hardcover) $17.99

Grades: K 1 2 3   92

    1. Opera 2. African American singers 3. Sopranos (Singers) --

United States -- Biography

    ISBN 0375856064; 9780375956065; 9780385392464; 9780375856068

LC 2013048068

Author Carole Boston Weatherford presents a "picture-book biography of iconic African American opera star Leontyne Price. While racism made it unlikely that a poor black girl from the South would pursue an opera career, Leontyne's wondrous voice and unconquerable spirit prevailed. Leontyne was soon recognized and celebrated for her leading roles at the Metropolitan Opera and around the world." (Publisher's note)

"The watercolor and pencil drawings seem to vibrate off the page, especially in the form of rainbow-colored musical notes that often envelop the work's subject. An author's note includes more information on other singers for whom Price paved the way." SLJ

Quimby, Harriet, 1875-1912

Moss, Marissa. **Brave** Harriet; the first woman to fly the English Channel. illustrated by C.F. Payne. Silver Whistle Bks. 2001 un il $16

Grades: K 1 2 3   92

    1. Air pilots 2. Women air pilots 3. English Channel 4. Aeronautics -- Flights 5. Women air pilots -- United States -- Biography

    ISBN 0-15-202380-1

LC 99-50463

The first American woman to have received a pilot's license describes her April 1912 solo flight across the English Channel, the first such flight by any woman. "Ages five to nine." (Bull Cent Child Books)

"Moss writes effectively in first person, putting readers in touch with Quimby's dreams and determination through direct, vivid language. The mixed media artwork combines paints and pastels in a series of beautiful scenes." Booklist

Whitaker, Suzanne. The **daring** Miss Quimby; by Suzanne George Whitaker; illustrated by Catherine Stock. Holiday House 2009 un il $16.95

Grades: 1 2 3   92

    1. Air pilots 2. Women air pilots

    ISBN 978-0-8234-1996-8; 0-8234-1996-7

LC 2008022569

A biography of Harriet Quimby, who, in 1911 "became the first American woman to earn a pilot's license. . . . Whitaker's spare, engaging narrative and Stock's lively watercolors bring this little-known female adventurer to life." Booklist

Reagan, Ronald, 1911-2004

Burgan, Michael. **Ronald** Reagan; a photographic story of a life. DK Pub. 2011 128p il (DK biography) $14.99; pa $5.99

Grades: 5 6 7 8   92

    1. Actors 2. Governors 3. Presidents 4. Presidents -- United States

    ISBN 978-0-7566-7075-7; 0-7566-7075-6; 978-0-7566-7074-0 pa; 0-7566-7074-8 pa

"Burgan's survey covers the basic facts in a positive but not propagandistic introduction. . . . Featuring small but clear photos or boxed commentary on every page and capped with a substantial . . . multimedia resource list, this compact volume . . . gives readers a broad picture of his achievements and a sense of his compelling personal style." Booklist

Includes bibliographical references

Marsico, Katie. **Ronald** Reagan. Marshall Cavendish Benchmark 2011 112p il (Presidents and their times) lib bdg $23.95

Grades: 5 6 7 8   92

    1. Actors 2. Governors 3. Presidents 4. Presidents -- United

States

ISBN 978-0-7614-4814-3; 0-7614-4814-4

LC 2009044590

This offers information on President Ronald Reagan and places him within his historical and cultural context. Also explored are the formative events of his times and how he responded.

"The abundant sidebars provide a good deal of background information that will be helpful to students. . . . Attractive . . . as well as useful." Booklist

Includes glossary and bibliographical references

Ream, Vinnie, 1847-1914

★ Fitzgerald, Dawn. **Vinnie** and Abraham; [by] Dawn Fitzgerald; illustrated by Catherine Stock. Charlesbridge 2007 un il lib bdg $15.95

Grades: 2 3 4   92

1. Artists 2. Sculptors 3. Women artists

ISBN 978-1-57091-658-8 lib bdg; 1-57091-658-6 lib bdg

LC 2006009033

"This picture-book biography presents Vinnie Ream as a young woman who transcended the conventions of her time through determination and a remarkable talent for sculpture. . . . After Lincoln's assassination, Congress commissioned her to sculpt a marble statue of the late president, which is still on display in the Capital rotunda. Fitzgerald's clearly written narrative portrays Vinnie as a hardworking, resolute person who succeeded through her own gifts and the help of others who believed in her. Stock's watercolor paintings light up the pages." Booklist

Rector, Sarah, 1902-1967

Bolden, Tonya. **Searching** for Sarah Rector; the richest black girl in America. Tonya Bolden. Abrams Books for Young Readers 2014 80 p. $21.95

Grades: 4 5 6 7 8   92

1. Rich 2. African American women 3. Creek County (Okla.) -- Biography 4. Creek Indians -- Oklahoma -- Creek County -- Biography 5. Women millionaires -- Oklahoma -- Creek County -- Biography 6. Petroleum industry and trade -- Oklahoma -- History -- 20th century 7. African American women -- Oklahoma -- Creek County -- Biography

ISBN 1419708465; 9781419708466

LC 2012039254

Author Tonya Bolden presents a biography of Sarah Rector, who "turned 18 in 1920, [and] the young black woman had amassed a fortune estimated at $1 million. In telling her story, Bolden makes a largely unknown portion of American history accessible to young readers. Rector and her family were 'Creek freedmen,' black citizens of the Creek Indian nation." (School Library Journal)

Includes bibliographical references and index

Reeves, Bass, 1838-1910

★ Nelson, Vaunda Micheaux. **Bad** news for outlaws; the remarkable life of Bass Reeves, deputy U.S. Marshal. illustrations by R. Gregory Christie. Carolrhoda Books 2009 un il lib bdg $17.95

Grades: 3 4 5   92

1. Law enforcement 2. Frontier and pioneer life 3. Oklahoma 4. Sheriffs 5. West (U.S.) -- History 6. African Americans -- Biography

ISBN 978-0-8225-6764-6 lib bdg; 0-8225-6764-4 lib bdg

LC 2008001188

ALA EMIERT Coretta Scott King Author Award (2010)

This is a biography of Bass Reeves, a former slave who was recruited as a deputy United States Marshal in the area that was to become Oklahoma. Chronology. Glossary. Bibliography. "Grades three to six." (Bull Cent Child Books)

"Kids will have no trouble loping into this picture-book biography. Born a slave, Reeves became one of the most feared and respected Deputy U.S. Marshals to tame the West. . . . The text, especially, gets into the tall-tale spirit of things. . . . An exciting subject captured with narrative panache and visual swagger." Booklist

Reinhardt, Django, 1910-1953

★ Christensen, Bonnie. **Django**. Roaring Brook Press 2009 un il $17.99

Grades: 1 2 3 4   92

1. Guitarists 2. Jazz musicians

ISBN 978-1-59643-422-6; 1-59643-422-8

ALA Schneider Family Book Award (2010)

"Richly expressive paint and ink illustrations portray the hard-earned successes of Django Reinhardt, whose childhood was spent traveling with his impoverished gypsy family, where music was a constant and illuminating presence. . . . Christensen's soft, rhythmic prose echoes her evocative images as Django explores the music scene of 1920s Paris, before suffering serious burns on his hands and leg when his wagon catches fire. Despite his injuries, Reinhardt teaches himself to play again. . . . A sensuous tribute to an illustrious musician." Publ Wkly

Reiss, Johanna

★ Reiss, Johanna. The **upstairs** room. Crowell 1972 273p hardcover o.p. pa $5.99

Grades: 3 4 5 6 7 8   92

1. Authors 2. Holocaust survivors 3. Children's authors 4. Jews -- Netherlands 5. World War, 1939-1945 -- Jews 6. Holocaust, 1933-1945 -- Personal narratives 7. Netherlands -- History -- 1940-1945, German occupation

ISBN 0-690-85127-8; 0-06-440370-X pa

A Newbery Medal honor book, 1973

"In a vital, moving account the author recalls her experiences as a Jewish child hiding from the Germans occupying her native Holland during World War II. . . . Ten-year-old Annie and her twenty-year-old sister Sini, . . . are taken in by a Dutch farmer, his wife, and mother who hide the girls in an upstairs room of the farm house. Written from the perspective of a child the story affords a child's-eye-view of the war." Booklist

Followed by The journey back

Renoir, Auguste, 1841-1919

Somervill, Barbara A. **Pierre**-Auguste Renoir; [by] Barbara Somervill. Mitchell Lane 2007 48p il (Art profiles for kids) lib bdg $29.95

Grades: 5 6 7 8   92

1. Artists 2. Painters 3. Artists, French

ISBN 978-1-58415-566-9 lib bdg; 1-58415-566-3 lib bdg

LC 2007000661

Profiles the famous French artist best known for his portraits and his paintings such as "The Luncheon of the Boating Party" that depict people enjoying themselves

"The glossy pages allow for good reproductions of paintings as well as a few photos. . . . Back matter includes a glossary, chronology, chapter notes for quotes, lists of books and Internet sites, and a Timeline in History . . . offers a concise, readable account of the artist's life." Booklist

Includes glossary and bibliographical references

Revere, Paul, 1735-1818

★ Fritz, Jean. **And** then what happened, Paul Revere? pictures by Margot Tomes. Coward, McCann & Geoghegan 1973 45p il $16.99; pa $5.99

Grades: 2 3 4   92

1. Artisans 2. Metalworkers 3. Revolutionaries 4. United States

-- History -- 1775-1783, Revolution
ISBN 0-399-23337-7; 0-698-11351-9 pa
This "description of Paul Revere's ride to Lexington is funny, fast-paced, and historically accurate; it is given added interest by the establishment of Revere's character: busy, bustling, versatile, and patriotic, a man who loved people and excitement. The account of his ride is preceded by a description of his life and the political situation in Boston, and it concludes with Revere's adventures after reaching Lexington." Bull Cent Child Books

Giblin, James. The **many** rides of Paul Revere; by James Cross Giblin. Scholastic Press 2007 85p il map $17.99
Grades: 4 5 6 7   **92**
1. Artisans 2. Metalworkers 3. Revolutionaries 4. United States -- History -- 1775-1783, Revolution
ISBN 978-0-439-57290-3; 0-439-57290-8
                                                              LC 2006-38369
"This well-organized biography presents a lucid account of Revere's childhood, his limited education, his training in his father's workshop, his brief military career, and his adult life as a silversmith, family man, and Revolutionary War leader. . . . Giblin presents salient facts and intriguing details to create a well-rounded and credible image of the man. Among the many illustrations are period portraits, narrative paintings, engravings, drawings, and maps as well as photos of significant sites and artifacts." Booklist
Includes bibliographical references

Mortensen, Lori. **Paul** Revere's ride; illustrated by Craig Orback. Picture Window Books 2010 32p il map (Our American story) lib bdg $23.99
Grades: 2 3 4   **92**
1. Artisans 2. Metalworkers 3. Revolutionaries 4. Statesmen -- United States 5. United States -- History -- 1775-1783, Revolution
ISBN 978-1-4048-5537-3; 1-4048-5537-8
                                                               LC 2009-6893
Highlights the life and accomplishments of Paul Revere, including the events leading up to his famous ride to warn of the British attack on Concord.
This book is "illustrated with well-executed, full-page, color illustrations, maps, and photos. . . . [It has] accurate, clearly written information that students can use for either leisure reading or reports." SLJ
Includes glossary and bibliographical references

Rey, H. A. (Hans Augusto), 1898-1977
★ Borden, Louise. The **journey** that saved Curious George; the true wartime escape of Margret and H. A. Rey. illustrated by Allan Drummond. Houghton Mifflin 2005 72p il $17
Grades: 3 4 5 6   **92**
1. Artists 2. Authors 3. Illustrators 4. Jewish refugees 5. Authors, American 6. Children's authors
ISBN 0-618-33924-8
                                                              LC 2004-01015
This is the story of how Margret and H.A. Rey "escaped occupied Paris in 1940 on bicycles to save both their lives and the manuscript of a book that would become Curious George. . . . A partial bibliography of books by Margret and H. A. Rey is included. . . . Grades three to six." (Bull Cent Child Books)
This "book tells the story of Margret and H. A. Rey. Part 1 concerns their childhoods in Germany, their lives together in Rio de Janeiro and Paris in the 1920s and 1930s, and the growing menace after war broke out in 1939. As German-born Jews, they were suspect in many quarters. Part 2 recalls the Reys' flight from Paris and the couple's escape to Lisbon, Rio, and finally New York. They were carrying several illustrated manuscripts, including The Adventures of FiFi, later retitled Curi-

ous George. Photos, reproductions of documents, and artwork appear throughout the book, as do Drummond's spirited ink-and-watercolor illustrations, brimming with action and details. The text . . . reads well." Booklist

Rey, Margret
★ Borden, Louise. The **journey** that saved Curious George; the true wartime escape of Margret and H. A. Rey. illustrated by Allan Drummond. Houghton Mifflin 2005 72p il $17
Grades: 3 4 5 6   **92**
1. Artists 2. Authors 3. Illustrators 4. Jewish refugees 5. Authors, American 6. Children's authors
ISBN 0-618-33924-8
                                                              LC 2004-01015
This is the story of how Margret and H.A. Rey "escaped occupied Paris in 1940 on bicycles to save both their lives and the manuscript of a book that would become Curious George. . . . A partial bibliography of books by Margret and H. A. Rey is included. . . . Grades three to six." (Bull Cent Child Books)
This "book tells the story of Margret and H. A. Rey. Part 1 concerns their childhoods in Germany, their lives together in Rio de Janeiro and Paris in the 1920s and 1930s, and the growing menace after war broke out in 1939. As German-born Jews, they were suspect in many quarters. Part 2 recalls the Reys' flight from Paris and the couple's escape to Lisbon, Rio, and finally New York. They were carrying several illustrated manuscripts, including The Adventures of FiFi, later retitled Curious George. Photos, reproductions of documents, and artwork appear throughout the book, as do Drummond's spirited ink-and-watercolor illustrations, brimming with action and details. The text . . . reads well." Booklist

Ride, Sally
Macy, Sue, 1954- **Sally** Ride; life on a mission. by Sue Macy. Aladdin 2014 160 p. illustrations (Real-life story) (hardback) $17.99
Grades: 4 5 6 7 8   **92**
1. Astronauts 2. Women astronauts 3. Physicists
ISBN 1442488549; 9781442488540; 9781442488557
                                                             LC 2014016685
"Sally Ride was more than the first woman in space--she was a real-life explorer and adventurer whose life story is a true inspiration for all those who dream big. . . . She was also a nationally ranked tennis player, a physicist who enjoyed reading Shakespeare, a university professor, the founder of a company that helped inspire girls . . . , and a recipient of the Presidential Medal of Freedom." (Publisher's note)
"The extensive backmatter provides scholarly data, while the writing imparts the drive and character of this famous woman. Macy's slim, empathetic account makes readers see the woman behind the achievement." Kirkus
Includes bibliographical references and index

O'Shaughnessy, Tam. **Sally** Ride; a photo biography of America's pioneering woman in space. Tam O'Shaughnessy. Roaring Brook Press 2015 153 p. illustrations (some color) (hardcover) $19.99
Grades: 4 5 6 7 8   **92**
1. Women astronauts 2. Astronauts -- United States -- Biography 3. Astronauts -- United States -- Pictorial works 4. Women astronauts -- United States -- Biography 5. Women astronauts -- United States -- Pictorial works
ISBN 9781596439948; 1596439947
                                                             LC 2015004913
This biography of Sally Ride, by Tam O'Shaughnessey, "is an intimate journey from her formative years to her final moments. Before she earned a Ph.D. in physics, she was called an underachiever by her high school classmates. After her first historic space flight-she took a second

in 1984-Sally continued to break ground as an inspirational advocate for space exploration, public policy, and science education." (Publisher's note)

"Ride was notoriously private, and this glimpse into her life and background will be both eye-opening and inspiring for many young readers. The irresistible photos and appealing page layouts make it an especially good pick for reluctant readers." Booklist

Ringgold, Faith

Venezia, Mike. **Faith** Ringgold; written and illustrated by Mike Venezia. Children's Press 2008 32p il (Getting to know the world's greatest artists) lib bdg $28

Grades: 3 4 5   **92**

1. Artists 2. Authors 3. Illustrators 4. Women artists 5. African American artists 6. Children's authors 7. Artists -- United States
ISBN 978-0-531-18526-1 lib bdg; 0-531-18526-5 lib bdg

LC 2007016125

This examines the work and life of Faith Ringgold, an African American artist who works in a variety of mediums including textiles, paintings, and prints, and is best known for her story quilts.

"Though the [text is] simply written, [this title contains] a wealth of information. . . . [The book has] many reproductions of the [artist's] works as well as those of the masters who influenced [her]. To help illustrate his points, Venezia has incorporated his own cartoon-style illustrations." SLJ

Rivera, Diego, 1886-1957

★ Tonatiuh, Duncan. **Diego** Rivera; his world and ours. Abrams Books for Young Readers 2011 32p il $15.95

Grades: K 1 2 3   **92**

1. Artists 2. Painters 3. Artists, Mexican
ISBN 978-0-8109-9731-8; 0-8109-9731-2

LC 2010032618

"Tonatiuh relates key moments in the famous muralist's life and ponders what would capture his interest if he were alive today. The stylized brown figures are shown in profile with open mouths, exaggerated features, and heads that seem hinged to the bodies. . . . In scenes both thoughtful and humorous, Tonatiuh contrasts interpretations of Rivera's work with renderings of imagined work today. . . . An inspired approach that combines child appeal, cultural anthropology, and art history." SLJ

Robeson, Paul, 1898-1976

Greenfield, Eloise. **Paul** Robeson; illustrated by George Ford. Lee & Low Books 2009 un il $18.95; pa $9.95

Grades: 2 3 4 5   **92**

1. Actors 2. Singers 3. Football players 4. Political activists 5. Civil rights activists 6. African Americans -- Biography
ISBN 978-1-60060-256-6; 1-60060-256-8; 978-1-60060-262-7 pa; 1-60060-262-2 pa

LC 2008030420

First published 1975 by HarperCollins

"Vibrant, monochromatic acrylic illustrations . . . use shading and depth to convey tremendous emotion. Powerful movements and vivid expressions enhance the narrative. . . . This book offers a fully developed portrayal of the man." SLJ

Robinson, Jackie, 1919-1972

Amoroso, Cynthia. **Jackie** Robinson; by Cynthia Amoroso and Robert B. Noyed. Child's World 2010 24p il (Basic biographies) lib bdg $22.79

Grades: PreK K 1   **92**

1. Baseball players 2. African American athletes 3. Army officers

4. Baseball -- Biography
ISBN 978-1-60253-342-4; 1-60253-342-3

LC 2009029371

This biography of Jackie Robinson "pairs intelligent, brief text with abundant photos. Simple but never basic." Booklist
Includes bibliographical references

★ Burleigh, Robert. **Stealing** home; written by Robert Burleigh; illustrated by Mike Wimmer. Simon & Schuster Books for Young Readers 2007 un il $16.99

Grades: 1 2 3 4   **92**

1. Baseball players 2. African American athletes 3. Army officers

4. Baseball -- Biography
ISBN 978-0-689-86276-2; 0-689-86276-8

LC 2006-01048

"Burleigh employs two narrative voices, one a spare, lyrical moment-by-moment replay of [Jackie] Robinson's bold steal home from third base in the first game of the 1955 World Series against the New York Yankees. . . . Historical sidebars on each spread supplement this dramatic, immediate account, providing anecdotes about the era, Robinson's struggles . . . plus highlights of his baseball career . . . and personal life. Wimmer's textured, animated oil paintings depict the game action at close range and with lifelike clarity." Publ Wkly

O'Sullivan, Robyn. **Jackie** Robinson plays ball; by Robyn O'Sullivan. National Geographic 2007 40p il (National Geographic history chapters) lib bdg $17.90

Grades: 2 3 4   **92**

1. Baseball players 2. African American athletes 3. Army officers

4. Baseball -- Biography
ISBN 978-1-4263-0190-2

LC 2007007893

This biography of Jackie Robinson is "nicely illustrated with photos. . . . [It is] just right for emerging chapter-book readers. . . . Useful . . . for reports . . . and interesting pleasure reading." SLJ
Includes glossary and bibliographical references

Robinson, Sharon. **Promises** to keep: how Jackie Robinson changed America. Scholastic 2004 64p il $16.95

Grades: 4 5 6 7   **92**

1. Baseball players 2. African American athletes 3. Army officers

4. Baseball -- Biography
ISBN 0-439-42592-1

LC 2003-42709

"Robinson's daughter, Sharon, describes her father's youth, his rise to become major-league baseball's first African American player, and his involvement in the civil rights movement. . . . Her private view of her father's accomplishments, placed within the context of American sports and social history, makes for absorbing reading. An excellent selection of family and team photographs and other materials . . . illustrate this fine tribute." Booklist

Robinson, Sharon, 1950- **Testing** the ice: a true story about Jackie Robinson; illustrated by Kadir Nelson. Scholastic Press 2009 un il $16.99

Grades: 1 2 3 4   **92**

1. Baseball players 2. African American athletes 3. Army officers

4. Baseball -- Biography
ISBN 0-545-05251-3; 978-0-545-05251-1

LC 2008-38838

Jackie Robinson's daughter shares memories of him, from his baseball career to the day he tests the ice for her, her brothers, and their friends. "Ages seven to ten." (N Y Times Book Rev)

"Robinson neatly sums up the significance of her father's achievements while depicting him as a loving family man. Nelson's large paintings, done in pencil, watercolor, and oils, dramatically convey Robinson's public persona, the intensely competitive athlete, and contrasts that with the relaxed, yet commanding father Sharon and her brothers knew." SLJ

Roget, Peter Mark, 1779-1869

★ Bryant, Jen. The **right** word; Roget and his thesaurus. by Jen Bryant; illustrated by Melissa Sweet. Eerdmans Books for Young Readers 2014 42 p. color illustrations $17.50

Grades: 1 2 3 4   **92**

1. Authors 2. Reference books 3. Philologists -- Great Britain -- Biography 4. Lexicographers -- Great Britain -- Biography

ISBN 0802853854; 9780802853851

LC 2013044348

Robert F. Sibert Informational Book Award (2015)

Caldecott Honor Book (2015)

Kirkus Prize Finalist (2014)

Written by Jen Bryant and illustrated by Melissa Sweet, this children's book tells how "for shy young Peter Mark Roget, books were the best companions--and it wasn't long before Peter began writing his own book. But he didn't write stories; he wrote lists. Peter took his love for words and turned it to organizing ideas and finding exactly the right word to express just what he thought. His lists grew . . . turning into one of the most important reference books of all time." (Publisher's note)

"Bryant's and Sweet's talents combine to make the lowly thesaurus fascinating in this beautifully illustrated picture-book biography of Peter Mark Roget. . . . In brilliant pages teeming with enthusiasm for language and learning, Bryant and Sweet . . . joyfully celebrate curiosity, the love of knowledge, and the power of words." (Booklist)

includes bibliographical references

Romo, Tony, 1980-

Sandler, Michael. **Tony** Romo. Bearport Pub. 2010 24p il (Football heroes making a difference) lib bdg $22.61

Grades: 2 3 4   **92**

1. Football players 2. Football -- Biography

ISBN 978-1-936087-60-0 lib bdg; 1-936087-60-X lib bdg

LC 2009031216

A look at the life and career of the football star.

Includes bibliographical references

Roosevelt, Eleanor, 1884-1962

★ Cooney, Barbara. **Eleanor.** Viking 1996 un il $15.99; pa $6.99

Grades: K 1 2 3   **92**

1. Diplomats 2. Columnists 3. Humanitarians 4. Social activists 5. Spouses of presidents 6. United Nations officials 7. Presidents' spouses -- United States

ISBN 0-670-86159-6; 0-14-055583-8 pa

LC 96-7723

"There are many biographies of Eleanor Roosevelt but this one is special. Not only does it boast Cooney's artwork, but it also gets to the heart of a young girl, which in many ways is as interesting as Roosevelt's later, well-known accomplishments." Booklist

Fleming, Candace. **Our** Eleanor; a scrapbook look at Eleanor Roosevelt's remarkable life. Atheneum Books for Young Readers 2005 176p il $19.95

Grades: 5 6 7 8   **92**

1. Diplomats 2. Columnists 3. Humanitarians 4. Social activists 5. Spouses of presidents 6. United Nations officials 7. Presidents'

spouses -- United States

ISBN 0-689-86544-9

LC 2004-22825

Told in scrapbook style, this biography looks behind the politics to present First Lady Eleanor Roosevelt in her many roles: wife and mother, United Nations delegate, popular columnist, civil rights crusader, and champion of the underprivileged.

"Each of the seven chapters leads readers through the subject's busy life with short sections of text filled with well-documented first-person accounts and direct quotes. . . . Not a spread goes by without incredible archival photographs or reproductions, newspaper and magazine clippings, handwritten letters, and diary entries. . . . They all provide relevant and fascinating insight." SLJ

★ Rappaport, Doreen. **Eleanor,** quiet no more; written by Doreen Rappaport; illustrated by Gary Kelley. Hyperion 2009 un il $16.99

Grades: 2 3 4 5   **92**

1. Diplomats 2. Columnists 3. Humanitarians 4. Social activists 5. Spouses of presidents 6. United Nations officials 7. Presidents' spouses -- United States

ISBN 978-0-7868-5141-6; 0-7868-5141-4

"The narrative moves swiftly through the important moments in [Eleanor] Roosevelt's life . . . but along with accomplishments, Rappaport does something more subtle—she shows the way Eleanor grew into herself. Crisp sentences focus the narrative and are bolstered by the quotes that end each page. . . . The accompanying art is composed of rich, beautifully crafted paintings that also catch Roosevelt's growing sense of purpose." Booklist

Roosevelt, Franklin D. (Franklin Delano), 1882-1945

Krull, Kathleen. A **boy** named FDR; how Franklin D. Roosevelt grew up to change America. illustrated by Steve Johnson & Lou Fancher. Alfred A. Knopf 2010 un il $17.99; lib bdg $20.99

Grades: 3 4 5   **92**

1. Governors 2. Presidents 3. People with disabilities 4. Philatelists 5. Presidents -- United States

ISBN 978-0-375-85716-4; 0-375-85716-8; 978-0-375-95716-1 lib bdg; 0-375-95716-2 lib bdg

LC 2009-22089

Focuses on Franklin D. Roosevelt's childhood years and summarizes his achievements as president.

"Full-page, painterly artwork evokes the times and the determination of FDR, and Krull has a knack for ferreting out interesting anecdotes that humanize the facts. Informative backmatter provides a dated list of his life and famous words and sources. Well done." Kirkus

Panchyk, Richard. **Franklin** Delano Roosevelt for kids; his life and times with 21 activities. [by] Richard Panchyk. Chicago Review Press 2007 147p il pa $14.95

Grades: 4 5 6 7   **92**

1. Governors 2. Presidents 3. People with disabilities 4. Philatelists 5. Presidents -- United States 6. United States -- Politics and government -- 1933-1945

ISBN 978-1-55652-657-2 pa; 1-55652-657-1 pa

LC 2007003484

"There are many interesting photos . . . and they are all sufficiently captioned. . . . Information about the Roosevelts [is] presented in a lively, engaging manner." SLJ

Includes bibliographical references

St. George, Judith. **Make** your mark, Franklin Roosevelt; [by] Judith St. George; illustrated by Britt Spencer. Philomel Books 2007 un il $16.99

Grades: 2 3 4   92
1. Governors 2. Presidents 3. People with disabilities 4. Philatelists 5. Presidents -- United States
ISBN 978-0-399-24175-8; 0-399-24175-2

LC 2006008921

"This illustrated biography . . . explores . . . . the influences that shaped Roosevelt's life with stories that will delight young readers. . . . Throughout, Spencer's spirited watercolor, gouache, and ink illustrations bring to life the culture and background of this American icon." SLJ

Includes bibliographical references

Roosevelt, Theodore, 1858-1919
★ Brown, Don. **Teedie**; the story of young Teddy Roosevelt. Houghton Mifflin Books for Children 2009 un il $16
Grades: 2 3 4   92
1. Governors 2. Presidents 3. Vice-presidents 4. Nobel laureates for peace 5. Presidents -- United States
ISBN 978-0-618-17999-2; 0-618-17999-2

LC 2008033879

"Teedie led a privileged life in one of New York City's wealthiest households, but was a sickly child. His asthma didn't stop him from being curious or from reading widely. . . . Teedie became Teddy when he entered Harvard University in 1876. After graduation, Roosevelt sought his own way. . . . He traveled, became an outdoorsman, a politician, and ultimately the youngest president of the United States. Line and wash illustrations add movement and a playful tone to the serious text, which generously incorporates quotes from Roosevelt." SLJ

Includes bibliographical references

Elish, Dan. **Theodore** Roosevelt; by Dan Elish. Marshall Cavendish Benchmark 2008 96p il (Presidents and their times) lib bdg $22.95
Grades: 5 6 7 8   92
1. Governors 2. Presidents 3. Vice-presidents 4. Nobel laureates for peace 5. Presidents -- United States
ISBN 978-0-7614-2429-1

LC 2006012987

A biography of the president
"Primary-source materials and quotes, helpful insets, and carefully selected photographs and/or reproductions bring history to life and help make [this] clearly written [biography] highly readable." SLJ

Includes glossary and bibliographical references

Fritz, Jean. **Bully** for you, Teddy Roosevelt! illustrations by Mike Wimmer. Putnam 1991 127p il hardcover o.p. pa $5.99
Grades: 5 6 7 8   92
1. Governors 2. Presidents 3. Vice-presidents 4. Nobel laureates for peace 5. Presidents -- United States
ISBN 0-399-21769-X; 0-698-11609-7 pa

LC 90-8142

Follows the life of the twenty-sixth president, discussing his conservation work, hunting expeditions, family life, and political career
"Jean Fritz gives a rounded picture of her subject and deftly blends the story of a person and a picture of an era." Bull Cent Child Books
Includes bibliographical references

Harness, Cheryl. The **remarkable,** rough-riding life of Theodore Roosevelt and the rise of empire America; painstakingly written and illustrated by Cheryl Harness. National Geographic 2007 144p il map $16.95; lib bdg $25.90
Grades: 4 5 6 7   92
1. Governors 2. Presidents 3. Vice-presidents 4. Nobel laureates

for peace 5. Presidents -- United States
ISBN 978-1-4263-0008-0; 1-4263-0008-5; 978-1-4263-0009-7 lib bdg; 1-4263-0009-3 lib bdg

LC 2006029039

"Animated writing and intricate black-and-white illustrations drive this biography of the ever-enthusiastic twenty-sixth president of the United States. An extensive running timeline at the bottom of the pages emphasizes the dramatic changes that occurred during Roosevelt's life. The book is jam-packed with information." Horn Book Guide

Includes bibliographical references

Hollihan, Kerrie Logan. **Theodore** Roosevelt for kids; his life and times + 21 activities. Chicago Review Press 2010 133p il pa $16.95
Grades: 5 6 7 8   92
1. Governors 2. Handicraft 3. Presidents 4. Vice-presidents 5. Nobel laureates for peace 6. Presidents -- United States 7. United States -- Politics and government -- 1898-1919
ISBN 978-1-55652-955-9 pa; 1-55652-955-4 pa

"What stands out in this volume is the writing, which presents history as an engaging and informative story. . . . The projects are interesting and accessible. . . . Both useful and entertaining, this is a worthy addition to most collections." SLJ

Keating, Frank. **Theodore**; illustrated by Mike Wimmer. Simon & Schuster Books for Young Readers 2006 un il $16.95
Grades: K 1 2 3   92
1. Governors 2. Presidents 3. Vice-presidents 4. Nobel laureates for peace 5. Presidents -- United States
ISBN 0-689-86532-5

LC 2003-17046

A picture book biography of the 26th president of the United States
"This handsome, well-researched biography is as dignified as its subject. Using a spare, readable style, the author captures Roosevelt's spirit and determination." SLJ

★ Kerley, Barbara. **What** to do about Alice? how Alice Roosevelt broke the rules, charmed the world, and drove her father Teddy crazy! illustrated by Edwin Fotheringham. Scholastic Press 2008 un il $16.99
Grades: K 1 2 3   92
1. Presidents -- United States -- Family 2. White House (Washington, D.C.)
ISBN 978-0-439-92231-9; 0-439-92231-3

LC 2006-38372

Boston Globe-Horn Book Award honor book: Nonfiction (2008)
"The daughter of Theodore Roosevelt, . . . Alice had a joie de vivre that she called 'eating up the world.' . . . Kerley's text has the same rambunctious spirit as its subject. . . . The large format gives Fotheringhame . . . plenty of room for spectacular art, which includes use of digital media." Booklist

★ Rappaport, Doreen, 1939- **To** dare mighty things; the life of Theodore Roosevelt. written by Doreen Rappaport; illustrated by C. F. Payne. Disney-Hyperion 2013 48 p. (hardback) $17.99
Grades: 2 3 4 5 6   92
1. Presidents -- United States 2. Presidents -- United States -- Biography
ISBN 142312488X; 9781423124887

LC 2013010691

This picture book, by Doreen Rappaport and illustrated by C. F. Payne, is a biography of American president Theodore Roosevelt. "As an American president, he left [a] . . . mark upon his country. He promised a 'square deal' to all citizens, he tamed big businesses, and protected the nation's wildlife and natural beauty. His . . . leadership assured that he would always be remembered." (Publisher's note).

St. George, Judith. **You're** on your way, Teddy Roosevelt! illustrated by Matt Faulkner. Philomel Books 2004 un il $16.99
Grades: 2 3 4   **92**
1. Governors 2. Presidents 3. Vice-presidents 4. Nobel laureates for peace 5. Presidents -- United States
ISBN 0-399-23888-3

LC 2003-21534

"St. George's skill in presenting information with a light touch keeps the pace lively, while Faulkner's gouache illustrations . . . further animate the narrative." Horn Book Guide
Includes bibliographical references

Wade, Mary Dodson. **Amazing** president Theodore Roosevelt. Enslow Publishers 2009 24p il (Amazing Americans) lib bdg $21.26
Grades: 1 2 3   **92**
1. Governors 2. Presidents 3. Vice-presidents 4. Nobel laureates for peace 5. Presidents -- United States
ISBN 978-0-7660-3284-2 lib bdg; 0-7660-3284-1 lib bdg

LC 2008-24892

"Colorful photos are found throughout, with a timeline, dictionary, websites concerning the topic, as well as an index making . . . [this] book a wonderful introduction to nonfiction features." Libr Media Connect
Includes glossary

Wadsworth, Ginger. **Camping** with the president; illustrated by Karen Dugan. Calkins Creek 2009 32p il $16.95
Grades: 3 4 5   **92**
1. Authors 2. Governors 3. Presidents 4. Naturalists 5. Vice-presidents 6. Environmental movement 7. National parks and reserves 8. Writers on nature 9. Nobel laureates for peace 10. Presidents -- United States 11. Yosemite National Park (Calif.)
ISBN 978-1-59078-497-6; 1-59078-497-9

LC 2008024155

"Inspired by conservationist John Muir's nature essays, President Theodore Roosevelt traveled west, visiting national parks and learing more about their resources. Wadsworth's well written, lively account highlights the pair's 1903 exploration of the Yosemite wilderness, as well as America's early conservation movement, in an accessible and engaging picture book for older readers. Dugan's abundant, intricately rendered watercolors portray the stunning vistas and wildlife and are set against white backgrounds." Booklist
Includes bibliographical references

Ross, Betsy, 1752-1836
White, Becky. **Betsy** Ross; illustrated by Megan Lloyd. Holiday House 2011 il $16.95
Grades: K 1 2   **92**
1. Generals 2. Presidents 3. Dressmakers 4. Needleworkers 5. Flags -- United States 6. United States -- History -- 1775-1783, Revolution
ISBN 0-8234-1908-8; 978-0-8234-1908-1

LC 2009054296

"Fourteen spreads with four to six rhythmic words on each one tell the story of the first American flag. . . . The large, simple text, paired with the irresistible appliqué art, makes this a perfect introduction to the Stars and Stripes. Using cotton fabric, embroidery thread, dye, paint, and linoleum-block prints, Lloyd captures the period, hard work, and ingenuity of this favorite colonial figure." SLJ

Rothschild, Lionel Walter Rothschild, Baron, 1868-1937
Judge, Lita. **Strange** creatures; the story of Walter Rothschild and his museum. Hyperion 2011 un il $17.99
Grades: 1 2 3   **92**
1. Zoology 2. Zoologists 3. Members of Parliament 4. Natural History Museum at Tring (England)
ISBN 1-4231-1389-6; 978-1-4231-1389-8

This is a biography of the British zoologist and banker. Rothschild "used his own income to finance [zoological] expeditions and ultimately built a museum to house his collection on the family's grounds. . . . Ages five to eight." (Bull Cent Child Books)

"Walter Rothschild, the shy eldest son of Lord Nathan Rothschild, never took an interest in the family banking business, instead developing an all-consuming veneration for the wild; at age seven, he began collecting living animals like kangaroos and kiwi birds for his 'museum.' Judge's expressive watercolors convey Rothschild's inquisitiveness and his parents' angst over such mishaps as a giant lizard escape. . . . Children should get a kick out of this 19th-century misfit who relentlessly pursued his unconventional passion." Publ Wkly

Rowling, J. K.
Peterson-Hilleque, Victoria. **J.K.** Rowling, extraordinary author. ABDO Pub. Company 2010 112p il (Essential lives) $32.79
Grades: 5 6 7 8   **92**
1. Authors 2. Novelists 3. Women authors 4. Fantasy writers 5. Authors, English 6. Children's authors 7. Young adult authors
ISBN 978-1-61613-517-1; 1-61613-517-4

LC 2010000503

This biography of author J. K. Rowling "toggles between the subject's personal and professional life. . . . [The book] offers sidebar . . . definitions of particular characters or events in the 'Harry Potter' series. The writing is accessible, the format is open, and full-color photos appear throughout." SLJ
Includes glossary and bibliographical references

Rudolph, Wilma, 1940-1994
★ Krull, Kathleen. **Wilma** unlimited: how Wilma Rudolph became the world's fastest woman; illustrated by David Diaz. Harcourt Brace & Co. 1996 un il $17; pa $7
Grades: 2 3 4   **92**
1. Women athletes 2. African American athletes 3. Olympic athletes 4. Runners (Athletes) 5. Track athletics -- Biography
ISBN 0-15-201267-2; 0-15-202098-5 pa

LC 95-32105

A biography of the African-American woman who overcame crippling polio as a child to become the first woman to win three gold medals in track in a single Olympics

"Brightly colored paintings contrast with sepia-toned photographic backgrounds, creating juxtapositions that extend both the text and the pictures in the foreground. Krull's understated conversational style is perfectly suited to Rudolph's remarkable and inspiring story." Horn Book Guide

Wade, Mary Dodson. **Amazing** Olympic athlete Wilma Rudolph. Enslow Publishers 2009 24p il (Amazing Americans) lib bdg $21.26
Grades: 1 2 3   **92**
1. Women athletes 2. Track athletics 3. African American athletes 4. Olympic athletes 5. Runners (Athletes)
ISBN 978-0-7660-3282-8 lib bdg; 0-7660-3282-5 lib bdg

LC 2008-24890

"The book features a design that is clear and inviting with a full-page photo on every double-page spread." Booklist
Includes glossary and bibliographical references

Rustin, Bayard, 1910-1987

★ Brimner, Larry Dane. **We** are one: the story of Bayard Rustin. Calkins Creek 2007 48p il $17.95

Grades: 5 6 7 8   **92**

1. Civil rights activists 2. African Americans -- Biography 3. African Americans -- Civil rights

ISBN 1-59078-498-7

"Brimner sets Rustin's personal story against the history of segregation in his time and focuses on his leadership role . . . in the struggle for civil rights. On each page, the clearly written, informal text is accompanied by eloquently captioned archival photos." Booklist

Includes bibliographical references

Ruth, Babe, 1895-1948

Yomtov, Nelson. The **Bambino** : the story of Babe Ruth's legendary 1927 season; illustrated by Tim Foley. Capstone Press 2011 32p il (Graphic library: American graphic) lib bdg $29.32; pa $7.95

Grades: 4 5 6 7   **92**

1. Baseball players 2. Biographical graphic novels 3. Baseball -- Biography

ISBN 978-1-4296-5473-9 lib bdg; 1-4296-5473-2 lib bdg; 978-1-4296-6265-9 pa; 1-4296-6265-4 pa

LC 2010024764

In graphic novel format, follows Babe Ruth through the 1927 season and describes his attempt to break his own home run record.

"The illustrations are eye-catching and the narration is presented simply, yet compellingly. . . . Fact-filled, entertaining, and accessible." SLJ

Includes glossary and bibliographical references

Sís, Peter, 1949-

★ Sis, Peter, 1949- The **wall**; growing up behind the Iron Curtain. Farrar, Straus and Giroux 2007 un il $18

Grades: 4 5 6 7 8 9 10   **92**

1. Artists 2. Authors 3. Cold war 4. Animators 5. Illustrators 6. Set designers 7. Children's authors 8. Prague (Czech Republic)

ISBN 978-0-374-34701-7; 0-374-34701-8

LC 2006-49149

Boston Globe-Horn Book Award: Nonfiction (2008)

"The author pairs his remarkable artistry with journal entries, historical context and period photography to create a powerful account of his childhood in Cold War-era Prague." Publ Wkly

Sacagawea

Green, Carl R. **Sacagawea**; courageous American Indian guide. by William R. Sanford and Carl R. Green. Enslow Publishers 2013 48 p. ill., map (library) $21.26

Grades: 5 6 7 8   **92**

1. Native Americans -- United States 2. Shoshoni women -- Biography 3. Shoshoni Indians -- Biography

ISBN 0766040062; 9780766040069

LC 2011048291

This book, part of the Courageous Heroes of the American West series, looks at Sacagawea. "Throughout Lewis and Clark's journey in the uncharted American West, this young America Indian woman proved to be an invaluable member of the expedition. Sacagawea served as translator and guide, all while caring for her infant son." (Publisher's note)

Includes bibliographical references (p. 47) and index.

Nelson, Maria. The **life** of Sacagawea; Maria Nelson. Gareth Stevens Pub. 2012 24 p. ill. (chiefly col.) (library binding) $22.60; (paperback) $8.15

Grades: 2 3 4   **92**

1. Native American women 2. United States -- History 3. Native Americans -- Biography 4. Shoshoni women -- Biography 5. Shoshoni Indians -- Biography

ISBN 9781433963575; 9781433963599

LC 2011035145

Author Maria Nelson presents information on "one of the most famous Native Americans in US history--Sacagawea. Though much of her life remains a mystery, this book will explore the story of the . . . woman who helped Lewis and Clark explore the American West. . . . [Nelson also includes] a timeline of important events [for children.]" (Publisher's note)

Includes bibliographical references (p. 23) and index.

Norwich, Grace. **I** am Sacagawea. Scholastic 2012 128 p. ill., map

Grades: 2 3 4   **92**

ISBN 0545405742; 9780545405744

Author Grace Norwich's biography of "Shoshoni Indian Sacagawea, known for guiding the Lewis and Clark expedition across the western half of the United States from 1804 to 1806," discusses "her childhood and kidnapping by the Hidatsa tribe, her marriage to Toussaint Charbonneau, and the mystery surrounding her death." (yabookscentral.com)

Includes bibliographical references (pages 124-125) and index.

Sagan, Carl, 1934-1996

★ Sisson, Stephanie Roth. **Star** stuff; Carl Sagan and the mysteries of the cosmos. Stephanie Roth Sisson. Roaring Brook Press 2014 40 p. color illustrations (hardcover) $17.99

Grades: K 1 2 3   **92**

1. Astronomers -- Biography 2. Astronomers -- United States -- Biography

ISBN 1596439602; 9781596439603

LC 2013048396

Orbis Pictus Award for Outstanding Nonfiction for Children Honor Book (2014)

This children's book, by Stephanie Roth Sisson, is "the story of a curious boy who never stopped wondering: Carl Sagan. . . . [This book] follows Carl from his days star gazing from the bedroom window of his Brooklyn apartment, through his love of speculative science fiction novels, to his work as an internationally renowned scientist who worked on the Voyager missions exploring the farthest reaches of space." (Publisher's note)

"Told in narrative format, this beautifully designed and illustrated picture book gives readers a glimpse into the childhood wonderings Sagan experienced as he looked at the night sky and imagined the possibilities...Children will easily relate to and may even see themselves in Sagan's youthful exuberance. Detailed notes illustrate the solid research and facts behind the narrative. A gorgeous, informative offering for biography and science collections." SLJ

Includes bibliographical references

Saint-Exupery, Antoine de, 1900-1944

★ Sis, Peter, 1949- The **Pilot** and the Little Prince; the Life of Antoine de Saint-Exupery. Peter Sis. Frances Foster Books, Farrar Straus Giroux 2014 48 p. (hardcover) $18.99

Grades: 1 2 3 4 5 6   **92**

1. Air pilots -- Biography 2. Air travel 3. Air pilots -- France -- Biography 4. Authors, French -- 20th century -- Biography

ISBN 0374380694; 9780374380694

LC 2013027732

"Antoine de Saint-Exupéry was born in France in 1900, when airplanes were just being invented. Antoine dreamed of flying and grew up to be a pilot--and that was when his adventures began. . . . From his plane, Antoine looked down on the earth and was inspired to write about his life and his pilot-hero friends in memoirs and in fiction. Peter Sís's .

.. biography celebrates the author of 'The Little Prince,' one of the most beloved books in the world." (Publisher's note)

"The main text, a fairly clear line through Saint-Exupery's life, is supplemented with myriad facts about his world, arranged in delicate circles around the edges of Sís's signature illustrated medallions. Here you can find information on Saint-Exupery's family tree or the perfume inspired by his book Night Flight or pithy anecdotes about his writing life." Horn Book

Saint-Georges, Joseph Boulogne, chevalier de, 1745-1799

Brewster, Hugh. The **other** Mozart; the life of the famous Chevalier de Saint George. [by] Hugh Brewster; illustrated by Eric Velasquez. Abrams Books for Young Readers 2007 48p il $18.95

Grades: 4 5 6 7   **92**

1. Nobility 2. Composers 3. Violinists 4. Racially mixed people
ISBN 978-0-8109-5720-6; 0-8109-5720-5

LC 2006-07488

"Born to a white plantation owner and a black slave in eighteenth-century Guadeloupe, Joseph Bologne grew up to become the Chevalier de Saint-George, one of France's most accomplished composers. In this picture-book biography for middle-graders, Brewster introduces his subject's fascinating life.... Archival images and Velasquez's arresting full-page portraits will captivate many young readers." Booklist

★ Cline-Ransome, Lesa. **Before** there was Mozart: the story of Joseph Boulogne, Chevalier de Saint-George; illustrated by James Ransome. Schwartz & Wade Books 2011 un il $17.99; lib bdg $20.99

Grades: 1 2 3 4   **92**

1. Nobility 2. Composers 3. Violinists 4. Racially mixed people
ISBN 978-0-375-83600-8; 0-375-83600-4; 978-0-375-93621-0 lib bdg; 0-375-93621-1 lib bdg

LC 2008-48825

"Born in Guadeloupe, Joseph Boulogne was the son of a black slave and a white plantation owner of French nobility. When Joseph's family moved to France, he enrolled in school and, despite facing racial prejudice, devoted himself to mastering the violin.... Joseph composed six operas (as well as other pieces of music), stood before audiences on the same stages as Mozart, and performed before Louis XVI and Marie Antoinette. Ransome's mixed-media paintings join tropical motifs with the sumptuous colors and prints of affluent Paris society, and his faces glow with vitality. Readers will likely marvel at why such a compelling figure has not received more attention." Publ Wkly

Sanghvi, Ruchi, 1982-

Waxman, Laura Hamilton. **Computer** engineer Ruchi Sanghvi; Laura Hamilton Waxman. Lerner Publications 2015 32 p. (STEM trailblazer bios) (lib. bdg. : alk. paper) $26.60

Grades: 4 5 6 7   **92**

1. Engineers 2. Computer programming 3. Computer engineers -- United States -- Biography 4. Women computer engineers -- United States -- Biography
ISBN 1467757942; 9781467757942; 9781467761192

LC 2014015878

This book by Laura Hamilton Waxman profiles Ruchi Sanghvi. "Sanghvi was the first female engineer at Facebook, and it wasn't easy blazing a trail for women in her field. But nothing stopped her from following her dreams. Her contributions at Facebook helped connect people from around the globe. Discover how this young female immigrant became a top-notch engineer who changed the tech world forever." (Publisher's note)

"Their names may not be familiar, but their work is recognizable around the world. These titles in the STEM Trailblazer Bios series introduce cutting-edge engineers and scientists through accessible text and high-quality color photographs.... Computer Engineer Ruchi Sanghvi

describes how she left India to study in the U.S., eventually changing the platform of Facebook and starting her own software tech company.... With a focus on modern engineers and scientists, this series fills a gap in STEM collections." Booklist

Includes bibliographical references and index

Santos-Dumont, Alberto, 1873-1932

Griffith, Victoria. The **fabulous** flying machines of Alberto Santos-Dumont; illustrated by Eva Montanari. Abrams Books for Young Readers 2011 il $16.95

Grades: 1 2 3 4   **92**

1. Airships 2. Engineers 3. Inventors 4. Air pilots 5. Aeronautics -- History
ISBN 978-1-4197-0011-8; 1-4197-0011-1

LC 2010048781

"Dumont is credited as being the first one to get an airplane off the ground under its own power, in 1906. In this fictionalized account, readers learn of the man's idiosyncratic and highly inventive nature. Although he was born in Brazil, he later made Paris his home where he became a larger-than-life personality, partly because of his reputation for—and the spectacle of—his chosen mode of transportation to run everyday errands: a dirigible. His quest to move through the air at a faster pace and for greater distances led to his invention of a biplane. ... Montanari captures the look, dress, and formality of the era in her splendid, impressionistic pastel, chalk, and oil paintings. The endnotes add details and facts about the life of this charismatic, adventurous man and mark his place in aviation history." SLJ

Includes bibliographical references

Sarg, Tony, 1882-1942

★ Sweet, Melissa. **Balloons** over Broadway; the true story of the puppeteer of Macy's Parade. Houghton Mifflin Books for Children 2011 40p il $16.99

Grades: K 1 2   **92**

1. Artists 2. Parades 3. Illustrators 4. Thanksgiving Day 5. Puppets and puppet plays 6. Puppeteers
ISBN 978-0-547-19945-0; 0-547-19945-7

LC 2010044181

Flora Stieglitz Straus Award (2012); Golden Kite Award: Picture Book Illustration (2011); Lupine Award (Maine): Picture Book (2011); Robert F. Sibert Informational Book Medal (2012)

"Tony Sarg ... the man who invented the giant balloons of the Macy's Thanksgiving Day Parade, has found a worthy biographer in ... Sweet.... With lighthearted watercolors, fanciful scrapbooking, and collaged typography, Sweet shows how Sarg, a self-taught immigrant, combined an indomitable curiosity with an engineer's know-how and a forever-young imagination. The story walks readers through each stage of Sarg's development as a master of puppetry—his childhood fascination with mechanics and marionettes, his first big break as a developer of window displays for Macy's, and his early earthbound parade creations (essentially air-filled rubber bags that were steered down the street)... . Sweet captures it all in what is truly a story for all ages." Publ Wkly

Sasaki, Sadako, 1943-1955

Coerr, Eleanor. **Sadako**; illustrated by Ed Young. Putnam 1993 un il $17.95; pa $6.99

Grades: 1 2 3 4   **92**

1. Children 2. Leukemia 3. Leukemia patients 4. Atomic bomb -- Physiological effect 5. Hiroshima (Japan) -- Bombardment, 1945
ISBN 0-399-21771-1; 0-698-11588-0 pa

LC 92-41483

"This is the same story as the author's Sadako and the Thousand Paper Cranes, told through an entirely new text. In this abbreviated version, the beautiful, limpid prose and crisp dialogue further telescope Sadako's fight with leukemia. . . . Young's pastels vividly capture all the moods of the narrative, place, and characters. . . . A masterful collaboration." SLJ

★ Coerr, Eleanor. **Sadako** and the thousand paper cranes; paintings by Ronald Himler. Putnam 1977 64p il $16.99; pa $5.99
Grades: 3 4 5 6   **92**
   1. Children 2. Leukemia 3. Leukemia patients 4. Atomic bomb -- Physiological effect 5. Hiroshima (Japan) -- Bombardment, 1945
   ISBN 0-399-20520-9; 0-698-11802-2 pa
                                                           LC 76-9872
   "A story about a young girl of Hiroshima who died from leukemia ten years after the dropping of the atom bomb. Her dreams of being an outstanding runner are dimmed when she learns she has the fatal disease. But her spunk and bravery, symbolized in her efforts to have faith in the story of the golden crane, are beautifully portrayed by the author." Babbling Bookworm

Savage, Augusta Christine, 1892-1962
   Schroeder, Alan, 1961- **In** her hands; the story of sculptor Augusta Savage. illustrated by JaeMe Bereal. Lee & Low Books 2009 un il $19.95
Grades: 3 4 5 6   **92**
   1. Artists 2. Sculptors 3. Women artists 4. Harlem Renaissance 5. African American artists
   ISBN 1-60060-332-7; 978-1-60060-332-7
                                                      LC 2009003859
   "Young readers will . . . find this a solid introduction to the art world and a daring but lesser-known African American artist. Bereal's . . . expansive, richly hued one and two-page spreads fit nicely with the text and deftly capture the emotions of the story." Booklist

Schaller, George B.
   Turner, Pamela S. A **life** in the wild; George Schaller's struggle to save the last great beasts. Farrar, Straus and Giroux 2008 103p il map $21.95
Grades: 5 6 7 8   **92**
   1. Zoologists 2. Wildlife conservation 3. Nonfiction writers
   ISBN 978-0-374-34578-5; 0-374-34578-3
                                                      LC 2007-42844
   "The author interviewed Schaller and had access to his photos, which allowed her to capture beautifully the spirit of Schaller's work. The book is organized chronologically, and each chapter covers a geographic area and the principal animals that Schaller studied there. . . . Animal lovers and conservation-minded students will enjoy this excellent introduction to Schaller and his ideals." Voice Youth Advocates
   Includes bibliographical references

Schiaparelli, Elsa, 1890-1973
   Rubin, Susan Goldman. **Hot** pink; the life and fashions of Elsa Schiaparelli. Susan Goldman Rubin. Abrams Books For Young Readers 2015 56 p. illustrations (chiefly color) (hardcover) $21.95
Grades: 5 6 7 8 9   **92**
   1. Fashion design 2. Fashion -- France -- History -- 20th century
   ISBN 9781419716423
                                                      LC 2014032527
   This book, by Susan Goldman Rubin, explores how "shocking pink—hot pink, as it is called today—was the signature color of Elsa Schiaparelli (1890–1973) and perhaps her greatest contribution to the fashion world. Schiaparelli was one of the most innovative designers in the early 20th century. Many design elements that are taken for granted today she created and brought to the forefront of fashion." (Publisher's note)
   "With accessible text, an inviting format, and a comprehensive list of multimedia resources in the back matter, this concise biography is well

suited to classroom use, particularly for students who prefer to approach history through art." Booklist

Schliemann, Heinrich, 1822-1890
   ★ Schlitz, Laura Amy. The **hero** Schliemann; the dreamer who dug for Troy. illustrated by Robert Byrd. Candlewick Press 2006 72p il $12.23
Grades: 4 5 6   **92**
   1. Archeologists 2. Excavations (Archeology) 3. Archaeologists 4. Troy (Extinct city)
   ISBN 0-7636-2283-4
                                                      LC 2005046916
   This is a biography of the archaeologist who rediscovered ancient Troy. "Intermediate." (Horn Book)
   "In this slim biography, Schlitz introduces Heinrich Schliemann, a nineteenth-century "storyteller, archaeologist, and crook," who led a search for the lost cities of Homer's epic poems." Booklist
   Includes bibliographical references

Schulz, Charles M.
   Amoroso, Cynthia. **Charles** Schulz; by Cynthia Amoroso and Robert B. Noyed. Child's World 2010 24p il (Basic biographies) lib bdg $22.79
Grades: PreK K 1   **92**
   1. Cartoonists
   ISBN 978-1-60253-340-0; 1-60253-340-7
                                                      LC 2009029366
   A biography of the cartoonist who created Charlie Brown in the strip "Peanuts."
   This "pairs intelligent, brief text with abundant photos. Simple but never basic." Booklist
   Includes bibliographical references

   ★ Gherman, Beverly. **Sparky** : the life and art of Charles Schulz. Chronicle Books 2010 125p il $16.99
Grades: 5 6 7 8   **92**
   1. Cartoonists
   ISBN 978-0-8118-6790-0; 0-8118-6790-0
   A look at the life and influences of Charles Schulz, creator of the beloved comic strip Peanuts.
   "Gherman's clear and direct prose is just right for portraying the life of the famous cartoonist for young readers. The splashy, bright design, with multicolored pages and several of Schulz's cartoons included, makes this a cheery read that may well introduce the Peanuts comic strip to a new generation, who likely know Charlie Brown mostly through the holiday TV specials. An informative yet lighthearted look at the life of an American icon." Kirkus

Schumann, Clara, 1819-1896
   ★ Reich, Susanna. **Clara** Schumann; piano virtuoso. Clarion Bks. 1999 118p il $18; pa $9.95
Grades: 5 6 7 8   **92**
   1. Pianists 2. Women composers
   ISBN 0-395-89119-1; 0-618-55160-3 pa
                                                      LC 98-24510
   Describes the life of the German pianist and composer who made her professional debut at age nine and who devoted her life to music and to her family
   "This thoroughly researched book draws on primary sources, both Clara's own diaries and her voluminous correspondence with her husband. . . . Reich's lucid, quietly passionate biography is liberally illustrated with photographs and reproductions." Horn Book Guide

Scidmore, Eliza Ruhamah, 1856-1928

Zimmerman, Andrea. **Eliza's** cherry trees; Japan's gift to America. illustrated by Ju Hong Chen. Pelican Pub. Co. 2011 un il $16.99

Grades: 3 4 5 6   **92**

1. Photographers 2. Cherry trees 3. Travel writers 4. Washington (D.C.)

ISBN 1-58980-954-8; 978-1-58980-954-3

LC 2010046163

"This is an inspiring, heartwarming story of determination and spirit. The writing flows well, and the lush illustrations are reminiscent of Impressionist paintings." SLJ

Scieszka, Jon, 1954-

Scieszka, Jon. **Knucklehead**; tall tales and mostly true stories of growing up Scieszka. Viking 2008 106p il $16.99; pa $12.99

Grades: 4 5 6 7   **92**

1. Authors 2. Authors, American 3. Children's authors

ISBN 978-0-670-01106-3; 0-670-01106-1; 978-0-670-01138-4 pa; 0-670-01138-X pa

LC 2008-16870

"Scieszka . . . has written an autobiography about boys, for boys and anyone else interested in baseball, fire and peeing on stuff. . . . The text is divided into two- to three- page nonsequential chapters and peppered with scrapbook snapshots and comic-book-ad reproductions. . . . By themselves, the chapters entertain with abrupt, vulgar fun. Taken together, they offer a look at the makings of one very funny author." Booklist

Scott, Wendell, 1921-1990

Weatherford, Carole Boston. **Racing** against the odds; the story of Wendell Scott, stock car racing's African-American champion. illustrated by Eric A. Velasquez. Marshall Cavendish Children 2009 un il $17.99

Grades: 3 4 5   **92**

1. Automobile racing 2. African American athletes 3. Automobile racing drivers

ISBN 978-0-76145-465-6; 0-76145-465-9

LC 2008010711

"In this stirring biography of Scott, the only black race car driver to win a NASCAR race, Velasquez's expressive pastels showcase the driver's determination and resourcefulness. . . . With as much attention paid to Scott's life off the track as on, readers won't need to be racing fans to be drawn in." Publ Wkly

Seeger, Pete, 1919-2014

Reich, Susanna. **Stand** up and sing! Pete Seeger, folk music, and the path to justice. by Susanna Reich; illustrated by Adam Gustavson. Bloomsbury 2017 48 p. illustrations (some color) (hardcover) $17.99

Grades: 1 2 3 4   **92**

1. Folk musicians -- United States -- Biography 2. Folk singers -- United States -- Biography

ISBN 9780802738127; 9781681191973; 9781681191980

LC 2016022360

This biography of Pete Seeger, by Susanna Reich, illustrated by Adam Gustavson, "celebrates his legacy, showing kids of every generation that no cause is too small and no obstacle too large if, together, you stand up and sing! . . . Coming of age during the Great Depression, Pete saw poverty and adversity that would forever shape his worldview, but it wasn't until he received his first banjo that he found his way to change the world." (Publisher's note)

"Gustavson's digitized gouache, watercolor, pencil, and oil paintings offer scenes from Seeger's life in both full-page color and spot-art accompaniments. While not a comprehensive treatment of Seeger's life, this is an excellent introduction; read and sing along—loudly." Kirkus

Silvey, Anita. **Let** your voice be heard; The Life and Times of Pete Seeger. Anita Silvey. Clarion Books 2016 112 p. illustrations (hardcover) $17.99

Grades: 5 6 7 8   **92**

1. Folk musicians 2. Folk singers -- United States -- Biography

ISBN 9780547330129

LC 2015034787

In this book by Anita Silvey, "Pete Seeger, the iconic folk musician and multiple Grammy winner, discovered early in life that what he wanted to do was make music. His amazing career as singer, songwriter, and banjo player spanned seven decades. . . . An activist and protester, Seeger crusaded for the rights of labor, the rights of people of color, and the First Amendment right to let his voice be heard, and launched the successful campaign to clean up the Hudson River." (Publisher's note)

"A lively, unique contribution to the biography shelves." Booklist

Includes bibliographical references and index

Selkirk, Alexander, 1676-1721

★ Kraske, Robert. **Marooned**; the strange but true adventures of Alexander Selkirk, the real Robinson Crusoe. illustrated by Robert Andrew Parker. Clarion Books 2005 120p il map $15

Grades: 5 6 7 8   **92**

1. Sailors 2. Survival after airplane accidents, shipwrecks, etc.

ISBN 0-618-56843-3

LC 2004-28769

"In 1704, English sailing master Alexander Selkirk was marooned on Juan Fernandez, an isolated Pacific island. . . . In 1709, two English ships rescued him, hired him as a second mate, and later captured a Spanish treasure ship. . . . Kraske offers a well-focused look at life in several quite different settings during the early eighteenth century as well as an absorbing telling of Selkirk's story." Booklist

Includes glossary and bibliographical references

Sellins, Fannie, 1870 or 1872-1919

Farrell, Mary Cronk. **Fannie** never flinched; One Woman's Courage in the Struggle for American Labor Union Rights. Mary Cronk Farrell. Abrams Books for Young Readers 2016 56 p. illustrations (ebook) $15.54; (hardcover) $19.95

Grades: 4 5 6 7 8   **92**

1. Labor -- United States -- History 2. Women labor leaders -- United States -- Biography 3. Labor unions -- United States -- History 4. Labor unions -- Organizing -- United States -- History

ISBN 9781613129722; 9781419718847

LC 2015040020

This book by Mary Cronk Farrell is about "Fannie Sellins (1872-1919), [who] lived during the Gilded Age of American Industrialization, when the Carnegies and Morgans wore jewels while their laborers wore rags. Fannie dreamed that America could achieve its ideals of equality and justice for all, and she sacrificed her life to help that dream come true. Fannie became a union activist, helping to create St. Louis, Missouri, Local 67 of the United Garment Workers of America. (Publisher's note)

"A cogent, well-documented, handsomely designed treatment of a heretofore forgotten hero of labor." Kirkus

Includes bibliographical references and index

Sendler, Irena, 1910-2008

★ Rubin, Susan Goldman. **Irena** Sendler and the children of the Warsaw Ghetto; illustrated by Bill Farnsworth. Holiday House 2011 40p il $18.95

Grades: 3 4 5 6   **92**

1. Jews -- Poland 2. Warsaw (Poland) 3. Holocaust, 1933-1945 4. World War, 1939-1945 -- Poland 5. World War, 1939-1945 -- Jews

-- Rescue
ISBN 978-0-8234-2251-7; 0-8234-2251-8

LC 2010-23667

"Irena Sendler stands out on the list of righteous Gentiles for her incredibly daring methods of hiding and transporting nearly 400 babies and children out of Nazi-occupied Poland. . . . Rubin's documentary-style narrative is smoothly interspersed with dialogue taken from interviews conducted with many of the now-adult survivors. . . . Farnsworth's moody oil renditions authentically capture the tension, fear, despair and darkness of the period." Kirkus

Vaughan, Marcia. **Irena's** jars of secrets; illustrated by Ron Mazellan. Lee & Low Books 2011 il $18.95
Grades: 3 4 5   92
1. Humanitarians 2. Jews -- Poland 3. Warsaw (Poland) 4. Holocaust, 1933-1945 5. World War, 1939-1945 -- Children 6. World War, 1939-1945 -- Jews -- Rescue
ISBN 978-1-60060-439-3; 1-60060-439-0

LC 2011016386

"Vaughan tells the true story without embellishment, employing stark, unadorned syntax that never wavers into pathos, sentiment or myth. It is a definition of quiet heroism. Mazellan's very dark, deeply shadowed oil paintings capture the unabated terror and sorrow. Children should read this work with an adult who is armed with some knowledge of the material. Powerful." Kirkus

Sequoyah, 1770?-1843
★ Rumford, James. **Sequoyah**; the Cherokee man who gave his people writing. Houghton Mifflin 2004 un il $16
Grades: 1 2 3 4   92
1. Cherokee Indians 2. Artisans 3. Metalworkers 4. Indian leaders
ISBN 0-618-36947-3

LC 2004-00980

"Rumford presents the seminal events in Sequoyah's life, culminating in his invention of the Cherokee syllabary. The author writes with a concise eloquence that echoes the oral tradition and makes this one of those rare gems of read-aloud nonfiction. . . . Done in ink, watercolor, pastel, and pencil, the illustrations were adhered to a rough piece of wood, and its textures were highlighted through the use of chalk and colored pencil. . . . The parallel text in Cherokee . . . makes this beautiful book readily accessible to Cherokee children in their own language." SLJ

Wade, Mary Dodson. **Amazing** Cherokee writer Sequoyah. Enslow Publishers 2009 24p il (Amazing Americans) lib bdg $21.26
Grades: 1 2 3   92
1. Cherokee Indians 2. Artisans 3. Metalworkers 4. Indian leaders
ISBN 978-0-7660-3285-9 lib bdg; 0-7660-3285-X lib bdg

LC 2008-24893

"Colorful photos are found throughout, with a timeline, dictionary, websites concerning the topic, as well as an index making . . . [this] book a wonderful introduction to nonfiction features." Libr Media Connect
Includes glossary

Sessions, Kate Olivia, 1857-1940
Hopkins, H. Joseph. The **tree** lady; H. Joseph Hopkins; illustrated by Jill McElmurry. Beach Lane Books 2013 32 p. (hardcover) $16.99
Grades: 2 3 4   92
1. Picture books for children 2. Horticulturists -- California -- San Diego -- Biography
ISBN 1442414022; 9781442414020

LC 2012032903

This "picture book biography recalls the life and contributions of a horticulturist in the late 19th century. Kate Sessions populated San

Diego's landscape with not lupines but trees. Her love for nature dated back to her childhood, where, in school, 'she liked studying wind and rain, muscles and bones, plants and trees. Especially trees.'" (Publishers Weekly)

Seuss, Dr., 1904-1991
Cohen, Charles D. The **Seuss,** the whole Seuss, and nothing but the Seuss; a visual biography of Theodor Seuss Geisel. Random House 2004 390p il $35; lib bdg $36.99
Grades: Adult Professional   92
1. Artists 2. Authors 3. Humorists 4. Illustrators 5. Authors, American 6. Children's authors
ISBN 0-375-82248-8; 0-375-92248-2 lib bdg

LC 2003-20526

This is a "profile of the creator of Horton, the Grinch, and the Cat in the Hat. . . . Crisp full-color illustrations on every page of the coffee-table volume will pull readers into Cohen's accessible recap of Theodore Geisel's career, which is enhanced with just enough personal information to bring everything together. . . . [The volume includes] clear reproductions of posters, book illustrations, newspaper cartoons, and book pages, with intriguing background information." Booklist

★ Krull, Kathleen. The **boy** on Fairfield Street: how Ted Geisel grew up to become Dr. Seuss; paintings by Steve Johnson and Lou Fancher; with decorative illustrations by Dr. Seuss. Random House 2004 43p il $16.95; lib bdg $18.99
Grades: K 1 2 3   92
1. Artists 2. Authors 3. Humorists 4. Illustrators 5. Authors, American 6. Children's authors
ISBN 0-375-82298-4; 0-375-92298-9 lib bdg

LC 2003-1754

Introduces the life of renowned children's author and illustrator Ted Geisel, popularly known as Dr. Seuss, focusing on his childhood and youth in Springfield, Massachusetts

"Johnson and Fancher's lovely, full-page illustrations are supplemented by samples of Dr. Seuss's artwork. . . . Krull's work is a terrific look at the boyhood of one of the most beloved author/illustrators of the 20th century." SLJ

Sewall, May Wright, 1844-1920
Boomhower, Ray E. **Fighting** for equality; a life of May Wright Sewall. [by] Ray E. Boomhower. Indiana Historical Society Press 2007 160p il $17.95
Grades: 4 5 6   92
1. Feminism 2. Educators 3. Reformers 4. Suffragists 5. Lecturers 6. Pacifists
ISBN 978-0-87195-253-0; 0-87195-253-X

LC 2007008517

"This accessible volume tells of the life and work of suffragist and educator [May] Wright Sewall. . . . Archival black-and-white photos enhance the text." Horn Book Guide
Includes bibliographical references

Shakur, Tupac
Harris, Ashley Rae. **Tupac** Shakur; multi-platinum rapper. ABDO Pub. Co. 2010 112p il (Lives cut short) lib bdg $32.79
Grades: 5 6 7 8   92
1. Poets 2. Actors 3. Hip-hop 4. Rap music 5. African American musicians 6. Rap musicians
ISBN 978-1-60453-791-8; 1-60453-791-4

This discusses Tupac Shakur's early life, "providing details that give insight into later success and troubles and maintaining a laudatory tone that focuses on the individual's artistic achievements and hard work to achieve fame. Details [such as] explaining . . . that Tupac Shakur was a standout student in high school are bound to resonate with readers. Numerous photos and sidebars appear throughout. [A] worthwhile [resource] for reports as well as popular reading." SLJ

Shiner, Michael, 1805-1880

Bolden, Tonya. **Capital** days; Michael Shiner's journal and the growth of our nation's capital. by Tonya Bolden. Abrams Books for Young Readers 2015 90 p. (hardback) $21.95

Grades: 4 5 6   92

1. Washington (D.C.) -- History 2. African Americans -- Biography 3. Washington (D.C.) -- Biography 4. Slaves -- Maryland -- Biography 5. Freedmen -- Washington (D.C.) -- Biography 6. Washington (D.C.) -- History -- 19th century 7. African Americans -- Washington (D.C.) -- Biography 8. Washington (D.C.) -- Race relations -- History -- 19th century

ISBN 1419707337; 9781419707339

LC 2014024668

This book, by Tonya Bolden, "introduces young readers to Washington, D.C., during the early to mid-19th century. Spanning more than 60 years, the story of Michael Shiner (c. 1804–1880) highlights a period of immense change in our country and its capital." Topics include the burning of the city during the War of 1812, the rebuilding of the Capitol and White House, the raising of the Washington Monument . . . the Civil War, [and] the end of slavery." (Publisher's note)

Includes bibliographical references and index

Shuster, Joe, 1914-1992

Nobleman, Marc Tyler. **Boys** of steel; the creators of Superman. illustrated by Ross MacDonald. Knopf 2008 un il $16.99; lib bdg $19.99

Grades: 1 2 3   92

1. Artists 2. Cartoonists 3. Illustrators 4. Comic book writers 5. Superman (Fictional character)

ISBN 978-0-375-83802-6; 0-375-83802-3; 978-0-375-93802-3 lib bdg; 0-375-93802-8 lib bdg

LC 2007041606

"This book brings the young men behind the Man of Steel to a picture-book audience. Along with the compressed account of the partnership between nerdy high-school outcasts Joe Shuster and Jerry Siegel, Nobleman includes insights about superheroes' cultural significance and the chord struck by Superman. . . . It's hard to imagine a better sidekick for the text than MacDonald's illustrations, which capture the look of 1930s comics with their sepia-toned, stylized imagery." Booklist

Siegel, Jerry, 1914-1996

Nobleman, Marc Tyler. **Boys** of steel; the creators of Superman. illustrated by Ross MacDonald. Knopf 2008 un il $16.99; lib bdg $19.99

Grades: 1 2 3   92

1. Artists 2. Cartoonists 3. Illustrators 4. Comic book writers 5. Superman (Fictional character)

ISBN 978-0-375-83802-6; 0-375-83802-3; 978-0-375-93802-3 lib bdg; 0-375-93802-8 lib bdg

LC 2007041606

"This book brings the young men behind the Man of Steel to a picture-book audience. Along with the compressed account of the partnership between nerdy high-school outcasts Joe Shuster and Jerry Siegel, Nobleman includes insights about superheroes' cultural significance and the chord struck by Superman. . . . It's hard to imagine a better sidekick for the text than MacDonald's illustrations, which capture the look of 1930s comics with their sepia-toned, stylized imagery." Booklist

Sikorsky, Igor

Wyckoff, Edwin Brit. **Helicopter** man: Igor Sikorsky and his amazing invention. Enslow 2010 32p il (Genius at work! Great inventor biographies) lib bdg $22.60

Grades: 4 5 6   92

1. Helicopters 2. Aeronautical engineers 3. Aeronautics -- History 4. Aircraft industry executives

ISBN 978-0-7660-3445-7; 0-7660-3445-3

LC 2009-15881

This is the story of Igor Sikorsky's life, and how he built the first successful helicopter.

Includes glossary and bibliographical references

Sitting Bull, Dakota Chief, 1831-1890

Bruchac, Joseph. A **boy** called Slow: the true story of Sitting Bull; illustrated by Rocco Baviera. Philomel Bks. 1994 un il $16.99; pa $6.99

Grades: 1 2 3   92

1. Dakota Indians 2. Indian chiefs

ISBN 0-399-22692-3; 0-698-11616-X pa

LC 93-21233

The author "recounts the early years of the young Lakota boy who grows from an unprepossessing child named 'Slow,' to a youth whose careful and deliberate actions bring honor to the name, to a young warrior whose courage in defeating the Crow earns him his father's vision name Tatan'ka Iyota'ke—Sitting Bull." Bull Cent Child Books

★ Nelson, S. D. **Sitting** Bull; Lakota warrior and defender of his people. by S. D. Nelson. Abrams Books for Young Readers 2015 55 p. illustrations (chiefly color) (hardcover) $19.95

Grades: 4 5 6   92

1. Dakota Indians 2. Hunkpapa Indians -- History 3. Hunkpapa Indians -- Kings and rulers -- Biography

ISBN 9781419707315

LC 2014045761

In this children's book, S. D. Nelson, "an enrolled member of the Standing Rock Sioux Tribe in the Dakotas, presents Sitting Bull's life as an entry point into that period of history. . . . The book is . . . told in the first person, with Sitting Bull describing his childhood training to be a warrior and a hunter." (School Library Journal)

"A tragic true story told in powerfully subdued tones." Booklist

Turner, Ann Warren. **Sitting** Bull remembers; paintings by Wendell Minor. HarperCollinsPublishers 2007 un il $16.99; lib bdg $17.89

Grades: 3 4 5 6   92

1. Dakota Indians 2. Little Bighorn, Battle of the, 1876 3. Indian chiefs

ISBN 978-0-06-051399-3; 0-06-051399-3; 978-0-06-051400-6 lib bdg; 0-06-051400-0 lib bdg

LC 2006-29870

"In this first-person, fictionalized account, Sitting Bull is living in captivity near the end of his life and remembering his past. . . . Turner's writing is lyrical, almost poetic. The story is poignant and sympathetic to the plight of the Native peoples who were driven from their land and forced to live on tiny reservations. . . . The well-crafted art adds drama and depth to the story." SLJ

Smalls, Robert, 1839-1915

Halfmann, Janet. **Seven** miles to freedom; the Robert Smalls story. by Janet Halfmann; illustrated by Duane Smith. Lee & Low Books 2008 un il $17.95

Grades: 3 4 5   92

1. Slaves 2. State legislators 3. Members of Congress 4. Planter (Steamship) 5. Slavery -- United States 6. African Americans --

Biography 7. African Americans -- Civil rights 8. United States -- History -- 1861-1865, Civil War
ISBN 978-1-60060-232-0; 1-60060-232-0

LC 2007029274

This "will grab readers with exciting action. . . . Spacious, impressionistic oil paintings accompany [the] text." Booklist

Smith, Elinor, 1911-2010

★ Brown, Tami Lewis. **Soar,** Elinor! pictures by François Roca. Farrar Straus Giroux 2010 un il $16.99

Grades: 2 3 4 5　　　　　　　　　　　　　　　**92**
1. Air pilots 2. Women air pilots 3. New York (N.Y.) -- History
ISBN 978-0-374-37115-9; 0-374-37115-6

LC 2008-30405

"Elinor Smith began talking flying lessons in 1921 when she was only 10 years old. At 16, she was the youngest person in the U.S., man or woman, to earn a pilot's license. The climax of this picture-book biography is when Smith achieved acclaim as the first person to fly a plane under . . . four of New York City's bridges. . . . Brown's narration is fluent, engaging, and full of dialogue. . . . [The book features] realistic oil illustrations. . . . Roca uses minimal background detail and skillfully arranges scenes to focus attention on the emotions and faces of the characters while still maintaining historical and geographical accuracy." SLJ
Includes bibliographical references

Smith, Louise, 1916-2006

★ Rosenstock, Barbara. **Fearless**; the story of racing legend Louise Smith. [by] Barb Rosenstock; illustrated by Scott Dawson. Dutton Children's Books 2010 un il $16.99

Grades: K 1 2　　　　　　　　　　　　　　　**92**
1. Automobile racing 2. Automobile drivers 3. Automobile racing drivers
ISBN 978-0-525-42173-3; 0-525-42173-4

LC 2009-53252

"Dawson's gorgeous, light-infused acrylics convey Louise's self-assured nature, while race scenes capture the rush of adrenaline in a blur of glinting metal. Rosenstock's upbeat prose finishes on a high note, with aging Louise flying down a country road. . . . This debut for both author and illustrator is a winner." Publ Wkly

Sneve, Virginia Driving Hawk

Sneve, Virginia Driving Hawk. The **Christmas** coat; memories of my Sioux childhood. illustrated by Ellen Beier. Holiday House 2011 un il $16.95

Grades: K 1 2 3　　　　　　　　　　　　　　**92**
1. Authors 2. Christmas 3. Novelists 4. Dakota Indians 5. Clothing and dress 6. Christmas stories 7. Children's authors 8. Young adult authors 9. Native Americans -- Biography
ISBN 978-0-8234-2134-3; 0-8234-2134-1

LC 2010029562

Virginia's coat is too small and hardly protects her from the frigid South Dakota winter. As Christmas approaches, all the children on the Sioux reservation look forward to receiving boxes full of clothing sent by congregations in the East. Virginia spots a beautiful gray fur coat but holds back tears as it is claimed by one of her classmates. Later, Virginia can't believe what Mama brings home. Based on an event from the author's childhood.

"Virginia's personality shines through in this poignant story that entertains and informs without recourse to sterotypes." Kirkus

Snyder, Grace, 1882-1982

Warren, Andrea. **Pioneer** girl; a true story of growing up on the prairie. with a new afterword by the author. University of Nebraska Press 2009 104p il map pa $14.95

Grades: 5 6 7 8　　　　　　　　　　　　　　**92**
1. Frontier and pioneer life 2. Quiltmakers 3. Centenarians
ISBN 978-0-8032-2526-8 pa; 0-8032-2526-1 pa

LC 2009-20883

First published 1998 by Morrow Junior Books
Biography of Nebraska homesteader, Grace McCance Snyder
"This new edition offers an afterword that includes information about black homesteaders, Native Americans, and the specific tasks of women, especially quilting. . . . Although it is written for younger readers than a teen audience, readability and intense subject matter should make the book popular with those readers." Voice Youth Advocates
Includes bibliographical references

Sockalexis, Louis, 1871-1913

Wise, Bill. **Louis** Sockalexis; Native American baseball pioneer. by Bill Wise; illustrated by Bill Farnsworth. Lee & Low Books 2007 un il $16.95

Grades: 2 3 4 5　　　　　　　　　　　　　　**92**
1. Baseball players 2. Baseball -- Biography 3. Native Americans -- Biography
ISBN 978-1-58430-269-8

LC 2006017730

"This picture book offers a rousing introduction to the life of the first Native American to play major league baseball. . . . Wise and Farnsworth collaborate to great effect in rendering this story both informative and poignant. The color-drenched paintings do an excellent job of bringing this period to life and capturing the intense emotion of the ballpark drama." SLJ
Includes bibliographical references

Soto, Gary

Abrams, Dennis. **Gary** Soto; foreword by Kyle Zimmer. Chelsea House Pubs. 2008 120p bibl il por (Who wrote that?) $30

Grades: 5 6 7 8　　　　　　　　　　　　　　**92**
1. Poets 2. Authors 3. Novelists 4. Mexican American authors 5. Essayists 6. College teachers 7. Authors, American 8. Children's authors 9. Young adult authors 10. Mexican Americans -- Biography
ISBN 978-0-7910-9529-4; 0-7910-9529-0

LC 2007045509

A biography of the popular Mexican American author for children and young adults.
Includes bibliographical references

Sotomayor, Sonia, 1954-

Gitlin, Marty. **Sonia** Sotomayor; Supreme Court justice. by Martin Gitlin. ABDO Pub. Co. 2011 112p il (Essential lives) $32.79

Grades: 5 6 7 8　　　　　　　　　　　　　　**92**
1. Judges 2. Women judges 3. District attorneys 4. Supreme Court justices 5. Hispanic Americans -- Biography
ISBN 978-1-61613-518-8; 1-61613-518-2

LC 2010000499

This biography of Supreme Court Justice Sonia Sotomayor "toggles between the subject's personal and professional life; [it] offers sidebar explanations of legal issues. . . . The writing is accessible, the format is open, and full-color photos appear throughout." SLJ
Includes glossary and bibliographical references

McElroy, Lisa Tucker. **Sonia** Sotomayor; first Hispanic U.S. Supreme Court justice. Lerner Publications 2010 48p il lib bdg $26.60

Grades: 5 6 7 8　　　　　　　　　　　　　　**92**
1. Judges 2. Women judges 3. District attorneys 4. Supreme

Court justices 5. Hispanic Americans -- Biography
ISBN 978-0-7613-5861-9 lib bdg; 0-7613-5861-7 lib bdg
LC 2009037703
"Well organized and straightforward, this biography is appealing with its bright photographs and bold, easy-to-read font. Starting with Sotomayor's childhood in the Bronx, the author covers the justice's life and career up to her nomination to the Supreme Court. . . . An informative, interesting, and, most of all, inspiring read." SLJ
Includes bibliographical references

Winter, Jonah. **Sonia** Sotomayor; a judge grows in the Bronx. illustrated by Edel Rodriguez. Atheneum Books for Young Readers 2009 un il $16.99
Grades: K 1 2 3   92
1. Judges 2. Women judges 3. District attorneys 4. Supreme Court justices 5. Hispanic Americans -- Biography 6. Bilingual books -- English-Spanish
ISBN 978-1-4424-0303-1; 1-4424-0303-9
LC 2009031659
A biography of the Bronx-born Latina Supreme Court justice.
"This timely, accessible picture-book biography, which features both English and Spanish text on every page, brings Sotomayor's exciting rags-to-riches story to young readers. . . . Winter lets the small details convey the drama, which is amplified in the mixed-media illustrations in warm shades of red and brown." Booklist

Spinelli, Jerry
★ Spinelli, Jerry. **Knots** in my yo-yo string; the autobiography of a kid. Knopf 1998 148p il hardcover o.p. pa $10.95
Grades: 4 5 6 7   92
1. Authors 2. Magazine editors 3. Authors, American 4. Children's authors
ISBN 0-679-88791-1 pa; 0-679-98791-6
LC 97-30827
This Italian-American Newbery Medalist presents a humorous account of his childhood and youth in Norristown, Pennsylvania
"There is an 'everyboy' universality to Spinelli's experiences, but his keen powers of observation and recall turn the story into a richly rewarding personal history." Horn Book Guide

Squires, Emily Swain, 19th cent.
Hailstone, Ruth. The **white** ox; the journey of Emily Swain Squires. [illustrations by] Dan Burr; [written by] Ruth Hailstone. Calkins Creek 2009 un il $18.95
Grades: 2 3 4   92
1. Mormons 2. Immigrants 3. Frontier and pioneer life 4. Pioneers
ISBN 978-1-59078-555-3; 1-59078-555-X
LC 2008024154
Hailstone's "narrative describes the real-life journey of ten-year-old Emily Swain Squires (her great-great grandmother), who traveled ahead of her family from England to Salt Lake City around 1863. During the hardest part of the journey, walking across the plains, she befriended a weary white ox, which gave her enough strength to complete the long trek. Burr uses a digital version of oil painting in Photoshop, applied to a traditional surface, to create 15 stunning and dramatic spreads that appear historically accurate in every detail. Children will be swept up by the lovely art and the tale of Emily's remarkable journey." Kirkus

Standish, Myles, 1584?-1656
Harness, Cheryl. The **adventurous** life of Myles Standish; and the amazing-but-true survival story of Plymouth Colony. painstakingly written and illustrated by Cheryl Harness. National Geographic 2006 144p il map (Cheryl Harness history) $16.95; lib bdg $25.90

Grades: 4 5 6 7   92
1. Pilgrims (New England colonists) 2. Colonists 3. Pilgrim fathers 4. Colonial leaders 5. Massachusetts -- History -- 1600-1775, Colonial period
ISBN 978-0-7922-5918-3; 0-7922-5918-1; 978-0-7922-5919-0 lib bdg; 0-7922-5919-X lib bdg
"Harness chronicles the history of the Plymouth Pilgrims from their troubles in England to their first years in North America, with the focus on Standish. Separating documented history from speculation, the narrative explains religious movements, introduces key figures, and gives a balanced account of Pilgrim-Indian relationships. . . . The tone is casual. . . . A reader-friendly approach to history." Booklist
Includes bibliographical references

Stanton, Elizabeth Cady, 1815-1902
★ Stone, Tanya Lee. **Elizabeth** leads the way; Elizabeth Cady Stanton and the right to vote; illustrations by Rebecca Gibbon. Henry Holt & Co. 2008 un il $16.95
Grades: 1 2 3   92
1. Feminism 2. Suffragists 3. Women -- Suffrage
ISBN 978-0-8050-7903-6; 0-8050-7903-3
LC 2007002833
This is "a short, incisive biography covering some of the high points of Stanton's life, beginning with her shocking realization about how unfairly the law treated women, which translated into Stanton's work for women's suffrage. . . . The child-pleasing artwork features characters a bit reminiscent of clothespin dolls, but the cameos of action, matched by full-page pictures, make the history accessible." Booklist

Stein, Gertrude, 1874-1946
Winter, Jonah. **Gertrude** is Gertrude is Gertrude is Gertrude; written by Jonah Winter; illustrated by Calef Brown. Atheneum Books for Young Readers 2009 un il $16.99
Grades: K 1 2 3   92
1. Poets 2. Authors 3. Novelists 4. Women authors 5. Essayists 6. Memoirists 7. Literary critics 8. Authors, American
ISBN 978-1-4169-4088-3; 1-4169-4088-X
LC 2007-01447
Winter "crafts a Steinesque 'word portrait' of the modernist author. Stein wears a serene smile in Brown's . . . patchy acrylic images, and by her side is an enigmatic Alice B. Toklas. . . . Winter's nonlinear prose echoes The Autobiography of Alice B. Toklas, and his fugues suit a poet fond of repetition (and babble). Brown's idiosyncratic visuals and complementary palette . . . befit this impresario of experimental artists and writers on the Rive Gauche." Publ Wkly

Stengel, Casey
Winter, Jonah. **You** never heard of Casey Stengel?! Jonah Winter, Barry Blitt. Schwartz & Wade Books 2015 40 p. color illustrations $17.99
Grades: K 1 2 3 4   92
1. Baseball managers 2. New York Yankees (Baseball team) 3. Baseball managers -- United States -- Biography
ISBN 9780375870132; 9780375970139
LC 2014005746
This children's book, by Jonah Winter, illustrated by Barry Blitt, profiles "legendary baseball manager Casey Stengel [who] worked with such greats as Joe DiMaggio and Mickey Mantle; . . . led the New York Yankees to a record-breaking ten pennants and seven World Series in twelve years; . . . invented 'platooning,' a way to use players that revolutionized the game; . . . [and] was a prankster." (Publisher's note)
"Blitt's softly colored pen, ink, and watercolor illustrations, in a variety of perspectives, perfectly convey Stengel's baseball world, and

the portraits of Stengel are amazingly accurate and lifelike. A charming, endearing introduction to a baseball icon." Kirkus

Stowe, Harriet Beecher, 1811-1896

Adler, David A. A **picture** book of Harriet Beecher Stowe; illustrated by Colin Bootman. Holiday House 2003 un il $17.95; pa $6.95
Grades: K 1 2 3   **92**
1. Authors 2. Novelists 3. Abolitionists 4. Women authors 5. Authors, American 6. Children's authors 7. Nonfiction writers 8. Short story writers
ISBN 0-8234-1646-1; 0-8234-1878-2 pa

LC 2002-27626

Details the life and achievements of abolitionist Harriet Beecher Stowe whose book, Uncle Tom's Cabin, is said to have started the Civil War
"This biography offers easily accessible information supported by realistic, evocative oil paintings." SLJ
Includes bibliographical references

Fritz, Jean. **Harriet** Beecher Stowe and the Beecher preachers. Putnam 1994 144p il $15.99; pa $5.99
Grades: 5 6 7 8   **92**
1. Authors 2. Novelists 3. Abolitionists 4. Women authors 5. Authors, American 6. Children's authors 7. Nonfiction writers 8. Short story writers
ISBN 0-399-22666-4; 0-698-11660-7 pa

LC 93-6408

This is a biography of the abolitionist author of "Uncle Tom's Cabin" with an emphasis on the influence of her preacher father and her family on her life and work.
"Written with vivacity and insight, this readable and engrossing biography is an important contribution to women's history as well as to the history of American letters." Horn Book
Includes bibliographical references

Su, Shih, 1036 or 7-1101

Demi. **Su** Dongpo; Chinese genius. Lee & Low Books 2006 un il map $24
Grades: 4 5 6 7   **92**
1. Poets 2. Authors 3. Authors, Chinese 4. Calligraphers
ISBN 978-1-58430-256-8; 1-58430-256-9

LC 2005030437

"In reverent tribute to a 'statesman, philosopher, poet, painter, engineer, architect, and humanitarian' born nearly ten centuries ago, Demi offers a text in which quoted passages of poetry and references to 'mystical painting skills' mingle with biographical detail. She pairs this with her trademark scenes of dignified, finely detailed figures floating through luminescent clouds in traditional dress. Though she sounds a false note near the end with a dismissive description of Hainan Island as 'a place inhabited only by natives,' this portrait of a 'knight-errant,' who shone brightly in both the literary and political arenas while surviving several severe reversals of fortune, presents an exemplary role model. In the author's view, he still stands at the 'heart and soul of Chinese culture.'" Kirkus
"Beautifully designed and produced, the book features delicately limned, brilliantly colored paintings of scenes from Su Dongpo's life, outlined in scarlet and bordered with thin bands of gold. A visually striking introduction to the man sometimes referred to as Su Shi or Su Tungpo." Booklist

Sullivan, Anne, 1866-1936

Amoroso, Cynthia. **Helen** Keller; by Cynthia Amoroso and Robert B. Noyed. Child's World 2010 24p il (Basic biographies) lib bdg $22.79

Grades: PreK K 1   **92**
1. Deaf 2. Blind 3. Authors 4. Memoirists 5. Humanitarians 6. Teachers of the deaf 7. Inspirational writers 8. Teachers of the blind 9. Social welfare leaders
ISBN 978-1-60253-341-7; 1-60253-341-5

LC 2009029369

This biography of Helen Keller "pairs intelligent, brief text with abundant photos. Simple but never basic." Booklist
Includes bibliographical references

Delano, Marfe Ferguson. **Helen's** eyes; a photobiography of Annie Sullivan, Helen Keller's teacher. [foreword by Keller Johnson Thompson] National Geographic 2008 63p il map $17.95; lib bdg $27.90
Grades: 4 5 6 7   **92**
1. Deaf 2. Blind 3. Authors 4. Teachers 5. Memoirists 6. Humanitarians 7. Teachers of the deaf 8. Inspirational writers 9. Teachers of the blind 10. Social welfare leaders
ISBN 978-1-4263-02-9-1; 1-4263-0209-6; 978-1-4263-0210-7 lib bdg; 1-4263-0210-X lib bdg
"There are many biographies of Helen Keller and Annie Sullivan, but this one is very nicely done. . . . The book is honest in its portrayals, especially of Sullivan. . . . What makes this oversize book so appealing is the clean design, with large typeface. The many fascinating photographs are sometimes placed over historical documents." Booklist
Includes bibliographical references

Suzuki, Hiromi

★ Barasch, Lynne. **Hiromi's** hands. Lee & Low Books 2007 un il $17.95
Grades: K 1 2 3   **92**
1. Cooks 2. Cooking 3. Gender role 4. Japanese Americans 5. Sex role
ISBN 978-1-58430-275-9

LC 2006017283

This picture book biography tells the story of sushi chef Hiromi Suzuki. "Primary." (Horn Book)
"Ink-and-watercolor scenes are rendered in salmon and grays; each childhood is captured in black-and-white snapshots. . . . An inspiring story." SLJ

Tallchief, Maria

Tallchief, Maria. **Tallchief**; America's prima ballerina. by Maria Tallchief with Rosemary Wells; illustrations by Gary Kelley. Viking 1999 un il $15.99
Grades: 3 4 5   **92**
1. Ballet 2. Ballet dancers 3. Native American women 4. Dance teachers
ISBN 0-670-88756-0

LC 98-35783

Ballerina Maria Tallchief describes her childhood on an Osage reservation, the development of her love of dance, and her rise to success in that field
"Through eloquent words, readers are immediately drawn into the first-person narrative. . . . As beautiful as the text is, so too are Kelley's pictures. The large illustrations, several covering double-page spreads, are rendered in soft pastels." SLJ

Tatum, Art, 1910-1956

★ Parker, Robert Andrew. **Piano** starts here: the young Art Tatum. Schwartz & Wade Books 2008 un il $16.99; lib bdg $19.99

Grades: K 1 2 3   92
1. Pianists 2. Jazz musicians 3. African American musicians
ISBN 978-0-375-83965-8; 0-375-83965-8; 978-0-375-93965-5
lib bdg; 0-375-93965-5 lib bdg
LC 2006-102105
This is a "a biography of famed jazz pianist Art Tatum. . . . A subtle
sophistication shines through Parker's easygoing yet dynamic watercolors. . . . Parker's unhurried account could inspire visions of jazz greatness among young musicians." Publ Wkly
Includes bibliographical references

Taylor, Annie Edson, 1838-1921
★ Van Allsburg, Chris, 1949- **Queen** of the Falls. Houghton Mif-
flin Harcourt 2011 un il $18.99
Grades: 3 4 5   92
1. Teachers 2. Stunt performers 3. Niagara Falls (N.Y. and Ont.)
ISBN 0-547-31581-3; 978-0-547-31581-2
LC 2010006780
This picture book tells the story of how "a retired sixty-two-year-old
charm school instructor named Annie Edson Taylor, seeking fame and
fortune, decided to . . . go over Niagara Falls in a wooden barrel." (Publisher's note) "Primary, intermediate." (Horn Book)
"Any kid who has beheld Niagara Falls—or even taken a good
look at pictures of it—will be suitably gobsmacked by the true story of
charm-school teacher Annie Edson Taylor, who, at age 62, decided on a
whim to fund her golden years by being the first person over the falls. . . .
On October 24, 1901, [a] reinforced and padded 160-pound [barrel] was
dropped into the water in front of thousands of nervous spectators. Van
Allsburg's trademark framed illustrations have the unnerving stillness of
old-timey photos." Booklist

Taylor, Major, 1878-1932
Brill, Marlene Targ. **Marshall** Major Taylor; world champion bicyclist, 1899-1901. by Marlene Targ Brill. Twenty-First Century Books
2008 112p il (Trailblazer biography) lib bdg $31.93
Grades: 5 6 7 8   92
1. Bicycle racing 2. African American athletes 3. Cyclists
ISBN 978-0-8225-6610-6 lib bdg; 0-8225-6610-9 lib bdg
LC 2006003883
"Marshall Taylor, an African American bicyclist who, despite fac-
ing prejudice in racing and in life, achieved world renown at the turn of
the last century. . . . Brill's accessible, personable prose vividly relates
Taylor's experiences." Booklist
Includes bibliographical references

Tenzing Norgay, 1914-1986
Burleigh, Robert. **Tiger** of the snows; Tenzing Norgay; the boy
whose dream was Everest. [by] Robert Burleigh and [illustrated by] Ed
Young. Simon & Schuster 2006 un il $16.95
Grades: 3 4 5 6   92
1. Mountaineering 2. Mountaineers 3. Mount Everest (China and
Nepal)
ISBN 0-689-83042-4
LC 2005-00469
Presents the true story of Nepalese Sherpa Tenzing Norgay who, re-
alizing his own dreams, helped Sir Edmund Hillary reach the summit of
Mount Everest.
"Young's hauntingly beautiful illustrations capture the mystery
and grandeur of these dangerously high peaks with somber-hued pas-
tels, predominantly blues and purples, set against black backgrounds. .
. . A stunning and lyrical ode to a contemplative man and his amazing
achievement." SLJ

Tharp, Marie
Burleigh, Robert. **Solving** the puzzle under the sea; Marie Tharp
maps the ocean floor. Robert Burleigh; illustrated by Raúl Colón. Si-
mon & Schuster Books for Young Readers 2016 40 p. color illustra-
tions (hardcover) $17.99
Grades: K 1 2 3 4   92
1. Map drawing 2. Submarine topography 3. Cartographers --
United States -- Biography 4. Geomorphologists -- United States
-- Biography 5. Women cartographers -- United States -- Biography
ISBN 9781481416009
LC 2014010158
This juvenile biography by Robert Burleigh, illustrated by Raúl
Colón, "shares the story of female scientist, Marie Tharp. . . . Marie
Tharp was always fascinated by the ocean. Taught to think big by her
father who was a mapmaker, Marie wanted to do something no one
had ever done before: map the bottom of the Atlantic Ocean." (Pub-
lisher's note)
"An ideal introduction to a lesser-known scientist and an important
understanding about how the Earth works." Kirkus

Thurman, Howard, 1900-1981
Jackson Issa, Kai. **Howard** Thurman's great hope; by Kai Jackson
Issa; illustrated by Arthur L. Dawson. Lee & Low Books 2008 un il
$16.95
Grades: 2 3 4 5   92
1. Clergy 2. Theologians 3. College teachers 4. Inspirational
writers
ISBN 978-1-60060-249-8; 1-60060-249-5
LC 2007050093
"Reds, blues, and yellows pop against brown wood desks or white-
washed walls in vivid, realistic oil paintings. The author drew from
Thurman's memoir and papers to create this accessible, engaging bi-
ography." SLJ

Tillage, Leon, 1936-
★ Tillage, Leon. **Leon's** story; [by] Leon Walter Tillage; collage
art by Susan L. Roth. Farrar, Straus & Giroux 1997 107p il hardcover
o.p. pa $6.95
Grades: 4 5 6 7 8 9 10   92
1. African Americans -- Biography 2. North Carolina -- Race
relations
ISBN 0-374-34379-9; 0-374-44330-0 pa
LC 96-43544
The son of a North Carolina sharecropper recalls the hard times
faced by his family and other African Americans in the first half of the
twentieth century and the changes that the civil rights movement helped
bring about
The author's "voice is direct, the words are simple. There is no rhetoric, no commentary, no bitterness. . . . This quiet drama will move readers of all ages . . . and may encourage them to record their own family
stories." Booklist

Tingle, Tim
★ Tingle, Tim. **Saltypie**; a Choctaw journey from darkness into
light. with illustrations by Karen Clarkson. Cinco Puntos Press 2010
40p il
Grades: 2 3 4 5   92
1. Blind 2. Grandmothers 3. Choctaw Indians 4. Storytellers
ISBN 1933693673; 9781933693675
"Tingle tells his family's story from their origins in Oklahoma Choctaw country to their life in Texas. The account spans generations and
weaves in ghosts from the past to the present day. . . . The author was
six that he learned that his grandmother was blind. Tingle was a junior
in college when he got word that Mawmaw was having surgery. As the

family gathered at the hospital, they told stories about their past, and he heard about her days as an orphan at an Indian boarding school and the discrimination she encountered living in Texas. . . . The large, full-spread illustrations are vibrant and vital in moving the story along. A lovely piece of family history." SLJ

Toulouse-Lautrec, Henri de, 1864-1901

Burleigh, Robert. **Toulouse**-Lautrec; the Moulin Rouge and the City of Light. Abrams 2005 32p il $17.95

Grades: 3 4 5   **92**

1. Artists 2. Painters 3. Lithographers 4. Artists, French

ISBN 0-8109-5867-8

This "volume introduces the life and art of Toulouse-Lautrec. . . . Burleigh relates the facts in a way that is comprehensible to children, without talking down to them. . . . The book's format allows for many illustrations, including period photos and paintings of Paris by artists such as Pissarro and Renoir, which are cleverly mingled with reproductions of Toulouse-Lautrec's arresting drawings, paintings, and lithographs, many in color. . . . A beautifully designed book that provides a lively, accessible introduction to the artist's life and work." Booklist

Toussaint Louverture, 1743?-1803

★ Rockwell, Anne F. **Open** the door to liberty!: a biography of Toussaint L'Ouverture; illustrated by R. Gregory Christie. Houghton Mifflin Books for Children 2009 64p il $18

Grades: 5 6 7 8   **92**

1. Generals 2. Revolutionaries 3. Haiti -- History 4. Blacks -- Biography 5. Slavery -- West Indies

ISBN 978-0-618-60570-5; 0-618-60570-3

LC 2007-25746

"In this eye-opening biography, Rockwell makes a strong case that Toussaint L'Ouverture is one of the most overlooked heroes of the eighteenth century. A freed slave of the French colony of St. Domingue (what we now know as Haiti), L'Ouverture was 48 when he was so inspired by his people's uprising against the French that he joined them and, through his oratory and strategical skills, became their leader. In 1793, he led history's first triumphant slave rebellion, but the resulting freedom would not last long. . . . Evocative paintings in primary colors help tell the story." Booklist

Includes bibliographical references

Truth, Sojourner, d. 1883

Clinton, Catherine. **When** Harriet met Sojourner; illustrated by Shane W. Evans. Katherine Tegen Books 2008 un il $16.99; lib bdg $17.89

Grades: K 1 2 3   **92**

1. Abolitionists 2. Memoirists 3. Slavery -- United States 4. African American women -- Biography

ISBN 978-0-06-050425-0; 0-06-050425-0; 978-0-06-050426-7 lib bdg; 0-06-050426-9 lib bdg

LC 2006-19099

"Clinton imagines what might have been said during a meeting between Harriet Tubman and Sojourner Truth, who both found themselves in Boston one day in October 1864. Their meeting is the climax of this picture book, which tells the stories of the two heroes in clear, simple words on alternating double-page spreads. Evans' dramatic collage-style illustrations evoke the quilts the women worked on, piecing together their history." Booklist

★ Pinkney, Andrea Davis. **Sojourner** Truth's step-stomp stride; [by] Andrea Davis Pinkney & Brian Pinkney. Disney Jump at the Sun Books 2009 un il $16.99

Grades: K 1 2 3   **92**

1. Feminism 2. Abolitionists 3. Memoirists 4. African American

women -- Biography

ISBN 978-0-7868-0767-3; 0-7868-0767-9

The Pinkneys "collaborate on an upbeat yet nuanced picture biography of Sojourner Truth, whose slave name was Isabella. . . . Andrea Davis Pinkney's narrative adopts a confidential, admiring tone, tracing Truth's years of enslaved toil, her subsequent escape, deep religious faith and narration of her life story to abolitionist Olive Gilbert. . . . Brian Pinkney's watercolors, in washes of ochre and slate blue contoured in inky black, utilize a dry-brush technique well suited for depicting Truth's hardscrabble youth and unyielding commitment to justice." Kirkus

Rockwell, Anne F. **Only** passing through: the story of Sojourner Truth; by Anne Rockwell; illustrated by Gregory Christie. Knopf 2000 un il $16.95; lib bdg $18.99

Grades: 3 4 5   **92**

1. Feminism 2. Abolitionists 3. Memoirists 4. African American women -- Biography

ISBN 0-679-89186-2; 0-679-99186-7 lib bdg

LC 00-35736

Rockwell's narrative "is both conversational and immediately riveting. . . . The semi-abstract paintings are inspirational rather than representational, their authority residing in the presence Christie imparts to this heroine." Bull Cent Child Books

Turner, Ann. **My** Name Is Truth; The Life of Sojourner Truth. Ann Turner; illustrated by James Ransome. Harpercollins Childrens Books 2015 40 p. color illustrations $17.99

Grades: 1 2 3 4   **92**

1. Civil rights 2. African American women 3. African American -- Biography 4. African American abolitionists -- Biography 5. Social reformers -- United States -- Biography

ISBN 0060758988; 9780060758981

Author Ann Turner presents the "true story of how former slave Isabella Baumfree transformed herself into the preacher and orator Sojourner Truth. An iconic figure of the abolitionist and women's rights movements, Sojourner Truth famously spoke out for equal rights roughly one hundred years before the civil rights movement." (Publisher's note)

"This picture book biography tackles the life of former slave and abolitionist Isabella Baumfree, better known as Sojourner Truth. Turner details the life of this pivotal figure, who was born into slavery in the late-18th century in New York, along with 11 siblings, all of whom were sold off...Those who are already somewhat familiar with Truth will get the most out of this book, and educators will find the author's note helpful in explaining this historical figure to students. A wonderful addition to collections of African American history that will also work well as a read-aloud." SLJ

Tubman, Harriet, 1820?-1913

Clinton, Catherine. **When** Harriet met Sojourner; illustrated by Shane W. Evans. Katherine Tegen Books 2008 un il $16.99; lib bdg $17.89

Grades: K 1 2 3   **92**

1. Abolitionists 2. Memoirists 3. Slavery -- United States 4. African American women -- Biography

ISBN 978-0-06-050425-0; 0-06-050425-0; 978-0-06-050426-7 lib bdg; 0-06-050426-9 lib bdg

LC 2006-19099

"Clinton imagines what might have been said during a meeting between Harriet Tubman and Sojourner Truth, who both found themselves in Boston one day in October 1864. Their meeting is the climax of this picture book, which tells the stories of the two heroes in clear, simple words on alternating double-page spreads. Evans' dramatic collage-style illustrations evoke the quilts the women worked on, piecing together their history." Booklist

Turner, Glennette Tilley. An **apple** for Harriet Tubman; [by] Glennette Tilley Turner; illustrated by Susan Keeter. Albert Whitman & Co. 2006 un il $15.95

Grades: 2 3 4   **92**

1. Apples 2. Abolitionists 3. Slavery -- United States 4. African American women -- Biography

ISBN 978-0-8075-0395-9; 0-8075-0395-9

LC 2005037360

"At age seven, Tubman's job was to care for the baby of an unkind white woman, who whipped her. Later, the overseer of an orchard lashes her for eating an apple. . . . Ketter's unframed, thickly painted pictures depict the slave child's cruel working conditions and her brave escape and rescue, culminating as Tubman buys a house and plants apple trees, which produce fruit for everyone to share. The story, with its concrete details, works as both fact and metaphor, bringing the transformation full circle—from the scars of suffering to the fruit of freedom." Booklist

Includes bibliographical references

★ Weatherford, Carole Boston. **Moses**; when Harriet Tubman led her people to freedom. illustrated by Kadir Nelson. Hyperion 2006 un il $15.99

Grades: 2 3 4   **92**

1. Abolitionists 2. Underground railroad 3. African American women -- Biography

ISBN 0-7868-5175-9

A Caldecott Medal honor book, 2007

Describes Tubman's spiritual journey as she hears the voice of God guiding her north to freedom on that very first trip to escape the brutal practice of forced servitude.

This is a "handsome, poetic account. . . . Shifting perspectives and subtle details . . . underscore the narrative's spirituality. . . . Tubman's beautifully furrowed face is expressive and entrancing." SLJ

Tutankhamen, King of Egypt

Demi. **Tutankhamun**; written and illustrated by Demi. Marshall Cavendish Children 2009 un il map $19.99

Grades: 4 5 6 7   **92**

1. Kings and rulers 2. Kings 3. Egypt -- History

ISBN 978-0-7614-5558-5; 0-7614-5558-2

LC 2008029313

"The unmistakable designs and opulent glitter of ancient Egyptian art gleam on every page of Demi's picture-book introduction to Tutankhamun. Beginning with King Tut's great-grandfather, Demi presents the broad historical context surrounding the young monarch's reign. . . . Demi's language, organized into brief but pithy paragraphs, is clear. . . . It's the beautiful illustrations that will attract and hold a young audience most, and as usual, Demi incorporates artistic motifs and materials appropriate to her subject." Booklist

Twain, Mark, 1835-1910

★ Burleigh, Robert. The **adventures** of Mark Twain by Huckleberry Finn; with considerable help from Robert Burleigh and [illustrated by] Barry Blitt. Atheneum Books for Young Readers 2011 un il

Grades: 2 3 4   **92**

1. Authors 2. Humorists 3. Novelists 4. Essayists 5. Satirists 6. Memoirists 7. Travel writers 8. Authors, American 9. Short story writers

ISBN 0689830416; 9780689830419

LC 2010006512

This is a biography of Mark Twain told from the perspective of one of his characters. "Grades two to five." (Bull Cent Child Books)

"The neat switcheroo in this picture-book biography has the story of Mark Twain's life told by one of his most endearing characters, Huck Finn. . . . Although Huck's narration is almost overwhelmingly folksy, his undeniably cheery tone is infectious. . . . Blitt . . . provides jaunty, cartoony pen-and-watercolor artwork, with exaggerated, tall-tale figures and period charm aplenty." Booklist

★ Fleischman, Sid. The **trouble** begins at 8; a life of Mark Twain in the wild, wild West. Greenwillow Books 2008 224p il $18.99; lib bdg $19.89

Grades: 5 6 7 8   **92**

1. Authors 2. Humorists 3. Novelists 4. Essayists 5. Satirists 6. Memoirists 7. Travel writers 8. Authors, American 9. Short story writers

ISBN 0-06-134431-1; 0-06-134432-X lib bdg; 978-0-06-134431-2; 978-0-06-134432-9 lib bdg

LC 2007-37891

This biography of Mark Twain focuses on his travels. Chronology. Index. "Grades five to nine." (Bull Cent Child Books)

"Fleischman writes a charming biography of Samuel Clemens before he became Mark Twain, the great American novelist. . . . Written with a sense of humor and wit that honors Twain, this book is sprinkled with famous Twain quotes, excerpts of his writing, and pictures of Twain and other primary documents from the era Clemens spent both on the Mississippi River and in the West." Voice Youth Advocates

Includes bibliographical references

★ Kerley, Barbara. The **extraordinary** Mark Twain (according to Susy) illustrated by Edwin Fotheringam. Scholastic Press 2010 un il $17.99

Grades: 2 3 4 5   **92**

1. Authors 2. Biography 3. Humorists 4. Novelists 5. Authorship 6. Essayists 7. Satirists 8. Memoirists 9. Travel writers 10. Authors, American 11. Short story writers

ISBN 978-0-545-12508-6; 0-545-12508-1

LC 2009-04752

"Wanting to present a portrait of her papa beyond that of just humorist and author, Mark Twain's 13-year-old daughter Susy spent a year chronicling her observations and reflections. . . . Kerley contextualizes the teenager's admiring musings with vivid familial backdrops. . . . Minibooklets titled 'Journal' appear in the fold of many spreads, containing excerpts from Susy's notebook. . . . Adding dynamic flair to the limited palettes of each digitally created scene are curlicues representing words, which emanate wildly from pen tips, pages, and mouths. Author notes about Susy and her father, a time line of Twain's life, and tips for writing an 'extraordinary biography' complete this accessible and inventive vision of a American legend." Publ Wkly

Velázquez, Diego, 1599-1660

Venezia, Mike. **Diego** Velazquez; written and illustrated by Mike Venezia. Children's Press 2004 32p il (Getting to know the world's greatest artists) lib bdg $26; pa $6.95

Grades: K 1 2 3   **92**

1. Artists 2. Painters 3. Artists, Spanish

ISBN 0-516-22580-4 lib bdg; 0-516-26980-1 pa

LC 2003-4590

Describes the life and career of the seventeenth-century Spanish artist famous for his portraits of royalty.

"The unusually abundant full-color reproductions more than justify this series' longevity, as do Venezia's lighthearted cartoons, which foster welcome associations between 'art appreciation' and 'fun.'" Booklist

Vivaldi, Antonio, 1678-1741

Shefelman, Janice Jordan. **I,** Vivaldi; written by Janice Shefelman; illustrated by Tom Shefelman. William B. Eerdmans Pub. Co. 2007 un il $18

Grades: 3 4 5   **92**

1. Composers 2. Violinists

ISBN 978-0-8028-5318-9; 0-8028-5318-8

LC 2006-20120

This is a picture book "biography of composer Antonio Vivaldi. . . . The first-person narration offers an accessible and personable view of Vivaldi's intense passion for music. . . . Stunning ink-and-watercolor scenes evoke the ornate, shadowy church interiors and gilded ornamentation of 17th century Venice." Publ Wkly

Wagner, Honus, 1874-1955

★ Yolen, Jane. **All** star! Honus Wagner and the most famous baseball card ever. illustrated by Jim Burke. Philomel Books 2010 un il $17.99

Grades: 2 3 4   **92**

1. Baseball cards 2. Baseball players 3. Baseball coaches 4. Baseball managers 5. Baseball -- Biography 6. Pittsburgh Pirates (Baseball team)

ISBN 978-0-399-24661-6; 0-399-24661-4

LC 2009-15066

Biography of Honus Wagner and an explanation of why his baseball card is worth almost $3 million.

"The treatment of Wagner's hardscrabble early years . . . is particularly masterful. . . . An eloquently understated tribute to that archetypal American combination of stoicism, decency, drive, and sheer talent." Publ Wkly

Waldman, Neil, 1947-

Waldman, Neil. **Out** of the shadows; an artist's journey. Boyds Mills Press 2006 144p il $21.95

Grades: 5 6 7 8   **92**

1. Artists 2. Authors 3. Illustrators 4. Jews -- Biography 5. Children's authors 6. Artists -- United States

ISBN 1-59078-411-1

Neil Waldman reveals how his passion for art emerged in the kitchen of his family's apartment, where he discovered the work of Vincent Van Gogh and the ability to use illustration as a means to escape the sadness that plagued his home.

"Young artists, as well as readers who wonder about the person behind the pictures they have seen, will appreciate every element of this book: well-constructed story, visual richness, and uncompromising honesty." Booklist

Walker, C. J., Madame, 1867-1919

Lasky, Kathryn. **Vision** of beauty: the story of Sarah Breedlove Walker; illustrated by Nneka Bennett. Candlewick Press 2000 un il $14.99

Grades: 3 4 5   **92**

1. Philanthropists 2. African American businesspeople 3. Cosmeticians 4. Cosmetics industry executives 5. African American women -- Biography

ISBN 9780763664282

LC 99-19594

This is a biography of the African American entrepreneur who founded a cosmetics company and became a millionaire. "Grades three to five." (Bull Cent Child Books)

"Lasky's engaging account moves smoothly through events in Walker's life. . . . The illustrations . . . are attractive and rich in historical detail." Booklist

Walker, Mary Edwards, 1832-1919

Harness, Cheryl. **Mary** Walker wears the pants; the true story of the doctor, reformer, and Civil War hero. Cheryl Harness; illustrated by Carlo Molinari. Albert Whitman & Co. 2013 32 p. (reinforced) $16.99

Grades: 2 3 4 5   **92**

1. Picture books for children 2. Women physicians 3. Physicians -- United States -- Biography 4. Suffragists -- United States -- Biography 5. Women physicians -- United States -- Biography 6. United States -- History -- Civil War, 1861-1865 -- Women 7. United States -- History -- Civil War, 1861-1865 -- Medical care

ISBN 0807549908; 9780807549902

LC 2012019531

This children's picture book focuses on the life of 19th-century "women's rights advocate, doctor, and abolitionist Mary Walker," who was "one of the first women doctors and the first woman to receive the Medal of Honor for her 'services and sufferings' during wartime." A "volunteer for the Union Army during the Civil War, her hard work and determination finally led to her appointment as an assistant surgeon in 1863, the first woman doctor in the U.S. Army." (School Library Journal)

Walking Coyote

Bruchac, Joseph, 1942- **Buffalo** song; by Joseph Bruchac; illustrated by Bill Farnsworth. Lee & Low Books 2008 un il $17.95

Grades: 1 2 3   **92**

1. Bison 2. Kalispel Indians 3. Wildlife conservation 4. Animal rescue workers 5. Native Americans -- Biography

ISBN 978-1-58430-280-3; 1-58430-280-1

LC 2007024912

This biography is "partly fictionalized. . . . Bruchac's long, eloquent afterword fills in the facts. . . . [It is illustrated with] Farnsworth's beautiful, full-bleed oil paintings." Booklist

Walton, Sam

Blumenthal, Karen. **Mr.** Sam; how Sam Walton built Wal-Mart and became America's richest man. Penguin Group 2011 183p il $17.99

Grades: 5 6 7 8   **92**

1. Businessmen 2. Discount stores 3. Retail executives 4. Wal-Mart Stores, Inc.

ISBN 978-0-670-01177-3; 0-670-01177-0

LC 2010049520

"This spectacular success story tracks Walton's rise from lower-middle-class origins to, by the mid-1980s, the top of the 'America's Richest' list. . . . Written in a fluid, journalistic style and enhanced by photos, boxed-out 'Sam stories,' charts tracking changes in Americans' spending habits, and a lavish source list, this account of the man who created what is today the world's largest company makes compelling reading." Booklist

Warhol, Andy, 1928?-1987

★ Christensen, Bonnie. **Fabulous!** a portrait of Andy Warhol. Henry Holt and Co. 2011 un il $16.99

Grades: 3 4 5 6   **92**

1. Artists -- United States 2. Pop art

ISBN 978-0-8050-8753-6; 0-8050-8753-2

LC 2010027840

"Spanning Warhol's rise to fame, this thoughtful account begins and ends with brief, fictionalized scenes that take place in 1966, illuminating the pop artist's popularity and success in contrast to the challenges he overcame to achieve recognition. The bulk of the narrative is fact-based, tracing major milestones in Warhol's personal and professional life through well-organized chronological flashbacks. . . . The differences between fine and commercial art, and Warhol's success in melding the two styles, are addressed in a way that is easy to understand even for someone with no background in art history. Christensen skillfully conveys emotion and mood through vivid, bold collage illustrations." SLJ

Includes bibliographical references

★ Rubin, Susan Goldman. **Andy** Warhol; pop art painter. H.N. Abrams 2006 48p il $18.95

Grades: 4 5 6 7   **92**

1. Artists 2. Pop art 3. Artists -- United States 4. Motion picture directors

ISBN 0-8109-5477-X

LC 2005-13238

"Andy Warhol was a colorful figure who revolutionized how the world looks at art. Rubin's coherent and interesting narrative is filled with quotes by the artist and people who knew him.... Excellent-quality black-and-white and full-color photographs of Warhol and his family and reproductions of his paintings and those of others who influenced him appear throughout." SLJ

Washington, Booker T., 1856-1915

Brimner, Larry Dane. **Booker** T. Washington; getting into the schoolhouse. Marshall Cavendish Benchmark 2009 41p il (American heroes) lib bdg $20.95

Grades: 2 3 4   **92**

1. Slaves 2. Authors 3. Educators 4. African American educators 5. Memoirists 6. Nonfiction writers 7. Tuskegee Institute 8. Civil rights activists 9. African Americans -- Biography

ISBN 978-0-7614-3063-6

LC 2008002870

A biography of Booker T. Washington, who rose from slavery to become a great African-American leader and educator

This "concise and well-written [title covers] key biographical facts without overwhelming young readers, and [includes] captioned illustrations and reproductions, most of which are in color. Text is large, and the layout is age-appropriate and attractive, with wide margins." SLJ

Includes glossary and bibliographical references

Washington, George, 1732-1799

Adler, David A. **George** Washington; an illustrated biography. by David A. Adler. Holiday House 2004 274p il map $24.95

Grades: 5 6 7 8   **92**

1. Generals 2. Presidents 3. Presidents -- United States

ISBN 0-8234-1838-3

LC 2003-67606

This "look at America's premier founding father literally spans his lifetime and attempts to focus . . . on how Washington's early character formation impacted his decisions as a military officer and later as president. . . . The illustrations are largely engravings from the late 19th century. . . . The writing style is accessible without ever falling prey to oversimplification." SLJ

Allen, Kathy. **President** George Washington; illustrated by Len Ebert. Picture Window Books 2010 32p il (Our American story) lib bdg $23.99

Grades: 2 3 4   **92**

1. Generals 2. Presidents 3. Presidents -- United States

ISBN 978-1-4048-5539-7; 1-4048-5539-4

LC 2009-6894

Highlights the life and accomplishments of the Commander in Chief of the Continental Army and first president of the United States.

This title is "illustrated with well-executed, full-page, color illustrations, maps, and photos. . . . [It has] accurate, clearly written information that students can use for either leisure reading or reports." SLJ

Includes glossary and bibliographical references

Dolan, Edward F. **George** Washington; [by] Edward F. Dolan. Marshall Cavendish Benchmark 2008 96p il (Presidents and their times) lib bdg $32.79

Grades: 5 6 7 8   **92**

1. Generals 2. Presidents 3. Presidents -- United States

ISBN 978-0-7614-2427-7 lib bdg; 0-7614-2427-X lib bdg

LC 2006037802

This biography of the first president of the United States "is illustrated with color photos and contains boxed descriptions of key historical events, artwork, and political concepts experienced during the time period. . . . This . . . will be of great use both for biographical research and for enriching the curriculum." Libr Media Connect

Includes glossary and bibliographical references

Harness, Cheryl. **George** Washington. National Geographic Soc. 2000 48p il $17.95

Grades: 3 4 5   **92**

1. Generals 2. Presidents 3. Presidents -- United States

ISBN 0-7922-7096-7

LC 99-29920

Presents the life of George Washington, focusing on the Revolutionary War years and his presidency

"Detailed paintings, full of action and rich with color, portray Washington as well as important moments in American history. . . . This heavily illustrated biography serves as a good introduction to Washington." Booklist

Includes bibliographical references

Malaspina, Ann. **Phillis** sings out freedom; the story of George Washington and Phillis Wheatley. illustrated by Susan Keeter. Albert Whitman 2010 un il $16.99

Grades: 2 3 4   **92**

1. Poets 2. Slaves 3. Authors 4. Generals 5. Presidents 6. Women poets 7. African American authors 8. Poets, American 9. Presidents -- United States 10. African American women -- Biography 11. United States -- History -- 1775-1783, Revolution

ISBN 978-0-8075-6545-2; 0-8075-6545-8

"Camped in Cambridge in the fall of 1775, General Washington despairs that his soldiers won't ever be able to defeat the British. In Providence, freed slave Phillis Wheatley pens a poem of encouragement to Washington. Malaspina intertwines information about Wheatley's early life with wartime events. . . . Keeter's rich oil paintings are full of period details that help to clarify both the war scenes and Wheatley's life." Booklist

Miller, Brandon Marie. **George** Washington for kids; his life and times with 21 activities. [by] Brandon Marie Miller. Chicago Review Press 2007 130p il pa $14.95

Grades: 4 5 6 7   **92**

1. Generals 2. Presidents 3. Presidents -- United States

ISBN 1-55652-655-5 pa; 978-1-55652-655-8 pa

This book covers Washington's life and includes 21 hands-on projects based on his experiences and the times in which he lived.

This is "accessible and absorbing . . . clearly written and informative. . . . Primary quotes are interposed throughout, and illustrations, photographs, and visual aids are plentiful and well placed." SLJ

Mooney, Carla. **George** Washington; 25 great projects you can build yourself. illustrated by Samuel Carbaugh. Nomad 2011 121p il (Build it yourself) $21.95; pa $15.95

Grades: 4 5 6 7   **92**

1. Generals 2. Handicraft 3. Presidents 4. Presidents -- United

States
ISBN 978-1-934670-64-4; 1-934670-64-2; 978-1-934670-63-7 pa pa; 1-934670-63-4 pa

"The life of George Washington lends itself remarkably well to a variety of kid-friendly crafts that don't require old-fashioned materials or 18th-century skills. . . . The projects separate biographical chapters that are thorough and clear. . . . Sidebars with vocabulary words, quotes, interesting facts about the man and his time, and 'What if?' questions regarding pivotal moments in Washington's life add to the text. These sidebars, as well as amusing cartoon illustrations, make the subject light and approachable." SLJ

Includes glossary and bibliographical references

★ Rockwell, Anne F. **Big** George: how a shy boy became President Washington; [by] Anne Rockwell; illustrated by Matt Phelan. Harcourt 2009 un il $17

Grades: K 1 2 3   **92**

1. Generals 2. Presidents 3. Presidents -- United States
ISBN 0-15-216583-5; 978-0-15-216583-3

LC 2002-4984

Portrays George Washington as a shy boy who wasn't afraid of anything except talking to people, but who grew up to lead an army against the British and serve as president of the new nation

This "adulatory biography offers plenty for contemporary kids to connect with. . . . But it's Phelan's . . . extraordinary artwork that cements the bond with readers. As his pencil-and-gouache scenes review Washington's life up to the presidency, his scenes bristle with immediacy, dramatic tension and emotional insight." Publ Wkly

White, Becky. **Betsy** Ross; illustrated by Megan Lloyd. Holiday House 2011 il $16.95

Grades: K 1 2   **92**

1. Generals 2. Presidents 3. Dressmakers 4. Needleworkers 5. Flags -- United States 6. United States -- History -- 1775-1783, Revolution
ISBN 0-8234-1908-8; 978-0-8234-1908-1

LC 2009054296

"Fourteen spreads with four to six rhythmic words on each one tell the story of the first American flag. . . . The large, simple text, paired with the irresistible appliqué art, makes this a perfect introduction to the Stars and Stripes. Using cotton fabric, embroidery thread, dye, paint, and linoleum-block prints, Lloyd captures the period, hard work, and ingenuity of this favorite colonial figure." SLJ

Weber, EdNah New Rider

Weber, EdNah New Rider. **Rattlesnake** Mesa; stories from a native American childhood. by EdNah New Rider Weber; photographs by Richela Renkun. Lee & Low Books 2004 132p il $18.95

Grades: 4 5 6 7   **92**

1. Artisans 2. Memoirists 3. Storytellers 4. Native Americans -- Biography
ISBN 1-58430-231-3

LC 2004-2385

"Weber describes her experiences with warmth and affection in this unusually compelling memoir. Striking black-and-white photos . . . add to the book's appeal." Horn Book Guide

Webster, Noah, 1758-1843

Ferris, Jeri Chase. **Noah** Webster and his words; by Jeri Chase Ferris; illustrated by Vincent X. Kirsch. Houghton Mifflin Harcourt 2012 32 p. col. ill. (reinforced) $16.99

Grades: 2 3 4   **92**

1. English language -- Spelling 2. Educators -- United States --

Biography 3. Lexicographers -- United States -- Biography
ISBN 0547390556; 9780547390550

LC 2011013018

In this picture-book biography, author Jeri Chase Ferris tells the story of Noah Webster, who "entered Yale University and became a teacher [at age 15]. When the Revolutionary War was over, he wanted to write . . . an American spelling book that would systematize American spelling. . . . He followed his speller with a grammar text, and eventually, at age 70, published his American Dictionary of the English Language." (Kirkus Reviews)

Maurer, Tracy Nelson. **Noah** Webster's fighting words; by Tracy Nelson Maurer; illustrated by Mircea Catusanu. Millbrook Press 2016 40 p. color illustrations (lb : alk. paper) $19.99

Grades: 3 4 5   **92**

1. Educators -- United States -- Biography 2. Lexicographers -- United States -- Biography
ISBN 9781467794107

LC 2016019759

This book, by Tracy Nelson Maurer, illustrated by Mircea Catusanu, presents a biography of "Noah Webster, famous for writing the first dictionary of the English language as spoken in the United States. [Noah] was known in his day for his bold ideas and strong opinions about, well, everything. Spelling, politics, laws, you name it he had something to say about it. He even commented on his own opinions!" (Publisher's note)

Includes bibliographical references

Wells-Barnett, Ida B., 1862-1931

Dray, Philip. **Yours** for justice, Ida B. Wells; the daring life of crusading journalist. written by Philip Dray; illustrated by Stephen Alcorn. Peachtree Publishers 2008 un il $18.95

Grades: 2 3 4   **92**

1. Authors 2. Journalists 3. Essayists 4. Nonfiction writers 5. Newspaper executives 6. Civil rights activists 7. United States -- Race relations 8. African Americans -- Civil rights 9. African American women -- Biography
ISBN 978-1-56145-417-4; 1-56145-417-6

LC 2007-4016

"Dray introduces this civil rights crusader and journalist who campaigned tirelessly to end the practice of lynching. . . . Alcorn's ink-and-watercolor illustrations have a fluid quality, conveying both action within the story and movement from one scene to the next. . . . This makes a good choice for middle-grade readers." Booklist

Includes bibliographical references

★ Myers, Walter Dean, 1937-2014. **Ida** B. Wells; let the truth be told. illustrated by Bonnie Christensen. HarperCollinsPublishers 2008 37p il $16.99; lib bdg $17.89

Grades: 2 3 4 5   **92**

1. Authors 2. Journalists 3. Essayists 4. Nonfiction writers 5. Newspaper executives 6. Civil rights activists 7. United States -- Race relations 8. African Americans -- Civil rights 9. African American women -- Biography
ISBN 978-0-06-027705-5; 0-06-027705-X; 978-0-06-027706-2 lib bdg; 0-06-027706-8 lib bdg

LC 2007-40107

"Myers deals with Wells-Barnett's career—from child of slaves, to teacher, to writer and organizer in the causes of anti-lynching and women's suffrage—in a style accessible to younger elementary audiences. . . . Each spread features a limited amount of text, and sourced quotations from Well-Barnett are frequently appended in red. Christensen's shaggy line and watercolor illustrations soften the rougher edges of the drama without straying into cartoonishness." Bull Cent Child Books

West, Benjamin, 1738-1820

Brenner, Barbara. The **boy** who loved to draw: Benjamin West; illustrated by Olivier Dunrea. Houghton Mifflin 1999 un il $15; pa $6.99

Grades: K 1 2 3   **92**

1. Artists 2. Painters 3. Artists -- United States 4. United States -- History -- 1600-1775, Colonial period

ISBN 0-395-85080-0; 0-618-31089-4 pa

LC 97-5183

Recounts the life story of the Pennsylvania artist who began drawing as a boy and eventually became well known on both sides of the Atlantic

"Naive in style and reminiscent of some colonial art, the illustrations present clear visual expressions of the activities and emotions related in the story. . . . A fascinating look at art in colonial times, and a likable portrait of the artist as a young boy." Booklist

Wheatley, Phillis, 1753-1784

Clinton, Catherine. **Phillis's** big test; written by Catherine Clinton; illustrated by Sean Qualls. Houghton Mifflin 2008 un il $16

Grades: 1 2 3 4   **92**

1. Poets 2. Slaves 3. Authors 4. Women poets 5. African American authors 6. Poets, American 7. Slavery -- United States

ISBN 978-0-618-73739-0; 0-618-73739-1

LC 2007-13241

"This picture-book biography deals with a transformative moment in the life of Phillis Wheatley, the first African American to publish a book of poetry. In 1772, 18 members of the intelligentsia from the Massachusetts Bay Colony . . . gathered to question the 17-year-old slave to ascertain the authorship of the poems she claimed were her own. . . . Qualls's uncluttered acrylic and collage compositions employ strong diagonal lines, swirling ribbons of thought, and a combination of opaque images and outlined, transparent figures over washes of color to create visual interest. . . . A formal tone, an occasional quaint turn of phrase, and a typeface with an irregular impression create the flavor of a time past. Clinton and Qualls offer an elegant introduction to an important individual." SLJ

Lasky, Kathryn. A **voice** of her own: the story of Phillis Wheatley, slave poet; illustrated by Paul Lee. Candlewick Press 2003 un il $17.99; pa $7.99

Grades: 3 4 5   **92**

1. Poets 2. Slaves 3. Authors 4. Women poets 5. African American authors 6. Poets, American 7. Slavery -- United States

ISBN 0-7636-0252-3; 0-7636-2878-6 pa

LC 2001-47139

A biography of an African girl brought to New England as a slave in 1761 who became famous on both sides of the Atlantic as the first Black poet in America

Written "in evocative language that's rich with historical detail. . . . This will serve as a good introduction to Wheatley's life and times for young children, who will appreciate Lee's full-page, historically accurate acrylics." Booklist

Malaspina, Ann. **Phillis** sings out freedom; the story of George Washington and Phillis Wheatley. illustrated by Susan Keeter. Albert Whitman 2010 un il $16.99

Grades: 2 3 4   **92**

1. Poets 2. Slaves 3. Authors 4. Generals 5. Presidents 6. Women poets 7. African American authors 8. Poets, American 9. Presidents -- United States 10. African American women -- Biography 11. United States -- History -- 1775-1783, Revolution

ISBN 978-0-8075-6545-2; 0-8075-6545-8

"Camped in Cambridge in the fall of 1775, General Washington despairs that his soldiers won't ever be able to defeat the British. In Providence, freed slave Phillis Wheatley pens a poem of encouragement to Washington. Malaspina intertwines information about Wheatley's early life with wartime events. . . . Keeter's rich oil paintings are full of period details that help to clarify both the war scenes and Wheatley's life." Booklist

White, E. B. (Elwyn Brooks), 1899-1985

★ Sweet, Melissa. **Some** writer!: the story of E. B. White; The Story of E. B. White. by Melissa Sweet. Houghton Mifflin Harcourt 2016 176 p. illustrations (some color) $18.99

Grades: 3 4 5 6   **92**

1. Children's stories -- Authorship 2. White, E. B. (Elwyn Brooks), 1899-1985 3. Authors, American -- 20th century -- Biography

ISBN 9780544319592

LC 2015002079

This book offers a tribute to author E. B. White, "focusing especially on his three children's classics: Stuart Little (1945), Charlotte's Web (1952), and The Trumpet of the Swan (1970) . . . , combining . . . intricate watercolor-and-collage illustrations; photographs, excerpts of White's writings, and ephemera that evoke farm and barn life. Chapters on the children's books offer fascinating glimpses into the origins of the tales." (Kirkus Reviews)

"This beautiful piece of bookmaking with enchanting artwork will easily draw in young readers, and the warm account of the adored author will keep them turning pages." Booklist

Includes bibliographical references (pages 152-156) and index.

Whitfield, Simon, 1975-

Whitfield, Simon. **Simon** says gold: Simon Whitfield's pursuit of athletic excellence; by Simon Whitfield with Cleve Dheensaw. Orca Publishers 2009 118p il pa $14

Grades: 5 6 7 8   **92**

1. Athletes 2. Track athletics 3. Triathletes

ISBN 978-1-55469-141-8 pa; 1-55469-141-9 pa

"In 2000, Whitfield won a gold medal in the inaugural triathlon race held in the Sydney Summer Olympics. . . . He tells his story with candor, and he sheds light on the dark side of early success and the pressures athletes face. Sidebars offer more information on the sport of triathlon, and scrapbook-style color photographs enliven the tale." SLJ

Whitman, Narcissa Prentiss, 1808-1847

Harness, Cheryl. The **tragic** tale of Narcissa Whitman and a faithful history of the Oregon Trail; written and illustrated by Cheryl Harness. National Geographic Society 2006 144p il map (Cheryl Harness history) $16.95; lib bdg $25.90

Grades: 4 5 6 7   **92**

1. Frontier and pioneer life 2. Overland journeys to the Pacific 3. Pioneers 4. Missionaries

ISBN 0-7922-5920-3; 0-7922-7890-9 lib bdg

LC 2005-30930

This "introduces a nineteenth-century pioneer and missionary. . . . [She and her husband Marcus Whitman] journeyed along the Oregon Trail to the Waiilatpu Mission, where they ministered to the Cayuse. . . . Harness' chatty, conversational style makes the pair accessible to modern readers, and frequent quotes from Narcissa's diaries and letters and a time line help to frame the story in light of world and national events. Harness' black-line illustrations . . . help to break up the text for younger readers." Booklist

Includes bibliographical references

Whitman, Walt, 1819-1892

★ Kerley, Barbara. **Walt** Whitman; words for America. illustrated by Brian Selznick. Scholastic Press 2004 un il $16.95

Grades: 4 5 6 7   92
1. Poets 2. Authors 3. Essayists 4. Poets, American
ISBN 0-439-35791-8

LC 2003-20085

A biography of the American poet whose compassion led him to nurse soldiers during the Civil War, to give voice to the nation's grief at Lincoln's assassination, and to capture the true American spirit in verse

"Delightfully old-fashioned in design, [the book's] oversized pages are replete with graceful illustrations and snippets of poetry. The brilliantly inventive paintings add vibrant testimonial to the nuanced text." SLJ

Wiesenthal, Simon
★ Rubin, Susan Goldman. The **Anne** Frank Case: Simon Wiesenthal's search for the truth; illustrated by Bill Farnsworth. Holiday House 2009 40p il $18.95
Grades: 4 5 6 7   92
1. Authors 2. Architects 3. Holocaust survivors 4. Essayists 5. Memoirists 6. Nazi hunters 7. Jewish leaders 8. Jews -- Biography 9. Holocaust, 1933-1945
ISBN 978-0-8234-2109-1; 0-8234-2109-0

LC 2007-28396

"In 1958, Holocaust deniers disrupted a theater performance of The Diary of Anne Frank. In response, the well-known Nazi hunter Simon Wiesenthal vowed to prove Anne's story true. . . . This 'hook' is the framing story for a picture-book biography chronicling Wiesenthal's experiences during World War II and illustrating the development of his unusual career." SLJ

Includes glossary and bibliographical references

Wilder, Laura Ingalls, 1867-1957
Anderson, William T. **Pioneer** girl: the story of Laura Ingalls Wilder; by William Anderson; illustrated by Dan Andreasen. HarperCollins Pubs. 1998 un il hardcover o.p. pa $6.99
Grades: 2 3 4   92
1. Authors 2. Novelists 3. Women authors 4. Frontier and pioneer life 5. Western writers 6. Authors, American 7. Children's authors 8. Young adult authors
ISBN 0-06-027243-0; 0-06-027244-9 lib bdg; 0-06-446234-X pa
LC 96-31203

Recounts the life story of the author of the "Little House" books, from her childhood in Wisconsin to her old age at Rocky Ridge Farm

"Laura Ingalls Wilder's many fans will delight in this inviting biographical overview in a picture-book format, graced by Andreasen's dreamy landscapes, glowing prairie skies and warm character portraits." Publ Wkly

Berne, Emma Carlson. **Laura** Ingalls Wilder; by Emma Carlson Berne. ABDO Pub. 2008 112p il map $22.95
Grades: 4 5 6 7   92
1. Authors 2. Novelists 3. Women authors 4. Frontier and pioneer life 5. Western writers 6. Authors, American 7. Children's authors 8. Young adult authors
ISBN 978-1-59928-843-7; 1-59928-843-5
LC 2007012513

"Beginning in 1929 with the events that led up to the publication of Little House in the Big Woods, this readable biography further amplifies Wilder's life and correlates it with her books. . . . This volume is packed with relevant material, a time line, archival photographs, quotes from primary sources, and an official Web site." SLJ

Includes glossary and bibliographical references

Wilder, Laura Ingalls. A **Little** House traveler; writings from Laura Ingalls Wilder's journeys across America. by Laura Ingalls Wilder. HarperCollins 2006 344p il $16.99; pa $7.99
Grades: 5 6 7 8   92
1. Authors 2. Novelists 3. Women authors 4. Western writers 5. Authors, American 6. Children's authors 7. Young adult authors 8. United States -- Description and travel
ISBN 978-0-06-072491-7; 0-06-072491-9; 978-0-06-072492-4 pa; 0-06-072492-7 pa
LC 2005014975

"This volume combines three Wilder travel diaries: On the Way Home, recounting the 1894 trip from South Dakota to Missouri, with husband Almanzo and daughter Rose; West from Home, featuring letters written by Laura to Almanzo during her 1915 solo visit to Rose in San Francisco; and The Road Back, highlighting Laura's previously unpublished record of a 1931 trip with Almanzo to De Smet, South Dakota, and the Black Hills. . . . This offers an amazing look at a beloved author, as well as a fascinating account of travel before interstate highways and air-conditioning." Booklist

Wilder, Laura Ingalls. **West** from home; letters of Laura Ingalls Wilder to Almanzo Wilder, San Francisco, 1915. edited by Roger Lea MacBride; historical setting by Margot Patterson Doss. Harper & Row 1974 124p il hardcover o.p. pa $5.99
Grades: 6 7 8 9   92
1. Authors 2. Novelists 3. Women authors 4. Western writers 5. Authors, American 6. Children's authors 7. Young adult authors
ISBN 0-06-024110-1; 0-06-440081-6 pa
LC 73-14342

This collection is "edited from letters sent to her beloved husband while Laura spent two months in late 1915 visiting their daughter and immersing herself in the sights of bustling San Francisco and the exciting Panama-Pacific Exposition. Wilder readers of all ages will lose themselves in this trip—the adults with nostalgia and wholesome pleasure, the youth with wonder and awe over the sights vividly described in her inimitable combination of homespun literary and journalistic styles." Child Book Rev Serv

Williams, Daniel Hale, 1856-1931
Venezia, Mike, 1945- **Daniel** Hale Williams; surgeon who opened hearts and minds. written and illustrated by Mike Venezia. Children's Press 2010 32p il (Getting to know the world's greatest inventors & scientists) lib bdg $28
Grades: 2 3 4   92
1. Surgeons 2. Physicians 3. Writers on medicine 4. African Americans -- Biography
ISBN 0-531-23729-X lib bdg; 978-0-531-23729-8 lib bdg

This book by Mike Venezia, part of the "Getting to Know the World's Greatest Inventors and Scientists" series, looks at "Daniel Hale Williams, founder of the first non-segregated hospital in the United States. . . . One of Williams' most significant contributions to the field of medicine was being one of the first surgeons to operate on the area around the heart." (Children's Literature)

Venezia "describes the life of Daniel Hale Williams, a pioneering physician working during the late 19th and early 20th centuries who achieved fame as one of the first open-heart surgeons. The book tells an inspiring story. . . . The colorful cartoons and historical photographs . . . complement the text well." Sci Books Films

Williams, J. W., 1929-
Barbour, Karen. **Mr.** Williams. Henry Holt and Co. 2005 29p il $16.95

Grades: K 1 2 3   **92**
1. Farmers 2. Country life 3. African Americans 4. Louisiana
ISBN 0-8050-6773-6

LC 2004-22182

"Recounting stories told by J. W. Williams, a friend of her mother's, Barbour captures the essence of a black Louisiana farmer's life in the early 20th century. . . . The words are succinct but evocative of a larger picture. . . . The ink-and-gouache illustrations, punctuated with well-placed bits of fabric collage, are perfect." SLJ

Williams, Lindsey, 1987-

Houle, Michelle E. **Lindsey** Williams; gardening for impoverished families. [by] Michelle Houle. KidHaven Press 2008 48p il (Young heroes) lib bdg $27.45

Grades: 4 5 6 7   **92**
1. Gardening 2. Food relief 3. Social action 4. Gardeners 5. Humanitarians
ISBN 978-0-7377-3867-4 lib bdg; 0-7377-3867-7 lib bdg

LC 2007022923

This "introduces 20-year-old Lindsey Williams, who has won numerous awards, including the International Eco-Hero Award, for her groundbreaking work with agriculture and hunger issues. . . . Williams has developed growing techniques that produce more food using fewer natural resources. . . . The straightforward text, with many quotes from Williams, will draw children into the science and environmental issues." Booklist

Includes glossary and bibliographical references

Williams, Roger, 1604?-1683

Avi. **Finding** Providence; the story of Roger Williams; story by Avi; illustrations by James Watling. HarperCollins Pubs. 1997 46p il (I can read chapter book) hardcover o.p. pa $3.99

Grades: 2 3 4   **92**
1. Clergy 2. Colonial leaders 3. Writers on religion 4. Rhode Island -- History 5. United States -- History -- 1600-1775, Colonial period
ISBN 0-06-025179-4; 0-06-444216-0 pa

LC 95-46360

After being forced to leave the Massachusetts Bay Colony, Roger Williams travels south and, with the help of the Narragansett Indians, founds Providence, Rhode Island

"Plentiful dialogue speeds the action along, and even the philosophical issues are cogently presented for young readers in the form of Williams' interrogation at the trial. Watling's watercolors have a roughhewn quality appropiate to the early colonies, and his grave figures are charged with tension." Bull Cent Child Books

Williams, Ted, 1918-2002

Bowen, Fred. **No** easy way; the story of Ted Williams and the last .400 season. illustrations by Charles S. Pyle. Dutton Children's Books 2010 un il lib bdg $16.99

Grades: 1 2 3   **92**
1. Baseball players 2. Baseball managers 3. Baseball -- Biography
ISBN 978-0-525-47877-5 lib bdg; 0-525-47877-9 lib bdg

LC 2009-17920

This recounts the 1941 baseball season in which Ted Williams hit .406 for the Boston Red Sox.

"Unlike many decades-old baseball stories, this one hasn't lost its appeal over the years, and Bowen makes the most of it in terms kids will understand. Pyle's illustrations, combined with vintage photographs, capture the drama of Williams at bat." Booklist

Williams, William Carlos, 1883-1963

★ Bryant, Jennifer. A **river** of words: the story of William Carlos Williams; written by Jen Bryant; illustrated by Melissa Sweet. Eerdmans Books for Young Readers 2008 un il $17

Grades: 1 2 3 4   **92**
1. Poets 2. Authors 3. Physicians 4. Essayists 5. Poets, American 6. Short story writers
ISBN 978-0-8028-5302-8; 0-8028-5302-1

LC 2007-49347

A Caldecott Medal honor book, 2009

This picture book biography of William Carlos Williams traces childhood events that lead him to become a doctor and a poet.

Bryant's "simple, spare language matches her subject well. Sweet's mixed-media collages will draw varying age groups. . . . [This is an] inspiring title." Booklist

Wilson, Teddy, 1912-1986

Cline-Ransome, Lesa. **Benny** Goodman & Teddy Wilson; taking the stage as the first black and white jazz band in history. by Lesa Cline-Ransome; illustrated by James E. Ransome. Holiday House 2014 32 p. (hardcover) $16.95

Grades: 2 3 4 5   **92**
1. Jazz musicians -- Biography 2. Race relations -- History -- 20th century 3. Jazz musicians -- United States -- Biography
ISBN 082342362X; 9780823423620

LC 2010048154

"In 1936, the Benny Goodman Trio became the first interracial band to perform in public, with Benny Goodman (the son of Jewish immigrants) on clarinet and African-American Teddy Wilson on piano (Gene Krupa, on drums, completed the trio). Writing in punchy free verse that echoes the bounce of both men's music," author Lesa Cline-Ransome, "traces Goodman and Wilson's parallel--but separate--paths to jazz fame, before eventually meeting in 1935." (Publishers Weekly)

"Goodman grew up in Chicago, a working-class Jewish boy; Wilson lived in Tuskegee, Alabama, a middle-class African American boy. The story of how the two jazz musicians met and formed the Benny Goodman Trio (the "first interracial band to perform publicly") is recounted in short bursts of text, almost like jazz riffs, accompanied by pencil and watercolor illustrations that capture distinctive moments. Timeline." Horn Book

Wilson, Woodrow, 1856-1924

Marsico, Katie. **Woodrow** Wilson. Marshall Cavendish Benchmark 2011 112p il (Presidents and their times) $23.95

Grades: 5 6 7 8   **92**
1. Governors 2. Presidents 3. College presidents 4. Nobel laureates for peace 5. Presidents -- United States
ISBN 978-0-7614-4815-0; 0-7614-4815-2

LC 2009041116

This offers information on President Woodrow Wilson and places him within his historical and cultural context. Also explored are the formative events of his times and how he responded.

"The abundant sidebars provide a good deal of background information that will be helpful to students. . . . Attractive . . . as well as useful." Booklist

Includes glossary and bibliographical references

Winfrey, Oprah

Weatherford, Carole Boston. **Oprah**; the little speaker. illustrated by London Ladd. Marshall Cavendish Children 2010 un il $17.99

Grades: K 1 2 3   **92**
1. Entertainers 2. Philanthropists 3. Television personalities 4. Talk show hosts 5. Television producers 6. African American

women -- Biography
ISBN 978-0-7614-5632-2; 0-7614-5632-5

LC 2009006339

This picture book biography of Oprah Winfrey "focuses solely on her childhood. An author's note at the beginning sets the stage for the true rags-to-riches story about a poor girl on a Mississippi pig farm who became an entertainer, entrepreneur, and philanthropist. . . . The narrative portrays a bright, spunky child . . . while the soft-edged, acrylic illustrations paint a determined, sober-faced girl." Booklist

Wong, Anna May, 1905-1961

Yoo, Paula. **Shining** star: the Anna May Wong story; by Paula Yoo; illustrated by Lin Wang. Lee & Low Books 2009 un il $17.95
Grades: 2 3 4 5   92
1. Actors 2. Chinese Americans -- Biography
ISBN 1-60060-259-2; 978-1-60060-259-7

LC 2008042673

"Lin Wang's . . . elegant paintings in muted hues capture the actress's emotions in her expressive eyes framed by dark bangs. . . . The conversational narrative uses many descriptive vignettes. . . . A fascinating account of the life of a determined actress." Publ Wkly

Woodhull, Victoria C., 1838-1927

Krull, Kathleen. A **woman** for president; the story of Victoria Woodhull. illustrations by Jane Dyer. Walker & Co 2004 un il $16.95; lib bdg $17.85
Grades: 3 4 5   92
1. Feminism 2. Suffragists 3. Women in politics 4. Feminists 5. Presidential candidates
ISBN 0-8027-8908-0; 0-8027-8909-9 lib bdg

LC 2004-49483

"Woodhull is a fascinating figure, and Krull's lively and astute writing does her justice. . . . The watercolors, cast with a golden glow, are handsome." Booklist

Includes bibliographical references

Woodson, Jacqueline

★ Woodson, Jacqueline. **Brown** girl dreaming; Jacqueline Woodson. Nancy Paulsen Books 2014 336 p. illustrations, photographs (hardback) $16.99
Grades: 4 5 6 7 8   92
1. African American women -- Biography 2. American poetry -- African American authors 3. African American women authors -- Biography -- Poetry 4. Authors, American -- 20th century -- Biography -- Poetry
ISBN 0399252517; 9780399252518

LC 2014021346

Robert F. Sibert Honor Book (2015)
Newbery Honor Book (2015)
National Book Award: Young People's Literature (2014)
Coretta Scott King Author Award (2015)
Boston Globe-Horn Book Honor: Nonfiction (2015)

"Raised in South Carolina and New York, [author Jacqueline] Woodson always felt halfway home in each place. In vivid poems, she shares what it was like to grow up as an African American in the 1960s and 1970s, living with the remnants of Jim Crow and her growing awareness of the Civil Rights movement." (Publisher's note)

"Here is a memoir-in-verse so immediate that readers will feel they are experiencing the author's childhood right along with her." Horn Book

Wright, David, 1982-

Rappoport, Ken. **David** Wright; a baseball star who cares. Enslow 2011 il (Sports stars who care) $23.93

Grades: 3 4 5   92
1. Baseball players 2. Baseball -- Biography
ISBN 978-0-7660-3775-5; 0-7660-3775-4

A biography of the all-star third baseman for the New York Mets who has worked with charities and who established the David Wright Foundation.

This is "especially good for book reports." Booklist

Wright, Orville, 1871-1948

Collins, Mary. **Airborne** : a photobiography of Wilbur and Orville Wright. National Geographic Soc. 2003 63p il maps $18.95
Grades: 4 5 6 7   92
1. Inventors 2. Aeronautics -- History 3. Aircraft industry executives
ISBN 0-7922-6957-8

LC 2002-5279

Examines the lives of the Wright brothers and discusses their experiments and triumphs in the field of flight

"The well-chosen photos give readers a feel for Kitty Hawk—windy, sandy, solitary. This is an exceptionally well-informed picture of the Wright brothers and what their 100-year-old achievement really meant." SLJ

★ Freedman, Russell. The **Wright** brothers: how they invented the airplane; with original photographs by Wilbur and Orville Wright. Holiday House 1991 129p il hardcover o.p. pa $14.95
Grades: 5 6 7 8 9 10   92
1. Inventors 2. Aeronautics -- History 3. Aircraft industry executives
ISBN 0-8234-0875-2; 0-8234-1082-X pa

LC 90-48440

A Newbery Medal honor book, 1992

In this "combination of photography and text, Freedman reveals the frustrating, exciting, and ultimately successful journey of these two brothers from their bicycle shop in Dayton, Ohio, to their Kitty Hawk flights and beyond. . . . An essential purchase for younger YAs." Voice Youth Advocates

Includes bibliographical references

O'Sullivan, Robyn. The **Wright** brothers fly; by Robyn O'Sullivan. National Geographic 2007 40p il (National Geographic history chapters) lib bdg $17.90
Grades: 2 3 4   92
1. Inventors 2. Aeronautics -- History 3. Aircraft industry executives
ISBN 978-1-4263-0188-9

LC 2007007895

This history of the Wright brothers is "nicely illustrated with photos. . . . [It is] just right for emerging chapter-book readers. . . . Useful . . . for reports . . . and interesting pleasure reading." SLJ

Includes glossary and bibliographical references

Venezia, Mike. The **Wright** brothers; inventors whose ideas really took flight. written and illustrated by Mike Venezia. Children's Press 2010 32p il (Getting to know the world's greatest inventors & scientists) lib bdg $28
Grades: 2 3 4   92
1. Inventors 2. Aeronautics 3. Aircraft industry executives
ISBN 978-0-531-23732-8 lib bdg; 0-531-23732-X lib bdg

LC 2009030222

This "explores the development of the Wright brothers by way of their early childhood environment and interests, which ultimately contributed to their successful attainment of the first powered aircraft. . . . Young readers will gain insights into the brothers' inventive and entrepreneurial lives from a humanistic perspective, as well as developing a sense of the qualities that are associated with contributors to advancements in technology." Sci Books Films

Wright, Patience Lovell, 1725-1786

★ Shea, Pegi Deitz. **Patience** Wright; America's first sculptor, and revolutionary spy. [by] Pegi Deitz Shea; illustrated by Bethanne Andersen. Henry Holt 2007 un il $17.95

Grades: 4 5 6   92

1. Spies 2. Artists 3. Sculptors 4. Women artists 5. United States -- History -- 1775-1783, Revolution

ISBN 978-0-8050-6770-5; 0-8050-6770-1

LC 2005021696

A biography of Patience Wright, born in 1725, who became a sculptor and a spy for the American colonies

"Shea writes with a dynamic simplicity that brings Wright to life. At the same time, she seamlessly incorporates information about the war and events leading up to it into her text." Booklist

Wright, Richard, 1908-1960

★ Miller, William. **Richard** Wright and the library card; illustrated by Gregory Christie. Lee & Low Bks. 1997 un il hardcover o.p. pa $6.95

Grades: K 1 2 3   92

1. Authors 2. Novelists 3. Dramatists 4. Essayists 5. Nonfiction writers 6. Short story writers 7. Libraries -- Fiction 8. African Americans -- Fiction 9. Books and reading -- Fiction

ISBN 1-880000-57-1; 1-880000-88-1 pa

LC 97-6847

Based on a scene from Wright's autobiography, Black boy, in which the seventeen-year-old African-American borrows a white man's library card and devours every book as a ticket to freedom

"Christie's powerful impressionistic paintings in acrylic and colored pencil show the harsh racism in the Jim Crow South. . . . Words and pictures express the young man's loneliness and confinement and, then, the power he found in books." Booklist

Wright, Wilbur, 1867-1912

Collins, Mary. **Airborne** : a photobiography of Wilbur and Orville Wright. National Geographic Soc. 2003 63p il maps $18.95

Grades: 4 5 6 7   92

1. Inventors 2. Aeronautics -- History 3. Aircraft industry executives

ISBN 0-7922-6957-8

LC 2002-5279

Examines the lives of the Wright brothers and discusses their experiments and triumphs in the field of flight

"The well-chosen photos give readers a feel for Kitty Hawk—windy, sandy, solitary. This is an exceptionally well-informed picture of the Wright brothers and what their 100-year-old achievement really meant." SLJ

★ Freedman, Russell. The **Wright** brothers: how they invented the airplane; with original photographs by Wilbur and Orville Wright. Holiday House 1991 129p il hardcover o.p. pa $14.95

Grades: 5 6 7 8 9 10   92

1. Inventors 2. Aeronautics -- History 3. Aircraft industry executives

ISBN 0-8234-0875-2; 0-8234-1082-X pa

LC 90-48440

A Newbery Medal honor book, 1992

In this "combination of photography and text, Freedman reveals the frustrating, exciting, and ultimately successful journey of these two brothers from their bicycle shop in Dayton, Ohio, to their Kitty Hawk

flights and beyond. . . . An essential purchase for younger YAs." Voice Youth Advocates

Includes bibliographical references

O'Sullivan, Robyn. The **Wright** brothers fly; by Robyn O'Sullivan. National Geographic 2007 40p il (National Geographic history chapters) lib bdg $17.90

Grades: 2 3 4   92

1. Inventors 2. Aeronautics -- History 3. Aircraft industry executives

ISBN 978-1-4263-0188-9

LC 2007007895

This history of the Wright brothers is "nicely illustrated with photos. . . . [It is] just right for emerging chapter-book readers. . . . Useful . . . for reports . . . and interesting pleasure reading." SLJ

Includes glossary and bibliographical references

Venezia, Mike. The **Wright** brothers; inventors whose ideas really took flight. written and illustrated by Mike Venezia. Children's Press 2010 32p il (Getting to know the world's greatest inventors & scientists) lib bdg $28

Grades: 2 3 4   92

1. Inventors 2. Aeronautics 3. Aircraft industry executives

ISBN 978-0-531-23732-8 lib bdg; 0-531-23732-X lib bdg

LC 2009030222

This "explores the development of the Wright brothers by way of their early childhood environment and interests, which ultimately contributed to their successful attainment of the first powered aircraft. . . . Young readers will gain insights into the brothers' inventive and entrepreneurial lives from a humanistic perspective, as well as developing a sense of the qualities that are associated with contributors to advancements in technology." Sci Books Films

Yaccarino, Dan

★ Yaccarino, Dan. **All** the way to America; the story of a big Italian family and a little shovel. Alfred A. Knopf 2011 un il $16.99; lib bdg $19.99

Grades: K 1 2 3   92

1. Artists 2. Authors 3. Genealogy 4. Illustrators 5. Italian Americans 6. Authors, American 7. Children's authors 8. United States -- Immigration and emigration

ISBN 0-375-86642-6; 0-375-96642-0 lib bdg; 978-0-375-86642-5; 978-0-375-96642-2 lib bdg

LC 2010017549

"In this picture book, Yaccarino shares his family history. Starting with his great-grandfather Michele Iaccarino's immigration to America, he gives a simplified rundown of each generation's career and family life. Advice passed from parent to child creates a narrative connection among generations. . . . The text is clear and simple . . . [and] readers' interest will be held fast by the bright illustrations. In his typical retro style, Yaccarino creates a world of friendly, rounded people set against stylized background scenery. . . . The story will make an excellent family-history discussion starter." SLJ

Yasui, Sachiko

★ Stelson, Caren. **Sachiko**; A Nagasaki Bomb Survivor's Story. by Caren B. Stelson. Carolrhoda Books 2016 144 p. illustrations (some color) (lib : alk. paper) $19.99; (ebook) $19.99

Grades: 5 6 7 8   92

1. Atomic bomb victims 2. World War, 1939-1945 -- Japan 3. Nagasaki (Japan) -- Bombardment, 1945 4. Nagasaki-shi (Japan) -- History -- Bombardment, 1945 5. World War, 1939-1945 -- Japan -- Nagasaki-shi (Japan) 6. Atomic bomb victims -- Japan -- Nagasaki-

shi -- Biography

ISBN 9781467789035; 9781512408935

LC 2015043908

Sibert Honor Book (2017)

This book, by Caren B. Stelson, "tells the true story of six-year-old Sachiko Yasui's survival of the Nagasaki atomic bomb on August 9, 1945, and the heartbreaking and lifelong aftermath. Having conducted extensive interviews with Sachiko Yasui, . . . Stelson chronicles Sachiko s trauma and loss as well as her long journey to find peace." (Publisher's note)

"This powerful narrative account of one person finding her voice after insufferable trauma encapsulates a grim era in global history." Pub Wkly

Includes bibliographical references and index

Yeboah, Emmanuel Ofosu, 1977-

★ Thompson, Laurie Ann. **Emmanuel's** dream; the true story of Emmanuel Ofosu Yeboah. by Laurie Ann Thompson; illustrated by Sean Qualls. Schwartz & Wade Books 2015 40 p. (glb) $20.99

Grades: PreK K 1 2 3   92

1. People with physical disabilities 2. Ghana -- Biography 3. Cyclists -- Ghana -- Biography 4. People with disabilities -- Ghana -- Biography

ISBN 0449817458; 9780449817445; 9780449817452

LC 2014005767

Schneider Family Book Award, Children (2016)

"Born in Ghana, West Africa, with one deformed leg, he was dismissed by most people--but not by his mother, who taught him to reach for his dreams. As a boy, Emmanuel hopped to school more than two miles each way, learned to play soccer, left home at age thirteen to provide for his family, and, eventually, became a cyclist." (Publisher's note)

York, ca. 1775-ca. 1815

★ Pringle, Laurence P. **American** slave, American hero; York of the Lewis and Clark Expedition. [by] Laurence Pringle; illustrations by Cornelius Van Wright and Ying-Hwa Hu. Calkins Creek Books 2005 40p il $17.95

Grades: 3 4 5   92

1. Slaves 2. Explorers 3. Lewis and Clark Expedition (1804-1806) 4. Slavery -- United States 5. West (U.S.) -- Exploration

ISBN 978-1-59078-282-8; 1-59078-282-8

LC 2005037352

"With a detailed text and handsome watercolor paintings, this illustrated biography celebrates the heroic role of Clark's personal slave on the famous expedition out west in 1804, with the horror of slavery in the background." Booklist

Includes bibliographical references

Young, Ed

★ Young, Ed. The **house** Baba built; an artist's childhood in China. Little, Brown and Co. 2011 48p il $17.99

Grades: 2 3 4 5   92

1. Artists 2. Authors 3. Illustrators 4. Authors, American 5. Children's authors 6. Artists -- United States 7. Chinese Americans -- Biography

ISBN 978-0-316-07628-9; 0-316-07628-7

LC 2011005396

"In this picture book memoir by the Caldecott Medalist, which opens in 1931 (the year he was born), the stock market has crashed, and China is in turmoil. Young's father, Baba, persuades a landowner in Shanghai to let him construct a huge brick house on his land; Baba promises to return the house after 20 years, long enough to keep his family safe until WWII ends. Young's creation, shaped with help from author Libby Koponen, is as complex and labyrinthine as Baba's house, with foldout

pages that open to reveal drawings, photos, maps, and memories. Tender portraits of his siblings, torn-paper collages showing tiny figures at play, and old photos of stylish adults intermingle, as if they'd been found forgotten in a drawer." Publ Wkly

Yousafzai, Malala, 1997-

McCormick, Patricia, 1956- **I** am Malala; how one girl stood up for education and changed the world. Malala Yousafzai with Patricia McCormick. Young readers edition Little Brown & Co 2014 230 p. illustrations, map (hardback) $17

Grades: 5 6 7 8   92

1. Women -- Education 2. Children's rights -- Pakistan 3. Young women -- Education -- Pakistan -- Biography

ISBN 031632793X; 9780316327930

LC 2014015881

"Malala Yousafzai was only ten years old when the Taliban took control of her region. . . . They said girls couldn't go to school. Raised in a once-peaceful area of Pakistan transformed by terrorism, Malala was taught to stand up for what she believes. So she fought for her right to be educated." (Publisher's note)

"Young education activist and Taliban victim Malala Yousafzai recounts her Pakistani childhood in this deftly adapted memoir. Domestic and academic tales illustrate her unusual maturity and resilience in the face of increasing Taliban threats. Yousafzai's moving narrative and engaging, sincere voice may provide an entryway to international awareness for middle-grade readers; a map and a thorough timeline provide additional political context." Horn Book

Yunus, Muhammad, 1940-

Yoo, Paula. **Twenty-**two cents; Muhammad Yunus and the Village Bank. by Paula Yoo; illustrated by Jamel Akib. First edition Lee & Low Books Inc. 2014 40 p. color illustrations (hardcover) $18.95

Grades: 3 4 5 6   92

1. Microfinance 2. Bankers 3. Economists 4. Grameen Bank 5. Microfinance -- Developing countries

ISBN 9781600606588; 160060658X

LC 2013041045

"Growing up in Bangladesh, Muhammad Yunus witnessed extreme poverty all around and was determined to eradicate it. . . . Muhammad founded Grameen Bank where people could borrow small amounts of money to start a job. . . . Over the next few years, Muhammad's compassion and determination changed the lives of millions of people by loaning the equivalent of more than ten billion US dollars in micro-credit." (Publisher's note)

"Akib's grainy, jewel-toned chalk pastels contrast a sense of scarcity and deprivation with one of warmth and humanity. Yoo makes the significance of Yunus's contributions understandable, relevant, and immediate." Pub Wkly

Includes bibliographical references

Zaharias, Babe Didrikson, 1911-1956

Freedman, Russell. **Babe** Didrikson Zaharias; the making of a champion. Clarion Bks. 1999 192p il hardcover o.p.; pbk $10.99

Grades: 5 6 7 8 9 10   92

1. Women athletes 2. Golfers 3. Hurdlers 4. High jumpers 5. Javelin throwers 6. Olympic athletes

ISBN 0-395-63367-2; 9780544104914; 0544104919

LC 98-50208

A biography of Babe Didrikson, who broke records in golf, track and field, and other sports, at a time when there were few opportunities for female athletes

"Freedman's measured yet lively style captures the spirit of the great athlete.... Plenty of black-and-white photos capture Babe's spirit and dashing good looks; the documentation ... is impeccable." Horn Book

Includes bibliographical references

Van Natta, Don, 1964- **Wonder** girl; the magnificent sporting life of Babe Didrikson Zaharias. Little, Brown and Co. 2011 403p il $27.99

Grades: 5 6 7 8   92

1. Women athletes 2. Golfers 3. Hurdlers 4. High jumpers 5. Javelin throwers 6. Olympic athletes

ISBN 978-0-316-05699-1; 0-316-05699-5

LC 2010041794

Describes the life and times of LPGA founder Babe Didrikson, the Texas woman who achieved All-American status in basketball, won gold medals in track and field in the 1932 Olympics, and became the first woman to play against men in a PGA tournament.

This is an "engaging biography.... Van Natta marvelously narrates the forgotten life of the 'greatest all-around athlete of all time,' a story that every American sport fan should relish." Publ Wkly

Includes bibliographical references

Wallace, Rich. **Babe** conquers the world; the legendary life of Babe Didrikson Zaharias. Rich Wallace, Sandra Neil Wallace. Calkins Creek 2014 272 p. (Includes bibliographical references (page 266-268) and index.) $16.95

Grades: 4 5 6 7 8   92

1. Women athletes -- Biography

ISBN 1590789814; 9781590789810

LC 2013953471

This book, by Rich Wallace and Sandra Neil Wallace, is a biography of Babe Didrikson Zaharias. "A champion basketball player, an Olympic track-and-field star, and career golfer, Babe didn't let obstacles stand in the way of her success. The authors detail her trajectory from the daughter of a Norwegian immigrant born in a working-class Texas neighborhood to record wins at the 1932 Olympics (still not broken to this day) to her last days as she fought cancer." (School Library Journal)

"Babe Didrikson Zaharias is perhaps the most accomplished athlete that young people have never heard of. She was an Olympic track star in the 1932 games, a noted professional basketball player, and a formative member of the LPGA...This is part sports journalism, part narrative nonfiction, and part proof that professional athletes can be exemplary role models for young people." Booklist

Zhu, Xiao-Mei

LeBlanc, Andre. The **red** piano; [illustrated by] Barroux; translated by Justine French. Wilkins Farago 2010 40p il $16.99

Grades: 2 3 4 5   92

1. Pianists 2. Music teachers 3. China -- History -- 1949-1976

ISBN 978-0-9806070-1-7; 0-9806070-1-9

"The experiences of Chinese-born French pianist Khu Xiao-Mei inspire this poignant, picture-book biography set during the Cultural Revolution. Separated from her family and forbidden to pursue classical music studies, a young girl in exile clandestinely collects Bach preludes and practices the piano in a hut on the outskirts of her rural village. When she and her accomplice, an elderly villager who hides the piano, are discovered, they are tortured and ridiculed, and the piano is destroyed. An ambiguous ending sends the girl from the camp into a murky sunset with her secreted music notebooks in tow. Leblanc's clipped, elegant phrases tell a woeful, abstracted story that is well-matched with Barroux's arresting paintings in inky brown and shocking red.... The dramatic imagery offers an accessible, vivid picture of life during the time of Chairman Mao." Booklist

Zitkala-Sa, 1876-1938

★ Pearce, Q. L. **Red** Bird sings: the story of Zitkala-Sa; by Gina Capaldi & Q.L. Pearce; illustrated by Gina Capaldi. Carolrhoda Books 2011 32p il lib bdg $17.95

Grades: 3 4 5 6   92

1. Authors 2. Women authors 3. Women musicians 4. Yankton Indians 5. Political activists 6. Essayists 7. Indian leaders 8. Authors, American 9. Short story writers 10. Native Americans -- Biography

ISBN 978-0-7613-5257-0; 0-7613-5257-0

LC 2011003014

This children's biography describes the life of "Gertrude Simmons Bonnin of the Yankton Sioux, later known as Zitkala-Sa [who] bridged the nineteenth and twentieth centuries, and the white and Indian cultures ... readers follow her school days, her later career as a political advocate for Indian rights, and her struggle to reconcile her determination for personal advancement with feelings of guilt for abandoning her family." The book includes "[f]irst-person narration adapted from Zitkala-Sa's own writings and supplemented with "additional primary and secondary sources"". (Bulletin of the Center for Children's Books)

"Capaldi and Pearce document the life of Gertrude Simmons, an author, musician, and activist best known by her pen name, Zitkala-Sa (Red Bird). Drawing from semiautobiographical stories that Zitkala-Sa wrote for the Atlantic Monthly in the early 1900s, Capaldi and Pearce eloquently describe her experience at a Quaker boarding school, where she laments the loss of her culture, but also develops passions for violin and women's suffrage.... Capaldi's understated illustrations integrate solid colors and doll-like characterizations with reproductions of period materials, while appended information on Sitkala-Sa rounds out this fascinating portrait." Publ Wkly

Includes bibliographical references

Zuckerberg, Mark

Woog, Adam. **Mark** Zuckerberg, Facebook creator. KidHaven Press 2009 48p il map (Innovators) $28.25

Grades: 4 5 6 7   92

1. Businesspeople 2. Facebook Inc. 3. Internet executives

ISBN 978-0-7377-4566-5; 0-7377-4566-5

LC 2009013458

"This brisk, readable [biography the creator of Facebook] ... presents an appealing picture of the shy, lonely future billionaire ... This is fascinating and relevant stuff." Booklist

Includes bibliographical references

920   Biography, genealogy, insignia

Adler, David A.

Heroes for civil rights; by David A. Adler; illustrated by Bill Farnsworth. Holiday House 2007 32p il $16.95

Grades: 3 4 5   920

1. African Americans -- Biography 2. African Americans -- Civil rights

ISBN 978-0-8234-2008-7

LC 2006038185

"Adler presents biographical sketches of several individuals and the defining actions or events in their lives as they relate to the roles they played during the Civil Rights Movement.... The format is attractive, with the easy-to-read text facing a full-page illustration. Farnsworth's oil paintings complement the simple presentations by featuring a large portrait of each individual, with one or more smaller pictures of a significant moment superimposed on it." SLJ

Includes bibliographical references

Bausum, Ann

★ **Our** country's first ladies; [by] Ann Bausum; with a foreword by First Lady Laura Bush. National Geographic 2007 127p il $19.95; lib bdg $28.90

Grades: 5 6 7 8   **920**

1. Presidents' spouses -- United States

ISBN 978-1-4263-0006-6; 978-1-4263-0007-3 lib bdg

LC 2006021284

"A well-researched, thoughtfully written, attractive account. Fact boxes provide basic information such as birth and death dates, marriage dates, and children's names; a 'Did You Know' section shares interesting personal tidbits. Periodic time lines help to place the women's lives within the broader events of history. There is enough information here for simple reports. Interesting facts and anecdotes will hold readers' attention. . . . An excellent layout and clear, colorful photographs and reproductions will further entice readers." SLJ

Includes bibliographical references

Beccia, Carlyn

The **raucous** royals; test your royal wits: crack codes, solve mysteries, and deduce which royal rumors are true. Houghton Mifflin 2008 64p il $17

Grades: 4 5 6 7   **920**

1. Nobility 2. Historiography 3. Kings and rulers

ISBN 978-0-618-89130-6; 0-618-89130-7

LC 2008-298419

"Thirteen beliefs about rulers receive an acerbic and irreverent interrogation in this blend of royal-watching and skeptical investigation. The royal rumors, arranged chronologically, start with the real story behind Prince Dracula and Richard III's murderous ways, stopping en route at Napoleon's short stature and Marie Antoinette's 'let them eat cake' utterance, and finish up with Catherine the Great's death and King George's madness. . . . The energy and gleefully gossipy nature makes this a fine companion for Krull's Lives of . . . series, while its verve particularly recommends it as an entrée into historiography and critical thinking." Bull Cent Child Books

Includes bibliographical references

Bolden, Tonya

★ **Pathfinders**; The Journeys of 16 Extraordinary Black Souls. Tonya Bolden. Abrams Books for Young Readers 2017 124 p. $24.95; (ebook) $18.65

Grades: 5 6 7 8   **920**

1. African Americans -- Biography 2. Successful people -- United States -- Biography

ISBN 9781419714559; 9781613129739

LC 2015043356

This book, by Tonya Bolden, "is a collective biography of sixteen diverse American men and women of African descent who made their mark on American history in the 18th to 20th centuries. . . . Bolden offers an insightful look at these figures, from Venture Smith, who bought his freedom; to Sadie Alexander, who contributed to the Civil Rights movement in the United States; to Katherine Johnson, who helped the United States land on the moon." (Publisher's note)

"A well-researched book introducing a varied group of African Americans who excelled in their own, individual ways." Booklist

Includes bibliographical references and index

Portraits of African-American heroes; paintings by Ansel Pitcairn. Dutton Children's Books 2003 88p il $18.99; pa $11.99

Grades: 4 5 6 7   **920**

1. African Americans -- Biography

ISBN 0-525-47043-3; 0-14-240473-X pa

LC 2002-75911

"Each profile lists expected biographical information, but offers even more by way of keen insights into a subject's personality based on interviews and information drawn from personal memoirs. . . . Pitcairn's beautifully rendered sepia-toned portraits make each subject jump from the page, beckoning children to come ever closer and learn." Booklist

Bragg, Georgia

How they choked; failures, flops, and flaws of the awfully famous. by Georgia Bragg; illustrated by Kevin O'Malley. Bloomsbury/Walker 2014 208 p. (pbk.) $18.89

Grades: 5 6 7 8   **920**

1. Inventions 2. Celebrities 3. Decision making

ISBN 0802734898; 9780802734884; 9780802734891

LC 2013039127

This book, by Georgia Bragg, "knocks fourteen famous achievers off their pedestals to reveal the human side of history. Successful 'failures' include: Marco Polo, Queen Isabella of Spain, Montezuma II, Ferdinand Magellan, Anne Boleyn, Isaac Newton, Benedict Arnold, Susan B. Anthony, George Armstrong Custer, Thomas Alva Edison, Vincent Van Gogh, J. Bruce Ismay, 'Shoeless Joe' Jackson, [and] Amelia M. Earhart." (Publisher's note)

"On the heels of How They Croaked: The Awful Ends of the Awfully Famous (2011), Bragg seeks to reconcile what she sees as a major flaw of the biography genre—that authors ignore the human potential for error. Her compendium is unapologetically full of bad news, criticism, and belly flops...The snarkily entertaining narratives are illustrated with caricatures of each subject. For better or worse, subjects are rarely as one-dimensional as most biographies paint them, and this book proves that nobody is perfect." Booklist

★ **How** they croaked; the awful ends of the awfully famous. Walker & Co. 2011 178p il $17.99; lib bdg $18.89

Grades: 5 6 7 8   **920**

1. Death 2. Biography 3. Celebrities -- Death

ISBN 978-0-8027-9817-6; 0-8027-9817-9; 978-0-8027-9818-3 lib bdg; 0-8027-9818-7 lib bdg

LC 2010-08659

"Bragg chronicles with ghoulish glee the chronic or fatal maladies that afflicted 19 historical figures. Nonsqueamish readers will by entranced by her riveting descriptions. . . . The author tucks quick notes on at least marginally relevant topics, such as leeching, scurvy, presidential assassins, and mummy eyes . . . between the chapters. . . . O'Malley's cartoon portraits and spot art add just the right notes of humor to keep the contents from becoming too gross." Booklist

Bryan, Ashley

★ **Freedom** over me; Eleven Slaves, Their Lives and Dreams Brought to Life by Ashley Bryan. by Ashley Bryan. Atheneum Books for Young Readers 2016 56 p. color illustrations (ebook) $15.99; (hardback) $17.99

Grades: 1 2 3 4   **920**

1. Slavery 2. African Americans

ISBN 9781481456913; 9781481456906; 1481456903

LC 2016002468

Kirkus Prize Finalist: Young Readers' Literature (2016)

Coretta Scott King (Illustrator) Honor Book (2017)

Coretta Scott King (Author) Honor Book (2017)

Newbery Honor Book (2017)

This children's book by Ashley Bryan shows "how a slave is given a monetary value by the slave owner. . . . Inspired by the actual will of a plantation owner that lists the worth of each and every one of his 'workers', Bryan has created that collages around document. . . . He imagines and interprets each person's life on the plantation, as well as . . . their dreams and pride in knowing that they were worth far more than an Overseer or Madam ever would guess." (Publisher's note)

"There are few first-person accounts of slaves, and these imagined words will strike a chord with even the youngest readers." Pub Wkly

Cook, Michelle

★ **Our** children can soar; a celebration of Rosa, Barack, and the pioneers of change. illustrations by Cozbi A. Cabrera . . . [et al.]; foreword by Marian Wright Edelman. Bloomsbury 2009 un il $16.99; lib bdg $17.89

Grades: K 1 2   920

1. African Americans -- History 2. African Americans -- Biography
ISBN 978-1-59990-418-4; 1-59990-418-7; 978-1-59990-419-1 lib bdg; 1-59990-419-5 lib bdg

LC 2009-1730

"The spreads understandably represent an array of artistic styles and media, yet they form a cohesive and affecting collective portrait. . . . Additional images from Leo and Diane Dillon, James Ransome, E.B. Lewis, Eric Velasquez and others, corroborate Children's Defense Fund founder Marian Wright Edelman's assertion, in the book's foreword, that African-American history is 'the story of hope.'" Publ Wkly

Cotter, Charis

Born to write; the remarkable lives of six famous authors. Annick Press 2009 167p il $24.95; pa $14.95

Grades: 5 6 7 8   920

1. Authors
ISBN 978-1-55451-192-1; 1-55451-192-5; 978-1-55451-191-4 pa; 1-55451-191-7 pa

A collective biography of authors Lucy Maud Montgomery, Christopher Paul Curtis, C. S. Lewis, E.B. White, Madeleine L'Engle, and Philip Pullman

"Younger readers will find the presentation of the book appealing, with many colorful photographs and illustrations; however, more mature readers will gain the most enjoyment as they discover the backgrounds and inspirations of some of their favorite writers. . . . An excellent resource for reports and pleasure reading." SLJ

Kids who rule; the remarkable lives of five child monarchs. Annick Press 2007 120p il map $24.95; pa $14.95

Grades: 5 6 7 8   920

1. Queens 2. Emperors 3. Kings and rulers 4. Kings 5. Buddhist leaders 6. Political leaders 7. Nobel laureates for peace
ISBN 978-1-55451-062-7; 1-55451-062-7; 978-1-55451-061-0 pa; 1-55451-061-9 pa

This "book discusses five people who became monarchs as children: Tutankhamen of Egypt, Mary Queen of Scots, Queen Christina of Sweden, China's Emperor Puyi, and the fourteenth Dalai Lama. . . . The illustrations, many in color, include portrait paintings, engravings, and maps as well as photos of people, places, and artifacts. . . . This appealing collective biography presents five unusual children whose stories are well worth reading." Booklist

Cummins, Julie

★ **Women** daredevils; thrills, chills, and frills. illustrated by Cheryl Harness. Dutton Children's Books 2008 48p il $17.99

Grades: 3 4 5 6   920

1. Stunt performers 2. Women -- Biography
ISBN 978-0-525-47948-2; 0-525-47948-1

LC 2007-18102

"Cummins introduces 10 women stunt performers, active from 1880 to 1929. . . . Each story includes broad historical context with facts about women's status and societal expectations. . . . Cummins' lively text provides a sense of each individual by including quotes and physical

descriptions. . . . Harness' richly colored, detailed illustrations . . . are expressive, realistic, and filled with action." Booklist

Donovan, Sandy

Lethal leaders and military madmen; by Sandy Donovan. Lerner Publications Company 2013 32 p. col. ill. (library) $26.60

Grades: 5 6 7 8   920

1. Picture books for children 2. Kings and rulers 3. Dictators 4. Dictatorship 5. Military government
ISBN 1467706094; 9781467706094

LC 2012018444

This book by Sandy Donovan is part of the Shockzone Villains series and looks at political and military leaders. "Some of history's most ruthless leaders are headed your way. Some of these rulers schemed their way to the top. Others just conquered everything around them." (Publisher's note)

Drucker, Malka

Portraits of Jewish American heroes; by Malka Drucker; illustrated by Elizabeth Rosen. Dutton Children's Books 2008 96p il $22.99

Grades: 4 5 6   920

1. Jews -- United States -- Biography
ISBN 978-0-525-47771-6; 0-525-47771-3

LC 2007-028481

"From Albert Einstein and Bella Abzug to Ruth Bader Ginsburg, Hank Greenberg, and Steven Spielberg, this invitingly illustrated collective biography celebrates 20 Jewish American heroes in all their diversity. . . . The nicely designed volume includes full-page portraits of the subjects in various media. . . . Drucker's eloquent, chatty style opens up big issues about Judaism as a source of idealism and for a just, compassionate society." Booklist

Includes bibliographical references

Fortey, Jacqueline

Great scientists; written by Jacqueline Fortey. DK Pub. 2007 72p il map (DK eyewitness books) $15.99

Grades: 5 6 7 8   920

1. Scientists
ISBN 978-0-7566-2974-8; 0-7566-2974-8

LC 2007-298205

This introduces readers to the great scientists and their discoveries from ancient history to modern times.

"An accompanying CD provides clip art taken from the book; this art can prove invaluable to both teachers and students. . . . A very fine book for elementary and middle school students and those who teach them." Sci Books and Films

Fradin, Dennis B.

The **founders**; the 39 stories behind the U.S. Constitution. [by] Dennis Brindell Fradin; illustrated by Michael McCurdy. Walker & Co. 2005 162p il map $22.95; lib bdg $23.95

Grades: 4 5 6 7   920

1. Statesmen -- United States 2. United States -- Constitution 3. United States -- Politics and government -- 1783-1809
ISBN 0-8027-8972-2; 0-8027-8973-0 lib bdg

"The makers of the U.S. Constitution are profiled in two or three pages each, in sections introduced by a brief note about their home states. McCurdy's black-and-white scratchboard illustrations are properly stately and engaging. Readers will find great nuggets of fact." Booklist

Includes bibliographical references

★ **Funny** business; conversations with writers of comedy. compiled and edited by Leonard S. Marcus. Candlewick Press 2009 214p il $21.99

Grades: 5 6 7 8 9 10   **920**

1. Authors 2. Authorship 3. Wit and humor

ISBN 978-0-7636-3254-0; 0-7636-3254-6

This book comprises interviews with writers of humorous books for young people: Judy Blume, Beverly Cleary, Sharon Creech, Christopher Paul Curtis, Anne Fine, Daniel Handler, Carl Hiaasen, Norton Juster, Dick King-Smith, Hilary McKay, Daniel Pinkwater, Louis Sachar, and Jon Scieszka. Index. "Intermediate, middle school." (Horn Book)

"In 12 entertaining interviews . . . Marcus's compilation explores the childhoods, writing processes and senses of humor of well-known writers for children, including Judy Blume, Beverly Cleary, Daniel Handler, Norton Juster and Jon Scieszka. Marcus's evident knowledge of his subjects' writing makes for some intriguing questions and answers. . . . Photographs, manuscript pages and even e-mail chains between the writers and their editors add fascinating tidbits." Publ Wkly

George-Warren, Holly

Honky-tonk heroes & hillbilly angels; the pioneers of country & western music. words by Holly George-Warren; pictures by Laura Levine. Houghton Mifflin 2006 32p il $16

Grades: 3 4 5 6   **920**

1. Musicians 2. Country music

ISBN 0-618-19100-3

LC 2003-5364

Profiles important and influential performers of country and western music, including the Carter Family, Roy Acuff, Gene Autry, Bill Monroe, Patsy Cline, and Loretta Lynn.

"Concise but thorough. . . . Colorful, stylized, folk art of the performers and/or their instruments is included." SLJ

Gifford, Clive

10 inventors who changed the world; written by Clive Gifford; illustrated by David Cousens. Kingfisher 2009 63p il $14.99

Grades: 4 5 6 7   **920**

1. Inventors 2. Inventions

ISBN 978-0-7534-6259-1; 0-7534-6259-1

"The innovative efforts of nine men and one woman are presented here. Some of the names will be familiar (Galileo, Franklin, Edison, Curie) while others will prove less so (Isambard Kingdom Brunel, Glenn Curtiss, Sergei Korolev). Starting in ancient times with Archimedes, the chronology ends in modern times with Korolev, a Soviet-era rocket designer. Each section offers a succinct yet thorough biography of the inventors. Striking graphic-novel-style art is a visual aid to draw readers into each setting and era." SLJ

10 kings & queens who changed the world; written by Clive Gifford; illustrated by David Cousens. Kingfisher 2009 63p il map $14.99

Grades: 4 5 6 7   **920**

1. Kings and rulers

ISBN 978-0-7534-6252-2; 0-7534-6252-4

"Cousens' bright graphic novel-style artwork is the grabber here; he uses theatrical angles to portray each historical figure as a chiseled or beautiful adventurer. . . . The writing is clear, packed with information, and presented in agile paragraphs that twist around the scenes of war, plotting, and murder." Booklist

Haven, Kendall F.

Reluctant heroes; true five-minute-read adventure stories for boys. Libraries Unlimited 2008 169p pa $30

Grades: Adult Professional   **920**

1. Heroes and heroines

ISBN 978-1-59158-749-1 pa; 1-59158-749-2 pa

LC 2008014017

"These 25 true stories are divided into three sections: 'Stories from History,' 'Stories from the Modern World,' and 'Stories from the Natural World.' Each one offers a short history or explanation to place events in context and concludes with suggestions for further reading. . . . Appropriate as partnered works to nonfiction topics, these brief entries create useful classroom writing prompts or simply entertaining read-alouds. Quick-moving action and dialogue place readers squarely in the midst of dangerous, momentous events." SLJ

Includes bibliographical references

Hearst, Michael

Extraordinary people; a semi-comprehensive guide to some of the world's most fascinating individuals. by Michael Hearst; illustrated by Aaron Scamihorn. Chronicle Books 2015 110 p. color illustrations (hardback) $16.99

Grades: 4 5 6 7 8   **920**

1. Curiosities and wonders 2. Biography

ISBN 1452127093; 9781452127095

LC 2014020931

This juvenile book, by Michael Hearst, illustrated by Aaron Scamihorn, presents "stories of 50 extraordinary people such as: Evel Knievel, who jumped his motorcycle over 14 Greyhound buses, The Iceman, the most well-preserved human, found in the ice after 5,300 years, Sam Patch, who jumped Niagara Falls for $75, Helen Thayer, who walked to the North Pole alone, [and] Roy Sullivan, who was struck by lightning 7 times." (Publisher's note)

"This is a welcome antidote to traditional biography-assignment fare." Booklist

Herrera, Juan Felipe, 1948-

★ **Portraits** of Hispanic American heroes; by Juan Felipe Herrera; pictures by Raul Colon. Dial Books for Young Readers 2014 96 p. color illustrations (hardback) $19.99

Grades: 4 5 6 7 8   **920**

1. Biography 2. Latinos (U.S.)

ISBN 0803738099; 9780803738096

LC 2013044661

Pura Belpré (Author) Honor Book (2015)

This book by Juan Felipe Herrera "showcases twenty Hispanic and Latino American men and women who have made outstanding contributions to the arts, politics, science, humanitarianism, and athletics. Biographies of Cesar Chavez, Sonia Sotomayor, Ellen Ochoa, Roberto Clemente, and many more [are included]." (Publisher's note)

"Herrera packs relevant info and kid-appropriate details . . . without overwhelming the work, infusing the narratives with engaging text. Colon's portraits are luminous." SLJ

Includes bibliographical references

Hodgkins, Fran

Champions of the ocean; illustrations by Cris Arbo. Dawn Publications 2009 144p il (Earth heroes) pa $11.95

Grades: 5 6 7 8   **920**

1. Scientists 2. Oceanography 3. Environmentalists

ISBN 978-1-58469-119-8 pa; 1-58469-119-0 pa

LC 2009-17926

This is a collective biography of oceanographers William Beebe, Archie Carr, Jacques-Yves Cousteau, Margaret Wentworth Owings, Eugenie Clark, Roger Payne, Sylvia Earle, and Tierney Thys.

This is illustrated with "black-and-white photographs and illustrations. [The book] provides young readers with fascinating facts and insights. . . . This volume is an excellent introduction to the biography genre, as well as a terrific research book." Sci Books Films

Includes bibliographical references

Housel, Debra J.

Ecologists; from Woodward to Miranda. Compass Point Books 2009 40p il (Mission: science) lib bdg $26.60

Grades: 4 5 6 **920**

1. Ecology 2. Environmentalists

ISBN 978-0-7565-4076-0 lib bdg; 0-7565-4076-3 lib bdg

LC 2008-35733

Profiles ecologists John Woodward, Aldo Leopold, Rachel Carson, Ruth Patrick, Eugene Odum, Lan Lubchenco, and Neo Martinez

Includes glossary and bibliographical references

Jankowski, Connie

Astronomers; from Copernicus to Crisp. Compass Point Books 2009 40p il (Mission: science) lib bdg $26.60

Grades: 4 5 6 **920**

1. Astronomers

ISBN 978-0-7565-3965-8 lib bdg; 0-7565-3965-X lib bdg

LC 2008-8325

Explores the lives and discoveries of noted astronomers from the fifteenth to the twenty-first century.

Includes glossary and bibliographical references

Jokulsson, Illugi

Stars of the World Cup; Illugi Jökulsson. Abbeville Kids 2014 63 p. (World soccer legends) (hardback) $12.95

Grades: 5 6 7 8 **920**

1. Soccer 2. Soccer teams 3. World Cup (Soccer) 4. Soccer players -- Biography

ISBN 0789212110; 9780789212115

LC 2014014490

In this book, by Illugi Jokulsson, "learn all about twenty-eight of the best players competing for the 2014 FIFA World Cup, from unstoppable scorers like Messi and Ronaldo to crafty playmakers like Iniesta and Modric, and ironclad defenders like Philipp Lahm and Thiago Silva." (Publisher's note)

"Young soccer fans will find plenty to enjoy in this visually dynamic introduction to 28 world-class soccer players... Readers will enjoy the information-packed text, but it's the eye-catching color photos (usually action shots) that will draw them to this attractive sports book." Booklist

Includes bibliographical references and index

Kiernan, Denise

★ **Signing** our lives away; the fame and misfortune of the men who signed the Declaration of Independence. by Denise Kiernan & Joseph D'Agnese. Quirk 2009 255p $19.95

Grades: 5 6 7 8 **920**

1. Statesmen -- United States 2. United States -- Declaration of Independence 3. United States -- Politics and government -- 1775-1783, Revolution

ISBN 978-1-59474-330-6; 1-59474-330-4

"Kiernan and D'Agnese present readers with astonishing individual portraits of all the signers [of the Declaration of Independence] in an attempt both to dispel some of the mythology surrounding the document as well as to establish a place in the historical discourse for those men not named Jefferson, Hancock, Franklin, or Adams. The marvelously arranged work lends itself to either straightforward reading or skipping around. . . . An entertaining and effective narrative of about three to five pages per individual is presented." SLJ

Includes bibliographical references

Kimmel, Elizabeth Cody

Ladies first; 40 daring American women who were second to none. [by] Elizabeth Cody Kimmel; foreword by Stacy Allison. National Geographic 2006 192p il $18.95

Grades: 5 6 7 8 **920**

1. Women -- Biography 2. United States -- Biography

ISBN 0-7922-5393-0

LC 2005005113

This offers "introductions to forty of America's most brilliant and courageous women. Each essay is three pages in length and includes a fourth full-page portrait of the woman being introduced. . . . The women chosen achieved greatness in a wide range of endeavors, from athletics to the arts to politics. . . . Students will find these excellent essays useful as an introduction to the women portrayed and as a good jumping off point for further research." Voice Youth Advocates

Includes bibliographical references

Krull, Kathleen

The **brothers** Kennedy; John, Robert, Edward. illustrated by Amy June Bates. Simon & Schuster Books for Young Readers 2010 40p il $16.99

Grades: 2 3 4 **920**

1. Brothers 2. Statesmen 3. Presidents 4. Senators 5. Attorneys general 6. Political leaders 7. Members of Congress 8. Siblings of presidents 9. Presidential candidates

ISBN 978-1-4169-9158-8; 1-4169-9158-1

"Focusing on John, Robert, and Edward, the book describes the Kennedys' early family life and highlights a pivotal event for each featured sibling. . . . The stylized artwork [is] rendered in pencil, watercolor, and gouache. . . . The likenesses are strong, and the images set a historic tone." Booklist

Includes bibliographical references

★ **Lives** of extraordinary women; rulers, rebels (and what the neighbors thought) written by Kathleen Krull; illustrated by Kathryn Hewitt. Harcourt 2000 95p il $21

Grades: 4 5 6 7 **920**

1. Queens 2. Saints 3. Diplomats 4. Empresses 5. Explorers 6. Travelers 7. Suffragists 8. Abolitionists 9. Prime ministers 10. Women in politics 11. Regents 12. Feminists 13. Pacifists 14. Columnists 15. Dissenters 16. Memoirists 17. Humanitarians 18. Indian chiefs 19. Archaeologists 20. Indian leaders 21. Cabinet members 22. Social activists 23. Political leaders 24. Nonfiction writers 25. Women -- Biography 26. Members of Congress 27. Spouses of presidents 28. Human rights activists 29. United Nations officials 30. Nobel laureates for peace

ISBN 0-15-200807-1

LC 99-6840

"Each entry offers a tightly written biography, often filled with delicious anecdote. . . . Each biographical essay is accompanied by one of Hewitt's full-page, full-color caricatures. Both artful and witty, the illustrations provide perfect accompaniments to the often breezy and accessible text." N Y Times Book Rev

Includes bibliographical references

Lives of the explorers; discoveries, disasters (and what the neighbors thought) Kathleen Krull; illustrated by Kathryn Hewitt. HMH Books for Young Readers 2014 96 p. col. ill., col. maps (hardback) $20.99

Grades: 4 5 6 7 **920**

1. Explorers 2. Exploration 3. United States -- Exploration 4. Discoveries in geography 5. Adventure and adventurers

ISBN 0152059105; 9780152059101

LC 2013037697

"Krull introduces middle-grade readers to a diverse cast of 17 explorers in this latest offering from her series. A short, two-to five page chapter is devoted to each explorer, incorporating a biographical sketch and a short discussion of the explorer's contributions. The subjects are presented chronologically, beginning in the medieval period with the Norseman Leif Ericson and finishing with the astronaut Sally Ride." (School Library Journal)

"The straightforward, accessible prose makes for fast reading, and Krull doesn't shy away from some deplorable, stomach-turning facts, which kids will devour and use to spice up staid homework assignments." Kirkus

Includes bibliographical references

★ **Lives** of the musicians; good times, bad times (and what the neighbors thought) written by Kathleen Krull; illustrated by Kathryn Hewitt. Harcourt Brace Jovanovich 1993 96p il $21; pa $12; pa $8.99

Grades: 4 5 6 7   **920**

1. Authors 2. Singers 3. Pianists 4. Composers 5. Dramatists 6. Violinists 7. Librettists 8. Folk musicians 9. Jazz musicians 10. Conductors (Music) 11. Memoirists 12. Songwriters 13. Music teachers 14. Classical musicians 15. Theatrical directors

ISBN 0-15-248010-2; 0-15-216436-7 pa; 9780544238060

LC 91-33497

"Twenty (including both Gilbert and Sullivan) composers, from Vivaldi to Gershwin, are here profiled in a series of irreverent, anecdotal vignettes, each stylishly illustrated with an elegant caricature." Bull Cent Child Books

Includes glossary and bibliographical references

★ **Lives** of the presidents; fame, shame (and what the neighbors thought) written by Kathleen Krull; illustrated by Kathryn Hewitt. updated ed.; Harcourt Children's Books 2011 104p il $21

Grades: 4 5 6 7   **920**

1. Presidents -- United States

ISBN 978-0-547-49809-6; 0-547-49809-8

First published 1998

"This new edition is sure to be even more popular than the original title (Harcourt, 1998) as it includes Presidents George W. Bush and Barack Obama, who are given the same cheeky-but-respectful treatment as their predecessors. . . . [Krull] provides further information on ex-Presidential activity since 1998, such as Jimmy Carter's Nobel Prize, Ronald Reagan's passing, and the Clintons' post-White House work. All other entries and art are virtually unaltered. Guaranteed to inject some levity into the ubiquitous presidential biography assignment, the 2011 Lives of the Presidents is a must-have for elementary schools and public libraries." SLJ

Includes bibliographical references

Malnor, Bruce

Champions of the wilderness; by Bruce and Carol L. Malnor; illustrated by Anisa Claire Hovemann. Dawn Publications 2009 143p il (Earth heroes) pa $11.95

Grades: 5 6 7 8   **920**

1. Environmentalists

ISBN 978-1-58469-116-7 pa; 1-58469-116-6 pa

LC 2008-53670

"This is a short gem of a book that includes short biographies of eight 'heroes' who have championed the preservation and/or conservation of wilderness areas around the world over the past two centuries. Henry David Thoreau, John Muir, Teddy Roosevelt, Aldo Leopold, Richard St. Barbe Baker, Mardy Murie, David Suzuki, and Wangari

Maathai are the heroes in question. The storytelling is fluent and engaging." Sci Books Films

Includes bibliographical references

Malnor, Carol

Champions of wild animals; by Carol L. and Bruce Malnor; illustrations by Anisa Claire Hovemann. Dawn Publications 2010 144p il (Earth heroes) pa $11.95

Grades: 5 6 7 8   **920**

1. Naturalists 2. Endangered species 3. Wildlife conservation

ISBN 978-1-58469-123-5 pa; 1-58469-123-9 pa

LC 2010-16030

This describes "the youth and careers of eight of the world's greatest environmentalists who championed the protection of wildlife, including William Hornaday (saved the bison from extinction), Ding Darling (A Duck's Best Friend), Rachel Carson (author of Silent Spring), Roger Tory Peterson (Inventor of the Modern Field Guide), R.D. Lawrence (Storyteller for Wolves), E.O. Wilson (Lord of the Ants), Jane Goodall (Champion for Chimps), and Ian and Saba Douglas-Hamilton (Saving the Elephants)." Publisher's note

Includes bibliographical references

Nathan, Amy

Meet the dancers; from ballet, Broadway, and beyond. Henry Holt 2008 231p il $18.95

Grades: 5 6 7 8   **920**

1. Dance 2. Dancers

ISBN 978-0-8050-8071-1; 0-8050-8071-6

LC 2007-27589

"This collective biography reveals the paths that 16 diverse dancers followed to become professionals and to join prestigious companies. . . . The tone of the text is conversational. . . . The pictures dramatically capture how talented these performers are. Anyone, whether considering a career in dance or not, will be inspired and educated by these up-close-and-personal accounts." SLJ

Pinkney, Andrea Davis

★ **Let** it shine; stories of Black women freedom fighters. illustrated by Stephen Alcorn. Harcourt 2000 107p il $20

Grades: 4 5 6 7   **920**

1. Slaves 2. Authors 3. Midwives 4. Educators 5. Journalists 6. Abolitionists 7. Philanthropists 8. Essayists 9. Memoirists 10. Political leaders 11. Nonfiction writers 12. Members of Congress 13. Newspaper executives 14. Presidential advisers 15. African American women 16. Civil rights activists 17. Organization officials 18. Political party leaders 19. Presidential candidates 20. United States -- Race relations 21. African Americans -- Civil rights 22. African American women -- Biography 23. African Americans -- Civil rights -- History 24. African American women civil rights workers -- Biography

ISBN 0-15-201005-X

LC 99-42806

This is a collection of "sketches celebrating the contributions of 10 women who moved forward the cause of civil rights in America. . . . They include Harriet Tubman, Mary McLeod Bethune and Rosa Parks, as well as Biddy Mason, Ida B. Wells-Barnett, Ella Josephine Baker, Dorothy Irene Height and Fannie Lou Hamer." (SLJ) Bibliography. "Grades three to six." (Bull Cent Child Books)

This "collective biography tells of 10 extraordinary black women. From Sojourner Truth to Shirley Chisholm, this is also a view of African American history through individual lives. . . . Stephen Alcorn's allegorical oil portraits are dramatic and beautiful. . . . The immediacy of the text and the spacious design of the large volume make this a natural for reading aloud." Booklist

Includes bibliographical references

Rappaport, Doreen

★ **We** are the many; a picture book of American Indians. illustrated by Cornelius Van Wright and Ying-Hwa Hu. HarperCollins Pubs. 2002 28p il hardcover o.p. lib bdg $17.89

Grades: 2 3 4   920

1. Native Americans -- Biography
ISBN 0-688-16559-1; 0-06-001139-4 lib bdg

LC 2001-39820

"One incident from each person's life is re-created, giving a quick, snapshot-style view of the individual's contribution to the world. . . . The text is large, and sentences are accessible to emerging readers. . . . There is some fictionalizing . . . but it is limited and does not detract from the overall worth of the title." SLJ

Rivera, Raquel

Arctic adventures; tales from the lives of Inuit artists. pictures by Jirina Marton. Groundwood Books/House of Anansi Press 2007 47p il $18.95

Grades: 3 4 5 6   920

1. Artists 2. Sculptors 3. Inuit artists 4. Printmakers 5. Inuit -- Art 6. Artists, Inuit
ISBN 978-0-88899-714-2; 0-88899-714-0

"This dynamic picture book draws on memoir, legend, art, and history to tell true dramatized events in the lives of four modern Inuit artists. . . . Beautiful illustrations in colored pencil and mixed media show the individual people and creatures in the Arctic landscape. . . . After each story, there is a brief, straightforward biography of the artist, a photo, and a reproduction of his or her work." Booklist

Includes glossary and bibliographical references

Roberts, Cokie

Founding mothers; remembering the ladies. by Cokie Roberts and illustrated by Diane Goode and edited by Alyson Day. HarperCollins 2014 40 p. (hardcover bdg.) $17.99

Grades: 3 4 5 6 7   920

1. Women -- United States -- History 2. United States -- History -- 1775-1783, Revolution
ISBN 0060780029; 9780060780029; 9780060780036

LC 2013936887

This book, by Cokie Roberts and illustrated by Diane Goode, "reveals the incredible accomplishments of the women who orchestrated the American Revolution behind the scenes. Roberts traces the stories of heroic, patriotic women such as Abigail Adams, Martha Washington, Phillis Wheatley, Mercy Otis Warren, Sarah Livingston Jay, and others. Details are gleaned from their letters, private journals, lists, and ledgers." (Publisher's note)

"Most children know that the "Founding Fathers" are the men who helped the 13 colonies develop into the United States. What about the women of the time period?...Grammarians may not appreciate the author's colloquial style, but the conversational tone is appealing. Beautifully intricate illustrations, rendered with antique pens, sepia ink, and watercolors, suit the text well. Thoughtful design, well-chosen facts, and an approachable format combine to make a book readers will enjoy and appreciate.□" (SLJ)

Roop, Peter

Tales of famous heroes; by Peter and Connie Roop; illustrated by Rebecca Zomchek. Scholastic 2010 106p il $17.99

Grades: 3 4 5 6   920

1. Heroes and heroines
ISBN 978-0-545-23750-5; 0-545-23750-5

"The lives of inspirational figures are presented in such an engaging manner that readers will not be able to stop after reading just one. The 17 profiles highlight important events from the individual's childhood, demonstrating how each was set on course for greatness. Current famous people, such as Sonia Sotomayor, Barack Obama, and Nelson Mandela, are included, as well as historical figures like Winston Churchill and Sojourner Truth. . . . The book is illustrated with caricature-type portraits superimposed on archival photographs. Each biography is made up of easy-to-read paragraphs designed for beginners or less capable older readers. An engaging collective biography." SLJ

Rosenberg, Aaron

The **Civil** War; one event, six people. Scholastic 2011 160p il map (Profiles) $14.99

Grades: 5 6 7 8   920

1. Nurses 2. Slaves 3. Authors 4. Lawyers 5. Generals 6. Presidents 7. Abolitionists 8. Photographers 9. Memoirists 10. Police officials 11. State legislators 12. College presidents 13. Members of Congress 14. Red Cross officials 15. Social welfare leaders 16. United States -- History -- 1861-1865, Civil War -- Biography
ISBN 978-0-545-28926-9; 0-545-28926-2

"This collective biography . . . introduces Abraham Lincoln, Frederick Douglass, Clara Barton, George McClellan, Robert E. Lee, and Matthew Brady. Single paragraph summaries of each subject's historical relevance are followed by resumes of their lives that focus on how each affected and was affected by the Civil War and that point out connections between them all. . . . Archival photographs are instuctive." Booklist

Includes bibliographical references

Stout, Glenn

Yes she can! women's sports pioneers. Houghton Mifflin Harcourt 2011 117p il (Good sports) pa $5.99

Grades: 4 5 6 7   920

1. Women athletes
ISBN 978-0-547-41725-7; 0-547-41725-X

"In chapters devoted to swimmer Trudy Ederle, runners Louise Stokes and Tidye Pickett, jockey Julie Krone, and Indy car driver Danica Patrick, Stout covers each woman's hard work, setbacks, and triumphs without minimizing the challenges and disappointments along the way. . . . Accessible and inspirational." Publ Wkly

Thimmesh, Catherine

★ **Girls** think of everything; illustrated by Melissa Sweet. Houghton Mifflin 2000 57p $16; pa $6.95

Grades: 5 6 7 8   920

1. Admirals 2. Chemists 3. Students 4. Inventors 5. Inventions 6. Physicists 7. Women inventors 8. Computer scientists 9. Home economists 10. Clothing industry executives 11. Office supply industry executives
ISBN 0-395-93744-2; 0-618-19563-7 pa

LC 99-36270

"Ten women and two girls are given a few pages each. Included are Mary Anderson, who invented the windshield wiper (after she was told it wouldn't work); Ruth Wakefield, who, by throwing chunks of chocolate in her cookie batter, gave Toll House cookies to the world; and young Becky Schroeder, who invented Glo-paper because she wanted to write in the dark. The text is written in a fresh, breezy manner, but it is the artwork that is really outstanding." Booklist

Waldman, Neil

A **land** of big dreamers; voices of courage in America. selected and illustrated by Neil Waldman. Millbrook Press 2010 32p il lib bdg $16.95

Grades: 3 4 5   **920**

1. Courage 2. American national characteristics 3. United States -- Biography

ISBN 978-0-8225-6810-0; 0-8225-6810-1

LC 2010001185

"Thirteen prominent American men and women are briefly profiled in this collection. Chronologically ranging from Thomas Jefferson to Barack Obama, each entry features an inspiring quote from its subject and a concise explanation of his or her context in history. Opposite each page of text is a watercolor painting by the author depicting an image or montage of the notable individual and illustrating the work they achieved or how they lived. Each one evokes the emotions the book is meant to inspire: courage, strength and determination." Kirkus

Winter, Jeanette

Malala, a brave girl from Pakistan/Iqbal, a brave boy from Pakistan; by Jeanette Winter. Beach Lane Books 2014 40 p. color illustrations (hardback) $17.99

Grades: 1 2 3 4   **920**

1. Pakistanis 2. Boys -- Pakistan -- Biography 3. Girls -- Education -- Pakistan 4. Girls -- Pakistan -- Biography 5. Heroes -- Pakistan -- Biography 6. Child slaves -- Pakistan -- Biography

ISBN 1481422944; 9781481422949

LC 2014009720

Author Jeanette Winter's children's book tells the true stories of "two heroes of Pakistan who stood up for the rights to freedom and education. Iqbal Masih and Malala Yousafzai. Each was unafraid to speak out. He, against inhumane child slavery in the carpet trade. She, for the right of girls to attend school. Both were shot by those who disagreed with them. Iqbal was killed instantly; Malala miraculously survived and continues to speak out around the world." (Publisher's note)

"This picture book introduces two Pakistani children who fought for peace and justice and suffered violence: one side is Malala Yousafzai's story; flip it for Iqbal Masih's. Iqbal was killed in 1995; Malala was shot by the Taliban (but survived) in 2012 "for speaking out for the right of girls to attend school." A great place to begin a young activist's education." Horn Book

Malala, a brave girl from Pakistan
Iqbal, a brave boy from Pakistan

Winter, Jonah

The **Founding** Fathers; Jonah Winter; illustrated by Barry Blitt. Atheneum Books for Young Readers 2014 48 p. color illustrations (hardcover) $17.99

Grades: 2 3 4 5   **920**

1. Founding Fathers of the United States 2. Constitutional history -- United States 3. United States -- History -- 1775-1783, Revolution 4. Founding Fathers of the United States

ISBN 1442442743; 9781442442740; 9781442442757

LC 2012030311

This children's book by Jonah Winter is a "look at our Founding Fathers. . . . It seems that Ben Franklin, Thomas Jefferson, and their co-horts sometimes agreed on NOTHING . . . except the thing that mattered most: creating the finest constitution in world history, for the brand-new United States of America. The men we now call America's Founding Fathers were a motley bunch of characters who fought a lot and made mistakes and just happened to invent a whole new kind of nation." (Publisher's note)

"Winter includes quotations from each man, as well as lists of stats with categories including their wealth, political party, 'Stance on France,' and 'Opinion on Boston Tea Party' (Benjamin Rush was a 'huge fan'). Blitt's pen-and-ink caricatures are right in line with Winter's playful tone, as he pokes fun at Washington, Franklin, Paine, and others, while giving readers a strong understanding of why these figures' contributions to the developing nation were so significant." Pub Wkly

Peaceful heroes; illustrated by Sean Addy. Arthur A. Levine Books 2009 56p il $17.99

Grades: 4 5 6 7   **920**

1. Peace 2. Heroes and heroines

ISBN 978-0-439-62307-0; 0-439-62307-3

LC 2008-48311

"Starting off with Jesus, Gandhi, King, and Sojourner Truth, this collective biography goes on to profile many less well-known peace activists across the world. . . . The detailed portraits never deny the horrifying realities that the peace-seeking leaders are fighting against. With the chatty interactive text, there are handsome full-page pictures of each activist, rendered in oil, acrylic, and collage in shades of red and brown." Booklist

Wild women of the Wild West; illustrated by Susan Guevara. Holiday House 2011 il $16.95

Grades: 2 3 4   **920**

1. Women -- Biography 2. West (U.S.) -- History 3. Frontier and pioneer life -- West (U.S.)

ISBN 978-0-8234-1601-1; 0-8234-1601-1

LC 2010030911

"This book introduces 16 figures who made their mark between the California Gold Rush and the end of the 19th century. . . . Each page-long biographical sketch is written in a delightful colloquial style that gives the text verve and sparkle. Each biography is accompanied by a full-page, watercolor and ink portrait of the subject. All are based on historical photos and show the women as strong and powerful." SLJ

Includes bibliographical references

Wishinsky, Frieda

Freedom heroines; Susan B. Anthony, Elizabeth Cady Stanton, Jane Addams, Ida B. Wells, Alice Paul, Rosa Parks. by Frieda Wishinsky. Scholastic Inc. 2012 144 p. ill. (some col.) (Profiles) (pbk.) $6.99

Grades: 4 5 6   **920**

1. Women's rights -- History 2. African Americans -- Civil rights 3. Women -- United States -- Biography 4. Civil rights workers -- United States 5. Feminists -- United States -- Biography 6. Suffragists -- United States -- Biography 7. African American women civil rights workers -- Biography

ISBN 0545425182; 9780545425186

LC 2012285016

Amelia Bloomer Project (2014)

Written by Frieda Wishinsky and part of the Profiles series, this book focuses "on Civil Champions--some of the incredible women who worked tirelessly to ensure equal rights for all." Women discussed include "Susan B. Anthony, Elizabeth Cady Stanton, Ida B. Wells, Alice Paul, Rosa Parks, and Jane Addams." (Publisher's note)

"The writing is matter-of-fact, with the design shouldering a lot of the load to distinguish each woman. Photos and reproductions of printed items, mostly black-and-white, lend context." Booklist

Includes bibliographical references and index

Yolen, Jane

Sea queens; women pirates around the world. illustrated by Christine Joy Pratt. Charlesbridge 2008 103p il $18.95

Grades: 4 5 6 7 **920**

1. Women pirates 2. Women -- Biography

ISBN 978-1-58089-131-8; 1-58089-131-4

LC 2007026983

This offers "12 portraits of sword-swinging, seafaring women throughout history, from Artemisia, in 500 B.C.E. Persia, to Madame Ching, an early nineteenth-century Chinese woman and named here as 'the most successful pirate in the world.' . . . The scratchboard illustrations work well as portraits. . . . The book is filled with fascinating, dramatically told stories and sidebars." Booklist

Includes bibliographical references

920.003 Dictionaries, encyclopedias, concordances of biography as a discipline

Biography for beginners: women who made a difference. Favorable Impressions 2011 $49

Grades: 3 4 5 6 **920.003**

1. Reference books 2. Women -- Biography

ISBN 978-1-931360-43-2

LC 2011017258

This is a "collection of 60 biographies of women who made an impact in their fields. . . . Each 6- to 10-page article is accompanied by well-chosen illustrations of the women. . . . The articles . . . are written at the appropriate level for elementary-school to middle-grade students and divided into sections that use bold type for the first few words to catch the reader's eye. The use of quotes from the subjects and others enhances the biographies and makes them more personal. . . . The biographies . . . serve as solid resources for young readers." Booklist

Includes glossary and bibliographical references

Rockman, Connie C.

Tenth book of junior authors and illustrators; edited by Connie C. Rockman. Wilson, H.W. 2008 803p autog il por (Junior authors & illustrators series) hardcover o.p. $120

Grades: Adult Professional **920.003**

1. Reference books 2. Authors -- Dictionaries 3. Illustrators -- Dictionaries 4. Children's literature -- Bio-bibliography

ISBN 978-0-8242-1066-3; 0-8242-1066-2

LC 2008043312

This volume covers some 200 authors and illustrators of books for children and young adults including David Almond, Blue Balliett, Terry Pratchett, and Laura Vaccaro Seeger. For 17 authors and artists whose careers include significant new works and honors since their profile in earlier editions of the series, newly written entries are featured

"Standard resource for libraries serving young readers and students studying children's and young adult literature." Booklist

Includes bibliographical references

Something about the author; facts and pictures about authors and illustrators of books for young people. Gale Res. il

Grades: Adult Professional **920.003**

1. Reference books 2. Authors -- Dictionaries 3. Illustrators -- Dictionaries 4. Children's literature -- Bio-bibliography

First published 1971. Frequency varies

"This important series gives comprehensive coverage of the individuals who write and illustrate books for children. Each new volume adds about 100 profiles. Entries include career and personal data, a bibliography of the author's works, information on works in progress and references to further information." Safford. Guide to Ref Materials for Sch Libr Media Cent. 5th edition

Something about the author: autobiography series. Gale Res. il

Grades: Adult Professional **920.003**

1. Reference books 2. Authors -- Dictionaries 3. Illustrators -- Dictionaries 4. Children's literature -- Bio-bibliography

First published 1986

An "ongoing series in which juvenile authors discuss their lives, careers, and published works. Each volume contains essays by 20 established writers or illustrators (e.g., Evaline Ness, Nonny Hogrogian, Betsy Byars, Jean Fritz) who represent all types of literature, preschool to young adult. . . . Some articles focus on biographical information, while others emphasize the writing career. Most, however, address young readers and provide family background, discuss the writing experience, and cite some factors that influenced it. Illustrations include portraits of the authors as children and more recent action pictures and portraits. There are cumulative indexes by authors, important published works, and geographical locations mentioned in the essays." Safford. Guide to Ref Books for Sch Libr Media Cent. 5th edition

920.72 Women

Branzei, Sylvia

Adventurers; Sylvia Branzei; illustrated by Melissa Sweet. Running Press 2011 96 p. ill., maps (ebook) $10.95; (paperback) $10.95

Grades: 3 4 5 6 7 **920.72**

1. Women 2. Adventure and adventurers 3. Women -- Biography 4. Women adventurers -- Biography 5. Adventure and adventurers -- Biography

ISBN 9780762443857; 0762436964; 9780762436965

LC 2009923889

This book "provides 6- to 8-page biographical sketches of 12 women who are 'the stuff of legends.' Each one is identified with a character trait, e.g. balloonist Sophie Blanchard is 'Intrepid' and Margaret Bourke-White is 'Relentless,' although most of the adjectives could apply to every subject, as [Sylvia] Branzei makes plain." Among those included are Amelia Earhart, Nellie Bly, Susan Butcher, and Kit Deslauriers. (School Library Journal)

Cowgirls; by Sylvia Branzei; illustratrated by Melissa Sweet. Running Press Kids 2011 96 p. ill. (some col.), map (paperback) $10.95

Grades: 3 4 5 6 7 **920.72**

1. Picture books for children 2. Cowgirls 3. Ranch life -- West (U.S.) 4. Cowgirls -- West (U.S.) -- History 5. Cowgirls -- West (U.S.) -- Biography

ISBN 0762436956; 9780762436958

LC 2009923890

This book "profiles 12 sketches of working cowgirls and rodeo riders from the 19th century through the present day. The term 'cowgirl' also covers other Western types: stagecoach driver Mary Fields is here, along with outlaw Sally Skull and 'Little Sure-Shot' Annie Oakley. 'Lady cowboy poet' Georgie Sicking will probably be new to most readers; one of her poems is included." (School Library Journal)

Includes bibliographical references (p. 92-96)

León, Vicki

★ **Outrageous** women of the Middle Ages; by Vicki Leon. Wiley 1998 ix, 118 p.p ill., maps hardcover o.p. (paperback) $14.95; (prebind) $23.95

Grades: 4 5 6 7 8 **920.72**

1. Middle Ages 2. Women -- History 3. Women -- Biography 4. Women -- History -- Middle Ages, 500-1500 5. Civilization, Medieval 6. Biography -- Middle Ages, 500-1500

ISBN 9780471170044; 9781435280090

LC 97030307

In this book, Vicki Leon looks at women of the Middle Ages. She "tells of a Viking killed by a severed head, a queen who knew the meaning of congregating frogs, and much more. The stories and sidebars provide a detailed picture of the times. . . . The women profiled lived in the 6th through 14th centuries in Europe, Asia, and Africa. Their spheres included everything from astronomy to warfare. They were nomads and empresses." (School Library Journal)

Includes bibliographical references (p. 115-117).

McCann, Michelle Roehm

Girls who rocked the world; heroines from Sacagawea to Natalie Portman. Michelle Roehm McCann and Amelie Welden. Simon & Schuster 2012 p. cm. (hardcover : alk. paper) $18.99

Grades: 5 6 7 8   **920.72**

1. Feminism 2. Women -- History 3. Women -- Biography 4. Girls -- Biography 5. Heros -- Biography 6. Women heros -- Biography

ISBN 9781582703022; 9781582703619

LC 2011050502

Author Michelle Roehm McCann presents "examples of strong, independent female role models, all of whom first impacted the world as teenagers or younger." The book "spans a variety of achievements, interests, and backgrounds, from Harriet Tubman and Coco Chanel to S.E. Hinton and Maya Lin--each with her own incredible story of how she created life-changing opportunities for herself and the world." (Publisher's note)

Includes bibliographical references and index.

929 Genealogy, names, insignia

Johnson, Mary J.

Your fascinating family history; super smart information strategies. by Mary J. Johnson. Cherry Lake Publishing 2011 32 p. (lib. bdg.) $28.50

Grades: 3 4 5 6   **929**

1. Family 2. Genealogy

ISBN 1610801229; 9781610801225

LC 2011000641

In this book, by Mary J. Johnson, readers can "learn how to research, understand, and arrange information about [their] ancestors." (Publisher's note) The book "provides ideas for beginning a genealogy search, explaining how to get started, where to find family information, and the value of oral histories and suggests creative ideas for putting everything together and sharing." (School Library Journal)

Includes bibliographical references and index

Ollhoff, Jim

Beginning genealogy; expert tips to help you trace your own ancestors. ABDO Pub. Co. 2011 32p il (Your family tree) $18.95

Grades: 4 5 6 7   **929**

1. Research 2. Genealogy

ISBN 978-1-61613-460-0; 1-61613-460-7

LC 2009050812

This is "great . . . for kids interested in genealogy. . . . [It does] a wonderful job of presenting the fundamentals of genealogical research in a clear and exciting manner. . . . Understanding and properly using primary documents is stressed throughout. . . . [An] attractive, spacious [layout]; full-color, sharp images; clearly labeled diagrams; and scattered maps add information and appeal." SLJ

Includes glossary

Collecting primary records. ABDO Pub. Co. 2011 32p il (Your family tree) $18.95

Grades: 4 5 6 7   **929**

1. Research 2. Genealogy

ISBN 978-1-61613-461-7; 1-61613-461-5

LC 2009050811

This describes how to collect primary records for geneological research.

This is "great . . . for kids interested in genealogy. . . . [It does] a wonderful job of presenting the fundamentals of genealogical research in a clear and exciting manner. . . . Understanding and properly using primary documents is stressed throughout. . . . [An] attractive, spacious [layout]; full-color, sharp images; clearly labeled diagrams; and scattered maps add information and appeal." SLJ

Includes glossary

DNA; window to the past: how science can help untangle your family roots. ABDO Pub. Co. 2011 32p il map (Your family tree) $18.95

Grades: 4 5 6 7   **929**

1. Genetics 2. Genealogy

ISBN 978-1-61613-462-4; 1-61613-462-3

LC 2009050808

This explains how DNA is used in geneology.

This is "great . . . for kids interested in genealogy. . . . [It does] a wonderful job of presenting the fundamentals of genealogical research in a clear and exciting manner. . . . Understanding and properly using primary documents is stressed throughout. . . . [An] attractive, spacious [layout]; full-color, sharp images; clearly labeled diagrams; and scattered maps add information and appeal." SLJ

Includes glossary

Filling the family tree. ABDO Pub. Co. 2011 32p il (Your family tree) lib bdg $18.95

Grades: 4 5 6 7   **929**

1. Research 2. Genealogy

ISBN 978-1-61613-464-8; 1-61613-464-X

LC 2009050806

This is "great . . . for kids interested in genealogy. . . . [It does] a wonderful job of presenting the fundamentals of genealogical research in a clear and exciting manner. . . . Understanding and properly using primary documents is stressed throughout. . . . [An] attractive, spacious [layout]; full-color, sharp images; clearly labeled diagrams; and scattered maps add information and appeal." SLJ

Using your research; how to check your facts and use your information. ABDO Pub. Co. 2011 32p il (Your family tree) lib bdg $18.95

Grades: 4 5 6 7   **929**

1. Research 2. Genealogy

ISBN 978-1-61613-465-5; 1-61613-465-8

LC 2009050805

Presents a brief guide on how to check facts and use other information in genealogical research.

This is "great . . . for kids interested in genealogy. . . . [It does] a wonderful job of presenting the fundamentals of genealogical research in a clear and exciting manner. . . . Understanding and properly using primary documents is stressed throughout. . . . [An] attractive, spacious [layout]; full-color, sharp images; clearly labeled diagrams; and scattered maps add information and appeal." SLJ

Includes glossary

Waddell, Dan

Who do you think you are? be a family tree detective. Candlewick Press 2011 24p il $19.99

Grades: 2 3 4 5   929
  1. Genealogy
  ISBN 978-0-7636-5547-1; 0-7636-5547-3
                                                                                  LC 2010050054
"This guide to genealogy . . . takes readers through the steps of trac-
ing their origins, starting with a who's who of possible extended family
members and an explanation of genes. Waddell provides oral history interview tips, Internet search guidelines, and suggestions such as consulting censuses for clues about deceased relatives. Flaps and other interactive features hold additional information. . . . Those with an interest in
the topic should discover useful insights, ideas, and tips for conducting
research." Publ Wkly

929.9   Forms of insignia and identification

Allen, Kathy
  The **first** American flag; illustrated by Siri Weber Feeney. Picture
Window Books 2010 32p il map (Our American story) lib bdg $23.99
Grades: 2 3 4   929.9
  1. Flags -- United States
  ISBN 978-1-4048-5541-0 lib bdg; 1-4048-5541-6 lib bdg
                                                                                   LC 2009-6892
An introduction to the American flag and its symbolism discusses
the features and history of early American flags
  This title is "illustrated with well-executed, full-page, color illustra-
tions, maps, and photos. . . . [It has] clearly written information that
students can use for either leisure reading or reports." SLJ
  Includes glossary and bibliographical references

Bateman, Teresa
  ★ **Red,** white, blue, and Uncle who? the stories behind some of
America's patriotic symbols. illustrated by John O'Brien. Holiday
House 2001 64p il $16.95; pa $6.95
Grades: 4 5 6 7   929.9
  1. National emblems 2. National monuments
  ISBN 0-8234-1285-7; 0-8234-1784-0 pa
                                                                                   LC 00-57258
This "volume presents 17 'patriotic symbols,' an umbrella term that
encompasses everything from the flag to Uncle Sam, from Mount Rushmore to the Korean War Memorial. Bateman finds plenty of interesting
information to share about each symbol or site, and browsers will be
entertained by the many stories of origination, construction, and history." Booklist
  Includes bibliographical references

Jackson, Donna M.
  The **name** game; a look behind the labels. illustrated by Ted Stearn. Viking 2009 64p il $16.99
Grades: 4 5 6 7 8   929.9
  1. Names
  ISBN 978-0-670-01197-1; 0-670-01197-5
                                                                                  LC 2008-37705
"All kinds of entertaining and random facts are found in this quirky
book. Tips for naming pets and companies are given, in a chapter each,
along with hints for remembering people's names, explanations of
conventions in other countries, and the system of choosing hurricane
monikers. Sports, people, and geographic locations all have different
sections. Black-and-white cartoons add a bit of humor. Students will
navigate this book with ease." SLJ

Znamierowski, Alfred, 1940-
  The **World** Encyclopedia of Flags; The definitive guide to international, flags, banners, standards and ensigns, with over 1400 illustration.
by Alfred Znamierowski. Lorenz Books 2013 256 p. $16.99
Grades: 5 6 7 8 9 10 11 12 Adult   929.9
  1. Flags
  ISBN 0754826295; 9780754826293
  This book, by Alred Znamierowski, presents "a directory of flags
and a fascinating history of their development and usage, featuring over
600 flags including military signs, royal standards, civic flags, ensigns
and national flags, expertly illustrated throughout." (Publisher's note)

930   History of ancient world (to ca. 499)

Adams, Simon
  The **Kingfisher** atlas of the ancient world; illustrated by Katherine
Baxter. Kingfisher 2006 44p il $15.95
Grades: 4 5 6 7   930
  1. Reference books 2. Ancient civilization 3. Historical geography
  ISBN 978-0-7534-5914-0; 0-7534-5914-0
"Featuring seventeen . . . hand-illustrated maps and . . . with . . .
information about ancient civilizations and peoples, this is [a] . . . pictorial guide to what the world was like between 10,000 B.C. and A.D.
1000. Each . . . map shows the major sites from a particular civilization or group of civilizations. . . . Feature spreads use photographs of
cultural and architectural artifacts, as well as additional information, to
focus in greater depth on the key cultures of Egypt, Greece, and Rome."
Publisher's note

930.1   Archaeology

Barber, Nicola
  Lost cities; by Nicola Barber. Capstone Raintree 2013 48 p. col.
ill. (Treasure hunters) (hardcover) $29.33; (paperback) $8.99
Grades: 5 6 7 8   930.1
  1. Picture books for children 2. Extinct cities 3. Legends 4.
  Civilization, Ancient 5. Archaeology -- History
  ISBN 1410949524; 1410949591; 9781410949523;
  9781410949592
                                                                                  LC 2012012891
This book by Nicola Barber is part of the Treasure Hunters series and
looks at lost cities. This entry "examines the search for lost cities and
the important artefacts within them that can offer us an extraordinary
window on to the past. . . . Cities covered in the book include Pompeii,
Troy, the desert city of Ubar, and the Inca city of Machu Picchu." (Publisher's note)
  Includes bibliographical references (p. 46-47) and index.

  Tomb explorers; by Nicola Barber. Capstone Raintree 2013 48
p. ill. (mostly col.) (Treasure hunters) (library) $29.33; (paperback)
$8.99
Grades: 5 6 7 8   930.1
  1. Tombs 2. Archeology 3. Antiquities 4. Treasure troves 5.
  Civilization, Ancient 6. Archaeology -- History
  ISBN 1410949559; 9781410949554; 9781410949622
                                                                                  LC 2012012894
This book by Nicola Barber "examines the hunt for and discovery of
ancient tombs, and the valuable treasures they hold. . . . Part of the Treasure Hunters series, 'Tomb Explorers' offers a crosscurricular mix of science & technology and history & civilizations. . . . Tombs covered in the
book include that of Tutankhamun, the Sumerian royal tombs of Ur, the

Terracotta Army of ancient China, and the Mayan tombs of Palanque in the Mexican Rainforest, and the Oseberg ship burial." (Publisher's note)
Includes bibliographical references and index.

Compoint, Stephane

Buried treasures; uncovering secrets of the past. Abrams Books for Young Readers 2011 72p il $19.95
Grades: 5 6 7 8   **930.1**
1. Archeology 2. Antiquities 3. Ancient civilization
ISBN 978-0-8109-9781-3; 0-8109-9781-9

LC 2010021626

"Showcasing the work of a specialist in archaeological photography, this loosely themed album offers a broad range of eye candy for fans of ancient artifacts, fossils, remote natural locales, and rare animals. . . . Confined to captions and a few introductory paragraphs, the text supplies useful background. . . . The photos are . . . dramatically lit, sharply reproduced, and tellingly angled. . . . Casual browsers will consider this book a real find." Booklist

Croy, Anita

Exploring the past. Marshall Cavendish Benchmark 2010 48p il (Invisible worlds) $28.50
Grades: 4 5 6 7   **930.1**
1. Fossils 2. Archeology 3. Human origins 4. Prehistoric peoples 5. Ancient civilization
ISBN 978-0-7614-4194-6; 0-7614-4194-8

The narrative is "clear, well written, broken down into manageable pieces, and peppered with eye-opening facts. The numerous photographs are so phenomenal that they will inspire kids to read the text . . . so that they can wrap their minds around what they see." SLJ
Includes glossary and bibliographical references

Hunter, Nick

Ancient treasures; by Nick Hunter; edited by Laura Knowles ... [et al.]; illustrated by Martin Bustamante. Raintree 2013 48 p. col. ill., col. maps (Treasure hunters) (hardcover) $29.33; (paperback) $8.99
Grades: 5 6 7 8   **930.1**
1. Archeology 2. Buried treasure 3. Ancient civilization 4. Treasure troves 5. Archaeology -- History
ISBN 1410949508; 9781410949509; 9781410949578

LC 2012012757

"Part of the Treasure Hunters series, 'Ancient Treasures' offers a crosscurricular mix of science & technology and history. . . .Treasures covered in the book include the Roman Hoxne Hoard, the Anglo-Saxon Staffordshire Hoard, the extraordinary discoveries of the Rosetta Stone and Dead Sea Scrolls, and the South American treasures of Lake Guatavita. The book also looks at the motives for these searches, and the importance of responsible archaeology." (Publisher's note)
Includes bibliographical references (p. 46-47) and index.

Matthews, Rupert

Ancient mysteries. QEB Pub. 2011 32p il (Unexplained) lib bdg $28.50
Grades: 4 5 6 7   **930.1**
1. Legends 2. Ancient civilization 3. Curiosities and wonders
ISBN 978-1-59566-854-7; 1-59566-854-3

LC 2010014189

This discusses mysteries in the ancient world.
"This well-written and thoughtfully designed [book] features [an] engrossing [topic]. . . . Though the pages are profusely illustrated with large, well-reproduced photographs and drawings, the layout is not cluttered. This [book] just might inspire kids to seek out more in-depth materials." SLJ

Panchyk, Richard

Archaeology for kids; uncovering the mysteries of our past: 25 activities. Chicago Review Press 2001 146p il map pa $14.95
Grades: 5 6 7 8   **930.1**
1. Archeology 2. Antiquities 3. Ancient civilization
ISBN 1-55652-395-5

LC 2001-42134

Twenty five activities support an overview of the science of archaeology as well as some of the secrets it has revealed from ancient civilizations throughout the world
"Panchyk explains things clearly and vividly. . . . Illustrations are plentiful, and suggested activities are practical and illuminate the subject matter well." Booklist
Includes bibliographical references

931   China to 420

Ball, Jacqueline A.

★ **Ancient** China; archaeology unlocks the secrets of China's past. by Jacqueline Ball and Richard Levey, Robert Murowchick, consultant. National Geographic 2006 64p il (National Geographic investigates) hardcover o.p. lib bdg $27.90; $17.95
Grades: 5 6 7 8   **931**
1. China -- Antiquities 2. China -- Civilization
ISBN 9780792278566 lib bdg; 9780792277835

"This volume spotlights archaeological finds from Ancient China. . . . While the discussions of archaeology will hold readers' interest, the accompanying illustrations steal the show." Booklist

Liu-Perkins, Christine

At home in her tomb; Lady Dai and the ancient Chinese treasures of Mawangdui. Christine Liu-Perkins; illustrated by Sarah Brannen. Charlesbridge 2013 80 p. (reinforced for library use) $19.95
Grades: 5 6 7 8   **931**
1. Tombs 2. Excavations (Archeology) -- China 3. China -- History -- Han dynasty, 202 B.C.-220 A.D. 4. Treasure troves -- China -- Changsha (Hunan Sheng) 5. Material culture -- China -- Changsha (Hunan Sheng)
ISBN 1580893708; 9781580893701; 9781607346159

LC 2012024630

This book, by Christine Liu-Perkins, "unearths the mysteries of the Mawangdui tombs, one of China's top archaeological finds of the last century. Miniature servants, mysterious silk paintings, scrolls of long-lost secrets, and the best preserved mummy in the world (the body of Lady Dai) are just some of the artifacts that shed light upon life in China during the Han dynasty." (Publisher's note)
"In 1971, the tomb of "Lady Dai" was discovered, virtually intact and of enormous archaeological significance. Here, buried in 158 BCE, was her still-soft body and more than a thousand artifacts. Liu-Perkins describes the discovery in fascinating detail; brief imagined scenes supplement the evidence. Illustrative materials include maps and well-captioned photos as well as Brannen's watercolors of the fictionalized scenes. Timeline. Bib., glos., ind." Horn Book
Includes bibliographical references and index

O'Connor, Jane

★ **The emperor's** silent army; terracotta warriors of Ancient China. Viking 2002 48p il $17.99
Grades: 4 5 6 7   **931**
1. Emperors 2. China -- Antiquities
ISBN 0-670-03512-2

LC 2001-46900

Describes the archaeological discovery of thousands of life-sized terracotta warrior statues in northern China in 1974, and discusses the emperor who had them created and placed near his tomb

"This intriguing book is enhanced by beautiful illustrations—pictures of stone engravings, colorful paintings, drawings, and maps—while numerous photographs show the clay soldiers from different perspectives. . . . The author's writing style is entertaining, yet informative." Book Rep

Includes bibliographical references

Shuter, Jane

Ancient China; [by] Jane Shuter. Heinemann Library 2006 48p il map (Excavating the past) lib bdg $31.43

Grades: 4 5 6   **931**

1. China -- Antiquities 2. China -- Civilization 3. Excavations (Archeology) -- China

ISBN 1-4034-5995-9

LC 2005009178

"Ancient China covers the region's history from the first single kingdom dynasty, Xia (2205 B.C.E. to 1700 B.C.E), to the conquering of China by Mongols in C.E.1279. Shuter includes a history of archaeology conducted by Westerners and by the Chinese government. Artifacts and a few well-preserved burial sites reveal lifestyles of the powerful and wealthy. Short chapters describe living conditions of the poor and of skilled workers as well." SLJ

Includes bibliographical references

932 Egypt to 640

Ancient Egypt; edited by Sherman Hollar. Britannica Educational Pub. in association with Rosen Educational Services 2011 87p il map (Ancient civilizations) lib bdg $31.70

Grades: 5 6 7 8   **932**

1. Egypt -- History 2. Egypt -- Civilization

ISBN 978-1-61530-523-0; 1-61530-523-8

LC 2011004714

This book provides "enough information about the development, way of life, accomplishments, and decline of [Ancient Egypt] without overwhelming readers. Maps; full-color illustrations and photographs, many full page; and sidebars provide additional focus. . . . The use of the Nile and its influence on the development of this civilization is emphasized. . . . The building of the great pyramids and the art of mummification are also mentioned. A detailed discussion of the everyday lives of the rich and the poor provide valuable insight." SLJ

Includes glossary and bibliographical references

Bolton, Anne

Pyramids and mummies. Simon & Schuster 2008 un il map $21.99

Grades: 3 4 5 6   **932**

1. Mummies 2. Pyramids 3. Egypt

ISBN 978-1-4169-5873-4; 1-4169-5873-8

LC 2008-299284

"The illustrations are an alluring mix of gold, images from ancient walls, cutaway views, and dried-out bodies. Almost hidden beneath all the visual glamour is a . . . text that begins with the death(s) of Osiris, ends with a game of 'Asps and Ladders,' and in between touches on the preparation of mummies, the history and purposes of Egyptian pyramids, animal mummies, sphinxes, King Tut, and other related topics. All in all, an ephemeral but artfully designed showstopper." SLJ

Hartland, Jessie

★ How the sphinx got to the museum. Blue Apple Books 2010 un il $17.99

Grades: 1 2 3 4   **932**

1. Queens 2. Museums 3. Sphinxes (Mythology) 4. Egypt -- Antiquities 5. Metropolitan Museum of Art (New York, N.Y.)

ISBN 978-1-609050-32-0; 1-609050-32-0

LC 2010-31603

How the seven-ton sphinx of the Pharaoh Hatshepsut got to the Metropolitan Museum of Art in New York City is described "with exhaustive, dizzying, yet crystal clear detail. . . . Before it's over we'll meet art movers, curators, conservators, riggers, registrars, retouchers, and more . . . Eye-openers abound." Booklist

Hawass, Zahi A.

★ Tutankhamun; the mystery of the boy king. by Zahi Hawass. National Geographic 2005 64p il $17.95; lib bdg $27.90

Grades: 3 4 5 6   **932**

1. Kings 2. Egypt -- History 3. Egypt -- Civilization

ISBN 0-7922-8354-6; 0-7922-8355-4 lib bdg

LC 2004-15002

"Hawass, director of excavations at the Giza pyramids and head of Egypt's archaeological council, . . . offers a solid summary . . . of the complex and controversial 18th dynasty in which Tut lived. . . . Black-and-white shots from the past join rich color photographs that almost glow. Especially marvelous is a stunning recreation, employing current reconstructive techniques, of what Tut might have looked like. . . . A first-rate investigation enriched by beautiful artwork." SLJ

Includes bibliographical references

Henzel, Cynthia Kennedy

Pyramids of Egypt. ABDO Pub. Co. 2011 32p il (Troubled treasures: world heritage sites) $25.65

Grades: 3 4 5   **932**

1. Pyramids 2. Egypt -- Antiquities

ISBN 978-1-61613-566-9; 1-61613-566-2

LC 2010021308

This "book describes in general terms [the Egyptian pyramids'] construction, . . . distinctive features, and history, as well as threats to its continued existence and both current and past restoration initiatives. Revealing color photos taken from different heights and angles are supplemented by maps and by graphic reconstructions. . . . Henzel's distinctive approach gives this [book] unusual value for both assignment and general reading." SLJ

Includes glossary

Jestice, Phyllis G.

Ancient Egyptian warfare. Gareth Stevens 2010 32p il map (Ancient warfare) lib bdg $26

Grades: 3 4 5 6   **932**

1. Egypt -- History 2. Military art and science -- History

ISBN 978-1-4339-1971-8 lib bdg; 1-4339-1971-0 lib bdg

LC 2009006189

Ancient Egyptian warfare "is presented in a well-organized, contextualized manner. The [author discusses] the overarching history of the times and then [gets] to specifics about weapons and military tactics. . . . A strong purchase for reports and pleasure reading." SLJ

Includes glossary and bibliographical references

Kennett, David

★ Pharaoh; life and afterlife of a God. Walker & Company 2008 48p il map $18.95; lib bdg $19.85

Grades: 3 4 5 6   932

1. Egypt -- Religion 2. Egypt -- Civilization
ISBN 978-0-8027-9567-0; 0-8027-9567-6; 978-0-8027-9568-7
lib bdg; 0-8027-9568-4 lib bdg

LC 2007-24236

"This extraordinarily handsome [book] delves deeply into the various roles of the pharoah, and, in the process, gives readers a much fuller understanding of Egyptian life. . . . One of the best things about this is the way the narrative moves simply and logically from topics such as flooding to farming and trading. But as fine as the text is, it more than meets its match in the masterful artwork. . . . There is much to see here, and children will want to look at the book again and again." Booklist

Kerrigan, Michael

Egyptians. Marshall Cavendish Benchmark 2010 64p il (Ancients in their own words) $32.79
Grades: 5 6 7 8   932

1. Egypt -- Civilization
ISBN 978-1-60870-064-6; 1-60870-064-X

Features "Numerous photographs provide visual interest, with text describing the images to give details and background. Translations of the writings offer primary sources to accompany the secondary material presented. . . . The text is interesting enough to read cover to cover while the table of contents' descriptive chapter titles and the comprehensive index enable the . . . [book] to be used for specific research." Libr Media Connect

Includes bibliographical references

Logan, Claudia

★ The **5,000**-year-old puzzle; solving a mystery of Ancient Egypt. illustrated by Melissa Sweet. Farrar, Straus & Giroux 2001 41p il $17
Grades: 2 3 4   932

1. Curators 2. Archaeologists 3. Egypt -- Civilization 4. Excavations (Archeology) -- Egypt
ISBN 0-374-32335-6

LC 00-60243

An account of Dr. George Reisner's 1925 discovery and excavation of a secret tomb in Giza, Egypt, based on archival documents and records, but told through the fictionalized experiences of a young boy named Will who accompanies his father on the dig.

"There's considerable value to the sidebar information . . . and the journal-style exposition of the excavation's painstaking pace. Snapshots and photographed artifacts from the expedition mingle with Sweet's golden acrylic and watercolor scenes, and readers who patiently sift through the fictional bits will be rewarded with an intriguing glimpse of an important excavation." Bull Cent Child Books

Malam, John

The **Egyptians**. PowerKids Press 2011 30p il map (Dig it: history from objects) lib bdg $25.25
Grades: 3 4 5   932

1. Egypt -- Antiquities 2. Egypt -- Civilization
ISBN 978-1-4488-3283-5; 1-4488-3283-7

LC 2010023834

Uses artifacts and other archaeological evidence to describe daily life in ancient Egypt, including their homes and towns, clothes, rulers, religion, and how they fought in war.

"The information is well-written and easily understood, well suited to the curriculum and national standards. Website links are intriguing and students will enjoy adding this piece to their research." Libr Media Connect

Includes glossary and bibliographical references

Rubalcaba, Jill

★ **Ancient** Egypt; archaeology unlocks the secrets of Egypt's past. by Jill Rubalcaba. National Geographic 2007 64p il map (National Geographic investigates) $17.95; lib bdg $27.90
Grades: 5 6 7 8   932

1. Egypt -- Antiquities 2. Egypt -- Civilization 3. Excavations (Archeology) -- Egypt
ISBN 0-7922-7784-8; 978-0-7922-7784-2; 0-7922-7857-7 lib bdg; 978-0-7922-7857-3 lib bdg

LC 2006032111

This describes how archeologists have learned about Ancient Egypt.

This offers "the beautiful photography and illustrations characteristic of the National Geographic Society, [a] well-written [text] and sidebars, and information on recent archaeological finds." SLJ

Includes bibliographical references

Sabuda, Robert

Tutankhamen's gift; written and illustrated by Robert Sabuda. Atheneum Pubs. 1994 un il $17; pa $6.99
Grades: K 1 2 3   932

1. Kings 2. Egypt -- Antiquities
ISBN 0-689-31818-9; 0-689-81730-4 pa

LC 93-5401

"His tutor foresees that little Tutankhamen's 'gift for the gods' will someday be revealed. That day comes sooner than expected, when the young boy becomes pharaoh after his brother's death and rebuilds the beautiful temples created by his father and destroyed by his brother. Bold pictures outlined in black against a background of painted, handmade Egyptian papyrus illustrate the book, and an afterword provides historical details." Horn Book Guide

Smith, Miranda

Ancient Egypt. Kingfisher 2010 48p (Navigators) $12.99
Grades: 4 5 6 7   932

1. Egypt -- Civilization
ISBN 978-0-7534-6429-8; 0-7534-6429-2

"Ancient Egypt opens with prominent pharaohs and continues with life at home, within a palace, and amidst the construction of a pyramid. Although it includes such typical subjects as religion, mummification, and tomb raiders, it also comprises female rulers, taxes, and extensive trading expeditions... a good first stop in the research process." Booklist

Stanley, Diane

★ **Cleopatra**; [by] Diane Stanley, Peter Vennema; illustrated by Diane Stanley. Morrow Junior Bks. 1994 un il map hardcover o.p. pa $7.99
Grades: 4 5 6 7   932

1. Queens 2. Egypt -- History
ISBN 0-688-10413-4; 0-688-10414-2 lib bdg; 0-688-15480-8 pa

LC 93-27032

This is a biography of the ancient Egyptian queen

"Lucid writing combines with carefully selected anecdotes, often attributed to the Greek historian Plutarch to create an engaging narrative. . . . Stanley's stunning, full-color gouache artwork is arresting in its large, well-composed images executed in flat Greek style." SLJ

Includes bibliographical references

Twist, Clint

Cleopatra; Queen of Egypt. by Clint Twist and Ian Andrew. Candlewick Press 2012 30 p. (reinforced) $19.99
Grades: 4 5 6   932

1. Queens 2. Queens -- Egypt 3. Egypt -- Civilization
ISBN 0763660957; 9780763660956

LC 2012942304

This book by Clint Twist presents a biography of Egyptian ruler Cleopatra. It covers topics "such as her complicated relationships with both Julius Caesar and, later, Mark Antony. Her role in the Ptolemy family is described. . . . Illustrated flaps to lift and explore and sidebars offer up . . . details about hairstyles, jewelry, battles, and religion." (School Library Journal)

Van Vleet, Carmella

Great Ancient Egypt projects you can build yourself. Nomad 2006 122p il (Build it yourself series) pa $14.95

Grades: 4 5 6   **932**

1. Handicraft 2. Egypt -- Civilization
ISBN 0-9771294-5-4

"The fascinating text in this collection of 30 projects is supplemented by sepia-colored illustrations or photos on each page. . . . The projects are tied to many aspects of this civilization, including the Nile River, agriculture, craftsmanship, pyramids, mummies, family, farming, bartering, the Egyptian calendar, Royal Library of Alexandria, temples, hieroglyphs, and more." SLJ

Includes bibliographical references

Weitzman, David L.

★ **Pharaoh's** boat; written and illustrated by David Weitzman. Houghton Mifflin Harcourt 2009 un il map $17

Grades: 4 5 6 7   **932**

1. Ships 2. Kings 3. Egypt -- Civilization
ISBN 978-0-547-05341-7; 0-547-05341-X

LC 2008036081

"Weitzman recounts the construction of a boat made for the Pharaoh Cheops and discusses its rediscovery and restoration in the 20th century. He weaves the history, texts, mythology, and customs of ancient Egypt into an effective narrative. . . . The volume's stylized illustrations are inspired by the two-dimensional depictions from ancient Egyptian art. The paintings' earth tones, accentuated by bright greens and blues, are both appropriate for the subject matter and pleasing to the eye." SLJ

Whiting, Jim

Threat to ancient Egyptian treasures; by Jim Whiting. Mitchell Lane Publishers 2007 32p il (On the verge of extinction: crisis in the environment) lib bdg $25.70

Grades: 3 4 5   **932**

1. Egypt -- Antiquities
ISBN 978-1-58415-588-1

LC 2007000817

This describes dangers to ancient Egyptian archeological sites and artifacts, including sand storms, air pollution, flooding, and human activity.

"Short chapters, large font, and pronunciation guides to key words engage children doing research, but the depth of information is not compromised. . . . Colorful, up-close photographs are accompanied by satisfying explanatory captions." SLJ

Includes glossary and bibliographical references

935   Mesopotamia to 637 and Iranian Plateau to 637

Gruber, Beth

★ **Ancient** Iraq; archaeology unlocks the secrets of Iraq's past. by Beth Gruber; Tony Wilkinson, consultant. National Geographic 2007 64p il map (National Geographic investigates) $17.95; lib bdg $27.90

Grades: 5 6 7 8   **935**

1. Iraq -- Antiquities 2. Iraq -- Civilization 3. Excavations

(Archeology) -- Iraq
ISBN 978-0-7922-5382-2; 978-0-7922-5383-9 lib bdg

LC 2006032109

This explores the "world of ancient Iraq, in the region once known as Mesopotamia, the cradle of civilization. Join scientists as they study the Citadel in northern Iraq; explore the ancient city of Nineveh; and see how ancient treasures help scientists reassemble the mosaic-like puzzle of Iraq's past." Publisher's note

Includes bibliographical references

Jestice, Phyllis G.

Ancient Persian warfare. Gareth Stevens 2010 32p il map (Ancient warfare) lib bdg $26

Grades: 3 4 5 6   **935**

1. Iran -- History 2. Military art and science -- History
ISBN 978-1-4339-1973-2 lib bdg; 1-4339-1973-7 lib bdg

LC 2009006199

Ancient Persian warfare "is presented in a well-organized, contextualized manner. The [author discusses] the overarching history of the times and then [gets] into specifics about weapons and military tactics. . . . A strong purchase for reports and pleasure reading." SLJ

Includes glossary and bibliographical references

Kerrigan, Michael

Mesopotamians. Marshall Cavendish Benchmark 2010 64p il (Ancients in their own words) lib bdg $32.79

Grades: 5 6 7 8   **935**

1. Iraq -- Civilization
ISBN 978-1-60870-066-0; 1-60870-066-6

"Numerous photographs provide visual interest, with text describing the images to give details and background. Translations of the writings offer primary sources to accompany the secondary material presented. . . . The text is interesting enough to read cover to cover while the table of contents' descriptive chapter titles and the comprehensive index enable the . . . [book] to be used for specific research." Libr Media Connect

Includes bibliographical references

936   Europe north and west of Italian Peninsula to ca. 499

Aronson, Marc

★ **If** stones could speak; unlocking the secrets of Stonehenge. by Marc Aronson; with Mike Parker Pearson and the Riverside Project. National Geographic 2010 64p il map $17.95; lib bdg $26.90

Grades: 4 5 6 7   **936**

1. Archeology 2. Archaeologists 3. College teachers 4. Stonehenge (England) 5. Excavations (Archeology) -- England
ISBN 978-1-4263-0599-3; 1-4263-0599-0; 978-1-4263-0600-6 lib bdg; 1-4263-0600-8 lib bdg

"Aronson investigates the work of archaeologist Mike Parker Pearson and his controversial theory that Stonehenge is but one end of a memorial ritual pathway that would have had an equivalent wood structure at the other end. . . . Time lines, resource lists, and photos of researchers at work add even more value to this informative, thought-provoking study. A uniquely perceptive look at how real science works." Booklist

Includes bibliographical references

Green, Jen

★ **Ancient** Celts; archaeology unlocks the secrets of the Celts' past. by Jen Green; Bettina Arnold, consultant. National Geographic 2008 64p il map (National Geographic investigates) $17.95; lib bdg $27.90

Grades: 4 5 6 7   **936**

1. Celts 2. Celtic civilization 3. Ireland -- Antiquities 4. Great

Britain -- Antiquities 5. Excavations (Archeology) -- Europe
ISBN 978-1-4263-0225-1; 1-4263-0225-8; 978-1-4263-0226-8
lib bdg; 1-4263-0226-6 lib bdg

LC 2007047836

This describes ancient Celtic civilization and how archeologists have found out about it.

"With excellent-quality photographs and a well-written text, this is a thorough presentation of the most up-to-date knowledge about this ancient European culture." SLJ

Includes glossary and bibliographical references

Millard, Anne

A **street** through time; written by Anne Millard; illustrated by Steve Noon. Revised ed. DK Pub. 2012 32p col il $17.99
Grades: 4 5 6 7   **936**
    1. Cities and towns
    ISBN 0-7894-3426-1

LC 98-3226

"The time-line construct is a useful demonstration for children, and the busy vistas would make a fine spring-board for encouraging students to create scenes of local history." Horn Book Guide

937   Italian Peninsula to 476 and adjacent territories to 476

Ancient Rome; edited by Michael Anderson. Britannica Educational
    Pub. in association with Rosen Educational Services 2011 88p il
    map (Ancient civilizations) lib bdg $31.70
Grades: 5 6 7 8   **937**
    1. Rome -- History 2. Rome -- Civilization
    ISBN 978-1-61530-522-3; 1-61530-522-X

LC 2011004749

This book provides "enough information about the development, way of life, accomplishments, and decline of [Ancient Rome] without overwhelming readers. Maps; full-color illustrations and photographs, many full page; and sidebars provide additional focus. . . . [The book] discusses the military expertise of Caesar and Pompey and the winning of the Punic Wars that led to world domination. The Romans' genius in engineering is highlighted." SLJ

Includes glossary and bibliographical references

Beller, Susan Provost

Roman legions on the march; soldiering in the ancient Roman
Army. by Susan Provost Beller. Twenty-First Century Books 2008
112p il map (Soldiers on the battlefront) lib bdg $33.26
Grades: 5 6 7 8   **937**
    1. Soldiers -- Rome 2. Rome -- Civilization
    ISBN 978-0-8225-6781-3

LC 2006037829

"The format is inviting with a variety of fonts at the beginning of each chapter, quotations, and a multitude of illustrations. . . . The text is clear and to the point, and chapters are divided into short topics." SLJ

Includes bibliographical references

Bingham, Jane

How people lived in ancient Rome. PowerKids Press 2009 30p il
map (How people lived) lib bdg $25.25; pa $10.60
Grades: 4 5 6 7   **937**
    1. Rome -- Social life and customs
    ISBN 978-1-4042-4432-0 lib bdg; 1-4042-4432-8 lib bdg; 978-1-
    4358-2622-9 pa; 1-4358-2622-1 pa

LC 2007-40221

Describes everyday life among the ancient Romans, covering family life, marriage, leisure, education, clothing, food and drink, warfare, religion, and funerals

"Clear, readable narrative is supplemented by large color and b&w reproductions of Roman art and artifacts. . . . It will hold the attention of both readers and reasearchers, and is a good choice for collections that serve elementary and younger middle level students." Libr Media Connect

Includes bibliographical references

Deem, James M.

★ **Bodies** from the ash. Houghton Mifflin 2005 50p il $16
Grades: 4 5 6 7   **937**
    1. Pompeii (Extinct city)
    ISBN 0-618-47308-4

LC 2004-26553

"On August 24, 79 C.E., the long-silent Mt. Vesuvius erupted, and volcanic ash rained down on the 20,000 residents of Pompeii. This photo-essay explains what happened when the volcano exploded—and how the results of this disaster were discovered hundreds of years later. . . . [This offers an] enormous amount of information. . . . But the jewels here are the numerous . . . photographs, especially those featuring the plaster casts and skeletons of people in their death throes. . . . Excellent for browsers as well as researchers." Booklist

James, Simon

Ancient Rome; written by Simon James. rev ed.; DK Pub. 2008
72p il map (DK eyewitness books) $15.99
Grades: 4 5 6 7   **937**
    1. Rome -- Antiquities 2. Rome -- Civilization
    ISBN 978-0-7566-3766-8; 0-7566-3766-X

LC 2008-276034

First published 1990 by Knopf

A photo essay documenting ancient Rome and the people who lived there as revealed through the many artifacts they left behind, including shields, swords, tools, toys, cosmetics, and jewelry

Includes glossary

Kerrigan, Michael

Romans. Marshall Cavendish Benchmark 2010 64p il (Ancients
in their own words) lib bdg $32.79
Grades: 5 6 7 8   **937**
    1. Rome -- Civilization
    ISBN 978-1-60870-067-7; 1-60870-067-4

"Numerous photographs provide visual interest, with text describing the images to give details and background. Translations of the writings offer primary sources to accompany the secondary material presented. . . . The text is interesting enough to read cover to cover while the table of contents' descriptive chapter titles and the comprehensive index enable the . . . [book] to be used for specific research." Libr Media Connect

Includes bibliographical references

Lassieur, Allison

★ The **ancient** Romans; written by Allison Lassieur. Franklin
Watts 2004 112p il map (People of the ancient world) lib bdg $30.50;
pa $9.95
Grades: 5 6 7 8   **937**
    1. Rome -- Civilization
    ISBN 0-531-12338-3 lib bdg; 0-531-16742-9 pa

LC 2004-1955

"This attractive, thorough, and comprehensible book . . . offers a stellar introduction to life in ancient Rome." Booklist

Includes bibliographical references

Malam, John

The **Romans**. PowerKids Press 2011 30p il map (Dig it: history from objects) lib bdg $25.25

Grades: 3 4 5   **937**

1. Rome -- Antiquities 2. Rome -- Civilization

ISBN 978-1-4488-3285-9; 1-4488-3285-3

LC 2010023832

This book about the Romans includes information about "homes and towns, daily life, clothing, religion, and entertainment. . . . The layout is crisp and the object illustrations and photographs, plus the 'What does it tell us' section provide visual understanding. These qualities will assist the teacher who needs to differentiate instruction. The information is well-written and easily understood, well suited to the curriculum and national standards. Website links are intriguing and students will enjoy adding this piece to their research." Libr Media Connect

Includes glossary and bibliographical references

Mann, Elizabeth

★ The **Roman** Colosseum; with illustrations by Michael Racz. Mikaya Press 1998 45p il (Wonders of the world) $19.95

Grades: 4 5 6   **937**

1. Rome -- Antiquities 2. Colosseum (Rome, Italy)

ISBN 0-9650493-3-7

LC 98-20060

Describes the building of the Colosseum in ancient Rome, and tells how it was used

This offers "a clear, well-written text and full-color drawings and paintings." SLJ

Includes glossary

Murrell, Deborah Jane

Gladiator; written by Deborah Murrell. QEB Pub. 2010 32p il map (QEB warriors) lib bdg $28.50

Grades: 4 5 6 7   **937**

1. Gladiators

ISBN 978-1-59566-736-6 lib bdg; 1-59566-736-9 lib bdg

LC 2009-3540

"Bold, comprehensible type and full-color and black-and-white illustrations; reproductions; and photographs will make this offering a hit with its target audience, including reluctant readers." SLJ

Includes glossary

Park, Louise

The **Roman** gladiators; by Louise Park and Timothy Love. Marshall Cavendish Benchmark 2009 32p il (Ancient and medieval people) $19.95

Grades: 4 5 6   **937**

1. Gladiators 2. Rome -- History 3. Rome -- Social life and customs

ISBN 978-0-7614-4443-5; 0-7614-4443-2

This title has "a simple and elegant design with the proper balance of quality writing and quantity of information. . . . Handy time lines, well-chosen photos of ruins and artifacts, quality illustrations, inset 'Quick Facts,' and 'What You Should Know About' features will grab reluctant readers and captivate even those with short attention spans." SLJ

Includes glossary

Rice, Rob S.

Ancient Roman warfare. Gareth Stevens 2010 32p il map (Ancient warfare) lib bdg $26

Grades: 3 4 5 6   **937**

1. Rome -- History 2. Military art and science -- History

ISBN 978-1-4339-1974-9 lib bdg; 1-4339-1974-5 lib bdg

LC 2009006201

Ancient Roman warfare "is presented in a well-organized, contextualized manner. The [author discusses] the overarching history of the times and then [gets] into specifics about weapons and military tactics. . . . A strong purchase for reports and pleasure reading." SLJ

Includes glossary and bibliographical references

Riggs, Kate

Gladiators. Creative Education 2011 24p il (Great warriors) $24.25; pa $8.99

Grades: K 1 2   **937**

1. Gladiators

ISBN 978-1-60818-000-4; 1-60818-000-X; 978-0-89812-571-9 pa; 0-89812-571-5 pa

LC 2010019599

An introduction to the Roman warriors known as gladiators, including their history, lifestyle, weapons, and how they remain a part of today's culture through sports such as wrestling.

This title makes gladiators "accessible to students just beginning to read on their own. The text and design of the [book is] spare, and vocabulary words are introduced unobtrusively. . . . The concepts are simple, but introduced without oversimplification that might lead to misunderstandings. [This is an] excellent [introduction]—and fun to read aloud." SLJ

Includes glossary and bibliographical references

Sonneborn, Liz

Pompeii; by Liz Sonneborn. Twenty-First Century Books 2008 80p il map (Unearthing ancient worlds) lib bdg $30.60

Grades: 5 6 7 8   **937**

1. Pompeii (Extinct city) 2. Rome (Italy) -- Antiquities 3. Excavations (Archeology) -- Italy

ISBN 978-0-8225-7505-4 lib bdg; 0-8225-7505-1 lib bdg

LC 2007022058

This describes the excavation of the Roman city buried in lava and ash when the volcano Mount Vesuvius erupted in A.D. 79.

This "clearly written [title is] illustrated with large photographs and period artwork, and the pages are broken up with text boxes featuring quotes and interesting anecdotes." SLJ

Includes glossary and bibliographical references

938   Greece to 323

Ancient Greece; edited by Michael Anderson. Britannica Educational Pub. in association with Rosen Educational Services 2012 88p il (Ancient civilizations) lib bdg $31.70

Grades: 5 6 7 8   **938**

1. Greece -- Civilization

ISBN 978-1-61530-513-1; 1-61530-513-0

LC 2011000086

This book provides "enough information about the development, way of life, accomplishments, and decline of [Ancient Greece] without overwhelming readers. Maps; full-color illustrations and photographs, many full page; and sidebars provide additional focus. . . . The system of city-states is explained. Literature, art, and architecture and their lasting influence are described in detail." SLJ

Includes glossary and bibliographical references

Kerrigan, Michael

Greeks. Marshall Cavendish Benchmark 2010 64p il (Ancients in their own words) lib bdg $32.79

Grades: 5 6 7 8   **938**

1. Greece -- Civilization

ISBN 978-1-60870-065-3; 1-60870-065-8

"Numerous photographs provide visual interest, with text describing the images to give details and background. Translations of the writings offer primary sources to accompany the secondary material presented. . . . The text is interesting enough to read cover to cover while the table of contents' descriptive chapter titles and the comprehensive index enable the . . . [book] to be used for specific research." Libr Media Connect

Includes bibliographical references

Malam, John

The **Greeks**. PowerKids Press 2011 30p il map (Dig it: history from objects) lib bdg $25.25

Grades: 3 4 5   **938**

1. Greece -- Antiquities 2. Greece -- Civilization

ISBN 978-1-4488-3284-2; 1-4488-3284-5

                     LC 2010023833

This book about the ancient Greeks includes information about "homes and towns, daily life, clothing, religion, and entertainment. . . . The layout is crisp and the object illustrations and photographs, plus the 'What does it tell us' section provide visual understanding. These qualities will assist the teacher who needs to differentiate instruction. The information is well-written and easily understood, well suited to the curriculum and national standards. Website links are intriguing and students will enjoy adding this piece to their research." Libr Media Connect

Includes glossary and bibliographical references

McGee, Marni

★ **Ancient** Greece; archaeology unlocks the secrets of Greece's past. by Marni McGee; Michael Shanks, consultant. National Geographic 2007 64p il map (National Geographic investigates) $17.95; lib bdg $27.90

Grades: 5 6 7 8   **938**

1. Greece -- Antiquities 2. Greece -- Civilization 3. Excavations (Archeology) -- Greece

ISBN 978-0-7922-7826-9; 0-7922-7826-7; 978-0-7922-7872-6 lib bdg; 0-7922-7872-0 lib bdg

                     LC 2006032108

This describes how archeologists have found out about Ancient Greek civilization

This offers "the beautiful photography and illustrations characteristic of the National Geographic Society, [a] well-written [text] and sidebars, and information on recent archaeological finds." SLJ

Includes bibliographical references

Park, Louise

The **Spartan** hoplites; by Louise Park and Timothy Love. Marshall Cavendish Benchmark 2009 32p il map (Ancient and medieval people) $19.95

Grades: 4 5 6   **938**

1. Soldiers 2. Sparta (Extinct city) 3. Athens (Greece) -- History

ISBN 978-0-7614-4449-7; 0-7614-4449-1

                     LC 2008-55779

This title has "a simple and elegant design with the proper balance of quality writing and quantity of information. . . . Handy time lines, well-chosen photos of ruins and artifacts, quality illustrations, inset 'Quick Facts', and 'What You Should Know About' features will grab reluctant readers and captivate even those with short attention spans." SLJ

Includes glossary

Reynolds, Susan

The **first** marathon: the legend of Pheidippides; by Susan Reynolds; illustrated by Daniel Minter. Albert Whitman & Company 2006 un il $16.95

Grades: 2 3 4   **938**

1. Marathon running 2. Marathon, Battle of, 490 B.C. 3. Runners

(Athletes)

ISBN 978-0-8075-0867-1; 0-8075-0867-5

                     LC 2005024618

The author tells the "story of how the Greeks fought off the mighty Persian army on the plains of Marathon, and how the young long-distance runner Pheidippides ran 140 miles in 36 hours to Sparta to ask for help, then ran back without stopping, fought in the battle, ran to tell Athens of the victory, and died. Now marathons are named for his heroic run. The dramatic, full-color, double-page illustrations, with heavy black accents, show the strong, rhythmic movement of the brave young athlete, the battle scenes, and then runners across the world today." Booklist

Rice, Rob S.

Ancient Greek warfare. Gareth Stevens 2010 32p il map (Ancient warfare) lib bdg $26

Grades: 3 4 5 6   **938**

1. Greece -- History 2. Military art and science -- History

ISBN 978-1-4339-1972-5 lib bdg; 1-4339-1972-9 lib bdg

                     LC 2009006198

Ancient Greek warfare "is presented in a well-organized, contextualized manner. The [author discusses] the overarching history of the times and then [gets] into specifics about weapons and military tactics. . . . A strong purchase for reports and pleasure reading." SLJ

Includes glossary and bibliographical references

Steele, Phillip

Ancient Greece; by Philip Steele. Kingfisher 2011 48 p. ill. (hardcover) $12.99

Grades: 4 5 6 7   **938**

1. Greece -- History 2. Greece -- Civilization

ISBN 0753465795; 9780753465790

In this "look at ancient Greece," author Philip Steele "offers young readers insight into the origins of all things Greek. Two page spreads cover Minoan civilization, the rise of the Mycenaean, war with Troy, the establishment of city-states, and the spread of the Hellenistic empire in a somewhat chronological order. Digital illustrations merge with historical artifacts, maps, works of art, and photographs." (Children's Literature)

939   Other parts of ancient world

Cline, Eric H., 1960-

★ **Digging** for Troy; from Homer to Hisarlik. [by] Jill Rubalcaba and Eric H. Cline; with illustrations by Sarah S. Brannen. Charlesbridge 2011 74p il map $17.95; pa $9.95

Grades: 5 6 7 8   **939**

1. Trojan War 2. Troy (Extinct city) 3. Greece -- Civilization 4. Excavations (Archaeology) -- Turkey 5. Archaeologists

ISBN 978-1-58089-326-8; 1-58089-326-0; 978-1-58089-327-5 pa; 1-58089-327-9 pa

                     LC 2010-07586

"Rubalcaba teams up with a noted archaeologist to make sense of the complicated, controversial, contradictory history and remains of the Turkish site called Hisarlik, better known as Troy. . . . The book begins with a brief but exciting retelling of the Trojan War . . . and goes on to profile Heinrich Schliemann. . . . After Schliemann, generations of archaeologists have excavated Hisarlik: along with the history of the excavations, readers are given an overview of technological developments in the field. . . . Source notes and an impressive bibliography attest to meticulous research and guide readers to journal articles, books, and online museum exhibits. Elegant illustrations mimicking Greek red-figure pottery are lovely and appropriate. Extraordinarily readable, gracefully laid out, and speckled with lines from The Iliad, this book will inspire young people interested in solving the mysteries of the past." SLJ

Includes bibliographical references

Sherrow, Victoria

★ **Ancient** Africa; archaeology unlocks the secrets of Africa's past. by Victoria Sherrow; James Denbow, consultant. National Geographic Society 2007 64p il map (National Geographic investigates) $17.95

Grades: 4 5 6 7   **939**

1. Africa -- Antiquities 2. Africa -- Civilization

ISBN 978-0-7922-5384-6; 0-7922-5384-1

LC 2007277594

This describes archeological discoveries about ancient peoples of Africa including the Dogon people of Mali, the ancient city of Jenne-jeno, and the Kushite temples at Jebel Barkal.

Includes bibliographical references

940   History of Europe

Feed the children first; Irish memories of the Great Hunger. edited by Mary E. Lyons. Atheneum Bks. for Young Readers 2002 43p il pbk. $22.99

Grades: 5 6 7 8   **940**

1. Famines 2. Ireland -- History

ISBN 9781442482920

LC 00-49606

The editor presents extracts from memoirs of the Irish famine period. Bibliography. "Intermediate, middle school." (Horn Book)

Lyons "compiles quotations from Irish citizens on the devastating effects of the potato famine that ravaged Ireland between 1845 and 1852." Publ Wkly

940.1   Europe--Early history to 1453

Adkins, Jan

★ **What** if you met a knight? [by] Jan Adkins, scribe and illuminator. Roaring Brook Press 2006 32p il $16.95

Grades: 3 4 5 6   **940.1**

1. Medieval civilization 2. Knights and knighthood

ISBN 1-59643-148-2; 978-1-59643-148-5

LC 2005-29163

"Adkins sets out to debunk some common misconceptions about knights, and he does so with style and wit. . . . Light in approach but quite informative, the text ably explains the feudal system, the business of knighthood, and the origins of legends such as King Arthur and dragons, and also discusses castles, arms, and the Crusades. Throughout the book, colorful, detailed illustrations and captions provide information even as they open windows on the medieval world." Booklist

Aliki

★ **A medieval** feast; written and illustrated by Aliki. Crowell 1983 un il hardcover o.p. pa $6.95

Grades: 2 3 4 5   **940.1**

1. Courts and courtiers 2. Medieval civilization 3. Dining -- History 4. Festivals -- History

ISBN 0-690-04246-9 lib bdg; 0-06-446050-9 pa

LC 82-45923

"In pictures of minute, charming detail and vibrant, translucent colors, Aliki takes us through the ritual of preparation and the enthusiastic consumption of a medieval feast served to a king and his retinue when they stop for a few days at Camdenton Manor. Not to be outdone by

the art, the text has its own various facets. There is the fictional story set in type outside the art and there is within the paintings a collection of delightful historical, gastronomical, agricultural, and zoological facts printed by hand. And throughout the spendid whole are border decorations worthy of the great illuminated manuscripts." Child Book Rev Serv

Ashman, Linda

★ **Come** to the castle! a visit to a castle in thirteenth-century England. illuminated by S.D. Schindler. Roaring Brook Press 2009 un il $17.95

Grades: 3 4 5   **940.1**

1. Castles 2. Stories in rhyme 3. Medieval civilization

ISBN 978-1-59643-155-3; 1-59643-155-5

"Wit meets historical accuracy in a pitch-perfect mix of laugh-out-loud text and entertaining image." Kirkus

Boyer, Crispin

Everything castles; capture these facts, photos, and fun to be king of the castle! 2011 64p il (National Geographic kids) lib bdg $25.90; pa $12.95

Grades: 3 4 5 6   **940.1**

1. Castles 2. Medieval civilization

ISBN 978-1-4263-0804-8 lib bdg; 1-4263-0804-3 lib bdg; 978-1-4263-0803-1 pa; 1-4263-0803-5 pa

This describes the history of medieval castles and their inhabitants.

"Exploding with astounding full-color photographs and written in an appealing conversational tone, [this book is] for every kid. . . . The [text] will keep kids interested and turning pages to discover more and more facts. . . . [This] compelling, browseable, and completely engrossing [title] will delight readers." SLJ

Includes glossary and bibliographical references

Corbishley, Mike

The **Middle** Ages; 3rd ed.; Chelsea House 2007 96p il map (Cultural atlas for young people) $35

Grades: 5 6 7 8   **940.1**

1. Middle Ages 2. Medieval civilization

ISBN 978-0-8160-6825-8; 0-8160-6825-9

First published 1989

Maps, charts, illustrations, and text explore the history and culture of the Middle Ages.

"The maps are excellent, precise, clear, and easy to read and understand, and the illustrations, particularly those of works of art, are wonderful. . . . This attractive volume provides an intriguing cross-cultural look at the medieval world. An excellent addition." SLJ

Includes glossary and bibliographical references

Durman, Laura

Castle life; by Laura Durman. Arcturus Pub. 2013 32 p. col. ill. (library) $28.50

Grades: 4 5 6   **940.1**

1. Castles 2. Medieval civilization

ISBN 1848585608; 9781848585607

LC 2011051440

In this book, author "[Laura] Durman presents young readers with a . . . view of what life was really like for everyday people in the Middle Ages. Bound by the strict societal system known as feudalism, peasants, knights, and nobles shared space . . . in castles. Readers take a room by room tour, learning how castles functioned both day-to-day, when under siege, and at times of feasting and banqueting." (Children's Literature)

Knights; by Laura Durman. Arcturus Pub. 2012 32 p. col. ill. (Knights and castles) (library) $28.50

Grades: 4 5 6   **940.1**
1. Picture books for children 2. Knights and knighthood 3. Civilization, Medieval

ISBN 1848585616; 9781848585614

LC 2011051452

This book by Laura Durman is part of the Knights and Castles series and looks at knights. The "books cover a wide range of topics such as weapons, castle construction, food, religion, and the structure and hierarchy of society." Full-color photographs and illustrations are included. (School Library Journal)

Includes bibliographical references (p. 31) and index.

Galloway, Priscilla
★ **Archers,** alchemists, and 98 other medieval jobs you might have loved or loathed; art by Martha Newbigging. Annick Press 2003 96p il lib bdg $24.95; pa $14.95

Grades: 3 4 5 6   **940.1**
1. Medieval civilization

ISBN 1-55037-811-2 lib bdg; 1-55037-810-4 pa

"Galloway introduces medieval Europe from 1000 to 1500 not by recounting dates, wars, and rulers but by discussing the occupations available in the society.... The jaunty, cartoonlike ink drawings, brightened with color washes, heighten the informal, upbeat tone of the informative text." Booklist

Includes bibliographical references

Helget, Nicole
Barbarians; Nicole Helget. Creative Education 2012 48 p. (alk. paper) $35.65

Grades: 5 6 7 8   **940.1**
1. Huns 2. Nomads 3. Vikings 4. Teutonic peoples 5. Classical civilization 6. Middle Ages 7. Migrations of nations 8. Europe -- History -- 392-814

ISBN 1608181820; 9781608181827

LC 2011035798

This book by Nicole Lea Helget "focuses on the transient, adaptable Gelts, Franks, Goths, Huns, and Vikings, collectively known as 'barbarians,' and their differing warring skills against the Greek and Roman Empires." (Booklist) "Viewed as threats by the Romans in particular, the barbarian people were often co-opted or conquered and then integrated into the Empire. Eventually, as the Roman Empire waned, the pressure of nomadic barbarians proved too much to withstand and Rome fell." (Children's Literature)

Includes bibliographical references and index

Kroll, Steven
★ **Barbarians!** illustrated by Robert Byrd. Dutton Children's Books 2009 48p il $18.99

Grades: 3 4 5   **940.1**
1. Huns 2. Goths 3. Mongols 4. Vikings 5. Middle Ages

ISBN 978-0-525-47958-1; 0-525-47958-9

LC 2008-39210

"Kroll introduces four notable groups referred to by their enemies as barbarians: the Goths, the Huns, the Vikings, and the Mongols.... Showing clear differences among the four groups, the many detailed, energetic ink-and-watercolor illustrations show the barbarians at home and at war.... This handsome volume will fill a collection gap while providing warrior-loving browsers with an informative and brightly illustrated book to enjoy." Booklist

Langley, Andrew
Medieval life; written by Andrew Langley; photographed by Geoff Brightling. rev ed; DK Pub. 2011 72p il (DK eyewitness books) lib bdg $19.99

Grades: 4 5 6 7   **940.1**
1. Medieval civilization

ISBN 9780756682828 lib bdg

First published 1996 by Knopf

An illustrated look at various aspects of life in medieval Europe, covering everyday life, religion, royalty, and more.

Park, Louise
The **medieval** knights; by Louise Park and Timothy Love. Marshall Cavendish Benchmark 2009 32p il map (Ancient and medieval people) $19.95

Grades: 4 5 6   **940.1**
1. Medieval civilization 2. Knights and knighthood

ISBN 978-0-7614-4444-2; 0-7614-4444-0

LC 2008-55777

This title has "a simple and elegant design with the proper balance of quality writing and quantity of information.... Handy time lines, well-chosen photos of ruins and artifacts, quality illustrations, inset 'Quick Facts', and 'What You Should Know About' features will grab reluctant readers and captivate even those with short attention spans." SLJ

Includes glossary

Riggs, Kate
Knights. Creative Education 2011 24p il (Great warriors) $16.98; pa $8.99

Grades: K 1 2   **940.1**
1. Medieval civilization 2. Knights and knighthood

ISBN 978-1-60818-001-1; 1-60818-001-8; 978-0-89812-572-6 pa; 0-89812-572-3 pa

LC 2010019604

An introduction to the European warriors known as knights, including their history, lifestyle, weapons, and how they remain a part of today's culture through books and films.

This title makes knights "accessible to students just beginning to read on their own. The text and design of the [book is] spare, and vocabulary words are introduced unobtrusively.... The concepts are simple, but introduced without oversimplification that might lead to misunderstandings. [This is an] excellent [introduction] and fun to read aloud." SLJ

Includes glossary and bibliographical references

Schlitz, Laura Amy
★ **Good** masters! Sweet ladies! voices from a medieval village. [by] Laura Amy Schlitz; illustrated by Robert Byrd. Candlewick Press 2007 85p il $19.99; pa $9.99

Grades: 5 6 7 8   **940.1**
1. Monologues 2. Middle Ages -- Drama

ISBN 978-0-7636-1578-9; 0-7636-1578-1; 978-0-7636-4332-4 pa; 0-7636-4332-7 pa

Awarded the Newbery Medal, 2008

A collection of short one-person plays featuring characters, between ten and fifteen years old, who live in or near a thirteenth-century English manor

"Designed for performance and excellent for use in interdisciplinary history classrooms, the book offers students an incredibly approachable format for learning about the Middle Ages that makes the period both realistic and relevant.... Byrd's illustrations evoke the era and give dramatists ideas for appropriate costuming and props." SLJ

940.3   World War I, 1914-1918

Adams, Simon

World   War I;   written by Simon Adams; photographed by Andy Crawford.   rev ed.; DK Pub. 2007 72p il (DK eyewitness books) $15.99

Grades: 4 5 6 7   **940.3**

1. World War, 1914-1918

ISBN 978-0-7566-3007-2; 0-7566-3007-X

LC 2007279476

First published 2001

This look at World War I examines life in the trenches and the devastation of Europe by the Great War

Swain, Gwenyth

World   War I; an interactive history adventure. by Gwenyth Swain; consultant: Timothy Solie. Capstone Press 2012 112 p. ill. (some col.) (library) $31.32; (paperback) $6.95

Grades: 3 4 5 6   **940.3**

1. World War, 1914-1918

ISBN 1429679972; 9781429660204; 9781429679978

LC 2011033624

This book by Gwenyth Swain is part of the You Choose series. "At the bottom of many pages, you are asked to make a decision about what to do or where to go. Subsequent decisions take you to the adventure's end, at which point readers may choose to go back and begin again and find out where an alternate path might have led. . . . [In] Belgium . . . student nurses must decide whether to stay at their hospital or flee. Later, a British teen has to choose whether to enlist or wait." (Booklist)

Includes bibliographical references (p. 111) and index.

940.4   Military history of World War I

Bausum, Ann

Stubby   the War Dog; The True Story of World War I's Bravest Dog. by Ann Bausum. Natl Geographic Soc Childrens books 2014 80 p. $26.90

Grades: 4 5 6 7   **940.4**

1. Dogs -- War use 2. World War, 1914-1918 -- United States 3. Stubby (Dog) 4. Dogs -- War use -- United States 5. United States. Army. Infantry Regiment, 102nd -- Mascots

ISBN 1426314868; 1426314876; 9781426314865; 9781426314872

This book, by Ann Bausum, is the story of "Stubby, a terrier of unknown origin, [who] found his way to the training grounds in New Haven, CT, as recruits were preparing to ship off to . . . World War I. . . . He attached himself to J. Robert Conroy, one of the recruits, and they became an inseparable team for the rest of Stubby's life. . . . [T]he dog lived the life of any soldier: sleeping in trenches, dodging bullets in the heat of battle, and ferreting out enemy combatants." (School Library Journal)

"The popularity of tales about dogs in war stems from the inherent poignancy—sweet, loyal, sad-eyed canines entered into the mad chaos of man-made destruction. But enter they occasionally do, and none more famously than Stubby... The speedy story is surrounded by evocative period photos, including plenty of the goofy-faced Stubby, and leads up to his later careers as a vaudeville star and a football mascot, and his eventual taxidermied inclusion in the Smithsonian. A triumph on three fronts: educational, emotional, and inspirational. For older teens, suggest Bausman's adult title, Sergeant Stubby." Booklist

Beller, Susan Provost

The   doughboys   over there; soldiering in World War I. by Susan Provost Beller. Twenty-First Century Books 2008 112p il map (Soldiers on the battlefront) lib bdg $33.26

Grades: 5 6 7 8   **940.4**

1. World War, 1914-1918 2. Soldiers -- United States

ISBN 978-0-8225-6295-5 lib bdg; 0-8225-6295-2 lib bdg

LC 2006026249

The is an account of the U.S. soldiers who fought in Europe in the First World War.

"The format is inviting with a variety of fonts at the beginning of each chapter, quotations, and a multitude of illustrations. . . . The text is clear and to the point, and chapters are divided into short topics." SLJ

Includes bibliographical references

Burleigh, Robert

Fly,   Cher Ami, fly! the pigeon who saved the lost battalion. by Robert Burleigh; illustrated by Robert MacKenzie. Abrams Books for Young Readers 2008 un il $16.95

Grades: K 1 2 3   **940.4**

1. Pigeons 2. World War, 1914-1918

ISBN 978-0-8109-7097-7; 0-8109-7097-X

"Burleigh tells the true story of the last flight of a U.S. Army Signal Corps carrier pigeon, which took place in France during World War I. Cher Ami was the last hope for the 'Lost Battalion' of the 77th Division in the Battle of Argonne. . . . Burleigh's short text clearly depicts the story's action, while MacKenzie's full-page golden-hued yet somber illustrations add to the account by showing the drama from a variety of perspectives." Booklist

Greenwood, Mark

The   donkey   of Gallipoli; a true story of courage in World War I. [by] Mark Greenwood; illustrated by Frane Lessac. Candlewick Press 2008 un il map $16.99

Grades: 2 3 4   **940.4**

1. Donkeys 2. Sailors 3. Soldiers 4. World War, 1914-1918 5. Gallipoli campaign, 1915

ISBN 978-0-7636-3913-6; 0-7636-3913-3

LC 2007032525

This is a "stirring picture book. . . . In folk-art style, the paintings, in shades that reflect the heat of a sandy landscape, show the heroic soldier and the gentle animal amid the slaughter of war." Booklist

Murphy, Jim

★ Truce; the day the soldiers stopped fighting. Scholastic Press 2009 116p il map $19.99

Grades: 5 6 7 8   **940.4**

1. World War, 1914-1918

ISBN 978-0-545-13049-3; 0-545-13049-2

LC 2008-40500

"By December 1918, the western front of World War I featured two parallel trenches stretching from the North Sea to the Alps. . . . On Christmas Day, an informal peace broke out in many locations along the front. . . . Murphy's excellent telling of this unusual war story begins with an account of the events that led to WWI and follows the shift in the soldiers' mind-sets. . . . Printed in tones of sepia, the illustrations in this handsome volume include many period photos as well as paintings and maps. . . . Well organized and clearly written, this presentation vividly portrays the context and events of the Christmas Truce." Booklist

Includes bibliographical references

940.53   World War II, 1939-1945

Adams, Simon

World War II; written by Simon Adams; photographed by Andy Crawford. rev ed.; DK Pub. 2007 72p il (DK eyewitness books) $16.99

Grades: 4 5 6 7   **940.53**

1. World War, 1939-1945

ISBN 978-0-7566-3008-9; 0-7566-3008-8

LC 2008273315

First published 2000

Provides a concise history of World War II including information about the Holocaust, the code-breaking Enigma, and the deadly V2 rocket

Adler, David A.

Hiding from the Nazis; illustrated by Karen Ritz. Holiday House 1997 un il $15.95; pa $6.95

Grades: 2 3 4   **940.53**

1. Holocaust survivors 2. Jews -- Netherlands 3. Holocaust, 1933-1945 4. World War, 1939-1945 -- Jews

ISBN 0-8234-1288-1; 0-8234-1666-6 pa

LC 96-38451

The true story of Lore Baer who as a four-year-old Jewish child was placed with a Christian family in the Dutch farm country to avoid persecution by the Nazis

"Adler includes a lot of factual information about the history of the time and about the people in the story, before and after the war. Ritz's realistic watercolors in warm shades of brown focus on the small girl whose childhood games of hide-and-seek become a terrifying reality." Booklist

Ambrose, Stephen E.

★ The good fight; how World War II was won. Atheneum Bks. for Young Readers 2001 96p il maps $19.95

Grades: 5 6 7 8   **940.53**

1. World War, 1939-1945

ISBN 0-689-84361-5

LC 00-49600

"An excellent balance between the big picture and the humanizing details, well supported by fact boxes, tinted photographs, and battlefield maps that are both simple and clear. . . . Ambrose's style is authoritative and warm." Booklist

Includes glossary and bibliographical references

Callery, Sean

★ World War II; Visual history of the world's darkest days. by Sean Callery. 1st ed. Scholastic 2013 105 p. ill. (some col.), col. maps (paperback) $15.99

Grades: 5 6 7 8   **940.53**

1. Military history 2. World War, 1939-1945

ISBN 0545479754; 9780545479752

LC 2012285678

This book presents "World War II in a nutshell. The text is divided into five chapters: 'The Path to War,' 'Europe & the Atlantic War,' the Pacific theater, Africa & the Middle East, and the end of the war. Each section is divided into several two-page topics. The title page of each chapter asks three questions that are answered in the text. It is followed by a two-page time line with boxed information and vintage photos." (School Library Journal)

Finkelstein, Norman H.

Remember not to forget; a memory of the Holocaust. [by] Norman H. Finkelstein; illustrated by Lois and Lars Hokanson. Jewish Publication Society 2004 31p il pa $9.95

Grades: 4 5 6 7   **940.53**

1. Jews -- History 2. Holocaust, 1933-1945

ISBN 0-82760-770-9

LC 2004556462

A reissue of the title first published 1985 by Watts

"This spare, starkly illustrated book explains what the Holocaust was and how it is remembered on Yom Hashoa, Holocaust Remembrance Day. The explanation reaches back to the explusion of the Jews from Jerusalem in A.D. 70 and describes how Jews . . . became targets of anti-Semitism, which culminated in the systematic murder of six million by the Nazis in World War II. The tone is straightforward and matter-of-fact. Black-and-white woodcuts accompany the text with somber scenes reflective of the narrative." Booklist [review of 1985 edition]

Greenfeld, Howard

★ The hidden children. Ticknor & Fields Bks. for Young Readers 1993 118p il hardcover o.p. pa $9.99

Grades: 4 5 6 7   **940.53**

1. Jews -- Europe 2. Holocaust, 1933-1945 -- Personal narratives

ISBN 0-395-66074-2; 0-395-86138-1 pa

LC 93-20326

Describes the experiences of those Jewish children who were forced to go into hiding during the Holocaust and survived to tell about it

"Illustrated with black-and-white photographs, the moving stories and dramatic facts make inspiring, and often troubling, reading. A lovely, important book about heroism and survival." Horn Book Guide

Includes bibliographical references

Hodge, Deborah

Rescuing the children; the story of the kindertransport. Deborah Hodge. Tundra Books of Northern New York 2012 60 p. (hardcover) $17.95

Grades: 4 5 6   **940.53**

1. Holocaust, 1939-1945 2. Jewish children in the Holocaust 3. World War, 1939-1945 -- Children 4. World War, 1939-1945 -- Refugees 5. Child refugees -- Great Britain -- History

ISBN 1770492569; 9781770492561

LC 2011938776

This children's book, by Deborah Hodge, "tells the story of how ten thousand Jewish children were rescued out of Nazi Europe just before the outbreak of World War 2. They were saved by the Kindertransport--a rescue mission that transported the children (or Kinder) from Nazi-ruled countries to safety in Britain. The book includes real-life accounts of the children and is illustrated with archival photographs . . . and original art by the Kinder commemorating their rescue." (Publisher's note)

Hurwitz, Johanna

Anne Frank: life in hiding; illustrated by Vera Rosenberry. Jewish Publ. Soc. 1988 62p il map $13.95

Grades: 3 4 5   **940.53**

1. Children 2. Diarists 3. Holocaust victims 4. Jews -- Netherlands 5. Holocaust, 1933-1945 6. World War, 1939-1945 -- Jews 7. Netherlands -- History -- 1940-1945, German occupation

ISBN 0-8276-0311-8

LC 87-35263

The author "gives a concise explanation of the political and economic background to the Holocaust and provides a map of Europe and a chronology. She ably covers the events of Anne's life before, during, and after the period covered by the 'Diary of Anne Frank,' explaining the significance and importance of the 'Diary' throughout the world." SLJ

Kacer, Kathy

Hiding Edith; a true story. Second Story 2006 120p (Holocaust remembrance book for young readers) pa $10.95

Grades: 4 5 6 7   **940.53**

1. Holocaust survivors 2. Jews -- France 3. Holocaust, 1933-1945

ISBN 1-897187-06-8

"Kacer recounts some extraordinary history: in Moissac, France, under Nazi occupation, a French Jewish couple hid 100 Jewish refugee children—with the support of the townspeople. Kacer, who based her account on interviews, tells the story of one child, Edith Schwalb. Captioned black-and-white photos on almost every page show Edith at home in Vienna before the war, then in Belgium, and then, separated from her parents, living with the rescuers." Booklist

Levine, Karen

Hana's suitcase; a true story. Whitman, A. 2003 111p il lib bdg $15.95

Grades: 4 5 6 7   **940.53**

1. Holocaust victims 2. Holocaust, 1933-1945

ISBN 0-8075-3148-0

LC 2002-27439

First published 2002 in Canada

A biography of a Czech girl who died in the Holocaust, told in alternating chapters with an account of how the curator of a Japanese Holocaust center learned about her life after Hana's suitcase was sent to her

"The account, based on a radio documentary Levine did in Canada . . . is part history, part suspenseful mystery, and always anguished family drama, with an incredible climactic revelation." Booklist

Meltzer, Milton

★ **Rescue** : the story of how Gentiles saved Jews in the Holocaust. Harper & Row 1988 168p maps hardcover o.p. pa $9.99

Grades: 6 7 8 9   **940.53**

1. Holocaust, 1933-1945 2. World War, 1939-1945 -- Jews -- Rescue

ISBN 0-06-024210-8; 0-06-446117-3 pa

LC 87-47816

A recounting drawn from historic source material of the many individual acts of heroism performed by righteous gentiles who sought to thwart the extermination of the Jews during the Holocaust

"This is an excellent portrayal of a difficult topic. Meltzer manages to both explain without accusing, and to laud without glorifying. . . . The discussion of the complicated relations between countries are clear, but not simplistic. An impressive aspect of this book is its lack of didacticism." Voice Youth Advocates

Includes bibliographical references

Mochizuki, Ken

★ **Passage** to freedom; the Sugihara story. written by Ken Mochizuki; illustrated by Dom Lee; afterword by Hiroki Sugihara. Lee & Low Bks. 1997 un il $15.95

Grades: 3 4 5 6   **940.53**

1. Diplomats 2. Humanitarians 3. Holocaust, 1933-1945 4. World War, 1939-1945 -- Jews -- Rescue

ISBN 1-880000-49-0

LC 96-35359

"Lee's stirring mixed-media illustrations in sepia shades are humane and beautiful. . . . The immediacy of the narrative will grab kids' interest and make them think." Booklist

Rol, Ruud van der

Anne Frank, beyond the diary; a photographic remembrance. by Ruud van der Rol and Rian Verhoeven; in association with the Anne Frank House; translated by Tony Langham and Plym Peters; with an introduction by Anna Quindlen. Viking 1993 113p il map hardcover o.p. pa $10.99

Grades: 5 6 7 8   **940.53**

1. Children 2. Diarists 3. Holocaust victims 4. Jews -- Netherlands 5. Holocaust, 1933-1945 6. World War, 1939-1945 -- Jews 7. Netherlands -- History -- 1940-1945, German occupation

ISBN 0-670-84932-4; 0-14-036926-0 pa

LC 92-41528

Original Dutch edition, 1992

Photographs, illustrations, and maps accompany historical essays, diary excerpts, and interviews, providing an insight to Anne Frank and the massive upheaval which tore apart her world

"Readers will become absorbed in the richness of the detail and careful explanation which revisit and expand the familiar, well-loved story." Horn Book

Rubin, Susan Goldman

The **flag** with fifty-six stars; a gift from the survivors of Mauthausen. illustrated by Bill Farnsworth. Holiday House 2005 39p il $16.95

Grades: 3 4 5   **940.53**

1. Jews -- Germany 2. Holocaust, 1933-1945 3. Flags -- United States 4. World War, 1939-1945 -- Germany

ISBN 0-8234-1653-4

LC 2004-47457

"In the spring of 1945, U.S. troops marched into the Mauthausen concentration camp in Austria to liberate surviving prisoners and were given an American flag that had been secretly made by a group of detainees there. This is an inspiring account of the camp, its survivors, and its liberators. . . . Nazi atrocities are muted here, but the sorrow, hunger, hopelessness, and, finally, optimism shine through in the pictures and in the text." SLJ

Includes bibliographical references

Ruelle, Karen Gray

★ The **grand** mosque of Paris; a story of how Muslims saved Jews during the Holocaust. by Karen Gray Ruelle and Deborah Durland DeSaix. Holiday House 2009 40p il $17.95

Grades: 3 4 5 6   **940.53**

1. Muslims 2. Jewish-Arab relations 3. Holocaust, 1933-1945 4. World War, 1939-1945 -- France 5. World War, 1939-1945 -- Jews -- Rescue 6. France -- History -- 1940-1945, German occupation

ISBN 978-0-8234-2159-6; 0-8234-2159-7

LC 2008-17209

"Although few documents remain, substantial evidence supports this fascinating and courageous story. . . . Realistic oil paintings complement the lengthy text. . . . A must read." Kirkus

Russo, Marisabina

★ **Always** remember me; how one family survived World War II. [by] Marisabina Russo. Atheneum Books for Young Readers 2005 un il $16.95

Grades: 3 4 5   **940.53**

1. Jews -- Germany 2. Holocaust, 1933-1945

ISBN 0-689-86920-7

LC 2004-4228

"Russo tells her Jewish family's story of Holocaust survival. She remembers herself as a small child visiting her grandmother, Oma, who tells Russo the family history with photos stretching back to Oma's youth and marriage before World War I . . . . Russo personalizes the history with photo-album entries printed on the endpapers, and her gouache illustrations, framed like photos, show the individuality and strength of family members." Booklist

Includes glossary

Samuels, Charlie

Home front; by Charlie Samuels. Brown Bear Books 2012 48 p.
ill. (some col.) (World War II sourcebook) (library) $35.65

Grades: 5 6 7 8   **940.53**

1. Military history   2. World War, 1939-1945 -- Social aspects   3.
World War, 1939-1945 -- Economic aspects

ISBN 1936333228; 9781936333226

LC 2011007054

This book by Charlie Samuels is part of the World War II Sourcebook series and focuses on the home front. "Each page is illustrated.
Little-known facts and, sometimes, direct narratives are presented with
the information given to the reader. . . . Each book has the same timeline of World War II, maps of both the European and Pacific theaters,
interesting biographical snapshots of people involved, and a list of websites that students may use to further explore World War II." (Library
Media Connection)

Life under occupation; by Charlie Samuels. Brown Bear Books
2011 48 p. ill. (chiefly col.), col. maps (World War II sourcebook)
(library) $35.65

Grades: 5 6 7 8   **940.53**

1. World War, 1939-1945   2. World War, 1939-1945 -- Occupied
territories   3. World War, 1939-1945 -- Europe   4. World War,
1939-1945 -- Atrocities   5. World War, 1939-1945 -- Pacific Area
6. World War, 1939-1945 -- Occupied territories

ISBN 1936333260; 9781936333264

LC 2011007055

This book by Charlie Samuels, part of the World War II Sourcebook
series, and focuses on life under occupation. "Each page is illustrated.
Little-known facts and, sometimes, direct narratives are presented with
the information given to the reader. . . . Each book has the same timeline
of World War II, maps of both the European and Pacific theaters, . . . biographical snapshots of people involved, and a list of websites." (Library
Media Connection)

Includes bibliographical references and index.

Taylor, Peter Lane

The **secret** of Priest's Grotto; a Holocaust survival story. [by] Peter
Lane Taylor with Christos Nicola. Kar-Ben Pub. 2007 64p il map lib
bdg $10.95; pa $8.95

Grades: 5 6 7 8 9 10 11 12   **940.53**

1. Caves   2. Jews -- Ukraine   3. Holocaust, 1933-1945

ISBN 978-1-58013-260-2 lib bdg; 1-58013-260-X lib bdg; 978-
1-58013-261-9 pa; 1-58013-261-8 pa

LC 2006-21709

"This volume relays the tale of 38 Ukrainian Jews who sought refuge
in a local cave to escape the invading Nazis in fall of 1942 and remained
there for 344 days. . . . At once sobering and uplifting, this is an astounding story of survival, powerfully told." Publ Wkly

Thomson, Ruth

★ **Terezin**; voices from the Holocaust. Candlewick Press 2011
64p il $18.99

Grades: 5 6 7 8   **940.53**

1. Jews -- Czechoslovakia   2. Holocaust, 1933-1945 -- Personal
narratives   3. Holocaust, Jewish (1939-1945)

ISBN 0-7636-4963-5; 978-0-7636-4963-0

LC 2010-39164

"Between 1941 and 1945, Nazi Germany turned the small town of
Terezín, Czechoslovakia, into a ghetto, and then into a transit camp for
thousands of Jewish people. It was a 'show' camp, where inmates were
forced to use their artistic talents to fool the world about the truth of gas
chambers and horrific living conditions for imprisoned Jews. Here is

their story, told through the firsthand accounts of those who were there."
(Publisher's note) Index. "Grades five to eight." (Bull Cent Child Books)

"Two years after the Nazi invasion of Czechoslovakia, the small fortress village of Terezin was converted into a Jewish ghetto, and over the
next four years, ten of thousands of Jews were transported there while
in transit to death camps in the east. The history of Terezin is fascinating: the camp housed many noted artists. . . . Much of the art created at
Terezin survived the Holocaust, and a generous sampling is included in
this volume. Thomson opts to tell the story of Terezin almost entirely in
the voices of those who lived there. . . . This is an accessible, carefully
researched work that effectively uses primary-source material to make
the experience of the Jews of Terezin come alive for today's students."
Bull Cent Child Books

Includes glossary and bibliographical references

Warren, Andrea

★ **Surviving** Hitler; a boy in the Nazi death camps. HarperCollins
Pubs. 2001 146p il hardcover o.p. pa $6.99

Grades: 5 6 7 8   **940.53**

1. Holocaust, 1933-1945

ISBN 0-688-17497-3; 0-06-029218-0 lib bdg; 0-06-000767-2 pa

LC 00-38899

"Simply told, Warren's powerful story blends the personal testimony
of Holocaust survivor Jack Mandelbaum with the history of his time,
documented by stirring photos from the archives of the U.S. Holocaust
Memorial Museum. . . . An excellent introduction for readers who don't
know much about the history." Booklist

Includes bibliographical references

940.54   Military history of World War II

Allen, Thomas B.

★ **Remember** Pearl Harbor; American and Japanese survivors tell
their stories. foreword by Robert D. Ballard. National Geographic Soc.
2001 57p il maps $17.95

Grades: 5 6 7 8   **940.54**

1. Pearl Harbor (Oahu, Hawaii), Attack on, 1941   2. World War,
1939-1945 -- Personal narratives

ISBN 0-7922-6690-0

LC 2001-796

Personal accounts of the Japanese attack on Pearl Harbor, with
background information.

"Eyewitness testimony of Japanese and American men and women
from various backgrounds enriches this balanced treatment of World
War II. . . . The first-person voices along with dozens of black-and-white
photos and several full-color maps make this a draw for both browsers
and World War II buffs." Booklist

Includes bibliographical references

Drez, Ronald J.

★ **Remember** D-day; the plan, the invasion, survivor stories. National Geographic Books 2004 61p il map $17.95; lib bdg $27.90

Grades: 5 6 7 8   **940.54**

1. World War, 1939-1945 -- Campaigns -- France

ISBN 0-7922-6666-8; 0-7922-6965-9 lib bdg

LC 2003-17733

Discusses the events and personalities involved in the momentous
Allied invasion of France on June 6, 1944

"This well-organized, clearly written account provides a solid overview for readers unfamiliar with the subject. A first-rate purchase." SLJ

Includes bibliographical references

Hama, Larry
★ The **battle** of Iwo Jima; guerilla warfare in the Pacific. by Larry Hama; illustrated by Anthony Williams. Rosen Pub. 2007 48p il map (Graphic battles of World War II) lib bdg $29.25

Grades: 5 6 7 8 9   **940.54**
    1. Graphic novels 2. World War, 1939-1945 -- Graphic novels 3. Iwo Jima, Battle of, 1945 -- Graphic novels
    ISBN 978-1-4042-0781-3 lib bdg; 1-4042-0781-3 lib bdg
                              LC 2006007645
"Using a graphic novel to introduce the battle for Iwo Jima makes it very accessible. Before the graphic-novel section of the book begins, Hama provides a short, informative background piece describing the run-up to World War II, the significance of the Japanese war machine, and the importance of the tiny island of Iwo Jima. Then the graphic novel, illustrated by Williams in camouflage colors, does a terrific job of examining the ups and downs of the battle as well as the horror of so many losses—on both sides." Booklist
    Includes bibliographical references

Hopkinson, Deborah
Dive! World War II Stories of Sailors & Submarines in the Pacific: The Incredible Story of U.S. Submarines in WWII. by Deborah Hopkinson. Scholastic Press 2016 384 p. illustrations, map $17.99

Grades: 4 5 6 7 8   **940.54**
    1. World War, 1939-1945 -- Naval operations -- Submarine 2. World War, 1939-1945 -- Campaigns -- Pacific Ocean 3. World War, 1939-1945 -- Naval operations, American
    ISBN 9780545425582
                              LC 2015040229
This book by Deborah Hopkinson "tells the incredible story of America's little known 'war within a war' -- US submarine warfare during World War II. Following the attack on Pearl Harbor, the US entered World War II in December 1941 with only 44 Naval submarines -- many of them dating from the 1920s. With the Pacific battleship fleet decimated after Pearl Harbor, it was up to the feisty and heroic sailors aboard the US submarines to stop the Japanese invasion across the Pacific." (Publisher's note)
    "With a fascinating blend of submarine mechanics and tales of courage, readers will dive in deep." Booklist
    Includes bibliographical references and index

Lawton, Clive
Hiroshima; the story of the first atom bomb. [by] Clive A. Lawton. Candlewick Press 2004 48p il map $18.99

Grades: 5 6 7 8   **940.54**
    1. Atomic bomb 2. World War, 1939-1945 -- Japan 3. Hiroshima (Japan) -- Bombardment, 1945
    ISBN 0-7636-2271-0
                              LC 2004-45166
"Engaging text and powerful photographs are intricately woven together to make a long-lasting impact on readers." Libr Media Connect

Manning, Mick
Tail-end Charlie; [by] Mick Manning and Brita Granström. Frances Lincoln Children's Books 2009 un il $16.95

Grades: 3 4 5   **940.54**
    1. World War, 1939-1945 -- Aerial operations
    ISBN 978-1-84507-651-1; 1-84507-651-6
    "The remembrances of Manning's father, a British Air Force gunner during World War II, are vividly presented through comic strips, watercolor-and-ink illustrations, and memorabilia such as ration books, postcards, and photographs. . . . Reluctant readers will be drawn to the graphic format and quickly engaged by the authentic voice." SLJ

Nicholson, Dorinda Makanaõnalani
The **school** the Aztec Eagles built; by Dorinda Makanaonalani Nicholson. Lee & Low Books Inc. 2015 48 p. (hardcover : alkaline paper) $19.95

Grades: 4 5 6   **940.54**
    1. World War, 1939-1945 -- Aerial operations -- Mexico 2. World War, 1939-1945 -- Campaigns -- Philippines -- Luzon 3. School buildings -- Mexico -- Tepoztlán -- Design and construction -- History -- 20th century 4. Mexico. Fuerza Aérea Expedicionaria Mexicana. Escuadrón Aérea de Pelea 201 -- History 5. Airmen -- Mexico -- Biography 6. Teachers -- Mexico -- Tepoztlán -- Biography 7. World War, 1939-1945 -- Aerial operations, Mexican 8. Tepoztlán (Mexico) -- History -- 20th century 9. World War, 1939-1945 -- Aerial operations, American
    ISBN 1600604404; 9781600604409
                              LC 2014047757
This children's book by Dorinda Makanaonalani Nicholson is a "tribute to Air Fighter Squadron 201 (the Aztec Eagles) and Sgt. Ángel Bocanegra del Castillo, whose actions ensured the building of a school in the village of Tepoztlán, Mexico. . . . By the time the squadron returned to Mexico at the end of World War II, the school had been built and named after the squadron. . . . The text briefly describes the military action in which the squadron was involved." (School Library Journal)
    Includes bibliographical references

Samuels, Charlie
Propaganda; by Charlie Samuels. Brown Bear Books 2011 48 p. ill. (chiefly col.), col. maps (World War II sourcebook) (library) $35.65

Grades: 5 6 7 8   **940.54**
    1. World War, 1939-1945 -- Propaganda
    ISBN 1936333236; 9781936333233
                              LC 2011010241
This book by Charlie Samuels on propaganda is part of the World War II Sourcebook series. "Each page is illustrated. Little-known facts and, sometimes, direct narratives are presented with the information given to the reader. . . . Each book has the same timeline of World War II, maps of both the European and Pacific theaters, interesting biographical snapshots of people involved, and a list of websites that students may use to further explore World War II." (Library Media Connection)
    Includes bibliographical references and index.

Soldiers; [Charlie Samuels] Brown Bear Books 2011 48 p. ill. (some col.), maps (col.) (World War II sourcebook) (library binding) $35.65

Grades: 5 6 7 8   **940.54**
    1. Soldiers 2. World War, 1939-1945 3. Soldiers -- History -- 20th century
    ISBN 1936333244; 9781936333240
                              LC 2011007057
This book by Charlie Samuels, part of the World War II Sourcebook series, "Describes the life of a soldier in World War II, from recruitment efforts around the world, to the daily life during the fighting." (Publisher's note)
    Includes bibliographical references (p. 47) and index

Spying and security; by Charlie Samuels. Brown Bear Books 2012 48 p. ill. (some col.) (World War II Sourcebook) (library binding) $35.65

Grades: 5 6 7 8   **940.54**
    1. Police -- History -- 20th century 2. World War, 1939-1945 -- Secret service 3. Spies -- History -- 20th century 4. Espionage -- History -- 20th century 5. World War, 1939-1945 -- Cryptography
    ISBN 1936333252; 9781936333257
                              LC 2011007058

This book by Charlie Samuels, part of the World War II Sourcebook, provides a history of spying and security for young readers. It "Describes the role spies and police played around the world during World War II, from controlling riots to gathering intelligence from the enemy." (Publisher's note)

Seiple, Samantha

Ghosts in the fog; the untold story of Alaska's WWII invasion. Scholastic 2011 221p il map $16.99

Grades: 5 6 7 8   **940.54**

1. Alaska 2. World War, 1939-1945 -- Campaigns 3. Japan. -- Kaigun -- History -- World War, 1939-1945

ISBN 978-0-545-29654-0; 0-545-29654-4

LC 2011027821

"A little-known story from World War II shows the unique role played by a small group of military personal and native civilians in a remote region of the county. The role of Alaska in World War II following the attack on Pearl Harbor is not often told. . . . The story illuminates the cultural differences between the American and Japanese cultures at that time as well as the reluctance of the U.S. government to treat the native Alaskans as full citizens. The narrative is full of details, and . . . the text is supported by many photographs of those involved. Maps, including a strategic military map, increase the level of specificity." Kirkus

Includes bibliographical references

Sheinkin, Steve

★ The **Port** Chicago 50; disaster, mutiny, and the fight for civil rights. Steve Sheinkin. Roaring Brook Press 2014 208 p. illustrations (hardcover : alk. paper) $19.99

Grades: 5 6 7 8 9   **940.54**

1. United States. Navy 2. African American sailors 3. African Americans -- Civil rights 4. World War, 1939-1945 5. Port Chicago Mutiny, Port Chicago, Calif., 1944

ISBN 1596437960; 9781596437968

LC 2013013452

Boston Globe-Horn Book Award: Nonfiction (2014)

National Book Award Shortlist: Young People's Literature (2014)

YALSA Award for Excellence in Nonfiction for Young Adults: Finalist (2015)

Author Steve Sheinkin tells how "on July 17, 1944, a massive explosion rocked the segregated Navy base at Port Chicago, California. On August 9th, 244 men refused to go back to work until unsafe and unfair conditions at the docks were addressed. Fifty were charged with mutiny." (Publisher's note)

"An unusual entry point for the study of WWII and the nascent civil rights movement. Photographs are helpful, and documentation is thorough." (Horn Book)

Includes bibliographical references and index

Stanley, Jerry

I am an American; a true story of Japanese internment. Crown 1994 102p il maps $15/Can$19; lib bdg $15.99 **940.54**

1. World War, 1939-1945 -- United States 2. Japanese Americans -- Evacuation and relocation, 1942-1945

ISBN 0-517-59786-1; 0-517-59787-X lib bdg

LC 93-41330

The author discusses "the internment of Japanese-Americans during World War II. He has spun a cogent narrative of the shameful events, focusing them through the experiences of Shi Nomura, a high school student sent with his family to Manzanar in 1942. . . . This is a first-rate, readable introduction to this particular part of history, and it's complemented by a spacious page design, numerous black-and-white photos, an exemplary bibliographic note, and an index." Bull Cent Child Books

Stone, Tanya Lee

★ **Courage** has no color, the true story of the Triple Nickles; America's first black paratroopers. Tanya Lee Stone. Candlewick Press 2013 160 p. $24.99

Grades: 5 6 7 8   **940.54**

1. Parachute troops 2. United States. Army 3. World War, 1939-1945 4. African American soldiers

ISBN 0763651176; 9780763651176

LC 2012942315

Orbis Pictus Awards Honor Book (2014)

YALSA Award for Excellence in Nonfiction for Young Adults: Finalist (2014)

This book tells the "untold story of the 555th Parachute Infantry Battalion, America's first black paratroopers." Enlisted black men "faced the tyranny of racial discrimination on the homefront. . . . When 1st Sgt. Walter Morris, whose men served as guards at The Parachute School at Fort Benning, saw white soldiers training to be paratroopers, he knew his men would have to train and act like them to be treated like soldiers." (Kirkus Reviews)

941   British Isles

Dillon, Patrick

The **story** of Britain from the Norman Conquest to the European Union; illustrated by P.J. Lynch. Candlewick Press 2011 341p il map $21.99

Grades: 5 6 7 8   **941**

1. Great Britain -- History

ISBN 978-0-7636-5122-0; 0-7636-5122-2

LC 2010038883

"This well-written, thoughtfully illustrated volume [is] an indispensible tool for European history buffs." Horn Book Guide

Dunn, James

ABC UK; illustrated by Helen Bate. Frances Lincoln 2009 un il $16.95

Grades: K 1 2 3   **941**

1. Alphabet 2. Great Britain

ISBN 978-1-84507-696-2; 1-84507-696-6

"Featuring historical and cultural highlights of Great Britain (Giant's Causeway, punk music, vindaloo), each letter of the alphabet gets a uniquely stylized treatment in Bate's mixed media art. . . . The diversity of subjects makes it a prime pick for Anglophiles of all ages." Publ Wkly

Indovino, Shaina C.

United Kingdom; by Rae Simons and Shaina C. Indovino. Mason Crest Publishers 2012 64 p. col. ill., col. maps (library) $22.95

Grades: 5 6 7 8   **941**

1. Great Britain 2. Northern Ireland 3. European Union -- Great Britain 4. European Union -- Northern Ireland

ISBN 1422222616; 9781422222614; 9781422222928

LC 2010051852

This book on the United Kingdom by Rae Simons and Shaina Carmel Indovino "covers Modern Issues, History and Government, The Economy, People and Culture, and Looking to the Future. . . Identical information on "The Formation of the European Union" appears in every book" in the series. (Library Media Connection) Also covered are "issues like immigration and the global financial crisis". (Publisher's note)

Includes bibliographical references (p. 60) and index.

941.5 Ireland

McQuinn, Colm

★ **Ireland**; [by] Anna and Colm McQuinn; Elizabeth Malcolm and John McDonagh, consultants. National Geographic 2008 64p il map (Countries of the world) lib bdg $27.90

Grades: 4 5 6 7 **941.5**

1. Ireland

ISBN 978-1-4263-0299-2 lib bdg; 1-4263-0299-1 lib bdg

This describes the geography, nature, history, people and culture, government, and economy of Ireland.

Includes glossary and bibliographical references

941.508 1800-1899

Fradin, Dennis Brindell

The **Irish** potato famine; by Dennis Fradin. Marshall Cavendish Benchmark 2012 32 p. (Great escapes) (library) $34.21

Grades: 5 6 7 8 **941.508**

1. Famines 2. Ireland -- History -- Famine, 1845-1852 3. Escapes -- Ireland -- History -- 19th century 4. Irish -- Migrations -- History -- 19th century 5. Disaster victims -- Ireland -- History -- 19th century 6. Ireland -- Emigration and immigration -- History -- 19th century

ISBN 1608704734; 9781608704736

LC 2010018788

This book, part of the Great Escapes series, focuses on the Irish Potato Famine. "Each book begins with an introduction to an individual who escaped, followed by the history of the precipitating events, the escape itself, and a follow-up on what happened after the escape. Each title includes a timeline, notes, and additional information on the topic." (Library Media Connection)

Includes bibliographical references and index.

941.7 Republic of Ireland

Blashfield, Jean F.

Ireland; Enchantment of the World. by Jean F. Blashfield. Children's Press; an imprint of Scholastic Inc. 2014 144 p. (Enchantment of the world--second series) (library binding) $40

Grades: 5 6 7 8 **941.7**

1. Ireland

ISBN 0531236765; 9780531236765

LC 2013002015

This book, by Jean F. Blashfield, focuses on Ireland. The book focuses on "country's culture, history, and geography are explored in detail. . . . Sidebars highlight especially interesting people, places, and events. . . . Recipes give readers the opportunity to experience foreign cuisine." (Publisher's note)

"Many students turn to the Internet for writing reports, but for reliably accurate, attractively presented and well-calibrated information, the long-standing Enchantment of the World series remains a superior choice. Each volume has been completely rewritten from a previous edition—in many cases to startling effect given recent political events. Although the basic structure holds true to past versions, the updated photographs are truly eye-popping and take care to portray the countries as modern often opting for showing, say, a surgeon at work rather than a rural farmer. It might not be necessary for libraries to replace Ireland, since it hasn't changed radically, but this is a solid offering with updated

statistics. Each volume in this reliable series includes extensive back matter with a detailed index." Booklist.

Includes bibliographical references and index

942 England and Wales

Banting, Erinn

England; by Erinn Banting; edited by Sarah Cairns; illustrated by Jeff Crosby, Dianne Eastman, and David Wysotski. Revised ed. Crabtree Pub. Co. 2012 32 p. ill. (some col.) (Lands, peoples, and cultures) (library) $26.60; (paperback) $8.95; (ebook) $26.60

Grades: 4 5 6 **942**

1. Culture 2. England 3. England -- Civilization 4. England -- Social life and customs

ISBN 0778798283; 9780778798286; 9780778798316; 9781427180056 pdf

LC 2012013776

This book by Erinn Banting is part of the Lands, Peoples and Cultural Series and looks at the culture of England. The books offer information about "folktales, sports, and history." Also included are "a table of contents, short glossary (words highlighted in test) and index." (Catholic Library World)

Includes index

Blashfield, Jean F.

England; by Jean F. Blashfield. Children's Press 2013 144 p. ill. (some col.), col. maps (Enchantment of the world) (library) $40.00

Grades: 4 5 6 7 **942**

1. England

ISBN 9780531275429

LC 2012000503

This book by Jean F. Blashfield, part of the "Enchantment of the World" series, "describes the geography, history, economy, language, religions, culture, people, plants, and animals of England." (Publisher's note) It includes "topics as recent as the 2012 Olympics and 2012 Grammy winners, as well as the latest royal wedding." (Children's Literature)

Includes bibliographical references (p. 134-135) and index.

Platt, Richard

★ **London**; illustrated by Manuela Cappon. Kingfisher 2009 45p il (Through time) $16.95

Grades: 3 4 5 **942**

1. London (England) -- History

ISBN 978-0-7534-6255-3; 0-7534-6255-9

This "book explores the history of London from 'Neolithic camp' to the modern city it is today. . . . Cutaway views of various structures and concise but engaging text effectively capture the changing face of a city over time." Publ Wkly

Rubbino, Salvatore

★ **A walk** in London. Candlewick Press 2011 40p il $16.99

Grades: PreK K 1 2 3 4 **942**

1. London (England)

ISBN 978-0-7636-5272-2; 0-7636-5272-5

LC 2010038769

"A mother and daughter get off a double-decker bus in central London for a day of sightseeing. . . . Playful yet realistic mixed-media illustrations, drawn from different perspectives, give the reader a real sense of what it's like to visit London. . . . Highly informative, visually stunning, and jam-packed with things for young readers to look at." Horn Book

942.05   England--Period of House of Tudor, 1485-1603

Hollihan, Kerrie Logan

Elizabeth I--the people's queen; her life and times: 21 activities. Chicago Review Press 2011 129p il (For kids) pa $16.95

Grades: 4 5 6 7 8   **942.05**

1. Queens 2. Great Britain -- History -- 1485-1603, Tudors

ISBN 978-1-56976-349-0; 1-56976-349-6

LC 2010047647

This is an interactive biography of Queen Elizabeth I.

"The writing is clear and suited to readers with no previous knowledge of the topic. The activities vary in difficulty, from reading The Faerie Queen, to creating a family coat of arms, to growing a knot garden. The book is well illustrated with black-and-white reproductions of portraits, engravings, and paintings depicting major events in the Tudors' lives. . . . This well-organized book succeeds at being interesting and scholarly at the same time." SLJ

Includes bibliographical references

942.9   Wales

Hestler, Anna

Wales; [by] Anna Hestler and Jo-Ann Spilling. 2nd ed.; Marshall Cavendish Benchmark 2011 144p il map (Cultures of the world) lib bdg $42.79

Grades: 5 6 7 8   **942.9**

1. Wales

ISBN 978-1-6087-0457-6; 1-6087-0457-2

LC 2010030339

First published 2001

Provides information on the geography, history, wildlife, governmental structure, economy, cultural diversity, peoples, religion, and culture of Wales.

"Plentiful color photographs accompany substantial amounts of information." Booklist

Includes glossary and bibliographical references

943   Germany and neighboring central European countries

Freedman, Russell, 1929-

We will not be silent; the White Rose student resistance movement that defied Adolf Hitler. Russell Freedman. Clarion Books 2016 112 p. illustrations (hardback) $17.99

Grades: 5 6 7 8   **943**

1. Students -- Political activity 2. Germany -- History -- 1933-1945 3. World War, 1939-1945 -- Underground movements 4. Weisse Rose (Resistance group) 5. Anti-Nazi movement -- Germany -- Munich 6. Munich (Germany) -- History -- 20th century 7. Universität München -- Riot, 1943 8. College students -- Political activity -- Germany -- Munich -- History -- 20th century

ISBN 0544223799; 9780544223790

LC 2015020439

Sibert Honor Book (2017)

This book, authored by Russell Freedman, "tells the story of Austrian-born Hans Scholl and his sister Sophie. They belonged to Hitler Youth as young children, but began to doubt the Nazi regime. As older students, the Scholls and a few friends formed the White Rose, a campaign of active resistance to Hitler and the Nazis. Risking imprisonment or even execution, the White Rose members distributed leaflets urging Germans to defy the Nazi government." (Publisher's note)

"A thorough and accessible introduction to the Holocaust and the students who dared to take a stand against evil." Kirkus

Includes bibliographical references (pages 93-95) and index.

Indovino, Shaina C.

Germany; by Ida Walker and Shaina C. Indovino. Mason Crest Publishers 2013 64 p. ill. (some col.), col. maps (Major European nations) (library) $22.95

Grades: 5 6 7 8   **943**

1. Germany 2. Germany -- Politics and government 3. Germany -- History 4. European Union -- Germany 5. German -- Description and travel 6. Germany -- Social life and customs

ISBN 1422222438; 9781422222430

LC 2010051291

This book on Germany by Ida Walker and Shaina Carmel Indovino is part of the "Major European Nations" series, which "stresses the modern relationships, goals, and problems of the European Union. . . . Chapters begin with 'Modern Issues' and a brief summary of the country's history and government, followed by chapters on economy, people and culture, and 'Looking to the Future.' In addition, there is a time line and a few suggestions for finding out more." (School Library Journal)

Russell, Henry

★ **Germany**; [by] Henry Russell; Benedict Kork and Antje Schlottmann, consultants. National Geographic 2007 64p il map (Countries of the world) lib bdg $27.90

Grades: 4 5 6 7   **943**

1. Germany

ISBN 978-1-4263-0059-2

LC 2007024677

Describes the geography, nature, history, people and culture, government and economy of Germany.

This "appealing [title has] wonderful photographs and maps. . . . The [book offers] reliable sources for country research, and the interesting and current material holds browsing potential as well." SLJ

Includes glossary and bibliographical references

943.6   Austria and Liechtenstein

Grahame, Deborah A.

Austria; [by] Deborah Grahame. Marshall Cavendish Benchmark 2007 48p il map (Discovering cultures) lib bdg $28.50

Grades: 2 3 4   **943.6**

1. Austria

ISBN 978-0-7614-1984-6 lib bdg; 0-7614-1984-5 lib bdg

LC 2006011471

An introduction to the geography, history, people, and culture of Austria

Includes glossary and bibliographical references

Indovino, Shaina C.

Austria; by Jeanine Sanna and Shaina C. Indovino. Mason Crest Publishers 2012 64 p. col. ill., col. maps (library) $22.95

Grades: 5 6 7 8   **943.6**

1. Austria -- History 2. Austria 3. European Union -- Austria

ISBN 1422222322; 9781422222324

LC 2010051075

This book, part of the Major European Union Nations series, focuses on Austria. In "addition to history, the book details government, economy, culture, and prospects for the future. There is a glossary and an index and a nice chronology in the back of the book as well as a brief bibliography and a list of photo credits." (Children's Literature)

Includes bibliographical references (p. 57) and index.

943.7 Czech Republic and Slovakia

Docalavich, Heather

Czech Republic; by Heather Docalavich and Shaina C. Indovino. Mason Crest Publishers 2013 64 p. col. ill, col. maps (library) $22.95; (ebook) $28.95

Grades: 5 6 7 8 **943.7**

1. Czech Republic 2. European Union -- Czech Republic
ISBN 1422222373; 9781422222379; 9781422222683; 9781422292648

LC 2010051083

This book by Heather Docalavich is part of the Major European Union Nations series and focuses on the Czech Republic. "The Czech Republic is one of the newest countries in the world. It's also new to the EU—it joined in 2004. People have lived in what we now call the Czech Republic for thousands of years, however. This land has a long history and is moving forward while dealing with challenges like the recent global recession." (Publisher's note)

Includes bibliographical references (p. 57-58, 63) and index.

Sioras, Efstathia

Czech Republic; [by] Efstathia Sioras and Michael Spilling. Marshall Cavendish Benchmark 2010 144p il map (Cultures of the world) lib bdg $42.79

Grades: 5 6 7 8 **943.7**

1. Czech Republic
ISBN 978-0-7614-4476-3 lib bdg; 0-7614-4476-9 lib bdg

LC 2009003185

This describes the geography, history, wildlife, governmental structure, economy, cultural diversity, peoples, religion, and culture of the Czech Republic

Includes glossary and bibliographical references

943.8 Poland

Deckker, Zilah

★ Poland; [by] Zilah Deckker; Richard Butterwick and Iwona Sagan, consultants. National Geographic 2008 64p il map (Countries of the world) lib bdg $27.90

Grades: 4 5 6 7 **943.8**

1. Poland
ISBN 978-1-4263-0201-5

LC 2007047823

This describes the geography, nature, history, people and culture, government, and economy of Poland.

Includes glossary and bibliographical references

Docalavich, Heather

Poland; by Healther Docalavich and Shaina C. Indovino. Mason Crest Publishers 2013 64 p. col. ill., col. maps (library) $22.95

Grades: 5 6 7 8 **943.8**

1. Poland 2. European Union -- Poland
ISBN 1422222543; 9781422222546

LC 2010051465

This book by Heather Docalavich and Shaina C. Indovino is part of the Major European Union Nations series and looks at Poland. "It joined the EU in 2004 . . . . For long time, Poland has been home to scientific thinkers, artists, and musicians. Today, it is one of the countries that have weathered the global recession the best, proving this nation's strength." (Publisher's note)

Includes bibliographical references and index

Mara, Wil

Poland; by Wil Mara. Children's Press, an imprint of Scholastic Inc. 2014 144 p. illustrations and maps (library binding) $40

Grades: 5 6 7 8 **943.8**

1. Poland
ISBN 0531220168; 9780531220160

LC 2013026061

This book, by Wil Mara, focuses on Poland. The book discusses the "country's culture, history, and geography are explored in detail, allowing readers a chance to see how people live. . . . Sidebars highlight especially interesting people, places, and events . . . [and] easy recipes give readers the opportunity to experience foreign cuisine first-hand." (Publisher's note)

Includes bibliographical references and index

944 France and Monaco

Dubowski, Mark

Discovery in the cave; by Mark Dubowski; illustrated by Bryn Barnard. Random House 2010 48 p. col. ill.

Grades: 1 2 3 **944**

1. Caves 2. Prehistoric art 3. Cave drawings and paintings 4. Lascaux Cave (France) 5. Montignac (Dordogne, France) -- Antiquities 6. Cave paintings -- France -- Montignac (Dordogne) 7. Art, Prehistoric -- France -- Montignac (Dordogne) 8. Magdalenian culture -- France -- Montignac (Dordogne)
ISBN 0375858938; 0375958932; 9780375858932; 9780375958939

LC 2009007099

This book tells the "true adventure story about the discovery of the Lascaux Cave. . . . In 1940, four teenage boys and a dog dropped themselves into a hole in the forest floor. Using a flaming grease gun as a torch, they ventured deep underground, eventually coming to a huge cave, the walls of which were covered with life-size paintings of animals. Whole herds of horses! Deer with horns as big as tree branches! Giant bison! The boys were amazed by their discovery. They'd stumbled upon the world's finest examples of prehistoric painting!" (Publisher's note)

Indovino, Shaina C.

France; by Jeanine Sanna and Shaina C. Indovino. Mason Crest Publishers 2013 64 p. col. ill., col. maps (hardcover) $22.95

Grades: 5 6 7 8 **944**

1. France
ISBN 142222242X; 9781422222423

LC 2010051290

This book by Liz Sonneborn is part of the Enchantment of the World series and looks at France. It covers "history, government, geography, natural resources, economics, the arts, and culture. . . . Maps, charts, sidebars highlighting items of interest, a time line, and a 'Fast Facts' section add to the presentation." (School Library Journal)

Includes bibliographical references (p. 59) and index.

King, David C.

Monaco; [by] David C. King. Marshall Cavendish Benchmark 2008 144p il map (Cultures of the world) lib bdg $42.79

Grades: 5 6 7 8 **944**

1. Monaco
ISBN 978-0-7614-2567-0

LC 2006030238

This describes the geography, history, government, economy, environment, people, and culture of Monaco

Includes glossary and bibliographical references

Rubbino, Salvatore

A **Walk** in Paris; Salvatore Rubbino. Candlewick Press 2014 40 p. color illustrations $16.99

Grades: PreK K 1 2 3 4   **944**

1. Paris (France)

ISBN 0763669849; 9780763669843

LC 2013943083

This children's book, by Salvatore Rubbino, "follows a girl and her grandfather through the streets of Paris. . . . The girl narrates excitedly while her grandfather offers occasional details about the Place Saint-Michel, the Louvre, and more. Brief informational captions about Parisian landmarks, cuisine, and language are tucked throughout the mixed-media illustrations." (Publishers Weekly)

"A girl and her grandpa tour Parisian sites old and new. They finally arrive, in a foldout, at the Eiffel Tower, "fizzing with lights!" It's an amiable amble, the child's travelogue nicely extended with extra facts in discreetly tiny type. The evocative art features gentle tones enlivened with verdant greens and inviting raspberry-reds. An endpaper map details the route." Horn Book

Sonneborn, Liz

France; by Liz Sonneborn. Children's Press 2013 144 p. ill., maps (library) $40

Grades: 5 6 7 8   **944**

1. France

ISBN 0531256006; 9780531256008

LC 2012047113

Includes bibliographical references (page 134) and index

Tidmarsh, Celia

France. Sea-to-sea Publications 2009 32p il map (Facts about countries) lib bdg $28.50

Grades: 3 4 5   **944**

1. France

ISBN 978-1-59771-115-9 lib bdg; 1-59771-115-2 lib bdg

Describes the geography, history, industries, education, government, and cultures of France

"The attractive layout includes color photographs and charts of current statistics as well as maps illustrating main farming regions, natural resources, or the literacy rates of girls and boys. The [text is] clear and succinct." SLJ

944.04   France since 1789

Riggs, Kate

The **French** Revolution. Creative Education 2009 48p il map (Days of change) lib bdg $32.80

Grades: 5 6 7 8   **944.04**

1. France -- History -- 1789-1799, Revolution

ISBN 978-1-58341-734-8 lib bdg; 1-58341-734-6 lib bdg

LC 2008009728

"With elegant design and mature prose, the Days of Change series is an ideal starting point for all manner of school projects. . . . The political pressures at the center of The French Revolution are difficult to dramatize, but Riggs carefully lays out the factions and civil disobedience that led to the Declaration of the Rights of Man and of The Citizen—and then the emperor's reign that overthrew everything." Booklist

Includes bibliographical references

945   Italy, San Marino, Vatican City, Malta

Blashfield, Jean F.

Italy; by Jean F. Blashfield. Children's Press, an imprint of Scholastic Inc. 2014 144 p. (library binding) $40

Grades: 5 6 7 8   **945**

1. Italy -- History 2. Italy -- Civilization 3. Italy -- Economic conditions 4. Italy -- Politics and government 5. Italy -- Social life and customs

ISBN 0531236773; 9780531236772

LC 2013000087

This book, by Jean F. Blashfield, focuses on Italy. The book discusses the "country's culture, history, and geography are explored in detail, allowing readers a chance to see how people live. . . . Sidebars highlight especially interesting people, places, and events . . . [and] recipes give readers the opportunity to experience foreign cuisine firsthand." (Publisher's note)

"Many students turn to the Internet for writing reports, but for reliably accurate, attractively presented and well-calibrated information, the long-standing Enchantment of the World series remains a superior choice. Each volume has been completely rewritten from a previous edition—in many cases to startling effect given recent political events. Although the basic structure holds true to past versions, the updated photographs are truly eye-popping and take care to portray the countries as modern often opting for showing, say, a surgeon at work rather than a rural farmer. It might not be necessary for libraries to replace [this title], since it hasn't changed radically, but this is a solid offering with updated statistics. Each volume in this reliable series includes extensive back matter with a detailed index." Booklist

Includes bibliographical references and index

Indovino, Shaina C.

Italy; by Ademola O. Sadik and Shaina C. Indovino. Mason Crest Publishers 2013 64 p. ill. (col. ill.), maps (library) $22.95

Grades: 5 6 7 8   **945**

1. Italy 2. European Union -- Italy

ISBN 1422222489; 9781422222485

LC 2010051333

This book by Ademola O. Sadek and Shaina C. Indovino is part of the Major European Nations series and looks at Italy. "Chapters begin with "Modern Issues" and a brief summary of the country's history and government, followed by chapters on economy, people and culture, and 'Looking to the Future.'" The texts "liken Italy's treatment of the "Roma" (Gypsies) to the U.S. treatment of the American Indian; the social standing of Italy's women is examined." (School Library Journal)

Nivola, Claire A.

★ **Orani**; my father's village. Farrar Straus Giroux 2011 un il $16.99

Grades: 2 3 4   **945**

1. Artists 2. Illustrators 3. Italy

ISBN 978-0-374-35657-6; 0-374-35657-2

LC 2009047598

"Nivola's charming primitive-style art works well in both the up-close images as well as in the broad landscape scenes that she loving captures. A book to inspire young writers and artists to interview and write about their own parents' (or grandparents') lives." SLJ

945.8   Sicily and adjacent islands

Sheehan, Sean

Malta; by Sean Sheehan and Yong Jui Lin. 2nd ed. Marshall Cavendish Benchmark 2010 144 p. col. ill. (library) $47.07

Grades: 5 6 7 8   **945.8**
1. Malta   2. Culture   3. Malta -- Social life and customs
ISBN 1608700240; 9781608700240

LC 2010000733

This book by Sean Sheehan is part of the Cultures of the World series and looks at Malta. The books in the series provide "broad overviews of each country's culture, geography, and history. The . . . texts discuss government, economy, people, lifestyles, religion, language, arts and leisure, festivals, and food." (School Library Journal)

Includes bibliographical references (p. 142) and index.

946   Spain, Andorra, Gibraltar, Portugal

Augustin, Byron
Andorra; by Byron D. Augustin. Marshall Cavendish Benchmark 2009 144p il map (Cultures of the world) lib bdg $42.79
Grades: 5 6 7 8   **946**
1. Andorra
ISBN 978-0-7614-3122-0 lib bdg; 0-7614-3122-5 lib bdg

LC 2007040356

"Provides comprehensive information on the geography, history, governmental structure, economy, cultural diversity, peoples, religion, and culture of Andorra." Publisher's note

Includes glossary and bibliographical references

Croy, Anita
Spain. National Geographic 2010 64p il map (Countries of the world) lib bdg $27.90
Grades: 4 5 6 7   **946**
1. Spain
ISBN 978-1-4263-0633-4 lib bdg; 1-4263-0633-4 lib bdg

This describes the geography, nature, history, people and culture, government and economy of Spain

"The information is substantial but not overwhelming. The [text is] clear, and the discussion points are well chosen. . . . [The text is] complemented with stunning photographs." SLJ

Includes glossary and bibliographical references

Hanks, Reuel R.
Spain; by Zoran Pavlovic and Reuel Hanks. Chelsea House 2006 104 p. col. ill., col. maps (library) $35.00; (hardcover) $35
Grades: 5 6 7 8   **946**
1. Spain
ISBN 9780791066973 out of print; 1617530476; 9781617530470

LC 2006002218

This book by Zoran Pavlovic is part of the Modern World Nations series and looks at Spain. "Although Spain is now part of a unified Europe, . . . it is also a land divided by a combination of its own history, ethnicity, and geography." This entry "offers readers a wealth of information about this nation, touching on a variety of topics such as Spanish geography, history, political evolution, and ethnic issues." (Publisher's note)

Includes bibliographical references (p. 96) and index.

Indovino, Shaina C.
Spain; by Rae Simons and Shaina C. Indovino. Mason Crest Publishers 2013 64 p. col. ill., col. maps (library) $22.95
Grades: 5 6 7 8   **946**
1. Spain   2. European Union -- Spain
ISBN 9781422222904; 1422222594; 9781422222591

LC 2010051847

This book by Rae Simons is part of the Major European Union Nations series and looks at Spain. "Spain has it all: beaches, modern cities, soaring architecture, mountains, and more. It has been a member of the EU since 1986. From the ancient Celts to the Moors to the Christian kings and queens, many people have influenced Spain. It has recently taken a step back in the current financial crisis, but this proud nation is slowly getting back on its feet." (Publisher's note)

946.9   Portugal

Deckker, Zilah
★ Portugal. National Geographic 2009 64p il map (Countries of the world) lib bdg $27.90
Grades: 4 5 6 7   **946.9**
1. Portugal
ISBN 978-1-4263-0390-6 lib bdg; 1-4263-0390-4 lib bdg

LC 2009275584

This describes the geography, nature, history, people and culture, government and economy of Portugal

Includes glossary and bibliographical references

Etingoff, Kim
Portugal; by Kim Etingoff and Shaina C. Indovino. Mason Crest Publishers 2013 64 p. col. ill. (library) $22.95
Grades: 5 6 7 8   **946.9**
1. Portugal
ISBN 1422222551; 9781422222553

LC 2010051466

This book by Kim Etingoff and Shaina C. Indovino is part of the Major European Union Nations series and looks at Portugal. "Long ago, Portugal was one of the world's most powerful countries, as it explored and conquered places far from home. Today, it is a nation that has had some economic and social struggles, but also some triumphs. It joined the EU in 1986." (Publisher's note)

947   Russia and neighboring east European countries

Robinson, Anthony
Hamzat's journey; a refugee diary. by Anthony Robinson and AnneMarie Robinson; illustrated by June Allan. Frances Lincoln Books 2010 un il (Refugee diary) $17.95
Grades: 3 4 5   **947**
1. Refugees   2. Children with physical disabilities   3. Chechnya (Russia)
ISBN 978-1-84780-030-5; 1-84780-030-0

"In 2001, eight-year-old Hamzat stepped on a land mine on the way to school with two friends in Grozny, Chechnya. His friends died, but Hamzat survived with a shattered leg. In his spare, quiet first-person narrative, Hamzat describes the horrific struggle of civilians in wartime. . . . Clear, detailed back matter offers more facts about Chechnya's geography and long, troubled history, while occasional small, color family photos add even more immediacy." Booklist

Stanley, Diane
★ Peter the Great. Morrow Junior Bks. 1999 32p il $16
Grades: 4 5 6 7   **947**
1. Emperors   2. Russia -- Kings and rulers
ISBN 0-688-16708-X

LC 98-45250

A reissue of the title first published 1986 by Four Winds Press

A biography of the tsar who began the transformation of Russia into a modern state in the late seventeenth-early eighteenth centuries

The author's "material is presented with a modicum of oversimplification and a plethora of details that are sure to fascinate children. But what really makes this biography shine are its breathtaking illustrations. The meticulously researched, vivid scenes of Russian life during Peter's reign—courts, countryside, architecture, costumes—are beautifully rendered." Publ Wkly

Yomtov, Nel

    Russia; by Nel Yomtov. Children's Press 2012 144 p. col. ill., col. maps (library) $40

Grades: 5 6 7 8   **947**

    1. Russia   2. Russia (Federation)

    ISBN 0531275450; 9780531275450

                               LC 2012000520

    This children's book, by Nel Yomtov, describes the geography and culture of Russia as part of the "Enchantment of the World" series. The book includes "colourful photos . . . [with] views of foreign cities and landscapes," facts and statistics on "interesting people, places, and events" in Russian history, and "delicious, easy recipes [to] give readers the opportunity to experience foreign cuisine firsthand." (Publisher's note)

    Includes bibliographical references and index

947.5   Caucasus

Dhilawala, Sakina

    Armenia; [by] Sakina Dhilawala. 2nd ed.; Marshall Cavendish Benchmark 2008 144p il map (Cultures of the world) lib bdg $39.93

Grades: 5 6 7 8   **947.5**

    1. Armenia

    ISBN 978-0-7614-2029-3

                               LC 2007014890

    First published 1997

    "Provides comprehensive information on the geography, history, wildlife, governmental structure, economy, cultural diversity, peoples, religion, and culture of Armenia." Publisher's note

    Includes glossary and bibliographical references

947.7   Ukraine

Bassis, Volodymyr

    Ukraine; [by] Volodymyr Bassis & Sakina Dhilawala. 2nd ed.; Marshall Cavendish Benchmark 2008 144p il map (Cultures of the world) lib bdg $42.79

Grades: 5 6 7 8   **947.7**

    1. Ukraine

    ISBN 978-0-7614-2090-3

                               LC 2007019179

    First published 1997

    "Provides comprehensive information on the geography, history, wildlife, governmental structure, economy, cultural diversity, peoples, religion, and culture of Ukraine." Publisher's note

    Includes glossary and bibliographical references

947.93   Lithuania

Kagda, Sakina

    Lithuania; [by] Sakina Kagda & Zawiah Abdul Latif. 2nd ed.; Marshall Cavendish Benchmark 2008 144p il map (Cultures of the world) lib bdg $42.79

Grades: 5 6 7 8   **947.93**

    1. Lithuania

    ISBN 978-0-7614-2087-3

                               LC 2007016290

    First published 1997

    "Provides comprehensive information on the geography, history, wildlife, governmental structure, economy, cultural diversity, peoples, religion, and culture of Lithuania." Publisher's note

    Includes glossary and bibliographical references

947.96   Latvia

Barlas, Robert

    Latvia; [by] Robert Barlas and Winnie Wong. 2nd ed.; Marshall Cavendish Benchmark 2010 144p il map (Cultures of the world) lib bdg $42.79

Grades: 5 6 7 8   **947.96**

    1. Latvia

    ISBN 978-0-7614-4857-0 lib bdg; 0-7614-4857-8 lib bdg

                               LC 2009046001

    First published 2000

    This offers information on the geography, history, wildlife, governmental structure, economy, cultural diversity, peoples, religion, and culture of Latvia

    Includes glossary and bibliographical references

947.98   Estonia

Spilling, Michael

    Estonia; 2nd ed.; Marshall Cavendish Benchmark 2010 142p il map (Cultures of the world) lib bdg $42.79

Grades: 5 6 7 8   **947.98**

    1. Estonia

    ISBN 978-0-7614-4846-4 lib bdg; 0-7614-4846-2 lib bdg

                               LC 2009021201

    First published 1999

    This describes the geography, history, wildlife, governmental structure, economy, cultural diversity, peoples, religion, and culture of Estonia

    Includes glossary and bibliographical references

948   Scandinavia

Gunderson, Jessica

    Vikings; Jessica Gunderson. 1st ed. Creative Education 2013 48 p. ill. (some col.) (library) $35.65

Grades: 3 4 5   **948**

    1. Vikings

    ISBN 1608181855; 9781608181858

                               LC 2011035801

    This children's book, by Jessica Gunderson, explores the history of the Vikings, as part of the "Fearsome Fighters" series. The book "covers the beginnings of the people, weaponry, war tactics, and famous leaders, and examines the current perception of the group in popular culture. . . . Historical reproductions, primary documents, photographs, maps, and film stills [also] appear throughout." (School Library Journal)

    Includes bibliographical references (p. 48) and index

Higgins, Nadia

    National Geographic Kids everything Vikings; all the incredible facts and fierce fun you can plunder. by Nadia Higgins. National Geographic Society 2015 63 p. col. ill., color map (library binding : alk. paper) $25.9

Grades: 3 4 5 6 **948**

1. Vikings

ISBN 9781426320767; 9781426320774

LC 2015019561

This children's book, by Nadia Higgins, presents a historical overview of Viking civilization. "Hats with horns, flying dragons . . . , you may think you know everything there is to know about Vikings, but think again! With stunning visuals and energetic, impactful design, and full of fun facts and surprises, readers won't stop until they've learned everything about Vikings." (Publisher's note)

"Historical reenactments and pop-culture references help make content relevant, as do interactive features that allow readers to determine which Viking god they are most like, create a saga-worthy nickname, decipher runes, or choose how to settle a dispute." Booklsit

Includes bibliographical references and index

Malam, John

The **Vikings**. PowerKids Press 2011 30p il (Dig it: History from objects) lib bdg $25.25

Grades: 3 4 5 **948**

1. Vikings

ISBN 978-1-4488-3286-6; 1-4488-3286-1

LC 2010023867

This book about the Vikings includes information about "homes and towns, daily life, clothing, religion, and entertainment.... The layout is crisp and the object illustrations and photographs, plus the 'What does it tell us' section provide visual understanding. These qualities will assist the teacher who needs to differentiate instruction. The information is well-written and easily understood, well suited to the curriculum and national standards. Website links are intriguing and students will enjoy adding this piece to their research." Libr Media Connect

Includes glossary and bibliographical references

Park, Louise

The **Scandinavian** Vikings; by Louise Park and Timothy Love. Marshall Cavendish Benchmark 2009 32p il map (Ancient and medieval people) $19.95

Grades: 4 5 6 **948**

1. Vikings 2. Scandinavia -- Civilization

ISBN 978-0-7614-4445-9; 0-7614-4445-9

This title has "a simple and elegant design with the proper balance of quality writing and quantity of information.... Handy time lines, well-chosen photos of ruins and artifacts, quality illustrations, inset 'Quick Facts', and 'What You Should Know About' features will grab reluctant readers and captivate even those with short attention spans." SLJ

Includes glossary

Raum, Elizabeth

What did the Vikings do for me? Heinemann Library 2010 32p il map (Heinemann infosearch: linking past to present) lib bdg $29; pa $7.99

Grades: 3 4 5 **948**

1. Vikings

ISBN 978-1-4329-3745-4 lib bdg; 1-4329-3745-6 lib bdg; 978-1-4329-3752-2 pa; 1-4329-3752-9 pa

LC 2009039662

"Children will likely know the Vikings primarily as marauding warriors, and although they won't stop thinking that after reading this title, ... they will also have a nicely balanced understanding of the other significant aspects and lasting impact of their civilization. Small chunks of text ... sit alongside a grab bag of digital illustrations, maps, paintings, and photographs." Booklist

Includes glossary and bibliographical references

948.5   Sweden

Docalavich, Heather

Sweden; by Heather Docalavich and Shaina C. Indovino. Mason Crest Publishers 2013 64 p. col. ill., col. maps (library) $22.95

Grades: 5 6 7 8 **948.5**

1. Sweden   2. European Union -- Sweden

ISBN 1422222608; 9781422222607; 9781422222911

LC 2010051848

This book by Heather Docalavich is part of the Major European Union Nations series and looks at Sweden. "A member of the EU since 1995, Sweden is one of the most stable and [peaceful] countries in the world. It takes caring for its people and the environment very seriously." The 2008-2009 financial crisis is discussed. (Publisher's note)

Includes bibliographical references (p. 57-58) and index

Grahame, Deborah A.

Sweden; [by] Deborah Grahame. Marshall Cavendish Benchmark 2007 48p il map (Discovering cultures) lib bdg $28.50

Grades: 2 3 4 **948.5**

1. Sweden

ISBN 978-0-7614-1985-3 lib bdg; 0-7614-1985-3 lib bdg

LC 2006011474

An introduction to geography, history, government, and culture of Sweden

Includes glossary and bibliographical references

Heinrichs, Ann

Sweden; by Ann Heinrichs. Children's Press, an Imprint of Scholastic Inc. 2014 144 p. color illustrations (library binding) $40

Grades: 5 6 7 8 **948.5**

1. Sweden

ISBN 0531220176; 9780531220177

LC 2013022562

This book, by Ann Heinrichs, focuses on Sweden. The "country's culture, history, and geography are explored in detail, allowing readers a chance to see how people live.... Sidebars highlight especially interesting people, places, and events [and] recipes give readers the opportunity to experience foreign cuisine first-hand." (Publisher's note)

"Introduces Sweden, describing its geography, history, animals, government, economy, food, religion, cities, culture, and family life." Baker & Taylor

Includes bibliographical references and index

Phillips, Charles

★ **Sweden**; [by] Charles Phillips; Susan C. Brantly and Eric Clark consultants. National Geographic 2009 64p il map (Countries of the world) lib bdg $27.90

Grades: 4 5 6 7 **948.5**

1. Sweden

ISBN 978-1-4263-0389-0 lib bdg; 1-4263-0389-0 lib bdg

LC 2009275585

This describes the geography, nature, history, people & culture, and government & economy of Sweden

Includes glossary and bibliographical references

948.9 Denmark and Finland

Docalavich, Heather
Denmark; by Heather Docalavich and Shaina C. Indovino. Mason Crest Publishers 2013 64 p. col. ill., col. maps (hardcover) $22.95
Grades: 5 6 7 8   **948.9**
1. Denmark 2. European Union -- Denmark
ISBN 1422222381; 9781422222386
LC 2010051090

This book by Heather Docalavich and Shaina Carmel Indovino is part of the Major European Union Nations series and focuses on Denmark. "Denmark is a peaceful northern country that joined the EU in 1973. From the Vikings to the modern day, Denmark has a long [history]. Today, Denmark is a very environmentally conscious nation with a lot going on. It also must figure out how to deal with issues of immigration and the global recession as it looks to the future." (Publisher's note)

Includes bibliographical references (p. 57) and index

948.97 Finland

Tan, Chung Lee
★ Finland; [by] Tan Chung Lee. 2nd ed.; Marshall Cavendish Benchmark 2007 144p il map (Cultures of the world) lib bdg $39.93
Grades: 5 6 7 8   **948.97**
1. Finland
ISBN 978-0-7614-2073-6 lib bdg; 0-7614-2073-8 lib bdg
LC 2006015897

First published 1996

This provides "information on the geography, history, governmental structure, economy, cultural diversity, peoples, religion, and culture of Finland." Publisher's note

Includes glossary and bibliographical references

949.12 Iceland

McMillan, Bruce
Going fishing; written and photo-illustrated by Bruce McMillan. Houghton Mifflin Co. 2005 32p il $16
Grades: 2 3 4   **949.12**
1. Fishing 2. Iceland
ISBN 0-618-47201-0
LC 2004-15506

"This narrative photo-essay follows a young boy from Reykjavik to the fishing village where his two grandfathers live. Each takes his grandson out on his own boat to catch a type of fish important to Iceland. . . . The clarity of the color photos brings the people, their surroundings, and the process of fishing sharply into focus. . . . A delightfully illustrated presentation of fishing, family, and, of course, Iceland." Booklist

Somervill, Barbara A.
Iceland; by Barbara A. Somervill. Children's Press 2013 144 p. ill., maps (library) $40
Grades: 5 6 7 8   **949.12**
1. Iceland 2. Icelandic language
ISBN 0531256022; 9780531256022
LC 2012047117

This book by Barbara A. Somervill is part of the Enchantment of the World series and looks at Iceland. A discussion is offered of "how this land near the Arctic Circle came to be. . . . Maps and illustrations show the variety in the terrain and the areas of major geological activity. . . .

Chapters [are] devoted to history, the economy, the government and the flora and fauna." (Children's Literature)

Includes bibliographical references (page 134) and index.

949.2 Netherlands

Docalavich, Heather
The Netherlands; by Heather Docalavich and Shaina Carmel Indovino. Mason Crest Publishers 2013 64 p. col. ill. (library) $22.95; (ebook) $28.95
Grades: 5 6 7 8   **949.2**
1. Netherlands
ISBN 9781422222539; 9781422222843; 9781422292716
LC 2010051464

This book on the Netherlands by Heather Docalvich and Shaina Carmel Indovino is part of the "Major European Union Nations" series. It presents an "overview of some of the successes and challenges that the Netherlands has faced and continues to face." Topics include "history, one on government, the economy, people and culture, and . . . global climate change." (Children's Literature)

Includes bibliographical references (p. 57-58, 63) and index.

949.304 Belgium 1909-

Indovino, Shaina C.
Belgium; by Ida Walker and Shaina C. Indovino. Mason Crest Publishers 2012 64 p. col. ill., col. maps (library) $22.95
Grades: 5 6 7 8   **949.304**
1. Belgium 2. European Union -- Belgium
ISBN 1422222330; 9781422222331
LC 2010051078

This book, "part of the 'Modern World Nations' series, is an . . . introduction to the kingdom of Belgium. For middle school and high school readers, the chapters are descriptive of the physical features, the history, people, government, and economy. There is a chapter about the future of the nation as well as a description of life in the country today." (Children's Literature)

Includes bibliographical references and index.

949.35 Luxembourg

Sheehan, Patricia
Luxembourg; by Patricia Sheehan & Sakina Dhilawala. 2nd ed.; Marshall Cavendish Benchmark 2008 144p il map (Cultures of the world) lib bdg $42.79
Grades: 5 6 7 8   **949.35**
1. Luxembourg
ISBN 978-0-7614-2088-0
LC 2007014891

First published 1997

Discusses the geography, history, government, economy, and customs of the smallest of the Benelux countries

Includes glossary and bibliographical references

949.4   Switzerland

Harris, Pamela K.

Welcome to Switzerland; by Pamela K. Harris and Brad Clemmons. Child's World 2008 32p il map (Welcome to the world) lib bdg $27.07

Grades: 1 2 3 4   **949.4**
1. Switzerland
ISBN 978-1-59296-980-7 lib bdg; 1-59296-980-1 lib bdg
LC 2007038146

This briefly describes the geography, history, people, and culture of Switzerland.

"Report writers and browsers will appreciate [this book]. . . . The captioned, color photographs have a balanced gender representation. Maps, fast facts, and recipes round out excellent offerings." SLJ
Includes glossary and bibliographical references

Seavey, Lura Rogers

Switzerland; by Lura Rogers Seavey. Children's Press, an imprint of Scholastic Inc. 2017 144 p. color ill., color maps (library binding) $40

Grades: 5 6 7 8   **949.4**
1. Switzerland 2. Switzerland
ISBN 0531218872; 9780531218877
LC 2016000985

In this book, by Lura Rogers Seavey, "Switzerland has become known as a place of peace and prosperity. Readers will explore this European nation's fascinating history and find out how it came to occupy such a unique position in the world. They will learn how the country is governed and what makes its economy so strong. They will also explore its beautiful cities and mountainous landscapes and sample its rich culture." (Publisher's note)

"With stunning, high-quality photos that reflect the richness of cultures around the globe, the Enchantment of the World series earns its name." Booklist
Includes bibliographical references and index

949.5   Greece

Etingoff, Kim

Greece; by Kim Etingoff and Shaina C. Indovino. Mason Crest Publishers 2013 64 p. ill. (library) $22.95

Grades: 5 6 7 8   **949.5**
1. Greece
ISBN 1422222446; 9781422222447; 9781422222751
LC 2010051304

This book by Kim Etingoff and Shaina C. Indovino is part of the Major European Union Nations series and looks at Greece. The series "stresses the modern relationships, goals, and problems of the European Union. . . . , Chapters begin with 'Modern Issues' and a brief summary of the country's history and government, followed by chapters on economy, people and culture, and 'Looking to the Future.'" (School Library Journal)

Green, Jen

★ **Greece;** [by] Greg Anderson and Kostas Vlassopoulos, consultants. National Geographic 2009 64p il map (Countries of the world) lib bdg $27.90

Grades: 4 5 6 7   **949.5**
1. Greece
ISBN 978-1-4263-0470-5 lib bdg; 1-4263-0470-6 lib bdg

This describes the geography, nature, history, people and culture, government and economy of Greece
Includes glossary and bibliographical references

Heinrichs, Ann

Greece; by Ann Heinrichs. Children's Press 2012 144 p. col. ill., col. maps (library) $40

Grades: 5 6 7 8   **949.5**
1. Greece -- History 2. Greece -- Civilization 3. Greece
ISBN 0531275434; 9780531275436
LC 2012000519

This book, part of the Enchantment of the World series, focuses on Greece. The books in the series each feature 10 "chapters, several maps, a fast-facts section, and a few references to other sources, including a referral to a Scholastic website . . . . The chapters cover geography, natural environment, history, politics, people and culture." (School Library Journal)
Includes bibliographical references and index

Vanvoorst, Jennifer Fretland

The **Byzantine** Empire; by Jenny Fretland VanVoorst. Compass Point Books 2013 48 p. ill. (chiefly col.), col. map (library) $28.65; (paperback) $8.95

Grades: 6 7 8   **949.5**
1. Byzantine Empire -- Civilization
ISBN 075654565X; 0756545862; 9780756545659; 9780756545864
LC 2012001994

This children's nonfiction book, by Jennifer Fretland VanVoorst, profiles the Byzantine Empire as part of the "Exploring the Ancient World" series. "The Byzantine Empire, which thrived from 395 to 1453, was a fascinating place. Its people thought of themselves as Romans, spoke Greek, and hailed from all across Europe and Asia. . . . It was a Christian empire that preserved and developed Europe's intellectual heritage at a time when western Europe was in decline." (Publisher's note)
Includes bibliographical references (p. 46-47) and index.

949.65   Albania

Knowlton, MaryLee

Albania; by MaryLee Knowlton. Marshall Cavendish Benchmark 2005 144p il map (Cultures of the world) lib bdg $42.79

Grades: 5 6 7 8   **949.65**
1. Albania
ISBN 0-7614-1852-0
LC 2004-22236

An overview of the history, culture, peoples, religion, government, and geography of Albania
Includes glossary and bibliographical references

949.7   Serbia, Croatia, Slovenia, Bosnia and Hercegovina, Montenegro, Macedonia

Cooper, Robert

Croatia; [by] Robert Cooper and Michael Spilling. 2nd ed; Marshall Cavendish Benchmark 2011 144p il map (Cultures of the world) lib bdg $42.79

Grades: 5 6 7 8   **949.7**
1. Croatia
ISBN 978-1-6087-0215-2; 1-6087-0215-4
LC 2010019626

First published 2001

Provides information on the geography, history, wildlife, governmental structure, economy, cultural diversity, peoples, religion, and culture of Croatia.

"Plentiful color photographs accompany substantial amounts of information." SLJ

Includes glossary and bibliographical references

Halilbegovich, Nadja

My childhood under fire; a Sarajevo diary. Kids Can Press 2006 120p il $14.95

Grades: 5 6 7 8   **949.7**

1. Yugoslav War, 1991-1995 2. Sarajevo (Bosnia and Hercegovina)

ISBN 1-55337-797-4

"In 1992, when the bombing started in Sarajevo, Halilbegovich, 12, kept a diary of her terrifying daily life under siege. Her terse vignettes replay the horror of her comfortable home torn apart." Booklist

Knowlton, MaryLee

Macedonia; by MaryLee Knowlton. Benchmark Books 2005 144p il map (Cultures of the world) lib bdg $42.79

Grades: 5 6 7 8   **949.7**

1. Macedonia (Republic)

ISBN 0-7614-1854-7

LC 2004-22735

Describes the geography, history, government, economy, people, and culture of Macedonia

Includes glossary and bibliographical references

950   History of Asia

Law, Felicia

Atlas of Southwest and Central Asia. Picture Window Books 2008 32p il map (Picture Window Books world atlases) lib bdg $27.93; pa $7.95

Grades: 2 3 4   **950**

1. Asia 2. Middle East

ISBN 978-1-4048-3884-0 lib bdg; 1-4048-3884-8 lib bdg; 978-1-4048-3892-5 pa; 1-4048-3892-9 pa

This introduction to the geography of Southwest and Central Asia offers maps and information about countries, landforms, bodies of water, climate, plants, animals, population, people and customs, places of interest, industries, transportation, and Mount Everest

Includes glossary

Atlas of the Far East and Southeast Asia. Picture Window Books 2008 32p il map (Picture Window Books world atlases) lib bdg $27.93; pa $7.95

Grades: 2 3 4   **950**

1. Asia

ISBN 978-1-4048-3883-3 lib bdg; 1-4048-3883-X lib bdg; 978-1-4048-3891-8 pa; 1-4048-3891-0 pa

This introduction to the geography of the Far East and Southeast Asia offers maps and information about countries, landforms, bodies of water, climate, plants, animals, population, people and customs, places of interest, industries, transportation, and the Pacific Islands

Includes glossary

951   China and adjacent areas

Demi, 1942-

The **great** voyages of Zheng He; by Demi. Shen's Books 2012 64 p. col. ill., col. map (hardcover) $21.95

Grades: 3 4 5   **951**

1. China -- History 2. Explorers -- China -- Biography

ISBN 1885008457; 9781885008459

LC 2012000934

This book is "Demi's account of 15th-century Chinese explorer Zheng He," demonstrating the "dazzling wealth his fleet carried back to China: 'Precious ambergris used for medicine, cowrie shells, sapphires, rubies, oriental topaz, and Persian carpers filled the Forbidden City.' His 62 'Treasure Ships' were the largest the world had ever seen, but Zheng He also displayed a wealth of intellect and imagination that allowed him to embrace religious tolerance and open-mindedness." (Publishers Weekly)

Henzel, Cynthia Kennedy

Great Wall of China. ABDO Pub. Co. 2011 32p il (Troubled treasures: world heritage sites) $25.65

Grades: 3 4 5   **951**

1. Great Wall of China

ISBN 978-1-61613-565-2; 1-61613-565-4

LC 2010021309

This "book describes in general terms [the Great Wall of China's] construction, . . . distinctive features, and history, as well as threats to its continued existence and both current and past restoration initiatives. Revealing color photos taken from different heights and angles are supplemented by maps and by graphic reconstructions. . . . Henzel's distinctive approach gives this [book] unusual value for both assignment and general reading." SLJ

Includes glossary

Keister, Douglas

To grandmother's house; a visit to old-town Beijing. Gibbs Smith, Publisher 2008 un $15.95

Grades: K 1 2 3 4   **951**

1. China 2. Beijing (China) 3. Bilingual books -- English-Chinese

ISBN 978-1-4236-0283-5; 1-4236-0283-8

LC 2007033167

"Through an engaging bilingual narrative and lovely, full-color photos, Zhang Yue gives readers a tour of her hometown, beautiful and historic Beijing. She starts the day with a visit to her grandmother in a hutong , or neighborhood, in the old part of the city. Along the way she introduces the sights and shops in a voice that is natural and interesting, inviting readers to experience all of the little details that make Beijing unique. The photographs wonderfully capture the splendor of the major monuments as well as the fascinating bustle of the outdoor markets." SLJ

Levy, Patricia

Tibet; [by] Patricia Levy & Don Bosco. 2nd ed.; Marshall Cavendish Benchmark 2007 144p il map (Cultures of the world) lib bdg $42.79

Grades: 5 6 7 8   **951**

1. Tibet (China)

ISBN 978-0-7614-2076-7 lib bdg; 0-7614-2076-2 lib bdg

LC 2006015826

First published 1996

This provides "information on the geography, history, wildlife, governmental structure, economy, diversity, peoples, religion, and culture of Tibet." Publisher's note

Includes glossary and bibliographical references

Lewin, Betsy, 1937-

★ **Horse** song; the Naadam of Mongolia. [by] Ted and Betsy Lewin. Lee & Low Books 2008 un il $19.95

Grades: 2 3 4 5   **951**

1. Nomads 2. Festivals 3. Horse racing 4. Mongolia -- Social life and customs

ISBN 978-1-58430-277-3; 1-58430-277-1

LC 2007025899

"In simple, captivating language, the Lewins describe their long journey. . . . Throughout, clearly presented cultural specifics mix with vivid sensory perceptions . . . but it's the color-washed sketches and beautiful full-page spreads . . . that will truly capture readers' attention." Booklist

Mara, Wil

People's Republic of China; by Wil Mara. Children's Press 2012 144 p. ill., maps (library) $40

Grades: 5 6 7 8   **951**

1. China -- Economic conditions 2. China

ISBN 053125352X; 9780531253526

LC 2011011308

This book, part of the Enchantment of the World, offers an "introduction to China. The book covers geography, climate, history, language, different ethnic groups, religion, government structure, and the arts. Frequent text boxes and large, bright photographs add extra information and deeper context. There is a heavy focus on the Chinese economy and recent strides made in human rights." (School Library Journal)

Includes bibliographical references and index.

Marx, Trish

Elephants and golden thrones; inside China's Forbidden City. written by Trish Marx; photographs and photograph selection by Ellen B. Senisi; foreword by Li Ji. Abrams Books for Young Readers 2008 48p il $18.95

Grades: 4 5 6 7   **951**

1. China 2. Forbidden City (Beijing, China)

ISBN 978-0-8109-9485-0; 0-8109-9485-2

LC 2007-022413

Introduces Beijing's Forbidden City, recounting some of the most famous incidents from its past, and describing its rooms, their function, and some of the daily rituals of palace life.

The author "brings the Forbidden City to life by telling stories about six different royal inhabitants from Zhengde, 'one of the worst emperors in Chinese history,' to Puyi, who became a pawn of the invading Japanese. . . . Beautiful drawings and photographs, some provided by the Palace Museum and some taken for this book, lend color and provide additional information. Of particular note are the photos of the interiors of buildings, a number of which are not regularly open to the public." Booklist

Includes bibliographical references

Riehecky, Janet

China; by Janet Riehecky. Lerner Publications Company 2008 48p il (Country explorers) lib bdg $27.93

Grades: 2 3 4   **951**

1. China

ISBN 978-0-8225-7129-2

LC 2006036731

This introduction to China covers "all of the areas of interest to students, including animals, sports, foods, celebrations, storytime, and even a few words in the country's native language. Small amounts of information are surrounded by current photographs, maps, charts, and illustrations. . . . Sure to grab the attention of even reluctant readers." SLJ

Includes glossary and bibliographical references

Sis, Peter

★ **Tibet**; through the red box. Farrar, Straus & Giroux 1998 un il maps $25

Grades: 4 5 6 7   **951**

1. Tibet (China)

ISBN 0-374-37552-6

LC 97-50175

A Caldecott Medal honor book, 1999

"When Sis opens the red lacquered box that has sat on his father's table for decades, he finds the diary his father kept when he was lost in Tibet in the mid-1950s. The text replicates the diary's spidery handwriting, while the illustrations depict elaborate mazes and mandalas, along with dreamlike spreads that are filled with fragmented details of the father's and son's lives. . . . Impeccably designed and beautifully made, the book has a dreamlike quality that will keep readers of many ages coming back to find more in its pages." Booklist

951.05 China--Period of People's Republic, 1949-

Chen, Jiang Hong

Mao and me; the Little Red Guard. [by] Chen Jiang Hong; [translated by Claudia Zoe Bedrick] Enchanted Lion Books 2008 77p il $19.95

Grades: 3 4 5   **951.05**

1. Children -- China 2. China -- History -- 1949-1976 -- Personal narratives

ISBN 978-1-59270-079-0; 1-59270-079-9

LC 2008037650

Originally published in French

Chen's "picture book memoir of growing up during the Cultural Revolution is not easy to read, but stands out for its epic sweep and unflinching honesty. Rendered in large panels, his ink and wash paintings document everything from the making of dumplings to the public humiliation of cherished neighbors. . . . [This shows] excellence in representing political upheaval." Publ Wkly

Jiang, Ji-li

Red scarf girl; a memoir of the Cultural Revolution. foreword by David Henry Hwang. HarperCollins Pubs. 1997 285p $16.99; pa $6.99

Grades: 6 7 8 9 10   **951.05**

1. Communism -- China 2. China -- History -- 1949-1976 -- Personal narratives

ISBN 0-06-027585-5; 0-06-446208-0 pa

LC 97-5089

"This is an autobiographical account of growing up during Mao's Cultural Revolution in China in 1966. . . . Jiang describes in terrifying detail the ordeals of her family and those like them, including unauthorized search and seizure, persecution, arrest and torture, hunger, and public humiliation. . . . Her voice is that of an intelligent, confused adolescent, and her focus on the effects of the revolution on herself, her family, and her friends provides an emotional focal point for the book, and will allow even those with limited knowledge of Chinese history to access the text." Bull Cent Child Books

951.25 Hong Kong

Kagda, Falaq

Hong Kong; [by] Falaq Kagda & Magdalene Koh. 2nd ed.; Marshall Cavendish Benchmark 2008 144p il map (Cultures of the world) lib bdg $42.79

Grades: 5 6 7 8   **951.25**
1. Hong Kong (China)
ISBN 978-0-7614-3034-6 lib bdg; 0-7614-3034-2 lib bdg
LC 2007048285
First published 1998
Surveys the geography, history, government, economy, and culture of Hong Kong
Includes glossary and bibliographical references

951.5 Tibet

Sonneborn, Liz
Tibet; by Liz Sonneborn. Children's Press, an imprint of Scholastic Inc. 2017 144 p. color ill., color maps (library binding) $40
Grades: 5 6 7 8   **951.5**
1. Tibet (China) 2. Tibet Autonomous Region (China)
ISBN 9780531218884
LC 2015048619
In this children's book in the Enchantment of the World series, by Liz Sonneborn, "despite Tibet's official status as a part of China, the country's people widely consider it to be an independent nation. Readers will trace Tibet's long history to discover how this conflict came to be. Along the way, they will find out how Tibet's people live, how the region is governed, and much more. They will also get a close-up look at its beautiful landscapes and diverse wildlife." (Publisher's note)
"With stunning, high-quality photos that reflect the richness of cultures around the globe, the Enchantment of the World series earns its name." Booklist
Includes bibliographical references and index

951.7 Mongolia

Pang, Guek-Cheng, 1950-
Mongolia; Pang Guek Cheng. Marshall Cavendish Benchmark 2010 144 p. col. ill., col. maps (Cultures of the world) (library) $42.79
Grades: 5 6 7 8   **951.7**
1. Mongolia
ISBN 9780761448495; 0761448497
LC 2009022643
This describes the geography, history, wildlife, governmental structure, economy, cultural diversity, peoples, religion, and culture of Mongolia
Includes bibliographical references and index.

951.73 Outer Mongolia

Bjorkland, Ruth
Mongolia; by Ruth Bjorklund. Children's Press, an Imprint of Scholastic Inc. 2017 144 p. color ill., color maps (library binding : alk. paper) $40
Grades: 5 6 7 8   **951.73**
1. Mongolia
ISBN 0531218848; 9780531218846
LC 2015043526
This book, by Ruth Bjorklund, focuses on Mongolia. "Situated directly between China and Russia, the country of Mongolia long had close ties to its larger neighbors. However, since the early 1990s it has become increasingly independent, and many Mongolians have worked to rediscover a national culture that existed long before Chinese or Rus-

sian rule. Readers will explore this Mongolia's amazing history and find out what makes its culture so unique." (Publisher's note)
"With stunning, high-quality photos that reflect the richness of cultures around the globe, the Enchantment of the World series earns its name." Booklist
Includes bibliographical references and index

951.9 Korea

Bowler, Ann Martin
All about Korea; stories, songs, crafts, and more. illustrated by Soosoonam Barg. Periplus Editions 2011 64p il $16.95
Grades: 3 4 5 6   **951.9**
1. Korea
ISBN 978-0-8048-4012-5; 0-8048-4012-1 (hardcover)
LC 2010040845
Introduces Korea, describing its history, culture, everyday life, food, sports, and holidays, as well as providing examples of Korean poems, songs, handicrafts, writing, legends, and folkore.
Includes bibliographical references

Cheung, Hyechong
K is for Korea; [by] Hyechong Chung, Prodeepta Das. Frances Lincoln 2008 un il $16.95
Grades: K 1 2 3   **951.9**
1. Alphabet 2. Korea
ISBN 978-1-84507-789-1; 1-84507-789-X
"This attractive book presents several aspects of Korea: its culture, traditional practices, national treasures, wildlife, food, and dress. Nicely designed pages showcase the excellent color photos. . . . Although other books speak more precisely of South Korea, North Korea, and the Korean peninsula, few are as accessible to primary-grade children as this one." Booklist

Santella, Andrew
The **Korean** War; by Andrew Santella. Compass Point Books 2007 48p il map (We the people) lib bdg $25.26; pa $8.95
Grades: 4 5 6 7   **951.9**
1. Korean War, 1950-1953
ISBN 978-0-7565-2027-4 lib bdg; 0-7565-2027-4 lib bdg; 978-0-7565-2039-7 pa; 0-7565-2039-8 pa
LC 2006006767
This "begins by explaining how North and South Korea became divided; the involvement of the United Nations and the United States; conflict between President Harry Truman and General Douglas MacArthur; eventual peace talks; and the division still occurring today. Accessible and straightforward, this book is an excellent one for the intended audience." SLJ
Includes bibliographical references

951.93 North Korea (People's Democratic Republic of Korea)

Kummer, Patricia K.
North Korea; by Patricia K. Kummer. Children's Press 2008 144p il map (Enchantment of the world, second series) lib bdg $38
Grades: 5 6 7 8 9   **951.93**
1. Korea (North)
ISBN 978-0-531-18485-1 lib bdg; 0-531-18485-4 lib bdg
LC 2007025693

In this introduction to North Korea "geography is the focus, but Kummer also discusses ancient and recent history, . . . the economy, religion, sports, education, and more. Without discounting the rich culture, the book doesn't shy away from more sensitive issues. . . . The open design will draw readers, with clear type on thick, high-quality paper; numerous maps and color photos and spacious back matter are also included." Booklist

Includes bibliographical references

Sonneborn, Liz

North Korea; by Liz Sonneborn. Children's Press; an imprint of Scholastic Inc. 2014 144 p. illustrations. maps (Enchantment of the world. Second series) (library binding) $40

Grades: 5 6 7 8 **951.93**
1. Korea (North)
ISBN 0531236781; 9780531236789

LC 2013003650

This book, by Liz Sonneborn, is part of the Enchantment of the World Series. "Each volume has been completely rewritten from a previous edition. . . . 'North Korea' has a new author and a strong political focus, discussing life under the new leader, Kim Jong-un. . . . Each volume in this . . . series includes extensive back matter with a detailed index." (Booklist)

Includes bibliographical references and index

951.95 South Korea (Republic of Korea)

Ryan, Patrick

Welcome to South Korea; by Patrick Ryan. The Child's World 2008 32p il map (Welcome to the world) lib bdg $27.07

Grades: 1 2 3 4 **951.95**
1. Korea (South)
ISBN 978-1-59296-978-4 lib bdg; 1-59296-978-X lib bdg

LC 2007036354

This briefly describes the geography, history, people, and culture of South Korea.

"Report writers and browsers will appreciate [this book]. . . . The captioned, color photographs have a balanced gender representation. Maps, fast facts, and recipes round out excellent offerings." SLJ

Includes glossary and bibliographical references

952 Japan

★ Art and life in rural Japan; Toho village through the eyes of its youth. Rolbin, Cyrus, editor. Next Generation Press 2011 176p il map $29.95; pa $24.95

Grades: 3 4 5 6 **952**
1. Japan 2. Country life -- Japan 3. Bilingual books -- English-Japanese
ISBN 978-0-9815595-4-4; 978-0-9815595-3-7 pa

"This gem of a book takes readers . . . into a small mountain community. . . . Simple, often poignant sentences in English and Japanese tell Toho's story, rich in history and culture. Stunning, full-color pictures capture verdant rice fields, jubilant school scenes, a lively festival, and expressive portraits of Toho's citizens. . . . A fascinating window into a vanishing way of life, this book holds appeal for both pleasure reading and reports." SLJ

Blumberg, Rhoda

★ Commodore Perry in the land of the Shogun. Lothrop, Lee & Shepard Bks. 1985 144p il map $21.99; pa $8.99

Grades: 5 6 7 8 **952**
1. Naval officers 2. Japan -- History 3. Japan -- Foreign relations -- United States 4. United States -- Foreign relations -- Japan 5. United States Naval Expedition to Japan (1852-1854)
ISBN 0-688-03723-2; 0-06-008625-4 pa

LC 84-21800

A Newbery Medal honor book, 1986

This "is a well-written story of Matthew Perry's expedition to open Japan to American trade and whaling ports. The account is sensitive to the extreme cultural differences that both the Japanese and Americans had to overcome. Especially good are the chapters and paragraphs explaining Japanese feudal society and culture. The text is marvelously complemented by the illustrations, almost all reproductions of contemporary Japanese art." SLJ

Includes bibliographical references

Moore, Willamarie

All about Japan; stories, songs, crafts, and more. illustrated by Kazumi Wilds. Tuttle Pub. 2011 63p il $16.95

Grades: 3 4 5 6 **952**
1. Japan
ISBN 978-4-8053-1077-9; 4-8053-1077-4

LC 2010040843

"In this treasure-trove of information, two children, one a Tokyo urbanite and the other from a rural village, introduce readers to their country and its culture, including geography, language, traditional arts, costume, etiquette, sports, and festivals. The dual narrators' conversational descriptions of their homes and daily routines will engage young readers while highlighting the differences between the Westernized big-city existence and the traditional way of life in Japan's countryside, deftly demonstrating the rich variety of lifestyles within this island nation. The scope of this book is remarkably comprehensive, covering almost anything a child would want to know." SLJ

Includes bibliographical references

Phillips, Charles

★ Japan; [by] Charles Phillips; Gil Latz and Kyohei Shibata, consultants. National Geographic 2007 64p il map (Countries on the world) lib bdg $27.90

Grades: 4 5 6 7 **952**
1. Japan
ISBN 1-4263-0029-8 lib bdg; 978-1-4263-0029-5 lib bdg

LC 2007296571

A basic overview of the history, geography, climate and culture of Japan.

This "clear, succinct [overview] will support assignments without overwhelming casual readers. . . . A good selection of recent, high quality color photographs gives the [book] visual appeal." SLJ

Includes glossary and bibliographical references

Riggs, Kate

Samurai. Creative Education 2011 24p il (Great warriors) $16.95; pa $8.99

Grades: K 1 2 **952**
1. Samurai
ISBN 978-1-60818-003-5; 1-60818-003-4; 978-0-89812-574-0 pa; 0-89812-574-X pa

LC 2010019612

A simple introduction to the Japanese warriors known as samurai, including their history, lifestyle, weapons, and how they remain a part of today's culture through the martial arts

This title makes samurai "accessible to students just beginning to read on their own. The text and design of the [book is] spare, and vocabulary words are introduced unobtrusively. . . . The concepts are simple, but introduced without oversimplification that might lead to misunderstandings. [This is an] excellent [introduction] and fun to read aloud." SLJ

Includes glossary and bibliographical references

Somervill, Barbara A.

Japan; by Barbara A. Somervill. Children's Press 2012 144 p. ill., maps (library) $40

Grades: 5 6 7 8   **952**

1. Japan   2. Japan -- Social life and customs

ISBN 0531253546; 9780531253540

            LC 2011009503

This book is part of the Enchantment of the World series and focuses on Japan. "Topics such as climate, wildlife, history, government, pop culture, and the arts are all addressed, providing a . . . look at Japan's past and present. With content revised considerably from previous editions, this book goes beyond facts and statistics to give readers an intimate glimpse at typical Japanese youth through fictionalized anecdotes detailing moments in their daily lives." (School Library Journal)

Includes bibliographical references and index.

Takabayashi, Mari

★ I live in Tokyo; written & illustrated by Mari Takabayashi. Houghton Mifflin 2001 un il map $16

Grades: K 1 2 3   **952**

1. Tokyo (Japan) 2. Japan -- Social life and customs

ISBN 0-618-07702-2

            LC 00-5964

"Seven-year-old narrator Mimiko takes readers on a month-by-month tour of contemporary Tokyo, briefly describing one or two festivals, customs, or facets of life each month. The narrative remains consistently childlike throughout. . . . This book is a model of efficiency and elegance, cramming numerous details into a small space in a compact and attractive manner." Horn Book

953   Arabian Peninsula and adjacent areas

King, David C.

★ The United Arab Emirates; [by] David C. King. 2nd ed; Marshall Cavendish Benchmark 2008 144p il map (Cultures of the world) lib bdg $42.79

Grades: 5 6 7 8   **953**

1. United Arab Emirates

ISBN 978-0-7614-2565-6

            LC 2006030237

This describes the geography, history, government, economy, environment, people, and culture of the United Arab Emirates.

Includes glossary and bibliographical references

953.3   Yemen

Hestler, Anna

Yemen; by Anna Hestler and Jo-Ann Spilling. 2nd ed.; Marshall Cavendish Benchmark 2010 144p il map (Cultures of the world) lib bdg $42.79

Grades: 5 6 7 8   **953.3**

1. Yemen

ISBN 978-0-7614-4850-1 lib bdg; 0-7614-4850-0 lib bdg

            LC 2009021200

First published 1999

This describes the geography, history, wildlife, governmental structure, economy, cultural diversity, peoples, religion, and culture of Yemen

Includes glossary and bibliographical references

O'Neal, Claire

We visit Yemen; by Claire O'Neal. Mitchell Lane Publishers 2012 63 p. ill. (chiefly col.), col. maps (library) $33.95; (ebook) $33.95

Grades: 4 5 6 7 8   **953.3**

1. Yemen -- Description and travel   2. Yemen (Republic) 3. Yemen (Republic)

ISBN 1584159618; 1612281060; 9781584159612; 9781612281063

            LC 2011016773

This book on Yemen by Claire O'Neal is part of the "Your Land and My Land: The Middle East" series, which "provides an . . . introduction to the history and geography of several Middle Eastern and Southeast Asian countries from a tourist's perspective." Also included are a "recipe and a . . . craft project representing the country." (Booklist)

Includes bibliographical references and index.

953.53   Oman

Ejaz, Khadija

We visit Oman; by Khadija Ejaz. Mitchell Lane Publishers 2012 63 p. col. ill., col. maps (library) $33.95; (ebook) $33.95

Grades: 4 5 6 7 8   **953.53**

1. Oman -- Description and travel

ISBN 1584159626; 1612281044; 9781584159629; 9781612281049

            LC 2011000724

This book on Oman by Khadija Ejaz is part of the "Your Land and My Land: The Middle East" series, which "provides an . . . introduction to the history and geography of several Middle Eastern and Southeast Asian countries from a tourist's perspective." Also included are a "recipe and a . . . craft project representing the country." (Booklist)

Includes bibliographical references (p. 59-61) and index.

953.6   Persian Gulf States

Cooper, Robert

Bahrain; [by] Robert Cooper and Jo-Ann Spilling. 2nd ed.; Marshall Cavendish Benchmark 2011 144p il map (Cultures of the world) lib bdg $42.79

Grades: 5 6 7 8   **953.6**

1. Bahrain

ISBN 978-1-6087-0213-8; 1-6087-0213-8

            LC 2010019621

First published 2000

Provides information on the geography, history, wildlife, governmental structure, economy, cultural diversity, peoples, religion, and culture of Bahrain.

Includes glossary and bibliographical references

Orr, Tamra

Qatar; [by] Tamra Orr. Marshall Cavendish Benchmark 2008 144p il map (Cultures of the world) lib bdg $42.79

Grades: 5 6 7 8   **953.6**

1. Qatar

ISBN 978-0-7614-2566-3; 0-7614-2566-7

            LC 2006033626

This describes the geography, history, government, economy, environment, people, and culture of Qatar

Includes glossary and bibliographical references

953.67 Kuwait

O'Shea, Maria

Kuwait; by Maria O'Shea and Michael Spilling. 2nd ed.; Marshall Cavendish Benchmark 2010 144p il map (Cultures of the world) lib bdg $42.79

Grades: 5 6 7 8   953.67

1. Kuwait

ISBN 978-0-7614-4479-4 lib bdg; 0-7614-4479-3 lib bdg

LC 2009007069

First published 1999

Provides information on the geography, history, wildlife, governmental structure, economy, cultural diversity, peoples, religion, and culture of Kuwait

Includes glossary and bibliographical references

Sonneborn, Liz

Kuwait; Enchantment of the World. by Liz Sonneborn. Children's Press, an imprint of Scholastic Inc. 2014 144 p. ill., maps. (library binding) $40

Grades: 5 6 7 8   953.67

1. Kuwait

ISBN 053122015X; 9780531220153

LC 2013026062

This book, by Liz Sonneborn, focuses on Kuwait. The book discusses the "country's culture, history, and geography are explored in detail, allowing readers a chance to see how people live. . . . Sidebars highlight especially interesting people, places, and events . . . [and] easy recipes give readers the opportunity to experience foreign cuisine first-hand." (Publisher's note)

"Many students turn to the Internet for writing reports, but for reliably accurate, attractively presented and well-calibrated information, the long-standing Enchantment of the World series remains a superior choice. Each volume has been completely rewritten from a previous edition—in many cases to startling effect given recent political events. Although the basic structure holds true to past versions, the updated photographs are truly eye-popping and take care to portray the countries as modern often opting for showing, say, a surgeon at work rather than a rural farmer. It might not be necessary for libraries to replace [this title], since it hasn't changed radically, but this is a solid offering with updated statistics. Each volume in this reliable series includes extensive back matter with a detailed index." Booklist

Includes bibliographical references and index

Tracy, Kathleen

We visit Kuwait; by Kathleen Tracy. Mitchell Lane Publishers 2012 63 p. ill. (chiefly col.), col. maps (Your land and my land. The Middle East) (library bound) $33.95; (ebook) $33.95

Grades: 4 5 6 7 8   953.67

1. Kuwait -- Description and travel

ISBN 1584159588; 1612281001; 9781584159582; 9781612281001

LC 2011002756

This book on Kuwait by Kathleen Tracy is part of the "Your Land and My Land: The Middle East" series, which "provides an . . . introduction to the history and geography of several Middle Eastern and Southeast Asian countries from a tourist's perspective." Also included are a "recipe and a . . . craft project representing the country." (Booklist)

Includes bibliographical references (p. 58-61) and index.

953.8 Saudi Arabia

Klepeis, Alicia Z.

Understanding Saudi Arabia today; Alicia Klepeis. Mitchell Lane Publishers 2014 63 p. (library bound) $33.95

Grades: 4 5 6 7   953.8

1. Saudi Arabia

ISBN 1612286518; 9781612286518

LC 2014020464

This book on Saudi Arabia by Alicia Klepeis is part of the "A Kid's Guide to the Middle East" series. It "explores the Middle Eastern nation of Saudi Arabia with a focus on the country as it is today: current issues, culture, and lifestyle." It "includes a native recipe and craft for students to create. Elementary students are encouraged to consider evidence from informational texts to support analysis, reflection, and research." (Publisher's note)

"Trying to sort through the Middle East can be difficult for even the most educated adults, but the titles in A Kid's Guide to the Middle East series breaks down the culture and ongoing conflict into manageable portions. . . . Understanding Saudi Arabia Today describes its transition from desert nomads to skyscrapers, the importance of Islam, and the benefits and challenges of being an oil-producing country. Extensive back matter includes a recipe, craft, time line, glossary, and area facts. An essential series to help children appreciate and understand the rich diversity of this region." Booklist

Includes bibliographical references and index

Tracy, Kathleen

We visit Saudi Arabia; by Kathleen Tracy. Mitchell Lane Publishers 2011 63 p. col. ill., map (library) $33.95

Grades: 4 5 6 7 8   953.8

1. Persian Gulf region 2. Saudi Arabia

ISBN 1584159634; 9781584159636

LC 2011000728

This book by Kathleen Tracy is part of the Social Studies series and looks at Saudi Arabia. "One of the most socially conservative countries on earth, Saudi Arabia is defined by Islam and ancient traditions. At the same time, its vast oil fields have helped build glistening, modern cities filled with world-class restaurants and designer shops." (Publisher's note)

Includes bibliographical references and index.

954 India and neighboring south Asian countries

Apte, Sunita

India. Children's Press 2009 48p il map (True book) lib bdg $26

Grades: 3 4 5   954

1. India

ISBN 978-0-531-16890-5 lib bdg; 0-531-16890-5 lib bdg

LC 2008014786

This "attractive [work covers] the geography, history, people, customs, and economy of [India]. . . . [The book has] large-size print and colorful pictures. [It] contains a section about current political challenges such as the recent terrorist attacks in Mumbai, India." SLJ

Includes glossary and bibliographical references

Arnold, Caroline

★ Taj Mahal; by Caroline Arnold and Madeleine Comora; illustrated by Rahul Bhushan. Carolrhoda Books 2007 un il lib bdg $17.95

Grades: 4 5 6 7   954

1. Mogul Empire 2. Taj Mahal (Agra, India)

ISBN 978-0-7613-2609-0 lib bdg; 0-7613-2609-X lib bdg

LC 2001006685

Recounts the love story behind the building of the Taj Mahal in India, discussing how it was constructed and providing information on Indian culture.

"The small, detailed paintings are . . . set on beautifully constructed pages resembling those of illuminated manuscripts. . . . The book is sumptuous in appearance and presents a bit of history not often told for children." SLJ

Dalal, A. Kamala

★ **India**; [by] A. Kamala Dalal; Ramesh C. Dhussa and Pradyumna P. Karan, consultants. National Geographic 2007 64p il map (Countries of the world) lib bdg $27.90

Grades: 4 5 6 7   **954**

1. India

ISBN 978-1-4263-0127-8 lib bdg; 1-4263-0127-8 lib bdg

LC 2007039552

This describes the geography, nature, history, people and culture, government and economy of India

"What helps [this book] stand out from the pack is [its] high-quality, rich photography. . . . The photos provide as much information as the [text]. . . . The writing is straightforward and solid." SLJ

Includes glossary and bibliographical references

Mann, Elizabeth

★ **Taj** Mahal; a story of love and empire. by Elizabeth Mann; with illustrations by Alan Witschonke. Mikaya 2008 47p il (Wonders of the world) $22.95

Grades: 4 5 6 7   **954**

1. Mogul Empire 2. Taj Mahal (Agra, India)

ISBN 1-931414-20-3; 978-1-931414-20-3

LC 2008060054

This is a "dramatic retelling of the construction of the Taj Mahal. Mann begins with two pages of prose that relay the commonly told legend, but then proceeds to explode that legend with descriptive writing, colorful illustrations, ancient paintings, maps, and photographs." Booklist

Includes bibliographical references

954.03   India--Period of British rule, 1785-1947

McGinty, Alice B.

Gandhi. Amazon Childrens Pub 2013 40 p. (hardcover) $17.99

Grades: 1 2 3 4 5   **954.03**

1. Civil disobedience 2. India -- History -- 1765-1947, British occupation

ISBN 1477816445; 9781477816448

This children's picture book by Alice B. McGinty "tells . . . [the] present-tense story of Mohandas Gandhi's 24-day march to the sea in 1930 in search of freedom and peaceful change for the people of India. . . . His goal is to challenge 200 years of British rule by breaking the law prohibiting Indians from collecting salt from the sea." (Kirkus Reviews)

954.9   Other jurisdictions

NgCheong-Lum, Roseline, 1962-

Maldives; 2nd ed.; Marshall Cavendish Benchmark 2011 144p il map (Cultures of the world) lib bdg $42.79

Grades: 5 6 7 8   **954.9**

1. Maldives

ISBN 978-1-6087-0217-6; 1-6087-0217-0

LC 2010019746

First published 2001

Provides information on the geography, history, wildlife, governmental structure, economy, cultural diversity, peoples, religion, and culture of Maldives.

Includes glossary and bibliographical references

Taylor-Butler, Christine

Sacred mountain; Everest. Lee & Low Books 2009 48p il $19.95

Grades: 5 6 7 8   **954.9**

1. Mount Everest (China and Nepal)

ISBN 978-1-60060-255-9; 1-60060-255-X

LC 2008-30423

"The informative text is amply illustrated with well-chosen black-and-white and color photographs." SLJ

Includes glossary

954.91   Pakistan

Hinman, Bonnie

We visit Pakistan; by Bonnie Hinman. Mitchell Lane Publishers 2012 63 p. ill. (chiefly col.), col. maps (Your land and my land. The Middle East) (library) $33.95

Grades: 4 5 6 7 8   **954.91**

1. Pakistan

ISBN 158415960X; 9781584159605

LC 2011030763

This book on Pakistan by Bonnie Hinman is part of the "Your Land and My Land: The Middle East" series, which "provides an . . . introduction to the history and geography of several Middle Eastern and Southeast Asian countries from a tourist's perspective." Topics such as "terrorism and al-Qaeda" are covered along with "descriptions of the country's history and attractions." Also included are a "recipe and a . . . craft project representing the country." (Booklist)

Includes bibliographical references (p. 59-61) and index.

Kwek, Karen

Pakistan; [written by Karen Kwek and Jameel Haque] Marshall Cavendish Benchmark 2010 48p il map (Welcome to my country) $19.95

Grades: 2 3 4 5   **954.91**

1. Pakistan

ISBN 978-1-60870-158-2; 1-60870-158-1

This is an introduction to Pakistan's culture, history, sports, religions, and foods.

"Beautifully illustrated. . . . The writing is clear. . . . [This title] will work well for reports and will be enjoyed by browsers." SLJ

Includes glossary and bibliographical references

Sonneborn, Liz

Pakistan; by Liz Sonneborn. Children's Press 2013 144 p. ill. (mostly col.), col. maps. (Enchantment of the world, second series) (library) $40

Grades: 5 6 7 8   **954.91**

1. Pakistan -- Description and travel

ISBN 0531275442; 9780531275443

LC 2012000505

This book, by Liz Sonneborn, is part of the "Enchantment of the World" series. In it the author provides information and photographs showcasing the people, places and events surrounding the South Asian country of Pakistan. Contents include photographs of Pakistani cities and landscapes, statistics describing the nation's features, and traditional Pakistani recipes.

Includes bibliographical references and index

954.92   Bangladesh

March, Michael

Bangladesh. Sea-to-sea Publications 2009 32p il map (Facts about countries) $28.50

Grades: 3 4 5   **954.92**

1. Bangladesh

ISBN 978-1-59771-113-5; 1-59771-113-6

Describes the geography, history, industries, education, government, and cultures of Bangladesh

"The attractive layout includes color photographs and charts of current statistics as well as maps illustrating main farming regions, natural resources, or the literacy rates of girls and boys. The [text is] clear and succinct." SLJ

Includes glossary

955   Iran

DiPrimio, Pete

We visit Iran; by Pete DiPrimio. Mitchell Lane Publishers 2012 63 p. col. ill., maps (library) $33.95

Grades: 4 5 6 7 8   **955**

1. Iran -- History

ISBN 1584159545; 9781584159544

LC 2011016765

This book by Pete DiPrimio looks at Iran. "It is a Middle Eastern country with European (not Arabian) founders. It was the home of one of the ancient world's greatest empires, the Persian Empire. Its many ancient ruins include the palace complex of Persepolis, which was so big it took 150 years to finish. While the nation develops nuclear technology, its government—called an Islamic Republic—dictates people's lives, from the clothing they wear to the news they hear." (Publisher's note)

Includes bibliographical references and index.

Mara, Wil

Iran; [by] Wil Mara. Marshall Cavendish Benchmark 2007 48p il map (Discovering cultures) lib bdg $28.50

Grades: 2 3 4   **955**

1. Iran

ISBN 978-0-7614-1986-0 lib bdg; 0-7614-1986-1 lib bdg

LC 2006011476

An introduction to the geography, history, people, and culture of Iran

Includes glossary and bibliographical references

956.04   Middle East--1945-1980

Marx, Trish

★ **Sharing** our homeland; Palestinian and Jewish Children at summer Peace Camp. photographs by Cindy Karp. Lee & Low Books 2010 47p il $19.95

Grades: 3 4 5 6   **956.04**

1. Palestinian Arabs 2. Jewish-Arab relations 3. Israel

ISBN 978-158430-260-5; 1-58430-260-7

"Alya, an Israeli Palestinian girl in a Muslim family, chooses to wear a hijab. Yuval, an Israeli Jewish boy, lives in a moshav farming community. In this picture-book photo-essay, crisp color images show the kids at home and then having fun at Peace Camp, where they swim, make arts and crafts, and do other universal summer-camp activities. Field trips introduce some kids to places they've never been, including a museum, a kibbutz, and an Arab village. . . . Marx weaves in detailed history of the Holy Land, from ancient times to 1948 and the establishment of the Jewish state and then the 1967 War. Throughout, she is frank about the continuing violence and conflict, and a contemporary image shows that the tall West Bank safety wall is also a divider between cultures. Realistic and upbeat, this moves beyond stereotypes and notions of the 'other.'" Booklist

Senker, Cath

The **Arab**-Israeli conflict; [by] Cath Senker. new ed.; Arcturus Pub. 2008 48p il map (Timelines) lib bdg $32.80

Grades: 5 6 7 8   **956.04**

1. Israel-Arab conflicts

ISBN 978-1-84193-725-0 lib bdg; 1-84193-725-8 lib bdg

LC 2007-7547

First published 2005 by Smart Apple Media

This describes current conditions in Israel and the occupied territories and includes a history of major events and political developments.

"A complex situation is clearly explained. . . . [This is] well-illustrated. . . . Throughout, the tone is nonjudgmental." SLJ [review of 2005 edition]

Includes bibliographical references

956.1   Turkey

LaRoche, Amelia

We visit Turkey; by Amelia LaRoche. Mitchell Lane Publishers 2012 63 p. ill. (chiefly col.), col. maps (library) $33.95

Grades: 4 5 6 7 8   **956.1**

1. Turkey -- Description and travel

ISBN 1584159561; 9781584159568

LC 2011030765

This book on Turkey by Amelia Laroche is part of the "Your Land and My Land: The Middle East" series, which "provides an . . . introduction to the history and geography of several Middle Eastern and Southeast Asian countries from a tourist's perspective." It "similarly mentions but does not dwell upon the rise of Islam and the hijab controversy." Also included are a "recipe and a . . . craft project representing the country." (Booklist)

Includes bibliographical references (p, 59-61) and index.

Shields, Sarah D.

★ **Turkey**; [by] Sarah Shields. National Geographic 2009 64p il map (Countries of the world) lib bdg $27.90

Grades: 4 5 6 7   **956.1**

1. Turkey

ISBN 978-1-4263-0387-6 lib bdg; 1-4263-0387-4 lib bdg

LC 2009275583

This describes the geography, nature, history, people and culture, government and economy of Turkey

Includes glossary and bibliographical references

956.7   Iraq

Falvey, David

Letters to a soldier; by First Lieutenant David Falvey and Mrs. Julie Hutt's fourth-grade class. Marshall Cavendish Children 2009 un il $16.99

Grades: 3 4 5   **956.7**

1. Soldiers 2. Children's writings 3. Contractors 4. Army officers 5. Iraq War, 2003- -- Personal narratives

ISBN 978-0-7614-5637-7; 0-7614-5637-6

LC 2008050268

"While serving in Iraq in 2008, First Lieutenant David Falvey received a packet of letters from Julie Hutt's fourth-grade class in Roslyn, NY. The children's correspondences and drawings, paired with Falvey's thoughtful answers and photographs from his deployment, are reproduced in an inviting, child-friendly format." SLJ

Goldish, Meish

Baghdad pups. Bearport Pub. 2011 32p il (Dog heroes) lib bdg $25.27

Grades: 3 4 5 **956.7**

1. Dogs 2. Iraq War, 2003- -- Personal narratives

ISBN 978-1-6177-2150-2; 1-6177-2150-6

LC 2010035187

This book "explores how a special division of the Society for the Prevention of Cruelty to Animals International (SPCAI) has been rescuing dogs who have befriended service people in Iraq, despite the clear disapproval of the United States military, which has strict laws about removing property, including animals, from war zones. . . . [This book is] engaging not just because the content is so compelling, but also because the [author has] highlighted specific dogs currently working in [this field]. The use of real names and full-color photographs on every page, many contributed by the individuals who work with these dogs, makes reading [this book] a personal experience. . . . [An] excellent [introduction] to [this] new [development] in service-dog training." SLJ

Includes bibliographical references

Malhotra, Sonali

Iraq. Marshall Cavendish Benchmark 2010 48p il map (Welcome to my country) $19.99

Grades: 2 3 4 5 **956.7**

1. Iraq

ISBN 978-1-60870-155-1; 1-60870-155-7

LC 2010006405

An overview of the history, geography, government, economy, language, people, and culture of Iraq.

"Beautifully illustrated. . . . The writing is clear. . . . [This title] will work well for reports and will be enjoyed by browsers." SLJ

Includes glossary and bibliographical references

O'Neal, Claire

We visit Iraq; by Claire O'Neal. Mitchell Lane Publishers 2012 63 p. ill. (chiefly col.), col. maps (library bound) $33.95

Grades: 4 5 6 7 8 **956.7**

1. Persian Gulf region 2. Iraq

ISBN 1584159553; 9781584159551

LC 2011016771

This book by Claire O'Neal is part of the Social Studies series and looks at Iraq. "Iraq's Tigris and Euphrates rivers turned this Middle Eastern desert into the world's first farmland. Over six millenia, Iraq's civilizations have laid foundations for the rest of the world. They built great stone ziggurats and soaring mosques. They invented the wheel, the calendar, and the written word. With their riches, they also attracted war." (Publisher's note)

Includes bibliographical references (p. 59-61) and index.

Samuels, Charlie

★ **Iraq**; [by] Charlie Samuels; Sarah Shields and Shakir Mustafa, consultants. National Geographic 2007 64p il map (Countries of the world) lib bdg $27.90

Grades: 4 5 6 7 **956.7**

1. Iraq

ISBN 978-1-4263-0061-5

LC 2007024675

This describes the geography, nature, history, people and culture, government and economy of Iraq.

Includes glossary and bibliographical references

Wilkes, Sybella

Out of Iraq; refugees' stories in words, paintings and music. Evans 2010 70p il map $17.99

Grades: 4 5 6 7 **956.7**

1. Refugees 2. Iraq

ISBN 978-0-237-53930-6; 0-237-53930-6

"Provides an concise overview of events before and during the invasion, interspersed with first-person narratives of Iraqi refugees, gathered while Wilkes worked with the United Nations Refugee Agency in Syria. . . . Moving photographs and artwork, quotations from political figures, and accessible language form a harrowing window into lives rarely paid witness." Publ Wkly

956.91 Syria

Yomtov, Nel

Syria; Nel Yomtov. Children's Press, an imprint of Scholastic Inc. 2013 144 p. color illustrations (library binding) $40

Grades: 5 6 7 8 **956.91**

1. Syria

ISBN 053123679X; 9780531236796

LC 2013000088

This book, by Nel Yomtov, focuses on Syria. The "country's culture, history, and geography are explored in detail, allowing readers a chance to see how people live. . . . Sidebars highlight especially interesting people, places, and events [and] recipes give readers the opportunity to experience foreign cuisine first-hand." (Publisher's note)

"Many students turn to the Internet for writing reports, but for reliably accurate, attractively presented and well-calibrated information, the long-standing Enchantment of the World series remains a superior choice. Each volume has been completely rewritten from a previous edition—in many cases to startling effect given recent political events. Although the basic structure holds true to past versions, the updated photographs are truly eye-popping and take care to portray the countries as modern—often opting for showing, say, a surgeon at work rather than a rural farmer. Syria obviously can't be completely up-to-date because of the ongoing rebellion, but it does a good job of explaining the roots of the unrest, along with the usual topics of food, religion, and customs. Each volume in this reliable series includes extensive back matter with a detailed index." Booklist

Includes bibliographical references and index

956.92 Lebanon

Perdew, Laura

Understanding Lebanon today; by Laura Perdew. Mitchell Lane Publishers 2015 63 p. col. ill., col map (A kid's guide to the Middle East) (library bound) $33.95

Grades: 4 5 6 7 **956.92**

1. Lebanon

ISBN 1612286534; 9781612286532

LC 2014008837

This children's book by Laura Perdew "is an accurate and contemporary presentation that explores the Middle Eastern nation of Lebanon with a focus on the country as it is today: current issues, culture, and lifestyle." (Publisher's note)

"Understanding Lebanon Today discusses the first prosperous civilization, established by the Phoenicians, and the sectarian tension that currently threatens peace. Extensive back matter includes a recipe, craft, time line, glossary, and area facts." Booklist

Includes bibliographical references and index

Sheehan, Sean

Lebanon; [by] Sean Sheehan & Zawiah Abdul Latif. 2nd ed.; Marshall Cavendish Benchmark 2008 144p il map (Cultures of the world) lib bdg $42.79

Grades: 5 6 7 8   956.92

1. Lebanon

ISBN 978-0-7614-2081-1 lib bdg; 0-7614-2081-9 lib bdg

LC 2006101735

First published 1997

"Provides comprehensive information on the geography, history, wildlife, governmental structure, economy, cultural diversity, peoples, religion, and culture of Lebanon." Publisher's note

Includes bibliographical references

956.93   Cyprus

Spilling, Michael

Cyprus; [by] Michael Spilling and Jo-Ann Spilling. 2nd ed.; Marshall Cavendish Benchmark 2010 144p il map (Cultures of the world) lib bdg $42.79

Grades: 5 6 7 8   956.93

1. Cyprus

ISBN 978-0-7614-4855-6 lib bdg; 0-7614-4855-1 lib bdg

LC 2009045689

First published 2000

This offers information on the geography, history, wildlife, governmental structure, economy, cultural diversity, peoples, religion, and culture of Cyprus

Includes glossary and bibliographical references

956.94   Palestine; Israel

Bowden, Rob, 1973-

Jerusalem; [by] Rob Bowden. World Almanac Library 2006 48p il map (Great cities of the world) lib bdg $31

Grades: 3 4 5 6   956.94

1. Jerusalem

ISBN 0-8368-5051-3

LC 2005043586

This describes the geography, cultures, work, play, history, and religions of Jerusalem

This is "attractive, informative . . . straightforward and objective." SLJ

Includes bibliographical references

Ellis, Deborah

Three wishes; Palestinian and Israeli children speak. Groundwood Bks. 2004 110p il map hardcover o.p. pa $9.99

Grades: 5 6 7 8   956.94

1. Palestinian Arabs 2. Israel-Arab conflicts

ISBN 0-88899-608-X; 0-88899-645-4 pa

"An excellent presentation of a confusing historic struggle, told within a palpable, perceptive and empathetic format." SLJ

Includes bibliographical references

Saul, Laya

We visit Israel; by Laya Saul. Mitchell Lane Publishers 2012 63 p. ill., maps (library) $33.95

Grades: 4 5 6 7 8   956.94

1. Israel -- Description and travel

ISBN 158415957X; 9781584159575

LC 2011024706

This book on Israel by Laya Saul is part of the "Your Land and My Land: The Middle East" series, which "provides an . . . introduction to the history and geography of several Middle Eastern and Southeast Asian countries from a tourist's perspective. . . . 'We Visit Israel' is clearly written from a Jewish Israeli perspective, but Saul makes sure to mention areas of conflict and controversy." Also included are a "recipe and a . . . craft project representing the country." (Booklist)

Includes bibliographical references (p. 60-61) and index.

Young, Emma

★ Israel; [by] Emma Young; Zvi Ben-Dor Benite, George Kanazi, and Aviva Halamish, consultants. National Geographic 2008 64p il map (Countries of the world) lib bdg $27.90

Grades: 4 5 6 7   956.94

1. Israel

ISBN 978-1-4263-0258-9 lib bdg; 1-4263-0258-4 lib bdg

This describes the geography, nature, history, people and culture, government, and economy of Israel.

Includes glossary and bibliographical references

956.95   Jordan and West Bank

Lusted, Marcia Amidon

Understanding Palestine today; by Marcia Amidon Lusted. Mitchell Lane Publishers 2015 63 p. col. ill., col. map (A kid's guide to the Middle East) (library bound) $33.95

Grades: 4 5 6 7   956.95

1. Palestine

ISBN 1612286550; 9781612286556

LC 2014008838

This book, by Marcia Amidon Lusted "is an accurate and contemporary presentation that explores the Middle Eastern nation of Lebanon with a focus on the country as it is today: current issues, culture, and lifestyle." (Publisher's note)

"Understanding Palestine Today explains the area's legacy as a sacred religious crossroad, the creation of Israel, and why violence continues between Israel and Palestine. Extensive back matter includes a recipe, craft, time line, glossary, and area facts." Booklist

Includes bibliographical references and index

Perdew, Laura

Understanding Jordan today; by Laura Perdew. Mitchell Lane Publishers 2014 63 p. (A kid's guide to the Middle East) $33.95

Grades: 4 5 6 7   956.95

1. Jordan

ISBN 1612286542; 9781612286549

LC 2014020462

This children's book, by Laura Perdew, part of the "Kid's Guide to the Middle East" series, "is an accurate and contemporary presentation that explores the Middle Eastern nation of Jordan with a focus on the country as it is today: current issues, culture, and lifestyle. The book is written in an easy-to-read enjoyable narrative form for elementary readers grades 3-6." (Publisher's note)

"Trying to sort through the Middle East can be difficult for even the most educated adults, but the titles in A Kid's Guide to the Middle East series breaks down the culture and ongoing conflict into manageable portions...Extensive back matter includes a recipe, craft, time line, glossary, and area facts. An essential series to help children appreciate and understand the rich diversity of this region." Booklist

Includes bibliographical references and index

Other recommended titles in the series are:

Understanding Afghanistan Today (2014)
Understanding Iran Today (2014)
Understanding Iraq Today (2014)
Understanding Israel Today (2014)
Understanding Lebanon Today (2015)
Understanding Palestine Today (2015)
Understanding Saudi Arabia Today (2014)
Understanding Syria Today (2014)
Understanding Turkey Today (2015)

958.1   Afghanistan

Ali, Sharifah Enayat

Afghanistan; by Sharifah Enayat Ali. 2nd ed.; Marshall Cavendish Benchmark 2006 144p il map (Cultures of the world) lib bdg $42.79

Grades: 5 6 7 8   **958.1**

1. Afghanistan

ISBN 978-0-7614-2064-4 lib bdg; 0-7614-2064-9 lib bdg

LC 2005034789

First published 1995

This is "well organized, informative, and entertaining. . . . Excellent-quality full-color photographs and reproductions show the people, landforms, buildings, and everyday activities of [Afghanistan]." SLJ [review of 1995 edtion]

Includes glossary and bibliographical references

Bjorklund, Ruth

Afghanistan; by Ruth Bjorklund. Children's Press 2012 144 p. col. ill., col. maps (library) $40

Grades: 5 6 7 8   **958.1**

1. Afghanistan -- Description and travel

ISBN 0531253503; 9780531253502

LC 2011013627

This book by Ruth Bjorklund is part of the Enchantment of the World series and looks at Afghanistan. In each book, "colourful photos provide . . . views of foreign cities and landscapes," "sidebars highlight especially interesting people, places, and events," and "recipes give readers the opportunity to experience foreign cuisine firsthand." (Publisher's note)

Includes bibliographical references (p. 134-135) and index.

Fordyce, Deborah

Afghanistan; [written by Deborah Fordyce] Marshall Cavendish Benchmark 2010 48p il map (Welcome to my country) $19.95

Grades: 2 3 4 5   **958.1**

1. Afghanistan

ISBN 978-1-60870-149-0; 1-60870-149-2

This is an introduction to Afghanistan's culture, history, sports, religions, and foods.

"Beautifully illustrated. . . . The writing is clear. . . . [This title] will work well for reports and will be enjoyed by browsers." SLJ

Includes glossary and bibliographical references

O'Brien, Tony

★ **Afghan** dreams; young voices of Afghanistan. by Tony O'Brien and Mike Sullivan; photographs by Tony O'Brien. Bloomsbury Children's Books 2008 69p il map $18.99; lib bdg $19.89

Grades: 3 4 5 6   **958.1**

1. Afghanistan 2. Children -- Afghanistan 3. Teenagers --

Afghanistan

ISBN 978-1-59990-287-6; 1-59990-287-7; 978-1-59990-321-7 lib bdg; 1-59990-321-0 lib bdg

LC 2008-07004

"This handsome photo-essay features contemporary Afghan children ranging in age from 8 to 18 years. They were asked about their families, lives, and hopes for the future. The young people's straightforward statements tell much about the devastating effects of decades of war." SLJ

Whitfield, Susan

Afghanistan; [by] Susan Whitfield; Thomas Barfield and Maliha Zulfacar, consultants. National Geographic 2008 64p il map (Countries of the world) lib bdg $27.90

Grades: 4 5 6 7   **958.1**

1. Afghanistan

ISBN 978-1-4263-0256-5 lib bdg; 1-4263-0256-8 lib bdg

This describes the geography, nature, history, people and culture, government, and economy of Afghanistan.

Includes glossary and bibliographical references

958.104   Afghanistan--1919-

Lunis, Natalie

The **takedown** of Osama bin Laden; by Natalie Lunis. Bearport Publishing 2012 32 p. (Special ops) (lib. bdg.) $25.27

Grades: 4 5 6 7   **958.104**

1. United States. Navy 2. Terrorism 3. Terrorists -- Biography 4. United States. Navy. SEALs

ISBN 1617724599; 9781617724596

LC 2011040472

In this book by Natalie Lunis on U.S. Navy SEALS "young readers will follow this elite group of soldiers on their raid and explore the context for their mission, from the 9/11 attacks by Al Qaeda to the war against terrorists in Afghanistan. Large, full-color photos, grade-appropriate text, and a narrative format [are designed to] keep kids turning the pages as they learn about [the U.S.] military." (Publisher's note)

Includes bibliographical references (p. 31) and index

958.4   Turkestan

King, David C.

Kyrgyzstan; [by] David C. King. Marshall Cavendish Benchmark 2005 144p il map (Cultures of the world) lib bdg $42.79

Grades: 5 6 7 8   **958.4**

1. Kyrgyzstan

ISBN 0-7614-2013-4

LC 2005001314

Describes the geography, history, government, economy, people, and culture of Kyrgyzstan

Includes glossary and bibliographical references

Pang, Guek-Cheng, 1950-

Kazakhstan; 2nd ed.; Marshall Cavendish Benchmark 2011 144p il map (Cultures of the world) lib bdg $42.79

Grades: 5 6 7 8   **958.4**

1. Kazakhstan

ISBN 978-1-6087-0455-2; 1-6087-0455-6

First published 2001

This offers information on the geography, history, wildlife, governmental structure, economy, cultural diversity, peoples, religion, and culture of Kazakhstan.

958.5 Turkmenistan

Knowlton, MaryLee

Turkmenistan; [by] MaryLee Knowlton. Marshall Cavendish Benchmark 2006 144p il map (Cultures of the world) lib bdg $42.79
Grades: 5 6 7 8   **958.5**
1. Turkmenistan
ISBN 0-7614-2014-2

LC 2005006455

Describes the geography, history, government, economy, people, and culture of Turkmenistan

Includes glossary and bibliographical references

958.6 Tajikistan

Abazov, Rafis

Tajikistan; [by] Rafis Abazov. Marshall Cavendish Benchmark 2006 144p il map (Cultures of the world) lib bdg $42.79
Grades: 5 6 7 8   **958.6**
1. Tajikistan
ISBN 0-7614-2012-6

LC 2005001166

Describes the geography, history, government, economy, people, and culture of the former Soviet republic of Tajikistan

Includes glossary and bibliographical references

959.3 Thailand

Morris, Ann

★ **Tsunami**; helping each other. by Ann Morris & Heidi Larson. Millbrook Press 2005 32p il map $15.95
Grades: 3 4 5   **959.3**
1. Tsunamis 2. Indian Ocean earthquake and tsunami, 2004 3. Thailand
ISBN 0-7613-9501-6

LC 2005-13616

The story of how one family in Thailand survived the tsunami of December 26, 2004, and, with the help of others, began to rebuild their lives.

"The brisk and straightforward text is enhanced by many excellent well-captioned color photos." Horn Book Guide

Rau, Dana Meachen

Thailand; [by] Dana Meachen Rau. Marshall Cavendish Benchmark 2007 48p il map (Discovering cultures) lib bdg $28.50
Grades: 2 3 4   **959.3**
1. Thailand
ISBN 978-0-7614-1989-1 lib bdg; 0-7614-1989-6 lib bdg

LC 2006011475

An introduction to the geography, history, people, and culture of Thailand

Includes glossary and bibliographical references

959.4 Laos

Dalal, A. Kamala

★ **Laos**; [by] A. Kamala Dalal. National Geographic 2009 64p il (Countries of the world) lib bdg $27.90

Grades: 4 5 6 7   **959.4**
1. Laos
ISBN 978-1-4263-0388-3 lib bdg; 1-4263-0388-2 lib bdg

This describes the geography, nature, history, people and culture, and govenment and economy of Laos

Includes glossary and bibliographical references

959.5 Malaysia, Brunei, Singapore

Foo Yuk Yee

Malaysia; by Heidi Munan, Foo Yuk Yee, and Jo-Ann Spilling. 3rd ed. Marshall Cavendish Benchmark 2012 144 p. col. ill., col. maps (library) $47.07
Grades: 5 6 7 8   **959.5**
1. Culture 2. Malaysia
ISBN 1608707857; 9781608707850

LC 2011004468

This book by Heidi Munan is part of the Cultures of the World series and looks at Malaysia. The "geography, history, economy and culture are all covered . . . . An entire chapter is devoted to the festivals, which are many because of the ethnic diversity of Malaysia. This is also made apparent in the section about food and manners, as the Muslims do not eat pork and the Hindus and Sikhs cannot eat beef, making it necessary to prepare various dishes for parties." (Children's Literature)

Includes bibliographical references and index.

959.57 Singapore

Layton, Leslie

Singapore; by Lesley Layton, Pang Guek Cheng,and Jo-Ann Spilling. 3rd ed. Marshall Cavendish Benchmark 2012 144 p. (library) $47.07
Grades: 5 6 7 8   **959.57**
1. Singapore
ISBN 1608707873; 9781608707874

LC 2011004479

This book is part of the Cultures of the World series and looks at Singapore. "Singapore is a small but mighty nation. Thanks to its strategic position and the energy of its people—the Malays, and migrant Chinese, Indians, and Eurasians—it is now the world's number one airport and sea port, a regional financial center, a telecommunications hub, and a favored tourist destination." (Publisher's note)

Includes bibliographical references and index.

959.6 Cambodia

Sobol, Richard

The **mysteries** of Angkor Wat; exploring Cambodia's ancient temple. Candlewick Press 2011 42p il map (Traveling photographer) $17.99
Grades: 3 4 5 6   **959.6**
1. Temples 2. Angkor (City) 3. Cambodia -- Antiquities 4. Angkor Wat (Angkor: Ancient city)
ISBN 978-0-7636-4166-5; 0-7636-4166-9

LC 2010041479

"This ancient temple, located in the jungles of Cambodia, has long been a source of mystery, reverence, and wonder. Sobol takes readers on a journey into the heart of the 1000-year-old ruins and presents a fascinating look at the history of the temple, the people who built it and worshiped there, and the current culture surrounding it. A good amount of information is presented while keeping the text conversational and accessible for young people. . . . The handsome book contains captioned color photographs on each page; they give interesting glimpses into the modern lives of the people living around this ancient site and a fascinating look at the ruins themselves. " SLJ

Includes glossary

Sonneborn, Liz

The **Khmer** Rouge; by Liz Sonneborn. Marshall Cavendish Benchmark 2012 80 p. ill. (some col.), col. map (library) $34.21; (ebook) $34.21

Grades: 5 6 7 8   **959.6**

1. Dith Pran, 1942-2008   2. Genocide -- Cambodia   3. Parti communiste du Kampuchea   4. Cambodia -- History -- 1975-1979   5. Political atrocities -- Cambodia   6. Journalists -- Cambodia -- Biography   7. Political refugees -- Cambodia -- Biography

ISBN 1608704742; 9781608704743; 9781608706952 pdf

LC 2011005595

This book "tells the story of Dith Pran, a Cambodian journalist and translator who provided support to Sydney Schanberg, a New York Times correspondent. . . . Sadly, when Schanberg evacuated, Pran was forced to remain behind where he fell into captivity. Over a three year time period Dith Pran survived horrendous conditions but ultimately escaped and fled to Thailand. There, in a refugee camp, Pran was rescued by Schanberg and relocated to the United States." (Children's Literature)

Includes bibliographical references and index.

959.7   Vietnam

Green, Jen

Vietnam; [by] Jen Green. National Geographic 2008 64p il map (Countries of the world) lib bdg $27.90

Grades: 4 5 6 7   **959.7**

1. Vietnam

ISBN 978-1-4263-0202-2

LC 2007047832

This describes the geography, nature, history, people and culture, government, and economy of Vietnam.

Includes glossary and bibliographical references

Guile, Melanie

Culture in Vietnam; [by] Melanie Guile. Raintree 2005 32p il map lib bdg $29.29

Grades: 4 5 6 7   **959.7**

1. Vietnam

ISBN 1-4109-1135-7

LC 2004-16651

This "title includes a map and picture of the nation's flag as well as color photographs that bring to life the wide range of topics addressed. Two to four-page chapters briefly cover languages, history, people, religions, holidays and festivals, customs, minority groups, costumes and clothing, food, and arts and crafts, providing students with lots of cultural information. Text is well spaced in an overall neat and pleasing manner." SLJ

Includes bibliographical references

McNab, Chris

50 things you should know about the Vietnam War; Chris McNab. Motorbooks Intl 2016 80 p. color ill., color maps $15.95

Grades: 4 5 6 7 8   **959.7**

1. Military history   2. Vietnam War, 1961-1975

ISBN 1609929616; 9781609929619

This children's book by Chris McNab from the "50 Things You Should Know About" series "is packed full of infographics, illustrations, maps, and color photographs from the period. Not only identifying major political and military figures from both sides of the conflict with the 'Who's Who' pages, this title also documents the significance of medical workers, protesters, and civilians caught in the crossfire." (Publisher's note)

"An excellent starting point for understanding the Vietnam War, presented as a conflict that commenced with French colonial occupation and continues even today." Kirkus

959.704   Vietnam--1945-

Skrypuch, Marsha Forchuk, 1954-

Last airlift; a Vietnamese orphan's rescue from war. Marsha Forchuk Skrypuch. Pajama Press 2012 120 p. $17.95

Grades: 3 4 5 6   **959.704**

1. Orphans   2. Aeronautics -- Flights   3. International adoption   4. Evacuation of civilians -- Vietnam   5. Vietnam War, 1961-1975 -- Children

ISBN 098694954X; 9780986949548

This book "tells the story of the last Canadian airlift [from Vietnam] through the memories of one child, Son Thi Anh Tuyet. Nearly 8 years old, the sad-eyed girl . . . had lived nearly all her life in a Catholic orphanage." When "she and a number of the institution babies were taken away, placed on an airplane and flown to a new world. . . . she assumed that John and Dorothy Morris had chosen her to help with their three children; instead, she had acquired a family." (Kirkus Reviews)

959.8   Indonesia and East Timor

Cooper, Robert

Indonesia; by Gouri Mirpuri and Robert Cooper. 3rd ed. Marshall Cavendish Benchmark 2012 144 p. ill., maps (library) $47.07

Grades: 5 6 7 8   **959.8**

1. Indonesia -- History

ISBN 1608707830; 9781608707836

LC 200128607

First published 1990

This "nonfiction book in the 'Cultures of the World' series presents a . . . story of the physical, social and historical characteristics of Indonesia. . . . Throughout the book, also, there are textboxes that add . . . information to the subject matter and include . . . drawings of native musical instruments, weapons, foods and other" things. (Children's Literature)

"The pictures are lush, with captions in tiny print offering much additional information. The text is written smoothly and readably, and it contains a substantial amount of information." Booklist

Includes bibliographical references and index.

959.803   Historical periods for Indonesia and East Timor together, for Indonesia alone

Nagara, Innosanto

My night in the planetarium; by Innosanto Nagara. Seven Stories Press, Triangle Square Books 2016 24 p. color illustrations $17.95

Grades: 2 3 4 5   **959.803**

1. Children -- Indonesia -- Biography   2. Indonesia -- History -- 1966-1998

ISBN 9781609807009

LC 2016017210

In this children's book, by Innosanto Nagara, "Innosanto's father, a famous . . . playwright, is in trouble with the government for his newest play's unfavorable portrayal of governmental power and corruption. After a rousing performance at a large theater complex which also houses the Jakarta Planetarium, Innosanto's father manages to sneak out of town to avoid arrest while Innosanto and his mother spend an exciting night sleeping under the stars in the Jakarta Planetarium." (Publisher's note)

"It's a stirring tribute to the power of the arts to challenge injustice, recounted with the confidence of a practiced storyteller." Pub Wkly

960 History of Africa

Bowden, Rob, 1973-

★ **African** culture; [by] Rob Bowden and Rosie Wilson. Heinemann Library 2009 48p il map (Africa focus) $30; pa $8.99

Grades: 4 5 6   960

1. Africa -- Civilization 2. Africa -- Social life and customs

ISBN 978-1-4329-2440-9; 1-4329-2440-0; 978-1-4329-2445-4 pa; 1-4329-2445-1 pa

LC 2008-48310

This book "presents a clear and timely overview of the diverse and complex continent. The full-color photographs are of exceptional quality. [The] book also includes interesting fact boxes, sidebars, maps, and a time line. [It] focuses on traditions and how they are relevant for today. Highlights include family and daily life; religion, beliefs, and customs; and the performing and visual arts." SLJ

Includes bibliographical references

★ **Ancient** Africa; [by] Rob Bowden and Rosie Wilson. Heinemann Library 2008 48p il map (Africa focus) $30; pa $8.99

Grades: 4 5 6   960

1. Africa -- History

ISBN 978-1-4329-2439-3; 1-4329-2439-7; 978-1-4329-2444-7 pa; 1-4329-2444-3 pa

LC 2008-48306

This book "presents a clear and timely overview of the diverse and complex continent. The full-color photographs are of exceptional quality. [The] book also includes interesting fact boxes, sidebars, maps, and a time line. . . . [It] begins with the origin of humankind and continues through the beginning of the slave trade in Europe and America. Early civilizations such as Egypt, ancient Ghana, the Mali Empire, Great Zimbabwe, and Kongo are represented. Invasions and explorations are discussed, as is slavery and colonialism." SLJ

Includes bibliographical references

★ **Changing** Africa; [by] Rob Bowden and Rosie Wilson. Heinemann Library 2009 48p il map (Africa focus) $30; pa $8.99

Grades: 4 5 6   960

1. Africa -- Social conditions 2. Africa -- Economic conditions

ISBN 978-1-4329-2437-9; 1-4329-2437-0; 978-1-4329-2442-3 pa; 1-4329-2442-7 pa

LC 2008-48277

This book "presents a clear and timely overview of the diverse and complex continent. The full-color photographs are of exceptional quality. [The] book also includes interesting fact boxes, sidebars, maps, and a time line. . . . [It] presents recent positive and negative changes. The rise of poverty and slums is explored, as is the lowered life expectancy due to the spread of malaria and HIV/AIDS. Positive changes include the freedom that voting has brought." SLJ

Includes bibliographical references

★ **Modern** Africa; [by] Rosie Wilson and Rob Bowden. Heinemann Library 2009 48p il map (Africa focus) $30; pa $8.99

Grades: 4 5 6   960

1. Africa

ISBN 978-1-4329-2438-6; 1-4329-2438-9; 978-1-4329-2443-0 pa; 1-4329-2443-5 pa

This book "presents a clear and timely overview of the diverse and complex continent. The full-color photographs are of exceptional quality. [The] book also includes interesting fact boxes, sidebars, maps, and a time line. . . . [It] chronicles the history of colonial Africa to independence, and the changes that have arisen and continue to manifest themselves. Topics include apartheid and recent and ongoing violence in Rwanda, Darfur, and the Congo. While corrupt leaders continue to hamper Africa's attempts at advancement, the exportation of oil as well as aid from missionaries and international organizations are presented as hopes for the future." SLJ

Mooney, Carla

Amazing Africa; projects you can build yourself. illustrated by Megan Stearns. Nomad Press 2010 122p il (Build it yourself) pa $15.95

Grades: 4 5 6 7   960

1. Handicraft 2. Africa

ISBN 978-1-934670-41-5; 1-934670-41-3

"Casual and informative, this large, attractive, browsable paperback . . . offers a view of contemporary African life that reaches far beyond the usual scenery-and-wildlife tourists' perspective. Blending history, culture, and tradition with politics and life in both cities and rural areas, the chapters begin with a look at natural wonders and dangerous wildlife that will grab readers, then move on to historical discussions of humankind's birthplace and early civilizations. . . . The open design includes sketches on every page. . . . The craft projects [include making] your own Maasai beaded necklace, kente cloth, woven basket, galimoto doll, and . . . more." Booklist

Murray, Jocelyn

Africa; updated by Brian A. Stewart. 3rd ed.; Chelsea House 2007 96p il map (Cultural atlas for young people) $35

Grades: 5 6 7 8   960

1. Africa -- History 2. Africa -- Civilization

ISBN 978-0-8160-6826-5; 0-8160-6826-7

First published 1990

Presents information on the history and various regions and cultures of Africa.

Includes glossary and bibliographical references

Musgrove, Margaret

★ **Ashanti** to Zulu: African traditions; pictures by Leo and Diane Dillon. Dial Bks. for Young Readers 1976 un il $21.99; pa $6.99

Grades: 3 4 5 6   960

1. Ethnology -- Africa 2. Africa -- Social life and customs

ISBN 0-8037-0357-0; 0-14-054604-9 pa

Awarded the Caldecott Medal, 1977

"In brief texts arranged in alphabetical order, each accompanied by a large framed illustration, the author introduces 'the reader to twenty-six African peoples by depicting a custom important to each.' . . . In most of the paintings the artists 'have included a man, a woman, a child, their living quarters, an artifact, and a local animal' and have, in this way, stressed the human and the natural ambience of the various peoples depicted." Horn Book

961.1 Tunisia

Brown, Roslind Varghese

Tunisia; [by] Roslind Varghese Brown & Michael Spilling. 2nd ed.; Marshall Cavendish Benchmark 2008 144p il map (Cultures of the world) lib bdg $42.79

Grades: 5 6 7 8   **961.1**

1. Tunisia

ISBN 978-0-7614-3037-7 lib bdg; 0-7614-3037-7 lib bdg

LC 2007050798

First published 1998

"Provides comprehensive information on the geography, history, wildlife, governmental structure, economy, cultural diversity, peoples, religion, and culture of Tunisia." Publisher note

Includes glossary and bibliographical references

962 Egypt, Sudan, South Sudan

Heinrichs, Ann

The **Nile**. Marshall Cavendish Benchmark 2008 96p il map (Nature's wonders) lib bdg $24.95

Grades: 5 6 7 8   **962**

1. Nile River 2. Nile River valley

ISBN 978-0-7614-2854-1

LC 2007019187

"It's tough to make a river interesting, but this . . . does an admirable job of it. . . . Crisp, full-color photos and original artwork decorate nearly every page. . . . [This is a] well-thought-out natural history." Booklist

Includes glossary and bibliographical references

962.05 Egypt since 1922

Abouraya, Karen Leggett

★ **Hands** around the library; protecting Egypt's treasured books. by Susan L. Roth and Karen Leggett Abouraya; collages by Susan L. Roth. Dial Books for Young Readers 2012 40 p. (hardcover) $16.99

Grades: 1 2 3   **962.05**

1. Libraries 2. Arab Spring, 2010- 3. Picture books for children 4. Cultural property -- Protection 5. Egypt -- History -- 21st century 6. Libraries -- Egypt -- Alexandria 7. Aliksandrina; (Library) -- History 8. Libraries -- Destruction and pillage -- Egypt -- Alexandria

ISBN 0803737475; 9780803737471

LC 2011038198

Author Susan L. Roth's book shows the "days of the Arab Spring when Egyptians marched to bring down their government, [and] youthful demonstrators and library staff stood together to protect the Bibliotheca Alexandrina, contemporary counterpart to the Great Library of Alexandria, from vandalism. Roth's . . . collages capture these heady moments, blending photos, papers and fabrics to bring the people's positive actions and the building's intriguing facade together in a celebration of patriotism and libraries." (Kirkus Reviews)

963 Ethiopia and Eritrea

Gish, Steven

Ethiopia; [by] Steven Gish & Winnie Thay & Zawiah Abdul Latif. 2nd ed.; Marshall Cavendish Benchmark 2007 144p il map (Cultures of the world) lib bdg $42.79

Grades: 5 6 7 8   **963**

1. Ethiopia

ISBN 978-0-7614-2025-5 lib bdg; 0-7614-2025-8 lib bdg

LC 2006020819

First published 1996

This provides "information on the geography, history, governmental structure, economy, cultural diversity, peoples, religion, and culture of Ethiopia." Publisher's note

Includes glossary and bibliographical references

963.5 Eritrea

NgCheong-Lum, Roseline, 1962-

Eritrea; 2nd ed.; Marshall Cavendish Benchmark 2011 144p il map (Cultures of the world) lib bdg $42.79

Grades: 5 6 7 8   **963.5**

1. Eritrea

ISBN 978-1-6087-0454-5; 1-6087-0454-8

LC 2010035973

First published 2001

Provides information on the geography, history, wildlife, governmental structure, economy, cultural diversity, peoples, religion, and culture of Eritea.

"Plentiful color photographs accompany substantial amounts of information." SLJ

Includes glossary and bibliographical references

964 Morocco, Ceuta, Melilla, Western Sahara, Canary Islands

Seward, Pat

Morocco; [by] Pat Seward & Orin Hargraves. 2nd ed.; Marshall Cavendish Benchmark 2006 144p il map (Cultures of the world) lib bdg $42.79

Grades: 5 6 7 8   **964**

1. Morocco

ISBN 0-7614-2051-7

LC 2005020782

First published 1995

Describes the geography, history, government, economy, people, and culture of Morocco

Includes glossary and bibliographical references

965 Algeria

Kagda, Falaq

Algeria; [by] Falaq Kagda & Zawiah Abdul Latif. 2nd ed.; Marshall Cavendish Benchmark 2008 144p il map (Cultures of the world) lib bdg $42.79

Grades: 5 6 7 8   **965**

1. Algeria

ISBN 978-0-7614-2085-9 lib bdg; 0-7614-2085-1 lib bdg

LC 2007014888

First published 1997

"Provides comprehensive information on the geography, history, wildlife, governmental structure, economy, cultural diversity, peoples, religion, and culture of Algeria." Publisher's note

Includes glossary and bibliographical references

966.1 Mauritania

Blauer, Ettagale

Mauritania; [by] Ettagale Blauer & Jason Lauré. Marshall Cavendish Benchmark 2009 144p il map (Cultures of the world) lib bdg $42.79

Grades: 5 6 7 8   **966.1**

1. Mauritania

ISBN 978-0-7614-3116-9

This describes the geography, history, government, economy, environment, people, and culture of Mauritania

966.2 Mali, Burkina Faso, Niger

Blauer, Ettagale

Mali; [by] Ettagale Blauer & Jason Lauré. 2nd ed.; Marshall Cavendish Benchmark 2008 144p il map (Cultures of the world) lib bdg $42.79

Grades: 5 6 7 8   **966.2**

1. Mali

ISBN 978-0-7614-2568-7

First published 1997

This describes the geography, history, government, economy, environment, people, and culture of Mali

Includes glossary and bibliographical references

McKissack, Pat, 1944-2017

The **royal** kingdoms of Ghana, Mali, and Songhay; life in medieval Africa. [by] Patricia and Fredrick McKissack. Holt & Co. 1993 142p il maps hardcover o.p. pa $12.99

Grades: 5 6 7 8   **966.2**

1. Ghana Empire 2. Songhai Empire 3. Mali -- History

ISBN 0-8050-4259-8 pa

LC 93-4838

Examines the civilizations of the Western Sudan which flourished from 700 to 1700 A.D., acquiring such vast wealth that they became centers of trade and culture for a continent

"The McKissacks are careful to distinguish what is known from what is surmised; they draw on the oral tradition, eyewitness accounts, and contemporary scholarship; and chapter source notes discuss various conflicting views of events." Booklist

Includes bibliographical references

966.3 Senegal

Berg, Elizabeth

Senegal; by Elizabeth L. Berg and Ruth Lau. 2nd ed.; Marshall Cavendish Benchmark 2009 144p il map (Cultures of the world) lib bdg $42.79

Grades: 5 6 7 8   **966.3**

1. Senegal

ISBN 978-0-7614-4481-7 lib bdg; 0-7614-4481-5 lib bdg

LC 2009007067

First published 1999

Describes the geography, history, wildlife, governmental structure, economy, cultural diversity, peoples, religion, and culture of Senegal

Includes glossary and bibliographical references

966.4 Sierra Leone

LeVert, Suzanne

Sierra Leone; [by] Suzanne LeVert. Marshall Cavendish Benchmark 2007 144p il map (Cultures of the world) lib bdg $42.79

Grades: 5 6 7 8   **966.4**

1. Sierra Leone

ISBN 978-0-7614-2334-8 lib bdg; 0-7614-2334-6 lib bdg

LC 2005035964

This provides "information on the geography, history, governmental structure, economy, cultural diversity, peoples, religion, and culture of Sierra Leone." Publisher's note

Includes glossary and bibliographical references

966.68 Cote d'Ivoire (Ivory Coast)

Sheehan, Patricia

Cote d'Ivoire; [by] Patricia Sheehan and Jacqueline Ong. 2nd ed.; Marshall Cavendish Benchmark 2010 144p il map (Cultures of the world) lib bdg $42.79

Grades: 5 6 7 8   **966.68**

1. Ivory Coast

ISBN 978-0-7614-4854-9 lib bdg; 0-7614-4854-3 lib bdg

LC 2009045688

First published 2000

This offers information on the geography, history, wildlife, governmental structure, economy, cultural diversity, peoples, religion, and culture of Cote d'Ivoire

Includes glossary and bibliographical references

966.7 Ghana

Levy, Patricia

Ghana; [by] Patricia Levy and Winnie Wong. 2nd ed.; Marshall Cavendish Benchmark 2010 144p il map (Cultures of the world) lib bdg $42.79

Grades: 5 6 7 8   **966.7**

1. Ghana

ISBN 978-0-7614-4847-1 lib bdg; 0-7614-4847-0 lib bdg

First published 1999

Introduces the geography, history, government, economy, culture, and people of Ghana

Includes glossary and bibliographical references

966.9 Nigeria

Giles, Bridget

★ **Nigeria**; [by] Bridget Giles. National Geographic 2007 64p il map (Countries of the world) lib bdg $27.90

Grades: 4 5 6 7   **966.9**

1. Nigeria

ISBN 978-1-4263-0124-7

LC 2007024729

This describes the geography, nature, history, people and culture, government, and economy of Nigeria

"What helps [this book] stand out from the pack is [its] high-quality, rich photography. . . . The photos provide as much information as the [text]. . . . The writing is straightforward and solid." SLJ

Includes glossary and bibliographical references

Oluonye, Mary N.

Nigeria; by Mary N. Oluonye. Lerner Publications Company 2007 48p il map (Country explorers) lib bdg $27.93; pa $8.95

Grades: 2 3 4 **966.9**

1. Nigeria

ISBN 978-0-8225-7131-5 lib bdg; 978-0-8225-8509-1 pa

LC 2006035846

"With short, chatty sentences and a lively, contemporary color photo on every page, this title . . . gives a brief overview of the history, geography, and culture of Nigeria. . . . The current information is not oversimplified." Booklist

Onyefulu, Ifeoma

Ikenna goes to Nigeria. Frances Lincoln 2007 33p il map hardcover o.p. $16.95

Grades: K 1 2 3 **966.9**

1. Nigeria

ISBN 978-1-84507-585-9; 1-84507-585-4; 978-1-84507-960-4 pa; 1-84507-960-4 pa

"Onyefulu delivers another photo-essay filled with vivid, colorful photographs, accompanied by brief, clear text about the land, people, and culture of her native Nigeria. The text is narrated by the author's son. . . . An outline map of the country shows the location of the cities/towns/villages that Ikenna will visit during the course of his trip. . . . The clear images contain a wealth of detail and provide valuable visual insight into the people and culture." SLJ

967.11 Cameroon

Sheehan, Sean

Cameroon; [by] Sean Sheehan and Josie Elias. 2nd ed.; Marshall Cavendish Benchmark 2011 144p il map (Cultures of the world) lib bdg $42.79

Grades: 5 6 7 8 **967.11**

1. Cameroon

ISBN 978-1-6087-0214-5; 1-6087-0214-6

LC 2010019623

First published 2001

Provides information on the geography, history, wildlife, governmental structure, economy, cultural diversity, peoples, religion, and culture of Cameroon.

Includes glossary and bibliographical references

967.3 Angola

Sheehan, Sean

Angola; [by] Sean Sheehan and Jui Lin Yong. 2nd ed.; Marshall Cavendish Benchmark 2010 144p il map (Cultures of the world) lib bdg $42.79

Grades: 5 6 7 8 **967.3**

1. Angola

ISBN 978-0-7614-4845-7 lib bdg; 0-7614-4845-4 lib bdg

LC 2009021203

"Provides comprehensive information on the geography, history, wildlife, governmental structure, economy, cultural diversity, peoples, religion, and culture of Angola." Publisher's note

Includes glossary and bibliographical references

967.43 Chad

Kneib, Martha

Chad; [by] Martha Kneib. Marshall Cavendish Benchmark 2007 144p il map (Cultures of the world) lib bdg $42.79

Grades: 5 6 7 8 **967.43**

1. Chad

ISBN 978-0-7614-2327-0 lib bdg; 0-7614-2327-3 lib bdg

LC 2005027079

This provides "information on the geography, history, governmental structure, economy, cultural diversity, peoples, religion, and culture of Chad." Publisher's note

Includes glossary and bibliographical references

967.51 Democratic Republic of the Congo

Heale, Jay

Democratic Republic of the Congo; by Jay Heale and Yong Jui Lin. 2nd ed.; Marshall Cavendish Benchmark 2009 144p il map (Cultures of the world) lib bdg $42.79

Grades: 5 6 7 8 **967.51**

1. Congo (Republic)

ISBN 978-0-7614-4478-7 lib bdg; 0-7614-4478-5 lib bdg

LC 2009003195

First published 1999

Describes the geography, history, government, economy, people, lifestyle, religion, languages, arts, leisure, festivals, and food of The Democratic Republic of the Congo

Includes glossary and bibliographical references

967.571 Rwanda

King, David C.

Rwanda; [by] David C. King. Marshall Cavendish Benchmark 2007 144p il map (Cultures of the world) lib bdg $42.79

Grades: 5 6 7 8 **967.571**

1. Rwanda

ISBN 978-0-7614-2333-1 lib bdg; 0-7614-2333-8 lib bdg

LC 2005031817

This provides "information on the geography, history, governmental structure, economy, cultural diversity, peoples, religion, and culture of Rwanda." Publisher's note

Includes glossary and bibliographical references

967.61 Uganda

Barlas, Robert

Uganda; [by] Robert Barlas and Yong Jui Lin. 2nd ed.; Marshall Cavendish Benchmark 2010 144p il map (Cultures of the world) lib bdg $42.79

Grades: 5 6 7 8 **967.61**

1. Uganda

ISBN 978-0-7614-4859-4 lib bdg; 0-7614-4859-4 lib bdg

LC 2009046002

First published 2000

This offers information on the geography, history, wildlife, governmental structure, economy, cultural diversity, peoples, religion, and culture of Uganda

Includes glossary and bibliographical references

967.62 Kenya

Tanguay, Bridget

Kenya; Bridget Tanguay; Chege Githiora and Tabitha Otieno, consultants. National Geographic 2006 p. cm. **967.62**

1. Kenya

ISBN 978-0-7922-7628-9 (hardcover : alk. paper); 978-0-7922-7668-5 (lib bdg: alk. paper)

LC 2006029047

Includes bibliographical references

Williams, Karen Lynn

Beatrice's dream; a story of Kibera slum. photographs by Wendy Stone. Frances Lincoln 2011 il $17.95

Grades: 3 4 5 6 **967.62**

1. Kenya

ISBN 978-1-84780-019-0; 1-84780-019-X

"Beatrice, a 13-year-old orphan who lives with her brother and his wife in a Kenyan slum, describes her current life and her hopes for the future. She touches on her 30-minute walks to school, her classes, and helping her brother in his shop. Vivid color photographs give readers a firsthand glimpse into a world about which they are likely to know nothing. . . . Although the book deals with difficult subject matter, it does so in an upbeat and positive way. . . . A unique and important addition." SLJ

967.73 Somalia

Hassig, Susan M.

Somalia; by Susan M. Hassig & Zawiah Abdul Latif. 2nd ed.; Marshall Cavendish Benchmark 2008 144p il map (Cultures of the world) lib bdg $42.79

Grades: 5 6 7 8 **967.73**

1. Somalia

ISBN 978-0-7614-2082-8 lib bdg; 0-7614-2082-7 lib bdg

LC 2006102270

First published 1997

"Provides comprehensive information on the geography, history, wildlife, governmental structure, economy, cultural diversity, peoples, religion, and culture of Somalia." Publisher's note

Includes glossary and bibliographical references

967.8 Tanzania

Heale, Jay

Tanzania; by Jay Heale & Winnie Wong. 2nd ed.; Marshall Cavendish Benchmark 2009 144p il map (Cultures of the world) lib bdg $42.79

Grades: 5 6 7 8 **967.8**

1. Tanzania

ISBN 978-0-7614-3417-7 lib bdg; 0-7614-3417-8 lib bdg

LC 2008028802

First published 1998

"Provides comprehensive information on the geography, history, wildlife, governmental structure, economy, cultural diversity, peoples, religion, and culture of Tanzania." Publisher's note

Includes glossary and bibliographical references

967.9 Mozambique

King, David C.

Mozambique; [by] David C. King. Marshall Cavendish Benchmark 2007 144p il map (Cultures of the world) lib bdg $42.79

Grades: 5 6 7 8 **967.9**

1. Mozambique

ISBN 978-0-7614-2331-7 lib bdg; 0-7614-2331-1 lib bdg

LC 2006002302

This provides "information on the geography, history, wildlife, governmental structure, economy, cultural diversity, peoples, religion, and culture of Mozambique." Publisher's note

Includes glossary and bibliographical references

968 Republic of South Africa and neighboring southern African countries

Mace, Virginia

★ South Africa; [by] Virginia Mace; Kate Rowntree and Vukile Khumalo, consultants. National Geographic 2008 64p il map (Countries of the world) lib bdg $27.90

Grades: 4 5 6 7 **968**

1. South Africa

ISBN 978-1-4263-0203-9

LC 2007047835

This describes the geography, nature, history, people and culture, government, and economy of South Africa.

"Through its numerous maps and standout photographs, this book provides a general overview of South Africa that will satisfy the basic needs of upper-elementary research paper writers." Horn Book Guide

Includes glossary and bibliographical references

968.06 South Africa--Period as Republic, 1961-

Brownlie, Ali

South Africa in our world; [by] Ali Brownlie Bojang. Smart Apple Media 2010 32p il (Countries in our world) lib bdg $28.50

Grades: 5 6 7 8 **968.06**

1. South Africa

ISBN 978-1-59920-444-4 lib bdg; 1-59920-444-4 lib bdg

LC 2009043163

This "contains relevant information presented in a visually appealing layout. Large colorful photographs inform readers about the past, present, and future of the country. . . . The book gives an honest view of apartheid, poverty, and government conflicts. At the same time, it is hopeful about recent changes, such as the hosting of the World Cup and the growing economy." SLJ

Includes glossary and bibliographical references

Cooper, Floyd

Mandela; from the life of the South African statesman. written and illustrated by Floyd Cooper. Philomel Bks. 1996 un il hardcover o.p. pa $6.99

Grades: 2 3 4 **968.06**

1. Presidents 2. Political prisoners 3. Political leaders 4. Human rights activists 5. Nobel laureates for peace 6. South Africa -- Race relations 7. South Africa -- Politics and government

ISBN 0-399-22942-6; 0-698-11816-2 pa

LC 95-19639

"Cooper's oil paintings are infused with golden light. Elegant composition and subtle shifts in perspective add emotional value to the carefully focused account." SLJ

Includes bibliographical references

McDonough, Yona Zeldis

★ **Peaceful** protest: the life of Nelson Mandela; illustrations by Malcah Zeldis. Walker & Co. 2002 un il hardcover o.p. pa $8.95

Grades: 2 3 4 5   **968.06**

1. Presidents 2. Political prisoners 3. Political leaders 4. Human rights activists 5. Nobel laureates for peace 6. South Africa -- Race relations 7. South Africa -- Politics and government

ISBN 0-8027-8821-1; 0-8027-8823-8 lib bdg; 0-8027-8948-X pa

LC 2002-23462

A biography of the black South African leader who became a civil rights activist, political prisoner, and president of South Africa

This is an "easy-to-read but engaging biography.... Zeldis's brightly colored folk-art illustrations reflect her subject's life and struggle with candid simplicity." SLJ

Includes bibliographical references

Nelson, Kadir

★ **Nelson** Mandela; Kadir Nelson. Katherine Tegen Books 2013 40 p. (hardcover bdg.) $17.99

Grades: 1 2 3   **968.06**

1. Stories in rhyme 2. South Africa -- History 3. Mandela, Nelson, 1918-2013

ISBN 0061783749; 9780061783746; 9780061783760

LC 2012025492

Coretta Scott King Honor Book: Illustrator (2014)

This illustrated children's book by illustrator Kadir Nelson is a biography in verse of Nelson Mandela. "It is the story of a young boy's determination to change South Africa and of the struggles of a man who eventually became the president of his country by believing in equality for people of all colors." (Publisher's note)

968.94   Zambia

Holmes, Timothy

Zambia; by Timothy Holmes & Winnie Wong. rev ed.; Marshall Cavendish Benchmark 2008 144p il map (Cultures of the world) lib bdg $42.79

Grades: 5 6 7 8   **968.94**

1. Zambia

ISBN 978-0-7614-3039-1 lib bdg; 0-7614-3039-3 lib bdg

LC 2007050794

First published 1998

Describes the geography, history, government, economy, people, lifestyle, religion, language, arts, leisure, festivals, and food of Zambia

Includes glossary and bibliographical references

969.1   Madagascar

Heale, Jay

Madagascar; [by] Jay Heale & Zawiah Abdul Latif. 2nd ed.; Marshall Cavendish Benchmark 2008 144p il map (Cultures of the world) lib bdg $42.79

Grades: 5 6 7 8   **969.1**

1. Madagascar

ISBN 978-0-7614-3036-0 lib bdg; 0-7614-3036-9 lib bdg

LC 2007048288

First published 1998

"Provides comprehensive information on the geography, history, wildlife, governmental structure, economy, cultural diversity, peoples, religion, and culture of Madagascar." Publisher's note

Includes glossary and bibliographical references

970   History of North America

Foster, Karen

Atlas of North America. Picture Window Books 2008 32p il map (Picture Window Books world atlases) lib bdg $27.93; pa $7.95

Grades: 2 3 4   **970**

1. North America

ISBN 978-1-4048-3885-7 lib bdg; 1-4048-3885-6 lib bdg; 978-1-4048-3893-2 pa; 1-4048-3893-7 pa

This introduction to the geography of North America offers maps and information about countries, landforms, bodies of water, climate, plants, animals, population, people and customs, places of interest, industries, transportation, and the Mississippi River

This book offers "well-organized, easy-to-access information.... Small photographs or colorful text boxes draw readers' attention to points of interest or fun facts. Maps and legends are simple, yet disseminate information clearly." SLJ

Includes glossary

970.004   North American native peoples

Andre, Julie-Ann

We feel good out here; by Julie-Ann Andre and Mindy Willett; photographs by Tessa Macintosh. Fitzhenry & Whiteside 2008 32p il (The land is our storybook) $16.95

Grades: 3 4 5 6   **970.004**

1. Northwest Territories 2. Native Americans -- Canada

ISBN 978-1-89725-233-8; 1-89725-233-1

This title focuses on the land and culture "of Canada's Northwest Territories and is replete with sharp and attractive full-color photographs. In [this book] a local woman describes her life with her husband and two daughters. Julie-Ann is a Canadian Ranger who studies business management but, more importantly, she is a student of Gwich'in language and culture. She was sent to a residential school at age seven and has spent the last 10 years reestablishing her people's traditional practices and beliefs. A boxed area, 'Our Words,' gives a few words in English and in Gwichya Gwich'in.... [This title provides] some useful information for reports and [is an] interesting [addition] for general reading." SLJ

Arnold, Caroline

★ **The** **ancient** cliff dwellers of Mesa Verde; photographs by Richard Hewett. Clarion Bks. 1992 64p il hardcover o.p. pa $7.95

Grades: 4 5 6 7   **970.004**

1. Pueblo Indians

ISBN 0-395-56241-4; 0-618-05149-X pa

LC 91-8145

Discusses the native Americans known as the Anasazi, who migrated to southwestern Colorado in the first century A.D. and mysteriously disappeared in 1300 A.D. after constructing extensive dwellings in the cliffs of the steep canyon walls

"A thorough and attractive introduction to the Anasazi people with outstanding photographs of the dramatic vistas and ceremonial chambers within this national park." SLJ

Includes glossary

Baylor, Byrd

★ **When** clay sings; illustrated by Tom Bahti. Scribner 1972 un il hardcover o.p. pa $6.99

Grades: 1 2 3 4   **970.004**

1. Pottery 2. Native American art 3. Native Americans -- Southwestern States

ISBN 0-684-18829-5; 0-689-71106-9 pa

A Caldecott Medal honor book, 1973

"A lyrical tribute to an almost forgotten time of the prehistoric Indian of the desert West presents broken bits of pottery from this ancient time. The designs and drawings, done in rich earth tones, are derived from prehistoric pottery found in the American Southwest." Read Ladders for Hum Relat. 6th edition

Bjornlund, Lydia D.

The **Trail** of Tears; the relocation of the Cherokee Nation. Lucent Books 2010 104p il map (American history) lib bdg $33.45

Grades: 5 6 7 8   **970.004**

1. Cherokee Indians 2. Native Americans -- Relocation

ISBN 978-1-4205-0211-4; 1-4205-0211-5

LC 2010001549

Describes the Federal government's seizure of Cherokee lands in Georgia and the forced migration of the Cherokee Nation to Oklahoma along the route that came to be known as the Trail of Tears.

This is "well written and [includes] primary sources, photographs, reproductions, and maps." SLJ

Includes bibliographical references

★ A **Braid** of lives; Native American childhood. edited by Neil Philip. Clarion Bks. 2000 81p il $20

Grades: 4 5 6 7   **970.004**

1. Native Americans

ISBN 0-395-64528-X

LC 00-21343

"This is an excellent choice for curriculum support and brief read-aloud material." Booklist

Includes bibliographical references

Bruchac, Joseph

★ The **Trail** of Tears; illustrated by Diana Magnuson. Random House 1999 46p il (Step into reading) hardcover o.p. pa $3.99

Grades: 2 3 4   **970.004**

1. Cherokee Indians 2. Native Americans -- Relocation

ISBN 0-679-99052-6 lib bdg; 0-679-89052-1 pa

LC 98-36199

Recounts how the Cherokees, after fighting to keep their land in the nineteenth century, were forced to leave and travel 1200 miles to a new settlement in Oklahoma, a terrible journey known as the Trail of Tears

"Magnuson's colorful pictures, packed with people and action, are a little bright for the subject, but strong new readers will find that nonfiction can tell a powerful story." Booklist

Connolly, Sean

★ The **Americas** and the Pacific. Zak Books 2009 48p il map (History of the world) lib bdg $34.25

Grades: 4 5 6 7 8   **970.004**

1. Maoris 2. Aboriginal Australians 3. Native Americans -- History

ISBN 978-88-60981-61-5 lib bdg; 88-60981-61-1 lib bdg

LC 2008008404

"Artists' renderings show groups of people engaged in representative activities, but it's the reproductions of artifacts . . . that will pull readers and browsers most. . . . [This is an] engaging overview." Booklist

Includes bibliographical references

Cunningham, Kevin

The **Cheyenne**; [by] Kevin Cunningham and Peter Benoit. Children's Press 2011 48p il map (True books: American Indians) lib bdg $28; pa $6.95

Grades: 3 4 5   **970.004**

1. Cheyenne Indians

ISBN 978-0-531-20759-8 lib bdg; 0-531-20759-5 lib bdg; 978-0-531-29301-0 pa; 0-531-29301-7 pa

LC 2010049082

An introduction to the Cheyenne people, explaining who they are, reviewing the history of the Cheyenne, looking at how the Cheyenne lived, their beliefs, and rituals, and discussing the Council of Forty-Four.

Includes bibliographical references

The **Comanche**; [by] Kevin Cunningham and Peter Benoit. Children's Press 2011 48p il (True book: American Indians) lib bdg $28; pa $6.95

Grades: 3 4 5   **970.004**

1. Comanche Indians

ISBN 978-0-531-20770-3 lib bdg; 0-531-20770-6 lib bdg; 978-0-531-29312-6 pa; 0-531-29312-2 pa

LC 2010049081

This book "covers cultural basics such as diet, clothing, lifestyle, and child rearing for [the Comanche]. Relevant historical events are also covered simply and clearly, including a time line of highlights in each group's history. This balance between history and culture keeps the series dynamic and interesting. Photos, paintings, and drawings—as well as occasional contemporary illustrations—add visual interest to the well-designed package and keep the [title] from feeling formulaic. The [book] traces the historical changes in Comanche life and their causes, from the 1600s to the twentieth century." Booklist

Includes bibliographical references

The **Inuit**; [by] Kevin Cunningham and Peter Benoit. Children's Press 2011 48p il (True book: American Indians) lib bdg $28; pa $6.95

Grades: 3 4 5   **970.004**

1. Inuit

ISBN 978-0-531-20760-4 lib bdg; 978-0-531-29302-7 pa

LC 2010049080

This book "covers cultural basics such as diet, clothing, lifestyle, and child rearing for [the Inuit]. Relevant historical events are also covered simply and clearly, including a time line of highlights in each group's history. This balance between history and culture keeps the series dynamic and interesting. Photos, paintings, and drawings-as well as occasional contemporary illustrations-add visual interest to the well-designed package and keep the [title] from feeling formulaic." Booklist

Includes bibliographical references

The **Navajo**; [by] Kevin Cunningham and Peter Benoit. Children's Press 2011 48p il map (True book: American Indians) lib bdg $28; pa $6.95

Grades: 3 4 5   **970.004**

1. Navajo Indians

ISBN 978-0-531-20762-8 lib bdg; 0-531-20762-5 lib bdg; 978-0-531-29304-1 pa; 0-531-29304-1 pa

LC 2010050837

An exploration of the Navajo Indians, discussing the nation's relationship with Spaniards and settlers, culture, crafts, and more.

The "balance between history and culture keeps the [book] dynamic and interesting. Photos, paintings, and drawings—as well as occasional contemporary illustrations—add visual interest to the well-designed package and keep the [title] from feeling formulaic." Booklist

Includes bibliographical references

The **Pueblo**; [by] Kevin Cunningham and Peter Benoit. Children's Press 2011 48p il map (True book: American Indians) lib bdg $28; pa $6.95

Grades: 3 4 5   **970.004**

1. Pueblo Indians

ISBN 978-0-531-20763-5 lib bdg; 0-531-20763-3 lib bdg; 978-0-531-29305-8 pa; 0-531-29305-X pa

LC 2010050838

An introduction to the Pueblo people, explaining who they are, reviewing the history of the Pueblo, examining key aspects of Pueblo culture, and looking at Pueblo traditions that continue into the twenty-first century.

Includes bibliographical references

The **Sioux**; [by] Kevin Cunningham and Peter Benoit. Children's Press 2011 48p il map (True book: American Indians) lib bdg $28; pa $6.95

Grades: 3 4 5   **970.004**

1. Teton Indians

ISBN 978-0-531-20768-0 lib bdg; 0-531-207684- lib bdg; 978-0-531-29310-2 pa; 0-531-29310-6 pa

LC 2010049083

An introduction to the Sioux people, explaining who they are, reviewing the history of the Sioux, telling the story of Little Bighorn, and examining key parts of Sioux culture.

Includes bibliographical references

The **Zuni**; [by] Kevin Cunningham and Peter Benoit. Children's Press 2011 48p il map (True book: American Indians) $28; pa $6.95

Grades: 3 4 5   **970.004**

1. Zuni Indians

ISBN 978-0-531-20761-1; 978-0-531-29303-4 pa

LC 2010050846

This book "covers cultural basics such as diet, clothing, lifestyle, and child rearing for [the Zuni]. Relevant historical events are also covered simply and clearly, including a time line of highlights in each group's history. This balance between history and culture keeps the [book] dynamic and interesting. Photos, paintings, and drawings-as well as occasional contemporary illustrations-add visual interest to the well-designed package and keep the [title] from feeling formulaic." Booklist

Includes bibliographical references

Dennis, Yvonne Wakim

★ **Children** of native America today; [by] Yvonne Wakim Dennis & Arlene Hirschfelder; with a foreword by Buffy Sainte-Marie. Charlesbridge Pub. 2003 64p il map lib bdg $19.95

Grades: 3 4 5 6   **970.004**

1. Native Americans

ISBN 1-57091-499-0

LC 2002-2272

"This photo-essay features 25 of the more than 500 native cultures of the U.S. as well as a section on urban Indians. In this 'book of few words and many pictures,' the clear, captioned photographs speak eloquently of contemporary Native American young people. . . . An excellent resource for multicultural studies, this handsome album will also attract browsers." Booklist

Includes glossary and bibliographical references

★ A **kid's** guide to native American history; more than 50 activities. by Yvonne Wakim Dennis and Arlene Hirschfelder. Chicago Review Press 2009 226p il pa $16.95

Grades: 3 4 5 6   **970.004**

1. Games 2. Cooking 3. Handicraft 4. Native Americans -- History

ISBN 978-1-55652-802-6 pa; 1-55652-802-7 pa

LC 2009015832

"This two-in-one history and activity book does an excellent job of explaining Native American history in easy-to-understand language while stressing the differences between and diversity among tribes. The book is divided by region. . . . Activities are kid-friendly . . . and encourage exploration of the text. . . . Clear illustrations accompany each activity." SLJ

Includes glossary and bibliographical references

Dolbear, Emily J.

The **Iroquois**; [by] Emily J. Dolbear and Peter Benoit. Children's Press 2011 48p il map (True book: American Indians) lib bdg $28; pa $6.95

Grades: 3 4 5   **970.004**

1. Iroquois Indians

ISBN 978-0-531-20771-0 lib bdg; 0-531-20771-4 lib bdg; 978-0-531-29313-3 pa; 0-531-29313-0 pa

LC 2010049079

This covers cultural basics of the Iroquois such as diet, clothing, lifestyle, and child rearing as well as relevant historical events.

Includes bibliographical references

Enzoe, Pete

The **caribou** feed our soul; [by] Pete Enzoe and Mindy Willett; photographs by Tessa Macintosh. Fitzhenry & Whiteside 2011 26p il (The land is our storybook) $16.95

Grades: 3 4 5 6   **970.004**

1. Caribou 2. Chipewyan Indians 3. Wildlife conservation

ISBN 978-1-89725-267-3; 1-89725-267-6

LC 2010-9045793

"This informative first-person narrative cleanly captures the Dénésôliné (Chipewyan) culture's dependence on and reverence for the caribou, the predominant symbol of the tribe's existence. . . . Enzoe, a Native spokesperson, teacher, and hunter, explains aspects of his tribe's daily life in the Northwest Territories. He speaks of the mysticism of the caribou and illustrates its importance in feeding and clothing the tribe. . . . The book is thoughtfully illustrated with a variety of engaging photographs of the area and its people, immersed in the daily goings-on of their lives. The aerial photography gives readers a grand view of the stunning geography." SLJ

Includes glossary and bibliographical references

Goble, Paul

All our relatives; traditional Native American thoughts about nature. compiled and illustrated by Paul Goble. World Wisdom 2005 un il $15.95

Grades: 5 6 7 8   **970.004**

1. Native Americans 2. Philosophy of nature

ISBN 0-941532-77-1; 978-0-941532-77-8

LC 2005004285

"The pages of this book are chock-full of quotations, songs, and brief stories that exemplify Native American attitudes toward nature. . . . Black Elk, Standing Bear, Brave Buffalo, and others observe the importance of various animals and the sacred qualities of all living things. . . . The spaces between text blocks are filled with Goble's familiar illustrations based on traditional Native American designs and colors." SLJ

Includes bibliographical references

Hicks, Terry Allan

The **Chumash**; by Terry Allan Hicks. Marshall Cavendish Benchmark 2008 48p il map (First Americans) lib bdg $29.93

Grades: 2 3 4   **970.004**

1. Chumash Indians

ISBN 978-0-7614-2678-3 lib bdg; 0-7614-2678-7 lib bdg

LC 2006034101

This describes Chumash "history and culture, way of life, beliefs, present status, and future outlook. Colorful modern photographs appear throughout, as do paintings, photos, and maps. [The] volume includes a simple craft . . . as well as a Native recipe. . . . [The] book has a helpful, easy-to-read graphical time line. Clear writing and attractive [layout makes this book] accessible and appealing." SLJ

Includes glossary and bibliographical references

King, David C.

First people; an illustrated history of American Indians. DK Pub. 2008 192p il map $19.99

Grades: 5 6 7 8   **970.004**

1. Native Americans

ISBN 978-0-7566-4092-7; 0-7566-4092-X

"This rich pictorial work serves as an entertaining, informative, and visually appealing introduction to American Indian culture and history. Each of the seven chapters covers a different time period in chronological order. . . . The glossy photographs, colorful drawings, and easily accessible paragraphs . . . make for an easy-to-use overall package." SLJ

The **Huron**. Marshall Cavendish Benchmark 2007 48p il (First Americans) lib bdg $31.36

Grades: 2 3 4   **970.004**

1. Huron Indians

ISBN 978-0-7614-2251-8 lib bdg; 0-7614-2251-X lib bdg

LC 2006011970

Provides information on the background, lifestyle, beliefs, and present-day lives of the Huron people

Includes glossary and bibliographical references

Kissock, Heather

Apache; American Indian art and culture. [by] Heather Kissock and Jordan McGill. Weigl Publishers Inc. 2010 24p il (American Indian art and culture) lib bdg $25.70; pa $9.95

Grades: 2 3 4   **970.004**

1. Apache Indians

ISBN 978-1-60596-991-6 lib bdg; 1-60596-991-5 lib bdg; 978-1-60596-992-3 pa; 1-60596-992-3 pa

LC 2010005331

Introduces the history, housing, clothing, agriculture, culture, art, and recipes of the Apache Indians.

This "provides early elementary students with an outstanding overview of the art and culture of [the Apache]. . . . Perfect for beginning readers, the content is straightforward and concise. Full-color up close photographs are integral to . . . [the] book, visually clarifying each idea and extending the text to aid in the student's understanding." Libr Media Connect

Includes glossary

Caddo; [by] Heather Kissock and Rachel Small. Weigl Publishers Inc. 2011 24p il (American Indian art and culture) lib bdg $25.70; pa $9.95

Grades: 2 3 4   **970.004**

1. Caddo Indians

ISBN 978-1-60596-979-4 lib bdg; 1-60596-979-6 lib bdg; 978-1-60596-980-0 pa; 1-60596-980-X pa

LC 2010005334

Highlights the traditional ways of the Caddo.

This "provides early elementary students with an outstanding overview of the art and culture of [the Caddo]. . . . Perfect for beginning readers, the content is straightforward and concise. Full-color up close photographs are integral to . . . [the] book, visually clarifying each idea and extending the text to aid in the student's understanding." Libr Media Connect

Includes glossary

Cherokee; American Indian art and culture. [by] Heather Kissock and Rachel Small. Weigl Publishers Inc. 2011 24p il (American Indian art and culture) lib bdg $25.70; pa $9.95

Grades: 2 3 4   **970.004**

1. Cherokee Indians

ISBN 978-1-60596-994-7 lib bdg; 1-60596-994-X lib bdg; 978-1-60596-995-4 pa; 1-60596-995-8 pa

LC 2010005335

Introduces the history, housing, clothing, agriculture, culture, art, and recipes of the Cherokee Indians

This "provides early elementary students with an outstanding overview of the art and culture of [the Cherokee Indians]. . . . Perfect for beginning readers, the content is straightforward and concise. Full-color up close photographs are integral to . . . [the] book, visually clarifying each idea and extending the text to aid in the student's understanding." Libr Media Connect

Includes glossary

Comanche; American Indian art and culture. Weigl Publishers Inc. 2011 24p il (American Indian art and culture) lib bdg $25.70; pa $9.95

Grades: 2 3 4   **970.004**

1. Comanche Indians

ISBN 978-1-60596-988-6 lib bdg; 1-60596-988-5 lib bdg; 978-1-60596-989-3 pa; 1-60596-989-3 pa

LC 2010005336

Introduces the history, housing, clothing, agriculture, culture, art, and recipes of the Comanche Indians

This "provides early elementary students with an outstanding overview of the art and culture of [the Comanche]. . . . Perfect for beginning readers, the content is straightforward and concise. Full-color up close photographs are integral to . . . [the] book, visually clarifying each idea and extending the text to aid in the student's understanding." Libr Media Connect

Includes glossary

Tigua; [by] Heather Kissock and Jordan McGill. Weigl Publishers Inc. 2011 24p il (American Indian art and culture) lib bdg $25.70; pa $9.95

Grades: 2 3 4   **970.004**

1. Tigua Indians

ISBN 978-1-60596-982-4 lib bdg; 1-60596-982-6 lib bdg; 978-1-60596-983-1 pa; 1-60596-983-4 pa

LC 2010005355

Introduces the history, housing, clothing, agriculture, culture, art, and recipes of the Tigua Indians.

This "provides early elementary students with an outstanding overview of the art and culture of [the Tigua Indians]. . . . Perfect for beginning readers, the content is straightforward and concise. Full-color up close photographs are integral to . . . [the] book, visually clarifying each idea and extending the text to aid in the student's understanding." Libr Media Connect

Includes glossary

McLeod, Tom

The **Delta** is my home; by Tom McLeod and Mindy Willett; photographs by Tessa Macintosh. Fitzhenry & Whiteside 2008 26p il (The land is our storybook) $16.95

Grades: 4 5 6 7   **970.004**

1. Northwest Territories 2. Mackenzie River (N.W.T.) 3. Native Americans -- Canada

ISBN 978-1-8972-5232-1; 1-8972-5232-3

"An 11-year-old boy who lives in the Mackenzie Delta region with his family tells about life there. His father is a renewable resource officer and has taught him how to hunt, fish, trap, and drive a boat. Readers also learn about his language, schooling, and clothing as well as the important role that storytelling plays in the culture. [This title provides] some useful information for reports and [is an] interesting [addition] for general reading." SLJ

McNeese, Tim

The **fascinating** history of American Indians; the age before Columbus. Enslow Publishers 2009 128p il map (America's living history) lib bdg $31.93

Grades: 5 6 7 8   **970.004**

1. Native Americans

ISBN 978-0-7660-2938-5 lib bdg; 0-7660-2938-7 lib bdg

"This thorough discussion of Native American life prior to Columbus's arrival combines theories of archaeologists, anthropologists, historians, and scientists to provide an engaging portrayal of the daily experiences of regional tribes. Based mostly on archaeological discoveries, the accessible text is supported by archival photographs, maps, and sidebars." Horn Book Guide

Includes glossary and bibliographical references

Murdoch, David Hamilton

North American Indian; written by David Murdoch; chief consultant, Stanley A. Freed; photographed by Lynton Gardiner. rev ed; DK Pubs. 2005 72p il (DK eyewitness books) $16.99; lib bdg $19.99

Grades: 4 5 6 7   **970.004**

1. Native Americans

ISBN 0-7566-1081-8; 0-7566-1082-6 lib bdg

First published 1995 by Knopf

This is a guide to the civilizations of North American Indians including full-color photographs of artifacts and descriptions ceremonies and customs.

Pokiak, James

Proud to be Inuvialuit; by James Pokiak and Mindy Willett; illustrated by Tessa Macintosh. Fitzhenry & Whiteside 2010 26p il pa $16.95

Grades: 3 4 5   **970.004**

1. Inuit 2. Native Americans -- Northwest Coast of North America

ISBN 1-89725-259-5; 978-1-89725-259-8

"Pokiak introduces his people, the Inuvialuit . . . to readers by having them meet his own family and their community of 900 people on the Arctic coast of Canada's Northwest Territories. Though they live in modern houses, have cell phones, and enjoy an indoor swimming pool, the people of Tuktoyaktuk still hunt beluga whales for subsistence as their ancestors did. . . . Text, illustrations, and captions work together well to present the Inuvialuit way of life. Illustrations include a large map and small paintings as well as many clear, color photos. . . . An informative introduction to an Inuit community today." Booklist

Terry, Michael Bad Hand

Daily life in a Plains Indian village, 1868. Clarion Bks. 1999 48p il map hardcover o.p. pa $9.95

Grades: 4 5 6 7   **970.004**

1. Native Americans -- Great Plains

ISBN 0-395-94542-9; 0-395-97499-2 pa

LC 98-32382

Depicts the historical background, social organization, and daily life of a Plains Indian village in 1868, presenting interiors, landscapes, clothing, and everyday objects

"The author presents short paragraphs of fascinating information accompanied by visuals that explain even more than the text." SLJ

Includes glossary

Zimmerman, Dwight Jon

Saga of the Sioux; an adaptation of Dee Brown's Bury My Heart at Wounded Knee. [adapted] by Dwight Jon Zimmerman. Henry Holt and Company 2011 208p il map $18.99

Grades: 5 6 7 8   **970.004**

1. Dakota Indians 2. West (U.S.) -- History 3. Native Americans -- Wars

ISBN 978-0-8050-9364-3; 0-8050-9364-8

LC 2011004792

"Dwight Jon Zimmerman has created a masterful adaptation of Dee Brown's Bury My Heart at Wounded Knee, presenting late nineteenth century history from a Native American viewpoint. While Brown's book traces the fates of several Native American tribes in the western United States, Zimmerman's adaptation focuses solely on the Sioux. . . . Historical figures central to the narrative, both Native American and white, are portrayed as real people, rather than caricatures. Rather than simply describing what happened, the book looks at why it happened. Individuals' motivations, strengths, and flaws are all explored in relation to how historical events unfolded. The book includes numerous photographs, illustrations, and maps that aid understanding and create visual appeal. . . . This is a must-have addition to any United States history collection serving teens." Voice Youth Advocates

Includes glossary and bibliographical references

Zoe, Therese

Living stories; [by] Therese Zoe, Philip Zoe and Mindy Willett; photographs by Tessa Macintosh. Fitzhenry & Whiteside 2009 32p il (The land is our storybook) $16.95

Grades: 3 4 5 6   **970.004**

1. Northwest Territories 2. Native Americans -- Canada 3. Native Americans -- Folklore

ISBN 978-1-89725-244-4; 1-89725-244-7

"Therese Zoe is a Tlicho woman from Gamèti in the Northwest Territories. . . . [In this book she] shares her love for her community and translates the sacred stories and traditional wisdom of her brother-in-law, Philip Zoe, and his sister, Elizabeth Chocolate. . . . Join Tlicho young people, Shelinda, Forest, and Bradley, as they learn about making dry-fish, bows and arrows, and birchbark baskets; the practices of old-time healers; as well as the sacred stories that tell the history of the Tlicho people." Publisher's note

970.01 North America--Early history to 1599

Bodden, Valerie

Columbus reaches the New World. Creative Education 2009 48p il (Days of change) lib bdg $32.80

Grades: 5 6 7 8   **970.01**

1. Explorers 2. America -- Exploration

ISBN 978-158341-732-4; 1-58341-732-X

LC 2008009163

"With elegant design and mature prose, the Days of Change series is an ideal starting point for all manner of school projects. . . . Columbus

Reaches the New World intelligently explains the famous sailor's motivations for forging a new trade route. . . . Anti-Columbus Day sentiments are mostly relegated to sidebars, but Bodden doesn't surgarcoat the enslavement and death that followed discovery." Booklist

Includes bibliographical references

Demi, 1942-
Columbus; by Demi. Marshall Cavendish 2012 64 p. ill. (hardcover) $19.99
Grades: 3 4 5 6   970.01
1. America -- Exploration   2. Columbus, Christopher, 1451-1506
3. Explorers -- Spain -- Biography   4. Explorers -- America -- Biography   5. America -- Discovery and exploration -- Spanish
ISBN 0761461671; 9780761461678
                                          LC 2011036019
This book on Christopher Columbus was written and illustrated by the children's book author Demi. "From his childhood in Italy to his death in Spain, this biography presents a detailed view of the explorer's life. . . .Columbus's faults and accomplishments are both presented, acknowledging that his drive to explore furthered Europeans' knowledge of other lands, but that his mistreatment of Native peoples devastated their lives and culture." (School Library Journal)

Englar, Mary
French colonies in America. Compass Point Books 2009 48p il (We the people) lib bdg $26.60
Grades: 4 5 6   970.01
1. French Americans 2. French Canadians 3. France -- Colonies
4. America -- Exploration
ISBN 978-0-7565-3839-2
                                          LC 2008007209
This is a history of French exploration and colonization in North America.
This provides "solid background matter and [introduces] key people and vocabulary." SLJ

Gunderson, Jessica
Conquistadors; by Jessica Gunderson. Creative Education 2011 48 p. (alk. paper) $35.65
Grades: 5 6 7 8   970.01
1. United States -- History 2. Soldiers 3. Military art and science -- History 4. Soldiers -- Spain -- History   5. Military art and science -- History   6. America -- Discovery and exploration -- Spanish
ISBN 1608181839; 9781608181834
                                          LC 2011035799
Author Jessica Gunderson's book "covers the beginnings of the people, weaponry, war tactics, and famous leaders, and examines the current perception of the group in popular culture in an appealing, detailed, and evenhanded manner. Historical reproductions, primary documents, photographs, maps, and film stills appear throughout" the "explorations of history." (Publisher's note)
Includes bibliographical references and index

Harrison, David L.
Mammoth bones and broken stones; the mystery of North America's first people. with illustrations by Richard Hilliard and archaeological photographs. Boyds Mills Press 2010 48p il map $18.95
Grades: 4 5 6 7   970.01
1. Prehistoric peoples 2. North America -- Antiquities
ISBN 978-1-59078-561-4; 1-59078-561-4
                                          LC 2009020247
"How and when the Western Hemisphere . . . came to be populated continues to be both mysterious and controversial for scientists. . . . Har-

rison does a good job setting the issue in context. He describes the earliest efforts to identify the original inhabitants of the continents, exploring the Clovis culture. . . . After clearly explaining how scholars decided that they were the first, he then lists the arguments against this hypothesis. . . . The narrative is aided by both photographs and original illustrations that imagine scenes from both the distant past and the field experiences." Kirkus

Includes glossary and bibliographical references

Hernandez, Roger E.
Early explorations: the 1500s. Marshall Cavendish Benchmark 2009 79p il map (Hispanic America) lib bdg $34.21
Grades: 4 5 6 7   970.01
1. Explorers 2. Spain -- Colonies 3. America -- Exploration 4. Southern States -- History 5. Southwestern States -- History
ISBN 978-0-7614-2937-1 lib bdg; 0-7614-2937-9 lib bdg
"Provides comprehensive information on the history of Spanish exploration in the United States." Publisher's note
Includes glossary and bibliographical references

Huey, Lois Miner
American archaeology uncovers the Vikings. Marshall Cavendish Benchmark 2009 64p il map (American archaeology) lib bdg $21.95
Grades: 4 5 6 7   970.01
1. America -- Antiquities 2. America -- Exploration 3. Vikings -- North America 4. Excavations (Archeology) -- Canada 5. Excavations (Archeology) -- United States
ISBN 978-0-7614-4270-7 lib bdg; 0-7614-4270-7 lib bdg
                                          LC 2008050266
This describes how archeologists have learned about the Vikings in America.
This is "both intriguing and engaging for young readers. . . . A welcomed addition to classroom and school libraries." Libr Media Connect
Includes glossary and bibliographical references

Lilly, Alexandra
Spanish colonies in America. Compass Point Books 2009 48p il map (We the people) lib bdg $26.60
Grades: 4 5 6   970.01
1. Explorers 2. Spain -- Colonies 3. America -- Exploration 4. Spaniards -- United States
ISBN 978-0-7565-3840-8 lib bdg; 0-7565-3840-8 lib bdg
                                          LC 2008011727
This is a history Spanish exploration, conquest, and colonization in North America.
This provides "solid background matter and [introduces] key people and vocabulary." SLJ

Maestro, Betsy
★ The discovery of the Americas; by Betsy and Giulio Maestro. Lothrop, Lee & Shepard Bks. 1990 48p il maps hardcover o.p. pa $6.95
Grades: 2 3 4   970.01
1. America -- Exploration
ISBN 0-688-06837-5; 0-688-11512-8 pa
                                          LC 89-32375
Discusses both hypothetical and historical voyages of discovery to America by the Phoenicians, Saint Brendan of Ireland, the Vikings, and such later European navigators as Columbus, Cabot, and Magellan
"The dazzlingly clean and accurate prose and the exhilarating beauty of the pictures combine for an extraordinary achievement in both history and art." SLJ

Mann, Charles C.

★ **Before** Columbus; the Americas of 1491. Atheneum Books for Young Readers 2009 117p il map $24.99

Grades: 5 6 7 8 9 10   **970.01**

1. America -- Antiquities 2. Native Americans -- Origin 3. Native Americans -- History

ISBN 978-1-4169-4900-8; 1-4169-4900-3

LC 2009007691

Adapted from 1491, published 2006 by Knopf for adults

"Mann paints a superb picture of pre-Columbian America. In the process, he overturns the misconceived image of Natives as simple, widely scattered savages with minimal impact on their surroundings. Well-chosen, vividly colored graphics and photographs of mummies, pyramids, artifacts, and landscapes as well as the author's skillful storytelling will command the attention of even the most reluctant readers." SLJ

Includes glossary and bibliographical references

Mooney, Carla

Explorers of the New World; discover the golden age of exploration; with 22 projects. illustrated by Tom Casteel. Nomad 2011 120p il map (Build it yourself) pa $15.95 **970.01**

1. Explorers 2. America -- Exploration

ISBN 978-1-936313-44-0; 1-936313-44-8

Provides twenty-two step-by-step projects to help readers learn about the explorers that discovered America and their voyages.

"This informative, entertaining activity book takes readers on a fascinating voyage of their own. . . . Each chapter concludes with 'Make Your Own' activities that bring life to the history with instructions for the construction of a logbook, clay activities, recipes, games, etc. Some may require the assistance of an adult but are not complicated or time consuming." SLJ

Includes glossary and bibliographical references

Wyatt, Valerie

★ **Who** discovered America? with illustrations by Howie Woo. Kids Can Press 2008 40p il map $17.95; pa $8.95

Grades: 4 5 6   **970.01**

1. America -- Antiquities 2. America -- Exploration

ISBN 978-1-55453-128-8; 1-55453-128-4; 978-1-55453-129-5 pa; 1-55453-129-2 pa

"With interesting sidebars and engaging illustrations and photos, this 'whodunit' of sorts describes, on a spread each, evidence for the journeys of various groups who discovered, or claimed to have discovered, [the North American] continent. . . . Wyatt writes clearly about how scientists unlock clues to how and when various groups could have made landfall. . . . Raising perhaps more questions than it answers, this book leaves it to readers to decide the solution to the mystery." SLJ

Includes glossary

970.02   North America 1600-1699

Maestro, Betsy

★ **The new** Americans; colonial times, 1620-1689. illustrated by Giulio Maestro. Lothrop, Lee & Shepard Bks. 1998 48p il map hardcover o.p. pa $7.99

Grades: 2 3 4   **970.02**

1. Canada -- History -- 0-1763 (New France) 2. United States -- History -- 1600-1775, Colonial period

ISBN 0-688-13448-3; 0-06-57572-7 pa

LC 95-19636

Traces the competition among the American Indians, French, English, Spanish, and Dutch for land, furs, timber, and other resources of North America

This is "accessibly written and meticulously illustrated. . . . Giulio Maestro's carefully detailed watercolor and color-pencil art includes maps, closely focused spot illustrations and dramatic spreads, which together provide a vivid picture of the century's pivotal events." Publ Wkly

971   Canada

Baker, Stuart

In the Arctic. Marshall Cavendish Benchmark 2010 32p il map (Climate change) lib bdg $19.95

Grades: 5 6 7 8   **971**

1. Arctic regions 2. Greenhouse effect

ISBN 978-0-7614-4437-4 lib bdg; 0-7614-4437-8 lib bdg

LC 2009-5767

The book about climate change in the Arctic "is perfectly organized for students. . . . Unique layout features serve as signposts and will help focus readers' attention. . . . [The book] features an outstanding chart of possible effects of global warming on the area in question, listing 'Possible Event,' 'Predicted Result,' and 'Impact' in short, bulleted statements." SLJ

Includes glossary

Bowers, Vivien

Hey Canada! by Vivien Bowers; illustrated by Milan Pavlovic. Tundra Books of Northern New York 2012 72 p. ill. (chiefly col.), maps (hardcover) $19.95

Grades: 3 4 5   **971**

1. Canada 2. Travelers 3. Voyages and travels

ISBN 1770492550; 9781770492554

LC 2011923470

This children's picture book by Vivien Bowers presents "a young traveler's . . . account of a quick province-by-province drive across Canada." The "9-year-old narrator [travels] to cities, roadside attractions and natural wonders from Cape Spear to Iqaluit." The book also provides information "about regional foods . . . and other artifacts of European settlement." (Kirkus Reviews)

Coulter, Laurie

★ **Ballplayers** and bonesetters; one hundred ancient Aztec and Maya jobs you might have adored or abhorred. [written] by Laurie Coulter; illustrated by Martha Newbigging. Annick Press 2008 96p il $25.95; pa $16.95

Grades: 4 5 6   **971**

1. Mayas 2. Aztecs

ISBN 978-1-55451-141-9; 1-55451-141-0; 978-1-55451-140-2 pa; 1-55451-140-2 pa

"Following a readable and humorous overview of the highly developed Aztec and Maya civilizations, this lively text lists 100 jobs that a young person might have held or aspired to during the Late Postclassic period in Mesoamerica (1350 to 1521). . . . Taken as a whole, the descriptions of the vocations yield a rich view of the culture, and the breezy text makes this as much a browsing as a reference title. The colorful cartoon illustrations enhance the text, adding just the right artistic complement." SLJ

Greenwood, Barbara

★ **A pioneer** sampler; the daily life of a pioneer family in 1840. illustrated by Heather Collins. Ticknor & Fields Bks. for Young Readers 1995 240p il hardcover o.p. pa $15

Grades: 4 5 6 7 **971**

1. Frontier and pioneer life 2. Ontario
ISBN 0-395-71540-7; 0-395-88393-8 pa

LC 94-12829

First published 1994 in Canada with title: A pioneer story

"Using a combination of fiction and fact-filled supplementary commentary, with illustrations inspired by Garth Williams, the author tells the story of the Robertsons, a large, hardworking farm family. Good projects for school or home." N Y Times Book Rev

★ **Junior** Worldmark encyclopedia of the Canadian provinces; [Timothy L. Gall and Susan Bevan Gall, editors] 5th ed.; U.X.L 2007 294p il map $70

Grades: 5 6 7 8 9 10 **971**

1. Reference books 2. Canada
ISBN 978-1-4144-1060-9; 1-4144-1060-3

LC 2007003908

First published 1997

"Arranged by 40 . . . subheadings . . . this . . . resource provides . . . information on all of Canada's provinces and territories. [It includes] details on Canada's arts, climate, government, health, languages, notable persons, ethnic groups and . . . more." Publisher's note

Includes bibliographical references

Penn, Briony

The **kids** book of Canadian geography; written and illustrated by Briony Penn. Kids Can Press 2008 56p il map $19.95

Grades: 3 4 5 6 **971**

1. Canada
ISBN 978-1-55074-890-1; 1-55074-890-4

This "traces the continents' formation, touching on Canada's ancient landscapes, evolving climate, continent shaping and life on the land including human settlement, plus a geographical coast to coast tour and much more." Publisher's note

Sonneborn, Liz

Canada; by Liz Sonneborn. Children's Press 2012 144 p. col. ill.. col. maps (library) $40

Grades: 5 6 7 8 **971**

1. Canada 2. Canada -- Social life and customs
ISBN 0531253511; 9780531253519

LC 2011011970

This book by Liz Sonneborn is part of the Enchantment of the World series and looks at Canada. The introduction focuses on Canadian Terry Fox. Sonneborn "covers geography, natural resources, environment, history, government, diversity, religions, culture, and everyday life. She includes details like 'poutine' (fries, cheese curds, and gravy) and 'Timmies' (a coffee and doughnut chain)." (School Library Journal)

Includes bibliographical references (p. 134) and index.

Walker, Sally M.

★ **Blizzard** of glass; the Halifax explosion of 1917. Henry Holt 2011 xii, 145p il $18.99

Grades: 5 6 7 8 **971**

1. World War, 1914-1918 -- Naval operations 2. Halifax (N.S.) -- History -- Explosion, 1917
ISBN 978-0-8050-8945-5; 0-8050-8945-4

LC 2011005914

"The text reads smoothly with unfamiliar words defined in the text. Illustrations consist of two full-page maps and numerous black-and-white photos. The final chapter revisits the featured families and their descendants, thus tying up the loose ends. . . . This tragic, but well-told story belongs in most collections." SLJ

Includes bibliographical references

Williams, Brian

★ **Canada**; [by] Brian Williams; Tom Carter and Ben Cecil, consultants. National Geographic 2007 64p il map (Countries of the world) lib bdg $27.90; pa $12.95

Grades: 4 5 6 7 **971**

1. Canada
ISBN 978-1-4263-0025-7 lib bdg; 978-1-4263-0573-3 pa

LC 2007296572

A basic overview of the history, geography, climate and culture of Canada

This "clear, succinct [overview] will support assignments without overwhelming casual readers. . . . A good selection of recent, high-quality color photographs gives the [book] visual appeal." SLJ

Includes glossary and bibliographical references

971.01 Canada -- Early history to 1763

Worth, Richard

New France, 1534-1763; featuring the region that now includes all or parts of Michigan, Minnesota, Wisconsin, Illinois, Indiana, Ohio, Pennsylvania, Vermont, Maine, and Canada from Manitoba to Newfoundland. by Richard Worth. National Geographic Society 2007 109p il map (Voices from colonial America) $21.95; lib bdg $32.90

Grades: 5 6 7 8 **971.01**

1. Mississippi River valley -- History 2. Canada -- History -- 0-1763 (New France)
ISBN 978-1-4263-0147-6; 1-4263-0147-2; 978-1-4263-0148-3 lib bdg; 1-4263-0148-0 lib bdg

LC 2007-29544

"Worth presents the history of the vast French colony known as New France. Clearly written, the book is studded with quotes from people living in the colony and illustrated with colorful paintings, prints, and maps from a variety of periods. . . . This nicely designed introduction to a historically significant area fills a gap in many colonial history series and library collections." Booklist

Includes bibliographical references

971.1 British Columbia

Ritchie, Scot

Qwuni and the Salmon Festival; Scot Ritchie. Groundwood Books 2015 32 p. color illustrations $18.95

Grades: K 1 2 **971.1**

1. Salmon fishing 2. Chehalis Indians
ISBN 1554987180; 9781554987184

"It's the day of the first salmon ceremony, and P'ésk'a is excited to celebrate. His community, the Sts'ailes people, give thanks to the river and the salmon it brings by commemorating the first salmon of the season." (Publisher's note)

972 Mexico, Central America, West Indies, Bermuda

Apte, Sunita

The **Aztec** empire. Children's Press 2009 48p il map (True book) lib bdg $26; pa $6.95

Grades: 3 4 5 **972**

1. Aztecs
ISBN 978-0-531-25227-7 lib bdg; 0-531-25227-2 lib bdg; 978-0-531-24108-0 pa; 0-531-24108-4 pa

LC 2009000299

In this book the Aztec empire is "outlined for young readers with care and precision. . . . Loaded with access points such as captions, pull-outs, a time line, and a map, and with better-than-usual reproductions of well-chosen primary sources and art, the [book sports] a bright, peppy design. . . . [This book is] rigorous in distinguishing fact from theory, and conscientious about presenting competing theories where they exist." SLJ

Includes glossary and bibliographical references

Cooke, Tim

★ **Ancient** Aztec; archaeology unlocks the secrets of Mexico's past. National Geographic 2007 64p il map (National Geographic investigates) $17.95; lib bdg $27.90

Grades: 4 5 6 7   972

1. Aztecs 2. Mexico -- Antiquities 3. Excavations (Archeology) -- Mexico

ISBN 978-1-4263-0072-1; 1-4263-0072-7; 978-1-4263-0073-8 lib bdg; 1-4263-0073-5 lib bdg

LC 2007024813

This describes ancient Aztec origins, technology, major archeological sites, civilization, and connections to the present

"Pithy and appealing. . . . Aerial photos, time [line], informative sidebars, an interview with an archaeologist, and excellent maps augment rigorously supported [text] that [asks] and [answers] interesting questions." SLJ

Gruber, Beth

★ **Mexico**; [by] Beth Gruber; Gary S. Elbow and Jorge Zamora, consultants. National Geographic 2007 64p il map (Countries of the world) lib bdg $27.90; pa $12.95

Grades: 4 5 6 7   972

1. Mexico

ISBN 0-7922-7669-8 lib bdg; 1-4263-0566-4 pa

LC 2004026452

"This volume introduces Mexico's geography, history, wildlife, culture, and government. The many excellent color photos and maps are a striking feature of the series. . . . This will be a useful addition to many libraries." Booklist

Includes glossary and bibliographical references

Harris, Nathaniel

★ **Ancient** Maya; archaeology unlocks the secrets to the Maya's past. by Nathaniel Harris; Elizabeth Graham, consultant. National Geographic 2008 64p il map (National Geographic investigates) $17.95; lib bdg $27.90

Grades: 4 5 6 7   972

1. Mayas 2. Mexico -- Antiquities 3. Excavations (Archeology) -- Mexico

ISBN 978-1-4263-0227-5; 1-4263-0227-4; 978-1-4263-0228-2 lib bdg; 1-4263-0228-2 lib bdg

LC 2007047837

This describes ancient Mayan civilization and how archeologists found out about it.

Includes glossary and bibliographical references

Heinrichs, Ann

The **Aztecs**; by Ann Heinrichs. Benchmark Books 2011 64 p. (Technology of the ancients) (print) $32.79

Grades: 4 5 6 7   972

1. Aztecs 2. Technological innovations -- History 3. Aztecs

ISBN 1608707652; 9781608707539; 9781608707652

LC 2011018348

This book, by Ann Heinrichs, includes "presentations of [the Aztec's] ancient cultures, emphasiz[ing] governance and material culture

(clothing, crafts, architecture). The book [does] not cover the origins of the empires or try to explain how they became so powerful." (School Library Journal)

★ **Junior** Worldmark encyclopedia of the Mexican states; [Timothy L. Gall and Susan Bevan Gall, editors] 2nd ed.; U.X.L,Thomson/Gale 2007 423p il map $70

Grades: 5 6 7 8 9 10   972

1. Reference books 2. Mexico

ISBN 978-1-4144-1112-5

LC 2007003906

First published 2004

"Arranged by 28 . . . subheadings . . . Junior Worldmark Encyclopedia of the Mexican States provides . . . information on each of Mexico's 31 states. Topics covered include climate, plants and animals, population and ethnic groups, religions, transportation, history, state and local governments, political parties, judicial system, economy, education, arts, media, tourism, sports, famous people and . . . more." Publisher's note

Includes bibliographical references

Kent, Deborah

Mexico; by Deborah Kent. Children's Press 2012 144 p. cil. ill., photographs (library) $40

Grades: 5 6 7 8   972

1. Mexico 2. Culture 3. Mexico -- History

ISBN 0531253554; 9780531253557

LC 2011010812

This book by Deborah Kent is part of the Enchantment of the World series and looks at Mexico. The books in the series offer 10 "chapters, several maps, a fast-facts section, and a few references to other sources, including a referral to a Scholastic website (new). The chapters cover geography, natural environment, history, politics, people and culture." (School Library Journal)

Includes bibliographical references and index.

Kops, Deborah

Palenque; by Deborah Kops. Twenty-First Century Books 2008 80p il (Unearthing ancient worlds) lib bdg $30.60

Grades: 5 6 7 8   972

1. Mayas 2. Mexico -- Antiquities 3. Palenque site (Mexico) 4. Excavations (Archeology) -- Mexico

ISBN 978-0-8225-7504-7 lib bdg; 0-8225-7504-3 lib bdg

LC 2007021323

This describes the discovery of the ancient Mayan site of Palenque in 1840 by John Stephens and Frederick Catherwood, and the mid-20th century excavations of the site by Alberto Ruz Lhuillier, who discovered the tomb of the Mayan king Pakal, who died in 683 A.D., inside a pyramid

This "clearly written [title is] illustrated with large photographs and period artwork, and the pages are broken up with text boxes featuring quotes and interesting anecdotes." SLJ

Includes glossary and bibliographical references

Lourie, Peter

Hidden world of the Aztec. Boyds Mills Press 2006 48p il map $17.95

Grades: 4 5 6 7   972

1. Aztecs 2. Excavations (Archeology) -- Mexico

ISBN 978-1-59078-069-5; 1-59078-069-8

The author takes a "look at the Aztecs from the perspective of archaeological digs at the Great Temple in modern-day Mexico City and at the Pyramid of the Moon in Teotihuacan. . . . The writing style is clear, informative, and interesting." SLJ

Includes glossary and bibliographical references

McDaniel, Melissa

New Mexico; [by] Melissa McDaniel, Ettagale Blauer, and Jason Laure. 2nd ed.; Marshall Cavendish Benchmark 2008 144p il map (Celebrate the states) lib bdg $39.93

Grades: 4 5 6 7 **972**

1. New Mexico

ISBN 978-0-7614-2719-3; 0-7614-2719-8

LC 2007-9273

First published 1999

"Provides comprehensive information on the geography, history, wildlife, governmental structure, economy, cultural diversity, peoples, religion, and landmarks of New Mexico." Publisher's note

Includes bibliographical references

972.81   Guatemala

Croy, Anita

★ Guatemala. National Geographic 2009 64p il map (Countries of the world) lib bdg $27.90

Grades: 4 5 6 7 **972.81**

1. Guatemala

ISBN 978-1-4263-0471-2 lib bdg; 1-4263-0471-4 lib bdg

This describes the geography, nature, history, people and culture, government and economy of Guatemala

Includes glossary and bibliographical references

Mann, Elizabeth

★ Tikal; the center of the Maya world. with illustrations by Tom McNeely. Mikaya Press 2002 47p il map (Wonders of the world) $19.95

Grades: 4 5 6 7 **972.81**

1. Mayas -- Antiquities

ISBN 1-931414-05-X

LC 2002-29599

A history of the Maya Indians in the city of Tikal, founded in 800 B.C.

"Mann's narrative flows smoothly, and frequent, full-color illustrations . . . help to clarify the details mentioned in the text." Booklist

Includes glossary

Ollhoff, Jim

Mayan and Aztec mythology; by Jim Ollhoff. ABDO Publishing Company 2011 32p. ill. (The world of mythology) lib bdg $27.07

Grades: 5 6 7 8 **972.81**

1. Mythology 2. Mayas -- Folklore 3. Aztecs -- Folklore 4. Mayas -- Religion 5. Aztecs -- Religion

ISBN 1617147249; 9781617147241

LC 2010042976

This describes the history of myths of the Maya and Aztecs, their meaning, and their gods and goddesses including Itzamna, Xolotl, the Aztec feathered serpent god Quetzalcoatl,and the Mayan rain god Chac.

"Ollhoff writes in a clear and engaging fashion, presenting complex issues in a way that will be easy for youngsters to grasp. . . . The photographs and reproductions of art tie directly to the [text]." SLJ

972.82   Belize

Jermyn, Leslie

Belize; [by] Leslie Jermyn and Yong Jui Lin. 2nd ed.; Marshall Cavendish Benchmark 2012 144p il map (Cultures of the world) lib bdg $42.79

Grades: 5 6 7 8 **972.82**

1. Belize

ISBN 978-1-60870-452-1; 1-60870-452-1

LC 2010035966

Provides information on the geography, history, wildlife, governmental structure, economy, cultural diversity, peoples, religion, and culture of Belize.

"The concise writing offers enough material for report writers without overwhelming them. Numerous full-color and black-and-white photos of interest, a clean layout, and use of pastels to highlight headings and sidebars contribute to the attractiveness of . . . [this presentation]." SLJ

Includes glossary and bibliographical references

972.83   Honduras

McGaffey, Leta

Honduras; [by] Leta McGaffey and Michael Spilling. 2nd ed.; Marshall Cavendish Benchmark 2010 144p il map (Cultures of the world) lib bdg $42.79

Grades: 5 6 7 8 **972.83**

1. Honduras

ISBN 978-0-7614-4848-8 lib bdg; 0-7614-4848-9 lib bdg

LC 2009022642

First published 1999

"Provides comprehensive information on the geography, history, wildlife, governmental structure, economy, cultural diversity, peoples, religion, and culture of Honduras." Publisher's note

Includes glossary and bibliographical references

Shields, Charles J., 1951-

Honduras; Charles J. Shields. Mason Crest Publishers 2016 64 p. illustrations, map (library binding) $22.95

Grades: 5 6 7 8 **972.83**

1. Honduras 2. Geography

ISBN 1422232905; 9781422206492; 9781422207161; 9781422232903

LC 2008031996

"Once a center for the Mayan civilization, Honduras was colonized by Spain during the 16th century. Three centuries of colonial rule produced a civilization that blended Spanish and native customs and culture. Since gaining independence from Spain in 1821, Honduras has experienced a great deal of political instability." (Publisher's note)

972.84   El Salvador

Foley, Erin

El Salvador; [by] Erin Foley, Rafiz Hapipi. 2nd ed.; Benchmark Bks. 2005 144p il map (Cultures of the world) lib bdg $42.79

Grades: 5 6 7 8 **972.84**

1. El Salvador

ISBN 0-7614-1967-5

LC 2005009360

First published 1994

This describes the geography, history, government, economy, environment, people, lifestyle, religion, language, arts, leisure, festivals, and food of El Salvador

Includes glossary and bibliographical references

972.85　Nicaragua

Kott, Jennifer

★ Nicaragua; [by] Jennifer Kott, Kristi Streiffert. 2nd ed.; Benchmark Bks. 2005 144p il map (Cultures of the world) lib bdg $42.79
Grades: 5 6 7 8　　　　　　　　　　**972.85**
1. Nicaragua
ISBN 0-7614-1969-1

LC 2005009240
First published 1994
An illustrated overview of the geography, economy, history, government, politics, and culture of Nicaragua
Includes glossary and bibliographical references

972.86　Costa Rica

Foley, Erin

Costa Rica; [by] Erin Foley and Barbara Cooke. 2nd ed.; Marshall Cavendish Benchmark 2008 144p il map (Cultures of the world) lib bdg $42.79
Grades: 5 6 7 8　　　　　　　　　　**972.86**
1. Costa Rica
ISBN 978-0-7614-2079-8 lib bdg; 0-7614-2079-7 lib bdg

LC 2006101736
First published 1997
This offers "information on the geography, history, wildlife, governmental structure, economy, cultural diversity, peoples, religion, and culture of Costa Rica." Publisher's note
Includes glossary and bibliographical references

Yomtov, Nel

★ Costa Rica; by Nel Yomtov. Scholastic Library Pub 2014 144 p. illustrations, color maps (library binding) $40
Grades: 5 6 7 8　　　　　　　　　　**972.86**
1. Costa Rica
ISBN 0531220141; 9780531220146

LC 2013022563
This book, by Nel Yomtov, focuses on Costa Rica. The "country's culture, history, and geography are explored in detail, allowing readers a chance to see how people live in faraway nations.... Sidebars highlight especially interesting people, places, and events ... [and] easy recipes give readers the opportunity to experience foreign cuisine first-hand." (Publisher's note)
Includes bibliographical references and index

972.87　Panama

Hassig, Susan M.

Panama; [by] Susan Hassig & Lynette Quek. 2nd ed.; Marshall Cavendish Benchmark 2007 144p il map (Cultures of the world) lib bdg $42.79
Grades: 5 6 7 8　　　　　　　　　　**972.87**
1. Panama
ISBN 978-0-7614-2028-6 lib bdg; 0-7614-2028-2 lib bdg

LC 2006020824
First published 1996
This provides "information on the geography, history, wildlife, governmental structure, economy, cultural diversity, peoples, religion, and culture of Panama." Publisher's note
Includes glossary and bibliographical references

972.9　West Indies (Antilles) and Bermuda

Kras, Sara Louise

Antigua and Barbuda; [by] Sara Louise Kras. Marshall Cavendish Benchmark 2008 144p il map (Cultures of the world) lib bdg $42.79
Grades: 5 6 7 8　　　　　　　　　　**972.9**
1. Antigua and Barbuda
ISBN 978-0-7614-2570-0

LC 2006031537
This describes the geography, history, government, economy, environment, people, and culture of Antigua and Barbuda
Includes glossary and bibliographical references

972.91　Cuba

Green, Jen

★ Cuba; [by] Jen Green; Damián Fernández and Alejandro de la Fuente, consultants. National Geographic 2007 64p il map (Countries of the world) lib bdg $27.90
Grades: 4 5 6 7　　　　　　　　　　**972.91**
1. Cuba
ISBN 978-1-4263-0057-8

LC 2007026468
This describes the geography, nature, history, people & culture, government & economy of Cuba.
Includes glossary and bibliographical references

Sheehan, Sean

Cuba; [by] Sean Sheehan, Leslie Jermyn. 2nd ed.; Benchmark Bks. 2005 144p il map (Cultures of the world) lib bdg $42.79
Grades: 5 6 7 8　　　　　　　　　　**972.91**
1. Cuba
ISBN 0-7614-1965-9

LC 2005009362
First published 1994
This describes the geography, history, government, economy, population, lifestyle, religion, language, arts, leisure, festivals, and food of Cuba
Includes glossary and bibliographical references

Stein, R. Conrad

Cuban Missile Crisis; in the shadow of nuclear war. Enslow Publishers 2009 128p il map (America's living history) lib bdg $31.93
Grades: 5 6 7 8　　　　　　　　　　**972.91**
1. Cuban Missile Crisis, 1962 2. Soviet Union -- Foreign relations -- United States 3. United States -- Foreign relations -- Soviet Union
ISBN 978-0-7660-2905-7 lib bdg; 0-7660-2905-0 lib bdg

LC 2008-4703
"Discusses the Cuban missile crisis, a thirteen-day struggle between the United States and the Soviet Union, including the causes of the conflict, the leaders faced with important decisions, and the final resolution to avoid nuclear war." Publisher's note
Includes glossary and bibliographical references

Tracy, Kathleen

We visit Cuba. Mitchell Lane Publishers 2010 63p il (Your land and my land) lib bdg $33.95
Grades: 4 5 6 7　　　　　　　　　　**972.91**
1. Cuba
ISBN 978-1-58415-890-5 lib bdg; 1-58415-890-5 lib bdg

LC 2010006558
"With an inviting format that includes bright color photos on every spread, this title ... offers an appealing overview of Cuba's history, ge-

ography, culture and lifestyle, politics, economics, and more. . . . A good starting point for research as well as for personal interest." Booklist

Includes glossary and bibliographical references

972.92 Jamaica and Cayman Islands

Green, Jen

★ **Jamaica**; [by] Jen Green; David J. Howard and Joel Frater, consultants. National Geographic 2008 64p il map (Countries of the world) lib bdg $27.90

Grades: 4 5 6 7   **972.92**

1. Jamaica

ISBN 978-1-4263-0300-5 lib bdg; 1-4263-0300-9 lib bdg

This describes the geography, nature, history, people and culture, government, and economy of Jamaica.

Includes glossary and bibligraphical references

Sheehan, Sean

Jamaica; Sean Sheehan, Debbie Nevins, Angela Black. Cavendish Square Publishing 2015 144 p. (library binding) $47.07

Grades: 5 6 7 8   **972.92**

1. Jamaica 2. Geography

ISBN 1502600773; 9781502600776

LC 2014037926

Introduces the geography, history, religion, government, economy, and culture of Jamaica

Includes bibliographical references and index

972.93 Dominican Republic

Foley, Erin

Dominican Republic; [by] Erin Foley & Leslie Jermyn. 2nd ed; Marshall Cavendish Benchmark 2005 144p (Cultures of the world) lib bdg $42.79

Grades: 5 6 7 8   **972.93**

1. Dominican Republic

ISBN 0-7614-1966-7

First published 1995

"The material is well organized in easily readable sections, accurately illustrated with well-placed, full-color photographs on every page." SLJ

972.94 Haiti

Aronin, Miriam

Earthquake in Haiti. Bearport Pub. 2011 32p il map (Code red) lib bdg $25.27

Grades: 4 5 6 7   **972.94**

1. Earthquakes 2. Haiti

ISBN 978-1-936088-66-9; 1-936088-66-5

LC 2010011126

Describes the devastating earthquake that occurred in Haiti on January 12, 2010.

"The text is written from the points of view of some of the people involved, including primary source direct quotes. Some of the pictures are necessarily graphic, which adds to the authenticity. . . . This title will be used for browsing as well as for reports." Libr Media Connect

Includes glossary and bibliographical references

Benoit, Peter

The **Haitian** earthquake of 2010. Children's Press 2011 48p il (True book: disasters) lib bdg $28; pa $6.95

Grades: 3 4 5   **972.94**

1. Earthquakes 2. Haiti

ISBN 978-0-531-25420-2 lib bdg; 0-531-25420-8; 978-0-531-26625-0 pa; 0-531-26625-7 pa

LC 2011007912

This book about the earthquake in Haiti in 2010 and its aftermath is "thoughtfully designed. . . . The information . . . is right on target: concise, accurate, and thorough. . . . The photographs . . . are especially effective at putting a human face on large-scale devastation." Booklist

Includes glossary and bibliographical references

NgCheong-Lum, Roseline, 1962-

Haiti; [by] Roseline Ng Cheong-Lum & Leslie Jermyn. 2nd ed; Marshall Cavendish Benchmark 2005 144p il map (Cultures of the world) lib bdg $42.79

Grades: 5 6 7 8   **972.94**

1. Haiti

ISBN 0-7614-1968-3

First published 1995

Describes the geography, history, government, economy, culture, peoples, and religion of Haiti

Includes glossary and bibliographical references

Oelschlager, Vanita

I came from the water; one Haitian boy's incredible tale of survival. VanitaBooks 2012 $8.95

Grades: K 1 2   **972.94**

1. Haiti 2. Orphans 3. Picture books for children

ISBN 0983290458; 9780983290452

In this book, Vanita Oelschlager "shares the real-life story of an eight-year-old Haitian boy who, as an infant, was packed into a basket during a catastrophic flood, rescued, and sent to a children's village, where he was named Moses. . . . Moses describes the priest who runs the village . . . and the new children who arrived after the great earthquake of 2012" 'I am one of the strong ones,' he says. 'I must help those who are not as strong.'" (Publishers Weekly)

Yomtov, Nel

Haiti; by Nel Yomtov. Children's Press 2012 144 p. col. ill. (library) $40

Grades: 5 6 7 8   **972.94**

1. Haiti

ISBN 0531253538; 9780531253533

LC 2011010048

This book is part of the Enchantment of the World series and focuses on Haiti. This series presents "factual information against a backdrop of brightly colored pictures and maps. . . . Each book provides a timeline, Fast Facts, and embassies." The books also include "brief chapters that follow real people in their daily lives." (Library Media Connection)

Includes bibliographical references and index.

972.95 Puerto Rico

DaSilva-Gordon, Maria

Puerto Rico; past and present. Rosen Central 2011 48p il map (The United States: past and present) lib bdg $26.50; pa $11.75

Grades: 3 4 5 6   **972.95**

1. Puerto Rico

ISBN 978-1-4358-9502-7 lib bdg; 1-4358-9502-9 lib bdg; 978-1-4358-9529-4 pa; 1-4358-9529-0 pa

LC 2010005891

This describes the history, culture, economy, and geography of the island of Puerto Rico.

Includes bibliographical references

Schwabacher, Martin

Puerto Rico; by Martin Schwabacher and Steve Otfinoski. 2nd ed.; Marshall Cavendish Benchmark 2010 144p il map (Celebrate the states) $42.79

Grades: 5 6 7 8   **972.95**

1. Puerto Rico

ISBN 978-0-7614-4734-4; 0-7614-4734-2

LC 2009007066

First published 2001

This offers information on the geography, history, wildlife, governmental structure, economy, cultural diversity, peoples, religion, and landmarks of Puerto Rico.

Includes bibliographical references

Stille, Darlene R., 1942-

Puerto Rico; by Darlene R. Stille. Revised edition Children's Press, an Imprint of Scholastic Inc. 2014 144 p. illustrations, maps (library binding : alk. paper) $40

Grades: 4 5 6 7   **972.95**

1. Puerto Rico 2. United States -- History 3. Puerto Rico

ISBN 0531282902; 9780531282908

LC 2013044805

"Not quite an independent nation, yet not quite a state, either, Puerto Rico enjoys a unique relationship with the United States. Readers will learn how Puerto Rico was first settled and how it came to be a part of the United States. They will also learn about its rich cultural heritage and how its people live today. In addition, detailed descriptions of the island's topography and wildlife give readers an up-close tour of Puerto Rico's wilderness." (Publisher's note)

Includes bibliographical references(pages 133-137)and index

972.96   Bahama Islands

Hintz, Martin

The **Bahamas**; by Martin Hintz. Children's Press 2013 144 p. col. ill., col. maps (Enchantment of the world. Second series) (library) $40

Grades: 5 6 7 8   **972.96**

1. Bahamas 2. Bahamas -- Description and travel

ISBN 0531275418; 9780531275412

LC 2012000513

This book, by Martin Hintz, is part of the "Enchantment of the World" series. In it the author provides information and photographs showcasing the people, places and events surrounding the Caribbean island chain of the Bahamas. Contents include photographs of Bahaman cities and landscapes, statistics describing the islands' features, and traditional Bahaman recipes.

Includes bibliographical references and index

972.98   Windward and other southern islands

Elias, Marie Louise

Barbados; [by] Marie Louise Elias and Josie Elias. 2nd ed.; Marshall Cavendish Benchmark 2010 144p il map (Cultures of the world) lib bdg $42.79

Grades: 5 6 7 8   **972.98**

1. Barbados

ISBN 978-0-7614-4853-2 lib bdg; 0-7614-4853-5 lib bdg

LC 2009044592

First published 2000

This offers information on the geography, history, wildlife, governmental structure, economy, cultural diversity, peoples, religion, and culture of Barbados

Includes glossary and bibliographical references

Orr, Tamra

Saint Lucia; [by] Tamra Orr. 2nd ed.; Marshall Cavendish Benchmark 2008 144p il map (Cultures of the world) lib bdg $42.79

Grades: 5 6 7 8   **972.98**

1. Saint Lucia

ISBN 978-0-7614-2569-4

First published 1997

This describes the geography, history, government, economy, environment, people, and culture of Saint Lucia

Includes glossary and bibliographical references

Pang, Guek-Cheng, 1950-

Grenada; 2nd ed.; Marshall Cavendish Benchmark 2011 144p il map (Cultures of the world) lib bdg $42.79

Grades: 5 6 7 8   **972.98**

1. Grenada

ISBN 978-1-6087-0216-9; 1-6087-0216-2

LC 2010019807

First published 2001

Provides information on the geography, history, wildlife, governmental structure, economy, cultural diversity, peoples, religion, and culture of Grenada.

Includes glossary and bibliographical references

973   United States

Addasi, Maha

A **kid's** guide to Arab American history; more than 50 activities. by Yvonne Wakim Dennis and Maha Addasi. 1st ed. Chicago Review Press 2013 xx, 204 p.p ill. (paperback) $16.95

Grades: 4 5 6 7   **973**

1. Arab Americans -- History 2. Arab Americans -- Social life and customs 3. Arab Americans -- History -- Study and teaching -- Activity programs

ISBN 1613740174; 9781613740170

LC 2012035758

This book by Yvonne Wakim Dennis and Maha Addasi "provides a contemporary as well as historical look at the people and experiences that have shaped Arab American culture. Each chapter focuses on a different group of Arab Americans including those of Lebanese, Syrian, Palestinian, Jordanian, Egyptian, Iraqi, and Yemeni descent and features more than 50 fun activities that highlight their distinct arts, games, clothing, and food." (Publisher's note)

America the Beautiful, third series. Children's Press 2007 52v il map lib bdg set $851.20

Grades: 4 5 6 7   **973**

1. United States

ISBN 978-0-531-20407-8 lib bdg; 0-531-20407-3 lib bdg

Replaces America the Beautiful, second series, published 1998-2001; Original series published 1987-1992

This series describes the geography, history, people, economy, and government of each state

"Most students should be able to satisfy their information needs with these polished new editions, and the copious extras and lively presentation will help keep them interested too." Booklist

Armstrong, Jennifer

★ The **American** story; 100 true tales from American history. illustrated by Roger Roth. Alfred A. Knopf 2006 358p il map $34.95; lib bdg $39.99

Grades: 4 5 6 7   **973**

1. United States -- History

ISBN 0-375-81256-3; 0-375-91256-8 lib bdg

LC 2005-34822

"This large, fully illustrated compendium features 100 stories, familiar and lesser known, drawn from America's past and arranged in chronological order. . . . Thanks to writing that is consistently good and sometimes excellent, the tales will certainly hold readers' attention, and brightening nearly every page are lively drawings enhanced by watercolor washes." Booklist

Includes bibliographical references

Bockenhauer, Mark H.

★ **Our** fifty states; by Mark H. Bockenhauer and Stephen F. Cunha; foreword by former president Jimmy Carter. National Geographic Society 2004 239p il map $25.95; lib bdg $45.90

Grades: 4 5 6 7   **973**

1. Reference books 2. United States

ISBN 0-7922-6402-9; 0-7922-6992-6 lib bdg

LC 2004-1190

This "book is organized by regions: the Northeast, Southeast, Midwest, Southwest, and West, with a map of each region and a short history. Four pages are devoted to each state and include basic facts and a map. The full-color photographs are outstanding. Reproductions of archival illustrations depict four important events from each state's history. The final sections offer a paragraph about each of the territories and a page of facts and figures about the United States." SLJ

Includes bibliographical references

Bolden, Tonya

How to build a museum; Tonya Bolden. Viking Childrens Books 2016 64 p. color illustrations (hardcover) $17.99; (ebook) $53.97

Grades: 5 6 7 8   **973**

1. Historical museums -- Washington (D.C.) 2. African Americans -- Museums -- Washington (D.C.) 3. National Museum of African American History and Culture (U.S.) 4. Historical museums -- Washington (D.C.) -- Design and construction

ISBN 9780451476371; 9780698403826

LC 2016011612

In this book, author Tonya Bolden explains that "the campaign to set up a museum honoring black citizens is nearly 100 years old. . . . Assembling its incredibly far-reaching collections is a modern story that involves all kinds of people, from educators and activists, to politicians, architects, curators, construction workers, and ordinary Americans who donated cherished belongings to be included in NMAAHC's thematically-organized exhibits." (Publisher's note)

"A well-organized and informative book introducing this significant new historical center." Booklist

Buckley, Susan

★ **Journeys** for freedom; a new look at America's story. [by] Susan Buckley and Elspeth Leacock; illustrations by Rodica Prato. Houghton Mifflin Co. 2006 48p il map $17

Grades: 4 5 6 7   **973**

1. United States -- History

ISBN 978-0-618-22323-7; 0-618-22323-1

LC 2004000974

This "history focuses on 20 individuals' quest for freedom across U.S. history. Some . . . will be familiar, but most will not. The stories, both varied and fascinating, often go beyond the personal. . . . Running along the bottom of each double-page spread is a pictorial map keyed to the text. . . . The authors make excellent use of primary sources. . . . As powerful as it is useful." Booklist

Kids make history; a new look at America's story. [by] Susan Buckley and Elspeth Leacock; Illustrations by Randy Jones. Houghton Mifflin 2006 48p il $17

Grades: 4 5 6 7   **973**

1. United States -- History

ISBN 978-0-618-22329-9; 0-618-22329-0

LC 2005036309

"This book introduces 20 children in extraordinary times, starting in 1607 with Pocahontas and ending in 2001 with 9/11 as experienced by high school senior Jukay Hsu. Laura Ingalls Wilder; John Rankin, Jr.; and Susie Baker, a young slave celebrating her independence in 1863, are among those included. The text and the highly detailed watercolor illustrations are married with numbers in small red boxes keyed to both elements for clarification. . . . A good browsing choice for children interested in American history." SLJ

Croy, Elden

United States. National Geographic 2010 64p il map (Countries of the world) lib bdg $27.90

Grades: 4 5 6 7   **973**

1. United States

ISBN 978-1-4263-0632-7 lib bdg; 1-4263-0632-6 lib bdg

This describes the geography, nature, history, people and culture, government and economy of the United States.

"The information is substantial but not overwhelming. The [text is] clear, and the discussion points are well chosen. . . . [The text is] complemented with stunning photographs." SLJ

Hoose, Phillip M.

★ **We** were there, too! young people in U.S. history. [by] Phillip Hoose. Farrar, Straus & Giroux 2001 264p il $28

Grades: 5 6 7 8   **973**

1. Youth 2. Children 3. United States -- History

ISBN 0-374-38252-2

LC 99-89052

National Book Award Finalist: Young People's Literature (2001)

Biographies of dozens of young people who made a mark in American history, including explorers, planters, spies, cowpunchers, sweatshop workers, and civil rights workers

"A treasure chest of history come to life, this is an inspired collection. . . . Because the book is packed with historical documents, evocatively illustrated . . . and full of eyewitness quotations, it should prove valuable to young historians and researchers." SLJ

Includes bibliographical references

Isaacs, Sally Senzell

Colonists and independence. Kingfisher 2011 32p il map (All about America)

Grades: 3 4 5 6   **973**

1. United States -- History -- 1783-1809 2. United States -- History -- 1775-1783, Revolution 3. United States -- History -- 1600-1775, Colonial period

ISBN 0-7534-6513-2 pa; 0-7534-6581-7; 978-0-7534-6513-4 pa; 978-0-7534-6581-3

This book covers U.S. history from 1600 to 1800.

This "visually appealing [title] effectively [combines] paintings, engravings, primary documents, and photographs with cartoon illustrations. The eye-catching [layout includes] different font sizes, bold type, and text boxes to highlight different pieces of information. The content is interesting and pithy." SLJ

Includes glossary and bibliographical references

Johnston, Robert D.

★ The making of America; the history of the United States from 1492 to the present. Robert D. Johnston; with a foreword by Douglas Brinkley. Revised ed. National Geographic 2010 240 p. ill. (chiefly col.), col. maps (hardcover) $29.95; (library) $38.90

Grades: 5 6 7 8   **973**

1. United States -- History

ISBN 9781426306631; 1426306636; 9781426306655; 1426306652

                                                        LC 2011401219

First published 2002

Includes bibliographical references (p. 226-234) and index.

"This energetically written and profusely illustrated history remains one of the top-drawer single-volume accounts of the founding and growth of the U.S. for middle grade students. The previous edition ended with 9/11; here, into the same page count, Johnston fits Hurricane Katrina, the wars in Iraq and Afghanistan, Barack Obama's election, and other major events." Booklist

Kuntz, Lynn

★ Celebrate the USA; hands-on history activities for kids. [by] Lynn Kuntz; illustrated by Mark A. Hicks. Gibbs Smith, Publisher 2007 80p il map pa $7.95

Grades: 3 4 5   **973**

1. United States -- History

ISBN 978-1-58685-846-9 pa; 1-58685-846-7 pa

                                                        LC 2006021953

This is a "fact-filled, fun-to-read compendium of American history and 25 related activities. . . . Many topics and fascinating facts are covered in brief, sometimes humorous explanations. Coverage includes the early immigrants, how America got its name, Native Americans, the 13 colonies, currency, songs, and holidays." SLJ

Lapham, Steven Sellers

Philip Reid saves the statue of freedom; Written by Steven Sellers Lapham and Dr. Eugene Walton; Illustrated by R. Gregory Christie. Sleeping Bear Press 2013 40 p. color illustrations $16.99

Grades: 2 3 4   **973**

1. Slaves -- United States -- 19th century 2. United States Capitol (Washington, D.C.) 3. African Americans 4. Foundry workers -- United States

ISBN 1585368199; 9781585368198

                                                        LC 2013002586

"Born into slavery, Philip Reid grew up on a South Carolina farm, helping various craftsmen such as the blacksmith and the potter. Eventually, he was sold to a man named Clark Mills, who was opening a foundry in Washington, D.C. Mr. Mills's foundry is contracted to cast

the Freedom statue but the project is jeopardized when a seemingly unsolvable puzzle arises." (Publisher's note)

"Acrylic gouache artwork adds a visual richness to the story, and endpapers include primary source documents. Only the addition of a source list could have strengthened this already strong book." Lib Med Con

Leacock, Elspeth

★ Journeys in time; a new atlas of American history. [by] Elspeth Leacock and Susan Buckley; illustrations by Rodica Prato. Houghton Mifflin 2001 48p il maps $15; pa $6.95

Grades: 4 5 6 7   **973**

1. United States -- History 2. United States -- Historical geography

ISBN 0-395-97956-0; 0-618-31114-9 pa

                                                        LC 00-40803

Each double-page spread of this book "takes an individual who was part of a historic movement (such as the Underground Railroad or immigration) and gives a brief narrative outlining his or her circumstances. Added to the text are sequential numbers that indicate major events in each of the twenty journeys. A double-page location map traces the routes each took, using illustrative vignettes marked with corresponding numbers that reference the text." Horn Book

Leedy, Loreen

Celebrate the 50 states; written and illustrated by Loreen Leedy. Holiday House 1999 32p il maps hardcover o.p. pa $6.95

Grades: K 1 2 3   **973**

1. United States

ISBN 0-8234-1431-0; 0-8234-1631-3 pa

                                                        LC 99-10986

Introduces statistics, emblems, notable cities, products, and other facts about the fifty states, United States territories, and Washington, D.C.

"Brightly colored and amusingly designed, this is a simple yet winning introduction to the U.S." Booklist

Moberg, Julia

Presidential pets; by Julia Moberg; illustrated by Jeff Albrecht. Charlesbridge Pub. 2012 95 p. col. ill. (reinforced) $14.95

Grades: 3 4 5   **973**

1. Presidents' pets -- United States 2. Pets -- United States 3. Presidents -- United States -- Biography

ISBN 9781936140794

                                                        LC 2011047785

In this book by Julia Moberg readers "will discover that all our chief executives but one, from Washington to Obama, have owned a variety of pets -- and, in some cases, been owned by them. In addition to the familiar dogs, cats and birds, some unusual First Animals have included goats, mice, bears, zebras, hyenas, lions, snakes, rats and tigers. . . . Brief details about each president's life and term [and] a 'Tell Me More!' feature with tidbits of trivia . . . supplement the pet facts." (Kirkus)

Pinkney, Andrea Davis

Hand in hand; ten Black men who changed America. by Andrea Davis Pinkney; paintings by Brian Pinkney. Disney/Jump at the Sun 2012 243 p. $19.99

Grades: 4 5 6 7   **973**

1. Biography 2. United States -- History 3. African Americans -- Biography 4. African Americans -- Biography 5. African American men -- Biography 6. Social change -- United States -- History

ISBN 1423142578; 9781423142577

                                                        LC 2011051348

Boston Globe-Horn Book Honor: Nonfiction (2013).

Coretta Scott King Author Book Award (2013)

In this book, Andrea Davis Pinkney profiles "ten influential black men--including Frederick Douglass, W.E.B. Du Bois, Thurgood Marshall, Jackie Robinson, and Martin Luther King Jr." She presents "descriptions of each man's influence on civil rights, culture, art, or politics. . . . An examination of Barack Obama's life and presidential election carries readers into the present day, placing the achievements of those who came before him into perspective." (Publishers Weekly)

Includes bibliographical references and index.

Provensen, Alice

The **buck** stops here; the presidents of the United States. 20th anniversary ed.; Viking 2010 un il $18.99

Grades: 2 3 4   973

1. United States -- History 2. Presidents -- United States

ISBN 978-0-670-01252-7; 0-670-01252-1

First published 1990

"Provensen updates her compendium of presidential portraits to include Clinton, Bush, and Obama. Rhyming couplets serve as footers beneath detailed earth-toned watercolor illustrations that fill each page with miniature scenes featuring campaign slogans, historical events with time line dates, and major accomplishments and inopportune failures. . . . This is an excellent introduction to America's leaders." SLJ

Rubel, David

★ **Scholastic** encyclopedia of the presidents and their times; David Rubel; with a foreword by James M. McPherson. Updated edition Scholastic 2013 248 p. illustrations, maps $24.99

Grades: 5 6 7 8   973

1. United States -- History 2. Presidents -- United States

ISBN 9780545499859

This encyclopedia "documents the tenure of each of the American presidents. It also includes information about the headlines, people, and fads that defined America during each presidency." (Publisher's note)

Smith, Charles R.

28 days; moments in Black history that changed the world. Charles Smith, Shane Evans. Roaring Brook Press 2015 56 p. color illustrations

Grades: K 1 2 3 4 5   973

1. African Americans 2. Heroes and heroines 3. African Americans -- History 4. African Americans -- Biography 5. Heroes -- United States -- Biography 6. Successful people -- United States -- Biography

ISBN 9781596438200

LC 2014009898

In this illustrated children's book, by Charles Smith, illustrated by Shane Evans, "each day features a different influential figure in African-American history, from Crispus Attucks, the first man shot in the Boston Massacre, sparking the Revolutionary War, to Madame C. J. Walker, who after years of adversity became the wealthiest black woman in the country, as well as one of the wealthiest black Americans, to Barack Obama, the country's first African-American president." (Publisher's note)

" Fueled by childhood memories of hearing the same Black History Month stories about the same people and events told the same way over and over, Smith sought to convey the importance and relevance of African American contributions and milestones in a fresh, engaging manner...Evans' buoyant and colorful illustrations have the look of cut-paper collage, and their expressive movement and joyfulness only add to the overall feeling of celebration. The book ends with the final day's exhortation: words of inspiration for young readers to make the most of every day. An inspiring, fresh take on a perennial topic." Booklist

Twenty-eight days

Smith, David J.

★ If America were a village; a book about the people of the United States. written by David J. Smith; illustrated by Shelagh Armstrong. Kids Can Press 2009 32p il $18.95

Grades: 3 4 5   973

1. United States

ISBN 978-1-55453-344-2; 1-55453-344-9

This "offers a thought-provoking perspective on the people who make up America. Organized by overarching questions such as 'Where do we come from?' and 'What do we use?' the text illustrates the ethnic divisions, income levels and material consumption (among other categories) of Americans—were a theoretical village containing only 100 people. . . . Armstrong's cheerful, smudgy paintings balance the text's heaviness." Publ Wkly

Talbott, Hudson

★ **United** tweets of America; 50 state birds; their stories, their glories. [by] Hudson Talbott. G.P. Putnam's Sons 2008 un il $17.99

Grades: 3 4 5   973

1. State birds 2. United States

ISBN 978-0-399-24520-6; 0-399-24520-0

LC 2007019419

"In this sly, comic, and irreverent book, loaded with hilarious puns and parodies about our 50 state birds, words and images deliver bits of history, folklore, and geography about each state. . . . Talbott's colored pencil and mixed-media illustrations ably combine the cartoon uproar with a sense of the individuality of the feathered creatures. . . . Clever, refeshing, and fun." Booklist

Tarrant-Reid, Linda

★ **Discovering** Black America; from the age of exploration to the twenty-first century. Linda Tarrant-Reid. Abrams Books for Young Readers 2012 xi, 244 p.p ill. (some col.), col. maps (hardcover) $29.95

Grades: 5 6 7 8 9 10   973

1. Blacks -- History 2. United States -- History -- 1775-1783, Revolution 3. United States -- History -- 1861-1865, Civil War 4. African Americans -- History 5. African Americans -- Biography

ISBN 0810970988; 9780810970984

LC 2011052201

Author Linda Tarrant-Reid presents a book on "African-American history, beginning with accounts of black explorers before the settlement of North America . . . [The book] includes major historical events . . . [such as] the American Revolution . . . [and] the period following the Civil War and Reconstruction . . . The societal changes brought on by World War II and the civil rights movement [are presented] . . . [E]xchanges between Malcolm X and Martin Luther King . . . [and] the election of President Barack Obama and the challenges facing the first black president" are also described. (Kirkus)

Includes bibliographical references and index.

The **United** States: past and present [series] Rosen Central 2010 52v. il map $1,378

Grades: 3 4 5 6   973

1. United States

ISBN 978-1-4358-9573-7

"These attractive overviews cover the geography, history, government, economy, and famous people in each state. . . . The writing is clear, and facts are plainly stated. . . . Good-quality photos, portraits and relevant paintings illustrate the texts." SLJ

Yorinks, Adrienne

Quilt of states; quilts by Adrienne Yorinks; written by Adrienne Yorinks and 50 librarians from across the nation; librarian contributions compiled and edited by Jeanette Larson. National Geographic 2005 122p il $19.95

Grades: 5 6 7 8   **973**

1. United States -- History

ISBN 0-7922-7285-4

LC 2004-17796

"The United States is stitched together chronologically in this stunning book that features a quilted spread for each state. Yorinks enlisted a librarian from each state to contribute a short entry to point up a few significant facts that add to the tapestry of the emerging nation. . . . The quilted representations are not only artistically intricate and beautiful, but also informative. A handsome book to linger over and learn from." SLJ

973.03   United States -- Encyclopedias

★ **Junior** worldmark encyclopedia of the states; Drew Johnson and Cynthia Johnson, editors; Kathleen J. Edgar, project editor. 6th edition UXL 2013 4v illustrations (set : alk. paper) $354

Grades: 5 6 7 8 9 10   **973.03**

1. Reference books 2. United States -- Encyclopedias

ISBN 9781414498645; 9781414498591

LC 2012050641

First published 1996

This encyclopedia, edited by Drew Johnson, Cynthia Johnson, and Kathleen J. Edgar, explores the states of the United States as well as its dependencies and broader territories. "Entries cover the geography, history, politics, economy and other facts about each state or area profiled. Alphabetically arranged entries feature consistent subheadings for each state so students can quickly find comparative information." (Publisher's note)

King, David C.

★ **Children's** encyclopedia of American history; by David C. King. Revised and updated DK Publishing, in association with the Smithsonian Institution 2014 320 p. illustrations (some color) (hardcover) $29.99

Grades: 4 5 6   **973.03**

1. United States -- History 2. United States -- History -- Encyclopedias, Juvenile

ISBN 1465428437; 9781465428431

LC 2015302320

"This revised edition takes a look at U.S. history, from the exploration of the New World in the 1400s to the present day. . . . New content includes the Boston bombing of 2013, the War on Terror, the death of Osama Bin Laden, and a focus on globalization and sports. Natural disasters, such as Hurricane Katrina, and additional environmental concerns are detailed. Presidential coverage is expanded to incorporate the election of Barack Obama, while other new topics include the growth of the Tea Party Movement and controversy regarding guns." SLJ

American history

973.09   Presidents--United States

Bausum, Ann

★ **Our** Country's Presidents; All You Need to Know About the Presidents, From George Washington to Barack Obama. by Ann Bausum; foreword by President Barack Obama. 4th ed. National Geographic 2013 223 p. ill., maps (hardcover) $24.95

Grades: 5 6 7 8   **973.09**

1. Presidents -- United States -- Encyclopedias

ISBN 1426310897; 9781426310898

LC 2009290293

First published 2001

This book by Ann Bausum looks at U.S. presidents. The text shares "facts about the men's personal lives, humorous incidents, political backgrounds, records, struggles, battles, successes, what they are most famous for, events that occurred during their administrations, and memorable quotes." (School Library Journal)

"This exceedingly attractive offering is . . . chock-full of information, presented . . . in such an inviting manner that children will enjoy paging through, even if there's no school report looming. . . . Full of interesting tidbits as well as solid information." Booklist

Includes bibliographical references

Gherman, Beverly

First mothers; written by Beverly Gherman; illustrated by Julie Downing. Clarion Books 2012 60 p. col. ill. (hardcover) $17.99

Grades: 3 4 5   **973.09**

1. Biography 2. Mother-child relationship 3. Presidents -- United States

ISBN 0547223013; 9780547223018

LC 2012930747

Author Beverly Gherman presents information on the mothers of past U.S. presidents. "Franklin Pierce's mother loved to shock her Puritan neighbors in New Hampshire . . . William McKinley's mother snatched roses from a train car to carry to her son's inauguration. The mother of five-star general Dwight Eisenhower was a pacifist. These are among the details Gherman . . . unearths in this collection of profiles of the mothers of each of the U.S. presidents." (Publishers Weekly)

Krull, Kathleen

A kid's guide to America's first ladies; Kathleen Krull; illustrated by Anna Divito. HarperCollins 2017 256 p. illustrations (hardcover) $16.99; (ebook) $6.99

Grades: 4 5 6 7 8   **973.09**

1. Women -- United States -- Biography 2. Presidents' spouses -- United States -- Biography

ISBN 9780062381064; 9780062381071; 9780062381088

LC 2016940933

This book in the Kids' Guide to American History series, by Kathleen Krull, illustrated by Anna Divito, "introduces readers to the women of the White House. . . . Find out what our country's First Ladies thought, did, and advocated for as they moved into the White House. Why did the Patriots love Martha Washington? What causes did Eleanor Roosevelt support and lead? What did Jacqueline Kennedy do to establish her legacy long after she left the White House?" (Publisher's note)

"Gathering momentum as it rolls along chronologically through American history, this lively book profiles the women who have enjoyed, to varying degrees, the unique privileges and challenges of being first lady." Booklist

Includes bibliographical references (pages 239-240) and index.

Rhatigan, Joe

White House kids; the perks, pleasures, problems, and pratfalls of the Presidents' children. Joe Rhatigan; with illustrations by Jay Shin. Charlesbridge Pub. 2012 96 p. ill. (chiefly col.) $14.95

Grades: 5 6 7 8   **973.09**

1. United States. White House Office 2. Presidents -- United States -- Family 3. Presidents -- United States -- Children 4. Children of presidents -- United States 5. Children of presidents -- United

States -- Biography
ISBN 1936140802; 9781936140800

LC 2011045090

This book presents "an overview of the young occupants of the White House . . . [and] details the perks and downfalls of being a president's child. Information on pets, favorite games and activities . . . and education of presidential offspring is . . . presented. [Joe] Rhatigan explores the press's and the public's fascination with the children . . . as well as the scrutiny and negative press endured by Amy Carter and Chelsea Clinton." (School Library Journal)

"An inviting collection of insightful, interesting and often wacky and weird facts and stories about U.S. presidents and their families." Kirkus

Includes bibliographical references and index

Time for kids presidents of the United States; the editors of Time for Kids. Time Inc. Books 2017 80 p. color illustrations $15.95
Grades: 3 4 5 6   **973.09**
1. United States -- History   2. Presidents -- United States -- Biography   3. United States -- Politics and government
ISBN 1683300009; 9781683300007

LC 2016955036

This book, by the editors of Time for Kids, "invites the reader inside the White House to discover fascinating facts about the U.S. commanders-in-chief--their origins, accomplishments, and place in history-as told through famous quotes, important historical dates, and a timeline of events. Special sections cover the election process, the branches of government, and the role of presidents in the expansion of our nation from before the 13 colonies through westward expansion." (Publisher's note)

"Accessible, direct, and even-handed, it's a handy guide for readers looking to get a better sense of American politics past and present." Pub Wkly

973.1   Early history to 1607

Hernandez, Roger E.
   New Spain: 1600-1760s. Marshall Cavendish Benchmark 2009 79p il map (Hispanic America) lib bdg $34.21
Grades: 4 5 6 7   **973.1**
1. Southern States -- History 2. Spaniards -- United States 3. Southwestern States -- History
ISBN 978-0-7614-2936-4 lib bdg; 0-7614-2936-0 lib bdg
"Provides comprehensive information on the history of Spanish exploration in the United States." Publisher's note
Includes glossary and bibliographical references

973.2   United States--Colonial period, 1607-1775

Colonial America and the Revolutionary War; the story of the people of the colonies, from early settlers to revolutionary leaders. Laurie Lanzen Harris, editor. Favorable Impressions 2009 399p il map (Biography for beginners) $49
Grades: 2 3 4 5   **973.2**
1. Reference books 2. United States -- Biography 3. United States -- History -- 1775-1783, Revolution 4. United States -- History -- 1600-1775, Colonial period
ISBN 978-1-931360-34-0; 1-931360-34-0

LC 2008-49193

"This volume is highly recommended for public and school library collections. The affordable price, well-organized basic information, and user-friendly format make it a valuable resource for young researchers." Booklist
Includes glossary

Fishkin, Rebecca Love
   English colonies in America. Compass Point Books 2009 48p il map (We the people) lib bdg $26.60
Grades: 4 5 6   **973.2**
1. United States -- History -- 1600-1775, Colonial period
ISBN 978-0-7565-3838-5

LC 2008007210

This is a history of English colonies in North America.
This provides "solid background matter and introduce key people and vocabulary." SLJ
Includes glossary and bibliographical references

Heinrichs, Ann
   The **Shipbuilder**; Ann Heinrichs. Marshall Cavendish 2013 48 p. (Colonial people) (print) $29.93
Grades: 3 4 5 6   **973.2**
1. Shipbuilding -- United States -- History 2. United States -- History -- 1600-1775, Colonial period 3. Shipwrights -- United States
ISBN 0761400052; 9780761400059; 9781608709878

LC 2011028344

This book on shipbuilders and shipbuilding in colonial America, by Christine Petersen, is part of the Colonial People series. It "introduces the master shipbuilder as well as the many skilled tradespeople needed to make a sailing ship." It includes "a description of the craftsman's process" and is "illustrated with tinted engravings and paintings from earlier eras as well as . . . color photos of artifacts and replicas." (Booklist)

"These excellent titles provide context about when people working during the colonial period would have first come to America and why, how they fit into the community, and the skills and tools required for their jobs. The authors emphasize various aspects related specifically to each spotlighted role..." (School Library Journal)

Includes bibliographical references and index

Huey, Lois Miner
   American archaeology uncovers the earliest English colonies. Marshall Cavendish Benchmark 2009 64p il map (American archaeology) lib bdg $31.36
Grades: 4 5 6 7   **973.2**
1. America -- Antiquities 2. America -- Exploration 3. Jamestown (Va.) -- History 4. Roanoke Island (N.C.) -- History 5. Great Britain -- Colonies -- America 6. Excavations (Archeology) -- United States
ISBN 978-0-7614-4264-6 lib bdg; 0-7614-4264-2 lib bdg

LC 2008050259

This describes how archeologists have learned about the history of early English colonists in America at Jamestown, Popham Colony, and Roanoke

"Huey enthusiastically brings . . . [this era] to life through artifacts and field research. . . . [The volume begins with an] introduction that defines 'historical archaeology' and explains its value in terms simple enough for lower-elementary readers to comprehend, yet detailed enough for older children to enjoy, an approach followed in the remaining chapters. . . . Huey's focus on American history, which is broken down into small, manageable chunks, is sure to entice budding historians." SLJ

Includes glossary and bibliographical references

Mara, Wil

The **farmer**. Marshall Cavendish Benchmark 2010 48p il (Colonial people) lib bdg $29.93

Grades: 3 4 5 6   **973.2**

1. Farm life -- United States 2. United States -- History -- 1600-1775, Colonial period

ISBN 978-0-7614-4797-9; 0-7614-4797-0

LC 2009019580

This describes the life of a colonial farmer and his importance to the community, as well as everyday life, responsibilities, and social practices during that time.

"The type font, just slightly larger than usual, makes the text very visually appealing. . . . [The] book is liberally illustrated with artwork dating from the colonial period . . . [and] information boxes offer supplemental material." Libr Media Connect

Includes glossary and bibliographical references

McNeese, Tim

Colonial America, 1543-1763. Chelsea House 2010 136p il map (Discovering U.S. history) $35

Grades: 5 6 7 8   **973.2**

1. United States -- History -- 1600-1775, Colonial period

ISBN 978-1-60413-349-3; 1-60413-349-X

LC 2008055170

This history of Colonial America "begins with a chapter on 'Rivals for North America' and ends with 'The Fight for the Ohio Country.' . . . [The] book has an excellent chronology; rich sidebars; and numerous well-captioned illustrations, maps, and photos that enhance the texts. [This book provides a] satisfying [introduction] to American history for students." SLJ

Includes glossary and bibliographical references

Petersen, Christine

The **wheelwright**; Christine Petersen. 1st ed. Benchmark Books 2013 48 p. (Colonial people) (print) $29.93

Grades: 3 4 5 6   **973.2**

1. Colonial Williamsburg (Williamsburg, Va.) 2. United States -- History 3. United States -- Social life and customs -- 1600-1775, Colonial period 4. United States -- Social life and customs -- To 1775 5. Wheelwrights -- United States -- History -- 17th century 6. United States -- History -- Colonial period, ca. 1600-1775 7. Carriage and wagon making -- United States -- History -- 18th century

ISBN 160870419X; 9781608704194; 9781608709885

LC 2011028345

This book, by Christine Petersen, is part of the Colonial People series. "Besides explaining the uses and the construction of wheels in colonial times, 'The Wheelwright' includes instructions for making a replica wheel using Styrofoam and craft sticks. In each book, the informative text is illustrated with tinted engravings and paintings from earlier eras as well as excellent color photos of artifacts and replicas and reenactments of historical trades in Colonial Williamsburg." (Booklist)

Includes bibliographical references and index

Tunis, Edwin

★ **Colonial** living; written and illustrated by Edwin Tunis. Johns Hopkins Univ. Press 1999 155p il pa $18.95

Grades: 5 6 7 8   **973.2**

1. United States -- Social life and customs -- 1600-1775, Colonial period

ISBN 0-8018-6227-2

LC 99-22591

A reprint of the title first published 1957 by World Pub. Co.

"Common everyday aspects of colonial living from 1564-1770 are highlighted by the detailed descriptions and numerous black and white illustrations of items such as tools, home furnishings, clothing, etc." N Y Public Libr. Ref Books for Child Collect

Voices from colonial America [series] National Geographic 2005 18v il map

Grades: 5 6 7 8   **973.2**

1. United States -- History -- 1600-1775, Colonial period

Each volume in this series describes the colonial history of a state illustrated with historical maps and reprints of period artwork, and includes excerpts from first-person accounts.

"Presented in clear, succinct text . . . this resource, containing a great deal of information, will be a welcome addition to history classes and a great source for report writers." Booklist [review of New Jersey volume]

Includes bibliographical references

973.3   United States--Periods of Revolution and Confederation, 1775-1789

Allen, Thomas B.

Remember Valley Forge; patriots, Tories, and Redcoats tell their stories. [by] Thomas B. Allen. National Geographic 2007 61p il map $17.95; lib bdg $27.90

Grades: 5 6 7 8   **973.3**

1. Generals 2. Presidents 3. Valley Forge (Pa.) -- History 4. United States -- History -- 1775-1783, Revolution

ISBN 978-1-4263-0149-0; 978-1-4263-0150-6 lib bdg

LC 2007024821

The author "recounts here the activities of Washington and his soldiers during the winter of 1777-8, spent regrouping at Valley Forge, Pennsylvania. . . . Allen's strength is his attention to military details and strategies, but his account is clearly presented and succinctly written as well. . . . Illustrated with reproductions of period artwork, drawings, maps, and a few contemporary photographs." Booklist

Anderson, Laurie Halse

★ **Independent** dames; what you never knew about the women and girls of the American Revolution. by Laurie Halse Anderson; illustrated by Matt Faulkner. Simon & Schuster Books for Young Readers 2008 37p il $16.99

Grades: 3 4 5   **973.3**

1. Women -- United States -- History 2. United States -- History -- 1775-1783, Revolution

ISBN 978-0-689-85808-6; 0-689-85808-6

LC 2007042643

"The stories of 22 'Revolutionary Grandmothers' take center stage in this well-illustrated volume. . . . Faulkner's ink-and-watercolor illustrations are exuberant, often amusing, and filled with crosshatching and dialogue balloons. The spreads are busy and information-packed, and readers will be both engaged by and educated about this critical period." SLJ

Includes bibliographical references

Blair, Margaret Whitman

Liberty or death; the surprising story of runaway slaves who sided with the British during the American Revolution. National Geographic 2010 64p il map lib bdg $27.90

Grades: 5 6 7 8   **973.3**

1. African American soldiers 2. Slavery -- United States 3. United States -- History -- 1775-1783, Revolution

ISBN 978-1-4263-0590-0 lib bdg; 1-4263-0590-7 lib bdg

LC 2009-26853

"Blair provides a well-researched account of slaves in Virginia who, beginning in 1775, fled to the British. . . . Though told in a matter-of-fact tone, the story is often heart-wrenching. . . . Colorful reproductions of period paintings, prints, and documents illustrate the clearly written text. . . . A fine and singular addition to American history collections." Booklist

Includes bibliographical references

Bobrick, Benson

★ **Fight** for freedom; the American Revolutionary War. Atheneum Books for Young Readers 2004 96p il map $22.95

Grades: 5 6 7 8   **973.3**

  1. United States -- History -- 1775-1783, Revolution

  ISBN 0-689-86422-1

LC 2003-25548

"This large-format volume profiles significant individuals and discusses the progress of the Revolutionary War. . . . Printed in color, most of the illustrations are period paintings and prints. . . . Students will find the book a well-organized and clearly written introduction to the war." Booklist

Includes glossary and bibliographical references

Brenner, Barbara

★ **If** you were there in 1776. Bradbury Press 1994 136p il $17.95

Grades: 3 4 5 6   **973.3**

  1. United States -- Social life and customs 2. United States -- Declaration of Independence

  ISBN 0-02-712322-7

LC 93-24060

Demonstrates how the concepts and principles expressed in the Declaration of Independence were drawn from the experiences of living in America in the late eighteenth century, with emphasis given to how children lived on a New England farm, a Southern plantation, and the frontier

"The author's inclusion of details of how peoples' lives began to change as a result of the Revolution and her accessible style are the selling points here. Both budding historians and report writers will find this title worth their time." SLJ

Includes bibliographical references

Brown, Don

★ **Henry** and the cannons; an extraordinary true story of the American Revolution. Don Brown. Roaring Brook Press 2013 32 p. (hardcover) $16.99

Grades: K 1 2 3 4   **973.3**

  1. Picture books for children 2. United States -- History -- 1775-1783, Revolution 3. Military roads -- Massachusetts -- History -- 18th century 4. Massachusetts -- History -- Revolution, 1775-1783 -- Campaigns 5. United States -- History -- Revolution, 1775-1783 -- Campaigns 6. Massachusetts -- History -- Revolution, 1775-1783 -- Artillery operations 7. United States -- History -- Revolution, 1775-1783 -- Artillery operations

  ISBN 1596432667; 9781596432666

LC 2012013450

This children's picture book recounts the difficulties faced by the American armies in the winter of 1775. "British soldiers occupy Boston, and the Americans have no way to dislodge them. Despite the seeming impossibility of transporting heavy cannons over snowy roads, across icy lakes and through forbidding forests, young Henry Knox, a bookseller and militia member, volunteered to get the job done." (Kirkus)

★ **Let** it begin here! April 19, 1775, the day the American Revolution began. Roaring Brook Press 2008 un il (Actual times) $17.95

Grades: 2 3 4   **973.3**

  1. Concord (Mass.), Battle of, 1775 2. Lexington (Mass.), Battle of, 1775 3. United States -- History -- 1775-1783, Revolution

  ISBN 978-1-59643-221-5; 1-59643-221-7

LC 2008-11221

"Brown distills the fairly complex story of the beginning of the American Revolution in a manner that deftly balances information and intrigue. . . . Equally impressive and vital to the success of this picture book are Brown's compositions which sometimes dramatically, sometimes whimsically intersect with the text. . . . [This is] rousing, accessible, and splendidly executed." Booklist

Carson, Mary Kay

Did it all start with a snowball fight? and other questions about the American Revolution. by Mary Kay Carson. Sterling Pub. Co., Inc. 2012 31 p. $12.95

Grades: 3 4 5   **973.3**

  1. Boston Massacre, 1770 2. Picture books for children 3. United States -- History -- 1775-1783, Revolution

  ISBN 1402796269; 9781402787348; 9781402796265

LC 2011019963

This children's book offers information about the American Revolution. "Starting with the Boston Massacre (the snowball fight in question) and ending with the Treaty of Paris, the facts are related in a question-and-answer format, in an arrangement that's more topical than chronological (though there is a . . . time line at the end). Each spread has one or two questions and answers on one side and a captioned, colorful full-page painting or cartoon on the other." (School Library Journal)

Includes bibliographical references and index

Crompton, Samuel Willard

The **Boston** Tea Party; colonists protest the British government. by Russell Freeman; illustrated by Peter Malone. Holiday House 2011 39 p. (hardcover) $17.95

Grades: 3 4 5   **973.3**

  1. Boston (Mass.) -- History 2. Boston Tea Party, 1773 3. United States -- History -- 1775-1783, Revolution

  ISBN 9780823422661; 0823422666

LC 2010028726

This children's book, by Russell Freedman, illustrated by Peter Malone, tells the story of the Boston Tea Party. "[T]he Boston Tea Party of 1773 has come to stand for the determination of American colonists to control their own destinies." The book tells the events from "the arrival of the ships full of controversial taxed tea in Boston Harbor, through the . . . protest meetings at the Old South Church, to the . . . dumping 226 chests of fine tea into the harbor on December 16." (Publisher's note)

Includes bibliographical references and index.

Decker, Timothy

For liberty; the story of the Boston Massacre. Calkins Creek 2009 un il $17.95

Grades: 4 5 6   **973.3**

  1. Boston Massacre, 1770

  ISBN 978-1-59078-608-6; 1-59078-608-4

"This handsomely designed picture book begins the story of the Boston Massacre by filling in the background. . . . The book concludes with the soldiers' trial and their lawyer, John Adams, reflecting on the protection of liberty. . . . The book does quite a good job of conveying how the actions and emotions of those on both sides escalated toward violence and death. Using parallel lines, crosshatching, and other texturing effects, the black-and-white drawings hold attention. . . . A fine, balanced look at an important event." Booklist

Figley, Marty Rhodes

John Greenwood's journey to Bunker Hill; illustrated by Craig Orback. Millbrook Press 2010 48p il (History speaks: picture books plus reader's theater) lib bdg $27.93

Grades: 2 3 4 **973.3**

1. Readers' theater 2. Bunker Hill (Boston, Mass.), Battle of, 1775 3. United States -- History -- 1775-1783, Revolution

ISBN 978-1-58013-673-0 lib bdg; 1-58013-673-7 lib bdg

LC 2009050063

This tells the story of fifteen-year-old John Greenwood, who fought at the Battle of Bunker Hill.

This "title begins with a well-illustrated narrative and concludes with a tip sheet for performing Reader's Theater as well as a list of characters, a script, and a pronunciation guide. . . . [This book will] make history come alive in a unique and interesting way." Libr Media Connect

Includes bibliographical references

Fradin, Dennis B.

The **Declaration** of Independence; [by] Dennis Brindell Fradin. Marshall Cavendish Benchmark 2007 45p il map (Turning points in U.S. history) lib bdg $31.36

Grades: 3 4 5 **973.3**

1. United States -- Declaration of Independence 2. United States -- Politics and government -- 1775-1783, Revolution

ISBN 978-0-7614-2129-0 lib bdg; 0-7614-2129-7 lib bdg

LC 2005016023

This "describes the unrest that led up to the signing of the famous document, how Jefferson composed it, and the uncertainty surrounding the vote for independence. . . . The clear, concise, and dynamic style of writing simplifies the information without dumbing it down. . . . The photos, paintings, and maps . . . add a wealth of information." SLJ

Includes glossary and bibliographical references

Let it begin here! Lexington & Concord: first battles of the American Revolution. [by] Dennis Brindell Fradin; illustrations by Larry Day. Walker & Co. 2005 un il maps $16.95; lib bdg $17.85

Grades: 2 3 4 **973.3**

1. Concord (Mass.), Battle of, 1775 2. Lexington (Mass.), Battle of, 1775

ISBN 0-8027-8945-5; 0-8027-8946-3 lib bdg

LC 2004-49473

This is an "account of Paul Revere's actions on the night of April 18, 1775, and the battles in Lexington and Concord on the following day. . . . Well-composed double-page illustrations, ink drawings with watercolor and gouache, highlight the human drama implicit in the text." Booklist

Includes bibliographical references

★ The **signers**; the fifty-six stories behind the Declaration of Independence. [by] Dennis Brindell Fradin; illustrations by Michael McCurdy. Walker & Co. 2002 164p il map $22.95; lib bdg $23.85

Grades: 4 5 6 7 **973.3**

1. Statesmen -- United States 2. United States -- Declaration of Independence 3. United States -- Politics and government -- 1775-1783, Revolution

ISBN 0-8027-8849-1; 0-8027-8850-5 lib bdg

LC 2002-66364

Profiles each of the fifty-six men who signed the Declaration of Independence, giving historical information about the colonies they represented. Includes the text of the Declaration and its history

"Fradin gives brief, fascinating glimpses into the people who have been overlooked as well as those with whom readers might be familiar. . . . An excellent resource for report writing." SLJ

Includes bibliographical references

Freedman, Russell, 1929-

★ Give me liberty! the story of the Declaration of Independence. Holiday House 2000 90p il $24.95; pa $14.95

Grades: 5 6 7 8 9 10 **973.3**

1. United States 2. United States -- Declaration of Independence 3. United States -- Politics and government -- 1775-1783, Revolution 4. United States -- Politics and government -- 1775-1783

ISBN 0-8234-1448-5; 0-8234-1753-0 pa

LC 99-57513

This book describes the events leading up to the Declaration of Independence as well as the personalities and politics behind its framing. Chronology. Annotated bibliography. Index. "Grades five to eight." (Bull Cent Child Books)

"Handsomely designed with a generous and thoughtful selection of period art, the book is dramatic and inspiring." Horn Book

Includes bibliographical references

★ **Washington** at Valley Forge. Holiday House 2008 100p il map $24.95

Grades: 5 6 7 8 9 **973.3**

1. Generals 2. Presidents 3. Pennsylvania -- History 4. Valley Forge (Pa.) -- History 5. United States -- History -- 1775-1783, Revolution

ISBN 978-0-8234-2069-8; 0-8234-2069-8

LC 2007-52467

NCTE Orbis Pictus Award honor book (2009)

"With his usual clarity of focus and keen eye for telling quotations, Freedman documents how Washington struggled to maintain morale despite hunger, near-nakedness, and freezing conditions. . . . Throughout, high-quality reproductions depict Washington among the men, and with the numerous other influential people who played crucial roles." Booklist

Harness, Cheryl

The **revolutionary** John Adams; written and illustrated by Cheryl Harness. National Geographic Soc. 2003 39p il map $17.95; pa $7.95

Grades: 3 4 5 6 **973.3**

1. Presidents 2. Vice-presidents 3. Presidents -- United States 4. United States -- History -- 1775-1783, Revolution

ISBN 0-7922-6970-5; 0-7922-5491-0 pa

LC 2002-11271

A biography of John Adams with emphasis on his role in the American Revolution

"Harness' warm, friendly, mixed-media illustrations, which range from full-color, double-page spreads to labeled diagrams to black-line silhouettes, will delight children, and quotes from Adams' letters, including many letters to his wife, Abigail, are a bonus. A fascinating book for young history buffs." Booklist

Includes bibliographical references

Herbert, Janis

★ The **American** Revolution for kids; a history with 21 activities. Chicago Review Press 2002 139p il pa $14.95

Grades: 4 5 6 **973.3**

1. United States -- History -- 1775-1783, Revolution

ISBN 1-55652-456-0

LC 2002-7938

Discusses the events of the American Revolution, from the hated Stamp Act and the Boston Tea Party to the British surrender at Yorktown and the writing of the Constitution. Activities include making a tricorn hat and discovering local history

"Achieving a good balance between textual material, illustration, and projects, the book immerses children in the milieu of these years.

... The directions are detailed enough and adequately illustrated with pencil drawings to make them exciting and easy to follow." SLJ

Includes glossary and bibliographical references

Jules, Jacqueline

Unite or die; how thirteen states became a nation. illustrated by Jef Czekaj. Charlesbridge 2009 48p il $16.95; pa $7.95

Grades: 2 3 4 5   **973.3**

1. United States -- History -- 1783-1809 2. United States -- Constitution 3. United States -- History -- 1783-1815 4. Constitutional history -- United States 5. United States -- Politics and government -- 1783-1789

ISBN 1-58089-189-6; 1-58089-190-X pa; 978-1-58089-189-9; 978-1-58089-190-5 pa

LC 2008-07229

"Using the conceit of a school play, Unite or Die traces the challenges, conflicts, and compromises that shaped the United States Constitution and brought unity to the states. [Bibliography.] Ages nine to twelve." (Publisher's note)

"This presentation is written as if it were a school play about the 13 colonies becoming a nation. Told through colorful comic-book illustrations, it stars students dressed as states humorously explaining the path to the writing of the Constitution. The brief text is accompanied by speech balloons expressing the states' multiple, often competing, views. . . . The vividly colored spreads will hold the interest of even middle school students and would be useful to introduce how our form of government was created." SLJ

Includes bibliographical references

Kostyal, K. M.

1776; a new look at revolutionary Williamsburg. by K.M. Kostyal with the Colonial Williamsburg Foundation; photographs by Lori Epstein. National Geographic 2009 48p il $17.95; lib bdg $27.90

Grades: 4 5 6   **973.3**

1. Williamsburg (Va.)--History--Revolution, 1775-1783 2. United States -- History -- 1775-1783, Revolution

ISBN 978-1-4263-0517-7; 1-4263-0517-6; 978-1-4263-0518-4 lib bdg; 1-4263-0518-4 lib bdg

LC 2009-18002

"Clear, distinctive photos add visual appeal to this short history of the American Revolution, written from the point of view of those living in Williamsburg, Virginia's capital in 1776. Kostyal blends political and social history into a readable account of the period, bolstered by informative sidebars, a chronology, and a closing note about the restoration of colonial Williamsburg. . . . The increasing inclusion of nonwhite colonists in the illustrations as well as the text is a welcome trend." Booklist

Includes bibliographical references

Leavitt, Amie Jane

The **Declaration** of Independence in translation; what it really means. by Amie Jane Leavitt. Capstone Press 2009 32p il (Fact finders. Kids' translations) lib bdg $23.93; pa $7.95

Grades: 3 4 5   **973.3**

1. United States -- Declaration of Independence 2. United States -- Politics and government -- 1775-1783, Revolution

ISBN 978-1-4296-1929-5 lib bdg; 1-4296-1929-5 lib bdg; 978-1-4296-2844-0 pa; 1-4296-2844-8 pa

LC 2008-3229

Provides "a nearly line-by-line translation that makes . . . the written word accessible and meaningful." SLJ

Includes glossary and bibliographical references

Maestro, Betsy

A **new** nation; the United States, 1783-1815. illustrated by Giulio Maestro. HarperCollins Publishers 2009 64p il map (American story series) $17.99; lib bdg $18.89

Grades: 3 4 5 6   **973.3**

1. United States -- History -- 1783-1865

ISBN 978-0-688-16015-9; 0-688-16015-8; 978-0-688-16016-6 lib bdg; 0-688-16016-6 lib bdg

LC 2008-26947

"The Maestros . . . cover a jam-packed 32 years that saw the country more than double in population and, with the Lousiana Purchase, double in size. . . . The abundant pastel artwork breaks up the pages and provides nifty images of the times. . . . Interesting for history buffs, useful for researchers." Booklist

McNeese, Tim

Revolutionary America, 1764-1789; consulting editor, Richard Jensen. Chelsea House 2010 128p il map (Discovering U.S. history) $35

Grades: 5 6 7 8   **973.3**

1. United States -- History -- 1775-1783, Revolution

ISBN 978-1-60413-350-9; 1-60413-350-3

LC 2008-55179

"The information is accurate and easy to understand. Pictures are well placed, and primary sources are included. . . . The maps are well done and there are sidebars with additional information. . . . [This would be good] to have on hand for reports as it is well laid out and easy to use." Libr Media Connect

Includes glossary and bibliographical references

Micklos, John

The **brave** women and children of the American Revolution; [by] John Micklos, Jr. Enslow Publishers 2008 48p il (The Revolutionary War library) lib bdg $17.95

Grades: 3 4 5 6   **973.3**

1. Children -- United States 2. Women -- United States -- History 3. United States -- History -- 1775-1783, Revolution

ISBN 978-0-7660-3019-0 lib bdg; 0-7660-3019-9 lib bdg

LC 2007048510

This describes the roles of women and children in the American Revolution, at home, in business, as spies and messengers, and on the battlefield.

This is "illustrated with historical engravings and photographs. . . . The many sidebars are informative. . . . The well-written text is studded with footnotes, and the appended time line is helpful." Booklist

Includes glossary and bibliographical references

Miller, Brandon Marie

Declaring independence; life during the American Revolution. by Brandon Marie Miller. Lerner Publications Co. 2005 112p il map (People's history) lib bdg $31.93

Grades: 5 6 7 8   **973.3**

1. United States -- Social conditions 2. United States -- History -- 1775-1783, Revolution

ISBN 0-8225-1275-0

LC 2004-17917

This describes the lives of American colonists in the late 1700s and the fight for independence from Great Britain with emphasis on "first-hand accounts, contemporary writings, and official documents. Miller does a good job of chronicling the history, presenting the information in a clear, concise, and well-organized manner." SLJ

Includes bibliographical references

Minor, Wendell

Yankee Doodle America; the spirit of 1776 from A to Z. [by] Wendell Minor. G.P. Putnam's Sons 2006 un il $16.99

Grades: 2 3 4   **973.3**

1. Alphabet 2. United States -- History -- 1775-1783, Revolution

ISBN 0-399-24003-9

LC 2005025174

"In colonial America, the public houses served as the news hubs of their surrounding areas. . . . Using hand-carved replicas of the signs for these inns and taverns to share facts about the American Revolution, Minor, in concert with master woodworker John Reichling, has created an unusual alphabet book. . . . The factual material is correct, clearly stated, and intriguing." SLJ

Includes bibliographical references

Murphy, Jim

★ The **crossing**; how George Washington saved the American Revolution. Scholastic Press 2010 96p il map $21.99

Grades: 5 6 7 8   **973.3**

1. Generals 2. Presidents 3. Trenton (N.J.), Battle of, 1776 4. United States -- History -- 1775-1783, Revolution

ISBN 978-0-439-69186-4; 0-439-69186-9

LC 2009-11561

Murphy "again digs into the well of history, this time emerging with a well-researched, absorbing account of the early battles of the Revolutionary War with General George Washington at their center. Enhanced by numerous sepia maps of troop movements, prints, paintings, and portraits of prominent figures, the blow-by-blow narrative begins with the shots fired at Lexington and Concord in 1775 and continues until the tide-turning battles at Trenton and Princeton in early 1777." Publ Wkly

Includes bibliographical references

★ A **young** patriot; the American Revolution as experienced by one boy. Clarion Bks. 1996 101p il maps $16; pa $7.95

Grades: 5 6 7 8   **973.3**

1. Soldiers 2. United States -- History -- 1775-1783, Revolution

ISBN 0-395-60523-7; 0-395-90019-0 pa

LC 93-38789

"Using Joseph Plumb Martin's first person account of his participation in the Revolutionary War as primary source material, Murphy intertwines this story of one teenager's life as a soldier with broader information about the Revolution, to put Martin's story in context. The handsome, informative, and fascinating look at American history is illustrated with many period reproductions." Horn Book Guide

Includes bibliographical references

Otfinoski, Steven

The **new** republic: 1760-1840s. Marshall Cavendish Benchmark 2009 79p il map (Hispanic America) lib bdg $23.95

Grades: 4 5 6 7   **973.3**

1. Latinos (U.S.) 2. Mexico -- History 3. Florida -- History 4. Hispanic Americans 5. Spaniards -- United States 6. United States -- History -- 1775-1783, Revolution

ISBN 978-0-7614-2938-8 lib bdg; 0-7614-2938-7 lib bdg

LC 2007-45958

"Provides comprehensive information on the history of the Spanish exploring the United States." Publisher's note

Includes glossary and bibliographical references

Rockwell, Anne F.

They called her Molly Pitcher; by Anne Rockwell; illustrated by Cynthia von Buhler. Knopf 2002 un il $16.95; lib bdg $17.99

Grades: 3 4 5   **973.3**

1. Soldiers 2. Revolutionaries 3. United States -- History -- 1775-

1783, Revolution

ISBN 0-679-89187-0; 0-679-99187-5 lib bdg

LC 2001-29422

A biography of the woman who was named a sergeant in the Continental Army by George Washington for her bravery in the Battle of Monmouth

"The language is inviting, the story, exciting. Von Buhler's illustrations, which appear crackled, as if they were painted during this period, make the book shine." SLJ

Sanders, Nancy I.

America's black founders; revolutionary heroes & early leaders with 21 activities. Chicago Review Press 2010 150p il $16.95

Grades: 4 5 6 7   **973.3**

1. African Americans -- History 2. United States -- History -- 1775-1783, Revolution

ISBN 978-1-55652-811-8; 1-55652-811-6

"This activity-based guide reveals how African Americans played crucial roles in helping the United States gain its independence. Sanders includes well-known figures such as Phillis Wheatley, Crispus Attucks, and James Forten in her narrative, but also enriches traditional accounts of the period by explaining the contributions of lesser-known patriots. . . . Most of the activities help make this period real to young people. . . . Sanders makes excellent use of primary sources." SLJ

Schanzer, Rosalyn

★ **George** vs. George; the American Revolution as seen from both sides. National Geographic 2004 60p il maps $16.95

Grades: 3 4 5 6   **973.3**

1. Generals 2. Presidents 3. Kings 4. United States -- History -- 1775-1783, Revolution

ISBN 0-7922-7349-4

LC 2003-20843

This book explores how the characters and lives of King George III of England and George Washington affected he progress and outcome of the American Revolution. Bibliography. Index. "Grades four to six." (Bull Cent Child Books)

"A carefully researched, evenhanded narrative with well-crafted, vibrant, watercolor illustrations. . . . This is a lovely book, showing historical inquiry at its best." SLJ

Includes bibliographical references

Sheinkin, Steve

★ **King** George: what was his problem? everything your schoolbooks didn't tell you about the American Revolution. Roaring Brook Press 2008 195p il map $19.95

Grades: 4 5 6   **973.3**

1. United States -- History -- 1775-1783, Revolution

ISBN 978-1-59643-319-9; 1-59643-319-1

LC 2007-39999

First published 2005 in paperback by Summer Street Press, in series Storyteller's History, with title: The American Revolution

This history of the American Revolution "features many droll line drawings that suit the tone of the writing and source notes for the extensive quotes. Sheinkin clearly conveys the gravity of events during the Revolutionary period, but he also has the knack of bringing historical people to life and showing what was at stake for them as individuals as well as for the new nation. . . . Vivid storytelling makes this an unusually readable history book." Booklist

Includes bibliographical references

St. George, Judith

★ The **journey** of the one and only Declaration of Independence; illustrated by Will Hillenbrand. Philomel Books 2005 un il $16.99

Grades: 2 3 4 **973.3**

1. United States -- Declaration of Independence 2. United States -- Politics and government -- 1775-1783, Revolution
ISBN 0-399-23738-0

LC 2004-13567

This describes how the Declaration of Independence was written and how the document was preserved and displayed throughout American history

"Readers will learn fascinating details. . . . Hillenbrand's lively mixed-media illustrations are a perfect match for the text, filling the pages with visual energy and humor. . . . This well-researched, readable, and well-illustrated book belongs on the shelves of all public and school libraries." SLJ

Includes bibliographical references

Winters, Kay

★ **Colonial** voices; hear them speak. [by] Kay Winters; illustrated by Larry Day. Dutton Children's Books 2008 un il map $17.99

Grades: 3 4 5 6 **973.3**

1. Boston Tea Party, 1773 2. Boston (Mass.) -- History 3. United States -- History -- 1775-1783, Revolution
ISBN 0-525-47872-8; 978-0-525-47872-0

LC 2007-28480

It's December 16, 1773 in Boston and "King George has decided to tax the colonists' tea. . . . Ethan, the printer's errand boy, is running through town to deliver a message about an important meeting. As he stops along his route—at the bakery, the schoolhouse, [and] the tavern—. . . [the workers talk] about living under Britain's rule." (Publisher's note) "Grades three to five." (Bull Cent Child Books)

"Colonial Bostonians introduce themselves through free-verse vignettes that describe their work and their feelings about the current political situation. As errand boy Ethan moves about the city, he links the people together. . . . The watercolor and ink illustrations add humor and drama through shifting perspectives and well-detailed settings full of period details. . . . A unique presentation for all libraries." SLJ

Includes bibliographical references

973.4 United States--Constitutional period, 1789-1809

Brown, Don, 1949-

Aaron and Alexander; the most famous duel in American history. Don Brown. Roaring Brook Press 2015 32 p. color illustrations (hardcover) $17.99

Grades: 2 3 4 5 **973.4**

1. Dueling 2. Burr-Hamilton Duel, Weehawken, N.J., 1804
ISBN 159643998X; 9781596439986

LC 2015003616

This children's book, written and illustrated by Don Brown, tells the story of how "Aaron Burr and Alexander Hamilton were both fierce patriots during the Revolutionary War, but the politics of the young United States of America put them in constant conflict. Their extraordinary story of bitter fighting and resentment culminates in their famous duel." (Publisher's note)

Delano, Marfé Ferguson

Master George's people; George Washington, his slaves, and his revolutionary transformation. By Marfe Ferguson Delano. National Geographic 2013 64 p. (hardcover : alk. paper) $18.95

Grades: 4 5 6 **973.4**

1. Slaves 2. Slaves -- Virginia -- Mount Vernon (Estate) 3. Slavery -- Virginia -- Mount Vernon (Estate) 4. Mount Vernon (Va. : Estate)

-- Race relations
ISBN 1426307594; 9781426307591; 9781426307607

LC 2012024295

This book, by Marfé Ferguson Delano, explores the lives of the slaves owned by U.S. President George Washington at "his Virginia plantation, Mount Vernon. . . . [The book] gives us . . . portraits of cooks, overseers, valets, farm hands, and more . . . interwoven with an extraordinary examination of the conscience of the Father of Our Country." (Publisher's note)

Includes bibliographical references and index

Fradin, Dennis Brindell

★ **Duel!** Burr and Hamilton's deadly war of words. by Dennis Brindell Fradin; illustrated by Larry Day. Walker & Co. 2008 un il $16.95; lib bdg $17.85

Grades: 3 4 5 6 **973.4**

1. Statesmen 2. Vice-presidents 3. Secretaries of the treasury 4. Burr-Hamilton Duel, Weehawken, N.J., 1804
ISBN 0-8027-9583-8; 0-8027-9584-6 lib bdg; 978-0-8027-9583-0; 978-0-8027-9584-7 lib bdg

LC 2007-37994

This is an account of the duel in 1804 which took Alexander Hamilton's life. Bibliography. "Grades three to five." (Bull Cent Child Books)

"Even children who don't know much about Aaron Burr . . . and Alexander Hamilton . . . will be hooked by this dramatic picture-book account of their deadly quarrel. . . . When Fradin deals with the divisive politics, Day's ink, watercolor, and gouache illustrations ably show the body language as the enemies furiously confront one another. . . . The words and art humanize the history for children." Booklist

Jurmain, Suzanne

★ The **worst** of friends; Thomas Jefferson, John Adams, and the true story of an American feud. illustrated by Larry Day. Dutton Children's Books 2011 32p il $16.99

Grades: 1 2 3 **973.4**

1. Architects 2. Presidents 3. Vice-presidents 4. Essayists 5. Presidents -- United States 6. United States -- History -- 1783-1809 7. United States -- History -- 1775-1783, Revolution -- Biography
ISBN 978-0-525-47903-1; 0-525-47903-1

LC 2011005190

"In zingy prose, Jurmain tells how Thomas Jefferson and John Adams 'were as different as pickles and ice cream.' . . . Yet she emphasizes that the two were best friends who worked together to shape America before parting ways when Jefferson backed the Republicans and Adams the Federalists. Entertaining anecdotes about both presidents' personal and political lives are energized by Day's lightly caricatured watercolor cartoons, which flesh out their personalities. . . . This entertaining and character-driven slice of history also offers a clear message about friendship." Publ Wkly

Includes bibliographical references

Kerley, Barbara

★ **Those** rebels, John and Tom; illustrated by Edwin Fotheringham. Scholastic Press 2012 il $17.99

Grades: 3 4 5 **973.4**

1. Architects 2. Presidents 3. Vice-presidents 4. Essayists 5. Presidents -- United States 6. United States -- History -- 1783-1809 7. United States -- History -- 1775-1783, Revolution
ISBN 978-0-545-22268-6; 0-545-22268-0

LC 2011002131

"Kerley and Fotheringham . . . cleverly contrast two diverse founding fathers and early presidents, Thomas Jefferson and John Adams. Entertaining verse and droll illustrations parlay their differences and similarities into a lens through which to view the start of the American

Revolution. . . . A playful tone also is reflected in the typeface, with certain phrases enlarged for shout-out emphasis, and in the caricatured artwork. Skillfully rendered and decidedly modern in a patriotic palette of red, white, blue, and brown, the digitally created scenes mirror and enhance the text's wit." Publ Wkly

Includes bibliographical references

Yasuda, Anita

The **Louisiana** Purchase through the eyes of Thomas Jefferson; Anita Yasuda. Abdo Pub. 2016 48 p. illustrations, map $32.79

Grades: 4 5 6   **973.4**

1. Louisiana Purchase 2. Presidents -- United States

ISBN 9781680780321

LC 2015945405

In this book, by Anita Yasuda, "experience the Louisiana Purchase from President Thomas Jeffersons perspective. Learn about the challenges he faced, how he responded to difficult issues, and how he shaped the country during this pressing time in office." (Publisher's note)

"Interesting and insightful complements to American history units." SLJ

Includes bibliographical references (page 47) and index.

973.6   United States--1845-1861

Kimmel, Allison Crotzer

A **primary** source history of slavery in the United States; by Allison Crotzer Kimmel. Capstone Press 2015 32 p. (lib bdg) $26.65; (pbk) $7.95

Grades: 3 4 5 6   **973.6**

1. Slavery -- United States 2. African Americans -- History

ISBN 1491418397; 9781491418390; 9781491418437

"For more than 100 years, slavery was a way of life in the United States. Many people believed slavery was necessary and right. Many others fought tirelessly to end it. Hear the words they spoke. Read the words they read. And see the differing points of view about slavery through the eyes of the people who lived it." (Publisher's Note)

"Well designed and informative, these books are ideal for those new to primary source documents. The fonts--large, plain, and bold--are offset by plain backgrounds. An apt and clearly captioned photograph appears on each page." SLJ

Includes bibliographical references and index

973.7   Administration of Abraham Lincoln, 1861-1865

Adler, David A., 1947-

Harriet Tubman and the Underground Railroad; by David A. Adler. Holiday House 2013 140 p. ill. (hardcover) $18.95

Grades: 5 6 7 8   **973.7**

1. Underground Railroad   2. African American women -- Biography   3. Slaves -- United States -- Biography

ISBN 0823423654; 9780823423651

LC 2012006582

This book, by David A. Adler, gives a biography of the ex-slave Harriet Tubman. "She escaped from her owners in Maryland on the Underground Railroad in 1849 and then fearlessly returned . . . to help guide . . . others to freedom as the most famous conductor of the Underground Railroad. . . . During and after the war, she helped hundreds of freed slaves begin new lives, and she later founded a home for elderly former slaves and became active in the women's suffrage movement." (Publisher's note)

Includes bibliographical references

Beller, Susan Provost

Billy Yank and Johnny Reb; soldiering in the Civil War. Twenty-First Century Books 2008 112p il map (Soldiers on the battlefront) lib bdg $33.26

Grades: 5 6 7 8   **973.7**

1. Soldiers -- United States 2. United States -- History -- 1861-1865, Civil War

ISBN 978-0-8225-6803-2 lib bdg; 0-8225-6803-9 lib bdg

LC 2006010240

First published 2000.

Describes military life for the average soldier in the Civil War, including camp life, diseases, and conditions for the wounded and prisoners of war. Includes excerpts from first-person accounts, letters, and diaries

The author "presents a good deal of solid information in an interesting manner. . . . Good black-and-white reproductions, mainly of photographs from the 1860s, appear throughout the book." Booklist [review of 2000 ed]

Includes bibliographical references

Benoit, Peter

The **surrender** at Appomattox; by Peter Benoit. Children's Press 2012 64 p. chiefly col. ill., col. map (library) $30.00; (paperback) $8.95

Grades: 4 5 6   **973.7**

1. Appomattox Campaign, 1865   2. United States -- History -- 1861-1865, Civil War -- Peace   3. United States -- History -- Civil War, 1861-1865 -- Peace

ISBN 0531250415; 9780531250419; 9780531265666

LC 2011011967

This book by Peter Benoit, part of the "Cornerstones of Freedom" series, describes the events leading up to the end of the U.S. Civil War. It "sketches the events of the Battle of the Wilderness and the capture of Richmond as well as the meeting between [Ulysses S.] Grant and [Robert E.] Lee on April 9, 1865." (School Library Journal)

Includes bibliographical references (p. 61) and index.

Brown, Don, 1949-

★ **He** has shot the president! April 14, 1865 : the day John Wilkes Booth killed President Lincoln. By Don Brown. First edition Roaring Brook Press 2014 64 p. (Actual times) (hardcover) $17.99

Grades: 2 3 4   **973.7**

ISBN 1596432241; 9781596432246

LC 2013016334

This book, by Don Brown, "is . . . [an] account of the assassination of President Lincoln. [John Wilkes] Booth 'believed that robbing the Union of the president's leadership would cripple the North and save the South.' . . . The assassination takes place early on, and the brunt of the book follows Booth's attempted flight, Lincoln's death, and the 'relentless, sweeping investigation' to find Booth and his conspirators." (Publishers Weekly)

"Brown introduces both major actors, Lincoln and Booth, and then begins the tricky task of chronologically following each man to his death. He does so successfully, switching back and forth with impeccable transitions. The text is matter-of-fact and detailed, and the illustrations, in Brown's slightly impressionistic style and rendered in somber shades of brown, blue, and gray, create drama. Bib."

A **Civil** War scrapbook; I was there too! History Colorado. Fulcrum Pub. 2012 64 p. ill. (some col.), maps (paperback) $14.95

Grades: 4 5 6 7 8   **973.7**

1. United States -- History -- 1861-1865, Civil War

ISBN 1555916686; 9781555916688

LC 2011042043

This book is "a multicultural Civil War history for children. The book . . . feature[es] chronological information" and "focus[es] on the different types of people and their place in the war. This . . . book emphasizes the roles of the children, women, minorities, and even pets that became mascots in the war." Also included are "historical photographs, drawings, maps, games, and primary quotes from children." (Publisher's Note)

Includes bibliographical references (p. 62-63) and index.

★ The **Civil** War: a visual history. DK Pub. 2011 360p il map $40
Grades: 5 6 7 8   **973.7**
1. United States -- History -- 1815-1861 2. United States -- History -- 1865-1898 3. United States -- History -- 1861-1865, Civil War -- Pictorial works
ISBN 978-0-7566-7185-3; 0-7566-7185-X

"A stunning, large-format pictorial history. The seven chapters are arranged chronologically, beginning with an overview of slavery in the United States, 1815 to 1860, and ending with a survey of the legacies of the conflict during the period 1865 to 1877. . . . Chapter introductions are followed by illustrated time lines and by short topical divisions that include biographies, maps, original documents or eyewitness accounts, illustrations, historical photographs, artifacts, and reproductions of paintings. Page layouts and the use of color are superb, and sidebars abound, adding to this extraordinary book." SLJ

Clinton, Catherine
★ **Hold** the flag high; illustrated by Shane W. Evans. Katherine Tegen Books 2005 un il $15.99; lib bdg $16.89
Grades: 2 3 4   **973.7**
1. Soldiers 2. African American soldiers 3. Postal employees 4. United States -- History -- 1861-1865, Civil War
ISBN 0-06-050428-5; 0-06-050429-3 lib bdg
LC 2003-11956

Describes the Civil War battle of Morris Island, South Carolina, during which Sargeant William H. Carney became the first African American to earn a Congressional Medal of Honor

"The story captures the fear and horror of battle as well as the bravery of the soldiers. . . . Evans' paintings convey the emotions of the characters as well as their actions." Booklist
Includes bibliographical references

Evans, Shane W.
★ **Underground**; [by] Shane W. Evans. Roaring Brook Press 2010 1 v. col. ill. $16.99
Grades: K 1 2   **973.7**
1. Abolitionists 2. Underground railroad 3. Slavery -- United States 4. Fugitive slaves
ISBN 1596435380; 9781596435384
LC 2010007735

Coretta Scott King Award (Illustrators) (2012)
This picture book portrays fugitive slaves escaping to freedom through the Underground Railroad. "Preschool, primary." (Horn Book)
"Powerfully expressive imagery will sweep young viewers into this suspenseful journey along the Underground Railroad. Accompanied by a commentary of, usually, just two or three words per spread, the scenes track a small group of escapees stealing through darkness beneath a thin crescent moon. . . . Underscoring the sense of fear and urgency with broad, slanted strokes of thinly applied paint, Evans limns his hunched, indistinct figures in dark lines and adds weight with scribbled fill and jagged bits of paper or cloth. . . . Lengthier accounts of travel on the Underground Railroad abound, but few if any portray the experience with such compelling immediacy." Kirkus

Fradin, Dennis Brindell
★ The **price** of freedom; how one town stood up to slavery. by Judith Bloom Fradin & Dennis Brindell Fradin; illustrated by Eric Velasquez. Walker & Co. 2013 48 p. (hardback) $16.99
Grades: 1 2 3   **973.7**
1. Fugitive slaves 2. Oberlin-Wellington Rescue, 1858 3. Underground railroad -- Ohio -- History 4. Quakers -- Ohio -- History -- 19th century 5. Fugitive slaves -- Ohio -- History -- 19th century
ISBN 0802721664; 9780802721662; 9780802721679
LC 2012015781

This juvenile history book, by Dennis Brindell Fradin and Judith Bloom Fradin, with illustrations by Eric Velasquez, describes how "an Ohio community successfully defied the 1850 Fugitive Slave Act. In 1856, John Price and two other Kentucky slaves crossed the Ohio River to freedom in Oberlin. . . . Two years later, when slave hunters tracked him down and captured him, the citizens of the town banded together to defend him." (Kirkus Reviews)

Gregory, Josh
Gettysburg; by Josh Gregory. Children's Press 2012 64 p. chiefly col. ill. (library) $30.00; (paperback) $8.95
Grades: 4 5 6   **973.7**
1. Gettysburg, Battle of, 1863
ISBN 0531250342; 9780531250341; 9780531265598
LC 2011010751

In this book on the 1863 Battle of Gettysburg, "[Josh] Gregory takes his readers back to the precursor events that set the stage for this meeting engagement pitting General [Robert E.] Lee's Army of Northern Virginia against General [George] Meade's oft times defeated Union Army of the Potomac. In the end the efforts of Lee's seemingly indomitable veterans were not enough to overcome the forces of fate and tactics." (Children's Literature)
Includes bibliographical references (p. 61) and index.

Hernandez, Roger E.
The **Civil** War, 1840s-1890s. Marshall Cavendish Benchmark 2008 80p il map (Hispanic America) lib bdg $34.21
Grades: 4 5 6 7   **973.7**
1. Latinos (U.S.) 2. Hispanic Americans 3. United States -- Ethnic relations 4. United States -- History -- 1861-1865, Civil War
ISBN 978-0-7614-2939-5 lib bdg; 0-7614-2939-5 lib bdg
LC 2007049525

Discusses Hispanic participation during the Civil War
Includes glossary and bibliographical references

Holzer, Harold
The **president** is shot! the assassination of Abraham Lincoln. Boyds Mills Press 2004 181p il $17.95
Grades: 5 6 7 8   **973.7**
1. Lawyers 2. Presidents 3. State legislators 4. Members of Congress
ISBN 1-56397-985-3

"A page-turner of a text, a fascinating array of photos and archival illustrations, and an event that changed the course of history: all these elements combine in this strong, highly readable book." Booklist
Includes bibliographical references

Huey, Lois Miner
American archaeology uncovers the Underground Railroad. Marshall Cavendish Benchmark 2009 64p il map (American archaeology) lib bdg $21.95
Grades: 4 5 6 7   **973.7**
1. Abolitionists 2. Underground railroad 3. Slavery -- United

States 4. Excavations (Archeology) -- United States
ISBN 978-0-7614-4267-7 lib bdg; 0-7614-4267-7 lib bdg

LC 2009003168

This describes how archeologists have learned about the history of the Underground Railroad.

This is "both intriguing and engaging for young readers.... A welcomed addition to classroom and school libraries." Libr Media Connect

Includes glossary and bibliographical references

Jordan, Anne Devereaux

The **Civil** War; by Anne Devereaux Jordan; with Virginia Schomp. Marshall Cavendish Benchmark 2007 72p il (Drama of African-American history) lib bdg $34.21

Grades: 5 6 7 8   **973.7**

1. African Americans -- History 2. United States -- History -- 1861-1865, Civil War
ISBN 978-0-7614-2179-5 lib bdg; 0-7614-2179-3 lib bdg

LC 2006012472

Describes the role of African Americans during the Civil War (1861-1865)

Includes glossary and bibliographical references

Kneib, Martha

The **Civil** War through the eyes of Abraham Lincoln; by Martha Kneib; content consultant, John M. Sacher, Chair, Department of History, University of Central Florida. Core Library, an imprint of Abdo Publishing 2016 48 p. illustrations, maps (hardback) $32.79

Grades: 4 5 6   **973.7**

1. United States -- History -- 1861-1865, Civil War 2. Presidents -- United States
ISBN 1680780301; 9781680780307

LC 2015945402

This juvenile book, by Martha Kneib, with John M. Sacher, helps children "experience the Civil War from President Abraham Lincolns perspective. [Through the book, they will] learn about the challenges he faced, how he responded to difficult issues, and how he shaped the country during this pressing time in office." (Publisher's note)

"Interesting and insightful complements to American history units." SLJ

Includes bibliographical references (page 47) and index

Kostyal, K. M.

1862, Fredericksburg; a new look at a bitter Civil War battle. National Geographic 2011 48p (National Geographic kids)

Grades: 3 4 5 6   **973.7**

1. United States -- History -- 1861-1865, Civil War -- Campaigns
ISBN 1-4263-0835-3; 1-4263-0836-1 lib bdg; 978-1-4263-0835-2; 978-1-4263-0836-9 lib bdg

LC 2011011798

Details the Civil War battle of Fredericksburg, Virginia, and profiles some of the key figures involved in what was a decisive victory for the Confederacy.

"Realistic, full-color pictures of modern-day re-enactors mix with clear language to bring the action to life. The text is interspersed with personal accounts.... Brief chapters tell the war's story from the perspective of what happened at Fredericksburg in a concise manner.... A valuable resource for classrooms, libraries, and travelers to Fredericksburg and the surrounding area." SLJ

Landau, Elaine

Fleeing to freedom on the Underground Railroad; the courageous slaves, agents, and conductors. Twenty-First Century Books 2006 88p il map (People's history) lib bdg $26.60

Grades: 5 6 7 8   **973.7**

1. Abolitionists 2. Underground railroad 3. Slavery -- United States
ISBN 978-0-8225-3490-7 lib bdg; 0-8225-3490-8 lib bdg

LC 2005020358

"Landau discusses the history of slavery in the United States, slave life, the Underground Railroad, and the leaders, both black and white, of antislavery organizations. Three chapters outline specifics of slaves' escapes.... An outstanding feature of this book is the use of primary sources and quotes from former slaves, contemporary newspaper accounts, and reminiscences of escaped slaves.... Excellent historical photographs and illustrations enhance the text." SLJ

Includes bibliographical references

Levy, Debbie

Soldier song; A True Story of the Civil War. by Debbie Levy; illustrated by Gilbert Ford. Disney Hyperion 2017 80 p. color illustrations $18.99

Grades: 3 4 5   **973.7**

1. United States -- History -- 1861-1865, Civil War 2. United States -- History -- Civil War, 1861-1865 -- Music and the war
ISBN 1484725980; 9781484725986

LC 2015019787

In this book, by Debbie Levy, illustrated by Gilbert Ford, "both Union and Confederate soldiers were urged onward by song.... And there was one song that reminded them all of what they hoped to return to after the war. Defeated in the battle of Fredericksburg, Virginia, the Union soldiers retreated across the river. There, a new battle emerged as both armies volleyed competing songs back and forth." (Publisher's note)

"A moving tale of ordinary soldiers in a great conflict who find solace in music." Kirkus

Includes bibliographical references.

McNeese, Tim

The **Civil** War era, 1851-1865; consulting editor, Richard Jensen. Chelsea House 2010 144p il map (Discovering U.S. history) $35

Grades: 5 6 7 8   **973.7**

1. United States -- History -- 1861-1865, Civil War
ISBN 978-1-60413-352-3; 1-60413-352-X

LC 2009-3660

"The information is accurate and easy to understand. Pictures are well placed, and primary sources are included.... The maps are well done and there are sidebars with additional information.... [This would be good] to have on hand for reports as it is well laid out and easy to use." Libr Media Connect

Includes glossary and bibliographical references

McPherson, James M.

★ **Fields** of fury; the American Civil War. Atheneum Bks. for Young Readers 2002 96p il map $22.95

Grades: 5 6 7 8   **973.7**

1. United States -- History -- 1861-1865, Civil War
ISBN 0-689-84833-1

LC 2001-46048

Examines the events and effects of the American Civil War

"McPherson writes with authority, offering a broad overview as well as many details and anecdotes that give his account a human dimension. ... The many fine illustrations include period photographs, paintings, prints, some excellent maps." Booklist

Includes glossary and bibliographical references

Murphy, Jim

★ The **boys'** war; Confederate and Union soldiers talk about the Civil War. Clarion Bks. 1990 110p il hardcover o.p. pa $8.95

Grades: 5 6 7 8 9 10   **973.7**

1. United States -- History -- 1861-1865, Civil War

ISBN 0-89919-893-7; 0-395-66412-8 pa

LC 89-23959

This book includes diary entries, personal letters, and archival photographs to describe the experiences of boys, sixteen years old or younger, who fought in the Civil War.

"An excellent selection of more than 45 sepia-toned contemporary photographs augment the text of this informative, moving work." SLJ

Includes bibliographical references

★ The **long** road to Gettysburg. Clarion Bks. 1992 116p il maps $17; pa $7.95

Grades: 5 6 7 8 9 10   **973.7**

1. Gettysburg (Pa.), Battle of, 1863

ISBN 0-395-55965-0; 0-618-05157-0 pa

LC 90-21881

Describes the events of the Battle of Gettysburg in 1863 as seen through the eyes of two actual participants, nineteen-year-old Confederate lieutenant John Dooley and seventeen-year-old Union soldier Thomas Galway. Also discusses Lincoln's famous speech delivered at the dedication of the National Cemetery at Gettysburg

The author "uses all of his fine skills as an information writer—clarity of detail, conciseness, understanding of his age group, and ability to find the drama appealing to readers—to frame a well-crafted account of a single battle in the war." Horn Book

Includes bibliographical references

★ A **savage** thunder; Antietam and the bloody road to freedom. Margaret K. McElderry Books 2009 103p il map $17.99

Grades: 5 6 7 8 9   **973.7**

1. Generals 2. Governors 3. Antietam (Md.), Battle of, 1862 4. College presidents 5. Presidential candidates 6. United States -- History -- 1861-1865, Civil War

ISBN 978-0-689-87633-2; 0-689-87633-5

LC 2008-32738

"Murphy provides readers with a lucid and compelling narrative, drawn mainly from firsthand accounts. . . . Replete with excellent-quality archival photos, reproductions, and maps, this is an outstanding account of a battle." SLJ

Includes bibliographical references

Norwich, Grace

I am Harriet Tubman; by Grace Norwich; illustrated by Ute Simon. Scholastic 2013 127 p. ill. (paperback) $5.99

Grades: 3 4 5   **973.7**

1. Slavery -- United States

ISBN 0545484367; 9780545484367

This book is part of the I Am series and focuses on Harriet Tubman, "the legendary Underground Railroad conductor. Prefaced by a time line and a page introducing important individuals to the story, [Grace] Norwich's narrative provides information as well as insight into how that information has come down to us. . . . Tubman's early life in slavery is . . . described, as are her brave efforts to escape." (Booklist)

O'Connor, Jim

What was the Battle of Gettysburg? by Jim O'Connor; illustrated by John Mantha. Grosset & Dunlap 2013 106 p. (hc) $15.99

Grades: 3 4 5 6   **973.7**

1. Gettysburg (Pa.), Battle of, 1863 2. United States -- History

-- 1861-1865, Civil War

ISBN 0448465752; 9780448462868; 9780448465753

LC 2012027557

This book, by Jim O'Connor, John Mantha, and James Bennett, "offers a strongly contextualized account of the bloodiest engagement of the Civil War and a mostly chronological discussion of the battle. Chapters, each beginning with a historical date, tell the story in a narrative format, but the story is effectively broken up with boxed biographies of such figures as Mathew Brady, Jeb Stuart, and Abraham Lincoln." (Booklist)

Includes bibliographical references (p. 106)

Raatma, Lucia

The **Underground** Railroad; by Lucia Raatma. Children's Press 2011 64 p. col. ill. (library) $30.00; (paperback) $8.95

Grades: 4 5 6   **973.7**

1. Fugitive slaves 2. Underground Railroad 3. Fugitive slaves -- United States -- History -- 19th century 4. Antislavery movements -- United States -- History -- 19th century

ISBN 0531250431; 9780531250433; 9780531265680

LC 2011009493

This book by Lucia Raatma is part of the Cornerstones of Freedom series and looks at the Underground Railroad. The entry "explains how the system worked, the journey, and important people who guided slaves such as Harriet Tubman and Levi and Catherine White Coffin of Indiana, who helped about 2,000 slaves reach freedom." (School Library Journal)

Includes bibliographical references (p. 61) and index.

Rossi, Ann

Freedom struggle; the anti-slavery movement in America 1830-1865. National Geographic 2005 40p il (Crossroads America) $12.95; lib bdg $21.90

Grades: 4 5 6   **973.7**

1. Abolitionists 2. Slavery -- United States

ISBN 0-7922-7828-3; 0-7922-8061-X lib bdg

LC 2003-19824

This discusses the Abolitionist Movement in the United States, profiling some of its leaders and its role in the Civil War.

"Period photographs, drawings, and cartoons; primary-source material; and biographical content make [this] introductory [title] interesting and accessible." SLJ

Includes glossary

Sheinkin, Steve

Lincoln's Grave Robbers. Scholastic 2013 224 p. $16.99

Grades: 5 6 7 8   **973.7**

1. Grave robbing 2. Counterfeits and counterfeiting

ISBN 0545405726; 9780545405720

This book is an "account of the attempted heist of Abraham Lincoln's body in 1876." Steve Sheinkin first "delv[es] into the history of counterfeiting. . . . James Kennally, leader of one of the largest counterfeiting rings in the Midwest, masterminded the plot to steal the late president's body from the Lincoln Monument," intending "to ransom the purloined corpse" and extort "the government for a tidy sum of money and the freedom of his jailed, top-notch engraver." (Publishers Weekly)

★ **Two** miserable presidents; everything your schoolbooks didn't tell you about the Civil War. illustrated by Tim Robinson. Roaring Brook Press 2008 246p il $19.95

Grades: 4 5 6 7   **973.7**

1. United States -- History -- 1861-1865, Civil War

ISBN 978-1-59643-320-5; 1-59643-320-5

LC 2007-33115

"Chatty and accessible, this book does double duty: it introduces Civil War history for readers who don't know much about it and supplies browsable commentary for those familiar with the big picture. . . . [Sheinkin's] fast-paced narrative is broken into short, tersely titled vignettes." Booklist

Includes bibliographical references

Turner, Ann Warren

Abe Lincoln remembers; [by] Ann Turner; pictures by Wendell Minor. HarperCollins Pubs. 2001 un il hardcover o.p. pa $6.99

Grades: K 1 2 3   **973.7**

1. Lawyers 2. Presidents 3. State legislators 4. Members of Congress 5. Presidents -- United States 6. United States -- History -- 1861-1865, Civil War

ISBN 0-06-027577-4; 0-06-027578-2 lib bdg; 0-06-051107-9 pa

LC 98-50937

A simple description of the life of Abraham Lincoln, presented from his point of view

"Turner's free-verse reminiscence gracefully ties images and themes from Lincoln's youth to those of his adult years. . . . Minor's well-composed paintings, best seen from a little distance, effectively portray the man as he ages." Booklist

Weber, Jennifer L.

Summer's bloodiest days; the Battle of Gettysburg as told from all sides. foreword by James M. McPherson. National Geographic 2010 61p il map $17.95; lib bdg $27.90

Grades: 5 6 7 8   **973.7**

1. Gettysburg (Pa.), Battle of, 1863 2. United States -- History -- 1861-1865, Civil War

ISBN 978-1-4263-0706-5; 1-4263-0706-3; 978-1-4263-0707-2 lib bdg; 1-4263-0707-1 lib bdg

"This colorful book tells of the Battle of Gettysburg, a dramatic event that becomes even more compelling because the text is laced with pertinent quotes from those who were there. Weber's vivid, pithy writing packs a great deal of information and many anecdotes into a relatively short account. . . . Many battle maps, short, informative sidebars, and the use of modern realistic paintings and photos of artifacts as well as period photographs . . . illustrate the book." Booklist

Includes bibliographical references

Williams, Carla

The **Underground** Railroad. Child's World 2009 32p il (Journey to freedom) lib bdg $28.50

Grades: 4 5 6   **973.7**

1. Underground railroad 2. Slavery -- United States

ISBN 978-1-60253-139-0 lib bdg; 1-60253-139-0 lib bdg

LC 2008031946

"Underground Railroad describes how this secret system worked and introduces key figures. Williams discusses relevant laws and amendments as well as the advent and conclusion of the Civil War. The facts, presented through stories, historical news accounts, and biographical sketches of Harriet Tubman and Levi Weeks, capture the desperation of the enslaved as well as the abolitionists' commitment to them. The [book is] concise and direct, yet the writing remains sophisticated. Vibrant personal stories accompanied by striking photographs of historical figures and artifacts provide a sense of the subjects' hopes and dreams." SLJ

Includes glossary and bibliographical references

973.8   United States--Reconstruction period, 1865-1901

Howell, Brian

The **US** Civil War and Reconstruction. Cherry Lake Pub. 2011 il (Language arts explorer: history digs) $18.95; pa $14.95

Grades: 3 4 5 6   **973.8**

1. Reconstruction (1865-1876) 2. United States -- History -- 1861-1865, Civil War

ISBN 978-1-61080-201-7; 978-1-61080-289-5 pa

LC 2011015126

"This compact volume is narrated by an unnamed child, who is helping a museum curator set up a Civil War museum. The first boxes that the narrator unpacks hold documents and exhibits about slavery. Each day, the child learns more about the origins of the war, its battles, and Reconstruction. Through simply told prose in first person, the book provides a great deal of information presented in ways that kids can understand. It also gives solid background in how research is done. . . . Photographs and numerous reproductions of historical documents add to the usefulness of this slim book." Booklist

McNeese, Tim

The **Gilded** Age and Progressivism, 1891-1913; Tim McNeese; consulting editor, Richard Jensen. Chelsea House 2010 136 p. ill. (some col.) (Discovering U.S. history) (library) $35.00

Grades: 5 6 7 8   **973.8**

1. Progressivism (United States politics) 2. United States -- History -- 1865-1921 3. United States -- Social conditions -- 1865-1918 4. United States -- Politics and government -- 1901-1953 5. Progressivism (United States politics) -- History -- 19th century 6. Progressivism (United States politics) -- History -- 20th century

ISBN 1604133554; 9781604133554

LC 2009015012

McNeese "discusses the people, politics, economic conditions, and foreign affairs of [the U.S. from 1891 to 1913], objectively explaining how the attitudes, perceptions, and expectations of the American people and their leaders shaped the development of the country. . . . Color period art and photos, maps, and cutaway drawings supplement the [text]." SLJ

Includes bibliographical references and index.

Stroud, Bettye

The **Reconstruction** era; by Bettye M. Stroud with Virginia Schomp. Marshall Cavendish Benchmark 2007 70p il (Drama of African-American history) lib bdg $34.21

Grades: 5 6 7 8   **973.8**

1. Reconstruction (1865-1876) 2. African Americans -- History

ISBN 978-0-7614-2181-8 lib bdg; 0-7614-2181-5 lib bdg

LC 2006012149

"Traces the history of Reconstruction, from the end of the Civil War in 1865 to 1877, when federal troops were removed from the South." Publisher's note

Includes glossary and bibliographical references

Todras, Ellen H.

Wagon trains and settlers. Kingfisher 2011 32p il (All about America) pa $9.99; $19.89

Grades: 3 4 5 6   **973.8**

1. Frontier and pioneer life 2. Overland journeys to the Pacific 3. West (U.S.) -- History

ISBN 0-7534-6511-6 pa; 0-7534-6583-3; 978-0-7534-6511-0 pa; 978-0-7534-6583-7

This describes westward migration and pioneer life in the United States in the 19th century.

This "visually appealing [title] effectively [combines] paintings, engravings, primary documents, and photographs with cartoon illustrations. The eye-catching [layout includes] different font sizes, bold type, and text boxes to highlight different pieces of information. The content is interesting and pithy." SLJ

Includes glossary and bibliographical references

Walker, Paul Robert

★ **Remember** Little Bighorn; Indians, soldiers, and scouts tell their stories. [by] Paul Robert Walker; [foreword by John A. Doerner] National Geographic Society 2006 61p il map $17.95; lib bdg $27.90
Grades: 5 6 7 8 **973.8**
1. Little Bighorn, Battle of the, 1876
ISBN 0-7922-5521-6; 0-7922-5522-4 lib bdg
LC 2005030929

This "volume gives an almost blow-by-blow account of the famous battle that came to be known as Custer's Last Stand. Walker concentrates on the battle itself, fought on the Great Plains in 1876, and the book includes diagrams of each side's tactics. . . . Walker's exhaustive research . . . [brings] together the conflicting viewpoints of the whites and the Lakota Sioux, Cheyenne, and Arapaho fighters, documenting everything in source notes. The handsome book design, with thick paper, clear type, maps, stirring photos, and archival images, will attract readers to the battle story and then start them thinking about lasting historical issues." Booklist

Includes bibliographical references

973.9 United States--1901-

Sandler, Martin W.

★ The **Dust** Bowl through the lens; how photography revealed and helped remedy a national disaster. Walker & Co. 2008 96p il map $15.99; lib bdg $20.89
Grades: 5 6 7 8 **973.9**
1. Dust storms 2. Documentary photography 3. Great Plains -- History
ISBN 978-0-8027-9547-2; 0-8027-9547-1; 978-0-8027-9548-9 lib bdg; 0-8027-9548-X lib bdg
LC 2008-55979

"This excellent photo-essay traces the history of the Dust Bowl from its causes to its resolution. In tandem, Sandler treats the role of the budding field of photojournalism. Forty-four spreads feature a page of clear, direct text with a large, well-reproduced image, many of which are set on color pages. . . . Seldom has the connection between the arts and the general quality of life been made so clear. The text deals equally with those who fled the decimated Bread Basket for California and those who waited out the devastation and dust. Throughout, the use of primary sources is superb, with quotations from affected citizens, the photojournalists themselves, political and entertainment figures, and writers, giving a multifaceted picture of a seminal time in United States history." SLJ

973.91 United States--1901-1953

Bingham, Jane

The **Great** Depression; the Jazz Age, Prohibition, and the Great Depression, 1921-1937. Chelsea House 2011 64p il (A cultural history of women in America) $35
Grades: 5 6 7 8 **973.91**
1. Great Depression, 1929-1939 2. Women -- United States 3.

Women -- United States -- History
ISBN 978-1-60413-933-4; 1-60413-933-1
LC 2010044889

An "eye-catching [layout] with good use of color, photographs, and informative sidebars, many of which use primary-source quotations, are the highlights of [this] appealing [volume]. . . . After a succinct overview of contemporary events, the chapters describe women's lives at home, at work, in education, in politics, in the arts, and their role in the general culture. . . . [This book] surveys an era after women won the right to vote and when the nation's economic crash placed new hardships on families." SLJ

Includes glossary and bibliographical references

Corrigan, Jim

The **1900s** decade in photos; a decade of discovery. Enslow Publishers 2010 64p il (Amazing decades in photos) lib bdg $27.93
Grades: 4 5 6 7 **973.91**
1. United States -- History -- 20th century
ISBN 978-0-7660-3129-6 lib bdg; 0-7660-3129-2 lib bdg
LC 2008042900

This highlights the important world, national, and cultural developments of the 1900s.

This is illustrated with "large, well-chosen black-and-white and color photos. . . . Captions provide specific information about the photos and supplement, rather than repeat, information in the [narrative]. Attractive and readable, this . . . will be popular with browsers and beginning researchers." SLJ

Includes glossary and bibliographical references

The **1910s** decade in photos; a decade that shook the world. Enslow Publishers 2010 64p il (Amazing decades in photos) lib bdg $27.93
Grades: 4 5 6 7 **973.91**
1. United States -- History -- 20th century
ISBN 978-0-7660-3130-2 lib bdg; 0-7660-3130-6 lib bdg
LC 2008042902

This highlights the important world, national, and cultural developments of the decade 1910-1919, including the sinking of the Titanic, the establishment of the Boy Scouts and Girl Scouts, immigration, income tax, Hollywood feature films, World War I, the Lusitania sinking, and more.

Includes glossary and bibliographical references

The **1920s** decade in photos; the Roaring Twenties. Enslow Publishers 2010 64p il (Amazing decades in photos) lib bdg $27.93
Grades: 4 5 6 7 **973.91**
1. United States -- History -- 1919-1933
ISBN 978-0-7660-3131-9 lib bdg; 0-7660-3131-4 lib bdg
LC 2008042903

This highlights the important world, national, and cultural developments of the decade 1920-1929, including Prohibition, jazz music, women's suffrage, the rise of Mussolini, flappers fashions, the KKK, U.S. Presidents Harding and Coolidge, the Teapot Dome Scandal, the rise of the Nazi Party, and more.

Includes glossary and bibliographical references

Kimmelman, Leslie

Hot dog! Eleanor Roosevelt throws a picnic. written by Leslie Kimmelman; illustrated by Victor Juhasz. Sleeping Bear Press 2014 40 p. color illustrations $16.99
Grades: 2 3 4 5 **973.91**
1. World history 2. Royal visitors -- United States 3. Royal visitors -- Great Britain 4. Visits of state -- United States 5. Presidents'

spouses -- United States
ISBN 158536830X; 9781585368303

LC 2013024897

In this illustrated history book for children, "when King George and Queen Elizabeth decided to visit the U.S.--the first time a British monarch had set foot on U.S. shores--Mrs. Roosevelt decided that, among other entertainments, a picnic in Hyde Park was in order. But when she said that she wanted to serve that quintessential American food, hot dogs, her menu choice became a subject of national discussion." (Booklist)

"Kimmelman's straightforward storytelling incorporates some basic explanatory facts and deftly brings this bit of Americana to life. An author's note provides further context along with a statement that quoted correspondence can be found at Hyde Park; it is silent, however, on the authenticity of the Roosevelts' dialogue. A captivating introductory piece for budding history buffs." Kirkus

Stanley, George Edward
An **emerging** world power (1900-1929) [by] George E. Stanley. World Almanac Library 2005 48p il (Primary source history of the United States) lib bdg $30

Grades: 5 6 7 8   **973.91**
1. United States -- Foreign relations 2. United States -- History -- 1919-1933 3. United States -- Politics and government -- 1919-1933
ISBN 0-8368-5828-X

LC 2004-61501

The author describes United States politics and foreign relations in the 1920s.

"Stanley explains and connects events utilizing clear language and a blending of text, images, and primary accounts. . . . Well-organized, highly attractive." SLJ

Includes bibliographical references

973.917   Administration of Franklin Delano Roosevelt, 1933-1945

Cooper, Michael L.
★ **Dust** to eat; drought and depression in the 1930's. Clarion Books 2004 81p il map hardcover o.p. $15

Grades: 4 5 6 7   **973.917**
1. Droughts 2. Migrant labor 3. Great Depression, 1929-1939
ISBN 0-618-15449-3

LC 2003-17807

This book begins "with the 1929 stock market crash that ushered in the Great Depression and {continues} with the severe drought in the Midwest, known as the Dust Bowl." (Publisher's note) Index. "Grades six to nine." (Bull Cent Child Books)

This includes "lots of stunning black-and-white archival photos and a clear, spacious text that draws on eloquent eyewitness reports—including comments from John Steinbeck and Woody Guthrie. . . . This is an excellent historical account." Booklist

Includes bibliographical references

Corrigan, Jim
The **1930s** decade in photos; Depression and hope. Enslow Publishers 2010 64p il (Amazing decades in photos) lib bdg $27.93

Grades: 4 5 6 7   **973.917**
1. Great Depression, 1929-1939 2. United States -- History -- 1919-1933 3. United States -- History -- 1933-1945
ISBN 978-0-7660-3132-6 lib bdg; 0-7660-3132-2 lib bdg

LC 2008042904

This highlights the important world, national, and cultural developments of the decade 1930-1939, including the Great Depression, the Lindbergh kidnapping, the administration of FDR, the New Deal, jazz and swing music, the rise of Nazism, the repeal of Prohibition and more.
Includes glossary and bibliographical references

The **1940s** decade in photos; a world at war. Enslow Publishers 2010 64p il (Amazing decades in photos) lib bdg $27.93

Grades: 4 5 6 7   **973.917**
1. World War, 1939-1945 2. United States -- History -- 1933-1945 3. United States -- History -- 1945-1953
ISBN 978-0-7660-3133-3 lib bdg; 0-7660-3133-0 lib bdg

LC 2008042910

This covers the important world, national, and cultural developments of the decade 1940-1949, focusing on World War II.

This is illustrated with "large, well-chosen black-and-white and color photos. . . . Captions provide specific information about the photos and supplement, rather than repeat, information in the [narrative]. Attractive and readable, this . . . will be popular with browsers and beginning researchers." SLJ

Includes glossary and bibliographical references

Freedman, Russell
★ **Eleanor** Roosevelt; a life of discovery. Clarion Bks. 1993 198p il hardcover o.p. pa $11.95

Grades: 5 6 7 8 9 10   **973.917**
1. Diplomats 2. Columnists 3. Humanitarians 4. Social activists 5. Spouses of presidents 6. United Nations officials 7. Presidents' spouses -- United States
ISBN 0-89919-862-7; 0-395-84520-3 pa

LC 92-25024

A Newbery Medal honor book, 1994

"This impeccably researched, highly readable study of one of this country's greatest First Ladies is nonfiction at its best. . . . Approximately 140 well-chosen black-and-white photos amplify the text." Publ Wkly

Includes bibliographical references

★ **Franklin** Delano Roosevelt. Clarion Bks. 1990 200p il hardcover o.p. pa $9.95

Grades: 5 6 7 8 9 10   **973.917**
1. Governors 2. Presidents 3. People with disabilities 4. Philatelists 5. Presidents -- United States 6. United States -- Politics and government -- 1933-1945
ISBN 0-89919-379-X; 0-395-62978-0 pa

LC 89-34986

The author "traces the personal and public events in a life that led to the formation of one of the most influential and magnetic leaders of the twentieth century." Horn Book

Includes bibliographical references

Garland, Sherry
Voices of the dust bowl; by Sherry Garland; illustrated by Judith Hierstein. Pelican Pub. Co. 2011 p. cm.

Grades: 4 5 6   **973.917**
1. Great Plains -- History 2. Droughts -- United States 3. Dust Bowl Era, 1931-1939 4. Middle West -- History -- 20th century 5. Great Plains -- History -- 20th century 6. Farmers -- Great Plains -- History -- 20th century 7. Droughts -- Great Plains -- History -- 20th century 8. Dust storms -- Great Plains -- History -- 20th century
ISBN 9781589809642

LC 2011002670

This book, by Sherry Garland, presents "[v]oices from those who lived through the largest environmental catastrophe in American history. From 1931 to 1940, a combination of drought and soil erosion destroyed the fragile ecology and economy of the Great Plains." Illustrations are given along with accounts such as "a farmer's wife, a banker, and a child who had never seen rain." (Publisher's note)

Includes bibliographical references

McNeese, Tim

The **Great** Depression, 1929-1940; consulting editor Richard Jensen. Chelsea House 2010 136p il map (Discovering U.S. history) $35

Grades: 5 6 7 8   **973.917**

1. Economic conditions 2. Great Depression, 1929-1939 3. United States -- History -- 1933-1945

ISBN 978-1-60413-357-8; 1-60413-357-0

LC 2009-22090

"The information is accurate and easy to understand. Pictures are well placed, and primary sources are included. . . . The maps are well done and there are sidebars with additional information. . . . [This would be good] to have on hand for reports as it is well laid out and easy to use." Libr Media Connect

Includes glossary and bibliographical references

973.92   United States--1953-2001

Corrigan, Jim

The **1990s** decade in photos; the rise of technology. Enslow Publishers 2010 64p il (Amazing decades in photos) lib bdg $27.93

Grades: 4 5 6 7   **973.92**

1. World history -- 20th century 2. United States -- History -- 1989-

ISBN 978-0-7660-3138-8 lib bdg; 0-7660-3138-1 lib bdg

LC 2008054648

This highlights the important world, national, and cultural developments of the decade 1990-1999, including Operation Desert Storm in 1991, race riots in Los Angeles, the election of President Clinton, the 1993 bombing of the World Trade Center, the Human Genome Project, the end of Apartheid, massacres in Bosnia and Rwanda, the Oklahoma City bombing, the O.J. Simpson murder trial, the Columbine High School shootings, and more

Includes glossary and bibliographical references

McNeese, Tim

Modern America, 1964-present; consulting editor, Richard Jensen. Chelsea House 2010 144p il map (Discovering U.S. history) $35

Grades: 5 6 7 8   **973.92**

1. United States -- History -- 1989- 2. United States -- History -- 1961-1974 3. United States -- History -- 1974-1989

ISBN 978-1-60413-361-5; 1-60413-361-9

"Through a good balance of social and political topics, McNeese capably covers a diverse range of subjects in [this] volume. . . . Modern America discusses civil rights, terrorism, and Barack Obama's first year as president. [The] book has an excellent chronology; rich sidebars; and numerous well-captioned illustrations, maps, and photos that enhance the [text]. [This book provides a] satisfying [introduction] to American history for students." SLJ

Includes glossary and bibliographical references

973.921   Administration of Dwight David Eisenhower, 1953-1961

Corrigan, Jim

The **1950s** decade in photos; the American decade. Enslow Publishers 2010 64p il (Amazing decades in photos) lib bdg $27.93

Grades: 4 5 6 7   **973.921**

1. United States -- History -- 1945-1953 2. United States -- History

-- 1953-1961

ISBN 978-0-7660-3134-0 lib bdg; 0-7660-3134-9 lib bdg

LC 2008042994

This highlights the important world, national, and cultural developments of the decade 1950-1959, including the Korean War, McCarthyism, the Baby Boom generation, the execution of the Rosenbergs, the Beat Generation, the polio epidemic and vaccine, the Montgomery Bus Boycott, the Suez Crisis, the beginning of rock music, the launching of Sputnik, and the Cuban Revolution

Includes glossary and bibliographical references

973.922   Administration of John Fitzgerald Kennedy, 1961-1963

Adler, David A.

A **picture** book of John F. Kennedy; illustrated by Robert Casilla. Holiday House 1991 un il $16.95; pa $6.95

Grades: 1 2 3   **973.922**

1. Presidents 2. Senators 3. Members of Congress 4. Presidents -- United States

ISBN 0-8234-0884-1; 0-8234-0976-7 pa

LC 90-23589

Depicts the life and career of John F. Kennedy

"Adler presents a brief, clearly written text that provides basic information about his subject in an appealing format. . . . Casilla's watercolors are full-color copies of famous photographs." SLJ

Nardo, Don

Assassination and its aftermath; how a photograph reassured a shocked nation. by Don Nardo. Compass Point Books, a Capstone imprint 2013 64 p. (Captured history) (library binding) $33.99

Grades: 6 7 8 9   **973.922**

1. Presidents -- United States -- Pictorial works 2. Kennedy, John F. (John Fitzgerald), 1917-1963 -- Assassination 3. Photojournalists -- United States -- History -- 20th century 4. Presidents -- Succession -- United States -- History -- 20th century

ISBN 0756546923; 9780756546922; 9780756546984

LC 2012051716

In this book, by Don Nardo, "vice president, Lyndon Baines Johnson, took the presidential oath of office on Air Force One just hours after the assassination [of U.S. President John F. Kennedy] . . . Cecil Stoughton's iconic photo [of this moment] showed the world that the smooth and orderly transfer of power called for in the U.S. Constitution had occurred." According to the book, "his photo helped ease the shock, tension, and fear in an anxious country." (Publisher's note)

Includes bibliographical references and index

973.923   Administration of Lyndon Baines Johnson, 1963-1969

Corrigan, Jim

The **1960s** decade in photos; love, freedom, and flower power. Enslow Publishers 2010 64p il (Amazing decades in photos) lib bdg $27.93

Grades: 4 5 6 7   **973.923**

1. United States -- History -- 1961-1974

ISBN 978-0-7660-3135-7 lib bdg; 0-7660-3135-7 lib bdg

LC 2008042996

This highlights the important world, national, and cultural developments of the decade 1960-1969, including the U-2 spy plane, the election and assassination of JFK, the beginnings of manned space exploration, the Bay of Pigs invasion, the Vietnam War, the Cuban Missile Crisis, the British invasion in rock music, the Civil Rights movement, the Six-Day War in the Middle East, the assassinations of RFK and Martin Luther King, and Hippie culture

Includes glossary and bibliographical references

Donohue, Moira Rose

The **Civil** Rights Movement through the eyes of Lyndon B. Johnson; Moira Rose Donohue. Abdo Publishing 2016 48 p. illustrations $32.79

Grades: 4 5 6   **973.923**

1. Civil rights -- United States -- History

ISBN 9781680780291

LC 2015945401

This book, by Moira Rose Donohue, "[goes] inside the Oval Office during the Civil Rights Movement to see the challenges faced by President Lyndon B. Johnson, how he responded to difficult issues, and how he shaped the country during this pressing time in office." (Publisher's note)

"Interesting and insightful complements to American history units." SLJ

Includes bibliographical references (page 47) and index.

973.924   Administration of Richard Milhous Nixon, 1969-1974

Corrigan, Jim

The **1970s** decade in photos; protest and change. Enslow Publishers 2010 64p il (Amazing decades in photos) lib bdg $27.93

Grades: 4 5 6 7   **973.924**

1. United States -- History -- 1961-1974 2. United States -- History -- 1974-1989

ISBN 978-0-7660-3136-4 lib bdg; 0-7660-3136-5 lib bdg

LC 2008042998

This highlights the important world, national, and cultural developments of the decade 1970-1979, including protests against the Vietnam War, terrorist airplane hijackings, the thawing of the Cold War, the deaths of rock musicians Jimi Hendrix, Janice Joplin, and Jim Morrison, the attack at the Munich Olympics, Watergate and the resignation of President Nixon, Three Mile Island, and more.

Includes glossary and bibliographical references

973.927   Administration of Ronald Reagan, 1981-1989

Corrigan, Jim

The **1980s** decade in photos; the triumph of democracy. Enslow Publishers 2010 64p il (Amazing decades in photos) lib bdg $27.93

Grades: 4 5 6 7   **973.927**

1. World history -- 20th century 2. United States -- History -- 1974-1989

ISBN 978-0-7660-3137-1 lib bdg; 0-7660-3137-3 lib bdg

LC 2008052627

This highlights the important world, national, and cultural developments of the decade 1980-1989, including the 1980 Winter Olympics, the presidency of Ronald Reagan, the Iran hostage crisis, the Space Shuttle, MTV, the War on Drugs, AIDS, the rise of the computer, fashion, the Chernobyl nuclear disaster, the Iran-Contra Affair, the massacre in Tiananmen Square, the fall of the Berlin Wall, and the U.S. invasion of Panama

Includes glossary and bibliographical references

973.93   United States--2001-

Corrigan, Jim

The **2000s** decade in photos; a new millennium. Enslow Publishers 2010 64p il (Amazing decades in photos) lib bdg $27.93

Grades: 4 5 6 7   **973.93**

1. World history -- 21st century 2. United States -- History -- 21st century

ISBN 978-0-7660-3139-5 lib bdg; 0-7660-3139-X lib bdg

LC 2008054644

This highlights the important world, national, and cultural developments of the first decade of the 21st century, including the disputed presidential election of 2000, the attacks of September 11, 2001, the Iraq War, digital technology and gadgets, the drop in stock market prices of internet companies, steroid use in sports, the Space Shuttle disaster of 2003, the tsunami of 2004, Hurricane Katrina, the massacre at Virginia Tech, the energy crisis, and the 2008 presidential election

Includes glossary and bibliographical references

973.931   Administration of George W. Bush, 2001-2009

Brown, Don

★ **America** is under attack; September 11, 2001: the day the towers fell. Roaring Brook Press 2011 un il $16.99

Grades: 2 3 4   **973.931**

1. Terrorism 2. September 11 terrorist attacks, 2001 3. War on terrorism

ISBN 978-1-5964-3694-7; 1-5964-3694-8

LC 2010045417

"Brown's compelling narrative chronologically recounts the morning's events in a tone both straightforward and compassionate, without resorting to sensationalism. Brown's watercolor illustrations, covering most of each spread, mirror this voice, conveying the day's chaos and despair without unnecessarily frightening readers." SLJ

Burgan, Michael

George W. Bush; Michael Burgan. Marshall Cavendish Benchmark 2012 112 p. $34.21

Grades: 5 6 7 8   **973.931**

1. Terrorism 2. Presidents -- United States 3. Presidents -- United States -- Biography

ISBN 1608701840; 9781608701841

LC 2010014801

This book "in the 'Presidents and Their Times' series provides . . . information about George W. Bush and how he handled critical situations (e.g., domestic spying vis-a-vis telephone records to highlight the difficulty battling terrorism and the effect of Bush's response to Hurricane Katrina). . . . Personal information is also provided about his early years, including his marriage to Laura, entry into politics, relationships with other family members, a decision to stop drinking, and his choice to become a Christian fundamentalist." Also included are "color and older black and white photos" and back matter such as "a timeline, chapter notes with complete citations, a glossary, books and websites for additional information, bibliography (books, articles, media), and index." (Children's Literature)

Includes bibliographical references and index

Fradin, Dennis B.

September 11, 2001; by Dennis Brindell Fradin. Marshall Cavendish Benchmark 2009 47p il map (Turning points in U.S. history) lib bdg $21.95

Grades: 3 4 5   **973.931**

1. September 11 terrorist attacks, 2001 2. War on terrorism 3.

United States -- Social conditions 4. United States -- Politics and government -- 2001-

ISBN 978-0-7614-4259-2 lib bdg; 0-7614-4259-6 lib bdg

LC 2008038267

This book provides "accurate, nonsensationalized information in [a] well-organized, clearly written, and politically neutral [text]. The photos are crisp, and, due to the subject matter, heartrending." SLJ

Includes glossary and bibliographical references

Murray, Laura K.

The **9** /11 terror attacks; Laura K. Murray. Creative Education 2016 48 p. (hardcover : alk. paper) $39.95

Grades: 6 7 8 9 **973.931**

1. September 11 terrorist attacks, 2001

ISBN 9781608187508

LC 2016002146

This children's book in the Turning points series, by Laura K. Murray, presents "a historical account of the 9/11 terrorist attacks, including the events leading up to that day, the people involved, the monumental rescue and recovery efforts, and the lingering aftermath." (Publisher's note)

"This highly readable and balanced account places events in a global context while handling the tragedy with respect." Booklist

Includes bibliographical references and index

September 11 terror attacks

973.932 Administration of Barack Obama, 2009-2017

Staake, Bob

The **First** Pup; the real story of how Bo got to the White House. Feiwel and Friends 2010 un il $16.99

Grades: 1 2 3 **973.932**

1. Dogs 2. Lawyers 3. Presidents 4. Senators 5. State legislators 6. Nobel laureates for peace 7. Presidents -- United States -- Family

ISBN 978-0-312-61346-4; 0-312-61346-6

"Staake chronicles President Obama's 2008 victory speech and the ensuing media blitz surrounding the new puppy promised that night to his daughters. The pop-culture tale includes the well-known details of how Senator Ted Kennedy suggested a Texas-born Portuguese water dog, a sibling of one of his own dogs, when that puppy's first home didn't work out." (School Library Journal)

Weatherford, Carole Boston

First pooch; the Obamas pick a pet. Illustrated by Amy Bates. Marshall Cavendish 2009 un il $16.99

Grades: PreK K 1 2 **973.932**

1. Dogs 2. Lawyers 3. Presidents 4. Senators 5. State legislators 6. Nobel laureates for peace 7. Presidents -- United States -- Family

ISBN 978-0-7614-5636-0; 0-7614-5636-8

LC 2009006117

"This brief, lighthearted chronicle of the Obama family's search for a suitable puppy to fulfill candidate Obama's promise to his daughters focuses on Malia and Sasha. But it also brings in information about promises made by previous presidents, various breeds of dogs that lived in the White House, whimsical duties of a first dog.... Lively watercolor, pencil, and gouache illustrations featuring a smiling Obama family happy in their endeavors, portraits of select past presidents, and a lineup of adorable potential first pooches add to the telling." Booklist

974 Specific states of United States

Bruchac, Joseph, 1942-

The **hunter's** promise; an Abenaki tale. by Joseph Bruchac; illustrated by Bill Farnsworth. Wisdom Tales 2015 32 p. color illustrations (hardcover : alk. paper) $16.95

Grades: 1 2 3 4 **974**

1. Folklore 2. Hunting -- Fiction 3. Abenaki Indians -- Folklore

ISBN 1937786439; 9781937786434

LC 2015009727

In this book "Joseph Bruchac retells this traditional story of love, loyalty, trust, and magic, which can be found in various forms among many of the indigenous nations of the northeast, both Iroquoian and Algonquin. The hunter had quickly fallen in love with the mysterious woman, and together they had become their own little family. But when spring arrived and it was time to return to the village, she disappeared just as suddenly as she had arrived. Would he ever see his love again?" (Publisher's note)

"The narrative itself is elliptical, offering literal readers a story of loyalty but founding it on a subtle exploration of the spirit world and its relation to ours. Bruchac and Farnsworth honor the Indians of the Northeast, the written versions of the tale, and the elders and Wabanaki tellers who keep this story alive." Kirkus

Rylant, Cynthia

★ **Appalachia**; the voices of sleeping birds. illustrated by Barry Moser. Harcourt Brace Jovanovich 1991 21p il $17; pa $6

Grades: 4 5 6 7 **974**

1. Appalachian region

ISBN 0-15-201605-8; 0-15-201893-X pa

LC 90-36798

"Taking her subtitle from a passage by James Agee, the author conveys with a marvelous economy of words the essence of the very special part of America where she was raised. A poetic text projects emotion as well as information.... Moser's watercolors capture the scene perfectly. ... The book is a treasure—simply a beautiful combination of text and art." Horn Book

974.1 Maine

Dornfeld, Margaret

Maine; by Margaret Dornfeld and Joyce Hart. 2nd ed.; Marshall Cavendish Benchmark 2010 144p il map (Celebrate the states) lib bdg $42.79

Grades: 5 6 7 8 **974.1**

1. Maine

ISBN 978-0-7614-4726-9; 0-7614-4726-1

LC 2009002583

This offers information on the geography, history, wildlife, governmental structure, economy, cultural diversity, peoples, religion, and landmarks of Maine.

Includes bibliographical references

Heinrichs, Ann

Maine; By Ann Heinrichs. Revised edition Children's Press, A Division of Scholastic Inc. 2014 144 p. (library binding) $40

Grades: 4 5 6 7 **974.1**

1. Maine 2. Geography

ISBN 0531248879; 9780531248874

LC 2013032187

"Located in the far northeast corner of the country, Maine is known for its breathtaking natural beauty. Readers will trace the history of this remarkable state from its earliest settlement to its latest developments.

They will also dive into the local culture, see the state's many fascinating sights, and learn about its economy." (Publisher's note)

Includes bibliographical references and index

Peterson, Judy Monroe

Maine; past and present. Rosen Central 2011 48p il map (The United States: past and present) lib bdg $26.50; pa $11.75

Grades: 3 4 5 6   **974.1**

1. Maine

ISBN 978-1-4358-9484-6 lib bdg; 1-4358-9484-7 lib bdg; 978-1-4358-9511-9 pa; 1-4358-9511-8 pa

LC 2009048769

Presents the history, geography, government, economy, and people of Maine, as well as general facts about the state.

Includes glossary and bibliographical references

974.2   New Hampshire

Auden, Scott

New Hampshire, 1603-1776; [by] Scott Auden; with Alan Taylor, consultant. National Geographic Society 2007 109p il map (Voices from colonial America) $21.95; lib bdg $32.90

Grades: 5 6 7 8   **974.2**

1. New Hampshire -- History

ISBN 978-1-4263-0034-9; 1-4263-0034-4; 978-1-4263-0035-6 lib bdg; 1-4263-0035-2 lib bdg

LC 2006-36055

Provides a look at the long and changing colonial history of the state of New Hampshire through a review of its borders, founding fathers, motto, and more, complete with archival images, period maps, and various first-person accounts.

Offers " thorough, well-documented information about the struggles and successes of early non-native settlers [in New Hampshire]. . . . Many reproductions of period illustrations (both color and sepia) and some photos of archival documents and maps enhance the text." Horn Book Guide

Includes bibliographical references

Ciarleglio, Lauren

New Hampshire; past and present. Rosen Central 2011 48p il map (The United States: past and present) lib bdg $26.50; pa $11.75

Grades: 3 4 5 6   **974.2**

1. New Hampshire

ISBN 978-1-4358-9489-1 lib bdg; 1-4358-9489-8 lib bdg; 978-1-4358-9516-4 pa; 1-4358-9516-9 pa

LC 2009053334

Presents the history, geography, government, economy, and people of New Hampshire, as well as general facts about the state.

Includes bibliographical references

Kent, Deborah, 1948-

New Hampshire; [by] Deborah Kent. Revised edition Children's Press, an imprint of Scholastic Inc. 2015 144 p. illustrations, maps (library binding : alk. paper) $40

Grades: 4 5 6 7   **974.2**

1. New Hampshire 2. United States -- History

ISBN 0531282848; 9780531282847

LC 2013044358

"As one of the earliest English colonies in North America, New Hampshire played a major role in the formation of the United States. Readers will learn how this small New England state impacted the nation's development and why it remains a vital part of the country today. They will also tour New Hampshire's beautiful towns and wilderness

areas, discover the local wildlife, and sample the state's rich traditions." (Publisher's note)

Includes bibliographical references(pages 133-137)and index

Otfinoski, Steven

New Hampshire; [by] Steve Otfinoski. 2nd ed.; Marshall Cavendish Benchmark 2008 144p il map (Celebrate the states) lib bdg $39.93

Grades: 4 5 6 7   **974.2**

1. New Hampshire

ISBN 978-0-7614-2718-6; 0-7614-2718-X

LC 2007-9944

First published 1999

"Provides comprehensive information on the geography, history, wildlife, governmental structure, economy, cultural diversity, peoples, religion, and landmarks of New Hampshire." Publisher's note

Includes bibliographical references

974.3   Vermont

Heinrichs, Ann

Vermont; by Ann Heinrichs. Revised edition Children's Press 2015 144 p. illustrations, maps (library binding : alk. paper) $40

Grades: 4 5 6 7   **974.3**

1. Vermont 2. Geography

ISBN 9780531282960; 0531282961

LC 2013046228

"A small state of small towns, Vermont preserves a New England heritage that reaches back many generations. Readers will find out what it is like to make homemade maple syrup and attend county fairs as they explore Vermont's history and culture. They will also learn about the state's government, wildlife, and economy." (Publisher's note)

Includes bibliographical references and index

Sommers, Michael

Vermont; past and present. Rosen Central 2011 48p il map (The United States: past and present) lib bdg $26.50; pa $11.75

Grades: 3 4 5 6   **974.3**

1. Vermont

ISBN 978-1-4358-9498-3 lib bdg; 1-4358-9498-7 lib bdg; 978-1-4358-9525-6 pa; 1-4358-9525-8 pa

LC 2009053185

Presents the history, geography, government, economy, and people of Vermont, as well as general facts about the state.

Includes bibliographical references

974.4   Massachusetts

Freedman, Jeri

Massachusetts; past and present. Rosen Central 2010 48p il map (The United States: past and present) lib bdg $26.50; pa $11.50

Grades: 3 4 5 6   **974.4**

1. Massachusetts

ISBN 978-1-4358-5294-5 lib bdg; 1-4358-5294-X lib bdg; 978-1-4358-5586-1 pa; 1-4358-5586-8 pa

LC 2008-54229

Presents the history, geography, government, economy, and people of Massachusetts, as well as general facts about the state.

Includes glossary and bibliographical references

Fritz, Jean

★ **Who's** that stepping on Plymouth Rock? illustrated by J. B. Handelsman. Coward, McCann & Geoghegan 1975 30p il hardcover o.p. pa $6.99

Grades: 2 3 4 **974.4**

1. Plymouth Rock

ISBN 0-698-20325-9; 0-698-11681-X pa

"Both a delightful story and a perceptive commentary on how the mythmaking process works in American history." N Y Times Book Rev

Greenwood, Mark

The **Mayflower**; by Mark Greenwood; illustrated by Frane Lessac. Holiday House 2014 38 p. color illustrations (hardcover) $16.95

Grades: PreK K 1 2 3 **974.4**

1. Pilgrims (New England colonists) 2. Massachusetts -- History -- 1600-1775, Colonial period 3. Mayflower (Ship) 4. Mayflower Compact (1620 5. Pilgrims (New Plymouth Colony) 6. Massachusetts -- History -- New Plymouth, 1620-1691

ISBN 0823429431; 9780823429431

LC 2013011144

This picture book, by Mark Greenwood and illustrated by Frane Lessac, "narrates the historic journey of the one hundred and two passengers aboard the Mayflower and their settlement at Plymouth Harbor. The three-thousand-mile trip was crowded and dangerous, with families cramped next to animals and stormy seas along the way. Trouble continued when the passengers settled in Plymouth for a bitter, cold winter. However, their determination was ultimately rewarded." (Publisher's note)

"Clear text describes the famous 1620 journey from England to what is now Massachusetts, as well as the difficulties of establishing a new home in the New World. Gouache paintings in deep hues interpret the oft-told story with a folk-art feel; images capturing the ocean voyage, especially one depicting a small ship in the desolate nighttime sea, are particularly arresting. Timeline. Bib." Horn Book

Krensky, Stephen

What's the big idea? four centuries of innovation in Boston. [by] Stephen Krensky. Charlesbridge 2008 64p il lib bdg $18.95; pa $9.95

Grades: 4 5 6 **974.4**

1. Boston (Mass.) -- History

ISBN 978-1-58089-310-7 lib bdg; 1-58089-310-4 lib bdg; 978-1-58089-311-4 pa; 1-58089-311-2 pa

LC 2006021255

This "title combines a short history of Boston with brief biographies of some of the city's major figures in diverse fields. . . . Each page includes a well-captioned illustration, many in color, and the book is effectively laid out, making for pleasant browsing. . . . Teachers and students . . . will find some well-presented and useful information here." Booklist

Includes bibliographical references

Lynch, P. J.

The **boy** who fell off the Mayflower, or John Howland's True Story; P. J. Lynch. Candlewick Press 2015 64 p. illustrations $17.99

Grades: 2 3 4 5 6 **974.4**

1. Voyages and travels 2. Mayflower (Ship)

ISBN 0763665843; 9780763665845

LC 2014952482

Author P.J. Lynch presents this "volume offers a dramatic personal story of the Pilgrim's voyage on the Mayflower and their early experiences in America. Based on historical sources, the narrative is laced with well-imagined characterizations and conversations. The book's wide format showcases Lynch's dramatic and richly atmospheric watercolor and gouache paintings." (Kirkus Reviews)

Sewall, Marcia

★ The **pilgrims** of Plimoth; written and illustrated by Marcia Sewall. Atheneum Pubs. 1986 48p il hardcover o.p. pa $6.99

Grades: 3 4 5 6 **974.4**

1. Pilgrims (New England colonists) 2. Massachusetts -- History -- 1600-1775, Colonial period

ISBN 0-689-31250-4; 0-689-80861-5 pa

LC 86-3362

"Translating narrative and descriptive details into visual images, the illustrations accompany every page of text, occasionally overspreading double pages for panoramic effects. Combining subtle, modulating color with a spiritual as well as an actual luminosity, the paintings—done in gouache—are vibrant with the daily pulse of life among an energetic, enterprising people." Horn Book

Trueit, Trudi Strain

Massachusetts; by Trudi Strain Trueit. Revised edition Children's Press, a Division of Scholastic Inc. 2014 144 p. (library binding) $40

Grades: 4 5 6 7 **974.4**

1. Massachusetts 2. Geography

ISBN 0531248895; 9780531248898

LC 2013032353

"As the origin point of the American Revolution, Massachusetts is home to some of the nation's oldest and most treasured historical sites. Readers will trace the history of this remarkable state from its earliest settlement to its latest developments. They will also dive into the local culture, see the state's many fascinating sights, and learn about its economy." (Publisher's note)

Includes bibliographical references and index

Waters, Kate

Sarah Morton's day; a day in the life of a pilgrim girl. photographs by Russ Kendall. Scholastic 1989 32p il hardcover o.p. pa $5.99

Grades: 2 3 4 **974.4**

1. Pilgrims (New England colonists) 2. Massachusetts -- History -- 1600-1775, Colonial period

ISBN 0-590-42634-6; 0-590-47400-6 pa

LC 88-35581

Text and photographs of Plimoth Plantation follow a pilgrim girl through a typical day as she milks the goats, cooks and serves meals, learns her letters, and adjusts to her new stepfather

Includes glossary

974.5 Rhode Island

Burgan, Michael

Rhode Island; by Michael Burgan. Revised edition Children's Press, a Division of Scholastic Inc. 2014 144 p. illustrations, maps (library binding : alk. paper) $40

Grades: 4 5 6 7 **974.5**

1. Rhode Island 2. United States -- History

ISBN 0531282910; 9780531282915

LC 2013044802

"Nestled between Connecticut and Massachusetts along the Atlantic Coast, Rhode Island is the smallest state in the nation. Readers will visit the state's lush forests, rocky coastline, and charming towns. They will find out how the state was settled and how it is governed today. They will also get a taste of Rhode Island's cuisine and culture as they learn about some of the state's local heroes." (Publisher's note)

Includes bibliographical references and index

Furgang, Adam

   Rhode Island; past and present. Rosen Central 2011 48p il map (The United States: past and present) lib bdg $26.50; pa $11.95

Grades: 3 4 5 6   **974.5**

   1. Rhode Island

   ISBN 978-1-4358-9494-5 lib bdg; 1-4358-9494-4 lib bdg; 978-1-4358-9521-8 pa; 1-4358-9521-5 pa

                                     LC 2010001451

   Presents the history, geography, government, economy, and people of Rhode Island, as well as general facts about the state.

   Includes bibliographical references

974.6   Connecticut

Burgan, Michael

   Connecticut, 1614-1776. National Geographic Society 2007 109p il map (Voices from colonial America) $21.95; lib bdg $32.90

Grades: 5 6 7 8   **974.6**

   1. Connecticut -- History -- 1600-1775, Colonial period

   ISBN 978-1-4263-0068-4; 1-4263-0068-9; 978-1-4263-0069-1 lib bdg; 1-4263-0069-7 lib bdg

                                     LC 2007-3123

   A history of Connecticut from its beginning as an English colony to 1788 when it became the fifth state.

   Offers " thorough, well-documented information about the struggles and successes of early colonial settlers and settlements..... Many reproductions of period illustrations and some photographs of period documents and maps with relevant captions are included." Horn Book Guide

   Includes bibliographical references

Kent, Zachary

   Connecticut; by Zachary Kent. Revised edition Children's Press, an Imprint of Scholastic Inc. 2014 144 p. color illustrations, maps (library binding) $40

Grades: 4 5 6 7   **974.6**

   1. Connecticut

   ISBN 0531248798; 9780531248799

                                   LC 2013031193

   "Connecticut takes its name from a Native American word meaning 'land on the long tidal river.' Readers will trace the history of this remarkable state from its earliest settlement to its latest developments. They will also dive into the local culture, see the state's many fascinating sights, and learn about its economy." (Publisher's note)

   Includes bibliographical references (page 138) and index

La Bella, Laura

   Connecticut; past and present. Rosen Central 2011 48p il map (The United States: past and present) lib bdg $26.50; pa $11.75

Grades: 3 4 5 6   **974.6**

   1. Connecticut

   ISBN 978-1-4358-9478-5 lib bdg; 1-4358-9478-2 lib bdg; 978-1-4358-9505-8 pa; 1-4358-9505-3 pa

                                   LC 2010000401

   Presents the history, geography, government, economy, and people of Connecticut, as well as general facts about the state.

   Includes glossary and bibliographical references

974.7   New York

Bial, Raymond

   ★ **Tenement**; immigrant life on the Lower East Side. Houghton Mifflin 2002 48p il $16

Grades: 4 5 6 7   **974.7**

   1. Poor 2. Immigrants -- United States 3. Lower East Side (New York, N.Y.)

   ISBN 0-618-13849-8

                                     LC 2002-00407

   Presents a view of New York City's tenements during the peak years of foreign immigration, discussing living conditions, laws pertaining to tenements, and the occupations of their residents

   "The writing is particularly clear and sharp. Calling upon and quoting the writing of reformer Jacob Riis (and featuring his compelling photographs), Bial explains simply, yet engagingly, what tenement life was like. . . . Along with Riis' photographs, Bial provides some of his own, taken at the Lower East Side Tenement Museum in New York City." Booklist

   Includes bibliographical references

Burgan, Michael

   New York, 1609-1776; [by] Michael Burgan; with Timothy J. Shannon, consultant. National Geographic Society 2006 109p il map (Voices from colonial America) $21.95; lib bdg $32.90

Grades: 5 6 7 8   **974.7**

   1. New York (State) -- History

   ISBN 978-0-7922-6390-6; 0-7922-6390-1; 978-0-7922-6860-4 lib bdg; 0-7922-6860-1 lib bdg

                                     LC 2005-22033

   Presents a brief history of colonial New York, from 1609 to 1776, and contains illustrations, historical maps, and first-person accounts from explorers, Native Americans, and colonists on early settlements.

   Includes bibliographical references

Englar, Mary

   Dutch colonies in America. Compass Point Books 2009 48p il map (We the people) lib bdg $26.60

Grades: 4 5 6   **974.7**

   1. Dutch Americans 2. New York (State) -- History -- 1600-1775, Colonial period

   ISBN 978-0-7565-3837-8

                                     LC 2008007211

   This is a history of Dutch exploration and colonization in North America.

   This provides "solid background matter and [introduces] key people and vocabulary." SLJ

   Includes glossary and bibliographical references

Glaser, Linda

   ★ **Emma's** poem; the voice of the Statue of Liberty. with paintings by Claire A. Nivola. Houghton Mifflin Books for Children 2010 un il $17

Grades: K 1 2 3   **974.7**

   1. Poets 2. Authors 3. Novelists 4. Philanthropists 5. Social reformers 6. Immigrants -- United States 7. Statue of Liberty (New York, N.Y.) 8. Biography, Individual 9. Statue of Liberty (New York, N.Y.) 10. United States -- Emigration and immigration -- History

   ISBN 0-547-17184-6; 978-0-547-17184-5

                                     LC 2009026924

   This is an account of how the poet and social reformer Emma Lazarus came to write the sonnet, 'The New Colossus,' now on the pedestal of The Statue of Liberty. The text of the poem is appended. "Primary." (Horn Book)

"The art and words are moving in this picture book, which pairs free verse with detailed, full-page paintings in watercolor, ink, and gouache to tell the history behind Lazarus' famous inscription on the Statue of Liberty." Booklist

Huey, Lois Miner

American archaeology uncovers the Dutch colonies. Marshall Cavendish Benchmark 2009 64p il map (American archaeology) lib bdg $21.95

Grades: 4 5 6 7 **974.7**

1. Dutch Americans 2. America -- Antiquities 3. Netherlands -- Colonies -- America 4. Excavations (Archeology) -- United States

ISBN 978-0-7614-4263-9 lib bdg; 0-7614-4263-4 lib bdg

LC 2008050187

This describes how archeologists have learned about the history of Dutch settlers in America

"The text is quite chatty in this attractive title. . . . An inviting design with clear type includes several paintings of the period by a modern artist as well as maps and photos of excavation sites." Booklist

Includes glossary and bibliographical references

Kalman, Maira

Fireboat; the heroic adventures of the John J. Harvey. Putnam 2002 un il $16.99

Grades: K 1 2 3 **974.7**

1. September 11 terrorist attacks, 2001 2. John J. Harvey (Fireboat)

ISBN 0-399-23953-7

LC 2002-2423

Boston Globe-Horn Book Award: Nonfiction (2003)

A fireboat, launched in 1931, is retired after many years of fighting fires along the Hudson River, but is saved from being scrapped and then called into service again on September 11, 2001. "Primary." (Horn Book)

"Among the many literary tributes to 9-11 heroism, Kalman's is particularly exciting, uplifting, and child-sensitive." Bull Cent Child Books

Maestro, Betsy

The **story** of the Statue of Liberty; [by] Betsy & Giulio Maestro. Lothrop, Lee & Shepard Bks. 1986 39p il hardcover o.p. pa $5.95

Grades: K 1 2 3 **974.7**

1. Artists 2. Sculptors 3. Statue of Liberty (New York, N.Y.)

ISBN 0-688-08746-9 pa

LC 85-11324

"Although Maestro simplifies the story—including only the most important people's names, for example—she still presents an accurate account of what happened. The exceptional drawings are visually delightful—primarily in the blue-green range, although they are in full color—and cover most of every page. Human figures—workers, tourists—are included in many drawings, indicating the statue's tremendous scale. Further, the drawings involve viewers through the use of unusual perspectives and angles and by placing the statue in scenes of city life." SLJ

Includes bibliographical references

Mann, Elizabeth

Statue of Liberty; a tale of two countries. with illustrations by Alan Witschonke. Mikaya Press 2011 47p il map (Wonders of the world) $22.95

Grades: 4 5 6 7 **974.7**

1. Artists 2. Authors 3. Lawyers 4. Sculptors 5. National monuments 6. Children's authors 7. Fairy tale writers 8. Members of Parliament 9. Statue of Liberty (New York, N.Y.) 10. Statue of

Liberty (New York, N.Y.)

ISBN 978-1-931414-43-2; 1-931414-43-2

"The story of how Lady Liberty was conceived, constructed and bestowed makes a compelling tale. Pointing to the disparate long-term outcomes of the American and French revolutions to explain why the U.S. system of government became so admired in France, Mann takes the statue from Edouard Laboulaye's pie-in-the-sky proposal at a dinner party in 1865 to the massive opening ceremonies in 1886. . . . Witschonke supplements an array of period photos and prints with full-page or larger painted reconstructions of Bartholdi's studio and workshop, of the statue's piecemeal creation and finally of the Lady herself, properly copper colored as she initially was, presiding of New York's crowded harbor. As she still does." Kirkus

Includes bibliographical references

Marrin, Albert, 1936-

★ **Flesh** & blood so cheap; the Triangle fire and its legacy. Alfred A. Knopf 2011 182p il map $19.99; lib bdg $22.99

Grades: 5 6 7 8 **974.7**

1. Fires 2. Italian Americans 3. Jews -- United States 4. Labor -- United States 5. New York (N.Y.) -- History 6. Triangle Shirtwaist Company, Inc. 7. Industrial safety 8. United States -- Immigration and emigration

ISBN 978-0-375-86889-4; 0-375-86889-5; 978-0-375-96889-1 lib bdg; 0-375-96889-X lib bdg

LC 2010-21533

National Book Award Finalist: Young People's Literature (2011)

"Published to coincide with the centennial anniversary of the 1911 fire that erupted in the Triangle Shirtwaist Factory, this powerful chronicle examines the circumstances surrounding the disaster, which resulted in the deaths of 146 workers, mostly young Italian and Jewish women. . . . B&W photographs and illustrations reveal immigrant families' impoverished living environments, while testimonials describe the 'humiliating' work rules and unsafe conditions of factories like Triangle. . . . A concluding description of a Bangladeshi garment factory fire in 2010 offers contemporary parallels. Marrin's message that protecting human dignity is our shared responsibility is vitally resonant." Publ Wkly

Includes bibliographical references

McKendry, Joe

One Times Square; a century of change at the crossroads of the world. written & illustrated by Joe McKendry. David R. Godine 2011 64 p. ill. (chiefly col.), col. maps (hardcover : alk. paper) $19.95

Grades: 4 5 6 **974.7**

1. Times Square (New York, N.Y.) -- History 2. New York (N.Y.) -- History

ISBN 156792364X; 9781567923643

LC 2011027379

This children's book by Joe McKendry "takes readers on a journey through 100 years of shifts and changes to . . . Times Square. . . . Beginning in 1904 when the 'New York Times' headquarters was built and forever changed the name of this small plot of land, McKendry accompanies the text with a . . . painting of the Square from a specific point of view. . . . as buildings and technology sprout and change." (Kirkus)

Includes bibliographical references and index

Melmed, Laura Krauss

New York, New York; the Big Apple from A to Z. illustrated by Frané Lessac. HarperCollins Pub. 2005 un il $16.99; lib bdg $17.89; pa $6.99

Grades: K 1 2 3 **974.7**

1. Alphabet 2. New York (N.Y.)

ISBN 0-06-054674-6; 0-06-054876-2 lib bdg; 0-06-054877-0 pa

"From the American Museum of Natural History to the Bronx Zoo, each letter is accompanied by a peppy eight-line poem as well as multiple sidebars, factoids, and tidbits about the sights described. Melmed brilliantly touches on all the major sights of NYC." SLJ

Mills, J. Elizabeth

New York; past and present. Rosen Central 2010 48p il map (The United States: past and present) lib bdg $26.50; pa $11.75

Grades: 3 4 5 6   **974.7**

1. New York (State)

ISBN 978-1-4358-5285-3 lib bdg; 1-4358-5285-0 lib bdg; 978-1-4358-5568-7 pa; 1-4358-5568-X pa

LC 2008054256

Presents the history, geography, government, economy, and people of New York, as well as general facts about the state.

Includes bibliographical references

Murphy, Jim

The **giant** and how he humbugged America; by Jim Murphy. Scholastic Press 2012 112 p. (hardcover : alk. paper) $19.99

Grades: 5 6 7 8   **974.7**

1. Relics 2. Sculpture 3. Impostors and imposture 4. Cardiff giant 5. Cardiff (N.Y.) -- Antiquities 6. New York (State) -- Antiquities 7. Forgery of antiquities -- New York (State) -- Cardiff

ISBN 0439691842; 9780439691840

LC 2011036798

In this book, "[Jim] Murphy traces the checkered career of the 'Cardiff Giant,' a 10-foot-long stone figure unearthed in 1869 in an upstate New York farmyard. The giant was a national sensation until its unmasking as a hoax a few months later. Almost from the outset, both educated and popular opinion was divided over whether the figure was a fossilized human or a carving, an ancient relic or a modern 'humbug.' Murphy shows how the controversy itself fueled the giant's notoriety." (Booklist)

Includes bibliographical references and index

Platt, Richard

New York City; an illustrated history of the Big Apple. illustrated by Manuela Cappon. Kingfisher 2010 45p il map (Through time) $16.99

Grades: 4 5 6 7   **974.7**

1. New York (N.Y.) -- History

ISBN 978-0-7534-6416-8; 0-7534-6416-0

This is a history of New York City from its Native American origins to the present.

"In this magnificently illustrated work, historical happenings and intriguing offshoots are showcased like stars on Broadway. . . . A wealth of information in an engaging format." Booklist

Rappaport, Doreen

★ **Lady** Liberty; a biography. illustrated by Matt Tavares. Candlewick Press 2008 un il $17.99

Grades: 2 3 4 5   **974.7**

1. Statue of Liberty (New York, N.Y.)

ISBN 978-0-7636-2530-6; 0-7636-2530-2

LC 2007-40723

This presents the story of the Statue of Liberty including "its conception and construction in France, the efforts to raise funds on both sides of the Atlantic, preparations for her arrival in New York, and the celebration culminating in her unveiling in 1886. Rappaport tells the story in a series of free-verse poems representing the reflections of individuals. . . . The first-person narratives effectively convey the personal significance the statue has had for many people. Large in scale and monumental in

effect, the watercolor, ink, and pencil illustrations . . . offer often beautiful views of her many-faceted story." Booklist

Includes bibliographical references

Schomp, Virginia

New York; [by] Virginia Schomp. 2nd ed.; Benchmark Books 2006 144p il map (Celebrate the states) lib bdg $39.93

Grades: 4 5 6 7   **974.7**

1. New York (State)

ISBN 978-0-7614-1738-5; 0-7614-1738-9

LC 2004-853

First published 1997

This book about New York covers "standard facts: geography, history, government, economy, landmarks, and regions. . . . [It is] attractively illustrated with clear maps, charts, and pie graphs. Photos and reproductions of original documents add to overall effectiveness. . . . . Excellent additions for reports or general interest." SLJ

Includes bibliographical references

Shea, Pegi Deitz

★ **Liberty** rising; the story of the Statue of Liberty. illustrated by Wade Zahares. Henry Holt 2005 un il $17.95

Grades: 2 3 4   **974.7**

1. Artists 2. Sculptors 3. Statue of Liberty (New York, N.Y.)

ISBN 0-8050-7220-9

LC 2004-24279

In this account of the building of the Statue of Liberty "Shea introduces the size and scale of creating such a large object. . . . Each step in the process . . . is told in simple text. . . . The book is easy to read, with three-quarter spreads of illustration and single columns of text. The stylized graphic art is fairly realistic with bold colors and unusual angles to create a sense of excitement." SLJ

Includes bibliographical references

Somervill, Barbara A.

New York; by Barbara A. Somervill. Revised edition Children's Press 2014 144 p. illustrations, maps (library binding) $40

Grades: 4 5 6 7   **974.7**

1. New York (State) 2. United States -- History

ISBN 053124895X; 9780531248959

LC 2013032830

"Located in the northeastern United States, along the border with Canada, New York is home to the country's largest city. Readers will trace the history of this remarkable state from its earliest settlement to its latest developments. They will also dive into the local culture, see the state's many fascinating sights, and learn about its economy." (Publisher's note)

Includes bibliographical references and index

Talbott, Hudson

★ **River** of dreams; the story of the Hudson River. G. P. Putnam's Sons 2009 un il map $17.99

Grades: 4 5 6 7   **974.7**

1. Hudson River (N.Y. and N.J.)

ISBN 978-0-399-24521-3; 0-399-24521-9

Talbott offers a "compelling blend of political and natural history in this beautifully illustrated celebration of the Hudson River. Combining delicate watercolor-and-pencil illustrations with accessible text, the spreads move briskly through the Hudson's River's history." Booklist

Vila, Laura

★ **Building** Manhattan. Viking 2008 un il $16.99

Grades: K 1 2 3 **974.7**

   1. Manhattan (New York, N.Y.) 2. New York (N.Y.) -- History

ISBN 978-0-670-06284-3; 0-670-06284-7

                    LC 2007-38119

"Tracing the growth of Manhattan from a time 'before maps or words were used' to the present day, . . . author/artist Vila employs many lenses—geography, sociology, politics, ethnography. Likewise, her radiantly dramatic mural-like paintings present a wide range of visual styles and approaches. . . . While her paintings are lavish, it takes her only one pithy sentence on each spread to convey both a specific moment and a sense of history and human ambitions." Publ Wkly

974.8   Pennsylvania

Hasan, Heather

   Pennsylvania; past and present. Rosen Central 2010 48p il map (The United States: past and present) lib bdg $26.50; pa $11.50

Grades: 3 4 5 6 **974.8**

   1. Pennsylvania

ISBN 978-1-4358-5291-4 lib bdg; 1-4358-5291-5 lib bdg; 978-1-4358-5580-9 pa; 1-4358-5580-9 pa

                    LC 2008-54214

Presents the history, geography, government, economy, and people of Pennsylvania, as well as general facts about the state.

Includes glossary and bibliographical references

Magaziner, Henry J.

   ★ **Our** Liberty Bell; by Henry Jonas Magaziner; illustrated by John O'Brien. Holiday House 2007 32p il $15.95; pa $5.95

Grades: 2 3 4 **974.8**

   1. Liberty Bell

ISBN 978-0-8234-1892-3; 0-8234-1892-8; 978-0-8234-2081-0 pa; 0-8234-2081-7 pa

                    LC 2004054196

"Written with clarity and verve. . . . O'Brien's imaginative and sometimes witty ink drawings illustrate with finesse." Booklist

Includes glossary and bibliographical references

Somervill, Barbara A.

   Pennsylvania; by Barbara A. Somervill. Revised edition Children's Press, A Division of Scholastic Inc. 2015 144 p. illustrations, maps (library binding : alk. paper) $40

Grades: 4 5 6 7 **974.8**

   1. Pennsylvania 2. United States -- History

ISBN 0531282899; 9780531282892

                    LC 2013044801

"On July 4, 1776, members of the Continental Congress signed the Declaration of Independence in Philadelphia, making Pennsylvania the birthplace of the United States. Since then, Pennsylvania has continued to play an integral role in the nation's history. Readers will learn how the state has changed over time, how it is governed, and what it is like to live there today. They will also explore its breathtaking outdoor areas and vibrant cities." (Publisher's note)

Includes bibliographical references (page 138) and index

Staton, Hilarie

   Independence Hall. Chelsea Clubhouse 2010 48p il (Symbols of American freedom) $30

Grades: 3 4 5 **974.8**

   1. Philadelphia (Pa.) 2. Independence Hall (Philadelphia, Pa.) 3. United States -- Politics and government -- 1783-1809 4. United

States -- Politics and government -- 1775-1783, Revolution

ISBN 978-1-60413-521-3; 1-60413-521-2

                    LC 2009-12824

This book about Independence Hall in Philadelphia "provides nearly as much information as a guided tour by a park ranger. [It begins] with the story of how the place came to be, and where it fits into U.S. history. Information boxes offer additional background and some surprising facts. . . . The final chapter shows the landmark today and includes maps and photographs of the visitors' center and some of the things individuals might see or do while visiting the site. Much information is packed into [this] slim [book]. Excellent . . . for state reports or to complement U.S. history units." SLJ

Includes glossary

974.9   New Jersey

Doak, Robin S.

   New Jersey 1609-1776; y. [by] Robin Doak with Brendan McConville. National Geographic 2005 109p il map (Voices from colonial America) $21.95; lib bdg $32.90

Grades: 5 6 7 8 **974.9**

   1. New Jersey -- History

ISBN 978-0-7922-6385-2; 0-7922-6385-5; 978-0-7922-6680-8 lib bdg; 0-7922-6680-3 lib bdg

                    LC 2004-26242

"This book gives detailed descriptions of family life and working in a Colonial village and the fight for independence. It also includes information about the Native people, early settlers, and first developments. . . . Paintings, maps, woodcuts, portraits, and reproductions accompany the well-written text. . . . An excellent resource." SLJ

Includes bibliographical references

Kent, Deborah, 1948-

   New Jersey; by Deborah Kent. Revised edition Children's Press 2014 144 p. illustrations, maps (library binding) $40

Grades: 4 5 6 7 **974.9**

   1. New Jersey 2. United States -- History

ISBN 0531248941; 9780531248942

                    LC 2013032829

"Though New Jersey is nicknamed the Garden State, it is actually one of the most urban and densely populated states in the country. Readers will trace the history of this remarkable state from its earliest settlement to its latest developments. They will also dive into the local culture, see the state's many fascinating sights, and learn about its economy." (Publisher's note)

Includes bibliographical references and index

Mattern, Joanne

   New Jersey; past and present. Rosen Central 2010 48p il map (The United States: past and present) lib bdg $26.50; pa $11.75

Grades: 3 4 5 6 **974.9**

   1. New Jersey

ISBN 978-1-4358-3525-2 lib bdg; 1-4358-3525-5 lib bdg; 978-1-4358-8500-4 pa; 1-4358-8500-7 pa

                    LC 2009026985

Presents the history, geography, government, economy, and people of New Jersey, as well as general facts about the state.

Includes bibliographical references

Moragne, Wendy

   New Jersey; by Wendy Moragne and Tamra B. Orr. 2nd ed.; Marshall Cavendish Benchmark 2009 144p il map (Celebrate the states) lib bdg $39.93

Grades: 4 5 6 7   **974.9**
   1. New Jersey
   ISBN 978-0-7614-3006-3; 0-7614-3006-7

                     LC 2007-38642
   First published 2000
"Provides comprehensive information on the geography, history, wildlife, governmental structure, economy, cultural diversity, peoples, religion, and landmarks of New Jersey." Publisher's note
   Includes bibliographical references

975.1   Delaware

King, David C.
   Delaware; [by] David C. King, Brian Fitzgerald. 2nd ed.; Marshall Cavendish Benchmark 2010 90p il map (It's my state) lib bdg $31.36
Grades: 3 4 5   **975.1**
   1. Delaware
   ISBN 978-1-6087-0048-6; 1-6087-0048-8

                     LC 2010003920
   Surveys the history, geography, government, and economy of Delaware as well as the diverse ways of life of its people.

Price, Karen
   Delaware, 1638-1776; [by] Karen Hossell, with Karin Wulf, consultant. National Geographic Society 2006 109p il map (Voices from colonial America) $21.95; lib bdg $32.90
Grades: 5 6 7 8   **975.1**
   1. Delaware -- History
   ISBN 978-0-7922-6408-8; 0-7922-6408-8; 978-0-7922-6864-2 lib bdg; 0-7922-6864-4 lib bdg

                     LC 2006-13444
   "The text is . . . written in full paragraphs, making up chronological chapters. These are divided into topical sections, which are clearly marked by large headings. This lovely, calm layout is liberally sprinkled with primary source illustrations, including reproductions of period maps, pamphlets, paintings, and drawings. . . . An essential purchase for schools with a colonies research project . . . and for the public libraries that support their communities." Voice Youth Advocates
   Includes bibliographical references

Schuman, Michael
   Delaware; by Michael Schuman and Marlee Richards. 2nd ed.; Marshall Cavendish Benchmark 2009 144p il map (Celebrate the states) lib bdg $42.79
Grades: 4 5 6 7   **975.1**
   1. Delaware
   ISBN 978-0-7614-3399-6; 0-7614-3399-6

                     LC 2008-5369
   First published 2000
"Provides comprehensive information on the geography, history, wildlife, governmental structure, economy, cultural diversity, peoples, religion, and landmarks of Delaware." Publisher's note
   Includes bibliographical references

Wolny, Philip
   Delaware; past and present. Rosen Central 2010 48p il map (The United States: past and present) lib bdg $26.50; pa $11.75
Grades: 3 4 5 6   **975.1**
   1. Delaware
   ISBN 978-1-4358-3526-9 lib bdg; 1-4358-3526-3 lib bdg; 978-1-4358-8502-8 pa; 1-4358-8502-3 pa

                     LC 2009024554

Presents the history, geography, government, economy, and people of Delaware, as well as general facts about the state.
   Includes glossary and bibliographical references

975.2   Maryland

Blashfield, Jean F.
   Maryland; By Jean F. Blashfield. Revised edition Children's Press, A Division of Scholastic Inc. 2014 144 p. color illustrations (library binding) $40
Grades: 4 5 6 7   **975.2**
   1. Maryland 2. Geography
   ISBN 0531248887; 9780531248881

                     LC 2013032188
   "From the dense population of Baltimore to the untouched forests of the Appalachian region, Maryland is a land of incredible diversity. Readers will trace the history of this remarkable state from its earliest settlement to its latest developments. They will also dive into the local culture, see the state's many fascinating sights, and learn about its economy." (Publisher's note)
   Includes bibliographical references and index

Doak, Robin S.
   Maryland, 1634-1776. National Geographic 2007 105p il map (Voices from colonial America) $21.95; lib bdg $32.90
Grades: 5 6 7 8   **975.2**
   1. Maryland -- History
   ISBN 978-1-4263-0143-8; 1-4263-0143-x; 978-1-4263-0144-5 lib bdg; 1-4263-0144-8 lib bdg

                     LC 2007-27886
   Offers "thorough, well-documented information about the struggles and successes of early colonial settlers and settlements. . . . Many reproductions of period illustrations and some photographs of period documents and maps with relevant captions are included." Horn Book Guide
   Includes bibliographical references

Friddell, Claudia
   ★ Goliath; hero of the great Baltimore fire. illustrated by Troy Howell. Sleeping Bear Press 2010 un il (True stories) $17.95
Grades: K 1 2 3 4 5   **975.2**
   1. Fire 2. Horses 3. Fire fighting 4. Working animals 5. Baltimore (Md.) -- History
   ISBN 978-1-58536-455-8; 1-58536-455-X

                     LC 2009036941
   "The Great Baltimore Fire of 1904 was one of the most destructive in U.S. history. Friddell brings the event to life through the true story of a huge horse from Engine Company 15. Goliath bore the full brunt of an explosion and then heroically pulled an entire fire rig to safety by himself. The text builds suspense. . . . Howell's expressive, sepia-toned illustrations interplay with the text to keep readers in the moment. Exciting, historically accurate, and visually appealing." SLJ
   Includes glossary and bibliographical references

Mattern, Joanne
   Maryland; past and present. Rosen Central 2010 48p il map (The United States: past and present) lib bdg $26.50; pa $11.75
Grades: 3 4 5 6   **975.2**
   1. Maryland
   ISBN 978-1-4358-3519-1 lib bdg; 1-4358-3519-0 lib bdg; 978-1-4358-8488-5 pa; 1-4358-8488-4 pa

                     LC 2009025517

Presents the history, geography, government, economy, and people of Maryland, as well as general facts about the state.

Includes glossary and bibliographical references

975.3 District of Columbia (Washington)

Aretha, David

The **story** of the civil rights march on Washington for jobs and freedom in photographs; David Aretha. Enslow Publishers, Inc. 2014 48 p. illustrations (some color) (The story of the civil rights movement in photographs) library $25.27

Grades: 5 6 7 8 **975.3**
1. March on Washington for Jobs and Freedom (1963 : Washington, D.C.) 2. African Americans -- Civil rights 3. Civil rights demonstrations -- Washington (D.C.) 4. March on Washington for Jobs and Freedom (1963 : Washington, D.C.) -- Pictorial works
ISBN 0766042383; 9780766042384

LC 2013004860

Author "David Aretha explores the 'greatest demonstration for freedom' in American history. On August 28, 1963, more than 250,000 people descended on Washington, D.C. They came by bus, car, and bicycle. Some even walked hundreds of miles to be there. On that day, the massive crowd gathered to march, protest, sing, and support the Civil Rights Movement and to demonstrate that the time had come to end segregation in the South." (Publisher's note)

"This series explores key events of the Civil Rights Movement through historical primary source pictures and documents. The books dramatically carry the reader from early 1963 Birmingham to sit-ins, marches, and protests. Through dramatic photographs along with descriptive captions, the reader feels the raw emotions of the times." Lib Med Con

Elish, Dan

Washington, D.C. by Dan Elish. 2nd ed.; Marshall Cavendish Benchmark 2007 144p il map (Celebrate the states) lib bdg $39.93

Grades: 4 5 6 7 **975.3**
1. Washington (D.C.)
ISBN 978-0-7614-2352-2; 0-7614-2352-4

LC 2006-13838

First published 1998

"Provides comprehensive information on the geography, history, wildlife, governmental structure, economy, cultural diversity, peoples, religion, and landmarks of Washington, D.C." Publisher's note

Includes bibliographical references

House, Katherine L.

The **White** House for kids; a history of a home, office, and national symbol : with 21 activities. Katherine L. House. Chicago Review Press 2014 144 p. illustrations, plans (For kids series) (pbk.) $16.95

Grades: 4 5 6 7 **975.3**
1. Presidents -- United States 2. White House (Washington, D.C.) 3. Washington (D.C.) -- Buildings, structures, etc.
ISBN 1613744617; 9781613744611

LC 2013038108

This children's book, by Katherine L. House, offers an "educates young readers on the White House. Blending facts from numerous primary sources with engaging anecdotes . . . , this book provides the complete story of the presidents' home. Details on the many changes, updates, renovations, and redecorations that have occurred over the years are featured as well as a look at the daily lives of the White House's inhabitants." (Publisher's note)

"Chapter organization enhances interest by covering seven subjects and including examples from multiple historical periods. From the pur-

poses and architecture of the building to the nature of multiple jobs performed, this book shows the varied functions of the White House." VOYA

Includes bibliographical references and index

Kenney, Karen Latchana

The **White** House; illustrated by Judith A. Hunt. Magic Wagon 2011 32p il (Our nation's pride) lib bdg $28.50

Grades: 2 3 4 **975.3**
1. White House (Washington, D.C.)
ISBN 978-1-61641-154-1; 1-61641-154-6

LC 2010014010

In this title about the White House "the author describes how the land was chosen, how the White House was built, the fact in burned down in 1814 and was rebuilt in 1817, and that it takes 570 buckets of white paint to cover the outside. . . . The full-color artwork not only explains the text but also gives the most photographic renderings of the [topic]." SLJ

Kent, Deborah, 1948-

Washington, D.C. by Deborah Kent. Revised edition Children's Press 2015 144 p. illustrations, maps (library binding) $40

Grades: 4 5 6 7 **975.3**
1. Washington (D.C.) 2. Geography
ISBN 9780531282984; 0531282988

LC 2013044317

"The nation's capital city is located in a small space between Virginia and Maryland, but it is not a part of either state. Readers will discover why the District of Columbia was chosen to be the center of the U.S. government and how the city was planned and constructed. They will also learn about the vibrant local culture and traditions as they find out what it is like to live in D.C. today." (Publisher's note)

Includes bibliographical references and index

★ **Our** White House; looking in, looking out. created by The National Children's Book and Literacy Alliance; introduction by David McCullough. Candlewick Press 2008 241p il $29.99

Grades: 5 6 7 8 **975.3**
1. White House (Washington, D.C.) 2. Short stories -- Collections 3. Presidents -- United States -- Family 4. United States -- Politics and government
ISBN 0-7636-2067-X; 978-0-7636-2067-7

This is a collection of essays, personal accounts, historical fiction, and poetry devoted to the history of the White House. Index. "Age ten and up." (N Y Times Book Rev)

"The White House is the focus of this handsome, large-format compendium of writings, both factual and fictional, and illustrations. . . . Poems and essays, stories and memoirs—all combine to create a mosaic of impressions of the house's residents and visitors and of the important events that occurred there. . . . The often-spectacular, beautifully reproduced on glossy paper, is particularly striking." Booklist

Rinaldo, Denise

White House Q & A. Smithsonian/Collins 2008 47p il (Smithsonian Q & A) lib bdg $16.99; pa $7.99

Grades: 3 4 5 **975.3**
1. Washington (D.C.) 2. Presidents -- United States 3. White House (Washington, D.C.)
ISBN 978-0-06-089966-0 lib bdg; 0-06-089966-2 lib bdg; 978-0-06-089965-3 pa; 0-06-089965-4 pa

LC 2006102994

"The history and functions of the presidential residence are unveiled in the typical series format. The questions are organized so that the story of the White House unfolds logically—first with a definition of what it is, how it came to be, some of its history, how to visit, special rooms, and, of course, a look at how the first families live. Anecdotes are plentiful and child-centered. . . . The elegant page layout includes full-color, full-bleed illustrations from Smithsonian archives and some presidential libraries." SLJ

Includes glossary and bibliographical references

Slade, Suzanne

The **house** that George built; Suzanne Slade; illustrated by Rebecca Bond. Charlesbridge 2012 48 p. col. ill. (reinforced for library use) $16.95

Grades: 1 2 3   **975.3**

1. Presidents -- United States -- Homes 2. Presidents -- United States -- History 3. White House (Washington, D.C.) -- History 4. Washington (D.C.) -- Buildings, structures, etc.

ISBN 1580892620; 9781580892629

LC 2011025781

This book by Suzanne Slade "describes how George Washington chose the design for what would become the White House and supervised its construction. Rhyming verses, interspersed with background paragraphs to fill out the narrative, describe how Washington found the site and held a contest to get design submissions. African American and white surveyors and laborers are included in the pictures." (School Library Journal)

Sonneborn, Liz

District of Columbia; past and present. Rosen Central 2011 48p il map (The United States: past and present) lib bdg $26.50; pa $11.75

Grades: 3 4 5 6   **975.3**

1. Washington (D.C.)

ISBN 978-1-4358-9501-0 lib bdg; 1-4358-9501-0 lib bdg; 978-1-4358-9528-7 pa; 1-4358-9528-2 pa

LC 2009053986

This describes life in the U.S. capitol city, Washington D.C.

Includes glossary and bibliographical references

975.4   West Virginia

Byers, Ann

West Virginia; past and present. Rosen Central 2011 48p il map (The United States: past and present) lib bdg $26.50; pa $11.75

Grades: 3 4 5 6   **975.4**

1. West Virginia

ISBN 978-1-4358-9499-0 lib bdg; 1-4358-9499-5 lib bdg; 978-1-4358-9526-3 pa; 1-4358-9526-6 pa

LC 2010002514

Presents the history, geography, government, economy, and people of West Virginia, as well as general facts about the state.

Includes bibliographical references

Hoffman, Nancy

West Virginia; [by] Nancy Hoffman and Joyce Hart. 2nd ed.; Marshall Cavendish Benchmark 2007 144p il map (Celebrate the states) lib bdg $39.93

Grades: 4 5 6 7   **975.4**

1. West Virginia

ISBN 978-0-7614-2562-5; 0-7614-2562-4

LC 2006-29393

First published 1999

Relates the history and describes the geographic features, places of interest, government, industry, environmental concerns, and life of the people of West Virginia.

Includes bibliographical references

975.5   Virginia

Chorao, Kay

D is for drums; a Colonial Williamsburg ABC. [by] Kay Chorao. Harry N. Abrams 2004 un il $16.95

Grades: K 1 2 3   **975.5**

1. Alphabet 2. Colonial Williamsburg (Williamsburg, Va.)

ISBN 0-8109-4927-X

LC 2003-25793

"Chorao has created a large, visually charming, and fact-rich look at Colonial Williamsburg. Endpaper maps of the city's streets show everything from a shoemaker's shop to the Governor's Palace. Each page in between displays a huge capital letter decorated with drawings that showcase an alliterative list of words. . . . Chorao selected items to foster chuckles and amazement. Her pen-and-ink and watercolor drawings of children and animals add energy to the stunning layouts." SLJ

Demarest, Chris L.

Arlington; the story of our nation's cemetery. written and illustrated by Chris Demarest. Roaring Brook Press/Flash Point 2010 un il $17.99

Grades: 3 4 5 6   **975.5**

1. Arlington National Cemetery (Va.)

ISBN 978-1-59643-517-9; 1-59643-517-8

"This handsome volume presents the history of Arlington National Cemetery. [It tells and illustrates] the story with quiet dignity. . . . Demarest writes clearly, organizes the information well, and illustrates the story in nicely composed, sometimes luminous paintings." Booklist

Kent, Deborah, 1948-

Virginia; by Deborah Kent. Revised edition Children's Press 2014 144 p. illustrations, maps (library binding) $40

Grades: 4 5 6 7   **975.5**

1. Virginia 2. Geography

ISBN 9780531248997; 0531248992

LC 2013033044

"First colonized by Europeans with the founding of Jamestown in 1607, Virginia is home to some of the oldest continuous settlements in the country. Readers will trace the history of this remarkable state from its earliest settlement to its latest developments. They will also dive into the local culture, see the state's many fascinating sights, and learn about its economy." (Publisher's note)

Includes bibliographical references and index

Lange, Karen E.

★ **1607**; a new look at Jamestown. photography by Ira Block. National Geographic 2007 48p il $17.95; lib bdg $27.90

Grades: 3 4 5 6   **975.5**

1. Virginia -- History 2. Jamestown (Va.) -- History 3. United States -- History -- 1600-1775, Colonial period

ISBN 1-4263-0012-3; 1-4263-0013-1 lib bdg

LC 2006-05824

"In 1994, scientists unearthed important new evidence about the original Jamestown fort. The work . . . has changed many established ideas about the early settlers. 1607 incorporates these findings and offers a fascinating look at archaeology in action. Color photographs of costumed interpreters and recreated buildings from the Jamestown Settlement living-history museum depict both English and Native American ways of life." SLJ

Pobst, Sandy

Virginia, 1607-1776; [by] Sandy Pobst with Kevin D. Roberts, consultant. National Geographic Society 2005 109p il map (Voices from colonial America) $21.95; lib bdg $32.90

Grades: 5 6 7 8   **975.5**
1. Virginia -- History
ISBN 978-0-7922-6388-3; 0-7922-6388-X; 978-0-7922-6771-3 lib bdg; 0-7922-6771-0 lib bdg

LC 2005-8885

"This title discusses the colony's founding, life on the Tidewater plantations, the struggles to survive, and the desire for independence. Full of period maps; portraits; photographs; and first-person accounts from masters and slaves, explorers, Native Americans, servants, and other residents, this is narrative nonfiction at its best. . . . An excellent resource." SLJ

Includes bibliographical references

Porterfield, Jason
   Virginia; past and present. Rosen Central 2009 48p il map (The United States: past and present) lib bdg $26.50; pa $11.50
Grades: 3 4 5 6   **975.5**
1. Virginia
ISBN 978-1-4358-5289-1 lib bdg; 1-4358-5289-3 lib bdg; 978-1-4358-5576-2 pa; 1-4358-5576-0 pa

LC 2008-54403

Presents the history, geography, government, economy, and people of Virginia, as well as general facts about the state.

Includes glossary and bibliographical references

975.6   North Carolina

Cannavale, Matthew C.
   North Carolina, 1524-1776; by Matthew C. Cannavale; with Patrick Griffith, consultant. National Geographic Society 2007 109p il map (Voices from colonial America) $21.95; lib bdg $32.90
Grades: 5 6 7 8   **975.6**
1. North Carolina -- History
ISBN 978-1-4263-0032-5; 1-4263-0032-8; 978-1-4263-0033-2 lib bdg; 1-4263-0033-6 lib bdg

LC 2006-36004

A history of colonial North Carolina.
Includes bibliographical references

Fritz, Jean
   ★ The Lost Colony of Roanoke; illustrated by Hudson Talbott. G.P. Putnam's Sons 2004 58p il map $16.99
Grades: 3 4 5 6   **975.6**
1. Roanoke Island (N.C.) -- History
ISBN 0-399-24027-6

LC 2002-152000

Describes the English colony of Roanoke, which was founded in 1585, and discusses the mystery of its disappearance.
"Talbott's softly colored watercolor illustrations . . . are at once detailed and impressionistic. Clever touches of humor abound. . . . Fritz has scored again, making history breathe while showing both historians and archaeologists at their reconstructive best." SLJ

Heinrichs, Ann
   North Carolina; by Ann Heinrichs. Revised edition Children's Press 2014 144 p. illustrations, maps (library binding) $40
Grades: 4 5 6 7   **975.6**
1. North Carolina 2. United States -- History
ISBN 0531248968; 9780531248966

LC 2013032831

"From its wet marshlands and the towering Appalachian Mountains to cities such as Raleigh and Charlotte, North Carolina is home to a diverse range of environments. Readers will trace the history of this remarkable state from its earliest settlement to its latest developments. They will also dive into the local culture, see the state's many fascinating sights, and learn about its economy." (Publisher's note)

Includes bibliographical references (p. 138) and index

Lew, Kristi
   North Carolina; past and present. Rosen Central 2011 48p il map (The United States: past and present) lib bdg $26.50; pa $11.75
Grades: 3 4 5 6   **975.6**
1. North Carolina
ISBN 978-1-4358-9491-4 lib bdg; 1-4358-9491-X lib bdg; 978-1-4358-9518-8 pa; 1-4358-9518-5 pa

LC 2009054264

Presents the history, geography, government, economy, and people of North Carolina, as well as general facts about the state.

Includes glossary and bibliographical references

Miller, Lee
   Roanoke; the mystery of the Lost Colony. Scholastic Nonfiction 2007 112p il map $18.99
Grades: 4 5 6 7   **975.6**
1. Roanoke Island (N.C.) -- History 2. United States -- History -- 1600-1775, Colonial period
ISBN 0-439-71266-1; 978-0-439-71266-8

LC 2005-51820

"Miller, author of Roanoke: solving the mystery of the Lost Colony (2001), here reprises for a young audience her historical theory that a certain man sabotaged the expedition eventually known as the Lost Colony. . . . Miller does an exceptional job of preseneting the Native American culture and viewpoint. . . . This handsomely designed book features one or two illustrations on each spread, many in color, including reproductions or period drawings, paintings, and maps, as well as modern photos of sites and wildlife." Booklist

Includes bibliographical references

Reed, Jennifer
   Cape Hatteras National Seashore; adventure, explore, discover. [by] Jennifer Reed. MyReportLinks.com Books 2008 128p il map (America's national parks) lib bdg $33.27
Grades: 5 6 7 8   **975.6**
1. Cape Hatteras National Seashore (N.C.) 2. National parks and reserves -- United States
ISBN 978-1-59845-086-6 lib bdg; 1-59845-086-7 lib bdg

LC 2006102321

This "informative, well-written book contains a physical description of the park; a summary of its history including the Native peoples of the area; activities such as hiking trails, campsites, and visitor centers; information about the park's plants, animals, and weather; full-color photographs; and numerous approved links available through the publisher's Web page. . . . Thorough, useful, and appealing, this . . . is a great update for collections." SLJ

Includes glossary and bibliographical references

975.7   South Carolina

Doak, Robin S.
   South Carolina, 1540-1776; by Robin Doak with Robert Olwell. National Geographic Society 2007 109p il map (Voices from colonial America) $21.95; lib bdg $32.90

Grades: 5 6 7 8   **975.7**
1. South Carolina -- History
ISBN 978-1-4263-0066-0; 1-4263-0066-2; 978-1-4263-0067-7
lib bdg; 1-4263-0067-0 lib bdg

LC 2007-3120

A history of South Carolina from its beginning as an English colony
to 1788 when it became the eighth state.

Offers "thorough, well-documented information about the struggles
and successes of early colonial settlers and settlements. . . . Many reproductions of period illustrations and some photographs of period documents and maps with relevant captions are included" Horn Book Guide

Includes bibliographical references

Harmon, Dan

South Carolina; past and present. [by] Daniel E. Harmon. Rosen
Central 2011 48p il (The United States: past and present) lib bdg
$26.50; pa $11.75
Grades: 3 4 5 6   **975.7**
1. South Carolina
ISBN 978-1-4358-9495-2 lib bdg; 1-4358-9495-2 lib bdg; 978-1-
4358-9522-5 pa; 1-4358-9522-3 pa

LC 2010002586

Presents the history, geography, government, economy, and people
of South Carolina, as well as general facts about the state.

Includes bibliographical references

Somervill, Barbara A.

South Carolina; by Barbara A. Somervill. Revised edition Children's Press, an Imprint of Scholastic Inc. 2015 144 p. illustrations,
maps (library binding : alk. paper) $40
Grades: 4 5 6 7   **975.7**
1. South Carolina 2. United States -- History
ISBN 0531282929; 9780531282922

LC 2013044804

"With its low-lying swamps, forested foothills, and ocean beaches,
South Carolina is home to a variety of landscapes. Readers will explore
the state's rich history and learn how it has grown to be the place it is today. They will also learn about South Carolina's Southern culture, from
delicious local dishes to traditional celebrations." (Publisher's note)

Includes bibliographical references (page 138) and index

975.8   Georgia

Doak, Robin S.

Georgia, 1521-1776. National Geographic Society 2006 109p il
map (Voices from colonial America) $21.95; lib bdg $32.90
Grades: 5 6 7 8   **975.8**
1. Georgia -- History
ISBN 978-0-7922-6389-0; 0-7922-6389-8; 978-0-7922-6858-1
lib bdg; 0-7922-6858-X lib bdg

LC 2005-22141

Provides a history of Georgia from the arrival of European explorers
in the sixteenth century to its becoming a state in 1788.

Includes bibliographical references

Prentzas, G. S.

Georgia; by G.S. Prentzas. Revised ed. Children's Press 2014 144
p. ill. (chiefly col.), col. maps $40
Grades: 4 5 6 7   **975.8**
1. Georgia 2. United States -- History
ISBN 053124881X; 9780531248812

"The last of the 13 original colonies to be established, Georgia is the
largest state east of the Mississippi River. Readers will trace the history

of this remarkable state from its earliest settlement to its latest developments. They will also dive into the local culture, see the state's many
fascinating sights, and learn about its economy." (Publisher's note)

Includes bibliographical references and index

Watson, Stephanie

Georgia; past and present. Rosen Central 2010 48p il map (The
United States: past and present) lib bdg $26.50; pa $11.50
Grades: 3 4 5 6   **975.8**
1. Georgia
ISBN 978-1-4358-5292-1 lib bdg; 1-4358-5292-3 lib bdg; 978-1-
4358-5582-3 pa; 1-4358-5582-5 pa

LC 2008-54225

Presents the history, geography, government, economy, and people
of Georgia, as well as general facts about the state.

Includes glossary and bibliographical references

975.9   Florida

Cannavale, Matthew C.

Florida, 1513-1821; [by] Matthew C. Cannavale with Robert Olwell, consultant. National Geographic 2006 109p il map (Voices from
colonial America) $21.95; lib bdg $32.90
Grades: 5 6 7 8   **975.9**
1. Florida -- History
ISBN 978-0-7922-6409-5; 0-7922-6409-6; 978-0-7922-6866-6
lib bdg; 0-7922-6866-0 lib bdg

LC 2006-20505

Offers "thorough, well-documented information about the struggles
and successes of early nonnative settlers [in Florida]. . . . Many reproductions of period illustrations (both color and sepia) and some photos
of archival documents and maps enhance the text." Horn Book Guide

Includes bibliographical references

George, Jean Craighead

★ Everglades; paintings by Wendell Minor. HarperCollins Pubs.
1995 un il hardcover o.p. pa $6.95
Grades: 2 3 4   **975.9**
1. Everglades (Fla.)
ISBN 0-06-021228-4; 0-06-446194-7 pa

LC 92-9517

"The story and the art create a mystical tale that flows from a serene
start to a powerful conclusion." SLJ

Jankowski, Susan

Everglades National Park; adventure, explore, discover. [by] Susan Jankowski. MyReportLinks.com Books 2009 128p il map (America's national parks) lib bdg $33.27
Grades: 5 6 7 8   **975.9**
1. Everglades National Park (Fla.) 2. National parks and reserves
-- United States
ISBN 978-1-59845-091-0 lib bdg; 1-59845-091-3 lib bdg

LC 2007-38262

This "informative, well-written book contains a physical description
of the park; a summary of its history including the Native peoples of the
area; activities such as hiking trails, campsites, and visitor centers; information about the park's plants, animals, and weather; full-color photographs; and numerous approved links available through the publisher's
Web page. . . . Thorough, useful, and appealing, this . . . is a great update
for collections." SLJ

Includes glossary and bibliographical references

Marsico, Katie

★ The **Everglades**; by Katie Marsico. Cherry Lake Pub. 2013 32 p. (It's cool to learn about America's waterways) (lib. bdg.) $28.50

Grades: 3 4 5 **975.9**

1. Picture books for children 2. Everglades (Fla.) 3. Everglades National Park (Fla.)

ISBN 1624310176; 9781624310171; 9781624310416; 9781624310652

LC 2012034738

This book by Katie Marsico is part of the Social Studies Explorer: It's Cool to Learn About America's Water-Ways series and looks at the Everglades. In the books, the "first chapter introduces the waterway and provides basic geographic information about the surrounding area; the second chapter discusses the wildlife; the third chapter supplies a history, including today's tourism and agriculture; and the final chapter moves on to conservation and environmental activism." (Booklist)

Includes bibliographical references and index

Orr, Tamra B.

Florida; by Tamra B. Orr. Revised edition Children's Press 2014 144 p. ill. (chiefly col.), col. maps (America the beautiful, third series) $40

Grades: 4 5 6 7 **975.9**

1. Florida

ISBN 0531248801; 9780531248805

"Thanks to its warm weather and plentiful beaches, Florida is often called the Sunshine State. Readers will trace the history of this remarkable state from its earliest settlement to its latest developments. They will also dive into the local culture, see the state's many fascinating sights, and learn about its economy." (Publisher's note)

Includes bibliographical references (p. 137-138) and index

Sawyer, Sarah

Florida; past and present. Rosen Central 2010 48p il map (The United States: past and present) lib bdg $26.50; pa $11.50

Grades: 3 4 5 6 **975.9**

1. Florida

ISBN 978-1-4358-5288-4 lib bdg; 1-4358-5288-5 lib bdg; 978-1-4358-5574-8 pa; 1-4358-5574-4 pa

LC 2008-54223

Presents the history, geography, government, economy, and people of Florida, as well as general facts about the state.

Includes glossary and bibliographical references

Turner, Glennette Tilley

★ **Fort** Mose; and the story of the man who built the first free black settlement in Colonial America. Abrams Books for Young Readers 2010 42p il map $18.95

Grades: 5 6 7 8 **975.9**

1. Army officers 2. Florida -- History 3. Fort Mose site (Fla.) 4. Slavery -- United States 5. African Americans -- History 6. United States -- History -- 1600-1775, Colonial period

ISBN 978-0-8109-4056-7; 0-8109-4056-6

LC 2009-52205

"In the 18th century, some Africans escaped slavery in England's southern colonies to find freedom in the Spanish colony of Florida. As a leader of St. Augustine's community, African-born Francisco Menendez helped establish Fort Mose, the first free black community on North American soil. Turner does an excellent job of explaining how the residents of Fort Mose probably blended African, English, and Spanish traditions to create a unique—and uniquely American—culture." SLJ

Includes glossary and bibliographical references

976.1 Alabama

Heos, Bridget

Alabama; past and present. Rosen Central 2010 48p il map (The United States: past and present) lib bdg $26.50; pa $11.75

Grades: 3 4 5 6 **976.1**

1. Alabama

ISBN 978-1-4358-3518-4 lib bdg; 1-4358-3518-2; 978-1-4358-8486-1 pa; 1-4358-8486-8 pa

LC 2009021850

Presents the history, geography, government, economy, and people of Alabama, as well as general facts about the state.

Includes bibliographical references

Shirley, David

Alabama; by David Shirley and Joyce Hart. 2nd ed.; Marshall Cavendish Benchmark 2009 144p il map (Celebrate the states) lib bdg $39.93

Grades: 4 5 6 7 **976.1**

1. Alabama

ISBN 978-0-7614-3397-2; 0-7614-3397-X

LC 2008-4601

First published 2000

"Provides comprehensive information on the geography, history, wildlife, governmental structure, economy, cultural diversity, peoples, religion, and landmarks of Alabama." Publisher's note

Includes bibliographical references

Somervill, Barbara A.

Alabama; by Barbara A. Somervill. Children's Press 2008 144p il map (America the beautiful, third series) lib bdg $38

Grades: 4 5 6 7 **976.1**

1. Alabama

ISBN 978-0-531-18556-8; 0-531-18556-7

LC 2006-37697

Describes the history, geography, ecology, people, economy, cities, and sights of the state of Alabama.

Includes glossary and bibliographical references

976.2 Mississippi

Casil, Amy Sterling

Mississippi; past and present. Rosen Central 2011 48p il map (The United States: past and present) lib bdg $26.50; pa $11.75

Grades: 3 4 5 6 **976.2**

1. Mississippi

ISBN 978-1-4358-9485-3 lib bdg; 1-4358-9485-5; 978-1-4358-9512-6 pa; 1-4358-9512-6 pa

LC 2009054262

Presents the history, geography, government, economy, and people of Mississippi, as well as general facts about the state.

Includes glossary and bibliographical references

Dell, Pamela

Mississippi; by Pamela Dell. Revised edition Children's Press, A Division of Scholastic Inc. 2014 144 p. (library binding) $40

Grades: 4 5 6 7 **976.2**

1. Mississippi 2. Geography

ISBN 0531248917; 9780531248911

LC 2013032478

"Bordered by the incredible river than shares its name, Mississippi a land of small towns and sprawling farmland. Readers will trace the history of this remarkable state from its earliest settlement to its latest developments. They will also dive into the local culture, see the state's many fascinating sights, and learn about its economy." (Publisher's note)

Includes bibliographical references and index

976.3   Louisiana

Benoit, Peter

Hurricane Katrina. Children's Press 2011 48p il (True book: disasters) lib bdg $28; pa $6.95

Grades: 3 4 5 **976.3**

1. Hurricane Katrina, 2005

ISBN 978-0-531-25421-9 lib bdg; 0-531-25421-6; 978-0-531-26626-7 pa; 0-531-26626-5 pa

LC 2011007145

This book about Hurricane Katrina in 2005 and its aftermath is "thoughtfully designed. . . . The information . . . is right on target: concise, accurate, and thorough. . . . The photographs . . . are especially effective at putting a human face on large-scale devastation." Booklist

Includes glossary and bibliographical references

Freedman, Jeri

Louisiana; past and present. Rosen Central 2011 48p il map (The United States: past and present) lib bdg $26.50; pa $11.75

Grades: 3 4 5 6 **976.3**

1. Louisiana

ISBN 978-1-4358-9483-9 lib bdg; 1-4358-9483-9 lib bdg; 978-1-4358-9510-2 pa; 1-4358-9510-X pa

LC 2010001616

Presents the history, geography, government, economy, and people of Louisiana, as well as general facts about the state.

Includes glossary and bibliographical references

Lassieur, Allison

Louisiana; by Allison Lassieur. Revised edition Children's Press, A Division of Scholastic Inc. 2014 144 p. (library binding) $40

Grades: 4 5 6 7 **976.3**

1. Louisiana 2. Geography

ISBN 0531248860; 9780531248867

LC 2013032186

"In 2005, Louisiana met with disaster when Hurricane Katrina struck the Gulf Coast. Since then, the state has been working to rebuild and recover. Readers will trace the history of this remarkable state from its earliest settlement to its latest developments. They will also dive into the local culture, see the state's many fascinating sights, and learn about its economy." (Publisher's note)

Includes bibliographical references and index

Worth, Richard

Louisiana, 1682-1803. National Geographic Society 2005 109p il map (Voices from colonial America) $21.95; lib bdg $32.90

Grades: 5 6 7 8 **976.3**

1. Louisiana -- History

ISBN 978-0-7922-6544-3; 0-7922-6544-0; 978-0-7922-6850-5 lib bdg; 0-7922-6850-4 lib bdg

LC 2005-16225

This "history of Louisiana begins in 1682 when Sieur de La Salle claimed the region for France. After that time, the region was governed under several different flags, including France, Spain, and Great Britain. . . . Thomas Jefferson purchased the land for the United States in 1803." Publisher's note

Includes bibliographical references

976.4   Texas

Chemerka, William R.

Juan Seguin; Tejano leader. William R. Chemerka; illustrations by Don Collins. Bright Sky Press 2012 64 p. ill. $16.95

Grades: 3 4 5 6 **976.4**

1. Texas -- History 2. Political activists 3. Soldiers -- Texas -- Biography 4. Politicians -- Texas -- Biography 5. Texas -- History -- Republic, 1836-1846 6. Alamo (San Antonio, Tex.) -- Siege, 1836 7. Texas -- History -- Revolution, 1835-1836 -- Biography

ISBN 1933979798; 9781933979793

LC 2011052720

This book is a biography of Texan Juan Seguin by William R. Chemerka. Despite "having been forced to flee to Mexico and die in obscurity, Tejano Juan Seguin is recognised as a Texas hero. From his family's early support of settlers such as Stephen F. Austin to his years in the Texas Senate and as mayor of Bexar, this biography celebrates the life of Juan Seguin and his . . . efforts in securing Texas' independence." (WorldCat)

Fradin, Dennis B.

The **Alamo**; [by] Dennis Brindell Fradin. Marshall Cavendish Benchmark 2007 45p il map (Turning points in U.S. history) lib bdg $29.93

Grades: 3 4 5 **976.4**

1. Texas -- History 2. Alamo (San Antonio, Tex.)

ISBN 978-0-7614-2127-6 lib bdg; 0-7614-2127-0 lib bdg

LC 2005016022

This "includes the background to the battle, as well as an account of its aftermath and some information on famous combatants. . . . The clear, concise, and dynamic style of writing simplifies the information without dumbing it down. . . . The photos, paintings, and maps . . . add a wealth of information." SLJ

Includes glossary and bibliographical references

Green, Carl R.

Davy Crockett; courageous hero of the Alamo. by William R. Sanford and Carl R. Green. Rev. ed. Enslow Publishers 2013 48 p. col. ill., map (library) $21.26; (paperback) $7.95

Grades: 5 6 7 8 **976.4**

1. Alamo (San Antonio, Tex.) -- History -- Siege, 1836 2. Alamo 3. Pioneers -- Tennessee -- Biography 4. Legislators -- United States -- Biography 5. United States. Congress. House -- Biography

ISBN 0766040054; 9780766040052; 9781464400865

LC 2011037749

This book by William Sanford is part of the Courageous Heroes of the American West series and focuses on Davy Crockett. "The courageous Texans chose to defend the fort in San Antonio against more than two thousands Mexican soldiers. . . . Although his brave deeds at the Alamo made him legendary, Crockett had already gained fame as a hunter, soldier, and U.S. Congressman." (Publisher's note)

Includes bibliographical references (p. 47) and index.

Sam Houston; courageous Texas hero. by William R. Sanford and Carl R. Green. Enslow Publishers 2013 48 p. ill., map (library) $21.26; (paperback) $7.95

Grades: 5 6 7 8 **976.4**

1. Picture books for children 2. Governors -- Texas -- Biography 3. Legislators -- United States -- Biography 4. United States. Congress. Senate -- Biography

ISBN 0766040097; 9780766040090; 9781464400926

LC 2011051265

This book, part of the Courageous Heroes of the American West series, looks at Sam Houston. "One of the founders of Texas, Sam Houston served the state as governor and senator—but he is most remembered as an American hero" for defeating the Mexican army. "Surprising the Mexican troops with their bold attack, . . . the fiery Texans rallied to an overwhelming victory, claiming their independence." (Publisher's note)

Includes bibliographical references (p. 47) and index.

Melmed, Laura Krauss

Heart of Texas; a Lone Star ABC. Illustrated by Frané Lessac. Collins 2009 un il $17.99; lib bdg $18.89

Grades: 1 2 3 4   **976.4**

1. Alphabet 2. Texas

ISBN 978-0-06-114283-3; 0-06-114283-2; 978-0-06-114285-7 lib bdg; 0-06-114285-9 lib bdg

LC 2008026948

"From Alamo to Ziller Park, Melmed and Lessac provide a tour of places to visit, people to know, and historic events to remember about Texas. Each entry begins with an eight-line poem with an impeccable rhythmic beat that slips off the tongue for reading aloud. . . . [Lessac's] detailed and colorful folk art perfectly conveys the multicultural panorama of the second-largest state." Booklist

Nagle, Jeanne

Texas; past and present. [by] Jeanne Nagle. Rosen Central 2010 48p il map (The United States: past and present) lib bdg $26.50; pa $11.50

Grades: 3 4 5 6   **976.4**

1. Texas

ISBN 978-1-4358-5287-7 lib bdg; 1-4358-5287-7 lib bdg; 978-1-4358-5572-4 pa; 1-4358-5572-8 pa

LC 2008-50962

Presents the history, geography, government, economy, and people of Texas, as well as general facts about the state.

Includes glossary and bibliographical references

Somervill, Barbara A.

Texas; by Barbara A. Somervill. Revised edition Children's Press 2014 144 p. illustrations, maps (library binding) $40

Grades: 4 5 6 7   **976.4**

1. Texas 2. United States -- History

ISBN 0531248984; 9780531248980

LC 2013033041

"Second in size only to Alaska, Texas is famed for its huge cattle ranches, oil fields, and several major cities. Readers will trace the history of this remarkable state from its earliest settlement to its latest developments. They will also dive into the local culture, see the state's many fascinating sights, and learn about its economy." (Publisher's note)

Includes bibliographical references and index

Spradlin, Michael P.

Texas Rangers; legendary lawmen. [by] Michael P. Spradlin; illustrations by Roxie Munro. Walker & Co. 2008 un il $16.95; lib bdg $17.85

Grades: 2 3 4   **976.4**

1. Frontier and pioneer life 2. Texas Rangers 3. Texas -- History 4. West (U.S.) -- History

ISBN 978-0-8027-8096-6; 0-8027-8096-2; 978-0-8027-8097-3 lib bdg; 0-8027-8097-0 lib bdg

LC 2007020139

"This picture-book account of the nearly 200-year history of the Texas Rangers begins in 1823. . . . The bulk of the book covers the 1800s, when the Rangers fought Indian tribes; participated in the war against Mexico; and defended settlers from bank robbers, cattle rustlers,

and horse thieves. . . . There is a brief section on modern Rangers. . . . Munro's colorful illustrations provide a look at the lawmen, depict the action and locales, and portray the changing times. They're sure to entice youngsters and keep them turning the pages." SLJ

Teitelbaum, Michael

Texas, 1527-1836. National Geographic Society 2005 109p il map (Voices from colonial America) $21.95; lib bdg $32.90

Grades: 5 6 7 8   **976.4**

1. Texas -- History

ISBN 978-0-7922-6387-6; 0-7922-6387-1; 978-0-7922-6682-2 lib bdg; 0-7922-6682-X lib bdg

LC 2005-11450

"Presents the history of Texas, including life in Spanish Texas, the arrival of American settlers, and The Texas Republic and statehood." Publisher's note

Includes bibliographical references

Wade, Mary Dodson

Henrietta King, la patrona; by Mary Dodson Wade; illustrated by Bill Farnsworth. Bright Sky Press 2012 23 p. $16.95

Grades: 4 5 6 7   **976.4**

1. Women ranchers -- Biography 2. Women philanthropists -- Biography 3. King Ranch (Tex.) 4. Texas -- Biography 5. Ranchers -- Texas -- Biography 6. Women ranchers -- Texas -- Biography 7. Philanthropists -- Texas -- Biography 8. Women philanthropists -- Texas -- Biography

ISBN 1933979631; 9781933979632

LC 2011052721

This book by Mary Dodson Wade "examines the . . . life of one of Texas's foremost frontier women and philanthropists, Henrietta Maria Morse Chamberlain King. . . . Henrietta accompanied her missionary father on his travels and later settled with her husband Richard King in the untamed frontiers of the south Texas gulf coast. . . . Under her stewardship, the family ranch went from . . . $500,000 in debt at her husband's death to a debt-free enterprise of more than one million acres." (Publisher's note)

Walker, Paul Robert

★ **Remember** the Alamo; Texians, Tejanos, and Mexicans tell their stories. by Paul Robert Walker. National Geographic 2007 61p il map $17.95; lib bdg $27.90

Grades: 5 6 7 8   **976.4**

1. Texas -- History 2. Alamo (San Antonio, Tex.)

ISBN 978-1-4263-0010-3; 978-1-4263-0011-0 lib bdg

LC 2006034497

"Opening with clear context about why tensions between Texas residents and the Mexican government were brought to a head, the book then chronicles events directly leading to the siege of the Alamo and its immediate aftermath, following up with an epilogue on the decisive battle of San Jacinto 10 months later. Bringing the history to life is a healthy selection of dramatic, modern paintings along with plenty of archival drawings, maps, and old photos." Booklist

Includes bibliographical references

Winter, Jonah

Born and bred in the Great Depression. Schwartz & Wade Books 2011 un il $17.99

976.4

1. Great Depression, 1929-1939 2. Texas

ISBN 978-0-375-86197-0; 0-375-86197-1

Jonah Winter offers an "account of his father's hardscrabble Depression-era childhood. He softens the rough edges and sees the beauty of the East Texas country where Grandpa Winter lives with his wife and eight children. Directly addressing his father in second-person narration, Winter pulls no punches about the humiliation Grandpa Winter faced to keep his family fed. . . . Winters writing is thoughtful and deeply felt. Root's portraits of the boy's solitary exploration convey the force of Winter's message about 'learning to love those things/ that didn't cost a single penny.'" Publ Wkly

976.6   Oklahoma

Dorman, Robert L.

   Oklahoma; past and present. Rosen Central 2011 48p il map (The United States: past and present) lib bdg $26.50; pa $11.75

Grades: 3 4 5 6   976.6

   1. Oklahoma

   ISBN 978-1-4358-9493-8 lib bdg; 1-4358-9493-6 lib bdg; 978-1-4358-9520-1 pa; 1-4358-9520-7 pa

                       LC 2010002591

Presents the history, geography, government, economy, and people of Oklahoma, as well as general facts about the state.

   Includes bibliographical references

Orr, Tamra B.

   Oklahoma; by Tamra B. Orr. Revised edition Children's Press, an imprint of Scholastic Inc. 2014 144 p. illustrations, maps (lib. bdg.) $40

Grades: 4 5 6 7   976.6

   1. Oklahoma 2. United States -- History

   ISBN 0531248976; 9780531248973

                       LC 2013033040

"Admitted in 1907 as the 46th state in the union, Oklahoma is home to one of the country's largest Native American populations. Readers will trace the history of this remarkable state from its earliest settlement to its latest developments. They will also dive into the local culture, see the state's many fascinating sights, and learn about its economy." (Publisher's note)

   Includes bibliographical references (page 138) and index

976.7   Arkansas

Altman, Linda Jacobs

   Arkansas; [by] Linda Jacobs Altman, Ettagale Blauer, and Jason Laure. 2nd ed.; Marshall Cavendish Benchmark 2009 144p il map (Celebrate the states) lib bdg $42.79

Grades: 4 5 6 7   976.7

   1. Arkansas

   ISBN 978-0-7614-3001-8; 0-7614-3001-6

   First published 2000

"Provides comprehensive information on the geography, history, wildlife, governmental structure, economy, cultural diversity, peoples, religion, and landmarks of Arkansas." Publisher's note

   Includes bibliographical references

Levy, Janey

   Arkansas; past and present. Rosen Central 2011 48p il map (The United States: past and present) lib bdg $26.50; pa $11.75

Grades: 3 4 5 6   976.7

   1. Arkansas

   ISBN 978-1-4358-9476-1 lib bdg; 1-4358-9476-6 lib bdg; 978-1-4358-9504-1 pa; 1-4358-9504-5 pa

                       LC 2009052310

Presents the history, geography, government, economy, and people of Arkansas, as well as general facts about the state.

   Includes glossary and bibliographical references

Prentzas, G. S.

   Arkansas. Children's Press 2009 144p il map (America the beautiful, third series) lib bdg $39

Grades: 4 5 6 7   976.7

   1. Arkansas

   ISBN 978-0-531-18596-4; 0-531-18596-6

                       LC 2007044423

Presents an introduction to the geography, natural resources, history, economy, important sites, daily life, and people Arkansas.

   Includes glossary and bibliographical references

976.8   Tennessee

Graham, Amy

   Great Smoky Mountains National Park; adventure, explore, discover. [by] Amy Graham. MyReportLinks.com Books 2009 128p il map (America's national parks) lib bdg $33.27

Grades: 5 6 7 8   976.8

   1. Great Smoky Mountains National Park (N.C. and Tenn.) 2. National parks and reserves -- United States

   ISBN 978-1-59845-093-4 lib bdg; 1-59845-093-X lib bdg

                       LC 2007-13456

This "informative, well-written book contains a physical description of the park; a summary of its history including the Native peoples of the area; activities such as hiking trails, campsites, and visitor centers; information about the park's plants, animals, and weather; full-color photographs; and numerous approved links available through the publisher's Web page. . . . Thorough, useful, and appealing, this . . . is a great update for collections." SLJ

   Includes glossary and bibliographical references

Somervill, Barbara A.

   Tennessee; by Barbara A. Somervill. Revised edition Children's Press, an Imprint of Scholastic Inc. 2014 144 p. illustrations, maps (library binding : alk. paper) $40

Grades: 4 5 6 7   976.8

   1. Tennessee 2. United States -- History

   ISBN 0531282945; 9780531282946

                       LC 2013046226

"Known for its diverse and robust music scene, down-home cooking, and breathtaking vistas, Tennessee has developed a rich and unique culture throughout its history. Readers will journey through the state's most exciting locations as they learn about its history, geography, and government. They will also read about the state's most famous residents and local tradition." (Publisher's note)

   Includes bibliographical references and index

976.9   Kentucky

Cook, C.

   Kentucky; past and present. [by] Colleen Ryckert Cook. Rosen Central 2011 48p il map (The United States: past and present) lib bdg $26.50; pa $11.95

Grades: 3 4 5 6   **976.9**
   1. Kentucky
   ISBN 978-1-4358-9482-2 lib bdg; 1-4358-9482-0 lib bdg; 978-1-4358-9509-6 pa; 1-4358-9509-6 pa
                                                               LC 2010002507
   Presents the history, geography, government, economy, and people of Kentucky, as well as general facts about the state.
   Includes bibliographical references

Green, Carl R.
   Daniel Boone; courageous frontiersman. by William R. Sanford and Carl R. Green. Enslow Publishers 2013 48 p. col. ill., map (library) $21.26; (paperback) $7.95
Grades: 5 6 7 8   **976.9**
   1. Frontier and pioneer life -- United States   2. Kentucky -- Biography   3. Pioneers -- Kentucky -- Biography   4. Frontier and pioneer life -- Kentucky
   ISBN 076604002X; 9780766040021; 9781464400858; 9781464509926; 9781464609923
                                                               LC 2011037736
   This book by William Sanford is part of the Courageous Heroes of the American West series and focuses on Daniel Boone. "Through the untamed wilderness, Daniel Boone marched forward. He was leading a group of workers to carve out the Wilderness Road. Over hills, through dense forests, along stony paths, and fending off American Indian attacks, Boone never quit. He opened the way for thousands of settlers to move west, establishing the settlement of Boonesborough in 1775." (Publisher's note)
   Includes bibliographical references (p. 47) and index.

Santella, Andrew
   Kentucky; by Andrew Santella. Revised edition Children's Press 2014 144 p. col. ill., col. maps (library binding) $40
Grades: 4 5 6 7   **976.9**
   1. Kentucky 2. Geography
   ISBN 0531248852; 9780531248850
                                                               LC 2013031928
   "Kentucky is famed for its horse races and rolling expanses of farmland. Readers will trace the history of this remarkable state from its earliest settlement to its latest developments. They will also dive into the local culture, see the state's many fascinating sights, and learn about its economy." (Publisher's note)
   Includes bibliographical references and index

977   North central United States

Kummer, Patricia K.
   The **Great** Lakes; [by] Patricia K. Kummer. Marshall Cavendish Benchmark 2008 96p il map (Nature's wonders) lib bdg $35.64
Grades: 5 6 7 8   **977**
   1. Great Lakes
   ISBN 978-0-7614-2853-4 lib bdg; 0-7614-2853-4 lib bdg
                                                               LC 2007019728
   "Provides comprehensive information on the geography, history, wildlife, peoples, and environmental issues of the Great Lakes." Publisher's note
   Includes glossary and bibliographical references

Marsico, Katie
   ★ The **Mississippi** River; by Katie Marsico. Cherry Lake Pub. 2013 32 p. (It's cool to learn about America's waterways) (lib. bdg.) $28.50

Grades: 3 4 5   **977**
   1. Picture books for children 2. Mississippi River
   ISBN 1624310117; 9781624310119; 9781624310355; 9781624310591
                                                               LC 2012037581
   This book by Katie Marisco is part of the Social Studies Explorer: It's Cool to Learn About America's Water-Ways series and looks at the Everglades. In the books, the "first chapter introduces the waterway and provides basic geographic information about the surrounding area; the second chapter discusses the wildlife; the third chapter supplies a history, including today's tourism and agriculture; and the final chapter moves on to conservation and environmental activism." (Booklist)

977.1   Ohio

Lew, Kristi
   Ohio; past and present. Rosen Central 2010 48p il map (The United States: past and present) lib bdg $26.50; pa $11.50
Grades: 3 4 5 6   **977.1**
   1. Ohio
   ISBN 978-1-4358-5286-0 lib bdg; 1-4358-5286-9 lib bdg; 978-1-4358-5570-0 pa; 1-4358-5570-1 pa
                                                               LC 2008-54234
   Presents the history, geography, government, economy, and people of Ohio, as well as general facts about the state.
   Includes glossary and bibliographical references

Stille, Darlene R., 1942-
   Ohio; by Darlene R. Stille. Revised edition Children's Press, an imprint of Scholastic Inc. 2015 144 p. illustrations, maps (library binding : alk. paper) $40
Grades: 4 5 6 7   **977.1**
   1. Ohio 2. United States -- History
   ISBN 0531282872; 9780531282878
                                                               LC 2013044360
   "Located in the heart of the Midwest, Ohio is nicknamed the Buckeye State, after its once plentiful buckeye trees. Readers will get an up-close look at the state, from the rolling hills of the northwest to the rugged cliffs of the southeast. They will also learn about Ohio's history, government, and local culture." (Publisher's note)
   Includes bibliographical references (pages 138) and index

977.2   Indiana

Brezina, Corona
   Indiana; past and present. Rosen Central 2010 48p il map (The United States: past and present) lib bdg $26.50; pa $11.75
Grades: 3 4 5 6   **977.2**
   1. Indiana
   ISBN 978-1-4358-3521-4 lib bdg; 1-4358-3521-2; 978-1-4358-8492-2 pa; 1-4358-8492-2 pa
                                                               LC 2009023685
   Presents the history, geography, government, economy, and people of Indiana, as well as general facts about the state.
   Includes bibliographical references

Stille, Darlene R., 1942-
   Indiana; by Darlene R. Stille. Revised edition Children's Press 2014 144 p. col. ill., col. maps (library binding) $40

Grades: 4 5 6 7   **977.2**
1. Indiana 2. Geography
ISBN 0531248844; 9780531248843

LC 2013031926

"Located in the heart of the Midwest, Indiana is often described as the Crossroads of America. Readers will trace the history of this remarkable state from its earliest settlement to its latest developments. They will also dive into the local culture, see the state's many fascinating sights, and learn about its economy." (Publisher's note)

Includes bibliographical references and index

977.3   Illinois

Burgan, Michael
Illinois; by Michael Burgan. Revised edition Children's Press, a division of Scholastic Inc. 2014 144 p. ill. (chiefly color), col. map (lib. bdg.) $40
Grades: 4 5 6 7   **977.3**
1. Illinois 2. Geography
ISBN 0531248836; 9780531248836

LC 2013031925

"As the home state of one of the nation's most beloved presidents, Illinois is nicknamed the Land of Lincoln. Readers will trace the history of this remarkable state from its earliest settlement to its latest developments. They will also dive into the local culture, see the state's many fascinating sights, and learn about its economy." (Publisher's note)

Includes bibliographical references (page 138) and index

Hurd, Owen
Chicago history for kids; triumphs and tragedies of the Windy city, includes 21 activities. [by] Owen Hurd. Chicago Review Press 2007 182p il map $14.95
Grades: 5 6 7 8   **977.3**
1. Chicago (Ill.) -- History
ISBN 978-1-55652-654-1; 1-55652-654-7

LC 2006031807

"This attractive overview begins with geography and moves to the colorful stories that characterize the city. Hurd tapped local experts and collections, using primary and secondary sources and the responses of young readers to craft this engaging resource. . . . Excellent-quality photos, maps, illustrations, or boxed facts appear on every page." SLJ

Includes bibliographical references

Mattern, Joanne
Illinois; past and present. Rosen Central 2010 48p il map (The United States: past and present) lib bdg $26.50; pa $11.50
Grades: 4 5 6   **977.3**
1. Illinois
ISBN 978-1-4358-5284-6 lib bdg; 1-4358-5284-2 lib bdg; 978-1-4358-5566-3 pa; 1-4358-5566-3 pa

LC 2008-50577

Presents the history, geography, government, economy, and people of Illinois, as well as general facts about the state.

Includes glossary and bibliographical references

Murphy, Jim
★ The **great** fire. Scholastic 1995 144p il maps $16.95; pa $12.99
Grades: 5 6 7 8 9 10   **977.3**
1. Fires -- Chicago (Ill.)
ISBN 0-590-47267-4; 0-439-20307-4 pa

LC 94-9963

Newbery honor book, 1996

"Firsthand descriptions by persons who lived through the 1871 Chicago fire are woven into a gripping account of this famous disaster. Murphy also examines the origins of the fire, the errors of judgment that delayed the effective response, the organizational problems of the city's firefighters, and the postfire efforts to rebuild the city. Newspaper lithographs and a few historical photographs convey the magnitude of human suffering and confusion." Horn Book Guide

Includes bibliographical references

Price-Groff, Claire
Illinois; [by] Claire Price-Groff, Elizabeth Kaplan. 2nd ed.; Marshall Cavendish Benchmark 2010 90p il map (It's my state) lib bdg $31.36
Grades: 3 4 5   **977.3**
1. Illinois
ISBN 978-1-6087-0050-9; 1-6087-0050-X

LC 2010003923

First published 2003

Surveys the history, geography, government, and economy of Illinois as well as the diverse ways of life of its people

977.4   Michigan

Levy, Janey
Michigan; past and present. Rosen Central 2010 48p il map (The United States: past and present) lib bdg $26.50; pa $11.75
Grades: 3 4 5 6   **977.4**
1. Michigan
ISBN 978-1-4358-3523-8 lib bdg; 1-4358-3523-9 lib bdg; 978-1-4358-8496-0 pa; 1-4358-8496-5 pa

LC 2009028025

Presents the history, geography, government, economy, and people of Michigan, as well as general facts about the state.

Includes glossary and bibliographical references

Raatma, Lucia
Michigan; by Lucia Raatma. Revised edition Children's Press 2014 144 p. ill. (chiefly col.), col maps (library binding) $40
Grades: 4 5 6 7   **977.4**
1. Michigan 2. Geography
ISBN 0531248909; 9780531248904

LC 2013032355

"Located amid the waters of the Great Lakes, Michigan takes its name from a Native American word meaning "large lake." Readers will trace the history of this remarkable state from its earliest settlement to its latest developments. They will also dive into the local culture, see the state's many fascinating sights, and learn about its economy." (Publisher's note)

Includes bibliographical references and index

977.5   Wisconsin

Blashfield, Jean F.
Wisconsin; by Jean F. Blashfield. Revised edition Children's Press 2014 144 p. illustrations, maps (library binding) $40
Grades: 4 5 6 7   **977.5**
1. Wisconsin 2. Geography
ISBN 9780531248744; 0531248747

LC 2013033045

"Thanks to its large number of dairy farms, Wisconsin is the nation's top cheese producer. Readers will trace the history of this remarkable state from its earliest settlement to its latest developments. They will also dive into the local culture, see the state's many fascinating sights, and learn about its economy." (Publisher's note)

Includes bibliographical references and index

Dornfeld, Margaret

Wisconsin; [by] Margaret Dornfeld and Richard Hantula. 2nd ed.; Marshall Cavendish Benchmark 2010 90p il map (It's my state!) lib bdg $31.36

Grades: 3 4 5 **977.5**

1. Wisconsin

ISBN 978-1-6087-0062-2; 1-6087-0062-3

LC 2010003937

First published 2003

Surveys the history, geography, economy, and people of Wisconsin.

Heos, Bridget

Wisconsin; past and present. Rosen Central 2010 48p il map (The United States: past and present) lib bdg $26.50; pa $11.50

Grades: 3 4 5 6 **977.5**

1. Wisconsin

ISBN 978-1-4358-5293-8 lib bdg; 1-4358-5293-1 lib bdg; 978-1-4358-5584-7 pa; 1-4358-5584-1 pa

LC 2009-3906

Includes glossary and bibliographical references

977.6 Minnesota

Harmon, Dan

Minnesota; past and present. [by] Daniel E. Harmon. Rosen Central 2010 48p il map (The United States: past and present) lib bdg $26.50; pa $11.75

Grades: 3 4 5 6 **977.6**

1. Minnesota

ISBN 978-1-4358-3524-5 lib bdg; 1-4358-3524-7 lib bdg; 978-1-4358-8498-4 pa; 1-4358-8498-1 pa

LC 2009028024

Presents the history, geography, government, economy, and people of Minnesota, as well as general facts about the state.

Includes glossary and bibliographical references

Schwabacher, Martin

Minnesota; [by] Martin Schwabacher and Patricia K. Kummer. 2nd ed.; Marshall Cavendish Benchmark 2008 144p il map (Celebrate the states) lib bdg $39.93

Grades: 4 5 6 7 **977.6**

1. Minnesota

ISBN 978-0-7614-2716-2; 0-7614-2716-3

LC 2007-2895

First published 1999

"Provides comprehensive information on the geography, history, wildlife, governmental structure, economy, cultural diversity, peoples, religion, and landmarks of Minnesota." Publisher's note

Includes bibliographical references

977.7 Iowa

Blashfield, Jean F.

Iowa; by Jean F. Blashfield. Revised edition Children's Press, an Imprint of Scholastic Inc. 2015 144 p. illustrations, maps (library binding) $40

Grades: 4 5 6 7 **977.7**

1. Iowa 2. Geography

ISBN 0531282791; 9780531282793

LC 2013044318

"Flanked on either side by two of the nation's mightiest rivers, Iowa's fertile rolling hills have made it one of the country's leading sources of agriculture. Readers will discover what grows in Iowa's vast, sprawling fields. They will also learn how the state was founded, what role it has played in U.S. history, and what life is like today in the Hawkeye State." (Publisher's note)

Includes bibliographical references (page 138) and index

Freedman, Jeri

Iowa; past and present. Rosen Central 2010 48p il map (The United States: past and present) lib bdg $26.50; pa $11.75

Grades: 3 4 5 6 **977.7**

1. Iowa

ISBN 978-1-4358-3517-7 lib bdg; 1-4358-3517-4 lib bdg; 978-1-4358-8485-4 pa; 1-4358-8485-X pa

LC 2009024564

Presents the history, geography, government, economy, and people of Iowa, as well as general facts about the state.

Includes bibliographical references

977.8 Missouri

Bennett, Michelle

Missouri; by Michelle Bennett and Joyce Hart. 2nd ed.; Marshall Cavendish Benchmark 2010 144p il map (Celebrate the states) lib bdg $42.79 **977.8**

1. Missouri

ISBN 978-0-7614-4727-6; 0-7614-4727-X

LC 2009005754

First published 2001

This offers information on the geography, history, wildlife, governmental structure, economy, cultural diversity, peoples, religion, and landmarks of Missouri.

Includes bibliographical references

Blashfield, Jean F.

Missouri; by Jean F. Blashfield. Revised edition Children's Press, A Division of Scholastic Inc. 2015 144 p. (library binding : alk. paper) $40

Grades: 4 5 6 7 **977.8**

1. Missouri 2. Geography

ISBN 0531282821; 9780531282823

LC 2013044325

"From the skyscrapers of St. Louis and Kansas City to the sprawling natural landscapes of the Ozarks and the Osage Prairie, Missouri is home to a breathtaking range of environments. Readers will learn how the area was first settled thousands of years ago by Native Americans and how it came to be part of the United States. They will also learn what it is like to live there today." (Publisher's note)

Includes bibliographical references(pages 138) and index

Bullard, Lisa

The **Gateway** Arch. Lerner Publications 2010 32p il map (Lightning Bolt Books. Famous places) lib bdg $25.26

Grades: 2 3 4 **977.8**

1. Monuments 2. Gateway Arch (Saint Louis, Mo.)

ISBN 978-0-8225-9406-2; 0-8225-9406-4

LC 2008-30640

Discusses the history, design, and construction of the Gateway Arch in Saint Louis, Missouri.

This book uses "high-quality photos, illustrations, maps, and diagrams. . . . Readers will enjoy learning about [the Gateway Arch] . . . and the challenges of building and maintaining large structures." SLJ

Includes glossary and bibliographical references

Roza, Greg

Missouri; past and present. Rosen Central 2010 48p il map (The United States: past and present) lib bdg $26.50; pa $11.75

Grades: 3 4 5 6   **977.8**

1. Missouri

ISBN 978-1-4358-3520-7 lib bdg; 1-4358-3520-4; 978-1-4358-8490-8 pa; 1-4358-8490-6 pa

LC 2009025520

Presents the history, geography, government, economy, and people of Missouri, as well as general facts about the state.

Includes bibliographical references

978   Western United States

Adler, David A.

A picture book of Sacagawea; illustrated by Dan Brown. Holiday House 2000 un il $16.95; pa $6.95

Grades: 1 2 3   **978**

1. Shoshoni Indians 2. Lewis and Clark Expedition (1804-1806) 3. Interpreters 4. Guides (Persons) 5. West (U.S.) -- Exploration 6. Native Americans -- Biography

ISBN 0-8234-1485-X; 0-8234-1665-8 pa

LC 99-37135

A biography of the Shoshone woman who joined the Lewis and Clark Expedition

"The narrative is clear, direct, and never fictionalized. . . . The soft watercolor art is more successful in depicting landscapes than human figures." Booklist

Includes bibliographical references

Bodden, Valerie

Through the American West; by Valerie Bodden. Creative Education 2011 48 p. col. ill. (Great Expeditions) (library) $34.25

Grades: 5 6 7 8   **978**

1. Lewis and Clark Expedition (1804-1806)   2. West (U.S.) -- Discovery and exploration

ISBN 1608180654; 9781608180653

LC 2010033413

This book by Valerie Bodden is part of the "Great Expeditions" series. It describes an expedition "led by William Clark and Meriwether Lewis to explore the wilderness to the west and look for an all water route to the Pacific Ocean. They were aided by Sacagawea, a Shoshone Indian. The adventures and hardships of the arduous three-year journey include both the achievements and the disappointments encountered along the way". (Children's Literature)

Includes bibliographical references (p. 46-47) and index.

Burgan, Michael

The Arapaho. Marshall Cavendish Benchmark 2009 48p il map (First Americans) lib bdg $31.36

Grades: 2 3 4   **978**

1. Arapaho Indians

ISBN 978-0-7614-3017-9 lib bdg; 0-7614-3017-2 lib bdg

LC 2007-33675

Provides information on the background, lifestyle, beliefs, and present-day lives of the Arapaho people

Includes glossary and bibliographical references

Croy, Anita

Ancient Pueblo; archaeology unlocks the secrets of America's past. by Anita Croy; J. Jefferson Reid, consultant. National Geographic 2007 64p il map (National Geographic investigates) $17.95; lib bdg $27.90

Grades: 4 5 6 7   **978**

1. Archeology 2. Pueblo Indians 3. Southwestern States -- Antiquities

ISBN 978-1-4263-0130-8; 978-1-4263-0131-5 lib bdg

LC 2007024800

This describes the prehistoric sites of the American Southwest, and what archeologists have learned from them about the lives of ancient Pueblo peoples.

Includes glossary and bibliographical references

Freedman, Russell

★ The life and death of Crazy Horse; drawings by Amos Bad Heart Bull. Holiday House 1996 166p il maps $22.95

Grades: 5 6 7 8 9 10   **978**

1. Oglala Indians 2. Indian chiefs 3. Native Americans -- Biography

ISBN 0-8234-1219-9

LC 95-33303

A biography of the Oglala Indian leader who relentlessly resisted the white man's attempt to take over Indian lands.

This is "a compelling biography that is based on primary source documents and illustrated with pictographs by a Sioux band historian." Voice Youth Advocates

Includes bibliographical references

Friedman, Mel

The Oregon Trail. Children's Press 2010 il map (True book) lib bdg $26; pa $6.95

Grades: 3 4 5   **978**

1. Oregon Trail 2. Frontier and pioneer life 3. Overland journeys to the Pacific

ISBN 978-0-531-20584-6; 0-531-20584-3; 978-0-531-21247-9 pa; 0-531-21247-5 pa

LC 2009014186

This introduction to the Oregon Trail provides "readers with clear explanations, maps, illustrations, time lines, and engaging reproductions of primary resources. [This] volume contains eye-catching quick facts; illustrations and photographs are representational of regional Native Americans, pioneers, and explorers. This is ideal material for reports on the Westward expansion." SLJ

Includes bibliographical references

George-Warren, Holly

The cowgirl way; hats off to America's women of the West. Houghton Mifflin Books for Children 2010 112p il $18

Grades: 4 5 6 7   **978**

1. Cowhands 2. Women -- West (U.S.)

ISBN 978-0-618-73738-3; 0-618-73738-3

"With ample dynamic photos and lively quotes throughout, George-Warren presents a thoroughly absorbing overview of the history of cowgirls up to the present. . . . Famous figures such as Belle Starr, Calamity Jane, and Annie Oakley are discussed in brief, but the real delights here are the anecdotes on lesser-known figures such as Lucille Mulhall, the first woman to be dubbed a cowgirl in print. . . . The introduction of women as rodeo and trick riders and their contributions to the sports in the 1920s and '30s are covered in fascinating detail, as are the film and singing sensations of the 1940s and '50s." SLJ

Grupper, Jonathan

Destination: Rocky Mountains. National Geographic Soc. 2001 31p il $16.95

Grades: 3 4 5 6   **978**

1. Rocky Mountains 2. Natural history -- West (U.S.)

ISBN 0-7922-7722-8

LC 00-55926

"A hypothetical trek up the Rocky Mountains provides the framework for . . . information about its animals and the vegetation that sustains them at elevations beyond fourteen thousand feet. Each animal— from huge grizzly bear to tiny pika—has a double-page spread, lavishly illustrated with well-chosen color photographs. The text and graphics work well together." Horn Book Guide

Huey, Lois Miner

American archaeology uncovers the westward movement. Marshall Cavendish Benchmark 2009 64p il map (American archaeology) lib bdg $21.95

Grades: 4 5 6 7   **978**

1. Historical geography 2. West (U.S.) -- History 3. United States -- Territorial expansion 4. Frontier and pioneer life -- West (U.S.) 5. Excavations (Archeology) -- United States

ISBN 978-0-7614-4265-3 lib bdg; 0-7614-4265-0 lib bdg

LC 2009003167

This describes how archeologists have learned about the history of the American West.

"The visually pleasing . . . [book is] replete with maps, paintings, and photographs, all appropriately placed and thoughtfully captioned. . . . Huey's focus on American history, which is broken down into small, manageable chunks, is sure to entice budding historians." SLJ

Includes glossary and bibliographical references

King, David C.

★ **Pioneer** days; discover the past with fun projects, games, activities, and recipes. Wiley 1997 118p il (American kids in history) pa $12.95

Grades: 3 4 5 6   **978**

1. Cooking 2. Handicraft 3. West (U.S.) -- Social life and customs 4. Frontier and pioneer life -- West (U.S.)

ISBN 0-471-16169-1

LC 96-37495

This book is an "assortment of history, culture, crafts, and stories to teach about the daily life of the pioneers. . . . [Crafts and recipes include] air-dried flowers, toys and games, homemade soda pop, johnny-cakes, and various holiday ornaments. The author's research is evident, and the presentation of the activities and recipes is so engaging that the book will appeal to a wide audience." SLJ

Includes glossary and bibliographical references

Olson, Tod

How to get rich on a Texas cattle drive; afterword by Marc Aronson; illustrations by Scott Allred & Gregory Proch. National Geographic 2010 47p il map $18.95

Grades: 4 5 6 7   **978**

1. Cowhands 2. West (U.S.) -- History 3. Frontier and pioneer life -- West (U.S.)

ISBN 978-1-4263-0524-5; 1-4263-0524-9

"This book provides one of the better true-to-life insider accounts of what happens on a cattle drive: why the cattle are being driven, where they're being driven to and from, and the multitude of daily chores and unforeseen obstacles along the way. Period photos and artwork, as well as original drawings, make for a lively design, and an ongoing ledger keeps track of the main character's mostly modest finances." Booklist

★ **How** to get rich on the Oregon Trail; my adventures among cows, crooks & heroes on the road to fame and fortune. [illustrations by Scott Allred & Gregory Proch; afterword by Marc Anonson] National Geographic 2009 47p il (How to get rich) $18.95; lib bdg $27.90

Grades: 4 5 6 7   **978**

1. Oregon Trail 2. Frontier and pioneer life 3. Overland journeys to the Pacific 4. West (U.S.) -- History 5. Oregon Trail -- History 6. Western States -- Discovery and exploration

ISBN 1-4263-0412-9; 1-4263-0413-7 lib bdg; 978-1-4263-0412-5; 978-1-4263-0413-2 lib bdg

This is a follow-up to How to Get Rich in the California Gold Rush (2008). "The fictional William Reed gives readers a historical portrait of the hardships of life on the journey west, as well as the ingenuity, skill, and trickery used to overcome such challenges." (Publisher's note) "Grades four to seven." (Bull Cent Child Books)

"The action follows young Will Reed and his family as they set off from Illinois to find their fortune along the 2,000-mile Oregon Trail. . . . Informing Will's impish sketches and wry journal entries is a wealth of information about life along the trail. . . . An ongoing ledger calculates the family's balance as it fluctuates from $10.70 to $3,021.70, but it's clear that this journey is more about survival than riches. The illustrations, historical anecdotes, and run-ins with everyone from the Mormons to escaped slaves to Abraham Lincoln form a perfect blend of history and humbuggery." Booklist

Patent, Dorothy Hinshaw

The **horse** and the Plains Indians; a powerful partnership. Dorothy Hinshaw Patent; photographs by William Munoz. Clarion Books 2012 xiii, 98 p.p ill. (chiefly col.) $17.99

Grades: 4 5 6 7 8   **978**

1. Domestic animals 2. Native Americans -- Great Plains 3. Horses -- Great Plains -- History 4. Human-animal relationships -- Great Plains -- History 5. Indians of North America -- Domestic animals -- Great Plains

ISBN 9780547125510

LC 2011025954

This book explores the relationship between Plains Indians and horses. The "Plains Indians and the horse were not always inseparable. Once, Native Americans used dogs to help carry their goods, and even after the Spaniards introduced the horse to the Americas," the Spanish hoarded the valuable animals. But "soon horses escaped from Spanish settlements, and Native Americans quickly learned how valuable the horse could be as a hunting mount, beast of burden, and military steed." (Publisher's note)

Includes bibliographical references and index

Perritano, John

The **Lewis** and Clark Expedition. Children's Press 2010 48p il (True book) lib bdg $26; pa $6.95

Grades: 3 4 5   **978**

1. Explorers 2. Lewis and Clark Expedition (1804-1806) 3. Territorial governors 4. West (U.S.) -- Exploration

ISBN 978-0-531-20582-2 lib bdg; 0-531-20582-7 lib bdg; 978-0-531-21245-5 pa; 0-531-21245-9 pa

LC 2009014183

This introduction to the Lewis and Clark Expedition provides "elementary readers with clear explanations, maps, illustrations, time lines, and engaging reproductions of primary resources. [This] volume contains eye-catching quick facts; illustrations and photographs are representative of regional Native Americans, pioneers, and explorers. This is ideal material for reports on the Westward expansion." SLJ

Includes bibliographical references

Sheinkin, Steve

★ **Which** way to the wild West? everything your schoolbooks didn't tell you about America's westward expansion. illustrated by Tim Robinson. Roaring Brook Press 2009 260p il map $19.95

Grades: 5 6 7 8　　　　　　　　　　　　　　　　　978

1. West (U.S.) -- History 2. United States -- Territorial expansion 3. Frontier and pioneer life -- West (U.S.)

ISBN 978-1-59643-321-2; 1-59643-321-3

Presents the greatest adventures of America's Westward expansion, from the Louisiana Purchase and the gold rush to the Indian wars and life of the cowboy, as well as the everyday happenings that defined living on the frontier

"An engaging storyteller, the author uses humor and little-known anecdotes to make such subjects as Manifest Destiny, the Mexican-American War, the Gold Rush and Custer's Last Stand entertaining for readers. His chatty, informal style . . . will appeal to young readers turned off to history by stale textbooks. Robinson's cartoons complement the text. . . . An accessible and engaging historical overview." Kirkus

Includes bibliographical references

Staton, Hilarie

Cowboys and the wild West. Kingfisher 2011 32p il map (All about America)

Grades: 3 4 5 6　　　　　　　　　　　　　　　　　978

1. Cowhands 2. West (U.S.) -- History 3. Frontier and pioneer life -- West (U.S.)

ISBN 0-7534-6510-8 pa; 0-7534-6582-5; 978-0-7534-6510-3 pa; 978-0-7534-6582-0

This is a history of cowboys and the American West from the early 1800s to around 1890.

This "visually appealing [title] effectively [combines] paintings, engravings, primary documents, and photographs with cartoon illustrations. The eye-catching [layout includes] different font sizes, bold type, and text boxes to highlight different pieces of information. The content is interesting and pithy." SLJ

Includes glossary and bibliographical references

Waldman, Stuart

The last river; John Wesley Powell & the Colorado River Exploration Expedition. by Stuart Waldman; illustrated by Gregory Manchess. Mikaya Press 2005 47p il map (Great explorers book) $19.95

Grades: 3 4 5 6　　　　　　　　　　　　　　　　　978

1. Explorers 2. Geologists 3. West (U.S.) -- Exploration 4. Colorado River (Colo.-Mexico)

ISBN 1-931414-09-2

LC 2005041580

"In 1869 the Colorado River Exploring Expedition set forth from Green River City led by John Wesley Powell, a one-armed explorer who was determined to reach the Colorado's canyons to study their geology. . . . Waldman relates their story clearly in the main text, while occasional sidebars carry short excerpts from the men's journals and letters. Illustrations include clear nineteenth-century photos as well as handsome full and double-page paintings. . . . Rich in color, strong in composition, and beautifully executed, these often-dramatic paintings bring the story to life." Booklist

Includes bibliographical references

Yasuda, Anita

Explore the wild west! Anita Yasuda; illustrated by Alex Kim. Nomad Press 2012 92 p. ill. (paperback) $12.95; (prebind) $21.95; (ebook) $9.99

Grades: 3 4 5　　　　　　　　　　　　　　　　　978

1. West (U.S.) -- History 2. Frontier and pioneer life -- West (U.S.)

3. United States -- History -- 19th century

ISBN 1936749718; 9781936749713; 9781451777307; 9781936749720

Author Anita Yasuda presents "a fun and educational journey through time [that] invites young readers to experience the spirit of the Wild West . . . [Yasuda provides a history of] Wild West legends, gold miners, settlers and frontier towns, Native American and cowboy cultures, cattle drives, and the peacekeepers and lawbreakers . . . [The book also includes f]un facts, trivia, jokes, and riddles." (Publisher's note)

978.02　　Western United States, 1800-1899

Fleming, Candace

Presenting Buffalo Bill; The Man Who Invented the Wild West. Candace Fleming. Roaring Brook Press 2016 288 p. illustrations (hardcover) $19.99; (ebook) $60

Grades: 6 7 8 9 10　　　　　　　　　　　　　　978.02

1. Pioneers -- West (U.S.) -- Biography 2. Buffalo Bill's Wild West Show -- History 3. Entertainers -- United States -- Biography

ISBN 9781596437630; 9781626727472

LC 2015035540

In this book, by Candace Fleming, "everyone knows the name Buffalo Bill, but few these days know what he did or, in some cases, didn't do. . . . This [is] the first significant biography of Buffalo Bill Cody for younger readers in many years. . . . With copious archival illustrations and a handsome design, [it] makes the great showman come alive for new generations. Extensive back matter, bibliography, and source notes complete the package." (Publisher's note)

"Illustrated with archival material and supplemented with extensive backmatter, this is a thoroughly engaging portrait of a fascinating, larger-than-life figure." Kirkus

Includes bibliographical references

978.1　　Kansas

Bailey, Diane

Kansas; past and present. Rosen Central 2011 48p il map (The United States: past and present) lib bdg $26.50; pa $11.75

Grades: 3 4 5 6　　　　　　　　　　　　　　　　978.1

1. Kansas

ISBN 9781435894815 lib bdg; 1-4358-9481-2 lib bdg; 978-1-4358-9508-9 pa; 1-4358-9508-8 pa

LC 2010000816

Presents the history, geography, government, economy, and people of Kansas, as well as general facts about the state.

Includes bibliographical references

Cannarella, Deborah

Kansas; by Deborah Cannarella. Revised edition Children's Press, a Division of Scholastic Inc. 2014 144 p. ill. (chiefly col.), col. map (library binding) $40

Grades: 4 5 6 7　　　　　　　　　　　　　　　　978.1

1. Kansas 2. Geography

ISBN 0531282805; 9780531282809

LC 2013044321

"Lying in the heart of the United States, Kansas is a sprawling landscape of rolling prairies and rugged hills. Readers will learn how the state was first settled thousands of years ago by ancient Paleo-Indians and find out how it came to be part of the United States. They will also explore the rich and varied culture of modern Kansas, from the crowded streets of Kansas City to the rural farms of the Great Plains." (Publisher's note)

Includes bibliographical references (pages 133-137)and index

978.2 Nebraska

Bjorklund, Ruth

Nebraska; [by] Ruth Bjorklund and Marlee Richards. 2nd ed.; Marshall Cavendish Benchmark 2010 144p il map (Celebrate the states) $42.79

Grades: 5 6 7 8 **978.2**

1. Nebraska

ISBN 978-0-7614-4732-0; 0-7614-4732-6

"Every school library should purchase this." Voice Youth Advocates

Bringle, Jennifer

Nebraska; past and present. Rosen Central 2011 48p il map (The United States: past and present) lib bdg $26.50; pa $11.75

Grades: 3 4 5 6 **978.2**

1. Nebraska

ISBN 978-1-4358-9487-7 lib bdg; 1-4358-9487-1 lib bdg; 978-1-4358-9514-0 pa; 1-4358-9514-2 pa

LC 2010002545

Presents the history, geography, government, economy, and people of Nebraska, as well as general facts about the state.

Includes bibliographical references

Heinrichs, Ann

Nebraska; by Ann Heinrichs. Revised edition Children's Press 2014 144 p. (library binding) $40

Grades: 4 5 6 7 **978.2**

1. Nebraska 2. Geography

ISBN 0531248925; 9780531248928

LC 2013032479

"Known for its wide expanses of flat farmlands, Nebraska is one of the most sparsely populated states in the country. Readers will trace the history of this remarkable state from its earliest settlement to its latest developments. They will also dive into the local culture, see the state's many fascinating sights, and learn about its economy." (Publisher's note)

Includes bibliographical references (p. 138) and index

978.3 South Dakota

Burgan, Michael

South Dakota; by Michael Burgan. Revised edition Children's Press, an Imprint of Scholastic Inc. 2014 144 p. illustrations, maps (library binding : alk. paper) $40

Grades: 4 5 6 7 **978.3**

1. South Dakota 2. United States -- History

ISBN 0531282937; 9780531282939

LC 2013044803

"Often called 'The Land of Infinite Variety,' South Dakota is home to sprawling plains, broad river valleys, and majestic mountains. Readers will get a look at landmarks such as Mount Rushmore and the Black Hills while finding out what it is like to live in South Dakota. They will also learn about the state's rich history, abundant wildlife, and bustling economy." (Publisher's note)

Includes bibliographical references(pages 133-137)and index

Kelley, True

Where is Mount Rushmore? by True Kelley; illustrated by John Hinderliter. Grosset & Dunlap 2015 108 p. illustrations, maps (Where is ... ?) (pbk) $5.99

Grades: 3 4 5 6 **978.3**

1. National monuments 2. Mount Rushmore National Memorial (S.D.)

ISBN 0448483564; 9780448483566

LC 2014042867

This book by True Kelley, illustrated by John Hinderliter and David Groff, examines how "it was world-famous sculptor Gutzon Borglum's dream to carve sixty-foot-high likenesses of four presidents on a granite cliff in South Dakota. Borglum faced a lot of opposition and problems at every turn; the blasting and carving carried out through the years of the Great Depression when funding for anything was hard to come by. Yet Mount Rushmore now draws almost three million visitors . . . every year." (Publisher's note)

"A strong addition to history collections for its inclusion of Native American history and the author's willingness to address the controversial legacy of this landmark." SLJ

Includes bibliographical references

Kenney, Karen Latchana

Mount Rushmore; illustrated by Judith A. Hunt. Magic Wagon 2011 32p il (Our nation's pride) lib bdg $28.50

Grades: 2 3 4 **978.3**

1. Mount Rushmore National Memorial (S.D.)

ISBN 978-1-61641-153-4; 1-61641-153-8

LC 2010014009

This book "tells of the sculptor who came to work on the carving, how men were lowered on special harnesses to do the work, and how dynamite specialists and drillers prepared the mountain. . . . The full-color artwork not only explains the text but also gives almost photographic renderings of the [topic]." SLJ

Petersen, Christine

South Dakota; past and present. Rosen Central 2011 48p il (The United States: past and present) lib bdg $26.50; pa $11.75

Grades: 3 4 5 6 **978.3**

1. South Dakota

ISBN 978-1-4358-9496-9 lib bdg; 1-4358-9496-0 lib bdg; 978-1-4358-9523-2 pa; 1-4358-9523-1 pa

LC 2010002584

Presents the history, geography, government, economy, and people of South Dakota, as well as general facts about the state.

Includes glossary and bibliographical references

Thomas, William

Mount Rushmore; by William David Thomas. Chelsea Clubhouse 2010 48p il (Symbols of American freedom) $30

Grades: 3 4 5 **978.3**

1. Mount Rushmore National Memorial (S.D.)

ISBN 978-1-60413-515-2; 1-60413-515-8

LC 2009-13027

This book about Mount Rushmore "provides nearly as much information as a guided tour by a park ranger. [It begins] with the story of how the place came to be, and where it fits into U.S. history. Information boxes offer additional background and some surprising facts, such as . . . the origin of the name of Mount Rushmore. The final chapter shows the landmark today and includes maps and photographs of the visitors' center and some of the things individuals might see or do while visiting the site. Much information is packed into [this] slim [book]. Excellent . . . for state reports or to complement U.S. history units." SLJ

Includes glossary

978.4 North Dakota

Lewis, Mark J.

North Dakota; past and present. Rosen Central 2011 48p il map (United States: past and present) lib bdg $26.50; pa $11.75
Grades: 3 4 5 6 **978.4**
1. North Dakota
ISBN 978-1-4358-9492-1 lib bdg; 1-4358-9492-8 lib bdg; 978-1-4358-9519-5 pa; 1-4358-9519-3 pa
LC 2010002697
This describes the geography, history, government, economy, and famous people of North Dakota.
Includes bibliographical references

McDaniel, Melissa

North Dakota; by Melissa McDaniel and Sara Louise Kras. 2nd ed.; Marshall Cavendish Benchmark 2010 144p il map (Celebrate the states) lib bdg $42.79
Grades: 5 6 7 8 **978.4**
1. North Dakota
ISBN 978-0-7614-4733-7; 0-7614-4733-4
LC 2009002584
First published 2001
This offers information on the geography, history, wildlife, governmental structure, economy, cultural diversity, peoples, religion, and landmarks of North Dakota.
Includes bibliographical references

Stille, Darlene R., 1942-

North Dakota; by Darlene R. Stille. Revised edition Children's Press, an imprint of Scholastic Inc. 2015 144 p. illustrations, maps (library binding : alk. paper) $40
Grades: 4 5 6 7 **978.4**
1. North Dakota 2. United States -- History
ISBN 0531282864; 9780531282861
LC 2013044357
"North Dakota's rich soil and abundant natural resources have made it one of the United States' most important centers of agriculture and mining. Readers will learn how the area was first settled and how it became a state. They will also learn how North Dakota is governed today, how its people celebrate local traditions, and which plants and animals can be found in the state's beautiful wilderness." (Publisher's note)
Includes bibliographical references and index

978.6 Montana

Bennett, Clayton

Montana; by Clayton Bennett and Wendy Mead. 2nd ed.; Marshall Cavendish Benchmark 2010 144p il map (Celebrate the states) $42.79
Grades: 5 6 7 8 **978.6**
1. Montana
ISBN 978-0-7614-4731-3; 0-7614-4731-8
LC 2009007939
First published 2001
This offers information on the geography, history, wildlife, governmental structure, economy, cultural diversity, peoples, religion, and landmarks of Montana.
Includes bibliographical references

Porterfield, Jason

Montana; past and present. Rosen Central 2011 48p il map (The United States: past and present) lib bdg $26.50; pa $11.75

Grades: 3 4 5 6 **978.6**
1. Montana
ISBN 978-1-4358-9486-0 lib bdg; 1-4358-9486-3 lib bdg; 978-1-4358-9513-3 pa; 1-4358-9513-4 pa
LC 2010000415
Presents the history, geography, government, economy, and people of Montana, as well as general facts about the state.
Includes bibliographical references

Stein, Conrad R.

Montana; by R. Conrad Stein. Revised edition Children's Press, an Imprint of Scholastic Inc. 2014 144 p. (library binding : alk. paper) $40
Grades: 4 5 6 7 **978.6**
1. Montana 2. Geography
ISBN 053128283X; 9780531282830
LC 2013044324
"Montana is one of the nation's largest states, but it is home to very few large towns or cities. Rather, it is defined by its vast wilderness areas, which range from the high peaks of the Rocky Mountains to the rolling hills and flatlands of the Great Plains. Readers will find out how Montana was settled and what role it has played in U.S. history. They will also explore the state's rich culture and traditions." (Publisher's note)
Includes bibliographical references and index

978.7 Wyoming

Baldwin, Guy

Wyoming; [by] Guy Baldwin and Joyce Hart. 2nd ed.; Marshall Cavendish Benchmark 2008 144p il map (Celebrate the states) lib bdg $39.93
Grades: 4 5 6 7 **978.7**
1. Wyoming
ISBN 978-0-7614-2563-2; 0-7614-2563-2
LC 2007-19560
First publsihed 1999
"Provides comprehensive information on the geography, history, wildlife, governmental structure, economy, cultural diversity, peoples, religion, and landmarks of Wyoming." Publisher's note
Includes bibliographical references

Byers, Ann

Wyoming; past and present. Rosen Central 2011 48p il map (The United States: past and present) lib bdg $26.50; pa $11.75
Grades: 3 4 5 6 **978.7**
1. Wyoming
ISBN 978-1-4358-9500-3 lib bdg; 1-4358-9500-2 lib bdg; 978-1-4358-9527-0 pa; 1-4358-9527-4 pa
LC 2010002519
Presents the history, geography, government, economy, and people of Wyoming, as well as general facts about the state.
Includes glossary and bibliographical references

Prentzas, G. S.

Wyoming; by G.S. Prentzas. Revised edition Children's Press 2015 144 p. illustrations, maps (library binding : alk. paper) $40
Grades: 4 5 6 7 **978.7**
1. Wyoming 2. Geography
ISBN 9780531283004; 0531283003
LC 2013046232
"From the amazing geysers of Yellowstone National Park and the heights of the Rocky Mountains to the sprawling grasslands of the Great Plains, Wyoming offers some of the most incredible sights the United

States has to offer. Readers will learn about the state's history, government, and economy as they tour its towns, cities, and wilderness. They will also explore the state's culture and cuisine as they see what it is like to live in Wyoming today." (Publisher's note)

Includes bibliographical references and index

978.8   Colorado

Heos, Bridget

Colorado; past and present. Rosen Central 2011 48p il map (The United States: past and present) lib bdg $26.50; pa $11.75

Grades: 3 4 5 6   **978.8**

1. Colorado

ISBN 978-1-4358-9477-8 lib bdg; 1-4358-9477-4 lib bdg; 978-1-4358-9530-0 pa; 1-4358-9530-4 pa

LC 2010000419

Presents the history, geography, government, economy, and people of Colorado, as well as general facts about the state.

Includes glossary and bibliographical references

Lowery, Linda

★ **Aunt** Clara Brown; official pioneer. illustrations by Janice Lee Porter. Carolrhoda Bks. 1999 48p il (On my own biography) lib bdg $19.93; pa $5.95

Grades: 2 3 4   **978.8**

1. Slaves 2. Frontier and pioneer life 3. Pioneers 4. African American women -- Biography

ISBN 1-57505-045-5 lib bdg; 1-57505-416-7 pa

LC 98-24259

A biography of the freed slave who made her fortune in Colorado and used her money to bring other former slaves there to begin new lives

"The well-defined primitivist shapes, canvas-y textures, and muted earth tones of the illustrations perfectly evoke the roughness of the terrain and the historical period, as well as the powerful basic emotions motivating the characters. The straightforward text allows the facts speak for themselves. . . . A good story and a solid resource." Bull Cent Child Books

Marsico, Katie

★ The **Rio** Grande; by Katie Marsico. Cherry Lake Publishing 2013 32 p. (lib. bdg.) $28.50

Grades: 3 4 5   **978.8**

1. Rivers 2. Rio Grande valley 3. Rio Grande (Colo.-Mexico and Tex.)

ISBN 1624310125; 9781624310126; 9781624310362; 9781624310607

LC 2012035444

This book by Katie Marsico presents "a tour of the Rio Grande and its surrounding area." It is part of a series that provides "information regarding each waterway's history, geographical characteristics, wildlife, and influence on the development of nearby towns and cities. Conservation is emphasized in all the titles. The importance of each waterway commercially and recreationally is also discussed. Vocabulary words are set apart in bold font and defined in the glossary." (Publisher's note)

Includes bibliographical references and index

Quigley, Mary

Mesa Verde; [by] Mary Quigley. Heinemann Library 2006 48p il (Excavating the past) lib bdg $31.43

Grades: 4 5 6   **978.8**

1. Native Americans -- Antiquities 2. Mesa Verde National Park

(Colo.) 3. Excavations (Archeology) -- United States

ISBN 1-4034-5997-5

LC 2005009179

"Mesa Verde explains how these ancient people reached North and South America using the land bridge and settled down to farm in the Four Corners area. Quigley uses the term Ancestral Puebloans rather than the sometimes derogatory Anasazi and explains why. She describes the daily lives of the people and includes current theories about why they may have abandoned this site. Activities and discoveries by the Wetherill brothers and other archaeologists as well as cultural information from modern-day people bring knowledge about the ancients up to date. This [is an] excellent title." SLJ

Includes bibliographical references

Somervill, Barbara A.

Colorado; by Barbara A. Somervill. Revised edition Children's Press 2014 144 p. (library binding) $40

Grades: 4 5 6 7   **978.8**

1. Colorado

ISBN 053124878X; 9780531248782

LC 2013031192

"With half of its territory lying within the Rocky Mountains, Colorado is known for its breathtaking natural features. Readers will trace the history of this remarkable state from its earliest settlement to its latest developments. They will also dive into the local culture, see the state's many fascinating sights, and learn about its economy." (Publisher's note)

Includes bibliographical references and index

978.9   New Mexico

Brezina, Corona

New Mexico; past and present. Rosen Central 2011 48p il map (The United States: past and present) lib bdg $26.50; pa $11.75

Grades: 3 4 5 6   **978.9**

1. New Mexico

ISBN 978-1-4358-9490-7 lib bdg; 1-4358-9490-1; 978-1-4358-9517-1 pa; 1-4358-9517-7 pa

LC 2010003059

Presents the history, geography, government, economy, and people of New Mexico, as well as general facts about the state.

Includes bibliographical references

Burgan, Michael

New Mexico; land of enchantment. World Almanac Library 2003 48p il map (World Almanac Library of the states) $31; pa $14.05

Grades: 4 5 6 7   **978.9**

1. New Mexico

ISBN 978-0-8368-5156-4; 0-8368-5156-0; 978-0-8368-5327-8 pa; 0-8368-5327-X pa

LC 2002-191008

Text and illustrations present the history, geography, people, politics and government, economy, customs, and attractions of New Mexico

Includes bibliographical references

979.1   Arizona

Brezina, Corona

Arizona; past and present. Rosen Central 2010 48p il map (The United States: past and present) lib bdg $26.50; pa $11.75

Grades: 3 4 5 6   **979.1**
   1. Arizona
   ISBN 978-1-4358-3516-0 lib bdg; 1-4358-3516-6 lib bdg; 978-1-4358-8483-0 pa; 1-4358-8483-3 pa
                               LC 2009017004
Presents the history, geography, government, economy, and people of Arizona, as well as general facts about the state.
   Includes glossary and bibliographical references

McDaniel, Melissa
   Arizona; by Melissa McDaniel and Wendy Mead. 2nd ed.; Marshall Cavendish Benchmark 2009 144p il map (Celebrate the states) lib bdg $39.93
Grades: 4 5 6 7   **979.1**
   1. Arizona
   ISBN 978-0-7614-3398-9; 0-7614-3398-8
                               LC 2008-6212
First published 2000
   "Provides comprehensive information on the geography, history, wildlife, governmental structure, economy, cultural diversity, peoples, religion, and landmarks of Arizona." Publisher's note
   Includes bibliographical references

Somervill, Barbara A.
   Arizona; by Barbara A. Somervill. Revised edition Children's Press, an Imprint of Scholastic Inc. 2015 144 p. illustrations, maps (library binding) $40
Grades: 4 5 6 7   **979.1**
   1. Arizona
   ISBN 0531282759; 9780531282755
                               LC 2013044319
   "With its soaring mountains, deep canyons, vast deserts, and remarkable rock formations, Arizona is a land of dramatic scenery. Readers will explore the state's incredible landscapes and get an up-close look at its plants and wildlife. They will also explore Arizona's rich history and get a taste of the state's vibrant culture." (Publisher's note)
   Includes bibliographical references (page 138) and index

979.2   Utah

Ching, Jacqueline
   Utah; past and present. Rosen Central 2011 48p il map (The United States: past and present) lib bdg $26.50; pa $11.75
Grades: 3 4 5 6   **979.2**
   1. Utah
   ISBN 978-1-4358-9497-6 lib bdg; 1-4358-9497-9 lib bdg; 978-1-4358-9524-9 pa; 1-4358-9524-X pa
                               LC 2010002493
Presents the history, geography, government, economy, and people of Utah, as well as general facts about the state.
   Includes bibliographical references

Kent, Deborah, 1948-
   Utah; by Deborah Kent. Revised edition Children's Press 2015 144 p. illustrations, maps (library binding : alk. paper) $40
Grades: 4 5 6 7   **979.2**
   1. Utah 2. Geography
   ISBN 9780531282953; 0531282953
                               LC 2013046227
   "Utah's dazzling rock formations and stunning canyons make it one of the highlights of the Southwestern United States. Readers will find out how the state was settled, first by ancient Paleo-Indians and later by Spanish Missionaries and Mormon travelers. They will tour some of the

state's most interesting locations, meet its most influential residents, and learn how it is governed. They will also get a close look at the state's wildlife and a taste of its local culture." (Publisher's note)
   Includes bibliographical references and index

Stefoff, Rebecca
   Utah; by Rebecca Stefoff and Wendy Mead. 2nd ed.; Marshall Cavendish Benchmark 2010 144p il map (Celebrate the states) lib bdg $42.79
Grades: 5 6 7 8   **979.2**
   1. Utah
   ISBN 978-0-7614-4035-2; 0-7614-4035-6
                               LC 2008040026
   This offers information on the geography, history, wildlife, governmental structure, economy, cultural diversity, peoples, religion, and landmarks of Utah.
   Includes bibliographical references

979.3   Nevada

Heinrichs, Ann
   Nevada; Ann Heinrichs. Revised edition Children's Press 2014 144 p. (library binding) $40
Grades: 4 5 6 7   **979.3**
   1. Nevada 2. United States -- History
   ISBN 0531248933; 9780531248935
                               LC 2013032828
   "As one of the driest states in the country, Nevada has few residents outside of cities such as Las Vegas and Reno. Readers will trace the history of this remarkable state from its earliest settlement to its latest developments. They will also dive into the local culture, see the state's many fascinating sights, and learn about its economy." (Publisher's note)
   Includes bibliographical references and index

Roza, Greg
   Nevada; past and present. Rosen Central 2011 48p il map (The United States: past and present) lib bdg $26.50; pa $11.75
Grades: 3 4 5 6   **979.3**
   1. Nevada
   ISBN 978-1-4358-9488-4 lib bdg; 1-4358-9488-X; 978-1-4358-9515-7 pa; 1-4358-9515-0 pa
                               LC 2010001980
Presents the history, geography, government, economy, and people of Nevada, as well as general facts about the state.
   Includes bibliographical references

Stefoff, Rebecca
   Nevada; 2nd ed.; Marshall Cavendish Benchmark 2010 144p il map (Celebrate the states) lib bdg $42.79
Grades: 5 6 7 8   **979.3**
   1. Nevada
   ISBN 978-0-7614-4728-3; 0-7614-4728-8
                               LC 2009007137
   This offers information on the geography, history, wildlife, governmental structure, economy, cultural diversity, peoples, religion, and landmarks of Nevada.
   Includes bibliographical references

979.4   California

Brown, Don

★ **Gold!** Gold from the American River! Roaring Brook Press 2011 un il map (Actual times) $17.99

Grades: 2 3 4   **979.4**

1. California -- History 2. California -- Gold discoveries 3. Frontier and pioneer life -- California

ISBN 978-1-59643-223-9; 1-59643-223-3

LC 2010-14375

"Brown here takes a look at the 1849 California gold rush. [This is written] with easygoing prose and revealing quotes from forty-niners and historians alike. . . . The inventive page compositions and scratchy watercolor cartoon figures carry small, telling dramas . . . and sweeping landscapes come into full relief, bringing not only visual context but a sense of playfulness to the book." Booklist

Includes bibliographical references

Calabro, Marian

★ The **perilous** journey of the Donner Party. Clarion Bks. 1999 192p il maps $20

Grades: 5 6 7 8   **979.4**

1. Donner party 2. Overland journeys to the Pacific 3. Frontier and pioneer life -- West (U.S.)

ISBN 0-395-86610-3

LC 98-29610

Uses materials from letters and diaries written by survivors of the Donner Party to relate the experiences of that ill-fated group as they endured horrific circumstances on their way to California in 1846-47

"Calabro's offering is a fine addition to the Donner Party canon and particularly well suited to its young audience, for whom the story of hardship and survival will be nothing short of riveting. . . . From the haunting cover with its lonely campfire to the recounting of a survivors' reunion, this is a page-turner." Booklist

Includes bibliographical references

Doak, Robin S.

California, 1542-1850; by Robin Doak; Andres Resendez, consultant. National Geographic Society 2006 109p map il (Voices from colonial America) $21.95; lib bdg $32.90

Grades: 5 6 7 8   **979.4**

1. California -- History

ISBN 978-0-7922-6391-3; 0-7922-6391-X; 978-0-7922-6861-1 lib bdg; 0-7922-6861-X lib bdg

LC 2005-30920

"The text is not written in sound bites but in full paragraphs, making up chronological chapters. These are divided into topical sections, which are clearly marked by large headings. This lovely, calm layout is liberally sprinkled with primary source illustrations, including reproductions of period maps, pamphlets, paintings, and drawings. . . . An essential purchase for schools with a colonies research project . . . and for the public libraries that support their communities." Voice Youth Advocates

Includes bibliograhical references

Freedman, Russell, 1929-

★ **Angel** Island; gateway to Gold Mountain. Russell Freedman; Chinese poems translated by Evans Chan. Clarion Books 2013 96 p. (hardcover) $17.99

Grades: 4 5 6 7 8   **979.4**

1. Immigrants -- United States 2. Angel Island Immigration Station (San Francisco, Calif.) 3. Angel Island (Calif.) -- History 4. Asia -- Emigration and immigration -- History 5. United States -- Emigration and immigration -- History 6. San Francisco Bay Area

(Calif.) -- Emigration and immigration -- History

ISBN 0547903782; 9780547903781

LC 2012036532

This book is a "history of Angel Island and its legacy in the American immigration narrative. Detailed descriptions of the island, the actual building, the events that took place there, and the people who passed through its doors are sprinkled with the emotional poems, quotes, and other writings that were discovered covering the walls of the areas where the detainees were housed." (School Library Journal)

Includes bibliographical references

Krensky, Stephen

Lizzie Newton and the San Francisco earthquake; illustrated by Jeremy Tugeau. Millbrook Press 2010 48p il (History speaks: picture books plus reader's theater) lib bdg $27.93

Grades: 2 3 4   **979.4**

1. Earthquakes 2. Readers' theater 3. San Francisco (Calif.) -- History

ISBN 978-0-8225-9031-6 lib bdg; 0-8225-9031-X lib bdg

LC 2009049597

Ten-year-old Lizzie Newton, having helped take her grandmother to the hospital after the 1906 San Francisco earthquake, sets off on her own to find her parents. Includes a readers' theater script and performance tips.

This "title begins with a well-illustrated narrative and concludes with a tip sheet for performing Reader's Theater as well as a list of characters, a script, and a pronunciation guide. . . . [This book will] make history come alive in a unique and interesting way." Libr Media Connect

Includes bibliographical references

La Bella, Laura

California; past and present. Rosen Central 2010 48p il map (The United States: past and present) lib bdg $26.50; pa $11.50

Grades: 3 4 5 6   **979.4**

1. California

ISBN 978-1-4358-5290-7 lib bdg; 1-4358-5290-7 lib bdg; 978-1-4358-5578-6 pa; 1-4358-5578-7 pa

LC 2008-55151

Presents the history, geography, government, economy, and people of California, as well as general facts about the state.

Includes glossary and bibliographical references

Olson, Tod

★ **How** to get rich in the California Gold Rush; an adventurer's guide to the fabulous riches discovered in 1848 . . . illustrations by Scott Allred; afterword by Marc Aronson. National Geographic 2008 47p il map (How to get rich) $16.95; lib bdg $25.90

Grades: 4 5 6 7   **979.4**

1. Gold mines and mining 2. California -- Gold discoveries 3. Prospecting 4. Frontier and pioneer life -- California 5. California -- History

ISBN 1-4263-0315-7; 1-4263-0316-5 lib bdg; 978-1-4263-0315-9; 978-1-4263-0316-6 lib bdg

LC 2008-19601

This is a personal account of the California Gold Rush from the point-of-view of the fictitious character Thomas Hartley. "Grades four to seven." (Bull Cent Child Books)

This "deftly blends story with history to not only give readers an understanding of a gold rush but also to provide a lighthearted and engaging entry point into frontier life. . . . Period lithographs are reproduced alongside original illustrations. . . . A ledger on each page tracks the young men's finances in a genuinely exciting way, adding a sly ele-

ment of math to this well-conceived and compulsively appealing book."
Booklist

Includes bibliographical references

Orr, Tamra B.

California; by Tamra B. Orr. Revised edition Children's Press 2014 144 p. ill. (chiefly col.), col. maps $40

Grades: 4 5 6 7   **979.4**

1. California

ISBN 9780531248775; 0531248771

"Located along the coast of the Pacific Ocean, California is famed for its sunny weather, beaches, and incredible cities. Readers will trace the history of this remarkable state from its earliest settlement to its latest developments. They will also dive into the local culture, see the state's many fascinating sights, and learn about its economy." (Publisher's note)

Includes bibliographical references (page 138) and index

Rosenstock, Barb

The **camping** trip that changed America; Theodore Roosevelt, John Muir, and our national parks. by Barbara Rosenstock; illustrated by Mordicai Gerstein. Dial Books for Young Readers 2012 32 p. col. ill. (hardcover) $16.99

Grades: 1 2 3 4   **979.4**

1. Picture books for children 2. National parks and reserves -- United States 3. Yosemite National Park (Calif.) -- History 4. Environmentalism -- United States -- History 5. National parks and reserves -- United States -- History

ISBN 0803737106; 9780803737105

LC 2011021927

This children's picture book, by Barb Rosenstock and illustrated by Mordicai Gerstein, "captures the majestic redwoods of Yosemite in this little-known but important story from our nation's history. In 1903, President Theodore Roosevelt joined naturalist John Muir on a trip to Yosemite. Camping by themselves in the uncharted woods, the two men saw sights and held discussions that would ultimately lead to the establishment of our National Parks." (Publisher's note)

"Brimming with fun and fact, this book recounts a 1903 camping trip in which Roosevelt asked Muir to convince him that conservation mattered. Soon after the trip, Roosevelt enacted legislation that marked the nascency of America's national park system. Ink and watercolor illustrations, with a studied messiness, match the folksy tone of the text. " SLJ

Includes bibliographical references.

Ryan, Pam Munoz

Our California; by Pam Munoz Ryan; illustrated by Rafael Lopez. Charlesbridge 2008 un il $17.95; pa $7.95

Grades: PreK K 1 2   **979.4**

1. California

ISBN 978-1-58089-116-5; 978-1-58089-117-2 pa

"A whirlwind loop tour whisks readers through the Golden State, starting with the beaches of San Diego, heading up to L.A. and beyond to Gold Country, then swinging down through Yosemite (depicted in a stunning nighttime vertical spread) and Death Valley before ending up poolside at Palm Springs. . . . López's illustrations, paintings rendered on wood and sometimes distressed, remain fresh and surprising as he finds ways to express wonder and affection. . . . This title is virtually certain to inspire California dreamin' in readers of all ages." Publ Wkly

Walker, Paul Robert

Gold rush and riches. Kingfisher 2011 32p il map (All about America)

Grades: 3 4 5 6   **979.4**

1. California -- History 2. California -- Gold discoveries 3.

Frontier and pioneer life -- California

ISBN 0-7534-6512-4 pa; 0-7534-6584-1; 978-0-7534-6512-7 pa; 978-0-7534-6584-4

This book looks at California and its neighboring states starting in 1848, with the discovery of gold and other precious metals.

This "visually appealing [title] effectively [combines] paintings, engravings, primary documents, and photographs with cartoon illustrations. The eye-catching [layout includes] different font sizes, bold type, and text boxes to highlight different pieces of information. The content is interesting and pithy." SLJ

Includes glossary and bibliographical references

Yep, Laurence, 1948-

The **lost** garden; Laurence Yep. 1st Beech Tree ed. Beech Tree Books 1996 xi, 116 p.p ill. (paperback) $6.99

Grades: 5 6 7 8   **979.4**

1. Authors 2. Novelists 3. College teachers 4. Authors, American 5. Children's authors 6. Young adult authors 7. Chinese Americans -- Biography

ISBN 9780688137014 reprint; 0688137016

LC 95053801

First published 1991 by Julian Messner

The author describes how he grew up as a Chinese American in San Francisco and how he came to use his writing to celebrate his family and his ethnic heritage

"The writing is warm, wry, and humorous. . . . The Lost Garden will be welcomed as a literary autobiography for children and, more, a thoughtful probing into what it means to be an American." SLJ

Zuehlke, Jeffrey

The **Golden** Gate Bridge. Lerner Publications 2010 32p il map (Lightning bolt books. Famous places) lib bdg $25.26

Grades: 2 3 4   **979.4**

1. Golden Gate Bridge (San Francisco, Calif.)

ISBN 978-0-8225-9407-9; 0-8225-9407-2

LC 2008-30641

Describes the Golden Gate Bridge that connects Marin County to the city of San Francisco, including information about its history, design, and construction.

This book uses "high-quality photos, illustrations, maps, and diagrams. . . . Readers will enjoy learning about [the Golden Gate Bridge] . . . and the challenges of building and maintaining large structures." SLJ

Includes glossary and bibliographical references

979.5   Oregon

Kent, Deborah, 1948-

Oregon; by Deborah Kent. Revised edition Children's Press, an imprint of Scholastic Inc. 2014 144 p. illustrations, maps (library binding : alk. paper) $40

Grades: 4 5 6 7   **979.5**

1. Oregon 2. United States -- History

ISBN 0531282880; 9780531282885

LC 2013044361

"From the peak of Mount Hood to the depths of Crater Lake, Oregon is home to some of the United States' most beautiful outdoor areas. Readers will take a tour of the state as they learn about its history, geography, and wildlife. They will also learn what life is like for the people of Oregon, whether they live in a big city such as Portland or a rural farm east of the Cascade Range." (Publisher's note)

Includes bibliographical references (pages 133-137) and index

Roza, Greg

Oregon; past and present. Rosen Central 2010 48p il map (The United States: past and present) lib bdg $26.50; pa $11.75

Grades: 3 4 5 6   **979.5**

1. Oregon

ISBN 978-1-4358-3515-3 lib bdg; 1-4358-3515-8 lib bdg; 978-1-4358-8480-9 pa; 1-4358-8480-9 pa

LC 2009016193

Presents the history, geography, government, economy, and people of Oregon, as well as general facts about the state.

Includes bibliographical references

979.6   Idaho

Kent, Deborah, 1948-

Idaho; by Deborah Kent. Revised edition Children's Press, an Imprint of Scholastic Inc. 2015 144 p. col. ill., col. maps $40

Grades: 4 5 6 7   **979.6**

1. Idaho 2. Geography

ISBN 9780531282786; 0531282783

LC 2013044327

"As the country's leading potato provider, Idaho produces around 12 billion pounds of spuds every year. Readers will travel through Idaho's remarkable farms, as well as its cities, forests, and mountains, as they explore the state's rich history. They will also get a taste of modern Idaho culture as they learn about the state's traditions, cuisine, and local heroes." (Publisher's note

Includes bibliographical references (page 138) and index

Stanley, John

Idaho; past and present. Rosen Central 2011 48p il map (The United States: past and present) lib bdg $26.50; pa $11.75

Grades: 3 4 5 6   **979.6**

1. Idaho

ISBN 978-1-4358-9480-8 lib bdg; 1-4358-9480-4 lib bdg; 978-1-4358-9507-2 pa; 1-4358-9507-X pa

LC 2009049391

Presents the history, geography, government, economy, and people of Idaho, as well as general facts about the state.

Includes glossary and bibliographical references

Stefoff, Rebecca

Idaho; by Rebecca Stefoff. 2nd ed.; Marshall Cavendish Benchmark 2008 144p il map (Celebrate the states) lib bdg $39.93

Grades: 4 5 6 7   **979.6**

1. Idaho

ISBN 978-0-7614-3003-2; 0-7614-3003-2

LC 2007-29496

First published 2000

"Provides comprehensive information on the geography, history, wildlife, governmental structure, economy, cultural diversity, peoples, religion, and landmarks of Idaho." Publisher's note

Includes bibliographical references

979.7   Washington

Harmon, Dan

Washington; past and present. [by] Daniel E. Harmon. Rosen Central 2010 48p il map (The United States: past and present) lib bdg $26.50; pa $11.50

Grades: 3 4 5 6   **979.7**

1. Washington (State)

ISBN 978-1-4358-5295-2 lib bdg; 1-4358-5295-8 lib bdg; 978-1-4358-5588-5 pa; 1-4358-5588-4 pa

LC 2008-54236

Presents the history, geography, government, economy, and people of Washington, as well as general facts about the state.

Includes glossary and bibliographical references

Jankowski, Susan

Olympic National Park; adventure, explore, discover. [by] Susan Jankowski. MyReportLinks.com Books 2009 128p il map (America's national parks) lib bdg $33.27

Grades: 5 6 7 8   **979.7**

1. Olympic National Park (Wash.) 2. National parks and reserves -- United States

ISBN 978-1-59845-092-7 lib bdg; 1-59845-092-1 lib bdg

LC 2007-17341

This "informative, well-written book contains a physical description of the park; a summary of its history including the Native peoples of the area; activities such as hiking trails, campsites, and visitor centers; information about the park's plants, animals, and weather; full-color photographs; and numerous approved links available through the publisher's Web page. . . . Thorough, useful, and appealing, this . . . is a great update for collections." SLJ

Includes glossary and bibliographical references

Otfinoski, Steven

Washington; [by] Steven Otfinoski and Tea Benduhn. 2nd ed.; Marshall Cavendish Benchmark 2010 90p il map (It's my state!) lib bdg $31.93

Grades: 3 4 5   **979.7**

1. Washington (State)

ISBN 978-1-6087-0061-5; 1-6087-0061-5

LC 2010003935

First published 2003

Surveys the history, geography, economy, and people of the state of Washington.

Stefoff, Rebecca

Washington; [by] Rebecca Stefoff. 2nd ed.; Marshall Cavendish Benchmark 2008 144p il map (Celebrate the states) lib bdg $39.93

Grades: 4 5 6 7   **979.7**

1. Washington (State)

ISBN 978-0-7614-2561-8; 0-7614-2561-6

LC 2006-32436

First published 1999

"Provides comprehensive information on the geography, history, wildlife, governmental structure, economy, cultural diversity, peoples, religion, and landmarks of Washington." Publisher's note

Includes bibliographical references

979.8   Alaska

Mattern, Joanne

Alaska; past and present. Rosen Central 2011 48p il map (The United States: past and present) lib bdg $26.50; pa $11.75

Grades: 3 4 5 6   **979.8**

1. Alaska

ISBN 978-1-4358-9475-4 lib bdg; 1-4358-9475-8 lib bdg; 978-1-4358-9503-4 pa; 1-4358-9503-7 pa

LC 2009046615

This describes the history, culture, geography and people of Alaska.
Includes bibliographical references

Miller, Debbie S.
Big Alaska; journey across America's most amazing state. illustrations by Jon Van Zyle. Walker 2006 un il map $17.95; lib bdg $18.85
Grades: 2 3 4 **979.8**
1. Alaska
ISBN 978-0-8027-8069-0; 0-8027-8069-5; 978-0-8027-8070-6 lib bdg; 0-8027-8070-9 lib bdg

LC 2005-24086

"Miller's text follows a bald eagle's flight across Alaska, beginning with Admiralty Island and circling back to the Chilkat Bald Eagle Preserve. . . . Zyle's acrylic paintings perfectly suit the grandeur of the subject. . . . Back matter includes Alaska Facts, State Symbols, Climate Records, and Alaska's Special Places, which has additional information on the locations described in the text. . . . The book . . . is a special treasure both for readers already interested in the subject and newcomers." SLJ
Includes bibliographical references

Orr, Tamra B.
Alaska; by Tamra B. Orr. Children's Press 2008 144p il map (America the beautiful, third series) lib bdg $38
Grades: 4 5 6 7 **979.8**
1. Alaska
ISBN 978-0-531-18569-8; 0-531-18569-9

LC 2007-22220

Describes the history, geography, ecology, people, economy, cities, and sights of the state of Alaska.
Includes glossary and bibliographical references

Alaska; Tamra B. Orr. Revised edition Children's Press 2014 144 p. color illustrations (library binding) $40
Grades: 4 5 6 7 **979.8**
1. Alaska
ISBN 0531248763; 9780531248768

LC 2013030722

"Far to the north of the rest of the country, Alaska became the union's 49th state in 1959. Readers will trace the history of this remarkable state from its earliest settlement to its latest developments. They will also dive into the local culture, see the state's many fascinating sights, and learn about its economy." (Publisher's note)
Includes bibliographical references and index

980   History of South America

Foster, Karen
Atlas of South America. Picture Window books 2008 32p il map (Picture Window Books world atlases) lib bdg $27.93
Grades: 2 3 4 **980**
1. South America
ISBN 978-1-4048-3887-1 lib bdg; 1-4048-3887-2 lib bdg
This introduction to the geography of South America offers maps and information about countries, landforms, bodies of water, climate, plants, animals, population, people and customs, places of interest, industries, transportation, and Lake Titicaca.
Includes glossary

Gorrell, Gena K.
★ **In** the land of the jaguar; South America and its people. illustrated by Andrej Krystoforski. Tundra Books 2007 149p il $22.95

Grades: 5 6 7 8 9 **980**
1. South America
ISBN 978-0-88776-756-2
"This beautifully designed volume, with an engaging narrative, combines a highly informative overview of the continent with country-by-country detail. . . . The spacious design includes big maps, clear type on thick paper, and small, beautiful, fully captioned illustrations." Booklist

981   Brazil

Berkenkamp, Lauri
Discover the Amazon; the world's largest rainforest. illustrated by Blair Shedd. Nomad Press 2008 90p il map pa $16.95
Grades: 4 5 6 7 **981**
1. Amazon River valley
ISBN 978-1-9346702-7-9 pa; 1-9346702-7-8 pa
"Berkenkamp's introduction to the [Amazon] river basin incorporates maps, drawings, and photos in various shades of green and brown on recycled paper. . . . The conversational style provides a 'you are there' feeling, conveying information and anecdotes while stressing outdoor survival skills. . . . Even readers who never travel to Amazonia will appreciate the region's complexity and significance after perusing this book." SLJ

Deckker, Zilah
★ **Brazil**; [by] Zilah Deckker; David Robinson and Joao Cezar de Castro Rocha, consultants. National Geographic 2008 64p il (Countries of the world) lib bdg $27.90
Grades: 4 5 6 7 **981**
1. Brazil
ISBN 978-1-4263-0298-5 lib bdg; 1-4263-0298-3 lib bdg
This describes the geography, nature, history, people and culture, government, and economy of Brazil.
Includes glossary and bibliographical references

Heinrichs, Ann
★ **Brazil**; by Ann Heinrichs. Children's Press, an imprint of Scholastic Inc. 2013 144 p. illustrations, color maps (library binding) $40
Grades: 5 6 7 8 **981**
1. Brazil
ISBN 0531236757; 9780531236758

LC 2013000089

This book, by Ann Heinrichs, focuses on Brazil. The "country's culture, history, and geography are explored in detail, allowing readers a chance to see how people live. . . . Sidebars highlight especially interesting people, places, and events . . . [and] recipes give readers the opportunity to experience foreign cuisine first-hand." (Publisher's note)
"Many students turn to the Internet for writing reports, but for reliably accurate, attractively presented and well-calibrated information, the long-standing Enchantment of the World series remains a superior choice...Each volume in this reliable series includes extensive back matter with a detailed index." Booklist
Includes bibliographical references (page 134), filmography (page 134), and index.

982   Argentina

Lourie, Peter
Tierra del Fuego; a journey to the end of the earth. Boyds Mills Press 2002 47p il map $19.95

Grades: 4 5 6 7 **982**

1. Tierra del Fuego (Argentina and Chile)
ISBN 1-56397-973-X

LC 2001-96395

The author describes his travels in Tierra del Fuego and provides historical background on the area

"Lourie's smooth, first-person narrative mixes history, adventure, and personal insights, while glorious photographs of the remarkable land at the southernmost point of the world enhance his travelogue. . . . Highly informative for reports, this fascinating account will also appeal to young readers with wanderlust." SLJ

983 Chile

Burgan, Michael

Chile; by Michael Burgan. Children's Press, an imprint of Scholastic Inc. 2017 144 p. color ill., color maps (library binding) $40
Grades: 5 6 7 8 **983**
1. Chile
ISBN 0531218856; 9780531218853

LC 2015048543

This book on Chile, by Michael Burgan, part of the Enchantment of the World series, "includes maps, timelines, fast facts, charts, vivid four-color photographs, and a to find out more section. . . . Straightforward, unbiased, and probing prose will provoke readers to think like historians; engaging text will take readers on a virtual tour of the country." (Publisher's note)

"With stunning, high-quality photos that reflect the richness of cultures around the globe, the Enchantment of the World series earns its name." Booklist

Includes bibliographical references and index

Rau, Dana Meachen

Chile. Marshall Cavendish Benchmark 2007 48p il map (Discovering cultures) lib bdg $28.50
Grades: 2 3 4 **983**
1. Chile
ISBN 978-0-7614-1988-4 lib bdg; 0-7614-1988-8 lib bdg
An introduction to the geography, history, people, and culture of Chile

Includes glossary and bibliographical references

984 Bolivia

Pateman, Robert

Bolivia; [by] Robert Pateman & Marcus Cramer. 2nd ed.; Marshall Cavendish Benchmark 2006 144p il map (Cultures of the world) lib bdg $42.79
Grades: 5 6 7 8 **984**
1. Bolivia
ISBN 978-0-7614-2066-8 lib bdg; 0-7614-2066-5 lib bdg

LC 2006002425

First published 1995

This is "well organized, informative, and entertaining. . . . Excellent-quality full-color photographs and reproductions show the people, landforms, buildings, and everyday activities." SLJ

Includes bibliographical references

985 Peru

Calvert, Patricia

★ The **ancient** Inca; written by Patricia Calvert. Franklin Watts 2004 128p il (People of the ancient world) lib bdg $30.50; pa $9.95
Grades: 5 6 7 8 **985**
1. Incas
ISBN 0-531-12358-8 lib bdg; 0-531-16740-2 pa

LC 2004-1956

This "well-written, attractive [title has] extensive collections of quality color photographs of ruins and artifacts." SLJ

Includes bibliographical references

Gruber, Beth

★ **Ancient** Inca; archaeology unlocks the secrets of the Inca's past. by Beth Gruber; Johan Reinhard, consultant. National Geographic 2007 64p il map (National Geographic investigates) $17.95; lib bdg $27.90
Grades: 5 6 7 8 **985**
1. Incas 2. Peru -- Antiquities 3. Excavations (Archeology) -- Peru
ISBN 978-0-7922-7827-6; 978-0-7922-7873-3 lib bdg

LC 2006032104

This describes how archeologists have found out about ancient Incan civilization.

This offers "the beautiful photography and illustrations characteristic of the National Geographic Society, [a] well-written [text] and sidebars, and information on recent archaeological finds." SLJ

Includes bibliographical references

Krebs, Laurie

Up and down the Andes; a Peruvian festival tale. [by] Laurie Krebs, Aurelia Fronty. Barefoot Books 2008 un il $16.99
Grades: K 1 2 3 **985**
1. Inti Raymi Festival 2. Andes 3. Festivals -- Peru 4. Native Americans -- Peru 5. Peru -- Social life and customs
ISBN 978-1-84686-203-8; 1-84686-203-5

LC 2008020722

This is a "picture book about the Peruvian Inti Raymi Festival as children travel from all over southern Peru, by bus, train, boat, mule, and truck, to the city of Cusco to celebrate with feasting and fun in their traditional costumes. The simply rhyming text and the bright, clear, beautiful unframed acrylic paintings express a strong sense of the rich traditions that are still part of contemporary life." Booklist

Lewin, Ted

★ **Lost** city; the discovery of Machu Picchu. Philomel Bks. 2003 un il $16.99
Grades: 2 3 4 **985**
1. Machu Picchu (Peru)
ISBN 0-399-23302-4

LC 2002-4461

In 1911, Yale professor Hiram Bingham discovers a lost Incan city with the help of a young Peruvian boy

"The language is graceful and uncomplicated, weaving in bits of background history along the way. . . . Full-page watercolors spreads of the stunning vistas and thick forests contrast with dark, intimate views of Bingham inside homes and walking along walled city streets. . . . An exciting, eye-catching story." Booklist

Newman, Sandra

The **Inca** empire. Children's Press 2009 48p il map (True book) lib bdg $26; pa $6.95

Grades: 3 4 5   **985**

1. Incas

ISBN 978-0-531-25228-4 lib bdg; 0-531-25228-0 lib bdg; 978-0-531-24109-7 pa; 0-531-24109-2 pa

LC 2009000293

In this book the Inca civilization is "outlined for young readers with care and precision. . . . Loaded with access points such as captions, pull-outs, a time line, and a map, and with better-than-usual reproductions of well-chosen primary sources and art, the [book sports] a bright, peppy design. . . . [This book is] rigorous in distinguishing fact from theory, and conscientious about presenting competing theories where they exist." SLJ

986.1   Colombia

Croy, Anita

★ **Colombia**; [by] Anita Croy; Ulrich Oslender and Mauricio Pardo, consultants. National Geographic 2008 64p il map (Countries of the world) lib bdg $27.90

Grades: 4 5 6 7   **986.1**

1. Colombia

ISBN 978-1-4263-0257-2 lib bdg; 1-4263-0257-6 lib bdg

This describes the geography, nature, history, people and culture, government, and economy of Colombia

Includes glossary and bibliographical references

Yomtov, Nel

★ **Colombia**; by Nel Yomtov. Children's Press, an imprint of Scholastic Inc. 2014 144 p. illustrations, color maps (library binding) $40

Grades: 5 6 7 8   **986.1**

1. Colombia

ISBN 0531220133; 9780531220139

LC 2013026060

This book, by Nel Yomtov, focuses on Colombia. The "country's culture, history, and geography are explored in detail, allowing readers a chance to see how people live in faraway nations. . . . Sidebars highlight especially interesting people, places, and events . . . [and] easy recipes give readers the opportunity to experience foreign cuisine first-hand." (Publisher's note)

Includes bibliographical references and index

986.6   Ecuador

Ecuador; Third Edition Marshall Cavendish Benchmark 2016 144p chiefly color illustrations lib bdg $47.07; (ebook) $47.07

Grades: 5 6 7 8   **986.6**

1. Ecuador

ISBN 9781502617019; 9781502617026

LC 2005022671

"Situated in South America very close to the Equator, Ecuador is a country known for its vibrant culture and ecotourism. This book discusses the history of Ecuador, what its people and cities are like, and examines how it became the country it is today" (Publisher's Note)

Includes bibliographical references (pages 141-142) and index.

Henzel, Cynthia Kennedy

Galapagos Islands. ABDO Pub. Co. 2011 32p il (Troubled treasures: world heritage sites) $25.65

Grades: 3 4 5   **986.6**

1. Galapagos Islands

ISBN 978-1-61613-563-8; 1-61613-563-8

LC 2010021311

This "book describes in general terms [the Galapagos Islands'] . . . creation, distinctive features, and history, as well as threats to its continued existence and both current and past restoration initiatives. Revealing color photos taken from different heights and angles are supplemented by maps and by graphic reconstructions. . . . Henzel's distinctive approach gives this [book] unusual value for both assignment and general reading." SLJ

Includes glossary

Kras, Sara Louise

The **Galapagos** Islands; [by] Sara Louise Kras. Marshall Cavendish Benchmark 2008 96p il map (Nature's wonders) lib bdg $35.64

Grades: 5 6 7 8   **986.6**

1. Galapagos Islands

ISBN 978-0-7614-2856-5 lib bdg; 0-7614-2856-9 lib bdg

LC 2007020416

"Provides comprehensive information on the geography, history, wildlife, peoples, and environmental issues of the Galapagos Islands." Publisher's note

Includes glossary and bibliographical references

988.1   Guyana

Jermyn, Leslie

Guyana; by Leslie Jermyn and Winnie Wong. Marshall Cavendish Benchmark 2010 144 p. col. ill., col. maps (library) $47.07

Grades: 5 6 7 8   **988.1**

1. Guyana

ISBN 1608700232; 9781608700233

LC 2010000724

This book by Leslie Jermyn is part of the Cultures of the World series and looks at the South American nation of Guyana. "Touching upon everything from its history to religion to architecture, this book . . . highlights the country's rich diversity and unique qualities. With a population that includes many different ethnic groups, the author . . . examines the contributions of each to Guyana's development and to its present culture." (Children's Literature)

Includes bibliographical references (p.142) and index.

989.2   Paraguay

Jermyn, Leslie

Paraguay; [by] Leslie Jermyn and Yong Jui Lin. 2nd ed.; Marshall Cavendish Benchmark 2010 144p il map (Cultures of the world) lib bdg $42.79

Grades: 5 6 7 8   **989.2**

1. Paraguay

ISBN 978-0-7614-4858-7 lib bdg; 0-7614-4858-6 lib bdg

LC 2009046495

First published 2000

This offers information on the geography, history, wildlife, governmental structure, economy, cultural diversity, peoples, religion, and culture of Paraguay

Includes glossary and bibliographical references

989.5 Uruguay

Jermyn, Leslie

Uruguay; by Leslie Jermyn and Winnie Wong. 2nd ed.; Marshall Cavendish Benchmark 2009 144p il map (Cultures of the world) lib bdg $42.79

Grades: 5 6 7 8 **989.5**

1. Uruguay

ISBN 978-0-7614-4482-4 lib bdg; 0-7614-4482-3 lib bdg

LC 2009007127

First published 1999

Provides information on the geography, history, wildlife, governmental structure, economy, cultural diversity, peoples, religion, and culture of Uruguay

Includes glossary and bibliographical references

993 New Zealand

Jackson, Barbara

★ New Zealand; [by] Barbara Jackson; Vaughan Wood and Simon Milne, consultants. National Geographic 2008 64p il map (Countries of the world) lib bdg $27.90

Grades: 4 5 6 7 **993**

1. New Zealand

ISBN 978-1-4263-0301-2 lib bdg; 1-4263-0301-7 lib bdg

This describes the geography, nature, history, people and culture, government, and economy of New Zealand.

Smelt, Roselynn

New Zealand; by Roselynn Smelt. 2nd ed.; Marshall Cavendish Benchmark 2009 128p il map (Cultures of the world) lib bdg $42.79

Grades: 5 6 7 8 **993**

1. New Zealand

ISBN 978-0-7614-3415-3 lib bdg; 0-7614-3415-1 lib bdg

LC 2008028792

First published 1998

"Provides comprehensive information on the geography, history, wildlife, governmental structure, economy, cultural diversity, peoples, religion, and culture of New Zealand." Publisher's note

Includes glossary and bibliographical references

994 Australia

Arnold, Caroline

★ Uluru, Australia's Aboriginal heart; photographs by Arthur Arnold. Clarion Books 2003 64p il $16

Grades: 5 6 7 8 **994**

1. Aboriginal Australians 2. Australia 3. Uluru-Kata Tjuta National Park (Australia)

ISBN 0-618-18181-4

LC 2002-15542

Describes Uluru, formerly known as Ayers Rock, in Australia's Uluru-Kata Tjuta National Park, its plant and animal life, and the country's Aboriginal people for whom the site is sacred

"The book's greatest accomplishment . . . is to give readers a sense of the ongoing spiritual importance of Uluru to the Anangu, who have lived around it for 10,000 years. Clear, colorful photos of Uluru and its surroundings appear on nearly every page, illustrating the text with beauty and finesse." Booklist

Foster, Karen

Atlas of Australia. Picture Window Books 2008 32p il map (Picture Window Books world atlases) lib bdg $27.93

Grades: 2 3 4 **994**

1. Australia

ISBN 978-1-4048-3881-9 lib bdg; 1-4048-3881-3 lib bdg

This introduction to the geography of Australia offers maps and information about landforms, bodies of water, climate, plants, animals, population, people and customs, places of interest, industries, transportation, and the Great Barrier Reef.

This book offers "well-organized, easy-to-access information. . . . Small photographs or colorful text boxes draw readers' attention to points of interest or fun facts. Maps and legends are simple, yet disseminate information clearly." SLJ

Includes glossary

Rau, Dana Meachen

Australia. Sea-to-Sea Publications 2009 32p il map (Facts about countries) lib bdg $28.50

Grades: 3 4 5 **994**

1. Australia

ISBN 978-1-59771-112-8 lib bdg; 1-59771-112-8 lib bdg

LC 2008004630

Describes the geography, history, industries, education, government, and cultures of Australia

"The attractive layout includes color photographs and charts of current statistics as well as maps illustrating main farming regions, natural resources, or the literacy rates of girls and boys. The [text is] clear and succinct." SLJ

Includes glossary

Turner, Kate

★ Australia; [by] Kate Turner; Elaine Stratford and Joseph Powell, consultants. National Geographic 2007 64p il map (Countries of the world) lib bdg $27.90

Grades: 4 5 6 7 **994**

1. Australia

ISBN 978-1-4263-0055-4

Describes the geography, nature, history, people and culture, government and economy of Australia

This "appealing [title has] wonderful photographs and maps. . . . [This book is a] reliable [source] for country research, and the interesting current material hold browsing potential as well." SLJ

Includes glossary and bibliographical references

995.3 Papua New Guinea

Gascoigne, Ingrid

Papua New Guinea; [by] Ingrid Gascoigne. 2nd ed.; Marshall Cavendish Benchmark 2009 144p il map (Cultures of the world) lib bdg $42.79

Grades: 5 6 7 8 **995.3**

1. Papua New Guinea

ISBN 978-0-7614-3416-0 lib bdg; 0-7614-3416-X lib bdg

LC 2008028794

First published 1998

"Provides comprehensive information on the geography, history, wildlife, governmental structure, economy, cultural diversity, peoples, religion, and culture of Papua New Guinea." Publisher's note

Includes glossary and bibliographical references

996 Polynesia and other Pacific Ocean islands

NgCheong-Lum, Roseline, 1962-
Tahiti; [by] Roseline NgCheong-Lum. 2nd ed.; Marshall Cavendish Benchmark 2008 144p il map (Cultures of the world) lib bdg $42.79
Grades: 5 6 7 8 **996**
1. Tahiti (French Polynesia)
ISBN 978-0-7614-2089-7

LC 2007014901

"Provides comprehensive information on the geography, history, wildlife, governmental structure, economy, cultural diversity, peoples, religion, and culture of Tahiti." Publisher's note
Includes glossary and bibliographical references

996.9 Hawaii and neighboring north central Pacific Ocean islands

Feeney, Stephanie
Sun and rain; exploring seasons in Hawaii. University of Hawaii Press 2008 un il $13.95
Grades: K 1 2 3 **996.9**
1. Rain 2. Seasons 3. Sun 4. Hawaii
ISBN 978-0-8248-3088-5; 0-8248-3088-1

LC 2008272547

"Readers learn that Hawaii has only two seasons: wet and dry. Easy-to-read text and large, inviting photographs show the changing seasons and explain how humans, animals, and plants are affected. . . . Back matter includes additional information for adults." Horn Book Guide

Kent, Deborah
Hawai'i; by Deborah Kent. Revised edition Children's Press 2014 144 p. col ill, col maps $40
Grades: 4 5 6 7 **996.9**
1. Hawaii 2. United States -- Geography
ISBN 0531248828; 9780531248829
Includes bibliographical references (page 138) and index

"Added to the union in August 1959, Hawaii is the youngest member of the United States. Readers will trace the history of this remarkable state from its earliest settlement to its latest developments. They will also dive into the local culture, see the state's many fascinating sights, and learn about its economy." (Publisher's note)

Mattern, Joanne
Hawaii; past and present. Rosen Central 2011 48p il map (The United States: past and present) lib bdg $26.50; pa $11.75
Grades: 3 4 5 6 **996.9**
1. Hawaii
ISBN 978-1-4358-9479-2 lib bdg; 1-4358-9479-0 lib bdg; 978-1-4358-9506-5 pa; 1-4358-9506-1 pa

LC 2009050544

Presents the history, geography, government, economy, and people of Hawaii, as well as general facts about the state.
Includes glossary and bibliographical references

998 Arctic islands and Antarctica

Bledsoe, Lucy Jane
★ **How** to survive in Antarctica; written and photographed by Lucy Jane Bledsoe. Holiday House 2006 101p il map $16.95

Grades: 5 6 7 8 **998**
1. Antarctica
ISBN 0-8234-1890-1

LC 2004-60639

"Bledsoe, who made three trips to study Antarctica, bases her informal, chatty narrative on her thrilling adventure, bringing close the amazing science and geography as well as the gritty facts of human survival in the frigid environment. . . . Bledsoe's own black-and-white photos . . . will grab students across the curriculum." Booklist
Includes glossary

Foster, Karen
Atlas of the Poles and Oceans. Picture Window Books 2008 32p il map (Picture Window Books world atlases) lib bdg $27.93
Grades: 2 3 4 **998**
1. Ocean 2. Antarctica 3. Arctic regions
ISBN 978-1-4048-3886-4 lib bdg; 1-4048-3886-4 lib bdg
This introduction to the geography of the Arctic, Antarctic, and the oceans offers maps and information about plants, animals, people, and protecting the environment.
Includes glossary

Goodman, Susan
★ **Life** on the ice; [by] Susan E. Goodman; with photographs by Michael J. Doolittle. Millbrook Press 2006 32p il lib bdg $22.60
Grades: 3 4 5 **998**
1. Arctic regions 2. Polar regions
ISBN 978-0-7613-2775-2 lib bdg; 0-7613-2775-4 lib bdg

LC 2005-06141

This book is "about the ice caps of both the North and South Poles. [Index.] Grades five to six." (Sci Books Films)
"This fully illustrated book introduces a few aspects of the Earth's polar regions. Topics presented include the difficulties of flying to and landing at the poles, scientific research done at each pole, and the challenge of human survival in the extreme cold." Booklist

Lourie, Peter
Arctic thaw; the people of the whale in a changing climate. Boyds Mills Press 2007 47p il map $17.95
Grades: 5 6 7 8 **998**
1. Inupiat 2. Whaling 3. Human ecology 4. Alaska 5. Greenhouse effect
ISBN 978-1-59078-436-5; 1-59078-436-7

LC 2006-20045

"A somewhat sobering, yet upbeat examination of the probable effects of global warming on the culture of the Iñupiaq whale hunters of Alaska's North Slope. . . . [Lourie's] lively, straightforward text describes the mixture of traditional and modern ways of the present-day Iñupiaq, as well as the work of [Paul] Shepson and his team to record weather and climate changes and to predict what effect they will have locally and globally." SLJ
Includes bibliographical references

Markle, Sandra
Animals Robert Scott saw; an adventure in Antarctica. Chronicle Books 2008 45p il (Explorers) $16.99
Grades: 2 3 4 5 **998**
1. Explorers 2. Animals -- Antarctica 3. Antarctica -- Exploration
ISBN 978-0-8118-4918-0; 0-8118-4918-X

LC 2006-20920

"Well illustrated with acrylic paintings and archival photos, this volume . . . traces the two Antarctic expeditions of English explorer Robert Falcon Scott, who reached the South Pole with his companions in 1912, 35 days after Amundsen's Norwegian expedition. The story may be Scott's, but the focus continually turns to animals. . . . Children fascinated by both explorers and animals are the natural audience for this." Booklist

Includes glossary and bibliographical references

Thompson, Gare

Roald Amundsen and Robert Scott race to the South Pole; by Gare Thompson. National Geographic 2007 48p il (National Geographic history chapters) lib bdg $17.90

Grades: 2 3 4   **998**

1. Explorers 2. South Pole 3. Antarctica -- Exploration
ISBN 978-1-4263-0187-2

LC 2007007898

This "presents the dramatic, tragic story of the South Pole's dueling explorers. . . . Crisp, informatively captioned photographs, some presumably taken by the doomed men, lend immediacy to the facts." Booklist

Wade, Rosalyn

Polar worlds. Simon & Schuster Books for Young Readers 2011 64p il (Insiders) $16.99

Grades: 4 5 6 7   **998**

1. Antarctica 2. Arctic regions
ISBN 978-1-4424-3275-8; 1-4424-3275-6

This "takes a look at the nether regions of the globe in this browser-friendly resource. . . . 'Introducing' opens with a geographic look at the Arctic and Antarctic regions, then moves on to the related topics of icebergs, plant and animal life, exploration, survival measures, and environmental threats. The 'In Focus' section zeroes in on 12 specific animals found in polar regions. . . . Each spread is dominated by a sharply rendered, often dramatic digital illustration. . . . A fine introduction to the world's deep freezers." Booklist

E EASY BOOKS

Ackerman, Karen

Song and dance man; illustrated by Stephen Gammell. Knopf 1988 un il lib bdg $17.99; pa $6.99

Grades: K 1 2 3   **E**

1. Entertainers -- Fiction 2. Grandfathers -- Fiction
ISBN 0-394-99330-6 lib bdg; 0-679-81995-9 pa

LC 87-3200

Awarded the Caldecott Medal, 1989

The illustrator "captures all the story's inherent joie de vivre with color pencil renderings that fairly leap off the pages." Booklist

Ada, Alma Flor, 1938-

I love Saturdays y domingos; by Alma Flor Ada; illustrated by Elivia. 1st ed; Atheneum Books for Young Readers 1998 32 p. $18.99

Grades: PreK K 1 2   **E**

1. Family life 2. Grandparent-grandchild relationship 3. Grandparents -- Fiction 4. Mexican Americans -- Fiction
ISBN 0689318197; 9780689318191

LC 94003362

Americas Award for Children's and Young Adult Literature. Commended

In this children's book by Alma Flor Ada and illustrated by Elivia Salvadier, "Saturdays and Sundays are very special days for the child in this story. On Saturdays, she visits Grandma and Grandpa, who come from a European-American background, and on Sundays -- los domingos -- she visits Abuelito y Abuelita, who are Mexican-American. This affirmation of both heritages [is designed to] speak to all children who

want to know more about their own families and ethnic backgrounds." (Publisher's note)

"A little girl visits her Grandpa and Grandma, her father's parents, on Saturdays and her "abuelito y abuelita," her mother's parents, on "los domingos." Dearly cherished by both sets of grandparents, the little girl delights in the unique differences of the two households and moves with ease between the two cultures...Together, Ada and Savadier have created a picture book that gracefully embraces and celebrates a young child's involvement in her dual heritages. Especially recommended for libraries serving Latino and multicultural communities." Booklist

With love, Little Red Hen; illustrated by Leslie Tryon. Atheneum Books for Young Readers 2001 40 p. col il $17.99

Grades: PreK K 1 2 3   **E**

1. Chickens -- Fiction 2. Neighbors -- Fiction 3. Letters 4. Characters in literature
ISBN 0689825811; 9780689825811

LC 00042021

In this children's book by Alma Flor Ada and illustrated by Leslie Tryon "Hidden Forest has a new resident. Little Red Hen and her seven little chicks have moved into a cottage and plan to grow a bountiful crop of corn in the nearby field. The problem is that none of the Red Hen's neighbors are willing to help with the hard work. So Goldilocks . . . comes up with a neighborly idea: Why don't all the residents of Hidden Forest chip in and work on the garden? Why not make it a surprise?" (Publisher's note)

"In this third collection of letters back and forth between the storybook residents of Hidden Forest, the wolf bad guys are turning their attention to poultry. The format is the same as the first two books: each double-page spread comprises a personal letter and a lively pen-and-ink and watercolor illustration. In addition to being a creative letter-writing lesson, this book offers readers a chance to spend some time with old friends." Horn Book

Addasi, Maha

Time to pray; Arabic translation by Nuha Albitar; illustrated by Ned Gannon. Boyds Mills Press 2010 un il $17.95

Grades: 1 2 3 4   **E**

1. Islam -- Fiction 2. Prayer -- Fiction 3. Muslims -- Fiction 4. Grandmothers -- Fiction 5. Bilingual books -- English-Arabic
ISBN 978-1-59078-611-6; 1-59078-611-4

LC 2010005090

When young Yasmin goes for a visit, her grandmother teaches her a Muslim's daily prayers, makes special prayer clothes, and gives a gift that will help Yasmin remember when to pray. Includes facts about prayer customs.

"This is a beautifully woven tale of grandparent affection and spiritual development. Gannon's illustrations present a warm and authentic balance of Islamic geometric designs and Arab architecture and culture. . . Familiarizing Islamic prayer through realistic fiction makes this a fine choice for most collections." SLJ

The white nights of Ramadan; [by] Maha Addasi; illustrated by Ned Gannon. Boyds Mills Press 2008 un il $16.95

Grades: 1 2 3 4   **E**

1. Kuwait -- Fiction 2. Muslims -- Fiction 3. Ramadan -- Fiction
ISBN 978-1-59078-523-2; 1-59078-523-1

LC 2008002637

"This story is centered around Girgian, a Muslim celebration observed mostly in the Arabian Gulf states during the middle of the month of Ramadan. When Noor, who lives in Kuwait, sees the almost-full moon rise, she knows it's time to prepare for the festival. The family makes candy from honey, sugar, and nuts to share with the children in the neighborhood, wrapping it with cellophane and colorful bows. . . .

Shimmering with moonlit hues, the attractive illustrations are done in a style that reflects one of many Muslim cultures. A helpful author's note and glossary are appended. An excellent choice for units on diversity and multiculturalism." SLJ

Adler, David A.

The **Babe** & I; written by David A. Adler; illustrated by Terry Widener. Harcourt Brace & Co. 1999 un il $17; pa $7

Grades: K 1 2 3   E

1. Baseball players 2. Great Depression, 1929-1939 -- Fiction
ISBN 0-15-201378-4; 0-15-205026-4 pa

LC 97-37580

While helping his family make ends meet during the Depression by selling newspapers, a boy meets Babe Ruth

"Widener's illustrations evoke the ambiance of the period in this book that is carefully paced and remarkable for its unified focus." Horn Book Guide

★ **Don't** throw it to Mo! by David A. Adler; illustrated by Sam Ricks. Viking, published by Penguin Group 2015 32 p. color illustrations $14.99

Grades: PreK K 1 2   E

1. Size -- Fiction 2. Football -- Fiction
ISBN 9780670016310; 0670016314

LC 2014030505

Theodor Seuss Geisel Award (2016)

"Mo is the youngest kid on the Robins, his football team. His classmates don't mind, but the kids on their rival team tease him for being a 'butterfingers' who's too tiny to catch the ball. But Mo's coach has a plan to turn Mo's little size into a big win for the Robins!" (Publisher's note)

"Laid out in simple words, large type, and wide-spaced lines, the text is illustrated with colorful, jaunty line-and-wash illustrations that portray the diverse characters with energy and style. The simply told story features an appealing underdog with enough skill to catch the ball and enough humility to give his coach some credit." Booklist

It's time to sleep, it's time to dream; illustrated by Kay Chorao. Holiday House 2009 un il $16.95

Grades: PreK K   E

1. Bedtime -- Fiction 2. Seasons -- Fiction
ISBN 978-0-8234-1924-1; 0-8234-1924-X

LC 2008022570

A parent lulls a child to sleep with visions of soft spring breezes, lazy summer days, cool autumn winds, and moon-lit winter nights

"Chorao's gouache-and-watercolor illustrations lend a new-fashioned slant to a bedtime book. . . . The softly infused color pictures pair well with the spare text. . . . Kids will be drawn to the comforting cover image of a cute tyke cuddling his toy bunny." Booklist

Young Cam Jansen and the 100th day of school mystery; illustrated by Susanna Natti. Viking 2009 31p il (Viking easy-to-read) $13.99

Grades: K 1 2   E

1. School stories 2. Mystery fiction
ISBN 978-0-670-06172-3; 0-670-06172-7

To celebrate their 100th day of school, Cam and Eric's class party will have snacks that start with "P"-pretzels, popcorn, pineapple juice, and pizza. But when the pizza disappears from the kitchen, it's up to Cam and her photographic memory to solve this delicious mystery.

"Colorful, small-scale line-and-wash illustrations brighten the pages of this entertaining . . . book." Booklist

★ **Young** Cam Jansen and the dinosaur game; illustrated by Susanna Natti. Viking 1996 32p il (Viking easy-to-read) $13.99; pa $3.99

Grades: K 1 2 3   E

1. Mystery fiction
ISBN 0-670-86399-8; 0-14-037779-4 pa

LC 95-46463

"At Jane's birthday party, everyone guesses the number of toy dinosaurs in a big jar. Jennifer 'the Camera' Jansen's photographic memory helps her nab Robert, who has cheated in order to win all the dinosaurs. Observant readers can follow Cam's reasoning and solve the mystery, too." Horn Book Guide

Other easy-to-read titles about Cam Jansen are:

Young Cam Jansen and the 100th day of school mystery (2009)
Young Cam Jansen and the baseball mystery (1999)
Young Cam Jansen and the double beach mystery (2002)
Young Cam Jansen and the ice skate mystery (1998)
Young Cam Jansen and the library mystery (2001)
Young Cam Jansen and the lions' lunch mystery (2007)
Young Cam Jansen and the lost tooth (1997)
Young Cam Jansen and the Molly shoe mystery (2008)
Young Cam Jansen and the missing cookie (1996)
Young Cam Jansen and the new girl mystery (2004)
Young Cam Jansen and the pizza shop mystery (2000)
Young Cam Jansen and the speedy car mystery (2010)
Young Cam Jansen and the substitute mystery (2005)
Young Cam Jansen and the zoo note mystery (2003)

Adler, Victoria

★ **All** of baby, nose to toes; pictures by Hiroe Nakata. Dial Books for Young Readers 2009 un il $14.99

Grades: PreK   E

1. Stories in rhyme 2. Infants -- Fiction
ISBN 978-0-8037-3217-9; 0-8037-3217-1

LC 2008-30971

Rhyming text celebrates everything about a beloved baby, from eyes to toes

"Adler's sunny poem and Nakata's ebullient watercolors demonstrate not only a baby's exploratory joy but also the palpable delight a baby brings to a family." Publ Wkly

Baby, come away; pictures by David Walker. Farrar Straus Giroux 2011 un il $16.99

Grades: PreK K 1   E

1. Stories in rhyme 2. Animals -- Fiction 3. Infants -- Fiction
ISBN 978-0-374-30480-5; 0-374-30480-7

LC 2010036234

A bird, a cat, a dog, and a fish each imagines an ideal day spent with a baby.

"This offering is destined to become a cherished favorite. [It has] utterly charming paintings. . . . Full of rhyme, alliteration, and playful wording, the text lends itself to group reading or one-on-one sharing equally well." SLJ

Adoff, Arnold

★ **Black** is brown is tan; pictures by Emily Arnold McCully. HarperCollins Pubs. 2002 un il $17.99; pa $6.99

Grades: PreK K 1 2   E

1. Family life -- Fiction 2. Racially mixed people -- Fiction
ISBN 0-06-028776-4; 0-06-443644-6 pa

LC 00-44864

A newly illustrated edition of the title first published 1973

Describes in verse a family with a brown-skinned mother, white-skinned father, two children, and their various relatives

"Children everywhere will love the simple, joyful rhythmic words in Adoff's signature 'shaped speech' style, with McCully's beautiful dancing watercolors." Booklist

Agee, Jon

★ **It's** only Stanley; written and illustrated by Jon Agee. Dial Books for Young Readers 2014 32 p. color illustrations (hardcover) $17.99

Grades: K 1 2 3   E

1. Dogs -- Fiction 2. Rockets (Aeronautics) -- Fiction 3. Humorous stories 4. Stories in rhyme

ISBN 0803739079; 9780803739079

LC 2013042652

Boston Globe-Horn Book Honor: Picture Book (2015)

"Mysterious noises keep waking up the Wimbledon family. When [Mr. Wimbledon] returns from checking on the sounds, he's always reassuring: 'It's only Stanley.' But what Stanley the dog is actually doing while his oblivious family goes back to bed is deliciously absurd: he's turning the house into a rocket ship to zoom himself and his family to another planet for an alien encounter." (Publisher's note)

"Agee understands the drama of the page turn better than anyone, with vignettes of the increasingly crowded Wimbledon family bed giving way to full-bleed double-page spreads of Stanley's machinations until it all comes together ('KAPOW!') to make everybody jump." Horn Book

Life on Mars; Jon Agee. Dial Books for Young Readers 2017 32 p. color illustrations (hardcover) $17.99

Grades: PreK K 1   E

1. Astronauts -- Fiction 2. Mars (Planet) -- Fiction 3. Humorous fiction -- Fiction 4. Mars (Planet) -- Fiction 5. Life on other planets -- Fiction

ISBN 0399538526; 9780399538520

LC 2015049804

In this book, by Jon Agee, "a young astronaut is absolutely sure there is life to be found on Mars. . . . But when he arrives, equipped with a package of cupcakes as a gift, he sees nothing but a nearly barren planet. Finally, he spies a single flower and packs it away to take back to Earth as proof that there is indeed life on Mars. But as he settles in for the journey home, he cracks open his cupcakes—only to discover that someone has eaten them all!" (Publisher's note)

"Bursting with quiet wit and gorgeous Martian vistas. Simply masterful." Kirkus

Lion lessons; Jon Agee. Dial Books for Young Readers 2016 32 p. color illustrations (hardcover) $17.99

Grades: PreK K 1 2   E

1. Lion -- Fiction

ISBN 9780803739086

LC 2015022743

This book, by Jon Agee, "teaches kids just what it takes to be a great lion. There are seven steps to becoming a proper lion, including Looking Fierce, Roaring, Prowling Around, and Pouncing. Our young hero, a rather meek and scrawny human boy, does his best to learn the necessary skills during his training with a master instructor (who just happens to be a real lion)." (Publisher's note)

"The text's well-timed humor and pacing work seamlessly with the expressive art to create an outstanding read-aloud and a rewarding story." Horn Book

★ **Little** Santa; Jon Agee. Dial Books for Young Readers, an imprint of Penguin Group (USA) Inc. 2013 40 p. (hardcover) $17.99

Grades: PreK K 1   E

1. Picture books for children 2. Santa Claus -- Fiction

ISBN 0803739060; 9780803739062

LC 2012031855

In this children's picture book, "Little Santa is the youngest child of a hardworking family eking out a hardscrabble existence at the North Pole. The whole family, except for Santa, hates their hard life, and they decide they will relocate to Florida. When a major blizzard buries everyone inside, brave Santa takes his snowshoes and a sack of food and goes up the chimney to seek help." He finds flying reindeer and magic elves, and soon the reader understands Santa's origins. (Kirkus Reviews)

Milo's hat trick; story and pictures by Jon Agee. Hyperion Bks. for Children 2001 un il $15.95

Grades: PreK K 1 2   E

1. Magic tricks 2. Bears -- Fiction 3. Magicians -- Fiction

ISBN 0-7868-0902-7

Milo, a second-rate magician, who can only pull a mouse from his hat rather than a rabbit, is rescued from mediocrity by "a good-natured bear who can jump in and out of hats with ease. . . . In the end, the resourceful bear shares with the conjurer a simple secret and the act becomes a great success. . . . Age three and up." (N Y Times Book Rev)

"Agee's bold, angular pencil-and-paint illustrations drive this warm story about perseverance, luck, and courage." Booklist

Mr. Putney's quacking dog. Michael Di Capua Books 2010 un il $16.95

Grades: PreK K 1   E

1. Puns -- Fiction

ISBN 978-0-545-16203-6; 0-545-16203-3

"Clue-packed pictures add to the fun. Agee fills out the spreads with thick-lined, soft-colored, comedic pictures. A great choice for fans of punnery." SLJ

My rhinoceros. Scholastic 2011 un il $16.95

Grades: PreK K 1   E

1. Pets -- Fiction 2. Rhinoceros -- Fiction

ISBN 978-0-545-29441-6; 0-545-29441-X

"Adopting a rhinoceros, in and of itself, would be absurd enough for most storytellers. For Agee, . . . it is simply the first in a series of weird narrative curveballs. . . . When two bank robbers attempt a getaway, using a hot-air balloon and a hang-glider, does the rhinoceros prove its mettle, springing into superheroic action and demonstrating a third, even more surprising ability. Agee's deadpan voice and blocky, India-ink-and-watercolor pictures play into the inherent oddity of the story." Publ Wkly

Nothing. Hyperion Books for Children 2007 un il $16.99

Grades: K 1 2 3   E

ISBN 978-0-7868-3694-9; 0-7868-3694-6

LC 2007-25191

When Suzie Gump, the richest lady in town, walks into Otis's empty antique shop and insists on buying nothing, she starts a fad that has everyone buying nothing and emptying their homes and stores to make room for it—until Suzie realizes things have gone too far.

"In illustrations that possess a timeless air, Agee contrasts cluttered, patterned spaces with airy rooms, outlines chunky, geometric areas with firm charcoal lines and tints broad surfaces with transparent watercolor wash. . . . This timely parable is certainly something worth having." Publ Wkly

★ **Terrific;** story and pictures by Jon Agee. Hyperion Books for Children 2005 un il $15.95

Grades: PreK K 1 2   E

1. Parrots -- Fiction 2. Shipwrecks -- Fiction

ISBN 0-7868-5184-8

LC 2004-117133

"Terrific," says Eugene when he wins an all-expenses-paid cruise to Bermuda. "I'll probably get a really nasty sunburn." But Eugene's luck is much worse than that. His ship sinks, and he ends up stranded on a tiny island. "Preschool." (Publisher's note)

"With pithy humor and a knack for comic timing, Agee has created a character who will endear himself to readers despite his curmudgeonly exterior and posturing.... The cartoon illustrations feature strong lines and soft colors that contrast wonderfully with the story line." SLJ

★ **Why** did the chicken cross the road? [by] Jon Agee ... [et al.] Dial Books for Young Readers 2006 un il $16.99
Grades: 1 2 3 4   E
1. Chickens -- Fiction
ISBN 0-8037-3094-2

LC 2005-16196

"What is perhaps the world's most tired joke becomes fresh and inspired in this lively collection of work by well-known contemporary children's book artists. On each double-page spread, a different contributor offers a new, illustrated punch line to the title question.... Lots of fun for young children, this collection, which demonstrates the impressive artistic range and talent featured in today's picture books, will also attract older art students and children's book enthusiasts." Booklist

Ahlberg, Allan

★ The **baby** in the hat; written by Allan Ahlberg; illustrations by Andre Amstutz. Candlewick Press 2008 un il $16.99
Grades: K 1 2   E
1. Seafaring life -- Fiction 2. Great Britain -- History -- 19th century -- Fiction
ISBN 978-0-7636-3958-7; 0-7636-3958-3

LC 2007-52029

Catching a baby in his hat sets off a series of adventures for a young nineteenth-century English boy as he becomes a sea captain and finds a surprising mate.

"Ahlberg and Amstutz ... overlook few opportunities for humor in this tall tale.... Witty, detailed gouaches dotted with dialogue balloons lend a theatricality to the picaresque tale." Publ Wkly

Hooray for bread; Allan Ahlberg, illustrated by Bruce Ingman. Candlewick Press 2013 32 p. ill. (reinforced) $15.99
Grades: PreK K 1   E
1. Bread -- Fiction
ISBN 0763663115; 9780763663117

LC 2012942661

In this children's story, by Allan Ahlberg, illustrated by Bruce Ingman, "early in the morning the baker bakes a delicious loaf of bread. So delicious, in fact, that by the time the sun goes down it has been gobbled up! Who eats it all? ... The baker's wife eats some toast for breakfast, and the baker's son gets a cheese and ham sandwich for lunch. And let's not forget the dog! As the loaf gets smaller, slice by slice and crumb by crumb, everyone eats their fill." (Publisher's note)

★ The **pencil**; [illustrated by] Bruce Ingman. Candlewick Press 2008 un il $16.99
Grades: PreK K 1 2   E
1. Drawing -- Fiction
ISBN 978-0-7636-3894-8; 0-7636-3894-3

LC 2007-51885

A lonely pencil timidly draws a boy, a dog, and other items but soon faces a problem as his creations begin demanding changes, and when he draws an eraser to make them happy, the real trouble begins.

"Both clever and suspenseful, this surefire delight tells the story of a pencil who must deal with the consequences of his inventions. ... The book's comical, unexpected plot and wry narrator keep the story fresh throughout." Publ Wkly

Previously; [by] Allan Ahlberg; [illustrated by] Bruce Ingman. Candlewick Press 2007 un il $16.99
Grades: PreK K 1 2   E
1. Fairy tales
ISBN 978-0-7636-3542-8; 0-7636-3542-1

LC 2006-51831

The adventures of various nursery rhyme and fairy tale characters are retold in backward sequence with each tale interrelated to the other. Includes Goldilocks, Jack and the beanstalk, Jack and Jill, the frog prince, Cinderella, and the gingerbread man.

"The jazzy, colorful pictures display substantive variety.... Children will delight in this energetic, amusing, and very approachable tale." SLJ

Ahlberg, Janet

The **jolly** postman; or other people's letters. [by] Janet and Allan Ahlberg. Little, Brown Books for Young Readers 2001 un il $17.99
Grades: PreK K 1 2   E
1. Fairy tales 2. Stories in rhyme 3. Letters -- Fiction 4. Postal service -- Fiction
ISBN 978-0-316-12644-1; 0-316-12644-6
A reissue of the title first published 1986

A Jolly Postman delivers letters to several famous fairy-tale characters such as the Big Bad Wolf, Cinderella, and the Three Bears. Each letter may be removed from its envelope page and read separately.

"The story of the postman's travels is told in charming verse; the pictures are delightful, full of clever detail; and the results are frequently hilarious." Publ Wkly

Aigner-Clark, Julie

You are the best medicine; [by] Julie Aigner Clark; illustrated by Jana Christy. Balzer + Bray 2010 un il $16.99
Grades: PreK K 1 2   E
1. Sick -- Fiction 2. Cancer -- Fiction 3. Mother-child relationship -- Fiction
ISBN 978-0-06-195644-7; 0-06-195644-9

A mother who has cancer gently informs her child of what the effects will be, and reminds her little one of all the special times they have shared, and will continue to share, even while she undergoes treatment.

"Here's a much-needed book, and one that's done with lots of love. ... Soft-edge illustrations, tender in feel and comforting in color, add sweetness." Booklist

Ain, Beth

★ **Starring** Jules (as herself) Beth Ain; illustrated by Anne Keenan Higgins. Scholastic Press 2013 160 p. (hardcover) $14.99
Grades: 2 3 4 5   E
1. Acting -- Fiction 2. Schools -- Fiction 3. Auditions -- Fiction 4. Friendship -- Fiction 5. Elementary schools -- Fiction
ISBN 0545443520; 9780545443524

LC 2012017678

This children's story, by Beth Ain, is the first book in the "Starring Jules" series. "Seven-year-old Jules has been asked to audition for a television commercial. But she needs help. ... But Jules is in the middle of a mean fight with her former best friend, Charlotte.... But with the opportunity of a lifetime four days away, Jules doesn't have the time to stay angry with Charlotte." (Kirkus Reviews)

Ainsworth, Kimberly

Hootenanny! a festive counting book. illustrated by Jo Brown. Little Simon 2011 un il $12.99

Grades: PreK K   E
1. Counting 2. Owls -- Fiction 3. Parties -- Fiction
ISBN 978-1-4424-2273-5; 1-4424-2273-4; 978-1-4424-3490-5 e-book; 1-4424-3490-2 e-book

LC 2011006557

"Five owls help youngsters learn to count from one to five as they get ready for a party at the top of an old oak tree. . . . The text is printed in a large, easy-to-read font with each numeral highlighted in a different color. The bright spreads feature a rainbow of colors, smiling characters, and some humorous details. With its jazzy vocabulary and cheerful illustrations, the book lives up to its title." SLJ

Akbarpour, Ahmad

Good night, Commander; pictures by Morteza Zahedi; translated by Shadi Eskandani and Helen Mixter. Groundwood Books 2010 un il $17.95

Grades: 3 4 5   E
1. Iran-Iraq War, 1980-1988 -- Fiction 2. Children with physical disabilities -- Fiction
ISBN 978-0-88899-989-4; 0-88899-989-5

"This picture book with difficult concepts could possibly be used with younger students who need a fiction bridge to their own reality. This is a brief and powerful story about the impact of war on the youngest inhabitants of the country." Libr Media Connect

Alalou, Ali

The **butter** man; [by] Elizabeth Alalou and Ali Alalou; illustrated by Julie Klear Essakalli. Charlesbridge 2008 un il lib bdg $14.95

Grades: K 1 2 3   E
1. Morocco -- Fiction
ISBN 978-1-58089-127-1 lib bdg; 1-58089-127-6 lib bdg

LC 2007-02278

While Nora waits for the couscous her father is cooking to be finished, he tells her a story about his youth in the High Atlas Mountains of Morocco. "Ages seven to ten." (Bull Cent Child Books)

The authors "write in descriptive language that speaks directly to children. . . . The folk-art paintings, created by a textile designer, feature whimsical characters and cozy domestic scenes, while the ochre, gold, and rust palette evokes the feeling of the dusty, sunlit landscape." Booklist

Alborough, Jez

★ **Duck** in the truck. HarperCollins Pubs. 2000 un il hardcover o.p. pa $7.95; bd bk $8.99

Grades: PreK K 1   E
1. Stories in rhyme 2. Ducks -- Fiction 3. Animals -- Fiction
ISBN 0-06-028685-7; 1-933605-76-6 pa; 978-1-929132-83-6 bd bk; 1-929132-83-2 bd bk

LC 99-60934

"A rhyming text relates the troubles of a duck whose truck gets stuck in the muck. . . . The art makes the most of the story's physical comedy, with exaggerated humor and an engaging animal cast, including a frog, a sheep, and a goat who all come to help out." Horn Book Guide

Other titles about Duck are:
Captain Duck (2003)
Duck's key, where can it be (2005)
Fix-it Duck (2002)
Hit the ball Duck (2006)
Super Duck (2009)

Where's my teddy? Candlewick Press 1992 un il hardcover o.p. pa $6.99

Grades: PreK K   E
1. Stories in rhyme 2. Bears -- Fiction 3. Teddy bears -- Fiction
ISBN 1-5640-2048-7; 1-5640-2280-3 pa

When a small boy named Eddie goes searching for his lost teddy in the dark woods, he comes across a gigantic bear with a similar problem.

"Alborough's verse adroitly employs kid-pleasing rhythms and repetitions, while his watercolor, crayon and pencil drawings underscore the broad comedy of this perfectly satisfying scenario of scary fun." Publ Wkly

Alda, Arlene

Did you say pears? Tundra Books 2006 31p il $16.95

Grades: K 1 2 3   E
1. English language -- Homonyms
ISBN 0-88776-739-7

"A marvelously imaginative pairing (sorry) of homonyms (words that sound alike but have different meanings and the same spelling) and homophones (words that sound alike but have different meanings and different spellings), wrapped up in a rhyme of amazingly few words and terrific offbeat photographs." Booklist

Hello, good-bye. Tundra Books 2009 un il $16.95

Grades: PreK K   E
1. Opposites
ISBN 978-0-88776-900-9; 0-88776-900-4

"Exceptionally fine color photographs bring clarity as well as beauty to this book of opposites. Alda . . . creates images that are striking in themselves and meaningful when paired with their opposites. . . . This offers plenty of opportunities for interaction between young children and those reading to them." Booklist

Alderson, Brian

Thumbelina; [by] Hans Christian Andersen; retold by Brian Alderson; illustrated by Bagram Ibatoulline. Candlewick Press 2009 un il $17.99

Grades: 1 2 3 4   E
1. Authors 2. Novelists 3. Dramatists 4. Fairy tales 5. Children's authors 6. Short story writers
ISBN 978-0-7636-2079-0; 0-7636-2079-3

LC 2008-27721

A tiny girl no bigger than a thumb is stolen by a great ugly toad and subsequently has many adventures and makes many animal friends, before finding the perfect mate in a warm and beautiful southern land.

"This retelling of Andersen's classic tale remains close to the original. . . . Alderson retells these adventures and misadventures with a wry wit, moving the plot quickly through each scene. . . . Ibatoulline's illustrations are lavishly composed in watercolor and gouache." Bull Cent Child Books

Alemagna, Beatrice

★ The **Wonderful** Fluffy Little Squishy; Beatrice Alemagna; translated from the French by Claudia Zoe Bedrick. Enchanted Lion Books 2015 48 p. color illustrations $18.95

Grades: PreK K 1 2   E
1. Gifts -- Fiction 2. Neighborhood -- Fiction
ISBN 1592701809; 9781592701803
Mildred L. Batchelder Award (2016)

In this children's story, by Beatrice Alemagna, translated by Claudia Zoe Bedrick, "Eddie is five and a half, and thinks she is the only one in her family who isn't really good at something. So when she hears her little sister say 'birthday, Mommy, fluffy, little, squishy,' it's extra important for her to find this amazing present before anyone else does. So . . . little Eddie goes all around the neighborhood . . . to find one." (Publisher's note)

"Colored pencil and collage techniques come together in whimsical illustrations that reflect the story's French origin, as well as the sweetness and quirkiness of Eddie's gift-finding mission." Booklist

Alexander, Kwame

Acoustic Rooster and his barnyard band; written by Kwame Alexander; illustrated by Tim Bowers. Sleeping Bear Press 2011 il $15.95
Grades: K 1 2 3   E
   1. Stories in rhyme 2. Contests -- Fiction 3. Musicians -- Fiction 4. Jazz music -- Fiction 5. Domestic animals -- Fiction
   ISBN 978-1-58536-688-0; 1-58536-688-9
                                 LC 2010053709

Acoustic Rooster forms a jazz band with Duck Ellington, Bee Holliday, and Pepe Ernesto Cruz to compete in the annual Barnyard Talent Show against such greats as Thelonius Steer, Mules Davis, and Ella Finchgerald. Includes glossary, notes on the characters and songs, and jazz timeline.

This is a "delightful picture book. . . . The large illustrations are done in bold colors and have humorous, jazzy details." SLJ

Surf's Up; by Kwame Alexander; illustrated by Daniel Miyares. NorthSouth 2016 32 p. color illustrations (hardcover) $17.95
Grades: PreK K 1 2   E
   1. Frogs -- Fiction 2. Surfing -- Fiction 3. Books and reading -- Fiction
   ISBN 9780735842205; 0735842205

In this children's story, by Kwame Alexander, illustrated by Daniel Miyares, frogs "Bro and Dude have very different ideas about how to spend the day at the beach. But as Bro continues to gasp and cheer as he reads his book (Moby Dick), Dude can't help but get curious. Before you can shout 'Surf's up!' both frogs are sharing the same adventure, that is, until they get to the beach." (Publisher's note)

"With their strategic use of color and line, the illustrations work well with Alexander's snappy, spare text (all in dialogue) to create a high-energy tribute to the power of a good book." Horn Book

Alexander, Lloyd

The fortune-tellers; illustrated by Trina Schart Hyman. Dutton Children's Bks. 1992 un il hardcover o.p. pa $6.99
Grades: K 1 2 3   E
   1. Cameroon -- Fiction 2. Fortune telling -- Fiction
   ISBN 0-525-44849-7; 0-14-056233-8 pa
                                   LC 91-30684

A carpenter goes to a fortune teller and finds the predictions about his future coming true in an unusual way

"Alexander's rags-to-riches story combines universal elements of the trickster character and the cumulative disaster tale. Hyman's pictures set it all in a vibrant community in Cameroon, West Africa. . . . The energetic, brilliantly colored paintings are packed with people and objects that swirl around the main characters. . . . With its ups and downs, this is a funny, playful story that evokes the irony of the human condition." Booklist

Alexander, Martha G.

Max and the dumb flower picture; [by] Martha Alexander with James Rumford. Charlesbridge 2009 un il $9.95
Grades: PreK K 1 2   E
   1. School stories 2. Artists -- Fiction 3. Mother's Day -- Fiction
   ISBN 978-1-58089-156-1; 1-58089-156-X
                                   LC 2008007251

Despite his teacher's entreaties that it would be perfect for Mother's Day, Max refuses to color in the same flower picture as the rest of the class

"Before her death in 2006, Alexander . . . left her manuscript and sketches in the hands of James Rumford. . . . The tender result honors both Alexander and the children for whom she wrote for 40 years. . . . The soft sketches are color washed digitally and by hand, and with Rumford's collaboration, still bear Alexander's simple, expressive style." Publ Wkly

Alexander, William

Goblin secrets; William Alexander. Margaret K. McElderry Books 2012 223 p.
Grades: 5 6 7 8   E
   1. Fantasy fiction 2. Goblins -- Fiction 3. Witches -- Fiction 4. Brothers -- Fiction 5. Missing persons -- Fiction 6. Fantasy 7. Magic -- Fiction 8. Masks -- Fiction 9. Entertainers -- Fiction
   ISBN 9781442427266; 9781442427280
                                   LC 2011015491

National Book Award: Young People's Literature (2012)

In this book, a "tempestuous river divides the city of Zombay into two parts: the wealthy, aristocratic Northside, run by the Mayor and his gearworked Guard, and the Southside, whose impoverished residents are under the control of Graba, a powerful, cruel witch who takes in orphans to be her servants. . . . Rownie . . . learns that [his brother] Rowan was to play an essential part in a ritual meant to save the town from an impending flood." (Bulletin of the Center for Children's Books)

Alexie, Sherman, 1966-

★ Thunder Boy Jr. by Sherman Alexie; illustrated by Yuyi Morales. Little, Brown & Co. 2016 40 p. color illustrations (hardcover) $17.99
Grades: K 1 2 3 4   E
   1. Personal names -- Fiction 2. Identity -- Fiction 3. Native Americans -- Fiction 4. Father-son relationship -- Fiction
   ISBN 9780316013727; 0316013722
                                   LC 2015020263

Boston Globe Horn Book Honor Book: Picture Books (2016)
Kirkus Prize Finalist: Young Readers' Literature (2016)

In this children's book by Sherman Alexie, illustrated by Yuyi Morales, "'Thunder Boy Jr.' is named after his dad, but he wants a name that's all his own. Just because people call his dad Big Thunder doesn't mean he wants to be Little Thunder. He wants a name that celebrates something cool he's done, like Touch the Clouds, Not Afraid of Ten Thousand Teeth, or Full of Wonder." (Publisher's note)

"An expertly crafted, soulful, and humorous work that tenderly explores identity, culture, and the bond between father and son." Kirkus

Aliki

All by myself! written and illustrated by Aliki. HarperCollins Pubs. 2000 un il $14.95; lib bdg $14.89; pa $6.99
Grades: K 1 2 3   E
   ISBN 0-06-028929-5; 0-06-028930-9 lib bdg; 0-06-446253-2 pa
                                   LC 99-51672

A child shows all the things he has learned to do all on his own

"Aliki's colorful illustrations closely match the moods and energy levels of a five- or six-year-old. . . . The text has a hand-printed appearance, large and easy to read. . . . A good choice for story-hours and beginning readers." SLJ

★ Painted words: Marianthe's story one. Greenwillow Bks. 1998 un il $16.99; lib bdg $17.89
Grades: K 1 2 3   E
   1. School stories 2. Immigrants -- Fiction
   ISBN 0-688-15661-4; 0-688-15662-2 lib bdg
                                   LC 97-34653

Two separate stories, the first telling of Mari's starting school in a new land, and the second describing village life in her country before she and her family left in search of a better life

"In simple, understated language, Aliki has captured the emotions and experiences of many of today's children. Colored-pencil and crayon illustrations in soft primary and secondary colors reinforce the mood of the text." SLJ

★ A **play's** the thing; written and illustrated by Aliki. HarperCollins 2005 32p il $16.99; lib bdg $17.89
Grades: K 1 2 3   E
1. School stories 2. Theater -- Fiction
ISBN 0-06-074355-7; 0-06-074356-5 lib bdg
LC 2004-22101
When Miss Brilliant's class puts on a performance of "Mary had a little lamb," all the children are eager to participate except for the uncooperative José—until Miss Brilliant assigns him the role of teacher. "Primary." (Horn Book)

"When Miss Brilliant's class decides to put on a fractured version of [Mary Had a Little Lamb], José must learn to work with his classmates and overcome his antisocial tendencies. . . . This is . . . the type of work that children will be drawn to again and again because they recognize their world so aptly captured in both word and art. Each time they revisit, they will find something new in the colorful cartoon illustrations." SLJ

★ **Push** button. Greenwillow Books 2010 un il $16.99; lib bdg $17.89
Grades: PreK   E
1. Stories in rhyme 2. Play -- Fiction
ISBN 978-0-06-167308-5; 0-06-167308-0; 978-0-06-167309-2 lib bdg; 0-06-167309-9 lib bdg
LC 2008047690
A little boy who loves pushing buttons of all kinds ends up with such a sore finger that he must play with other things.

"Against the clean white backgrounds, Aliki's familiar style of mixing pencils, watercolors, ink, and markers give the tousle-headed protagonist a vivid, crayon-colored expressiveness. . . . Rhyming text and sound effects add wry touches." Booklist

Quiet in the garden; written and illustrated by Aliki. Greenwillow Books 2009 un il lib bdg $18.89
Grades: PreK K   E
1. Animals -- Fiction 2. Gardens -- Fiction
ISBN 978-0-06-155207-6; 0-06-155207-0; 978-0-06-155208-3 lib bdg; 0-06-155208-9 lib bdg
LC 2008-12641
Sitting quietly in his garden, a little boy observes the eating habits of birds, bugs, butterflies, and other small animals. Includes instructions on how to make your own garden and a detailed illustration of plants typically found in a garden.

"With spare words and a balance of line and color against white backgrounds framed with lacey branches, Aliki deftly portrays the benefits of observing nature." SLJ

The **two** of them; written and illustrated by Aliki. Greenwillow Bks. 1979 un il hardcover o.p. pa $6.99
Grades: PreK K 1 2   E
1. Death -- Fiction 2. Grandfathers -- Fiction
ISBN 0-688-07337-9 pa
LC 79-10161
Describes the relationship of a grandfather and his granddaughter from her birth to his death

"The eloquent illustrations in muted full color and the smaller soft-pencil drawings show the life the two shared as well as the tenderness and pure pleasure implicit in their relationship." Horn Book

We are best friends. Greenwillow Bks. 1982 un il hardcover o.p. $16.99; pa $5.99
Grades: PreK K 1 2   E
1. Friendship -- Fiction
ISBN 0-688-00822-4; 0-688-07037-X pa
LC 81-6549
When Robert's best friend Peter moves away, both are unhappy, but they learn that they can make new friends and still remain best friends

"Brightly lit pictures in cheerful primary colors portray with just a stroke of the pen the misery of losing a friend who must move away and the tentative beginnings of a new companionship. . . . Details of school and home abound in the lively pictures." Horn Book

Allard, Harry
★ **Miss** Nelson is missing! [by] Harry Allard, James Marshall. Houghton Mifflin 1977 32p il $16; pa $5.95
Grades: PreK K 1 2   E
1. School stories 2. Teachers -- Fiction
ISBN 0-395-25296-2; 0-395-40146-1 pa
LC 76-55918
"The kids in room 207 were so fresh and naughty that they lost their sweet-natured teacher, the blonde Miss Nelson, and got in her place the sour-souled Miss Swamp." N Y Times Book Rev

"Humor and suspense fill the pages of [this book]." Christ Sci Monit
Other titles about Miss Nelson are:
Miss Nelson has a field day (1985)
Miss Nelson is back (1982)

Allegra, Mike
Sarah gives thanks; how Thanksgiving became a national holiday. by Mike Allegra; illustrated by David Gardner. Albert Whitman & Co. 2012 32 p. col. ill.
Grades: 2 3 4   E
1. Thanksgiving Day -- History -- Fiction
ISBN 080757239X; 9780807572399
LC 2011034161
This book by Mike Allegra, illustrated by David Gardner, tells the story of Sarah Josepha Hale, who "dedicated her life to making Thanksgiving a national holiday, all while raising a family and becoming a groundbreaking writer and women's magazine editor . . . [d]uring the nineteenth century. . . . Sarah Hale's . . . story, accompanied by . . . watercolor illustrations, tells the tale of one woman who wouldn't take no for an answer." (Publisher's note)

Allen, Debbie
Dancing in the wings; pictures by Kadir Nelson. Dial Bks. for Young Readers 2000 un il $16.99; pa $6.99
Grades: PreK K 1 2   E
1. Ballet -- Fiction 2. African Americans -- Fiction
ISBN 0-8037-2501-9; 0-14-250141-7 pa
LC 99-462181
Sassy tries out for a summer dance festival in Washington, D.C., despite the other girls' taunts that she is much too tall

"Allen's dialogue is realistic, and Nelson's illustrations of the predominantly African-American cast ably capture Sassy's love of dance and her lively personality." Horn Book Guide

Allen, Elanna
★ **Itsy** Mitsy runs away. Atheneum Books for Young Readers 2011 un il $16.99

Grades: PreK K 1 2   E
1. Runaway children -- Fiction 2. Father-daughter relationship -- Fiction
ISBN 978-1-4424-0671-1; 1-4424-0671-2

LC 2010004418

When Mitsy decides to run away, her father helps her pack.

"Mitsy may be itsy, but she has no shortage of energy or determination. She's also a sartorial standout, wearing lime green, dinosaur-style footie/hoodie pajamas and bright orange goggles. . . . Allen . . . has a breezy drawing style and a cheery disdain for logic reminiscent of 1950s-era cartoons. . . . Yet the freewheeling art stays anchored by Allen's very funny text, which combines rhythmic, cumulative passages with Mitsy's irreverent, precocious voice." Publ Wkly

Allen, Jonathan

I'm not Santa! Hyperion Books for Children 2008 un il $14.99
Grades: PreK K   E
1. Owls -- Fiction 2. Rabbits -- Fiction 3. Christmas -- Fiction 4. Santa Claus -- Fiction
ISBN 978-1-4231-1300-3; 1-4231-1300-4

When Baby Hare mistakes Baby Owl for Santa Claus, it takes a visit from St. Nick himself to straighten things out.

"With almost no background illustration, the two cartoon-style characters face off from opposite pages, their growing frustration evident in their body language. . . . This will . . . have appeal for children at the stage where Christmas is all about Santa sightings." Booklist

I'm not scared! Hyperion Books for Children 2007 un il $14.99
Grades: PreK K   E
1. Fear -- Fiction 2. Owls -- Fiction 3. Animals -- Fiction
ISBN 978-0-7868-3722-9

When Baby Owl takes his stuffed Owly out for a walk in the moonlit woods, he insists that he is not afraid of the other animals that keep popping up and making them jump.

"The cartoon illustrations are painted in dusky hues with black outlines, and the glossy quality of the light-infused colors makes the art look like animation cels. . . . The expressive visuals, brief text, and protagonist's believably childlike behavior are just right for young audiences." SLJ

The **little** rabbit who liked to say moo. Boxer Books 2008 un il $14.95
Grades: PreK K 1   E
1. Sound -- Fiction 2. Animals -- Fiction 3. Rabbits -- Fiction
ISBN 978-1-905417-78-0; 1-905417-78-0

"Little Rabbit likes to say 'moo,' because rabbits don't have a big noise. The little creature also likes to say 'baa,' 'oink,' 'heehaw,' and 'quack,' and gets the other young farm animals to join the refrain until a surprise ending reveals the bunny's favorite sound. The illustrations are large, uncluttered, simple, and bold, made of black lines and computer air-brushed color. . . . With its large print and natural repetition, this cumulative tale will be useful for building early literacy skills." SLJ

Alsdurf, Phyllis

★ **It's** milking time; by Phyllis Alsdurf; illustrations by Steve Johnson & Lou Fancher. Random House 2012 40 p. col. ill. (hardcover) $16.99
Grades: K 1 2 3   E
1. Milk -- Fiction 2. Farms -- Fiction 3. Farm life -- Fiction 4. Milk supply -- Fiction 5. Father-daughter relationship -- Fiction 6. Cows -- Fiction
ISBN 0375869115; 9780375869112; 9780375899935; 9780375969119

LC 2010047772

In this children's book by Phyllis Alsdurf, illustrated by Steve Johnson and Lou Fancher, "a little girl and her father begin the evening milking. They work side by side, fanning out beds of straw, bringing in the cows, and hooking up the milkers. . . . The fresh dairy product isn't just for them--other families will buy their milk, butter, and cheese at stores and farmers' markets near and far, connecting the little girl's farm to the world beyond." (Publisher's note)

Alter, Anna

Abigail spells. Alfred A. Knopf 2009 un il $16.99; lib bdg $19.99
Grades: K 1 2   E
1. Friendship -- Fiction 2. Spelling bees -- Fiction
ISBN 978-0-375-85617-4; 0-375-85617-X; 978-0-375-95617-1 lib bdg; 0-375-95617-4 lib bdg

LC 2008024529

George helps his best friend Abigail practice for the city spelling bee, then cheers her up when she makes a mistake.

"Alter's folk-style acrylics done in warm, muted shades beautifully complement this steady-paced, conversational story." SLJ

A **photo** for Greta. Alfred A. Knopf 2011 un il $16.99; lib bdg $19.99
Grades: PreK K 1   E
1. Rabbits -- Fiction 2. Photographers -- Fiction 3. Father-daughter relationship -- Fiction
ISBN 978-0-375-85618-1; 0-375-85618-8; 978-0-375-95618-8 lib bdg; 0-375-95618-2 lib bdg

LC 2010036001

"Greta, a young rabbit, loves her father, a photographer who 'travels all around the world taking pictures of very important people.' Admiring the framed pictures he's taken . . . she wishes to be famous and photo-ready herself. . . . Alter displays notable sensitivity to children's insecurities and doubts, while providing reassurance of their worth. Her acrylics have a comforting sturdiness, and readers who similarly take pride in their parents' professions, even as they miss them in their absence, will relate both to Greta's role-playing when her father is away and their tender time together when he comes home." Publ Wkly

Altes, Marta

My grandpa; by Marta Altes. Abrams Books for Young Readers 2013 32 p. ill. (reinforced) $15.95
Grades: PreK K 1   E
1. Picture books for children 2. Senile dementia -- Fiction 3. Bears -- Fiction 4. Old age -- Fiction 5. Grandfathers -- Fiction
ISBN 1419705881; 9781419705885

LC 2012015616

This children's picture book is "narrated by a young bear whose grandfather is exhibiting signs of advanced age and dementia. The simple text uses single sentences that vacillate between the joy of the pair's loving bond and the young bear's honest look at Grandpa's decline." (School Library Journal)

Alvarez, Julia

A **gift** of gracias; the legend of Altagracia. written by Julia Alvarez; illustrated by Beatriz Vidal. Knopf 2005 un il $15.95; lib bdg $17.99
Grades: K 1 2 3   E
1. Saints -- Fiction 2. Oranges -- Fiction 3. Dominican Republic -- Fiction
ISBN 0-375-82425-1; 0-375-92425-6 lib bdg

Maria's family is almost forced to leave their farm on the new island colony, until a mysterious lady appears in Maria's dream

"Rich in cultural authenticity and brimming with the magical realism that is characteristic of Hispanic literature, this elegantly woven tale introduces the legend of Our Lady of Altagracia, the patron saint of the Dominican Republic. . . . With an exquisite use of watercolor and gouache, Vidal has painted colorful, yet warm illustrations that add depth to the story." SLJ

Amado, Elisa

Tricycle; [by] Elisa Amado; [illustrated by] Alfonso Ruano. Groundwood Books/House of Anansi Press 2007 un il $17.95

Grades: 1 2 3 4   **E**

1. Theft -- Fiction 2. Friendship -- Fiction 3. Social classes -- Fiction 4. Truthfulness and falsehood -- Fiction

ISBN 978-0-88899-614-5; 0-88899-614-4

"This book tells of rich and poor from the viewpoint of young Margarita, who climbs a tree on her rich family's estate and sees the shacks on the other side of the hedge, where her friend Rosario lives. Margarita watches as Rosario and her brother take her tricycle, but she doesn't say anything about it, even when her mother's lunch guests spew prejudice. . . . The text is spare, and the richly colored acrylic art . . . is just on the edge of magical realism. Although there is no overt message, there is much to talk about." Booklist

What are you doing? pictures by Manuel Monroy. Groundwood Books/House of Anansi Press 2011 un il $16.95

Grades: PreK K 1 2   **E**

1. Books and reading -- Fiction

ISBN 978-1-55498-070-3; 1-55498-070-4

"Everywhere Chepito goes in his little village, there are people reading. He questions the readers on their motives . . . and receives a variety of responses. . . . When he starts school, he's drawn to the classroom's big shelf of books. . . . He takes one home to share with his sister, who then asks him why he wants to read to her. . . . Monroy's digitally enhanced colored pencil and watercolor illustrations offer simple renderings of Chepito's conversations around town. . . . This is a thoughtful offering for soon-to-be literates that just may get them thinking about the power of reading." Bull Cent Child Books

Anderson, AnnMarie

★ The **Nutcracker**; pictures by Alison Jay. Dial Books for Young Readers 2010 un il $16.99

Grades: K 1 2 3   **E**

1. Fairy tales 2. Nutcracker (Ballet) 3. Christmas -- Fiction 4. Ballet -- Stories, plots, etc.

ISBN 978-0-8037-3285-8; 0-8037-3285-6

LC 2009051657

After rescuing her Christmas nutcracker from an army of angry toys, Marie and her brother are rewarded by the nutcracker, now a prince, with a fantastic nighttime journey to a realm of dancing fairies, beautiful palaces, and wonderful things to eat.

"Jay's delicate crackle-varnish oil paintings—equal parts elegant and whimsical-distinguish this edition of Hoffman's Nutcracker, based on Balanchine's staging of the ballet. . . . Jay's gleaming marzipan palace, pink spun-sugar trees, and peppermint-stick gates are the stuff of holiday visions, indeed" Publ Wkly

Andersen, Hans Christian

The **emperor's** new clothes; designed and illustrated by Virginia Lee Burton. Houghton Mifflin 2004 44p il $16

Grades: K 1 2 3   **E**

1. Fairy tales

ISBN 0-618-34421-7

A reissue of the edition first published 1949

Weavers convince the vain emperor that the clothing they make for him can only be seen by those who are not fools, but only the child recognizes the truth

"Burton's sense of pageantry sets forth in beautiful colors the magnificence of the Emperor's domain and entourage; her sense of humor brings out rightly the ridiculous situation with all its implications." Horn Book Guide

★ The **nightingale**; [by] Hans Christian Andersen; adapted and illustrated by Jerry Pinkney. Phyllis Fogelman Bks. 2002 un il $16.99

Grades: 2 3 4   **E**

1. Authors 2. Novelists 3. Dramatists 4. Fairy tales 5. Children's authors 6. Short story writers 7. Nightingales -- Fiction

ISBN 0803724640

LC 2001-47601

Despite being neglected by the emperor for a jewel-studded bird, the little nightingale revives the dying ruler with its beautiful song. A retelling set in Morocco

This "is a pleasing version of the classic, fresh in its interpretation but true to the spirit of the original. . . . Each double-page spread is illuminated by artwork that glows with rich colors and teems with lively details. Done in graphic, gouache, and watercolor, the large, gracefully composed illustrations feature a profusion of patterns." Booklist

The **nightingale**; illustrated by Pirkko Vainio. North South Books 2011 un il $16.95

Grades: K 1 2 3   **E**

1. China -- Fiction 2. Nightingales -- Fiction

ISBN 978-0-7358-4029-4; 0-7358-4029-6

Though the emperor banishes the nightingale in preference of a jeweled mechanical imitation, the little bird remains faithful and returns years later when the emperor is near death and no one else can help him.

"A fresh version of Andersen's tender tale is illustrated with delicate watercolors. . . . This retelling, first published in Switzerland . . . is straightforward, allowing the soft, muted artwork to accent the details and ambiance." Kirkus

★ The **Snow** Queen; a retelling of the fairy tale. by Hans Christian Andersen; illustrated by Bagram Ibatoulline. HarperCollins 2013 40 p. (hardcover) $17.99

Grades: K 1 2   **E**

1. Friendship -- Fiction 2. Blessing and cursing -- Fiction 3. Fairy tales

ISBN 0062209507; 9780062209504

LC 2012011533

Author Hans Christian Andersen and illustrator Bagram Ibatoulline present a story of "friendship, love, and bravery. Best friends Kai and Gerda would do anything for each other. When Kai starts to behave cruelly and disappears, Gerda sets out on an epic quest to save Kai from the evil Snow Queen. But can Gerda break the Snow Queen's enchantment and complete the final task?" (Publisher's note)

★ **Thumbeline**; illustrated by Lisbeth Zwerger; translated by Anthea Bell. North-South Bks. 2000 un il hardcover o.p. pa $6.95

Grades: K 1 2 3   **E**

1. Fairy tales

ISBN 0-7358-1213-6; 0-7358-2236-0 pa

LC 99-57073

A reissue of 1985 edition published by Picture Book Studio

The adventures of a tiny girl no bigger than a thumb and her many animal friends

"The book's squarish design . . . draws the reader's attention to the exceptional art. Lovely, lean, lithe lines combine with a palette of tawny earth tones to create a minimalist world redolent with grace and rich with imagination." Horn Book Guide

The **ugly** duckling; [illustrated by] Pirkko Vainio. NorthSouth 2009 un il $16.95
Grades: PreK K 1 2   E
   1. Fairy tales 2. Ducks -- Fiction 3. Swans -- Fiction
   ISBN 978-0-7358-2226-9; 0-7358-2226-3
"Andersen's timeless story is lovingly revisited in this modest yet engaging retelling. With the sound and feel of a classic in the very best sense, the familiar tale has been reworked but not oversimplified, making it particularly appealing for children who might be too young for some of the harsher elements of the original. But what makes this version particularly appealing is the lovely watercolor artwork, which, like the text, exudes a feeling of tradition and familiarity." SLJ

Anderson, Liam

  Monster chefs; Brian and Liam Anderson. Roaring Brook Press 2014 32 p. (hardcover : alk. paper) $16.99
Grades: PreK K 1 2   E
   1. Humorous fiction 2. Monsters -- Fiction 3. Kings and rulers -- Fiction 4. Diet -- Fiction 5. Cooks -- Fiction 6. Humorous stories 7. Kings, queens, rulers, etc. -- Fiction
   ISBN 1596438088; 9781596438088
                  LC 2012046930
In this book, by Brian and Liam Anderson, "the horribly horrible monster king summoned his four equally horrible chefs. . . . Trembling with fear, they each set off in a different direction to look for something truly scrumptious. But what, besides eyeballs and ketchup, could a monster king possibly want to eat? A rabbit? A fish? A snake? What one finally brings back may change dinnertime in the kingdom forever." (Publisher's note)
"A monster king tells his monster chefs that he wants to eat more than eyeballs and ketchup, so they set off in search of alternatives. Only one finds a solution, via a pastry chef: eyeball cupcakes (recipe included). Several layouts are cramped, and the backgrounds could be more interesting, but the setup is fresh and the execution riotous." Horn Book

Andreae, Giles, 1966-

  I love my mommy; [by] Giles Andreae and [illustrated by] Emma Dodd. Hyperion/Disney 2011 un il $12.99
Grades: PreK   E
   1. Mother-child relationship -- Fiction
   ISBN 978-1-4231-4327-7; 1-4231-4327-2
First published 2010 in the United Kingdom with title: I love my mummy
"This appealing oversize book has a rhyming text and a huggable-looking toddler who clutches a purple toy duck. He lists some of the reasons he loves his mother. . . . The bright illustrations are set against pastel backgrounds with close-ups of the child and Mom outlined in black. . . . This is a tale oft told, but with its cheerful, familiar scenarios, it will be a hit at storytimes." SLJ

Andreasen, Dan

  The **baker's** dozen; [by] Dan Andreasen. Henry Holt 2007 un il $16.95
Grades: PreK K   E
   1. Counting 2. Stories in rhyme 3. Baking -- Fiction
   ISBN 978-0-8050-7809-1; 0-8050-7809-6
                  LC 2006031372
The reader is invited to count from one to thirteen as a jolly baker makes delectable treats from one mouthwatering eclair to twelve luscious cupcakes, and serves them to invited guests

This offers "a simple rhyme and clear, mouthwatering illustrations." Booklist

The **giant** of Seville; a tall tale based on a true story. Abrams Books for Young Readers 2007 un il $15.95
Grades: K 1 2 3   E
   1. Giants 2. Army officers 3. Circus performers
   ISBN 978-0-8109-0988-5; 0-8109-0988-X
                  LC 2006-13579
"Seville, Ohio, is so quiet that you can 'hear the corn grow' until a giant comes to town. Nearly eight feet tall, Captain Martin Van Buren is searching for a friendly community in which to settle down. Seville's residents welcome him, but accommodating a guest of his stature proves difficult. . . . An endnote introduces the historical people and events that inspired the story, and Andreasen extends the tale's old-fashioned feel in detailed, color-washed ink drawings of townspeople in nineteenth-century dress." Booklist

The **treasure** bath. Henry Holt and Co. 2009 un il $16.99
Grades: PreK   E
   1. Stories without words 2. Baths -- Fiction 3. Imagination -- Fiction
   ISBN 978-0-8050-8686-7; 0-8050-8686-2
                  LC 2008-38224
A wordless picture book in which a young boy explores a creature-filled world beneath the bubbles in his bathtub
"Andreasen borrows motifs from comic-book art—extra gleam on objects, squared-off, blunt-cut hair and the humans' doll-like postures—and combines them with Disney-esque cheer to create amiable scenarios with just a hint of irony." Publ Wkly

Andrews, Julie

  The **very** fairy princess; by Julie Andrews & Emma Walton Hamilton; [illustrations by Christine Davenier] Little, Brown Books for Young Readers 2010 un il $16.99
Grades: PreK K 1 2   E
   1. Princesses -- Fiction
   ISBN 0-316-04050-9; 978-0-316-04050-1
                  LC 2009-19307
Despite her scabby knees and dirty fingernails, Geraldine knows that she is a princess inside and shows it through her behavior at home and in school.
"Davenier's whimsical ink-and-colored-pencil illustrations enchant. . . . The mother-daughter team successfully demonstrates an understanding of that magical stage of childhood in which determination, desire and dreams can transform reality." Kirkus
Another title about Geraldine is:
The very fairy princess takes the stage (2011)

The **very** fairy princess; graduation girl. by Julie Andrews & Emma Walton Hamilton; illustrated by Christine Davenier. Little, Brown & Co. 2014 32 p. color illustrations (The very fairy princess) (reinforced) $18
Grades: PreK K 1 2   E
   1. School stories 2. Princesses -- Fiction 3. Change -- Fiction 4. Schools -- Fiction 5. Teachers -- Fiction
   ISBN 0316219606; 9780316219600
                  LC 2013014112
In this story, "the end of the school year is here, and Very Fairy Princess Gerry is getting ready to graduate! She always loves a celebration, but can't help but feel a little sad as she empties her cubby, takes down her art projects, and says goodbye to her class pet, Houdini the hamster." (Publisher's note)

"Davenier's ink-and-colored-pencil illustrations neatly capture Gerry's feelings, making them stand out against the rest of her class' more joyful faces.Though the cover is bedecked in sparkles, Gerry's sparkle is just as internal as it is external—her essential self-confidence shines." Kirkus

Andros, Camille

Charlotte the scientist is squished; Camille Andros; illustrated by Brianne Farley. Clarion Books, Houghton Mifflin Harcourt 2017 40 p. color illustrations (hardcover) $16.99

Grades: 1 2 3   E

1. Rabbits -- Fiction 2. Scientists -- Fiction 3. Family life -- Fiction 4. Brothers and sisters -- Fiction 5. Brothers and sisters -- Fiction 6. Science -- Experiments -- Fiction 7. Science -- Methodology -- Fiction

ISBN 9780544785830

LC 2015045603

In this book, by Camille Andros, illustrated by Brianne Farley, "Charlotte is a serious scientist. She solves important problems by following the scientific method. She has all the right equipment: protective glasses, a lab coat, a clipboard, and a magnifying glass. What she doesn't have is space. She has so many brothers and sisters (she is a rabbit, after all) that she is too squished to work on her experiments! Can she use science to solve her problem?" (Publisher's note)

Angleberger, Tom

★ **Crankee** Doodle; by Tom Angleberger; illustrations by Cece Bell. Clarion Books 2013 32 p. ill. (hardcover) $16.99

Grades: PreK K 1   E

1. Picture books for children 2. Historical fiction -- Fiction 3. Humorous stories 4. Ponies -- Fiction 5. Mood (Psychology) -- Fiction

ISBN 0547818548; 9780547818542

LC 2012001346

In this children's picture book, "when a colonial-era Yankee announces that he's bored, his pony suggests the pair could go to town. 'Town?' replies the man. 'No way. I hate going to town. There are too many people in town.' For each subsequent nudge from the pony . . . , the Yankee has a long-winded and highly opinionated rant against the idea." (Publishers Weekly)

Anholt, Laurence

Cezanne and the apple boy. Barron's 2009 un il

Grades: PreK K 1   E

1. Artists 2. Painters 3. Artists -- Fiction 4. Father-son relationship -- Fiction

ISBN 0-7641-6282-9; 978-0-7641-6282-4

Paul's father, the artist Paul Cézanne has been away from home for so long that the boy hardly recognizes his father when he returns. But the two soon become fast friends. The local townspeople laugh at the artist's pictures. But young Paul likes the art. An influential art dealer comes from Paris the lives of the artist and his son change dramatically.

"Evocative, realistic illustrations mix with reproductions of Cézanne works and, along with the young character, will draw kids into this enjoyable, informative portrayal of Cézanne as both a father and an influential artist." Booklist

Anno, Mitsumasa

★ **Anno's** counting book. Crowell 1977 un il $17.99; lib bdg $18.89; pa $6.99

Grades: PreK K 1   E

1. Counting 2. Stories without words 3. Seasons -- Fiction

ISBN 0-690-01287-X; 0-690-01288-8 lib bdg; 0-06-443123-1 pa

LC 76-28977

Original Japanese edition, 1975

"A distinctive, beautifully conceived counting book in which twelve full-color doublespreads show the same village and surrounding countryside during different hours (by the church clock) and months. Both the seasons and community changes are studied, as such components of the scene as flowers, trees, animals, people, and buildings increase from one to twelve." LC. Child Books, 1977

Antle, Bhagavan

Suryia swims! : the true story of how an orangutan learned to swim; Bhagavan "Doc" Antle, with Thea Feldman; photographs by Barry Bland. Henry Holt 2012 32 p. (hc) $16.99

Grades: 1 2 3   E

1. Swimming 2. Orangutan -- Fiction 3. Animal behavior 4. Swimming -- Fiction 5. Orangutan -- Fiction 6. Wildlife refuges -- Fiction 7.

ISBN 0805093176; 9780805093179

LC 2011029047

This book, by Bhagavan Antle, illustrated by Barry Bland, narrated by Thea Feldman, describes an episode in the life of the orangutan Suryia. "Suryia is not your average orangutan. In the first book about him, . . . Suryia found an unusual best friend: a dog named Roscoe. Now Suryia jumps into an unusual new hobby: swimming! Orangutans don't swim; it doesn't come naturally to them. But Suryia shows that adventures await those who are willing to try something new." (Publisher's note)

Antony, Steve

Please, Mr. Panda; Steve Antony. Scholastic Press 2015 32 p. color illustrations $16.99

Grades: PreK K   E

1. Etiquette 2. Doughnuts -- Fiction 3. Pandas -- Fiction 4. Pandas -- Fiction 5. Etiquette -- Fiction 6. Courtesy -- Fiction 7. Etiquette -- Fiction

ISBN 0545788927; 9780545788922

LC 2014022891

In this children's book by Steve Antony "Mr. Panda asks the animals he comes across if they would like a doughnut. A penguin, a skunk, and a whale all say yes, but they do not remember to say 'please' and 'thank you.' Is anyone worthy of Mr. Panda's doughnuts?" (Publisher's note)

"Simply stated--and slightly aggressive--this etiquette book lays down the law." Booklist

Another title in this series is:
I'll Wait, Mr. Panda (2016)

Appelt, Kathi

★ **Bats** around the clock; illustrated by Melissa Sweet. HarperCollins Pubs. 2000 un il $15.99; lib bdg $16.89

Grades: PreK K 1 2   E

1. Stories in rhyme 2. Bats -- Fiction 3. Rock music -- Fiction

ISBN 0-688-16469-2; 0-688-16470-6 lib bdg

LC 99-15502

Click Dark hosts a special twelve-hour program of American Bat Stand where the bats rock and roll until the midnight hour ends.

"The rhymes are delightful and the narrative jives right along." SLJ

Other titles about the bats are:
The bat jamboree (1996)
Bats on parade (1999)

Brand-new baby blues; words by Kathi Appelt; illustrations by Kelly Murphy. HarperCollins Publishers 2010 un il $16.99

Grades: PreK K 1 2   E
1. Stories in rhyme 2. Infants -- Fiction 3. Siblings -- Fiction
ISBN 978-0-06-053233-8; 0-06-053233-5; 978-0-06-053234-5
lib bdg; 0-06-053234-3 lib bdg

LC 2008-05796

The arrival of a new little brother has his big sister singing the blues.

"Funny and concise, the rollicking rhyme bounces along, accepting the frustration natural to the situation, while gently allowing the girl's love of and appreciation for her brother. . . . The process is complemented by the illustrations, which modulate in palette from angry blues and greens to sunny yellows, while serene compositions replace off-kilter ones. Older brothers and sisters will easily identify with this jaunty heroine and profit from her realizations—an excellent choice for a new older sibling." Kirkus

Counting crows; Kathi Appelt; illustrated by Rob Dunlavey. Atheneum Books for Young Readers 2015 40 p. color illustrations (hardcover) $17.99
Grades: PreK K 1   E
1. Counting 2. Crows -- Fiction 3. Stories in rhyme
ISBN 1442423277; 9781442423275

LC 2014002094

In this story by Kathi Appelt, illustrated by Rob Dunlavey, "hungry crows avoid a feline foe. . . . Crows in a tree . . . fly out of their nest with snacking in mind . . . , but before they have time to complain about bellyaches, they have a bigger problem: a cat has been eyeing them...as potential snacks! Can these well-fed crows become well-FLED crows?" (Publisher's note)

"Writing a fresh counting rhyme calls for the poet to hear the numbers in a new way, and that's just what Appelt . . . has done. She tweaks sequences, varies rhythms, and punctuates her lines with piquant sound words." Pub Wkly

★ **Mogie**; the heart of the house. Kathi Appelt; illustrated by Marc Rosenthal. Atheneum Books for Young Readers 2014 40 p. (hardcover) $17.99
Grades: PreK K 1 2 3   E
1. Sick -- Fiction 2. Charities -- Fiction 3. Dogs -- Fiction 4. Animals -- Infancy -- Fiction 5. Ronald McDonald House Charities -- Fiction
ISBN 1442480548; 9781442480544

LC 2013018100

In this children's book, written by Kathi Appelt and illustrated by Marc Rosenthal, "Mogie, a labradoodle with a trademarked name who lives at the Ronald McDonald House in Houston, has his story fictionally told. . . . While seemingly not cut out for other canine careers, [he] bonds instantly with Gage, a . . . boy at the house who has lost his 'mojo.' The two become fast friends, and once Gage finally recovers from his unstated illness and moves out, Mogie turns his affection to Antonia." (Booklist)

"In this touching story, rambunctious Mogie fails as a service dog, at search-and-rescue work, and in the show ring, but when he wanders into a Ronald McDonald House (unnamed in the main text), he discovers his true calling as a comfort dog. Colored-in pencil and charcoal illustrations depict Mogie's exuberance and affection as he helps once-energetic young patients get their "mojo" back." Horn Book

Oh my baby, little one; pictures by Jane Dyer. Harcourt Brace & Co. 2000 un il $16; pa $3.99
Grades: PreK K   E
1. Stories in rhyme 2. Mother-child relationship -- Fiction
ISBN 0-15-200041-0; 0-15-206031-6 pa

LC 99-6363

"The light, bright pictures will charm young listeners, who will find this book best enjoyed while cuddled up next to Mama." Booklist

★ **When** Otis courted Mama; Kathi Appelt; illustrated by Jill McElmurry. Houghton Mifflin Harcourt 2014 40 p. col. ill. $16.99
Grades: PreK K 1 2 3   E
1. Single mothers -- Fiction 2. Children of divorced parents 3. Coyote -- Fiction 4. Stepfathers -- Fiction 5. Fathers and sons -- Fiction 6. Mothers and sons -- Fiction
ISBN 0152166882; 9780152166885

LC 2007029880

In this children's book by Kathi Appelt and illustrated by Jill McElmurry "Cardell's life is mostly wonderful. He knows he's loved . . . by his perfectly good mama and his perfectly good daddy. They live in different parts of the desert, but that's okay--Cardell is mostly used to it. Then Otis comes calling. . . . Cardell waits for Mama to say "Adiós, Otis." But what will happen if she doesn't?" (Publisher's note)

"Aside from a few sticker burrs and occasional sand fleas, Cardell, a little coyote, has a mostly wonderful life. He has a perfectly good mama and a perfectly good daddy, and even though his daddy lives in a different part of the desert, Cardell still gets to see him... And gradually, Cardell's "grrrs" get softer until they stop altogether. Like Otis, Appelt is a gifted storyteller, and families whose circumstances echo Cardell's will welcome this gentle story, which is nicely augmented by illustrator McElmurry's gouache pictures, with their vivid desert colors. " Booklist

Applegate, Katherine

The **buffalo** storm; illustrated by Jan Ormerod. Clarion Books 2007 32p il $16
Grades: 2 3 4   E
1. Fear -- Fiction 2. Grandmothers -- Fiction 3. Frontier and pioneer life -- Fiction 4. Overland journeys to the Pacific -- Fiction
ISBN 978-0-618-53597-2; 0-618-53597-7

LC 2006-15661

When Hallie and her parents join a wagon train to Oregon and leave her grandmother behind, Hallie must learn to face the storms that frighten her so, as well as other, newer fears, with just her grandmother's quilt to comfort her.

"Ormerod's . . . textured watercolors and pastels employ billowy swaths of color to suggest the vastness of the setting. . . . Vivid imagery makes this lyrical tale an accessible, fresh addition to the children's pioneer genre as it tackles themes of change, courage and home." Publ Wkly

Archer, Dosh

Big Bad Wolf; Dosh Archer. Albert Whitman & Company 2013 48 p. color illustrations (Urgency emergency!) (hardback) 48 p.
Grades: K 1 2 3   E
1. Wolves -- Fiction 2. Hospitals -- Fiction 3. Humorous stories 4. Animals -- Fiction 5. Asphyxia -- Fiction 6. Medical care -- Fiction 7. Characters in literature -- Fiction
ISBN 0807583529; 9780807583524

LC 2013005440

Cybil Award: Early Reader (2013)

In this children's book, written and illustrated by Dosh Archer, "A choking wolf is rushed to City Hospital, and a lost little girl in a red coat has been found, looking for her missing granny. What on earth did the wolf eat?" The book is an "animal hospital adventure story" for "young readers." (Publisher's note)

"New readers are in for a treat with these British imports. Both are set in an emergency room where Doctor Glenda (a dog) and Nurse Percy (a rooster) assist their nursery-rhyme- and fairy-tale-character patients. Muted colors and droll cartoon-style illustrations keep the action light and to the point. Limited, easy-to-decode vocabulary in a large typeface will support emerging readers." Horn Book

Urgency emergecy! Itsy bitsy spider; written and illustrated by Dosh Archer. Albert Whitman & Company 2013 48 p. (hardback) $12.99

Grades: K 1 2   E

1. Hospitals -- Fiction 2. Spiders -- Fiction 3. Humorous stories 4. Animals -- Fiction 5. Medical care -- Fiction 6. Wounds and injuries -- Fiction

ISBN 0807583588; 9780807583586

LC 2013005442

In this book by Dosh Archer "a spider arrives at City Hospital with some strange head injuries. How did this happen? And does it have anything to do with all the water rushing down the water spout? This animal hospital adventure story [includes] bright color illustrations on every page, minimal easy-to-read text and a . . . fast-paced plot." (Publisher's note)

Armand, Glenda

Love twelve miles long; illustrated by Colin Bootman. Lee & Low Books 2011 il $17.95

Grades: K 1 2   E

1. Slaves 2. Authors 3. Abolitionists 4. Memoirists 5. Slavery -- Fiction 6. Mother-son relationship -- Fiction

ISBN 978-1-60060-245-0; 1-60060-245-2

LC 2011014275

In 1820s Maryland, Frederick's mother, who is a slave on a different plantation, walks twelve miles each way for a nighttime visit with her son, during which she recounts what each mile of the journey represents. Based on the childhood of Frederick Douglass.

"Armand's debut reveals a poignant conversation between young Frederick and his mother, paired with Bootman's arresting and emotive paintings. . . . Bootman . . . deftly uses candlelight and moonlight to give his art a lovely iridescence, and presents intimate portraits of mother and son." Pub Wkly

Armstrong, Jennifer

★ **Once** upon a banana; illustrated by David Small. Simon & Schuster Books for Young Readers 2006 un il $16.95

Grades: PreK K 1 2   E

1. Stories without words 2. City and town life -- Fiction

ISBN 0-689-84251-1; 978-0-689-84251-1

LC 2005-08567

"A street juggler's pet monkey runs off and steals a deli's outdoor stall. . . . The monkey tosses the banana peel on the sidewalk, thus triggering a book-long, slapstick-rich chase that covers an entire city center and ensnares a cavalcade of characters. . . . Small's loose yet precise ink lines and watercolor wash seem ideal for these crowded streets where anarchy abounds. . . . The pages overflow with enough pratfalls and comic asides to reward many readings." Publ Wkly

Armstrong, Matthew S.

Jane and Mizmow; by Matthew S. Armstrong. Harper 2011 il

Grades: PreK K 1   E

1. Monsters -- Fiction 2. Friendship -- Fiction

ISBN 0061177199; 9780061177194

LC 2010012628

Jane and her best friend, a monster named Mizmow, are best friends in spite of their differences, and nothing can keep them apart.

"A palette of fall colors mirrors the warmth of their friendship, while the expressive faces of the two characters reinforce both mood and action. Emerging readers will be able to read much of the simple text, but

the illustrations really tell the tale. . . . A solid choice that youngsters will enjoy time and time again." SLJ

Arndt, Michael

Cat says meow; and other animalopoeia. by Michael Arndt. Chronicle Books LLC 2014 36 p. col. ill. (alk. paper) $12.99

Grades: PreK K   E

1. Animal sounds 2. English language -- Terms and phrases 3. Animal sounds -- Fiction

ISBN 1452112347; 9781452112343

LC 2013003270

In this book by Michael Arndt, "animals and the sounds they make are paired up in playfully compelling ways . . . featuring bold colors and an engaging use of onomatopoeia. Kids and parents [can discover] the ways in which the letters that spell out each animal's sound are key elements of that animal's illustration." (Publisher's note)

"Each page turn reveals a new graphic in a bold color, with a pleasing variety of single- and double-page spreads, as well as subtle changes in composition. This is one of those rare picture books with something for everyone to enjoy, beginning with colors, sounds and shapes for the youngest." Kirkus

Arnold, Tedd

Dirty Gert; by Tedd Arnold. Holiday House 2013 40 p. (hardcover) $16.95

Grades: K 1 2 3   E

1. Stories in rhyme 2. Trees -- Fiction 3. Humorous fiction 4. Humorous stories

ISBN 0823424049; 9780823424047

LC 2012006578

This children's story, by Tedd Arnold, follows a girl who becomes a tree. "Gert loves dirt. . . . Then one day while making mud pies in the rain, Gert becomes reorganized: she grows branches, leaves and roots. Gert is delighted . . . until camera crews televise her, botanists analyze her, and Hollywood tries to immortalize her. The child is traumatized! But Mom and Dad know what to do to protect their offbeat plant-child." (Publisher's note)

Fix this mess! Tedd Arnold. Holiday House 2014 32 p. color illustrations (I like to read) (hardcover) $14.95

Grades: PreK K 1 2   E

1. Cleaning 2. Robots -- Fiction 3. Orderliness -- Fiction

ISBN 0823429423; 9780823429424

LC 2013009565

In this children's book, part of the I Like to Read series, written and illustrated by Tedd Arnold, "Robug [the robot] tries to obey when Jake instructs it to 'fix this mess' but somehow manages to make things worse. . . . Robug comes up with a solution: Jake can fix his own mess." (Publisher's note)

"Jake turns Robug ("Remote Operating Basic Utility Gizmo") on and commands it to 'fix this mess.' Robug energetically fires into action, but things don't quite turn out right. Funny details in Arnold's characteristic cartoon-style illustrations build momentum from page to page, and the vocabulary is simple enough to allow the newest readers to enjoy it all on their own." Horn Book

Fly guy presents; space. by Tedd Arnold. Scholastic 2013 32 p. $3.99

Grades: PreK K 1 2   E

1. Comets 2. Space vehicles 3. Outer space 4. Readers (Elementary) 5. Outer space -- Exploration -- History

ISBN 0545564921; 9780545564922

In this book, author Tedd Arnold "brings nonfiction to life. . . . During a visit to a space museum, Fly Guy and Buzz learn all about planets, space crafts, space suits, and even dirty snowballs (i.e. comets!)! With straightforward . . . facts, . . . illustrations of Fly Guy and Buzz, and vivid photographs throughout." (Publisher's note)

Green Wilma, frog in space. Dial Books for Young Readers 2009 un il $16.99

Grades: K 1 2   E

1. Stories in rhyme 2. Frogs -- Fiction 3. Space flight -- Fiction 4. Extraterrestrial beings -- Fiction

ISBN 978-0-8037-2698-7; 0-8037-2698-8

LC 2008039497

Green Wilma the frog is mistaken for an alien child and taken on a trip through space.

This is written "in perfect rhyme. . . . The illustrations explode across the pages with frantic innocence. . . . To say that the pictures complement the text is like declaring that the Sun complements the Earth. Children will adore Wilma." SLJ

Another title about Green Wilma is:

Green Wilma (1993)

Hi, Fly Guy! Scholastic 2005 30p il $5.99; pa $3.99

Grades: PreK K 1 2   E

1. Pets -- Fiction 2. Flies -- Fiction

ISBN 0-439-63903-4; 0-439-85311-7 pa; 978-0-439-63903-3; 978-0-439-85311-8 pa

LC 2004-20553

When Buzz captures a fly to enter in The Amazing Pet Show, his parents and the judges tell him that a fly cannot be a pet, but Fly Guy proves them wrong. "Grades one to three." (Bull Cent Child Books)

"Suitably wacky cartoon art accompanies the text, which is simple enough for beginning readers." Publ Wkly

Other titles in this series are:

Super Fly Guy (2006)

Shoo Fly Guy (2006)

There was an old lady who swallowed Fly Guy (2007)

Fly high, Fly Guy (2008)

Hooray for Fly Guy! (2008)

I spy Fly Guy! (2009)

Fly Guy meets Fly Girl! (2010)

Buzz Boy and Fly Guy (2010)

Fly Guy vs. the flyswatter! (2011)

There's a Fly Girl in My Soup (2012)

Ride Fly Guy Ride (2012)

Fly Guy and the Frankenfly (2013)

Fly Guy's Amazing Tricks (2014)

Prince Fly Guy (2015)

Fly Guy's Ninja Christmas (2016)

I spy Fly Guy. Scholastic 2009 30p il $5.99

Grades: PreK K 1 2   E

1. Flies -- Fiction

ISBN 978-0-545-11028-0; 0-545-11028-9

LC 2008042956

ALA ALSC Geisel Award Honor Book (2010)

While playing hide-and-seek with Buzz, Fly Guy is taken away by a garbage man

This is "outrageously funny. . . . There's no mistaking Arnold's hilarious cartoon illustrations, and . . . there are plenty of them to enjoy." SLJ

A **pet** for Fly Guy; Tedd Arnold. Orchard Books 2014 32 p. $16.99

Grades: PreK K 1 2   E

1. Pets -- Fiction 2. Flies -- Fiction 3. Humorous fiction 4.

Humorous stories

ISBN 0545316154; 9780545316156

LC 2013035044

In this children's book, by Tedd Arnold, "Buzz tries to help Fly Guy find the right pet. It seems that everyone else at the park has a pet, so Fly Guy wants one, too. A dog licked Fly Guy. A frog chased Fly Guy. A cricket was too jumpy. Who will be the best pet for Fly Guy?" (Publisher's note)

"Fly Guy's latest adventure is in picture-book format. While on a picnic at the park, Buzz and Fly Guy watch people playing with their zany pets...This humorous selection is fun to read aloud but is also well designed for new readers. The simple text is well placed on each page, including occasional thought and speech bubbles that are easy to follow. Children who have enjoyed other books about Buzz and Fly Guy will love this one, too." SLJ

Vincent paints his house; by Tedd Arnold. Holiday House 2015 32 p. color illustrations (hardcover) $16.95

Grades: PreK K 1 2 3   E

1. Color -- Fiction 2. House painting -- Fiction 3. Animals -- Fiction

ISBN 0823432106; 9780823432103

LC 2014006045

This children's story, written and illustrated by Tedd Arnold, pays "homage to artist Vincent van Gogh. . . . Vincent is ready to paint his house. The only problem is choosing the color. . . . Before long, Vincent has a list of requests: the termite wants orange, the caterpillar loves yellow and the ladybug insists on purple. With a little creativity and a lot of color Vincent does a brilliant job!" (Publisher's note)

"Arnold, best known for his Fly Guy series, uses a simple, engaging formula to introduce readers to different colors and reinforces this palette with appealing, cartoonish illustrations." Booklist

Arnosky, Jim

At this very moment. Dutton Children's Books 2011 un il $16.99

Grades: K 1 2   E

1. Stories in rhyme 2. Nature -- Fiction 3. Animals -- Fiction

ISBN 978-0-525-42252-5; 0-525-42252-8

LC 2010037711

Identifies some of the things happening in nature while one goes about an ordinary day, such as a shark circling a reef while one brushes one's teeth, or puffins eating fresh-caught fish while one eats dinner.

"With a gentle rhythm, unforced rhymes and near rhymes and perfect pacing, this bedtime story encourages children to think, dream and wonder about the lives of animals in the wild." Kirkus

★ **Babies** in the bayou; [by] Jim Arnosky. G. P. Putnam's Sons 2007 un il $16.99

Grades: PreK K   E

1. Wetlands 2. Animal babies

ISBN 978-0-399-22653-3; 0-399-22653-2

LC 2006011910

There are many babies in the bayou, and even though they might have sharp white teeth, hard shells, webbed feet, or quick claws, their mothers still need to protect them.

"This is a wonderful resource to use with children to illuminate the ways of nature; it's economical and rhythmic in text, and beautifully and clearly illustrated. Arnosky uses simple language and a repeated refrain to describe the animals that live in a lush Southern environment." SLJ

Dolphins on the sand; by Jim Arnosky. G.P. Putnam's Sons 2008 un il $16.99

Grades: PreK K 1 2   **E**
  1. Dolphins -- Fiction 2. Wildlife conservation -- Fiction
  ISBN 978-0-399-24606-7; 0-399-24606-1
                                       LC 2007045384
  A dozen dolphins, led by their eldest member and her youngster, become stranded on a sandbar and must be helped to safety by humans.
  This "juxtaposes a straightforward narrative with particularly colorful paintings. . . . Arnosky reflects the simple beauty of the dolphins of the dolphins' happy existence in tropical pinks, oranges, and aquas, moving to a more somber palette of grays and blacks as danger sets in. He includes all manner of flora and fauna in his illustrative arc." Booklist

I'm a turkey! Scholastic Press 2009 un il $16.99
Grades: PreK K 1   **E**
  1. Stories in rhyme 2. Turkeys -- Fiction
  ISBN 978-0-439-90364-6; 0-439-90364-5
                                     LC 2008-38335
  "Arnosky's illustrations manage to be both autumnal and bright. . . . Arnosky gives [the birds] personality and charm." Booklist

Aronson, Billy

The **chicken** problem; Jennifer Oxley & Billy Aronson. Random House 2012 25 p. col. ill. (hardcover) $16.99; (library) $16.99
Grades: PreK K   **E**
  1. Picture books for children 2. Chickens -- Fiction 3. Counting -- Fiction 4. Farm life -- Fiction 5. Problem solving -- Fiction
  ISBN 0375869891; 9780375869891; 9780375969898
                                     LC 2011031249
  In this children's picture book by Jennifer Oxley, "Peg (a girl) and her pal Cat (a cat) are getting ready 'to have a perfect picnic with a pig' when they realize that they've cut one too many pieces of pie. Cat retrieves a little chicken (for the little piece of pie) from the nearby chicken coop, but she leaves the door to the coop wide open. . . . Peg and Cat eventually manage to return the errant poultry to the coop." (Bulletin of the Center for Children's Books)

Aruego, Jose

★ The **last** laugh; [by] Jose Aruego & Ariane Dewey. Dial Books for Young Readers 2006 un il $12.99
Grades: PreK K 1 2   **E**
  1. Stories without words 2. Ducks -- Fiction 3. Snakes -- Fiction
  ISBN 0-8037-3093-4
                                     LC 2005-48461
  A wordless tale in which a clever duck outwits a bullying snake
  "In comic-strip panels, Aruego and Deweys signature pen-and-ink and gouache art is droll and accessible. . . . Young readers will find the format and the karmic justice of this story appealing." SLJ

Asch, Frank

The **Daily** Comet; boy saves Earth from giant octopus. written by Frank Asch; illustrated by Devin Asch. Kids Can Press 2010 un il $16.95
Grades: K 1 2 3   **E**
  1. Octopuses -- Fiction 2. Journalists -- Fiction 3. Father-son relationship -- Fiction
  ISBN 978-1-55453-281-0; 1-55453-281-7
  When Hayward Palmer accompanies his father, a reporter for the sensationalistic Daily Comet, on a "Go to Work with a Parent Day," he has a rational explanation for all the weird and wacky things they encounter until he finally comes face to face with an enormous octopus.
  "The dialogue is brisk, and visual quotes from Hollywood abound; Devin Asch's digital illustrations portray Hayward's father as a Gregory Peck look-alike and his photographer sidekick is an Elvis clone; dozens of other retro elements whirl at high speed. . . . It's a strangely believable tall tale." Publ Wkly

Happy birthday, Moon. Simon & Schuster Books for Young Readers 2000 un il pa $6.99
Grades: PreK K 1   **E**
  1. Moon -- Fiction 2. Bears -- Fiction 3. Birthdays -- Fiction
  ISBN 978-0-689-83544-5; 0-689-83544-2
  First published 1982 by Prentice Hall
  Bear travels to the highest mountaintop to find out what to give the Moon for its birthday and discovers a delightful surprise—the Moon has the same birthday as Bear. Or so it seems.
  Other titles in this series are:
  Mooncake (1983)
  Moongame (1984)
  Moonbear's shadow (1985)

Like a windy day; [by] Frank Asch & Devin Asch. Harcourt 2002 un il $16; pa $7
Grades: PreK K   **E**
  1. Winds -- Fiction
  ISBN 0-15-216376-X; 0-15-206403-6 pa
                                     LC 2001-5260
  A young girl discovers all the things the wind can do, by playing and dancing along with it
  Written "in a poetic text. . . . The brief story is filled with action verbs. . . . The exciting pen-and-ink illustrations were colorized in Adobe Photoshop. Broad and sweeping spreads are filled with movement." SLJ

The **sun** is my favorite star. Harcourt 2001 un il $15; pa $7
Grades: PreK K 1   **E**
  1. Sun -- Fiction
  ISBN 0-15-202127-2; 0-15-206397-8 pa
                                     LC 98-46383
  Celebrates a child's love of the sun and the wondrous ways in which it helps the earth and the life upon it
  "Asch strikes just the right tone for his audience. . . . With colors as warm as a summer day, he creates a series of large-scale illustrations that reflect the direct unaffected tone of the writing." Booklist

Ashburn, Boni

I had a favorite dress; pictures by Julia Denos. Abrams 2011 un il $16.95
Grades: PreK K 1 2   **E**
  1. Clothing and dress -- Fiction
  ISBN 978-1-4197-0016-3; 1-4197-0016-2
  "When the unnamed narrator's favorite dress is suddenly a size too small, she is not a happy camper; she wears that dress every Tuesday, which is her favorite day of the week. Then her mother transforms the too-small dress into the perfect shirt. As the child's favorite day of the week changes so does her garment as she grows out of it. It becomes a tank top . . . a skirt . . . a scarf . . . socks . . . a hair bow . . . and, finally, a picture of the original dress by the narrator herself. . . . Some of Ashburn's text is playfully placed in and around the art to good effect. . . . Denos's multimedia illustrations, a combination of collages, watercolors, and graphite and colored pencil artwork, reinforce the narrator's vibrant personality and the amazing transformations of the dress while capturing the action and emotion of the story." SLJ

Over at the castle; illustrated by Kelly Murphy. Abrams 2010 un il $15.95
Grades: PreK K 1 2   **E**
  1. Counting 2. Stories in rhyme 3. Castles -- Fiction 4. Dragons

-- Fiction 5. Middle Ages -- Fiction

ISBN 978-0-8109-8414-1; 0-8109-8414-8

"The familiar rhythm of the folk song Over in the Meadow finds a new setting as over at the castle, on the hill in the sun, an old mother dragon tries to teach her little dragon patience as they laze about near a castle. . . . Richly textured paintings in subtle hues that fit the medieval period convey the chores of the occupants of the castle, and comedic touches throughout . . . deepen the story and will have children flipping back through the pages." Booklist

Ashdown, Rebecca

Bob and Flo; by Rebecca Ashdown. Houghton Mifflin Harcourt 2015 32 p. color illustrations $16.99

Grades: PreK K   E

1. School stories 2. Penguins -- Fiction 3. Friendship -- Fiction 4. Schools -- Fiction 5. Nursery schools -- Fiction

ISBN 0544444302; 9780544444300

LC 2014017544

In this children's story, by Rebecca Ashdown, "it's Flo's first day of preschool. She has her lunch in a bucket and a new bow--but soon her bucket disappears! Does her classmate Bob have anything to do with the bucket mystery? How two irresistible little penguins find both Flo's bucket and a new friendship makes for a preschool charmer." (Publisher's note)

"On the first day of preschool, Flo, a little penguin, meets a classmate who is fascinated by her pink lunch bucket. While Flo is busy painting, Bob purloins her pail. . . .Pair this title with Antoinette Portis's Not a Box (HarperCollins, 2007) for an imaginative toddler storytime." SLJ

Ashman, Linda

All We Know; by Linda Ashman; illustrated by Jane Dyer. Harpercollins Childrens Books 2016 40 p. color illustrations $17.99

Grades: PreK K 1   E

1. Mother-child relationship -- Fiction

ISBN 0061689580; 9780061689581

This book, by Linda Ashman, illustrated by Jane Dyer, is a "story of a mother's unconditional love for her child. A seed knows how to sprout. A lamb knows how to bleat. A bee knows where the nectar is to make the honey sweet. Stars shine, seasons change, and waves rise and fall. Invoking the majestic beauty of the natural world, a mother affectionately explains that some things just come naturally—like a parent's love." (Publisher's note)

"A gentle, heartwarming celebration of the continuity of life and of a parent's love." Pub Wkly

★ **Babies** on the go; illustrated by Jane Dyer. Harcourt 2003 un il $16

Grades: PreK K 1   E

1. Animal babies 2. Animal locomotion

ISBN 0-15-201894-8

LC 2002-6310

Illustrations and rhyming text show how different animals carry their babies when they are on the move

"The large, soft watercolor illustrations and rhyming text make this celebration of parent/child love a natural for toddler storytime, and it's also perfect for one-on-one sharing." SLJ

Castles, caves, and honeycombs; illustrated by Lauren Stringer. Harcourt 2001 un il $16

Grades: PreK K 1   E

1. Home 2. Stories in rhyme 3. Animals -- Habitations

ISBN 0-15-202211-2

LC 99-50801

Describes some of the unique places where animals build their homes such as in a heap of twigs, on a castle tower, in a cave, or in the hollow space inside a tree

"The concise text and womb-like illustrations convey the feelings of love, safety, and security that a home should have." Horn Book Guide

★ **Mama's** day; [illustrated by] Jan Ormerod. Simon & Schuster Books for Young Readers 2006 un il $15.95

Grades: PreK K 1   E

1. Stories in rhyme 2. Mother-child relationship -- Fiction

ISBN 0-689-83475-6

LC 00-45063

In rhyming text, mothers and their babies are described sharing in a variety of activities, from playing at the ocean to reading books and taking a bath

"Ashman's skillful verse and Ormerod's cozy ink-and-gouache artwork improve upon many other picture-book fulminations on mother love. A lilting line of verse appears on each spread, illustrated by a neatly framed scene of a different mother-child pair (including a demure image of breastfeeding) as well as a crew of charming, multicultural babies." Booklist

No dogs allowed! [ilustrated by] Kristin Sorra. Sterling 2011 un il $14.95

Grades: PreK K 1   E

1. Dogs -- Fiction 2. Pets -- Fiction 3. Animals -- Fiction 4. Restaurants -- Fiction

ISBN 978-1-4027-5837-9; 1-4027-5837-5

When Alberto turns away people with pets from his restaurant, they gather in the street and buy treats from a street vendor.

"Digital artwork with plenty of captivating details essentially tells this story; the only text appears in speech bubbles and changing restaurant signage. . . . This lively picture book is a good choice for one-on-one sharing; the details in the art could serve as a visual stimulus to initiate conversations about what is happening." SLJ

Rain! written by Linda Ashman; illustrated by Christian Robinson. Houghton Mifflin Books for Children 2013 32 p. col. ill. (reinforced) $16.99

Grades: PreK K 1   E

1. Rain -- Fiction 2. Picture books for children 3. Neighbors -- Fiction 4. Mood (Psychology) -- Fiction 5. Rain and rainfall -- Fiction

ISBN 054773395X; 9780547733951

LC 2011042039

This children's picture book is set on a rainy day. "Two strangers have very different views about the weather: one is an elderly man who grumbles and complains throughout the day, and the other is a little boy who makes the most of the puddles on the sidewalk. When they meet at the Rain or Shine Café, the child finds himself momentarily brought down by the man's sullen demeanor until a mix-up with their hats brings out the old man's smile and optimism." (School Library Journal)

★ **Samantha** on a roll; pictures by Christine Davenier. Farrar, Straus & Giroux 2011 un il $16.99

Grades: K 1 2   E

1. Stories in rhyme 2. Roller skating -- Fiction

ISBN 978-0-374-36399-4; 0-374-36399-4

"Samantha decides to try out her roller skates for the first time, despite her mother's admonition to wait. She likes skating so much in the house that she hungers for the wide open spaces of the great outdoors. She sneaks outside, and the fun begins. . . . The rhyming text makes this delightful story tons of fun to read aloud. Davenier's illustrations aptly capture the action with bold colors and plenty of lines indicating motion." SLJ

Stella, unleashed; notes from the doghouse. illustrated by Paul Meisel. Sterling Pub. Co. 2008 40p il $14.95
Grades: K 1 2   E
   1. Stories in rhyme 2. Dogs -- Fiction 3. Family life -- Fiction
ISBN 978-1-4027-3987-3; 1-4027-3987-7
                                    LC 2007036499
The family dog describes her life in a series of rhymes.
"Ashman aptly captures life with a pup, balancing the sweet (lap naps) with the sour (shedding). . . . Meisel's realistic acrylic, gouache, and pencil illustrations are filled with a variety of people and pups. . . . This collection of rhymes is ideal for family read-alouds." SLJ

Asper-Smith, Sarah
   Have you ever seen a smack of jellyfish? an alphabet book. Sasquatch Books 2010 un il $16.95
Grades: PreK K   E
   1. Animals 2. Alphabet
ISBN 978-1-57061-687-7; 1-57061-687-6
"Asper-Smith's background in graphic design is evident in this ABC book devoted to collective nouns. Crisp, eye-popping silhouettes put the animals' shapes . . . in high relief. A murder of crows perches on a tree's spindly blue branches against a neon green sky . . . while the yellow-on-pink victim of a 'scourge of mosquitoes' makes their descriptor feel all the more apt. Clean design, attention to detail, and intriguing animal selections . . . make this an elegant primer." Publ Wkly

   I would tuck you in; Sarah Asper-Smith. Sasquatch Books 2012 32 p. $16.99
Grades: K 1 2   E
   1. Picture books for children 2. Bedtime -- Fiction 3. Animal behavior 4. Love -- Fiction 5. Mother and child -- Fiction 6. Animals -- Alaska -- Fiction 7. Animals -- Infancy -- Fiction
ISBN 1570618445; 9781570618444
                                    LC 2012032054
This children's picture book features drowsy animals alongside scientific explanations of animal behavior. "Each two-page spread features an illustration of an adult/child animal pair and a sweet, nonrhyming promise . . . . The feel-good sentiment is then explained in scientific terms via smaller text at the bottom of the page." (Booklist)

Aston, Dianna Hutts
   ★ **Dream** something big; the story of the Watts Towers. Dial Books for Young Readers 2011 un il $16.99
Grades: K 1 2 3   E
   1. Artists 2. Folk artists 3. Watts Towers Arts Center (Los Angeles, Calif.)
ISBN 978-0-8037-3245-2; 0-8037-3245-7
                                    LC 2010028797
"Aston pays tribute to the creative genius of an Italian immigrant and tile worker who, in the 1920s, begins a unique project on his Watts, Calif., property that takes 34 years to complete. Simon Rodia uses only re-bar, cement, broken tiles, shells, and other found items to build towering spires, some almost a hundred feet tall, decorated with mosaic designs. A fictional neighbor girl, Marguerite, provides lyrical first-person narration as she watches the towers take shape throughout her childhood. The subject lends itself perfectly to the collage illustrations. Employing mostly paper, but also bits of pottery, cloth, clay and string, Roth stunningly recreates bold, stylized versions of the towers. This book beautifully illuminates a little-known story of imagination and perseverance that resulted in a national landmark." Publ Wkly

   ★ **Moon** over Star; pictures by Jerry Pinkney. Dial Books for Young Readers 2008 un il $17.99
Grades: PreK K 1 2 3   E
   1. Farm life -- Fiction 2. African Americans -- Fiction 3. Apollo 11 (Spacecraft) -- Fiction 4. Space flight to the moon -- Fiction
ISBN 978-0-8037-3107-3; 0-8037-3107-8
                                    LC 2007050703
Coretta Scott King honor book for illustration, 2009
On her family's farm in the town of Star, eight-year-old Mae eagerly follows the progress of the 1969 Apollo 11 flight and moon landing and dreams that she might one day be an astronaut, too.
"Spaced vertically in phrases like free verse alongside the large illustrations, the text combines dignity and immediacy in a clean, spare telling of events. Pinkney's evocative artwork, created using graphite, ink, and watercolor, depicts a black family captivated, and perhaps subtly changed, by the moon landing in 1969." Booklist

   An **orange** in January; [by] Dianna Hutts Aston; illustrated by Julie Maren. Dial Books for Young Readers 2007 un il $16.99
Grades: PreK K 1   E
   1. Oranges -- Fiction
ISBN 978-0-8037-3146-2
                                    LC 2006014488
An orange begins its life as a blossom where bees feast on the nectar, and reaches the end of its journey, bursting with the seasons inside it, in the hands of a child.
This is a "poetic tale. . . . Like the text, the glowing acrylic paintings are artfully simple and make beautiful use of color." SLJ

Atinuke (Author)
   Double Trouble for Anna Hibiscus; by Atinuke; illustrated by Lauren Tobia. Kane Miller, A Division of EDC Pub. 2015 32 p. color illustrations (hardcover) $20.99
Grades: PreK K   E
   1. Infants -- Fiction 2. Brothers and sisters -- Fiction
ISBN 1610673670; 9781610673679
                                    LC 2014947160
In this picture book, by Atinuke, illustrated by Lauren Tobia, "Anna Hibiscus welcomes not one but two new baby brothers. . . . It's going to be a big adjustment for everyone, especially Anna Hibiscus. Luckily, her family knows that while two babies mean double the trouble, it also means double the love." (Publisher's note)

   Splash! Anna hibiscus; Atinuke. Kane Miller, A Division of EDC Pub. 2013 32 p. (hardcover) $17.95
Grades: PreK K   E
   1. Ocean waves 2. Beaches -- Fiction
ISBN 1610671732; 9781610671736
                                      LC 2012954083
In this picture book, by Atinuke and illustrated by Lauren Tobia, "Anna Hibiscus is at the beach and all she wants to do is SPLASH! . . . But everyone, including Grandmother and Grandfather, Chocolate, Benz, Wonderful, Joy, Clarity and Common Sense, is much too busy to wave-jump! So, it's just Anna Hibiscus and the white waves." (Publisher's note)

Auch, Mary Jane
   Beauty and the beaks; a Turkey's cautionary tale. [by] Mary Jane and Herm Auch. Holiday House 2007 un il $16.95; pa $6.95
Grades: K 1 2 3   E
   1. Turkeys -- Fiction 2. Chickens -- Fiction 3. Thanksgiving Day

-- Fiction

ISBN 978-0-8234-1990-6; 0-8234-1990-8; 978-0-8234-2164-0 pa; 0-8234-2164-3 pa

LC 2006049468

When Lance, a very pretentious turkey, arrives on the farm and boasts that he is the only bird invited to a special feast, no hen is impressed, but when Beauty learns that Lance is the main course, she convinces the others to save him

"Wonderfully creative handmade characters and sets are the highlight of this over-the-top chicken tale. . . . The author made chicken mannequins with polymer eyes, beaks, and shoes, as well as wool wings and yarn feathers. Her husband designed the sets, built them, and photographed the images, adjusting their size. A humorous story about dressing a turkey, but not in the usual manner." SLJ

The **buk** buk buk festival; by Mary Jane and Herm Auch. Holiday House 2015 32 p. color illustrations (hardcover) $16.95

Grades: PreK K 1 2   E

1. Humorous fiction 2. Chickens -- Fiction 3. Authorship -- Fiction 4. Humorous stories 5. Books and reading -- Fiction

ISBN 0823432017; 9780823432011

LC 2014017137

In this children's story, by Mary Jane and Herm Auch, "thrilled to have her picture book published, Henrietta is all aflutter with excitement when she's invited to a local book festival. However, the event organizers did not count on having a chicken show up to sign books. Luckily, just when the festival director gives chase, Henrietta comes up with a clever plan to make herself heard and be respected." (Publisher's note)

"The numerous references to the writing and publishing process for authors coupled with the double-entendre wordplay and vivid digitally created illustrations are an imaginative way to enlighten children while simultaneously giving adults an appreciative chuckle." Kirkus

The **plot** chickens; by Mary Jane and Herm Auch. Holiday House 2009 un il $16.95

Grades: PreK K 1 2   E

1. Chickens -- Fiction 2. Authorship -- Fiction 3. Books and reading -- Fiction

ISBN 978-0-8234-2087-2; 0-8234-2087-6

LC 2007011234

Henrietta the chicken loves to read so much that she decides to write a book herself, but first no one will publish a book written by a chicken, and then, when she publishes it herself and it gets a terrible review in "The Corn Book," Henrietta is devastated

"The illustrations, a combination of oil paints and digital technology, are bold and colorful. . . . A droll chicken with a repeating line adds to the humor. This offering works on two levels. It's a funny picture book that could be used as a manual on writing." SLJ

Austin, Mike

★ **Fire** engine no. 9; by Mike Austin. Random House Inc 2015 40 p. color illustrations (hardcover : alk. paper) $16.99

Grades: PreK K 1   E

1. Fire engines -- Fiction 2. Fire fighters -- Fiction

ISBN 0553510959; 9780375974281; 9780553510959

LC 2014016610

This children's story, by Mike Austin, "told almost entirely in sound words, [offers a] . . . day-in-the-life look at firefighters and their fire truck. . . . Mike Austin evokes the excitement of a 911 call as we follow firefighters sliding down the fire pole, racing through town, and up the ladder truck. Includes fire safety tips from the Federal Emergency Management Agency." (Publisher's note)

"On a bright sunny day, Engine No. 9 responds to the fire at the corner of Fourth and Main. The first of three dramatic vertical spreads shows the firemen sliding down the pole. They suit up and rush to the engine, the rings of the alarm ("BRRRRIIING!") are repeated over and over in various letter sizes. . . . The exceptionally fine, full-color graphic artwork combined with the sound and action words make this book a surefire winner." SLJ

Fire engine number nine

Rescue squad no. 9; by Mike Austin. Random House Childrens Books 2017 40 p. color illustrations (hardcover) $16.99

Grades: PreK K 1   E

1. Rescue work -- Fiction

ISBN 9781101936658; 9781101936641; 1101936622; 9781101936627; 9781101936634

LC 2015039782

In this book, by Mike Austin, "Rescue Squad No. 9 must spring into action when a young sailor and her dog are stranded during a storm! Follow the crew as they scramble aboard their helicopter and speedboat, racing to the rescue through the waves and winds. The high action is communicated through minimal sound words and bold, graphic art reminiscent of that in Donald Crews's transportation books." (Publisher's note)

"A brilliant little book not just for emergency services fans. Highly recommended." SLJ

Averbeck, Jim

Except if. Atheneum Books for Young Readers 2011 un il $12.99

Grades: PreK K 1   E

1. Eggs -- Fiction 2. Animals -- Fiction

ISBN 978-1-4169-9544-9; 1-4169-9544-7

LC 2009-52489

An egg is just an egg, except if, after hatching it becomes something else.

"Averbeck's simple shapes are outlined in pastel, a coloring-book style nicely suited to the deadpan narration. . . . It's a book in which the action unfolds in the mind as much as it does on the page." Publ Wkly

★ **In** a blue room; [by] Jim Averbeck; illustrated by Trica Tusa. Harcourt 2008 un il $16

Grades: PreK K 1 2   E

1. Color -- Fiction 2. Bedtime -- Fiction 3. Mother-daughter relationship -- Fiction

ISBN 978-0-15-205992-7; 0-15-205992-X

LC 2006034453

Alice wants everything in her bedroom to be blue before she falls asleep

"Prose and pictures partner each other effortlessly all the way to the last page." Publ Wkly

One word from Sophia; Jim Averbeck; illustrated by Yasmeen Ismail. Atheneum Books for Young Readers 2015 40 p. Averbeck, Jim (hardcover) $17.99

Grades: PreK K 1 2 3   E

1. Negotiation -- Fiction 2. Humorous fiction -- Fiction 3. Humorous stories 4. Giraffe -- Fiction 5. Birthdays -- Fiction 6. Family life -- Fiction 7. Interpersonal communication -- Fiction

ISBN 1481405144; 9781481405140

LC 2014024661

In this children's story, written by Jim Averbeck and illustrated by Yasmeen Ismail, "Sophia tries varied techniques to get the giraffe she wants more than anything. . . . But she has Four Big Problems in the way: Mom, Dad, Uncle Conrad . . . and Grand-mama. . . . Turns out, all it takes is one word." (Publisher's note)

"Poor Sophia. Her birthday is coming, and she only has One True Desire (a pet giraffe), but four major obstacles stand in her way, namely her mother (a judge), father (a businessman), uncle (a politican), and grandmother (a strict disciplinarian). She gives each member of her biracial family an individualized presentation including visuals and supporting material, but each one says no and critiques her presentation as being too wordy.... An amusing story to which kids and adults can relate. Plus it's nice to see a biracial family and female judge in the same book." SLJ

Avi

Silent movie; Avi, the author; C.B. Mordan, the illustrator. Atheneum Bks. for Young Readers 2002 un il $16.95

Grades: K 1 2 3   E

1. Immigrants -- Fiction 2. Silent films -- Fiction

ISBN 0-689-84145-0

LC 2001-33025

In the early years of the twentieth century, a Swedish family encounters separation and other hardships upon immigrating to New York City until the son is cast in a silent movie, in a picture book that evokes an actual silent movie

"Clear, beautiful ink-on-clayboard illustrations; white type on thick, glossy black paper; and cinematic lighting effects combine to evoke the historical period." Booklist

Avraham, Kate Aver

What will you be, Sara Mee? illustrated by Anne Sibley O'Brien. Charlesbridge 2010 un il $16.95; pa $7.95

Grades: PreK K 1   E

1. Parties -- Fiction 2. Siblings -- Fiction 3. Birthdays -- Fiction 4. Korean Americans -- Fiction

ISBN 978-1-58089-210-0; 1-58089-210-8; 978-1-58089-211-7 pa; 1-58089-211-6 pa

LC 2009-1708

At her Tol, the first birthday party, Sara Mee plays the traditional Korean prophecy game—Toljabee—while her extended family and friends watch.

"The illustrations are ink brush line with watercolor and done in vibrant colors. The love among family and friends is evident in these pictures, depicting their joy about this important event." SLJ

Axtell, David

We're going on a lion hunt; [illustrated by] David Axtell. Holt & Co. 2000 un il $15.95

Grades: PreK K 1 2   E

1. Lions -- Fiction 2. Africa -- Fiction

ISBN 0-8050-6159-2

LC 98-47507

First published 1999 in the United Kingdom

Two girls set out bravely in search of a lion, going through long grass, a swamp, and a cave before they find what they're looking for

"Axtell takes a storytime classic to the African savanna. . . . [His] sun-soaked, impressionistic oil paintings offer beautiful landscapes and engaging details. . . . Large figures on the page make this a good choice for storytimes as well as lap times." SLJ

Aylesworth, Jim

★ The **full** belly bowl; illustrated by Wendy Halperin. Atheneum Bks. for Young Readers 1998 un il $16.95

Grades: K 1 2 3   E

1. Fairy tales

ISBN 0-689-81033-4

LC 98-14052

In return for the kindness he showed a wee small man, a very old man is given a magical bowl that causes problems when it is not used properly

"From the dainty pictures on the endpapers to the stunning artwork inside, this book is a feast for the eyes. The story . . . is just as good, smoothly blending folktale conventions with touches of magic and a dusting of comedy." Booklist

Little Bitty Mousie; [by] Jim Aylesworth; illustrated by Michael Hague. Walker 2007 un il $16.95; lib bdg $17.85

Grades: PreK K 1   E

1. Alphabet 2. Stories in rhyme 3. Mice -- Fiction

ISBN 978-0-8027-9637-0; 0-8027-9637-0; 978-0-8027-9638-7 lib bdg; 0-8027-9638-9 lib bdg

LC 2007002366

Little Bitty Mousie sneaks into a house one night and discovers many tantalizing new things, as well as one very scary thing.

"The alphabet-related words are in boldface, the bouncy rhymes are fun, and the cute periodic refrain . . . will encourage listener participation. . . . Enchanting, vividly colored pictures, created in pencil and then digitally colored, set the sweet miss mouse in the middle of realistic, detailed close-ups of familiar household objects." Booklist

My grandfather's coat; retold by Jim Aylesworth; illustrated by Barbara McClintock. Scholastic Press 2014 32 p. col. ill. (hardcover : alk. paper) $17.99 E

1. Coats 2. Folklore 3. Grandfathers 4. Coats -- Folklore 5. Folklore -- Europe, Eastern

ISBN 0439925452; 9780439925457

LC 2011012226

This children's book, written by Jim Aylesworth and illustrated by Barbara McClintock, "chronicles four generations . . . from a boy's arrival at Ellis Island . . . to his story being shared with a great-grandson." (Publishers Weekly) "He made a coat for his wedding and wore it for years until it was ragged and torn, at which point he cut it down to make a jacket. The pattern continues, with each item becoming smaller." (Kirkus Reviews)

"Aylesworth extends the Yiddish folksong's events over four generations. "My grandfather," a tailor, made his own blue wedding coat; while his daughter's a baby, it serves for a jacket. Soon it's reduced to a vest, then a tie, then a toy for "you" (his great-grandchild). The old-timey, inviting book has well-paced pages, spreads, and vignettes that nicely celebrate one family's ongoing affection and continuity." Horn Book

Old black fly; illustrations by Stephen Gammell. Holt & Co. 1992 un il $16.95; pa $6.95

Grades: K 1 2 3   E

1. Alphabet 2. Stories in rhyme 3. Flies -- Fiction

ISBN 0-8050-1401-2; 0-8050-3924-4 pa

LC 91-26825

Rhyming text and illustrations follow a mischievous old black fly through the alphabet as he has a very busy bad day landing where he should not be

Aylesworth's "snappy couplets constitute a waggish presentation of a basic concept. . . . Gammell's paintings are exuberant splashes of mayhem—rainbows of splattered hues from which truly memorable characters emerge. His appropriately bug-eyed (and cross-eyed) fly and gap-toothed humans sporting crazy hairdos provide a level of dementia that children will relish." Publ Wkly

Baasansuren, Bolormaa

My little round house; adapted by Helen Mixter. Groundwood Books 2009 un il $18.95

Grades: K 1 2 3   E

1. Infants -- Fiction 2. Mongolia -- Fiction 3. Family life -- Fiction

ISBN 978-0-88899-934-4; 0-88899-934-8

"The little round house of the title is a large tent, or ger, home to the nomadic people of Mongolia. In a spare first-person narrative, baby Jilu recounts his first year and introduces readers to the rhythm of his loving family's nomadic life. . . . Attractive full-page gouache illustrations by the Mongolian writer/illustrator Baasansuren show the round house's interior as well as the characters' clothes, including elaborate details such as painted woodwork, embroidery, and the texture of fabrics." SLJ

Bachelet, Gilles

My cat, the silliest cat in the world; written and illustrated by Gilles Bachelet. Abrams 2006 un il $16.95
Grades: PreK K 1 2   E
    1. Cats -- Fiction 2. Elephants -- Fiction
    ISBN 0-8109-4913-X; 978-0-8109-4913-3
                                                    LC 2005-27837
"While the text is a completely conventional list of a cat's habits, the very, very, large cat in the pictures is, in fact, an elephant. The straight-faced humor becomes all the funnier because Bachelet captures a cat's peculiar postures and behavior exactly. The paintings are filled with visual wit." Horn Book Guide
    Another title about the silliest cat is:
    When the silliest cat was small (2007)

Badescu, Ramona

Pomelo begins to grow; illustrated by Benjamin Chaud; translated from French by Claudia Bedrick. Enchanted Lion Books 2011 un il $16.95
Grades: 1 2 3   E
    1. Growth -- Fiction 2. Elephants -- Fiction
    ISBN 978-1-59270-111-7; 1-59270-111-6
                                                    LC 2010053472
When his favorite dandelion looks surprisingly small, Pomelo the garden elephant discovers that he is growing and then wonders about the mysterious process called growth.
"The author and illustrator demonstrate a brilliant marriage of text and illustration. Chaud's charming paintings of Pomelo in his landscape of dandelions, strawberries, and smiling potatoes—set simply against oversize white pages—breathe life and humor into Badescu's big-picture questions, while playing with scale." SLJ

Pomelo explores color; Ramona Badescu; [illustrated by] Benjamin Chaud. Enchanted Lion Books 2012 120 p.
Grades: K 1 2   E
    1. Color -- Fiction 2. Emotions -- Fiction 3. Elephants -- Fiction
    ISBN 1592701264; 9781592701261
                                                    LC 2012022766
This book by Ramona Badescu and illustrated by Benjamin Chaud "is all about exploration and the experience of seeing color anew. . . . Pomelo discovers colors in all their nuance. He encounters the infinite white of falling snow, the hypnotizing red of love, and the shadowy blue of the unknown. The colors describe our concrete world, but also reflect emotional states, as well as the curious, oddball sensibility of our dear Pomelo." (Publisher's note)

Pomelo's Opposites; by Ramona Badescu and illustrated by Benjamin Chaud. Enchanted Lion Books 2013 120 p. $15.95
Grades: K 1 2   E
    ISBN 1592701329; 9781592701322
In this book, written by Ramona Badescu and illustrated by Benjamin Chaud, "Pomelo . . . is here again in a surprisingly comic and playful book of opposites. True to the concept, there are classic oppositions such as left/right, thin/fat, up/down. There are also philosophical opposites, such as with/without, dream/reality, and possible/impossible.

And then there are silly, surreal, and laugh-out-loud opposites for the reader to discover on his or her own!" (Publisher's note)

Bae, Hyun-Joo

★ New clothes for New Year's Day. Kane/Miller 2007 un il $15.95
Grades: K 1 2 3   E
    1. Korea -- Fiction 2. New Year -- Fiction 3. Clothing and dress -- Fiction
    ISBN 978-1-933605-29-6
A young Korean girl describes the new clothes that she will be wearing to celebrate the new year.
"Simple words and inventively composed pictures depict each step in donning the elaborate, traditional costume. . . . Bae's delicate illustrations move smoothly between depictions of mishaps as the child wrestles with troublesome accessories and grand, wordless portraits." Booklist

Baeten, Lieve

The curious Little Witch. North-South 2010 un il $16.95
Grades: PreK K 1 2   E
    1. Witches -- Fiction
    ISBN 978-0-7358-2305-1; 0-7358-2305-7
    First published 1992
"A young blonde witch and her cat decide to investigate a house, but the witch's broomstick breaks. As she explores the house, flaps reveal each of the residents: the Music Witch, who creates 'sublime' sounds; the Kitchen Witch, who prepares delicious food; and the Bedroom Witch, with soporific powers. Luckily, the Tinkering Witch is able to fix her broom-while adding rocket power. The cozy, cluttered details on every floor lend the book warmth and charm." Publ Wkly
    Other titles about Little Witch are:
    Up and away with the Little Witch (2011)
    Happy Birthday, Little Witch (2011)

Bagley, Jessixa

Before I leave; Jessixa Bagley. Roaring Brook Press 2016 40 p. color illustrations (hardcover) $17.99
Grades: PreK K 1 2   E
    1. Moving -- Fiction 2. Hedgehogs -- Fiction 3. Friendship -- Fiction 4. Moving, Household -- Fiction
    ISBN 9781626720404
                                                    LC 2015004009
This children's book, by Jessixa Bagley, asks "How do you say goodbye to your best friend? When a little hedgehog's family tells her they're moving far away, she and her anteater best friend decide to play one last time, like nothing is changing. And though it's hard, they discover that while some things have to change, the most important things find a way of working out." (Publisher's note)
"The pen and watercolor illustrations are filled with homey details that children will enjoy, and enhance the poignant tone of the story, particularly the picture of large Aaron trying to pack himself in Zelda's tiny suitcase... A sweet and tender moving story that makes a fine addition to most collections." SLJ

★ Boats for Papa; Jessixa Bagley. Roaring Brook Press 2015 40 p. (hardcover) $17.99
Grades: PreK K 1 2   E
    1. Grief -- Fiction 2. Fathers -- Fiction 3. Boats and boating -- Fiction 4. Handicraft -- Fiction 5. Mother and child -- Fiction
    ISBN 1626720398; 9781626720398
                                                    LC 2014031479
In this children's book by Jessixa Bagley "Buckley and his Mama live in a cozy cabin by the ocean. He loves to carve boats out of the driftwood he finds on the beach nearby. He makes . . . each one more

beautiful than the last, and sends them out to sea. If they don't come back, he knows they've found their way to his papa, whom he misses very much. Bagley explores the subtle and deep emotions associated with loss." (Publisher's note)

"They didn't have much, but they always had each other." So begins this spare tale of longing and acceptance...The only thing better than this title for anyone who has experienced loss is the redemptive nature of time." SLJ

Laundry day; Jessixa Bagley. Roaring Brook Press 2017 40 p. (ebook) $60; (hardback) $17.99

    Grades: PreK K 1   E

    1. Badgers -- Fiction 2. Laundry -- Fiction 3. House cleaning -- Fiction

    ISBN 9781250153500; 1626723176; 9781626723177

                      LC 2016002012

This book, by Jessixa Bagley, asks "what do two bored badgers do when they've done everything, including driving their mother around the bend? Laundry, of course. What could possibly go wrong? In this spirited picture book, Tic and Tac, two adorable badgers, get a little carried away while helping their mom out with the laundry." (Publisher's note)

"This tale of badger mischief is excellent both as a read-aloud and as a book for beginning readers." Kirkus

Baker, Barbara

    ★ **Digby** and Kate and the beautiful day; pictures by Marsha Winborn. Dutton Children's Bks. 1998 48p il hardcover o.p. pa $3.99

Grades: PreK K 1 2   E

    1. Cats -- Fiction 2. Dogs -- Fiction

    ISBN 0-525-45855-7; 0-14-240035-4 pa

Digby the dog and Kate the cat disagree about many things but they remain best friends

"The artwork . . . together with the cheerful stories make up good, light fare for beginning readers." Horn Book Guide

    Other titles about Digby and Kate are:

    Digby and Kate (1988)

    Digby and Kate 1 2 3 (2004)

    Digby and Kate again (1989)

    One Saturday evening; pictures by Kate Duke. Dutton Children's Books 2007 48p il hardcover o.p. $13.99

Grades: K 1 2 3   E

    1. Bears -- Fiction 2. Family life -- Fiction

    ISBN 978-0-525-47103-5; 0-525-47103-0

                      LC 2006-24785

On a Saturday evening, the members of a bear family busy themselves with cleaning up the kitchen, taking baths, and reading.

"The chapter structure and short, basic sentences are well tuned to newly confident readers, and the reassuringly familiar scenarios, nicely extended in Duke's expressive ink-and-watercolor pictures, will draw children into the cozy nighttime mayhem." Booklist

    Another title about the bear family is:

    One Saturday morning (1994)

Baker, Jeannie

    Circle; Jeannie Baker. Candlewick Press 2016 48 p. color illustrations $17.99

Grades: PreK K 1 2 3   E

    1. Birds -- Migration

    ISBN 0763679666; 9780763679668

                    LC 2014960102

This book, by Jeannie Baker, "follows the epic flight of an extraordinary bird. Each year, bar-tailed godwits undertake the longest unbroken migration of any bird, flying from their breeding grounds in the Arctic to

Austrlia and New Zealand and back again. They follow invisible pathways—pathways that have been followed for thousands of years—while braving hunger and treacherous conditions to reach their destination." (Publisher's note)

"It's hard to imagine a more powerful treatment of migration: Baker conveys the strength of the birds and the fragility of their habitat with equal care." Pub Wkly

    Home. Greenwillow Books 2004 un il $15.99

Grades: PreK K 1 2   E

    1. City and town life 2. Stories without words

    ISBN 0-06-623935-4

                    LC 2003-49287

A wordless picture book that observes the changes in a neighborhood from before a girl is born until she is an adult, as it first decays and then is renewed by the efforts of the residents

"Baker uses natural materials to create detailed, arresting collages that tell a story in which words are superfluous. Children can pore over these pages again and again and make fresh discoveries with each perusal." SLJ

    ★ **Mirror**. Candlewick Press 2010 un il $18.99

Grades: PreK K 1 2   E

    1. Stories without words 2. Markets -- Fiction 3. Morocco -- Fiction 4. Australia -- Fiction

    ISBN 978-0-7636-4848-0; 0-7636-4848-5

                    LC 2009-50391

In Sydney, Australia, and in Morocco, two boys and their families have a day of shopping. Readers are invited to compare illustrations in two wordless stories that are intended to be read one from left to right and the other from right to left.

"Baker's entrancing collages, packed with visual information and created with fabric, sand, vegetation, and other unusual materials, have the power to bring back child and adult viewers for infinite 'readings.' Perfectly spectacular." Kirkus

    Where the forest meets the sea; story and pictures by Jeannie Baker. Greenwillow Bks. 1988 un il $16

Grades: PreK K 1 2   E

    1. Australia -- Fiction 2. Rain forests -- Fiction

    ISBN 0-688-06363-2

                    LC 87-7551

First published 1987 in the United Kingdom

On a camping trip in an Australian rain forest with his father, a young boy thinks about the history of the plant and animal life around him and wonders about their future

The illustrations "are relief collages 'constructed from a multitude of materials, including modeling clay, papers, textured materials, preserved natural materials, and paints.' Integrated by the artist's vision, the collages create three-dimensional effects on two-dimensional pages drawing the reader into each scene as willing observer and explorer." Horn Book

    Window. Greenwillow Bks. 1991 un il lib bdg $17.89

Grades: PreK K 1 2   E

    1. Stories without words 2. Australia -- Fiction 3. Human ecology -- Fiction

    ISBN 0-688-08918-6

                    LC 90-3922

"Filled with marvelous detail, the textured collages make an affecting statement about the erosion of the planet Earth." SLJ

Baker, Keith

    Hickory dickory dock; [by] Keith Baker. Harcourt 2007 un il $16

Grades: PreK K 1 2   E
1. Stories in rhyme 2. Animals -- Fiction 3. Clocks and watches
-- Fiction
ISBN 978-0-15-205818-0; 0-15-205818-4

LC 2006003257

"The nursery rhyme 'Hickory Dickory Dock' gets new life as it goes
through 12 hours of the day. . . . As each hour chimes, another creature
appears, often completing an action initiated in the previous spread. .
. . With a bouncy, easy-to-enjoy text and child-appealing collage-style
pictures, this is a book that will work well one-on-one or with groups."
Booklist

Just how long can a long string be!? Arthur A. Levine Books 2009
un il hardcover o.p. $16.99
Grades: PreK K 1 2   E
1. Stories in rhyme 2. Ants -- Fiction 3. Birds -- Fiction
ISBN 978-0-545-08661-5; 0-545-08661-2; 978-0-545-08662-2
pa; 0-545-08662-0 pa

LC 2008027344

Be it tied to a balloon, or kite, or hanging a picture, or stringing a
banjo or a mop, a bird explains to an ant how long a string needs to be
"By using pale overlapping images, Baker creates a sense of movement in many of the illustrations. A palette of pastels captures the beauty
of spring. . . . [This is a] lovely book . . . for a fine spring storytime." SLJ

★ **LMNO** peas. Beach Lane Books 2010 un il $16.99
Grades: PreK K 1 2   E
1. Alphabet 2. Stories in rhyme 3. Occupations -- Fiction
ISBN 978-1-4169-9141-0; 1-4169-9141-7

LC 2009012672

Busy little peas introduce their favorite occupations, from astronaut
to zoologist.
"With its digital illustrations' luminous colors, buoyant spirit, and
engaging characters, this handsome picture book is definitely worth a
second look, even in the overcrowded field of alphabet books." Booklist

★ **Meet** Mr. and Mrs. Green. Harcourt 2004 71p il hardcover
o.p. pa $5.95
Grades: K 1 2   E
1. Alligators -- Fiction
ISBN 0-15-204954-1; 0-15-204955-X pa

LC 2001-1955

First published 2002
A loving alligator couple enjoy going camping, eating pancakes, and
visiting the county fair
"The acrylic illustrations have a loud, oversized presence that is
complemented by the strong text." SLJ
Other titles about Mr. and Mrs. Green are:
Lucky days with Mr. and Mrs. Green (2005)
More Mr. and Mrs. Green (2004)
On the go with Mr. and Mrs. Green (2006)

★ **No** two alike. Beach Lane Books 2011 un il $16.99
Grades: PreK K 1   E
1. Stories in rhyme 2. Birds -- Fiction 3. Winter -- Fiction
ISBN 978-1-4424-1742-7; 1-4424-1742-0

LC 2010044659

Follows a pair of birds on a snowflake-filled journey through a winter landscape, where everything everywhere, from branches and leaves
to forests full of trees, is unique.
"Brief rhyming couplets, printed in large type and each requiring a
page turn for completion, describe the birds' discoveries. . . . The engaging, digitally rendered avian characters stand out against the wintry

landscape, and their many antics as they navigate their surroundings will
sustain readers' interest." SLJ

Potato Joe; [by] Keith Baker. Harcourt 2008 un il $16
Grades: PreK K 1   E
1. Nursery rhymes 2. Counting -- Fiction
ISBN 978-0-15-206230-9; 0-15-206230-0

LC 2007005930

Potato Joe leads the other spuds from the familiar nursery rhyme,
"One Potato, Two Potato," in various activities, from a game of tic-tac-
toe to a rodeo.
"The fuzzy-edged, childlike illustrations were done in Adobe Photoshop and complement the bouncy tone of the text. This will be fun to
share, and even young children will soon have the rhyme committed to
memory." SLJ

Baldacchino, Christine
★ **Morris** Micklewhite and the Tangerine Dress; by Christine Baldacchino; illustrated by Isabelle Malenfant. Pgw 2014 32 p. color
illustrations $16.95
Grades: PreK K 1 2   E
1. School stories 2. Imagination -- Fiction 3. Outer space -- Fiction
4. Clothing and dress -- Fiction
ISBN 1554983479; 9781554983476
Stonewall Honor Book: Children's & Young Adult Literature (2015)
In this book by Christine Baldacchino, "Morris is a little boy who
loves using his imagination. But most of all, Morris loves wearing the
tangerine dress in his classroom's dress-up center. The children in Morris's class don't understand. Dresses, they say, are for girls. . . . One day
when Morris feels all alone and sick from their taunts, his mother lets
him stay home from school. Morris dreams of a fantastic space adventure with his cat, Moo." (Publisher's note)
"Baldacchino's gentle story sensitively depicts gender nonconform-
ing children, offering them reassurance and, one hopes, acceptance by
introducing other children to the concept. An excellent book for discussion." Booklist

Balouch, Kristen
Feelings. Little Simon 2011 un il bd bk $6.99
Grades: PreK   E
1. Board books for children 2. Animals -- Fiction 3. Emotions
-- Fiction
ISBN 978-1-4424-1199-9; 1-4424-1199-6
"Familiar animals convey common emotions through body language
and facial expressions. A lion's frown, curled-in tail, and droopy mane
communicate his sadness, . . . while a crocodile with a sly smile is feeling sneaky about planning a surprise. . . . Vivid colors, relatable examples, and a compact trim size should appeal to toddlers." Publ Wkly

★ The **little** little girl with the big big voice. Little Simon 2011
un il $12.99
Grades: PreK K 1   E
1. Play -- Fiction 2. Voice -- Fiction 3. Friendship -- Fiction
ISBN 1-4424-0808-1; 978-1-4424-0808-1
A loud little girl has trouble finding a jungle friend to play with because of her booming voice, until at last, she meets the one jungle animal
whose roar is louder than hers. "Preschool." (Horn Book)
"Exuberant, stylized illustrations in bright pink, peach, coral, lime,
orange and lemon effectively portray this girl and her energy. . . . Young
readers can practically hear this little, little girl's big, big voice from
where they're sitting, and most pre-schoolers will know exactly how
she feels." Kirkus

Bancroft, Bronwyn

Kangaroo and crocodile; my big book of Australian animals. Bronwyn Bancroft. Little Hare Books 2011 48 p. (hbk) $19.99

Grades: 1 2 3   E

1. Australia 2. Animals -- Australia 3. Picture books for children

ISBN 1921714255; 9781921714252

     LC 2012405708

This children's picture book looks at Australian animals. "Most of the double-page spreads feature two often-related animals (bottlenose dolphin and great white shark, for instance), although a few . . . concentrate on one animal. There are also several spreads with four different animals." (Kirkus)

W is for wombat; my first Australian word book. Little Hare 2010 un il bd bk $8.99

Grades: PreK   E

1. Alphabet 2. Board books for children 3. Animals -- Australia

ISBN 978-1-921541-17-9 bd bk; 1-921541-17-2 bd bk

"This ABC book features Australian Aboriginal motifs. Creatures like a koala, platypus, and quokka are thickly outlined in paint and decorated with multicolored dots, making them resemble ornate masks, while a river, sun, and tree take on an elemental quality. It's an aesthetically striking guide to Australian wildlife." Publ Wkly

Bandy, Michael S.

White water; [by] Michael S. Bandy and Eric Stein; illustrated by Shadra Strickland. Candlewick Press 2011 40p il $16.99

Grades: K 1 2 3   E

1. Segregation -- Fiction 2. African Americans -- Fiction

ISBN 978-0-7636-3678-4; 0-7636-3678-9

     LC 2010040343

After tasting the warm, rusty water from the fountain designated for African Americans, a young boy questions why he cannot drink the cool, refreshing water from the 'Whites Only' fountain. Based on a true experience co-author Michael S. Bandy had as a boy.

"Strickland's watercolor-and-ink illustrations extend the story. . . . Inspirational in tone, this is a strong introduction for young listeners and readers to the American Civil Rights movement." Kirkus

Bang, Molly

All of me! a book of thanks. Blue Sky Press 2009 un il $16.99

Grades: PreK K   E

1. Human body -- Fiction

ISBN 978-0-545-04424-0; 0-545-04424-3

     LC 2008-49692

A celebration of how the body's parts work together, from hands and eyes to lips and heart, allowing one to exist in the wondrous universe. Includes instructions for making a book.

"Bang's artwork incorporates cut paper and fabric, photographed elements, red crayon, and paints. . . . Unusual, uneven, creative, and challenging." Booklist

★ The **paper** crane. Greenwillow Bks. 1985 un il $16.99; pa $6.99

Grades: K 1 2 3   E

ISBN 0-688-04108-6; 0-688-07333-6 pa

     LC 84-13546

"Every detail of the restaurant interior, from the strawberries on the cake to the floral centerpieces, is a delight to the eye and imagination. . . . The book successfully blends Asian folklore themes with contemporary Western characterization." Horn Book

★ **When** Sophie gets angry--really, really angry. Blue Sky Press (NY) 1999 un il $16.99; pa $6.99

Grades: PreK K 1   E

1. Anger -- Fiction

ISBN 0-590-18979-4; 0-439-59845-1 pa

     LC 97-42209

A Caldecott Medal honor book, 2000

"The text is appropriately brief, for it is Bang's double-page illustrations, vibrating with saturated colors, that reveal the drama of the child's emotions." SLJ

Another book about Sophie is:

When Sophie's feelings are really, really hurt (2015)

Bang-Campbell, Monika

Little Rat makes music; [by] Monika Bang-Campbell; illustrated by Molly Bang. Harcourt 2007 un il $15

Grades: 1 2 3   E

1. Rats -- Fiction 2. Music -- Fiction 3. Violins -- Fiction

ISBN 978-0-15-205305-5; 0-15-205305-0

     LC 2005-27536

Little Rat loves the violin but hates to practice, until her teacher suggests she perform a duet with one of the advanced students at the holiday concert.

"The jewel-toned watercolor-and-gouache artwork will help keep readers engaged. A realistic and meaningful look at the satisfying results of hard work and perseverance." SLJ

Banks, Kate

★ **And** if the moon could talk; pictures by Georg Hallensleben. Foster Bks. 1998 un il $15

Grades: PreK K 1 2   E

1. Moon -- Fiction 2. Night -- Fiction 3. Bedtime -- Fiction

ISBN 0-374-30299-5

     LC 97-29770

As evening progresses into nighttime, the moon looks down on a variety of nocturnal scenes, including a child getting ready for bed

"The deeply saturated tones of the lovely, impressionistic oil paintings perfectly match the somnolent feeling of the text." SLJ

Baboon; pictures by Georg Hallensleben. Farrar, Straus & Giroux 1997 un il $14

Grades: PreK K 1 2   E

1. Baboons -- Fiction

ISBN 0-374-30474-2

     LC 96-20888

Original French edition, 1994

"Visible brush-strokes give texture to the impressionistic paintings, and adept lighting evokes sunlight and shadow. The simple, eloquent text is as subtly understated." Horn Book Guide

The **bear** in the book; Kate Banks; pictures by Georg Hallensleben. Frances Foster Books 2012 36 p. $16.99

Grades: PreK K 1 2   E

1. Bears -- Fiction 2. Bedtime -- Fiction 3. Hibernation -- Fiction 4. Reading -- Fiction

ISBN 0374305919; 9780374305918

     LC 2011036691

In this children's book by Kate Banks, illustrated by Georg Hallensleben, "it's time for bed, and a little boy chooses his favorite book for his mother to read to him. The bear in the book is preparing for his own deep slumber, hibernating through the winter while humans and other animals explore the snowy landscape around him. Just when the bear wakes up to greet the spring, the boy drifts off to sleep. . . . This bedtime read . . . will carry young readers through the seasons." (Publisher's note)

The **cat** who walked across France; pictures by Georg Hallensleben. Farrar, Straus and Giroux 2004 un il $16
Grades: PreK K 1 2   E
1. Cats -- Fiction 2. France -- Fiction
ISBN 0-374-39968-9
LC 2002-25091

After his owner dies, a cat wanders across the countryside of France, unable to forget the home he had in the stone house by the edge of the sea

"Banks uses simple, lovely words to tell the elemental story of an outcast's journey home. . . . The paintings are exquisite . . . but what kids will like best is the cat's adventure and the loving welcome he receives." Booklist

★ **Close** your eyes; pictures by Georg Hallensleben. Foster Bks. 2002 un il $16
Grades: PreK K 1   E
1. Sleep -- Fiction 2. Dreams -- Fiction 3. Tigers -- Fiction
ISBN 0-374-31382-2
LC 99-46430

A mother tiger entices her child to sleep by telling of all that can be seen with one's eyes closed

"Banks' language will delight young children with its delicious rhythms, patterned sounds, and the mystery in the poetic imagery. . . . Hallensleben's thick, expressive brush strokes occasionally blur shapes and details, but the vividly colored dreamscapes . . . will capture young imaginations and reassure children who . . . harbor secret fears of falling asleep." Booklist

The **eraserheads**; pictures by Boris Kulikov. Farrar, Straus and Giroux 2010 un il $16.99
Grades: PreK K 1 2   E
1. Adventure fiction 2. Drawing -- Fiction
ISBN 978-0-374-39920-7; 0-374-39920-4
LC 2008024144

Three eraserheads that live with a boy in the land of pencils, paper, rulers, numbers, letters, and drawings become trapped in one of his pictures while trying to correct mistakes

"Kulikov combines loving attention to detail . . . with beguiling portraits of the erasers in various attitudes of dismay and distress. In the story's dueling realities, the 'real life' sections of the spreads feature three-dimensional figures, while the boy's drawings are done in gawky crayon." Publ Wkly

Max's math; Kate Banks; pictures by Boris Kulikov. Frances Foster Books, Farrar Straus Giroux 2015 40 p. color illustrations (Max's Words) (hardcover) $17.99
Grades: PreK K 1 2   E
1. Shape -- Fiction 2. Mathematics -- Fiction 3. Numbers -- Fiction 4. Arithmetic -- Fiction
ISBN 0374348758; 9780374348755
LC 2014015873

In this book by Kate Banks, illustrated by Boris Kulikov, part of the Max's Words series, "Max and his two brothers hop into a car and go looking for problems they can solve. They cruise down highway number 4 on their way to Shapeville, but they see an abandoned number along the way. Is it a 6? Is it a 9? And what's it doing on the side of the road? Once the trio reach Shapeville, there's another problem: a flood washed away all of the squares." (Publisher's note)

"All too often, math content in books for children feels contrived or tacked on, or it smacks of reconstituted textbook material--and didacticism reigns. Here, Banks's characters experience math more organically; the boys play with numbers and shapes--encouraging readers to do likewise." Horn Book

★ **Max's** words; pictures by Boris Kulikov. Farrar, Straus and Giroux 2006 un il $16
Grades: PreK K 1 2   E
1. Storytelling -- Fiction 2. English language -- Fiction 3. Collectors and collecting -- Fiction
ISBN 978-0-374-39949-8; 0-374-39949-2

When Max cuts out words from magazines and newspapers, collecting them the way his brothers collect stamps and coins, they all learn about words, sentences, and storytelling

"Imaginative, softly colored illustrations reveal the gathered words scattered all over the pages. . . . This tale pays homage to the written word and may get children thinking about cutting and pasting their own stories or creating concrete poetry." SLJ

Other titles about Max are:
Max's dragon (2008)
Max's castle (2011)

Monkeys and dog days; pictures by Tomek Bogacki. Farrar, Straus and Giroux 2008 48p il $14.95
Grades: 1 2 3   E
1. Dogs -- Fiction 2. Pets -- Fiction 3. Brothers -- Fiction 4. Chimpanzees -- Fiction
ISBN 0-374-35029-9; 978-0-374-35029-1
LC 2007060726

When Max and Pete get a new dog, they learn that taking care of a pet is not as easy as they thought.

"The story, divided into four chapters, includes a sprinkling of fun facts about dogs and emphasizes important lessons about responsibility, loyalty, and cooperation. Muted pastel illustrations show the brothers and their new pet." SLJ

★ The **night** worker; pictures by Georg Hallensleben. Farrar, Straus & Giroux 2000 un il $16
Grades: PreK K 1 2   E
1. Work -- Fiction 2. Night -- Fiction 3. Building -- Fiction
ISBN 0-374-35520-7
LC 99-27595

Alex wants to be a "night worker" like his father who goes to work at a construction site after Alex goes to bed

"Banks' elegant, simple words and poetic images and rhythms evoke the book's exciting activity and the secure comfort Alex feels with his father. With thick brush strokes and deep, satisfying primary and earth colors, Hallensleben's paintings extend the story's balance of exhilarating intensity and reassuring calm." Booklist

This baby; pictures by Gabi Swiatkowska. Farrar, Straus and Giroux 2010 il $16.99
Grades: PreK K 1 2   E
1. Infants -- Fiction 2. Siblings -- Fiction
ISBN 978-0-374-37514-0; 0-374-37514-3
LC 2009009299

While waiting for it to be born, a young child wonders what its new sibling will be like.

"Swiatkowska . . . pivots easily between the real and the magical . . . [and] Banks . . . acknowledges the gravity of children's thoughts and the depth of their love; it's a quiet, idiosyncratic celebration of new life." Publ Wkly

What's coming for Christmas? pictures by Georg Hallensleben. Farrar, Straus and Giroux 2009 un il $15.99
Grades: PreK K 1   E
1. Christmas -- Fiction 2. Domestic animals -- Fiction
ISBN 978-0-374-39948-1; 0-374-39948-4
LC 2008-20753

While a farm family bustles about, preparing for the arrival of Christmas, they do not notice the great anticipation spreading among the animals, who know that something very special is on its way.

"The muted colors and quality of Hallensleben's illustrations create a dreamlike feeling, matched by the quiet, lyrical text, with its simple, repeated refrains that create a mounting sense of mysterious expectation." Kirkus

Bannerman, Helen

★ The **story** of Little Babaji; illustrated by Fred Marcellino. HarperCollins Pubs. 1996 un il $16.99; pa $7.95
Grades: PreK K 1 2   E
1. India -- Fiction 2. Tigers -- Fiction
ISBN 0-06-205064-8; 0-06-008093-0 pa

In this edition of the Story of Little Black Sambo, originally published 1899, the characters have been given Indian names

Babaji gives his new clothing to tigers who threaten to eat him, but they chase one another around a tree until they turn to butter

"Marcellino has set the story of Little Black Sambo in India. . . . Except for a change of names . . . Bannerman's text is essentially unaltered, retaining the narrative rhythm that has always paced a tightly patterned plot. Marcellino's watercolor paintings project a toy-like quality that emphasizes humor over suspense." Bull Cent Child Books

Bansch, Helga

Brava, mimi! NorthSouth 2010 un il $16.95
Grades: PreK K 1 2   E
1. Mice -- Fiction 2. Acting -- Fiction 3. Dancers -- Fiction 4. Singing -- Fiction 5. Theater -- Fiction
ISBN 978-0-7358-2322-8; 0-7358-2322-7

"Mimi the mouse wants to be on stage, but she doesn't think she is talented or beautiful enough. As she seeks advice and lessons from friends, she prepares herself for an audition. . . . The scale of the illustrations portray the size of Mimi in comparison to her environment. Budding ballerinas will recognize the tutus on the cover; this is sure to delight all who love to read about performing in theater." Libr Media Connect

I want a dog! North-South 2009 un il $16.95
Grades: K 1 2   E
1. Dogs -- Fiction
ISBN 978-0-7358-2255-9; 0-7358-2255-7

"A dog is all young Lisa yearns for, but whether wheedles or tantrums, the parental answer is the same: 'Our apartment is still too small for a dog.' Finally, the clever girl puts up signs in the park asking for a dog to borrow, whereupon Mr. Lewis shows up at her door with sausage hound Rollo. . . . Bausch writes with a dry humor even as the text effectively conveys Lisa's longing, and the solution is both a reasonable and creative one." Bull Cent Child Books

Odd bird out; translated from the German by Monika Smith. Gecko Press 2011 il $17.95
Grades: K 1 2   E
1. Ravens -- Fiction
ISBN 978-1-8774-6708-0; 1-8774-6708-1

Robert is different from all other ravens. He is a happy bird. But when he laughs and tells jokes, the other birds don't like it at all. Nor do they like his colorful clothes and they hold their ears when he tries to sing.

"The conversational text is paired with paintings that perfectly capture the raven's nature. Who knew birds could have so many facial expressions and disapproving postures? In his wildly colored outfits and high-heeled shoes, Robert shines amid the status quo." SLJ

Banyai, Istvan

The **other** side. Chronicle Books 2005 un il $15.95
Grades: K 1 2 3   E
1. Stories without words
ISBN 0-8118-4608-3   LC 2004-63448

"This is a challenging book, one that allows for creative speculation. The graphite-rendered artwork is quirky as well as infinitely interesting." SLJ

Barbieri, Gladys E.

A **Charmed** Life/ Una Vida Con Suerte; Gladys Barbieri. Piñata Books 2016 32 p. color illustrations $17.95
Grades: PreK K 1 2   E
1. Hope -- Fiction 2. Curiosity -- Fiction
ISBN 155885827X; 9781558858275

In this children's book, by Gladys Barbieri, "Felicia always feels very small when she and her mom walk by the huge homes and beautiful gardens to the house where her mother works as a cleaning lady. But Felicia gets bored, and in spite of her mother's warnings, begins to explore. When Mrs. Fitzpatrick comes outside, Felicia can't help but wonder if the woman knows she was roaming through the house. To her surprise, . . . the two realize that even though they live in different worlds they have something in common." (Publisher's note)

"With illustrations that suggest a sunny memory, Felicia's story shows the ways that she's part of a continuing cycle, rather than an outsider, and does it without belaboring the point." Kirkus

Barclay, Jane

Proud as a peacock, brave as a lion; illustrated by Renné Benoit. Tundra Books 2009 un il $18.95
Grades: PreK K 1 2   E
1. Memory -- Fiction 2. Veterans -- Fiction 3. Grandfathers -- Fiction 4. World War, 1939-1945 -- Fiction
ISBN 978-0-88776-951-1; 0-88776-951-9

"A small boy has fun with his grandfather as they page through an old photo album, and Poppa tells how, at age 17, he lied about his age so that he could join the army. Small photos in sepia shades evoke the past. . . . Opposite the wartime photos, large, bright, unframed pictures in watercolor and gouache show the boy and Poppa in the present, talking about the soldier's feelings—proud as a peacock, pretending to be brave as a lion—and the lively animal images in the words are also part of the pictures. . . . The blend of grim reality, heroic battle, and playful fantasy will speak to kids." Booklist

Bardhan-Quallen, Sudipta

Chicks run wild; [by] Sudipta Bardhan; illustrated by Ward Jenkins. Simon & Schuster Books for Young Readers 2011 un il
Grades: PreK K 1   E
1. Stories in rhyme 2. Bedtime -- Fiction 3. Chickens -- Fiction 4. Mother-child relationship -- Fiction
ISBN 1-4424-0673-9; 978-1-4424-0673-5

When her little chicks refuse to settle down for the night, Mama decides to surprise them with an unusual request.

"The pencil and digitally painted illustrations carry the folksy tale in an able fashion. An entertaining selection for bedtime." SLJ

Duck, Duck, Moose! by Sudipta Bardhan-Quallen; illustrated by Noah Z. Jones. Disney-Hyperion Books 2014 32 p. color illustrations $16.99
Grades: PreK K 1   E
1. Ducks -- Fiction 2. Moose -- Fiction 3. Parties -- Fiction 4.

Humorous stories 5. Surprise -- Fiction 6. Roommates -- Fiction
ISBN 1423171101; 9781423171102

LC 2013012211

In this children's book by Sudipta Bardhan-Quallen, "Duck and Duck are preparing for a party, and each step of the way, Moose inadvertently messes things up. When he disappears in shame, Duck and Duck must go find him so he can join in the party-which was for him!" (Publisher's note)

"Jones' cartoon artwork tells the story with detailed, precise drawings of the ducks outlined in black against a clean white background. The moose's antics, in contrast, are chaotic, with colors and spillage abounding. All three faces are wonderfully expressive." Kirkus

Tyrannosaurus wrecks! by Sudipta Bardhan-Quallen; illustrated by Zachariah OHora. Abrams Books for Young Readers 2014 32 p. $14.95
Grades: PreK K 1   E
1. Dinosaurs -- Fiction 2. Stories in rhyme 3. Behavior -- Fiction 4. Tyrannosaurus rex -- Fiction
ISBN 1419710354; 9781419710353

LC 2013022197

Written by Sudipta Bardhan-Quallen and illustrated by Zachariah O'Hora, "in this read-along picture book, a classroom full of young dinosaurs plays with toys, does art projects, and reads books. But each activity is another opportunity for the over-enthusiastic Tyrannosaurus Rex to wreak havoc. . . . The format is extra vertical in order to accommodate T. Rex's biggest messes." (Publisher's note)

"All is harmony in the dinosaur classroom, except for one member with a self-control issue: "Apatosaurus colors. Pteranodon inspects. Velociraptor glitters. Tyrannosaurus...WRECKS!" Naively drawn dinosaurs with bold outlines and flat, digitally added colors pop from white pages. A text consisting primarily of simple subjects and verbs builds tension until the students band together to reform the disruptive dino. A satisfyingly high-energy, primal read-aloud." Horn Book

Bardoe, Cheryl
The **ugly** dinosaur; a prehistoric tale. illustrated by Doug Kennedy. Abrams Books for Young Readers 2011 un il $16.95
Grades: PreK K 1   E
1. Ducks -- Fiction 2. Dinosaurs -- Fiction
ISBN 978-0-8109-9739-4; 0-8109-9739-8

LC 2010021624

In this take on "The Ugly Duckling," a tyrannosaurus rex is hatched in a nest of ducklings. Includes facts about dinosaurs.

"Kennedy's cartoonish watercolors nicely balance the ugly 'duckling's' good intentions with his slightly threatening appearance and clumsiness, helping readers empathize with him. . . . A sure winner for those dino-hungry readers." Kirkus

Includes bibliographical references

Bardos, Magli
★ **100** Bears. Flying Eye Books 2014 104 p. $19.95
Grades: K 1 2 3   E
1. Counting 2. Bears -- Fiction
ISBN 190926315X; 9781909263154

This illustrated children's counting book, written and illustrated by Magali Bardos is a "real bear caper." The book presents "a a wacky, . . . anarchic tale of hunters, feasts, and marauding beasts, [in which] we chase the numbers 1-100 through mountains, forests, and cities." (Publisher's note)

Barner, Bob
★ **Bug** safari. Holiday House 2004 un il $16.95

Grades: PreK K 1 2   E
1. Ants -- Fiction 2. Insects -- Fiction
ISBN 0-8234-1707-7

LC 2003-56619

"The bright, cut-paper collages will appeal to the youngest bug lovers, but the funny, dramatically told story is tailored to a more sophisticated young entomologist." Booklist

Barnett, Mac
Billy Twitters and his big blue whale problem; Mac Barnett, author; Adam Rex, illustrator. Disney/Hyperion Books 2009 un il $16.99
Grades: PreK K 1 2   E
1. School stories 2. Whales -- Fiction 3. Family life -- Fiction
ISBN 978-0-7868-4958-1; 0-7868-4958-4

LC 2009-11203

When Billy Twitters' mother follows through on her threat to buy him a blue whale if he refuses to obey, he finds himself the owner of an enormous pet that he must take with him everywhere, which does not make him popular at school.

"Young readers will likely enjoy the ridiculous premise, and the many whale facts worked seamlessly into the tale." SLJ

Count the monkeys; by Mac Barnett; illustrated by Kevin Cornell. 1st ed. Disney Hyperion 2013 32 p. ill. (reinforced) $16.99
Grades: PreK K 1   E
1. Counting 2. Picture books for children 3. Humorous stories 4. Animals -- Fiction 5. Monkeys -- Fiction
ISBN 1423160657; 9781423160656

LC 2012020299

In this children's picture book, readers are asked to count the monkeys. "But on the first page, one king cobra has scared them off. Next, two mongooses frighten off the cobra, and so on, with ever-increasing numbers of wacky animals and people until '10 polka-dotted rhinoceroses with bagpipes and bad breath' are called upon to get rid of 9 lumberjacks and the book runs out of pages, leaving 0 monkeys." (School Library Journal)

★ **Extra** yarn; written by Mac Barnett; illustrated by Jon Klassen. Balzer & Bray 2012 il $16.99
Grades: PreK K 1 2   E
1. Yarn -- Fiction 2. Magic -- Fiction 3. Knitting -- Fiction
ISBN 978-0-06-195338-5; 0-06-195338-5

LC 2010015945

Caldecott Honor Book (2013); Boston Globe-Horn Book Award: Picture Book (2012)

With a supply of yarn that never runs out, Annabelle knits for everyone and everything in town until an evil archduke decides he wants the yarn for himself.

"Klassen . . . uses inks, gouache and colorized scans of a sweater to create a stylized, linear design of dark geometric shapes against a white background. . . . Barnett . . . maintains a folkloric narrative that results in a traditional story arc complete with repetition, drama and a satisfying conclusion. A quiet story of sharing with no strings attached." Kirkus

Guess again! illustrated by Adam Rex. Simon & Schuster Books for Young Readers 2009 un il $16.99
Grades: 1 2 3 4   E
1. Stories in rhyme
ISBN 978-1-4169-5566-5; 1-4169-5566-6

LC 2008-12882

"A rhymed text joins with hinting illustrations to encourage readers to fill in the last word of the verse. A page turn, however, unveils an answer that's an absurd breach of expectation. . . . The confounding of expectations is pleasingly goofy. . . . Rex partners the rhyme with robust and solid gouache scenes that are comedic in their own right. . . . This would be particularly useful as a quick pick for reluctant readers, who'll warm to the combination of corniness and sophistication in the satirically unguessable guessing game." Bull Cent Child Books

★ **Leo**; by Mac Barnett; illustrated by Christian Robinson. Chronicle Books 2015 52 p. color illustrations (alk. paper) $16.99
Grades: PreK K 1   E
  1. Friendship -- Fiction 2. Ghost stories -- Fiction 3. Ghost stories 4. Ghosts -- Fiction 5. Friendship -- Fiction
  ISBN 1452131562; 9781452131566
                                                              LC 2014024417
This children's story, by Mac Barnett, illustrated by Christian Robinson, follows the ghost boy Leo. "When a new family moves into his home and Leo's efforts to welcome them are misunderstood, Leo decides it is time to leave and see the world. That is how he meets Jane, a kid with a tremendous imagination and an open position for a worthy knight. That is how Leo and Jane become friends." (Publisher's note)
  " In an empty house on the edge of a city lives Leo, the ghost of a young boy. He has been alone in the house a long time, and when a family moves in, he's delighted to have company, immediately rushing out to greet them with tea and toast. But not all families appreciate ghosts; when the tray comes floating toward them, they panic and call in the experts to dehaunt their house. . . . Despite the blue tones and Leo's initial loneliness, this is a tender, touching story of friendship and the power of imagination. And it is sure to warm hearts." Booklist

Mustache! illustrations by Kevin Cornell. Disney/Hyperion Books 2011 un il $16.99
  Grades: 1 2 3   E
  1. Kings and rulers -- Fiction 2. Personal appearance -- Fiction
  ISBN 978-1-4231-1671-4; 1-4231-1671-2
                                                              LC 2011008462
When extremely good-looking King Duncan builds more and more tributes to his handsome face, neglecting kingdom projects and repairs, his loyal subjects find a mustachioed solution.
  "The large cartoon illustrations, mostly spreads, are framed in gold with a peacock motif along the bottom. The brief, humorous text appears in scrolls superimposed on the paintings. . . . This royal romp of a story contains some subtle messages behind the hilarity." SLJ

Noisy night; Mac Barnett; illustrated by Brian Biggs. Roaring Brook Press 2016 32 p. color illustrations (hardback) $16.99; (ebook) $60
Grades: PreK K 1 2   E
  1. Night -- Fiction 2. Bedtime -- Fiction 3. Apartment houses
  ISBN 9781596439672; 9781250157270
                                                              LC 2016002016
In this children's book, by Mac Barnett, illustrated by Brian Biggs, "it's a noisy night in this city building! The residents of each floor can hear their neighbors above them, and are wondering what's going on above their heads. Climb floor by floor and page by page to find out whose singing, dancing, cheering, and cooing are keeping a grumpy old man awake." (Publisher's note)
  "Children will want to return to this witty cover to catch glimpses of all the characters they've met ascending from floor to floor." Booklist

Oh no! Not again! (or how I built a time machine to save history) (or at least my history grade) written by Mac Barnett; illustrated by Dan Santat. Disney-Hyperion 2012 40 p. col. ill. $17.99
Grades: K 1 2 3   E
  1. Belgium -- Fiction 2. Time travel -- Fiction 3. Picture books for children 4. Humorous stories 5. Cave dwellers -- Fiction 6. Cave

paintings -- Fiction
  ISBN 1423149122; 9781423149125
                                                              LC 2011011111
In this book, part of the "Oh No!" series "[Mac] Barnett's overachiever has a new dilemma: Her history test is returned with one point off for an incorrect answer. Noting that 'Belgium' is not the country where the oldest prehistoric cave paintings exist . . . she builds a time machine to alter history. After a few glitches . . . she finds her Belgian cavemen. . . . The duo gives the transporter a spin while the frustrated scholar decorates the cave herself." (Kirkus Reviews)

★ **Oh** no!, or, How my science project destroyed the world; written by Mac Barnett; illustrated by Dan Santat. Disney Hyperion Books 2010 un il $16.99
Grades: K 1 2   E
  1. Robots -- Fiction 2. Science projects -- Fiction
  ISBN 978-1-4231-2312-5; 1-4231-2312-3
                                                              LC 2010004516
After winning the science fair with the giant robot she has built, a little girl realizes that there is a major problem.
  "Santat's brilliantly hued digital illustrations are the perfect foil for Barnett's almost-wordless tale of a science project gone awry. . . . Comic-book, picture-book and movie styles come together in a well-designed package that includes a movie poster on the reverse side of the jacket, an old-time computation book as the inside cover and detailed scientific drawings on the endpapers. . . . A must-have." Kirkus

President Taft is stuck in the bath; Mac Barnett, illustrated by Chris Van Dusen. Candlewick Press 2014 32 p. color illustrations $16.99
Grades: 1 2 3 4   E
  1. Presidents -- United States
  ISBN 0763663174; 9780763663179
                                                              LC 2013943103
"Mac Barnett begins with a historically unconfirmed rumor that President Taft once got stuck in his bathtub. While President Taft gets increasingly louder and more frustrated, the First Lady remains calm. He calls on the vice-president and his Cabinet members, each of them offering a self-serving or unworkable solution. Finally, his wife suggests that they use their muscle to get the President out and he is quickly freed." (Library Media Connection)
  "The combination of Barnett's repetitive assonance . . . and Van Dusen's gouache caricature illustrations (with strategically placed water and bubbles) sets the hilarious tone." Booklist

Rules of the house; by Mac Barnett; illustrated by Matt Myers. Disney-Hyperion Books 2015 48 p. color illustrations (hardcover) $17.99
Grades: K 1 2 3   E
  1. Monsters -- Fiction 2. Rules (Philosophy) -- Fiction 3. Brothers and sisters -- Fiction
  ISBN 9781423185161; 1423185161
                                                              LC 2014015780
In this children's story, by Mac Barnett, illustrated by Matt Myers, "Ian is thrilled when the house where his family is vacationing posts a tidy list of rules. But when Jenny breaks them all, the house itself decides it's time for payback. The rug, the stove, and the bathtub are hungry for rulebreaker soup. . . . Now Ian is faced with a thorny question: What if saving your sister means breaking the rules?" (Publisher's note)
  "A scary but silly sibling story about times when breaking the rules might just be okay. The perfect read to prepare for a stay at a vacation house." SLJ

★ **Sam** and Dave dig a hole; Mac Barnett, illustrated by Jon Klassen. First edition Candlewick Press 2014 40 p. $16.99

Grades: PreK K 1 2   **E**
1. Humorous fiction -- Fiction 2. Adventure and adventurers -- Fiction 3. Holes 4. Imagination 5. Humorous stories
ISBN 0763662291; 9780763662295
LC 2013955959
Caldecott Honor Book (2015)
In this children's book, by Mac Barnett and illustrated by Jon Klassen, "Sam and Dave are on a mission. A mission to find something spectacular. So they dig a hole. And they keep digging. And they find . . . nothing. Yet the day turns out to be pretty spectacular after all." (Publisher's note)
"Sam and Dave, each wearing baseball caps and wielding long-handled shovels, set out to dig a hole. How big a hole? 'We won't stop digging until we find something spectacular,' says Dave, so off they go, digging ever deeper while their little dog follows their progress. A cross section of their dig reveals that Sam and Dave come awfully close to their prize, but they keep digging and missing treasure until they decide to take a nap, during which they tumble right through the earth." Booklist

The **skunk**; Mac Barnett; illustrated by Patrick McDonnell. Roaring Brook Press 2015 32 p. color illustrations (hardback) $17.99
Grades: K 1 2 3   **E**
1. Skunks -- Fiction 2. City and town life 3. Human-animal relationship -- Fiction 4. Humorous stories
ISBN 1596439661; 9781596439665
LC 2014032753
"When a skunk first appears in the tuxedoed man's doorway, it's a strange but possibly harmless occurrence. But then the man finds the skunk following him, and the unlikely pair embark on an increasingly frantic chase through the city, from the streets to the opera house to the fairground. What does the skunk want?" (Publisher's note)
"Clever visual motifs, sly storytelling, and tight pacing make this a picture book that will be enjoyed by children and their grown-ups." SLJ

Triangle; by Mac Barnett and Jon Klassen. Candlewick Press 2017 48 p. color illustrations $15.99
Grades: PreK K 1   **E**
1. Humorous fiction 2. Shape -- Fiction 3. Picture books for children
ISBN 076369603X; 9780763696030
In this book, illustrator Jon Klassen's "minimalist visuals make for beautiful, surreal landscapes as the shapes go back and forth; [author Mac] Barnett's even-more-minimalist narrative leaves gaps of many shapes and sizes for readers to ponder. Children will be intrigued by the fairy-tale quality of this narrative and may enjoy debating the motivations of its peculiar characters." (Kirkus Reviews)

Barrett, Judi
Cloudy with a chance of meatballs; written by Judi Barrett and drawn by Ron Barrett. Aladdin Paperbacks 1982 un il pa $6.99
Grades: PreK K 1 2   **E**
1. Food -- Fiction 2. Weather -- Fiction
ISBN 0-689-70749-5
LC 87-29643
First published 1978
Life is delicious in the town of Chewandswallow where it rains soup and juice, snows mashed potatoes, and blows storms of hamburgers—until the weather takes a turn for the worse.

★ **Never** take a shark to the dentist and other things not to do; [by] Judi Barrett; illustrated by John Nickle. Atheneum Books for Young Readers 2007 un il $16.99

Grades: PreK K 1 2   **E**
1. Animals -- Fiction
ISBN 978-1-4169-0724-4; 1-4169-0724-6
LC 2006000153
A list of things one should not do with various animals, such as "hold hands with a lobster"
"Nickle, working in hyper-detailed acrylics, enhances the comical phrases with surreal imagery. . . . Kids will revel in the absurd humor." Publ Wkly

Santa from Cincinnati; How a Little Boy Named Santa Grew up to Become the Real Thing. Judi Barrett; illustrated by Kevin Hawks. Atheneum Books for Young Readers 2012 48 p. (hardcover) $16.99
Grades: K 1 2 3   **E**
1. Christmas -- Fiction 2. Santa Claus -- Fiction 3. Humorous fiction -- Fiction 4. Santa Claus -- Fiction
ISBN 9781442429932; 9781442429949; 1442429933
LC 2011050810
This children's book, by Judi Barrett, illustrated by Kevin Hawkes, tells the story of Santa Claus' childhood. "His first words were 'ho ho ho!' By five he was wearing a fake beard and mustache, and could rarely be found without his favorite stuffed reindeer. . . . Despite this, his parents went to great lengths to keep the normalcy in his life. . . . But there was no stopping Santa from being Santa, and one winter, he began to make his lists." (Publisher's note)

Barrett, Mary Brigid
Shoebox Sam; illustrated by Frank Morrison. Zonderkidz 2011 un il $15.99
Grades: K 1 2   **E**
1. Shoes -- Fiction 2. Christian life -- Fiction 3. Homeless persons -- Fiction
ISBN 978-0-310-71549-8; 0-310-71549-0
On Saturdays, Delia and Jesse help Shoebox Sam, who teaches them about charity and love by not only repairing shoes for paying customers, but also giving poor and homeless people the dignity—and footwear—they need.
"Even in quieter poses, Morrison's bright-eyed, rubber-limbed figures look like they are dancing, and they perfectly reflect the lively sounds and rhythms of Barrett's language." Booklist

Barretta, Gene
Timeless Thomas; how Thomas Edison changed our lives. Gene Barretta. Henry Holt 2012 37 p.
Grades: 2 3 4   **E**
1. Inventions -- History 2. Inventions
ISBN 0805091084; 9780805091083
LC 2011034057
In this children's book, by Gene Barretta, the life and inventions of Thomas Edison are described. "Edison is most famous for inventing the incandescent lightbulb, but at his landmark laboratories in Menlo Park & West Orange, New Jersey, he also developed many other staples of modern technology. Despite many failures, Edison persevered. And good for that, because it would be very difficult to go through a day without using one of his life-changing inventions." (Publisher's note)
Includes bibliographical references

Zoola Palooza; a book of homographs. Henry Holt 2011 un il $16.99
Grades: K 1 2   **E**
1. Animals -- Fiction 2. Concerts -- Fiction 3. Musicians -- Fiction 4. English language -- Homonyms
ISBN 0-8050-9107-6; 978-0-8050-9107-6
LC 2010025833

Written and illustrated by Gene Barretta, "this picture book uses pairs of homographs to describe a silly Zoola Palooza animal concert. For example, Carmen Chameleon's entrance will entrance the audience, as she can produce a bowl of produce and blend into it. Colorful, energetic illustrations capture the fun, while capitalized text emphasizes the homographs in the story." (Booklist)

"While teachers are sure to reach for this entertaining resource again and again, the humor, illustrations, wordplay and story are strong enough that casual readers will pick this up, chuckle and even . . . learn." Kirkus

Barron, T. A.

Ghost hands; a story inspired by Patagonia's Cave of the Hands. illustrated by William Low. Philomel Books 2011 un il $18.99
Grades: PreK K 1   E
1. Courage -- Fiction 2. Native Americans -- Fiction 3. Cave drawings and paintings -- Fiction 4. Patagonia (Argentina and Chile) -- Fiction
ISBN 978-0-399-25083-5; 0-399-25083-2
LC 2010010648

Auki, a young member of the Tehuelche tribe in Patagonia, wants to prove himself as a hunter but when he sets out on his own to face the puma, he stumbles upon a sacred cave and its guardian.

"As in Barron and Low's previous collaboration . . . tightly connected visuals and text provoke curiosity and awe about a phenomenon at once mysterious and accessible." Kirkus

Barros, Bruna

The **carpenter**; Bruna Barros; [edited by] Michelle Branson. Gibbs M. Smith Inc. 2017 40 p. chiefly color illustrations (jacketed hardcover) $12.99
Grades: PreK K 1   E
1. Storytelling -- Fiction 2. Adventure and adventurers -- Fiction
ISBN 1423646762; 9781423646761
LC 2016945725

This book, by Bruna Barros, "shares its story without a single word. . . . Barros' beautiful, creative illustrations will capture children's imaginations, showing readers that even the simplest, most common objects can start a wonderful adventure. This book also offers opportunities to foster discussions and spontaneous story telling." (Publisher's note)

"A quality selection to put into the hands of emergent readers to help them expand their imagination and prepare for reading." SLJ

Barrow, David

Have You Seen Elephant? David Barrow. Lerner Pub Group 2016 32 p. color illustrations (hardcover) $16.99
Grades: PreK K   E
1. Elephants -- Fiction 2. Hide-and-seek -- Fiction
ISBN 9781776570089; 1776570081

In this children's story, by David Barrow, "a small child plays hide-and-seek with a surprisingly elusive (except to viewers) elephant. . . . The dark-skinned, springy-haired, and increasingly confused-looking child fruitlessly searches house and yard for the pachyderm—who positively dominates each scene whether 'hiding' beneath curtains, under a coverlet on top of the bed, or behind a skinny tree." (Kirkus Reviews)

"Beyond the sheer absurdity, children will delight in details, such as the wide-screen TV the elephant holds in one scene, the child's dad so focused on the soccer game on the screen that he asks, 'What elephant?' and the sly alterations to the family portraits on the rear endpapers." Kirkus

Bartlett, T. C.

Tuba lessons; illustrated by Monique Felix. Creative Editions 2009 un il $25.65

Grades: PreK K 1   E
1. Stories without words 2. Animals -- Fiction 3. Musical instruments -- Fiction
ISBN 978-1-56846-209-7; 1-56846-209-3
LC 2009-3834

First published 1997 by Harcourt, Brace and Company

While walking through the woods on his way to his tuba lesson, a boy becomes sidetracked by all the animals that want to hear him play.

"This text is not only for storytimes, but can be used as a catalyst to get young readers and writers to create their own words to enhance the imaginative, playful illustrations. Friendship, music and the journey are the themes in this picture tale." Libr Media Connect

Bartoletti, Susan Campbell

★ **Naamah** and the ark at night. Candlewick Press 2011 un il $16.99
Grades: PreK K 1 2   E
1. Lullabies 2. Stories in rhyme 3. Children's poetry 4. Night -- Fiction 5. Animals -- Fiction 6. Noah's ark -- Fiction
ISBN 978-0-7636-4242-6; 0-7636-4242-8
LC 2010040398

"Bartoletti shapes his verse form into a gentle litany . . . centerd on Naamah's lulling song. . . . Meade's watercolor collages are a fine complement. . . . A lovely lullaby, in a beautiful, masterfully integrated book." Horn Book

Barton, Byron

★ **Dinosaurs**, dinosaurs. Crowell 1989 un il $16.99; lib bdg $17.89; pa $6.99; bd bk $7.99
Grades: PreK K   E
1. Dinosaurs -- Fiction
ISBN 0-694-00269-0; 0-690-04768-1 lib bdg; 0-06-443298-X pa; 0-694-400625-4 bd bk
LC 88-22938

This book examines the many different kinds of dinosaurs, big and small, those with spikes and those with long, sharp teeth

"Barton conveys the primordial sense of excitement that draws children to these beasts. . . . The endpapers identify the creatures by scientific name and pronunciation. Barton wisely keeps his text simple, describing dinosaurs only by size and physical features." SLJ

My bike; Byron Barton. Greenwillow Books, an imprint of HarperCollinsPublishers 2015 40 p. color illustrations hbk $16.99
Grades: PreK K 1   E
1. Circus -- Fiction 2. Bicycles -- Fiction 3. Bicycles and bicycling -- Fiction
ISBN 0062336991; 9780062336996
LC 2014013919

In this picture book by Byron Barton, "Tom . . . is the proud owner of a bright green bicycle. After Tom describes all the parts of his bike, he rides the bike to work. He rides along busy roads and bustling streets, past cars and buses and animals and people, until he arrives at the circus, changes into his work clothes, and goes to work. It turns out that Tom is a clown, and his job is to ride a unicycle on a high wire under the big top!" (Publisher's note)

★ **My** bus; Byron Barton. First edition Greenwillow Books, an imprint of HarperCollinsPublishers 2014 40 p. (trade ed.) $16.99
Grades: PreK K   E
1. Pets -- Fiction 2. Buses -- Fiction 3. Mathematics -- Fiction 4. Transportation -- Fiction
ISBN 0062287362; 9780062287366
LC 2013007869

This book, by Byron Barton, "is a lively celebration of vehicles and transportation, occupations, pets, and basic math concepts. The busy bus driver . . . has a job to do. He drives his bus along his route, picks up the cat and dog passengers waiting at the bus stops, and delivers them to their destinations--which in this case include the airport, the harbor, and the train station. Along the way, children are introduced to the concepts of addition, subtraction, and sets." (Publisher's note)

"In a companion volume to My Car, Joe drives Bus #123 across a bold-hued landscape populated with feline and canine passengers. The book ingeniously and subtly introduces the basic concepts of cardinal and ordinal numbers, addition, subtraction, and sets. Illustrated in Barton's signature style, with bold, flat colors and with only the most important visual details included, there are sure to be re-readings." Horn Book

★ **My** car. Greenwillow Bks. 2001 un il $14.95; pa $6.99; bd bk $7.99
Grades: PreK K   E
1. Automobiles -- Fiction
ISBN 0-06-029624-0; 0-06-029625-9 lib bdg; 0-06-058940-X pa; 0-06-056045-2 bd bk
            LC 00-50334

Sam describes in loving detail his car and how he drives it
"The chunky blocks of color and minimalist text will withstand countless readings." Publ Wkly

Barton, Chris

★ **Shark** vs. train; by Chris Barton & [illustrated by] Tom Lichtenheld. Little, Brown 2010 un il $16.99
Grades: PreK K 1   E
1. Sharks -- Fiction 2. Railroads -- Fiction
ISBN 978-0-316-00762-7; 0-316-00762-5
            LC 2009-17961

A shark and a train compete in a series of contests on a seesaw, in hot air balloons, bowling, shooting baskets, playing hide-and-seek, and more.

"This is a genius concept. . . . Lichtenheld's . . . watercolor cartoons have a fluidity and goofy intensity that recalls Mad magazine, while Barton . . . gives the characters snappy dialogue throughout." Publ Wkly

Bartone, Elisa

★ **Peppe** the lamplighter; illustrations by Ted Lewin. Lothrop, Lee & Shepard Bks. 1993 un il $17.99; pa $6.99
Grades: K 1 2 3   E
1. New York (N.Y.) -- Fiction 2. Italian Americans -- Fiction
ISBN 0-688-10268-9; 0-688-15469-7 pa
            LC 92-1397

A Caldecott Medal honor book, 1994

Peppe's father is upset when he learns that Peppe has taken a job lighting the gas street lamps in his New York City neighborhood

"Peppe's quiet quest for familial respect and pleasure in his work is touching and rhythmically written. The early-American city scenes are dark but have a nice period luminescence in the myriad street and table lamps, and the earth-toned watercolors lend the bustling streets and interiors of Little Italy an air both somber and lively." Bull Cent Child Books

Bartram, Simon

Bob's best ever friend. Templar Books 2009 un il $16.99
Grades: K 1 2   E
1. Dogs -- Fiction 2. Moon -- Fiction 3. Astronauts -- Fiction 4. Friendship -- Fiction
ISBN 978-0-7636-4425-3; 0-7636-4425-0

"Bob, an astronaut who travels daily from Earth to the Moon to entertain tourists, is lonely: there are no visitors this Tuesday and his friends have gone off to Pluto. The next day, he begins to look for a 'best-ever friend' and decides that it could be a pet. One day he sees something amazing pop out of a crater: a dog. Bartram's detailed acrylics give readers comic relief while Bob is on his quest. . . . The artwork is reminiscent of books from the 1950s and is done in electric blues, yellows, and reds." SLJ

Another title about Bob is:
Man on the moon (2002)

Baruzzi, Agnese

The **true** story of Little Red Riding Hood; [by] Agnese Baruzzi and Sandro Natalini. Templar Books 2009 un il $14.99
Grades: K 1 2 3   E
1. Fairy tales 2. Pop-up books
ISBN 978-0-7636-4427-7

"In this fractured fairy tale, the wolf asks for help rehabilitating his reputation. Little Red Riding Hood's advice (become a vegetarian) works—for a while. The book overflows with lift-the-flaps; envelopes with tiny letters inside and a fabric shower curtain and apron are also included. The boldly colored naive-style paintings are enhanced by collage elements, including rickrack borders." Horn Book Guide

Base, Graeme

★ **Animalia**; Graeme Base. H.N. Abrams 1993 32 p. $12.95
Grades: PreK K 1 2 3   E
1. Animals -- Fiction 2. Alphabet -- Fiction 3. Animals -- Pictorial works 4. English language -- Alphabet
ISBN 0810919397; 9780810919396

In this children's book, author Graeme Base "has created an ABC book that goes far beyond a simple listing of items in alphabetical order. There are captions or headlines accompanying each letter's scene, such as 'Eight Enormous Elephants Expertly Eating Easter Eggs,' or 'Two Tigers Taking the 10:20 Train to Timbuktu.' Each picture is replete with an apparently random choice of objects that have in common (on every page but the one for the letter X) their first letters." (Publishers Weekly)

★ The **Jewel** Fish of Karnak. Abrams Books for Young Readers 2011 un il
Grades: K 1 2 3   E
1. Magic -- Fiction 2. Thieves -- Fiction 3. Egypt -- History -- Fiction 4. Kings and rulers -- Fiction
ISBN 1-4197-0086-3; 978-1-4197-0086-6
            LC 2010050080

Two thieves, caught stealing from an Egyptian market, are brought before the Cat Pharaoh, who agrees to pardon them if they bring back a treasure that was stolen from her, without taking anything else and without getting the precious Jewel Fish wet.

Base "doesn't disappoint his sleuthing fans, providing decodable hieroglyphic messages on painted stone tablets across the bottom of each spread. This tale packs in plenty of puzzle solving and Egyptology amid the boldly animated scenes; the illustrations' exquisite details—right down to the comical facial expressions of the bumbling thieves—tell much of the story." Publ Wkly

The **water** hole; Graeme Base. Harry N. Abrams 2001 32 p. col. ill. $19.95
Grades: PreK K 1 2 3   E
1. Counting 2. Habitat (Ecology)
ISBN 0810945681; 9780810945685
            LC 00066378

In this children's book, author Graeme Base "takes the reader on a journey of discovery, from the plains of Africa and the jungles of the Amazon to the woodlands of North America and the deserts of the Australian outback. . . . Page by page the numbers increase as the animals come to their water hole to drink. But at the same time, the cast of frogs frolicking by the water hole is diminishing. What is going on?" (Publisher's note)

"One rhino, two tigers, and other animals up to ten kangaroos come to drink from a water hole, a die-cut hole that shrinks through successive pages. Why are animals on different continents shown drinking from the same water hole? Why is the water hole shrinking? Don't ask--just enjoy searching the detailed paintings for hidden animal images and a family of sartorially savvy frogs." Horn Book

Basher, Simon

★ **ABC** Kids. Kingfisher Books 2011 un il $17.99
Grades: PreK K   E
  1. Alphabet
  ISBN 978-0-7534-6495-3; 0-7534-6495-0

"This ABC book provides a stylish introduction to the alphabet while building vocabularies. [Basher's] chunky cartoon illustrations are front and center, joined by heavily alliterative sentences. . . . Full-bleed pastel backdrops give the book the feel of a cheerily illustrated sheaf of construction paper; with inventive vocab on left-hand pages opposite pages focusing on one stand-alone image, . . . the book is appropriate for both beginning and developing readers. Smart fun." Publ Wkly

Go! go! Bobo: colors. Kingfisher 2011 un il bd bk $6.99
Grades: PreK   E
  1. Color 2. Board books for children
  ISBN 978-0-7534-6493-9; 0-7534-6493-4

Bouncy Bobo can't sit still. He just has to bounce his way across the pages of this book, painting everything he sees. From yellow ducks, to blue butterflies, orange carrots, pink piggies, red roses, and green apples.

"A great title in encourage toddlers' interactive play. . . . Kids will want to move from the book to the real world and name the colors all around them." Booklist

Bass, L. G.

Boom boom go away! by Laura Geringer; illustrated by Bagram Ibatoulline. Atheneum 2010 un il $15.99
Grades: PreK K 1   E
  1. Toys -- Fiction 2. Music -- Fiction 3. Bedtime -- Fiction
  ISBN 978-0-689-85093-6; 0-689-85093-X

"Each time a parent tells a boy to go to bed, the toys in his room delay the process by playing their instruments and saying they can't be disturbed. . . . The rhythmical text has an appealing cadence and a catchy refrain. Ibatoulline's watercolor and acrylic-gouache spreads of the child's room are wonderfully designed." SLJ

Basseches, K. B.

ABeCedarios; Mexican folk art ABCs in English and Spanish. [by] Cynthia Weill and K.B. Basseches; wood sculptures from Oaxaca by Moises and Armando Jimenez. Cinco Puntos Press 2008 un il $14.95
Grades: PreK K 1 2 3 4   E
  1. Alphabet 2. Folk art 3. Mexican art 4. Animals in art 5. Animals 6. Bilingual books -- English-Spanish
  ISBN 1-933693-13-4; 978-1-933693-13-2

                                          LC 2007019441
This bilingual picture book "introduces the alphabet, using painted wooden sculptures of animals made by the Jiménez family." (Publisher's note) "Preschool to grade three." (MultiCult Rev)

"Mexican folk-art figures are the focus of this colorful alphabet book. Each page presents a small Oaxacan woodcarving of an animal done in a rainbow of colors. The only text is the animals' names in Spanish and in English. . . . The sculpted figures display personality and enough vibrant energy to leap off the pages." SLJ

Bastianich, Lidia

Nonna's birthday surprise; Lidia Bastianich. Running Press Kids 2013 60 p. (hardcover) $16.95
Grades: K 1 2 3   E
  1. Birthdays -- Fiction 2. Farm life -- Fiction
  ISBN 0762446552; 9780762446551

                                          LC 2012944237
In this children's story, by Lidia Bastianich, illustrated by Renée Graef, "It's Nonna Mima's birthday, and Nonna Lidia and her grandkids are determined to throw her a surprise feast! While planning the evening's menu, Nonna Lidia shares her memories of growing up on the farm during each season of the year, gardening her own fruits and vegetables, and being surrounded by animals of all kinds." (Publisher's note)

Bataille, Marion

10. Roaring Brook Press 2011 un il $14.99
Grades: 1 2 3 4 5   E
  1. Numbers 2. Pop-up books
  ISBN 978-1-59643-682-4; 1-59643-682-4

"Housed within a shiny red slipcase, this minimalist counting book can be viewed in multiple ways. By turning the pages once from left to right, readers can count from '01' to '10,' the black numerals appearing on the left side of each white spread. By proceeding through the book and unfolding each page twice, however, the numbers transform—the top of the '2' swivels, losing its base to become a '9,' for example—so readers can count down to '01.' . . . the sleek construction should appeal to pop-up fans of any age." Publ Wkly

★ **ABC3D**. Roaring Brook Press 2008 un il $19.95
Grades: 1 2 3 4 5   E
  1. Alphabet 2. Pop-up books
  ISBN 978-1-59643-425-7; 1-59643-425-2

                                          LC 2008-08933
"From the lenticular cover to the jazzy use of a red, white and black color scheme, this hand-size French alphabet book is as stylish as a pop-up can be. Letters here not only pop up, they move and transform. . . . Many letters are three-dimensional (i.e., the legs of H are hollow paper rectangles), and gain extra glamour from high-contrast backgrounds (white on black; red or black on white). A-plus for drama and innovation." Publ Wkly

Bateman, Teresa

April foolishness; illustrated by Nadine Bernard Westcott. Albert Whitman & Co. 2004 un il $15.95
Grades: PreK K 1 2   E
  1. Stories in rhyme 2. Farm life -- Fiction 3. April Fools' Day -- Fiction
  ISBN 0-8075-0404-1

                                          LC 2004-825
"Bateman's verse prances along in a pleasing way, never sounding a false note or tripping over its metric feet. Bright with colorful washes, Westcott's ink drawings illustrate the action with equal lightness and grace. . . . Zany and inventive, the artwork amplifies the story's humor." Booklist

★ **Keeper** of soles; illustrated by Yayo. Holiday House 2006 un il $16.95
Grades: K 1 2 3   E
  1. Death -- Fiction 2. Shoes -- Fiction 3. Shoemakers -- Fiction
  ISBN 0-8234-1734-4

                                          LC 2004-52297
When Death comes for a shoemaker's soul, he outwits him by making shoes for him, giving him soles instead of souls.

"Bateman pairs the cadences of a traditional folktale with contemporary humor. The scenes are imbued with suspense without being macabre. Yayo's full-bleed acrylics provide large expanses of rich, layered colors as foils for the smaller, whimsical details." SLJ

Bates, Janet Costa

Seaside dream; illustrated by Lambert Davis. Lee & Low Books 2010 un il $17.95

Grades: K 1 2　　　　　　　　　　　　　　　　　　　　E

1. Gifts -- Fiction 2. Birthdays -- Fiction 3. Cape Verde -- Fiction 4. Grandmothers -- Fiction

ISBN 978-1-60060-347-1; 1-60060-347-5

LC 2009-17049

At a birthday celebration on the beach, Cora gives her grandmother a special gift and encourages her to make a trip back to her home country, Cape Verde.

"This poignant tale of a special relationship between a young girl and her grandmother showcases the joy of gift giving as well as the importance of family connections. . . . Color-drenched illustrations in deep-blue tones effectively evoke the summery coastal setting." Booklist

Battersby, Katherine

Squish Rabbit. Viking 2011 un il $12.99

Grades: PreK K　　　　　　　　　　　　　　　　　　　E

1. Size -- Fiction 2. Rabbits -- Fiction 3. Friendship -- Fiction 4. Loneliness -- Fiction

ISBN 978-0-670-01267-1; 0-670-01267-X

LC 2010042227

A lonely little rabbit wants to make a friend.

"Battersby's expert, ample distribution of white space provides room on each page for readers to luxuriate in her impressive, evocative ink, watercolor and collage illustrations—and to absorb a small rabbit's feelings. Rough papers and textured fabrics add depth, creating an almost tactile reading experience. . . . Minimal, moving and adorable, little Squish makes a big impression." Kirkus

Battut, Eric

★ The fox and the hen. Boxer 2010 un il $16.95

Grades: PreK K　　　　　　　　　　　　　　　　　　　E

1. Eggs -- Fiction 2. Foxes -- Fiction 3. Domestic animals -- Fiction

ISBN 978-1-907152-02-3; 1-907152-02-4

"Henrietta Hen lays her first egg and innocently trades it to Red Fox for a worm. The other farm animals quickly tell her that she must get her precious egg back and go with her to make the trade. . . . Each time Red Fox refuses and thinks of a new way to eat the egg. . . . Henrietta finds an enormous stone that her friends paint white, and Red Fox eagerly trades her egg for this bigger one. . . . The animals are outlined in thick, black line and dabs of white highlight the vibrant red and orange palette. . . . With great economy, Battut gives each animal an expressive face and moves the story to a satisfying conclusion." SLJ

Little Mouse's big secret. Sterling 2011 un il $12.95

Grades: PreK K　　　　　　　　　　　　　　　　　　　E

1. Mice -- Fiction 2. Trees -- Fiction 3. Apples -- Fiction 4. Animals -- Fiction

ISBN 978-1-4027-7462-1; 1-4027-7462-1

LC 2010019689

Little Mouse refuses to reveal his secret despite being questioned by his friends.

"The urge to hoard treats is a common one, and Battut's . . . brisk, spare treatment of the problem has the feel of a classic. . . . Elemental text and artwork effectively convey the lesson about Mouse's best-laid

plans, while his obliviousness to the tree's growth provides suspense and satisfaction." Publ Wkly

Bauer, Marion Dane

The longest night; illustrated by Ted Lewin. Holiday House 2009 un il $17.95

Grades: K 1 2 3　　　　　　　　　　　　　　　　　　　E

1. Night -- Fiction 2. Winter -- Fiction 3. Animals -- Fiction

ISBN 978-0-8234-2054-4; 0-8234-2054-X

LC 2008022575

One very long night, a crow, a moose, and a fox all claim they can bring back the sun, but the wind knows that only one little creature has what is needed to end the darkness.

"This stunningly crafted tale, written in the language of the storyteller, realistically pictures, in both words and paintings, the phenomenon that is the winter solstice. . . . There is plenty of moonlight in Lewin's watercolor paintings created with just blue, brown, and green." SLJ

Thank you for me! illustrated by Kristina Stephenson. Simon & Schuster Books for Young Readers 2010 un il $14.99

Grades: PreK K 1　　　　　　　　　　　　　　　　　　E

1. Human body -- Fiction

ISBN 978-0-689-85788-1; 0-689-85788-8

LC 2006023872

Rhythmic text enumerates what various body parts can do, including hands to clap and a body to twirl, then expresses thanks for each of those parts—and for the whole.

"Bauer's lilting text matches the jubilant energy in Stephenson's watercolor rainbow palette." SLJ

Bauer, Marion Dane, 1938-

In like a lion, out like a lamb; illustrated by Emily Arnold McCully. Holiday House 2011 un il $16.95

Grades: PreK K 1 2　　　　　　　　　　　　　　　　　E

1. Stories in rhyme 2. Lions -- Fiction 3. Sheep -- Fiction 4. Spring -- Fiction

ISBN 0-8234-2238-0; 978-0-8234-2238-8

LC 2010007892

"In Bauer's capable hands, the age-old simile of March coming in like a lion and going out like a lamb is made quite literal. . . . While the text provides the skeleton, McCully's pen, ink and watercolor illustrations truly bring the old song to life. Her lion is a wonderful cross between a fierce foe . . . and a party pooper. . . . Meanwhile, the lamb is a perfect ball of fluff. . . . A good addition to the spring shelf, it is sure to find its way, roaring and bleating, to classrooms studying similes." Kirkus

Bean, Jonathan

★ At night. Farrar, Straus and Giroux 2007 un il $15

Grades: PreK K 1　　　　　　　　　　　　　　　　　　E

1. Night -- Fiction 2. Sleep -- Fiction 3. City and town life -- Fiction

ISBN 0-374-30446-7; 978-0-374-30446-1

LC 2006-48403

Boston Globe-Horn Book Award: Picture Book (2008)

A sleepless city girl imagines what it would be like to get away from snoring family members and curl up alone with one's thoughts in the cool night air under wide-open skies.

"The artist supplies luminous aerial scenes of the roof garden amid a friendly, well-lit cityscape. . . . The story breathes reassurance and adventure at the same time." Publ Wkly

★ **Building** our house; Jonathan Bean. Farrar, Straus and Giroux 2013 48 p. (reinforced) $17.99

Grades: PreK K 1 2   E
1. Houses 2. House construction 3. Picture books for children 4. Building -- Fiction 5. Dwellings -- Design and construction -- Fiction

ISBN 0374380236; 9780374380236

LC 2007027681

Boston Globe-Horn Book Award: Picture Book (2013)

In this children's picture book, Jonathan Bean tells the story of his "back-to-the-land parents, who built his childhood home in the 1970s. . . . Frontmatter depicts [the family] packing and leaving the city, Ensuing spreads detail how they live in a trailer on their new property while slowly building the house: setting the corners of the foundation; digging out the basement; gathering rocks and using them in the foundation; measuring, marking and cutting timber for the frame; and so on." (Kirkus)

"The watercolor-and-ink illustrations invite close examination for narrative details such as these while also providing ample visual information about construction." Kirkus

★ **This** is my home, this is my school; Jonathan Bean. Farrar, Straus & Giroux 2015 48 p. color illustrations (hardback) $18.99
Grades: PreK K 1 2   E
1. Home schooling -- Fiction 2. Home and school -- Fiction 3. Family life -- Fiction

ISBN 0374380201; 9780374380205

LC 2014040682

In this book, "drawing from his own childhood experiences, [author and illustrator] Jonathan Bean takes the autobiographically inspired family he introduced in 'Building Our House' through the special rhythms and routines of a homeschooling day. For young Jonathan and his sisters, Mom is the teacher and a whole lot more, and Dad is the best substitute any kid could want." (Publisher's note)

"This will delight homeschooled children, who will identify with Jonathan and his sisters, and captivate others not familiar with the home-schooled experience." Booklist

Beard, Alex
The **jungle** grapevine. Abrams Books for Young Readers 2009 un il $16.95
Grades: K 1 2 3   E
1. Africa -- Fiction 2. Animals -- Fiction 3. Communication -- Fiction

ISBN 978-0-8109-8001-3; 0-8109-8001-0

LC 2008046197

When Turtle makes an off-hand remark to Bird at the watering hole one day, Bird's misunderstanding starts a series of rumors that stirs up the other animals.

"Young children will easily understand the moral of the story. This book will be constantly circulating, thanks to the dialogue, storyline, and artwork." Libr Media Connect

Monkey see monkey draw. Abrams Books for Young Readers 2010 un il $16.95
Grades: PreK K 1   E
1. Play -- Fiction 2. Africa -- Fiction 3. Monkeys -- Fiction 4. Elephants -- Fiction

ISBN 978-0-8109-8970-2; 0-8109-8970-0

Elephant leads a troupe of monkeys into a cave they have been afraid to explore, and after admiring the paintings found on the walls they make their own art with mud, squabbling over whose painting is best until Elephant explains that this is not a game to win or lose.

"Bold, imaginative and very comical pen, ink and watercolor illustrations rely on line, color, pattern and thumbprints to produce surreal, gangly blue monkeys frenetically cavorting and clambering across the pages. . . . Beard aptly conjures the look and feel of prehistoric cave

paintings, inspiring readers to create their own. Wild and wonderful." Kirkus

Beaton, Kate
King Baby; Kate Beaton. Arthur A. Levine Books, an imprint of Scholastic Inc. 2016 40 p. color illustrations (hardcover : alk. paper) $17.99
Grades: PreK K 1 2   E
1. Humorous fiction 2. Infants -- Fiction 3. Kings and rulers -- Fiction 4. Babies -- Fiction 5. Parent and child -- Fiction

ISBN 9780545637541

LC 2015045685

In this children's book by Kate Beaton, the chief character King Baby "greets his adoring public with giggles and wiggles and coos, posing for photos and allowing hugs and kisses. But this royal ruler also has many demands, and when his subjects can't quite keep up, King Baby takes matters into his own tiny hands." (Publisher's note)

"It's less a story than an extended riff, but Beaton offers a sly, hilarious dig at the way young parents bow to their child's every desire." Pub Wkly

★ The **princess** and the pony; Kate Beaton. Arthur A. Levine Books 2015 40 p. (hardcover : alk. paper) $17.99
Grades: PreK K 1 2   E
1. Horses -- Fiction 2. Princesses -- Fiction 3. Humorous stories 4. Ponies -- Fiction

ISBN 0545637082; 9780545637084

LC 2014030927

In this children's book by Katie Beaton "Princess Pinecone knows exactly what she wants for her birthday this year. A BIG horse. A STRONG horse. A horse fit for a WARRIOR PRINCESS! But when the day arrives, she doesn't quite get the horse of her dreams." (Publisher's note)

"Rambunctious Princess Pinecone is the smallest warrior in her kingdom, but what she lacks in size, she makes up for in enthusiasm. Tired of receiving novelty sweaters for her birthday, Pinecone asks her parents for a big, strong battle horse—and receives a chubby little pony with a vacant expression, and incurable flatulence, instead...A highly recommended, charmingly illustrated tale of teamwork and tenderness." SLJ

Beaty, Andrea
Ada Twist, scientist; by Andrea Beaty; illustrated by David Roberts. Abrams Books for Young Readers 2016 32 p. color illustrations (ebook) $15.54; (hardback) $17.95
Grades: PreK K 1   E
1. Science -- Fiction 2. Curiosity -- Fiction 3. Scientists -- Fiction 4. Perseverance -- Fiction 5. Stories in rhyme 6. Curiosity -- Fiction 7. Science -- Experiments -- Fiction

ISBN 9781613129685; 9781419721373

LC 2016000588

In this children's book by Andrea Beaty, illustrated by David Roberts, young scientist Ada, "a character of color, has a boundless imagination and has always been hopelessly curious. . . . When her house fills with a horrific, toe-curling smell, Ada knows it's up to her to find the source. . . . Not afraid of failure, Ada embarks on a fact-finding mission and conducts scientific experiments, all in the name of discovery." (Publisher's note)

Doctor Ted; [illustrated by] Pascal Lemaitre. Atheneum Books for Young Readers 2008 32p il $14.99
Grades: PreK K 1   E
1. Bears -- Fiction 2. Physicians -- Fiction 3. Imagination --

Fiction
ISBN 978-1-4169-2820-1; 1-4169-2820-0

LC 2006-03191

After bumping his knee one morning, Ted the bear cub decides to become a doctor, but he has only one problem—he has no patients!

This is "a breezy story about pretend play that's laugh-out-loud funny. . . . The pictures' chunky ink lines and almost neon-like digital colors give every page plenty of punch." Publ Wkly

Other titles about Ted are:
Firefighter Ted (2009)
Artist Ted (2012)

Happy Birthday, Madame Chapeau; by Andrea Beaty; illustrated by David Roberts. Harry N Abrams Inc 2014 32 p. color illustrations $16.95

Grades: K 1 2 3   E
1. Hats -- Fiction 2. Birthdays -- Fiction 3. Paris (France) -- Fiction 4. Millinery -- fiction 5. Friendship -- Fiction
ISBN 1419712195; 9781419712197

LC bl2014037828

This children's book, by Andrea Beaty and illustrated by David Roberts, tells "the tale of a lonely hat maker who matches customers to the perfect hat but lacks her own perfect match in life. Once a year, on her birthday, Madame Chapeau ventures out in her favorite bonnet to dinner. This time, a crow snatches her hat and flies away." (Publisher's note)

"Madame Chapeau is the world's finest hat maker. She's also lonely. Once a year, she treats herself to a posh birthday dinner, wearing her finest gown and a beloved hat made especially for her. When a crow steals it from her head, Madame Chapeau endures the loss of her treasured hat but then enjoys the misguided generosity of so many—presumably satisfied customers—who offer her their own lids. . . . Although there are some abrupt shifts in the storytelling, the effervescent cadence of Beaty's rhyming text compensates, as do Roberts' quirky, doll-like characters. An artist's note reveals that Roberts, who worked as a milliner himself, has included many famous hats and styles among Chapeau's repertoire. Hats off to a story brimming with charm and panache." Booklist

★ **Iggy** Peck, architect; by Andrea Beaty; illustrated by David Roberts. Abrams Books for Young Readers 2007 il $15.95

                                                                       E
1. Stories in rhyme. 2. Schools -- Fiction. 3. Building -- Fiction. 4. School field trips -- Fiction.
ISBN 978-0-8109-1106-2; 0-8109-1106-X

LC 2006013574

Rosie Revere, engineer; by Andrea Beaty; illustrated by David Roberts. Abrams Books for Young Readers 2013 32 p. (alk. paper) $16.95

Grades: K 1 2   E
1. Picture books for children 2. Women engineers -- Fiction 3. Stories in rhyme 4. Engineers -- Fiction 5. Inventions -- Fiction 6. Failure (Psychology) -- Fiction 7. Perseverance (Ethics) -- Fiction
ISBN 1419708457; 9781419708459

LC 2012048268

This children's picture book conveys "the story of a girl who likes to build things but is shy about it. . . . Rosie picks up trash and oddments where she finds them, stashing them in her attic room to work on at night. Once, she made a hat for her favorite zookeeper uncle to keep pythons away, and he laughed so hard that she never made anything publicly again. But when her great-great-aunt Rose comes to visit and reminds Rosie of her own past building airplanes," Rosie is inspired. (Kirkus Reviews)

Beaty, Daniel

★ **Knock** knock; my dad's dream for me. by Daniel Beaty; illustrated by Bryan Collier. Little, Brown and Company 2014 40 p. $18
Grades: K 1 2 3   E
1. Father-son relationship -- Fiction 2. Fathers and sons -- Fiction 3. African Americans -- Fiction 4. Separation (Psychology) -- Fiction
ISBN 0316209171; 9780316209175

LC 2012043088

Coretta Scott King Book Award: Illustrator (2014)
Boston Globe-Horn Book Honor: Picture Book (2014)
In this book, by Daniel Beaty, a father and son play knock knock every morning. "But what happens when, one day, that 'knock knock' doesn't come? This . . . book shows the love that an absent parent can leave behind, and the strength that children find in themselves as they grow up and follow their dreams." (Publisher's note)

Beaumont, Karen

★ **Baby** danced the polka; pictures by Jennifer Plecas. Dial Books for Young Readers 2004 un il $12.99
Grades: PreK K 1 2   E
1. Infants -- Fiction
ISBN 0-8037-2587-6
"What a happy, rollicking baby. And what a rolling, rhythmic text. . . . The sprightly pen-and-watercolor artwork bears a very strong resemblance to the work of Helen Oxenbury." Booklist

Crybaby; Karen Beaumont; illustrated by Eugene Yelchin. Henry Holt & Co. 2015 40 p. color illustrations (hardback) $17.99
Grades: PreK K 1 2   E
1. Crying -- Fiction 2. Dogs -- Fiction 3. Bedtime -- Fiction 4. Infants -- Fiction 5. Family life -- Fiction
ISBN 0805089748; 9780805089745

LC 2014036094

In this children's book, by Karen Beaumont, illustrated by Eugene Yelchin, a "black Labrador retriever is the only family member who can soothe a crying baby. . . . Each family member tries a different tactic to help quiet the baby, from rocking to a bottle feeding to changing the baby's diaper. . . . Faithful Roy the retriever keeps offering the baby's stuffed lamb, and eventually the baby reaches down for her toy, solving her crying spell." (Kirkus Reviews)

" On the title page, a pooch perks up his ears—a hint that the peaceful scene on the next spread of a moonlit block awash in dreamy blues is about to explode. On this quiet street, "a not-so-quiet baby cried . . . W-A-A-A-A!" The retriever, Roy, is first to arrive cribside in this clever, rhyming cumulative tale that uses plenty of repetition and pleasing onomatopoeia. . . . With irresistible refrains and one hilariously expressive dog, this pitch-perfect tale will make a raucous read-aloud." Booklist

Duck, duck, goose! a coyote's on the loose! illustrated by Jose Aruego and Ariane Dewey. HarperCollins Pubs. 2004 un il $15.95; lib bdg $16.89
Grades: PreK K 1 2   E
1. Stories in rhyme 2. Animals -- Fiction
ISBN 0-06-050802-7; 0-06-050804-3 lib bdg

LC 2003-8734

Several farm animals try to evade a coyote that they think is dangerous
"Aruego and Dewey use bold paints as varied as a child's imagination to color their comically rendered farmyard animals. A suspenseful romp that will strike a chord with children." SLJ

★ **I** ain't gonna paint no more! illustrated by David Catrow. Harcourt 2005 un il $16

Grades: PreK K 1 2   E
1. Stories in rhyme 2. Painting -- Fiction
ISBN 0-15-202488-3

LC 2003-27739

"Catrow splashes color all over, uses white space cleverly, and includes playful flourishes. . . . Elongated figures and exaggerated expressions match the silly tone of the story. . . . With rhymes that invite audience participation and scenes that draw the eye, this is a strong storytime choice." SLJ

Move over, Rover; [by] Karen Beaumont; illustrated by Jane Dyer. Harcourt 2006 un il $16
Grades: PreK K 1 2   E
1. Stories in rhyme 2. Dogs -- Fiction 3. Rain -- Fiction 4. Animals -- Fiction
ISBN 978-0-15-201979-2; 0-15-201979-0

LC 2005014557

When a storm comes, Rover expects to have his doghouse all to himself but finds that various other animals, including a skunk, come to join him.

This offers "marvelously textured watercolor-and-acrylic illustrations. . . . The repetition of key phrases, the rhythmic text, and the cumulative structure of the narrative make this book an ideal read-aloud." SLJ

★ **No** sleep for the sheep! illustrated by Jackie Urbanovic. Houghton Mifflin Harcourt 2011 un il $16.99
Grades: PreK K 1   E
1. Stories in rhyme 2. Sleep -- Fiction 3. Sounds -- Fiction 4. Domestic animals -- Fiction
ISBN 978-0-15-204969-0; 0-15-204969-X

LC 2009007978

A sheep wants nothing but to go to sleep in the big red barn on the farm, but each time he closes his eyes, another animal moos or neighs or peeps to come in.

"Beaumont's playful, repetitive text, with its loud animal sounds, will have children chanting along to the beat." Kirkus

Shoe-la-la! illustrated by Leuyen Pham. Scholastic Press 2011 un il $16.99
Grades: PreK K 1 2   E
1. Stories in rhyme 2. Shoes -- Fiction
ISBN 978-0-545-06705-8; 0-545-06705-7

LC 2010007848

Four girls go in search of the perfect pair of party shoes.

"The sparkly jacket is an irresistible draw, depicting the girls vamping in dress-up clothes and high heels, as are the humorously expressive, cartoonlike illustrations rendered in full-color with lots of girl-pleasing pink and purple. Pure fun." SLJ

Another title in this series is:
Hats off to you! (2017)

Where's my t-r-u-c-k? pictures by David Catrow. Dial Books for Young Readers 2011 un il $16.99
Grades: PreK K 1   E
1. Stories in rhyme 2. Dogs -- Fiction 3. Toys -- Fiction 4. Trucks -- Fiction 5. Lost and found possessions -- Fiction
ISBN 978-0-8037-3222-3; 0-8037-3222-8

LC 2010045689

"This peppy picture book relates in rhyming verse the story of a boy's expansive search for his favorite toy—a riding truck. . . . A raucous and rotund dog finally digs a huge hole and reveals the treasure, which lies amid other items, including an iPod and a set of false teeth. Beaumont's refrain promises that listeners will know how to spell 'truck' by tale's end and is perfectly paced for expressive pauses and exclama-

tions. Catrow's jam-packed pencil and watercolor scenes are masterworks of detail and humor." SLJ

Who ate all the cookie dough? [by] Karen Beaumont; illustrated by Eugene Yelchin. Henry Holt and Company 2008 un il $16.95
Grades: PreK K 1   E
1. Stories in rhyme 2. Animals -- Fiction 3. Lost and found possessions -- Fiction
ISBN 978-0-8050-8267-8; 0-8050-8267-0

LC 2007012733

Kanga and her friends try to discover who ate all of her cookie dough
"Infectious repetitive rhyming verse, eye-catching gouache illustrations with ample white space, and a lift-the-flap surprise combine to create a joyful tale." Horn Book Guide

Bechtold, Lisze
Sally and the purple socks; [by] Lisze Bechtold. Philomel Books 2008 un il $15.99
Grades: PreK K 1   E
1. Size -- Fiction 2. Clothing and dress -- Fiction
ISBN 978-0-399-24734-7; 0-399-24734-3

LC 2007023649

When her tiny purple socks start to expand, Sally turns them into a scarf and then curtains, but things soon get out of hand.

"The quirky, playful, and ultimately warm illustrations, coupled with the simple text and a plot with just the right amount of suspense, make the book spot-on for sharing with young audiences." Booklist

Beck, Andrea
Pierre Le Poof! written and illustrated by Andrea Beck. Orca Book Publishers 2009 un il $19.95
Grades: PreK K 1 2   E
1. Dogs -- Fiction
ISBN 978-1-55469-028-2; 1-55469-028-5

"Lapdog Pierre Le Poof, 'a pedigreed pooch,' lives a pampered life with Miss Murphy but longs to frolic with the dogs in the park. At a practice session for a dog championship, Pierre makes his escape . . . but soon longs for the comforts of home. . . . Dog and owner bear a strong resemblance to each other in airy ink-and-watercolor pictures that delightfully go for the laughs." Booklist

Other titles about Pierre are:
Pierre's friends (2010)
Pierre in the air! (2011)

Becker, Aaron
★ **Journey**; Aaron Becker. Candlewick Press 2013 40 p. color illustrations hbk $15.99
Grades: K 1 2 3   E
1. Magic -- Fiction 2. Drawing -- Fiction 3. Stories without words 4. Picture books for children
ISBN 9780763660536; 0763660531

LC 2012947264

Caldecott Honor Book (2014)

In this book by Aaron Becker "a lonely girl draws a magic door on her bedroom wall and through it escapes into a world where wonder, adventure, and danger abound. Red marker in hand, she creates a boat, a balloon, and a flying carpet that carry her on a spectacular journey toward an uncertain destiny. When she is captured by a sinister emperor, only an act of tremendous courage and kindness can set her free." (Publisher's note)

"An imaginative adventure story whose elaborate illustrations inspire wonder, careful examination and multiple reads." Kirkus

★ **Quest**; Aaron Becker. First edition Candlewick Press 2014 40 p. color illustrations $15.99

Grades: K 1 2 3   **E**

1. Adventure and adventurers 2. Kings and rulers -- Fiction 3. Maps -- Fiction 4. Magic -- Fiction 5. Drawing -- Fiction

ISBN 0763665959; 9780763665951

LC 2013952837

Sequel to: Journey (2013)

"A king emerges from a hidden door in a city park, startling two children sheltering from the rain. No sooner does he push a map and some strange objects into their hands than he is captured by hostile forces that whisk him back through the enchanted door. Just like that, the children are caught up in a quest to rescue the king and his kingdom from darkness, while illuminating the farthest reaches of their imagination. Colored markers in hand, they make their own way through the portal, under the sea, through a tropical paradise, over a perilous bridge, and high in the air with the help of a winged friend." (Publisher's note)

"In addition to the winning adventure of the silent story, Becker manages to evolve his imagery with more sophisticated designs and ideas that draw readers into the narrative ever more deeply, proving once again that lush details, a meticulous sense of motion and action, and a boundless love of fun are worth all the words in the world." Booklist

★ **Return**; Aaron Becker. Candlewick Press 2016 40 p. color illustrations $15.99

Grades: K 1 2 3   **E**

1. Fantasy fiction 2. Girls -- Fiction 3. Imaginary places 4. Magic -- Fiction

ISBN 9780763677305

LC 2015940258

In this book, by Aaron Becker, "failing to get the attention of her busy father, a lonely girl turns back to a fantastic world for friendship and adventure. It's her third journey into the enticing realm of kings and emperors, castles and canals, exotic creatures and enchanting landscapes. This time, it will take something truly powerful to persuade her to return home, as a gripping backstory is revealed that will hold readers in its thrall." (Publisher's note)

"A fantastic final leg to a reading journey that altered, expanded, and enriched the landscape of children's literature—and surely many young people's lives." Kirkus

Becker, Bonny

A **Library** book for bear; Bonny Becker, illustrated by Kady MacDonald Denton. Candlewick Press 2014 32 p. color illustrations $16.99

Grades: PreK K 1 2   **E**

1. Mice -- Fiction 2. Bears -- Fiction 3. Libraries -- Fiction

ISBN 0763649244; 9780763649241

LC 2013952827

In this children's book, by Bonny Becker, "Bear does not want to go to the library. He is quite sure he already has all the books he will ever need. Yet the relentlessly cheery Mouse, small and gray and bright-eyed, thinks different. When Bear reluctantly agrees to go with his friend to the big library, neither rocket ships nor wooden canoes are enough for Bear's picky tastes. How will Mouse ever find the perfect book for Bear?" (Publisher's note)

"The hooray-for-books message is served subtly. Bear's grouchiness and Mouse's joie de vivre come through in Denton's expressive lines." Horn Book

A **visitor** for Bear; illustrated by Kady MacDonald Denton. Candlewick Press 2008 un il $16.99

Grades: PreK K 1 2   **E**

1. Mice -- Fiction 2. Bears -- Fiction 3. Friendship -- Fiction

ISBN 978-0-7636-2807-9; 0-7636-2807-7

LC 2006-51850

Bear's efforts to keep out visitors to his house are undermined by a very persistent mouse.

This offers "watercolor, ink and gouache illustrations in a soft color palette. . . . The characters are highly expressive . . . and the dramatic text will lend itself to reading aloud." Booklist

Other titles about Bear are:

A birthday for Bear (2009)

A bedtime for Bear (2010)

The sniffles for Bear (2011)

Becker, Helaine

Juba this, juba that; illustrated by Ron Lightburn. Tundra 2011 il $17.95

Grades: PreK K   **E**

1. Cats -- Fiction 2. Fairs -- Fiction

ISBN 978-0-88776-975-7; 0-88776-975-6

"This modern-day version of a traditional African chant imagines an adventure that happens one evening when a dark-skinned boy follows a yellow cat to the fair. They laugh at their reflections in the House of Mirrors, take a spooky fun-house ride, and generally have a wonderful time before returning home to bed. Becker's simple rhyme plays with opposites and is just right for clapping and bouncing along. Lightburn's lively illustrations perfectly capture the joy of the nighttime escapade and extend the story." SLJ

Becker, Suzy

★ **Manny's** cows; the Niagara Falls tale. written and illustrated by Suzy Becker. HarperCollins 2006 un il lib bdg $16.89

Grades: PreK K 1 2   **E**

1. Cattle -- Fiction 2. Vacations -- Fiction 3. Niagara Falls (N.Y. and Ont.) -- Fiction

ISBN 978-0-06-054152-1; 0-06-054152-0; 978-0-06-054153-8 lib bdg; 0-06-054153-9 lib bdg

LC 2005-14508

For his summer vacation, Manny takes his five hundred cows to Niagara Falls.

"The over-the-top story, full of fun and laced with amusing visual and verbal details, . . . is accompanied by occasional sidebar facts about dairy cattle. The cows' outrageous comments and antics are bolstered by free-spirited ink drawings brightened with color." Booklist

Bee, William

And the cars go... William Bee. First U.S. edition Candlewick Press 2013 32 p. $15.99

Grades: PreK K   **E**

1. City traffic 2. Automobile travel -- Fiction 3. Automobiles -- Fiction

ISBN 0763665800; 9780763665807

LC 2012947829

This children's book by William Bee centers around a traffic jam where "everyone's in a hurry! There's the family in the paneled station wagon . . . packed to the roof rack with gear for the beach. There's the be-hatted Duke and Duchess, out for a drive in their ornate Rolls Royce. Not to mention a yellow school bus . . . an overheating race car . . . and other vehicles revving to go." (Publisher's note)

""Here is the traffic, all ground to a halt, / and the policeman calls out... / 'What's causing this holdup?'" The vehicles may be at a standstill, but the rhythmic text motors along as the officer investigates the problem. Bee's stylish compositions have a distinctly sixties vibe; the pages practically vibrate with eye-popping colors held in place with a lively, sure-handed line." Horn Book

And the train goes... Candlewick Press 2007 un il $15.99
Grades: PreK K   **E**
1. Sounds -- Fiction 2. Parrots -- Fiction 3. Railroads -- Fiction
ISBN 978-0-7636-3248-9; 0-7636-3248-1
    LC 2006-43857
As assorted passengers comment on their train ride, and the train itself goes "Clickerty click, clickerty clack," the station parrot is carefully listening to every sound

"Filled with sound effects galore, this rollicking read-aloud is perfect for transportation storytimes. . . . The train and the characters' clothing are depicted in glossy colors and covered with flat floral patterns and other graphic designs. . . . There are many details for children to pore over." SLJ

Beebe, Katy

Brother Hugo and the bear; by Katy Beebe; illustrated by S.D. Schindler. Eerdmans Books for Young Readers 2014 34 p. $17
Grades: 1 2 3 4   **E**
1. Bears -- Fiction 2. Monks -- Fiction 3. Middle Ages -- Fiction 4. Books and reading -- Fiction 5. Manuscripts -- Fiction
ISBN 0802854079; 9780802854070
    LC 2013031001
In this book, by Kathryne Beebe, "Brother Hugo can't return his library book - the letters of St. Augustine - because, it turns out, the precious book has been devoured by a bear! Instructed by the abbot to borrow another monastery's copy and create a replacement, the hapless monk painstakingly crafts a new book, copying it letter by letter and line by line. But when he sets off to return the borrowed copy, he finds himself trailed by his hungry new friend." (Publisher's note)

"According to detailed back matter, the author learned of a documented incident involving a book-eating bear and the subsequent letter written by Peter the Venerable to a neighboring French monastery requesting St. Augustine's letters. . . . Arches and columns cleverly frame the monk, creating sequential panels to portray his painstaking progress on what becomes, alas, another 'choice morsel' for the insatiable beast." SLJ

Beil, Karen Magnuson

Jack's house; illustrated by Mike Wohnoutka. Holiday House 2008 un il $16.95
Grades: PreK K 1 2   **E**
1. Dogs -- Fiction 2. House construction -- Fiction
ISBN 978-0-8234-1913-5; 0-8234-1913-4
    LC 2007014978
Cumulative text reveals who was really responsible for the house that Jack claims to have built, and all of the trucks involved, from the bulldozer used to clear the land to the van that brought a hammock for the back yard

"A wonderful twist on an age-old rhyme. . . . Wohnoutka's full-page acrylic paintings are large scale, but are also full of small details for readers to enjoy. . . . This beguiling book will be a hit both at storytimes and in circulating collections." SLJ

Bell, Cece

I yam a donkey; Cece Bell. Clarion Books, Houghton Mifflin Harcourt 2015 32 p. color illustrations (hbk.) $16.99
Grades: 1 2 3   **E**
1. Donkeys -- Fiction 2. English language -- Pronunciation 3. English language -- Grammar -- Fiction 4. Yams -- Fiction 5.

Humorous stories
ISBN 0544087208; 9780544087200
    LC 2014021781
In this children's book written and illustrated by Cece Bell, "An escalating series of misunderstandings leaves the yam furious and the clueless donkey bewildered by the yam's growing (and amusing) frustration. The yam finally gets his point across, but regrettably, he's made the situation a little bit too clear . . . and the story ends with a dark . . . funny twist." (Publisher's note)

"This irreverent, animated outing fairly begs to be read aloud, and children will demand repeat readings." Booklist

Itty bitty. Candlewick Press 2009 un il $9.99
Grades: PreK K 1   **E**
1. Dogs -- Fiction 2. Size -- Fiction
ISBN 978-0-7636-3616-6; 0-7636-3616-9
"Where does a tiny dog find just the right decor for his hollowed-out-bone house? Why, the 'teeny-weeny department' at a huge store downtown, of course! Such is the premise of this sweet and silly picture book that introduces a sunny pup of small size but big personality. . . . Bell's . . . crisp acrylic and ink artwork features blocks of color and simple stylized shapes on grainy, speckled backgrounds." Publ Wkly

Rabbit and Robot; the sleepover. Cece Bell. Candlewick 2012 56 p. (hardback) $14.99
Grades: K 1 2   **E**
1. Children's stories 2. Negotiation -- Fiction 3. Friendship -- Fiction 4. Humorous stories 5. Robots -- Fiction 6. Rabbits -- Fiction 7. Friendship -- Fiction 8. Sleepovers -- Fiction
ISBN 0763654752; 9780763654757
    LC 2011048365
Theodor Seuss Geisel Honor Book (2013)
This "book's four chapters . . . correspond to the plan for [Rabbit and Robot's] eagerly anticipated sleepover: make pizza, watch TV, play Go Fish, go to bed. But it's a list Rabbit generated without consulting his friend, so negotiations . . . are the order of the day. . . . Robot wants to play Old Maid in addition to Go Fish; Rabbit insists it's 'not on the list.' Robot . . . insists on taking apart Rabbit's furniture to get his favorite topping, nuts and bolts." (Publishers Weekly)

Belloc, Hilaire

Jim who ran away from his nurse and was eaten by a lion; a cautionary tale. pictures by Mini Grey. Alfred A. Knopf 2010 un il $19.99
Grades: 2 3 4   **E**
1. Stories in rhyme 2. Pop-up books 3. Zoos -- Fiction 4. Lions -- Fiction
ISBN 978-0-375-85970-0; 0-375-85970-5
Text originally published 1907; A newly illustrated edition of the title first published 1987 by Little Brown; this edition first published 2009 in the United Kingdom

Jim runs away from his nurse at the zoo and he is eaten by a lion.

"Grey's artwork is gorgeous and bold. . . . Fold-outs, pop-ups and lift-up flaps contribute to the over-the-top element that makes even little Jim's bloody, chewed-off head seem not as horrific as it might. . . . All but the most sensitive children (over eight) will laugh . . . especially if the book is read aloud with an English accent." Kirkus

Belton, Robyn

Herbert; the true story of a brave sea dog. Candlewick Press 2010 un il $15.99

Grades: PreK K 1 2   E
1. Sea stories 2. Dogs -- Fiction
ISBN 978-0-7636-4741-4; 0-7636-4741-1

LC 2009-46538

Herbert, a beloved, small dog who lives near the sea in New Zealand, sets out one fine day with his boy Tim's father on a boat that is beset by a sudden storm, which washes Herbert overboard.

"Belton's beautiful watercolor illustrations bring to life the dangerously changeable weather at sea without making it too scary. Reproductions of newspaper articles and letters about the incident, as well as Herbert's 'Iron Dog' medal, appear on the endpapers. These real-life documents give readers a fascinating taste of the true story behind the book and provide a nice balance to Belton's dreamy illustrations." Booklist

Bemelmans, Ludwig
★ **Madeline**; story and pictures by Ludwig Bemelmans. Viking 1985 un il $17.99; pa $7.99
Grades: PreK K 1 2   E
1. Stories in rhyme 2. Paris (France) -- Fiction
ISBN 0-670-44580-0; 0-14-056439-X pa
A reissue of the title first published 1939 by Simon & Schuster
A Caldecott Medal honor book, 1940
"Madeline is a nonconformist in a regimented world—a Paris convent school. This rhymed story tells how she made an adventure out of having appendicitis." Hodges. Books for Elem Sch Libr
Other titles about Madeline are:
Madeline and the bad hat (1957)
Madeline and the gypsies (1959)
Madeline in London (1961)
Madeline's Christmas (1985)
Madeline's rescue (1985)

Madeline and the bad hat; written and illustrated by Ludwig Bemelmans. Viking Press 1957 54p il $16.99; pa $7.99
Grades: PreK K 1 2   E
1. Stories in rhyme
ISBN 978-0-670-44614-8; 0-670-44614-9; 978-0-14-056648-2 pa; 0-14-056648-1 pa

LC 00-268562

When the Spanish ambassador moves in next door, Madeline and the rest of the twelve little girls discover that his son is not the best neighbor.

Madeline's rescue; story and pictures by Ludwig Bemelmans. Viking 1985 un il $16.99; pa $7.99
Grades: PreK K 1 2   E
1. Stories in rhyme 2. Dogs -- Fiction 3. Paris (France) -- Fiction
ISBN 0-670-44716-1; 0-14-056651-1 pa
First published 1953
Awarded the Caldecott Medal, 1954
A picture-story book with rhymed text about little Madeline in Paris. This time she falls into the Seine and is rescued by 'a dog that kept its head.' The dog, named Genevieve, was promptly adopted by Madeline's boarding school mistress and her twelve pupils. When Genevieve was turned out by snobbish trustees the little girls were inconsolable, until Genevieve solved their problem

Benchley, Nathaniel
★ A **ghost** named Fred; pictures by Ben Shecter. Harper & Row 1968 un il (I can read mystery book) lib bdg $17.89
Grades: K 1 2   E
1. Ghost stories
ISBN 0-06-020474-5
"More humorous than scary . . . this is a pleasing and acceptable ghost story for beginning readers." Booklist

Benjamin, A. H.
Oh No! Said Elephant; A.H. Benjamin, illustrated by Alireza Goldouzian. minedition 2016 48 p. color illustrations $17.99
Grades: PreK K 1 2   E
1. Games -- Fiction 2. Elephants -- Fiction
ISBN 9789888341078; 9888341073
In this book, by A.H. Benjamin, illustrated by Alireza Goldouzian, the animals are playing. "Though Elephant always wants to join in . . . he has trouble with the proposed games. His size makes concealing himself a challenge during hide-and-seek. He is too tall and heavy for leapfrog. . . . Until finally Elephant suggests a game--tug-of-war. Here, . . . elephant . . . has an opportunity to . . . shine among his playmates, defeating them all single-handedly." (School Library Journal)
"Readers will be drawn in immediately to try to figure out how the scores will relate to the story." Booklist

Bennett, Kelly
Dad and Pop; an ode to fathers & stepfathers. illustrated by Paul Meisel. Candlewick Press 2010 un il $15.99
Grades: PreK K 1 2   E
1. Fathers -- Fiction 2. Stepfathers -- Fiction 3. Father-daughter relationship -- Fiction
ISBN 978-0-7636-3379-0; 0-7636-3379-8
"A cheerful girl explains that Dad and Pop are different in many ways, but the same in their love for her. . . . Dad is the girl's biological father and . . . Pop is her step-father. . . . This is a positive and playful portrayal of a blended family. . . . Expressive faces and gentle humor add charm to the pictures." SLJ

Your daddy was just like you; illustrated by David Walker. G. P. Putnam's Sons 2010 un il $16.99
Grades: PreK K 1   E
1. Fathers -- Fiction 2. Grandmothers -- Fiction
ISBN 978-0-399-24798-9; 0-399-24798-X

LC 2008053644

A grandmother describes to her grandson how his father was just like him when he was a child, never wanting to take a bath, fearing the dark, and swooping through the house in a cape and mask.
"Characters' facial expressions and body language successfully capture emotions, actions, and reactions. . . . The humorous text is in perfect sync with the simple illustrations." SLJ

Your mommy was just like you; illustrated by David Walker. G. P. Putnam's Sons 2011 un il $16.99
Grades: PreK K   E
1. Mothers -- Fiction 2. Grandmothers -- Fiction
ISBN 978-0-399-24798-9; 0-399-24798-X
"A grandmother looks at an old photo album with her granddaughter, telling her stories about her mother when she was little. . . . The illustrations are soft and gentle, complementing each milestone mentioned in the story. Perfect for intergenerational sharing." SLJ

Bently, Peter
Captain Jack and the pirates; Peter Bently; illustrated by Helen Oxenbury. Dial Books for Young Readers 2016 32 p. color illustrations (hardcover) $17.99 E
1. Adventure fiction 2. Pirates -- Fiction 3. Imagination -- Fiction 4. Sea stories 5. Stories in rhyme 6. Pirates -- Fiction 7. Adventure and adventurers -- Fiction
ISBN 9780525429500; 0525429506

LC 2015001884

In this children's book, by Peter Bently and illustrated by Helen Oxenbury, "Jack, Zack, and Caspar are building a ship--on the beach, out of sand. When they set sail on their imaginary adventure, Jack spies an enemy pirate ship nearby. They chase after the pirates, but a storm wrecks their ship and sweeps them up on a desert island. The island isn't totally deserted, though—their pirate enemies are there too." (Publisher's note)

"Perfect for a lap-sit, where a child has plenty of time to search for details, identify with the characters, and fall into the rhythm of the story, but useful, too, in a small group, where readers can predict the end to each rhyming verse." SLJ

★ **King** Jack and the dragon. Dial Books for Young Readers 2011 un il $17.99

Grades: PreK K   E
1. Stories in rhyme 2. Play -- Fiction 3. Imagination -- Fiction
ISBN 978-0-8037-3698-6; 0-8037-3698-3
LC 2011001273

"Bently's verse never misses a beat, and Oxenbury shifts between monochromatic, engraving-like drawings and pale watercolors; the images feel as if they were drawn from a classic fairy tale book and contemporary life simultaneously. It's an enchanting tribute to both full-throttle pretend play and the reassurance of a parent's embrace." Publ Wkly

Berger, Carin

Finding spring; Carin Berger. Greenwillow Books, an imprint of HarperCollinsPublishers 2015 40 p. color illustrations (hardcover) $17.99

Grades: PreK K 1   E
1. Bears -- Fiction 2. Spring -- Fiction 3. Winter -- Fiction 4. Seasons -- Fiction
ISBN 0062250191; 9780062250193
LC 2014003155

"Instead of hibernating as he should, a little bear cub goes out in search of spring—and he thinks he's found it! Gloriously illustrated with dioramas and cut-paper collages by the award-winning designer and illustrator Carin Berger, this stunning picture book celebrates the changing of the seasons." (Publisher's Note)

"Winter is coming, but little bear Maurice, excited about his first spring, imagines springtime flowers. Instead of sleeping, he leaves his den to look for spring . . . . Eager to share his discovery, Maurice takes his mother and friends back over his path, this time passing blooming trees and green buds. 'Everything had changed.' They do, indeed, find spring—and spring flowers. Chock-full of visual cues and information, this is a charming exploration of seasonal changes." Booklist

Forever friends. Greenwillow Books 2010 un il $16.99; lib bdg $17.89

Grades: PreK K   E
1. Birds -- Fiction 2. Rabbits -- Fiction 3. Seasons -- Fiction 4. Friendship -- Fiction
ISBN 978-0-06-191528-4; 0-06-191528-9; 978-0-06-191529-1 lib bdg; 0-06-191529-7 lib bdg
LC 2009-18758

In the spring, a blue bird awakens a rabbit and invites him to play, and they enjoy every day together until it is time for the bird to fly south for the winter, with a promise to return again next spring.

"Berger's superb, stylized cut-paper collage illustrations, constructed from lined and graph paper and magazines, depict sylvan landscapes with graceful curves and airy compositions that echo the simplicity and gentleness of the tale. A reassuring, poetic story that will give young children much to ponder any time of the year." Booklist

The **little** yellow leaf. Greenwillow Books 2008 un il $16.99; lib bdg $17.89

Grades: PreK K 1 2   E
1. Trees -- Fiction 2. Autumn -- Fiction 3. Leaves -- Fiction
ISBN 978-0-06-145223-9; 0-06-145223-8; 978-0-06-145224-6 lib bdg; 0-06-145224-6 lib bdg
LC 2007-39191

A yellow leaf is not ready to fall from the tree when autumn comes, but finally, after finding another leaf still on the tree, the two let go together.

"In Berger's eye-catching collage illustrations, pieced background papers in shades of yellow, green, blue, and beige show off stylized forms of naked tree branches, leaves, and sun created by clipping and pasting (sometimes tiny) segments of various papers—faded, lined ledger, and graph paper; colored and printed magazine pages—and adding touches of paint." SLJ

★ **OK** go. Greenwillow Books 2009 un il $17.99; lib bdg $18.89

Grades: K 1 2 3   E
1. Automobiles -- Fiction 2. Environmental protection -- Fiction
ISBN 978-0-06-157666-9; 0-06-157666-2; 978-0-06-157669-0 lib bdg; 0-06-157669-7 lib bdg
LC 2008-14681

In this almost wordless picture book, car drivers stuck in traffic under smoggy skies seek "greener" alternatives to driving, including riding bicycles, walking, and playing

"Berger's simple environmental message is delivered through clever, innovative illustrations that make her point without being didactic. Idiosyncratic creatures decked out in fabric pieces, buttons, and tall imaginative hats sail along in even more idiosyncratic vehicles that are variously colored and decorated with stickers and decals." SLJ

Berger, Lou

Dream dog; by Lou Berger; illustrated by David J. Catrow. 1st ed. Schwartz & Wade Books 2013 40 p. ill. (hardcover) $17.99; (library) $20.99

Grades: PreK K 1 2   E
1. Dogs -- Fiction 2. Picture books for children 3. Imaginary playmates -- Fiction 4. Imagination -- Fiction 5. Fathers and sons -- Fiction
ISBN 0375866558; 9780375866555; 9780375966552
LC 2011048582

In this children's picture book, "Harry wants a dog, but Dad has allergies. So Harry puts on his X-35 Infra-Rocket Imagination Helmet and conjures up his own perfect pet, a dream dog named Waffle. This new pet is huge and fuzzy, all light blue and white like cumulous clouds, and only Harry can see him. Waffle and Harry become best pals, with Harry's dad playing along with the idea of the imaginary dog. . . . When Dad's allergies suddenly improve, he brings home a real dog." (Kirkus Reviews)

Berger, Samantha

Crankenstein; by Samantha Berger; illustrated by Dan Santat. 1st ed. Little, Brown and Co. 2013 40 p. ill. (reinforced) $16.99

Grades: PreK K   E
1. Anger -- Fiction 2. Bad behavior -- Fiction 3. Behavior -- Fiction
ISBN 031612656X; 9780316126564
LC 2012029480

This book, written by Samantha Berger and illustrated by Dan Santat, features Crankenstein, "a monster of grumpiness. He may look like any ordinary boy, but when faced with a rainy day, a melting popsicle, or an early bedtime, one little boy transforms into a mumbling, grumbling Crankenstein! When Crankenstein meets his match in a fellow Crankenstein, the results could be catastrophic--or they could be just what he needs to brighten his day." (Publisher's note)

Martha doesn't say sorry! illustrated by Bruce Whatley. Little, Brown and Co. 2009 un il $15.99
Grades: PreK K 1 2   E
    1. Otters -- Fiction
    ISBN 978-0-316-06682-2; 0-316-06682-6
                                                        LC 2008-16769
Young Martha learns that she must apologize for her bad behavior if she wants people to cooperate with her.

"The watercolor and colored pencil artwork encapsulates Martha's girliness, her better-than-thou attitude and her internal struggle with her conscience. Whatley's representation of body language and facial expression powerfully complement the text. An enjoyable introduction to what could be a new beloved character." Kirkus

Another title about Martha is:
Martha doesn't share (2010)

Bergman, Mara
    Lively Elizabeth! what happens when you push; illustrated by Cassia Thomas. Albert Whitman 2010 un il
Grades: PreK K 1 2   E
    1. School stories
    ISBN 0807547026; 9780807547021
Describes a chain reaction that is caused by Elizabeth pushing her classmate Joe.

"The text is placed in and around the illustrations for maximum effect. . . . Thomas's illustrations make the whole thing work. The action is clear, as are the consequences of that ill-fated push. The myriad children wear wacky costumes, have expressive faces, and are awash in detail that makes multiple readings a joy." SLJ

Bergstein, Rita M.
    Your own big bed; by Rita M. Bergstein; illustrated by Susan Kathleen Hartung. Viking 2008 un il $15.99
Grades: PreK K 1   E
    1. Beds -- Fiction 2. Growth -- Fiction
    ISBN 978-0-670-06079-5; 0-670-06079-8
                                                        LC 2007-17902
Introduces how different animals and even human babies grow from being newly-hatched or born, through being carried everywhere, to having their own special place to sleep.

"The absence of the anxiety, whining, or excuses common to books of this ilk is refreshing. . . . This sweet book provides a gentle, matter-of-fact introduction to a sometimes-difficult transition." SLJ

Berk, Ari
    Nightsong; by Ari Berk and illustrated by Loren Long. Simon & Schuster Books for Young Readers 2012 48 p. (hardcover : alk. paper) $17.99
Grades: 1 2 3   E
    1. Bats -- Fiction 2. Senses and sensation in animals 3. Mother-son relationship -- Fiction 4. Echolocation (Physiology) -- Fiction
    ISBN 1416978860; 9781416978862
                                                        LC 2009026608
Author Ari Berk and illustrator Loren Long present a picture book "about a young bat setting off into the world using only his good sense! Chiro's mother sends him off into the night for the first time alone. It's an adventure, but how will he find his way? And how will he find his way home? As the young bat discovers, navigating the world around him is easy as long as he uses his good sense." (Publisher's note)

Berkes, Marianne
    Over in the forest; come and take a peek. by Marianne Berkes; illustrated by Jill Dubin. Dawn Publications 2012 32 p. (hardback) $16.95
Grades: PreK K 1 2   E
    1. Counting 2. Stories in rhyme 3. Forest animals -- Poetry 4. Nature 5. Forest animals -- Fiction 6. Animals -- Infancy -- Fiction
    ISBN 9781584691624; 9781584691631; 158469162X
                                                        LC 2011030879
This nature book by Marianne Berkes allows children to "follow the tracks of ten woodland animals. . . . Children learn the ways of forest animals to the rhythm of 'Over in the Meadow' as they leap like a squirrel, dunk like a raccoon, and pounce like a fox. They . . . also count the babies and search for ten hidden forest animals. . . . Marianne [also] provides [multiple] ideas for activities and curriculum extensions about forest animals, literature, and writing." (Publisher's note)

Berne, Jennifer
    Calvin can't fly; the story of a bookworm birdie. illustrated by Keith Bendis. Sterling 2010 un il $14.95
Grades: PreK K 1 2   E
    1. Birds -- Fiction 2. Books and reading -- Fiction
    ISBN 978-1-4027-7323-5; 1-4027-7323-4
                                                        LC 2009050797
A young starling chooses to read books when his cousins are learning to fly, and the knowledge he acquires comes in handy when a hurricane threatens the flock's migration.

"The irresistible story of a proud bookworm will put smiles on the faces of readers of all ages. . . . The illustrations are wildly original and full of funny details." Kirkus

Bernheimer, Kate
    The **girl** in the castle inside the museum; [illustrated by] Nicoletta Ceccoli. Schwartz & Wade Books 2008 un il $16.99; lib bdg $19.99
Grades: K 1 2 3   E
    1. Castles -- Fiction 2. Museums -- Fiction
    ISBN 978-0-375-83606-0; 978-0-375-83606-7 lib bdg
                                                        LC 2006-101854
"In an eclectic toy museum, children are drawn to a snow globe where it is said that, if they look hard enough, they can see the little girl who lives in the castle therein. To their delight, she is visible, as is her entire enchanted world. The girl is lonely when the museum empties, and she dreams of other children visiting her. . . . Using media as varied as clay sculpture and photography, Ceccoli has created a world that beckons young readers inside. . . . This unusual book will jump-start the imaginations of all who are lucky enough to enter it." SLJ

Bernstrom, Daniel
    ★ **One** day in the eucalyptus, eucalyptus tree; written by Daniel Bernstrom; illustrated by Brendan Wenzel. Katherine Tegen Books, an imprint of HarperCollins Publishers 2016 32 p. color illustrations (hardback) $17.99
Grades: PreK K 1 2   E
    1. Stories in rhyme 2. Hunger -- Fiction 3. Snakes -- Fiction 4. Humorous stories 5. Animals -- Fiction
    ISBN 9780062354853
                                                        LC 2015023148
This book, by Daniel Bernstrom, illustrated by Brendan Wenzel, is a "tale of a plucky little boy who is gobbled up by a giant snake. Consuming his victims at an alarming rate, this snake doesn't realize that his captives are planning their escape." (Publisher's note)

Berry, Lynne

★ **Duck** skates; illustrated by Hiroe Nakata. Henry Holt and Co. 2005 un il $15.95

Grades: PreK K E

1. Stories in rhyme 2. Snow -- Fiction 3. Ducks -- Fiction

ISBN 978-0-8050-7219-8; 0-8050-7219-5

LC 2004-22176

Five little ducks skate, romp, and play in the snow.

"The illustrations follow the text exactly, allowing children to count the ducks engaged in each activity. The watercolor-and-ink pictures convey the playfulness in warm, cozy tones, and a surprising amount of expression is conveyed in simple lines." SLJ

Other titles about these ducks are:

Duck dunks (2008)

Duck tents (2009)

Ducking for apples (2010)

Pig and Pug; Lynne Berry; illustrated by Gemma Correll. Simon & Schuster Books for Young Readers 2015 40 p. color illustrations (hardcover) $16.99

Grades: PreK K 1 2 E

1. Dogs -- Fiction 2. Pigs -- Fiction 3. Miniature pigs as pets -- Fiction

ISBN 148142131X; 9781481421317

LC 2014025503

In this children's story, by Lynne Berry and illustrated by Gemma Correll, "Pig and Pug are petite and portable pets--one in a pocket, one in a purse. They are also two spunky spirits: Pug, rather pugnacious; Pig, a bit pigheaded. When these two meet, bickering, chasing, and even some mud wrestling ensue. But after some creative compromises, Pig and Pug manage to settle their differences and become friends." (Publisher's note)

"Pug (who travels around in a lady's handbag) and Pig (who travels around in a man's shirt pocket) recognize a kindred spirit in each other. That is, until they start talking. Pug repeatedly asks Pig if he is a pug. He calls him "Pig, the pudgy pug," which Pig resents. Pig demands an apology, which is not forthcoming and leads to much chasing and hollering until Pug falls into a mud puddle. . . . The alliterative language and wordplay with pug and pig lend themselves to reading aloud and will appeal to children who like their humor on the slapsticky side." Booklist

What floats in a moat? by Lynne Berry; illustrated by Matthew Cordell. 1st ed. Simon & Schuster Books for Young Readers 2013 48 p. col. ill. (hardcover) $17.99

Grades: K 1 2 3 E

1. Floating bodies -- Fiction 2. Science -- Experiments 3. Goats -- Fiction 4. Stories in rhyme 5. Chickens -- Fiction 6.

ISBN 1416997636; 9781416997634

LC 2010002844

This children's book by Lynne Berry is "inspired by Archimedes' principle. "Archie . . . the goat and Skinny the hen need to deliver three barrels of buttermilk to the queen . . . in her moated castle. Rejecting the drawbridge in the name of 'Science!' they embark on a process of trial and error to float the barrels across the moat." (Kirkus Reviews)

Berry, Matt

Up on Daddy's shoulders; by Matt Berry; illustrated by Lucy Corvino. Scholastic 2006 un il $6.99

Grades: PreK K 1 2 E

1. Size -- Fiction 2. Father-son relationship -- Fiction

ISBN 0-439-67045-4

LC 2005023626

While riding on his father's shoulders, a young boy feels taller than everything in his house, his neighborhood, and the world.

"Corvino's sunny paintings fill each double-page spread. . . . Easy on the eyes and ears, this title's rhythm and attractiveness make it a fine read-aloud choice." Booklist

Bertrand, Diane Gonzales

Adelita and the veggie cousins; illustrations by Christina Rodriguez; Spanish translation by Gabriela Baeza Ventura. Pinata Books/Arte Publico Press 2011 il

Grades: PreK K 1 E

1. School stories 2. Vegetables -- Fiction 3. Bilingual books -- English-Spanish

ISBN 1-55885-699-4; 978-1-55885-699-8

LC 2010054521

On her first day at a new school, Adelita makes new friends through a lesson on vegetables, including how some vegetables are 'cousins' because they share certain characteristics.

"The dual message of nutrition and diversity will probably find its place in today's curriculum and can certainly augment units on food, language and culture." Kirkus

Beskow, Elsa

Princess Sylvie. 2011 il $17.95

Grades: PreK K 1 E

1. Dogs -- Fiction 2. Rabbits -- Fiction 3. Princesses -- Fiction 4. Father-daughter relationship -- Fiction

ISBN 978-086315-813-1; 0-86315-813-7

First published 1934

Princess Sylvie persuades her father, the king, to leave the palace gardens and walk in the woods. The king is unsure. What might be in the woods? Then Sylvie's dog Oskar runs off after a long-eared hare and Sylvie's adventures begin.

"The bear looks like a very large teddy, the 'wild' wood is spacious and airy and Sylvie never loses her tiny crown or musses her dress. . . . Old-fashioned in all the senses of the word, but quite charming in its art-deco shapes and vintage colors." Kirkus

Best, Cari

Beatrice spells some lulus and learns to write a letter; by Cari Best; illustrated by Giselle Potter. Margaret Ferguson Books 2013 40 p. ill. (reinforced) $16.99

Grades: K 1 2 3 E

1. Spelling -- Fiction 2. Grandparent-grandchild relationship -- Fiction 3. Schools -- Fiction 4. Show-and-tell presentations -- Fiction 5. English language -- Spelling -- Fiction

ISBN 0374399042; 9780374399047

LC 2012015337

This children's picture book by Cari Best "tell[s] the story of a girl named Beatrice whose initially rocky relationship with spelling (she spells her name ABCTERIE) turns into a full-fledged romance. Although Beatrice's family doesn't share her interest in spelling ('Leo had his ant farm, June had gymnastics, and her parents had their music'), she discovers a fellow word lover in her grandmother." (Publishers Weekly)

Easy as pie; [pictures by Melissa Sweet] Farrar, Straus and Giroux 2010 un il $16.99

Grades: K 1 2 3 E

1. Pies -- Fiction 2. Baking -- Fiction

ISBN 0-374-39929-8; 978-0-374-39929-0

LC 2008-16803

Jacob watches his favorite television show, Baking with Chef Monty, and bakes a beautiful peach pie, which he gives to his parents on their anniversary. "Ages six to nine." (Bull Cent Child Books)

"With pencil and watercolor illustrations done in a palette of soft colors, Sweet captures the warmth and security Jacob feels in the kitchen. . . . Important themes abound—love, security, cooperation, warmth, respect—and somehow all are tied to the simple acts of cooking and eating together. A delicious book for all collections." SLJ

Goose's story; pictures by Holly Meade. Farrar, Straus & Giroux 2002 un il hardcover o.p. pa $6.99

Grades: PreK K 1 2   E

    1. Geese -- Fiction

    ISBN 0-374-32750-5; 0-374-40032-6 pa

                                 LC 2001-27285

A young girl finds a Canada goose with a badly injured foot and looks for her each day to see how she is doing

   "Holly Meade's animated paper collage enhances Best's poignant story. . . . Best tells the story from the girl's point of view, and her language is appropriately childlike and empathetic." Horn Book

★ **My** three best friends and me, Zulay; Cari Best; illustrated by Vanessa Newton. Farrar Straus & Giroux 2015 40 p. color illustrations (hardback) $17.99

Grades: K 1 2 3   E

    1. Running 2. Friendship -- Fiction 3. Blind -- Fiction 4. Schools -- Fiction 5. People with disabilities -- Fiction

    ISBN 0374388199; 9780374388195

                                   LC 2014021833

In this children's book by Cari Best "Zulay and her three best friends are all in the same first grade class and study the same things, even though Zulay is blind. When their teacher asks her students what activity they want to do on Field Day, Zulay surprises everyone when she says she wants to run a race. With the help of a special aide and the support of her friends, Zulay does just that." (Publisher's note)

   "Best friends Maya, Nancy, Chyng, and Zulay laugh and sing and help one another with homework. When their first-grade teacher, Ms. Seeger, surprises them with an announcement about an upcoming field day, excitement fills the air...This story is a great read-aloud for younger students due to the length of the text, but just right as independent reading for second and third graders. This picture book is a great way to continue building diverse library collections for all readers." SLJ

★ **Sally** Jean, the Bicycle Queen; pictures by Christine Davenier. Farrar, Straus and Giroux 2005 un il $16

Grades: PreK K 1 2   E

    1. Cycling -- Fiction 2. Bicycles -- Fiction

    ISBN 0-374-36386-2

                                   LC 2004-40461

When Sally Jean outgrows her beloved bicycle, Flash, she experiments with various ideas for acquiring a new, bigger one.

   "Davenier's ink-and-watercolor illustrations are light and airy and convey a variety of emotions and delightful details. Sally Jean is a real charmer, and children will appreciate her resourcefulness and tenacity." SLJ

★ **Three** cheers for Catherine the Great! illustrated by Giselle Potter. Sunburst ed.; Farrar, Straus and Giroux 2003 un il pa $7.99

Grades: PreK K 1 2   E

    1. Gifts -- Fiction 2. Parties -- Fiction 3. Birthdays -- Fiction 4. Grandmothers -- Fiction 5. Russian Americans -- Fiction

    ISBN 0-374-47551-2

                                     LC 2002040804

First published 1999 by DK Pub.

Sara's Russian grandmother has requested that there be no presents at her seventy-eighth birthday party so Sara must think of a gift from her heart.

   "In lively, lyrical prose, Best celebrates a special family relationship, and conveys the unique challenges and joys of an immigrant's new life.

. . . Potter's festive, whimsical artwork is an irresistible play of vibrant colors and patterns, filled with rich detail and diverse, expressive characters." Booklist

   Another title about Sara and her grandmother is:

   When Catherine the Great and I were eight! (2003)

What's so bad about being an only child? [by] Cari Best; pictures by Sophie Blackall. Farrar, Straus and Giroux 2007 un il $16

Grades: PreK K 1 2   E

    1. Pets -- Fiction 2. Only child -- Fiction

    ISBN 0-374-39943-3; 978-0-374-39943-6

                                    LC 2005-51232

Rosemary Emma Angela Lynette Isabel Iris Malone grows tired of being an only child, but eventually finds a way to feel less alone.

   "Kids should applaud this self-reliant, spunky heroine." Publ Wkly

Bevis, Mary Elizabeth

   Wolf song; [by] Mary Bevis; illustrated by Consie Powell. Raven Productions 2007 un il $18.95; pa $12.95

Grades: K 1 2 3   E

    1. Uncles -- Fiction 2. Wolves -- Fiction

    ISBN 978-0-9794202-0-7; 978-0-9794202-1-4 pa

                                    LC 2007027953

At twilight, Nell and her Uncle Walter go into the north woods, hoping to hear—and join—the howling of the wolves. Includes facts about wolves and howling expeditions.

   "The text and illustrations both convey the wonder and mystery of nature." SLJ

Biddulph, Rob

   Blown away; written and illustrated by Rob Biddulph. Harper, an imprint of HarperCollinsPublishers 2015 40 p. color illustrations (hardback) $17.99

Grades: PreK K 1 2   E

    1. Home -- Fiction 2. Flight -- Fiction 3. Penguins -- Fiction 4. Tropics -- Fiction 5. Arctic regions -- Fiction 6. Voyages and travels -- Fiction 7. Animals -- Arctic regions -- Fiction

    ISBN 0062367242; 9780062367242

                                    LC 2014022227

In this book, "when Penguin Blue flies his kite, it ends up flying him, along with some penguin pals who try to help. Then Wilbur, a seal, and Clive, a polar bear in a fishing raft, also find themselves towed along by the kite until it runs out of wind power over a remote, shark-encircled jungle island. Fortunately, Penguin Blue rigs up a parasaillike contraption from leaves and vines and attaches it to Clive's raft, and the wayward group makes it home." (Bulletin of the Center for Children's Books)

   "Crisp, formal, and understated, newcomer Biddulph's images give evidence of his training as a graphic designer (as well as his sense of humor). He begins with a simple idea—a kite that carries its owner into the sky—and develops it with tongue-in-cheek charm...With the book's gentle ending and the kind of narrative voice that gives readers the sense that everything's well in hand, children will demand repeat reads." PW

Biedrzycki, David

   Ace Lacewing, bug detective: the big swat. Charlesbridge 2010 un $16.95

Grades: K 1 2   E

    1. Mystery fiction 2. Insects -- Fiction

    ISBN 978-1-57091-747-9; 1-57091-747-7

Me and my dragon. Charlesbridge 2011 un il $16.95; pa $7.95

Grades: PreK K E
1. Pets -- Fiction 2. Dragons -- Fiction
ISBN 1-58089-278-7; 1-58089-279-5 pa; 978-1-58089-278-0;
978-1-58089-279-7 pa

A child tells all the reasons a small, fire-breathing dragon would make an excellent pet, and the ways to take proper care of it.

"The Adobe Photoshop artwork abounds with expressions of surprise and alarm when others see the dragon. . . . While the brief text is a boon for early readers, this clever, funny book will delight young dragon lovers at storytimes." SLJ

Biggs, Brian

By sea; by Brian Biggs. Balzer + Bray 2013 56 p. color illustrations (Everything goes) (hardcover) $14.99
Grades: PreK K 1 E
1. Sailing -- Fiction 2. Vehicles -- Fiction 3. Boats and boating -- Fiction 4. Ships -- Fiction
ISBN 9780061958113; 0061958115

LC 2012051820

Author and illustrator Brian Biggs presents "the third picture book in the Everything Goes series of picture books, board books, and I Can Reads, [which] is a wonderful celebration of sailboats, submarines, and many other interesting sea vehicles. Featuring . . . mini-story lines, seek-and-find activities, tons of . . . details, and . . . cutaways, 'Everything Goes: By Sea' is an interactive book." (Publisher's note)

"The pleasingly busy cartoon illustrations are packed with details and visual jokes, including some comedic bits from the earlier books, which should delight the series' frequent visitors. . . . Biggs navigates this nautical lesson with a steady hand." Horn Book

Bildner, Phil

★ The **Hallelujah** Flight; illustrated by John Holyfield. G.P. Putnam's Sons 2010 un il $16.99
Grades: K 1 2 3 E
1. Air pilots 2. Mechanics (Persons) 3. Flight -- Fiction 4. Air pilots -- Fiction 5. African Americans -- Fiction
ISBN 978-0-399-24789-7; 0-399-24789-0

LC 2009-10362

In 1932, James Banning, along with his co-pilot Thomas Allen, make history by becoming the first African Americans to fly across the United States, relying on the generosity of people they meet in the towns along the way who help keep their 'flying jalopy' going.

"Based on both fictional and nonfiction sources, the story is briskly told in Allen's voice, with plenty of imagined dialogue. Holyfield's gorgeous . . . paintings are done on textured backgrounds in a palette of blues and browns." Kirkus

Marvelous Cornelius; Hurricane Katrina and the spirit of New Orleans. by Phil Bildner; illustrations by John Parra. Chronicle Books LLC 2015 44 p. color illustrations (alk. paper) $16.99
Grades: PreK K 1 2 E
1. African Americans -- Fiction 2. New Orleans (La.) -- Fiction 3. Hurricane Katrina, 2005 -- Fiction 4. Refuse collectors -- Fiction
ISBN 9781452125787

LC 2013043742

This book, by Phil Bildner, illustrated by John Parra, is a "modern-day folktale about Cornelius Washington, a real-life figure who was a dynamic street sweeper in New Orleans. The working man, aka Marvelous Cornelius, can be seen doing fun tricks and flips while sweeping the streets of the Quarter. When Hurricane Katrina hits the city, Cornelius is overwhelmed by the cleanup, but volunteers come from everywhere to help." (Publisher's note)

★ **Shoeless** Joe & Black Betsy; illustrated by C.F. Payne. Simon & Schuster Bks. for Young Readers 2002 un il $17
Grades: K 1 2 3 E
1. Baseball players 2. Baseball -- Fiction
ISBN 0-689-82913-2

LC 99-40563

Shoeless Joe Jackson, said by some to be the greatest baseball player ever, goes into a hitting slump just before he is to start his minor league career, so he asks his friend to make him a special bat to help him hit

This is "told in a folksy, Southern voice, with many of the stylistic elements of a tall tale. . . . The mixed-media illustrations are layered and rich in texture, qualities that add depth and drama." SLJ

The **soccer** fence; a story of friendship, hope, and apartheid in South Africa. by Phil Bildner; illustrated by Jesse Joshua Watson. G. P. Putnam's Sons 2014 40 p. color illustrations $16.99
Grades: K 1 2 3 E
1. Soccer -- Fiction 2. Apartheid -- Fiction 3. South Africa -- History 4. Race relations -- Fiction 5. Johannesburg (South Africa) 6. Blacks -- South Africa -- Fiction
ISBN 0399247904; 9780399247903

LC 2013014675

"Hector loved playing soccer in his small Johannesburg township. He dreamed of playing on a real pitch with the boys from another part of the city, but apartheid made that impossible. Then, in 1990, Nelson Mandela was released from prison, and apartheid began to crumble. . . When the beloved Bafana Bafana national soccer team won the African Cup of Nations, Hector realized that dreams once impossible could now come true." (Publisher's note)

"Bildner and Watson offer young readers an informative snapshot of a divided land through the lens of boys who just want to play." Kirkus

Includes bibliographical references

Turkey Bowl; [by] Phil Bildner; illustrated by C.F. Payne. Simon & Schuster Books for Young Readers 2008 un il $15.99
Grades: 1 2 3 E
1. Snow -- Fiction 2. Football -- Fiction 3. Family life -- Fiction 4. Thanksgiving Day -- Fiction
ISBN 9780-689-87896-1; 0-689-87896-6

LC 2005020139

Ethan looks forward to the Thanksgiving Day when he and his friends are finally old enough to play in the annual family football game, but that day arrives full of snow and icy roads

"Payne's muted, full-color illustrations capture the disappointment and joy the characters experience and feature plenty of gridiron action. Perfect for reading aloud at holiday time, this lively story will resonate year-round with sports fans." SLJ

Billingsley, Franny

★ **Big** Bad Bunny; story by Franny Billingsley; art by G. Brian Karas. Atheneum Books for Young Readers 2008 un il $16.99
Grades: PreK K 1 E
1. Mice -- Fiction 2. Mother-child relationship -- Fiction
ISBN 978-1-4169-0601-8; 1-4169-0601-0

LC 2006-32754

When Baby Boo-Boo, a mouse dressed in a bunny suit, becomes lost in the forest, his mother follows the sound of his cries to locate him.

Billingsley "extends her plot with satisfying onomatapoeia; the oversize format, too, marks this for a readaloud. Karas . . . strategically deploys mixed-media to render the id-gone-wild scenes with comic abandon." Publ Wkly

Bingham, Kelly

Circle, square, Moose; by Kelly Bingham; pictures by Paul O. Zelinsky. First edition. Greenwillow Books, an imprint of HarperCollinsPublishers 2014 48 p. color illustrations (trade ed.) $17.99

Grades: PreK K 1 2   E

1. Humorous fiction 2. Moose -- Fiction 3. Shape -- Fiction 4. Zebras -- Fiction 5. Friendship -- Fiction 6. Humorous stories 7. Behavior -- Fiction

ISBN 0062290037; 9780062290038; 9780062290045

LC 2013019534

In this children's book, by Kelly Bingham & illustrated by Paul O. Zelinsky, "Moose infiltrates a book about shapes (because he loves shapes, naturally) and it is up to his best friend, Zebra, to restore order and save the day." (Publisher's note)

"Moose is back! Hooray—unless you are a book about circles and squares. The simple concept book starts off well enough with a button representing a circle and a sandwich representing a square. And then mischief and mayhem erupt as Moose takes an enormous bite out of the sandwich. Admonitions from the book follow, and then it attempts to continue with a wedge of cheese and a slice of pie to illustrate triangles. Alas, Moose interrupts again, presenting a cat with triangular ears. Leave the book, they are told. More Moose antics ensue with rectangles and diamonds.... It is a great joy to watch Bingham and Zelinsky, who brilliantly collaborated on Z Is for Moose (2012), once more let Moose loose to naughtily and enthusiastically disrupt reading. ... Hilarious fun." Kirkus

★ Z is for Moose; by Kelly Bingham; illustrations by Paul O. Zelinsky. Greenwillow Books 2012 32 p.

Grades: PreK K 1 2   E

1. Moose -- Fiction 2. Zebras -- Fiction 3. Children's stories 4. Alphabet -- Fiction 5. Books and reading -- Fiction 6. Humorous stories 7. Behavior -- Fiction

ISBN 9780060799847; 9780060799854

LC 2011002148

In this illustrated children's book, "[c]lipboard-bearing Zebra is in charge of getting the players on and off the stage in an item-by-item alphabetical pageant. ... [Then] the excited Moose ... pops onto the stage for D, leaving the distressed Duck fluttering in frustration. ... Moose then tantrums through the rest of the book, ... defacing other subjects with crayoned-on antlers and claiming ... that R and S are also for Moose." (Bulletin of the Center for Children's Books)

Birdsall, Jeanne

★ Flora's very windy day; illustrated by Matt Phelan. Clarion Books 2010 un il $16

Grades: K 1 2   E

1. Winds -- Fiction 2. Siblings -- Fiction

ISBN 978-0-618-98676-7; 0-618-98676-6

LC 2008-56061

When a big wind blows her annoying little brother away, Flora decides to save him despite the many tempting offers she gets for him from, among others, a cloud, an eagle, the man in the moon, and the wind itself.

"This is a gem of a book that will resonate with older siblings everywhere." SLJ

My favorite pet by Gus W. for Ms. Smolinski's class; by Jeanne Birdsall; illustrated by Harry Bliss. Alfred A. Knopf 2016 40 p. color illustrations $16.99

Grades: K 1 2 3   E

1. Humorous fiction 2. Sheep -- Fiction 3. Humorous stories 4. Behavior -- Fiction

ISBN 9780385755702; 9780385755719

LC 2014033875

This book, by Jeanne Birdsall, illustrated by Harry Bliss, is "about one child's outrageous school essay on his 'pet' sheep. Things to know about sheep: Sheep live outside. Sheep have wool. Sheep will not learn to ride a skateboard. Sheep will not climb a tree. Sheep will come into the house...but this will get you into trouble. Seventeen sheep plus one Gus means that life is never dull on the farm!" (Publisher's note)

"A thoroughly engaging book that children are bound to giggle through." SLJ

Birtha, Becky

Far Apart, Close in Heart; Being a Family when a Loved One is Incarcerated. by Becky Birtha, illustrated by Maja Kastelic. Albert Whitman & Co 2017 32 p. color illustrations $16.99

Grades: PreK K 1 2   E

1. Children of prisoners

ISBN 0807512753; 9780807512753

In this book on incarcerated family members, by Becky Birtha, illustrated by Maja Kastelic, "young readers will learn that even when it feels like nothing can get better again, there are ways they can improve their circumstances. Sending letters, talking to a trusted grown-up about their feelings, and even visiting a parent in jail or prison can help keep a parent close in their hearts." (Publisher's note)

★ Grandmama's pride; illustrated by Colin Bootman. Albert Whitman 2005 un il $16.95

Grades: K 1 2 3   E

1. Segregation -- Fiction 2. Grandmothers -- Fiction 3. African Americans -- Fiction

ISBN 0-8075-3028-X

LC 2005003991

While on a trip in 1956 to visit her grandmother in the South, six-year-old Sarah Marie experiences segregation for the first time, but discovers that things have changed by the time she returns the following year.

"The strong, sensitive writing is enhanced by beautiful watercolor paintings filled with chips of light." SLJ

★ Lucky beans; illustrated by Nicole Tadgell. Albert Whitman 2010 un il $16.99

Grades: 1 2 3   E

1. Beans -- Fiction 2. Mathematics -- Fiction 3. African Americans -- Fiction 4. Great Depression, 1929-1939 -- Fiction

ISBN 0-8075-4782-4; 978-0-8075-4782-3

During the Great Depression, an African American boy named Marshall uses lessons learned in arithmetic class to figure out how many beans are in a jar to win his mother a sewing machine.

"Math and wry comedy mix in this lively historical story. ... The expressive watercolor paintings show both the racism that Marshall and his family endure as well as his final triumph, and Tadgell folds in humor." Booklist

Bitterman, Albert

Fortune cookies; illustrated by Chris Raschka. Beach Lane Books 2011 un il $14.99

Grades: PreK K   E

1. Fortune telling -- Fiction

ISBN 978-1-4169-6814-6; 1-4169-6814-8

LC 2008-20158

Seven fortune cookies foretell a child's fortunes for each day of the week.

"A tidy, perfectly paced story with subtle grace and a kernel of wisdom." Publ Wkly

Bjorkman, Steve

Dinosaurs don't, dinosaurs do. Holiday House 2011 un il (I like to read) $14.95

Grades: PreK K 1   E

1. Dinosaurs -- Fiction 2. Etiquette -- Fiction
ISBN 978-0-8234-2355-2; 0-8234-2355-7

LC 2010032832

This book "deftly [combines] text and art to create a positive experience for new readers. [It is] larger than typical easy readers, leaving plenty of room for uncluttered, colorful cartoon illustrations and clear, large fonts. . . . Björkman uses repetitive text and playful pictures to introduce appropriate behavior. 'Dinosaurs don't run here' is demonstrated by a dismayed dinosaur in front of glassware falling from a china cabinet; opposite, 'Dinosaurs do run here' shows two smiling creatures running through a playground. . . . [This title has] similar-sounding vowels and consonants, popular sight words, and short, simple sentences with clear punctuation, making [it a] successful [entry] in the beginning-reader canon." SLJ

Black, Michael Ian

Chicken cheeks; illustrated by Kevin Hawkes. Simon & Schuster Books for Young Readers 2009 un il $15.99

Grades: PreK K 1 2   E

1. Stories in rhyme 2. Animals -- Fiction
ISBN 1-4169-4864-3; 978-1-4169-4864-3

LC 2007-16872

Illustrations and text describe the back ends of various animals. "Ages five to seven." (Bull Cent Child Books)

This "features the hind quarters of animals, complete with silly names for them. . . . The closeup, color-saturated illustrations—which are at the same time obviously hilarious and sneakily deadpan—tell a story. A brown bear stands poised atop a ladder, gazing thoughtfully up the skinny trunk of a tall, branch-free tree. He grabs a duck and sets it on his head. . . . Sixteen animals later, children can only laugh helplessly at the absurd ladder of animals balanced parallel to the tree trunk. . . . Filled with visual jokes and amusing details, ChickenCheeks is a lot more than a list of words for kids to snicker at." SLJ

★ A **pig** parade is a terrible idea; illustrated by Kevin Hawkes. Simon & Schuster Books for Young Readers 2010 un il $16.99

Grades: PreK K 1 2   E

1. Pigs -- Fiction 2. Parades -- Fiction
ISBN 978-1-4169-7922-7; 1-4169-7922-0

LC 2008-51562

Explains precisely why, although it may sound like a good idea, gathering hundreds of pigs to march in a parade through one's hometown is inadvisable.

"If this book's arch-toned text wasn't flat-out funny enough, Hawkes' deliciously down-and-dirty art takes the concept to a whole other level." Booklist

Blackaby, Susan

★ **Brownie** Groundhog and the February fox; illustrated by Carmen Segovia. Sterling 2010 un il $16.99

Grades: PreK K 1   E

1. Foxes -- Fiction 2. Winter -- Fiction 3. Marmots -- Fiction
ISBN 978-1-4027-4336-8; 1-4027-4336-X

Brownie the groundhog encounters a fox while waiting for winter to be over, and through clever maneuvering—and tasty snacks—the two become friends.

"Segovia's acrylic paints and inks elevate the simple-seeming story, truly driving home the bone-penetrating chill of a typical February day. Blackaby is as tricky as her heroine, economically developing two dis-

tinct and likable characters and delivering plenty of chuckles and word-play. Elegant." Kirkus

Followed by: Brownie Groundhog and the wintry surprise (2013)

Blackall, Sophie

★ **Are** you awake? Henry Holt 2011 un il $12.99

Grades: PreK K 1   E

1. Night -- Fiction 2. Bedtime -- Fiction 3. Mother-son relationship -- Fiction
ISBN 978-0-8050-7858-9; 0-8050-7858-4

LC 2010026946

Persistent young Edward has many questions for his sleepy mother, many of which are answered, "Because it's night time."

Blackall's "palette starts out gray, warming to sunlit yellow as the bedside clock hands rotate and dawn breaks. Dialogue moves from speech balloons to type and back again, while watercolor panels offer affectionate closeups of Edward, his mother, and night scenes from their apartment window. Edward's antics hit the mark. . . . while Blackall's arch voice . . . makes this a solid candidate for the favorites pile." Publ Wkly

★ The **baby** tree; Sophie Blackall. Nancy Paulsen Books, an imprint of Penguin Group (USA) Inc. 2014 40 p. $17.99

Grades: PreK K 1 2   E

1. Children's stories 2. Reproduction 3. Humorous stories 4. Babies -- Fiction 5. Pregnancy -- Fiction 6. Questions and answers -- Fiction 7. Sex instruction for children -- Fiction
ISBN 0399257187; 9780399257186

LC 2013036309

"Revealing the basics of reproduction in an age-appropriate way, award-winning Sophie Blackall has created a beautiful picture book full of playful details to amuse and engage readers. . . . Join a curious little boy who asks everyone from his babysitter to the mailman, getting all sorts of funny answers along the way, before his parents gently set him straight." (Publisher's note)

"After learning he's going to be a big brother, a boy asks various grownups (babysitter, teacher, grandfather) where babies come from. At bedtime, Mom and Dad provide a very basic, concise explanation. Blackall's text is straightforward, calm, and reassuring. Her Chinese-ink and watercolor illustrations feature cherubic, rosy-cheeked, cute-as-a-button babies of different ethnicities. An appended page provides suggestions for adults addressing the same question." Horn Book

Blackford, Andy

Bill's bike; illustrated by Hannah Wood. Crabtree Pub. Co. 2011 21p il (Tadpoles) lib bdg $21.27; pa $6.95

Grades: PreK K 1   E

1. Wheels -- Fiction 2. Bicycles -- Fiction
ISBN 978-0-7787-0575-8 lib bdg; 0-7787-0575-7 lib bdg; 978-0-7787-0586-4 pa; 0-7787-0586-2 pa

LC 2010052360

"Bill starts off with four wheels on his bike but finds that he only needs two. . . . The [story is] gently funny with supportive illustrations that offer a solid structure within which kids can begin to read on their own. . . . [This book offers] characters with personality and scenes full of action." SLJ

The **hungry** little monkey; illustrated by Gabriele Antonini. Crabtree Pub. Co. 2011 21p il (Tadpoles) lib bdg $21.27; pa $6.95

Grades: PreK K 1   E

1. Animals -- Fiction 2. Monkeys -- Fiction
ISBN 978-0-7787-0581-9 lib bdg; 0-7787-0581-1 lib bdg; 978-0-7787-0592-5 pa; 0-7787-0592-7 pa

LC 2010052367

"A little monkey gets advice from the other animals on how to eat his banana, . . . but the right answer eventually comes from his mother. The [story is] gently funny with supportive illustrations that offer a solid structure within which kids can begin to read on their own. . . . [This book offers] characters with personality and scenes full of action." SLJ

Blackford, Cheryl

Hungry Coyote; Cheryl Blackford; illustrated by Laurie Caple. Minnesota Historical Society Press 2015 32 p. color illustrations (cloth : alk. paper) $16.95

Grades: PreK K 1 2   E

1. Animals -- Food 2. Cities and towns -- Fiction 3. Coyotes -- Fiction 4. Seasons -- Fiction 5. Urban animals -- Fiction

ISBN 0873519647; 9780873519649

LC 2014042450

In this children's book by Cheryl Blackford, illustrated by Laurie Caple, "Coyote makes his deliberate way through the seasons in his urban habitat. Across the pages, Coyote sneaks, skulks, and scurries in his constant quest to feed himself and his growing family. While Coyote hunts nearby, people enjoy a city park. At the lake, in the marsh, among the trees, children jump, twirl, and play, oblivious to his secret life." (Publisher's note)

"Readers follow the eponymous coyote across four seasons in his city park habitat. The creature is introduced in winter, where people in colorful coats play in the snow unaware of the nearby coyote unsuccessfully hunting for his dinner. Spring finds him at the same lake, now marshy and teeming with dining options. . . . An afterword details the lives of city coyotes, focusing on their habitats and eating habits, as well as advice on what do during an encounter. The gorgeous watercolors depicting wildlife in its urban park setting are strikingly realistic. VERDICT An interesting and informative read." SLJ

Blackstone, Stella

My granny went to market; a round-the-world counting rhyme. written by Stella Blackstone; illustrated by Christopher Corr. Barefoot Books 2005 un il $16.99

Grades: PreK K 1 2   E

1. Counting 2. Stories in rhyme 3. Grandmothers -- Fiction 4. Voyages and travels -- Fiction

ISBN 1-84148-792-9

LC 2004-17394

A child's grandmother travels around the world, buying things in quantities that illustrate counting from one to ten.

"The brightly colored gouache illustrations have the feel of Mexican folk art, and endpaper maps route Granny's travels, with a one-page legend showing her purchases—from one carpet to 10 llamas. A cheery, global shopping trip, fun to read alone and also useful in the classroom." Booklist

Blackwood, Freya

★ Ivy loves to give. Arthur A. Levine Books 2010 un il $15.99

Grades: PreK K 1   E

1. Gifts -- Fiction

ISBN 978-0-545-23467-2; 0-545-23467-0

First published 2009 in Australia

Ivy loves to give presents, and although they are not always appropriate, they are always given with enthusiasm and generosity.

Blackwood's "text—five sentences total—is brilliant in its economy, empathy, and pacing; the same can be said for the subtle and slyly funny family characterizations of her delicate pencil and watercolor drawings, rendered on a creamy white backdrop with minimal propping." Publ Wkly

Blake, Robert J.

Painter and Ugly. Philomel Books 2011 un il $16.99

Grades: K 1 2 3   E

1. Dogs -- Fiction 2. Alaska -- Fiction 3. Friendship -- Fiction 4. Sled dog racing -- Fiction

ISBN 978-0-399-24323-3; 0-399-24323-2

LC 2010005395

Painter and Ugly, two sled dogs who are inseparable best friends, are put on different teams for the Junior Iditarod, but they manage to find their way back to one another for the big race.

"Blake paints the dogs' heavy coats and eager faces in painstaking detail, and does a notably good job of narrating from a dog's point of view. His portrait of this specialized world will lure even those who have never been part of it." Publ Wkly

Blake, Stephanie

I don't want to go to school! written and illustrated by Stephanie Blake. Random House 2009 un il $12.99; lib bdg $15.99

Grades: PreK K   E

1. School stories 2. Rabbits -- Fiction

ISBN 0-375-85688-9; 0-375-95688-3 lib bdg; 978-0-375-85688-4; 978-0-375-95688-1 lib bdg

LC 2008011256

Original French edition 2007

Simon the rabbit does not want to go to his first day of school, but by the time his mother comes to take him home, he is having such a good time that he does not want to leave

"This title has a standard premise that is instantly understandable and reassuring, and the naive-style art, rendered in bold outlines and primary colors, is appealing and expressive." Booklist

Another title about Simon the Rabbit is:

A deal's a deal (2011)

Blake, Robert J.

★ Togo. Philomel Bks. 2002 un il $16.99

Grades: K 1 2 3   E

1. Dogs -- Fiction 2. Alaska -- Fiction

ISBN 0-399-23381-4

LC 2001-45926

In 1925, Togo, a Siberian husky who loves being a sled dog, leads a team that rushes to bring diphtheria antitoxin from Anchorage to Nome, Alaska

The author "paints a vivid word-picture of bitter, deadly conditions and the grueling effort required to surmount them, reinforcing it with dramatic art." Booklist

Blechman, Nicholas, 1967-

Night light; Nicholas Blechman. Scholastic 2013 48 p. ill. (reinforced) $16.99

Grades: PreK K 1   E

1. Counting 2. Picture books for children 3. Light -- Fiction 4. Stories in rhyme 5. Counting -- Fiction 6. Vehicles -- Fiction

ISBN 0545462630; 9780545462631

LC 2012024221

This children's picture book is "a counting book about big vehicles . . . with an extra . . . twist. [Nicholas Btechman] invites readers to identify the vehicles with a turn-the-page guessing game. First, spreads of pure black show only the vehicles' distinctive signature of lights. '1 light, shining bright?' reads the first black spread, a small, die-cut circle on the right side creating a single white dot. A page turn uncovers the answer: 'train.'" (Publishers Weekly)

Bledsoe, Josh

Hammer and nails; written by Josh Bledsoe; illustrated by Jessica Warrick. Flashlight Press 2016 32 p. color illustrations (hardback) $17.95

Grades: PreK K 1 2   **E**

1. Play -- Fiction 2. Father-daughter relationship -- Fiction 3. Fathers and daughters -- Fiction

ISBN 9781936261369; 9781936261840

LC 2015024217

In this book, by Josh Bledsoe, illustrated by Jessica Warrick, "Darcy has plans. She and her friend are going to play dress up, do each other's hair, and polish their nails. Daddy has plans, too. He's going to read the paper, mow the lawn, and fix the fence. When Darcy's friend cancels and she's sure her day is ruined, Daddy suggests that they tackle their to-do lists together with a Darcy-Daddy Day." (Publisher's note)

"This spunky, relatable read offers a heartwarming look at the bond between fathers and their daughters." Booklist

Blessing, Charlotte

New old shoes; written by Charlotte Blessing; illustrated by Gary R. Phillips. Pleasant St. Press 2009 un il $16.95

Grades: K 1 2   **E**

1. Shoes -- Fiction 2. Africa -- Fiction

ISBN 978-0-9792035-6-5; 0-9792035-6-2

"This story is narrated by a pair of red sneakers and follows their journey from their first home with a young boy in America to children in Africa. . . . The color-saturated illustrations provide a vibrant background to this touching story." SLJ

Blexbolex

★ **People**; [translated by Claudia Bedrick] Enchanted Lion Books 2011 il $19.95

Grades: K 1 2   **E**

1. Occupations -- Fiction

ISBN 978-1-59270-110-0; 1-59270-110-8

LC 2011001132

Explores, through brief text and illustrations, various sorts of people, the jobs they do, and the connections among them.

"German artist Blexbolex's captivating silk-screens explore human archetypes using a 1960s-era design aesthetic. Powder-blue type identifies each figure. As with its predecessor, the book's brilliance lies in the intriguing ways in which the images mimic, challenge, and inform one another. . . . Readers will form new associations and make new discoveries upon each revisiting." Publ Wkly

★ **Seasons**; translated by Claudia Bedrick. Enchanted Lion Books 2010 un il $19.95

Grades: K 1 2   **E**

1. Seasons -- Fiction

ISBN 978-1-59270-095-0; 1-59270-095-0

LC 2010001114

Original French edition, 2009

Explores, through brief text and illustrations, various aspects of each season of the year.

"This thick volume is both beautiful and intriguing—artist's portfolio, concept book, and word book rolled into one. The words, in huge, vividly pink block capitals, caption full pages and spreads for which seasons are the organizing principle. . . . These sophisticated images are sure to stimulate creative thought." Horn Book

Bley, Anette

And what comes after a thousand? Kane/Miller 2007 un il $15.95

Grades: PreK K 1 2   **E**

1. Death -- Fiction 2. Friendship -- Fiction 3. Bereavement --

Fiction

ISBN 978-1-933605-27-2

"This tender tale about intergenerational friendship, love, and loss tells of the cozy relationship between a young girl and an old, hard-of-hearing man. . . . After he dies, she must learn to deal with her pain and feelings of abandonment. The closeness of the characters is portrayed in heartwarming illustrations. . . . This universal story will speak to many readers." SLJ

Bliss, Harry

★ **Bailey**. Scholastic 2011 un il $16.99

Grades: PreK K 1 2   **E**

1. School stories 2. Dogs -- Fiction

ISBN 978-0-545-23344-6; 0-545-23344-5

LC 2010045096

Although he is a dog, Bailey goes to school where his canine abilities enliven an ordinary day.

"Deceptively simple cartoon illustrations belie the brilliance of the story. . . . From the facial expressions to the titles of the books Bailey reads, no opportunity is lost for fleshing out this character; and laughs abound on every page." SLJ

Bloch, Serge

Butterflies in my stomach and other school hazards; by Serge Bloch. Sterling Pub. Co. 2008 un il $12.95

Grades: PreK K 1 2   **E**

1. School stories 2. English language -- Idioms -- Fiction

ISBN 978-1-4027-4158-6; 1-4027-4158-8

LC 2007-43372

On the first day of school, a student is confused by many of the phrases that are used, such as when the librarian says not to open a can of worms, or when the teacher says he expects the class to be busy bees doing their homework.

"Bloch's simple though imaginative pictures and clean visual style invite discussion of the deeper meanings of these oft-used phrases, making this an ideal book for the classroom or for one-on-one sharing." SLJ

Snowed under and other Christmas confusions. Sterling 2011 il $12.95

Grades: PreK K 1   **E**

1. Christmas -- Fiction

ISBN 978-1-4027-7131-6; 1-4027-7131-2

LC 2010037056

A snow storm the day before Christmas causes a boy many worries, which are not helped by such confusing phrases as "Don't be a wet blanket" and "That's the way the cookie crumbles."

"The illustrations are creatively composed with effective use of white space, shadows and perspective along with motion and sight gags. As all kids know, 'time flies when you're having fun,' even on Christmas Eve. This is more fun than a barrel of monkeys." Kirkus

Bloom, Suzanne

Alone together; Suzanne Bloom. Boyds Mills Press 2014 32 p. color illustrations (Goose and bear) $16.95

Grades: PreK K   **E**

1. Bears -- Fiction 2. Foxes -- Fiction 3. Friendship -- Fiction 4. Geese -- fiction

ISBN 162091736X; 9781620917367

LC 2014931586

In this children's book, author Suzanne Bloom "crafts a story about her beloved Goose, Bear, and Fox that focuses on the simple emotional truths of childhood. Bear is quietly sitting by himself so Fox wonders if Bear is sad or mad or lonely. But no, Bear just occasionally enjoys a little quiet time alone. Not to be outdone, Fox decides that she would like quiet time alone, too—with Bear! Needless to say, Fox's version of quiet time is very different from Bear's." (Publisher's note)

"Large white lettering over a deep blue background presents the sparse text, perfectly worded for a beginning reader to figure out or for a preschooler to memorize. . . . Short on words and long on expressive artwork--a charming addition to a winning series for little ones." Kirkus

Feeding friendsies. Boyds Mills Press 2011 un il $16.95
Grades: PreK K   **E**
1. Play -- Fiction 2. Gardens -- Fiction
ISBN 978-1-59078-529-4; 1-59078-529-0

Baby and friends are busy in the garden making lunch that includes puddle-water soup, mud pie, and dandelion-and-dirt dessert.

"Bloom's sunny, naive watercolor illustrations show the children joyfully playing in the dirt while a shaggy dog and a black cat watch with curiosity. . . . This celebration of imaginative, outdoor fun is a tasty treat." SLJ

★ A **splendid** friend, indeed; written and illustrated by Suzanne Bloom. Boyds Mills Press 2005 un il $15.95
Grades: PreK K 1   **E**
1. Geese -- Fiction 2. Friendship -- Fiction 3. Polar bear -- Fiction
ISBN 1-59078-286-0
     LC 2004-10780

Other titles about Bear and Goose are:
Treasure (2007);
What about Bear? (2010);
Oh! What a surprise! (2012);
Fox forgets (2013);
Alone together (2014)

When a studious polar bear meets an inquisitive goose, they learn to be friends.

"The cool palette of the pastel illustrations, consisting of shades of blue and white and touches of violet, sets a quiet, friendly tone, and the animals' priceless expressions tell all. The gentle humor will elicit giggles." SLJ

Blue, Rose

Ron's big mission; [by] Rose Blue and Corinne J. Naden; illustrated by Don Tate. Dutton Childrens Books 2009 un il $16.99
Grades: K 1 2 3   **E**
1. Astronauts 2. Physicists 3. Libraries -- Fiction 4. Segregation -- Fiction 5. South Carolina -- Fiction 6. African Americans -- Fiction 7. Books and reading -- Fiction
ISBN 978-0-525-47849-2; 0-525-47849-3
     LC 2007050563

One summer day in 1959, nine-year-old Ron McNair, who dreams of becoming a pilot, walks into the Lake City, South Carolina, public library and insists on checking out some books, despite the rule that only white people can have library cards. Includes facts about McNair, who grew up to be an astronaut

"Vibrant illustrations portray a cozy small town. . . . Tate's figures feature oversized heads with very expressive faces that vividly convey well-meant kindness and the frustrations of injustice. . . . This will make a good choice for reading aloud and discussing." Booklist

Bluemle, Elizabeth

★ **How** do you wokka-wokka? illustrated by Randy Cecil. Candlewick Press 2009 un il $15.99
Grades: PreK K 1   **E**
1. Stories in rhyme 2. Dance -- Fiction
ISBN 978-0-7636-3228-1; 0-7636-3228-7
     LC 2008-27715

A young boy who likes to "wokka-wokka, shimmy-shake, and shocka-shocka" gathers his neighbors together for a surprise celebration.

"The sketchy, full-color oil illustrations in muted colors feature cartoon children cavorting alternately against stark white backgrounds or cityscapes as they join a giant block party. This bouncy book is a joy as a read-aloud." SLJ

Tap tap boom boom; Elizabeth Bluemle, illustrated by G. Brian Karas. Candlewick Press 2014 32 p. color illustrations $16.99
Grades: PreK K 1   **E**
1. Thunderstorms 2. City and town life 3. Picture books for children
ISBN 0763656968; 9780763656966
     LC 2013943093

In this children's picture book, by Elizabeth Bluemle and illustrated by G. Brian Karas, "as a thunderstorm rolls in, people of all stripes race down to the subway to get away from the crackling rain and wind. With quirky wordplay and . . . rhymes, Elizabeth Bluemle crystallizes an unexpected moment of community." (Publisher's note)

"The poetic rhythm of the language mimics the stages of the storm and the tempo of the citizens' footsteps. Though minimal, the text is powerful, and works well with the illustrations to create positive feelings about the weather." Lib Med Con

Blume, Judy

★ The **Pain** and the Great One; illustrations by Irene Trivas. rev format ed; Atheneum Books for Young Readers 2002 un il $17.95; pa $6.99
Grades: K 1 2 3   **E**
1. Siblings -- Fiction
ISBN 0-689-85507-9; 0-440-40967-5 pa
First published 1984 by Bradbury Press

A six-year-old (The Pain) and his eight-year-old sister (The Great One) see each other as troublemakers and the best-loved in the family

"Young readers, depending on their position within the family, will readily identify with either character and may learn empathy for the other. Used in a group, this will provide much healthy discussion. . . . Trivas' vibrant colors add depth and humor to a valuable book on sibling relationships." SLJ

Blumenthal, Deborah

The **blue** house dog; illustrated by Adam Gustavson. Peachtree 2010 un il $15.95
Grades: K 1 2 3   **E**
1. Dogs -- Fiction
ISBN 978-1-56145-537-9; 1-56145-537-7

"After his owner dies, Bones [a dog] roams the streets until young Cody acknowledges his grief over losing his own pet and persuades Bones to trust him. Perceptive art and emotive, free verse-style text work well together." Booklist

Bodeen, S. A.

★ **Elizabeti's** doll; illustrated by Christy Hale. Lee & Low Bks. 1998 un il $15.95
Grades: K 1 2 3   **E**
1. Siblings -- Fiction 2. Tanzania -- Fiction
ISBN 1-880000-70-9
     LC 98-13086

When a young Tanzanian girl gets a new baby brother, she finds a rock, which she names Eva, and makes it her baby doll

"Vibrant patterns and soft watercolor backgrounds evoke a sense of place and familial love." SLJ

Other titles about Elizabeti are:
Elizabeti's school (2002)

Mama Elizabeti (2000)

A **small,** brown dog with a wet, pink nose; by Stephanie Stuve-Bodeen; [illustrations by Linzie Hunter] Little Brown Books for Young Readers 2009 un il $16.99
Grades: K 1 2   E
1. Dogs -- Fiction 2. Parent-child relationship -- Fiction
ISBN 978-0-316-05830-8; 0-316-05830-0
LC 2008039298
Amelia will stop at nothing to convince her parents to let her adopt a very special dog.

"The concepts are complicated but clear, and Hunter's patterned illustrations are appropriately unpredictable, with nearly every page design different from the last. Plenty for kids to pore over." Booklist

Boelts, Maribeth
Before you were mine; story by Maribeth Boelts; pictures by David Walker. Putnam 2007 un il $15.99
Grades: PreK K 1 2   E
1. Dogs -- Fiction
ISBN 978-0-399-24526-8; 0-399-24526-X
LC 2006-20525
A young boy imagines what his rescued dog's life might have been like before he adopted him.

"Cozy, soft-edged pictures of an adorable dog characterize this warmhearted book. . . . The pastel illustrations use a variety of layouts to infuse the story with emotion." Booklist

A **Bike** Like Sergio's; Maribeth Boelts, illustrated by Noah Z. Jones. Candlewick Press 2016 40 p. color illustrations $15.99
Grades: K 1 2 3   E
1. Bicycles -- Fiction 2. Money 3. Poverty
ISBN 0763666491; 9780763666491
LC 2016909440
In this picture book by Maribeth Boelts, illustrated by Noah Z. Jones, "Ruben feels like he is the only kid without a bike. . . . So when Ruben sees a dollar bill fall out of someone's purse, he picks it up and puts it in his pocket. But when he gets home, he discovers it's not one dollar, or even five or ten-it's a hundred-dollar bill, more than enough for a new bike. . . . [But] what about the woman who lost her money?" (Publisher's note)

"The resolution is realistic for a kid with a loving, supportive family, and it leaves plenty of room for talking about what is most important in life from an authentically childlike perspective." Horn Book

Dogerella; illustrated by Donald Wu. Random House 2008 48p il (Step into reading) lib bdg $11.99; pa $3.99
Grades: 1 2 3   E
1. Fairy tales 2. Dogs -- Fiction
ISBN 978-0-375-93393-6 lib bdg; 0-375-93393-X lib bdg; 978-0-375-83393-9 pa; 0-375-83393-5 pa
LC 2007-15229
With the help of her fairy dogmother, Dogerella attends Princess Bea's ball where she competes with other dogs to become the princess's royal pet

"The combination of dozens of dogs, an earnest princess and a touch of magic add up to a charming whole." Kirkus

Those shoes; [by] Maribeth Boelts; illustrated by Noah Z. Jones. Candlewick Press 2007 un il $15.99; pa $6.99

Grades: K 1 2 3   E
1. Shoes -- Fiction 2. Grandmothers -- Fiction
ISBN 978-0-7636-2499-6; 0-7636-2499-3; 978-0-7636-4284-6 pa; 0-7636-4284-3 pa
LC 2006-51839
Jeremy, who longs to have the black high tops that everyone at school seems to have but his grandmother cannot afford, is excited when he sees them for sale in a thrift shop and decides to buy them even though they are the wrong size.

"Jones' mixed-media, digitally assembled pictures cleverly capture how thoroughly the shoe craze permeates every aspect of Jeremy's life. . . . Boelts and Jones create a work with broad appeal." Bull Cent Child Books

Bogan, Paulette
★ **Goodnight** Lulu. Bloomsbury Children's Bk. 2003 un il hardcover o.p. pa $6.95
Grades: PreK K 1 2   E
1. Bedtime -- Fiction 2. Chickens -- Fiction
ISBN 1-58234-803-0; 1-58234-983-5 pa
LC 2002-27825
When her mother tucks her in for the night, Lulu the chicken worries what would happen if a bear or a tiger or an alligator should come in during the night

This is a "funny, original, and reassuring tale. . . . The saturated watercolor and ink spreads deftly capture the night's ominous as well as cozy qualities." Horn Book Guide
Another title about Lulu is:
Lulu the big little chick (2009)

Bogart, Jo Ellen
Big and small, room for all; illustrated by Gillian Newland. Tundra Books 2009 un il $18.95
Grades: PreK K 1 2   E
1. Size -- Fiction
ISBN 978-0-88776-891-0; 0-88776-891-1
"A young girl sitting on a low tree branch views the vast mountains, sky, and fields around her. As the book progresses, realistic watercolor illustrations show the universe, the solar system, and a mountain range, as the spare text labels each concept in comparison to the size of the one before it. . . . Youngsters will delight in the awe-inspiring illustrations. . . . Word choice is highly suitable for the earliest independent readers." SLJ

★ The **White** Cat and the Monk; A Retelling of the Poem "Pangur Ban" by Jo Ellen Bogart; illustrated by Sydney Smith. Groundwood Books 2016 32 p. color illustrations $18.95
Grades: K 1 2 3   E
1. Cats -- Fiction 2. Monks -- Fiction
ISBN 1554987806; 9781554987801
This book, by Jo Ellen Bogart, illustrated by Sydney Smith, "is a retelling of the classic Old Irish poem 'Pangur Bán.' With Jo Ellen Bogart's simple and elegant narration and Sydney's Smith's classically inspired images, this contemplative story pays tribute to the wisdom of animals and the wonders of the natural world." (Publisher's note)

"The tale begins wordlessly with watercolor-and-ink compositions framed in sequential panels of varying size. . . . The voice is lyrical yet easily understood. . . . Reminiscent of the succinct storytelling and expressive brushwork of Chris Raschka and Kevin Henkes, this quiet, historical gem will charm children and adults alike." Kirkus

Boiger, Alexandra
Max and Marla; Alexandra Boiger. Penguin Group USA 2015 32 p. color illustrations $17.99

Grades: PreK K 1   E
  1. Olympic games 2. Sledding -- Fiction 3. Friendship -- Fiction
ISBN 0399175040; 9780399175046

                        LC 2015020237

In this children's book by Alexandra Boiger "Max and Marla are best friends. And aspiring Olympians! With their eyes on the prize, they know exactly what it'll take to reach sledding success: preparation, practice and perseverance. So when rusty blades, strong winds and difficult slopes get in their way, Max and Marla realize true joy lies not in winning but in friendship. Obstacles turn into victories!." (Publisher's note)

"Author/illustrator Boiger's story is graceful, and her limited-palette watercolor illustrations in well-designed combinations—including spot illustrations, full-page bleeds, and double-page spreads—effectively keep readers' attention on the story and do not overwhelm with gratuitous detail. A fun-filled story that delivers the true nature of the Olympian spirit." Kirkus

Boisrobert, Anouck
Popville; [by] Anouck Boisrobert & Louis Rigaud. Roaring Brook Press 2010 un il lib bdg $16.99
Grades: K 1 2 3   E
  1. Stories without words 2. Pop-up books 3. City and town life -- Fiction
ISBN 1-59643-593-3 lib bdg; 978-1-59643-593-3 lib bdg

Successive pop-up scenes show the progress as a rural area is built up into a busy city. "Ages four to eight." (N Y Times Book Rev)

"Using crisp, appealing pop-ups in a long, thin binding, [this book] chronicles a city's evolution from a bucolic, perhaps lonely, country church to an urban landscape. . . . 'Popville' has a clever central mechanism that tells the story quietly: a window cut out right through the book allows all the successive buildings to stay popped up even when the pages turn. The artwork is uncluttered and stylized, using muted, solid colors with a fabric-like texture to create clean geometric shapes." New York Times

Bolden, Tonya
Beautiful moon; a child's prayer. by Tonya Bolden; illustrated by Eric Velasquez. Abrams Books for Young Readers 2014 32 p. color illustrations $16.95
Grades: K 1 2 3   E
  1. Prayer -- Fiction 2. Bedtime -- Fiction 3. Moon -- Fiction 4. City and town life -- Fiction
ISBN 1419707922; 9781419707926

                        LC 2013031976

In this children's book, by Tonya Bolden, illustrated by Eric Velasquez, "a young boy wakes. He has forgotten to say his prayers. Outside his window, a beautiful harvest moon illuminates the city around him and its many inhabitants. As the moon slowly makes its way across the heavens, the boy offers a simple prayer for the homeless, the hungry, and others." (Publisher's note)

"Bolden (Maritcha: A 19th Century American Girl) expands a pleasingly simple premise into a depiction of the profound possibility of prayer. It's night. An 'amber orb'—the moon—floats above the city, and a boy startles awake in bed, having forgotten to say his nightly prayers. Velasquez (My Uncle Martin's Big Heart) shows the subjects of the boy's prayers: 'people with no homes,' the hungry, the lonely, 'for wars to end.' . . . Velasquez's illustrations, done in mixed media and oil on watercolor paper, convey mostly urban scenes in dark blues and browns, each illuminated by moonlight, which are both peaceful and full of detail. The book offers young readers plenty to look at, along with a simple message about the way prayer unites everyone, as the multicultural subjects in Velasquez's gorgeous illustrations make clear." Pub Wkly

Boldt, Mike
123 versus ABC; by Mike Boldt. Harper, an imprint of HarperCollinsPublishers 2013 32 p. color illustrations (hardcover) $17.99
Grades: K 1 2 3   E
  1. Alphabet 2. Numbers -- Fiction 3. Alphabet -- Fiction 4. Counting 5. Humorous stories
ISBN 0062102990; 9780062102997

                        LC 2012025494

This book, written by Mike Boldt, asks "which is more important, numbers or letters? Numbers and letters, the colorful characters in this story, compete to be the stars of this book. Their debate escalates when funny animals and props arrive—starting with 1 alligator, 2 bears, and 3 cars." (Publisher's note)

Bond, Felicia
Big hugs, little hugs. Philomel Books 2012 un il $16.99
Grades: PreK K   E
  1. Animals -- Fiction 2. Hugging -- Fiction
ISBN 978-0-399-25614-1; 0-399-25614-8

                        LC 2010053139

"This jubilant ode to the joys of hugging boldly announces its message on the first page: 'Everyone hugs all over the world.' What follows are tidy snippets of text that declare what animals like to hug, . . . as well as where, how, and when this hugging takes place. Bond . . . works in torn and cut-paper collage, her cheerful animal families showing various happy emotions. . . . The book's many whimsical touches should prove both comforting and entertaining." Publ Wkly

Bond, Rebecca
Pig & Goose and the first day of spring; Rebecca Bond. Charlesbridge 2017 48 p. color illustrations (reinforced for library use) $12.99
  Grades: K 1 2 3   E
  1. Pigs -- Fiction 2. Geese -- Fiction 3. Spring -- Fiction 4. Picnics -- Fiction 5. Friendship -- Fiction
ISBN 9781580895941

                        LC 2016013778

In this children's book, by Rebecca Bond, "Pig is happy. She loves to dance. She loves to eat. But she cannot fly. And she cannot swim. Goose can fly like a bird. Goose can glide across the water beautifully. But he cannot tell stories or host a party like Pig can. Pig and Goose are very different. But what they do have in common is that they like each other. And they love springtime." (Publisher's note)

Bonsall, Crosby Newell
★ The **case** of the hungry stranger; by Crosby Bonsall. HarperCollins Pubs. 1992 64p il (I can read book) hardcover o.p. pa $3.99
Grades: K 1 2 3   E
  1. Mystery fiction
ISBN 0-06-020571-7 lib bdg; 0-06-444026-5 pa

                        LC 91-13345

A reissue of the title first published 1963. This edition has full color illustrations

Wizard and his friends are clueless when they are sent on the trail of a blueberry pie thief, until Wizard hits on a plan that is sure to nab the sweet-toothed pilferer

This offers "suspense and humor." Horn Book

Other titles in this series are:

The case of the cat's meow (1965)

The case of the double cross (1980)

The case of the dumb bells (1966)

The case of the scaredy cats (1971)

★ The **day** I had to play with my sister; story and pictures by Crosby Bonsall. newly il ed; HarperCollins Pubs. 1999 32p il (My first I can read book) hardcover o.p. pa $3.99

Grades: K 1 2   E

1. Siblings -- Fiction

ISBN 0-06-028181-2; 0-06-444253-5 pa

LC 98-20342

A newly illustrated edition of the title first published 1972

A young boy becomes very frustrated when he tries to teach his little sister to play hide-and-seek

"The extremely simple text . . . is one with which children can readily identify. . . . The realistic atmosphere makes Bonsall's book an excellent addition to the very early reading shelves." SLJ

★ **Mine's** the best; newly il ed; HarperCollins Pubs. 1996 32p il (My first I can read book) lib bdg $16.89; pa $3.99

Grades: K 1 2   E

1. Balloons -- Fiction 2. Friendship -- Fiction

ISBN 0-06-027091-8 lib bdg; 0-06-444213-6 pa

LC 95-12405

A newly illustrated edition of the title first published 1973

Two little boys meet at the beach, each sure that his balloon is better

"The playful illustrations tell their own story; the extremely brief text (not to mention the head start provided by the two initial wordless spreads) will give new readers a sense of accomplishment." Horn Book Guide

★ **Who's** afraid of the dark? by Crosby Bonsall. Harper & Row 1980 32p il (Early I can read book) lib bdg $16.89; pa $3.99

Grades: K 1 2   E

1. Fear -- Fiction 2. Night -- Fiction

ISBN 0-06-020599-7 lib bdg; 0-06-444071-0 pa

LC 79-2700

"A little boy describes to a friend the nighttime fears of his dog Stella. Stella shivers in the dark, he claims; she sees shapes and hears scary sounds. The doubting but sympathetic friend offers a suggestion—hug Stella in the night and comfort her until her fears go away. . . . The illustrations in shades of light blue and brown are filled with as much life and warmth as ever." Horn Book

Bootman, Colin

Steel pan man of Harlem. Carolrhoda Books 2009 un il lib bdg $16.95

Grades: K 1 2 3   E

1. Rats -- Fiction 2. Harlem (New York, N.Y.) -- Fiction 3. Steel drum (Musical instrument) -- Fiction

ISBN 978-0-8225-9026-2 lib bdg; 0-8225-9026-3 lib bdg

LC 2008039654

A mysterious man appears in Harlem and promises to rid the city of its rats by playing the steel pan drum

Bootman "triumphs with this gorgeously moody, thoroughly cinematic retelling of the Pied Piper of Hamelin. . . . The oil paintings conjure up a gritty, workaday world where magic has taken hold." Publ Wkly

Borando, Silvia

Black cat, white cat; Silvia Borando. Candlewick Press 2015 48 p. illustrations $14

Grades: PreK K   E

1. Cats -- Fiction 2. Opposites -- Fiction 3. Day -- Fiction 4. Night -- Fiction

ISBN 0763681067; 9780763681067

LC 2014957053

In this children's story, by Silvia Borando, "Black Cat--black from the tips of his ears to the tip of his tail--only ever goes out in the day. But White Cat--white from her whiskers to her four furry paws--only ever goes out at night. He picks daisies, while she gazes at the stars. When they both feel the urge to explore a world beyond their own, Black Cat and White Cat go on a journey of discovery and meet for the very first time." (Publisher's note)

"Black Cat is completely black, from the tip of his nose to the tip of his tail. He goes out only during the day. By contrast, White Cat is utterly white from tip to tip and ventures forth only by night. Each savors the particular delights of the diurnal or nocturnal lifestyle, but each is also very curious about the time of day he/she is missing. . . . A highly recommended charmer for storytimes in all libraries, exploring concepts of opposites and friendship. This will be a big hit, especially when adult readers draw out that startling reveal at the end." SLJ

Near, Far; A Minibombo Book. Silvia Borando. Candlewick Press 2016 48 p. color illustrations (Minibombo book) (hardcover) $14

Grades: PreK K 1   E

1. Size 2. Shape 3. Animals

ISBN 0763687839; 9780763687830

LC 2015937227

In this children's book by Silvia Borando, "no words are needed in [the] . . . colorful exploration of animal shapes. Bold graphic forms create a playful exercise in visual perception. At first glance, that green bump might be a grassy hill. . . . Step back (turn the page) to see a little more. Now there are two green loopy humps. What could it be? Turn one more page to reveal—of course, the squiggles of a snake! Preschoolers will see animals in a new way." (Publisher's note)

"Borando aims for a high level of visual acuity and sophistication, demanding sharp eyes and a vivid imagination. Grown-ups and little ones will want to experience the fun again and again." Kirkus

Now You See Me, Now You Don't; A Minibombo Book. Silvia Borando. Candlewick Press 2016 28 p. color illustrations (Minibombo) (hardcover) $14

Grades: PreK K 1   E

1. Color 2. Animals

ISBN 0763687820; 9780763687823

LC 2015937229

This wordless book by Silvia Borando "invites children to explore the concept of visibility. . . . When the background color changes with each turn of the page, a different animal (almost) vanishes—and another seems to appear on every spread. Who blends in with the fallen leaves? What about the trees of the forest? Brimming with visual humor, this attractive play on color and camouflage is sure to delight keen-eyed youngsters." (Publisher's note)

"Artistic simplicity and visual play spark unfettered fun in this charming little book." Kirkus

Borden, Louise

The **A** + custodian; illustrated by Adam Gustavson. Margaret K. McElderry Books 2004 un il $15.95

Grades: K 1 2 3   E

1. School stories 2. Janitors -- Fiction

ISBN 0-689-84995-8

LC 2002-12029

The students and teachers at Dublin Elementary School make banners, posters, and signs for their school custodian to show how much they appreciate him and all the work he does

"The simple, unrhymed poetic words and the realistic oil paintings create a strong sense of a diverse school community and a man in flannel shirt and worn leather shoes." Booklist

A. Lincoln and me; illustrated by Ted Lewin. Scholastic 1999 un il hardcover o.p. pa $5.99

Grades: K 1 2 3   E

1. Lawyers 2. Presidents 3. State legislators 4. Members of Congress

ISBN 0-590-45714-4 pa

LC 98-51921

With the help of his teacher, a young boy realizes that he not only shares his birthday and similar physical appearance with Abraham Lincoln, but that he is like him in other ways as well

"Borden's text flows nicely, creating imagery of the physical presence of the man. Lewin's distinctive watercolors lend style and substance to the book, producing a treat for the eyes." SLJ

Big brothers don't take naps; art by Emma Dodd. Margaret K. McElderry Books 2011 un il $16.99

Grades: PreK K 1   E

1. Infants -- Fiction 2. Brothers -- Fiction 3. Siblings -- Fiction

ISBN 978-1-4169-5503-0; 1-4169-5503-8

"Nicholas admires and pays great attention to everything his big brother does. . . . James is a patient teacher and role model for his younger sibling. . . . When the two boys work together on a list of names for a 'special event' to take place in June, the older boy lets his brother make the definitive choice. Of course, the surprise is a baby sister, which makes Nicholas a big brother himself. Bright pastel, digitally rendered illustrations span autumn, winter, and spring and show the brothers and their ever-present dogs in a loving, noncompetitive relationship." SLJ

Baseball is... Louise Borden; illustrated by Raul Colon. Margaret K. McElderry Books, an imprint of Simon & Schuster Children's Pub. Division 2013 48 p. (hardcover) $17.99

Grades: 2 3 4 5   E

1. Baseball

ISBN 141695502X; 9781416955023

LC 2013008621

This picture book presents a free-verse tribute to baseball. Author Louise Borden "enumerates the elements of the game, including ballparks and fans, plays and players. . . . A fold-out page gives special attention to Babe Ruth, Jackie Robinson, and Roberto Clemente. The author also mentions the 'long ago' Negro leagues and the women's league; and notes baseball's ability to bring diverse people together. Emphasis is placed on patriotic elements." (School Library Journal)

"America's national pastime gets a treatment that is both lively and knowledgeable in this oversize, fact-filled volume...This is due in no small part to Colón's signature colored-pencil artwork, which impressively captures baseball moments big and small. A neat vehicle for getting an intergenerational conversation going over a shared passion." Booklist

Off to first grade; illustrated by Joan Rankin. Margaret K. McElderry Books 2008 un il $16.99

Grades: PreK K 1   E

1. School stories

ISBN 978-0-689-87395-9; 0-689-87395-6

LC 2005-02320

Each member of a first grade class, as well as their teacher, principal, and a bus driver, expresses excitement, worry, or hope as the first day of school begins.

"The sequence is gentle yet genuinely perceptive in its documentation of the varying responses to the dramatic transition from home to school." Bull Cent Child Books

Boswell, Addie K.

The **rain** stomper. Marshall Cavendish 2008 un il $16.99

Grades: PreK K 1 2   E

1. Rain -- Fiction 2. Parades -- Fiction

ISBN 978-0-7614-5393-2; 0-7614-5393-8

When it begins to rain and storm on the day of her big parade, Jazmin stomps, shouts, and does all she can think of to drive the rain away.

"Velasquez's large oils impart a sense of the girl's disappointment as well as the feel of a driving rain and eventual pleasure. Large letters in white, black, or red and in different sizes emphasize the sounds and rhythm of the rain and thunder. . . . A delightful read-aloud that deals with making the best of a disappointing situation." SLJ

Bottner, Barbara

★ An **annoying** ABC; illustrated by Michael Emberley. Alfred A. Knopf 2011 un il $17.99; lib bdg $20.99

Grades: PreK K 1 2   E

1. Alphabet 2. School stories

ISBN 978-0-375-86708-8; 0-375-86708-2; 978-0-375-96708-5 lib bdg; 0-375-96708-7 lib bdg; 978-0-375-98469-3 e-book

LC 2011011843

"Adelaide annoys Bailey when she runs at him wearing her tiger costume, scaring him and causing him to let the gerbil out of its cage. So begins a rollicking preschool/early elementary romp featuring kids who appear in alphabetical order with a corresponding action. . . . The hilarity lies in the illustrations, typical Emberley style, done in mechanical pencil and watercolors. . . . One read-through will simply not be enough to enjoy all the fun." Kirkus

Bootsie Barker bites; illustrated by Peggy Rathmann. Putnam 1992 un il $17.99; pa $5.99

Grades: K 1 2 3   E

1. Bullies -- Fiction

ISBN 0-399-22125-5; 0-698-11427-2 pa

LC 91-12182

"Bottner's tone is a model of simplicity and matter-of-factness, sometimes droll but never coy. Rathmann's neon-bright, full-color artwork extends the emotional tenor and the humor of the text." Booklist

Another title about Bootsie is:

Bootsie Barker ballerina (1997)

★ **Miss** Brooks loves books (and I don't) story by Barbara Bottner; illustrations by Michael Emberley. Alfred A. Knopf 2010 un il $17.99; lib bdg $20.99

Grades: PreK K 1 2   E

1. School stories 2. Librarians -- Fiction 3. Books and reading -- Fiction

ISBN 978-0-375-84682-3; 0-375-84682-4; 978-0-375-94682-0 lib bdg; 0-375-94682-9 lib bdg

LC 2009-02305

A first-grade girl who does not like to read stubbornly resists her school librarian's efforts to convince her to love books until she finds one that might change her mind.

"Children will delight in Emberley's spirited watercolor and ink renderings of literary favorites. . . . Bottner's deadpan humor and delicious prose combine with Emberley's droll caricatures to create a story sure to please those who celebrate books—and one that may give pause to those who don't (or who work with the latter)." SLJ

Miss Brooks' Story Nook; (where tales are told and ogres are welcome) by Barbara Bottner; illustrated by Michael Emberley. Alfred A. Knopf 2014 40 p. color illustrations (trade) $16.99

Grades: PreK K 1 2   E

1. Bullies -- Fiction 2. Librarians -- Fiction 3. Storytelling --

Fiction

ISBN 0449813282; 9780449813287; 9780449813294

LC 2013013799

Companion to: Miss Brooks loves books! (and I don't)

In this book by Barbara Bottner, illustrated by Michael Emberley, "Missy loves her librarian, Miss Brooks. And she loves to go to Miss Brooks' before-school story time. But to get to Story Nook, she has to pass Billy Toomey's house--and she does not love Billy Toomey. . . . And that's when Missy has a brainstorm. She sees a way to use her made-up story to deal with her real-life bully." (Publisher's note)

"Capably constructed and full of lively dialogue, the story is well served by Emberley's many expressive drawings of the characters, including a sympathetic, symbolic portrayal of Missy burdened by her nemesis." Booklist

★ **Priscilla** gorilla; by Barbara Bottner; illustrated by Michael Emberley. Atheneum Books for Young Readers 2017 40 p. color illustrations (ebook) $15.99; (hardback) $17.99

Grades: PreK K 1 2   E

1. Bad behavior -- Fiction 2. Cooperativeness -- Fiction 3. Helping behavior -- Fiction

ISBN 9781481458986; 9781481458979

LC 2016032027

In this children's book, written by Barbara Bottner and illustrated by Michael Emberley, "when a whole class goes gorilla, they learn the importance of balancing passion and creativity with cooperation." (Publisher's note)

"A precious and precocious primate parable sure to please." Kirkus

Includes bibliographical references and index

Boudreau, Helene

I dare you not to yawn; Helene Boudreau, illustrated by Serge Bloch. Candlewick Press 2013 32 p. (reinforced) $15.99

Grades: PreK K 1   E

ISBN 9780763650704

LC 2012942415

"'Yawns are like colds. They spread!' And you don't want to catch one. If you do, your parents will have you jammied-up and shipped off to bed in no time flat. So when the cat or your big sister starts to yawn, there's only one thing to do: 'LOOK AWAY!' This picture book, which speaks directly to the audience as an instructional guide of sorts, teaches kids how to avoid the pitfalls of being sent to bed prematurely." (Booklist)

Bourguignon, Laurence

Heart in the pocket; by Laurence Bourguignon; illustrated by Valerie d'Heur. Eerdmans Books for Young Readers 2008 un il $16.50

Grades: PreK K 1 2   E

1. Kangaroos -- Fiction 2. Mother-child relationship -- Fiction

ISBN 978-0-8028-5343-1; 0-8028-5343-9

LC 2007049348

A baby kangaroo is reluctant to leave the comfort of his mother's pocket, where he is safe and warm and can always hear her heartbeat, until he finds out that her heart is not actually in her pocket.

"The gentle, well-crafted text is sweet, but not overly so. The watercolor illustrations have a soft palette dominated by yellowish tans and light blues, and expressively portray a wise and loving mother with her shy, slightly fearful child." SLJ

Boyd, Lizi

Big bear little chair; by Lizi Boyd. Chronicle Books LLC 2015 36 p. color illustration (alk. paper) $16.99

Grades: PreK K 1   E

1. Size -- Fiction 2. Animals -- Fiction 3. Opposites -- Fiction 4.

Polarity -- Fiction

ISBN 1452144478; 9781452144474

LC 2015001412

New York Times Best Illustrated Children's Books (2015)

In this children's book, author Lizi Boyd "has created a compendium of unexpected opposites that is also a charming and emotionally warm story about Big Bear, little bear, and the stories that bring them together." (Publisher's note)

"In this dynamic visual journey, opposites in size receive a striking comparison, though only a few brief words pepper each page. Boyd uses blacks, whites, and grays, and splashes of red to emphasize visual details. Each examination highlights two items of contrasting proportions with a rolling rhythm, such as "big zebra/little broom/big rock/little butterfly/big elephant/little trick/big moon/little star." . . . Opposites receive a fresh interpretation in this stylish selection." SLJ

Flashlight; by Lizi Boyd. Chronicle Books 2014 40 p. color illustrations (reinforced) $16.99

Grades: PreK K 1   E

1. Boys -- Fiction 2. Night -- Fiction 3. Stories without words 4. Flashlights -- Fiction

ISBN 9781452118949; 1452118949

LC 2013029635

"In this wordless picture book" by Lizi Boyd, "a child camping at night in a forest uses a flashlight to explore the flora and fauna of the area; when he trips over a rock and drops the flashlight, the animals take their turn with the light, highlighting various parts of the child and eventually helping him find his way to his tent." (Bulletin of the Center for Children's Books)

"With each successive page, more color appears, even outside of the beam of light, as knowledge of and comfort with the woodland surroundings grows, and the final endpapers feature bits of color, whereas the opening endpapers had none. Children will enjoy repeatedly poring over the many details and creating their own nighttime narratives." Booklist

Inside outside; by Lizi Boyd. Chronicle Books 2012 40 p. (reinforced) $15.99

Grades: PreK K   E

1. Stories without words 2. Play -- Fiction 3. Board books 4. Dogs -- Fiction 5. Play -- Fiction 6. Toy and movable books -- Specimens

ISBN 1452106444; 9781452106441

LC 2012015430

This children's picture book, by Lizi Boyd, explores the differences between inside and outside. "What is happening outside today? Peek through the window to find out. What is happening inside? Peek again!" The story shows diverse scenes of different rooms within a house and outside, with several details to focus on. (Publisher's note)

Boyer, Cecile

Woof, meow, tweet-tweet. Seven Footer Kids 2011 un il $15.95

Grades: PreK K 1   E

1. Cats -- Fiction 2. Dogs -- Fiction 3. Birds -- Fiction

ISBN 978-1-934734-60-5; 1-934734-60-8

Presents a humorous account of the differences between dogs, cats, and birds, from the sounds they make, how they behave, and what happens when they all meet.

"The book's unique juxtaposition of text, clean graphic images, and font changes might also encourage older readers, noting its text-as-art or perhaps a few new vocabulary words. . . . This simple yet cleverly executed story can be used in multiple ways in various classes and individual settings." SLJ

Boyle, Bob

Hugo and the really, really, really long string. Random House 2010 un il $15.99; lib bdg $18.99

Grades: PreK K 1 2   E

1. Stories in rhyme 2. Animals -- Fiction

ISBN 978-0-375-83423-3; 0-375-83423-0; 978-0-375-93423-0 lib bdg; 0-375-93423-5 lib bdg

LC 2006016303

Hugo follows a mysterious red string through his town, collecting a series of new friends along the way, all of them knowing that something special must be at the end of the string.

"This is a great story that can lead to a discussion of friends and neighborhoods. Written in rhyme, it is an entertaining story. The geometric style used in the artwork will be familiar to students as Boyle is the author/illustrator who created the Nick Jr. television show, WOW! WOW! Wubbzy!" Libr Media Connect

Boynton, Sandra

★ **Happy** Hippo, angry Duck; a book of moods. Little Simon 2011 un il $5.99

Grades: PreK K   E

1. Board books for children 2. Animals -- Fiction 3. Emotions -- Fiction

ISBN 978-1-4424-1731-1; 1-4424-1731-5

"With her familiar brand of gentle absurdity, Boynton creates similes that ascribe moods to various animals. . . . Part of the book's pleasure is that Boynton doesn't rely on clichéd animal personifications. . . . Even kids in the stoniest of moods will feel the effect of this pick-me-up." Publ Wkly

Bradby, Marie

★ **Momma,** where are you from? illustrated by Chris K. Soentpiet. Orchard Bks. 2000 un il $16.95

Grades: K 1 2 3   E

1. African Americans -- Fiction 2. Mother-daughter relationship -- Fiction

ISBN 0-531-30105-2

LC 99-23068

Momma describes the special people and surroundings of her childhood, in a place where the edge of town met the countryside, in a time when all the children at school were brown.

"Soentpiet's detailed, beautifully lit paintings freeze the mother's vivid memories, culminating in a dreamy, gray-toned montage of all the previous scenes. Children will be inspired by the mother's eloquent, proud answer to her daughter's essential question." Booklist

★ **More** than anything else; story by Marie Bradby; pictures by Chris K. Soentpiet. Orchard Bks. 1995 un il $15.95

Grades: K 1 2 3   E

1. Slaves 2. Authors 3. Educators 4. Memoirists 5. Nonfiction writers 6. Civil rights activists 7. African Americans -- Fiction 8. Books and reading -- Fiction

ISBN 0-531-09464-2

LC 94-48804

Nine-year-old Booker works with his father and brother at the saltworks, but dreams of the day when he'll be able to read.

"An evocative text combines with well-crafted, dramatic watercolors to provide a stirring, fictionalized account of the early life of Booker T. Washington." Horn Book

Bradford, Wade

Why do I have to make my bed? or, a history of messy rooms. illustrations by Johanna Van der Sterre. Tricycle Press 2011 un il $16.99

Grades: K 1 2   E

1. Home economics -- Fiction 2. Mother-son relationship -- Fiction

ISBN 978-1-58246-327-8; 1-58246-327-1

When a boy asks his mother why he must make his bed, she tells him a story about his ancestors who posed the same question through the centuries, going all the way back to a caveboy and his mother.

"While playing up the timelessness and universality of the human condition (at least as far as chores are concerned), the text and pictures underscore the evolving demands and trappings of domestic life. With its clever premise, keenly observed visual comedy, and easygoing pedagogy . . . this book deserves a place next to the Magic School Bus series." Publ Wkly

Bradley, Kimberly Brubaker

Ballerino Nate; illustrated by R.W. Alley. Dial Books for Young Readers 2006 un il $16.99

Grades: PreK K 1 2   E

1. Ballet -- Fiction 2. Sex role -- Fiction

ISBN 0-8037-2954-5

LC 2004-17822

After seeing a ballet performance, Nate decides he wants to learn ballet but he has doubts when his brother Ben tells him that only girls can be ballerinas.

"Bradley writes smoothly and insightfully about Nate's experiences. . . . Alley's watercolor-and-pencil contributions, portraying an entirely canine universe, capture both the warm family dynamics and Nate's zooming, irrepressible energy. " Booklist

Brallier, Jess M.

Tess's tree; pictures by Peter H. Reynolds. Harper 2009 un il $16.99

Grades: PreK K 1   E

1. Trees -- Fiction 2. Bereavement -- Fiction

ISBN 978-0-06-168752-5; 0-06-168752-9

LC 2009014580

When nine-year-old Tess invites her friends, family, and neighbors to celebrate her beloved maple tree's life before it must be cut down, she learns that it has meant a lot to other people, as well.

"Reynolds's soft watercolor vignettes extend the quiet story. Wispy lines portray a subtle vulnerability; washes of muted blue effectively provide emotional depth as Tess survives grief's powerful storm." Kirkus

Brannen, Sarah S.

Uncle Bobby's wedding; [by] Sarah S. Brannen. G. P. Putnam's Sons 2008 32p il $15.99

Grades: PreK K 1 2   E

1. Uncles -- Fiction 2. Weddings -- Fiction 3. Guinea pigs -- Fiction 4. Homosexuality -- Fiction

ISBN 978-0-399-24712-5; 0-399-24712-2

LC 2007-16550

Chloë the guinea pig is jealous and sad when her favorite uncle announces that he will be getting married, but as she gets to know Jamie better and becomes involved in planning the wedding, she discovers that she will always be special to Uncle Bobby—and to Uncle Jamie, too.

"Warmly affectionate watercolor and graphite illustrations accompany this genial story of same-sex marriage." Horn Book Guide

Braun, Sebastien

★ **Back** to bed, Ed! Peachtree Publishers 2010 un il $15.95

Grades: PreK K 1   E

1. Mice -- Fiction 2. Sleep -- Fiction 3. Bedtime -- Fiction 4. Parent-child relationship -- Fiction

ISBN 978-1-56145-518-8; 1-56145-518-0

First published 2009 in the United Kingdom

Ed the mouse will not sleep in his own bed, until eventually his exasperated and tired parents find a way to keep him from joining them in the middle of the night.

"Braun's clean illustrations in India ink with markers and colored pencils are bright and bold. . . . They show all the emotions of the characters and many interesting details. . . . The simple text works in tandem with the illustrations to produce a great story that's fun to read." SLJ

Meeow and the big box. Boxer Books 2009 un il lib bdg $12.95
Grades: PreK   E
1. Cats -- Fiction 2. Play -- Fiction 3. Imagination -- Fiction
ISBN 978-1-906250-86-7 lib bdg; 1-906250-86-3 lib bdg

"Braun shows a wide-eyed black cat in a red scarf playing with a box. The omniscient narrator carries on a one-way dialogue, describing imaginative Meeow's actions and intentions as he transforms the box into a bright red fire engine. . . . The book is simple and direct, and pulls together all the ingredients (box, red paint, green scissors) in the same methodical way that toddlers hard at work would. Uncluttered pages and primary colors make this a highly attractive book, as does the tactile jacket that allows readers to stroke fuzzy Meeow." SLJ

Other titles about Meeow are:
Meeow and the little chairs (2009)
Meeow and the pots and pans (2010)
Meeow and the blue table (2010)

On our way home. Boxer 2009 un il $14.95
Grades: PreK K   E
1. Bears -- Fiction 2. Father-child relationship -- Fiction
ISBN 978-1-906250-59-1; 1-906250-59-6

"With unadorned, heartfelt prose and idyllic images, Braun . . . conveys just how wonderful it feels to spend a day alone with Daddy. . . . Braun's acrylic pictures strike a lovely balance, as he places his genial, naïf-styled characters within majestically scaled landscapes." Publ Wkly

The **ugly** duckling. Boxer Books 2010 il (A Story House book) lib bdg $16.95
Grades: PreK K   E
1. Authors 2. Novelists 3. Dramatists 4. Fairy tales 5. Ducks -- Fiction 6. Swans -- Fiction 7. Children's authors 8. Short story writers
ISBN 978-1-907152-04-7; 1-907152-04-0

A retelling of Hans Christian Andersen's tale of the ugly little duckling who grows up to become a beautiful swan.

"This text presents the highlights of the story in a straightforward fashion that perserves the formal feel of the original. . . . The expressive pictures, though rendered with ink and colored pencil, have the careful lines and bold edges that give them the feel of woodcuts. . . . The large format, combined with bright, bold illustrations and simplified language, makes this ideal for storytime sharing." SLJ

Who can swim? Sebastien Braun. Candlewick Press 2014 14 p. $6.99
Grades: PreK   E
1. Swimming 2. Aquatic animals
ISBN 0763667528; 9780763667528

LC 2013943102

In this children's board book, author and illustrator Sebastien Braun asks "who can swim? . . . Dive with a dolphin, wallow with a whale, and paddle with a polar bear. Who else might be in the water?" (Publisher's note)

Other titles in the series include:
Who can Jump?
Who's Hiding?

Breathed, Berke
Pete & Pickles; [by] Berkeley Breathed. Philomel Books 2008 un il $17.99
Grades: 2 3 4   E
1. Pigs -- Fiction 2. Elephants -- Fiction 3. Friendship -- Fiction
ISBN 978-0-399-25082-8; 0-399-25082-4

LC 2007-50044

When Pickles the elephant turns his life upside-down, Pete the pig comes to realize that a perfectly predictable, practical, and uncomplicated life is not always preferable.

"This heartwarming tale is packed with adventure, imagination, and the all-important message of accepting differences. The illustrations alternate from naturalistic renderings of fantastical scenarios to flat compositions reminiscent of traditional comic strips." SLJ

Breen, Steve
Stick; [by] Steve Breen. Dial Books For Young Readers 2007 un il $16.99
Grades: PreK K 1 2 3   E
1. Frogs -- Fiction 2. Dragonflies -- Fiction
ISBN 978-0-8037-3124-0

LC 2006046318

An independent young frog goes on a wild adventure when he accidentally gets carried away by a dragonfly.

"Breen generates plenty of fun and suspense in the skillfully rendered, animated pictures." Booklist

Violet the pilot; [by] Steve Breen. Dial Books for Young Readers 2008 un il $16.99
Grades: K 1 2 3   E
1. Dogs -- Fiction 2. Air pilots -- Fiction
ISBN 978-0-8037-3125-7

LC 2007022367

Young Violet's only friend is her dog, Orville, until one of her homemade flying machines takes her to the rescue of a Boy Scout troop in trouble.

"An engaging story of a spunky girl who follows her dreams. . . . Done in watercolors, acrylics, and Photoshop, the lively cartoon artwork evokes a nostalgic setting. Violet's various inventions are clever and amusing." SLJ

Woodpecker wants waffles; by Steve Breen. Harper, an imprint of HarperCollinsPublishers 2016 32 p. color illustrations (hardcover) $17.99
Grades: PreK K 1 2   E
1. Food -- Fiction 2. Woodpeckers -- Fiction 3. Animals -- Fiction 4. Food habits -- Fiction 5. Pancakes, waffles, etc. -- Fiction 6. Determination (Personality trait) -- Fiction
ISBN 9780062342577

LC 2014041209

In this children's story, written and illustrated by Steve Breen, "One day Benny the woodpecker awakens to the best tummy-rumbling smell ever and discovers it's something called waffles. . . . Each time Benny tries, he just can't seem to get to those delicious waffles. The other forest animals laugh at him: 'Woodpeckers don't eat waffles!' they say. But Benny has a brilliant plan." (Publisher's note)

"His attempts (and final success) will have preschoolers giggling and begging for a second helping. Ink, watercolors, colored pencils, and 'artistic genius' were used to make the cartoon illustrations that add the perfect subtle and slapstick humor to Benny's quest." Kirkus

Brendler, Carol
Not very scary; Carol Brendler; pictures by Greg Pizzoli. Farrar, Straus and Giroux 2014 40 p. color illustrations (hardcover) $12.99

Grades: PreK K 1   E
1. Fear -- Fiction 2. Parties -- Fiction 3. Monsters -- Fiction 4. Halloween -- Fiction 5. Surprise -- Fiction
ISBN 0374355479; 9780374355470

LC 2013011139

In this children's book, by Carol Brendler, "Melly is a brave little monster who is not afraid of anything. She loves surprises, and when her fun-loving cousin invites her over for a big surprise, Melly excitedly sets out for a visit. On her way, she notices skittish skeletons, a coal-black cat, and even ghoulish goblins following her. But Melly is not scared, no she's not! Well, maybe just a teensy bit." (Publisher's note)

"In a delightful Halloween romp that's part counting book, part tongue twister, Brendler and Pizzoli introduce a green-skinned monster named Melly who is heading to her cousin Malberta's house for a 'surprise.' Along the way, Melly realizes an entourage is growing behind her, starting with a 'coal-black cat with an itchy-twitchy tail," which Melly dismisses as "not the least bit scary.' But then come 'two skittish skeletons,' 'four mournful ghosts,' and 'seven frenzied fruit bats,' and suddenly Melly isn't feeling so brave. Pizzoli crams the pages with comically ghoulish chaos, and his smiley creatures (Melly included) are more cute than bloodcurdling. Amid the mounting tension (which results in an epic party), readers also get a crash course in adverbs: 'Not significantly scary!' says Melly when six mummies show up. 'Not especially scary!' she shouts on the next page." Pub Wkly

Winnie Finn, worm farmer. Farrar Straus Giroux 2009 un il $15.99
Grades: PreK K 1 2   E
1. Worms -- Fiction
ISBN 978-0-374-38440-1; 0-374-38440-1

LC 2008004255

Winnie Finn raises earthworms, which help her neighbors win prizes at the county fair. Includes instructions on making a worm farm.

"Nimble lines and cool colors depict the energy of the active outdoor scenes. Humorous details abound through animated expressions. . . . Winnie's spunky, good-natured heart anchors a gentle and entertaining read." SLJ

Includes bibliographical references

Brennan, Eileen
Dirtball Pete. Random House 2010 un il $15.99; lib bdg $18.99
Grades: K 1 2 3   E
1. School stories 2. Theater -- Fiction 3. Cleanliness -- Fiction
ISBN 978-0-375-83425-7; 0-375-83425-7; 978-0-375-93425-4 lib bdg; 0-375-93425-1 lib bdg

LC 2006022433

"It's tough to make a book sardonic and heartwarming at the same time, but Brennan nails it." Publ Wkly

Brennan, Rosemarie
Willow; written by Denise Brennan Nelson and Rosemarie Brennan; illustrated by Cyd Moore. Sleeping Bear Press 2008 un il $16.95
Grades: K 1 2 3   E
1. Art -- Fiction 2. Painting -- Fiction 3. Imagination -- Fiction
ISBN 978-1-58536-342-1; 1-58536-342-1

LC 2007034588

In art class, neatness, conformity, and imitation are encouraged, but when Willow brings imagination and creativity to her projects, even straight-laced Miss Hawthorn is influenced

"Soft-toned watercolors contrast colorful, autumn trees with all-the-same green ones. . . . Expressive faces show wonderment and joy as teacher and students discover . . . the intese power of imagination." SLJ

Another title about Willow is:
Willow and the snow day dance (2011)

Brennan-Nelson, Denise
Leopold the Lion; by Denise Brennan-Nelson; illustrated by Ruth McNally Barshaw. Sleeping Bear Press 2015 32 p. color illustrations $16.99
Grades: PreK K 1 2   E
1. Pets -- Fiction 2. Lions -- Fiction 3. Food habits -- Fiction 4. Lions as pets -- Fiction 5. Brothers and sisters -- Fiction
ISBN 1585368288; 9781585368280

LC 2015001570

In this children's book by Denise Brennan-Nelson, illustrated by Ruth McNally Barshaw, "hen Jack and Ella come across a friendly--and talented!--lion in their backyard they are thrilled to take him in as their pet. And they're positive they know just how to care for their new pet, ignoring Grandpa's cheeky asides. But soon Leopold the Lion grows despondent and chubby. Even the circus who lost him won't take him back! Do Jack and Ella know what to do to get Leopold healthy again?" (Publisher's note)

"A whimsical story that could spark healthy living discussions." SLJ

Brenner, Barbara
Good morning, garden; illustrated by Denise Ortakales. Northword Press 2004 un il $15.95
Grades: K 1 2 3   E
1. Stories in rhyme 2. Gardens -- Fiction
ISBN 1-55971-888-9

Upon entering a garden one morning, a child greets the flowers, plants, insects, and animals there.

"The alliterative tone and subtle rhyme scheme continue throughout this joyful celebration. . . . Ortakales works with sculpted paper to convey the depth and detail of a garden replete with luscious plants and friendly creatures." SLJ

★ **Wagon** wheels; story by Barbara Brenner; pictures by Don Bolognese. newly il ed; HarperCollins Pubs. 1993 64p il (I can read book) hardcover o.p. pa $3.99
Grades: K 1 2   E
1. African Americans -- Fiction 2. Frontier and pioneer life -- Fiction
ISBN 0-06-444052-4 pa

LC 92-18780

A newly illustrated edition of the title first published 1978

Shortly after the Civil War a black family travels to Kansas to take advantage of the free land offered through the Homestead Act

"The based-on-fact story . . . is as fascinating as ever. Beautifully narrated with sensitivity, compassion, and just the right amount of suspense, and featuring new full-color illustrations." Horn Book Guide

Brenner, Tom
And then comes Christmas; Tom Brenner, illustrated by Jana Christy. Candlewick Press 2014 32 p. color illustrations $15.99
Grades: PreK K 1 2   E
1. Winter -- Fiction 2. Christmas -- Fiction
ISBN 076365342X; 9780763653422

LC 2013953455

This children's book, by Tom Brenner, is a "lyrical invitation to watch for signs of the approaching season--and revel in the homespun rituals that warm a family celebration. From icicles clinging to roofs and houses strung with colorful lights to visiting Santa and hunting for the perfect tree, this classic-in-the-making celebrates all of the holiday's excitement." (Publisher's note)

"In Brenner's inviting story, chilly weather, holiday decorations, delicious baked goods, and all the other trappings of Christmas act as guideposts for a brother and sister as they eagerly await Christmas morning. Soft-focus digital illustrations in vibrant hues reflect the season's coziness and industry. Those looking for an accessible book about secular celebration of Christmas will enjoy this warm-hearted offering." Horn Book

And then comes Halloween; illustrated by Holly Meade. Candlewick Press 2009 un il $16.99
Grades: PreK K 1 2   E
1. Autumn -- Fiction 2. Halloween -- Fiction
ISBN 978-0-7636-3659-3; 0-7636-3659-2

"When autumn arrives, a group of suburban children and their parents rake leaves, carve pumpkins, decorate yards and porches, and make Halloween costumes. The big day comes at last, and the children go trick-or-treating. . . . The descriptions beautifully evoke the feeling of fall. . . . The watercolor and collage art contributes to the autumnal mood, and the varied perspectives and page design make the story more dynamic. The text and illustrations are a perfect complement to one another." SLJ

And then comes summer; by Tom Brenner, illustrated by Jaime Kim. Candlewick Press 2017 32 p. color illustrations $16.99
Grades: PreK K 1 2   E
1. Summer -- Fiction
ISBN 076366071X; 9780763660710

In this book, by Tom Brenner, illustrated by Jaime Kim, "when the days stretch out like a slow yawn, and the cheerful faces of Johnny-jump-ups jump up . . . then it's time to get ready for summer! From flip-flops and hide-and-seek to fireworks and ice-cream trucks, from lemonade stands and late bedtimes to swimming in the lake and toasting marshmallows, there's something for everyone in this bright and buoyant celebration of the sunny season." (Publisher's note)

Brett, Jan
Cinders; a chicken Cinderella. Jan Brett. G.P. Putnam's Sons, an imprint of Penguin Group (USA) Inc. 2013 32 p.
Grades: K 1 2 3   E
1. Folklore 2. Fairy tales
ISBN 9780399257834
LC 2012048973

The **Easter** egg. G.P. Putnam's Sons 2010 un il $17.99
Grades: PreK K   E
1. Eggs -- Fiction 2. Easter -- Fiction 3. Rabbits -- Fiction 4. Contests -- Fiction
ISBN 978-0-399-25238-9; 0-399-25238-X
LC 2009-08234

Hoppi the bunny wants to win the egg-decorating contest so the Easter Bunny will choose him to help distribute Easter eggs, but instead, while everyone else is working on their decorations, he finds himself guarding an egg that has fallen from a robin's nest.

"Brett's large watercolors include a few visual puns . . . and lots of woodland detail. . . . A satisfying, gentle tale whose text and images can be enjoyed multiple times over." Booklist

Gingerbread friends; [by] Jan Brett. G.P. Putnam's Sons 2008 un il $17.99
Grades: PreK K 1 2   E
1. Cookies -- Fiction 2. Friendship -- Fiction
ISBN 978-0-399-25161-0; 0-399-25161-8
LC 2007042829

Lonely Gingerbread Baby, having set out to find a friend, enters a bakery where he tries to talk to different cookies and other figures, but winds up leading a crowd back to his house on a chase similar to the one in the familiar tale.

"Brett's highly detailed, luscious illustrations do a fine job telling this story for nonreaders, while readers and listeners will enjoy Gingerbread Baby's energy and enthusiasm." SLJ

★ The **hat**. Putnam 1997 un il $16.95
Grades: PreK K 1 2   E
1. Animals -- Fiction 2. Hedgehogs -- Fiction 3. Clothing and dress -- Fiction
ISBN 0-399-23101-3
LC 96-54015

When Lisa hangs her woolen clothes in the sun to air them out for winter, the hedgehog, to the amusement of the other animals, ends up wearing a stocking on his head

This story "has charm and humor. . . . The setting is the Danish countryside (detailed down to the moss on a tree) on a day when the first snow begins to fall, and Brett conveys the season with such loving spirit that children will almost wish for winter." Booklist

★ **Honey** . . . honey . . . lion! a story from Africa. G.P. Putnam's Sons 2005 un il $16.99
Grades: PreK K 1 2   E
1. Africa -- Fiction 2. Badgers -- Fiction 3. Honeyguides (Birds) -- Fiction
ISBN 0-399-24463-8
LC 2005-00449

After working together to obtain honey, the African honey badger always shares it with his partner, the honeyguide bird, until one day when the honey badger becomes greedy and his feathered friend decides to teach him a lesson.

"Brett has created another lush winner with beautifully detailed illustrations of the animals and a clear, fast-paced story." SLJ

On Noah's ark. Putnam 2003 un il $16.99
Grades: K 1 2 3   E
1. Biblical characters 2. Noah's ark -- Fiction
ISBN 0-399-24028-4
LC 2003-1281

Noah's granddaughter helps him bring the animals onto the ark, calm them down, and get them to sleep

"The words are basic and effective; it's the detailed watercolors of the animals that are the real attraction here. In precise brushstrokes and vivid colors, Brett creates incredibly textured feathers and fur." Booklist

The **turnip**; Jan Brett. G. P. Putnam's Sons, an Imprint of Penguin Group (USA) 2015 32 p. color illustrations $17.99
Grades: PreK K 1   E
1. Animals -- Fiction 2. Vegetables -- Fiction 3. Animals -- Fiction 4. Turnips -- Fiction
ISBN 0399170707; 9780399170706
LC 2015000708

In this children's story, by Jan Brett, "a badger family and their friends, Hedgie, Mr. Ram and Vanya, the horse, struggle to pull up a giant turnip. A cocky rooster steps in and pulls, sending him into the air, holding onto the turnip. No one knows that a mother bear in her underground den has kicked the turnip up through the soil to give the family room to sleep through the winter." (Publisher's note)

"Richly colored and lavishly detailed, the watercolor-and-gouache paintings on each page include large, central pictures framed by intricate decorative borders that incorporate small, turnip-shaped vignettes." Booklist

Brian, Janeen
I'm a dirty dinosaur; Janeen Brian. Kane Miller, A Division of EDC Pub. 2014 22 p. col. ill. (hardcover) $11.99

Grades: PreK K 1   **E**
1. Color 2. Dinosaurs -- Fiction
ISBN 1610672968; 9781610672962

LC 2013949620

In this children's book by Janeen Brian and Ann James "the prehistoric protagonist is drawn with magic pencil (which creates a thin
rainbow-hued line) and minimal detail. Slowly, through onomatopoetic,
brightly colored, rhyming text, he begins to color himself in with mud."
(School Library Journal)

"A buoyant dinosaur revels in the mud in this paper-over-board
story, first published in Australia. Brian's repeating rhymes take on the
cadence of a song—almost like a mud-themed version of the "Hokey
Pokey"—as the raptorlike dinosaur becomes increasingly muddy...Bri-
an's narrative lends itself to reading aloud, and it invites both chiming
in and imitating the dinosaur's movements (preferably sans mud). Better still, the sturdy pages are sufficiently coated for easy wiping off if
muddy fingers do happen to turn them." PW

Briant, Ed

If you lived here you'd be home by now. Roaring Brook Press 2009
un il $17.99
Grades: PreK K 1 2   **E**
1. Stories without words 2. Leaves -- Fiction 3. Animals -- Fiction
ISBN 978-1-59643-420-2; 1-59643-420-1

"Crisp colors and bold outlines make the illustrations sing, and tell
the story without any words. The linear time line is easy to follow." SLJ

Bridges, Shirin Yim

★ Mary Wrightly, so politely; by Shirin Bridges; illustrated by
Maria Monescillo. Houghton Mifflin Harcourt 2013 32 p. (reinforced)
$16.99
Grades: PreK K   **E**
1. Etiquette -- Fiction 2. Assertiveness (Psychology) -- Fiction
ISBN 9780547342481

LC 2012019633

"Every child will enjoy joining in on this book's irresistible refrain...
Understated and sunny." Kirkus

★ Ruby's wish; illustrated by Sophie Blackall. Chronicle Bks.
2002 un il $15.95
Grades: K 1 2 3   **E**
1. China -- Fiction 2. Sex role -- Fiction 3. Education -- Fiction
ISBN 0-8118-3490-5

LC 2001-7406

In China, at a time when few girls are taught to read or write, Ruby
dreams of going to the university with her brothers and male cousins

"This true story about Bridges' own grandmother has a gentle momentum.... Blackall's gouache illustrations have a quietly historical air,
their palette subtly shaded with smoky inks and highlighted with touches
of brilliant red." Bull Cent Child Books

The Umbrella Queen; illustrations by Taeeun Yoo. Greenwillow
Books 2008 un il $16.99; lib bdg $17.89
Grades: K 1 2 3   **E**
1. Painting -- Fiction 2. Thailand -- Fiction 3. Umbrellas and
parasols -- Fiction
ISBN 978-0-06-075040-4; 0-06-075040-5; 978-0-06-075041-1
lib bdg; 0-06-075041-3 lib bdg

LC 2005-35730

In a village in Thailand where everyone makes umbrellas, young
Noot dreams of painting the most beautiful one and leading the annual
parade as Umbrella Queen, but her unconventional designs, depicting
elephants instead of flowers and butterflies, displease her parents.

"Yoo's orange, green, and black colored linoleum prints wonderfully
establish the tone for the story, which is related through gracefully told
text." SLJ

Bridwell, Norman

★ Clifford, the big red dog board book; a board book. Norman
Bridwell. Scholastic 1997 32 p. $6.99
Grades: PreK K 1 2   **E**
1. Board books for children 2. Dogs -- Fiction
ISBN 0590341251; 9780590341257

"To celebrate Clifford's 35th anniversary, this durable board book
edition of the first Clifford storybook invites the youngest readers into
the happy world of the Big Red Dog and his friends." (Publisher's note)

Other titles in the Clifford the Big Red Dog series are:

Clifford takes a trip
Clifford's tricks
Clifford, the small red puppy
Clifford's riddles
Clifford at the circus
Clifford goes to Hollywood
Clifford's Christmas
Clifford's family
Clifford's kitten
Clifford and the grouchy neighbors
Clifford's good deeds
Clifford's pals
Count on Clifford
Clifford's Halloween
Clifford's manners
Clifford's birthday party
Clifford's puppy days
Where is Clifford?
Clifford gets a job
Clifford's word book
Clifford, we love you
Clifford's Thanksgiving visit
Clifford, the firehouse dog
Clifford's big book of stories
Clifford's first Christmas
Clifford's happy Easter
Clifford and the big storm
Clifford's first Halloween
Clifford's sports day
Clifford's first autumn
Clifford's first Valentine's Day
Clifford's spring clean-up
Clifford and the big parade
Clifford's first snow day
Clifford grows up
Clifford keeps cool
Clifford's first school day
Cooking with Cliford
Oops, Clifford
Clifford to the rescue
Clifford visits the hospital
Clifford's best friend
Clifford's happy Mother's Day
Clifford goes to dog school
Clifford's busy week
Clifford the champion
Clifford goes to kindergarten

Briggs, Raymond

★ The **snowman**. Random House 1978 un il $17; pa $6.99; bd bk $4.99

Grades: PreK K 1 2   **E**

1. Stories without words 2. Snow -- Fiction 3. Dreams -- Fiction

ISBN 0-394-83973-0; 0-394-88466-3 pa; 0-375-81067-6 bd bk

LC 78-55904

"The pastel-toned pencil-and-crayon pictures in their neat rectangular frames will hold the attention of primary 'readers.'" SLJ

Bright, Paul

The **not**-so-scary Snorklum; [illustrations by] Jane Chapman. Good Books 2011 un il $16.99

Grades: PreK K 1   **E**

1. Fear -- Fiction 2. Animals -- Fiction 3. Mythical animals -- Fiction

ISBN 978-1-56148-728-8; 1-56148-728-7

LC 2011007764

First published in the United Kingdom

As the scary Snorklum stomps home to his cave, he encounters a mole, a rabbit, and a badger, who see through his attempts to frighten them.

"Brisk and bright, yet subtle in its message." Kirkus

Brimner, Larry Dane

Trick or treat, Old Armadillo; illustrated by Dominic Catalano. Boyds Mills Press 2010 un il $16.95

Grades: K 1 2 3   **E**

1. Animals -- Fiction 2. Halloween -- Fiction 3. Armadillos -- Fiction 4. Spanish language -- Vocabulary

ISBN 978-1-59078-758-8; 1-59078-758-7

LC 2010004342

On Halloween, Old Armadillo sits inside his little house waiting for his friends to come trick-or-treating.

"Brimner infuses this tale with humor and Southwestern flavor. Spanish words are sprinkled throughout and defined in a glossary at the beginning of the book. . . . Catalano's dark pastel illustrations work well with the text." SLJ

Another title about Old Armadillo is:

Merry Christmas, Old Armadillo (1995)

Brisson, Pat

I remember Miss Perry; illustrated by Stéphane Jorisch. Dial Books for Young Readers 2006 un il $16.99

Grades: K 1 2 3   **E**

1. School stories 2. Death -- Fiction 3. Teachers -- Fiction 4. Bereavement -- Fiction

ISBN 0-8037-2981-2

LC 2004-24070

When his teacher, Miss Perry, is killed in a car accident, Stevie and his elementary school classmates take turns sharing memories of her, especially her fondest wish for each day.

"The delicate pen-and-ink, watercolor, and gouache illustrations reflect the varied emotions evoked by this treasured individual." SLJ

Broach, Elise

Barnyard baby; Elise Broach, illustrated by Cori Doerrfeld. Little Brown & Co 2013 14 p. col. ill. (Baby Seasons) $7.99

Grades: PreK   **E**

1. Barns -- Fiction 2. Autumn -- Fiction 3. Infants -- Fiction 4. Stories in rhyme 5. Lift-the-flap books 6. Toy and movable books

ISBN 0316212032; 9780316212038

LC 2012947193

In this children's book by Elise Broach and Cori Doerrfeld, readers join "baby during a day full of fall fun, from hayrides to apple picking. This interactive novelty board book features large lift-the-flaps on each spread, hiding . . . surprises underneath." (Publisher's note)

"The endearing rhymes scan well and read quickly, a great combination for keeping little ones interested." Kirkus

Gumption! with pictures by Richard Egielski. Atheneum Books for Young Readers 2010 un il $16.99

Grades: PreK K   **E**

1. Africa -- Fiction 2. Uncles -- Fiction 3. Animals -- Fiction 4. Jungles -- Fiction

ISBN 978-1-4169-1628-4; 1-4169-1628-8

LC 2008-49048

"Peter is thrilled when his uncle Nigel invites him on an expedition in search of a rare African gorilla, but making it through the jungle involves lots of challenges. Nigel leads the way, surmounting each obstacle . . . but Egielski's ink-and-watercolor illustrations show a parallel story. As Nigel charges ahead, Peter is swept along by a succession of wild animals. . . . Egielski plays up the comedy with clever, small details, and Broach's repetitive text, with its occasionally vocabulary, is well suited for dramatic read-alouds." Booklist

Brooks, Erik

Polar opposites; written and illustrated by Erik Brooks. Marshall Cavendish 2010 un il $16.99

Grades: PreK K 1   **E**

1. Opposites 2. Penguins -- Fiction 3. Polar bear -- Fiction

ISBN 978-0-7614-5685-8; 0-7614-5685-6

LC 2009005214

Ambrose, a polar bear, and Zina, a penguin, are very different but they can still find ways to meet in the middle

"The cheerful pencil, charcoal, and watercolor illustrations brim with energy and engaging details. . . . A natural for storytimes or as a lapsit." Booklist

Brosgol, Vera

★ **Leave** me alone; Vera Brosgol. Roaring Brook Press 2016 40 p. illustrations (chiefly color) (hardback) $17.99

Grades: PreK K 1 2   **E**

1. Knitting -- Fiction 2. Solitude -- Fiction 3. Grandmothers -- Fiction 4. Picture books

ISBN 1626724415; 9781626724419

LC 2016002024

Caldecott Honor Book (2017)

In this children's book by Vera Brosgol, "a grandmother shouts, 'LEAVE ME ALONE!' and leaves her tiny home and her very big family to journey to the moon and beyond to find peace and quiet to finish her knitting. Along the way, she encounters ravenous bears, obnoxious goats, and even hordes of aliens! But nothing stops grandma from accomplishing her goal--knitting sweaters for her many grandchildren to keep them warm and toasty for the coming winter." (Publisher's note)

"The fizzy collision of old-fashioned fairy tale elements with space-age physics is delightful, and even the most extroverted readers will recognize that sometimes you just need a little space." Pub Wkly

Brown, Alan

Love-a-duck; by Alan James Brown; illustrated by Francesca Chessa. Holiday House 2010 un il $16.95

Grades: PreK K 1 2   **E**

1. Toys -- Fiction 2. Baths -- Fiction 3. Ducks -- Fiction

ISBN 978-0-8234-2263-0; 0-8234-2263-1

After falling out of the window and spending an unforgettable day outdoors, a plastic duck is returned home safely, just in time for little Jane's bath.

"Cheerful, bright illustrations help relate this humorous escapade. Call-and-response portions of the book will engage young listeners." SLJ

Brown, Barbara

Hanukkah in Alaska; Barbara Brown; illustrated by Stacey Schuett. Henry Holt and Company 2013 32 p. (hardcover) $16.99

Grades: K 1 2 3   E

1. Picture books for children 2. Hanukkah -- Fiction 3. Moose -- Fiction 4. Alaska -- Fiction 5. Winter -- Fiction 6. Auroras -- Fiction 7. Jews -- United States -- Fiction

ISBN 0805097481; 9780805097481

LC 2013003166

In this children's picture book set in Alaska, a girl and her family want to watch the aurora borealis, or northern lights. Things are complicated by the fact that in their backyard, "a moose has taken up residence. . . . While beautiful, the moose can also be dangerous. Luring him away with apples and carrots does not work, but . . . a trail of latkes on the snow tempts the moose away from the swing," and the family can watch the lights on the last night of Hanukkah. (Kirkus Reviews)

Brown, Calef

Boy wonders. Atheneum Books for Young Readers 2011 un il $16.99

Grades: K 1 2   E

1. Stories in rhyme 2. Questions and answers

ISBN 978-1-4169-7877-0; 1-4169-7877-1

LC 2010020976

A young boy's questions lead to more and more questions, but there do not seem to be any answers.

"The connotations of everyday words and sayings are pondered and turned inside out and upside down in this wholly original paeon to intellectual curiosity. . . . The artist's trademark stylized illustrations, flat, hip, and jazzy, are rendered in a palette of predominantly blue/green/yellow acrylics." SLJ

Pirateria; the wonderful plunderful pirate emporium. written and illustrated by Calef Brown. Atheneum Books for Young Readers 2012 304 p. col. ill. (hardcover) $16.99

Grades: PreK K 1 2   E

1. Stories in rhyme 2. Pirates -- Fiction 3. Picture books for children 4. Stores, Retail -- Fiction

ISBN 141697878X; 9781416978787

LC 2011034023

This rhyming children's book "extols the virtues of the Pirateria," a "one-stop shop [that] carries everything from 'solid maple walking planks' to 'fresh lime quinine/to ward off the scurvy' to eye patches in colors such as 'plunder plum' and 'cannonball black.' However, Pirateria is more than just a store: it provides night classes in subjects such as chart reading, smuggling molasses, and spyglass making." (School Library Journal)

Brown, Heather

The **robot** book. Accord Pub. 2010 un il bd bk $16.99

Grades: PreK K   E

1. Board books for children 2. Robots -- Fiction

ISBN 978-0-7407-9725-5 bd bk; 0-7407-9725-5 bd bk

"'A robot is made of so many parts,' begins this modest board book with movable components. Each spread focuses on a specific feature of a humble red robot that looks very DIY. . . . It's an elegantly simple design with care paid to every detail." Publ Wkly

Brown, Jeff

★ **Flat** Stanley; by Jeff Brown; illustrated by Scott Nash. Harper-Collins Pubs. 2006 un il $16.99

Grades: K 1 2 3   E

ISBN 978-0-06-112904-9; 0-06-112904-6

LC 2006019547

Based on the original Flat Stanley by Jeff Brown c1964

A bulletin board falls on Stanley while he is sleeping, and he finds that being flat has its advantages

"Full-page, cartoon illustrations in watercolor and crayon enhance the story while remaining true to the original. This version of an old favorite will introduce a beloved character to a new generation of younger children." SLJ

Brown, Lisa

How to be. HarperCollins Pubs. 2006 un il $15.99

Grades: PreK K 1   E

1. Animals -- Fiction 2. Conduct of life -- Fiction

ISBN 0-06-054635-2

LC 2005-15147

"A girl and a younger boy take turns imitating different animals, including a bear, a snake, and a dog. . . . The final chapter, How to be a PERSON, shows both children embodying all the positive characteristics of the critters with the animals shadowing their actions. . . . The spare text matches the black-and-white drawings, supplemented with well-placed smatterings of bright paint." SLJ

Vampire boy's good night. Harper 2010 un il $16.99

Grades: PreK K 1 2   E

1. Witches -- Fiction 2. Vampires -- Fiction 3. Halloween -- Fiction

ISBN 978-0-06-114011-2; 0-06-114011-2

When Morgan, a young vampire, and his witchy friend Bela set out one night to see if human children really exist, they find themselves at a Halloween party.

"The use of speech balloons adds to the intimacy of Brown's detail-rich scenes, and the absence of parental figures contributes to an exultant mood. The lyrical, understated prose and clever outsider's perspective on the holiday might make this a new seasonal favorite." Publ Wkly

Brown, Marc

★ **In** New York; by Marc Brown. First edition Alfred A. Knopf 2014 40 p. (hardcover) $17.99

Grades: PreK K 1 2 3   E

1. New York (N.Y.)

ISBN 0375864547; 9780375864544; 9780375964541

LC 2013020158

In this book, author Marc Brown "shares his love for all that the city [of New York] has to offer and all that it stands for, including the way it's always changing and evolving. From its earliest days as New Amsterdam to the contemporary wonders of Central Park, the Statue of Liberty, and the Empire State Building, to the kid-appealing subway, High Line, and so much more, Marc's . . . text and . . . illustrations showcase what he's come to adore about New York." (Publisher's note)

"Just about all of Manhattan's child-pleasing sites get a place in Brown's stupendously detailed gouache and watercolor pictures showing a little boy and his father touring NYC. The text is minimal but inviting ("wherever you walk in New York, you'll see a great parade of people passing by"); endpapers offer additional vignettes and facts. Appended information includes phone numbers and websites for the highlights." Horn Book

Brown, Marc Tolon

Arthur's eyes; [by] Marc Brown. Little, Brown 1979 un il hardcover o.p. pa $6.99

Grades: PreK K 1 2   **E**
   1. Aardvark -- Fiction 2. Eyeglasses -- Fiction
   ISBN 0-316-11063-9; 0-316-11069-8 pa

LC 79-11734

His friends tease Arthur when he gets glasses, but he soon learns to wear them with pride.

★ **Arthur's** nose; 25th aniversary limited edition. [by] Marc Brown. Little, Brown and Company 2001 un il $15.95
Grades: PreK K 1 2   **E**
   1. Nose -- Fiction 2. Aardvark -- Fiction
   ISBN 0-316-11884-2

LC 00-106832

A reissue of the title first published 1976
Unhappy with his nose, Arthur the aardvark visits the rhinologist to get a new one. In this edition "Brown shows the evolution of his drawings of Arthur from 1976 to the present, along with a sidebar of 'Fun Facts,' . . . followed by a photo gallery of Brown's family with some pretty clear correlations between the author's relatives and Arthur's. Aspiring writers and artists also get a peek at the original manuscript and sketches for Arthur's Nose." Publ Wkly
   Arthur's nose

★ **D.W.** all wet; [by] Marc Brown. Little, Brown 1988 un il hardcover o.p. pa $5.95
Grades: PreK K 1 2   **E**
   1. Beaches -- Fiction 2. Aardvark -- Fiction 3. Siblings -- Fiction
   ISBN 0-316-11268-2; 0-316-11077-9 pa

LC 87-15752

"A simple, even predictable vignette, but entertaining nonetheless because of Brown's warm pictures." Booklist
   Other titles about D.W. are:
   D.W. flips (1987)
   D.W. go to your room! (1999)
   D.W. rides again (1993)
   D.W. the picky eater (1995)
   D.W. thinks big (1993)
   D.W.'s guide to perfect manners (2006)
   D.W.'s guide to preschool (2003)
   D.W.'s library card (2001)
   D.W.'s lost blankie (1998)

Brown, Margaret Wise

★ **Another** important book; pictures by Chris Raschka. HarperCollins Pubs. 1999 un il $15.99; lib bdg $16.89
Grades: PreK K 1   **E**
   1. Counting 2. Stories in rhyme 3. Growth -- Fiction
   ISBN 0-06-026282-6; 0-06-026283-4 lib bdg

LC 98-7212

Illustrations and simple rhyming text describe how a child grows from ages one through six.
"Raschka assigns each age group a geometric shape: a simple circle represents age one, pairs of stacked squares indicate two, a five-pointed star signifies five and so on. . . . It's a pleasure to hear the organic rhythms of Brown's prose . . . and Raschka paints in boisterous surprises." Publ Wkly

Big red barn; pictures by Felicia Bond. newly il ed; Harper & Row 1989 un il $16.99; lib bdg $17.89; bd bk $7.99
Grades: PreK K 1 2   **E**
   1. Stories in rhyme 2. Animals -- Fiction 3. Farm life -- Fiction
   ISBN 0-06-020748-5; 0-06-020749-3 lib bdg; 0-694-00624-6 bd bk

LC 85-45814

A newly illustrated edition of the title first published 1956
Rhymed text and illustrations introduce the many different animals that live in the big red barn
"The large illustrations are somewhat stylized, but still have a strong sense of detail and reality. The bright colors will attract young readers. The short text on each page is superimposed on the picture, but always in a way that is easy to read. Children will enjoy studying each of the pages as the day progresses from early morning to night." SLJ

A **Celebration** of the Seasons; Goodnight Songs. by Margaret Wise Brown. Sterling Pub Co Inc. 2015 36 p. $17.95
Grades: PreK K 1 2   **E**
   1. Children's songs 2. Seasons -- Fiction 3. Lullabies
   ISBN 145490447X; 9781454904472

This children's picture book, by Margaret Wise Brown, "celebrates the beauty and wonder of nature all year long. . . . From a little bear singing one morning in May to a soft snowfall, mysterious, deep, and glowing, each song is magical." (Publisher's note)
"Following 2014's Goodnight Songs (Sterling), this second volume of previously unpublished poems and songs by the legendary Brown is just as enchanting and handsomely produced as the first. Twelve poems about the seasons are brought to life through art and music. . . . As in the first book, an included CD features Tom Proutt and Emily Gary's musical renditions of each of Brown's songs. Their lilting folk harmonies, country- and jazz-infused rhythms, accompanied on various tracks by mandolin, accordion, tympani, bass clarinet, and harmonica, elevate the verses and offer listeners a more complete sensory experience. VERDICT Whether read or sung aloud, this essential collection is made to be shared—and no doubt will be, again and again." SLJ

A **child's** good morning book; illustrated by Karen Katz. newly illustrated ed.; HarperCollins 2009 un il $17.99; lib bdg $18.89
Grades: PreK   **E**
   1. Animals -- Fiction 2. Morning -- Fiction
   ISBN 978-0-06-128864-7; 0-06-128864-0; 978-0-06-128861-6 lib bdg; 0-06-128861-6 lib bdg

LC 2008000786

A newly illustrated edition of the title first published 1952
As the sun rises, birds, horses, rabbits, flowers, bugs, and finally children get up to start their day.
"Katz has reinterpreted the text in her warm and rounded style. . . . Brightly colored patterns and use of collage add interest to each page. This book has been popular over the years." SLJ

The **Dead** Bird; Margaret Wise Brown, illustrated by Christian Robinson. Harpercollins Childrens Books 2016 32 p. color illustrations (hardcover) $17.99
Grades: PreK K 1   **E**
   1. Children and death 2. Grief -- Fiction
   ISBN 9780060289317; 0060289317

In this children's story, by Margaret Wise Brown, illustrated by Christian Robinson, "one day, the children find a bird lying on its side with its eyes closed and no heartbeat. They are very sorry, so they decide to say good-bye. In the park, they dig a hole for the bird and cover it with warm sweet-ferns and flowers. Finally, they sing sweet songs to send the little bird on its way." (Publisher's note)
"The original text is timeless, and the modern, cheerful illustrations will help resurrect this classic for a new generation of readers." Booklist

Doctor Squash, the doll doctor; illustrated by David Hitch. Golden Books 2010 un il $17.99; lib bdg $20.99

Grades: PreK K 1   **E**

1. Dolls -- Fiction 2. Physicians -- Fiction

ISBN 978-0-375-84800-1; 0-375-84800-2; 978-0-375-95623-2 lib bdg; 0-375-95623-9 lib bdg

A revised and newly illustrated edition of the title first published 1952

"When dolls are sick or in pain, there's really only one doctor to call: the good Doctor Squash, who attends to their every need. . . . And when the doc falls ill, the dolls take care of him in return. . . . Playing doctor with dolls never falls out of style, and Hitch's retro style and modern toy updates work overtime to ensure that this book becomes a classic all over again. Entertaining and charming." Kirkus

★ The **fierce** yellow pumpkin; story by Margaret Wise Brown; pictures by Richard Egielski. HarperCollins Pubs. 2003 un il $15.99; lib bdg $16.89

Grades: PreK K 1   **E**

1. Pumpkin -- Fiction

ISBN 0-06-024479-8; 0-06-024481-X lib bdg

LC 2002-8338

A little pumpkin dreams of the day when he will be a big, fierce, yellow pumpkin who frightens away the field mice as the scarecrow does

"Egielski's artwork features subtle shadings and interesting juxtapositions of colors. . . . The story rolls along smoothly with a clear plot line and some nice phrasing." Booklist

★ **Goodnight** moon; by Margaret Wise Brown; pictures by Clement Hurd. rev ed; HarperCollins Publishers 2005 un il $17.99

Grades: PreK K   **E**

1. Stories in rhyme 2. Bedtime -- Fiction 3. Rabbits -- Fiction

ISBN 978-0-06-077585-8; 0-06-077585-8

LC 2005281602

A reissue of the title first published 1947

A little bunny bids goodnight to all the objects in his room before falling asleep

"Rhythmic, gently lulling words combined with warm and equally lulling pictures make this beloved classic an ideal bedtime book." Christ Sci Monit

Goodnight moon ABC; an alphabet book. based on the book by Margaret Wise Brown; pictures by Clement Hurd. Harper 2010 un il $16.99

Grades: PreK K   **E**

1. Alphabet 2. Bedtime -- Fiction

ISBN 978-0-06-189484-8; 0-06-189484-2

"Familiar objects in the classic story are arranged in alphabetical order and accompanied by upper and lowercase letters in the original style and palette. . . . Endpapers show the entire alphabet being investigated by two mice. The book conveys the timeless appeal of the original, and the literacy skill building will appeal to adults." SLJ

The **little** island; with illustrations by Leonard Weisgard. Doubleday Bks. for Young Readers 2003 un il $14.95

Grades: PreK K 1 2   **E**

1. Islands -- Fiction

ISBN 0-385-74640-7

A reissue of the title first published 1946 under the pseudonym Golden MacDonald

Awarded the Caldecott Medal, 1947

There was a little island in the ocean and his book is about how the seasons and the storm and the day and night changed it, how the lobsters and seals and gulls and everything else lived on it, and what the kitten who came to visit found out about it

The **little** scarecrow boy; pictures by David Diaz. newly il ed; HarperCollins Pubs. 1998 un il $15.99; lib bdg $16.89; pa $6.99

Grades: PreK K 1 2   **E**

1. Scarecrows -- Fiction

ISBN 0-06-026284-2; 0-06-026290-7 lib bdg; 0-06-77891-1 pa

LC 97-32558

Early one morning, a little scarecrow whose father warns him that he is not fierce enough to frighten a crow goes out into the cornfield alone

"Diaz provides wonderful illustrations for a story Brown wrote in the 1940s. . . . Brown's masterful use of repetition and rhythm creates a fine read-aloud story. The warm watercolor illustrations incorporate straw and patchwork." SLJ

North, South, East, West; Margaret Wise Brown, Greg Pizzoli; [edited by] Nanci Intelli. HarperCollins 2017 40 p. (hardcover) $17.99

Grades: PreK K 1 2   **E**

1. Birds -- Fiction 2. Birds -- Flight -- Fiction

ISBN 9780060262785

LC 2016936056

"It's time for a little bird to fly away to the north, the south, the east, and the west. Which direction will she like best? In a never-before-published story from beloved children's author Margaret Wise Brown, a little bird's first journey is brought to life by Geisel Award-winning illustrator Greg Pizzoli." (Publisher's note)

"A bittersweet ending makes this homecoming feel altogether real. Equal parts wistful and uplifting—a small triumph." Kirkus

★ The **runaway** bunny; pictures by Clement Hurd. HarperCollins Publishers 2005 un il $16.99; lib bdg $17.89

Grades: PreK K   **E**

1. Rabbits -- Fiction

ISBN 0-06-077582-3; 0-06-077583-1 lib bdg

A reissue, with some illustrations redrawn, of the title first published 1942

"The text has the simplicity of a folk tale and the illustrations are black and white or double page drawings in startling colour." Ont Libr Rev

Sleepy ABC; illustrated by Karen Katz. HarperCollinsPublishers 2010 un il $16.99; lib bdg $17.89

Grades: PreK   **E**

1. Alphabet 2. Stories in rhyme 3. Bedtime -- Fiction

ISBN 978-0-06-128863-0; 0-06-128863-2; 978-0-06-128865-4 lib bdg; 0-06-128865-9 lib bdg

LC 2008051781

Simple rhymes for each letter of the alphabet are illustrated with an array of toddlers and babies saying goodnight.

"Katz's interpretation of Brown's text . . . is joyful and energetic and features her trademark, round-faced, multicultural children, rendered in collage-like art. . . . Likely to be just what little not-yet-sleeping beauties will want." Booklist

★ **Two** little trains; pictures by Leo and Diane Dillon. HarperCollins Pubs. 2001 un il $15.95; lib bdg $15.89; pa $6.99

Grades: PreK K 1 2   **E**

1. Railroads -- Fiction

ISBN 0-06-028376-9; 0-06-028377-7 lib bdg; 0-06-443568-7 pa

LC 00-40798

A newly illustrated edition of the title first published 1949 by Scott

Two little trains, one streamlined, the other old-fashioned, puff, puff, puff, and chug, chug, chug, on their way West

"The rhythms, the word sounds and the resonant echo of folk song set up a veritable hypnotic chant. . . . [The] soft-grained paintings . . . are beautifully composed in both form and color. A handsome reinterpretation." Booklist

★ **Where** have you been? pictures by Leo and Diane Dillon. HarperCollins 2004 un il $15.99; lib bdg $16.89
Grades: PreK K 1   E
  1. Stories in rhyme 2. Animals -- Fiction
  ISBN 0-06-028378-5; 0-06-028379-3 lib bdg
                                                          LC 2003-49981
A newly illustrated edition of the title first published 1952 by Crowell
In rhyming verse, various animals tell where they have been.
"Children fond of call-and-response will enjoy this humorous nursery rhyme. ... The illustrations are as lively as they are charming, and have enough detail to keep children interested." SLJ

Brown, Monica
  Chavela and the Magic Bubble; illustrated by Magaly Morales. Clarion Books 2010 un il $16
Grades: K 1 2 3   E
  1. Magic -- Fiction 2. Chewing gum -- Fiction 3. Grandmothers -- Fiction 4. Mexican Americans -- Fiction
  ISBN 0-547-24197-6; 978-0-547-24197-5
                                                          LC 2009015819
When Chavela blows a bubble with a strange new gum, she floats away to Mexico, where her great-grandfather once worked harvesting the tree sap that makes gum chewy.
"Kids will want to chew their own bubblegum as they listen to this exciting, magical journey, handsomely illustrated in brilliantly colored double-page spreads." Booklist

  Lola Levine is not mean! by Monica Brown. Little, Brown & Co. 2015 96 p. illustrations (hc) $15
Grades: 1 2 3 4   E
  1. School stories 2. Teasing -- Fiction 3. Friendship -- Fiction 4. Schools -- Fiction 5. Teasing -- Fiction 6. Family life -- Fiction
  ISBN 9780316258364
                                                          LC 2014041416
"Lola is fierce on the field, but when a soccer game during recess gets too competitive, she accidentally hurts her classmate Juan Gomez. Now everyone is calling her Mean Lola Levine! Lola feels terrible, but with the help of her family, her super best friend, Josh Blot, and a little 'pencil power,' she just might be able to turn it all around." (Publisher's note)
"The appealing protagonist is energetic and enthusiastic, and her family is atypical. Her father, a ponytailed artist, works at home, and her mom writes for a newspaper. They celebrate both their Peruvian and Jewish roots and encourage the use of peaceful words." Booklist
Another title in this series is:
  Lola Levine drama queen (2016)

  Waiting for the BiblioBurro; illustrations by John Parra. Tricycle Press 2011 un il $16.99; lib bdg $19.99
Grades: PreK K 1   E
  1. Reading teachers 2. Colombia -- Fiction 3. Libraries -- Fiction 4. Elementary school teachers 5. Books and reading -- Fiction
  ISBN 978-1-58246-353-7; 1-58246-353-0; 978-1-58246-398-8 lib bdg; 1-58246-398-0 lib bdg
                                                          LC 2010024183
When a man brings to a remote village two burros, Alfa and Beto, loaded with books the children can borrow, Ana's excitement leads her to write a book of her own as she waits for the BiblioBurro to return. Includes glossary of Spanish terms and a note on the true story of Columbia's BiblioBurro and mobile libraries in other countries.
"Parra's naïve-styled acrylics brim with scenes of country life. A palette of salmon pinks and turquoise and sky blues, painted on board,

give the book a roughhewn, handmade quality and an innocent, childlike appeal." Publ Wkly

Brown, Peter
  ★ **Children** make terrible pets. Little, Brown 2010 un il $16.99
Grades: PreK K 1   E
  1. Pets -- Fiction 2. Bears -- Fiction
  ISBN 978-0-316-01548-6; 0-316-01548-2
                                                          LC 2010-04982
When Lucy, a young bear, discovers a boy lost in the woods, she asks her mother if she can have him as a pet, only to find him impossible to train. "Ages three to six." (N Y Times Book Rev)
"Appealing and humorous, with a lesson to boot!" SLJ
Another title about Lucy the bear is:
  You will be my friend! (2011)

  ★ The **curious** garden. Little, Brown 2009 un il
Grades: K 1 2 3   E
  1. Gardens -- Fiction 2. City and town life -- Fiction
  ISBN 0-316-01547-4; 978-0-316-01547-9
                                                          LC 2008029165
Liam discovers a hidden garden and with careful tending spreads color throughout the gray city.
This "is a quiet but stirring fable of urban renewal, sure to capture imaginations. ... In Brown's utopian vision, the urban and the pastoral mingle to joyfully harmonious effect." Publ Wkly

  ★ **Mr.** Tiger goes wild; written and illustrated by Peter Brown. Little Brown & Co 2013 48 p. ill. (reinforced) $18
Grades: PreK K 1 2   E
  1. Tigers -- Fiction 2. Picture books for children 3. Etiquette -- Fiction 4. CIty and town life -- Fiction
  ISBN 0316200638; 9780316200639
                                                          LC 2012048429
Boston Globe-Horn Book Award: Picture Book (2014)
"Mr. Tiger walks upright and wears a top hat and a handsome coat with a bow tie, fitting in with the rest of society. But his orange fur provides the only spot of color in the very drab, very proper community, and Mr. Tiger is bored: 'He wanted to loosen up. He wanted to be...wild.' And so, Mr. Tiger drops to all fours and for the first time looks happy. As he gets progressively wilder, roaring and shedding his confining clothes, the town animal-folk are appalled and banish him to the wilderness--which, he decides, is 'a magnificent idea.'" (Horn Book)

Brown, Peter, 1979-
  Chowder; [by] Peter Brown. Little, Brown 2006 un il $15.99
Grades: PreK K 1 2   E
  1. Dogs -- Fiction
  ISBN 978-0-316-01180-8; 0-316-01180-0
                                                          LC 2005035616
Chowder the bulldog has never fit in with the other neighborhood canines, but he sees a chance to make friends with the animals at the local petting zoo
"The tongue-in-cheek humor melds delightfully with Brown's distinctive acrylic-and-pencil artwork." Booklist
Another title about Chowder is:
  The fabulous bouncing Chowder (2007)

  ★ **My** teacher is a monster! (no, I am not) by Peter Brown. Little Brown & Co 2014 40 p. $18
Grades: PreK K 1 2   E
  1. Monsters -- Fiction 2. Teachers -- Fiction 3. Schools -- Fiction

4. Monsters -- Fiction 5. Teachers -- Fiction
ISBN 0316070297; 9780316070294

LC 2013016664

"A young boy named Bobby has the worst teacher. She's loud, she yells, and if you throw paper airplanes, she won't allow you to enjoy recess. She is a monster! Luckily, Bobby can go to his favorite spot in the park on weekends to play. Until one day . . . he finds his teacher there! Over the course of one day, Bobby learns that monsters are not always what they seem." (Publisher's note)

"Bobby's teacher, Ms. Kirby, is a roaring, teeth-gnashing, galumphing giant green monster. Really! (And it has nothing to do with her reaction to that paper airplane Bobby threw.)...This playful, eye-catching story goes a long way to humanize both teachers and students." Booklist

Brown, Ruth

★ A **dark,** dark tale; story and pictures by Ruth Brown. Dial Bks. for Young Readers 1981 un il hardcover o.p. pa $6.99
Grades: PreK K 1 2   E
1. Cats -- Fiction
ISBN 0-14-054621-9 pa
"The book's mysterious power is engendered by the illustrations of weed-choked gardens and abandoned, echoing halls, of mullioned windows and blowing curtains." Time

Gracie the lighthouse cat. Andersen Press USA 2011 un il $16.95
Grades: K 1 2 3   E
1. Cats -- Fiction 2. Storms -- Fiction 3. Shipwrecks -- Fiction 4. Lighthouses -- Fiction
ISBN 978-0-7613-7454-1; 0-7613-7454-X

LC 2010032950

"Gracie, a cat whose home is in a lighthouse, relaxes alongside her little kitten while in the background Grace, the lighthouse keeper's daughter, spots a ship in trouble on the rocks. The two stories about bravery during a raging storm in 1838 unfold simultaneously. Gracie's story is described in the text, while the human drama is portrayed primarily in the artwork. Attractive, painterly renditions of the treacherous sea as well as the emotional features on the faces of the animals will draw children into the suspenseful tale." SLJ

Brown, Stephanie Gwyn

Bang! Boom! Roar! a busy crew of dinosaurs. by Nate Evans and Stephanie Gwyn Brown; illustrated by Christopher Santoro. Harpercollins Childrens Books 2012 40 p. (trade bdg.) $15.99
Grades: PreK K 1   E
1. Alphabet -- Fiction 2. Picture books for children 3. Dinosaurs -- Fiction 4. Alphabet 5. Stories in rhyme 6. Building -- Fiction 7. Playgrounds -- Fiction 8. Construction workers -- Fiction
ISBN 0060879602; 9780060879600; 9780060879624

LC 2009005244

In this book by Nate Evans, "[a] teeming dino crew in hard hats and safety vests create organized if frenetic chaos on a mucky construction . . . [A] swarm of grimacing, toothy cartoon monsters convert a trash-filled empty lot into an urban playground. . . . Whether peeking out of a port-a-potty . . . [or] racing lumbering earth movers . . . the well-larded laborers are easily identifiable . . . [a]long with the aforementioned hidden alphabet." (Kirkus)

Brown, Tameka Fryer

Around our way on neighbors' day; illustrated by Charlotte Riley-Webb. Abrams 2010 un il $16.95
Grades: PreK K 1 2   E
1. African Americans -- Fiction 2. City and town life -- Fiction
ISBN 978-0-8109-8971-9; 0-8109-8971-9

"As an African American girl bounces around her urban neighborhood celebrating Neighbors' Day, when everyone comes together for celebration and community bonding, she shares her energetic and enthusiastic observations. . . . The acrylic art is saturated with rich color, energetic movement, and abstract figures and shapes, all reminiscent of Jacob Lawrence's art. Most scenes are double-page spreads that, together with the words, demonstrate the size and diversity of a joyful world." Booklist

My cold plum lemon pie bluesy mood; by Tameka Fryer Brown; illustrated by Shane Evans. Viking 2013 32 p. (hardcover) $16.99
Grades: PreK K   E
1. Stories in rhyme 2. African Americans -- Fiction 3. Mood (Psychology) -- Fiction
ISBN 9780670012855

LC 2012016781

"A boy describes each of the varying emotions he experiences in terms of color. Listening to music puts him in a purple kind of mood, while being evicted from the couch by his two bossy older brothers makes him feel gray. When his little sister asks him to draw a dragon, a gentle green feeling comes over him, which turns black when his siblings snatch the picture and tease: 'Awww-it's cwayon time.'" (School Library Journal)

"In a free-wheeling style and going far beyond the usual pairings of colors with moods, Jamie describes his day's emotional path. . . . This isn't the easiest scansion to read aloud, but it's worth it. Figurative and grounded--a nicely sophisticated exploration." Kirkus

Browne, Anthony

The **little** bear book; Anthony Browne. 1st Candlewick Press ed. Candlewick Press 2014 [22] p. col. ill. $15.99
Grades: PreK K   E
1. Bears -- Fiction 2. Drawing -- Fiction
ISBN 0763670073; 9780763670078
First published 1988

In this book, "[a] little white bear and his magic pencil make wonderful things happen. . . . As a bear strolls through the forest, he meets a lonely gorilla, a noisy crocodile, a lion, and even an elephant. They all look as if they are missing something, so the bear steps in to save the day, using his magic pencil to draw just what they are looking for." (Publisher's note)

"In this simple yet matter-of-factly bizarre picture book first published in the UK in 1988, Browne makes the surreal accessible. The text consists almost entirely of Bear's musings, which are reminiscent of a young child at play." Horn Book

Little Beauty. Candlewick Press 2008 un il $16.99
Grades: PreK K 1 2 3   E
1. Cats -- Fiction 2. Zoos -- Fiction 3. Gorillas -- Fiction 4. Sign language -- Fiction
ISBN 978-0-7636-3959-4; 0-7636-3959-1

LC 2007051887

When a gorilla who knows sign language tells his keepers that he is lonely, they bring him a small kitten and he names her Beauty

Browne "tells a picture-book story with exquisitely detailed art that blends magic and realism." Booklist

★ **Me** and you. Farrar Straus Giroux 2010 un il
Grades: PreK K 1 2 3   E
1. Fairy tales 2. Bears -- Fiction 3. Social classes -- Fiction
ISBN 0-374-34908-8; 978-0-374-34908-0
Original French edition 2009

In this retelling of "The Three Bears, Goldilocks is a modern-day have-not, while the three bears are haves; their stories unfold separately and receive distinct visual treatments. . . . Primary." (Horn Book) Originally published in France in 2009 under the title Une autre histoire.

This "is a work that's both playfully interpretive and interestingly thought-provoking at a youthful level, raising some easily discussable questions." Bull Cent Child Books

★ **My** brother; [by] Anthony Browne. Farrar, Straus & Giroux 2007 un il $16
Grades: PreK K 1   E
1. Brothers -- Fiction
ISBN 978-0-374-35120-5; 0-374-35120-1
LC 2006050262

"To the younger brother, the older one is coolness personified. . . . Browne . . . takes this universal theme of sibling idolatry and interprets it visually with economy and verve." Booklist

★ **My** dad. Farrar, Straus & Giroux 2001 un il $16
Grades: PreK K 1 2   E
1. Fathers -- Fiction
ISBN 0-374-35101-5
LC 00-37951

First published 2000 in the United Kingdom
A child describes the many wonderful things about "my dad," who can jump over the moon, swim like a fish, and be as warm as toast

"The offhand affection is genuinely moving as well as funny." Booklist

★ **My** mom. Farrar, Straus & Giroux 2005 un il $16; pa $6.95
Grades: PreK K 1 2   E
1. Mothers -- Fiction
ISBN 0-374-35098-1; 0-374-40026-1 pa
LC 2004-47173

A child describes the many wonderful things about "my mom," who can make anything grow, roar like a lion, and be as comfy as an armchair

"Browne's paintings hold attention, whether depicting images true to life or flights of fancy, and the honesty of the narrator's emotions and Mom's devotion shine through." Booklist

Piggybook. Knopf 1986 un il hardcover o.p. pa $7.99
Grades: PreK K 1 2   E
1. Mothers -- Fiction 2. Family life -- Fiction
ISBN 0-679-80837-X pa
LC 86-3008

When Mrs. Piggott unexpectedly leaves one day, her demanding family begins to realize just how much she did for them

"As in most of Browne's art, there is more than a touch of irony and visual humor here, bringing off the didactic with a light touch and turning the lesson into satire." Bull Cent Child Books

Silly Billy. Candlewick Press 2006 un il $15.99
Grades: PreK K 1 2   E
1. Dolls -- Fiction 2. Worry -- Fiction
ISBN 0-7636-3124-8
LC 2005-55305

To help with his anxiety, Billy uses the worry dolls his grandmother recommends, but he finds that they do not quite solve his problem.

"The pictures are amazing. In counterpoint to the monochromatic worry scenes are pictures so vivid and colorful they ease concern and spread cheer with each turn of the page." Booklist

★ **Voices** in the park. DK Ink 1998 un il hardcover o.p. pa $7.99

Grades: PreK K 1 2   E
1. Gorillas -- Fiction
ISBN 978-0-7894-8191-7 pa; 978-0-7894-2522-5
LC 97-48730

"A simple outing is described by two parents and two children, each with a different point of view and emotional outlook. Intriguing illustrations of the gorilla characters and surreal touches add layers of visual humor." SLJ

★ **What** if...? Anthony Browne. Candlewick Press 2014 32 p. $16.99
Grades: PreK K 1 2 3   E
1. Anxiety -- Fiction 2. Children's parties -- Fiction 3. Worry -- Fiction 4. Birthday parties -- Fiction
ISBN 0763674192; 9780763674199
LC 2013952843

This illustrated children's story, by Anthony Browne, the main character struggles with anxiety only to be reassured at the end. "What if Joe doesn't like the party he's going to? What if he doesn't like the food or the games or the people? As Joe and his mom walk down the darkening street, Joe's imagination starts to run wild." (Publisher's note)

"Young Joe is apprehensive about attending his friend Tom's evening birthday party. He lost the invitation, remembers the street name, but forgot the house number. His mother assures him they'll find Tom's home if they just walk along the street and look in windows...he common fear of dealing with a new situation is handled well, and Browne's treatment of the topic will have readers nodding with understanding." SLJ

Browning, Diane
★ **Signed,** Abiah Rose; written & illustrated by Diane Browning. Tricycle Press 2009 un il $15.99
Grades: 1 2 3   E
1. Artists -- Fiction 2. Sex role -- Fiction 3. Frontier and pioneer life -- Fiction
ISBN 978-1-58246-311-7; 1-58246-311-5
LC 2009-22172

In pioneer days, a young girl who is a talented artist is encouraged to paint portraits, Bible scenes, and other pictures, but told never to sign her work, either because it would be a sign of pride or because artists are expected to be men.

"In an engaging narrative, Abiah Rose tells of her experiences. . . . In Browning's pleasing colored-pencil-and-acrylic illustrations, the formal composition and decorative elements are reminiscent of folk art, while the softer, more natural depiction of the characters is all her own." Booklist

Broyles, Anne
Priscilla and the hollyhocks; [by] Anne Broyles; illustrated by Anna Alter. Charlesbridge 2008 un il $15.95
Grades: 2 3 4   E
1. Slavery -- Fiction 2. Native Americans -- Fiction 3. African Americans -- Fiction
ISBN 978-1-57091-675-5
LC 2007002281

A young African American girl is sold away from her mother as a slave, and then later is sold to a Cherokee Indian, but eventually she is bought by a white man who not only sets her free, but adopts her into his family of fifteen children. Based on a true story; includes instructions for making a hollyhock doll.

"Told in descriptive language accompanied by engaging acrylic paintings, this fictionalized story about a real child . . . offers a unique perspective on slavery." SLJ

Bruchac, Joseph

Crazy Horse's vision; illustrated by S.D. Nelson. Lee & Low Bks. 2000 un il pa $9.95

Grades: K 1 2 3   E

1. Indian chiefs 2. Oglala Indians -- Fiction
ISBN 9781584302827

LC 99-47451

This is "a fictionalized account of the early life of Lakota leader Crazy Horse. . . . Grades three to six." (Bull Cent Child Books)

"Bruchac has created a memorable tale about Crazy Horse's childhood. . . . In beautiful illustrations inspired by the ledger book style of the Plains Indians, Sioux artist Nelson fills the pages with both action and quiet drama." Booklist

Bruel, Nick

★ **Bad** Kitty; Nick Bruel. Roaring Brook Press 2005 1 v. (unpaged) $15.95

Grades: 2 3 4   E

1. Alphabet 2. Cats -- Fiction 3. Food -- Fiction 4. Behavior -- Fiction 5. English language -- Alphabet
ISBN 1596430699; 9781596430693; 1-59643-069-9; 978-1-59643-069-3

LC 2004024456

When a kitty discovers there is no cat food in the house, she decides to become very, very bad. (N Y Times Book Rev)

"After Kitty discovers that the only food in the house consists of 26 kinds of vegetables (asparagus, beets, cauliflower and on through zucchini), her mood turns blacker than her scraggly fur coat. She unleashes her own alphabet of woe that will have youngsters howling with laughter. . . . Even readers who've mastered their ABCs will laugh at Bruel's gleefully composed litanies and the can-you-top-this spirit that animates every page." Publ Wkly

Other Bad Kitty picture books are:
Poor Puppy and Bad Kitty (2007)
A Bad Kitty Christmas (2011)
Bad Kitty, scaredy-cat (2016)

A **Bad** Kitty Christmas. Roaring Brook Press 2011 un il $15.99

Grades: 2 3 4   E

1. Stories in rhyme 2. Cats -- Fiction 3. Christmas stories 4. Christmas -- Fiction
ISBN 978-1-59643-668-8; 1-59643-668-9

LC 2010037814

After destroying all of the gifts and decorations at home, Bad Kitty escapes from the car on Christmas Eve and finds a new friend, who helps her learn the true meaning of Christmas.

"Kitty's zany antics, three romps through the alphabet, and a warm reunion make this a gift indeed for Bad Kitty fans." Publ Wkly

Bad Kitty goes to the vet; Nick Bruel. Roaring Brook Press 2016 144 p. illustrations (hardback) $13.99

Grades: 2 3 4   E

1. Cats -- Fiction 2. Veterinarians -- Fiction 3. Humorous stories
ISBN 1596439777; 9781596439771

LC 2015014997

In this children's book by Nick Bruel "Kitty looks terrible and she is not eating. When she gets to the vet, she does her best to be bad, but the vet knows how to handle a bad kitty. After a short exam, the vet gives Kitty a shot that, she thinks, means the end—Kitty finds herself waking up in Puppy Paradise because of her poor treatment of dogs on Earth. She is sent back, however, with the warning that the choices she makes in her world can have serious consequences for eternity." (School Library Journal)

"Die-hard fans of this naughty feline will love this new story, and newcomers will be in for a treat. Even the most reluctant reader will have trouble putting this one down." SLJ

Little red bird; by Nick Bruel. Roaring Brook Press 2008 un il $16.95

Grades: PreK K 1 2   E

1. Stories in rhyme 2. Birds -- Fiction
ISBN 978-1-59643-339-7; 1-59643-339-6

LC 2007-13198

After escaping from her cage to see the world, a little red bird finds it difficult to decide whether to stay free or to go home and never fly again.

"The rhyming narrative, . . . is appealingly bouncy and will draw children through the small hero's exciting peregrinations until the final page, which hints at a satisfying conclusion while leaving room to wonder." Booklist

A **wonderful** year; Nick Bruel. Roaring Brook Press 2015 40 p. color illustrations (hardback) $17.99

Grades: PreK K 1   E

1. Year -- Fiction 2. Humorous fiction 3. Seasons -- Fiction 4. Humorous stories
ISBN 1596436115; 9781596436114

LC 2014009904

This children's book, by Nick Bruel, is a "comics-style look at the seasons. . . . A girl is excited to play in the snow. However, everyone reminds her to bundle up. Key characters seen again in later stories all pop in to suggest what to wear (the most obvious of her advisers being her mother and father, but a large purple hippo, a tree, a refrigerator and a can of beans weigh in as well). Alas, when she has finally put on all of the clothing, the weather has changed to spring." (Kirkus Reviews)

"Bruel takes readers on a walk through the seasons with a girl and her animal friends . . . The stylized cartoon illustrations are vividly colored and the panels are easy to follow. This clever, engaging introduction to visual storytelling will hold up through multiple readings." SLJ

Bruel, Robert O.

Bob and Otto; pictures by Nick Bruel. Roaring Brook Press 2007 un il $15.95

Grades: PreK K 1 2   E

1. Worms -- Fiction 2. Friendship -- Fiction 3. Butterflies -- Fiction 4. Caterpillars -- Fiction
ISBN 978-1-59643-203-1; 1-59643-203-9

LC 2006012008

Otto the worm is shocked to discover that his best friend Bob is actually a caterpillar who emerges one day as a butterfly.

"Along with the engaging story, the science in the illustrations and text is quite accurate; there are rich, not-to-be missed visual details." Horn Book

Bruins, David

The **legend** of Ninja Cowboy Bear; illustrated by Hilary Leuny. Kids Can Press 2009 un il $16.95

Grades: PreK K 1 2   E

1. Bears -- Fiction 2. Ninja -- Fiction 3. Cowhands -- Fiction
ISBN 978-1-55453-486-9; 1-55453-486-0

The ninja, the cowboy and the bear do everything together. But when a contest among themselves leads to resentment, they soon learn that the only way to stop disagreeing is to be considerate of their differences and appreciate one another.

"Readers can take the story a step further with the Ninja Cowboy Bear Game, which is strongly reminiscent of Rock Paper Scissors. The digital-cartoon illustrations are set in comic panels; the art and the occasional Japanese word bubble give the story an anime feel. A fun purchase with a solid message." SLJ

Other titles in this series are:

The way of the ninja (2010)

The call of the cowboy (2011)

Brun-Cosme, Nadine

★ **Big** Wolf & Little Wolf; illustrated by Olivier Tallec. Enchanted Lion Books 2009 un il $16.95

Grades: PreK K 1   E

1. Wolves -- Fiction 2. Loneliness -- Fiction

ISBN 978-1-5927-0084-4; 1-5927-0084-5

LC 2008054040

ALA ALSC Batchelder Award Honor Book (2010)

Big Wolf has always lived alone at the top of a hill under a tree, so when a little wolf suddenly arrives one day, he does not know what to think.

"Tallec's colorful illustrations play off the quiet dignity of the text, revealing emotion through the characters' stances and expressions, employing a sketchy painting style that brims with light." SLJ

Other titles about Big Wolf & Little Wolf are:

Big Wolf & Little Wolf, the little leaf that wouldn't fall (2009)

Big Wolf & Little Wolf, such a beautiful orange! (2011)

Brunhoff, Jean de

★ The **story** of Babar, the little elephant; translated from the French by Merle S. Haas. Random House 1937 47p il $15.95; lib bdg $17.99

Grades: PreK K 1 2   E

1. Elephants -- Fiction

ISBN 0-394-80575-5; 0-394-90575-X lib bdg

Original French edition, 1931; this is a reduced format version of the 1933 United States edition

"Babar runs away from the jungle and goes to live with an old lady in Paris, where he adapts quickly to French amenities. Later he returns to the jungle and becomes king. Much of the charm of the story is contributed by the author's gay pictures." Hodges. Books for Elem Sch Libr

Other titles about Babar are:

Babar and Father Christmas (1940)

Babar and his children (1938)

Babar the king (1935)

Bonjour, Babar (2000)

Travels of Babar (1934)

Bryant, Jennifer

Abe's fish; a boyhood tale of Abraham Lincoln. by Jen Bryant; illustrated by Amy June Bates. Sterling 2009 un il $15.95

Grades: PreK K 1 2   E

1. Lawyers 2. Presidents 3. State legislators 4. Members of Congress 5. Presidents -- United States -- Fiction

ISBN 978-1-4027-6252-9; 1-4027-6252-6

LC 2008028597

Young Abe Lincoln learns the meaning of selflessness and freedom when he encounters a soldier on a country road and gives up his prized possession: a fish he caught for the family's evening meal. Includes author's note on the early life of the sixteenth president.

"Bates's lively watercolors have rich detail, depicting Abe as a boy in a coonskin hat, still too small to lift his father's ax. The full-spread, sepia-toned paintings capture his rustic lifestyle, the Kentucky landscape, and the reactions of Abe's family to his generosity." SLJ

Includes bibliographical references

Buck, Nola

A **Christmas** goodnight; illustrated by Sarah Jane Wright. Katherine Tegen Books 2011 un il $12.99; lib bdg $13.89

Grades: PreK K   E

1. Stories in rhyme 2. Christmas stories 3. Bedtime -- Fiction 4. Christmas -- Fiction

ISBN 978-0-06-166491-5; 0-06-166491-X; 978-0-06-166492-2 lib bdg; 0-06-166492-8 lib bdg

Illustrations and rhyming text portray characters from the Nativity story, from doves in the stable to the wise men, as they go to sleep on Christmas Eve.

"The double-page-spread format makes this a fine read-aloud for a group of little ones, but it's also a cozy choice as a December bedtime story. A terrific introduction for preschoolers who are just learning about the Nativity story." Kirkus

Buckley, Michael

Kel Gilligan's daredevil stunt show; semiprofessional daredevil. pictures by Dan Santat; written by Michael Buckley. Abrams Books for Young Readers 2012 35 p. (alk. paper) $16.95

Grades: PreK K 1   E

1. Vegetables -- Fiction 2. Picture books for children 3. Toilet training -- Fiction 4. Humorous stories 5. Courage -- Fiction

ISBN 141970379X; 9781419703799

LC 2012001285

In his debut children's picture book, Michael Buckley tells the story of "a child who just loves danger. . . . [Protagonist Kel Gilligan] earnestly recollects his past triumphs in pictures designed to look like freeze frames of his life," discussing the times he successfully ate his broccoli and used the toilet. (School Library Journal)

Budnitz, Paul

The **hole** in the middle; illustrated by Aya Kakeda. Disney/Hyperion Books 2011 un il $16.99

Grades: PreK K 1   E

1. Friendship -- Fiction

ISBN 978-1-4231-3761-0; 1-4231-3761-2

LC 2010036236

Morgan was born with a big hole through his middle that gives him a strange, empty feeling all of the time, but when his good friend Yumi becomes ill, he finds that helping her makes him feel whole.

"The colorful, cheerful spreads depict all sorts of amusements and feature whimsical details that add to the brief text. . . . Focusing on the needs of others is a time-honored solution for those dissatisfied with their own lot in life; here is a motivating parable for contemporary kids." Kirkus

Buehner, Caralyn

Fanny's dream; pictures by Mark Buehner. Dial Bks. for Young Readers 1996 un il $16.99; pa $6.99

Grades: K 1 2 3   E

1. Marriage -- Fiction 2. Farm life -- Fiction

ISBN 0-8037-1496-3; 0-14-250060-7 pa

LC 94-31910

Fanny Agnes is a sturdy farm girl who dreams of marrying a prince, but when her fairy godmother doesn't show up, she decides on a local farmer instead

"Fanny Agnes is a delight: a feminist with a wry sense of humor, she balances her dreams with common sense and a loving heart. What's more, there's plenty for youngsters to enjoy in the robust, bucolic pictures, which seem almost to jump off the page." Booklist

Snowmen all year; pictures by Mark Buehner. Dial Books for Young Readers 2010 un il $16.99

Grades: PreK K 1 2   **E**
1. Stories in rhyme 2. Snow -- Fiction 3. Year -- Fiction
ISBN 978-0-8037-3383-1; 0-8037-3383-6

LC 2009-51658

A child imagines what it would be like if a snowman, made of magical snow, could be a companion throughout the year.

"Caralyn Buehner's rhyming text . . . sets the scene nicely, while Mark Buehner paints the scenery in gorgeously luminous oils and acrylics. With changing perspectives, places, and details that show off the illustrator's skill and imagination, every spread explodes with glee." SLJ

★ **Snowmen** at night; pictures by Mark Buehner. Phyllis Fogelman Bks. 2002 un il $15.99
Grades: PreK K 1 2   **E**
1. Stories in rhyme 2. Snow -- Fiction
ISBN 0-8037-2550-7

LC 2001-33517

Snowmen play games at night when no one is watching

The "text has bouncy rhymes, but it's the artwork that is spectacular. Acrylic-over-oil paintings feature fat, happy snowpeople who practically jump—or sled—off the pages." Booklist

Other titles about the snowmen are:
Snowmen at Christmas (2005)
Snowmen all year (2010)

★ **Superdog**; the heart of a hero. illustrated by Mark Buehner. HarperCollins 2004 un il $15.99; lib bdg $16.89
Grades: PreK K 1 2   **E**
1. Dogs -- Fiction
ISBN 0-06-623620-7; 0-06-623621-5 lib bdg

LC 2002-3540

Tired of being overlooked because he is so small, a big-hearted dog named Dexter transforms himself into a superhero

"Solid shapings, surprising perspectives, and thick paints in dynamic colors combine for artwork that practically jumps off the page. There's plenty of wit, too." Booklist

Buhler, Cynthia von
But who will bell the cats? Houghton Mifflin Books for Children 2009 un il $16
Grades: K 1 2   **E**
1. Bats -- Fiction 2. Cats -- Fiction 3. Mice -- Fiction 4. Princesses -- Fiction
ISBN 978-0-618-99718-3; 0-618-99718-0

LC 2008050165

While a princess spoils her eight cats, a mouse and his friend, a brown bat, live on scraps in the castle cellar, but Mouse decides to place bells on the cats necks so that he and Brown Bat might live comfortably, as well. Includes the Aesop fable on which the story is based.

"Dark, complicated mixed-media illustrations bring a humorously creepy feel to the tale." Horn Book

Buitrago, Jairo
★ **Jimmy** the greatest! Jairo Buitrago; Rafael Yockteng, illustrator; Elisa Amado, translator. Groundwood Books/House of Anansi Press 2012 48 p. ill. $18.95
Grades: K 1 2 3   **E**
1. Boxing -- Fiction 2. Poverty -- Fiction 3. Picture books for children
ISBN 1554981786; 9781554981786

In this book, "[w]ide-eyed Jimmy lives in a ramshackle, tin-roofed village, painted by [illustrator Rafael] Yockteng . . . . Jimmy finds out about Muhammad Ali from a boxful of old newspapers and, galvanized, starts training in the local gym. 'He wasn't thinking about what he didn't

have anymore. . . . He didn't need much stuff to run.' . . . But it's Jimmy's trainer, Don Apolinar, who leaves for the big city, while Jimmy stays behind; he ends up coaching kids at the gym." (Publishers Weekly)

Two White Rabbits; by Jairo Buitrago; illustrated by Rafael Yockteng; translated by Elisa Amado. Groundwood Books 2015 32 p. color illustrations $18.95
Grades: K 1 2 3 4   **E**
1. Immigrants -- Fiction 2. Migrant labor -- Fiction 3. Father-daughter relationship -- Fiction
ISBN 1554987415; 9781554987412

In this children's book, by Jairo Buitrago, illustrated by Rafael Yockteng, "a young child describes what it is like to be a migrant as she and her father travel north toward the U.S. border. They travel mostly on the roof of a train known as The Beast, but the little girl doesn't know where they are going. . . . [S]ometimes they are forced to stop and her father has to earn more money before they can continue their journey." (Publisher's note)

"Older readers will appreciate the allegory, and younger ones the simplicity of this spare immigration tale. The digital illustrations use saturated earth tones to render these anonymous people beautifully real." Booklist

Walk With Me; Jairo Buitrago, illustrated by Rafael Yockteng. Groundwood Books 2017 35 p. color illustrations $18.95
Grades: PreK K 1 2   **E**
1. Parents -- Fiction 2. Friendship -- Fiction 3. Imagination -- Fiction 4. Emotions in children -- Fiction
ISBN 1554988578; 9781554988570

In this children's book, by Jairo Buitrago, illustrated by Rafael Yockteng, a "girl conjures up an imaginary companion, a lion, who will come with her on the long walk home from school. He will help her to pick up her baby brother from daycare and shop at the store, . . . and he'll keep her company all along the way until she is safe at home. He will always come back when she needs him, unlike the father whom she sees only in a photograph." (Publisher's note)

Bulla, Clyde Robert
★ The **chalk** box kid; illustrated by Thomas B. Allen. Random House 1987 un il hardcover o.p. pa $3.99
Grades: K 1 2 3   **E**
1. Gardens -- Fiction 2. Artists -- Fiction 3. Imagination -- Fiction
ISBN 0-394-99102-8; 0-394-89102-3 pa

LC 87-4683

"Bulla manages a poignant depth within the confines of simple style and narrative. Understated and easy to read, this nevertheless tackles problems that are not easy to solve without exercising the imagination." Bull Cent Child Books

Bunting, Eve
Baby can; [by] Eve Bunting; illustrated by Maxie Chambliss. Boyds Mills Press 2007 un il $15.95
Grades: PreK   **E**
1. Growth -- Fiction 2. Infants -- Fiction 3. Brothers -- Fiction
ISBN 978-1-59078-322-1

LC 2006011485

Every time his family gets excited over something Baby James can do, big brother Brendan demonstrates that he can do even better, from burping to rolling over to walking

"The watercolor illustrations match the light touch of the spare text." Booklist

The **Banshee**; illustrated by Emily Arnold McCully. Clarion Books 2009 un il $16

Grades: K 1 2 3   **E**
1. Fear -- Fiction 2. Ireland -- Fiction 3. Family life -- Fiction 4. Superstition -- Fiction
ISBN 978-0-618-82162-4; 0-618-82162-7

LC 2008-14581

When Terry wakes up in the middle of the night to horrible screeching, he thinks the Banshee has come to pay his family a visit.

"This picture book creates a convincing story of bravery in the face of vividly imagined danger. Not a word is wasted in the first-person text, and the ink-and-watercolor illustrations show Terry's emotions with clarity and sensitivity." Booklist

Big Bear's big boat; by Eve Bunting; illustrated by Nancy Carpenter. Clarion Books 2013 32 p. (hardcover) $12.99
Grades: PreK K 1   **E**
1. Bears -- Fiction 2. Boats and boating -- Fiction 3. Bears -- Fiction 4. Boats and boating -- Fiction
ISBN 0618585370; 9780618585373

LC 2012003974

In this book by Eve Bunting "Big Bear outgrew his little boat, so he is building himself a big boat and can't wait till he's rowing, fishing, and relaxing in it. When his friends start suggesting improvements, Big Bear obligingly follows their advice. To his dismay, his big boat is turning out all wrong. It's because he hasn't followed his own dream, and he knows exactly how to fix it." (Publisher's note)

★ The **bones** of Fred McFee; illustrated by Kurt Cyrus. Harcourt 2002 un il hardcover o.p. pa $6
Grades: K 1 2 3   **E**
1. Stories in rhyme 2. Halloween -- Fiction
ISBN 0-15-202004-7; 0-15-205423-5 pa

LC 2001-2414

A toy skeleton at Halloween provides menace and mystery

"The story, told in rhyme keeps readers on the edge of their seats. . . . Cyrus's detailed, realistic illustrations, done in scratchboard and watercolor, are appropriately dark and are a perfect complement to the subtly scary mood of the text." SLJ

Butterfly house; illustrated by Greg Shed. Scholastic Press 1999 un il $17.99
Grades: K 1 2 3   **E**
1. Stories in rhyme 2. Butterflies -- Fiction 3. Grandfathers -- Fiction
ISBN 0-590-84884-4

LC 98-16349

With the help of her grandfather, a little girl makes a house for a larva and watches it develop before setting it free, and every summer after that butterflies come to visit her

"Shed's gouache-on-canvas paintings evoke feelings of warmth and nostalgia suited to the quiet story. Earth tones predominate, especially the browns and oranges found in this species. Appended with directions for raising a butterfly." Booklist

Cheyenne again; illustrated by Irving Toddy. Clarion Bks. 1995 un il $16; pa $5.95
Grades: K 1 2 3   **E**
1. School stories 2. Cheyenne Indians -- Fiction
ISBN 0-395-70364-6; 0-618-19465-7 pa

LC 94-43287

Young Bull, "a young Cheyenne boy tells how he's taken from his parents on the reservation in the late 1880s and sent to a boarding school, where he's forced to learn white ways. . . . This is a picture book for older readers, a grim story of painful separation and forced assimilation. . . . The short, spare lines of free verse are illustrated by double-page-

spread oil and acrylic paintings that contrast the open landscape with the stiffness of figures forced into uniform and regimentation." Booklist

Christmas cricket; illustrated by Timothy Bush. Clarion Bks. 2002 32p il $15
Grades: K 1 2 3   **E**
1. Crickets -- Fiction 2. Christmas -- Fiction
ISBN 0-618-06554-7

LC 2001-55266

On Christmas Eve, a little cricket finds its way into a house where its singing is thought to be the voice of an angel

"Bush's watercolor pictures celebrate the story's cheerful warmth while their varying sizes and shapes create a cinematic effect that cleverly captures both the rhythm of the text and a cricket's kinetic spirit." Booklist

★ **Flower** garden; written by Eve Bunting; illustrated by Kathryn Hewitt. Harcourt Brace & Co. 1994 un il $16; pa $7; bd bk $10.95
Grades: K 1 2 3   **E**
1. Stories in rhyme 2. Flowers -- Fiction 3. Birthdays -- Fiction
ISBN 0-15-228776-0; 0-15-202372-0 pa; 0-15-206516-4 bd bk

LC 92-25766

"The simple rhymed verse, which skips along in pace with the child's anticipation, is smoothly integrated with the vibrant, lifelike paintings." Booklist

★ **Fly** away home; illustrated by Ronald Himler. Clarion Bks. 1991 32p il $16; pa $6.99
Grades: K 1 2 3   **E**
1. Airports -- Fiction 2. Homeless persons -- Fiction
ISBN 0-395-55962-6; 0-395-66415-2 pa

LC 90-42353

A homeless boy who lives in an airport with his father, moving from terminal to terminal and trying not to be noticed, is given hope when he sees a trapped bird find its freedom

"Himler's quiet paintings echo the economy and the touching quality of the story, which is all the more effective in depicting the plight of the homeless because it is so low-keyed." Bull Cent Child Books

Frog and friends; written by Eve Bunting; illustrated by Josee Masse. Sleeping Bear Press 2011 37p il (I am a reader!)
Grades: 1 2   **E**
1. Frogs -- Fiction 2. Ponds -- Fiction 3. Animals -- Fiction 4. Friendship -- Fiction
ISBN 1-58536-548-3; 1-58536-689-7 pa; 978-1-58536-548-7; 978-1-58536-689-7 pa

LC 2010053706

Frog and his friends are alarmed by a strange object that appears on his pond, share a thoughtful—if scratchy—gift, and meet a hippopotamus that has run away from the zoo.

"This clever beginning reader is divided into three chapters. . . . Repetition, white space, and a large font help prepare children for tackling a smattering of more challenging vocabulary. Bright cartoon illustrations provide some picture clues. Readers will enjoy feeling superior to Frog and his friends." SLJ

Girls A to Z; illustrated by Suzanne Bloom. Boyds Mills Press 2002 un il $15.95
Grades: PreK K 1 2   **E**
1. Alphabet 2. Occupations
ISBN 1-56397-147-X

Girls with names ranging from Aliki to Zoe imagine themselves in various fun and creative professions

"Bunting has created a winning alphabet book that is playful, inventive, and (coincidentally) politically correct. Accompanied by Bloom's exuberant watercolor portraits." SLJ

★ **Have** you seen my new blue socks? by Eve Bunting; illustrated by Sergio Ruzzier. Clarion Books 2013 32 p. (hardcover) $16.99
Grades: PreK K 1   E
1. Stories in rhyme 2. Ducks -- Fiction 3. Lost and found possessions -- Fiction 4. Socks -- Fiction 5. Animals -- Fiction
ISBN 0547752679; 9780547752679
LC 2012012192
This rhyming children's book, by Eve Bunting, illustrated by Sergio Ruzzier, "spin[s] the tale of a small duck who waddles through the countryside, forlornly searching for his blue socks. . . . Finally, a sharp-eyed peacock sees a bit of blue peeking out of duck's lace-up shoes and the mini-mystery is solved!" (Publisher's note)

Hey diddle diddle; illustrated by Mary Ann Fraser. Boyds Mills Press 2011 un il $16.95
Grades: PreK K   E
1. Stories in rhyme 2. Animals -- Fiction 3. Musicians -- Fiction
ISBN 978-1-59078-768-7; 1-59078-768-4
In this variation on the traditional nursery rhyme, the cat plays the fiddle, the cow plays the silver trombone, and other animals play other musical instruments and join in a band, which is revealed in the end to be a music box wound by a small child.
"Pure whimsy . . . is what [Bunting] delivers here. . . . Fraser's accompanying artwork is cheery and saturated, the colors running from cool to hot. . . . The music made here will be in a sing-along read-aloud, with accompanying guffaws to mark the time." Kirkus

★ **How** many days to America? a Thanksgiving story. illustrated by Beth Peck. Clarion Bks. 1988 un il lib bdg $16; pa $5.95
Grades: K 1 2 3   E
1. Refugees -- Fiction 2. Thanksgiving Day -- Fiction
ISBN 0-89919-521-0 lib bdg; 0-395-54777-6 pa
LC 88-2590
Refugees from an unnamed Caribbean island embark on a dangerous boat trip to America where they have a special reason to celebrate Thanksgiving
"Bunting's simple tale focuses on the hardships of the journey and on the American ideals of freedom and safety. She wisely leaves aside the issues of politics in the homeland or in this country. Her prose is poetically spare. . . . Peck's richly colored crayon drawings yield added enjoyment. . . . A poignant story and a thought-provoking discussion starter." SLJ

Jin Woo; illustrated by Chris K. Soentpiet. Clarion Bks. 2001 30p il $16
Grades: K 1 2 3   E
1. Adoption -- Fiction 2. Brothers -- Fiction 3. Korean Americans -- Fiction
ISBN 0-395-93872-4
LC 00-38408
Davey is dubious about having a new adopted brother from Korea, but when he finds out that his parents still love him, he decides that having a baby brother will be fine
"Soentpiet's watercolors are suffused with light and perfectly capture the characters' expressions. . . . The story's emotional veracity will speak to any new sibling." SLJ

The **memory** string; pictures by Ted Rand. Clarion Bks. 2000 32p il $15

Grades: K 1 2 3   E
1. Memory -- Fiction 2. Stepmothers -- Fiction
ISBN 0-395-86146-2
LC 99-42771
While still grieving for her mother and unable to accept her stepmother, Laura clings to the memories represented by forty-three buttons on a string
"Rand's realistic artwork concentrates on the faces of the family and the emotions that cross them. Some children will find this touches them very deeply." Booklist

Mr. Goat's valentine; Eve Bunting; illustrated by Kevin Zimmer. Sleeping Bear Press 2016 32 p. color illustratios $16.99
Grades: K 1 2   E
1. Gifts -- Fiction 2. Goats -- Fiction 3. Valentine's Day -- Fiction
ISBN 9781585369447; 1585369446
LC 2015027634
In this children's book, by Eve Bunting and illustrated by Kevin Zimmer, "after reading in the newspaper that it's Valentine's Day, Mr. Goat sets out in search of very special gifts for his first love. But just what would a goat choose as the perfect gifts to show how he feels? Readers will be in for a surprise at Mr. Goat's nontraditional selections." (Publisher's note)
"Zimmer's large, vibrant cartoonlike illustrations complement the story and its characters. Readers will be drawn to their eyes, which are sizable and full of expression." SLJ

My dog Jack is fat; illustrated by Michael Rex. Marshall Cavendish Children 2011 un il $16.99
Grades: PreK K 1   E
1. Dogs -- Fiction 2. Weight loss -- Fiction
ISBN 978-0-7614-5809-8; 0-7614-5809-3
LC 2010018271
Carson does his best to help his dog, Jack, lose weight, with unexpected results.
"This appealing take on a common problem has understated, smooth writing and colorful, digitally rendered cartoons enlivened by Rex's characteristic humor." SLJ

One candle; illustrated by K. Wendy Popp. HarperCollins Pubs. 2002 un il hardcover o.p. pa $6.99
Grades: K 1 2 3   E
1. Jews -- Fiction 2. Hanukkah -- Fiction 3. Holocaust, 1933-1945 -- Fiction
ISBN 0-06-028115-4; 0-06-028116-2 lib bdg; 0-06-008560-6 pa
LC 2001-47205
Every year a family celebrates Hanukkah by retelling the story of how Grandma and her sister managed to mark the day while in a German concentration camp
"Popp invests her art with all the emotion of Bunting's heartfelt text. . . . A gentle but forthright opening for discussion about the Holocaust." Booklist

★ **One** green apple; illustrated by Ted Lewin. Clarion Books 2006 un il $16
Grades: K 1 2 3   E
1. School stories 2. Apples -- Fiction 3. Muslims -- Fiction 4. Immigrants -- Fiction
ISBN 0-618-43477-1
LC 2005011378
While on a school field trip to an orchard to make cider, a young immigrant named Farah gains self-confidence when the green apple she picks perfectly complements the other students' red apples

"Young readers will respond as much to Bunting's fine first-person narrative as to Lewin's double-page, photorealistic watercolors." Booklist

Our library; by Eve Bunting; illustrated by Maggie Smith. Clarion Books 2008 32p il $16
Grades: K 1 2   E
   1. Animals -- Fiction 2. Raccoons -- Fiction 3. Libraries -- Fiction 4. Books and reading -- Fiction
   ISBN 978-0-618-49458-3; 0-618-49458-8
                          LC 2006009519
   A raccoon and his friends go to great lengths to make sure they will always have a library from which to borrow books.
   "Bunting's style has a graceful simplicity, descriptive enough to be evocative without overwhelming. . . . Smith's watercolor and acrylic illustrations are charming and should have most children longing to enter the buttercup-yellow library with the grass-green door. An excellent vehicle for discussing the importance of libraries, books, reading, and teamwork." SLJ

Pirate boy; illustrated by Julie Fortenberry. Holiday House 2011 un il $16.95
Grades: PreK K   E
   1. Pirates -- Fiction 2. Imagination -- Fiction 3. Mother-son relationship -- Fiction
   ISBN 978-0-8234-2321-7; 0-8234-2321-2
                          LC 2010029446
   As Colin imagines himself in a series of adventures beginning with joining a pirate crew, his mother assures him that she will always be there to help if he needs her.
   "Layers of color and heavily worked figures give Fortenberry's . . . digital art a thick, substantial feel. . . . The book reads like a conversation Bunting . . . might once have had with one of her own children; it's a warmhearted portrait of an endlessly patient parent, ready to help her child work through his fears and desires." Publ Wkly

★ **Pop's** bridge; written by Eve Bunting; illustrated by C. F. Payne. Harcourt, Inc. 2006 un il $17
Grades: 1 2 3 4   E
   1. Fathers -- Fiction 2. San Francisco (Calif.) -- Fiction 3. Golden Gate Bridge (San Francisco, Calif.) -- Fiction
   ISBN 0-15-204773-5
                          LC 2004-23774
   Robert and his friend Charlie are proud of their fathers, who are working on the construction of San Francisco's Golden Gate Bridge.
   "Distinguished by its lovely, understated text and Payne's lavish and affectionate mixed-media pictures, this picture book does a quietly successful job of humanizing one of the most important feats of civil engineering in American history." Booklist

★ **Smoky** night; written by Eve Bunting; illustrated by David Diaz. Harcourt Brace & Co. 1994 un il $17; pa $7
Grades: K 1 2 3   E
   1. Riots -- Fiction 2. Korean Americans -- Fiction 3. African Americans -- Fiction 4. Los Angeles (Calif.) -- Fiction
   ISBN 0-15-269954-6; 0-15-201884-0 pa
                          LC 93-14885
   Awarded the Caldecott Medal, 1995
   When the Los Angeles riots break out in the streets of their neighborhood, Daniel and his mother, African Americans, make friends with Mrs. Kim, a Korean grocer from across the street
   "Thick black lines border vibrant acrylic paintings. . . . Diaz places these dynamic paintings on collages of real objects that, for the most part, reinforce the narrative action. . . . Both author and illustrator insist on a headlong confrontation with the issue of rapport between different races, and the result is a memorable, thought-provoking book." Horn Book

So far from the sea; illustrated by Chris K. Soentpiet. Clarion Bks. 1998 30p il $16; pa $7.99
Grades: K 1 2 3   E
   1. Japanese Americans -- Evacuation and relocation, 1942-1945 -- Fiction
   ISBN 0-395-72095-8; 0-547-23752-9 pa
                          LC 97-28176
   When seven-year-old Laura and her family visit Grandfather's grave at the Manzanar War Relocation Center, the Japanese American child leaves behind a special symbol
   "Soentpiet's impressionistic watercolors perfectly complement Bunting's evocative text." SLJ

That's what leprechauns do; illustrated by Emily Arnold McCully. Clarion Books 2005 32p il $16
Grades: K 1 2 3   E
   1. Ireland -- Fiction 2. Leprechauns -- Fiction
   ISBN 0-618-35410-7
   When leprechauns Ari, Boo, and Col need to place the pot of gold at the end of the rainbow, they cannot help getting into mischief along the way.
   "McCully graces this lighthearted story with her characteristically expressive and charming watercolors that eloquently capture the verdant beauty of the Irish countryside and the irrepressible personalities." SLJ

★ **Tweak,** tweak; illustrated by Sergio Ruzzier. Clarion Books 2011 40p il $14.99
Grades: PreK K 1   E
   1. Elephants -- Fiction 2. Mother-child relationship -- Fiction
   ISBN 978-0-618-99851-7; 0-618-99851-9
                          LC 2010024651
   While out for a walk, Mama Elephant answers her child's questions about a monkey, a frog, a songbird, a butterfly, and a crocodile, all the while teaching about Little Elephant too.
   "Young children will enjoy following Little Elephant's fantasies, depicted in the uncluttered, double-page spreads, all the way to the story's climax, which celebrates what Little Elephant really is, as well as the big, strong creature she will grow up to be. Along with imaginative silliness, the nuturing parent-child tenderness is the core of the story." Booklist

Walking to school; by Eve Bunting; illustrated by Michael Dooling. Clarion Books 2008 32p il $16
Grades: 2 3 4   E
   1. Prejudices -- Fiction 2. Belfast (Northern Ireland) -- Fiction
   ISBN 978-0-618-26144-4; 0-618-26144-3
   "The book does an excellent job of presenting the situation from a child's perspective without demonizing either side. . . . Dooling's oil-on-canvas illustrations are realistic enough to resemble stills from documentary footage." SLJ

★ The **Wall**; illustrated by Ronald Himler. Clarion Bks. 1990 un il $16; pa $5.95
Grades: K 1 2 3   E
   1. Vietnam Veterans Memorial (Washington, D.C.) -- Fiction
   ISBN 0-395-51588-2; 0-395-62977-2 pa
                          LC 89-17429
   "A father and his young son come to the Vietnam Veterans Memorial to find the name of the grandfather the boy never knew. This moving account is beautifully told from a young child's point of view; the

watercolors capture the impressive mass of the wall of names as well as the poignant reactions of the people who visit there." Horn Book Guide

Washday; by Eve Bunting; illustrated by Brad Sneed. Holiday House 2014 32 p. (hardcover) $16.95

Grades: K 1 2 3   E

1. Laundry -- Fiction 2. Grandmothers -- Fiction 3. Frontier and pioneer life -- Fiction

ISBN 0823428680; 9780823428687

LC 2012040347

"Lizzie helps her grandma on washday and gets rewarded with a tea party in this historical story celebrating family tradition and hard work," written by Eve Bunting and illustrated by Brad Sneed. (Publisher's note)

"Historical details like hairstyles and sturdy black shoes combine with phrases like 'Grandma's dog...has the misery in his back' to make the story feel genuine. An appealing snapshot of rough-hewn life that might well make kids appreciate washing machines." Kirkus

The **Wednesday** surprise; illustrated by Donald Carrick. Clarion Bks. 1989 un il lib bdg $16; pa $5.95

Grades: K 1 2 3   E

1. Reading -- Fiction 2. Grandmothers -- Fiction

ISBN 0-89919-721-3 lib bdg; 0-395-54776-8 pa

LC 88-12117

"Bunting's writing is simple and warm and direct. . . . Carrick's pictures echo the warmth, especially in the faces of the family, painted in realistically detailed watercolors with a careful attention to familial resemblance. A gentle charmer." Bull Cent Child Books

Will it be a baby brother? illustrated by Beth Spiegel. Boyd Mills Press 2010 un il $16.95

Grades: PreK K   E

1. Infants -- Fiction 2. Siblings -- Fiction

ISBN 978-1-59078-439-6; 1-59078-439-1

A little boy is certain that his expectant mother will give birth to a baby brother.

"The large, bright, watercolor-and-ink cartoon-style pictures skillfully convey the boy's feelings. . . . This warm, reassuring story is about a child's fear of displacement as much as his longing for a sibling just like him." Booklist

Yard sale; Eve Bunting, illustrated by Lauren Castillo. Candlewick Press 2015 32 p. color illustrations $15.99

Grades: PreK K 1   E

1. Garage sales -- Fiction 2. Moving -- Fiction

ISBN 9780763665425; 0763665428

LC 2014939360

In this children's book, by Eve Bunting, "[a]lmost everything Callie's family owns is spread out in their front yard—their furniture, their potted flowers, even Callie's bike. They can't stay in this house, so they're moving to an apartment in the city. The new place is 'small but nice,' Mom says, and most of their things won't fit, so today they are having a yard sale. But it's kind of hard to watch people buy your stuff, even if you understand why it has to happen." (Publisher's note)

You were loved before you were born; [by] Eve Bunting & [illustrated by] Karen Barbour. Blue Sky Press 2008 un il $16.99

Grades: PreK   E

1. Love -- Fiction 2. Family life -- Fiction

ISBN 978-0-439-04061-7; 0-439-04061-2

LC 2007-9703

A mother shares with her child all the ways in which family members and friends were loving and welcoming before the child was even born

"A marvelous integration of color, image and verbal rhythm sure to delight and to become a must-purchase for newborns and their parents." Kirkus

Burell, Sarah

Diamond Jim Dandy and the sheriff; illustrated by Bryan Langdo. Sterling Pub. 2010 un il $14.95

Grades: K 1 2   E

1. Infants -- Fiction 2. West (U.S.) -- Fiction 3. Rattlesnakes -- Fiction

ISBN 978-1-4027-5737-2; 1-4027-5737-9

LC 2008013767

When a friendly and talented rattlesnake slithers into Dustpan, Texas, he must prove his value to the residents of the town before the sheriff will allow him to stay.

"This charming tale has bright, appealing, kid-friendly illustrations. The lively dialogue combined with the satisfying ending will serve as an excellent storytime read-aloud." SLJ

Burgess, Mark

Where teddy bears come from; written by Mark Burgess; illustrated by Russell Ayto. Peachtree 2009 un il $16.95

Grades: PreK K 1 2   E

1. Wolves -- Fiction 2. Teddy bears -- Fiction

ISBN 978-1-56145-487-7; 1-56145-487-7

LC 2008052705

When Little Wolf cannot fall asleep, he decides that he needs a teddy bear and goes into the woods to see if he can find out where to get one.

"This charming story plays with the conventions of familiar nursery tales. . . . With its lively, bold watercolors filled with humorous details, this tale is likely to be a storytime hit." SLJ

Burkert, Rand

★ **Mouse** & Lion; [by] Aesop; retold by Rand Burkert; picutres by Nancy Ekholm Burkert. Michael di Capua Books 2011 un il $17.95

Grades: 2 3 4 5 6   E

1. Fables 2. Mice -- Fiction 3. Lions -- Fiction 4. Africa -- Fiction

ISBN 978-0-545-10147-9; 0-545-10147-6

This is "a book rich with [Nancy Ekholm Burkert's] signature meticulous brush lines, compelling display of color, and carefully delineated detail. Each page offers dramatic delight that extends the story. In an unusual but fascinating variation on the Aesop tale, Rand Burkert places Mouse at center stage. . . . The illustrations for this spirited tale are nothing less than spectacular. . . . Choosing the Aha Hills (between Botswana and Namibia) for her setting, the artist imbues the scenes with the fauna and flora of this region." SLJ

Burleigh, Robert

Clang-clang! Beep-beep! listen to the city. illustrated by Beppe Giacobbe. Simon & Schuster Books for Young Readers 2009 un il $14.99

Grades: PreK K 1   E

1. Stories in rhyme 2. Noise -- Fiction 3. Sound -- Fiction 4. City and town life -- Fiction

ISBN 978-1-4169-4052-4; 1-4169-4052-9

LC 2007-45844

From morning until night, a city is filled with such sounds as the roars and snores of a subway ride, the flutters and coos of pigeons, and the shouts and beeps of drivers in traffic

"The rhymes that accompany the story are short but evocative. . . . The artist uses a vivid mix of primary and secondary colors to set the stage." SLJ

Good-bye, Sheepie; illustrated by Peter Catalanotto. Marshall Cavendish 2010 un il $16.99
Grades: K 1 2   E
  1. Dogs -- Fiction 2. Death -- Fiction 3. Father-son relationship -- Fiction
  ISBN 978-0-7614-5598-1; 0-7614-5598-1

LC 2009-5955

A father teaches his young son about death and remembrance as he buries their beloved dog.

"Catalanotto's gentle watercolor-and-gouache paintings give off a yellow glow suggestive of warm sunshine on an autumn day, and are well suited to Burleigh's quiet text." Booklist

Zoom, zoom; sounds of things that go in the city. Robert Burleigh; illustrated by Tad Carpenter. Simon & Schuster Books for Young Readers 2014 32 p. color illustrations (hardcover) $16.99
Grades: PreK K 1   E
  1. Noise -- Fiction 2. Stories in rhyme 3. City and town life -- Fiction 4. Sound -- Fiction 5. Vehicles -- Fiction
  ISBN 1442483156; 9781442483163; 9781442483156

LC 2012041015

In this children's book, by Robert Burleigh, illustrated by Tad Carpenter, "the sounds of the city come to life in this vivid picture book that's ready-made for repetition and perfect for preschool. From . . . an alarm clock in the morning to the . . . subway and . . . streaming traffic, all the way to the . . . hush of evening, the exciting and lively sounds of the city are vibrantly expressed." (Publisher's note)

"Carpenter's . . . carefree scenes, digitally rendered and saturated in primary colors, are the very picture of urban hustle and bustle, with a jaunty look of 1960s animation. Visual sound effect cues abound in dynamic display type." Pub Wkly

Burn, Doris

Andrew Henry's meadow; Doris Burn. Philomel Books 2012 48 p. ill. $14.99
Grades: K 1 2   E
  1. Picture books for children 2. Runaway children -- Fiction 3. Building -- Fiction 4. Self-acceptance -- Fiction
  ISBN 0399256083; 9780399256080

LC 2011017476

First published by Coward, McCann (1965)

In this chlidren's picture book reissue, "Andrew Henry has two younger brothers, who are always together, and two older sisters, who are always together. But Andrew Henry is in the middle—and he's always with himself. He doesn't mind this very much, because he's an inventor. But when Andrew Henry's family doesn't appreciate him or his inventions, he decides it's time to run away." (Publisher's note)

Burningham, John

Edwardo; the horriblest boy in the whole wide world. Alfred A. Knopf 2006 un il $16.99; lib bdg $19.99
Grades: PreK K 1 2 3   E
  ISBN 978-0-375-84053-1; 0-375-84053-2; 978-0-375-94053-8 lib bdg; 0-375-94053-7 lib bdg

LC 2006-03681

Each time he does something a little bit bad, Edwardo is told that he is very bad and soon his behavior is awful, but when he accidentally does good things and is complimented, he becomes much, much nicer.

"Fans of Burningham will delight in his witty, winsome pictures, so full of animation and expression." SLJ

★ **It's** a secret. Candlewick Press 2009 un il $16.99

Grades: PreK K 1   E
  1. Cats -- Fiction 2. Night -- Fiction
  ISBN 978-0-7636-4275-4; 0-7636-4275-4
  Boston Globe-Horn Book Honor: Picture Book (2010)

"Marie Elaine wonders what her cat, Malcolm, does at night that causes him to sleep all day. When she goes down to the kitchen late one night and finds him all dressed up to go out, she asks to come along. . . He takes her and her neighbor Norman to a secret cat party on the rooftops, where they dance, feast, and meet the queen of the cats. Burningham's signature sketchy mixed-media illustrations are a good fit for the dreamlike story, as is the off-kilter logic of the text." SLJ

John Patrick Norman McHennessy; the boy who was always late. Alfred A. Knopf 2008 un il $16.99
Grades: PreK K 1 2   E
  1. School stories 2. Teachers -- Fiction 3. Truthfulness and falsehood -- Fiction
  ISBN 978-0-375-85220-6; 0-375-85220-4
  First published 1987 by Crown Publishers

A teacher regrets his decison to disbelieve a student's outlandish excuses for being tardy.

"Burningham uses mixed media here to create boldly-colored illustrations which do a marvelous job of reinforcing the text. The storyline is a simple one, but it is filled with irony." SLJ

Motor miles; John Burningham. Candlewick Press 2016 32 p. color illustrations $16.99
Grades: PreK K 1   E
  1. Dogs -- Fiction 2. Friendship -- Fiction 3. Automobiles -- Fiction
  ISBN 9780763690649

LC 2016943941

In this picture book by John Burningham, the dog "Miles does not come when he is called. He does not like going for walks, his food, other dogs, or the rain. What Miles does like is going for drives in the car. So when Mr. Huddy makes Miles a car of his own, Miles becomes a much happier dog. And now he and his friend Norman can go on all sorts of adventures!" (Publisher's note)

"Burningham's matter-of-fact text and blithely inked illustrations embrace the comedy of the premise while capturing the close-knit relationship between boy and dog—especially when they're tooling across an empty beach at sunrise." Pub Wkly

Mr. Gumpy's motor car. Crowell 1976 un il lib bdg $18.89
Grades: PreK K 1   E
  1. Animals -- Fiction 2. Automobiles -- Fiction
  ISBN 0-690-00799-X

LC 75-4582

First published 1973 in the United Kingdom

"The strength here is in the rural simplicity and in the colorful illustrations of amiable animals, the countryside in sunshine and under lowering clouds. Those things and the bold type which carries words and phrases for the reader to chew on and roll around on the tongue." N Y Times Book Rev

Another available title in the author's series about Mr. Grumpy

★ **Mr.** Gumpy's outing. Holt & Co. 1971 un il $17.95; pa $7.99; bd bk $6.95
Grades: PreK K 1   E
  1. Animals -- Fiction
  ISBN 0-8050-0708-3; 0-8050-1315-6 pa; 0-8050-6629-2 bd bk
  First published 1970 in the United Kingdom

"Mr. Gumpy is about to go off for a boat ride and is asked by two children, a rabbit, a cat, a dog, and other animals if they may come.

To each Mr. Gumpy says yes, if—if the children don't squabble, if the rabbit won't hop, if the cat won't chase the rabbit or the dog tease the cat, and so on. Of course each does exactly what Mr. Gumpy forbade, the boat tips over, and they all slog home for tea in friendly fashion." Sutherland. The Best in Child Books

Another title about Mr. Gumpy is:

Mr. Gumpy's motor car (1976)

★ **Picnic**; John Burningham. First U.S. Edition Candlewick Press 2014 32 p. color illustrations (reinforced) $16.99
Grades: PreK K   **E**
1. Animals -- Fiction 2. Picnics -- Fiction 3. Friendship -- Fiction
ISBN 9780763669454; 0763669458
LC 2013944024

First U.S. edition

"One day, Boy and Girl head down the hill with a picnic basket and meet a fancily dressed Sheep, Pig, and Duck. They all set off to find the perfect place to sit outside--until they see Bull coming! A short-lived chase segues into a gentle interactive text as the friends wend their way from an idyllic outdoor world to a welcoming house on a hill. (Can you find Pig's ball? Shall we find your bed?)" (Publisher's note)

"Picnic has an interactive quality that encourages readers to find objects easily hidden in the pictures. Each painting is done in bold and bright colors that catch viewers' attention. Reminiscent of a simpler day, this book is a breath of fresh air--a time out of a busy schedule to enjoy the beauty of a picture book with a young child." SLJ

★ **There's** going to be a baby; [illustrated by] Helen Oxenbury. Candlewick Press 2010 un il $16.99
Grades: PreK K 1   **E**
1. Infants -- Fiction 2. Siblings -- Fiction 3. Imagination -- Fiction
ISBN 978-0-7636-4907-4; 0-7636-4907-4
LC 2009-51509

A young boy imagines what life will be like when his new sibling arrives.

"The handsome, clear-lined images may seem retro at first, but the crispness acts as a containing presence for displacement fears and a source of narrative momentum—all the while allowing Oxenbury to exercise the full power of her visual image." Publ Wkly

The **way** to the zoo; John Burningham. Candlewick Press 2014 40 p. color illustrations $15.99
Grades: PreK K   **E**
1. Zoos -- Fiction 2. Humorous fiction 3. Animals -- Fiction 4. Imagination -- Fiction
ISBN 076367317X; 9780763673178
LC 2013952847

"What if you noticed a door in your bedroom that wasn't there before? And what if it led to a passage to . . . the zoo? You might want to take just one little bear back to your room with you, or maybe just all the smaller animals. But how could you resist the penguins and the tigers and the birds?" (Publisher's note)

"Sylvie discovers a door to the zoo in her bedroom and begins bringing animals home, but--being an orderly child--just a few at a time. When she forgets to close the door, a crowd of creatures troops in to watch television. Sylvie's arrangements have both the childlike logic and the solid reality of the best fantasy. Masterfully limned drawings feature harmonious hues." Horn Book

Burton, Virginia Lee

Katy and the big snow; story and pictures by Virginia Lee Burton. Houghton Mifflin 1943 32p il $16; pa $6.95

Grades: PreK K 1   **E**
1. Snow -- Fiction 2. Tractors -- Fiction
ISBN 0-395-18155-0; 0-395-18562-9 pa

"Katy was a beautiful red crawler tractor. In summer she wore a bulldozer to push dirt with. In winter she wore a snowplow. She was big and strong and the harder the job the better she liked it. When the Big Snow covered the city of Geoppolis like a thick blanket, Katy cleared the city from North to South and East to West." Ont Libr Rev

★ The **little** house; story and pictures by Virginia Lee Burton. Houghton Mifflin 1942 40p il $14.95; pa $5.95
Grades: PreK K 1   **E**
1. Houses -- Fiction 2. City and town life -- Fiction
ISBN 0-395-18156-9; 0-395-25938-X pa
Awarded the Caldecott Medal, 1943

"The little house was very happy as she sat on the quiet hillside watching the changing seasons. As the years passed, however, tall buildings grew up around her, and the noise of city traffic disturbed her. She became sad and lonely until one day someone who understood her need for twinkling stars overhead and dancing apple blossoms moved her back to just the right little hill." Child Books Too Good to Miss

★ **Mike** Mulligan and his steam shovel; story and pictures by Virginia Lee Burton. Houghton Mifflin 1939 un il $16; pa $6.95
Grades: PreK K 1   **E**
1. Steam-shovels -- Fiction
ISBN 0-395-16961-5; 0-395-25939-8 pa

"One of the most convincing personifications of a machine ever written. Lively pictures, dramatic action, and a satisfying conclusion." Adventuring with Books. 2d edition

Butler, Dori Hillestad

My grandpa had a stroke; written by Dori Hillestad Butler; illustrated by Nicole Wong. Magination Press 2007 31p il $14.95; pa $8.95
Grades: K 1 2   **E**
1. Stroke -- Fiction 2. Fishing -- Fiction 3. Grandfathers -- Fiction
ISBN 978-1-59147-806-5; 1-59147-806-5; 978-1-59147-807-2 pa; 1-59147-807-3 pa
LC 2006034528

"Ryan loves spending Saturdays fishing with his grandfather. But when Grandpa suffers a stroke, everything changes. . . . The book, illustrated in soft-edged watercolors, ends on a hopeful note. . . . With quiet prose, this covers most of the emotional and practical hurdles faced by both patient and child." Booklist

Butler, John

Bedtime in the jungle; [written and illustrated by John Butler] Peachtree 2009 un il $16.95
Grades: PreK K   **E**
1. Counting 2. Stories in rhyme 3. Animals -- Fiction 4. Bedtime -- Fiction
ISBN 978-1-56145-486-0; 1-56145-486-9
LC 2008040592

As dusk falls in the jungle, animal babies and their parents prepare for bedtime

"What distinguishes this title is its stunning illustrations. . . . The animals are depicted in their natural settings in soothing shades that are sure to bring about the calm that encourages sleep. A lovely addition." SLJ

Butler, M. Christina

The **smiley** snowman; illustrations by Tina Macnaughton. Good Books 2010 un il $16.99
Grades: PreK K   **E**
1. Snow -- Fiction 2. Bears -- Fiction 3. Foxes -- Fiction 4.

Rabbits -- Fiction
ISBN 978-1-56148-696-0; 1-56148-696-5

LC 2010004916

A bear, a fox, and a rabbit build a snowman, but their efforts to keep it happy and warm almost bring about its demise.

"Silvery blue-green glitter makes the snowman appear to twinkle. And as the lovable animal friends play in the snowy woods, they make winter seem cozy and fun. This book would be a pleasant read-aloud for a winter-themed storytime." SLJ

Button, Lana

Willow's whispers; illustrated by Tania Howells. Kids Can Press 2010 il $16.95

Grades: PreK K 1   E

1. Voice -- Fiction
ISBN 978-1-55453-280-3; 1-55453-280-9

Buxton, Jane

The **littlest** llama; by Jane Buxton; illustrated by Jenny Cooper. Sterling 2008 un il $9.95

Grades: K 1 2   E

1. Stories in rhyme 2. Play -- Fiction 3. Andes -- Fiction 4. Llamas -- Fiction
ISBN 978-1-4027-5277-3; 1-4027-5277-6

LC 2007036396

High in the Andes Mountains, the littlest llama wants to play but his mother, sisters, gran, and aunt are busy, and so he leaves the herd to seek a playmate and finds adventure, instead.

"The descriptive rhyming text will make a lively read-aloud, while the beautiful, intricately detailed color illustrations extend each scenario." Booklist

Buzzeo, Toni

Adventure Annie goes to work; illustrated by Amy Wummer. Dial 2009 un il lib bdg $16.99

Grades: PreK K 1   E

1. Superheroes -- Fiction 2. Lost and found possessions -- Fiction
ISBN 978-0-8037-3233-9; 0-8037-3233-3

When she goes to work with her mother on a Saturday, Adventure Annie uses her own special methods to help find a missing report.

"The bright, full-color pencil and watercolor pictures are set against ample white space and show the warm relationship between mother and daughter. This is an office adventure that children will want to experience and a heroine they'll love meeting." SLJ

Another title about Adventure Annie is:

Adventure Annie goes to kindergarten (2010)

Inside the books; readers and libraries around the world. Toni Buzzeo; illustrations by Jude Daly. Upstart Books 2012 32 p. col. ill. (hardcover) $17.95

Grades: K 1 2   E

1. Libraries 2. Stories in rhyme 3. Libraries -- Fiction 4. Bookmobiles -- Fiction 5. Books and reading -- Fiction
ISBN 1602130582; 9781602130586

LC 2011287827

This children's book by Toni Buzzeo and illustrated by Jude Daly presents a "gentle homage to books and libraries. . . . [Buzzeo] reminds us of the extraordinary possibilities that lie inside every book and introduces us to many unique places these treasures can be found." (Publisher's note)

My Bibi always remembers; by Toni Buzzeo; illustrated by Mike Wohnoutka. Disney-Hyperion 2014 32 p. color illustrations $16.99

Grades: PreK K 1   E

1. Elephants -- Fiction 2. Animals -- Infancy -- Fiction
ISBN 1423183851; 9781423183853

LC 2013007146

"Little Tembo, a baby elephant, is thirsty and her herd cannot find any water. But Bibi, the matriarch, 'remembers the way to wet.' As Bibi leads them across the parched savannah, Tembo happily follows, every now and then getting distracted by her own memories of games she loves to play." (Publisher's note)

"Wohnoutka's lovely illustrations, in tans, purples and grays, convey the vastness of the setting, along with accurate depictions of the elephants and the other watchful animals.A gentle, loving picture of interaction among generations." Kirkus

★ **One** cool friend; pictures by David Small. Dial Books for Young Readers 2012 32 p. (reinforced) $16.99

Grades: K 1 2   E

1. Pets -- Fiction 2. Penguins -- Fiction 3. Father-son relationship -- Fiction
ISBN 0803734131; 9780803734135

LC 2011021637

Caldecott Honor Book (2013)

In this book, "[a]fter Elliott convinces his father to allow him to bring home a penguin (Dad thinks he means a toy) from the aquarium, he sets Magellan (named after the explorer who discovered the species) up in style, creating an ice rink in his bedroom using a wading pool, the garden hose, and the lowest air-conditioning setting. Elliott reads up on his new pet, . . . feeds him anchovy pizza, and lets him hang out in the freezer and the bathtub." (Bulletin of the Center for Children's Books)

Penelope Popper, book doctor; illustrations by Jana Christy. Upstart Books 2011 un il $17.95

Grades: 1 2 3   E

1. Libraries -- Fiction 2. Books -- Conservation and restoration -- Fiction
ISBN 978-1-60213-054-8; 1-60213-054-X

LC 2011283516

In all corners of the library, there are books that need care and Penelope immediately dedicates herself to learning how to mend them.

"The upbeat narrative is . . . enlivened by cheerful illustrations depicting Penelope, an earnest girl with red hair and freckles, in her bright and pleasant classroom and school library. With its soft edges and palette of springtime colors, each painting reflects the positive tone of the story." SLJ

Byars, Betsy Cromer

Boo's surprise; [by] Betsy Byars; illustrated by Erik Brooks. Henry Holt and Co. 2009 45p il $15.99

Grades: K 1 2   E

1. Siblings -- Fiction 2. Dinosaurs -- Fiction 3. Imagination -- Fiction
ISBN 978-0-8050-8817-5; 0-8050-8817-2

LC 2008048849

Sequel to: Boo's dinosaur (2006)

Boo finds an egg that hatches into a new dinosaur.

"Lively black-and-white drawings extend the fun, with a climactic double-page illustration at the end of each chapter." Booklist

★ The **Golly** sisters go West; by Betsy Byars; pictures by Sue Truesdell. Harper & Row 1986 64p il (I can read book) lib bdg $16.89; pa $3.99

Grades: K 1 2   E

1. West (U.S.) -- Fiction 2. Entertainers -- Fiction 3. Frontier and

pioneer life -- Fiction
ISBN 0-06-020884-8 lib bdg; 0-06-444132-6 pa

LC 84-48474

May-May and Rose, the singing, dancing Golly sisters, travel west by covered wagon, entertaining people along the way

"The dialogue and antics are convincingly like those of rivalrous young siblings anywhere on the block. The story lines are cleverer than much easy-to-read fare, and the old-West setting adds flair. The accompanying watercolors, too, add a generous dollop of humor." Bull Cent Child Books

Other titles about the Golly sisters are:
The Golly sisters ride again (1994)
Hooray for the Golly sisters! (1990)

Bynum, Eboni
Jamari's drum; [by] Eboni Bynum and Roland Jackson; pictures on glazed tiles by Baba Wagué Diakité. Groundwood Books 2004 un il $16.95
Grades: K 1 2 3   E
1. Drums -- Fiction 2. Africa -- Fiction 3. Volcanoes -- Fiction
ISBN 0-88899-531-8

When Jamari forgets to heed Baba Mdogo's warning to play the drum in the village every day, he narrowly averts disaster from a volcano.

"The beautifully executed, folk-style artwork swirls with bold lines and bright patterns, incorporating backgrounds that blend earth tones with the blues and purples of the sky. . . . This book makes an excellent read-aloud." SLJ

Bynum, Janie
Kiki's blankie. Sterling Pub. 2009 un il $14.95
Grades: PreK   E
1. Monkeys -- Fiction 2. Blankets -- Fiction 3. Lost and found possessions -- Fiction
ISBN 978-1-4027-5910-9; 1-4027-5910-X

LC 2008-26837

Kiki the monkey has many daring adventures with her polka-dot 'blankie,' but when it sails away without her and lands above a sleeping crocodile, she may not be brave enough to come to the rescue.

"Brightly colored, uncluttered illustrations are set on large areas of white space, making the objects and action easy for young children to find and follow. Preschoolers will relate to Kiki, her blankie attachment, and to her energy and creative play." SLJ

Byrne, John
Donald & Benoit; written and illustrated by John Patrick Byrne. Rizzoli 2011 un il $17.95
Grades: 2 3 4 5   E
1. Cats -- Fiction 2. Drums -- Fiction
ISBN 978-0-7893-2084-1; 0-7893-2084-3

"Benoît, the son of a sailor, and Donald, his new kitten, live in an idyllic fishing village. . . . When Benoît's father, Jean-Kiki, disappears at sea and they're left to support themselves, Donald's love of drumming and the timely help of a library book . . . wins him resounding professional triumph—which Jean-Kiki reappears in time to enjoy. With a nod to early cubism, Byrne paints bulky, curvy figures whose swoops and angles have the rhythmic energy of Donald's drums; their impact is heightened by the book's large trim size. Dreamy, melancholy hand-lettering and graceful design add even more charm." Publ Wkly

Cabral, Olga
The **seven** sneezes; illustrated by Bruce Ingman. Golden Books 2009 unp il

Grades: PreK K 1 2   E
1. Animals -- Fiction 2. Sneezing -- Fiction
ISBN 9780375835940; 9780375935947 lib bdg

A newly illustrated edition of the title first published 1948

What happens when the local rag man sneezes? The kitten's ears end up on the bunny. The bunny's ears end up on the kitten. The dog meows, the cat barks. But with a little concentration—and a lot of pepper—the rag man tries to sneeze everything right

"At the conclusion of this sweet tale, one feels fully satisfied, as a topsy-turvy situation is resolved and order is regained. First published in 1948, this version preserves the original charm of Cabral's text and introduces Ingman's fresh illustrations, which combine splashes of bright color with simple line drawings." SLJ

Cabrera, Jane
Here we go round the mulberry bush. Holiday House 2010 un il $16.95
Grades: PreK   E
1. Day -- Fiction 2. Dogs -- Fiction
ISBN 978-0-8234-2288-3; 0-8234-2288-7

LC 2009048137

"This old favorite gets a sprightly new workout in Cabrera's adorable offering. The duo going around the mulberry bush 'on a cold and frosty morning' is a small spotted puppy and an even younger sibling. Lots of verses are added to the familiar refrain. . . . A fun read-aloud, or more aptly put, read-along, because children will want to pick up on the chant." Booklist

★ **If** you're happy and you know it. Holiday House 2005 un il hardcover o.p. board book $7.95
Grades: PreK K   E
1. Songs 2. Animals -- Fiction
ISBN 0-8234-1881-2; 978-0-8234-2227-2 board book

LC 2004-47264

An elephant, a monkey, and a giraffe join other animals to sing different verses of this popular song that encourages everyone to express their happiness through voice and movement.

"Cheerful painterly pictures in a kaleidoscope of colors enhance the jovial mood of the song." SLJ

★ **Mommy,** carry me please! Holiday House 2006 un il $16.95
Grades: PreK K   E
1. Animals -- Fiction 2. Mother-child relationship -- Fiction
ISBN 0-8234-1935-5

LC 2004048862

"On each spread of this warm lapsit book, a baby animal asks its mother to carry me please. Each mother accommodates by transporting the youngster in that animals special way: lemur under its belly, kangaroo in a pouch, tiger in its mouth, crocodile in teeth, penguin on its feet, and so on until the cozy ending when a human child is carried in the mothers arms. The art features Cabrera's trademark breezy, blocky, and bold animals in bright and energetic colors that focus childrens eye and attention." SLJ

One, two, buckle my shoe. Holiday House 2009 un il $16.95
Grades: PreK   E
1. Counting 2. Stories in rhyme 3. Animals -- Fiction 4. Parties -- Fiction 5. Birthdays -- Fiction
ISBN 978-0-8234-2230-2; 0-8234-2230-5

LC 2008055303

Four chicks have fun hiding while Rabbit and Mommy Hen prepare a party for the little pigs' birthday.

Cabrera's "version of this familiar schoolyard song takes readers all the way up through the number 20. . . . The lively images, thick with paint strokes, create a cheerful atmosphere. Additionally, the opening challenge to find four small chicks on each spread will keep readers entertained as they read along." Publ Wkly

There was an old woman who lived in a shoe; Jane Cabrera. Holiday House 2016 32 p. color illustrations (hardcover) $16.95
Grades: PreK   E
1. Stories in rhyme   2. Nursery rhymes -- Fiction   3. Mother-child relationship -- Fiction   4. Mother and child -- Fiction
ISBN 9780823435548

LC 2015016727

In this children's book, by Jane Cabrera, "a favorite rhyme gets an ecofriendly spin. This old woman and her household of high-spirited children and talented pets are resourceful. Together they repair their broken furniture, find alternative modes of transportation when the car breaks down and remake worn clothing with colorful patches. Sheet music for piano, voice and guitar are included in the book." (Publisher's note)

"The rhyming text is bouncy and lively, making it suitable for sharing aloud with a group. This is a charming reimagining of an originally more cynical nursery rhyme." SLJ

Twinkle, twinkle, little star; by Jane Cabrera. 1st American ed. Holiday House 2012 1 v. (unpaged) ill. (hardcover) $16.95
Grades: PreK K 1   E
ISBN 9780823425198

LC 2011044969

Cadena, Beth

Supersister; illustrated by Frank W. Dormer. Clarion Books 2009 un il $16
Grades: K 1 2   E
1. Pregnancy -- Fiction   2. Mother-daughter relationship -- Fiction
ISBN 978-0-547-01006-9; 0-547-01006-0

LC 2008-11618

A young girl does all kinds of things around the house to help her pregnant mother, proud that when the new baby comes she is going to be 'a super sister.'

"Lively yet thoughtful text and bright, funny illustrations combine beautifully to settle into a pleasing conclusion: a supersister dream that features a superbrother. Highly recommended for children with siblings on the way." Kirkus

Cadow, Kenneth M.

Alfie runs away; pictures by Lauren Castillo. Frances Foster Books 2010 un il $16.99
Grades: PreK K   E
1. Runaway children -- Fiction   2. Mother-son relationship -- Fiction
ISBN 978-0-374-30202-3; 0-374-30202-2

LC 2008024146

Told he must give up his favorite, now too-small, shoes, Alfie leaves home, but not before his mother persuades him to take all of the things he might need while he is gone

"Castillo's . . . spreads, comfortingly rendered in muted colors, are just right for Cadow's even-tempered narration." Publ Wkly

Calhoun, Mary

★ **Cross**-country cat; illustrated by Erick Ingraham. Morrow 1979 un il hardcover o.p. pa $6.99
Grades: K 1 2 3   E
1. Cats -- Fiction
ISBN 0-688-22186-6; 0-698-06519-8 pa

LC 78-31718

When he becomes lost in the mountains, Henry, a cat with the unusual ability of walking on two legs finds his way home on cross-country skis

"Only the careful blending of skills by a talented author and illustrator could turn such a farfetched plot into a warm, rich, and rewarding story. The realistic illustrations seem to be enveloped in a glowing light and invite the reader to step right into the story." Child Book Rev Serv
Other titles about Henry the cat are:
Blue-ribbon Henry (1999)
Henry the Christmas cat (2004)
Henry the sailor cat (1994)
High-wire Henry (1991)
Hot-air Henry (1981)

Cali, Davide

The **enemy**; a book about peace. written by Davide Cali and illustrated by Serge Bloch. Schwartz & Wade Books 2009 un il $15.99; lib bdg $18.99
Grades: 1 2 3 4   E
1. War stories   2. Soldiers -- Fiction
ISBN 978-0-375-84500-0; 0-375-84500-3; 978-0-375-93752-1 lib bdg; 0-375-93752-8 lib bdg

LC 2007047974

After watching an enemy for a very long time during an endless war, a soldier finally creeps out into the night to the other man's hole and is surprised by what he finds there.

"Bloch pairs pen-and-ink cartoons with collage elements like family photos, and gives readers a bird's-eye view from which to observe the men's similarities. The point will not be lost on readers." Publ Wkly

I love chocolate; illustrated by Evelyn Daviddi. Tundra Books 2009 un il $12.95
Grades: PreK K   E
1. Chocolate -- Fiction
ISBN 0-88776-912-8; 978-0-88776-912-2
Original Italian edition 2001

"'Why do I love chocolate?' a boy asks as he is about to take a colossal bite of a candy bar. He then lists all the reasons: it crunches and melts, and it can make bad times better. . . . The text captures the essence of chocolate—its varying incarnations and textures—and it will leave everyone salivating. In addition to being a great candidate for programs, the book has potential as an easy reader as well. The art has a European flair." SLJ

Calmenson, Stephanie

Jazzmatazz! by Stephanie Calmenson; illustrated by Bruce Degen. HarperCollinsPublishers 2008 un il $16.99; lib bdg $17.89
Grades: PreK K 1   E
1. Stories in rhyme   2. Mice -- Fiction   3. Animals -- Fiction   4. Musicians -- Fiction   5. Jazz music -- Fiction
ISBN 978-0-06-077289-5; 0-06-077289-1; 978-0-06-077290-1 lib bdg; 0-06-077290-5 lib bdg

LC 2007009133

When a mouse scurries into a house and starts to play jazz music, other animals join in, one by one, each using his or her own particular talent

"This cheerful book . . . is full of color and sound. . . . Degen fills the white space . . . with colorful zigzags, curlicues, stars, and other patterns to show how the music is connecting and joining all of the characters together." SLJ

Late for school! by Stephanie Calmenson; illustrated by Sachiko Yoshikawa. Carolrhoda Books 2008 un il lib bdg $16.95
Grades: K 1 2   E
1. School stories   2. Stories in rhyme   3. Teachers -- Fiction   4.

Transportation -- Fiction

ISBN 978-1-57505-935-8 lib bdg; 1-57505-935-5 lib bdg

LC 2007034776

When Mr. Bungles the teacher oversleeps, he goes to great lengths, trying every form of transportation he can find to get to school on time.

"Cartoon characters in scenes of collage and mixed media follow Mr. Bungles's efforts to watch the clock and avoid breaking his own rule, 'Never, ever, ever be late for school!' A colorful selection for all libraries." SLJ

Calvert, Pam

Multiplying menace; the revenge of Rumpelstiltskin. illustrated by Wayne Geehan. Charlesbridge Pub. 2006 32p il $16.95; pa $6.95

Grades: 3 4 5 6   E

1. Fairy tales 2. Multiplication -- Fiction

ISBN 1-57091-889-9; 1-57091-890-2 pa

LC 2004-23072

Ten years after being tricked, Rumpelstiltskin returns to the royal family to wreak vengeance using multiplication. Includes nonfiction math notes about multiplying by whole numbers and by fractions.

"Calvert has created an interesting vehicle for teaching children about the differences between multiplying with whole numbers and multiplying with fractions.... Calvert has written an enjoyable teaching tool, and Geehan's luminous and expressive paintings are perfect for this fairy-tale world." SLJ

Princess Peepers; illustrated by Tuesday Mourning. Marshall Cavendish 2008 un il $16.99

Grades: K 1 2 3   E

1. Eyeglasses -- Fiction 2. Princesses -- Fiction

ISBN 978-0-7614-5437-3; 0-7614-5437-3

LC 2007022134

When the other princesses make fun of her for wearing glasses, Princess Peepers vows to go without, but after several mishaps—one of which is especially coincidental—she admits that she really does need them if she wants to see.

"Mourning's graphite and digital/collage illustrations combine figures in traditional costumes from different eras with lush backgrounds. The palette of pinks keeps the emphasis on sweet, even when some of the characters are not. Princess Peepers will circulate well and bring laughs during storytimes." SLJ

Another title about Princess Peepers is:

Princess Peepers picks a pet (2011)

Campbell, Bebe Moore

Stompin' at the Savoy; [by] Bebe Moore Campbell; illustrated by Richard Yarde. Philomel Books 2006 un il $16.99

Grades: K 1 2 3   E

1. Dance -- Fiction 2. Jazz music -- Fiction 3. African Americans -- Fiction 4. Harlem (New York, N.Y.) -- Fiction

ISBN 0-399-24197-3

LC 2005025044

On the night of her jazz dance recital Mindy feels too nervous to go, until a magical drum whisks her away to the Savoy Ballroom in Harlem where she finds her "happy feet"

"Rhythmic gouache and pastel paintings depicting swinging dancers and jiving musicians perfectly complement the lyrical energy and magical realism of the cadenced prose." SLJ

Campbell, K. G.

Lester's dreadful sweaters; Keith Campbell. Kids Can Press 2012 32 p. $16.95

Grades: PreK K 1 2   E

1. Cousins -- Fiction 2. Picture books for children 3. Sweaters

-- Fiction

ISBN 1554537703; 9781554537709

In this book, "it's Cousin Clara who knits the dramatically awful, humiliating sweaters of the title. Lester's parents compel him to wear them. . . . One is a 'less-than-pleasant yellow' hoodie with a trailing sleeve and purple pom-poms . . .; another has knitted feathers and striped feet. . . . When a group of performing clowns fall in love with the sweaters . . . , Lester is able to offload his entire collection--and Cousin Clara." (Publishers Weekly)

The **Mermaid** and the Shoe; by K G Campbell. Kids Can Pr 2014 32 p. $16.95

Grades: PreK K 1 2   E

1. Mermaids and mermen -- Fiction 2. Mermaids -- Fiction 3. Curiosity -- Fiction

ISBN 1554537711; 9781554537716

In this book, by K G Campbell, "each of King Neptune's 50 mermaid daughters boasts a special talent, except for little Minnow, who seems to be good only at asking questions. When she finds a strange object, Minnow follows her questions to a wondrous place and finds answers, including the answer to the most important question of all: Who am I?" (Publisher's note)

"When a shoe drops into the sea, little mermaid Minnow (least exceptional of King Neptune's fifty daughters) investigates. What she discovers is "an odd creature...a landmaid." Minnow tells her family, and the kingdom's newfound storyteller-adventurer is born. Campbell's tale shows that a little imagination and a lot of inquisitiveness go a long way. The watercolor and pencil-crayon illustrations have a sense of motion and playfulness." Horn Book

Campbell, Nicola I.

Shi-shi-etko; pictures by Kim La Fave. Groundwood Books 2005 un il $16.95

Grades: K 1 2 3   E

1. Canada -- Fiction 2. Native Americans -- Fiction

ISBN 0-88899-659-4

"This is a moving story set in Canada about the practice of removing Native children from their villages and sending them to residential schools to learn the English language and culture.... Shi-shi-etko counts down her last four days before going away.... The vivid, digital illustrations rely on a red palette, evoking not only the land but also the sorrow of the situation and the hope upon which the story ultimately ends." SLJ

Campbell, Scott

Hug machine; by Scott Campbell. 1st ed Atheneum Books for Young Readers 2014 40 p. color illustrations (hardcover) $16.99

Grades: PreK K 1   E

1. Machinery 2. Hugging -- Fiction 3. Hugging -- Fiction

ISBN 1442459352; 9781442459359

LC 2013019664

"Much like cats, young children can be quite persnickety about whom they embrace and when. Not so with this story's protagonist, aka the Hug Machine. This boy takes it upon himself to calm and cheer everyone, and everything (rocks, trees), he encounters with a warm hug. He takes his work quite seriously and no challenge is too tough (a porcupine) or large (a whale) for him to wrap his arms around." (School Library Journal)

"A feel-good ride, full of droll artistic asides and an abundance of caring.... Unadorned, hand-lettered text and deliberately muted watercolors increase the warmth of this adorable little fellow." Kirkus

Campisi, Stephanie

The **ugly** dumpling; Stephanie Campisi; illustrated by Shahar Kober. Mighty Media Kids 2016 32 p. color illustrations (hardback) $15.95

Grades: PreK K 1 2   E

1. Friendship -- Fiction 2. Self-esteem -- Fiction

ISBN 9781938063671; 9781938063695

LC 2015040899

In this book, by Stephanie Campisi, illustrated by Shahar Kober, "It's not easy being the ugliest dumpling in a dim sum restaurant. Uneaten and ignored, the ugly dumpling is down in the dumps. But when an encouraging cockroach sees the dumpling's inner beauty, this unlikely duo embarks on an eye-opening adventure, leading the ugly dumpling to discover its true identity and realize that being different is beautiful after all." (Publisher's note)

"The use of anthropomorphic food takes some getting used to, but the ultimate end, about accepting people because of their differences, adds an extra moral to this timeless tale. The bright illustrations are detailed and full of energy—never has food been so expressive!—and the concept is just odd enough to succeed." Booklist

Cannon, A. E.

Sophie's fish; by A.E. Cannon; illustrated by Lee White. Viking 2012 32p.

Grades: PreK K 1 2   E

1. Pets -- Fiction 2. Fishes -- Fiction 3. Children's stories 4. Picture books for children 5. Humorous stories 6. Worry -- Fiction

ISBN 9780670012916

LC 2011016227

In this picture book, "[w]hen schoolmate Sophie asks Jake to care for her fish, Yo-Yo, for a weekend, he agrees, because '[h]ow hard can it be to babysit a fish?' But while waiting for Yo-Yo to arrive, Jake begins to worry. 'What kind of snacks do fish like to eat?' he frets. [Illustrator Lee] White presents a massive Strawberry Worm Cake as a possible fish snack; standing atop the highest layer, Jake offers a slice to a laughing blue fish he finds sitting upright on a wire chair. The fish is as big as Jake. Next, Jake wonders, '[w]hat if Yo-Yo wants to play a game?' Here, the portrayed fish is several times Jake's size, dressed as a pirate and riding an enormous rubber ducky." (Kirkus)

Cannon, Janell

★ **Crickwing**; written and illustrated by Janell Cannon. Harcourt 2000 un il $16; pa $7

Grades: K 1 2 3   E

1. Ants -- Fiction 2. Cockroaches -- Fiction

ISBN 0-15-201790-9; 9780152050610

LC 99-50456

A lonely cockroach named Crickwing has a creative idea that saves the day for the leaf-cutter ants when their fierce forest enemies attack them

"An amusing tale lightly rooted in natural history. . . . Cannon's illustrations skillfully blur the line between fact and fancy." Publ Wkly

★ **Stellaluna**. Harcourt Brace Jovanovich 1993 un il $17

Grades: K 1 2 3   E

1. Bats -- Fiction

ISBN 0-15-280217-7

LC 92-16439

After she falls headfirst into a bird's nest, a baby bat is raised like a bird until she is reunited with her mother

"Cannon's delightful story is full of gentle humor. . . . [She] provides good information about bats in the story, amplifying it in two pages of notes at the end of the book. Her full-page colored-pencil-and-acrylic paintings fairly glow." Booklist

Cantrell, Charlie

A **friend** for Einstein; the smallest stallion. by Charlie Cantrell and Rachel Wagner. Disney/Hyperion 2011 un il $16.99

Grades: PreK K 1 2   E

1. Dogs -- Fiction 2. Size -- Fiction 3. Horses -- Fiction

ISBN 978-1-4231-4563-9; 1-4231-4563-1

"With hooves the size of quarters, Einstein, a mini minature horse, is the smallest horse ever born. . . . Einstein is not tall enough to keep up with other equines, even his fellow miniature horses. The fascinating facts lead into a fictional story line as the presumably lonely horse searches for a playmate. . . . Einsten meets a dog named Lilly . . . who is just his size. Although Lilly and Einstein are actual friends, children will care less about the reality of their meeting and more about this unusual horse and the color photographs. . . . No doubt little Einstein will appeal to big hearts everywhere." Booklist

Caple, Kathy

Duck & Company. Holiday House 2007 32p il $14.95; pa $4.95

Grades: K 1 2   E

1. Rats -- Fiction 2. Ducks -- Fiction 3. Booksellers and bookselling -- Fiction

ISBN 978-0-8234-1993-7; 0-8234-1993-2; 978-0-8234-2125-1 pa; 0-8234-2125-2 pa

LC 2006-12118

Rat and Duck run a bookshop and work to find the right book for each of their customers.

"There are tons of visual clues embedded in the ink and goauche illustrations to help burgeoning readers. . . . Young readers will appreciate both the humor and the diversity of the five included tales." Bull Cent Child Books

Another title about Duck and Rat is:

Duck & Company Christmas (2011)

The **friendship** tree. Holiday House 2000 48p il (Holiday House reader) lib bdg $15.95

Grades: K 1 2   E

1. Sheep -- Fiction 2. Trees -- Fiction 3. Friendship -- Fiction

ISBN 0-8234-1376-4

LC 98-39043

This book "includes four little stories about trees. Best friends Blanche and Otis are sheep who live next door to each other and share their sorrows and joys. . . . The line-and-watercolor illustrations reflect the sweet, gentle tone of the text with the soft, pastel shades." Booklist

Capucilli, Alyssa

Biscuit; pictures by Pat Schories. HarperCollins Pubs. 1996 26p il (My first I can read book) $12.95

Grades: PreK K 1 2   E

1. Dogs -- Fiction

ISBN 0-06-026197-8; 0-06-026198-6 lib bdg

LC 95-9716

A little yellow dog wants ever one more thing before he'll go to sleep

★ **Biscuit's** new trick; story by Alyssa Satin Capucilli; pictures by Pat Schories. HarperCollins Pubs. 2000 24p il (My first I can read book) $12.95; lib bdg $15.89; pa $3.99

Grades: PreK K 1 2   E

1. Dogs -- Fiction

ISBN 0-06-028067-0; 0-06-028068-9 lib bdg; 0-06-444308-6 pa

LC 99-23004

"While his owner tries to teach him to fetch a ball, Biscuit the dog chews his bone or chases the cat—that is, until the ball lands in a mud puddle. . . . The simple language . . . and playful watercolor illustrations make this an appealing choice for beginning readers." Horn Book Guide

Other titles about Biscuit are:

Bathtime for Biscuit (1998)

Biscuit (1996)

Biscuit and the baby (2005)

Biscuit and the lost teddy bear (2011)

Biscuit finds a friend (1997)

Biscuit goes to school (2002)

Biscuit visits the big city (2006)

Biscuit wants to play (2001)

Biscuit wins a prize (2004)

Biscuit's big friend (2003)

Biscuit's day at the farm (2007)

Biscuit's picnic (1998)

Happy birthday, Biscuit! (1999)

Hello, Biscuit! (1998)

Pedro's burro; story by Alyssa Satin Capucilli; pictures by Pau Estrada. HarperCollinsPublishers 2007 32p il (I can read!) $15.99; lib bdg $16.89

Grades: PreK K 1   E

1. Mexico -- Fiction 2. Donkeys -- Fiction

ISBN 978-0-06-056031-7; 0-06-056031-2; 978-0-06-056032-4 lib bdg; 0-06-056032-0 lib bdg

LC 2006036323

Pedro and his papa go to the market to look for the perfect burro

"This winning story is enhanced by Estrada's colorful, inviting illustrations. . . . Featuring repetition and humor, the simple story is set in large type with ample white space." SLJ

Capucilli, Alyssa Satin

Katy Duck and the tip-top tap shoes; by Alyssa Satin Capucilli; illustrated by Henry Cole. Simon Spotlight 2013 24 p. (Ready-to-read. Level one) (hardcover) $15.99

Grades: K 1 2   E

1. Dance -- Fiction 2. Ducks -- Fiction 3. Sharing -- Fiction 4. Dance -- Fiction 5. Ducks -- Fiction 6. Ballet -- Fiction 7. Tap dancing -- Fiction

ISBN 1442452455; 1442452463; 1442452471; 9781442452459; 9781442452466; 9781442452473

LC 2011052608

In this book by Alyssa Satin Capucilli "There's a new student in Mr. Tutu's dance class! When dancing diva Katy Duck meets Alice, she thinks Alice has forgotten her ballet slippers! Instead, Alice is ready to make some noise in a pair of tip-top tap shoes! Together, Katy and Alice learn that sharing can be fun—and that there is always more to learn!" (Publisher's note)

Carbone, Elisa

★ **Heroes** of the surf; by Elisa Carbone. Viking 2012 40 p.

Grades: 2 3 4   E

1. Shipwrecks -- Fiction 2. Rescue work -- Fiction 3. Picture books for children 4. New Jersey -- History -- Fiction 5. United States. Life-Saving Service -- Fiction 6. New Jersey -- History -- 19th century -- Fiction

ISBN 0670063126; 9780670063123

LC 2011012218

The book is "based on a true story of shipwreck and rescue . . . with narration by Anthony, a venturesome lad whose penchant for playing pirates helps him through the harrowing event" aboard the steamship Pliny, which was wrecked in a storm near New Jersey in 1882. Elisa Carbone describes Anthony's rescue with his friend Pedro from the sinking ship: "'I swing out into open space. Below me, waves crash and twist like angry snakes. Will the ropes hold?" Illustrator Nancy Carpenter de-

picts the scene with "a seagoing palette of blue, gray, brown and ochre, crosshatched in black." (Kirkus)

★ **Night** running; how James escaped with the help of his faithful dog; based on a true story. [by] Elisa Carbone; illustrated by E.B. Lewis. Alfred A. Knopf 2008 un il $16.99; lib bdg $19.99

Grades: 2 3 4   E

1. Dogs -- Fiction 2. Slavery -- Fiction 3. African Americans -- Fiction

ISBN 0-375-82247-X; 978-0-375-82247-6; 0-375-92247-4 lib bdg; 978-0-375-92247-3 lib bdg

LC 2003014502

A runaway slave makes a daring escape to freedom with the help of his faithful hunting dog, Zeus. Based on the true story of James Smith's journey from Virginia to Ohio in the mid-1800s.

"The watercolor paintings beautifully evoke the sun-drenched cotton fields. Deep purples and rich, dark greens capture the moonlit night. . . . A vividly realized narrative, based on a true story." SLJ

Carle, Eric

★ **10** little rubber ducks. HarperCollins 2005 un il $21.99; bd bk $11.99

Grades: PreK K 1 2   E

1. Counting 2. Toys -- Fiction

ISBN 0-06-074075-2; 0-06-074078-7 bd bk

LC 2004-1420

When a storm strikes a cargo ship, ten rubber ducks are tossed overboard and swept off in ten different directions. Based on a factual incident

"Carle's signature cut-paper collages burst with color, texture, light, and motion, delighting the eye and bringing out the text's nuances." SLJ

★ **The artist** who painted a blue horse. Philomel Books 2011 un il $17.99

Grades: PreK K 1   E

1. Artists 2. Painters 3. Color -- Fiction 4. Animals -- Fiction 5. Artists -- Fiction 6. Painting -- Fiction

ISBN 978-0-399-25713-1; 0-399-25713-6

LC 2011000662

Rather than use the same old colors, a child paints animals and objects in a variety of different hues. Includes biographical information about the German painter Franz Marc, who created unconventional animal paintings in the early 1900s.

"While Carle's creatures are constructed from his familiar, brilliantly colored painted-paper shapes, it is the strength and sinew of their forms that impresses. . . . An homage to Marc becomes testimony to Carle's gifts, too. A short afterword about Marc's life is included." Publ Wkly

★ **Do** you want to be my friend? Crowell 1971 un il $17.99; lib bdg $18.89; pa $6.99; bd bk $7.99

Grades: PreK K   E

1. Stories without words 2. Mice -- Fiction

ISBN 0-690-24276-X; 0-690-01137-7 lib bdg; 0-06-443127-4 pa; 0-694-00709-9 bd bk

"Good material for discussion and guessing games. . . . The pictures tell an amusing story and they are good to look at as well." Times Lit Suppl

Friends; written and illustrated by Eric Carle. Philomel Books 2013 32 p. $17.99

Grades: PreK K   E

1. Picture books for children 2. Voyages and travels -- Fiction 3. Friendship -- Fiction 4. Voyages and travels -- Fiction

ISBN 0399165339; 9780399165337

LC 2012048850

In this book, a "describes his devoted affection for a friend with whom he plays, dances, and shares secrets. Then she moves away, and he is all alone. He misses her terribly and vows to find her. Readers will cheer his bravery as he crosses a swift river, climbs over a steep mountain, and travels through a dewy meadow and shadowy forest to find her. Ultimately, he stumbles across a flower garden. With a bouquet in hand, he finds his friend, reunites with her and (playfully) marries her." (School Library Journal)

★ The **grouchy** ladybug. HarperCollins Pubs. 1996 un il $17.99; lib bdg $18.89; pa $7.99; bd bk $8.99

Grades: PreK K 1   E

1. Ladybugs -- Fiction

ISBN 0-06-027087-X; 0-06-027088-8 lib bdg; 0-06-443450-8 pa; 0-694-01320-X bd bk

LC 95-26581

A reissue of the title first published 1977 by Crowell

A grouchy ladybug, looking for a fight, challenges everyone she meets regardless of their size or strength

"The finger paint and collage illustrations—as bold as the feisty hero—are satisfyingly placed on pages sized to suit the successive animals that appear. . . . Tiny clocks show the time of each enjoyable encounter, with the sun rising and setting as the action proceeds." SLJ

★ A **house** for Hermit Crab. Picture Bk. Studio 1988 un il $18.99; pa $7.99; bd bk $8.99

Grades: PreK K 1   E

1. Crabs -- Fiction

ISBN 0-88708-056-1; 0-689-84894-3 pa; 0-689-87064-7 bd bk

LC 87-29261

"The bright illustrations in Carle's familiar style, which seems particularly suited to undersea scenes, and the cumulative story are splendid." Horn Book

★ **Mister** Seahorse. Philomel Books 2004 un il $17.99; bd bk $8.99

Grades: PreK K 1   E

1. Fishes -- Fiction 2. Fathers -- Fiction 3. Sea horses -- Fiction

ISBN 0-399-24269-4; 978-0-399-25490-1 bd bk

LC 2003-17125

After Mrs. Seahorse lays her eggs on Mr. Seahorse's belly, he drifts through the water, greeting other fish fathers who are taking care of their eggs

"With each encounter comes a delightful surprise: an acetate overlay camouflages the sea creatures as Mister Seahorse passes by. . . . Awash with the wonders of undersea life, this is a stunning, ingeniously conceived lesson in nature as well as a celebration of fatherly affection." Booklist

★ The **mixed**-up chameleon. Crowell 1984 un il $17.99; lib bdg $18.89; pa $6.99; bd bk $8.99

Grades: PreK K 1   E

1. Chameleons -- Fiction

ISBN 0-690-04396-1; 0-690-04397-X lib bdg; 0-06-443162-2 pa; 0-694-01147-9 bd bk

LC 83-45950

A revised and newly illustrated edition of the title first published 1975

The author "has replaced the heavy-lined, childlike, scrawled colors with crisp, appealing collages and has streamlined the text. The cutaway pages have been retained, and none of the humor has been lost. The simpler text results in a smoother flow, and children will enjoy the resulting repetition." Booklist

★ The **Nonsense** Show; Eric Carle. Philomel Books, an imprint of Penguin Group (USA) 2015 40 p. color illustrations (hardback) $18.99

Grades: PreK K 1 2   E

1. Picture books for children 2. Imagination -- Fiction 3. Humorous stories 4. Stories in rhyme 5. Surrealism -- Fiction

ISBN 039917687X; 9780399176876

LC 2015006416

This children's picture book by Eric Carle explores surrealism. It "combine[s] verbal and visual jokes to provide 'something downright preposterous'. 'The Nonsense Show' is the final part of a trilogy of Carle homages to art, along with 'The Artist Who Painted a Blue Horse' and 'Friends'. (The Telegraph)

"Nonsense indeed! A rabbit pulls a boy out of a hat, a mouse chases a cat, and a girl plays tennis with an apple instead of a ball. These are just a few of the goofy images readers will find in Carle's latest picture book. . . . A sure hit as a read-aloud and a definite purchase for picture book collections." SLJ

Papa, please get the moon for me. Simon & Schuster Books for Young Readers 1991 un il $6.99

Grades: PreK K 1   E

1. Moon -- Fiction

ISBN 0-8870-8177-0

LC 91014561

First published 1986 by Picture Book Studio

Monica's father fulfills her request for the moon by taking it down after it is small enough to carry, but it continues to change in size. Some pages fold out to display particularly large pictures.

This is "drawn in thick, brilliant brushstrokes of blues and greens and reds that dazzle the eye. . . . A splendid introduction to the monthly lunar cycle, this is also a wondrous work of art that will stand up to countless readings." Publ Wkly

★ **Slowly,** slowly, slowly, said the sloth. Philomel Bks. 2002 un il $16.99; pa $7.99

Grades: PreK K 1   E

1. Sloths -- Fiction 2. Animals -- Fiction

ISBN 0-399-23954-5; 0-14-240847-6 pa

LC 2002-16057

Challenged by the other jungle animals for its seemingly lazy ways, a sloth living in a tree explains the many advantages of his slow and peaceful existence

"Carle's art is at its best with a brightly colored selection of painted tissue-paper collage that captures 25 rain-forest denizens." SLJ

★ The **very** busy spider. Philomel Bks. 1984 un il $21.99; bd bk $11.99; oversized bd bk $15.99

Grades: PreK K 1   E

1. Spiders -- Fiction

ISBN 0-399-21166-7; 0-399-21592-1 pa; 0-399-22919-1 bd bk; 978-0-399-25601-1 oversized bd bk

LC 84-5907

The farm animals try to divert a busy little spider from spinning her web, but she persists and produces a thing of both beauty and usefulness

This book "has a disarming ingenuousness and a repetitive structure that will capture the response of pre-school audiences. Of special note is the book's use of raised lines for the spider, its web, and an unsuspecting fly. Both sighted and blind children will be able to follow the action with ease." Booklist

★ The **very** clumsy click beetle. Philomel Bks. 1999 un il $22.99

Grades: PreK K 1   **E**
1. Animals -- Fiction 2. Beetles -- Fiction
ISBN 0-399-23201-X

LC 97-33417

A clumsy young click beetle learns to land on its feet with encouragement from various animals and a wise old beetle. An electronic chip with a built-in battery creates clicking sounds to accompany the story

"Done in colored tissue-paper collage, the illustrations burst from the pages and are charmingly rendered. . . . A well-crafted story, joyfully illustrated." SLJ

★ The **very** hungry caterpillar. Philomel Bks. 1981 un il $21.99; bd bk $10.99
Grades: PreK K 1   **E**
1. Caterpillars -- Fiction
ISBN 0-399-20853-4; 0-399-22690-7 bd bk
First published 1970 by World Publishing Company

"This caterpillar is so hungry he eats right through the pictures on the pages of the book—and after leaving many holes emerges as a beautiful butterfly on the last page." Best Books for Child, 1972

★ The **very** lonely firefly. Philomel Bks. 1995 un il $22.99; bd bk $11.99
Grades: PreK K 1   **E**
1. Fireflies -- Fiction
ISBN 0-399-22774-1; 0-399-23427-6 bd bk

LC 94-27827

A lonely firefly goes out into the night searching for other fireflies

"The illustrations are painted cut-paper collages, designed to draw the eye to the page. This is a compelling accomplishment." SLJ

★ The **very** quiet cricket. Philomel Bks. 1990 un il $22.99; bd bk $12.99
Grades: PreK K 1   **E**
1. Crickets -- Fiction
ISBN 0-399-21885-8; 0-399-22684-7 bd bk

LC 89-78317

A very quiet cricket who wants to rub his wings together and make a sound as do so many other animals finally achieves his wish

"The text is skillfully shaped; the illustrations convey energy and immediacy; and, in a surprise ending, a microchip inserted in the last page replicates the cricket's chirp." Horn Book Guide

What's your favorite animal? Eric Carle and friends, Nick Bruel, Lucy Cousins, Susan Jeffers, Steven Kellogg, Jon Klassen, Tom Lichtenheld, Peter McCarty, Chris Raschka, Peter Sís, Lane Smith, Erin Stead, Rosemary Wells, Mo Willems. Henry Holt and Company 2014 40 p. (hardback) $17.99
Grades: PreK K 1 2   **E**
1. Animals in art 2. Animals -- Pictorial works
ISBN 0805096418; 9780805096415

LC 2013018841

This book, by Eric Carle, explains that "everybody has a favorite animal. Some like little white dogs or big black cats or hoppy brown bunnies best. Others prefer squishy snails or tall giraffes or sleek black panthers. With . . . illustrations and . . . personal stories, 14 children's book artists share their favorite animals and why they love them." (Publisher's note)

"Eric Carle and his friends bring a consideration of What's Your Favorite Animal? to the pages of this fine-looking book. Each of fourteen illustrators gets a double-page spread to devote to his or her favorite. Grown-up picture book enthusiasts will appreciate this souvenir of the

artists in their singular styles; children will enjoy perusing the spaciously designed pages to decide their own favorites." (Horn Book)

★ **Where** are you going? To see my friend! [by] Eric Carle & Kazuo Iwamura. Orchard Bks. 2003 un il $19.95
Grades: PreK K 1   **E**
1. Animals -- Fiction 2. Friendship -- Fiction 3. Bilingual books -- English-Japanese
ISBN 0-439-41659-0

LC 2002-70396

Original Japanese edition, 2001

This "bilingual picture book is told in dialogue, with rebuslike symbols used to identify speakers. It details an energetic romp with a dog, cat, rooster, goat, rabbit, and a child, all of whom become friends. Carle's familiar collage technique is employed in the book's first half, while Iwamura's gentle watercolor illustrations, combined with the Japanese text, make up the second half. . . . An irresistible, spirited ode to friendship." SLJ

Carling, Amelia Lau
★ **Mama** & Papa have a store; story and pictures by Amelia Lau Carling. Dial Bks. for Young Readers 1998 un il $16.99
Grades: K 1 2 3   **E**
1. Chinese -- Fiction 2. Guatemala -- Fiction 3. Retail trade -- Fiction
ISBN 0-8037-2044-0

LC 97-10217

A little girl describes what a day is like in her parents' Chinese store in Guatemala City

"Carling's lovingly detailed watercolors in candy-box colors illustrate [the author's] memories. . . . A pleasant family story that should enrich library collections, especially those looking for multicultural themes." SLJ

Carlson, Nancy L.
★ **Get** up and go! by Nancy Carlson. Viking 2006 un il $15.99
Grades: PreK K   **E**
1. Exercise 2. Pigs -- Fiction 3. Rabbits -- Fiction
ISBN 0-670-05981-1

LC 2005003864

Text and illustrations encourage readers, regardless of shape or size, to turn off the television and play games, walk, dance, and engage in sports and other forms of exercise.

"Bright and sassy, the clearly delineated drawings with vivid washes provide a light, sometimes-comical tone that makes the lessons easier to take. With a short, simple text and a cheerful look, this will suit preschool and kindergarten teachers looking for an accessible book on exercise." Booklist

Henry and the Valentine surprise; [by] Nancy Carlson. Viking 2008 un il $15.99
Grades: PreK K 1 2   **E**
1. School stories 2. Mice -- Fiction 3. Animals -- Fiction 4. Teachers -- Fiction 5. Valentine's Day -- Fiction
ISBN 978-0-670-06267-6; 0-670-06267-7

LC 2008001283

When Henry the mouse and his first-grade classmates notice a heart-shaped box on their teacher's desk the day before Valentine's Day, they try to find out if he has a girlfriend.

"Told with mounting suspense, this mystery has a delightful and satisfying conclusion. Brightly colored comic illustrations portray the excitement at school as the special day approaches." SLJ

Other titles about Henry are:
Henry's show and tell (2004)

Henry's 100 days of kindergarten (2005)
Henry's amazing imagination! (2008)
Start saving, Henry! (2009)
Henry and the bully (2010)

I like me! [by] Nancy Carlson. Viking Kestrel 1988 un il lib bdg $16.99; pa $6.99
Grades: PreK K 1   E
1. Pigs -- Fiction
ISBN 0-670-82062-8 lib bdg; 0-14-050819-8 pa

LC 87-32616

By admiring her finer points and showing that she can take care of herself and have fun even when there's no one else around, a charming pig proves the best friend you can have is yourself

This book is "visually interesting, with sturdy animals drawn in a deliberately artless style. Simple shapes, strong lines, and clear colors, with lots of pattern mixing, show what is not described in the minimal text. The text is hand-lettered." SLJ

Another title about this pig is:
ABC I like me! (1997)

Carlstrom, Nancy White

It's your first day of school, Annie Claire. Abrams Books for Young Readers 2009 un il $15.95
Grades: PreK K   E
1. School stories 2. Stories in rhyme 3. Dogs -- Fiction 4. Mother-daughter relationship -- Fiction
ISBN 978-0-8109-4057-4; 0-8109-4057-4

LC 2009-2124

Annie Claire the puppy, excited but nervous about her first day of school, is reassured by her mother, whose love always goes with her.

"Sweet, gentle illustrations pair with reassuring text." Booklist

★ **Jesse** Bear, what will you wear? illustrations by Bruce Degen. Macmillan 1986 un il $16.95; pa $6.99; bd bk $7.99
Grades: PreK K   E
1. Stories in rhyme 2. Bears -- Fiction
ISBN 0-02-717350-X; 0-689-80623-X pa; 0-689-80930-1 bd bk

LC 85-10610

"The big, cheerful watercolor paintings show the baby bear in loving relation to his family and world. Without crossing the line into sentimentality, this offers a happy, humorous soundfest that will associate reading aloud with a sense of play." Bull Cent Child Books

Other titles about Jesse Bear are:
Better not get wet, Jesse Bear (1988)
Climb the family tree, Jesse Bear (2004)
Guess who's coming, Jesse Bear (1998)
Happy birthday, Jesse Bear (1994)
How do you say it today, Jesse Bear? (1992)
It's about time, Jesse Bear, and other rhymes (1990)
Let's count it out, Jesse Bear (1996)
What a scare, Jesse Bear! (1999)
Where is Christmas, Jesse Bear? (2000)

Carluccio, Maria

I'm 3! look what I can do. Henry Holt 2010 un il $10.99
Grades: PreK   E
1. Growth -- Fiction 2. Siblings -- Fiction
ISBN 978-0-8050-8313-2; 0-8050-8313-8

"The accomplishments of two young siblings are presented, from morning to night. Short, declarative sentences announce, 'I can sleep in my bed,' 'I can eat with my fork and spoon,' 'I can try different foods.' At preschool, the twins 'read,' paint, and demonstrate social skills such as sharing. At the end of the day they put on their pajamas and kiss

their family good night. The bright, cheery digital collages have an eye-catching variety of textures and patterns. An exuberant celebration of three-year-old milestones." SLJ

The **sounds** around town; by Maria Carluccio. Barefoot Books 2008 un il $16.99
Grades: PreK   E
1. Stories in rhyme 2. Day -- Fiction 3. Sound -- Fiction 4. City and town life -- Fiction
ISBN 978-1-905236-28-2; 1-905236-28-X

LC 2007025044

Reveals many things a child might hear during the day, from the singing of birds at dawn to the soft sounds of sleep.

"The text is alive with onomatopoeia, and the visually stimulating cut-paper collages provide myriad sources of the sounds to share and enjoy." Horn Book Guide

Carnesi, Mônica

Sleepover with Beatrice and Bear; Mônica Carnesi. Nancy Paulsen Books, an imprint of Penguin Group (USA) 2014 32 p. col. ill. $15.99
Grades: PreK K 1   E
1. Bears -- Fiction 2. Rabbits -- Fiction 3. Friendship -- Fiction 4. Winter -- Fiction 5. Hibernation -- Fiction 6. Best friends -- Fiction
ISBN 0399256679; 9780399256677

LC 2013034624

In this children's picture book, "Beatrice and Bear meet one spring day and become best buddies. They play together through summer and fall. Then winter comes and Beatrice can't find Bear anywhere. She hears he's gone to hibernate--but where on earth is that? When Beatrice learns that hibernation is not a place and that Bear will be sleeping all winter long, she fears it will be a lonely season . . . unless she comes up with a brilliant plan to share winter with Bear too." (Publisher's note)

"Carnesi's sweet illustrations perfectly capture the joys of friendship, the frustration at being left behind, and the satisfaction in making something for a friend. The spare text is an excellent complement to the lively illustrations, and the addition of speech balloons for Beatrice's big emotions really lets her perky personality shine." SLJ

Carr, Jan

Greedy Apostrophe; a cautionary tale. by Jan Carr; illustrated by Ethan Long. Holiday House 2007 un il $16.95
Grades: K 1 2 3   E
1. Punctuation -- Fiction
ISBN 978-0-8234-2006-3; 0-8234-2006-X

LC 2006012114

"All the punctuation marks stumble into the Hiring Hall one morning, sipping cocoa and discussing their job prospects. Each receives an important assignment, even Greedy Apostrophe, who has a well-deserved reputation for his bad attitude. . . . Students are asked to be vigilant and to take Greedy away from all the places where he inserts himself but doesn't really belong. With jazzy colors and cartoon-style characters, the upbeat artwork gives personality to the inanimate while underscoring the witty, vivacious tone of the text." Booklist

Carrer, Chiara

Otto Carrotto; written and illustrated by Chiara Carrer. Eerdmans Books for Young Readers 2011 un il $15.99
Grades: K 1 2   E
1. Carrots -- Fiction 2. Rabbits -- Fiction
ISBN 978-0-8028-5393-6; 0-8028-5393-5

LC 2010049546

Otto the rabbit decides to eat nothing but carrots, causing unexpected consequences.

"Sophisticated readers will pore over the thumbnail drawings and speech bubbles within the intricate collage illustrations, and the boldface text emphasizing repetitive words adds visual interest." SLJ

Carrick, Carol

★ **Patrick's** dinosaurs; pictures by Donald Carrick. Clarion Bks. 1983 un il lib bdg $16; pa $5.95
Grades: PreK K 1 2   E
   1. Brothers -- Fiction 2. Dinosaurs -- Fiction
   ISBN 0-89919-189-4 lib bdg; 0-89919-402-8 pa
                                     LC 83-2049
When his older brother talks about dinosaurs during a visit to the zoo, Patrick is afraid, until he discovers they all died millions of years ago.

"The Carricks do a particularly good job of creating an impressive array of creatures both in text and illustrations—realistic pencil drawings washed in muted greens, browns and oranges." SLJ

Other titles about Patrick's dinosaurs are:
Patrick's dinosaurs on the Internet (1999)
What happened to Patrick's dinosaurs? (1986)

Carter, David A.

600 black spots. Little Simon 2007 un il $19.99
Grades: 2 3 4 5 6   E
   1. Puzzles 2. Counting 3. Pop-up books
   ISBN 1-4169-4092-8; 978-1-4169-4092-0
In this pop-up book, readers are encouraged to search for the black spots throughout the pages

"This is both simple and stunning. . . . It takes a sophisticated artistic taste to appreciate the modern-art-style creations. . . . Older children will have an interesting time interpreting the artwork and marveling at the skill involved in the construction." Booklist

Blue 2; a pop-up book for children of all ages. Little Simon 2006 un il $10.95
Grades: 2 3 4 5 6   E
   1. Puzzles 2. Pop-up books
   ISBN 1-4169-1781-0
Each page contains an original piece of artwork that challenges the reader to find the a blue 2.

"Mobiles pop from the pages and readers spin pinwheels and pull tabs to find each elusive numeral two. Another enchanting creation from the inventive paper engineer." Publ Wkly

Hide and Seek. Harry N Abrams Inc 2012 20 p. (hardcover) $25
Grades: K 1 2 3 4 5   E
   1. Paper crafts 2. Stories in rhyme 3. Picture books for children
   ISBN 1849761019; 9781849761017
This pop-up book "offers six . . . new constructs—each hiding a handful of small cutouts or printed shapes to find. . . . Tallies along the margins invite viewers to spot a 'yellow splat, a red vine, a car and a star.' / . . . A sleepy head, in bed, with a red thread on his forehead' and like prizes. These are attached to, dangling from or hidden within the bursts of paper swirls, interlocking mazes and geometrical structures that rise up as each spread opens." (Kirkus)

Lots of bots; a counting pop-up book. Random House/Corey 2011 un il $14.99
Grades: PreK K 1   E
   1. Counting 2. Stories in rhyme 3. Pop-up books 4. Robots -- Fiction
   ISBN 978-0-375-86509-1; 0-375-86509-8
This is "a counting book that introduces an eclectic cast of specialized robots that sport antennae, springs, wheels, pincers, and other handy apparatuses. Using a question-and-answer format to count up to

10, the book asks energetic, reader-directed questions like 'Who makes you happy when you are sad?' with the answers appearing in verse. . . . Carter's quirky robots . . . should have effortless appeal for the preschool audience." Publ Wkly

★ **One** red dot; a pop-up book for children of all ages. Little Simon 2005 un il $19.95
Grades: 2 3 4 5 6   E
   1. Puzzles 2. Counting 3. Pop-up books
   ISBN 0-689-87769-2
Original Italian edition 2004
"A graphically bold pop-up book that entices readers to find the one red dot that is hidden on each paper sculpture. Going from 1 to 10, Carter creates a visual hide-and-seek game, ranging from flip-flop flaps to fluttering flicker clickers that really click to orbs that tower above the page. Bold primary colors and a silver-black text give the book a very slick, modern feel." SLJ

White noise; a pop-up book for children of all ages. Little Simon 2009 un il $22.99
Grades: 2 3 4 5 6   E
   1. Pop-up books 2. Noise -- Fiction
   ISBN 978-1-4169-4094-4; 1-4169-4094-4
"Each spread, designed to make crackly, crinkly, creaky, tinkling or snapping noises as the pages are turned, evokes children's construction-paper cutouts. . . . Carter's creations are akin to fireworks displays, each building in pyrotechnical intensity until the most impressive burst at the end." NY Times Book Rev

Yellow square; a pop-up book for children of all ages. Little Simon 2008 un il $19.99
Grades: 2 3 4 5 6   E
   1. Pop-up books
   ISBN 978-1-4169-4093-7; 1-4169-4093-6
"A yellow square hides in plain sight in or within the paper engineering on each spread; sometimes, the creation of the yellow square is entirely up to the reader. On the first spread, for example, that square exists only when the reader peers through a die-cut while holding the book at the correct angle-in other words, perspective is everything. Captions are variously enigmatic . . . or childlike. . . . Carter confines himself to primary colors, black and white; even with this palette, he alludes to a number of artists, among them Agam, . . . Christo, . . . Miro, and Calder. . . . Not all the spreads are equally impressive, but the best are dazzlers." Publ Wkly

Casanova, Mary

The **day** Dirk Yeller came to town; illustrated by Ard Hoyt. Farrar, Straus and Giroux 2011 un il $16.99
Grades: PreK K 1 2   E
   1. Tall tales 2. Libraries -- Fiction 3. West (U.S.) -- Fiction 4. Books and reading -- Fiction
   ISBN 978-0-374-31742-3; 0-374-31742-9
"Dangerous outlaw Dirk Yeller looms into town . . . terrifying even the tumbleweeds. . . . Only one small boy, the narrator of the tale, stands up to Dirk and leads him to, of all places, the public library. . . . The sandy-hued illustrations are packed with details and humor. . . . Hoyt's marvelous caricatures are worth thousands of words, making this hilarious tall tale not only a plug for books and reading but an outsized winner." Kirkus

Utterly otterly day; by Mary Casanova; illustrated by Ard Hoyt. Simon & Schuster Books for Young Readers 2008 un il $16.99

Grades: PreK K 1   E
1. Stories in rhyme 2. Otters -- Fiction
ISBN 978-1-4169-0868-5; 1-4169-0868-4

LC 2007041428

After a day out on his own, Little Otter realizes that he still needs his family no matter how big he grows

"The pen-and-ink-and-watercolor illustrations . . . emphasize the quick, exciting movement of the forest's animals, while the text hops with made-up rhyming words. . . . The adventurous otter and his caring family prove fairly irresistable." Booklist

Another title about Little Otter and his family is:

Utterly Otter night (2011)

Casarosa, Enrico

La Luna; story and illustrations by Enrico Casarosa, words by Kiki Thorpe. Disney Press 2012 40 p. $14.99
Grades: PreK K 1   E
1. Moon -- Fiction 2. Picture books for children 3. Intergenerational relations -- Fiction
ISBN 1423137663; 9781423137665

This children's book is based on a "Pixar film with an Academy Award nomination for Best Animated Short. . . . [T]hree characters, a boy, his hugely mustachioed father and his hugely bearded grandfather take their little boat, La Luna, out. . . . This family's job is to clean up the moon. . . . A huge star crashes into the moon, and while his father and grandfather argue about how to deal with it, the boy taps it. The star breaks into . . . tiny stars, and the three sweep them all up." (Kirkus)

Caseley, Judith

★ **On** the town; a community adventure. Greenwillow Bks. 2002 un il $15.95; lib bdg $15.89
Grades: PreK K 1 2   E
1. Community life -- Fiction
ISBN 0-06-029584-8; 0-06-029585-6 lib bdg

LC 2001-23896

Charlie and his mother walk around the neighborhood doing errands so that Charlie can write in his notebook about the people and places that make up his community

"Written from a child's perspective, the story has a cheerful tone and enough variety to keep the expedition interesting. The lively ink, watercolor, and colored-pencil illustrations are full of intriguing details." Booklist

Cash, Megan Montague

★ **Bow**-Wow's nightmare neighbors; Mark Newgarden, Megan Montague Cash. Roaring Brook Press 2014 64 p. chiefly color illustrations (hardcover) $17.99 E
1. Dogs -- Fiction 2. Theft -- Fiction 3. Halloween -- Fiction 4. Neighbors -- Fiction 5. Stories without words
ISBN 1596436409; 9781596436404

LC 2013028312

"As Bow-Wow naps, his neighbors creep in and steal his cozy green bed. When the expressive pup tries to get it back, colorful chaos ensues as the house next door might not be exactly what he thought.'" (Publisher's note)

"In this completely wordless picture book, Newgarden and Cash cue readers with various techniques taken from comics. In some scenes, a series of smaller frames builds to a dramatic turn of events, and page turns are never predictable." Kirkus

Castellucci, Cecil

Grandma's gloves; illustrated by Julia Denos. Candlewick Press 2010 un il $15.99

Grades: PreK K 1 2   E
1. Death -- Fiction 2. Gardening -- Fiction 3. Grandmothers -- Fiction
ISBN 978-0-7636-3168-0; 0-7636-3168-X

LC 2009015139

When her grandmother, a devoted gardener, dies, a little girl inherits her gardening gloves and feels closer to her memory.

"Castellucci's narrative details give voice to the perspicacity of a sensitive child—the smells, gestures, and alterations of experience that are noticed but rarely articulated. Denos's watercolor, pencil, and digital collage illustrations are bright and charming." SLJ

Odd Duck; by Cecil Castellucci, illustrated by Sara Varon. First Second 2013 96 p. (hardcover) $15.99
Grades: 1 2 3 4 5   E
1. Ducks -- Fiction 2. Friendship -- Fiction 3. Eccentrics and eccentricities -- Fiction
ISBN 1596435577; 9781596435575

In this book by Cecil Castellucci, illustrated by Sara Varon, "Theodora is a perfectly normal duck. She may swim with a teacup balanced on her head and stay north when the rest of the ducks fly south for the winter, but there's nothing so odd about that. Chad, on the other hand, is one strange bird. Theodora quite likes him, but she can't overlook his odd habits. It's a good thing Chad has a normal friend like Theodora to set a good example for him." (Publisher's note)

Castillo, Lauren

Melvin and the boy. Henry Holt 2011 un il $16.99
Grades: PreK K 1   E
1. Pets -- Fiction 2. Turtles -- Fiction
ISBN 978-0-8050-8929-5; 0-8050-8929-2

LC 2010038103

When a boy finds a turtle basking in the sun at the park he thinks he has found the perfect pet, but the turtle only seems happy at bath time. Includes facts about turtles.

"Castillo's . . . gently outlined drawings help to soften a potentially disappointing situation. . . . The boy's parents offer surprising support, allowing their son to bring Melvin home from the park, but the decision to return Melvin is the boy's own. . . . It's an honest account of a small, manageable failure, with a lemonade-from-lemons moment at the end." Publ Wkly

★ **Nana** in the city; by Lauren Castillo. Clarion Books, Houghton Mifflin Harcourt 2014 40 p. (hardcover) $16.99
Grades: PreK K 1   E
1. Grandmothers -- Fiction 2. Cities and towns -- Fiction 3. Courage -- Fiction 4. City and town life -- Fiction
ISBN 0544104439; 9780544104433

LC 2013043953

Caldecott Honor Book (2015)

In this children's book by Lauren Castillo, "a young boy spends an overnight visit with his nana and is frightened to find that the city where she lives is filled with noise and crowds and scary things. But then Nana makes him a special cape to help him be brave, and soon the everyday sights, sounds, and smells of the city are not scary--but wonderful."

""I love my nana," a boy explains, "but I don't love the city." She greets him with a hug, but he's still nervous. "The city is busy," he says (crowds press in). "The city is loud" (a whistle shrieks). "The city is filled with scary things" (the boy shrinks from a homeless man holding out a cup). "It is no place for a nana to live," he concludes. While he sleeps, nana knits him a gift—a big red cape. A series of vignettes shows him wearing it the next morning, striking delighted poses. With new courage, the boy discovers a city he hasn't seen before—one full of life, wonder, and pretzels for homeless men..." PW

The **troublemaker**; by Lauren Castillo. Clarion Books, Houghton Mifflin Harcourt 2014 48 p. (hardcover) $16.99

Grades: PreK K 1   E

1. Bad behavior 2. Toys -- Fiction 3. Siblings -- Fiction 4. Lost and found possessions -- Fiction 5. Behavior -- Fiction

ISBN 054772991X; 9780547729916

LC 2012039686

In this children's book by Lauren Castillo, "bored and restless on a summer day, a little boy steals his sister's bunny and sends it on an adventure. He is well satisfied with the results--until his own stuffed animal disappears. Could it be that he is not the only troublemaker around . . . ? A case of sibling rivalry is neatly resolved with the 'assistance' of a hilarious raccoon." (Publisher's note)

"The narrator kidnaps his sister's stuffed rabbit, lashes it to his toy boat, and sets it sail on the lake. The boat capsizes, and sister and mom are angry; later when the bunny disappears--again!--they understandably suspect the narrator. (Readers will see that a wild raccoon is the real culprit.) With boldly rendered spreads, the book is at once handsome and child friendly." Horn Book

Caswell, Deanna

Guess who, haiku! Deanna Caswell; Illustrated by Bob Shea. Abrams Appleseed 2016 24 p. color illustrations (ebook) $14.95; (hardcover) $14.95

Grades: PreK K   E

1. Haiku 2. Stories in rhyme 3. Questions and answers -- Fiction

ISBN 9781613129074; 9781419718892

LC 2015016274

This book in the Guess Who Haiku series by Deanna Caswell, illustrated by Bob Shea, "offers clues about the creatures hiding on every page in this creative and clever picture book of charmingly illustrated poems for the very young. As readers meet a cow, a bee, a horse, a bird, a frog, a fish, a mouse, a cat, and a dog, they will be delighted to learn that they are the subject of the final poem." (Publisher's note)

"Overall, a superb introduction to this potent poetic form, teaching pre-readers both the evocative power of description and the reward for listening closely. Not to be missed: gorgeous poetry, vibrant illustrations, and masterful use of the page turn." Kirkus

Train trip; written by Deanna Caswell; illustrated by Dan Andreasen. Disney Hyperion 2011 un il $16.99

Grades: PreK K   E

1. Railroads -- Fiction

ISBN 978-1-4231-1837-4; 1-4231-1837-5

"A young boy sets off on a solo train trip. As he climbs aboard, he takes in the new sights and sounds. . . . The staccato stop and start iambic verse mimics the rhythm of the train. . . . At the final station, he finds his grandmother waiting. Andreasen's cartoon illustrations have a sentimental, homespun appeal. The anthropomorphized train has a wide, smiling face and even the whistle has goggle eyes and gives a friendly toot. . . . The excitement of the journey rings true." SLJ

Catalanotto, Peter

Emily's art. Atheneum Bks. for Young Readers 2001 un il $16

Grades: PreK K 1   E

1. Artists 2. Artists -- Fiction 3. Winning and losing 4. Contests -- Fiction

ISBN 0-689-83831-X

LC 00-29293

Emily paints four pictures and enters one in the first-grade art contest, but the judge interprets Emily's entry as a rabbit instead of a dog. "Ages five to eight." (Bull Cent Child Books)

"Filled with touches of humor and authentically childlike emotions, this book explores the subjectivity of opinion and the importance of personal conviction." Horn Book Guide

Monkey and Robot; Peter Catalanotto. Atheneum Books for Young Readers 2013 64 p. (hardcover) $12.99

Grades: 1 2   E

1. Robots -- Fiction 2. Monkeys -- Fiction 3. Friendship -- Fiction

ISBN 144242978X; 9781442429789; 9781442430600

LC 2012003044

This children's chapter book, by Peter Catalanotto, presents four stories which follow a monkey and robot who are friends. "They simply belong together, and it never matters that silly Monkey is furry, or that kind Robot can rust. What matters is their sharing: movies and popcorn, games of hide-and-seek, a fish tank for . . . a hippopotamus?" (Publisher's note)

More of Monkey & Robot; Peter Catalanotto. Atheneum Books for Young Readers 2014 64 p. (hardcover) $14.99

Grades: 1 2   E

1. Adventure and adventurers 2. Robots -- Fiction 3. Monkeys -- Fiction 4. Friendship -- Fiction 5. Best friends -- Fiction

ISBN 144245251X; 9781442452510

LC 2012051501

In this book, by Peter Catalanatto, "Monkey and Robot . . . return. . . . Divided into four stand-alone chapters, the stories provide kids with . . . antics of two unlikely pals as they plan for Halloween, enjoy a day at the beach, make a new friend, and figure out if it's time for breakfast or bedtime." (School Library Journal)

"In four chapters for new independent readers, Monkey (Monkey & Robot) continues to make a mess, and Robot helps him fix things, at the beach, in the front yard, on Halloween, and while telling time. Catalanotto has created two distinct and likable characters--unlikely pals who understand each other. Black-and-white pencil illustrations provide helpful visual cues for the easy-to-decode text." Horn Book

More of Monkey and Robot

Question Boy meets Little Miss Know-It-All. Atheneum Books for Young Readers 2012 il $16.99

E

1. Humorous fiction 2. Curiosity -- Fiction

ISBN 978-1-4424-0670-4; 1-4424-0670-4

LC 2011000496

A curious boy with non-stop questions meets a girl who seems to know all the answers.

Catchpool, Michael

The **cloud** spinner; by Michael Catchpool; illustrations by Alison Jay. Alfred A. Knopf 2012 32 p.

Grades: K 1 2 3   E

1. Fairy tales 2. Clouds -- Fiction 3. Weaving -- Fiction 4. Kings and rulers -- Fiction 5. Conservation of natural resources -- Fiction 6. Kings, queens, rulers, etc. -- Fiction

ISBN 9780375870118; 9780375970115; 9780375987397

LC 2011000894

In this book, a "young boy spins clouds into thread, . . . then weaves the thread into cloth. . . . [The] king . . . requests a scarf from the boy, then goes on to demand more and more clothing. . . . [The] king's daughter has been paying attention, and when the king's greedy consumption . . . results in the disappearance of all the clouds and . . . rain, she brings the clothes back to the spinner so that they can be reverted to clouds." (Bulletin of the Center for Children's Books)

Cate, Annette LeBlanc

The **magic** rabbit; [by] Annette LeBlanc Cate. Candlewick Press 2007 un il $15.99
Grades: K 1 2 3   E
  1. Rabbits -- Fiction 2. Magicians -- Fiction 3. Lost and found possessions -- Fiction
  ISBN 978-0-7636-6685-9; 978-0-7636-2672-3; 0-7636-2672-4
                                                                            LC 2007022789
When Bunny becomes separated from Ray, a magician who is his business partner and friend, he follows a crowd to a park where he has a lovely afternoon, and after the people leave and darkness falls, the lonely and frightened Bunny finds a glittering trail of hope

"Embellished only with the gold of 'glittering stars,' Cate's black-and-white drawings perfectly evoke an urban setting in this tale of lost and found." SLJ

Cates, Karin

★ The **Secret** Remedy Book; a story of comfort and love. illustrated by Wendy Anderson Halperin. Orchard Bks. 2003 un il $16.95
Grades: K 1 2 3   E
  1. Aunts -- Fiction
  ISBN 0-439-35226-6
                                                                            LC 2002-35475
Although Lolly loves to visit her Auntie Zep's house, she feels homesick when she actually gets there, and so Auntie Zep retrieves the Secret Remedy Book from an old trunk

"This wonderfully warm and satisfying story is paired with Halperin's lovely illustrations. Her trademark details and patterns abound, with softened edges, muted colors, and quiet landscapes." SLJ

Catrow, David

Dinosaur hunt. Orchard Books 2009 un il (Max Spaniel) $6.99
Grades: K 1 2   E
  1. Dogs -- Fiction 2. Dinosaurs -- Fiction
  ISBN 978-0-545-05748-6; 0-545-05748-5
                                                                            LC 2008-30144
Max Spaniel searches for dinosaurs in his back yard.

"Washed with colors, the exaggerated, cartoonlike drawings create a zany mood that energizes and extends the deadpan text." Booklist

Other titles about Max Spaniel are:
Funny lunch (2010)
Best in show (2011)

Cauley, Lorinda Bryan

Clap your hands. Putnam 1992 un il hardcover o.p. pa $6.99; bd bk $7.99
Grades: PreK K   E
  1. Stories in rhyme 2. Animals -- Fiction
  ISBN 0-399-22118-2; 0-698-11428-0 pa; 0-399-237100 bd bk
                                                                            LC 91-12863
Rhyming text instructs the listener to find something yellow, roar like a lion, give a kiss, tell a secret, spin in a circle, and perform other playful activities along with the human and animal characters pictured

"The illustrations feature glowing colors and make good use of Cauley's gift for characterization. . . . Some parts of the book would be fun as action rhymes for preschool story time." Booklist

Cave, Kathryn

One child, one seed; a South African counting book. photographs by Gisèle Wulfsohn. Holt & Co. 2003 un il $16.95

Grades: PreK K 1 2   E
  1. Pumpkin 2. Counting 3. South Africa -- Social life and customs
  ISBN 0-8050-7204-7
                                                                            LC 2002-24098
"Children count from 1 to 10 with Nothando as she plants a pumpkin seed that grows to bear fruit for a delicious stew. . . . In a harmonious partnership of narrative and crisp, beautifully composed photographs that show the individuality of each person, readers get a glimpse into the life of an extended family living in a rural South African community. . . . The recipe for isijingi, the pumpkin stew, is included as are some basic geographical facts and a simple map. The writing has good rhythm, and reads aloud well." SLJ

Cazet, Denys

Minnie and Moo and the haunted sweater; [by] Denys Cazet. HarperCollinsPublishers 2007 45p il (I can read!) $15.99; lib bdg $16.89
Grades: 1 2 3   E
  1. Cattle -- Fiction 2. Birthdays -- Fiction
  ISBN 978-0-06-073016-1; 0-06-073016-1; 978-0-06-073017-8 lib bdg; 0-06-073017-X lib bdg
                                                                            LC 2006036246
Minnie and Moo want to give special presents to the Farmer for his birthday, but something goes awry when Moo knits him a sweater.

This is "an outlandishly hilarious romp. . . . Nonstop action and a clever plot place this title at the top of the list for young readers ready for a slightly more complex story." SLJ

★ **Minnie** and Moo, wanted dead or alive. HarperCollinsPublishers 2006 47p il (I can read book) hardcover o.p. lib bdg $16.89; pa $3.99
Grades: 1 2 3   E
  1. Cattle -- Fiction 2. Thieves -- Fiction
  ISBN 0-06-073010-2; 978-0-06-073010-9; 0-06-073011-0 lib bdg; 978-0-06-073011-6 lib bdg; 978-0-06-073012-3 pa; 0-06-073012-9 pa
                                                                            LC 2005-14526
Trying to help Mr. Farmer with his finances, Minnie and Moo (dressed in trenchcoats, ties, and gray fedoras) go to the bank to ask for money and are mistaken for the Bazooka sisters, dangerous outlaws. "Preschool, primary." (Horn Book)

"Cazet's watercolor illustrations of cows dressed as gangsters and cows driving a tractor extend the story's absurd humor and will help move emerging readers through eight chapters of text." Booklist

★ The **octopus**; Grandpa Spanielson's Chicken pox stories, story #1. HarperCollins 2005 46p il (I can read!) $15.99; lib bdg $16.89
Grades: PreK K 1 2   E
  1. Dogs -- Fiction 2. Octopuses -- Fiction 3. Chickenpox -- Fiction
  ISBN 0-06-051088-9; 0-06-051089-7 lib bdg
                                                                            LC 2003-26557
Grandpa Spanielson helps his favorite grandpup to avoid scratching his chicken pox by telling how he once had to fight off an octopus during a terrible storm.

"Beginning readers will love the humor, action, and compassion in this story, brought to life in the fun-filled text and superb cartoon illustrations." SLJ

Other titles in Grandpa Spanielson's Chicken pox stories series are:
A snout for chocolate (2006)
The shrunken head (2007)

★ **Will** you read to me? story and pictures by Denys Cazet. Atheneum Books for Young Readers 2007 un il $16.99

Grades: PreK K 1 2   **E**
1. Pigs -- Fiction 2. Books and reading -- Fiction
ISBN 978-1-4169-0935-4; 1-4169-0935-4

LC 2005024144

Hamlet enjoys reading books and writing poetry, not playing in the mud and fighting over supper like the other pigs, but he finally finds someone who appreciates him just as he is

"Kids will enjoy the uproarious pigsty scenes.... But Cazet's simple poetry and soft-toned watercolor-and-colored-pencil spreads also show the beauty of the quiet night . . . and the farm community in solitude. This is not only a celebration of reading but also a moving story about not fitting in, even at home." Booklist

Cech, John
The **nutcracker**; based on the story by E.T.A. Hoffmann; retold by John Cech; illustrated by Eric Puybaret. Sterling 2009 un il $17.95
Grades: 2 3 4 5   **E**
1. Fairy tales 2. Christmas -- Fiction
ISBN 978-1-4027-5562-0; 1-4027-5562-7

LC 2008043084

In this retelling of the original 1816 German story, Godfather Drosselmeier gives young Marie a nutcracker for Christmas, and she finds herself in a magical realm where she saves a boy from an evil curse

"This beautifully illustrated rendition . . . is wordier than some picture-book adaptations. . . . The language is accessible, though, and lustrous, richly colored paintings cover half, sometimes more, of nearly every spread, providing valuable visual breaks." Booklist

The **princess** and the pea; by Hans Christian Andersen; retold by John Cech; illustrated by Bernhard Oberdieck. Sterling Pub. 2007 un il $14.95
Grades: K 1 2 3   **E**
1. Authors 2. Novelists 3. Dramatists 4. Fairy tales 5. Children's authors 6. Short story writers
ISBN 978-1-4027-3065-8; 1-4027-3065-9

LC 2006007033

A girl proves that she is a real princess by feeling a pea through twenty mattresses and twenty featherbeds. Includes historical notes about Hans Christian Anderson and the original fairy tale.

"Cech's fluid text sparkles in this well-crafted retelling. . . . The illustrations, created with colored pencils, pastels, and acrylics, glow with lustrous yellow-gold, blue, and green tones." SLJ

Cecil, Randy
Duck; [by] Randy Cecil. Candlewick Press 2008 un il $15.99
Grades: PreK K 1   **E**
1. Ducks -- Fiction
ISBN 978-0-7636-3072-0

LC 2007040407

Companion volume to: Gator (2007)

Duck happily raises a duckling that has wandered into the amusement park where she is a carousel animal, but finds that she cannot teach what she herself has always longed to do—fly—and sets out to find real ducks to instruct him

"Cecil's illustrations . . . are done in oils. Duck, with her bright, striped scarf, stands out against soft green and gold hues. Many of the paintings are in circles of various sizes on a white background with a gold frame. . . . A beautifully realized friendship story with a happy ending." SLJ

Celenza, Anna Harwell
Duke Ellington's Nutcracker suite; illustrated by Don Tate. Charlesbridge 2011 il lib bdg $19.95

Grades: K 1 2 3   **E**
1. Pianists 2. Composers 3. Band leaders 4. Music arrangers 5. Jazz music -- Fiction 6. Jazz musicians -- Fiction 7. African Americans -- Fiction
ISBN 978-1-57091-700-4; 1-57091-700-0

LC 2010023060

Tells the story of how jazz composer and musician Duke Ellington, along with Billy Strayhorn, created his jazz composition based on Tchaikovsky's famous Nutcracker Suite ballet.

"This fictionalization of Ellington and Strayhorn's daring collaboration is well told, and the illustrations convey the hip, cool feeling of the time. An author's note provides more information, and a CD of the piece is included." SLJ

Gershwin's Rhapsody in Blue; [by] Anna Harwell Celenza; illustrated by JoAnn E. Kitchel. Charlesbridge 2006 un il $19.95
Grades: 1 2 3 4   **E**
1. Composers 2. Music -- Fiction 3. Composers -- Fiction
ISBN 978-1-57091-556-7; 1-57091-556-3

LC 2005006009

In January of 1924, a twenty-six-year-old pianist, George Gershwin, finds himself slated to compose, in only five weeks, a concerto that defines "American music," and the result is his masterpiece, Rhapsody in Blue.

"Celenza's tale, complete with invented dialogue, brings the composer to life. . . . An author's note contains Gershwin's words describing the rhythm of the train ride that freed his mental block. . . . Kitchel's sensitivity to this source material is especially evident in her spread of multifaceted patterns and images. . . . An accompanying CD features Gershwin himself (courtesy of a piano roll)." SLJ

Chabon, Michael, 1963-
★ The **astonishing** secret of Awesome Man; illustrated by Jake Parker. Balzer + Bray 2011 un il $17.99
Grades: K 1 2   **E**
1. Family life -- Fiction 2. Imagination -- Fiction 3. Superheroes -- Fiction
ISBN 978-0-06-191462-1; 0-06-191462-2

LC 2010041192

A young superhero describes his awesome powers, which he then demonstrates as various foes arrive on the scene.

"Chabon's first picture book discharges delectable language. . . . Things are more likely to skloosh and skarunch than not. Verbiage like this nudges the story into read-aloud territory, and children will be swooping around the room as they listen. But if they stop long enough to peek at the pages, they'll enjoy the way Parker kicks it up another notch with hyperkinetic, hypercolored comic-book action scenes." SLJ

Chaconas, Dori
★ **Cork** & Fuzz; illustrated by Lisa McCue. Viking 2005 32p il (Viking easy-to-read) $13.99
Grades: K 1 2   **E**
1. Muskrats -- Fiction 2. Opossums -- Fiction 3. Friendship -- Fiction
ISBN 0-670-03602-1

LC 2004-13613

A possum and a muskrat become friends despite their many differences.

"The story's repeated words and entire sentences will help beginning readers feel successful. McCue's endearing drawings add personality and humor to the animals' faces. An excellent addition to easy-reader collections." SLJ

Other titles about Cork & Fuzz are:
Cork & Fuzz: short and tall (2006)

Cork & Fuzz: good sports (2007)
Cork & Fuzz: the collectors (2008)
Cork & Fuzz: finder's keepers (2009)
Cork & Fuzz: the babysitters (2010)
Cork & Fuzz: the swimming lesson (2011)

Don't slam the door! illustrated by Will Hillenbrand. Candlewick Press 2010 un il $15.99
Grades: PreK K 1 2   E
1. Stories in rhyme 2. Doors -- Fiction 3. Animals -- Fiction
ISBN 978-0-7636-3709-5; 0-7636-3709-2

LC 2009015254

A cumulative, rhyming tale of a slamming door which wakes a cat, setting into motion an absurd chain of events and resulting in chaos.

"The author's bouncy couplets are rhythmically consistent all the better for reading aloud. Hillenbrand's mixed-media illustrations with characteristic domestic details and expressive faces on both animal and human figures are a spot-on match to the narrative." SLJ

Mousie love; illustrated by Josee Masse. Bloomsbury U.S.A. Children's Books 2009 un il $16.99; lib bdg $17.89
Grades: K 1 2   E
1. Love -- Fiction 2. Mice -- Fiction
ISBN 978-1-59990-111-4; 1-59990-111-0; 978-1-59990-368-2 lib bdg; 1-59990-368-7 lib bdg

LC 2008-39888

After falling in love at first sight, Tully the mouse strives to prove his devotion to Frill every day—while avoiding the cat—but never gives her a chance to respond to his marriage proposal

"Masse's bright, cheerful acrylic-and-gel illustrations complement the text . . . [and] courtship vignettes alternate with humorous, action-packed chase scenes from a mouse-eye perspective. Mousie love triumphs through adversity in this fetching little romance." Kirkus

Chall, Marsha Wilson

Pick a pup; [by] Marsha Chall; illustrated by Jed Henry. Margaret K. McElderry Books 2011 un il $16.99
Grades: PreK K 1   E
1. Stories in rhyme 2. Dogs -- Fiction 3. Pets -- Fiction 4. Grandmothers -- Fiction
ISBN 978-1-4169-7961-6; 1-4169-7961-1

After observing different types of dogs in his neighborhood, Sam and Gram go to the local pet shelter to choose a puppy.

"Terrific for sharing, with bouncing and memorable phrasing and appealing, energetic illustrations, this sweet and satisfying tale showcases the charm and special qualities of dogs as well as the tenderness of a grandparent-grandchild relationship." Kirkus

Chandra, Deborah

★ **George** Washington's teeth; written by Deborah Chandra & Madeleine Comora; pictures by Brock Cole. Farrar, Straus & Giroux 2003 un il $16
Grades: PreK K 1 2   E
1. Teeth 2. Generals 3. Presidents
ISBN 0-374-32534-0

LC 2002-25086

A rollicking rhyme portrays George Washington's lifelong struggle with bad teeth. A timeline taken from diary entries and other nonfiction sources follows

This is written "with wit, verve, and a generous amount of sympathy for poor Washington and his dental woes. . . . Illustrator Cole is at his absolute best here, totally at ease with human gesture and expression." Booklist

Chapman, Jane

I'm not sleepy! Jane Chapman. Good Books 2012 32 p. col. ill. (hardcover : alk. paper) $16.99
Grades: PreK K 1   E
1. Grandmothers -- Fiction 2. Owls -- Fiction 3. Bedtime -- Fiction
ISBN 1561487651; 9781561487653

LC 2012000185

In author Jeffrey Frank's book, "a little owlet employs a big bag of tricks when Grandma tries to get him to settle down to sleep." Grandma comes "up with a plan. She will go to sleep, and Mo, after putting her to bed, can play to his heart's content. Mo is delighted, but he finds that the effort of arranging a nest for Grandma and flying down to get her bedtime snack has made him...sleepy." (Kirkus Reviews)

Charest, Emily MacLachlan

Before you came; by Patricia MacLachlan & Emily MacLachlan Charest; illustrated by David Diaz. Katherine Tegen Books 2011 un il $16.99; lib bdg $17.89
Grades: PreK K 1   E
1. Mother-child relationship -- Fiction
ISBN 978-0-06-051234-7; 0-06-051234-2; 978-0-06-051235-4 lib bdg; 0-06-051235-0 lib bdg

A mother relates how she spent time before her child arrived, then passes on a gift of days paddling a red canoe, reading in a pillow-filled hammock until dark, and watching the moon rise at night.

"Iridescent light, tropical colors, and entwined, nature-themed patterns distinguish Caldecott Medalist Diaz's . . . lavish art, which is the bedrock of this resplendent book. . . . Details of their mothers' and fathers' lives before they became parents are a constant source of fascination for children, and this talented team celebrates the 'before', while emphasizing (and reassuring) that the 'now' is even better." Publ Wkly

Charles, Veronika Martenova

The **birdman**; illustrated by Annouchka Gravel Galouchko & Stéphan Daigle. Tundra Books 2006 un il $17.95
Grades: K 1 2 3   E
1. Birds -- Fiction 2. India -- Fiction 3. Bereavement -- Fiction
ISBN 978-0-88776-740-1; 0-88776-740-0

"In the crowded streets of Calcutta, Nobi, a tailor, works hard to support his family. Then his wife and children are killed. . . . After weeks of immobilizing anguish, Nobi buys some caged birds at the market, sets them free, and finds some of his weighty sorrow released. . . . Charles, who based her vivid, poetic text on a true story (explained in a lengthy afterword), is frank about the pain of loss, but focuses on the uplifting message that acts of kindness can ease grief. The illustrators extend the story's spirit-healing themes in vibrant folk-art paintings, gloriously patterned with flowers, Hindu symbols, and soaring birds." Booklist

Charlip, Remy

Fortunately; written and illustrated by Remy Charlip. Aladdin Books 1993 un il pa $6.99
Grades: PreK K 1   E
1. Chance -- Fiction 2. Travel -- Fiction
ISBN 0-689-71660-5; 978-0-689-71660-7

LC 92-22794

First published 1964 by Four Winds Press

Good and bad luck accompany Ned from New York to Florida on his way to a surprise party.

★ A **perfect** day; [by] Remy Charlip. Greenwillow Books 2007 un il $16.99; lib bdg $17.89

Grades: PreK K 1 2   **E**
1. Stories in rhyme 2. Father-son relationship -- Fiction
ISBN 0-06-051972-X; 0-06-051973-8 lib bdg
LC 2004-52350

A father and son's "perfect day consists of doing ordinary things—going for a walk, picnicking with friends, watching the clouds, reading books. . . . The simple illustrations resemble something a youngster might draw, and the palette of soft pastel colors supports the story's comforting atmosphere and the love between these two. . . . Charlip has crafted a cozy story that is a perfect example of parent and child bonding." SLJ

Chase, Kit

Oliver's tree; Kit Chase. G. P. Putnam's Sons 2014 32 p. color illustrations $16.99
Grades: PreK K   **E**
1. Elephants -- Fiction 2. Owls -- Fiction 3. Rabbits -- Fiction 4. Friendship -- Fiction 5. Hide-and-seek -- Fiction
ISBN 0399257004; 9780399257001
LC 2013014667

In this children's book, written and illustrated by Kit Chase, "Oliver, Charlie, and Lulu love to play outside together. Their favorite game is hide-and-seek, but it's not fun for Oliver when his friends hide in the trees--he can't reach them! So the friends set off to find a tree that Oliver can play in." (Publisher's note)

"Suffused with warmth and gentle humor, this deceptively simple story demonstrates the power of friendship, the importance of working together and problem-solving, while simultaneously introducing basic concepts (high/low, tall/short) in a pleasing, organic way." Kirkus

Chast, Roz

★ **Too** busy Marco. Atheneum Books for Young Readers 2010 un il $16.99
Grades: PreK K 1 2   **E**
1. Birds -- Fiction 2. Bedtime -- Fiction
ISBN 978-1-4169-8474-0; 1-4169-8474-7
LC 2009052481

"Cartoonist Chast brings her affectionate, anxious line and fascination with the eccentrically ordinary to an original riff on bedtime avoidance." Horn Book

Chatelain, Jeremy

May the stars drip down; by Jeremy Chatelain; illustrated by Nikki McClure. Abrams Books for Young Readers 2014 40 p. $17.95
Grades: PreK K 1   **E**
1. Lullabies 2. Songs 3. Children's songs, English -- United States -- Texts
ISBN 1419710249; 9781419710247
LC 2013008241

This book, by musician Jeremy Chatelain, is a "lullaby . . . adapted into a . . . bedtime book with illustrations by . . . cut-paper artist Nikki McClure. McClure's . . . intricate images, inspired by nature and the intense bond between parent and child, . . . complement . . . Chatelain's . . . lyrics. An audio download of the song is also included." (Publisher's note)

"In this achingly loving interpretation of the indie band Cub Country's lullaby, a mother cuddles her sleepy son, picturing his dream wanderings in the natural world and wishing him well on his nighttime journeys...A richly imagined dreamscape in a feat of paper artistry." Kirkus

Chaud, Benjamin

The **bear's** sea escape; Benjamin Chaud. Chronicle Books LLC 2014 32 p. color illustrations $17.99

Grades: PreK K 1 2   **E**
1. Sea stories 2. Bears -- Fiction 3. Hibernation -- Fiction 4. Lost children -- Fiction 5. Father and child -- Fiction
ISBN 1452127433; 9781452127439
LC 2013037654

"When the bears seek warmth from their chilly perch atop the Paris Opera House, Little Bear is mistaken for a toy bear and whisked away . . . to a tropical island! Papa Bear sets out on a frenzied journey to find Little Bear, traveling to a bustling wharf, beneath a sea brimming with coral and mermaids, onto a busy beach, and all the way to a sun-drenched island." (Publisher's note)

"In delightfully crowded, oversize spreads that jostle with activity and eye-catching colors, Chaud offers another absorbing and cheerful visual feast." Booklist

★ The **bear's** song; by Benjamin Chaud. Chronicle Books 2013 32 p. (alk. paper) $17.99
Grades: PreK K 1 2   **E**
1. Bears -- Fiction 2. Cities and towns -- Fiction 3. Fathers and sons -- Fiction
ISBN 1452114242; 9781452114248
LC 2012046877

Author Benjamin Chaud presents a "immersive picture book about two bears on a big-city adventure. Papa Bear is searching for Little Bear, who has escaped the den. Little Bear is following a bee, because where there are bees, there is honey! When the quest leads both bears into the bustling city and a humming opera house, theatrical hijinks ensue." (Publisher's note)

Other titles in this series are:
The bear's escape (2014)
The bear's surprise (2015)

Chen, Chih-Yuan

★ **Guji** Guji. Kane/Miller 2004 un il $15.95
Grades: PreK K 1 2   **E**
1. Ducks -- Fiction 2. Crocodiles -- Fiction
ISBN 1-929132-67-0

Crocodile Guji Guji, who was raised by a family of ducks, meets three crocodiles who tell him that he was not a duck. When the crocodiles ask Guji Guji to help them trap the ducks he saves the duck family.

"This beautifully written story has much to say about appreciating families and differences. . . . Chen's unique illustrations are compelling. . . . The rich blues and earth tones and dramatic page layouts create moving scenes, but the quirky details and characters' expressions are hilarious." SLJ

On my way to buy eggs; written and illustrated by Chih-Yuan Chen. Kane/Miller 2003 un il hardcover o.p. pa $7.99
Grades: PreK K 1 2   **E**
1. Imagination -- Fiction
ISBN 1-929132-49-2; 1-933605-41-3 pa
LC 2002-117381

First published 2001 in Taiwan

"Sent to the local store to buy eggs, Shau-yu takes a circuitous walk through her neighborhood, 'balancing' on the shadow thrown on the sidewalk by a rooftop, scuffing through fallen leaves, looking at the world through a marble so that everything is transformed into 'a blue ocean world.' . . . Preschool. Primary." (Horn Book)

"A young girl's errand to the store turns into a sensory adventure. . . . After a make-believe game with the shopkeeper and more adventures along the way, Shau-yu returns home to her loving dad. The story is basic, but the simple words and phrases easily show Shau-yu's delight in transforming small things. The earth-tone colors in the crisp paper-and-pencil collages are as quiet as the story." Booklist

Chen, Yong

A **gift**. Boyds Mills Press 2009 un il $16.95

Grades: K 1 2 3　　　　　　　　　　　　　　　E

1. Aunts -- Fiction 2. China -- Fiction 3. Uncles -- Fiction 4. Chinese New Year -- Fiction 5. Chinese Americans -- Fiction

ISBN 978-1-59078-610-9; 1-59078-610-6

LC 2009012794

Amy receives a gift for the Chinese New Year from her aunt and uncles who live far away in China.

"Chen's text is spare but, combined with her luscious watercolors, evokes a vivid portrait of rural Chinese culture." SLJ

Cherry, Lynne

★ The **great** kapok tree; a tale of the Amazon rainforest. Harcourt Brace Jovanovich 1990 un il $16; pa $7

Grades: K 1 2 3　　　　　　　　　　　　　　　E

1. Rain forests -- Fiction

ISBN 0-15-200520-X; 0-15-202614-2 pa

LC 89-2208

The many different animals that live in a great kapok tree in the Brazilian rainforest try to convince a man with an ax of the importance of not cutting down their home

"A carefully researched picture book. . . . Cherry captures the Amazonian proportions of the plants and animals that live there by using vibrant colors, intricate details, and dramatic perspectives. . . . The writing is simple and clear." Booklist

How Groundhog's garden grew. Blue Sky Press (NY) 2003 un il $15.95

Grades: PreK K 1 2　　　　　　　　　　　　　E

1. Marmots -- Fiction

ISBN 0-439-32371-1

LC 2002-3428

Squirrel teaches Little Groundhog how to plant and tend a vegetable garden

The author "tells a charming and also informative story about plants, gardening, and environmental respect. Her beautiful, full-color illustrations—realistic and wonderfully detailed—often incorporate spot-art borders of labeled seedlings and plants, highlighting a diverse array of wildlife." Booklist

The **sea,** the storm, and the mangrove tangle. Farrar, Straus and Giroux 2004 un il $16

Grades: K 1 2 3　　　　　　　　　　　　　　　E

1. Ecology -- Fiction 2. Wetlands -- Fiction 3. Marine animals -- Fiction 4. Caribbean region -- Fiction

ISBN 0-374-36482-6

LC 2002-29705

A seed from a mangrove tree floats on the sea until it comes to rest on the shore of a faraway lagoon where, over time, it becomes a mangrove island that shelters many birds and animals, even during a hurricane.

"Cherry paints lustrous, detailed scenes that, together with her accessible narrative, will spark children's interest in a magnificent, endangered ecosystem." Booklist

Chichester-Clark, Emma

Little Miss Muffet counts to ten. Andersen Press 2010 un il pa $9.99

Grades: K 1 2　　　　　　　　　　　　　　　　E

1. Counting 2. Stories in rhyme 3. Animals -- Fiction 4. Nursery rhymes -- Fiction

ISBN 978-1-84270-955-9; 1-84270-955-0

"The text is spot-on as Clark keeps the rhyming pattern of the original nursery rhyme and makes it her own. . . . The whimsical illustrations

show plenty of activity as the number of characters increases, but they never descend into overwhelming busyness and many invite closer inspection. Perfect for storytime or individual sharing." SLJ

Melrose and Croc: an adventure to remember. Walker & Co. 2008 un il $16.95; lib bdg $17.85

Grades: PreK K 1 2　　　　　　　　　　　　　E

1. Dogs -- Fiction 2. Birthdays -- Fiction 3. Crocodiles -- Fiction

ISBN 978-0-8027-9774-2; 0-8027-9774-1; 978-0-8027-9775-9 lib bdg; 0-8027-9775-X lib bdg

LC 2007-037146

A friendly crocodile receives the best birthday present ever when he rescues his dear companion, Melrose the dog, during a storm at sea

"This simple story, set in a European seaside village, celebrates two caring individuals who think only of one another. Its gentle, affectionate message and expressive illustrations are a wonderful, reassuring way to lull any child into a peaceful sleep in which all is right with the world." SLJ

Other titles about Melrose and Croc are:

Melrose and Croc: a Christmas to remember (2006)

Melrose and Croc beside the sea (2009)

Melrose and Croc find a smile (2009)

Melrose and Croc: friends for life (2009)

Melrose and Croc go to town (2009)

Piper; [written and illustrated by] Emma Chichester Clark. Eerdmans Books for Young Readers 2007 un il $17

Grades: PreK K 1 2　　　　　　　　　　　　　E

1. Dogs -- Fiction

ISBN 978-0-8028-5314-1

LC 2006008548

A young dog runs away from its cruel master, but finds a new home after saving the life of an old woman

"Both honorable and adorable, Piper will inspire strong reactions from kids, and Clark's always-impressive watercolors effectively capture both the happy and the dark moments of the tale." Booklist

Child, Lauren

★ **I** am too absolutely small for school. Candlewick 2004 un il $16.99; pa $6.99

Grades: PreK K 1 2　　　　　　　　　　　　　E

1. School stories 2. Siblings -- Fiction

ISBN 0-7636-2403-9; 0-7636-2887-5 pa

LC 2003-65576

When Lola is worried about starting school, her older brother Charlie reassures her

"The children's relationship is refreshingly noncombative. . . . Incorporating photos, fabric, and appealingly childlike cartoon renderings of the siblings, the mixed-media illustrations are a visual treat of color and texture." SLJ

Other titles about Lola and Charlie are:

Absolutely one thing (2016)

But excuse me that is my book (2006)

I am not sleepy and I will not go to bed (2001)

I will never not eat a tomato (2000)

Say cheese (2007)

Slightly invisible (2011)

Snow is my favorite and my best (2006)

Maude the not-so-noticeable Shrimpton; Lauren Child, Trisha Krauss. Candlewick Press 2013 32 p. $16.99

Grades: 1 2 3   E
1. Picture books for children 2. Dysfunctional families -- Fiction
ISBN 0763665150; 9780763665159

LC 2012947262

This children's picture book focuses on the dramatic and sometimes ostentatious Shrimpton family. "Readers first see them in a framed photograph, as they ensure their best sides are showing while jostling each other for prominence. Mrs. Shrimpton favors extraordinary hats . . . , her husband has a dramatic mustache, and three of their four children are talented and/or beautiful. Middle daughter Maude is the exception—she literally blends in with the scenery." (Publishers Weekly)

The **New** small person; Lauren Child. Candlewick Press 2015 32 p. $17.99
Grades: PreK K 1 2   E
1. Family -- Fiction 2. Brothers and sisters -- Fiction
ISBN 0763678104; 9780763678104

LC 2014939346

In this children's book by Lauren Child, "Elmore Green starts life as an only child, as many children do. He has a room to himself, where he can line up his precious things and nobody will move them one inch. But one day everything changes. When the new small person comes along, it seems that everybody might like it a bit more than they like Elmore. Then, one night, everything changes." (Publisher's note)

Chinn, Karen
Sam and the lucky money; illustrated by Cornelius Van Wright, and Ying-Hwa Hu. Lee & Low Bks. 1995 un il hardcover o.p. pa $7.95
Grades: PreK K 1 2   E
1. Chinese New Year -- Fiction 2. Chinese Americans -- Fiction
ISBN 1-880000-13-X; 1-880000-53-9 pa

LC 94-11766

"The illustrators masterfully combine Chinatown's exotic setting with the universal emotions of childhood through expressive portraits of the characters." SLJ

Chocolate, Debbi
El barrio; illustrated by David Diaz. Henry Holt 2009 un il $16.95
Grades: PreK K 1 2   E
1. Community life -- Fiction 2. City and town life -- Fiction 3. Hispanic Americans -- Fiction
ISBN 978-0-8050-7457-4; 0-8050-7457-0

LC 2008013422

A young boy explores his vibrant Latino neighborhood, with its vegetable gardens instead of lawns, Nativity parades, quinceanera parties, and tejana and salsa music.

"Thick lines surround the woodcut-like artwork imbued with a rainbow of glowing colors. Fascinating mixed-media collages (toy skulls, rocks, beads, shells) border each spread. The whole is an exuberant cacophony of colors and sights." Booklist

Chodos-Irvine, Margaret
Best best friends; [by] Margaret Chodos-Irvine. Harcourt 2006 un il $16
Grades: PreK K 1   E
1. School stories 2. Birthdays -- Fiction 3. Friendship -- Fiction
ISBN 0-15-205694-7

LC 2005002251

Mary and Clare do everything together at preschool, but Mary's birthday celebration puts a strain on the girls' friendship.

"In spot-on words and crisp, gaily patterned prints, the [author-illustrator] captures the unselfconscious affection and quicksilver shifts in mood that characterize preschool friendships." Booklist

★ **Ella** Sarah gets dressed. Harcourt 2003 un il $16; bd bk $10.95
Grades: PreK K 1   E
1. Clothing and dress -- Fiction
ISBN 0-15-216413-8; 0-15-206486-9 bd bk

LC 2002-5097

A Caldecott Medal honor book, 2004

Despite the advice of others in her family, Ella Sarah persists in wearing the striking and unusual outfit of her own choosing

"With minimal words and her signature art marked by bright, bold prints, Chodos-Irvine perfectly captures a universal childhood struggle." Booklist

Choldenko, Gennifer
Dad and the dinosaur; Gennifer Choldenko; illustrated by Dan Santat. G.P. Putnam's Sons 2017 40 p. (hardback) $17.99
Grades: K 1 2 3   E
1. Dinosaurs -- Fiction 2. Fear in children -- Fiction 3. Father-son relationship -- Fiction 4. Fear -- Fiction 5. Toys -- Fiction 6. Dinosaurs -- Fiction 7. Fathers and sons -- Fiction
ISBN 9780399243530

LC 2016009819

In this children's book, by Gennifer Choldenko, illustrated by Dan Santat, "Nicholas was afraid of the dark outside his door, the bushes where the giant bugs live, and the underside of manhole covers. . . . Nicholas wants to be as brave as his dad, but he needs help. . . . With his toy dinosaur, Nicholas can scale tall walls, swim in deep water, even score a goal against the huge goalie everyone calls Gorilla. But when the dinosaur goes missing, everything is scary again." (Publisher's note)

"Her knowing, understated storytelling and Santat's warm, expressive spreads give full credence to the fears that weigh on kids, as well as the presences—both real and imagined—that can help alleviate them." Pub Wkly

A **giant** crush; illustrated by Melissa Sweet. G.P. Putnam's Sons 2011 un il $16.99
Grades: PreK K 1 2   E
1. School stories 2. Rabbits -- Fiction 3. Shyness -- Fiction 4. Valentine's Day -- Fiction
ISBN 978-0-399-24352-3; 0-399-24352-6

LC 2009040110

"Jackson, a young rabbit, has a giant crush on Cami, a bunny in his class, but he's too shy to tell her he likes her. Instead, he leaves her a flower, candy, and a giant valentine. . . . Sweet's watercolor, gouache, and mixed-media illustrations are sunny and expressive, and bring the characters and their world to life. The lighthearted pictures are a perfect match for the breezy text." SLJ

Chorao, Kay
Ed and Kip; Kay Chorao. Holiday House 2014 32 p. color illustrations (I like to read) (hardcover) $14.95
Grades: PreK K 1   E
1. Insects -- Fiction 2. Elephants -- Fiction 3. Friendship -- Fiction 4. Play -- Fiction 5. Rocks -- Fiction 6. Jungle animals -- Fiction
ISBN 0823429032; 9780823429035

LC 2012045920

This children's book, written and illustrated by Kay Chorao, focuses on the adventures of two elephants and their insect friend. "When elephants Ed and Kip get into mischief, their friend Bug uses some quick thinking [and] . . . big brains . . . to get them out of Crocodile's pond . . . [and] save the day!" (Publisher's note)

"Elephants, monkeys, bugs, and crocodiles play games, interact, and experience emotions together in the jungle. Though the text is simple, the panel illustrations tell a more complex story, allowing new readers to enjoy the book on multiple levels. The soft, pastel-colored illustrations in watercolor, gouache, and ink imbue the eponymous elephants with personality. This is an easy reader with substance." Horn Book

Christelow, Eileen

The **desperate** dog writes again. Clarion Books 2010 32p il $16.99

Grades: PreK K 1 2   E

1. Dogs -- Fiction

ISBN 978-0-547-24205-7; 0-547-24205-0

When a new girlfriend comes between Emma the dog and her owner George, Emma e-mails "Ask Queenie," an advice column for dogs having problems with difficult humans.

"Christelow's bright, cartoon-like illustrations in comic-book panels humorously display the antics while dialogue bubbles abet easy reading. Pitch perfect for those children adjusting to a new person in their lives." Kirkus

★ **Five** little monkeys jumping on the bed; retold and illustrated by Eileen Christelow. Clarion Bks. 1989 un il $15; pa $5.95; bd bk $11.99

Grades: PreK K 1 2   E

1. Counting 2. Monkeys -- Fiction

ISBN 0-89919-769-8; 0-395-55701-1 pa; 0-547-13176-3 bd bk

LC 88-22839

A counting book in which one by one the five little monkeys jump on the bed only to fall off and bump their heads

"Squiggling, swirling lines of color capture the sense of unbridled motion as the monkeys bounce and, one by one, topple from the bed. After all five bandaged youngsters finally fall asleep, a relaxed mama gratefully retires to her room . . . to bounce on 'her' bed. An amusingly presented counting exercise." Booklist

Other titles about the five little monkeys are:

Don't wake up Mama! (1992)

Five little monkeys go shopping (2007)

Five little monkeys play hide and seek (2004)

Five little monkeys reading in bed (2011)

Five little monkeys sitting in a tree (1991)

Five little monkeys wash the car (2000)

Five little monkeys with nothing to do (1996)

Letters from a desperate dog; [by] Eileen Christelow. Clarion Books 2006 32p il $16

Grades: PreK K 1 2   E

1. Dogs -- Fiction

ISBN 978-0-618-51003-0; 0-618-51003-6

LC 2005032744

Feeling misunderstood and unappreciated by her owner, Emma the dog asks for advice from the local canine advice columnist.

"This is a delightful romp, and Christelow shows Emma's story off to great advantage in an oversize format with comic-book-style watercolor art." Booklist

Another title about Emma the dog is:

The desperate dog writes again (2010)

Christensen, Bonnie

★ **Plant** a little seed; Bonnie Christensen. Roaring Brook Press 2012 32 p.

Grades: 2 3 4 5   E

1. Seeds -- Fiction 2. Seasons -- Fiction 3. Gardening -- Fiction 4. Picture books for children 5. Community gardens -- Fiction

ISBN 159643550X; 9781596435506

LC 2011005202

In this picture book, "a girl narrates the cycle of working a community-garden plot over three productive seasons. She and her friend (a boy) plan, plant, tend and harvest fruits, veggies and flowers. . . . [Bonnie] Christensen's pictures . . . convey visual affirmations of friendship, co-operation and patience through changing seasons. Basic biological facts about plants, arranged on seed packets scattered across a final page, are reinforced visually throughout." (Kirkus Reviews)

Christian, Cheryl

Witches; illustrated by Wish Williams. Star Bright Books 2011 24p il pa $5.95

Grades: PreK   E

1. Stories in rhyme 2. Witches -- Fiction 3. Halloween -- Fiction

ISBN 978-1-59572-283-6; 1-59572-283-1

LC 2010050909

"Children dressed as witches are gathered around a kitchen table putting all sorts of food from the cupboards and refrigerator in a giant black cauldron. This image sets the scene for a very simple story of children (or witches) getting ready for their Halloween outing. The whimsical and vibrant colors in Williams's pictures make this story great fun to view and help to move the rhyming text forward." SLJ

Chung, Arree

Ninja! Arree Chung. Henry Holt & Co. 2014 40 p. color illustrations (hardback) $16.99

Grades: PreK K 1 2   E

1. Ninja -- Fiction 2. Comic books, strips, etc. 3. Play -- Fiction 4. Brothers and sisters -- Fiction

ISBN 0805099115; 9780805099119

LC 2013043353

"Readers follow the main character through comic-book-style panels as he moves with stealthlike precision, covertly navigating each room and the furniture, to fulfill his mission of capturing his prize: his sister's snack. Silent as a spider, this cartoonish little guy is regaled in makeshift black ninja fashion (where is Dad's necktie?), with only his wide eyes (and several teeth) visible to his enemies." (School Library Journal)

"Told through a blend of traditional picture-book illustrations and comic-book-style panels, this seamlessly hybridizes the two forms, creating the perfect jumping-in point for readers interested in ninjas and comics." Kirkus

Ninja! attack of the clan; Arree Chung. Henry Holt and Company 2016 40 p. color illustrations (hardback) $16.99

Grades: PreK K 1 2   E

1. Play -- Fiction 2. Ninja -- Fiction 3. Family life -- Fiction

ISBN 9780805099164

LC 2015014270

In this book, by Arree Chung, "a ninja must be ready for anything! Maxwell is a strong, courageous, silent ninja, but he also wants somebody to play with. Mama, Papa, and little sister Cassy are all too busy, leaving Maxwell disappointed and alone. When Maxwell gets called to dinner, he finds an empty dining room. Could his ninja clan be up to something?" (Publisher's note)

"Readers will happily creep, meditate, and spar along with ninja Maxwell. A clever, laugh-out-loud story for a broad audience." Kirkus

Church, Caroline

One more hug for Madison; by Caroline Jayne Church. Orchard Books 2010 un il lib bdg $16.99

Grades: PreK K   E

1. Mice -- Fiction 2. Bedtime -- Fiction 3. Mother-child
relationship -- Fiction
ISBN 978-0-545-16179-4 lib bdg; 0-545-16179-7 lib bdg
LC 2008-52691

Madison the mouse keeps asking her patient mother for just one
more thing before she goes to sleep.

Clanton, Ben

Mo's mustache; Ben Clanton. Tundra Books of Northern New
York 2013 32 p. (hardcover) $17.95
Grades: PreK K 1   E

1. Picture books for children 2. Monsters -- Fiction 3. Mustaches
-- Fiction
ISBN 177049538X; 9781770495388; 9781770495401
LC 2012955642

In this children's picture book, Mo the monster gets a mustache. "All
the other monsters are impressed" and soon "each of the monsters appears, be-mustached. Each hairy facial adornment is different." Mo is
annoyed and decides to trade his mustache for a scarf. "Every monster
follows suit. . . . 'WHY IS EVERYBODY COPYING ME?!' And all the
monsters confess that they emulate him because they respect his taste
and his style." (Kirkus Reviews)

Clayton, Dallas

An **awesome** book! Dallas Clayton. Harper 2012 64 p. (trd.
bdg.) $16.99
Grades: PreK K 1 2   E

1. Stories in rhyme 2. Creative thinking 3. Dreams -- Fiction
ISBN 0062114689; 9780062114686
LC 2011935482

Author and illustrator Dallas Clayton presents a children's picture
book about imagination and dreams demonstrated through monsters.

Cleary, Beverly

The **hullabaloo** ABC; illustrated by Ted Rand. rev ed; Morrow
Junior Bks. 1998 un il $17.99
Grades: PreK K 1 2   E

1. Alphabet 2. Stories in rhyme 3. Noise -- Fiction 4. Farm life
-- Fiction
ISBN 0-688-15182-5
LC 97-6457

A revised and newly illustrated edition of the title first published
1960 by Parnassus Press

An alphabet book in which two children demonstrate all the fun that
is to be had by making and hearing every kind of noise as they dash
about on the farm

"Rand's expert watercolor illustrations on crisp white backgrounds
bring the action to life with just the slightest touch of nostalgia." SLJ

Cleland, Jo

Getting your zzzzs; Jo Cleland; [edited by] Precious McKenzie.
Rourke Pub. 2012 24 p. $22.79
Grades: K 1 2   E

1. Sleep 2. Children's songs 3. Picture books for children
ISBN 1618100858; 9781618100856
LC 2011944395

This children's book from Jo Cleland is part of the "Sing and Read:
Healthy Habits series, which sets healthful reminders to familiar tunes."
Here, the tune of "If You're Happy and You Know It" is used to remind
children about the immune system-boosting effects of getting enough
sleep. (Booklist)

Clement, Nathan

★ **Drive**; [by] Nathan Clement. Front Street 2008 un il $16.95
Grades: PreK K   E

1. Trucks -- Fiction 2. Fathers -- Fiction
ISBN 978-1-59078-517-1
LC 2007037469

In brief text with illustrations, a boy describes his father's work as
a truck driver

"Working in big, streamlined shapes; flat, bright colors; and shiny,
airbrushed-like surfaces, [Clement] evokes a deco-esque world. . . . Unusual and often cinematic perspectives . . . plunge readers into the action
and give the compositions a red-blooded energy." Publ Wkly

Job site. Boyds Mills Press 2011 un il
Grades: PreK K 1   E

1. Building -- Fiction 2. Vehicles -- Fiction
ISBN 1-59078-769-2; 978-1-59078-769-4

"Over the course of a day on the job, a burly construction foreman,
referred to only as 'Boss,' makes good on his name and bosses around a
bulldozer, excavator, dump truck, and other vehicles. . . . Featuring . . .
bold digital artwork, . . . this book . . . makes excellent use of perspective
to play up the machines' immensity and power." Publ Wkly

Clements, Andrew

Circus family dog; illustrated by Sue Truesdell. Clarion Bks. 2000
32p il $16
Grades: PreK K 1 2   E

1. Dogs -- Fiction 2. Circus -- Fiction
ISBN 0-395-78648-7
LC 99-52657

Grumps is content to do his one trick in the center ring at the circus,
until a new dog shows up and steals the show—temporarily

"The combination of Clements's impeccable storyteller pacing and
Truesdell's creative and whimsical cartoons create a reading and visual
experience second only to actually being at the circus. The illustrator
uses a mixture of watercolors with pen and ink to bring the action to life
in vibrant colors." SLJ

The **handiest** things in the world; photographs by Raquel Jaramillo. Atheneum 2010 un il $16.99
Grades: PreK K 1 2   E

1. Stories in rhyme 2. Hand -- Fiction
ISBN 978-1-416-96166-6; 1-416-96166-6

"This unusual concept book looks at all the things that hands can do
and the tools that help do them better. On a typical double-page spread,
two short rhyming sentences are paired with photos. The first shows a
child's hands performing a job, while the next shows them using a tool.
. . . In the first picture, a girl untangles her hair with her fingers; in the
next, with a comb. . . . Excellent color photos of different children engaged in everyday activities enhance the book's appeal." Booklist

Cleminson, Katie

Cuddle up, goodnight. Disney Hyperion Books 2011 un il $15.99
Grades: PreK K   E

1. Stories in rhyme 2. Day -- Fiction 3. Toddlers -- Fiction
ISBN 978-1-4231-3844-0; 1-4231-3844-9
LC 2010004890

First published 2010 in the United Kingdom with title: Wake up!
Follows, in rhymed text and illustrations, a little boy's activities
from the time he wakes up in the morning until he goes to bed at night.

"Boldly outlined illustrations effectively employ spare brush strokes
and soft-shaded colors to playfully depict characters, objects, and irre-
pressibly goofy experiences, such as a hippo slurping spaghetti at the

table. . . . Children will enjoy the unexpected antics as well as the reassuring sense of a daily routine." Booklist

Clifton-Brown, Holly

Annie Hoot and the knitting extravaganza. Andersen Press USA 2010 un il $16.95

Grades: PreK K 1 2   E

1. Owls -- Fiction 2. Knitting -- Fiction

ISBN 978-0-7613-6444-3; 0-7613-6444-7

Annie Hoot, an owl, loves to knit, but the other owls in the woods will not wear the clothes she makes for them so she goes off in search of other animals that will appreciate her knitwear.

"The exuberant and joyful tale about finding one's bliss is accompanied by watercolor illustrations full of whimsical details." Horn Book Guide

Climo, Liz

Rory the dinosaur; me and my dad. by Liz Climo. Little, Brown & Co. 2015 40 p. color illustrations (hardcover) $17

Grades: PreK K 1   E

1. Dinosaurs -- Fiction 2. Father-son relationship -- Fiction 3. Adventure and adventurers -- Fiction 4. Islands -- Fiction 5. Self-reliance -- Fiction 6. Fathers and sons -- Fiction

ISBN 0316277282; 9780316277280

LC 2014015126

In this children's book, by Liz Climo, "Rory is a young dinosaur who loves to do things with his dad, but when his father takes some time to relax, Rory decides to set off on a solo adventure. . . . He hatches a plan to leave their island home in search of fun. Readers will notice his father not far behind." (Kirkus Reviews)

"Bright colors and clean lines help bring these whimsical characters, previously seen in Climo's comic blog, to life. Climo's hand lettering lends a folksy quality to the otherwise sleek style of her digital artwork. Ample white space on each page and small pieces of text make this a read-aloud option with broad appeal." SLJ

Rory the dinosaur wants a pet; by Liz Climo. Little, Brown & Co. 2016 40 p. color illustrations (hardcover) $16.99

Grades: PreK K 1   E

1. Pets -- Fiction 2. Dinosaurs -- Fiction

ISBN 9780316277297

LC 2015008689

In this picture book, by Liz Climo, "when Rory meets his friend Sheldon's pet crab, he realizes he wants a pet of his own. He searches high and low--from tree tops to sand pits--for a creature to love. It's at the end of a long day, when Rory least expects it, that he meets George." (Publisher's note)

"The cartoon-style illustrations, achieved with 'digital magic,' are set off with plenty of white space, and with just a sentence or two per page, it is an appealing read-aloud.Children just developing a sense of humor will appreciate the innocent silliness of the tale." Kirkus

Cline-Ransome, Lesa

Light in the darkness; a story about how slaves learned in secret. by Lesa Cline-Ransome; illustrations by James E. Ransome. Disney/Jump at the Sun Books 2013 40 p. $16.99

Grades: 2 3 4   E

1. Books and reading -- Fiction 2. Slavery -- United States -- Fiction 3. African Americans -- History -- Fiction 4. Reading -- Fiction 5. Slavery -- Fiction 6. Learning -- Fiction 7. Southern States -- History -- 1775-1865 -- Fiction

ISBN 1423134958; 9781423134954

LC 2012001834

This children's story, by Lesa Cline-Ransome, illustrated by James E. Ransome, is a historical story of 19th century life in slavery. "Rosa and her mama go to school . . . in the dark of night, silently, afraid that any noise they hear is a patroller on the lookout for escaped slaves. . . . If the Master catches them, it'll mean a whipping--one lash for each letter. No matter how slow and dangerous the process might be, Rosa is determined to learn, and pass on her learning to others." (Publisher's note)

Cobb, Jane

What'll I do with the baby-o? Nursery rhymes, songs and stories for babies. Jane Cobb; illustrated by Kathryn Shoemaker. Black Sheep Press 2012 255 p. ill. (paperback) $39.95; (ebook) $29.95

Grades: Adult Professional   E

1. Children's libraries 2. Children's literature 3. Infants -- Development 4. Early childhood education

ISBN 0969866615; 9780969866619; 9780969866640

This book by Jane Cobb presents "rhymes, songs, and stories . . . to engage . . . babies throughout their first two years of development. All of the activities recommended encourage bonding, fun, and brain and emotional development. . . . This resource contains . . . chapters on a baby's brain, early language, and literacy development; program planning and presentation tips; 350 rhymes and songs arranged by type . . . and other resources and bibliographies for further reading." (Publisher's note)

"Extensive preliminary chapters cover such things as identifying the audience, considering the developmental needs of the babies, and selecting and teaching the rhymes and books. The remainder of the book contains thoughtful suggestions of specific rhymes and songs, as well as comments to use with parents. . . . A musical CD provides samples of songs. . . . This book is a must-have for those embarking upon 'Baby and Me' or 'Mother Goose'-type programs." SLJ

Cobb, Rebecca

★ **Missing** mommy; Rebecca Cobb. Henry Holt and Co. 2013 32 p. (hardcover) $16.99

Grades: K 1 2   E

1. Mother-son relationship 2. Bereavement -- Fiction 3. Death -- Fiction 4. Grief -- Fiction 5. Mothers -- Fiction

ISBN 0805095071; 9780805095074

LC 2011052417

This children's book, by Rebecca Cobb, "explores the many emotions a bereaved child may experience, from anger and guilt to sadness and bewilderment. Ultimately, [the story] focuses on the positive--the recognition that the child is not alone but still part of a family that loves and supports him." (Publisher's note)

"Told from a young child's point of view, Cobb's moving story respectfully explores the complex emotions a little one may experience while grieving the loss of a parent. ... The artwork, done in a primary palette, skillfully emulates the innocence of a child's drawings... Accessible and tender, this story gives young children a voice and shows how to hold the memory of a loved one close." Kirkus

Cocca-Leffler, Maryann

Princess K.I.M. and the lie that grew. Albert Whitman & Co. 2009 32p $16.99

Grades: PreK K 1 2   E

1. Truthfulness and falsehood -- Fiction

ISBN 978-0-8075-4178-4; 0-8075-4178-8

LC 2008-28056

After new girl Kim tells her classmates she is from a royal family, her lie grows and grows.

"The brightly colored artwork brings the story to life. . . . Varying layouts effectively convey the action." SLJ

Another title about Kim is:

Princess Kim and too much truth (2011)

Rain brings frogs; a little book of hope. Harper 2011 un il $9.99
Grades: PreK K 1   **E**
  1. Hope -- Fiction 2. Happiness -- Fiction
  ISBN 978-0-06-196106-9; 0-06-196106-X

"Nate sees everything in a positive light. When Charlie says, 'Keep Out!'/Nate says, 'Room for All.' When Mom says, 'I Hate Rain.' Nate says, 'Rain Brings Frogs!' Green frog endpapers enhance the cheerful colors and cartoonlike characters surrounded by plenty of white space. The font is large, and the narrative waves through the pages showing action and movement." SLJ

A **vacation** for Pooch; Maryann Cocca-Leffler. Christy Ottaviano Books 2013 32 p. (hardcover) $16.99
Grades: K 1 2 3   **E**
  1. Dogs -- Fiction 2. Girls -- Fiction 3. Vacations -- Fiction 4. Dogs -- Fiction 5. Vacations -- Fiction
  ISBN 0805091068; 9780805091069
                LC 2012011271

This children's story, by Maryann Cocca-Leffler, follows a girl and her pet dog going on separate vacations. Violet is "going on vacation to sunny Florida. She packed her bag very carefully. . . ." Pooch is "going on vacation to Grandpa's snowy farm. Violet packed his bag very carefully, too. . . . When their bags get mixed up, Violet thinks Pooch's vacation will be miserable. But Pooch is having a grand old time, so all is very well!" (Publisher's note)

Cochran, Bill

My parents are divorced, my elbows have nicknames, and other facts about me; illustrated by Steve Björkman. HarperCollins 2009 un il $17.99; lib bdg $18.89
Grades: K 1 2 3   **E**
  1. Divorce -- Fiction
  ISBN 978-0-06-053942-9; 0-06-053942-9; 978-0-06-053943-6 lib bdg; 0-06-053943-7 lib bdg

While describing his not-so-weird life with his divorced parents, a young boy also describes some other things about himself that could be considered weird.

"This story uses humor to help children cope with the issue of divorce. . . . Ted has a believable voice that children will recognize. . . . The colorful cartoons add to the upbeat nature of the story and make a serious subject a little easier to swallow." SLJ

Codell, Esmé Raji, 1968-

Fairly fairy tales; illustrated by Elisa Chavarri. Aladdin 2011 un il
Grades: PreK K 1   **E**
  1. Fairy tales 2. Books and reading -- Fiction
  ISBN 1-4169-9086-0; 978-1-4169-9086-4
                LC 2009-16475

This book reimagines six familiar fairy tales. "Ages four to seven." (Bull Cent Child Books)

"In this fanciful collection, Codell takes six familiar fairy tales, lists three known attributes for each . . . then throws in a novel element . . . which provides impetus for a fanciful revisioning depicted in the following spread. . . . It's a great gimmick, and the 'what if?' approach to fairy tales offers heaps of potential for classroom projects and discussions. . . . Chavarri's splashy, digitally rendered illustrations are most notable for their attention to detail: the wordless alternative-story spreads are chock full of minutiae that add considerable humor to the simple text." Bull Cent Child Books

Coelho, Rogério

Boat of dreams; Rogerio Coelho. Tilbury House Publishers 2017 80 p. color illustrations (hardcover) $22.95
Grades: 1 2 3 4   **E**
  1. Stories without words 2. Dreams -- Fiction 3. Boats and boating -- Fiction
  ISBN 9780884485285; 9780884485346
                LC 2016951433

This wordless picture book, by Rogerio Coelho, "opens with an elderly man waking up. He goes outside and we discover he lives at the seaside. After a floating bottle beaches, he opens it to find a piece of paper. He begins to draw: a picture of a boat. He places the paper back in the bottle and returns it to the sea. The action then shifts to a city, where a small boy finds an envelope at his doorstep. Inside is the drawing." (Booklist)

"A nuanced physical and emotional landscape aimed to capture experienced readers but likely to snag the occasional neophyte as well." Kirkus

Coerr, Eleanor

The **big** balloon race; pictures by Carolyn Croll. Harper & Row 1981 62p il (I can read book) hardcover o.p. pa $3.99
Grades: K 1 2   **E**
  1. Balloons -- Fiction
  ISBN 0-06-444053-2 pa
                LC 80-8368

The author "recounts the winning of a hydrogen balloon race by Carlotta Myers, a famous aeronaut, and her stowaway daughter Ariel. Balloon facts are slipped naturally and painlessly into the story, which moves cogently along. The novel subject matter, straightforward mother-daughter relationship, and clear composition of the orange, blue and gray illustrations . . . . make for a high-flying new look at a piece of the past." SLJ

The **Josefina** story quilt; pictures by Bruce Degen. Harper & Row 1986 64p il (I can read book) hardcover o.p. pa $3.99
Grades: K 1 2 3   **E**
  1. Quilts -- Fiction 2. Overland journeys to the Pacific -- Fiction
  ISBN 0-06-021348-5; 0-06-444129-6 pa
                LC 85-45260

While traveling west with her family in 1850, a young girl makes a patchwork quilt chronicling the experiences of the journey and reserves a special patch for her pet hen Josefina

"The story makes the history go down easily, and an author's note at the end fills in facts about the western trip and the place of quilts as pioneer diaries. The charcoal and blue/yellow wash illustrations are clear and natural. . . . A good introduction to historical fiction that children can read for themselves." SLJ

Coffelt, Nancy

Catch that baby! illustrated by Scott Nash. Aladdin 2011 un il $16.99
Grades: PreK K   **E**
  1. Baths -- Fiction 2. Infants -- Fiction 3. Family life -- Fiction
  ISBN 978-1-4169-9148-9; 1-4169-9148-4
                LC 2009-34934

Everyone from Mom to Grandpa joins the chase when baby Rudy decides he does not want to get dressed after his bath.

"Ebullient in tone and sassy in spirit, this is a romp where both family and action seem quite real." Booklist

★ **Fred** stays with me; illustrated by Tricia Tusa. Little, Brown 2007 un il $16.99

Grades: PreK K 1 2   E
1. Dogs -- Fiction 2. Divorce -- Fiction
ISBN 0-316-88269-0

LC 2005-07973
Boston Globe-Horn Book Award honor book: Picture Book (2008)
A child describes how she lives sometimes with his mother and sometimes with his father, but his dog is his constant companion.
"Coffelt and Tusa have teamed up to create a charming book that meshes text and illustrations seamlessly. .... Tusa uses gold and brown hues with occasional splashes of red to create a warm tone." SLJ

Cohen, Barbara
  ★ **Molly's** pilgrim; illustrated by Daniel Mark Duffy. Lothrop, Lee & Shepard Bks. 1998 un il $17.99; pa $3.95
Grades: K 1 2 3   E
1. School stories 2. Jews -- Fiction 3. Immigrants -- Fiction 4. Thanksgiving Day -- Fiction
ISBN 0-688-16279-7; 0-688-16280-0 pa

LC 98-9227
A newly illustrated edition of the title first published 1983
Told to make a Pilgrim doll for the Thanksgiving display at school, Molly is embarassed when her mother tries to help her out by creating a doll dressed as she herself was dressed before leaving Russia to seek religious freedom

Cohen, Caron Lee
  Broom, zoom! illustrated by Sergio Ruzzier. Simon & Schuster Books for Young Readers 2010 un il $12.99
Grades: PreK K 1   E
1. Brooms -- Fiction 2. Goblins -- Fiction 3. Witches -- Fiction
ISBN 978-1-4169-9113-7; 1-4169-9113-1

LC 2009000581
One beautiful, starry night, a little witch wants to go for a ride on a broom but first she must help a little monster clean up a mess.
"The text is simple enough for beginning readers, as the characters speak in one and two-word sentences. The illustrations were digitally created in flat, singular colors. .... Although Witch and Monster give the story a Halloween feel, it is a simple tale of cooperation and friendship, and youngsters will respond to it as such." SLJ

Cohen, Deborah Bodin
  Engineer Ari and the sukkah express; illustrated by Shahar Kober. Kar-Ben Pub. 2010 p. cm. il lib bdg $17.95; pa $7.95
Grades: PreK K 1 2   E
1. Jews -- Fiction 2. Israel -- Fiction 3. Sukkot -- Fiction 4. Railroads -- Fiction
ISBN 978-0-7613-5126-9 lib bdg; 0-7613-5126-4 lib bdg; 978-0-7613-5128-3 pa; 0-7613-5128-0 pa

LC 2009001876

  Nachshon, who was afraid to swim; a Passover story. by Deborah Bodin Cohen; illustrations by Jago. Kar-Ben Pub. 2009 un il lib bdg $17.95; pa $8.95
Grades: 1 2 3 4   E
1. Fear -- Fiction 2. Jews -- Fiction 3. Courage -- Fiction 4. Slavery -- Fiction 5. Passover -- Fiction
ISBN 978-0-8225-8764-4 lib bdg; 0-8225-8764-5 lib bdg; 978-0-8225-8765-1 pa; 0-8225-8765-3 pa

LC 2007048359
When the Israelites flee Egypt, Nachshon exhibits great courage by being the first to step into the Red Sea, even though he cannot swim.
"The digitally prepared, mixed-media illustrations utilize muted yellow, orange, and brown tones to depict the sweltering heat of the desert and bright blue and green tones to illustrate the celebration of freedom.

They complement and enhance the text marvelously. A wonderful, unique addition." SLJ

Cohen, Miriam
  ★ **First** grade takes a test; by Miriam Cohen; illustrated by Ronald Himler. Star Bright Books 2006 un il $15.95; pa $5.95
Grades: PreK K 1 2   E
1. School stories 2. Examinations -- Fiction
ISBN 978-1-59572-054-2; 1-59572-054-5; 978-1-59572-055-9 pa; 1-59572-055-3 pa

LC 2006020488
A revised and newly illustrated edition of the title first published 1980 by Greenwillow Bks.
"One day the first-graders are given a special multiple-choice test by the principal. Some kids find the questions puzzling. Then, suddenly, time's up. Anna Maria announces, 'That was easy.' But many kids are confused and upset, and 'You're a dummy!' echoes through the class, which only settles down when the kindly teacher reminds the children of all the things they do understand. .... Cohen's sensitivity to children's feelings and reactions really shows here. ... Himler's loose-lined, pencil-and-watercolor pictures skillfully use body language and facial expressions to chart the children's emotional highs and lows." Booklist

  My big brother; art by Ronald Himler. Star Bright 2005 un il $15.95
Grades: K 1 2 3   E
1. Brothers -- Fiction 2. Soldiers -- Fiction 3. Family life -- Fiction
ISBN 1-59572-007-3

LC 2004-16056
When his big brother leaves to become a soldier, a boy does what he can to take his place in the family.
"This quiet picture book packs a strong emotional wallop. Himler's artwork, pencil with watercolor washes, sensitively depicts each character's emotions through body language and facial expressions." Booklist

  ★ **Will** I have a friend? by Miriam Cohen; illustrated by Ronald Himler. Star Bright Books 2009 un il $15.95
Grades: PreK K 1   E
1. School stories 2. Friendship -- Fiction
ISBN 978-1-59572-069-6; 1-59572-069-3

LC 2008036957
A newly illustrated edition of the title first published 1967 by Macmillan
Jim's anxieties on his first day of school are happily forgotten when he makes a new friend.
The art is "fresh and new. .... Himler's soft watercolors are ... contemporary in look, with touches like a recycle mark on the trash bin. ... Great for combating new-kid-in-school blues." Booklist

Cohn, Diana
  Namaste! illustrated by Amy Cordova; with an Afterward by Ang Rita Sherpa of the Mountain Institute. SteinerBooks 2009 un il $17.95
Grades: K 1 2   E
1. Nepal -- Fiction
ISBN 978-0-88010-625-2; 0-88010-625-5

LC 2009003216
Whenever Nima meets someone on her long walk to the market village in Nepal, she brings her hands together with her fingers almost touching her chin, bows her head slightly, and says "Namaste," which means "the light in me meets the light in you." Includes information on the geography, culture, and people of Nepal
"The vibrant folk-art illustrations showing the details of Nima's life in her village support the simple story perfectly. This beautiful book will

appeal to primary readers and make an ideal addition to multicultural collections." SLJ

Colato Lainez, Rene

Mamá the alien; story, René Colato Laínez; illustrations, Laura Lacámara; Spanish translation by René Colato Laínez = Mamá la extraterrestre / cuento, René Colato Laínez; ilustraciones, Laura Lacámara. Children's Book Press, an imprint of Lee & Low Books Inc. 2016 32 p. (hardcover : alk. paper) $17.95

Grades: K 1 2 3   E

1. Bilingual books 2. Citizenship -- Fiction 3. Hispanic Americans -- Fiction 4. Immigrants -- Fiction 5. Immigrants -- Fiction 6. Spanish language materials -- Bilingual

ISBN 9780892392988

LC 2015024643

In this book, by Rene Colato Lainez, illustrated by Laura Lacamara, "when Mama's purse falls on the floor, Sofia gets a peek at Mama's old Resident Alien card and comes to the conclusion that Mama might be an alien from outer space. Sofia heads to the library to learn more about aliens. Some are small and some are tall. Some have four fingers on each hand and some have large, round eyes. Their skin can be gray or blue or green. But Mama looks like a human mother! Could she really be an alien?" (Publisher's note)

Mamá la extraterrestre

My shoes and I; illustrations by Fabricio Vanden Broeck. Boyds Mills Press 2010 un il $16.95

Grades: K 1 2 3   E

1. Shoes -- Fiction 2. Travel -- Fiction 3. Immigrants -- Fiction 4. Central America -- Fiction 5. Father-son relationship -- Fiction

ISBN 978-1-59078-385-6; 1-59078-385-9

LC 2008-30003

As Mario and his Papa travel from El Salvador to the United States to be reunited with Mama, Mario's wonderful new shoes help to distract him from the long and difficult journey.

"Vanden Broeck's color-drenched illustrations on weathered backgrounds add immediacy and detail. This moving, heartfelt tale of courage and perseverance will be embraced by a wide audience of readers, young and old." SLJ

Señor Pancho had a rancho; by René Colato Laínez; illustrated by Elwood Smith. Holiday House 2013 (hardcover) $16.95

Grades: PreK K 1   E

1. Farms -- Fiction 2. Bilingual books -- English-Spanish 3. Stories in rhyme 4. Bilingualism -- Fiction 5. Animal sounds -- Fiction 6. Domestic animals -- Fiction

ISBN 0823426327; 9780823426324

LC 2012007672

In this book, by René Colato Laínez, "the barnyard animals on Old MacDonald's and Senor Pancho's farms have a hard time communicating. MacDonald's rooster says cock-a-doodle-doo! While Senor Pancho's gallo says quiquirquí. The English-speaking chick says peep, peep, but el pollito says pio, pio. Then the cow says moo and la vaca says mu! Maybe they're not so different after all! So all the animals come together for a barnyard fiesta, because dancing is a universal language." (Publisher's note)

"Old MacDonald has a farm; Seqor Pancho has a rancho. You'll hear "cock-a-doodle-doo" and "peep" on the farm; Pancho's gallo says "quiquiriqum" and his pollito says "pmo." But when the cow and una vaca get together: "Here a moo, there a muu. / Everywhere a moo muu." The energetic illustrations are a good match for the lively reworked lyrics, which include Spanish words and animal sounds." (Horn Book)

The **Tooth** Fairy meets El Raton Perez; illustrations by Tom Lintern. Tricycle Press 2010 un il $15.99; lib bdg $18.99

Grades: PreK K 1   E

1. Mice -- Fiction 2. Teeth -- Fiction 3. Fairies -- Fiction 4. Mexican Americans -- Fiction

ISBN 978-1-58246-296-7; 1-58246-296-8; 978-1-58246-342-1 lib bdg; 1-58246-342-5 lib bdg

LC 2009-16782

When Miguel loses a tooth, two legendary characters come to claim it—one who is responsible for collecting teeth in the United States and one who has collected the teeth of the boy's parents and grandparents.

"Lainez's creative story approaches the topic of cultural identity with humor and grace, while newcomer Lintern's colored pencil illustrations give it a sense of nocturnal whimsy." Publ Wkly

Cole, Brock

★ **Buttons.** Farrar, Straus & Giroux 2000 un il hardcover o.p. $16

Grades: K 1 2 3   E

1. Father-daughter relationship -- Fiction

ISBN 0-374-31001-7; 0-374-41013-5 pa

LC 99-27162

Boston Globe-Horn Book Award Honor: Picture Book (2000)

When their father eats so much that he pops the buttons off his britches, each of his three daughters tries a different plan to find replacements

"A delectable tall tale. . . . Cole's narrative has a humorous lilt that's as much fun as his rollicking illustrations." Horn Book Guide

★ **Good** enough to eat. Farrar, Straus & Giroux 2007 un il $16

Grades: K 1 2 3   E

1. Fairy tales 2. Orphans -- Fiction 3. Homeless persons -- Fiction

ISBN 978-0-374-32737-8; 0-374-32737-8

LC 2006-37368

When an Ogre comes to town demanding a bride, the mayor sacrifices the homeless girl with no name that everyone thinks is a pest and a bother, but she finds a way to outwit them all.

The illustrations offer "lively line and delicate use of color. The cadenced language and blithe illustrations work perfectly together. . . . With the structure of a fairy tale and the freshness of an original story, Good Enough to Eat is satisfying fare indeed." Horn Book

★ **Larky** Mavis. Farrar, Straus & Giroux 2001 un il $16

Grades: K 1 2 3   E

1. Infants -- Fiction

ISBN 0-374-34365-9

LC 00-51419

Having found a tiny baby in a peanut shell, Larky Mavis calls him Heart's Delight and carries him around as he grows bigger, to the confusion and anger of the adults around her

"The prose is lyrical, peppered with quaint speech patterns and lively dialogue that is a delight to read aloud. . . . The rumpled, animated line-and-watercolor illustrations extend the charming story beyond his tightly constructed prose." SLJ

★ The **money** we'll save. Farrar Straus & Giroux 2011 un il $16.99

Grades: K 1 2   E

1. Christmas stories 2. Turkeys -- Fiction 3. Christmas -- Fiction 4. Apartment houses -- Fiction 5. New York (State) -- Fiction

ISBN 978-0-374-35011-6; 0-374-35011-6

LC 2010037760

In nineteenth-century New York City, when Pa brings home a young turkey in hopes of saving money on their Christmas dinner, his family faces all sorts of trouble—and expense—in their tiny apartment.

"The cleverly constructed text is full of understated humor and witty dialogue, with a satisfying conclusion describing the family's simple but happy Christmas celebration. Cole's loose watercolor-and-ink illustrations skillfully evoke the old-fashioned setting and busy life of a New York tenement community." Kirkus

Cole, Henry

Big bug; Henry Cole. Little Simon 2014 32 p. color illustrations (hc : alk. paper) $14.99

Grades: PreK K 1 2   E

1. Size -- Fiction 2. Farm life -- Fiction 3. English language -- Comparison -- Fiction

ISBN 1442498978; 9781442498976

LC 2013020626

"Beginning with a . . . close-up of a 'big' ladybug, this book," by author and illustrator Henry Cole, "depicts the concept of scale. The book zooms out from the bug, to a flower, to a cow, all the way to an expansive spread of sky. Then . . . zooms back in from that sky, to a tree, to a house, to a window, all the way to the end where [a] . . . dog is taking a 'little' nap." (Publisher's note)

"The concept of scale is brilliantly depicted on the title page (where tiny ladybugs crawl over the title of the book in large font) as well as the endpapers. The different font sizes further highlight the use of scale in his breathtaking illustrations. Big Bug is a unique reading experience with broad appeal." SLJ reviews

Jack's garden; Henry Cole. Greenwillow Bks. 1995 24 p. $17.99

Grades: PreK K 1   E

1. Gardening -- Fiction 2. Picture books for children

ISBN 0688135013; 9780688135010

LC 94006249

Author and illustrator Henry Cole features a rhyming children's book that focuses on how to create and maintain a garden. The book chronicles a little boy named Jack as he constructs and plants a flower garden, complete with birds and butterflies. Cole also presents additional and more specific gardening suggestions and guidelines at the back of the book.

The **littlest** evergreen. Katherine Tegen Books 2011 un il $16.99; lib bdg $18.89

Grades: PreK K 1 2   E

1. Trees -- Fiction 2. Christmas stories 3. Christmas trees -- Fiction 4. Conservation of natural resources -- Fiction

ISBN 978-0-06-114619-0; 0-06-114619-6; 978-0-06-114620-6 lib bdg; 0-06-114620-X lib bdg

LC 2008022630

"The littlest evergreen, Cole's narrator, is dug out of the earth . . . by men searching for Christmas trees. They forgo using their chainsaw on it, believing it 'too small to make much of a tree,' but a young family purchases it and, after Christmas, replants the pine, which thrives. . . . Preschool, primary." (Horn Book)

"Told from the perspective of a small evergreen, this tale begins with the narrator as a sprout and continues through the seasons until men come with their chainsaws. Luckily, the tree's size saves it from being cut down. . . . Taken to a Christmas tree lot, it is taken home by a family where it is decorated with ornaments and begins to feel loved. After a few weeks, the evergreen is replanted in the yard, where it grows big and strong. Illustrations are of a contemporary setting with nature's beauty brought forth through the lush greenery. A fine Christmas choice with an environmental message." SLJ

★ **On** Meadowview Street; [by] Henry Cole. Greenwillow Books 2007 un il $17.99; lib bdg $18.89

Grades: K 1 2 3   E

1. Nature -- Fiction 2. Meadows -- Fiction 3. Suburban life -- Fiction

ISBN 978-0-06-056481-0; 0-06-056481-4; 978-0-06-056482-7 lib bdg; 0-06-056482-2 lib bdg

LC 2006023761

Upon moving to a new house, young Caroline and her parents encourage wildflowers to grow and birds and animals to stay in their yard, which soon has the whole suburban street living up to its name

"Cole's understated watercolors match the tale's gentle tone." Booklist

On the way to the beach. Greenwillow Bks. 2003 un il $16.99

Grades: PreK K 1 2   E

1. Nature -- Fiction 2. Ecology -- Fiction 3. Senses and sensation -- Fiction

ISBN 0-688-17515-5

LC 2002-23537

On a walk through the woods and a marsh to the seashore, the reader is encouraged to notice all sorts of plants, animals, insects, and shells

"Each locale . . . is gloriously depicted in a three-page foldout that is entered through a die-cut. . . . The outstanding realistic acrylic illustrations depict the scenes in an almost three-dimensional perspective. . . . This beautiful, interactive book encourages discussion, develops observation skills, and provides a learning experience that will bring children closer to nature." SLJ

Trudy. Greenwillow Books 2009 un il $17.99; lib bdg $18.89

Grades: PreK K 1 2   E

1. Snow -- Fiction 2. Goats -- Fiction

ISBN 978-0-06-154267-1; 0-06-154267-9; 978-0-06-154268-8 lib bdg; 0-06-154268-7 lib bdg

LC 2007-47641

It seems as though Trudy the goat knows when to expect snow, but it turns out that she is really expecting something completely different.

"Cole's acrylic paintings are rounded and soft. They juxtapose muted, earth-toned colors of the environment with the bright, primary colors of manmade objects. . . . The steady pace of the text combined with its loosely repetitive structure creates a calm, reassuring mood, making the book an excellent bedtime read." SLJ

★ **Unspoken**; a story from the Underground Railroad. by Henry Cole. Scholastic Press 2012 40 p. (hardcover : alk. paper) $16.99

Grades: 2 3 4 5   E

1. Fugitive slaves -- Fiction 2. Underground railroad -- Fiction 3. United States -- History -- 1861-1865, Civil War -- Fiction 4. African Americans -- Fiction

ISBN 0545399971; 9780545399975

LC 2011043583

In this wordless picture book about the Underground Railroad by Henry Cole, "a farm child and a fugitive [slave] make an unspoken connection" during the American "Civil War. Going about her chores after watching a detachment of mounted soldiers beneath a Confederate flag trot by, the child is startled and fearful to realize that someone is hiding in a pile of cornstalks in the storehouse. . . . She courageously ventures out by herself, carrying small gifts of food." (Kirkus Reviews)

Cole, Kathryn

That Uh-oh Feeling; A Story About Touch. by Kathryn Cole, illustrated by Qin Leng. Orca Book Publishers 2016 24 p. color illustrations (hardcover) $15.95

Grades: K 1 2 3   E

1. Touch -- Fiction 2. Children -- Conduct of life

ISBN 1927583918; 9781927583913

In this children's story, by Kathryn Cole, illustrated by Qin Leng, part of the "I'm a Great Little Kid" series, "Claire is feeling uncomfortable about the attention her soccer coach is giving her. Too much flattery and too much contact give her that uh-oh feeling. By seeking help from others and talking about her feelings, the situation is resolved happily." (Publisher's note)

"Leng employs great identity and ethnic diversity in the cast of characters through bright, expressive, and simple illustrations perfect for young readers." SLJ

Collard, Sneed B.

Butterfly count; illustrated by Paul Kratter. Holiday House 2002 un il $16.95

Grades: K 1 2 3   E

1. Prairies -- Fiction 2. Butterflies -- Fiction 3. Wildlife conservation -- Fiction

ISBN 0-8234-1607-0

LC 2001-24114

Amy and her mother look for a very special butterfly while attending the annual Fourth of July Butterfly Count at a prairie restoration site. Includes factual information about butterflies and how to attract and watch them

"A gentle family story with an environmental message. . . . Soft watercolor illustrations of prairie grasses, plants, and butterflies quietly illuminate this tranquil tale." SLJ

Collier, Bryan

★ **Uptown.** Holt & Co. 2000 un il $16.95

Grades: K 1 2 3   E

1. African Americans -- Fiction 2. Harlem (New York, N.Y.) -- Fiction

ISBN 0-8050-5721-8

LC 99-31774

Coretta Scott King Award for illustration

A tour of the sights of Harlem, including the Metro-North Train, brownstones, shopping on 125th Street, a barber shop, summer basketball, the Boy's Choir, and sunset over the Harlem River as narrated by a young boy. "Ages six to nine." (Bull Cent Child Books)

"Collier's evocative watercolor-and-collage illustrations create a unique sense of mood and place. Bold color choices for text as well as background pages complement engagingly detailed pictures of city life." SLJ

Collins, Pat Lowery

The **Deer** watch; Pat Lowery Collins, illustrated by David Slonim. Candlewick Press 2013 32 p. ill. (reinforced) $15.99

Grades: K 1 2 3   E

1. Deer -- Fiction 2. Father-son relationship -- Fiction

ISBN 0763648906; 9780763648909

LC 2012942667

In this children's story, by Pat Lowery Collins, illustrated by David Slonim, "a father promises his young son that this summer they will see a deer. They set out over the dunes, through the marsh, and into the woods, searching for a white-flag tail or a set of leaping legs. But deer are hard to find, especially if your feet want to dance and your nose tickles until you sneeze." (Publisher's note)

Collins, Ross

Dear Vampa; written and illustrated by Ross Collins. Katherine Tegen Books 2009 un il $16.99

Grades: K 1 2   E

1. Letters -- Fiction 2. Vampires -- Fiction

ISBN 978-0-06-135534-9; 0-06-135534-8

LC 2008-22631

A young vampire writes a letter to his grandfather bemoaning his new neighbors

"Collins's . . . black, angular vampires lace the comedy with a drop of real creepiness. . . . Young vampire fans will enjoy (and perhaps be secretly relieved by) the vampires' beleaguered state." Publ Wkly

Doodleday. Albert Whitman 2011 un il $16.99

Grades: PreK K   E

1. Drawing -- Fiction 2. Mother-son relationship -- Fiction

ISBN 978-0-8075-1683-6; 0-8075-1683-X

LC 2010-31128

First published in the United Kingdom

Despite his mother's warning, young Harvey draws on Doodleday, but when his drawings come to life in frightening ways, only his mother can help.

"Collins brings to life the always intriguing notion of art brought to life, giving it a movie-blockbuster level of entertaining disaster. Spare, exclamatory text keeps the focus squarely on the action. . . . Any kid who's put crayon to paper will relish the notion that there's having waiting to be caused thereby." Bull Cent Child Books

There's a Bear on My Chair; by Ross Collins. Candlewick Press 2016 32 p. color illustrations $16.99

Grades: PreK K 1   E

1. Mice -- Fiction 2. Bears -- Fiction

ISBN 0763689424; 9780763689421

In this book, by Ross Collins, "poor Mouse! A bear has settled in his favorite chair, and that chair just isn't big enough for two. Mouse tries all kinds of tactics to move pesky Bear, but nothing works. Once Mouse has gone, Bear gets up and walks home. But what's that? Is that a mouse in Bear's house?" (Publisher's note)

"A must-purchase and instant classic for storytime and one-on-one sharing. Sure to become a favorite." SLJ

Collins, Suzanne, 1962-

Year of the jungle; memories from the home front. by Suzanne Collins; illustrated by James Proimos. Scholastic Press 2013 40 p. color illustrations (hc) $17.99

Grades: K 1 2 3   E

1. Vietnam War, 1961-1975 2. Picture books for children 3. Fathers and daughters 4. Separation (Psychology)

ISBN 0545425166; 9780545425162

LC 2012015346

This children's picture book "recounts, through the author's eyes as a child, the year of her father's military tour of duty in Viet Nam. The youngest of four kids growing up in a safe, loving family, Suzy is first seen listening to her dad read Ogden Nash's poem about Custard, the dragon who stays brave despite his inner fears. Thus the stage is set for her father's imminent deployment," a challenge for Suzy and her father alike. (School Library Journal)

Colon, Edie

Good-bye, Havana! Hola, New York! illustrated by Raúl Colón. Simon & Schuster Books for Young Readers 2011 un il $16.99

Grades: PreK K 1   E

1. Cuba -- Fiction 2. Immigrants -- Fiction 3. Cuban Americans -- Fiction 4. Bronx (New York, N.Y.) -- Fiction

ISBN 978-1-4424-0674-2; 1-4424-0674-7; 9781442406742; 1442406747

LC 2010020932

When Fidel Castro's government takes over their restaurant in 1960, six-year-old Gabriella and her parents move from Cuba to New York City.

"In his signature, almost pointillist style, Raúl Colón's earth-toned artwork imbues the story with a comforting texture and warmth, closely depicting the clothing, hair, and décor of the era. The dialogue is smoothly rendered in Spanish and English, and many Spanish words are defined on the final page. This gentle look back at an important time will also speak to contemporary children whose families are starting anew in the United States." Publ Wkly

Colón, Raúl, 1952-

★ **Draw!** Raul Colon; illustrated by Raul Colon. SSBFYR 2014 40 p. (hardcover) $17.99

Grades: PreK K 1 2 3   E

1. Safaris 2. Art 3. Drawing -- Fiction 4. Animals -- Fiction 5. Stories without words 6. Imagination -- Fiction

ISBN 1442494921; 9781442494923

LC 2013043781

In this children's book by Raúl Colón, "A boy named Leonardo begins to imagine and then draw a world afar - first a rhinoceros, and then he meets some monkeys, and he always has a friendly elephant at his side. Soon he finds himself in the jungle and carried away by the sheer power of his imagination, seeing the world through his own eyes and making friends along the way." (Publisher's note)

"A boy in bed, asthma inhaler within reach, sketchbook at his side, looking at a book about Africa, is not confined by the walls of his room. As he begins to draw, he takes a journey. The palette changes from subdued pen-and-ink with wash in the bedroom to vibrant hues textured with scratched-in lines that seem to pulse, capturing the landscape and animals of Africa...Youngsters will pore over each spread in wonder, soaking up the details...A true celebration of where our imaginations can take us." (Booklist)

Comden, Betty

What's new at the zoo? by Betty Comden and Adolph Green; illustrations by Travis Foster; with an introduction by Phyllis Newman. Blue Apple Books 2011 un il $16.99

Grades: K 1 2 3   E

1. Songs 2. Animals -- Songs

ISBN 978-1-60905-088-7; 1-60905-088-6

LC 2011019080

Presents the lyrics to a song from the Broadway musical, 'Do Re Mi,' in which animals in an overcrowded zoo beg to be let out while accidentally stepping on one anothers trunks, quills, and toes.

"With fun lift-the-flap details and tummy-tickling rhymes, this book will appeal to fans of slapstick humor. The cartoon illustrations really bring the silliness to life." SLJ

Compestine, Ying Chang

★ **Boy** dumplings; illustrated by James Yamasaki. Holiday House 2009 un il $16.95

Grades: PreK K 1 2   E

1. Ghost stories 2. China -- Fiction 3. Cooking -- Fiction

ISBN 978-0-8234-1955-5; 0-8234-1955-X

LC 2006050064

When a hungry ghost threatens to gobble up a plump little boy, the boy tricks the ghost by convincing him to prepare an elaborate recipe first.

"In keeping with the tale's brisk pacing and light tone, Yamasaki depicts the beaming, succulent boy and the menacing but increasingly beleaguered ghost with particularly comical faces in his cartoon illustrations. . . . [This is a] crowd-pleaser." Booklist

★ **The runaway** rice cake; pictures by Tungwai Chau. Simon & Schuster Bks. for Young Readers 2001 un il $16.95

Grades: K 1 2 3   E

1. China -- Fiction 2. Chinese New Year -- Fiction

ISBN 0-689-82972-8

LC 99-462168

After chasing the special rice cake, Nian Gao, that their mother has made to celebrate the Chinese New Year, three poor brothers share it with an elderly woman and have their generosity richly rewarded

"Compestine's engaging tale brims with intriguing details of the traditions that surround the holiday. . . . Chau makes a splash with vibrant acrylics whose textured surface and controlled, sophisticated blending of shades mimic the look of pastels." Publ Wkly

★ **The runaway** wok; a Chinese New Year tale. illustrated by Sebastià Serra. Dutton Children's Books 2011 un il $16.99

Grades: K 1 2 3   E

1. China -- Fiction 2. Magic -- Fiction 3. Chinese New Year -- Fiction

ISBN 978-0-525-42068-2; 0-525-42068-1

LC 2010013473

On Chinese New Year's Eve, a poor man who works for the richest businessman in Beijing sends his son to market to trade their last few eggs for a bag of rice, but instead he brings home an empty—but magic—wok that changes their fortunes forever. Includes information about Chinese New Year and a recipe for fried rice.

"Inspired by the Danish folktale, The Talking Pot, Compestine's . . . jaunty story takes place long ago in Beijing, which Serra . . . portrays as a bustling, cheerful village. . . . The sight of the insouciant wok carrying away the miserly family . . . will make kids snicker. They'll also chime in, since the wok's refrain begs for audience participation." Publ Wkly

Conahan, Carolyn

The **big** wish. Chronicle Books 2011 il $16.99

Grades: PreK K 1   E

1. Wishes -- Fiction

ISBN 978-0-8118-7040-5; 0-8118-7040-5

LC 2010027353

When Molly's neighbor, Pie, tries to mow down her dandelions, Molly insists that dandelions aren't weeds they're wishes in the making! Molly is convinced that if she grows enough dandelions she can make the world's biggest wish ever, a world record!

"Conahan's whimsical watercolors, full of swirl and movement, complement her gentle fable of community harmony. Quirky and full of heart." Kirkus

Connor, Leslie

Miss Bridie chose a shovel; illustrated by Mary Azarian. Houghton Mifflin 2004 un il $16

Grades: K 1 2 3   E

1. Immigrants -- Fiction

ISBN 0-618-30564-5

LC 2003-12290

Miss Bridie emigrates to America in 1856 and chooses to bring a shovel, which proves to be a useful tool throughout her life.

"Azarian's sturdy woodcuts are an excellent choice to illustrate daily life in mid-nineteenth-century America, and her pictures catch some of the emotions that the text shies away from. . . . This is a simple pleasure that will be truly appreciated by those old enough to understand the message." Booklist

Conway, David

The **great** nursery rhyme disaster; illustrated by Melanie Williamson. Tiger Tales 2009 un il $15.95

Grades: PreK K 1 2 **E**

1. Nursery rhymes -- Fiction
ISBN 978-1-58925-080-2; 1-58925-080-X
First published 2008 in the United Kingdom

Little Miss Muffet is bored. So she goes off to find a new nursery rhyme to be in. No rhyme seems quite right for Little Miss Muffet. Suddenly life with a scary little spider doesn't seem so bad after all.

"Witty prose and updated interpretations are complemented by Williamson's exuberant illustrations. Colorful, comical, and energetic, the characters race through the pages to the story's end." SLJ

Lila and the secret of rain; [by] David Conway; illustrated by Jude Daly. Frances Lincoln Children's 2007 un il $16.95
Grades: PreK K 1 2 **E**

1. Rain -- Fiction 2. Kenya -- Fiction 3. Droughts -- Fiction
ISBN 978-1-84507-407-4; 1-84507-407-6

Lila's village in Kenya is experiencing a terrible drought. When Lila's grandfather tells her the secret of rain, she sets off on her own to save her village.

"This quiet story offers inspiration and hope. . . . The illustrations are quite lovely. A huge orange sun in a brilliant blue sky dominates most pages. The prominence of the brown baked earth intensifies the unwanted result of the lack of rain. . . . This story will work well both as a read-aloud and for sharing one-on-one." SLJ

Cooke, Trish

Full, full, full of love; illustrated by Paul Howard. Candlewick Press 2003 un il hardcover o.p. pa $3.99
Grades: PreK K 1 **E**

1. Grandmothers -- Fiction 2. African Americans -- Fiction
ISBN 0-7636-1851-9; 0-7636-3883-8 pa

LC 2001-43761

For young Jay Jay, Sunday dinner at Gran's house is full of hugs and kisses, tasty dishes, all kinds of fishes, happy faces, and love

"Howard's generous, full-bleed illustrations capture the loving, bountiful spirit of a big family meal with a colorful palette and expressive eyes and smiles." Booklist

Coombs, Kate

The **secret**-keeper; story by Kate Coombs; paintings by Heather M. Solomon. Atheneum Books for Young Readers 2006 un il $16.95
Grades: 1 2 3 4 **E**

1. Fairy tales
ISBN 0-689-83963-4

LC 2003-24695

The people of Maldinga and the surrounding area bring their deep, dark secrets to Kalli, who keeps them all safe until they become too much for her to bear.

"This original fairy tale is elegantly and tenderly told. . . . Solomon's watercolor and oil paintings are lushly colored. . . . The intricate details . . . slow and eye and invite repeated viewings." Bull Cent Child Books

Cooney, Barbara

Chanticleer and the fox; adapted and illustrated by Barbara Cooney. Crowell 1958 un il $16.99; lib bdg $17.89; pa $7.99
Grades: K 1 2 3 **E**

1. Poets 2. Fables 3. Authors 4. Foxes -- Fiction
ISBN 0-690-18561-8; 0-690-18562-6 lib bdg; 0-06-443087-1 pa
Adaptation of the 'Nun's Priest's Tale' from the Canterbury Tales.
Verso of title page

Awarded the Caldecott Medal, 1959

This adaptation "retains the spirit of the original in its telling and in the beautiful, strongly colored illustrations softened by detailed lines. . . . [It] will be excellent for reading aloud to children." Libr J

Cooper, Elisha

★ **Beach**. Orchard Books 2006 un il $16.99
Grades: PreK K 1 2 **E**

1. Beaches -- Fiction 2. Seashore -- Fiction
ISBN 0-439-68785-3

LC 2005-20195

Women, men, boys, and girls spend a day at the beach enjoying a variety of activities on the sand and in the water.

"Cooper opens with a gorgeous stretch of sand in sun-flecked, amber-white watercolors. . . . His fondness for his subject is evident and infectious." SLJ

Bear dreams. Greenwillow Books 2006 un il $16.99; lib bdg $17.89
Grades: PreK K 1 2 **E**

1. Bears -- Fiction 2. Sleep -- Fiction
ISBN 0-06-087428-7; 0-06-087429-5 lib bdg

After a bear cub persuades his friends to play with him instead of hibernating, he gets very tired and falls asleep

"The watercolor-and-pencil illustrations softly portray the transition from fall to winter as well as from wakefulness to slumber. . . . This quiet book with its dreamlike quality is ideal for bedtime sharing." SLJ

Beaver is lost. Schwartz & Wade Books 2010 un il $17.99; lib bdg $20.99
Grades: PreK K 1 **E**

1. Beavers -- Fiction
ISBN 978-0-375-85765-2; 0-375-85765-6; 978-0-375-95765-9 lib bdg; 0-375-95765-0 lib bdg

LC 2009-24915

A lost beaver looks for the way home.

"Beaver's saga unfolds entirely through Cooper's splendid watercolor-and-pencil illustrations. . . . Stunning in their simplicity, these pictures speak a thousand words." Kirkus

★ **Big** cat, little cat; Elisha Cooper. Roaring Brook Press 2017 40 p. illustrations (some color) (ebook) $60; (hardback) $16.99
Grades: PreK K 1 **E**

1. Cats -- Fiction 2. Friendship -- Fiction
ISBN 9781250155979; 9781626723719

LC 2016002014

In this children's book, by Elisha Cooper, "there was a cat who lived alone. Until the day a new cat came. . . . And so a story of friendship begins, following two cats through their days, months, and years until one day, the older cat has to go. And he doesn't come back. This a poignant story, told in measured text and bold black-and-white illustrations about life and the act of moving on." (Publisher's note)

"A hard book to read for anyone who has lost a feline family member but a heart-healing message all the same." Kirkus

★ **Farm**. Orchard Books 2010 un il $17.99
Grades: K 1 2 3 **E**

1. Farm life -- Fiction
ISBN 0-545-07075-9; 978-0-545-07075-1

LC 2009-04342

This book describes the activities on a family farm from the spring when preparations for planting begin to the autumn when the cats grow winter coats and the cold rains begin to fall. "Ages five to nine." (Bull Cent Child Books)

"Working in his signature style of loosely rendered figures and simple compositions in pencil and watercolor, Cooper combines beautiful expansive views of the farm . . . with small, individual images. . . . Filled with sensory details, the brief text has a poetic, stripped-down simplicity that matches the stark images and will read aloud well." Booklist

A **good** night walk. Orchard Books 2005 un il $16.99
Grades: PreK K 1 2   E
  1. Bedtime -- Fiction 2. Walking -- Fiction
  ISBN 0-439-68783-7
                     LC 2004-23571
The reader is taken on a journey through a neighborhood and shown the sights, sounds, and smells as evening approaches.
  "The clear, unfussy compositions echo the poetic words' soothing, elemental sounds . . . which beautifully capture the soft, slowdown rhythms of dusk. Children will find much that's cozy, reassuring, and familiar in the scenes, . . . depicted in luminous watercolors and firmly penciled shapes" Booklist

  ★ **Homer**; Elisha Cooper. Greenwillow Books 2012 32 p. col. ill. (trade bdg.) $16.99
Grades: PreK K 1 2   E
  1. Dogs -- Fiction 2. Family -- Fiction 3. Picture books for children 4. Contentment -- Fiction 5. Human-animal relationships -- Fiction
  ISBN 0062012487; 9780062012487
                     LC 2011013453
This picture book tells the story of "an aging yellow Lab named Homer . . . [and his] love for his family. . . . At daybreak Homer is already lying on the front porch. . . . As the family members . . . pass by Homer on their way out, they all invite him to come along to play in the water, dig in the sand or bike to the store. Homer replies to each in turn that he is happy to stay right there on the porch. . . . Homer finally curl[s] up in a cozy armchair for the night, content because 'I have everything I want.'" (Kirkus Reviews)

  ★ **Magic** thinks big. Greenwillow Books 2004 un il $14.99; lib bdg $15.89
Grades: PreK K 1 2   E
  1. Cats -- Fiction
  ISBN 0-06-058164-6; 0-06-058165-4 lib bdg
                     LC 2003-12566
A cat sits in the doorway and tries to decide whether to go inside where he might get fed again, go outside where he might have an adventure, or stay where he is.
  "The simple text is full of dry humor and whimsy. The dreamy pencil-and-watercolor illustrations are a pleasing mixture of soft colors and thick lines." SLJ

  ★ **Train**; by Elisha Cooper. Orchard Books 2013 40 p. $17.99
Grades: PreK K 1 2 3   E
  1. Travel 2. Railroads 3. Railroad trains -- Fiction 4. Voyages and travels -- Fiction
  ISBN 0545384958; 9780545384957
                     LC 2012049336
In this book, by Elisha Cooper, readers can "experience [the] sights, sounds, smells [of trains]--and the engineers and conductors who make them go--as they roll across the country. Climb aboard a red-striped Commuter Train in the East. Switch to a blue Passenger Train rolling through midwestern farmland. Then hop on a Freight Train, soar over mountains on an Overnight Train, and finish on a High-Speed Train as it races to the West Coast." (Publisher's note)
  "As five trains (commuter, freight, etc.) overtake each other, we travel with them across the country. Cooper varies his composition throughout, showing close-up interiors, long landscapes, or several vignettes on one spread. He makes sure we hear the trains, too (the passenger train leaving: "like the da dum da dum of a beating heart"). Ideal for poring over. Glos." (Horn Book)

Cooper, Floyd
  Max and the tag-along moon; Floyd Cooper. Philomel Books 2012 32 p. ill. (reinforced) $16.99
Grades: PreK K 1   E
  1. Picture books for children 2. Grandparent-grandchild relationship -- Fiction 3. Moon -- Fiction 4. Grandfathers -- Fiction
  ISBN 0399233423; 9780399233425
                     LC 2011049784
In this children's picture book, "it's hard to leave Granpa's house, but he has a promise for young Max" the 'big fine moon' in the sky 'will always shine for you . . . on and on!' Granpa seems right for most of the 'swervy-curvy' trip home. . . . Then storm clouds turn the sky dark," and Max begins to worry. "When moon reappears, Max has a deeper understanding of what Granpa's promise means: love, like the moon's light, goes 'on and on.'" (Publishers Weekly)

  ★ **Willie** and the All-Stars; [by] Floyd Cooper. Philomel Books 2008 un il $16.99
Grades: PreK K 1   E
  1. Baseball -- Fiction 2. Chicago (Ill.) -- Fiction 3. Race relations -- Fiction 4. African Americans -- Fiction
  ISBN 978-0-399-23340-1; 0-399-23340-7
                     LC 2007042101
In 1934 Chicago, Willie sees a game between the Negro League All-Star team and the Major League All-Stars, and realizes that his dream of becoming a professional baseball player could come true.
  "By looking at race relations through the prism of baseball, Cooper will draw readers. . . . The soft-focus sepia-touched artwork, vintage Cooper, is a nice mix of action and nostalgia." Booklist

Cooper, Helen
  ★ **Dog** biscuit. Farrar Straus Giroux 2009 un il $16
Grades: PreK K 1   E
  1. Dogs -- Fiction 2. Imagination -- Fiction
  ISBN 978-0-374-31812-3; 0-374-31812-3
                     LC 2008-24124
"One day, while Bridget is at Mrs. Blair's house being looked after, she eats a biscuit she finds in the shed—a dog biscuit. Mrs. Blair jokes that she will 'go bowwow and turn into a dog,' and Bridget begins to believe it. . . . A handsome and thoughtfully done layout uses different fonts and sizes for the text, and Cooper's illustrations alternate quiet, ordinary scenes with wild scenes of Bridget's imagination. . . . This is a beautiful and imaginative book for anyone who loves a good story." SLJ

  ★ **Pumpkin** soup. Farrar, Straus & Giroux 1999 un il hardcover o.p. pa $6.95
Grades: PreK K 1 2   E
  1. Cats -- Fiction 2. Ducks -- Fiction 3. Cooking -- Fiction 4. Squirrels -- Fiction
  ISBN 0-374-36164-9; 0-374-46031-0 pa
                     LC 98-18677
First published 1998 in the United Kingdom
  The Cat and the Squirrel come to blows with the Duck in arguing about who will perform what duty in preparing their pumpkin soup, and they almost lose the Duck's friendship when he decides to leave them
  "Cooper serves up a well-rounded tale told with storyteller's cadences. . . . Rich autumn colors and enchanting details on large spreads and spot illustrations embellish characterizations and setting." SLJ
  Other titles about Cat, Squirrel and Duck are:
  A pipkin of pepper (2005)
  Delicious! (2007)

Cooper, Ilene

The **golden** rule; by Ilene Cooper; illustrated by Gabi Swiatowska. Abrams Books for Young Readers 2007 un il $16.95

Grades: K 1 2 3   E

    1. Conduct of life -- Fiction

ISBN 978-0-8109-0960-1; 0-8109-0960-X

LC 2006013333

Grandpa explains that the golden rule is a simple statement on how to live that can be practiced by people of all ages and faiths, then helps his grandson figure out how to apply the rule to his own life.

"The rich, golden paintings and large format reinforce the importance of the topic. . . . Swirling patterns of animal shapes and symbols from various traditions are reminders that the topic is as abstract as the art, with much room for interpretation. This is less a story than a discussion starter, and teachers, parents, and religious leaders will welcome it as a clear introduction to an important subject." SLJ

Copeland, Misty, 1982-

★ **Firebird**; ballerina Misty Copeland shows a young girl how to dance like the firebird. Misty Copeland; illustrated by Christopher Myers. First edition G.P. Putnam's Sons, an imprint of Penguin Group (USA) 2014 40 p. (hardback) $17.99

Grades: 2 3 4 5 6   E

    1. Ballerinas -- Fiction 2. Girls -- Fiction 3. Dance -- Fiction 4. Ballet dancing -- Fiction 5. Self-confidence -- Fiction 6. African Americans -- Fiction

ISBN 0399166157; 9780399166150

LC 2014008878

Coretta Scott King (Illustrator) Book Award (2015)

"In her debut picture book, [author] Misty Copeland tells the story of a young girl--an every girl--whose confidence is fragile and who is questioning her own ability to reach the heights that Misty has reached. Misty encourages this young girl's faith in herself and shows her exactly how, through hard work and dedication, she too can become 'Firebird.'" (Publisher's note)

"Think you can simply write off celebrity books? Think again. American Ballet Theatre soloist Copeland is just as graceful with words as she is with her body....Myers's stunning collages layer strips of thickly painted paper to echo the wings of a firebird (Copeland's signature role), whether they are illustrating the stage curtains or a cloudy sky. His deep, rich colors make even the portraits of the dancers at rest dramatic, and when the dancers are on stage, they seem to fly." Horn Book

Copp, Jim

Jim Copp, will you tell me a story? three uncommonly clever tales. as told by Jim Copp; illustrated by Lindsay duPont. Harcourt 2008 54p il $17.95

Grades: 2 3 4   E

    1. Short stories 2. Stories in rhyme

ISBN 978-0-15-206331-3; 0-15-206331-5

LC 2007033969

"This collection contains three short stories that were originally recordings by Copp, who died in 1999. The humorous tales, some rhyming, have definite kid appeal. In the first, feisty Kate Higgins refuses to take her medicine and suffers the consequences in the morning. . . . [In] 'Miss Goggins and the Gorilla,' . . . a fourth-grade class is saved from a cruel teacher by a visitor in a gorilla suit. In the last story, forgetful Martha Matilda O'Toole has to keep returning home to get school supplies she's left behind—until her teacher reminds her that it is Sunday. . . . DuPont's pen-and-ink and watercolor illustrations are a perfect match for the quirky stories. . . . Copp's narration on the accompanying CD are a refreshing contrast to the commercialized sound of much of today's children's music." SLJ

Cora, Cat

A **suitcase** surprise for Mommy; pictures by Joy Allen. Dial Books for Young Readers 2011 un il $16.99

Grades: PreK K   E

    1. Mother-son relationship -- Fiction

ISBN 978-0-8037-3332-9; 0-8037-3332-1

Mommy must travel for business, and Zoran is not happy—he will miss her too much! But what if he gives Mommy one of his special things to take with her so that she will have a part of him with her when she goes?

"The story's concepts and emotions ring true and are accessibly related through the descriptive narrative, which is filled with realistic dialogue and interactions. . . . The brightly colored, cartoon-style, gouache-and-pencil illustrations include many playful touches that reinforce the comforting tone." Booklist

Cordell, Matthew

★ **Another** brother; written and illustrated by Matthew Cordell. Feiwel and Friends 2012 un il $16.99

Grades: PreK K 1 2   E

    1. Sheep -- Fiction 2. Brothers -- Fiction 3. Family life -- Fiction

ISBN 978-0-312-64324-9; 0-312-64324-1

LC 2011001135

Davy the sheep wishes he had time alone with his parents, as he did before his twelve brothers came along and started imitating his every move, but when his wish comes true Davy misses playing with the youngsters.

"This is not just another new-baby book: Cordell's humorous text and mischievously silly, expressive cartoon art will have readers bleating to read it again and again." Kirkus

Trouble gum. Feiwel & Friends 2009 un il $16.99

Grades: K 1 2 3   E

    1. Pigs -- Fiction 2. Brothers -- Fiction 3. Chewing gum -- Fiction

ISBN 978-0-312-38774-7; 0-312-38774-1

Playing indoors with his little brother on a rainy day, a rambunctious young pig causes a ruckus and then breaks his mother's three chewing gum rules.

"The simple story line and liberal use of white space open plenty of opportunities for Cordell's winsome art to generate laughs. Even better are the sound effects bouncing around each page." Booklist

★ **Wolf** in the snow; Matthew Cordell. Feiwel & Friends 2017 48 p. color illustrations (hardcover) $17.99; (ebook) $60

Grades: PreK K 1 2   E

    1. Snow -- Fiction 2. Girls -- Fiction 3. Wolves -- Fiction

ISBN 9781250076366; 9781250148308

LC 2016937562

In this picture book, by Matthew Cordell, "a girl is lost in a snowstorm. A wolf cub is lost, too. How will they find their way home? Paintings rich with feeling tell this satisfying story of friendship and trust." (Publisher's note)

"What distinguishes this book are the many feelings that Cordell's pen-and-ink-with-watercolor illustrations capture so well—cold, fear, courage, exhaustion, relief—keeping readers hooked to the end. Deeply satisfying" Kirkus

Corderoy, Tracey

The **little** white owl; illustrated by Jane Chapman. Good Books 2010 un il $16.99

Grades: PreK K 1   E

    1. Owls -- Fiction 2. Imagination -- Fiction 3. Storytelling -- Fiction

ISBN 978-1-56148-693-9; 1-56148-693-0

"Living all alone in a snowy landscape under a starry sky, a little white owl imagines himself as a knight or as a rocket, blasting off to the moon. Those empowering fantasies inspire him to take off one day . . . until he reaches a group of big beautiful owls in bright-jewel colors. . . . After he tells the snotty birds his magical stories, . . . they are . . . smitten. . . . [The book offers] tropically hued, textured illustrations. . . . Young children will recognize the pain of loneliness, the power of solitude, and the bliss of imaginative play." Booklist

Cordsen, Carol Foskett

★ **Market** day; illustrated by Douglas B. Jones. Dutton Children's Books 2008 un il $16.99
Grades: PreK K 1   E
1. Stories in rhyme 2. Cattle -- Fiction 3. Markets -- Fiction 4. Farm life -- Fiction
ISBN 978-0-525-47883-6; 0-525-47883-3

LC 2007-28489

The Benson family is so busy preparing for their day at a farmers' market that they not only forget to feed the cow, they leave the farmyard gate open and the hungry cow follows them, making a mess of the market.

"It's not often that words and art mesh as well as they do here. . . . The retro-style artwork . . . mixes striking compositions with tints of glowing peach, vegetable green, honey yellow, and other luscious colors. A delightful read-aloud." Booklist

Corey, Shana

Players in pigtails; illustrated by Rebecca Gibbon. Scholastic Press 2003 un il $16.95
Grades: K 1 2 3   E
1. Baseball -- Fiction 2. Sex role -- Fiction 3. All-American Girls Professional Baseball League -- Fiction
ISBN 0-439-18305-7

LC 2002-3445

Katie Casey, a fictional character, helps start the All-American Girls Professional Baseball League, which gave women the opportunity to play professional baseball while America was involved in World War II

"Kids, both girls and boys, will revel in the energy and joy Corey packs into her story. Gibbon's pictures look straight out of the 1940s, with vintage details and an evocative color palette. They also possess a winsome charm that plays nicely with the text." Booklist

The **secret** subway; Shana Corey; Red Nose Studio. Schwartz & Wade Books 2016 40 p. illustrations $17.99
Grades: K 1 2 3 4   E
1. Transportation -- Fiction 2. New York (N.Y.) -- History -- Fiction 3. New York (N.Y.) -- History -- 1865-1898 -- Fiction 4. Subways -- New York (State) -- New York -- Fiction
ISBN 9780375870712; 9780375970719

LC 2014025770

This book, by Shana Corey, illustrated by Red Nose Studio, tells the "story of New York City's first subway. . . . You see, way back in 1860, there were no subways, just cobblestone streets. That is, until Alfred Ely Beach had the idea for a fan-powered train that would travel underground. On February 26, 1870, after fifty-eight days of drilling and painting and plastering, Beach unveiled his masterpiece—and throngs of visitors took turns swooshing down the track." (Publisher's note)

"The incredibly inventive multimedia illustrations match the text perfectly and add detail, dimension, and pizazz... Absolutely wonderful in every way." Kirkus

Includes bibliographical references

Cornwall, Gaia

Jabari Jumps; by Gaia Cornwall. Candlewick Press 2017 32 p. color illustrations $15.99
Grades: PreK K 1 2   E
1. Diving -- Fiction 2. Swimming -- Fiction
ISBN 0763678384; 9780763678388

This book, by Gaia Cornwall, "Jabari is definitely ready to jump off the diving board. He's finished his swimming lessons and passed his swim test, and he's a great jumper, so he's not scared at all. . . . But when his dad squeezes his hand, Jabari squeezes back. He needs to figure out what kind of special jump to do anyway, and he should probably do some stretches before climbing up onto the diving board." (Publisher's note)

Cosentino, Ralph

Superman: the story of the man of steel; written and illustrated by Ralph Cosentino; Superman created by Jerry Siegel & Joe Shuster. Viking 2010 33p il $16.99
Grades: 1 2 3   E
1. Superheroes -- Fiction 2. Superman (Fictional character)
ISBN 978-0-670-06285-0; 0-670-06285-5

"Cosentino acquaints the youngest readers with a comic-book legend. . . . Cosentino presents snapshots that provide a groundwork for understanding Supe's endless print, TV, and movie iterations. Thick-lined new-retro cartoon art in startling primary colors sets off the . . . block-jawed hero. . . . A flashback follows his escape from Krypton, and his boyhood with the Kents features many beloved touchstones. . . . The lineup of his Daily Planet cohorts . . . is followed by the evildoers, who get one double-page spread apiece: Luthor, Metallo, Braniac, and Bizarro." Booklist

Wonder Woman; the story of the Amazon princess. written and illustrated by Ralph Cosentino. Viking 2011 un il $16.99
Grades: 1 2 3   E
1. Superheroes -- Fiction 2. Wonder Woman (Fictitious character)
ISBN 978-0-670-06256-0; 0-670-06256-1

LC 2010024540

Wonder Woman tells how she came to be the protector of humankind, who her enemies are, and how she keeps her identity secret.

"The bold retro artwork has vivid colors and thick black outlines. It's a mix that will work well for the intended audience." SLJ

Cossi, Olga

Pemba Sherpa; Olga Cossi; illustrated by Gary Bernard. Odyssey Books 2009 32p $15.95
Grades: PreK K 1 2   E
1. Siblings -- Fiction 2. Gender role -- Fiction 3. Tibet (China) -- Fiction 4. Himalaya Mountains -- Fiction
ISBN 9780976865582

LC 2009934415

This book take place "[i]n a Himalayan village in Tibet, [where] a young boy rises before dawn to collect firewood. His younger sister, Yang Ki, longs to join him in his task, which is part of the training to be a Sherpa, but the boy scoffs: it isn't girls' work. One morning, . . . Yang Ki disregards her brother's . . . command to stay home, follows him along the steep mountain path, and saves his life when he loses his footing. When Yang Ki carries his heavy load of firewood home, the villagers are astonished, and she . . . grow[s] up to be a famous guide. . . . [T]his . . . story . . . embeds specifics of Tibetan culture as it captures a child's . . . feelings of frustration when she is . . . underestimated, her determination, and her final pleasure when she triumphs." (Booklist)

Costello, David

I can help; [by] David Hyde Costello. Farrar, Straus & Giroux 2010 un il $12.99

Grades: PreK   E

1. Animals -- Fiction 2. Helping behavior -- Fiction

ISBN 978-0-374-33526-7; 0-374-33526-5

LC 2005044321

When a duck gets lost and a monkey helps him find his way, it starts a chain reaction in which all the young animals help each other solve their problems.

"The ink-and-watercolor artwork features simply drawn, brightly colored focal characters set against landscaped backgrounds. . . . Spare, repetitive text and attractive artwork make this an ideal story hour choice for even the squirmiest group." Booklist

Cote, Genevieve

Goodnight, You; Genevieve Cote, illustrated by Genevieve Cote. Kids Can Press 2014 32 p. $16.95

Grades: PreK K   E

1. Bedtime -- Fiction 2. Monsters -- Fiction 3. Fear -- Fiction 4. Swine -- Fiction 5. Rabbits -- Fiction

ISBN 1771380500; 9781771380508

In this children's book, written and illustrated by Genevieve Cote, part of the Piggy and Bunny series, "the two friends explore what scares them as they prepare for their first campout together. When Bunny admits to being frightened of monsters, Piggy responds that 'even if there WAS a monster, I wouldn't scream like you!' . . . Then, one by one, all of Bunny's questions about what to do if a monster came near are countered confidently by Piggy." (Publisher's note)

"Two friends, a rabbit and a pig, appear in their fourth picture book adventure by the Canadian author/illustrator. As in the earlier titles, this one addresses preschool emotions, in this case, fear . . . The book's square format is appealing, and the multimedia illustrations—in a simple, soft palette—are charming. The art has a childlike quality and should appeal to the target audience." SLJ

Other titles in the series include:

Me and You (2009)

Starring Me and You (2014)

Without You (2011)

Mr. King's castle; Genevieve Cote. Kids Can Press 2013 32 p. $16.95

Grades: PreK K 1 2   E

1. Castles -- Fiction 2. Conservation of natural resources -- Fiction

ISBN 1554539722; 9781554539727

In this children's picture book by author Genevieve Cote, 'a lion-turned' real estate developer recklessly undermines his own foundations. Fixed on expanding his house into a 'BIG castle' . . . Mr. King chips block-shaped pieces from the surrounding BIG hill. . . . Feeling 'very small' at seeing the hill's other animal residents gathered to protest . . . Mr. King joins in to reassemble the cutout pieces into seamless slopes." (Kirkus Reviews)

Starring Me and You; by Genevieve Cote. Kids Can Press 2014 32 p. $16.95

Grades: PreK K   E

1. Pigs -- Fiction 2. Rabbits -- Fiction 3. Emotions -- Fiction 4. Children's plays -- Fiction 5. Swine -- Fiction 6. Friendship -- Fiction

ISBN 1894786394; 9781894786393

In this children's story, "two animal friends, a bunny and a pig, explore the world of their emotions as they attempt to put on a play together. Along the way, they must face a few challenges, such as when the bunny wants them to 'be sunflowers and sing a duet,' while the pig would rather 'be pirates on a shipwreck.' As they work their way to a successful collaboration, they take turns describing the different ways they act when they are shy, scared, eager, angry and sad." (Publisher's note)

"The duo from Me and You (2009) and Without You (2011) is back and ready to put on a play. That is, once they get all ready and decide if the play is about pirates or flowers...The illustrations are a simple yet charming mix of crayon and watercolors. Fans of other buddy books, such as the Elephant and Piggie series by Mo Willems or Suzanne Bloom's A Splendid Friend, Indeed (2005), will cheer this team of unlikely friends." Booklist

Cotten, Cynthia

Rain play; [by] Cynthia Cotten; illustrated by Javaka Steptoe. Henry Holt & Co. 2008 un il $16.95

Grades: PreK K 1 2   E

1. Stories in rhyme 2. Play -- Fiction 3. Rain -- Fiction 4. African Americans -- Fiction

ISBN 978-0-8050-6795-8; 0-8050-6795-7

LC 2007012734

Most people leave the park when rain begins to fall, while others enjoy the sights, sounds, and feel of the cool water—until thunder and lightening come near

"The text is written in rhythmic two-line rhymes. . . . Steptoe's cut-paper collages are filled with texture and motion. Facial features rendered in paint show the joy that the youngsters feel. . . . These African-American kids exuberantly jump, splash, run, and puddle-stomp all around the playground." SLJ

This is the stable; illustrated by Delana Bettoli. Holt 2006 un il lib bdg $16.95

Grades: PreK K 1 2   E

1. Stories in rhyme

ISBN 0-8050-7556-9

LC 2005-19904

Recalls, in rhyming text and illustrations, the Nativity story, from the brown and dusty stable to the star shining brightly above.

"This lovely picture book combines beautiful artwork and a seamless, thoughtful . . . style. . . . The rhyme is sweet but never forced. Bettoli uses a mixture of pastels, primary colors, and earth tones." SLJ

Cotter, Bill

Beard in a Box; Bill Cotter. Knopf Books for Young Readers 2016 40 p. color illustrations (trade) $17.99

Grades: PreK K 1 2   E

1. Beards -- Fiction 2. Father-son relationship -- Fiction 3. Fathers and sons -- Fiction 4. Swindlers and swindling -- Fiction

ISBN 0553508369; 9780553508352; 9780553508369

LC 2014047471

In this children's book, by Bill Cotter, "a young boy longs for a beard like Dad's, and when he discovers a hair-growth product called Beard in a Box, he must have it! He rips open the package, plants the beard seeds, and waits . . . and waits . . . and waits." (Publisher's note)

"The droll, expressive illustrations hit just the right tone and include visual celebrations of facial hair... Young readers—both boys and girls—will appreciate this humorous homage to dads." Booklist

Cottin, Menena

★ The **black** book of colors; by Menena Cottin and Rosana Faria; translated by Elisa Amado. Groundwood/Anansi Books 2008 un il $17.95

Grades: 1 2 3 4   E

1. Blind -- Fiction 2. Color -- Fiction

ISBN 978-0-88899-873-6; 0-88899-873-2

Original Spanish edition 2006

"With entirely black pages and a bold white text, this is not your typical color book. Meant to be experienced with the fingers instead of the eyes, this extraordinary book allows sighted readers to experience colors the way blind people do: through the other senses. The text, in both print and Braille, presents colors through touch . . . taste . . . smell . . . and sound. . . . Faría's distinctive illustrations present black shapes embossed on a black background for readers to feel instead of see. . . . Fascinating, beautifully designed, and possessing broad child appeal, this book belongs on the shelves of every school or public library committed to promoting disability awareness and accessibility." SLJ

Cottringer, Anne

Eliot Jones, midnight superhero; illustrated by Alex T. Smith. Tiger Tales 2009 un il $15.95; pa $7.95

Grades: PreK K 1 2　　　　　　　　　　　　　　　　　　　E

　1. Superheroes -- Fiction

　ISBN 978-1-58925-083-3; 1-58925-083-4; 978-1-58925-416-9 pa; 1-58925-416-3 pa

"By day, Eliot is a quiet boy who likes to read, but when the clock strikes midnight, he becomes a superhero. . . . Eliot's adventures are fast-paced and exciting. A variety of fonts are used, making the text feel integrated into the action-packed illustrations. Done in vibrant pastel hues, the collage-style spreads match the tone of each adventure and include many details that youngsters will enjoy exploring." SLJ

Cousins, Lucy

Hooray for Birds! written and illustrated by Lucy Cousins. Candlewick Press 2017 40 p. color illustrations $15.99

　Grades: PreK K　　　　　　　　　　　　　　　　　　　　E

　1. Birds -- Fiction

　ISBN 0763692654; 9780763692650

This book, by Lucy Cousins, "invites little ones to imagine themselves as brilliant birds. Birds of all feathers flock together in a fun, rhyme-filled offering by the creator of Maisy. From the rooster's 'cock-a-doodle-doo' at dawn to the owl's nighttime 'tuwit, tuwoo,' the cheeps and tweets of many bright and beautiful avian friends will have children eager to join in as honorary fledglings." (Publisher's note)

★ **Hooray** for fish! Candlewick Press 2005 un il $14.99; $8.99

Grades: PreK K 1　　　　　　　　　　　　　　　　　　　E

　1. Fishes -- Fiction

　ISBN 0-7636-2741-0; 978-0-7636-3918-1

Little Fish has all sorts of fishy friends in his underwater home, but loves one of them most of all

"This winning title . . . features . . . bright hues and cheerful, child-like creatures. The stars here are fish, and Cousins matches a gloriously decorated assortment of them with rhyming text that encourages children to look carefully and think about similarities and differences." Booklist

★ **I'm** the best. Candlewick Press 2010 un il $14.99

Grades: PreK K 1　　　　　　　　　　　　　　　　　　　E

　1. Dogs -- Fiction 2. Animals -- Fiction 3. Friendship -- Fiction

　ISBN 978-0-7636-4684-4; 0-7636-4684-9

When Dog's constant boasting makes his friends sad, they find a way to teach him what it means to be a good friend.

"The book's large format gives plenty of range for Cousins' naive, expressive pencil-and-ink illustrations. From the exuberant text to the bold, colorful artwork, a joyous spirit pervades this picture book and its fallible yet lovable protagonist." Booklist

Maisy goes to preschool. Candlewick Press 2009 un il $12.99

Grades: PreK　　　　　　　　　　　　　　　　　　　　　E

　1. School stories 2. Mice -- Fiction

　ISBN 978-0-7636-4254-9; 0-7636-4254-1

"Maisy is confident and acquainted with the routines of preschool. She clearly has no separation issues. She hangs up her coat, joins in making music, listens to a story, and so on. Throughout the day, the young mouse and her friends have a good time. As always, Cousins's bright color illustrations are simple and appealing." SLJ

　Other Maisy First Experiences books are:

　Maisy, Charley, and the wobbly tooth (2006)

　Maisy goes on a plane (2015)

　Maisy goes on vacation (2010)

　Maisy goes to the hospital (2007)

　Maisy goes to the library (2005)

　Maisy goes to the local bookstore (2017)

　Maisy goes to the movies (2014)

　Maisy goes to the museum (2008)

　Maisy learns to swim (2013)

　Maisy plays soccer (2014)

　Maisy's field day (2016)

Maisy plays soccer; Lucy Cousins. Candlewick Press 2014 32 p. color illustrations (Maisy first experiences) (hardcover) $12.99; (pbk.) $6.99

Grades: PreK　　　　　　　　　　　　　　　　　　　　　E

　1. Soccer -- Fiction 2. Friendship -- Fiction

　ISBN 0763672289; 9780763672287; 9780763672386

　　　　　　　　　　　　　　　　　　　　　　LC 2013944013

"Maisy and her friends can't wait to play soccer! Maisy puts on her uniform, laces up her sneakers, and heads to the field. Charlie, Tallulah, and Dotty are on the blue team, while Maisy, Cyril, and Eddie are on the red. Let's play! Soon enough the game heats up, with plenty of action, excitement, and suspense." (Publisher's note)

"The best thing about these books is the distinctive, colorful illustrations. Drenched in primary and secondary colors, the animal characters all display personality and humor." SLJ

Coville, Bruce

Hans Brinker; inspired by the novel by Mary Mapes Dodge; retold by Bruce Coville; illustrated by Laurel Long. Dial Books for Young Readers 2007 un il $16.99

Grades: 3 4 5　　　　　　　　　　　　　　　　　　　　E

　1. Siblings -- Fiction 2. Ice skating -- Fiction 3. Netherlands -- Fiction

　ISBN 978-0-8037-2868-4

　　　　　　　　　　　　　　　　　　　　　　LC 2006027109

A Dutch brother and sister work toward two goals, finding the doctor who can restore their father's memory and winning the competition for the silver skates.

"The story's climax . . . is unglamorous yet satisfying. . . . The book's highlight is Long's glowing oil paintings, which are equally effective in illustrating Holland's snowy, glittering landscape and the story's warmer, more intimate family moments." Horn Book

Cowen-Fletcher, Jane

Hello puppy! Candlewick Press 2010 un il $12.99

Grades: PreK K 1　　　　　　　　　　　　　　　　　　E

　1. Dogs -- Fiction

　ISBN 978-0-7636-4303-4; 0-7636-4303-3

A child spends time with her new puppy, learning what it means when puppy yawns, stretches, and sniffs.

"The simple sentences are paired with cozy pastel illustrations. The youngster explores the puppy's behavior indoors and out with a special emphasis on play and fun. The story gives young readers a good sense of the responsibility of taking care of a pet." SLJ

Cox, Judy

Carmen learns English; illustrated by Angela N. Dominguez. Holiday House 2010 un il $16.95
Grades: PreK K 1 2   E
1. School stories 2. Sisters -- Fiction 3. Immigrants -- Fiction 4. English language -- Fiction 5. Mexican Americans -- Fiction 6. Spanish language -- Vocabulary
ISBN 978-0-8234-2174-9; 0-8234-2174-0
        LC 2008048462
"Older sister Carmen tells Lupita, who is about to enter kindergarten, about her first day of school, when she could speak only Spanish. She recalls other children teasing her about saying the wrong words or mocking her accent. Yet with a kind teacher's help, Carmen mastered English well enough to teach her new language to Lupita and then to begin to use it at school, where classmates learn Spanish from her. Dominguez's . . . paintings convey a childlike energy and effectively express Carmen's moods. This charming celebration of bilingualism captures both the fears and delights of learning a new tongue." SLJ

Go to sleep, Groundhog! illustrated by Paul Meisel. Holiday House 2004 un il $16.95
Grades: PreK K 1 2   E
1. Marmots -- Fiction 2. Groundhog Day -- Fiction
ISBN 0-8234-1645-3
        LC 2002-24124
When Groundhog is unable to sleep, he experiences autumn and winter holidays he never knew about, and then he finally falls asleep before Groundhog Day
"An endnote discussing the tradition of using critters as meteorologists makes this a useful as well as a charming answer to the scarcity of engaging material on Groundhog Day." Booklist

My family plays music; illustrated by Elbrite Brown. Holiday House 2003 un il $17.95
Grades: PreK K 1 2 3   E
1. Musicians -- Fiction 2. Family life -- Fiction 3. Musical instruments -- Fiction
ISBN 0-8234-1591-0
        LC 00-44903
A musical family with talents for playing a variety of instruments enjoys getting together to celebrate
"The paper-cut illustrations vibrate with color and—almost—with sound. The multiracial family with its rainbow of skin tones is not only a lovely multicultural statement but also a vivid reflection of contemporary families and musical tastes." Booklist

One is a feast for Mouse; a Thanksgiving tale. illustrated by Jeffrey Ebbeler. Holiday House 2008 un il $16.95; pa $6.95
Grades: PreK K 1 2   E
1. Cats -- Fiction 2. Mice -- Fiction 3. Thanksgiving Day -- Fiction
ISBN 978-0-8234-1977-7; 0-8234-1977-0; 978-0-8234-2231-9 pa; 0-8234-2231-3 pa
        LC 2007-13972
On Thanksgiving Day while everyone naps, Mouse spots one pea, a perfect feast, but he cannot help adding all of the fixings—until Cat spots him
"Whimsical, large-scale illustrations drawn in acrylics, pastels, and colored pencils are a perfect complement to the story. Plenty of action and humor as well as a thoroughly satisfying ending make this a wonderful holiday read-aloud." SLJ
Other titles about Mouse are:
Cinco de Mouse-O! (2010)
Haunted house, haunted Mouse (2011)

Cox, Lynne

Elizabeth, queen of the seas; Lynne Cox; illustrated by Brian Floca. Schwartz & Wade Books 2014 48 p. $17.99
Grades: K 1 2 3   E
1. New Zealand 2. Seals (Animals) 3. Human-animal relationship 4. Elephant seals -- New Zealand 5. Human-animal relationships -- New Zealand 6. Christchurch (N.Z.) -- Social life and customs
ISBN 0375858881; 9780375858888; 9780375958885
        LC 2011023586
This book, by Lynne Cox, "is the incredible story of Elizabeth, a real-life elephant seal who made her home in the Avon River in the city of Christchurch, New Zealand. When Elizabeth decides to stretch out across a two-lane road, the citizens worry she might get hurt or cause traffic accidents, so a group of volunteers tows her out to sea. But Elizabeth swims all the way back to Christchurch. The volunteers catch her again and again . . . but, still, Elizabeth finds her way back home." (Publisher's note)
"Cox opens this fact-based story on just the right note: 'There was once a lovely elephant seal who lived in the city.'...Especially effective is a page where Michael, who after nearly three months without his friend, wishes on the stars reflected in the river's water; the page turn reveals the seal's head poking through radiating rings of water while the boy shouts, 'Welcome home, Elizabeth!' Children are likely to request multiple readings of this compelling told and lovingly illustrated true story." SLJ

Coy, John

★ **Strong** to the hoop; illustrations by Leslie Jean-Bart. Lee & Low Bks. 1999 un il hardcover o.p. pa $8.95
Grades: 2 3 4 5   E
1. Basketball -- Fiction
ISBN 1-880000-80-6; 1-58430-178-3 pa
        LC 98-33264
Ten-year-old James tries to hold his own and prove himself on the basketball court when the older boys finally ask him to join them in a game
"Coy's text moves with all the free-wheeling speed of playground ball. . . . Best of all, though, are Jean-Bart's collage-style illustrations, produced by combining Polaroid photographs and scratchboard drawings." Booklist

Craig, Lindsey

Dancing feet! illustrations by Marc Brown. Knopf 2010 un il $16.99
Grades: PreK   E
1. Stories in rhyme 2. Dance -- Fiction 3. Animals -- Fiction
ISBN 978-0-375-86181-9; 0-375-86181-5
"Children are asked to guess who's dancing across a spread by looking at clues in the artwork and listening to the rhymes. . . . Brown uses hand-painted paper collage and primary shapes to create all of the happy dancers. A surprise pairing of partners ends this cheerful story and acts as a motivator to get children moving." SLJ

Farmyard beat; illustrations by Marc Brown. Alfred A. Knopf 2011 un il $15.99; lib bdg $18.99
Grades: PreK K   E
1. Stories in rhyme 2. Bedtime -- Fiction 3. Domestic animals -- Fiction
ISBN 978-0-375-86455-1; 0-375-86455-5; 978-0-375-96455-8 lib bdg; 0-375-96455-X lib bdg
        LC 2010016123
The sounds of the farm animals create a lively beat that keep Farmer Sue, the chicks, sheep, and other farm animals awake.

"The repetition, rhythm, and sounds of the words are a big part of the fun in this picture book and will have toddlers chanting along." Booklist

Crangle, Claudine

Woolfred cannot eat dandelions; a tale of being true to your tummy. by Claudine Crangle. Magination Press 2015 32 p. color illustrations (hardcover) $14.95

Grades: 1 2 3   **E**

1. Sheep -- Fiction 2. Dandelions -- Fiction 3. Food intolerance -- Fiction

ISBN 1433816725; 1433816733; 9781433816727; 9781433816734

LC 2013048306

"Here's a slightly disguised episode designed for sharing with children who have food intolerances (as opposed to allergies). All the other sheep eat dandelions. Woolfred can't . . . but they look so good and (as it turns out) taste so good, too. . . . A closing spread of advice from a psychologist for parents and caregivers adds definitions as well as techniques for support and discussion." Booklist

Crews, Donald

★ **Harbor**. Greenwillow Bks. 1982 un il hardcover o.p. pa $6.99

Grades: PreK K 1   **E**

1. Ships 2. Harbors

ISBN 0-688-00862-3 lib bdg; 0-688-07332-8 pa

LC 81-6607

This book "is an exciting, educational and beautiful show-and-tell. . . . The full-page, full-color paintings will delight children." Publ Wkly

★ **Night** at the fair; pictures and words by Donald Crews. Greenwillow Bks. 1998 un il $17.99

Grades: PreK K 1 2   **E**

1. Fairs -- Fiction

ISBN 0-688-11483-0

LC 96-48780

Nighttime is a wonderful time to enjoy the lights, the games, and the rides at a fair

"Each borderless double-page spread bursts with color and light and action and noise. . . . A minimal text acts for the most part as captioning or clues us in to what's coming next in this truly spectacular visual experience." Horn Book Guide

★ **Parade**. Greenwillow Bks. 1983 un il hardcover o.p. pa $6.99

Grades: PreK K 1   **E**

1. Parades

ISBN 0-688-01996-X lib bdg; 0-688-06520-1 pa

LC 82-20927

Illustrations and brief text present the various elements of a parade-the spectators, street vendors, marchers, bands, floats, and the cleanup afterwards.

The author/illustrator's "refined poster-art approach to evoking an event works again here. . . . A polished assembly of crisp shapes, effective compositions, and pure, bright color." Booklist

★ **Sail** away. Greenwillow Bks. 1995 un il $17.99; pa $6.99

Grades: PreK K 1   **E**

1. Sailing -- Fiction

ISBN 0-688-11053-3; 0-688-17517-1 pa

LC 94-6004

A family takes an enjoyable trip in their sailboat and watches the weather change throughout the day

"To read any Crews book is to be immersed in sights and sounds vividly rendered and perfectly phrased, and this book proves no excep-

tion. The paintings move and swell; the words are haiku-like in their efficiency and implication." Horn Book

★ **School** bus. Greenwillow Bks. 1984 un il $16.99; lib bdg $17.89; pa $6.99; bd bk $7.99

Grades: PreK K 1   **E**

1. School stories 2. Buses -- Fiction

ISBN 0-688-02807-1; 0-688-02808-X lib bdg; 0-688-12267-1 pa; 0-694-01690-X bd bk

LC 83-18681

Follows the progress of school buses as they take children to school and bring them home again

"The author-artist cleverly avoids monotony in his subject matter by using different size buses and a pleasing variety of background, perspectives, and the directions in which they travel. . . . The . . . yellow of the buses provides both a unifying element and a contrast for the cheerful colors of the children's clothing and for the bustle of city streets." Horn Book

★ **Shortcut**. Greenwillow Bks. 1992 un il $17.99; lib bdg $18.89; pa $6.99

Grades: K 1 2   **E**

1. Railroads -- Fiction 2. African Americans -- Fiction

ISBN 0-688-06436-1; 0-688-06437-X lib bdg; 0-688-813576-5 pa

LC 91-36312

Children taking a shortcut by walking along a railroad track find excitement and danger when a train approaches

"The story . . . is a perfect foil for the artist's masterful renderings of trains. . . . Scenes portraying the frightened children are equally effective in this out of the ordinary drama set forth with uncommon artistry." Publ Wkly

Ten black dots; rev ed; Greenwillow Bks. 1986 un il $16.99; lib bdg $17.89; pa $6.99; bd bk $7.99 **E**

1. Counting 2. Stories in rhyme

ISBN 0-688-06067-6; 0-688-06068-4 lib bdg; 0-688-13574-9 pa; 978-0-06-185779-9 bed bk

LC 85-14871

A revision of the title first published 1968

"In this basic counting book . . . large black dots appear as an integral part of each illustrated subject. For example, 'Five dots can make buttons on a coat . . . or the port-holes of a boat.' This simple concept succeeds admirably through the bold, flat colors and briskly delineated graphics of Crews' illustrations." Booklist

★ **Truck**. Greenwillow Bks. 1980 un il $16.99; lib bdg $17.89; pa $6.99; bd bk $7.99

Grades: PreK K 1   **E**

1. Stories without words 2. Trucks -- Fiction

ISBN 0-688-80244-3; 0-688-84244-5 lib bdg; 0-688-10481-9 pa; 0-688-15597-9 bd bk

LC 79-19031

A Caldecott Medal honor book, 1981

"Although there is no text, the story is far from wordless; trucks, buses, and vans are emblazoned with letters and emblems, the streets are lined with familiar traffic signs, and a truck stop is festooned with advertisements in neon lights. . . . [This is] an imaginative, almost pop-art view of mobile America." Horn Book

Crews, Nina

Below. Henry Holt 2006 un il $16.95

Grades: PreK K 1 2   E
1. Toys -- Fiction 2. Imagination -- Fiction
ISBN 0-8050-7728-6; 978-0-8050-7728-5

LC 2005-12128

"Crews uses digitally manipulated photos and line drawings along with brief text to relate the adventures of Jack and his action-figure toy, Guy. . . . One day Guy falls through a hole in the stairs. . . . The child uses his crane and other action figures to effect a rescue. . . . This story . . . will surely inspire young readers to see everyday objects in a new light." SLJ

Another title about Guy is:
Sky-high Guy (2010)

Crimi, Carolyn
Dear Tabby; illustrated by David Roberts. Harper 2011 un il $16.99
Grades: PreK K 1 2   E
1. Cats -- Fiction 2. Animals -- Fiction 3. Journalists -- Fiction
ISBN 978-0-06-114245-1; 0-06-114245-X

LC 2007041935

A feline advice columnist assists other animals with their problems, such as a parrot whose owners complain that he talks too much, a groundhog who feels the pressure of predicting the weather, and a cat who objects to being pampered.

"Roberts' playful artwork provides many details that extend and enhance Crimi's clever text." Booklist

Rock 'n' roll Mole; pictures by Lynn Munsinger. Dial Books for Young Readers 2011 il $16.99
Grades: PreK K 1   E
1. Musicians -- Fiction 2. Rock music -- Fiction 3. Moles (Animals) -- Fiction
ISBN 978-0-8037-3166-0; 0-8037-3166-3

LC 2010028796

Mole has a "rock-and-roll soul" and the groupies to prove it, but when his friend Pig organizes a talent show, Mole's stagefright may prevent him from performing.

"Munsinger's charming band of characters includes a break-dancing pig, a skateboarding raccoon, and a trio of swooning chicks. The watercolor illustrations are full of witty details." SLJ

Cronin, Doreen
The **Chicken** Squad; The First Misadventure. Doreen Cronin; illustrated by Kevin Cornell. Atheneum Books for Young Readers 2014 92 p. illustrations (A Chicken Squad adventure) $12.99
Grades: 1 2 3   E
1. Mystery fiction 2. Chickens -- Fiction 3. Dogs -- Fiction 4. Humorous stories 5. Squirrels -- Fiction 6. Chickens -- Fiction 7. Mystery and detective stories
ISBN 1442496762; 9781442496767

LC 2012276490

"Meet the Chicken Squad: Dirt, Sugar, Poppy, and Sweetie. These chicks are not your typical barnyard puffs of fluff, and they are not about to spend their days pecking chicken feed and chasing bugs. No sir, they're too busy solving mysteries and fighting crime." (Publisher's note)

"With its shorter text and larger type, the book will suit somewhat younger readers, those just moving up to chapter books. As in the previous series, some chapters are written in third person, while others are narrated by the dog. Cornell's comical gray-wash illustrations magnify the story's mild humor." - Booklist

Click, clack, boo; Doreen Cronin; illlustrated by Betsy Lewin. Atheneum Books for Young Readers 2014 40 p. (hardcover) $16.99

Grades: PreK K 1   E
1. Farm life -- Fiction 2. Halloween -- Fiction 3. Animals -- Fiction 4. Halloween -- Fiction 5. Domestic animals -- Fiction
ISBN 1442465530; 9781442465534; 9781442465541

LC 2012014537

In this Halloween-themed children's book, "Farmer Brown leaves a bowl of candy on the porch . . . puts up a "Do Not Disturb" sign, and prepares to sleep through the holiday, but his animals have other plans for the evening. . . . When he spies a dark, lurking figure through the window, he realizes that his animal friends are at it again. His candy has disappeared and a new note appears on his door--'Halloween Party at the Barn!'" (School Library Journal)

Click, clack, ho ho ho! Doreen Cronin; illustrated by Betsy Lewin. Atheneum Books for Young Readers 2015 40 p. color illustrations (hardcover) $17.99
Grades: PreK K 1 2 3   E
1. Ducks -- Fiction 2. Christmas -- Fiction 3. Farm life -- Fiction 4. Christmas stories 5. Animals -- Fiction 6. Santa Claus -- Fiction
ISBN 1442496738; 9781442496736

LC 2014043594

In this children's story, by Doreen Cronin, illustrated by Betsy Lewin, "it's the night before Christmas and . . . Farmer Brown is busy decorating his home in preparation for Santa's arrival on Christmas Eve! All seems calm in the barnyard, but Farmer Brown isn't the only one who is getting ready. . . . Once again, Duck has gotten the whole barnyard stuck in quite a predicament!" (Publisher's note)

"If the sight of Duck—outfitted with night-vision goggles, climbing spurs, and a Santa hat—ziplining across a cold winter's night toward Farmer Brown's chimney doesn't provoke laughs and smiles, then the War on Christmas is as good as over. . . . Echoes of Moore's "Visit from St. Nicholas" can be sensed throughout ('A few creatures are stirring' as the book opens, and Farmer Brown rushes to the window as he senses Santa's approach), but Cronin and Lewin make this slapstick story all their own, leaving readers (and the farm's human and animal residents) with a big dose of holiday cheer." PW

★ **Click,** clack, moo; cows that type. pictures by Betsy Lewin. Simon & Schuster Bks. for Young Readers 2000 un il $15
Grades: PreK K 1 2   E
1. Cattle -- Fiction 2. Farm life -- Fiction
ISBN 0-689-83213-3

LC 97-29718

A Caldecott Medal honor book, 2001

When Farmer Brown's cows find a typewriter in the barn they start making demands, and go on strike when the farmer refuses to give them what they want

"A laugh-out-loud look at life on a very funny farm. . . . Lewin's hilarious cartoons deftly capture the farmer's exasperation and the animals' sheer determination." SLJ

Other titles about Farmer Brown's animals are:
Giggle, giggle, quack (2002)
Click, clack, quackity quack (2005)
Click, clack, splish, splash (2006)
Dooby, dooby, moo (2006)
Thump, quack, moo (2008)
Click, clack, surprise (2016)

★ **Diary** of a fly; pictures by Harry Bliss. Joanna Cotler Books 2007 un il $15.99; lib bdg $16.89

Grades: PreK K 1 2   E
1. Flies -- Fiction
ISBN 978-0-06-000156-8; 0-06-000156-9; 978-0-06-000157-5
lib bdg; 0-06-000157-7 lib bdg

LC 2006-36064

A young fly discovers, day by day, that there is a lot to learn about being an insect, including the dangers of flyswatters and that heroes come in all shapes and sizes.

"The attention to detail . . . and a lively layout that has a comic-book vibe are sure to appeal." SLJ

★ **Diary** of a spider; pictures by Harry Bliss. Joanna Cotler Books 2005 un il $15.99; lib bdg $16.89
Grades: PreK K 1 2   E
1. Spiders -- Fiction
ISBN 0-06-000153-4; 0-06-000154-2 lib bdg

LC 2004-11549

A young spider discovers, day by day, that there is a lot to learn about being a spider, including how to spin webs and avoid vacuum cleaners.

"The amusing pen-and-ink and watercolor cartoons, complete with funny asides in dialogue balloons, expand the sublime silliness of some of the scenarios." SLJ

★ **Diary** of a worm; pictures by Harry Bliss. HarperCollins Pubs. 2003 un il $15.99; lib bdg $16.89
Grades: PreK K 1 2   E
1. Worms -- Fiction
ISBN 0-06-000150-X; 0-06-000151-8 lib bdg

LC 2002-7949

A young worm discovers, day by day, that there are some very good and some not so good things about being a worm in this great big world

"Bliss's droll watercolor illustrations are a marvel. He gives each worm an individual character with a few deft lines. . . . Inventive and laugh-out-loud funny, this worm's-eye view of the world will be a sure-fire hit." Publ Wkly

★ **Duck** for President; illustrated by Betsy Lewin. Simon & Schuster Books for Young Readers 2004 un il $15.95
Grades: PreK K 1 2   E
1. Ducks -- Fiction 2. Elections -- Fiction
ISBN 0-689-86377-2

LC 2003-21923

When Duck gets tired of working for Farmer Brown, his political ambition eventually leads to his being elected President.

"Lewin's characteristic humorous watercolors with bold black outlines fill the pages with color and jokes. Cronin's text is hilarious for kids and adults and includes a little math and quite a bit about the electoral process." SLJ

Into the wild; yet another misadventure. Doreen Cronin; illustrated by Jessica Warrick. Atheneum Books for Young Readers 2016 112 p. illustrations (Chicken Squad) (hardback) $12.99
Grades: 2 3 4   E
1. Chickens -- Fiction 2. Humorous fiction -- Fiction
ISBN 9781481450461; 9781481450478

LC 2015033467

In this children's story, by Doreen Cronin and illustrated by Jessica Warrick, the "fluffy, fearless young detectives are back out sleuthing because there's a new cage in the yard, and the Chicken Squad is determined to figure out just who this new addition is. . . . So equipped with the latest surveillance gear—which apparently includes copious amounts of marshmallows—the chicks venture into the wild to get answers." (Publisher's note)

"Many illustrations and frequent word repetition (not to mention the giggle-inducing high jinks) make this series a great choice for those new to chapters." Kirkus

Smick; by Doreen Cronin; illustrated by Juana Medina. Viking, published by Penguin Group 2015 40 p. color illustrations (hardcover) $16.99
Grades: PreK K 1 2 3   E
1. Dogs -- Fiction 2. Animals -- Fiction 3. Friendship -- Fiction
4. Stories in rhyme 5. Chickens -- Fiction 6. Animals -- Infancy
-- Fiction
ISBN 0670785784; 9780670785780

LC 2014015658

This book by Doreen Cronin follows a dog named Smick. "Ordered to fetch a stick, Smick complies. . . . Then Smick hears Chick clucking. He curiously approaches the little bird to investigate and receives an alarmed 'No, Smick, no!' As Smick and Chick check each other out, Chick perches on Smick's head until Smick resumes chasing the stick. Eventually, the unlikely pair bond and companionably share the stick as well as a friendly lick." (Kirkus Reviews)

"On wide expanses of cream-colored spreads sits Smick, and just a few strokes of black ink outline him--a big old dog with floppy ears. . . . The oversize format makes this great for story time, but independent new readers will also enjoy the story, which may provide their only opportunity to read the word Smick." Booklist

★ **Wiggle**; art by Scott Menchin. Atheneum Books for Young Readers 2005 un il $12.95
Grades: PreK K 1   E
1. Stories in rhyme 2. Dogs -- Fiction
ISBN 0-689-86375-6

LC 2004-3326

"A spotted dog on the cover, vigorously working a hula hoop, leads children through a wiggling world. . . . The delightful cartoon-style, ink-and-watercolor artwork is highlighted by tidbits of collage. . . . Every candy-colored page features the funny, frenetic dog involved in some furious activity, and the sense of motion and movement is palpable each time." Booklist

Other titles about this dog are:
Bounce (2007)
Stretch (2009)

Crosby, Jeff
Wiener wolf. Hyperion Books 2011 32p il $15.99
Grades: PreK K 1   E
1. Dogs -- Fiction 2. Pets -- Fiction 3. Wolves -- Fiction
ISBN 978-1-4231-3983-6; 1-4231-3983-6

Weiner Dog's life of leisure has lost its bite. So when he hears the call of the wild one day, he answers! Thus Weiner Dog becomes Weiner Wolf.

"Crosby employs an array of techniques in his visual storytelling, from the way Wiener Dog appears to run right out of spot illustrations to the hilarious contrast between the turtleneck sweater wearing dog and the slavering wolves. This wiener's a winner." Publ Wkly

Crow, Kristyn
★ **Cool** Daddy Rat; [by] Kristyn Crow; illustrated by Mike Lester. Putnam 2008 un il $16.99
Grades: PreK K 1 2   E
1. Stories in rhyme 2. Rats -- Fiction 3. Musicians -- Fiction 4. Jazz music -- Fiction 5. New York (N.Y.) -- Fiction
ISBN 978-0-399-24375-2; 0-399-24375-5

LC 2006020533

A young rat hides in his father's bass case and tags along as he plays and scats around the big city.

This "hip ode to jazz (and scat in particular) will sweep up its audience in its catchy beat as kinetic cartoon art adds verve and wit. . . . Lester's . . . computer-assisted watercolor illustrations in a heady palette show characters seemingly in perpetual motion." Publ Wkly

The **middle**-child blues; illustrated by David Catrow. G.P. Putnam's Sons 2009 un il $16.99
Grades: K 1 2   E
    1. Stories in rhyme 2. Siblings -- Fiction 3. Birth order -- Fiction 4. Blues music -- Fiction
    ISBN 978-0-399-24735-4; 0-399-24735-1
                             LC 2008-30591
A boy named Lee sings about all the miserable aspects of being a middle child.

"Catrow's trademark pencil and watercolor illustrations are perfect for this story. Heads are oversized, and facial expressions exaggerated. The colorful illustrations dance all over the pages. This book is a winner." SLJ

Zombelina; by Kristyn Crow and illustrated by Molly Idle. Walker & Company 2013 32 p. (hardback) $16.99
Grades: PreK K 1 2   E
    1. Ballet -- Fiction 2. Zombies -- Fiction 3. Stories in rhyme
    ISBN 0802728030; 9780802728036; 9780802728043
                             LC 2012027333
In this book by Kristyn Crow "Zombelina loves to dance. When Zombelina enrolls in a ballet class for real girls, her dancing gives everyone the chills! But when her first recital brings on a case of stage fright, her zombie moans and ghoulish groans scare her audience away. Only her devoted family's cheers, in their special spooky way, help Zombelina dance the ballet." (Publisher's note)

"Rhymed couplets chronicle a young zombie girl's progression from dancing at home to ballet classes (her detachable limbs give her amazing extension) to a recital. Although Zombelina has a moment of stage fright during her performance, her supportive family's shrieking, howling, and cheering see her through. The charming, funny, and technically accurate dance illustrations outshine the somewhat hokey text." (Horn Book)

Other titles about Zombelina are:
Zombelina dances the Nutcracker (2015)
Zombelina school days (2017)

Crowley, Ned
    Nanook & Pryce; gone fishing. pictures by Larry Day. HarperCollinsPublishers 2009 un il $16.99
Grades: PreK K 1 2   E
    1. Stories in rhyme 2. Adventure fiction 3. Friendship -- Fiction 4. Marine animals -- Fiction 5. Voyages and travels -- Fiction
    ISBN 978-0-06-133641-6; 0-06-133641-6; 978-0-06-133642-3 lib bdg; 0-06-133642-4 lib bdg
                             LC 2008032095
Parka-clad friends Nanook and Pryce and their dog Yukon encounter many different types of ocean life and adventure on an unexpected voyage.

"Crowley's perfectly rhymed narrative about an accidental adventure is both minimal and evocative, and Day's watercolor and line illustrations turn some very funny text into a hilarious book." SLJ

Crowther, Robert
    Amazing pop-up trucks. Candlewick Press 2011 il $17.99
Grades: PreK K   E
    1. Trucks 2. Pop-up books
    ISBN 978-0-7636-5587-7; 0-7636-5587-2

"Crowther offers formidable pop-ups of a car transporter, a cement mixer, a monster truck, a 'rubbish' truck, and truck trains. Each spread contains a description of the featured vehicle and its primary function, while flaps offer photographs along with additional information about how the trucks operate. . . . The brightly colored vehicles, which include working door/window flaps, and real-life details should give truck enthusiasts a gratifying peek into the world of big rigs." Publ Wkly

The **most** amazing hide-and-seek alphabet book. Candlewick Press 2010 un il $12.99
Grades: PreK K 1   E
    1. Alphabet 2. Animals -- Fiction
    ISBN 978-0-7636-5030-8; 0-7636-5030-7
    First published 1999
This "pull-the-tab [book features a] clean, attractive [cover] and sturdy paper-on-board construction. The solid black letters . . . on white pages reveal colorful creatures when tabs are pulled and animals peek out. [The book is] cleverly designed and visually appealing." Horn Book Guide

The **most** amazing hide-and-seek numbers book. Candlewick Press 2010 un il $12.99
Grades: PreK K 1   E
    1. Numbers 2. Animals -- Fiction
    ISBN 978-0-7636-5029-2; 0-7636-5029-3
    First published 1999
This "pull-the-tab [book features a] clean, attractive [cover] and sturdy paper-on-board construction. The solid black . . . numbers on white pages reveal colorful creatures when tabs are pulled and animals peek out. [The book is] cleverly designed and visually appealing." Horn Book Guide

★ **Opposites**. Candlewick Press 2005 un il $12.99
Grades: PreK K 1   E
    1. Opposites
    ISBN 0-7636-2783-6
"Each page features a word and readers must take some action—pulling a tab or turning a wheel—to discover its opposite. The pictures incorporate easy-to-understand examples in creative ways. . . . Warmly colored backgrounds and simply rendered images keep kids' attention focused on the task at hand, and the volume's sturdy pages and reinforced tabs will survive lots of use." SLJ

Robert Crowther's pop-up dinosaur ABC; Robert Crowther. Candlewick Press 2015 10 p. color illustrations $19.99
Grades: PreK K 1 2 3   E
    1. Alphabet 2. Dinosaurs
    ISBN 0763672963; 9780763672966
                             LC 2013957284
This pop-up book, by Robert Crowther, "[presents] a stylish alphabet of dinosaurs. . . . Turn the pages to say each letter of the alphabet, then lift the flaps to reveal fascinating prehistoric beasts." (Publisher's note)

"The final page offers a chart showing the relative size of each dino, as well as a brief vocab list. Dino-lovers will be delighted by the surprising pop-ups and sated by the abundance of facts." Booklist

Croza, Laurel
    From there to here. Pgw 2014 36 p. $18.95
Grades: K 1 2 3   E
    1. Moving -- Fiction 2. Friendship -- Fiction 3. Family life -- Fiction 4. Toronto (Ont.) -- Fiction 5. Country life -- Fiction 6. Moving, Household -- Fiction
    ISBN 1554983657; 9781554983650
    Sequel to: I Know Here (2010)

"A little girl and her family have just moved across the country by train. Their new neighborhood in the city of Toronto is very different from their home in the Saskatchewan bush, and at first everything about "there" seems better than "here". The little girl's dad has just finished building a dam across the Saskatchewan River, and his new project is to build a highway through Toronto...Then one day there is a knock on the door. It is Anne, who lives kitty-corner and is also eight, going on nine, and suddenly living in Toronto takes on a whole new light. Laurel Croza and Matt James have beautifully captured the voice and intense feelings of a young child who, in the midst of upheaval, finds hope in her new surroundings." (Publisher's Note)

"In a lovely companion story to 2010's I Know Here, Croza's heroine and her family have settled in Toronto. While the girl's references to "here" meant their rural Saskatchewan dwelling in the previous book, Toronto is "here" for her family now, and their former home has become "there."... Croza doesn't avoid the reality that some things were perhaps better in the country ("Here. No stars, no northern lights"), but readers will come to understand that while "here" and "there" are different, different is OK, especially when you have the support of a new friend." PW

I know here; pictures by Matt James. Groundwood Books 2010 un il $18.95
Grades: K 1 2 3   E
1. Moving -- Fiction 2. Saskatchewan -- Fiction
ISBN 978-0-88899-923-8; 0-88899-923-2
Boston Globe-Horn Book Award: Picture Book (2010)
A tale about a young girl whose family moves from the forests of northeastern Saskatchewan to a strange new place called "Toronto."

"James's vividly colored, naive-style scenes capture the bright intensity of the child's inner and outer landscapes and also the unaffected way in which she observes them. Good for sharing." Kirkus

Cruise, Robin
Bartleby speaks! pictures by Kevin Hawkes. Farrar, Straus and Giroux 2009 un il $16.99
Grades: PreK K 1   E
1. Growth -- Fiction 2. Family life -- Fiction 3. Grandfathers -- Fiction
ISBN 978-0-374-30514-7; 0-374-30514-5
LC 2008-17235
As he grows from infancy to three-years of age, Bartleby Huddle remains quiet, not speaking a word, until the day Grampy Huddle arrives and discovers the solution

"Hawkes accompanies Cruise's gently pointed text with characteristically comic line-and-color cartoons, varying vignettes with full and double-page spreads that focus readers' attention exactly where it needs to be, modulating noise and silence through artful pacing. A sweetly underscored paean to the beauty of quiet." Kirkus

Little Mama forgets; illustrated by Stacey Dressen-McQueen. Farrar, Straus and Giroux 2006 32p il $16
Grades: PreK K 1 2   E
1. Memory -- Fiction 2. Family life -- Fiction 3. Grandmothers -- Fiction 4. Mexican Americans -- Fiction
ISBN 0-374-34613-5
LC 2004-40462
Although her Mexican-American grandmother now forgets many things, Luciana finds that she still remembers the things that are important to the two of them. Includes glossary of Spanish words used

"The story is bittersweet, but Lucy's ability to look on the bright side, and the obvious love that she and Little Mama share, wrap the events in affection and warmth. Dressen-McQueen's artwork is outstanding. . . . The Mexican family . . . comes alive in pictures that show the vibrancy of the happy household." Booklist

Crum, Shutta
Dozens of cousins; by Shutta Crum; illustrated by David Catrow. Clarion Books 2013 32 p. col. ill. (reinforced) $16.99
Grades: PreK K 1 2   E
1. Family reunions -- Fiction 2. Cousins -- Fiction 3. Cousins -- Fiction 4. Behavior -- Fiction
ISBN 061815874X; 9780618158744
LC 2012005010
This book, written by Shutta Crum and illustrated by David Catrow, focuses on an "annual family reunion, and . . . dozens of cousins are running wild. They hug fluttering aunts and soft-spoken elders, play in the creek, shimmy up trees [and] take 'double-dog dares.' Hilarious side stories unfold in Catrow's . . . colorful, chaotic spreads that gambol and splash with comical caricatures of grinning kinfolk large and small." (Publisher's note)

★ **Mine!** story by Shutta Crum; pictures by Patrice Barton. Knopf 2011 32 p. il $16.99
Grades: PreK   E
1. Sharing -- Fiction 2. Infants -- Fiction 3. Siblings -- Fiction
ISBN 0375867112; 9780375867118
LC 2011283841
This book, written by Shutta Crum and illustrated by Patrice Barton, is a "playful, picture-based book about two very young children and an adorable dog navigating the troubles and triumphs of sharing." (Publisher's note)

"When a baby and a toddler confront a pile of toys, the elder says "Mine," grabbing every plaything in sight. By the end of this giggle-inducing book--all the more so because of a feisty dog and its water bowl--the baby has the final word. Barton hits the bull's-eye with her illustrations of round-bellied, plump-tushied tots." Horn Book

★ **Thunder-**Boomer! illustrated by Carol Thompson. Clarion Books 2009 32p il $16
Grades: PreK K 1 2   E
1. Farm life -- Fiction 2. Family life -- Fiction 3. Thunderstorms -- Fiction
ISBN 978-0-618-61865-1; 0-618-61865-1
LC 2008-10478
A farm family scurries for shelter from a violent thunderstorm that brings welcome relief from the heat and also an unexpected surprise.

"Thompson's illustrations, done in pastels, ink, and watercolor, are full of motion and capture the sensations. . . . The free-verse storytelling is light, airy, and perfectly matched to the drawings." SLJ

Crummel, Susan Stevens
★ The **Little** Red Pen; written by Janet Stevens and Susan Stevens Crummel; illustrated by Janet Stevens. Harcourt Children's Books 2011 un il $16.99
Grades: PreK K 1 2   E
1. School stories 2. Office equipment and supplies -- Fiction
ISBN 978-0-15-206432-7; 0-15-206432-X
LC 2010009062
When a little red pen accidentally falls into the waste basket while trying to correct papers all by herself, the other classroom supplies must cooperate to rescue her.

"Steven's humor-filled watercolors are busy and active, especially since each character is a familiar object with its own personality, facial and body expressions, color, and even typeface. . . . A rollicking read-aloud." Horn Book

Ten-Gallon Bart beats the heat; illustrated by Dorothy Donohue. Marshall Cavendish 2010 il $17.99

Grades: K 1 2 3   E
1. Dogs -- Fiction 2. Animals -- Fiction 3. Blizzards -- Fiction
ISBN 978-0-7614-5634-6

       LC 2009006342

Tired of the blistering heat in Dog City, Ten-Gallon Bart departs for the frozen north, where he gets lost in a blizzard.

Cuevas, Michelle

The **uncorker** of ocean bottles; Michelle Cuevas; illustrated by Erin Stead. Dial Books for Young Readers 2016 40 p. color illustrations (hardback) $17.99

Grades: K 1 2 3   E
1. Friendship -- Fiction 2. Ocean bottles -- Fiction
ISBN 9780803738683

       LC 2015032353

In this book, by Michelle Cuevas, illustrated by Erin Stead, "The Uncorker of Ocean Bottles, who lives alone atop a hill, has a job of the utmost importance. It is his task to open any bottles found at sea and make sure that the messages are delivered. He loves his job, though he has always wished that, someday, one of the letters would be addressed to him. One day he opens a party invitation—but there's no name attached." (Publisher's note)

"Readers will find both consolation and encouragement on every visit to this emotionally resonant, evocative story." Kirkus

Cummings, Pat

Harvey Moon, museum boy; written and illustrated by Pat Cummings. HarperCollinsPublishers 2008 un il $16.99; lib bdg $17.89

Grades: PreK K 1 2   E
1. Stories in rhyme 2. Lizards -- Fiction 3. Museums -- Fiction 4. African Americans -- Fiction
ISBN 978-0-688-17889-5; 0-688-17889-8; 978-0-06-057861-9 lib bdg; 0-06-057861-0 lib bdg

       LC 2004030056

When Harvey and his pet lizard Zippy go on a school field trip, Zippy gets loose in the museum and they have a harrowing adventure

"A lively read-aloud." Booklist

Another title about Harvey Moon is:

Clean your room, Harvey Moon (1991)

Cummings, Phil

Boom bah! [text by Phil Cummings; illustrations by Nina Rycroft] Kane Miller 2010 un il $15.99

Grades: PreK K   E
1. Music -- Fiction 2. Orchestra -- Fiction 3. Domestic animals -- Fiction
ISBN 1-935279-22-X; 978-1-935279-22-8

First published 2008 in Australia

After a tiny mouse taps a cup with a spoon and creates a noise, everyone wants to join in. Follow the band as it gathers and grows from a solo perfomance to an explosive, full-scale orchestra.

"Cummings's minimal text moves along in clipped phrases, punctuated by onomatopoeic effects, creating a splendid read-aloud chant. Rycroft's buoyant watercolors, arranged gracefully against expansive white space, add zest. Even the youngest readers should be able to handle the simple text and catch the rhythm." Kirkus

Cummings, Troy

The **eensy** weensy spider freaks out (big time!) written and illustrated by Troy Cummings. Random House 2010 un il $16.99; lib bdg $19.99

Grades: 1 2 3   E
1. Fear -- Fiction 2. Spiders -- Fiction 3. Ladybugs -- Fiction
ISBN 978-0-375-86582-4; 0-375-86582-9; 978-0-375-96582-1 lib bdg; 0-375-96582-3 lib bdg

Frightened after the scary waterspout incident, the Eensy Weensy Spider needs some encouragement from her friend the ladybug before she will try climbing again.

"The lively text and whimsical, cartoon-style illustrations include periodic word balloons . . . that advance the story line. The vibrant settings and expressive insects have a retro flair, while the varying perspectives add to the fun." Booklist

Giddy-up, daddy! written and illustrated by Troy Cummings. 1st ed. Random House Inc. 2013 40 p. col. ill. (library) $19.99; (hardcover) $16.99

Grades: PreK K 1 2   E
1. Picture books for children 2. Father-child relationship -- Fiction 3. Play -- Fiction 4. Humorous stories 5. Imagination -- Fiction 6. Father and child -- Fiction
ISBN 0375971297; 9780375971297; 9780307978561

       LC 2012009236

In this children's picture book, the "childhood game of 'horsey' leaps into outlandish territory as a bespectacled, bald, and very accommodating father eagerly bounds about with his daughter and diapered son riding on his back. . . . When two horse rustlers lure Dad away with sugar cubes, it's up to the kids to rescue him from the rodeo, after which their adventures take them to the Kentucky Derby, a polo match, the circus, and exotic—Canada." (Publishers Weekly)

Cummins, Lucy Ruth

A **hungry** lion, or, a dwindling assortment of animals; Lucy Ruth Cummins. Atheneum Books for Young Readers 2016 40 p. color illustrations (hardcover) $16.99

Grades: PreK K 1 2   E
1. Lions -- Fiction 2. Friendship -- Fiction 3. Animals -- Fiction 4. Surprise -- Fiction 5. Predatory animals -- Fiction
ISBN 9781481448895; 1481448897

       LC 2015000523

In this children's book, by Lucy Ruth Cummins, "the very hungry lion is all set to enjoy an exciting day with his other animal pals. But all of a sudden his friends start disappearing at an alarming rate! Is someone stealing the hungry lion's friends, or is the culprit a little…closer to home?" (Publisher's note)

"Cummins's dizzy meta-tale has just enough wink and cheek to assure readers that it's all in good fun, and her visual style—sketchbook playful, slyly spiking sweet-seeming scenes with moments of menace and fear—should leave them hungering (in a nice way) for her next book." Pub Wkly

Cumpiano, Ina

Quinito's neighborhood; story Ina Cumpiano; illustrations by José Ramirez. Children's Book Press 2005 22p il $16.95

Grades: PreK K 1 2   E
1. Occupations -- Fiction 2. Bilingual books -- English-Spanish
ISBN 0-89239-209-6

Quinito not only knows everyone in his neighborhood, he also knows that each person in his community has a different, important occupation

"Ramírez's vibrant acrylic-on-canvas paintings bring this community to life, the primitive forms fairly bursting from the book's pages with their deep hues and sense of emotional warmth. The simple text, equally good in both English and Spanish, is in a font that resembles a child's printing." SLJ

Another title about Quinito is:

Quinito, day and night (2008)

Cunnane, Kelly

★ **Chirchir** is singing. Schwartz & Wade Books 2011 un il $17.99

Grades: PreK K 1 2   **E**

1. Kenya -- Fiction 2. Singing -- Fiction 3. Family life -- Fiction

ISBN 978-0-375-86198-7; 0-375-86198-X

This book, set in Kenya, is "given depth by lyrical prose. . . . Chirchir tries but fails to help her elders and is sent away time after time. . . . Not until Chirchir finds her baby brother, Kip-rop, crying untended does she discover a task she can do as well as the grownups. In an afterword, Cunnane explains that Chirchir is a member of the Kalenjin tribe; the story contains a great deal of information about Kalenjin life, language, customs, and Kenyan flora and fauna. . . . Daly's . . . softly shaded acrylics have much to teach, too. . . . Images of security, dependability, and plenty offer a fresh picture of African life." Publ Wkly

★ **Deep** in the Sahara; Kelly Cunnane; illustrated by Hoda Hadadi. Schwartz & Wade Books 2013 40 p. (g.l.b.) $20.99

Grades: K 1 2 3   **E**

1. Picture books for children 2. Veils -- Religious aspects -- Islam 3. Sahara -- Fiction 4. Muslims -- Fiction 5. Africa, West -- Fiction 6. Coming of age -- Fiction 7. Clothing and dress -- Fiction

ISBN 0375970347; 9780375870347; 9780375970344

LC 2011050245

This book shows "a Mauritanian girl who's fascinated with the malafa, the veil the women in her family wear. The second-person narration . . . presents the veil as desirable rather than confining and describes the girl's wish to wear it so she can be beautiful . . . [and] mysterious. . . . Her relatives reject these superficial reasons. It's not until the girl shows she understands the malafa as a sign of Muslim belief . . . that Mama gives the girl one of her own." (Publishers Weekly)

★ **For** you are a Kenyan child; [by] Kelly Cunnane; art by Ana Juan. Atheneum Books for Young Readers 2005 un il $16.95

Grades: PreK K 1 2   **E**

1. Kenya -- Fiction

ISBN 0-689-86194-X

LC 2004-17060

From rooster crow to bedtime, a Kenyan boy plays and visits neighbors all through his village, even though he is supposed to be watching his grandfather's cows.

This story is told "through vivid, descriptive text. . . . The brilliant, colorful, and humorous illustrations stand out against the white backgrounds and are large enough for group viewing. A gentle story about family, responsibility, and a curious little boy." SLJ

Curato, Mike

Little Elliot, big city; Mike Curato. Henry Holt & Co. (BYR) 2014 40 p. color illustrations (hardback) $16.99

Grades: PreK K 1   **E**

1. Animals -- Fiction 2. Friendship -- Fiction 3. City and town life -- Fiction 4. Mice -- Fiction 5. Size -- Fiction 6. Elephants -- Fiction

ISBN 0805098259; 9780805098259

LC 2014009173

This children's book by Mike Curato follows "Little Elliot . . . a cuddly-looking elephant with pastel polka dots all over his body, all the more . . . incongruous in that he lives in a 1930s-esque version of New York City filled with big, busy people wearing hats. For the diminutive elephant, it is a challenge being so small. . . . Elliot loves cupcakes, but the shopkeeper at the bakery never notices him at the counter. After doing a favor for an even-smaller mouse, Elliot . . . is able to get his treat." (Horn Book Magazine)

Other titles in this series are:

Little Elliot, big family (2015)

Little Elliot, big family; story and pictures by Mike Curato. Henry Holt & Co. 2015 40 p. color illustrations (hardcover) $17.99

Grades: PreK K 1   **E**

1. Mice -- Fiction 2. Elephants -- Fiction 3. Friendship -- Fiction 4. Family life -- Fiction 5. Families -- Fiction

ISBN 0805098267; 9780805098266

LC 2014044996

In this book, by Mike Curato, "when Mouse heads off to a family reunion, Little Elliot decides go for a walk. As he explores each busy street, he sees families in all shapes and sizes. In a city of millions, Little Elliot feels very much alone-until he finds he has a family of his own!" (Publisher's note)

"The art creates an inviting atmosphere that draws readers in and keeps them lingering on each page, while the text tells an appealing story of family and friendship." SLJ

Curtis, Gavin

★ The **bat** boy & his violin; illustrated by E.B. Lewis. Simon & Schuster Bks. for Young Readers 1998 un il hardcover o.p. pa $7.99

Grades: K 1 2 3   **E**

1. Baseball -- Fiction 2. Violinists -- Fiction 3. African Americans -- Fiction 4. Father-son relationship -- Fiction

ISBN 0-689-80099-1; 0-689-84115-9 pa

LC 97-25417

Reginald is more interested in practicing his violin than in his father's job managing the worst team in the Negro Leagues, but when Papa makes him the bat boy and his music begins to lead the team to victory, Papa realizes the value of his son's passion

"Lewis's soft watercolor illustrations portray the characters with depth and beauty, resulting in a very special book." SLJ

Curtis, Jamie Lee

★ **Big** words for little people; illustrated by Laura Cornell. Joanna Cotler Books 2008 un il $16.99; lib bdg $17.89

Grades: PreK K 1   **E**

1. Stories in rhyme 2. Conduct of life -- Fiction

ISBN 978-0-06-112759-5; 0-06-112759-0; 978-0-06-112760-1 lib bdg; 0-06-112760-4 lib bdg

LC 2008011856

A big sister teaches her younger siblings some important words, like "responsibility," "perseverance," and "respect"

"Curtis once again demonstrates her trademark sensibility for childhood's simultaneously awkward and silly moments while focusing on the positive values learned from these experiences. Cornell keeps the tone ever lighthearted with her charmingly busy illustrations." SLJ

★ **I'm** gonna like me; letting off a little self-esteem. illustrated by Laura Cornell. HarperCollins Pubs. 2002 un il $16.99; lib bdg $17.89

Grades: PreK K 1 2   **E**

1. Stories in rhyme

ISBN 0-06-028761-6; 0-06-028762-4 lib bdg

LC 2002-1300

"Though the message is both catchy and effective in its delivery, it's Cornell's humorous, detailed, ink-and-watercolor illustrations that give this volume true pizzazz." Publ Wkly

★ **Is** there really a human race? illustrated by Laura Cornell. Joanna Cotler Books 2006 un il $16.99; lib bdg $17.89

Grades: PreK K 1 2   E

1. Stories in rhyme 2. Conduct of life -- Fiction

ISBN 978-0-06-075346-7; 0-06-075346-3; 978-0-06-075348-1 lib bdg; 0-06-075348-X lib bdg

LC 2006-00274

While thinking about life as a race, a child wonders whether it is most important to finish first or to have fun along the way.

"Curtis writes so very well, in infectious toe-tapping poetic form, of the inner thoughts and worries that children struggle with all too frequently. . . . Cornell's ink-and-color wash cartoons are a perfect match to Curtis's lilting text." SLJ

My mommy hung the moon; a love story. [by] Jamie Lee Curtis & Laura Cornell. HarperCollins 2010 un il $16.99

Grades: PreK K 1   E

1. Stories in rhyme 2. Mothers -- Fiction

ISBN 978-0-06-029016-0; 0-06-029016-1

A hardworking mother's extraordinary accomplishments are listed by her devoted child.

"This is a lively homage to mothers that children and parents alike will enjoy." Booklist

★ **Tell** me again about the night I was born; illustrated by Laura Cornell. HarperCollins Pubs. 1996 un il $16.99; pa $5.99; bd bk $7.99

Grades: PreK K 1 2   E

1. Infants -- Fiction 2. Adoption -- Fiction

ISBN 0-06-024528-X; 0-06-443581-4 pa; 0-694-01215-7 bd bk

LC 95-5412

"The young female narrator asks her adoptive parents to 'tell me again' the story of her birth and introduction into the family she is now a part of. . . . The humorous, cartoon-style pictures by Laura Cornell . . . are a perfect visual counterpart to the text." Horn Book

Cushman, Doug

Christmas Eve good night. Henry Holt 2011 un il $12.99

Grades: PreK K 1   E

1. Stories in rhyme 2. Christmas stories 3. Bedtime -- Fiction 4. Christmas -- Fiction

ISBN 978-0-8050-6603-6; 0-8050-6603-9

LC 2010038058

On Christmas Eve, animals at the North Pole, gingerbread men, robots, and more say good night to their mommas, papas, and buddies.

"Cushman's watercolor-and-ink illustrations are full of witty details and hints about the conclusion, but it is his dramatic pacing and skilled balance between art and text that makes this Christmas offering sparkle." Kirkus

Dirk Bones and the mystery of the haunted house; story and pictures by Doug Cushman. HarperCollinsPublishers 2006 31p il (I can read book) $15.99; lib bdg $16.89

Grades: K 1 2   E

1. Ghost stories 2. Mystery fiction

ISBN 978-0-06-073764-1; 0-06-073764-6; 978-0-06-073765-8 lib bdg; 0-06-073765-4 lib bdg

LC 2005019484

"Daily Tombs" newspaper reporter Dirk Bones, who also happens to be a skeleton, investigates when a family of ghosts fears that they are being haunted.

"Cushman's illustrations are delightfully silly and spirited; his hilarious plot will please youngsters who often claim that they want horror but are relieved to get humor instead." SLJ

Another title about Dirk Bones is:

Dirk Bones and the mystery of the missing books (2009)

Halloween goodnight. Henry Holt & Co. 2010 un il $12.99

Grades: PreK K 1   E

1. Bedtime -- Fiction 2. Monsters -- Fiction 3. Halloween -- Fiction

ISBN 978-0-8050-8928-8; 0-8050-8928-4

On Halloween night, monsters, from hairy werewolves on the moors to scaly swamp creatures in a black lagoon, say goodnight to their mommies and daddies.

"The watercolor and ink drawings are colorful and clever. . . . The delightful illustrations make these seasonal monsters not-so-scary for very young readers. This book will fly off your holiday shelves." SLJ

★ **Inspector** Hopper; story and pictures by Doug Cushman. HarperCollins Pubs. 2000 64p il (I can read book) hardcover o.p. pa $3.99

Grades: K 1 2   E

1. Mystery fiction 2. Insects -- Fiction

ISBN 0-06-028382-3; 0-06-028383-1 lib bdg; 0-06-444260-8 pa

LC 99-30878

Inspector Hopper and his perpetually hungry assistant McBugg solve three mysteries for their insect friends

"Beginning readers will find a familiar structure, natural language, compelling plot, supporting illustrations, and engaging characters. . . . The light watercolors define the characters as soft-boiled while slyly playing on stereotypes out of film noir." Horn Book Guide

Another title about Inspector Hopper is:

Inspector Hopper's mystery year (2003)

Mystery at the Club Sandwich; written and illustrated by Doug Cushman. Clarion Books 2004 un il $15

Grades: K 1 2 3   E

1. Mystery fiction 2. Animals -- Fiction 3. Elephants -- Fiction

ISBN 0-618-41969-1

LC 2004-537

When Lola, famous singer at the Club Sandwich, loses her lucky marbles, elephant detective Nick Trunk, lover of peanut butter, takes the case

"Readers will guess the villain early on but that won't interfere with their enjoyment of the droll story, which is greatly enhanced by delightful illustrations. Cushman uses black watercolor washes, colored pencil, and pastel against a stark white background, suggesting the silver nitrate photographs and popular black-and-white movies of the gumshoe era." SLJ

Pigmares; porcine poems of the silver screen. Doug Cushman. Charlesbridge 2012 40 p. col. ill.

Grades: 2 3 4   E

1. Pigs -- Poetry 2. Children's poetry 3. Monsters -- Poetry 4. Swine -- Juvenile poetry 5. Children's poetry, American

ISBN 1580894011; 9781580894012

LC 2011025703

This book of children's poems by Doug Cushman "versifies classic movie and literary monsters in 18 single-page poems with accompanying movie-poster-inspired watercolor illustrations starring, of course, pigs rather than people. Plants from outer space (Pigweed), the Yeti (Abominable Snow Pig) and Pig Kong all enjoy the spotlight in turn. All entries are rhymed . . . and each has a humorous twist beyond the punny titles." (Kirkus)

Cutbill, Andy

The **cow** that laid an egg; [by] Andy Cutbill; illustrated by Russell Ayto. HarperCollins Publishers 2008 un il $16.99

Grades: PreK K 1 2   **E**
1. Eggs -- Fiction 2. Cattle -- Fiction 3. Chickens -- Fiction
ISBN 978-0-06-137295-7; 0-06-137295-1
First published 2006 in the United Kingdom

Marjorie the cow "has no special talents like the rest of the herd, so the chickens hatch a plan. One morning, Marjorie shrieks, 'I've laid an egg!' ... The bovine endures the taunts of the suspicious cows and the support of the ever-present, silent chickens, until the egg finally hatches a chick with an astonishing 'moo' voice. Cutbill's writing is spare and amusing, and Ayto's goofy, mixed-media collages are a perfect match." SLJ

Another title about Marjorie the cow is:
The cow that was the best moo-ther (2009)

Cutler, Jane
Guttersnipe; pictures by Emily Arnold McCully. Farrar Straus Giroux 2009 un il $16.95
Grades: K 1 2 3   **E**
1. Jews -- Fiction 2. Canada -- Fiction 3. Poverty -- Fiction 4. Immigrants -- Fiction
ISBN 978-0-374-32813-9; 0-374-32813-7
        LC 2007034417

In Canada early in the twentieth century, Ben, the youngest in a family of Jewish immigrants struggling to make ends meet, decides to help out but when a hat maker gives him a chance, disaster strikes and Ben nearly loses hope.

"Detailed watercolors reflect Ben's exhilaration and evoke the early-twentieth-century setting of this unusual story based on true events." Horn Book Guide

★ **Rose** and Riley; pictures by Thomas F. Yezerski. Farrar Straus Giroux 2005 48p il $15
Grades: PreK K 1 2   **E**
1. Friendship -- Fiction
ISBN 0-374-36340-4
        LC 2003-54887

Together, Rose, a vole, and Riley, a groundhog, figure out how to prepare for the possibility of rain, how to celebrate un-birthdays, and what to do with worries.

"Soft pastel illustrations add to the warmth of the text while repetition eases the decoding. A sweet, thoughtful offering with two memorable characters." SLJ

Another title about Rose and Riley is:
Rose and Riley come and go (2005)

Cuyler, Margery
100th day worries; illustrated by Arthur Howard. Simon & Schuster Bks. for Young Readers 2000 un il $16
Grades: K 1 2   **E**
1. Counting 2. School stories 3. Worry -- Fiction
ISBN 0-689-82979-5
        LC 98-52887

Jessica worries about collecting 100 objects to take to class for the 100th day of school

"Energetic pen-and-ink squiggles and bright watercolors fill the pages with round-eyed figures and striped, dotted, and floral patterns as the groups of objects are described and counted." Booklist

Other titles about Jessica are:
Stop, drop, and roll (2001)
Hooray for Reading Day! (2008)
Bullies never win (2009)

The **bumpy** little pumpkin; illustrated by Will Hillenbrand. Scholastic Press 2005 un il $15.95

Grades: PreK K 1 2   **E**
1. Pumpkin -- Fiction
ISBN 0-439-52835-6
        LC 2004-12179

Little Nell chooses an unusual pumpkin for her Halloween jack-o-lantern, despite her big sisters' criticisms

"Cuyler's infectious, repetitive text, with its recurrent use of BIG, is perfectly paced for participatory read-alouds, and Hillenbrand's cheery, whimsical mixed-media illustrations show Little Nell's perspective." Booklist

Another title about Little Nell is:
The biggest, best snowman (1998)

Guinea pigs add up; illustrated by Tracey Campbell Pearson. Walker Books for Young Readers 2010 un il $16.99
Grades: PreK K 1   **E**
1. School stories 2. Stories in rhyme 3. Pets -- Fiction 4. Guinea pigs -- Fiction 5. Mathematics -- Fiction
ISBN 978-0-8027-9795-7; 0-8027-9795-4

"After a teacher announces that a new animal is coming, his young students imagine a giraffe, an elephant, and a snake. What they find, though, is a guinea pig, and the students enjoy petting and feeding him. Because he is lonely, they get him a playmate, who gives birth to three babies, and the numbers start growing. ... The pen-and-ink, watercolor, and acrylic-gouache pictures show the classroom chaos. ... The arithmetic exercises—addition, subtraction, multiplication—are woven into the story, and there are surprises right up to the end." Booklist

Hooray for Reading Day! by Margery Cuyler; illustrated by Arthur Howard. Simon & Schuster Books for Young Readers 2008 un il $15.99
Grades: K 1 2   **E**
1. School stories 2. Dogs -- Fiction 3. Worry -- Fiction 4. Reading -- Fiction
ISBN 978-0-689-86188-8; 0-689-86188-5
        LC 2007005191

First-grader Jessica, a big worrier, is especially afraid that she will make a mistake when she is reading in front of her class and parents on Reading Theater Day, but after lots of practice reading to her dog Wiggles, she performs perfectly.

"Cuyler acknowledges Jessica's insecurity and shows a practical solution while offering bits of humor along the way. Amusing cartoon-style ink drawings with colorful washes help create the right tone for this encouraging picture book." Booklist

The **little** dump truck; illustrated by Bob Kolar. Henry Holt and Co. 2009 un il $12.99
Grades: PreK K 1   **E**
1. Stories in rhyme 2. Trucks -- Fiction
ISBN 978-0-8050-8281-4; 0-8050-8281-6
        LC 2008036811

A happy little dump truck, driven by Hard Hat Pete, hauls stones, rocks, and debris from a construction site to a landfill.

"The digital artwork will appeal to young children, who will look for the face depicted on each of the various trucks. The endpapers show all of the vehicles that play a part in the illustrations. The heavy-duty pages are perfect for curious youngsters. Preschoolers will love this book." SLJ

Monster mess! [by] Margery Cuyler; illustrated by S.D. Schindler. Margaret K. McElderry Books 2008 40p il $14.99

Grades: PreK K 1   E
1. Stories in rhyme 2. Monsters -- Fiction 3. Cleanliness -- Fiction
ISBN 0-689-86405-1; 978-0-689-86405-6

LC 2005-012762

A monster sneaks into a boy's room and cleans up while the boy is asleep.

"The watercolor illustrations at times show only part of the creature as its head or other body parts extend off the page. . . . Rhyming, repetitive text and whimsical images whirl on the pages, making this a fun read-aloud." SLJ

Princess Bess gets dressed; illustrated by Heather Maione. Simon & Schuster Books for Young Readers 2009 un il $15.99
Grades: PreK K 1   E
1. Stories in rhyme 2. Princesses -- Fiction 3. Clothing and dress -- Fiction
ISBN 978-1-4169-3833-0; 1-4169-3833-8

LC 2007-25915

A fashionably dressed princess reveals her favorite clothes at the end of a busy day.

This "story brims over with little-girl appeal. Princess Bess [is] depicted in debut artist Maione's zesty ink-and-watercolor art. . . . The well-crafted rhymes roll easily off the tongue; Maione's droll pictures, balancing fashion-loving detail with Bess's brio, are a skillful accompaniment." Publ Wkly

Skeleton hiccups; illustrated by S.D. Schindler. Margaret K. McElderry Books 2002 un il $14.95; pa $6.99
Grades: PreK K 1   E
1. Ghost stories 2. Hiccups -- Fiction 3. Skeleton -- Fiction
ISBN 0-689-84770-X; 1-4169-0276-7 pa

LC 2001-44121

Ghost tries to help Skeleton get rid of the hiccups

"This simple story begs to be read aloud. . . . Schindler's gouache, watercolor, and ink pictures make the most out of each situation, instilling humor in every scene." SLJ

Tick tock clock; pictures by Robert Neubecker. HarperCollins Children's Books 2012 il (My first I can read) $16.99; pa $3.99
Grades: PreK K 1   E
1. Stories in rhyme 2. Time -- Fiction 3. Twins -- Fiction 4. Sisters -- Fiction 5. Grandmothers -- Fiction
ISBN 978-0-06-1363092-; 0-06-136309-X; 978-0-06-136311-5 pa; 0-06-136311-1 pa

LC 2008051780

"Grandma spends a busy day with her twin granddaughters in a day filled with action, rhythm and rhyme. . . . Neubecker's sunny illustrations, in rich reds, yellows and greens, perfectly reflect the spare, very easy-to-read text. Each illustration is set on a white, unframed background and is set apart from the text, making it nicely legible. The repetition of words . . . helps beginning readers build confidence." Kirkus

Cyrus, Kurt
★ **Big** rig bugs. Walker 2010 un il $16.99; lib bdg $17.89
Grades: PreK K 1   E
1. Stories in rhyme 2. Insects -- Fiction 3. Construction workers -- Fiction
ISBN 978-0-8027-8674-6; 0-8027-8674-X; 978-0-8027-8688-3 lib bdg; 0-8027-8688-X lib bdg

"Digital illustrations explore perspective as a crew of insects joins together to clean up a construction worker's littered tuna-fish sandwich. Rhymed couplets . . . feature creatures such as an ant, a weevil, a pick-leworm, an earwig, and a dragonfly. The oversize views of bugs will delight many children, as will the construction analogy." SLJ

Billions of bricks; A Counting Book About Building. Kurt Cyrus. Henry Holt & Co. 2016 32 p. color illustrations (hardback) $17.99
Grades: PreK K 1 2   E
1. Bricks -- Fiction 2. Picture books for children 3. Building -- Fiction 4. Counting -- Fiction 5. Construction workers -- Fiction 6. Stories in rhyme 7. Construction workers -- Fiction
ISBN 9781627792738; 9781250138248

LC 2015030945

This rhyming picture book by Kurt Cyrus "leads readers through a day in the life of a construction crew building with bricks. A brick may seem like just a simple block, but in groupings of ten, twenty, and more, it can create many impressive structures, from hotels to schools to skyscrapers." (Publisher's note)

"This impressive melding of illustrations and text that celebrates hard work and building deserves a place in general collections and on read-aloud shelves." SLJ

★ **Tadpole** Rex; by Kurt Cyrus. Harcourt 2008 un il $16
Grades: K 1 2 3   E
1. Stories in rhyme 2. Frogs -- Fiction 3. Growth -- Fiction 4. Dinosaurs -- Fiction
ISBN 978-0-15-205990-3; 0-15-205990-3

LC 2006033825

A tiny primordial tadpole grows into a frog, feeling just as strong and powerful as the huge tyrannosaurus rex that stomps through the mud

"The rhyming text is image-rich, informational, and fun to read aloud. . . . Cyrus's oversize artwork conveys information spectacularly. . . . Created in scratchboard and then colored digitally, the illustrations are luminous and striking." SLJ

★ The **voyage** of Turtle Rex; written and illustrated by Kurt Cyrus. Harcourt Children's Books 2011 $16.99
Grades: PreK K 1 2   E
1. Stories in rhyme 2. Sea turtles -- Fiction 3. Marine animals -- Fiction 4. Prehistoric animals -- Fiction
ISBN 978-0-547-42924-3; 0-547-42924-X; 054742924X; 9780547429243

LC 2010019226

"A tiny prehistoric ancestor to modern sea turtles hatches from a buried egg, scuttles across a beach into the sea, survives multiple hazards to grow into a mighty two-ton Archelon and then in season returns to shore to lay a clutch of her own. Injecting plenty of drama into his beach and sunlit undersea scenes with sudden close-ups and changes of scale, the illustrator vividly captures the hatchling's vulnerability. . . . Like it's subject, the rhymed text moves with grand deliberation, carrying the primeval story line to a clever transition between that ancient era and ours." Kirkus

Czekaj, Jef
Call for a new alphabet. Charlesbridge 2011 un il lib bdg $12.95; pa $5.95
Grades: K 1 2 3   E
1. Alphabet -- Fiction 2. English language -- Fiction
ISBN 978-1-58089-228-5 lib bdg; 1-58089-228-0 lib bdg; 978-1-58089-229-2 pa; 1-58089-229-9 pa

LC 2010007534

Tired of being near the end of the alphabet, starting few words, and being governed by grammar rules, X calls for a vote on a new Alphabet Constitution, then dreams of how life would be if he became a different letter.

"Written with sly wit and wordplay that will appeal to the target audience, this little book delves into constitutional government as well as spelling rules. . . . The upbeat text and brightly colored, cartoon-like illustrations propel the story, while the personified letters' grievances will draw a sympathetic response from children struggling with the order of letters as they learn to read." Booklist

Cat secrets. Balzer + Bray 2011 un il $16.99
Grades: PreK K 1   E
1. Cats -- Fiction
ISBN 978-0-06-192088-2; 0-06-192088-6
LC 2009-49424
Important secrets about how best to live a cat's life will be revealed only to those who can prove that they are genuine cats.

"Although the appeals for reader interaction may make for a rowdy read-aloud, Czekaj cleverly slows the book's pace at the end by demanding that readers take a catnap. It's easy to see this one being read just before preschool naptime." Publ Wkly

Hip & Hop, don't stop. Disney/Hyperion 2010 un il $16.99
Grades: K 1 2   E
1. Rabbits -- Fiction 2. Turtles -- Fiction 3. Contests -- Fiction 4. Rap music -- Fiction
ISBN 978-1-4231-1664-6; 1-4231-1664-X
LC 2009-20022
A fast rabbit named Hip and a slow turtle named Hop defy convention when they team up to win a rap music contest in spite of their differences.

"Speech balloons and short rhymes are seamlessly incorporated into the story line. Red text means read fast and green text means read slowly. . . . The bright colors and engaging characters will grab children's attention." SLJ

Oink-a-doodle-moo; written and illustrated by Jef Czekaj. Balzer + Bray 2012 32 p. (tr. bdg.) $16.99
Grades: PreK K 1   E
1. Games -- Fiction 2. Picture books for children 3. Domestic animals -- Fiction 4. Humorous stories 5. Animal sounds -- Fiction 6. Domestic animals -- Fiction
ISBN 0062060112; 9780062060112
LC 2011010065
This barnyard story "is propelled by an old-fashioned game of telephone. 'I have a secret,' a bubble-gum pink pig whispers, hoof to mouth, to a blank-eyed rooster: 'Oink. Pass it on.' The rooster, in turn, relays an 'Oink-a-doodle-doo' to a cow, whose 'Oink-a-doodle-moo' becomes a frog's 'Oink-a-ribbit-moo,' and so on." (Publishers Weekly)

D'Amico, Carmela

Ella the Elegant Elephant; by Carmela & Steven D'Amico. Arthur A. Levine Books 2004 un il $16.95
Grades: PreK K 1 2   E
1. School stories 2. Hats -- Fiction 3. Elephants -- Fiction
ISBN 0-439-62792-3
LC 2003-28081
Ella is nervous about the first day of school in her new town, but wearing her grandmother's good luck hat makes her feel better—until the other students tease her and call her names.

"Combining a fairy-tale quality with elements in story and setting that will be familiar to children, this has a charming protagonist, as well as lovely, whimsical art, in a soft rich palette. . . . The text is simple, descriptive, and often lively, making a good read-aloud." Booklist
Other titles about Ella are:
Ella takes the cake (2005)
Ella sets the stage (2006)

Ella sets sail (2008)

Suki, the very loud bunny; [by] Carmela & Steven D'Amico. Dutton Children's Books 2011 un il $16.99
Grades: PreK K 1   E
1. Noise -- Fiction 2. Rabbits -- Fiction
ISBN 978-0-525-42230-3; 0-525-42230-7
LC 2010013470
Unlike most bunnies, Suki loves shouting and playing in the mud, but when she disobeys her mother and leaves the burrow one day, her loud voice is what saves her.

"Appealing for reading in a lap but also well suited to storytimes, this tale of a bunny whose most troublesome traits save the day will ring true with children who have ever been scolded for being noisy or curious." SLJ

D'Aulaire, Ingri

Foxie; the singing dog. [by] Ingri and Edgar Parin d'Aulaire. New York Review Books 2007 un il (New York Review Books children's collection) $14.95
Grades: K 1 2   E
1. Dogs -- Fiction
ISBN 978-1-59017-264-3; 1-59017-264-7
LC 2007-27028
First published 1949
A lost dog's luck makes him fat and famous, but when given a chance he proves he still thinks there is no place like home.

"Foxie's adventures are illustrated in delightful color." Horn Book Guide

The **two** cars; [by] Ingri & Edgar Parin d'Aulaire. New York Review Books 2007 un il (The New York Review children's collection) $14.95
Grades: PreK K 1   E
1. Fables 2. Automobiles -- Fiction
ISBN 978-1-59017-234-6; 1-59017-234-5
LC 2007-2636
First published 1955 by Doubleday
On a magic moonlit night, the sleek, shiny automatic new car and the beat-up old car with many miles on its speedometer go for a drive to see which car is the best.

"A modern adaptation of The Tortoise and the Hare, in which safe and courteous driving wins the day. Delicate pencil illustrations and a plot delivered at a pace fit for a turnpike should prove as enchanting to today's automotively inclined children as when the book was first published in 1955." Pub Wkly

Da Costa, Deborah

Hanukkah moon; [illustrated by] Gosia Mosz. Kar-Ben Pub. 2007 un il lib bdg $17.95; pa $7.95
Grades: PreK K 1 2   E
1. Jews -- Fiction 2. Moon -- Fiction 3. Aunts -- Fiction 4. Hanukkah -- Fiction 5. Rosh Hodesh -- Fiction 6. Mexican Americans -- Fiction
ISBN 978-1-58013-244-2 lib bdg; 1-58013-244-8 lib bdg; 978-1-58013-245-9 pa; 1-58013-245-6 pa
LC 2006-27430
When Isobel visits her Aunt Luisa, who has just arrived from Mexico, she celebrates Hanukkah with a dreidel-shaped piñata and learns how to celebrate Rosh Hodesh, the women's holiday of the new moon

This is "a valuable contribution to the canon of holiday literature. . . . Mosz's mixed-media pictures . . . feature a cast of doe-eyed, stylized characters golden as Hanukkah lights against the deep purple of moonless night." Bull Cent Child Books

DaCosta, Barbara

★ **Nighttime** Ninja; by Barbara DaCosta; illustrated by Ed Young. Little, Brown 2012 32 p. (hardback) $16.99

Grades: PreK K 1   E

1. Ninja -- Fiction 2. Suspense fiction 3. Picture books for children 4. Bedtime -- Fiction 5. Imagination -- Fiction

ISBN 031620384X; 9780316203845

LC 2012005492

This children's picture book features a "ninja, a black silhouette, [who] breaks into a house and makes his way silently toward some unknown object: 'He crept down the twisting moonlit hallway, and knelt in the dark shadows, listening.' Suddenly, a huge mother-shaped shadow flicks the light on, and the ninja is revealed as a boy sneaking into the kitchen for ice cream." (Publishers Weekly)

Dahl, Michael

Nap time for Kitty; illustrated by Oriol Vidal. Picture Window Books 2011 un il (Hello genius) bd bk $7.99

Grades: PreK   E

1. Board books for children 2. Cats -- Fiction 3. Sleep -- Fiction

ISBN 978-1-4048-5216-7; 1-4048-5216-6

LC 2010032115

"Toddlers will see themselves in this kitten who just doesn't want to take a nap. When Mama calls him in, he has been busy ogling a bird—and leaping into the birdbath. . . . The cute cats have a slightly stylized and digitized look. Minimal text and plenty of action are just right for the intended age group." Booklist

Daly, Cathleen

Emily's blue period; Cathleen Daly; illustrated by Lisa Brown. Roaring Brook Press 2014 56 p. color illustrations $17.99

Grades: PreK K 1 2 3   E

1. Child artists 2. Art -- Fiction 3. Divorce -- Fiction

ISBN 1596434694; 9781596434691

LC 2013016727

"Emily wants to be an artist. She likes painting and loves the way artists like Pablo Picasso mixed things up. Emily's life is a little mixed up right now. Her dad doesn't live at home anymore, and it feels like everything around her is changing. 'When Picasso was sad for a while,' says Emily, 'he only painted in blue. And now I am in my blue period.' It might last quite some time." (Publisher's note)

"This is a heartfelt, relatable, and even sometimes funny picture book. . . . It's also empowering for readers struggling with similar situations, as Emily figures out a way to redefine her idea of home." Horn Book

★ **Prudence** wants a pet. Roaring Brook Press 2011 un il $16.99

Grades: PreK K 1   E

1. Pets -- Fiction

ISBN 978-1-59643-468-4; 1-59643-468-6

LC 2010022001

"Small pen-and-ink and watercolor illustrations on a white background reveal a time progression in vignettes that are spread across the pages. The humorous consequences of Prudence's experiments make this a lighthearted read about never giving up on one's dreams." SLJ

Daly, Jude

Sivu's six wishes; a Taoist tale. retold and illustrated by Jude Daly. Eerdmans Books for Young Readers 2010 un il

Grades: K 1 2   E

1. Africa -- Fiction 2. Taoism -- Fiction 3. Wishes -- Fiction 4. Happiness -- Fiction 5. Stonecutting -- Fiction 6. Folklore

ISBN 0-8028-5369-2; 978-0-8028-5369-1

LC 2010001619

Sivu, an African stonecarver, is not paid well for his work, but through his wishes to become more powerful and live as different people, like the mayor, and things, like the wind, he discovers where real power lies.

"Daly's stylized art, in a rich, clear palette, is quietly stunning. . . . Repetition in both text . . . and art . . . helps make the story easy to follow, and the modern embellishments never obscure its meaning." Horn Book

Daly, Niki

★ **Pretty** Salma; a Red Riding Hood story from Africa. Clarion Books 2007 29p $16

Grades: K 1 2 3   E

1. Fairy tales 2. Ghana -- Fiction

ISBN 978-0-618-72345-4; 0-618-72345-5

LC 2006-04249

In this version of "Little Red Riding Hood," set in Ghana, a young girl fails to heed Granny's warning about the dangers of talking to strangers.

"The cartoon-style paintings capture the sights and flavor of the setting and add dimension and humorous details to this modern version of a timeless tale." SLJ

A **song** for Jamela; story and pictures by Niki Daly. Frances Lincoln Children's Books 2010 un il $16.95

Grades: K 1 2   E

1. Singers -- Fiction 2. Celebrities -- Fiction 3. Beauty shops -- Fiction 4. South Africa -- Fiction

ISBN 978-1-84507-871-3; 1-84507-871-3

It is summer vacation and Jamela is bored, until her Aunt Beauty asks her to come and help her get her hair salon ready for a special client, who turns out to be "Afro-Idols" contestant Miss Bambi Chaka Chaka.

"Daly's humorous and colorful illustrations reflect everyday South African scenes from a child's point of view. The illustrations [are made] utilizing digital art." SLJ

Other titles about Jamela are:

Jamela's dress (1999)

What's cooking Jamela? (2001)

Where's Jamela? (2004)

Happy birthday, Jamela! (2006)

★ **Welcome** to Zanzibar Road; story and pictures by Niki Daly. Clarion Books 2006 31p il $16

Grades: PreK K 1 2   E

1. Africa -- Fiction 2. Chickens -- Fiction 3. Elephants -- Fiction

ISBN 0-618-64926-3

LC 2005021758

After moving into the house on Zanzibar Road that her neighbors helped her build, Mama Jumbo the elephant decides to share it with Little Chico the chicken.

"Through his warm, expressive watercolors, Daly teaches readers about some of the important things in life—friendship, family, and how to make a house into a home. Details abound, and the animals' patterned clothing adds texture and variety to the pages." SLJ

Danneberg, Julie

The **big** test; illustrated by Judy Love. Charlesbridge 2011 un il $16.95; pa $6.95

Grades: K 1 2   E

1. School stories

ISBN 1580893600; 1580893619 pa; 9781580893602; 9781580893619 pa; 978-1-58089-360-2; 1-58089-360-0; 978-1-58089-361-9 pa; 1-58089-361-9 pa

Mrs. Hartwell is concerned that preparing her students to take the Big Test is only making them nervous, and so she thinks of a way to help them relax.

"Mrs. Hartwell's students . . . are not sure they can deal with the Big Test. . . . The kids worry and get headaches, stomachaches, and other maladies. On Thursday, Mrs. Hartwell lines up her class and marches them down the hall to the library. The sign on the door says, 'Library Closed: Students Testing.' But inside it's a test party. The students get to play and relax and eat. This works so well that no one is sick anymore and they breeze through the actual Big Test on Friday. The illustrations, done in ink and transparent dyes on watercolor paper, are priceless. The children's faces clearly express all the agony that the situation requires." SLJ

Monet paints a day; Julie Danneberg; illustrated by Caitlin Heimerl. Charlesbridge 2012 48 p. col. ill. (reinforced) $15.95
Grades: 2 3 4   E
   1. Plein-air painting 2. Impressionism (Art)
   ISBN 1442435798; 9781580892407

                 LC 2011025789
This book by Julie Danneburg is "written in the voice of the artist and drawn from the letters of the noted French Impressionist Claude Monet. . . . One day, so absorbed in painting as much as he could within a seven-to-15-minute window . . . Monet was actually swept away by a high tide, supplies and all. . . . [Danneburg] integrates details from Monet's letters and minifacts about Impressionism and the exciting practice of plein-air painting." (Kirkus)

Danticat, Edwidge, 1969-
   ★ **Eight** days; a story of Haiti. pictures by Alix Delinois. Orchard Books 2010 un il
Grades: K 1 2 3   E
   1. Play -- Fiction 2. Haiti -- Fiction 3. Earthquakes -- Fiction 4. Imagination -- Fiction
   ISBN 0-545-27849-X; 978-0-545-27849-2

                 LC 2010035981
Junior tells of the games he played in his mind during the eight days he was trapped in his house after the devastating January 12, 2010 earthquake in Haiti. Includes author's note about Haitian children before the earthquake and her own children's reactions to the disaster.
   This is illustrated with "beautiful, bright artwork, in acrylics, pastel, and collage. . . . The narrative's powerful rhythm echoes the Genesis Creation story, giving it even more gravity. . . . Never too sentimental, the story works because of the clear presence of great sadness and loss." Booklist

Mama's nightingale; a story of immigration and separation. by Edwidge Danticat; illustrated by Leslie Staub. Dial Books, an imprint of Penguin Group (USA) Inc. 2015 32 p. color illustrations (hardcover) $17.99
Grades: K 1 2 3   E
   1. Children of prisoners -- Fiction 2. Immigrants -- United States -- Fiction 3. Mother-daughter relationship -- Fiction 4. Haitian Americans -- Fiction 5. Detention of persons -- Fiction 6. Mothers and daughters -- Fiction 7. Separation (Psychology) -- Fiction 8. Emigration and immigration -- Fiction
   ISBN 0525428097; 9780525428091

                 LC 2014039868
In this children's story, by Edwidge Danticat and illustrated by Leslie Staub, "After Saya's mother is sent to an immigration detention center, Saya finds comfort in listening to her mother's warm greeting on their answering machine. To ease the distance between them while she's in jail, Mama begins sending Saya bedtime stories inspired by Haitian folklore on cassette tape." (Publisher's note)
   "Danticat's immigration story is compelling. Saya's mother is in a detention center because she doesn't have the right 'papers,' and while Saya can visit her, she wants Mama HOME. Papa's letters to elected

officials and news outlets get no response, but when Saya writes to the paper, amazing things happen. . . . right, comforting blues dominate the double-page spreads, and Mama floats above her worldly problems. The inclusion of Haitian phrases adds to the personal nature of the story, whose happy ending is deserved by all. Danticat's endnotes remind us that this is a story based in reality." Booklist

Danziger, Paula
   ★ **It's** Justin Time, Amber Brown; illustrated by Tony Ross. Putnam 2001 48p il (A is for Amber) $12.99; pa $3.99
Grades: K 1 2 3   E
   1. Time -- Fiction 2. Birthdays -- Fiction 3. Clocks and watches -- Fiction
   ISBN 0-399-23470-5; 0-698-11907-X pa

                 LC 99-89396
Unlike her best friend Justin, Amber Brown loves to measure time and hopes to receive a watch on her seventh birthday
   "The illustrations capture the mood of the story, which is playful and spirited. Beginning readers will enjoy sharing Amber's pre-birthday anticipation and older readers may want to go back and see the early years of the characters they know and love." SLJ
   Other easy-to-read titles about Amber Brown are:
   Get ready for second grade, Amber Brown (2002)
   It's a fair day, Amber Brown (2002)
   Orange you glad it's Halloween, Amber Brown (2005)
   Second grade rules, Amber Brown (2004)
   What a trip, Amber Brown (2001)

Darrow, Sharon
   Yafi's family; an Ethiopian boy's journey of love, loss, and adoption. by Linda Pettitt and Sharon Darrow; illustrated by Jan Spivey Gilchrist. Amharic 2010 un il
Grades: PreK K 1 2   E
   1. Adoption -- Fiction 2. Ethiopia -- Fiction 3. Family life -- Fiction
   ISBN 0-979748-14-3; 978-0-979748-14-1
   "With his new family in America, Yafi, six, remembers when they first came to his orphanage in Ethiopia. . . . Mom remembers too. . . . They talk about his first mother, who died, and his grandma Elsa, who raised him until she could no longer care for him. . . . Gilchrist's beautiful sepia-toned portraits depict the love Yafi feels for his American family and also his warm remembrances of his birth family. Both words and pictures effectively convey the strong familial ties." Booklist

Daugherty, James Henry
   ★ **Andy** and the lion; by James Daugherty. Viking 1938 un il hardcover o.p. pa $6.99
Grades: PreK K 1 2   E
   1. Lions -- Fiction
   ISBN 0-14-050277-7 pa
   A Caldecott Medal honor book, 1939
   A modern picture story of Androcles and the lion in which Andy, who read a book about lions, was almost immediately plunged into action. The next day he met a circus lion with a thorn in his paw. Andy removed the thorn and earned the lion's undying gratitude
   "This is a tall tale for little children. It is typically American in its setting and its fun. The large full page illustrations are in yellow, black and white and the brief, hand-lettered text on the opposite page is clear and readable." Libr J

Davies, Jacqueline
   The **night** is singing; illustrations by Kyrsten Brooker. Dial Books for Young Readers 2006 un il $16.99

Grades: PreK K 1   E
1. Stories in rhyme 2. Night -- Fiction 3. Sound -- Fiction
ISBN 0-8037-3004-7; 978-0-8037-3004-5
                                                                    LC 2004-14161
Rhyming text tells of lullabies that can be heard in the sounds of
the night, such as a radiator's hiss, a cat's shadowboxing, and a rainstorm's drumming

This is a "perfect bedtime read. . . . Attractive, full-page folk-art
illustrations that combine collage and oil paint on gessoed watercolor
paper lend an old-fashioned charm." SLJ

★ **Tricking** the Tallyman; illustrated by S. D. Schindler. Alfred A.
Knopf 2009 un il $17.99; lib bdg $20.99
Grades: 1 2 3 4   E
1. Census -- Fiction 2. Vermont -- Fiction 3. United States --
History -- 1783-1809 -- Fiction
ISBN 978-0-375-83909-2; 0-375-83909-7; 978-0-375-93909-9
lib bdg; 0-375-93909-1 lib bdg
                                                                    LC 2007-45488
In 1790, the suspicious residents of a small Vermont town try to trick
the man who has been sent to count their population for the first United
States Census.

"This lively, engaging picture book is an outstanding introduction
to the concept of census taking and its role in the implementation of the
new United States Constitution. . . . Schindler's exceptional illustrations,
mainly in earth tones, depict indoor and outdoor scenes that are full of
activity. . . . Charming and humorous." SLJ

Davies, Matt

Ben draws trouble; Matt Davies. Roaring Brook Press 2015 32 p.
color illustrations (hardback) $17.99
Grades: PreK K 1 2 3   E
1. Drawing -- Fiction 2. Lost and found possessions -- Fiction 3.
Ability -- Fiction 4. Schools -- Fiction
ISBN 1596437952; 9781596437951
                                                                    LC 2014009905
In this children's story, by Matt Davies, "Ben loved drawing more
than anything else in the world (with the possible exception of riding his
bicycle). He drew boats as well as bicycles, sharks and spaceships. But
most of all he loved drawing people. When Ben loses his sketchbook
his world is turned upside down. Who will find it? And how will they
react?" (Publisher's note)

"Through the succinct text and emotionally charged illustrations,
children will feel Ben's panic and anguish over losing his sketchbook,
his fear of punishment for the caricatures, and his satisfaction at the
happy ending." Booklist

Another book about Ben is:
Ben Rides On (2013)

Ben rides on; Matt Davies. 1st ed. Roaring Brook Press 2013 32
p. (reinforced) $16.99
Grades: PreK K 1 2 3   E
1. Picture books for children 2. Bullies -- Fiction 3. Bullies --
Fiction 4. Stealing -- Fiction 5. Conduct of life -- Fiction 6.
Bicycles and bicycling -- Fiction
ISBN 1596437944; 9781596437944
                                                                    LC 2012013101
In this children's picture book, when "Adrian Underbite takes Ben's
bicycle for a joyride and hurtles off a cliff, Ben leans over the edge
and sees Adrian clinging to a tiny branch. 'How extraordinarily terri-
ble,' Ben thinks, though his toothy grin conveys quite another emotion.
But Ben's conscience smites him, and he goes back to rescue Adrian."
(Publishers Weekly)

Davies, Nicola

Outside your window; a first book of nature. Nicola Davies; illus-
trated by Mark Hearld. Candlewick Press 2012 105 p. il
Grades: K 1 2   E
1. Nature poetry 2. Nature -- Fiction
ISBN 076365549X; 9780763655495
                                                                    LC 2011046637
This book of poetry has as its subject "the seasons. . . . The year
starts with spring (featuring aspects such as 'Bulbs,' 'Lambs' Tails,' and
'Planting Seeds') and goes on through summer (a bird's 'Summer Song,'
a farm's 'Making Hay') and on to fall ('Acorn,' 'Harvest,' 'Berry Picking') and finally winter ('Winter Trees,' 'Snow Song'). The verses, in
different forms ranging from prose poems (including craft instructions)
to tightly metered rhymes, . . . offer . . . observations ('In the morning,
you'll find the snow has kept a diary/ of things that happened when you
were asleep'—'Snow Song') or invit[e] humor (one of the 'Five Reasons to Keep Chickens' is 'They look very silly when they are taking a
dust bath')." (Bulletin of the Center for Children's Books)

Perfect; by Nicola Davies, illustrated by Cathy Fisher. Trafalgar
Square Books 2016 36 p. color illustrations $14.99
Grades: PreK K 1 2 3 4 5   E
1. Love -- Fiction 2. Siblings -- Fiction
ISBN 1910862460; 9781910862469
This book, by Nicola Davies, illustrated by Cathy Fisher, "is a story
of anticipation, disappointment, acceptance, and, ultimately, love. Suf-
fused with natural imagery, [it] is an ideal way to open up the subject of
disability with children, as well as being a great story in its own right."
(Publisher's note)

"An emotionally vivid, hopeful illustration of unpredictability, disappointment, and acceptance—recommended for children and parents
alike." Kirkus

★ **Surprising** Sharks; by Nicola Davies and illustrated by James
Croft. Candlewick 2005 29 p. il $6.99
Grades: K 1 2 3   E
1. Sharks
ISBN 0763621854; 0763627429; 9780763627423
                                                                    LC 200340943
Boston Globe-Horn Book Award Honor: Nonfiction (2004)
This book, by Nicola Davies and illustrated by James Croft, presents
"illustrations, and captivating facts [designed to] reveal that sharks come
in all shapes and sizes—and probably should be more afraid of humans
than we are of them." (Publisher's note)

What happens next? Nicola Davies, illustrated by Marc Boutavant.
Candlewick Press 2012 24 p. $9.99
Grades: PreK K 1   E
1. Picture books for children 2. Animal behavior -- Fiction 3.
Animals 4. Toy and movable books -- Specimens
ISBN 076366264X; 9780763662646
                                                                    LC 2012942306
Author Nicola Davies' "lift-the-flap book reveals surprises in the
animal kingdom. A hungry chameleon spies a juicy grasshopper. Turn
the half-page. His long tongue shoots out to catch it. Going on, Davies
presents other unexpected animal behaviors. . . . The final spread in this
sequencing exercise offers a matching game to remind young viewers of
the actions described." (Kirkus Reviews)

What will I be? by Nicola Davies and illustrated by Marc Boutavant. Candlewick 2012 32 p. (alk. paper) $9.99

Grades: PreK K   E
    1. Life cycles (Biology) 2. Animals 3. Animal life cycles
    ISBN 0763658030; 9780763658038

                                        LC 2011047178

In this book, by Nicola Davies and illustrated by Marc Boutavant, readers "Peek under each large flap and look at colorful spreads to find out how each animal develops. A final spread invites readers to match each fullgrown creature with its beginning stage." (Publisher's note)
    Includes bibliographical references and index

    ★ White owl, barn owl; illustrated by Michael Foreman. Candlewick Press 2007 29p il $16.99; pa $6.99
Grades: PreK K 1 2 3   E
    1. Owls -- Fiction
    ISBN 978-0-7636-3364-6; 0-7636-3364-X; 978-0-7636-4143-6 pa; 0-7636-4143-X pa

"Simple facts about the hunting and nesting habits of barn owls intertwine with the story of two humans who put a nesting box for them high in a tree. Narrated by a girl whose grandfather explains owl behavior as the two watch for avian visitors in the evenings, the story also contains insets of information bits. Well-chosen design elements move both fiction and fact along with clarity and ease. . . . Foreman's artwork includes lovely watercolor and pastel paintings of the birds." SLJ

    Who lives here? Nicola Davies, illustrated by Marc Boutavant. Candlewick Press 2012 24 p. $9.99
Grades: PreK K 1   E
    1. Children's literature 2. Animals -- Habitations 3. Toy and movable books -- Specimens
    ISBN 0763662631; 9780763662639

                                        LC 2012942307

In this children's book by Nicola Davies, illustrated by Marc Boutavant, readers can "lift the flaps and learn about animal life. . . . The jungle is warm and steamy. What kind of animal might live there, a snow goose or a sloth? What about a still, cool pond -- could that be home for a howler monkey? Find out why meerkats like dry sunny grasslands (hint: they like to dig holes to hide in) or why clown fish feel right at home in a coral reef." (Publisher's note)

Davies, Stephen
    Don't spill the milk; by Stephen Davies; illustrated by Christopher Corr. Andersen Press 2013 32 p. (trade hard cover : alk. paper) $16.95
Grades: PreK K   E
    1. Love -- Fiction 2. Responsibility -- Fiction 3. Africa -- Fiction
    ISBN 1467720283; 9781467720281

                                        LC 2012049659

Author Stephen Davies presents an illustrated children's picture book about the relationship between a girl and her father in the mountains. "Up the downy dunes, across the dark, wide river and up and down the steep, steep mountain, Penda lovingly carries a bowl of milk to her father in the grasslands. But will she manage to get it there without spilling a single drop?" (Publisher's note)

Davis, Anne
    No dogs allowed! words and pictures by Anne Davis. HarperCollins Children's Books 2011 un il $16.99
Grades: PreK K 1 2   E
    1. Cats -- Fiction 2. Dogs -- Fiction 3. Friendship -- Fiction
    ISBN 978-0-06-075353-5; 0-06-075353-6

                                        LC 2010007028

Bud the cat is not happy when his feline companion Gabby befriends a dog.

"Charming illustrations add humor, and young readers will note small details. . . . The kindness-wins-out theme is perfect for storytime." Booklist

Davis, Aubrey
    Kishka for Koppel; illustrated by Sheldon Cohen. Orca Book Publishers 2011 il $19.95
Grades: K 1 2 3   E
    1. Jews -- Fiction 2. Wishes -- Fiction
    ISBN 978-1-55469-299-6; 1-55469-299-7

"In this Jewish retelling of the Grimm Brothers' 'Three Wishes,' Koppel finds a wish-granting meat grinder. The junk man and his wife, Yetta, dream of all the riches they'll wish for, but inevitably they end up wishing for kishka (a kind of sausage), and subsequently wishing it onto and off Koppel's nose. All ends well as the meat grinder points out how lucky they are to have each other (plus a delicious kishka). The naive, folksy cartoon illustrations are expressive and lend a lighthearted air with their varying perspectives and bright acrylic colors. The storytelling is lively and humorous." SLJ

Davis, David
    Fandango stew; illustrated by Ben Galbraith. Sterling Pub. 2011 un il
Grades: PreK K 1 2   E
    1. Folklore 2. West (U.S.) -- Fiction
    ISBN 1402765274; 9781402765278

                                        LC 2010004775

Penniless Slim and his grandson Luis ride into the unwelcoming western town of Skinflint, and manage to rustle up a delicious meal for all its citizens out of one lone bean.

"Witty illustrations featuring warm tones and amusing details effectively complement the text. Either alone or paired with a traditional version, this will make for an appealing read and an even better read-aloud, especially when audiences join in on the chorus: 'Chili's good,/ so is barbecue,/ but nothing's finer than/ fandango stew!'" Libr Media Connect

Davis, Jill
    The **first** rule of little brothers; illustrated by Sarah McMenemy. Alfred A. Knopf 2008 un il $16.99; lib bdg $19.99
Grades: PreK K 1   E
    1. Brothers -- Fiction
    ISBN 978-0-375-84046-3; 0-375-84046-X; 978-0-375-94046-0 lib bdg; 0-375-94046-4 lib bdg

                                        LC 2007-44314

A young boy learns that, while his little brother's constant mimicking may be annoying, it is also a sign of admiration.

"Davis makes her point—siblings can drive eachother crazy but also have fun together—credibly and sympathetically with plenty of humor as well. . . . McMenemy's mixed-media art (which looks to incorporate watercolor, ink, and torn paper collage) is sunny and vivid, with lots of crisp white space surrounding the brightly colored figures and backgrounds." Bull Cent Child Books

Davis, Katie
    Little Chicken's big day; [by] Katie Davis and Jerry Davis. Margaret K. McElderry Books 2011 un il $14.99
Grades: PreK K   E
    1. Chickens -- Fiction 2. Mother-child relationship -- Fiction
    ISBN 978-1-4424-1401-3; 1-4424-1401-4

                                        LC 2010011826

Little Chicken is tired of being told what to do by Big Chicken, but when they become separated he misses all of the clucking.

"Done in bold lines, simple shapes, and bright colors, the chunky poultry are set against unadorned, mainly white backgrounds. . . . This look at a busy mom and preschooler perfectly echoes a child's experience." SLJ

Dawson, Willow

★ The **Wolf**-birds; by Willow Dawson. Owlkids Books 2015 40 p. colour illustrations $17.95

Grades: K 1 2   E

1. Ravens 2. Wolves 3. Hunting

ISBN 1771470542; 9781771470544

This children's book, by Willow Dawson, "is based on observers' reports of ravens alerting hunters--both humans and wolves--to potential prey. . . .The ravens watch a wolf pack chase a buffalo; the buffalo gets away but not without delivering a fatal kick to one of the wolves. The hunt continues until the birds see an injured deer and summon the wolves. This second chase is more successful. 'One animal's life helps many others live.'" (Kirkus Reviews)

"Wolves and ravens work together (an author's note explains "mutualism") when the birds alert the pack to an injured deer. The ravens and the pack pursue the creature, then feast and share the bounty with their families. Earth-toned acrylic paintings, with stylized, flat forms, avoid graphic detail, focusing instead on the creatures' survival. Matter-of-fact language describes the hunt and feast. Bib." Horn Book

Day, Alexandra

Carl and the puppies; story and pictures by Alexandra Day. Square Fish 2011 un il (My readers) $15.99; pa $3.99

Grades: PreK K 1   E

1. Dogs -- Fiction

ISBN 978-0-312-62482-8; 0-312-62482-4; 978-0-312-62483-5 pa; 0-312-62483-2 pa

"Carl dog-sits three active pups. Large print, controlled vocabulary, simple sentences and story [arc], supportive pictures, and plentiful white space make [this] a good choice for the newest readers." Horn Book Guide

★ **Carl's** sleepy afternoon. Farrar, Straus and Giroux 2005 un il $12.95

Grades: PreK K 1   E

1. Dogs -- Fiction

ISBN 0-374-31088-2

Carl's owners have many errands to do and expect Carl to sleep the entire afternoon. Instead, Carl the rottweiler roams the town assisting many people in their daily chores

"The entertaining story is told through the gently detailed, warmly realistic paintings." SLJ

Other titles about Carl are:

Carl and the baby duck (2011)

Carl and the puppies (2011)

Carl goes shopping (1990)

Carl goes to daycare (1993)

Carl makes a scrapbook (1994)

Carl's afternoon in the park (1991)

Carl's birthday (1995)

Carl's Christmas (1990)

Carl's masquerade (1992)

Carl's snowy afternoon (2009)

Carl's summer vacation (2008)

Follow Carl (1998)

Good dog, Carl (1985)

Good dog Carl and the baby elephant (2016)

Frank and Ernest. Green Tiger Press 2010 un il $15.95

Grades: PreK K 1 2   E

1. Bears -- Fiction 2. Elephants -- Fiction 3. Restaurants -- Fiction

ISBN 978-1-59583-424-9; 1-59583-424-9

LC 2010010747

A reissue of the title first published 1988 by Scholastic

An elephant and a bear take over a diner and find out about responsibility and food language.

"Day's mock-dignified illustrations, lush and attractive, add dimension to the entertaining story. A diner glossary is included to aid comprehension." Horn Book Guide

Another title about Frank and Ernest is:

Frank and Ernest play ball (2011)

Frank and Ernest play ball. Green Tiger Press 2011 un il $15.95

Grades: PreK K 1 2   E

1. Bears -- Fiction 2. Baseball -- Fiction 3. Elephants -- Fiction

ISBN 978-1-59583-438-6; 1-59583-438-9

LC 2010048046

A reissue of the title first published 1990 by Scholastic

With the help of a baseball dictionary so they can learn the necessary language, an elephant and a bear take over the management of a baseball team.

"Sports fans will enjoy the text with its in-the-know lingo. . . . Day's play-it-straight paintings—except for the elephant and bear in the infield—convey much of the spirit of baseball." Horn Book Guide

Day, Nancy Raines

On a windy night; illustrated by George Bates. Abrams Books for Young Readers 2009 un il $16.95

Grades: PreK K 1   E

1. Stories in rhyme 2. Fear -- Fiction 3. Halloween -- Fiction

ISBN 978-0-8109-3900-4; 0-8109-3900-2

LC 2008-52532

On a windy Halloween night as a boy is returning home through the woods after trick-or-treating, he hears scary noises behind him.

Bates's "pen-and-ink drawings push and pull, creating scariness with forceful hatching and eerie lighting. . . . There's enough Halloween fright to satisfy adventurous young readers, and a comforting ending for those with jangled nerves." Publ Wkly

Daywalt, Drew

The **day** the crayons came home; by Drew Daywalt; pictures by Oliver Jeffers. Philomel Books, an imprint of Penguin Group (USA) 2015 48 p. color illustrations (hardback) $18.99

Grades: PreK K   E

1. Color -- Fiction 2. Crayon drawing -- Fiction 3. Crayons -- Fiction 4. Postcards -- Fiction

ISBN 0399172750; 9780399172755

LC 2015003512

In this children's book by Drew Daywalt, illustrated by Oliver Jeffers, "having soothed the hurt feelings of one group who threatened to quit, Duncan now faces a whole new group of crayons asking to be rescued. From Maroon Crayon, who was lost beneath the sofa cushions and then broken in two after Dad sat on him; to poor Turquoise, whose head is now stuck to one of Duncan's stinky socks after they both ended up in the dryer together." (Publisher's note)

"A brilliant, colorful tale that begs to be read aloud and a must-have for all collections." SLJ

★ The **day** the crayons quit; Drew Daywalt; illustrated by Oliver Jeffers. Philomel Books 2013 40 p. $17.99

Grades: PreK K   E

1. Color -- Fiction 2. Crayon drawing -- Fiction 3. Crayons --

Fiction 4. Letters -- Fiction
ISBN 0399255370; 9780399255373

LC 2012030384

In this children's picture book, by Drew Daywalt, illustrated by Oliver Jeffers, "a schoolboy finds a mysterious parcel of letters addressed to him in what looks just like a child's handwriting. The letters, it turns out, are from his crayons, who deeply resent being typecast according to color. Red is tired of drawing apples and fire engines, Green is bored of coloring dinosaurs and frogs, and so on." (New York Times Book Review)

"Daywalt composes droll missives that express aggravation and aim to persuade, while Jeffers's . . . crayoned images underscore the waxy cylinders' sentiments: each spread features a facsimile of a letter scrawled, naturally, in the crayon's hue; a facing illustration evidences how Duncan uses the crayon. . . . These memorable personalities will leave readers glancing apprehensively at their own crayon boxes." Pub Wkly

Followed by: The day the crayons came home (2015)

The **legend** of rock paper scissors; Drew Daywalt; illustrated by Adam Rex. Balzer & Bray 2017 48 p. color illustrations $17.99

Grades: PreK K 1   E

1. Games -- Fiction 2. Humorous fiction -- Fiction
ISBN 0062438891; 9780062438898

This picture book, by Drew Daywalt, illustrated by Adam Rex, is about the tale of the classic game Rock, Paper, Scissors. "Long ago, . . . [in] the Kingdom of Backyard, there lived a warrior named Rock [who] . . . travels far and wide searching for an adversary that might best him. Meanwhile, in the Empire of Mom's Home Office and the Kitchen Realm, . . . Paper and Scissors set out on similar quests." (Kirkus Review)

De Groat, Diane

Ants in your pants, worms in your plants! (Gilbert goes green) Harper 2011 un il $16.99

Grades: K 1 2 3   E

1. School stories 2. Opossums -- Fiction 3. Earth Day -- Fiction 4. Environmental protection -- Fiction
ISBN 978-0-06-176511-7; 0-06-176511-2

LC 2010009396

Gilbert seems to be the only one in his class who cannot think of any ideas for an Earth Day project.

"The cartoon illustrations add detail to the story, and fans of Gilbert and friends will enjoy reading about their Earth-friendly plans." SLJ

Brand-new pencils, brand-new books. HarperCollins Publishers 2005 il lib bdg $16.89

Grades: K 1 2 3   E

1. School stories
ISBN 0-06-072615-6

LC 200404179

Gilbert's excitement over starting first grade turns to worry that the teacher will be mean, the work too hard, and his classmates too unfriendly, but throughout the day there are pleasant surprises.

"With its charming, detailed watercolor illustrations, this story has significant child appeal." SLJ

No more pencils, no more books, no more teacher's dirty looks! HarperCollins 2006 un il lib bdg $18.89; pa $6.99

Grades: K 1 2 3   E

1. School stories 2. Friendship -- Fiction
ISBN 978-0-06-079115-5 lib bdg; 0-06-079115-2 lib bdg; 978-0-06-079116-2 pa; 0-06-079116-0 pa

LC 2005008783

Gilbert and his first-grade classmates are nervous about their performance on the last day of school, curious about the awards they will receive, sad to be leaving their teacher, and excited about summer vacation.

"The bright, cheery watercolor illustrations, with their sizeable cast of lovable, expressive characters, will draw youngsters into Gilbert's comfortable small-town suburban environment." Booklist

★ **Trick** or treat, smell my feet. Morrow Junior Bks. 1998 un il hardcover o.p. pa $4.95

Grades: K 1 2 3   E

1. Siblings -- Fiction 2. Halloween -- Fiction
ISBN 0-688-15766-1; 0-688-15767-X lib bdg; 0-688-17061-7 pa

LC 97-32916

"De Groat's funny watercolor pictures capture the various animal creatures' very human expressions and body language." Booklist

Other titles about Gilbert are:
Ants in your pants, worms in your plants! (2011)
April fool!, watch out at school! (2009)
Brand-new pencils, brand-new books (2005)
Good night, sleep tight, don't let the bedbugs bite! (2002)
Happy birthday to you, you belong in the zoo (1999)
Jingle, bells, homework smells (2000)
Last one in is a rotten egg! (2007)
Liar, liar, pants on fire (2003)
Mother, you are the best! (2008)
No more pencils, no more books, no more teacher's dirty looks! (2006)
Roses are pink, your feet really stink (1996)
We gather together, now please get lost! (2001)

De la Peña, Matt

★ **Last** stop on Market Street; by Matt de la Pena; illustrated by Christian Robinson. G.P. Putnam's Sons, an imprint of Penguin Group (USA) 2015 32 p. color illustrations (hardback) $16.99

Grades: PreK K 1 2   E

1. City and town life 2. Grandparent-grandchild relationship -- Fiction 3. Buses -- Fiction 4. Grandmothers -- Fiction 5. African Americans -- Fiction 6. City and town life -- Fiction
ISBN 0399257748; 9780399257742

LC 2014019913

Newbery Medal (2016)
Caldecott Honor Book (2016)
Coretta Scott King Illustrator Honor Book (2016)

In this children's book by Matt De La Peña and illustrated by Christian Robinson "every Sunday after church, CJ and his grandma ride the bus across town. CJ wonders why they don't own a car like his friend Colby. Why doesn't he have an iPod like the boys on the bus? How come they always have to get off in the dirty part of town? Each question is met with an encouraging answer from grandma, who helps him see the beauty--and fun--in their routine and the world around them." (Publisher's note)

"After church on Sundays, CJ and his nana wait for the bus. It's a familiar routine, but this week CJ is feeling dissatisfied . . . . This is an excellent book that highlights less popular topics such as urban life, volunteerism, and thankfulness, with people of color as the main characters. A lovely title." SLJ

De Mouy, Iris

Naptime; Iris de Mouy; translated by Shelley Tanaka. Groundwood Books 2014 28 p. $16.95

Grades: PreK K   E

1. Sleep -- Fiction 2. Jungle animals -- Fiction
ISBN 1554984874; 9781554984879

In this children's book by Iris de Moüy "all of the animals in the jungle are grumpy--no, they will not take a nap! But one little girl may know just what to do to make sure these creatures can get some much-needed shut-eye. Fortunately for these sleepy creatures, a little girl appears who knows the secret to a good snooze: first close one eye, then close the other one." (Publisher's note)

"It's naptime, but none of the savannah animals is sleepy--that is, until a small girl tricks them into simply shutting their eyes. The book's wide, horizontal orientation suggests the act of lying down, while bold colors evoke sunset on the horizon. Spare text emphasizes the animals' stubbornness, inviting anyone familiar with the trials of naptime to delight in this short, clever story." Horn Book

De Regniers, Beatrice Schenk

★ **May** I bring a friend? illustrated by Beni Montresor. Atheneum Pubs. 1964 un il hardcover o.p. pa $7.99
Grades: PreK K   E
1. Animals -- Fiction
ISBN 0-689-20615-1; 0-689-71353-3 pa
Awarded the Caldecott Medal, 1965

"Rich color and profuse embellishment adorn an opulent setting. Absurdities and contrasts are so imaginatively combined in a hilarious comedy of manners that the merriment can be enjoyed on several levels." Horn Book

De Roo, Elena

The **rain** train; illustrated by Brian Lovelock. Candlewick Press 2011 un il $15.99
Grades: PreK K   E
1. Rain -- Fiction 2. Night -- Fiction 3. Railroads -- Fiction
ISBN 978-0-7636-5313-2; 0-7636-5313-6
     LC 2010039174

A young boy watches and listens as the Rain Train takes him on a ride past city lights, over rivers, and through tunnels one rainy night.

"De Roo's rhyming, lyrical text never derails; the onomatopoeic verse rolls rhythmically along, both lulling listeners and moving the action forward. . . . Lovelock's misty watercolor and ink illustrations, dominated by dusky purples and blues, convey the excitement of a special nighttime journey." Horn Book

De Seve, Randall

The **Duchess** of Whimsy; an absolutely delicious fairy tale. [by] Randall de Seve; [illustrated by] Peter de Seve. Philomel Books 2009 un il $17.99
Grades: PreK K 1   E
1. Fairy tales
ISBN 978-0-399-25095-8; 0-399-25095-6
     LC 2009-2637

The Duchess of Whimsy has absolutely no interest in the Earl of Norm until he makes a sandwich that causes her to look at him in an entirely different way

"Pages burst to life with rich colors whenever the duchess appears and then become comically dull whenever the earl shows up. With a romantic story and smooth art, this charming picture book will appeal to sophisticated young readers who will find the happily-ever-after whimsically ordinary." Booklist

De Smet, Marian

I have two homes; Marian De Smet; [illustrated by] Nynke Talsma. Clavis 2011 32 p. col. ill. $15.95
Grades: PreK K 1 2   E
1. Divorce -- Fiction 2. Picture books for children 3. Children of divorced parents -- Fiction
ISBN 1605371025; 9781605371023

In this children's picture book, "Nina's parents have divorced, and she is dealing with the changes in her life . . . . When they decide to have separate homes, Nina notices changes in their behavior toward her. She misbehaves in an attempt to get their attention but they are often preoccupied. She talks about missing each parent while she is in the home of the other. . . . She finally concludes that her parents aren't happy with each other but they are happy with her." (School Library Journal)

De Sève, Randall

A **fire** truck named Red; Randall de Sève; pictures by Bob Staake. Farrar, Straus & Giroux 2015 40 p. color illustrations (hardback) $16.99
Grades: PreK K 1 2   E
1. Toys -- Fiction 2. Fire engines -- Fiction 3. Grandfathers -- Fiction
ISBN 9780374300739; 0374300739
     LC 2015030358

In this children's book, by Randall de Sève and illustrated by Bob Straake, "a young boy has his heart set on a brand-new toy fire truck, so he is disappointed when he gets his grandfather's rusty old fire truck, Red, instead. But working together, the boy and his grandfather patch Red right up while Grandpa tells his grandson all about the adventures he had with Red when he was a boy." (Publisher's note)

"De Sève ... and Staake ... are an inspired pairing, and the brisk storytelling and funny segues ... give the graphic, posterlike images a deep warmth and narrative energy. Clearly Rowan isn't the only one swept away by Papa's tale." Pub Wkly

Peanut and Fifi have a ball; by Randall de Sève; illustrations by Paul Schmid. Dial Books for Young Readers 2013 40 p. (hardcover) $15.99
Grades: PreK K   E
1. Toys -- Fiction 2. Sharing -- Fiction 3. Sisters -- Fiction 4. Balls (Sporting goods) -- Fiction
ISBN 0803735782; 9780803735781
     LC 2012014355

In this book, "Peanut . . . the little girl is delighted with her new toy. . . . Her sister, pigtailed Fifi, yearns for a piece of the action, but grabbing for the ball, begging, and suggesting shared games don't melt Peanut's resolve to hang on to her toy. Finally Fifi gets wise and presents an attraction all her own: a seal named Bob, and a planned trip around the world for Bob, Fifi, Peanut, and the ball." (Bulletin of the Center for Children's Books)

Deacon, Alexis

I am Henry Finch; Alexis Deacon, Viviane Schwarz. Candlewick Press 2015 40 p. color illustrations $16.99
Grades: 1 2 3   E
1. Reason 2. Family -- Fiction 3. Dinosaurs -- Fiction
ISBN 0763678120; 9780763678128
     LC 2014949717

In this children's book by Alexis Deacon, illustrated by Viviane Schwarz, "Henry Finch and his loving family . . . live in a tree. The Beast--a green dinosaur--comes and terrifies the finches. Henry . . . flies directly toward the creature when it shows up, and is promptly eaten. In the Beast's stomach, he hears its' thoughts about finding its food and feeding its family. After the wily bird escapes, he returns to his family and is an inspiration to them for how things can be better." (School Library Journal)

"A fun, well-illustrated look at how standing up for yourself can be scary but rewarding." SLJ

★ A **place** to call home; Alexis Deacon; illustrated by Viviane Schwarz. Candlewick Press 2011 1 v. col. ill. $15.99

Grades: PreK K 1   **E**
1. Adventure fiction 2. Hamsters -- Fiction 3. Picture books for children 4. Voyages and travels -- Fiction 5. Home -- Fiction 6. Brothers -- Fiction
ISBN 0-7636-5360-8; 9780763653606

LC 2010040125

This book tells the story of "hamsterlike creatures bumbling across a junkyard . . . [as] they embark on a search for a new home. They cross an ocean (readers can see it's a puddle), a 'desert,' and make their way to the edge of the world--the top of an old dryer. In [various] scenes, . . . [illustrator Viviane] Schwarz's . . . furry animals squabble, fret, and cheer each other on; in sequential panels, their running commentary appears in word balloons above their heads. When the junkyard dog grabs one of them, they balk, . . . but taking courage from all they've done so far, they tackle the dog and rescue their sibling." (Publishers Weekly)

"In scenes bursting with physical comedy, Schwarz's . . . furry animals squabble, fret, and cheer each other on; in sequential panels, their running commentary appears in word balloons above their heads. . . . While the creatures may trip over themselves, blundering through their tiny lives not knowing quite where they are headed, Deacon . . . and Schwarz never put a foot wrong. Children will clamor for repeats." Publ Wkly

Deedman, Heidi
   Too many toys; Heidi Deedman. Candlewick Press 2015 32 p. color illustrations $15.99
Grades: PreK K 1   **E**
1. Toys -- Fiction 2. Teddy bears -- Fiction
ISBN 0763678619; 9780763678616

LC 2014949928

In this children's story, by Heidi Deedman, "ever since Lulu was a little baby, she's had Jupiter, her cuddly and most-favorite-ever teddy bear. But with each new birthday she gets new toys. And every Christmas she gets even more toys. Lulu's toys are absolutely everywhere! And now she can't even fit into her own bed. So Lulu decides to throw a very special party for all her toys--and all her friends." (Publisher's note)

"Children will be captivated by the later pictures of all those toys— individually good-natured little dolls and animals that become an overwhelming crowd cavorting about Lulu's room at bedtime." Booklist

Deedy, Carmen Agra
   The **rooster** who would not be quiet! by Carmen Agra Deedy; illustrated by Eugene Yelchin. Scholastic Press 2017 48 p. color illustrations (hardcover : alk. paper) $17.99
Grades: PreK K 1 2   **E**
1. Noise -- Fiction 2. Singing -- Fiction 3. Roosters -- Fiction 4. Villages -- Fiction
ISBN 9780545722889

LC 2016013458

In this children's book, by Carmen Agra Deedy, illustrated by Eugene Yelchin, "La Paz is a happy, but noisy village. A little peace and quiet would make it just right. So the villagers elect the bossy Don Pepe as their mayor. Before long, singing of any kind is outlawed. Even the teakettle is afraid to whistle! But there is one noisy rooster who doesn't give two mangos about this mayor's silly rules. Instead, he does what roosters were born to do." (Publisher's note)

"Deedy's message about speaking up and speaking out rings as clearly as a bell." Pub Wkly

DeFelice, Cynthia C.
   Cold feet; illustrated by Robert Andrew Parker. Dorling Kindersley 2000 32 p. col. ill. $16.99

Grades: 2 3 4   **E**
1. Boots -- Fiction 2. Bagpipers -- Fiction 3. Boots 4. Bagpipers
ISBN 0789426366; 9780789426369

LC 00021279

Boston Globe-Horn Book Award: Picture Book (2001)

In this book, by Cynthia DeFelice, illustrated by Robert Andrew Parker, "Willie McPhee has fallen on hard times. . . . Now, wandering near--shoeless in the dark heart of the cold woods, Willie McPhee has fallen on something else-- . . . a DEAD man, lying in the snow. . . . That body is wearing a fine--looking pair of boots. Soon Willie's feet are warm... but who's that tapping on the door?" (Publisher's note)

"The blotted impressionistic colors and scrawled lines are both edgy and amusing, while the cool gray tones create an appropriately chilly backdrop for the spooky antics." Pub Wkly

★ **Old** Granny and the bean thief; pictures by Cat Bowman Smith. Farrar, Straus and Giroux 2003 un il $16
Grades: K 1 2 3   **E**
1. Thieves -- Fiction 2. Grandmothers -- Fiction
ISBN 0-374-35614-9

LC 2002-20770

After a thief steals Old Granny's beans while she is asleep at night, she gets some surprising help with catching him.

"The down-home narrative is folksy and fun to read aloud. . . . Smith uses a Southwestern palette in her cartoon-style paintings." SLJ

★ **One** potato, two potato; pictures by Andrea U'Ren. Farrar, Straus and Giroux 2006 un il $16
Grades: K 1 2 3   **E**
1. Magic -- Fiction 2. Potatoes -- Fiction
ISBN 978-0-374-35640-8; 0-374-35640-8

LC 2004-47217

A very poor, humble couple live so simple a life they share everything, until the husband discovers a pot with magical powers buried under the very last potato in the garden.

"U'Ren's large pen-and-gouache illustrations infuse the couple's grim situation with humor. . . . An entertaining tale." SLJ

Degen, Bruce
   ★ **Jamberry**; story and pictures by Bruce Degen. Harper & Row 1983 un il $17.99; pa $7.99; bd bk $7.99
Grades: PreK K 1 2   **E**
1. Stories in rhyme 2. Berries -- Fiction
ISBN 0-06-021416-3; 0-06-443068-5 pa; 0-694-00651-3 bd bk

LC 82-47708

"Berries and jam are roundly celebrated in a lilting rhyme that, coupled with the jaunty colored pictures, makes it . . . a good pick for sharing one on one, or fun to read aloud as a poetry introduction." Booklist

Degennaro, Sue
   The **pros** and cons of being a frog; Sue deGennaro. Simon & Schuster Books for Young Readers 2016 40 p. color illustrations (hardcover) $17.99
Grades: K 1 2 3   **E**
1. Frogs -- Fiction 2. Friendship -- Fiction 3. Individuality -- Fiction
ISBN 1481471309; 9781481471305

LC 2015039967

In this book, by Sue deGennaro, "two shy kids discover the power of friendship. . . . A boy likes to dress as a cat, but his best friend's dog objects. What will he dress as now? A giraffe? A fox? A shark? When his best friend, Camille, suggests a frog, they work together to make the frog costume...until Camille runs out of patience. So the boy makes a list of the pros and cons of being a frog." (Publisher's note)

"The visuals surrounding their endearing embrace show how unspoken layers contribute to communication and reconciliation. This celebration of differences displays great respect for readers' intelligence and yields more with each reading." Kirkus

Degman, Lori

1 zany zoo. Simon & Schuster Books for Young Readers 2010 un il $15.99

Grades: PreK K 1   E

1. Counting 2. Stories in rhyme 3. Zoos -- Fiction 4. Animals -- Fiction

ISBN 978-1-4169-8990-5; 1-4169-8990-0

LC 2009003776

When one fearless fox grabs the zookeeper's keys and opens all the cages, increasing numbers of animals behave in most unusual ways.

"Kids will enjoy hearing the catchy rhymes read multiple times. Digital cartoon images, made to appear like hand-drawn ink sketches, capture the swift movement and playful mood." SLJ

Dek, Maria

A **walk** in the forest; written and illustrated by Maria Dek. Princeton Architectural Press 2017 48 p. illustrations $17.95

Grades: PreK K 1 2   E

1. Forests and forestry -- Fiction

ISBN 9781616895693

LC 2016023509

This book, by Maria Dek, "is a stunning invitation to discover the woods as a place for both imaginative play and contemplation: collect pinecones, feathers, or stones; follow the tracks of a deer; or listen to the chirping of birds and the whisper of trees. Build a shelter and play hide-and-seek. Pretend the woods are a jungle, or shout out loud to stir up the birds!" (Publisher's note)

Del Rizzo, Suzanne

My beautiful birds; Suzanne Del Rizzo. Pajama Press 2017 32 p. color illustrations $17.95

Grades: K 1 2 3 4 5   E

1. Birds -- Fiction 2. Refugees -- Fiction 3. Art therapy -- Fiction

ISBN 1772780103; 9781772780109

In this book, by Suzanne Del Rizzo, "behind Sami, the Syrian skyline is full of smoke. The boy follows his family and all his neighbours in a long line, as they trudge through the sands and hills to escape the bombs that have destroyed their homes. But all Sami can think of is his pet pigeons—will they escape too? When they reach a refugee camp and are safe at last, everyone settles into the tent city. But . . . can't forget his birds and what his family has left behind." (Publisher's note)

Delessert, Etienne

Big and Bad; [by] Etienne Delessert. Houghton Mifflin 2008 32p il $17

Grades: 1 2 3 4   E

1. Cats -- Fiction 2. Pigs -- Fiction 3. Wolves -- Fiction 4. Animals -- Fiction

ISBN 978-0-618-88934-1; 0-618-88934-5

LC 2007019291

In this variation on the classic tale of the three little pigs, two clever cats decide to rid their locale of a vicious wolf whose hunger threatens the entire planet, and enlist the help of assorted animals to build houses for the bait—three exquisitely pink pigs.

"Surreal watercolor and colored-pencil scenes are rendered in the artist's signature earthy tones against white backgrounds.... Delessert's direct, sophisticated language and unnerving closeups of the 'marauding' felines and their predator are not for the faint of heart, but the mes-

sage—that the powerless can reverse their fortunes if they unite and use their wits—will resonate with many readers." SLJ

Moon theater. Creative Editions 2009 un il $17.95

Grades: K 1 2 3   E

1. Moon -- Fiction 2. Theater -- Fiction

ISBN 978-1-56846-208-0; 1-56846-208-5

LC 2008-53991

To prepare for the moon's nightly rising, a young stagehand performs such tasks as dressing the birds in long dark coats, training wild dogs to howl, and watering the stars.

"Delessert's distinctive, sophisticated style and a dark palette evoke a nighttime theme that turns the onset of evening into a theatrical production. . . . Inventive and dramatic, this has more child appeal than usual from Delessert; although other man-in-the-moon tales exist, they wane alongside this numinous performance." Booklist

Demarest, Chris L.

All aboard! a traveling alphabet. concept by Chris L. Demarest; illustrated by Bill Mayer. Simon & Schuster 2008 un il $17.99

Grades: PreK K 1 2   E

1. Alphabet 2. Travel -- Fiction

ISBN 978-0-689-85249-7; 0-689-85249-5

LC 2006103006

An alphabet book provides a presentation of the common structures one sees and uses while getting from place to place, using such images as an 'O' for a looped overpass and a 'B' to denote the arches of a bridge.

"Mayer is a master of airbrush and bold design, using striking perspectives and dynamic angles, often evoking a strong sense of motion in this homage to travel posters of the 1920s." Horn Book Guide

Demas, Corinne

Always in trouble; written by Corinne Demas & pictures by Noah Z. Jones. Scholastic Press 2009 un il $16.99

Grades: K 1 2 3   E

1. Dogs -- Fiction

ISBN 978-0-545-02453-2; 0-545-02453-6

LC 2007-36079

Even after attending obedience school, Emma's dog Toby misbehaves until she takes him back to become a "specially trained dog."

"The story is great for reading aloud, but the many humorous details in the cartoon-style illustrations make it fun for individual reading as well. Text, illustration, and design all work together to create a delightful story." SLJ

Pirates go to school; illustrated by John Manders. Orchard Books 2011 un il $16.99

Grades: K 1 2   E

1. School stories 2. Stories in rhyme 3. Pirates -- Fiction

ISBN 978-0-545-20629-7; 0-545-20629-4

LC 2010031394

A rhyming tale of pirates who go to school accompanied by their parrots, learn arithmetic and letters, and want to hear sea stories at storytime.

"Boldly colored scenes in watercolor, gouache, and colored pencil are paired with a nonthreatening ensemble, introducing imaginative readers to a typical school day. . . . A humorous read and a general purchase for most libraries." SLJ

Saying goodbye to Lulu; illustrated by Ard Hoyt. Little, Brown 2004 un il hardcover o.p. pa $6.99

Grades: PreK K 1 2   E
1. Dogs -- Fiction 2. Death -- Fiction 3. Bereavement -- Fiction
ISBN 0-316-70278-1; 0-316-04749-X pa

LC 2003-44690

When her dog Lulu dies, a girl grieves but then continues with her life

"Hoyt's expressive illustrations, ink-and-colored-pencil drawings washed with watercolors, reflect the tone of the text and show the child's sadness without sentimentality. . . . A sensitive, hopeful portrayal." Booklist

Valentine surprise; [by] Corinne Demas; illustrations by R. W. Alley. Walker & Co. 2008 un il $12.95
Grades: PreK K 1   E
1. Valentine's Day -- Fiction 2. Mother-daughter relationship -- Fiction
ISBN 978-0-8027-9664-6; 0-8027-9664-8

LC 2007020143

A little girl tries to create the perfect heart-shaped valentine for her mother on Valentine's Day.

"The language is simple enough for beginning readers, and the story will also work well for group sharing. The typeface changes to reflect the adjective relating to each valentine. Cartoon illustrations in pencil, watercolor, and gouache show Lily in a frenzy of activity." SLJ

Another title about Lily is:
Halloween surprise (2011)

Demers, Dominique

Today, maybe; illustrated by Gabrielle Grimard; translated by Sheila Fischman. Orca Book Publishers 2011 un il $19.95
Grades: K 1 2 3   E
1. Fairy tales
ISBN 978-1-55469-400-6; 1-55469-400-0

"A little girl lives alone in a small house in a big forest, where she waits for someone. She doesn't know for whom she waits, nor why. . . . Then a parade of strangers arrives. . . . The girl sends them off . . . explaining that she is waiting for someone else. And, at last, that someone comes. . . . [This] is a work of clever, poetic sweetness, with familiar folktale imagery giving way to tender surprise." Booklist

Demi

★ The **boy** who painted dragons; [by] Demi. Margaret K. McElderry Books 2007 un il $21.99
Grades: 1 2 3 4   E
1. Artists -- Fiction 2. Courage -- Fiction 3. Dragons -- Fiction
ISBN 978-1-4169-2469-2; 1-4169-2469-8

LC 2005033679

Ping, a painter of dragons—of which he is secretly afraid—is challenged to seek the truth, find the truth, and dare to be true

"Each page contains paintings of gilt-colored creatures and swatches of delicate Chinese silk brocade. The colors range from rich purples and vibrant reds to cool blues and muted beiges. . . . An elegantly told tale, enhanced by exquisite illustrations." SLJ

★ The **emperor's** new clothes; a tale set in China. Margaret K. McElderry Bks. 2000 un il $19.95
Grades: K 1 2 3   E
1. Authors 2. Novelists 3. Dramatists 4. Fairy tales 5. China -- Fiction 6. Children's authors 7. Short story writers
ISBN 0-689-83068-8

LC 99-24883

In this retelling of Hans Christian Andersen's tale, two rascals sell a vain Chinese emperor an invisible suit of clothes

"Demi's retelling is lucid, graceful, and true to the original. . . . Figures are delicately outlined; they are painted with flat, jewel-like colors and metallic gold and set against subtly patterned grounds that resemble silk damask. . . . A lovely and meticulously wrought rendition." Horn Book Guide

The **girl** who drew a phoenix; [by] Demi. Margaret K. McElderry Books 2008 un il $21.99
Grades: 1 2 3   E
1. China -- Fiction 2. Drawing -- Fiction 3. Phoenix (Mythical bird) -- Fiction
ISBN 978-1-4169-5347-0; 1-4169-5347-7

LC 2007015411

A young Chinese girl acquires the qualities of the miraculous phoenix—wisdom, clear sight, generosity, and right judgment—by practicing drawing the mythical bird

"Created in paint, ink, and Chinese silk brocade, swirling images of phoenixes with long, feathery tails fill the pages, including elegant horizontal foldouts." Booklist

The **greatest** power. Margaret K. McElderry Bks. 2004 un il $19.95
Grades: K 1 2 3   E
1. China -- Fiction 2. Power (Social sciences) -- Fiction
ISBN 0-689-84503-0

LC 2002-10869

Companion volume to The empty pot

Long ago, a Chinese emperor challenges the children of his kingdom to show him the greatest power in the world, and all are surprised at what is discovered

"The text and the handsomely designed, richly colored artwork, which is touched with gold leaf, are set within a circular motif that reinforces the idea of eternity. As usual, Demi ably combines striking artwork and a meaningful story, with quiet dignity and wisdom." Booklist

The **magic** pillow; written and illustrated by Demi. Margaret K. McElderry Books 2008 un il $19.99
Grades: K 1 2   E
1. China -- Fiction 2. Magic -- Fiction 3. Dreams -- Fiction
ISBN 978-1-4169-2470-8; 1-4169-2470-1

LC 2006-029213

A poor young boy in China yearns for wealth and power, until a magician gives him a magic pillow that brings dreams of what would happen if his wishes came true.

"Demi's dainty, jewel-like art is the perfect vehicle for this story, adoped from a Shen Jiji story. Rendered in traditional Chinese paints and inks and framed in her characteristic gold borders." Booklist

Dempsey, Kristy

A **dance** like starlight; one ballerina's dream. Kristy Dempsey; illustrated by Floyd Cooper. Philomel Books 2014 32 p. $16.99
Grades: K 1 2   E
1. Ballerinas -- Fiction 2. Harlem (New York, N.Y.) -- Fiction 3. Ballet dancing -- Fiction 4. Discrimination -- Fiction 5. African Americans -- Fiction 6. New York (N.Y.) -- History -- 1951- -- Fiction
ISBN 0399252843; 9780399252846

LC 2013009520

This book, by Kristy Dempsey and illustrated by Floyd Cooper, "tell[s] the story of one little ballerina who was inspired by Janet Collins, [the first African-American prima ballerina] to make her own dreams come true." (Publisher's note) "When the Ballet Master at the ballet school where Mama works cleaning and sewing costumes notices the girl mimicking dancers backstage, he takes notice" and allows her to join lessons, though she is not allowed to perform with the white students. (Booklist)

"An African American girl from Harlem dreams of becoming a prima ballerina in this beautifully written narrative, which is also a tribute to Janet Collins, who, in 1951, was the "first colored prima ballerina" to perform at the Metropolitan Opera...though the narrator is imagined, the inspirational message is real. Cooper's art incorporates his signature subtractive process and mixed media in tones of brown and pink to achieve illustrations as beautiful and transporting as the text. Pair this title with Pam Munoz Ryan and Brian Selznick's When Marian Sang (Scholastic, 2002), and use this poetic offering for units on black history or women's history." (SLJ)

Me with you; illustrated by Christopher Denise. Philomel Books 2009 un il $16.99
Grades: PreK K 1   **E**
1. Stories in rhyme 2. Bears -- Fiction 3. Grandfathers -- Fiction
ISBN 978-0-399-25017-0; 0-399-25017-4
LC 2008-11751
A little girl bear describes her relationship with her beloved grandfather.

"While the rhyming text is delightful, it is the lush, computer-generated illustrations and the two cozy, endearing characters that children will treasure. The enticing, picturesque scenes will make readers want to climb right into the pages to participate in each charming episode." Booklist

Mini racer; illustrated by Bridget Stevens-Marzo. Bloomsbury USA Children's Books 2011 un il $16.99; lib bdg $17.89
Grades: PreK K 1   **E**
1. Stories in rhyme 2. Racing -- Fiction 3. Animals -- Fiction 4. Vehicles -- Fiction
ISBN 978-1-59990-170-1; 1-59990-170-6; 978-1-59990-591-4 lib bdg; 1-59990-591-4 lib bdg
LC 2010006950
Animals in a variety of fanciful vehicles, including a snail on a skateboard and rabbits in a carrot-car, race over a difficult course with a suspenseful and surprising outcome.

"Dempsey's rapid text helps spur readers to keep the pages turning. . . Full of zooming action and fender-bender drama, it has definite appeal for youngsters." Kirkus

Surfer Chick; by Kristy Dempsey; illustrated by Henry Cole. Abrams Books for Young Readers 2012 32 p.
Grades: PreK K 1 2 3   **E**
1. Stories in rhyme 2. Picture books for children 3. Surfing -- Fiction 4. Chickens -- Fiction 5. Father-daughter relationship -- Fiction 6. Surfing -- Fiction 7. Roosters -- Fiction 8. Fathers and daughters -- Fiction
ISBN 1419701886; 9781419701887
LC 2011031798
This children's rhyming picture book tells a story with extensive use of surfing slang of a chicken father and his young daughter "who take to the beach so she can finally learn how to surf." The daughter learns perseverance and how to face new discouraging challenges. "At first Chick's mood is foul as she struggles through some [difficult] waters, but soon she is catching waves on her own board and even doing . . . just like her . . . dad!" (Publisher's note)

Dempsey, Sheena
Bye-bye baby brother! Sheena Dempsey. Candlewick Press 2013 32 p. (reinforced) $15.99

Grades: PreK K 1 2   **E**
1. Imagination -- Fiction 2. Sibling rivalry -- Fiction
ISBN 0763662410; 9780763662417
LC 2012942659
In this children's story, by Sheena Dempsey, "Ruby loves nothing more than playing, especially with Mom. But Mom is always so busy with Oliver, Ruby's baby brother . . . and Ruby is tired of waiting. . . . Maybe if Ruby puts her imagination to work, she can invent a way to make Oliver disappear to a place far, far away. Or would it be even more fun if she and Mom climbed aboard and went along for the ride?" (Publisher's note)

Denise, Anika
Bella and Stella come home; [illustrated] by Christopher Denise. Philomel Books 2010 un il $16.99
Grades: PreK K 1 2   **E**
1. Moving -- Fiction 2. Imaginary playmates -- Fiction
ISBN 978-0-399-24243-4; 0-399-24243-0
"Bella, an endearing girl with a big imagination and lots of personality, is nervous about moving to a new home. Fortunately, her trusted stuffed elephant, Stella, who looms large and lifelike in the child's mind, remains at her side through the upcoming uncertainties. . . . The sweet narrative, told from Bella's point of view, perfectly captures the little girl's psyche. The story is enhanced by luminous, almost photographic illustrations drawn in shades of pink, ivory, and gold." SLJ

Monster trucks; by Anika Denise; illustrated by Nate Wragg. Harper, an imprint of HarperCollinsPublishers 2016 32 p. color illustrations $17.99
Grades: PreK K 1 2   **E**
1. Monsters -- Fiction 2. Automobile racing -- Fiction 3. Monster trucks -- Fiction
ISBN 0062345222; 9780062345226
LC 2016299713
This book, by Anika Denise, illustrated by Nate Wragg, is "perfect for Halloween and year round! Ready, set, go! The monster truck race is on in this frightfully delightful picture book. On a spooky speedway, Monster Trucks moan! Monster Trucks grumble! Monster Trucks groan! Join Frankentruck, Zombie Truck, Ghost Truck, and more as they race to the finish line. But one of these trucks isn't quite who you think." (Publisher's note)

"Wragg's acrylic-and-digital illustrations are sufficiently dark and creepy, filled with greens, purples, and yellows, and the anthropomorphized trucks truly suit their names. Monster-truck fans won't want to miss this Halloween showdown." Kirkus

DePalma, Mary Newell
Bow-wow wiggle waggle; written and illustrated by Mary Newell DePalma. Eerdmans Books for Young Readers 2012 32 p. col. ill. (reinforced : alk. paper) $14.00
Grades: PreK K 1 2   **E**
1. Dogs -- Fiction 2. Animals -- Fiction 3. Picture books for children 4. Stories in rhyme
ISBN 0802854087; 9780802854087
LC 2011035827
This story is "told exclusively with onomatopoetic narrative and watercolor illustrations." In it, "a boy and his dog encounter other animals while playing outdoors," including a cat, a frog, a butterfly, and other animals. "Geese chase them from the pond, a snake and then rabbits appear from under the bushes, and the dog wanders off from the boy to chase a cat." (School Library Journal)

A grand old tree. Arthur A. Levine Books 2005 un il $16.99

Grades: K 1 2 3   E
1. Trees -- Fiction
ISBN 0-439-62334-0
"For many years a tree flourishes. . . . After the old tree dies, it still provides a home to animals and insects as it slowly decomposes. . . . Neither sentimental nor unfeeling, this appealing picture book offers an appreciation of the cycle of life through a story that is accessible to young children." Booklist

The **Nutcracker** doll. Arthur A. Levine Books 2007 un il $16.99
Grades: K 1 2   E
1. Ballet -- Fiction
ISBN 0-439-80242-0; 978-0-439-80242-0
     LC 2006-16466
Kepley, a young ballerina, gets to play a flower doll in a professional production of "The Nutcracker."
"Airy pen-and-wash illustrations convey moments both large and small. The text thoughtfully keeps the spotlight on the young dancer's feelings." Horn Book Guide

The **perfect** gift. Arthur A. Levine Books 2010 un il $16.99
Grades: PreK K 1   E
1. Gifts -- Fiction 2. Animals -- Fiction 3. Parrots -- Fiction 4. Grandmothers -- Fiction 5. Books and reading -- Fiction
ISBN 978-0-545-15402-4; 0-545-15402-2
     LC 2009006769
Lori the lorikeet wants to give her grandmother a present, but after dropping her beautiful red berry into the river, she and her friends must try to retrieve the berry or find another gift.
"While DePalma uses delightfully expressive, rhythmic language to tell her accessible tale, her acrylic illustrations are the standout." SLJ

Uh-oh! William B. Eerdmans 2011 un il
Grades: PreK K 1   E
1. Dinosaurs -- Fiction
ISBN 0-8028-5372-2; 978-0-8028-5372-1
     LC 2010048403
"A young dinosaur gets himself into all kinds of trouble in this clever, nearly wordless book. The little terror is jumping on the couch, which leads to knocking over his siblings' blocks and a plant. This begins a chain of events that culminates in an overflowing dishwasher washing the youngster out the window. . . . The plot is humorously appealing, if deceptively sophisticated. Despite the lack of text, it is likely to appeal most to older preschoolers and early elementary children who will understand the humor." SLJ

dePaola, Tomie, 1934-
    Andy & Sandy and the first snow; Tomie dePaola; cowritten with Jim Lewis. Simon & Schuster Books for Young Readers 2016 32 p. color illustrations (hardcover) $8.99; (ebook) $12.99
Grades: K 1 2   E
1. Snow -- Fiction 2. Friendship -- Fiction
ISBN 1481441590; 9781481441599; 9781481441605
     LC 2016014289
In this children's picture book in the Andy & Sandy series by Tomie dePaola with Jim Lewis, "when the first big snow of winter hits, Sandy wants to play outside--but Andy isn't so sure. After all, snow is very wet and very cold! But Sandy drags Andy along to make a snowman, go sledding, and make snow angels. Will Andy discover that snow can be fun--despite being wet and cold?" (Publisher's note)

The **art** lesson; written and illustrated by Tomie dePaola. Putnam 1989 un il hardcover o.p. pa $5.99

Grades: PreK K 1 2   E
1. Art -- Fiction
ISBN 0-399-21688-X; 0-698-11572-4 pa
     LC 88-27617
Having learned to be creative in drawing pictures at home, young Tommy is dismayed when he goes to school and finds the art lesson there much more regimented
This is "engrossing reading. DePaola's characteristic bright illustrations complement and enliven his tale of growing up." Horn Book

The **baby** sister; written and illustrated by Tomie dePaola. Putnam 1996 un il $16.99; pa $5.99
Grades: PreK K 1 2   E
1. Infants -- Fiction 2. Siblings -- Fiction 3. Grandmothers -- Fiction
ISBN 0-399-22908-6; 0-698-11773-5 pa
     LC 94-37218
"Tommy's mother is expecting a baby. Tommy helps get the baby's room ready and longs for a sister with a red ribbon in her hair. He's thrilled when the baby is a girl, but while his mother is away in the hospital, his Italian grandmother comes to stay, and he finds it hard to get along with her. . . . Simple lines and warm colors convey the affection in the extended family and the special closeness between Tommy and his parents." Booklist

Four friends at Christmas. Aladdin 2009 un il $12.99
Grades: PreK K 1 2   E
1. Frogs -- Fiction 2. Animals -- Fiction 3. Christmas -- Fiction 4. Friendship -- Fiction
ISBN 978-1-4169-9175-5; 1-4169-9175-1
A reissue of the edition published 2002; previously published 1977, in different form, as the chapter entitled Winter in Four Stories for Four Seasons
Mister Frog has slept through Christmas every year and is determined to celebrate this one with his three best friends. But when he takes a short nap that turns into a very long sleep, he wakes up late on Christmas Eve, and there's no one to celebrate with!
"The tale of Frog's first Christmas is charming in its simplicity. The four animal friends' unique personalities come through in dePaola's trademark cozy illustrations." Horn Book Guide

★ **Guess** who's coming to Santa's for dinner? written and illustrated by Tomie dePaola. Putnam's 2004 un il $16.99
Grades: PreK K 1 2   E
1. Christmas -- Fiction 2. Family life -- Fiction 3. Santa Claus -- Fiction
ISBN 0-399-24271-6
     LC 2003-26638
A houseful of relatives turns "Mrs. C." and Santa's Christmas into a string of surprises, from the arrival of a pet polar bear to Cousin James B.'s flaming plum pudding.
"The part comic strip-style format cleverly reflects the busy, everyone-talk-at-once hum of a big family gathering and serves up plenty of funny asides. Warm and wonderful as Christmas cake fresh out of the oven, dePaola's softly hued, rounded illustrations shine with holiday spirit." Booklist

Jack; Tomie dePaola. Nancy Paulsen Books, an imprint of Penguin Group (USA) 2014 40 p. color illustrations (hbk.) $17.99
Grades: PreK K 1   E
1. Animals -- Fiction 2. Friendship -- Fiction 3. Dwellings -- Fiction
ISBN 9780399161544; 0399161546
     LC 2013036653

"When Jack sets out to see the world and find a place of his own, he's surprised to attract a following of enthusiastic animal friends eager to join him on his quest. Jack and his entourage all have high hopes that they will find just what they are looking for as they travel on their merry way." (Publisher's note)

"DePaola dresses the journey in his most sumptuous colors, the carrot-topped hero and his ever-growing group of friends traversing a landscape of deep greens and grays and purple farmhouses to their new home, bright pink in the heart of the city. Storytime audiences will enjoy the trip as well as the sly cameo appearances by nursery-rhyme favorites such as Jack and Jill and Miss Muffet's eight-legged friend." Horn Book

★ **Jamie** O'Rourke and the pooka. Putnam 2000 un il $16.99; pa $6.99
Grades: PreK K 1 2 3   E
1. Ireland -- Fiction
ISBN 0-399-23467-5; 0-698-11974-X pa
LC 99-22469
While his wife is away, lazy Jamie O'Rourke relies on a pooka to clean up the messes that he and his friends make

"DePaola's cozy, colorful illustrations are a good match for the light-hearted, rhythmic text." Horn Book Guide

Look and be grateful; by Tomie dePaola. Holiday House 2015 32 p. color illustrations (hardcover) $16.95
Grades: PreK K 1 2   E
1. Nature 2. Children 3. Gratitude 4. Gratitude -- Fiction
ISBN 0823434435; 9780823434435
LC 2014044525
In this children's book by Tomie DePaola "a young boy awakens with the dawn, opens his eyes and looks closely at his world. He admires all that surrounds him, large and small, from the radiant sun to a tiny, but exquisite, lady bug." (Publisher's note)

"A useful book on a topic rarely attempted for this age group, this should prove popular with parents and religious-school teachers hoping to encourage this virtue in their young charges." Booklist

Meet the Barkers; Morgan and Moffat go to school. written and illustrated by Tomie dePaola. Putnam 2001 un il $13.99; pa $5.99
Grades: PreK K 1 2   E
1. School stories 2. Dogs -- Fiction 3. Twins -- Fiction
ISBN 0-399-23708-9; 0-14-250083-6 pa
LC 00-55355
Bossy Moffie (a dog) and her quiet twin brother Morgie both enjoy starting school, especially getting gold stars and making new friends

"Genuinely expressive, lovable characters, depicted in warm tones on handmade watercolor paper, make this a great read-aloud." SLJ

Other titles about the Barkers are:
Boss for a day (2001)
Hide-and-seek all week (2001)
A new Barker in the house (2002)
Trouble in the Barkers' class (2003)

★ **Nana** Upstairs & Nana Downstairs; written and illustrated by Tomie dePaola. Putnam 1998 un il $16.99; pa $6.99
Grades: PreK K 1 2   E
1. Death -- Fiction 2. Grandmothers -- Fiction
ISBN 0-399-23108-0; 0-698-11836-7 pa
LC 96-31908
A newly illustrated edition of the title first published 1973

"The illustrations are vintage dePaola, and the warm palette conveys the boy's love for his elderly relatives." Horn Book Guide

★ The **night** of Las Posadas; written and illustrated by Tomie dePaola. Putnam 1999 un il $15.99; pa $6.99
Grades: K 1 2 3   E
1. Saints 2. Christmas -- Fiction 3. Santa Fe (N.M.) -- Fiction
ISBN 0-399-23400-4; 0-698-11901-0 pa
LC 98-36405
At the annual celebration of Las Posadas in old Santa Fe, the husband and wife slated to play Mary and Joseph are delayed by car trouble, but a mysterious couple appear who seem perfect for the part

"DePaola's talent for crafting folktales is honed to near-perfection, and his pages glow with the soft sun-washed hues of the Southwest." Publ Wkly

Now one foot, now the other. G. P. Putnam's Sons 2005 un il $14.99; pa $7.99
Grades: PreK K 1 2   E
1. Stroke -- Fiction 2. Grandfathers -- Fiction
ISBN 0-399-24259-7; 0-14-240104-8 pa
A newly illustrated edition of the title first published 1981
When his grandfather suffers a stroke, Bobby teaches him to walk, just as his grandfather had once taught him.

"The illustrations have been digitally colorized in this welcome new edition." Horn Book Guide

Pascual and the kitchen angels; written and illustrated by Tomie dePaola. G.P. Putnam 2004 un il hardcover o.p. pa $5.99
Grades: PreK K 1 2   E
1. Angels -- Fiction 2. Cooking -- Fiction 3. Christian life -- Fiction
ISBN 0-399-24214-7; 0-14-240536-1 pa
LC 2003-8521
Pascual, a boy blessed by angels at his birth, receives divine help when the Franciscan monks make him their cook

"Acrylic illustrations with soft pastel backgrounds show Pascual as a little boy. . . . The winsome paintings capture his serene spirituality as he and the creatures lift their voices toward heaven. Simple, well-chosen words reflect the youngster's sincere love for God and all of His creatures." SLJ

★ The **song** of Francis; [by] Tomie dePaola. G.P. Putnam's Sons 2009 un il $16.99
Grades: PreK K 1 2   E
1. Saints 2. Birds -- Fiction 3. Saints -- Fiction 4. Writers on religion
ISBN 978-0-399-25210-5; 0-399-25210-X
LC 2008018578
Francis, the Little Poor One, is so filled with the love of God that he bursts into song, and he is joined by birds of every color.

"De Paola's tropical-hued collages convey the magic of this religious interpretation in an appealing way." SLJ

★ **Stagestruck**; written and illustrated by Tomie dePaola. G.P. Putnam's Sons 2005 un il $16.99
Grades: PreK K 1 2   E
1. School stories 2. Theater -- Fiction
ISBN 0-399-24338-0
LC 2004-9261
Although Tommy fails to get the part of Peter Rabbit in the kindergarten play, he still finds a way to be the center of attention on stage

"The gently delivered lesson at the end does not dampen the fun of watching this aspiring thespian get carried away. . . . With its warm palette, rounded shapes, and clarity of expression, dePaola's signature style makes Tommy's world an inviting place to visit." Booklist

Strega Nona does it again; written and illustrated by Tomie de-Paola. Nancy Paulsen Books 2013 40 p. $17.99

Grades: PreK K 1 2 3   E

1. Cousins -- Fiction 2. Courtship -- Fiction 3. Witches -- Fiction

ISBN 0399257810; 9780399257810

LC 2012048224

In this book by Tomie dePaola "Angelina is so beautiful that all the young men in the village are chasing her, but the one she has eyes for doesn't know she exists. At his wits' end, her father sends her to his dear cousin--Strega Nona. Strega Nona, Big Anthony and Bambolona are excited to have a houseguest, but they're in for a surprise. Angelina is a spoiled young lady used to being boss. It's up to Strega Nona to devise a plan that will make everyone happy." (Publisher's note)

★ **Strega** Nona: an old tale. Simon & Schuster 1988 un il $18.99; pa $7.99

Grades: PreK K 1 2   E

1. Italy -- Fiction 2. Witches -- Fiction

ISBN 0-671-66283-X; 0-671-66606-1 pa

LC 88-11438

A reissue of the title first published 1975 by Prentice-Hall

A Caldecott Medal honor book, 1976

"Tomie de Paola has used simple colors, simple line, and medieval costume and architecture in his spaciously composed humorous pictures." Bull Cent Child Books

Other titles about Strega Nona are:

Big Anthony and the magic ring (1979)
Big Anthony: his story (1998)
Brava, Strega Nona (2008)
Merry Christmas, Strega Nona (1986)
Strega Nona: her story (1996)
Strega Nona meets her match (1993)
Strega Nona takes a vacation (2000)
Strega Nona's gift (2011)
Strega Nona's harvest (2009)
Strega Nona's magic lessons (1982)

When Andy met Sandy; Tomie dePaola. Simon & Schuster Books for Young Readers 2016 32 p. color illustrations (hardcover) $8.99

Grades: K 1 2   E

1. Friendship -- Fiction 2. Playgrounds -- Fiction

ISBN 9781481441551

LC 2014047505

In this book, by Tomie dePaola, "Andy is small. Sandy is tall. Andy is quiet. Sandy is LOUD. But when these two seemingly opposites meet at a playground one day, it might just be the beginning of a beautiful friendship. Written in simple words and short, declarative sentences, this book is perfect for little ones just learning to read on their own." (Publisher's note)

"The scenario and supportive, insightful approach will likely resonate with many kids, especially shyer ones, highlighting how reaching out can bring rewards like fun and friendship." Booklist

Other titles in this series are:

Andy & Sandy's Anything Adventure (2016)
Andy & Sandy and the First Snow (2016)
Andy & Sandy and the Big Talent Show (2017)

Derby, Sally

No mush today; by Sally Derby; illustrated by Nicole Tadgell. Lee & Low 2008 un il $16.95

Grades: PreK   E

1. Infants -- Fiction 2. Siblings -- Fiction 3. African Americans -- Fiction

ISBN 978-1-60060-238-2; 1-60060-238-X

"Nonie, a young African-American girl, sits at the breakfast table with her parents and a wailing baby, sulking: 'Not gonna eat my mush. Not gonna eat it!' I say. 'Squishy, yucky, yellow stuff-mush is baby food.' She puts on her shiny black shoes, and, with her chin poked out, stomps off to live with Grandma (next door). . . . The spare text deftly conveys Nonie's reactions and emotions, which are clearly reflected in Tadgell's realistic, folksy watercolors sweeping across double pages." SLJ

Dernavich, Drew

It's not easy being Number Three; Drew Dernavich. Henry Holt & Co. 2016 40 p. color illustrations (hardcover) $16.99

Grades: PreK K 1 2   E

1. Numbers -- Fiction 2. Contentment -- Fiction 3. Three (The number) -- Fiction

ISBN 1627792082; 9781627792080

LC 2015004516

In this children's book by Drew Dernavich "the Number Three is having an identity crisis-there are so many other things he could do with his life; why stop at being just a number? He tries being a ship's anchor, a spatula, even a shiny bronze sculpture, and he won't listen when the other numbers beg him to come back to the lineup. But after awhile, Number Three starts to realize that what he enjoys most is the job no one else can do: being the Number Three." (Publisher's note)

"An acclaimed cartoonist in the adult world has created a solid hit for children." Kirkus

It is not easy being Number Three

Derom, Dirk

Pigeon and Pigeonette; [text by] Dirk Derom; [illustrations by] Sarah Verroken. Enchanted Lion Books 2009 un il $16.95

Grades: K 1 2   E

1. Flight -- Fiction 2. Pigeons -- Fiction 3. Friendship -- Fiction 4. Physical disabilities -- Fiction

ISBN 978-1-59270-087-5; 1-59270-087-X

LC 2009-20779

An old, blind pigeon and a young, deformed pigeon become friends as they persevere in their quest to fly.

"The bold woodcuts and limited color palette convey the setting of the woods throughout the seasons. The boot-wearing pigeons are stylized and encourage closer examination. This is a story of overcoming odds and obstacles, and, despite an occasional adult tone, it delivers a positive and important message." SLJ

Derrick, David G.

Animals don't, so I won't! by David G. Derrick. Immedium 2012 36 p. (hardcover) $15.95

Grades: PreK K 1   E

1. Conduct of life -- Fiction 2. Animal behavior -- Fiction 3. Mother-child relationship -- Fiction 4. Behavior -- Fiction 5. Imagination -- Fiction 6. Mother and child -- Fiction 7. Animals -- Habits and behavior -- Fiction

ISBN 159702029X; 9781597020299

LC 2011052797

Author David G. Derrick, Jr. presents a "knowledgeable mother turns the tables on her balky son by pointing out what animals DO. . . . Animal-loving Ben likes to pretend he's wild himself. He won't clean his room until his mother reminds him that as a beetle, he'll have to clean up elephant dung. He pretends to be a penguin that won't eat his lasagna until his mother pretends to barf up fish for him. And so forth . . . [When the story is about to end with] baby chimps rocking in their bedtime nests, there's a surprise: Dawn comes early for roosters." (Kirkus)

Desrosiers, Sylvie

Hocus Pocus. Kids Can Press 2011 un il
Grades: PreK K 1   **E**
   1. Stories without words 2. Dogs -- Fiction 3. Rabbits -- Fiction
   ISBN 1-55453-577-8; 978-1-55453-577-4

"This wordless book features a Wile E. Coyote vs. Road Runner-like
battle between a rabbit, Hocus Pocus, and a hapless canine. Mr. Magic
arrives home one day with a bag of peanuts, greens, and carrots. When
he and his pooch settle down for a nap, his rabbit decides to bolt from the
magic hat he left on the bureau. . . . The digitally rendered illustrations
are suggestive of '60s cartoon storyboards. The drawings are colorful,
and the amusing facial expressions and antics of Dog and Hocus Pocus
will appeal to children." SLJ

Detlefsen, Lisl H.

Time for cranberries; Lisl H. Detlefsen; illustrated by Jed Henry.
Roaring Brook Press 2015 32 p. color illustrations (hardback) $17.99
Grades: PreK K 1 2   **E**
   1. Farm life -- Fiction 2. Cranberries -- Fiction 3. Harvesting
-- Fiction
   ISBN 9781626720985
                                                     LC 2015003615
In this book, by Lisl H. Detlefsen, illustrated by Jed Henry, "join
Sam and his family as they harvest a classic American fruit. When the
vines hang heavy with berries that the autumn winds have turned deep
red, it's time for cranberries, and Sam is finally old enough to help with
the harvest!" (Publisher's note)

"The author, who lives on a marsh, calls this a love letter to the
cranberry-growing community, but it is also an enlightening, joyful celebration of a little-explored agricultural endeavor." Kirkus

Devlin, Jane

Hattie the bad; [pictures by] Joe Berger. Dial Books for Young
Readers 2010 un il $16.99
Grades: PreK K 1   **E**
   1. Good and evil -- Fiction
   ISBN 978-0-8037-3447-0; 0-8037-3447-6
                                                     LC 2009-09281
A little girl tries to be good but soon discovers that being bad is ever
so much more fun.

"Berger's zesty, orange-splashed illustrations hum with energy and
comic hyperbole, in perfect sync with the text. . . . This is a romp worth
reading time and again." Publ Wkly

Dewan, Ted

One true bear. Walker 2009 un il $14.99
Grades: 1 2 3   **E**
   1. Teddy bears -- Fiction
   ISBN 978-0-8027-8495-7; 0-8027-8495-X
                                                     LC 2009001807
A brave teddy bear puts his fur on the line when he goes to live with
a boy who has a long history of destroying his toys.

"Wonderfully rich and detailed illustrations clearly show an active,
rambunctious boy who is also capable of some quiet time with his bear.
The placement of the text in and around the illustrations reinforces how
well they complement one another." SLJ

Dewdney, Anna

Llama, llama red pajama; by Anna Dewdney. Viking 2005 un
il $15.99
Grades: PreK K   **E**
   1. Stories in rhyme 2. Llamas -- Fiction 3. Bedtime -- Fiction 4.

Mother-child relationship -- Fiction
   ISBN 0-670-05983-8
                                                     LC 2004-25149
At bedtime, a little llama worries after his mother puts him to bed
and goes downstairs.

"Dewdney gives a wonderfully fresh twist to a familiar nighttime
ritual with an adorable bugeyed baby llama, staccato four-line rhymes,
and page compositions that play up the drama. The simple rhymes call
out for repeating." Booklist
   Other titles about Llama are:
   Llama Llama mad at Mama (2007)
   Llama Llama misses Mama (2009)
   Llama Llama holiday drama (2010)
   Llama Llama home with Mama (2011)
   Llama Llama time to share (2012)
   Llama Llama and the bully goat (2013)
   Llama Llama Gram and Grandpa (2015)

Nobunny's perfect; by Anna Dewdney. Viking Childrens Books
2008 32p il $12.99
Grades: PreK K 1   **E**
   1. Stories in rhyme 2. Rabbits -- Fiction 3. Etiquette -- Fiction
   ISBN 978-0-670-06288-1; 0-670-06288-X
                                                     LC 2007-24008
Bunnies, who slurp their juice, forget to say "please," and bite their
friends, learn about good manners.

"Dewdney's straightforward text, written in short sentences and
rhyme, flows well. Full-color artwork effectively captures the facial expressions, conveys the bunnies' changing emotions, and recreates the
activity described in the text." SLJ

Roly Poly pangolin. Viking 2010 un il $16.99
Grades: PreK K   **E**
   1. Stories in rhyme 2. Shyness -- Fiction 3. Pangolins -- Fiction
   ISBN 978-0-670-01160-5; 0-670-01160-6

"In this short rhyming story, a small pangolin is afraid of new experiences, including meeting other animals. When he hears an unexpected
sound, he runs off in a panic, trips, and rolls into a tight ball to keep
himself safe. . . . Dewdney has created a lovable childlike character with
whom most preschoolers can easily identify. Textured full-bleed pages
interspersed with some small action drawings on white space convey
movement. Expressive closeup illustrations aptly portray Roly Poly's
feelings." SLJ

Dewey, Ariane

Splash! [by] Ariane Dewey and Jose Aruego. Harcourt 2001 un il
(Green Light readers) $10.95; pa $3.95
Grades: PreK K 1 2   **E**
   1. Bears -- Fiction 2. Fishing -- Fiction
   ISBN 0-15-216256-9; 0-15-216262-3 pa
                                                     LC 00-9723
Two clumsy bears join in fishing fun at the river

"This combines big, silly ink-and-watercolor pictures with two or
three lines of text on each page. New readers will enjoy the slapstick .
. . and the sounds of such words as splash and slip add to the fun of the
story." Booklist

Dewey, Jennifer

Once I knew a spider; [by] Jennifer Owens Dewey; illustrated by
Jean Cassels. Walker & Co. 2002 un il $16.95; lib bdg $17.85
Grades: PreK K 1 2   **E**
   1. Spiders -- Fiction
   ISBN 0-8027-8700-2; 0-8027-8701-0 lib bdg
                                                     LC 2001-26345

An expectant mother watches as an orb weaver spider spins a web, lays her eggs, and stays with them over the winter

An "eloquent meditation on the cycle of life. The muted tones of Cassels's . . . austere interiors and the detailed paintings of the spider's behavior complement the calm, contemplative tone of the journal-like text." Publ Wkly

Diakite, Penda

★ **I** lost my tooth in Africa; by Penda Diakité and Baba Wagué Diakité; illustrated by Baba Wagué Diakité. Scholastic Press 2006 un il $16.99

Grades: PreK K 1 2 3   E

1. Mali -- Fiction 2. Teeth -- Fiction 3. Chickens -- Fiction 4. Family life -- Fiction

ISBN 0-439-66226-5

LC 2004-01933

While visiting her father's family in Mali, a young girl loses a tooth, places it under a calabash, and receives a hen and a rooster from the African Tooth Fairy.

"The vivid ceramic-tile illustrations expand the text, revealing a range of animals, houses, and greenery. At the end are the words to Grandma's Good Night Song, the recipe for African Onion Sauce, and a glossary of Bambara words, all of which add to the authentic feel of the story." SLJ

DiCamillo, Kate

★ **Great** joy; illustrated by Bagram Ibatoulline. Candlewick Press 2007 un il $16.99

Grades: PreK K 1 2   E

1. Christmas -- Fiction 2. Homeless persons -- Fiction

ISBN 978-0-7636-2920-5; 0-7636-2920-0

LC 2007-29934

Just before Christmas, when Frances sees a sad-eyed organ grinder and his monkey performing near her apartment, she cannot stop thinking about them, wondering where they go at night, and wishing she could do something to help.

"The plotline is simplicity itself, and the text lacks any sentimentality or fluff, allowing the acrylic paintings . . . to enrich and expand the story." SLJ

★ **Louise**; the adventures of a chicken. written by Kate DiCamillo; pictures by Harry Bliss. Joanna Cotler Books 2008 un il $17.99; lib bdg $18.89

Grades: PreK K 1 2   E

1. Adventure fiction 2. Pirates -- Fiction 3. Chickens -- Fiction

ISBN 978-0-06-075554-6; 0-06-075554-7; 978-0-06-075555-3 lib bdg; 0-06-075555-5 lib bdg

LC 2008-20091

Longing for adventure, intrepid Louise the chicken leaves her comfortable nest and goes to sea.

"DiCamillo's brisk, comic narrative crackles with read-aloud savoriness, and her respect for Louise makes the book all the funnier. . . . Bliss creates a thrilling sense of place and puts his wide-eyed heroine front and center. An enlarged format does justice to the details in the art—and to the grand sweep of the storytelling." Publ Wkly

Dickinson, Rebecca

Over in the hollow; illustrated by Stephan Britt. Chronicle Books 2009 un il $15.99

Grades: PreK K 1 2   E

1. Counting 2. Stories in rhyme 3. Monsters -- Fiction 4. Halloween -- Fiction

ISBN 978-0-8118-5035-3; 0-8118-5035-8

LC 2009000955

A counting book that features a variety of spooky Halloween creatures, from one spider to thirteen ghosts.

"The rhyme and rhythm flow well, making this a good choice for reading aloud. The mixed-media illustrations have a retro cartoon feel and are spooky, but not scary—just like the text." SLJ

Dickson, Irene

Blocks; by Irene Dickson. Candlewick Press 2016 32 p. color illustrations $14.99

Grades: PreK   E

1. Toys -- Fiction 2. Color -- Fiction 3. Sharing -- Fiction

ISBN 0763686565; 9780763686567

In this children's picture book, by Irene Dickson, "Ruby has red blocks and Benji has blue blocks. They both build with their blocks, until Benji takes one of Ruby's red blocks and, in the tussle that follows, all the blocks CRASH to the floor. But now Benji has blue and red blocks, and Ruby has red and blue blocks, and together they build and build . . . until Guy comes with his green blocks!" (Publisher's note)

"Its entertaining approach to problem-solving and large-format illustrations make this book a terrific pick for preschool story time, hopefully followed by a building activity" Booklist

Diesen, Deborah

The **pout**-pout fish; illustrated by Dan Hanna. Farrar, Straus & Giroux 2008 un il $16

Grades: PreK K 1   E

1. Stories in rhyme 2. Fishes -- Fiction 3. Marine animals -- Fiction

ISBN 978-0-374-36096-2; 0-374-36096-0

LC 2007-60730

The pout-pout fish believes he only knows how to frown, even though many of his friends suggest ways to change his expression, until one day a fish comes along that shows him otherwise.

"The bouncy rhythm is appealing [and] . . . the cartoon illustrations of undersea life are bright and clean and the protagonist's exaggerated expressions are entertaining. The layout is attractive, and the three-panel sequences showing the fish moping around during the refrain are especially well done." SLJ

Other titles about the pout-pout fish are:

The pout-pout fish in the big-big dark (2010)

The pout-pout fish goes to school (2014)

The not very merry pout-pout fish (2015)

The pout-pout fish, far, far from home (2017)

The **pout**-pout fish goes to school; a Pout-pout fish adventure. Deborah Diesen; pictures by Dan Hanna. Farrar Straus & Giroux 2014 32 p. (hardcover) $16.99

Grades: PreK K 1   E

1. School stories 2. Fishes -- Fiction 3. Stories in rhyme 4. Schools -- Fiction 5. Self-confidence -- Fiction 6. First day of school -- Fiction

ISBN 0374360952; 9780374360955

LC 2013001317

In this children's book by Deborah Diesen, illustrated by Daniel X. Hanna, "Mr. Fish is nervously awaiting his first day of school, and he frets about not knowing how to write his name, how to draw shapes, and how to do math--until he's reassured that school is the perfect place to learn how to master all of these new skills, in Pout-Pout Fish Goes to School from Deborah Diesen and Dan Hanna." (Publisher's note)

"In Mr. Fish's latest rhymed tale, he reflects on his first experience at school, where he had to try several different classrooms before he found the right one (marked "Brand-new fish"). Hanna comes through with illustrations of the unlikely hero--just look at the pitiful/hilarious one of an upside-down school-age Mr. Fish trying to negotiate a mind-melting math problem." Horn Book

Diggs, Taye, 1971-

Chocolate me! illustrated by Shane W. Evans. Feiwel and Friends 2011 40p il $16.99

Grades: PreK K 1 2   E

1. Race relations -- Fiction 2. African Americans -- Fiction

ISBN 978-0-312-60326-7; 0-312-60326-6

The boy is teased for looking different than the other kids. His skin is darker, his hair curlier. He tells his mother he wishes he could be more like everyone else. And she helps him to see how beautiful he really, truly is.

"The cartoonlike illustrations are done in bold colors. . . . With its universal themes of wanting to fit in, self-acceptance, and self-esteem, this read-aloud offering is sure to strike a chord with many young readers/listeners, and on a variety subjects, not just race." SLJ

Dipucchio, Kelly

★ **Antoinette**; words by Kelly DiPuccio; pictures by Christian Robinson. Atheneum Books for Young Readers 2017 40 p. color illustrations (hardcover) $17.99

Grades: PreK K 1 2   E

1. Dogs -- Fiction 2. Ability -- Fiction 3. Bulldog -- Fiction 4. Poodles -- Fiction

ISBN 1481457837; 9781481457835

LC 2015024845

"Antoinette's three burly brothers each have a special talent. . . . Mrs. Bulldog reassures Antoinette that there is something extra special about her. . . . One day, while Antoinette plays in the park with her friend Gaston, Gaston's sister Ooh-La-La goes missing. Antoinette feels a tug in her heart and a twitch in her nose. She must find Ooh-La-La." (Publisher's note)

"DiPucchio and Robinson don't miss a comedic beat, creating a playful and funny tale full of warmth that deftly explores complex themes of belonging, self-worth, and purpose. Robinson's seemingly simple artwork belies his masterful ability to imbue his characters and the places they live with an authenticity and humanity that move readers beyond the surface of the page." Kirkus

Clink; manufactured by Kelly DiPucchio and [illustrated by] Matthew Myers. Balzer & Bray 2011 un il

Grades: PreK K 1   E

1. Robots -- Fiction

ISBN 006192928X; 9780061929281

While newer, fancier robots are quickly purchased, Clink, an old-fashioned robot who can only make toast and music, gathers dust and feels downhearted until a young boy enters the shop looking for something special.

"The witty text, occasionally interspersed with colorful onomatopoeic robot-centric words . . . is ideal for reading aloud. . . . Myer's paintings . . . burst with loud colors and an energy that's perfect for a store—and story—full of bopping robots and smiling clientele." Horn Book

★ **Crafty** Chloe; illustrated by Heather Ross. Atheneum Books for Young Readers 2012 il $16.99

Grades: PreK K 1 2   E

1. Gifts -- Fiction 2. Birthdays -- Fiction 3. Handicraft -- Fiction

ISBN 978-1-4424-2123-3; 1-4424-2123-1

LC 2010042811

Chloe is very good at sewing and crafts and when her best friend's birthday approaches, she creates a fabulous gift but also saves the day for a classmate who had been unkind to her.

"DiPucchio is to be commended for providing a simple and strong story with a loving solution that will surprise readers. Strong pacing and fanciful illustrations full of happy yellow highlights capture a delightfully determined and winning child." Kikus

Dragon was terrible; Kelly DiPucchio; pictures by Greg Pizzoli. Farrar, Straus & Giroux 2016 40 p. color illustrations (hardcover) $16.99

Grades: PreK K 1 2 3   E

1. Dragons -- Fiction 2. Emotions -- Fiction 3. Animal behavior -- Fiction 4. Behavior -- Fiction 5. Temper tantrums -- Fiction 6. Books and reading -- Fiction

ISBN 9780374300494

LC 2014025065

This book by Kelly DiPucchio with pictures by Greg Pizzoli tells a tale of a disobedient dragon, "we all know dragons are terrible, but this one is especially terrible. He scribbles in books. He steals candy from baby unicorns. He even burps in church. Seriously, who does that? Dragon, that's who. The king, the knights, and the villagers are desperate to take down this beast once and for all. But sometimes it's up to the unlikeliest of heroes to tame a dragon this terrible." (publisher's note)

"This is one terribly good dragon tale that will leave readers laughing and with an appreciation for the healing power of a good book." Kirkus

★ **Gaston**; words by Kelly DiPucchio; pictures by Christian Robinson. First edition Atheneum Books for Young Readers 2014 40 p. (hardcover) $16.99

Grades: PreK K 1 2   E

1. Dogs -- Fiction 2. Individuality -- Fiction 3. Bulldog -- Fiction 4. Poodles -- Fiction

ISBN 1442451025; 9781442451025

LC 2012031987

This children's book, written by Kelly DiPucchio and illustrated by Christian Robinson, "is the story of four puppies: Fi-Fi, Foo-Foo, Ooh-La-La, and Gaston. Gaston works the hardest at his lessons on how to be a proper pooch. . . . But a chance encounter with a bulldog family in the park - Rocky, Ricky, Bruno, and Antoinette - reveals there's been a mix-up, and so Gaston and Antoinette switch places. The new families look right - but they don't feel right." (Publisher's note)

"Bumptious Gaston looms over his elegant poodle sisters. At the park, they meet a family like theirs but in reverse: bulldogs Rocky, Ricky, and Bruno and their petite sister Antoinette. Were Gaston and Antoinette switched at birth? Should they trade families? DiPucchio's lively text was made to be read aloud. Robinson's elegant illustrations feature dogs with minimal yet wonderfully expressive facial details." (Horn Book)

Gilbert Goldfish wants a pet; by Kelly DiPucchio; pictures by Bob Shea. Dial Books for Young Readers 2011 un il $16.99

Grades: PreK K 1   E

1. Pets -- Fiction 2. Fishes -- Fiction 3. Animals -- Fiction 4. Goldfish -- Fiction

ISBN 978-0-8037-3394-7; 0-8037-3394-1

LC 2010028806

Gilbert has everything a goldfish could want except a pet of his own, but none of the animals who come near his fishbowl seem quite right until Fluffy, with his long tail and whiskers, appears.

"The clever text stands on its own, but Shea's bold, expressive illustrations elevate this title to a higher plane. Wavy orange endpapers establish the watery setting and bright palette. Gilbert exudes emotion. . . . Gilbert Goldfish is a perfect choice for storytime and bedtime." SLJ

Grace for president; written by Kelly DiPucchio; pictures by LeUyen Pham. Hyperion Books for Children 2008 un il $15.99

Grades: K 1 2 3   E

1. Elections -- Fiction

ISBN 0-7868-3919-8; 978-0-7868-3919-3

When Grace discovers that there has never been a female U.S. president, she decides to run for school president.

"The illustrations are colorful, and depict the various aspects of political campaigns. While the readership of this title is elementary students, Social Studies teachers at upper levels might consider this as a good way to introduce a concept that isn't always easily understood. This is a timely title, with a likeable heroine." Libr Media Connect

DiSalvo, DyAnne

A **castle** on Viola Street. HarperCollins Pubs. 2001 un il $16.95; lib bdg $16.89

Grades: K 1 2 3   E

1. Houses -- Fiction

ISBN 0-688-17690-9; 0-688-17691-7 lib bdg

LC 00-40889

A hardworking family gets their own house at last by joining a community program that restores old houses

"DiSalvo-Ryan shares an uplifting story of the importance and impact of community pride and support. . . . The colorful gouache, pen, and pencil pictures are folksy and warm." Booklist

City green; DyAnne DiSalvo-Ryan. Morrow Junior Bks. 1994 32 p. col il $17.99

Grades: K 1 2 3   E

1. Community gardens -- Fiction 2. City and town life -- Fiction

ISBN 0688127878; 068812786X; 9780688127862

LC 93027117

In this book, by DyAnne DiSalvo-Ryan, "when an abandoned house on her street is torn down, Marcy feels saddened by its loss. But then an idea strikes her: She enlists the aid of several grown-up neighbors and rents the vacant lot from the city for the price of $1. Working together with materials like leftover yellow paint and surplus wood, the residents create a community garden and plant it with a variety of flowers, fruits, and vegetables." (Kirkus Reviews)

A **dog** like Jack. Holiday House 1999 un il hardcover o.p. $17.95

Grades: K 1 2 3   E

1. Dogs -- Fiction 2. Death -- Fiction

ISBN 0-8234-1369-1; 0-8234-1680-1 pa

LC 97-41949

After a long life of chasing squirrels, licking ice cream cones, and loving his adoptive family, an old dog comes to the end of his days

"Thoughtful words and tender pictures beautifully convey the special relationship between a young boy and his dog." Booklist

Uncle Willie and the soup kitchen. Morrow Junior Bks. 1991 un il hardcover o.p. pa $5.99

Grades: K 1 2 3   E

1. Uncles -- Fiction 2. Poverty -- Fiction

ISBN 0-688-15285-6 pa

LC 90-6375

A boy spends the day with Uncle Willie in the soup kitchen where he works preparing and serving food for the hungry

"The color-pencil and wash illustrations observe . . . [a] balance between attracting the viewer with softly blended colors and avoiding the sentimentality of glamorizing an essentially sad situation. Without sacrifice of story, the total effect leaves young listeners with new considerations of society and social service, a theme too often neglected in picture books." Bull Cent Child Books

Ditchfield, Christin

Shwatsit! illustrated by Rosalind Beardshaw. Golden Books 2009 un il $15.99

Grades: PreK K 1   E

1. Siblings -- Fiction 2. Toddlers -- Fiction

ISBN 978-0-375-84181-1; 0-375-84181-4

As Baby points at everything in sight, she has just one thing to say: "Shwatsit!" But what on earth does it mean? Finally, her older brother solves the mystery.

"The well-designed, expressive illustrations expand on the rhyming text by showing the toddler throughout her day." SLJ

DiTerlizzi, Angela

★ **Some** bugs; words by Angela DiTerlizzi; bugs by Brendan Wenzel. First edition Beach Lane Books 2014 32 p. (hardcover) $17.99

Grades: PreK K   E

1. Stories in rhyme 2. Insects -- Fiction 3. Insects -- Fiction

ISBN 1442458801; 9781442458802

LC 2013006303

This picture book, written by Angela DiTerlizzi and illustrated by Brendan Wenzel, focuses on the "buggy natural world. With minimal words cajoled into loose rhyme . . . each page of this . . . book introduces a different bug's proclivity . . . while a small ladybug saunters past, serving as a cohesive visual element." (Kirkus Reviews)

"'Stinging, biting, stinking, fighting, hopping, gliding, swimming, hiding....' Jaunty rhymes describe the many activities of a variety of bugs. The scansion is unstrained, begging to be chanted aloud, and Wenzel's spirited mixed-media illustrations match the text's tone, clarify its meaning, and imbue the bugs with personality. Readers won't hesitate to follow the ending injunction to "find some bugs in your backyard!" Horn Book

Divakaruni, Chitra Banerjee, 1956-

Grandma and the great gourd; a Bengali folk tale. retold by Chitra Divakaruni; illustrated by Susy Waters. Roaring Brook Press 2013 32 p. (hardcover) $17.99

Grades: PreK K 1 2   E

1. Fairy tales 2. Picture books for children 3. Folklore -- India -- Bengal 4. Bengali (South Asian people) -- Folklore

ISBN 1596433787; 9781596433786

LC 2012001392

This children's picture book sets a retelling of "Little Red Riding Hood" in India, "where the forest hides a fox, a bear, and a tiger. Grandma talks the three predators out of eating her during her first trip ("I'll be a lot fatter on my way back from my daughter's house because she's such a good cook"), but she has to innovate on her way back. Grandma rolls herself home in a giant gourd, singing cheerfully," and continues to elude the predators. (Publishers Weekly)

Dobbins, Jan

Driving my tractor; [text by] Jan Dobbins; [illustrations by] David Sim. Barefoot Books 2009 un il $16.99

Grades: PreK K   E

1. Counting 2. Stories in rhyme 3. Color -- Fiction 4. Tractors -- Fiction 5. Domestic animals -- Fiction

ISBN 978-1-84686-358-5; 1-84686-358-9

LC 2008051065

The reader is invited to count the animal passengers riding in a tractor traveling on a bumpy road.

"This tale is ideal for storytime with its rhyming text, fun sounds, and refrain, 'Chug, chug, clank, clank, toot! It's a very busy day.' This is a jolly read-aloud, and the accompanying CD with a jazzy version adds to the charm, with both an instrumental track and SteveSongs (of PBS fame) singing the text." SLJ

Docherty, Helen

The **Snatchabook**; by Helen Docherty; illustrated by Thomas Docherty. Sourcebooks Jabberwocky 2013 32 p. (hc : alk. paper) $16.99

Grades: PreK K 1　　　　　　　　　　　　　　　　　　E

1. Bedtime 2. Books -- Fiction 3. Thieves -- Fiction 4. Stories in rhyme 5. Bedtime -- Fiction 6. Forest animals -- Fiction 7. Books and reading -- Fiction

ISBN 1402290829; 9781402290824

LC 2013012468

In this book by Helen Docherty, "it's bedtime in the woods of Burrow Down, and all the animals are ready for their bedtime story. But books are mysteriously disappearing. [Rabbit] Eliza Brown decides to stay awake and catch the book thief. It turns out to be a little creature called the Snatchabook who has no one to read him a bedtime story. All turns out well when the books are returned and the animals take turns reading bedtime stories to the Snatchabook." (Publisher's note)

Docherty, Thomas

Big scary monster. Candlewick Press 2010 un il

Grades: PreK K　　　　　　　　　　　　　　　　　　E

1. Fear -- Fiction 2. Monsters -- Fiction 3. Self-perception -- Fiction

ISBN 978-0-7636-4787-2; 0-7636-4787-X

LC 2009047397

Big Scary Monster learns some surprising things about himself when he goes down his mountain to find the creatures he has frightened away.

"The full-spread watercolor illustrations in deep colors add to the 'scary' element of the story. . . . The style of these pictures will give young readers an early lesson in perspective. Great as a read-aloud, this book will engage young monster lovers." SLJ

Little boat. Templar Books 2009 un il $15.99

Grades: PreK K　　　　　　　　　　　　　　　　　　E

1. Boats and boating -- Fiction

ISBN 978-0-7636-4428-4; 0-7636-4428-5

Setting off into the big, wide world, Little Boat runs into treacherous waters, turbulent tides, and seafaring friends. After all his nautical adventures, he finds out that he's no longer such a little boat.

"This simple story of friendship and self-esteem is beautifully illustrated in ink-and-watercolor paintings with a wistful, nostalgic flavor." Booklist

To the beach. Templar Books 2009 un il $15.99

Grades: PreK K 1　　　　　　　　　　　　　　　　　　E

1. Imagination -- Fiction 2. Voyages and travels -- Fiction

ISBN 978-0-7636-4429-1; 0-7636-4429-3

"A boy packs up all of the necessary gear for a day at the beach, like goggles, snorkel, flippers, bathing suit, and, of course, a big yellow inner tube. The only problem is: it's raining. His imagination then takes over as he secures an airplane, a sailboat, a truck, a camel, and some sand, and finally arrives at the sea. . . . This clever book is complemented by beautiful ink and watercolor drawings of the landscapes that the boy has created. The simple narrative encourages youngsters to think for themselves and never to limit the places their imaginations will take them." SLJ

Dockray, Tracy

The **lost** and found pony; illustrated by Paul Bachem. Feiwel and Friends 2011 85p il $16.99

Grades: PreK K 1 2　　　　　　　　　　　　　　　　　　E

1. Horses -- Fiction

ISBN 978-0-312-59259-2; 0-312-59259-0

"The little pony at the heart of this surprisingly affecting story is thrilled when he becomes a little girl's perfect birthday present. He loves jumping and running with her on his back—until the day he encounters a jump too high. The little girl falls, and he is declared too small for her. Her parents sell him to the circus, where he brings joy to thousands of children, but he never forgets his first owner. When the circus closes down and he is sold at auction, who should buy him but the little girl, now an adult and running a stable of her own. . . . The simple, straightforward narrative in the pony's voice, combined with Dockray's soft, expressive watercolor and ink illustrations, makes it truly heartwarming." SLJ

Dodd, Emma

Forever; Emma Dodd. Candlewick Press 2013 24 p. $12.99

Grades: PreK K　　　　　　　　　　　　　　　　　　E

1. Picture books for children 2. Parent-child relationship -- Fiction

ISBN 0763671320; 9780763671327

LC 2013943157

Author and illustrator Emma Dodd's picture book for children focuses on the message that "love between parent and child lasts a lifetime." The book features a family of polar bears and explores the relationships between parents and children and the bonds that tie them together. The book's main idea is that a parent's love lasts forever. (Publisher's note)

Foxy; Emma Dodd. Harper 2012 40 p. (trade bdg.) $14.99

Grades: PreK K 1　　　　　　　　　　　　　　　　　　E

1. Foxes -- Fiction 2. Magic -- Fiction 3. Picture books for children 4. First day of school -- Fiction

ISBN 0062014196; 9780062014191

LC 2010045555

In this children's picture book, "Emily cannot go to sleep because she is worried that she won't have all the things she needs for . . . school. Her friend, Foxy, is sure that he can help her with his magic tail, and . . . waves it at Emily's every wish--only, the tail doesn't always work as he hopes. Emily needs a pencil and Foxy's . . . tail produces a penguin. . . . However, second tries work better, and so Emily goes to sleep with all her supplies in her book pack." (School Library Journal)

I am small. Cartwheel Books 2011 il $8.99

Grades: PreK K　　　　　　　　　　　　　　　　　　E

1. Penguins -- Fiction

ISBN 978-0-545-35370-0; 0-545-35370-X

"A penguin chick ponders the big, fast, long, steep world around him and notes how small he is in comparison. But when he is with his mother, he knows he is safe. . . . The simple text and easy-to-read block printing make this a good choice for beginning readers. Dodd uses a palette of black, white, and slate blue with touches of silver to evoke the freezing Antarctic habitat." SLJ

★ **I** don't want a cool cat! Little, Brown 2010 un il $15.99

Grades: PreK K 1　　　　　　　　　　　　　　　　　　E

1. Cats -- Fiction

ISBN 978-0-316-03674-0; 0-316-03674-9

A little girl "knows what she does not want: 'A stuffy cat. A huffy, over-fluffy cat.' . . . The true-to-life hilarity of the text commands attention, especially when mixed with such smart art. With a combination of paint and collage, the images have a three-dimensional feel as they sit on their smooth, candy-colored backgrounds. . . . Combine the art with the pithy text, and you're got a book that's perfect to read aloud to groups." Booklist

I love bugs. Holiday House 2010 un il $16.95

Grades: PreK K 1 2　　　　　　　　　　　　　　　　　　E

1. Insects -- Fiction 2. Spiders -- Fiction

ISBN 978-0-8234-2280-7; 0-8234-2280-1

LC 2009-32814

"The text juggles sounds and rhymes skillfully. . . . Varied in composition, palette, and scale, the illustrations have great vitality. . . . Easy to see from a distance, this would be an excellent choice for group sharing." Booklist

Meow said the cow. Arthur A. Levine Books 2011 un il $16.99

Grades: PreK K 1   E
 1. Stories in rhyme 2. Magic -- Fiction 3. Domestic animals -- Fiction
 ISBN 978-0-545-31861-7; 0-545-31861-0

            LC 2010034247

A noisy rooster causes a disgruntled cat to cast a magic spell that creates confusion among the other farm animals.

"The rollicking text is paired with large, colorful digitally produced art that has the kinetic animals fairly popping off the spreads." SLJ

No matter what; [by] Emma Dodd. Dutton Children's Books 2008 un il $10.99

Grades: PreK   E
 1. Stories in rhyme 2. Elephants -- Fiction 3. Parent-child relationship -- Fiction
 ISBN 978-0-525-47932-1; 0-525-47932-5

            LC 2007019207

In rhyming text, a baby elephant is assured of being loved unconditionally.

"Each phrase is supported by a stylized African landscape in muted colors, but with bright touches. . . . The young elephant is simply rendered, too, and quite charming. The art, and the padded cover with metallic accents, is appealing, and the comforting text is perfect for toddlers." SLJ

Dodds, Dayle Ann

Minnie's Diner; a multiplying menu. illustrated by John Manders. Candlewick Press 2004 un il hardcover o.p. pa $6.99

Grades: K 1 2 3   E
 1. Stories in rhyme 2. Restaurants -- Fiction 3. Multiplication -- Fiction
 ISBN 0-7636-1736-9; 0-7636-3313-5 pa

            LC 2002-34756

Rhyming tale of five boys and their father who forget about their chores on the farm to enjoy Minnie's good cooking, each requesting double what the previous one ordered

"Told in jaunty rhymes with varied type sizes for emphasis, this funny story is illustrated with colorful cartoons done in gouache. Children will appreciate the humor and groan with delight when they recognize the math pattern." SLJ

The **prince** won't go to bed; pictures by Kyrsten Brooker. Farrar, Straus & Giroux 2007 un il $16

Grades: PreK K 1 2   E
 1. Stories in rhyme 2. Bedtime -- Fiction 3. Princes -- Fiction
 ISBN 0-374-36108-8; 978-0-374-36108-2

            LC 2005051234

When the young prince refuses to go to bed, assorted members of the royal household offer their ideas on exactly what he needs, but it is his sister, Princess Kate, who learns the truth.

Dodd's "rhymed text abounds with the kind of repetitions in structure and language that make children want to join in. . . . The fonts grow larger and Brooker's hilarious, cock-eyed collages ever more frantic with each repetition." Publ Wkly

Teacher's pets; illustrated by Marylin Hafner. Candlewick Press 2006 un il $15.99

Grades: PreK K 1 2   E
 1. School stories 2. Pets -- Fiction
 ISBN 0-7636-2252-4

A teacher invites her students to bring their pets in each Monday for sharing day, but by the end of the year, she has a classroom full of "forgotten" animals.

"This gentle and humorous story has charming watercolor illustrations that reinforce the emotions of the children, the animals, and, of course, the warmhearted teacher." SLJ

Doerrfeld, Cori

Maggie and Wendel; imagine everything. Cori Doerrfeld. Simon & Schuster Books for Young Readers 2016 48 p. color illustrations (hardcover) $17.99

Grades: PreK K   E
 1. Play -- Fiction 2. Elephants -- Fiction 3. Imagination -- Fiction 4. Brothers and sisters -- Fiction
 ISBN 9781481439749

            LC 2014045472

In this book, by Cori Doerrfeld, "brother and sister elephants come together for an afternoon of epic adventures as they let their big imaginations take them to the wildest of places! When it comes to playtime, Maggie and Wendel's imaginations are limitless. Whether the elephant siblings are pretending to rescue a pal from a burning building, buying a pet dragon at the pet store, or going on a wild jungle safari, no adventure is too far-fetched." (Publisher's note)

" Most of the story lies in the illustrations, and the text is accessible enough for early readers. Maggie and Wendel's imaginative games, not to mention their sometimes-rocky sibling dynamic, will resonate with lots of little ones." Booklist

Penny loves pink. Little, Brown 2011 un il $15.99

Grades: PreK K 1   E
 1. Color -- Fiction 2. Infants -- Fiction 3. Siblings -- Fiction
 ISBN 978-0-316-05458-4; 0-316-05458-5

            LC 2010008632

A little girl who loves pink more than anything must learn to accept the color blue when her baby brother arrives.

"The illustrations are bright and lively. . . . A sweet, satisfying story." SLJ

Dokas, Dara

Muriel's red sweater; illustrations by Bernadette Pons. Dutton Children's Books 2009 un il $16.99

Grades: PreK K 1   E
 1. Gifts -- Fiction 2. Animals -- Fiction 3. Birthdays -- Fiction 4. Clothing and dress -- Fiction
 ISBN 978-0-525-47962-8; 0-525-47962-7

            LC 2008020605

"Unbeknownst to duck Muriel, her sweater is unraveling as she delivers invitations to her birthday party. Luckily, her friends have already been working on the perfect present: a new sweater. The cheery illustrations do a good deal of storytelling; readers can spot hints about the new sweater and chuckle at the uses Muriel's friends find for yarn from the old one." Horn Book Guide

Dolan, Elys

Weasels; Elys Dolan. Candlewick Press 2014 32 p. $17.99

Grades: K 1 2 3 4   E
 1. Weasels -- Fiction 2. Machinery -- Fiction 3. Conspiracies -- Fiction 4. Humorous stories
 ISBN 0763671002; 9780763671006

            LC 2013943084

In this children's picture book, by Elys Dolan, "ultracaffeinated weasels plotting world domination face a setback when their room-sized, Rube Goldberg-ian machine breaks down. They scurry to troubleshoot, many of them inappropriately insistent on deploying tools like a blow torch, saws and a large electric drill. Luckily, the Health and Safety officer prevails, and the gang repairs to the laboratory to tinker." (Kirkus Reviews)

Dolan fills her pages with visual and verbal jokes about coffee obsessions, tech geeks, bureaucracy, and unsafe workplace practices. PW

Dolphin, Ray

Wall; Tom Clohosy Cole. Candlewick Press 2014 32 p. color illustrations $16.99

Grades: K 1 2 3 4   E

1. Family life -- Fiction 2. Berlin Wall (1961-1989) -- Fiction 3. Cold War -- Fiction

ISBN 0763675601; 9780763675608

LC 2013957276

This children's story, written and illustrated by Tom Clohosy Cole, is being released "on the 25th anniversary of the fall of the Berlin Wall. A young boy and his mother and sister were separated from their father when the Berlin Wall was built between East and West Germany. This story shows the family's struggle as they try to cross the wall so they can be together again." (Publisher's note)

"Although the jacket calls it a story about the Berlin Wall, the book proper does not provide any such identification (probably wise, given its ahistorical conclusion). Digital illustrations reinforce the story's fabular nature, with tenderly cartooned characters set against ominous silhouettes and the monumental wall." Horn Book

Dominguez, Angela

Let's go, Hugo! story and pictures by Angela Dominguez. Dial Books for Young Readers 2013 40 p. col. ill. (hardcover) $16.99

Grades: PreK K   E

1. Fear -- Fiction 2. Birds -- Fiction 3. Artists -- Fiction

ISBN 9780803738645

LC 2012003561

Maria had a little llama/ María tenía una llamita; Angela Dominguez. Henry Holt and Company 2013 28 p. (hardcover) $16.99

Grades: PreK K 1 2   E

1. Nursery rhymes 2. Stories in rhyme 3. Llamas as pets -- Fiction 4. Spanish language materials -- Bilingual

ISBN 0805093338; 9780805093339

LC 2012013530

Pura Belpre Illustrator Honor Book (2014)

This book, by Angela Dominguez, is a "bilingual presentation of a classic children's rhyme, set in rural Peru. Dominguez presents a straightforward version of the familiar rhyme, adding just enough new elements to transform it into a story. The text flows rhythmically in both the English and the Spanish, which are placed together on the page with the English in bold and positioned above the Spanish." (Kirkus Reviews)

María tenía una llama pequeña

Santiago stays; by Angela Dominguez. Abrams Books 2013 32 p. bcol. ill. $12.95

Grades: PreK K   E

1. Dogs 2. Siblings 3. Dogs -- Fiction

ISBN 141970821X; 9781419708213

LC 2012041376

In this children's book, written and illustrated by Angela Dominguez, "Santiago [the French bulldog] stays . . . , despite the growing disappointment of the little boy who is trying to engage him. After several futile attempts, the boy's frustration bubbles over into a yell, which

wakes the baby, and the reader realizes whom Santiago has been resolutely guarding all along." (Publisher's note)

"The illustrations, in pencil, marker, ink, tissue paper, and digital color, capture the boy's persistence and the bulldog's dug-in resistance; the warm palette is perfect for this affection-filled, simple, and satisfying family story." - Horn book

Domney, Alexis

Splish, splat! written by Alexis Domney; illustrated by Alice Crawford. Second Story Press 2011 un il $15.95

Grades: PreK K 1   E

1. Deaf -- Fiction 2. Painting -- Fiction 3. Sign language -- Fiction

ISBN 978-1-897187-88-3; 1-897187-88-2

"Colin is having nightmares in his yolk-colored room. As he sleeps, eggs over easy zoom around like alien spaceships. It is time for a new paint job, and his mother opts for professionals to do the work. She gets the message relay number of Deaf painters and, via an interpreter, makes an appointment. Whereas this could simply be a didactic picture book on Deaf and hearing etiquette, the humor imbued makes it a delightful story about the joy of communication. The unique collage illustrations add warmth and render the two women painters in realistic signing stances." SLJ

Don, Lari

Little Red Riding Hood; Lari Don; illustrated by Celia Chauffrey. Barefoot Books 2012 32 p. $16.99

Grades: K 1 2 3   E

1. Fairy tales 2. Wolves -- Fiction 3. Children and strangers -- Fiction 4. Folklore

ISBN 1846867665; 9781846867668

LC 2012009603

In this book by Lari Don, "Little Red Riding Hood loves to visit her Granny's cottage in the forest. Her mother warns her to go straight to Granny's, but when she meets a handsome grey wolf, she doesn't see the harm in stopping for a chat." (Publisher's note) "Although the two leading ladies are gobbled up, legs last, the hunter comes to the rescue. He is rewarded with cakes, Granny learns to lock her door, and Red 'never turned round to talk to strangers again.'" (School Library Journal)

Donaldson, Julia

The **fish** who cried wolf; [by] Julia Donaldson & Axel Scheffler. Arthur A. Levine Books 2008 un il $15.99

Grades: PreK K 1 2   E

1. Stories in rhyme 2. Fishes -- Fiction 3. Storytelling -- Fiction

ISBN 978-0-439-92825-0; 0-439-92825-7

LC 2007-12308

Tiddler the fish is always telling tall tales about why he is late for school, but when he is actually caught in a net and taken far from home, it is his stories that help him find his way back.

"Donaldson's rhyming text is crisp and clean, leaving plenty of metaphorical room for Scheffler's expansively imagined art." Publ Wkly

The **giant** jumperee; Julia Donaldson; illustrated by Helen Oxenbury. Dial Books for Young Readers 2017 32 p. color illustrations (hardcover) $17.99

Grades: PreK K   E

1. Fear -- Fiction 2. Animals -- Fiction 3. Frogs -- Fiction

ISBN 9780735227972

LC 2016016406

In this book, by Julia Donaldson, illustrated by Helen Oxenbury, "Rabbit arrives home one day to hear a loud voice coming from inside his burrow: I'm the Giant Jumperee and I'm scary as can be!" shouts the stranger. Rabbit's friends Cat, Bear, and Elephant come to help, but they're no match for the mysterious, booming voice. But who is the Giant Jumperee?" (Publisher's note)

★ The **gruffalo**; Julia Donaldson; pictures by Axel Scheffler. Dial Books for Young Readers 1999 32 p. $6.99

Grades: PreK K 1 2 3   E

1. Mice -- Fiction 2. Animals -- Fiction 3. Stories in rhyme

ISBN 0803723865; 9780803723863; 9789992142226; 9992142227

LC 98033893

"A mouse is taking a stroll through the deep, dark wood when along comes a hungry fox, then an owl, and then a snake. The mouse is good enough to eat but smart enough to know this, so he invents . . . the gruffalo! As Mouse explains, the gruffalo is a creature with terrible claws, and terrible tusks in its terrible jaws, and knobbly knees and turned-out toes, and a poisonous wart at the end of its nose. But Mouse has no worry to show. After all, there's no such thing as a gruffalo. . . ." (Publisher's Note)

The **Highway** Rat; a tale of stolen snacks. by Julia Donaldson and illustrated by Axel Scheffler. 1st American ed. Arthur A. Levine Books 2013 32 p. (reinforced) $16.99

Grades: PreK K 1 2   E

1. Theft -- Fiction 2. Picture books for children 3. Rats -- Fiction 4. Stories in rhyme 5. Animals -- Fiction 6. Robbers and outlaws -- Fiction

ISBN 0545477581; 9780545477581

LC 2012009889

This children's picture book is the tale "of a swashbuckling rat with mask and cape who stops hapless travelers and takes their food at sword point. . . . A brave duck in a red kerchief lures the thief to a distant cave, supposedly full of biscuits and buns. While he follows the echoes of his own voice deeper and deeper into the dark, the duck jumps on Rat's horse and takes the stolen food back to her hungry friends." (School Library Journal)

One Ted falls out of bed; illustrated by Anna Currey. Henry Holt 2006 un il $15.95

Grades: PreK K 1 2   E

1. Counting 2. Stories in rhyme 3. Toys -- Fiction 4. Teddy bears -- Fiction

ISBN 978-0-8050-7787-2; 0-8050-7787-1

LC 2005-12173

"In this rhythmic counting book, a sleeping child's teddy bear falls out of bed and can't climb back up. Three mice invite him to play, racing four cars, counting five stars, sipping tea with six dolls, and so on. . . . The toys in the airy illustrations that sweep across the pages are packed with personality. Perfect for storytimes or one-on-one lapsits, this book can be counted on for a gentle, cozy read." SLJ

Stick Man; illustrated by Axel Scheffler. Arthur A. Levine Books 2009 un il $16.99

Grades: PreK K 1   E

1. Stories in rhyme 2. Christmas -- Fiction 3. Santa Claus -- Fiction

ISBN 978-0-545-15761-2; 0-545-15761-7

LC 2008-48323

First published 2008 in the United Kingdom

Stick Man ends up far away from his family tree when he is fetched by a dog, thrown by a child, used as a snowman's arm, and even put on a fire, but finally Santa Claus steps in to make sure that Stick Man and his family have a joyous Christmas.

"Scheffler's engaging illustrations, Donaldson's irresistible rhyming text and repeated refrains make this a winning read-aloud that will stick around long after the holiday season." Kirkus

Superworm; by Julia Donaldson; illustrated by Axel Scheffler. First American Edition Arthur A. Levine Books 2014 32 p. (hardcover : alk. paper) $16.99

Grades: K 1 2 3   E

1. Stories in rhyme 2. Worms -- Fiction 3. Superheroes -- Fiction 4. Heroes -- Fiction 5. Insects -- Fiction 6. Lizards -- Fiction 7. Wizards -- Fiction

ISBN 0545591767; 9780545591768

LC 2013001546

This book, by Julia Donaldson, features a worm superhero who "rescues toads and beetles from peril and young bees from boredom. The insects clap and cheer for their very own invertebrate champion, inciting the ire of the Wizard Lizard and his henchman crow, who kidnap Superworm for their own sinister devices. The toads, slugs, earwigs, and other bugs band together to rescue the hero." (School Library Journal)

Tyrannosaurus Drip; [by] Julia Donaldson; [illustrations by] David Roberts. Feiwel and Friends 2008 un il $16.95

Grades: K 1 2   E

1. Stories in rhyme 2. Dinosaurs -- Fiction

ISBN 978-0-312-37747-2; 0-312-37747-9

LC 2007-40511

A duckbilled dinosaur, accidentally raised by fierce tyrannosauruses who would eat duckbills if only they could reach them, tries to be like his "family" but finally gives up, runs away, and finds a real home with others of his kind.

"The dinosaurs are rendered in an Art Deco-influenced style, and the lines roll off the tongue like the rhymes of Dr. Seuss. Children will enjoy the repetitive lilt, and adults will appreciate how naturally it reads. Expressive characters enhance the humor, and the limited palette helps emphasize just how different the creatures' worlds are. An enjoyable group read-aloud." SLJ

What the ladybug heard; illustrated by Lydia Monks. Henry Holt and Company 2010 un il $16.99

Grades: PreK K 1   E

1. Stories in rhyme 2. Sounds -- Fiction 3. Thieves -- Fiction 4. Ladybugs -- Fiction 5. Domestic animals -- Fiction

ISBN 978-0-8050-9028-4; 0-8050-9028-2

LC 2009005266

First published 2009 in the United Kingdom

Although much quieter than the farm animals that moo, cluck, or oink, a gentle ladybug is instrumental in foiling a plan to steal the farm's prize-winning cow.

"Filled with drama, lively action, and a large supporting cast of characters, this is a mini play more than a fully fleshed story. The appealing and brightly colored collage illustrations, rhyming text, and assorted animal sounds make it a natural for individual or group read-alouds." Booklist

Donofrio, Beverly

Where's Mommy? Beverly Donofrio; illustrations by Barbara McClintock. Schwartz & Wade Books 2013 32 p. color illustrations (trade) $17.99

Grades: PreK K 1   E

1. Mice -- Fiction 2. Mothers -- Fiction 3. Friendship -- Fiction 4. Human-animal relationship -- Fiction

ISBN 0375844236; 9780375844232; 9780375944567

LC 2011050242

In this companion to the children's book "Mary and the Mouse, the Mouse and Mary," by Beverly Donofrio, "Maria (Mary's daughter) and Mouse Mouse (Mouse's daughter) are looking for their mothers. They're not in their bedrooms, their car and cart are still in the driveway, and they are not in the gazebo or under the mushroom! Where could they be?" (Publisher's note)

"Donofrio and McClintock offer a companion to 2007's Mary and the Mouse, the Mouse and Mary that's every bit as charming as its predecessor. In the human-scale rooms of her midcentury modern home, Maria spends time with her family; in the subfloor, Mouse Mouse lives with her own. Maria and Mouse Mouse keep their friendship hush-hush, for they fear the adults might acquire a cat. . . . McClintock pictures the cozy, twinned environments in low-lit panels, and her eggshell-white backgrounds and uncluttered pages allow a pleasurable comparison of human and nonhuman habitats (whereas Maria stands on a stool at the kitchen counter, Mouse Mouse's chairs are jam jars and pill bottles around a plastic berry container). Fans of the original book will revel in the resolution (and the abundance of visual hints), yet the story is no less delightful for newcomers." Pub Wkly

Donovan, Jane Monroe

Small, medium & large; [written and illustrated by] Jane Monroe Donovan. Sleeping Bear Press 2010 un il $15.95
Grades: PreK K 1   E
1. Stories without words 2. Gifts -- Fiction 3. Christmas -- Fiction
ISBN 978-1-58536-447-3; 1-58536-447-9

"A girl who has just moved to a new house mails a letter to Santa, and on Christmas Day her wishes appear under the tree in three appropriately sized boxes–a cat, a dog, and a miniature horse. The new friends play in the snow, make Christmas cookies, and finally snuggle in bed together after a long, wonderful day. This wordless story [is] told in full and half-page illustrations. . . . It's a sure bet that this supersweet yet cozy story will have kids adding 'a cat, a dog, and a horse–REAL ones' to their Christmas lists." SLJ

Doodler, Todd H.

What color is Bear's underwear? Blue Apple Books 2011 il bd bk $9.99
Grades: PreK K   E
1. Color 2. Stories in rhyme 3. Board books for children 4. Bears -- Fiction 5. Underwear -- Fiction
ISBN 978-1-60905-096-2; 1-60905-096-7
     LC 2011018924
Bear wears different colored underwear for every day of the week.
"It's about as an irreverently silly guide to colors as one could want." Publ Wkly

Doremus, Gaetan

Bear despair; Gaetan Doremus. Enchanted Lion Books 2012 32 p. (alk. paper) $14.95
Grades: PreK K 1 2   E
1. Bears -- Fiction 2. Theft -- Fiction 3. Teddy bears -- Fiction
ISBN 1592701256; 9781592701254
     LC 2012931209
This book by Gaetan Doreumus, part of the Stories Without Words series, was designated a 2012 "New York Times" Best Illustrated Children's Book. "[B]ear is napping when his teddy bear is taken by a fox who leads him on a merry chase. . . . Since neither animal is particularly good at conflict resolution, bear swallows the fox whole. As he searches, bear is taunted by a series of creatures that play keep-away with his toy. Furious, bear swallows each one." (Children's Literature)

Empty Fridge; by Gaetan Doremus. Trafalgar Square Books 2013 40 p. ill. (hardcover) $19.99

Grades: PreK K 1   E
1. Food -- Fiction 2. Sharing -- Fiction 3. Neighbors -- Fiction
ISBN 0987109936; 9780987109934
In this picture book by Gaetan Doremus,"the many and varied occupants of an apartment house in a French city have been . . . so busy . . . that . . .no one has remembered to buy any food! In a . . . chain of visits, each . . . character makes a trip up to the next floor to explore how they can pool the paltry ingredients they have scavenged to make a meal that everyone can share. . . . A cozy quiche-baking party ensues." (Kirkus Reviews)

Dormer, Frank W.

★ **Firefighter** duckies! words and pictures by Frank W. Dormer. Atheneum 2017 40 p. color illustrations (hardcover) $17.99
Grades: PreK K 1   E
1. Ducks -- Fiction 2. Rescue work -- Fiction 3. Fire fighters -- Fiction 4. Humorous fiction -- Fiction 5. Animals -- Fiction
ISBN 9781481460903
     LC 2015051070
This picture book, by Frank W. Dormer, is "full of wacky charm and perfect for little duckies of all dispositions. The Firefighter Duckies are brave and strong. They rescue: Gorillas in chef hats! Whales in trees! Dinosaurs on bicycles! But when the emergencies requiring their attention become a little overwhelming, the Firefighter Duckies realize that they don't have to be brave and strong to be helpful and kind." (Publisher's note)

The **obstinate** pen; Frank W. Dormer. Henry Holt 2012 32 p. (hardcover : alk. paper) $16.99
Grades: K 1 2 3   E
1. Writing -- Fiction 2. Picture books for children 3. Bad behavior -- Fiction 4. Pens -- Fiction 5. Obstinacy -- Fiction
ISBN 0805092951; 9780805092950
     LC 2010031794
In this children's story, by Frank W. Dormer, a pen writes what it wants instead of what the writer decides. The pen "speaks the truth to a series of self-involved townsfolk" after it is delivered to Uncle Flood and then passes from person to person through the town, correcting and insulting all who try to use it. (Kirkus)

Socksquatch; words and pictures by Frank W. Dormer. Henry Holt 2010 un il $14.99
Grades: PreK K 1   E
1. Monsters -- Fiction
ISBN 978-0-8050-8952-3; 0-8050-8952-7
     LC 2009-27413
Socksquatch tries to find a sock to warm his cold foot.
"The palette contrasts warm-toned monsters with soothing backgrounds of aqua or plain white, and Dormer uses scrawled ink motion and texture lines to great effect to add movement and dimension to the artwork. While youngsters will definitely enjoy listening to this one in a crowd, don't be surprised if they borrow it afterwards to reenact with a friend." Bull Cent Child Books

Dorros, Alex

Numero uno; by Alex Dorros and Arthur Dorros; illustrated by Susan Guevara. Abrams Books for Young Readers 2007 un il $16.95
Grades: K 1 2 3   E
1. Mexico -- Fiction 2. Spanish language -- Vocabulary
ISBN 0-8109-5764-7
Tired of listening to strong Hercules and smart Socrates constantly argue over who is more important to their village, the townspeople devise a test to settle the question once and for all.

"The battle between brains and brawn is entertainingly pitched here. . . . The Spanish dialogue is simple . . . and punctuates the story-hour-ready text with verve. Guevara's tropically accented pastoral oil paintings provide contrast to the often slapstick goings-on but also do their share of storytelling." Horn Book

Dorros, Arthur

★ **Abuela**; illustrated by Elisa Kleven. Dutton Children's Bks. 1991 un il $16.99; pa $7.99
Grades: PreK K 1 2   E
1. Flight -- Fiction 2. Imagination -- Fiction 3. Grandmothers -- Fiction 4. New York (N.Y.) -- Fiction 5. Hispanic Americans -- Fiction
ISBN 0-525-44750-4; 0-14-056225-7 pa
LC 90-21459

While riding on a bus with her grandmother, a little girl named Rosalba imagines that they are carried up into the sky and fly over the sights of New York City

"Each illustration is a masterpiece of color, line, and form that will mesmerize youngsters. . . . The smooth text, interpresed with Spanish words and phrases, provides ample context clues, so the glossary, while helpful, is not absolutely necessary." Booklist

Another title about Rosalba and her grandmother is:
Isla (1995)

Julio's magic; collages by Ann Grifalconi. HarperCollins 2005 32p il $15.99; lib bdg $16.89
Grades: PreK K 1 2   E
1. Mexico -- Fiction 2. Wood carving -- Fiction
ISBN 0-06-029004-8; 0-06-029005-6 lib bdg
LC 2004-6616

A young artist in a Mexican village discovers the power of friendship when he helps his mentor win a prestigious wood-carving contest

"Grifalconi's photorealistic collages capture the texture, color, and feel of village life. This book will be excellent for art and social studies classrooms. . . . It is also a compassionate intergenerational story." SLJ

Mama and me; pictures by Rudy Gutierrez. Rayo 2011 un il $16.99; lib bdg $17.89
Grades: PreK K 1 2   E
1. Mother's Day -- Fiction 2. Spanish language -- Vocabulary 3. Mother-daughter relationship -- Fiction
ISBN 0-06-058160-3; 0-06-058161-1 lib bdg; 978-0-06-058160-2; 978-0-06-058161-9 lib bdg

A girl and her mother spend a day together gardening, making cookies, and visiting a neighbor. Includes Spanish words interspersed in the text.

"The first person point of view and smooth integration of informal Spanish terms and phrases provide a comfortable intimacy with the characters, and the vibrant magic realism of the full-page spreads includes elements of street art." Booklist

Papa and me; by Arthur Dorros; illustrated by Rudy Gutierrez. HarperCollinsPublishers 2008 un il $16.99; lib bdg $17.89
Grades: PreK K   E
1. Hispanic Americans -- Fiction 2. Spanish language -- Vocabulary 3. Father-son relationship -- Fiction
ISBN 978-0-06-058156-5; 978-0-06-058157-2 lib bdg
LC 2007011868

A Pura Belpre Illustrator Award honor book, 2009

"From the time they wake up in the morning, a Latino boy and his father have fun. . . . The simple words, in both Spanish and English, and the bright, exuberant unframed double-page pictures celebrate the loving connection between parent and child. . . . The big, swirling circles in the artwork embrace the characters within the widening arcs of sky and waves." Booklist

Dotlich, Rebecca Kai

One day, the end. short, very short, shorter-than-ever stories. Rebecca Kai Dotlich, Illustrations by Fred Koehler. Boyds Mills Press 2015 32 p. chiefly color illustrations $16.95
Grades: PreK K 1   E
1. Picture books for children
ISBN 9781620914519
LC 2014958544

Boston Globe Horn Book Honor Book: Picture Books (2016)

This book, by Rebecca Kai Dotlich, with Illustrations by Fred Koehler, presents a "series of cleverly crafted tales involving a precocious girl doing ordinary things in a creative and energetic manner. Nine 'shorter-than-ever' stories of a dozen words or less become considerably more sophisticated when readers delve into Koehler's dynamic cartoon illustrations. While brief, the text plays an integral role in each story." (Publisher's note)

"Ultimately, this entertaining collection shows that storytelling can be easily accomplished and can consist of more than just words." Booklist

Doughty, Rebecca

Oh no! Time to go! a book of goodbyes. Schwartz & Wade 2009 un il $15.99; lib bdg $18.99
Grades: PreK K 1 2   E
1. Stories in rhyme 2. Family life -- Fiction
ISBN 978-0-375-84981-7; 0-375-84981-5; 978-0-375-95696-6 lib bdg; 0-375-95696-4 lib bdg
LC 2008022462

A young boy presents the different ways his family members and others say goodbye, then describes the worst goodbye he ever experienced.

"Opaque, brightly colored illustrations outlined in black ink are rendered in a spare, stylized manner. . . . This satisfying tale conveys an important truth about how life's goodbyes often lead to new hellos." SLJ

Dowdy, Linda Cress

All kinds of kisses; [illustrated] by Priscilla Lamont. Cartwheel Books 2010 un il bd bk $8.99
Grades: PreK   E
1. Stories in rhyme 2. Board books for children 3. Kissing -- Fiction
ISBN 978-0-545-14599-2 bd bk; 0-545-14599-6 bd bk
LC 2010010215

Simple, rhyming text explores different kinds of kisses.

"The padded cover, Lamont's dusky palette, and Dowdy's simple rhymes convey a cozy, loving world, making this a ready choice for easing into bedtime." Publ Wkly

Downing, Julie

No hugs till Saturday; [by] Julie Downing. Clarion Books 2008 31p il lib bdg $16
Grades: PreK K 1   E
1. Week -- Fiction 2. Dragons -- Fiction 3. Hugging -- Fiction 4. Mother-son relationship -- Fiction
ISBN 978-0-618-91078-6 lib bdg; 0-618-91078-6 lib bdg
LC 2007010030

When Felix the dragon declares that there will be no hugs, snuggles, or super squeezes for a whole week, both he and his mama have a hard time.

"The soft-edged paintings show a lovable green dragon and humorously depict his antics. . . . Featuring a believably childlike protagonist, a cozy parent-child relationship, and a satisfying resolution, it is a delight-fully warmhearted choice for most collections." SLJ

Doyen, Denise

★ **Once** upon a twice; illustrated by Barry Moser. Random House Children's Books 2009 un il $16.99; lib bdg $19.99

Grades: PreK K 1   E

1. Nonsense verses 2. Stories in rhyme 3. Mice -- Fiction 4. Conduct of life -- Fiction

ISBN 978-0-375-85612-9; 0-375-85612-9; 978-0-375-95612-6 lib bdg; 0-375-95612-3 lib bdg

LC 2008011125

"Doyen's utterly sound and alive story is paired with the perfect il-lustrator, whose deft touch provides all the eeriness that it begs for. . . . With gloriously nonsensical words and phrases . . . . the author manages to get the point across that there is much to fear in the night.. . . .This wonderful book is a marvelous read-aloud that children will want to hear again and again." SLJ

Doyle, Eugenie

Sleep tight, farm; A Farm Prepares for Winter. by Eugenie Doyle; illustrated by Becca Stadtlander. Chronicle Books Llc 2015 36 p. color illustrations (ebook) $14.29; (ebook) $14.29; (alk. paper) $16.99

Grades: PreK K 1 2   E

1. Winter -- Fiction 2. Farm life -- Fiction 3. Farm families -- Fiction 4. Winter -- Fiction 5. Family life -- Fiction 6. Rural families -- Fiction

ISBN 9781452153377; 9781452153353; 9781452129013

LC 2013043751

This book, by Eugenie Doyle, illustrated by Becca Stadtlander, is an "exploration of how a family gets a farm ready for the snow of winter. . . . [It] paints a fascinating picture of what winter means to the farm year and to the family that shares its seasons, from spring's new growth, sum-mer's heat, and fall's bounty to winter's well-earned rest. All year long the farm has worked to shelter us, feed us, keep us warm, and now it's time to sleep." (Publisher's note)

"Front and back endpapers show a stand of trees, first in their autumn reds and golds and then bare and covered in snow; but each is bookended with a page of field flowers in glorious summer colors, reminding read-ers that winter doesn't last forever." Horn Book

Doyle, Malachy

Get happy; illustrated by Caroline Uff. Walker & Co. 2011 un il $15.99

Grades: PreK K   E

1. Stories in rhyme 2. Happiness -- Fiction

ISBN 978-0-8027-2271-3; 0-8027-2271-7

LC 2010031000

Simple, rhyming text urges the reader to be happy by making such choices as teasing less and tickling more, or groaning less and giggling more.

"With a short, powerful text and endearing, recognizable children, this book is an excellent discussion starter for the youngest children." Booklist

Dragonwagon, Crescent

All the awake animals are almost asleep; written by Crescent Drag-onwagon; illustrated by David McPhail. Little, Brown 2012 40 p. $16.99

Grades: PreK   E

1. Sleep -- Fiction 2. Animals -- Fiction 3. Picture books for children 4. Alphabet 5. Stories in rhyme 6. Bedtime -- Fiction

ISBN 0316070459; 9780316070454

LC 2011042734

Author Crescent Dragonwagon "introduces a familiar bedtime battle of wills between a child who resists slumber and a mother trying to lull him to sleep. This introductory section adopts a rhythmic, rhyming text . . . [and e]nsuing pages go through the alphabet using alliterative lan-guage to describe animals going to sleep, from" antelopes to zebras. (Kirkus)

Drummond, Allan

Liberty! Farrar, Straus & Giroux 2002 un il pa $6.95

Grades: K 1 2 3   E

1. Statue of Liberty (New York, N.Y.) -- Fiction

ISBN 0-374-34385-3; 0-374-44397-1 pa

LC 2001-18777

"Drummond tells the story of October 28, 1886, the day the Statue of Liberty was first unveiled in New York harbor. A boy, whose name is now lost, is on the ground, ready to signal Bartholdi, the statue's sculp-tor, to release the tricolor veil that covers the Lady of Liberty's face. . . . This is an unusual offering. Drummond takes a kernel of history . . . and turns it into both a thoughtful lesson and a visual pageant. Scenes of the construction of France's gift to the U.S. are shown in finely wrought, energetic, pen-and-wash images that swirl through the text." Booklist

Drummond, Ree

Charlie the ranch dog; illustrations by Diane deGroat. HarperCol-lins 2011 un il $16.99

Grades: PreK K 1 2   E

1. Dogs -- Fiction 2. Ranch life -- Fiction

ISBN 978-0-06-199655-9; 0-06-199655-6

LC 2010018435

While Charlie, a sleepy basset hound, tells about the busy life of a ranch dog, his best friend Suzie, a Jack Russell terrier, is getting the work done.

"Charlie seems unaware of the impish chipmunk that deGroat, with characteristic humor, sneaks into each spread. Her paintings drolly por-tray the discrepancy between reality and Charlie's perceptions of his day. . . . Kids should find it irresistible." Publ Wkly

Dubosarsky, Ursula

The **terrible** plop; pictures by Andrew Joyner. Farrar, Straus and Giroux 2009 un il $15.95

Grades: PreK K   E

1. Stories in rhyme 2. Fear -- Fiction 3. Animals -- Fiction 4. Courage -- Fiction 5. Rabbits -- Fiction

ISBN 978-0-374-37428-0; 0-374-37428-7

LC 2008043323

When a mysterious sound sends the whole forest running away in fear, only the littlest rabbit is courageous enough to discover what really happened.

"Basic, fun rhymes and repetitive, excitable text lend themselves to reading aloud, and the recurring appearance of the word PLOP provides an explosive entree for children to chime in while soaking up Joyner's bouyant mixed-media artwork. In addition, kids will appreciate the easy absurdity of the situation, enjoy the role-reversal in the end, and maybe even come away knowing that most things aren't so scary once you look a little closer." Booklist

Dubuc, Marianne

Animal masquerade; Marianne Dubuc. Kids Can Press 2012 120 p.

Grades: PreK K 1   E

1. Animals -- Fiction 2. Costume -- Fiction 3. Picture books for children

ISBN 1554537827; 9781554537822

In this children's picture book, "[i]t's time for the animal masquerade, and lion begins considering his costume. He settles on . . . an elephant. But what will the elephant be? A parrot. And which costume will the parrot choose? A turn of the page reveals all. Simple text, translated from French, accompanies . . . colored-pencil illustrations of an assortment of animals in and out of costume on white backgrounds. . . . For the most part, each spread features an animal in disguise." (Kirkus)

The **bus** ride; Marianne Dubuc. Kids Can Press 2015 40 p. (hardcover) $15.95

Grades: PreK K 1 2 3   E
1. Animals -- Fiction 2. Automobile travel -- Fiction
ISBN 9781771382090; 1771382090

In this children's story, written and illustrated by Marianne Dubuc, translated by Yvonne Ghione, "while the bus is taking her down the streets, through a forest and into a pitch-black tunnel, the little girl encounters an assortment of animal characters who enliven her journey, including a goat who offers her a flower from a bouquet, a wolf child with whom she happily shares her cookies and a fox who attempts to pickpocket a bear." (Publisher's note)

In front of my house; translated from the French by Yvette Ghione. Kids Can Press 2010 un il $18.95

Grades: PreK K 1 2   E
1. Imagination -- Fiction
ISBN 978-1-55453-641-2; 1-55453-641-3

"In an excursion that starts and ends with a little house on a hill, a child's imagination soars, moving from a rosebush and a bird outside to discover things 'behind the window' and 'in my room,' including a book of fairy tales in which a dragon, a frog prince, and the Big Bad Wolf dwell, as well as the Abominable Snowman, a werewolf, a ghost, and a vampire. Finally, the adventure leads into outer space. . . . While this small picture book is thick, the childlike text is brief. . . . Its size is perfect for one-on-one interaction, and youngsters will enjoy the twists and turns of the trip. . . . The illustrations, rendered in pencil crayon, are appropriately simple. . . . This little gem has everything." SLJ

★ The **lion** and the bird; Marianne Dubuc; translated from the French by Claudia Z. Bedrick. First American edition. Enchanted Lion Books 2014 64 p. (hardback) $17.95

Grades: PreK K 1   E
1. Lion -- Fiction 2. Birds -- Fiction 3. Seasons -- Fiction 4. Friendship -- Fiction
ISBN 1592701515; 9781592701513

LC 2014000317

In this children's book by Marianne Dubuc, "One autumn day, a lion finds a wounded bird in his garden. With the departure of the bird's flock, the lion decides that it's up to him to care for the bird. He does and the two become fast friends. Nevertheless, the bird departs with his flock the following autumn. What will become of Lion and what will become of their friendship?"

"The intimacy of friendship, as well as the bittersweet sweep of time, is exquisitely rendered in this spare story of a kindly lion who rescues an injured bird flying south for winter . . . The charming depiction of Lion's home will delight sharp-eyed children, and the gentle pace of the story, which takes its time as surely as the plants in Lion's garden take their time to grow, is reassuring. A much needed antidote to the speed of the world, this picture book by French Canadian Dubuc is one to savor." Booklist

Mr. Postmouse's Rounds; by Marianne Dubuc. Kids Can Press 2015 24 p. color illustrations $17.95

Grades: PreK K 1 2   E
1. Mice -- Fiction 2. Postal service -- Fiction 3. Animals -- Fiction
ISBN 1771385723; 9781771385725

In this children's book, by Marianne Dubuc, "Mr. Postmouse has loaded up his wagon and is ready to deliver the mail. From the lofty heights of the Birds' tree houses to the inky depths of Mrs. Octopus's ship, the intrepid letter carrier lets nothing stand in the way of his deliveries. Each spread features . . . detailed interiors of creatures' homes." (Publisher's note)

"Friendly and efficient Mr. Postmouse starts his Monday mail rounds, toting a letter sack and pulling a wagon of packages. But it's not the spare text that tells the real story. Fans of Richard Scarry will enjoy the adorable, detailed mixed-media illustrations that provide inside views of each creature's dwelling, reveal fun traits, and even set up visual jokes." Booklist

Another title about Mr. Postmouse is:
Mr. Postmouse Takes a Trip (2017)

Duffy, Carol Ann

The **gift**; [text] by Carol Ann Duffy and [illustrations] by Rob Ryan. Barefoot Books 2010 un il $16.99

Grades: 2 3 4   E
1. Wishes -- Fiction
ISBN 978-1-84686-355-4; 1-84686-355-4

After meeting a magical old woman in a clearing in the woods and trading her daisy chain for the granting of a wish, a little girl grows into a young woman and the clearing begins to fill with the loveliest flowers, the most fragrant herbs, and the most perfect stones.

"This original tale is told in simple language and has a clarity and beauty all its own. Ryan's silhouette illustrations are created using hand-cut paper that is painted and photographed, a technique that makes effective use of color and shadows." Booklist

Duke, Kate

Ready for pumpkins; Kate Duke. Knopf Books for Young Readers 2012 40 p. col. ill.

Grades: K 1 2   E
1. Gardens -- Fiction 2. Pumpkin -- Fiction 3. Gardening -- Fiction 4. Guinea pigs -- Fiction
ISBN 0375870687; 9780307974549; 9780375870682; 9780375970689

LC 2011044615

In this children's book by Kate Duke "Hercules, a classroom guinea pig, has a revelation when he watches the first graders grow plants from seeds. He wants to grow things, too! And during summer vacation (spent with the teacher's dad), he gets his chance. With the help of a friendly rabbit, Herky prepares the soil, carefully plants pumpkin seeds, and waits. . . . [I]n October, the teacher's dad arrives with a big pumpkin for her class--that just mysteriously grew in his yard!" (Publisher's note)

Dumon Tak, Bibi

★ **Mikis** and the donkey; by Bibi Dumon Tak; illustrated by Philip Hopman; translated by Laura Watkinson. Eerdmans Books for Young Readers 2014 93 p. illustrations $13

Grades: 2 3 4   E
1. Greece -- Fiction 2. Donkeys -- Fiction 3. Grandfathers -- Fiction 4. Corfu Island (Greece) -- Fiction 5. Family life -- Greece -- Fiction
ISBN 9780802854308

LC 2013044666

Mildred L. Batchelder Award (2015)

In this book by Bibi Dumon Tak, "one day, Mikis's grandfather has a surprise for him: a new donkey waiting! Mikis falls in love with the creature, but his grandparents tell him that the donkey is a working animal, not a pet. However, they still let Mikis choose her name--Tsaki-- and allow the two of them to spend their Sundays together. Mikis and Tsaki soon become fast friends, and together the two have some grand adventures." (Publisher's note)

A "quiet story filled with endearing characters, believable situations, and a sense of the importance of caring for other creatures. Short chapters and frequent pencil drawings make the story accessible for beginning chapter-book readers." Booklist

Dumont, Jean-François, 1959-
The **chickens** build a wall; written and illustrated by Jean Francois Dumont. Eerdmans Books for Young Readers 2013 33 p. ill. (reinforced) $16.00
Grades: PreK K 1   E
 1. Walls -- Fiction 2. Chickens -- Fiction 3. Toleration -- Fiction 4. Domestic animals -- Fiction
 ISBN 9780802854223

LC 2012038991

"The chickens at the farm are building a wall, and no one is quite sure why. But they know one thing: the hedgehog that wandered in must be trouble. So all winter they build and build, until they have a wall that towers over the barn. When spring comes, though, they find that everything hasn't gone quite according to plan." (Publisher's note)

Dumont "crafts a clever barnyard commentary on protectionism, xenophobia, and overreaction. . . . Adult readers won't have to look hard to spot parallels to contemporary discourse on immigration and other hot-button topics, and the target audience will easily see the chickens' folly thanks to a drily funny ending and the comedy that runs throughout Dumont's prose and sly characterizations." Pub Wkly

Dunbar, Polly
 ★ **Penguin**. Candlewick Press 2007 un il $15.99
Grades: PreK K   E
 1. Toys -- Fiction 2. Penguins -- Fiction
 ISBN 0-7636-3404-2

"A pajama-clad toddler opens his present to find a toy penguin. Much to Ben's chagrin, the bird doesn't say anything, no matter how hard the boy tries to engage it. . . . It isn't until a blue lion chomps on the child that Penguin jumps into action and rescues his new pal. . . . The attractive, spare illustrations in mixed media are focused and centered on a white background." SLJ

Where's Tumpty? Candlewick Press 2009 un il $12.99
Grades: PreK   E
 1. Animals -- Fiction 2. Elephants -- Fiction 3. Friendship -- Fiction
 ISBN 978-0-7636-4273-0; 0-7636-4273-8

"After several unsuccessful attempts at hiding, Tumpty the elephant is able to trick his friends into thinking he has disappeared. . . . There are many amusing situations involving Tilly, a little girl, and her animal friends. . . . The background consists of a variety of muted tones, which contrast with the brighter mixed-media drawings. The illustrations are whimsical and detailed. . . . Young children and beginning readers are sure to gravitate to this delightful story that celebrates the joy of friendship." SLJ

Other titles about Tilly and her friends are:
Doodle bites (2009)
Good night, Tiptoe (2009)
Happy Hector (2008)
Hello, Tilly (2008)
Pretty Pru (2009)

Dunklee, Annika
 ★ **My** name is Elizabeth! written by Annika Dunklee; illustrated by Matthew Forsythe. Kids Can Press 2011 un il $14.95
Grades: PreK K 1 2   E
 1. Personal names -- Fiction
 ISBN 978-1-55453-560-6; 1-55453-560-3

Elizabeth is not not amused when people insist on using nicknames like "Lizzy" and "Beth." She bears her frustration in silence until an otherwise ordinary autumn day, when she discovers her power to change things once and for all.

"Forsythe's restrained color palette and expressive line contribute to his brilliant rendering of Elizabeth's character, and his whimsical inclusion of a pet duck (unmentioned in the text) adds another layer of idiosyncratic delight." Kirkus

Dunrea, Olivier
 Bear Noel. Farrar, Straus & Giroux 2000 un il hardcover o.p. pa $5.95
Grades: PreK K 1 2   E
 1. Bears -- Fiction 2. Animals -- Fiction 3. Christmas -- Fiction
 ISBN 0-374-39990-5; 0-374-40001-6 pa

LC 99-27600

The animals of the North Woods react with excitement as they hear Bear Noel coming to bring them Christmas

"Dunrea beautifully creates the effect of falling snow throughout the pictures and uses a limited palette of browns, grays, and greens with flashes of fox red to lend a celebratory feel." Booklist

A **Christmas** tree for Pyn. Philomel Books 2011 un il $16.99
Grades: PreK K   E
 1. Trees -- Fiction 2. Christmas stories 3. Christmas -- Fiction 4. Father-daughter relationship -- Fiction
 ISBN 978-0-399-24506-0; 0-399-24506-5

LC 2010041653

Little Pyn finally persuades her gruff father to find the perfect Christmas tree in the snowy forest and, after bringing it home, decorates it with him.

Dun-rea's "talent for capturing a mood of majestic stillness in snowy landscapes shines yet again, as does his skill at creating cozy, rustic details—bushy fur coats and boots, tree-stump beds, a stone hearth—that suggest a mythical time. Pyn and Papa's warming relationship is one to celebrate any time of year." Publ Wkly

 Gideon; Olivier Dunrea. Houghton Mifflin Books for Children 2012 1 v. (unpaged) col. ill.
Grades: K 1 2 3   E
 1. Geese -- Fiction 2. Children's stories 3. Picture books for children 4. Domestic animals -- Fiction 5. Animals -- Fiction
 ISBN 9780618436613

LC 2010044359

This children's book tells the story of "Gideon, 'a small, ruddy gosling who likes to play,' [who] joins Gossie and the other goslings on Dunrea's farm. Always on the move, Gideon chases a piglet, plays 'tag-the-mole,' leaps over a frog, and listens to bees buzzing in their hive— always with his octopus toy in tow. No naps for Gideon, no matter what mother goose says, but a day of barnyard shenanigans has a way of tiring out a gosling." (Publishers Weekly)

 Gideon and Otto; Olivier Dunrea. Houghton Mifflin Harcourt 2012 1 v. (unpaged) col. ill.
Grades: K 1 2 3   E
 1. Children's stories 2. Friendship -- Fiction 3. Picture books for children 4. Domestic animals -- Fiction 5. Toys -- Fiction 6.

Geese -- Fiction 7. Rabbits -- Fiction
ISBN 9780618436620

LC 2010045844

This children's book tells the story of "Gideon [who] is a 'small ruddy gosling who likes to play. All day.' . . . After climbing to the top of a haystack and snuggling down in the straw, sleepiness wins out. In Gideon and Otto, children meet the gosling's favorite friend. When the toy octopus goes missing, a search of the leaf pile and pond ensues. Otto's triumphant return is on the back of a turtle." (SLJ)

★ **Gossie**. Houghton Mifflin 2002 un il $9.95
Grades: PreK K 1   E
1. Geese -- Fiction
ISBN 0-618-17674-8

LC 2002-214

Gossie is a gosling who likes to wear bright red boots every day, no matter what she is doing, and so she is heartbroken the day the boots are missing and she can't find them anywhere. "Ages two to four." (Bull Cent Child Books)

The succinct text uses "repetition and predictability with great skill and will therefore work equally well with early independent readers and preschoolers. . . . The illustrations, focused against restful white space, are spare and expressive, models of composition and clarity." Horn Book

Other titles about Gossie and her friends are:
BooBoo (2004)
Gossie & Gertie (2002)
Merry Christmas, Ollie (2008)
Ollie (2003)
Ollie the stomper (2003)
Ollie's Easter eggs (2010)
Ollie's Halloween (2010)
Peedie (2004)

★ **It's** snowing! Farrar, Straus & Giroux 2002 un il hardcover o.p. pa $6.99
Grades: PreK K 1   E
1. Snow -- Fiction 2. Infants -- Fiction 3. Mothers -- Fiction
ISBN 0-374-39992-1; 0-312-60216-2 pa

LC 00-42172

A mother shares the magic of a snowy night with her baby
"The gentle, rhythmical rocking of the text conveys a reassuring message that's beautifully supported by Dunrea's spare, snow-dappled gouache illustrations." Horn Book

Jasper & Joop; Olivier Dunrea. Houghton Mifflin Books for Children 2013 32 p. col. ill. (reinforced) $9.99
Grades: PreK K 1   E
1. Geese -- Fiction 2. Friendship -- Fiction
ISBN 9780547867625

LC 2012018964

"Jasper likes to be neat. Each morning he tidies his nest and puts on his cap and bow tie. Joop likes to be messy! Each morning he rumples his nest and musses his feathers. Despite their differences, Jasper and Joop are two very good friends--birds of a feather! But what will happen when one friend gets into trouble with some busy bees?" (Publisher's note)

Little Cub; Olivier Dunrea. Philomel 2012 32 p. (hardback) $16.99
Grades: PreK K 1 2   E
1. Adoption -- Fiction 2. Bears -- Fiction 3. Picture books for children 4. Bears -- Fiction 5. Loneliness -- Fiction 6. Foster

home care -- Fiction
ISBN 039924235X; 9780399242359

LC 2012015126

In this book, "Little Cub is sad and lonely. He has no one to take care of him, teach him how to catch fish, help him get honey, and be with him during the long dark nights. Old Bear is sad and lonely. He has no one to teach, share his food with, and keep him company during the long dark nights. One day he finds Little Cub . . . . Old Bear names him, takes him home, feeds him, puts him to bed, tells him a story, and the rest is history." (School Library Journal)

Merry Christmas, Ollie! [by] Olivier Dunrea. Houghton Mifflin 2008 un il $12.95
Grades: PreK K 1   E
1. Geese -- Fiction 2. Christmas -- Fiction 3. Santa Claus -- Fiction
ISBN 978-0-618-53242-1; 0-618-53242-0

LC 2004025126

On Christmas Eve, Ollie and the other goslings anxiously await the arrival of Father Christmas Goose.

"First-time readers and those already familiar with Dunrea's goslings will be delighted by this simple story. . . . Remaining true to his uncomplicated watercolor style, Dunrea maintains an element of charm to Ollie's waiting, depicting his impatience as sweet and subdued." SLJ

★ **Old** Bear and his cub. Philomel Books 2010 un il $16.99
Grades: PreK K 1 2   E
1. Bears -- Fiction 2. Parent-child relationship -- Fiction
ISBN 978-0-399-24507-7; 0-399-24507-3

LC 2008-00663

Although they love each other, Old Bear and his little Cub have a tug of war over which one knows best in a variety of situations.

"The adult-child give-and-take in this charming bedtime story will be quite familiar and is bound to bring smiles to both ages. Simplicity at its best." Kirkus

Ollie's Halloween. Houghton Mifflin Books for Children 2010 un il $12.99
Grades: PreK K 1   E
1. Stories in rhyme 2. Geese -- Fiction 3. Halloween -- Fiction
ISBN 978-0-618-53241-4; 0-618-53241-2

LC 2009-49699

Dressed in their costumes, Ollie and his siblings go out on Halloween night and have a scary but fun adventure.

"As with the previous titles starring this gosling crew, Dunrea's ink and watercolor images beget an understandable and cozy world, this time with just a hint of spookiness and autumnal gloom." Publ Wkly

Dunston, Marc

The **magic** of giving; illustrated by Katie Cantrell; foreword by Wally Amos. Pelican 2010 32p il $16.99
Grades: K 1 2   E
1. School stories 2. Contests -- Fiction 3. Magic tricks -- Fiction
ISBN 978-1-58980-805-8; 1-58980-805-3

LC 2010014648

Little Marc is determined to win his school's talent contest and use the prize money to buy Thanksgiving dinner for his neighbors, but first he must pick a talent and master it.

"The positive, uplifting message encourages children to read and develop their talents not to just help themselves, but to help others. Cantrell's illustrations are bright and sunny and feature a multigenerational, multiethnic cast of characters. The foreward is written by literacy advocate Wally Amos. Literacy awareness is stressed below the storyline on each page with the placement of vocabulary development tools." Libr Media Connect

Durand, Hallie

Mitchell goes bowling; Hallie Durand; illustrated by Tony Fucil. Candlewick Press 2013 40 p. col. ill. $15.99

Grades: PreK K 1   E

1. Bowling -- Fiction 2. Father-son relationship -- Fiction 3. Bowling alleys -- Fiction 4. Picture books for children

ISBN 0763660493; 9780763660499

LC 2012947730

"One Saturday, when Mitchell almost knocks down his dad, his dad catches him and puts him in the car. And when they step into the bowling alley, Mitchell feels right at home. Pizza! Giant crashing noises! Special shoes!" (Publisher's note)

"The story is played for laughs, but, in the process, readers will enjoy the father/son relationship and subtlely learning about being a sport. Mitchell's frustration and anger issues are addressed and his dad's patience pays off." SLJ

Mitchell's license; illustrated by Tony Fucile. Candlewick Press 2011 un il $15.99

Grades: PreK K 1   E

1. Bedtime -- Fiction 2. Father-son relationship -- Fiction

ISBN 978-0-7636-4496-3; 0-7636-4496-X

LC 2010039181

Mitchell never wants to go to bed until, at the age of three years, nine months, and five days he gets his license so that he can drive there—at least until he and the car have a disagreement about what fuel goes in the tank.

"Durmand's text will appeal to the active and car obsessed, but Fucile's masterful illustrations, full of expressive characters, great physical comedy and wonderful warmth, will engage readers young and old. . . , An incredibly entertaining ride." Kirkus

Durango, Julia

Cha-cha chimps; illustrated by Eleanor Taylor. Simon & Schuster Books for Young Readers 2006 un il $15.95

Grades: PreK K 1   E

1. Stories in rhyme 2. Dance -- Fiction 3. Chimpanzees -- Fiction

ISBN 0-689-86456-6

In this counting book, "10 little chimps sneak out of their tree house to go dancing at Mambo Jambas, where a pig band plays music all night long. . . . The rhymes roll easily off the tongue, making the text fun to read aloud. . . . Done in watercolor and pencil, the illustrations are bright and lively." SLJ

Durant, Alan

I love you, Little Monkey; by Alan Durant; illustrated by Katharine McEwen. Simon & Schuster Books for Young Readers 2007 un il $15.99

Grades: PreK K   E

1. Love -- Fiction 2. Monkeys -- Fiction

ISBN 978-1-4169-2481-4; 1-4169-2481-7

First published 2006 in the United Kingdom

"Little Monkey gets into mischief when Big Monkey is too busy to play with him. . . . Little Monkey fears that he is no longer loved when he is sent to bed for punishment, but is reassured that Big Monkey loves him always, even when naughty. . . . The familiar message is always on target for small children. . . . Lively cartoon drawings in watercolor and pencil depict the mischievous animals at play in a colorful jungle setting." SLJ

Duval, Kathy

The **Three** Bears' Halloween; by Kathy Duval; illustrated by Paul Meisel. Holiday House 2007 un il $16.95

Grades: PreK K 1   E

1. Bears -- Fiction 2. Halloween -- Fiction

ISBN 978-0-8234-2032-2; 0-8234-2032-9

LC 2006012120

Is it a witch or a blonde little girl hiding in the bushes of the spooky house when the three bears go trick or treating?

This is a "delightfully presented story, rich with folk-art warmth and whimsical humor." SLJ

Duvoisin, Roger

★ **Petunia**; fiftieth anniversary edition; Knopf 2000 un il $15.95; pa $6.99

Grades: PreK K 1   E

1. Geese -- Fiction 2. Books and reading -- Fiction

ISBN 0-394-90865-7; 0-394-90865-1 lib bdg; 0-440-41754-6 pa

A reissue of the title first published 1950

Petunia, the goose, learns that possessing knowledge involves more than just carrying a book around under her wing

"Duvoisin's energetic drawings perfectly capture Petunia's growing arrogance." Horn Book Guide

DwellStudio (Firm)

Good morning, toucan; by DwellStudio. Blue Apple Books 2011 un il bd bk $8.99

Grades: PreK   E

1. Board books for children 2. Morning -- Fiction 3. Rain forest animals -- Fiction

ISBN 978-1-60905-085-6; 1-60905-085-1

LC 2010046649

Simple text invites the reader to look under lift-up flaps to find various creatures as they awaken in the rain forest.

This is "engaging. . . . [This] visually appealing [book features a] very basic [layout] and graphic-style illustrations that resemble Colorforms, which allow youngsters to focus on the guessing game in [the] book." SLJ

Goodnight, owl; by DwellStudio. Blue Apple Books 2011 un il bd bk $8.99

Grades: PreK   E

1. Board books for children 2. Night -- Fiction 3. Bedtime -- Fiction 4. Forest animals -- Fiction

ISBN 978-1-60905-083-2; 1-60905-083-5

LC 2010046819

Simple text invites the reader to look under lift-up flaps to find various creatures as they go to sleep at night in the forest.

This is "engaging. . . . [This] visually appealing [book features a] very basic [layout] and graphic-style illustrations that resemble Colorforms, which allow youngsters to focus on the guessing game in [the] book." SLJ

Dyckman, Ame

Boy and Bot; by Ame Dyckman; illustrated by Dan Yaccarino. Alfred A. Knopf 2012 32 p.

Grades: PreK K   E

1. Boys -- Fiction 2. Robots -- Fiction 3. Friendship -- Fiction 4. Picture books for children

ISBN 9780375867569; 9780375987243

LC 2011016682

This picture book tells the story of a friendship between a boy and a robot "that prevails over confusion." During the course of author Ame Dyckman's plot, Boy mistakes Bot for another child and later Bot thinks that Boy is also a robot, until an inventor steps in and explains the situation. Illustrator Dan Yaccarino's "stylized gouache paintings" include "final, nearly wordless spreads depicting the two wide-awake friends' happy, ongoing companionship." (Kirkus)

Horrible bear! by Ame Dyckman; illustrated by Zachariah OHora. Little, Brown & Co. 2016 40 p. color illustrations (hardcover : alk. paper) $16.99
Grades: PreK K 1 2   E
  1. Bears -- Fiction 2. Apologizing -- Fiction 3. Friendship -- Fiction
  ISBN 9780316282833
LC 2015015518

In this children's story, by Ame Dyckman, illustrated by Zachariah O'Hora, "Bear didn't mean to break a little girl's kite, but she's upset anyway--upset enough to shout "HORRIBLE BEAR!" Bear . . . doesn't think he's horrible! Then Bear gets a truly Horrible Bear idea. . . . As Bear prepares to live up to his formerly undeserved reputation, the girl makes a mistake of her own, and realizes that maybe . . . Bear isn't as horrible as she had thought." (Publisher's note)

"Dyckman and Ohora portray genuine forgiveness without a hint of moralizing." Pub Wkly

★ **Tea** party rules; by Ame Dyckman; illustrated by K.G. Campbell. Viking, published by Penguin Group 2013 40 p. (hardcover) $16.99
Grades: PreK K 1   E
  1. Bears -- Fiction 2. Afternoon teas -- Fiction 3. Tea -- Fiction 4. Parties -- Fiction 5. Etiquette -- Fiction 6. Animals -- Infancy -- Fiction
  ISBN 0670785016; 9780670785018
LC 2012046989

Ezra Jack Keats New Illustrator Honor Award (2014)
Ezra Jack Keats New Writer Award (2014)

In this children's picture book, by Ame Dyckman, illustrated by K. G. Campbell, "Cub discovers a backyard tea party--with cookies! He is just about to dig in when the hostess of the tea party shows up. And she has several strong opinions on how Tea Party must be played. Cub tries to follow her rules . . . but just how much can one bear take, even for cookies?" (Publisher's note)

"Strong storytelling, pacing, emotive illustrations that match the deceptive plot and an exuberant sense of fun make this little gem a winner." Kirkus

Wolfie the bunny; Ame Dyckman; illustrated by Zachariah OHora. Little Brown & Co 2015 40 p. illustrations (hardcover) $17
Grades: PreK K 1 2   E
  1. Adoption -- Fiction 2. Wolves -- Fiction 3. Rabbits -- Fiction 4. Animal babies -- Fiction
  ISBN 0316226149; 9780316226141
LC 2013034213

"The Bunny family has adopted a wolf son, and daughter Dot is the only one who realizes Wolfie can--and might--eat them all up! Dot tries to get through to her parents, but they are too smitten to listen. A new brother takes getting used to, and when (in a twist of fate) it's Wolfie who's threatened, can Dot save the day?" (Publisher's note)

Dyer, Sarah
  Batty. Frances Lincoln Children's Books 2011 un il $16.95
Grades: PreK K 1 2   E
  1. Bats -- Fiction 2. Zoos -- Fiction 3. Animals -- Fiction
  ISBN 978-1-84780-084-8; 1-84780-084-X

"Batty is a zoo-dwelling, long-eared bat. . . . Zoo visitors tend to drift past Batty toward the more popular, talented animals; he tries hanging out with the eager-to-groom gorillas and the raucous birds in the aviary . . . but he doesn't fit in. . . . The spreads in which Batty watches the

other animals are upside-down, as a hanging bat would see them, with intervening spreads right-side-up—an entertaining way of representing Batty's point of view. . . . Dyer's understated humor, both in her text and artwork, makes for a winning take on the be-true-to-yourself theme." Publ Wkly

Monster day at work. Frances Lincoln 2010 un il
Grades: PreK K 1   E
  1. Monsters -- Fiction
  ISBN 1-84780-069-6; 978-1-84780-069-5

Little monster spends a day at work with his father.

"Wide-set eyes, squat statures and two horns that look like party hats worn askew make these monsters anything but scary. Detailed spreads filled with other oddball creatures and quirky touches . . . complete this offbeat monster landscape." Kirkus

Eastman, P. D.
  ★ **Are** you my mother? written and illustrated by P. D. Eastman. Beginner Bks. 1960 63p il $8.99; lib bdg $12.99; bd bk $4.99
Grades: PreK K 1   E
  1. Birds -- Fiction 2. Mother-child relationship -- Fiction
  ISBN 0-394-80018-4; 0-394-90018-9 lib bdg; 0-679-89047-5 bd bk

"A small bird falls from his nest and searches for his mother. He asks a kitten, a hen, a dog, a cow, a boat, [and] a plane . . . 'Are you my mother?' Repetition of words and phrases and funny pictures are just right for beginning readers." Chicago. Public Libr

★ **Go,** dog, go! Beginner Books 2010 64p il $8.99
Grades: PreK K 1 2   E
  1. Dogs -- Fiction
  ISBN 978-0-394-80020-2; 0-394-80020-6

A reissue of the title first published 1961

Eaton, Jason Carter
  The **catawampus** cat; by Jason Carter Eaton; illustrated by Gus Gordon. Crown Books for Young Readers 2017 32 p. illustrations (chiefly color) $16.99
Grades: PreK K 1   E
  1. Cats -- Fiction 2. Individuality -- Fiction 3. City and town life -- Fiction
  ISBN 9780553509717; 9780553509724; 9780553509748
LC 2016008919

In this book, by Jason Carter Eaton, illustrated by Gus Gordon, "the catawampus cat walks with a slant. And his skewed point of view has everyone in town looking at everything with fresh eyes. Even Bushy Brows Billiam who never notices anything, including what time class is over, spots the catawampus cat, and now he's a star student! . . . The catawampus cat is in town and everything is about to change." (Publisher's note)

★ **How** to train a train; by Jason Carter Eaton and illustrated by John Rocco. Candlewick Press 2013 48 p. $16.99
Grades: PreK K 1 2   E
  1. Pets 2. Railroads
  ISBN 0763663077; 9780763663070
LC 2012947747

This book on railroad trains, by Jason Carter, "written as a guidebook for new owners, . . . incorporates language usually associated with pet ownership and child rearing. Digitally colored illustrations [by John Rocco] . . . capture the expressiveness and playfulness of the pet trains." (School Library Journal)

"The ultimate dream for railroad fanatics: pet trains! Eaton offers humorously detailed instructions on how to locate and catch a wild train, with tips on naming and helping your locomotive adjust to life among humans. Digitally colored graphite illustrations have energy and excitement in this fantastical picture book that's sure to be on heavy rotation in train-loving households." (Horn Book)

Eaton, Maxwell

★ **Best** buds; [by] Maxwell Eaton III. Alfred A. Knopf 2007 un il (The adventures of Max and Pinky) $12.99; lib bdg $14.99
Grades: PreK K 1   E
1. Pigs -- Fiction 2. Friendship -- Fiction
ISBN 978-0-375-83803-3; 0-375-83803-1; 978-0-375-93803-0 lib bdg; 0-375-93803-6 lib bdg
LC 2006-02037

Best friends Max and Pinky the pig have an adventure together every Saturday, but one week Max looks everywhere and cannot find Pinky.

"The book is offbeat, irreverent, and affectionate, contrasting the pared-down simplicity of the main text with cheerful dialogue in the speech balloons and the sturdy simplicity of of the flat-planed, digitally colored art with the eccentric actions they depict." Horn Book

Other titles about Max and Pinky are:
Superheroes (2007)
The mystery (2008)

Two dumb ducks. Alfred A. Knopf 2010 un il $12.99; lib bdg $15.99
Grades: PreK K 1 2   E
1. Anger -- Fiction 2. Ducks -- Fiction 3. Gulls -- Fiction 4. Bullies -- Fiction
ISBN 978-0-375-84576-5; 0-375-84576-3; 978-0-375-94576-2 lib bdg; 0-375-94576-8 lib bdg
LC 2010-04959

Steve and Carl, two ducks, decide to get even when the seagulls call them "dumb."

This "is utterly genuine in both its humor and pain; Eaton's bold cartooning and dead-pan, economic storytelling make every page a treat." Publ Wkly

Edmundson, Chris

Yeti, turn out the light! by Greg Long and Chris Edmundson and illustrated by Wednesday Kirwan. Chronicle Books 2013 36 p. (alk. paper) $12.99
Grades: PreK K   E
1. Yeti -- Fiction 2. Sleep -- Fiction 3. Monsters -- Fiction 4. Bedtime -- Fiction 5. Shadows -- Fiction
ISBN 1452111588; 9781452111582
LC 2012049298

In this book, by Greg Long and Chris Edmundson and illustrated by Wednesday Kirwan, "all Yeti wants to do after a long day in the woods is to close his eyes and go to sleep. But something is not right! Shadows lurk, sounds creak, and there are monsters...or are there? This . . . bedtime book featuring the fierce and frenetic GAMAGO Yeti [is designed to] amuse and delight kids, all while encouraging them to turn out the light and go to sleep!" (Publisher's note)

Edwards, David

The **pen** that Pa built; by David Edwards; illustrations by Ashley Wolff. Tricycle Press 2007 un il $14.95
Grades: PreK K 1 2   E
1. Stories in rhyme 2. Wool -- Fiction 3. Sheep -- Fiction 4. Weaving -- Fiction
ISBN 978-1-58246-153-3; 1-58246-153-8
LC 2006101994

A cumulative, illustrated tale describing the process of raising sheep and using their wool to make warm woolen blankets.

"The language is pleasant and the rhymes clever. What really works here are Wolff's highly textured gesso-and-gouache illustrations." Booklist

Edwards, Karl Newsom

I **got** a new friend; Karl Newsom Edwards. Alfred A. Knopf 2017 32 p. color illustrations (lib. bdg.) $19.99
Grades: PreK K 1   E
1. Dogs -- Fiction 2. Friendship -- Fiction 3. Animal babies -- Fiction 4. Dogs -- Fiction 5. Friendship -- Fiction 6. Animals -- Infancy -- Fiction
ISBN 9780399557002; 9780399557019
LC 2016005552

In this book, by Karl Newsom Edwards, "when a little girl gets a new puppy, they have a lot to learn about each other. The new friends can be shy, messy, and sometimes get into trouble. They get lost, but they always get found. Their friendship may be a lot of work—but at the end of the day, they love each other!" (Publisher's note)

Edwards, Michelle

A **hat** for Mrs. Goldman; a story about knitting and love. by Michelle Edwards; illustrated by G. Brian Karas. Schwartz & Wade Books 2016 40 p. color illustrations (ebook) $53.97; (hardcover) $17.99
Grades: PreK K 1   E
1. Girls -- Fiction 2. Knitting -- Fiction 3. Neighbors -- Fiction 4. Jewish women -- Fiction 5. Old age -- Fiction 6. Knitting -- Fiction 7. Neighbors -- Fiction 8. Mexican Americans -- Fiction 9. Jews -- United States -- Fiction
ISBN 9780553497120; 9780553497106; 0553497103; 9780553497113
LC 2015036747

In this picture book for children by Michelle Edwards, illustrated by G. Brian Karas, "Mrs. Goldman always knits hats for everyone in the neighborhood, and Sophia, who thinks knitting is too hard, helps by making the pom-poms. But now winter is here, and Mrs. Goldman herself doesn't have a hat. . . . It's up to Sophia to buckle down and knit a hat for Mrs. Goldman. . . . Sophia is devastated until she gets an idea that will make Mrs. Goldman's hat the most wonderful of all." (Publisher's note)

"Instructions for knitting the hat and decorating it are included, and every beginning (and experienced) knitter will find it a perfect project. Knit a hat and love thy neighbor." Kirkus

★ **Papa's** latkes; illustrated by Stacey Schuett. Candlewick Press 2004 un il $15.99
Grades: PreK K 1 2   E
1. Jews -- Fiction 2. Hanukkah -- Fiction 3. Bereavement -- Fiction
ISBN 0-7636-0779-7
LC 00-69801

On the first Hanukkah after Mama died, Papa and his two daughters try to make latkes and celebrate without her.

"The poignant text with touches of humor is nicely matched with warm and richly colored oil paintings. . . . A touching and uplifting story." SLJ

Edwards, Pamela Duncan

Jack and Jill's treehouse; illustrated by Henry Cole. Katherine Tegen Books 2008 un il $16.99; lib bdg $17.89
Grades: PreK K 1   E
1. Birds -- Fiction 2. Building -- Fiction 3. Tree houses -- Fiction
ISBN 978-0-06-009077-7; 0-06-009077-4; 978-0-06-009078-4 lib bdg; 0-06-009078-2 lib bdg

A cumulative tale about Jack and Jill who build a treehouse, as a pair of robins make their own home in the same tree.

"Color, spirit, and a sense of satisfaction fill the soft illustrations, which depict idyllic days spent in outdoor amusement.... The large images lend themselves well to group sharing, and the text includes small rebus pictures of each added item, allowing listeners to chant along." SLJ

The **leprechaun's** gold; illustrated by Henry Cole. Katherine Tegen Books 2004 un il $15.99; lib bdg $16.89; pa $6.99
Grades: K 1 2 3   E
1. Ireland -- Fiction 2. Musicians -- Fiction 3. Leprechauns -- Fiction
ISBN 0-06-623974-5; 0-06-623975-3 lib bdg; 0-06-443878-3 pa
LC 2002-3150

A leprechaun intervenes with gold and magic when a greedy, boastful young harpist gains an unfair advantage for a royal harping contest

"Cole's imaginative illustrations are a good match for the story, displaying both realism and fantasy.... An appealing tale that need not be limited to St. Patrick's Day storytime." Booklist

★ The **mixed**-up rooster; written by Pamela Duncan Edwards; illustrated by Megan Lloyd. Katherine Tegen Books 2006 un il lib bdg $16.89
Grades: PreK K 1 2   E
1. Chickens -- Fiction 2. Roosters -- Fiction
ISBN 978-0-06-028999-7; 0-06-028999-6; 978-0-06-029000-9 lib bdg; 0-06-029000-5 lib bdg
LC 2005014401

Ned the rooster is fired from his job because he cannot wake up in the morning, but he restores his reputation after discovering his usefulness as a night bird

"This lighthearted story is written in an uncomplicated, comical style and has vibrant illustrations that are full of personality and charm." SLJ

The **neat** line; scribbling through Mother Goose. illustrated by Diana Cain Bluthenthal. Katherine Tegen Books 2004 un il hardcover o.p. lib bdg $16.89
Grades: PreK K 1 2   E
1. Nursery rhymes -- Fiction
ISBN 0-06-623970-2; 0-06-623971-0 lib bdg
LC 2002-153424

A young scribble matures into a neat line, then wriggles into a book of nursery rhymes where he transforms himself into different objects to assist the characters he meets there

This is a "brilliantly creative romp.... The large cartoon paintings ... are appropriately outlined with thick, bold lines and are framed by book pages on either side." SLJ

The **old** house; [by] Pamela Duncan Edwards; illustrated by Henry Cole. Dutton Children's Books 2007 un il $16.99; pa $6.99
Grades: PreK K 1   E
1. Houses -- Fiction
ISBN 978-0-525-47796-9; 0-14-241480-8 pa
LC 2006102950

An old empty house feels sorry for itself because it has no family living inside, but with the help of some good friends, its dreams come true

"Edwards colloquial text is accessible for young readers to tackle on their own and would make a lively read-aloud. Cole's energetic cartoon-style artwork gives oodles of personality to this house waiting to shine." SLJ

Princess Pigtoria and the pea; illustrated by Henry Cole. Orchard Books 2010 un il $16.99

Grades: PreK K 1   E
1. Fairy tales 2. Pigs -- Fiction 3. Princesses -- Fiction
ISBN 978-0-545-15625-7; 0-545-15625-4
LC 2008-52693

To make her pigsty of a palace picturesque again, penniless Princess Pigtoria tries to get the pompous porker Prince Proudfoot to propose marriage.

"Fun for listeners and readers alike... The scale of the artwork make this a good choice for storytime." Booklist

Some smug slug; illustrated by Henry Cole. HarperCollins Pubs. 1996 32p il $17.99; pa $6.99
Grades: PreK K 1 2   E
1. Animals -- Fiction 2. Slugs (Mollusks) -- Fiction
ISBN 0-06-024789-4; 0-06-443502-4 pa
LC 94-18682

"A slug senses a slope and saunters on up, against the advice of a sparrow, a spider, and a skink, among others, and meets with a sudden, spontaneous demise. Such is the life of a slug told with a multitude of common and not so common 'S' words.... Realistically detailed, earth-toned illustrations focus attention on each scene.... This slug is so appealing and full of personality that it will certainly garner sympathy." SLJ

While the world is sleeping; illustrated by Dan Kirk. Orchard Books 2010 un il lib bdg $16.99
Grades: PreK K 1   E
1. Stories in rhyme 2. Night -- Fiction 3. Animals -- Fiction 4. Bedtime -- Fiction
ISBN 978-0-545-01756-5; 0-545-01756-4
LC 2007040283

A sleepy child is flown through the night sky to see foxes hunting, rabbits playing, raccoons scrounging, and other animals that are active while people sleep.

"Kirk's illustrations are big and bold, featuring the shimmering light of the moon, animals whose every hair seems distinct, and playful faux-Rousseau forests. The book's mix of the realistic and fantastic seems like a perfect prelude to dream time." Booklist

Edwards, Wallace

Uncle Wally's old brown shoe; Wallace Edwards. Orca Book Publishers 2012 32 p. (hardcover) $19.95
Grades: 3 4 5   E
1. Shoes -- Fiction 2. Picture books for children 3. Animals -- Fiction
ISBN 1459801547; 9781459801547; 9781459801554
LC 2012935414

The protagonist of this book by Wallace Edwards "is a tiger, resplendent in red-and-white-striped pyjamas and a solitary brown oxford. His missing shoe has all the fun in this story, as it is driven by a kitten, who is tickled by a pig in a fancy hat, who is chased by a limber frog on stilts, who—well, you get the idea. Eventually, the reader is treated to the revelation of how the shoe has come to pass through the possession of a menagerie of animals." (Quill & Quire)

Egan, Tim

Dodsworth in London; written and illustrated by Tim Egan. Houghton Mifflin Harcourt 2009 un il $15
Grades: K 1 2   E
1. Ducks -- Fiction 2. London (England) -- Fiction 3. Voyages and travels -- Fiction
ISBN 978-0-547-13816-9; 0-547-13816-4
LC 2008-40464

Despite a dart-throwing episode at a local pub and a case of mistaken identity, Dodsworth and his mischievous duck companion receive a royal invitation to stay at Buckingham Palace during their trip to London.

"As usual, Egan's wit is as sharp as the fashion sense of the assorted animals populating his droll ink-and-watercolor illustrations." Horn Book

★ **Dodsworth** in New York; written and illustrated by Tim Egan. Houghton Mifflin 2007 un il $15

Grades: K 1 2   E

1. Ducks -- Fiction 2. New York (N.Y.) -- Fiction 3. Voyages and travels -- Fiction

ISBN 978-0-618-77708-2; 0-618-77708-3

LC 2006-34522

When Dodsworth sets out for adventure, including a stop in New York City before going to Paris, London, and beyond, he does not expect a crazy duck to stow away in his suitcase and lead him on a merry chase.

"Egan favors a palette of golds and clay-browns, and draws pillowy shapes in a gentle, never rigid line. . . . Egan keeps the hijinks low-key, preferring long pauses and slow burns to nutty slapstick." Publ Wkly

Other titles about Dodsworth are:

Dodsworth in Paris (2008)

Dodsworth in London (2009)

Dodsworth in Rome (2011)

Dodsworth in Paris; written and illustrated by Tim Egan. Houghton Mifflin Co. 2008 un il $15

Grades: K 1 2   E

1. Ducks -- Fiction 2. Paris (France) -- Fiction 3. Voyages and travels -- Fiction

ISBN 978-0-618-98062-8; 0-618-98062-8

LC 2007-47732

When Dodsworth and the duck vacation in Paris, they have a grand time despite running out of money and accidentally riding their bicycles in the Tour de France.

"An out-of-the-ordinary offering for new readers that moves them to new places, both literally and literarily." Booklist

Dodsworth in Rome; written and illustrated by Tim Egan. Houghton Mifflin Harcourt 2011 un il $14.99

Grades: K 1 2   E

1. Ducks -- Fiction 2. Italy -- Fiction 3. Rome (Italy) -- Fiction 4. Voyages and travels -- Fiction

ISBN 978-0-547-39006-2; 0-547-39006-8

LC 2010007024

Dodsworth and his duck companion have a lovely time in Rome, even though the duck tries to improve the ceiling of the Sistine Chapel and takes all the coins from the Trevi Fountain.

"Egan's understated, hilarious travelogue continues." Kirkus

The **pink** refrigerator; [by] Tim Egan. Houghton Mifflin 2007 un il $16

Grades: K 1 2   E

1. Mice -- Fiction

ISBN 978-0-618-63154-4; 0-618-63154-2

LC 2006009816

Dodsworth the mouse does as little work as he can, collecting items from a junkyard and placing them in his thrift store for sale, until he happens upon a pink refrigerator that spurs him to do much more with his life.

"The ink-and-watercolor art mirrors the laid-back tone of the narrative. . . . This offbeat tale is perfect for reading aloud, but will also be appreciated as a read-alone and lap-sit." SLJ

Egielski, Richard

★ **Captain** Sky Blue. Michael Di Capua Books 2010 un il $17.95

Grades: PreK K 1 2   E

1. Adventure fiction 2. Toys -- Fiction 3. Christmas -- Fiction 4. Air pilots -- Fiction

ISBN 978-0-545-21342-4; 0-545-21342-8

Jack's best toy pal is Captain Sky Blue, a pilot. After a thunderstorm separates Sky and his buddy, Sky is abducted by a whale, then left alone to wander a frigid ocean floor until he chances upon a very special place, a place where he's been before.

Egielski "is in top form in this story. . . . From start to finish, it has the feel of an old-fashioned adventure. . . . Egielski's boldly outlined artwork lends the story a cinematic scope. . . . Airplane-obsessed readers will be thrilled with the aeronautical jargon Sky uses." Publ Wkly

The **sleepless** little vampire. Arthur A. Levine Books 2011 un il $16.99

Grades: PreK K 1   E

1. Bedtime -- Fiction 2. Vampires -- Fiction

ISBN 978-0-545-14597-8; 0-545-14597-X

LC 2010032096

A young vampire, unable to sleep, tries to figure out whether it is the howling of a werewolf, the clacking of skeletons, or something else that is keeping him awake.

"The book closes on a satisfying note, with everyone safe and sound. Egielski's watercolor/ink paintings are superbly executed, with strong colors and bold, expressive lines." SLJ

Ehlert, Lois

Boo to you! Beach Lane Books 2009 un il $17.99

Grades: PreK K 1   E

1. Stories in rhyme 2. Cats -- Fiction 3. Mice -- Fiction 4. Parties -- Fiction

ISBN 978-1-4169-8625-6; 1-4169-8625-1

LC 2008-44352

When the neighborhood cat tries to crash the mice's harvest party, the mice have a plan to scare the intruder away

"Ehlert's use of paper, fruit, seeds, and string is labyrinthine enough to have young children tracing their routes, and so vivid they'll want to touch the page to make sure it's not real." Booklist

★ **Circus**. HarperCollins Pubs. 1992 un il $17.99

Grades: PreK K 1   E

1. Circus -- Fiction 2. Animals -- Fiction

ISBN 0-06-020252-1

LC 91-12067

Leaping lizards, marching snakes, a bear on the high wire, and others perform in a somewhat unusual circus

"The book approximates a light show in visual intensity, with neon-bright illustrations set against black or bold backgrounds. . . . The sprightly rhythm of Ms. Ehlert's text complements her Day-Glo palette. Echoing a ringmaster's speech, she's afraid of neither alliteration . . . nor hyperbole." N Y Times Book Rev

★ **Feathers** for lunch. Harcourt Brace Jovanovich 1990 un il $17; pa $7

Grades: PreK K 1 2   E

1. Stories in rhyme 2. Cats -- Fiction 3. Birds -- Fiction

ISBN 0-15-230550-5; 0-15-200986-8 pa

LC 89-29459

"Ehlert has attempted many things in these pages—for instance, the birds are all drawn life-size—and has succeeded in all of them; her lavish use of bold color against generous amounts of white space is graphically appealing, and the large type, nearly one-half-inch tall, invites attempts by those just beginning to read. An engaging, entertaining, and recognizably realistic story." Horn Book

★ **Hands**; growing up to be an artist. Harcourt 2004 un il $14.95
Grades: PreK K 1 2   E
   ISBN 0-15-205107-4
                          LC 2004-1237
A reformatted edition of the title first published 1997

When a child works alongside her parents doing carpentry, sewing, and gardening, she thinks of being an artist as well when she grows up

This edition offers "slightly reworked trimmings, but keeps the same die-cut pages—in the shapes of scissors, seed packets and more—as well as a 'paint box' that opens." Publ Wkly

★ **Leaf** Man. Harcourt 2005 un il $16
Grades: PreK K 1 2   E
   1. Winds -- Fiction 2. Leaves -- Fiction
   ISBN 0-15-205304-2
                          LC 2004-9981
Boston Globe-Horn Book Award: Picture Book (2006)

A man made of leaves blows away, traveling wherever the wind may take him.

This is an "eye-popping book.... Scalloped edgings on the tops of the pages, cut at varying heights, artfully give the effect of setting the action against a three-dimensional landscape." Booklist

★ **Lots** of spots. Beach Lane Books 2010 un il $17.99
Grades: PreK K 1   E
   1. Animals
   ISBN 978-1-4424-0289-8; 1-4424-0289-X
                          LC 2009034361
"Each of the 50 featured creatures in Ehlert's ... offering sports distinctive markings.... Each spread features a beautiful collage illustration of an animal, accompanied by a poem of four, short, catchy lines. ... Children will enjoy paging through and identifying the multitude of brilliantly hued animals that make up this visual zoo." Booklist

★ **Market** day; a story told with folk art. written and designed by Lois Ehlert. Harcourt 2000 un il $17; pa $7
Grades: PreK K 1 2   E
   1. Stories in rhyme 2. Markets -- Fiction 3. Farm life -- Fiction
   ISBN 0-15-202158-2; 0-15-216820-6 pa
                          LC 99-6252
On market day, a farm family experiences all the fun and excitement of going to and from the farmers' market

"The very young will enjoy the spare, simple rhymes.... All ages will appreciate the illustrations, comprising images of folk art, primitive art, and textiles from around the world. An annotated inventory of the featured items is included." Horn Book Guide

★ **Nuts** to you! Harcourt Brace Jovanovich 1993 un il $17; pa $7
Grades: PreK K 1 2   E
   1. Stories in rhyme 2. Squirrels -- Fiction
   ISBN 0-15-257647-9; 0-15-205064-7 pa
                          LC 92-19441
"A frisky squirrel digs up bulbs and steals birdseed from a nearby feeder; in his boldest act, he enters the young narrator's apartment through a tear in the window screen. The quick-thinking child entices the mischievous squirrel back outside with some peanuts.... The story, told in brisk rhyme, is a fast-paced romp, and the large, dramatically

styled collages will dazzle even the largest audiences.... The four concluding pages offer basic information about squirrels." Horn Book

Oodles of animals. Harcourt 2008 un il $17
Grades: PreK K 1 2   E
   1. Stories in rhyme 2. Animals -- Fiction
   ISBN 978-0-15-206274-3; 0-15-206274-2
                          LC 2007-17018
Short, easy to read rhymes reveal what is unique about various animals, from ape to wolf.

"The artist uses scissors, pinking shears, and a hole punch to transform brightly colored papers into squares, rectangles, triangles, circles, diamonds, half circles, ovals, hearts, and teardrops of different sizes, which she then fashions into a menagerie guaranteed to spark readers' imaginations. Each creature is coupled with a short, humorous poem that is sure to delight." SLJ

★ **Pie** in the sky. Harcourt 2004 un il $16
Grades: PreK K 1 2   E
   1. Pies -- Fiction 2. Cherries -- Fiction
   ISBN 0-15-216584-3
                          LC 2003-4986
A father and child watch the cherry tree in their back yard, waiting until there are ripe cherries to bake in a pie. Includes a recipe for cherry pie

"The vibrant collage illustrations, made with an eclectic combination of materials—from paint and handmade papers to sheet metal, wires, and tree branches—celebrate the colors and simplified shapes of birds, insects, the cherry tree, and, yes, kitchen implements." Booklist

★ **Planting** a rainbow; written and illustrated by Lois Ehlert. Harcourt Brace Jovanovich 1988 un il $17; pa $7; bd bk $6.95
Grades: PreK K 1   E
   1. Flowers -- Fiction 2. Gardening -- Fiction
   ISBN 0-15-262609-3; 0-15-262610-7 pa; 0-15-204633-X bd bk
                          LC 87-8528
A mother and daughter plant a rainbow of flowers in the family garden

"The stylized forms of the plants are clearly and beautifully designed, and the primary, blazing colors of the blossoms dazzle in their resplendence. The minimal text, in very large print, is exactly right to set off the glorious illustrations, making a splendid beginning book of colors and flowers cleverly arranged for young readers." Horn Book

Rain fish; Lois Ehlert. Beach Lane Books 2016 40 p. color illustrations (hardback) $17.99
Grades: PreK K 1 2   E
   1. Stories in rhyme 2. Fishes -- Fiction 3. Fishes -- Fiction 4. Imagination -- Fiction 5. Rain and rainfall -- Fiction
   ISBN 9781481461528; 9781481461535
                          LC 2015022828
This children's book, by Lois Ehlert, "through lyrical text and ... mixed-media collage illustrations ... introduces readers to 'rain fish'— the varied, colorful, and unique little collections of materials that float along on streams of rain water during storms. From a scrap of newspaper with a seashell eye and feather smile to a piece of cardboard with an orange peel eye and a leaf for a fin, Ehlert's rain fish come in all shapes and sizes." (Publisher's note)

"Vivid colors, varied textures, and expressive language inspire further contemplation. As an exploration of creativity and inventiveness, the book serves as a challenge to readers." SLJ

★ **Rrralph**. Beach Lane Books 2011 32p il $17.99

Grades: PreK K 1 2 3   E
1. Dogs -- Fiction
ISBN 1-4424-1305-0; 978-1-4424-1305-4

LC 2010006866

The narrator describes discovering how Ralph the dog can talk, appropriately saying words such as "roof," "rough," "bark," and "wolf."

"Created with realia as well as painted and textured papers, the three-dimensional collage illustrations feature zippers for Ralph's mouth, a metal pop-top for his nose, buttons for the bird's eyes, and actual bark for the tree's trunk. The pages, colored in hot-pink, grass-green, and pumpkin, magnify the visual energy of the artwork and graphics. . . . With its appealing jacket art, clever text, and vibrant illustrations, this amusing picture book is a pleasure to read aloud." Booklist

★ The **scraps** book; notes from a colorful life. Lois Ehlert. First edition Beach Lane Books 2013 72 p. (hardcover) $17.99
Grades: K 1 2 3 4   E
1. Autobiographies 2. Illustration of books 3. Picture books for children 4. Illustrators -- United States 5. Illustrators -- United States -- Biography
ISBN 1442435712; 9781442435711

LC 2012041869

Author Lois Ehlert "employs her signature collage technique and images from her past work to explore her lifelong relationship with creating art in this . . . picture book memoir. The journey begins with Ehlert's early creative inklings, . . . accompanied by family photos, images of the tools she uses today, . . . and a glimpse of her vibrant studio space. She shares thoughts on her varied sources of inspiration . . . and illustrates how those ideas are translated to the page." (Publishers Weekly)

"In a generously illustrated picture book memoir, Ehlert speaks directly to her audience, particularly readers who like collecting objects and making things. The book is jam-packed with her art and photos from her life: her parents, the house she grew up in, and the small table where she was encouraged to pursue her art; along the way, we see how autobiographical her books have been." Horn Book

★ **Top** cat. Harcourt Brace & Co. 1998 un il $17; pa $7
Grades: PreK K 1 2   E
1. Stories in rhyme 2. Cats -- Fiction
ISBN 0-15-201739-9; 0-15-202425-5 pa

LC 97-8818

The top cat in a household is reluctant to accept the arrival of a new kitten but decides to share various survival secrets with it

"Ehlert creates a memorable cat duo in her trademark cut-paper collage style. . . . Children and other feline fans will quickly warm to this spunky story of rivalry and acceptance." Publ Wkly

★ **Wag** a tail; [by] Lois Ehlert. Harcourt, Inc. 2007 un il $16
Grades: PreK K 1 2   E
1. Stories in rhyme 2. Dogs -- Fiction
ISBN 978-0-15-205843-2

LC 2006013318

Assorted graduates of the Bow Wow School meet at a farmers market and a dog park, where most of them remember their obedience training.

"This simple story has a rhythmic, jazzy quality that begs to be read aloud. . . . Collages composed of brightly colored buttons and scraps of paper stand out on vivid green backgrounds." SLJ

Ehrhardt, Karen
★ **This** Jazz man; pictures by R. G. Roth. Harcourt 2006 un il $16
Grades: K 1 2 3   E
1. Counting 2. Stories in rhyme 3. Jazz musicians -- Fiction 4.

African Americans -- Fiction
ISBN 0-15-205307-7

LC 2004-21094

This introduction to jazz is set to the rhythm of the traditional song This Old Man. "Ages five to nine." (Bull Cent Child Books)

"The candy-colored collages burst from the pages, making this addition just right as an up-tempo introduction for youngest music lovers." Publ Wkly

Ehrlich, Amy
Baby Dragon; [by] Amy Ehrlich; illustrated by Will Hillenbrand. Candlewick Press 2008 un il $16.99
Grades: PreK K 1 2   E
1. Animals -- Fiction 2. Dragons -- Fiction 3. Mother-child relationship -- Fiction
ISBN 978-0-7636-2840-6; 0-7636-2840-9

LC 2007051883

All day, Baby Dragon turns down other animals' offers to go play or find a snack while he waits for his mother to return for him, but at nightfall, he agrees to go with Crocodile to find her

"Hillenbrand's illustrations, done with ink, colored pencil, finger paint, gouache, and collage, and digitally manipulated, bring to life Baby Dragon's misty tropical forest where water buffaloes wander and storks splash in the river." SLJ

★ The **girl** who wanted to dance; by Amy Ehrlich; illustrated by Rebecca Walsh. Candlewick Press 2009 un il $17.99
Grades: 2 3 4   E
1. Fairy tales 2. Dance -- Fiction 3. Loss (Psychology) -- Fiction
ISBN 978-0-7636-1345-7; 0-7636-1345-2

"Both a haunting fairy tale and a parable for families separated by divorce or death, this lyrically rendered story also presents art as a vehicle for transcending pain. . . . Working in a representational style, Walsh . . . adds lush paintings of an idealized old world, and her nighttime scenes glow." Publ Wkly

★ **Thumbelina**; by Hans Christian Andersen; retold by Amy Ehrlich; [illustrated by Susan Jeffers] Dutton Children's Books 2005 32p il $16.99
Grades: K 1 2 3   E
1. Fairy tales
ISBN 0-525-47508-7

LC 2004028979

A reissure of the edition published 1979 by Dial Books for Young Readers

A retelling of Hans Christian Andersen's classic fairy tale about a girl who is only one inch tall.

"This sumptuous picture book version the classic Andersen story has been an adapted text that shows some softening of the tale's harsher edges. . . . [Readers will] be caught up in the action as depicted in Jeffers' striking, pastel-dominated pictures." Booklist

Ehrlich, Fred
Does an elephant take a bath? pictures by Emily Bolan. Blue Apple Books 2005 un il (Early experiences) lib bdg $13.50; pa $5.95
Grades: PreK K   E
1. Baths 2. Animals 3. Cleanliness
ISBN 1-59354-111-2 lib bdg; 1-59354-123-5 pa

"The humor is just right for the audience . . . and, like the text, the uncluttered illustrations . . . are both informative and amusing." Horn Book Guide

Other titles in the Early experiences series are:
Does a baboon sleep in a bed? (2005)
Does a chimp wear clothes? (2005)

Does a hippo say ahh? (2006)

Does a lion brush? (2005)

Does a panda go to school? (2006)

Does a pig flush? (2005)

Does a seal smile? (2006)

Does a tiger open wide? (2006)

Does a yak get a haircut? (2006)

Ehrlich, H. M.

★ **Louie's** goose; illustrated by Emily Bolam. Houghton Mifflin 2000 un il $15

Grades: PreK K 1   E

1. Toys -- Fiction 2. Beaches -- Fiction

ISBN 0-618-03023-9

LC 99-28566

While spending the summer at the beach with his parents, Louie has a wonderful time playing with his toy goose and even rescues her from a big wave

"This true-to-life look at a preschooler growing more independent is low-key and natural. . . . Bolam's sunny paintings capture the seashore experience of a charming, lovable family." Booklist

Another title about Louie is:

Gotcha, Louie! (2002)

Eichenberg, Fritz

Ape in a cape; an alphabet of odd animals. Harcourt Brace & Co. 1952 un il hardcover o.p. pa $8

Grades: PreK K 1   E

1. Animals 2. Alphabet

ISBN 0-15-607830-9 pa

A Caldecott Medal honor book, 1953

"The skill of a craftsman distinguishes this picture book illustrated with bold and lively drawings printed in three colors." N Y Public Libr

Elffers, Joost

Do you love me? [by] Joost Elffers + Curious Pictures. Bowen Press 2009 un il $14.99

Grades: PreK K 1   E

1. Stories in rhyme 2. Love -- Fiction

ISBN 978-0-06-166799-2; 0-06-166799-4

LC 2008005939

Playful creatures called Snuzzles explore the idea of unconditional love

"The gentle, rhyming text is the straightforward stuff of bedtime rituals. But while the questions are expected, the answers feel fresh. . . . Set against high-contrast, single-color backgrounds, the action takes place at close range, so that just their heads, or parts of their heads, are visible." Publ Wkly

Elkin, Mark

Samuel's baby; illustrations by Amy Wummer. Tricycle Press 2010 un il $15.99

Grades: PreK K 1   E

1. School stories 2. Infants -- Fiction 3. Siblings -- Fiction

ISBN 978-1-58246-301-8; 1-58246-301-8

LC 2009-7548

Samuel announces during show-and-tell that he is having a baby and soon his kindergarten classmates are expecting everything from twins to puppies, but while Samuel teaches them how to hold and diaper a newborn, he has some qualms about becoming a big brother.

"A standout original title among new-baby picture books. . . . Wummer's pencil and watercolor illustrations effectively utilize facial expressions to communicate voice and personality." SLJ

Ellery, Amanda

If I were a jungle animal; illustrated by Tom Ellery. Simon & Schuster Books for Young Readers 2009 un il $15.99

Grades: PreK K 1   E

1. Animals -- Fiction 2. Baseball -- Fiction 3. Imagination -- Fiction

ISBN 978-1-4169-3778-4; 1-4169-3778-1

While playing baseball, a boy wonders what it would be like to be different jungle animals.

"Amanda Ellery's tale is simple but delicious, and accessible to very young readers. Husband Tom's expressive, Bill Peet-esque illustrations-in colored pencil, pen and ink-are all they should be: funny, original and so lively they virtually jump off the page." Kirkus

Elliot, David

Henry's map; by David Elliot. Philomel Books 2013 40 p. ill. (reinforced) $16.99

Grades: PreK K 1 2   E

1. Farms -- Fiction 2. Picture books for children 3. Maps -- Fiction 4. Pigs -- Fiction 5. Farm life -- Fiction 6. Domestic animals -- Fiction

ISBN 0399160728; 9780399160721

LC 2012035391

This children's picture book stars a very organized pig named Henry, who "decries the messy state of the farm. . . . Henry decides to draw a map to sort things out and, armed with pencil and paper, makes his way across the barnyard. All the animals are excited to be included, falling in line behind the earnest cartographer." His efforts are less than successful, however, and ultimately all the animals stay where they were originally, "to the relief of all concerned." (Publishers Weekly)

Elliott, David

Finn throws a fit; illustrated by Timothy Basil Ering. Candlewick Press 2009 un il $16.99; pa $6.99

Grades: PreK K 1   E

1. Anger -- Fiction

ISBN 978-0-7636-2356-2; 0-7636-2356-3; 978-0-7636-5604-1 pa; 0-7636-5604-6 pa

LC 2008-21174

A cranky toddler has an enormous tantrum.

"Elliott . . . and Ering . . . operate like the left and right hands of a single comic mind; each tongue-in-cheek line of text is deftly countered with raw charcoal scrawls, wild strokes of paint and crazed scribbles. Small readers will giggle at the realization of their angry feelings—complete with rippling lengths of toilet paper, floods of tears and flying crockery—while parents will blanch at the brilliant exposition of the power their children hold over them." Publ Wkly

Knitty Kitty; illustrated by Christopher Denise. Candlewick Press 2008 un il $16.99

Grades: PreK K 1 2   E

1. Cats -- Fiction 2. Winter -- Fiction

ISBN 978-0-7636-3169-7; 0-7636-3169-8

LC 2007-52160

Knitty Kitty is knitting a scarf, a hat, and some mittens for her kittens, but when night falls and the snow comes down, the kittens request a blanket to keep them warm Knitty Kitty has a better idea.

"The full-bleed illustrations in acrylic and ink portray an idyllic cottage in a snow-covered countryside. Inside the warmth is made evident with soft golds, browns, and touches of soft color here and there." SLJ

★ **On** the farm; [by] David Elliott; illustrated by Holly Meade. Candlewick Press 2008 un il $16.99; pa $6.99

Grades: PreK K 1 2   E
1. Domestic animals
ISBN 978-0-7636-3322-6; 0-7636-3322-4; 978-0-7636-5591-4 pa
LC 2007060857

"Elliott looks at a rooster, a cow, a pony, a dog, sheep, a barn cat, a goat, a pig, a snake, bees, a bull, a turtle, a duck, a hen, and a rabbit in verses that are rich in vocabulary and, for the most part, written in rhyme. Large, black typeface mirrors the black lines in Meade's beautiful, color woodblock prints that superbly reflect the mood and action in the poetry." SLJ

One little chicken; a counting book. by David Elliott; illustrated by Ethan Long. Holiday House 2007 un il $16.95
Grades: PreK K   E
1. Counting 2. Dance -- Fiction 3. Chickens -- Fiction
ISBN 978-0-8234-1983-8
LC 2006037046

"For each number up to 10, funny flapping fowls dance up a storm of different steps—from the hula to the cha cha. . . . The computer-generated cartoon art adds shimmy to the text, with egg-eyed pullets wearing silly attire and equally silly expressions." Booklist

This orq. (he cave boy.) (he cave boy) David Elliott. Boyds Mills Press, an imprint of Highlights 2014 40 p. $15.95
Grades: PreK K 1 2   E
1. Mammoths -- Fiction 2. Cave dwellers -- Fiction 3. Woolly mammoth -- Fiction 4. Pets -- Behavior -- Fiction 5. Saber-toothed tigers -- Fiction
ISBN 1620915219; 9781620915219
LC 2014931588

In this children's book by David Elliott, illustrated by Lori Nichols, readers will "Meet Orq, cave boy. And Woma, woolly mammoth. Orq love Woma. Only one problem: Mom is not a fan of Woma, who sheds and smells and is definitely not cave-trained. How can Orq convince his mother that Woma belongs with them? Orq has a plan to get Woma back in the cave." (Publisher's note)

"Orq struggles to endear his woolly mammoth Woma to Mother. Then Woma saves Orq from becoming a meal for a saber-toothed tiger and finally wins Mother's heart. Succinct Paleolithic "prose" (Mother's objections: "Woma shed. Woma smell") allows room for plenty of visual humor. This silly tale of unconditional love between a cave boy and his pet mammoth is one for the ages." Horn Book

What the grizzly knows; [by] David Elliott; illustrated by Max Grafe. Candlewick Press 2008 un il $16.99
Grades: PreK K   E
1. Stories in rhyme 2. Bears -- Fiction 3. Teddy bears -- Fiction
ISBN 978-0-7636-2778-2; 0-7636-2778-X
LC 2007052158

When night falls magical things begin to happen to Teddy, taking the reader on an adventure around the countryside and seeing the world through the senses of a bear

"The simple, rhyming text is paired with noteworthy, realistically rendered watercolor art that glows with a dreamlike quality. . . . An engaging fantasy." Booklist

Elliott, Laura
A **string** of hearts; by Laura Malone Elliott; illustrations by Lynn Munsinger. Katherine Tegen Books 2010 un il $16.99; lib bdg $17.89
Grades: PreK K 1   E
1. Valentine's Day -- Fiction
ISBN 978-0-06-000085-1; 0-06-000085-6; 978-0-06-000086-8 lib bdg; 0-06-000086-4 lib bdg

Sam's friend Mary Ann helps him make a special valentine for Tiffany, but when Tiffany does not even notice it, Sam realizes who is really special. Includes facts about the history of Valentine's Day.

"The cheery artwork illustrating this heartwarming love triangle shows fluffy, well-dressed animals in bright colors. Their expressive faces mirror the emotions explored in the narrative. A lovely Valentine story about the real meaning of friendship." SLJ

Elliott, Rebecca
★ **Just** because. Trafalgar 2011 un il $14.99
Grades: K 1 2 3   E
1. Children with disabilities -- Fiction 2. Love -- Fiction 3. Siblings -- Fiction
ISBN 978-0-7459-6267-2; 0-7459-6267-X

Toby describes all the fun he has with Clemmie, his beloved big sister who "can't walk, talk, [or] move around much."

"An endearing and enduring picture book about sibling love. . . . Clemmie's wheelchair plays only a minor role in this story. . . . The double-page spreads burst forth in vibrant colors and energetic streaks and swirls. . . . Full of unconditional love, this is a must-have title." Kirkus

Zoo girl; Rebecca Elliott. Lion Children's 2012 26 p. col. ill $14.99
Grades: PreK K 1   E
1. Zoos -- Fiction 2. Orphans -- Fiction 3. Picture books for children 4. Adopted children -- Fiction 5. Families -- Fiction 6. Loneliness -- Fiction
ISBN 0745963234; 9780745963235
LC 2012392527

This children's picture book is the story of a "lonely orphan girl [who] finds her true friends within the walls of the zoo. . . . While the other children play on the swing set and slide outside the orphanage, she sits huddled on the grass far away from them. But the mere sight of the animals at the zoo brings a big smile to her face." After a night where she is accidentally left behind at the zoo, she is adopted by "the pair of zoo workers who find her." (Kirkus)

Elliott, Zetta
Bird; illustrated by Shadra Strickland. Lee & Low Books Inc. 2008 un il $18.95
Grades: 2 3 4 5   E
1. Novels in verse 2. Death -- Fiction 3. Drawing -- Fiction 4. Drug abuse -- Fiction 5. Family life -- Fiction 6. African Americans -- Fiction
ISBN 978-1-60060-241-2; 1-60060-241-X
LC 2007-49039

Bird, an artistic young African American boy, expresses himself through drawing as he struggles to understand his older brother's drug addiction and death, while a family friend, Uncle Son, provides guidance and understanding

"This picture book tells a poignant story. . . . A complicated weaving of impressive watercolor, gouache, charcoal and ink drawings amplifies the metaphors and action of the poetic text as it combines black-and-white with color." Publ Wkly

Ellis, Carson
★ **Du** Iz Tak? Carson Ellis. Candlewick Press 2016 48 p. color illustrations $16.99
Grades: PreK K 1 2   E
1. Insects -- Fiction 2. Growth (Plants) -- Fiction
ISBN 0763665304; 9780763665302
LC 2015934273
Caldecott Honor Book (2017)

In this book written and illustrated by Carson Ellis, "using intricate illustrations supported by spare dialogue in an invented language, Ellis elegantly weaves the tale of several square feet of ground in the insect world as the seasons pass. Multiple story lines intersect: a mysterious plant bursting from the soil, the rise and fall of a spectacular fort, and a caterpillar's quiet then triumphant metamorphosis into a shimmering moth." (School Library Journal)

"Effortlessly working on many levels, Ellis' newest is outstanding." Booklist

Ellis, Sarah

Ben over night; illustrated by Kim LaFave. Fitzhenry & Whiteside 2005 un il $16.95

Grades: PreK K 1   E

1. Fear -- Fiction

ISBN 1-55041-807-6

"Little Ben loves to play at his friend Peter's house across the street, but every time he tries to sleep over, he wakens in the night and chickens out. His supportive parents suggest that he take his flashlight and security blanket, but nothing works until his big sister comes up with more imaginative ideas. Ellis tells Ben's story with economy and understanding.... With fresh colors and energetic line work, the apparently digital illustrations do a good job of expressing the characters' emotions as well as defining their actions." Booklist

Elvgren, Jennifer Riesmeyer

Josias, hold the book; [by] Jennifer Riesmeyer Elvgren; illustrated by Nicole Tadgell. Boyds Mills Press 2006 un il $15.95

Grades: PreK K 1 2   E

1. Haiti -- Fiction 2. Education -- Fiction 3. Gardening -- Fiction

ISBN 1-59078-318-2

LC 2005024989

Each day Chrislove, who lives in Haiti, asks his friend Josias when he will "hold the book," or join them at school, but Josias can only think of tending the bean garden so that his family will have enough food

"Elvgren has crafted a matter-of-fact snapshot of rural Haitian life. Tadgells muted watercolor spreads set the tone and enhance the text. Emotions are clearly depicted, giving the characters added dimension and believability." SLJ

Elwell, Peter

Adios, Oscar! a butterfly fable. The Blue Sky Press 2009 un il $16.99

Grades: K 1 2   E

1. Moths -- Fiction 2. Caterpillars -- Fiction 3. Books and reading -- Fiction

ISBN 978-0-545-07159-8; 0-545-07159-3

LC 2007050842

Despite his friends' teasing, Oscar the caterpillar studies to prepare for becoming a butterfly and migrating to Mexico, so when things do not turn out as he expects, he is still able to make his dream come true.

"This charming story about loving oneself and pursuing one's dreams sends an important message to children without being preachy or pedantic. The bright colors and cartoon-style illustrations enhance its ebullient, optimistic tone." SLJ

Elya, Susan Middleton

Adios, tricycle; illustrated by Elisabeth Schlossberg. G. P. Putnam's Sons 2009 un il $16.99

Grades: PreK K   E

1. Stories in rhyme 2. Growth -- Fiction 3. Cycling -- Fiction 4. Garage sales -- Fiction 5. Hispanic Americans -- Fiction 6. Spanish language -- Vocabulary

ISBN 978-0-399-24522-0; 0-399-24522-7

LC 2008006562

Even though he has outgrown his tricycle, a young pig hides it at his family's yard sale until just the right smaller child comes along.

"Peppy, rhyming text filled with Spanish vocabulary words tells this entertaining, supportive story.... Schlossberg's pastel illustrations capture the mixed emotions in scenes of the diverse animal characters." Booklist

★ **Bebe** goes shopping; illustrated by Steven Salerno. Harcourt 2006 un il $16

Grades: PreK K 1   E

1. Stories in rhyme 2. Infants -- Fiction 3. Shopping -- Fiction 4. Spanish language -- Vocabulary

ISBN 0-15-205426-X

Rhyming text describes a trip to the grocery store for a mamá and her baby boy. Includes Spanish words.

"Almost all the words can be understood from the context or from the pictures.... Using gouache, watercolors, colored inks, and pencils, Salerno evokes the hip, retro style of 1950s cartoon-style advertisements.... Salerno is also a master at getting motion into his pictures, and his spreads rumble and tumble." Booklist

Another title about Bebé is:

Bebé goes to the beach (2008)

Cowboy Jose; illustrated by Tim Raglin. Putnam's 2005 un il $15.99

Grades: PreK K 1 2   E

1. Stories in rhyme 2. Mexico -- Fiction 3. Cowhands -- Fiction 4. Spanish language -- Vocabulary

ISBN 0-399-23570-1

LC 2003-26636

A poor cowboy enters a rodeo to win a date from a pretty señorita, but afterwards wonders if he should spend his winnings on the girl, who is only interested in the money, or on his trusty horse, whose encouragement helped him win.

"Elya's engaging text features snappy rhymes and plenty of contextual clues for the Spanish words that appear in bold type.... Raglin's watercolor-and-colored-pencil artwork features bright south-of-the-border colors and characters in traditional dress to accentuate the story's Mexican setting." SLJ

★ **F** is for fiesta; illustrated by G. Brian Karas. G.P. Putnam's Sons 2006 un il $11.99

Grades: PreK K 1 2   E

1. Alphabet 2. Birthdays 3. Stories in rhyme 4. Spanish language -- Vocabulary

ISBN 0-399-24225-2

LC 2004-20478

A rhyming book that outlines the preparations for and celebration of a young boy's birthday, with Spanish words for each letter of the alphabet translated in a glossary.

"At their best, Elya's verses bounce as easily between languages as they did in Oh, No, Gotta Go! (2003), which was also buoyantly illustrated by Karas." Booklist

Fairy trails; a story told in English and Spanish. illustrated by Mercedes McDonald. Bloomsbury Children's Books 2005 un il $17.99

Grades: PreK K 1 2   E

1. Fairy tales 2. Stories in rhyme 3. Spanish language -- Vocabulary

ISBN 1-58234-927-4

Miguel and Maria meet various fairy tale characters as they walk to their aunt's house. Includes some Spanish words

"Done in pastels, the warm and colorful illustrations have an appealing folk-art quality. . . . A glossary of the Spanish words is included, but the rhyming text provides ample context clues so that the story is accessible to non-Spanish speakers. Overall, Fairy Trails would be a great storytime choice for both bilingual and English-only audiences." SLJ

Fire! Fuego! Brave bomberos; by Susan Elya; illustrated by Dan Santat. Bloomsbury Children's Books 2012 40 p. (reinforced : alk. paper) $17.89

Grades: PreK K 1 2   E

1. Spanish language 2. Stories in rhyme 3. Fire fighters -- Fiction

ISBN 1599907593; 9781599904610; 9781599907598

LC 2011004934

This picture book depicts the story of a group of firefighters, "four bomberos and el capitán," as they "race to gear up and get to the fire after the alarm sounds." The book describes various firefighting themes such as the fire station Dalmatian, the fire pole, and rescuing a cat. Author Susan Middleton Elya incorporates Spanish vocabulary words into the text, and adds "context clues as well as words that are close to English [to] make most of the Spanish vocabulary easy to decode." (Kirkus Reviews)

"With more than 20 picture books to her name, Elya has built her career on stories that deftly incorporate Spanish vocabulary words into English verse...The meanings of most of the Spanish words can be inferred from context, and a glossary is also included. The firefighters' determination, grit, and camaraderie—all fully evident in Santat's cinematically action-packed scenes—are sure to bolster childhood ambitions of joining their ranks." PW

Little Roja Riding Hood; Susan Middleton Elya; illustrated by Susan Guevara. G.P. Putnam's Sons 2014 32 p. color illustrations (hardcover) $16.99

Grades: PreK K 1 2   E

1. Folklore 2. Fairy tales 3. Stories in rhyme

ISBN 039924767X; 9780399247675

LC 2012022545

Pura Belpré (Illustrator) Honor Book (2015)

In this book, by Susan Middleton Elya, "while Roja picks flowers on the way to her grandma's, a mean wolf sneaks away with her cape to surprise Abuelita. But Grandma's no fool and Roja's no ordinary chica. They send that hungry lobo packing with a caliente surprise! This . . . retelling of Little Red Riding Hood has accessible Spanish rhymes." (Publisher's note)

"Elya remains a master at blending Spanish and English to create clever, lively verse, and she and Guevara give the story of Little Red Riding Hood an entertaining and thoroughly modern spin." Pub Wkly

N is for Navidad; by Susan Middleton Elya and Merry Banks; illustrated by Joe Cepeda. Chronicle Books 2007 un il $14.95

Grades: PreK K 1   E

1. Alphabet 2. Stories in rhyme 3. Christmas -- Fiction 4. Hispanic Americans -- Fiction 5. Spanish language -- Vocabulary

ISBN 978-0-8118-5205-0; 0-8118-5205-9

LC 2006008169

A rhyming book that outlines the preparations for and celebration of the Christmas season, with Spanish words for each letter of the alphabet translated in a glossary.

"Cepeda's lively paintings take a colorful, dynamic look at a warm Latino neighborhood celebration of the holiday season. . . . This book has potential to provide a springboard for discussion of holiday traditions while keeping children entertained visually." SLJ

No more, por favor; pictures by David Walker. G.P. Putnam's Sons 2010 un il $16.99

Grades: PreK K 1 2   E

1. Stories in rhyme 2. Food -- Fiction 3. Rain forest animals -- Fiction 4. Spanish language -- Vocabulary

ISBN 978-0-399-24766-8; 0-399-24766-1

LC 2008048411

Rain forest parents come up with a solution when all their children become picky eaters at the same time. Spanish words interspersed in the rhyming text are defined in a glossary.

"Walker's acrylic paintings in rich, primary rainforest colors add appeal to the bouncy, sometimes uneven rhyme. Kids with picky palates will appreciate the message and discover new tasty options while training their tongues with morsels of Spanish." Kirkus

Oh no, gotta go! illustrated by G. Brian Karas. Putnam 2003 un il $14.99

Grades: PreK K 1 2   E

1. Stories in rhyme 2. Bathrooms -- Fiction 3. Spanish language -- Vocabulary

ISBN 0-399-23493-4

LC 2002-17703

As soon as she goes out for a drive with her parents, a young girl needs to find a bathroom quickly. Text includes some Spanish words and phrases

"The unexpected rhyming of the English and boldface Spanish words give the rhythmic text an ebullient humor enhanced by Karas' understated gouache, acrylic, pencil, and collage illustrations." Bull Cent Child Books

Another title is:

Oh no, gotta go! #2 (2007)

Emberley, Barbara

Night's nice; [by] Barbara and Ed Emberley. Little, Brown Children 2008 un il $12.99

Grades: PreK K   E

1. Night -- Fiction

ISBN 978-0-316-06623-5; 0-316-06623-0

First published 1962 by Doubleday Books

Moonlit treetops, city lamps aglow, bright fireworks bursting in a dark July sky, and other wondrous illuminated evening sights are captured in a colorful picture book with a die-cut moon and silver foil title type on the cover.

"An inviting exploration of the wonders of nighttime. . . . Thin, sketchlike black line drawings, awash in sumptuous jewel-toned colors, work in tandem with this soothing tale sure to diminish night frights for youngsters concerned about the dark." SLJ

Emberley, Ed

Ed Emberley's bye-bye, big bad bullybug! Little, Brown & Co. 2007 un il $10.99

Grades: PreK K 1 2   E

1. Bullies -- Fiction 2. Insects -- Fiction 3. Monsters -- Fiction

ISBN 978-0-316-01762-6; 0-316-01762-0

LC 2006-15423

Die-cut pages reveal "a mean and scary 'Big Bad Bullybug' from outer space who threatens to bite, pinch, and tickle itty-bitty baby bugs. Luckily for the small fliers, a human with a huge sneaker is willing to do away with the pink-polka-dotted meanie. The cobolt blue backgrounds create a grand contrast for the electric greens, oranges, and yellows." SLJ

★ **Go** away, big green monster! Little, Brown 1992 un il $10.99

Grades: PreK K 1   **E**
1. Fear -- Fiction 2. Bedtime -- Fiction 3. Monsters -- Fiction
ISBN 0-316-23653-5

LC 9206231

"Using die-cut, black pages, the book begins with the monster's 'two big yellow eyes' glowing through round holes. Each flip of a page displays more features shining in electric colors through new holes—'a long blue nose/ a big red mouth with sharp white teeth/ two little squiggly ears . . .,' and so on—until the narrator announces, 'You don't scare me! So GO AWAY scraggly purple hair . . .,' and dismisses the monster page by page, feature by feature, like the departing Cheshire Cat." (Booklist) "Preschool." (SLJ)

"In the first half of this fear-dispelling book, graphically distinctive die-cut pages reveal, bit by bit, a monster with 'sharp white teeth' and 'scraggly purple hair.' The process is then reversed as the text commands each scary feature to 'go away,' until there is nothing at all left of the monster but a black page instructing 'Don't Come Back! Until I say so.' Entertaining and empowering for young children." Horn Book Guide

Mice on ice; by Rebecca Emberley and Ed Emberley. Holiday House 2012 32 p. (I like to read) (hardcover) $14.95
Grades: K 1 2   **E**
1. Ice skating -- Fiction 2. Cats -- Fiction 3. Mice -- Fiction 4. Stories in rhyme
ISBN 0823425762; 9780823425761

LC 2011038812

Authors and illustrators Rebecca Emberley and Ed Emberley present a children's rhyming book about a cat and some mice ice-skating. "Mice skate on ice. As they skate, their blades leave lines that depict a cat. Magically, the cat appears, colorful, graphic, and three-dimensional. What happens next? Why, the cat and the mice skate together!" (Publisher's note)

Nighty night, little green monster; Ed Emberley. Little Brown & Co 2013 32 p. $8.99
Grades: PreK K   **E**
1. Bedtime -- Fiction 2. Monsters -- Fiction 3. Color -- Fiction 4. Toy and movable books -- Specimens
ISBN 0316210412; 9780316210416

LC 2012947183

In this picture book, by Ed Emberley, "each turn of the page . . . reveal[s] Little Green Monster's little yellow eyes, his little red mouth, and even a . . . tiny white monster tooth. Then, when the stars begin to appear, it's time for bed... so, nighty night, little yellow eyes. Nighty night, little red mouth. Nighty night, . . . little white tooth. Sweet dreams!" (Publisher's note)

Thanks, Mom! Little, Brown 2003 un il $11.95
Grades: PreK K 1   **E**
1. Mice -- Fiction 2. Animals -- Fiction
ISBN 0-316-24022-2

LC 2001-50715

Kiko the mouse finds some delicious cheese and gets help from his mother when a group of various animals tries to take it

"Using sunny yellow highlights and creatures constructed from bold, geometric shapes, Emberley creates an exciting, chaotic chase with sparse text and an impressive sense of graphic design." SLJ

Where's my sweetie pie? LB Kids 2010 un il $7.99
Grades: PreK   **E**
1. Stories in rhyme 2. Board books for children
ISBN 978-0-316-01891-3; 0-316-01891-0

"The book's title becomes a refrain for the short, rhyming text, encouraging kids to lift the flap and discover what's hidden. . . . Bold and

colorful, the simple forms that make up the digital illustrations show up clearly against the white backgrounds. . . . As rewarding as a good game of peekaboo." Booklist

Emberley, Rebecca
★ The **ant** and the grasshopper; Rebecca Emberley and Ed Emberley. Roaring Brook Press 2012 32 p. (alk. paper) $16.99
Grades: PreK K 1 2 3   **E**
1. Fables 2. Ants -- Fiction 3. Grasshoppers -- Fiction 4. Ants -- Fiction 5. Insects -- Fiction 6. Bands (Music) -- Fiction
ISBN 1596434937; 9781596434936

LC 2011033800

This children's story, by Rebecca Emberley, illustrated by Ed Emberley, retells the fable of the ant and the grasshopper. "While hard at work on her chores, an ant hears the wonderful clickety click chirrup of music coming from the distance. Although she knows she should focus on the task at hand, she can't help but explore the joyful noise!" (Publisher's note)

★ **If** you're a monster and you know it; by Rebecca Emberley & Ed Emberley. Orchard Books 2010 un il $16.99
Grades: PreK K 1   **E**
1. Monsters -- Fiction
ISBN 978-0-545-21829-0; 0-545-21829-2

"In this rollicking interpretation of 'If You're Happy and You Know It,' brightly colored, digitally created monsters . . . run amok, wriggling and roaring, stomping and twitching. The never-frightening creatures are rendered in eye-popping psychedelic colors against a flat black background and feature horns. antennae, claws, teeth and any number of eyes. . . . This will be a favorite with adults and children alike, allowing for both imaginative play and a raucous but structured outpouring of energy." Kirkus

The **lion** and the mice; by Rebecca Emberley and Ed Emberley. Holiday House 2011 un il (I like to read picture book) $14.95
Grades: PreK K 1 2   **E**
1. Mice -- Fiction 2. Size -- Fiction 3. Lions -- Fiction
ISBN 978-0-8234-2357-6; 0-8234-2357-3

LC 2010044205

"Aesop's lion and mouse (or mice, as this case has it) have never looked more stylish. . . . A wacky-hued lion sleeps. But when a tiny mouse, resplendent in olive-green heels and a tuft of electric-blue fur, finds herself next to the lion, he wakes up. The wry narrator intones . . . 'Uh-oh.' But . . . the lion lets the mouse go, with the mouse squeaking in reply, 'One day I will help you.'. . . The mouse returns, with the help of many fashion-forward rodent friends, and fits a key into a never-before-seen padlock. . . . Fantastic visual fun." Kirkus

Ten little beasties; [by] Rebecca Emberley and Ed Emberley. Roaring Brook Press 2011 un il $12.99
Grades: PreK K 1   **E**
1. Counting 2. Monsters -- Fiction
ISBN 978-1-59643-627-5; 1-59643-627-1

LC 2010028118

"Begin with one weird and wacky, black-and-white beastie, then add an additional, but very different-looking one, to each subsequent page, and you have the Emberleys' newest offering, done with their inimitable twist and style. . . . Each creature is fantastical and geometric, but with a splotch of color to add to the exotic designs each one sports. Each spread is of a different vibrant color." SLJ

★ **There** was an old monster! [by] Rebecca, Adrian, & Ed Emberley. Orchard Books 2009 un il lib bdg $16.99

Grades: PreK K   E
1. Songs 2. Monsters -- Fiction
ISBN 978-0-545-10145-5; 0-545-10145-X

LC 2008007191

In this variation on the traditional cumulative rhyme, a monster swallows ants, a lizard, a bat, and other creatures to try to cure a stomach ache than began when he swallowed a tick.

"Individual readers will pore over the illustrations and enjoy the repetition in the text while the large pictures make this a natural to share with groups. With the song provided as a free download at the publisher's Web site, this jazzy crowd-pleaser will have kids begging for repeat reads." SLJ

Emmett, Jonathan
Leaf trouble; illustrated by Caroline Jayne Church. Chicken House 2009 un il $16.99
Grades: PreK K 1 2   E
1. Autumn -- Fiction 2. Leaves -- Fiction 3. Squirrels -- Fiction
ISBN 978-0-545-16070-4; 0-545-16070-7

LC 2009008268

A young squirrel panics when the leaves on his tree change color and fall, but he feels better when his mother tells him about autumn.

"The colorful and endearing ink illustrations, placed in a layered collage using a variety of textures and perspectives, are a delight." SLJ

The **princess** and the pig; by Jonathan Emmett; illustrated by Poly Bernatene. Bloomsbury Distributed to the trade by Macmillan 2011 32 p. col. ill. (hardcover) $16.99
Grades: PreK K 1 2 3 4   E
1. Humorous fiction 2. Pigs -- Fiction 3. Princesses -- Fiction
ISBN 0802723349; 9780802723345

LC 2010049549

In this children's picture book by Jonathan Emmett, "There's been a terrible mix-up in the royal nursery. Priscilla the princess has accidentally switched places with Pigmella, the farmer's new piglet. The kindly farmer and his wife believe it's the work of a good witch, while the ill-tempered king and queen blame the bad witch. . . . While Priscilla grows up on the farm, poor yet very happy, things don't turn out quite so well for Pigmella." (Publisher's note)

Empson, Jo
Never Ever; by Jo Empson. Childs Play Intl Ltd 2013 32 p. $7.99
Grades: PreK K 1   E
1. Children's stories 2. Animals -- Fiction 3. Girls -- Fiction 4. Animals -- Pictorial works -- Fiction
ISBN 184643551X; 9781846435515

In this picture book, by Jo Empson, "a little girl clutches her toy rabbit and goes for a walk. As a pig with wings takes to the air, she says, 'Nothing exciting ever happens to me! Never, ever!' Her eyes are downcast, seeing nothing. . . . Even the youngest readers . . . will see what the child does not. . . . Humor builds as the simple text is repeated, leading the way to the next encounter." (School Library Journal)

Endle, Kate
Bunny Rabbit in the sunlight; [by] Kate Endle & Casper Babypants. Sasquatch Books 2011 il bd bk $9.99
Grades: PreK   E
1. Board books for children 2. Sun -- Fiction 3. Animals -- Fiction
ISBN 978-1-57061-749-2; 1-57061-749-X

"Eye-catching collages depict gentle animals whose habitats are brightened by different light sources. . . . Endle varies her compositions with warm and cool colors; visual textures suggest smoothness of glass and the roughness of gravel. When it's time to turn off the lights, readers will likely request a rereading. A recording by Babypants (aka Chris

Ballew, lead singer for the Presidents of the United States of America) is available for download." Publ Wkly

Engelbreit, Mary
Night of great joy; Mary Engelbreit. Zonderkidz 2016 32 p. color illustrations (hardback) $16.99; (ebook) $14.99
Grades: PreK K 1   E
1. Christmas 2. Jesus Christ -- Nativity
ISBN 9780310743545; 9780310744290

LC 2016018075

This picture book by Mary Engelbreit "tells the story of the nativity through the performance of a children's Christmas pageant. With adorable illustrations and simple storytelling, Engelbreit paints a wonderful picture of the night that Jesus was born. . . . From the arrival of Mary and Joseph in Bethlehem to the gathering of many before the baby Jesus, this holiday treasure leads children through the tale of the birth of Jesus, guiding them with the star of Bethlehem." (Publisher's note)

"With the spotlight on the rounded forms of rosy-cheeked, costumed kids drawn in Engelbreit's signature style, this colorful picture book will please her adult fans while holding the interest of many children." Booklist

Engle, Margarita
Drum dream girl; how one girl's courage changed music. by Margarita Engle; illustrated by Rafael López. Houghton Mifflin Harcourt 2015 48 p. color illustrations $16.99
Grades: K 1 2 3   E
1. Drums -- Fiction 2. Girls -- Fiction 3. Sex role -- Fiction 4. Dance music -- Fiction 5. Drummers (Musicians) -- Fiction 6. Cuba -- History -- 1909-1933 -- Fiction
ISBN 0544102290; 9780544102293

LC 2014015056

Pura Belpre Illustrator Award (2016)

In this book by Margarita Engle, illustrated by Rafael Lopez, "girls cannot be drummers. Long ago on an island filled with music, no one questioned that rule--until the drum dream girl. In her city of drumbeats, she dreamed of pounding tall congas and tapping small bongós. She had to keep quiet. She had to practice in secret. But when at last her dream-bright music was heard, everyone sang and danced and decided that both girls and boys should be free to drum and dream." (Publisher's note)

"A talented young girl with a passion for drumming dreams of playing music in this upbeat story based on the life of Cuban musician Millo Castro Zaldarriaga. . . . Vibrant, warm, and hopeful, this expressive story shows the power of perseverance and importance of following your dreams. Engle's prose flows easily, with clean but evocative language that will be accessible to a range of young readers." Booklist

Includes bibliographical references

Orangutanka; a story in poems. Margarita Engle; illustrated by Renée Kurilla. Henry Holt & Co. 2015 40 p. color illustrations (hardback) $17.99
Grades: PreK K 1 2   E
1. Sleep -- Fiction 2. Stories in rhyme 3. Waka 4. Orangutans -- Fiction 5. Naps (Sleep) -- Fiction 6. Familial behavior in animals -- Fiction
ISBN 0805098399; 9780805098396

LC 2014019224

In this children's story, by Margarita Engle, illustrated by Renée Kurilla, "all the orangutans are ready for a nap in the sleepy depths of the afternoon . . . all except one. This little orangutan wants to dance! A hip-hop, cha-cha-cha dance full of somersaults and cartwheels. But who will dance with her?" (Publisher's note)

"A sprightly introduction to orangutans through nimble wordplay and attractive book design. Kurilla's pen-and-ink illustrations frame

Engle's tanka verses, which relate a simple story of an orangutan family in an animal sanctuary in Borneo." SLJ

Includes bibliographical references

English, Karen

★ The **baby** on the way; pictures by Sean Qualls. Farrar, Straus and Giroux 2005 un il $16

Grades: PreK K 1 2   E

1. Infants -- Fiction 2. Childbirth -- Fiction 3. Grandmothers -- Fiction 4. African Americans -- Fiction

ISBN 0-374-37361-2

LC 2003-49047

Jamal, a young African American boy, asks his grandmother if she was ever a baby; she tells him the story of how she was born.

"The intimate artwork, in earth colors with pencil-thin line details, shows the loving bond between family members stretching back in time and into the future." Booklist

★ **Hot** day on Abbott Avenue; illustrated by Javaka Steptoe. Clarion Books 2004 32p il $15

Grades: PreK K 1 2   E

1. Summer -- Fiction 2. Friendship -- Fiction 3. Rope skipping -- Fiction 4. African Americans -- Fiction

ISBN 0-395-98527-7

LC 2002-09043

After having a fight, two friends spend the day ignoring each other, until the lure of a game of jump rope helps them to forget about being mad.

"Steptoe's found-object and cut-paper collages highlight facial features and depict oppressive summertime weather to perfection. . . . English's simple narrative consists mostly of two to three sentences per page and ends on a gratifying note." SLJ

★ **Speak** to me; (and I will listen between the lines) pictures by Amy June Bates. Farrar Straus Giroux 2004 un il $16

Grades: 2 3 4 5   E

1. School stories 2. African Americans -- Fiction 3. San Francisco (Calif.) -- Fiction

ISBN 0-374-37156-3

LC 2002-192895

Describes events of one day at a San Francisco Bay Area school as perceived by different second-graders, from the observations of first to arrive on the playground to the walk home.

"English's rich descriptions and insights bring readers into the world of six inner-city . . . students. . . . Bates's watercolor-and-ink illustrations capture the characters' expressions and moods vividly." SLJ

Ericsson, Jennifer A.

A **piece** of chalk; by Jennifer A. Ericsson; illustrated by Michelle Shapiro. Roaring Brook Press 2007 un il $16.95

Grades: PreK K 1   E

1. Drawing -- Fiction

ISBN 978-1-59643-057-0; 1-59643-057-5

LC 2006032178

A little girl creates a colored chalk drawing on her driveway

"This simple, sunny offering captures the delight and escape a child finds in art. . . . The words and rhythms read like poetry, but there are no bouncy rhymes to distract from the story's quiet joy. Shapiro effectively mirrors the girl's art with a childlike style and an appealing palette of bright, opaque colors, muted with chalk white." Booklist

Ering, Timothy Basil

The **Almost** fearless Hamilton Squidlegger; Timothy Basil Ering. Candlewick Press 2013 48 p. $16.99

Grades: PreK K 1 2   E

1. Fear -- Fiction 2. Frogs -- Fiction 3. Bedtime -- Fiction 4. Father-son relationship -- Fiction 6. Fathers and sons -- Fiction

ISBN 0763623571; 9780763623579

LC 2012947714

This book, by Timothy Basil Ering, is "an endearing tale of a boy overcoming his bedtime fears with a little help from Dad--and the promise of wormcake in the morning. Hamilton Squidlegger is fearless! Well, almost. During the day he can best all the frackensnappers, skelecragons, and bracklesneeds in the swamp, but at night he quakes in terror. Will his father be able to help Hamilton remain fearless in his own mud all night?" (Publisher's note)

"Hamilton is "the rippingest, roaringest Squidlegger in the scrintalberry swamp," but his kryptonite is bedtime, when he fears the bracklesneed will strike. Hamilton's father's attempt to bribe him with a double-decker grasshopper worm cake succeeds following a nighttime (or dreamtime? It's rather confusing) multivillain romp in which Hamilton, who resembles a Muppet guppy, cavorts in Ering's fantastically fantastical acrylics." Horn Book

The **unexpected** love story of Alfred Fiddleduckling; Timothy Basil Ering. Candlewick Press 2017 48 p. color illustrations $15.99

Grades: PreK K 1   E

1. Ducks -- Fiction 2. Storms -- Fiction 3. Violins -- Fiction

ISBN 9780763664329

LC 2016951796

In this book, by Timothy Basil Ering, "Captain Alfred is sailing home with new ducks for his farm when his little boat is caught in . . . [a] storm. Everything aboard . . . is flung to the . . . sea, including . . . [a] very special . . . duck egg. . . . But . . . the little duckling stumbles out of his shell and discovers Captain Alfred's fiddle, floating . . . in the waves. And when the duckling embraces the instrument with all his heart, what happens next is pure magic." (Publisher's note)

"Exuding a zest for living and loving, this nautical narrative is an ode to joy." Kirkus

Ernst, Lisa Campbell

The **Gingerbread** Girl. Dutton Children's Books 2006 un il $16.99

Grades: PreK K 1 2   E

1. Fairy tales

ISBN 0-525-47667-9; 978-0-525-47667-2

LC 2006004193

Like her older brother, the Gingerbread Boy, who was eventually devoured by a fox, the Gingerbread Girl eludes the many people who would like to eat her but also has a plan to escape her sibling's fate.

"Ernst's familiar art . . . utilizes the oversize format to best advantage, with large characters leaping out of their frames." Booklist

Followed by: Gingerbread Girl goes animal crackers (2011)

The **Gingerbread** Girl goes animal crackers. Dutton Childrens Books 2011 un il $16.99

Grades: PreK K 1 2   E

1. Foxes -- Fiction 2. Cookies -- Fiction 3. Birthdays -- Fiction

ISBN 978-0-525-42259-4; 0-525-42259-5

LC 2011005244

Sequel to: The Gingerbread Girl (2006)

The Gingerbread Girl, who once escaped the fox that devoured her brother, must now try to save from a similar fate the animal crackers she received as a birthday gift.

"Ernst's pastel palette is well-suited to this lively story of 'Animal Crackers gone wild,' which, with words like 'menagerie' and 'brouhaha,' scattered throughout, offers a bit of a vocabulary lesson, too." Publ Wkly

Round like a ball! by Lisa Campbell Ernst. Blue Apple Books 2008 un il $15.95

        E

1. Earth -- Fiction

ISBN 978-1-934706-01-5; 1-934706-01-9

Everyone tries to guess what is round and warm and cold and strong and fragile, until they finally realize it is Earth

"The clues are placed in large letters on the left side of a double-page spread, encircling progressively larger cutout circles. The cutout on each successive page offers a glimpse of the next article guessed. When the pages are flipped, a rainbow of cutout circles, large and small, is created on the previous page. . . . The distinctive illustrations, the guessing element, and the showstopping foldout of the Earth will work well for individual or group viewing." Booklist

Sam Johnson and the blue ribbon quilt. Lothrop, Lee & Shepard Bks. 1983 32p il lib bdg $17.89; pa $6.99

Grades: K 1 2 3   **E**

1. Quilts -- Fiction 2. Sex role -- Fiction

ISBN 0-688-01517-4 lib bdg; 0-688-11505-5 pa

LC 82-9980

While mending the awning over the pig pen, Sam discovers that he enjoys sewing the various patches together but meets with scorn and ridicule when he asks his wife if he could join her quilting club

The illustrations "bring an old-timey, bucolic scene to life and show steps in an equal-rights issue." Publ Wkly

Sylvia Jean, scout supreme. Dutton Children's Books 2010 un il $16.99

Grades: PreK K 1 2   **E**

1. Pigs -- Fiction 2. Costume -- Fiction 3. Scouts and scouting -- Fiction

ISBN 978-0-525-47873-7; 0-525-47873-6

LC 2009017919

Sylvia Jean disguises herself in order to assist a neighbor who does not want her enthusiastic help, but she still might be the only one in her Pig Scout Troop who will not earn a Good Deed Badge.

"Expressive faces enhance the gentle narrative; thin lines indicate a quiet vulnerability. Ernst's scenes feature her signature pastel palette even as humorous details advance the energetic tale." Kirkus

Another title about Sylvia Jean is:

Sylvia Jean, drama queen (2005)

The **turn**-around upside-down alphabet book. Simon & Schuster Books for Young Readers 2004 un il $15.95

Grades: PreK K 1 2   **E**

1. Alphabet

ISBN 0-689-85685-7

LC 2003-16318

"With touches of humor and a great deal of creativity, Ernst fashioned this book out of cut paper and surrounded each block with a thick black border that sets off white words. Children will enjoy tilting the pages to see the transformations and will be motivated to come up with ideas of their own." SLJ

Zinnia and Dot. Viking 1992 un il $16.99; pa $5.99

Grades: PreK K 1 2   **E**

1. Chickens -- Fiction

ISBN 0-670-83091-7; 0-14-054199-3 pa

LC 91-36178

Zinnia and Dot, self-satisfied hens who bicker constantly about who lays better eggs, put aside their differences to protect a prime specimen from a marauding weasel.

"Ernst has an easy storytelling style and a flair for grouchy dialogue that clucks to be read aloud, and her line-and-wash paintings, lighted with gentle yellow tones, warm the comedy." Bull Cent Child Books

Esbaum, Jill

I hatched! by Jill Esbaum; pictures by Jen Corace. Dial Books for Young Readers 2014 40 p. (hardcover) $16.99

Grades: PreK   **E**

1. Chickens -- Fiction 2. Animal babies -- Fiction 3. Birds -- Fiction 4. Stories in rhyme 5. Animals -- Infancy -- Fiction

ISBN 0803736886; 9780803736887

LC 2012006100

In this book, by Jill Esbaum, "a baby chick bursts from his egg and into the world with . . . enthusiasm, awe, and I-can't-help-myself energy. . . . Jen Corace's . . . artwork is alive with critters and curiosities and surprises--the biggest of which? The hatching of a new baby sister, to the absolute delight of her now 'expert' big brother!" (Publisher's note)

Stanza; illustrated by Jack E. Davis. Harcourt Children's Books 2009 un il $16

Grades: PreK K 1 2   **E**

1. Stories in rhyme 2. Dogs -- Fiction 3. Poetry -- Fiction 4. Contests -- Fiction

ISBN 978-0-15-205998-9; 0-15-205998-9

LC 2007051078

Stanza the dog and his two rotten brothers terrorize the streets by day, but at night Stanza secretly writes poetry.

"The message, though well seasoned, is refreshed by lively characterizations of Stanza, his brothers, and the people around them. Children will delight in the details that are often hidden on the page. Rhyming verse makes this an especially fine read-aloud, but the real fun is in up-close scrutiny of the illustrations." SLJ

Teeny Tiny Toady; Jill Esbaum, illustrated by Keika Yamaguchi. Sterling Pub Co Inc 2016 40 p. chiefly color illustrations (hardcover) $14.95

Grades: 1 2 3   **E**

1. Size -- Fiction 2. Frogs -- Fiction

ISBN 9781454914549; 1454914548

In this children's story, by Jill Esbaum and illustrated by Keika Yamaguchi, "when a giant hand scoops up her mama and puts her in a pail, a terrified tiny toad named Teeny . . . begs her big, clumsy brothers [to help.] . . . But as the boys rush headlong to the rescue, pushing their little sister aside, it becomes clear: brawn isn't always better than brains—and the smallest of the family may just be the smartest one of all." (Publisher's note)

"Yamaguchi's illustrations are every bit as adorable as Teeny, her wee pink form hilarious when juxtaposed with her brothers', who resemble warty tennis balls with limbs. A triumphant reaffirmation of the truth that large hearts can beat in small chests, told in playful verse that gallops along with nary a stumble." Kirkus

To the big top; [by] Jill Esbaum; pictures by David Gordon. Farrar Straus Giroux 2008 un il $16.95

Grades: PreK K 1 2   **E**

1. Circus -- Fiction 2. Friendship -- Fiction

ISBN 0-374-39934-4; 978-0-374-39934-4

LC 2006053530

When the circus comes to the small town of Willow Grove in the early 1900s, best friends Benny and Sam enjoy an exciting day helping set up the tent, admiring the various animals, and anticipating the big show.

"Gordon's joyful illustrations capture the appeal traveling entertainers had for small-town residents of the early twentieth century. . . . Esbaum . . . provides a nostalgic trip down memory lane that will give children . . . a good idea of what it was like back then." Booklist

Tom's tweet; illustrated by Kyle M. Stone. Alfred A. Knopf 2010 il $16.99; lib bdg $19.99
Grades: PreK K 1   E
   1. Cats -- Fiction 2. Birds -- Fiction
   ISBN 978-0-375-85171-1; 0-375-85171-2; 978-0-375-95171-8 lib bdg; 0-375-95171-7 lib bdg
                  LC 2009017262
When a cat finds a bedraggled baby bird that has fallen from its nest, an unlikely friendship develops between the two.
"Esbaum's tweet tale will have listeners in stitches (especially the wormy bits), and Santat's Photoshopped cartoon illustrations of bulky Tom and the goggle-eyed tweets are as expressive as they are goofy. Totally tweet-rific." Kirkus

Escoffier, Michael
Rabbit and the Not-So-Big-Bad Wolf; by Michaël Escoffier; illustrated by Kris Di Giacomo. Holiday House 2013 32 p.
Grades: PreK K   E
   1. Wolves -- Fiction 2. Rabbits -- Fiction
   ISBN 9780823428137
                  LC 2012027931

Where's the Baboon? by Michaël Escoffier; illustrated by Kris Di Giacomo. Enchanted Lion Books 2015 40 p. $17.95
Grades: K 1 2 3 4   E
   1. Animals -- Fiction 2. Hide-and-seek -- Fiction
   ISBN 1592701892; 9781592701896
                  LC 2015030850
This children's book, by Michaël Escoffier, illustrated by Kris Di Giacomo, "will PROVE to you that a snake can hide in a snowflake, that pigs can paint, and that the ones who copy the most are not necessarily cats! Prepare to be AMAZED by the game of hide-n-seek the words play! These tricksters are true experts in the art of camouflage!" (Publisher's note)
"The interplay on the pages is whimsical, charming, and overflowing with fun. In a word: outstanding." Kirkus

Eszterhas, Suzi
Brown bear; by Suzi Eszterhas. Frances Lincoln Children's Books 2012 32 p. ill. (hardcover) $15.99
   Grades: K 1 2   E
   1. Brown bear
   ISBN 1847803024; 9781847803023
This book, part of the Eye on the Wild series, "introduces two little brown bears, . . . and follows them for several years as they grow up and become independent. First seen as cubs closely guarded by their mother, the sisters . . . play fight, and nap under her watchful eye. After more than two years of teaching them how to hunt for food and protect themselves, their mother leaves. They hibernate together before going their separate ways to start families of their own." (Booklist)

Ets, Marie Hall
Play with me; story and pictures by Marie Hall Ets. Viking 1955 31p il hardcover o.p. pa $5.99
Grades: PreK K   E
   1. Animals -- Fiction
   ISBN 0-14-050178-9 pa
A Caldecott Medal honor book, 1956
On a sunny morning in the meadow an excited little girl tries to catch the meadow creatures and play with them. But, one by one, they all

run away. Finally, when she learns to sit quietly and wait, there is a happy ending
The "pictures done in muted tones of brown, gray and yellow . . . accurately reflect the little girl's rapidly changing moods of eagerness, bafflement, disappointment and final happiness." N Y Times Book Rev

Eugenie
Kitten's autumn; [written and illustrated by] Eugenie Fernandes. Kids Can Press 2010 un il $14.95
Grades: PreK   E
   1. Stories in rhyme 2. Cats -- Fiction 3. Autumn -- Fiction
   ISBN 978-1-55453-341-1; 1-55453-341-4
Autumn has settled on the farm, but fallen laeaves aren't the only signs of the season. Find out what animals kitten sees preparing themselves for winter.
"The self-hardening clay, acrylic paint and mixed-media collage illustrations . . . are . . . intricate and eye-catching. . . . A fine addition to seasons and kitty collections." Kirkus

Kitten's spring; [written and illustrated by] Eugenie Fernandes. Kids Can Press 2010 un il $14.95
Grades: PreK   E
   1. Stories in rhyme 2. Cats -- Fiction 3. Spring -- Fiction
   ISBN 978-1-55453-340-4; 1-55453-340-6
"It is spring on the farm, and Kitten is out exploring and visiting the new babies. The feline sees the bees on the flowers, the redwing blackbird by its nest, a chick, a duckling hatching, and more. At the end of a busy day, the cat returns to a house and settles down for a night of sweet dreams. . . . The illustrations are filled with delightful images and the brief text will appeal to the very young." SLJ

Kitten's summer; [by] Eugenie Fernandes. Kids Can Press 2011 un il $14.95
Grades: PreK   E
   1. Stories in rhyme 2. Cats -- Fiction 3. Summer -- Fiction
   ISBN 978-1-55453-342-8; 1-55453-342-2
"As rain begins to fall, Kitten dashes home. . . . Using rhyming couplets, the text tracks her progress and the critters she passes by. . . . Fernandes's clay, acrylic paint, and mixed-media collage artwork creates a unique look for the forest and its denizens. There is a tremendous amount of detail and charm in these realistic vignettes." SLJ
   Other titles about Kitten are:
   Kitten's autumn (2010)
   Kitten's spring (2010)
   Kitten's winter (2011)

Kitten's winter; written and illustrated by Eugenie Fernandes. Kids Can Press 2011 un il $14.95
Grades: PreK K 1   E
   1. Stories in rhyme 2. Cats -- Fiction 3. Winter -- Fiction
   ISBN 978-1-55453-343-5; 1-55453-343-0
Winter comes to Kitten's world, and the little calico leaves her cozy home for an afternoon of exploration and discovery.

Evans, Cambria
Bone soup. Houghton Miffin 2008 un il lib bdg $16
Grades: K 1 2 3   E
   1. Monsters -- Fiction 2. Halloween -- Fiction
   ISBN 978-0-618-80908-0 lib bdg; 0-618-80908-2 lib bdg
                  LC 2008001862
The skeletal Finnigin tricks a town's witches, ghouls, and zombies into helping him make soup
"Even the zombies are lovable in Evans's charming Halloween-themed rendition of 'Stone Soup.' . . . Seasoned with sprightly, lumines-

cent watercolors and the perfect dose of gross-out factor, this tale has all the right ingredients for a hearty storytime." SLJ

Evans, Freddi Williams

★ **Hush** harbor; praying in secret. illustrated by Erin Bennett Banks. Carolrhoda Books 2008 un il lib bdg $16.95

Grades: K 1 2 3   **E**

1. Slavery -- Fiction 2. Religion -- Fiction 3. Christian life -- Fiction 4. African Americans -- Fiction

ISBN 978-0-8225-7965-6 lib bdg; 0-8225-7965-0 lib bdg

LC 2007-34777

While Simmy watches for danger from high in a tree, other slaves gather in a hidden spot in the woods to sing and pray together in their own way, risking their lives in pursuit of religious freedom. Includes historical facts about hush, or brush, arbors and the churches that grew from them

This is "a moving narrative. . . . Illustrated with extremely stylized pictures that don't prettify their subjects, this captures some of the fear and horror associated with slavery." Booklist

Evans, Kristina

What's special about me, Mama? words by Kristina Evans; pictures by Javaka Steptoe. Hyperion 2011 un il $16.99

Grades: PreK K   **E**

1. African Americans -- Fiction 2. Mother-child relationship -- Fiction

ISBN 978-0-7868-5274-1; 0-7868-5274-7

A child wonders what exactly makes him unique. Mama lists her son's many good traits, from physical attributes to behavior. He dismisses each quality as just a little thing, until Mama explains that there is nothing little about love.

"Evans's dialogue swings with an easy back-and-forth rhythm between a mother and her son, and Steptoe's collage illustrations, in deep rich colors, effectively position the characters, harmoniously connecting the two. . . . A heartfelt, comforting tale." SLJ

Evans, Lezlie

Who loves the little lamb? illustrated by David McPhail. Disney-Hyperion Books 2010 un il $15.99

Grades: PreK   **E**

1. Stories in rhyme 2. Animals -- Fiction 3. Mother-child relationship -- Fiction

ISBN 978-1-4231-1659-2; 1-4231-1659-3

LC 2009015896

Rhyming text reveals that, although baby animals are not always perfect, their mothers love them and help them through difficult moments.

"This has two things going for it that set it apart: Evans' uncommonly clever text and artwork by McPhail. . . . What's so terrific about this . . . is the motherly diversity shown in the art." Booklist

Evans, Michael

Poggle and the treasure. Egmont 2011 il $16.99

Grades: PreK K   **E**

1. Dragons -- Fiction

ISBN 978-1-4052-4811-2; 1-4052-4811-4

"Poggle is a teddy-bearish blue dragon with a best friend named Henry, who's equally cuddly but of a less determinate species. Inhabiting a cheery world that's given depth and texture by crayon-y black shading, Poggle lives at the beach. . . . It's an ideal setting for making important discoveries, like a mysterious pink egg that the duo uncovers while playing pirates. . . . Evans deftly sidesteps treacle and spins out his stories with a light and distinctly British touch; a few novelty elements . . . provide additional interest. Sweet, expressive, and reassuring." Publ Wkly

Evans, Shane W.

We march; Shane W. Evans. Roaring Brook Press 2012 32 p.

Grades: PreK K 1 2 3   **E**

1. Family -- Fiction 2. Civil rights demonstrations -- Fiction 3. African Americans -- Civil rights -- Fiction 4. African Americans -- Fiction 5. March on Washington for Jobs and Freedom, Washington, D.C., 1963 -- Fiction

ISBN 9781596435391

LC 2010046862

This illustrated children's book tells the story of "[a]n African-American family [which] awakens before dawn to prepare for the historic March on Washington in August, 1963. In this . . . companion to "Underground" (2011), [author and illustrator Shane W.] Evans captures a pivotal event in the struggle for equality and civil rights in America. The family joins neighbors to pray at their church, paint signs and travel by bus to Washington. They walk and sing and grow tired but "are filled with hope" as they stand together at the Washington Monument to listen to Dr. King speak of dreams and freedom. . . . The March has become synonymous with Dr. King's . . . speech, but Evans reminds readers that ordinary folk were his determined and courageous audience." (Kirkus)

Eversole, Robyn Harbert

East Dragon, West Dragon; story by Robyn Eversole; pictures by Scott Campbell. Atheneum Books for Young Readers 2012 un il $16.99

Grades: PreK K 1 2   **E**

1. Dragons -- Fiction 2. Prejudices -- Fiction

ISBN 978-0-689-85828-4; 0-689-85828-0

LC 2010039609

East Dragon and West Dragon are suspicious of one another although they have never met, but when the western king is captured in the Eastern Kingdom and West Dragon goes to rescue him, they find they have much in common.

"Eversole's spare narrative mixes tongue-in-cheek exaggeration, childhood fears and adventure, inspiring Campbell to contrast the rough and the refined, designing detailed watercolor worlds brimming with humor and beauty. This primer on friendship wrapped in hijinks is paced for maximum pleasure." Kirkus

Evert, Lori

The **Christmas** wish; by Lori Evert. Random House Inc 2013 48 p. (trade) $17.99

Grades: PreK K 1 2   **E**

1. Elves -- Fiction 2. Christmas -- Fiction 3. Santa Claus -- Fiction 4. Arctic regions -- Fiction 5. Tundra animals -- Fiction 6. Voyages and travels -- Fiction

ISBN 0449816818; 9780375971730; 9780375981562; 9780449816813; 9780449819425

LC 2012035529

This book, by Lori Evert, presents the story of "a brave little girl named Anja [who] wanted to be one of Santa's elves. So she leaves a note for her family and helps her elderly neighbor prepare for the holiday, then she straps on her skis, and heads out into the snowy landscape. From a red bird to a polar bear to a reindeer, a menagerie of winter animals help Anja make her way to Santa." (Publisher's note)

Ewart, Claire

Fossil; [by] Claire Ewart. Walker 2004 un il $16.89; lib bdg $17.85

Grades: PreK K 1 2   **E**

1. Stories in rhyme 2. Fossils -- Fiction 3. Pterosaurs -- Fiction

ISBN 0-8027-8890-4; 0-8027-8891-2 lib bdg

LC 2003-53469

Upon finding a special stone, a child imagines the life of a pterosaur, the ancient flying reptile that lived, died, and was fossilized into that stone. Includes facts about fossils and how they are formed.

"Ewart's inviting text and dramatic artwork work nicely together to describe the fossilization process in an engrossing way." SLJ

Includes bibliographical references

Fackelmayer, Regina

The **gifts**; illustrated by Christa Unzner. North-South Books 2009 un il $16.95

Grades: K 1 2 3   **E**

1. Gifts -- Fiction 2. Christmas -- Fiction

ISBN 978-0-7358-2265-8; 0-7358-2265-4

"Mia buys a turkey for dinner, gifts for her dog and cat, a hat for herself, and a Christmas tree. Stopping to help an old man who has slipped on the ice, she leaves her tree outdoors. . . . The story is written with clarity and restraint. . . . The sensitive artwork includes a delicately spattered effect that textures all the illustrations and works particularly well in the snowy outdoor scenes." Booklist

Fagan, Cary

Book of big brothers; pictures by Luc Melanson. Groundwood Books 2010 un il $18.95

Grades: PreK K 1 2   **E**

1. Brothers -- Fiction

ISBN 978-0-88899-977-1; 0-88899-977-1

"In this fictionalized story, the author reminisces about what it was like to live with two older brothers. The trio will make readers giggle with delight as the boys' escapades, teasing, and love capture the warmth and fireworks of sibling dynamics. The 1970s retro-style illustrations reflect the mood and tone, and color choices accent the setting, creating a shared story from the past. . . . This fresh approach to fraternal relationships makes a welcome purchase." SLJ

A **Cage** Went in Search of a Bird; by Cary Fagan, illustrated by Banafsheh Erfanian. Groundwood Books 2017 32 p. color illustrations $18.95

Grades: PreK K 1 2   **E**

1. Birds -- Fiction 2. Friendship -- Fiction 3. Loneliness -- Fiction

ISBN 1554988616; 9781554988617

This book, by Cary Fagan, illustrated by Banafsheh Erfanian, is an "unusual tale of friendship and belonging. . . . A long-empty birdcage takes a chance and leaves behind its attic home to find a bird to keep. Out in the world, the cage encounters many birds and offers shelter to each of them. One by one, they refuse, explaining why they belong elsewhere. The cage feels lonelier than ever–until the cage in search of a bird finds a bird in search of a cage." (Publisher's note)

Ella May and the wishing stone; illustrated by Geneviève Côté. Tundra Books 2011 un il $17.95

Grades: PreK K 1 2   **E**

1. Wishes -- Fiction 2. Friendship -- Fiction

ISBN 978-1-77049-225-7; 1-77049-225-9

Ella May finds a stone and makes a wish on it, then refuses to share it with friends who then turn against her, but she finds a way to win them back.

"Fagan believably captures the delicate balance of friendship in the very young and lets the story [play] out with welcome complexity. Côté's illustrations are simple without being cartoonish, demonstrating the same warm understanding of childhood." Kirkus

Mr. Zinger's hat; Cary Fagan. Tundra Books of Northern New York 2012 32 p. (hardcover) $17.95

Grades: K 1 2   **E**

1. Imagination -- Fiction 2. Storytelling -- Fiction

ISBN 1770492534; 9781770492530

LC 2011938764

In this children's book, by Cary Fagan and illustrated by Dusan Petricic, "when old Mr. Zinger's windblown hat lands atop young Leo, the elder's suggestion . . . leads the pair to make up a tale about a rich but bored lad who offers half his possessions to anyone who can cheer him up. . . . Zinger then departs, leaving Leo to continue playing alone . . . until a new friend named Sophie shows up to share both the ball and the creation of a brand new story." (Kirkus Reviews)

Falatko, Julie

Snappsy the alligator (did not ask to be in this book!) words by Julie Falatko; pictures by Tim Miller. Viking, published by Penguin Group 2016 40 p. color illustrations (hardback) $16.99

Grades: PreK K 1 2   **E**

1. Books and reading -- Fiction 2. Alligators -- Fiction 3. Humorous fiction -- Fiction 4. Humorous stories 5. Storytelling -- Fiction

ISBN 9780451469458

LC 2015016653

In this book, by Julie Falatko, illustrated by Tim Miller, "Snappsy the alligator is having a normal day when a pesky narrator steps in to spice up the story. Is Snappsy reading a book ... or is he making CRAFTY plans? Is Snappsy on his way to the grocery store ... or is he PROWLING the forest for defenseless birds and fuzzy bunnies? Is Snappsy innocently shopping for a party ... or is he OBSESSED with snack foods that start with the letter P? What's the truth?" (Publisher's note)

"Falatko's debut picture book is a truly laugh-out-loud, mischievous romp, made gleefully goofier by Miller's straitlaced, deadpan animal characters." Booklist

Falconer, Ian

★ **Olivia**; written and illustrated by Ian Falconer. Atheneum Bks. for Young Readers 2000 un il $17.99; bd bk $7.99

Grades: PreK K 1 2   **E**

1. Pigs 2. Behavior 3. Pigs -- Fiction

ISBN 0-689-82953-1; 0-689-87472-3 bd bk

LC 99-24003

A Caldecott Medal honor book, 2001

Whether at home getting ready for the day, enjoying the beach, or at bedtime, Olivia is a young pig who has too much energy for her own good. "Ages three to seven." (Christ Sci Monit)

"The spacious design of the book; the appeal of the strong, clever art; and the humor that permeates every page make this a standout. . . . Falconer . . . renders Olivia's world in charcoal with dollops of red brightening the pages." Booklist

Other titles about Olivia are:

Olivia . . . and the missing toy (2003)

Olivia forms a band (2006)

Olivia goes to Venice (2010)

Olivia helps with Christmas (2007)

Olivia saves the circus (2001)

Olivia the fairy princess (2015)

Olivia the spy (2017)

Olivia and the fairy princesses; Ian Falconer. Atheneum Books for Young Readers 2012 40 p. (hardback) $17.99

Grades: PreK K 1 2   **E**

1. Pigs -- Fiction 2. Princesses -- Fiction 3. Professions -- Fiction 4. Individuality -- Fiction

ISBN 1442450274; 9781442450271; 9781442450288

LC 2011053046

In this book, the piglet Olivia is "suffering from an identity crisis. While all the other girls she knows, and even some of the boys, dress as ruffled pink princesses for parties and desperately want to be fairy princess ballerinas, Olivia's aspirations are more" unique. Dressed like choreographer Martha Graham, "Olivia explains that she is 'trying to develop a more stark, modern style'...Her ultimate choice is quintessentially Olivia." (Kirkus Reviews)

"Fans will be pleased with this addition to the series." (Booklist)

Olivia goes to Venice; written and illustrated by Ian Falconer. Atheneum Books for Young Readers 2010 un il $17.99
Grades: PreK K 1 2   E
1. Pigs -- Fiction 2. Italy -- Fiction 3. Vacations -- Fiction 4. Venice (Italy) -- Fiction
ISBN 978-1-4169-9674-3; 1-4169-9674-5
LC 2010009589

On a family vacation in Venice, Olivia indulges in gelato, rides in a gondola, and finds the perfect souvenir. "Ages three to seven." (N Y Times Book Rev)

"The contrast between the antic lines of the charcoal and gouache paintings superimposed over gorgeous color photographs provides much hilarity.... Falconer's understated text is both witty and subtle." Publ Wkly

Falkenstern, Lisa
A **dragon** moves in; written and illustrated by Lisa Falkenstern. Marshall Cavendish Children 2011 il $16.99; ebook $16.99
Grades: PreK K   E
1. Houses -- Fiction 2. Dragons -- Fiction 3. Rabbits -- Fiction 4. Hedgehogs -- Fiction
ISBN 978-0-7614-5947-7; 0-7614-5947-2; 978-0-7614-5995-8 e-book; 0-7614-5995-2 e-book
LC 2011001122

When Rabbit and Hedgehog bring home a newly-hatched dragon they all have a wonderful time together, but soon the dragon baby grows too big for their house.

"Falkerstern's oils have depth and warmth, and, though her animals are anthropomorphized, they're closer in authenticity to nature photos than cartoons. Gentle country concoction, two parts Beatrix Potter and one part Cressida Cowell." Kirkus

Faller, Regis
★ The **adventures** of Polo. Roaring Brook Press 2006 75p il $16.95
Grades: PreK K 1 2 3   E
1. Stories without words 2. Dogs -- Fiction
ISBN 978-1-59643-160-7; 1-59643-160-1
LC 2005055261

Polo the dog sets out from his home and enjoys many adventures, including sailing his boat on top of a whale, roasting hot dogs over a volcano, and taking a ride in a spaceship built from a mushroom.

"Young readers will be charmed by this hound, and be awed by his ingenuity. Somewhat similar to a graphic-novel format, this wordless picture book contains bold, colorful, cartoon panels that are sure to captivate even the most finicky youngster." SLJ

Other titles about Polo are:
Polo: the runaway book (2006)
Polo and the magic flute (2009)
Polo and Lily (2009)
Polo and the dragon (2009)
Polo and the magician (2009)

Falwell, Cathryn
David's drawings; story and pictures by Cathryn Falwell. Lee & Low Bks. 2001 un il hardcover o.p. pa $8.95
Grades: PreK K 1 2   E
1. School stories 2. Drawing -- Fiction 3. Friendship -- Fiction 4. African Americans -- Fiction
ISBN 1-58430-031-0; 1-58430-261-5 pa
LC 2001-16450

A shy African American boy arriving at a new school makes friends with his classmates by drawing a picture of a tree

"The cut-paper-and-fabric collages are a good choice for the story. . . Both theme and execution make this a fine choice for classroom read-alouds." Booklist

Gobble, gobble. Dawn Publications 2011 un il
Grades: PreK K 1   E
1. Stories in rhyme 2. Turkey -- Fiction
ISBN 1-58469-148-4; 1-58469-149-2 pa; 978-1-58469-148-8; 978-1-58469-149-5 pa
LC 2011011698

"After discovering a flock of turkeys in her yard in the spring, Jenny continues to watch them thoughout the year. With simple text, mostly rhyming couplets, the young nature watcher describes the turkeys' appearance and behavior as they nest and raise their young in the woods nearby. . . . Falwell augments her multimedia (cut and torn paper and found natural materials) images with overlaid block prints. Leaf prints add further texture. These charming illustrations also show other animals. . . . The author includes suggestions for artwork and other activities." Kirkus

Pond babies. Down East 2011 un il $15.95
Grades: PreK K 1   E
1. Ponds -- Fiction 2. Animals -- Fiction
ISBN 978-0-89272-920-3; 0-89272-920-1
LC 2010043117

"This offering focuses on creatures that live in or near ponds, with a human child included at the end. A simple question-and-answer format presents a single physical characteristic of each one and then inquires, 'Whose baby is this?' Children will quickly catch on to the pattern and the idea that a page turn is necessary to learn the answer. Whether it is white spots that indicate a fawn or a wiggly tail to represent a tadpole, Falwell's colorful collages incorporate the given features. . . . The soft hues of the illustrations evoke the wonder of springtime." SLJ

★ **Scoot!** Greenwillow Books 2008 un il $16.99; lib bdg $17.89
Grades: PreK K 1 2   E
1. Stories in rhyme 2. Ponds -- Fiction 3. Turtles -- Fiction
ISBN 978-0-06-128882-1; 0-06-128882-9; 978-0-06-128883-8 lib bdg; 0-06-128883-7 lib bdg
LC 2007-18355

Six silent turtles sit still as stones on a log, as energetic movement by the other animals in the pond happens all around them

"Extraordinary paper collages accompany a high-spirited romp. . . . Strong, predictable rhymes bounce across the pages. . . . Unusual, lively words extend vocabulary." SLJ

Shape capers; [by] Cathryn Falwell. Greenwillow Books 2007 un il $16.99; lib bdg $17.89
Grades: PreK K   E
1. Stories in rhyme 2. Shape -- Fiction 3. Imagination -- Fiction
ISBN 978-0-06-123699-0; 978-0-06-123700-0 lib bdg
LC 2006043061

A group of children shakes shapes out of a box and discovers the fun of using circles, squares, triangles, semicircles, rectangles, and their imaginations

This is a "bright, playful book, illustrated in whimsical cut-paper collage." Booklist

★ **Turtle** splash! countdown at the pond. Greenwillow Bks. 2001 un il $15.95; lib bdg $15.89

Grades: PreK K 1 2   **E**

1. Counting 2. Stories in rhyme 3. Turtles -- Fiction

ISBN 0-06-029462-0; 0-06-029463-9 lib bdg

LC 00-30918

As they are startled by the activities of other nearby creatures, the number of turtles on a log in a pond decreases from ten to one

"The rhyming, alliterative text is energized with a rolling rhythm, suspense, and vivid, descriptive words. . . . Evocative woodland scenes spring to life with well-defined animals that are described in a final appended section." Booklist

Fan, Terry

The **Night** Gardener; by Terry Fan and Eric Fan. Schuster Books for Young Readers 2016 48 p. color illustrations (hardcover : alk. paper) $17.99

Grades: K 1 2 3   **E**

1. Color -- Fiction 2. Gardeners -- Fiction 3. Topiary work -- Fiction

ISBN 1481439782; 9781481439787

LC 2014041306

In this juvenile picture book, by Terry Fan and Eric Fan, "one day, William discovers that the tree outside his window has been sculpted into a wise owl. In the following days, more topiaries appear, and each one is more beautiful than the last. . . . And though the mysterious night gardener disappears as suddenly as he appeared, William—and his town—are changed forever." (Publisher's note)

"An economic text punctuated with commas, questions, and ellipses leads readers forward; highly textured graphite and deepening, digitally colored compositions surprise and delight. Visual pleasure abounds." Kirkus

Fancher, Lou

Star climbing; by Lou Fancher; paintings by Steve Johnson and Lou Fancher. Laura Geringer Books 2006 un il hardcover o.p. lib bdg $16.89

Grades: PreK K   **E**

1. Stars -- Fiction 2. Bedtime -- Fiction 3. Imagination -- Fiction 4. Constellations -- Fiction

ISBN 978-0-06-073901-0; 0-06-073901-0; 978-0-06-073902-7 lib bdg; 0-06-073902-9 lib bdg

LC 2005005048

When he cannot sleep, a little boy imagines himself on a nighttime journey across the sky where he can run and dance with star constellations

"Ethereal, textured paintings accompany Fancher's rhythmic, lyrical poem." Publ Wkly

Farber, Norma

How the hibernators came to Bethlehem; by Norma Farber; illustrated by Barbara Cooney. Walker 2006 un il $9.95

Grades: K 1 2 3   **E**

1. Animals -- Fiction 2. Christmas -- Fiction 3. Hibernation -- Fiction

ISBN 0-8027-9610-9

A reissue of the title first published 1980

The Star of Bethlehem awakens the winter-sleeping creatures, such as Bear, Badger, and Raccoon, to send them to visit a newborn baby.

"The simple, unabashed realism of Cooney's art . . . along with Farber's respectful text, celebrates the hibernators as part of a divine plan." Horn Book Guide

Farley, Brianne

★ **Ike's** incredible ink; Brianne Farley. Candlewick Press 2013 32 p. $16.99

Grades: 1 2 3   **E**

1. Ink -- Fiction 2. Writer's block

ISBN 0763662968; 9780763662967

LC 2012947261

In this children's picture book by Brianne Farley, "Ike--an inkblot . . . is also a blocked writer. Like many before him, he procrastinates . . . and then he decides that his story demands ink made from exceptional ingredients: shadows, the feathers of a booga-bird, and the essence of the dark side of the moon. . . . After some chaotic concocting . . . Ike sits down to write and, sure enough, a story inspired by his ink quest materializes." (Publishers Weekly)

Secret tree fort; Brianne Farley. Candlewick Press 2016 32 p. color illustrations (hardcover) $16.99

Grades: PreK K 1 2   **E**

1. Play -- Fiction 2. Children -- Books and reading -- Fiction

ISBN 9780763662974; 0763662976

LC 2015934269

In this children's story, by Brianne Farley, "when two sisters are ushered outside to play, one sits under a tree with a book while the other regales her with descriptions of a cool fort in a tree that grows ever more fantastical in the telling. What will it take to get the older sister to look up?" (Publisher's note)

"Like a beloved box rattling with tiny, precious, ferreted things, this delightful picture book holds small, wonderfully specific insights into childhood imaginings, feelings, and frustrations." Kirkus

Farley, Robin

Mia and the too big tutu; pictures by Aleksey and Olga Ivanov. HarperCollins 2010 32p il (I can read) $16.99; pa $3.99

Grades: PreK K 1   **E**

1. Cats -- Fiction 2. Ballet -- Fiction

ISBN 978-0-06-173302-4; 0-06-173302-4; 978-0-06-173301-7 pa; 0-06-173301-6 pa

LC 2010021960

Mia the kitten is so excited about her first day of ballet class that she accidentally brings her big sister's tutu instead of her own.

"Large, colorful illustrations and an easy-to-read typeface make [this book] visually appealing." SLJ

Farmer, Jacqueline

Valentine be mine; Jacqueline Farmer; illustrated by Megan Halsey and Sean Addy. Charlesbridge 2013 32 p. (reinforced) $17.95; (paperback) $7.95

Grades: 1 2 3   **E**

1. Valentine's Day

ISBN 1580893902; 9781580893893; 9781580893909

LC 2011049504

This children's book, by Jacqueline Farmer, discusses the history of Valentine's Day. "Influenced by kings, poets, and religious customs, Valentine's Day has changed over the centuries from its origins in ancient Rome. Readers of all ages will learn the history of Valentine's Day as well as its past and present traditions in this informative dual-level text." (Publisher's note)

Farooqi, Musharraf
The **cobbler's** holiday, or, why ants don't have shoes; illustrated by Eugene Yelchin. Roaring Brook Press 2008 un il $16.95
Grades: K 1 2 3   E
   1. Ants -- Fiction 2. Shoes -- Fiction 3. Fashion -- Fiction
ISBN 978-1-59643-234-5; 1-59643-234-9
LC 2007044046

At a time when every ant has at least fifteen pairs of shoes and disputes over footwear are common, the one and only ant cobbler decides to take some time off, which leads to many tears until the Red Ant provides an elegant solution.

This is "a dainty, droll fable. . . , Farooqi builds scenarios ripe with comedy. . . . Yelchin . . . contributes decorative initial caps and a modish Jazz Age aesthetic; his spiky-looking ant flappers and dandies sport ritzy top hats and beaded caps, tailored and fur-collared coats, monocles and, of course, elaborate footwear." Publ Wkly

Farrell, Darren
Doug-Dennis and the flyaway fib; words and pictures by Darren Farrell. Dial Books for Young Readers 2010 un il $16.95
Grades: K 1 2   E
   1. Sheep -- Fiction 2. Circus -- Fiction 3. Honesty -- Fiction 4. Friendship -- Fiction 5. Truthfulness and falsehood -- Fiction
ISBN 978-0-8037-3437-1; 0-8037-3437-9
LC 2009-12141

Having fibbed about stealing his best friend's popcorn at the circus, Doug-Dennis the sheep finds himself carried far away to a place filled with lies and liars of all sorts and must discover a way to return.

"Sharp-edged irony and wacky cartoon visuals provide newcomer Farrell's moral tale with some serious wattage. . . . Despite the antifib message, the fibs are where all the entertainment is ('I invented the interweb,' declares a spider), and the ethically unsteady Doug-Dennis has plenty of Homer Simpson–like appeal." Publ Wkly

Stop following me Moon! Darren Farrell. Dial Books for Young Readers, an imprint of Penguin Group (USA) 2016 40 p. color illustrations (hardcover) $17.99
Grades: PreK K   E
   1. Moon -- Fiction 2. Bears -- Fiction 3. Behavior -- Fiction
ISBN 9780803741591
LC 2014045700

In this children's story, by Darren Farrell, "bear is hungry. So hungry that when he spies a squirrel's berry snack, he can't help taking the whole berry bush. Then, when he wanders past a busy beehive, Bear knows he's hit the jackpot. But someone is on to him—the moon! Or so Bear thinks. Before he knows it, Bear is on the run with his stolen snacks, causing a whole lot of trouble for the other animals in the forest." (Publisher's note)

"Not only will Bear make readers laugh out loud, but he illustrates how sharing can build a community. Bear's hilarious adventure begs for multiple readings." Kirkus

Thank you, Octopus; story and pictures by Darren Farrell. Dial Books for Young Readers 2014 40 p. color illustrations (hardcover) $16.99
Grades: PreK K 1   E
   1. Humorous fiction 2. Bedtime -- Fiction 3. Octopuses -- Fiction
ISBN 0803734387; 9780803734388
LC 2013027093

"It's bedtime, and Octopus is here to help his buddy get ready. First up is a bath (Thank you, Octopus)...in egg salad (No, thank you, Octopus)! Then it's time to brush teeth with paint brushes! And don't worry, Octopus made sure there were no monsters under the bed...because they're all in the closet! No, thank you, Octopus!" (Publisher's note)

"Prepare for escalating giggles as a well-meaning octopus takes on bedtime routines with hilarious ineptness. . . . Each page-turn extends the jokes, and the simple recurring refrain adds opportunities for kids to join in." Booklist

Faulkner, Matt
A **taste** of colored water. Simon & Schuster 2008 un il $16.99
Grades: K 1 2 3   E
   1. Cousins -- Fiction 2. Civil rights demonstrations -- Fiction 3. African Americans -- Segregation -- Fiction
ISBN 978-1-4169-1629-1; 1-4169-1629-6

In the 1960s two cousins hear of a water fountain labelled "Colored" and imagine a multicolored drink, but they discover the true meaning of the sign when they encounter a Civil Rights demonstration.

"Watercolors decorated with ink crosshatching ably contrast the sweet pastoral fun the children experience with their sudden, terrifying wake up. Faulkner's personal note about his growing up in the north, where segregation was not official but prejudice was always there, will spark discussion." Booklist

Fearing, Mark
The **great** Thanksgiving escape; Mark Fearing. First edition Candlewick Press 2014 32 p. color illustrations $15.99
Grades: K 1 2 3   E
   1. Cousins -- Fiction 2. Thanksgiving Day -- Fiction
ISBN 0763663069; 9780763663063
LC 2013955664

"It's another Thanksgiving at Grandma's. Gavin expects a long day of boredom and being pestered by distantly related toddlers, but his cousin Rhonda has a different idea: make a break for it--out of the kids' room to the swing set in the backyard! Gavin isn't so sure, especially when they encounter vicious guard dogs (in homemade sweaters)." (Publisher's note)

"Playing with perspective, Fearing's digitally created cartoons show long lines of pantyhosed legs and an aerial shot of outstretched manicured hands reaching for a hug. Funny play-by-play running commentary describes the action as it unfolds." SLJ

Fearnley, Jan
Martha in the middle; [by] Jan Fearnley. Candlewick Press 2008 40p il $16.99
Grades: PreK K 1   E
   1. Mice -- Fiction 2. Frogs -- Fiction 3. Siblings -- Fiction 4. Family life -- Fiction
ISBN 978-0-7636-3800-9; 0-7636-3800-5

Martha, a young mouse with a sensible big sister and a cute little brother, begins to feel invisible and decides to run away, but at the end of the garden she meets a wise frog who points out just how special the middle can be.

"Fearnley's nimble use of line and uncluttered watercolors focus on character and plenty of action. . . . Witty details . . . ramp up the fun." Publ Wkly

Milo Armadillo. Candlewick Press 2009 un il $15.99
Grades: PreK K 1 2   E
   1. Toys -- Fiction 2. Armadillos -- Fiction
ISBN 978-0-7636-4575-5; 0-7636-4575-3
LC 2009004231

When no one can find a pink, fluffy rabbit to give to Tallulah for her birthday, her grandmother knits her a pink, fluffy 'thing' that they name Milo Armadillo, which proves to be a great present.

"Mixed-media collages pay homage to all things handmade by incorporating worked yarn and fabric into the illustrations. This candy-colored picture book tells a simple, sweet story about learning to love what you have." SLJ

Mr. Wolf's pancakes; [by] Jan Fearnley. Tiger Tales 2001 un il $15.95; pa $6.95
Grades: PreK K 1 2 3   E
  1. Fairy tales 2. Wolves -- Fiction
  ISBN 1-58925-004-4; 1-58925-354-X pa

LC 2001-834

First published 1999 in the United Kingdom
"Mr. Wolf seeks assistance from his neighbors, but Chicken Little, Wee Willy Winkle, the Gingerbread Man, Little Red Riding Hood and the Three Little Pigs all nastily refuse. Of course, when Mr. Wolf eventually whips up the pancakes all by himself, they demand a share of his culinary creation. Mr. Wolf . . . lets the marauders into the kitchen-and then gobbles them all up. . . . Chipper watercolors depict a sunny storybook town. . . . A gleeful twist on a nursery staple." Publ Wkly

Another title about Mr. Wolf is:
Mr. Wolf and the three bears (2002)

Feder, Jane
  Spooky friends; starring Scarlet and Igor. by Jane Feder and illustrated by Julie Downing. Scholastic Press 2013 40 p. (Spooky friends) (hardcover : alk. paper) $16.99
Grades: K 1 2   E
  1. Mummies -- Fiction 2. Vampires -- Fiction 3. Friendship -- Fiction 4. Friendship -- Fiction 5. Best friends -- Fiction
  ISBN 0545478154; 9780545478151; 9780545478168

LC 2012014786

In this book by Jane Feder and illustrated by Julie Downing "Scarlet is a feisty little Vampire, and her best friend, Igor, is a roly-poly little Mummy. Together, they star in three humorous, heartwarming stories about two friends who never agree on anything. That is--until they discover different ideas can become even better ideas when they cooperate." (Publisher's note)

Federle, Tim
  Tommy can't stop; by Tim Federle; pictures by Mark Fearing. Disney-Hyperion 2015 32 p. color illustrations $16.99
Grades: PreK K 1   E
  1. Boys -- Fiction 2. Tap dancing -- Fiction 3. Family life -- Fiction
  ISBN 1423169174; 9781423169178

LC 2014015781

In this illustrated children's story, by Tim Federle with pictures by Mark Fearing, about an active child finding a place for his energy, "Tommy bounces, and he leaps. Tommy clomps, and he bulldozes. Nothing tires Tommy out, and his family can't keep up! But then his sister has an idea: could tap class be just right for Tommy?" (Publisher's note)

"The story is a fabulous reminder that all of the qualities that make one unique, even those that seem troublesome, can be used to fulfill a higher purpose. The story also reinforces that boys can dance, too. Gorgeously illustrated in bright colors and cartoonish characters, the pictures add humor and allure to the kid-friendly text." SLJ

Feelings, Muriel
  ★ **Jambo** means hello; Swahili alphabet book. pictures by Tom Feelings. Dial Bks. for Young Readers 1981 un il hardcover o.p. pa $6.99
Grades: PreK K 1 2   E
  1. Alphabet 2. Swahili language 3. East Africa
  ISBN 0-14-054652-1 pa
  A Caldecott Medal honor book, 1975

"Integrated totally in feeling and mood, the book has been engendered by an intense personal vision of Africa—one that is warm, all-enveloping, quietly strong and filled with love." Horn Book

★ **Moja** means one; Swahili counting book. pictures by Tom Feelings. Dial Bks. for Young Readers 1971 un il hardcover o.p. pa $6.99
Grades: PreK K 1 2   E
  1. Counting 2. Swahili language 3. East Africa
  ISBN 0-14-054662-6 pa
  A Caldecott Medal honor book, 1972

"A short introduction explaining the importance of Swahili and providing a map of the areas in which it is spoken expands the book's use beyond the preschool level of the text into the first three school grades." SLJ

Feiffer, Jules, 1929-
  ★ **Bark,** George; Jules Feiffer. HarperCollins Publishers 1999 30 p. il $17.99
Grades: PreK K 1 2   E
  1. Animal sounds 2. Dogs -- Fiction 3. Humorous fiction -- Fiction 4. Dogs -- Fiction 5. Humorous stories
  ISBN 0062051857; 9780062051851

LC 98074468

This children's book, by Jules Feiffer, "is a story about a pup whose mother is trying to teach him to bark, but George will only meow, quack, oink and moo. Preschool to grade two." (School Library Journal)

"Feiffer's characters are unforgettable, the text is brief and easy to follow, and the pictures burst with the sort of broad physical comedy that a lot of children just love." Booklist

Rupert Can Dance; Jules Feiffer. Farrar Straus & Giroux 2014 32 p. color illustrations $17.95
Grades: PreK K 1 2   E
  1. Cats -- Fiction 2. Dance -- Fiction
  ISBN 0374363633; 9780374363635

LC 2013908976

In this children's book by Jules Feiffer, "Rupert has a big secret. When his owner, Mandy, is fast asleep, he likes to slip on her dancing shoes and dance the night away. Then one night Mandy catches Rupert in the act. She's not upset; she's thrilled! And she's determined to give Rupert dancing lessons so he can hone his talent. Rupert is horrified. Lessons are for dogs. Cats like to do things their own way." (Publisher's note)

"This warmly humorous book may resonate most with those familiar with the love of dance or the delicate dignity of cats, but the story of friendship and shared passion at its heart will appeal to any reader." Horn Book

Feiffer, Kate
  But I wanted a baby brother! illustrated by Diane Goode. Simon & Schuster Books for Young Readers 2010 un il $16.99
Grades: PreK K 1   E
  1. Infants -- Fiction 2. Siblings -- Fiction 3. Family life -- Fiction
  ISBN 978-1-4169-3941-2; 1-4169-3941-5

Oliver Keaton wants a baby brother more than anything but when he gets a baby sister instead, he sets out with his dog Chaplin to trade his sister for the perfect baby brother.

"Both text and breezy cartoon illustrations are laced with humor, making this an excellent choice for reading aloud. . . . Feiffer's book is a cut above many of its kind." Booklist

Double pink; illustrated by Bruce Ingman. Simon & Schuster Books for Young Readers 2005 un il $15.95

Grades: PreK K 1   E
  1. Color -- Fiction
  ISBN 0-689-87190-0

LC 2004--06582

Madison covers and surrounds herself with her favorite color, pink, until the day her mother has trouble finding her.

"Feiffer's simple text reads easily, and Ingman's playful acrylic-and-ink paintings take a light approach to this look at childhood obsession." SLJ

Henry, the dog with no tail; illustrated by Jules Feiffer. Simon & Schuster Books for Young Readers 2007 un il $16.99
Grades: PreK K 1 2   E
  1. Dogs -- Fiction
  ISBN 978-1-4169-1614-7; 1-4169-1614-8

LC 2006-13418

Envious of the other dogs that have tails, Henry goes in search of a tail of his own, but in the end he decides he is happy the way he is.

"Feiffer's story features droll humor, wonderfully outlandish plot twists, and a satisfying journey of self-discovery. . . . The charcoal and watercolor illustrations use loose lines and color splashes to convey the action and capture the characters' personalities." SLJ

★ **My** mom is trying to ruin my life; [by] Kate Feiffer; illustrated by Diane Goode. Simon & Schuster Books for Young Readers 2009 un il $16.99
Grades: PreK K 1 2   E
  1. Father-daughter relationship -- Fiction 2. Mother-daughter relationship -- Fiction
  ISBN 978-1-4169-4100-2; 1-4169-4100-2

LC 2007045351

A young girl describes all the ways in which her mother and father conspire to ruin her life

"Feiffer and Goode . . . give the old chestnut of a story line an urbane sheen. . . . [Goode's] watercolor vignettes are gems of wry intelligence and comic understatement." Publ Wkly

★ **My** side of the car; illustrated by Jules Feiffer. Candlewick Press 2011 un il $16.99
Grades: PreK K 1 2   E
  1. Rain -- Fiction 2. Automobile travel -- Fiction 3. Father-daughter relationship -- Fiction
  ISBN 978-0-7636-4405-5; 0-7636-4405-6

LC 2010039184

Sadie and her father have been planning a trip to the zoo for a long time but something always gets in the way, so when they finally start out and her father sees some raindrops, Sadie insists there is no rain on her side of the car.

"Feiffer's sweet and loopy watercolor-and-pencil drawings follow Sadie's imaginings and explanations for wet car windows. . . . Sadie's cheerful sass and her father's obvious respect for and indulgence of the force of her imagination make this a keeper." Publ Wkly

President Pennybaker; [by] Kate Feiffer; illustrated by Diane Goode. Simon & Schuster Books for Young Readers 2008 un il $16.99
Grades: PreK K 1 2   E
  1. Politics -- Fiction
  ISBN 978-1-4169-1354-2; 1-4169-1354-8

LC 2007004815

Tired of the unfairness of life, young Luke Pennybaker decides to run for president, with his dog Lily as his running mate

"Deadpan narration allows the absurdity of the premise to carry the day, with plenty of help from the illustrations. Goode's breezy watercolors set just the right tone. . . . The humor is deftly understated, both

visually and verbally, making this an amusing and appealing send-up of politics and children's chores." SLJ

Feldman, Eve

★ **Billy** and Milly, short and silly! written by Eve Feldman; pictures by Tuesday Mourning. G.P. Putnam's Sons 2009 un il $16.99
Grades: PreK K 1 2   E
  1. Stories in rhyme
  ISBN 978-0-399-24651-7; 0-399-24651-7

LC 2008-26143

"This picture book presents 13 short rhyming stories about Billy and Milly. Most of them are four words long; some, only three. Every word in each selection rhymes. . . . The bright cartoon illustrations done in mixed-media collage are the keys to understanding the stories and the humor. . . . Both clever and slapstick, this book can be read for pleasure or used as a jumping-off point for thinking about rhyme, language, and story." SLJ

Feldman, Thea

Harry Cat and Tucker Mouse: Harry to the rescue! Square Fish 2011 47p (My readers) $15.99; pa $3.99
Grades: 1 2 3   E
  1. Cats -- Fiction 2. Mice -- Fiction 3. New York (N.Y.) -- Fiction
  ISBN 978-0-312-62507-8; 0-312-62507-3; 978-0-312-62509-2 pa; 0-312-62509-X pa

Tucker Mouse spotted a lost penny in the shoeshine store, so he ran in to get it for his collection. Now the store is closed up tight, and Tucker is trapped. Can Harry Cat find a way to get him out?

Harry Cat and Tucker Mouse: starring Harry. Square Fish 2011 32p (My readers) $15.99; pa $3.99
Grades: K 1 2   E
  1. Cats -- Fiction 2. Mice -- Fiction 3. Theater -- Fiction 4. Friendship -- Fiction 5. New York (N.Y.) -- Fiction
  ISBN 978-0-312-68168-5; 978-0-312-68169-2 pa

LC 2010048674

Harry Cat loves the theater, but when he becomes the star of a Broadway play he and his best friend Tucker Mouse miss one another terribly.

Harry Cat and Tucker Mouse: Tucker's beetle band. Square Fish 2011 47p il (My readers) $15.99; pa $3.99
Grades: 1 2 3   E
  1. Cats -- Fiction 2. Mice -- Fiction 3. Beetles -- Fiction 4. Crickets -- Fiction 5. Bands (Music) -- Fiction 6. New York (N.Y.) -- Fiction
  ISBN 978-0-312-62575-7; 0-312-62575-8; 978-0-312-62576-4 pa; 0-312-62576-6 pa

"Tucker Mouse, Harry Cat, and Chester Cricket contend with a beetle rock band disturbing their sleep under Times Square. The band is practicing to win the Battle of the Bug Bands competition and travel the country. . . . The Ivanovs' intricate ink and watercolor illustrations reflect the charm of Garth Williams's characters and original setting and add many details including varied visual perspectives and characters that exude facial and kinesthetic expression. . . . This well-told tale will appeal to the many young readers and their friends whose family members are in bands, and it serves as a wonderful introduction to the beloved characters in George Selden's The Cricket in Times Square." SLJ

Other titles in this series are:
Harry Cat and Tucker Mouse: Harry to the rescue! (2011)
Harry Cat and Tucker Mouse: Starring Harry! (2011)

Fenske, Jonathan

A **pig,** a fox, and a box; by Jonathan Fenske. Penguin Young Readers, an imprint of Penguin Group (USA) LLC 2015 30 p. (hc) $14.99

Grades: PreK K 1 2   **E**
1. Pigs -- Fiction 2. Foxes -- Fiction 3. Friendship -- Fiction 4. Boxes -- Fiction
ISBN 0448485117; 9780448485102; 9780448485119
    LC 2014044337
Geisel Honor Book (2016)
This illustrated children's story, written and illustrated by Jonathan Fenske, "tells three humorous stories of two friends, Pig and Fox, and their shenanigans with a cardboard box (all of which involved Pig accidentally crushing Fox in the box)." (Publisher's note)

Fenton, Joe
What's under the bed? written and illustrated by Joe Fenton. Simon & Schuster for Young Readers un il $15.99
Grades: PreK K 1 2   **E**
1. Stories in rhyme 2. Fear -- Fiction 3. Bedtime -- Fiction
ISBN 978-1-4169-4943-5; 1-4169-4943-7
When Fred lays down his head, he imagines there is something monstrous under his bed.
"The narrative is accessible, using uncomplicated rhymes. . . . The brooding illustrations would be more unnerving if Fred, diminutive in outsize glasses, weren't so adorably disarming." Horn Book Guide

Ferber, Brenda A.
The **yuckiest**, stinkiest, best Valentine ever; by Brenda A. Ferber; pictures by Tedd Arnold. Dial Books for Young Readers 2012 32 p. col. ill. (hardcover) $16.99
Grades: PreK K 1 2   **E**
1. Love -- Fiction 2. Valentine's Day -- Fiction
ISBN 0803735057; 9780803735057
    LC 2011047668
In this children's picture book, "Leon makes a very special valentine for his crush, Zoey Maloney, but the valentine has a mind and life of its own. The valentine tells Leon not to tell Zoey that he loves her. In a gingerbread man-like fashion, the valentine dashes out of the house with Leon running after it. During the chase, Leon and the valentine come across different groups of kids who share their opinions about Leon's declaration of love." (Children's Literature)

Fergus, Maureen
★ **Buddy** and Earl; by Maureen Fergus, illustrated by Carey Sookocheff. Groundwood Books 2015 32 p. color illustrations $16.95
Grades: PreK K 1 2   **E**
1. Dogs -- Fiction 2. Hedgehogs -- Fiction 3. Friendship -- Fiction
ISBN 1554987121; 9781554987122
In this children's story, by Maureen Fergus and illustrated by Carey Sookocheff, pet dog "Buddy does not know what is in the box that Meredith carries into the living room. But when the small, prickly creature says he is a pirate--and that Buddy is a pirate too--the two mismatched friends are off on a grand adventure. In this . . . book . . . a dog who likes to play by the rules meets a hedgehog who knows no limits." (Publisher's note)
"On a rainy afternoon Buddy the dog is bored and lonely, trapped in the house with his family. Watching the raindrops fall, he is surprised when his owner Meredith brings in a box that contains an odd looking object. The new "thing" is indeed alive and introduces itself as Earl. Since Buddy is not sure what type of thing Earl could be, the two begin a guessing game to solve the mystery. . . . A simple story for animal loving readers and proponents of imaginative play." SLJ
Other titles about Buddy and Earl are:
Buddy and Earl Go Exploring (2015)
Buddy and Earl and the Great Big Baby (2016)
Buddy and Earl Go to School (2017)

Buddy and Earl and the great big baby; by Maureen Fergus; illustrated by Carey Sookocheff. Groundwood Books 2016 32 p. color illustrations (Buddy and Earl) $16.95
Grades: PreK K 1 2   **E**
1. Infants -- Fiction 2. Adventure fiction -- Fiction
ISBN 1554987164; 9781554987160
In this book, by Maureen Fergus, illustrated by Carey Sookocheff, "Mom's friend Mrs. Cunningham is coming for a visit, and she's bringing her baby! While Buddy tries to explain the ins and outs of babydom to Earl, neither of them is prepared for the chaos the small and adorable creature brings with it. When the baby manages to escape from its cage—which Buddy gently suggests is really just a playpen—it's up to our favorite odd couple to save the day." (Publisher's note)
"This sweet story showcases qualities of friendship, love, and imagination." SLJ

Buddy and Earl go exploring; Maureen Fergus; illustrated by Carey Sookocheff. Groundwood Books 2016 32 p. color illustrations $16.95
Grades: PreK K 1 2   **E**
1. Animals -- Fiction 2. Friendship -- Fiction
ISBN 1554987148; 9781554987146
In this children's book, by Maureen Fergus and illustrated by Carey Sookocheff, "Buddy and Earl are safely tucked in for the night; Buddy on his blanket and Earl in his cage. But just as Buddy settles in for a nice, long sleep, Earl says it's time to say 'Bon voyage.' Soon these mismatched pals are at it again, exploring the wilds of the kitchen and defending a lovely lady hedgehog -- who may or may not be Mom's hairbrush -- from imminent danger." (Publisher's note)
"Sookocheff's acrylic and gouache illustrations in subdued gray, lavender, blue, and beige tones perfectly capture the quiet feel of a nighttime kitchen. Her cartoonish portrayal of Buddy and Earl is both amusing and expressive, wonderfully complementing Fergus's humorous prose." SLJ

Fern, Tracey E.
★ **Buffalo** music; illustrated by Lauren Castillo. Clarion Books 2008 31p il $16
Grades: 1 2 3 4   **E**
1. Teachers 2. Conservationists 3. Ranchers 4. Bison -- Fiction 5. Texas -- Fiction 6. Frontier and pioneer life -- Fiction
ISBN 978-0-618-72341-6; 0-618-72341-2
    LC 2007-18435
After hunters kill off the buffalo around her Texas ranch, a woman begins raising orphan buffalo calves and eventually ships four members of her small herd to Yellowstone National Park, where they form the beginnings of newly thriving buffalo herds. Based on the true story of Mary Ann Goodnight and her husband Charles; includes author's note about her work, with websites and a bibliography.
"Fern's lyrical text and Castillo's folk-style artwork beautifully capture the era and events. Done in warm, earthy hues, the mixed-media illustrations depict a rugged landscape of grays and browns speckled with touches of color-wildflowers or bright blooms on a tree." SLJ

★ **Pippo** the Fool; [by] Tracey E. Fern; illustrated by Pau Estrada. Charlesbridge 2009 un il $15.95
Grades: 1 2 3   **E**
1. Artists 2. Sculptors 3. Architects 4. Florence (Italy) -- Fiction 5. Italy -- History -- 0-1559 -- Fiction 6. Santa Maria del Fiore (Cathedral: Florence, Italy) -- Fiction
ISBN 978-1-57091-655-7; 1-57091-655-1
    LC 2007002283
In fifteenth-century Florence, Italy, a contest is held to design a magnificent dome for the town's cathedral, but when Pippo the Fool claims

he will win the contest, everyone laughs at him. Based on the true story of Filippo Brunelleschi.

This is "told with a great deal of charm and buttressed by understated humor. . . . Estrada's timeless art highlights Florence's orange-roofed architecture and colorfully attired citizens." Booklist

Ferrell, Sean

I don't like Koala; Sean Ferrell; illustrated by Charles Santoso. Atheneum Books for Young Readers 2015 40 p. color illustrations (hardcover) $17.99

Grades: PreK K 1 2   E

1. Toys -- Fiction 2. Koalas -- Fiction

ISBN 1481400681; 9781481400688

LC 2013015976

In this children's book by Sean Ferrell, illustrated by Charles Santoso, "when Adam opens a striped gift box and discovers a plush koala bear, he takes an immediate dislike to the stuffed animal. The young boy's parents, who do not understand his aversion, urge him to take good care of the toy. At bedtime, the little boy suddenly has a change of heart when he realizes that Koala's watching eyes will keep him safe from monsters in the dark." (Publisher's note)

"Slightly creepy, funny and fun." Kirkus

The **Snurtch**; words by Sean Ferrell; pictures by Charles Santoso. Atheneum Books for Young Readers 2016 40 p. color illustrations (hardcover) $17.99

Grades: PreK K 1 2 3   E

1. Emotions -- Fiction 2. Imaginary playmates -- Fiction 3. Behavior -- Fiction

ISBN 9781481456562

LC 2015017875

In this book, by Sean Ferrell, illustrated by Charles Santoso, "Ruthie has a problem at school. It is not the students. It is not the classroom. It is not the reading or the writing or the math. It is something scribbly, scrunchy, grabby, burpy, and rude. It is the Snurtch." (Publisher's note)

"Original in its visual and linguistic presentation of behavioral problems, this important call for understanding should sit on library, classroom, and bedrooms shelves—the high ones, just above a Snurtch's reach." Kirkus

Ferry, Beth

Pirate's Perfect Pet; by Beth Ferry; illustrated by Matt Myers. Candlewick Press 2016 32 p. color illustrations $15.99

Grades: PreK K 1 2   E

1. Pets -- Fiction 2. Pirates -- Fiction 3. Friendship -- Fiction 4. Human-animal relationships -- Fiction

ISBN 0763672882; 9780763672881

LC 2015940264

In this children's book by Beth Ferry, illustrated by Matt Myers, "brave Captain Crave can check off most items on the handy Be Your Best Buccaneer checklist. . . . Only one thing is missing: Captain Crave doesn't have a pet. . . . The captain and his crew race and chase critters . . . from the beach . . . to the zoo to a pet shop, causing a commotion wherever they go. But just when all seems lost, the search party stumbles on the most perfectly perfect pet for Captain Crave." (Publisher's note)

"Animated readers may find a new favorite read-aloud in this book. The illustrations will delight kids, who will find something new every time they pick it up." SLJ

Stick and Stone; by Beth Ferry; illustrated by Tom Lichtenheld. Houghton Mifflin Harcourt 2015 48 p. $16.99

Grades: PreK K 1 2   E

1. Stories in rhyme 2. Friendship -- Fiction 3. Stones -- Fiction 4. Friendship -- Fiction 5. Best friends -- Fiction 6. Staffs (Sticks, canes, etc.) -- Fiction

ISBN 054403256X; 9780544032569

LC 2014012651

In this story by Beth Ferry, illustrated by Tom Lichtenheld, "when Stick rescues Stone from a prickly situation with a Pinecone, the pair becomes fast friends. But when Stick gets stuck, can Stone return the favor? . . . [This] warm, rhyming text . . . includes a subtle anti-bullying message even the youngest reader will understand." (Publisher's note)

Finchler, Judy

★ **Miss** Malarkey leaves no reader behind. Walker & Company 2006 un il $16.95; lib bdg $17.85

Grades: K 1 2 3   E

1. School stories 2. Teachers -- Fiction 3. Books and reading -- Fiction

ISBN 978-0-8027-8084-3; 0-8027-8084-9; 978-0-8027-8085-0 lib bdg; 0-8027-8085-7 lib bdg

LC 2005037182

Miss Malarkey vows to find each of her students a book to love by the end of the school year, but one video-game loving boy proves to be a challenge.

"O'Malley's illustrations, done in markers and colored pencils, enhance the text with expressive pictures. . . . A must-have for all libraries." SLJ

Other titles about Miss Malarkey are:

Congratulations, Miss Malarkey! (2009)

Miss Malarkey doesn't live in Room 10 (1995)

Miss Malarkey won't be in today (1998)

Miss Malarkey's field trip (2004)

Testing Miss Malarkey (2000)

You're a good sport, Miss Malarkey (2002)

Fine, Edith Hope

Armando and the blue tarp school; [by] Edith Hope Fine & Judith Pinkerton Josephson; illustrated by Hernan Sosa. Lee & Low 2007 un il lib bdg $16.95

Grades: K 1 2 3   E

1. School stories 2. Mexico -- Fiction 3. Poverty -- Fiction

ISBN 978-1-58430-278-0

"This poignant picture book . . . is based on a true story. . . . [It is illustrated with] clear, unframed, double-page pictures in watercolor and ink with thick white outlines. . . . Without melodrama, Armando's story shows what poverty means and the hope that things can change." Booklist

Fischer, Scott M.

Jump! [by] Scott Fischer. Simon & Schuster Books for Young Readers 2010 un il $14.99

Grades: PreK K   E

1. Stories in rhyme 2. Fear -- Fiction 3. Animals -- Fiction

ISBN 978-1-4169-7884-8; 1-4169-7884-4

LC 2008025861

From bugs and frogs to alligators and whales, frightened animals always move out of the way of a larger opponent.

"With simple, rhyming text and action-packed artwork, this picture book will appeal to young preschoolers. . . . Even after kids have figured out what is coming, they will enjoy the animals' shifts in power roles, all depicted in lively drawings, rendered in thick black lines and strong, bright colors against blank white space." Booklist

Fisher, Aileen Lucia

The **story** goes on; illustrated by Mique Moriuchi. Roaring Brook Press 2004 un il $16.95

Grades: PreK K 1 2   E
  1. Stories in rhyme 2. Food chains (Ecology)
  ISBN 1-59643-037-0

LC 2003-18143

An illustrated poem about the cycle of life—bug eats plant, frog eats bug, snake eats frog, hawk eats snake, and so on

"With bright colors, rhyming text, and collage illustrations, this circular tale points out the interdependence of life. . . . This offering is a visual treat and an engaging opportunity to introduce the cycle of life to young readers." SLJ

Fisher, Carolyn

The **Snow** Show; with Chef Kelvin. producer, Carolyn Fisher. Harcourt 2008 un il $17
Grades: K 1 2 3   E
  1. Snow -- Fiction 2. Cooking -- Fiction 3. Television programs -- Fiction
  ISBN 978-0-15-206019-0; 0-15-206019-7

LC 2007031724

A cooking show goes on location to the North Pole to demonstrate the recipe for making snow.

"The visually dynamic, digitally created art features lettering that helps tell the story. . . . Fisher includes collage, dialogue asides, arrows, onomatopoeic descriptors, and fact boxes, yet maintains clarity, cohesion, and purpose." SLJ

Fisher, Valorie

Everything I need to know before I'm five. Schwartz & Wade 2011 un il $17.99; lib bdg $20.99
Grades: PreK K 1   E
  1. Color 2. Numbers 3. Seasons 4. Alphabet 5. Concepts 6. Geometry 7. Opposites
  ISBN 978-0-375-86865-8; 0-375-86865-8; 978-0-375-96865-5 lib bdg; 0-375-96865-2 lib bdg

LC 2010031265

Fisher "gives preschoolers a leg up on need-to-know information in this energetic collection. In candy-colored multimedia collages, . . . she presents such topics as weather, seasons, and numbers up to 20. . . . Considering all the titles on just one of these topics, these vintage/tacky photo-spreads are worth several books in one, even as they display the vast potential in rummage sales and vending machines." Publ Wkly

My big brother. Atheneum Bks. for Young Readers 2002 un il $15.95
Grades: PreK K 1   E
  1. Brothers -- Fiction
  ISBN 0-689-84327-5

LC 2001-22947

Photographs and simple text depict a big brother from the point of view of his baby sibling

"The design is clean and strong, and the colors, textures, and lines all lead the eye to the important parts of the story. Together the text and the pictures tell a funny, very tender story of sibling relationships." Booklist

Fitzpatrick, Marie-Louise

There. Roaring Brook Press 2009 un il $17.95
Grades: K 1 2   E
  1. Questions and answers 2. Growth -- Fiction
  ISBN 978-1-59643-087-7; 1-59643-087-7

LC 2008-54266

A young girl asks questions about growing up as she walks over rolling hills, climbs a ladder up to the stars, and meets a dragon.

This "is a book for rumination, a rare permission to ask the unanswerable questions. The thoughts that propel it and the images that illuminate it make this volume a small wonder for children." SLJ

Flack, Marjorie

Ask Mr. Bear. Macmillan 1958 un il $15.95; pa $6.99
Grades: PreK K 1   E
  1. Animals -- Fiction 2. Birthdays -- Fiction
  ISBN 0-02-735390-7; 0-02-043090-6 pa
  First published 1932

Danny did not know what to give his mother for a birthday present, so he set out to ask various animals—the hen, the duck, the goose, the lamb, the cow and others, but he met with very little success until he met Mr. Bear

This "will have a strong appeal to very young children because of its repetition, its use of the most familiar animals, its gay pictures and the cumulative effect of the story." N Y Times Book Rev

Flaherty, Alice

The **luck** of the Loch Ness monster; a tale of picky eating. [by] A. W. Flaherty; illustrated by Scott Magoon. Houghton Mifflin 2007 un il $16
Grades: K 1 2 3   E
  1. Scotland -- Fiction 2. Ocean travel -- Fiction 3. Loch Ness monster -- Fiction
  ISBN 978-0-618-55644-1; 0-618-55644-3

LC 2006026083

"A girl is traveling alone to visit her grandmother in Scotland. . . . She tosses her dreaded morning oatmeal overboard, only to attract the attention of a tiny sea worm that gobbles it up and immediately quadruples in size. . . . This pourquoi tale about how the Loch Ness Monster came to be has a lot of imagination and wonderful storytelling techniques. Dark, cartoonlike watercolors exhibit an excellent use of perspective." SLJ

Fleischman, Paul

The **animal** hedge; illustrated by Bagram Ibatoulline. Candlewick Press 2003 un il $16.99
Grades: K 1 2 3   E
  1. Animals -- Fiction 2. Farmers -- Fiction
  ISBN 0-7636-1606-0

LC 2002-23751

A newly illustrated edition of the title first published 1983 by Dutton

After being forced to sell the animals he loves, a farmer cuts his hedge to look like them and teaches his sons about following their hearts

"Ibatoulline's watercolor-and-gouache illustrations, inspired by 19th-century American folk-art paintings, are the perfect complement to this simple allegory." SLJ

The **birthday** tree; illustrated by Barry Root. Candlewick Press 2008 un il $16.99
Grades: K 1 2 3   E
  1. Trees -- Fiction
  ISBN 978-0-7636-2604-4

LC 2007-32344

A newly illustrated edition of the title first published 1979 by Harper & Row

When Jack goes to sea, his parents watch as the tree planted at his birth reflects his fortunes and misfortunes

"Precisely worded and fluid in the telling, the story has a timeless quality that is echoed in the expressive watercolor artwork." Booklist

★ The **Matchbox** diary; Paul Fleischman, illustrated by Bagram Ibatoulline. Candlewick Press 2013 40 p. $16.99

Grades: 1 2 3 4 5 **E**

1. Memory -- Fiction 2. Diaries -- Fiction 3. Immigrants -- United States -- Fiction

ISBN 0763646016; 9780763646011

LC 2012942613

In this children's story, by Newbery Medalist Paul Fleischman and illustrated by Bagram Ibatoulline, "when a little girl visits her great-grandfather at his curio-filled home, she chooses an unusual object to learn about: an old cigar box. What she finds inside surprises her: a collection of matchboxes making up her great-grandfather's diary. . . . Together they tell of his journey from Italy to a new country, before he could read and write." (Publisher's note)

Sidewalk circus; presented by Paul Fleischman and Kevin Hawkes. Candlewick Press 2004 un il $15.99

Grades: PreK K 1 2 3 **E**

1. Stories without words 2. Circus -- Fiction 3. City and town life -- Fiction

ISBN 0-7636-1107-7

LC 2002-74168

"As posters advertising the world-renowned Garibaldi circus are put up along a busy city block, a girl waiting for a bus watches the circus of everyday life unfold. There is no actual text to the book, just the words of store signs, a scrolling theater marquee, and the show bills. What the girl imagines is revealed through the playful shadows of the people on the street and the corresponding circus flyers. . . . Hawkes's richly colored acrylic paintings sustain interest and pacing throughout the book. . . . This delightful book will fascinate children and help them to see their world with new eyes." SLJ

★ **Weslandia**; illustrated by Kevin Hawkes. Candlewick Press 1999 un il $15.99; pa $5.99

Grades: K 1 2 3 **E**

1. Plants -- Fiction 2. Gardening -- Fiction

ISBN 0-7636-0006-7; 0-7636-1052-6 pa

LC 98-30240

Wesley's garden produces a crop of huge, strange plants which provide him with clothing, shelter, food, and drink, thus helping him create his own civilization and changing his life

"This story about a nonconformist creating his own reality resonates with imagination and humor. . . . His natural creativity is reflected in Hawkes' vivid recreations of Wesley's altered environment, lush illustrations that have a realistic whimsy." Bull Cent Child Books

Fleming, Candace

★ **Boxes** for Katje; pictures by Stacey Dressen-McQueen. Farrar, Straus & Giroux 2003 un il $16

Grades: K 1 2 3 **E**

1. Netherlands -- Fiction 2. World War, 1939-1945 -- Fiction

ISBN 0-374-30922-1

LC 2002-20027

After a young Dutch girl writes to her new American friend in thanks for the care package sent after World War II, she begins to receive increasingly larger boxes

The story is "moving, and Dressen-McQueen's lively illustrations, in colored pencil, oil pastel, and acrylic, pack lots of color, pattern, and historical details onto every expansive page." Booklist

Bulldozer's big day; Candace Fleming; illustrated by Eric Rohmann. Atheneum Books for Young Readers 2015 40 p. color illustrations (hardcover) $17.99

Grades: PreK K 1 **E**

1. Bulldozers (Machines) 2. Birthdays -- Fiction 3. Parties -- Fiction 4. Bulldozers -- Fiction 5. Construction equipment --

Fiction

ISBN 1481400975; 9781481400978

LC 2013038526

In this children's book by Candace Fleming, illustrated by Eric Rohmann, "It's Bulldozer's big day--his birthday! But around the construction site, it seems like everyone is too busy to remember. Bulldozer wheels around asking his truck friends if they know what day it is, but they each only say it's a work day. . . . But when the whistle blows at the end of the busy day, Bulldozer discovers a construction site surprise, especially for him!" (Publisher's note)

"Fleming and Rohmann team up for their second picture book in celebration of Bulldozer's birthday. He zooms across the construction site in joyous anticipation of his big day only to discover that every construction truck he greets is too busy to acknowledge anything more than the jobs that need to be done. . . . The heavyweight matte paper and relief lettering on the dust jacket add satisfying tactile details to the engaging text and playful illustrations. VERDICT This masterfully crafted story will become a favorite read-aloud choice." SLJ

★ **Clever** Jack takes the cake; written by Candace Fleming; illustrated by G. Brian Karas. Schwartz & Wade Books 2010 un il **E**

Grades: K 1 2 3

1. Fairy tales 2. Cake -- Fiction 3. Birthdays -- Fiction 4. Princesses -- Fiction 5. Storytelling -- Fiction

ISBN 0375849793; 0375956972 lib bdg; 9780375849794; 9780375956973 lib bdg

LC 2009030030

A poor boy named Jack struggles to deliver a birthday present worthy of the princess. "Ages five to eight." (Bull Cent Child Books)

"Jack accidentally receives an invitation to the princess's birthday party. He . . . bakes a wonderful cake. On his way to the castle, the cake is slowly demolished by crows, a troll, a spooky forest, a dancing bear, and even a palace guard, until the only present Jack has to offer . . . is the story of the cake's demise. . . . This entertaining adventure is packed with action. Karas's scratchy gouache and pencil cartoon illustrations are as detail-rich as the text itself." SLJ

The **hatmaker's** sign; a story. by Benjamin Franklin; retold by Candace Fleming; illustrated by Robert Andrew Parker. Orchard Bks. 1998 un il $16.95; lib bdg $17.99

Grades: K 1 2 3 **E**

1. Authors 2. Diplomats 3. Inventors 4. Statesmen 5. Scientists 6. Vice-presidents 7. Essayists 8. Writers on science 9. Members of Congress

ISBN 0-531-30075-7; 0-531-33075-3 lib bdg

LC 97-27596

To heal the hurt pride of Thomas Jefferson as Congress makes changes to his Declaration of Independence, Benjamin Franklin tells his friend the story of a hatmaker and his sign

"Based on an anecdote in The Papers of Thomas Jefferson, the story has a folktale-like quality that lends itself to being read aloud. The illustrations give dimension to the characters and a sense of times past." Horn Book Guide

★ **Imogene's** last stand; written by Candice Fleming; illustrated by Nancy Carpenter. Schwartz & Wade Books 2009 un il $16.99; lib bdg $19.99

Grades: K 1 2 **E**

1. United States -- History -- Fiction

ISBN 978-0-375-83607-7; 0-375-83607-1; 978-0-375-93607-4 lib bdg; 0-375-93607-6 lib bdg

LC 2008-22458

Enamored of history, young Imogene Tripp tries to save her town's historical society from being demolished in order to build a shoelace factory.

"Fleming's sense of small-town space is impeccable; Carpenter's pen-and-ink art enjoyably scribbly; and the historical facts and quotes that bookend the story are just the thing to get new Imogenes fired up." Booklist

★ **Muncha!** Muncha! Muncha! illustrated by G. Brian Karas. Atheneum Bks. for Young Readers 2002 un il $16; lib bdg $18.63
Grades: PreK K 1 2   E
  1. Rabbits -- Fiction 2. Gardening -- Fiction
  ISBN 0-689-83152-8; 0-689-93652-X lib bdg
LC 99-24882

After planting the garden he has dreamed of for years, Mr. McGreely tries to find a way to keep some persistent bunnies from eating all his vegetables

"Fleming's text is lilting and deftly paced, with sound effects . . . strategically and enjoyably employed. . . . Karas' mixed-media (gouache, acrylic, and pencil) illustrations offer a cornucopia of plot-enriching details." Bull Cent Child Books

Another title about Mr. Greely and the bunnies is:
Tippy-tippy-tippy-hide! (2007)

★ **Oh**, no! Candace Fleming; [illustrations by Eric Rohmann] Schwartz & Wade Books 2012 40 p. $17.99
Grades: PreK K 1 2   E
  1. Rescue work -- Fiction 2. Jungle animals -- Fiction 3. Picture books for children 4. Stories in rhyme 5. Animals -- Fiction
  ISBN 0375842713; 9780375842719; 9780375945571
LC 2009045564

In this book, when a "frog falls into a deep hole . . . , a . . . mouse, . . . loris, . . . sun bear, and . . . monkey all tumble down after him during unsuccessful rescue attempts. . . . The animals face a lurking tiger eager to snack on the helpless group," who, in the end, is himself caught in the hole, seeking help. (School Library Journal)

Papa's mechanical fish; by Candace Fleming; pictures by Boris Kulikov. 1st ed. Margaret Ferguson Books 2013 40 p. ill. (chiefly col.) (reinforced) $16.99
Grades: 2 3 4   E
  1. Picture books for children 2. Submarines -- Fiction 3. Inventors -- Fiction 4. Family life -- Fiction
  ISBN 0374399085; 9780374399085
LC 2012029659

This children's picture book "profiles a would-be inventor and his indulgent family. Out fishing one day, daughter and narrator Virena happens to ask, "Papa . . . have you ever wondered what it's like to be a fish?'" At this, her "inspired father races for his workshop. To a refrain of 'Clink! Clankety-bang! Thump-whirrrr!' Papa sets to building a series of submarines, which he tests in Lake Michigan." (Publishers Weekly)

Seven hungry babies; illustrated by Eugene Yelchin. Atheneum Books for Young Readers 2010 un il $16.99
Grades: PreK K 1   E
  1. Stories in rhyme 2. Birds -- Fiction
  ISBN 978-1-4169-5402-6; 1-4169-5402-3
LC 2008-53481

A mother bird frantically tries to keep her seven baby birds fed.

"Fleming's playful text features endearments that will tickle listeners . . . and a rhythm that sweeps the story along. The fresh gouache illustrations are awash in blues and white with fire-bright red and yellow birds and feature expressive faces on the avian stars." SLJ

Sunny Boy! the life and times of a tortoise. pictures by Anne Wilsdorf. Farrar, Straus and Giroux 2005 un il $16
Grades: PreK K 1 2   E
  1. Turtles -- Fiction
  ISBN 0-374-37297-7
LC 2004-40451

In this fictionalized account, Sunny Boy, a 100-year-old tortoise, describes various events in his long life including the dangerous barrel ride over Niagara Falls that he takes with his daredevil owner on July 5, 1930

"This saga makes for wildly entertaining reading. . . . The comical cartoon narrative . . . enhances the textual flow of the story. Not to be missed is the author's fascinating historical note." SLJ

★ **This** is the baby; pictures by Maggie Smith. Farrar, Straus and Giroux 2004 un il $16.50
Grades: PreK K 1   E
  1. Stories in rhyme 2. Infants -- Fiction 3. Clothing and dress -- Fiction
  ISBN 0-374-37486-4
LC 2002-70941

A cumulative rhyme enumerating all the items of clothing that go on the baby who hates to be dressed, from the diaper often a mess to the jacket woolen and plaid.

"Smith's naive and rosy-cheeked characters, cozy textures, and crayon-box colors are a perfect accompaniment to Fleming's well-constructed, cumulative, 'House That Jack-Built' patterned story that positively insists on reader interaction." SLJ

Fleming, Denise

5 little ducks; Denise Fleming. Beach Lane Books 2015 40 p. color illustrations (hardcover) $17.99; (ebook) $15.99
Grades: PreK K   E
  1. Nursery rhymes 2. Ducks -- Fiction 3. Counting -- Fiction 4. Stories in rhyme
  ISBN 9781481424226; 9781481424233
LC 2014042898

In this preschool picture book, written and illustrated by Denise Fleming, "featuring a flock of oh-so-adorable fuzzy ducklings, this delightfully fresh take on the classic 'Five Little Ducks' nursery rhyme emphasizes numbers and the days of the week—and these lucky ducklings are doted on by a loving Papa Duck as well as the traditional Mama. Young readers won't be able to resist counting—and quacking—along!" (Publisher's note)

"Whether it's a panorama of farmland or a shadowy woodland glade, each double-page spread offers plenty of intriguing details limned in bright colors. Packed with personality and charm, these five ducklings will waddle their ways into the hearts of readers and listeners." Kirkus

★ **Barnyard** banter. Holt & Co. 1994 un il $17.95; pa $7.95; bd bk $7.95
Grades: PreK K 1 2   E
  1. Stories in rhyme 2. Animals -- Fiction
  ISBN 0-8050-1957-X; 0-8050-5581-9 pa; 0-8050-6594-6 bd bk
LC 93-11032

All the farm animals are where they should be, clucking and mucking, mewing and cooing, except for the missing goose

"Strong rhythm and rhyme, plus fun onomatopoetic animal sounds, demand reading aloud. But even more delightful than the engaging text are Fleming's spectacular illustrations. . . . They create realistically textured, bold, bright settings for the whimsical critters to romp through." SLJ

★ **Beetle** bop. Harcourt 2007 un il $16

Grades: PreK K   E
1. Stories in rhyme 2. Beetles -- Fiction
ISBN 978-0-15-205936-1

LC 2006-09756

Illustrations and rhyming text reveal the great variety of beetles and their swirling, humming, crashing activities.

"Fleming creates a vibrant exciting portrait of often-overlooked creatures. Here she uses expertly crafted fiber collage to celebrate beetles, and both words and pictures vibrate with the relentless energy of the subject." Booklist

Buster. Holt & Co. 2003 un il $16.95; pa $6.95
Grades: PreK K 1 2   E
1. Cats -- Fiction 2. Dogs -- Fiction
ISBN 0-8050-6279-3; 0-8050-8757-5 pa

LC 2002-10857

Buster the dog thinks his perfect life is spoiled when Betty the cat comes to live with him, until he learns not to be afraid of cats

"Fleming's trademark handmade-paper artwork is awash with vibrant colors and dazzling details." SLJ

Another title about Buster is:
Buster goes to Cowboy Camp (2008)

Buster goes to Cowboy Camp. Henry Holt 2008 un il $16.95
Grades: PreK K 1 2   E
1, Dogs -- Fiction 2. Camps -- Fiction 3. West (U.S.) -- Fiction
ISBN 978-0-8050-7892-3; 0-8050-7892-4

LC 2007-12368

When Buster the dog's owner goes away for a few days, he sends Buster to Sagebrush Kennels for Cowboy Camp, where Buster is homesick at first, but then has fun herding balls into the corral, gathering sticks for a campfire, and making wanted posters with his pawprints.

"This sweet, simple story is steeped in the stuff of the Wild West. . . . Fleming extracts remarkable expression from her signature paper-pulp illustrations." Booklist

★ The **cow** who clucked. Henry Holt 2006 un il $16.95
Grades: PreK K 1 2   E
1. Cattle -- Fiction 2. Animals -- Fiction
ISBN 978-0-8050-7265-5; 0-8050-7265-9

LC 2005-22676

When a cow loses her moo, she searches to see if another animal in the barn has it

"The gentle inside jokes, the animal sounds, and the repetitive phrase constitute only a fraction of this book's appeal. Fleming is, after all, a thrilling illustrator whose pulp-painting technique brings subtlety and texture to densely colored art. . . . The layers of subtle humor and visual splendor are truly impressive." SLJ

★ The **everything** book. Holt & Co. 2000 64p il $18.95
Grades: PreK K   E
ISBN 0-8050-6292-0

LC 99-53626

Fleming offers an illustrated introduction to such concepts as colors, shapes, numbers, animals, food, and seasons. "Ages two to five." (N Y Times Book Rev)

"The book includes everything needed to make it an anthology of preschool interests and concerns. . . . The very attractive illustrations, done in Fleming's characteristic bold and energetic style, were produced by pouring cotton pulp through hand-cut stencils, the result being simple forms that are attractively textured, with edges that are just fuzzy enough to look soft and friendly." SLJ

★ The **first** day of winter. Henry Holt and Co. 2005 un il $16.95

Grades: PreK K 1   E
1. Snow -- Fiction 2. Winter -- Fiction
ISBN 0-8050-7384-1

LC 2004-22181

A snowman is built and is given special gifts to put on by his best friend each day for ten days with cumulative items of gifts

"Fleming captures the tranquility and light of snowy days with her unique artistic style. Her paper-pulp and stencil illustrations depict a winter wonderland in which vibrant striped scarves, blue mittens, and red hats provide the color in a white, uncluttered landscape. . . . Quietly told and thoughtfully illustrated." SLJ

Go, shapes, go! Denise Fleming. Beach Lane Books 2013 40 p. color illustrations (hardcover) $17.99
Grades: PreK K 1   E
1. Adventure fiction 2. Mice -- Fiction 3. Shape -- Fiction 4. Locomotion -- Fiction
ISBN 9781442482401; 1442482400

LC 2013004899

In this children's book by Denise Fleming, readers join a "creative adventure with a gang of saucy shapes--and a mischievous mouse who wants to play too. Meet circles, rectangles, ovals, arcs, and a triangle and a square as well. Wait till you see what this crowd can make when they're all working together!" (Publisher's note)

"Tiny paper-collage Mouse gives various cut-paper shapes their marching—and rolling, bouncing, and slithering—orders in Fleming's (Underground) celebration of concepts and perception...The shapes themselves, snipped from decorative handmade paper, are labeled, helping to introduce or reinforce readers' familiarity with them." PW

★ In the small, small pond. Holt & Co. 1993 un il $17.95; pa $7.95
Grades: PreK K 1   E
1. Stories in rhyme 2. Pond ecology -- Fiction
ISBN 0-8050-2264-3; 0-8050-5983-0 pa

LC 92-25770

A Caldecott Medal honor book, 1994
Illustrations and rhyming text describe the activities of animals living in and near a small pond as spring progresses to autumn

"The brilliant, primitive illustrations were made by pouring colored cotton pulp through hand-cut stencils. Against the eye-catching colors, the four-word rhymes in bold black print dance, each double-page spread picturing and describing a different creature. Text, pictures, layout, and design are all beautifully done." SLJ

★ In the tall, tall grass. Holt & Co. 1991 un il $17.95; pa $7.99
Grades: PreK K 1   E
1. Stories in rhyme 2. Animals -- Fiction
ISBN 0-8050-1635-X; 0-8050-3941-4 pa

LC 90-26444

Rhymed text (crunch, munch, caterpillars lunch) presents a toddler's view of creatures found in the grass from lunchtime till nightfall, such as bees, ants, and moles

"Boldly colored in grassy greens, sunny yellows, and evening blues, the impressionistic illustrations make this a real treat for eyes as well as ears." Booklist

★ **Lunch**. Holt & Co. 1993 un il $17.99; pa $7.99; bd bk $7.95
Grades: PreK K 1   E
1. Color 2. Mice -- Fiction
ISBN 0-8050-1636-8; 0-8050-4646-1 pa; 0-8050-5696-3 bd bk

LC 92-178

"Fleming continues to work in the medium of handmade paper built from layers of colored pulp that has been forced through a stencil. A huge typeface and the judicious use of large blocks of bold, solid color give this book a fresh look. Delectable fun, and, with its simple yet engaging plot, sure to be requested over and over by the youngest readers." Horn Book

Maggie and Michael get dressed; Denise Fleming. Henry Holt & Co. 2016 40 p. color illustrations (hardback) $17.99
Grades: PreK K   E
1. Color -- Fiction 2. Clothing and dress -- Fiction 3. Brothers and sisters -- Fiction 4. Dogs -- Fiction
ISBN 9780805087949

LC 2015005807
In this book, by Denise Fleming, "it's time for Michael to get dressed! Maggie will help. Michael knows where each piece of colorful clothing should go. Yellow socks on feet, brown hat on head. But who will end up wearing the blue pants?" (Publisher's note)
"Fleming captures audience attention with page after page of hilarious scenes aptly combined with large text and color-coordinated words. A terrific pick for storytime." Booklist
Time to get dressed!

★ **Mama** cat has three kittens. Holt & Co. 1998 un il $17.95; pa $7.95
Grades: PreK K 1   E
1. Cats -- Fiction
ISBN 0-8050-5745-5; 0-8050-7162-8 pa

LC 98-12249
While two kittens copy everything their mother does, their brother naps
"Fleming's kittens, created by pouring colored cotton pulp through hand-cut stencils, are large and bold and set against colorful backdrops. An excellent choice for reading aloud to groups." SLJ

★ **Pumpkin** eye. Holt & Co. 2001 un il $16.99; pa $7.95
Grades: PreK K 1   E
1. Stories in rhyme 2. Halloween -- Fiction
ISBN 0-8050-6681-0; 0-8050-7635-2 pa

LC 00-44850
Simple rhymes describe the sights, sounds, and smells of Halloween
"Fleming's homemade paper landscapes set off their midnight-blue—well, probably eight-o'clock blue—backdrops with glowing orange and white accents as well as with the rainbow of colors represented in the trick-or-treaters' costumes. . . . This will be just the shivery ticket for kids looking to move from Halloween giggles to genuine spookiness." Bull Cent Child Books

Shout! Shout it out! Henry Holt 2011 40p il $16.99
Grades: PreK K   E
1. Alphabet 2. Counting 3. Mice -- Fiction 4. Vocabulary -- Fiction
ISBN 978-0-8050-9237-0; 0-8050-9237-4

LC 2010011691
Mouse invites the reader to shout out what he or she knows as they review numbers, letters, and easy words.
"Fleming brings new dimension to her signature pulp-painting technique, using swatches of patterned paper collage and marker accents on her figures. . . . Children just learning their colors, animals, and ABCs will be invigorated, and those who have already mastered these basics will still enjoy the top-of-their lungs review." Publ Wkly

★ **Sleepy,** oh so sleepy. Henry Holt and Company 2010 un il $16.99
Grades: PreK   E
1. Animals -- Fiction 2. Bedtime -- Fiction 3. Mother-child

relationship -- Fiction
ISBN 978-0-8050-8126-8; 0-8050-8126-7

LC 2009006151
Depicts a number of animal babies sleeping as a mother puts her own baby to bed.
"Formed using Fleming's signature medium of 'pulp painting,' which simultaneously creates the image and the paper that bears it, and accented with pastel pencil, the large-scale illustrations are bold in form and rich in color. With mesmerizing words rolling along, this large-format book does its job so well that it's hard to repress a contented yawn when the story winds down to its quiet ending." Booklist

★ **Time** to sleep. Holt & Co. 1997 un il $17.95; pa $7.95
Grades: PreK K 1   E
1. Winter -- Fiction 2. Animals -- Fiction 3. Hibernation -- Fiction
ISBN 0-8050-3762-4; 0-8050-6767-1 pa

LC 96-37553
When Bear notices that winter is nearly here he hurries to tell Snail, after which each animal tells another until finally the already sleeping Bear is awakened in his den with the news
"Fleming's simple text is ripe with astute observations of the natural world and animal behavior. . . . Fleming's 'pulp painting' style results in lushly textured handmade paper compositions saturated with earthy browns, reds and golds." Publ Wkly

Underground; Denise Fleming. Beach Lane Books 2012 40 p. (hardcover) $17.99
Grades: PreK K   E
1. Stories in rhyme 2. Animals -- Fiction 3. Burrowing animals -- Fiction 4. Underground areas -- Fiction
ISBN 1442458828; 9781442458826; 9781442458833

LC 2012007083

Fletcher, Ashlee
My dog, my cat. Tanglewood Press 2011 un il $13.95
Grades: PreK K 1   E
1. Cats -- Fiction 2. Dogs -- Fiction
ISBN 978-1-933718-22-4; 1-933718-22-6; 1933718226; 9781933718224

LC 2010032919
A child points out the differences between a dog and a cat, but finds something they have in common, as well.
"Fletcher outlines the friendly blue dog and orange cat in thick, dark lines and surrounds each picture with a wide squiggly frame. The trim size, simple text, predictable story pattern, and obvious picture clues make this book a fine choice for beginning readers." SLJ

Fletcher, Ralph
The **Sandman**; [by] Ralph Fletcher; illustrated by Richard Cowdrey. Henry Holt and Company 2008 un il $16.95
Grades: PreK K 1 2   E
1. Sleep -- Fiction 2. Bedtime -- Fiction 3. Dragons -- Fiction
ISBN 978-0-8050-7726-1; 0-8050-7726-X

LC 2007002831
A tiny little man discovers that sand made from a dragon's scale will send him to dreamland, and begins carrying this magical sand to children each night to give them the gift of sleep
"Fletcher's smoothly written story flows in a thoroughly plausible way and is beautifully served by Cowdrey's vibrant acrylic paintings." SLJ

Fletcher, Susan
Dadblamed Union Army cow; [by] Susan Fletcher; illustrated by Kimberly Bulcken Root. Candlewick Press 2007 un il $16.99

Grades: 2 3 4 5   E
1. Cattle -- Fiction 2. United States -- History -- 1861-1865, Civil War -- Fiction
ISBN 978-0-7636-2263-3; 0-7636-2263-X
LC 2006051833

During the Civil War, a devoted cow follows her owner when he joins the Union Army and, despite all his efforts to send her home, stays with him and his regiment until the end of the war. Based on a true story

"Root's pencil and watercolor drawings vividly render the Civil War landscape. . . . A terrific read-aloud, and a marvelous approach to history." Publ Wkly

Flett, Julie
Wild berries; by Julie Flett; translated by Earl N. Cook. Simply Read Books 2013 32 p. $16.95
Grades: PreK K 1 2 3   E
1. Berries -- Fiction 2. Bilingual books -- English-Cree 3. Grandmothers -- Fiction
ISBN 1897476892; 9781897476895

In this picture book, by Julie Flett, "spend the day picking wild blueberries with Clarence and his grandmother. Meet ant, spider, and fox in a . . . woodland landscape. . . . This book is written in both Enlglish and Cree, in particular the n-dialect, also known as Swampy Cree from the Cumberland House area." (Publisher's note)

"Clarence and his grandma pick "wild berries / pikaci-minisa." Each double-page spread describes the sights and sounds and also uses one word in a dialect of Cree (the "n" dialect, known as Swampy Cree), highlighted in red font. The muted earth tones of the watercolor and collage illustrations perfectly complement the quiet story. A pronunciation guide and glossary are appended." (Horn Book)

Floca, Brian
Five trucks; Brian Floca. Simon & Schuster 2014 32 p. il $17.99
Grades: PreK K 1 2   E
1. Counting 2. Trucks -- Fiction 3. Airports -- Fiction
ISBN 1481405934; 9781481405935
LC 9819834

This book, by Brian Floca, "features airport vehicles rarely seen in preschool books as well as the trucks' diverse drivers (men and women of various ethnicities). Unlike most counting books, the story introduces ordinal numbers (first, second, etc.) rather than cardinals (one, two, three). On the second appearance of each truck, the text counts back from the fifth to the first truck, adding another concept covered in the book." (School Library Journal)

"Five drivers for five trucks" begins this concept book, as five workers head out across a tarmac to prepare an airplane for take-off. At close inspection, there's more to see--a boy, his dad, and an overstuffed, rainbow-colored plaid suitcase pop up in various illustrations. The book's simplicity is engaging and age appropriate--even those who are vague about airport operations will catch on quickly." Horn Book

Flood, Nancy Bo
Cowboy up! ride the navajo rodeo. Nancy Bo Flood. WordSong 2013 48 p. (hardcover) $17.95
Grades: 1 2 3 4 5   E
1. Rodeos 2. Navajo Indians
ISBN 1590788931; 9781590788936
LC 2012949009

This book looks at the "history and tradition of the Navajo rodeo" through a day-in-the-life account. "Short narrative poems accompany each spread, recounting the anticipation, determination, danger, and excitement of the day. . . . An announcer guides readers through the book (and each individual event) page by page." (School Library Journal)

Flora, James
The day the cow sneezed; story and pictures by James Flora. Enchanted Lion Books 2010 un il $16.95
Grades: K 1 2 3   E
1. Tall tales 2. Cattle -- Fiction 3. Animals -- Fiction 4. Sneezing -- Fiction
ISBN 978-1-59270-097-4; 1-59270-097-7
LC 2010025866

First published 1957 by Harcourt, Brace & World, Inc
A cow sneezes and sets off a series of ridiculous events.

"Flora's illustrations are rich and varied. It doesn't take long to read the text, but children will spend hours with the pictures." Horn Book Guide

Florian, Douglas
★ Shiver me timbers; Douglas Florian; illustrated by Robert Neubecker. Beach Lane Books 2012 32 p.
Grades: 2 3 4   E
1. Pirates -- Poetry
ISBN 1442413212; 9781442413214
LC 2010048963

In this collection of "pirate poems and paintings" for children by Douglas Florian, illustrated by Robert Neubecker, "readers will meet scoundrels, scalawags, and scurvy dogs (human and canine). They'll partake in battles, treasure hunts, and some pirate-style grub (flounder, anyone?)" (Publisher's note)

Florian, Douglas, 1950-
Pig is big on books; Douglas Florian. Holiday House 2015 24 p. color illustrations (I like to read) (hardcover) $14.95
Grades: PreK K 1 2   E
1. Pigs -- Fiction 2. Books and reading -- Fiction
ISBN 0823433935; 9780823433933
LC 2014032162

In this children's book by Douglas Florian "Pig loves to read. He's never without a big stack of books! He reads them one after another. His friends know they'll find him with his snout in a book, whether he's at home, on the bus or even at the beach. But one day, Pig has no books. He looks everywhere and can't find a single thing to read! Instead of panicking, Pig has a great idea. He knows just how to solve this problem . . . Pig will write his own book!" (Publisher's note)

"A perfect ode to the joys of reading and writing."

Flournoy, Valerie
The patchwork quilt; pictures by Jerry Pinkney. Dial Bks. for Young Readers 1985 un il $16.99
Grades: K 1 2 3   E
1. Quilts -- Fiction 2. Family life -- Fiction 3. African Americans -- Fiction
ISBN 0-8037-0097-0
LC 84-1711

Coretta Scott King Award for illustration
Using scraps cut from the family's old clothing, Tanya helps her grandmother and mother make a beautiful quilt that tells the story of her Afro-American family's life

"Plentiful full-page and double-page paintings in pencil, graphite and watercolor are vivid yet delicately detailed. . . . Giving a sense of dramatization to the text, . . . the illustrations provide just the right style and mood for the story." SLJ

Foggo, Cheryl
Dear baobab; written by Cheryl Foggo; illustrated by Qin Leng. Second Story 2011 il $15.95

Grades: K 1 2 3   E

1. Trees -- Fiction 2. Orphans -- Fiction 3. Immigrants -- Fiction 4. Africans -- United States -- Fiction

ISBN 978-1-8971-8791-3; 1-8971-8791-2

"Maiko used to live in a village in Africa. He misses his home and the 2000-year-old baobab tree beneath which he and other village children sat. . . . Now, since the death of his parents, the lonely child lives in what appears to be a North American city. . . . He likes to sit on the stone steps outside his red brick house where a little spruce tree has sprung up. . . . When its roots begin to threaten the foundation of the house, something needs to be done. . . . The tree is moved and replanted elsewhere, just as Maiko has been. Leng's colorful, cartoonlike watercolor illustrations impart a sense of warmth and emotion to this story of a child's bewildering sense of loss and loneliness, as well as new beginnings." SLJ

Fogliano, Julie

★ **And** then it's spring; Julie Fogliano; illustrated by Erin E. Stead. Roaring Brook Press 2012 32 p.

Grades: PreK K 1   E

1. Seeds -- Fiction 2. Spring -- Fiction 3. Gardening -- Fiction 4. Picture books for children 5. Gardens -- Fiction

ISBN 9781596436244

LC 2010049379

Boston Globe-Horn Book Honor: Picture Book (2012)

This picture book is about a boy who gardens and explores the seasonal changes of "spring. . . . Amid the brown "all around," he plants seeds, and he waits hopefully for the miracle of their growth; he trudges through in the rain and squelches out in the post-rain puddles to check, but there's no sign of progress. As the weeks of waiting go by and the earth remains stubbornly brown, the boy fears that disaster ("maybe it was the birds . . . or maybe it was the bears and all that stomping") has befallen his would-be crop. Eventually, though, spring, real spring, comes, greening up the earth and sprouting the young gardener's young seedlings." (Bulletin of the Center for Children's Books)

★ **If** you want to see a whale; Julie Fogliano; Erin E. Stead. 1st ed. Roaring Brook Press 2013 32 p. ill. (hardcover) $16.99

Grades: PreK K 1   E

1. Patience -- Fiction 2. Whale-watching -- Fiction

ISBN 1596437316; 9781596437319

LC 2012012988

This children's book by Julie Fogliano presents a "story about a boy, his animal friends (a basset hound and a bird) and practicing patience. Whale watching requires lots of resolve to avoid distractions like birds, roses, pirate ships, clouds, pelicans and so on. . . . The poem's unresolved ellipses at the conclusion suggest an unending whale hunt, but [illustrator Erin] Stead's final two images silently deliver what we've been waiting for." (Kirkus Reviews)

★ **Old** dog baby baby; Julie Fogliano; illustrated by Chris Raschka. Roaring Brook Press 2016 32 p. color illustrations (ebook) $60; (hardcover) $17.99

Grades: PreK K   E

1. Dogs -- Fiction 2. Infants -- Fiction 3. Human-animal relationships -- Fiction 4. Stories in rhyme

ISBN 9781626729766; 9781596438538

LC 2015042624

In this book, by Julie Fogliano, illustrated by Chris Raschka, "those privileged to have known a mild-mannered dog, a martyr to baby love, a dog that will withstand any annoyance from an infant and still adore him, will appreciate this sweet story told in verse. Fogliano's spare, pitch-perfect rhymes capture the joyful meeting between a blond-haired diapered baby and a shaggy dog on the kitchen floor." (Publisher's note)

"Text and pictures are seamlessly complementary and interdependent, and little ones and their grown-ups will laugh with delight. Tender, joyous, and altogether wonderful." Kirkus

Foley, Greg

I miss you Mouse. Viking 2010 un il $12.99

Grades: PreK K   E

1. Mice -- Fiction 2. Bears -- Fiction 3. Friendship -- Fiction

ISBN 978-0-670-01238-1; 0-670-01238-6

After receiving a special note from her friend Bear, Mouse searches everywhere for Bear because she has something important to tell him.

"The simple illustrations are as endearing as Mouse and Bear themselves. . . . The sweetness of the characters, their obvious fondness for one another, and the message of friendship freshen the story." SLJ

Purple Little Bird. Balzer + Bray 2011 un il $14.99

Grades: PreK K 1 2   E

1. Birds -- Fiction 2. Color -- Fiction 3. Houses -- Fiction 4. Animals -- Fiction 5. Happiness -- Fiction

ISBN 978-0-06-200828-2; 0-06-200828-5

LC 2010030617

Purple Little Bird leaves his almost-perfect purple home in search of a better place, but although Brown Bear, Yellow Camel, and others live in very nice places, none is quite right for him.

"The economical text packs in a surprising amount. . . . Foley uses a crayon palette to good effect, with warm hues and quick strokes that color outside the friendly cartoon lines and fill the page. . . . Satisfying for the very youngest." Kirkus

Thank you Bear; by Greg Foley. Viking 2007 un il $15.99

Grades: PreK K   E

1. Mice -- Fiction 2. Bears -- Fiction 3. Boxes -- Fiction 4. Gifts -- Fiction

ISBN 978-0-670-06165-5

LC 2006016881

Despite the criticism of others, a bear finds the perfect gift for his mouse friend

"Bear's journey from euphoria to doubt to euphoria again is gently rendered. . . . Pastels provide the backdrop for the text, while Bear and his detractors stand in contrast on a white page, carrying the story with their expressions and body language." SLJ

Other titles about Bear are:

Don't worry Bear (2008)

Good luck Bear (2009)

I miss you Mouse (2010)

★ **Willoughby** & the lion. Bowen Press 2009 un il $17.99; lib bdg $18.89

Grades: PreK K 1 2   E

1. Lions -- Fiction 2. Magic -- Fiction 3. Wishes -- Fiction 4. Friendship -- Fiction

ISBN 978-0-06-154750-8; 0-06-154750-6; 978-0-06-154751-5 lib bdg; 0-06-154751-4 lib bdg

LC 2008000430

When Willoughby moves to a new house far away from his friends, he meets an enchanted lion who shows him what is truly important in life

Foley "scores points for unique visual presentation in this sumptuously produced, two-color book, instantly distinguished by its heavily embossed jacket. . . . With every wish, the ratio of gold to gray increases and Foley's compositions, mingling line drawings with digitally manipulated b&w photos, become more complex. . . . The elegant combination of the two basic colors boosts the visual impact exponentially." Publ Wkly

Another title about Willoughby is:

Willoughby & the moon (2010)

Folgueira, Rodrigo

Ribbit! written by Rodrigo Folgueira; illustrated by Poly Berna-tene. Alfred A. Knopf 2013 32 p. (library) $18.99

Grades: PreK K 1   E

1. Pigs -- Fiction 2. Animals -- Fiction 3. Friendship -- Fiction

ISBN 9780307981462; 9780307981479; 9780307981509

LC 2012012718

Ford, Bernette

★ **First** snow; illustrated by Sebastien Braun. Holiday House 2005 un il $16.95

Grades: PreK K 1 2   E

1. Snow -- Fiction 2. Night -- Fiction 3. Rabbits -- Fiction

ISBN 0-8234-1937-1

LC 2004-55257

A family of young rabbits goes into a meadow at night to explore and play in winter's first snow.

"Ford's text has a poetic rhythm that emphasizes the senses as the rabbits explore their wintry world. . . . Braun's illustrations . . . are particularly engaging and complement the story wonderfully." SLJ

No more blanket for Lambkin. Boxer Books 2009 un il $12.95

Grades: PreK   E

1. Ducks -- Fiction 2. Sheep -- Fiction 3. Blankets -- Fiction 4. Friendship -- Fiction

ISBN 978-1-906250-28-7; 1-906250-28-6

"One day Lambkin's friend Ducky comes to visit and decides that they should play laundry day, immediately zeroing in on her friend's much-loved and rather-soiled blanket. Lambkin is none too happy, but she decides it is worth it to play with Ducky. Once the blanket is washed, it's cleaner, but it's also smaller and has some holes. Lambkin is upset, but Ducky surprises her by turning the blanket into a little toy lamb. This is a good story to read to young children when it is nearing the time to give up their blankets. . . . The overall feel is one of gentleness, from the soft style of illustrations to the tone of the dialogue between the two friends." SLJ

No more bottles for Bunny! [by] Bernette Ford and [illustrations by] Sam Williams. Sterling Pub. 2007 un il $12.95

Grades: PreK   E

1. Pigs -- Fiction 2. Ducks -- Fiction 3. Growth -- Fiction 4. Rabbits -- Fiction 5. Bottle feeding -- Fiction

ISBN 978-1-905417-34-6; 1-905417-34-9

LC 2007006856

Bunny gives up his bottle so he can have tea and cookies just like the big kids

"This tough topic is handled subtly but the point is made. Complementing this endearing tale are expressive, bright watercolor illustrations with black outlines that make them jump out from the page." SLJ

No more diapers for Ducky! [by] Bernette Ford and [illustrations by] Sam Williams. Sterling Pub. 2006 un il $12.95

Grades: PreK   E

1. Ducks -- Fiction 2. Toilet training -- Fiction

ISBN 1-905417-08-X

When Piggy can't come out to play because he is using the potty, Ducky decides it's time for him to learn to use the potty too.

"The interaction between these toddlers and their implicit support of one another is charming. The dynamic characters, done in thick charcoal outlines and watercolor, are set against a white background." SLJ

Ford, Christine

Ocean's child; by Chistine Ford and Trish Holland; illustrated by David Diaz. Golden Books 2009 un il $15.99; lib bdg $18.99

Grades: PreK K 1 2   E

1. Inuit -- Fiction 2. Bedtime -- Fiction 3. Marine animals -- Fiction

ISBN 978-0-375-84752-3; 0-375-84752-9; 978-0-375-95752-9 lib bdg; 0-375-95752-9 lib bdg

"As an Inuit mother paddles her baby home at dusk, she identifies baby ocean animals as they prepare for night. . . . The language is warm and assuring bedtime fare with two free-verse lines introducing each animal, followed by a refrain. . . . Close inspection of mother and child's parkas reveal delicate indigenous designs. . . . The soothing flow of rhythmic language and elegant images creates a serenity just right for bedtimes." Booklist

Fore, S. J.

Read to Tiger; illustrated by R.W. Alley. Viking 2010 un il $15.99

Grades: PreK K 1   E

1. Noise -- Fiction 2. Tigers -- Fiction 3. Books and reading -- Fiction

ISBN 978-0-670-01140-7; 0-670-01140-1

LC 2009-35147

A little boy who wants to read his book keeps being distracted by a tiger who is busy chomping on gum, growling, and practicing karate kicks.

"Fore and Alley play with sound effects and comic expressions, which will please a read-aloud audience. The spare ink drawings expand on Tiger's amusing antics." SLJ

Another title about Tiger is:

Tiger can't sleep (2006)

Foreman, Jack

Say hello; [by] Jack & Michael Foreman. Candlewick Press 2008 un il $15.99

Grades: PreK K 1 2   E

1. Stories in rhyme 2. Dogs -- Fiction 3. Friendship -- Fiction

ISBN 978-0-7636-3657-9; 0-7636-3657-6

"A simple story about loneliness and the power of friendliness. Spare charcoal, pastel, and colored pencil drawings illustrate [this book]." SLJ

Foreman, Mark

Grandpa Jack's tattoo tales; [by] Mark Foreman. Farrar, Straus & Giroux 2007 un il $16

Grades: PreK K 1 2   E

1. Sea stories 2. Tattooing -- Fiction 3. Grandfathers -- Fiction 4. Storytelling -- Fiction

ISBN 978-0-374-32768-2; 0-374-32768-8

LC 2006040853

Chloe loves to spend time at her grandparents' restaurant, where she gets to hear Grandpa Jack's stories about the many tattoos that commemorate events in his life at sea

The illustrations are "done in bright crisp watercolors . . . and the pictures are filled with minute details. . . . Children will relish this amusing tall tale and delight in its visual elements." SLJ

Foreman, Michael

Fortunately, unfortunately. Andersen Press 2011 un il $16.95

Grades: PreK K 1 2   E

1. Adventure fiction

ISBN 0-7613-7460-4; 978-0-7613-7460-2

LC 2010032952

On his way to return his grandmother's umbrella, Milo has a series of unlikely adventures, some more fortunate than others.

"Brightly colored, cartoon-style characters (some large but not too ominous) cavorting across the oversize pages convey the lively action. These eye-catching illustrations and the briskly paced text make this a natural for group sharing." Booklist

The **little** ships; the heroic rescue at Dunkirk in World War II. illustrated by Michael Foreman. Margaret K. McElderry Bks. 1997 un il hardcover o.p. pa $6.99
Grades: K 1 2 3   E
1. World War, 1939-1945 -- Fiction 2. Dunkerque (France), Battle of, 1940 -- Fiction
ISBN 0-689-80827-5; 0-689-85396-3 pa
LC 95-52557

A young English girl and her father take their sturdy fishing boat and join the scores of other civilian vessels crossing the English Channel in a daring attempt to rescue Allied and British troops trapped by Nazi soldiers at Dunkirk

"Borden's descriptive style is potent, and Foreman's watercolors perfectly express the dulled and watery scenes of devastation, the exhausted and hopeful soldiers awaiting rescue." Horn Book Guide

The **littlest** dinosaur's big adventure; written and illustrated by Michael Foreman. Walker & Co. 2009 un il $16.99
Grades: PreK K 1 2   E
1. Size -- Fiction 2. Dinosaurs -- Fiction
ISBN 978-0-8027-9545-8; 0-8027-9545-5
LC 2008-40297

The littlest dinosaur discovers the advantages of being small as he frolics among the lily pads with his new frog friends, and then bravely finds his way home after getting lost in the woods

"Foreman's soft and gentle cartoon-style illustrations are tailored for young eyes and hearts. Sharing the book aloud will invite discussion as Foreman leaves readers a well-marked trail for inference and reflection, while the twists and turns of the plot will keep even the youngest audiences riveted." SLJ

Another title about the littlest dinosaur is:

The littlest dinosaur (2008)

Mia's story; a sketchbook of hopes and dreams. Candlewick Press 2006 un il $15.99
Grades: 1 2 3   E
1. Dogs -- Fiction 2. Chile -- Fiction 3. Flowers -- Fiction
ISBN 0-7636-3063-2
LC 2005-53183

"Mia's father harvests scrap metal from the nearby dump and sells it in the city. When Mia's dog Poco disappears one winter day, she rides a horse into the mountains to look for him, gathers some flowering plants she has never seen before, and brings them back to her village, where they change the landscape and her fortunes for the better. . . . This unusual book offers an engaging story, graceful illustrations, and a rare glimpse of a child's life in contemporary Chile." Booklist

Foreman, Michael, 1938-
Friends; Michael Foreman. Lerner Pub. Group 2012 32 p. (trade hard cover : alk. paper) $16.95
Grades: PreK K 1   E
1. Picture books for children 2. Animal behavior -- Fiction 3. Conduct of life -- Fiction 4. Cats -- Fiction 5. Fishes -- Fiction 6. Friendship -- Fiction
ISBN 1467703176; 9781467703178
LC 2011051456

Author Michael Foreman presents a picture book on the relationship between a goldfish and a cat. "Bubble is a goldfish who swims around and around unhappily in his tank. Cat is his friend and wishes he could show him the world. One day, Cat has an idea to set Bubble free. But is Bubble ready to swim off into the world and leave his friend behind?" (Publisher's note)

Forler, Nan
Bird child. Tundra Books 2009 un il $19.95
Grades: K 1 2 3   E
1. Bullies -- Fiction 2. Friendship -- Fiction
ISBN 0-88776-894-6; 978-0-88776-894-1

"Silently, Eliza observes new girl Lainey's ostracism due to her unusual appearance, watching as the bullying increases, refraining from intervention when Lainey is brutally pushed in the snow. The authentic voice portrays bullying's devastating impact. . . . Eliza's mother gently guides her daughter to a moral decision. The symbolism of flight is woven through the narrative. Thisdale's vibrant mixed-media art plays with dominance and size in its compositions; drawings, paintings and digital images add layers of context. . . . This is a sensitive account through an empowered youngster's eyes." Kirkus

Formento, Alison
These bees count! Alison Formento; illustrated by Sarah Snow. Albert Whitman & Co. 2012 32 p.
Grades: PreK K 1 2   E
1. Counting 2. Field trips 3. Bees -- Fiction 4. Honeybee -- Fiction 5. Beekeepers -- Fiction 6. School field trips -- Fiction 7. Human-animal communication -- Fiction
ISBN 0807578681; 9780807578681
LC 2011008567

This children's story by Alison Formento, illustrated by Sarah Snow, provides a lesson both in basic counting and in the ecological importance of bees. "How do bees count? The bees at the Busy Bee Farm buzz through the sky as one big swarm, fly over two waving dandelions, find three wild strawberries dripping tasty nectar" As the children in Mr. Tate's class listen, they learn how bees work to produce honey and make food and flowers grow. Bees count--they're important to us all. (Publisher's note)

This tree counts! illustrated by Sarah Snow. Albert Whitman 2010 un il $16.99
Grades: PreK K 1 2   E
1. Counting 2. Trees -- Fiction 3. Ecology -- Fiction
ISBN 0-8075-7890-8; 978-0-8075-7890-2

As Mr. Tate's class prepares to plant saplings, they hear the giant oak tree in their schoolyard tell about all the animal life it supports.

"Snow's collage illustrations add texture and natural beauty to the story. . . . The picture of the industrious kids working together in the grassy field under a bright blue sky epitomizes the story's theme of cooperation and friendship." SLJ

Forward, Toby
What did you do today? the first day of school. illustrated by Carol Thompson. Clarion Books 2004 29p il $15
Grades: PreK K 1   E
1. School stories 2. Mother-child relationship -- Fiction
ISBN 0-618-49586-X
LC 2004-2467

A child describes the events of the first day of school, from making sandwiches for lunch to holding a parent's hand on the walk home

"The parallels between a child's day at school and his mother's day at work are shown with insight and love in this cleverly designed book.

... Thompson varies her pen-and-watercolor illustrations in surprising and eye-catching ways." Booklist

Fox, F. G.

Jean Laffite and the big ol' whale; pictures by Scott Cook. Farrar, Straus & Giroux 2003 un il $16

Grades: K 1 2 3   E

1. Tall tales 2. Whales -- Fiction 3. Mississippi River -- Fiction

ISBN 0-374-33669-5

LC 99-43733

When a huge white whale gets stuck between the banks of the Mississippi River causing the water to stop flowing, Jean Laffite finds a way to get the river moving again

"This rollicking good yarn is brought to life with Cook's warm, glowing oil paintings full of action and humor." SLJ

Fox, Lee

Ella Kazoo will not brush her hair; illustrated by Jennifer Plecas. Walker & Co. 2010 un il $15.99; lib bdg $16.89

Grades: PreK K 1   E

1. Stories in rhyme 2. Hair -- Fiction

ISBN 978-0-8027-8836-8; 0-8027-8836-X; 978-0-8027-8755-2 lib bdg; 0-8027-8755-X lib bdg

LC 2009-13329

First published 2007 in Australia

A little girl refuses to brush her hair until it becomes so unruly that it takes over everything.

"Plecas's creative illustrations bring out quirky Ella and her story of stubbornness. The use of rhyme and its overall energy make this book a terrific read-aloud. . . . This book will definitely find fans in libraries serving the young and the young at heart." Libr Media Connect

Fox, Mem

The **goblin** and the empty chair; [illustrated by] Leo & Diane Dillon. Beach Lane Books 2009 un il $17.99

Grades: K 1 2 3   E

1. Monsters -- Fiction

ISBN 978-1-4169-8585-3; 1-4169-8585-9

LC 2008041862

A goblin who for many years has been hiding himself so that he does not frighten anyone finally finds a family

"The all-star team of Fox and the Dillons brings poise and sensitivity to this folksy tale of the pitfalls of self-perception. . . . The ink-and-watercolors are rigidly confined to uniform frames, but even these frames are ornately festooned with not-so-monstrous faces, further developing the story's theme." Booklist

Good night, sleep tight; written by Mem Fox; illustrated by Judy Horacek. Orchard Books 2013 32 p. ill. (reinforced) $16.99

Grades: PreK   E

1. Nursery rhymes -- Fiction 2. Storytelling -- Fiction 3. Nursery rhymes 4. Stories in rhyme 5. Bedtime -- Fiction 6. Babysitters -- Fiction 7. Bedtime -- Fiction 8. Babysitters -- Fiction

ISBN 0545533708; 9780545533706

LC 2012032174

In this book, written by Mem Fox and illustrated by Judy Horacek, Bonnie and Ben's favorite babysitter tells them nursery rhymes at bedtime--including "It's raining! It's pouring! The old man is snoring"; "This little piggy went to market"; and more. Bonnie and Ben enjoy the stories so much that they don't want to go to sleep; they want to hear each one again! Instead the babysitter tells them new nursery rhymes until, finally, all three of them fall fast sleep." (Publisher's note)

★ **Hattie** and the fox; illustrated by Patricia Mullins. Bradbury Press 1987 un il $16.95; pa $6.99

Grades: PreK K 1 2   E

1. Foxes -- Fiction 2. Chickens -- Fiction

ISBN 0-02-735470-9; 0-689-71611-7 pa

LC 86-18849

First published 1986 in Australia

"Bright, whimsical tissue collage and crayon illustrations add zest to this simple cumulative tale, and reveal more action than is expressed by the text alone." SLJ

★ **Hello** baby! illustrated by Steve Jenkins. Beach Lane Books 2009 un il $15.99

Grades: PreK K 1   E

1. Stories in rhyme 2. Animals -- Fiction 3. Infants -- Fiction 4. Animals -- Infancy

ISBN 978-1-4169-8513-6; 1-4169-8513-1

LC 2008-34421

A baby encounters a variety of young animals, including a clever monkey, a hairy warthog, and a dusty lion cub, before discovering the most precious creature of all.

This "has all the marks of a lap-sit classic. . . . While Fox is cooing as only she can, Jenkins . . . works his usual magic with cut paper. In many of his large-scale closeups . . . his subjects' big, expressive eyes seem locked in a gaze with the reader." Publ Wkly

Hunwick's egg; illustrated by Pamela Lofts. Harcourt 2005 un il $16

Grades: PreK K 1 2   E

1. Australia -- Fiction 2. Bandicoots -- Fiction

ISBN 0-15-216318-2

LC 2003-16385

When a wild storm sends a beautiful egg to Hunwick the bandicoot's burrow, he decides to give it a home and become its friend.

"This slightly offbeat story . . . is accompanied by glowing watercolor pencil illustrations in orange, pink, and violet tones that showcase the flora and fauna of the Australian landscape, adding an interesting element to this charming title." SLJ

★ **Koala** Lou; illustrated by Pamela Lofts. Harcourt Brace Jovanovich 1989 un il $16.95; pa $6.99

Grades: PreK K 1 2   E

1. Koalas -- Fiction

ISBN 0-15-200502-1; 0-15-200076-3 pa

LC 88-26810

First published 1988 in Australia

"A reassuring story for the child who feels neglected when siblings arrive." Child Book Rev Serv

Let's count goats! illustrated by Jan Thomas. Beach Lane Books 2010 un il $16.99

Grades: PreK K   E

1. Counting 2. Stories in rhyme 3. Goats -- Fiction

ISBN 978-1-4424-0598-1; 1-4424-0598-8

LC 2009-41627

The reader is invited to count goats of many shapes, sizes, hobbies, and professions.

"The traditional counting format receives a charming update as playfully expressive goats mimic human behavior. . . . Fox, an early-literacy specialist to the core, gets each rhyme just right. . . . Thomas's trademark digital spreads provide punch through chunky, dark outlines and zany off-kilter expressions. . . . These wacky goats guarantee a goofy good time." Kirkus

Night noises; written by Mem Fox; illustrated by Terry Denton. Harcourt Brace Jovanovich 1989 un il $16; pa $6
Grades: PreK K 1 2   **E**
   1. Night -- Fiction 2. Sleep -- Fiction
   ISBN 0-15-200543-9; 0-15-257421-2 pa

                                 LC 89-2162
Old Lily Laceby dozes by the fire with her faithful dog Butch Aggie at her feet as strange night noises herald a surprising awakening

"With an almost joltingly bright palette . . . Denton has divided up many of the double-page spreads into three scenes: the main one depicting Lily Laceby and Butch Aggie in various stages of alertness, another showing the chronology of Lily's life, and the third cleverly revealing clues to the mysterious activity outdoors. The text, in Mem Fox's Houdini-like hands, reads beautifully—the language, pacing, tension, and sparks of excitement absolutely at one with the artwork." Horn Book

A **particular** cow; [by] Mem Fox; illustrated by Terry Denton. Harcourt 2006 un il $16
Grades: PreK K 1 2   **E**
   1. Cattle -- Fiction
   ISBN 0-15-200250-2

                             LC 2004030060
"When a cow decides to take her usual Saturday constitutional, she accidentally steps through a clothesline and ends up with a pair of bloomers covering her head. Unable to see and running off in a panic, the poor bovine wreaks havoc. . . . The story is told with a dry wit and an economy of words, and the illustrations interpret the action with panache." SLJ

★ **Sleepy** bears; illustrated by Kerry Argent. Harcourt Brace & Co. 1999 un il $16; pa $6
Grades: PreK K 1 2   **E**
   1. Stories in rhyme 2. Bears -- Fiction 3. Bedtime -- Fiction
   ISBN 0-15-202016-0; 0-15-216542-8 pa

                             LC 98-42640
"Mother Bear tucks in her six cubs, sending them off on dreamy adventures. Baxter dreams of pirates, Bella of the circus, Winifred of the jungle, Tosca of kingdoms, Ali of divine foods, and Baby Bear of moonbeams. . . . The rhymes are well written, and the charming pictures, done in gouache, watercolor, and colored pencil, are full of funny details." SLJ

Sophie; illustrated by Aminah Brenda Lynn Robinson. Harcourt Brace & Co. 1994 un il hardcover o.p. pa $7
Grades: PreK K 1 2   **E**
   1. Grandfathers -- Fiction 2. African Americans -- Fiction
   ISBN 0-15-277160-3; 0-15-201598-1 pa

                             LC 94-1976
First published 1989 in Australia

"The artwork is rich, expressionist, heavily lined oil. . . . The oversized hands depicted in many drawings exemplify the handholding theme, and the sunny hues of earth and garden convey with warmth a loving and extended African-American family." Bull Cent Child Books

★ **Ten** little fingers and ten little toes; [illustrations by] Helen Oxenbury. Harcourt 2008 un il $16
Grades: PreK K   **E**
   1. Stories in rhyme 2. Infants -- Fiction
   ISBN 978-0-15-206057-2; 0-15-206057-X

                             LC 2007-10692
Rhyming text compares babies born in different places and in different circumstances, but they all share the commonality of ten little fingers and ten little toes.

"Given their perfect cadences, the rhymes feel as if they always existed in our collective consciousness and were simply waiting to be written down. . . . Oxenbury . . . once again makes multiculturalism feel utterly natural and chummy. As her global brood of toddlers grows . . . readers can savor each addition both as beguiling individualist and giggly, bouncy co-conspirator." Publ Wkly

Tough Boris; illustrated by Kathryn Brown. Harcourt Brace & Co. 1994 un il pa $6; $16
Grades: PreK K 1 2   **E**
   1. Parrots -- Fiction 2. Pirates -- Fiction
   ISBN 0-15-201891-3 pa; 0-15-289612-0

                             LC 92-8015
Boris von der Borch is a tough pirate but he weeps when his parrot dies

"The text is deceptively simple, but the observant child will quickly fill in the details, aptly provided in the illustrations. The reassuring message, although understated, is clear and effective." Horn Book Guide

Two little monkeys; Mem Fox; illustrated by Jill Barton. Beach Lane Books 2010 32 p.
Grades: PreK K 1   **E**
   1. Stories in rhyme 2. Picture books for children 3. Monkeys -- Fiction 4. Leopards -- Fiction 5. Leopard -- Fiction 6. Monkeys -- Fiction
   ISBN 1416986871; 9781416986874

                             LC 2009021995
This preschool children's rhyming picture book by Mem Fox, illustrated by Jill Barton, follows two monkeys hiding from a predator "[w]ith the . . . rhythm of a nursery-school finger game. . . . [T]he text . . . [tells] this story of two little monkeys and their escapades on the plains. Playing among the high grasses and dirt, Cheeky and Chee are frightened by something prowling and take refuge in a nearby tree. . . . Hidden in the landscape are hints of the action to come: a tail in the grass or leopard spots in the brush." (Kirkus)

Where is the green sheep? [by] Mem Fox and [illustrated by] Judy Horacek. Harcourt 2004 un il $15
Grades: PreK K 1 2   **E**
   1. Stories in rhyme 2. Sheep -- Fiction
   ISBN 0-15-204907-X

                             LC 2003-4990
A story about many different sheep, and one that seems to be missing.

"Until the lost sheep turns up, children will have fun with the other sheep that make an appearance and perhaps, unbeknownst to them, also get lessons in colors and comparisons. . . . In this neat and satisfying wedding of text and art, the squat, square format uses wool-white backgrounds to display much of the amusing pen-and-watercolor pictures." Booklist

Where the giant sleeps; [by] Mem Fox; pictures by Vladimir Radunsky. Harcourt 2007 un il $16
Grades: PreK K 1 2   **E**
   1. Stories in rhyme 2. Sleep -- Fiction 3. Bedtime -- Fiction
   ISBN 978-0-15-205785-5

                             LC 2006020539
Illustrations and rhyming text portray the different residents of fairyland and where each one goes to sleep.

"The paintings and multifaceted structure of the book inventively translate the puckish text, conjuring misty visions of magical realms." Publ Wkly

Fox, Paula
   Traces. Front Street 2008 un il $16.95

Grades: K 1 2 3   E
1. Nature -- Fiction
ISBN 978-1-932425-43-7; 1-932425-43-8
           LC 2006-11739
Looks at the traces left behind by a turtle on the sand, a jet in the sky, and even a long-gone dinosaur in loose soil.

Fox "gives the book an energetic and distilled poetry. . . . The charming medallion sun, torn-paper clouds and watercolor ribbon of the horizon found on these spreads all feel like the naive and studious work of a dedicated seven-year-old. . . . The pictures are much fun and fit the story perfectly." Publ Wkly

Fox, Tamar
No baths at camp; by Tamar Fox; illustrated by Natalia Vasquez. Kar-Ben Pub. 2013 32 p. col. ill. (reinforced) $17.95
Grades: PreK K 1 2   E
1. Baths -- Fiction 2. Camps -- Fiction 3. Sabbath -- Fiction 4. Jews -- United States -- Fiction
ISBN 9780761381204
           LC 2012009498
"It's bath time, but Max is none too enthused, telling his mother he wishes he were back at camp, because 'there are NO BATHS AT CAMP! No baths for a whole week.' Max then recounts his week at camp with pals, as they climb a rock wall, produce a play, and learn Israeli dances--and while they may get dirty, 'there are NO BATHS AT CAMP.' But Friday at camp means prepping for Shabbat, which includes cleaning bunks and taking showers. The book's conclusion finds Max in a bubble-filled bath at home, still asserting that camp is better, including Shabbat, because, well, you know." (Booklist)

Frame, Jeron Ashford
★ Yesterday I had the blues; illustrations by R. Gregory Christie. Tricycle Press 2003 un il $14.95
Grades: K 1 2 3   E
1. Emotions -- Fiction 2. Family life -- Fiction 3. African Americans -- Fiction
ISBN 1-58246-084-1
           LC 2002-155295
A young African American boy ponders a variety of emotions and how different members of his family experience them, from his own blues to his father's grays and his grandmother's yellows

"Vibrant acrylic-and-gouache spreads give rhythm and meaning to this child's interpretation of everyday life, his neighborhood, and his family. The illustrations effectively express each individual's mood and beautifully capture the cultural and artistic aspects of the family's life, while the expressive text is engaging." SLJ

Franceschelli, Christopher
(oliver) Lemniscaat 2011 un il bd bk $12.95
Grades: PreK K   E
1. Board books for children 2. Eggs -- Fiction 3. Chickens -- Fiction
ISBN 978-1-9359-5401-9; 1-9359-5401-6
First published in Holland
In this board book, Oliver the egg can't do much but roll from one side to the other, until a miracle happens and he becomes a chick.

This book "contains crisp, attractive text and drawings, using space, light, and dark elegantly. Small children will delight in pulling open the sturdy pages and experiencing Oliver's transformation over and over." SLJ

Alphablock; by Christopher Franceschelli. Appleseed 2013 104 p. $16.95

Grades: K 1 2   E
1. Alphabet 2. Toy and movable books 3. Toy and movable books -- Specimens
ISBN 1419709364; 9781419709364
           LC 2012047783
In this ABC board book, by Christopher Franceschelli, "thick pages [are] cut into the shape of each letter. Sprinkles, hot fudge, and cherries hint at I's ice cream sundae, while aquarium accessories hint at F's fish. As readers interact with the pages, they will familiarize themselves not only with the 26 letters and associated words, but also with each letter's physicality angles, holes, and curves, both front and back." (Publisher's note)

Franco, Betsy
Bird songs; a backwards counting book. [by] Betsy Franco; [illustrated by] Steve Jenkins. Margaret K. McElderry Books 2006 un il $16.99
Grades: PreK K 1 2   E
1. Counting 2. Day -- Fiction 3. Birds -- Fiction 4. Birdsongs -- Fiction
ISBN 0-689-87777-3; 978-0-689-87777-3
           LC 2004-25056
Throughout the day and into the night various birds sing their songs, beginning with the woodpecker who taps a pole ten times and counting down to the hummingbird who calls once.

"In his vivid, realistic-looking collages, Jenkins uses accurate textures and colors for each species, and creates the appearance of depth, light, and warmth. . . . The writing is lyrical and engaging, and quick 'feathery facts' about the creatures are appended." SLJ

Double play! monkeying around with addition. illustrations by Doug Cushman. Tricycle Press 2011 un il $15.99; lib bdg $18.99
Grades: PreK K 1   E
1. Addition 2. School stories 3. Stories in rhyme 4. Play -- Fiction 5. Monkeys -- Fiction
ISBN 978-1-58246-384-1; 1-58246-384-0; 978-1-58246-396-4 lib bdg; 1-58246-396-4 lib bdg
           LC 2010024347
Monkey friends Jill and Jake play together at recess, and each game they play provides practice in doubling. Each page displays the matching addition problem.

"The large watercolor illustrations show a joyous romp. . . . Young students will enjoy the book for its play aspect, not realizing that the math lesson is built into it." SLJ

Pond circle; illustrated by Stefano Vitale. Margaret K. McElderry Books 2009 un il $16.99
Grades: PreK K 1 2 3   E
1. Animals -- Fiction 2. Ecology -- Fiction 3. Pond ecology -- Fiction 4. Food chains (Ecology) -- Fiction
ISBN 978-1-4169-4021-0; 1-4169-4021-9
           LC 2008016268
In the pond by Anna's house, a food chain begins with algae which is eaten by a mayfly nymph which is eaten by a beetle which is eaten by a bullfrog.

"Vitale's rich, colorful oil-on-wood illustrations are as poetic as the text in their depiction of the natural world. . . . A clear, child-friendly look at ecology." SLJ

Frank, John
How to catch a fish; by John Frank; illustrated by Peter Sylvada. Roaring Brook Press 2007 un il $17.95

Grades: K 1 2   E

1. Stories in rhyme 2. Fishing -- Fiction

ISBN 978-1-59643-163-8; 1-59643-163-6

LC 2006032184

Rhyming text and illustrations describe the ways fish are caught in various locations around the world

"The handsome, full-page oil paintings are rendered in an impressionistic style that evokes the atmospheres of watery, misty, aquatic environments. . . . Resonating poetic vignettes spawn a glinting, striking catch." Booklist

Franson, Scott E.

Un-brella. Roaring Brook Press 2007 un il $15.95

Grades: PreK K   E

1. Stories without words 2. Magic -- Fiction 3. Weather -- Fiction 4. Umbrellas and parasols -- Fiction

ISBN 978-1-59643-179-9; 1-59643-179-2

LC 2006047658

In this wordless book, a little girl uses her magic umbrella to give her the weather she wants, regardless of what the conditions really are outside.

"The crisp, clean pictures have bright colors, exceptional detail, fun patterns, sly repetition, and heaps of whimsy." SLJ

Fraser, Mary Ann

Heebie-Jeebie Jamboree. Boyds Mills Press 2011 un il

Grades: PreK K 1   E

1. Siblings -- Fiction 2. Festivals -- Fiction 3. Halloween -- Fiction

ISBN 1-59078-857-5; 978-1-59078-857-8

"Dressed as a witch and a ghost, Sam and Daphne pull tickets out of thin air to the Heebie-Jeebie Jamboree on Halloween night. They are treated to a magical, good time. . . . Then, in the midst of the festivities, Sam goes missing. . . . The full-bleed illustrations in vibrant colors feature Halloween creatures of all sorts (but none frightening), and the pages are packed with action and energy. Children will love poring over the many details." SLJ

Pet shop follies. Boyd Mills Press 2010 un il $16.95

Grades: PreK K   E

1. Pets -- Fiction 2. Theater -- Fiction

ISBN 978-1-59078-619-2; 1-59078-619-X

"All the pet-shop animals mix and mingle in the front window anxiously awaiting customers, yet no one comes in. The clever hamster takes matters in hand and devises a brilliant plan to get visitors: 'Let's put on a show!' he squeaks. . . . The creamy, rich gouache double-page spreads are uncluttered, allowing each amazing feat its moment in the spotlight while remaining developmentally appropriate for young readers." Kirkus

Pet shop lullaby. Boyds Mills Press 2009 un il $16.95

Grades: PreK K   E

1. Pets -- Fiction 2. Animals -- Fiction 3. Bedtime -- Fiction

ISBN 978-1-59078-618-5; 1-59078-618-1

LC 2009019661

When the pet store closes for the night, a hamster's activities keep the other animals awake as they try to think of some way to put him to sleep.

"Fraser's tale is brief and to the point, and the comical gouache illustrations infuse energy into the telling. Fun touches abound." SLJ

Another title about the pet shop is:

Pet shop follies (2010)

Frasier, Debra

★ A **birthday** cake is no ordinary cake; written and illustrated by Debra Frasier. Harcourt 2006 un il $16

Grades: PreK K 1 2   E

1. Cake -- Fiction 2. Year -- Fiction 3. Birthdays -- Fiction

ISBN 978-0-15-205742-8; 0-15-205742-0

A lyrical recipe using the changes in the natural world to explain to a child the time that passes between one birthday and the next. Includes recipe for more traditional birthday cake.

"Pop-off-the-page, vibrant-colored cut-paper collage illustrations capture the fanciful and factual concepts." SLJ

A **fabulous** fair alphabet. Beach Lane Books 2010 un il $16.99

Grades: PreK K 1   E

1. Alphabet 2. Fairs -- Fiction

ISBN 978-1-4169-9817-4; 1-4169-9817-9

LC 2009038329

Letters of the alphabet in various graphic styles accompany words associated with fairs.

"Despite the flat graphic style, the pages seem to sparkle and blink with the bright lights of a midway. The endpapers are bold collages of photos of signs at fairs. As alphabet books go, this one is delightful. As graphic art goes, it's alive with evocative, almost magical examples." SLJ

★ **On** the day you were born. Harcourt Brace Jovanovich 1991 un il $16

Grades: K 1 2 3 4   E

1. Childbirth 2. Earth

ISBN 0-15-302160-8

LC 90-36816

This combination of text and paper-collage graphics depicts the earth's preparation for, and celebration of, the birth of a newborn baby

"The text reads like unrhymed poetry, and both parents and educators will find themselves wanting to share this book over and over with individuals and with groups. A three-page appendix that includes miniature versions of each spread elaborates on natural phenomena for older readers—migrating animals, spinning Earth, rising tide, falling rain, growing trees, and more." SLJ

Frazee, Marla

★ **Boot** & Shoe; Marla Frazee. Beach Lane Books 2012 40 p. (hardcover) $16.99

Grades: PreK K 1 2   E

1. Dogs -- Fiction 2. Solitude -- Fiction 3. Squirrels -- Fiction 4. Dogs -- Fiction 5. Solitude -- Fiction

ISBN 1442422475; 9781442422476

LC 2011035990

In this children's picture book by Marla Frazee "Two adorably floppy dogs confront unexpected change. . . . Boot and Shoe were born into the same litter, and now they live in the same house. . . . But they spend their days apart--Boot on the back porch because he's a back porch kind of dog, and Shoe on the front porch because he's a front porch kind of dog. . . . Then a crazy neighborhood squirrel arrives . . . and everything goes topsy-turvy!" (Publisher's note)

★ The **boss** baby. Beach Lane Books 2010 un il $16.99

Grades: PreK K 1   E

1. Infants -- Fiction

ISBN 978-1-4424-0167-9; 1-4424-0167-2

From the moment he arrives, it is obvious that the new baby is boss and he gets whatever he wants, from drinks made-to-order around the clock to his executive gym.

"Cartoon vignettes in pencil-streaked gouache hum with a funky, retro style seen in sleek furnishings and the '50s fashions of the accommodating but increasingly exhausted parents. . . . Clever and empathetic." Publ Wkly

★ The **bossier** baby; Marla Frazee. Beach Lane Books 2016 40 p. color illustrations (ebook) $15.99; (hardback) $17.99
Grades: PreK K 1   E
1. Infants -- Fiction 2. Humorous fiction -- Fiction 3. Brothers and sisters -- Fiction 4. Humorous stories 5. Babies -- Fiction 6. Brothers and sisters -- Fiction
ISBN 9781481471633; 9781481471626
LC 2015045579
In this picture book, by Marla Frazee, "change is in the air—the Boss Baby's staff has stopped taking his direction! It seems that there is a new CEO in town; from the moment she comes home, Boss Baby's little sister is extremely loud and demanding all sorts of corporate perks he never got. Can the Boss Baby and his staff get used to the new corporate structure?" (Publisher's note)
"Elder siblings and parents alike will recognize the tensions that come with a growing family, and the just-sweet-enough resolution proves that this CEO knows how to negotiate a takeover with savvy." Pub Wkly

★ A **couple** of boys have the best week ever; [by] Marla Frazee. Harcourt 2008 32p il $16
Grades: K 1 2 3   E
1. Beaches -- Fiction 2. Vacations -- Fiction 3. Friendship -- Fiction 4. Grandparents -- Fiction
ISBN 978-0-15-206020-6
LC 2006-25781
A Caldecott Medal honor book, 2009
Friends James and Eamon enjoy a wonderful week at the home of Eamon's grandparents during summer vacation. "Ages six to nine." (Bull Cent Child Books)
"After Eamon enrolls in nature camp, he spends nights with his grandparents, Bill and Pam, at their beach cottage. Eamon's friend James joins the sleepover. . . . Humorous contradictions arise between the hand-lettered account . . . and voice-bubble exchanges between the boys. . . . Frazee's narrative resembles a tongue-in-cheek travel journal, with plenty of enticing pencil and gouache illustrations of the characters knocking about the shoreline." Publ Wkly

★ The **farmer** and the clown; Marla Frazee. Beach Lane Books 2014 32 p. color illustrations (hardcover) $17.99
Grades: PreK K 1 2   E
1. Circus -- Fiction 2. Clowns -- Fiction 3. Farmers -- Fiction 4. Stories without words
ISBN 1442497440; 9781442497443
LC 2013019361
Boston Globe-Horn Book Award: Picture Book (2015)
In this picture book, by Marla Frazee, "a baby clown is separated from his family when he accidentally bounces off their circus train and lands in a lonely farmer's vast, empty field. The farmer reluctantly rescues the little clown, and over the course of one day together, the two of them make some surprising discoveries about themselves--and about life!" (Publisher's note)
"Frazee's controlled palette of subdued golds, browns, and grays offers a fitting backdrop for the hard-working farmer foregrounded in this wordless tale. . . . This is a tender look at light and shadow, the joy and comfort in companionship, the lift that laughter provides, and the friendship possible among generations (and species)." SLJ

★ **Roller** coaster. Harcourt 2003 un il

Grades: PreK K 1 2   E
1. Roller coasters
ISBN 0-15-204554-6
LC 2002-7805
Twelve people set aside their fears and ride a roller coaster, including one who has never done so before. "Ages three to seven." (Christ Sci Monit)
"Frazee does an extraordinary job of conveying motion by the placement of her images, her use of white space, bright colors, and swooshing speed lines. . . . What will keep children coming back for extra looks, however, is Frazee's clever, dramatic depiction of the 12 riders and their wildly and amusingly different reactions to the stomach-churning experience." Booklist

★ **Santa** Claus, the world's number one toy expert. Harcourt 2005 $16
Grades: PreK K 1 2   E
1. Christmas -- Fiction 2. Santa Claus -- Fiction
ISBN 0-15-204970-3; 0152049703
LC 2004005228
Santa Claus has his own ways of knowing more about children and toys than anyone else in the world. "Ages four to eight." (Bull Cent Child Books)
"Frazee, a master at creating scenes and moods in her energetic drawings and spare text, fills these pages with details and vignettes that readers will want to explore repeatedly." SLJ

★ **Walk** on! a guide for babies of all ages. Harcourt, Inc. 2006 un il $16
Grades: PreK K 1 2   E
1. Infants -- Fiction 2. Walking -- Fiction
ISBN 0-15-205573-8
LC 2004-29895
"In this how-to for little ones, a baby learns to walk for the first time. . . . The pencil-and-gouache art has the delightful feel of self-help pamphlets from an earlier era. . . . This is one of those rare books that speaks to crawling and walking babies who like to look at pictures of creatures like themselves, preschoolers who enjoy stories about what they were like when they were little, and older children and adults who will appreciate the wry humor." SLJ

Frazier, Craig
Bee & Bird. Roaring Brook Press 2011 un il $16.99
Grades: PreK K 1   E
1. Adventure fiction 2. Stories without words 3. Bees -- Fiction 4. Birds -- Fiction 5. Travel -- Fiction
ISBN 978-1-59643-660-2; 1-59643-660-3
LC 2010013012
In this wordless picture book, a bumblebee and a bird embark on a travel adventure.
Frazier "uses perspective to great advantage in creating mystery and drawing readers into the story. . . . The vividly colored artwork will immediately snag young readers' attention; the perplexing views will entice them into the plot; and subtle clues . . . will help them make sense of the details in subsequent viewings." Booklist

★ **Hank** finds inspiration; [by] Craig Frazier. Roaring Brook Press 2008 un il $16.95
Grades: K 1 2   E
1. Snakes -- Fiction
ISBN 978-1-59643-358-8; 1-59643-358-2
LC 2007047919
Hank the snake and his human friend, Stanley, each go to the city in search of inspiration, but Hank's journey is a failure until he returns home

"Frazier's crisp graphics draw the eye to varied perspectives with bold splashes of color and sharply defined silhouettes and shadings. An 'inspired' addition for all libraries." SLJ

Lots of dots. Chronicle Books 2010 un il
Grades: PreK K 1   E
1. Stories in rhyme 2. Shape -- Fiction
ISBN 0811877159; 9780811877152

Circular shapes are spotted in familiar objects and everyday situations. Buttons are dots. Wheels are dots. Stars are dots. Ladybugs have dots and so do the fried eggs on your plate. Lots of dots!

"Frazier maintains an upbeat tone with tight rhyme and meter throughout; with the exception of one night scene, with dots for stars, the backgrounds are plain white, giving the pages a freshly washed, contemporary feel." Publ Wkly

Frederick, Heather Vogel
Babyberry pie; [illustrations by] Amy Schwartz. Harcourt Children's Books 2010 un il $16.99
Grades: PreK K 1   E
1. Stories in rhyme 2. Bedtime -- Fiction 3. Infants -- Fiction
ISBN 978-0-15-205927-9; 0-15-205927-X

In illustrations and rhyming text, gives the recipe for making "babyberry pie," from picking a baby from the babyberry tree and popping him in the tub to putting powdered sugar on his nose and toes and tucking him into pie crust covers.

"Schwartz brings out her best with these vivid gouache and pen-and-ink illustrations of a family getting a toddler ready for bed. . . . Frederick's rhyming text, repetition, and wordplay amplify the fun in this yummy mix of old-fashioned cozy and modern setting." SLJ

Hide-and-squeak; illustrated by C.F. Payne. Simon & Schuster Books for Young Readers 2011 un il $16.99
Grades: PreK K 1   E
1. Stories in rhyme 2. Mice -- Fiction 3. Bedtime -- Fiction 4. Father-child relationship -- Fiction
ISBN 978-0-689-85570-2; 0-689-85570-2
LC 2008039648

A mouse baby leads his father on a merry game of hide-and-squeak at bedtime.

"Payne's settings, amplifying the baby mouse's inexhaustible energy and giddy transgressiveness, while buoying Frederick's . . . rock solid, somewhat quaint rhymes. . . . The spreads are small masterpieces of composition, yet they never feel static; rather, it's as if someone has hit the pause button to briefly allow readers to savor the image's beauty before the story continues on its rollicking way to the bedtime wrap-up." Publ Wkly

Freedman, Claire
Gooseberry Goose; illustrated by Vanessa Cabban. Tiger Tales 2003 un il $15.95
Grades: PreK K 1 2   E
1. Geese -- Fiction 2. Winter -- Fiction 3. Animals -- Fiction
ISBN 1-58925-030-3
LC 2003-12960

As Gooseberry Goose practices flying on a beautiful fall morning, his friends are preparing for winter, causing Gooseberry to wonder if there is something else he should be doing

"The text is brought to life through the illustrations, which are loose and lovely. Vibrant red and gold leaves enliven the pages. Gooseberry is a bundle of expression. . . . Readers will be captivated by this irrepressible gosling's infectious charm." SLJ

Freedman, Deborah
★ **Blue** chicken. Viking 2011 un il $15.99
Grades: PreK K 1   E
1. Chickens -- Fiction 2. Farm life -- Fiction 3. Domestic animals -- Fiction
ISBN 978-0-670-01293-0; 0-670-01293-9
LC 2011001502

An enterprising chicken attempts to help an artist paint the barnyard and accidentally turns the whole picture blue.

"Watercolor washes and splashes, from pale blue to dark, create wonderful, wet patterns; their liquid edges contrast alluringly with fine pencil lines and shadings. . . . Delicate and durable, visually sophisticated yet friendly: simply exquisite." Kirkus

This house, once; Deborah Freedman. Atheneum Books for Young Readers 2017 40 p. color illustrations (ebook) $15.99; (hardcover) $17.99
Grades: PreK K 1 2   E
1. Houses -- Fiction 2. Nature -- Fiction 3. Nature -- Fiction 4. Dwellings -- Fiction
ISBN 9781481442855; 9781481442848
LC 2015011937

Author "Deborah Freedman's masterful new picture book is at once an introduction to the pieces of a house, a cozy story to share and explore, and a dreamy meditation on the magic of our homes and our world. . . . This poetically simple, thought-provoking, and gorgeously illustrated book invites readers to think about where things come from and what nature provides." (Publisher's note)

"The arc emphasizes shelter but also human use of nature, so the feelings of warmth, safety, and coziness hold the faintest tinge of melancholy and loss. Tender, comforting, and complex." Kirkus

Freeman, Don
★ **Corduroy;** 40th anniversary edition; Viking Press 2008 32p il $19.99
Grades: PreK K 1   E
1. Teddy bears -- Fiction
ISBN 978-0-670-06336-9; 0-670-06336-3

A reissue of the title first published 1968

A toy bear in a department store wants a number of things, but when a little girl finally buys him he finds what he has always wanted most of all. This edition includes copies of letters and the original manuscript.

"The art and story are direct and just right for the very young who like bears and escalators." Book World

Another title about Corduroy is:
A pocket for Corduroy (1978)

Earl the squirrel. Viking 2005 un il $15.99
Grades: PreK K 1   E
1. Squirrels -- Fiction
ISBN 0-670-06019-4
LC 2005-03929

Earl the squirrel learns to gather acorns on his own.

"The pictures are full of energy and detail, and Earl is both cheeky and endearing. . . . The story is gentle, innocent, and funny." SLJ

Quiet! there's a canary in the library; by Don Freeman. Viking Children's Books 2007 un il $15.99
Grades: PreK K 1   E
1. Animals -- Fiction 2. Libraries -- Fiction
ISBN 978-0-670-06230-0; 0-670-06230-8
LC 2006-37904

A reissue of the title first published 1969 by Golden Gate

Cary imagines a special day at the library when she invites only animals and birds to browse.

"Freeman contrasts more detailed drawings of the actual library with childlike crayoned depictions of Cary's daydreamed adventures." Horn Book Guide

Freeman, Martha

Mrs. Wow never wanted a cow; by Martha Freeman; illustrated by Steven Salerno. Random House 2006 un il (Beginner books) $8.99; lib bdg $11.99
Grades: K 1 2   E
   1. Cats -- Fiction 2. Dogs -- Fiction 3. Cattle -- Fiction
   ISBN 0-375-83418-4; 0-375-93418-9 lib bdg
LC 2005006000
When Mrs. Wow takes in a stray cow, her lazy dog and cat hope to train the new household member to catch mice and intimidate the mailman

"The mostly one-syllable words with regular phonetic patterns are spare and natural, and Salerno's brightly colored cartoon illustrations amplify the text's humor." SLJ

Freeman, Tor

Olive and the big secret; Tor Freeman. Candlewick Press 2012 32 p. $15.99
Grades: PreK K 1 2   E
   ISBN 076366149X; 9780763661496
LC 2012938740
"When Molly shares a secret with Olive, the urge to tell is just too great! Olive tells Joe who tells Matt who tells Lola. But Lola is best friends with Molly. Uh-oh, the secret is out, and Olive is in for it!" (Publisher's note)

French, Jackie

Christmas wombat; by Jackie French; illustrated by Bruce Whatley. Clarion Books 2012 32 p. (hardback) $16.99
Grades: PreK K 1 2   E
   1. Holidays -- Fiction 2. Animals 3. Human-animal relationships
   -- Fiction 4. Diaries -- Fiction 5. Wombats -- Fiction 6. Christmas
   -- Fiction
   ISBN 0547868723; 9780547868721
LC 2011052112
Author Jackie French's story centers on a wombat. "A bearlike Australian animal, the wombat likes to sleep, hide in holes and eat. This wombat especially likes to eat carrots, and the . . . plot focuses on the wombat's intensive search for more and more carrots." The book "describes the wombat's activities and its discovery of carrots set out for some 'strange creatures' (Santa's reindeer). The wombat chomps every carrot in sight, stows away in Santa's sleigh and beats the reindeer to their carrot treats at stops around the world." (Kirkus Reviews)

Diary of a baby wombat; written by Jackie French; illustrated by Bruce Whatley. Clarion Books 2010 un il $16.99
Grades: PreK K 1 2   E
   1. Wombats -- Fiction
   ISBN 978-0-547-43005-8; 0-547-43005-1
LC 2009050452
Through a week of diary entries, a wombat describes his life of sleeping, playing, and helping his mother look for a bigger hole in which to make their home.

"Economy of voice is reflected in the understated illustrations. . . . This will be read over and over, providing new laughs each time." Horn Book

★ **Diary** of a wombat; illustrated by Bruce Whatley. Clarion Bks. 2003 un il $14
Grades: PreK K 1 2   E
   1. Wombats -- Fiction
   ISBN 0-618-38136-8
LC 2003-829
First published 2002 in Australia
In his diary, a wombat describes his life of eating, sleeping, and getting to know some new human neighbors

The story is presented in "simple sentences and hilarious yet realistic acrylic illustrations. . . . Whatley gives a sublime balance of the adorable charm of the creature, along with its drawbacks as an acquaintance." SLJ

Another title about the wombat is:
Diary of a baby wombat (2010)

Pete the sheep-sheep; illustrated by Bruce Whatley. Clarion Books 2005 32p il $14
Grades: PreK K 1 2   E
   1. Dogs -- Fiction 2. Sheep -- Fiction
   ISBN 0-618-56862-X
LC 2004-30935
First published 2004 in Australia with title: Pete the sheep
The sheep-shearers in Shaggy Gully all have a sheep dog, but the new guy Shaun uses an extremely polite sheep named Pete.

"Cleanly designed illustrations work well with French's understated text. Strong lines focus attention on the expressive characters." Horn Book Guide

French, Vivian

The **Daddy** Goose treasury; as told to Vivian French; illustrated by AnnaLaura Cantone . . . [et al.] Scholastic 2006 93p il $18.99
Grades: K 1 2 3   E
   1. Nursery rhymes -- Fiction
   ISBN 0-439-79608-3
"French includes 12 untold stories that give background and context for such familiar rhymes as Little Miss Muffet, Georgie Porgie, Old King Cole, and Hickory, Dickory, Dock. . . . Four European illustrators contribute lively, colorful, and witty illustrations that adeptly articulate the cozy narratives." SLJ

The **most** wonderful thing in the world; Vivian French, Angela Barrett. Candlewick Press 2015 32 p. color illustrations $18.99
Grades: K 1 2 3 4 5   E
   1. Arranged marriage -- Fiction 2. Princesses -- Fiction 3. Kings
   and rulers -- Fiction
   ISBN 9780763675011
LC 2014953065
In this book, by Vivian French, illustrated by Angela Barrett, "a king and a queen promise to marry their daughter to the young man who can show them the most wonderful thing in the world. Suitors arrive at the palace, one after the other, with elaborate gifts, . . . but nothing feels quite right. . . . It is only when a shy young man, who isn't a suitor at all, steps forward that the king and queen finally understand what the most wonderful thing in the world actually is." (Publisher's note)

"Children will enjoy the well-told story for its own sake, and the beautifully composed pictures for their intricacy and their sometimes surprising details." Booklist

★ **Yucky** worms; illustrated by Jessica Ahlberg. Candlewick Press 2010 28p il $16.99; pa $6.99
Grades: PreK K 1 2   E
   1. Worms -- Fiction 2. Gardening -- Fiction 3. Grandmothers --

Fiction 4. Earthworms

ISBN 978-0-7636-4446-8; 0-7636-4446-3; 978-0-7636-5817-5 pa

LC 2009-17307

While helping Grandma in the garden, a child learns about the important role of the earthworm in helping plants grow.

"The cheerful pencil-and-gouache artwork shows scenes both above and below the ground and weaves facts into each image, as well as humorous cartoon speech bubbles. . . . Friendly and interactive, this is a great choice for sharing at home and in the classroom." Booklist

Freymann, Saxton

★ **Fast** food; written and illustrated by Saxton Freymann. Arthur A. Levine Books 2006 32p il $12.99

Grades: PreK K 1 2 3   E

1. Transportation

ISBN 0-439-11019-X

"This picture book takes a theme (here, transportation) and illustrates it with exceptionally clear color photos of ephemeral, sometimes whimsical sculptures created from fruits and vegetables. As quietly witty as its title, the book is narrated by a little mushroom man who suggests different ways of getting about. . . . The playful text gallops along smoothly in rhymed couplets, while the illustrations work their inimitable charm." Booklist

★ **Food** for thought; the complete book of concepts for growing minds. written and illustrated by Saxton Freymann. Arthur A. Levine Books 2005 61p il $14.95

Grades: PreK K 1 2 3   E

1. Alphabet 2. Concepts 3. Counting

ISBN 0-439-11018-1

This "covers basic shapes, colors, numbers, letters, and opposites—all introduced through images of artfully manipulated fruits and vegetables. . . . The simple, clean design is ideal for demonstrating the concepts. . . . But it's the playful, wonderfully clever transformation of familiar foods that will win an audience." Booklist

Friedlaender, Linda K.

Look! look! look! by Nancy Elizabeth Wallace with Linda K. Friedlaender; illustrated by Nancy Elizabeth Wallace. Marshall Cavendish 2006 un il $16.95

Grades: K 1 2 3   E

1. Art -- Fiction 2. Mice -- Fiction

ISBN 978-0-7614-5282-9; 0-7614-5282-6

LC 2005016934

Three mice "borrow" a postcard which is a reproduction of a painting, and from it they learn about color, pattern, line, and shape. Includes instructions for making and sending a postcard.

This picture book tells the story of three mice exploring a sculpture exhibit in a museum. "Three frisky mice, sensibilities honed by an exposure to painting in [Linda K. Friedlaender's] 'Look! Look! Look!' (2006), give 3-D art a similarly close once over. The story is centered on an abstract work in slate by Barbara Hepworth in the Yale Center for British Art (where Friedlaender is a curator), but it features sharp color photos of 20 other sculptures from as many eras and cultures." (Kirkus)

"This is not only an amusing, creative story, but also an adventure into art that encourages originality while inspiring creativity." SLJ

Friedman, Caitlin

How do you feed a hungry giant? a munch-and-sip pop-up book. illustrated by Shaw Nielsen. Workman 2011 un il $18.95

Grades: PreK K 1 2   E

1. Pop-up books 2. Giants -- Fiction

ISBN 978-0-7611-5752-6; 0-7611-5752-2

"A gentle giant clothed in patchwork clothing appears in a boy's front yard carrying a sign that says, 'Food Please.' The giant gobbles an entire pizza, slurps up 15 bottles of chocolate milk from a kiddie pool, and consumes 197 cookies, but remains hungry. Luckily, the boy's mother is willing to help. The well-integrated interactive elements—popups, tabs, and flaps—add an extra touch of fun to this lighthearted story." Publ Wkly

Friedman, Darlene

Star of the Week; a story of love, adoption, and brownies with sprinkles. story by Darlene Friedman; illustrations by Roger Roth. HarperCollins 2009 un il $17.99; lib bdg $18.89

Grades: PreK K 1 2 3   E

1. School stories 2. Adoption -- Fiction 3. Chinese Americans -- Fiction

ISBN 978-0-06-114136-2; 0-06-114136-4; 978-0-06-114137-9 lib bdg; 0-06-114137-2 lib bdg

LC 2008-22581

As her turn to be "Star of the Week" in her kindergarten class approaches, Cassidy-Li puts together a poster with pictures of her family, friends, and pets, and wonders about her birthparents in China.

"Roth's vibrant illustrations capture the personality of Cassidy-Li, the six-year-old narrator who tells her story in unaffected language that will appeal to children." SLJ

Friedman, Ina R.

How my parents learned to eat; illustrated by Allen Say. Houghton Mifflin 1984 30p il hardcover o.p. pa $6.99

Grades: K 1 2 3   E

1. Japan -- Fiction 2. Dining -- Fiction

ISBN 0-395-35379-3; 0-395-44235-4 pa

LC 83-18553

An American sailor courts a Japanese girl and each tries, in secret, to learn the other's way of eating

"The illustrations have precise use of line and soft colors, and the composition is economical. A warm and gentle story of an interracial family." Bull Cent Child Books

Friend, Catherine

Eddie the raccoon; illustrated by Wong Herbert Yee. Candlewick Press 2004 40p il (Brand new readers) hardcover o.p. pa $5.99

Grades: K 1 2   E

1. Raccoons -- Fiction

ISBN 0-7636-2331-8; 0-7636-2334-2 pa

LC 2003-69717

"Pleasant watercolors . . . provide ample visual clues to the accompanying sentence—usually comprising four or five basic vocabulary words. . . . Each setup packs a gently humorous punch that's easy enough for children to grasp and sweet enough to make their adult helpers chuckle." Booklist

The **perfect** nest; illustrated by John Manders. Candlewick Press 2007 un il $16.99

Grades: K 1 2   E

1. Cats -- Fiction 2. Chickens -- Fiction

ISBN 978-0-7636-2430-9; 0-7636-2430-6

LC 2006047518

Jack the cat gets much more than he bargained for when he decides to build the perfect nest to attract the perfect chicken

This is "highly comical yet heartwarming tale. . . . Manders's gouache illustrations are a perfect complement to the text." SLJ

Friend, David

With any luck, I'll drive a truck; David Friend; illustrated by Michael Rex. Nancy Paulsen Books, an imprint of Penguin Group (USA) 2016 32 p. color illustrations (hbk.) $16.99

Grades: PreK K   E

1. Stories in rhyme 2. Trucks -- Fiction 3. Imagination -- Fiction 4. Trucks -- Fiction 5. Imagination -- Fiction

ISBN 9780399169564

LC 2015009191

This children's book, by David Friend, illustrated by Michael Rex, is a "celebration of big rigs and big imaginations. Bulldozers and backhoes, pavers and plows, trailers and tractors--the world is filled with so many types of trucks! Imagine the fun you could have if you could drive them all! And what if you could bring your best friends along with you? Hop along for a thrilling ride!" (Publisher's note)

"The rhythmic, rhyming text has just enough detail to keep kids engaged without slowing down the pace. Drawn in ink and digitally colored, the illustrations feature the boy, his dressed-animal helpers, and his powerful trucks and other equipment." Booklist

Friester, Paul

Owl howl; [illustrated by] Philippe Goossens; [English translation by Erica Stenfalt] NorthSouth Books 2011 un il (Tuff books) pa $6.95

Grades: PreK K   E

1. Owls -- Fiction 2. Forest animals -- Fiction

ISBN 978-0-7358-4017-1; 0-7358-4017-2

"In response to a little owl's howling, various forest animals take turns trying to determine the problem and stop her tears. The bulbous-eyed owl is uncommonly sympathetic thanks to Goossens's illustrations on sturdy, glossy pages. When the owl is back under her mom's wings, readers will exhale with relief—before they grin at the punch line." Horn Book Guide

Frisch, Aaron

A **night** on the range; written by Aaron Frisch; illustrated by Chris Sheban. Creative Editions 2010 un il $25.65

Grades: K 1 2 3   E

1. Fear -- Fiction 2. Camping -- Fiction 3. Cowhands -- Fiction 4. Imagination -- Fiction

ISBN 978-1-56846-205-9; 1-56846-205-0

LC 2008016595

"Young cowboy-wannabe Cole daydreams about roping strays and hunting down rustlers. He's beyond excited for his first camping experience—that is, until it gets dark. . . . Dreamy, expansive illustrations distinguish between Cole's wild imagination and his reality—a suburban backyard—in this well-done ode to self-fulfillment." Horn Book Guide

Frost, Helen

Sweep up the sun; Helen Frost, illustrated by Rick Leider. Candlewick Press 2015 32 p. $15.99

Grades: PreK K 1 2 3   E

1. Birds 2. Nature photography

ISBN 0763669040; 9780763669041

LC 2013957345

In this book by Helen Frost, here "commonly seen birds in their natural settings, captured in photographs of rare beauty and grace. In perfect synchrony, a lyrical narrative evokes images of play and flight, perseverance and trust.At the end, readers will find profiles of the featured species. This stunning book is an ideal gift for bird lovers of all ages, graduates, or anyone embarking on an adventure." (Publisher's note)

Fucile, Tony

★ **Let's** do nothing! Candlewick Press 2009 un il $16.99; pa $6.99

Grades: PreK K 1 2   E

1. Imagination -- Fiction

ISBN 978-0-7636-3440-7; 0-7636-3440-9; 978-0-7636-5269-2 pa

LC 2008-935654

"Frankie and Sal are bored . . . and now there is nothing—which is exactly what they will attempt to do for ten whole seconds. In a series of increasingly hilarious spreads, the two boys . . . are deterred everytime by Frankie's overactive imagination. . . . The imagined scenes employ vibrant color, in effective contrast with the reality sequences. . . . Fucile's figures, ink line with acrylic paints, . . . have a retro touch in their period hues and springy drafting." Bull Cent Child Books

Poor Louie; Tony Fucile. Candlewick Press 2017 40 p. color illustrations $16.99

Grades: PreK K 1 2   E

1. Dogs -- Fiction 2. Infants -- Fiction 3. Family life -- Fiction

ISBN 0763658286; 9780763658281

In this book, author Tony Fucile "provides a creative and comic look at the arrival of a new sibling. His expressive cartoon artwork is funny and endearing and the perfect complement to the spare text. A great read-aloud for any apprehensive older sibling and a fun storytime selection. Children will enjoy chiming in with the 'Poor Louie' refrain." (School Library Journal)

Fuge, Charles

Astonishing animal ABC. Sterling 2011 un il $14.95

Grades: PreK K 1   E

1. Alphabet 2. Stories in rhyme

ISBN 978-1-4027-8645-7; 1-4027-8645-X

An alphabet book featuring rhyming text and all sorts of animals.

"The rhyming text is abundant with adjectives and alliteration. Fuge's animals communicate a variety of emotions (fear, happiness and worry), but when they gather together to see the animal that starts with the letter Z zoom past them, they all look surprised. Readers will likely express a similar sentiment." SLJ

Fuller, Sandy Ferguson

My cat, coon cat; illustrated by Jeannie Brett. Islandport 2011 il $17.95

Grades: PreK K 1 2   E

1. Stories in rhyme 2. Cats -- Fiction

ISBN 978-1-934031-32-2; 1-934031-32-1

When a young girl moves into a new home, she slowly wins the affection of a shy Maine coon cat, as he meets the girl's kitten, chases dragonflies, and explores the neighborhood.

"The illustrations are full of color and character, capturing with equal charm the bucolic background and the winsome feline. . . . Any reader who has ever known the love of a cat will find much to relate to in this cozy book." SLJ

Funk, Josh

Dear dragon; a pen pal tale. by Josh Funk; illustrated by Rodolfo Montalvo. Viking, published by Penguin Group 2016 40 p. color illustrations (hardback) $16.99; (ebook) $50.97

Grades: PreK K 1   E

1. Stories in rhyme 2. Dragons -- Fiction 3. Letters -- Fiction 4. Pen pals -- Fiction 5. Friendship -- Fiction 6. Dragons -- Fiction 7. Letters -- Fiction 8. Pen pals -- Fiction 9. Friendship -- Fiction

ISBN 0451472306; 9780451472304; 9780698180574

LC 2015048168

In this story in rhyme by Josh Funk, illustrated by Rodolfo Montal-vo, "George and Blaise are pen pals, and they write letters to each other about everything: their pets, birthdays, favorite sports, and science fair projects. There's just one thing that the two friends don't know: George is a human, while Blaise is a dragon! What will happen when these pen pals finally meet face-to-face?" (Publisher's note)

"Montalvo's visual irony skillfully paces alongside Funk's gamboling rhymes, rendering readers' investigations of each spread just as rewarding as the page turns. A playful celebration of difference (and poetry)." Kirkus

Funke, Cornelia Caroline

★ The **princess** knight; by Cornelia Funke; illustrations by Kerstin Meyer; translated by Anthea Bell. Chicken House/Scholastic 2004 un il $15.95
Grades: PreK K 1 2   E
1. Princesses -- Fiction 2. Knights and knighthood -- Fiction
ISBN 0-439-53630-8
Original German edition 2001
"Raised by a widowed king, Princess Violetta is put through the same paces (swordplay, riding, jousting) as her older, brawnier brothers. Her practice pays off when her father holds a tournament—with Violetta as the grand prize—and she handily scuttles his plans. Bell translates Funke's story from the German with aplomb . . . and Meyer's effervescent line-and-watercolor artwork, as funny as it is lovely, stretches across each spread in horizontal strips." Booklist

Princess Pigsty; by Cornelia Funke; illustrated by Kerstin Meyer; translated by Chantal Wright. Chicken House/Scholastic 2007 un il $16.99
Grades: K 1 2   E
1. Fairy tales 2. Princesses -- Fiction
ISBN 0-439-88554-X
                                                                    LC 2006006294
"Sick of her pampered existence, Princess Isabella tosses aside her tiara, declaring, 'I want to get dirty!' The outraged king prescribes tours of duty in the kitchens and pigsty, but Isabella merely revels in the good, honest work and good, honest mess. . . . Most kids will relate to her spirit of rebellion, especially as embodied in Meyer's ebullient watercolors of the beaming, disheveled girl." Booklist

The **wildest** brother; [by] Cornelia Funke; illustrated by Kerstin Meyer; translated by Oliver Latsch. The Chicken House/Scholastic 2006 un il $16.99
Grades: PreK K 1 2   E
1. Siblings -- Fiction
ISBN 0-439-82862-7
When it comes to protecting his big sister, Anna, young Ben is as brave as a lion. But when the day is over and darkness falls, Ben suddenly doesn't feel quite so brave. Sometimes, he realizes, it's Anna who does the protecting

"Wright's wonderfully expressive acrylic paintings elevate this simple glimpse of sibling play into something special. The animated scenes, filled with Ben's imagined foes, perfectly capture the wild-eyed, physical fun." Booklist

Fusco Castaldo, Nancy

★ **Pizza** for the queen; by Nancy Castaldo; illustrated by Mélisande Potter. Holiday House 2005 un il $16.95
Grades: PreK K 1 2 3   E
1. Italy -- Fiction 2. Pizza -- Fiction 3. Cooking -- Fiction
ISBN 0-8234-1865-0
                                                                    LC 2004-58134

In 1889 Napoli, Italy, Raffaele Esposito prepares a special pizza for Queen Margherita. Based on a true story. Includes a recipe.

"The richly toned, detailed illustrations . . . extend the action and the sense of history in busy scenes in the kitchen and on the picturesque streets." Booklist

Fyleman, Rose, 1877-1957

Mice; Rose Fyleman; illustrated by Lois Ehlert. Beach Lane Books 2012 p. cm.
Grades: PreK K 1   E
1. Stories in rhyme 2. Mice -- Fiction 3. Picture books for children 4. Mice -- Fiction
ISBN 9781442456846; 9781442456860
                                                                    LC 2011020555
In this book, "a 1932 poem from [Rose] Fyleman (1877–1957) serves as a springboard for [Lois] Ehlert's artwork. As "the mice scamper across the pages ('They nibble things they shouldn't touch') Ehlert labels the items they find, turning the story into an introduction to art supplies, household items, and food items that range from mangos and avocadoes to cereal and desserts." (Publishers Weekly)

Gag, Wanda

★ **Millions** of cats. Putnam 2004 un il $13.99
Grades: PreK K 1   E
1. Cats -- Fiction
ISBN 0-399-23315-6
A reissue of the title first published 1928 by Coward-McCann
A Newbery Medal honor book, 1929
It is "a perennial favorite among children and takes a place of its own, both for the originality and strength of its pictures and the living folktale quality of its text." NY Her Trib Books

Gaiman, Neil

Chu's day; Neil Gaiman, Adam Rex; [edited by] Rosemary Brosnan. HarperCollins 2013 32 p. (hardcover bdg.) $17.99
Grades: PreK K 1   E
1. Mystery fiction 2. Sneezing -- Fiction 3. Picture books for children
ISBN 0062017810; 9780062017819
                                                                    LC 2012942557
In this children's picture book, "[Neil] Gaiman builds suspense from the . . . opening sentence ('When Chu sneezed, bad things happened')." Trips to a dusty library and a diner with peppery air make "Chu's anxious parents ask, 'Are you going to sneeze?' . . . That evening, under a big top . . . , Chu cannot resist, and his true power is revealed." (Publishers Weekly)

Chu's day at the beach; written by Neil Gaiman; illustrated by Adam Rex. Harper, an imprint of HarperCollins Publishers 2015 32 p. color illustrations (hardback) $17.99
Grades: PreK K 1   E
1. Beaches -- Fiction 2. Sneezing -- Fiction 3. Pandas -- Fiction
ISBN 0062223992; 9780062223999
                                                                    LC 2014034091
"Chu and his family are going to the beach! Chu is excited. He will get to play in the sand and wade in the water. But what will happen if Chu sneezes at the beach? And what will happen if he doesn't?" (Publisher's note)

"In the third tale about Chu, the little panda and his parents visit the beach. . . . Bright colors and the assortment of creatures will enchant children who enjoy poring over pictures, while the type size and short sentences make this a good fit for early readers." Booklist

Crazy hair; illustrated by Dave McKean. HarperCollins Publishers 2009 un il $18.99; lib bdg $19.89

Grades: PreK K 1 2 3   E

1. Stories in rhyme 2. Hair -- Fiction

ISBN 978-0-06-057908-1; 0-06-057908-0; 978-0-06-057909-8 lib bdg; 0-06-057909-9 lib bdg

LC 2008012791

Bonnie encounters all sorts of exotic animals and marvelous things inside a man's crazy hair.

This is a "chaotic picture book popping with bright collage and multimedia imagery. . . . Each page is a veritable feast for the eyes, with frazzled clumps of hair competing for attention with outlandish elements. . . . There's something a little unsettling and unhinged about the imagery, just on the safe side of nightmarish; but the text, for the most part, is delightful and glib." Booklist

The **dangerous** alphabet; by Neil Gaiman; illustrated by Gris Grimly. HarperCollinsPublishers 2008 un il $17.99; lib bdg $18.89

Grades: 2 3 4 5   E

1. Stories in rhyme 2. Pirates -- Fiction 3. Alphabet -- Fiction 4. Monsters -- Fiction

ISBN 978-0-06-078333-4; 0-06-078333-8; 978-0-06-078334-1 lib bdg; 0-06-078334-6 lib bdg

LC 2007-10893

As two children and their pet gazelle sneak out of the house in search of treasure, they come across a world beneath the city that is inhabited with monsters and pirates.

"A sophisticated, interactive alphabet tale in which even the letters break the expected pattern. . . . Skillful narrative and visual storytelling combine to present a complex adventure that unravels through multilayered text and illustrations, challenging readers to ponder the numerous levels of plot. . . . The gothic illustrations, done in sepia tones and faded color washes, ensure that readers remain riveted throughout the story." SLJ

Instructions; written by Neil Gaiman; illustrated by Charles Vess. Harper 2010 un il $14.99; lib bdg $15.89

Grades: 1 2 3 4   E

1. Poetry 2. Voyages and travels -- Poetry

ISBN 978-0-06-196030-7; 0-06-196030-6; 978-0-06-196031-4 lib bdg; 0-06-196031-4 lib bdg

The poem first published 2000 in A Wolf at the Door published by Simon & Schuster

Go on a journey to unknown, but strangely familiar, lands and then travel home again.

"Vess's compositions are distinguished by elegant, winding lines-gnarled vines, plumes of smoke, dragon tails-and intimate frames that evoke moments of gentle wisdom. Young readers should relish the chimerical vision while older Gaiman fans should grasp the underlying suggestion that the compass used to navigate fairy tales can also guide us in the real world." Publ Wkly

The **wolves** in the walls; written by Neil Gaiman; illustrated by Dave McKean. HarperCollins Pubs. 2003 un il $16.99

Grades: 2 3 4   E

1. Wolves -- Fiction

ISBN 0-380-97827-X

LC 2002-192194

Lucy is sure there are wolves living in the walls of her house, although others in her family disagree, and when the wolves come out, the adventure begins

"Gaiman's text rings with energetic confidence and an inviting tone. . . . McKean . . . expertly matches the tale's funny-scary mood . . . against shadow-filled backdrops that blend paint, digital manipulation

and photography, his stylized human figures look right at home. His pen-and-inks of the wolves . . . suggest that they inhabit a world apart—or perhaps unreal?" Publ Wkly

Gal, Susan

Day by day; Susan Gal. Alfred A. Knopf 2012 40 p. col. ill. (hardback) $16.99

Grades: PreK K 1 2   E

1. Pigs -- Fiction 2. Family -- Fiction 3. Picture books for children 4. Family life -- Fiction 5. Neighborhoods -- Fiction

ISBN 037586959X; 9780375869594; 9780375969591; 9780375984334

LC 2011042371

In this children's picture book, "[a]cross a golden prairie, a family of pigs heads west. Their small actions grow in significance as bricks become a house, beloved paraphernalia create a home, neighbors are welcomed and friendships begin." Through daily hard work, "a community is built" and at the end of the book, the pigs gather "under a festive tree at twilight to enjoy the bounty they have grown." (Kirkus)

★ **Night** lights. Alfred A. Knopf 2009 un il $14.99; lib bdg $17.99

Grades: PreK K 1   E

1. Light -- Fiction 2. Night -- Fiction

ISBN 978-0-375-85862-8; 0-375-85862-8; 978-0-375-95862-5 lib bdg; 0-375-95862-2 lib bdg

LC 2008-50909

While preparing for bedtime, a little girl and her dog note all the different kinds of lights that brighten up the night, from headlights to moonlight.

"An appropriately dark palette complements the 15 types of illumination named in this nearly wordless story. Young children will enjoy poring over the rich details in the cozy charcoal and digital collage spreads as they learn to read the simple text." SLJ

Please take me for a walk. Alfred A. Knopf 2010 un il $15.99; lib bdg $18.99

Grades: PreK K 1   E

1. Dogs -- Fiction

ISBN 0375858636; 0375958630 lib bdg; 9780375858635; 9780375958632; 978-0-375-85863-5; 0-375-85863-6; 978-0-375-95863-2 lib bdg; 0-375-95863-0 lib bdg

A dog gives many good reasons it likes to go for a walk—to chase away the neighbor's cat, to greet people on the street, to watch guys shooting hoops, and to feel the wind lifting its ears.

"Gal celebrates the joys of perambulating the neighborhood in simple sentences and mixed-media collage illustrations featuring expressive canines and humans, as well as inventive details." Booklist

Galbraith, Kathryn Osebold

Arbor Day square; written by Kathryn Galbraith; illustrated by Cyd Moore. Peachtree Publishers 2010 un $16.95

Grades: K 1 2 3   E

1. Trees -- Fiction 2. Arbor Day -- Fiction 3. Frontier and pioneer life -- Fiction 4. Father-daughter relationship -- Fiction

ISBN 978-1-56145-517-1; 1-56145-517-2

LC 2009017017

In the mid-nineteenth century, as young Katie and her father help plant and tend trees in their booming frontier town, she doubts that the spindly saplings will ever grow big. Includes facts about Arbor Day.

"Galbraith's poetic text and Moore's soft watercolor and colored-pencil illustrations recreate those spring days on the prairie when planting trees was cause for celebration." SLJ

Boo, bunny! [by] Kathryn O. Galbraith; illustrated by Jeff Mack. Harcourt 2008 un il $16

Grades: PreK K   **E**

1. Stories in rhyme 2. Fear -- Fiction 3. Rabbits -- Fiction 4. Halloween -- Fiction

ISBN 978-0-15-216246-7; 0-15-216246-1

LC 2007021426

Two small bunnies face their fears while trick-or-treating on Halloween night

"With very simple, shivery rhyme and bright shapes on black double-page spreads, this picture book brings toddlers the creepy fun of Halloween." Booklist

Galindo, Renata

My new mom and me; Renata Galindo. Schwartz & Wade Books 2016 32 p. $16.99

Grades: PreK K 1 2   **E**

1. Adoption -- Fiction 2. Mother-child relationship -- Fiction 3. Adoption -- Fiction 4. Families -- Fiction 5. Mother and child -- Fiction

ISBN 9780553521344; 9780553521351

LC 2015005374

This children's story, by Renata Galindo, is "about adoption, diversity, and acceptance. Told from the point of view of a puppy who is adopted by a cat, . . . when the puppy comes to live with his new mom, he is nervous. After all, his mom has stripes and he doesn't. But his mom says she likes that they look different, and soon the puppy likes it, too. (And who cares what anyone else thinks!)" (Publisher's note)

"The presentation of a single mother is also unusual and valuable. Throughout, digital illustrations employ a soft, flat aesthetic rendered in a muted palette that meets the gentle text's tone. A welcome addition." Kirkus

Galing, Ed

Tony; Ed Galing, Erin E. Stead (illustrator) Roaring Brook Press 2017 32 p. color illustrations (hardcover) $16.99

Grades: PreK K 1 2 3 4   **E**

1. Horses -- Fiction 2. Children and animals -- Fiction

ISBN 9781626723085

LC 2016942447

This children's book, by Ed Galing, illustrated by Erin E. Stead, presents the tale of a boy and his friendship with a horse. "The muted pencil drawings are gorgeous and soft, a comfort simply to view. The gray and aqua coloring puts readers in predawn's light, with the yellow highlights perfectly yielding a sense of warmth. The illustrations and text work together perfectly, conveying a story for readers of all ages." (School Library Journal)

"A lovely tribute to a bygone service, especially for equine fans." Booklist

Gall, Chris

Dear fish; written and illustrated by Chris Gall. Little, Brown 2006 un il $16.99

Grades: 1 2 3 4   **E**

1. Fishes -- Fiction 2. Beaches -- Fiction

ISBN 0-316-05847-5; 978-0-316-05847-6

LC 2005-03828

One afternoon at the beach, a small boy puts an invitation to the fish to come for a visit in a bottle and throws it into the ocean, and the results are unprecedented.

"The text has a rich vocabulary. . . . Boldly colored illustrations combine clay-engraved art with digital effects to give the pages a three-dimensional look. Readers who enjoy poring over pictures that are layered

with meaning on both the literal and figurative levels will find much to explore here." SLJ

★ **Dinotrux**. Little, Brown 2009 un il $16.99

Grades: PreK K 1 2   **E**

1. Trucks -- Fiction 2. Dinosaurs -- Fiction

ISBN 978-0-316-02777-9; 0-316-02777-4

LC 2008-27531

Millions of years ago, the prehistoric ancestors of today's trucks, such as garbageadon, dozeratops, and craneosaurus, roamed the Earth until they rusted out and became extinct.

"Blending the endless appeal of dinosaurs and trucks in one hilarious volume, this title will be hard to keep on the shelves." SLJ

★ **Dog** vs. Cat; Chris Gall. Little Brown & Co 2014 32 p. (hardcover) $17

Grades: PreK K 1 2   **E**

1. Cats -- Fiction 2. Dogs -- Fiction 3. Friendship -- Fiction 4. Individuality -- Fiction 5. Cats -- Fiction 6. Dogs -- Fiction 7. Friendship -- Fiction 8. Individuality -- Fiction

ISBN 0316238015; 9780316238014

LC 2013015639

In this children's book, by Chris Gall, "Dog and Cat do not get along. But when they're forced to share a room, they agree to be on their best behavior...until Dog won't stop sniffing. Cat won't stop primping. Dog won't stop howling. Cat won't stop scratching. And when it comes to the litter-box...sharing is not an option! What will it take to bring Dog and Cat together?" (Publisher's note)

"Starting with illustrations on the endpapers, readers know immediately that they are in for a treat with this picture book...The colored-pencil illustrations are remarkable, and the animals' dialogue, expressions, and body language are priceless, as is the funny conclusion. A terrific addition to any friendship or pet storytime." SLJ

Dog versus Cat

★ **NanoBots**; Chris Gall. Little, Brown & Co. 2016 40 p. color illustrations (ebook) $30; (hardcover) $16.99

Grades: 1 2 3   **E**

1. Size -- Fiction 2. Robots -- Fiction 3. Size -- Fiction 4. Robots -- Fiction

ISBN 9780316271035; 9780316375528

LC 2015007825

In this book, by Chris Gall, "a boy inventor creates the ultimate in high-tech superheroes that could one day save the world--but they have some smaller problems to take on first! NanoBots are . . . too small to see, but they can each do a unique and important job: Medibot makes sure their Inventor never catches a cold.... Chewbots gobble up that gum the Inventor trampled into the carpet... [and] Binobot scans the scene of a crime for clues the Inventor could never see." (Publisher's note)

"Action oriented with a sci-fi feel, this will have robot-obsessed readers clamoring for more." Kirkus

Revenge of the Dinotrux; Chris Gall. Little, Brown & Co 2012 32 p.

Grades: PreK K 1 2   **E**

1. Picture books for children 2. Trucks -- Fiction 3. Dinosaurs -- Fiction 4. Mythical animals -- Fiction 5. Trucks -- Fiction 6. Behavior -- Fiction 7. Imaginary creatures -- Fiction

ISBN 0316132888; 9780316132886

LC 2011025118

This picture book by Chris Gall is a sequel to his earlier children's book 'Dinotrux!' in which the metal dinosaurs escape from their museum. "Exploding through the dino-museum's wall in the wake of a particularly stressful Kindergarten Day, enraged Tyrannosaurus Trux rolls off to climb a skyscraper. . . . Further chaos threatens when they burst out again, though, taking along the children who have introduced them to the wonders of (truck) books and other reading." Gall illustrates the dinotrux as "towering massively atop heavy-duty tires, with wide, headlight eyes and toothy maws agape." (Kirkus)

★ **Substitute** Creacher. Little, Brown 2011 un il $16.99
Grades: K 1 2   E
   1. School stories 2. Stories in rhyme 3. Monsters -- Fiction 4. Teachers -- Fiction
   ISBN 978-0-316-08915-9; 0-316-08915-X
                          LC 2010019758
   Mr. Creacher, a multi-tentacled substitute teacher, warns his prankish students not to misbehave, recounting rhyming cautionary tales of the weird, spooky, and unexpected.
   Gall "illustrates in explosive, cinematic panels; retro Ben-Day dot patterns allude to classic funnies. If the dire warnings fail to inspire repentance, Mr. Creacher's dilemma—and a conclusion that breaks the spell—may warm the cold hearts of defiant substitute baiters." Publ Wkly

There's nothing to do on Mars; written and illustrated by Chris Gall. Little, Brown 2008 un il $16.99
Grades: PreK K 1 2   E
   1. Science fiction 2. Mars (Planet) -- Fiction
   ISBN 978-0-316-16684-3; 0-316-16684-7
                          LC 2006025290
   After moving to Mars with his family, Davey complains of being bored until he begins exploring the planet with his dog Polaris and uncovers a most unusual "treasure"
   "The illustrations, created with an engraving technique, are precisely drawn and appropriately painted in scorching reds and oranges. . . . Amusing details . . . extend the text and play off the deadpan humor." SLJ

Gammell, Stephen
   ★ **Mudkin**. Carolrhoda Books 2011 un il
Grades: PreK K 1   E
   1. Play -- Fiction 2. Rain -- Fiction 3. Imagination -- Fiction
   ISBN 0-7613-5790-4 lib bdg; 978-0-7613-5790-2 lib bdg
                          LC 2010026373
   While playing outside on a rainy day, a little girl peers into a puddle and sees Mudkin, who invites her to become her queen.
   "Kids love mud, and here's a picture book that positively revels in all its gleefully gloppy glory. . . . The girl has a few lines of dialogue, but Mudkin's responses are all a scrawl of indecipherable brown smears, offering a neat chance for kids to engage and fill in their own ideas for what he's saying. But what will really bring on the squeals is the joyfully messy watercolors that look composed of thick, overhand tosses of mud splatters and heartily ground-in grass stains." Booklist

Once upon MacDonald's farm; rev format ed; Simon & Schuster Bks. for Young Readers 2000 un il $15
Grades: PreK K 1 2   E
   1. Animals -- Fiction 2. Farm life -- Fiction
   ISBN 0-689-82885-3
                          LC 99-30691
   First published 1981 by Four Winds Press
   MacDonald tries farming with exotic circus animals, but has better luck with his neighbor's cow, horse, and chicken—or does he?
   "The accomplished, shaded pencil drawings are well suited to this slyly humorous tale with an unexpected twist." Horn Book Guide

Gannij, Joan
   Topsy-turvy bedtime; by Joan Levine; illustrated by Tony Auth. Candlewick 2008 un il $14.99
Grades: PreK K 1   E
   1. Bedtime -- Fiction 2. Parent-child relationship -- Fiction
   ISBN 978-0-7636-3008-9; 0-7636-3008-X
   "Arathusela hates going to bed. Her parents are exhausted by day's end, so they reverse roles with her. . . . Kids will appreciate the tables-turned humor ('You forgot to sing us a song') and the reasuring resolution. Auth has a light touch; his watercolors display the particular coziness of domestic life at night." Horn Book Guide

Gantos, Jack
   ★ **Rotten** Ralph; written by Jack B. Gantos; illustrated by Nicole Rubel. Houghton Mifflin 1976 un il lib bdg $16; pa $7.95
Grades: PreK K 1 2   E
   1. Cats -- Fiction
   ISBN 0-395-24276-2 lib bdg; 0-395-29202-6 pa
   The "bright watercolor scenes . . . capturing Ralph's demonic meanness and his family's chagrin are a perfect complement to the text." SLJ
   Other titles about Rotten Ralph are:
   Back to school for Rotten Ralph (1998)
   Best in show for Rotten Ralph (2005)
   Happy birthday Rotten Ralph (1990)
   The nine lives of Rotten Ralph (2009)
   Not so Rotten Ralph (1994)
   Practice makes perfect for Rotten Ralph (2002)
   Rotten Ralph helps out (2001)
   Rotten Ralph's rotten Christmas (1984)
   Rotten Ralph's rotten romance (1997)
   Rotten Ralph's show and tell (1989)
   Rotten Ralph's trick or treat! (1986)
   Three strikes for Rotten Ralph (2011)
   Wedding bells for Rotten Ralph (1999)
   Worse than rotten, Ralph (1978)

   Rotten Ralph feels rotten; written by Jack Gantos; illustrated by Nicole Rubel. Farrar Straus Giroux 2004 47p il $15.99
Grades: PreK K 1 2   E
   1. Cats -- Fiction 2. Sick -- Fiction
   ISBN 0-374-36357-9
                          LC 2003-49252
   Rotten Ralph comes to appreciate Sarah's healthy cat food after he gets sick from eating out of trash cans.
   "The Magic-Marker intensity of Rubel's palette and the undulating quality of her lines are ideal for showing the quavery misery of nausea. . . . Beginning readers will gobble up this third installment of the Rotten Ralph Rotten Reader series." Booklist

   Rotten Ralph's rotten family; written by Jack Gantos; illustrated by Nicole Rubel. Farrar Straus & Giroux 2014 48 p. color illustrations (hardback) $16.99
Grades: 1 2 3   E
   1. Bad behavior 2. Cats -- Fiction 3. Family -- Fiction 4. Behavior -- Fiction 5. Families -- Fiction
   ISBN 0374363536; 9780374363536
                          LC 2013022076
   In this children's book, by Jack Gantos, "Rotten Ralph's owner, Sarah, is fed up with her red rascal's behavior. Ralph is tired of Sarah trying to change him. He misses his cat family, which never made him alter a thing about himself. But in this . . . adventure for newly independent readers, the world's favorite rotten red cat gets tripped up when he runs away for a journey down memory lane." (Publisher's note)

"After finding an old photo album, Ralph visits his family. His mother treats him well, but the other relatives heap humiliation on him. Ralph realizes the reason he is so rotten is that his own family was rotten to him. The longer early-chapter-book format serves Ralph well, allowing a more sophisticated story line to emerge. Lively tongue-in-cheek illustrations extend the action." Horn Book

Three strikes for Rotten Ralph; written by Jack Gantos; illustrated by Nicole Rubel. Farrar Straus Giroux 2011 47p il $16.99
Grades: 1 2 3   E
1. Baseball -- Fiction 2. Squirrels -- Fiction
ISBN 978-0-374-36354-3; 0-374-36354-4

Before he tries out for the new Fighting Squirrels baseball team, Rotten Ralph is sure he is going to be a superstar. Never mind that he doesn't have any skills and doesn't want to practice.

"There is never a dull moment in this colorful and appealing early reader." SLJ

Ganz-Schmitt, Sue

Planet Kindergarten; by Sue Ganz-Schmitt; illustrated by Shane Prigmore. Chronicle Books 2014 40 p. (alk. paper) $16.99
Grades: PreK K 1   E
1. School stories 2. Outer space -- Fiction 3. Kindergarten -- Fiction 4. Imagination -- Fiction 5. First day of school -- Fiction
ISBN 1452118930; 9781452118932
                                                    LC 2013011773

This children's book by Sue Ganz-Schmitt, illustrated by Shane Prigmore, encourages "young explorers to boldly go where they have never gone before: Planet Kindergarten. Suit up for a daring adventure as our hero navigates the unknown reaches and alien inhabitants of this strange new world. Hilarious and confidence-boosting, this exciting story will have new kindergarteners ready for liftoff!" (Publisher's note)

"A child bids farewell to his parents (who are sent back to their own planets) and begins his first mission on Planet Kindergarten... With the help of Prigmore's superpowered animation-style illustrations, she offers a story that will help readers understand that kindergarten really is out of this world." SLJ

Another title in this series is:
Another Day in Orbit (2016)

Garcia, Emma

Tap tap bang bang. Boxer Books 2010 un il $16.95
Grades: PreK K   E
1. Tools -- Fiction 2. Sounds -- Fiction 3. Building -- Fiction
ISBN 978-1-907152-00-9; 1-907152-00-8

"A lively introduction to tools and the sounds that they make. . . . They all work together to make a bright, cherry-red go-kart. . . . Garcia's artwork is clear and colorful, and all of the tools stand out against the stark white backgrounds. . . . There are plenty of opportunities to stretch vocabulary with these building-tool words." SLJ

Garden, Nancy

Molly's family; pictures by Sharon Wooding. Farrar Straus Giroux 2004 un il $16
Grades: PreK K 1 2   E
1. School stories 2. Lesbians -- Fiction 3. Family life -- Fiction
ISBN 0-374-35002-7
                                                    LC 2002-29784

When Molly draws a picture of her family for Open School Night, one of her classmates makes her feel bad because he says she cannot have a mommy and a momma

"By tying this specific household to the general diversity within all families, Garden manages to celebrate them all. The soft colored-pencil drawings with their many realistic details depict a room full of active kindergartners." SLJ

Garland, Michael

Grandpa's tractor. Boyds Mills Press 2011 un il $16.95
Grades: PreK K 1   E
1. Farm life -- Fiction 2. Grandfathers -- Fiction
ISBN 978-1-59078-762-5; 1-59078-762-5

Grandpa Joe brings his grandson Timmy back to the site of the family farm, where the old house and a ramshackle barn still stand. The visit evokes many memories for Grandpa Joe, which he shares with Timmy.

"Garland's artistic genius has never been shown to such advantage as in this book. . . . The text . . . complements the vivid and folksy digitally enhanced artwork. . . . The pictures and text together compose a loving tribute to the heyday of small farms in America." SLJ

Super snow day: seek and find. Dutton Children's Books 2010 un il $16.99
Grades: PreK K 1 2 3   E
1. Picture puzzles 2. Literary recreations 3. Snow -- Fiction 4. Aunts -- Fiction
ISBN 978-0-525-42245-7; 0-525-42245-5
                                                    LC 2009-53245

When a heavy snowfall causes schools and businesses to close, Tommy follows a series of notes from his Aunt Jeanne as he explores the frozen landscape, makes new friends, and participates in winter sports. Artwork includes over 200 objects for the reader to find and count.

"Garland's computer-generated illustrations are eye-catching and surreal. . . . They're characterized by bright colors, Claymation-style figures, and an admirable restraint when it comes to clutter." SLJ

Garland, Michael, 1952-

Fish had a wish; by Michael Garland. Holiday House 2012 24p
Grades: PreK K 1 2   E
1. Fishes -- Fiction 2. Wishes -- Fiction 3. Children's stories 4. Picture books for children 5. Animals -- Fiction 6. Contentment -- Fiction 7. Self-acceptance -- Fiction
ISBN 9780823423941
                                                    LC 2010050124

In this children's picture book, "Fish has a wish to be some creature other than what he is: a bird, so he can fly high in the sky; a turtle, so he can nap on a sunny rock; a skunk, so he can make a big stink; or a bobcat, a bee, a beaver, a butterfly or a snake. But when a mayfly lands on the water, Fish eats it in one bite and declares: 'That was so good! . . . I wish to stay a fish.' . . . The double-page spreads have wood-grain backgrounds . . . evok[ing] Fish's woodland pond environment." (Kirkus)

Garland, Sarah

Eddie's garden; and how to make things grow. Frances Lincoln 2004 40p il hardcover o.p. pa $8.95
Grades: K 1 2   E
1. Siblings -- Fiction 2. Gardening -- Fiction
ISBN 1-8450-7015-1; 978-1-8450-7089-2 pa

"Watching their mother dig in her garden, Eddie and his little sister, Lily, ask for their own. During the next few months, Eddie plants seeds, waters them, helps Lily, watches their plants grow, hunts slugs, harvests vegetables, and eats the home-grown produce. Bits of humor in the telling and appealing visual elements such as a bean-pole teepee will help keep children involved in the story. This book ends with four helpful pages explaining how to grow 'Eddie's plants,' such as carrots, nasturtiums, and sunflowers, as well as discussing soil, seeds, pests, hazards, and gardening indoors and in containers. . . . This picture book offers plenty of genial details in the bright, engaging colored artwork." Booklist

Eddie's kitchen; and how to make good things to eat. Frances Lincoln 2008 un il $16.95

Grades: K 1 2   **E**

1. Cooking -- Fiction 2. Birthdays -- Fiction 3. Grandfathers -- Fiction

ISBN 978-1-84507-58-0; 1-84507-88-9

"Grandad phones at 2 p.m., sings happy birthday to himself, and then announces, 'I'll see you at six o'clock for my birthday party.' Mum is horrified; the date has completely slipped her mind. But with a lot of help from her kids, capable Eddie and mischievous toddler Lily, she plans the meal, assembles the ingredients, . . . cooks a festive dinner and finally sits down by the fire. . . . Garland cleverly weaves some playful patterns into the smoothly written story. . . . The accessible pictures convey an atmosphere of warmth and cheerful dishevelment. Readers will find recipes for the special dinner at the end of the book; the steps are clearly described, and the dishes look nutritious and tasty." SLJ

Eddie's toolbox; and how to make and mend things. Frances Lincoln 2011 un il $17.95

Grades: K 1 2   **E**

1. Tools -- Fiction 2. Friendship -- Fiction

ISBN 978-1-84780-053-4; 1-84780-053-X

"Eddie is hoping a boy his age will move in next door, but when he sees the new family unpack, he notices that the only child is a girl his younger sister's age. When the two families meet . . . the two girls form an instant bond. . . . Tilly's dad asks him if he'd like to help him with chores that need to be done. . . . Tom teaches him how to use a saw, a hammer, and a screwdriver. . . . Soon, the two families are completing projects together. . . . This is a lovely story about friendship between neighbors. Garland's watercolor illustrations show scenes in which everyone is helping one another. These two families make lending a hand look fun and rewarding." SLJ

Other titles about Eddie are:

Eddie's kitchen (2004)

Eddie's garden (2008)

Garland, Sherry

The **buffalo** soldier; by Sherry Garland; illustrated by Ronald Himler. Pelican Pub. Co. 2006 un il $15.95

Grades: 2 3 4   **E**

1. West (U.S.) -- Fiction 2. African American soldiers -- Fiction

ISBN 978-1-58980-391-6

LC 2006012484

Realizing that his future lies in owning land, not just being free, a young man raised as a slave becomes a buffalo soldier—a member of an all-black cavalry regiment formed to protect white settlers from Indians, bandits, and outlaws, and that later fought in the Spanish American War. Includes historical note

"Himler's vibrant illustrations capture the broad vistas of western landscape, the excitement of horseback pursuit, and the hardships of the work, at the same time conveying respect for the loyal soldiers who endured it all." Booklist

Includes bibliographical references

Gary, Meredith

Sometimes you get what you want; art by Lisa Brown; words by Meredith Gary. HarperCollinsPublishers 2008 un il $16.99; lib bdg $17.89

Grades: PreK K   **E**

1. School stories 2. Siblings -- Fiction 3. Conduct of life -- Fiction

ISBN 978-0-06-114015-0; 978-0-06-114016-7 lib bdg

LC 2007041933

A brother and sister spend a day in preschool learning lessons about boundaries, such as that it is sometimes okay to make a lot of noise, but at other times one must be quiet.

"Gary's concise text conveys an important life lesson about the need to balance fun, responsibility, and respect for others. . . . Appealing illustrations depict each scenario and keep the tone light. Background scenery, props, and adult characters are portrayed in black lines and white and gray shades, while the children are fully fleshed out with a variety of skin tones and bright-hued clothing." SLJ

Garza, Cynthia Leonor

Lucia the luchadora; Cynthia Leonor Garza; illustrated by Alyssa Bermudez. Pow! 2017 32 p. color illustrations $16.99

Grades: PreK K 1 2   **E**

1. Superheroes -- Fiction

ISBN 9781576878279

LC 2016954881

In this book, by Cynthia Leonor Garza, illustrated by Alyssa Bermudez, "Lucía zips through the playground in her cape just like the boys, but when they tell her 'girls can't be superheroes,' suddenly she doesn't feel so mighty. That's when her beloved abuela reveals a dazzling secret: Lucía comes from a family of luchadoras, the bold and valiant women of the Mexican lucha libre tradition." (Publisher's note)

Garza, Xavier

Juan and the Chupacabras; by Xavier Garza; illustrations by April Ward; Spanish translation by Carolina Villarroel. Pinata Books 2006 un il $15.95

Grades: K 1 2 3   **E**

1. Monsters -- Fiction 2. Grandfathers -- Fiction 3. Bilingual books -- English-Spanish

ISBN 978-1-55885-454-3; 1-55885-454-1

After hearing about their grandfather's boyhood encounter with the Chupacabras, a green, winged creature with glowing eyes, Juan and his cousin Luz decide to find out if the story could be true.

"The English and Spanish texts appear on the same page, separated by a narrow illustration. The full-page illustration moves the action along nicely. An excellent choice for storytime and classroom sharing." SLJ

Gauch, Patricia Lee

Aaron and the Green Mountain Boys; pictures by Margot Tomes. Boyds Mills Press 2005 64p il $16.95; pa $9.95

Grades: K 1 2   **E**

1. United States -- History -- 1775-1783, Revolution -- Fiction

ISBN 1-59078-335-2; 1-59078-354-9 pa

A reissue of the title first published 1972 by Coward, McCann & Geohegan

In 1777 nine-year-old Aaron would rather help the Green Mountain Boys fight the British than stay home and bake bread for them.

★ **Tanya** and the red shoes; illustrated by Satomi Ichikawa. Philomel Bks. 2002 un il $16.99

Grades: PreK K 1 2   **E**

1. Ballet -- Fiction

ISBN 0-399-23314-8

LC 2001-33916

"Tanya confides her dreams of dancing en pointe like the dancer in the movie The Red Shoes. She finally gets her wish but discovers that the seemingly effortless beauty of the dance requires much work (and produces many blisters). The use of the present tense underscores the conversational tone, adding verisimilitude matched by Ichikawa's marvelously agile, expressive illustrations." Horn Book

Other titles about Tanya are:
Bravo Tanya (1992)
Dance Tanya (1989)
Presenting Tanya the Ugly Duckling (1999)
Tanya and the magic wardrobe (1997)

Gauch, Sarah

Voyage to the Pharos; illustrated by Roger Roth. Viking 2009 un il $16.99

Grades: 1 2 3   E

1. Sea stories 2. Egypt -- Fiction 3. Lighthouses -- Fiction
ISBN 978-0-670-06254-6; 0-670-06254-5

LC 2009012345

A young boy in ancient times embarks on an adventurous sea voyage to Alexandria, Egypt, home of the famous Pharos Lighthouse.

"Large-scale illustrations capture the drama of the events to full effect. . . . Roth varies his palette to increase the intensity of the perilous scenes and to highlight the joy of surviving unharmed." SLJ

Gay, Marie-Louise

Caramba and Henry. Groundwood Books 2011 $17.95

Grades: PreK K 1   E

1. Cats -- Fiction 2. Flight -- Fiction 3. Siblings -- Fiction
ISBN 978-1-55498-097-0; 1-55498-097-6; 9781554980970; 1554980976

"Caramba, a zebra-striped cat who lives in a world where cats can fly, has always wanted a brother—but not the one he gets. Henry screams and cries all of the time and, unlike Caramba, Henry isn't having any trouble flying. To Caramba's chagrin, his mother puts him in charge of making sure Henry's fledgling flights don't end in disaster. . . . Gay's watercolors, laced with feathery pencil lines, bring warmth to this fresh spin on a story about learning how to be an older sibling." Publ Wkly

Another title about Caramba is:
Caramba (2005)

Princess pistachio; Marie-Louise Gay; translated from French by Jacob Homel. Pajama Press 2015 46 p. color illustrations hardcover $10.95

Grades: K 1 2 3   E

1. Birthdays -- Fiction 2. Princesses -- Fiction
ISBN 192748569X; 9781927485699

"Pistachio has always known she was a princess. When a mysterious gift turns up on her birthday, she's sure it's only a matter of time before her real parents, the king and queen of Papua, arrive to take her away. But in the meantime, she still has to eat her spinach and get up for school." (Publisher's note)

"The skillful combination of text and illustrations addresses many serious concerns of early childhood--and even of parenthood--without straying from the book's tone of fun and frivol ity. (Among the issues so adeptly addressed are adoption, sibling relationships, classmate rejection and a missing child.)" Kirkus

Another title in this series is:
Princess Pistachio and the pest (2015)

★ **Roslyn** Rutabaga and the biggest hole on earth; by Marie-Lou Gay. Groundwood Books/House of Anansi Press 2010 un il $18.95

Grades: PreK K   E

1. Rabbits -- Fiction 2. Father-daughter relationship -- Fiction
ISBN 978-0-88899-994-8; 0-88899-994-1

"The whimsical illustrations, created on Kraft paper and handmade Japanese paper with watercolor, acrylic, pastels, aquarelle crayons, pen-

cil, and collage, are busy without being overdone. Imaginative and adventurous children will identify with Roslyn in this simple, fun story." SLJ

★ **When** Stella was very very small. Groundwood Books 2009 un il $16.95

Grades: PreK K 1 2   E

1. Size -- Fiction 2. Growth -- Fiction
ISBN 978-0-88899-906-1; 0-88899-906-2

"Stella explores her vantage points from each developmental stage to date. As a crawler, she's eye to eye with a turtle. . . . A goldfish and dog phase follow. Gay's sensitivity to the rich inner life of childhood flows into her art and language. . . . Gay's mixed-media scenes dance with the energy of scribbled butterflies on the walls, teetering objects, and a blanket-turned-turban. . . . Subtle and sweet, yet full of life and humor, the child's world is a place kids will want to visit again and again." SLJ

Other titles about Stella are:
Stella, star of the sea (1999)
Stella, queen of the snow (2000)
Stella, fairy of the forest (2002)
Stella, princess of the sky (2004)

Geeslin, Campbell

★ **Elena's** serenade; written by Campbell Geeslin; illustrated by Ana Juan. Atheneum Books for Young Readers 2004 un il $16.95

Grades: K 1 2 3   E

1. Mexico -- Fiction 2. Sex role -- Fiction 3. Glassblowing -- Fiction
ISBN 0-689-84908-7

LC 2002-3233

In Mexico a little girl disguised as a boy sets out for Monterrey determined to master the art of glassblowing, and in the process, experiences self-discovery along the way

"The story flows well and Spanish words are smoothly incorporated into the text. The alluring acrylic-and-crayon illustrations have a stylized folk-art quality that helps to set the stage for the tale." SLJ

Geisert, Arthur

Country road ABC; an illustrated journey through America's farmland. Houghton Mifflin Harcourt 2010 un il $17

Grades: K 1 2 3   E

1. Alphabet 2. Farm life -- Fiction
ISBN 978-0-547-19469-1; 0-547-19469-2

LC 2009045450

Arthur Geisert takes readers on a literal journey following a real road in Iowa through the ins and outs of America's farmland.

"Pastoral charm is not Geisert's aim: . . . he begins with 'A is for ammonia fertilizer.' His finely worked etchings, colored in muted shades, sweep across a sprawl of fields and roads. . . . Much visual information about farming is provided for lovers of tractors and farm animals, but it's more than a simple picture book; it's a deeply personal account." Publ Wkly

Hogwash. Houghton Mifflin 2008 32p il $16

Grades: K 1 2 3   E

1. Stories without words 2. Pigs -- Fiction 3. Machinery -- Fiction 4. Cleanliness -- Fiction
ISBN 978-0-618-77332-9; 0-618-77332-0

LC 2007-21731

Illustrations without words depict the enormous and complicated contraption that Mama Pig uses to get her little piglets clean.

This is illustrated with "intricately detailed colored etchings. . . . A master of the 'page turn,' only Geisert could take a one-word title and create such an engaging scenario." Booklist

★ **Ice**. Enchanted Lion Books 2011 un il $14.95
Grades: K 1 2   E
1. Stories without words 2. Ice -- Fiction 3. Pigs -- Fiction
ISBN 978-1-59270-098-1; 1-59270-098-5
LC 2010-942321
This wordless tale depicts a community of pigs that suffer from the heat and go in search of ice despite the odds against them.
"This is an especially satisfying Geisert title, because the task is essential for the pigs' survival and they carry it off with such élan. And the air-schooner, a charming marriage of sailing and balloon technology, is a standout among Geisert's many contraptions." Publ Wkly

★ **Lights** out. Houghton Mifflin Co. 2005 32p il $16
Grades: 1 2 3 4   E
1. Pigs -- Fiction 2. Bedtime -- Fiction 3. Inventions -- Fiction
ISBN 0-618-47892-2
LC 2005-00555
Told by his parents that his light must be out at eight o'clock, a young piglet who is afraid of the dark devises an ingenious solution to the problem.
"Fans of roller-coaster construction, marble runs, and contraption-like machines will be immediately engaged, and the problem-solving humor is for everyone. The fine lines and small scale of Geisert's color art work perfectly to give an effect that is intimate, energetic, and delightful." SLJ

Thunderstorm; Arthur Geisert. 1st ed. Enchanted Lion Books 2013 32 p. (hardcover) $17.95
Grades: PreK K 1 2   E
1. Farm life 2. Thunderstorms
ISBN 1592701337; 9781592701339
LC 2012952191
This picture book by Arthur Geisert "follows the course of a storm through midwestern farm country minute-by-minute, hour-by-hour, from late morning into late afternoon." (Publisher's note) "Cutaway views show the interiors of buildings and, in the ground below, the burrows of rabbits and foxes. The story follows a single farming family driving a red pickup truck hauling a trailer-load of hay; timestamps ('3:00 pm') are the only text." (Publishers Weekly)

Gellman, Ellie B.
Netta and her plant; by Ellie Gellman; illustrated by Natascia Ugliano. Kar-Ben Publishing 2014 32 p. color illustrations (lib. bdg) $17.95
Grades: PreK K   E
1. Jews -- Fiction 2. Growth -- Fiction 3. Plants -- Fiction 4. Tu bi-Shevat -- Fiction
ISBN 9781467704229; 1467704229
LC 2013002192
"One Tu B'Shevat day in Israel, little Netta brings a plant home from preschool. Over time, Netta grows, and the plant grows too. Soon it is time for both of them to find new homes and new friends." (Publisher's note)
"A pale springlike palette of greens, yellows and blues in the soft-edged drawings reinforces the symbolism of new growth. A welcome addition to the Judaica and ecology shelves." Kirkus

Genechten, Guido van
Kai-Mook. Clavis Pub. 2011 il $16.95
Grades: PreK K   E
1. Zoos -- Fiction 2. Animals -- Fiction 3. Elephants -- Fiction
ISBN 978-1-60537-096-5; 1-60537-096-7
"When a baby elephant is born, all the animals are smitten. . . . Each creature takes a turn to point out similarities with the new baby and all declare her 'cute.' At last the new baby says, 'I AM NOT CUTE,'. . . 'I AM KAI-MOOK!' The friendly collage and pastel cartoon-style animals are just right for toddlers and preschoolers. . . . Bright-eyed, smiling faces and interesting texturing provide visual appeal that earns this book a spot among the pack of baby-in-the-jungle tales." SLJ

No ghost under my bed. Clavis Pub. 2010 un il $17.95
Grades: PreK K 1 2   E
1. Fear -- Fiction 2. Bedtime -- Fiction 3. Penguins -- Fiction 4. Father-child relationship -- Fiction
ISBN 978-1-60537-069-9; 1-60537-069-X
When a little penguin named Jake becomes afraid of strange noises in his room at night, he calls his father to check out the situation, and when everything from the curtain to the wardrobe and toy box has been checked, Jake feels comforted that all of the ghosts are gone and prepares to sleep.
"This story is kept lighthearted with the addition of animated stuffed animals and humorous illustrations of Jake's father looking for ghosts. . . . Told mostly through dialogue between parent and child, this picture book starring two charming penguins dispels bedtime fears by replacing them with belief in a father's love." SLJ

George, Jean Craighead
★ **Goose** and Duck; illustrated by Priscilla Lamont. Laura Geringer Books 2008 48p il (I can read!) $16.99; lib bdg $17.89
Grades: PreK K 1 2   E
1. Ducks -- Fiction 2. Geese -- Fiction
ISBN 978-0-06-117076-8; 0-06-117076-3; 978-0-06-117077-5 lib bdg; 0-06-117077-1 lib bdg
LC 2006-21715
A young boy becomes the "mother" to a goose, who becomes "mother" to a duck, as they learn about the rhythms of nature together.
"Lamont's colorful illustrations combine sensitive line work with appealing color washes. . . . The clearly written story is well suited to beginning readers and, as a read-aloud." Booklist

Luck; the story of a sandhill crane. by Jean Craighead George; paintings by Wendell Minor. Laura Geringer Books 2006 un il $16.99; lib bdg $17.89
Grades: 1 2 3   E
1. Cranes (Birds) -- Fiction
ISBN 0-06-008201-1; 0-06-008202-X lib bdg
LC 2004-15628
A young sandhill crane, Luck, finds his place in the ancient crane migration from northern Canada to the Platte River
"Minor's beautifully painted spreads of Luck, including many pictures of the birds in flight, increase the sense of awe that the birds' miraculous journey inspires. A fine title to prompt discussion about local wildlife." Booklist

Morning, noon, and night; paintings by Wendell Minor. Harper-Collins Pubs. 1999 un il $16.99; lib bdg $17.89
Grades: K 1 2 3   E
1. Day -- Fiction 2. Animals -- Fiction
ISBN 0-06-023628-0; 0-06-023629-9 lib bdg
LC 97-28796
Each day as the sun makes its dawn-to-dusk journey from the Eastern seaboard to the Pacific coast, the animals perform their daily activities

This offers "rhythmic, lyrical text. . . . Minor's lushly detailed paintings capture the beauty of both animals and landscape, elucidating the subtle journey the book makes from east coast to west." Horn Book Guide

Nutik, the wolf pup; illustrated by Ted Rand. HarperCollins Pubs. 2001 un il hardcover o.p. lib bdg $18.89
Grades: K 1 2 3   E
  1. Inuit -- Fiction 2. Wolves -- Fiction 3. Arctic regions -- Fiction
  ISBN 0-06-028164-2; 0-06-028165-0 lib bdg
                                                              LC 99-10501
When his older sister Julie brings home two small wolf pups, Amaroq takes care of the one called Nutik and grows to love it, even though Julie tells him it cannot stay
  "Rand's realistic paintings establish the Alaska setting and capture the affection between boy and pup. . . . First told in Julie's Wolf Pack (1997), the story is skillfully telescoped into a picture book with heart-tugging appeal." Booklist
  Another title about Nutik and Amaroq is:
  Nutik & Amaroq play ball (2001)

George, Kallie
  Secrets I know; Kallie George; illustrations by Paola Zakimi. Schwartz & Wade Books 2017 32 p. color illustrations $17.99
Grades: PreK K 1 2 3   E
  1. Secrets -- Fiction 2. Friendship -- Fiction
  ISBN 9781101938935
                                                              LC 2016019456
This book, by Kallie George, illustrated by Paola Zakimi, is a "charming, whimsical story about one imaginative little girl's magical world is sure to enchant readers young and old. Follow the girl throughout a day spent in her own backyard, and you'll discover lots of secrets only she can tell. For example, did you know that whispers hide in trees? Or that trees make great umbrellas?" (Publisher's note)

George, Kristine O'Connell
  Hummingbird nest; a journal of poems. illustrated by Barry Moser. Harcourt 2004 un il $16
Grades: 2 3 4   E
  1. Stories in rhyme 2. Hummingbirds -- Fiction
  ISBN 0-15-202325-9
                                                              LC 99-50909
When a mother hummingbird builds a nest on a family's porch, they watch and record her actions and the birth and development of her fledglings.
  "Moser's quiet, exquisitely detailed pictures show the people watching and the small, delicate creatures. . . . The long, beautifully written notes with astonishing facts about hummingbirds make this a fine choice for both language arts and science classes." Booklist

  Up! illustrated by Hiroe Nakata. Clarion Books 2005 32p il $15
Grades: PreK K   E
  1. Stories in rhyme 2. Father-daughter relationship -- Fiction
  ISBN 0-618-06489-3
                                                              LC 2004-10729
Rhyming text and illustrations animate the feeling of "up" as experienced by a little girl with her father.
  "Nakata's airy, spirited watercolors beautifully expand on the words' carefree, physical elation with skewed angles, glorious fruit-juice colors, and leaping, tumbling toys and figures." Booklist

George, Lindsay Barrett
  ★ **Inside** mouse, outside mouse. Greenwillow Books 2004 un il $15.99; lib bdg $16.89

Grades: PreK K 1 2   E
  1. Mice -- Fiction
  ISBN 0-06-000466-5; 0-06-000467-3 lib bdg
                                                              LC 2003-48497
Two mice, one who sleeps inside the house in a clock and one who sleeps outside the house in a stump, follow complicated but strangely parallel paths and meet each other at a window.
  "The pictures are packed with interesting details just waiting to be explored. The simple text . . . compares and contrasts the animals' environments and lifestyles. The overall effect is mesmerizing" SLJ

  Maggie's ball. Greenwillow Books 2010 un il $16.99
Grades: PreK K   E
  1. Dogs -- Fiction
  ISBN 978-0-06-172166-3; 0-06-172166-2
                                                              LC 2008052482
When Maggie the dog goes searching for her missing ball, she finds a lot of different things—including a new friend.
  "The illustrations are bright and big, as is the minimal text, making the oversize book a winner for preschool storytimes as well as for individual perusings where the ample small details will fascinate children." SLJ

  That pup! Greenwillow Books 2011 un il $16.99
Grades: PreK   E
  1. Dogs -- Fiction 2. Squirrels -- Fiction
  ISBN 978-0-06-200413-0; 0-06-200413-1
                                                              LC 2010012641
After having fun digging up acorns, a little dog decides to bury them all again.
  "There is a real story here about taking things that don't belong to you and putting things right after a misunderstanding, right on target for younger preschoolers. Gouache illustrations of the appealing puppy and concerned squirrel use simple layouts and lots of white space." Kirkus

George, Lucy M.
  Back to school Tortoise; written by Lucy M. George; illustrated by Merel Eyckerman. Albert Whitman 2011 un il $15.99
Grades: PreK K 1   E
  1. School stories 2. Turtles -- Fiction 3. Teachers -- Fiction
  ISBN 978-0-8075-0510-6; 0-8075-0510-2
                                                              LC 2010046344
Summer is over and Tortoise must summon the courage to go back to school.
  "The precisely worded text and amiable mixed-media illustrations work well together. An empathetic read-aloud choice, this book offers a welcome antidote for first-day-of-school jitters." Booklist

George, William T.
  Box Turtle at Long Pond; pictures by Lindsay Barrett George. Greenwillow Bks. 1989 un il $17.99
Grades: PreK K 1 2   E
  1. Turtles -- Fiction
  ISBN 0-688-08184-3
                                                              LC 88-18787
On a busy day at Long Pond, Box Turtle searches for food, basks in the sun, and escapes a raccoon
  "A beautifully illustrated book that introduces a pond environment. . . . The reader learns of other plants, animals, and insects that inhabit the pond." Sci Child
  Other titles about Long Pond are:
  Beaver at Long Pond (1988)
  Christmas at Long Pond (1992)
  Fishing at Long Pond (1991)

Geras, Adele

★ **Little** ballet star; by Adèle Geras; pictures by Shelagh Mc-Nicholas. Dial Books for Young Readers 2008 un il $16.99

Grades: PreK K 1 2   **E**

1. Aunts -- Fiction 2. Ballet -- Fiction

ISBN 978-0-8037-3237-7; 0-8037-3237-6

Tilly is thrilled when she gets to see her aunt perform in the ballet, "The Sleeping Beauty," especially because she gets to go backstage and even on the stage itself.

"This picture book will charm aspiring young dancers. The large format allows plenty of space for the expressive pencil illustrations, tinted with washes in pastel shades." Booklist

Another book about about Tilly is:

Time for ballet (2004)

Gerber, Carole

Leaf jumpers; by Carole Gerber; [illustrated by] Leslie Evans. Charlesbridge 2004 32 p. col ill. $7.95

Grades: PreK K 1 2   **E**

1. Autumn 2. Leaves

ISBN 1570914974; 1570914982; 9781570914980

LC 200315846

This book, by Carole Gerber, illustrated by Leslie Evans, "celebrates the beauty of autumn leaves, while the . . . text at the end explains why leaves change color. Readers learn how to identify all sorts of leaves from red maple to sycamore by their color, shape, and other characteristics. A great choice for science units and autumn displays." (Publisher's note)

"Gerber's poetic text describes colors, shapes, and characteristics with an abundance of similes and metaphors. . . . Evans' vibrant hand-colored linoleum prints feature scenes of a brother and sister with the family dog enjoying traditional fall activities." Booklist

Seeds, bees, butterflies, and more! poems for two voices. poems by Carole Gerber; illustrated by Eugene Yelchin. 1st ed. Henry Holt and Co. 2013 32 p. col. ill. (reinforced) $17.99

Grades: 2 3 4   **E**

1. Nature poetry 2. Children's poetry

ISBN 0805092110; 9780805092110

LC 2012011490

This book by Carole Gerber presents a "collection of nature- and spring-themed poems designed to be recited by two readers. The poems' alternating parts are differentiated by color, with multicolored phrases intended to be read in unison." They contain "information about flowers, berries, bugs, and more, as well as topics including germination and pollination." (Publishers Weekly)

Gerdner, Linda

Grandfather's story cloth; written by Linda Gerdner and Sarah Langford; illustrated by Stuart Loughridge. Shen's Books 2008 29p il $16.95

Grades: 2 3 4   **E**

1. Quilts -- Fiction 2. Grandfathers -- Fiction 3. Laotian Americans -- Fiction 4. Alzheimer's disease -- Fiction 5. Hmong (Asian people) -- Fiction 6. Bilingual books -- English-Hmong

ISBN 978-1-885008-34-3; 1-885008-34-1

Ten-year-old Chersheng helps his beloved grandfather cope with his failing memory, brought on by Alzheimer's disease, by showing him the story quilt Grandfather made after fleeing his homeland, Laos, during wartime.

"The English and Hmong texts face paintings that express the many moods of the characters. Endpapers and the back cover feature numerous geometric patterns that are common in Hmong handicrafts. . . . [The book includes] background information on Alzheimer's disease and the Hmong refugees and their story cloths. . . . A strong family story about difficult social issues relevant to today's society." SLJ

Gerritsen, Paula

Nuts; [by] Paula Gerritsen. Front Street 2006 un il $15.95

Grades: PreK K 1 2   **E**

1. Mice -- Fiction 2. Nuts -- Fiction 3. Storms -- Fiction

ISBN 1-932425-66-7

LC 2005021491

Original Dutch edition 2005

Mouse braves many dangers while trying to collect nuts before winter sets in, including a sudden storm that first brings her disappointment, then a delightful surprise

"The words are well chosen and the repeated refrain will delight readers. The pencil-and-pastel illustrations are charming, displaying the textures and colors of fall and the foreboding energy of the storm." SLJ

Gershator, Phillis

★ **Listen,** listen; [by] Phillis Gershator; [illustrated by] Alison Jay. Barefoot Books 2007 un il $16.95

Grades: K 1 2 3   **E**

1. Stories in rhyme 2. Sound -- Fiction 3. Nature -- Fiction 4. Seasons -- Fiction

ISBN 978-1-84686-084-3

LC 2006100351

Illustrations and rhyming text explore the sights and sounds of nature in each season of the year.

"Jay's magical and occasionally eerie crackle-glaze oil paintings furnish a visual feast. The text is built around a series of rhyming, gentile directives to attune one's ears." Publ Wkly

Moo, moo, brown cow, have you any milk? illustrated by Giselle Potter. Random House Children's Books 2011 32p il $16.99; lib bdg $19.99

Grades: PreK K 1   **E**

1. Stories in rhyme 2. Bedtime -- Fiction 3. Domestic animals -- Fiction

ISBN 978-0-375-86744-6; 0-375-86744-9; 978-0-375-96744-3 lib bdg; 0-375-96744-3 lib bdg

LC 2010018767

Through rhyming text, farm animals are asked if they have items needed to prepare for a snack and bedtime, such as wool for a blanket, down for a pillow, and milk to drink.

"Gershator uses rhyme and the melodic rhythm of 'Baa, Baa, Black Sheep' in her dialogue, making the tale fit for either singing or speaking. Potter uses soft colors for day and rich cobalt and chocolate for night in her folksy paintings." SLJ

Sky sweeper; pictures by Holly Meade. Farrar, Straus & Giroux 2007 un il $16

Grades: 1 2 3 4   **E**

1. Work -- Fiction 2. Japan -- Fiction 3. Gardens -- Fiction 4. Buddhism -- Fiction

ISBN 978-0-374-37007-7; 0-374-37007-9

LC 2005-49762

Despite criticism for his lack of "accomplishments," Takiboki finds contentment sweeping flower blossoms and raking the sand and gravel in the monks' temple garden. Includes a note on the art and beauty of Japanese gardens

"This is a complex, challenging story. . . . But Meade's beautiful collage illustrations of the earthly garden and glorious afterlife greatly enhance the story's accessibility and will help kids get closer to the text's religious and philosophical themes." Booklist

Who's awake in springtime? [by] Phillis Gershator and Mim Green; illustrated by Emilie Chollat. Henry Holt & Co. 2010 un il $16.99

Grades: PreK K 1 2   E

   1. Stories in rhyme 2. Spring -- Fiction 3. Animals -- Fiction 4. Bedtime -- Fiction

   ISBN 978-0-8050-6390-5; 0-8050-6390-0

                   LC 2009009224

Describes, in rhymed cumulative text and illustrations, how various young animals and one small human prepare for sleep at the end of a spring day.

"This cumulative tale is simple and accessible by young readers. . . Adults who share this book with children can engage the students with the rhythmic text, and repetition throughout the book begs for call-backs and other participation activities. . . . Chollat's illustrations offer bold colors and clear lines and strongly support the story." Libr Media Connect

Who's in the forest? [illustrations by] Jill McDonald. Barefoot Books 2010 un il bd bk $14.99

Grades: PreK K   E

   1. Stories in rhyme 2. Board books for children 3. Forest animals -- Fiction

   ISBN 978-1-84686-476-6; 1-84686-476-3

                   LC 2010009438

"Simple rhymes tell listeners that the deep and dark forest is home to bears, foxes, squirrels, and all types of birds. The collage illustrations are colorful and childlike, and every other page has a cutout circle that highlights a particular animal. . . . Toddlers, especially, will love the rhyming couplets and enjoy finding the creatures revealed with each page turn of this large-format board book." SLJ

Gershator, Phillis, 1942-

Time for a hug; by Phillis Gershator & Mim Green; illustrated by David Walker. Sterling Pub. Co. 2012 24 p. $9.95

Grades: PreK K   E

   1. Stories in rhyme 2. Hugging -- Fiction 3. Rabbits -- Fiction

   ISBN 1402778627; 9781402778629

                   LC 2011021209

In this children's book, by Phillis Gershator & Mim Green, "two bunnies, one small and orange and the other bigger and gray, wake up at 8:00 to begin a day chock-full of activities that preschoolers will recognize. Washing faces, getting dressed, baking a pie, playing with puppets, reading a book, bathing, brushing teeth and hopping off to bed are all portrayed in [David] Walker's softly colored full-page and double-page spreads or vignettes." (Kirkus Reviews)

"Hour by hour, this bouncy rhyme follows a rabbit parent and child through their day. Every so often, they pause in their many activities-indoors and out--to share a hug. "A hug feels good. / Let's hug again. / We'll hug at nine. / We'll hug at ten." The energetic illustrations, rendered in delicate pastel colors, often include a clock to show the time." Horn Book

Gerstein, Mordicai, 1935-

  ★ A **book**. Roaring Brook 2009 un il

Grades: PreK K 1 2   E

   1. Authorship -- Fiction 2. Books and reading -- Fiction

   ISBN 1-59643-251-9; 978-1-59643-251-2

"Among a family who lives in a book, the youngest daughter is the only one who doesn't have a story to belong to, so she sets out among fairy tales, adventures, mysteries, histories, science fiction, and others to track down her story." (Publisher's note) "Grades two to four." (Bull Cent Child Books)

"This charming story follows a young girl and her family who live in a book, . . . though she doesn't know what kind of story her book is. . . .

She dashes though spreads that take her into nursery rhymes, on the trail of a mystery, across pirate waters, and even into outer space before she ultimately decides to write her own story, which is, of course, this story. . . . The concept is executed with . . . cleverness and gentleness." Booklist

  ★ **Carolinda** clatter! Roaring Brook Press 2005 un il $16.95

Grades: PreK K 1 2 3   E

   1. Fairy tales 2. Giants -- Fiction

   ISBN 1-59643-063-X

                   LC 2004-24258

The excessively quiet town of Pupickton and the sleeping lovesick giant upon which it was built, are both awakened by the joyful noise of a little girl's songs.

"Gerstein tells his whimsical tale with direct humor, and his lovely paint-and-ink illustrations extend the comedy." Booklist

The **first** drawing; by Caldecott Medalist Mordicai Gerstein. Little Brown & Co 2013 40 p. $17

Grades: PreK K 1   E

   1. Picture books for children 2. Cave drawings and paintings -- Fiction 3. Drawing -- Fiction 4. Imagination -- Fiction 5. Cave dwellers -- Fiction 6. Cave paintings -- Fiction 7. Prehistoric peoples -- Fiction

   ISBN 0316204781; 9780316204781

                   LC 2013001269

In this picture book, Caldecott Medalist Mordicai Gerstein tells the tale "of a boy living 30,000 years ago with his pet wolf and his very extended family. Using narrative direct address . . . to effectively bridge the gap between prehistoric times and the present, the story follows the boy on his fanciful discoveries of wooly mammoths in clouds, bears in stones and horses galloping on cave walls." (Kirkus Reviews)

How to bicycle to the moon to plant sunflowers; a simple but brilliant plan in twenty-four easy steps. Mordicai Gerstein. Roaring Brook Press 2013 40 p. (hardcover) $16.99

Grades: K 1 2 3   E

   1. Moon -- Fiction 2. Picture books for children 3. Voyages and travels -- Fiction

   ISBN 1596435127; 9781596435124

                   LC 2012013787

In this book from Caldecott Medalist Mordicai Gerstein, a "boy with spiky red hair and glasses shares his 24-step plan for planting sunflowers on the moon to cheer it up." The expedition "involves creating a giant sling-shot to launch a flag pole/anchor harpoon into the moon . . .; then, wearing a spacesuit kindly donated by NASA, one can simply bicycle up to the moon on the 238,900 miles of garden hose attached to the harpoon." (Publishers Weekly)

Leaving the nest. Farrar, Straus and Giroux 2007 un il $16

Grades: K 1 2 3   E

   1. Cats -- Fiction 2. Birds -- Fiction 3. Growth -- Fiction 4. Squirrels -- Fiction

   ISBN 978-0-374-34369-9; 0-374-34369-1

                   LC 2005-51228

The lives of a baby jaybird, a young girl, a kitten, and a small squirrel intersect as they venture out into the world.

"Using dialogue bubbles to reveal conversations and thoughts, Gerstein's realistic illustrations set the backyard stage and choreograph the frenzied acts of the drama, adding touches of humor without diminishing the tension." Booklist

Minifred goes to school. HarperCollins 2009 un il $17.99

Grades: PreK K 1 2   E
1. School stories 2. Cats -- Fiction 3. Animals -- Fiction
ISBN 978-0-06-075889-9; 0-06-075889-9; 978-0-06-075890-5
lib bdg; 0-06-075890-2 lib bdg
LC 2008-13861

When Mr. Portly finds a kitten, he and his wife raise her like a child, but unlike a typical child, Minifred the kitten does not like to follow rules at home or at school.

"Gerstein matches the story's lighthearted mood with action-packed scenes, using playful colors, caricatured figures, and sometimes multiple scenes per page, increasing the sense of action." SLJ

★ The **night** world; by Mordicai Gerstein. Little, Brown & Co. 2015 40 p. (hc) $18
Grades: PreK K 1   E
1. Color -- Fiction 2. Night -- Fiction 3. Cats -- Fiction 4. Animals -- Fiction 5. Sun -- Rising and setting -- Fiction
ISBN 0316188220; 9780316188227
LC 2014006903

In this juvenile story, by Mordicai Gerstein, "the shadows of a summer night sing the promise of morning to a boy and his cat as they venture out into the dark yard surrounding their house. . . . [His cat,] Sylvie, it soon appears, is not ready for sleep and meows insistently until the two tiptoe through the sleeping house and out into the nighttime shadows." (School Library Journal)

"Gerstein is at the top of his game here, capturing a nearly inexpressible mood. Beginning with the very darkest shades while the boy is in the house . . . makes readers look and look again, and once they are outside, the animals' stirrings will have children pointing at the darkened pages with delight." Booklist

Sparrow Jack. Frances Foster Bks. 2003 un il $16
Grades: PreK K 1 2 3   E
1. Photographers 2. Sparrows -- Fiction 3. Immigrants -- Fiction
ISBN 0-374-37139-3
LC 2001-23829

In 1868, John Bardsley, an immigrant from England, brought one thousand sparrows from his home country back to Philadelphia, where he hoped they would help save the trees from the inch-worms that were destroying them

"Though a few imaginative liberties are taken with the facts, Gerstein's cheerful tale is based on a true story. The humor of his whimsically witty text is beautifully captured and expanded by drawings that are filled with comic action and droll details." Booklist

★ The **white** ram; a story of Abraham and Isaac. Holiday House 2006 un il $16.95
Grades: 1 2 3 4   E
1. Prophets 2. Sheep -- Fiction 3. Biblical characters 4. Rosh ha-Shanah -- Fiction
ISBN 0-8234-1897-9; 978-0-8234-1897-8
LC 2005-46001

A white ram, made on the sixth day of creation, waits patiently in the garden of Eden until the time is right, then runs to save a certain child in fulfillment of God's plan.

"This stunningly illustrated picture book is based on a Midrash. . . . The art, done in pen and ink, oils, and colored pencil, is mesmerizing. [This is told] with a captivating use of language along with true drama." SLJ

Ghahremani, Susie
Stack the cats; Susie Ghahremani. Harry N Abrams Inc 2017 32 p. color illustrations $14.95

Grades: PreK K   E
1. Cats 2. Counting
ISBN 1419723499; 9781419723490
LC 2016954851

In this picture book, by Susie Ghahremani, "One cat sleeps. Two cats play. Three cats stack! Cats of all shapes and sizes scamper, stretch and yawn across the pages of this adorable counting book. And every now and then, they find themselves in the purrfect fluffy stack!" (Publisher's note)

Ghigna, Charles
Barn storm; by Charles Ghigna and Debra Ghigna; illustrated by Diane Greenseid. Random House 2010 32p il (Step into reading) lib bdg $12.99; pa $3.99
Grades: 1 2 3   E
1. Stories in rhyme 2. Farm life -- Fiction 3. Tornadoes -- Fiction
ISBN 978-0-375-96114-4 lib bdg; 0-375-96114-3 lib bdg; 978-0-375-86114-7 pa; 0-375-86114-9 pa
LC 2009033321

When a tornado touches down in a pond on Farmer Brown's property, it sets off a chain of events among the barnyard animals that soon has every creature displaced, but not unhappy

"The Ghignas' silly rhymes bounce along; Greenseid's textured illustrations will elicit giggles." Horn Book Guide

Gibfried, Diane
Brother Juniper; illustrated by Meilo So. Clarion Books 2006 un il $16
Grades: K 1 2 3   E
1. Saints 2. Clergy -- Fiction 3. Writers on religion
ISBN 0-618-54361-9; 978-0-618-54361-8
LC 2005-10038

Worried about having left the overly-generous Brother Juniper in charge of their chapel when they went out to preach, Father Francis of Assisi and the other friars are not prepared for what they find upon their return.

"Filled with delicate details and gentle humor, the accomplished watercolor paintings add greatly to the book's appeal. . . . This is an excellent choice to open discussion about generosity." SLJ

Giff, Patricia Reilly
Watch out, Ronald Morgan! illustrated by Susanna Natti. Viking Kestrel 1985 24p il hardcover o.p. pa $5.99
Grades: PreK K 1 2   E
1. School stories 2. Eyeglasses -- Fiction
ISBN 0-14-050638-1 pa
LC 84-19623

Ronald has many humorous mishaps until he gets a pair of eyeglasses. Includes a note for adults about children's eye problems

"Told in a forthright manner but with appreciation for children's candor, the book's dialogue rings true with catchy humor. . . . Natti's illustrations show the characters to be bright, colorful informal figures who move with the text." SLJ

Other titles about Ronald Morgan are:
Good luck, Ronald Morgan (1996)
Happy birthday, Ronald Morgan! (1986)
Ronald Morgan goes to bat (1988)
Ronald Morgan goes to camp (1995)
Today was a terrible day (1980)

Gilani-Williams, Fawsia
★ **Nabeel's** new pants; an Eid tale. retold by Fawzia Gilani-Williams; illustrations by Proiti Roy. Marshall Cavendish Children 2010 un il $15.99

Grades: K 1 2 3   **E**
1. Turkey -- Fiction 2. Muslims -- Fiction 3. Id al-Adha -- Fiction 4. Family life -- Fiction
ISBN 978-0-7614-5629-2; 0-7614-5629-5
First published 2007 in India

"Turkish shoemaker Nabeel buys Eid gifts for his family. . . . The shopkeeper also persuades Nabeel to buy himself new pants, but the pants are too long. His wife, mother, and daughter are all too busy cooking for Eid to shorten his pants, so he cuts a few inches off himself. Later, the women in the house feel guilty and each secretly trims the pants more. . . . Roy's cheerful gouache, watercolor, and ink illustrations show the bonds among family members as they follow their traditions together. Kids will laugh right along with the loving characters." Booklist

Includes glossary

Gilchrist, Jan Spivey

My America; illustrations by Ashley Bryan and Jan Spivey Gilchrist; poem by Jan Spivey Gilchrist. HarperCollins Pubs. 2007 un il $16.99; lib bdg $17.89
Grades: PreK K 1 2   **E**
1. United States -- Poetry
ISBN 978-0-06-079104-9; 0-06-079104-7; 978-0-06-079105-6 lib bdg; 0-06-079105-5 lib bdg

LC 2006029867

"This unusual tribute celebrates America's diversity in its landscapes, both urban and rural, its wildlife, but most of all its people. . . . Both Bryan and Gilchrist illustrate the poem in alternating spreads: his signature color swirls work in tandem with her muted, blue-toned tableaux and faces. . . . The words have the potential for choral reading or dramatization." Booklist

Gilman, Grace

Dixie; pictures by Sarah McConnell. HarperCollins 2011 30p il (I can read!) $16.99; pa $3.99
Grades: PreK K 1   **E**
1. School stories 2. Dogs -- Fiction 3. Theater -- Fiction
ISBN 978-0-06-171914-1; 0-06-171914-5; 978-0-06-171913-4 pa; 0-06-171913-7 pa

LC 2010015979

Dixie the puppy plays with Emma every day after school until Emma starts memorizing her lines for the school play.

This "should make for a successful experience for the brand-new reader. The simple sentences are accompanied by uncluttered, realistic, brightly colored paintings that complement the story and provide clues to help the reader decipher the text." Booklist

Ginsburg, Mirra

★ The **chick** and the duckling; translated [and adapted] from the Russian of V. Suteyev; pictures by Jose & Ariane Aruego. Macmillan 1972 un il hardcover o.p. pa $6.99
Grades: PreK K   **E**
1. Ducks -- Fiction 2. Chickens -- Fiction
ISBN 0-689-71226-X pa

"The sunny simplicity of the illustrations is just right for a slight but engaging text, and they add a note of humor that is a nice foil for the bland directness of the story." Bull Cent Child Books

Good morning, chick; by Mirra Ginsburg, adapted from a story by Korney Chukovsky; pictures by Byron Barton. Greenwillow Bks. 1980 un il hardcover o.p. pa $6.99

Grades: PreK K   **E**
1. Chickens -- Fiction
ISBN 0-688-84284-4 lib bdg; 0-688-08741-8 pa

LC 80-11352

"Based upon a tale by the great Russian poet and storyteller, the totally childlike picture book for the very young employs an engaging device: The text, illustrated with a bright vignette, appears on each of the left-hand pages; then, after pausing briefly and leading the eye to the right, a sentence runs to completion on the opposite page with two words contained in a large storytelling picture done in bold, brilliant color." Horn Book

Giovanni, Nikki

★ The **grasshopper's** song; an Aesop's fable revisited. by Nikki Giovanni; illustrated by Chris Raschka. Candlewick Press 2008 44p il $16.99
Grades: K 1 2 3   **E**
1. Ants -- Fiction 2. Trials -- Fiction 3. Grasshoppers -- Fiction
ISBN 978-0-7636-3021-8; 0-7636-3021-7

Every year the Grasshoppers sing and play their instruments and the Ants work in rhythm to the music. But when winter comes, the Ants turn their backs on the Grasshoppers, and Jimmy Grasshopper finds this unfair. He's hired Robin, Robin, Robin, and Wren to sue Abigail and Nestor Ant for what he deserves—R-E-S-P-E-C-T—and a one-half share of the harvest. But will a jury of his peers agree about the worth of art?

"To illustrate Giovanni's detailed and insightful prose, Raschka . . . creates evocative, earth-tone watercolors that suggest camouflage." Publ Wkly

Glaser, Linda

Hoppy Hanukkah! illustrated by Daniel Howarth. Albert Whitman 2009 un il $15.99
Grades: PreK K   **E**
1. Rabbits -- Fiction 2. Hanukkah -- Fiction 3. Family life -- Fiction
ISBN 978-0-8075-3378-9; 0-8075-3378-5

LC 2008-55696

Two young bunnies learn about the customs of Hanukkah from their parents and grandparents before they light the menorahs, eat potato latkes, and play dreidel.

"Howarth's soft, bright illustrations of an extended floppy-eared family offer details of a Judaic home in this gentle introduction to the rituals of a traditional celebration that young families can follow as they create a Hanukkah atmosphere in their own homes." Kirkus

Hoppy Passover! illustrated by Daniel Howarth. Albert Whitman 2011 un il $15.99
Grades: PreK K   **E**
1. Jews -- Fiction 2. Rabbits -- Fiction 3. Passover -- Fiction
ISBN 978-0-8075-3380-2; 0-8075-3380-7

LC 2010024111

Two young bunnies learn about the customs of the Passover seder from their parents and grandparents as they all celebrate the holiday meal.

"Howarth's cozy and colorful illustrations portray a warm and loving family enjoying this holiday and passing their traditions along to a new generation." Booklist

Another title about this rabbit family is:
Hoppy Hanukkah! (2009)

Glass, Beth Raisner

Blue-ribbon dad; illustrated Margie Moore. Harry N Abrams Inc. 2011 un il $14.95

Grades: PreK K 1   **E**

1. Fathers -- Fiction 2. Squirrels -- Fiction
ISBN 978-0-8109-9727-1; 0-8109-9727-4

"A young squirrel hustles to get a surprise ready before his father comes home. While working on an arts-and-crafts project that necessitates glue, glitter, sequins, stickers, and more, the squirrel reflects on everything his father does for him. . . . Moore's delicately outlined watercolors mirror the coziness of the text." Publ Wkly

Glass, Eleri

The **red** shoes; by Eleri Glass; illustrated by Ashley Spires. Simply Read 2008 un il $16.95
Grades: PreK K 1 2   **E**

1. Shoes -- Fiction 2. Shopping -- Fiction
ISBN 978-1-894965-78-1; 1-894965-78-7

"Shopping for shoes, a little girl knows that her mother will pick the practical, very dull, lace-ups. Even the palette that Spires uses is dark and drab, and the child's body language screams disappointment. But when she gets to the store, she sees the most wonderful pair of red shoes and wants them more than anything. . . . This sweet story will appeal to little girls who count shoes as something very important indeed." SLJ

Gleeson, Libby

★ **Clancy** & Millie, and the very fine house; [illustrated by] Freya Blackwood. Little Hare Books 2009 un il $16.99
Grades: 1 2   **E**

1. Moving -- Fiction
ISBN 978-1-921541-19-3; 1-921541-19-9

LC 2010399372

"Australians Gleeson and Blackwood . . . portray with sensitivity a small boy's ambivalence about moving to a new house. . . . Blackwood exaggerates the building's imposing exterior and its rooms, with towering walls, windows that seem miles away, and chilly gray expanses of floor, emphasizing the enormity of the move for Clancy. . . . Though the story deals with a particular childhood dilemma, Clancy's feelings are conveyed with a dignity that should appeal to a wide audience." Publ Wkly

The **great** bear; [illustrations by Armin Greder] Candlewick Press 2011 il $16.99
Grades: PreK K 1   **E**

1. Bears -- Fiction 2. Freedom -- Fiction
ISBN 978-0-7636-5136-7; 0-7636-5136-2

LC 2010040288

A bear imprisoned in a medieval circus is forced to perform night after night before a mocking crowd, but she finally can no longer stand the torment and determines to set herself free.

"Greder's darkly beautiful charcoal-and-pastel illustrations carry the weight of the storytelling . . . and are abetted by a unique design. . . . Subtle—yet spectacular and deeply moving" Kirkus

★ **Half** a world away; by Libby Gleeson; illustrated by Freya Blackwood. Arthur A. Levine Books 2007 un il hardcover o.p. $15.99
Grades: PreK K 1 2   **E**

1. Moving -- Fiction 2. Friendship -- Fiction
ISBN 0-439-88977-4; 0-439-88978-2 pa

LC 2006007712

When Louie's best friend Amy moves to the other side of the world, Louie must find a way to reconnect with her

"Blackwood's tender, realistic watercolors reinforce the friends' sweet closeness and magic. . . . Subtle, direct, and profound." Booklist

Glenn, Sharlee Mullins

Just what Mama needs; [by] Sharlee Glenn; illustrated by Amiko Hirao. Harcourt 2008 un il lib bdg $16
Grades: PreK K 1 2   **E**

1. Dogs -- Fiction 2. Week -- Fiction 3. Imagination -- Fiction
ISBN 978-0-15-205759-6; 0-15-205759-5

LC 2005-25440

Abby the dog assumes a different identity for each day of the week until Sunday, when she is just herself.

"Glenn's descriptive text and use of onomatopoeia provide an ideal read-aloud [and] . . . Hirao's collage and colored-pencil art, expressed on a variety of paper surfaces, alternates stark views as Abby introduces a costume, followed by busy scenes of her imagination and the real-life labors. . . . There's something to please nearly everyone in this tale." SLJ

Gliori, Debi

No matter what. Harcourt Brace & Co. 1999 un il $16; bd bk $6.95
Grades: PreK K 1   **E**

1. Stories in rhyme 2. Foxes -- Fiction 3. Parent-child relationship -- Fiction
ISBN 0-15-202061-6; 0-15-206343-9 bd bk

LC 98-47277

Small, a little fox, seeks reassurance that Large will always provide love, no matter what

"Gliori's whimsical illustrations use warm, inviting color to invoke the same sense of emotional security as the rhyming text." Booklist

Stormy weather; written and illustrated by Debi Gliori. Walker & Co. 2009 un il $15.99; lib bdg $16.89
Grades: PreK K   **E**

1. Stories in rhyme 2. Foxes -- Fiction 3. Animals -- Fiction 4. Bedtime -- Fiction 5. Mother-child relationship -- Fiction
ISBN 978-0-8027-9419-2; 0-8027-9419-X; 978-0-8027-9422-2 lib bdg; 0-8027-9422-X lib bdg

LC 2008043523

As nighttime approaches, a baby fox and his mother imagine all the different animals around the world preparing for bed and falling asleep.

"The story's lulling pace enhances the quiet bedtime read-aloud. . . . Watercolor-and-ink spreads utilize warm earth tones within the family homes to contrast the sometimes threatening outside elements or cool night backdrops. Nimble lines support the comforting images, and swirling designs and twinkling stars add unique details." SLJ

The **trouble** with dragons; [by] Debi Gliori. Walker & Co. 2008 un il $16.99; lib bdg $17.89
Grades: PreK K 1   **E**

1. Stories in rhyme 2. Dragons -- Fiction 3. Environmental protection -- Fiction 4. Conservation of natural resources -- Fiction
ISBN 978-0-8027-9789-6; 0-8027-9789-X; 978-0-8027-9790-2 lib bdg; 0-8027-9790-3 lib bdg

LC 2008005389

When dragons cut down too many trees, blow out too much hot air, and do other environmental damage, the future looks grim, but other animals advise them on how to mend their ways and save the planet

This "is magical, thanks to the playful artwork and bouncy rhymes. Though the text sticks to the basics of taking care of the Earth, the illustrations offer fodder for discussion." SLJ

What's the time, Mr. Wolf? by Deb Gliori. Walker 2012 32 p.
Grades: PreK K 1   **E**

1. Time -- Fiction 2. Wolves -- Fiction 3. Characters and

characteristics in literature 4. Characters in literature -- Fiction
ISBN 0802734324; 9780802734327

LC 2012014710

This book by Debi Gliori is "told from the point of view of Mr. Wolf on his birthday. Four and twenty black birds wake him up at seven o'clock, tweeting, 'What's the time, Mr. Wolf?' . . . Little Red Riding Hood, Hickory Dickory Dock . . . Humpty Dumpty, and other favorite nursery rhyme characters make an appearance in the text and/or pictures. Mr. Wolf's day is not going well until six o'clock when his friends surprise him with a birthday party." (School Library Journal)

★ Global baby girls; a Global Fund for Children Book. Global Fund for Children. Charlesbridge 2013 16 p. (board book) $6.95
Grades: PreK   E
1. Girls 2. Board books for children 3. Picture books for children 4. Board books 5. Girls -- Fiction 6. Girls -- Fiction
ISBN 1580894399; 9781580894395

LC 2012007368

Amelia Bloomer List (2014)

This is a children's board book from the nonprofit Global Fund for Children. The "babies' smiling faces and bright-colored clothing (which ranges from everyday jumpers to, in the case of one Russian child, a fur suit) are attention-grabbing, and the overall message ('Baby girls can grow up to change the world') is empowering." (Publishers Weekly)

Global Fund for Children (Organization)

American babies; developed by the Global Fund for Children. Charlesbridge 2010 un il $6.95
Grades: PreK   E
1. Infants 2. Board books for children
ISBN 978-1-58089-280-3; 1-58089-280-9

"This appealing board book offers 17 closeup photos of babies. . . . [It] has a brief text, really a single sentence divided into phrases. . . . From the Hawaiian child on the cover to the African-American girl on the last page, all the babies pictured are beyond early infancy. Their expressive faces and emotions are as varied as their family backgrounds, surroundings, and activities. . . . The pleasing layout places each colorful, full-page photo opposite a page with a slightly smaller photo and large-type text on its bright, solid-color border." Booklist

Global babies; developed by the Global Fund for Children. Charlesbridge 2007 un il $6.95
Grades: PreK   E
1. Infants 2. Board books for children
ISBN 978-1-58089-174-5

This board book offers color photographs of babies from 17 cultures around the world.

Goble, Paul

Beyond the ridge; story and illustrations by Paul Goble. Bradbury Press 1989 un il hardcover o.p. pa $6.99
Grades: 2 3 4   E
1. Native Americans -- Fiction
ISBN 0-689-71731-8 pa

LC 87-33113

At her death an elderly Plains Indian woman experiences the afterlife believed in by her people, while the surviving family members prepare her body according to their custom

"Goble's illustrations—in a double spread of gray rocks, smoothly surfaced in a skyscape of flying vultures—make a dignified context for a moving, direct discussion of death." Bull Cent Child Books

Death of the iron horse; story and illustrations by Paul Goble. Bradbury Press 1987 un il hardcover o.p. pa $7.99

Grades: K 1 2 3   E
1. Railroads -- Fiction 2. Cheyenne Indians -- Fiction
ISBN 0-689-71686-9 pa

LC 85-28011

The author "has taken several accounts of the 1867 Cheyenne attack of a Union Pacific freight train . . . and combined them into a story from the Indians' viewpoint. As the Cheyenne Prophet Sweet Medicine had foretold, strange hairy people were invading the land, killing women and children and driving off the horses. Descriptions of the iron horse inspired curiosity and fear in the young braves who decided to go out and protect their village from this new menace. Keeping fairly close to actual Indian accounts, Goble presents the braves' bold attack on the train, glossing over the deaths of the train crew." SLJ

Godden, Rumer

The **story** of Holly & Ivy; [by] Rumer Godden; [pictures by] Barbara Cooney. Viking 2006 31p il $17.99
Grades: K 1 2 3   E
1. Dolls -- Fiction 2. Orphans -- Fiction 3. Christmas -- Fiction
ISBN 0-670-06219-7; 978-0-670-06219-5

First published 1957; a reissue of the newly illustrated edition published 1985

Orphaned Ivy finds her Christmas wish fulfilled with the help of a lonely couple and a doll named Holly.

"Texturally rich and evocatively wintry, this reissue is timeless." Horn Book Guide

Godin, Thelma Lynne

The **hula** hoopin' queen; by Thelma Lynne Godin; illustrated by Vanessa Brantley-Newton. Lee & Low Books Inc. 2014 40 p. color illustrations (hardcover) $18.95
Grades: K 1 2 3 4   E
1. City and town life -- Fiction 2. Intergenerational relations -- Fiction 3. Parties -- Fiction 4. Birthdays -- Fiction 5. Responsibility -- Fiction 6. African Americans -- Fiction 7. Harlem (New York, N.Y.) -- Fiction 8. Competition (Psychology) -- Fiction
ISBN 1600608469; 9781600608469

LC 2013015548

"A spunky girl has a hula-hooping competition with her friends in Harlem, and soon everyone in the neighborhood--young and old alike--joins in on the fun. . . . Kameeka's disappointed to be stuck at home and can only think about the hoopin' competition. Distracted, Kameeka accidentally ruins Miz Adeline's birthday cake, and has to confess to her that there won't be a cake for her special day." (Publisher's note)

"First-time picture book author Godin's empathic prose and Brantley-Newton's emotionally telegraphic art capture the lively and nurturing Harlem neighborhood and the thrill of competition, whether age nine or 90." Pub Wkly

Godwin, Laura

★ **Happy** and Honey; written by Laura Godwin; pictures by Jane Chapman. Margaret K. McElderry Bks. 2000 un il (Happy Honey) $12.95
Grades: PreK K 1   E
1. Cats -- Fiction 2. Dogs -- Fiction
ISBN 0-689-83406-3

LC 99-46923

Honey the cat is determined to play with Happy the dog, even though he is trying to sleep

"The text is short and effective, and the delightful acrylic paintings, which are set against an expanse of white space, center on Happy and Honey, keeping children as focused on the goings-on as does the just-right text." Booklist

Other titles about Happy and Honey are:

The best fall of all (2002)
Happy Christmas, Honey (2002)
Honey helps (2000)

One moon, two cats; illustrated by Yoko Tanaka. Atheneum Books for Young Readers 2011 un il $16.99

Grades: PreK K 1   **E**

1. Stories in rhyme 2. Cats -- Fiction 3. Country life -- Fiction 4. City and town life -- Fiction

ISBN 978-1-4424-1202-6; 1-4424-1202-X

LC 2009053697

Two cats, one in the city and one in the country, chase mice before going to sleep.

"The brief, rhymed text changes size to match the rhythms of the cats' adventures, and the rich acrylic paintings create an air of nighttime mystery. An ably told and atmospheric romp." SLJ

Owl sees owl; by Laura Godwin; illustrated by Rob Dunlavey. Schwartz & Wade Books 2016 40 p. color illustrations (hardback) $17.99

Grades: PreK K 1   **E**

1. Owls -- Fiction

ISBN 9780553497823; 9780553497830

LC 2015036751

This picture book by Laura Godwin, illustrated by Rob Dunlavey, "follows a baby owl one night as he leaves the safety of his nest . . . and explores the starry world around him. . . . Inspired by reverso poetry, the words reverse in the middle when the baby owl is startled upon seeing his reflection in the pond. . . . Afraid of it, little owl takes off toward home, soaring over farms and forests . . . until he is finally safely home again." (Publisher's note)

"Luminous blue-and-black-toned multimedia illustrations, rendered in soft shapes and rich colors, convey the quiet, dark beauty of an autumn night. Simple yet stirring, this is perfect for preschooler bedtimes." Booklist

Goembel, Ponder

Animal fair; adapted and illustrated by Ponder Goembel. Marshall Cavendish Children 2010 un il $12.99

Grades: PreK K 1   **E**

1. Stories in rhyme 2. Animals -- Fiction

ISBN 978-0-7614-5642-1; 0-7614-5642-2

LC 2009005937

"Based on the children's song Animal Fair, Goembel's adaptation adroitly posits the wild imaginings of a child: what might go on at a fair apparently run by animals? The answer is nonsense, as virtually nothing the animals do makes a whit of sense. That, of course, is what will make young listeners squeal with glee. The text is wonderfully wordy and tied to an irresistible rhythm. . . . Goembel's ink and acrylic-wash artwork has an appealing orderliness to it." Booklist

Goetz, Steve

Old Macdonald had a truck; by Steve Goetz; illustrated by Eda Kaban. Chronicle Books LLC 2016 40 p. color illustrations $16.99

Grades: PreK K   **E**

1. Farmers -- Fiction 2. Trucks -- Fiction 3. Folk songs -- United States 4. Construction equipment -- Fiction 5. Trucks -- Songs and music 6. Earthmoving machinery -- Songs and music 7. Folk songs, English -- United States -- Texts

ISBN 9781452132600

LC 2014047555

In this book, by Steve Goetz, illustrated by Eda Kaban, a "couple make their way down a road in a dilapidated pickup carrying an unidentifiable pile of metal. Old MacDonald and, presumably, his wife are greeted by a construction crew of farm animals ready to start their day. . . . While her spouse directs the digging, Mrs. MacDonald calmly rebuilds the truck's engine. . . . By day's end, the two of them drive off, this time with the wife in the driver's seat." (Kirkus Reviews)

"Vibrant gouache-and-pencil illustrations incorporate stylized and cartoon elements with witty details, while the text encourages lively sing-alongs... A fun, entertaining intersection of song and topic that both respective fan bases ought to enjoy." Booklist

Going, K. L. (Kelly L.), 1973-

Dog in charge; by K.L. Going; illustrated by Dan Santat. Dial Books for Young Readers 2012 40 p. col. ill. (hardcover) $16.99

Grades: PreK K 1 2   **E**

1. Cats -- Fiction 2. Dogs -- Fiction 3. Picture books for children 4. Cats -- Fiction 5. Dogs -- Fiction

ISBN 0803734794; 9780803734791

LC 2011035211

This is "Printz-winner [K.L.] Going['s] . . . picture-book debut." It's a 'saga of a tutu-wearing bulldog who is the designated cat-sitter while the humans are at the store. Once the car leaves the driveway, five cats of varying breeds skedaddle from the sofa to spill milk, stir up fireplace ash, empty the hamper, disrupt a vanity, and more. Dog worries that their raucous acting out will reflect badly on him: 'Would he still be a good Dog, a smart Dog, the very best Dog?' His idea to entice good behavior with kibbles disappears with his own hunger. As he naps, the cats remember that they love Dog and bring the house back to perfect order as the family arrives." (School Library Journal)

Golan, Avirama

Little Naomi, Little Chick; by Avirama Golan; illustrated by Raaya Karas. Eerdmans Books for Young Readers 2013 34 p. illustrations (color) (hbk.) $17

Grades: PreK K   **E**

1. Chickens -- Fiction 2. Farm life -- Fiction 3. School stories -- Fiction 4. Schools -- Fiction 5. Chickens -- Fiction 6. Farm life -- Fiction 7. Nursery schools -- Fiction 8. Animals -- Infancy -- Fiction

ISBN 0802854273; 9780802854278

LC 2013000492

In this book, by Avirama Golan, "Little Naomi has a busy day! She gets ready for school, plays with all her friends, builds with blocks, bakes mud pies, colors pictures, eats lunch, and helps mom with the shopping. Little Chick has to stay at home with the other barnyard animals, but that doesn't stop him from having adventures of his own." (Publisher's note)

Gold, August

★ **Thank** you, God, for everything; by August Gold; illustrated by Wendy Anderson Halperin. G.P. Putnam's Sons 2009 un il $16.99

Grades: PreK K 1 2   **E**

1. God -- Fiction 2. Religious life -- Fiction

ISBN 978-0-399-24049-2; 0-399-24049-7

LC 2008016801

As Daisy watches her parents thanking God everyday, she begins to look at everything around her and realizes she is also thankful for many things.

Gold's "goal here is to 'show young readers how to develop their own thankful eyes.' Both she and artist Halperin do that beautifully in this story. . . . In her signature softly colored style . . . Halperin takes everyday doings and elevates them." Booklist

Goldfinger, Jennifer P.

My dog Lyle. Clarion Books 2007 un il $16

Grades: PreK K 1 2   E
1. Dogs -- Fiction
ISBN 978-0-618-63983-0; 0-618-63983-7

LC 2006-07146

A child provides an ever-increasing list of characteristics that make Lyle a very special dog, despite appearances.

"The lively text matches perfectly with the vibrant, playful illustrations, done in bold, richly hued acrylics and oils." SLJ

Goldin, Barbara Diamond
Cakes and miracles; a Purim tale. [illustrated by] Jaime Zollars. Marshall Cavendish 2010 un il $17.99
Grades: PreK K 1   E
1. Jews -- Fiction 2. Blind -- Fiction 3. Purim -- Fiction
ISBN 978-0-7614-5701-5; 0-7614-5701-1

A revised and newly illustrated edition of the title first published 1991

Young, blind Hershel finds that he has special gifts he can use to help his mother during the Jewish holiday of Purim. Includes author's notes about the holiday and its origins

"Edited significantly from the 1991 edition, the new text is more accessible to a younger audience and works better as a read-aloud. Rich, full-spread illustrations in collage and acrylic paint warmly depict the Eastern European shtetl setting with expression and dimension." SLJ

Goldin, David
Meet me at the art museum; a whimsical look behind the scenes. by David Goldin. Abrams Books for Young Readers 2012 33 p. (hardback) $18.95
Grades: K 1 2 3   E
1. Museums 2. Picture books for children 3. Art museums
ISBN 1419701878; 9781419701870

LC 2012019355

In this book, an "anthropomorphized name tag named Daisy gives a discarded 'Admit One' ticket stub (named Stub) a tour of an art museum--doing the same for readers in the process. . . . As Daisy guides Stub through the galleries, she discusses the museum's layout, operations (including security systems and temperature controls), and various staff responsibilities, from conservators to archivists." (Publishers Weekly)

Includes bibliographical references and index

Goldman, Judy
Uncle monarch and the Day of the Dead; [by] Judy Goldman; illustrated by Rene King Moreno. Boyds Mills Press 2008 un il $16.95
Grades: K 1 2 3   E
1. Death -- Fiction 2. Mexico -- Fiction 3. Uncles -- Fiction 4. Butterflies -- Fiction 5. All Souls' Day -- Fiction 6. Spanish language -- Vocabulary
ISBN 978-1-59078-425-9; 1-59078-425-1

LC 2007049322

Upon the death of her beloved Tio Urbano, who has taught her that monarch butterflies are the souls of the dead, young Lupita gains a deeper understanding of Dia de los Muertos, the Day of the Dead, as it is observed in rural Mexico. Includes glossary of Spanish terms and facts about the Day of the Dead

"This lovely picture book effectively blends a poignant story about losing a beloved relative with a lucid description of Día de Muertos. . . . [This features] lovely, bright-hued colored-pencil illustrations. . . . Spanish words are integrated into the text." SLJ

Goldsaito, Katrina
★ The **sound** of silence; by Katrina Goldsaito; art by Julia Kuo. Little, Brown & Co. 2016 40 p. (hardcover) $17.99
Grades: K 1 2 3 4   E
1. Japan -- Fiction 2. Sound -- Fiction 3. Silence -- Fiction 4.

Tokyo (Japan) -- Fiction 5. Japan -- Fiction 6. Tokyo (Japan) -- Fiction
ISBN 9780316203371

LC 2014007229

In this book, by Katrina Goldsaito, art by Julia Kuo, "Yoshio lives in Tokyo, Japan: a giant, noisy, busy city. He hears shoes squishing through puddles, trains whooshing, cars beeping, and families laughing. Tokyo is like a symphony hall! Where is silence? Join Yoshio on his journey through the hustle and bustle of the city to find the most beautiful sound of all." (Publisher's note)

"An inviting tale that will stretch inquisitive and observant young minds--and may even lead children to a greater appreciation of that golden commodity, silence." Kirkus

Goldstone, Bruce
Awesome autumn; Bruce Goldstone. 1st ed. Henry Holt and Co. 2012 48 p. ill. (hardcover) $16.99
Grades: K 1 2   E
1. Climate 2. Seasons -- Encyclopedias 3. Autumn
ISBN 0805092102; 9780805092103

LC 2011029043

This book is an educational resource for learning about the Autumn season. "Leaves change color. Animals fly south or get ready to hibernate. People harvest crops and dress up as scary creatures for Halloween. . . . With . . . photographs, . . . explanations, and . . . craft ideas, Bruce Goldstone has created a[n] . . . exploration of autumn." (Publisher's note)

Golenbock, Peter
ABC's of baseball; by Peter Golenbock; illustrated by Dan Andreasen. Dial Books for Young Readers 2012 48 p. col. ill. (reinforced) $16.99
Grades: 3 4 5   E
1. Alphabet 2. Baseball
ISBN 0803737114; 9780803737112

LC 2011021928

In this book, "[Peter] Golenbock defines several baseball terms and phrases for each letter of the alphabet, the entries and their definitions appearing in . . . sidebars that let [illustrator Dan] Andreasen's artwork take center stage. Figures like Babe Ruth and Alexander Cartwright . . . are mentioned alongside terms like 'bases loaded,' 'fielder's choice,' 'line drive' and 'southpaw,' which all receive brief definitions." (Publishers Weekly)

Golson, Terry
Tillie lays an egg; [by] Terry Golson; with photographs by Ben Fink. Scholastic Press 2009 un il $16.99
Grades: PreK K 1 2   E
1. Chickens -- Fiction
ISBN 978-0-545-00537-1; 0-545-00537-X

LC 2008011737

In search of the perfect place to lay her egg, Tillie the chicken leaves the barnyard and explores the farmhouse

"The photographed scenes are packed with Golson's own chicken-motif treasures—glassware, tins, vintage board games—and invite close exploration. Text and photos appear in bordered boxes; these are set against pastel wallpapers with country patterns—a pleasant contrast to Fink's crisp photography. . . . Full of charm." Publ Wkly

Gomi, Taro, 1945-
The **great** day; by Taro Gomi. Chronicle Books LLC. 2014 40 p. color illustrations $16.99
Grades: PreK   E
1. Boys -- Fiction 2. Play -- Fiction 3. Picture books for children

4. Day -- Fiction
ISBN 9781452111254; 1452111251

LC 2013011767

Previously published under the title: First comes Harry

This children's picture book, written and illustrated by Tarō Gomi, depicts "a boy, . . . the first to wake up, get dressed, brush his teeth, eat breakfast, leap out the door, jump over a trash can and run up a slide. . . . He is the first to argue, the first to make up, and the first to march and do a handstand. His frantically busy day tires him out, so naturally, he is the first to finish dinner and the first to fall asleep." (Kirkus Reviews)

"Simple sentences invite readers into the child's daily routine. Gomi's bold, clean design features warm colors and appealing, round-headed characters. A charming celebration of the pleasures of an ordinary day." SLJ

Over the ocean; Taro Gomi. Chronicle Books Llc 2016 36 p. color illustrations $16.99
Grades: PreK K 1   E
1. Imagination -- Fiction
ISBN 9781452145150; 1452145156

LC 2015045044

Originally published in Japan in 1979

Batchelder Honor Book (2017)

In this children's picture book, by Taro Gomi, "a young girl gazes out to where the water meets the sky and wonders what lies beyond the waves. Boats filled with toys? Skyscrapers filled with people? Houses filled with families? Or, maybe, over the ocean stands someone not so different from the girl herself, returning her gaze." (Publisher's note)

"The book's elegant simplicity lends itself not only to pointing out visual details but also to encouraging a listening child's own speculations." SLJ

Peekaboo! by Taro Gomi. Chronicle Books 2013 16 p. (alk. paper) $6.99
Grades: PreK K   E
1. Children's costumes 2. Children's literature 3. Board books 4. Toy and movable books 5. Animals -- Fiction 6. Toy and movable books -- Specimens
ISBN 1452108358; 9781452108353

LC 2012011703

In this book by Taro Gomi "every spread includes a funny fact about featured creatures, from bears to robots. And young readers will squeal in surprise to find that when this board book is opened, the eye-sized die-cuts allow each spread to become a mask! Kids will have a blast posing as a fly-eating frog or a mouse-chasing cat." (Publisher's note)

Presents through the window; A Taro Gomi Christmas Book. Taro Gomi. Chronicle Books Llc 2016 36 p. color illustrations (ebook) $12.99; $15.99
Grades: PreK K   E
1. Christmas -- Fiction 2. Picture books for children 3. Santa Claus -- Fiction 4. Picture books 5. Christmas stories
ISBN 9781452163178; 9781452151380

LC 2015027032

In this children's book, by Taro Gomi, "[he] may not be your ordinary Santa, but it's still a daunting Christmas Eve challenge! There are so many presents to deliver, and so little time. It's a good thing Santa has a plan. He'll just peek into every window and toss in a gift. Done! The trouble is, Santa is moving much too quickly to see who really lives in each house." (Publisher's note)

"There's a subtle lesson here to slow down and evaluate before making a decision. But with this book, a snap judgement holds up—it's a winner." Kirkus

Gonzalez, Maya Christina

Call me tree; Maya Christina Gonzalez; translation/traducción, Dana Goldberg. Children's Book Press, an imprint of Lee & Low Books Inc. 2014 24 p. color illustrations (hardcover : alk. paper) $17.95
Grades: PreK K 1 2 3   E
1. Stories in rhyme 2. Trees -- Fiction 3. Bilingual books -- English-Spanish 4. Spanish language materials -- Bilingual
ISBN 0892392940; 9780892392940

LC 2014008759

In this bilingual book, by Maya Christina Gonzalez, "we join a child on a journey of self-discovery. Finding a way to grow from the inside out, just like a tree, the child develops as an individual comfortable in the natural world and in relationships with others. . . . Young readers will be inspired to dream and reach, reach and dream . . . and to be as free and unique as trees." (Publisher's note)

"This bilingual story is an anthem to the innate strength and individuality of children and trees...Many of the children are portrayed in variations of the yoga tree pose—providing an opportunity for inquisitive readers to ask questions in regards to yoga and its practice. Gonzalez's art and text invite reader participation on multiple levels, thereby appealing to a wider audience." SLJ

Llámame árbol

★ **My** colors, my world. Children's Book Press 2007 23p il $16.95
Grades: PreK K 1 2   E
1. Color -- Fiction 2. Deserts -- Fiction 3. Hispanic Americans -- Fiction 4. Bilingual books -- English-Spanish
ISBN 978-0-89239-221-6; 0-89239-221-5

LC 2007005297

A Pura Belpré Award honor book, 2008

Maya, who lives in the dusty desert, opens her eyes wide to find the colors in her world, from Papi's black hair and Mami's orange and purple flowers to Maya's red swing set and the fiery pink sunset

Goode, Diane

The **most** perfect spot; by Diane Goode. HarperCollins 2006 un il $16.99; lib bdg $17.89
Grades: PreK K 1 2   E
1. Parks -- Fiction 2. Mother-son relationship -- Fiction 3. Brooklyn (New York, N.Y.) -- Fiction
ISBN 0-06-072697-0; 0-06-072698-9 lib bdg

LC 2004030058

"Young Jack wants to go on a picnic with his mother and thinks that he knows the perfect spot in Prospect Park. Maybe it is, but getting there is fraught with problems. . . . When the rain begins to pour down, Mama and Jack decide there's only one perfect spot for a picnic—back home. . . . Goode's art was inspired by the early years of the last century. . . . Full of amusing details and nice touches . . . this book will sustain more readings than one might expect." Booklist

★ **Thanksgiving** is here! HarperCollins Pubs. 2003 un il $15.99; lib bdg $16.89
Grades: PreK K 1 2   E
1. Family life -- Fiction 2. Thanksgiving Day -- Fiction
ISBN 0-06-051588-0; 0-06-051589-9 lib bdg

LC f002-151781

A family gathers to celebrate Thanksgiving at Grandma's house

"The humorously detailed, pen-and-ink and watercolor, cartoon artwork is exuberant, mischievous, and full of surprises. This Thanksgiving book has something for everyone." SLJ

Goodhart, Pippa

Three little ghosties; illustrated by AnnaLaura Cantone. Bloomsbury Children's Books 2007 un il $16.95
Grades: PreK K 1 2   E
1. Ghost stories 2. Stories in rhyme
ISBN 978-1-58234-711-0; 1-58234-711-5
LC 2007-02610
Three mischievous ghosts love scaring little children, until the children decide to take matters into their own hands.
"Goodhart's engagingly silly rhymes are paired with mixed-media illustrations that use dark and spooky colors but feature goofy-looking ghosts." Horn Book

Goodrich, Carter

The **hermit** crab. Simon & Schuster Books for Young Readers 2009 un il $16.99
Grades: K 1 2 3   E
1. Crabs -- Fiction 2. Marine animals -- Fiction
ISBN 978-1-4169-3892-7; 1-4169-3892-3
LC 2007045240
Absorbed in his search for food, a shy hermit crab, disguised in a fancy new shell, inadvertently rescues a flounder caught beneath a trap and wins the admiration of the other marine animals.
"The personal tone engages the audience, bringing immediacy to the plot, and serves as a warm contrast to the cool illustrations. Goodrich's colored pencil and watercolor spreads predominately feature greens and blues to convey the watery depth of the sea." SLJ

Mister Bud wears the cone; Carter Goodrich. Simon & Schuster Books for Young Readers 2014 48 p. color illustrations (hardcover) $16.99
Grades: PreK K 1 2   E
1. Dogs -- Fiction
ISBN 1442480882; 9781442480889
LC 2012040030
"Mister Bud has to wear a dreaded cone to keep him from scratching an itch on his back. It blocks his view and makes it difficult for him to eat, drink, and play with Zorro, the precocious pug with whom he shares a household. Zorro teases and taunts Mister Bud and delights in getting into all kinds of doggie mischief." (School Library Journal)
"Goodrich's watercolors excel at squat doggie bodies, especially the abstract shape of Bud's faceless conehead. This third book featuring the duo is delightfully light on morals and anthropomorphizing. Just weirdo dogs being weird. And therein lies the joy." Booklist

★ **Say** hello to Zorro! Simon & Schuster Books for Young Readers 2010 un il $15.99
Grades: PreK K 1 2   E
1. Dogs -- Fiction
ISBN 978-1-4169-3893-4; 1-4169-3893-1
LC 2009-11484
Mister Bud, the family dog, has a satisfying routine to his life, but when another dog joins the family and disrupts his schedule, Mister Bud must learn to adapt.
"Goodrich has a delightfully economical and humorous voice: trim yet filled with barely contained emotion—kind of like a dog. . . . And the artwork is arresting, done in watercolors of enormous personality and quality." Kirkus

We forgot Brock! Carter Goodrich. Simon & Schuster Books for Young Readers 2015 48 p. color illustrations (hardcover : alk. paper) $17.99
Grades: PreK K 1 2   E
1. Friendship -- Fiction 2. Imaginary playmates -- Fiction 3. Best

friends -- Fiction 4. Missing children -- Fiction 5. Imaginary playmates -- Fiction
ISBN 1442480904; 9781442480902
LC 2014015991
In this children's story, by Carter Goodrich, "Phillip and Brock are best friends. Everyone can see Phillip, but only Phillip can see Brock. A night at the Big Fair is all fun and games until Phillip gets sleepy, heads home, and forgets Brock! Brock misses Phillip. And Phillip misses Brock. Will they reunite? With the help of another pair of pals, they just might. Because even imaginary friends get lost sometimes." (Publisher's note)
"Hilarious and heartwarming in equal measure." Booklist

Zorro gets an outfit; Carter Goodrich. Schuster Books for Young Readers 2012 48 p. col. ill. (hardcover) $15.99
Grades: PreK K 1 2   E
1. Dogs -- Fiction 2. Clothing and dress -- Fiction
ISBN 1442435356; 9781442435360; 9781442435353
LC 2011029153
"Zorro and an unwanted gift of a hooded cape similar to that worn by the masked outlaw. When Zorro's owner puts the cape on her dog, the precocious pug hangs his head in embarrassment. . . . The situation improves dramatically with the arrival of Dart, a dashing dog in a striped coat and bandanna, who makes wearing an outfit seem cool." (Kirkus Reviews)
"With his enormous nose, easygoing mutt Mister Bud supplies the perfect comedic counterpoint to Napoleonic dynamo Zorro in this tale of self-perception and acceptance." Booklist

Gorbachev, Valeri

★ **Christopher** counting; [by] Valeri Gorbachev. Philomel Books 2008 un il $15.99
Grades: PreK K 1   E
1. Animals -- Fiction 2. Rabbits -- Fiction 3. Counting -- Fiction
ISBN 978-0-399-24629-6
LC 2007023642
When Christopher Rabbit learns to count in school, he enjoys it so much that he counts everything in sight, including how many baskets his friends make when they play basketball and how many peas and carrots are on his plate.
"The simplicity of this charming story is what sets it apart from others that aim to introduce this concept. The text's deliberate pace is a perfect match for the pen, ink, and watercolor illustrations." SLJ

Dragon is coming! Harcourt Children's Books 2009 un il $16
Grades: PreK K 1 2   E
1. Fear -- Fiction 2. Mice -- Fiction 3. Clouds -- Fiction 4. Animals -- Fiction 5. Thunderstorms -- Fiction
ISBN 978-0-15-205196-9; 0-15-205196-1
LC 2006101580
Mouse frightens all of the animals she sees by shouting that a dragon is going to eat the sun, and then come after them.
"While the story is familiar, Gorbachev's illustrations revive it with delightful details and humorous poses." SLJ

Me too! by Valeri Gorbachev. Holiday House 2013 32 p. (I like to read) (hardcover) $14.95
Grades: PreK K 1   E
1. Friendship -- Fiction 2. Snow -- Fiction 3. Snow -- Fiction 4. Bears -- Fiction 5. Chipmunks -- Fiction
ISBN 0823427447; 9780823427444
LC 2012039294
In this book, by Valeri Gorbachev, "Chipmunk and Bear have a lot in common, despite their difference in size. And Chipmunk is determined

to emulate his big friend. The two dig a path through the snow, build a jolly snowman, have fun skating and skiing—although Chipmunk does need a bit of help from time to time. Warmth and humor fill the snowy-day adventures of two friends who, despite their physical differences, share work and play and true companionship." (Publisher's note)

The **missing** chick. Candlewick Press 2009 un il $15.99
Grades: PreK K 1   E
    1. Ducks -- Fiction 2. Chickens -- Fiction
    ISBN 978-0-7636-3676-0; 0-7636-3676-2

"Mother Hen and her seven chicks are hanging the laundry one sunny morning when neighborly Mrs. Duck observes that one chick is missing. Goat, Sheep, and Dog help to search the premises before being joined by the firefighters and the police on the ground and in helicopters. Amid all this noisy commotion, the missing chick wakes up from its napping spot in the laundry basket. . . . The story's simple premise, just-enough page-turning tension, and comical watercolor and ink illustrations add up to a gentle and satisfying tale that will hold up to repeated readings." SLJ

Molly who flew away. Philomel Books 2009 un il $16.99
Grades: PreK K 1 2   E
    1. Mice -- Fiction 2. Fairs -- Fiction 3. Animals -- Fiction 4. Balloons -- Fiction
    ISBN 978-0-399-25211-2; 0-399-25211-8
                                                    LC 2008-32607

Molly the mouse buys so many balloons for all her animal friends at the fair, she gets carried away into the air.

"Pen-and-ink and watercolor illustrations carry this simple friendship story along to the climactic end. Molly's flight is especially well shown, with a double-page spread with three ascending panels followed by a bird's eye view of the frightened mouse high over the scenery and her friends running to the rescue down below." Booklist

Another title about Molly is:
What's the big idea, Molly? (2010)

★ **Ms.** Turtle the babysitter. HarperCollins Pubs. 2005 64p il (I can read book) hardcover o.p. pa $3.99
Grades: PreK K 1 2   E
    1. Frogs -- Fiction 2. Turtles -- Fiction 3. Babysitters -- Fiction
    ISBN 0-06-058073-9; 0-06-058074-7 lib bdg; 0-06-058075-5 pa
                                                    LC 2004-6234

Ms. Turtle babysits for three little frogs when their parents go out for the evening

"Beginning readers will enjoy this chapter-style book. . . . The pen-and-ink and watercolor cartoons seamlessly complement the text. The expressions on the faces of these endearing frogs are priceless." SLJ

Shhh! Philomel Books 2011 un il $16.99
Grades: PreK K 1   E
    1. Play -- Fiction 2. Noise -- Fiction 3. Sleep -- Fiction 4. Brothers -- Fiction
    ISBN 978-0-399-25429-1; 0-399-25429-3
                                                    LC 2010041652

A little boy tries hard to be quiet while his little brother takes a nap.

"The illustrations, done in watercolors, gouache, and ink, are cheerfully rendered in soft tones that capture the calm, then playful, actions in the story. This is a fine book about how a child should behave while a younger sibling is asleep." SLJ

★ **That's** what friends are for. Philomel Books 2005 un il $15.99

Grades: PreK K 1 2
    1. Pigs -- Fiction 2. Goats -- Fiction 3. Friendship -- Fiction
    ISBN 0-399-23966-9
                                                    LC 2004-18118

When Goat finds his friend Pig crying, he imagines all the terrible things that might have happened to cause his distress

"The book is a warm display of friendship and a caution against unnecessary worry. Soft-colored drawings supply details for the simple text." Horn Book Guide

★ **Turtle's** penguin day; [by] Valeri Gorbachev. Alfred A. Knopf 2008 un il $16.99; lib bdg $19.99
Grades: PreK K 1   E
    1. School stories 2. Animals -- Fiction 3. Turtles -- Fiction 4. Penguins -- Fiction
    ISBN 978-0-375-84374-7; 0-375-84374-4; 978-0-375-94564-9 lib bdg; 0-375-94564-4 lib bdg
                                                    LC 2007037078

After hearing a bedtime story about penguins, Turtle dresses as a penguin for school and soon the entire class is having a penguin day.

"Cheerful watercolors and expressive line art imbue the matter-of-fact narrative with personality. . . . This nurturing tale celebrates the inspiration and information found in books, the invention bubbling up from a child who is read to, and the quality of learning that is possible when a teacher seizes the moment." SLJ

Two little chicks. NorthSouth Books 2011 un il (Tuff books) $6.95
Grades: PreK   E
    1. Fear -- Fiction 2. Chickens -- Fiction 3. Playgrounds -- Fiction
    ISBN 978-0-7358-4018-8; 0-7358-4018-0
    First published 2001 with title: Chicken chickens

When two little chicks go to the playground for the very first time, everything looks scary—the seesaw, the merry-go-round, the swings, even the slide. But it takes just one slide down to turn two frightened little chicks into two brave little chicks.

"The new 'Tuff Books' edition of the story . . . sports a smaller trim size and glossy, heavy paper suitable for young hands." Horn Book Guide

What's the big idea, Molly? Philomel Books 2010 un il $16.99
Grades: PreK K 1 2   E
    1. Mice -- Fiction 2. Gifts -- Fiction 3. Animals -- Fiction 4. Seasons -- Fiction 5. Turtles -- Fiction 6. Birthdays -- Fiction 7. Books and reading -- Fiction
    ISBN 978-0-399-25428-4; 0-399-25428-5

Molly Mouse and her friends struggle to come up with ideas for birthday gifts for their friend Turtle and decide to make a book about the four seasons.

"Written and illustrated with verve and affection, this . . . features a sympathetic protagonist. . . . A fitting tribute to the art of storytelling." Booklist

Gordon, Domenica More
    Archie; by Domenica More Gordon. Bloomsbury Childrens Books 2012 48 p. (hardcover) $17.99
Grades: PreK K 1   E
    1. Sewing -- Fiction 2. Success -- Fiction 3. Clothing and dress 4. Dogs -- Fiction 5. Humorous stories 6. Stories without words 7. Fashion design -- Fiction
                                                    LC 2012009329

Author Domenica More Gordon's character "Archie, a well-dressed dog, receives a sewing machine as a gift. He takes to it immediately, creating smart outfits for his own pet dog, his friends' dogs, and his friends.

His phone is ringing off the hook by book's end--the final call comes from a canine monarch with a crown, handbag, and pet corgi .... Even without the success Archie finds, his life as a clothing designer living alone with his dog is a winning premise." (Publishers Weekly)

Archie's vacation; by Domenica More Gordon; illustrated by Domenica More Gordon. Bloomsbury USA Childrens 2014 32 p. color illustrations (hardback) $17.99

Grades: PreK K 1   E

    1. Wit and humor 2. Dogs -- Fiction 3. Vacations -- Fiction 4. Humorous stories 5. Stories without words 6. Luggage -- Packing -- Fiction

ISBN 1619631903; 9781619631908; 9781619631915

LC 2013036177

In this children's book, by Domenica More Gordon, "Archie is taking some much needed some time off. As he prepares for his vacation at the beach, he packs the usual things. But at night he dreams of rain, of snorkeling, and of other fun adventures, convincing him that he'll need to pack everything–just in case! But will his suitcase fit it all?" (Publisher's note)

"In this follow-up to Archie, the dashing canine fashionisto prepares for his coming vacation. But travel anxiety plagues him, causing him to pack for best- and worst-case scenarios until his overflowing suitcase bursts open in a four-page foldout spread. Gordon's loose watercolor illustrations and hand-lettered text capture the excitement and apprehension one often feels before a big trip." Horn Book

Gordon, Gus

    ★ **Herman** and Rosie; by Gus Gordon. Roaring Brook Press 2013 32 p. (hardcover : alk. paper) $17.99

Grades: K 1 2 3   E

    1. Friendship -- Fiction 2. Jazz music -- Fiction 3. Animals -- Fiction 4. Deer -- Fiction 5. Crocodiles -- Fiction 6. Loneliness -- Fiction 7. New York (N.Y.) -- Fiction

ISBN 1596438568; 9781596438569

LC 2012037557

In author Gus Gordon's book, "once upon a time in a very busy city, on a very busy street, in two very small apartments, lived...Herman and Rosie. Herman liked playing the oboe, the smell of hot dogs in the winter, and watching films about the ocean. Rosie liked pancakes, listening to old jazz records, and watching films about the ocean. They both loved the groovy rhythm of the city, but sometimes the bustling crowds and constant motion left them lonely, until one night" something happens. (Publisher's note)

"In New York City, neighbors Herman (a crocodile) and Rosie (a deer) work boring day jobs but express their true talents at night as a musician and singer. Their disenchantment and the series of romantic comedy style near-misses that stall their meeting will charm adults more than kids. Mixed-media illustrations combine city maps and postcards with quirky drawings of the menagerie of city dwellers." (Horn Book)

Gore, Leonid

    Danny's first snow; by Leonid Gore. Atheneum 2007 un il $16.99

Grades: PreK K   E

    1. Snow -- Fiction 2. Rabbits -- Fiction 3. Imagination -- Fiction

ISBN 1-4169-1330-0

When he ventures outside to experience his first snowfall, a young rabbit discovers that his world has greatly changed.

"The exquisite illustrations in this story . . . will delight young readers. . . . Gore achieves remarkable shapes and surfaces, with green pines transformed into bears that gradually melt away as the day advances." Publ Wkly

Mommy, where are you? [by] Leonid Gore. Atheneum Books for Young Readers 2009 un il $16.99

Grades: PreK K 1   E

    1. Mice -- Fiction 2. Mother-child relationship -- Fiction

ISBN 978-1-4169-5505-4; 1-4169-5505-4

LC 2008-25994

A little mouse wakes up one day and, when he cannot find his mother, goes in search of her.

"Gore skillfully provides both repetition and variety for his audience, so both young listeners and their adults will find the story engaging as well as easy to follow. . . . Acrylic illustrations are simply composed, and the layered colors . . . and textured application of the paint . . . add pleasing depth and sophistication to the images." Bull Cent Child Books

When I grow up. Scholastic Press 2009 un il $16.99

Grades: PreK   E

    1. Growth -- Fiction 2. Father-son relationship -- Fiction

ISBN 978-0-545-08597-7; 0-545-08597-7

LC 2008014313

At his drawing table on a rainy day, a boy imagines all the ways in which different things might grow up, and comes to the conclusion that he will grow up to be just like his dad.

"The simple and poetic artwork was done in acrylic and mixed media on die-cut pages. . . . The exploration of his world gives this father-and-son selection a refreshing take on a familiar theme." SLJ

The wonderful book. Scholastic Press 2010 un il

Grades: PreK K 1   E

    1. Forest animals -- Fiction 2. Books and reading -- Fiction

ISBN 0-545-08598-5; 978-0-545-08598-4

LC 2009026348

When various forest animals discover a mysterious object in the woods, they each use it for a different purpose, until a boy reads stories from it, much to the animals' delight. "Ages three to five." (Bull Cent Child Books)

"Unpretentious watercolor-and-ink illustrations on textured paper suit well, because both text and pictures have a light, unfussy vibe—even while puns lurk unstated, such as the fox treating sheets of paper as bedsheets. Children just beginning to recognize books as objects will appreciate the animals' confusion and their own advanced understanding." Kirkus

Worms for lunch? Scholastic Press 2011 un il $16.99

Grades: PreK K   E

    1. Food -- Fiction 2. Animals -- Fiction 3. Animals -- Food

ISBN 0-545-24338-6; 978-0-545-24338-4

LC 2010004023

In this picture book, readers "follow a curious worm through die-cut pages to discover what different animals like to eat for lunch. 'Who on earth would eat worms for lunch?' the curious little leaf-loving worm wants to know... Not the mouse who likes cheese. Not the little girl, who loves spaghetti and ice cream! Not the cow, nor the bee, nor the monkey... But when a fish reveals what he most desires for lunch, . . . our little worm goes quickly on his way." (Publisher's note) "Preschool." (Horn Book)

"In this entertaining primer about what animals like to eat, Gore's bright acrylic paintings are reminiscent of the artwork of Carle and Lionni in their simplicity, textures, and whimsical humor. . . . The clever and effective die-cuts will easily keep readers' interest." Publ Wkly

Gormley, Greg

    ★ **Dog** in boots; illustrated by Roberta Angaramo. Holiday House 2011 un il $17.95

Grades: PreK K 1

E

1. Dogs -- Fiction 2. Shoes -- Fiction

ISBN 978-0-8234-2347-7; 0-8234-2347-6

LC 2010029889

After reading "Puss in Boots," an adventurous dog sets out to find the perfect pair of shoes to suit his every need.

"Children will identify with Dog's good-natured struggle through trial and error, fall in love with the evocative and funny illustrations and laugh out loud at the satisfying ending. A truly enjoyable selection and a nice follow-up to a favorite fairy tale, just right for reading aloud." Kirkus

Gourley, Robbin

★ **Bring** me some apples and I'll make you a pie; a story about Edna Lewis. Clarion Books 2009 45p il $16

Grades: PreK K 1 2

E

1. Cooks 2. Food -- Fiction 3. Cookbook writers 4. Cooking -- Fiction 5. Virginia -- Fiction 6. Farm life -- Fiction 7. Family life -- Fiction 8. African Americans -- Fiction

ISBN 978-0-618-15836-2; 0-618-15836-7

LC 2007-46978

Edna and members of her family gather fruits, berries, and vegetables from the fields, garden, and orchard on their Virginia farm and turn them into wonderful meals. Includes facts about the life of Edna Lewis, a descendant of slaves who grew up to be a famous chef, and five recipes.

"The cheery watercolor spreads follow Edna and various relatives . . . from spring to first snow. . . . Folk sayings or songs accompany mention of each new food. . . . Dynamic paintings, increasingly lush as summer intensifies, add vigor." Publ Wkly

Gow, Nancy

Ten big toes and a prince's nose; illustrated by Stephen Costanza. Sterling Pub. 2010 un il $14.95

Grades: PreK K 1 2

E

1. Stories in rhyme 2. Princes -- Fiction 3. Princesses -- Fiction

ISBN 978-1-4027-6396-0; 1-4027-6396-4

LC 2008031835

A lovely princess with enormous feet and a charming prince with a huge nose meet on a ski lift and, while their flaws are hidden, fall in love.

"Told in chatty rhyme, . . . this cleverly plotted tale conveys its message . . . with aplomb. The saturated colors and folk-like feel of the artwork are just right for this jaunty tale." Kirkus

Gower, Catherine

Long-Long's New Year; a story about the Chinese spring festival. illustrated by He Zhihong. Tuttle 2005 un il $16.95

Grades: K 1 2 3

E

1. China -- Fiction 2. Grandfathers -- Fiction 3. Chinese New Year -- Fiction

ISBN 0-8048-3666-3

LC 2004-111580

"Gower's simple, appealing story aptly captures the details of the festival as well as specifics of Chinese life. Zhihong's softly colored, detailed drawings on tan rice paper evoke both the bustle of a preholiday marketplace as well as the gentle warmth shared by grandfather and grandchild." SLJ

Graber, Janet

Muktar and the camels. Henry Holt and Co. 2009 un il $16.99

Grades: K 1 2 3

E

1. School stories 2. Kenya -- Fiction 3. Camels -- Fiction 4.

Orphans -- Fiction 5. Refugees -- Fiction

ISBN 978-0-8050-7834-3; 0-8050-7834-7

LC 2008038217

Muktar, an eleven-year-old refugee living in a Kenyan orphanage, dreams of tending camels again, as he did with his nomadic family in Somalia, and has a chance to prove himself when a traveling librarian with an injured camel arrives at his school.

"Muktar longs to live the life that is in his blood, and Graber tells his story well. . . . Mack's oil-on-canvas paintings evoke the sun and dust of Kenya, giving readers an impression of the landscape." SLJ

Graegin, Stephanie

Little fox in the forest; by Stephanie Graegin. Schwartz & Wade Books 2017 40 p. color illustrations (hardback) $17.99

Grades: PreK K 1 2

E

1. Stories without words 2. Foxes -- Fiction 3. Magic -- Fiction

ISBN 9780553537895; 9780553537901

LC 2016006970

In this children's book, by Stephanie Graegin, "when a young girl brings her beloved stuffed fox to the playground, . . . a real fox takes off with it! The girl chases the fox into the woods with her friend, . . . but soon the two children lose track of the fox. Wandering deeper and deeper into the forest, they come across a . . .marvelous village of miniature stone cottages, tiny treehouses, and, most extraordinary of all, woodland creatures of every shape and size." (Publisher's note)

"Young children will pore over this wordless picture book again and again, finding something new to enjoy each time. A wordless picture book that makes a great read." Kirkus

Graff, Lisa

It is not time for sleeping; (a bedtime story) Lisa Graff; illustrated by Lauren Castillo. Clarion Books, Houghton Mifflin Harcourt 2016 40 p. color illustrations (ebook) $16.99; (hardcover) $16.99

Grades: PreK K

E

1. Bedtime -- Fiction 2. Parent-child relationship -- Fiction 3. Parent and child -- Fiction

ISBN 9780544319332; 9780544319301

LC 2015020441

In this book, by Lisa Graff, illustrated by Lauren Castillo, "bedtime draws near. But the little boy in this book is quite sure it is NOT time for sleeping. As each piece of his evening routine is completed--helping with the dishes, playing with the dog, getting into pajamas, brushing teeth with Dad, being tucked in by Mom, and listening to a story--he becomes a little more certain: it is definitely not time for sleeping. The question is, when WILL it be time for sleeping?" (Publisher's note)

"The pictures look downright magical at book's end when luminous wallpaper—a rich blue with golden stars and crescent moons—fills up the background of cozy closing images, creating interior starry splendor. A very good goodnight book." Kirkus

Graham, Bob

★ **April** and Esme, tooth fairies. Candlewick Press 2010 un il $16.99

Grades: PreK K 1 2

E

1. Teeth -- Fiction 2. Fairies -- Fiction 3. Sisters -- Fiction

ISBN 978-0-7636-4683-7; 0-7636-4683-0

On their first assignment, two young tooth fairy sisters journey by night into the huge world of humans to collect Daniel Dangerfield's tooth and fly it safely home.

"Young audiences will linger over the detailed illustrations that bring to life Graham's gentle tale." Horn Book

A **bus** called Heaven; written and illustrated by Bob Graham. Candlewick Press 2012 40p. ill. $16.99

Grades: PreK K 1   E

1. Friendship 2. Neighborhood 3. Buses -- Fiction
ISBN 978-0-7636-5893-9

LC 2011278839

This book tells the story of "[a] city neighborhood" which "takes shape around an abandoned school bus." (Kirkus) The bus "becomes a hub of activity. People come together to hold meetings, play games and share stories. . . . But one day a tow truck arrives and threatens to take away not just the bus, but everything everyone has worked so hard to create. . . . This is . . . [a] story about friendship, the strength of a community and a little girl who . . . comes into her own." (Publisher's note)

Dimity Dumpty; the story of Humpty's little sister. Candlewick Press 2006 un il $15.99

Grades: PreK K 1 2   E

1. Eggs -- Fiction 2. Circus -- Fiction 3. Siblings -- Fiction 4. Nursery rhymes -- Fiction
ISBN 0-7636-3078-0

LC 2005-55306

Humpty Dumpty's little sister is too shy to be part of her family's circus act, but she finds courage when her brother needs her help.

"The full-color watercolor illustrations are a delight. . . . The language is lyrical . . . and makes a perfect read-aloud." SLJ

How the sun got to Coco's house; Bob Graham. Candlewick Press 2015 40 p. color illustrations $17.99

Grades: PreK K 1   E

1. Sun -- Fiction
ISBN 0763681091; 9780763681098

LC 2014955416

In this children's story, by Bob Graham, "while Coco sleeps far away, the sun creeps over a hill and skids across the water, touching a fisherman's cap. It heads out over frozen forests, making shadows in a child's footprints, and balances on an airplane's wing for a little boy to see. The sun crosses cities and countrysides, wakes furry creatures, makes a desert rainbow, and barges into Coco's room to follow her through a day of play." (Publisher's note)

"It's great to be able to count on something; readers can count on both the sun and Graham." Kirkus

★ **How** to heal a broken wing. Candlewick Press 2008 un il $16.99

Grades: PreK K 1 2   E

1. Birds -- Fiction 2. Rescue work -- Fiction
ISBN 978-0-7636-3903-7; 0-7636-3903-6

LC 2007-40622

When Will finds a bird with a broken wing, he takes it home and cares for it, hoping in time it will be able to return to the sky.

This is a "sparsely worded story. . . . Graham breaks his watercolor-and-ink cartoons into full-bleed spreads and large and small comics-like panels, enabling him to dwell on each moment of tender loving care and to preach patience." Publ Wkly

Let's get a pup, said Kate. Candlewick Press 2001 un il hardcover o.p. pa $6.99

Grades: PreK K 1 2   E

1. Dogs -- Fiction 2. Animal shelters -- Fiction
ISBN 0-7636-1452-1; 0-7636-2193-5 pa

LC 00-57208

Boston Globe-Horn Book Award: Picture Book (2002)

When Kate and her parents visit the animal shelter, an adorable puppy charms them, but it is very hard to leave an older dog behind

"Bob Graham's cozy watercolors, lightly held in place by loose, sketchy outlines, contribute to this story's feelings of warmth, family, and belonging." Horn Book

Another title about Kate and her dog is:

"The trouble with dogs," said Dad (2007)

★ **Oscar's** half birthday. Candlewick Press 2005 un il $16.99

Grades: PreK K 1 2   E

1. Birthdays -- Fiction 2. Family life -- Fiction 3. Racially mixed people -- Fiction
ISBN 0-7636-2699-6

LC 2004-57041

"A mixed-race family sets out for a picnic in the park to celebrate baby Oscar's half birthday. . . . The warm, expressive illustrations show a family apartment in which a mop, shoes, and toys all share floor space. . . . This is an effortlessly multicultural story, full of the joy of childhood, family, and community." SLJ

★ The **silver** button; written and illustrated by Bob Graham. Candlewick Press 2013 32 p. $16.99

Grades: PreK K 1   E

1. Drawing -- Fiction 2. Walking -- Fiction 3. Everyday life
ISBN 0763664375; 9780763664374

LC 2012947825

In this book, by Bob Graham, "at the same moment that Jodie's baby brother takes his first step, a city's worth of moments unfold. From an ordinary scene of an apartment strewn with child's artwork and toys to a bird's-eye view of a city morning pulsing with life, Bob Graham celebrates a whole world-vision in a single moment, encouraging readers to stop, observe, and savor the world around them." (Publisher's note)

Vanilla ice cream; Bob Graham. Candlewick Press 2014 40 p. color illustrations (reinforced) $16.99

Grades: PreK K 1 2   E

1. Birds -- Fiction 2. Sparrows -- Fiction
ISBN 9780763673772; 0763673773

LC 2013952841

In this book, written and illustrated by Bob Graham, "following some food, a curious young sparrow stows away in the back of a truck and takes an unusual voyage south--through the lush rice paddies of India, across the rough sea, and all the way into a bright new day. As the sun rises high over the city, he finds little Edie at a café with her grandma and granddad, and for a fleeting instant, his world meets up with hers and changes her life in the most delightful way." (Publisher's note)

Graham's "signature theme, that of connection, remains vibrant and joyous, and we are treated again to his particular loving portraits of people of all shapes, sorts, and conditions." Horn Book

Gralley, Jean

The **moon** came down on Milk Street; written and illustrated by Jean Gralley. Holt 2004 un il $16.95

Grades: PreK K 1 2   E

1. Stories in rhyme 2. Moon -- Fiction 3. Rescue work -- Fiction
ISBN 0-8050-7266-7

When the moon comes down in pieces, different helpers work to set things right again, including the Fire Chief, rescue workers, and helper dogs.

"Gralley presents a perceptive look at how individuals react to an unexpected crisis. . . . Done in gouache and mixed media, the large, uncluttered illustrations on white backgrounds contribute to the gentle nature of the story." SLJ

Gramatky, Hardie

Little Toot; pictures and story by Hardie Gramatky. G.P. Putnam's Sons 2007 86p il $17.99

Grades: PreK K   E

1. Tugboats -- Fiction

ISBN 978-0-399-24713-2; 0-399-24713-0

First published 1939

Little Toot the tugboat conquers his fear of rough seas when he singlehandedly rescues an ocean liner during a storm

"Mr. Gramatky tells his story with humor and enjoyment, giving, too, a genuine sense of the water front in both pictures and story." Horn Book

Grambling, Lois G.

T. Rex and the Mother's Day hug; by Lois G. Grambling; illustrated by Jack E. Davis. HarperCollins 2008 un il $16.99; lib bdg $17.89

Grades: K 1 2   E

1. Dinosaurs -- Fiction 2. Mother's Day -- Fiction

ISBN 978-0-06-053126-3; 0-06-053126-6; 978-0-06-053127-0 lib bdg; 0-06-053127-4 lib bdg

LC 2007-6882

Eager to do something special for Mother's Day, T. Rex decides to surprise his mother by decorating her car.

"Davis's jaunty cartoon illustrations bring these less-than-extinct dinosaurs alive. This fun read-aloud will tickle young children as they prepare for Mother's Day themselves." SLJ

Other titles in this series are:

Here comes T. Rex Cottontail (2007)

T. Rex trick-or-treats (2005)

Grandits, John

★ **Ten** rules you absolutely must not break if you want to survive the school bus; illustrated by Michael Allen Austin. Clarion Books 2011 32p il $16.99

Grades: K 1 2   E

1. School stories 2. Buses -- Fiction 3. Brothers -- Fiction

ISBN 978-0-618-78822-4; 0-618-78822-0

Before Kyle rides a school bus for the first time, his older brother gives him a list of rules he must follow but after breaking every single one the first day, Kyle discovers the rule his brother left out.

"Austin's acrylic artwork is amazingly lifelike. He is at his best when he illustrates scenes from Kyle's vivid imagination, which has a tendency toward the metaphor. Kyle's every thought and feeling are manifest on the page. . . . Worthy of being shelved next to Jon Scieszka's funniest." Kirkus

The **travel** game; illustrated by R. W. Alley. Clarion Books 2009 32p il $16

Grades: K 1 2 3   E

1. Aunts -- Fiction 2. Games -- Fiction 3. Tailoring -- Fiction 4. Imagination -- Fiction 5. Buffalo (N.Y.) -- Fiction 6. Polish Americans -- Fiction 7. Hong Kong (China) -- Fiction

ISBN 978-0-618-56420-0; 0-618-56420-9

LC 2005017646

To avoid a nap, Tad plays his favorite quiet game with his aunt and together their imaginations take them from their home in Buffalo, New York, to Hong Kong.

"Alley's cheery and busy street, home, and shop scenes in ink, watercolor, and acrylic are filled with the sorts of details that are fully appreciated over multiple readings. Children will be charmed by the warmth and humor of Grandits's wonderful tribute to family memories and the power of imagination." SLJ

Grandpré, Mary, 1954-

Cleonardo, the little inventor; written and illustrated by Mary GrandPré. Arthur A. Levine Books, an imprint of Scholastic Inc. 2016 48 p. color illustrations (hardcover : alk. paper) $18.99

Grades: PreK K 1 2   E

1. Inventors -- Fiction 2. Inventions -- Fiction 3. Father-daughter relationship -- Fiction 4. Contests -- Fiction 5. Contests -- Fiction 6. Competition (Psychology) -- Fiction 7. Fathers and daughters -- Fiction

ISBN 9780439357647

LC 2015043457

In this book by Mary Grandpre, "Cleonardo's father is an inventor. So was her grandfather, her great-grandfather, and all the great-greats before them. Cleo wants to be an inventor too. She tries to help her father in his workshop, but he never uses her great ideas. Can Cleo invent something big and important and perfect all by herself? This imaginative story of a father and his daughter brings the magic of creativity to little inventors everywhere." (Publisher's note)

"Rooted in intelligence and love, GrandPré's story will enthrall, empower, and encourage creation." Booklist

The **sea** chest; illustrated by Mary GrandPré. Dial Bks. for Young Readers 2002 un il $16.99

Grades: K 1 2 3   E

1. Maine -- Fiction 2. Islands -- Fiction 3. Sisters -- Fiction 4. Lighthouses -- Fiction

ISBN 0-8037-2703-8

LC 2001-28255

A young girl listens as her great-aunt, a lighthouse keeper's daughter, tells of her childhood living on a Maine island, and of the infant that washed ashore after a storm

"GrandPré's oil paintings create the dramatic effects of the story. . . . This lovely book has an intimacy that is enhanced by reading it aloud." SLJ

Granstrom, Brita

Baby knows best; illustrated by Brita Granström. Little, Brown 2002 un il $15.95

Grades: PreK K 1 2   E

1. Stories in rhyme 2. Infants -- Fiction

ISBN 0-316-60580-8

LC 00-107325

First published 2001 in the United Kingdom

"The rhyming text is short and fun, and Granström's colorful watercolor illustrations get the point across." Booklist

Grant, Judyann

★ **Chicken** said, Cluck! by Judyann Ackerman Grant; pictures by Sue Truesdell. HarperCollins 2008 32p il (My first I can read book) $16.99; lib bdg $17.89

Grades: K 1 2   E

1. Chickens -- Fiction 2. Gardening -- Fiction 3. Grasshoppers -- Fiction

ISBN 978-0-06-028723-8; 0-06-028723-3; 978-0-06-028724-5 lib bdg; 0-06-028724-1 lib bdg

LC 2001-24016

A Geisel Award honor book, 2009

Earl and Pearl do not want Chicken's help in the garden, until a swarm of grasshoppers arrives and her true talent shines

"This easy reader has short sentences, a variety of verb tenses, and vowel and consonant blends and digraphs. . . . Emergent readers may chime in with their own 'Shoo, Shoos' and 'Cluck, Cluck.' The funny, expressive pen-and-ink drawings support the reading with simple clarity." SLJ

Grant, Karima

Sofie and the city; [by] Karima Grant; illustrated by Janet Monte-
calvo. Boyds Mills Press 2006 un il $15.95

Grades: PreK K 1 2   E

1. Friendship -- Fiction 2. Immigrants -- Fiction 3. African
Americans -- Fiction 4. City and town life -- Fiction

ISBN 1-59078-273-9

LC 2005020116

When Sofie calls her grandmother in Senegal on Sundays, she complains about the ugliness of the city she now lives in, but her life changes
when she makes a new friend

"Told in simple language, with dialogue matching that of a child
learning English, the text and art show how upsetting any move can be
and how it feels to be small in a large and unfamiliar place." SLJ

Graves, Keith

Chicken Big. Chronicle Books 2010 un il $16.99

Grades: PreK K 1 2   E

1. Size -- Fiction 2. Chickens -- Fiction

ISBN 978-0-8118-7237-9; 0-8118-7237-8

"Compared to panicky Chicken Little, Chicken Big is unflappable. .
. . This newborn towers over four fellow chickens, who decide he must
be an elephant. . . . When something drops on the smallest hen, she
yelps 'The sky is falling!' Chicken Big calmly says, 'It's only an acorn.
They're actually quite tasty.' He is equally placid and helpful when the
ditsy chickens freak out over the rain and wind. . . . Graves . . . renders
his fowl in a palette of gray-blue, taupe, and wheat yellow, with exuberant voice bubbles that highlight the ridiculousness of the smaller chickens' assertions." Publ Wkly

The **monsterator**; Keith Graves. Roaring Brook Press 2014 40 p.
color illustrations (hardcover) $17.99

Grades: K 1 2 3 4   E

1. Stories in rhyme 2. Monsters -- Fiction 3. Halloween -- Fiction
4. Toy and movable books

ISBN 159643855X; 9781596438552

LC 2013016728

In this Halloween-themed children's book, written by Keith Graves,
"join Master Edgar Dreadbury as he discovers the Monsterator, a machine that changes people into monsters." (Publisher's note)

"Underwhelmed by Halloween costume choices, Master Edgar
Dreadbury wants to be "something screamingly scary." The "monsterator" machine fulfills his wish, transforming him into a multicolored
creature with fur, horns, fangs, claws, and a tail. Graves's acrylics accentuate the contrast between Edgar's vibrant appearance and his dull
surroundings. A five-creature partitioned flipbook creatively extends the
humorous rhyming tale so readers can "monsterate" Edgar themselves."
Horn Book

Second banana; Keith Graves. Henry Holt & Co 2015 32 p. color
illustrations (hardback) $17.99

Grades: K 1 2 3   E

1. Humorous fiction 2. Circus -- Fiction 3. Monkeys -- Fiction 4.
Gorillas -- Fiction

ISBN 1596438835; 9781596438835

LC 2014009899

This children's book, written and illustrated by Keith Graves, is
"about Oop, a gorilla, who is second banana to The Amazing Mr. Bubbles, a monkey, until one day, Mr. Bubbles finds himself in trouble and
Oop has to save the day." (Publisher's note)

"Amazing Bubbles is the star of the circus. This monkey is dramatic.
He's stylish—he's Top Banana! His sidekick, a gorilla named Oop, is
Second Banana...This goofy story about the friendship between a mon-
key and a gorilla (and a mouse) is a delight." SLJ

Gravett, Emily

Again! Emily Gravett. Simon & Schuster Books for Young Readers
2013 32 p. (hardcover : alk. paper) $17.99

Grades: PreK K 1   E

1. Dragons -- Fiction 2. Storytelling -- Fiction 3. Bedtime --
Fiction 4. Books and reading -- Fiction

ISBN 1442452315; 9781442452312

LC 2012003322

In this book, by Emily Gravett, "it's nearly Cedric the dragon's bedtime, and for Cedric, bedtime means storytime! When his mother reads
him his favorite book, he likes the story so much that he wants to hear it
again. Cedric's mom understands that the best stories are ripe for repetition, and she tries very hard to be patient. But sometimes dragons will be
dragons." (Publisher's note)

"Readers get the feeling that things are not what they appear when
a dragon, clutching a book, winks at them. The creature snuggles in to
hear its bedtime story--a tale of a dragon who has "never, / His whole
life, / (Not once) been to bed." With surprising die-cuts and satisfying
metafictive elements, Gravett takes that I-don't-want-to-go-to-sleep
trope to a new level." (Horn Book)

Bear & Hare -- share! Emily Gravett. Simon & Schuster Books
for Young Readers 2016 32 p. color illustrations (hardback) $16.99

Grades: PreK K   E

1. Bears -- Fiction 2. Rabbits -- Fiction 3. Friendship -- Fiction 4.
Hares -- Fiction 5. Stories in rhyme 6. Sharing -- Fiction

ISBN 1481462172; 9781481462174

LC 2015027727

In this children's story, by Emily Gravett, "friends Bear and Hare go
for a walk to look for things to do. But Hare is finding it hard to share
anything they come across. Will Hare ever learn that playing together is
more fun than yelling 'Mine!'?" (Publisher's Note)

"With short sentences, simple vocabulary, and word repetition, this
dryly comic story will appeal to both beginning independent readers as
well as kids in a group story time." Booklist

Blue chameleon. Simon & Schuster Books for Young Readers
2011 un il $16.99

Grades: PreK K 1   E

1. Chameleons -- Fiction 2. Friendship -- Fiction

ISBN 1-4424-1958-X; 978-1-4424-1958-2

Chameleon can turn himself into anything and appear to fit in anywhere, but it seems that neither the swirly snail, the green grasshopper
nor the striped sock want to be friends. Will he ever find someone to talk
to? Someone just like him?

"Gravett's art charms; colored pencil lines on rough paper give the
pages warmth, and the chameleon's 'disguises' repay attention as readers spot similarities to and differences from the things the chameleon
mimics." Publ Wkly

Little Mouse's big book of fears. Simon & Schuster Books for
Young Readers 2008 un il $17.99

Grades: K 1 2 3   E

1. Fear -- Fiction 2. Mice -- Fiction

ISBN 978-1-4169-5930-4; 1-4169-5930-0

LC 2008-61104

First published 2007 in the United Kingdom with title: Emily Gravett's big book of fears

Little Mouse draws pictures of some of the many things he is afraid
of, including creepy crawlies, sharp knives, and having accidents, and
provides the correct scientific name for each of his fears

"Spare text and delightful illustrations chronicle this nervous rodent's journey. . . . The striking mixed-media art captures the humorous
adventures of the white mouse and his red pencil." SLJ

Another title in this series is:
Little Mouse's big book of beasts (2016)

Matilda's cat; Emily Gravett. Simon & Schuster Books for Young Readers 2013 32 p. ill. (hardcover) $16.99
Grades: PreK K 1   E
   1. Cats -- Fiction 2. Pets -- Fiction
ISBN 1442475277; 9781442475274
                  LC 2012049731

In this book, by Emily Gravett, "Matilda is desperate to figure out what her cat will enjoy. She tries everything she can think of: climbing trees, playing with wool, even tea parties and dress-up games, but as Matilda gets more and more creative in her entertainment attempts, her cat moves from unimpressed to terrified. Will Matilda ever figure out what her cat likes?" (Publisher's note)

"A master of animal countenance, Gravett pairs an expressive cat with a busy kid and winks at the difference between textual and visual message. Matilda likes many things, including riding bikes, climbing trees, funky hats and fighting foes. Each spread shows Matilda playing at one thing while the text claims that her orange tabby enjoys it. "Matilda's cat likes playing with wool," it begins, as rosy-cheeked Matilda romps inside a huge, multicolored wool tangle and launches a ball of yarn toward the cat. . . . On the next page, the words "playing with wool" are neatly crossed out and replaced by the word "boxes." . . . Matilda sports a head-to-toe tabby suit, linking cat and girl all along; the shrewd and skillful art implies sly underlying affection even when the cat's nonplussed, worried or asleep." Kirkus.

Meerkat mail. Simon & Schuster Books for Young Readers 2007 un il $17.99
Grades: PreK K 1   E
   1. Africa -- Fiction 2. Meerkats -- Fiction
ISBN 978-1-4169-3473-8; 1-4169-3473-1
                  LC 2007001569

Through a series of flip-up postcards addressed to his family, Sunny Meerkat documents his travels as he searches for the perfect place for him to live.

"Gravett neatly incorporates facts about meerkats, mongooses, and their habitats. She employs a spare narrative, allowing Sunny's postcards to tell most of the story through both the character's distinctive voice and each post card's illustrations." Horn Book

★ **Monkey** and me. Simon & Schuster 2008 un il $15.99
Grades: PreK K   E
   1. Toys -- Fiction 2. Animals -- Fiction 3. Imagination -- Fiction
ISBN 978-1-4169-5457-6; 1-4169-5457-0

"A little girl pretends that she and her adored stuffed monkey fit right in with tribes of penguins, kangaroos, bats, elephants and . . . monkeys. A catchy refrain sets up each scenario. . . . Working in pencil and watercolor, with a palette limited to red, black and brown, Gravett . . . portrays the action in a series of exuberant spot sketches set against a white sweep." Publ Wkly

★ The **odd** egg. Simon & Schuster Books for Young Readers 2009 un il $15.99
Grades: PreK K 1   E
   1. Eggs -- Fiction 2. Birds -- Fiction 3. Ducks -- Fiction 4. Alligators -- Fiction
ISBN 978-1-4169-6872-6; 1-4169-6872-5
                  LC 2008-61108
Duck is trying to hatch the oddest egg of all.

"Using visual suspense and few words, Gravett depicts an alligator bursting from the shell, snapping its jaws and scattering the naysayers. . . . A witty salute to both nature and nurture." Publ Wkly

★ **Orange** pear apple bear. Simon & Schuster Books for Young Readers 2007 un il $12.99
Grades: PreK K   E
   1. Bears -- Fiction 2. Color -- Fiction 3. Shape -- Fiction
ISBN 978-1-4169-3999-3; 1-4169-3999-7
                  LC 2006-17964

A "bear changes color and shape as he balances, juggles, and eventually eats the three pieces of fruit before loping off. The front endpapers show oranges, green pears, and green apples with rosy tinges in a line leading readers into the simple and appealing story. . . . Beautiful, softly hued watercolor illustrations loosely outlined in black pen and ink are delightful." SLJ

★ The **rabbit** problem. Simon & Schuster Books for Young Readers 2010 un il $17.99
Grades: K 1 2   E
   1. Counting 2. Months -- Fiction 3. Rabbits -- Fiction 4. Seasons -- Fiction 5. Family life -- Fiction
ISBN 978-1-4424-1255-2; 1-4424-1255-0
                  LC 2010009751

In Fibonacci's Field, Lonely and Chalk Rabbit meet, snuggle together, and then spend a year trying to cope with their ever-increasing brood and the seasonal changes that bring a new challenge each month. Presented in calendar format with one pop-up illustration and other special features.

"Whimsical ideas proliferate as fast as rabbits in Gravett's splendid sendup of Fibonacci's query. . . . The only drawback to Graver's delicious creation is that the moving parts and magnificent final pop-ups are likely to fall prey to small hands. Solution: purchase a duplicate." Publ Wkly

★ **Spells**. Simon & Schuster Books for Young Readers 2009 un il $16.99
Grades: K 1 2 3 4   E
   1. Frogs -- Fiction 2. Magic -- Fiction
ISBN 978-1-4169-8270-8; 1-4169-8270-1
                  LC 2008-941243

"A small green frog stumbles on a book of spells, . . . tries to turn himself into a handsome prince, but suffers a series of glitches. Frog transforms himself into a snake, bird, rabbit and other creatures before getting it right. . . . The five pages that show Frog's new forms are cut in half horizontally, and children will delight in turning the half-pages, reading the new spells that appear on the left side of each spread and seeing the combined creatures that emerge (a half-prince, half-newt "prewt," for instance)." Publ Wkly

Tidy; Emily Gravett. Simon & Schuster Books for Young Readers 2017 40 p. color illustrations (ebook) $15.99; (hardcover) $17.99
Grades: PreK K 1 2   E
   1. Badgers -- Fiction 2. Cleanliness -- Fiction 3. Orderliness -- Fiction 4. Badgers -- Fiction 5. Cleanliness -- Fiction 6. Orderliness -- Fiction
ISBN 9781481480208; 9781481480192
                  LC 2016000239

In this children's story written and illustrated by Emily Gravett, "Pete the badger likes everything to be neat and tidy at all times, but what starts as the collecting of one fallen leaf escalates quickly and ends with the complete destruction of the forest. Will Pete realize the error of his ways and reverse his tidying habit?" (Publisher's note)

"With a humorous narrative and charming artwork—plus a playful message of moderation and the value of environmental conservation—this is an all-around delight." Booklist

Wolf won't bite! Emily Gravett. Simon & Schuster Books for Young Readers 2012 32 p.
Grades: PreK K   E
1. Pigs -- Fiction 2. Circus -- Fiction 3. Picture books for children 4. Wolves -- Fiction
ISBN 1442427639; 9781442427631
LC 2011000773

In this illustrated children's book by Emily Gravett, "three pigs have captured a wild wolf, and now he's the star of their little circus production as the ringmaster gloatingly presents his patient submission: 'I can stand him on a stool! I can dress him in a bow. . . I can ride him like a horse but WOLF WON'T BITE!' When the trio attempts to place their heads 'between his mighty jaws,' however, they have tried the wolf 's patience too far (. . . not to a fatal degree, as the endpapers show the wolf pursuing the three with a bit of the ringmaster pig's jacket in his mouth)." (Bulletin of the Center for Children's Books)

Wolves; [by] Emily Grrrabbett [i.e. Gravett] Simon & Schuster Books for Young Readers 2006 un il $15.95
Grades: 1 2 3   E
1. Wolves -- Fiction 2. Rabbits -- Fiction 3. Books and reading -- Fiction
ISBN 978-1-4169-1491-4; 1-4169-1491-9
LC 2005027540

Boston Globe-Horn Book Honor: Picture Book (2007)
When a young rabbit checks out a library book about wolves, he learns much more about their behavior than he wanted to know
"This imaginative, cleverly designed story unfolds in a delectable blend of spare text and eloquent multimedia illustrations." SLJ

Gray, Kes

Frog on a log? Kes Gray and Jim Field. Scholastic Press 2015 32 p. 32 plates; color illustrations (hbk.) $16.99
Grades: PreK K 1 2   E
1. Stories in rhyme 2. Frogs -- Fiction 3. Cats -- Fiction 4. Animals -- Fiction
ISBN 9780545687911; 0545687918
LC 2014043290

In this children's story, by Kes Gray and Jim Field, a "frog does not want to sit on a log. Doing his best to find an alternative place to sit, the frog asks the cat a litany of questions. For every answer the cat has, the frog has another question--until the frog finds out what dogs sit on!" (Publisher's note)
"The eyes of each animal reflect its emotions, including confusion (seal), annoyance (gorilla), and obliviousness (mole). And their awkward poses are hilarious, particularly mule perched precariously on a stool. The clever and skillful artwork is highlighted by the pure, bright background colors, making this an eye-catcher for groups. Expect lots of laughter—especially at the twisty ending—and some creative additions." Booklist
Another title in this series is:
Dog on a frog? (2017)

Gray, Libba Moore

★ **My** mama had a dancing heart; illustrated by Raúl Colón. Orchard Bks. 1995 un il hardcover o.p. pa $6.99
Grades: K 1 2 3   E
1. Dance -- Fiction 2. Seasons -- Fiction 3. Mother-daughter

relationship -- Fiction
ISBN 0-531-09470-7; 0-531-08770-0 lib bdg; 0-531-07142-1 pa
LC 94-48802

"In spring, summer, fall and winter, a mother leads her young daughter in dancing a celebratory ballet, a hymn to the season. When the girl is older, she is a ballerina and remembers that her mother gave her a dancing heart. . . . Colón's etched watercolors in earth and muted jewel tones give the book an old-fashioned ambiance. . . . Gray's writing lends itself to reading aloud, but independent readers will also enjoy it." SLJ

Gray, Luli

★ **Ant** and Grasshopper; written by Luli Gray; illustrated by Giuliano Ferri. Margaret K. McElderry Books 2011 un il $16.99
Grades: K 1 2   E
1. Ants -- Fiction 2. Grasshoppers -- Fiction
ISBN 1-4169-5140-7; 978-1-4169-5140-7

"Industrious Ant and pesty, music-loving Grasshopper move beyond Aesop's pointed lesson on negligence to a quite different moral as Gray further develops their relationship in this engaging, extended story. . . . Ferri expands the fun in fulsome watercolor scenes of Ant's glowing home and the changing seasons beyond his door and windows. The sturdy comic insects . . . have expressive eyes and body language. . . . The old tale has a new implied moral about empathy and friendship as the two unlikely fellows learn to care for each other. . . . The humorous, fluent telling and pictures would pair well with terse Aesop versions and stand on their own, offering especially nice read-aloud fare." SLJ

Gray, Rita

Have you heard the nesting bird? by Rita Gray; illustrated by Kenard Pak. Houghton Mifflin Books for Children 2014 32 p. color illustrations $16.99
Grades: PreK K 1 2   E
1. Birds -- Behavior 2. Birdsongs 3. Birds -- Nests
ISBN 054410580X; 9780544105805
LC 2013017621

This children's book, written by poet Rita Dove and illustrated by Kenard Pak, features "all the different bird calls in counterpoint to the pervasive quiet of a mama bird waiting for her eggs to hatch. Fun and informative back matter takes the shape of an interview so that readers learn more right from the bird's bill." (Publisher's note)
"It's a fine first book about watching living beings in the wild, and it also serves as a beginning birders' guide, identifying the features and cries of common backyard birds." Pub Wkly

Green, Alison

The fox in the dark; illustrated by Deborah Allwright. Tiger Tales 2010 un il $15.95
Grades: PreK K 1   E
1. Fear -- Fiction 2. Foxes -- Fiction 3. Animals -- Fiction
ISBN 978-1-58925-091-8; 1-58925-091-5

Rabbit, Duck, Mouse and Lamb squish into Rabbit's house to hide from Fox.
"Allwright's warm and comforting mixed-media illustrations are full of soft lines and earth tones, which balance the threat felt by the animals and make Rabbit's home a safe haven. Young children will squeal every time they hear the knock at the door, but will be relieved by the gentle ending." SLJ

Green, Dan

Wild alphabet; an A to zoo pop-up book. [by] Dan Green, [illustrated by] Mike Haines and Julia Frohlich. Kingfisher 2010 un il $19.99
Grades: PreK K 1 2   E
1. Animals 2. Alphabet 3. Pop-up books
ISBN 978-0-7534-6472-4; 0-7534-6472-1

"On each spare, uncluttered spread, a short poem, a small color photo, and a creative paper construction introduce a different animal for each letter of the alphabet. . . . The letters are clearly presented, opening this to a broad audience of both new ABC learners and elementary students, who will appreciate the whimsical, action-filled verse and artistry in the images." Booklist

Greenberg, David

Crocs! by David T. Greenberg; illustrated by Lynn Munsinger. Little, Brown 2008 un il $16.99

Grades: K 1 2 3   E

1. Stories in rhyme 2. Crocodiles -- Fiction

ISBN 978-0-316-07306-6; 0-316-07306-7

LC 2006020571

Having moved from the city to a tropical island to escape such horrifying creatures as bugs and cats, a boy encounters a horde of friendly crocodiles, who drink Tabasco sauce, get tangled in dental floss, and turn the house into a swamp

"The zany illustrations—done in mixed-media, soft-palette watercolors with pen and ink—use plenty of white space and add humor and charm to the perfect-pitch verses." SLJ

Enchanted lions; by David T. Greenberg; illustrated by Kristina Swarner. Dutton Children's Books 2009 un il $16.99

Grades: PreK K 1 2   E

1. Stories in rhyme 2. Constellations -- Fiction 3. Outer space -- Exploration -- Fiction

ISBN 978-0-525-47938-3; 0-525-47938-4

LC 2008-34215

One evening, Rose climbs on the back of an enchanted lion who takes her on a tour of outer space, where they race with Monoceros the unicorn, pass by Pegasus and Pisces, and are rescued from a black hole by Cetus the whale.

"The gentle, rhyming text and the mottled, softly colored scratchboardlike illustrations work together to convey a quiet, calm tone for this heavenly romp." Booklist

Greene, Stephanie

Princess Posey and the first grade boys; Stephanie Greene; illustrated by Stephanie Roth Sisson. G.P. Putnam's Sons, an imprint of Penguin Group (USA) 2014 84 p. illustrations (Princess Posey) (hardcover) $13.99

Grades: K 1 2   E

1. Bad behavior 2. School stories 3. Bullies -- Fiction 4. Schools -- Fiction 5. Teasing -- Fiction 6. Behavior -- Fiction

ISBN 0399163646; 9780399163647

LC 2013020941

In this book, by Stephanie Greene, "will Posey ever be able to get along with boys? Probably not. They barely ever sit still, they make lots of rude noises, and they are just plain annoying. But when Posey teases Henry for being a 'weirdo,' Miss Lee tells her that she's being a (gasp!) bully. Only by calling on the help of the Pink Princess can Posey step back and see that boys have feelings as well. And maybe, in the end, she can be friends with the boys too." (Publisher's note)

Part of the "Princess Posey" series.

Greenfield, Eloise

Africa dream; illustrated by Carole Byard. Crowell 1977 un il hardcover o.p. pa $6.99

Grades: PreK K 1 2   E

1. Africa -- Fiction

ISBN 0-690-04776-2 lib bdg; 0-06-443277-7 pa

LC 77-5080

Coretta Scott King Award for text

"As ethereal as the title implies, this sparsely worded prose-poem relates the benign dream experience of a young child who transports her mind to 'Long-ago Africa.'" Booklist

Grandpa's face; illustrated by Floyd Cooper. Philomel Bks. 1988 un il lib bdg $16.99; pa $6.99

Grades: PreK K 1 2   E

1. Actors -- Fiction 2. Grandfathers -- Fiction

ISBN 0-399-21525-5 lib bdg; 0-399-22106-9 pa

LC 87-16729

"Tamika fears that her grandfather, an actor, is incapable of loving her when she sees him practicing a cruel expression. The young girl's turmoil and its resolution are keenly felt through evocative text and striking pictures." SLJ

Gregorich, Barbara

Waltur paints himself into a corner and other stories; by Barbara Gregorich; illustrated by Kristin Sorra. Houghton Mifflin 2007 un il $15

Grades: K 1 2 3   E

1. Bears -- Fiction 2. Animals -- Fiction 3. Proverbs -- Fiction

ISBN 978-0-618-74796-2; 0-618-74796-6

LC 2006102370

Walter the bear learns more lessons from his friend Matilda, such as "do not put the cart before the horse" and "let sleeping dogs lie."

"Gregorich creates some deliciously sticky, comical situations. . . . Sorra's pen-and-ink and watercolor artwork is a lively mix of spread and panels." Booklist

Another title about Walter is:

Walter buys a pig in a poke and other stories (2006)

Gregory, Nan

Pink; [illustrated by] Luc Melanson. Groundwood 2007 32p il $17.95

Grades: PreK K 1 2   E

1. Dolls -- Fiction

ISBN 978-0-88899-781-4

Vivi loves the color pink. She is working and saving her money in order to buy a pink doll from the store. How does she feel when the doll is sold to someone else?

"Gregory writes with precision and creates apt, sometimes surprising phrases that capture the characters' feelings. Melanson's painterly, digitally assisted pictures create a distinctive look though the elongated forms and faces of the characters." Booklist

Gretz, Susanna

★ **Riley** and Rose in the picture. Candlewick Press 2005 un il $16.99

Grades: PreK K 1 2   E

1. Cats -- Fiction 2. Dogs -- Fiction 3. Friendship -- Fiction

ISBN 0-7636-2681-3

LC 2004-54569

On a rainy day Reilly the dog and Rosa the cat decide to stay indoors and draw a picture together but have trouble agreeing on how to do it

"The lively text is read-aloud friendly, incorporating child-familiar dialogue, interactions, and humor. The colorful gouache art is charming, too, filling the pages with expressive characters and distinctive childlike artwork that perfectly matches the story." Booklist

Gretzky, Glen

Great; Glen Gretzky (Author), Lauri Holomis (Author), Kevin Sylvester (Illustrator), Wayne Gretzky (Foreword) Penguin Random House Canada Childrens Group 2016 32 p. (hardcover) $16.99

Grades: PreK K 1 2   **E**
1. Hockey -- Fiction 2. Hockey players -- Fiction
ISBN 0670069906; 9780143194941; 9780143194958;
9780143194965; 9780670069903
LC 2016932994

In this children's book by Glen Gretzky and Lauri Holomis, illustrated by Kevin Sylvester and with a foreword by Wayne Gretzky, "Taylor is so excited when he makes the hockey team -- and not just any team, but HIS team. The boy they are already calling The Great One. Taylor wants to be great too, but he's still got a lot to learn. Lucky for him, Coach Wally is . . . guiding him through the ups and downs of being part of a hockey team, and being the best player he can be." (Publisher's note)

"While the message is one that kids on sports teams hear repeatedly, this fictional narrative delivers it in a more enjoyable way. An easy choice for libraries serving hockey players and fans." Booklist

Grey, Mini

★ The **adventures** of the dish and the spoon. Knopf 2006 un il $16.95; lib bdg $18.99
Grades: PreK K 1 2   **E**
1. Tableware -- Fiction 2. Nursery rhymes -- Fiction
ISBN 0-375-83691-8; 0-375-93691-2 lib bdg
LC 2005017548

Having run away together, the Dish and the Spoon from the nursery rhyme "The Cat and the Fiddle" become vaudeville stars before turning to a life of crime

"The narrative is packed with tongue-in-cheek humor. The rich art mingles paint with collage, featuring framed scenes and a palette of lush browns dotted with primary reds and blues." Bull Cent Child Books

Egg drop. Alfred A. Knopf 2009 un il $16.99; lib bdg $19.99
Grades: 1 2 3   **E**
1. Eggs -- Fiction 2. Flight -- Fiction
ISBN 978-0-375-84260-3; 0-375-84260-8; 978-0-375-94260-0 lib bdg; 0-375-94260-2 lib bdg
LC 2008-24534

Tragedy strikes when an egg, eager to fly like birds, airplanes, and insects, steps off of a tall tower.

"The mixed-media and collage full-color art is quirky and inventive with multiple perspectives, and imbues the Egg with personality." SLJ

★ **Hermelin** the detective mouse; by Mini Grey. Alfred A. Knopf 2014 32 p. (hardcover) $17.99
Grades: PreK K 1 2 3   **E**
1. Detectives -- Fiction 2. Mice -- Fiction 3. Neighborhoods -- Fiction 4. Lost and found possessions -- Fiction
ISBN 0385754337; 9780385754330; 9780385754347
LC 2013019508

In this children's book by Mini Grey, "Hermelin is a special little mouse. He was born in a box of cheese and lives in an attic at 33 Offley Street. He can read books and type notes on his typewriter. Most importantly, Hermelin can solve mysteries. And the people of Offley Street are in need of a detective!" (Publisher's note)

"This winning picture book opens with a scene of a tiny community of attached houses on Offley Street, where the residents and their pets are engaged in all sorts of activities simultaneously... Some children will enjoy the challenge of solving the mini-mysteries using clues found in the illustrations, while others will be content to follow the adventures of the amiable mouse as his tale unfolds. An absorbing picture book with a small but worthy hero." SLJ

★ **Three** by the sea. Alfred A. Knopf 2011 un il $17.99; lib bdg $20.99

Grades: K 1 2   **E**
1. Cats -- Fiction 2. Dogs -- Fiction 3. Mice -- Fiction 4. Foxes -- Fiction 5. Happiness -- Fiction 6. Friendship -- Fiction 7. Cooperation -- Fiction
ISBN 978-0-375-86784-2; 0-375-86784-8; 978-0-375-96784-9 lib bdg; 0-375-96784-2 lib bdg
LC 2010004084

First published 2010 in the United Kingdom

Cat, Dog, and Mouse live together contentedly in a cottage by the sea, dividing the work between them, until A. Stranger, Esq., a fox from the Winds of Change company, arrives and stirs up trouble.

This is "a beguiling little parable. . . . The artwork is standard-issue outstanding for Grey, with creative dollops of collage, endearing animal characters, and detail-strewn settings. . . . [The] complex resolution . . . refreshingly eschews any simple message." Booklist

Traction Man and the beach odyssey; Mini Grey. Alfred A. Knopf 2012 32 p.
Grades: PreK K 1 2   **E**
1. Toys -- Fiction 2. Dolls -- Fiction 3. Beaches -- Fiction 4. Brooms and brushes -- Fiction 5. Action figures (Toys) -- Fiction
ISBN 0375969527; 9780375869525; 9780375969522; 9780375983641
LC 2011020102

In this children's book by Mini Grey, "the action-figure star . . . Traction Man and his trusty sidekick, Scrubbing Brush, are brought to the beach by their boy owner. They explore an underwater world of crabs and cockles, defend their picnic lunch from a hungry dog, and get swept out to sea by a vigorous wave. They're rescued by a girl and squirreled away in a sand castle, where they meet two towering sirens called the Dollies." (Booklist)

★ **Traction** Man is here! Knopf 2005 un il $15.95; lib bdg $17.99
Grades: PreK K 1 2   **E**
1. Toys -- Fiction 2. Imagination -- Fiction 3. Superheroes -- Fiction
ISBN 0-375-83191-6; 0-375-93191-0 lib bdg
LC 2004-4452

Boston Globe-Horn Book Award: Picture Book (2005)

Traction Man, a boy's courageous action figure, has a variety of adventures with Scrubbing Brush and other objects in the house

And "imaginative and very funny romp. . . . The angular, full-color art sweeps across the pages and perfectly animates the antics of Traction Man and his enemies." SLJ

Followed by: Traction Man meets Turbodog (2008)

Gribnau, Joe

Kick the cowboy; illustrated by Adrian Tans. Pelican Pub. Co. 2009 un il $15.95
Grades: PreK K 1 2   **E**
1. Tall tales 2. Texas -- Fiction 3. Cowhands -- Fiction
ISBN 978-1-58980-605-4; 1-58980-605-0
LC 2009-3950

A cowboy named Kick becomes a mean braggart, driving away all of his friends and terrorizing the people of his Texas town, until a nononsense little girl named Belle helps him to mend his ways.

"Gribnau has a real winner here. . . . This above average story will be a real hit with both kids and storytellers. . . . Tans' illustrations are terrific, making the reader really want to see what happens next. This is a fantastic children's story. . . . Highly Recommended." Libr Media Connect

Grifalconi, Ann

★ **Ain't** nobody a stranger to me; illustrated by Jerry Pinkney. Hyperion/Jump at the Sun 2007 un il $16.99

Grades: K 1 2 3   E

1. Slavery -- Fiction 2. Grandfathers -- Fiction 3. African Americans -- Fiction 4. Underground railroad -- Fiction

ISBN 978-0-7868-1857-0

This story spotlights both the loving rapport between a girl and her grandfather, and the story of his family's escape to freedom.

"Pinkney's watercolor double-paged spreads contrast the sepia-toned gloom of slavery and hiding with the abundant light-filled apple orchard today. . . . Caught by the action, children will hear Finger's shining words across time, race, and generations." Booklist

★ The **village** that vanished; illustrated by Kadir Nelson. Dial Bks. for Young Readers 2002 un il $16.99

Grades: 1 2 3 4   E

1. Escapes -- Fiction 2. Slave trade -- Fiction 3. Southern Africa -- Fiction 4. Yao (African people) -- Fiction

ISBN 0-8037-2623-6

LC 00-38416

In southeastern Africa, a young Yao girl and her mother find a way for their fellow villagers to escape approaching slave traders

"This story celebrating resourcefulness, quick thinking, and community solidarity may inspire and empower readers. Nelson's pencil drawings enhanced with oil paints are wonderfully evocative of place, mood, posture, and expression." SLJ

Griffin, Kitty

The **ride**; the legend of Betsy Dowdy. illustrated by Marjorie Priceman. Atheneum Books for Young Readers 2010 un il $16.99

Grades: 1 2 3   E

1. United States -- History -- 1775-1783, Revolution -- Fiction

ISBN 978-1-4169-2816-4; 1-4169-2816-2

"The year is 1775, and teenage Betsy Dowdy secretly sets off on an all-night horseback journey to alert colonial militia to the British advance upon her North Carolina island home. . . . Swirls of deep royal and swaths of magenta evoke the eerie nighttime setting. . . . Griffin's . . . direct yet descriptive narrative recounts the calamities that befall Betsy, while the characters' cartoon styling lessens the tension. Priceman's . . . trademark freeflowing lines speed the story's momentum." Publ Wkly

Griffin, Molly Beth

Loon baby; illustrated by Anne Hunter. Houghton Mifflin Harcourt 2011 un il $16.99

Grades: PreK K 1 2   E

1. Loons -- Fiction 2. Animals -- Fiction

ISBN 978-0-547-25487-6; 0-547-25487-3

LC 2010006770

A baby loon, afraid that his mother will not return, sets out on his own to find his way across a stormy lake to their home in the great north woods.

This offers "simple text . . . [and] loosely rendered watercolors in blues, greens and grays textured with pen-and-ink cross hatch. . . . Guaranteed to hit the mark with anyone who's ever felt lost and alone." Kirkus

Griffith, Gretchen

When Christmas feels like home; Gretchen Griffith; illustrated by Carolina Farias. Albert Whitman & Company 2013 32 p. $16.99

Grades: PreK K 1 2 3   E

1. Moving -- Fiction 2. Christmas -- Fiction 3. Immigrants -- United States -- Fiction 4. Immigrants -- Fiction 5. North Carolina -- Fiction 6. Mexican Americans -- Fiction 7. Moving, Household

-- Fiction 8. Expectation (Psychology) -- Fiction

ISBN 0807588725; 9780807588727

LC 2013010899

In this book, by Gretchen Griffith, "a little boy named Eduardo moves from a village in an unnamed Latin American country to a town in the United States. . . . Eduardo moves to the U.S. in the fall, bringing along his fútbol (soccer ball) and his family's box of Christmas decorations. . . . He makes friends and participates in family celebrations at Halloween and Thanksgiving. On Christmas, Eduardo sets out the family's Nativity set and announces, 'This is home.'" (Kirkus Reviews)

"Eduardo moves from a village where the kids play futbol to Sleepy Tree Lane, where the kids play football, ride school buses, eat Thanksgiving turkey, and put up Christmas trees. Homesickness aside, Eduardo's immigration experience is conflict-free; but warmly colored, comfortably rounded illustrations ably capture the change of the seasons and the happy anticipation that the wait for Christmas can provide."

Griffith, Helen V.

Moonlight; by Helen V. Griffith; illustrations by Laura Dronzek. Greenwillow Books 2012 1 v. (unpaged) col. ill.

Grades: PreK K   E

1. Stories in rhyme 2. Dreams -- Fiction 3. Rabbits -- Fiction 4. Picture books for children 5. Moon -- Fiction

ISBN 9780062032850; 9780062032867

LC 2011002149

This children's picture book "tell[s] the . . . story of a rabbit who--too sleepy to wait for the moon to appear-hops into his safe, grass-lined burrow. He dreams of a sky full of veggies, strawberries, and tender flowers, until the moon's buttery light seeps into his burrow, 'spatters him with moondrops/shakes him out of bed--' and draws him out into the bright, flowery field to dance. What Rabbit does not see is the small gray mouse outside his burrow, a raccoon family watching from their hollow tree, and a deer and fawn asleep in the moonlit grass." (School Libr J)

Griffiths, Andy

★ The **big** fat cow that goes kapow; illustrated by Terry Denton. Feiwel & Friends 2009 123p $14.99

Grades: 2 3 4   E

1. Animals -- Fiction

ISBN 978-0-312-36788-6; 0-312-36788-0

First published 2008 in Australia

In these ten easy-to-read stories there is a mixed-up cow that says "miaow," a mole called Noel who plays rock 'n' roll in a hole, and a boy named Mike who rides a bike with a very big spike

"Broad slapstick humor and galloping, Seuss-like rhymes are just part of the reason this . . . has strong child appeal. Denton's funny illustrations are full of action, and his use of stick figures and stink lines makes the book look as though it had been illustrated by a cheeky but talented kid." SLJ

The **cat** on the mat is flat; [by] Andy Griffiths; illustrated by Terry Denton. Feiwel & Friends 2007 166p il pa $9.95

Grades: 2 3 4   E

1. Stories in rhyme 2. Animals -- Fiction

ISBN 978-0-312-36787-9

This "innovative book for beginning readers collects nine short, intentionally silly snippets propelled by kid-pleasing, tongue-tripping verse. In the title tale, a cat sitting on a mat decides to chase a rat, who grabs a baseball bat. . . . Other protagonists also encounter tongue-in-cheek adversity. . . . Denton's edgy, stick-figure-filled sketches enhance the zaniness factor and the offbeat, ironic humor." Publ Wkly

Grigsby, Susan

In the garden with Dr. Carver; illustrated by Nicole Tadgell. Albert Whitman 2010 un il $16.99

Grades: 2 3 4   E

1. Botanists 2. Alabama -- Fiction 3. Gardening -- Fiction 4. African Americans -- Fiction

ISBN 978-0-8075-3630-8; 0-8075-3630-X

Sally is a young girl living in rural Alabama in the early 1900s, a time when people were struggling to grow food in soil that had been depleted by years of cotton production. One day, Dr. George Washington Carver shows up to help the grownups with their farms and the children with their school garden.

"Concepts like composting and planting are well conveyed through Sally's descriptive, sometimes lyrical narrative. . . . The colorful watercolor illustrations, featuring soft touches and historical details, depict the rural setting and expressive characters." Booklist

Grimes, Nikki

Oh, brother! [by] Nikki Grimes; illustrations by Mike Benny. 1st ed.; Greenwillow Books 2008 un il $16.99; lib bdg $17.89

Grades: 2 3 4   E

1. Brothers -- Fiction 2. Remarriage -- Fiction 3. Stepfamilies -- Fiction 4. Hispanic Americans -- Fiction

ISBN 978-0-688-17294-7; 0-688-17294-6; 978-0-688-17295-4 lib bdg; 0-688-17295-4 lib bdg

LC 2005035645

Xavier is unhappy when his mother remarries and he suddenly has a new stepbrother, as well as a stepfather, in his home.

"Snappy language and varied rhyme schemes energize Grimes's . . . verses. . . . Benny . . . intersperses surreal illustrations with more realistic scenes. . . . The art and poems capture and memorably convey a range of emotions." Publ Wkly

Grindley, Sally

It's my school; [by] Sally Grindley; illustrations by Margaret Chamberlain. Walker & Company 2006 un il $15.95; lib bdg $16.85

Grades: PreK K 1 2   E

1. School stories 2. Siblings -- Fiction

ISBN 978-0-8027-8086-7; 0-8027-8086-5; 978-0-8027-8087-4 lib bdg; 0-8027-8087-3 lib bdg

LC 2005037181

Tom is not happy that his younger sister, Alice, is starting kindergarten at his school

"The large illustrations . . . are depicted in soft pastel hues, capturing the siblings' facial expressions and the varying degress of emotion. . . . This is a new take on first-day-of-school stories, and a realistic choice to help children share their lives with a younger sibling." SLJ

Groom, Juliet

Silent night; [illustrated by] Tim Warnes. Good Books 2010 un il $16.99

Grades: PreK K 1 2   E

1. Songs 2. Carols 3. Bears -- Fiction

ISBN 978-1-56148-697-7; 1-56148-697-3

LC 2010004919

"This new interpretation of the beloved Christmas carol focuses on an enchanting pair of bears, a parent and cub. The text retains the familiar beginning and then moves on to new words celebrating the beauty of the mountain setting at night under a full moon, as well as peace among the animals and love between parent and child. . . . Warnes masterfully illustrates the charismatic bears, with intimate views of parent and child in close harmony with nature." Kirkus

Guarino, Deborah

Is your mama a llama? illustrated by Steven Kellogg. Scholastic 1989 un il hardcover o.p. pa $6.99; bd bk $6.99

Grades: PreK K   E

1. Stories in rhyme 2. Llamas -- Fiction 3. Animals -- Fiction

ISBN 0-590-41387-2 lib bdg; 0-439-59842-7 pa; 0-590-25938-5 bd bk

LC 87-32315

A young llama asks his friends if their mamas are llamas and finds out, in rhyme, that their mothers are other types of animals

"The lines are clean as well as exuberant, the colors well-blended as well as bright, and the compositions uncluttered as well as appealing. An ingenious page design invites choral participation, and the ending will encourage a cozy hiatus for bed/nap time." Bull Cent Child Books

Guback, Georgia

Luka's quilt. Greenwillow Bks. 1994 un il $16.99; lib bdg $13.93

Grades: K 1 2 3   E

1. Hawaii -- Fiction 2. Quilts -- Fiction 3. Grandmothers -- Fiction

ISBN 0-688-12154-3; 0-688-12155-1 lib bdg

LC 93-12241

When Luka's grandmother makes a traditional Hawaiian quilt for her, she and Luka disagree over the colors it should include

"Eye-catching collages of brightly painted papers, the illustrations express the characters' emotions and show a delight in the Hawaiian landscape and traditions. . . . An involving story that's all the more satisfying because the ending offers no mere emotional patch up but a real solution." Booklist

Gudeon, Adam

Me and Meow. Harper 2011 il

Grades: PreK K   E

1. Cats -- Fiction 2. Play -- Fiction

ISBN 0061998214; 9780061998218

LC 2010003095

A little girl and her cat enjoy a full day of playing together.

"The primitive figures are expertly posed and arranged with simple props on color-saturated spreads to reflect the joy and devotion the companions share. Children as young as two years will appreciate the brevity, rhythm, onomatopoeia, and repetition in the text. . . . Me and Meow may inspire children to talk about a special friend and events in their day." SLJ

Guest, Elissa Haden

Harriet's had enough; illustrated by Paul Meisel. Candlewick Press 2009 un il $15.99

Grades: PreK K 1 2   E

1. Raccoons -- Fiction 2. Family life -- Fiction

ISBN 978-0-7636-3454-4; 0-7636-3454-9

"Harriet refuses to pick up her toys, and her mother is angry. When she tells her grandmother and father that she will run away because 'Mama's mean', they explain that everyone has chores to complete. Grandma succinctly explains, 'That's life, honey-bun.' . . . Harriet's shifting emotions are conveyed through her varied expressions. Intricate strokes add depth and texture to this raccoon family. Soft watercolor, acrylic, and gouache illustrations suit the subject." SLJ

★ Iris and Walter; written by Elissa Haden Guest; illustrated by Christine Davenier. Harcourt 2000 43p il $15; pa $5.95

Grades: K 1 2   E

1. Friendship -- Fiction 2. Country life -- Fiction 3. City and town

life -- Fiction
ISBN 0-15-202122-1; 0-15-216442-1 pa

LC 99-6242

When Iris moves to the country, she misses the city where she formerly lived; but with the help of a new friend named Walter, she learns to adjust to her new home

"Christine Davenier's exuberant pen-and-ink drawings reveal all the delightful things Iris discovers with Walter. . . . An easy-to-read chapter book . . . just right for children ready to step up their skills." Booklist

Other titles about Iris and Walter are:
Iris and Walter and Baby Rose (2002)
Iris and Walter and Cousin Howie (2003)
Iris and Walter and the birthday party (2006)
Iris and Walter and the field trip (2005)
Iris and Walter and the substitute teacher (2004)
Iris and Walter, lost and found (2004)
Iris and Walter, the school play (2003)
Iris and Walter, the sleepover (2002)
Iris and Walter, true friends (2001)

Guidone, Thea
  Drum city; illustrations by Vanessa Newton. Tricycle Press 2010 un il $15.99
  Grades: PreK K 1 2   E
    1. Stories in rhyme 2. Drums -- Fiction
  ISBN 978-1-58246-308-7; 1-58246-308-5
  "Leaning against a tree and beating a kettle with a spoon and whisk, a smiling young drummer seems to be in the zone, mesmerized by his own beats. An exuberant, multicultural crowd quickly gathers, and as hundreds and hundreds of kid drummers march down the streets, they turn the heads of the ho-hum passersby. . . . Guidone's steadily rhythmic, rhyming text captures the allure of a beating drum, and Newton's catchy illustrations echo the cadences of people at work." Booklist

Guthrie, James
  ★ **Last** song; a poem. illustrated by Eric Rohmann. Roaring Brook Press 2010 un il $10.99
  Grades: PreK K   E
    1. Stories in rhyme 2. Squirrels -- Fiction 3. Family life -- Fiction
  ISBN 978-1-59643-508-7; 1-59643-508-9
  "Rohmann tenderly interprets a 30-word poem by Scotsman James Guthrie in this attractive offering with a small, easily held trim size and a die-cut cover. One bright day, two squirrels bounce out of their tree to frolic in the meadow, but after the sky darkens, they return home again, where another, parental squirrel awaits them. The watercolor artwork is warm and sweet but never cloying, and it pairs well with the rhythm of the poem. . . . The brevity and calmness of the words make this a good just-one-more book at bedtime, and the depictions of the circle of family love and the cycle of the day will inspire many just-one-more kisses before the lights go out." Booklist

Guy, Ginger Foglesong
  ★ **Fiesta!** pictures by Rene King Moreno. Greenwillow Bks. 1996 un il $15.99
  Grades: PreK K 1 2   E
    1. Counting 2. Parties -- Fiction 3. Bilingual books -- English-Spanish
  ISBN 0-688-14331-8

LC 95-35848

"Three children begin with una canasta (one basket) and proceed to fill it with scrumptious candies, trinkets, and toys in preparation for a Mexican fiesta. . . . A simple bilingual text provides numbers in English

and Spanish. The soft-edged full-color illustrations done in pencils, pastels, and watercolors have a subtle folkloric quality." SLJ

  ★ **Perros!** Perros! Dogs! Dogs! a story in English and Spanish. by Ginger Foglesong Guy; pictures by Sharon Glick. Greenwillow Books 2006 un il $15.99; lib bdg $16.89
  Grades: PreK K 1 2   E
    1. Opposites 2. Dogs -- Fiction 3. Bilingual books -- English-Spanish
  ISBN 978-0-06-083574-3; 0-06-083574-5; 978-0-06-083575-0 lib bdg; 0-06-083575-3 lib bdg
  This "title makes use of a wide array of breeds to demonstrate the concept of opposites. The story begins with a girl waking up in her bedroom. . . . As she looks out her window, an excited pack of dogs runs by. Big dog. Little dog. . . .Where are they going? . . . What the book lacks in plot development it makes up for in the sheer exuberance of the watercolor cartoons. A must for dog lovers and a good choice for beginning readers in either language." SLJ

Haas, Jessie
  Sugaring; pictures by Jos. A. Smith. Greenwillow Bks. 1996 un il $17.99
  Grades: PreK K 1 2   E
    1. Horses -- Fiction 2. Maple sugar -- Fiction 3. Grandfathers -- Fiction
  ISBN 0-688-14200-1

LC 95-38139

Nora wants to find a way to give the horses a special treat for helping her grandfather and her gather sap to make maple syrup

"The realistic watercolor illustrations effectively capture the scenes; color and texture are skillfully used to depict the cold, hard job of gathering the sap and the hot steamy atmosphere of the sugar house." SLJ

Haas, Rick de
  Peter and the winter sleepers. NorthSouth Books 2011 un il $16.95
  Grades: PreK K 1 2   E
    1. Snow -- Fiction 2. Animals -- Fiction 3. Lighthouses -- Fiction
  ISBN 978-0-7358-4033-1; 0-7358-4033-4
  "When a huge snowstorm hits, sounds of scratching bring Peter to the door of the lighthouse where he and his grandmother live. First one animal and then another is trapped in the deep snow and seeking shelter. Peter and Grandma invite them in, letting them sleep (except the nocturnal ones) in boxes set up along the stairs. . . . The story is simply told, yet charming. The illustrations are also inviting, and characters have expressive faces and animated movements." SLJ

Haber, Tiffany Strelitz
  The **monster** who lost his mean; Tiffany Strelitz Haber; illustrated by Kirstie Edmunds. Henry Holt 2012 36 p. (hc) $16.99
  Grades: PreK K 1 2   E
    1. Picture books for children 2. Monsters -- Fiction 3. Stories in rhyme 4. Conduct of life -- Fiction 5. Self-acceptance -- Fiction
  ISBN 0805093753; 9780805093759

LC 2011029046

In this children's picture book, "monsters are characterized . . . as Mean, Observant, Noisy, Super Strong, Tough-to-please, Envious, and Remarkable, but what happens if the letter M for Mean is missing? The multicolored monster crew of Monsterwood won't tolerate the chartreuse mutant, not even while eating eyeball soup. Try as he might to find the M and be mean . . . , Onster's behavior is altered. A new identity brings an array of friends that leave footprints on his heart." (Children's Literature)

Hacohen, Dean

★ **Tuck** me in! [by] Dean Hacohen & Sherry Scharschmidt. Candlewick Press 2010 un $9.99

Grades: PreK   E

   1. Animals -- Fiction 2. Bedtime -- Fiction

   ISBN 0-7636-4728-4; 978-0-7636-4728-5

"In a gentle, rhythmic nighttime chant, an unseen narrator asks, 'Who needs to be tucked in?' The next page reveals a pop-eyed cartoon baby animal, head on a pillow against a field of white. Readers turn a half-page which is revealed as a blanket and the baby is tucked in. The opposite page, night blue with yellow stars, displays the text 'Good night, baby' and the next request for who needs tucking. . . . The animals are rendered digitally in a sketchy, jazzy style with swaths of bright color. Youngsters will delight in covering the babies and chanting the text in this book that will be re-read endlessly as a comfy prelude to bedtime." SLJ

Haddon, Mark

★ **Footprints** on the Moon; illustrated by Christian Birmingham. Candlewick Press 2009 un il $16.99

Grades: K 1 2 3   E

   1. Space flight to the moon -- Fiction

   ISBN 978-0-7636-4440-6; 0-7636-4440-4

First published 1996 in the United Kingdom with title: The sea of tranquillity

A man remembers his boyhood fascination with the Moon and the night mankind first bounced through the dust in the Sea of Tranquillity.

"Birmingham's nostalgia-tinged illustrations have a dreamlike quality and provide readers a glimpse into both the boy's and astronauts' separate worlds until, in a wonderful spread, both worlds join as a third tiny astronaut is seen bouncing on the Moon with Armstrong and Aldrin. The pairing of text and art creates a wonderful read-aloud." SLJ

Hader, Berta

The **big** snow; by Berta and Elmer Hader. Macmillan 1948 un il $18.99; pa $7.99

Grades: PreK K 1   E

   1. Winter -- Fiction 2. Animals -- Fiction

   ISBN 0-02-737910-8; 0-689-71757-1 pa

   Awarded the Caldecott Medal, 1949

This book shows "the birds and animals which come for the food put out by an old couple after a big snow." Hodges. Books for Elem Sch Libr

Hafner, Marylin

M & M and the bad news babies; pictures by Marylin Hafner. Puffin Books 1985 46p il pa $4.99

Grades: K 1 2   E

   1. Twins -- Fiction 2. Babysitters -- Fiction

   ISBN 0-14-031851-8

   LC 84-16557

Mandy and Mimi discover a way to make the unruly twins for whom they babysit into perfect angels.

Hajdusiewicz, Babs Bell

Sputter, sputter, sput! by Babs Bell; illustrated by Bob Staake. HarperCollins 2008 un il $16.99; lib bdg $17.89

Grades: PreK K   E

   1. Stories in rhyme 2. Automobiles -- Fiction

   ISBN 978-0-06-056222-9; 0-06-056222-6; 978-0-06-056223-6 lib bdg; 0-06-056223-4 lib bdg

A driver happily cruising in his car sputters out of gas, refills his tank, and zooms right out of town.

"Staake's vibrant, computer-generated geometric art perfectly complements the playfulness of the simple, rhyming text. Certain to be a favorite among toddler vehicle enthusiasts." SLJ

Hakala, Marjorie

Mermaid dance; by Marjorie Rose Hakala; illustrated by Mark Jones. Blue Apple 2009 un il $16.99

Grades: PreK K 1 2   E

   1. Summer solstice -- Fiction 2. Mermaids and mermen -- Fiction

   ISBN 978-1-934706-47-3; 1-934706-47-7

   LC 2008042595

On the first night of summer when high tide brings the ocean to the edge of the forest, woodland animals watch mermaids frolicking under a full moon.

"Jones's pastel illustrations show the dreamlike festivities both above and below water. A magical fantasy to celebrate the summer solstice." SLJ

Hale, Nathan

The **twelve** bots of Christmas. Walker & Company 2010 un il $14.99; lib bdg $15.89

Grades: PreK K 1 2   E

   1. Robots -- Songs 2. Christmas -- Songs

   ISBN 978-0-8027-2237-9; 0-8027-2237-7; 978-0-8027-2238-6 lib bdg; 0-8027-2238-5 lib bdg

   LC 2010009541

In this variation on the folk song "The Twelve Days of Christmas," Robo-Santa gives gifts that consist of electronic gear, including a cartridge in a gear tree, three wrench hens, and nine droids a-dancing.

"The brightly colored digital artwork pays subtle homage to everything from Star Wars to Dr. Who and rewards careful study with fun details." SLJ

Hall, Bruce Edward

Henry and the kite dragon; illustrated by William Low. Philomel Books 2004 un il $15.99

Grades: K 1 2 3 4   E

   1. Kites -- Fiction 2. New York (N.Y.) -- Fiction 3. Chinese Americans -- Fiction 4. Italian Americans -- Fiction

   ISBN 0-399-23727-5

   LC 2003-16381

In New York City in the 1920s, the children from Chinatown go after the children from Little Italy for throwing rocks at the beautiful kites Grandfather Chin makes, not realizing that they have a reason for doing so.

The author "tells an engaging story about a vibrant community, which is beautifully captured in Low's detailed, dramatic paintings." Booklist

Hall, Donald

Ox-cart man; pictures by Barbara Cooney. Viking 1979 un il $16.99; pa $6.99

Grades: K 1 2 3   E

   1. New England -- Fiction

   ISBN 0-670-53328-9; 0-14-050441-9 pa

   LC 79-14466

   Awarded the Caldecott Medal, 1980

"The stunning combination of text and illustrations, suggesting early American paintings on wood, depict the countryside through which [the farmer] travels, the jostle of the marketplace, and the homely warmth of family life." Horn Book

Hall, Michael, 1954-

★ **Cat** tale; Michael Hall. Greenwillow Books 2012 40 p. col. ill. (trade ed.) $16.99

Grades: PreK K 1   **E**

1. Cats -- Fiction 2. Picture books for children 3. Puns 4. Stories in rhyme 5. Imagination -- Fiction

ISBN 0061915165; 9780061915161

LC 2011033654

In this story, three cats "try to keep up with . . . wordplay as [Michael] Hall . . . explores verbal puns. The . . . text is reinforced by . . . illustrations . . . . Each line ends with a . . . thump: 'They flee a steer. / They steer a plane. / They plane a board. / They board a train.' A huge, blue steer sends the cats dashing into a blobby purple plane. 'They plane a board' explains the verb 'to plane' with vivid red curls of wood; two cats do carpentry" while the third talks to the train driver. (Publishers Weekly)

It's an orange aardvark! Michael Hall. Greenwillow Books, an imprint of HarperCollinsPublishers 2014 40 p. (trade bdg.) $17.99

Grades: PreK K 1 2   **E**

1. Ants -- Fiction 2. Color -- Fiction 3. Toy and movable books 4. Imagination -- Fiction

ISBN 0062252062; 9780062252067; 9780062252081

LC 2013017265

In this children's book, author Michael Hall "delivers a . . . story about colors, ants, aardvarks, and rainbows. . . . Five carpenter ants at home in their tree stump hear a noise. What is it? One ant thinks it is a hungry aardvark lurking outside the stump, just waiting to eat them. One ant makes a hole in the stump to see. Orange light floods the stump—it's not an aardvark, proclaims the ant chorus. It's orange!" (Publisher's note)

"With an illustration style reminiscent of Lois Ehlert's and storytelling style similar to Eric Carle's, this tale of imagination succeeds in its bold simplicity...The use of color has application to early learning curricular needs, while the pace and flow of the text works well for read-aloud and storytime settings. Get ready to have another go-to favorite to pair with cherished titles like Carle's The Very Hungry Caterpillar (Penguin, 1969) and Ehlert's Color Zoo (HarperCollins, 1989)." SLJ

My heart is like a zoo. Greenwillow Books 2010 un il

Grades: PreK K 1   **E**

1. Stories in rhyme 2. Love -- Fiction 3. Animals -- Fiction

ISBN 0-06-191510-6; 0-06-191511-4 lib bdg; 978-0-06-191510-9; 978-0-06-191511-6 lib bdg

LC 2009017818

Depicts in rhyming text how love can be many different things, such as eager as a beaver, steady as a yak, or silly as a seal.

"The bold digital collages of zoo animals in this debut picture book are clear and bright, and the simple rhymes about feelings will have preschoolers savoring the words, joining in, and pointing at every playful zoo scene, each featuring one animal per page." Booklist

★ **Perfect** square. Greenwillow Books 2011 un il $16.99

Grades: PreK K 1 2   **E**

1. Shape -- Fiction 2. Square -- Fiction 3. Happiness -- Fiction 4. Color 5. Geometry

ISBN 978-0-06-191513-0; 0-06-191513-0

LC 2010004104

A perfect square that is perfectly happy is torn into pieces, punched with holes, crumpled, and otherwise changed but finds in each transformation that it can be something new, and just as happy.

"This near-perfect concept book incorporates an imaginative exploration of colors, a nice assortment of vivid words, and the tranformational possibilities of a simple-seeming square. . . . Just right for toddlers, but

also for those ready for the abstract theme of inventive self-empowerment: a book to revisit often, and with delight." Horn Book

Red; a crayon's story. Michael Hall. Greenwillow Books, an imprint of HarperCollinsPublishers 2015 40 p. color illustrations (trade bdg.) $17.99; (lib. bdg.) $18.89

Grades: PreK K 1 2 3   **E**

1. Color -- Fiction 2. Crayons -- Fiction 3. Identity -- Fiction

ISBN 0062252097; 9780062252074; 9780062252098

LC 2014010834

In this children's book by Michael Hall, "when a red-labeled crayon discovers he's actually blue, he finds joy, ebullience and acceptance.Red tries to be a quintessential red crayon, coloring fire trucks, strawberries, hearts and cherries, but no matter the object, they all turn blue. . . . Some say he needs to press harder or grow out of it; others say he's lazy or unintelligent. . . . Until Berry asks him to draw something blue. When Red succeeds, he feels free!" (Kirkus Reviews)

"The solid text is matched by the eye-catching artwork. Often placed against pages of shiny white or black, the crayons and their scribblings will charm children (who will also get the message that when it comes to creativity, strawberries and hearts can also be colored blue)." Booklist

Wonderfall; Michael Hall. Greenwillow Books, an imprint of HarperCollinsPublishers 2016 40 p. color illustrations (trade ed.) $17.99

Grades: PreK K 1 2 3   **E**

1. Trees -- Fiction 2. Autumn -- Fiction 3. Seasons -- Fiction

ISBN 9780062382986

LC 2016004139

This book, by Michael Hall, "follows a single tree through the changing of the seasons. People, animals, and vehicles pass in front of the tree, celebrating holidays, playing in its leaves, and getting ready for winter. Fifteen combined words . . . underscore the themes and concepts of the season, while the main attraction—the beautiful tree—drops acorns, loses leaves, and provides food and a home for a pair of scurrying squirrels." (Publisher's note)

"An excellent seasonal addition, great for storytime and as a catalyst for poetry writing or artwork." SLJ

Hallowell, George

Wagons ho! by George Hallowell and Joan Holub; illustrated by Lynne Avril. Albert Whitman 2011 il $16.99

Grades: K 1 2   **E**

1. Moving -- Fiction 2. Automobile travel -- Fiction 3. Overland journeys to the Pacific -- Fiction

ISBN 978-0-8075-8612-9; 0-8075-8612-9

LC 2010050422

Compares the experiences of Jenny Johnson and Katie Miller as their families move from Missouri to Oregon, one in 1846 and one in 2011.

"Carefully chosen facts make contrasts and similarities easy to comprehend. . . . Readers will relate to the travel activities and smile at the humor in the pen-and-ink and watercolor drawings. Together, the art and text make a good introduction to the Westward Movement." SLJ

Hamanaka, Sheila

All the colors of the earth. Morrow Junior Bks. 1994 un il $17.99; pa $6.99

Grades: 1 2 3 4   **E**

1. Stories in rhyme

ISBN 0-688-11131-9; 0-688-17062-5 pa

LC 93-27118

Reveals in verse that despite outward differences children everywhere are essentially the same and all are lovable

"A poetic picture book and an exemplary work of art. . . . Hamanaka's oil paintings are all double-page spreads filled with the colors of earth, sky, and water, and the texture of the artist's canvas shines through. The text is arranged in undulant waves across each painting." SLJ

Grandparents song. HarperCollins Pubs. 2003 un il $15.99; lib bdg $16.89

Grades: 1 2 3 4   E

1. Stories in rhyme 2. Grandparents -- Fiction 3. Racially mixed people -- Fiction

ISBN 0-688-17852-9; 0-688-17853-7 lib bdg

LC 00-47952

In verse "a young girl recounts the roots of her family tree. Fondly and respectfully, she describes her grandparents—one American Indian, one Irish, one Mexican, and one a descendent of African slaves. Beautifully rendered in calligraphy, the text is clean, simple, and lilting. . . . Filled with magnificent texture, Hamanaka's oil paintings are substantial and striking." SLJ

Hamburg, Jennifer

Hazy Bloom and the tomorrow power; Jennifer Hamburg; pictures by Jenn Harney. Farrar, Straus & Giroux 2017 176 p. illustrations (Hazy Bloom) (hardcover) $15.99; (ebook) $60

Grades: 2 3 4 5   E

1. Humorous fiction 2. Schools -- Fiction 3. Extrasensory perception -- Fiction

ISBN 9780374304942; 9780374304966

LC 2016024328

In this book in the Hazy Bloom series, by Jennifer Hamburg, illustrated by Jenn Harney, "Hazy realizes she has a strange new power to foresee a visual clue about trouble that's on its way within twenty-four hours. But seeing is not always understanding, and headstrong Hazy quickly discovers that 'tomorrow power' sometimes only gives her the ability to make a hilarious mess of things instead of saving the day." (Publisher's note)

"Hazy's irrepressible, hilarious narration... proves fast-paced and amusing... Likely to engage the primary school set with its madcap humor and unpredictable heroine." Kirkus

A **moose** that says moo; Jennifer Hamburg; pictures by Sue Truesdell. Farrar, Straus and Giroux 2013 32 p. (hardcover) $16.99

Grades: PreK K 1   E

1. Animals -- Fiction 2. Zoos -- Fiction 3. Humorous stories 4. Stories in rhyme 5. Zoo animals -- Fiction

ISBN 0374350582; 9780374350581

LC 2013000498

Author Jennifer Hamburg's book focuses on a pretend zoo. "From jump-roping skunks to book-reading sharks, the animals in this girl's make-believe zoo will do whatever she wants. Messing with nature is fun at first, until we see how hilariously wrong things go. Oinking otters! Picketing ground hogs! Stage-crashing pigs! What could be next?" (Publisher's note)

Hamilton, K. R.

★ **Police** officers on patrol; by Kersten Hamilton; pictures by R. W. Alley. Viking 2009 un il $15.99

Grades: PreK   E

1. Stories in rhyme 2. Police -- Fiction

ISBN 978-0-670-06315-4; 0-670-06315-0

LC 2008023240

"Sergeant Santole dispatches Officers Mike, Jan, and Carl to spots around town that require their expertise. Mike in his police car attends to a broken traffic light, Jan on horseback reconnects a small child with his mom, and Carl runs to a crime scene. . . . The hilarious cartoon illustra-

tions effectively convey excitement and brisk movement. . . . Preschoolers will be reassured that special people are there to assist in a variety of circumstances and see that their jobs require all kinds of cool tools." SLJ

★ **Red** Truck; by Kersten Hamilton; illustrated by Valeria Petrone. Viking Childrens Books 2008 un il $15.99

Grades: PreK K   E

1. Stories in rhyme 2. Buses -- Fiction 3. Trucks -- Fiction

ISBN 978-0-670-06275-1

LC 2007-22902

When a school bus gets stuck in the mud, Red Truck the tow truck saves the day by pulling it out.

"Strong, flowing lines and highly simplified forms create a certain retro look in the digital artwork. . . . With a well-crafted text spiced with sound effects, this appealing picture book is highly recommended for reading aloud to the truck-loving crowd." Booklist

Hamilton, Virginia

Wee Winnie Witch's Skinny; an original African American scare tale. engravings by Barry Moser. Blue Sky Press 2004 un il $16.95

Grades: 2 3 4 5   E

1. Witches -- Fiction 2. African Americans -- Fiction

ISBN 0-590-28880-6

LC 00-67999

James Lee and Uncle Big Anthony become victims of Wee Winnie Witch, who takes them on a ride up into the sky, but Mama Granny saves them.

This "is a wonderful horror story that draws on traditional beliefs about witches. . . . Moser's framed, colored wood engravings do a great job of bringing the wild, shivery adventure close to home, their black backgrounds and strong lines lit with garish Halloween images in green and red." Booklist

Hamlisch, Marvin, 1944-2012

Marvin makes music; Marvin Hamlisch; illustrated by Jim Madsen. Dial Books for Young Readers 2012 32 p. (hardcover) $17.99

Grades: 2 3 4   E

1. Anxiety 2. Picture books for children 3. Pianists -- Fiction 4. Composers -- Fiction

ISBN 0803737300; 9780803737303

LC 2011052317

This book, by Marvin Hamlisch, illustrated by Jim Madsen, is the "story of [the author,] . . . who, at the age of six, was . . . accepted into the Juilliard School. . . . Marvin loves to play the piano and compose his own songs. But performing music over and over that's composed by some old guys . . . just gives him knots in his stomach. When . . . he has an audition with the most prestigious music school, how can Marvin overcome his nerves and get swept away by the music?" (Publisher's note)

Hamm, Mia

Winners never quit! illustrated by Carol Thompson. HarperCollins 2004 un il $15.99; lib bdg $16.89

Grades: PreK K 1 2   E

1. Soccer -- Fiction

ISBN 0-06-074050-7; 0-06-074051-5 lib bdg

"Mia's favorite sport is soccer but she hates losing. In fact, she dislikes it so much that she quits in the middle of a game. . . . Mia learns quickly that there will be times when she will score a goal and those when she will not, but playing the game is the most fun of all. Bright, energetic cartoons depict the child's ups and downs." SLJ

Hammill, Matt

Sir Reginald's logbook. Kids Can Press 2008 un il $17.95

Grades: K 1 2 3   E
1. Adventure fiction 2. Imagination -- Fiction
ISBN 978-1-55453-202-5; 1-55453-202-7

"Sir Reginald is on a mission to find the Lost Tablet of Illusion. Readers will quickly realize, with the help of Hammill's illustrations, that his dangerous and mysterious quest into the deepest jungle is happening in his imagination. In actuality, he is only searching his home and yard for a missing TV remote control. . . . Hammill's keen sense of humor abounds in both the text and art." SLJ

Hanlon, Abby
Dory and the real true friend; by Abby Hanlon. Dial Books for Young Readers, an imprint of Penguin Group (USA) LLC 2015 160 p. (hardcover) $14.99
                                                                   E
1. Imagination -- Fiction 2. School stories -- Fiction 3. Female friendship -- Fiction
ISBN 0525428666; 9780525428664
                                                         LC 2014034036
In this children's book by Abby Hanlon, Dory's "older siblings, Luke and Violet, warn her to leave her imaginary friend, Mary, at home--or better yet, leave her whole imagination at home! Dory is determined to behave . . . but on her very first day she meets a new friend, a girl whose imagination and style are just about as wild as her own. Now she just has to convince her siblings that she's not making it all up!" (Publisher's note)

Hanson, Warren
Bugtown Boogie; illustrated by Steve Johnson and Lou Fancher. Laura Geringer Books 2008 un il $16.99; lib bdg $17.89
Grades: PreK K 1 2   E
1. Stories in rhyme 2. Dance -- Fiction 3. Insects -- Fiction 4. Parties -- Fiction
ISBN 978-0-06-059937-9; 0-06-059937-5; 978-0-06-059938-6 lib bdg; 0-06-059938-3 lib bdg
                                                         LC 2006029207
While strolling home through the woods one evening, a young boy happens upon a rollicking dancing party in Bugtown
This is written "in jazzy rhyming couplets. . . . Vibrant hues and frenetic energy suffuse the artwork." SLJ

It's Monday, Mrs. Jolly Bones; Warren Hanson; illustrated by Tricia Tusa. Beach Lane Books 2013 32 p. col. ill. (hardcover) $16.99
Grades: PreK K 1 2   E
1. Ballads 2. Week -- Fiction 3. Humorous stories 4. Stories in rhyme 5. Housekeeping -- Fiction
ISBN 1442412291; 9781442412293
                                                         LC 2010004309
This book-length ballad focuses on "Mrs. Jolly Bones [who] is a woman who keeps a serious housekeeping schedule--in her own peculiar way. Monday is for doing laundry, which concludes with throwing all the clothes out the window; Tuesday's gardening ends with a garden-wrecking dance . . .; Wednesday's housecleaning culminates in a toilet-bowl bath, etc. Finally Sunday comes, and a blissful day of rest comes to a celebratory finale." (Bulletin of the Center for Children's Books)
"Mrs. Jolly Bones's life is one of cheerful but determined rule breaking, and readers are guaranteed to laugh out loud at each gag." Pub Wkly

The **Sea** of Sleep; illustrations by Jim LaMarche. Scholastic Press 2010 un il $16.99
Grades: PreK K 1   E
1. Ocean -- Fiction 2. Sleep -- Fiction 3. Otters -- Fiction 4.

Bedtime -- Fiction
ISBN 978-0-439-69735-4; 0-439-69735-2
                                                         LC 2009032602
This "bedtime story follows an otter and its mother on a journey in the Sea of Sleep. They see the moon, myriad examples of marine life, and the personified sea herself. . . . Hanson's musician roots show in the text, which reads very much like lyrics, including a repeating chorus. . . . Young audiences . . . will appreciate the lilting, poetic language. The illustrations are done in restful blues and purples befitting a bedtime story." SLJ

Hardin, Melinda
Hero dad; [illustrations by] Bryan Langdo. Marshall Cavendish 2010 un il $12.99
Grades: PreK K 1 2   E
1. Soldiers -- Fiction 2. Heroes and heroines -- Fiction 3. Father-child relationship -- Fiction
ISBN 978-0-7614-5713-8; 0-7614-5713-5
A child demonstrates that while Dad differs from a traditional superhero, as an American soldier he is a superhero of a different kind.
"Langdo's watercolor-and-pencil illustrations have an appealing simplicity and texture, almost as if made by the boy narrator himself. . . . An important message, delivered with effective straightforwardness and an abundance of heart." Kirkus

Hardy, Aurelia
Dancers of the World; by Aurelia Hardy; illustrated by Sybile; edited by Rebecca Frazer; translated by Susan Allen Maurin. Innovative Logistics Llc 2013 32 p. ill. (hardcover) $19.95
Grades: 3 4 5   E
1. Dogs 2. Dance
ISBN 2733812335; 9782733812334
In this book by Aurelia Hardy, "fifteen young women worldwide enthusiastically describe the dance form they love and practice. Each one talks about the music, the steps, and the dance's history, and imagines herself in a particular role. In some cases, she describes a real performance. The styles vary greatly--ballet, ballroom, folk, Kabuki, Senegalese, Flamenco, Tahitian, etc." (School Library Journal)

Harley, Bill
Dirty Joe, the pirate; a true story. words by Bill Harley; pictures by Jack E. Davis. HarperCollinsPublishers 2008 un il $16.99; lib bdg $17.89
Grades: PreK K 1 2   E
1. Stories in rhyme 2. Pirates -- Fiction 3. Clothing and dress -- Fiction
ISBN 978-0-06-623780-0; 0-06-623780-7; 978-0-06-623781-7 lib bdg; 0-06-623781-5 lib bdg
                                                         LC 2007018377
Dirty Joe and his pirate crew terrorize the seven seas in their quest for dirty socks, but they meet their match in Stinky Annie, whose favorite loot is pilfered underwear
"Davis's balloon-headed, goofy characters are just right for the tale. The chaotic full-color pictures are jam-packed with pirates and dirty laundry. The crews, dressed in a hilarious mishmash of styles, will have readers poring over the pages to spot amusing details." SLJ

Harper, Charise Mericle
Gigi in the big city. Random House 2010 un il $12.99
Grades: K 1 2   E
1. City and town life -- Fiction
ISBN 978-0-375-84235-1; 0-375-84235-7
"With an arsenal of flaps, mini-booklets, and wheels, Harper demonstrates the possibilities cities have to offer, as readers follow Gigi on

a solo journey through a lively metropolis. Harper balances traditionally girly activities (shoe shopping! makeovers!) with basic information about art, literature, and more (one wheel rotates through birthstones, art movements, and mythical creatures; another simply lets Gigi try different hairstyles). Cheerful cartoons, surprises aplenty, and a smart design will keep young urbanites occupied." Publ Wkly

Henry's heart. Henry Holt 2011 un il $16.99 **E**
1. Dogs -- Fiction 2. Heart -- Fiction 3. Family life -- Fiction
ISBN 978-0-8050-8989-9; 0-8050-8989-6

LC 2010040321

When Henry falls in love with a puppy but his father will not buy it for him, his heart reacts strangely. Includes facts about the heart's role within the body.

"Harper's acrylic-and-collage artwork with its filled-in stick figures is a perfect match for the irreverent humor of the text." Kirkus

Includes bibliographical references

Mimi and Lulu; three sweet stories: one forever friendship. Balzer & Bray 2009 un il $16.99
Grades: PreK K 1 **E**
1. Friendship -- Fiction
ISBN 978-0-06-175583-5; 0-06-175583-4

Mimi and Lulu are best friends despite liking different colors and they love playing together, whether it's pretending to be on a phone or being princesses.

"The dramatic, fuming stand-offs and the fun when things turn around are playfully illustrated in the bright scenes of the cartoonish, animal-like figures, set against spacious white pages. A solid offering to add to the picture-book friendship canon." Booklist

Pink me up. Alfred A. Knopf 2010 un il $16.99; lib bdg $19.99
Grades: PreK K 1 **E**
1. Color -- Fiction 2. Father-daughter relationship -- Fiction
ISBN 978-0-375-85607-5; 0-375-85607-2; 978-0-375-95607-2 lib bdg; 0-375-95607-7 lib bdg

LC 2009-23168

When Mama is too sick to go to the Pink Girls Pink-nic with Violet, Daddy offers to take her place but, first, he needs to "pink-up" his clothes.

"Rendered in acrylics, the illustrations are humorous and lively." SLJ

The **power** of cute. Robin Corey Books 2011 un il $10.99
Grades: PreK K **E**
1. Size -- Fiction 2. Courage -- Fiction 3. Monsters -- Fiction
ISBN 978-0-375-85965-6; 0-375-85965-9

In this picture book with lift-the-flaps, pull-tabs, and simple pop-ups, a small teddy bear-like superhero claims he is unafraid of a monster because of his "power of cute."

Harper "knows a thing or two about cute; now she shows it's about being more than a pretty face." Publ Wkly

★ **When** Randolph turned rotten. Alfred A. Knopf 2007 un il $16.99; lib bdg $19.99
Grades: K 1 2 3 **E**
1. Geese -- Fiction 2. Beavers -- Fiction 3. Friendship -- Fiction
ISBN 978-0-375-84071-5; 978-0-375-94071-2 lib bdg

LC 2006-30572

Best friends Randolph, a beaver, and Ivy, a goose, do everything together until Ivy is invited to a girls-only birthday sleepover party and Randolph, full of bad feelings, tries to spoil her fun

This is "irreverent and fun thanks to Harper's exaggerated situations and signature art, with its brightly colored backgrounds and charmingly simple figures." Booklist

Harper, Dan
★ **Sit,** Truman! illustrated by Cara Moser & Barry Moser. Harcourt 2001 un il hardcover o.p. pa $6.99
Grades: PreK K 1 2 **E**
1. Dogs -- Fiction
ISBN 0-15-202616-9; 0-15-205068-X pa

LC 00-9298

A busy day in the life of Truman the big dog includes walks, play time, and a little dog named Oscar

"Harper's minimal text and the Mosers' watercolor paintings are perfectly paired. Slobbery canine Truman is both exasperating and lovable." SLJ

Harper, Jamie
Miles to go. Candlewick Press 2010 un il $12.99
Grades: PreK **E**
1. Automobiles -- Fiction
ISBN 978-0-7636-3598-5; 0-7636-3598-7

Although concerned about a broken horn, young Miles makes his way to preschool in his very own car, with Mom close at hand.

"The rosy-cheeked Miles marvelously embodies the exuberance, imagination and passions of a preschool boy. The block-print, watercolor, ink and cut-paper illustrations create a feast of colors and textures without being overbusy." Kirkus

Miles to the finish; Jamie Harper. Candlewick Press 2013 32 p. $12.99
Grades: PreK K 1 **E**
1. School stories 2. Racing -- Fiction 3. Conduct of life -- Fiction 4. Play -- Fiction 5. Automobile racing -- Fiction
ISBN 0763655627; 9780763655624

LC 2012950558

In this children's book, by Jamie Harper, "it's race day at the Red Apple School, and Miles and Otto can't wait. But what's that fancy Speedster doing here? It belongs to a girl named Indie, and the boys had better get in shape if they want to win the trophy! Soon everyone is off . . . and Miles takes an early lead. But then Indie is at his side, only to go off the track. Will Miles take his chance for an easy win?" (Publisher's note)

"It's race day, and Miles is pretty pumped, until he sees a new driver with an electric car in the lineup: Indie and her Speedster 660... The book is easy enough for beginning readers, has pictures large and clear enough for a small read-aloud session, and could be a good discussion starter." SLJ

Harper, Lee
The **Emperor's** cool clothes; written and illustrated by Lee Harper. Marshall Cavendish Children's 2011 il $16.99
Grades: PreK K 1 2 **E**
1. Authors 2. Novelists 3. Dramatists 4. Fairy tales 5. Children's authors 6. Short story writers
ISBN 978-0-7614-5948-4; 0-7614-5948-0

LC 2010024234

Two rascally weavers convince the emperor they are making clothing that will make him look "cool" and will let him know who else is "cool," as well, but when he wears them during the Royal Parade, a child cries out that the emperor has nothing on. Includes author's note about the story's origins.

"Humorous details are scattered throughout, some seemingly for the benefit of adult audiences. He uses bright colors in his watercolor-and-pencil artwork and ably conveys the sad fact that the emperor's clothes, no matter how nice, cannot mask his lack of cool. The visual humor makes this a winner, and adults will appreciate the easy segue into conversations about honesty and what defines 'cool' that are sure to follow." Kirkus

Snow! Snow! Snow! Simon & Schuster Books for Young Readers 2009 un il $14.99
Grades: K 1 2 3 4   E
1. Dogs -- Fiction 2. Snow -- Fiction 3. Sledding -- Fiction 4. Father-son relationship -- Fiction
ISBN 978-1-4169-8454-2; 1-4169-8454-2
LC 2008051985

A dog father and his two sons spend a perfect day sledding together.
"Harper's watercolor illustrations are simple, yet effective. Readers get a good sense of the cold, crisp snow and billowing clouds, and the characters' faces are expressive." SLJ

Harrington, Janice N.
Busy-busy Little Chick; Janice Harrington; pictures by Brian Pinkney. Farrar Straus Giroux 2013 32 p. (hardcover) $15.99
Grades: PreK K 1   E
1. Birds -- Fiction 2. Picture books for children 3. Chickens -- Fiction 4. Perseverance (Ethics) -- Fiction
ISBN 0374347468; 9780374347468
LC 2012004871

This children's picture book is "based on a fable of the Nkundo people of Central Africa" about being self-reliant. Mama Nsoso's chicks need a new, warmer nest, but Mama keeps getting distracted by food and doesn't build one. It's up to "persistent, industrious Little Chick" to help. He works "alone and in secret on a new nest for the family. . . . When the nest is ready, Little Chick invites his brothers and sisters in for a good night's rest." (Kirkus Reviews)

★ The **chicken**-chasing queen of Lamar County; pictures by Shelley Jackson. Farrar, Straus and Giroux 2007 un il $16
Grades: K 1 2 3   E
1. Chickens -- Fiction 2. Farm life -- Fiction 3. African Americans -- Fiction
ISBN 0-374-31251-6; 978-0-374-31251-0
LC 2005-52768

A young farm girl tries to catch her favorite chicken, until she learns something about the hen that makes her change her ways.
"Both words and pictures elevate a simple story about a girl's sly barnyard game into a rollicking, well-told delight." Booklist

Going north; pictures by Jerome Lagarrigue. Farrar, Straus and Giroux 2004 un il $16
Grades: 2 3 4 5   E
1. Moving -- Fiction 2. African Americans -- Fiction
ISBN 0-374-32681-9

A young African American girl and her family leave their home in Alabama and head for Lincoln, Nebraska, where they hope to escape segregation and find a better life.
"Lagarrigue's paintings are subdued but powerful and well-suited to Harrington's somber, poetic narrative voice." SLJ

Harris, Joe
The **belly** book; [written and illustrated] by Joe Harris. Random House Children's Books 2008 un il (Beginner books) $8.99; lib bdg $12.99

Grades: PreK K 1   E
1. Stories in rhyme 2. Stomach -- Fiction
ISBN 978-0-375-84340-2; 0-375-84340-X; 978-0-375-94340-9 lib bdg; 0-375-94340-4 lib bdg
LC 2006016630

Bellies can be used for many things, such as dancing the hula and resting your cup, but it is important to feed them healthy foods, too
"This beginning reader has vibrant illustrations, ample white space, and just two to four lines of simple text per page. . . . [This is a] funny, fast-moving, and original romp." SLJ

Harris, John
Jingle bells; how the holiday classic came to be. written by John Harris; illustrated by Adam Gustavson. Peachtree 2011 un il $16.95
Grades: K 1 2   E
1. Clergy 2. Songs 3. Christmas 4. Christmas stories 5. College administrators
ISBN 978-1-56145-590-4; 1-56145-590-3
LC 2010052274

"In 1857, John Lord Pierpont sat down to write a song for his congregation's Thanksgiving program, despite the fact that he was in Savannah, Georgia, struggling with a miserable heat wave and a population that was troubled by his Unitarian church's position on slavery. Homesick for New England (and cool weather), Pierpont ended up writing an enduringly popular holiday song. This is a fictional retelling of the story behind the song's creation." (Publisher's note) "Primary." (Horn Book)
"The oil painting illustrations do right by the story . . . capturing the atmosphere of a community willing to stick together as they journey against the grain, whether that means bringing snow somehow to the South or standing by an unpopular belief." SLJ

Harris, Robie H.
★ The **day** Leo said I hate you; illustrated by Molly Bang. Little, Brown and Co. 2008 un il $16.99
Grades: PreK K 1 2   E
1. Love -- Fiction 2. Anger -- Fiction 3. Mother-son relationship -- Fiction
ISBN 978-0-316-06580-1; 0-316-06580-3
LC 2007-48371

Leo, upset he has been hearing the word "no" all day, lets three words slip out that he wishes he could take back.
The hero is "evoked via vibrant collages of photos and cut paper." Publ Wkly

★ **Goodbye,** Mousie; illustrated by Jan Ormerod. Margaret K. McElderry Bks. 2001 un il hardcover o.p. pa $6.99
Grades: PreK K   E
1. Mice 2. Pets 3. Death 4. Grief 5. Mice -- Fiction 6. Death -- Fiction
ISBN 0-689-83217-6; 0-689-87134-1 pa
LC 99-89167

A boy grieves for his dead pet Mousie, helps to bury him, and begins to come to terms with his loss. "Ages three to six." (Bull Cent Child Books)
"Ormerod's honest pictures, black-pencil line drawings with watercolor washes on buff-colored paper, capture the emotions of the situation and chronicle the boy's move from disbelief to acceptance. . . . This covers all the bases of a frequently asked-for subject." Booklist

I am not going to school today; illustrated by Jan Ormerod. Margaret K. McElderry Bks. 2003 un il $16.95

Grades: PreK K 1 2 E
1. School stories
ISBN 0-689-83913-8

LC 00-48053

A little boy decides to skip his very first day of school, because on the first day one doesn't know anything, but on the second, one knows everything

"Children with first-day jitters will take comfort in this story. . . . Ormerod's colorful, expressive illustrations capture a child's anxiety and the warmth of family with equal success." Booklist

★ **Mail** Harry to the moon! [illustrated by] Michael Emberley. Little, Brown and Co. 2008 un il $16.99
Grades: PreK K 1 2 E
1. Infants -- Fiction 2. Siblings -- Fiction
ISBN 978-0-316-15376-8; 0-316-15376-1

LC 2007-48369

Harry's older brother, unhappy that the new baby seems to have taken over, dreams up imaginative ways to get rid of him.

"Harris and Emberley . . . are old hands at striking the right balance between comic Sturm and Drang and genuine poignancy, and their considerable talents make this otherwise familiar tale feel fresh and funny—and psychologically true." Publ Wkly

Maybe a bear ate it! by Robie Harris; illustrated by Michael Emberley. Orchard Books 2007 un il lib bdg $15.99
Grades: PreK K 1 2 E
1. Animals -- Fiction 2. Bedtime -- Fiction 3. Books and reading -- Fiction
ISBN 978-0-439-92961-5

LC 2006102373

At bedtime, a young boy who cannot find his favorite book imagines the various creatures that might have taken it from him

"Plain white backgrounds allow Emberley, who obviously knows how toddlers move and react, to concentrate closely on his character, whose every beautifully calibrated movement and feeling blasts out across the page." Booklist

Harris, Teresa E.
Summer Jackson: grown up; illustrated by AG Ford. Katherine Tegen Books 2011 un il $16.99
Grades: PreK K 1 2 E
1. Parent-child relationship -- Fiction
ISBN 978-0-06-185757-7; 0-06-185757-2

LC 2010-15962

Seven-year-old Summer Jackson wants to be a grown-up, starting right now.

"Ford's charming and humorous cartoon illustrations are liberally sprinkled throughout the book, ranging from three pictures on a page to full-page images. Although predictable, this story should have wide appeal." SLJ

Harris, Trudy
The **clock** struck one; a time-telling tale. written by Trudy Harris; illustrations by Carrie Hartman. Millbrook Press 2009 31p il (Math is fun) lib bdg $16.95
Grades: K 1 2 E
1. Stories in rhyme 2. Time -- Fiction 3. Animals -- Fiction 4. Clocks and watches -- Fiction
ISBN 978-0-8225-9067-5 lib bdg; 0-8225-9067-0 lib bdg

LC 2008041583

Rhyming text expands on the nursery rhyme, "Hickory Dickory Dock," as a cat chases the mouse up the clock, followed by other ani-

mals, until midnight arrives and the tired creatures fall asleep. Includes facts about clocks and basic information about telling time

"The animated romp's peppy verse and colorful art capture the comical bedlam with flair. . . . An entertaining addition to beginning time-telling lessons." Booklist

Say something, Perico; illustrated by Cecilia Rebora. Millbrook Press 2011 un il lib bdg $21.27
Grades: PreK K E
1. Parrots -- Fiction 2. Bilingualism -- Fiction 3. Spanish language -- Fiction
ISBN 978-0-7613-5231-0; 0-7613-5231-7

LC 2011001114

Perico is a Spanish-speaking parrot who lives in a pet store, and although he works very hard to earn a new home, buyers keep returning him until the bird, now bilingual, finds the perfect owner. Includes Spanish glossary and pronunciation guide.

"The text is well assisted by Rebora's bright, wide-eyed illustrations, which bring out the humor and frustration of Perico's search for a home." Booklist

Tally cat keeps track; illustrated by Andrew N. Harris. Millbrook Press 2011 31p il lib bdg $22.60
Grades: K 1 2 3 E
1. Counting 2. Stories in rhyme 3. Cats -- Fiction 4. Friendship -- Fiction 5. Mathematics -- Fiction
ISBN 978-0-7613-4451-3; 0-7613-4451-9

LC 2009049586

Alley cat Tally McNally loves to tally and loves to win, but when his competitive streak gets him into trouble, he has to rely on his friends for help.

"The illustrations depict a bunch of street savvy, hip cats with great facial expressions. . . . This concept book would work equally well in the classroom or at storytime." SLJ

Harrison, David L.
A **monster** is coming! illustrated by Hans Wilhelm. Random House 2011 32p il (Step into reading) lib bdg $12.99; pa $3.99
Grades: PreK K 1 E
1. Fear -- Fiction 2. Food -- Fiction 3. Animals -- Fiction
ISBN 978-0-375-96677-4 lib bdg; 0-375-96677-3; 978-0-375-86677-7 pa; 0-375-86677-9 pa

LC 2010014513

When Inchworm overhears Mama Bug tell Baby Bug that she eats like a monster, he cries out in fear and sets off a chain reaction of animals trying to hide from the horrible beast they believe is coming.

"Beginning readers who crave suspense will be drawn to this gentle spin on the 'Chicken Little' motif. . . . Wilhelm's expressive, cheerfully colored cartoon illustrations reflect the fact that there is nothing to fear and provide a lot of picture clues to help decode the clever, descriptive text." SLJ

Harrison, Hannah E.
★ **Extraordinary** Jane; by Hannah E. Harrison. Dial Books for Young Readers 2014 40 p. (hardcover : alk. paper) $16.99
Grades: PreK K E
1. Dogs -- Fiction 2. Circus -- Fiction 3. Self-acceptance -- Fiction
ISBN 0803739141; 9780803739147

LC 2012009713

This book, by Hannah E. Harrison, is a "story set at the circus shows that quiet qualities like friendship, kindness, and loyalty are important and worthy. Jane is an ordinary dog in an extraordinary circus. She isn't strong, graceful, or brave like her family. When she tries to be those things, Jane just doesn't feel like herself, but she also doesn't feel special. Is she really meant for this kind of life? Her Ringmaster thinks so, but not for the reasons Jane believes." (Publisher's note)

"Jane, a small circus dog, doesn't measure up to her talented doggy parents and siblings who can get shot from a cannon, lift an elephant, tightrope walk, etc. The detailed acrylic illustrations set against white backgrounds distinguish the slight story; the colorful circus milieu and aerial perspectives convey Jane's ordinariness, which turns out to be enough for her ringmaster owner." Horn Book

Harrison, Joanna

Grizzly dad. David Fickling Books 2009 un il $16.99; lib bdg $19.99

Grades: PreK K 1   E
1. Bears -- Fiction 2. Father-son relationship -- Fiction
ISBN 978-0-385-75173-5; 0-385-75173-7; 978-0-385-75174-2 lib bdg; 0-385-75174-5 lib bdg
LC 2007049461

First published 2008 in the United Kingdom

One morning Dad wakes up in such a bad mood that he turns into a bear

This "combines appealing text told from the children's point of view with hilarious illustrations that will ring true to parents and caregivers." Booklist

Harshman, Marc

Only one neighborhood; by Marc Harshman & Barbara Garrison; illustrated by Barbara Garrison. Dutton Children's Books 2007 un il $15.99

Grades: PreK K 1 2   E
1. City and town life -- Fiction
ISBN 978-0-525-47468-5
LC 2006035908

Explores a neighborhood that has only one of several kinds of buildings, but within each there are many things, such as different kinds of breads in the bakery, then shows that the neighborhood itself is just one of many in a world united by a single wish

"Like the best celebrations of unity, this picture book is about the exciting diversity that enriches everyone, and the collagraph illustrations, in warm colors, establish the details and the connections." Booklist

Hartfield, Claire

Me and Uncle Romie; a story inspired by the life and art of Romare Bearden. paintings by Jerome Lagarrigue. Dial Bks. for Young Readers 2002 un il $16.99

Grades: 2 3 4   E
1. Artists 2. Uncles -- Fiction 3. Artists -- Fiction 4. African Americans -- Fiction
ISBN 0-8037-2520-5
LC 99-41390

A boy from North Carolina spends the summer in New York City visiting the neighborhood of Harlem, where his uncle, collage artist Romare Bearden, grew up. Includes a biographical sketch of Bearden and instructions on making a story collage

This is a "vibrant, evocative picture book. . . . Lagarrigue's lush, acrylic illustrations with collage elements recall the tones, brush strokes, and mixture of media that saturate Bearden's groundbreaking work." SLJ

Hartland, Jessie

Night shift. Bloomsbury Children's Books 2007 un il $16.95; lib bdg $17.85

Grades: PreK K 1 2   E
1. Night -- Fiction 2. Occupations -- Fiction
ISBN 978-1-59990-025-4; 1-59990-025-4; 978-1-59990-138-1 lib bdg; 1-59990-138-2 lib bdg
LC 2006-102092

Late at night after children have gone to bed, people who work the night shift, like street sweepers, window dressers, newspaper printers, road workers, and donut bakers, are doing their jobs.

"Quirky gouache paintings capture the mood of this alternative world with its vibrant life. . . . Text and illustrations are equally unique." SLJ

Harvey, Jeanne

My hands sing the blues; Romare Bearden's childhood journey. illustrated by Elizabeth Zunon. Marshall Cavendish 2011 40p il

Grades: K 1 2 3   E
1. Artists 2. Stories in rhyme 3. Artists -- Fiction 4. Blues music -- Fiction 5. North Carolina -- Fiction 6. Harlem (New York, N.Y.) -- Fiction
ISBN 0-7614-5810-7; 978-0-7614-5810-4

In Harlem, New York City, artist Romare Bearden follows the rhythms of blues music as he recalls his North Carolina childhood while painting, cutting, and pasting to make art.

"The talented Zunon's pictures intriguingly combine realistic faces, stylized landscapes and photo-collage that pays homage to Bearden's art. . . . The interplay of poetic and visual metaphor makes for a striking presentation; adults who can appreciate and chant the bluesy poem as well as sensitively interpret the pictures together with children are the ideal collaborators in savoring this intriguing work." Kirkus

Harvey, Matt

Shopping with Dad; [by] Matt Harvey and [illustrated by] Miriam Latimer. Barefoot Books 2008 un il $16.99

Grades: PreK K 1 2   E
1. Stories in rhyme 2. Shopping -- Fiction 3. Father-daughter relationship -- Fiction
ISBN 978-1-84686-172-7; 1-84686-172-1
LC 2007042763

A little girl and her father have a wonderful time in the grocery store until she nearly knocks over a display, then while trying her best to be good she lets out a big sneeze that results in chaos.

"The cartoon mixed-media illustrations depict a lively hubbub amid plenty of color. . . . Funny and warmhearted, this story will be enjoyed one-on-one and handy in classrooms." SLJ

Haseley, Dennis

Twenty heartbeats; [illustrated by] Ed Young. Roaring Brook Press 2008 un il $16.95

Grades: 2 3 4 5   E
1. Horses -- Fiction 2. Artists -- Fiction
ISBN 978-1-59643-238-3; 1-59643-238-1
LC 2007-13202

After waiting for decades for the portrait of his prize horse to be finished, an angry rich man decides to confront the artist.

"Based on a literary anecdote, the story, like its subject, contains only what is essential. Haseley's minimalist text leaves plenty of room for Young's marvelous collages to set the scene and develop the characters." SLJ

Hassett, Ann

★ **Come** back, Ben; by Ann & John Hassett. Holiday House 2013 32 p. (I like to read) (hardcover) $14.95

Grades: PreK K   E
   1. Balloons -- Fiction
   ISBN 0823425991; 9780823425990
                LC 2011049310

In this children's picture book, "happy-go-lucky Ben has a balloon that lifts him up and off the page. With a smile on her face, Ben's sister says, 'Bye, Ben'. . . . As Ben begins his ascent, the window bids him "Come back, Ben," as do the bees, the trees . . . and many more 'friends.' . . . When the child reaches the Moon, he cleverly arranges his descent and down he comes, past all of the friends who await his return." (School Library Journal)

Too many frogs; by Ann and John Hassett. Houghton Mifflin Harcourt 2011 un il $16.99
Grades: PreK K 1   E
   1. Frogs -- Fiction
   ISBN 978-0-547-36299-1; 0-547-36299-4
                LC 2010006783

With rapidly increasing numbers of frogs coming out of her basement, Nana Quimby asks assorted neighborhood children for help, but finally it is up to her to come up with a solution.

"Delicious to look at—with its explosion of acrobatic frogs, its primitivist-detail décor, its confectionery colors—and a treat to listen to." Horn Book

Hatanaka, Kellen
   Work; an occupational ABC. Groundwood Books 2014 40 p. $16.95
Grades: K 1 2 3 4 5   E
   1. Alphabet 2. Vocational guidance
   ISBN 1554984092; 9781554984091

"An alphabetical tour through the coolest jobs you can imagine and some you might never have heard of! With a sophisticated, minimalist design and visual jokes to interpret on every page, Work: An Occupational ABC introduces children both to the alphabet and to a range of alternative careers." (Publisher's Note)

Hatsue Nakawaki
   ★ **Wait!** wait! by Hatsue Nakawaki; illustrated by Komako Sakai; translated from the Japanese by Yuki Kaneko. 1st American ed. Enchanted Lion Books 2013 24 p. ill. (hardcover) $14.95
Grades: PreK   E
   1. Animals -- Fiction 2. Parent-child relationship -- Fiction 3. Animals -- Fiction 4. Parent and child -- Fiction
   ISBN 1592701388; 9781592701384
                LC 2013011003

This book by Hatsue Nawaki "follows a young child's discovery of other creatures. This discovery comes with the recognition that while other creatures can suddenly appear they can also go away and disappear just as quickly. But the delightful appearance of a dad and his playful swoop of his toddler up onto his shoulders will remind little ones that the people who love them will always be there and will never, ever not come back." (Publisher's note)

Haughton, Chris
   Goodnight everyone; Chris Haughton. Candlewick Press 2016 32 p. color illustrations $15.99
Grades: PreK K   E
   1. Bears -- Fiction 2. Animals -- Fiction 3. Bedtime -- Fiction
   ISBN 9780763690793
                LC 2016948035

In this children's book, by Chris Haughton, "the sun is setting, and everyone in the forest is getting sleepy. The mice, rabbits, and deer all give great big yawns as they snuggle up with their families for the night.

But someone isn't sleepy just yet. Little Bear thinks he can stay awake a bit longer. Can he do it?" (Publisher's note)
"A stunning picture book for sharing during storytimes or quiet times before bed, this is a must for all collections." SLJ

Little owl lost. Candlewick Press 2010 un il $14.99
Grades: PreK K   E
   1. Owls -- Fiction 2. Mothers -- Fiction 3. Forest animals -- Fiction
   ISBN 978-0-7636-5022-3; 0-7636-5022-6

While his mother is away finding food, a newborn owl falls out of his nest and anxiously tries to find her, receiving help from various forest animals.

"Haughton's pitch-perfect use of language flows smoothly to the satisfying end. The pencil and digitally rendered illustrations, which have the feel of a mix of woodblock and cut-paper collage, are done in intense, saturated colors of olive, red, orange, fuchsia, blue, and yellow." SLJ

Shh! we have a plan; Chris Haughton. Candlewick Press 2014 40 p. color illustrations $15.99
Grades: PreK K 1 2   E
   1. Bird watching 2. Hunting -- Fiction 3. Bird trapping -- Fiction
   ISBN 0763672939; 9780763672935
                LC 2013955701

In this book by Christ Haughton, "four friends creep through the woods, and what do they spot? An exquisite bird high in a tree! 'Hello birdie,' waves one. 'Shh! We have a plan,' hush the others. They stealthily make their advance, nets in the air. Ready one, ready two, ready three, and go! But as one comically foiled plan follows another, it soon becomes clear that their quiet, observant companion, hand outstretched, has a far better idea." (Publisher's note)

"In spare, humorous text and blocky digital illustrations, four hunters (three of them outfitted with nets) pursue a vibrantly red bird through blue-hued woods. The three larger hunters shush their smallest, netless cohort when he calls to the bird. Subsequent bird-catching attempts result in slapstick pratfalls, but the littlest hunter's methods prevail, charming not only that first red bird, but an entire multicolored flock." Horn Book

Hauman, George
   ★ The **little** engine that could; retold by Watty Piper; illustrated by George & Doris Hauman. Grosset & Dunlap 2009 un il $17.99
Grades: PreK K 1 2   E
   1. Toys -- Fiction 2. Railroads -- Fiction
   ISBN 978-0-448-45257-9; 0-448-45257-X
                LC 2009-9031

First published 1930
"When a train carrying good things to children breaks down, the little blue engine proves his courage and determination. The rhythmic, repetitive text encourages children to help tell the story." Hodges. Books for Elem Sch Libr

Havill, Juanita
   Call the horse Lucky; illustrated by Nancy Lane. Gryphon Press 2010 un il $15.95
Grades: K 1 2 3   E
   1. Horses -- Fiction
   ISBN 978-0-940719-10-1; 0-940719-10-X

"A girl helps a neglected horse in this heartfelt picture book about animal rescue. Bike riding in the country with her grandmother, Mel sees a despondent pinto alone in a corral. When she realizes that the horse is too skinny and moves painfully, her grandmother calls the Humane Society. Lucky, as Mel names him, is taken to a veterinarian and ultimately to a horse therapy ranch where he will live and work. Havill's conversational text keeps the story moving along swiftly without being hindered by a lot of detail, thus keeping the didacticism at a minimum. Lane's watercolor paintings deftly convey the emotions of both the horse and Mel." SLJ

Just like a baby; [by] Juanita Havill; [illustrated by] Christine Davenier. Chronicle Books 2009 un il $15.99
Grades: PreK K 1   E
1. Infants -- Fiction 2. Family life -- Fiction
ISBN 978-0-8118-5026-1; 0-8118-5026-9
LC 2008021971

Delighted by the arrival of baby Ellen, extended family members describe their plans for the young one, from becoming a fisherman to playing the saxophone, but baby Ellen prefers other activities.

"Lively dialogue and an upbeat refrain enhance the spare text. Davenier's watercolor-and-ink illustrations seamlessly blend colors; bursts of rosy reds lead to an arresting presentation." Kirkus

Hawkes, Kevin
Remy and Lulu; written and illustrated by Kevin Hawkes; with miniatures by Hannah Harrison. Alfred A. Knopf 2014 40 p. $17.99
Grades: K 1 2 3   E
1. Art -- Fiction 2. Dogs -- Fiction 3. Vision -- Fiction 4. Artists -- Fiction 5. Portraits -- Fiction
ISBN 0449810852; 9780449810859; 9780449810873; 9780449810897
LC 2012021740

In this children's book by Kevin Hawkes, illustrated by Hannah Harrison, "Lulu and her master, Remy, a passionate but struggling portrait painter, wander the French countryside looking for customers. They don't need much business--just enough for some figs and cheese to keep their bellies full--but not many people seem to appreciate Remy's abstract style. Before long, Lulu secretly lends a paw to Remy's work and . . . the pair are the most celebrated artists on the salon circuit." (Publisher's note)

"This is a delightful story that must be viewed and read several times to capture all of its wonderful details, humor, and charm. Remy is an artist who paints "the essence of a person, not their likeness," no doubt because of his very poor eyesight...Children and adults will enjoy giving the two types of paintings a close look and picking up the subtle humor in each. Hawkes has done the illustrations for the story, but Harrison is credited for creating Lulu's miniatures. The contrast of the two types of illustration is what make this book so clever." SLJ

The **wicked** big toddlah. Alfred A. Knopf 2007 un il $16.99; lib bdg $19.99
Grades: PreK K 1 2   E
1. Size -- Fiction 2. Maine -- Fiction 3. Infants -- Fiction
ISBN 978-0-375-82427-2; 0-375-82427-8; 978-0-375-92427-9 lib bdg; 0-375-92427-2 lib bdg
LC 2006-32209

A year in the life of a baby in Maine who is just like any other baby except that he is gigantic.

"Each lush spread . . . uses space and perspective to particular advantage. . . . The many bits of visual humor will keep youngsters poring back and forth over the pages." SLJ

Another title about the wicked big toddlah is:
The wicked big toddlah goes to New York (2011)

The **wicked** big toddlah goes to New York. Alfred A. Knopf 2011 un il $16.99; lib bdg $19.99
Grades: PreK K 1 2   E
1. Size -- Fiction 2. New York (N.Y.) -- Fiction 3. Missing children -- Fiction
ISBN 978-0-375-86188-8; 0-375-86188-2; 978-0-375-96189-2 lib bdg; 0-375-96189-5 lib bdg
LC 2009-48258

A Maine couple and their gigantic toddler take a trip to New York City, where despite his size, the 'wicked big toddlah' becomes lost.

"Hawkes pairs caricaturish sketches of Toddie with gorgeous blue summer skies and skillful renderings of iconic landmarks." Publ Wkly

Hayes, Geoffrey
A **poor** excuse for a dragon. Random House Children's Books 2011 47p il (Step into reading) $12.99; lib bdg $14.99; pa $3.99
Grades: K 1 2   E
1. Dragons -- Fiction
ISBN 978-0-375-87180-1; 0-375-87180-2; 978-0-375-96867-9 lib bdg; 0-375-96867-9 lib bdg; 978-0-375-86867-2 pa; 0-375-86867-4 pa; 978-0-375-89938-6 e-book
LC 2010025000

When Fred the dragon leaves home he learns that he is not very good at roaring or breathing fire and swallowing people only makes him ill, but with help from a witch, a giant, and a wise boy he finds his true calling.

"Entertaining black-line and colored pencil cartoon drawings enliven this Kuklapolitan-esque cast. Part-slapstick, part-fairy tale, the gently humorous plot has enough twists and turns to keep newly independent readers engaged." SLJ

Hayes, Joe
Don't say a word, mamá = No digas nada, mamá; No digas nada, mamá. by Joe Hayes; illustrations by Esau Andrade Valencia. Cinco Puntos Press 2013 32 p. (hardcover : alk. paper) $17.95
Grades: K 1 2 3   E
1. Gardens -- Fiction 2. Sisters -- Fiction 3. Generosity -- Fiction 4. Farm produce -- Fiction 5. Spanish language materials -- Bilingual
ISBN 1935955292; 9781935955290; 9781935955450
LC 2012004536

In this book, "Rosa and Blanca are loving sisters who grow up and live separately, one by herself and the other with a family, in close proximity to their mother's home. Both have bountiful gardens and decide to share their harvests, in secret, with one another. . . . Only Mamá knows of her daughters' generosity, and she is the recipient of the extra tomatoes and corn. The chile peppers are the last straw, and, finally, Mamá spills the beans about what has been going on." (School Library Journal)

Hayes, Karel
The **summer** visitors. Down East 2011 un il $16.95
Grades: K 1 2 3   E
1. Bears -- Fiction 2. Summer -- Fiction
ISBN 978-0-89272-918-0; 0-89272-918-X
LC 2011014445

During the summer a family of bears enjoys the comforts of life at a cottage by a lake, alongside the human visitors.

"The book is almost wordless. The humorous illustrations, done in pen and ink, cleverly highlight the puzzled family's expressions. Children will enjoy being in on the joke as they watch the bears' antics. A fine vacation choice, especially for one-on-one sharing." SLJ

The **winter** visitors; by Karel Hayes. Down East Books 2007 un il $15.95
Grades: K 1 2 3   E
1. Bears -- Fiction 2. Houses -- Fiction 3. Winter -- Fiction
ISBN 978-0-89272-750-6
LC 2007014051

When the summer visitors leave in the fall, a family of bears moves into the vacation cottage to spend the winter.

"Just five sentences of simple text, spread throughout the book, are a perfect accompaniment to the delightful pen-and-ink and watercolor artwork." SLJ

Hayes, Sarah

Dog day; by Sarah Hayes; illustrated by Hannah Broadway. Farrar Straus and Giroux 2008 un il $16.95

Grades: PreK K 1 2　　　　　　　　　　　　　E

1. School stories 2. Dogs -- Fiction 3. Teachers -- Fiction

ISBN 978-0-374-31810-9; 0-374-31810-7

Ben and Ellie's class has a new teacher, and it's a dog named Riff!

"Colorful full-page illustrations add to the doggone good fun. The placement of the illustrations and text lets readers' eyes scamper across the page." SLJ

Hays, Anna Jane

Kindergarten countdown; written by Anna Jane Hays; illustrated by Linda Davick. Alfred A. Knopf 2007 un il $8.99; lib bdg $11.99

Grades: PreK K　　　　　　　　　　　　　E

1. Counting 2. School stories 3. Stories in rhyme

ISBN 978-0-375-84252-8; 978-0-375-94252-5 lib bdg

LC 2006024249

Rhyming text follows an excited little girl as she counts down the days before the start of kindergarten

"Both the rhyming verse and the pictures are filled with humor and energy. . . . The computer-generated illustrations are detailed and vibrant." SLJ

★ **Ready**, set, preschool! illustrated by True Kelley. Knopf 2005 30p il $16.95; lib bdg $18.99

Grades: PreK　　　　　　　　　　　　　E

1. School stories

ISBN 0-375-82519-3; 0-375-92519-8 lib bdg

A collection of simple stories, poems, and picture games designed to prepare children for preschool

"With lots of cheerfully illustrated rhymes, stories, and interactive games, this big picture book is an excellent title to prepare kids for preschool." Booklist

Smarty Sara; by Anna Jane Hays; illustrated by Sylvie Wickstrom. Random House 2008 32p il (Step into reading) lib bdg $11.99; pa $3.99

Grades: K 1 2　　　　　　　　　　　　　E

1. Stories in rhyme 2. Diaries -- Fiction

ISBN 978-0-375-95054-4 lib bdg; 0-375-95054-0 lib bdg; 978-0-375-83512-4 pa; 0-375-83512-1 pa

LC 2007-11068

Everywhere Sara goes she brings along her journal where she jots notes, makes lists, draws pictures and maps, writes poems, and plans a big surprise for her friends.

"The casual, rhyming text has fun with the sound of words as well as their meaning, and the colorful, relaxed pictures, in thick line and watercolor, add to the celebration of reading and writing—not as a duty, but as play." Booklist

Hazen, Barbara Shook

★ **Digby**; story by Barbara Shook Hazen; pictures by Barbara J. Phillips-Duke. HarperCollins Pubs. 1996 32p il (I can read book) hardcover o.p. lib bdg $15.89; pa $4.99

Grades: K 1 2　　　　　　　　　　　　　E

1. Dogs -- Fiction 2. Old age -- Fiction

ISBN 0-06-026253-2; 0-06-026254-0 lib bdg; 0-06-444239-X pa

LC 95-1689

"A boy wants the family dog to play ball, but his big sister explains that Digby is too old now to run and catch. . . . The story of aging and of time passing is told in very simple conversation . . . and the bright contemporary pictures show the bond between the African American brother and sister and their beloved pet." Booklist

Heap, Sue

Danny's drawing book; by Sue Heap. Candlewick Press 2008 un il $9.99

Grades: PreK K 1　　　　　　　　　　　　E

1. Zoos -- Fiction 2. Africa -- Fiction 3. Animals -- Fiction 4. Drawing -- Fiction 5. Imagination -- Fiction

ISBN 978-0-7636-3654-8; 0-7636-3654-1

LC 2007040402

On a trip to the zoo with his friend Ettie, Danny draws pictures of some animals, who then lead the two on an imaginary adventure to Africa and back

This is a "charming picture book, illustrated in a childlike style. . . . Heap's colorful acrylic paintings and pencil sketches differentiate between reality and fantasy, but young children will easily recognize that . . . there's plenty of overlap between the worlds." Booklist

Heapy, Teresa

Very Little Cinderella; Teresa Heapy; illustrated by Sue Heap. Houghton Mifflin Harcourt 2015 32 p. color illustrations $16.99

Grades: PreK K 1 2　　　　　　　　　　　E

1. Toddlers -- Fiction

ISBN 054428223X; 9780544282230

In this children's book by Teresa Heapy, illustrated by Sue Heap, "Very Little Cinderella is upset when her ugly Sisters are off to a party without her. But her Fairy Godmother (the babysitter) comes to the rescue and takes her to the ball in her favorite blue dress. When the clock strikes midnight, she discovers she's lost her favorite "lello" boot. A happy playdate ensues when a young prince shows up the next day." (Publisher's note)

"With splashy watercolor-and-ink illustrations and a wonderfully tongue-in-cheek tone, Heapy and Heap celebrate the spirit of willful toddlers." Pub Wkly

Hector, Julian

The **Gentleman** Bug. Atheneum Books for Young Readers 2010 un il $16.99

Grades: PreK K 1　　　　　　　　　　　　E

1. Insects -- Fiction 2. Books and reading -- Fiction

ISBN 978-1-4169-9467-1; 1-4169-9467-X

LC 2009-13177

Teased because he likes to spend all of his time reading, the Gentleman Bug decides to change in order to catch the eye of the new Lady Bug in the garden, but she is not impressed until he goes back to being himself.

"Hector's crisp, utterly charming watercolor-and-colored pencil illustrations have a classic, timeless feel, and the spectacularly detailed scenes, which demand close-up viewing, do the bulk of the storytelling." Booklist

The **Little** Matador; words and pictures by Julian Hector. Hyperion Books for Children 2008 un il $15.99

Grades: PreK K 1 2 **E**
1. Spain -- Fiction 2. Artists -- Fiction 3. Bullfights -- Fiction
ISBN 978-1-4231-0779-8; 1-4231-0779-9

LC 2007042072

A young matador who would rather draw pictures than fight bulls finds a new way to entertain the townsfolk

"The old-time setting is well conveyed through illustrations using muted colors for the most part, with the hero in a bright red matador's outfit. The succinct text is enriched by numerous visual touches that help tell the story." SLJ

Heder, Thyra
The **bear** report; by Thyra Heder. Abrams Books for Young Readers 2015 40 p. color illustrations $17.95
Grades: PreK K 1 2 **E**
1. Homework -- Fiction 2. Polar bears -- Fiction 3. Arctic regions -- Fiction 4. Bears -- Fiction 5. Arctic regions -- Fiction 6. Zoology -- Arctic regions
ISBN 1419707833; 9781419707834

LC 2014038684

In this children's book, by Thyra Heder, "Sophie does not want to do her homework, a research report on polar bears. Bor-ing. They're big. They eat things. They're mean. What else is there to say about them anyway? As it turns out, plenty. And when a polar bear named Olafur swoops her away to the Arctic, she soon learns all about the playful bear's habits and habitat." (Publisher's note)

"A breezy, entertaining introduction to the Arctic." Booklist

Hegamin, Tonya
★ **Most** loved in all the world; illustrated by Cozbi Cabrera. Houghton Mifflin 2009 un il $17
Grades: PreK K 1 2 **E**
1. Slavery -- Fiction 2. African Americans -- Fiction 3. Mother-daughter relationship -- Fiction
ISBN 0-618-41903-9; 978-0-618-41903-6

LC 2004-13189

Even though Mama is an agent on the Underground Railroad, in order to help others she must remain a slave, but she teaches her daughter the value of freedom through a gift of love and sacrifice.

Cabrera's "broad sweeping paintings—filled with shadowy images, occasionally bordering on the abstract, with some pages merely washes of color—add a deeper note of somberness to the spare text, told in a child's voice." Publ Wkly

Heide, Florence Parry
Always listen to your mother; [by] Florence Parry Heide & Roxanne Heide; pictures by Kyle M. Stone. Disney/Hyperion Books 2010 un il $15.99
Grades: K 1 2 **E**
1. Monsters -- Fiction
ISBN 978-1-4231-1395-9; 1-4231-1395-0

LC 2010004519

When a new neighbor moves in next door, Ernest's mother, who always insists that he obey all the rules, encourages them to play together every day.

"Young readers will love the contrast in colors from Vlapid's bright and cheery home and the neighbors' dark gray home. This book creates a great opportunity to talk about following directions and how to make chores fun." Libr Media Connect

★ The **day** of Ahmed's secret; [by] Florence Parry Heide & Judith Heide Gilliland; illustrated by Ted Lewin. Lothrop, Lee & Shepard Bks. 1990 un il $16; pa $6.99

Grades: 1 2 3 4 **E**
1. Cairo (Egypt) -- Fiction
ISBN 0-688-08894-5; 0-688-14023-8 pa

LC 90-52694

"Ahmed has monumental news to share with his family, but first he must complete the age-old duties of a butagaz boy, delivering cooking gas to customers all over Cairo. . . . Enhanced by Lewin's distinguished photorealistic watercolors, the sights, sounds, and smells of the exotic setting come to life. . . . At home at last, surrounded by his loving family, Ahmed demostrates his newly acquired facility, proudly writing his name in Arabic." SLJ

The **one** and only Marigold; written by Florence Parry Heide; illustrated by Jill McElmurry. Schwartz & Wade Books 2009 un il $16.99; lib bdg $19.99
Grades: PreK K 1 2 **E**
1. Monkeys -- Fiction 2. Friendship -- Fiction 3. Family life -- Fiction 4. Hippopotamus -- Fiction
ISBN 978-0-375-84031-9; 0-375-84031-1; 978-0-375-94051-4 lib bdg; 0-375-94051-0 lib bdg

LC 2007-37840

Relates the misadventures of Marigold the monkey, who does not agree with anyone, as she shops with her mother for a coat, becomes interested in a new hobby, finds a way to "bug" her best friend, Maxine (a hippo), and imaginatively copes with finding the right outfit for the first day of school

"As depicted in McElmurry's . . . stylish spreads, a blend of up-to-the-minute humor and nostalgic, folklike patterning, Marigold has a long prehensile tail and spiky rust-colored hair that she sometimes wears in topknots. Heide . . . introduces a stubborn, potentially maddening character, but Marigold's sunny disposition and creativity make up for her mischief." Publ Wkly

★ **Princess** Hyacinth; (the surprising tale of a girl who floated) illustrated by Lane Smith. Schwartz & Wade Books 2009 un il $17.99; lib bdg $20.99
Grades: PreK K 1 2 **E**
1. Princesses -- Fiction
ISBN 978-0-375-84501-7; 0-375-84501-1; 978-0-375-93753-8 lib bdg; 0-375-93753-6 lib bdg

LC 2008-39923

Princess Hyacinth is bored and unhappy sitting in her palace every day because, unless she is weighed down by specially-made clothes, she will float away, but her days are made brighter when kite-flying Boy stops by to say hello.

"The quirky oil and watercolor illustrations seamlessly match Heide's wry, understated text." Publ Wkly

★ **Sami** and the time of the troubles; [by] Florence Parry Heide & Judith Heide Gilliland; illustrated by Ted Lewin. Clarion Bks. 1992 un il $16; pa $6.95
Grades: 1 2 3 4 **E**
1. Lebanon -- Fiction 2. Family life -- Fiction
ISBN 0-395-55964-2; 0-395-72085-0 pa

LC 91-14343

A ten-year-old Lebanese boy in Beirut goes to school, helps his mother with chores, plays with his friends, and lives with his family in a basement shelter when bombings occur and fighting begins on his street

This is "a powerful, poignant book. Heide and Gilliland's lyrically written, haunting story makes clear that war threatens not only physical existence but affects the human spirit as well. Lewin's watercolor illustrations capture contemporary Beirut with stunning clarity and drama." SLJ

Heide, Iris van der

A **strange** day; [by] Iris van der Heide; illustrations by Marijke ten Cate. Lemniscaat 2007 un il $15.95

Grades: K 1 2   E

1. Letters -- Fiction
ISBN 978-1-932425-94-9; 1-932425-94-2

LC 2006029265

Original Dutch edition 2006

Upset when an important letter does not arrive in the mail as expected, Jack wanders through the park not even noticing what he is doing and becomes an unwitting hero

"Dutch artist ten Cate's landscapes may be delicate and winsome, but they also brim with scenes of farce and slapstick. . . . It all adds up to a clever comedy of coincidences and misadventures, with ample rewards for attentive youngsters." Publ Wkly

Heilbroner, Joan, 1929-

A **pet** named Sneaker; by Joan Heilbroner; illustrated by Pascal Lemaitre. Random House Children's Books 2013 48 p. (Beginner books) (library binding) $12.99

Grades: K 1 2   E

1. Snakes as pets -- Fiction 2. Snakes as pets -- Fiction
ISBN 0375971165; 9780307975805; 9780375971167; 9780375981128

LC 2011047340

This children's book by Joan Heilbroner presents "the story of a pet-store snake who longs for a real home. When he is finally adopted by Pete . . . Sneaker not only proves himself a good pet, but proves to be a good student (sneaking into school with Pete and learning to read and write); a good citizen (saving a drowning toddler at a community pool); and a goodwill ambassador for the entire animal kingdom (inspiring the community to open the pool to all animals)!" (Publisher's note)

Heiligman, Deborah

Cool dog, school dog; illustrated by Tim Bowers. Marshall Cavendish Children 2009 un il $15.99

Grades: PreK K 1   E

1. School stories 2. Stories in rhyme 3. Dogs -- Fiction
ISBN 978-0-7614-5561-5; 0-7614-5561-2

LC 2008029398

When Tinka the dog follows her owner to school and creates havoc, the children discover a way to let her stay in the classroom and help

"Bowers's vivid acrylic illustrations are full of expression. . . . Youngsters will like learning with each turn of the page just what makes this dog so special." SLJ

Helakoski, Leslie Hebert

Big chickens; [by] Leslie Helakoski; illustrated by Henry Cole. Dutton Children's Books 2006 un il $15.99

Grades: PreK K 1 2   E

1. Fear -- Fiction 2. Chickens -- Fiction
ISBN 0-525-47575-3

LC 2005003282

While trying to escape from a wolf, four frightened chickens keep getting themselves into the very predicaments they are trying to avoid

"Bright pictures convey the comic events with an exaggerated style just right for the story line. There's a satisfying amount of silliness that will leave children giggling." SLJ

Other titles about the big chickens are:

Big chickens fly the coop (2008)

Big chickens go to town (2009)

Fair cow; written and illustrated by Leslie Helakoski. Marshall Cavendish 2010 un il $16.99

Grades: PreK K 1 2   E

1. Pigs -- Fiction 2. Cattle -- Fiction
ISBN 978-0-7614-5684-1; 0-7614-5684-8

LC 2009004789

Effie the cow dreams of winning a blue ribbon at the state fair, while her best friend Petunia the pig advises her to give up all that she truly enjoys in order to prepare for the big day.

"The acrylic on paper illustrations are large, bright, and humorous. The animals' faces are quite expressive. . . . This book will work well for storytimes about barnyard antics and for those always-be-yourself lessons. Besides that, it's just plain fun." SLJ

Helfer, Ralph

World's greatest lion; Ralph Helfer; illustrated by Ted Lewin. Philomel Books 2012 40 p.

Grades: 2 3 4   E

1. Lions 2. Mascots 3. Zamba (Lion) 4. Lion -- California -- Los Angeles -- Biography 5. Animal trainers -- California -- Los Angeles -- Biography 6. Animals in motion pictures -- California -- Los Angeles -- Biography
ISBN 039925417X; 9780399254178

LC 2011020681

This children's picture book, by Ralph Helfer, "opens in Zambia, where a woman in a safari camp rescues an orphaned lion cub and names him Zamba. . . . Animal behaviorist [Ralph] Helfer . . . brings the lion to his animal sanctuary in California. . . . He eventually becomes sufficiently gentle to star in Hollywood films. Zamba's heroism emerges in the book's final episode, in which he saves Helfer and the sanctuary animals during a flash flood." (Publishers Weekly)

Heller, Linda

How Dalia put a big yellow comforter inside a tiny blue box; and other wonders of tzedakah. illustrations by Stacey Dressen McQueen. Tricycle Press 2011 un il $16.99; lib bdg $19.99

Grades: K 1 2   E

1. Jews -- Fiction 2. Charity -- Fiction 3. Judaism -- Fiction 4. Siblings -- Fiction
ISBN 978-1-58246-378-0; 1-58246-378-6; 978-1-58246-402-2 lib bdg; 1-58246-402-2 lib bdg; 978-1-58246-382-7 e-book; 1-58246-382-4 e-book

LC 2010024325

After learning about the Jewish tradition of tzedakah boxes, Dalia shares her knowledge with her younger brother, Yossi, by telling him what her savings can help to provide for someone in need. Includes a note about the history and customs of tzedakah boxes.

"Dressen-McQueen's fully developed summer scenes in acrylic and oil pastel provide a vivid complement to the often-page-filling text, their naive, folk quality bringing great quantities of love and warmth to the tale." Kirkus

Today is the birthday of the world; by Linda Heller; illustrated by Allison Jay. Dutton Children's Books 2009 un il $16.99

Grades: PreK K 1   E

1. God -- Fiction 2. Animals -- Fiction 3. Birthdays -- Fiction
ISBN 978-0-525-47905-5; 0-525-47905-8

LC 2008-34216

On the birthday of the world, all of God's creatures pass before Him as He asks whether each has been the best giraffe, or bee, or child they could be, helping to make the world a better place.

Heller's "repeating form lends the soothing tone of a lullaby, well-matched by Jay's . . . bucolic scenes. . . . Readers will be left feeling connected to the larger world, as one of the 'dear little helpers' God praises." Publ Wkly

Helmore, Jim

Oh no, monster tomato! illustrated by Karen Wall. Egmont 2011 un il pa $8.99

Grades: K 1 2   E

1. Plants -- Fiction 2. Siblings -- Fiction 3. Tomatoes -- Fiction

ISBN 978-1-4052-4741-2; 1-4052-4741-X

"Marvin is the smallest child in his family, but when the Great Gris-lygust Grow-off comes around, he is determined to produce the tastiest tomatoes and win. His brother and sister bait and tease him . . . but he has a potion and a few songs up his sleeve. He grows a plant so large that it shoots its tomatoes—they are the size of beach balls—at his mean siblings. . . . Helmore uses alliteration to make the story sing . . . and the rollicking words dance across the pages. Wall's vibrant, cartoon-style, collage illustrations can seem as fast-growing as Marvin's plant." SLJ

Helquist, Brett

★ Bedtime for bear. Harper 2010 un il $16.99

Grades: PreK K 1   E

1. Bears -- Fiction 2. Winter -- Fiction 3. Bedtime -- Fiction 4. Hibernation -- Fiction

ISBN 978-0-06-050205-8; 0-06-050205-3

Just after the first snowfall, Bear is ready to go to sleep until spring but his friends encourage him to spend one last day playing with them.

"Helquist's sumptuous paintings and expansive sense of visual comedy make this otherwise familiar hibernation tale a keeper. . . . Reader's will want to jump right into these pages and join in the fun—and they'll close the book agreeing that Bear has truly earned his zzzzs." Publ Wkly

Hemingway, Edward

Bump in the night; [by] Edward Hemingway. G.P. Putnam's Sons 2008 un il $15.99

Grades: PreK K 1 2   E

1. Bedtime -- Fiction 2. Monsters -- Fiction

ISBN 978-0-399-24761-3; 0-399-24761-0

LC 2007013812

After Billy goes to bed one night he hears a scary noise, which, upon investigation turns out to be nothing but a sweet little monster named Bump.

"This lively story meets nighttime fears head-on with the right mix of silliness and reassurance. . . . The acrylic-on-wood illustrations create the perfect mood for this appealing bedtime story." SLJ

Henderson, Kathy

★ Look at you! a baby body book. illustrated by Paul Howard. Candlewick Press 2006 un il $15.99

Grades: PreK   E

1. Infants -- Fiction 2. Human body -- Fiction

ISBN 0-7636-2745-3

LC 2005-50792

This "commemorates a small child's amazing feats, from crawling to clapping to exploring food with their entire bodies. . . . The oversize pencil-and-watercolor illustrations are warm and soft, with perfectly captured body movements and facial expressions." SLJ

Hendrix, John

★ Shooting at the stars; the Christmas truce of 1914. John Hendrix. Abrams Books for Young Readers 2014 40 p. color illustrations (reinforced) $18.95

Grades: 3 4 5 6   E

1. Christmas -- Fiction 2. World War, 1914-1918 -- Fiction 3. Soldiers -- Fiction 4. Christmas Truce, 1914 -- Fiction

ISBN 9781419711756; 141971175X

LC 2013029535

Written by John Hendrix, "'Shooting at the Stars' is the moving story of a young British soldier on the front lines during World War I who experiences an unforgettable Christmas Eve. In a letter home to his mother, he describes how, despite fierce fighting earlier from both sides, Allied and German soldiers ceased firing and came together on the battlefield to celebrate the holiday. They sang carols, exchanged gifts, and even lit Christmas trees." (Publisher's note)

"A scene of miniature candlelit Christmas trees aglow above the German trench, as the lyrics to 'Silent Night' float across the page, is just one of several powerful images. An author's note, glossary, and bibliography may serve as jumping off points for budding history buffs." Pub Wkly

Includes bibliographical references

Henkes, Kevin

★ Birds; illustrated by Laura Dronzek. Greenwillow Books 2009 un il $17.99; lib bdg $18.89

Grades: PreK K 1 2   E

1. Birds -- Fiction

ISBN 978-0-06-136304-7; 0-06-136304-9; 978-0-06-136305-4 lib bdg; 0-06-136305-7 lib bdg

LC 2007-45084

Fascinated by the colors, shapes, sounds, and movements of the many different birds she sees through her window, a little girl is happy to discover that she and they have something in common.

"Henkes' spare, direct words have a lyrical magic, while Dronzek's bright acrylic paintings, in saturated primary color and heavy black outlines, reflect the text's plain elegance while carrying an exuberant energy all their own." Booklist

★ Chester's way. Greenwillow Bks. 1988 un il $16.99; lib bdg $17.89; pa $6.99

Grades: PreK K 1 2   E

1. Mice -- Fiction

ISBN 0-688-07607-6; 0-688-07608-4 lib bdg; 0-688-15472-7 pa

LC 87-14882

The mice Chester and Wilson share the same exact way of doing things, until Lilly moves into the neighborhood and shows them that new ways can be just as good

"Henkes' charming cartoons are drawn with pen-and-ink, washed over with cheerful watercolors. They give witty expressions to his characters." SLJ

★ Chrysanthemum. Greenwillow Bks. 1991 un il $16.99; lib bdg $17.89; pa $6.99

Grades: PreK K 1 2   E

1. School stories 2. Mice -- Fiction 3. Personal names -- Fiction

ISBN 0-688-09699-9; 0-688-09700-6 lib bdg; 0-688-814732-1 pa

LC 90-39803

Chrysanthemum, a mouse, loves her name, until she starts going to school and the other children make fun of it

"The text, precise and evocative, uses contrast and repetition to achieve rhythm and balance; the illustrations are forthright yet delicately colored, remarkable for the agility of the fine line which creates setting and characters." Horn Book

★ Egg; Kevin Henkes. Greenwillow Books, An Imprint of HarperCollins Publishers 2017 40 p. color illustrations (trade ed.) $17.99

Grades: PreK K 1 2   E

1. Eggs -- Fiction 2. Animal reproduction -- Fiction 3. Birth -- Fiction 4. Friendship -- Fiction 5. Animals -- Infancy -- Fiction

ISBN 0062408720; 9780062408723; 9780062408730

LC 2016005267

This children's story, by Kevin Henkes, "is a graphic novel for preschoolers about four eggs, one big surprise, and an unlikely friendship. . . . One is blue, one is pink, one is yellow, and one is green. Three of the eggs hatch, revealing three baby birds who fly away. But the green egg does not hatch. Why not? When the three birds return to investigate, they're in for a big surprise!" (Publisher's note)

"Another stunner from Henkes, who is able to evoke so much with few words and such seemingly simple illustrations. Gorgeous and thought-provoking." Kirkus

★ **A good** day. Greenwillow Books 2007 un il $16.99; lib bdg $17.89; bd bk $7.99

Grades: PreK K 1   E

1. Board books for children 2. Animals -- Fiction
ISBN 978-0-06-114018-1; 0-06-114018-X; 978-0-06-114019-8 lib bdg; 0-06-114019-8 lib bdg; 978-0-06-185778-2 bd bk; 0-06-185778-5 bd bk

LC 2005-35923

A bird, a fox, a dog, and a squirrel overcome minor setbacks to have a very good day

"This story works well in every way. As precise, unaffected, and easy for a young child to understand as the text, the illustrations feature forms cleanly defined with thick black lines and brightened with watercolors." Booklist

★ **Jessica**. Greenwillow Bks. 1989 un il $16.99; lib bdg $17.89; pa $6.99

Grades: PreK K 1 2   E

1. Imaginary playmates -- Fiction
ISBN 0-688-07829-X; 0-688-07830-3 lib bdg; 0-688-15847-1 pa

LC 87-38087

"A shy preschooler insists that her friend Jessica is not imaginary—and, in the end, she's absolutely correct. Henkes' depiction of play-alone and play-together time brims with buoyant camaraderie in this upbeat story of friendship fulfilled." SLJ

★ **Julius,** the baby of the world. Greenwillow Bks. 1990 un il $16.99; lib bdg $16.89; pa $5.99

Grades: PreK K 1 2   E

1. Mice -- Fiction
ISBN 0-688-08943-7; 0-688-08944-5 lib bdg; 0-688-14388-1 pa

LC 88-34904

"Magically, Henkes conveys a world of expressions and a wide range of complex emotions with a mere line or two upon the engaging mousey faces of Lilly and her family. A reassuring, funny book for all young children who suffer from new-sibling syndrome." SLJ

★ **Kitten's** first full moon. Greenwillow Books 2004 un il $17.99; lib bdg $16.89

Grades: PreK K 1   E

1. Cats -- Fiction 2. Moon -- Fiction
ISBN 0-06-058828-4; 0-06-058829-2 lib bdg

LC 2003-12564

Awarded the Caldecott Medal, 2005

When Kitten mistakes the full moon for a bowl of milk, she ends up tired, wet, and hungry trying to reach it

"Done in a charcoal and cream-colored palette, the understated illustrations feature thick black outlines, pleasing curves, and swiftly changing expressions that are full of nuance. The rhythmic text and delightful artwork ensure storytime success." SLJ

★ **Lilly's** purple plastic purse. Greenwillow Bks. 1996 un il $17.99; lib bdg $18.89

Grades: PreK K 1 2

1. School stories 2. Mice -- Fiction
ISBN 0-688-12897-1; 0-688-12898-X lib bdg

LC 95-25085

"Lilly loves everything about school. . . . But most of all, she loves her teacher, Mr. Slinger, who is a sharp dresser and greets his students with an uncharacteristic 'Howdy.' The little mouse will do anything for him—until he refuses to allow her to interrupt lessons to show the class her new movie-star sunglasses, three shiny quarters, and purple plastic purse. Seething with anger, she writes a mean story about him and places it in his book bag at the end of the day. But when she looks in her purse, she discovers that he has written her a kind note and even left her a bag of treats. Filled with remorse, Lilly sets out to make amends. . . . Preschool to grade two." (SLJ)

Another title about Lilly is:
Lilly's big day (2006)

★ **Little** white rabbit. Greenwillow Books 2011 un il $16.99; lib bdg $17.89

Grades: PreK K   E

1. Rabbits -- Fiction 2. Imagination -- Fiction
ISBN 978-0-06-200642-4; 0-06-200642-8; 978-0-06-200643-1 lib bdg; 0-06-200643-6 lib bdg

LC 2010011602

"The colored-pencil-and-acrylic art combines thick outlines with vibrant hues, here mostly in a soothing palette of green that fits the nature setting and the comforting tone." Booklist

★ **My** garden. Greenwillow Books 2010 un il $17.99; lib bdg $18.89

Grades: PreK K 1   E

1. Gardens -- Fiction 2. Imagination -- Fiction
ISBN 978-0-06-171517-4; 0-06-171517-4; 978-0-06-171518-1 lib bdg; 0-06-171518-2 lib bdg

LC 2008-42364

After helping her mother weed, water, and chase the rabbits from their garden, a young girl imagines her dream garden complete with jellybean bushes, chocolate rabbits, and tomatoes the size of beach balls

This is rendered with "thick outlines; boldly applied, ice-cream parlor colors; and simple declarative sentences. . . . [This book is] an enjoyable tour of an imaginary place and will plant creativity in young minds." Booklist

★ **Old** Bear. Greenwillow Books 2008 un il $17.99; lib bdg $18.89

Grades: PreK   E

1. Bears -- Fiction 2. Dreams -- Fiction 3. Seasons -- Fiction 4. Hibernation -- Fiction
ISBN 978-0-06-155205-2; 0-06-155205-4; 978-0-06-155206-9 lib bdg; 0-06-155206-2 lib bdg

LC 2007-35965

Boston Globe-Horn Book Award honor book: Picture Book (2009)

When Old Bear falls asleep for the winter, he has a dream that he is a cub again, enjoying each of the four seasons.

"Every word, line, color choice, and composition element feels essential and fits beautifully into a common theme. . . . The elemental words and graceful pacing make this a perfect read-aloud. . . . [The illustrations are] rendered in bold outlines and color washes." Booklist

★ **Owen**. Greenwillow Bks. 1993 un il $17.99; lib bdg $16.89

Grades: PreK K 1 2   E

1. Blankets -- Fiction
ISBN 0-688-11449-0; 0-688-11450-4 lib bdg

LC 92-30084

A Caldecott Medal honor book, 1994

Owen's parents try to get him to give up his favorite blanket before he starts school, but when their efforts fail, they come up with a solution that makes everyone happy

This is "imbued with Henkes's characteristically understated humor, spry text and brightly hued watercolor-and-ink pictures." Publ Wkly

★ **Penny** and her doll; by Kevin Henkes. Greenwillow Books 2012 32 p. $12.99

Grades: K 1 2   E

1. Mice -- Fiction 2. Dolls -- Fiction 3. Personal names -- Fiction 4. Picture books for children 5. Family life -- Fiction 6. Names, Personal -- Fiction

ISBN 0062081993; 9780062081995 (trade bdg.))

LC 2011030043

In this children's picture book, Penny the mouse "is delighted to receive a doll from her grandmother ('I love her already,' Penny tells her mother and father separately). But Penny faces a quandary when it comes to naming her doll. As her mother and father attend to 'the babies,' they offer suggestions, but nothing feels right until Penny stops thinking so hard and lets the name come to her." (Publishers Weekly)

★ **Penny** and her marble; by Kevin Henkes. Greenwillow Books 2012 48 p. $12.99

Grades: PreK K 1 2   E

1. Mice -- Fiction 2. Marbles -- Fiction 3. Lost and found possessions -- Fiction

ISBN 0062082035; 9780062082039; 9780062082046

LC 2012000708

Theodor Seuss Geisel Honor Book (2014)

In this children's book, written and illustrated by Kevin Henkes, the question of ownership is explored when a mouse finds a marble and discovers the lesson of finding objects which aren't yours. "When Penny spots a marble in Mrs. Goodwin's front yard, she picks it up, puts it in her pocket, and takes it home. . . . but does the marble really belong to Penny?" (Publisher's note)

"Henkes continues to plumb the emotional world of childhood as few author/illustrators can... Another gem." Kirkus

Penny and her song; by Kevin Henkes. Greenwillow Books 2012 32 p.

Grades: PreK K 1 2   E

1. Mice -- Fiction 2. Songs -- Fiction 3. Children's stories 4. Singing -- Fiction 5. Family life -- Fiction

ISBN 9780062081957; 9780062081964

LC 2011002154

In this book, "after dinner is done, Penny[, a mouse,] sings her song for her family. They like it so much that they ask her to sing it again, then join her in singing and, on a fourth round, put on silly costumes while belting the tune. In the end, it turns out that Penny's song helped the babies to fall asleep, as they have both dozed off in their basket." (Bulletin of the Center for Children's Books)

★ **Sheila** Rae, the brave. Greenwillow Bks. 1987 un il $16.99; lib bdg $17.89; pa $6.99

Grades: PreK K 1 2   E

1. Mice -- Fiction

ISBN 0-688-07155-4; 0-688-07156-2 lib bdg; 0-688-14738-0 pa

LC 86-25761

"Bouncy watercolors in spring-like colors with some pen-and-ink detailing highlight Sheila Rae's bravado in an engaging and amusing way, and Henkes provides Sheila Rae, Louise, and their school friends with highly expressive faces." SLJ

★ **So** happy! pictures by Anita Lobel. Greenwillow Books 2005 un il $15.99; lib bdg $16.89

Grades: PreK K 1 2   E

1. Seeds -- Fiction 2. Flowers -- Fiction 3. Rabbits -- Fiction

ISBN 0-06-056483-0; 0-06-056484-9 lib bdg

"Lobel's vigorous artwork, a riot of color that pays homage to Van Gogh, locates events in a sun-toasted, south-of-the-border landscape, and captures the rhythm of Henkes' splitting, braided narratives in triptychs alternating with cohesive scenes." Booklist

★ **Waiting**; Kevin Henkes. Greenwillow Books, an imprint of HarperCollinsPublishers 2015 32 p. (trade ed.) $17.99

Grades: PreK K   E

1. Animals -- Fiction 2. Patience -- Fiction 3. Animals -- Fiction 4. Waiting (Philosophy) -- Fiction

ISBN 0062368435; 9780062368430

LC 2014030560

Theodor Seuss Geisel Honor Book (2016)

Caldecott Honor Book (2016)

In this children's story, by Kevin Henkes, "five friends sit happily on a windowsill, waiting for something amazing to happen. The owl is waiting for the moon. The pig is waiting for the rain. The bear is waiting for the wind. The puppy is waiting for the snow. And the rabbit is just looking out the window because he likes to wait! What will happen? Will patience win in the end? Or someday will the friends stop waiting and do something unexpected?" (Publisher's note)

"Henkes never tells readers explicitly what he's up to, and several incidents are wide open to interpretation--and that's what makes this enigmatic, lovely book intriguing and inimitable." Pub Wkly

★ **Wemberly** worried. Greenwillow Bks. 2000 un il lib bdg $16.89

Grades: PreK K 1 2   E

1. School stories 2. Mice -- Fiction 3. Worry -- Fiction

ISBN 0-688-17028-5

LC 99-34341

A mouse named Wemberly, who worries about everything, finds that she has a whole list of things to worry about when she faces the first day of nursery school.

The author combines "good storytelling, careful characterization, and wonderfully expressive artwork to create an entertaining and reassuring picture book that addresses a common concern." SLJ

When spring comes; by Kevin Henkes; illustrated by Laura Dronzek. Greenwillow Books, an imprint of HarperCollinsPublishers 2016 40 p. color illustrations (trade ed.) $17.99

Grades: PreK K 1 2   E

1. Spring -- Fiction 2. Seasons -- Fiction 3. Spring -- Fiction 4. Seasons -- Fiction

ISBN 9780062331397; 9780062331403

LC 2014050050

In this book, by Kevin Henkes, illustrated by Laura Dronzek, "Before spring comes, the trees are dark sticks, the grass is brown, and the ground is covered in snow. But if you wait, leaves unfurl and flowers blossom, the grass turns green, and the mounds of snow shrink and shrink. Spring brings baby birds, sprouting seeds, rain and mud, and puddles. You can feel it and smell it and hear it—and you can read it!" (Publisher's note)

"Henkes and Dronzek make waiting almost as much fun—if not more so—than the payoff." Kirkus

Hennessy, B. G.

★ **Because** of you; [by] B.G. Hennessy; illustrated by Hiroe Nakata. Candlewick Press 2005 un il $15.99

Grades: PreK K 1   E
1. Kindness -- Fiction 2. Conduct of life -- Fiction
ISBN 0-7636-1926-4

LC 2004-45168

"'Because of you,' Hennessy writes, 'there is one more person who will grow and learn,' but also 'one more person who can teach others.'. . . In an empowering conclusion, Hennessy widens the child's sphere of influence, seeing the 'small and precious' acts at home as the first step toward world peace—an ambitious goal made less daunting by Nakata's billowy, cotton candy-hued watercolors of smiling characters exchanging gestures of help and affection." Booklist

Henrichs, Wendy

When Anju loved being an elephant; written by Wendy Henrichs; illustrated by John Butler. Sleeping Bear Press 2011 il
Grades: K 1 2 3   E
1. Elephants -- Fiction
ISBN 1-58536-533-5; 978-1-58536-533-3

LC 2010053708

Anju the Asian elephant recalls her childhood in Sumatra, and the American circuses and zoos in which she toiled for fifty years, when she is loaded into a trailer truck and taken to a sanctuary. Includes advice on helping elephants and 'Elephant Q&A'.

"Butler's realistic paintings in acrylic and colored pencil deliver a soft, hazy muted quality that provides balance to the gentle and often lyrical narration, which highlights Anju's flashback memories of her childhood life with fellow young elephant Lali. . . . This heartfelt, humane vignette provides just the right details to appeal to animal-loving children." Kirkus

Henry, Steve

Happy Cat; Steve Henry. Holiday House 2013 32 p. (hardcover) $14.95
Grades: PreK K   E
1. Cats -- Fiction 2. Gifts -- Fiction 3. Apartment houses -- Fiction 4. Animals -- Fiction
ISBN 0823426599; 9780823426591

LC 2012006579

In this children's picture book by Steve Henry, "on a cold night, a chilly kitty slides through the basement window of a house and encounters a rat. As he makes his way up the stairs, he comes upon the other animal residents: a dog, a rabbit, a bird, and an elephant. Each occupant is busy reading, painting, or playing music and presents the feline with a gift. When Cat reaches the top, he settles into his new home and is warm and happy." (School Library Journal)

Another title in this series is:
Cat got a lot (2015)

Henson, Heather

Grumpy Grandpa; written by Heather Henson; illustrated by Ross MacDonald. Atheneum Books for Young Readers 2009 un il $16.99
Grades: K 1 2   E
1. Fishing -- Fiction 2. Old age -- Fiction 3. Country life -- Fiction 4. Grandfathers -- Fiction
ISBN 978-1-4169-0811-1; 1-4169-0811-0

LC 2008-21543

Jack's grandfather is always grumpy, and a bit scary, too, but during a visit to the country house where "Grumpy Grandpa" lives with the brave Aunt Ellie and Uncle Wilbur, Jack learns that his grandfather was once very different.

"MacDonald's wonderful watercolors have his typical '50s look, and include comic scenes. . . . The pictures are a great match for the text,

where the modern elements sit comfortably alongside the old-fashioned ones." SLJ

★ **That** Book Woman; pictures by David Small. Atheneum Books for Young Readers 2008 un il $16.99
Grades: K 1 2 3   E
1. Librarians -- Fiction 2. Appalachian region -- Fiction
ISBN 978-1-4169-0812-8; 1-4169-0812-9

LC 2007-18156

A family living in the Appalachian Mountains in the 1930s gets books to read during the regular visits of the "Book Woman"—a librarian who rides a pack horse through the mountains, lending books to the isolated residents.

"Complementing Cal's authentically childlike thoughts, Small's deft, rough-edged lines and masterful watercolors convey even more than Henson's carefully honed text." Horn Book

Heo, Yumi

Ten days and nine nights; an adoption story. Schwartz & Wade Books 2009 un il $16.99; lib bdg $19.99
Grades: PreK K 1 2   E
1. Sisters -- Fiction 2. Adoption -- Fiction 3. Family life -- Fiction 4. Korean Americans -- Fiction
ISBN 978-0-375-84718-9; 0-375-84718-9; 978-0-375-94715-5 lib bdg; 0-375-94715-9 lib bdg

LC 2007044073

A young girl eagerly awaits the arrival of her newly-adopted sister from Korea, while her whole family prepares.

"The exquisite oil, pencil, and collage illustrations dovetail with the quiet, simple tone of the text." SLJ

Heos, Bridget

Mustache baby; Bridget Heos; [illustrations by] Joy Ang. Clarion Books 2013 40 p. col. ill. (hardcover) $16.99
Grades: PreK K 1 2   E
1. Mustaches -- Fiction 2. Bad behavior -- Fiction 3. Humorous stories 4. Babies -- Fiction 5. Behavior -- Fiction
ISBN 0547773579; 9780547773575

LC 2012008155

In this children's picture book by Bridget Heos, "[w]hen Baby Billy is born with a mustache, his family takes it in stride. They are reassured when he nobly saves the day in imaginary-play sessions as a cowboy or cop. . . . But as time passes, their worst fears are confirmed when little Billy's mustache starts to curl up at the ends in a suspiciously villainous fashion. Sure enough, 'Billy's disreputable mustache led him into a life of dreadful crime.'" (Publisher's note)

Herman, Charlotte

First rain; illustrated by Kathryn Mitter. Albert Whitman 2010 un il $16.99
Grades: 1 2 3   E
1. Rain -- Fiction 2. Israel -- Fiction 3. Grandmothers -- Fiction
ISBN 978-0-8075-2453-4; 0-8075-2453-0

When Abby moves with her family to Israel, she misses her grandmother and during the dry Israeli summer, she remembers the fun they used to have splashing in puddles together

"Besides being a realistic look at another culture, this well-written book is heartwarming and reassuring." SLJ

Herman, Emily

★ **Hubknuckles**; illustrated by Deborah Kogan Ray. Crown Pubs. 2010 un il $14.99; lib bdg $17.99

Grades: PreK K 1 2   E

1. Ghost stories 2. Halloween -- Fiction
ISBN 978-0-517-55646-7; 0-517-55646-4; 978-0-375-96687-3
lib bdg; 0-375-96687-0 lib bdg

A reissue of the title first published 1985

Lee, certain that the Halloween ghost that visits her family is just a
trick played by her mother or father, decides one year to go outside and
dance with Hubknuckles the ghost.

"Ray's black-and-white drawings of family scenes and costumed
children playing Halloween games are warm and friendly, while her
pictures o the spectral dance add just the right touch of mystery to the
story." Horn Book Guide

Hernandez, Leeza

Dog gone! Leeza Hernandez. G.P. Putnam's Sons 2012 40 p.
(hardcover) $15.99
Grades: PreK K 1 2   E

1. Dogs -- Fiction 2. Pets -- Fiction 3. Picture books for children
4. Lost and found possessions -- Fiction
ISBN 0399254471; 9780399254475

LC 2011013408

In this picture book, a "dog acts up at home and is reprimanded by
his human. He runs away, gets lost wandering the streets, and meets a
rough crowd of street cats and dogs. They are friendly to him and become envious when the boy comes to find him, using a big flashlight in
the pouring rain. As the boy and dog reunite, there are lots of big hugs
and sloppy kissing. The two fall asleep together in the boy's bed that
night." (School Library Journal)

Herold, Maggie Rugg

★ A **very** important day; illustrated by Catherine Stock. Morrow
Junior Bks. 1995 un il $17.99
Grades: K 1 2 3   E

1. Immigrants -- Fiction 2. Naturalization -- Fiction 3. New York
(N.Y.) -- Fiction
ISBN 0-688-13065-8

LC 94-16647

Two-hundred nineteen people from thirty-two different countries
make their way to downtown New York in a snowstorm to be sworn in
as citizens of the United States

"After the first quiet, gray-tone painting . . . this book bursts forth
in a riot of color and activity. . . . A glossary supplies guidance for pro-
nouncing names, and a clear, nicely detailed overview of the process of
naturalization rounds things out. Pictures and story combine to make the
joy of the day contagious." Booklist

Herthel, Jessica

I am Jazz! by Jessica Herthel and Jazz Jennings; pictures by Shelagh McNicholas. Dial Books for Young Readers 2014 32 p. color
illustrations (hardcover) $17.99
Grades: PreK K 1 2   E

1. Autobiographies 2. Transgender people 3. Transgenderism
ISBN 0803741073; 9780803741072

LC 2013031939

This children's book by Jessica Herthel and Jazz Jennings, illustrated by Shelagh McNicholas, describes how "from the time she was
two years old, Jazz knew that she had a girl's brain in a boy's body. She
loved pink and dressing up as a mermaid and didn't feel like herself in
boys' clothing. This confused her family, until they took her to a doctor
who said that Jazz was transgender and that she was born that way."
(Publisher's note)

"An autobiographical picture book describes trans-youth activist
Jazz Jennings' story of embracing and asserting her transgender identity.
. . . The story balances . . . acceptance with honest acknowledgement

of others' ongoing confusion and intermittent cruelty, and it briefly addresses Jazz's exclusion from girls' soccer in her state." Kirkus

Includes bibliographical references and index

Hesse, Karen

★ The **cats** in Krasinski Square; illustrated by Wendy Watson.
Scholastic Press 2004 un il $16.95
Grades: 2 3 4 5   E

1. Cats -- Fiction 2. Jews -- Fiction 3. Poland -- Fiction 4.
Holocaust, 1933-1945 -- Fiction
ISBN 0-439-43540-4

LC 2003-27775

Two Jewish sisters, escapees of the infamous Warsaw ghetto, devise
a plan to thwart an attempt by the Gestapo to intercept food bound for
starving people behind the dark Wall.

"In luminous free verse [this] book tells a powerful story. . . . In bold
black lines and washes of smoky gray and ochre, Watson's arresting images echo the pared-down language as well as the hope that shines like
glints of sunlight on Kraskinski Square." Booklist

★ **Come** on, rain! pictures by Jon J. Muth. Scholastic Press 1999
un il $15.95
Grades: PreK K 1 2   E

1. Rain -- Fiction 2. Summer -- Fiction
ISBN 0-590-33125-6

LC 98-11575

A young girl eagerly awaits a coming rainstorm to bring relief from
the oppressive summer heat

"Beautifully drafted watercolor paintings illustrate the lyrical text,
creating a wonderful sense of atmosphere." Horn Book Guide

★ **Spuds**; by Karen Hesse; illustrated by Wendy Watson. Scholastic Press 2008 un il $16.99
Grades: PreK K 1 2   E

1. Potatoes -- Fiction 2. Siblings -- Fiction 3. Country life --
Fiction 4. Great Depression, 1929-1939 -- Fiction
ISBN 978-0-439-87993-4; 0-439-87993-0

LC 2007-24046

Maybelle, Jack, and Eddie want to help Ma by putting something extra on the table, so they set out in the dark to take potatoes from a nearby
field, but when they arrive home and empty their potato sacks, they are
surprised by what they see.

"This beautifully crafted picture book features panoramic landscapes
and intimate pictures. Watson's pencil, ink, watercolor, and gouache illustrations, warmly rendered in earth tones, capture the small figures
trudging along under a huge full moon. . . . This sweetly understated
affirmation of hard work and honesty, neighborliness and family love,
will resonate with a wide audience." SLJ

Hesselberth, Joyce

Shape shift; Joyce Hesselberth. Christy Ottaviano Books, Henry
Holt & Co. 2016 32 p. color illustrations (hardback) $16.99
Grades: PreK K 1   E

1. Shape -- Fiction 2. Imagination -- Fiction
ISBN 9781627790574

LC 2015003032

In this book, by Joyce Hesselberth, "'Look around. What shapes
do you see?' This shape-shifting story reinforces the identification of
circles, squares, crescents, diamonds, triangles, rectangles, trapezoids,
and ovals while encouraging readers to pair shapes together to make new
forms." (School Library Journal)

"Most shape books ask readers to find shapes in the everyday world;
Hesselberth does the opposite and sparks children's imaginations."
Kirkus

Hest, Amy

★ **Charley's** first night; Amy Hest, Helen Oxenbury. Candlewick Press 2012 32 p. $15.99

Grades: PreK K 1   E

1. Dogs -- Fiction 2. Pets -- Fiction 3. Human-animal relationships -- Fiction

ISBN 0763640557; 9780763640552

LC 2012942295

In this children's picture book by Amy Hest, "on Charley's first night, Henry carries his new puppy . . . . all the way to his house. . . .Henry's parents are very clear about who will be walking and feeding Charley. . . .They are also very clear about where Charley will be sleeping . . . the kitchen. But when the crying starts in the middle of the night, Henry knows right away that it's Charley! And it looks like his parents' idea . . . may have to change." (Publisher's note)

★ The **dog** who belonged to no one; by Amy Hest; illustrated by Amy Bates. Abrams Books for Young Readers 2008 un il $15.95

Grades: PreK K 1   E

1. Dogs -- Fiction

ISBN 978-0-8109-9483-6; 0-8109-9483-6

LC 2007012763

The hard-working daughter of two bakers and a perfectly nice stray dog live lonely lives in the same town, until they meet one very stormy day.

"The pencil and watercolor illustrations, featuring a palette of golden earth tones, echo the gentle sentiment of the narrative. Lia in her blue dress, pinafore, and jaunty cap and the bright-eyed little dog evoke tender sympathy." SLJ

★ **Guess** who, Baby Duck! illustrated by Jill Barton. Candlewick 2004 un il $15.99

Grades: PreK K   E

1. Ducks -- Fiction 2. Grandfathers -- Fiction

ISBN 0-7636-1981-7

"Baby Duck has a cold and Grampa comes to visit, bringing a 'cheering-up present,' an album of her baby photos. Together they look at pictures of her on the day she was born, after her first bath, taking her first steps, and on her first birthday. She feels better and draws a picture of Grampa kissing her cheek, which is just what he does. . . . Barton's watercolor-and-pencil art is as warm and playful as Baby Duck herself." SLJ

Other titles about Baby Duck are:
Baby Duck and the bad eyeglasses (1996)
In the rain with Baby Duck (1995)
Make the team, Baby Duck (2003)
Off to school, Baby Duck (1999)
You're the boss, Baby Duck (1997)

Kiss good night; illustrated by Anita Jeram. Candlewick Press 2001 un il $15.99

Grades: PreK K   E

1. Bears -- Fiction 2. Bedtime -- Fiction

ISBN 0-7636-0780-0

LC 00-41372

Even after a story, being tucked in, and warm milk, Sam the bear is not ready to go to sleep until his mother kisses him good-night

"This is an enchanting little story, with homey illustrations that add to its appeal." SLJ

Other titles about Sam the bear are:
Don't you feel well, Sam? (2002)
You can do it, Sam (2003)

★ **Little** Chick; illustrated by Anita Jeram. Candlewick Press 2009 un il $17.99

Grades: PreK K   E

1. Aunts -- Fiction 2. Chickens -- Fiction

ISBN 978-0-7636-2890-1; 0-7636-2890-5

LC 2008-935296

"Old-Auntie the hen, endlessly patient, marvelously kind, helps Little Chick deal with frustration in three stories. As depicted in Jeram's . . . watercolor washes, Old-Auntie's feathered bulk dwarfs Little Chick, and her gestures . . . are infused with tenderness. Old-Auntie helps Little Chick deal with her eagerness to harvest the carrot she planted; helps Little Chick endure the long wait until her kite finally flies; and assures Little Chick that the star in the night sky that she wants is better off staying just where it is. . . . Hest's . . . light humor and Jeram's visual charm work . . . harmoniously together." Publ Wkly

★ **Mr.** George Baker; illustrated by Jon J. Muth. Candlewick Press 2004 un il hardcover o.p. pa $6.99

Grades: K 1 2 3   E

1. Old age -- Fiction 2. Reading -- Fiction 3. Friendship -- Fiction 4. African Americans -- Fiction

ISBN 0-7636-1233-2; 0-7636-3308-9 pa

Harry sits on the porch with Mr. George Baker, an African American who is one hundred years old but can still dance and play the drums, waiting for the school bus that will take them both to the class where they are learning to read.

This is "beautifully illustrated in subtle watercolors. Hest's understated, unhurried poetry echoes the syncopated rhythms of music. . . . Her book is a simple, sweet, moving portrait of a natural friendship between seniors and children." Booklist

The **purple** coat; pictures by Amy Schwartz. Four Winds Press 1986 un il hardcover o.p. pa $6.99

Grades: PreK K 1 2   E

1. Coats -- Fiction 2. Grandfathers -- Fiction

ISBN 0-02-743640-3; 0-689-71634-6 pa

LC 85-29186

"The artwork is full color, and the deep shades and vibrant colors (especially that purple) are arresting. The numerous details and patternings catch the eye and make for pictures that can be looked at over and over; each time the story's satisfying conclusion rings sweetly true." Booklist

When Charley Met Grampa; Amy Hest, illustrated by Helen Oxenbury. Candlewick Press 2013 40 p. $15.99

Grades: PreK K 1   E

1. Dogs -- Fiction 2. Picture books for children

ISBN 0763653144; 9780763653149

LC 2012954329

This book is a follow-up to Amy Hest's "Charley's First Night." Here, "Grampa, who admits that he is uncertain about getting to know Henry's puppy, is coming to visit and to meet Charley. The boy and puppy wait for him at the train station while snow gently covers the tracks and the town." When the wind blows Grampa's cap away, "Charley takes off into the white world and it's feared that he's lost in the snow. But the diminutive dog saves the day by bringing the cap back." (School Library Journal)

★ **When** you meet a bear on Broadway; pictures by Elivia Savadier. Farrar, Straus and Giroux 2009 un il $16.99

Grades: PreK K 1   E

1. Bears -- Fiction 2. New York (N.Y.) -- Fiction 3. Mother-child

relationship -- Fiction
ISBN 978-0-374-40015-6; 0-374-40015-6

LC 2008026053

When a little bear becomes separated from its mother in New York, a sympathetic child explains the proper steps that must be taken to reunite them.

"The repetitive beat in the sly, humorous words make this a perfect read-aloud, although the irresistible nuances in Savadier's artwork . . . are best viewed at close range." Booklist

Heyward, DuBose

The **country** bunny and the little gold shoes; as told to Jenifer; pictures by Marjorie Flack. Houghton Mifflin 1939 un il lib bdg $15; pa $5.95
Grades: PreK K   E

1. Easter -- Fiction 2. Rabbits -- Fiction
ISBN 0-395-15990-3 lib bdg; 0-395-18557-2 pa

This is an Easter story for young readers which grew out of a story the author has told and retold to his young daughter. It is of the little country rabbit who wanted to become one of the five Easter bunnies, and how she managed to realize her ambition

"It is really imaginative and well written. . . . The colored pictures are just right too." New Yorker

Hicks, Barbara Jean

Jitterbug jam; pictures by Alexis Deacon. Farrar, Straus and Giroux 2005 un il $16
Grades: K 1 2 3   E

1. Monsters -- Fiction
ISBN 0-374-33685-7

LC 2004-46981

First published 2004 in the United Kingdom

Grandpa Boo-Dad not only believes that Bobo has seen a pink-skinned boy with orange fur on his head hiding under the bed, he knows exactly how a little monster can scare off such a horrible creature

"Printed on luxurious, buff-colored paper, Deacon's line-and-watercolor artwork unites cleverly altered Victorian decorative elements . . . with the striking, varied design of contemporary graphic novels. . . . Hicks' folksy, slightly off-kilter language . . . keeps the sense of an exotic, alternate reality watertight." Booklist

Monsters don't eat broccoli; illustrated by Sue Hendra. Alfred A. Knopf 2009 un il $16.99; lib bdg $19.99
Grades: K 1 2   E

1. Stories in rhyme 2. Food -- Fiction 3. Monsters -- Fiction
ISBN 978-0-375-85686-0; 0-375-85686-2; 978-0-375-95686-7 lib bdg; 0-375-95686-7 lib bdg

LC 2008-24536

Illustrations and rhyming text reveal how imagination can spice up even the healthiest meal

"With a toe-tapping beat and loud, splashy spreads, this paean to mealtime chaos will charm small monsters everywhere. . . . Too much fun to limit to kids who don't like broccoli." Publ Wkly

Higgins, Ryan T.

Be quiet! written & illustrated by Ryan T. Higgins. Disney-Hyperion 2017 40 p. color illustrations (hardback) $17.99
Grades: PreK K 1 2   E

1. Mice -- Fiction 2. Noise -- Fiction 3. Animals -- Fiction 4. Humorous fiction -- Fiction 5. Books and reading -- Fiction 6. Books -- Fiction 7. Humorous stories
ISBN 148473162X; 9781484731628

LC 2016028507

In this book, written and illustrated by Ryan T. Higgins, "all Rupert the mouse wants is to star in a beautiful, wordless picturebook. One that's visually stimulating! With scenic pictures! And style! He has plenty of ideas about what makes a great book, but his friends just WON'T. STOP. TALKING." (Publisher's note)

Hotel Bruce; by Ryan T. Higgins. Disney-Hyperion 2016 48 p. color illustrations (hardcover) $17.99
Grades: PreK K 1   E

1. Bears -- Fiction 2. Forest animals -- Fiction 3. Hotels and motels -- Fiction 4. Humorous stories 6. Forest
ISBN 1484743628; 9781484743621

LC 2015044855

In this children's book, by Ryan T. Higgins, "when Bruce gets home from a southern migration trip with his goslings, he is tired. He is grumpy. And he is definitely not in the mood to share his home with the trio of mice who have turned his den into a hotel. There's a possum pillow fight wreaking havoc in one room, a fox luring guests into a stew in the kitchen, and a snuggly crew of critters hogging the bed. . . . [Will he] get his quiet, peaceful den back to himself?" (Publisher's note)

"A merry, witty celebration of chaos and grumpiness." Kirkus

Mother Bruce; by Ryan T. Higgins. Disney-Hyperion 2016 48 p. color illustrations (hardcover) $17.99
Grades: PreK K 1   E

1. Bears -- Fiction 2. Geese -- Fiction 3. Animal babies -- Fiction 4. Eggs -- Fiction 5. Bears -- Fiction 6. Geese -- Fiction 7. Animals -- Infancy -- Fiction
ISBN 9781484730881; 1484730887

LC 2014045992

In this children's story, written and illustrated by Ryan T. Higgins, "Bruce the bear likes to keep to himself. That, and eat eggs. But when his hard-boiled goose eggs turn out to be real, live goslings, he starts to lose his appetite. And even worse, the goslings are convinced he's their mother. Bruce tries to get the geese to go south, but he can't seem to rid himself of his new companions." (Publisher's note)

"Higgins' softly fascinating textures, deft lines, savvy use of scale, and luminous landscapes (which evoke traditional romantic landscape painting, atmospheric in air and light) make for gorgeous art. Visually beautiful, clever, edgy, and very funny." Kirkus

Highway, Tomson

Caribou Song; Tomson Highway, illustrated by John Rombough. Fifth House 2013 32 p. color illustrations $19.95
Grades: 1 2 3   E

1. Spiritualism 2. Caribou -- Fiction 3. Cree Indians -- Fiction
ISBN 1897252617; 9781897252611

American Indian Youth Literature Award: Picture Book (2014)

In this book by Tomson Highway, "Joe and Cody are young Cree brothers who follow the caribou all year long, tucked into their dog sled with Mama and Papa. To entice the wandering caribou, Joe plays his accordion and Cody dances. Bursting upon the boys, ten thousand animals fill the meadow. And yet what should be a moment of terror turns into something mystical and magical, as the boys open their arms and their hearts to embrace the caribou spirit." (Publisher's note)

"Bilingual in English and Cree, this story of the far north follows a family of four that has a spiritual connection to the caribou of the land. . . . [T]he illustrations forgo snowy whites for deep shades of purple, blue, and orange with shapes delineated by thick black lines; the effect is not unlike a stained-glass window." SLJ

Dragonfly kites; by Tomson Highway; illustrations by Brian Deines = Pimihákanisa / Tomson Highway, ohci; osisopéhikéwina Brian Deines. Midpoint Trade Books Inc. 2016 32 p. color illustrations $19.95

Grades: K 1 2 3   E

   1. Dragonflies -- Fiction 2. Cree Indians -- Fiction

ISBN 1897252633; 9781897252635

                   LC 2002491912

This book, by Tomson Highway, illustrated by Julie Flett, "has a bilingual text, written in English and Cree. . . . Joe and Cody, two young Cree brothers, along with their parents and their little dog Ootsie, are spending the summer by one of the hundreds of lakes in northern Manitoba. Summer means a chance to explore the world and make friends with an array of creatures, But what Joe and Cody like doing best of all is flying dragonfly kites." (Publisher's note)

"At once a celebration of heritage, the wilderness, and imagination, this book is a breath of fresh northern air." Kirkus

Hill, Isabel

Building stories; Isabel Hill. Star Bright Books 2012 40p. ill. (some col.) $17.95

Grades: 2 3 4   E

   1. Buildings 2. City and town life 3. Stories in rhyme

ISBN 9781595722805; 9781595722799

                   LC 2010050860

"Rhyming text and photographs of icons on buildings invite the reader to guess what was done or made in each building originally. Includes "stories characters and plots" of the buildings, as well as their settings." (Publisher's note)

"The sharp, clear pictures of the ornaments appear opposite those of the exterior and interior of the buildings on which they are found. . . . [This is a] good resource." SLJ

Hill, Susan

Ruby's perfect day; pictures by Margie Moore. HarperCollins 2006 32p il (I can read!) $15.99; lib bdg $16.89

Grades: PreK K 1 2   E

   1. Raccoons -- Fiction

ISBN 978-0-06-008982-5; 0-06-008982-2; 978-0-06-008983-2 lib bdg; 0-06-008983-0 lib bdg

                   LC 2005-14516

When Ruby Raccoon wants to share a perfectly sunny day with her busy woodland friends, she discovers that perfect days can be spent all by yourself.

This "book is perfect for beginning readers. A simple plot and good sentence structure provide repetition without being simplistic, and Ruby is indeed appealing." SLJ

Hill, Susanna Leonard

April Fool, Phyllis! illustrated by Jeffrey Ebbeler. Holiday House 2011 un il

Grades: K 1 2 3   E

   1. Snow -- Fiction 2. Marmots -- Fiction 3. Riddles -- Fiction 4. Maple sugar -- Fiction 5. April Fools' Day -- Fiction 6. Weather forecasting -- Fiction

ISBN 0-8234-2270-4; 978-0-8234-2270-8

                   LC 2010019878

When Punxsutawney Phyllis forecasts a blizzard on April Fools' Day—the same day as the Spring Treasure Hunt—the other groundhogs are convinced that Phyllis is pulling a prank. Includes information of the origins of April Fools' Day and how it is celebrated around the world.

"Warm acrylics, saturated in rich golden tones and creamy tans, offer a cozy look into this furry family's den. . . . Funny details abound. . . . Here's a lighthearted romp that highlights an often overlooked holiday." Kirkus

Can't sleep without sheep; illustrated by Mike Wohnoutka. Walker & Co. 2010 un il $16.99; lib bdg $17.89

Grades: PreK K 1 2   E

   1. Sheep -- Fiction 2. Sleep -- Fiction 3. Animals -- Fiction 4. Bedtime -- Fiction

ISBN 978-0-8027-2066-5; 0-8027-2066-8; 978-0-8027-2067-2 lib bdg; 0-8027-2067-6 lib bdg

                   LC 2009054215

When counting sheep does not help Ava fall asleep and the sheep complain that they are exhausted, they send in replacements, including cows, horses, penguins, and pigs, but none prove satisfactory.

"Hill's words are simple and effective, and leave room for the art to tell the story. . . . A book that is delightful for the eyes and soothing to the ears, Can't Sleep Without Sheep will quickly become a bedtime favorite." SLJ

Not yet, Rose; written by Susanna Leonard Hill; illustrated by Nicole Rutten. Eerdmans Books for Young Readers 2009 un il $16.50

Grades: PreK K   E

   1. Infants -- Fiction 2. Hamsters -- Fiction 3. Siblings -- Fiction 4. Imagination -- Fiction

ISBN 978-0-8028-5326-4; 0-8028-5326-9

                   LC 2008031736

While impatiently waiting for the birth of a new baby brother or sister, Rose the hamster imagines the things they will do together and how her life will change.

"Rutten's cheery watercolor illustrations, depicting the hamsters' life in their cozy country cottage and later in the hospital, are infused with subtle, appropriate humor. With its thoughtful text and playful art, this book gently helps older siblings confidently adjust to their new roles." SLJ

Punxsutawney Phyllis; illustrated by Jeffrey Ebbeler. Holiday House 2005 un il $16.95

Grades: K 1 2 3   E

   1. Marmots -- Fiction 2. Sex role -- Fiction 3. Groundhog Day -- Fiction

ISBN 0-8234-1872-3

                   LC 2003-67641

Although she can predict the weather much better than the boys in her family, no one thinks that Phyllis the groundhog has a chance of replacing the aging Punxsutawney Phil when Groundhog Day's official groundhog retires

"Details about the origins of Groundhog Day and Punxsutawney Phil are appended. Ebbeler's full-bleed acrylic illustrations show an exuberant Phyllis skipping through a brook, sunbathing, and munching on berries." SLJ

Another title about Punxsutawney Phyllis is:

April fool, Phyllis! (2011)

Hillenbrand, Will

All for a dime! a Bear and Mole story. Will Hillenbrand. Holiday House 2015 32 p. (hardcover) $16.95

Grades: PreK K   E

   1. Skunks -- Fiction 2. Bears -- Fiction 3. Moles (Animals) -- Fiction 4. Markets -- Fiction

ISBN 0823429466; 9780823429462

                   LC 2013038990

This children's book, by Will Hillenbrand, "introduces a delightful new friend. It's Market Day! Bear has picked delicious blueberries. Mole has dug up yummy worms. Their friend Skunk made a new kind of perfume she knows will be a gigantic hit. The trio can't wait to make big piles of dimes. But there are surprises both good and bad in store for the three friends as the farmers market gets underway." (Publisher's note)

"It's Market Day in Bear and Mole's fourth adventure, and they are ready to sell their wares, along with a female friend, Skunk. But Mole's "fresh hand caught worms" and Skunk's "highly aromatic perfume" aren't attracting buyers so much as

wrinkled noses and all-around disgust . . . Hillenbrand's mixed-media artwork should provoke plenty of giggles, as he plays up the smelly, squirmy disruptions Skunk and Mole inflict on the fair, as well as the joy they get out of their less-than-hot-ticket items." PW

Cock-a-doodle Christmas! by Will Hillenbrand. Marshall Cavendish 2007 un il $16.99

Grades: PreK K 1   E

1. Roosters -- Fiction 2. Christmas -- Fiction 3. Farm life -- Fiction

ISBN 978-0-7614-5354-3

LC 2006030236

Long ago in the town of Bethlehem, young Harold the rooster keeps failing to wake the other farm animals in the morning, but when a young woman gives birth to a very special baby in the stable, Harold is finally able to crow loudly and help spread the good news

"The text, matter-of-fact and unsentimental, reads like a folktale, making this an excellent story to read aloud, and the gouache, ink, and collage illustrations depict a humble but colorful farm." SLJ

Kite day; a Bear and Mole book. Will Hillenbrand. Holiday House 2012 32 p.

Grades: PreK K 1   E

1. Bears -- Fiction 2. Kites -- Fiction 3. Storms -- Fiction 4. Moles (Animals) -- Fiction 5. Picture books for children 6. Birds -- Fiction

ISBN 9780823416035

LC 2011007269

In this children's picture book, "Bear . . . and his friend Mole work together to construct a lovely yellow [kite] which soars . . . until a storm hits and snaps the kite's string. The two friends rush to extricate their storm-battered creation from a tree but change their minds when they see where it has landed: right above a nest of baby birds, who are now sheltered by its cover." (Bulletin of the Center for Children's Books)

★ **Louie!** Philomel Books 2009 un il $16.99

Grades: PreK K 1 2   E

1. Pigs -- Fiction 2. Artists -- Fiction 3. Drawing -- Fiction

ISBN 978-0-399-24707-1; 0-399-24707-6

LC 2008-19453

Louie the pig loves to draw but it gets him thrown out of every school he attends, so he goes to live with his aunt and uncle who help him realize he has a wonderful talent.

"Using the bare-bones outline of Ludwig Bemelmans's childhood, Hillenbrand brings to life the experience of countless children whose creativity sets them apart in structured environments, especially school. . . . Hillenbrand's gloriously colored, superbly executed illustrations—collages, fingerpaintings, gouache, inks, pencils—magnetically draw readers from page to page." SLJ

Off we go! a Bear and Mole story. Will Hillenbrand. Holiday House 2013 32 p. (hardcover) $16.95

Grades: PreK K   E

1. Bicycles -- Fiction 2. Friendship -- Fiction 3. Bears -- Fiction 4. Moles (Animals) -- Fiction 5. Bicycles and bicycling -- Fiction

ISBN 0823425207; 9780823425204

LC 2012045823

In this children's picture book by Will Hillenbrand, "Mole is ready to lose the training wheels on his bicycle. . . . After a shaky start, he's on his way. . . . 'Bump. Bump. Bump,' writes Hillenbrand as Mole careens through a field of cattle. 'Scramble. Scramble. Scramble,' he continues

as Mole narrowly misses a turtle. . . . All ends well, and Bear remains a supportive, concerned friend through the chaos." (Publishers Weekly)

Spring is here! Holiday House 2011 un il $16.95

Grades: PreK K 1   E

1. Bears -- Fiction 2. Spring -- Fiction 3. Moles (Animals) -- Fiction

ISBN 978-0-8234-1602-8; 0-8234-1602-X

LC 2010018883

Excited that spring has finally arrived, Mole tries—unsuccessfully—to wake up Bear, but then he comes up with the perfect plan.

"The repetition, ample onomatopoeia, and tender tone of the spare text, combined with heavily textured mixed-media renderings of this gentle pair of pals, create a sunny welcome to the season." Publ Wkly

Other titles about Bear and Mole are:

Kite day (2012)

Off we go! (2013)

All for a dime! (2015)

Hills, Tad

★ **Duck** & Goose; written and illustrated by Tad Hills. Schwartz & Wade Books 2006 un il $14.95; lib bdg $17.99

Grades: PreK K   E

1. Ducks -- Fiction 2. Geese -- Fiction

ISBN 0-375-83611-X; 0-375-93611-4 lib bdg

LC 2005010849

Duck and Goose learn to work together to take care of a ball, which they think is an egg

"While the narrative is fairly straightforward and has touches of childlike humor throughout, it's the bright and colorful artwork that will attract youngsters' attention. The cartoon-style oil paintings set against soft-focus, almost impressionistic backgrounds keep Duck and Goose center stage, and their expressions are priceless." SLJ

Other titles about Duck and Goose are:

Duck, duck, goose (2007)

Duck & Goose, 1, 2, 3 (2008)

What's up, Duck?: a book of opposites (2008)

Duck & Goose, how are you feeling? (2009)

Duck & Goose find a pumpkin (2009)

Duck & Goose: it's time for Christmas (2010)

Duck & Goose go to the beach; written and illustrated by Tad Hills. Schwartz & Wade 2014 40 p. (hardback) $17.99

Grades: PreK K   E

1. Ducks -- Fiction 2. Geese -- Fiction 3. Adventure fiction 4. Beaches -- Fiction 5. Friendship -- Fiction 6. Adventure and adventurers -- Fiction

ISBN 0385372353; 9780385372350; 9780385372374

LC 2013029728

In this book, "a contented Goose comments on the loveliness of the here and now moment in the meadow just as good friend Duck conceives of the idea to set off on an adventure. Goose joins him despite being largely unimpressed with the plan, but upon arriving at the sandy shore, there is a sudden shift in opinions: Duck is put off by the noise, the water, and the sand, while Goose is positively thrilled by their new environs." (Bulletin of the Center for Children's Books)

"Soft oils transport the impressively simple, silly little figures of Duck and Goose in their floppy sun hats across single- and double-page spreads, from the greens of the meadow to the blues, whites and tans of sky, water and sand, while their expressive eyes and postures amply convey comic emotion and visual back story." Kirkus

Duck & Goose, it's time for Christmas! Schwartz & Wade Books 2010 un il bd bk $6.99

Grades: PreK K   E

1. Board books for children 2. Snow -- Fiction 3. Ducks -- Fiction 4. Geese -- Fiction 5. Christmas -- Fiction

ISBN 978-0-375-86484-1 bd bk; 0-375-86484-9 bd bk

LC 2010007743

Goose is more interested in skating, sledding, and making snow angels than in helping Duck decorate their big Christmas tree

"Cheery holiday fare for pre-readers." SLJ

How Rocket learned to read. Schwartz & Wade Books 2010 un il

Grades: PreK K 1   E

1. Dogs -- Fiction 2. Birds -- Fiction 3. Reading -- Fiction

ISBN 0-375-85899-7; 0-375-95899-1 lib bdg; 978-0-375-85899-4; 978-0-375-95899-1 lib bdg

LC 2008051015

A little yellow bird teaches Rocket the dog how to read by first introducing him to the "wondrous, mighty, gorgeous alphabet."

The author "offers up an appealing picture of the learning-to-read process. . . . Hills' oil-paint and colored-pencil illustrations nicely capture both the sweetness of pupil and tutor and the prettiness of the changing seasons." Booklist

R is for rocket; an ABC book. Tad Hills. Schwartz & Wade Books 2015 32 p. color illustrations $17.99

Grades: PreK K 1   E

1. Alphabet 2. Dogs -- Fiction 3. Animals -- Fiction

ISBN 0553522280; 9780553522280; 9780553522297

LC 2014045439

In this children's alphabet book "Rocket the dog and Goose, from the 'Duck & Goose' series (Random), both appear in [Tad] Hills's latest picture book. As they play outside with their friends Bella the squirrel and Owl, they encounter a variety of animals whose activities are described in sentences that use alliteration." (Publisher's note)

"An endearing introduction to the alphabet." SLJ

★ **Rocket** writes a story; Tad Hills. Schwartz & Wade 2012 40 p. col. ill. (hardback) $17.99

Grades: PreK K 1 2   E

1. Dogs -- Fiction 2. Authorship -- Fiction 3. Picture books for children 4. Owls -- Fiction 5. Birds -- Fiction 6. Books and reading -- Fiction 7. FICTION -- Animals -- Dogs 8. FICTION -- Bedtime & Dreams 9. FICTION -- Family -- General (see also headings under Social Issues)

ISBN 0375870865; 9780307974914; 9780375870866; 9780375970863

LC 2011041233

Sequel to: How Rocket learned to read

In this book, "Rocket sniffs out . . . new words in his environment," and his bird friend "helps him create a . . . word tree. Now Rocket searches for ideas for his own story in which he can use his word collection. . . . It's not all smooth sailing; he writes, crosses out, and draws pictures, alternately wagging his tail and growling" but his "finished story wins rave reviews." (Kirkus Reviews)

Rocket's 100th day of school; Tad Hills. Schwartz & Wade Books 2014 32 p. color illustrations $12.99

Grades: K 1 2   E

1. School stories 2. Dogs -- Fiction 3. Squirrels -- Fiction 4. Schools -- Fiction 5. Friendship -- Fiction 6. Collectors and collecting -- Fiction

ISBN 0385390955; 9780385390958; 9780385390965; 9780385390972

LC 2014010940

In this children's book by Tad Hills "Rocket, the beloved dog from the . . . picture books 'How Rocket Learned to Read' and 'Rocket Writes a Story,' is busy collecting 100 things to take to school on his 100th day, and he has the perfect place to keep them safe. That is, until Bella, a squirrel who loves acorns, gets involved." (Publisher's note)

"In the fifth book about Rocket, we discover him searching for 100 things for the one hundredth day of school. He gets help from five friends, including Bella the squirrel, who allows him to store his treasures in her nest . . . The simple text uses short sentences, repetition, and illustrations that support the emerging reader when more difficult words are introduced. Pair this with 100th Day Worries, by Margery Cuyler, and Emily's First 100 Days of School, by Rosemary Wells (both 2000)." Booklist

Rocket's one hundredth day of school

Other titles in the series include:

How Rocket Learned to Read (2010)

Rocket Writes a Story (2012)

Rocket's Mighty Words (2013)

Drop it, Rocket! (2014)

Himmelman, John

10 little hot dogs. Marshall Cavendish 2010 un $12.99

Grades: PreK K 1   E

1. Counting 2. Dogs -- Fiction

ISBN 978-0-7614-5797-8; 0-7614-5797-6

LC 2009042307

One by one, ten excitable dachshunds pile onto a chair.

"Every page has a watercolor scene of the same chair and the changing number of lively dogs. This book will work well as a read-aloud with small groups, though the engaging puppies will encourage closer examination." SLJ

★ **Chickens** to the rescue. H. Holt 2006 un il $16.95

Grades: PreK K 1 2   E

1. Days -- Fiction 2. Chickens -- Fiction 3. Farm life -- Fiction

ISBN 978-0-8050-7951-7; 0-8050-7951-3

LC 2005-20044

Six days a week the chickens help the Greenstalk family and their animals recover from mishaps that occur on the farm, but they need one day to rest

"The simplicity of the text allows the sheer brilliance of the colored-pencil and watercolor illustrations to shine through. The details in each rescue scene will have everyone laughing." SLJ

Other titles in this series are:

Pigs to the rescue (2010)

Cows to the rescue (2011)

Cows to the rescue. Henry Holt 2011 un il $16.99

Grades: PreK K 1 2   E

1. Cattle -- Fiction 2. Farm life -- Fiction

ISBN 978-0-8050-9249-3; 0-8050-9249-8

LC 2010036880

After helping the Greenstalk family get to the county fair, the cows busy themselves finding solutions to many other problems that arise during the day.

"The pencil and watercolor illustrations are packed with plenty of personality and have enough detail to keep kids turning the pages to learn the outcome. Children will, of course, pipe up with the refrain 'Cows to the Rescue!' in group readings and during lapsits, and the mad antics of these friendly and very game rescuers will delight them." SLJ

Duck to the rescue; John Himmelman. Henry Holt and Co 2014 32 p. color illustrations (Barnyard Rescue) (hardcover) $16.99

Grades: PreK K 1 2 — E
1. Ducks -- Fiction 2. Farms -- Fiction 3. Humorous stories
ISBN 0805094857; 9780805094855

LC 2012027681

In this children's book, written and illustrated by John Himmelman, "when something goes wrong on the farm, someone is always ready to jump in, and this time Ernie the duck is determined to help out. But no matter how hard he tries, nothing goes quite right. It takes the clever trick of a kind little lamb for Ernie to finally get his chance to come to the rescue!" (Publishers' note)

"Himmelman's watercolors are sure, whether depicting the brewing crisis or Ernie's inevitable mortification. The artwork also has a comedic clarity that lifts the simple text, enlivening its deadpan humor." Kirkus

Frog in a bog. Charlesbridge 2004 un il $15.95; pa $6.95
Grades: K 1 2 3 — E
1. Marshes -- Fiction
ISBN 1-57091-517-2; 1-57091-518-0 pa

LC 2003-3737

"Himmelman leads children through natural events that occur on a typical day in a bog, beginning with a frog hopping into some moss. . . . Throughout, readers are introduced to plant, insect, and animal names that may not be commonly known and the idea that some events trigger others. Some classification lessons are included at the end of the book. The watercolor illustrations are definitely a draw: the effect is soft and delicate. Detail is beautifully rendered. . . . This book will have broad appeal." SLJ

Includes bibliographical references

Katie loves the kittens. Henry Holt & Co. 2008 un il $16.95
Grades: PreK K 1 2 3 — E
1. Cats -- Fiction 2. Dogs -- Fiction 3. Friendship -- Fiction
ISBN 978-0-8050-8682-9; 0-8050-8682-X

When Sara Ann brings home three little kittens, Katie the dog's enthusiasm frightens the kittens away, until she learns that quiet patience is sometimes needed to begin a friendship.

"Himmelman's charming watercolor-and-ink illustrations depict a character sure to earn the affection of young readers. Katie's expressive movements make both her excitement and her dismay palpable and adorable." SLJ

Hindley, Judy
★ **Baby** talk; a book of first words and phrases. illustrated by Brita Granström. Candlewick Press 2006 un il $15.99
Grades: PreK — E
1. Stories in rhyme 2. Infants -- Fiction
ISBN 0-7636-2971-5

Rhyming text describes the the activities in a baby's day and the words he says while going to the playground, eating dinner, and taking a bath.

"Hindley's unfussy rhyme offers on-target opportunities for concept development: low, high, bye, out. Granström's festive gouache-and-pencil cartoons shine." SLJ

Hines, Anna Grossnickle
★ **1,** 2, buckle my shoe. Harcourt 2008 un il $16
Grades: PreK — E
1. Counting 2. Nursery rhymes
ISBN 978-0-15-206305-4; 0-15-206305-6

LC 2007007022

A child learns to count with the help of a classic nursery rhyme

"The popular verse, included in numerous collections of nursery rhymes, gets the star treatment in this delightful picture book. Illustrated

entirely with quilt patches festooned with buttons, the ditty bounces along in bursts of color." SLJ

Daddy makes the best spaghetti. Clarion Bks. 1986 un il hardcover o.p. pa $5.95; bd bk $5.95
Grades: PreK K 1 2 — E
1. Father-son relationship -- Fiction
ISBN 0-89919-794-9 pa; 0-395-98036-4 bd bk

LC 85-13993

"Corey and his father enjoy a close relationship that is aptly demonstrated in picture and story. He teases Corey and they spend time together doing things such as shopping for groceries and making a pot of spaghetti or being silly at bath time and getting ready for bed. Hines' simple but warm pencil drawings play out the scenes by capitalizing on the incidents described in the text; the strong sense of family (Mother is here too) is evident." Booklist

I am a backhoe. Tricycle Press 2010 un il $12.99
Grades: PreK K — E
1. Play -- Fiction 2. Trucks -- Fiction
ISBN 978-1-58246306-3; 1-58246306-9

LC 2009007534

A young boy imagines himself to be different types of trucks as he plays in the sand.

"Richly colored, digitally enhanced spreads depict the boy at play, intermingled with illustrations of the actual vehicles. The text is set in white and includes plenty of action words. This is a worthy choice for preschoolers and kindergarteners with a big appetite for truck books." SLJ

I am a Tyrannosaurus. Tricycle Press 2011 un il $12.99; lib bdg $15.99
Grades: PreK K — E
1. Dinosaurs -- Fiction 2. Imagination -- Fiction
ISBN 978-1-58246-413-8; 1-58246-413-8; 978-1-58246-414-5 lib bdg; 1-58246-414-6 lib bdg

LC 2010024181

A boy mimics the actions of several different dinosaurs as he imagines he is one of them.

"Set against bright backdrops, Hines's digital illustrations focus on the boy, and in scenes where he appears with the various dinos, his poses mimic theirs. Kids are sure to follow suit." Publ Wkly

Hirst, Daisy
Alphonse, That Is Not Ok to Do! Daisy Hirst. Candlewick Press 2016 40 p. color illustrations $15.99
Grades: PreK K — E
1. Picture books for children 2. Monsters -- Fiction 3. Siblings -- Fiction 4. Conduct of life -- Fiction 5. Brothers and sisters -- Fiction
ISBN 0763681032; 9780763681036

In this children's book about sibling squabbles by Daisy Hirst, "once there was just Natalie. And then there was Alphonse, too. Natalie mostly doesn't mind Alphonse being there—they both like naming pigeons . . ., bouncing things off bunk beds, and sharing a story together on the chair. But Alphonse sometimes draws on things that Natalie has made. And when she finds him eating her favorite book, she's had enough: 'Alphonse, that is not OK to do!'" (Publisher's note)

"Hirst's screen-printed illustrations, bright primary palette, simple text, and even her bespoke, faux hand-printed typeface (WB Natalie Alphonse) suggest the work of a young child, giving her simple tale an authentic charm. Sweet and effective." Kirkus

Hissey, Jane

Old Bear; Jane Hissey. McClelland & Stewart Ltd 2013 36 p. color illustrations (hardcover) $17.95

Grades: PreK K   E

1. Rescue work -- Fiction 2. Teddy bears -- Fiction 3. Toys -- Fiction 4. Children's stories

ISBN 9781770494817; 1770494812

LC 2012939438

In this children's story, written and illustrated by Jane Hissey, "Old Bear has been up in the attic for a very long time, but he hasn't been forgotten. Bramwell Brown and his friends Little Bear, Duck, and Rabbit attempt to rescue Old Bear from the attic and bring him safely back home." (Publisher's note)

"A cast of well-worn stuffed animals populate this story about rescuing Old Bear from the attic. Though the plot lacks conflict, the animals' thwarted efforts and eventual victory are fun to follow, and Hissey's detailed pencil drawings will appeal to fans of old-fashioned toys. This new edition includes a scrapbook with more information about Hissey and the real Old Bear's history." Horn Book

Hoban, Lillian

★ **Arthur's** Christmas cookies; words and pictures by Lillian Hoban. Harper & Row 1972 63p il (I can read book) hardcover o.p. pa $3.99

Grades: PreK K 1 2   E

1. Christmas -- Fiction 2. Chimpanzees -- Fiction

ISBN 0-06-022368-5 lib bdg; 0-06-444055-9 pa

The characters are chimpanzees but "are endearingly like human children. . . . The Christmas setting is appealing, the plot has problem, conflict, and solution yet is not too complex for the beginning independent reader, and the simplicity and humor make the book an appropriate one for reading aloud to preschool children also." Bull Cent Child Books

Other titles about Arthur are:

Arthur's back to school day (1996)
Arthur's birthday party (1999)
Arthur's camp-out (1993)
Arthur's funny money (1981)
Arthur's great big valentine (1989)
Arthur's Halloween costume (1984)
Arthur's Honey Bear (1974)
Arthur's loose tooth (1985)
Arthur's pen pal (1976)
Arthur's prize reader (1978)

Silly Tilly's Thanksgiving dinner; story and pictures by Lillian Hoban. Harper & Row 1990 63p il (I can read book) hardcover o.p. pa $3.99

Grades: PreK K 1 2   E

1. Animals -- Fiction 2. Moles (Animals) -- Fiction 3. Thanksgiving Day -- Fiction

ISBN 0-06-022423-1 lib bdg; 0-06-444154-7 pa

LC 89-29287

Forgetful Silly Tilly Mole nearly succeeds in ruining her Thanksgiving dinner, but her animal friends come to the rescue with tasty treats

"Watercolors in vibrant autumn hues accentuate this comedy of errors with quirky characterizations and fine brushwork." Booklist

Other titles about Silly Tilly are:

Silly Tilly and the Easter Bunny (1987)
Silly Tilly's valentine (1998)

Hoban, Russell

★ **Bedtime** for Frances; pictures by Garth Williams. HarperCollins Pubs. 1995 31p il $16.99; lib bdg $17.89; pa $6.99

Grades: PreK K 1   E

1. Badgers -- Fiction 2. Bedtime -- Fiction

ISBN 0-06-027106-X; 0-06-027107-8 lib bdg; 0-06-443451-6 pa

LC 94-43809

A reissue of the title first published 1960

"The soft humorous pictures of these lovable animals in human predicaments are delightful." Horn Book

Other titles about Frances are:

A baby sister for Frances (1964)
A bargain for Frances (1970)
Best friends for Frances (1969)
A birthday for Frances (1968)
Bread and jam for Frances (1964)

Rosie's magic horse; Russell Hoban, illustrated by Quentin Blake. Candlewick Press 2013 40 p. $15.99

Grades: PreK K 1 2   E

1. Dreams -- Fiction 2. Picture books for children

ISBN 0763664006; 9780763664008

LC 2012942392

In this children's picture book, "Rosie finds a discarded ice-pop stick and adds it to the others collected in her cigar box. . . . The sticks discuss what they can be without their ice pops. 'Maybe a horse,' muses" one. "Meanwhile, Rosie overhears her parents say that they can't pay their bills. Longing to help, she falls asleep and dreams of Stickerino, a flying, talking horse that gallops out of the cigar box and takes her on a treasure hunt. The next morning, Rosie surprises her dad with . . . gold." (Booklist)

Hoban, Tana

★ **Black** on white. Greenwillow Bks. 1993 un il bd bk $5.99

Grades: PreK   E

1. Board books for children

ISBN 0-688-11918-2

LC 92-18897

Black illustrations against a white background depict such objects as an elephant, butterfly, and leaf

This board book features "the stunning, sophisticated photography of Tana Hoban. . . . Simply the best for babies." Horn Book Guide

★ **Is** it red? Is it yellow? Is it blue? an adventure in color. Greenwillow Bks. 1978 un il lib bdg $17.99; pa $6.99

Grades: PreK K   E

1. Size 2. Color 3. Shape

ISBN 0-688-84171-6 lib bdg; 0-688-07034-5 pa

LC 78-2549

Illustrations and brief text introduce colors and the concepts of shape and size

"The wordless book is simply designed and opens the eye to the marvelous world of color; each stark-white page contains one photograph which nearly fills it. In the bottom margin the predominant colors in the photograph are indicated by a row of corresponding circles." Horn Book

Over, under & through, and other spatial concepts. Macmillan 1973 un il hardcover o.p. pa $8.99

Grades: PreK K   E

1. Vocabulary

ISBN 0-02-744820-7; 1-4169-7541-1 pa

In brief text and photographs, the author depicts several spatial concepts—over, under, through, on, in, around, across, between, beside, below, against, and behind

"Children who are confused by these concepts may need help understanding that many of the pictures illustrate more than one concept. However, both the photographs and the format, with the words printed large on broad yellow bands at the beginning of each section, are uncluttered and appealing." Booklist

★ **White** on black. Greenwillow Bks. 1993 un il bd bk $6.99 **E**
1. Board books for children
ISBN 0-688-11919-0

LC 92-20092

In this board book, white illustrations against a black background depict such objects as a horse, baby bottle, and sailboat

"Hoban's compositions are so supple and her layouts so well balanced that she casts a kind of spell." Publ Wkly

Hobbie, Holly

A **cat** named Swan; Holly Hobbie. Random House Inc. 2017 32 p. illustrations (ebook) $53.97; (hardcover) $17.99
Grades: PreK K 1 **E**
1. Cats -- Fiction 2. Pets -- Fiction 3. Pet adoption -- Fiction
ISBN 9780553537468; 9780553537444; 9780553537451

LC 2015044010

This book, by Holly Hobbie, "presents the story of a rescue cat's adoption, the paradise he finds, and the transformative joy he brings to his new family. . . . Hobbie's intricate watercolors evoke the small kitten's hardscrabble life as powerfully as they do his blissful one. This story tugs the heartstrings and is a testament to the importance of pet adoption and the powerful ways that pets connect with their people." (Publisher's note)

"A luminous, heartwarming story of one kitten's transformative journey." Kirkus

★ **Everything** but the horse; a childhood memory. Little, Brown 2010 un il $16.99
Grades: PreK K 1 2 **E**
1. Horses -- Fiction 2. Farm life -- Fiction 3. Country life -- Fiction
ISBN 978-0-316-07019-5; 0-316-07019-X

LC 2010006907

When Holly's family moves from the city to a farm, she longs to get a horse for her birthday. Based on events in the author's childhood.

"The simple artwork, done in pen-and-ink and watercolor, beautifully depicts a time when life for a young farm girl was filled with rustic barns, fields, and delightful animals, while her heartwarming text conveys a sense of innocence and dreams." SLJ

Gem; Holly Hobbie. Little, Brown & Co. 2012 32 p.
Grades: PreK **E**
1. Girls -- Fiction 2. Toads -- Fiction 3. Spring -- Fiction 4. Gardens -- Fiction 5. Picture books for children
ISBN 0316203343; 9780316203340

This picture book "explores the wonders of spring through the eyes of a toad that survives the perils and pleasures of its trek to a country garden, where he encounters the author's granddaughter, Hope. Opening with a letter explaining how Hope's discovery of a toad named Gem inspired her to 'tell the story of Gem's spring journey,' [Holly] Hobbie wordlessly chronicles this odyssey in . . . watercolor, pen and ink illustrations. A palette of fresh greens and yellows heralds springtime, while varying frame sizes and perspectives allow readers to view the . . . toad's cross-country ramble from multiple angles." (Kirkus)

Toot & Puddle; 10th anniversary ed.; Little, Brown Books for Young Readers 2007 un il $16.99; pa $6.99
Grades: PreK K 1 2 **E**
1. Pigs -- Fiction 2. Voyages and travels -- Fiction
ISBN 978-0-316-16702-4; 0-316-16702-9; 978-0-316-08080-4 pa; 0-316-08080-2 pa
A reissue of the title first published 1997

Toot and Puddle pigs are best friends with very different interests, so when Toot spends the year travelling around the world, Puddle enjoys receiving his postcards.

"In Hobbie's expert watercolors are dozens of inventive touches. . . . The book and its heroes are endearing." Kirkus

Toot & Puddle: let it snow. Little, Brown & Co. 2007 un il $16.99
Grades: PreK K 1 2 **E**
1. Pigs -- Fiction 2. Snow -- Fiction 3. Gifts -- Fiction 4. Christmas -- Fiction 5. Friendship -- Fiction
ISBN 978-0-316-16686-7; 0-316-16686-3

Toot and Puddle celebrate Christmas and learn that the best kind of present for the best kind of friend is one that shows just how much you care.

"Hobbie infuses her holiday story of devoted friendship with cozy language . . . all evoked in Hobbie's signature watercolor illustrations." Horn Book

Other titles about Toot & Puddle are:
Toot & Puddle (1997)
Toot & Puddle: a present for Toot (1998)
Toot & Puddle: you are my sunshine (1999)
Toot & Puddle: Puddle's ABC (2000)
Toot & Puddle: I'll be home for Christmas (2001)
Toot & Puddle: top of the world (2002)
Toot & Puddle: charming Opal (2003)
Toot & Puddle: the new friend (2004)
Toot & Puddle: the one and only (2006)

Toot & Puddle: the new friend. Little, Brown 2004 un $16.99
Grades: PreK K 1 2 **E**
1. Pigs -- Fiction 2. Friendship -- Fiction
ISBN 978-0-316-36636-6; 0-316-36636-6

LC 2003054553

Opal's new friend Daphne seems to be the best at everything she does, but Toot and Puddle see another side of her.

"Hobbie's signature watercolors are delightfully warm and appealing. . . . A gentle, entertaining lesson showing that everyone is special." SLJ

Toot & Puddle: wish you were here. Little, Brown 2005 un $16.99
Grades: PreK K 1 2 **E**
1. Pigs -- Fiction 2. Sick -- Fiction 3. Plants -- Fiction 4. Friendship -- Fiction 5. Voyages and travels -- Fiction
ISBN 0-316-36602-1

LC 2004-9897

Toot travels to Wildest Borneo for exotic plants, but when he returns with the Violet Virus, it is up to Opal and Puddle to find a cure.

"The lovely watercolors sparkle with spring sunshine. The pigs' endearingly expressive faces, which convey myriad emotions, add much humor to the story." SLJ

Toot and Puddle: you are my sunshine. Little, Brown 1999 un il $16.99
Grades: PreK K 1 2 **E**
1. Pigs -- Fiction 2. Friendship -- Fiction 3. Thunderstorms -- Fiction
ISBN 0-316-36562-9

LC 98-3665

Puddle cannot make his friend Toot stop moping until a huge thunderstorm clears the air.

"The cartoon illustrations are right on target in portraying the gist of the story and the characters' emotions." SLJ

Hoberman, Mary Ann

I like old clothes; by Mary Ann Hoberman; illustrations by Patrice Barton. Alfred A. Knopf 2012 32 p. (hard cover) $16.99
Grades: PreK K 1   E
1. Play -- Fiction 2. Picture books for children 3. Clothing and dress -- Fiction 4. Stories in rhyme
ISBN 0375869514; 9780375869518; 9780375969515
LC 2010038292

This children's picture book was "[o]riginally published by Knopf in 1976 (with illustrations by Jacqueline Chwast)," using a poem from "Children's Poet Laureate Mary Ann Hoberman" as its text. The story features a "protagonist who likes old clothes for their 'history' and 'mystery.'" In the update, "[i]llustrator Patrice Barton" offers illustrations of a "little girl and her younger brother playing dress-up, making crafts, and happily treasuring their hand-me-downs." (Barnes and Noble)

The seven silly eaters; written by Mary Ann Hoberman; illustrated by Marla Frazee. Browndeer Press 1997 40 p. col. ill. $17
Grades: PreK K 1 2 3   E
1. Food -- Fiction 2. Stories in rhyme 3. Mothers -- Fiction 4. Birthdays -- Fiction 5. Food habits -- Fiction
ISBN 0152000968; 9780152000967
LC 95018186

In this book, by Mary Ann Hoberman, "Peter wants only milk, Lucy won't settle for anything but homemade lemonade, and Jack is stuck on applesauce. . . . What's a mother to do? Even though Mrs. Peters picks, peels, strains, scrapes, poaches, fries, and kneads, the requests for special foods keep coming. It isn't until her birthday arrives that a present from her children solves the problem with a hilarious surprise that pleases everyone." (Publisher's note)

The two sillies; illustrated by Lynne Cravath. Harcourt 2000 un il $16
Grades: PreK K 1 2   E
1. Stories in rhyme 2. Cats -- Fiction 3. Mice -- Fiction
ISBN 0-15-202221-X
LC 98-51844

"When Silly Lilly admires Sammy's cat and asks how to get one, he gives her step-by-step instructions that seem to make no sense at all. . . . Short sentences use mono-syllabic words and rhyme to great effect. The brightly colored cartoon-style art adds just the right touch of exaggerated humor." Horn Book Guide

★ You read to me, I'll read to you; very short fairy tales to read together (in which wolves are tamed, trolls are transformed, and peas are triumphant) illustrated by Michael Emberley. Little, Brown 2004 32p il $16.95
Grades: K 1 2 3   E
1. Fairy tales
ISBN 0-316-14611-0
LC 2003-47445

"The two voices join seamlessly together to create a truly delightful reading ensemble. Emberley's humorous illustrations feature expressive characters drawn in pen, watercolor, and pastel." SLJ

Hodges, Margaret

The wee Christmas cabin; retold by Margaret Hodges; illustrated by Kimberly Bulcken Root. Holiday House 2009 un il $16.95
Grades: K 1 2 3   E
1. Fairies -- Fiction 2. Ireland -- Fiction 3. Christmas -- Fiction
ISBN 978-0-8234-1528-1; 0-8234-1528-7
LC 00044877

A tinker's child who grows up helping everyone in her Irish village is rewarded in her old age with a cabin built by fairies on Christmas Eve.

"Hodges' elegant prose doesn't spell out exactly what happens to Oona, allowing children's imaginations to fill in the rest, and preserving the wonder of the story. Delicate watercolor paintings emphasize the cool dark blues and greens of wintry Ireland against the warm golds and reds of the cheery cabin's hearth." Booklist

Hodgkins, Fran

Who's been here? a tale in tracks. illustrated by Karel Hayes. Down East 2008 un il $15.95
Grades: PreK K 1 2   E
1. Dogs -- Fiction 2. Animal tracks -- Fiction
ISBN 978-0-89272-714-8; 0-89272-714-4
LC 2008015756

"Three children follow golden retriever Willy into the snowy outdoors, seeing not only his paw prints but also those animals he's tracked. Delicate illustrations of snow-covered forest include accurate animal tracks and woodsy borders. The spare text uses repetition effectively in this book for nature lovers." Horn Book Guide

Hodgkinson, Jo

The talent show. Andersen 2011 un il $16.95
Grades: PreK K 1   E
1. Stories in rhyme 2. Size -- Fiction 3. Birds -- Fiction 4. Animals -- Fiction
ISBN 0761374876; 9780761374879; 978-0-7613-7487-9; 0-7613-7487-6
LC 2010032965

A tiny red bird wants very much to win the upcoming talent show, but first he must prove that being small does not mean having little talent.

"The rhyming text and dynamic scenes in vivid colors keep the tale rocking. Panels in various sizes are simple compositions that encourage focus on the personalities depicted. From the crooning moose to the singing hippo in a boa, the illustrations don't miss a beat of humor." SLJ

Hodgkinson, Leigh

Limelight Larry. Tiger Tales 2011 un il $15.95
Grades: PreK K 1   E
1. Peacocks -- Fiction 2. Books and reading -- Fiction
ISBN 978-1-58925-102-1; 1-58925-102-4

Limelight Larry the peacock is delighted when he finds an empty book— he can be the star of the story! Then a whole host of storybook characters arrive and Larry, much to his outrage, is pushed out of the limelight.

"Prereaders should be captivated by this cacophony of type and images, and they will certainly identify with the willful peacock." Kirkus

Smile! Balzer & Bray 2010 un il $16.99
Grades: PreK K 1   E
1. Family life -- Fiction
ISBN 978-0-06-185269-5; 0-06-185269-4
LC 2009-14277

A little girl searches all over the house for the smile that seems to have deserted her.

"The childlike illustrations are done in bright colors with collage elements, occasional labels, and sometimes with sound effects. . . . Sunny's imagination enriches her search." SLJ

Hodson, Sally

Granny's clan; a tale of wild orcas. by Sally Hodson; illustrated by Ann Jones. Dawn Publications 2012 32 p. (hardback) $16.95
Grades: 2 3 4   E
1. Killer whales -- Fiction 2. Killer whale -- Behavior
ISBN 1584691719; 9781584691716; 9781584691723
LC 2011049431

In this book, Sally Hodson offers a "glimpse into the real world of a Pacific Northwest killer whale family or pod. Also known as an orca, 100-year-old granny and her family (the J-pod) interact with one another, just as humans do. Granny teaches her children, grandchildren and great-grandchildren, how and where to locate food, play nicely, avoid danger, sing orca songs, and coexist with people." (Children's Literature)

Hoefler, Kate

Real cowboys; written by Kate Hoefler and illustrated by Jonathan Bean. Houghton Mifflin Harcourt 2015 32 p. color illustrations (ebook) $16.99; $16.99

Grades: K 1 2 3   E

1. Cowboys -- Fiction

ISBN 9781328686107; 0544148924; 9780544148925

LC 2014048555

This book, written by Kate Hoefler and illustrated by Jonathan Bean, is a "realistic and poetic picture book debut about the wide open West, the myth of rowdy, rough-riding cowboys and cowgirls is remade. A timely and multifaceted portrayal reveals a lifestyle that is as diverse as it contrary to what we've come to expect." (Publisher's note)

Hoff, Syd

The **littlest** leaguer; story and pictures by Syd Hoff. HarperCollins Childrens Books 2008 48p il (I can read!) $16.99; pa $3.99

Grades: PreK K 1 2   E

1. Baseball -- Fiction

ISBN 978-0-06-053772-2; 0-06-053772-8; 978-0-06-053774-6 pa; 0-06-053774-4 pa

A reissue of the title first published 1976

Littlest of all the little leaguers, Harold has a hard time finding some way to really help his team.

"Hoff's ability to tell an interesting story with a minimum of words is unsurpassed." Horn Book Guide

Oliver; story and pictures by Syd Hoff. HarperCollins Pubs. 2000 64p il (I can read book) lib bdg $17.89; pa $3.99

Grades: PreK K 1 2   E

1. Circus -- Fiction 2. Elephants -- Fiction

ISBN 0-06-028709-8 lib bdg; 0-06-444272-1 pa

LC 99-25591

A newly illustrated edition of the title first published 1960

Oliver the elephant looks elsewhere for employment after learning that the circus already has enough elephants

"One of the most warm-hearted and appealing easy-to-read books available." SLJ

Sammy the seal; story and pictures by Syd Hoff. newly il ed; HarperCollins Pubs. 2000 64p il (I can read book) $16.99; lib bdg $16.89; pa $3.99

Grades: PreK K 1 2   E

1. Zoos -- Fiction 2. Seals (Animals) -- Fiction

ISBN 0-06-028545-1; 0-06-028546-X lib bdg; 0-06-444270-5 pa

LC 99-13805

A newly illustrated edition of the title first published 1959

Anxious to see what life is like outside the zoo, Sammy the seal explores the city, goes to school, and plays with the children but decides that there really is no place like home

"Happy adventures told in entertaining colored cartoonlike drawings and in simple vocabulary and short sentences which first graders can read with a minimum of help." Booklist

Hoffman, Mary

★ **Amazing** Grace; pictures by Caroline Binch. Dial Bks. for Young Readers 1991 un il $16.99

Grades: K 1 2 3   E

1. Theater -- Fiction 2. African Americans -- Fiction

ISBN 0-8037-1040-2

LC 90-25108

Although her classmates say that she cannot play Peter Pan in the school play because she is black and a girl, Grace discovers that she can do anything she sets her mind to do

"Gorgeous watercolor illustrations portraying a determined, talented child and her warm family enhance an excellent text and positive message of self-affirmation. Grace is an amazing girl and this is an amazing book." SLJ

Other picture book titles about Grace are:

Boundless Grace (1995)

Grace at Christmas (2011)

Princess Grace (2008)

The **color** of home; pictures by Karin Littlewood. Phyllis Fogelman Bks. 2002 un il $15.99

Grades: K 1 2 3   E

1. Somalia -- Fiction 2. Refugees -- Fiction 3. Immigrants -- Fiction

ISBN 0-8037-2841-7

LC 2001-7393

Hassan, newly-arrived in the United States and feeling homesick, paints a picture at school that shows his old home in Somalia as well as the reason his family had to leave

"Readers gain a realistic child's perspective on what it is like to be forced to emigrate from a war-torn country. . . . Littlewood's impressionistic watercolor illustrations . . . beautifully convey Hassan's sadness, fear, and ultimate happiness." SLJ

Grace at Christmas; illustrated by Cornelius Van Wright and Ying-Hwa Hu. Dial Books for Young Readers 2011 il $17.99

Grades: K 1 2 3   E

1. Christmas -- Fiction 2. Family life -- Fiction 3. African Americans -- Fiction

ISBN 978-0-8037-3577-4; 0-8037-3577-4

LC 2011004571

When her grandmother takes in a stranded family at Christmas, Grace is reluctant to share her favorite holiday with strangers, even though the visiting family includes a "real live ballerina."

"Hoffman's empathetic storytelling and Van Wright and Hu's naturalistic illustrations make the most of Grace's abundant humor and personality." Publ Wkly

Hogan, Jamie

Seven days of Daisy. Down East 2012 un il $14.95

Grades: PreK K   E

1. Islands -- Fiction 2. Grandmothers -- Fiction

ISBN 978-0-89272-919-7; 0-89272-919-8

"Counting down the days before Nana comes to visit her island home, young Daisy describes how she fills her time. Sailing, tea parties at the shore, rocking in the hammock, and playing tag all make the wait a bit less tedious. When Nana arrives, Daisy is ready to tell her about her various activities. . . . The simple sentences and childlike focus stay true to the narrator. . . . The realistic charcoals and pastels offer texture, and colors vary to reflect moods and times of day." SLJ

Hogrogian, Nonny

Cool cat. Roaring Brook Press 2009 un il $17.99

Grades: PreK K 1 2   E

1. Stories without words 2. Cats -- Fiction 3. Animals -- Fiction 4. Painting -- Fiction

ISBN 978-1-59643-429-5; 1-59643-429-5

"A vacant lot strewn with garbage is transformed by an artistic and imaginative black cat in this wordless picture book. Using paints and brushes from his wooden art box, the feline covers his drab surroundings with leaves and sky, enlisting the help of some birds and woodland creatures that take up brushes to add flowers, trees, and a pond. . . . Simple, almost childlike art in the lush colors of summer combines with brilliant composition to tell the story. . . . Both visually and conceptually, this is a gem." SLJ

Holabird, Katharine

★ **Angelina** Ballerina; story by Katharine Holabird; illustrations by Helen Craig. Viking 2006 un il $12.99

Grades: PreK K 1 2   E
  1. Mice -- Fiction 2. Ballet -- Fiction
  ISBN 0-670-06026-7

A reissue of the title first published 1983 by Potter

Angelina the mouse loves to dance and wants to become a ballerina more than anything else in the world.

"Touches of humor, attention to detail, a feel for dance and truly anthropomorphic mice make the illustrations a major part of the book." Child Book Rev Serv

  Other titles about Angelina are:
  Angelina and Alice (1987)
  Angelina and Henry (2002)
  Angelina and the princess (1984)
  Angelina and the royal wedding (2010)
  Angelina at the fair (1985)
  Angelina on stage (1986)
  Angelina, star of the show (2008)
  Angelina's baby sister (1991)
  Angelina's Christmas (1985)
  Angelina's Halloween (2000)

Hole, Stian

★ **Garmann's** summer. Eerdmans Books for Young Readers 2008 un il $17.50

Grades: 1 2 3   E
  1. Fear -- Fiction 2. Aunts -- Fiction 3. Summer -- Fiction 4. Old age -- Fiction 5. Family life -- Fiction
  ISBN 978-0-8028-5339-4; 0-8028-5339-0

Original Norwegian edition, 2006

Now that summer is nearly over, Garmann is afraid of starting school. He asks his elderly aunts, and his father, and his mother what they are afraid of.

"The illustrations, spacious, quirky mosaic collages comprising photos, old-fashioned etchings, and wallpaper samples are utterly without a trace of sentimentality. In a feat of deceptive simplicity, Hole has crafted an elegant, fanciful, wholly poetic exploration of the nature of fear and the strength and hope required to conquer it." Booklist

  Another title about Garmann is:
  Garmann's street (2010)

Holmberg, Bo R.

A **day** with Dad; illustrations by Eva Eriksson. Candlewick Press 2008 un il $15.99

Grades: K 1 2 3   E
  1. Divorce -- Fiction 2. Father-son relationship -- Fiction
  ISBN 978-0-7636-3221-2; 0-7636-3221-X

LC 2007034228

Tim waits with excitement for a train to bring his father, who lives in another town, then spends an entire day with him, doing all of their favorite things, until it is time for Dad to catch the train home.

"Eriksson's unfussy colored-pencil illustrations are a good match for Holmberg's straightforward text. . . . This gentle, poignant story offers comfort to readers in similar circumstances and leaves them with a hopeful message." Horn Book

Holmes, Janet A.

Have you seen Duck? [by] Janet A. Holmes and [illustrated by] Jonathan Bentley. Scholastic 2011 un il $8.99

Grades: PreK K   E
  1. Toys -- Fiction 2. Lost and found possessions -- Fiction
  ISBN 978-0-545-22488-8; 0-545-22488-8

LC 2010-20587

"Holmes offers a fresh spin on an old favorite—the child who can't be away from his stuffed animal. Here that child is the towheaded narrator, and the stuffie, a small yellow duck. But in the boy's mind, it's Duck who needs him. . . . The light, airy ink-and-watercolor artwork, brightened by yellows, keeps its focus on the boy and his duck. Perhaps not as dramatic as Knuffle Bunny (2004) but every bit as moving." Booklist

Holmes, Mary Tavener

A **giraffe** goes to Paris; by Mary Tavener Holmes and John Harris; illustrated by Jon Cannell. Marshall Cavendish 2010 31p il $16.95

Grades: K 1 2 3   E
  1. France -- Fiction 2. Giraffes -- Fiction 3. Voyages and travels -- Fiction
  ISBN 978-0-7614-5595-0; 0-7614-5595-7

LC 2009-19047

Recounts the 1827 journey of a young giraffe named Belle, a gift from the Pasha of Egypt to King Charles X of France, as she makes her way by boat and land to Paris, accompanied by her devoted caretaker, Atir.

"Loopy handwritten script is used for emphasis . . . while old maps, photographs, and potraits supplement Cannell's watercolor-and-ink drawings. . . . This is history for children as it ought to be written." Publ Wkly

Holt, Kimberly Willis

The **adventures** of Granny Clearwater & Little Critter; illustrated by Laura Huliska-Beith. Henry Holt and Company 2010 un il $16.99

Grades: K 1 2 3   E
  1. Tall tales 2. West (U.S.) -- Fiction 3. Grandmothers -- Fiction 4. Frontier and pioneer life -- Fiction
  ISBN 978-0-8050-7899-2; 0-8050-7899-1

LC 2009-27418

"When the Clearwaters start their journey west in a covered wagon, a mishap separates Granny and her grandson Little Critter from the others. They travel across the scorching-hot prairie in an effort to find their missing family members. . . . This is a wonderful tall tale, told with plenty of humor and enhanced by colorful collage illustrations. . . . A rip-roaring yarn." SLJ

Holub, Joan

Apple countdown; by Joan Holub; illustrated by Jan Smith. Albert Whitman & Co. 2009 un il $16.99

Grades: PreK K 1 2   E
  1. Counting 2. School stories 3. Stories in rhyme 4. Apples -- Fiction
  ISBN 978-0-8075-0398-0; 0-8075-0398-3

LC 2008031705

Rhyming text describes a school field trip to an apple orchard, where the students count down all the things they see, from twenty nametags to one apple pie.

"The vibrant watercolor illustrations are dominated by primary colors, and the excitement shows on the smiling faces of the students." SLJ

The **garden** that we grew; pictures by Hiroe Nakata. Viking 2001 un il (Viking easy-to-read) $13.99

Grades: K 1 2 **E**

1. Stories in rhyme 2. Pumpkin -- Fiction 3. Gardening -- Fiction
ISBN 0-670-89799-X

LC 00-10966

Children plant pumpkin seeds, water and weed the garden patch, watch the pumpkins grow, pick them, and enjoy them in various ways

"The text blossoms with the ample warmth, light, and gentle sense of humor in the pictures." Horn Book

★ **Little** Red Writing; by Joan Holub and illustrated by Melissa Sweet. Chronicle Books 2013 36 p. (alk. paper) $16.99

Grades: 1 2 3 **E**

1. Pencils -- Fiction 2. Adventure fiction -- Fiction 3. Humorous stories 4. Authorship -- Fiction 5. Creative writing -- Fiction
ISBN 0811878694; 9780811878692

LC 2012027737

In this book author Joan Holub and illustrator Melissa Sweet present a "retelling of 'Little Red Riding Hood,' in which a brave, little red pencil finds her way through the many perils of writing a story, faces a ravenous pencil sharpener (the Wolf 3000) . . . and saves the day." (Publisher's note) "Little Red is eager to begin, and knowing that a good story often involves a journey, she sets off, armed with a basket of words for help along the way." (Booklist)

Spring is here! a story about seeds. by Joan Holub; illustrated by Will Terry. Aladdin 2008 un il (Ready-to-read: Ant hill) hardcover o.p. pa $3.99

Grades: PreK K 1 **E**

1. Stories in rhyme 2. Ants -- Fiction 3. Seeds -- Fiction 4. Gardening -- Fiction
ISBN 978-1-4169-5132-2; 1-4169-5132-6 lib bdg; 978-1-4169-5131-5 pa; 1-4169-5131-8 pa

LC 2007-17677

In autumn, the little friends from Ant Hill find and plant some seeds, then patiently wait until spring to enjoy the plants that appear.

"The very few words of rhyming text on each spread are supplemented by the book's funny illustrations, which fill the pages and are integral to helping tell the stories. The rhymes and picture clues will help even the newest readers decipher these simplest of tales." Horn Book Guide

Zeus and the thunderbolt of doom; Joan Holub, Suzanne Williams. Aladdin, Simon and Schuster 2012 100 p. (paperback) $5.99; (hardcover) $15.99

Grades: 3 4 5 **E**

1. Greek mythology -- Graphic novels 2. Gods and goddesses -- Graphic novels
ISBN 1442457872; 9781442452633; 9781442457874

LC 2012939508

Authors Joan Hollub and Suzanne Williams present a children's story. "After 10-year-old Zeus is plucked from his childhood cave in Crete by armed 'Cronies' of the Titan king, Cronus, he is rescued by harpies. He then finds himself in a Grecian temple where he acquires a lightning bolt with the general personality of a puppy and receives hints of his destiny from an Oracle with fogged eyeglasses. Recaptured and about to be eaten by Cronus, Zeus hurls the bolt down the Titan's throat--causing the king to choke and . . . barf up several previously eaten Olympians." (Kirkus)

Hood, Susan

Mission: back to school; Back to School: Top-Secret Information. by Susan Hood; illustrated by Mary Lundquist. Random House Inc. 2016 32 p. color illustrations (hardcover) $16.99

Grades: PreK K 1 2 **E**

1. Social skills -- Fiction 2. Elementary schools -- Fiction 3. Preparatory schools -- Fiction 4. Schools -- Fiction 5. First day of school -- Fiction 6. First day of school -- Fiction
ISBN 9780375973499; 9780385384711

LC 2015013850

This children's book by Susan Hood, illustrated by Mary Lundquist presents the first day of school as a secret agent's mission with steps to complete. "After rendezvousing at the vehicle checkpoint (meeting at the bus stop), young agents will learn to build diplomatic relations (make new friends), conduct fieldwork (explore outside during science class), and develop new lines of communication (learn to read and play music)." (Publisher's note)

"Humorous details, diverse agents, and a full day's worth of elementary school fieldwork make this an excellent choice for students on the first day of school." SLJ

Pup and Hound hatch an egg; written by Susan Hood; illustrated by Linda Hendry. Kids Can Press 2007 32p il (Kids can read) $14.95; pa $3.95

Grades: PreK K 1 **E**

1. Stories in rhyme 2. Dogs -- Fiction 3. Turtles -- Fiction
ISBN 978-1-55337-974-4; 1-55337-974-8; 978-1-55337-975-1 pa; 1-55337-975-6 pa

"Pup finds an egg in the grass and tries to return it to Duck and then Mother Hen. Both mothers deny ownership, and when the egg eventually hatches, it turns out to be a baby turtle—a new friend for Pup and Hound. [The book has] appealing characters and all of the requisites for a successful beginning reader. . . . Bouncy rhymes add to the fun." SLJ

Other titles about Pup and Hound are:

Pup and Hound (2004)
Pup and Hound at sea (2006)
Pup and Hound catch a thief (2007)
Pup and Hound in trouble (2005)
Pup and Hound lost and found (2006)
Pup and Hound move in (2004)
Pup and Hound play copycats (2007)
Pup and Hound scare a ghost (2007)
Pup and Hound stay up late (2005)

Hooks, Bell

Grump groan growl; illustrated by Chris Raschka. Hyperion Books for Children 2008 un il $16.99

Grades: PreK K 1 **E**

1. Emotions -- Fiction
ISBN 978-0-7868-0816-8; 0-7868-0816-0

LC 2007022312

Rhythmic text exposes a bad mood on the prowl, and advises the reader not to hide, but to let those feelings be

"Expressionistic art and economical poetry combine smoothly to create an inspiring model of self-control. . . . Thick, almost tactile lines of paint are slathered onto the pages with gusto, capturing a feeling of movement and strong emotion." SLJ

Hooks, Gwendolyn

Pet costume party; a Pet Club story. illustrated by Mike Byrne. Stone Arch Books 2011 31p il (Stone Arch readers) lib bdg $21.32; pa $3.95

Grades: K 1 2 **E**

1. Pets -- Fiction 2. Fishes -- Fiction 3. Parties -- Fiction 4.

Halloween -- Fiction

ISBN 978-1-4342-2513-9 lib bdg; 1-4342-2513-5 lib bdg; 978-1-4342-3053-9 pa; 1-4342-3053-8 pa

LC 2010036339

"Andy and his pet goldfish are having a Halloween party and need costumes. They move through various choices but the fact that Nibbles can't talk complicates matters. . . . Byrne's vibrant cartoon drawings offer gentle humor to Hooks's giggle-worthy story. Basic vocabulary combined with dialogue and slightly more complex sentence structures will help stretch beginning readers while keeping them engaged with the familiar. An excellent addition to most collections." SLJ

Hopgood, Tim

Wow! said the owl. Farrar, Straus and Giroux 2009 un il $14.95

Grades: PreK K 1   E

1. Day -- Fiction 2. Owls -- Fiction 3. Color -- Fiction 4. Night -- Fiction

ISBN 978-0-374-38518-7; 0-374-38518-1

LC 2008044038

A curious little owl decides to stay awake to find out how the things he sees at night look during the daytime.

"Collage-style illustrations done in simple, bright shapes show little owl in her tree while the changing colors and perspectives keep each page turn 'WOW!'-worthy. . . . Straightforward and flowing, this title makes a satisfying introduction to the colors of the day." SLJ

Hopkins, Lee Bennett, 1938-

Full moon and star; illustrated by Marcellus Hall. Abrams Books for Young Readers 2011 un il $16.95

Grades: PreK K 1 2   E

1. Moon -- Fiction 2. Stars -- Fiction 3. Theater -- Fiction 4. Authorship -- Fiction 5. Friendship -- Fiction

ISBN 978-1-4197-0013-2; 1-4197-0013-8

"This winsome tale is just another preschool story of cooperation. Yet the focus on playwriting and performance, complete with script formatting and special punctuation, sets a new stage for this common tale. Perfect for budding thespians, this book in three acts would make an excellent springboard for classroom explorations of drama." Kirkus

Hopkinson, Deborah

★ **Abe** Lincoln crosses a creek; a tall, thin tale (introducing his forgotten frontier friend) pictures by John Hendrix. Schwartz & Wade Books 2008 un il $16.99; lib bdg $19.99

Grades: K 1 2 3   E

1. Lawyers 2. Presidents 3. State legislators 4. Members of Congress 5. Friendship -- Fiction

ISBN 0-375-83768-X; 0-375-93768-4 lib bdg; 978-0-375-83768-5; 978-0-375-93768-2 lib bdg

LC 2007-35149

This book is set in Knob Creek, Kentucky, in 1816. A seven-year-old Abe Lincoln falls into a creek and is rescued by his best friend, Austin Gollaher. "Ages seven to ten." (Bull Cent Child Books)

"Hopkinson has created a lively, participatory tale that will surely stand out. . . . Hendrix's illustrations have a naive and rustic flavor that's in perfect harmony with the gravelly, homespun narrator's voice." SLJ

★ **Apples** to Oregon; being the (slightly) true narrative of how a brave pioneer father brought apples, peaches, pears, plums, grapes, and cherries (and children) across the plains. illustrated by Nancy Carpenter. Atheneum Books for Young Readers 2004 un il map $15.95

Grades: 1 2 3 4   E

1. Tall tales 2. Fruit culture -- Fiction 3. Frontier and pioneer life

-- Fiction 4. Overland journeys to the Pacific -- Fiction

ISBN 0-689-84769-6

LC 2001-22949

A pioneer father transports his beloved fruit trees and his family to Oregon in the mid-nineteenth century. Based loosely on the life of Henderson Luelling

"Carpenter's oil paintings are filled with vivid shades that reflect the changing scenery. Amusing details abound, and the slightly exaggerated humor of the pictures is in perfect balance with the tone of the text." SLJ

★ **A band** of angels; a story inspired by the Jubilee Singers. illustrated by Raúl Colón. Atheneum Bks. for Young Readers 1999 un il hardcover o.p. pa $7.99

Grades: 1 2 3 4   E

1. Pianists 2. Choral conductors 3. Gospel music -- Fiction 4. African Americans -- Fiction 5. Jubilee Singers (Musical group) -- Fiction

ISBN 0-689-81062-8; 0-689-84887-0 pa

LC 96-20011

Based on the life of Ella Sheppard Moore. The daughter of a slave forms a gospel singing group and goes on tour to raise money to save Fisk University

"Lilting prose, poignant historical details and arresting portraits of trailblazing singers lost in song contribute to this triumphant tale." Publ Wkly

★ **Billy** and the rebel; based on a true Civil War story. illustrated by Brian Floca. Atheneum Books for Young Readers 2002 44p il map (Ready-to-read) $14.95

Grades: 1 2 3 4   E

1. Gettysburg (Pa.), Battle of, 1863 -- Fiction 2. United States -- History -- 1861-1865, Civil War -- Fiction

ISBN 0-689-83964-2

LC 2001-22982

During the Battle of Gettysburg in 1863, a mother and son shelter a young Confederate deserter. Includes a historical note on the incident.

"Based on the real William Bayly and his mother, Harriet Hamilton Bayly, [this book] . . . allows beginning readers and researchers some insight into life during the Civil War. Full-page, full-spread, and spot art, executed mainly in shades of yellow and tan, add detail and expression to this story of courage and an unlikely friendship." SLJ

★ **From** slave to soldier; based on a true Civil War story. illustrated by Brian Floca. Atheneum Books for Young Readers 2005 44p il $14.95

Grades: 1 2 3   E

1. Slavery -- Fiction 2. African American soldiers -- Fiction 3. United States -- History -- 1861-1865, Civil War -- Fiction

ISBN 0-689-83965-8

A boy who hates being a slave joins the Union Army to fight for freedom, and proves himself brave and capable of handling a mule team when the need arises

This is written "in simple sentences for those who have just begun to read proficiently. . . . Short chapters and detailed watercolors aid the transition to more difficult text, while an exciting plot . . . keeps readers interested." SLJ

Girl wonder; a baseball story in nine innings. with pictures by Terry Widener. Atheneum Bks. for Young Readers 2003 un il $16.95

Grades: 1 2 3 4   E

1. Baseball -- Fiction

ISBN 0-689-83300-8

LC 99-47052

In the early 1900s, Alta Weiss, a young woman who knows from an early age that she loves baseball, finds a way to show that she can play, even though she is a girl

"Hopkinson tells her story with practiced skill—vivid details, lively language, varied pacing. . . . The illustrations are . . . broad, somewhat exaggerated, but conveying much emotion and narrative content." Horn Book

The **humblebee** hunter; pictures by Jen Corace. Disney Hyperion Books 2010 un il $16.99
Grades: K 1 2   **E**
   1. Naturalists 2. Travel writers 3. Bees -- Fiction 4. Writers on science 5. Great Britain -- History -- 19th century -- Fiction
   ISBN 978-1-4231-1356-0; 1-4231-1356-X
                               LC 2009-33987
On a beautiful day, some of Charles Darwin's many children help him study humblebees (bumblebees) in the garden at their home in the English countryside.

"The delicate, stylized illustrations, outlined in black and washed in natural shades of green and brown with spots of color, depict an amiable country Victorian household. . . . [This is an] inspiring read-aloud." SLJ

Knit your bit; a World War One story. by Deborah Hopkinson; illustrated by Steven Guarnaccia. G.P. Putnam's Sons 2013 32 p. $16.99
Grades: 1 2 3 4   **E**
   1. Historical fiction 2. Knitting -- Fiction 3. Picture books for children 4. Sex role -- Fiction 5. World War, 1914-1918 -- United States -- Fiction 6. New York (N.Y.) -- History -- 1898-1951 -- Fiction 7. World War, 1914-1918 -- New York (State) -- New York -- Fiction
   ISBN 039925241X; 9780399252419
                               LC 2012009635
This children's picture book offers a "story highlighting a patriotic civilian initiative during WWI. After Pop goes overseas, Mikey scoffs at helping Mama and his sister knit clothing for soldiers . . . . But after his teacher announces a knitting competition to benefit soldiers (based on an actual 'Knit-In' held in New York City's Central Park in 1918), Mikey and two friends accept a boys vs. girls challenge to win the knitting bee." (Publishers Weekly)

A **letter** to my teacher; Deborah Hopkinson, illustrated by Nancy Carpenter. Schwartz & Wade Books, an imprint of Random House Children's Books 2015 40 p. color illustrations (hc) $17.99
   Grades: PreK K 1 2   **E**
   1. Letters -- Fiction 2. Teachers -- Fiction 3. Schools -- Fiction 4. Behavior -- Fiction
   ISBN 9780375868450; 9780375968457
                               LC 2013018299
This picture book, by "Deborah Hopkinson, illustrated by Nancy Carpenter," is "about a girl who prefers running and jumping to listening and learning-and the teacher who gently inspires her. . . . This book's young heroine would be a challenge to any teacher. But this teacher isn't just any teacher. By listening carefully and knowing just the right thing to say, she quickly learns that the girl's unruly behavior is due to her struggles with reading." (Publisher's note)

★ **Sky** boys; how they built the Empire State Building. [by] Deborah Hopkinson & James E. Ransome. Schwartz & Wade Books 2006 un il $16.95
Grades: K 1 2 3 4   **E**
   1. Building -- Fiction 2. New York (N.Y.) -- Fiction 3. Empire State Building (New York, N.Y.) -- Fiction
   ISBN 0-375-83610-1
                               LC 2005010852

Boston Globe-Horn Book Honor: Picture Book (2006)
In 1931, a boy and his father watch as the world's tallest building, the Empire State Building, is constructed, step-by-step, near their Manhattan home.

"Crisp, lyrical free verse and bold paintings celebrate the skill and daring of those who constructed the Empire State Building. . . . Ransome's powerful acrylic paintings show the building in all stages of construction, and includes the workers' perilous views. A unique, memorable title." Booklist

Steamboat school; inspired by a true story : St. Louis, Missouri: 1847. written by Deborah Hopkinson; illustrated by Ron Husband. Disney Hyperion 2016 40 p. illustrations $17.99
Grades: K 1 2 3   **E**
   1. Education -- Fiction 2. African Americans -- Fiction 3. African Americans -- Education
   ISBN 1423121961; 9781423121961
                               LC 2015016315
In this book, by Deborah Hopkinson, illustrated by Ron Husband, "when James first started school, his sister practically had to drag him there. . . . James knew everything outside was more exciting than anything he'd find inside. But his teacher taught him otherwise. . . . And through hard work and learning, they did, until their school was shut down by a new law forbidding African American education in Missouri." (Publisher's note)

"This fascinating story, illustrated in pen and ink with a color palette of browns and blacks with occasional pops of blue and red, draws readers into the historical era effectively and emphasizes what a privilege literacy was for African-Americans in the 19th century. An unforgettable story that needs to be known." Kirkus

Includes bibliographical references

★ **Sweet** Clara and the freedom quilt; paintings by James Ransome. Knopf 1993 un il hardcover o.p. pa $6.99
Grades: K 1 2 3 4   **E**
   1. Quilts -- Fiction 2. Slavery -- Fiction
   ISBN 0-679-82311-5; 0-679-92311-X lib bdg; 0-679-87472-0 pa
                               LC 91-11601
Clara, a young slave, stitches a quilt with a map pattern which guides her to freedom in the North

"The smooth, optimistic, first-person vernacular of the story is ably accompanied by Ransome's brightly colored, full-page paintings." Horn Book Guide

Another title about Clara is:
Under the quilt of night (2001)

Hoppe, Paul
Hat. Bloomsbury U.S.A Children's Books 2009 un il $14.99
Grades: PreK K 1   **E**
   1. Hats -- Fiction 2. Imagination -- Fiction 3. Lost and found possessions -- Fiction
   ISBN 978-1-59990-247-0; 1-59990-247-8; 978-1-59990-248-7 lib bdg; 1-59990-248-6 lib bdg
                               LC 2008-22357
When Henry finds a hat he is very excited by its possibilities, but becomes worried when he thinks that the hat might belong to someone else

"The text is simple but imaginative. The illustrations bring each imagined scenario to life, and the ink drawings have a slightly retro feel with their subdued colors. The story lends itself to being read aloud, and the red hat pops off the pages." SLJ

The **woods**. Chronicle Books 2011 un il $16.99
Grades: PreK K 1   **E**
   1. Boys -- Fiction 2. Fear -- Fiction 3. Toys -- Fiction 4. Animals

-- Fiction 5. Bedtime -- Fiction

ISBN 978-0-8118-7547-9; 0-8118-7547-4

LC 2010039393

"The refrain—'we weren't scared at all. Until...'—sets a comfortable pattern, and the fuzzy watercolors on thick creamy stock enhance the coziness of the tale. . . . Hoppe's delightfully quirky monsters enhance this pleasant tonic for bedtime fears." Kirkus

Horacek, Petr

Animal opposites; Petr Horacek. Candlewick Press 2013 20 p. $15.99

Grades: PreK K 1   E

1. Picture books for children 2. Animals 3. Opposites

ISBN 0763667765; 9780763667764

LC 2012950554

In this book from illustrator Petr Horacek, readers can "turn the pages, lift the flaps, and see animals of all shapes and sizes bring the world of opposites to life." Animals "from slow snail to fast cheetah, heavy hippo to light butterfly, smooth frog to prickly porcupine" are covered. (Publisher's note) "Horacek contrasts 20 animals, using flaps, pop-ups, and . . . mixed-media paintings to highlight the differences between them." (Publishers Weekly)

★ **Choo** choo. Candlewick Press 2008 un il $5.99

Grades: PreK   E

1. Board books for children 2. Railroads -- Fiction

ISBN 978-0-7636-3477-3; 0-7636-3477-8

"Horácek's cheerful acrylic collage artwork shines in this small, beautifully designed board book about a train that carries cars full of smiling children to the beach. From the sound effects that begin the single line on each spread . . . to the shaped pages that emphasize the curve of mountains or the spikes of treetops, this book begs for interaction." Booklist

Look out, Suzy Goose. Candlewick Press 2008 un il $14.99

Grades: PreK K 1 2   E

1. Geese -- Fiction 2. Animals -- Fiction

ISBN 978-0-7636-3803-0; 0-7636-3803-X

"Suzy Goose . . . finds herself feeling dissatisfied with her life. The incessant honking of her fellow geese sends her flip-flopping to the woods to find a quiet respite. . . . Soon she is unwittingly pursued by a fox, a wolf, and a bear—tiptoeing, creeping, and padding behind her. . . . Visually stimulating mixed-media illustrations, including textured paints and paper collage, evoke those fundamental emotions often found in stories involving the fabled 'woods.' . . . Despite its mildly scary content, this book is amusing, relatively short, and overall suitable for younger children." SLJ

★ **Silly** Suzy Goose. Candlewick Press 2006 un il $14.99

Grades: PreK K 1 2   E

1. Geese -- Fiction 2. Lions -- Fiction

ISBN 0-7636-3040-3

Suzy longs to be different from all the other geese, but learns that imitating a lion may not be the best way to express her individuality.

"Created in mixed media, the art jumps off the pages, a fitting verb for a clever, clever book, alive in every way." Booklist

Other titles about Suzy Goose are:

Look out, Suzy Goose (2008)

Suzy Goose and the Christmas star (2009)

One spotted giraffe; a counting pop-up book. Petr Horáček. Candlewick 2012 20 p. (hardback) $18.95

Grades: PreK   E

1. Counting 2. Toy and movable books 3. Numerals -- Fiction

4. Pop-up books 5. Animals -- Fiction 6. Numerals -- Fiction 7. Pop-up books -- Specimens

ISBN 0062234897; 9780763661571

LC 2011048376

This pop-up book by Petr Horacek is aimed at helping children "identify animals, count them, and discover numerals. . . . Spreads filled with realistic depictions of colorful creatures -- everything from pandas to lemurs -- entice readers to count the animals, then flip the flap to reveal a corresponding pop-up numeral. And then the surprise: the numeral looks just like the animal -- fur, spots, stripes, and all!" (Publisher's note)

Suzy Goose and the Christmas star. Candlewick Press 2009 un il $15.99

Grades: PreK K 1 2   E

1. Geese -- Fiction 2. Stars -- Fiction 3. Christmas -- Fiction

ISBN 978-0-7636-4487-1; 0-7636-4487-0

Silly Suzy Goose tries to get a star from the sky to put on the Christmas tree.

"The full-spread mixed-media illustrations depicting a textured snowy landscape against a starry night sky contrast with the friendly and determined figure of Suzy, with her orange beak glowing and her tiny eyes on the prize. Quiet and sweet–a fine choice for both storytime and family sharing." SLJ

Horning, Sandra

Chicks! by Sandra Horning; illustrated by Jon Goodell. Random House 2013 32 p. (Step into Reading. Step 1) (trade pbk.) $3.99

Grades: PreK K 1   E

1. Chickens -- Fiction 2. Animal babies 3. Animals -- Infancy -- Fiction

ISBN 0307932214; 9780307932211; 9780375971174; 9780375981142

LC 2011050438

In this children's book by Sandra Horning, "when a family brings home chicks from a local farm, they must do everything they can to make sure their feathered friends thrive in their new environment. With the help of their knowledgeable parents, the children provide the baby chicks with food, water, warmth, and proper shelter." (Publisher's note)

The **giant** hug; illustrated by Valeri Gorbachev. Knopf 2005 un il $15.95; lib bdg $17.99

Grades: PreK K 1 2   E

1. Pigs -- Fiction 2. Grandmothers -- Fiction 3. Postal service -- Fiction

ISBN 0-375-82477-4; 0-375-92477-9 lib bdg

LC 2003-25883

When Owen the pig sends a real hug to his grandmother for her birthday he inadvertently brings cheer to the postal workers as they pass the hug along

"Gorbachev's cast of animal characters, drawn with a . . . sense of whimsy, are well chosen to emphasize the relevant personality traits." Booklist

Horowitz, Dave

Twenty-six pirates; by Dave Horowitz. Nancy Paulsen Books 2013 32 p. col. ill. (reinforced) $16.99

Grades: PreK K 1   E

1. Pirates -- Fiction 2. Alphabet -- Fiction 3. Alphabet 4. Humorous stories 5. Stories in rhyme 6. Pirates -- Fiction

ISBN 9780399257773

LC 2012023866

This children's book by Dave Horowitz presents "an alphabetical parade of pirates -- by name! . . . Each pirate receives a full-page portrait that depicts him (they are all boys) engaged in the behavior described. Pirate Lee, who needs to pee, quivers outside the head, hands over his crotch. Pirate Quaid, who is not afraid, nevertheless looks a little dubious as giant octopus tentacles loom. Pirate Tony, who is fall of baloney, happily munches a sandwich." (Kirkus Reviews)

Twenty-six princesses. Putnam 2008 un il $15.99
Grades: PreK K 1 2　　　　　　　　　　　　　　　E
　1. Alphabet 2. Fairy tales 3. Princesses -- Fiction
　ISBN 978-0-399-24607-4; 0-399-24607-X
　　　　　　　　　　　　　　　LC 2007-13233
Twenty-six princesses, one for each letter of the alphabet, go to a party at the prince's castle.
　"Horowitz has a light, witty touch, and the text is rich with puns. The words and the pictures play off one another perfectly, encouraging children to pore over each humorously detailed portrait." SLJ
　Includes bibliographical references

Horrocks, Anita
　Silas' seven grandparents; story by Anita Horrocks; illustrations by Helen Flook. Orca Book Publishers 2010 un il $19.95
Grades: PreK K　　　　　　　　　　　　　　　E
　1. Family life -- Fiction 2. Grandparents -- Fiction
　ISBN 978-1-55143-561-9; 1-55143-561-9
Silas' Seven Grandparents is a fun and loving story about having multiple sets of grandparents and stepgrandparents. When Silas' parents go away on a business trip, all seven grandparents invite Silas to stay with them. How can he choose one without hurting the others' feelings?
　"The deftly drawn water-based ink illustrations reflect the story's upbeat tone and portray the widely diverse grandparents in ways that make them distinctive." Booklist

Horse, Harry
　Little Rabbit lost. Peachtree Pubs. 2002 un il $15.95; bd bk $9.95
Grades: PreK K 1　　　　　　　　　　　　　　　E
　1. Rabbits -- Fiction 2. Birthdays -- Fiction
　ISBN 1-56145-273-4; 1-56145-345-5 bd bk
　　　　　　　　　　　　　　　LC 2002-2697
On his birthday Little Rabbit thinks that he is now a big rabbit, until he gets lost at the Rabbit World amusement park.
　"The lovely ink-and-watercolor illustrations are filled with clever details kids will enjoy—carrot-shaped paddleboats and bunny rollercoaster cars. Children will welcome this charming story." Booklist
　Other titles about Little Rabbit are:
　Little Rabbit goes to school (2004)
　Little Rabbit runaway (2005)
　Little Rabbit's Christmas (2007)
　Little Rabbit's new baby (2008)

Horstman, Lisa
　Squawking Matilda. Marshall Cavendish Children 2009 un il $17.99
Grades: PreK K 1 2　　　　　　　　　　　　　　　E
　1. Aunts -- Fiction 2. Chickens -- Fiction 3. Farm life -- Fiction
　ISBN 978-0-7614-5463-2; 0-7614-5463-2
　　　　　　　　　　　　　　　LC 2008003657
Mae likes starting projects but never seems to finish them, and so when Aunt Susan asks her to take care of a feisty chicken Mae is soon distracted, then must find a way to make up for her neglect before Aunt Susan's visit.
　"Handcrafted puppets wearing cheery clothing are posed, photographed, and digitally colored to give this charming selection a down-to-earth quality that matches the story perfectly." SLJ

Horvath, David
　What dat? the great big Uglydoll book of things to look at, search for, point to, and wonder about. Random House 2011 il $14.99
Grades: PreK K 1 2 3　　　　　　　　　　　　　　　E
　1. Puzzles 2. Vocabulary
　ISBN 978-0-375-86434-6; 0-375-86434-2
　"Horvath and Kim have created a word book featuring the Uglyverse. Each spread has bright, labeled cartoon illustrations, and brief paragraphs ask readers to find different things on each page. The scenarios, while full, are not too busy, so the items are easy to find and the labels are easy to read. The scenes are funny, and some jokes are obviously intended for an older audience. . . . These jokes will be easily passed over by younger children as they are buried within the scenes. The popularity of the toys combined with the fun of a look-and-find word book should make this a popular choice." SLJ

Hosford, Kate
　Infinity and me; written by Kate Hosford; illustrations by Gabi Swiatkowska. Carolrhoda Books 2012 32 p. (lib. bdg. : alk. paper) $16.95
Grades: K 1 2 3 4 5　　　　　　　　　　　　　　　E
　1. Infinite 2. Mathematics 3. Picture books for children 4. Schools -- Fiction 5. Infinity -- Fiction 6. Grandmothers -- Fiction
　ISBN 0761367268; 9780761367260
　　　　　　　　　　　　　　　LC 2011044746
　In this book, protagonist "Uma's struggle with the meaning of infinity offers readers a[n] . . . introduction to the mathematical concept. When little Uma gazes at the vast night sky and wonders how many stars are there, she asks, 'How could I even think about something as big as infinity?' When friends, her grandmother, the school cook and the music teacher offer creative ways of describing infinity, Uma ends up feeling rather overwhelmed." (Kirkus Reviews)

Houston, Gloria
　Miss Dorothy and her bookmobile; illustrated by Susan Condie Lamb. Harper 2010 un il $16.99
Grades: K 1 2　　　　　　　　　　　　　　　E
　1. Librarians -- Fiction 2. Bookmobiles -- Fiction 3. Country life -- Fiction 4. Books and reading -- Fiction
　ISBN 978-0-06-029155-6; 0-06-029155-9
　　　　　　　　　　　　　　　LC 2005-18630
Dorothy has always wanted to work in a library like the red brick one of her girlhood, but after moving to rural North Carolina she discovers that the type of library is less important than the books and the people who read them.
　"Beautiful, soft landscapes of the rugged terrain throughout the seasons serve as a backdrop for this charming story of a librarian on the go." SLJ

　The **year** of the perfect Christmas tree; an Appalachian story. pictures by Barbara Cooney. Dial Bks. for Young Readers 1988 un il $15.99; pa $6.99
Grades: K 1 2 3　　　　　　　　　　　　　　　E
　1. Christmas -- Fiction 2. Appalachian region -- Fiction
　ISBN 0-8037-0299-X; 0-14-055827-2 pa
　　　　　　　　　　　　　　　LC 87-24551
　"It's 1918 in the mountains of North Carolina, and the custom in the village is for one family to select and donate the Christmas tree each year. In the spring Ruthie and her father select a perfect balsam high on a rocky crag. Then Father goes to war. Still, on Christmas Eve the tree is in the church and Ruthie plays the angel. The winning illustrations perfectly match the tone of this affecting story, which comes from the author's family." NY Times Book Rev

Hovland, Henrik

★ **John** Jensen feels different; by Henrik Hovland; illustrated by Torill Kove; translated by Don Bartlett. Eerdmans Books for Young Readers 2012 33 p. col. ill. (alk. paper) $16

Grades: PreK K 1 2   E

1. Picture books for children 2. Crocodiles -- Fiction 3. Individuality -- Fiction

ISBN 0802853994; 9780802853998

LC 2011022446

This children's picture book follows John Jensen, "a well-dressed, well-mannered crocodile living a civilized life in the human world" who worries constantly about being different. "When John Jensen trips and falls after binding up his bulky tail in a futile attempt to conceal it, he meets Dr. Field, whose huge ears and long trunk mean he knows a thing or two about being different. . . . John Jensen realizes that his tail—and his differentness in general—are all a question of attitude." (Publishers Weekly)

Howard, Arthur

Hoodwinked. Harcourt 2001 un il $16

Grades: PreK K 1   E

1. Pets -- Fiction 2. Witches -- Fiction

ISBN 0-15-202656-8

LC 00-8318

Mitzi, a young witch, searches for a creepy pet, but finds that a cute kitten is perfect for her

"The pictures are perfect for this lively story—lots of fangs and slimy, scaly, weird, and wiggly outlines fill the pages." SLJ

Howard, Elizabeth Fitzgerald

★ **Aunt** Flossie's hats (and crab cakes later) paintings by James Ransome. 10th anniversary ed; Clarion Books 2001 31p il $16; pa $6.95

Grades: K 1 2 3   E

1. Hats -- Fiction 2. Aunts -- Fiction 3. African Americans -- Fiction

ISBN 0-618-12038-6; 0-395-72077-X pa

LC 00-65757

A reissue of the title first published 1991

Sara and Susan share tea, cookies, crab cakes, and stories about hats when they visit their favorite relative, Aunt Flossie.

"This is an affecting portrait of a black American family. . . . Howard's quiet, sure telling is well matched by Ransome's art-elegant, expressive oil paintings that convey warmth, joy, tenderness and love." Publ Wkly

★ **Virgie** goes to school with us boys; illustrated by E.B. Lewis. Simon & Schuster Bks. for Young Readers 1999 un il $17.99; pa $7.99

Grades: K 1 2 3   E

1. African Americans -- Fiction

ISBN 0-689-80076-2; 0-689-87793-5 pa

LC 97-49406

In the post-Civil War South, a young African American girl is determined to prove that she can go to school just like her older brothers

"The story is a superb tribute to the author's great aunt, the inspiration for this book. . . . Lewis's watercolor illustrations capture the characters with warmth and dignity." SLJ

Howatt, Sandra J.

Sleepyheads; by Sandra J. Howatt; illustrated by Joyce Wan. Beach Lane Books 2014 32 p. col. ill. (hardcover) $16.99

Grades: PreK K 1   E

1. Animals -- Fiction 2. Bedtime -- Fiction 3. Sleep -- Fiction 4.

Stories in rhyme 5. Babies -- Fiction 6. Animals -- Sleep behavior -- Fiction

ISBN 1442422661; 9781442422667

LC 2013013607

"The sun has set, and sleepyheads all across the land are tucked into their cozy beds. Rabbit is snoozing in the weeds, and Duck is snuggled in the reeds. Bear is nestled in his cave, and Otter is rocking on a wave. But there's one little sleepyhead who's not in his bed. Where, oh where, could he be?" (Publisher's note)

"Gentle narration, soft exclamations and soothing 's' sounds surface again and again, streaming together sweetly. The earthy, mellow artwork, with its dusky greens and browns and thick linework, comforts too. Wan's many circular shapes (all those radiant stars, the creatures' rounded heads, ears, coiled bodies and tails—even dandelion seed-puffs and a lightning bug's glow) recall the warm curve of a caregiver's chest." - Kirkus

Howe, James

★ **Brontorina**; illustrated by Randy Cecil. Candlewick Press 2010 un il $15.99

Grades: PreK K 1 2   E

1. Ballet -- Fiction 2. Dinosaurs -- Fiction

ISBN 978-0-7636-4437-6; 0-7636-4437-4

"Initially turned away from Madame Lucille's Dance Academy for Boys and Girls because she is an enormous dinosaur, Brontorina counters, 'But in my heart I am a ballerina.' . . . Text and illustrations work beautifully together in this witty fantasy. . . . In Cecil's arresting oil paintings, the tawny orange dinosaur stands out boldly against slate blue or white backgrounds, and the unusual texture of the paint creates a distinctive effect." Booklist

★ **Horace** and Morris but mostly Dolores; written by James Howe; illustrated by Amy Walrod. Atheneum Bks. for Young Readers 1999 un il $16; pa $6.99

Grades: PreK K 1 2   E

1. Mice -- Fiction 2. Sex role -- Fiction 3. Friendship -- Fiction

ISBN 0-689-31874-X; 0-689-85675-X pa

LC 96-17645

"Three adventure-loving mice are best friends until gender stereotypes separate them, driving Horace and Morris into a rowdy boys-only clubhouse while Dolores reluctantly goes off to join the ultra-ladylike Cheese Puffs. The bold artwork suits the book's lively protest against conformity." Horn Book Guide

Other titles about Horace, Morris, and Dolores are:

Horace and Morris join the chorus (but what about Dolores?) (2002)

Horace and Morris say cheese (which makes Dolores sneeze!) (2009)

★ **Houndsley** and Catina; illustrated by Marie-Louise Gay. Candlewick Press 2006 36p il $14.99

Grades: PreK K 1 2   E

1. Cats -- Fiction 2. Dogs -- Fiction 3. Friendship -- Fiction

ISBN 0-7636-2404-7

LC 2005-50187

Houndsley, a dog, and Catina, a cat, run into trouble when they decide to prove that they are the best at cooking and writing, respectively.

"The lively, brisk writing is wonderfully extended in Gay's airy watercolor-and-pencil illustrations." Booklist

Other titles about Houndsley and Catina are:

Houndsley and Catina and the birthday surprise (2006)

Houndsley and Catina and the quiet time (2008)

Houndsley and Catina plink and plunk (2009)

Kaddish for Grandpa in Jesus' name, amen; [Illustrated by] Catherine Stock. Atheneum Books for Young Readers 2004 un il $16.95
Grades: K 1 2 3   **E**
  1. Death -- Fiction 2. Judaism -- Fiction 3. Christianity -- Fiction
  4. Grandfathers -- Fiction 5. Funeral rites and ceremonies -- Fiction
  ISBN 0-689-80185-8
                                                    LC 2002-11569
Five-year-old Emily tries to understand her grandfather's death by exploring the Christian and Jewish rituals that her family practices during and after his funeral
  "The soft watercolor illustrations, done in pastel colors, are a perfect accompaniment to the story. This book is a good vehicle to explain the rituals of death to children." SLJ

Otter and odder; James Howe; illustrated by Chris Raschka. 1st ed. Candlewick Press 2012 40 p. ill. (reinforced) $14
Grades: 2 3 4   **E**
  1. Otters -- Fiction 2. Picture books for children 3. Love -- Fiction
  4. Fishes -- Fiction
  ISBN 076364174X; 9780763641740
                                                    LC 2010048213
In this story, while Otter is hunting for food, "he realizes something unlikely has happened: 'I am in love with my food source.' Myrtle (as Otter hears the fish's name of Gurgle) has fallen for Otter as well, but despite their love the two can't make it work: 'I am no longer sure a fish can love an otter . . . when the way of the otter is to eat fish.' Fortunately, a wise beaver introduces Otter to vegetarianism, and the two 'lived happily ever after.'" (Bulletin of the Center for Children's Books)

★ **Pinky** and Rex; illustrated by Melissa Sweet. Atheneum Pubs. 1990 38p il $15; pa $3.99
Grades: K 1 2   **E**
  1. Toys -- Fiction 2. Museums -- Fiction 3. Friendship -- Fiction
  ISBN 0-689-31454-X; 0-689-82348-7 pa
                                                    LC 89-30786
"Sweet's gently washed, jovial illustrations reflect the unpretentious sincerity of Rex and Pinky's relationship, while Howe's readable text blending natural dialogue with narrative, is divided into individual chapters." Booklist
  Other titles about Pinky and Rex are:
  Pinky and Rex and the bully (1996)
  Pinky and Rex and the double-dad weekend (1995)
  Pinky and Rex and the just-right pet (2001)
  Pinky and Rex and the mean old witch (1991)
  Pinky and Rex and the new baby (1993)
  Pinky and Rex and the new neighbors (1997)
  Pinky and Rex and the perfect pumpkin (1998)
  Pinky and Rex and the school play (1998)
  Pinky and Rex and the spelling bee (1991)
  Pinky and Rex get married (1990)
  Pinky and Rex go to camp (1992)

Howland, Naomi
  ★ **Latkes,** latkes, good to eat; a Chanukah story. Clarion Bks. 1999 31p il $16; pa $5.95
Grades: PreK K 1 2   **E**
  1. Jews -- Fiction 2. Magic -- Fiction 3. Hanukkah -- Fiction
  ISBN 0-395-89903-6; 0-618-49295-X pa
                                                    LC 97-50616
In an old Russian village, Sadie and her brothers are poor and hungry until an old woman gives Sadie a frying pan that will make potato pancakes until it hears the magic words that make it stop
  "Howland effectively sets her story in a Russian shtetl, using words, intonation, and especially pictures. Working in gouache and colored

pencil, she offers a snowy landscape peopled with Jewish villagers who work hard and celebrate harder." Booklist

Princess says goodnight; illustrated by David Small. HarperCollins 2010 un il $16.99; lib bdg $17.89
Grades: PreK K 1 2   **E**
  1. Stories in rhyme 2. Bedtime -- Fiction 3. Princesses -- Fiction
  ISBN 978-0-06-145525-4; 0-06-145525-3; 978-0-06-145526-1
  lib bdg; 0-06-145526-1 lib bdg
Rhyming text presents what a princess might do between leaving the ball and saying goodnight.
  "Sweet and disarmingly infectious without being cloying, this is a bedtime story full of joy and imagination." Publ Wkly

Hubbell, Patricia
  Airplanes; soaring! diving! turning! by Patricia Hubbell; illustrated by Megan Halsey and Sean Addy. Marshall Cavendish Children 2008 un il $16.99
Grades: PreK K 1 2   **E**
  1. Stories in rhyme 2. Airplanes -- Fiction
  ISBN 978-0-7614-5388-8; 0-7614-5388-1
                                                    LC 2007011721
Illustrations and rhyming text celebrate different kinds of airplanes and what they can do
  "This picture book features . . . animated, whimsical art that will delight young would-be jet-setters. . . . The lively, descriptive prose . . . incorporates peppy sounds that amp up the energy that's echoed in the vibrant illustrations." Booklist

  ★ **Boats**; speeding! sailing! cruising! illustrated by Megan Halsey and Sean Addy. Marshall Cavendish 2009 un il $17.99
Grades: PreK K 1 2   **E**
  1. Stories in rhyme 2. Boats and boating -- Fiction
  ISBN 978-0-7614-5524-0; 0-7614-5524-8
                                                    LC 2007-49522
Illustrations and rhyming text celebrate different kinds of boats and what they can do.
  "The tight, surprisingly informative rhyming text works so well because it pairs with art that shows off each of these boats to best advantage. The fun part comes in the way the design and the mixed-media art . . . come together." Booklist

  Cars; rushing! honking! zooming! illustrated by Megan Halsey and Sean Addy. Marshall Cavendish Children 2006 un il $14.99
Grades: PreK K 1   **E**
  1. Stories in rhyme 2. Automobiles -- Fiction
  ISBN 978-0-7614-5296-6; 0-7614-5296-6
Illustrations and rhyming text celebrate different kinds of cars and what they can do
  "The rhyming text rolls smoothly along. . . . Color heightens the appeal of the clip art, stamps, etchings, maps, and original drawings, which come together in the paper-collage illustrations." Booklist

  Firefighters! speeding! spraying! saving! illustrated by Viviana Garofoli. Marshall Cavendish 2007 un il $14.99; bd bk $7.99
Grades: PreK K 1   **E**
  1. Stories in rhyme 2. Board books for children 3. Fire fighters -- Fiction
  ISBN 978-0-7614-5337-6; 0-7614-5337-7; 978-0-7614-5615-5
  bd bk; 0-7614-5615-5 bd bk
"The tale begins with the 'Clang! Clang! Clang!' of the alarm. The firefighters rush to get dressed and board their truck, along with Spot, the firehouse Dalmatian. Brief, pulsating, rhythmic text follows across the

pages. . . . The digital, cartoon-style artwork is simple. Done in vibrant hues of predominately primary colors." SLJ

Horses; Trotting! Prancing! Racing! illustrated by Joe Mathieu. Marshall Cavendish Children 2011 il $17.99
Grades: PreK K 1   **E**
   1. Stories in rhyme 2. Horses -- Fiction
   ISBN 978-0-7614-5949-1; 0-7614-5949-9; 978-0-7614-5997-2 e-book

                  LC 2010044929
"A simple, rhyming text introduces readers to horses—the different breeds, their abilities in providing transportation, and all else they do. . . . Lovely, action-packed illustrations done in watercolors and colored pencils highlight the different hues and patterns found on the horses' coats. . . . This is an excellent addition for any collection, and it will extend knowledge about transportation that isn't manmade." SLJ

My first airplane ride; by Patricia Hubbell; illustrated by Nancy Speir. Marshall Cavendish 2008 un il $16.99
Grades: PreK K 1   **E**
   1. Stories in rhyme 2. Airplanes -- Fiction
   ISBN 978-0-7614-5436-6; 0-7614-5436-5
"Short, rhyming phrases record the events as a boy takes his first plane ride. Every incident along the way is chronicled here: packing, driving to the airport, getting boarding passes, going through security in stocking feet, waiting at the gate, etc. . . . The level of detail is well calibrated to the target audience. . . . Colorful and reassuring." Booklist

Police: hurrying! helping! saving! Marshall Cavendish Children 2008 un il $14.99
Grades: PreK K 1   **E**
   1. Stories in rhyme 2. Police -- Fiction
   ISBN 978-0-7614-5421-2; 0-7614-5421-7
Illustrations and rhyming text celebrate police officers and what they do.
"A picture book with a rhyming text, bright colors, and plenty of action." SLJ

Shaggy dogs, waggy dogs; illustrated by Donald Wu. Marshall Cavendish 2011 un il $17.99
Grades: PreK K 1 2   **E**
   1. Dogs -- Fiction
   ISBN 978-0-7614-5957-6; 0-7614-5957-X
"An assortment of lovable-looking pooches is pictured in this charming ode to man's best friend. In perfect rhyme, Hubbell describes the canines by their characteristics rather than breeds: shaggy, waggy, thin, saggy, shy, bold, pretty, puppies, full-grown, and more. Next she offers a litany of the things dogs are good at doing. . . . Wu's detailed illustrations drawn with colored pencil over acrylic vividly depict the different textures of each animal's fur as it engages in typical doggie pastimes. Children who love animals will adore this fetching book." SLJ

Snow happy! Tricycle Press 2010 un il $15.99
Grades: PreK K 1   **E**
   1. Stories in rhyme 2. Snow -- Fiction
   ISBN 978-1-58246-329-2; 1-58246-329-8
"A rollicking verse about the joys of playing in the snow. Lively children and their parents and grandparents enjoy a day of sledding, making snow angels, building igloos, even shoveling. Hubbell's meter is bouncy. . . . The artwork matches the upbeat mood of the text. . . . The simple watercolor characters are full of activity." SLJ

Hubbell, Will
  Pumpkin Jack; written and illustrated by Will Hubbell. Whitman, A. 2000 un il $15.95
Grades: PreK K 1 2 3   **E**
   1. Pumpkin -- Fiction 2. Halloween -- Fiction
   ISBN 0-8075-6665-9

                  LC 00-8282
After Halloween, Tim discards Jack, his jack-o'lantern, in the garden and during the following year it sprouts, blooms, and grows new pumpkins
"Satisfying and surprisingly varied in approach and perspective, Hubbell's colored pencil drawings illustrate the simple story in a series of well-imagined scenes." Booklist

Huckabee, Mike
  Can't wait till Christmas; [illustrated by Jed Henry] G. P. Putnam's Sons 2010 un il $17.99
Grades: PreK K 1   **E**
   1. Gifts -- Fiction 2. Siblings -- Fiction 3. Christmas -- Fiction
   ISBN 978-0-399-25539-7; 0-399-25539-7
Mike is so eager to open his Christmas gifts that he convinces his older sister, Pam, to unwrap and play with them in advance, but when Christmas morning arrives they are unhappy about what they have done.
"Huckabee's lighthearted cautionary tale is buoyed by zippy digital illustrations that convey both its humor and warmth." Publ Wkly

Hucke, Johannes
  Pip in the Grand Hotel; illustrated by Daniel Müller. North-South 2009 un il $16.95
Grades: PreK K 1 2   **E**
   1. Mice -- Fiction 2. Hotels and motels -- Fiction
   ISBN 978-0-7358-2225-2; 0-7358-2225-5
Originally published in Sweden
Mary has a new pet, a mouse named Pip. When she opens the lid to his box, Pip is off straight into the Grand Hotel. The reader can search for Pip in the pictures.
"This lively escapade is heightened by ellipses at the end of each spread, which create dramatic page turns. As the children race through this bustling high-end hotel, Müller's detail-filled watercolor illustrations truly bring the caper to life." SLJ

Hudes, Quiara Alegria
  Welcome to my neighborhood! a barrio ABC. illustrated by Shino Arihara. Arthur A. Levine Books 2010 un il $16.99
Grades: PreK K   **E**
   1. Alphabet 2. Stories in rhyme 3. City and town life -- Fiction 4. Hispanic Americans -- Fiction
   ISBN 978-0-545-09424-5; 0-545-09424-0
"An expressive girl takes a friend on a poetic tour of her inner-city neighborhood. 'E is for the echo of the elevated train./ F is for the fire hydrant spraying summer rain.' Chalky, gouache washes capture both the vital and gently dilapidated elements of city life. . . . The subtle presence of the girl's personal narrative and her nuanced understanding of what makes her neighborhood home set this ABC book apart." Publ Wkly

Hudson, Katy
  Bear and duck; written and illustrated by Katy Hudson. Harper, an imprint of HarperCollinsPublishers 2015 32 p. (hardcover) $17.99
Grades: PreK K 1   **E**
   1. Bears -- Fiction 2. Ducks -- Fiction 3. Self-acceptance -- Fiction
   ISBN 0062320513; 9780062320513

                  LC 2013043137

In this children's story, written and illustrated by Katy Hudson, "Bear is sick and tired of being a bear. . . . But when he sees a line of happy yellow ducklings, he has a thought. What if he could be a duck? With a few duck lessons from Duck, Bear learns that being a duck is fun; but as it turns out, Bear realizes he makes a really good bear." (Publisher's note)

Huget, Jennifer LaRue

The **best** birthday party ever; illustrated by LeUyen Pham. Schwartz & Wade Books 2011 un il $16.99; lib bdg $19.99

Grades: PreK K 1 2   E

  1. Parties -- Fiction 2. Birthdays -- Fiction

  ISBN 978-0-375-84763-9; 0-375-84763-4; 978-0-375-95763-5 lib bdg; 0-375-95763-4 lib bdg

LC 2009-28010

A child plans an elaborate birthday party and eagerly counts the months, days, hours, and minutes before the celebration.

"Pham's watercolor illustrations perfectly capture the frivolity of the little girl's imagination. . . . Young birthday enthusiasts will readily identify with the considerable thought and energy involved in getting ready for the big day." Bull Cent Child Books

How to clean your room in 10 easy steps; illustrated by Edward Koren. Schwartz & Wade Books 2009 un il $16.99; lib bdg $19.99

Grades: K 1 2   E

  1. Home economics -- Fiction

  ISBN 978-0-375-84410-2; 0-375-84410-4; 978-0-375-96410-7 lib bdg; 0-375-96410-X lib bdg

LC 2008-48824

A young girl provides unique advice on how to tidy a bedroom.

"Children and their adults are in for a treat with this new showcase for Koren's illustrations. His wry, bushy, squiggly style is well-matched by Huget's puckish and not entirely serious advice. . . . Good for great giggles-and at the end, she promises even more awesome advice on fixing your hair." Kirkus

Thanks a LOT, Emily Post! written by Jennifer LaRue Huget; illustrated by Alexandra Boiger. Schwartz & Wade Books 2009 un il $16.99; lib bdg $19.99

Grades: K 1 2 3   E

  1. Novelists 2. Advice columnists 3. Mothers -- Fiction 4. Etiquette -- Fiction 5. Conduct of life -- Fiction

  ISBN 978-0-375-83853-8; 0-375-83853-8; 978-0-375-93853-5 lib bdg; 0-375-93853-2 lib bdg

LC 2008004994

When a mother instructs her children to behave according to Emily Post's rules of etiquette, they respond by insisting that Mother follow the rules, as well. Includes information about Post and selected items from her 1922 book.

"Written with clarity and wit. . . . The fresh, expressive watercolors dramatize events through distinctive characters playing out sometimes-chaotic scenes full of energy, elegance, and entertaining details." Booklist

Hughes, Shirley

Alfie and the big boys. Bodley Head 2007 un il $17.95

Grades: PreK K 1   E

  1. School stories 2. Friendship -- Fiction

  ISBN 978-0-370-32884-3; 0-370-32884-1

Alfie and his friends wish they could play with the bigger boys and one day they get a chance

This "sensitively portrays children's emotional lives through everyday events in familiar settings. Ink drawings, brightened with washes and strokes of color, have the narrative power to tell the basic story on their own. But the book is richer for the inclusion of a straightforward text." Booklist

★ **Annie** Rose is my little sister. Candlewick Press 2003 un il $15.99

Grades: PreK K 1 2   E

  1. Siblings -- Fiction

  ISBN 0-7636-1959-0

LC 2002-67695

Alfie describes all the things that he and his younger sister Annie Rose do together

"Few artists have recreated the young child's body language and surroundings as faithfully as Hughes. The gouache-and-oil pastel illustrations teem with well-observed details." Booklist

★ The **Christmas** Eve ghost. Candlewick Press 2010 un il $15.99

Grades: K 1 2 3   E

  1. Laundry -- Fiction 2. Christmas -- Fiction 3. Prejudices -- Fiction 4. Great Britain -- Fiction 5. Single parent family -- Fiction

  ISBN 978-0-7636-4472-7; 0-7636-4472-2

LC 2009051506

In 1930s Liverpool, England, Bronwen and Dylan live with their widowed mother, who works long hours doing other people's washing, and even though she sometimes must leave the children alone in the house, she cautions them not to speak to the O'Rileys next door, who go to a different church.

"A mixture of full-page and spot illustrations in watercolor and ink creates a nostalgic atmosphere. . . . The overall theme of the budding friendship between families of different faiths is subtly and effectively presented." Kirkus

★ **Don't** want to go! Candlewick Press 2010 un il $16.99

Grades: PreK K   E

  1. Babysitters -- Fiction

  ISBN 978-0-7636-5091-9; 0-7636-5091-9

LC 2010011454

Lily's mother is sick and her father must go to work, but she does not want to stay with a babysitter, even if it means playing with cute baby Sam, sweet little dog Ringo, and fun big brother Jack.

Hughes's "unadorned narration exudes empathy for the dislocated Lily. . . . And her densely textured, saturated gouache images . . . make a strong case that the right people can make any situation feel homey. . . . Lily's gradual acceptance of the situation unfolds naturally and believably." Publ Wkly

Ella's big chance; a Jazz-Age Cinderella. [by] Shirley Hughes. Simon & Schuster Books for Young Readers 2004 un il $16.95

Grades: K 1 2 3   E

  1. Fairy tales

  ISBN 0-689-87399-9

LC 2003-27274

In this version of the Cinderella tale set in the 1920s, Ella has two men courting her—the handsome Duke of Arc and Buttons the delivery boy

"Hughes's gouache-and-pen-line illustrations exhibit her usual meticulous attention to detail. . . . This insightful retelling also offers a fascinating visual peek at a glamorous time." SLJ

Jonadab and Rita. Red Fox 2011 il pa $11.99

Grades: PreK K 1   E

  1. Toys -- Fiction 2. Magic -- Fiction 3. Fairies -- Fiction

  ISBN 978-1-86-230313-3; 1-86-230313-4

Jonadab is a very special toy donkey who can fly. But Minnie has so many other toys that often Jonadab and his friend Rita the mouse find themselves sad and lonely and left behind in the toy box. One moonlit night, tired of being ignored, Jonadab flies away and joins a magical fairy feast. But then he can't get back in to Minnie's room.

"Colorful illustrations cover half of each page while the text is set off in rectangular boxes highlighted with small black pen-and-ink sketches featuring characters from the tale. . . . This quiet fantasy will be welcomed by [Hughes'] many fans." SLJ

Olly and me 1 2 3. Candlewick Press 2009 un il $16.99
Grades: PreK K 1 2   **E**
    1. Counting 2. Siblings -- Fiction
    ISBN 978-0-7636-4016-3; 0-7636-4016-6
                               LC 2008-934556
"Hughes warms up this counting book with appealing characters and colorful action scenes. On the first page, which begins with a big numeral 1 and one large dot, a little girl named Katie introduces herself. On the next, with the numeral 2 and two large dots, she is joined by her baby brother, Olly. . . . On the pages that follow, more family members, friends, neighbors, and pets join the siblings. . . . The line drawings depict characters with a certain air of rumpled reality that makes Hughes' artwork so endearing and enduring." Booklist

Hughes, Ted, 1930-1998
My brother Bert; pictures by Tracey Campbell Pearson. Farrar, Straus & Giroux 2009 un il $16.95
Grades: PreK K 1   **E**
    1. Stories in rhyme 2. Pets -- Fiction 3. Animals -- Fiction 4. Siblings -- Fiction
    ISBN 978-0-374-39982-5; 0-374-39982-4
                               LC 2007034415
Illustrations and rhyming text portray a hobby gone awry, as Bert's collection of exotic pets seems on the verge of breaking into a quarrel, and perhaps a rumpus, as well.

"Full of action, merriment, and wit, the pictures will occupy children with always one more thing to see. . . . Dizzying and delightful." Booklist

Hughes, Vi
Once upon a bathtime. Tradewind Books 2010 un il $17.95
Grades: PreK K 1   **E**
    1. Baths -- Fiction
    ISBN 978-1-896580-5-48; 1-896580-5-48
As a child takes a bath and gets ready for bed, characters from fairy tales accompany the child.

"This picture book is told in simple, elegant verse and illustrated with paper-cut collage artwork." SLJ

Huneck, Stephen
Sally goes to Heaven; Stephen Huneck. Abrams Books for Young Readers 2014 48 p. (Sally the dog) $18.95
Grades: PreK K 1 2 3   **E**
    1. Pets -- Fiction 2. Death -- Fiction 3. Dogs -- Fiction 4. Heaven -- Fiction
    ISBN 1419709690; 9781419709692
                               LC 2013010063
Written by Stephen Huneck, "'Sally Goes to Heaven' is a wonderful, joyous book to help provide gentle insight into the natural cycle of life of a pet, or to share with young children who have recently experienced the loss of a beloved animal. In this book, Sally passes away and goes to heaven, where she lives happily and helps her family on Earth find a new pet." (Publisher's note)

"Huneck, who died in 2010, takes Sally on one last adventure, a trip to heaven. There she finds her aches are gone, there are piles of dirty socks, and there are no fences or animal shelters...Young readers will be reassured that Sally expects to meet her human family in heaven someday, but in the meantime, she hopes they will find a dog to adopt who will look after them." Booklist
    Other titles include:
    Sally Gets a Job (2008)
    Sally Goes to the Beach (2000)
    Sally Goes to the Farm (2002)
    Sally Goes to the Mountains (2001)
    Sally Goes to the Vet (2004)
    Sally's Great Balloon Adventure (2009)
    Sally's Snow Adventure (2006)

★ **Sally** goes to the beach; written and illustrated by Stephen Huneck. Abrams 2000 un il $17.95
Grades: PreK K 1   **E**
    1. Dogs -- Fiction 2. Beaches -- Fiction
    ISBN 0-8109-4186-4
                               LC 99-28421
Sally, a black Labrador retriever, goes to the beach, where she enjoys various activities with other visiting dogs

"The playful pup's enjoyment is conveyed through a simple but engaging text and beautiful, full-page woodblock prints." SLJ
    Other titles about Sally are:
    Sally goes to the mountains (2001)
    Sally goes to the farm (2002)
    Sally goes to the vet (2004)
    Sally's snow adventure (2006)
    Sally gets a job (2008)
    Sally's great balloon adventure (2010)

Hunt, Julie
Precious Little; [by] Julie Hunt & Sue Moss; pictures by Gaye Chapman. Allen & Unwin 2011 un il $16.99
Grades: K 1 2 3   **E**
    1. Circus -- Fiction 2. Acrobats and acrobatics -- Fiction
    ISBN 978-1-74175-147-5; 1-74175-147-0
                               LC 2011290332
"A tatterdemalion heroine wearing rags and stars falls into a dream hole and flies through the heavens. Precious Little works for the Light Fantastics, watching the contortionists, Knots-RUs, and the fire-eaters, Flambé and the Infernos, but longing to fly. Her friends Fat Chance and Tough Luck draw a wire across the 'lucky dip,' and she begins to cross it. . . . The text swirls and makes loop-the-loops all over the pages, necessitating constant turning, all the better to pore over the spectacular art. . . . Children (and adults) can be lost for a long and pleasurable time amid the sparkles." Kirkus

Hunter, Anne
★ **Cricket** song; Anne Hunter. Houghton Mifflin Harcourt 2016 32 p. color illustrations $16.99
Grades: PreK K 1   **E**
    1. Sleep -- Fiction 2. Animal sounds -- Fiction 3. Animals -- Fiction 4. Bedtime -- Fiction
    ISBN 9780544582590; 0544582594
                               LC 2014048561
This children's book, by Anne Hunter, "connects two children on different continents through the evocation of sound and smell. Readers will [see] various creatures portrayed in the book and watching what they are doing as the two children begin to fall to sleep in their beds on seemingly opposite sides of the world." (Publisher's note)

"In a yellow house, in a blue bedroom decorated with planets and stars, a boy sleeps. He cuddles a sea otter toy, and on the wall behind a windblown curtain is the painting of a South Pacific island, volcanic, the ocean parted by a whale's tail. The tranquil spread is underlined with a long, narrow panel depicting his house, the stretch of the sea, and then another house on an island just like the one in his painting. . . . An evocative work in which readers can look at the pictures and hear the wind, the whales, and the crickets singing." SLJ

Hurd, Edith Thacher

★ **Johnny** Lion's book; pictures by Clement Hurd. new ed.; HarperCollins Pubs. 2001 63p il (I can read book) hardcover o.p. pa $3.99
Grades: PreK K 1   E
1. Lions -- Fiction
ISBN 0-06-029334-9 lib bdg; 0-06-444297-7 pa

A reissue of the title first published 1965

When his parents go out hunting, Johnny Lion stays home and experiences exciting adventures reading a book about a baby lion who goes out into the world and gets lost

"A subtle boost for the joys of reading in a story with engaging illustrations." Booklist

Other titles about Johnny Lion are:
Johnny Lion's bad day (1970)
Johnny Lion's rubber boots (1972)

Hurd, Thacher

★ **Art** dog. HarperCollins Pubs. 1996 un il $15.99; pa $6.99
Grades: PreK K 1 2   E
1. Dogs -- Fiction 2. Artists -- Fiction
ISBN 0-06-024424-0; 0-06-443489-3 pa

LC 95-31092

When the Mona Woofa is stolen from the Dogopolis Museum of Art, a mysterious character who calls himself Art Dog tracks down and captures the thieves

"This is exuberantly drawn by Hurd, who has imbued Art Dog with the flash and dash every artist feels at times; but Hurd also captures the shyness that comes with displaying your art. Kids will respond not just to the pictures but also to a story that does as well with characters as with plot." Booklist

Bad frogs. Candlewick Press 2009 un il $15.99
Grades: PreK K 1 2   E
1. Frogs -- Fiction
ISBN 978-0-7636-3253-3; 0-7636-3253-8

"Hurd's bad frogs—170 of them—revel in mischievous conduct and generate chaos wherever they go. Whether jumping in muck, slurping ice cream, burping at the dinner table, fighting with toothbrushes, or skateboarding down stair railings, the delightfully green, yellow-tinged characters prance across the pages in an array of costumes, entertaining viewers with their antics. The artwork gleams with Hurd's shiny bright colors, and his swinging text, presented in bold purple, trumpets the frogs' badness as they romp through the action-packed illustrations." SLJ

Mama don't allow; starring Miles and the Swamp Band. Harper & Row 1984 un il hardcover o.p. pa $5.99
Grades: PreK K 1 2   E
1. Alligators -- Fiction 2. Bands (Music) -- Fiction
ISBN 0-06-022690-0 lib bdg; 0-06-443078-2 pa

LC 83-47703

Miles and the Swamp Band have the time of their lives playing at the Alligator Ball, until they discover the menu includes Swamp Band soup

"The multi-colored full-spread watercolor illustrations are stunningly bright and full of movement, far outpacing the story line in energy and imagination." SLJ

The **weaver**; pictures by Elisa Kleven. Farrar Straus Giroux 2010 un il $16.99
Grades: PreK K 1 2   E
1. Dreams -- Fiction 2. Weaving -- Fiction
ISBN 978-0-374-38254-4; 0-374-38254-9

LC 2008028533

High above the world, a weaver spins thread from such things as clouds, dyes it with colors from the sky and grass, and weaves a cloth filled with the emotions she sees throughout the day to make a blanket of dreams.

"The fanciful illustrations reflect the story's sense of celebration, portraying children, their families, and friends sharing small but significant moments in a kaleidoscope of springtime colors. Tiny characters of all nationalities enjoy life in a sun-drenched landscape while the gentle weaver and her adorable gray kitten watch from above. This dreamy story offers a reassuring message of love and security." SLJ

Hurst, Carol Otis

Rocks in his head; pictures by James Stevenson. Greenwillow Bks. 2001 un il $15.99; lib bdg $15.89
Grades: PreK K 1 2   E
1. Rocks -- Collectors and collecting
ISBN 0-06-029403-5; 0-06-029404-3 lib bdg

LC 00-56197

Boston Globe-Horn Book Award Honor: Nonfiction (2001)

Hurst "recounts the story of her father, an avid rock collector from the time he was a boy. . . . Dominated by earth tones, Stevenson's artwork convincingly evokes both the personality of this endearing protagonist and the period in which he lived." Publ Wkly

★ **Terrible** storm; [illustrated by] S. D. Schindler. Greenwillow Books 2007 un il $16.99; lib bdg $17.89
Grades: K 1 2 3   E
1. Blizzards -- Fiction 2. Grandfathers -- Fiction 3. Massachusetts -- Fiction
ISBN 978-0-06-009001-2; 0-06-009001-4; 978-0-06-009002-9 lib bdg; 0-06-009002-2 lib bdg

LC 2005-35731

"Humor is everywhere, but the funniest pictures show the men shoveling out of the snow, passing one another through the drifts. This lively, clever story, based on a real storm, neatly captures both the oddities of nature and how differing natures view the same event." Booklist

Hurwitz, Johanna

New shoes for Silvia; illustrated by Jerry Pinkney. Morrow Junior Bks. 1993 un il $17.99; lib bdg $16.89
Grades: PreK K 1 2   E
1. Shoes -- Fiction 2. Latin America -- Fiction
ISBN 0-688-05286-X; 0-688-05287-8 lib bdg

LC 92-40868

Silvia receives a pair of beautiful red shoes from her Tia Rosita and finds different uses for them until she grows enough for them to fit

"This simple story, told in spare prose, speaks universally to the imagination and emotions. Pinkney's spirited watercolors animate the narrative and are large enough for group sharing." SLJ

Husband, Amy

Dear teacher. Sourcebooks Jabberwocky 2010 un il pa $8.99

Grades: K 1 2   E

1. School stories 2. Letters -- Fiction
ISBN 978-1-4022-4268-7 pa; 1-4022-4268-9 pa

"Each vertical, double-page spread in this inventive title is a letter from young Michael to his new teacher explaining why he may be late for the first day of school. . . . The wild, colorful illustrations show the imaginative play, and kids with back-to-school panic will find comic relief in these over-the-top scenes." Booklist

Hutchins, H. J.

Mattland; story by Hazel Hutchins and Gail Herbert; art by Dusan Petricic. Annick Press 2008 un il $19.95; pa $8.95

Grades: K 1 2   E

1. Moving -- Fiction 2. Friendship -- Fiction 3. Imagination -- Fiction
ISBN 978-1-55451-121-1; 1-55451-121-6; 978-1-55451-120-4 pa; 1-55451-120-8 pa

"Matt finds himself in yet another new home. Surrounded by an uninspiring landscape and lacking friends, he begins to poke at the mud outside his house. He quickly notices in his marks the beginning of a landscape. Bit by bit, a miniature world unfolds before Matt. . . . When a rainstorm threatens to flood the newly created 'Mattland,' helping hands appear to route the current safely away. Petricic's understated watercolors are an essential counterpart to Hutchins and Herbert's mature narrative. . . . The illustrator skillfully leads readers from gray, nondescript images to a detailed world brimming with color." SLJ

Hutchins, Pat

1 hunter. Greenwillow Bks. 1982 un il hardcover o.p. pa $6.99

Grades: PreK K 1 2   E

1. Counting 2. Animals -- Fiction
ISBN 0-688-00614-0; 0-688-06522-8 pa

LC 81-6352

"Humorous illustrations done in a flat, clear style make an outstanding counting book." Horn Book

★ The **doorbell** rang. Greenwillow Bks. 1986 un il $15.99; lib bdg $16.89; pa $5.99

Grades: PreK K 1 2   E

1. Cookies -- Fiction 2. Division -- Fiction
ISBN 0-688-05251-7; 0-688-05252-5 lib bdg; 0-688-09234-9 pa

LC 85-12615

"Bright, joyous, dynamic, this wonderfully humorous piece of realism for the young is presented simply but with style and imagination." Horn Book

★ **Rosie's** walk. Macmillan 1968 un il $16.95; pa $6.99

Grades: PreK K 1   E

1. Foxes -- Fiction 2. Chickens -- Fiction
ISBN 0-02-745850-4; 0-02-043750-1 pa

"Rosie the hen goes for a walk around the farm and gets home in time for dinner, completely unaware that a fox has been hot on her heels every step of the way. The viewer knows, however, and is not only held in suspense but tickled by the ways in which the fox is foiled at every turn by the unwitting hen. A perfect choice for the youngest." Booklist

Another book about Rosie is:

Where, oh where, is Rosie's chick (2016)

Ten red apples. Greenwillow Bks. 2000 un il $17.99; lib bdg $18.89

Grades: PreK K 1   E

1. Counting 2. Stories in rhyme 3. Apples -- Fiction 4. Domestic

animals -- Fiction
ISBN 0-688-16797-7; 0-688-16798-5 lib bdg

LC 99-25065

In rhyming verses, one animal after another neighs, moos, oinks, quacks and makes other appropriate sounds as each eats an apple from the farmer's tree

"A concept book that blends rhyming, counting, repetition, and animal sounds into a charming, folksy story. . . . The gouache paintings are bright and clear." SLJ

★ **We're** going on a picnic! Greenwillow Bks. 2002 un il $15.95; lib bdg $15.89

Grades: PreK K 1 2   E

1. Ducks -- Fiction 2. Chickens -- Fiction
ISBN 0-688-16799-3; 0-688-16800-0 lib bdg

LC 00-62225

"With an understated humor infusing both narrative and pictures, Hutchins successfully pulls off the child-pleasing contrivance of letting readers in on the secret." Publ Wkly

Hyde, Heidi Smith

Feivel's flying horses; illustrated by Johanna van der Sterre. KarBen Pub. 2010 un il lib bdg $17.95; pa $7.95

Grades: PreK K 1 2   E

1. Jews -- Fiction 2. Carousels -- Fiction 3. Immigrants -- Fiction 4. Wood carving -- Fiction 5. Coney Island (New York, N.Y.) -- Fiction
ISBN 978-0-7613-3957-1; 0-7613-3957-4; 978-0-7613-3959-5 pa; 0-7613-3959-0 pa

LC 2008033480

A Jewish immigrant who is saving money to bring his wife and children to join him in America creates ornate horses for a carousel on Coney Island, one for each member of his family.

"Watercolor illustrations with ink lines illustrate the immigrant experience on New York's Lower East Side in the late 1800s and help bring to life the magic of Coney Island." SLJ

Hyewon Yum

★ **Mom,** it's my first day of kindergarten! Hyewon Yum. Frances Foster Books 2012 40 p. col. ill. $16.99

Grades: PreK K   E

1. School stories 2. Picture books for children 3. Mother-son relationship -- Fiction 4. Worry -- Fiction 5. Schools -- Fiction 6. Kindergarten -- Fiction 7. Mothers and sons -- Fiction 8. First day of school -- Fiction
ISBN 0374350043; 9780374350048

LC 2011018294

This book "looks at the first day of school from two points of view—that of a little boy who is more than ready and a nervous mother not quite prepared to let him go. . . . [T]he 5-year-old shakes his mother awake on the first day of school." The text "enumerates her worries (that he won't have time to eat, she forgot some vital supply, he'll be late, he'll get lost, he won't have any friends)" but when "they reach his classroom door . . . [h]e quickly gets over it and has a great day at school." (Kirkus)

Puddle; Hyewon Yum. Farrar, Straus & Giroux 2016 40 p. color illustrations (hardback) $16.99

Grades: PreK K 1   E

1. Rain -- Fiction 2. Imagination -- Fiction 3. Imagination -- Fiction 4. Mothers and sons -- Fiction 5. Rain and rainfall -- Fiction
ISBN 9780374316952; 0374316953

LC 2015005288

In this children's book, by Hyewon Yum, "one rainy day, a little boy is upset because he can't go out and play. His mom comes up with a way to keep him entertained--by drawing a picture of herself and him going outside, playing in the rain, and splashing in a giant puddle. They have so much fun drawing themselves that they decide to venture out and make the most of the rainy weather." (Publisher's note)

"Yum deftly ties moods, weather, parenting, and the power of art together." Kirkus

This is our house; Hyewon Yum. Frances Foster Books 2013 40 p. (hardcover) $16.99

Grades: PreK K 1 2   **E**

1. Houses -- Fiction 2. Picture books for children 3. Home -- Fiction 4. Dwellings -- Fiction 5. Family life -- Fiction
ISBN 0374374872; 9780374374877

LC 2012029684

In this children's picture book, a "small girl with twin braids narrates her family's history with pride, starting with when her grandparents arrived at a brick rowhouse on a leafy street, coming from 'far away with just two suitcases in hand.' Since then, three generations have marked the seasons and personal milestones outside the house's front door . . . , found snug shelter within its walls . . . , and consumed homemade soup in its kitchen." (Publishers Weekly)

★ The **twins'** blanket. Farrar Straus Giroux 2011 un il $16.99

Grades: PreK K   **E**

1. Twins -- Fiction 2. Sisters -- Fiction 3. Blankets -- Fiction
ISBN 978-0-374-37972-8; 0-374-37972-6

Two twin girls, who have always shared everything, sleep in separate beds with their own blankets for the first time.

"It's an exquisitely designed book: lots of white space focuses attention on unexpected pleasures, like the feet of the twins as they stomp on the fabric in a wash basin. The book's inherent symmetry, with the twins mirroring each other on the left and right sides of the spreads, is a treat as well." Publ Wkly

The **twins'** little sister; Hyewon Yum. Frances Foster Books, Farrar Straus Giroux 2014 40 p. color illustrations (hardcover) $17.99

Grades: PreK K   **E**

1. Twins -- Fiction 2. Sisters -- Fiction 3. Babies -- Fiction 4. Mother and child -- Fiction
ISBN 0374379734; 9780374379735

LC 2013013078

Sequel to: The Twins' Blanket

"In 'The Twins' Little Sister' by . . . picture book author Hyewon Yum, being twins means having two of almost everything: two twin beds, two polka-dot dresses, two dolls. But these two little girls have only one mom. This is a big problem. Soon there will be an even bigger problem: Mom is having a baby, and the twins will have a little sister." (Publisher's note)

"Those strong-willed sisters from The Twins' Blanket are fighting over Mom's attention. The situation worsens when Mom brings home a new baby sister. Yum's twins are believably childlike in their directness and their unshakable belief that the world revolves around them. Collage elements add texture and interest to the gouache illustrations. This is a fresh take on both the sibling-rivalry and new-baby themes." Horn Book

Ian, Janis

Tiny Mouse; by Janis Ian, illustrated by Ingrid Schubert and Dieter Schubert. Lemniscaat USA 2013 32 p. $19.95

Grades: PreK K 1 2   **E**

1. Mice -- Fiction 2. Ocean travel -- Fiction
ISBN 193595430X; 9781935954309

This children's book, by Janis Ian and illustrated by Ingrid and Dieter Schubert, "follows the adventures of a bored mouse who decides to go to sea and narrowly escapes a grisly death. In his moment of truth, he

understands that it's better to be a whole mouse at home than someone's dinner at sea." (Publisher's note)

"In the singer-songwriter's first picture book, a mouse, bored with his life, stows away on a ship and has an encounter that makes him appreciate what he had. The lyrics don't quite work without the accompanying CD--the rhyming text's rhythms can be elusive, and some lines pointlessly repeat--but there's pleasure in Ian's punchy language and the verging-on-surreal illustrations. Sheet music included." (Horn Book)

Ichikawa, Satomi

★ **Come** fly with me; [by] Satomi Ichikawa. Philomel Books 2008 un il $15.99

Grades: PreK K 1   **E**

1. Dogs -- Fiction 2. Toys -- Fiction 3. France -- Fiction 4. Airplanes -- Fiction 5. Paris (France) -- Fiction
ISBN 978-0-399-24679-1

LC 2007023643

Woggy and Cosmos, a toy dog and a toy airplane, go on an adventure in Paris.

"The adventure element is perfectly keyed to the age group. . . . The charming watercolors with their everchanging scenes and skies will pull [children] in." Booklist

La La Rose. Philomel Books 2004 un il $15.99

Grades: PreK K 1 2   **E**

1. Gardens -- Fiction 2. Paris (France) -- Fiction 3. Lost and found possessions -- Fiction
ISBN 0-399-24029-2

LC 2002-15366

La La Rose, a young girl's stuffed rabbit, gets lost in Luxembourg Gardens in Paris.

"Ichikawa's ink-and-watercolor paintings are a wonderful mix of action and thoughtfulness, sweetness and subtlety that extend the story and give it life past a first reading. . . . A very satisfying story that also captures the magic and excitement of a special place." Booklist

My father's shop. Kane/Miller 2006 un il $15.95

Grades: K 1 2 3   **E**

1. Morocco -- Fiction 2. Roosters -- Fiction 3. Rugs and carpets -- Fiction 4. Father-son relationship -- Fiction
ISBN 1-929132-99-9

"When given a flawed carpet, Mustafa . . . drums up business for his merchant father by attracting first a similarly colored rooster, then numerous trourists who crow in their own languages: 'Co-co-ri-co!' 'Qui-qui-ri-qui!' and 'Cock-a-doodle-do!' The multicultural message is light and the humor contagious. Bright scenes of the crowded Moroccan marketplace amplify the story." Horn Book Guide

My little train. Philomel Books 2010 un il $15.99

Grades: PreK K 1   **E**

1. Toys -- Fiction 2. Animals -- Fiction 3. Railroads -- Fiction
ISBN 978-0-399-25453-6; 0-399-25453-6

A little train goes for a ride, taking all the stuffed animals where they want to go.

"Ichikawa's soft watercolors reveal destinations that are ripped from kids' playtime imaginations. . . . Repeated animal noises and train sounds encourage readers to lend their voices to this whimsical read-aloud." Publ Wkly

My pig Amarillo. Philomel Bks. 2003 un il $15.99

Grades: PreK K 1 2   **E**

1. Pigs -- Fiction 2. Guatemala -- Fiction
ISBN 0-399-23768-2

LC 2002-7318

Original French edition, 2002

Pablito, a Guatemalan boy whose pet pig Amarillo has disappeared, uses a kite to send him a message that he still loves him

"Ichikawa uses her Guatemalan setting very effectively, but she also wraps the story in universal emotions: love, longing, grief, hope. The pen-and-watercolor artwork brings children close to all facets of Pablito's story." Booklist

Idle, Molly

★ **Flora** and the flamingo; by Molly Idle. Chronicle Books 2013 44 p. col. ill. (reinforced) $16.99

Grades: PreK K 1   E

1. Stories without words 2. Dance -- Fiction 3. Picture books for children 4. Flamingos -- Fiction 5. Human-animal relationships -- Fiction 6. Human-animal relationships -- Fiction

ISBN 1452110069; 9781452110066

LC 2012014608

Caldecott Honor Book (2014)

"In this . . . wordless picture book with interactive flaps, [by Molly Idle,] Flora and her graceful flamingo friend explore the trials and joys of friendship through an elaborate synchronized dance. With a twist, a turn, and even a flop, these unlikely friends learn at last how to dance together in perfect harmony." (Publisher's note)

Flora and the peacocks; Molly Idle. Chronicle Books LLC 2016 40 p. color illustrations $17.99

Grades: PreK K 1   E

1. Dance -- Fiction 2. Lift-the-flap books 3. Peacocks -- Fiction 4. Stories without words 5. Toy and movable books 6. Human-animal relationship -- Fiction 7. Peafowl -- Fiction 8. Lift-the-flap books -- Specimens 9. Human-animal relationships -- Fiction

ISBN 9781452138169

LC 2015004521

In this book, by Molly Idle, "Flora is back, and this time she's found two new friends: a pair of peacocks! But amidst the fanning feathers and mirrored movements, Flora realizes that the push and pull between three friends can be a delicate dance. Will this trio find a way to get back in step?" (Publisher's note)

"Design, engineering, and art intersect to deliver a virtuoso interpretation of the pitfalls and pleasures of triads." Kirkus

Flora and the penguin; Molly Idle. Chronicle Books LLC 2014 40 p. color illustrations (alk. paper) $16.99

Grades: PreK K 1   E

1. Penguins -- Fiction 2. Stories without words 3. Ice skating -- Fiction 4. Dance -- fiction 5. Lift-the-flap books 6. Friendship -- Fiction 7. Toy and movable books 8. Conduct of life -- fiction 9. Lift-the-flap books -- Specimens 10. Human-animal relationships -- fiction

ISBN 145212891X; 9781452128917

LC 2013042455

In this children's story without words, written and illustrated by Molly Idle, "Flora takes to the ice and forms an unexpected friendship with a penguin. Twirling, leaping, spinning, and gliding, on skates and flippers, the duo mirror each other's graceful dance above and below the ice. But when Flora gives the penguin the cold shoulder, the pair must figure out a way to work together for uplifting results." (Publisher's note)

"Idle reprises the structure and format of her Caldecott Honor-winning Flora and the Flamingo in this wordless wintry companion, which is every bit as graceful a performance for both Flora and her creator. A thick sheet of ice serves as the canvas for Flora's skating performance with a penguin that has climbed up onto the ice; a cutaway view of the pale blue-violet water below shows a school of fish doing a dance of their own. Small glued-in flaps help create a sense of movement, and

also explore the brief rift that forms between Flora and the penguin after the bird dives back below the ice in pursuit of a fish. Once again, Idle's elegantly drafted scenes couldn't be more polished, and the fold-out sequence that brings this dance to a close feels like a real triumph." Pub Wkly

Tea Rex; by Molly Idle. Viking 2013 40 p. ill. (hardcover) $16.99

Grades: PreK K 1   E

1. Afternoon teas -- Fiction 2. Humorous fiction -- Fiction 3. Tyrannosaurus rex -- Fiction 4. Humorous stories 5. Parties -- Fiction 6. Dinosaurs -- Fiction 7. Etiquette -- Fiction 8. Tyrannosaurus rex -- Fiction

ISBN 0670014303; 9780670014309

LC 2012016443

This children's story, by Molly Idle, describes a tea party between children and a Tyrannosaurus rex. "Some tea parties are for grown-ups. Some are for girls. But this tea party is for a very special guest. And it is important to follow some rules . . . like providing comfortable chairs, and good conversation, and yummy food. But sometimes that is not enough for special guests, especially when their manners are more Cretaceous than gracious." (Publisher's note)

Imai, Ayano

Chester. Minedition 2007 un il $16.99

Grades: PreK K   E

1. Dogs -- Fiction

ISBN 978-0-698-40062-7

"Chester, a black-and-white dog with a serious mein, loves his family, but they seem to have forgotten about him. Unhappy, he puts his doghouse on his head and leaves. . . . Imai . . . has produced a small gem. The story . . . is illustrated in delicate watercolors that nonetheless project force both in action and emotion." Booklist

Ingalls, Ann

The **little** piano girl; by Ann Ingalls & Maryann Macdonald; illustrated by Giselle Potter. Houghton Mifflin Books for Children 2010 un il

Grades: K 1 2 3   E

1. Pianists 2. Composers 3. Pianists -- Fiction 4. Jazz musicians -- Fiction 5. African American musicians -- Fiction

ISBN 0-618-95974-2; 978-0-618-95974-7

LC 2008040457

This story depicts the life of the American pianist and composer. "Grades one to five." (SLJ)

Potter's "gouache paintings provide a vivid portrait of industrial Pittsburgh at the beginning of the 20th century, yet have an iconic quality too. Ingalls and MacDonald provide a touching memorial to a jazz great who is not a household name—a valuable contribution." Publ Wkly

Ingman, Bruce

When Martha's away. Candlewick Press 2010 un il $16.99

Grades: PreK K 1 2   E

1. Cats -- Fiction

ISBN 978-0-7636-5135-0; 0-7636-5135-4

A reissue of the title first published 1995 by Houghton Mifflin

Martha's cat reveals that he does not sleep all day, as she believes, but rather has a very busy schedule of activities.

"With humor and sponaneity, the large, spacious illustrations combine line drawings, simple shapes, and bright textured colors." Horn Book Guide

Intriago, Patricia

★ **Dot**. Farrar Straus Giroux 2011 un il $14.99

Grades: PreK K 1   **E**
1. Opposites
ISBN 978-0-374-31835-2; 0-374-31835-2
LC 2010019816
"Even two and three-year-olds will make astute observations. . . . Children will encounter ample ways to interact with this incredibly elegant, clever, and delightful concept book." SLJ

Isaacs, Anne
★ **Dust** Devil; illustrated by Paul O. Zelinsky. Schwartz & Wade 2010 un il $17.99
Grades: K 1 2 3   **E**
1. Tall tales 2. Montana -- Fiction 3. Frontier and pioneer life -- Fiction
ISBN 0-375-86722-8; 978-0-375-86722-4
Having moved to Montana from Tennessee in the 1830s, fearless Angelica Longrider—also known as Swamp Angel—changes the state's landscape, tames a wild horse, and captures some desperadoes.
"Isaac's far-fetched tall tale is again paired with Zelinsky's stunning American-primitive paintings, framed by the wood upon which they are painted. . . . Zelinsky's action-packed panoramas capture Angel's Paul Bunyanlike strength. . . . Isaacs wraps her narrative in exaggeration that will have kids howling." Publ Wkly

★ **Meanwhile,** back at the ranch; by Anne Isaacs and illustrated by Kevin Hawkes. First edition Schwartz & Wade 2014 56 p. color illustrations hardcover $17.99
Grades: K 1 2 3 4   **E**
1. Texas -- Fiction 2. Widows -- Fiction 3. Ranch life -- Fiction 4. Tall tales 5. Humorous stories 6. Courtship -- Fiction
ISBN 0375867457; 9780375867453
LC 2011046490
In this book, by Anne Issacs, "widow Tulip Jones of Bore, England, inherits a ranch in By-Golly Gully, Texas, and moves in with two trunks of tea, twelve pet tortoises, and three servants. The peaceful life suits the wealthy widow fine until word gets out and every unmarried man in Texas lines up to marry her. Widow Tulip and her small staff of three can't possibly run the farm and manage all the suitors, so she devises a plan." (Publisher's note)
"Lively storytelling in colorful, drawn-out sentences, Texas-style, makes for a splendid--albeit lengthy--read-aloud. Hawkes' extra-charming soft-focus acrylic-and-colored-pencil artwork on textured paper suits the cactus-filled desert landscape to a T-for-Texas." Kirkus

Pancakes for supper! illustrated by Mark Teague. Scholastic Press 2006 un il $15.99
Grades: PreK K 1   **E**
1. Animals -- Fiction 2. New England -- Fiction
ISBN 0-439-64483-6
LC 2005-14532
In the backwoods of New England, a young girl cleverly fends off the threats of wild animals by trading her clothes for her safety.
"Isaacs's clever, respectful take on an iconic tale is testament to its appeal. Teague's pictures are brilliant, cinematic full-bleed oil-paint dramas that capture the essence of a nascent New England spring." SLJ

★ **Swamp** Angel; illustrated by Paul O. Zelinsky. Dutton Children's Bks. 1994 un il $16.99; pa $6.99
Grades: K 1 2 3   **E**
1. Tall tales 2. Tennessee -- Fiction 3. Frontier and pioneer life -- Fiction
ISBN 0-525-45271-0; 0-14-055908-6 pa
LC 93-43956
A Caldecott Medal honor book, 1995

Along with other amazing feats, Angelica Longrider, also known as Swamp Angel, wrestles a huge bear, known as Thundering Tarnation, to save the winter supplies of the settlers in Tennessee
"Isaacs tells her original story with the glorious exaggeration and uproarious farce of the traditional tall tale and with its typical laconic idiom—you just can't help reading it aloud. . . . Zelinsky's detailed oil paintings in folk-art style are exquisite, framed in cherry, maple, and birch wood grains." Booklist
Another title about Swamp Angel is:
Dust Devil (2010)

Isaacs, Ronald H.
Farmer Kobi's Hanukkah match; by Karen Rostoker-Gruber and Rabbi Ron Isaacs; illustrations by CB Decker. Behrman House 2015 color illustrations (hardcover) $17.95
Grades: K 1 2   **E**
1. Jews -- Fiction 2. Humorous stories 3. Hanukkah -- Fiction 4. Farm life -- Fiction 5. Domestic animals -- Fiction 6. Dating (Social customs) -- Fiction 7. Human-animal relationships -- Fiction
ISBN 168115501X; 9781681155012
LC 2014027243
"Farmer Kobi's well-mannered goats, donkey, and sheep know just how to play host, and they give Polly, Kobi's Hanukkah guest, a gracious welcome. But when Polly isn't sure animals belong in a house, what will happen next?" (Publisher's note)

Isadora, Rachel
★ **Bea** at ballet; Rachel Isadora. Nancy Paulsen Books 2012 32 p. col. ill. (hardcover) $12.99
Grades: PreK K   **E**
1. Ballet -- Fiction 2. Picture books for children 3. Dance -- Study and teaching -- Fiction 4. Ballet dancing -- Fiction
ISBN 0399254099; 9780399254093
LC 2011046803
This children's picture book offers a "primer" about ballet for preschool children. The illustrations "present the preschoolers in black, white, and gray line with bursts of color in wardrobe and accessories, which [author Rachel Isadora] explains piece by piece, for each gender. The class instruction includes labels for the barre, mirror, piano, the five classic positions, and four foot movements (point, flex, flat, relevé)." (School Library Journal)

Bea in The Nutcracker; Rachel Isadora. Nancy Paulsen Books 2015 32 p. colour illustrations (hardback) $16.99
Grades: PreK K   **E**
1. Ballet -- Fiction 2. Friendship -- Fiction 3. Toddlers -- Fiction 4. Nutcracker (Choreographic work) -- Fiction
ISBN 0399252312; 9780399252310
LC 2014044934
In this children's book by Rachel Isadora "Bea and her friends are excited to put on their costumes and dance onstage in The Nutcracker! Bea is going to be Clara, and Sam is going to be the Prince. They will dance in the ballet's magical Land of Sweets." (Publisher's note)
"This is a standout in the crowded field of Nutcracker picture books." SLJ

★ **Ben's** trumpet. Greenwillow Bks. 1979 un il $17.99; pa $6.99
Grades: PreK K 1 2   **E**
1. Musicians -- Fiction 2. African Americans -- Fiction
ISBN 0-688-80194-3; 0-688-10988-8 pa
LC 78-12885
A Caldecott Medal honor book, 1980

This is the story of Ben, a boy whose dream is to be a jazz trumpeter but who is too poor to own an instrument until a real musician, remembering his own dreams, puts one into the boy's hands

"The art is astonishingly varied in its brilliant recreation—in the margins, in the urban backgrounds—of the commercial art of the 20's and 30's." N Y Times Book Rev

Happy belly, happy smile. Harcourt Children's Books 2009 un il $16

Grades: PreK K 1   E

1. Restaurants -- Fiction 2. Grandfathers -- Fiction 3. Chinese Americans -- Fiction

ISBN 978-0-15-206546-1; 0-15-206546-6

LC 2008046221

Sitting in the kitchen of his grandfather's Chinese restaurant, a young boy enjoys watching the chefs and waiters prepare and serve mouth-watering dishes

"Isadora's characteristic collage-and-oil illustrations [are] attractive as always. . . . This brief bite of Chinese cuisine will add flavor to cuisine-themed story hours." Booklist

I hear a pickle; (and smell, see, touch, and taste it, too!) Rachel Isadora. Nancy Paulsen Books 2016 32 p. color illustrations $16.99

Grades: PreK K 1   E

1. Pickles -- Fiction 2. Smell -- Fiction 3. Taste -- Fiction 4. Touch -- Fiction 5. Vision -- Fiction 6. Hearing -- Fiction 7. Perception -- Fiction 8. Senses and sensation -- Fiction 9. Senses and sensation -- Fiction

ISBN 0399160493; 9780399160493

LC 2015013960

This illustrated children's book by Rachel Isadora is an "introduction to the five senses. Hearing, smelling, seeing, touching, tasting--our five senses allow us to experience the world in so many ways! With our ears we hear the birds sing; with our nose we smell the stinky cheese; with our eyes we see the moon and stars (and sometimes glasses help us see even better!); with our skin we feel the rain (and learn not to touch the hot stove!); and with our tongue we can taste our favorite foods." (Publisher's note)

"Well designed for raising awareness of the senses, this is fine for reading aloud in a group setting and particularly effective one-on-one." Booklist

Jake at gymnastics; Rachel Isadora. Nancy Paulsen Books, an imprint of Penguin Group (USA) Inc. 2014 32 p. $14.99

Grades: PreK K   E

1. Toddlers -- Fiction 2. Gymnastics -- Fiction

ISBN 0399160485; 9780399160486

LC 2013024243

In this children's book, by Rachel Isadora, "Jake and his diverse group of friend[s] love their action-packed gymnastics class, where they stretch, tumble, balance, turn somersaults and so much more. This is the perfect book to introduce toddlers to the joy of movement and the fun of gymnastics." (Publisher's note)

"Isadora shows a group of roly-poly toddlers enjoying a beginning gymnastics class. Teachers lead five girls and four boys through activities such as stretching, tumbling, walking on a low balance beam, and hanging on a parallel bar. The text is minimal, but the real joy comes through Isadora's sprightly illustrations that combine pencil and ink line drawings with swathes of oil paint." Horn Book

★ **Lili** at ballet. Putnam 1993 un il hardcover o.p. pa $6.99

Grades: PreK K 1 2   E

1. Ballet -- Fiction

ISBN 0-399-22423-8; 0-698-11408-6 pa

LC 92-8429

Lili dreams of becoming a ballerina and goes to her ballet lessons four afternoons a week

"Isadora uses pastel shades of purple, pink, green, and blue with bold splashes of black. This is a prettily illustrated book that captures the magic and hard work involved in ballet." SLJ

Other titles about Lili are:

Lili backstage (1997)

Lili on stage (1995)

★ **Max**; story & pictures by Rachel Isadora. Macmillan 1976 un il hardcover o.p. pa $5.99

Grades: PreK K 1 2   E

1. Ballet -- Fiction 2. Baseball -- Fiction

ISBN 0-02-043800-1 pa

LC 76-9088

Max "is the star of his baseball team. On a Saturday morning, he has time to spare before his game and accepts (with some hidden disdain) the invitation of his sister, Lisa, to watch her ballet class in action. Max is surprised to find himself interested and happy to join the students at their teacher's suggestion. . . . The experience pays off at the ball park where Max hits a home run. Now he warms up for the game each week at Lisa's dancing class. The pictures are an ebullient combination of grace and comedy, with the leggy students dipping and soaring, in contrast to Max in his uniform." Publ Wkly

Old Mikamba had a farm; Rachel Isadora. Nancy Paulsen Books, An Imprint of Penguin Group (USA) Inc. 2013 40 p. $17.99

Grades: PreK K 1   E

1. Farmers 2. Animals -- Africa 3. Songs 4. Folk songs -- United States 5. Folk songs, English -- United States -- Texts

ISBN 0399257403; 9780399257407

LC 2012049555

"A familiar childhood song gets an African twist in [adaptor and illustrator Rachel] Isadora's latest picture book. She takes readers on safari to the plains of Africa to meet elephants, cheetahs, and dassies. . . . Old Mikamba's farm is a game park, so while there is some interaction between the two small children in the book and the animals, most of them are presented against a backdrop wilder and freer than any space Old MacDonald could offer his domestic stock." (Booklist)

Peekaboo bedtime. G.P. Putnam's Sons 2008 un il $16.99

Grades: PreK   E

1. Bedtime -- Fiction 2. Toddlers -- Fiction

ISBN 978-0-399-24384-4; 0-399-24384-4

LC 2007-34814

A toddler plays peekaboo with parents, grandparents, toys, and the moon while getting ready for bed.

"The pastel illustrations are a delight, a visual celebration of family. . . Perfect for laptime sharing or calm story hours." Kirkus

Say hello! G.P. Putnam's Sons 2010 un il $16.99

Grades: PreK K 1   E

1. City and town life -- Fiction 2. Language and languages -- Fiction

ISBN 978-0-399-25230-3; 0-399-25230-4

LC 2009011318

A little girl greets people in her neighborhood in many different languages.

"The text is paired down to essentials and the striking collage-style illustrations are colorful and dynamic. Richly patterned with oil paints as well as printed patterns, the cut-paper shapes show up vividly against the white backgrounds." Booklist

Ishida, Sanae

Little Kunoichi, the ninja girl; written and illustrated by Sanae Ishida. Little Bigfoot, an imprint of Sasquatch Books 2015 32 p. (hardback) $16.99

Grades: PreK K 1 2   **E**

1. Work ethic 2. Martial arts -- Fiction 3. Ninja -- Fiction 4. Contests -- Fiction 5. Cooperativeness -- Fiction 6. Determination (Personality trait) -- Fiction

ISBN 9781570619540

LC 2014031294

In this children's book by Sanae Ishida, "Little Kunoichi, a young ninja in training, is frustrated. Inspired by tiny Chibi Samurai's practice and skills, she works harder than ever and makes a friend. Together, they show the power of perseverance, hard work, and cooperation when they wow the crowd at the Island Festival. Ninja skills don't come easily to Little Kunoichi. She needs determination--and a special friend--to unleash her power!" (Publisher's note)

"Little Kunoichi is a ninja girl who lives and trains on a super secret island where she is not doing so well at learning her ninja skills until she meets a young samurai-in-training who inspires her to practice harder. Together, they perform at the Island Festival and although everything does not go perfectly, they have a wonderful time and are able to show off all of their new skills. . . . The tale's message of practice does not always have to equal perfection will resonate with young readers. VERDICT A fun title with great appeal." SLJ

Ismail, Yasmeen

Christmas for Greta and Gracie; Yasmeen Ismail. Candlewick Press 2016 32 p. color illustrations $15.99

Grades: PreK K 1 2   **E**

1. Sisters -- Fiction 2. Christmas -- Fiction

ISBN 9780763689438

LC 2016945891

In this picture book written and illustrated by Yasmeen Ismail, "Greta and Gracie are sisters. Greta is chatty while Gracie is quiet. . . . One day, everything changes. It's almost Christmas, and the sisters decorate the tree [and] shop for presents. . . . Then on Christmas Eve, while Greta is sleeping, Gracie hears a funny noise. She creeps downstairs to investigate, and the next morning her very special revelation leaves chitty-chatty Greta lost for words!" (Publisher's note)

"This one has it all: original characters, an exciting plot, dazzling illustrations, and the triumph of an underdog (or underbunny). More Greta and Gracie, please." Kirkus

Time for bed, Fred! Yasmeen Ismail. Bloomsbury/Walker 2014 32 p. color illustrations (hardcover) $14.99; (library reinforced) $15.89

Grades: PreK K 1   **E**

1. Dogs -- Fiction 2. Bedtime -- Fiction

ISBN 0802735983; 9780802735973; 9780802735980

LC 2013010711

In this children's story, written and illustrated by Yasmeen Ismail, "it's time for [the dog] Fred to go to bed . . . but Fred really, really doesn't want to! From hiding up in trees, to splashing in muddy puddles, to hiding behind bookshelves, Fred will do anything to avoid bedtime. He would even rather have a bath than go to bed . . . but all of this running couldn't possibly have possibly made Fred sleepy--could it?" (Publisher's note)

"The sophisticated and loose artwork is the ideal match for the simple, emotive text. A perfectly designed read-aloud for the bedtime staller." Kirkus

Isol, 1972-

Daytime visions; an alphabet. Isol; adapted into English by Isol and Elisa Amado. Enchanted Lion Books 2016 56 p. color illustrations (hardback) $17.95

Grades: PreK K 1 2   **E**

1. Alphabet -- Fiction

ISBN 9781592701957

LC 2015044309

This book, by Isol, is a "many-layered alphabet book. . . . Whether it's a kiwi who returns to a boy's shoulder or a little duck who can't sleep, the visions here are relatable to children and rich with possibility." (Publisher's note)

"Sometimes funny, occasionally eerie, often bizarre, such fantastic images keep readers alert, expectant, and excited. A visionary alphabet book that seeks to introduce not only letters, but nuanced narratives to eager, unfettered young minds." Kirkus

It's useful to have a duck; It's useful to have a boy. Groundwood Books 2009 un il $10

Grades: PreK K 1 2 3   **E**

1. Board books for children 2. Ducks -- Fiction

ISBN 978-0-88899-927-6; 0-88899-927-5

"Why on earth is it useful to have a duck? In a series of accordioned spreads on yellow board, a little boy reveals the answers, accompanied by swift line sketches that illustrate them. . . . The verso, on blue board, . . . is titled It's Useful to Have a Boy, [and] the identical images receive a very different gloss in the duck's voice. . . . Do not be deceived by the simple-looking board format: This is not for babies. Rather, it challenges children who have accepted the initial premise with developmentally appropriate narcissism to regard the world from the opposite perspective. Gently mind-bending, this playful Mexican import, packaged in a slipcase, will get readers thinking." Kirkus

The **Menino**; A Story Based on Real Events. by Isol, translated by Elisa Amado. Groundwood Books 2015 60 p. color illustrations $19.95

Grades: K 1 2 3   **E**

1. Child rearing 2. Infants -- Care

ISBN 1554987784; 9781554987788

This book, by Isol, translated by Elisa Amado, is "for babies and their parents about the whole new world that they both encounter when the baby arrives. . . . For babies, there's a rich range of images of babies and all their functions to look at. . . . For parents, this is a wonderful exploration of the new world this stranger-baby brings with him or her." (Publisher's note)

"The processes of elimination, regurgitation, nourishment, and other perfectly normal activities are illustrated clearly (and with humor)." Kirkus

Petit, the monster; words and pictures by Isol; translated by Elisa Amado. Groundwood Books 2010 un il $16.95

Grades: PreK K   **E**

1. Good and evil -- Fiction

ISBN 978-0-88899-947-4; 0-88899-947-X

"Poor Petit is a little confused: sometimes he's a good boy and sometimes he's a bad boy, and that's a hard contradiction to work out. . . . Argentinian author-illustrator Isol touches imaginatively on the challenging complexities of behavioral morality, and the book gains special traction from going into failed intentions and contrary correlations . . . while keeping the concept easily kid-accessible. Isol's quirky illustrations feature pencil and oil pastels . . . while computer planes of color fill in figures and backgrounds. . . . Kids will appreciate this playful approach to one of their biggest moral conundrums." Bull Cent Child Books

Isop, Laurie

How do you hug a porcupine? illustrated by Gwen Millward. Simon & Schuster Books for Young Readers 2011 il $15.99

Grades: PreK K 1   E

1. Stories in rhyme 2. Animals -- Fiction 3. Hugging -- Fiction 4. Porcupines -- Fiction

ISBN 978-1-4424-1291-0; 1-4424-1291-7

LC 2010006941

A child figures out the best way to hug a porcupine as he watches his friends hug other animals.

"The spare, interactive text and clear, uncluttered illustrations . . . make this a natural for group sharing." Booklist

Ives, Penny

★ **Celestine,** drama queen. Arthur A. Levine Books 2009 un il $16.99

Grades: PreK K   E

1. Ducks -- Fiction 2. Theater -- Fiction

ISBN 978-0-545-08149-8; 0-545-08149-1

Celestine the duck is sure that she is destined for stardom, but when her big break comes, she is temporarily stricken with stage fright.

Celestine "captures the essence of children, their emotions, and how they cope. Adorable, annoying, and utterly childlike, Celestine is appealingly portrayed in Ives' funny, sunny watercolors." Booklist

Iwai, Melissa

★ **Soup** day. Henry Holt 2010 un il $12.99

Grades: PreK K 1 2   E

1. Soups -- Fiction 2. Cooking -- Fiction 3. Vegetables -- Fiction 4. Mother-daughter relationship -- Fiction

ISBN 978-0-8050-9004-8; 0-8050-9004-5

LC 2009029314

A mother and daughter spend a snowy day together buying and preparing vegetables, assembling ingredients, and playing while their big pot of soup bubbles on the stove. Includes a recipe for "Snowy Day Vegetable Soup."

"With economical text and vivid, multitextured collages whose upbeat charm belies their sophistication, the process of preparing the dish unfolds. In one spread, Iwai cleverly offers lessons about numbers, colors, sizes, textures, and what various vegetables look like. . . . A perfect meal and a perfect book." SLJ

Iwamatsu, Atushi Jun

Crow Boy; [by] Taro Yashima. Viking 1955 37p il lib bdg $17.99; pa $5.99

Grades: PreK K 1 2   E

1. School stories 2. Japan -- Fiction

ISBN 0-670-24931-9 lib bdg; 0-14-050172-X pa

A Caldecott Medal honor book, 1956

"A moving story interpreted by the author's distinctive illustrations, valuable for human relations and for its picture of Japanese school life." Hodges. Books for Elem Sch Libr

Umbrella; [by] Taro Yashima. Viking 1958 30p il $16.99; pa $6.99

Grades: PreK K 1   E

1. Umbrellas and parasols -- Fiction

ISBN 0-670-73858-1; 0-14-050240-8 pa

A Caldecott Medal honor book, 1959

In this simple tale, young children "will be carried along by their identification with the actions of this very real little girl. . . . The beauty of the book makes this worthwhile." Horn Book

Iwamura, Kazuo

Bedtime in the forest. North-South Books 2010 un il $16.95

Grades: PreK K   E

1. Owls -- Fiction 2. Bedtime -- Fiction 3. Squirrels -- Fiction

ISBN 978-0-7358-2310-5; 0-7358-2310-3

Original Japanese edition 1982

Mick, Mack, and Molly, three young squirrels, find themselves awake and wanting to play all night like the owl children and learn that they should be going to bed instead.

"This unpretentious story with lovely art and endearing animals will be enjoyed by young children." SLJ

Jackson, Alison

The **ballad** of Valentine; illustrated by Tricia Tusa. Dutton Children's Bks. 2001 un il $16.99; pa $6.99

Grades: K 1 2 3   E

1. Stories in rhyme 2. Valentines -- Fiction

ISBN 0-525-46720-3; 0-14-240400-4 pa

LC 2001-42737

An ardent suitor tries various means of communication, from smoke signals to Morse code to skywriting, in order to get his message to his Valentine

"Tusa uses sketchy, wispy lines to create loads of droll details that are both funny and subtle. . . . Jackson and Tusa make perfect harmony here—the cadence and rhythm of text and the watercolor artwork are right on pitch." Booklist

Desert Rose and her highfalutin hog; illustrated by Keith Graves. Walker & Co. 2009 un il $16.99; lib bdg $17.89

Grades: K 1 2 3   E

1. Tall tales 2. Texas -- Fiction 3. Animals -- Fiction

ISBN 978-0-8027-9833-6; 0-8027-9833-0; 978-0-8027-9834-3 lib bdg; 0-8027-9834-9 lib bdg

LC 2009000206

Upon finding a large gold nugget on her pig farm, Desert Rose sets out to buy the biggest, fattest hog in Texas to enter in the state fair, but first she must get the hog to Laredo and every animal she asks for help is just as "ornery" as the hog

"The cartoon style of the acrylic illustrations accentuates the alliterative text. Youngsters will laugh out loud." SLJ

Thea's tree; [by] Alison Jackson; illustrated by Janet Pedersen. Dutton Children's Books 2008 un il $15.99

Grades: K 1 2 3   E

1. Plants -- Fiction 2. Science projects -- Fiction

ISBN 978-0-525-47443-2; 0-525-47443-9

LC 2007-5220

Thea Teawinkle plants an odd, purple, bean-shaped seed in her backyard for her class science project, with astonishing results that even the experts she writes to—including a botanist, an arborist, a museum curator, and a symphony director—cannot offer any explanations for.

"Pedersen's energetic, full-page watercolor illustrations capture the hilarious consequences of Thea's growing crisis." SLJ

Jackson, Ellen

Beastly babies; by Ellen Jackson; illustrated by Brendan Wenzel. Beach Lane Books 2015 32 p. color illustrations (hardcover) $17.99

Grades: PreK K 1   E

1. Stories in rhyme 2. Animal babies 3. Animals -- Infancy -- Fiction

ISBN 1442408340; 9781442408340

LC 2014009702

This rhyming children's story, by Ellen Jackson and illustrated by Brendan Wenzel, "introduce[s] readers to all sorts of mischievous baby animals--and the grown-ups who love them no matter what. Featuring puppies that slobber, kittens who spill, and young gorillas who won't sit still, this book is sure to resonate with beastly babies of all ages--and their exasperated moms and dads, too!" (Publisher's note)

"This anthropomorphic animal book introduces readers to a variety of patient moms and their "beastly," mischievous children. The babies' playfulness is reflected in both the rollicking rhyming text and mixed-media illustrations, both of which have plenty of funny details (e.g., as the little elephants butt into Mom's back: "there goes Mama's noontime nap!"). An ideal read-aloud for similarly active little ones." Horn Book

Jackson, Richard

All ears, all eyes; Richard Jackson; illustrated by Katherine Tillotson. Atheneum Books for Young Readers 2015 40 p. color illustrations (ebook) $15.99; (hardcover) $17.99

Grades: PreK K 1 2   E

1. Stories in rhyme 2. Bedtime -- Fiction 3. Animal sounds -- Fiction 4. Forest animals -- Fiction

ISBN 9781481415729; 9781481415712

LC 2014003384

This picture book for children, by Richard Jackson, illustrated by Katherine Tillotson, "takes us on a moonlit journey where the landscape shimmers with Fantasia--like beauty. Where if you look and listen, you might spy an owl, a deer, a chipmunk--or--what else!--before falling asleep." (Publisher's note)

"This lovely, evocative selection is a guessing game and a soothing bedtime offering that's perfect for reading aloud, especially to young animal and nature lovers." SLJ

★ **In** plain sight; Richard Jackson; illustrated by Jerry Pinkney. Roaring Brook Press 2016 40 p. color illustrations (hardback) $17.99

Grades: PreK K 1 2   E

1. Lost and found possessions -- Fiction 2. Grandparent-grandchild relationship -- Fiction 3. Games -- Fiction 4. Grandfathers -- Fiction 5. African Americans -- Fiction

ISBN 1481415905; 9781626722552

LC 2015034427

Coretta Scott King (Illustrator) Honor Book (2017)

"Sophie lives with Mama and Daddy and Grandpa, who spends his days by the window. Every day after school, it's Grandpa whom Sophie runs to. . . . As Sophie and her grandpa talk, he asks her to find items he's 'lost' throughout the day, guiding Sophie on a tour through his daily life and connecting their generations." (Publisher's note)

"There's one thing that's never missing from this gentle story about a special bond between the generations, and that's the love Grandpa and Sophie have for each other." Pub Wkly

Jackson, Shelley

★ **Mimi's** Dada Catifesto. Clarion Books 2009 41p il $17

Grades: 1 2 3 4   E

1. Cats -- Fiction 2. Dadaism -- Fiction

ISBN 978-0-547-12681-4; 0-547-12681-6

LC 2008-39486

In Zurich, Switzerland, an artistic cat finds the perfect owner in fellow Dadaist, Mr. Dada. Author's note provides background on the Dadaist art movement.

"Children . . . may not know much about the artistic movement Dada but . . . all (well perhaps not all) becomes clear through Jackson's zingy text and wildly inventive art. . . . With pictures inspired by many artists, including Marcel Duchamp, it's the art that will get kids to sit up and take notice. A mix of collage, fantastical and realistic drawings, and offbeat design work, the illustrations are played against a variety of fonts and typefaces, designed to keep the reader off balance." Booklist

Jacobs, Paul DuBois

Fire drill; [by] Paul DuBois Jacobs and Jennifer Swender; illustrated by Huy Voun Lee. Henry Holt and Company 2010 un il $15.99

Grades: PreK K 1   E

1. School stories 2. Stories in rhyme 3. Fire drills -- Fiction 4. Safety education -- Fiction

ISBN 978-0-8050-8953-0; 0-8050-8953-5

LC 2009005268

In this story told in brief rhyming text, students in a class follow the proper procedures during a fire drill.

"Simple rhyming text paired with colorful, upbeat art offer children an accessible overview of fire-drill rules. . . . Appealing, cheerful illustrations in elemental shapes and colors and vibrant patterns portray the multicultural group and familiar school settings." Booklist

Jadoul, Emile

Good night, Chickie. Eerdmans Books for Young Readers 2011 un il $13.99

Grades: PreK K   E

1. Bedtime -- Fiction 2. Chickens -- Fiction 3. Parent-child relationship -- Fiction

ISBN 978-0-8028-5378-3; 0-8028-5378-1

LC 2010024985

Mother Hen reassures Chickie, and Chickie's bunny, that she is near-by and keeping watch over them at bedtime.

"Jadoul is a minimalist, but his big, rounded shapes, thick ink out-lines, forceful brushstrokes, and expanses of bright colors do more visual and emotional work than a truckload of detail. . . . Jadoul strikes the right balance between flattering kids' independence and acknowledging their uncertainties." Publ Wkly

Jahn-Clough, Lisa

Felicity & Cordelia; a tale of two bunnies. Farrar Straus and Giroux 2010 un il $16.99

Grades: PreK K 1   E

1. Rabbits -- Fiction 2. Balloons -- Fiction 3. Friendship -- Fiction 4. Voyages and travels -- Fiction

ISBN 978-0-374-32300-4; 0-374-32300-3

LC 2009016143

Felicity Rose and Cordelia Bean are best friends, but they are separated when Felicity wants to go on a hot air balloon trip and Cordelia does not want to accompany her.

"Jahn-Clough's illustrations are, as ever, childlike, winsome, and boldly colored. Her story . . . reinforces the importance and interdependence of distinct personalities as well as the beauty of real friendship." SLJ

Little Dog; by Lisa Jahn-Clough. Houghton Mifflin 2006 un il $16

Grades: PreK K   E

1. Dogs -- Fiction 2. Artists -- Fiction

ISBN 978-0-618-57405-6; 0-618-57405-0

LC 2005020455

A lonely stray dog befriends a struggling artist, transforming her art and both their lives.

"The minimal text is accompanied by simple, childlike artwork, framed in and accented by heavy, black brush strokes." SLJ

Jain, Mahak

Maya; by Mahak Jain; illustrated by Elly MacKay. Owlkids Books 2016 32 p. color illustrations $16.95

Grades: PreK K 1 2 3 4   E

1. Fear of the dark -- Fiction 2. Mother-daughter relationship --

Fiction

ISBN 177147100X; 9781771471008

In this book, by Mahak Jain, illustrated by Elly MacKay, the "electricity in Maya's house has gone out again. Worse, she is afraid of the dark—and her fear has been even worse since her father died. . . . Maya's mother distracts her with a legend about the banyan tree, which saved the world from the first monsoon by drinking up the floodwaters, and growing tall and strong. Later that night, unsettled by the noises around her, Maya revisits the story in her imagination." (Publisher's note)

"Jain and MacKay's story and art work seamlessly to convey an important and subtle story of love, loss, beauty, and joy." Kirkus

Jalali, Reza

Moon watchers; Shirin's Ramadan miracle. illustrated by Anne Sibley O'Brien. Tilbury 2010 un il

Grades: 2 3 4   E

1. Maine -- Fiction 2. Muslims -- Fiction 3. Ramadan -- Fiction 4. Siblings -- Fiction 5. Family life -- Fiction

ISBN 0884483215; 9780884483212

Nine-year-old Shirin wants to join her family and other Muslims in fasting for Ramadan but is told she is too young, and so she seeks other ways to participate including, perhaps, getting along better with her older brother, Ali.

"O'Brien's watercolor illustrations evoke a culturally authentic Persian-American aesthetic, depicting warm characters in a family setting. An explanation of Ramadan and Eid is given in the back matter. This is another wonderful contribution to the slowly increasing collection of fictional books on the observance of Ramadan and a great resource for librarians and teachers." SLJ

James, Simon

★ **Baby** Brains. Candlewick Press 2004 un il $15.99; pa $6.99

Grades: PreK K 1 2   E

1. Infants -- Fiction

ISBN 0-7636-2507-8; 0-7636-3682-7 pa

LC 2003-65528

Even though the new baby of Mr. and Mrs. Brains is very intelligent, they realize that he is still just a baby

"This tongue-in-cheek tale will tickle the funny bones of young listeners. The loose and playful lines of the watercolor-and-ink illustrations are used judiciously and to great effect." SLJ

Other titles about Baby Brains are:

Baby Brains superstar (2005)

Baby Brains and RoboMom (2008)

George flies south. Candlewick Press 2011 un il $16.99

Grades: PreK K   E

1. Birds -- Fiction 2. Flight -- Fiction

ISBN 978-0-7636-5724-6; 0-7636-5724-7

LC 2010049468

George does not feel ready to learn to fly, leave his nest, and go south with the other birds, despite his mother's encouragement, but when a strong autumn wind gets hold of the nest, he may have no choice.

This is an "understated yet action-packed story. . . . Beige and pale blue dominate the subtle palette of James's . . . minimalist ink and watercolor pictures, arranged in square and rectangular panels, full-page scenarios, and—when George at last takes flight—a sprawling double-page vista." Publ Wkly

Little One Step. Candlewick Press 2003 un il $15.99; bd bk $6.99

Grades: PreK K 1   E

1. Ducks -- Fiction 2. Brothers -- Fiction

ISBN 0-7636-2070-X; 0-7636-3520-0 bd bk

LC 2002-71407

As three duckling brothers cross forest and field to return to their mother, the older ones encourage the youngest by teaching him a game that earns him the name of Little One Step

"Abundant white space surrounds the line drawings suffused with buttery yellow and peach watercolor tones. . . . This satisfying tale about perseverance will find an eager audience at storytimes, on a parent's lap, and with independent readers." SLJ

Nurse Clementine; Simon James. Candlewick Press 2013 40 p. (reinforced) $15.99

Grades: PreK K   E

ISBN 9780763663827

LC 2012942668

In this picture book, "young Clementine is thrilled with the nurse's kit she receives for her birthday, so pleased that she starts work immediately when her father bangs his toe on a door, bandaging his leg from toe to knee and admonishing him to keep the bandage on for a week. Her mom gets similar treatment for a headache, and Clementine eagerly waits for her risk-taking little brother, Tommy, to require her medical skills." (Bulletin of the Center for Children's Books)

Jane, Pamela

Little goblins ten; written by Pamela Jane; illustrated by Jane Manning. Harper 2011 un il $16.99; lib bdg $17.89

Grades: K 1 2   E

1. Counting 2. Stories in rhyme 3. Monsters -- Fiction 4. Halloween -- Fiction

ISBN 978-0-06-176798-2; 0-06-176798-0; 978-0-06-176800-2 lib bdg; 0-06-176800-6 lib bdg

LC 2010010169

Ghouls, goblins, ghosts, witches, and other scary creatures cavort in the forest on Halloween, introducing the numbers one through ten.

"Numerous titles interpreting 'Over in the Meadow' have been published, but trust the team of Jane and Manning to conjure up an impressive new vision in time for Halloween. Set in a fantastical land dominated by watery blues, greens and grays and punctuated by warm reds and yellows, Manning's tale presents ethereal ghosts, country-bumpkin werewolves, parading mummies, screeching witches, happy bats and boogieing skeletons that readers will instantly want to have as friends. . . . Truly satisfying." Kirkus

Janisch, Heinz

The **King** and the Sea. Lerner Pub Group 2015 48 p. color illustrations $16.99

Grades: 2 3 4 5   E

1. Authority 2. Kings and rulers -- Fiction

ISBN 1877579947; 9781877579943

Author Heinz Janisch and illustrator Wolf Erlbruch presents this short story collection. "In each story, the king has an encounter which he tries to rule over. But of course the rain doesn't stop just because a king orders it, and tired eyelids can be much stronger than a king's will. The king sees that his power has limits; the world is diverse and much of it operates under its own rules." (Publisher's note)

"The youngest readers will love the king's blissful, sleeping countenance after his losing battle against sleep. Occasionally the king finds his own capability, as when he lights a candle to solve an impasse with the night. This gem's childlike warmth, whimsy, and wisdom bring to mind The Little Prince." Kirkus

Janni, Rebecca

Every cowgirl needs a horse; illustrations by Lynne Avril. Dutton Children's Books 2010 un il $16.99

Grades: PreK K 1   E

1. Cycling -- Fiction 2. Cowhands -- Fiction 3. Birthdays -- Fiction 4. Imagination -- Fiction

ISBN 978-0-525-42164-1; 0-525-42164-5

                                         LC 2009-12278

Nellie Sue, who fancies herself a real cowgirl, wants a horse for her birthday, but she discovers that a brand new bicycle—her first—takes almost as much taming as a filly.

"The bright, sketchy, watercolor and ink illustrations are suffused with pinks and purples and capture a child who tries to live up to cowgirl ideals of helping others, looking on the bright side, and being strong. The lesson on dealing positively with disappointment is gently delivered." SLJ

Another title about Nellie Sue is:
Every cowgirl needs dancing boots (2011)

Every cowgirl needs dancing boots; illustrated by Lynne Avril. Dutton Children's Books 2011 un il $16.99

Grades: PreK K 1   E

1. Dance -- Fiction 2. Cowhands -- Fiction 3. Imagination -- Fiction

ISBN 978-0-525-42341-6; 0-525-42341-9

                                         LC 2010037712

Sequel to: Every cowgirl needs a horse (2010)

Nellie Sue hopes to make friends with her new neighbors by hosting a hoedown in her barn, but wonders if the 'glitter girls' will be able to dance in their ballet slippers, rather than in dancing boots like hers.

"Avril's line-and-watercolor cartoons keep the visual tone light. . . . A passel of fun activities—dancing, crafting, biking and dress up—are tucked into Janni's tonic tale of imagination and optimism." Kirkus

Janovitz, Marilyn

Baby baby baby! Sourcebooks 2010 un il bd bk $7.99

Grades: PreK   E

1. Stories in rhyme 2. Board books for children 3. Infants -- Fiction

ISBN 978-1-4022-4414-8 bd bk; 1-4022-4414-2 bd bk

"Nine stanzas of appealing verse show a baby playing with family members and pets, taking a bath, and going to bed. . . . [This board book's] bouncy verses will hold young children's attention with rhythm, rhyme, repeated phrases, and references to familiar things. . . . The digital artwork illustrates the cheerful characters in squiggly, black line drawings brightened with bold patterns and colors." Booklist

Jarka, Jeff

Love that kitty; the story of a boy who wanted to be a cat. Henry Holt 2010 un il $12.99

Grades: PreK K 1   E

1. Cats -- Fiction 2. Imagination -- Fiction

ISBN 978-0-8050-9053-6; 0-8050-9053-3

Tired of being an ordinary boy, Peter decides to become a cat.

"Jarka draws each character and setting with only a few well-placed lines filled in with bright solid colors. Peter's quirky confidence contrasts hilariously with his parents' bewilderment." SLJ

Love that puppy! the story of a boy who wanted to be a dog. Henry Holt 2009 un il $12.95

Grades: PreK K 1   E

1. Dogs -- Fiction 2. Imagination -- Fiction

ISBN 978-0-8050-8741-3; 0-8050-8741-9

                                         LC 2008018333

When his parents want him to change back into a human boy, Peter the dog comes up with a novel solution.

"Jarka's colorful comic-strip-style illustrations drive the humor with one visual joke after another. . . . Children will appreciate both the absurdity of Peter's behavior and Jarka's delivery." SLJ

Another title about Peter is:
Love that kitty (2010)

Jarrett, Clare

★ **Arabella** Miller's tiny caterpillar; [by] Clare Jarrett. Candlewick Press 2008 un il $16.99

Grades: PreK K 1 2   E

1. Butterflies -- Fiction 2. Caterpillars -- Fiction

ISBN 978-0-7636-3660-9; 0-7636-3660-6

Arabella Miller finds a tiny caterpillar and watches and cares for it until it becomes a butterfly

This is "an engaging, exceptional picture book. . . . Based on the verse about Little Arabella Miller, the story arc is simple but the charm lies in the sketchy, pencil-and-paper collage illustrations." Booklist

Javaherbin, Mina

★ **Goal!** illustrated by A.G. Ford. Candlewick Press 2010 un il $16.99; pa $6.99

Grades: 2 3 4   E

1. Soccer -- Fiction 2. Bullies -- Fiction 3. Friendship -- Fiction 4. South Africa -- Fiction

ISBN 0763645710; 9780763645717; 9780763658229

                                         LC 2008047266

In a dangerous alley in a township in South Africa, the strength and unity which a group of young friends feel while playing soccer keep them safe when a gang of bullies arrives to cause trouble.

"Illustrations rendered in oil are impressive. Large and colorful action shots, many full spread, keep the story moving at a quick pace." SLJ

Soccer star; Mina Javaherbin, illustrated by Renato Alarcao. Candlewick Press 2014 40 p. color illustrations (reinforced) $16.99

Grades: K 1 2 3   E

1. Brazil -- Fiction 2. Soccer -- Fiction 3. Brothers and sisters -- Fiction 4. Picture books for children

ISBN 9780763660567; 0763660566

                                         LC 2013944008

This children's book, by Mina Javaherbin, tells the "story of a Brazilian boy who dreams of being a soccer star--and the sister who steps in to help his team win a game. When Paulo Marcelo Feliciano becomes a soccer star, crowds will cheer his famous name! Then his mother won't have to work long hours, and he won't have to work all day on a fishing boat. . . . But when Jose falls on his wrist, will the team finally break the rules and let a girl show her stuff?" (Publisher's note)

"[I]t's downright refreshing to see illustrations that realistically relay the diversity of shades found among Brazilians. Javaherbin deftly handles Paulo and Maria's poverty with honesty while simultaneously refraining from sugarcoating, overemphasizing or romanticizing it." Kirkus

Javernick, Ellen

The **birthday** pet; illustrated by Kevin O'Malley. Marshall Cavendish 2009 un il $16.99

Grades: PreK K 1 2   E

1. Stories in rhyme 2. Pets -- Fiction 3. Turtles -- Fiction 4. Birthdays -- Fiction

ISBN 978-0-7614-5522-6; 0-7614-5522-1

                                         LC 2008010740

Danny can have a pet for his birthday and he knows exactly what he wants, but the other members of his family think differently.

"The colorful, animated illustrations incorporate exaggerated close-ups, unusual perspectives, and witty details that extend the humor in the words. Young readers and listeners will enjoy the simple, well-paced, rhyming text." Booklist

Jay, Alison

★ 1 2 3; a child's first counting book. Dutton Children's Books 2007 un il $15.99; bd bk $9.99
Grades: PreK K 1 2   E
   1. Counting
   ISBN 978-0-525-47836-2; 978-0-525-42165-8 bd bk
                                           LC 2006035905
"Jay takes readers on an enchanted journey from 1 to 10 and back again, with help from fairy tale figures. A quartet of self-satisfied frog princes impressively embody the number 4, while a plate of gingerbread men . . . represent the number 6. . . . The pictures are a wonder to behold: Jay's flattened perspectives, gently faded colors, crackle-glaze finishes and lean, angular characterizations vaguely evoke the dreamy, ambiguous narrative qualities of medieval art." Publ Wkly

★ ABC: a child's first alphabet book. Dutton Children's Bks. 2003 un il hardcover o.p. bd bk $9.99
Grades: PreK K 1 2   E
   1. Alphabet
   ISBN 0-525-46951-6; 0-525-47524-9 bd bk
                                           LC 2003-45218
In this alphabet book, a is for apple and z is for zoo
"This imaginative alphabet book offers visual clues to track and a story to tease out in its beautiful paintings. . . . Older children will flip from page to page, finding the simple story, drawing connections, and naming the letter-related objects. Younger ones can simply enjoy the delightful paintings with their crackle-glazed folk art look and touches of humor." Booklist

Red green blue; a first book of colors. Dutton Children's Books 2010 un il $16.99
Grades: PreK K 1   E
   1. Stories in rhyme 2. Color -- Fiction 3. Nursery rhymes -- Fiction
   ISBN 978-0-525-42303-4; 0-525-42303-6
                                           LC 2009-25098
Characters from nursery rhymes populate this tale, which highlights the colorful aspects of the familiar poems. Includes a key to the nursery rhymes referenced in the story.
"There are numerous opportunities for discussing colors, but as ever, it's Jay's luminous images that steal the show." Publ Wkly

Welcome to the zoo. Dial 2008 un il $16.99
Grades: PreK K 1 2   E
   1. Stories without words 2. Zoos -- Fiction 3. Animals -- Fiction
   ISBN 978-0-8037-3177-6; 0-8037-3177-9
"Jay creates a zoo without the usual barriers between the animals and their visitors. . . . The oil paintings reward close attention with amusing visual details and small wordless dramas that carry through from page to page. . . . Polished yet playful, this nearly wordless picture book is a engaging choice." Booklist

Jeffers, Oliver

The **great** paper caper; [by] Oliver Jeffers. Philomel Books 2009 un il $17.99
Grades: PreK K   E
   1. Trees -- Fiction 2. Animals -- Fiction
   ISBN 978-0-399-25097-2; 0-399-25097-2
                                           LC 2008026192

When tree branches begin disappearing and paper airplanes are left in their place, the forest creatures carry out an investigation to find the culprit who has been stealing their homes.
"Managed forestry is the theme of this book that features folk-art-style animals with funny little stick legs. The mixed-media illustrations nicely complement the spare yet eloquent text." SLJ

The **heart** and the bottle. Philomel Books 2010 un il $17.99
Grades: PreK K 1   E
   1. Death -- Fiction 2. Emotions -- Fiction 3. Bereavement -- Fiction
   ISBN 978-0-399-25452-9; 0-399-25452-8
After safeguarding her heart in a bottle hung around her neck, a girl finds the bottle growing heavier and her interest in things around her becoming smaller.
The "artwork is the sweetness in this bittersweet story. . . . While the subject of loss always has the potential to unsettle young readers, most should find this quietly powerful treatment of grief moving." Publ Wkly

The **Hueys** in The new sweater; Oliver Jeffers. Philomel Books 2012 32 p.
Grades: PreK K 1 2   E
   1. Children's stories 2. Sweaters -- Fiction 3. Individuality -- Fiction
   ISBN 0399257675; 9780399257674
                                           LC 2011048399
In this children's story by Oliver Jeffers ,"each Huey looks the same, thinks the same, and does the same exact things. So you can imagine the chaos when one of them has the idea of knitting a sweater! It seems like a good idea at the time--he is quite proud of it, in fact--but it does make him different from the others. So the rest of the Hueys, in turn, decide that they want to be different too! How? By knitting the exact same sweater, of course!" (Publisher's note)
Other titles about the Hueys are:
It wasn't me (2014)
None the number (2014)
What's the opposite (2016)

The **Hueys** in What's the opposite? Oliver Jeffers. Philomel Books, an imprint of Penguin Group (USA) 2016 32 p. color illustrations (hardback) $17.99
Grades: K 1 2   E
   1. Opposites -- Fiction 2. English language -- Synonyms and antonyms -- Fiction
   ISBN 9780399257704
                                           LC 2015011693
This children's counting book, by Oliver Jeffers, part of "The Hueys" series, asks "'What's the opposite of the beginning?' A sensible question to ask when opening a book that teaches the reader about opposites. But maybe we should start with something a little easier? For example, it's quite unlucky when a Huey finds himself stranded on a hot, deserted island—but how lucky it is when a fan arrives to provide some cool air!" (Publisher's note)
"It's not easy to be so very simple and so very clever, but Jeffers manages in this laugh-aloud offering that will get groups giggling." Booklist

The **incredible** book eating boy; by Oliver Jeffers. Philomel Books 2007 un il $16.99
Grades: PreK K 1 2 3   E
   1. Food -- Fiction 2. Books and reading -- Fiction
   ISBN 978-0-399-24749-1
                                           LC 2006026279

Henry loves to eat books, until he begins to feel quite ill and decides that maybe he could do something else with the books he has been devouring

"The simple cartoon illustrations twinkle with humor and feeling. Done in paint and pencil on smart backdrops—pages from old books—the pictures set the stage for the quirky story." SLJ

It wasn't me; written and illustrated by Oliver Jeffers. Philomel Books 2014 32 p. (The Hueys) (hardback) $17.99

Grades: PreK K 1 2   E

1. Debates and debating   2. Brothers and sisters -- Fiction   3. Individuality -- Fiction   4. Interpersonal relations -- Fiction

ISBN 0399257683; 9780399257681

LC 2013019164

Author Oliver Jeffers presents another book in his Hueys series. The "egg-shaped creatures may look the same, think the same, and even do the same things, but that doesn't mean they always agree. The only problem is, they can't seem to agree on what they disagreed on in the first place! Which ultimately leads to an even bigger disagreement!" (Publisher's note)

★ **Once** upon an alphabet; Short Stories for All the Letters. Oliver Jeffers. First American edition Philomel Books, an imprint of Penguin Group (USA) 2014 112 p. color illustrations (reinforced) $26.99

Grades: PreK K 1 2 3 4   E

1. Short stories -- Collections 2. Alphabet

ISBN 0399167919; 9780399167911

LC 2014021089

Boston Globe-Horn Book Honor: Picture Book (2015)

This children's book, written and illustrated by Oliver Jeffers, presents a collection of short stories from A to Z. "From an Astronaut who's afraid of heights, to a Bridge that ends up burned between friends, to a Cup stuck in a cupboard and longing for freedom, . . . this series of interconnected stories and characters explores the alphabet." (Publisher's note)

"With wry humor, equally droll ink illustrations, and a solid dose of alliteration, Jeffers (the Hueys series) creates delightful mini-narratives for each letter of the alphabet." Pub Wkly

★ **Stuck**. Philomel Books 2011 un il $16.99

Grades: PreK K   E

1. Kites -- Fiction

ISBN 978-0-399-25737-7; 0-399-25737-3

LC 2011016349

When Floyd's kite gets stuck in a tree, he tries to knock it down with increasingly larger and more outrageous things.

This is "an exuberantly absurd tale. . . . Jeffers . . . pictures the extravagant accumulation in abstract pencil-and-gouache doodles, with hand-lettered text to set a conversational tone." Publ Wkly

This moose belongs to me; Oliver Jeffers. Philomel Books 2012 32 p.

Grades: PreK K 1 2   E

1. Pets -- Fiction 2. Moose -- Fiction 3. Human-animal relationships -- Fiction 4. Pets -- Fiction 5. Moose as pets -- Fiction

ISBN 9780399161032

LC 2012020373

This children's picture book by Oliver Jeffers tells the "tale of a boy and his moose. Wilfred is a boy with rules. He lives a very orderly life. . . . There is, however, one rule that Wilfred's pet has difficulty following: Going whichever way Wilfred wants to go. Perhaps this is because Wilfred's pet doesn't quite realize that he belongs to anyone. . . . Fortunately, the two manage to work out a compromise." (Publisher's note)

★ **Up** and down. Philomel Books 2010 un il $16.99

Grades: PreK K 1   E

1. Flight -- Fiction 2. Penguins -- Fiction 3. Friendship -- Fiction

ISBN 978-0-399-25545-8; 0-399-25545-1

LC 2010011358

Even though the penguin and the boy are close friends and do many things together, the penguin decides that he wants to fly and he wants to do it on his own.

"Serene white backdrops highlight brilliant compositional choices, while full-page spreads of unconfined color depict dramatic moments with subtle force. Children will intuit, absorb and appreciate this soothing book's heart—the fast, offbeat friendship that makes it so singular and appealing." Kirkus

Another title about Penguin and the boy is:

Lost and found (2006)

The **way** back home; [by] Oliver Jeffers. Philomel Books 2008 un il $16.99

Grades: PreK K 1 2   E

1. Moon -- Fiction 2. Space flight -- Fiction 3. Extraterrestrial beings -- Fiction

ISBN 978-0-399-25074-3; 0-399-25074-3

LC 2007029570

Stranded on the moon after his extraordinary airplane takes him into outer space, a boy meets a marooned young Martian with a broken spacecraft, and the two new friends work together to return to their respective homes

"The charm of this story is how completely it maintains a childlike perspective. . . . This approach continues in the watercolor, graphite, and collage artwork. Figures consist of circle heads, box bodies, and stick legs; the backgrounds are flat colors with a few scribbled-in clouds or puffs of exhaust. Humorous details abound." SLJ

Jeffers, Susan

My Chincoteague pony. Hyperion Books for Children 2008 un il $16.99

Grades: PreK K 1 2 3   E

1. Horses -- Fiction 2. Chincoteague Island (Va.) -- Fiction

ISBN 1-4231-0023-9; 978-1-4231-0023-2

Julie's "fondest wish is to have a pony of her own. The child convinces her farm-dwelling parents to take her to Chincoteague Island for Pony Penning Day so that she can bid in the auction. Unfortunately, she is continually outbid and realizes that the money she's earned won't be enough. Then one pony is returned and several people in the crowd pitch in to make her dream come true. . . . The lovely illustrations capture Julie's love of horses, the beauty of the ponies, and the excitement of the roundup." SLJ

The **Nutcracker**; [retold and illustrated by] Susan Jeffers. HarperCollinsPublishers 2007 un il $16.99; lib bdg $17.89

Grades: K 1 2   E

1. Fairy tales 2. Toys -- Fiction 3. Magic -- Fiction 4. Christmas -- Fiction

ISBN 978-0-06-074386-4; 0-06-074386-7; 978-0-06-074387-1 lib bdg; 0-06-074387-5 lib bdg

LC 2007012489

An abridged version of the story of Marie Stahlbaum, who helps break the spell on her toy nutcracker and watches him change into a handsome prince

"Children who love the traditional Christmas ballet will enjoy this romantic illustrated edition. . . . The illustrations communicate the beauty and the emotional quality of the ballet." SLJ

The **twelve** days of Christmas; written and illustrated by Susan Jeffers. HarperCollins 2013 40 p. (hardcover bdgs) $17.99
Grades: PreK K 1 2   **E**
1. Christmas -- Fiction 2. Santa Claus -- Fiction 3. Gifts -- Fiction
4. Magic -- Fiction
ISBN 0062066153; 9780062066152; 9780062066169
LC 2012050675
In this book, by Susan Jeffers, "a little girl sneaks a look at a wrapped present on the night before Christmas-a snow globe of a partridge in a pear tree-and accidentally breaks it. Falling asleep, she dreams of Santa giving her a ride on his sled, during which he gives her two turtledoves and all the rest of the traditional gifts in the song. Arriving back at his workshop, he repairs the broken gift, and the girl wakes up to Christmas morning to a wrapped-up, unbroken snow globe." (School Library Journal)

Jenkins, Emily
  Daffodil, crocodile; pictures by Tomek Bogacki. Farrar, Straus & Giroux 2007 un il $16
Grades: PreK K 1 2   **E**
1. Sisters -- Fiction 2. Triplets -- Fiction 3. Imagination -- Fiction
ISBN 978-0-374-39944-3; 0-374-39944-1
LC 2005-40163
Tired of being one of three look-alike sisters that no one can tell apart, Daffodil puts on a papier mâché crocodile head and has her own individual adventures
"Daffodil's words and actions ring kidlike and true.... Colorful art, whimsical and expressive, fills the pages with fanciful patterns, perspectives, and details." Booklist

  Five creatures; pictures by Tomek Bogacki. Foster Bks. 2001 un il $16; pa $5.95
Grades: K 1 2 3   **E**
1. Cats -- Fiction 2. Family life -- Fiction
ISBN 0-374-32341-0; 0-374-42328-8 pa
LC 00-28771
Boston Globe-Horn Book Award Honor: Picture Book (2001)
In words and pictures, a girl describes the three humans and two cats that live in her house, and details some of the traits that they share
"This clever, multilayered book is as much for sharing and getting little ones on the path to deductive reasoning as it is for reading.... The text encourages readers to be observant.... Bogacki's colored chalk art ... is childlike in the best possible way—immediate, identifiable, and executed with soft colors and simple shapes." Booklist

  The **fun** book of scary stuff; Emily Jenkins; pictures by Hyewon Yum. Frances Foster Books, Farrar, Straus & Giroux 2015 32 p. color illustrations (hardback) $16.99
Grades: PreK K 1 2   **E**
1. Dogs -- Fiction 2. Fear -- Fiction
ISBN 0374300003; 9780374300005
LC 2014040679
In this picture book, by Emily Jenkins, illustrated by Hyewon Yum, "a boy and his two dogs go through a list of all the things, both real and imagined, that make the hair on the backs of their necks stand on end—and come up with a clever way to face their fears." (Publisher's note)
"A not-so-scary look at talking about and tackling fears together." SLJ

  ★ A **greyhound**, a groundhog; Emily Jenkins; illustrated by Chris Appelhans. Schwartz & Wade 2017 32 p. (glb) $20.99
Grades: PreK K 1   **E**
1. Tongue twisters 2. Stories in rhyme 3. Dogs -- Fiction 4.

Greyhounds -- Fiction 5. Woodchuck -- Fiction
ISBN 9780553498059; 9780553498066; 9780553498073
LC 2016000753
In this children's book, by Emily Jenkins, illustrated by Chris Appelhans, "when a greyhound meets a groundhog, wordplay and crazy antics ensue. The two animals, much like kids, work themselves into a frenzy as they whirl around and around one another. (Around, round hound. Around, groundhog!) The pace picks up (Around and around and astound and astound!), until they ultimately wear themselves out." (Publisher's note)
"This delightful story is a feast for the eyes and ears, and it will hold up well to repeated demands from eager young listeners." Kirkus

  Lemonade in winter; a book about two kids counting money. Emily Jenkins; illustrated by G. Brian Karas. Schwartz & Wade Books 2012 40 p. $16.99
Grades: PreK K 1 2   **E**
1. Siblings -- Fiction 2. Picture books for children 3. Entrepreneurship 4. Winter -- Fiction 5. Addition -- Fiction 6. Lemonade -- Fiction 7. Brothers and sisters -- Fiction 8. Moneymaking projects -- Fiction
ISBN 0375858830; 9780375858833; 9780375958830
LC 2010024135
In this children's picture book, "two young entrepreneurs, Pauline and John-John, ignore the naysayers (their parents) and set up a lemonade stand smack dab on the snowy sidewalk. The lemonade, limeade--and lemon-limeade--are ready. But there are no customers to be seen. Pauline and John-John aren't discouraged. Instead, they improvise by singing a catchy jingle, turning cartwheels to attract attention, decorating their stand and, finally, having a half-price sale." (Kirkus Reviews)
"This quirky tale is a boon for young entrepreneurs, who will enjoy looking at the humorous details in the pictures as much as working out the math after each sale. Abounding with teaching possibilities

  Skunkdog; pictures by Pierre Pratt. Farrar, Straus and Giroux 2008 un il $16.95
Grades: K 1 2 3   **E**
1. Dogs -- Fiction 2. Skunks -- Fiction
ISBN 0-374-37009-5; 978-0-374-37009-1
LC 2005-54701
Dumpling, a lonely dog with no sense of smell, moves with his family to the country and makes a new friend who takes some getting used to.
"Jenkins uses a lot of detail and repetition. Pratt's sunlit illustrations are done in oils and portray a white dog with an elongated nose and a furiously wagging black tail who complements the black-and-white skunk. Children will instantly relate to the pup's skunk encounters.... Important themes of loneliness, tolerance, friendship, and family emerge from this funny story." SLJ

  ★ **That** new animal; pictures by Pierre Pratt. Farrar, Straus and Giroux 2005 un il $16
Grades: PreK K 1 2   **E**
1. Dogs -- Fiction 2. Infants -- Fiction
ISBN 0-374-37443-0
LC 2003-44058
Boston Globe-Horn Book Honor: Picture Book (2005)
The lives of two dogs change after a new animal, a baby, comes to their house.
"Both the author and illustrator demonstrate wonderful insight into pet psychology and family dynamics, and the elongated style of the vibrantly colored artwork strikes just the right note of humor and whimsy." SLJ

Tiger and Badger; Emily Jenkins; illustrated by Marie-Louise Gay. Candlewick Press 2016 32 p. color illustrations $15.99
Grades: PreK K 1   E
  1. Animals -- Fiction 2. Friendship -- Fiction
  ISBN 0763666041; 9780763666040
                           LC 2015933236

In this children's story, by Emily Jenkins, illustrated by Marie-Louise Gay, "Tiger and Badger are best friends. Of course, sometimes even very best friends can get into disagreements—over a toy, or a chair, or even sharing some orange slices. But no matter what, after a bit of pouting and with the help of some very silly faces, they always make up." (Publisher's note)

"While picture books centering on pals coping with disagreements are common, this gentle and quirky addition is sure to please. A light-hearted yet spot-on look at friendship from a child's point of view." SLJ

Toys meet snow; being the wintertime adventures of a curious stuffed buffalo, a sensitive plush stingray, and a book-loving rubber ball. Emily Jenkins; Paul O. Zelinsky. Schwartz & Wade Books 2015 40 p. color illustrations (alk. paper) $17.99
Grades: PreK K 1 2   E
  1. Snow -- Fiction 2. Toys -- Fiction 3. Snow -- Fiction 4. Toys -- Fiction
  ISBN 0385373309; 9780385373302; 9780385373319
                           LC 2014010935

This children's story, by Emily Jenkins and illustrated by Paul O. Zelinsky, continues the authors' trilogy following a set of toys. "With their owner, the Little Girl, away for winter vacation, plush animals StingRay and Lumphy the buffalo, along with their pal Plastic the bouncy red ball, suit up . . . and head outside for their very first snow day." (Publisher's note)

"Simple and cozy with just the right amount of wonder, this story offers a look at the pleasures snow brings and its transformative effect on the world." Booklist

Water in the park; a book about water and the times of the day. Emily Jenkins. 1st ed. Schwartz & Wade Books 2013 40 p. ill. (hardcover) $16.99; (library) $19.99
Grades: PreK K 1   E
  1. Parks 2. Water -- Fiction
  ISBN 0375870024; 9780375870026 trade; 9780375970023
                           LC 2011050243

This children's picture book, by Emily Jenkins, illustrated by Stephanie Graegin, shows the readers "from the first orange glow on the water in the pond, to the last humans and animals running home from an evening rain shower, . . . a day-in-the-life of a city park, and the playground within it." (Publisher's note)

Jenkins, Steve

  ★ **Move!** [written by Steve Jenkins and Robin Page; illustrated by Steve Jenkins] Houghton Mifflin 2006 un il $16; bd bk $7.99
Grades: PreK K   E
  1. Animal locomotion
  ISBN 0-618-64637-X; 0-547-24000-7 bd bk
                           LC 2005-19082

In this "book illustrated with cut and torn-paper collages, animals leap, swim, slide, swing, and waddle. Each spread contains one action word and two animals for whom that behavior is typical. . . . Jenkins uses brief phrases as captions and provides a well-written, concise appendix. . . . This book is gorgeous and educational." SLJ

Jennings, Sharon

  A **Chanukah** Noel; a true story. written by Sharon Jennings; illustrated by Gillian Newland. Second Story Press 2010 un il $15.95

Grades: K 1 2   E
  1. Jews -- Fiction 2. Hanukkah stories 3. Christmas stories 4. France -- Fiction 5. Christmas -- Fiction 6
  ISBN 1897187742; 9781897187746

A young Jewish girl is fascinated by the traditions of Christmas when her family moves to a small town in France.

Jenson-Elliott, Cindy

  Weeds find a way; Cynthia Jenson-Elliott; illustrated by Carolyn Fisher. 1st ed. Beach Lane Books 2013 40 p. (hardcover) $16.99
Grades: PreK K 1 2   E
  1. Weeds 2. Plants
  ISBN 1442412607; 9781442412606
                           LC 2011018524

In this book, author Cindy Jenson-Elliott "celebrates weeds for their heartiness and ability to disseminate and adapt. More detailed information about how weeds can actually be useful despite their reputation can be found in the back matter, along with a list both identifying and offering further facts about the plants pictured in the book." (School Library Journal)

Jessell, Tim

  Falcon; by Tim Jessell. Random House Inc 2012 40 p. (trade : alk. paper) $17.99; (library) $20.99
Grades: 1 2 3   E
  1. Falcons 2. Flight -- Fiction 3. Imagination -- Fiction
  ISBN 0375868666; 9780375868665; 9780375968662
                           LC 2011012758

This book looks at falcons, inviting "readers to imagine taking wing. In a series of . . . paintings, [Tim] Jessell provides a bird's-eye view of the raptor in flight, as well as sweeping panoramas that show how it interacts with landscapes as diverse as mountains, sea cliffs, and skyscrapers." (School Library Journal)

Jesset, Aurore

  Loopy; by Aurore Jesset; illustrated by Barbara Korthues. NorthSouth 2008 un il $16.95; pa $7.95
Grades: PreK K 1   E
  1. Toys -- Fiction 2. Lost and found possessions -- Fiction
  ISBN 978-0-7358-2175-0; 0-7358-2175-5; 978-0-7358-2261-0 pa; 0-7358-2261-1 pa

"A child leaves her favorite toy at the doctor's office and ponders its fate should they fail to be reunited 'RIGHT NOW!' On each spread, Jesset's speculation about the beloved stuffed animal's current state is matched with Korthues's Tim Burton-esque illustrations rendered in vibrant colors, often muted to depict the nighttime setting. The simple, rhythmic prose recalls a small child's inner dialogue or storytelling voice." SLJ

Ji Zhaohua

  No! that's wrong! [by] Zhaohua Ji and Cui Xu. Kane Miller Book Pub. 2008 un il $15.95
Grades: PreK K 1 2   E
  1. Animals -- Fiction 2. Rabbits -- Fiction 3. Clothing and dress -- Fiction
  ISBN 978-1-933605-66-1; 1-933605-66-9

"A rabbit has a humorous encounter with a pair of red underpants. Rabbit's not sure how to wear the mysterious garment and tries it on as a hat. He offers the hat in turn to eight different animals until a donkey straightforwardly inquires why the rabbit is wearing underpants on his head. . . . The cartoon-style artwork and the text, consisting primarily of dialogue, work well together. . . . This entertaining picture book stimulates a bit of creative thinking and problem solving." SLJ

JiHyeon Lee

Pool; by JiHyeon Lee. Chronicle Books LLC 2015 56 p. color illustrations (alk. paper) $16.99

Grades: PreK K 1 2   E

1. Stories without words 2. Swimming pools -- Fiction 3. Magic -- Fiction 4. Friendship -- Fiction 5. Underwater exploration -- Fiction

ISBN 1452142947; 9781452142944

LC 2014045689

This picture book, by JiHyeon Lee, is a "wordless adventure [that] follows a timid boy's foray into a crowded public pool. Due to the crash of humanity cramming the water with their comical bulk and myriad of blow-up gear, the goggled hero dives deep and discovers a female counterpart, who leads him to a forest of fantastic aquatic creatures and plants." (Publisher's note)

"This unique and elegant wordless adventure follows a timid boy's foray into a crowded public pool. Due to the crash of humanity cramming the water with their comical bulk and myriad of blow-up gear, the goggled hero dives deep and discovers a female counterpart, who leads him to a forest of fantastic aquatic creatures and plants.... Lee's debut picture book is a swan dive." SLJ

Jimenez, Francisco

The **Christmas** gift: El regalo de Navidad; illustrated by Claire B. Cotts. Houghton Mifflin 2000 un il $15; pa $6.99

Grades: K 1 2 3   E

1. Christmas -- Fiction 2. Migrant labor -- Fiction 3. Mexican Americans -- Fiction 4. Bilingual books -- English-Spanish

ISBN 0-395-92869-9; 0-547-13364-2 pa

LC 99-26224

When his family has to move again a few days before Christmas in order to find work, Panchito worries that he will not get the ball he has been wanting

"This story, a version of which appeared in Jiménez's ... TheCircuit, is presented here in a bilingual picture book format with an excellent Spanish text.... Mural-like illustrations soulfully depict the hard life and strong people of the migrant labor camps." Horn Book Guide

Jocelyn, Marthe

Eats; [by] Marthe Jocelyn; [illustrations by] Tom Slaughter. Tundra Books 2007 un il $15.95; bd bk $7.95

Grades: PreK K 1 2   E

1. Animals -- Food

ISBN 978-0-88776-820-0; 978-0-88776-988-7 bd bk

"Painted paper cuts in jewel colors graphically portray the principal foods eaten by 14 different animals.... Using bold, simple, brightly colored shapes ... [and] placing them on backgrounds of equally bold contrasting colors, the animals and their dinners are easily identified and, thus, will have instant kid appeal." SLJ

★ **Ones** and twos; by Marthe Jocelyn and Nell Jocelyn. Tundra Books 2011 un il $15.95

Grades: PreK K 1   E

1. Numbers 2. Stories in rhyme 3. Birds -- Fiction 4. Friendship -- Fiction

ISBN 978-1-77049-220-2; 1-77049-220-8

"Deceptively simple text accompanied by highly textured, patterned, and colorful collages invite children to consider number relationships, opening with the spread 'One birds, two eggs. One girl, two legs.' The rhyming couplets, akin to terse verse, trace both bird and girl throughout the day.... Operating on two levels as a concept book that also tells a story, this delightful picture book will draw readers for many repeat visits." Booklists

Over under; [illustrated by] Tom Slaughter. Tundra Books 2005 un il $15.95; bd bk $7.95

Grades: PreK   E

1. Opposites

ISBN 0-88776-708-7; 0-88776-790-7 bd bk

"Minimal rhyming text and cut-paper illustrations of animals in six basic colors introduce opposites: e.g. 'big' and 'small' are represented by a black elephant and mouse on a vibrant red background." Horn Book Guide

Sam sorts; one hundred favorite things. Marthe Jocelyn. Tundra Books 2017 32 p. color illustrations (hardcover) $16.99

Grades: PreK K   E

1. Counting -- Fiction 2. Orderliness -- Fiction

ISBN 9781101918050; 9781101918067; 9781101918074

LC 2016933020

In this children's book, by Marthe Jocelyn, "Sam's things are in a heap. Time to tidy up! He starts to organize his things, but quickly runs into trouble. He can make a pile of black and white things. But the penguin also belongs in the things with wings pile. He can make a pile of rocks. But the round rock also belongs in the round things pile. How will he ever sort his 100 things?" (Publisher's note)

★ **Same** same; Tom Slaughter, illustrator. Tundra Books 2009 un il $15.95; bd bk $7.95

Grades: PreK K 1   E

1. Concepts 2. Classification

ISBN 978-0-88776-885-9; 0-88776-885-7; 978-0-88776-987-0 bd bk; 0-88776-987-X bd bk

"Jocelyn and Slaughter ... strikingly introduce the concept of classification. Slaughter's graphic cut-paper compositions command attention with their paintbox-bright colors. The first spread, for example, shows an apple, a blue-and-green planet Earth and a tambourine.... 'Round things,' reads the caption. The next pages show the tambourine again, now with a guitar and a bird. This spread is captioned 'things that make music.' Always carrying forward one of the three objects from the previous spread, Jocelyn delivers the vital lesson that everyday objects fall into many categories. The concept is clear and the delivery attractive." Publ Wkly

John, Jory

Penguin problems; by Jory John; illustrated by Lane Smith. Random House 2016 32 p. color illustrations (hardback) $17.99

Grades: PreK K 1 2   E

1. Humorous stories 2. Penguins -- Fiction

ISBN 0553513370; 9780375974656; 9780553513370

LC 2015036697

In this book, by Jory John, illustrated by Lane Smith, "a penguin levels with human readers about what penguin life is really like.... Have you ever considered running away to Antarctica? ... This penguin has come to tell you that his life down there is no more a picnic than yours is here. For starters, it is FREEZING. Also, penguins have a ton of natural predators. Plus, can you imagine trying to find your mom in a big ol' crowd of identical penguins? No, thank you." (Publisher's note)

"Well-paced, bursting with humor, and charmingly misanthropic." Kirkus

Johnson, Angela

★ **All** different now; Juneteenth, the first day of freedom. Angela Johnson; illustrated by E.B. Lewis. Simon & Schuster Books for Young Readers 2014 40 p. (hardcover) $17.99

Grades: K 1 2 3 4   E

1. Juneteenth 2. Slaves -- Emancipation 3. African Americans -- History -- Fiction 4. Slavery -- Fiction 5. Juneteenth -- Fiction

6. African Americans -- Fiction 7. Family life -- Texas -- Fiction 8. Texas -- History -- 1865-1950 -- Fiction

ISBN 068987376X; 9780689873768

LC 2011038273

Written by Angela Johnson and illustrated by E. B. Lewis, "'All Different Now' tells the story of the first Juneteenth, the day freedom finally came to the last of the slaves in the South. Since then, the observance of June 19 as African American Emancipation Day has spread across the United States and beyond." (Publisher's note)

"In exquisite, lyrical text, Johnson reimagines Juneteenth--the date slaves in Texas finally learned of their emancipation--from the perspective of one fictional family. The words build to a crescendo of emotions as these now-free people prepare for a new life. Lewis's soft watercolors mirror the emotion of the text--the sun reflects off the grateful faces, eyes face the future with clarity." Horn Book

The **day** Ray got away; illustrated by Luke LaMarca. Simon & Schuster 2010 un il $16.99

Grades: PreK K 1 2   E

1. Parades -- Fiction 2. Balloons -- Fiction

ISBN 978-0-689-87375-1; 0-689-87375-1

"In this lighthearted story, the fateful morning begins when Ray wakes up with a smile (he always does) and announces to his fellow balloons, 'Today is the day.' The parade begins the same as usual, until Ray makes his break and havoc ensues. Cheerful acrylic cartoon illustrations elevate the understated story, adding foreshadowing, drama, and much humor." SLJ

★ **I** dream of trains; illustrated by Loren Long. Simon & Schuster Bks. for Young Readers 2003 un il $16.95

Grades: K 1 2 3   E

1. Locomotive engineers 2. Railroads -- Fiction 3. African Americans -- Fiction

ISBN 0-689-82609-5

LC 98-52886

The son of a sharecropper dreams of leaving Mississippi on a train with the legendary engineer Casey Jones

"Long's moody acrylic paintings, mainly in subdued tones, are a sterling accompaniment to the book's provocative prose." SLJ

Just like Josh Gibson; written by Angela Johnson; illustrated by Beth Peck. Simon & Schuster Books for Young Readers 2004 un il $15.95; pa $6.99

Grades: K 1 2 3   E

1. Baseball -- Fiction 2. Grandmothers -- Fiction 3. African Americans -- Fiction

ISBN 0-689-82628-1; 1-4169-2728-X pa

LC 2001-49531

A young girl's grandmother tells her of her love for baseball and the day they let her play in the game even though she was a girl.

"Johnson tempers what could have been a sentimental tale with Grandmama's contagious enthusiasm and sense of empowerment, and her text has a baseball announcer's suspenseful rhythm.... Peck's angular pastels ... skillfully capture the nostalgic sports action and celebration." Booklist

Lottie Paris lives here; illustrated by Scott Fischer. Simon & Schuster Books for Young Readers 2011 un il $16.99

Grades: PreK K 1 2   E

1. Parks -- Fiction 2. Houses -- Fiction

ISBN 978-0-689-87377-5; 0-689-87377-8

"Award-winning author Angela Johnson and illustrator Scott Fischer take you inside the mind of a spunky girl and the imaginative world she lives in with this ... story now available as a Classic Board Book. Lot-

tie Paris may be precocious, but she still knows how to act like a kid. She dresses up, plays on the slide, and prefers to eat cookies instead of vegetables." (Publisher's note)

"Lottie Paris is an exuberant, imaginative, and mischievous girl... . Fischer's large gouache images created with brayer, linocut, stamping, airbrush, sandpaper and brush line are endearing. ... A universal story told through the eyes of a vivacious youngster." SLJ

Wind flyers; illustrated by Loren Long. Simon & Schuster 2006 un il $16.99

Grades: K 1 2 3   E

1. Air pilots -- Fiction 2. African Americans -- Fiction 3. World War, 1939-1945 -- Fiction

ISBN 0-689-84879-X

"In spare, poetic lines, a young African American boy introduces his great-great-uncle, who was a Tuskegee airman. ... Johnson introduces the history in oblique, pared-down words. ... Long's acrylics beautifully extend the evocative words." Booklist

Johnson, Crockett

★ **Harold** and the purple crayon. Harper & Row 1955 un il $15.99; lib bdg $15.89; pa $6.99

Grades: PreK K   E

1. Drawing -- Fiction

ISBN 0-06-022935-7; 0-06-022936-5 lib bdg; 0-06-443022-7 pa

"As Harold goes for a moonlight walk, he uses his purple crayon to draw a path and the things he sees along the way, then draws himself back home." Hodges. Books for Elem Sch Libr

Other titles about Harold are:

Harold's ABC (1963)

Harold's circus (1959)

Harold's fairy tale (1986)

Harold's trip to the sky (1957)

A picture for Harold's room (1960)

Johnson, D. B., 1944-

Magritte's marvelous hat; a picture book. by D.B. Johnson. Houghton Mifflin Harcourt 2012 32 p.

Grades: K 1 2 3 4   E

1. French painting 2. Hats -- Fiction 3. Dogs -- Fiction 4. Picture books for children 5. Magic -- Fiction 6. Painting, French -- Fiction

ISBN 9780547558646

LC 2011012242

This picture book "recasts René Magritte as a dapper, blue-eyed hound and incorporates the painter's surreal iconography. ... The black bowler hat (a familiar, recurrent image in Magritte's paintings) is characterized as a playful muse, engaging the artist in frisky games on walks." Author/illustrator D.B. Johnson depicts the story with "surreal elements," including "four see-through acetate pages .... [that] transform adjacent spreads," and images inspired by famous Magritte paintings. (Kirkus

Johnson, David

Snow sounds; an onomatopoeic story. [by] David A. Johnson. Houghton Mifflin Company 2006 un il $16

Grades: PreK K 1   E

1. Snow 2. Sound

ISBN 978-0-618-47310-6; 0-618-47310-6

LC 2006-00333

A nearly-wordless book in which a young boy, eager to reach a much-anticipated holiday party on time, listens to the sounds of the shovels, snow plow, and other equipment used to clear his way.

"Full-bleed watercolor spreads capture the light of a wintry morning perfectly. . . . This accomplished offering has a variety of uses and will appeal to a wide age range." SLJ

Johnson, Dinah

★ **Black** magic; illustrated by R. Gregory Christie. Henry Holt and Co. 2010 un il $15.99

Grades: PreK K 1 2   E

1. Black 2. African Americans -- Fiction

ISBN 978-0-8050-7833-6; 0-8050-7833-9

LC 2009-9219

"This expressive book combines well-matched text and pictures to pay tribute to the myriad qualities of blackness. Buoyant yet reflective, Johnson's . . . free-flowing verse presents an imaginative girl's musings on the essence of black, which she sees as containing multitudinous, even oppositional, dimensions. . . . With vibrant colors offsetting velvety black images, Christie's . . . acrylic gouache illustrations playfully tweak perspective and scale, echoing the verse's energy and fluidity. " Publ Wkly

Johnson, Donald B.

★ **Henry** hikes to Fitchburg; [by] D. B. Johnson. Houghton Mifflin 2000 un il $16; pa $6.95

Grades: PreK K 1 2   E

1. Authors 2. Naturalists 3. Essayists 4. Pacifists 5. Bears -- Fiction 6. Nature -- Fiction 7. Writers on nature 8. Nonfiction writers 9. Walking -- Fiction

ISBN 0-395-96867-4; 0-618-73749-9 pa

LC 99-35302

Boston Globe-Horn Book Award: Picture Book (2000)

While his friend works hard to earn the train fare to Fitchburg, Henry the bear walks the thirty miles through woods and fields, enjoying nature and the time to think great thoughts. Includes biographical information about Henry David Thoreau

"This splendid book works on several levels. Johnson's adaption of a paragraph taken from Thoreau's Walden (set down in an author's note) illuminates the contrast between materialistic and naturalistic views of life without ranting or preaching. His illustrations are breathtakingly rich and filled with lovingly rendered details." Booklist

Other titles about Henry the bear are:

Henry builds a cabin (2002)

Henry climbs a mountain (2003)

Henry works (2004)

Henry's night (2009)

Johnson, Lindsay Lee

Ten moonstruck piglets; illustrated by Carll Cneut. Clarion Books 2011 un il $16.99

Grades: PreK K 1 2   E

1. Counting 2. Stories in rhyme 3. Moon -- Fiction 4. Pigs -- Fiction

ISBN 0-618-86866-6; 978-0-618-86866-7

LC 2010-05443

On the night of the full moon, ten piglets go out adventuring while their mother is fast asleep. "Ages four to seven." (Bull Cent Child Books)

"The precise yet playful verse sets the tone and creates the story's structure. Cneut's acrylic paintings give individual traits to the piglets, create a magical moonlit setting, and brilliantly transform it when the moon disappears. . . . An amusing romp and a great opportunity to practice counting from 1 to 10." Booklist

Johnson, Paul Brett

★ **On** top of spaghetti; written and illustrated by Paul Brett Johnson; with lyrics by Tom Glazer. Scholastic Press 2006 un il $15.99

Grades: PreK K 1 2   E

1. Songs 2. Dogs -- Fiction 3. Animals -- Fiction 4. Meatballs -- Fiction

ISBN 0-439-74944-1

LC 2005-14311

"Expanding on the popular song, Johnson spins the tale of Yodeler Jones, a hound dog who serves nothing but meatballs and spaghetti at his dining establishment. When business begins to slow, Yodeler concocts a brand-new meatball, but before he can taste it, someone sneezes. . . . With original text printed in black and the lyrics sprinkled throughout in color, this story successfully marries the two. The loony illustrations, full of color and movement, effectively capture the zaniness." SLJ

Johnson, Stephen, 1964-

Alphabet school; Stephen T. Johnson. Simon & Schuster Books for Young Readers 2015 32 p. color illustrations (hardcover) $17.99

Grades: PreK K 1 2 3   E

1. Alphabet -- Fiction 2. Alphabet books

ISBN 141692521X; 9781416925217

LC 2014041731

In this book, illustrator Stephen T. Johnson "creates a graphic-alphabet book that will have students searching their own schools for letters. . . . A shadow on the fender of a yellow school bus forms a B; an ordinary double-paned window is an E when viewed from the side; the handle on a pencil sharpener is an L; two metal bookends next to one another form an M; an upturned toilet seat is a perfect U. " (Kirkus Review)

"Though alphabet books have proliferated in the years since Johnson published his Caldecott Honor book Alphabet City (Viking, 1999), his concept, which is about looking, not about language, remains distinctive. Twenty years after Johnson's initial foray into the genre, there are still very few alphabet books that are about visual discovery. . . . A highly recommended title." SLJ

Johnston, Lynn

Farley follows his nose; story by Lynn Johnston & Beth Cruikshank; illustrations by Lynn Johnston. Bowen Press 2009 un il $17.99

Grades: PreK K 1   E

1. Dogs -- Fiction 2. Smell -- Fiction

ISBN 978-0-06-170234-1; 0-06-170234-X

LC 2008-24713

Farley the dog follows his nose from one good smell to another all over town.

"Big-eyed, energetic Farley and his 'sniff snorfle SNUFF' nose will be a big hit with storytimers, and it won't matter a bit that they're too young to recognize the characters. A great addition to storytimes on baths, senses and dogs." Kirkus

Johnston, Tony

The **cat** with seven names; Tony Johnston; illustrated by Christine Davenier. Charlesbridge 2013 36 p. (reinforced for library use) $16.95

Grades: K 1 2 3   E

1. Cats -- Fiction 2. Picture books for children 3. Loneliness -- Fiction

ISBN 1580893813; 9781580893817; 9781607346029

LC 2012024434

This picture book shows "six lonely people [who] welcome a large, fat cat into their lives, each giving the feline a different name and enjoying his company for a while. There is a librarian who loves to read . . . , an old man with a walker, a Latino man and his dog, a policewoman, a homeless ex-soldier, and a mother and her daughter who are new to the area." Ultimately, the cat is found by his owner, but not before all the lonely people have met and begun friendships. (School Library Journal)

★ **Levi** Strauss gets a bright idea or; the positively true and unfabricated story of a pair of pants. written by Tony Johnston; illustrated by Stacy Innerst. Houghton Mifflin Harcourt 2011 il $16.99
Grades: PreK K 1 2   E
    1. Tall tales 2. California -- Fiction 3. Jeans (Clothing) -- Fiction 4. Clothing industry executives 5. Clothing and dress -- Fiction 6. Gold mines and mining -- Fiction
    ISBN 978-0-15-206145-6; 0-15-206145-2
                          LC 2010043402
Retells, in tall-tale fashion, how Levi Strauss went to California during the Gold Rush, saw the need for a sturdier kind of trouser, and invented jeans.

"Johnston creates an unrepentantly exaggerated version of events that is sure to entertain, offering more factual information about Strauss in an author's note. Using a bright idea of his own, Innerst . . . chronicles the raucous action in acrylic paintings on a canvas of, yes, old Levi's jeans. The denim's texture provides an appropriately rugged tone to the colorful proceedings." Kirkus

★ **My** abuelita; written by Tony Johnston; illustrated by Yuyi Morales; photographed by Tim O'Meara. Harcourt Children's Books 2009 un il $16
Grades: 1 2 3   E
    1. Grandmothers -- Fiction 2. Storytelling -- Fiction 3. Spanish language -- Vocabulary
    ISBN 978-0-15-216330-3; 0-15-216330-1
    ALA ALSC Belpre Illustrator Medal Honor Book (2010)
"A boy describes the morning routine he shares with his grandmother as she prepares for work. Flights of fancy enliven the tasks of bathing, eating breakfast, and dressing. When the pair arrive at her workplace, readers discover that Abuelita is a storyteller—a calling that her grandson shares. Spanish words are sprinkled throughout, often followed by brief definitions. . . . Johnston effectively engages young readers' interest. . . . Morales's bold, innovative illustrations brilliantly reinforce the text. . . . Characters molded from polymer clay are dressed in brightly patterned fabrics and placed among images that evoke Mexican art." SLJ

A **small** thing ... but big; Tony Johnston; illustrated by Hadley Hooper. Roaring Brook Press 2016 40 p. color illustrations (hardback) $17.99
Grades: PreK K 1 2   E
    1. Dogs -- Fiction 2. Friendship -- Fiction 3. Elderly men -- Fiction 4. Human-animal relationships -- Fiction 5. Older people -- Fiction 6. Self-confidence -- Fiction
    ISBN 9781626729919; 9781626722569
                          LC 2015042626
In this children's book by Tony Johnston, illustrated by Hadley Hooper, "Lizzie and her mom go to the park. That's where Lizzie meets an elderly man and his companion, Cecile, a dog about her size. But Lizzie is afraid of dogs, so she'll have to rely on her new friend to help her take things one step at a time." (Publisher's note)

"This intergenerational tale of kindred spirits facing fears and finding friendship is certain to inspire courage in readers. A sublime read-aloud for small group sharing." SLJ

Uncle Rain Cloud; illustrated by Fabricio Vanden Broeck. Charlesbridge Pub. 2001 un il $15.95; pa $7.95
Grades: PreK K 1 2   E
    1. Uncles -- Fiction 2. English language -- Fiction 3. Mexican Americans -- Fiction
    ISBN 0-88106-371-1; 0-88106-372-X pa
                          LC 99-54195

Carlos tries to help his uncle, who is frustrated and angry at his inability to speak English, adjust to their new home in Los Angeles

"Brisk pacing, sympathetic characters, and clear prose that uses embedded Spanish words effectively make a winner. VandenBroeck's acrylic and colored-pencil illustrations flesh out the narrative in soft, bright colors enhanced by dramatic shading." SLJ

Winter is coming; Tony Johnston; illustrated by Jim LaMarche. Simon & Schuster Books for Young Readers 2014 40 p. col. ill. (hard cover : alk. paper) $17.99
Grades: PreK K 1 2 3   E
    1. Winter -- Fiction 2. Seasons -- Fiction 3. Autumn -- Fiction 4. Forest animals -- Fiction
    ISBN 1442472510; 9781442472518
                          LC 2012040457
In this children's book by Tony Johnston, illustrated by Jim LaMarche, "Day after day, a girl goes to her favorite place in the woods and quietly watches from her tree house as the chipmunks, the doe, the rabbits prepare for the winter. As the temperature drops, sunset comes earlier and a new season begins. Silently she observes the world around her as it reveals its secrets. It takes time and patience to see the changes as, slowly but surely, winter comes." (Publisher's note)

"On a cold September day, a girl takes her binoculars, sketch pad, and pencils outdoors to draw the wildlife around her family's farm. She returns several times before late November, when the first snowflakes fall...Winter may be in the title, but this evocative picture book is best for reading aloud in the fall, when children can notice the subtle changes happening in their own outdoor spaces. A quiet, beautiful picture book to share." Booklist

Jonas, Ann
The **quilt**. Greenwillow Bks. 1984 un il $16.99
Grades: PreK K 1 2   E
    1. Quilts -- Fiction
    ISBN 0-688-03825-5
                          LC 83-25385
"The intricate illustrations in Jonas's book can be described only in superlatives. Backed by a length of golden-yellow calico imprinted with small red flowers, a quilt fashioned from squares in a variety of colors is the prize shown to readers by a dear little girl." Publ Wkly

Round trip. Greenwillow Bks. 1983 un il $15.99; pa $5.99
Grades: PreK K 1 2   E
    1. City and town life -- Fiction
    ISBN 0-688-01772-X; 0-688-09986-6 pa
                          LC 82-12026
Black and white illustrations and text record the sights on a day trip to the city and back home again to the country. The trip to the city is read from front to back and the return trip, from back to front, upside down

"Although one or two pictures too easily suggest their upside-down images and the device is occasionally strained, the author-artist displays a fine sense of graphic design and balance, and pictorial beauty is never sacrificed for mere cleverness." Horn Book

★ **Splash!** Greenwillow Bks. 1995 un il $16.99; pa $6.99
Grades: PreK K 1 2   E
    1. Counting 2. Animals -- Fiction
    ISBN 0-688-11051-7; 0-688-15284-8 pa
                          LC 94-4110
A little girl's turtle, fish, frogs, dog, and cat jump in and out of a backyard pond, constantly changing the answer to the question "How many are in my pond?"

"A clever concept book with physical humor and exciting acrylic paintings that capture the heat and drama of a sunny summer day." Booklist

Joosse, Barbara

Lovabye dragon; text by Barbara Joosse; illustrations by Randy Cecil. Candlewick 2012 32 p. (hardback) $15.99

Grades: PreK K 1 2   E

1. Dragons -- Fiction 2. Picture books for children 3. Friendship -- Fiction 4. Princesses -- Fiction

ISBN 0763654086; 9780763654085

LC 2011046647

In this children's picture book, "[w]hen the tears of a young princess trickle onto a dragon, a sweet friendship is born. . . . [Barbara] Joosse creates a friendship born out of loneliness and tears between a young princess who longs for a dragon and a friendly dragon who dreams of a girl for a friend." (Kirkus)

Another title in this series is:

Evermore Dragon (2015)

Joosse, Barbara M.

Friends (mostly) by Barbara Joosse; illustrated by Tomaso Milian. Greenwillow Books 2010 un il $16.99

Grades: K 1 2 3   E

1. Friendship -- Fiction

ISBN 978-0-06-088222-8; 0-06-088222-0

LC 2009-34951

Henry and Ruby are best friends forever, even though they do not always get along.

"This title provides an excellent springboard for conversations about friendship. . . . Joosse uses some of the text in a dialogue format, the characters responding as if they were being interviewed, providing this picture book with a pre-chapter-book feel. Sections are loosely separated by a rhyme. Lively watercolor illustrations express the children's moods and provide vibrancy to the theme." SLJ

Higgledy-piggledy chicks; by Barbara Joosse; pictures by Rick Chrustowski. Greenwillow Books 2010 un il $16.99; lib bdg $17.89

Grades: PreK K 1 2   E

1. Chickens -- Fiction

ISBN 978-0-06-075042-8; 0-06-075042-1; 978-0-06-075043-5 lib bdg; 0-06-075043-X lib bdg

LC 2007047594

Banty Hen keeps her seven new baby chicks safe, even though they like to go exploring.

"Chrustowski's illustrations—done in colorful torn-paper collages—effectively capture the energy of the roaming and curious chicks. Readers will delight in counting the seven chicks on each spread and in predicting what danger might be hiding on the following page." Booklist

★ Hot city; by Barbara Joosse; illustrated by R. Gregory Christie. Philomel Books 2004 un il $16.99

Grades: PreK K 1 2   E

1. Summer -- Fiction 2. Libraries -- Fiction 3. African Americans -- Fiction 4. City and town life -- Fiction

ISBN 0-399-23640-6

LC 2002-1254

Mimi and her little brother Joe escape from home and the city's summer heat to read and dream about princesses and dinosaurs in the cool, quiet library.

"This eloquently told story is boldly illustrated with evocative acrylic paintings in shades of orange, red, and yellow." SLJ

★ Papa, do you love me? illustrated by Barbara Lavallee. Chronicle Books 2005 un il $15.95

Grades: PreK K   E

1. Africa -- Fiction 2. Masai (African people) -- Fiction 3. Father-son relationship -- Fiction

ISBN 0-8118-4265-7

LC 2003-17344

When a Masai father in Africa answers his son's questions, the boy learns that his father's love for him is unconditional.

"Echoing the soothing rhythm of the poetic narrative, Lavallee's graceful watercolors feature a harmoniously balanced palette." Publ Wkly

Please is a good word to say; by Barbara Joosse; pictures by Jennifer Plecas. Philomel Books 2007 un il $12.99

Grades: PreK K 1 2   E

1. Etiquette -- Fiction

ISBN 978-0-399-24217-5

LC 2006034508

Harriet gives examples of polite words and expressions to use in various social situations to make them more pleasant.

"Joosse's effective use of speech bubbles in various fonts, in addition to the main text, makes for especially interesting and amusing reading. Plecas's ink-and-watercolor cartoons imbue the already spirited commentary with personality, dimension, and even more energy." SLJ

Roawr! illustrated by Jan Jutte. Philomel Books 2009 un il $16.99

Grades: PreK K   E

1. Bears -- Fiction

ISBN 978-0-399-24777-4; 0-399-24777-7

LC 2008-16907

When Liam hears a load roar in the middle of the night, he must use all his ingenuity to protect his sleeping mother from a hungry bear.

"This adrenaline-charged romp is, first and foremost, exciting. Jutte's lively cartoon artwork contrasts muted night colors to form powerful images." SLJ

Sleepover at gramma's house; illustrated by Jan Jutte. Philomel Books 2010 un il $17.99

Grades: PreK K 1   E

1. Elephants -- Fiction 2. Grandmothers -- Fiction

ISBN 978-0-399-25261-7; 0-399-25261-4

LC 2009-31549

A little girl and her grandmother have a rollicking good time during a sleepover.

"Jutte's illustrations are jam-packed full of details. Readers get a clear sense of the child's excitement and activity level, but they will never lose sight of the relationship being celebrated. The colors in the ink, watercolor and acrylic illustrations lend the artwork a retro feel, and the elephants may remind many readers of Babar." Kirkus

Wind-wild dog; written by Barbara Joosse; illustrated by Kate Kiesler. Henry Holt and Company 2006 un il $16.95

Grades: K 1 2 3   E

1. Dogs -- Fiction 2. Alaska -- Fiction

ISBN 978-0-8050-7053-8; 0-8050-7053-2

LC 2005020055

Ziva, a "wind-wild" young sled dog, decides whether to stay with the man who has trained her or to run free with the wolves and wind

"In spare, precise prose, Ziva's story drives with understated dramatic tension toward a satisfying conclusion. Kiesler's oil paintings capture the clean beauty of the rural Alaska setting as well as the unique qualities of Ziva and the man." Booklist

Jordan, Deloris

★ **Salt** in his shoes; Michael Jordan in pursuit of a dream. by Deloris Jordan with Roslyn M. Jordan; illustrated by Kadir Nelson. Simon & Schuster Bks. for Young Readers 2000 un il $16.95; pa $7.99

Grades: 2 3 4   E

    1. Basketball 2. Baseball players 3. Olympic athletes 4. Basketball players

    ISBN 0-689-83371-7; 0-689-83419-5 pa

                LC 00-20539

"This readable and entertaining story will delight the superstar's fans. Nelson's illustrations bring the right blend of vivid color, realism, and personality." SLJ

Jordan, Sandra

★ **Mr.** and Mrs. Portly and their little dog Snack; pictures by Christine Davenier. Farrar Straus Giroux 2009 un il $16.99

Grades: PreK K 1 2   E

    1. Art -- Fiction 2. Dogs -- Fiction

    ISBN 978-0-374-35089-5; 0-374-35089-2

                LC 2007046663

Snack is a very happy puppy when Mrs. Portly adopts him but when persnickety Mr. Portly returns from a fishing trip, he banishes Snack to a doghouse until their mutual love of art, and a thief, bring them together.

"Davenport's ink-and-watercolor drawings are a delightful mix of sizes and shapes. . . . Exuding warmth, both narrative and pictures transcend the basic plotline, turning this into an irresistible offering." Booklist

Jordan-Fenton, Christy

Not my girl. Firefly Books Ltd 2014 36 p. $21.95

Grades: 1 2 3 4   E

    1. Native American children 2. Mother-daughter relationship -- Fiction 3. Inuit women -- Biography 4. Inuit -- Cultural assimilation -- Canada

    ISBN 1554516250; 9781554516254

    Sequel to: When I was eight

In this children's book by Christy Jordan-Fenton and Margaret Pokiak-Fenton, illustrated by Gabrielle Grimard, "Two years ago, Margaret left her Arctic home for the outsiders' school. Now she has returned and can barely contain her excitement as she rushes towards her waiting family--but her mother stands still as a stone. This strange, skinny child, with her hair cropped short, can't be her daughter. 'Not my girl!' she says angrily." (Publisher's note)

"A poignant picture book memoir about an Inuit girl reconnecting with her culture...Culturally relevant, accurate, and soft, painterly illustrations depict the sequence of events and reinforce the bittersweet and tender reunion of Olemaun with her family...this is an excellent illustrated biography, overall." SLJ

Joubert, Beverly

African animal alphabet; by Beverly and Dereck Joubert. National Geographic 2011 48p il (National Geographic little kids) $16.95

Grades: PreK K 1 2   E

    1. Alphabet 2. Animals -- Africa

    ISBN 978-1-4263-0781-2; 1-4263-0781-0

"This alphabet book features vivid photographs of African animals. Readers will recognize a cheetah, elephant, and lion, but this husband-and-wife naturalist team also highlights unsung species like the tsessebe, the umbrette, and the dung beetle. . . . Appended animal facts and a glossary for words like 'vociferous' underscore the book's dual focus on diverse animal characteristics and language development." Publ Wkly

Joyce, William

Billy's booger; a memoir. Moonbot Studios and William Joyce. Atheneum Books for Young Readers 2015 40 p. color illustrations (hardcover : alk. paper) $17.99

Grades: K 1 2 3   E

    1. Drawing 2. Child authors 3. Schools -- Fiction 4. Contests -- Fiction 5. Authorship -- Fiction 6. Imagination -- Fiction 7. Books and reading -- Fiction

    ISBN 1442473517; 9781442473515

                LC 2014034955

This book by William Joyce is about a "young lad who would rather draw than do math, spell, or gargle finds the perfect outlet for his always-on imagination in this manifesto to creative joie de vivre, featuring a book within a book. Full of nostalgic references to a time when TV was black-and-white and Sunday newspapers had things called the funnies, this wildly fun story-within-a-story is based loosely on children's book legend William Joyce's third grade year." (Publisher's note)

"Creative, strange, energetic Billy (a young Joyce) finds an outlet for his imagination when he enters a school contest for the best kids' book. He's devastated to not win--until he discovers his entry (included as a book within this book) is the most circulated entry at the library. Budding writers and illustrators will find reassurance and inspiration, plus plenty of chuckles." Horn Book

A **day** with Wilbur Robinson; by William Joyce. Laura Geringer Books 2006 un il $16.99

Grades: PreK K 1 2   E

    1. Family life -- Fiction 2. Eccentrics and eccentricities -- Fiction

    ISBN 978-0-06-089098-8; 0-06-089098-3

                LC 2005037287

An expanded version of the title published 1990

While spending the day in the Robinson household, Wilbur's best friend joins in the search for Grandfather Robinson's missing false teeth and meets one wacky relative after another

"The real fun is in the tension between the deadpan words and the fantastical pictures. . . . Save this for small groups, which will most appreciate the wondrous visual details." Booklist

★ **Dinosaur** Bob and his adventures with the family Lazardo; new ed; HarperCollins Pubs. 1995 un il $16.99

Grades: K 1 2 3   E

    1. Dinosaurs -- Fiction

    ISBN 0-06-021074-5

                LC 94-19100

A revised and enlarged edition of the title first published 1988

"The Lazardo family goes on safari to Africa where they find a dinosaur. They name him Bob and take him back to Pimlico Hills. . . . Bob soon becomes famous because he can play the trumpet, dance, and most importantly play baseball." Child Book Rev Serv [review of 1988 edition]

The **fantastic** flying books of Mr. Morris Lessmore; William Joyce. Atheneum Books for Young Readers 2012 56 p. (hardback) $17.99

Grades: PreK K 1 2 3   E

    1. Fantasy 2. Libraries -- Fiction 3. Books and reading -- Fiction

    ISBN 1442457023; 9781442457027; 9781442464896

                LC 2012004465

This children's picture book "follows a dreamy bibliophile named Morris Lessmore, who loses his cherished book collection to a cataclysmic storm. . . . After meeting a 'lovely lady . . .' being pulled along by a festive squadron of flying books,' Morris finds an abandoned library whose books are alive and whose covers beat like the wings of birds. They flutter around him protectively, watch as he starts writing again, and care for him as he ages." (Publishers Weekly)

"The message-heavy narrative is lifted by Joyce's superb artwork, presenting nostalgic, picket-fence scenes with a modeled, dimensional feel built on the animation but given a lustrous polish for the printed page." Booklist

★ **George** shrinks; story and pictures by William Joyce. Harper & Row 1985 un il $16.99; pa $6.99
Grades: K 1 2 3   E
1. Fantasy fiction 2. Size -- Fiction
ISBN 0-06-023070-3; 0-06-443129-0 pa

LC 83-47697

"The colorful illustrations, executed with painstaking attention to detail, create a surreal landscape from an ordinary breakfast-cereal world, as familiar objects become monumental structures through which the diminutive George moves with panache." Horn Book

★ The **Man** in the Moon; edited by Laura Geringer Books. Atheneum Books for Young Readers 2011 un il (Guardians of childhood) $17.99
Grades: K 1 2 3   E
1. Fantasy fiction 2. Moon -- Fiction
ISBN 978-1-4424-3041-9; 1-4424-3041-9

LC 2010053985

When a newly orphaned baby in the moon makes friends with the children of Earth, he begins to shine as brightly as possible to ward off their fears.

This "is a rich, cinematic brew of steampunk fancies. [Joyce's] sumptuous spreads are crowded with rotund telescopes, Jules Verne rocket ships, and sherbet-bearing robots, all painted in a superb palette of indigo and gold. . . . Joyce combines elemental fairyland themes . . . into a tale that's warm and fuzzy, swashbuckling, and dazzling inventive all at the same time." Publ Wkly

Joyner, Andrew
Boris for the win; Andrew Joyner. Branches 2013 73 p. (Boris) $15.99
Grades: PreK K 1 2   E
1. Racing -- Fiction 2. Friendship -- Fiction 3. Competition (Psychology) -- Fiction 4. Racing -- Fiction 5. Schools -- Fiction 6. Warthog -- Fiction 7. Friendship -- Fiction 8. Running races -- Fiction
ISBN 0545484480; 9780545484480; 9780545484497

LC 2012046575

In this book, by Andrew Joyner, "it's Field Day, and Boris is ready to run like he's never run before. All he wants is to beat Eddie, who always wins everything. And all his friend Frederick wants is not to come in last...again. Who will make it across the finish line first? And when Boris is faced with a big decision, will he go for the gold or help a friend in need?" (Publisher's note)

Boris on the move; Andrew Joyner. Branches 2013 80 p. ill. (Boris) (library) $15.99
Grades: PreK K 1 2   E
1. Picture books for children 2. Voyages and travels -- Fiction 3. Parks -- Fiction 4. Warthog -- Fiction 5. Natural areas -- Fiction
ISBN 0545484421; 9780545484428

LC 2012034254

In this book, "Boris, a not-particularly-attractive hog, is frustrated. Although he and his parents live in a bus that once took them on fabulous vacations, now the old vehicle is permanently parked, and he longs for adventure. Finally, his empathetic parents fire up the engine to bring him on a journey that, it disappointingly turns out, is only across town to a nature preserve." Boris still manages to get lost. (Kirkus Reviews)

Juan, Ana
The **Night** Eater; by Ana Juan. Arthur A. Levine Books 2004 un il $16.95
Grades: K 1 2 3   E
1. Night -- Fiction
ISBN 0-439-48891-5

LC 2003-20197

The Night Eater, who brings each new day by gobbling up the darkness, decides he is too fat and stops eating, with dire consequences

"The sense of magic realism in this story is matched by in Juan's richly colored acrylic-and-wax paintings. . . . This delightful tale will definitely appeal to children's imaginations." SLJ

The **pet** shop revolution. Arthur A. Levine Books 2011 un il
Grades: 1 2 3   E
1. Pets -- Fiction 2. Animals -- Fiction 3. Animal rescue -- Fiction
ISBN 0-545-12810-2; 978-0-545-12810-0

LC 2010051325

Everyone is afraid of Mr. Walnut, the scowling owner of the biggest pet store in the city, who sells all kinds of animals to rich customers from out of town, but when Mina's pet rabbit goes missing she vows to do something about it.

"This intriguing and thought-provoking tale skillfully illustrates the benevolence that is born when one walks in the shoes of another. It may also generate some activist thinking among young readers. . . . Juan's beautifully stylized and deeply expressive acrylic and colored pencil drawings perfectly capture the somber tone that prevails throughout most of the book." SLJ

Judge, Lita
Flight school; by Lita Judge. Atheneum Books for Young Readers 2014 40 p. (hardcover) $16.99
Grades: PreK K 1 2   E
1. Animal flight 2. Flight -- Fiction 3. Penguins -- Fiction
ISBN 1442481773; 9781442481770

LC 2012046161

In this book, by Lita Judge, "a persevering penguin is determined to fly. . . . Although little Penguin has the soul of an eagle, his body wasn't built to soar. But Penguin has an irrepressible spirit, and he adamantly follows his dreams to flip, flap, fly! Even if he needs a little help with the technical parts, this penguin is ready to live on the wind." (Publisher's note)

"Penguin leaves the South Pole for flight school. Though the other birds are skeptical, Penguin is determined. When instead of soaring he plunges into the ocean, Penguin sadly admits defeat and gets ready to head home. Then Flamingo has an idea. Variations in perspective throughout Judge's soft watercolor and pencil illustrations add visual interest to the book, as do parts told entirely through the pictures." Horn Book

Good morning to me! Lita Judge. Atheneum Books for Young Readers 2015 40 p. color illustrations (hardcover) $17.99
Grades: PreK K 1 2   E
1. Morning -- Fiction 2. Parrots -- Fiction 3. Voice -- Fiction 4. Animals -- Fiction 5. Behavior -- Fiction
ISBN 1481403699; 9781481403696

LC 2014006270

In this children's book written and illustrated by Lita Judge, "it's a sleepy morning in the cottage, but Beatrix the parrot is wide AWAKE and she can't wait to start the day with her friends. [It's designed] children who can't contain their exuberance--and who might have a little, tiny, itty bit of trouble using indoor voices." (Publisher's note)

"All of her friends are sleeping, but Beatrix the parrot is wide awake. She knows she is supposed to be quiet and tries to talk softly but a loud

"GOOD MORNING, MOUSE!" wakes up the snoozing rodent. . . . Children who have a hard time with indoor voices will relate to Beatrix's enthusiastic nature." SLJ

Pennies for elephants. Hyperion Books for Children 2009 un il $16.99

Grades: PreK K 1 2   E

1. Zoos -- Fiction 2. Elephants -- Fiction 3. Boston (Mass.) -- Fiction

ISBN 978-1-4231-1390-4; 1-4231-1390-X

"In 1914, the children of Boston raised $6,000 to buy three trained elephants for the Franklin Park Zoo. But told through the eyes of siblings (and fund-raisers) Dorothy and Henry, the story expands into an inspired celebration of kid power. . . . Dollops of historical flavor abound, with watercolors of knickers-clad boys and streets bustling with people, horses and horseless carriages. Warm sepia tones lend atmosphere." Publ Wkly

Red hat; Lita Judge. Atheneum Books for Young Readers 2013 40 p. (hardcover) $16.99

Grades: PreK K 1 2   E

1. Hats -- Fiction 2. Picture books for children 3. Forest animals -- Fiction 4. Hats -- Fiction 5. Animals -- Infancy -- Fiction

ISBN 1442442328; 9781442442320; 9781442442337

LC 2012002600

In this children's picture book story, by Lita Judge, "it's spring-cleaning time now, so the child washes the red hat and hangs it out to dry. . . . When the critters spy the hat pinned to the line, . . . an energetic game of keep-away breaks out, with the accompanying sounds and exclamations of pursuit and merriment. . . . [Until] the animals' realiz[e] that the hat is now just one long red strand of yarn with a white pompom on the end." (Kirkus)

★ **Red** sled. Atheneum Books for Young Readers 2011 un il $16.99

Grades: PreK K 1 2   E

1. Sounds -- Fiction 2. Sledding -- Fiction 3. Forest animals -- Fiction

ISBN 978-1-4424-2007-6; 1-4424-2007-3

LC 2010033264

At night, a host of woodland creatures plays with a child's red sled.

"The premise of this book is simple; the execution is anything but. . . . Pencil and watercolor spreads create a basic wintry mountain environment, but the stars of the show are the expressive animals. Their childlike delight in each dynamic scene brings a sense of excitement to the story. The text consists entirely of sound effects, laid out on the page in varying font sizes to evoke a sense of movement." SLJ

Jules, Jacqueline

Duck for Turkey Day; illustrated by Kathyrn Mitter. Albert Whitman 2009 un il $16.99

Grades: K 1 2 3   E

1. School stories 2. Thanksgiving Day -- Fiction 3. Vietnamese Americans -- Fiction

ISBN 978-0-8075-1734-5; 0-8075-1734-8

LC 2008055537

When Tuyet finds out that her Vietnamese family is having duck rather than turkey for Thanksgiving dinner, she is upset until she finds out that other children in her class did not eat turkey either.

"Mitter's acrylic illustrations, in clear bright colors and simple shapes, capture the warmth of the holiday bustle and the affection among family members." Booklist

Jung Jin-Ho

Look up! Jin-ho Jung; English translation by My Hyun Kim. Holiday House 2016 32 p. chiefly illustrations (hardcover) $16.95; (ebook) $16.95

Grades: K 1 2 3   E

1. Neighborliness -- Fiction 2. Children with disabilities -- Fiction 3. People with disabilities -- Fiction 4. Perspective (Philosophy) -- Fiction

ISBN 9780823436521; 9780823437283

LC 2015050735

In this children's book, by Jin-ho Jung, translated by My Hyun Kim, "a girl in a wheelchair looks down from her balcony and calls to passers-by below: 'Look up!' Dog walkers, a bike rider, a kite flier, and dozens of commuters walk by without taking any notice. Then a boy stops and looks up. He lies on the sidewalk so the girl can see him better. A woman joins him. Soon nine people and one dog are lying down and looking up. The girl looks up at the reader and smiles." (Publisher's note)

"Conceptually sophisticated; especially inviting for young artists ready to explore new visual angles." Kirkus

Juster, Norton

★ The **hello,** goodbye window; story by Norton Juster; pictures by Chris Raschka. Hyperion Books for Children 2005 un il $15.95

Grades: PreK K 1 2   E

1. Grandparents -- Fiction

ISBN 0-7868-0914-0

Boston Globe-Horn Book Honor: Picture Book (2005)

"The window in Nanna and Poppy's kitchen is no ordinary window—it is the place where love and magic happens. . . . The first-person text is both simple and sophisticated, conjuring a perfectly child-centered world. . . . Using a bright rainbow palette of saturated color, Raschka's impressionistic, mixed-media illustrations portray a loving, mixed-race family." SLJ

Another title about Nanna and Poppy and their granddaughter is: Sourpuss and Sweetie Pie (2008)

★ **Neville**; [illustrations by G. Brian Karas] Schwartz & Wade Books 2011 un il $17.99; lib bdg $20.99

Grades: PreK K 1 2   E

1. Moving -- Fiction

ISBN 978-0-375-86765-1; 0-375-86765-1; 978-0-375-96765-8 lib bdg; 0-375-96765-6 lib bdg

LC 2010024119

When a boy and his family move to a new house, he devises an ingenious way to meet people in the neighborhood.

This is an "emotionally authentic tale. . . . Karas's melancholy illustrations brighten and expand as the mood improves; small, quiet type sets the sullen tone, until colorful hand-lettered display type implies the children's collective chatter. . . . Juster . . . identifies a common, stressful situation, and Karas handles the drama with compassion." Publ Wkly

★ The **odious** Ogre; story by Norton Juster; pictures by Jules Feiffer. Michael Di Capua Books 2010 un il $17.95

Grades: K 1 2 3   E

1. Fairy tales 2. Monsters -- Fiction

ISBN 978-0-545-16202-9; 0-545-16202-5

An ogre "rampages through the countryside, terrorizing (and eating) the residents with impunity. Until, that is, he is utterly 'confounded, overcome, and undone' by the unexpected kindness and friendly advice of a young woman. . . . Kids might not pick up on all of the philosophical overtones, but they're sure to enjoy Juster's rich wordplay and happily ridiculous story and Feiffer's wonderfully scratchy and energetic watercolors." Kirkus

Kacer, Kathy

I Am Not a Number; written by Jenny Kay Dupuis and Kathy Kacer; illustrated by Gillian Newland. Orca Book Publishers 2016 32 p. color illustrations $18.95

Grades: 4 5 6   E

1. First Nations children -- Fiction 2. First Nations -- Residential schools -- Fiction

ISBN 1927583942; 9781927583944

LC 2016048303

In this children's book, by Jenny Kay Dupuis and Kathy Kacer, illustrated by Gillian Newland, "when Irene is removed from her First Nations family to live in a residential school, she is confused, frightened and terribly homesick. She tries to remember who she is and where she came from despite being told to do otherwise. When she goes home for summer holidays, her parents decide never to send her away again, but . . . what will happen when her parents disobey the law?" (Publisher's note)

"A moving glimpse into a not-very-long-past injustice." Kirkus

Kain, Karen

The Nutcracker; paintings by Rajka Kupesic. Tundra Books 2005 un il $18.95

Grades: K 1 2 3   E

1. Fairy tales 2. Christmas -- Fiction

ISBN 0-88776-696-X

This is a "striking staging of the classic ballet. . . . The narrative reads smoothly, but it's the art that steals the show. Peopled with doll-like folk-art figures, Kupesic's full-page illustrations . . . are intense with luminous colors." Booklist

Kalan, Robert

★ Jump, frog, jump! pictures by Byron Baron. Greenwillow Books 1995 un il $16.99; pa $6.99

Grades: PreK K 1   E

1. Stories in rhyme 2. Frogs -- Fiction

ISBN 0-688-13954-X; 0-688-09241-1 pa

A reissue of the title first published 1981

"When a frog catches a fly, he sets off a chain of predators. . . . The title answers the repeated refrain 'How did the frog get away?' and children will soon be chanting along with this cumulative tale enhanced by Barton's folk-art-style illustrations." Publ Wkly

Kaneko, Yuki

Into the Snow; Yuri Kaneko; illustrated by Masamitsu Saito. Enchanted Lion Books 2016 32 p. color illustrations $16.95

Grades: PreK K 1   E

1. Exploration -- Fiction 2. Mother-son relationship -- Fiction

ISBN 1592701884; 9781592701889

This children's book by Yuri Kaneko, illustrated by Masamitsu Saito "is an exuberant story told in the child's own voice. Celebrating immediacy and exploration, along with the tender bond between mother and child, this is a story that feels good, the way all real things do." (Publisher's note)

"There's no shortage of picture books about snowy days, but this one, with its playful art style and joyful celebration of winter, is particularly lovely." Booklist

Kanevsky, Polly

Sleepy boy; illustrated by Stephanie Anderson. Atheneum Books for Young Readers 2006 un il $15.95

Grades: PreK K   E

1. Bedtime -- Fiction 2. Father-son relationship -- Fiction

ISBN 0-689-86735-2

Unable to fall asleep, a little boy lying next to his father experiences the various sensations of his body and remembers a lion cub he saw that day at the zoo

"Simple, physical words and full-page, unframed, sepia-toned watercolor-and-charcoal images combine to create a portrait of blissful intimacy between a toddler and his father." Booklist

Kang, A. N.

The very fluffy kitty, Papillon; A. N. Kang. Disney-Hyperion 2016 40 p. color illustrations $16.99

Grades: PreK K 1 2   E

1. Cats -- Fiction 2. Humorous stories

ISBN 1484717988; 9781484717981

LC 2015019786

In this book, by A. N. Kang, "Papillon is a very fluffy kitty. So fluffy that he's lighter than air! His owner tries to weigh him down, but Papillon just wants to fly. One particularly sunny day, he floats right out the window! Exploring the wide world is exhilarating, but it's also a little scary. Will his new friend, a bird, be able to help him find his way home?" (Publisher's note)

"Puffy Papillon's the most charming puss to pop up in years!" Kirkus

Kang, Anna

You are (not) small; by Anna Kang; illustrated by Christopher Weyant. Two Lions 2014 32 p. color illustrations (trade pbk) $16.99

Grades: PreK K 1 2   E

1. Size 2. Animals -- Fiction

ISBN 9781477847725; 1477847723

LC 2013958332

Theodor Seuss Geisel Award (2015)

In this children's book by Anna Kang, "two bears argue about perspective. Each is convinced that the other is big or small in comparison to him and his friends ('I am not small. You are big.'; 'I am not big. See?'). Each group argues, until two other creatures (one even bigger and one even smaller) come along and shows them that they can be both big and small at the same time." (School Library Journal)

"While the story itself seems simple, the concepts are pertinent to several important social issues such as bullying and racism, as well as understanding point of view. Charming characters, a clever plot and a quiet message tucked inside a humorous tale." Kirkus

Kanninen, Barbara J.

A story with pictures; story by Barbara Kanninen; pictures by Lynn Rowe Reed. Holiday House 2007 un il $16.95

Grades: PreK K 1 2   E

1. Authorship -- Fiction 2. Illustration of books -- Fiction

ISBN 978-0-8234-2049-0; 0-8234-2049-3

LC 2006019535

An author forgets to give her manuscript to an illustrator who begins to paint whatever she herself wants, making the author a character in the book, along with a meddlesome duck and other creatures

Reed's "mixed-media compositions expertly contain the antic action. . . . The artist renders the characters in a childlike style, painting them with skewered proportions and in gumdrop-colored clothes, and enhances her spreads with collage elements. . . . Readers will enjoy the wild ride." Publ Wkly

Kantorovitz, Sylvie, 1960-

★ The very tiny baby; Sylvie Kantorovitz. Charlesbridge 2014 32 p. (reinforced for library use) $14.95

Grades: PreK K 1 2   E

1. Infants -- Fiction 2. Jealousy -- Fiction 3. Teddy bears -- Fiction 4. Sibling rivalry -- Fiction 5. Premature babies -- Fiction 6.

Jealousy in children -- Fiction
ISBN 1580894453; 9781580894456; 9781607346357

LC 2012038697

In this book, by Sylvie Kantorovitz, "Jacob learns that adults can be scared, too, when his new sibling is born prematurely. While Jacob has his grandma and his faithful teddy bear, Bob, with him at home while his parents are at the hospital, he still feels alone. The Book portrays the range of emotions older siblings often have about a new baby, including fear, anger, and resentment, along with the added challenges of the preemie's health concerns and parents' frequent absences." (Publisher's note)

"Jacob's parents are excited about their expected baby, but the child isn't so sure he wants to share the limelight. Then when the infant arrives too early and everyone-even grandma-is so preoccupied with its survival that they don't pay much attention to him, he's certain that the new baby is a bad idea . . . Pumping of breast milk, hospital visit precautions, and care of preemies are all depicted. This story can provide information and comfort to youngsters experiencing worry about a sibling born prematurely or even for those who are preparing to share parents with a new brother or sister." SLJ

Kaplan, Bruce Eric
★ **Monsters** eat whiny children. Simon & Schuster Books for Young Readers 2010 un il $15.99
Grades: PreK K 1   **E**
    1. Cooking -- Fiction 2. Monsters -- Fiction 3. Siblings -- Fiction
ISBN 1-4169-8689-8; 978-1-4169-8689-8

LC 2008-50434

Henry and Eve, having ignored their father's warning, are kidnapped by monsters who eat whiny children, but while increasing numbers of monsters argue over how to prepare them, the siblings begin to play nicely. Includes a recipe for cucumber sandwiches.

"For those who like their picture books with a little edge and offbeat humor, this is a surefire hit. . . . Kaplan's minimalist cartoon illustrations bring to mind Quentin Blake's work and complement the humorous, quirky text with its askew frames, thick black lines, and color accents." SLJ

Kaplan, Michael B.
Betty Bunny didn't do it; written by Michael B. Kaplan; illustrated by Stéphane Jorisch. Dial Books for Young Readers 2013 32 p. (hardcover) $16.99
Grades: PreK K 1   **E**
    1. Honesty 2. Rabbits -- Fiction 3. Conduct of life -- Fiction 4. Blame -- Fiction 5. Honesty -- Fiction 6. Behavior -- Fiction 7. Family life -- Fiction
ISBN 0803738587; 9780803738584

LC 2012014367

In this children's book, by Michael Kaplan, illustrated by Stephanie Jorisch, "the value of honesty as seen through the eyes of a . . . precocious preschooler. When Betty Bunny breaks a lamp, she blames it on the Tooth Fairy. Blaming someone else for something she had done seems like such a good idea to Betty Bunny. . . . But when a vase gets broken, everyone blames Betty Bunny, and no one believes her when she says that she really didn't do it." (Publisher's note)

"With humor and some delightful twists, Betty Bunny learns the importance of telling the truth. The peppy ink and watercolor illustrations give Betty and her siblings lots of personality." Horn Book

Betty Bunny did not do it

★ **Betty** Bunny loves chocolate cake; pictures by Stephane Jorisch. Dial Books for Young Readers 2011 un il $16.99
Grades: PreK K 1   **E**
    1. Cake -- Fiction 2. Food -- Fiction 3. Rabbits -- Fiction 4.

Family life -- Fiction
ISBN 978-0-8037-3407-4; 0-8037-3407-7

LC 2010-28799

From her first bite, young Betty Bunny likes chocolate cake so much that she claims she will marry it one day, and she has trouble learning to wait patiently until she can have her next taste.

"Readers will delight in feeling older and wiser than Betty, and both Jorisch . . . and debut talent Kaplan demonstrate a sure handle on feisty modern family dynamics." Publ Wkly

Karas, G. Brian
The **Village** Garage. Henry Holt and Company 2010 un il $16.99
Grades: PreK K 1 2 3   **E**
    1. Garages -- Fiction 2. Seasons -- Fiction 3. City and town life -- Fiction
ISBN 0-8050-8716-8; 978-0-8050-8716-1

LC 2009009223

Throughout the seasons the workers at the Village Garage are busy taking care of the town and its residents.

"Adding bits of fun along the way, the simple text explains [the workers'] tasks without too much detail. Nicely varied in composition, the appealing pencil, gouache, and acrylic illustrations offer wonderfully childlike depictions of the workers and their machines." Booklist

Kargman, Jill
Pirates & Princesses; by Jill Kargman & Sadie Kargman; illustrated by Christine Davenier. Dutton Childrens Books 2011 il $16.99
Grades: PreK K 1 2   **E**
    1. School stories 2. Play -- Fiction 3. Sex role -- Fiction 4. Friendship -- Fiction 5. Kindergarten -- Fiction
ISBN 978-0-525-42229-7; 0-525-42229-3

LC 2011005191

Ivy and Fletch have been best friends since they were born but now, at age five, the boys in their kindergarten play Pirates at recess while the girls play Princesses, and the duo is split apart.

"The mother-and-daughter team tells the story, but it's Davenier's energetic pencil-and-watercolor illustrations that give the story its heart. . . . Though the story ends as expected, it's nice to see that they figure out things for themselves, with no adult intervention, giving young readers some good ideas for when gender roles exert themselves in school. Teachers especially will turn to this good-natured story; it will help open up a discussion about friendship that many children will profit from." Kirkus

Kasbarian, Lucine
The **greedy** sparrow; an Armenian tale. illustrated by Maria Zaikina. Marshall Cavendish 2011 un il $17.99
Grades: PreK K 1 2   **E**
    1. Birds -- Fiction 2. Folklore -- Armenia
ISBN 978-0-7614-5821-0; 0-7614-5821-2

LC 2010-18172

A sparrow who is treated kindly by strangers repays each act of kindness with a trick to get more. Will the sparrow's greed get the best of him?

"Zaikina's expressive portrayals of both animal and human characters, rendered in bold outline and rich color, beautifully convey the tale's goofy fun. Her use of wax and oil paint in a kind of scratchboard technique smartly blends folk and cartoon styles." SLJ

Kasza, Keiko
★ The **dog** who cried wolf; [by] Keiko Kasza. G.P. Putnam's Sons 2005 un il $15.99; pa $6.99

Grades: K 1 2 3   **E**
1. Dogs -- Fiction 2. Wolves -- Fiction
ISBN 0-399-24247-3; 0-14-241305-4 pa

LC 2004-24737

Tired of being a house pet, Moka the dog moves to the mountains to become a wolf but soon misses the comforts of home.

"With an effective variety of page layouts, the expressive pen-and-watercolor pictures show [Moka] dashing off on his adventures. . . . Thanks to excellent pacing, children will get caught up in the childlike Moka's emotions." SLJ

Finders keepers; Keiko Kasza. G. P. Putnam's Sons 2015 32 p. color illustrations $16.99
Grades: PreK K 1   **E**
1. Hats -- Fiction 2. Forest animals -- Fiction 3. Humorous stories 4. Animals -- Fiction 5. Lost and found possessions -- Fiction
ISBN 0399168982; 9780399168987

LC 2014022119

In this children's book by Keiko Kasza, "squirrel claims an acorn for himself declaring, "Finders, keepers," unaware that the hat he uses to mark his buried treasure will take on a new life wherever it lands. After the squirrel leaves his find, wind blows the hat into a tree where a bird uses it for a nest. Next it becomes a boat for an ant, then a clown nose for a bear. But the nose tickles the bear whose sneeze sends the hat flying until it lands back over the squirrel's hole." (School Library Journal)

"Squirrel rejoices when he discovers an acorn, which he buries and then marks with his jaunty red hat. Picture book veterans might expect that another critter will come along and find that hat, but instead, the wind blows it away until it lands wedged between two branches to make "a terrific nest!" . . . Unlike the more cynical (if hilarious) I Want My Hat Back (rev. 11/11) by Klassen, this ends with two hats and two happy animals but will still leave the audience laughing." Horn Book

A **mother** for Choco; Keiko Kasza. Putnam 1992 32 p. col il $16.99
Grades: PreK K 1   **E**
1. Mothers 2. Self-acceptance 3. Mothers -- Fiction
ISBN 0399218416; 9780399218415

LC 91012361

In this children's book by Keiko Kasza "Choco wishes he had a mother, but who could she be? He sets off to find her, asking all kinds of animals, but he doesn't meet anyone who looks just like him. He doesn't even think of asking Mrs. Bear if she's his mother-but then she starts to do just the things a mommy might do. And when she brings him home, he meets her other children-a piglet, a hippo, and an alligator-and learns that families can come in all shapes and sizes and still fit together." (Publisher's note)

"Fans of Kasza's previous picture books will welcome this latest effort. Cheerful, energetic illustrations decorate the simple but charming tale of a youngster's search for a loving parent. . . . The emphasis on caring and sharing despite superficial differences will surely find a wide audience. A multicultural message may also be read into this satisfying story with appealing illustrations and a very happy ending." SLJ

★ **My** lucky day. Putnam 2003 un il $15.99; pa $5.99
Grades: PreK K 1 2   **E**
1. Pigs -- Fiction 2. Foxes -- Fiction
ISBN 0-399-23874-3; 0-14-240456-X pa

LC 2001-57874

When a young pig knocks on a fox's door, the fox thinks dinner has arrived, but the pig has other plans

"Kasza's gouache art is as buoyant and comical as her narrative." Publ Wkly

Ready for anything. G.P. Putnam's Sons 2009 un il $16.99
Grades: PreK K 1 2   **E**
1. Ducks -- Fiction 2. Worry -- Fiction 3. Raccoons -- Fiction
ISBN 978-0-399-25235-8; 0-399-25235-5

LC 2008033615

Raccoon is nervous about all of the things that could spoil a picnic, from bees to dragons, until Duck convinces him that surprises can be fun.

"The characters' dialogue is lively and fun to read aloud; Kasza's affable gouache illustrations spotlight action and emotions." Horn Book

★ The **wolf's** chicken stew. Putnam 1987 un il $16.99; pa $6.99
Grades: K 1 2 3   **E**
1. Wolves -- Fiction 2. Chickens -- Fiction
ISBN 0-399-21400-3; 0-399-22000-9 pa

LC 86-12303

"Kasza combines quivery line and shaded color to turn Wolf and Chicken into scuptural forms. Landscape images are treated similarly. . . . Wolf is comically and suspensefully visualized, making the flimflamming refrains sound just right." Wilson Libr Bull

Katz, Alan

Stalling; illustrated by Elwood H. Smith. Margaret K. McElderry Books 2010 un il $16.99
Grades: PreK K 1 2   **E**
1. Stories in rhyme 2. Bedtime -- Fiction
ISBN 978-1-4169-5567-2; 1-4169-5567-4

"Katz's exuberant, ebulliently punctuated tale is enhanced by Smith's humorous art. Cartoon drawings intermixed with digitally collaged items create a visual rhythm for the catchy rhyme." Kirkus

Katz, Bobbi

Nothing but a dog; illustrated by Jane Manning. Dutton Children's Books 2010 un il $16.99
Grades: PreK K 1 2   **E**
1. Dogs -- Fiction
ISBN 978-0-525-47858-4; 0-525-47858-2

LC 2009017918

"A young girl wishes for a dog while she engages in everyday activities, exclaiming that once the longing for a pup sets in, nothing stops it. Each page gives examples of other kinds of fun . . . but 'a dog is something else.' Subtle images of canines appear in the delightful watercolor illustrations. . . . This is a sweet addition to the child/pet genre." SLJ

Katz, Karen

How Does Baby Feel? A Karen Katz Lift-the-Flap Book. [Karen Katz] Simon & Schuster Merchandise 2013 14 p. $6.99
Grades: PreK K   **E**
1. Infants -- Fiction 2. Emotions in children 3. Picture books for children 4. Infants -- Fiction 5. Emotions -- Fiction 6. Board books -- Fiction 7. Lift-the-flap books -- Specimens 8. Toy and movable books -- Specimens 9. Emotions in infants -- Fiction 10. Lift-the-flap books -- Specimens -- Fiction
ISBN 1442452048; 9781442452046

LC 2012277019

In this book, "'Baby wants milk and crackers. How does baby feel?' Lift the picture of a toddler stretching for the goodies on the counter top of the facing page. Now she's in her high chair enjoying her repast under the word 'Hungry.' 'Baby is yawning. How does baby feel?' The little boy in the stroller is clearly 'Sleepy,' as evidenced by his contented snore as he snoozes beneath the picture flap." (Bulletin of the Center for Children's Literature)

My first Chinese New Year; [by] Karen Katz. H. Holt 2004 un il $14.95

Grades: PreK K   E

1. Chinese New Year -- Fiction 2. Chinese Americans -- Fiction

ISBN 0-8050-7076-1

LC 2003-23488

In this "picture book, a young girl prepares for and celebrates the Chinese New Year with her extended family. . . . The tale radiates warmth. . . . The collage illustrations, cut from paper with colorful Asian designs, also include paint and other media to capture the joyful celebrants." SLJ

My first Ramadan; [by] Karen Katz. Henry Holt & Co. 2007 un il $14.95

Grades: PreK K   E

1. Muslims -- Fiction 2. Ramadan -- Fiction

ISBN 978-0-8050-7894-7; 0-8050-7894-0

LC 2006030768

"A young Muslim boy describes the ways his family celebrates the holy month of Ramadan, explaining some of the rituals and symbols of the holiday. Straightforward, easy-to-read text and bright, friendly collage and mixed-media illustrations make this a solid, approachable resource." Horn Book Guide

Now I'm big; Karen Katz. Margaret K. McElderry Books 2013 32 p. (hardcover) $15.99

Grades: PreK   E

1. Babies -- Fiction 2. Growth -- Fiction

ISBN 9781416935476

LC 2011047256

In this picture book, "a multiracial cast of children who note ways they've grown up from babyhood to toddlers/preschoolers. 'I used to be a baby,' the first speaker begins, setting up a pattern: on each spread, the verso lists something the child did as a baby ('When I was a baby, I had to wear diapers') while the recto offers a contrasting ability of the older child ('NOW I'M BIG! I can wear real underpants and poo in the toilet')." (Bulletin of the Center for Children's Books)

Princess Baby; [by] Karen Katz. Schwartz & Wade Books 2008 un il $14.99; lib bdg $17.99

Grades: PreK   E

1. Nicknames -- Fiction 2. Princesses -- Fiction

ISBN 978-0-375-84119-4; 0-375-84119-9; 978-0-375-94119-1 lib bdg; 0-375-94119-3 lib bdg

LC 2007001913

A little girl does not like any of the nicknames her parents have for her she wants to be called by her "real" name, Princess Baby

"Katz has drawn the human and stuffed-animal characters with perfectly rounded heads, and she uses other softly curving lines in rendering motions. . . . The [predominant] color is fuchsia, while other bright hues complement the rosy tones. . . . Toddlers will ask for repeated readings of this cheerful view of a youngster's world." SLJ

Other titles about Princess Baby are:

Princess Baby, night-night (2009)

Princess Baby on the go! (2010)

Ten tiny babies; [by] Karen Katz. Margaret K. McElderry Books 2008 un il $14.99

Grades: PreK K 1   E

1. Counting 2. Stories in rhyme 3. Infants -- Fiction

ISBN 978-1-4169-3546-9; 1-4169-3546-0

LC 2007-36061

Babies from one to ten enjoy a bouncy, noisy, jiggly day until they are finally fast asleep at night

"The second half of every couplet is split by a page turn, providing a gentle tease that encourages readers to flip the page and complete the rhyme. Ideally suited for read-aloud in both cadence and content." Publ Wkly

Katz, Susan

ABC, baby me! by Susan B. Katz; illustrated by Alicia Padrón. Robin Corey Books 2010 un il bd bk $7.99

Grades: PreK   E

1. Alphabet 2. Board books for children 3. Infants -- Fiction

ISBN 978-0-375-86679-1 bd bk; 0-375-86679-5 bd bk

"This alphabet book is comprised of activities and actions that are presented from the perspective of several babies. For each letter, a simple scene features a child and caregiver from 'Adore me' to 'Zzzz, I'm fast asleep.' The soft-focus watercolor and pencil artwork is done in a predominately pastel palette. The text is simple with a lilting rhyme scheme that will encourge reading aloud." SLJ

Kat, Yukiko, 1936-

In the meadow; illustrated by Komako Sakai. Enchanted Lion Books 2011 un il $16.99

Grades: PreK   E

1. Sound -- Fiction 2. Nature -- Fiction 3. Meadows -- Fiction

ISBN 978-1-59270-108-7; 1-59270-108-6

LC 2010051988

A little girl named Yu hears the sounds of nature all around her when she follows a butterfly into a meadow.

This is illustrated with "expressionistic acrylic and oil-pencil illustrations in a palette of soft greens, browns, and blues. . . . With her fascination with nature and her first steps into independence and back again, Yu is a relatable, believable preschooler; and illustrator Sakai . . . eloquently captures the facial expressions and postures of the very young." Horn Book

Kaufman, Elliott, 1946-

Numbers everywhere; by Elliott Kaufman. 1st ed. Abbeville Kids 2013 32 p. (hardback) $12.95

Grades: PreK K 1   E

1. Numbers 2. Photography 3. Shape 4. Numbers in art 5. Mathematical notation 6. Photography of mathematical notation

ISBN 0789211572; 9780789211576

LC 2013027822

This book, by Elliott Kaufman, "reveals how digits and mathematical symbols can be found in the world around us--if we know how to look for them. Kaufman reveals the 'secret' life of numbers through his photographs, showing how they can be found in things we encounter everyday. Each number is represented by multiple images, unintentionally created by the intersection of architectural details, shadows, light, or natural elements." (Publisher's note)

Kay, Verla

Covered wagons, bumpy trails; illustrated by S.D. Schindler. Putnam 2000 un il $15.99

Grades: K 1 2 3   E

1. Stories in rhyme 2. Frontier and pioneer life -- Fiction 3. Overland journeys to the Pacific -- Fiction

ISBN 0-399-22928-0

LC 96-37478

Illustrations and simple rhyming text follow a family as they make the difficult journey by wagon to a new home across the Rocky Mountains

"Schindler handsomely augments the clip-clop rhyme with sweeping vistas and close-up views of the wagons, animals, and people through various stages of the journey." Horn Book Guide

Hornbooks and inkwells; illustrated by S.D. Schindler. G.P. Putnam's Sons 2011 32p il $16.99

Grades: PreK K   E

1. School stories 2. Stories in rhyme 3. Frontier and pioneer life -- Fiction

ISBN 978-0-399-23870-3; 0-399-23870-0

LC 2010-13070

John Paul and his older brother Peter spend a year attending a one-room schoolhouse on the frontier.

"In both text and illustrations, the light narrative element is engaging. . . . Schindler's well-composed watercolor-and-gouache paintings offer appealing glimpses of a period that seems distant while portraying the characters as individuals behaving in ways that are wholly recognizable." Booklist

Keane, Dave

Daddy Adventure Day; illustrated by Sue Ramá. Philomel Books 2011 un il $15.99

Grades: PreK K   E

1. Baseball -- Fiction 2. Father-son relationship -- Fiction

ISBN 978-0-399-24627-2; 0-399-24627-4

LC 2010024077

Daddy Adventure Days are always special, and this one, featuring a boy's first visit to a baseball stadium, is no exception.

"Ramá's watercolor and digital collage illustrations capture the warm relationship between the wide-eyed boy and his ever-patient dad. . . . A satisfying story about spending time with loved ones." SLJ

Sloppy Joe; illustrated by Denise Brunkus. Harper 2009 un il $16.99; lib bdg $17.89

Grades: PreK K 1 2   E

1. Cleanliness -- Fiction

ISBN 978-0-06-171020-9; 0-06-171020-2; 978-0-06-171021-6 lib bdg; 0-06-171021-0 lib bdg

LC 2008020212

Sloppy Joe determines to do everything he can to surprise his family by becoming Neat Joe.

"The illustrations are hilarious. This charming picture book is a wonderful choice for most libraries." SLJ

Who wants a tortoise? by Dave Keane; illustrated by K.G. Campbell. Alfred A. Knopf 2015 40 p. color illustrations (hardcover) $17.99

Grades: PreK K 1 2   E

1. Pets -- Fiction 2. Turtles -- Fiction 3. Birthdays -- Fiction 4. Turtles -- Fiction 5. Testudinidae -- Fiction

ISBN 9780385754170; 9780385754187

LC 2015007166

In this book, by Dave Keane, illustrated by K.G. Campbell, "when the spunky, loveable narrator receives a tortoise for her birthday, instead of the cuddly puppy she's longed for her entire life, she's more than a little disappointed. But while her new lump of a pet isn't what she dreamed of, it doesn't take long . . . for the little girl to change her mind—sort of. But when her pet goes missing, all she wants is to be reunited with her new best friend." (Publisher's note)

"Carefully tracing the emotional journey from disappointment to love, Keane and Campbell allow readers wrestling with their own frustrations to imagine what change feels like." Pub Wkly

Kearney, Meg

Trouper; by Meg Kearney; illustrated by E. B. Lewis. Scholastic Press 2013 32 p. (hardcover : alk. paper) $16.99

Grades: K 1 2 3   E

1. Dogs -- Fiction 2. Animal shelters -- Fiction 3. Novels in verse

4. Feral dogs -- Fiction 5. Pet adoption -- Fiction

ISBN 0545100410; 9780545100410

LC 2012015730

This book, by Meg Kearney and illustrated by E. B. Lewis, is the "story of a three-legged stray dog who finds a loving boy to call his own. . . . Trouper ran with a mob of mutts. . . . One day, the dogs are captured from off the streets and put in cages in a shelter as they wait to be adopted. Trouper watches . . . as . . . each of his dog friends are chosen. He's the only one left until finally, one lucky day, just the right boy comes around." (Publisher's note)

"This tender story, sensitively illustrated by Lewis's luminous watercolors, is based on the true story of a rescued dog. Trouper himself narrates in free verse, telling of his life on the street and his desolate days and nights in the pound until he's adopted by a gentle boy who is as "skinny as a string bean." It's all quite heartwarming." (Horn Book)

Keats, Ezra Jack

Apt. 3. Viking 1999 un il hardcover o.p. pa $6.99

Grades: PreK K 1 2   E

1. Blind -- Fiction 2. Brothers -- Fiction 3. City and town life -- Fiction

ISBN 0-670-88342-5; 0-14-056507-8 pa

LC 98-41043

A reissue of the title first published 1971 by Macmillan

On a rainy day two brothers try to discover who is playing the harmonica they hear in their apartment building

"The well-paced text is illustrated with shadowy paintings that capably convey both the dingy surroundings and the brothers' affection." Horn Book Guide

Hi, cat! Viking 1999 un il $15.99

Grades: PreK K 1 2   E

1. Cats -- Fiction 2. African Americans -- Fiction

ISBN 0-670-88546-0

LC 98-37764

A reissue of the title first published 1970 by Macmillan

This book "tells the story of Peter's friend Archie and the inquisitive, nondescript, half-grown alley cat that tags after him and manages to make a shambles out of the boys' street carnival. The text provides an adequate framework for Keats's bold bright paintings of a lively city neighborhood." Horn Book Guide

Another title about Archie is:

Pet show! (1972)

Louie. Viking 2004 un il pa $6.99

Grades: PreK K 1 2   E

1. Puppets and puppet plays -- Fiction

ISBN 978-0-14-240080-7 pa; 0-14-240080-7 pa

LC 2003-11378

First published 1975 by Greenwillow Books

Susie and Roberto's puppet show is temporarily interrupted when Louis becomes fascinated by one of the puppets

"This story is illustrated with the same glowing colors . . . and with some of the postercollage that is the artist's trademark. The aura is touching without being maudlin, the writing simple and informal." Sutherland. The Best in Child Books

Other titles about Louie are:

Louie's search (1980)

Regards to the man in the moon (1981)

The trip (1978)

★ **Over** in the meadow; [written and] illustrated by Ezra Jack Keats. Viking 1999 un il $16.99; pa $6.99

Grades: PreK K 1 2   E
1. Counting 2. Nursery rhymes 3. Animals -- Poetry
ISBN 0-670-88344-1; 0-14-056508-6 pa

LC 98-47037

A reissue of the title first published 1971 by Four Winds Press
An old nursery poem introduces animals and their young and the
numbers one through ten
"The book features Keats's illustrations that show animals in lively
characteristic activity." Horn Book Guide

★ The **snowy** day. Viking 1962 31p il lib bdg $16.99; pa
$5.99; bd bk $6.99
Grades: PreK K 1 2   E
1. Snow -- Fiction
ISBN 0-670-65400-0 lib bdg; 0-14-050182-7 pa; 0-670-86733-0
bd bk
Awarded the Caldecott Medal, 1963
A small "boy's ecstatic enjoyment of snow in the city is shown in
vibrant pictures. Peter listens to the snow crunch under his feet, makes
the first tracks in a clean patch of snow, makes angels and a snowman.
At night in his warm bed he thinks over his adventures, and in the morn-
ing wakens to the promise of another lovely snowy day." Moorachian.
What is a City?
Other titles about Peter are:
Goggles (1969)
A letter to Amy (1968)
Peter's chair (1967)
Whistle for Willie (1964)

Keller, Holly
★ **Geraldine's** blanket. Greenwillow Bks. 1984 un il hardcover
o.p. pa $5.99
Grades: PreK K 1 2   E
1. Blankets -- Fiction
ISBN 0-688-07810-9 pa

LC 83-14062

"Simply but wonderfully expressive line drawings washed with pas-
tel colors capture the gentleness and humor of the story." SLJ
Other titles about Geraldine are:
Geraldine and Mrs. Duffy (2000)
Geraldine first (1996)
Geraldine's baby brother (1994)
Geraldine's big snow (1988)
Merry Christmas, Geraldine (1997)

Grandfather's dream. Greenwillow Bks. 1994 un il $16.99
Grades: PreK K 1 2   E
1. Vietnam -- Fiction 2. Grandfathers -- Fiction 3. Cranes (Birds)
-- Fiction
ISBN 0-688-12339-2

LC 93-18186

After the end of the war in Vietnam, a young boy's grandfather
dreams of restoring the wetlands of the Mekong delta, hoping that the
large cranes that once lived there will return
"Keller uses simple, direct storytelling and vivid watercolor and ink
illustrations to present a complex theme in a story of hope and rebirth."
Horn Book Guide

★ **Help!** a story of friendship. Greenwillow Books 2007 un il
$16.99; lib bdg $17.89

Grades: PreK K 1 2   E
1. Fear -- Fiction 2. Animals -- Fiction 3. Friendship -- Fiction
ISBN 978-0-06-123913-7; 0-06-123913-5; 978-0-06-123914-4
lib bdg; 0-06-123914-3 lib bdg

LC 2006-32116

Mouse hears a rumor that snakes do not like mice and while trying
to avoid his former friend, Snake, he falls into a hole from which neither
Hedgehog, Squirrel, nor Rabbit can help him out
"This story has the simplicity of a fable. The appealing art is done in
collographs, which are printed collages, and watercolors." SLJ

Miranda's beach day. Greenwillow Books 2009 un il $17.99;
lib bdg $18.89
Grades: PreK K   E
1. Beaches -- Fiction 2. Mother-daughter relationship -- Fiction
ISBN 978-0-06-158298-1; 0-06-158298-0; 978-0-06-158300-1
lib bdg; 0-06-158300-6 lib bdg

LC 2008012645

Miranda and Mama spend a fun day at the beach building castles and
catching sand crabs, and Miranda learns that just like the sand and the
sea, she and her mother will always be together
"Attractive illustrations in watercolors and printed collages on well-
designed spreads capture the children's activities and the vastness of
sand and sea. This is a disarmingly simple and reassuring selection." SLJ

Nosy Rosie; [by] Holly Keller. Greenwillow Books 2006 un il
$16.99; lib bdg $17.89
Grades: PreK K 1 2   E
1. Foxes -- Fiction 2. Smell -- Fiction 3. Personal names -- Fiction
ISBN 978-0-06-078758-5; 0-06-078758-9; 978-0-06-078759-2
lib bdg; 0-06-078759-7 lib bdg

LC 2005022183

Rosie the fox's excellent sense of smell is good for finding things,
but she stops using it after everyone begins to call her "Nosy Rosie"
"Keller takes on the subject of name calling in a gentle, simple, and
compassionate manner. . . . The heartfelt dialogue poignantly conveys
the little fox's hurt feelings and reads aloud perfectly. The colorful mixture of robust watercolors and simple black lines touchingly reveals each
character's attitude through expressive body movement." SLJ

Pearl's new skates. Greenwillow Books 2005 24p il $15.99
Grades: PreK K 1 2   E
1. Ice skating -- Fiction
ISBN 0-06-056280-3

LC 2004-576

Pearl's birthday skates have a single blade and learning to use them
is harder than she expects
"With her pitch-perfect text and uncluttered watercolor-and-ink pictures . . . Keller tells a tender story about accepting the failures and
frustrations that come with learning something new." Booklist

Keller, Laurie
Arnie the doughnut; cooked up by Laurie Keller. 1st ed; Henry
Holt 2003 1 v (unpaged) col il E
1. Doughnuts
ISBN 0-8050-6283-1 (alk. paper)

LC 2002-4357

Arnie the talking doughnut convinces Mr. Bing that not all doughnuts are meant to be eaten

★ **Do** unto otters; (a book about manners) by Laurie Keller. Henry
Holt 2007 un il $16.95

Grades: PreK K 1 2   E

    1. Otters -- Fiction 2. Rabbits -- Fiction 3. Etiquette -- Fiction
    ISBN 978-0-8050-7996-8; 0-8050-7996-3

LC 2006030505

Mr. Rabbit wonders if he will be able to get along with his new neighbors, who are otters, until he is reminded of the golden rule

"From the gleeful title pun to the kenetic illustrations, this clever book . . . introduces the golden rule with irresistible humor." Booklist

The **scrambled** states of America talent show. Henry Holt 2008 un il $16.95

Grades: PreK K 1 2   E

    1. United States -- Fiction
    ISBN 978-0-8050-7997-5; 0-8050-7997-1

LC 2007-40907

The states decide to get together and put on a show featuring their particular talents. Also includes facts about the history and geography of the states.

"The snappy dialogue flows effortlessly, the personalities are as winning as ever, and the pictures' energy never flags. It's e pluribus boffo." Publ Wkly

Kelley, Ellen A.

My life as a chicken; as told to Ellen A. Kelley; pictures by Michael Slack. Harcourt, Inc. 2007 un il $16

Grades: PreK K 1 2   E

    1. Stories in rhyme 2. Chickens -- Fiction
    ISBN 0-15-205306-2; 978-0-15-205306-2

LC 2005020051

After escaping the frying pan, Pauline the chicken has an adventure that includes pirates, a typhoon, and a balloon ride before landing happily in a petting zoo.

"Slack's digital mixed-media illustrations are wacky and cartoonish, and the text ripples with big, impressive words befitting the exaggerated nature of Pauline's adventures." SLJ

Kelley, Marty

Almost everybody farts; written and illustrated by Marty Kelley. Sterling Children's Books 2017 32 p. color illustrations $12.95

    Grades: PreK K 1 2   E

    1. Flatulence -- Fiction 2. Humorous fiction -- Fiction 3. Humorous stories 4. Stories in rhyme 5. Flatulence -- Fiction
    ISBN 9781454919544

LC 2016035334

This book, by Marty Kelley, "looks at a subject that's sure to make children laugh: farting. With silent farts, farts like horns, and rainbow farts from unicorns, [this book] comically captures the gassy scene." (Publisher's note)

★ **Twelve** terrible things. Tricycle Press 2008 un il $15.99

Grades: 1 2 3 4   E

    1. Courage -- Fiction 2. Monsters -- Fiction
    ISBN 978-1-58246-229-5; 1-58246-229-1

LC 2007-46795

Grownups who wax nostalgic about their youth are given a visual tour through twelve terrible experiences of childhood, including bedtime monsters and "atomic wedgies."

"Realistic, double-page watercolor illustrations use a clever first-person perspective to render readers the victims of horrors such as a cheek-pinching lady, an over-the-top birthday clown, and a hairy-moled lunch lady. . . . Minimal text and detailed artwork combine to convey a macabre humor that is bound to ensnare even the most hesitant of readers." SLJ

Kelley, True

Dog who saved Santa. Holiday House 2008 un il $16.95

Grades: PreK K 1 2   E

    1. Dogs -- Fiction 2. Christmas -- Fiction 3. Santa Claus -- Fiction
    ISBN 978-0-8234-2120-6; 0-8234-2120-1

LC 2007-041180

With the help of his take-charge dog Rodney and a self-help video, young Santa Claus mends his lazy and irresponsible ways.

"The cartoon artwork, done in acrylic, watercolors, and colored pencils, captures the endearing pup's antics and will give readers the giggles." SLJ

Kellogg, Steven

★ **Best** friends; story and pictures by Steven Kellogg. Dial Bks. for Young Readers 1986 un il $16.99; pa $6.99

Grades: PreK K 1 2   E

    1. Friendship -- Fiction
    ISBN 0-8037-0099-7; 0-14-054607-3 pa

LC 85-15971

Kathy feels lonely and betrayed when her best friend Louise goes away for the summer and has a wonderful time

"The watercolor and ink illustrations are appealingly bright and magical. Kathy and Louise's daydreams are vividly and flamboyantly portrayed, with 'reality' just as attractively pictured." SLJ

★ The **missing** mitten mystery; story and pictures by Steven Kellogg. Dial Bks. for Young Readers 2000 un il $15.99; pa $6.99

Grades: PreK K 1 2   E

    1. Lost and found possessions -- Fiction
    ISBN 0-8037-2566-3; 0-14-230192-2 pa

LC 99-54777

First published 1974 with title: The mystery of the missing red mitten

Annie searches the neighborhood for her red mitten, the fifth she's lost this winter

"Kellogg really outdoes himself with pictures that are filled with good cheer, warm spirits, and happy daydreams. . . . A book that's upbeat and touching by turns." Booklist

★ The **mysterious** tadpole; new illustrations and text by Steven Kellogg. 25th anniversary ed; Dial Bks. for Young Readers 2002 un il $16.99; pa $6.99

Grades: PreK K 1 2   E

    1. Pets -- Fiction
    ISBN 0-8037-2788-7; 0-14-240140-4 pa

LC 2001-53776

First published 1977

"Louis receives a birthday present from his uncle in Scotland: Alphonse, an amiable tadpole that outgrows his bowl, the bathtub, and even the apartment. . . . The new illustrations are bigger, bolder, brighter, and brimming with lively details." Booklist

The **Pied** Piper's magic. Dial Books for Young Readers 2009 un il $16.99

Grades: PreK K 1   E

    1. Fairy tales 2. Rats -- Fiction 3. Magic -- Fiction
    ISBN 978-0-8037-2818-9; 0-8037-2818-2

LC 2008-12267

In a story loosely based on The Pied Piper of Hamelin, an elf acquires from a miserable witch a magic pipe that allows him to transform things, including the mean-spirited Grand Duke who rules over a rat-infested town.

"Kellogg depicts the magic-making in bright, buoyant mixed media spreads that show streams of colorful text and corresponding animals pouring from the mouth of the pipe. . . . Far sunnier than the original, this slightly educational adaptation (thanks to the built-in spelling lessons within) should please parents and kids alike." Publ Wkly

★ **Pinkerton,** behave! story and pictures by Steven Kellogg. Dial Books for Young Readers 2002 un il $17.99; pa $6.99
Grades: PreK K 1 2   E
    1. Dogs -- Fiction
    ISBN 0-8037-2722-4; 0-14-230007-1 pa
A reissue of the title first published 1979
"Kellogg wittily captures expressions and movements of animal and human, wisely allowing the focal humor to emanate through the faces and action." Booklist
    Other titles about Pinkerton are:
    A penguin pup for Pinkerton (2001)
    Prehistoric Pinkerton (1987)
    A Rose for Pinkerton (1981)
    Tallyho, Pinkerton (1982)

Kelly, Mij
    Where giants hide; illustrated by Ross Collins. Sourcebooks/Jabberwocky 2010 un il
Grades: PreK K 1 2   E
    1. Imagination -- Fiction 2. Voyages and travels -- Fiction
    ISBN 1-4022-4270-0; 978-1-4022-4270-0
"A girl, convinced that all the world's magic has leaked away, is sad because she can't find any giants, fairies, goblins, unicorns, dragons, or genies. . . . By reading the pictures, young children will enjoy the visual joke and find satisfaction in figuring out the mismatch between the girl's narration and what is actually happening. The whimsical, detailed illustrations, dominated by bright red, yellow, and turquoise, add humor and capture the subtle message of the story" SLJ

Kelly, Sheila M.
    Yummy! good food makes me strong. by Shelley Rotner and Sheila M. Kelly; photographs by Shelley Rotner. Holiday House 2013 32 p. col. ill. (reinforced) $16.95
Grades: 1 2 3   E
    1. Food 2. Children -- Nutrition 3. Nutrition
    ISBN 082342426X; 9780823424269
                         LC 2012016564
This book by Shelley Rotner presents "color photos of children eating nourishing foods with enjoyment and helping to prepare them. The youngsters are shown in various indoor and outdoor settings, sometimes displaying brightly colored fruits and vegetables. Throughout, text boxes with nutrition tips are clearly meant for adults. The end page includes a handful of additional recommendations . . . and a ChooseMyPlate.gov diagram." (School Library Journal)

Kelsey, Elin
    You are stardust; Elin Kelsey, Soyeon Kim. Owlkids Books 2012 32 p. $18.95
Grades: K 1 2 3 4 5   E
    1. Nature 2. Human beings
    ISBN 1926973356; 9781926973357
                         LC 2011943505
This book by Elin Kelsey, illustrated by Soyeon Kim, "begins by introducing the idea that every tiny atom in our bodies came from a star that exploded long before we were born. From its opening pages, the book suggests that we are intimately connected to the natural world; it compares the way we learn to speak to the way baby birds learn to sing, and the growth of human bodies to the growth of forests." (Publisher's note)

Kempter, Christa
    Wally and Mae; by Christa Kempter; illustrated by Frauke Weldin. North-South 2008 un il $16.95
Grades: PreK K 1 2   E
    1. Bears -- Fiction 2. Rabbits -- Fiction 3. Friendship -- Fiction
    ISBN 978-0-7358-2208-5; 0-7358-2208-5
"A capricious bear named Mae befriends a sensible rabbit named Wally, and this unlikely pair shares an idyllic cottage in the woods. . . . Both of the animals are depicted with tenderness. The colors are bright and many of the scenes show one or both of the characters in full action." SLJ

    When Mama can't sleep; illustrated by Natascha Rosenberg. NorthSouth Books 2011 un il (Tuff books) $6.95
Grades: PreK   E
    1. Bedtime -- Fiction 2. Family life -- Fiction
    ISBN 978-0-7358-4015-7; 0-7358-4015-6
When worries keep Mama, Papa, and Max awake, they crawl into bed together with Max's teddy bear for comfort.
"The vibrant speads are filled with color, and the heavy, glossy paper will withstand toddler destruction. Comforting, soothing, and sure to be a hit." SLJ

Kenah, Katharine
    The **best** seat in second grade; story by Katharine Kenah; pictures by Abby Carter. HarperCollins Pubs. 2005 48p il (I can read book) $15.99; lib bdg $16.89; pa $3.99
Grades: K 1 2   E
    1. School stories 2. Hamsters -- Fiction
    ISBN 0-06-000734-6; 0-06-000735-4 lib bdg; 0-06-000736-2 pa
                         LC 2004-178
Sam's favorite thing about second grade is the class pet, a hamster named George Washington, so when the class goes on a field trip to a science museum, Sam cannot resist bringing George along
"Kenah has created an appealing cast of characters whose actions ring true. . . . Carter's watercolor illustrations add to the story's appeal." Booklist
    Other titles about this second grade are:
    The best teacher in second grade (2006)
    The best chef in second grade (2007)

Kennedy, Anne Vittur
    The **Farmer's** away! baa! neigh! Anne Vittur Kennedy. Candlewick Press 2014 32 p. color illustrations $15.99
Grades: PreK K 1   E
    1. Farms -- Fiction 2. Farm life -- Fiction 3. Domestic animals -- Fiction
    ISBN 0763666793; 9780763666798
                         LC 2013946622
This book, by Anne Vittur Kennedy, explores "what mischief . . . the animals get up to when the farmer's back is turned. . . . Kennedy lets us know in the animals' own words! There will be boating, of course, and a picnic, a rollercoaster ride, Jet Skiing, a hot-air balloon, ballroom dancing." (Publisher's note)
"Babies, toddlers and very young emergent readers will delight in the strong, playful rhythm and energetic and detailed illustrations in this introduction to the noisy world of animal sounds." Kirkus

    Ragweed's farm dog handbook; by Anne Vittur Kennedy. Candlewick Press 2015 32 p. color illustrations $15.99
Grades: PreK K 1   E
    1. Dogs -- Fiction 2. Farm life -- Fiction
    ISBN 0763674176; 9780763674175
                         LC 2014953086

This book, by Anne Vittur Kennedy, is a "tongue-in-cheek primer on how to be a good farm dog.... Being a farm dog is a tough job, but luckily, Ragweed's handbook will tell you everything you need to know. Step one: don't wake the farmer! You may really, really want to, but that's the rooster's job. Of course, if you do wake the farmer, you might just get a biscuit." (Publisher's note)

"This pup's irrepressible energy will win over plenty of readers and give them a fun look at life on a farm." SLJ

Kent, Jack

There's no such thing as a dragon. Golden Book 2005 un il hardcover o.p. pa $6.99

Grades: PreK K 1 2   E

1. Dragons -- Fiction

ISBN 0-375-83208-4; 0-375-85137-2 pa

LC 2004-6123

First published 1975 by Western Pub.

"When Billy Bixbee wakes up and finds a dragon in his room, his mother tells him there is no such thing. The neglected dragon grows larger and larger, eventually walking off with the house, and the Bixbee family is forced to admit his existence. Practically a classic... for its neat story line and humorous cartoons of expressively surprised characters." Horn Book Guide

Kerascoët (Illustrator)

Paul & Antoinette; Kerascoët, translated by Claudia Zoe Bedrick. Enchanted Lion Books 2016 40 p. color illustrations $17.95

Grades: PreK K 1 2 3   E

1. Pigs -- Fiction 2. Hygiene-- Fiction 3. Siblings -- Fiction 4. Orderliness -- Fiction

ISBN 1592701965; 9781592701964

In this children's book, by Kerascoët, translated by Claudia Zoe Bedrick, "Piggy siblings Paul and Antoinette get along well and are respectful of their dissimilarities. Antoinette likes her toast with jam and chocolate and offers to make some for Paul. He prefers just butter on his toast. Paul likes things to be clean and neat, and his sister likes to clear the table and lick the plates.... They are so different yet still take pleasure in each other's company." (Publisher's note)

"It's a gently funny and emotionally observant portrait of the rewards of spending time with people who aren't just carbon copies of yourself." Pub Wkly

Kerby, Mona

★ **Owney,** the mail-pouch pooch; pictures by Lynne Barasch. Farrar, Straus and Giroux 2008 un il $16.95

Grades: K 1 2 3   E

1. Dogs -- Fiction 2. Postal service -- Fiction 3. Voyages and travels -- Fiction

ISBN 0-374-35685-8; 978-0-374-35685-9

LC 2006-47605

In 1888, Owney, a stray terrier puppy, finds a home in the Albany, New York, post office and becomes its official mascot as he rides the mail train through the Adirondacks and beyond, criss-crossing the United States, into Canada and Mexico, and eventually traveling around the world by mail boat in 132 days.

"The author does an excellent job of introducing readers to the late-19th century and the system used by the postal service to send mail both nationally and internationally via horse-pulled wagons, trains, and steamships.... Barasch's ink and watercolor illustrations complement the narrative with period details. A pair of sepia-toned photographs at the end of the book adds to the authenticity of the tale." SLJ

Another title about Owney is:

The further adventures of a lucky dog: Owney, U.S. rail mail mascot (2009)

Kerley, Barbara

You and me together; moms, dads, and kids around the world. with a note by Marian Wright Edelman. National Geographic 2005 32p il $16.95; lib bdg $25.90

Grades: PreK K 1 2   E

1. Parent-child relationship

ISBN 0-7922-8297-3; 0-7922-8298-1 lib bdg

"Using a simple rhyming text, Kerley captures the essence of childhood's special moments, accompanied by superb full-color photos.... Diverse cultures in various locations around the world are represented. ... Children and parents engage in activities such as playing an instrument, taking a walk, making a meal, fishing, and dancing.... This book is an excellent tool for raising awareness of cultural differences and similarities." SLJ

Kerr, Judith

One night in the zoo. Kane Miller 2010 un il $15.99

Grades: PreK K   E

1. Counting 2. Stories in rhyme 3. Children's poetry 4. Zoos -- Fiction 5. Magic -- Fiction 6. Animals -- Fiction

ISBN 978-1-935279-37-2; 1-935279-37-8

One magical night an elephant jumped in the air and flew. Wild antics, high spirits and silly games of the other zoo animals also occur. Will anyone find out?

"Kerr's softly shaded pencil drawings depict the beasts and birds with all the charm of friendly animal characters come to life. Fresh and simple." Booklist

Kessler, Cristina

The **best** beekeeper of Lalibela; a tale from Africa. by Cristina Kessler; illustrated by Leonard Jenkins. Holiday House 2006 un il $16.95

Grades: K 1 2 3   E

1. Ethiopia -- Fiction 2. Sex role -- Fiction 3. Beekeeping -- Fiction

ISBN 978-0-8234-1858-9; 0-8234-1858-8

LC 2005046217

In the Ethiopian mountain village of Lalibela a young girl named Almaz determines to find a way to be a beekeeper despite being told that is something only men can do

"Jenkins follows the ups and downs of Almaz's labor in deep-hued, mixed-media scenes spread richly across double pages.... Kessler includes well-chosen details about the beekeeping project and a few words from the local Amharic and Tigringna languages." SLJ

Kessler, Leonard P.

★ **Here** comes the strikeout; newly il ed.; HarperCollins Pubs. 1992 64p il (I can read book) hardcover o.p. pa $3.99

Grades: K 1 2   E

1. Baseball -- Fiction

ISBN 0-06-023156-4; 0-06-444011-7 pa

LC 91-14717

A revised and newly illustrated edition of the title first published 1965

This "concerns a boy who can't hit a baseball until he follows the advice of a friend. 'Lucky helmets won't do it. Lucky bats won't do it. Only hard work will do it.'... A winner." Booklist

★ **Kick,** pass, and run; story and pictures by Leonard Kessler. newly il ed; HarperCollins Pubs. 1996 64p il (I can read book) hardcover o.p. pa $3.99

Grades: K 1 2   E

1. Football -- Fiction

ISBN 0-06-027105-1; 0-06-444210-1 pa

LC 95-6185

A newly illustrated edition of the title first published 1966

"After a group of animal friends watches a boys' football team play, they are eager to have their own game. An apple serves as a ball until Frog eats it; a paper-bag football works until Duck kicks and pops it. The game is kept alive when a real football from the boys' game sails into the animals' midst. [A] simply told story with plenty of sports action." Horn Book Guide

★ **Last** one in is a rotten egg; newly il ed; HarperCollins Pubs. 1999 64p il (I can read book) hardcover o.p. pa $3.99

Grades: K 1 2   E

1. Swimming -- Fiction

ISBN 0-06-028485-4; 0-06-444262-4 pa

LC 98-50882

A newly illustrated edition of the title first published 1969

After Freddy is pushed into deep water by a couple of toughs, he decides to learn to swim

"This lively . . . sports story has been newly illustrated with a multi-cultural cast in a New York City neighborhood." Booklist

Ketteman, Helen

Goodnight, Little Monster; illustrated by Bonnie Leick. Marshall Cavendish 2010 un il $16.99

Grades: PreK K   E

1. Stories in rhyme 2. Bedtime -- Fiction 3. Monsters -- Fiction 4. Mother-child relationship -- Fiction

ISBN 978-0-7614-5683-4; 0-7614-5683-X

LC 2009002185

Rhyming text describes a mother guiding her young monster through bedtime preparations, such as howling at the moon, snacking on worm juice and beetle bread, and choosing a bedtime story.

"While the text is quite fun to read, it is the watercolor illustrations that steal the show. Each page is filled with kid-friendly monster details." SLJ

Swamp song; illustrated by Ponder Goembel. Marshall Cavendish Children 2009 un il $17.99

Grades: PreK K 1 2   E

1. Stories in rhyme 2. Animals -- Fiction 3. Marshes -- Fiction

ISBN 978-0-7614-5563-9; 0-7614-5563-9

LC 2008013810

Down in the swamp where the cypress grows, the animals all come out to enjoy the day.

"The sunny illustrations are done with colored ink lines and acrylic wash paint against mostly white backgrounds. . . . Children will be tapping their toes with Old Man Gator and creating their own cacophony of swamp sounds as they learn about the inhabitants of this habitat." SLJ

The **three** little gators; illustrated by Will Terry. Albert Whitman 2009 un il $16.99

Grades: K 1 2 3   E

1. Folklore 2. Alligators -- Folklore

ISBN 978-0-8075-7824-7; 0-8075-7824-X

LC 2008028085

In this adaptation of the traditional folktale, three little gators each build their house in an east Texas swamp, hoping for protection from the Big-bottomed Boar.

"Ketteman's retelling, including a sassy Texas twang, makes the story hilarious and bright. . . . Terry's illustrations work well with the story. The colors are vibrant yet ominous and swampy." SLJ

Khan, Hena

★ **Night** of the Moon; a Muslim holiday story. illustrated by Julie Paschkis. Chronicle Books 2008 un il $16.99

Grades: PreK K 1 2   E

1. Islam -- Fiction 2. Muslims -- Fiction 3. Ramadan -- Fiction 4. Id al-Adha -- Fiction 5. Pakistani Americans -- Fiction

ISBN 978-0-8118-6062-8; 0-8118-6062-0

LC 2007024962

"A new moon is in the sky, and Yasmeen, identified on the jacket as a seven-year-old Pakistani-American, knows that it is time for the holidays of Ramadan and Eid. . . . Paschkis, borrowing from the arabesque motifs and jeweled colors of Islamic art, portrays the Muslim community as warm, welcoming and multiethnic. . . . Sweet and visually striking, this is a good choice both for children who celebrate these holidays and for others seeking a bridge to their culture." Publ Wkly

Khan, Rukhsana

★ **Big** red lollipop; illustrated by Sophie Blackall. Viking 2010 un il lib bdg $16.99

Grades: PreK K 1 2   E

1. Parties -- Fiction 2. Sisters -- Fiction 3. Birthdays -- Fiction 4. Pakistani Americans -- Fiction

ISBN 978-0-670-06287-4 lib bdg; 0-670-06287-1 lib bdg

LC 2009-22676

"Khan is of Pakistani descent, and this tale of clashing cultural customs is based on an incident from her childhood. The story (and its lesson) comes to like in Blackall's spot-on illustrations. . . . This is an honest, even moving, commentary on sisterly relationships." Booklist

★ **King** for a day; by Rukhsana Khan; illustrations by Christiane Krömer. Lee & Low Books, Inc. 2013 32 p. (hardcover : alk. paper) $17.95

Grades: PreK K 1 2   E

1. Kites -- Fiction 2. Picture books for children 3. Pakistan -- Fiction 4. Wheelchairs -- Fiction 5. Basant Festival -- Fiction 6. People with disabilities -- Fiction

ISBN 1600606598; 9781600606595

LC 2013007506

This children's picture book, set in Pakistan during Basant, "focuses on the strength and resourcefulness of a child in a wheelchair as he navigates the skies at the spring kite festival. Perched on the rooftop and assisted by his brother and sister, Malik launches his small but swift creation, named Falcon, into the stratosphere, where it defeats both of the kites that belong to the bully next door." (Kirkus Reviews)

★ **Silly** chicken; illustrated by Yunmee Kyong. Viking 2005 un il $15.99

Grades: K 1 2 3   E

1. Chickens -- Fiction 2. Pakistan -- Fiction

ISBN 0-670-05912-9

LC 2004-15830

In Pakistan, Rani believes that her mother loves their pet chicken Bibi more than she cares for her, until the day that a fluffy chick appears and steals Rani's own affections.

"This picture book clearly depicts a child's jealousy. . . . Kyong . . . paints in a naive style, using fresh, warm colors. A pleasing book with an unusual setting." Booklist

Kherdian, David

Come back, Moon; by David Kherdian; illustrated by Nonny Hogrogian. Beach Lane Books 2013 32 p. (hardcover) $16.99

Grades: PreK K 1 2   E

1. Moon -- Fiction 2. Picture books for children 3. Bears -- Fiction 4. Forest animals -- Fiction

ISBN 1442458879; 9781442458871

LC 2012037038

In this children's picture book, Bear can't sleep and blames the moon. "He steals it and stuffs it into his pillowcase. Other animals Fox, Skunk, Opossum and Raccoon miss the moon and speculate as to its whereabouts." When they realize Bear has it. "Crow tells Bear a slumber-inducing story, then he and Fox snatch the pillowcase and release the moon." (Kirkus Reviews)

Killen, Nicola

Not me! Egmont USA 2010 un il $13.99
Grades: PreK K 1   E
1. Cleanliness -- Fiction
ISBN 978-1-4052-4829-7; 1-4052-4829-7

Not one member of a group of friends admits to having made a big mess, or offers to pitch in to clean it up.

"The illustrations and typeface will melt hearts and delight and inspire potato-printing young readers. The simple, expressive shapes, mostly in muted tones with dapples of red to keep things cheery, are utterly fresh and warm, and the textures feel organic. Children will delight in this sweet-natured picture book." SLJ

Kim, Patti, 1970-

Here I am; by Patti Kim and illustrated by Sonia Sanchez. Capstone 2013 40 p. $14.95
Grades: 1 2 3   E
1. Picture books for children 2. Immigrants -- United States -- Fiction
ISBN 1623700361; 9781404882997; 9781479519316; 9781479519323; 9781623700362
LC 2012051009

In this book by Patti Kim and illustrated by Sonia Sanchez, "newly arrived from their faraway homeland, a boy and his family enter into the lights, noise, and traffic of a busy American city. The language is unfamiliar. Food, habits, games, and gestures are puzzling. They boy clings tightly to his special keepsake from home and wonders how he will find his way. How will he once again become the happy, confident kid he used to be?" (Publisher's note)

Kimmel, Elizabeth Cody

Glamsters; written by Elizabeth Cody Kimmel; illustrated by Jackie Urbanovic. Hyperion Books for Children 2008 un il $16.99
Grades: K 1 2   E
1. Hamsters -- Fiction
ISBN 978-1-4231-1148-1; 1-4231-1148-6
LC 2008029692

Harriet the hamster is desperate to be adopted, so she gives her sister Patricia and herself glamorous makeovers in hopes they will get more attention when Hamster World has its huge annual sale

"The story is filled with clever details and laugh-out-loud humor, but the underlying message of self-acceptance is an important one for children to hear." SLJ

My penguin Osbert; illustrated by H. B. Lewis. Candlewick Press 2004 un il $16.99; pa $6.99
Grades: PreK K 1 2   E
1. Penguins -- Fiction 2. Christmas -- Fiction
ISBN 0-7636-1699-0; 0-7636-5730-1 pa
LC 2003-40981

When a boy finally gets exactly what he wants from Santa, he learns that owning a real penguin may not have been a good idea after all

"Kimmel sneaks some sly humor into the well-told, nicely paced story, and Lewis' artwork, executed in watercolor and pastels and enhanced with digital renderings, has a soft look, colored in marshmallow tints." Booklist

Another title about Osbert the penguin is:

My penguin Osbert in love (2009)

The **top** job; by Elizabeth Cody Kimmel; illustrated by Robert Neubecker. Dutton Children's Books 2007 un il $16.99; pa $6.99
Grades: K 1 2 3   E
1. Occupations -- Fiction 2. New York (N.Y.) -- Fiction 3. Father-daughter relationship -- Fiction 4. Empire State Building (New York, N.Y.) -- Fiction
ISBN 978-0-525-47789-1; 0-525-47789-6; 978-0-14-241424-8 pa; 0-14-241424-7 pa
LC 2006039770

On Career Day, a young girl entertains the class with a description of her father's exciting job as light bulb changer at the top of the Empire State Building.

"The pacing and rhythm of the text is impeccable. . . . The stylized, cartoon-style illustrations, rendered in clear colors and bold black outlines, nicely extend the plot." Booklist

Kimmel, Eric A.

★ The **Golem's** latkes; adapted by Eric A. Kimmel; illustrated by Aaron Jasinski. Marshall Cavendish Children 2011 un il $17.99
Grades: K 1 2   E
1. Rabbis 2. Jews -- Fiction 3. Hanukkah -- Fiction 4. Czech Republic -- Fiction 5. Household employees -- Fiction 6. Prague (Czech Republic) -- Fiction
ISBN 978-0-7614-5904-0; 0-7614-5904-9
LC 2010020008

Rabbi Judah Loew ben Bezalel visits the Emperor, leaving a new housemaid to prepare for his Hanukkah party, but returns to find that she has misused the clay man he created. Includes historical and cultural notes.

"Kimmel's storytelling is effective in its use of suspense, humor, trope and repetition, making a fine read-aloud holiday treat." Kirkus

★ **Hershel** and the Hanukkah Goblins; written by Eric A. Kimmel; illustrated by Trina Schart Hyman. 25th anniversary edition Holiday House 2014 32 p. color illustrations (hardcover) $17.95
Grades: K 1 2 3   E
1. Goblins -- Fiction 2. Hanukkah -- Fiction 3. Jews -- Fiction 4. Jews -- Folklore 5. Fairies -- Fiction
ISBN 0823431649; 9780823431649
LC 2013048854

Originally published 1985

This book, by Eric A. Kimmel and illustrated by Trina Schart Hyman, is "the 25th anniversary edition of . . . [a] Caldecott Honor-winning classic. . . . On the first night of Hanukkah, a weary traveler named Hershel of Ostropol eagerly approaches the next village, where . . . the villagers are being tormented by a band of goblins who hate Hanukkah. Brave Hershel leaps to the villagers' rescue." (Publisher's note)

★ **Joha** makes a wish; a Middle Eastern tale. adapted by Eric A. Kimmel; illustrated by Omar Rayyan. Marshall Cavendish Children 2010 un il $17.99
Grades: 1 2 3   E
1. Wishes -- Fiction 2. Middle East -- Fiction
ISBN 978-0-7614-5599-8; 0-7614-5599-X
LC 2009006334

An original story, based on the Joha tales of the Arabic-speaking world, in which a hapless man finds a wishing stick that brings him nothing but bad luck. Includes an author's note about the history of Joha tales.

"Kimmel's well-paced text smoothly builds events and dialogue, leaving the character interpretation to the comic portrayals in Rayyan's energetic watercolors." SLJ

Little Britches and the rattlers; by Eric A. Kimmel; illustrated by Vincent Nguyen. Marshall Cavendish Children 2008 un il $16.99
Grades: PreK K 1 2   E
1. Texas -- Fiction 2. Cowhands -- Fiction 3. Rattlesnakes -- Fiction
ISBN 978-0-7614-5432-8; 0-7614-5432-2
LC 2007030155

As Little Britches, in her best attire, starts for the rodeo in town, she is waylaid by several rattlesnakes wanting to do her harm, but with some quick thinking she finds a way to outsmart them all

"Kimmel's little yarn makes good use of early counting concepts and introduces some western lingo in a leisurely repetitive structure. . . . Nguyen's artwork complements the glib silliness." Booklist

The **mysterious** guests; a Sukkot story. by Eric A. Kimmel; illustrated by Katya Krenina. Holiday House 2008 un il $16.95
Grades: K 1 2 3   E
1. Jews -- Fiction 2. Sukkot -- Fiction 3. Brothers -- Fiction
ISBN 978-0-8234-1893-0; 0-8234-1893-6
LC 2007-43208

Three mysterious guests appear at generous but impoverished Ezra's table on Sukkot and bless him, while they bring curses upon his rich but selfish brother Eben.

This is "a lyrically rendered tale. . . . Krenina's stylized, harvest-toned acrylics and thoughtful, dark-eyed characters evoke a world where the everyday and mystical are intertwined, and righteousness is clear-cut." Publ Wkly

Rip Van Winkle's return; adapted and retold by Eric A. Kimmel from Rip Van Winkle by Washington Irving; pictures by Leonard Everett Fisher. Farrar, Straus and Giroux 2007 un il $17
Grades: 1 2 3 4   E
1. New York (State) -- Fiction 2. Catskill Mountains (N.Y.) -- Fiction
ISBN 978-0-374-36308-6; 0-374-36308-0
LC 2005042922

A man who sleeps for twenty years in the Catskill Mountains wakes to a much-changed world

"Kimmel and Fisher take on an American literary treasure and make it accessible to young children. . . . The drama is nicely played out with Fisher's solid, strategically placed figures." Booklist

Simon and the bear; a Hanukkah tale. by Eric A. Kimmel; illustrated by Matthew Trueman. Disney-Hyperion Books 2014 40 p. $16.99
Grades: PreK K 1 2   E
1. Hanukkah -- Fiction 2. Polar bears -- Fiction 3. Survival after airplane accidents, shipwrecks, etc. -- Fiction 4. Jews -- Fiction 5. Bears -- Fiction 6. Miracles -- Fiction 7. Survival -- Fiction 8. Shipwrecks -- Fiction
ISBN 1423143558; 9781423143550
LC 2013046370

In this children's story, by Eric A. Kimmel, illustrated by Matthew Trueman, "Simon's mother knows he will need a miracle, so she reminds him to celebrate Hanukkah wherever he may be. Little does either of them know that Simon will spend the first night of Hanukkah on an ice floe after his ship sinks. . . . This fanciful Hanukkah tale . . . celebrates eight miracles: family, friendship, hope, selflessness, sharing, faith, courage, and love." (Publisher's note)

Stormy's hat; just right for a railroad man. pictures by Andrea U'Ren. Farrar, Straus and Giroux 2008 un il $16.95
Grades: PreK K 1 2   E
1. Hats -- Fiction 2. Sewing -- Fiction 3. Railroads -- Fiction
ISBN 0-374-37262-4; 978-0-374-37262-0
LC 2005-51233

As Stormy, a railroad engineer, searches for the perfect hat—one that will not blow off, get too hot, or shade his eyes too much—his wife, Ida, becomes increasingly annoyed that he will not let her help. Includes a historical note about the real Stormy and Ida Kromer.

"U'Ren's vibrant paintings capture the palette and motion of Midwestern landscapes and city scenes. . . . With a snappy, high-interest story and connections to hats, history, trains, gender equality, and industrialism, this book is a gem for libraries and classrooms." SLJ

The **three** little tamales; by Eric A. Kimmel; illustrated by Valeria Docampo. Marshall Cavendish 2009 un il $17.99
Grades: K 1 2 3   E
1. Fairy tales 2. Wolves -- Fiction 3. Hispanic Americans -- Fiction
ISBN 978-0-7614-5519-6; 0-7614-5519-1
LC 2008010738

In this variation of 'The Three Little Pigs' set in the Southwest, three little tamales escape from a restaurant before they can be eaten, and set up homes in the prairie, cornfield, and desert.

"Docampo's oil-on-paper illustrations add dimension to the story and bring the three little tamales to life. An excellent addition to collections of fairy-tale retellings." Booklist

★ **Zigazak!** a magical Hanukkah night. illustrated by Jon Goodell. Doubleday Bks. for Young Readers 2001 un il $15.95; lib bdg $19.99
Grades: K 1 2 3   E
1. Jews -- Fiction 2. Magic -- Fiction 3. Hanukkah -- Fiction
ISBN 0-385-32652-1; 0-385-90004-X lib bdg
LC 98-46269

Two evil spirits wreak havoc on the town of Brisk's Hanukkah celebration, until the town's wise rabbi puts a stop to their mischief

"The text is safely boxed away from the devilry in double-page spreads in which intricately detailed art realistically depicts the furnishings, clothing, facial features, and even the townspeople's pets. Storytellers will have fun with the surprise ending." Booklist

Kimmelman, Leslie
★ **Everybody** bonjours! by Leslie Kimmelman; illustrated by Sarah McMenemy. Alfred A. Knopf 2008 un il $16.99; lib bdg $19.99
Grades: PreK K   E
1. Stories in rhyme 2. Paris (France) -- Fiction
ISBN 978-0-375-84443-0; 978-0-375-94443-7 lib bdg
LC 2007006899

"On vacation with her parents . . . and little brother, a girl embraces her role as tourist, savoring all the places where one can say 'Bonjour': On a barge trip down the Seine, at the top of the Tour Eiffel and Notre Dame, in a chic boutique. . . . McMenemy's . . . mixed-media images, mostly full-page scenes of classic locations, are a stylish yet timeless mélange of fauvist whimsy and affectionate reportage." Publ Wkly

In the doghouse; an Emma and Bo story. by Leslie Kimmelman; illustrated by True Kelley. Holiday House 2006 30p il (Holiday House reader) $14.95
Grades: K 1 2   E
1. Dogs -- Fiction 2. Vacations -- Fiction
ISBN 0-8234-1882-0
LC 2004047466

When the Lewis family goes on vacation to the lake, Emily gets mad at her best friend Bo, the family dog, so he runs away to look for a new best friend

"Kimmelman writes with simplicity and wit, affectionately portraying the main characters' flaws, feelings, and pride. Kelley's cartoonlike ink drawings, brightened with colorful washes, have a carefree air that suits the vacation setting and the tone of the story." Booklist

Mind your manners, Alice Roosevelt! written by Leslie Kimmelman and illustrated by Adam Gustavson. Peachtree Publishers 2009 un il $16.95

Grades: K 1 2 3   E

1. Governors 2. Presidents 3. Vice-presidents 4. Socialites 5. Children of presidents 6. Nobel laureates for peace 7. Presidents -- United States -- Fiction

ISBN 978-1-5614-5492-1; 1-5614-5492-3

LC 2008052837

A brief, fictionalized account of what life was like for Theodore Roosevelt during his political career, with his oldest daughter, Alice, a strong-willed and somewhat wild young woman, who loved to do things that shocked the public, even when she lived in the White House

"Gustavson's energetic oil paintings do justice to Alice's shocking escapades, and parts of the text . . . are cleverly incorporated into the art." Booklist

The **three** bully goats; illustrated by Will Terry. Albert Whitman 2011 un il $16.99

Grades: PreK K 1   E

1. Goats -- Fiction 2. Bullies -- Fiction

ISBN 0-8075-7900-9; 978-0-8075-7900-8

LC 2010024274

Billy goat brothers Gruff, Ruff, and Tuff are bullies who rule their meadow, but when they cross Little Ogre's bridge and are mean to the baby animals on the other side, they are in for a surprise.

"Terry's brilliantly colored acrylics have a soft, out-of-focus look to them, but there is no mistaking the grouchy looks and mean personalities of his Bully Goats. . . . Kimmelman's version stands out even from other nontraditional versions, since the ogre/troll is the good guy and the goats are the villains. A good springboard for both bullying conversations and problem-solving sessions." Kirkus

Kimura, Ken

999 Frogs Wake Up; by Ken Kimura; illustrated by Yasunari Murakami. NorthSouth 2013 48 p. $17.95

Grades: PreK K 1   E

1. Sleep -- Fiction 2. Frogs

ISBN 073584108X; 9780735841086

In this children's book, by Ken Kimura, illustrated by Yasunari Murakami, "it's springtime in the swamp! As 999 young frogs awaken, they panic to find that all of the other animals are still asleep. First they wake the biggest frog . . . then the tortoise, the lizard, and the ladybugs. But when they hop down a hole and all pull together, they find someone they don't want to wake--a big, long snake." (Publisher's note)

★ **999** tadpoles. NorthSouth Books 2011 un $16.95

Grades: PreK K 1   E

1. Frogs -- Fiction 2. Hawks -- Fiction

ISBN 978-0-7358-4013-3; 0-7358-4013-X

Original Japanese edition, 2003

"This well-paced journey, with just enough tension to keep young listeners engaged, will be a solid storytime choice." Kirkus

Kinerk, Robert

Clorinda; illustrated by Steven Kellogg. Simon & Schuster Bks. for Young Readers 2003 un il $15.95; pa $6.99

Grades: PreK K 1 2   E

1. Stories in rhyme 2. Ballet -- Fiction 3. Cattle -- Fiction

ISBN 0-689-86449-3; 1-4169-3964-4 pa

LC 2003-4559

Defying the odds, Clorinda the cow follows her dream of becoming a ballet dancer

"As fine a mix of story and message as this is, it's the irrepressible art that makes this book shine. Kellogg is at the top of his game, finding the humor in every line." Booklist

Another title about Clorinda is:

Clorinda takes flight (2007)

King, Dedie

I see the sun in Afghanistan; illustration by Judith Inglese. Satya House Pub. 2011 40p il $12.95

Grades: PreK K 1   E

1. Afghanistan -- Fiction 2. Family life -- Fiction 3. Bilingual books -- English-Dari

ISBN 978-0-9818720-8-7; 0-9818720-8-5

"This simple story follows a young Afghani girl from sunrise to sunset. Living in Bamiyan, a relatively safe city, Habiba fetches water, attends school, and anticipates the arrival of her cousins, who have lost their home because of the war. The story captures the flavor of the culture, and the love and support of this close family is evident. The story is written in both English and Dari (Afghan Farsi), and an author's note provides supplemental information. Inglese's watercolor and collage illustrations are well composed, and color and pattern add richness and texture." SLJ

King, Stephen Michael

Leaf; ideas, sound effects, and pictures. Roaring Brook 2009 un il $14.95

Grades: K 1 2   E

1. Dogs -- Fiction 2. Hair -- Fiction 3. Dreams -- Fiction

ISBN 978-1-59643-503-2; 1-59643-503-8

"A mopheaded child faces a momlike figure with scissors in her hands—definitely time for a haircut. The child, however, has other ideas and runs out to frolic in the grass. . . . Wonderful squiggly line, patches of green and brown, gold and blue and fabulous use of negative white space make this a joy to reread." Kirkus

Mutt dog! words and pictures by Stephen Michael King. Harcourt 2005 un il $16

Grades: PreK K 1 2   E

1. Dogs -- Fiction 2. Homeless persons -- Fiction

ISBN 0-15-205561-4

First published 2004 in Australia

A lonely dog finally finds a home after he makes friends with a woman who works at a homeless shelter.

"The presentation is well done, and the gentle pen-and-ink and watercolor cartoons tell the story beautifully. . . . The book's oversize format and clear wash illustrations on white backgrounds make this a good choice for storytimes." SLJ

You. Greenwillow Books 2011 un il $14.99

Grades: PreK K 1 2   E

1. Birds -- Fiction 2. Rabbits -- Fiction 3. Friendship -- Fiction

ISBN 978-0-06-206014-3

LC 2010032237

Reveals the world as a colorful, musical, and exciting place where the most special thing of all is a best friend.

King "draws a pup with gravity-defying ears whose best chum is a tiny orange bird; together, they cavort through this free-verse paean to friendship. With curlicue lines and gentle watercolor tints, King creates a winning series of scenarios to accompany his text. . . . The text is good-tempered and reassuring, but it's King's pocket-size, whimsical characters that will endear his creation to readers." Publ Wkly

King-Smith, Dick

The **twin** giants; [by] Dick King-Smith; illustrated by Mini Grey. Candlewick Press 2008 67p il $16.99

Grades: K 1 2 3   E

1. Twins -- Fiction 2. Giants -- Fiction

ISBN 978-0-7636-3529-9; 0-7636-3529-4

Two twin giants do everything together, including looking for the perfect wives.

"This handsomely designed volume offers an original story accompanied by droll illustrations." Booklist

Kinney, Jessica

The **pig** scramble; written by Jessica Kinney; illustrated by Sarah S. Brannen. Islandport Press 2011 un il $17.95

Grades: PreK K 1   E

1. Pigs -- Fiction 2. Fairs -- Fiction 3. Brothers -- Fiction 4. Contests -- Fiction

ISBN 978-1-934031-61-2; 1-934031-61-5

"August is County Fair time in New England, and Clarence, the youngest of three brothers, is looking forward to the Pig Scramble, which involves 10 children and one wily piglet. . . . Clarence thinks that he can be the best, winning the contest and the pig. The story and illustrations match perfectly—they are both timeless and evocative of yesteryear. Brannen's watercolors are detailed. . . . The illustrations are many sizes, keeping the story flowing, and Brannen's pigs are bristly, adorable, and full of life." SLJ

Kinsey-Warnock, Natalie

★ **Nora's** ark; illustrated by Emily Arnold McCully. HarperCollins 2005 un il $15.99; lib bdg $16.89

Grades: K 1 2 3   E

1. Floods -- Fiction 2. Vermont -- Fiction 3. Farm life -- Fiction 4. Grandparents -- Fiction

ISBN 0-688-17244-X; 0-06-029517-1 lib bdg

LC 2004-3444

During the Vermont flood of 1927, a girl and her grandparents share their new hilltop house with neighbors and animals.

This is a "well-told tale, based on an incident from the author's life. . . . [A] stunning picture is the wild, rainy scene showing houses bobbing along as the water pours down." Booklist

Kipling, Rudyard, 1865-1936

Just So Stories; Volume 2. Rudyard Kipling; illustrated by Ian Wallace. Groundwood Books 2014 88 p. color illustrations (hbk.) $19.95

Grades: K 1 2 3 4 5   E

1. Animals -- Fiction 2. Children's stories

ISBN 1554982138; 9781554982134

In this collection of children's stories by Rudyard Kipling "illustrator Ian Wallace once again reinterprets the famous tales with luminous art, bringing Kipling to a new generation of young readers. Many of the tales are origin stories, explaining, for example, how an animal came to be, or the how the alphabet and writing began. They all display Kipling's vivid imagination, inventive vocabulary, and engaging wordplay." (Publisher's note)

"Six of Kipling's stories, including 'The Beginning of the Armadillos' and 'The Butterfly That Stamped' are featured in this work. Over

the years, these tales have delighted young readers with their imaginative pourquoi style, beautiful language, and clever wordplay. Wallace uses mixed media (watercolor, pencil crayon, pastel pencil and chalk) to create glowing, softly colored paintings that successfully capture the essence of the tales." SLJ

★ **Rikki**-tikki-tavi; by Rudyard Kipling; adapted and illustrated by Jerry Pinkney. Morrow Junior Bks. 1997 un il pa $6.99; $16.99

Grades: 1 2 3 4   E

1. Poets 2. Authors 3. Novelists 4. Memoirists 5. India -- Fiction 6. Cobras -- Fiction 7. Children's authors 8. Short story writers 9. Mongooses -- Fiction 10. Nobel laureates for literature

ISBN 0-06-058785-7 pa; 0-688-14320-2

LC 96-51194

This is a retelling of the story from Rudyard Kipling's The jungle book in which a mongoose saves an English boy and his family from cobras in their garden in India

"Dramatic in content, sensitive in line, and rich with color, the illustrations in this picture book make full use of the broad, double-page spreads. Children who are not familiar with the story will be captivated, those who have had the story read to them before will find new things to shiver over." Booklist

Kirk, Connie Ann

Sky dancers; illustrations by Christy Hale. Lee & Low Books 2004 un il $16.95

Grades: 1 2 3 4   E

1. Mohawk Indians -- Fiction 2. Steel construction -- Fiction 3. Father-son relationship -- Fiction 4. Empire State Building (New York, N.Y.) -- Fiction

ISBN 1-58430-162-7

LC 2004-1885

John Cloud, a Mohawk boy, lives in upstate New York, but he goes to visit his father who is working on the Empire State Building

"Rich, sunlit gouache illustrations establish the 1930s setting for this well-told story." Horn Book Guide

Kirk, Daniel

A **friend's** tale; Daniel Kirk. Abrams Books for Young Readers 2009 32 p. col. ill.

Grades: K 1 2 3   E

1. Mice -- Fiction 2. Authorship -- Fiction 3. Friendship -- Fiction 4. Libraries -- Fiction 5. Bashfulness -- Fiction

ISBN 0810989271; 9780810989276

LC 2008024686

In this book, "Sam, the perky creative mouse hero of 'Library Mouse,' returns. The Writers and Illustrators Club's next project at the library is to be a joint one. Each author is to collaborate with an illustrator. . . . One night, busy researching his next story, Sam falls asleep. He must hide when the children start arriving, and he leaves his notebook behind. Tom finds it. Suspicious, the boy follows inky footprints to Sam's mouse hole and realizes that the mysterious author must be a mouse. When Tom leaves cheese and a cracker for him, Sam hopes that the boy will forget about him. Instead, Tom is inspired to write a story about shy Sam. He leaves the story by the mouse hole, and Sam surprises Tom by illustrating it. Together, they keep the secret of Sam's identity." (Children's Literature)

Honk honk! Beep beep! words and pictures by Daniel Kirk. Disney/Hyperion Books 2010 un il $15.99

Grades: PreK K   E

1. Stories in rhyme 2. Toys -- Fiction 3. Vehicles -- Fiction

ISBN 978-1-4231-2486-3; 1-4231-2486-3

LC 2010010275

When a toy father and son set out early one morning for a cross-country drive in their jeep, they see all sorts of vehicles and pick up diverse passengers along the way.

"Bright colors, a rhythmic text, and an imaginative premise make this a winner for kids just starting to find fun in books. . . . The spacious layout and oversize typeface make the story accessible to the youngest readers and listeners, who will want to call out the noisy refrain." Booklist

Keisha Ann can! [by] Daniel Kirk. G.P. Putnam's Sons 2008 un il $15.99
Grades: PreK K 1 2   E
    1. School stories 2. Stories in rhyme
    ISBN 978-0-399-24179-6; 0-399-24179-5
                                  LC 2007-034815
Keisha Ann is proud of all the things she can do during her day at school.

The "rhyming text . . . is catchy and upbeat. . . . Gouache paintings done in a striking, childlike style are filled with motion and color. . . . The images are clear and crisp, making the book ideal for sharing aloud. The story ends on a positive, all-inclusive note." SLJ

Library mouse; home sweet home. Daniel Kirk. Abrams Books for Young Readers 2013 40 p. (alk. paper) $16.95
Grades: K 1 2 3   E
    1. Picture books for children 2. Architecture 3. Mice -- Fiction 4. Dwellings -- Fiction 5. Libraries -- Fiction
    ISBN 141970544X; 9781419705441
                                  LC 2012039261
This book is part of Daniel Kirk's Library Mouse series. Here, while "Sam the mouse's library is undergoing renovation, he and [his] best friend Sarah . . . want to build the perfect temporary house for themselves, but are having trouble finding it. Sam tries his hand at creating a classical Roman structure, a 'Tudor-style house,' and a bungalow; Sarah . . . gravitates toward a Mongolian yurt, a 'Vietnamese stilt house,' and a geodesic dome worthy of Buckminster Fuller." (Publishers Weekly)

Ten thank-yous; Daniel Kirk. Nancy Paulsen Books, An Imprint of Penguin Group (USA) 2014 32 p. color illustrations $16.99
Grades: PreK K 1 2   E
    1. Gratitude 2. Pigs -- Fiction 3. Rabbits -- Fiction 4. Friendship -- Fiction 5. Gratitude -- Fiction 6. Best friends -- Fiction 7. Thank-you notes -- Fiction
    ISBN 0399169377; 9780399169373
                                  LC 2013046403
In this children's book, by Daniel Kirk, "Pig is writing a thank-you note to his grandma when his friend Rabbit comes over to play. Eager to get in on the action, Rabbit writes one of his own . . . and another . . . and another . . . until his flurry of thank-you notes has Pig in a tizzy. Pig just wants to finish writing his note in peace! Fortunately, Rabbit's last thank-you note reminds Pig how lucky he is to have Rabbit as a friend." (Publisher's note)

"This pleasant follow-up to Ten Things I Love about You (2012) again features Pig and Rabbit learning another sweet lesson in thoughtfulness... Kirk's upbeat story is told through dialogue and letters, and his expert combination of old techniques (drawing with ink, painting plywood panels) with new ones (adding colors and textures with Photoshop) nicely highlights the perpetual value of appreciation." Booklist

Kirk, Katie
    Eli, no! Abrams Books for Young Readers 2011 un il $14.95
Grades: PreK K 1   E
    1. Dogs -- Fiction
    ISBN 978-0-8109-8964-1; 0-8109-8964-6

Eli is a sweet black dog with a knack for getting into huge messes. He makes his disastrous way through the house and the yard, at every turn disobeying his owners.

"There is a retro feel to the minimalist, bold illustrations that match the simple rhyming story. . . . Amusing details . . . make this a fun read-aloud for small groups and lapsits." SLJ

Kirsch, Vincent X.
    Forsythia & me. Farrar Straus Giroux 2011 un il $16.99
Grades: PreK K 1   E
    1. Friendship -- Fiction
    ISBN 978-0-374-32438-4; 0-374-32438-7
                                  LC 2009-53233
Chester has always been in awe of his best friend's accomplishments, but when she becomes ill, he discovers that he is capable of doing amazing things to entertain her while she is bed-ridden.

"The young audience will welcome the wild, imaginative play and the story of loyal friendship, all captured in the winsome ink, watercolor, and pencil illustrations." Booklist

Natalie & Naughtily. Bloomsbury Children's Books 2008 un il $16.99; lib bdg $17.89
Grades: K 1 2 3   E
    1. Twins -- Fiction 2. Sisters -- Fiction 3. Department stores -- Fiction
    ISBN 978-1-59990-269-2; 1-59990-269-9; 978-1-59990-320-0 lib bdg; 1-59990-320-2 lib bdg
                                  LC 2007-51098
Natalie and Naughtily Nopps live above their family's department store and love to play there, but one particularly busy day they discover that 'helping' is even better than playing.

"Readers will pore over the intricately detailed watercolor and pencil illustrations of each floor of the department store while chuckling over the girls' ideas of helpfulness." Horn Book Guide

Two little boys from Toolittle Toys. Bloomsbury 2010 un $16.99; lib bdg $17.89
Grades: PreK K 1 2 3   E
    1. Play -- Fiction 2. Toys -- Fiction 3. Brothers -- Fiction
    ISBN 978-1-59990-428-3; 1-59990-428-4; 978-1-59990-429-0 lib bdg; 1-59990-429-2 lib bdg
                                  LC 2009034583
The Toolittle Toy Company makes toys that children like to play with by making toys that like to play with children.

"Kirsch offers a clever story about the nature and rewards of play, and children will enjoy poring over the wild details of fanciful toys in the watercolor-and-pencil scenes, which culminate in a Toolittle Toy Company catalog at the back of the book." Booklist

Kirwan, Wednesday
    Minerva the monster. Sterling 2008 un il $14.95
Grades: PreK K 1 2   E
    1. Monsters -- Fiction 2. Family life -- Fiction
    ISBN 978-1-4027-5718-1; 1-4027-5718-2
                                  LC 2007043376
Feeling out of sorts, Minerva pretends to be a monster, but after realizing that monsters do not eat cookies, read stories, or sleep in nice warm beds, she decides to rejoin her family.

"The gouache and colored-pencil illustrations are crisp, bright, and full of mischief, much like Minerva herself. This book will be a hit with readers." SLJ

Another title about Minerva is:
    Nobody notices Minerva (2007)

Kitamura, Satoshi

Stone Age boy. Candlewick Press 2007 32p il $15.99

Grades: K 1 2 3   E

1. Stone Age -- Fiction 2. Prehistoric peoples -- Fiction

ISBN 978-0-7636-3474-2; 0-7636-3474-3

LC 2007025614

"A boy walking in the woods finds himself falling . . . through time and space, landing in the Stone Age. He befriends a girl named Om and learns about prehistoric society by watching her people make fire, prepare food, use tools, and celebrate a successful hunt. . . . Kitmaura makes Om's society come alive. . . . Sentences are concise and easy to read. . . . The well-designed pages make effective use of white space." Horn Book

Kladstrup, Kristin

★ The gingerbread pirates; illustrated by Matt Tavares. Candlewick Press 2009 un il $16.99

Grades: K 1 2 3   E

1. Cookies -- Fiction 2. Pirates -- Fiction 3. Christmas -- Fiction

ISBN 978-0-7636-3223-6; 0-7636-3223-6

LC 2007-23171

When Jim's gingerbread pirate, Captain Cookie, comes alive, the tasty treat prepares to battle Santa Claus, who likes to eat cookies on Christmas Eve.

"An exciting story and full-page, dramatically composed paintings depicting harrowing adventures with a mouse, a cat, and the crew imprisoned in a cookie jar make this a good holiday read-aloud." SLJ

Klassen, Jon

★ I want my hat back. Candlewick Press 2011 un il $15.99

Grades: PreK K 1 2   E

1. Hats -- Fiction 2. Bears -- Fiction 3. Animals -- Fiction 4. Lost and found possessions -- Fiction

ISBN 978-0-7636-5598-3; 0-7636-5598-8

LC 2010042793

"Digitally manipulated ink paintings show a slow-witted bear. . . . Unadorned lines of type, printed without quotation marks of attributions, parallel the sparse lines Klassen uses for the forest's greenery. . . . [Klassen creates] skillful characterizations. . . . Each animal emerges fully realized." Publ Wkly

★ This is not my hat; Jon Klassen. Candlewick Press 2012 40 p. col. ill. $15.99

Grades: K 1 2 3   E

1. Hats -- Fiction 2. Theft -- Fiction 3. Fishes -- Fiction

ISBN 0763655996; 9780763655990

LC 2012942300

Randolph Caldecott Medal (2013)

In this children's story, written and illustrated by Jon Klassen, a fish steals a hat from a larger fish. "When a tiny fish shoots into view wearing a round blue topper (which happens to fit him perfectly), trouble could be following close behind. So it's a good thing that enormous fish won't wake up. And even if he does, it's not like he'll ever know what happened." (Publisher's note)

★ We found a hat; by Jon Klassen. Candlewick Press 2016 56 p. color illustrations $17.99

Grades: PreK K 1 2 3   E

1. Hats -- Fiction 2. Humorous fiction 3. Turtles -- Fiction

ISBN 0763656003; 9780763656003

LC 2016947237

In this children's story, by Jon Klassen, "two turtles have found a hat. The hat looks good on both of them. But there are two turtles. And there is only one hat. . . . Evoking hilarity and sympathy, the shifting eyes tell the tale in this brilliantly paced story in three parts." (Publisher's note)

"The conclusion might surprise even those familiar with Klassen's twist endings, and the growing tensions, simple narrative, and intriguing details will endear this to many." Booklist

Klausmeier, Jesse

★ Open this little book; by Jesse Klausmeier; illustrated by Suzy Lee. Chronicle Books 2013 40 p. (alk. paper) $16.99

Grades: PreK K 1 2   E

1. Toy and movable books 2. Books and reading -- Fiction 3. Board books 4. Color -- Fiction 5. Animals -- Fiction 6. Colors -- Fiction 7. Animals -- Fiction 8. Books and reading -- Fiction 9. Toy and movable books -- Specimens

ISBN 0811867838; 9780811867832

LC 2012002129

Boston Globe-Horn Book Honor: Picture Book (2013).

This children's book, by Jesse Klausmeier, illustrated by Suzy Lee, features a series of nested smaller books within itself. The story revolves around a group of animals which each individually read about other animals reading more books until the end where they close their books and find another. The book gives tribute and attention to the joys of reading, colors, and friendship.

Kleber, Dori

More-igami; by Dori Kleber, illustrated by G. Brian Karas. Candlewick Press 2016 40 p. color illustrations (hardcover) $15.99

Grades: PreK K 1 2   E

1. Origami -- Fiction

ISBN 9780763668198; 0763668192

In this children's story, by Dori Kleber, illustrated by G. Brian Karas, "Joey loves things that fold: maps, beds, accordions, you name it. When a visiting mother of a classmate turns a plain piece of paper into a beautiful origami crane, his eyes pop. Maybe he can learn origami, too. It's going to take practice—on his homework, the newspaper, the thirty-eight dollars in his mother's purse." (Publisher's note)

"With engaging text, charming illustrations, and bonus instructions for an origami ladybug, this is a winner." Booklist

Kleven, Elisa

★ The apple doll; [by] Elisa Kleven. Farrar, Straus & Giroux 2007 un il $16

Grades: PreK K 1 2   E

1. School stories 2. Dolls -- Fiction 3. Apples -- Fiction

ISBN 978-0-374-30380-8; 0-374-30380-0

LC 2006040981

Lizzy is scared to start school, so she makes a doll out of an apple from her favorite tree to take with her on the first day and keep her company. Includes instructions for making an apple doll

"Kleven's lovely mixed-media collage illustrations . . . are filled with eye-catching detail and activity. A sweet story about accepting change, working together, and forming new friendships." SLJ

The friendship wish. Dutton Childrens Books 2011 un il $17.99

Grades: PreK K 1 2   E

1. Dogs -- Fiction 2. Angels -- Fiction 3. Moving -- Fiction 4. Animals -- Fiction 5. Friendship -- Fiction

ISBN 978-0-525-42374-4; 0-525-42374-5

LC 2011005248

Foley the dog has trouble making friends when he moves to a new home, but after an angel visits him in a dream, Foley's neighbors come to hear about the experience and they all begin to share their talents in hopes the angel will return.

Kleven "deftly interweaves fantastic and familiar elements, and kids will recognize how imagination, support, and shared activities can inspire fun and connection. The lively, lyrical prose is illustrated with colorful, intricate mixed-media artwork that includes droll details that invited close viewing." Booklist

Welcome home, Mouse. Tricycle Books 2010 un il $15.99; lib bdg $18.99

Grades: PreK K 1   E

1. Mice -- Fiction 2. Houses -- Fiction 3. Elephants -- Fiction
ISBN 978-1-58246-277-6; 1-58246-277-1; 978-1-58246-364-3 lib bdg; 1-58246-364-6 lib bdg

Stanley the elephant, who is very clumsy, accidentally smashes Mouse's house, then promises to try to make a new one.

"The fascinating illustrations made from watercolors, ink, pastels, and colored pencils feature two simply drawn plump gray elephants and a small tan mouse placed on intricately assembled collage backgrounds. . . . Using one's imagination, repairing a mistake, and making a new friend are some of the themes contained in this charming story." SLJ

Kling, Kevin

Big little brother; illustrations by Chris Monroe. Borealis Books 2011 il $17.95

Grades: PreK K 1 2   E

1. Size -- Fiction 2. Brothers -- Fiction
ISBN 978-0-87351-844-4; 0-87351-844-6

LC 2011018586

A four-year-old boy explains that his little brother is bigger than he is, follows him everywhere, and is annoying, but his presence becomes indispensible when bullies are around.

"Monroe's minimalist, boldly hued cartoons carefully and humorously depict the action. Big Brother's emotional ups and downs are subtly expressed, while Little Brother mostly maintains an even-tempered smile. A sweet-natured tale about negotiating sibling dynamics that is as comforting as a hug." Kirkus

Big little mother; Kevin Kling; illustrated by Chris Monroe. Borealis Books 2013 32 p. (cloth : alk. paper) $17.95

Grades: PreK K 1 2   E

1. Cats -- Fiction 2. Brothers and sisters -- Fiction
ISBN 0873519116; 9780873519113

LC 2013015999

In this book, by Kevin Kling and illustrated by Chris Monroe, "a younger brother has little choice but to look up to his older sister. . . . Big Sister . . . loves to share her knowledge, particularly with her best friend, Kittywumpus, the family cat. However . . . Kittywumpus runs away for a much-needed break, leaving Little Brother as the new target for Big Sister's ministrations. And while it's fun at first, . . . Little Brother think[s] that the cat might have had the right idea." (Publisher's note)

Klinting, Lars

What do you want? [translated from the Swedish by Maria Lundin] Groundwood Books/House of Anansi Press 2006 un il $15.95; board book $7.95

Grades: PreK   E

1. Board books for children 2. Wishes -- Fiction
ISBN 0-88899-636-5; 978-0-88899-988-7 board book
Original Swedish edition 2003

"This diminutive book is mesmerizing in its calm simplicity. Cream-colored pages provide the backdrop to clear, precise color illustrations that are executed with artistic aplomb." SLJ

Klise, Kate

Grammy Lamby and the secret handshake; Kate Klise; illustrated by M. Sarah Klise. Henry Holt 2012 32 p. (hc) $16.99

Grades: K 1 2   E

1. Storms -- Fiction 2. Grandmothers -- Fiction 3. Picture

books for children 4. Sheep -- Fiction 5. Repairing -- Fiction 6. Neighborliness -- Fiction
ISBN 0805093133; 9780805093131

LC 2011028532

This is the tale of "Grammy Lamby who arrives for a visit and swoops down on her little grandson Larry. Larry learns her secret handshake is meant to let him know Grammy loves him but he is more than a little intimidated by her. She's very energetic and a trifle overbearing," which "leaves Larry waiting for her visits to end. However, when a terrible storm descends and leaves the house in shambles, Grammy Lamby stays for a month, energetically fixing things." (Children's Literature)

★ **Shall** I knit you a hat? a Christmas yarn. illustrated by M. Sarah Klise. H. Holt 2004 un il $16.95; pa $6.99

Grades: PreK K 1 2   E

1. Hats -- Fiction 2. Animals -- Fiction 3. Rabbits -- Fiction 4. Christmas -- Fiction
ISBN 0-8050-7318-3; 0-312-37139-X pa

LC 2003-22497

When Mother Rabbit knits a warm winter hat for Little Rabbit, he likes it so much that he suggests they make hats for all of their friends as Christmas gifts

"The acrylic artwork glows with humor and radiates warmth." Booklist

Other titles about Little Rabbit are:
Why do you cry?: not a sob story (2006)
Imagine Harry (2007)
Little Rabbit and the night mare (2008)
Little Rabbit and the Meanest Mother on Earth (2010)

★ **Stand** straight, Ella Kate; the true story of a real giant. pictures by M. Sarah Klise. Dial Books for Young Readers 2010 un il $16.99

Grades: K 1 2 3   E

1. Giants -- Fiction
ISBN 978-0-8037-3404-3; 0-8037-3404-2

A fictionalized biography of Ella Kate Ewing, born in 1872, who was eight feet tall by the age of seventeen and who became financially independent by traveling the country for nearly twenty years appearing at museums, exhibitions, and in circus shows.

"The story is well told in straightforward prose with lots of dialogue, and Ella's strength of character shines through. The stylized acrylic illustrations add much to the text, using bright colors and emphasizing Ella's height from various perspectives." SLJ

Kloske, Geoffrey

Once upon a time, the end; (asleep in 60 seconds) by Geoffrey Kloske and Barry Blitt. Atheneum Books for Young Readers 2005 25p il $15.95

Grades: PreK K 1 2   E

1. Fairy tales 2. Bedtime -- Fiction
ISBN 0-689-86619-4

A tired father takes only a few sentences to tell a number of classic tales in order to get the persistent listener to fall asleep.

"Blitt's ink-and-watercolor illustrations are amusing, with fine lines and soothing colors underscoring the comedy in the characters and situations." SLJ

Knapman, Timothy

Guess what I found in Dragon Wood? by Timothy Knapman; illustrated by Gwen Millward. Bloomsbury Children's Books 2008 un il $16.95

Grades: PreK K 1 2   E

1. Dragons -- Fiction
ISBN 978-1-59990-190-9; 1-59990-190-0

LC 2007018847

A young dragon finds a boy and introduces him to his family, friends, and teacher, but it is clear that the boy would like to return to his faraway home

"Executed with humor and cozy, scaly charm. . . . The tidy linework in the line-and-watercolor art adds a certain comic formality to the dragonworld." Bull Cent Child Books

Mungo and the spiders from space; illustrated by Adam Stower. Dial Books for Young Readers 2008 un il $16.99

Grades: PreK K 1 2   E

1. Science fiction 2. Comic books, strips, etc. -- Fiction
ISBN 978-0-8037-3277-3; 0-8037-3277-5

First published 2007 in the United Kingdom

"Mungo discovers the last page is missing from his secondhand picture book; how will he learn what happens to Captain Galacticus and Gizmo? Mungo himself provides the ending when, suddenly, he is pulled into the book and saves the universe. The brightly colored comic-book format, busy with rocket ships, space creatures, and humorous details, weaves Mungo's story into this metafictional adventure." Horn Book Guide

Knapp, Ruthie

★ **Who** stole Mona Lisa? illustrations by Jill McElmurry. Bloomsbury Children's Books 2010 un il $17.99; lib bdg $18.89

Grades: K 1 2 3   E

1. Artists 2. Painters 3. Scientists 4. Writers on science 5. Art thefts -- Fiction
ISBN 978-1-59990-058-2; 1-59990-058-0; 978-1-59990-549-5 lib bdg; 1-59990-549-3 lib bdg

LC 2010005512

Tells the story of the famous Leonardo Da Vinci portrait known as the Mona Lisa, including its 1911 theft from the Louvre in Paris, from the point of view of the subject of the painting. Includes an author's note with facts about the painting.

"The engaging, rhythmic-but-not-rhyming text fuses deliciously with McElmurry's marvelous artwork—its flat, decorative style, skewed head angles, strong lines and rich gouache colors echo both illuminated manuscripts and the Sienese school of painting. . . . A gem." Kirkus

Kneen, Maggie

Chocolate moose. Dutton Children's Books 2011 un il $16.99

Grades: PreK K 1   E

1. Mice -- Fiction 2. Moose -- Fiction 3. Baking -- Fiction
ISBN 978-0-525-42202-0; 0-525-42202-1

LC 2010013464

When a chocolate-loving moose goes to work in Mrs. Mouse's bakery he does not fit in very well, but Mrs. Mouse discovers that he has other useful talents.

"This is a winsome offering, illustrated in soft-edged shapes and pastel colors. . . . The baby mice are delighted with Moose, and children will be too." Booklist

Knight, Hilary

Kay Thompson's Eloise; a book for precocious grown ups. drawings by Hilary Knight. Simon & Schuster 1995 65p il $17 **E**

1. New York (N.Y.) -- Fiction 2. Hotels and motels -- Fiction
ISBN 0-671-22350-X

LC 96-103190

A reissue of the title first published 1955

This is the "tale of the little girl who makes merry mayhem from her digs on the top floor of New York's Plaza Hotel." Horn Book

Other titles about Eloise are:

Eloise at Christmastime (1958)
Eloise in Paris (1957)
Eloise in Moscow (1959)
Eloise's guide to life (2000)
Eloise takes a bawth (2002)

Knowlton, Laurie Lazzaro

A **young** man's dance; [by] Laurie Knowlton; paintings by Layne Johnson. Boyds Mills Press 2006 un il $15.95

Grades: K 1 2 3   E

1. Old age -- Fiction 2. Grandmothers -- Fiction 3. Alzheimer's disease -- Fiction
ISBN 1-59078-259-3

LC 2005021138

Grandma Ronnie's grandson has a hard time adjusting to her needing a wheelchair, living in a nursing home, and not recognizing him when he comes to visit her

"Swirling, dancing colors, both muted and sunny, accompany this lyrical story. . . . Oil paintings reveal clear, expressive faces on soft, fluid backgrounds that breathe action." SLJ

Knudsen, Michelle

Argus; illustrated by Andrea Wesson. Candlewick Press 2011 un il $15.99

Grades: PreK K 1 2   E

1. School stories 2. Dragons -- Fiction 3. Chickens -- Fiction 4. Science -- Experiments -- Fiction
ISBN 978-0-7636-3790-3; 0-7636-3790-4

LC 2010-38721

Sallie's class is supposed to be raising chicks as a science project, but although Argus, the large, green, scaly creature that hatches from her egg, causes all sorts of trouble she worries about him when he disappears.

Wesson's "watercolors of the tubby Argus are wonderfully goofy. . . . Knudsen . . . never overplays her hand, but lets the story's laughs unfold naturally from the characters and circumstances. Her grasp of the life of the elementary school classroom is spot-on." Publ Wkly

Bugged! illustrated by Blanche Sims. Kane Press 2008 32p il (Science solves it!) pa $5.95

Grades: 1 2 3   E

1. Mosquitoes -- Fiction
ISBN 978-1-57565-259-7 pa; 1-57565-259-5 pa

LC 2007026567

Tired of being covered in itchy mosquito bites, Riley uses science to investigate why mosquitoes are more attracted to him than to his friends.

"Clear and simple sentences, colorful realistic illustrations, and diverse characters all contribute to this appealing easy reader. . . . Riley's activities serve as a great model of the research process as well as the scientific method." SLJ

★ **Library** lion; [by] Michelle Knudsen; illustrated by Kevin Hawkes. Candlewick Press 2006 un il $15.99; pa $6.99

Grades: PreK K 1 2   E

1. Lions -- Fiction 2. Libraries -- Fiction
ISBN 978-0-7636-2262-6; 0-7636-2262-1; 978-0-7636-3784-2 pa; 0-7636-3784-X pa

LC 2006042578

A lion starts visiting the local library but runs into trouble as he tries to both obey the rules and help his librarian friend

"Hawkes's deft acrylic-and-pencil pictures have appeal for generations of library lovers. They are rich with expression, movement, and detail. . . . This winsome pairing of text and illustration is a natural for storytime and a first purchase for every collection." SLJ

Marilyn's monster; Michelle Knudsen; illustrated by Matt Phelan. Candlewick Press 2015 40 p. $15.99

Grades: PreK K 1 2 3   E

  1. School stories 2. Monsters -- Fiction 3. Patience -- Fiction

  ISBN 0763660116; 9780763660116

LC 2014944904

In this children's book by Michelle Knudsen, illustrated by Matt Phelan, "some of the kids in Marilyn's class have monsters. Marilyn doesn't have hers yet, but she can't just go out and look for one. Your monster has to find you. That's just the way it works. Marilyn tries to be patient and the kind of girl no monster can resist, but her monster doesn't come. Could she go out and search for him herself? Even if that's not the way it works?" (Publisher's note)

Kobald, Irena

My two blankets; Irena Kobald; [illustrated by] Freya Blackwood. Little Hare 2014 32 p. color illustrations $16.99

Grades: K 1 2 3 4   E

  1. Homesickness -- Fiction 2. Children of immigrants -- Fiction 3. Immigrant children -- Fiction 4. Belonging (Social psychology) in children -- Fiction

  ISBN 0544432282; 192171476X; 9780544432284; 9781921714764

LC 2015376947

In this children's story, by Irena Kobald, illustrated by Freya Blackwood, "a young girl has moved to a new country with her auntie, and misses all she's ever known. . . . To comfort herself, she creates a safe place under her old blanket, which is made out of memories, thoughts, and reminders of home. After meeting a new friend in the park, the girl begins to weave a new blanket . . . , one to share with her new friend." (Publisher's note)

"The illustrations, a combination of watercolor and oils, heighten the effect of the thought-provoking story. Just the right format for children to think about immigrants and friendship." Booklist

Kockere, Geert De

★ **Willy**; illustrated by Carll Cneut. Eerdmans Books for Young Readers 2011 un il $14

Grades: K 1 2   E

  1. Elephants -- Fiction

  ISBN 978-0-8028-5395-0; 0-8028-5395-1

LC 2010049545

Willy the elephant has everything an elephant should have, from four sturdy legs to a tail with a little brush on the end.

"It is the unexpected turn that De Kockere takes at the story's end that is the showstopper. Suddenly we are all Willy, in one great inclusive hug." Kirkus

Koehler, Fred

How to cheer up dad; story and pictures by Fred Koehler. Dial Books for Young Readers, an imprint of Penguin Group (USA) Inc. 2014 32 p. (hardcover : alk. paper) $16.99

Grades: PreK K 1   E

  1. Elephants -- Fiction 2. Helping behavior -- Fiction 3. Father-child relationship -- Fiction 4. Behavior -- Fiction 5. Father and child -- Fiction 6. Mood (Psychology) -- Fiction

  ISBN 0803739222; 9780803739222

LC 2013008514

In this children's book, by Fred Koehler, "Little Jumbo's Dad is having a bad day. The cereal on the floor, the raisins stuck to the ceiling, and the game of hide-and-seek at bath time are not helping. Little Jumbo

spends his time-out thinking of a way to cheer him up. A hug, a game of catch, and some ice cream start to do the trick." (School Library Journal)

""Little Jumbo's dad was having a bad day." The joke is that the little elephant is cluelessly responsible for his dad's frustrations--e.g., Jumbo shoots the raisins intended for his oatmeal at the ceiling with his trunk (Dad "should have known what a mess that would make"). Plenty of white space and a modest palette foreground an entertaining father-child dynamic." Horn Book

Kohara, Kazuno

★ **Ghosts** in the house! [by] Kazuno Kohara. Roaring Brook Press 2008 un il $12.95

Grades: PreK K 1   E

  1. Ghost stories 2. Witches -- Fiction

  ISBN 978-1-59643-427-1; 1-59643-427-9

LC 2008018204

Tired of living in a haunted house, a young witch captures, washes, and turns her pesky ghosts into curtains and a tablecloth

"Kohara's wonderfully distinctive art, all orange and black, has the look of woodcuts. . . . A must-have for Halloween." Booklist

Here comes Jack Frost. Roaring Brook Press 2009 un il $12.99

Grades: PreK K 1   E

  1. Winter -- Fiction

  ISBN 978-1-59643-442-4; 1-59643-442-2

"A young boy has nobody to play with until a frosty figure named Jack appears. . . . All the boy has to do to ensure more fun is never mention anything warm. . . . The artwork is divine, beginning with the glittered jacket cover. . . . The simple yet creatively rendered shapes are all icy blues and snowy whites. . . . The artful design . . . is what will draw repeat viewers, young and old." Booklist

The **Midnight** Library; Kazuno Kohara. Roaring Brook Press 2014 32 p. color illustrations (hardcover) $16.99

Grades: PreK K 1   E

  1. Owls -- Fiction 2. Libraries -- Fiction 3. Animals -- Fiction 4. Books and reading -- Fiction 5. Nocturnal animals -- Fiction

  ISBN 1596439858; 9781596439856

LC 2013023154

"There is a little library that only opens at night. In the library there is a little librarian--and her three assistant owls--who helps everyone find the perfect book. The library is always peaceful and quiet . . . until one night when some of the animals stir up a little trouble (and a little fun!) in the Midnight Library." (Publisher's note)

"The jaunty, cartoonish illustrations depict happy animals enjoying the library for more than just reading, and cooperatively respecting everyone's space (is there a more important library lesson?). It goes without saying that this is perfect for storytime." Booklist

Kohuth, Jane

Anne Frank's chestnut tree; by Jane Kohuth; illustrated by Elizabeth Sayles. Random House 2013 48 p. (hardcover : alk. paper) $12.99

Grades: 1 2 3   E

  1. Nature 2. Amsterdam (Netherlands) -- Biography 3. Jews -- Netherlands -- Amsterdam -- Biography 4. Jewish children in the Holocaust -- Netherlands -- Amsterdam

  ISBN 0449812553; 9780307975799; 9780375971150; 9780375981135; 9780449812556

LC 2012034585

Author "Jane Kohuth explores Anne Frank's strong belief in the healing power of nature in this Step 3 leveled reader biography for newly independent readers ages 5-8," which is illustrated by Elizabeth Sayles. It describes how "hidden away in their Secret Annex in Amsterdam during World War II, Anne Frank and her family could not breathe fresh air or see the blue sky for years. . . . This small glimpse of nature gave Anne hope and courage." (Publisher's note)

"Nature, as represented by a chestnut tree outside the Secret Annex, serves as a continuing image for this easy reader. The tree's presence throughout Anne's life in hiding not only gives her a sense of peace but also provides readers a respite from her ordeal. Illustrations are somber except those depicting Anne's pre-war life or Annex visits from helpers bringing food and books." (Horn Book)

Includes bibliographical references and index

Duck sock hop; by Jane Kohuth; illustrated by Jane Porter. Dial Books for Young Readers 2012 32 p. col. ill. (hardcover) $16.99
Grades: PreK K 1   E
1. Ducks -- Fiction 2. Stories in rhyme 3. Picture books for children 4. Dance -- Fiction 5. Socks -- Fiction
ISBN 0803737122; 9780803737129
LC 2011029969

This children's picture book "stars a crew of dancing ducks whose webby feet are made even happier by donning all kinds of sprightly socks . . . . No matter that socks prove more of a hindrance than a help when it comes to dancing (the sock hop results in 'big duck flops!' and trips to the first-aid station); at book's end, the dancers are back at the Duck Sock Shop to pick up new pairs for the next soiree." (Publishers Weekly)

Ducks go vroom; illustrated by Viviana Garofoli. Random House 2011 31p il (Step into reading) lib bdg $12.99; pa $3.99
Grades: PreK K 1   E
1. Stories in rhyme 2. Ducks -- Fiction 3. Noise -- Fiction
ISBN 978-0-375-96567-8 lib bdg; 0-375-96567-X lib bdg; 978-0-375-86560-2 pa; 0-375-86560-8 pa
LC 2010002695

Relates three silly ducks' rather impolite visit to their Auntie Goose's house, introducing simple action and noise words.

"Concentrated colored backgrounds add to the visual appeal of the pages, which have either black or white text and bright cartoon illustrations. . . . A solid choice for libraries needing entry-level readers." SLJ

Kolanovic, Dubravka
Everyone needs a friend. Price Stern Sloan 2010 il $9.99
Grades: PreK K 1   E
1. Mice -- Fiction 2. Wolves -- Fiction 3. Friendship -- Fiction
ISBN 978-0-8431-9918-5; 0-8431-9918-0
Jack the wolf has been wishing for a friend, but Walter the dormouse may not be the right choice.

"This simple story is rendered in bright oil pastels, with thoughtful background details that give the illustrations a cozy feel. A tale of friendship that will fit nicely into most collections." SLJ

Kolar, Bob
Big kicks. Candlewick Press 2008 un il $16.99
Grades: PreK K 1 2   E
1. Bears -- Fiction 2. Soccer -- Fiction 3. Animals -- Fiction
ISBN 978-0-7636-3390-5; 0-7636-3390-9
"Biggie Bear's soccer-playing friends appear at his doorstep . . . begging him to join them. . . . Biggie is a jazz fan who collects stamps. . . . Despite his athletic shortcomings, the score is tied until the bear bends over to grasp a rare stamp on the ground and heads the ball into the net for the winning goal. . . . Kolar's soccer story is just rollicking enough for listeners. . . . Digital cartoons of rounded figures with exaggerated features are brightly hued and presented in detailed scenes that are balanced with less complex spreads." SLJ

Komako Sakai
Hannah's Night; Komako Sakai. Lerner Pub Group 2014 32 p. chiefly color illustrations $17.95
Grades: PreK K 1   E
1. Night -- Fiction 2. Bedtime -- Fiction
ISBN 1877579548; 9781877579547
In this book, written and illustrated by Komako Sakai, "when Hannah wakes up and discovers the quiet, exciting night-time world. When Hannah wakes suddenly in the night, she discovers a whole new world of adventure. With nobody awake to tell her off, she can do just as she pleases." (Publisher's note)

"The artist's smoothly drafted drawings capture with aching sweetness all the movements of a very young child the way Hannah's trip down the stairs is an expedition carried out step by step; the way she sits thoughtfully on her haunches to eat the cherries stolen from the refrigerator as Shiro laps milk; the way she reaches stealthily over her sleeping sister to take the older girl's doll. By keeping her focus tight and observing Hannah closely, Sakai's characterization feels natural, light, and true to life." Pub Wkly

Konagaya, Kiyomi
Beach feet; by Kiyomi Konagaya; illustrated by Masamitsu Saito. Enchanted Lion Books 2012 32 p. (hardback) $14.95
Grades: PreK K 1   E
1. Beaches -- Fiction 2. Picture books for children 3. Foot -- Fiction
ISBN 9781592701216
LC 2011052465

In this "installment in the 'Being in the World' series, Japanese collaborators [Kiyomi] Konagaya and [Masamitsu] Saito offer a[n] . . . account of a day in the life of a child at the beach. Cover art depicts . . . toes scrunching down into the sand, and the book opens to a first-person, stream-of-consciousness text detailing the child's seaside experience. It's never clear whether this child is a boy or a girl, but this doesn't matter, as from page to page those feet from the cover art feel the heat of sun-baked sand, the coolness of the ocean waters, and the hard pressure of a seashell underfoot. . . . [N]arration delivers the child's experiences in brief snippets of text that" describe the child's "experiences of the surroundings." (Kirkus)

Konnecke, Ole
Anton can do magic. Gecko Press 2011 il $17.95
Grades: PreK K 1 2   E
1. Magicians -- Fiction
ISBN 978-1-8774-6737-0; 1-8774-6737-5
"Young Anton dons a magician's turban and sets off to prove that he can make things disappear. Because his too-large turban keeps slipping down over his eyes, a few things do indeed go missing. . . . This story is told with a spare, easy-to-read text; it's the illustrations that tell the true story and add much humor." SLJ

Kono, Erin Eitter
Hula lullaby; [by] Erin Eitter Kono. Little, Brown 2005 un il $15.99
Grades: PreK K 1 2   E
1. Hawaii -- Fiction 2. Bedtime -- Fiction 3. Mother-child relationship -- Fiction
ISBN 0-316-73591-4
LC 2004-10270

Against the backdrop of a beautiful Hawaiian landscape, a young girl cuddles and sleeps in her mother's lap

"The rhyming text becomes almost hypnotic as night deepens around the two and, finally, the girl falls asleep. Glowing with warm colors, which seem all the more brilliant in the night scenes, the gouache-

and-pencil illustrations create an idyllic vision of Hawaiian culture." Booklist

Kontis, Alethea

Alpha oops! the day Z went first. [by] Alethea Kontis; illustrated by Bob Kolar. Candlewick Press 2006 un il $15.99

Grades: K 1 2   E

1. Alphabet -- Fiction

ISBN 978-0-7636-2728-7; 0-7636-2728-3

LC 2006042310

Chaos ensues when Z thinks that its time for him to go first in the alphabet for a change

"Reflecting the letters' saucy ways, the colorful, stylized artwork dramatizes the action and offers bits of comic byplay for the observant. An alphabet book with attitude." Booklist

★ **AlphaOops!**: H is for Halloween; illustrated by Bob Kolar. Candlewick Press 2010 un il $15.99

Grades: K 1 2 3   E

1. Alphabet 2. Halloween -- Fiction

ISBN 978-0-7636-3966-2; 0-7636-3966-4

LC 2009-14827

While putting on a Halloween pageant, the alphabet mixes things up with some spooky, and funny, results.

"Kontis's text is rhythmic and comical, and readers who are comfortable with the alphabet will delight in the silliness of this story. Kolar's illustrations are imbued with a sense of nighttime theater magic, and the slightly muted jewel-tone hues set the scene perfectly. A winsome union of humorous text and art." SLJ

Kooser, Ted, 1939-

Bag in the wind; illustrated by Barry Root. Candlewick 2010 un il

Grades: 1 2 3   E

1. Bags -- Fiction 2. Landfills -- Fiction 3. Recycling -- Fiction

ISBN 0-7636-3001-2; 978-0-7636-3001-0

One cold, spring morning, an ordinary grocery bag begins blowing around a landfill, then as it travels down a road, through a stream, and into a town, it is used in various ways by different people, many of whom do not even notice it.

"The muted, dappled colors of Root's gouache and watercolor illustrations are a perfect complement to Kooser's lengthy, meditative passages. . . . An excellent opener for discussions about creative reuse and recycling." Booklist

Kornell, Max

Bear with me. Putnam 2011 un il $15.99

Grades: PreK K 1   E

1. Bears -- Fiction 2. Family life -- Fiction

ISBN 978-0-399-25257-0; 0-399-25257-6

LC 2010-23202

A boy at first is angry when his parents suddenly welcome a giant bear named Gary into their family, but eventually he and Gary learn to get along.

"The pleasant watercolor, ink, and acrylic illustrations are expertly drawn, with an interesting use of outlining, perspectives, and layout. . . . This charming offering can be enjoyed even by those whose families are staying just the way they are." SLJ

Korngold, Jamie S., 1965-

Sadie and the big mountain; by Jamie Korngold; illustrated by Julie Fortenberry. Kar-Ben Pub. 2012 32 p. (lib. bdg. : alk. paper) $17.95 E

1. Jewish holidays -- Fiction 2. Jewish children -- Fiction 3. Schools -- Fiction 4. Shavuot -- Fiction 5. Nursery schools -- Fiction 6. Ten commandments -- Fiction 7. Jews -- United States

-- Fiction

ISBN 0761364927; 9780761364924

LC 2011018797

In this children's book by Jamie Korngold, illustrated by Julie Fortenberry, "When her preschool plans a Shavuot hike just like Moses took up Mt. Sinai, Sadie is afraid she is too little to make it to the top, and tries to think of ways to be absent. But when the day comes, she learns that anyone can climb high enough to reach God." (Publisher's note)

"To celebrate Shavuot, Sadie's class will go on a hike. But Sadie worries that she won't be able to "climb a mountain as big as the one Moses climbed." Unsurprisingly, the rabbi allays Sadie's fears, and she enjoys the day. The formulaic story lacks substance, though the pleasant illustrations suitably convey Sadie's anxiety. A brief explanation of the holiday is included." (Horn Book)

Sadie's almost marvelous menorah; by Jamie Korngold; illustrated by Julie Fortenberry. Kar-Ben Pub. 2013 24 p. $7.95

Grades: PreK K 1   E

1. Hanukkah -- Fiction 2. Jewish children -- Fiction 3. Menorah -- Fiction

ISBN 0761364935; 0761364951; 9780761364931; 9780761364955

LC 2011029042

In this book, "Sadie works hard to carefully sculpt and paint her clay menorah." She "is eager to show it to her mother on the last day of the week. In her rush, she trips and drops the menorah, which breaks into 'a million, zillion pieces.' Through tears and disappointment, Sadie and her mom realize that while the shattered menorah is not repairable, the shamas remains perfectly intact and becomes 'Sadie's Super Shammash' to light all the menorahs in the home each year." (Kirkus Reviews)

"Sadie has made her own menorah at school. She's thrilled to take home her pink and blue creation, but she trips, shattering the menorah into "a million, zillion pieces." Luckily the shammash remains intact--a Hanukkah miracle!--and a new tradition begins. Illustrations capture both the bustling and the quiet times of Sadie's classroom; light-infused pictures of the family at home radiate warmth." (Horn Book)

Kostecki-Shaw, Jenny Sue

My travelin' eye; [by] Jenny Sue Kostecki-Shaw. Henry Holt 2008 un il $16.95

Grades: K 1 2   E

1. Eye -- Fiction 2. Vision -- Fiction

ISBN 978-0-8050-8169-5; 0-8050-8169-0

LC 2007007224

Jenny Sue loves that her "travelin' eye" lets her see the world in a special way, and so she is not happy when her teacher suggests that her parents take her to an opthamologist to fix the lazy eye

"Bright colors and patterns warm the realistic story, while graphics-style artwork gives a since of [Jenny] Sue's vision." Booklist

Same, same, but different. Henry Holt 2011 un il $16.99

Grades: PreK K 1 2   E

1. Friendship -- Fiction

ISBN 978-0-8050-8946-2; 0-8050-8946-2

LC 2010030121

Pen pals Elliott and Kailash discover that even though they live in different countries—America and India—they both love to climb trees, own pets, and ride school buses.

"The imaginative multimedia illustrations, drawn in an animated, childlike style, add vibrant color and rich details to the story. Kostecki-Shaw presents a meaningful message of inclusivity in this engaging title." SLJ

Koster, Gloria

The **Peanut**-Free Cafe; illustrated by Maryann Cocca-Leffler. Whitman, A. 2006 un il $16.95

Grades: K 1 2 3   **E**

1. School stories 2. Allergy -- Fiction 3. Peanuts -- Fiction

ISBN 0-8075-6386-2

When a new classmate has a peanut allergy and has to sit in a special area of the lunchroom, Simon reconsiders his love for peanut butter.

"The cartoon-style art is fun, with some moments of exaggerated drama, as when Grant demonstrates what would happen to him if he ate just one peanut." Booklist

Kraegel, Kenneth

Green pants; written and illustrated by Kenneth Kraegel. Candlewick Press 2017 40 p. color illustrations $15.99

Grades: PreK K 1 2   **E**

1. Choice (Psychology) -- Fiction

ISBN 9780763688400

LC 2017931944

In this book, by Kenneth Kraegel, "Jameson only ever wears green pants. When he wears green pants, he can do anything. But if he wants to be in his cousin's wedding, he's going to have to wear a tuxedo, and that means black pants. It's an impossible decision: Jameson would love nothing more than to be in his cousin's wedding, but how can he not wear green pants?" (Publisher's note)

King Arthur's very great grandson; by Kenneth Kraegel. Candlewick 2012 40 p. (hardback) $15.99

Grades: PreK K 1 2   **E**

1. Dragons -- Fiction 2. Picture books for children 3. Knights and knighthood -- Fiction 4. Animals, Mythical -- Fiction 5. Adventure and adventurers -- Fiction 6. FICTION -- Animals -- Mythical 7. FICTION -- Historical -- Medieval 8. FICTION -- Action & Adventure -- General

ISBN 076365311X; 9780763653118

LC 2011046646

In this book, "Henry Alfred Grummorson, the great-great-great-great-great-great-great grandson of Arthur, King of Britain, goes in search of adventure. First, he challenges a fire-breathing Dragon that simply blows smoke rings. He announces his presence to the giant Cyclops who, instead of fighting, engages him in a staring contest. . . . Travelling far in search of a worthy adversary, his search leads him past the winged Griffin (who offers a game of chess) to the sea monster Leviathan. Has he finally found something worthy of a fight? . . . Despite the determined lack of conflict, Henry still manages to find a treasure he didn't know he was seeking." (Kirkus)

The **song** of Delphine; Kenneth Kraegel. Candlewick Press 2015 40 p. color illustrations $15.99

Grades: PreK K 1 2 3   **E**

1. Servants -- Fiction 2. Musicians -- Fiction 3. Princesses -- Fiction 4. Orphans -- Fiction 5. Singing -- Fiction

ISBN 0763670014; 9780763670016

LC 2014945455

In this children's book by Kenneth Kraegel, "Delphine . . . has no family and no friends, and as a servant in Queen Theodora's palace, her life is full of work. Delphine loves to sing. When young Princess Beatrice comes to live at the palace, . . . the unkind princess only makes Delphine's life more miserable. One night, as Delphine sings out her sorrows, she draws the attention of . . . giraffes! Delphine is delighted to have friends, but joining them on an outdoor adventure leads her to accidentally cross the princess." (Publisher's note)

"Delphine is a young orphan who scrubs floors in Queen Theodora's palace. When her spirits are low, she looks out across the savanna and

sings. The queen's niece, Princess Beatrice, comes to live at the palace, but the spiteful girl makes Delphine's life miserable. . . . The text works beautifully with the watercolor-and-ink artwork, which includes elements drawn with great simplicity and set against the richly textured backdrop of the savanna. Watercolors are applied with finesse. A quiet yet magical picture book that is just right for reading aloud." Booklist

Krall, Dan

The **great** lollipop caper; Dan Krall. 1st ed. Simon & Schuster Books for Young Readers 2013 48 p. col. ill. (hardcover) $16.99

Grades: PreK K 1 2   **E**

1. Lollipops -- Fiction 2. Humorous fiction -- Fiction 3. Humorous stories 4. Pickles -- Fiction 5. Lollipops -- Fiction 6. Contentment -- Fiction

ISBN 1442444606; 9781442444607; 9781442444614

LC 2012004041

In this children's story, by Dan Krall, "Mr. Caper . . . wants the children of the world to love him--just as much as they love the sweet, saccharine Lollipop. And thus a plot is hatched: Caper-flavored lollipops are dispatched throughout the world . . . and everything goes horribly wrong. Will Mr. Caper find a way to repair the havoc he's wreaked by over-reaching? Maybe, if Lollipop helps save the day!" (Publisher's note)

Includes bibliographical references and index

Krans, Kim, 1980-

ABC dream; by Kim Krans. Random House Inc 2016 48 p. color illustrations (hardcover) $16.99

Grades: K 1 2 3   **E**

1. Alphabet 2. Picture books for children

ISBN 9780553539295; 9780553539301

LC 2015008746

In this children's book, by Kim Krans, "a wordless alphabet book becomes an identification game. . . . On top of the letter A, for instance, are two arrows piercing a whole apple, while at the bottom, scads of ants attack an eaten apple core. Kids will easily name the apple, ants, and arrows but are likely to miss the argyle plaid that fills in the letter. Other letters are also textured with fabrics or wood." (Kirkus Reviews)

"Discoveries range from obvious to quite challenging, but there is a key to each letter in the back. The rich imagery and smart page design make this alphabet book a pleasure to spend time enjoying." SLJ

Krasnesky, Thad

I always, always get my way; illustrated by David Parkins. Flashlight 2009 un il $16.95

Grades: PreK K 1 2   **E**

1. Family life -- Fiction

ISBN 978-0-9799746-4-9; 0-9799746-4-X

"Three-year-old Emmy wreaks havoc on her entire household. . . . Krasnesky tells the story with flowing rhyme that accommodates the humor of the plot and heightens Parkins's comical cartoon illustrations." SLJ

That cat can't stay! illustrated by David Parkins. Flashlight 2010 il $16.95

Grades: K 1 2   **E**

1. Cats -- Fiction

ISBN 978-0-9799746-5-6; 0-9799746-5-8

"Poor dad is surrounded by a stray-cat collecting family. He finds all sorts of excuses to get rid of the pathetic cats, but always caves in. It begins with just one soaking wet kitty, and ends with a houseful of five. Dejected dad leaves the happy clan for a walk and returns with a smile and a dog." (Library Media Connection)

Kraus, Robert

★ **Whose** mouse are you? pictures by José Aruego. 30th anniversary ed.; Simon & Schuster Books for Young Readers 2000 un il $17.95
Grades: PreK K   E
   1. Stories in rhyme 2. Mice -- Fiction
   ISBN 0-689-84052-7
A reissue of the title first published 1970 by Macmillan
A lonely little mouse has to be resourceful in order to bring his family back together
"This is an absolute charmer of a picture book, original, tender, and childlike. The rhyming text is so brief, so catchy, and so right that a child will remember the words after one or two readings, and the large, uncluttered illustrations are gay and appealing." Booklist
   Other titles about the mouse and his family are:
   Come out and play, little mouse (1987)
   Mouse in love (2000)
   Where are you going, little mouse? (1986)

Krause, Ute

Oscar and the very hungry dragon. NorthSouth Books 2010 un il $16.95
Grades: PreK K 1 2   E
   1. Cooking -- Fiction 2. Dragons -- Fiction
   ISBN 978-0-7358-2306-8; 0-7358-2306-5
Original German edition, 2007
"When the earth trembles, the villagers at the bottom of the hill know it's time to send the dragon a princess to eat. One day, unfortunately, no princess is available; a child is the next best thing. Village elder Mr. Ballymore holds a lottery and young Oscar . . . is selected. . . . Packed with wit that never descends into camp and illustrated with verve and style in ink-and-watercolor cartoons, Krause's substantial, self-translated fractured fairy tale delights on every level." Kirkus

Krauss, Ruth

The **backward** day; story by Ruth Krauss; pictures by Marc Simont. New York Review Children's Collection 2007 un il (New York Review Children's Collection) $14.95
Grades: PreK K 1   E
   1. Family -- Fiction 2. Morning -- Fiction
   ISBN 978-1-59017-237-7; 1-59017-237-X
                    LC 2007-6747
A reissue of the title first published 1950 by Harper
Having decided that it is backward day, a boy dresses himself first in his coat, last in his socks, and continues in that way with the cooperation of his family.
"The silliness is enhanced by Simont's bold three-color illustrations showing everyone playing along. The universality of Krauss's work assures that a new generation will want to celebrate backward day." Horn Book Guide

★ **Bears**; story by Ruth Krauss; pictures by Maurice Sendak. HarperCollins Pubs. 2005 un il $14.95
Grades: PreK   E
   1. Bears -- Fiction
   ISBN 0-06-027994-X
A newly illustrated edition of the title first published 1948
"The 27-word text is full of possibility: 'Bears—Under chairs—Washing hairs—Giving stares—Collecting fares—.' . . . Sendak sets a full-color story in motion on the cover. In a scene both familiar and fresh, a boy in a wolf suit snuggles his stuffed bear in a themed room where the object of his affection is replicated on every conceivable sur-

face. . . . Sure to spark laughter and original wordplay, this is the marriage of two masters." SLJ

★ The **carrot** seed; pictures by Crockett Johnson. Harper & Row 1945 un il $14.99; pa $5.99; bd bk $6.99
Grades: PreK K   E
   1. Gardening -- Fiction
   ISBN 0-06-023350-8; 0-06-443210-6 pa; 0-06-443210-6 bd bk
Simple text and picture show how the faith of a small boy, who planted a carrot seed, was rewarded
"Crockett Johnson's pictures are perfect and the brief text is just right." Book Week

★ The **growing** story; by Ruth Krauss; illustrated by Helen Oxenbury. HarperCollins 2000 un il $16.99; lib bdg $17.89
Grades: PreK K   E
   1. Growth -- Fiction
   ISBN 0-06-024716-9; 0-06-024717-7 lib bdg
                    LC 97-42822
A newly illustrated edition of the title first published 1947
A little boy worries throughout the summer that he's not getting bigger, but at the end of the season he tries on his winter clothes and realizes that he has grown.
"The story gets right to a child's experiences as it expresses both wondering and wonderment. This comes out beautifully in art that captures the affection between a boy and his hardworking mother who makes a bountiful place of the land they farm." Booklist

A **very** special house; by Ruth Krauss; pictures by Maurice Sendak. HarperCollins 1981 un il $16.95
Grades: PreK K   E
   1. Imagination -- Fiction
   ISBN 0-06-028638-5
                    LC 2002511422
A reissue of the title first published 1953
A Caldecott Medal honor book, 1954
"The very special house is a house which exists in the imagination of a small boy—a house where the chairs are for climbing, the walls for writing on, and the beds for jumping on; a house where a lion, a giant, or a dead mouse is welcome, and where nobody ever says stop. Told in a chanting rhythm that demands participation by the reader; the imaginary characters, objects, and doings are pictured in line drawings almost as a child would scribble them while the real little boy stands out boldly in bright blue overalls." Booklist

Krebs, Laurie

The **Beeman**; [text by] Laurie Krebs; [illustrations by] Valeria Cis. Barefoot Books 2008 un il $16.99
Grades: PreK K 1 2   E
   1. Stories in rhyme 2. Bees -- Fiction 3. Grandfathers -- Fiction
   ISBN 978-1-84686-146-8; 1-84686-146-2
A newly illustrated edition of the title first published 2002 by National Geographic
In rhyming text, a child describes the work Grandpa does to take care of honeybees and harvest the honey they make.
"This charming book is visually enticing and just plain fun to read. . . . The acrylic illustrations are done in predominantly muted, pastel shades with occasional touches of bright colors." SLJ

Krensky, Stephen

Hanukkah at Valley Forge; illustrated by Greg Harlin. Dutton Children's Books 2006 un il $17.99
Grades: 1 2 3 4   E
   1. Generals 2. Presidents 3. Jews -- Fiction 4. Hanukkah -- Fiction

5. United States -- History -- 1775-1783, Revolution -- Fiction
ISBN 0-525-47738-1

During the Revolutionary War, a Jewish soldier from Poland lights the menorah on the first night of Hanukkah and tells General George Washington the story of the Maccabees and the miracle that Hanukkah celebrates. Based on factual events.

"Harlin's evocative paintings are rich with period details that successfully bring the settings to life. A well-told story." Booklist

★ **How** Santa got his job; illustrated by S.D. Schindler. Simon & Schuster Bks. for Young Readers 1998 un il hardcover o.p. pa $6.99
Grades: PreK K 1 2   E
1. Santa Claus -- Fiction
ISBN 0-689-80697-3; 0-689-84668-1 pa

LC 97-23474

This "peek at Santa's resumé reveals how various odd jobs, like chimney sweep and mail carrier, helped prepare him for his world-famous career. . . . [Schindler's] intricate pen-and-watercolor illustrations make Santa's evolution from boyish redhead to the familiar heavy-set, snowy-bearded character a joy to watch." Publ Wkly

Another title about Santa by this author and illustrator is:
How Santa lost his job (2001)

Noah's bark; illustrated by Roge. Carolrhoda Books 2010 un il lib bdg $16.95
Grades: K 1 2   E
1. Sounds -- Fiction 2. Animals -- Fiction 3. Biblical characters 4. Noah's ark -- Fiction
ISBN 978-0-8225-7645-7; 0-8225-7645-7

LC 2007010022

Noah is distracted by animals making whatever sound comes into their heads while he is trying to build, then pilot, the ark, and so he devises a way for each animal to choose only one sound.

"The stylized, brushstroked paintings are embellished with highlighted sound effects and subtle comic expressions. Inventive and sure to elicit a boatload of giggles." Booklist

★ **Play** ball, Jackie! illustrated by Joe Morse. Millbrook Press 2011 un il lib bdg $16.95
Grades: 2 3 4 5   E
1. Baseball players 2. Army officers 3. Baseball -- Fiction 4. Race relations -- Fiction 5. African Americans -- Fiction 6. Brooklyn Dodgers (Baseball team) -- Fiction
ISBN 978-0-8225-9030-9; 0-8225-9030-1

LC 2010027270

On April 15, 1947, Matt Romano and his father watch the Brooklyn Dodgers season-opener, during which Jackie Robinson, a twenty-eight-year-old rookie, breaks the "color line" that had kept black men out of Major League baseball. Includes facts about Jackie Robinson's life and career.

"Morse's dramatically grained, exaggerated artwork plays up the intensity of the era's racial tensions and the dynamism of the game, while Krensky adeptly moves between the action on Ebbets Field and Matty's conversations with his father. An intimate and powerful account of a historic day." Publ Wkly

Sisters of Scituate Light; by Stephen Krensky; illustrated by Stacey Schuett. Dutton Children's Books 2008 un il $16.99
Grades: 1 2 3   E
1. Sisters -- Fiction 2. Lighthouses -- Fiction 3. War of 1812 -- Fiction 4. Massachusetts -- Fiction
ISBN 978-0-525-47792-1; 0-525-47792-6

LC 2007028297

In 1814, when their father leaves them in charge of the Scituate lighthouse outside of Boston, two teenaged sisters devise a clever way to avert an attack by a British warship patrolling the Massachusetts coast

"Krensky's fine telling is well matched by Schuett's illustrations, which are especially effective in capturing the colors of the sea and sky." Booklist

Spark the firefighter; by Stephen Krensky; illustrated by Amanda Haley. Dutton Childrens Books 2008 un il $16.99
Grades: PreK K 1   E
1. Fear -- Fiction 2. Dragons -- Fiction 3. Fire fighters -- Fiction
ISBN 978-0-525-47887-4; 0-525-47887-6

LC 2007050565

Spark's fear of fire has kept him from being a proper dragon, so he takes a job with the Hardscrabble volunteer fire department in hopes of conquering his fear

"Simply told with bright cartoon pictures and a dragon to hold interest, the . . . story teaches fire safety in an appealing way." SLJ

★ **Too** many leprechauns; (or how that pot o' gold got to the end of the rainbow) illustrated by Dan Andreasen. Simon & Schuster Books for Young Readers 2007 un il $12.99
Grades: K 1 2 3   E
1. Ireland -- Fiction 2. Leprechauns -- Fiction
ISBN 0-689-85112-X

LC 2005-20659

Finn O'Finnegan returns home after a year in Dublin and when he finds his village taken over by leprechauns, he must devise a way to get them to leave without making them angry.

"The well-paced story moves along smoothly, enhanced by Andreasen's handsome oil paintings, which picture the setting and characters with equal verve and charm." Booklist

Krilanovich, Nadia
Chicken, chicken, duck! Tricycle Press 2011 un il $16.99
Grades: PreK K   E
1. Ducks -- Fiction 2. Games -- Fiction 3. Sounds -- Fiction 4. Domestic animals -- Fiction
ISBN 978-1-58246-385-8; 1-58246-385-9

LC 2010010773

"A feisty white duck coordinates an impressive stunt amid lots of barnyard noise in Krilanovich's rhythmic book for very young readers. Paintings of the duck with outstretched wings suggest her cheerleader role directing a flock of chickens, a cat, a dog, and assorted other barnyard animals as they prepare to form a Flying Wallendas-style pyramid. The animals appear in tight close-up against clean white pages; they'd look clinical if not for their obvious excitement, the intensity of their interactions, and the painterly attention Krilanovich . . . devotes to their feathers, whiskers, black noses, and furry tails." Publ Wkly

Moon child; illustrations by Elizabeth Sayles. Tricycle Press 2010 un il $15.99; lib bdg $18.99
Grades: PreK K 1   E
1. Moon -- Fiction 2. Animals -- Fiction 3. Bedtime -- Fiction
ISBN 978-1-58246-325-4; 1-58246-325-5; 978-1-58246-366-7 lib bdg; 1-58246-366-2 lib bdg

LC 2009032304

"Various animal babies interact with the full moon in this quiet charmer. Otter playfully 'catches' it in order to give the orb a big hug, a raccoon plays with the reflection of its light, and an owl smiles at the stars and pretends she can balance the moon on the tip of her nose. There is very little text—only one sentence per spread—but it works well for this subject matter and mood. Sayles has primarily used dark blue and brown pastels with acrylic ink to set the tone for this peaceful night where all is well. Sweet dreams are sure to follow. Perfect for bedtime or evening storytimes." SLJ

Krishnaswami, Uma

Monsoon; pictures by Jamel Akib. Farrar, Straus & Giroux 2003 un il $16

Grades: K 1 2 3   E

1. India -- Fiction 2. Monsoons -- Fiction

ISBN 0-374-35015-9

           LC 2001-54753

A child in India describes waiting for the monsoon rains to arrive and the worry that they will not come

"Krishnaswami's poetic text rides faithfully on the child's sensibilities. . . . Akib's impressionistic, pastel illustrations make stunning use of extreme perspectives." SLJ

★ **Out** of the way! Out of the way! story, Uma Krishnaswami; pictures, Uma Krishnaswamy. Groundwood Books/House of Anansi Press 2012 28 p. col. ill. $17.95

Grades: K 1 2 3   E

1. India -- Fiction 2. Picture books for children 3. Rural development -- Fiction

ISBN 1554981301 Groundwood Books; 9781554981304 Groundwood Books

In this picture book, "[a] boy in India sees a baby tree growing by the side of a dusty path, and, because he protects it, it flourishes throughout his lifetime despite the changes to the landscape around him." The illustrations "depict the path [by the tree] turning into a lane, then a street, then a road, signaling the rapid development that transforms the landscape from a quiet, sleepy village into a busy town. Meanwhile, the boy grows into a man, and the tree becomes a meeting place for local people." (Kirkus)

Kroll, Steven

The **Hanukkah** mice; by Steven Kroll; illustrated by Michelle Shapiro. Marshall Cavendish Children 2008 un il $14.99

Grades: PreK K 1 2   E

1. Mice -- Fiction 2. Hanukkah -- Fiction

ISBN 978-0-7614-5428-1; 0-7614-5428-4

           LC 2007035003

A family of mice enjoys the doll house and furnishings that Rachel receives as gifts on the eight nights of Hanukkah

"This book would make a wonderful addition to any holiday collection, and will most likely become a new holiday classic that will be cherished by students for years to come." Libr Media Connect

Stuff! reduce, reuse, recycle. illustrated by Steve Cox. Marshall Cavendish 2009 un il $16.99

Grades: PreK K 1 2   E

1. Rats -- Fiction 2. Recycling -- Fiction

ISBN 978-0-7614-5570-7; 0-7614-5570-1

           LC 2008-12915

Pinch is a pack rat who does not want to give up the possessions that are cluttering his house, but when he finally is persuaded to sell them at a neighborhood tag sale, he discovers the beauty of recycling. Includes tips on "reducing, reusing, and recycling."

"The bright, bold colors convey the friendly tone of the story and ably show the movement from cluttered to clean as Pinch relinquishes his possessions. An admirable introduction to beginning environmentalism for a young audience." Kirkus

Kroll, Virginia L.

Everybody has a teddy; [by] Virginia Kroll; illustrated by Sophie Allsopp. Sterling Pub. 2007 un il $12.95

Grades: PreK K   E

1. Stories in rhyme 2. Teddy bears -- Fiction

ISBN 978-1-4027-3580-6; 1-4027-3580-4

           LC 2006005154

A child describes teddy bears owned by other children, from Joshy's giant grizzly to the floppy bear Poppy's grandmother made from socks.

"This light, gentle offering celebrates individuality. . . . The text rolls along with the infectious, easy rhyme and rhythm of a children's song. . . . Cheerful illustrations capture the happy hum of a multicultural classroom filled with kids who paint, play, and look at books." Booklist

Krosoczka, Jarrett J.

Ollie the purple elephant. Knopf 2011 un il $16.99

Grades: PreK K   E

1. Elephants -- Fiction

ISBN 978-0-375-86654-8; 0-375-86654-X

"With bright, friendly acrylic art . . . the author offers a fast-paced and surreal tale with twists aplenty. After Mr. McLaughlin makes good on a silly promise that comes back to bite him ('that should they ever come across a purple elephant, they could keep him'), the McLaughlin family makes room for Ollie. . . . Good times and floor-shaking dance parties follow, upsetting the family cat and the downstairs neighbor, who collude to remove the unwanted pachyderm. . . . Krosoczka's story feels tailor-made for story time, thanks to kid-pleasing plot elements, . . . emphatic prose, . . . and emotive art." Publ Wkly

Krupinski, Loretta

Snow dog's journey. Dutton Children's Books 2010 un il $16.99

Grades: PreK K 1 2   E

1. Dogs -- Fiction 2. Love -- Fiction 3. Snow -- Fiction

ISBN 978-0-525-42246-4; 0-525-42246-3

           LC 2009-53237

Anna builds a dog of snow, which the Frost King admires and takes away with him, but when Anna's love and faith eventually reunite her with Snow Dog, they each get their fondest wish.

"Krupinski's delightful tale blends fantasy and reality in a familiar, shape-shifting animal story. . . . The softly textured illustrations smoothly convey the characters' individual perspectives and emotions." Booklist

Kruusval, Catarina

Franny's friends. R & S Books 2008 un il $16

Grades: PreK   E

1. Play -- Fiction 2. Toys -- Fiction 3. Imagination -- Fiction

ISBN 978-91-29-66836-0; 91-29-66836-0

"Franny is a sweet little girl who plans a picnic for her seven stuffed animals. The simple outing runs into trouble when the two smallest guests, Itty Bitty Kitty and Little Heddy, fall into a hole and can't get out. . . . Kruusval's pastel-shaded illustrations capture the story's charm. . . . Each animal is drawn with a liveliness that will seem wholly believable to a young child engaged in imaginative play." SLJ

Kubler, Annie

Humpty Dumpty; illustrated by Annie Kubler. Child's Play 2010 un il (Baby board books) bd bk $4.99

Grades: PreK   E

1. Nursery rhymes 2. Board books for children

ISBN 978-1-84643-339-9 bd bk; 1-84643-339-8 bd bk

"Kubler sets the familiar nursery rhyme in a jolly day-care setting peopled with a multiethnic cast of toddlers. . . . This is a splendid, slightly larger-than-usual contribution that is sure to see many repeated readings." Kirkus

Kuefler, Joseph

Rulers of the playground; Joseph Kuefler; [edited by] Alessandra Balzer. Balzer + Bray 2017 48 p. color illustrations (hardcover) $17.99

Grades: PreK K 1   E

1. Sharing -- Fiction 2. Friendship -- Fiction 3. Playgrounds -- Fiction

ISBN 9780062424327

LC 2016938958

In this book, by Joseph Kuefler, edited by Alessandra Balzer, "one morning, Jonah decided to become ruler of the playground. Everyone agreed to obey his rules to play in King Jonah's kingdom . . . Everyone except for Lennox . . . because she wanted to rule the playground, too. A gloriously rendered, hilariously deadpan tale of playground politics." (Publisher's note)

Kuhlman, Evan

Hank's big day; by Evan Kuhlman; illustrated by Chuck Groenink. Schwartz & Wade Books 2016 40 p. color illustrations (hardback) $16.99

Grades: PreK K 1 2 3   E

1. Woodlice -- Fiction 2. Friendship -- Fiction 3. Human-animal relationships -- Fiction 4. Play -- Fiction 5. Best friends -- Fiction

ISBN 9780553511505; 9780553511512

LC 2015036910

This picture book by Evan Kuhlman, illustrated by Chuck Groenink, "about a day in the life of a pill bug in suburbia is also about an unusual friendship. . . . Hank is a pill bug with a busy life. . . . His daily routine involves nibbling a dead leaf, climbing up a long stick, avoiding a skateboarder, and playing pretend with his best friend, a human girl named Amelia, in her backyard. And when day is done, Hank likes nothing better than returning home to his cozy rock." (Publisher's note)

"Excellent layout, text, and illustrations make for a thoroughly satisfying story." Kirkus

Kulka, Joe

★ **Wolf's** coming! [by] Joe Kulka. Carolrhoda Books 2007 un il lib bdg $15.95

Grades: PreK K 1   E

1. Wolves -- Fiction 2. Animals -- Fiction

ISBN 978-1-57505-930-3 lib. bdg; 1-57505-930-4 lib bdg

LC 2006013865

"The simple rhyming text describes the various ways in which the denizens of the forest prepare for Wolf's imminent arrival. . . . Saturated with color, the cartoonlike illustrations depict characters that are more human than animal, but will likely appeal to young children." SLJ

Kulling, Monica

In the bag! Margaret Knight wraps it up. Monica Kulling. Tundra Books of Northern New York 2011 32 p. ill. (Great idea) (hardcover) $17.95

Grades: K 1 2 3 4   E

1. Women inventors 2. Picture books for children 3. Inventors

ISBN 1770492399; 9781770492394

LC 2010938592

This children's picture book is a "portrait of [Margaret] Knight [that] chronicles her process in inventing the machine that made the flat-bottomed paper bag and, at the age of 12, the shuttle cover for cotton-mill machinery." It points out "the trouble facing female inventors in the 1800s." (School Library Journal)

This is written "in clean, straightforward prose. . . . [The text is] paired with Parkin's detailed and handsome pen-and-ink illustrations." Publ Wkly

The **Tweedles** Go Electric! by Monica Kulling and Marie Lafrance. Pgw 2014 32 p. $16.95

Grades: 1 2 3   E

1. Automobiles -- Fiction 2. Family life -- Fiction 3. Electric automobiles -- Fiction

ISBN 1554981670; 9781554981670

In this book, by Monica Kulling and Marie Lafrance, readers "meet the Tweedles: Papa, Mama, daughter Frances and her brother, Francis. It's the dawn of a new century--the twentieth century!--and the Tweedles have decided to buy a car. . . . Frances is the only member of her eccentric family who is not delighted when Papa decides they need an electric car. . . . But when Mr. Hamm is unable to get to the hospital because his car has run out of gas, Frances saves the day." (Publisher's note)

"In 1903, the Tweedle family eschews the new noisy, dirty, unreliable gas- and steam-powered automobiles, so Papa buys a quiet electric car. Mr. Hamm the butcher tells them to "get a real car," but when his car is out of gas during an emergency, a Tweedle helps out with their trusty electric. Energetic art accompanies the lighthearted story with contemporary relevance." Horn Book

Kumin, Maxine, 1925-2014

Oh, Harry! illustrated by Barry Moser. Roaring Brook Press 2011 un il $16.99

Grades: PreK K   E

1. Stories in rhyme 2. Horses -- Fiction

ISBN 978-1-59643-439-4; 1-59643-439-2

LC 2010024837

Harry the Horse excels at calming skittish equines in Adams & Son's show-horse barn, but he faces a different challenge when mischievous six-year-old Algernon Adams the Third arrives.

"Moser uses vibrant watercolors from multiple perspectives against dramatic white backgrounds to convey animal personality and movement in an uncluttered way. His Harry grins and rolls his eyes in ways that, like the text, are fanciful but grounded in reality. . . . Good fun for the preschool set and slightly beyond." Kirkus

Kupfer, Wendy

Let's hear it for Almigal. Handfinger Press 2012 32 p. $16.99

Grades: PreK K 1   E

1. Cochlear implants 2. Picture books for children

ISBN 0983829403; 9780983829409

This children's picture book follows deaf Amigal, who wants "to hear every single sound in the whole entire universe," so her "doctor suggests cochlear implants. . . . The book gently covers Almigal's trip to the hospital for the operation and the importance of handling the implants carefully. . . . The implants successfully help Almigal hear all the things she'd been missing." (Kirkus)

Kurtz, Jane

Faraway home; illustrated by E.B. Lewis. Harcourt Brace & Co. 2000 un il $16

Grades: PreK K 1 2   E

1. Ethiopia -- Fiction 2. African Americans -- Fiction 3. Father-daughter relationship -- Fiction

ISBN 0-15-200036-4

LC 96-47664

Desta's father, who needs to return briefly to his Ethiopian homeland, describes what it was like for him to grow up there

"Lewis captures the lyricism and rich imagery of the text with his evocative, realistic watercolors." SLJ

Water hole waiting; by Jane and Christopher Kurtz; illustrated by Lee Christiansen. Greenwillow Bks. 2002 un il $15.95; lib bdg $15.89

Grades: PreK K 1 2   **E**
1. Animals -- Fiction 2. Monkeys -- Fiction
ISBN 0-06-029850-2; 0-06-029851-0 lib bdg
LC 2001-23040

A thirsty monkey waits as the larger animals drink from the water hole on the African savanna

"Richly colored pastel drawings and precise, surprising word choices make this story a natural for sharing with a group." SLJ

Kushner, Lawrence

In God's hands; [by] Lawrence Kushner and Gary Schmidt; illustrated by Matthew J. Baek. Jewish Lights Pub. 2005 un il $16.99
Grades: K 1 2 3   **E**
1. Jews -- Fiction 2. Prayer -- Fiction 3. Miracles -- Fiction
ISBN 1-58023-224-8
LC 2005001669

While contemplating their problems in a synagogue, Jacob and David, one man rich, the other poor, come to realize their role in making miracles happen. Inspired by an ancient legend.

"This lovely piece of bookmaking combines a good tale with a strong, easily understood message. Baek's artwork, set against buff-colored pages and highlighted in shades of blue, uses a variety of angles, placements, and design elements to invite interest." Booklist

Kuskin, Karla

A boy had a mother who bought him a hat. Harper 2010 un il $16.99
Grades: PreK K 1   **E**
1. Stories in rhyme 2. Children's poetry 3. Mother-son relationship -- Fiction
ISBN 0-06-075330-7; 978-0-06-075330-6

A newly illustrated edition of the title first published 1976

This is a newly illustrated version of a rhyming cumulative tale, orginally published in 1976. "Preschool, primary." (Horn Book)

This "showcases the late poet's mastery of verse and her acute awareness of both children's sense of humore and the value they place on special belongings. . . . Hawkes' pictures . . . are skillfully executed and include some hidden surprises." Booklist

Green as a bean. Laura Geringer Books 2007 un il $16.99; lib bdg $17.89
Grades: PreK K 1 2   **E**
1. Stories in rhyme
ISBN 978-0-06-075332-0; 0-06-075332-3; 978-0-06-075334-4 lib bdg; 0-06-075334-X lib bdg
LC 2005017881

First published 1960 with title: Square as a house

Questions in verse about the many things you could be if you were square or soft or loud or red or small or fat or fierce or dark

This "is sure to inspire loud crowd participation. . . . Lines in expertly modulated rhyme and meter . . . are nicely extended in Iwai's bright, fanciful acrylic paintings." Booklist

I am me. Simon & Schuster Bks. for Young Readers 2000 un il $14.95
Grades: PreK K   **E**
1. Family life -- Fiction
ISBN 0-689-81473-9
LC 98-7911

After being told how she resembles other members of her family, a young girl states positively and absolutely that she is "NO ONE ELSE BUT ME"

"The illustrations set the story during a family trip to the beach, and in Wolcott's brightly colored double-page spreads, all the rhythmic curves . . . show the natural connections around us, the loving family embrace across generations, and the child's exuberant energy as her own individual self." Booklist

★ **So** what's it like to be a cat? Atheneum Books for Young Readers 2005 un il $15.95; pa $6.99
Grades: PreK K 1 2   **E**
1. Cats -- Fiction
ISBN 0-689-84733-5; 0-689-85930-9 pa
LC 2003-27338

A cat answers a young child's questions about such things as how much and where it sleeps, and whether or not it likes living with people.

"Lewin's charming, uncluttered watercolors extend the spare poetry's precise wit with swooping bold lines that beautifully capture both characters' movements and moods." Booklist

Kvasnosky, Laura McGee

Little wolf's first howling; by Laura McGee Kvasnosky and Kate Harvey McGee. Candlewick Press 2017 32 p. color illustrations $15.99
Grades: PreK K 1   **E**
1. Picture books for children 2. Wolves -- Fiction 3. Father-child relationship -- Fiction
ISBN 0763689718; 9780763689711

In this children's book, by Laura McGee Kvasnosky, illustrated by Kate Harvey McGee, "little Wolf can hardly wait. Tonight he will howl at the moon. . . . First, Big Wolf demonstrates traditional howling form. . . . Then it's Little Wolf's turn. He's sure he is ready, but when the big moment comes, something happens. Something unexpected, something wild, something unbe-beep-bop-believable!" (Publisher's note)

Really truly Bingo; [by] Laura McGee Kvasnosky. Candlewick Press 2008 un il $15.99
Grades: PreK K 1   **E**
1. Dogs -- Fiction 2. Imaginary playmates -- Fiction
ISBN 978-0-7636-3210-6; 0-7636-3210-4
LC 2007-40103

When Bea wants to play, her busy mother tells her to use her imagination—outside—and soon Bea and a talking dog, Bingo, are getting into all kinds of mischief.

"This book, with its child-sized problem and child-sized solution, is a fresh take on imaginary friends." Horn Book Guide

★ **Zelda** and Ivy, the runaways. Candlewick Press 2006 42p il $14.99; pa $4.99
Grades: PreK K 1 2   **E**
1. Foxes -- Fiction 2. Sisters -- Fiction
ISBN 0-7636-2689-9; 978-0-7636-2689-1; 0-7636-3061-6 pa; 978-0-7636-3061-4 pa
LC 2005-54282

In three short stories, fox sisters Zelda and Ivy run away from home, bury a time capsule, and take advantage of some creative juice.

"Bright, expressive cartoon illustrations complement the fine writing in this beginning reader." SLJ

Other titles about Zelda and Ivy are:
Zelda and Ivy (1998)
Zelda and Ivy and the boy next door (1999)
Zelda and Ivy one Christmas (2000)
Zelda and Ivy: keeping secrets (2009)
Zelda and Ivy: the big picture (2010)

Zelda and Ivy: the big picture. Candlewick Press 2010 42p il $14.99; pa $4.99

Grades: PreK K 1 2   E

1. Foxes -- Fiction 2. Camping -- Fiction 3. Sisters -- Fiction 4. Detectives -- Fiction

ISBN 978-0-7636-4180-1; 0-7636-4180-4; 978-0-7636-5645-4 pa; 0-7636-5645-3 pa

LC 2010007545

After fox sisters Zelda and Ivy and their best friend Eugene watch the new Secret Agent Fox movie, they are inspired to do some detective work then practice their new skills when rain threatens their campout plans.

"The distinctive gouache resist illustrations add lots of humorous details and textual clues for beginning readers. A wonderful addition to the series for existing fans or new readers." SLJ

Kwan, James

Dear Yeti; by James Kwan. Farrar, Straus & Giroux 2015 40 p. color illustrations (hardcover) $17.99

Grades: PreK K 1 2   E

1. Humorous fiction 2. Yeti -- Fiction 3. Hiking -- Fiction 4. Yeti -- Fiction 5. Humorous stories 6. Hiking -- Fiction 7. Letters -- Fiction

ISBN 9780374300456

LC 2015002575

In this children's book, by James Kwan, "[t]wo young hikers set out to look for Yeti one day . . . with the help of a bird friend. . . . But as their trip goes on, the hikers find that they have not prepared very well . . . and a snowstorm looms. Luckily Yeti is a friend they can rely on, and though he's not ready to come out of hiding, he sneakily finds a way to get the hikers exactly what they need when they need it." (Publisher's note)

"The spare text, consisting largely of the boys' notes, and the equally austere and stylized illustrations are perfectly matched, creating a lighthearted and comical tone." Booklist

Kwon, Yoon-Duck

My cat copies me. Kane/Miller 2007 un il $15.95

Grades: PreK K 1 2   E

1. Cats -- Fiction

ISBN 978-1-933605-26-5

Original Korean edition, 2005

"Kwon tells the story of a little girl and her cat. The pet may act coy and shy when the child seeks its affection, but when she turns away, the feline begins to follow her and mimics her actions. . . . The bright, colorful illustrations feature light gray outlining and accents that add a luminous quality and increase the imaginative nature of the drawings." SLJ

La Chanze

Little diva; illustrated by Brian Pinkney. Feiwel and Friends 2010 un il $16.99

Grades: PreK K   E

1. Theater -- Fiction 2. Mother-daughter relationship -- Fiction

ISBN 978-0-312-37010-7; 0-312-37010-5

"LaChanze, a star of stage and screen herself, supplies a peek at the life of a Broadway performer in this enticing story about a girl's dream of one day conquering the Great White Way. Nena relates her activities from morning to night as she works as a 'D.I.T.—Diva inTraining.' After trying on her mother's clothes, dancing and singing about the house, and watching her mother practice her yoga, the two spend the afternoon at the theater, where the woman is the star. . . . Pinkney catches the mood with sprawling thick black lines and swirling soft hues of pink, lavender, blue, and tawny, bringing a breezy lightness that fits this upbeat tale." SLJ

Labatt, Mary

Pizza for Sam; written by Mary Labatt; illustrated by Marisol Sarrazin. Kids Can Press 2003 32p il (Kids can read) $14.95; pa $3.95

Grades: PreK K 1 2   E

1. Dogs -- Fiction 2. Food -- Fiction

ISBN 1-55337-329-4; 1-55337-331-6 pa

"Sam the dog watches eagerly as [her] owners set out cakes, cookies, and pies for a party. . . . Sam's presented with traditional dog food, but [she] turns up [her] snout, preferring to go hungry . . . until a pizza arrives and he finds [her] perfect puppy chow. Winsome pastel illustrations combine with a few large-type sentences per page in an attractive, uncluttered layout. The basic, repetitive text is filled with action, noise, and enough suspense and silliness to engage new readers." Booklist

Other titles about Sam are:
A friend for Sam (2003)
A parade for Sam (2005)
Sam at the seaside (2006)
Sam finds a monster (2004)
Sam gets lost (2004)
Sam goes next door (2006)
Sam goes to school (2004)
Sam's first Halloween (2003)
Sam's snowy day (2005)

Lacamara, Laura

★ **Floating** on Mama's song; illustrated by Yuyi Morales. Katherine Tegen Books 2010 un il $16.99

Grades: K 1 2 3   E

1. Mothers -- Fiction 2. Singing -- Fiction 3. Bilingual books -- English-Spanish

ISBN 978-0-06-084368-7; 0-06-084368-3

Anita, a seven-year-old girl, is amazed when her mother's singing suddenly begins to make her listeners float, but Grandma says she must stop, making Mama terribly sad until her daughter makes her smile again.

"Lacámara's debut weaves together a stirring Caribbean tale inspired by her Cuban roots and her mother's opera singing. Both the English and Spanish versions of the story are fun and easy to read, and also well translated. The fusion of Morales's collage illustrations, with bright energetic colors, large warm brown characters, and real photographs interspersed with digitally enhanced foliage, will help children's imaginations take flight." SLJ

Laden, Nina

Peek-a zoo! by Nina Laden. Chronicle Books 2014 22 p. color illustrations (alk. paper) $6.99

Grades: PreK   E

1. Animals 2. Board books 3. Stories in rhyme 4. Animals -- Fiction 5. Toy and movable books

ISBN 1452111758; 9781452111759

LC 2013027686

In this book author Nina Laden presents "a companion to her . . . classic 'Peek-a Who?' Colorful pictures and a . . .rhyming text help children predict what animal is peeking through die-cut windows. The anticipation of what's hiding on the next page and the bright, engaging illustrations [are designed to] keep youngsters laughing and learning." (Publisher's note)

"The follow-up to the long-lived and much-loved Peek-a-Who? (2000) is finally here.As with the first book, a game of peekaboo plays out through die-cut holes that allow readers a glimpse through one right-hand page to the next...Laden's boldly colored gouache art, which has the look of prints, uses the signature style found in the original." Kirkus

Follow up to: Peek a Who? (2000)

★ **Peek**-a-who? by Nina Laden. Chronicle Books 2000 10 p. col. ill. $6.95

Grades: PreK   E

1. Stories in rhyme 2. Board books for children 3. Toy and movable books

ISBN 0811826023; 9780811826020

LC 99044248

The reader can look through die-cut pages for a visual clue to complete a game of peek-a-boo.

Lafaye, A.

Walking home to Rosie Lee; illustrated by Keith D. Shepherd. Cinco Puntos Press 2011 il $16.95

Grades: 2 3 4   E

1. Slavery -- Fiction 2. African Americans -- Fiction 3. Voyages and travels -- Fiction 4. Mother-son relationship -- Fiction 5. United States -- History -- 1865-1898 -- Fiction

ISBN 978-1-933693-97-2; 1-933693-97-5

LC 2010037397

At the end of the Civil War, young Gabe meets many other former slaves getting a feel for freedom whose kindness helps him in his quest to find his mother, who was sold away.

This "is distinguished by a vivid narrative voice and page-turning suspense. . . . Shepherd contributes big, dramatic spreads, thickly painted and filled with the blues of night and the yellow light of fires and lanterns." Publ Wkly

Lakritz, Deborah

Say hello, Lily; illustrated by Martha Aviles. Kar-Ben Pub. 2010 un il lib bdg $17.95; pa $7.95

Grades: PreK K 1 2   E

1. Old age -- Fiction 2. Shyness -- Fiction

ISBN 978-0-7613-4511-4 lib bdg; 0-7613-4511-6 lib bdg; 978-0-7613-4512-1 pa; 0-7613-4512-4 pa

LC 2009001873

Lily wants to go with her mother to visit the people who live at Shalom Home, an assisted living facility, but when they arrive she suddenly feels very shy.

"Pencil-and-gouache illustrations brightly delineate an elder community of kind, thoughtful faces. . . . A gentle and satisfying introduction to a senior residential situation." Kirkus

LaMarche, Jim

Lost and found. Chronicle Books 2009 un il $17.99

Grades: PreK K 1   E

1. Short stories 2. Dogs -- Fiction 3. Lost and found possessions -- Fiction

ISBN 978-0-8118-6401-5; 0-8118-6401-4

LC 2008-23009

"In the first story, Anna's retriever Molly leads the way home after the girl runs off in anger and gets lost; in the second, Jules enjoys a happy reunion with his pet Ginger after the scruffy dog disappears in the woods. Jack finds a husky named Yuki, whose owner gives Jack's single mother a fresh start in the final tale. . . . LaMarche's gentle artwork distinguishes this collection, gracefully rendering the special bond between dogs and children. . . . The soft colors of autumn unite the stories visually, and the pages are full of activity." Publ Wkly

Pond; Jim LaMarche. Simon & Schuster Books for Young Readers 2016 40 p. color illustrations (hardback) $17.99

Grades: PreK K 1 2   E

1. Ponds -- Fiction 2. Nature -- Fiction 3. Ecology -- Fiction 4. Seasons -- Fiction 5. Forests and forestry -- Fiction 6. Nature --

Effect of human beings on -- Fiction

ISBN 1481447351; 9781481447355

LC 2015045972

In this book, by Jim LaMarche, "when Matt is out for a late winter hike he sees a trickle of water in the old deserted and junk filled dirt pit at the edge of his neighborhood. With quiet appreciation, Matt can imagine the pond that must once have been there, shining in the early spring light, freezing in the winter for skating and the perfect place for swimming in the summer." (Publisher's note)

"A loving portrayal of a never-forgotten connection with the natural world." Kirkus

★ The **raft**. Lothrop, Lee & Shepard Bks. 2000 un il $15.99; pa $6.99

Grades: 2 3 4 5   E

1. Animals -- Fiction 2. Grandmothers -- Fiction 3. Rafting (Sports) -- Fiction

ISBN 0-688-13977-9; 0-06-443856-2 pa

LC 99-35546

Reluctuant Nicky spends a wonderful summer with Grandma who introduces him to the joy of rafting down the river near her home and watching the animals along the banks

"LaMarche introduces young readers to a visually resplendent, magical world. . . . Nicky's descriptive first-person narration supports the radiant, expressive illustrations." SLJ

Lamb, Albert

Tell me the day backwards. Candlewick Press 2011 un il $15.99

Grades: PreK K   E

1. Day -- Fiction 2. Bears -- Fiction 3. Bedtime -- Fiction 4. Mother-son relationship -- Fiction

ISBN 978-0-7636-5055-1; 0-7636-5055-2

LC 2010039177

"Gentle storytelling and a clever concept set this bedtime book apart from the pack. . . . McPhail's always playful and evocative illustrations set against a beautiful countryside perfectly capture this original way of remembering a day's events. An exceptional idea and a truly fine follow through." Kirkus

Laminack, Lester L.

Three hens and a peacock; written by Lester L. Laminack; illustrated by Henry Cole. Peachtree 2011 un il $15.95

Grades: PreK K 1 2   E

1. Dogs -- Fiction 2. Chickens -- Fiction 3. Peacocks -- Fiction 4. Farm life -- Fiction 5. Happiness -- Fiction

ISBN 978-1-56145-564-5; 1-56145-564-4

LC 2010031989

When life on the Tucker farm is disrupted by the arrival of a peacock, whose shrieking and strutting bring many welcome visitors, the hens complain that they are doing all of the work until the hound suggests a trade.

"Laminack's tale of barnyard envy is a fine addition to farm fables, but it's Cole's signature watercolor, ink, and pencil cartoon illustrations that charm here." Kirkus

Lamorisse, Albert

The **red** balloon. Doubleday 1957 un il $16.95; pa $12.95

Grades: PreK K 1 2   E

1. Balloons -- Fiction 2. Paris (France) -- Fiction

ISBN 0-385-00343-9; 0-385-14297-8 pa

Original French edition, 1956

"The chief feature of this book is the stunning photographs, many in color, which were taken during the filming of the French movie of the same name. A little French schoolboy Pascal catches a red balloon which turns out to be magic. The streets of Paris form a backdrop for a charming story and superb photographs." Libr J

Lamstein, Sarah Marwil

A **big** night for salamanders; [by] Sarah Marwil Lamstein; art by Carol Benioff. Boyds Mills Press 2010 un il $17.95

Grades: K 1 2 3   E

     1. Salamanders -- Fiction

     ISBN 978-1-9324-2598-7; 1-9324-2598-5

"One spring evening . . . spotted salamanders emerge from their winter burrows and make their way to a vernal pool. . . . Young Evan and his parents . . . carry salamanders across the road and even stop cars to ask drivers to slow down and watch out for their amphibian neighbors. . . . The dual text offers Evan's story in plain type and information about salamanders in italics. Readers intrigued by salamanders will learn plenty here and more in the back matter. . . . The gouache paintings add color and drama to this informative picture book." Booklist

Includes glossary and bibliographical references

Landry, Leo

Grin and bear it. Charlesbridge 2011 48p il lib bdg $12.95

Grades: K 1 2 3   E

     1. Bears -- Fiction 2. Comedians -- Fiction 3. Forest animals -- Fiction

     ISBN 978-1-57091-745-5; 1-57091-745-0

                                    LC 2010033633

Will stage fright prevent a very funny bear from becoming a stand-up comedian?

"A deft balance of punchy, dialogue-driven text and expressive, appealingly naïf pencil-and-watercolor pictures make this well suited to newly independent readers. With humor and subtlety, Landry's words and art impart a smart message about partnership, ingenuity, and pursuing one's goals." Publ Wkly

Space boy; written and illustrated by Leo Landry. Houghton Mifflin Company 2007 un il $16

Grades: PreK K 1   E

     1. Bedtime -- Fiction 2. Family life -- Fiction 3. Space flight to the moon -- Fiction

     ISBN 978-0-618-60568-2; 0-618-60568-1

                                    LC 2006-26081

Having decided not to go to bed because his home is too noisy, Nicholas flies his spaceship to the Moon, where he enjoys a snack, takes a moonwalk, and enjoys the quiet—until he realizes what he is missing at home.

"Simple lines and shapes become much more in the bright water-color-and-pen paintings. . . . Kids who love outer space and rockets will adore this quiet, imaginative adventure." SLJ

Landstrom, Lena

A **hippo's** tale; [by] Lena Landstrom; translated by Joan Sandin. R&S Books 2007 un il $15

Grades: PreK K 1 2   E

     1. Africa -- Fiction 2. Hippopotamus -- Fiction

     ISBN 978-91-29-66603-8; 91-29-66603-1

Original Swedish edition 1993

Deep in the middle of Africa, Mrs. Hippopotamus enjoys having quiet time all to herself, especially when bathing. But then a monkey shows up and disturbs her solitude.

"This quiet picture book manages to convey a wide range of human emotions through its hippo heroine. . . . The text is simple, and Landstrom's paintings create a pleasing setting and expressive characters with a minimum of fuss." Booklist

Other titles in this series are:

The little hippo's adventure (2002)

The new hippos (2003)

Pom and Pim; by Lena Landstrom; illustrated by Olof Landstrom. Lerner Pub Group 2014 32 p. $16.95

Grades: PreK K   E

     1. Luck -- Fiction 2. Adventure fiction 3. Friendship -- Fiction 4. Play -- Fiction 5. Fortune -- Fiction 6. Imagination -- Fiction

     ISBN 1877579661; 9781877579660

In this children's book, by Lena Landstrom, "Pom and Pim go outside. It' s hot. The sun is shining. What luck! Pom and Pim's day full of ups and downs, and luck both good and bad. Is eating a huge ice-cream truly a good idea? Is it really bad luck that it' s raining? Or is it good luck...?" (Publisher's note)

"In this simply written picture book, Pom and Pim enjoy the ups and downs of a day together. Pom, a young child, is inseparable from Pim, an unidentifiable stuffed animal with an egg-shaped body, two eyes, and four legs..." Booklist

Where is Pim? by Lean Landström; illustrated by Olof Landström. Lerner Pub Group 2015 32 p. (hardcover) $16.99

Grades: PreK K   E

     1. Pets -- Fiction 2. Hide-and-seek -- Fiction

     ISBN 1927271738; 9781927271735

In this children's story, by Lean Landström and illustrated by Olof Landström, "Pom and Pim are out in the park having fun--until a dog eagerly catches the flying Pim and gallops off. An upset Pom hunts high and low, with a little canine help, but finds only park detritus; fortunately, Pim's abductor happily romps back and reunites the two, then bounds off in the company of the pooch who assisted Pom." (Bulletin of the Center for Children's Books)

Lanthier, Jennifer

Hurry up, Henry; Jennifer Lanthier, illustrated by Isabelle Malenfant. Penguin Random House Canada Childrens Group 2016 32 p. color illustrations (hardcover) $16.99

Grades: PreK K 1 2   E

     1. Speed -- Fiction 2. Family life -- Fiction 3. Punctuality -- Fiction

     ISBN 0670068373; 9780143192572; 9780143192589; 9780670068371; 9781101918760

                                    LC 2016932995

In this picture book by Jennifer Lanthier, illustrated by Isabelle Malenfant, "Henry's mother and father and sister are always telling him to hurry up, and his best friend, Simon, never slows down. Henry doesn't like to be late. But he doesn't want to hurry, either. He likes to take his time and often sees things that his family misses in the rush. For Henry's birthday, Simon arranges for a special present that lets Henry take the time he needs -- with his whole family!" (Publisher's note)

"Malenfant's subtle color scheme and watercolor/pastel mixed media complement the text, varying vignettes and quiet double-page spreads to visually evoke the different paces of Henry's world. The repetition of clock motifs, fanciful flora and fauna, and changes in scale add a touch of magical realism that furthers the book's emotional themes." Kirkus

LaReau, Kara

The **infamous** Ratsos; Kara LaReau, illustrated by Matt Myers. Candlewick Press 2016 64 p. illustrations $14.99

Grades: 1 2 3 4   E

     1. Rats -- Fiction 2. Helping behavior -- Fiction

     ISBN 9780763676360; 0763676365

                                    LC 2016938103

Geisel Honor Book (2017)

In this book, by Kara LaReau, illustrated by Matt Myers, "Louie and Ralphie Ratso's dad, Big Lou, always says that there are two kinds of people: those who are tough and those who are soft. Louie and Ralphie are tough, tough, tough, just like Big Lou, and they're going to prove it. But every time they try to show just how tough they are, the Ratso brothers end up accidentally doing good deeds instead." (Publisher's note)

"LaReau keeps the action high and completely appropriate for readers embarking on chapter books. Each of the first six chapters features a new, failed attempt by Louie and Ralphie to be mean, and the final, seventh chapter resolves everything nicely. The humor springs from their foiled efforts and their reactions to their failures." Kirkus

Rabbit & Squirrel; a tale of war & peas. [by] Kara LaReau; Scott Magoon. Harcourt 2008 un il $16
Grades: K 1 2 3   E
  1. Rabbits -- Fiction 2. Gardening -- Fiction 3. Squirrels -- Fiction
ISBN 978-0-15-206307-8; 0-15-206307-2
LC 2006-101618
Rabbit and Squirrel are neighbors who never even say hello until someone starts damaging their gardens, and then they blame one another and start a fight that continues even after they meet the real culprit.

"The textured, earth-tone illustrations assist in identifying the real garden grabber [and] . . . both text and illustration suggest the bickering may become wearisome and the two may actually become friends." Libr Media Connect

LaRochelle, David
1 +1; illustrated by Brenda Sexton. Sterling Pub. Co. 2010 un il
Grades: K 1 2   E
  1. Mathematics -- Fiction
ISBN 1-4027-5995-9; 978-1-4027-5995-6
"This clever concept book asks children to take a fresh look at simple addition. Are there times when one plus one can equal three and not two? Yes—if you add one unicorn and one goat, you get three horns. Can one plus one ever equal five? Yes, because when you add one set of triplets and one set of twins, you get five babies. After sharing the numerous examples provided, children can be asked to stretch their imaginations and come up with their own quirky equations. Sexton's brightly colored digitally rendered cartoonlike illustrations are not only cheerful and attractive, but they also provide subtle clues." SLJ

How Martha saved her parents from green beans; by David LaRochelle; illustrated by Mark Fearing. Dial Books for Young Readers 2013 32 p. (hardcover) $16.99
Grades: K 1 2 3   E
  1. Food -- Fiction 2. Beans -- Fiction 3. Humorous fiction -- Fiction 4. Beans -- Fiction 5. Food habits -- Fiction 6. Parent and child -- Fiction
ISBN 0803737661; 9780803737662
LC 2012014361
In this juvenile story, by David LaRochelle, illustrated by Mark Fearing, "Martha hates green beans. When some mean, green bandits stroll into town, anyone who ever said 'Eat your green beans' is in big trouble. But when the beans kidnap Martha's parents, Martha is forced to take action. She can think of only one way to stop the villainous veggies from taking over her town, and it's not pretty . . . or tasty." (Publisher's note)

Moo! by David LaRochelle; illustrated by Mike Wohnoutka. Walker 2013 40 p. (hardcover) $16.99
Grades: PreK K 1   E
  1. Cattle 2. Automobile travel -- Fiction 3. Cows -- Fiction 4. Humorous stories 5. Behavior -- Fiction 6. Automobile driving

-- Fiction
ISBN 080273409X; 9780802734099; 9780802734105
LC 2013007463
Written by David LaRochelle and illustrated by Mike Wohnoutka, this book features "a complete story with just one word--MOO . . ." as an "imaginative picture book" that "will have readers laughing one moment and on the edge of their seats the next, as it captures the highs and lows of a mischievous cow's very exciting day." (Publisher's note)

Larsen, Andrew
The **imaginary** garden; [by] Andrew Larsen; [illustrated] by Irene Luxbacher. Kids Can Press 2009 un il $16.95
Grades: PreK K 1 2   E
  1. Gardens -- Fiction 2. Imagination -- Fiction 3. Grandfathers -- Fiction
ISBN 978-1-55453-279-7; 1-55453-279-5
"Theo's Poppa's new apartment has no garden, and the windy balcony does not promise to be a good growing spot. But Theo proposes an imaginary garden, and she and her grandfather begin to fill a large blank canvas with a stone wall for the vines to climb on, early springtime flowers, and a visiting robin. . . . The lively artwork is rendered in pen and ink and multimedia collage. The warmth of the grandparent/grandchild relationship is evident." SLJ

The **not**-so-faraway adventure; by Andrew Larsen; illustrated by Irene Luxbacher. Kids Can Press 2016 32 p. color illustrations $16.95
Grades: PreK K 1 2   E
  1. Beaches -- Fiction 2. Birthdays -- Fiction 3. Grandfathers -- Fiction 4. Adventure fiction -- Fiction
ISBN 1771380977; 9781771380973
In this book, by Andrew Larsen, illustrated by Irene Luxbacher, "Theo's Poppa was an explorer. He had been everywhere. He kept an old trunk packed with the pictures, postcards, maps and menus that he had collected on his adventures. Someday, Theo wants to be an explorer, too. For now, it's Poppa's birthday, and Theo has planned a special trip to the beach with him to celebrate. They plot out their course on a map they've drawn and then take the streetcar to the local beach." (Publisher's note)

"This quiet, sweet story is a gift for all—explorers, grandchildren, parents—any who celebrate the gift of discovering the world together." Kirkus

A **squiggly** story; by Andrew Larsen; illustrated by Mike Lowery. Kids Can Press 2016 32 p. color illustrations $16.95
Grades: PreK K 1 2   E
  1. Authorship -- Fiction 2. Storytelling -- Fiction 3. Brothers and sisters -- Fiction
ISBN 1771380160; 9781771380164
This picture book from award-winning author Andrew Larsen, illustrated by Mike Lowery, "imaginatively explores a young child's process of learning to express himself. It promotes the idea that stories are available for everyone to tell, whatever way we can, and will inspire prereaders to try writing stories of their own. . . . It beautifully highlights the exciting worlds that are opened up when children begin to read and write." (Publisher's note)

"This playful multilayered story about sparking the mind is loaded with opportunities for readers to consider different kinds of storytelling." Booklist

Lasky, Kathryn
Marven of the Great North Woods; written by Kathryn Lasky; illustrated by Kevin Hawkes. Harcourt Brace & Co. 1997 un il hardcover o.p. pa $7
Grades: K 1 2 3   E
  1. Jews -- Fiction 2. Minnesota -- Fiction 3. Lumber and lumbering

-- Fiction
ISBN 0-15-200104-2; 0-15-216826-5 pa

LC 96-2334

When his Jewish parents send him to a Minnesota logging camp to escape the influenza epidemic of 1918, ten-year-old Marven finds a special friend

"Inspired by her father's childhood, Lasky's handsomely crafted picture book is also a captivating survival story.... Contributing to the book's vivid sense of time and place are Hawkes' graphically accomplished paintings." Booklist

Latimer, Alex

The **boy** who cried ninja; written and illustrated by Alex Latimer. Peachtree 2011 un il $15.95

Grades: PreK K 1 2 E

1. Honesty -- Fiction
ISBN 978-1-56145-579-9; 1-56145-579-2

LC 2010034688

A young boy named Tim is accused of lying when he tells his parents that a ninja ate the last piece of cake and a sunburned crocodile landed on the roof, so he figures out a way to prove that he is telling the truth.

"Latimer has created offbeat digitally colored drawings brimming with quirky, diverse perspectives and hilarious details." SLJ

Laval, Thierry

★ **Colors**. Chronicle Books 2011 un il bd bk $6.99

Grades: PreK E

1. Color 2. Board books for children
ISBN 978-0-8118-7952-1; 0-8118-7952-6

LC 2010035582

Original French edition 2009

"This zesty book about colors offers genuine surprises. Each page features a flap with a die-cut shape that lets readers view the color and texture beneath.... Many of the revealed objects are thematically linked to the main scene.... Laval delivers the thrills that a peek-a-boo book should with his charmingly eccentric compositions." Publ Wkly

Lawson, Dorie McCullough

Tex; a book for little dreamers. Trafalgar Square Books 2011 un il $15.95

Grades: PreK K E

1. Cowhands -- Fiction 2. Ranch life -- Fiction
ISBN 978-1-57076-501-8; 1-57076-501-4

LC 2011014775

"Through full-color photographs, each one accompanied by a short sentence or phrase, Lawson tells the story of Luke, a boy who becomes 'Tex' in his dreams each night. He has all sorts of ranch duties like riding horses, digging irrigation trenches, checking the fence, and riding the tractor, and he relaxes for a bit in the pasture. The full-page photos will delight all cowhand enthusiasts." SLJ

Lawson, JonArno

Sidewalk flowers; by JonArno Lawson, illustrated by Sydney Smith. Groundwood Books 2015 32 p. illustrations $16.95

Grades: PreK K 1 2 3 E

1. Stories without words 2. Girls -- Fiction 3. Generosity -- Fiction
ISBN 1554984319; 9781554984312

In this book, by JonArno Lawson, illustrated by Sydney Smith, "a little girl collects wildflowers while her distracted father pays her little attention. Each flower becomes a gift, and whether the gift is noticed or ignored, both giver and recipient are transformed by their encounter." (Publisher's note)

Layton, Neal

The **tree**; Neal Layton. Candlewick Press 2017 40 p. color illustrations $16.99

Grades: PreK K 1 E

1. Animals -- Habitations 2. Trees -- Fiction
ISBN 0763689521; 9780763689520

LC 2016951795

In this book, by Neal Layton, "for the rabbits, birds, and squirrels, the big tree is home. But then come two new arrivals with wonderful plans, all ready to create their dream house. What will it mean for the animal families if their tree is cut down?" (Publisher's note)

Lazo Gilmore, Dorina K.

★ **Cora** cooks pancit; written by Dorina Lazo Gilmore; illustrated by Kristi Valiant. Shen's Books 2009 un il $17.95

Grades: PreK K 1 2 3 E

1. Cooking -- Fiction 2. Filipino Americans -- Fiction
ISBN 978-1-885008-35-0; 1-885008-35-X

LC 2008045836

When all her older siblings are away, Cora's mother finally lets her help make pancit, a Filipino noodle dish. Includes recipe for pancit.

"Clear expository prose explains how to perform kitchen tasks... These scenes effectively model how adults can introduce children to cooking. The simple, direct style also makes the book equally well suited as a read-aloud and for newly independent readers. The artwork nicely complements the text, as Valiant's warm hues of gold, red, and orange highlight the family's loving relationship." SLJ

Le Guin, Ursula K.

Cat dreams; illustrations by S.D. Schindler. Orchard Books 2009 un il lib bdg $16.99

Grades: PreK K 1 E

1. Stories in rhyme 2. Cats -- Fiction 3. Dreams -- Fiction
ISBN 978-0-545-04216-1 lib bdg; 0-545-04216-X lib bdg

LC 2008-46299

Presents a feline dreamland where it rains mice, all the dogs have run away, and a big bowl of kibbles and cream is waiting

"Easy rhyming text will be quickly memorized, but the realistic, full-bleed watercolor illustrations will keep youngsters turning the pages. A perfect fit for storytimes on cats, naps and dreams." Kirkus

Leaf, Munro, 1905-1976

★ The **story** of Ferdinand; by Munro Leaf; illustrated by Robert Lawson. 75th anniversary edition Viking Children's Books 2011 un illustrations pbk $4.99; hbk $21

Grades: PreK K 1 2 E

1. Bulls -- Fiction 2. Spain -- Fiction 3. Bullfights -- Fiction
ISBN 9780448456942; 0670013234; 044845694X; 9780670013234

Originally published 1936

"Ferdinand was a peace-loving little bull who preferred smelling flowers to making a reputation for himself in the bull ring. His story is told irresistibly in pictures and few words." Wis Libr Bull

"The drawings picture not only Ferdinand but Spanish scenes and characters as well." N Y Public Libr

Leathers, Philippa

The **Black** rabbit; Philippa Leathers. Candlewick Press 2013 40 p. (reinforced) $14

Grades: PreK K 1 2 E

1. Children's stories 2. Picture books for children 3. Rabbits -- Fiction 4. Shades and shadows -- Fiction
ISBN 076365714X; 9780763657147

LC 2012942317

In this children's book by Philippa Leathers, part of the Junior Library Guild Selection series, "rabbit has a problem. There's a large black rabbit chasing him. No matter where he runs--behind a tree, over the river--the shadowy rabbit follows. Finally in the deep, dark wood, Rabbit loses his nemesis--only to encounter a real foe!" (Publisher's note)

Lechner, John

The **clever** stick. Candlewick Press 2009 un il $14.99
Grades: K 1 2 3   E
1. Drawing -- Fiction 2. Communication -- Fiction
ISBN 978-0-7636-3950-1; 0-7636-3950-8

LC 2008024230

"A clever stick longs to express himself but can't find a way to make his thoughts understood. Discouraged, he drags himself home and discovers that the lines he creates in the sand make shapes and even pictures. . . . Lechner's gently funny ink and watercolor pictures convey the story's meaning." Horn Book Guide

Lee, Spike

Giant steps to change the world; [by] Spike and Tonya Lewis Lee; illustrated by Sean Qualls. Simon & Schuster Books for Young Readers 2011 un il $16.99
Grades: PreK K 1 2 3   E
1. Conduct of life -- Fiction
ISBN 978-0-689-86815-3; 0-689-86815-4

LC 2009-27622

"In plainspoken free verse directed right to kids, this title introduces individuals who took 'giant steps to make the world a better place.' . . . Rendered in paint, pencil, and collage, the artwork, featuring often-faceless figures, leaves space for young people to imagine their own stories and, like the poems, will inspire many children to match the pictures with the famous names and find out more." Booklist

Lee, YJ

The **little** moon princess; written and illustrated by YJ Lee. HarperCollins 2010 un il $16.99
Grades: K 1 2   E
1. Stars -- Fiction 2. Sparrows -- Fiction 3. Princesses -- Fiction
ISBN 978-0-06-154736-2; 0-06-154736-0

LC 2009-9294

With the help of a friendly sparrow, the Little Moon Princess, who is afraid of the dark, uses the jewels on the surface of her moon to light up the sky.

"Lee's stunning use of watercolor and ink creates the illusion of light, and her art offers readers a breathtaking view of the night sky. A lovely read-aloud." SLJ

Lee-Tai, Amy

A **place** where sunflowers grow; story, Amy Lee-Tai; illustrations by Felicia Hoshino; [Japanese translation, Marc Akio Lee] Children's Book Press 2006 31p il $16.95
Grades: 1 2 3   E
1. Bilingual books -- English-Japanese 2. Japanese Americans -- Evacuation and relocation, 1942-1945 -- Fiction
ISBN 0-8923-9215-0; 978-0-8923-9215-5

LC 2005032957

While she and her family are interned at Topaz Relocation Center during World War II, Mari gradually adjusts as she enrolls in an art class, makes a friend, plants sunflowers and waits for them to grow.

"The story is told in both English and Japanese, and the earth-toned illustrations, created using watercolors, ink, tissue paper, and acrylic paint, nicely detail the simple plot." SLJ

Leedy, Loreen

Crazy like a fox; a simile story. written and illustrated by Loreen Leedy. Holiday House 2008 un il lib bdg $16.95; pa $6.95
Grades: K 1 2   E
1. Foxes -- Fiction 2. Parties -- Fiction 3. Birthdays -- Fiction 4. English language -- Idioms
ISBN 978-0-8234-1719-3 lib bdg; 0-8234-1719-0 lib bdg; 978-0-8234-2248-7 pa; 0-8234-2248-7 pa

LC 2007-051016

"Rufus, a spunky fox in suspenders, rudely startles his friend Babette, a lamb, by roaring 'like...a lion.' She gets 'mad...as a hornet' and chases him, and he eventually leads her to her surprise birthday party. Leedy relates this narrative entirely through similes. Her illustrations emphasize the comparisons as each protagonist is amusingly transformed from one object into another. . . . [Leedy's] vivid illustrations, filled with movement and wide-eyed creatures, will entertain readers." SLJ

The **great** graph contest; written and illustrated by Loreen Leedy. Holiday House 2005 32p il $16.95; pa $6.95
Grades: 1 2 3   E
1. Graphic methods 2. Frogs -- Fiction 3. Snails -- Fiction 4. Lizards -- Fiction
ISBN 0-8234-1710-7; 0-8234-2029-9 pa

LC 2003-62549

Gonk the toad, Chester the snail, and Beezy the lizard hold a contest to see who can make better graphs

"A splashy and colorful offering designed to inform and entertain. . . . The lively text, delivered in large type and contained in dialogue and thought balloons, is engaging and well supported by the vivid, cartoon illustrations." SLJ

Lehman, Barbara

Museum trip. Houghton Mifflin 2006 un il $15
Grades: K 1 2 3   E
1. School stories 2. Stories without words 3. Art museums -- Fiction
ISBN 0-618-58125-1

LC 2005052840

In this wordless picture book, a boy imagines himself inside some of the exhibits when he goes on a field trip to an art museum.

"The sturdiness and clarity of the ink-lined, watercolor-and-gouache art juxtaposes wonderfully with the story's airy world of imagination." Booklist

Rainstorm. Houghton Mifflin 2007 un il $16
Grades: PreK K 1 2   E
1. Stories without words 2. Play -- Fiction
ISBN 978-0-618-75639-1; 0-618-75639-6

LC 2006-49318

In this wordless picture book, a boy finds a mysterious key which leads him on an adventure one rainy day.

"Lehman provides purely colored, precisely rendered artwork that capably captures both adventures and emotions." Booklist

★ The **red** book. Houghton Mifflin 2004 un il $12.95
Grades: K 1 2 3   E
1. Stories without words 2. Books and reading -- Fiction
ISBN 0-618-42858-5

A Caldecott Medal honor book, 2005

This "wordless book tells the complex story of a reader who gets lost, literally, in a little book that has the magic to move her to another place. . . . Done in watercolor, gouache, and ink, the simple, streamlined pictures are rife with invitations to peek inside, to investigate further, and—like a hall of mirrors—reflect, refract, repeat, and reveal. Lehman's story captures the magical possibility that exists every time readers open a book." SLJ

★ The **secret** box. Scholastic Press 2011 un il $15.99

Grades: PreK K 1   E

1. Stories without words 2. Boys -- Fiction 3. Photography -- Fiction

ISBN 978-0-547-23868-5; 0-547-23868-1

"Here, three boys discover a box in the top floor of their urban boarding school that holds decades-old sepia photographs of a schoolboy, a postcard, and a map leading to a location on the coast. Picking out features of the old landscape amid the built-up, modern city around them, the boys make their way to a boardwalk amusement park, where they find the schoolboy of the photograph with a crowd of children who presumably have made the same trip. . . . . A provocative example of the complexity that can be conveyed using only pictures." Publ Wkly

Trainstop. Houghton 2008 un il $16

Grades: PreK K 1 2   E

1. Stories without words 2. Railroads -- Fiction 3. Imagination -- Fiction

ISBN 0-618-75640-X

In this wordless picture book, a young girl takes a train and makes a stop at a most unusual place where she has an important task to perform.

Lehman "demonstrates her extraordinary knack for storytelling sans words. . . . Gouache, watercolor, and ink illustrations reveal a bleak cityscape and adults dressed in muted tones—all in pointed contrast to the girl's head-to-toe multicolored outfit. . . . Lehman's true talent is her spot-on depiction of a young child's capacity for criss-crossing the real with the imaginary." Horn Book

Lehrhaupt, Adam

I will not eat you; Adam Lehrhaupt; illustrated by Scott Magoon. Simon & Schuster Books for Young Readers 2016 40 p. color illustrations (ebook) $15.99; (hardcover) $17.99

Grades: PreK K 1   E

1. Animals -- Fiction 2. Dragons -- Fiction 3. Friendship -- Fiction

ISBN 9781481429344; 9781481429337

LC 2015029655

This children's book, by Adam Lehrhaupt, illustrated by Scott Magoon, focuses on "a creature who resists the urge to eat the animals that wander into his cave at least for now! Theodore thinks everything is a potential meal. Lucky for the bird, wolf, and tiger, who pass by his cave, Theodore isn't hungry yet. But then something new approaches. A boy. Has Theodore found a new favorite food? Or something more?" (Publisher's note)

"Highly recommended for storytime and one-on one sharing." SLJ

Warning: do not open this book! Adam Lehrhaupt; illustrated by Matthew Forsythe. Simon & Schuster Books for Young Readers 2013 40 p. color illustrations (hardcover) $16.99

Grades: PreK K 1   E

1. Monkeys -- Fiction 2. Picture books for children 3. Humorous stories 4. Toucans -- Fiction 5. Alligators -- Fiction

ISBN 9781442435827; 1442435828; 9781442435834

LC 2012014432

In this children's picture book, by Adam Lehrhaput, illustrated by Matthew Forsythe, "the narrator repeatedly warns readers not to open this book. Those who do not heed these pleas release a troop of artistic monkeys that wreak havoc on the book itself. Nothing is safe from these wild invaders--not the art and not the text. When the narrator again urges readers to turn back, toucans join the fracas." (Kirkus Reviews)

"The earth-tone digital illustrations well replicate the messy monkey business of painting all over the trees and pages, and the playful

arrangement of text adds greatly to the book's mayhem. Wonderful chaos." Booklist

Lepp, Bil

The **King** of Little Things; by Bil Lepp and illustrated by Daniel T. Wenzel. Peachtree Publishers 2013 32 p. $16.95

Grades: PreK K 1 2   E

1. Size -- Fiction 2. Kings and rulers -- Fiction

ISBN 1561457086; 9781561457083

LC 2012032584

In this book, by Bil Lepp, "when King Normous thinks he has finally become the ruler of all the world, he is enraged to learn that the King of Little Things still reigns happily in his tiny kingdom. Normous sends his army to defeat this upstart, but he finds he cannot outfight or outwit a king who holds sway over the little things of the world." (Publisher's note)

Leroy, Jean

A **well**-mannered young wolf; Jean Leroy, illustrated by Matthieu Maudet. Eerdmans Books for Young Readers 2016 30 p. color illustrations (hardback) $16

Grades: PreK K 1 2   E

1. Wolves -- Fiction 2. Etiquette -- Fiction 3. Manners and customs -- Fiction 4. Humorous stories

ISBN 9780802854797

LC 2015046911

This children's book by Jean Leroy, illustrated by Matthieu Maudet, tells "a hilarious story about why manners matter. One morning, a young wolf eagerly sets out on his first hunting trip. But before he can devour his prey, he must honor their final wishes, just as his parents taught him to do. But the wolf's would-be meals aren't quite as honorable as he is! Can common courtesy prove effective amidst the wild laws of nature?" (Publisher's note)

"A palette of rich reds, yellows, and browns against pages with plentiful white space contributes to this cockeyed tale of politeness gone awry. Jon Klassen fans rejoice—another twisted ending!" Booklist

Lester, Alison, 1952-

Noni the pony; Alison Lester. Beach Lane Books 2013 32 p. (hardback) $15.99

Grades: PreK K 1   E

1. Stories in rhyme 2. Horses -- Fiction 3. Friendship -- Fiction 4. Ponies -- Fiction

ISBN 144245959X; 9781442459595; 9781442459601

LC 2012004907

This rhyming children's book, by Alison Lester, introduces readers to "Noni, the friendliest, funniest, and friskiest pony you'll ever meet! When she's not racing and chasing with her best pals Dave Dog and Coco the Cat, she's busy making sure they feel cozy and loved. Because Noni isn't just heaps of fun--she's a great friend, too." (Publisher's note)

Noni the pony goes to the beach; Alison Lester. Beach Lane Books 2015 32 p. color illustrations (hardcover) $17.99

Grades: PreK K 1   E

1. Dogs -- Fiction 2. Ponies -- Fiction 3. Beaches -- Fiction 4. Friendship -- Fiction 5. Stories in rhyme

ISBN 9781481446259

LC 2014043640

In this book, by Alison Lester, "It's beach time for a playful pony and her friends in this light hearted celebration of friendship and loyalty. . . . Noni the Pony and her friends are off to the beach! Their playful day is going swimmingly—until Dave Dog follows a whale a bit too far out to sea. Luckily, Noni is there to rescue the poor pup and bring him back to safety and back to the fun!" (Publisher's note)

"A perfect blend of text and pictures makes this an outstanding offering for the youngest crowd." SLJ

★ **Running** with the horses. North South Books 2011 un il $16.95
Grades: 2 3 4 E
1. Horses -- Fiction 2. Austria -- Fiction 3. World War, 1939-1945 -- Fiction 4. Father-daughter relationship -- Fiction
ISBN 0-7358-4002-4; 978-0-7358-4002-7
First published 2009 in Australia
"Lester crafts a believable wartime adventure. . . . The illustrations, predominantly black-and-white drawings layered between photographic and colored-pencil back- and foregrounds, make the historical contemporary." Kirkus

Sophie Scott goes south; Alison Lester. Penguin 2012 [32] p. $17.99
Grades: 1 2 3 4 E
1. Antarctica -- Fiction 2. Exploration -- Fiction 3. Arctic regions -- Fiction 4. Antarctica
ISBN 0544088956; 9780544088955; 9780670880683
LC 2013433269
In this picture book, by Alison Lester, "nine-year-old Sophie is going on a month-long voyage to Antarctica, with her dad, the captain of an icebreaker. Sailing the frozen seas round-trip from Australia to Mawson Station in the South Pole, Sophie recounts the adventure of a lifetime in her own words, illustrations, and color photographs. She'll show us icebergs, penguins, seals, and whales!" (Publisher's note)

Lester, Helen
Happy birdday, Tacky! written by Helen Lester; illustrated by Lynn Munsinger. Houghton Mifflin Books for Children 2013 32 p. col. ill. (reinforced) $16.99
Grades: PreK K 1 2 E
1. Penguins -- Fiction 2. Birthdays -- Fiction 3. Dance -- Fiction 4. Parties -- Fiction 5. Penguins -- Fiction 6. Birthdays -- Fiction
ISBN 0547912285; 9780547912288
LC 2012014847
This children's picture book is part of the Tacky the Penguin series. Here, "everyone is deep into preparations for Tacky's Birdday Party. This includes baking, practicing the special song and making a whole slew of cards for their decidedly odd friend." However, the party goes awry due to Tacky's strange habits and another penguin's injury. Can the party be saved? (Kirkus)

★ **Hooway** for Wodney Wat; illustrated by Lynn Munsinger. Houghton Mifflin 1999 32p il $16; pa $5.95
Grades: PreK K 1 2 E
1. School stories 2. Speech disorders -- Fiction
ISBN 0-395-92392-1; 0-618-21612-X pa
LC 98-46149
All his classmates make fun of Rodney because he can't pronounce his name, but it is Rodney's speech impediment that drives away the class bully.
"Munsinger's watercolor with pen-and-ink illustrations positively bristle with humor and each rat, mouse, hamster, and capybara is fully realized as both rodent and child." SLJ
Another title about Rodney is:
Wodney Wat's wobot (2011)

The **Loch** Mess monster; written by Helen Lester and illustrated by Lynn Munsinger. Houghton Mifflin Books for Children, Houghton Mifflin Harcourt 2014 32 p. color illustrations $16.99

Grades: PreK K 1 E
1. Orderliness 2. Monsters -- Fiction 3. Scotland -- Fiction 4. Loch Ness monster -- Fiction 5. Humorous stories 6. Orderliness -- Fiction
ISBN 0544099907; 9780544099906
LC 2013017881
In this book, by Helen Lester and illustrated by Lynn Munsinger, "beware the Loch Mess monster! The legend of the Loch Ness monster is not exactly true. There is no single monster; there are three! Nessie, Fergus, and their wee laddie, Angus, live peacefully together beneath the surface of the lake, obeying proper monster etiquette by following five basic monster rules. All is well until Angus' untidy ways result in a grottie mess and break rule No. 2." (Kirkus Reviews)
"Legendary monster Nessie's son Angus is banished to his room for being messy. When his personal junk pile bursts through the surface of the loch, one look at 'land-monsters'--a goat, duck, and cow--scares Angus into cleaning up and remaining in the lake's depths where he belongs. Munsinger's watercolors further the silly humor. A Scottish glossary is included." Horn Book

The **sheep** in wolf's clothing; illustrated by Lynn Munsinger. Houghton Mifflin 2007 32p il $16
Grades: PreK K 1 2 E
1. Sheep -- Fiction 2. Wolves -- Fiction 3. Clothing and dress -- Fiction
ISBN 978-0-618-86844-5; 0-618-86844-5
LC 2007-00644
Clothing is important to Ewetopia, but her carefully-chosen wolf outfit fails to impress the other sheep at the Woolyones' costume ball until a real wolf appears dressed as a sheep, mistakes her for his mother, and throws a tantrum when she outsmarts him.
"The playful illustrations, suffused with expression and shades of pink, show sheep outfitted in tutus and an Elvis costume, and the wolf having a tantrum. Lester follows a familiar format in this clever tale." SLJ

Tacky and the haunted igloo; by Helen Lester; illustrated by Lynn Munsinger. Houghton Mifflin Harcourt 2015 32 p. color illustrations (Tacky the penguin) $16.99
Grades: PreK K 1 2 E
1. Penguins -- Fiction 2. Halloween -- Fiction 3. Fear -- Fiction 4. Haunted houses -- Fiction
ISBN 0544339940; 9780544339941
LC 2014009955
In this Halloween children's book, by Helen Lester, illustrated by Lynn Munsinger, "Goodly, Lovely, Angel, Neatly, and Perfect are planning the spookiest haunted igloo ever! They've decorated with spoohooky cobwebs, they've baked some awful waffle treats, and the only thing left to do is dress up as something scary to haunt the igloo. Everything is going spooktacularly . . . until ghostly hunters show up! They want all the penguins' snacks." (Publisher's note)
"A first purchase for general collections and holiday alike." SLJ

Three cheers for Tacky; illustrated by Lynn Munsinger. Houghton Mifflin 1994 32p il $16; pa $5.95
Grades: PreK K 1 2 E
1. Contests -- Fiction 2. Penguins -- Fiction 3. Cheerleading -- Fiction
ISBN 0-395-66841-7; 0-395-82-740-X pa
LC 93-14342
This "is a smooth, fun read. Munsinger's full-color illustrations are charming and subtle." SLJ
Other titles about Tacky are:
Tacky the penguin (1988)

Tacky in trouble (1998)
Tacky and the emperor (2000)
Tackylocks and the three bears (2002)
Tacky and the winter games (2005)
Tacky goes to camp (2009)
Tacky's Christmas (2010)
Happy birdday, Tacky! (2013)
Tacky and the haunted igloo (2015)

Wodney Wat's wobot; written by Helen Lester; illustrated by Lynn Munsinger. Houghton Mifflin Books for Children 2011 un il $16.99
Grades: PreK K 1 2   E
   1. School stories 2. Robots -- Fiction 3. Speech disorders -- Fiction
   ISBN 978-0-547-36756-9; 0-547-36756-2
                    LC 2010044363
When Wodney Wat, who cannot pronounce the letter R, gets a talking robot for his birthday, it turns out to be more than just a fun gift.
   "Wodney is a wonderfully quirky character with whom many children will connect. Munsinger's illustrations are joyful and humorous." SLJ

Lester, Julius
   ★ **Black** cowboy, wild horses; a true story. [by] Julius Lester, Jerry Pinkney. Dial Bks. 1998 un il $18.99
Grades: 2 3 4   E
   1. Horses -- Fiction 2. Cowhands -- Fiction 3. African Americans -- Fiction
   ISBN 0-8037-1787-3
                    LC 97-25210
A black cowboy is so in tune with wild mustangs that they accept him into the herd, thus enabling him singlehandedly to take them to the corral
   This story is told in "vivid, poetic prose. . . . Pinkney's magnificent earth-toned paintings bring to life the wild beauty of the horses and the western plains." Horn Book Guide

   Sam and the tigers; a new telling of Little Black Sambo. pictures by Jerry Pinkney. Dial Bks. for Young Readers 1996 un il $16.99; pa $6.99
Grades: K 1 2 3   E
   1. Tigers -- Fiction
   ISBN 0-8037-2028-9; 0-14-056288-5 pa
                    LC 95-43080
A boy named Sam, who lives in the land of Sam-sam-sa-mara, gives his new school clothes to tigers who threaten to eat him, but he re-claims them when the tigers chase one another until they turn into butter
   "The rolling, lilting narrative is a model of harmony, clarity, and meticulously chosen detail. . . . Pinkney's lively pencil-and-watercolor illustrations sprawl extravagantly across double spreads and are smoothly integrated with the narrative." SLJ

Leuck, Laura
   I love my pirate papa; [by] Laura Leuck; illustrated by Kyle M. Stone. Harcourt 2007 un il $16
Grades: PreK K 1 2   E
   1. Pirates -- Fiction 2. Father-son relationship -- Fiction
   ISBN 978-0-15-205664-3
                    LC 2006009240
A pirate's son shares the things he loves about his father, including climbing the mast together to yell "Land ho" and sharing the booty when they find buried treasure.
   This is written "in well cadenced, rhyming verses. . . . The stylized acrylic paintings, using exaggeration and comical details effectively, create one dramatic double-page scene after another." Booklist

Levert, Mireille
   A **wizard** in love; [written by] Mireille Levert; [illustrated by] Marie Lafrance. Tundra Books 2009 un il $17.95
Grades: PreK K 1 2   E
   1. Magic -- Fiction 2. Noise -- Fiction 3. Witches -- Fiction
   ISBN 978-0-88776-901-6; 0-88776-901-2
   Original French edition published 2007 in Canada
Hector, a retired wizard, lives happily and quietly with his cat, Poison, in a dilapidated house at the edge of the forest, until a noisy new neighbor moves into the abandoned house across the road, and things are never the same again.
   "Both verbally and visually entirely funny . . . this offbeat import is a sophisticated treat.." Kirkus

Levine, Arthur A.
   Monday is one day; illustrated by Julian Hector. Scholastic Press 2011 un il $16.99
Grades: PreK K 1   E
   1. Counting 2. Stories in rhyme 3. Day -- Fiction 4. Week -- Fiction 5. Family life -- Fiction
   ISBN 978-0-439-78924-0; 0-439-78924-9
                    LC 2009011575
A rhyming countdown of the days of the week as families find ways to spend time together while waiting for the weekend.
   "Hector's grinning cartoon-style illustrations are delightful, based in reality but accented with unexpected color. . . . But the book's greatest accomplishment might be its cross section of middle America: white, black, old, young, white-collar, blue-collar, straight, and gay. . . . It's that rare book perceptive enough to recognize that the random moments are those we treasure most." Booklist

Levine, Ellen
   ★ **Henry's** freedom box; illustrated by Kadir Nelson. Scholastic Press 2007 un il $16.99
Grades: 1 2 3   E
   1. Slaves 2. Magicians 3. Abolitionists 4. Slavery -- Fiction 5. African Americans -- Fiction 6. Underground railroad -- Fiction
   ISBN 0-439-77733-X
                    LC 2006-09487
A Caldecott Medal honor book, 2008
A fictionalized account of how in 1849 a Virginia slave, Henry "Box" Brown, escapes to freedom by shipping himself in a wooden crate from Richmond to Philadelphia.
   "According to the flap copy, an antique lithograph of Brown inspired Nelson's paintings, which use crosshatched pencil lines layered with watercolors and oil paints. . . . Transcending technique is the humanity Nelson imbues in his characters." Booklist

Levine, Gail Carson
   Betsy Red Hoodie; illustrated by Scott Nash. HarperCollins Publishers 2010 un il $16.99; lib bdg $17.89
Grades: K 1 2   E
   1. Sheep -- Fiction 2. Wolves -- Fiction 3. Grandmothers -- Fiction
   ISBN 978-0-06-146870-4; 0-06-146870-3; 978-0-06-146871-1 lib bdg; 0-06-146871-1 lib bdg
                    LC 2008-27456
In this variation of "Little Red Riding Hood," Betsy Red Hoodie goes to visit her grandma with her friend Zimmo the wolf and her flock of sheep, but Zimmo, her mother, and her grandma have a surprise planned.
   "Nash stages the shenanigans in an attractive country landscape, supporting Levine's light tone with comical pen drawings. . . . Good read-aloud fun." Horn Book

Betsy who cried wolf; illustrated by Scott Nash. HarperCollins Pubs. 2002 un lib bdg $16.89

Grades: PreK K 1 2   E

   1. Sheep -- Fiction 2. Wolves -- Fiction 3. Shepherds -- Fiction

   ISBN 0-06-028763-2; 0-06-028764-0 lib bdg

                         LC 00-54032

   Betsy, a serious young shepherd, finds that there is more than one way to keep a wolf from eating her sheep

   "Nash's cartoonlike illustrations, with their clean lines, crisp colors, and folk-art touches, add considerably to the story." SLJ

Levis, Caron

   Ida, always; written by Caron Levis; illustrated by Charles Santoso. Atheneum Books for Young Readers 2016 40 p. color illustrations (hardcover) $17.99

Grades: K 1 2 3   E

   1. Grief -- Fiction 2. Friendship -- Fiction 3. Polar bear -- Fiction 4. Loss (Psychology) -- Fiction 5. Central Park (New York, N.Y.) -- Fiction 6. Bears -- Fiction 7. Grief -- Fiction 8. Friendship -- Fiction 9. Polar bear -- Fiction 10. Best friends -- Fiction 11. New York (N.Y.) -- Fiction 12. Loss (Psychology) -- Fiction

   ISBN 9781481426404

                         LC 2014017409

   In this book, by Caron Levis, illustrated by Charles Santoso, "Gus lives in a big park in the middle of an even bigger city, and he spends his days with Ida. . . . Then one sad day, Gus learns that Ida is very sick, and she isn't going to get better. The friends help each other face the difficult news with whispers, sniffles, cuddles, and even laughs. Slowly Gus realizes that even after Ida is gone, she will still be with him—through the . . . memories that live in their favorite spots." (Publisher's note)

   "Although Gus experiences real loss upon Ida's death, the book ends on a hopeful note, emphasizing the strength of the friendship and Gus's memories of Ida... A tender and honest portrayal of coming to terms with death." SLJ

   Stuck with the Blooz; Caron Levis; illustrated by Jon Davis. Harcourt Children's Books 2012 40 p. $16.99

Grades: K 1 2 3   E

   1. Melancholy 2. Emotions -- Fiction 3. Monsters -- Fiction 4. Sadness -- Fiction 5. Monsters -- Fiction

   ISBN 0547745605; 9780547745602

                         LC 2011041938

   This children's book, by Caron Lewis, illustrated by Jon Davis, asks "What do you do when you're feeling blue--especially when your mood takes the form of a drippy, oozy monster called the Blooz? Do you ignore it? Do you ask it lots of questions? Do you give it an ice-pop and hope it goes away? Through trial and error, the child in this story discovers that while it may not be easy, it's not impossible to shake the Blooz." (Publisher's note)

Leviton, Michael

   My first ghost; illustrated by Stephanie Buscema; text by Margaret Miller & Michael Leviton. 1st ed. Disney/Hyperion Books 2012 40 p.

Grades: PreK K 1 2   E

   1. Wit and humor 2. Picture books for children 3. Ghosts -- Fiction

   ISBN 1423119495; 9781423119494

                         LC 2011017596

   This children's picture book, by Maggie Miller and Michael Leviton, illustrated by Stephanie Buscema, "comes with a free ghost! But, like any pet, ghosts need special care and attention. . . . [The book] teaches kids everything they need to know about taking care of their very own ghost. . . . [A]uthors Miller and Leviton offer humorous tips on feeding, grooming, and ghostly games which are complemented by . . . illustrations." (Publisher's note)

Levy, Debbie

   We Shall Overcome; The Story of a Song. by Debbie Levy; illustrated by Vanessa Brantley-Newton. Disney Press 2013 32 p. $16.99

Grades: 1 2 3 4   E

   1. Slavery -- United States -- Songs 2. African Americans -- Civil rights -- Songs 3. African American music

   ISBN 1423119541; 9781423119548

   This book, written by Debbie Levy and illustrated by Vanessa Brantley-Newton, focuses on the song "We Shall Overcome." "From the song's roots in America's era of slavery through to the civil rights movement of the 1960s and today, 'We Shall Overcome' has come to represent the fight for equality and freedom around the world." (Publisher's note)

   "A simple story explains how this rallying song for freedom became the watchword for the civil rights movement in the United States, and from there to countries around the world struggling with human rights issues. Lively digital and mixed-media illustrations convey a joyous mood. Although "No single day marks the birth of the song...", a timeline of highlights is included. Reading list, websites." (Horn Book)

Levy, Janice

   Gonzalo grabs the good life; written by Janice Levy; illustrated by Bill Slavin. Eerdmans Books for Young Readers 2009 un il $17.50

Grades: K 1 2 3   E

   1. Wealth -- Fiction 2. Roosters -- Fiction

   ISBN 978-0-8028-5328-8; 0-8028-5328-5

                         LC 2008009998

   When Gonzalo the rooster wins the lottery, he leaves his job at the farm in search of the good life.

   "Acrylic illustrations on gessoed paper animate the humor with fine-feathered cleverness, adding wry details. . . . A vocabulary list defines the six Spanish words sprinkled throughout. This is beak-in-cheek fun with an underlying message." Booklist

Lewin, Betsy, 1937-

   Good night, Knight; Betsy Lewin. Holiday House 2015 24 p. color illustrations (I like to read) (hardcover) $14.95

Grades: PreK K 1   E

   1. Cookies -- Fiction 2. Dreams -- Fiction 3. Knights and knighthood -- Fiction 4. Horses -- Fiction 5. Knights and knighthood -- Fiction

   ISBN 0823432068; 9780823432066

                         LC 2014007376

   In this picture book by Betsy Lewin "Knight and Horse are drifting off to sleep when Knight has a magical dream. In his vision, he sees the most scrumptious, soft golden cookies he has ever laid his eyes on. The delicious treats call to him: Go and find the golden cookies. When Knight wakes up, he gets Horse ready for their journey, and they go trotting along in search of the golden goods." (Publisher's note)

   "Lewin's latest entry in the I Like to Read series (You Can Do It!, 2013) stars a sleepy knight whose dream instructs him to "go and find the golden cookies." In folkloric fashion, Knight ("Clank! Clank!") and Horse ("Clip-clop!") set off, searching unsuccessfully in a tree, some bushes, and water before giving up and going home. . . . The simple, often repeating text is well placed on the page, allowing beginning readers to easily predict unfamiliar words from the context and the art. This should be popular with fans of Shelley Moore Thomas' Good Knight series." Booklist

   Puffling patrol; Ted and Betsy Lewin. Lee & Low Books 2012 56 p. (hardcover : alk. paper) $19.95

Grades: 2 3 4   E

   1. Puffins 2. Heimaey (Iceland) 3. Birds -- Protection 4. Children and animals 5. Wildlife rescue -- Iceland -- Heimaey (Westman Islands) 6. Atlantic puffin -- Infancy -- Iceland -- Heimaey

(Westman Islands)
ISBN 1600604242; 9781600604249

LC 2011032248

In this book, "husband and wife team Ted and Betsy Lewin detail their visit to the island of Heimaey (off the coast of Iceland). They accompany two child members of the 'Puffling Patrol' (who rescue newly hatched puffins that become disoriented and lost on their way to the sea) and observe as the children find, care for, and release the baby pufflings." (Bulletin of the Center for Children's Books)

Where is Tippy Toes? [written and] illustrated by Betsy Lewin. Atheneum Books for Young Readers 2010 un il $16.99
Grades: PreK K
E
1. Stories in rhyme 2. Cats -- Fiction
ISBN 978-1-4169-3808-8; 1-4169-3808-7

LC 2009-24455

Although everyone can see how Tippy Toes, a mischievous cat, spends his days, only one knows where he goes after dark.

"Oversize watercolors outlined in a thick black line add humor to the text . . . and the bright hues seen in the flowers, sun, and cat's fur enhance the changing backgrounds. Rhyming sentences come together with the turn of a page and continue to the satisfying page turn at the end. This cat's sun up to sun down routine makes an excellent choice for those looking for a new bedtime story." SLJ

★ **You** can do it! by Betsy Lewin. 1st ed. Holiday House 2013 32 p. (I like to read) (reinforced) $14.95
Grades: K 1 2
E
1. Racing -- Fiction 2. Crocodiles -- Fiction 3. Self-confidence -- Fiction 4. Racing -- Fiction 5. Alligators -- Fiction 6. Self-confidence -- Fiction
ISBN 0823425223; 9780823425228

LC 2011051992

This children's book, by Caldecott Honor-winning illustrator Betsy Lewin, is part of the "I Like to Read" series. "'Can I do it?' wonders the little crocodile when he sees a sign for Sunday's big swimming race. A mean, bigger crocodile tells him he cannot win, but the little crocodile's friend helps him train and tells him more than once that he can indeed succeed. On the day of the big race, the little crocodile is ready to prove himself." (Publisher's note)

"Limited, repetitive text invites new readers to adopt the same spirit of determination about reading that the protagonist alligator does about swimming... Lewin's restrained watercolor-and-ink artwork matches the control of the text...while delivering engaging and expressive characters. Subtle shifts in the placement of speech balloons provide humor while helping children decode. A winner of an early reader." Kirkus

Lewin, Ted
Animals work; by Ted Lewin. Holiday House 2014 28 p. col. ill., col. map (hardcover) $14.95
Grades: PreK K 1
E
1. Animals 2. Working animals
ISBN 0823430405; 9780823430406

LC 2013014333

"Bursting with detailed illustrations, this picture book not only teaches readers about the variety of work animals perform, but depicts the give-and-take dynamic of human/animal relationships." It "transports readers from an open field to a desert to a snowy tundra as animals of all kinds, from a shaggy pup to a group of camels, perform some very important tasks." (Publisher's note)

"The watercolor illustrations of the various locations and the people that inhabit them are stunningly lifelike, and a world map on the final spread shows where Lewin saw the animals. Easy enough for the very earliest readers." SLJ

Can you see me? by Ted Lewin. Holiday House 2014 32 p. (I like to read) (hardcover) $14.95
Grades: PreK K 1
E
1. Costa Rica 2. Rain forest animals 3. Animals -- Habitations
ISBN 0823429407; 9780823429400

LC 2013009555

In this children's book, by Ted Lewin, "readers are invited to spot various animals in the Costa Rican rain forest. Lewin . . . . displays . . . mammals, birds and reptiles in their natural habitats. Camouflage is the unspoken theme. . . . A pictorial guide identifies each of the animals by name." (Kirkus Reviews)

"Lewin camouflages an animal for youngsters to find in each of eleven rainforest scenes. The language ("I am a reptile. Can you see me?") is largely, and appropriately, repetitive, but the challenge of decoding the key word before finding the animal in the illustration adds an extra burden to the target audience of beginning readers. A picture guide with species names is appended." Horn Book

Lewis, J. Patrick
Big is big (and little, little) a book of contrasts. by J. Patrick Lewis; illustrated by Bob Barner. Holiday House 2007 un il $16.95
Grades: PreK K 1
E
1. Opposites 2. Animals -- Poetry
ISBN 978-0-8234-1909-8; 0-8234-1909-6

LC 2005050341

"Wordplay meets playful art in this clever look at opposites. Lewis's bouncy verse and Barner's rollicking illustrations show the contrasts between various animals. . . . Done in a combination of cut-paper collage, bright pastels, and bold black line, Barner's animals cavort against vivid backgrounds." SLJ

Face bug; by J. Patrick Lewis; illustrated by Kelly Murphy; photographs by Frederic B. Siskind. WordSong 2013 36 p. ill. (reinforced) $16.95
Grades: 3 4 5
E
1. Insects -- Poetry
ISBN 1590789253; 9781590789254

LC 2012943510

This book by J. Patrick Lewis "combines poetry, line drawings and scientific facts. . . . A collection of small bugs . . . visits the Face Bug Museum, where they learn to drill like a carpenter bee, experience the stinkbug's stench, sip on nectar at the snack bar and measure the speed of the green darner dragonfly. The insects on display at the 'museum' . . . are portrayed in . . . full-color micrographs by renowned nature photographer [Frederic B.] Siskind." (Kirkus Reviews)

The **snowflake** sisters; illustrated by Lisa Desimini. Atheneum Bks. for Young Readers 2003 un il $16.95
Grades: K 1 2 3
E
1. Snow -- Fiction 2. New York (N.Y.) -- Fiction
ISBN 0-689-85029-8

LC 2002-6138

Two snowflakes named Crystal and Ivory travel on Santa's sleigh and make their way through the wintry sky until they become part of a snowboy in Central Park

"The setting is New York City, captured through witty collage illustrations that make use of such materials as rice paper, maps, newsprint, and Scrabble letters. Lewis's elegant and fluid rhymed text offers surprises on every page." SLJ

World Rat day; J. Patrick Lewis, illustrated by Anna Raff. Candlewick Press 2013 40 p. (reinforced) $15.99

Grades: K 1 2 3   **E**

  ISBN 9780763654023

                             LC 2012942612

"Twenty-two obscure but entertaining holidays get their own poems, each one funny, playful, and even instructive." (Horn Book)

Lewis, Jill

Don't read this book! illustrated by Deborah Allwright. Tiger Tales 2010 un il $15.95

Grades: 2 3 4   **E**

  1. Fairy tales

  ISBN 978-1-58925-094-9; 1-58925-094-X

The king frantically rides throughout his kingdom trying to piece together fragments of his story.

"The collage pictures in blazing colors are just right for scenes of the king threatening to put the reader in the dungeon if he does not go away. . . . Not for the usual picture-book fairy-tale crowd, this is for readers who already know the classic stories and will enjoy the parodies and rebellious chaos, especially their own defiance just by turning the pages." Booklist

Lewis, Kevin

Not inside this house! illustrated by David Ercolini. Orchard Books 2011 un il $16.99

Grades: PreK K   **E**

  1. Stories in rhyme 2. Animals -- Fiction 3. Explorers -- Fiction 4. Mother-son relationship -- Fiction

  ISBN 978-0-439-43981-7; 0-439-43981-7

                             LC 2010033233

Rhyming text follows a young explorer as he discovers bugs and then increasingly larger creatures, brings them home to learn about them, and is warned by his mother that each is unwelcome.

"The precisely composed ink drawing, painting, and Photoshop illustrations, which set the tale in the halcyon age when men wore hats and women donned aprons, add an odd-fashioned charm and much humor to the story." SLJ

Lewis, Paeony

No more yawning! by Paeony Lewis; illustrated by Brita Granström. Chicken House/Scholastic 2008 un il $16.99

Grades: PreK K   **E**

  1. Toys -- Fiction 2. Sleep -- Fiction 3. Bedtime -- Fiction

  ISBN 0-545-02957; 978-0-545-02957-5

Companion volume to: No more cookies (2005)

Florence and her toy monkey Arnold try to fall asleep but Florence's big yawns keep them awake. Includes tips for falling asleep.

"Florence's childlike voice carries this charming story, and the repetition of her excuses . . . adds humor, as do her crayon drawings, which frequently appear superimposed on the watercolor-and-pencil scenes." Booklist

Lewis, Rose A.

Every year on your birthday; written by Rose Lewis; illustrated by Jane Dyer. Little, Brown 2007 un il $16.99

Grades: PreK K 1 2   **E**

  1. Adoption -- Fiction 2. Birthdays -- Fiction 3. Mother-daughter relationship -- Fiction

  ISBN 978-0-316-52552-7; 0-316-52552-9

                             LC 2006026467

Each year on the birthday of her adopted Chinese daughter, a mother recalls the moments they have shared, from the first toy to the friends left behind in China

"Expressive watercolors evoke vivid memories. . . . By story's end, readers see a matured parent, secure in her love for her child." Publ Wkly

I love you like crazy cakes; written by Rose Lewis; illustrated by Jane Dyer. Little, Brown 2000 un il $14.95; bd bk $6.99

Grades: PreK K 1 2   **E**

  1. Infants -- Fiction 2. Adoption -- Fiction

  ISBN 0-316-52538-3; 0-316-52576-6 bd bk

                             LC 99-34175

A woman describes how she went to China to adopt a special baby girl. Based on the author's own experiences

"Dyer's simple watercolor layouts with expressive characters make this a calming read, befitting the gentle affection in the text." SLJ

Lexau, Joan M.

Who took the farmer's [hat]? [by] Joan L. Nodset; pictures by Fritz Siebel. Harper & Row 1963 un il lib bdg $17.89; pa $6.99

Grades: PreK K   **E**

  1. Animals -- Fiction

  ISBN 0-06-024566-2 lib bdg; 0-06-443174-6 pa

"Away flew the farmer's hat. In his search for it he found that his hat could be many things to many animals including, most permanently, a bird's nest." Publ Wkly

Lichtenheld, Tom

★ **Bridget's** beret. Henry Holt and Company 2010 un il $16.99

Grades: K 1 2   **E**

  1. Hats -- Fiction 2. Artists -- Fiction 3. Drawing -- Fiction

  ISBN 0-8050-8775-3; 978-0-8050-8775-8

                             LC 2009-12220

When Bridget loses the beret that provides her with artistic inspiration like other great artists, she thinks she will never be able to draw again.

"This smart, saucy book, with its spacious cartoon-style art, is both a spur to artistic endeavor and a message about inspiration and hard work. Yet the motivations are cocooned by a crackin' good tale and tempered by a full-faceted heroine." Booklist

Cloudette. Henry Holt 2011 un il $16.99

Grades: PreK K 1   **E**

  1. Rain -- Fiction 2. Size -- Fiction 3. Clouds -- Fiction

  ISBN 978-0-8050-8776-5; 0-8050-8776-1

                             LC 2010011688

Cloudette, the littlest cloud, finds a way to do something big and important as the other clouds do.

"Sprinkled with punny jokes, Lichtenheld's polished spreads show Cloudette as a simple, scalloped-edged puff who looks mighty dejected as she tries to be useful. . . . Neatly constructed and nicely pitched, the message of self-reliance comes through as clear as a cloudless day." Publ Wkly

★ **E-mergency.** Chronicle Books 2011 il $16.99

Grades: 1 2 3   **E**

  1. Alphabet -- Fiction 2. English language -- Spelling -- Fiction

  ISBN 978-0-8118-7898-2; 0-8118-7898-8

                             LC 2010053591

"Though some of the jokes will be clear only to older brothers and sisters, readers who are in the thick of learning spelling rules will pore over the pages. Comprehensive, witty entertainment from A to Z." Publ Wkly

★ **Exclamation** mark; Amy Krouse Rosenthal, Tom Lichtenheld. Scholastic Press 2013 56 p. (reinforced) $17.99

Grades: PreK K 1 2   E
1. Self-acceptance -- Fiction 2. Identity (Psychology) -- Fiction
ISBN 0545436796; 9780545436793

LC 2012936803

This children's book, by Amy Krouse Rosenthal, illustrated by Tom Lichtenheld, is a story about an exclamation point that learns to be comfortable with its own identity, different from all the other periods around it. "It's not easy being seen. Especially when you're NOT like everyone else. Especially when what sets you apart is YOU. Sometimes we squish ourselves to fit in. We shrink. Twist. Bend. Until--!--a friend shows the way to endless possibilities." (Publisher's note)

Light, Kelly

Louise loves art; Kelly Light. Balzer + Bray, an imprint of HarperCollinsPublishers 2014 40 p. color illustrations (hardcover) $17.99
Grades: K 1 2 3   E
1. Imagination -- Fiction 2. Brothers and sisters -- Fiction 3. Art -- Fiction 4. Drawing -- Fiction
ISBN 0062248170; 9780062248176

LC 2013043069

In this children's book by Kelly Light, readers "meet Louise. Louise loves art more than anything. It's her imagination on the outside. She is determined to create a masterpiece. Louise also loves Art, her little brother. This is their story." (Publisher's note)

"Passion is contagious. Fun, focused, and full of flair, Louise anxiously works toward creating her masterpiece. Meanwhile her little brother, tagging along, wants her attention . . . Younger siblings will appreciate Louise's generosity that transcends the typical dominant older sibling dynamic. Most importantly, budding artists, those not only crazy for art but who have their eyes and heart open, will find a muse and a collaborator." SLJ

Another title about Louise is:
Louise and Andie (2016)

Light, Steve

★ The **Christmas** giant. Candlewick Press 2010 un il $15.99
Grades: PreK K 1   E
1. Giants -- Fiction 2. Christmas -- Fiction
ISBN 978-0-7636-4692-9; 0-7636-4692-X

When two best friends, a giant and an elf, grow Christmastown's holiday tree, disaster strikes.

"The pen, ink, and pastel artwork is truly lovely. Muted colors and swirly lines evoke old-fashioned folk art while retaining a fresh cartoon whimsy. . . . The story itself is sweet and economically told, capturing not only the spirit of Christmas, but also of friendship, persistence, and resourcefulness." SLJ

Have you seen my dragon? Steve Light. Candlewick Press 2014 48 p. $16.99
Grades: PreK K 1 2   E
1. Dragons -- Fiction 2. Cities and towns -- Fiction 3. Counting
ISBN 0763666483; 9780763666484

LC 2013943993

In this children's book, by Steve Light, readers "help a boy find his dragon while counting objects from hot dogs to traffic lights. In the heart of the city, among the taxis and towers, a small boy travels uptown and down, searching for his friend. . . . Is the dragon taking the crosstown bus, or breathing his fiery breath below a busy street? Maybe he took a taxi to the zoo or is playing with the dogs in the park." (Publisher's note)

"A dragon is on the loose in New York City, but rather than inciting terror, he provides an opportunity for a gentle quest and counting game. Light (Zephyr Takes Flight, 2012) takes readers on a tour of lower Manhattan with a little boy as he travels from spot to spot looking for his escaped pet . . . His cityscapes capture the bustle of New York City, and

children will have as much fun exploring the city as they do trying to spot the sneaky dragon hidden within. A rough map of the city serves as the book's endpapers, so little eyes can follow along." Booklist

Have you seen my monster? Steve Light. Candlewick Press 2015 48 p. ill (some col) reinforced $16.99
Grades: PreK K 1 2   E
1. Pets -- Fiction 2. Monsters -- Fiction 3. Lost and found possessions -- Fiction
ISBN 076367513X; 9780763675134

LC 2013957389

In this story by Steve Light, "a little girl gallivants through a county fair, searching for her furry friend. Readers will surely spot the friendly monster as well as twenty shapes, identified here by their proper names--trapezoids, ellipses, kites, and more--hidden among iconic fair attractions from the fun house to the Ferris wheel." (Publisher's note)

"Simple sentences in large print are prominently placed within the illustrations, and a black banner with white lettering announces the names of brightly colored shapes. A square, rectangle, triangle and circle each make an appearance, along with other familiar shapes. But watch for a quatrefoil, trapezium, nonagon and curvilinear triangle as well." Kirkus

★ **Planes** go; by Steve Light. Chronicle Books LLC 2014 16 p. color illustrations (board bk) $9.99
Grades: PreK   E
1. Airplanes 2. Airplanes -- Fiction
ISBN 1452128995; 9781452128993

LC 2013025008

In this children's book, by Steve Light, "the helicopter goes, 'PIT-TATATATA.' . . . The jumbo jet goes, 'Wheeeeeeee VRRRRRRRRRRRU-UUHHHHHHHHHMMM.' The propeller plane goes, 'HUK HUK HUK WHIRRRRRRR.' . . . Prepare for liftoff with 8 exciting aircraft and the noises they make in this . . . board book!" (Publisher's note)

"The bright and colorful watercolor illustrations zoom across the blue-and-white cloudy backgrounds on wide-trim pages. Buzzy, onomatopoeic sounds in splashy, expressive fonts make this one easily enjoyable with or without a grown-up." Booklist

Swap! Steve Light. Candlewick Press 2016 40 p. illustrations (some color) $16.99
Grades: PreK K 1 2   E
1. Barter -- Fiction 2. Pirates -- Fiction
ISBN 0763679909; 9780763679903

In this children's book, by Steve Light, "a peg-legged youngster sets out to help his captain repair his vessel. One button for three teacups. SWAP! Two teacups for four coils of rope. SWAP! And so it goes, until the little swashbuckler secures sails, anchors, a ship's wheel, and more . . . including a happy friend." (Publisher's note)

"The result is a delightful adventure with a sweet underlying message, and the treasure maps that grace the endpapers are a perfect final touch." Booklist

Trains go; Steve Light. Chronicle Books 2012 16 p. (board) $8.99
Grades: 1 2 3   E
1. Board books for children 2. Sounds 3. Locomotives 4. Board books 5. Railroad trains -- Fiction
ISBN 0811879429; 9780811879422

LC 2011008004

This children's story, by Steve Light, describes different types of trains and their sounds. "All aboard! Take a trip on eight noisy trains as they huff, puff, and toot-toot their way through this . . . board book!"

Trains described include steam engines, diesel trains, and magnetic high-speed commuter rails. (Publisher's note)

Zephyr takes flight; Steve Light. Candlewick 2012 40 p. (hardcover) $16.99

Grades: PreK K 1   E

1. Flight -- Fiction 2. Imagination -- Fiction 3. Adventure fiction -- Fiction

ISBN 076365695X; 9780763656959

LC 2011046669

This children's story, by Steve Light, follows "a clever girl's flight of fancy in a whimsical ode to free spirits, inventiveness, and flying pigs. Zephyr is a girl who loves airplanes . . . and hopes one day to fly one of her own. But when Gramma, Daddy, and Mom are too busy to play airplane with her, Zephyr's excess enthusiasm gets her sent to her room--where she discovers a secret door that leads to the most wondrous place she's ever seen!" (Publisher's note)

Lillegard, Dee

Tiger, tiger; illustrated by Susan Guevara. Putnam 2002 un il $16.99

Grades: PreK K 1   E

1. Magic -- Fiction 2. Tigers -- Fiction

ISBN 0-399-22633-8

LC 2002-272

A bored young boy uses a magic feather to form a tiger, and then must use the feather to save his village when the tiger gets hungry

"The suspenseful story reaches a dramatic climax, made all the more vivid by Guevara's highly charged artwork." Booklist

Lin, Grace

Bringing in the New Year; [by] Grace Lin. Alfred A. Knopf 2008 un il $15.99; lib bdg $18.99

Grades: PreK K 1 2   E

1. Chinese New Year -- Fiction 2. Chinese Americans -- Fiction

ISBN 978-0-375-83745-6; 0-375-83745-0; 978-0-375-93745-3 lib bdg; 0-375-93745-5

LC 2007011687

A Chinese American family prepares for and celebrates the Lunar New Year. End notes discuss the customs and traditions of Chinese New Year.

"The lustrous gouache illustrations are saturated with bold primary colors and deftly convey the joyousness of the festivities. . . . A wonderful and much-needed addition to Chinese New Year literature." SLJ

★ **Dim** sum for everyone! written and illustrated by Grace Lin. Knopf 2001 un il $14.95; pa $6.99

Grades: K 1 2 3   E

1. Restaurants -- Fiction 2. Chinese Americans -- Fiction

ISBN 0-375-81082-X; 0-440-41770-8 pa

LC 00-34813

A child describes the various little dishes of dim sum that she and her family enjoy on a visit to a restaurant in Chinatown

"Lin's paintings are graphically striking. They combine a simplicity of form and design with a delight of patterning that appears in clothing and in backgrounds. . . . Like the pleasures of dim sum, this is a compact treat." Booklist

Kite flying. Knopf 2002 un il hardcover o.p. pa $6.99

Grades: K 1 2 3   E

1. Kites -- Fiction

ISBN 0-375-81520-1; 0-553-11254-6 pa

LC 2001-33456

"A Chinese girl describes how the members of her family come together to make and fly a dragon kite. . . . The overall simplicity is effective and appealing, and the spare text is accentuated by bright gouache illustrations, in colorful shapes and painted fabric patterns." Booklist

Ling & **Ting**; together in all weather. by Grace Lin. Little, Brown & Co. 2015 43 p. color illustrations (hardcover) $16

Grades: K 1 2   E

1. Play -- Fiction 2. Twins -- Fiction 3. Asian Americans -- Fiction 4. Seasons -- Fiction 5. Sisters -- Fiction 6. Weather -- Fiction 7. Chinese Americans -- Fiction

ISBN 0316335495; 9780316335492

LC 2014040293

In this book, by author Grace Lin, "The adorable twins Ling and Ting from the Geisel Honor early reader series are back to have fun in Winter, Spring, Fall, and Summer, giving parents and educators the perfect opportunity to teach young readers about every season of the year." (Publisher's note)

"As always, the girls' personalities shine through in both text and illustrations." Horn Book

★ **Ling** & **Ting**: not exactly the same! Little, Brown 2010 43p il

Grades: K 1 2   E

1. Twins -- Fiction 2. Sisters -- Fiction

ISBN 031602452X; 9780316024525

"Sticking together through everything from getting haircuts and preparing dumplings to practicing magic tricks and using chopsticks, identical twin sisters Ling and Ting display distinctive differences in personality and preference despite their similar looks." (Publisher's note) "Primary." (Horn Book)

"Sisters Ling and Ting may be twins, but that doesn't mean they're 'exactly the same,' no matter what everyone says upon first meeting them. Children will come to their own conclusions after reading the six short, interconnected stories that make up this pleasing book for beginning readers. . . . Framed with narrow borders, the paintings illustrate the stories with restrained lines, vivid colors, and clarity." Booklist

Other titles in this series are:

Ling and Ting Share a Birthday (2013)
Ling and Ting: Twice as Silly (2014)
Ling and Ting: Together in All Weather (2016)

Thanking the moon; celebrating the Mid-Autumn Moon Festival. Alfred A. Knopf 2010 un il $16.99; lib bdg $19.99

Grades: PreK K 1 2   E

1. Food -- Fiction 2. Moon -- Fiction 3. China -- Fiction 4. Mid-autumn Day -- Fiction

ISBN 978-0-375-86101-7; 0-375-86101-7; 978-0-375-96101-4 lib bdg; 0-375-96101-1 lib bdg

LC 2009052349

Each member of a Chinese family contributes to the celebration of the Mid-Autumn Moon Festival.

"Lin fashions a child-friendly introduction to the mid-autumn harvest moon festival with engagingly simple text and colorful, oversize gouache illustrations. . . . The writing is concise and accessible, and an author's note adds further information on the holiday and its significance. The inviting nocturnal landscapes are vivid with interesting details" SLJ

Lindbergh, Reeve

Homer, the library cat; illustrated by Anne Wilsdorf. Candlewick Press 2011 un il

Grades: PreK K 1   E

1. Stories in rhyme 2. Cats -- Fiction 3. Libraries -- Fiction

ISBN 0-7636-3448-4; 978-0-7636-3448-3

LC 2010048130

A cat's quiet life is disrupted one day when a window is broken, and after several frustrating attempts to find a suitable place, he winds up in the perfect spot.

"Lindbergh's simple rhyming text makes a good match with Wilsdorf's exuberant ink-and-watercolor artwork, which captures all the fun of a cat on the loose." Booklist

Lindgren, Astrid

Goran's great escape; translated by Polly Lawson; illustrated by Marit Törnqvist. Floris 2011 il $17.95

Grades: PreK K 1 2   E

1. Bulls -- Fiction 2. Easter -- Fiction 3. Sweden -- Fiction 4. Farm life -- Fiction

ISBN 978-0-86315-793-6; 0-86315-793-9

Original Swedish edition published 1950 as part of a story collection; first English language edition published 1991 with title: The day Adam got mad

"Years ago in Sweden, on an Easter morning, Goran the bull escaped from his barn and might still be at large if 7-year-old Karl hadn't come by and offered to scratch his head. This charming story . . . gets new life with Lawson's translation, which smoothes and slightly modernizes the English. . . . Törnqvist's meticulous watercolor illustrations again complement the story. . . . There are lovely touches of humor. . . . From a beloved author, a tiny gem for reading aloud or reading alone." Kirkus

Lindsey, Kat

Sweet potato pie; by Kathleen D. Lindsey; illustrated by Charlotte Riley-Webb. Lee & Low Books 2003 un il $16.95; pa $7.95

Grades: K 1 2 3   E

1. Pies -- Fiction 2. Farm life -- Fiction 3. Family life -- Fiction 4. African Americans -- Fiction

ISBN 1-58430-061-2; 1-60060-277-0 pa

LC 2002-30164

During a drought in the early 1900s, a large loving African American family finds a delicious way to earn the money they need to save their family farm

"Lindsey's down-home storytelling quality is charming. . . . The artwork's broad, energetic strokes and strong color palette sweep children into this tasty tale, and the included pie recipe makes the experience complete." Booklist

Ling, Nancy Tupper

Double-happiness; by Nancy Tupper Ling; illustrations by Alina Chau. Chronicle Books LLC 2015 48 p. color illustrations (alk. paper) $16.99

Grades: K 1 2 3   E

1. Stories in rhyme 2. Moving -- Fiction 3. Grandmothers -- Fiction 4. Chinese Americans -- Fiction 5. Moving, Household -- Fiction 6. Chinese American children -- Fiction

ISBN 1452129185; 9781452129181

LC 2013039301

In this children's story in verse, by Nancy Tupper Ling with illustrations by Alina Chau, "Gracie and Jake are sad to leave the golden bridge, the trolley tracks, and Nai Nai. But they fill empty boxes with treasures . . . so happiness stays close, no matter where they go. . . . This lyrical picture book speaks to the difficulty of transition, and celebrates the ways in which love and family give us the strength to weather life's changes." (Publisher's note)

"Rendered in delicate watercolors and brush strokes, Chau's illustrations and calligraphy evoke calm in the midst of Gracie's anxieties and ethereal playfulness with Jake's ever present mystical dragon. A thoughtful and moving story of memory and change." Kirkus

Lionni, Leo

Alexander and the wind-up mouse; by Leo Lionni. Alfred A. Knopf 2006 un il $16.99; lib bdg $18.99; pa $6.99

Grades: PreK K 1 2   E

1. Mice -- Fiction

ISBN 0-394-80914-9; 0-394-90914-3 lib bdg; 0-394-82911-5 pa

A reissue of the title first published 1969 by Pantheon Books

A Caldecott Medal honor book, 1970

The author's "collage illustrations are dazzling in their color and bold design and contribute to a beautiful and appealing picture book." Booklist

★ **Fish** is fish. Alfred A. Knopf 2005 un il $15.95

Grades: PreK K 1 2   E

1. Frogs -- Fiction 2. Fishes -- Fiction

ISBN 0-394-80440-6

A reissue of the title first published 1970 by Pantheon Bks.

The frog tells the fish all about the world above the sea. The fish, however, can only visualize it in terms of fish-people, fish-birds and fish-cows.

"The story is slight but pleasantly and simply told, the illustrations are page-filling, deft, colorful, and amusing." Bull Cent Child Books

★ **Frederick**. Pantheon Bks. 1967 un il $16.95; lib bdg $18.99; pa $5.99

Grades: PreK K 1 2   E

1. Mice -- Fiction

ISBN 0-394-81040-6; 0-394-91040-0 lib bdg; 0-394-82614-0 pa

"This captivating book . . . sings a hymn of praise to poets in a gentle story that is illustrated with gaiety and charm." Saturday Rev

★ **Inch** by inch. Alfred A. Knopf 2010 un il $16.99; lib bdg $19.99

Grades: PreK K 1 2   E

1. Birds -- Fiction 2. Measurement -- Fiction 3. Caterpillars -- Fiction

ISBN 978-0-375-85764-5; 0-375-85764-8; 978-0-375-95764-2 lib bdg; 0-375-95764-2 lib bdg

LC 2009-1767

A reissue of the title first published 1960 by Astor-Honor

A Caldecott Medal honor book, 1961

To keep from being eaten, an inchworm measures a robin's tail, a flamingo's neck, a toucan's beak, a heron's legs, and a nightingale's song.

"This is a book to look at again and again. The semi-abstract forms are sharply defined, clean and strong, the colors subtle and glowing, and the grassy world of the inchworm is a special place of enchantment." N Y Times Book Rev

Little blue and little yellow; a story for Pippo and Ann and other children. 50th anniversary ed.; Alfred A. Knopf 2009 un il $15.99; lib bdg $18.99

Grades: PreK K 1 2   E

1. Color -- Fiction 2. Friendship -- Fiction

ISBN 978-0-375-86013-3; 0-375-86013-4; 978-0-375-96013-0 lib bdg; 0-375-96013-9 lib bdg

LC 2008035932

A reissue of the title first published 1959 by Astor-Honor

A little blue spot and a little yellow spot are best friends, and when they hug each other they become green.

"So well are the dots handled on the pages that little blue and little yellow and their parents seem to have real personalities. It should inspire interesting color play and is a very original picture book by an artist." N Y Her Trib Books

Six crows; a fable. Alfred A. Knopf 2010 un il $16.99; lib bdg $19.99

Grades: PreK K 1 2   E

1. Owls -- Fiction 2. Crows -- Fiction 3. Farm life -- Fiction

ISBN 978-0-375-84550-5; 0-375-84550-X; 978-0-375-94550-2 lib bdg; 0-375-94550-4 lib bdg

A reissue of the title first published 1988

An owl helps a farmer and some crows reach a compromise over the rights to the wheat crop.

"This brief, simple story works on a literal level as well as on a metaphoric one. It is illustrated with Lionni's usual handsome, colorful collages which project well for reading aloud to groups." SLJ

★ **Swimmy**. Pantheon Bks. 1973 un il $16; pa $5.99

Grades: PreK K 1 2   E

1. Fishes -- Fiction

ISBN 0-394-81713-3; 0-394-82620-5 pa

"To illustrate his clever, but very brief story, Leo Lionni has made a book of astonishingly beautiful pictures, full of undulating, watery nuances of shape, pattern, and color." Horn Book

Lipan, Sabine

Mom, there's a bear at the door; Sabine Lipan; illustrated by Manuela Olten. Eerdmans Books for Young Readers 2016 34 p. color illustrations $16

Grades: PreK K 1 2   E

1. Mother-son relationship 2. Bears -- Fiction 3. Bears -- Fiction 4. Humorous stories 5. Mother and child -- Fiction

ISBN 0802854605; 9780802854605

LC 2015022340

In this children's book, by Sabine Lipan and illustrated by Manuela Olten, "a mother is surprised when her son tells her that there is a bear standing outside their door. How did the bear get all the way from his cave in the forest to their eleventh-floor apartment? And what is it doing here in the middle of the city?" (Publisher's note)

"Olten's colorful, full-bleed artwork with reds and greens predominating imbues the characters with barrelfuls of personality. Verbal and visual humor abound." Kirkus

Lipson, Eden Ross

Applesauce season; illustrated by Mordicai Gerstein. Roaring Brook Press 2009 un il $17.99

Grades: PreK K 1 2   E

1. Apples -- Fiction 2. Family life -- Fiction

ISBN 978-1-59643-216-1; 1-59643-216-0

"Flavored with family tradition and spiced with Gerstein's cheerful illustrations, this account of one family's love of applesauce hits the spot. . . . In a crowded orchard of apple books, this one stands out for home or school apple and/or family-tradition projects. Applesauce recipe appended." Kirkus

Litchfield, David

The **bear** and the piano; by David Litchfield. Clarion Books, Houghton Mifflin Harcourt 2016 40 p. color illustrations (hardback) $16.99

Grades: PreK K 1 2 3   E

1. Bears -- Fiction 2. Piano music -- Fiction 3. Bears -- Fiction 4. Music -- Fiction 5. Piano -- Fiction 6. Friendship -- Fiction

ISBN 9780544674547

LC 2015020008

In this children's story, by David Litchfield, "one day, a bear cub finds something strange and wonderful in the forest. When he touches the keys, they make a horrible noise. Yet he is drawn back again and again. Eventually, he learns to play beautiful sounds, delighting his

woodland friends. Then the bear is invited to share his sounds with new friends in the city." (Publisher's note)

"Litchfield's poignant debut picture book celebrates both the wonders of wandering far in pursuit of one's dreams and the sweet comfort of returning home." Kirkus

Lithgow, John

Micawber; illustrated by C.F. Payne. Simon & Schuster Bks. for Young Readers 2002 un il $17.95; pa $6.99

Grades: PreK K 1 2   E

1. Stories in rhyme 2. Artists -- Fiction 3. Squirrels -- Fiction 4. New York (N.Y.) -- Fiction

ISBN 0-689-83341-5; 0-689-83542-6 pa

LC 2001-20919

Micawber, a squirrel fascinated by art, leaves the Metropolitan Museum of Art with an art student, secretly uses her supplies to make her own paintings, and starts his own art museum atop Central Park's carousel

"The rhymed text sparkles with pleasing sounds. . . . Lithgow's reading on the CD is brimming with texture and playful pomposity. The mixed-media illustrations depict an utterly fetching protagonist displaying a range of moods and poses." SLJ

Little, Jean

★ **Emma's** yucky brother; story by Jean Little; pictures by Jennifer Plecas. HarperCollins Pubs. 2001 63p il (I can read book) hardcover o.p. pa $3.99

Grades: PreK K 1 2   E

1. Adoption -- Fiction 2. Siblings -- Fiction

ISBN 0-06-028348-3; 0-06-444258-6 pa

LC 99-34515

Emma finds out how hard it is to be a big sister when her family adopts a four-year-old boy named Max

"Heartfelt and honest. . . . Little's simple words and Plecas' clear, expressive line-and-watercolor illustrations tell an intense story." Booklist

Other titles about Emma are:

Emma's magic winter (1998)

Emma's strange pet (2003)

Littlewood, Karin

Immi's gift; written and illustrated by Karin Littlewood. Peachtree 2010 un il $15.95

Grades: K 1 2   E

1. Inuit -- Fiction 2. Fishing -- Fiction

ISBN 978-1-56145-545-4; 1-56145-545-8

Day after day in the frozen north, a young Inuit girl catches brightly-colored objects while ice fishing and uses them to decorate her igloo, until the ice begins to melt and she drops in a gift of her own before leaving for the season.

"A fur-clad Inuit girl searches for the brightest objects she can find in a 'frozen white world,' rendered in smudgy watercolor and gouache with colored pencil detailing. Ice fishing, she finds a painted wooden bird, followed by an orange starfish, a green leaf, and a purple feather, which she uses to adorn her igloo. . . . It's a story with a quiet magic and beauty." Publ Wkly

Litwin, Eric

Pete the Cat; I love my white shoes. Harper 2010 un il $16.99

Grades: PreK K 1 2   E

1. Cats -- Fiction 2. Color -- Fiction 3. Shoes -- Fiction

ISBN 978-0-06-190622-0; 0-06-190622-0

Pete the Cat goes walking down the street wearing his brand-new white shoes. Along the way, his shoes change from white to red to blue to brown to WET as he steps in piles of strawberries, blueberries, and other big messes! But no matter what color his shoes are, Pete keeps movin' and groovin' and singing his song . . . because it's all good.

First published 2008 by Blue Whiskey Press
Other titles about Pete the Cat are:
Rocking in my School Shoes (2011)
Pete the Cat and His Four Groovy Buttons (2012)
Pete the Cat Saves Christmas (2012)
Pete the Cat and His Sunglasses (2013)
The First Thanksgiving (2013)
Valentine's Day is Cool (2013)
Big Easter Adventure (2014)
Peter the Cat and New Guy (2014)
Rock on Mom and Dad! (2015)
Construction Destruction (2015)
Peter the Cat's Groovy Guide to Life (2015)
Pete the Cat and the Bedtime Blues (2015)
Pete the Cat's Groovy Guide to Love (2015)
Pete the Cat and the Missing Cupcakes (2016)

Liu, Sylvia
A **morning** with grandpa; Sylvia Liu; illustrations by Christina Forshay. Lee & Low Books Inc. 2016 32 p. color illustrations (hardcover : alk. paper) $17.95
Grades: PreK K 1 2 3   E
1. Tai chi 2. Yoga -- Fiction 3. Grandfathers -- Fiction 4. Tai chi -- Fiction
ISBN 9781620141922; 1620141922
LC 2015018278
In this children's book, by Sylvia Liu and illustrated by Christina Forshay, "Mei Mei's grandpa is practicing tai chi in the garden, and Mei Mei is eager to join in. As Gong Gong tries to teach her the slow, graceful movements, Mei Mei enthusiastically does them with her own flair. Then Mei Mei takes a turn, trying to teach Gong Gong the yoga she learned in school. Will Gong Gong be able to master the stretchy, bendy poses?" (Publisher's note)
Includes bibliographical references

Liwska, Renata
★ **Red** wagon. Philomel Books 2011 un il $16.99
Grades: PreK K   E
1. Play -- Fiction 2. Work -- Fiction
ISBN 978-0-399-25237-2; 0-399-25237-1
LC 2010005393
When Lucy gets a new red wagon she wants to play with it immediately, but first she must use it to bring vegetables home from the market for her mother.
"Liwska's story stays true to the way children see the world, gives the gentlest of pushes toward cooperation, and offers respite from suburban anxiety and busyness." Publ Wkly

Ljungkvist, Laura
★ **Follow** the line; words and art by Laura Ljungkvist. Viking 2006 un il $16.99
Grades: PreK K 1 2   E
1. Counting
ISBN 0-670-06049-6
LC 2005-22701
Invites the reader to visit a wide variety of places and count different objects found in each, from fire hydrants in a big city in the morning, through starfish in the ocean during the day, to babies sleeping in a country village at night.
"An entrancing counting game with a search through detailed art, this title doubles as a vocabulary builder for the youngest readers and includes shapes, colors, and patterns in the search." SLJ

Other titles in this series are:
Follow the line through the house (2007)
Follow the line around the world (2008)
Follow the line to school (2011)

Lloyd, Jennifer
★ The **Best** Thing About Kindergarten. Simply Read Books 2013 36 p. $16.95
Grades: PreK K   E
1. Picture books for children 2. Kindergarten -- Fiction
ISBN 1897476825; 9781897476826
In this children's picture book, the "kids in Mrs. Appleby's kindergarten class are getting ready to graduate, but there's time for one last activity: 'Who can guess what is the best thing about kindergarten?' she asks. Guesses include the playhouse, the writing center, and recess, and Mrs. Appleby affirms each suggestion: 'You are a monkey bar superstar,' she tells a boy named Will, adding, 'We still haven't found the answer' (it turns out to be the children themselves)." (Publishers Weekly)

Lloyd, Sam
Mr. Pusskins and Little Whiskers; another love story. 1st U.S. ed.; Atheneum Books for Young Readers 2008 un il $15.99
Grades: PreK K 1 2   E
1. Cats -- Fiction
ISBN 978-1-4169-5796-6; 1-4169-5796-0
LC 2007031911
When Emily brings home a little kitten to be best friends with Mr. Pusskins, the older cat does not appreciate the gesture.
"The combination of bold colors, highly expressive characters, and slightly off-kilter illustrations will pull children in and keep them wanting more." SLJ
Another title about Mr. Pusskins is:
Mr. Pusskins: a love story (2007)

Lloyd-Jones, Sally
★ **How** to be a baby--by me, the big sister; [by] Sally Lloyd-Jones and [illustrated by] Sue Heap. Schwartz & Wade Books 2007 un il $15.99; lib bdg $18.99
Grades: PreK K 1 2   E
1. Infants -- Fiction 2. Siblings -- Fiction
ISBN 0-375-83843-0; 978-0-375-83843-9; 0-375-93843-5 lib bdg; 978-0-375-93843-6 lib bdg
LC 2006-02469
"A worldly wise big sister . . . reads from a book she has written for her new sibling. She itemizes a long list of things that babies cannot do. . . . Although she tends to focus on the negatives, in the end the unnamed protagonist admits that babies have some uses. . . . Heap uses acrylic paint, crayon, and felt-tip pen in a pleasing palette of pinks, blues, and yellows to enhance the story with childlike charm." SLJ
Other titles about this character are:
How to get married by me, the bride (2009)
How to get a job by me, the boss (2011)

How to get a job by me, the boss; [written by] Sally Lloyd-Jones and [illustrated by] Sue Heap. Schwartz & Wade Books 2011 un il $17.99; lib bdg $20.99
Grades: PreK K 1 2   E
1. Occupations -- Fiction
ISBN 978-0-375-86664-7; 0-375-86664-7; 978-0-375-96664-4 lib bdg; 0-375-96664-1 lib bdg
LC 2009050696
The narrator knows all about how to get a job, and she walks readers through the whole process: from deciding what you want to be all the way to acing the interview.

"The illustrations are perfectly rendered in childlike acrylic paint and crayons and show the fun details of imaginative play on a rainy day." SLJ

Poor Doreen; a fishy tale. by Sally Lloyd-Jones; illustrated by Alexandra Boiger. Schwartz & Wade 2013 40 p. color illustrations $17.99

Grades: PreK K 1 2   E

1. Fishes -- Fiction 2. Cousins -- Fiction 3. Fishing -- Fiction
ISBN 0375869182; 9780375869181; 9780375969188

LC 2012047195

In this children's book, written by Sally Lloyd-Jones and illustrated by Alexandra Boiger, "an Ample Roundy Fish called Mrs. Doreen Randolph-Potts is on a mission: to visit her second cousin twice removed who's just welcomed 157 babies. But when she spies what she thinks is a yummy dragonfly--and is actually bait--poor Doreen is lifted out of the water on a fishing pole. Luckily, Doreen is, shall we say, a wee bit clueless about the dire situation." (Publisher's note)

"Delightful illustrations in watercolor, gouache, and colored pencil show a smiling small blue and pink polka-dotted fish wearing a red babushka and sporting a red umbrella. A charming tale with an endearing—and enduring—heroine." -SLJ Reviews

Song of the stars; a Christmas story. illustrated by Alison Jay. Zonderkidz 2011 il $15.99

Grades: PreK K 1   E

1. Nature -- Fiction 2. Animals -- Fiction
ISBN 978-0-310-72291-5; 0-310-72291-8

LC 2011006762

Nature and the animal kingdom celebrate the birth of Jesus, while most people do not even notice that a miracle has occurred.

"A subtle, yet satisfying story. . . . Lloyd-Jones's lyrical language . . . and repetitive refrains make the text suitable for reading aloud. Jay's signature-style, crackle-varnish paintings are bright and effective in conveying a sense of eager anticipation and movement among the animals." SLJ

The **ultimate** guide to grandmas and grandpas; by Sally Lloyd-Jones; illustrated by Michael Emberley. HarperCollinsPublishers 2008 un il $14.99; lib bdg $15.89

Grades: PreK K 1 2 3   E

1. Family life -- Fiction 2. Grandparents -- Fiction
ISBN 978-0-06-075687-1; 0-06-075687-X; 978-0-06-075688-8 lib bdg; 0-06-075688-8 lib bdg

LC 2007020880

"In this story about how children should treat their elders, grandparents and grandchildren representing all kinds of animal species play together, enjoy snacks, take trips, tell stories, snuggle, and share secrets. Lloyd-Jones's text is both charming and tongue-in-cheek. . . . Emberley's enchanting illustrations mirror each character's personality." SLJ

Lobel, Anita

10 hungry rabbits; by Anita Lobel. Alfred A. Knopf 2012 24 p. (trade hardcover : alk. paper) $9.99

Grades: PreK K   E

1. Color 2. Counting 3. Rabbits -- Fiction 4. Hunger -- Fiction 5. Gardens -- Fiction
ISBN 037586864X; 9780375868641; 9780375968648; 9780375987564

LC 2011003514

In this book by Anita Lobel, "one by one, 10 very hungry rabbits find 10 very yummy vegetables for Mama Rabbit's soup pot. Lobel combines learning to count with color concepts in this . . . celebration of good things to eat. Lobel makes a delightful story for preschoolers

with the two most basic early learning concepts, counting and color." (Publisher's note)

"In this introduction to numbers and colors which also champions healthful eating poor Mama Rabbit doesn't have anything to feed her hungry brood, so Papa Rabbit sends the little ones out to find the makings for a delicious soup...However, it's the educational components that are rightly front and center here, with both numbers and colors prominently highlighted, close-ups of grouped items for counting, and simple lines of descriptive text (The seventh rabbit spotted SEVEN BROWN mushrooms). An early learning concept book is an obvious choice for one-on-one sharing, but the book's appealing scenes and petite size make it a good fit for little browsers, too." (Booklist)

★ **Hello,** day! Greenwillow Books 2008 un il $16.99; lib bdg $17.89

Grades: PreK   E

1. Sun -- Fiction 2. Animals -- Fiction 3. Morning -- Fiction
ISBN 978-0-06-078765-3; 0-06-078765-1; 978-0-06-078766-0 lib bdg; 0-06-078766-X lib bdg

LC 2007-18361

Various animals greet the sunrise in their own unique voices, except for the owl who welcomes the night.

"The luxuriantly hued, playfully textured portraits will rivet preschoolers and invite them to make animal sounds of their own; the minimal text, set in big, friendly type, may also encourage some simple word recognition." Publ Wkly

Lena's sleep sheep; a going-to-bed book. Anita Lobel. Alfred A. Knopf 2013 24 p. $11.99

Grades: PreK K   E

1. Sheep -- Fiction 2. Bedtime -- Fiction 3. Moon -- Fiction 4. Sheep -- Fiction 5. Bedtime -- Fiction
ISBN 0449810259; 9780449810255; 9780449810262; 9780449810279

LC 2012028378

In this children's picture book by Anita Lobel, "every evening Lena counts her sheep to help her fall asleep, but tonight they are afraid of the 'round monster' in the window. Lena tries to explain that it's just the Moon, but those silly creatures won't listen, so she convinces them to dress up in disguises to scare it away. When a bit of cloud covers it, the sheep finally line up so she can count them properly." (School Library Journal)

★ **One** lighthouse, one moon. Greenwillow Bks. 2000 40p il hardcover o.p. pa $6.99

Grades: PreK K 1 2   E

1. Counting 2. Days -- Fiction 3. Months -- Fiction
ISBN 0-688-15539-1; 0-06-000537-8 pa

LC 98-50790

This is a "three-part introduction to days, seasons, colors, counting, and other basics. The first section pictures a little girl's feet as they journey through a week, with a different colored shoe marking each day's activity. . . . The second section shows Nini the cat in postcard-size images that reflect those from the 12 months of the year. The title section presents the numbers 1 through 10 in serene images of shoreline activity. . . . The simple phrases are lyrical in places, and Lobel's beautiful paintings, with their rich patterns and textures, luxurious detail, and sophisticated palette, will inspire children to linger over the pages and connect new words with images." Booklist

Playful pigs from A to Z; Anita Lobel. Alfred A. Knopf 2015 40 p. color illustrations (lib. bdg. : alk. paper) $19.99

Grades: PreK K 1 2   **E**
1. Alphabet 2. Pigs -- Fiction 3. Pigs -- Fiction 4. Play -- Fiction
ISBN 0553508334; 9780553508338
           LC 2014033874

In this children's alphabet book Anita Lobel "twenty-six playful pigs wake in their pen ready for an adventure. They trot down a country road and discover a field full of surprises! By the time they return to their pen that night, the playful pigs have happily oinked their way through the alphabet." (Publisher's note)

"Despite the winning, whimsical artwork, this ABC book lacks the interest and punch to replace many current alphabet favorites." SLJ

Lobel, Arnold
★ **Frog** and Toad are friends. Harper & Row 1970 64p il (I can read book) $16.99; lib bdg $17.89; pa $3.99
Grades: K 1 2   **E**
1. Frogs -- Fiction 2. Toads -- Fiction 3. Friendship -- Fiction
ISBN 0-06-023957-3; 0-06-023958-1 lib bdg; 0-06-444020-6 pa
A Caldecott Medal honor book, 1971

Here are five stories . . . which recount the adventures of two best friends—Toad and Frog. The stories are: Spring; The story; A lost button; A swim; The letter

The stories are told "with humor and perception. Illustrations in soft green and brown enhance the smooth flowing and sensitive story." SLJ

Other titles about Frog and Toad are:
Days with Frog and Toad (1979)
Frog and Toad all year (1976)
Frog and Toad together (1972)

★ **Grasshopper** on the road. Harper & Row 1978 62p il (I can read book) lib bdg $17.89; pa $3.99
Grades: K 1 2   **E**
1. Animals -- Fiction 2. Grasshoppers -- Fiction
ISBN 0-06-023962-X lib bdg; 0-06-444094-X pa
           LC 77-25653

"The contemporary version of the fable of the ant and the grasshopper is told in a repetitive I-Can-Read text and extended in three-color illustrations which delicately capture the grasshopper's microcosmic world view." Horn Book

Ming Lo moves the mountain; written and illustrated by Arnold Lobel. Greenwillow Bks. 1982 un il hardcover o.p. pa $5.99
Grades: K 1 2 3   **E**
1. Houses -- Fiction 2. Mountains -- Fiction
ISBN 0-688-10995-0 pa
           LC 81-13327

"An original tale utilizing folkloric motifs, the book is Chinese-like rather than Chinese, for the artist has created an imagined landscape. The setting, shown in flowing lines and tones of delicate watercolors, provides a source of inspiration drawn from an ancient artistic tradition; particularly effective in conveying a sense of distance are the panoramic double-page spreads." Horn Book

★ **Mouse** soup. Harper & Row 1977 63p il (I can read book) $15.99; lib bdg $16.89; pa $3.99
Grades: K 1 2   **E**
1. Mice -- Fiction
ISBN 0-06-023967-0; 0-06-023968-9 lib bdg; 0-06-444041-9 pa
           LC 76-41517

"An artistic triumph with enough suspense, humor and wisdom to hold any reader who has a trace of curiosity and compassion. . . . The little one triumphs over the big one, and every child will rejoice. The exquisite wash drawings in mousey shades of grays, blues, greens and

golds, have enough humor and pathos to exact repeated scrutiny. Like the stories, they improve with each reading." N Y Times Book Rev

★ **Mouse** tales. Harper & Row 1972 61p il (I can read book) $15.99; lib bdg $16.89; pa $3.99
Grades: K 1 2   **E**
1. Mice -- Fiction
ISBN 0-06-023941-7; 0-06-023942-5 lib bdg; 0-06-444013-3 pa
Papa Mouse tells seven bedtime stories, one for each of his sons

"The illustrations have soft colors and precise, lively little drawings of the imaginative and humorous events in the stories. The themes are familiar to children: cloud shapes, wishing, a tall and a short friend who observe-and greet-natural phenomena on a walk, taking a bath, et cetera." Bull Cent Child Books

★ **On** Market Street; pictures by Anita Lobel; words by Arnold Lobel. Greenwillow Bks. 1981 un il $16.99; lib bdg $17.89; pa $6.99
Grades: K 1 2 3   **E**
1. Alphabet 2. Stories in rhyme 3. Shopping -- Fiction
ISBN 0-688-80309-1; 0-688-84309-3 lib bdg; 0-688-08745-0 pa
           LC 80-21418

A Caldecott Medal honor book, 1982

"The artist has adapted the style of old French trade engravings, infusing it with a wonderful sense of color and detail. . . . Arnold Lobel's words ring of old rhymes, but it is these intricate, lovely drawings that take the day, and truly make it brighter." N Y Times Book Rev

★ **Owl** at home. Harper & Row 1982 64p il (I can read book) lib bdg $16.89; pa $3.99
Grades: K 1 2   **E**
1. Owls -- Fiction
ISBN 0-06-023949-2 lib bdg; 0-06-444034-6 pa
Five stories describe the adventures of a lovably foolish owl

"A child reader or listener in a kind of one-upmanship over wide-eyed tufted Owl will bristle with anxiety to have him perceive what causes two bewildering bumps under the blanket at the foot of his bed. The best scope for Lobel's inventiveness in drawing is, however, the opening episode where 'poor old' Winter makes a pushy entry into Owl's home. Muted browns and greys are countered by an animation that fully reveals Owl's distresses and contentments." Wash Post Child Book World

★ **Small** pig; story and pictures by Arnold Lobel. Harper & Row 1969 63p il (I can read book) lib bdg $16.89; pa $3.99
Grades: K 1 2   **E**
1. Pigs -- Fiction
ISBN 0-06-023932-8 lib bdg; 0-06-444120-2 pa
This "is the story of a pig who, finding the clean farm unbearable, runs away to look for mud—and ends up stuck in cement. His facial expressions alone are worth the price of the book; the illustrations, in blue, green, and gold, are a perfect complement to the story. Humor, adventure, and short, simple sentences provide a real treat for beginning readers." SLJ

★ **Uncle** Elephant. Harper & Row 1981 62p il (I can read book) lib bdg $16.89; pa $3.99
Grades: K 1 2   **E**
1. Uncles -- Fiction 2. Elephants -- Fiction
ISBN 0-06-023980-8 lib bdg; 0-06-444104-0 pa
           LC 80-8944

Uncle Elephant takes care of his nephew whose parents are lost at sea. This book describes the way they lived together until the parents are rescued and little elephant rejoins them

"Nine gentle stories for the beginning independent reader; the soft grey, peach, and green tones of the deft pictures are an appropriate echo of the mood." Bull Cent Child Books

Lobel, Gillian

Moonshadow's journey; illustrated by Karin Littlewood. Albert Whitman & Co. 2009 un il $16.99

Grades: K 1 2 3 4   E

1. Death -- Fiction 2. Swans -- Fiction 3. Grandfathers -- Fiction 4. Birds -- Migration -- Fiction

ISBN 978-0-8075-5273-5; 0-8075-5273-9

LC 2009000004

When his beloved grandfather is killed in a storm while leading the swan flock south for the winter, Moonshadow is reassured by his father that the flock will go on with Grandfather always in their hearts

"Lobel skillfully moves the plot forward while creating appropriate character development for Moonshadow. . . . Littlewood's combination of watercolors and gouache on textured paper of light and dark hues adds to the moods and movement of the book. The pictures capture the elements of nature in both harsh and calm circumstances." SLJ

Loewen, Nancy

The **last** day of kindergarten; illustrated by Sachiko Yoshikawa. Marshall Cavendish 2011 un il $16.99

Grades: PreK K   E

1. School stories 2. Kindergarten -- Fiction

ISBN 978-0-7614-5807-4; 0-7614-5807-7

LC 2010001225

As she prepares for her graduation ceremony, a first grader-to-be remembers her enjoyable year in kindergarten.

"Included in the text are excellent discussion questions that focus on summer plans and first-grade privileges. Yoshikawa's irresistibly sweet illustrations are perfect for children ready to emerge from the kindergarten cocoon and rejoice in their achievements." SLJ

Logue, Mary

★ **Sleep** like a tiger; written by Mary Logue and illustrated by Pamela Zagarenski. Houghton Mifflin Harcourt 2012 40 p. $16.99

Grades: PreK K 1 2   E

1. Sleep -- Fiction 2. Tigers -- Fiction 3. Bedtime -- Fiction 4. Sleep -- Fiction 5. Bedtime -- Fiction 6. Animals -- Sleep behavior -- Fiction

ISBN 0547641028; 9780547641027

LC 2011044881

Caldecott Honor Book (2013)

This picture book features a "little girl" whose "wise parents sidestep her protestation of not being sleepy ('They nodded their heads and said she didn't have to go to sleep. But she had to put her pajamas on'), but once she's in bed she starts a new delaying tactic, inquiring about sleeping habits in the animal kingdom. After exploring the sleep habits of bats, whales, and tigers, she's inspired enough by their snoozes to fall asleep herself." (Bulletin of the Center for Children's Books)

London, Jonathan

Baby whale's journey; illustrated by Jon Van Zyle. Chronicle Bks. 1999 un il $15.95; pa $6.95

Grades: K 1 2 3   E

1. Whales -- Fiction

ISBN 0-8118-2496-9; 0-8118-5761-1 pa

LC 99-13020

Off the Pacific coast of Mexico, a baby sperm whale is born, feeds, speaks to her mother in clicks, and spends her days diving, spy-hopping, lob-tailing, and rolling as she grows and learns the ways of the sea

This book offers "London's lyrical text and Van Zyle's dramatic paintings dominated by blues and purples. . . . An informative afterword supplies additional facts about sperm whales, and a reader's guide offers thoughtful ideas for discussion of both the scientific and poetic aspects of the text." Horn Book Guide

Froggy goes to Hawaii; illustrated by Frank Remkiewicz. Viking 2010 un il $15.99

Grades: PreK K 1 2   E

1. Frogs -- Fiction 2. Hawaii -- Fiction 3. Vacations -- Fiction

ISBN 978-0-670-01221-3; 0-670-01221-1

LC 2010007323

When Froggy goes on vacation to Hawaii, he is too excited to pay much attention to his parents.

Froggy learns to swim; illustrated by Frank Remkiewicz. Viking 1995 un il $15.99; pa $5.99

Grades: PreK K 1 2   E

1. Frogs -- Fiction 2. Swimming -- Fiction

ISBN 0-670-85551-0; 0-14-055312-6 pa

LC 94-43077

Froggy is afraid of the water until his mother, along with his flippers, snorkle, and mask, help him learn to swim

"Vivid watercolor cartoons add the humor, showing the comical facial expressions and hilarious beachwear. Froggy's childlike dialogue and the sound words—'zook! zik!'; 'flop flop . . . splash!'—make this story a wonderful read-aloud." SLJ

Other titles about Froggy are:

Froggy bakes a cake (2000)
Froggy builds a treehouse (2011)
Froggy eats out (2001)
Froggy gets a doggy (2014)
Froggy gets dressed (1992)
Froggy goes to bed (2000)
Froggy goes to camp (2008)
Froggy goes to Hawaii (2011)
Froggy goes to school (1996)
Froggy goes to the doctor (2002)
Froggy goes to the library (2016)
Froggy plays in the band (2002)
Froggy plays T-Ball (2007)
Froggy plays soccer (1999)
Froggy's baby sister (2003)
Froggy's best Christmas (2000)
Froggy's birthday wish (2015)
Froggy's day with Dad (2004)
Froggy's first kiss (1998)
Froggy's Halloween (1999)
Froggy's sleepover (2005)
Froggy's worst playdate (2013)
Let's go, Froggy! (1994)

I'm a truck driver; illustrated by David Parkins. Henry Holt 2010 26p il $12.99

Grades: PreK K 1   E

1. Stories in rhyme 2. Trucks -- Fiction

ISBN 978-0-8050-7989-0; 0-8050-7989-0

LC 2009009220

"This is a wonderful picture book about trucks. . . . On every other spread, a girl and a boy take turns driving each of the vehicles. The trucks are described in rhyming couplets. . . . The alternating voices of the children help to enhance the rhythm and rhyme of the story. . . . The acrylic illustrations are vibrant, cartoonlike, and friendly." SLJ

A **plane** goes ka-zoom! illustrated by Denis Roche. Henry Holt & Co. 2010 un il $15.99

Grades: PreK   E

1. Airplanes -- Fiction

ISBN 978-0-8050-8970-7; 0-8050-8970-5

"Simple enough for toddlers, the rhythmic, rhyming text comments on what planes do as well as how they look, sound, and move. . . . The naive gouache paintings invite kids to stop along the way and talk about who's doing what in each colorful illustration. A engaging choice." Booklist

Long, Ethan

Bird & Birdie in a fine day. Ten Speed Press 2010 un il $14.99

Grades: PreK K 1   E

1. Birds -- Fiction 2. Friendship -- Fiction

ISBN 978-1-5824-6321-6; 1-5824-6321-2

"Three separate stories introduce two bug-eyed cartoon birds (Bird is blue, while Birdie, who is yellow, sports eyelashes and a pink ribbon) interacting over the course of a day. In 'A Beautiful Morning,' they meet, exchange pleasantries, are briefly separated by a storm, and happily join up again. In 'A Wonderful Afternoon,' Bird tries to concentrate on getting a worm out of the ground but is distracted by Birdie. In 'A Marvelous Night,' Birdie can't get comfortable in her nest until Bird helps out. . . . The fetching Bird and Birdie will hit the right note with many preschoolers and beginning readers." Booklist

The **Croaky** Pokey! Holiday House 2011 un il $14.95

Grades: PreK K 1   E

1. Frogs -- Fiction

ISBN 978-0-8234-2291-3; 0-8234-2291-7

"Inspired by a tasty-looking dragonfly, a group of frogs decides to perform their own version of the Hokey Pokey. The first part of the song is familiar ('Put your right hand in...'), but each verse is intended to end with a snack: 'Hop the Croaky Pokey/ As we chase a fly around,/ Right in the froggy's mouth!/ Whap!') The problem is, not a single member of the froggy chorus can catch the fly. . . . Long . . . has a gift for conveying manic, obsessive personalities . . . and he has found a great match in a song of relentless, rote cheeriness." Publ Wkly

In, over and on the farm; Ethan Long. G. P. Putnam's Sons, an imprint of Penguin Group (USA) 2015 40 p. chiefly color illustrations $15.99

Grades: PreK K 1 2   E

1. Humorous fiction 2. Farm life -- Fiction 3. Domestic animals -- Fiction 4. English language -- Prepositions -- Fiction 5. Humorous stories

ISBN 0399169075; 9780399169076

LC 2014022124

This book, by author Ethan Long, presents "humorous situations involving a hen, pig, goat, and cow with an emphasis on the concepts of "in and out" in chapter 1, "over and under" in chapter 2, and "on and off" in chapter 3." (School Library Journal)

Max & Milo go to sleep! by Heather & Ethan Long. Aladdin 2013 32 p. (hardcover edition) $14.99

Grades: PreK K 1 2   E

1. Bedtime -- Fiction 2. Brothers -- Fiction 3. Humorous fiction -- Fiction 4. Humorous stories 5. Beavers -- Fiction

ISBN 1442451432; 9781442451438

LC 2012011458

This children's story, by Heather Long and Ethan Long, follows "Max and Milo, two . . . beaver brothers who make going to sleep an up-all-night adventure. Milo can't get to sleep, . . . but no matter what helpful sleeping tip Max suggests, Milo turns it riotously on its head and

is as far from rest as ever. Will Milo finally get to sleep? Will he ever stop driving Max crazy?" (Publisher's note)

My dad, my hero. Sourcebooks Jabberwocky 2011 un il $12.99

Grades: PreK K 1   E

1. Father-son relationship -- Fiction

ISBN 978-1-4022-4239-7; 1-4022-4239-5

A child describes his dad, who may not have super powers, but is still wonderful.

"Powered by a Roy Lichtenstein meets Sunday funnies aesthetic and a self-effacing sense of humor, Long's story is sincere without being saccharine—which dads will appreciate." Publ Wkly

Pug; by Ethan Long. Holiday House 2016 24 p. color illustrations (ebook) $14.95; (hardcover) $14.95

Grades: PreK K 1   E

1. Pug -- Fiction 2. Dogs -- Fiction 3. Dog walking -- Fiction 4. Pug -- Fiction 5. Dogs -- Fiction 6. Dog walking -- Fiction

ISBN 9780823437405; 0823436454; 9780823436453

LC 2015040852

In this children's book in the I Like to Read series by Ethan Long, "Pug sees Peg through the window. He wants to join her! Why won't anyone take him on a wonderful snowy walk? Mom is just too comfortable in her recliner. Dad is tired from shoveling. That leaves lazy Tad, who is still sleeping. Yap, yap, yap! insists a determined and clever Pug." (Publisher's note)

"New readers will be happy to yap along with this pup. How about a sequel?" Kirkus

Up, tall and high; Ethan Long. G.P. Putnam's Sons 2012 p. cm.

Grades: K 1 2 3   E

1. Vocabulary 2. Birds -- Fiction 3. Altitudes -- Fiction

ISBN 9780399256110

LC 2011003291

Theodor Seuss Geisel Award (2013)

This children's picture book presents "three tiny tales of a flock of bird buddies. 'I Am Tall' centers on boasting about stature . . . . 'I Can Go High' finds the birds outdoing each other on altitude attempts . . . . In 'I Am Up,' two birds 'up' in a nest collapse the branch and are now decidedly 'down,' until their friends arrive to help them 'up' on their feet again . . . each tale's punchline is delivered with a visual gag revealed with a lifted or pulled flap." (Bulletin of the center for Children's Books)

Long, Loren

Little tree; Loren Long. Philomel Books, an imprint of Penguin Group (USA) 2015 40 p. illustrations (hardback) $17.99

Grades: PreK K 1 2 3   E

1. Leaves -- Fiction 2. Trees -- Fiction 3. Autumn -- Fiction 4. Trees -- Fiction 5. Change -- Fiction 6. Seasons -- Fiction 7. Forest animals -- Fiction

ISBN 0399163972; 9780399163975

LC 2015003514

In this children's book by Loren Long "Autumn arrives, and with it the cool winds that ruffle Little Tree's leaves. One by one the other trees drop their leaves, facing the cold of winter head on. But not Little Tree. Year after year Little Tree remains unchanged, . . . his leaves having long since turned brown and withered. As Little Tree sits in the shadow of the other trees . . . he remembers when they were all the same size. And he knows he has an important decision to make." (Publisher's note)

"Complementing the emotional complexity of the story is an abundance of friendly forest dwellers and the gentle narrative tone, which further makes the message go down easy. Understated and inviting, young readers will be entranced by Little Tree's difficult but ultimately rewarding journey." Booklist

★ **Otis.** Philomel Books 2009 un il $17.99; board bk $8.99
Grades: PreK K 1 2   E
    1. Tractors -- Fiction 2. Farm life -- Fiction
    ISBN 978-0-399-25248-8; 0-399-25248-7; 978-0-399-25600-4
    board bk; 0-399-25600-8 board bk
                            LC 2008-50020
When a big new yellow tractor arrives, Otis the friendly little tractor is cast away behind the barn, but when trouble occurs Otis is the only one who can help.

"Long's gouache and pencil artwork is stunning with a red and cream main character against a sepia-toned monochromatic background. The overall effect is nostalgic and comforting." SLJ

    Other books about Otis are:
    Otis and the Tornado (2012)
    Otis and the Puppy (2013)
    An Otis Christmas (2013)
    Otis and the Scarecrow (2014)
    Otis and the Kittens (2016)

Long, Melinda

★ **How** I became a pirate; written by Melinda Long; illustrated by David Shannon. Harcourt 2003 un il $16
Grades: K 1 2 3   E
    1. Pirates -- Fiction
    ISBN 0-15-201848-4
                            LC 2002-6308
Jeremy Jacob joins Braid Beard and his pirate crew and finds out about pirate language, pirate manners, and other aspects of their life. "Ages four to seven." (Bull Cent Child Books)

"Jeremy spies a pirate ship. When he's asked to join its crew, he can't resist. On board, he does all sorts of fun pirate stuff. . . . But, alas, Jeremy soon discovers, there's no goodnight kiss or bedtime story, so there's something to be said for home. . . . The rollicking tale is a charmer, with a lively, witty, first-person narrative, highly expressive characters, and farcical elements. . . . Shannon's acrylic art is marvelously animated, with bright, bold colors and extraordinary details." Booklist

    Another title about Jeremy is:
    Pirates don't change diapers (2007)

Long, Sylvia

Sylvia Long's Thumbelina. Chronicle Books 2010 un $17.99
Grades: 1 2 3 4   E
    1. Authors 2. Novelists 3. Dramatists 4. Fairy tales 5. Children's authors 6. Short story writers
    ISBN 978-0-8118-5522-8; 0-8118-5522-8
                            LC 2009-04369
A tiny girl no bigger than a thumb is stolen by a great ugly toad and subsequently has many adventures and makes many animal friends, before finding the perfect mate in a warm and beautiful southern land.

"While following the familiar story line of Hans Christian Andersen's original, Long effectively condenses the narrative and gives a contemporary touch to the wording. . . . Thumbelina's adventures with the beautifully drawn toad, beetles, mouse, mole, and swallow unfold in jewel-like colors, defined textures, and well-imagined details to complete the surroundings." SLJ

Longstreth, Galen Goodwin

Yes, let's; by Galen Goodwin Longstreth; illustrated by Maris Wicks. Tanglewood Publishing 2013 32 p. (hardcover) $15.95
Grades: PreK K 1 2   E
    1. Stories in rhyme 2. Camping -- Fiction 3. Family life -- Fiction

    4. Family life -- Fiction 5. Outdoor life -- Fiction 6. FICTION -- Sports & Recreation -- Camping & Outdoor Activities
    ISBN 1933718870; 9781933718873
                            LC 2012045312
This children's book, by Galen Goodwin Longstreth, illustrated by Maris Wicks, is "about a family's camping trip." Activities such as driving, singing, taking pictures and hiking are all included. "The . . . rhyming text is enhanced by comical illustrations. . . . This little book serves as a loving tribute to family togetherness." (Publisher's note)

Look, Lenore

★ **Brush** of the gods; by Lenore Look; illustrated by Meilo So Sandford. 1st ed. Schwartz & Wade Books 2013 40 p. ill. (hardcover) $17.99; (library) $20.99
Grades: K 1 2 3   E
    1. Picture books for children 2. Artists -- Fiction 3. Painting -- Fiction 4. China -- History -- Tang dynasty, 618-907 -- Fiction
    ISBN 0375870016; 9780375870019; 9780375970016
                            LC 2012006442
In this children's picture book, Lenore Look "blends mystical realism and biography to create a magical portrait of one of ancient China's famous artists, Wu Daozi. As a boy during the T'ang Dynasty in the seventh century, Daozi is unable to conform in calligraphy class. . . . Later known for his dynamic murals, Daozi paints subjects so realistically they seem to come alive." (Publishers Weekly)

★ **Henry's** first-moon birthday; illustrated by Yumi Heo. Atheneum Bks. for Young Readers 2001 un il $16
Grades: PreK K 1 2   E
    1. Infants -- Fiction 2. Grandmothers -- Fiction 3. Chinese Americans -- Fiction
    ISBN 0-689-82294-4
                            LC 98-21626
Jen helps her grandmother with preparations for the traditional Chinese celebration to welcome her new baby brother

"The words are clear and basic as well as creative . . . and Jen's chatty narration infuses the book with the cozy immediacy that's beautifully picked up in Heo's swirling paint-and-paper collages." Booklist

★ **Love** as strong as ginger; illustrated by Stephen T. Johnson. Atheneum Pubs. 1999 un il $15
Grades: PreK K 1 2   E
    1. Work -- Fiction 2. Grandmothers -- Fiction 3. Chinese Americans -- Fiction
    ISBN 0-689-81248-5
                            LC 96-43459
A Chinese American girl comes to realize how hard her grandmother works to fulfill her dreams when they spend a day together at the grandmother's job cracking crabs

"Inspired by the author's memories of her grandmother, this gentle story is carefully and precisely told. . . . Johnson's expressive pastel-and-watercolor illustrations are rendered in muted colors and set within wide, softly colored margins." SLJ

★ **Uncle** Peter's amazing Chinese wedding; illustrated by Yumi Heo. Atheneum Books for Young Readers 2006 un il $16.95
Grades: PreK K 1 2   E
    1. Uncles -- Fiction 2. Weddings -- Fiction 3. Chinese Americans -- Fiction
    ISBN 0-689-84458-1
                            LC 2002-10740
Companion volume to Henry's first-moon birthday
Jenny, a Chinese American girl, describes the festivities of her uncle's Chinese wedding and the customs behind them.

"Heo's child-inspired illustrations contribute to the story's strong appeal with lively colors, perspectives, and details that accentuate both Jenny's feelings and the wedding traditions. A delightful invitation to learn more about Chinese traditions." SLJ

Lopez, Mario

Mario and baby Gia; [illustrations by Maryn Roos] Celebra Childrens Books 2011 il $17.99

Grades: PreK K   E

1. Cousins -- Fiction 2. Infants -- Fiction 3. Birthdays -- Fiction 4. Babysitters -- Fiction 5. Family life -- Fiction

ISBN 978-0-451-23417-9; 0-451-23417-0

LC 2011005235

Unable to find anyone to play with, Mario agrees to help his Nana by watching cousin Gia, but caring for the toddler is challenging and Mario is near the end of his rope when he gets a reminder that spending time with family is a gift.

"Roos continues the commercial-looking cartoon-style illustrations from the earlier Mario book, which work well with the story, particularly during Mario's stories. A good choice for children with younger siblings and cousins, especially Latinos." Kirkus

Another title about Mario is:

Mud tacos (2009)

Lord, Cynthia

Happy birthday, Hamster; pictures by Derek Anderson. Scholastic Press 2011 un il $16.99

Grades: PreK K 1   E

1. Dogs -- Fiction 2. Hamsters -- Fiction 3. Birthdays -- Fiction 4. Friendship -- Fiction

ISBN 978-0-545-25522-6; 0-545-25522-8

LC 2010018989

Follows Hamster and his friend Dog as they prepare for a birthday party.

"Those who miss the clues the first time, should enjoy being privy to them upon rereading." Publy Wkly

Hot rod hamster; monster truck mania! by Cynthia Lord; pictures by Derek Anderson. Scholastic Press 2014 40 p. color illustrations (hardcover : alk. paper) $16.99

Grades: PreK K 1   E

1. Fairs -- Fiction 2. Hamsters -- Fiction 3. Amusement rides -- Fiction

ISBN 0545462614; 9780545462617

LC 2013008570

In this book, by Cynthia Lord and illustrated by Derek Anderson, "it's Fair Day, and Fearless Franco's famous Monster Truck Mania has come to town. Hot Rod Hamster and his friends are geared up for a roaring, soaring great time, so they set out to find the best ride at the fair. The water boats, spinning teacups, and bumper cars are great, but Hamster can't seem to find the BEST ride. That is, of course, until Fearless Franco needs a last-minute back-up driver for his monster truck." (Publisher's note)

"Hot Rod Hamster and his bulldog buddy (and readers, too) have myriad choices of rides and food at the fair: 'Slurp treats, lick treats, eat it on a stick treats. Which would you choose?' Ultimately, Hot Rod's biggest thrill is filling in for driver Fearless Franco in Monster Truck Mania. Colorful acrylics complement the peppy rhymes and the boisterous good time." Horn Book

Lord, Janet

★ **Albert** the Fix-it Man; story by Janet Lord; pictures by Julie Paschkis. Peachtree 2008 un il $15.95

Grades: PreK K 1 2   E

1. Repairing -- Fiction 2. Community life -- Fiction

ISBN 978-1-56145-433-4

LC 2007-29465

A cheerful repairman fixes squeaky doors, leaky roofs, and crumbling fences for his neighbors, who return the kindness when he catches a terrible cold

"Lord's rhythmic, simple text is perfectly cadenced for reading aloud, while Paschkis' cheerful illustrations, filled with scrolling designs and smiling friends, reinforce the sense of the close, busy community working together." Booklist

Here comes Grandma! [by] Janet Lord; illustrated by Julie Paschkis. Henry Holt and Co. 2005 un il $12.95

Grades: PreK K 1   E

1. Grandmothers -- Fiction 2. Transportation -- Fiction

ISBN 0-8050-7666-2

LC 2004-22179

Grandma is coming to visit and she will use any possible method of transport, including a horse and a hot air balloon, to get there

"The simple, rhythmic text suits the mood of the story, and the vivid gouache illustrations have a warm, folklike quality." SLJ

Where is Catkin? written by Janet Lord; illustrated by Julie Paschkis. Peachtree Publishers 2010 un il $16.95

Grades: PreK K 1   E

1. Cats -- Fiction 2. Animals -- Fiction

ISBN 978-1-56145-523-2; 1-56145-523-7

"In this picture-book hide-and-seek game, feline Catkin jumps off young Amy's lap and goes hunting into the grass, by a pond, through rocks, and up a tree, looking for Cricket, then Frog, Mouse, Snake, and Bird. Where are they? Children will enjoy searching through the busy, bright, stylized pictures in ink and gouache and pointing to the creatures hiding where Catkin doesn't see them." Booklist

Lord, John Vernon

The **giant** jam sandwich; story and pictures by John Vernon Lord, with verses by Janet Burroway. Houghton Mifflin 1973 32p il lib bdg $17; pa $6.95; bd bk $6.99

Grades: K 1 2 3   E

1. Stories in rhyme 2. Wasps -- Fiction

ISBN 0-395-16033-2 lib bdg; 0-395-44237-0 pa; 0-547-15077-6 bd bk

First published 1972 in the United Kingdom

"Highly amusing in the details of John Vernon Lord's illustrations. . . . The figures are deliciously grotesque, their expressions wickedly accurate and the colours cheerfully vivid." Jr Bookshelf

Loth, Sebastian

Clementine. North-South 2011 un il $14.95

Grades: PreK K 1 2   E

1. Shape -- Fiction 2. Worms -- Fiction 3. Snails -- Fiction

ISBN 978-0-7358-4009-6; 0-7358-4009-1

Clementine the snail loves all things round and dreams of flying to the moon. Her earthworm friend Paul helps her fly a rocket in orbit around the Earth, and she discovers that the Earth is round too.

"Loth's illustrations carry the weight of the offbeat story, featuring rich colors, beautiful compositions and a cinematic sense of movement." Kirkus

Remembering Crystal. NorthSouth 2010 un il $14.95

Grades: PreK K 1 2   E

1. Death -- Fiction 2. Ducks -- Fiction 3. Turtles -- Fiction 4.

Friendship -- Fiction
ISBN 978-0-7358-2300-6; 0-7358-2300-6
Zelda is a young duck that lives in the garden. Her friend Crystal is a turtle who is growing old. The two do many things together. One day Crystal is not in the garden. But friendship never dies.

"This gets high points for the simplicity of the text . . . and the handsomeness of the design. Buff, mottled pages serve as the background for illustrations that are elegant in their spareness. . . . Despite the somber subject, moments of humor escape into the art. . . . This story of a final friendship touches the heart." Booklist

Zelda the Varigoose; Sebastian Loth. NorthSouth Books 2012 32 p. $15.95
Grades: PreK K   E
1. Geese -- Fiction 2. Imagination -- Fiction 3. Picture books for children
ISBN 0735840768; 9780735840768
This children's picture book is about Zelda the goose who "enjoys changing her persona as she allows her imagination to take flight. The left side of each spread features a digitalized photo of the habitat of a different creature. Opposite, Zelda becomes a different animal through the assistance of an overlay. . . . After the little bird transforms into a 'Chamelegoose,' a 'Goosquid,' and so on, she is also perfectly content to just be herself." (School Library Journal)

Lottridge, Celia Barker
One watermelon seed. Fitzhenry & Whiteside 2008 un il $17.95
Grades: PreK K 1 2   E
1. Counting 2. Gardening -- Fiction
ISBN 978-1-55455-034-0; 1-55455-034-3
First published 1986 by Oxford University Press
"Numbers, colors, and gardening are combined in this vividly illustrated counting book. The story starts as Max and Josephine plant a garden, first 1 watermelon seed, then 2 pumpkin seeds, and so on all the way to 10. The phrase, 'and they grew' follows mention of each new set of seeds. The graphic-style illustrations depict the seedlings as they grow. . . . The vibrant colors and closeup views of the produce make it look delicious and irresistible." SLJ

Lotu, Denize
Running the road to ABC; by Denizé Lauture; illustrated by Reynold Ruffins. Simon & Schuster Bks. for Young Readers 1996 un il hardcover o.p. pa $6.99
Grades: PreK K 1 2   E
1. School stories 2. Haiti -- Fiction
ISBN 0-689-80507-1; 0-689-83165-X pa
LC 95-38290
A Coretta Scott King honor book for illustration, 1997
Long before the sun even thinks of rising the Haitian children run to school where they learn the letters, sounds, and words of their beautiful books
"The rich lyrical language used by the author, a Haitian poet, creates a strong sense of place. . . . The lush, green country and sense of hope are reflected and enhanced by stylized, warmly detailed gouache paintings." Horn Book

Low, William
★ **Machines** go to work in the city; William Low. 1st ed. Henry Holt and Company 2012 48 p.
Grades: PreK K   E
1. Vehicles -- Fiction 2. Cities and towns -- Fiction 3. Lift-the-flap books -- Specimens 4. Machinery
ISBN 0805090509; 9780805090505
LC 2011029045

This children's book by William Low focuses on "Trains, planes, trucks and cranes and the people who make them work [and] keep the city moving. . . . Low presents each vehicle, with an appropriate onomatopoetic sound, in two double-page spreads wherein a simply stated question is posed with the answer appearing on a gate-fold that enlarges the view even further." (Kirkus)

Lowry, Lois
★ **Crow** call; illustrated by Bagram Ibatoulline. Scholastic Press 2009 un il $16.99
Grades: 1 2 3 4   E
1. Crows -- Fiction 2. Hunting -- Fiction 3. Veterans -- Fiction 4. Pennsylvania -- Fiction 5. Father-daughter relationship -- Fiction
ISBN 978-0-545-03035-9; 0-545-03035-8
LC 2008-30158
Nine-year-old Liz accompanies the stranger who is her father, just returned from the war, when he goes hunting for crows in Pennsylvania farmland.
"Beautifully written. . . . Lowry's narrative, dense with sensory details, is based on her own life's events. Fittingly, Ibatoulline's muted, earth-toned palette is reminiscent of vintage, faded photographs." Kirkus

Lucas, David
A **Letter** for Bear; David Lucas. Flying Eye Books 2013 32 p. $14.95
Grades: PreK K 1   E
1. Bears -- Fiction 2. Postal service -- Fiction
ISBN 1909263133; 9781909263130
This picture book, written and illustrated by David Lucas, tells the story of Bear. "Come rain or shine, he works so hard delivering the post to all the animals of the wood but he never receives anything himself. Hardly surprising since he's never actually sent a message! One day Bear decides to write some mail of his own, inviting all the forest animals to a party." (Publisher's note)

The **Skeleton** pirate; David Lucas. Candlewick Press 2013 30 p. ill. (reinforced) $15.99
Grades: PreK K 1 2   E
1. Picture books for children 2. Pirates -- Fiction
ISBN 0763661074; 9780763661076
LC 2012942674
This children's picture book, by David Lucas, follows "the Skeleton Pirate . . . , and he'll never be beaten! That is, until he gets beaten by an unruly bunch of pirates and is thrown overboard. Down in the depths of the sea, he is rescued by a beautiful mermaid, only to be swallowed by a whale. But the whale has a tummy ache from all the other things he has swallowed--like a golden ship full of treasure." (Publisher's note)

Lucke, Deb
Sneezenesia. Clarion Books 2010 un il $17
Grades: K 1 2   E
1. Sneezing -- Fiction
ISBN 978-0-547-33006-8; 0-547-33006-5
Young Zack sneezes so hard, over and over, that he sneezes all memories out of his head, leaving everything he once knew standing before him, trying to figure out how to get back inside.
"The artwork, done in paint, collage, and Photoshop, jumps off the page and adds pace and animation to the story. The supermarket mothers are worth a giggle with their retro outfits and accessories. This funny read-aloud could be paired with any version of 'I Know an Old Lady Who Swallowed a Fly' for a rousing storytime." SLJ

Ludwig, Trudy

Better than you; illustrations by Adam Gustavson. Tricycle Press 2011 un il $15.99; lib bdg $18.99

Grades: PreK K 1 2   E

1. Friendship -- Fiction

ISBN 978-1-58246-380-3; 1-58246-380-8; 978-1-58246-407-7 lib bdg; 1-58246-407-3 lib bdg

LC 2010033224

Tyler's friend Jake continually boasts about his abilities, making Tyler feel bad about himself until his Uncle Kevin and new neighbor Niko help him see that Jake is the one with the problem.

"Focusing on a subject not often written about for children, Ludwig's story may be helpful to youngsters dealing with braggarts. . . . Well-executed paintings are appealing and portray the characters' emotions clearly." SLJ

★ The **invisible** boy; by Trudy Ludwig. Alfred A. Knopf Books for Young Readers 2013 40 p. (hardcover) $16.99; (library binding) $19.99

Grades: K 1 2 3   E

1. Picture books for children 2. School stories -- Fiction 3. Schools -- Fiction 4. Friendship -- Fiction 5. Popularity -- Fiction

ISBN 1582464502; 1582464510; 9780449818206; 9781582464503; 9781582464510

LC 2012042631

In this children's picture book, timid schoolchild "Brian wants to join in but is overlooked, even ostracized, by his classmates. . . . High-maintenance children get the teacher's attention; team captains choose kickball players by popularity and athletic ability; chatter about birthday parties indicates they are not inclusive events." Ultimately, Brian's creative drawings help him win his classmates' attention. (Kirkus Reviews)

Lum, Kate

What! cried Granny; an almost bedtime story. pictures by Adrian Johnson. Dial Bks. for Young Readers 1999 un il hardcover o.p. pa $6.99

Grades: K 1 2 3   E

1. Bedtime -- Fiction 2. Grandmothers -- Fiction

ISBN 0-8037-2382-2; 0-14-230092-6 pa

LC 98-19642

First published 1998 in the United Kingdom with title: What!

This "combines the deadpan and the surreal in wild words and neon-colored acrylic illustrations." Booklist

Lumry, Amanda

Safari in South Africa; by Amanda Lumry and Laura Hurwitz; illustrated by Sarah McIntyre. Scholastic 2008 32p il map (Adventures of Riley) $16.99; pa $6.99

Grades: 1 2 3 4   E

1. Game reserves 2. Animals -- Africa 3. South Africa -- Fiction 4. Wildlife conservation -- Fiction

ISBN 978-0-545-06827-7; 0-545-06827-4; 978-0-545-06826-0 pa; 0-545-06826-6 pa

First published 2003 by Eaglemont Press

Riley travels with his Uncle Max to check on the animal population at a South African game reserve.

"Combining whimsical cartoons and striking photographs of animals in the bush, this title is a marvelous intermingling of adventure and science. . . . Boxes presenting significant facts about the animals appear next to their photographs." SLJ

Other titles in this series are:

Amazon River rescue (2004)

Dolphins in danger (2009)

Mission to Madagascar (2005)

Operation Orangutan (2007)

Polar bear puzzle (2008)

Project Panda (2008)

Riddle of the reef (2009)

South Pole penguins (2008)

Tigers in Terai (2009)

Lund, Deb

Monsters on machines; [by] Deb Lund; illustrated by Robert Neubecker. Harcourt 2008 un il $16

Grades: PreK K 1 2   E

1. Stories in rhyme 2. Monsters -- Fiction 3. Construction workers -- Fiction 4. Construction equipment -- Fiction

ISBN 978-0-15-205365-9; 0-15-205365-4

LC 2006037393

Construction crew monsters arrive on the scene with tractors, cranes, and grader machines, and after a gruesome site is created as their routine, they straighten it up and leave everything clean.

"The India-ink drawings colored digitally in neon-bright hues exude a jazzy, busy look that brings to life the chaos that results when monsters and machines meet." SLJ

Lunde, Darrin

Monkey colors; Darrin Lunde; illustrated by Patricia J. Wynne. Charlesbridge 2011 48 p. col. ill.

Grades: PreK K 1 2   E

1. Color 2. Monkeys 3. Picture books for children 4. Monkeys -- Color

ISBN 1570917418; 9781570917417; 9781570917424

LC 2011000669

In this children's picture book, "[Darrin] Lunde and [Patricia] Wynne describe 12 monkey species in simple sentences. The monkeys are grouped into three categories: four whose fur is a single all-over color (yellow, red, brown, orange); four who have colorful features or stripes; and four whose colors vary with sex or age or gender or who are truly multicolored." (Kirkus)

Lunde, Stein Erik

★ **My** father's arms are a boat; Stein Erik Lunde; [illustrated by Oyvind Torseter; [translated by Kari Dickson] Enchanted Lion Books 2013 40 p. (hardback) $15.95

Grades: K 1 2 3   E

1. Death -- Fiction 2. Emotions -- Fiction 3. Father-son relationship -- Fiction 4. Fathers and sons -- Fiction

ISBN 1592701248; 9781592701247

LC 2012022767

Mildred L. Batchelder Honor Book (2014)

In author Stein Erik Lunde's book, "it's quieter than it's ever been. Unable to sleep, a young boy climbs into his father's arms. Feeling the warmth and closeness of his father, he begins to ask about the birds, the foxes . . . and whether his mother will ever wake up. Even in the face of absence and loss, the cycles of life continue unabated. We know in the end everything will somehow be all right." (Publisher's note)

Lundquist, Mary

Cat & Bunny; by Mary Lundquist. Balzer + Bray, an imprint of HarperCollins Publishers 2014 32 p. color illustrations (hardcover) $17.99

Grades: PreK K 1   E

1. Cats -- Fiction 2. Play -- Fiction 3. Rabbits -- Fiction 4. Friendship -- Fiction 5. Animals -- Fiction 6. Best friends -- Fiction

ISBN 006228780X; 9780062287809

LC 2013051219

This children's book, by Mary Lundquist, is about "Cat and Bunny. . . . It's always been just the two of them - daydreaming, having adventures, playing their special game. Until the day someone else asks, 'Can I play?'" (Publisher's note)

While developing independent identities and adjusting their expectations, Cat and Bunny demonstrate how to admit new friends into a tight circle." PW

Luxbacher, Irene

Mr. Frank; by Irene Luxbacher. Pgw 2014 32 p. mostly color illustrations $16.95

Grades: PreK K 1   E
  1. Sewing -- Fiction 2. Tailoring -- Fiction 3. Retirement -- Fiction
ISBN 1554984351; 9781554984350

LC bl2014038746

In this children's book, by Irene Luxbacher, "on his last day before retirement, Mr. Frank is sewing the most wonderful outfit of his long career. Who could it be for? In all his years working as a tailor, Mr. Frank has made all kinds of clothes. From the practical uniforms of the 1940s to the wild and weird designs of the 1960s and 1970s, he has seen (and sewn) just about everything. But today's project is especially close to Mr. Frank's heart." (Publisher's note)

"Outstanding mixed-media collages and a thoughtful text create a distinctive book that rises far above most tributes to grandparental love. "Mr. Frank was a tailor," proclaims the first page, in bold, unambiguous lettering. . . . The double-page spreads that follow are perfect examples of artwork extending text, as each decade of Mr. Frank's long career reveals the fashions he helped to create and promulgate. . . The entirely wordless climax hints that the book may be turning maudlin, until the turn of the page reveals a humorous and heartwarming denouement. It's a perfect ending to a perfect book. " Kirkus

Luyken, Corinna

The book of mistakes; Corinna Luyken. Dial Books for Young Readers 2017 56 p. chiefly color illustrations (hardback) $18.99

Grades: PreK K 1 2   E
  1. Errors -- Fiction 2. Drawing -- Fiction 3. Illustrators -- Fiction
ISBN 9780735227927

LC 2016028512

In this picture book, by Corinna Luyken, "as one artist incorporates accidental splotches, spots, and misshapen things into her art, she transforms her piece in quirky and unexpected ways, taking readers on a journey through her process. Told in minimal, playful text, this story shows readers that even the biggest 'mistakes' can be the source of the brightest ideas--and that, at the end of the day, we are all works in progress, too." (Publisher's note)

Lynn, Sarah

Tip-Tap Pop; illustrated by Valeria Docampo. Marshall Cavendish 2010 un il $17.99

Grades: PreK K 1   E
  1. Dance -- Fiction 2. Old age -- Fiction 3. Grandfathers -- Fiction
ISBN 978-0-7614-5712-1; 0-7614-5712-7

Emma and Pop have been tap dancing together since before she could talk, but Pop becomes very forgetful and can no longer dance until one special day when he hears Emma's steps and they find a way for him to join in.

"Short text and attention-grabbing words combine with colorful gouache and pencil illustrations. . . . With Docampo's inclusion of a gramophone, bowties, and suspenders, Tip-Tap Pop has a nostalgic feel and leisurely pace. A first purchase." SLJ

Lyon, George Ella

Boats float! George Ella Lyon and Ben Lyon; illustrated by Mick Wiggins. Atheneum Books for Young Readers 2015 40 p. illustrations, color (hardcover : alk. paper) $17.99

Grades: PreK K   E
  1. Stories in rhyme 2. Boats and boating -- Fiction
ISBN 148140380X; 9781481403801

LC 2014034649

This children's book, by George Ella Lyon and Ben Lyon, illustrated by Mick Wiggins, presents an overview of several kinds of boats in rhyming text. "Numerous boats of all kinds and sizes, from different cultures and parts of the world and used for a variety of purposes, including play and habitation, are introduced here. Young readers will be awash in vessels plying waterways from rivers to lakes, ponds to bathtubs, and pools to oceans." (Kirkus Reviews)

My friend, the starfinder; by George Ella Lyon; pictures by Stephen Gammell. Atheneum Books for Young Readers 2008 un il $16.99

Grades: PreK K 1 2   E
  1. Storytelling -- Fiction
ISBN 978-1-4169-2738-9; 1-4169-2738-7

LC 2006032026

A child relates some of the wondrous tales told by an old man who once found a falling star and stood at the end of a rainbow.

This is a "sumptuously illustrated book. . . . Text and art are sure to evoke wonder in young readers." Publ Wkly

The pirate of kindergarten; illustrated by Lynne Avril. Atheneum Books for Young Readers 2010 un il $16.99

Grades: PreK K 1 2   E
  1. School stories 2. Vision disorders -- Fiction
ISBN 978-1-4169-5024-0; 1-4169-5024-9

Ginny's eyes play tricks on her, making her see everything double, but when she goes to vision screening at school and discovers that not everyone sees this way, she learns that her double vision can be cured.

"Lyon's short, descriptive sentences set up the situation deftly, and Avril's astute chalk, pencil, and acrylic drawings of 'two of everything' provide a vivid window into Ginny's pretreatment world." SLJ

Planes fly! George Ella Lyon; illustrated by Mick Wiggins. Atheneum Books for Young Readers 2013 40 p. (hardcover : alk. paper) $17.99

Grades: PreK K   E
  1. Picture books for children 2. Air travel 3. Stories in rhyme 4. Airplanes -- Fiction
ISBN 1442450258; 9781442450257; 9781442450264

LC 2012030310

This children's picture book by George Ella Lyon looks at planes. Rhyming "text names aircraft parts, lists different kinds of planes, and describes passenger air-travel experiences, repeating the upbeat refrain, 'Planes fly!' throughout." A "reassuring rundown of events that happen between buckling the seatbelt and touching down for landing (including a snack and a nap) makes this title helpful to those new to flying." (School Library Journal)

Trucks roll! words by George Ella Lyon; art by Craig Frazier. Atheneum Books for Young Readers 2007 un il $14.99

Grades: PreK   E
  1. Stories in rhyme 2. Trucks -- Fiction
ISBN 978-1-4169-2435-7; 1-4169-2435-3

LC 2006-10811

Illustrations and simple, rhyming text reveal many different—and sometimes silly—items that trucks can haul.

"Solid, up-to-date information about a major preschool enthusiasm is leavened with lively verse and touch of whimsey." Horn Book

You and me and home sweet home; illustrated by Stephanie Anderson. Atheneum Books for Young Readers 2009 un il $17.99
Grades: PreK K 1 2 3   E
    1. Houses -- Fiction 2. Building -- Fiction 3. Volunteer work -- Fiction 4. African Americans -- Fiction
    ISBN 978-0-689-87589-2; 0-689-87589-4
                               LC 2008010414
Third-grader Sharonda and her mother help volunteers from their church to build the house that will be their very own.

"Sharonda narrates in clean, simple prose. . . . Varied in composition and perspective, the watercolor-and-pastel-pencil illustrations center on the nicely individualized characters . . . and readers will share Sharonda's quiet glow of happiness at the end." Booklist

Lyon, Tammie

Olive and Snowflake; written and illustrated by Tammie Lyon. Marshall Cavendish Children 2011 il
Grades: PreK K 1   E
    1. Dogs -- Fiction
    ISBN 0761459553; 9780761459552; 9780761460695 e-book
                               LC 2011001124
When her parents threaten to send away the dog if he cannot learn to behave, Olive is worried they will both be sent to live with a new family.

"Bold text and vibrant cartoon-style illustrations make this a great read-aloud or lap read. Children will delight in the happy ending and will appreciate this simple tale of love, responsibility, and growing up." SLJ

Lyons, Kelly Starling

Ellen's broom; Kelly Starling Lyons; illustrated by Daniel Minter. G. P. Putnam's Sons 2012 32 p.
Grades: K 1 2 3   E
    1. Brooms -- Fiction 2. Picture books for children 3. Reconstruction (1865-1876) -- Fiction 4. Slaves -- Emancipation -- Fiction 5. Marriage customs and rites -- Fiction 6. Slavery -- Fiction 7. Marriage -- Fiction 8. African Americans -- Fiction 9. Brooms and brushes -- Fiction 10. Reconstruction (U.S. history, 1865-1877) -- Fiction
    ISBN 9780399250033
                               LC 2011047101
Coretta Scott King Illustrator Honor Book (2013)
This picture book, "[s]et during Reconstruction, . . . [is] based on a historical event, [and] opens with a preacher's announcement to his black congregation that "all former slaves living as husband and wife shall be registered and seen as married in the eyes of the law." Young Ellen doesn't quite understand what this means until her mother explains to her that during slavery, slave couples like Ellen's mother and father were only allowed "broom weddings," wherein couples would jump over a broom. . . . Ellen grabs the marriage broom, . . . decorates it with flowers, and hands it to her parents during the[ir] ceremony. . . . [T]he story touches . . . on how formerly enslaved people . . . found . . . ways to celebrate their freedoms during . . . Reconstruction." (Bulletin of the Center for Children's Books)

Hope's gift; Kelly Starling Lyons; illustrated by Don Tate. G.P. Putnam's Sons 2012 32 p. (hardcover) $16.99
Grades: 1 2 3   E
    1. Slaves -- Emancipation -- Fiction 2. United States -- History -- 1861-1865, Civil War -- Fiction 3. Slavery -- Fiction 4. African Americans -- Fiction 5. Emancipation Proclamation -- Fiction
    ISBN 0399160019; 9780399160011
                               LC 2012014587

In this children's story, by Kelly Starling Lyons, illustrated by Don Tate, "it's 1862. . . . Hope's father . . . decides to join the Union army to fight for freedom. He slips away one tearful night, leaving Hope, . . . with only a conch shell for comfort. . . . But then Lincoln finally does it: on January 1, 1863, he issues the Emancipation Proclamation, freeing the slaves, and a joyful Hope finally spies the outline of a familiar man standing on the horizon." (Publisher's note)

Maass, Robert

A is for autumn. Henry Holt 2011 un il $16.99
Grades: PreK K 1 2   E
    1. Alphabet 2. Autumn -- Fiction
    ISBN 978-0-8050-9093-2; 0-8050-9093-2
                               LC 2010040333
Photographs and simple text present a variety of things seen in the fall.

"Vivid photography brings the autumn season to life in an alphabet book with thoughtful descriptions of nature, changing weather, and leisure activities. . . . Maass delivers a vibrant tribute to Autumn." Publ Wkly

Macaulay, David

Why the chicken crossed the road. Houghton Mifflin 1987 31p il lib bdg $16
Grades: 3 4 5   E
    1. Chickens -- Fiction
    ISBN 0-395-44241-9 lib bdg
                               LC 87-2908
"A ridiculous chicken sets off a circular story involving a herd of cows, a bridge, a train, a robber, the fire department and some hydrangeas. Chaos. The illustrations are suitably wild—painted with brilliant color and almost palpable energy." N Y Times Book Rev

Maccarone, Grace

★ **Miss** Lina's ballerinas; illustrated by Christine Davenier. Feiwel and Friends 2010 un il $16.99
Grades: PreK K 1   E
    1. Stories in rhyme 2. Ballet -- Fiction
    ISBN 0-312-38243-X; 978-0-312-38243-8
                               LC 2009-49367
Ballet instructor Miss Lina has a solution when her eight students, who always dance in pairs, are distraught when a ninth girl joins the class.
"The rhymic rhyming text flows beautifully throughout the book. . . . Davenier's free-spirited drawings and color washes add a sense of music as well as movement to the scenes." Booklist
Another title about Miss Lina is:
Miss Lina's ballerinas and the prince (2011)

Miss Lina's ballerinas and the prince; illustrated by Christine Davenier. Feiwel & Friends 2011 $16.99
Grades: PreK K 1   E
    ISBN 978-0-312-64963-0; 0-312-64963-0
Miss Lina's ballerinas have all learned how to dance as a group. But now Miss Lina has a new surprise for them—a boy will be joining their class and performing in their end-of-year show.

"Maccarone has fashioned another charming story in rhyme for young readers that integrates ballet terminology into the narrative and provides a very positive reinforcement for boys interested in the arts. The pastel drawings with swirls of crayon lines provide just the right touch of ambiance and energy." Kirkus

Macdonald, Suse

Circus opposites; an interactive extravaganza. Little Simon 2010 un il $11.99

Grades: PreK K 1 2 E
1. Opposites 2. Circus -- Fiction
ISBN 978-1-4169-7154-2; 1-4169-7154-8

"Macdonald's crisp trademark paper collages are the main event, as she uses the sights of the circus to explore the concept of opposites. Readers kick things off by pulling a tab to let 11 clowns 'out' of a tiny yellow car. They can also literally turn a clown's frown upside down. . . . The elaborate costumes and variety of interactive elements should prove kid-pleasing." Publ Wkly

Shape by shape. Simon & Schuster 2009 il $14.99
Grades: PreK K 1 E
1. Shape
ISBN 9781416971474; 1416971475

"Introducing a series of basic shapes, die-cuts on sturdy square pages reveal, piece by piece, a friendly dinosaur." (Booklist)

MacHale, D. J.

The **monster** princess; written by D.J. MacHale; illustrated by Alexandra Boiger. Aladdin Paperbacks 2010 un il $17.99
Grades: PreK K E
1. Stories in rhyme 2. Monsters -- Fiction 3. Princesses -- Fiction 4. Self-acceptance -- Fiction
ISBN 978-1-4169-4809-4; 1-4169-4809-0
LC 2008037933

Unhappy with her life in a dark cave, Lala longs to live like the princesses far, far above but after venturing into their world, she finds contentment at home.

"A potentially didactic story . . . is saved by a wry text . . . and endearing illustrations. . . . The resolution satisfies." Booklist

MacIver, Juliette, 1972-

The **Frog** who lost his underpants; written by Juliette MacIver, illustrated by Cat Chapman. Candlewick Press 2014 32 p. $14.99
Grades: PreK K 1 E
1. Frogs -- Fiction 2. Underwear -- Fiction 3. Stories in rhyme 4. Teddy bears -- Fiction 5. Jungle animals -- Fiction
ISBN 076366782X; 9780763667825
LC 2013944130

In this children's book by Juliette MacIver, illustrated by Cat Chapman, "Frog is in a frenzy, scattering the ants. . . . Poor Frog. Someone stole his underpants! Good thing Teddy Bear, Little Chimp, and Big Gray Elephant are there to help--although they may find it hard to hide their smiles. A jungle frog in underpants? Now that is something to see." (Publisher's note)

"The silliness begins with the book's title and cover image, which features a big teddy bear helping a woebegone frog through the jungle... When the elephant, chimpanzee, bear, and a hundred jungle frogs find the pair of red undies, chaos ensues, followed by a suitably silly solution. Frog distinguishes himself from the other jungle frogs not by his taste in skivvies but by the friendships he has made." Booklist

Mack, Jeff

Ah ha! Jeff Mack. Chronicle Books 2013 40 p. (alk. paper) $16.99
Grades: PreK K 1 E
1. Frogs -- Fiction 2. Picture books for children
ISBN 1452112657; 9781452112657
LC 2012040903

"This nearly wordless book . . . follows the adventures of a frog who is caught in a jar by a boy and his dog ('AH HA!'). Don't worry, he escapes ('AAHH!') but lands on the back of a hungry turtle ('AH HA!') from whom he leaps away to escape being eaten ('AAHH!'), only to find himself on the back of an even hungrier crocodile ('AH HA!'). And so

it goes from croc to flamingo leg and then back into the jar to the final escape ('AH HA!')." (School Library Journal)

Good news, bad news; Jeff Mack. Chronicle Books 2012 40 p. (alk. paper) $16.99
Grades: PreK K 1 E
1. Rain -- Fiction 2. Picnics -- Fiction 3. Picture books for children 4. Mice -- Fiction 5. Rabbits -- Fiction 6. Optimism -- Fiction 7. Pessimism -- Fiction
ISBN 1452101108; 9781452101101
LC 2011016710

In this book, "[w]hen optimistic Rabbit and unlucky Mouse go on a picnic, there is plenty of good news and bad news. Some good news-umbrella, apples, cake, cave. Some bad news-rain, worms, bees, bear. Unfortunately, all the bad seems to happen to Mouse, who eventually has a hissy fit that makes Rabbit cry. But as the sun breaks through the clouds, Mouse makes it all better with a peace offering of the picnic basket and a hug" (School Library Journal)

Hippo and Rabbit in three short tales. Scholastic/Cartwheel Books 2011 32p il pa $3.99
Grades: K 1 2 E
1. Graphic novels 2. Humorous graphic novels 3. Rabbits -- Fiction 4. Friendship -- Fiction 5. Hippopotamus -- Fiction
ISBN 978-0-545-27445-6; 0-545-27445-1
LC 2010-13567

Friends Hippo and Rabbit are very different in size, but they have fun together as they eat breakfast (Rabbit eats vegetables, Hippo has a cheeseburger), play on the swing (Rabbit has to try very hard to push Hippo), and then comfort each other during a thunderstorm at night.

"With a low word count and simple sentences [this is] suitable for newly independent readers. . . . The book can be used as a supplemental reader in the classroom, but the stories are fun enough for recreational reading at home. " Booklist

Another title in this series is:
Hippo and Rabbit in 3 more tales (2011)

Hush little polar bear; [by] Jeff Mack. Roaring Brook Press 2008 un il $16.95
Grades: PreK K E
1. Stories in rhyme 2. Adventure fiction 3. Dreams -- Fiction 4. Bedtime -- Fiction 5. Polar bear -- Fiction
ISBN 978-1-59643-368-7; 1-59643-368-X
LC 2007044049

A little girl invites her plush polar bear to dream of all of the places where sleeping bears go, from the high seas to a starry desert and back home

"The richly textured spreads are bright and imaginative, perfectly complementing the simple, lyrical text." SLJ

Look! Jeff Mack. Philomel Books, an imprint of Penguin Group (USA) 2015 32 p. color illustrations (hardback) $16.99
Grades: PreK K 1 E
1. Humorous fiction 2. Gorillas -- Fiction 3. Friendship -- Fiction 4. Books and reading -- Fiction 5. Humorous stories
ISBN 0399162054; 9780399162053
LC 2014020636

"Everyone needs a little attention from time to time. Just ask our gorilla who will stop at nothing to be noticed by the boy with his eyes glued to the TV set. . . . Using only two words--LOOK and OUT--[author] Jeff Mack relates an adorably hilarious story about an attention-loving gorilla, a television-loving boy, and a friendship that develops over books." (Publisher's note)

"Bright, mostly monochrome page backgrounds evoke clothbound book covers and distressed old pages; minimal set dressing (a door, a stool, the TV) keeps the focus on the zany interaction. The personalities and emotions of the chunky, fluffy ape and the TV-entranced boy nearly vibrate off the page." Kirkus

Playtime? Jeff Mack. Philomel Books 2016 32 p. color illustrations (hardback) $16.99
Grades: PreK K 1   E
   1. Gorillas -- Fiction 2. Play -- Fiction 3. Bedtime -- Fiction
   ISBN 9780399175985
                 LC 2015036920

This picture book, by Jeff Mack, is an "ode to the struggles of bedtime. . . . Bedtime can be a challenge for the best of us. But when you're a fun-loving, overactive pet gorilla, bedtime is downright hard. Who would want to go to sleep when Playtime is so much more fun? But the gorilla's responsible friend thinks enough is enough; no more fun and games. It's not Playtime--It's Bedtime!" (Publisher's note)

"A pleasant and action-filled going-to-sleep book, this selection may prove the perfect antidote for a sleepless night. A simple, fun-filled goodnight book." Kirkus

Mackall, Dandi Daley
   First day; illustrated by Tiphanie Beeke. Harcourt 2003 un il $16
Grades: PreK K   E
   1. School stories 2. Stories in rhyme
   ISBN 0-15-216577-0
                 LC 2002-933

The first day of school starts out filled with doubt, but after facing fear of the big kids, reciting the alphabet with ease, and learning about recess, a child can't help but look forward to day two.

"The rhyming text gives the story a sweet, singsong quality. . . . The softly colored, reassuring art works well with the simple text that is set on pastel backgrounds." SLJ

Macken, JoAnn Early
   Baby says moo! written by JoAnn Early Macken; illustrated by David Walker. Disney Hyperion Books 2011 un il lib bdg $15.99
Grades: PreK   E
   1. Stories in rhyme 2. Sounds -- Fiction 3. Animals -- Fiction 4. Infants -- Fiction
   ISBN 978-1-4231-3400-8 lib bdg; 1-4231-3400-1 lib bdg
                 LC 2009-52504

A cumulative, rhyming tale of a baby who sees many animals while out with her family, only one of which makes her favorite sound.

"The rhyming text reads smoothly, and the acrylic illustrations are childlike and cheerful, making the book exactly right for toddlers." SLJ

★ **Waiting** out the storm; illustrated by Susan Gaber. Candlewick Press 2010 un il $15.99
Grades: PreK K 1 2   E
   1. Stories in rhyme 2. Rain -- Fiction 3. Storms -- Fiction 4. Mother-child relationship -- Fiction
   ISBN 978-0-7636-3378-3; 0-7636-3378-X
                 LC 2008030746

A mother reassures her child about the wind, lightning, and thunder when a storm passes through.

"The text creates a natural-sounding rhythm and flow of dialogue. . . . Gaber's captivating artwork, combining watercolor, pencil, and charcoal with digital renderings, is simultaneously strong and delicate." Booklist

Mackintosh, David
   Marshall Armstrong is new to our school. Abrams 2011 il

Grades: PreK K 1 2   E
   1. School stories 2. Parties -- Fiction 3. Birthdays -- Fiction 4. Friendship -- Fiction
   ISBN 1-4197-0036-7; 978-1-4197-0036-1

Marshall Armstrong is new to school and definitely stands out from the crowd, with his pale skin, perpetual hats, and special "space food" lunches that come in silver wrappers. He doesn't play sports, and he doesn't watch television. So when he invites everyone in class over for his birthday party, it's sure to be a disaster. Or is it?

"Macintosh's beautifully underplayed text and genial drawings manage to be empathic to both the leery narrator and the serenely outré object of his misapprehension." Publ Wkly

MacLachlan, Patricia
   Barkus; by Patricia MacLachlan; illustrated by Marc Boutavant Chronicle Books Llc 2017 56 p. color illustrations (Barkus) (alk paper) $14.99
   Grades: PreK K 1 2   E
   1. Dogs -- Fiction
   ISBN 9781452111827
                 LC 201600699

In this book, by Patricia MacLachlan, illustrated by Marc Boutavant "meet Barkus. Barkus is loyal. Barkus is generous. Barkus is family. . . The accessible text is ideal for even the newest independent reader while the warm, humorous story and energetic illustrations will appea to picture book readers as well as advanced readers." (Publisher's note)

   Lala salama; a Tanzanian lullaby. illustrated by Elizabeth Zunon Candlewick Press 2011 il $16.99
   Grades: PreK K 1   E
   1. Lullabies 2. Tanzania -- Fiction 3. Family life -- Fiction 4 Mother-child relationship -- Fiction
   ISBN 978-0-7636-4747-6; 0-7636-4747-0
                 LC 201004046

A mother relates the events of a peaceful day along the banks of Lak Tanganyika to her baby, wrapped up and ready for sleep.

"Zunon's lush, softly textured oil paintings on watercolor paper re flect the warmth of the African setting and emotion-imbued prose. . . Share this with preschoolers who may enjoy a peek into another cul ture's family life or keep at hand for the tired child, who will most ap preciate this quietly sentimental offering." Kirkus

   Painting the wind; by Patricia MacLachlan & Emily MacLachlan illustrated by Katy Schneider. J. Cotler Bks. 2003 un il $15.99; p $7.99
   Grades: K 1 2 3   E
   1. Artists -- Fiction 2. Painting -- Fiction
   ISBN 0-06-029798-0; 0-06-443825-2 pa
                 LC 2001-4754

Several artists who paint different things, with different kinds o paint, and at different times of the day, all paint the same island that the visit each summer

"The gentle prose pairs well with handsome artwork that evoke warm, strong sensory impressions through a combination of thick brush work, texture, and a vibrant color palette." Booklist

The **Poet's** Dog; by Patricia MacLachlan. Harpercollins Children Books 2016 96 p. illustrations $14.99
   Grades: 1 2 3 4 5 6
   1. Stories in rhyme 2. Dogs -- Fiction 3. Poets -- Fiction
   ISBN 9780062292650; 0062292625; 9780062292629

In this book, by Patricia MacLachlan, "Teddy is a gifted dog. Raise in a cabin by a poet named Sylvan, he grew up listening to sonnets rea aloud. . . . Although Teddy understands words, Sylvan always told hi there are only two kinds of people in the world who can hear Teddy speak: poets and children. Then one day Teddy learns that Sylvan was right. When Teddy finds Nickel and Flora trapped in a snowstorm, he tells them that he will bring them home—and they understand him." (Publisher's note)

"Readers will find their own jewels in this gem of a book." Booklist

Your moon, my moon; a grandmother's words to a faraway child. illustrated by Bryan Collier. Simon & Schuster Books for Young Readers 2011 un il $16.99

Grades: PreK K 1 2   E

1. Africa -- Fiction 2. New England -- Fiction 3. Grandmothers -- Fiction

ISBN 978-1-4169-7950-0; 1-4169-7950-6

LC 2008050451

Although their homes are different, a grandmother in New England and her loving grandson in Africa share the same moon.

"Collier's vibrant illustrations are a blend of watercolor and his trademark collage. This is a wonderful book to contrast different life-styles." SLJ

Maclear, Kyo

Spork; written by Kyo Maclear; illustrated by Isabelle Arsenault. Kids Can Press 2010 un il $16.95

Grades: PreK K 1 2   E

1. Cutlery -- Fiction 2. Prejudices -- Fiction 3. Identity (Psychology) -- Fiction 4. Racially mixed people -- Fiction

ISBN 978-1-55337-736-8; 1-55337-736-2

His mum is a spoon. His dad is a fork. And he's a bit of both. He's Spork! The spoons think he's too pointy, while the forks find him too round.

"Maclear's text feels nearly effortless. The inanimate-object identifi-cation . . . pairs brilliantly with Arsenault's melding of mixed media and digital art. . . . A sublime little parable." Kirkus

MacLeod, Doug

Heather Fell in the Water; by Doug MacLeod; illustrated by Craig Smith. Independent Pub Group 2013 32 p. ill. (hardcover) $16.99

Grades: PreK K   E

1. Picture books for children 2. Swimming -- Fiction

ISBN 1742376487; 9781742376486

In this children's picture book, "everywhere Heather goes, from farms to art galleries, she falls in the water. As a result, her parents make her wear water wings at all times, even in bed. Then one day they deter-mine that their child needs to learn how to swim. Unsurprisingly, Heath-er is frightened, convinced that the water dislikes her. But she climbs into the shallow end of a pool with her mother and father," and finds that she loves the water and it loves her. (School Library Journal)

Mader, C. Roger

Stowaway in a sleigh; written and illustrated by Roger Mader. Houghton Mifflin Harcourt 2016 32 p. color illustrations (ebook) $17.99; $17.99

Grades: PreK K 1   E

1. Cats -- Fiction 2. Christmas -- Fiction 3. Santa Claus -- Fiction

ISBN 9781328664112; 9780544481749

LC 2015018705

In this book, by Roger Mader, "when Slipper finds Mr. Furry Boots in her house, she does what any cat would do and investigates. But cu-riosity gets the best of her when she finds herself on a trip she hadn't planned on taking . . . . Join Slipper as she discovers that there's no place like home—especially for Christmas." (Publisher's note)

"The succinct, perfectly paced text makes every carefully chosen word count. This stowaway is here to stay as a new Christmas classic." Kirkus

★ **Tiptop** cat; written and illustrated by C. Roger Mader. Hough-ton Mifflin Books for Children, Houghton Mifflin Harcourt 2014 40 p. color illustrations $17.99

Grades: PreK K 1 2   E

1. Cats -- Fiction

ISBN 0544147995; 9780544147997

LC 2013038998

In this children's book, by Roger Mader, "a curious cat plus a big fall leads to squashed confidence. How this cat bounces back will encourage readers everywhere to try, try again. Eye-catching art and crisp graphic paneling invite even the youngest of children to get back on their feet to explore the city alongside TipTop Cat." (Publisher's note)

"A Parisian cat that has enjoyed touring rooftops is terrified when he falls from a sixth-floor balcony, only to have his confidence later re-stored. Arresting, detailed pastels capture feline behavior and also steep heights and angles. The simple narrative's tone is light rather than didac-tic as we cheer on the unnamed hero's triumphant return to the "top of the world." Horn Book

Madison, Alan

Velma Gratch & the way cool butterfly; written by Alan Madison; illustrated by Kevin Hawkes. Schwartz & Wade Books 2007 un il $16.99; lib bdg $19.99

Grades: PreK K 1 2   E

1. School stories 2. Sisters -- Fiction 3. Butterflies -- Fiction

ISBN 978-0-375-83597-1; 978-0-375-93597-8 lib bdg

LC 2006030978

Velma starts first grade in the shadow of her memorable older sisters, and while her newfound interest in butterflies helps her to stand out, it also leads to an interesting complication

"With humorous wordplay and electric cartoon art, this is an uplift-ing and way-cool look at one child's metamorphosis." SLJ

Madrigal, Antonio Hernandez

Erandi's braids; written by Antonio Hernandez Madrigal; illus-trated by Tomie dePaola. Putnam 1999 un il $15.99; pa $6.99

Grades: K 1 2 3   E

1. Hair -- Fiction 2. Mexico -- Fiction 3. Mother-daughter relationship -- Fiction

ISBN 0-399-23212-5; 0-698-11885-5 pa

LC 97-49631

In a poor Mexican village, Erandi surprises her mother by offering to sell her long, beautiful hair in order to raise enough money to buy a new fishing net

"This tale of love and sacrifice is based on an actual Mexican prac-tice in the 1940s and 50s. The facial expressions in dePaola's warm il-lustrations add to the poignancy of the story." Horn Book Guide

Magoon, Scott

The boy who cried Bigfoot! Scott Magoon. Simon & Schuster Books for Young Readers 2012 48 p. color illustrations $16.99

Grades: PreK K 1   E

1. Yeti -- Fiction 2. Honesty -- Fiction

ISBN 1442412577; 9781442412576

LC 2010031149

In this children's book, written and illustrated by Scott Magoon, "a friendly Sasquatch narrates this twist on 'The Boy Who Cried Wolf,' relating his introduction to young Ben, who has a habit of making up stories about spying Bigfoot near the woods. When no Bigfoot ever ac-tually appears, Ben's believers predictably lose faith. As Ben sits dejectedly near the woods one evening, Bigfoot makes his presence known and borrows Ben's bike for a ride." (Bulletin of the Center for Children's Books)

"Digitally rendered illustrations are done in mostly green hues. Bigfoot is charming and goofy-looking with his smiles and manners, asking if he can 'borrow' Ben's bike, and the child's expressions are priceless." SLJ

Breathe; Scott Magoon. Simon & Schuster Books for Young Readers 2014 40 p. (hardcover) $16.99

Grades: PreK K 1   E

1. Whales -- Fiction 2. Whales -- Fiction 3. Animals -- Infancy -- Fiction

ISBN 1442412585; 9781442412583

LC 2013017696

This children's book, by Scott Magoon, "follows a young whale on a journey of discovery as he experiences his first day at sea on his own! He swims, explores, and makes friends in his marine habitat. After a day of independence, this little whale delights in returning home to his mother." (Publisher's note)

"With the encouragement of its mother, a young whale spends the day exploring, making new friends, finding shipwrecks, and swimming past glaciers, while intermittently pausing to "breathe" during its busy day...The minimal text is laid out in clear, big font, supporting the impressive illustrations without ever overshadowing them. With its succinct text and sprawling pictures, this story is perfectly suitable as a read-aloud." SLJ

Mahy, Margaret

17 kings and 42 elephants; pictures by Patricia MacCarthy. Dial Bks. for Young Readers 1987 26p il $16.99

Grades: K 1 2 3   E

1. Stories in rhyme 2. Animals -- Fiction

ISBN 0-8037-0458-5

LC 87-5311

A newly illustrated edition of the title first published 1972 in the United Kingdom

Seventeen kings and forty-two elephants romp with a variety of jungle animals during their mysterious journey through a wild, wet night

"This book takes you on a jungle journey you will never forget. . . . The text is lyrical, humorous, and full of nonsense and fantasy. Children and adults will be charmed by the melodic use of language and the beautiful batik illustrations." Child Book Rev Serv

Bubble trouble; illustrated by Polly Dunbar. Clarion Books 2009 37p il $16

Grades: PreK K 1   E

1. Stories in rhyme 2. Bubbles -- Fiction

ISBN 978-0-547-07421-4; 0-547-07421-2

LC 2008-07244

Boston Globe-Horn Book Award: Picture Book (2009)

Mabel blows a bubble that captures Baby and wafts him away, resulting in a wild chase that involves the whole neighborhood.

"Mahy is a master at creating verse that is as light and airy as the baby's bubble. Filled with lovely Briticisms, alliterative nonsense words, double, triple and internal rhymes, it's meant to be read aloud. . . . Dunbar's joyous watercolor-and-cut-paper illustrations are wonderfully expressive, a visual treat moving apace with the text." Kirkus

The **green** bath; Margaret Mahy; illustrated by Steven Kellogg. Arthur A. Levine Books 2013 40 p. (hardcover : alk. paper) $16.99

Grades: PreK K 1 2   E

1. Baths -- Fiction 2. Picture books for children 3. Pirates -- Fiction 4. Baths -- Fiction 5. Bathtubs -- Fiction 6. Adventure and

adventurers -- Fiction

ISBN 0545206677; 9780545206679; 9780545206686

LC 2012013239

In this children's picture book, Sammy's father buys a "clunky, green bathtub" at the flea market. "This is no ordinary tub: for one, it has an expressive, wide-eyed face, and Sammy hears the tub 'give a gurgle as if it were laughing.'" During Sammy's bath, the tub comes to life and "Sammy sails out to sea in the tub and, with the help of a friendly sea serpent, engages in 'a wonderful bath-and-buccaneer battle' with pirates." (Publishers Weekly)

The **man** from the land of Fandango; Margaret Mahy; illustrations by Polly Dunbar. Clarion Books 2012 32 p. (hardback) $16.99

Grades: PreK K 1 2   E

1. Picture books for children 2. Imagination -- Fiction 3. Adventure fiction -- Fiction 4. Stories in rhyme 5. Imagination -- Fiction

ISBN 0547819889; 9780547819884

LC 2011052109

In this children's book by Margaret Mahy, illustrated by Polly Dunbar, "two children paint Mr. Fandango to life, and together the trio has a tremendous adventure with baboons and bisons, dinosaurs and kangaroos . . . [in] a playful imaginary world. . . . Even the lines of type curve and tango." (Publisher's note)

Mair, J. Samia

The **perfect** gift; illustrated by Craigh Howarth. Kube Pub. 2010 29p il $8.95

Grades: 1 2 3 4   E

1. Gifts -- Fiction 2. Muslims -- Fiction 3. Id al-Adha -- Fiction 4. Family life -- Fiction

ISBN 978-0-86037-438-1; 0-86037-438-6

Sarah is sad because she cannot find an Eid gift for her mother, so she takes a walk along the secret path in the woods that always makes her feel better. There she finds the first flower of spring—God's perfect gift to the world. Leaving her gift in its place to share with her entire family, Sarah grows in her understanding and appreciation of nature and what it means to live in submission to God.

"Howarth's watercolor illustrations effectively portray a contemporary Muslim family living in North America or Europe. This realistic picture book, one of the few stories on Eid-ul-Adha, is a solid purchase for many collections." SLJ

Mak, Kam

★ **My** Chinatown; one year in poems. HarperCollins Pubs. 2002 un il $16.95

Grades: 2 3 4   E

1. Immigrants -- Fiction 2. Chinese Americans -- Fiction 3. Chinatown (New York, N.Y.) -- Fiction

ISBN 0-06-029190-7; 0-06-029191-5 lib bdg

LC 2001-16686

A boy adjusts to life away from his home in Hong Kong, in the Chinatown of his new American city

"Extraordinary photo-realistic paintings and spare, free-verse poems bring New York's Chinatown to life in this picture book with appeal to a wide age group." Booklist

Malaspina, Ann

★ **Heart** on fire; Susan B. Anthony votes for president. by Ann Malaspina; illustrated by Steve James. Albert Whitman & Co. 2012 32 p. col. ill. (hardcover) $16.99

Grades: 2 3 4   E

1. Elections 2. Voter registration 3. Women's rights -- History 4. Election law -- New York (State) -- Criminal provisions 5. Trials (Political crimes and offenses) -- New York (State) 6. Women --

Suffrage -- United States -- History -- 19th century
ISBN 080753188X; 9780807531884

LC 2011034179

Author Ann Malaspina tells the story of Susan B. Anthony. "On November 5, 1872, Susan B. Anthony made history--and broke the law--when she voted in the US presidential election, a privilege that had been reserved for men. She was arrested, tried, and found guilty . . . It wasn't until 1920 that women were granted the right to vote, but the civil rights victory would not have been possible without Susan B. Anthony's leadership and passion to stand up for what was right." (Publisher's note)

"Incisive storytelling and luminous oil paintings make for a memorable, important read." SLJ

Includes bibliographical references.

Maloney, Peter

★ **One** foot two feet; an exceptional counting book. [by] Peter Maloney & Felicia Zekauskas. G.P. Putnam's Sons 2011 un il $12.99
Grades: PreK K   E

1. Counting 2. English language -- Grammar
ISBN 978-0-399-25446-8; 0-399-25446-3

LC 2010028172

"Preschoolers will enjoy pointing at the pictures and turning the pages in this simple, interactive counting book that is also a game of wordplay. Along with the numbers, the spreads introduce the vocabulary changes from single to plural nouns. Each brightly colored page has a central cut-out window of a single object, beginning with one foot. Turn the page, and there are two feet. . . . The playful cartoon pictures on thick paper with lots of white space will draw kids with the humorous details." Booklist

Mandel, Peter

Jackhammer Sam; illustrated by David Catrow. Roaring Brook Press 2011 un il $16.99
Grades: PreK K 1 2   E

1. Stories in rhyme 2. Construction workers -- Fiction
ISBN 978-1-59643-034-1; 1-59643-034-6

LC 2010036341

A jackhammer operator boasts about his loud, sidewalk-blasting skills.

"The sing-song text is punctuated by onomatopoeia and nonsense words, and it is as loud and brash as the illustrations or, for that matter, a jackhammer." Horn Book

Manger; edited by Lee Bennett Hopkins; illustrated by Helen Cann. Eerdmans Books for Young Readers 2014 34 p. color illustrations $16
Grades: K 1 2 3   E

1. Children's poetry 2. Christmas -- Poetry 3. Jesus Christ -- Nativity -- Poetry
ISBN 0802854192; 9780802854193

LC 2013044516

This collection of children's poetry, selected by author Lee Bennett Hopkins, focuses on the "legend that describes how, at midnight on Christmas Eve, all creatures are granted the power of speech for one hour. . . . The poems represent a diverse group of animals, but all come together with one singular purpose: celebrating the joy of the miraculous event. This collection of graceful poems provides readers with a Nativity story unlike any other." (Publisher's note)

""What gifts have I / to give / this Child? // No gold, / no frankincense, / no myrrh, / only my quiet / soothing purr." Fourteen poems, each told from the perspective of an animal present at Jesus' birth, are here collected. The poems convey both the majesty and intimacy of that night; decorative mixed-media illustrations highlight each animal on its own double-page spread." Horn Book

Manley, Curtis

Shawn loves sharks; Curtis Manley; pictures by Tracy Subisak. Roaring Brook Press 2017 32 p. color illustrations (hardback) $17.99
Grades: K 1 2   E

1. Sharks -- Fiction 2. Friendship -- Fiction 3. Seals (Animals) -- Fiction 4. Schools -- Fiction 5. Imagination -- Fiction
ISBN 9781626721340

LC 2016025026

In this picture book, by Curtis Manley, illustrated by Tracy Subisak, "Shawn loves sharks. He loves their dark, blank eyes. He loves their big mouths full of sharp teeth. And he loves pretending to be a shark and chasing Stacy around the playground. Shawn loves sharks more than anything else in the world. But Predator Day at school is on Monday and Great White Shark isn't assigned to Shawn. It's assigned to . . . . Stacy." (Publisher's Note)

The **summer** Nick taught his cats to read; Curtis Manley; illustrated by Kate Berube. Simon & Schuster Books for Young Readers 2016 32 p. color illustrations (hardcover) $17.99
Grades: PreK K 1 2   E

1. Cats -- Fiction 2. Books and reading -- Fiction 3. Cats -- Fiction 4. Books and reading -- Fiction 5. Illustration of books -- Fiction
ISBN 9781481435697

LC 2014024861

In this book, written by Curtis Manley and illustrated by Kate Berube, "Nick loves to read books—and he loves to play with his cats, Verne and Stevenson. So naturally Nick decides it's a great idea to teach his cats to read. But Verne and Stevenson don't appreciate when Nick wakes them up with a flashcard that says NAP. Nick finally piques Verne's interest with words like MOUSE and FISH." (Publisher's note)

"A satisfying combination of original storytelling and amusing, affectionate artwork." Booklist

Mann, Jennifer K.

Two speckled eggs; Jennifer K. Mann. Candlewick Press 2014 32 p. $14.99
Grades: K 1 2 3   E

1. Birthdays -- Fiction 2. Self-acceptance -- Fiction 3. Eccentrics and eccentricities -- Fiction 4. Birthday parties -- Fiction
ISBN 0763661686; 9780763661687

LC 2013944009

In this book, by Jennifer K. Mann, "it's Ginger's birthday, and she has to invite all the girls in her class to her party, including Lyla Browning. Lyla isn't like the other girls. . . . But . . . . Ginger's party doesn't go quite the way she'd hoped. . . . By the time Lyla gives Ginger her present—a tiny homemade nest with two delicious malted-milk eggs—Ginger begins to wonder: is being different really such a bad thing?" (Publisher's note)

"Ginger does not want strange Lyla Browning to come to her birthday party. But when her other friends disrupt Ginger's party plans, she discovers that she and Lyla have some things in common after all. Mann infuses a simple text with humorous details and insights, and her art combines pencil, paint, and digital collage to produce a quietly complex backdrop that echoes the story." Horn Book

Manning, Jane

Millie Fierce Sleeps Out; by Jane Manning. Penguin Group USA 2014 32 p. $16.99
Grades: PreK K 1 2   E

1. Courage -- Fiction 2. Emotions -- Fiction 3. Temper -- Fiction 4. Camping -- Fiction 5. Sleepovers -- Fiction
ISBN 0399160930; 9780399160936

In this children's book, by Jane Manning, "Millie is strong. Millie is fierce. But Millie has learned to keep her fierceness in check. And since she's been sweet all summer long, Millie gets to have a sleepout with her friends. . . . [S]he tries her best to keep her fierceness inside. But when the scary dog from next door howls at the girls' tent, Millie's ferocity saves them all!" (Publisher's note)

"In this follow-up to Millie Fierce, the protagonist hosts a backyard sleepover for her friends. Millie is determined to control her temper and keep herself "fierce-free." She manages to do so until a snarling dog scares her friends (an authorial voice obtrusively ends the narrative with "Sometimes it takes a little ferocity to set things right"). Outdoorsy watercolor illustrations set the scene." Horn Book

Follow up to:
Millie Fierce (2012)

Manning, Maurie J.

Kitchen dance; by Maurie J. Manning. Clarion Books 2008 un il $16

Grades: PreK K 1   **E**
1. Dance -- Fiction 2. Bedtime -- Fiction 3. Family life -- Fiction 4. Hispanic Americans -- Fiction
ISBN 978-0-618-99110-5; 0-618-99110-7

LC 2007036838

"Drawn from their beds by noises downstairs, the narrator and her little brother, Tito, peer into the kitchen to find that their parents have turned dinner cleanup into a rambunctious, Latin-flavored song and dance number. . . . As the rounded, sculptural bodies of the couple move about the kitchen with humor and grace, the illustrations take on a cinematic sense of motion and space." Publ Wkly

Laundry day; by Maurie J. Manning. Houghton Mifflin Harcourt 2012 40 p.

Grades: K 1 2 3 4   **E**
1. Scarves 2. Picture books for children 3. City and town life -- Fiction 4. Lost and found possessions -- Fiction 5. New York (N.Y.) -- History -- Fiction 6. Graphic novels 7. Neighborhoods -- Fiction 8. Tenement houses -- Fiction 9. New York (N.Y.) -- History -- 1898-1951 -- Fiction
ISBN 0547241968; 9780547241968

LC 2010043252

This picture book depicts the events of "one windy day [when] a young shoeshine boy makes a world of new friends. Unable to make a sale, he looks up to see a long, bright-red scarf drifting down to him as he sits dejectedly on the curb. The story of his search for the owner is told with dialogue balloons in comic-book style. Text and illustrations are mutually dependent as one panel follows another, moving the story along. . . . [Maurie J.] Manning's . . . detailed digital pencil, watercolor and pastel drawings depict an unnamed but unmistakable turn-of-the-20th-century New York City. Laundry whips in the wind, and busy people on every floor of the buildings are shown from multiple perspectives." (Kirkus)

Mannis, Celeste Davidson

One leaf rides the wind; counting in a Japanese garden. by Celeste Davidson Mannis, pictures by Susan Kathleen Hartung. Viking 2002 un il $15.99; pa $6.99

Grades: PreK K 1 2   **E**
1. Haiku 2. Counting 3. Gardens -- Poetry
ISBN 0-670-03525-4; 0-14-240195-1 pa

LC 2002-1024

In this collection of haiku poems, a young girl walks through a Japanese garden and discovers many delights, from one leaf to ten stone lanterns. Includes notes about Japanese religion and philosophy

"The book as a whole is elegantly and respectfully presented and the counting aspect is especially well crafted, capturing the meandering focus of a small child. Mannis's simple verses are complemented by Hartung's pleasing and evocative pen-and-ink and watercolor art." SLJ

Manushkin, Fran

The **belly** book; illustrated by Dan Yaccarino. Feiwel and Friends 2011 il $16.99

Grades: PreK K   **E**
1. Stories in rhyme 2. Abdomen
ISBN 978-0-312-64958-6; 0-312-64958-4

"A meditation on the middle for beginning readers and younger listeners supports some appealingly merry illustrations. Manushkin's rhyming text is an invitation to a general celebration of abdomens— readers' own or other peoples', and occasionally those of beasts and birds. . . . The art. . . is the real treat here, Yaccarino's clever, energetic, lighthearted illustration. . . . His playful full-page gouaches zip nimbly from thought to thought and invest the whole with a generous dollop of whimsy." Kirkus

Happy in our skin; Fran Manushkin; illustrated by Lauren Tobia. Candlewick Press 2015 32 p. illustrations (hardcover) $15.99

Grades: PreK   **E**
1. Infants -- Fiction 2. Pluralism (Social sciences)
ISBN 9780763670023

LC 2014951411

In this children's book, by Fran Manushkin and illustrated by Lauren Tobia, celebrates racial diversity and skin color in children. "Just savor these bouquets of babies—cocoa-brown, cinnamon, peaches and cream. As they grow, their clever skin does too, enjoying hugs and tickles, protecting them inside and out, and making them one of a kind." (Publisher's note)

"Happy in Our Skin paints a picture of an ideal world that recognizes the value of diversity and shuns color blindness—a positive message for ears of every age and color." Booklist

Manzano, Sonia

★ **Miracle** on 133rd Street; Sonia Manzano; illustrated by Marjorie Priceman. Atheneum Books for Young Readers 2015 48 p. color illustrations (hardcover : alk. paper) $17.99

Grades: PreK K 1 2 3   **E**
1. Christmas -- Fiction 2. Neighbors -- Fiction 3. Cooking -- Fiction 4. Contentment -- Fiction 5. Puerto Ricans -- United States -- Fiction
ISBN 9780689878879

LC 2014035882

In this children's story, by Sonia Manzano, illustrated by Marjorie Priceman, "it's Christmas Eve and Mami has bought a delicious roast for a Christmas feast. But . . . it's too big to fit in the oven. Jose and Papa need to find an oven big enough to cook Mami's roast. As they walk from door to door through their apartment building, no one seems to be in the Christmas spirit. So they head down the street to find someone willing to help, and . . . holiday cheer manifests in ways most unexpected." (Publisher's note)

"Families will enjoy curling up with this warm story about finding home in community." SLJ

Marceau, Fani

★ **Panorama**; a foldout book. [illustrated by] Joëlle Jolivet. Abrams Books for Young Readers 2009 un il $19.95

Grades: 1 2 3   **E**
1. Travel -- Fiction 2. Voyages around the world -- Fiction
ISBN 978-0-8109-8332-8; 0-8109-8332-X

LC 2008022166

Original French edition 2007

Illustrations and simple text invite the reader to visit different places around the world, then to view the same scenes at night on the reverse of the fanfolded page.

This is a "stunning travelogue.... Each oversize page is grounded by a poetic fragment evoking each locale.... A faint ecological bent further enriches the descriptions. But the main event is the alternately dizzying and mysterious black-and-white woodcut illustrations. They can be flipped through like an ordinary book, though the full impact is felt only through unfurling all 15 pages so that they lay flat in a seamless panorama." Booklist

Marcellino, Fred

I, crocodile. HarperCollins Pubs. 1999 un il hardcover o.p. pa $6.99
Grades: 1 2 3 4   E
1. Emperors 2. Crocodiles -- Fiction
ISBN 0-06-205168-7; 0-06-008859-1 pa

"The text is reportorial in tone, a perfect complement to the extravagant, expressive illustrations.... A sophisticated picture book, this is one publication with appeal to many different audiences." Horn Book

Marciano, John Bemelmans

Madeline at the White House; story and pictures by John Bemelmans Marciano. Viking Children's Books 2011 un il $17.99
Grades: PreK K 1   E
1. Stories in rhyme 2. Easter -- Fiction 3. Orphans -- Fiction 4. Presidents -- Fiction 5. Washington (D.C.) -- Fiction
ISBN 978-0-670-01228-2; 0-670-01228-9
LC 2010025110
Madeline and the other orphans of the vine-covered house in Paris spend Easter at the White House visiting with the President's daughter.

"Based on an idea Bemelmans was working on at the time of his 1962 death, grandson Marciano has done a credible job copying the rhythms and artistic style of the originals." Booklist

Marcus, Kimberly

Scritch-scratch a perfect match; illustrated by Mike Lester. G.P. Putnam's Sons 2011 un il $16.99
Grades: PreK K   E
1. Stories in rhyme 2. Dogs -- Fiction 3. Fleas -- Fiction
ISBN 978-0-399-25004-0; 0-399-25004-2
LC 2008-30482
When a flea lands on a stray dog, it starts a chain of events that ends with the dog happily adopted by a pet-loving man.

"Abundant motion lines, copious scrawled hatch and crosshatch details, and heaps of sly character humor .... all work together to support the playful text. Those who like their friendship tales with a touch of chaos will gladly take a bite out of this mischievous offering." Bull Cent Child Books

Mariconda, Barbara

Sort it out! illustrated by Sherry Rogers. Sylvan Dell 2008 un il $16.95; pa $8.95
Grades: PreK K 1 2   E
1. Rats -- Fiction 2. Collectors and collecting -- Fiction
ISBN 978-1-934359-11-2; 1-934359-11-4; 978-1-934359-32-7 pa; 1-934359-32-7 pa

"When Pack rat comes home with a cart full of stuff—a locket, a book, an umbrella, a pinecone, and many more random items—his mother admonishes him to sort it all out and put it away. Packy does just that, cleverly sorting things with like characteristics such as where they're found, their color, shape, etc. . . . The illustrations are brightly colored, large, and very clear. Careful readers will notice a subplot in the pictures and find satisfaction in seeing its resolution on the final page. In

addition, the rhyming text prompts them to guess the word that defines each collection. Back matter has activities to extend the experience." SLJ

Ten for me; illustrated by Sherry Rogers. Sylvan Dell 2011 il $16.95; pa $8.95
Grades: 2 3 4   E
1. Stories in rhyme 2. Butterflies -- Fiction 3. Mathematics -- Fiction
ISBN 978-1-60718-074-6; 1-60718-074-X; 978-1-60718-085-2 pa; 1-60718-085-5 pa

"Rose and Ed learn much more than expected on their butterfly hunt. . . . Each day is seen as a double-page spread of the duo hunting in field and garden. As Rose's totals grow, Ed's shrink. The totals in the text are mirrored in a tally of 'Butterflies Captured and Released' in the illustrations. . . . An excellent rhyming tale that doubles as math lesson and triples as a butterfly-biology primer." Kirkus

Marino, Gianna

Following Papa's song; by Gianna Marino. Viking, published by Penguin Group 2014 40 p. (hardback) $16.99
Grades: PreK K   E
1. Whales -- Fiction 2. Father-child relationship -- Fiction 3. Humpback whale -- Fiction 4. Father and child -- Fiction 5. Animals -- Migration -- Fiction
ISBN 0670013153; 9780670013159
LC 2013024213
"Two whales swim together through the big ocean," in this children's book by Gianna Marino. "Little Blue has many questions for Papa, especially ones about the long migration. How will they know the way? Will he be able to keep up? What will they see along the way? Papa has answers for all these questions, but Little Blue remains curious as they begin their journey." (Publisher's note)

"Little Blue, a young humpback whale, is worried about his first long migration up the coast, and he is scared he will be separated from Papa in the big ocean. As with human families on adventures, Little Blue has many questions that need to be answered and needs to be reassured that everything will be fine . . . This is a story for all ages to enjoy. What a wonderful way to use science in the lower grades. A top choice for any library." SLJ

Meet me at the moon; by Gianna Marino. Viking 2012 40p. illustrations (hardcover) $16.99
Grades: PreK K   E
1. Elephants -- Fiction 2. Picture books for children 3. Mother-child relationship -- Fiction 4. Africa -- Fiction 5. Drought -- Fiction 6. Separation (Psychology) -- Fiction
ISBN 9780670013135
LC 2011013210
A "mother elephant tells her Little One that she must leave and 'climb the highest mountain to ask the skies for rain.' 'What if I can't hear you, Mama?' Little One asks. 'Listen for my sound on the wind,' she answers. . . . When rain finally arrives but Mama doesn't return, Little One is bereft until he remembers to 'sing the calling song' that brings her back." (Publishers Weekly)

"Marino impresses with her lyrical language, conveying it in a perfect tone to allay young readers' feelings of separation anxiety. The textured mixed-media art paired with the flowing text elevates this title above most missing-mama fare." Kirkus

Night animals; by Gianna Marino. Viking, Published by Penguin Group 2015 40 p. (hardcover) $16.99
Grades: PreK K   E
1. Fear of the dark -- Fiction 2. Nocturnal animals -- Fiction 3.

Fear -- Fiction 4. Opossums -- Fiction
ISBN 9780451469540; 0451469542

LC 2014028636

In this children's story, written and illustrated by Gianna Marino, "Possum is hiding in the woods when a friendly skunk comes along. Possum spreads a fear of 'night animals' to the skunk, then a wolf, and a bear. It takes a calm bat to explain to them that they are night animals." (School Library Journal)

"As Possum frantically attempts to hide from "night animals," he is joined by Skunk, then anxious Gray Wolf, and finally terrified Grizzly Bear, resulting in a humorous nighttime romp about a group of animals who don't realize that they are night creatures themselves. . . . The large illustrations, abundant silliness, and forest noises will make this a fun storytime selection that can be easily paired with other nighttime-adventures tales, such as the wordless Flashlight, by Lizi Boyd (2014)." Booklist

Markes, Julie
Good thing you're not an octopus! story by Julie Markes; pictures by Maggie Smith. HarperCollins Pubs. 2001 un il $14.95; pa $6.99
Grades: PreK K   E
1. Animals -- Fiction
ISBN 0-06-028465-X; 0-06-443586-5 pa

LC 99-37139

"A boy who complains about getting dressed, riding in his car seat, and more is answered with funny worst-case scenarios: 'You don't like to take a nap? It's a good thing you're not a bear. If you were a bear, you would have to nap all winter long!' The tone is silly, and the cheerful illustrations convey the absurdity in the text." Horn Book Guide

Shhhhh! Everybody's sleeping; illustrated by David Parkins. HarperCollins 2005 un il $14.99; lib bdg $15.89
Grades: PreK K 1   E
1. Stories in rhyme 2. Sleep -- Fiction 3. Bedtime -- Fiction
ISBN 0-06-053790-6; 0-06-053791-4 lib bdg

LC 2003-27854

A young child is encouraged to go to sleep by the thought of everyone else sleeping, from teacher to baker to postman

"The text satisfyingly moves along while the artwork soars. . . . Glowing with warm colors in subdued hues, the sturdy pictures stretch wide across double-page spreads, offering surprisingly energetic, varied compositions." Booklist

Markle, Sandra, 1946-
Butterfly tree; written by Sandra Markle; illustrated by Leslie Wu. Peachtree 2010 32 p. ill.
Grades: K 1 2   E
1. Clouds -- Fiction 2. Monarch butterflies 3. Lake Erie -- Fiction 4. Butterflies -- Fiction 5. Picture books for children 6. Erie, Lake -- Fiction
ISBN 1561455393; 9781561455393

LC 2009040526

In this picture book, "[a] black rain that becomes a mysterious orange cloud over Lake Erie is the beginning for of a magical encounter with monarch butterflies for Jilly, her dog, Fudge, and her mother. Veteran nature-writer [Sandra] Markle . . . offers a gentle free-verse narrative based on a never-to-be-forgotten experience from her own Ohio childhood. . . . At first, Jilly is worried, hesitant about following the cloud into the woods with her mother, wanting to turn back. [In illustrator Leslie] Wu's hazy pastel paintings . . . the monarchs explode from the tree where they were resting and Jilly realizes what they are. . . . Author's notes, a map showing monarch migration and a list of books and websites for further exploration add . . . information." (Kirkus)

"What looks dark and indistinct closeup shows surprisingly well at a distance; the text reads aloud smoothly, suiting this especially well for use with a group. Author's notes, a map showing monarch migration and a list of books and websites for further exploration add helpful information. Even collections with many monarch titles will want to add this one for its masterful evocation of a child's sense of wonder at the natural world." Kirkus
Includes bibliographical references

★ **Family** pack; illustrated by Alan Marks. Charlesbridge 2011 un il lib bdg $15.95
Grades: K 1 2 3   E
1. Wolves -- Fiction 2. Yellowstone National Park -- Fiction
ISBN 978-1-58089-217-9 lib bdg; 1-58089-217-5 lib bdg

LC 2010-07548

A young wolf, taken from her pack in Canada to Yellowstone National Park, struggles alone to master the skills of hunting and survival until she finds a lone male and begins a new pack with him.

"Without a hint of anthropomorphism but with vivid, poetic language, [Markle] shows readers the wolves bound only by nature. . . . The illustrator's watercolors add drama and energy. . . . An excellent story for wolf-lovers and a welcome addition to elementary-school science shelves." Kirkus

Race the wild wind; a story of the Sable Island horses. Sandra Markle; paintings by by Layne Johnson. Walker 2011 1 v. (unpaged) $17.99
Grades: K 1 2 3   E
1. Horses -- Fiction 2. Nova Scotia -- Fiction 3. Wild horses -- Fiction 4. Sable Island (N.S.) -- Fiction
ISBN 978-0-8027-9766-7; 0-8027-9766-0; 9780802797667; 9780802797674

LC 2010036013

"After being lowered into the frigid Atlantic by a schooner, a young stallion and his equine companions swim to Sable Island in this poetic tale that imagines how wild horses first came to live on this isolated island off of Nova Scotia. . . . Dramatic oil spreads depict his survival and transformation from domestic to wild horse amid this beautiful yet harsh environment." Booklist
Includes bibliographical references

Snow school; Sandra Markle; illustrated by Alan Marks. Charlesbridge 2013 32 p. (reinforced) $16.95
Grades: PreK K 1 2   E
1. Snow leopard 2. Animal behavior 3. Learning in animals 4. Snow leopard -- Infancy
ISBN 1580894100; 9781580894104

LC 2012000790

In this children's book, by Sandra Markle, illustrated by Alan Marks, "readers are introduced to twin snow leopard cubs and their mother from the Hindu Kush mountains of Pakistan. . . . Text and . . . watercolor illustrations lead readers through the struggles these snow leopards face from finding food to bearing harsh weather conditions and the lessons the young cubs learn as they prepare for a life on their own, out from underneath the watchful, caring eye of their mother." (Publisher's note)

"Here the title reflects the plot line: a snow leopard in Pakistan's Hindu Kush Mountains teaches her two cubs what they'll need to survive, such as how to hunt, take shelter, and 'No matter what, stay clear of humans.' Marks's illustrations effectively use watercolor for the snowy backgrounds and soft textured fur, with dark pencil for the animals' sharp features." Horn Book
Includes bibliographical references

What If You Had Animal Teeth? by Sandra Markle; illustrated by Howard McWilliam. Scholastic 2013 32 p. ill. (paperback) $3.99
Grades: K 1 2   E
  1. Teeth 2. Comparative anatomy
  ISBN 0545484383; 9780545484381
  In this book by Sandra Markle, readers "explore what it would be like if their own front teeth were replaced by those of a different animal. Featuring a dozen animals (beaver, great white shark, narwhal, elephant, rattlesnake, naked mole rat, hippopotamus, crocodile, and more), this book explores how different teeth are especially adapted for an animal's survival. At the end of the book, children will discover why their own teeth are just right for them." (Publisher's note)
  Other titles in this series are:
  What If You Had Animal Hair? (2014)
  What If You Had Animal Feet? (2015)
  What if You Had Animal Ears (2016)
  What if You Had Animal Noses? (2015)

Marko, Cyndi
Let's get cracking! by Cyndi Marko. Branches Scholastic Inc. 2014 80 p. (Kung Pow Chicken) (hardcover) $15.99
Grades: 1 2 3   E
  1. Chickens -- Fiction 2. Superheroes -- Fiction 3. Humorous stories 4. Cookies -- Fiction
  ISBN 0545610621; 9780545610612; 9780545610629
                                                            LC 2013018130
  In this book, by Cyndi Marko, "Gordon Blue transforms into Kung Pow Chicken, an avian superhero who fights crime in the city of Fowladelphia. The first book in the series kicks off when Gordon's birdy senses lead him to a festival. Suddenly, POOF! Feathers fill the air and shivering naked chickens are everywhere. Why have all these chickens lost their feathers? Forced to wear wooly sweaters, the city itches for a hero. Kung Pow Chicken hops into his Beakmobile to save the day!" (Publisher's note)

Marlow, Layn
★ **Hurry** up and slow down; [by] Layn Marlow. Holiday House 2009 un il $16.95
Grades: PreK K 1   E
  1. Bedtime -- Fiction 2. Rabbits -- Fiction 3. Turtles -- Fiction 4. Books and reading -- Fiction
  ISBN 978-0-8234-2178-7; 0-8234-2178-3
                                                            LC 2008010796
  First published 2008 in the United Kingdom
  Hare likes to hurry through the day, unlike Tortoise, but manages to slow down for his favorite bedtime story
  "This delightful spinoff of 'The Tortoise and the Hare' follows a typical day in the lives of these two friends. . . . The illustrations of Hare, Tortoise, their animal companions, and their environment are rounded and softly colored, creating a comforting world for young children. An endearing story that will no doubt become a bedtime favorite." SLJ

Marsalis, Wynton, 1961-
Squeak! rumble! whomp! whomp! whomp! a sonic adventure. Wynton Marsalis; illustrated by Paul Rogers. Candlewick 2012 40 p. (hardback) $15.99
Grades: PreK K 1   E
  1. Music -- Fiction 2. Sound -- Fiction 3. Neighborhood -- Fiction
  ISBN 9780763639914; 0763639915
                                                            LC 2011048367
  This children's book, by Wynton Marsalis, illustrated by Paul Rogers, explores various sounds in everyday life in a neighborhood. "What's that sound? The back door squeeeaks open, sounding like a noisy mouse

nearby--eeek, eeeek, eeeek! Big trucks on the highway rrrrrrrumble, just as hunger makes a tummy grrrrrumble." (Publisher's note)

Marshall, Edward
★ **Fox** and his friends; pictures by James Marshall. Dial Bks. for Young Readers 1982 56p il (Dial easy-to-read) hardcover o.p. pa $3.99
Grades: K 1 2   E
  1. Foxes -- Fiction
  ISBN 0-14-037007-2 pa
                                                            LC 81-68769
  "The sibling exchanges and situations are comically true to life. . . . The red, green and black illustrations . . . pick the story up and add character embellishment and humor." SLJ
  Other titles about Fox are:
  Fox in love (1982)
  Fox on wheels (1983)
  Fox at school (1983)
  Fox all week (1984)
  Fox on the job (1988)
  Fox be nimble (1990)
  Fox outfoxed (1992)
  Fox on stage (1993)

★ **Space** case; pictures by James Marshall. Dial Bks. for Young Readers 1980 un il hardcover o.p. pa $6.99
Grades: PreK K 1 2   E
  1. Science fiction 2. Halloween -- Fiction
  ISBN 0-8037-8005-2; 0-14-054704-5 pa
                                                            LC 80-13369
  "The open ending of the brief story is as satisfying as it is original, for the small space traveler is thoroughly childlike in its insouciance, curiosity, and concern for self-gratification. The text is an economical, tongue-in-cheek accompaniment to the various levels of humor depicted in the illustrations." Horn Book

Three by the sea; pictures by James Marshall. Dial Bks. for Young Readers 1981 48p il (Dial easy-to-read) hardcover o.p. pa $3.99
Grades: K 1 2   E
  1. Storytelling -- Fiction
  ISBN 0-14-037004-8 pa
  "The mild lunacy of the illustrations (an almost vertical hill, a neatly striped cat) with their ungainly, comical figures is nicely matched with the bland directness of the writing. This is good-humored and amusing." Bull Cent Child Books
  Other titles about Spider, Sam, and Lolly are:
  Four on the shore (1985)
  Three up a tree (1986)

Marshall, James
★ **George** and Martha; written and illustrated by James Marshall. Houghton Mifflin 1972 46p il lib bdg $16; pa $6.95
Grades: PreK K 1 2   E
  1. Friendship -- Fiction 2. Hippopotamus -- Fiction
  ISBN 0-395-16619-5 lib bdg; 0-395-19972-7 pa
  In these five short episodes which include a misunderstanding about split pea soup, invasion of privacy and a crisis over a missing tooth, two not very delicate hippopotamuses reveal various aspects of friendship
  "The pale pictures of these creatures and their adventures—in yellows, pinks, greens, and grays—capture the directness and humor of the stories." Horn Book
  Other titles about George and Martha are:
  George and Martha back in town (1984)
  George and Martha encore (1973)

George and Martha, one fine day (1978)

George and Martha rise and shine (1976)

George and Martha round and round (1988)

George and Martha, tons of fun (1980)

★ **Swine** Lake; [pictures by] Maurice Sendak. HarperCollins
Pubs. 1999 un il $16.95

Grades: PreK K 1 2   E

    1. Pigs -- Fiction 2. Ballet -- Fiction 3. Wolves -- Fiction

    ISBN 0-06-205171-7

                     LC 98-73253

A hungry wolf attends a performance of Swine Lake, performed by
the Boarshoi Ballet, intending to eat the performers, but he is so entranced by the story unfolding that he forgets about his meal

    "Both Marshall and Sendak are cleverly comic here . . . the text
shines. Sendak's art captures the nuance as well as all the humor of the
story." Booklist

Marshall, Linda Elovitz

    Talia and the rude vegetables; illustrated by Francesca Assirelli.
Kar-Ben 2011 un il lib bdg $16.95

Grades: PreK K 1 2   E

    1. Jews -- Fiction 2. Gardening -- Fiction 3. Vegetables -- Fiction
4. Rosh ha-Shanah -- Fiction

    ISBN 978-0-7613-5217-4; 0-7613-5217-1

                 LC 2010020301

City-girl Talia misunderstands her grandmother's request that she go
to the garden for "root vegetables" for a Rosh Hashanah stew but manages to find some she thinks are rude, as well as a good use for the rest
she harvests. Includes a recipe for Rude Vegetable Stew.

    "This laugh-out-loud title keeps the little jokes coming. . . . Quirky,
cool-palette color illustrations by Italian artist Assirelli perfectly convey
the whimsical narrative." Publ Wkly

    Another book about Talia is:

    Talia and the Very Yum Kippur (2015)

Marshall, Natalie

    Colors; Natalie Marshall. Little Brown & Co 2013 12 p. color
illustrations (My turn to learn) $6.99

Grades: PreK   E

    1. Color 2. Picture books for children

    ISBN 0316251631; 9780316251631

                 LC 2012953594

Written by Natalie Marshall and part of the My Turn to Learn series,
in this book "The tabbed edges and thick, strong pages make it easy for
young readers to flip through the book by themselves, revealing fun,
colorful answers on every spread." It offers "an interactive reading and
learning experience that can withstand even the most 'hands-on' readers." (Publisher's note)

    "Marshall's illustrations are a friendly jumble of clean lines and
mixed textures, and the tabs are tailor-made for little fingers to help turn
pages." Pub Wkly

    My turn to learn opposites; Natalie Marshall. Little, Brown and Co.
2013 12 p. color illustrations (My turn to learn) $6.99

Grades: PreK   E

    1. Opposites 2. Toy and movable books

    ISBN 0316251658; 9780316251655

                 LC 2012953392

In this book, part of the My Turn To Learn series, by Natalie Marshall, children can "explore the exciting world of numbers, brought to
life through this . . . tabbed board book." The book aims to "teach early

counting concepts." It is an "interactive reading and learning experience." (Publisher's note)

    My turn to learn shapes; Natalie Marshall. Little, Brown and Co.
2013 12 p. col. ill. (My turn to learn) $6.99

Grades: PreK   E

    1. Shape

    ISBN 0316251666; 9780316251662

                 LC 2012953593

In this book, part of the My Turn To Learn series, by Natalie Marshall, children can "explore the exciting world of numbers, brought to
life through this . . . tabbed board book." The book aims to "teach early
counting concepts." It is an "interactive reading and learning experience." (Publisher's note)

    Numbers; Natalie Marshall. Little Brown & Co 2013 12 p. $6.99

Grades: PreK   E

    1. Numbers 2. Counting 3. Children's literature

    ISBN 031625164X; 9780316251648

                 LC 2012953545

Written by Natalie Marshall and part of the My Turn to Learn series,
this book "uses simple, colorful images and bold, lively scenes to teach
early counting concepts. The tabbed edges and thick, strong pages make
it easy for young readers to flip through the book by themselves, revealing fun, colorful answers on every spread." (Publisher's note)

Martin, Amy

    Symphony city; written and illustrated by Amy Martin. McSwee-
ney's 2011 un il $17.95

Grades: 2 3 4 5   F

    1. Music -- Fiction 2. Sounds -- Fiction 3. City and town life
-- Fiction

    ISBN 978-1-936365-39-5; 1-936365-39-1

A young girl, lost in a big city, makes her way home by following the
rich and vibrant music of the streets.

    "The story is told visually through the gradual outpouring of color,
the division of space in surprising vertical and horizontal lines, with
cityscape backgrounds like blueprints; and colors layered as if silk
screened. . . . The economical text is a paean to music. . . . Craftsmanship
reigns in this title. A flock of birds embossed in gold flies from the back
to the front of the textured orange binding, and the jacket folds out into
two-sided poster. A perfect book for music lovers and bibliophiles." SL

Martin, Bill, 1916-2004

    Baby Bear, Baby Bear, what do you see? by Bill Martin, Jr.; pic-
tures by Eric Carle. Henry Holt & Co. 2007 un il $16.95; My first
reader ed. $8.99

Grades: PreK K   F

    1. Stories in rhyme 2. Bears -- Fiction 3. Animals -- Fiction

    ISBN 978-0-8050-8336-1; 0-8050-8336-7; 978-0-8050-9291-2

    My first reader ed.

                 LC 2006037767

Written by Bill Martin and illustrated by Eric Carle, part of the
Brown Bear and Friends series, "'Baby Bear, Baby Bear, What Do You
See?' is the final collaboration from this bestselling author-illustrator
team. Young readers will enjoy Baby Bear's quest to find Mama, and
they'll revel in identifying each of the native North American animals
that appear along the way. The central focus on the special bond between mama and baby makes a fitting finale to a beloved series." (Publisher's note)

    "Creative action words and renderings of the various creatures in
motion give the book a pleasing energy, while Mama Bear's obvious

delight at finding her cub provides an endearing poignancy. [An] elegant balance of art, text, emotion and exposition." Publ Wkly

Barn dance! by Bill Martin, Jr. and John Archambault; illustrated by Ted Rand. Holt & Co. 1986 un il $16.95; pa $6.95
Grades: PreK K 1 2   E
  1. Stories in rhyme 2. Dance -- Fiction 3. Country life -- Fiction
  ISBN 0-8050-0089-5; 0-8050-0799-7 pa
LC 86-14225
Unable to sleep on the night of a full moon, a young boy follows the sound of music across the fields and finds an unusual barn dance in progress
"The bouncy rhyme will be a pleasure for listeners and tellers as they pick up the twang and the barn-dance beat. Rand's raucous two-page watercolor spreads are as spirited as the story poem." Booklist

★ A **beasty** story; [written by] Bill Martin, Jr. & [illustrated by] Steven Kellogg. Harcourt Brace & Co. 1999 un il $16; pa $7
Grades: PreK K 1 2   E
  1. Stories in rhyme 2. Mice -- Fiction 3. Color -- Fiction
  ISBN 0-15-201683-X; 0-15-216560-6 pa
LC 97-49519
A group of mice venture into a dark, dark woods where they find a dark brown house with a dark red stair leading past other dark colors to a spooky surprise
"A rhymed narrative tells the story along the top of the pages, with the mice commenting in rhymed conversation as they move through the adventure. The silly resolution will appeal to young children. . . . Kellogg's lively ink-and-watercolor art strikes just the right note for the gently suspenseful story." Booklist

★ **Brown** bear, brown bear what do you see? pictures by Eric Carle. Holt & Co. 1992 un il $16.99; bd bk $7.95; $8.99
Grades: PreK K   E
  1. Stories in rhyme 2. Color -- Fiction 3. Animals -- Fiction
  ISBN 0-8050-1744-5; 0-8050-4790-5 bd bk; 978-0-8050-9244-8 My first reader ed.; 0-8050-9244-7 My first reader ed.
LC 91-29115
A newly illustrated edition of the title first published 1967 by Holt, Rinehart & Winston
A chant in which a variety of animals, each one a different color, answers the question, "What do you see?"
"Carle's large, brilliantly colored animals set against a white background make the book perfect for sharing with a group of preschoolers, while Martin's repetitive text is eminently chantable—a boon for beginning readers." Horn Book

★ **Chicka** chicka 1, 2, 3; [by] Bill Martin, Jr. & Michael Sampson; illustrated by Lois Ehlert. Simon & Schuster Books for Young Readers 2004 un il $15.95
Grades: PreK K 1   E
  1. Counting 2. Stories in rhyme
  ISBN 0-689-85881-7
LC 2003-19106
Numbers from one to one hundred climb to the top of an apple tree in this rhyming chant.
"The chanting rhyme and eye-popping images have a contagious energy youngsters will find irresistible." Booklist

★ **Chicka** chicka boom boom; [by] Bill Martin, Jr. and John Archambault; illustrated by Lois Ehlert. anniversary edition; Beach Lane Books 2009 un il $17.99 E
  1. Alphabet 2. Stories in rhyme
  ISBN 978-1-4169-9091-8; 1-4169-9091-7
LC 2009-626
A reissue of the title first published 1989
An alphabet rhyme/chant that relates what happens when the whole alphabet tries to climb a coconut tree.
"Ehlert's illustrations-bold, colorful shapes-are contained by broad polka-dotted borders, like a proscenium arch through which the action explodes. Tongue-tingling, visually stimulating, with an insistent repetitive chorus of 'chicka chicka boom boom,' the book demands to be read again and again and again." Horn Book

★ The **ghost**-eye tree; by Bill Martin, Jr. and John Archambault; illustrated by Ted Rand. Holt & Co. 1985 un il $16.95; pa $6.95
Grades: K 1 2 3   E
  1. Ghost stories 2. Fear -- Fiction
  ISBN 0-8050-0208-1; 0-8050-0947-7 pa
LC 85-8422
"On a dark and ghostly night a brother and sister are sent to fetch a pail of milk from the other end of town. They must pass the fearful ghost-eye tree, old and horribly twisted, looking like a monster, with a gap in the branches where the moon shines through like an eye. . . . The story is rhythmically told, sometimes rhyming, always moving ahead, sharp with the affectionate teasing of the brother and sister. The realistic watercolor illustrations are superb—strong, striking, very dark, with highlights of moonlight and lantern light that cast a spooky, scary spell. A splendidly theatrical book for storytelling and reading aloud." Horn Book

Kitty cat, kitty cat, are you going to sleep? by Bill Martin Jr. and Michael Sampson; illustrated by Laura J. Bryant. Marshall Cavendish Children's 2011 un il $15.99
Grades: PreK K   E
  1. Stories in rhyme 2. Cats -- Fiction 3. Bedtime -- Fiction
  ISBN 978-0-7614-5946-0; 0-7614-5946-4
LC 2010025274
A young cat is distracted by many things while getting ready for bed at night.
"A simple rhyming exchange alternates between parent and child as it playfully follows the usual bedtime routine and stall tactics. . . . Adorable colored pencil and watercolor illustrations support the conversation and take Kitty from wide awake to sleeping sooo tight. The soft palette and simple details have the perfect calming effect." SLJ

Kitty Cat, Kitty Cat, are you waking up? by Bill Martin Jr. & Michael Sampson; illustrated by Laura J. Bryant. Marshall Cavendish 2008 un il $14.99
Grades: PreK K 1   E
  1. Stories in rhyme 2. Cats -- Fiction
  ISBN 978-0-7614-5438-0; 0-7614-5438-1
LC 2007041987
Kitty Cat is distracted by many things as she gets ready for school in the morning
This is a "delightfully comic rhyming book. . . . A tiny mouse serves as an interested observer in each watercolor, until he becomes prey, and then a very relieved escapee, as the kitten is finally swept off to school." Booklist

★ **Knots** on a counting rope; by Bill Martin, Jr. and John Archambault; illustrated by Ted Rand. Holt & Co. 1987 un il $16.95; pa $6.95

Grades: K 1 2 3   E
1. Blind -- Fiction 2. Grandfathers -- Fiction 3. Native Americans -- Fiction
ISBN 0-8050-0571-4; 0-8050-5479-0 pa

LC 87-14858

A different version of the title illustrated by Joe Smith was published in 1966

"The powerful spare poetic text is done full justice by Rand's fine full-color illustrations, which capture both the drama and brilliance of vast southwestern space and the intimacy of starlit camp-fire scenes." Booklist

Panda bear, panda bear, what do you see? by Bill Martin Jr.; pictures by Eric Carle. Henry Holt & Co. 2003 un il $15.95; bd bk $7.95; My first reader ed. $8.99
Grades: PreK K   E
1. Stories in rhyme 2. Animals -- Fiction 3. Endangered species -- Fiction
ISBN 0-8050-1758-5; 0-8050-8078-3 bd bk; 978-0-8050-9292-9 My first reader ed.

LC 2002-10855

In this board book in the Bear series, "A Bald Eagle soars, a Spider Monkey swings, a Macaroni Penguin struts, and a Red Wolf sneaks through [author] Bill Martin Jr's rhythmic text and [illustrator] Eric Carle's vibrant images, and all are watched over by our best hope for the future--a dreaming child." (Publisher's note)

"The pictures, featuring animals strolling, splashing, and soaring, are brilliant lessons in the application of color, shape, form, and texture. . . . A fine read-aloud with a subtle, yet clear, message." Booklist

Polar bear, polar bear, what do you hear? by Bill Martin, Jr.; pictures by Eric Carle. Holt & Co. 1991 un il $16.95; bd bk $7.95
Grades: PreK K   E
1. Stories in rhyme 2. Animals -- Fiction
ISBN 0-8050-1759-3; 0-8050-5388-3 bd bk

LC 91-13322

Zoo animals from polar bear to walrus make their distinctive sounds for each other, while children imitate the sounds for the zookeeper

"Carle's characteristically inventive, jewel-toned artwork forms a seamless succession of images that fairly leap off the pages." Publ Wkly

Ten little caterpillars; [by] Bill Martin Jr.; illustrated by Lois Ehlert. Beach Lane Books 2011 40p il
Grades: PreK K   E
1. Stories in rhyme 2. Caterpillars -- Fiction
ISBN 1-4424-3385-X; 978-1-4424-3385-4

LC 2011002156

A newly illustrated edition of the title first published 1967

Illustrations and rhyming text follow ten caterpillars as one wriggles up a flower stem, another sails across a garden pool, and one reaches an apple leaf, where something amazing happens.

"Martin's caterpillar counting rhyme has been given new life with gorgeous and bold watercolor collages from . . . Ehlert. . . . This is a graphically sumptuously book, but the lesson is clear: nature is one tough town." Publ Wkly

★ **Trick** or treat? [by] Bill Martin, Jr. and Michael Sampson; illustrated by Paul Meisel. Simon & Schuster Bks. for Young Readers 2002 un il hardcover o.p. pa $6.99
Grades: PreK K 1 2   E
1. Magic -- Fiction 2. Halloween -- Fiction
ISBN 0-689-84968-0; 1-4169-0262-7 pa

LC 2002-70646

A child has a wonderful time collecting treats from the wacky neighbors until Magic Merlin decides that a trick would be more fun

"Meisel's cartoon illustrations take full advantage of the topsy-turvy story, adding lots of comic holiday detail to keep little ones alert. The fun is in the pictures, and the challenge is in figuring out the visual joke and the backward names." Booklist

Martin, David
Christmas tree; illustrated by Melissa Sweet. Candlewick Press 2009 un il bd bk $5.99
Grades: PreK   E
1. Board books for children 2. Trees -- Fiction 3. Christmas -- Fiction
ISBN 978-0-7636-3030-0 bd bk; 0-7636-3030-6 bd bk

At Christmastime, a tree from the outside comes inside, just waiting to be decorated

This "attractive board [book features] simple, [a] clear [concept] and delightful pencil-and-watercolor illustrations enhanced with patterned fabric swatches." SLJ

Hanukkah lights; illustrated by Melissa Sweet. Candlewick Press 2009 un il bd bk $5.99
Grades: PreK   E
1. Board books for children 2. Hanukkah -- Fiction
ISBN 978-0-7636-3029-4 bd bk; 0-7636-3029-2 bd bk

Children celebrate Hanukkah by lighting candles, eating latkes, spinning a dreidel, and giving presents

This "attractive board [book features] simple, clear concepts and delightful pencil-and-watercolor illustrations enhanced with patterned fabric swatches." SLJ

Peep and Ducky; David Martin, illustrated by David Walker. Candlewick Press 2013 32 p. (reinforced) $14.99
Grades: PreK K   E
1. Stories in rhyme 2. Play -- Fiction 3. Friendship -- Fiction
ISBN 0763650390; 9780763650391

LC 2012942391

In this children's book, by David Martin, illustrated by David Walker, "when Peep goes to the playground with his mommy and runs into Ducky and his daddy, the result is definitely lucky. In . . . rhyming verse the two encounter the usual highs and lows of playground adventures. . . After a long bout of play, it's time to go home, but the two don't whine, promising instead to play together another time." (Kirkus)

Piggy and Dad go fishing; illustrated by Frank Remkiewicz. Candlewick Press 2005 un il $14.99
Grades: PreK K 1 2   E
1. Pigs -- Fiction 2. Fishing -- Fiction 3. Father-son relationship -- Fiction
ISBN 0-7636-2506-X

LC 2004-5194

When his dad takes Piggy fishing for the first time and Piggy ends up feeling sorry for the worms and the fish, they decide to make some changes.

"The summery watercolor-and-pencil cartoon illustrations clue listeners into Piggy's emotions and create a bit of tension in the nicely paced story." Horn Book Guide
Other titles about Piggy and Dad are:
Piggy and Dad (2001)
Piggy and Dad play (2002)

Martin, Emily Winfield
Dream animals; by Emily Winfield Martin. Random House Inc 2013 32 p. (hc) $17.99

Grades: PreK K   E
1. Stories in rhyme 2. Dreams -- Fiction 3. Animals -- Fiction 4. Bedtime -- Fiction
ISBN 0449810801; 9780375971495; 9780375981371; 9780449810804

LC 2012029945

Author and illustrator Emily Winfield Martin "convinces children to close their eyes and discover who their dream animal might be--and what dream it might take them to." This rhyming picture book story for children also includes illustrations of multiple animals and acts as a bedtime story for children, parents, and readers of all ages. (Publisher's note)

Martin, Jacqueline Briggs
Grandmother Bryant's pocket; pictures by Petra Mathers. Houghton Mifflin 1996 48p il hardcover o.p. pa $5.95
Grades: K 1 2 3   E
1. Fear -- Fiction 2. Maine -- Fiction 3. Grandmothers -- Fiction
ISBN 0-395-68984-8; 0-618-03309-2 pa

LC 94-31309

"Appealingly structured in one-and two-page chapters, the book is illustrated with watercolor paintings. Executed in naive style, the artwork has an unassuming sweetness." Booklist

On Sand Island; illustrated by David Johnson. Houghton Mifflin 2003 un il $16
Grades: 1 2 3   E
1. Islands -- Fiction
ISBN 0-618-23151-X

LC 2002-5090

In 1916 on an island in Lake Superior, Carl builds himself a boat by bartering with the other islanders for parts and labor

"Martin's simple, poetic text deftly balances small, revealing details about the island's characters and Carl's life with the particulars of boat building. . . . The illustrations . . . capture the lake's translucent light and the story's nostalgic mood in expert, geometric line drawings washed with watery blue-green and sunset-orange colors." Booklist

Martin, Rafe
Will's mammoth; illustrated by Stephen Gammell. Putnam 1989 un il $16.99
Grades: K 1 2 3   E
1. Mammoths -- Fiction
ISBN 0-399-21627-8

LC 88-11651

Though his parents explain there have been no mammoths for over 10,000 years, Will goes out in the snow one day, certain he will meet some. "Preschool to grade two." (SLJ)

"Gammell's depiction of a child's rich imagination is illustrated in vivid colors. The fantasy spreads use winter whites and blues as background for subtly individualized animals who move energetically across the pages." Booklist

Martin, Ruth
Moon dreams; illustrated by Olivier Latyk. Templar Books 2010 un il $15.99
Grades: PreK K 1   E
1. Day -- Fiction 2. Moon -- Fiction 3. Night -- Fiction 4. Dreams -- Fiction
ISBN 978-0-7636-5012-4; 0-7636-5012-9

LC 2010003808

Published in the United Kingdom with title: Where on earth is the moon?

Luna, who loves to look at the moon, wonders where it goes during the day.

"Latyk's lush artwork, well-executed and incredibly tasteful, is a visual treat. Composed of graphic shapes in a retro-cool style, the digital illustrations flow with Martin's words as the story progresses. . . . A lovely, slumberous story." Kirkus

Martin, Steve
The **alphabet** from A to Y with bonus letter, Z! by Steve Martin & [illustrated by] Roz Chast. Doubleday/Flying Dolphin Press 2007 un il $17.95; lib bdg $17.95
Grades: K 1 2 3   E
1. Alphabet 2. Stories in rhyme
ISBN 978-0-385-51662-4; 978-0-385-52377-6 lib bdg

LC 2006102543

Presents a rhyming couplet featuring each letter of the alphabet, with such characters as David the dog-faced boy, who dons a derby despite being dirty, and Victor, whose frequent victories have made him vainglorious

"Martin and Chast show their mettle as each other's wacky sidekicks. . . . [A] peculiar and funny book." Publ Wkly

Martins, Isabel Minhós
My neighbor is a dog; Isabel Minhos Martins. Owlkids Books 2013 32 p. $16.95
Grades: K 1 2   E
1. Dogs -- Fiction 2. Picture books for children
ISBN 1926973682; 9781926973685

LC 2012943001

In this children's picture book, apartment building residents "are shocked when a blue dog moves into a vacant apartment. 'My parents thought it was very strange to have a dog as a neighbor,' says the young narrator. 'They said he would leave his hair all over the place . . . .' (Meanwhile, the dog's habits actually involve reading the newspaper and playing saxophone.) Additional animals move in, but while the girl befriends them, her parents are having none of it." (Publishers Weekly)

"Stylish and understated, this argument for tolerance is a welcome one." Kirkus

★ **Where** do we go when we disappear? Isabel Minhos Martins, Madalena Matoso. Abrams 2013 44 p. $14.95
Grades: K 1 2 3   E
1. Picture books for children 2. Change
ISBN 1849761604; 9781849761604

LC 2013933771

This children's picture book offers a "rumination on the idea that disappearance is really only change. For someone to disappear, [Isabel Minhós] Martins begins, someone else has to be left behind with questions: '"Where has she gone?" "Will we ever see each other again?"' But from leaves and rain puddles to the sand on beaches and the noise of children at play, everything in this world disappears, going somewhere else or taking some new form." (Kirkus Reviews)

The **World** in a Second; Isabel Minhos Martins, Bernardo P. Carvalho; translated from the Portuguese by Lyn Miller-Lachmann. Enchanted Lion Books 2015 56 p. color illustrations (alk. paper) $18.95
Grades: 2 3 4 5   E
1. Time -- Fiction
ISBN 9781592701575; 1592701574

LC 2015006960

This book, by Isabel Minhós Martins, illustrated by Bernardo Carvalho, and translated by Lyn Miller-Lachmann, "focuses on natural and human events happening all over the world in the same second. Talking about the world and how it's so different in places but also so similar and shared, . . . the books takes us to New York, Chicago, Mexico, Portugal, Angola, Turkey, Greece, Italy, Hungry, Brazil, and South Africa, among others." (Publisher's note)

"The flat, posterlike art features bright, matte colors and shapes defined by sure, black lines. In sequencing, the book resist s easy, time-zone chronology, taking readers from Papua New Guinea to Portugal to Angola to Turkey with successive turns of the page, creating an experience that is at once disorienting and immersive." Kirkus

Marzollo, Jean

Help me learn numbers 0-20; photographs by Chad Phillips. Holiday House 2011 un il $15.95

Grades: PreK K   E

1. Numbers 2. Counting

ISBN 978-0-8234-2334-7; 0-8234-2334-4

LC 2010029892

"Marzollo and Phillips team up for an idiosyncratic and eye-catching counting book featuring photographic compositions of miscellaneous objects including vintage toy cars, Dalmatian figurines, and rubber finger-puppet monsters. In one spread, 10 glass animals are clustered atop white steps, while the verse hints at the answer. . . . The playful displays suggest that number sense isn't just a classroom tool, but a way in which to explore and engage with one's environment." Publ Wkly

Mason, Margaret H.

These hands. Houghton Mifflin Harcourt 2011 un il $16.99

Grades: PreK K 1 2 3   E

1. Hand -- Fiction 2. Grandfathers -- Fiction 3. African Americans -- Fiction 4. African Americans -- Civil rights -- Fiction

ISBN 978-0-547-21566-2; 0-547-21566-5

LC 2010006782

"Cooper's signature style of softly blurred illustrations in sepia shades shows the bonds in a loving family. . . . The story's roots in rarely told history will widen the audience of this moving title to older readers, too." Booklist

Mathers, Petra

Lottie's new beach towel. Atheneum Bks. for Young Readers 1998 un il hardcover o.p. pa $6.99

Grades: PreK K 1 2   E

1. Beaches -- Fiction 2. Chickens -- Fiction

ISBN 0-689-81606-5; 0-689-84441-7 pa

LC 97-6689

Lottie the chicken has a number of adventures at the beach, during which her new towel, a gift from her friend Herbie the duck, comes in handy.

"Pure fun, with a resourceful, big-hearted main character; humor in both text and pictures; and a good story, elegantly shaped." Horn Book

Other titles about Lottie and Herbie are:

A cake for Herbie (2000)

Herbie's secret Santa (2002)

Lottie's new friend (1999)

When Aunt Mattie got her wings; by Petra Mathers. Beach Lane Books 2014 32 p. color illustrations (hardcover) $17.99

Grades: PreK K 1 2   E

1. Grief -- Fiction 2. Chickens -- Fiction 3. Death -- Fiction 4. Ducks -- Fiction 5. Friendship -- Fiction

ISBN 148141044X; 9781481410441

LC 2013037476

In this book, written and illustrated by Petra Mathers, "Aunt Mattie has died. But before she went, she got to say good-bye to Lottie. Then she got to follow a light to a bustling gate. (A gate that sounded a lot like a busy airport!) And there she found a crew of friends who were waiting

to take off with her on a new journey. Will Lottie and Herbie be able to overcome their sadness? They will, with time, and by taking a journey of their own." (Publisher's note)

"Lucid and insightful, Mathers presents death and grief as natural processes with compassion and great care." Kirkus

Matsuoka, Mei

★ **Footprints** in the snow. Henry Holt & Co. 2008 un il $16.95

Grades: PreK K 1 2 3   E

1. Wolves -- Fiction 2. Storytelling -- Fiction

ISBN 978-0-8050-8792-5; 0-8050-8792-3

Wolf is feeling offended and indignant: All the wolves he's ever read about are nasty, scary, and greedy! To set the record straight he decides to write a story about a nice wolf. But will his wolfish instincts get the better of him after all?

"Both plot and pictures . . . take a surprising turn, which will delight young readers. Replete with visual allusions to popular wold stories, the folk-art style illustrations set up the scenario for this story-within-stories." Booklist

Matthews, Tina

Out of the egg. Houghton Mifflin 2007 un il $12.95

Grades: K 1 2 3   E

1. Animals -- Fiction 2. Chickens -- Fiction

ISBN 978-0-618-73741-3; 0-618-73741-3

LC 2006-09812

When the barnyard animals who refused to help her plant and tend a seed ask to play under the "great green whispery tree" that Little Red Hen grew, she says no, but her chick thinks that answer is mean.

"This gritty, sharply graphic woodcut version of the time-honored tale sets our feathered friend and her slothful sidekicks squarely in the present. . . . Matthews's hand-painted Japanese woodblock illustrations black and white and red all over—with, of course, an important touch of green—are striking editorial panoramas." SLJ

Matthies, Janna

★ The **Goodbye** Cancer garden; illustrated by Kristi Valiant Albert Whitman 2011 un il $16.99

Grades: K 1 2 3   E

1. Cancer -- Fiction 2. Gardens -- Fiction 3. Gardening -- Fiction 4. Family life -- Fiction

ISBN 978-0-8075-2994-2; 0-8075-2994-X

LC 201002406

When a mother is diagnosed with breast cancer, she and her family plant a garden and watch it grow through the seasons as she undergoes treatments and gets better.

"Smoothly told in a reassuringly matter-of-fact and understated way . . . Details about the treatment and the woman's physical reactions to it are worked in unobtrusively. . . . Realistic emotions like her general sadness or Janie's brother's dismay at his mom's baldness are included but are downplayed. The sketchy illustrations are tender and sweet. . . . An uplifting, hopeful story, well told and beautifully illustrated." SLJ

Mattick, Lindsay

★ **Finding** Winnie; the true story of Winnie-the-Pooh. by Lindsay Mattick; illustrated by Sophie Blackall. Little, Brown & Co. 2015 56 p. color illustrations (hardcover) $18

Grades: PreK K 1 2 3   E

1. Bears -- Fiction 2. Soldiers -- Fiction 3. Winnipeg (Bear) -- Fiction 4. Winnie-the-Pooh (Fictitious character) -- Fiction

ISBN 0316324906; 9780316324908

LC 201404112

Caldecott Medal (2016)

This children's book, by Lindsay Mattick and illustrated by Sophie Blackall, tells the story of how "before Winnie-the-Pooh, there was a real bear named Winnie. In 1914, Harry Colebourn, a veterinarian on his way to tend horses in World War I, followed his heart and rescued a baby bear. He named her Winnie, after his hometown of Winnipeg, and he took the bear to war." (Publisher's note)

The visuals not only complement the fablelike cadences of Mattick's text but also include subtle details that enrich the story—the opening pages, for instance, recall a storybook forest before melting into the surroundings of Cole's bedroom, where he hears the story of Colebourn and Winnie. Little ones who love A. A. Milne's classic stories will be enchanted by this heartening account of the bear's real-life origins." Booklist

Mayer, Mercer

★ A **boy**, a dog, and a frog. Dial Bks. for Young Readers 1967 un il hardcover o.p. $6.99
Grades: PreK K 1   E
   1. Stories without words 2. Frogs -- Fiction
   ISBN 0-8037-2880-8

"Without the need for a single word, humorous, very engaging pictures tell the story of a little boy who sets forth with his dog and a net on a summer day to catch an enterprising and personable frog. Even very young preschoolers will 'read' the tiny book with the greatest satisfaction and pleasure." Horn Book

Other titles in this series are:
A boy, a dog, a frog, and a friend (1971)
Frog goes to dinner (1974)
Frog on his own (1973)
Frog, where are you? (1969)
One frog too many (1975)

The **bravest** knight; story and pictures by Mercer Mayer. Dial Books for Young Readers 2007 un il $16.99
Grades: PreK K 1 2   E
   1. Play -- Fiction 2. Knights and knighthood -- Fiction
   ISBN 978-0-8037-3206-3
                                         LC 2006021321
First published 1968 by Dial Press with title: Terrible Troll
A little boy imagines the adventures he would have if he lived a thousand years ago and was the squire of a bold knight who fought dragons and trolls.

"Funny details abound in every picture. . . . This fresh version of an old favorite should find a place in all picture-book collections." SLJ

Octopus soup. Marshall Cavendish Children 2011 un il $16.99
Grades: PreK K 1 2   E
   1. Stories without words 2. Animals -- Fiction 3. Octopuses -- Fiction
   ISBN 978-0-7614-5812-8; 0-7614-5812-3
                                         LC 2010021232
An octopus struggles with misadventure when he leaves home but is relieved to know how and where to find a safe haven.

"The artist's signature cartoons are colorful, whimsical, and entertaining. Mayer continues to enchant." SLJ

★ **There's** a nightmare in my closet. Dial Bks. for Young Readers 1968 un il $16.99; pa $6.99
Grades: PreK K 1   E
   1. Fear -- Fiction
   ISBN 0-8037-8682-4; 0-14-054712-6 pa
"Childhood fear of the dark and the resulting exercise in imaginative exaggeration are given that special Mercer Mayer treatment in this dryly

humorous fantasy. Young children will easily empathize with the boy and can be comforted by his experience." SLJ

Another title about this boy is:
There's an alligator under my bed (1987)

Too many dinosaurs. Holiday House 2011 un il $16.95
Grades: PreK K 1   E
   1. Pets -- Fiction 2. Dinosaurs -- Fiction
   ISBN 978-0-8234-2316-3; 0-8234-2316-6
                                         LC 2010029442
A little boy really wants a dog, but instead he gets dinosaurs!

"Mayer's colloquial text and unmistakable illustrative style are both present here. The illustrations are full-page or cutouts surrounded by white space and done in rich colors. The text is placed in and around them to good effect. Plenty of background details spice up the very funny scenes for observant readers, and wild action and chases abound." SLJ

Mayo, Margaret

Choo choo clickety-clack! written by Margaret Mayo; illustrated by Alex Ayliffe. Carolrhoda Books 2005 un il lib bdg $14.95
Grades: PreK K   E
   1. Noise -- Fiction 2. Transportation -- Fiction
   ISBN 1-57505-819-7
                                         LC 2004-11976
First published 2004 in the United Kingdom
Rhythmic sounds imitate trains, planes, and other busy transports that come and go

"Short and snappy, four lines of text encapsulate the excitement that comes with getting in a car, sailing on a lake, or floating in a hot-air balloon. The graphic-style artwork is executed in a melange of pure colors." Booklist

Mayr, Diane

Run, Turkey run; [by] Diane Mayr; illustrated by Laura Rader. Walker Pub. Co. 2007 un il $15.95; lib bdg $16.85
Grades: PreK K 1 2   E
   1. Turkeys -- Fiction 2. Thanksgiving Day -- Fiction
   ISBN 978-0-8027-9630-1; 0-8027-9630-3; 978-0-8027-9631-8 lib bdg; 0-8027-9631-1 lib bdg
                                         LC 2006036190
The day before Thanksgiving, Turkey tries to disguise himself as other animals in order to avoid being caught by the farmer.

"This fast-paced romp is as much fun to read as it is to listen to. . . . The illustrations are light and humorous." SLJ

McAlister, Caroline

Brave Donatella and the Jasmine thief; illustrated by Donald Hendricks. Charlesbridge 2010 un il $16.95
Grades: 1 2 3   E
   1. Princes 2. Love -- Fiction 3. Italy -- Fiction 4. Middle Ages -- Fiction
   ISBN 978-1-57091-729-5; 1-57091-729-9
In sixteenth-century Florence, in what would become Italy, Antonio and Donatella flee the wrath of Duke Cosimo de Medici from whom Antonio has stolen a sprig of jasmine, and they use that rare plant to make a fresh start. Includes facts about the duke and Italian history.

"The illustrations have a soft quality to them and fit the time period perfectly. . . . This story could be used in a world history class for older students, as well as in a class studying legends around the world. And of course, it can be read aloud to younger students." Libr Media Connect

McAllister, Angela

Little Mist; illustrated by Sarah Fox-Davies. Alfred A. Knopf 2011 un il $16.99; lib bdg $19.99

Grades: PreK K 1   E

1. Snow leopard -- Fiction

ISBN 978-0-375-86788-0; 0-375-86788-0; 978-0-375-96788-7 lib bdg; 0-375-96788-5 lib bdg

LC 2010-28822

Little Mist, a young snow leopard, is filled with wonder when his mother introduces him to the world for the first time.

"Young readers will be lulled by the incantatory quality of the text and drawn to the snow leopards, who look as friendly and welcoming as they do dignified." SLJ

My mom has x-ray vision; illustrated by Alex T. Smith. Tiger Tales 2011 un il $15.95; pa $7.95

Grades: PreK K 1 2   E

1. Mothers -- Fiction 2. Superheroes -- Fiction

ISBN 978-1-58925-097-0; 1-58925-097-0; 978-1-58925-428-2 pa; 1-58925-428-7 pa

"Matthew is certain that his mother has superhuman abilities. She might have 'ordinary hair, ordinary clothes, and a nice smile,' but she also seems to have x-ray vision. So Matthew decides to test his hypothesis. He disobeys her request to bring in the groceries and hides in a closet, waiting to see if she knows where he is. . . . Matthew's logical thought processes pull youngsters along through bright full-page cartoons with visual details like the dragon in his fantasies or a superhero costume hanging on the clothesline while font changes add emphasis. . . . Young readers will recognize this puzzled child's analysis of an age-old mystery." SLJ

Yuck! That's not a monster! illustrated by Alison Edgson. Good Books 2010 un il $16.99

Grades: PreK K   E

1. Monsters -- Fiction 2. Parent-child relationship -- Fiction

ISBN 978-1-56148-683-0; 1-56148-683-3

LC 2009-33696

As Mr. and Mrs. Monster's three eggs begin to hatch, they happily welcome the first two ugly little monsters to come out, but are shocked and disappointed when they see what pops out of their last egg.

"The large format and brightly colored cartoons lend themselves well to group sharing. Edgson's monsters are like plush toys with coy expressions, more funny than fierce. McAllister offers fresh descriptions touched with humor." SLJ

McAnulty, Stacy

101 reasons why I'm not taking a bath; by Stacy McAnulty; illustrated by Joy Ang. Random House Inc. 2016 40 p. color illustrations (hardcover) $17.99

Grades: PreK K 1 2   E

1. Baths -- Fiction 2. Children -- Health and hygiene 3. Baths -- Fiction 4. Humorous stories 5. Cleanliness -- Fiction

ISBN 9780375973659; 9780385391894

LC 2015023380

This children's book by Stacy McAnulty, illustrated by Joy Ang, demonstrates why "no one likes baths. What a waste of time! There's so much more important stuff to do! Plus, baths are super dangerous for a number of reasons. You want me to list a few? Most household accidents happen in the bathroom. Scientific fact! A kid in Texas turned into a prune after taking a bath. Scientific fact!" (Publisher's Note)

"Digitally created images and varying perspectives accentuate large eyes and raised eyebrows, while both visuals and text introduce his

grimy world, from dirt and water-smudged endpapers to the permanent marker on his colorful hands." SLJ

★ **Excellent** Ed; by Stacy McAnulty; illustrated by Julia Sarcone-Roach. Alfred A. Knopf 2016 32 p. color illustrations (hardback) $16.99

Grades: PreK K 1   E

1. Dogs -- Fiction 2. Humorous fiction 3. Ability -- Fiction 4. Family life -- Fiction 5. Humorous stories

ISBN 9780553510232; 9780553510249

LC 2015029134

In this book, by Stacy McAnulty, illustrated by Julia Sarcone-Roach, "Everyone in the Ellis family is excellent--except Ed. Ed wonders if this is why he isn't allowed to eat at the table or sit on the couch with the other children. So he's determined to find his own thing to be excellent at--only to be (inadvertently) outdone by a family member every time. Now Ed is really nervous--what if he's not excellent enough to belong in this family?" (Publisher's note)

"Rounded, loose lines and vivid splashes of color in acrylics, watercolor, crayon, and grease pencil make for a cheery depiction of life in a middle-class African-American household. A warm, welcome reminder that everyone is excellent at something." Kirkus

McBratney, Sam

★ **Guess** how much I love you; illustrated by Anita Jeram; paper engineering by Corina Fletcher. pop-up edition; Candlewick Press 2011 un il $19.99

Grades: PreK K   E

1. Pop-up books 2. Love -- Fiction 3. Rabbits -- Fiction 4. Father-son relationship -- Fiction

ISBN 978-0-7636-5378-1; 0-7636-5378-0

First published 1995

During a bedtime game, every time Little Nutbrown Hare demonstrates how much he loves his father, Big Nutbrown Hare gently shows him that the love is returned even more

"It's hard to believe that a pop-up wasn't the creators' original intention, so seamlessly do moveable parts dovetail into this modern classic's storyline. . . . The figures here move on every page, and with an unusually graceful naturalism to boot. . . . All of Little Nutbrown Hare's hops, stretches and small gestures serve the poetically spare text. . . . The book is available in just about every format—but this is the perfect one." Kirkus

McCanna, Tim

Watersong; Tim McCanna; illustrated by Richard Smythe. Simon & Schuster Books for Young Readers 2017 32 p. color illustration (ebook) $15.99; (hardback) $17.99

Grades: PreK K 1 2   E

1. Stories in rhyme 2. Rain -- Fiction 3. Animals -- Fiction 4. Foxes -- Fiction 5. Sounds, Words for 6. Rain and rainfall -- Fiction 7. English language -- Onomatopoeic words

ISBN 9781481468824; 9781481468817

LC 201601198-

This picture book, by Tim McCanna, illustrated by Richard Smythe, takes readers "on a dazzling journey as a fox seeks shelter from a rainstorm. . . . As the rain begins, a little fox seeks shelter. But then it builds and builds into to a torrential storm. . . . This stunning picture book showcases the power and beauty of nature." (Publisher's note)

"Backmatter introduces such concepts as ecosystems and the water cycle. Beautiful." Kirkus

McCardie, Amanda

Our very own dog; Taking Care of Your First Pet. Amanda McCardie, Salvatore Rubbino. Candlewick Press 2017 32 p. color illustrations $15.99

Grades: PreK K 1 2   E

1. Pets   2. Rescue dogs   3. Dogs -- Training

ISBN 9780763689483

LC 2016951634

In this children's book about getting a dog, by Amanda McCardie, illustrated by Salvatore Rubbino, "join Sophie's new human family as they prepare their home for her and introduce her to life as a beloved pet. Follow along as they learn about bedding and bowls, treats and training, walks and washing—and even an unexpected dog show! Factual notes run alongside the simple story, offering tips that will help turn tentative dog adopters into doting experts." (Publisher's note)

"Families in the early stages of bringing a dog into their lives should find this a reassuring guide to understanding their new pet." Pub Wkly

Includes bibliographical references and index.

McCarthy, Mary

★ **A closer** look. Greenwillow Books 2007 un il $16.99; lib bdg $17.89

Grades: PreK K 1 2   E

1. Nature -- Fiction

ISBN 978-0-06-124073-7; 0-06-124073-7; 978-0-06-124074-4 lib bdg; 0-06-124074-5 lib bdg

LC 2006-29459

Detailed collage illustrations accompanied by simple text present expanding views of familiar objects in nature, such as a bug and a flower.

"Rendered from handmade papers and collage, the bold artwork is elegant and eye-catching. The broad lines, simple graphic images, and textured details suit the magnified perspectives, while the more expansive scenes are beautifully composed." SLJ

McCarthy, Meghan

Daredevil; by Meghan McCarthy. 1st ed. Simon & Schuster Books for Young Readers 2013 48 p. col. ill. (reinforced) $16.99

Grades: K 1 2   E

1. Women air pilots   2. Skelton, Betty, 1926-2011   3. Air pilots -- United States -- Biography   4. Women air pilots -- United States -- Biography   5. Automobile racing drivers -- United States -- Biography   6. Women automobile racing drivers -- United States -- Biography

ISBN 1442422629; 9781442422629

LC 2012023603

This biographical "portrait of Betty June Skelton (1926-2011) reveals a woman who embodies a 'need for speed.' . . . She was obsessed with flying from an early age, and she made the newspapers for a solo flight on her 16th birthday--never mind that her father had already plopped her into a cockpit four years earlier. . . . Skelton went on to break records on land, sea, and air, and she even had a shot at becoming the first woman in space." (Publishers Weekly)

McCarty, Peter

Chloe; Peter McCarty. Balzer + Bray 2012 40 p.

Grades: PreK K 1   E

1. Play -- Fiction   2. Rabbits -- Fiction   3. Siblings -- Fiction   4. Television -- Fiction   5. Family life -- Fiction   6. Brothers and sisters -- Fiction

ISBN 0061142913; 9780061142918; 9780061142925

LC 2011019346

"Chloe is the middle rabbit child, with 10 older brothers and sisters and 10 younger. One of the best things about so many siblings is family fun time. When Dad brings home a television set, all the siblings are delighted except for Chloe and baby Bridget, who are less enthused. Why watch a piece of pound cake attack a city onscreen when you could do something else--like play inside the box the TV came in?" (Booklist)

First snow; Peter McCarty. Balzer + Bray, an imprint of HarperCollins Publishers 2015 40 p. color illustrations (hardcover) $16.99

Grades: PreK K 1   E

1. Snow -- Fiction 2. Cousins -- Fiction

ISBN 0062189964; 9780062189967

LC 2013037211

In this children's picture book, written and illustrated by Peter McCarty, "it's a day of firsts for Pedro . . . First snowfall. First snow angel. First taste of a snowflake. First sled run. First snowball fight!" (Publisher's note)

"Pedro, a young anthropomorphic dog, has traveled from far away, and his cousins Sancho, Bella, Lola, Ava, and Maria are eager to introduce him to snow—something he's never before experienced...Through it all, a message emphasizing the importance of trying new things is unobtrusively folded in, but most of all, readers will come away with a genuine sense of fun and the joy of family and friends. A delightful winter excursion." SLJ

★ **Henry** in love. Balzer & Bray 2009 un il $16.99; lib bdg $17.89

Grades: PreK K 1   E

1. School stories 2. Cats -- Fiction 3. Love -- Fiction 4. Rabbits -- Fiction

ISBN 978-0-06-114288-8; 0-06-114288-3; 978-0-06-114289-5 lib bdg; 0-06-114289-1 lib bdg

LC 2009-14412

On the first day of school, Henry the cat vies for the attention of the most amazing girl in class, Chloe Rabbit.

"This gentle, pitch-perfect romance will have readers' hearts thumping with the thrill of first love." Publ Wkly

★ **Hondo** and Fabian. Holt & Co. 2002 un il $16.95; pa $6.95

Grades: PreK K 1 2   E

1. Cats -- Fiction 2. Dogs -- Fiction

ISBN 0-8050-6352-8; 0-312-36747-3 pa

LC 2001-1884

A Caldecott Medal honor book, 2003

Hondo the dog gets to go to the beach and play with his friend Fred, while Fabian the cat spends the day at home.

"McCarty's staccato text, one line to a page, captures a lot of action in a few words, but it is the pencil-on-watercolor-paper art that makes this so arresting. Each carefully shaded picture, in muted tones, has a smooth, solid look." Booklist

Another title about Hondo and Fabian is:

Fabian escapes (2007)

Jeremy draws a monster. Henry Holt 2009 un il $16.99 E

1. Drawing -- Fiction 2. Monsters -- Fiction

ISBN 978-0-8050-6934-1; 0-8050-6934-8

LC 2008-36813

A young boy who spends most of his time alone in his bedroom makes new friends after the monster in his drawing becomes a monstrous nuisance.

"The finely rendered pen-and-ink and watercolor illustrations skillfully delineate characters and objects. . . . [This is] top-notch." Booklist

★ **Moon** plane; written and illustrated by Peter McCarty. Henry Holt 2006 un il $16.95

Grades: PreK K   E
1. Moon -- Fiction 2. Flight -- Fiction 3. Airplanes -- Fiction
ISBN 978-0-8050-7943-2; 0-8050-7943-2

LC 2005016244

A young boy looks at a plane in the sky and imagines flying one all the way to the moon

"Using pencils, McCarty creates soft-edged, silver-tone artwork notable for its elegant simplicity. . . . McCarty catches both the way children's imaginations work and the connections they make." Booklist

T is for terrible; written and illustrated by Peter McCarty. Henry Holt 2004 un il $15.95; pa $6.99
Grades: PreK K 1   E
1. Dinosaurs -- Fiction
ISBN 0-8050-7404-X; 0-312-38423-8 pa

LC 2003-18246

A tyrannosaurus rex explains that he cannot help it that he is enormous and hungry and is not a vegetarian.

"Filled with textured lines and soft shading, the artwork glows with warmth and vitality. This beautifully formatted and well-conceived offering has creamy ivory pages that frame the subtle illustrations and spare text." SLJ

McClatchy, Lisa
Dear Tyrannosaurus Rex; illustrated by John Manders. Random House 2010 un il $16.99; lib bdg $19.99
Grades: PreK K 1 2   E
1. Parties -- Fiction 2. Birthdays -- Fiction 3. Dinosaurs -- Fiction
ISBN 978-0-375-85608-2; 0-375-85608-0; 978-0-375-95608-9 lib bdg; 0-375-95608-5 lib bdg

LC 2009005038

Enamored of dinosaurs, Erin writes a letter inviting a real one to her sixth birthday party.

"Enthusiastic descriptions of games, treats, the cake, party favors, etc., are accompanied by large cartoonlike illustrations featuring the T. rex as if he were in attendance. Each spread is filled with humor. . . . Perfect for reading aloud." SLJ

McClements, George
★ **Dinosaur** Woods; can seven clever critters save their forest home? Beach Lane Books 2009 un il $16.99
Grades: PreK K 1 2   E
1. Animals -- Fiction 2. Dinosaurs -- Fiction 3. Endangered species -- Fiction 4. Environmental protection -- Fiction
ISBN 978-1-4169-8626-3; 1-4169-8626-X

LC 2008-33084

To save their homes from being destroyed by developers, a fanciful group of endangered animals constructs a fearsome dinosaur.

"This title's generous trim size, cleanly rendered illustrations, and fast-paced text are perfect for group read-alouds or one-on-one sharing." SLJ

Night of the Veggie Monster. Bloomsbury Children's Books 2008 un il $14.95; lib bdg $15.85
Grades: K 1 2 3   E
1. Food -- Fiction 2. Family life -- Fiction
ISBN 978-1-59990-061-2; 1-59990-061-0; 978-1-59990-234-0 lib bdg; 1-59990-234-6 lib bdg

LC 2007017850

Every Tuesday night, while his parents try to enjoy their dinner, a boy turns into a monster the moment a pea touches his lips

"Illustrations are a creative medley of photographed realia . . . cutout brown paper . . . and simple pastel lines and textural elements, . . .

resulting in a spare vigor that nicely supports the textual humor." Bull Cent Child Books

McClintock, Barbara
★ **Adele** & Simon. Farrar, Straus & Giroux 2006 un il $16
Grades: PreK K 1 2   E
1. Siblings -- Fiction 2. Paris (France) -- Fiction 3. Lost and found possessions -- Fiction
ISBN 0-374-38044-9

LC 2002-35311

When Adele walks her little brother Simon home from school he loses one more thing at every stop: his drawing of a cat at the grocer's shop, his books at the park, his crayons at the art museum, and more.

"Set in Paris during the early 20th century, this simple story is the basis for some remarkable illustrations. McClintock's pen-and-ink with watercolor technique has the feel of illustrated children's books from that period. . . . A beautiful example of bookmaking, with plenty to charm children, this is a visual delight." SLJ

Another title about Adele and Simon is:
Adele & Simon in America (2008)

Emma and Julia love ballet; Barbara McClintock. Scholastic Press 2016 32 p. color illustrations (hardcover : alk. paper) $17.99
Grades: PreK K 1 2   E
1. Ballet -- Fiction 2. Ballet dancers -- Fiction 3. Ballet -- Fiction 4. Ballet dancing -- Fiction 5. Dance recitals -- Fiction
ISBN 9780439894012

LC 2014026920

In this children's story, written and illustrated by Barbara McClintock, "Emma is little. Julia is big. . . . Emma takes ballet lessons. . . . Julia is a professional ballerina. They are both excited about the big performance in the theater tonight. Emma will be watching from the audience. Julia will be dancing onstage! And afterward, Emma will go backstage to meet her ballet hero!" (Publisher's note)

"McClintock makes effective use of white space and leaves the full-color spreads to the dramatic scenes of the performance hall and stage, where Emma and Julia's stories converge." SLJ

McCloskey, Robert
★ **Blueberries** for Sal. Viking 1948 54p il $16.99; pa $7.99
Grades: PreK K 1 2   E
1. Bears -- Fiction 2. Maine -- Fiction
ISBN 0-670-17591-9; 0-14-050169-X pa
A Caldecott Medal honor book, 1949

"The author-artist tells what happens on a summer day in Maine when a little girl and a bear cub, wandering away from their blueberry-picking mothers, each mistakes the other's mother for its own. The Maine hillside and meadows are real and lovely, the quiet humor is entirely childlike, and there is just exactly the right amount of suspense for small children." Wis Libr Bull

Another title about Sal is:
One morning in Maine (1952)

Lentil. Viking 1940 un il $18.99; pa $5.99
Grades: PreK K 1 2   E
1. Ohio -- Fiction 2. Harmonicas -- Fiction
ISBN 0-670-42357-2; 0-14-050287-4 pa

Picture-story book about a small boy who could not sing, but who could work wonders on a simple harmonica, especially on the day when the great Colonel Carter returned to his home town

"Big, vigorous, amusing pictures in black-and-white, with an Ohio small-town background." New Yorker

★ **Make** way for ducklings. Viking 1941 un il $17.99; pa $7.99

Grades: PreK K 1 2   E
1. Ducks -- Fiction 2. Boston (Mass.) -- Fiction
ISBN 0-670-45149-5; 0-14-056434-9 pa
Awarded the Caldecott Medal, 1942
"There are some very beautiful drawings in this book." Horn Book

★ **Time** of wonder. Viking 1957 63p il $18.99; pa $6.99
Grades: K 1 2 3   E
1. Maine -- Fiction
ISBN 0-670-71512-3; 0-14-050201-7 pa
Awarded the Caldecott Medal, 1958
"A summer on an island in Maine is described through the simple everyday experiences of children, but also reveals the author's deep awareness of an attachment to all the shifting moods of season and weather, and the salty, downright character of the New England people." Top News

McClure, Nikki
Apple; Nikki McClure. Abrams Appleseed 2012 40 p. $12.95
Grades: PreK K 1   E
1. Apples 2. Plants -- Growth 3. Picture books for children 4. Apples -- Fiction
ISBN 9781419703782
LC 2011052130
This picture book by cut-paper artist Nikki McClure "follows the life of an apple throughout the year, demonstrating the cyclical patterns in nature. . . . [R]eaders will . . . follow[. . .] the journey of the bright red apple—the only splash of color in the otherwise black-and-white illustrations—as it travels from tree, to harvest, to snack, to compost, and finally to sprout. A single word complements each illustration, urging early readers to reflect on each stage in the apple's life." (Amazon.com)

How to be a cat; Nikki McClure. Abrams Books for Young Readers 2013 40 p. $16.95
Grades: PreK K 1   E
1. Cats 2. Picture books for children 3. Cats -- Fiction 4. Animals -- Infancy -- Fiction
ISBN 1419705288; 9781419705281
LC 2012021633
This children's picture book from Nikki McClure includes cut-paper illustrations that "show nothing more than cats being cats, with a single word describing each of their actions." Words illustrated include "stretch," "wait," "find," "feast," and "dream." (Publishers Weekly)
"The expressive, striking cut-paper illustrations are entirely black and white except for well-placed touches of sky blue, which reinforce the natural setting. Very new readers will enjoy navigating the simple story arc on their own." Horn Book

In; by Nikki McClure. Abrams Appleseed 2015 36 p. illustrations hbk $16.95
Grades: PreK K   E
1. Play -- Fiction 2. Imagination -- Fiction 3. Contentment -- Fiction 4. English language -- Prepositions -- Fiction
ISBN 1419714864; 9781419714863
LC 2014027139
In this story by Nikki McClure, "for a boy and his toy giraffe, today is the perfect day to stay in. Snug in his pajamas, he reads books, bakes popovers, and plays with a big wicker basket--that he transforms into a rocket ship to fly in 'innerspace.' But soon, the outdoors is too tempting to resist, and he takes his wild imagination into nature. That is, until it's time to come inside again." (Publisher's note)
"Using only yellow, black, and white, McClure's cut-paper illustrations are filled with amazing detail. Readers will have fun spotting the yellow giraffe in every picture and following the boy from one activity to the next." Booklist

Mama, is it summer yet? Abrams Books for Young Readers 2010 un il $17.95
Grades: PreK K 1   E
1. Summer -- Fiction 2. Mother-son relationship -- Fiction
ISBN 978-0-8109-8468-4; 0-8109-8468-7
"Repetition of this book's title question ties together responses and scenes of a child and his mother as they wait for warmer weather. . . . The days pass with a graceful swirl as the most delicate of paper-cuts detail budding trees, squirrels nesting, soft earth for seedlings, young ducklings following their mother, swallows circling overhead, and blossoming trees, culminating in the anticipated delight of summer berries. . . . Simple black paper contrasts with a light, neutral background, highlighting spare use of digitally added color accents; solid-color sheets underscore the repeated text. . . . Children will appreciate the simple sentences and lyrical verse that relate the seasonal passing of time." SLJ

McCormack, Caren McNelly
The **fiesta** dress; a quinceanera tale. illustrated by Martha Aviles. Marshall Cavendish 2009 un il $17.99
Grades: K 1   E
1. Sisters -- Fiction 2. Family life -- Fiction 3. Hispanic Americans -- Fiction 4. Quinceañera (Social custom) -- Fiction
ISBN 0-7614-5467-5; 978-0-7614-5467-0
LC 2008-10781
While Eva and her family prepare for her quinceanera, no one is paying attention to her younger sister, but when the dog gets out of the laundry room and steals Eva's sash, her little sister comes to the rescue.
"Aviles incorporates a warm palette of roses, aquas, deep oranges and springy greens to illustrate the story; her acrylic and watercolor compositions have a somewhat old fashioned feel. . . . There is abundant joy in this tale of a big extended family preparing for an exciting event, and audience members will relish being included." Bull Cent Child Books

McCourt, Frank
Angela and the baby Jesus; illustrated by Raúl Colón. Simon & Schuster Books for Young Readers 2007 un il $17.99
Grades: K 1 2 3   E
1. Ireland -- Fiction 2. Christmas -- Fiction
ISBN 978-1-4169-3789-0; 1-4169-3789-7
"The six-year-old heroine is McCourt's mother, Angela, who is disturbed that the Baby Jesus must be cold as he lies outside in a Nativity scene. . . . Angela steals the baby so she get him home and warm him in her bed. . . . McCourt writes with the lilt of the Irish and the ability to get inside a child's mind. . . . Painted with a glow that comes from street lamps or candlelight, Colon's artwork showcases the warmth that a caring family radiates." Booklist

McCue, Lisa
Quiet Bunny. Sterling 2009 un il $14.95
Grades: PreK K   E
1. Sounds -- Fiction 2. Rabbits -- Fiction
ISBN 978-1-4027-5719-8; 1-4027-5719-0
LC 2008-32903
Quiet Rabbit enjoys listening to the night song of the other animals every evening and wishes he could join them, but no matter how hard he tries he is unable to copy their sounds.
"The text is full of onomatopoeic words, often incorporated into the illustrations, creating a pleasing link between story and picture." SLJ
Other titles about Quiet Bunny are:
Quiet Bunny's many colors (2011)

Quiet Bunny & Noisy Puppy (2011)

McCully, Emily Arnold

3, 2, 1, go! Emily Arnold McCully. Holiday House 2015 24 p.
illustrations (hardcover) $14.95

Grades: PreK K 1 2   E

1. Creative ability 2. Play -- Fiction 3. Sisters -- Fiction 4. Play
-- Fiction

ISBN 0823432882; 9780823432882

LC 2014013402

In this children's book by Emily Arnold McCully "Min is clever
and resourceful. She gets a board, a tube, a rope, and a rock and builds
and launches a rocket that catapults her right into the middle of her big
sister's playdate without stepping over the line! Beginning readers will
cheer underdog Min's triumphant landing in this easy-to-read book that
celebrates ingenuity and perseverance." (Publisher's note)

"McCully's signature pen-and-ink with watercolor illustrations appear throughout--some as inset drawings and others as double-page
spreads. . . . This succeeds both as entertainment and instruction; the
pachyderms' social interactions and STEM content are a delightful bonus." Booklist

Three, two, one, go!

Clara; the (mostly) true story of the rhinoceros who dazzled kings,
inspired artists, and won the hearts of everyone . . . while she ate her way
up and down a continent! Emily Arnold McCully. Schwartz & Wade
Books 2016 48 p. col. ill., col. map (hc : alk. paper) $17.99

Grades: K 1 2 3   E

1. Rhinoceros -- Fiction 2. Human-animal relationship -- Fiction

ISBN 9780553522464; 9780553522471

LC 2015011189

This picture book, by Emily Arnold McCully, "is based on the true
story of an eighteenth-century rhino who toured Europe. . . . McCully
shows Clara being introduced to Louis XV of France, Frederick the
Great of Germany, and others willing to pay for a chance to stroke her
soft lip. Her owner, a Dutch sea captain, keeps Clara fed . . . and watered
. . . and takes loving care of her until her death 17 years later." (Publisher's note)

"Clara's unusual story, which introduces readers to a time when attitudes to animals were much different than now, is a strong consideration
for most collections." SLJ

Includes bibliographical references.

★ **First** snow. HarperCollins Publishers 2004 un il $15.99

Grades: PreK K   E

1. Mice -- Fiction 2. Snow -- Fiction 3. Sledding -- Fiction

ISBN 0-06-623852-8

LC 2003-44971

A timid little mouse discovers the thrill of sledding in the first snow
of the winter.

"First published as a wordless picture book in 1985, First Snow is
back with a brief text, enhanced illustrations, and a larger trim size. . . .
This new edition has brighter, deeper colors. . . . Full of exuberance and
excitement." SLJ

Other titles about this young mouse are:

Picnic (2003)

School (2005)

★ The **grandma** mix-up; story and pictures by Emily Arnold
McCully. Harper & Row 1988 63p il (I can read book) hardcover
o.p. pa $5.99

Grades: PreK K 1 2   E

1. Grandmothers -- Fiction

ISBN 0-06-444150-4 pa

LC 87-29378

Young Pip doesn't know what to do when two very different grandmothers come to baby sit, each with her own way of doing things

"McCully's two-color, line-and-wash drawings emphasize the personality differences by consciously flouting stereotypes: Pip's laid-back
Grandma Sal has white hair and glasses, while his strict Grandma Nan
dresses like a teenager. Choice of words and sentence length will make
the sly humor easy for beginning readers to grasp." Booklist

Other titles about Pip and his grandmothers are:

Grandmas at bat (1993)

Grandmas at the lake (1990)

★ **Mirette** on the high wire. Putnam 1992 un il hardcover o.p.
pa $6.99

Grades: K 1 2 3   E

1. Paris (France) -- Fiction 2. Tightrope walking -- Fiction

ISBN 0-399-22130-1; 0-698-11443-4 pa

LC 91-36324

Awarded the Caldecott Medal, 1993

Mirette learns tightrope walking from Monsieur Bellini, a guest in
her mother's boarding house, not knowing that he is a celebrated tightrope artist who has withdrawn from performing because of fear

"With a rich palette of deep colors, the artist immerses the reader in
19th-century Paris. Colorful theatrical personalities . . . fill the glowing
interiors with robust life. And the exterior scenes . . . are filled with the
magic of a Paris night when anything can happen. . . . An exuberant and
uplifting picture book." N Y Times Book Rev

Other titles about Mirette and Bellini are:

Mirette & Bellini cross Niagra Falls (2000)

Starring Mirette and Bellini (1997)

★ The **secret** cave; discovering Lascaux. Farrar Straus Giroux
2010 un il $16.99

Grades: 1 2 3 4   E

1. France -- Fiction 2. Prehistoric art -- Fiction 3. Cave drawings
and paintings -- Fiction

ISBN 978-0-374-36694-0; 0-374-36694-2

"This mesmerizing look at the discovery of the prehistoric cave
paintings of Lascaux invites today's readers to experience the wonder
of the event. McCully has written and drawn a stunning fictionalized account based on historical records and interviews. The endpapers entice
with the rendering of the maps of the caves, and soft wide watercolor
strokes capture the essence of the prehistoric art. . . . The Caldecott winner gets the emotions of the secret decent for buried treasure just right."
Kirkus

Includes bibliographical references

★ **Wonder** horse. Henry Holt and Company 2010 un il $16.99

Grades: K 1 2 3   E

1. Slaves 2. Veterinarians 3. Animal trainers 4. Horses -- Fiction
5. African Americans -- Fiction

ISBN 978-0-8050-8793-2; 0-8050-8793-1

LC 2009006208

A fictionalized account of Bill "Doc" Key, a former slave who became a veterinarian, trained his horse, Jim Key, to recognize letters
and numbers and to perform in skits around the country, and moved
the nation toward a belief in treating animals humanely. Includes an author's note.

"McCully's storytelling is as sensitive, engaging, and well paced as
her brightly colored, expressive artwork." Booklist

Includes bibliographical references

McCutcheon, John

Flowers for Sarajevo; John McCutcheon; illustrated by Kristy Caldwell. Peachtree Publishers 2017 32 p. color illustrations $19.95

Grades: 1 2 3 4 5   E

1. War stories 2. Sarajevo (Bosnia and Hercegovina) -- Fiction 3. War -- Fiction 4. Cellists -- Fiction 5. Florists -- Fiction 6. Bosnia and Herzegovina -- Fiction 7. Sarajevo (Bosnia and Herzegovina) -- History -- Siege, 1992-1996 -- Fiction

ISBN 9781561459438

LC 2016025765

This book, by John McCutcheon, illustrated by Kristy Caldwell, presents the "story of a young boy who discovers the power of beauty and kindness during a time of war. Drasko helps his father sell flowers in Sarajevo, but when war threatens and his father is called to the battle-front, Drasko must take over the flower stall. One morning the boy's familiar routine is shattered when a mortar shell hits the bakery, killing twenty-two people." (Publisher's note)

McDermott, Gerald

Papagayo; the mischief maker. written and illustrated by Gerald McDermott. Harcourt Brace Jovanovich 1992 un il hardcover o.p. pa $8

Grades: 2 3 4   E

1. Parrots -- Fiction

ISBN 0-15-259465-5; 0-15-259464-7 pa

LC 91-40364

A reissue of the title first published 1980 by Windmill Bks.

Papagayo, the noisy parrot, helps the night animals save the moon from being eaten up by the moon dog

"McDermott's original story assumes folktale proportions. . . . Art for the story is striking; deep tropical colors seem intensified by glossy page surfaces, and they nearly vibrate against the intermittent deep-blue backdrop of a night sky." Booklist

McDonald, Megan

Ant and Honey Bee; a pair of friends at Halloween. illustrated by G. Brian Karas. new ed.; Candlewick Press 2010 44p il $14.99

Grades: K 1 2   E

1. Ants -- Fiction 2. Bees -- Fiction 3. Costume -- Fiction 4. Halloween -- Fiction 5. Friendship -- Fiction

ISBN 978-0-7636-4662-2; 0-7636-4662-8

LC 2009021485

A new edition of Ant and Honey Bee: what a pair! published 2005

Best friends Ant and Honey Bee, who think of themselves as quite a pair, become matching home appliances on Halloween.

"With its open format, large type, judious use of repetition, and plentiful, narrative-laden mixed-media illustrations, this book functions well both as a picture book and an easy reader." Horn Book Guide

Another titles about Ant and Honey Bee is:

Ant and Honey Bee: A pair of friends in winter (2013)

Hen hears gossip; illustrated by Joung Un Kim. HarperCollins 2008 un il $17.99; lib bdg $17.89

Grades: PreK K   E

1. Gossip -- Fiction 2. Animals -- Fiction

ISBN 978-0-06-113876-8; 0-06-113876-2; 978-0-06-113877-5 lib bdg; 0-06-113877-0 lib bdg

LC 2007027137

When Hen overhears some news on the farm, she runs to tell Duck, who tells another animal, and as the gossip is repeated from one animal to the next, it becomes unrecognizable

"The simple prose incorporates capitals and punctuation that offer guidance for animated read-alouds. The colorful, mixed-media collages

. . . blend bold, blocky shapes with vivid, intricate patterns and textures. Children will enjoy the farcical fun." Booklist

It's picture day today! illustrated by Katherine Tillotson. Atheneum Books for Young Readers 2009 un il $16.99

Grades: PreK K   E

1. School stories 2. Artists' materials -- Fiction

ISBN 978-1-4169-2434-0; 1-4169-2434-5

LC 2007-46435

A classroom of art supplies gathers for their picture day.

"Tillotson's collage work, both creative and endearingly clunky, will awaken the inner cutter-and-paster in almost any young child. An ideal book to pair with a craft session." Booklist

Jessica Finch in Pig Trouble; by Megan McDonald; illustrated by Erwin Madrid; based on the characters created by Peter H. Reynolds. Candlewick Press 2014 64 p. color illustrations (Judy Moody and Friends) (pbk) $4.99; (reinforced) $12.99

Grades: K 1 2   E

1. Pigs -- Fiction 2. Gifts -- Fiction 3. Birthdays -- Fiction 4. Female friendship -- Fiction

ISBN 9780763670276; 9780763657185; 0763657182; 0763670278

LC 2012947726

In this book, by Megan McDonald, "readers meet Jessica Finch, a friend of Judy Moody who loves pigs and hopes to get one as a pet for her upcoming birthday. Jessica asks Judy to snoop around and find out what her birthday present will be and is upset when she does not help her. When Judy later appears at the birthday party with a baby pot-bellied pig, Jessica realizes that Judy is her best friend ever." (School Library Journal)

"Full-bleed color illustrations (modeled after Peter H. Reynolds's originals) add to the fun. The easy-to-read books are great for newly independent readers not quite ready for the longer Judy Moody chapter books." Horn Book

Shoe dog; Megan McDonald; illustrated by Katherine Tillotson. Atheneum Books for Young Readers 2014 40 p. color illustrations (hardcover) $17.99

Grades: PreK K 1 2   E

1. Dogs 2. Dog adoption -- Fiction 3. Dogs -- Training -- Fiction

ISBN 1416979328; 9781416979326

LC 2012051499

In this book, by Megan McDonald, illustrated by Katherine Tillotson, "Shoe Dog likes to chew. And chew and chew. But he doesn't chew a boring old bone. Not a squeaky old toy. Not a smelly old sock. Nope. Shoe Dogs chews well, take a guess! Chewing shoes poses a problem, however, and Shoe Dog needs help to solve it. Good thing there's... Shoe Cat!" (Publisher's note)

"Tillotson's crayon, charcoal, and digital illustrations give it a goofy spark, depicting Shoe Dog as a zig-zag pattern that looks drawn from a single, thick line. This cool canine creation cavorts through an Escher-like home abstracted into furniture floating amid white space. Simple to relate to and easy to love." Booklist

McDonnell, Patrick

★ The **monsters'** monster; Patrick McDonnell. Little, Brown 2012 40 p. $16.99

Grades: PreK   E

1. Monsters -- Fiction 2. Conduct of life -- Fiction 3. Behavior -- Fiction

ISBN 0316045470; 9780316045476

LC 2011042742

In this children's picture book by Patrick McDonnell, a National Parenting Publications Award Silver Winner, a trio of monsters "bicker about who is the most impressive monster." When they decide to create "'the biggest, baddest monster EVER!'" they discover that "they cannot change their creation's pleasant nature . . . and learn that respectful, mannerly companionship can lead to fulfilling and sunny results." (Kirkus Reviews)

A **perfectly** messed-up story; by Patrick McDonnell. Little, Brown & Co. 2014 40 p. color illustrations (hardcover) $17
Grades: PreK K 1   E
1. Perfection 2. Storytelling -- Fiction 3. Orderliness -- fiction 4. Anger in children -- fiction 5. Books and reading -- Fiction 6. Characters and characteristics in literature
ISBN 0316222585; 9780316222587
LC 2013041668

In this children's story, written and illustrated by Patrick McDonnell, "little Louie's story keeps getting messed up, and he's not happy about it! What's the point of telling his tale if he can't tell it perfectly? But when he stops and takes a deep breath, he realizes that everything is actually just fine, and his story is a good one--imperfections and all." (Publisher's note)

"Here's an existential dilemma: What if you were a character in a book, and sandwich fillings fell onto your page from above? . . . The ultrarealistic digitally collaged PB&J splotches retain their exact shape from spread to spread; McDonnell also uses pen and ink, brush pen, crayon and watercolor. More messes deface the idyllic countryside—fingerprints, juice, scribbles and, worst of all, a paper towel that smears rather than cleaning—and Louie has a meltdown. The blank backgrounds that throw Louie's freakout in relief, the interplay between narrative text and Louie's frantic speech bubbles, and Louie's prostrate despair are all brilliant. Happily, the backgrounds reappear (clean, but what's that on the endpaper?), and so does Louie's equilibrium. A playful, funny and friendly treatment of anxiety and life's unpredictable messes." Kirkus

★ **South**; [by] Patrick McDonnell. Little, Brown and Co. 2008 un il $14.99
Grades: PreK K 1 2   E
1. Stories without words 2. Cats -- Fiction 3. Birds -- Fiction
ISBN 978-0-316-00509-8; 0-316-00509-6
LC 2007048373

Mooch the cat helps a lonely bird find its flock, which has flown south for the winter

"McDonnell's comfort with unfilled expanses, his beautifully balanced compositions, and the nature of his brushwork evoke the feel of traditional Chinese art. Tan recycled paper provides warmth in keeping with this tender, compact story." SLJ

Thank you and good night; Patrick McDonnell. Little, Brown & Co. 2015 40 p. 1 volume unnum pgs; col ills. (hardcover) $15.99
Grades: PreK K 1   E
1. Bedtime -- Fiction 2. Friendship -- Fiction 3. Sleepovers -- Fiction 4. Gratitude 5. Bedtime -- Fiction 6. Gratitude -- Fiction 7. Friendship -- Fiction 8. Sleepovers -- Fiction
ISBN 031633801X; 9780316338011
LC 2014035293

This book, by Patrick McDonnell, is a "bedtime book [that] captures the magic of a sleepover with friends, and reminds us to cherish life's simplest pleasures. During a fun pajama party, three animal friends dance and play, but at last everyone is getting sleepy. Is it time for bed yet? Not before taking the time to say thank you for the day, the night, and good friends." (Publisher's note)

"This delightful bedtime story extols the virtues of friendship and of gratitude for simple pleasures." SLJ

McElligott, Matthew
★ **Bean** thirteen. G. P. Putnam's Sons 2007 un il lib bdg $15.99
Grades: K 1 2 3   E
1. Insects -- Fiction 2. Division -- Fiction
ISBN 978-0-399-24535-0 lib bdg; 0-399-24535-9 lib bdg
LC 2006-26295

Two bugs, Ralph and Flora, try to divide thirteen beans so that the unlucky thirteenth bean disappears, but they soon discover that the math is not so easy.

"Done in pen and ink with digital effects, the cartoon illustrations feature bright hues and slightly off-kilter perspectives that will appeal to children. Youngsters will undoubtedly enjoy this funny tale; teachers will truly appreciate the connections it makes to their curriculum and the use of manipulatives in math." SLJ

Even monsters need haircuts. Walker & Co. 2010 un il $16.99
Grades: PreK K 1   E
1. Monsters -- Fiction 2. Barbers and barbershops -- Fiction
ISBN 978-0-8027-8819-1; 0-8027-8819-X

At night under a full moon, a child operates a barber shop with a monstrous clientele.

"With the distinctive combination of the freakish and the humdrum, it's a good candidate for the stack of battered bedtime favorites." Publ Wkly

The **lion's** share; [by] Matt McElligott. Walker & Co. 2009 un il $16.99; lib bdg $17.89
Grades: PreK K 1 2   E
1. Ants -- Fiction 2. Lions -- Fiction 3. Etiquette -- Fiction 4. Mathematics -- Fiction
ISBN 978-0-8027-9768-1; 0-8027-9768-7; 978-0-8027-9769-8 lib bdg; 0-8027-9769-5 lib bdg
LC 2008013358

Ant is honored to receive an invitation to lion's annual dinner party, but is shocked when the other guests behave rudely and then accuse her of thinking only of herself.

"McElligott's digitally touched ink-and-watercolor artwork combines expressive animal characters with clear groupings of objects that illustrated the embedded arithmetic exercises. While the story will find an obvious place in early elementary math or character education units, the lively illustrations amplify the story's slapstick humor and will easily entertain story hour crowds." Booklist

McElmurry, Jill
Mario makes a move; Jill McElmurry. Schwartz & Wade Books 2012 32 p. (glb) $19.99
Grades: K 1   E
1. Dance -- Fiction 2. Squirrels -- Fiction 3. Picture books for children
ISBN 0375968547; 9780375868542; 9780375968549
LC 2011011014

In this children's picture book, "Mario is a frenetic squirrel whose 'amazing' acrobatic high jinks impress his family but not his . . . friend Isabelle. Not only does she put down his best trick, but she also comes up with a more impressive one of her own and points out that everyone can have special moves. Crushed, Mario abandons his beloved but no longer unique hobby . . . . Isabelle persuades him to return to his spiffy move-making. Teaming up, they teach each other new stunts." (School Library Journal)

McGhee, Alison
Always; illustrated by Pascal Lemaitre. Simon & Schuster Books for Young Readers 2009 un il $15.99

Grades: PreK K 1   E
   1. Dogs -- Fiction
   ISBN 978-1-4169-7481-9; 1-4169-7481-4

LC 2008-42624

A loyal dog promises to protect his young mistress and her home from any danger.

"Succinct, funny and, in its way, action-packed, this is written in the universal language of affection—only the stonyhearted could withstand its charms." Publ Wkly

★ **Bye**-bye, crib; illustrated by Ross MacDonald. Simon & Schuster Books for Young Readers 2008 un il $16.99
Grades: PreK   E
   1. Beds -- Fiction 2. Growth -- Fiction
   ISBN 978-1-4169-1621-5; 1-4169-1621-0

LC 2006-10583

A big boy and his best stuffed friend seek the courage to move to a gigantic new bed.

"MacDonald's evocative art . . . . employs the comic-book conventions, visual wit, and pulp-art palette fans know and love, and the animation in both the text and the pictures turns what might have been a ho-hum tale of trepidation into a proactive adventure with a winsome wee hero." SLJ

The **case** of the missing donut; by Alison McGhee; pictures by Isabel Roxas. Dial Books for Young Readers 2013 32 p. (hardcover) $16.99
Grades: PreK K 1   E
   1. Food -- Fiction 2. Sheriffs -- Fiction 3. Donuts -- Fiction
   ISBN 0803739257; 9780803739253

LC 2012017460

In this book by Alison Mcghee and illustrated by Isabel Roxas "the sheriff and his deputy dog have been charged with a mission: to bring a dozen donuts home safely. The young sheriff peeks inside the box to check on the tasty treats. They're practically calling his name, and in the blink of an eye (and with just a few nibbles), a donut disappears! Wherever could that missing donut be? Luckily, this is one mystery the sheriff and his deputy are sure to bring to a close." (Publisher's note)

Little boy; [by] Alison McGhee and [illustrated by] Peter H. Reynolds. Atheneum Books for Young Readers 2008 un il $15.99
Grades: PreK K 1   E
   1. Father-son relationship -- Fiction
   ISBN 978-1-4169-5872-7; 1-4169-5872-X

LC 2007029625

A father reflects on how the future depends upon the all of the little things in his son's world, from his yellow drinking cup to a big cardboard box

"There is ample white space around the charming pen, ink, and watercolor illustrations. The artwork bursts with energy. . . . The straightforward text, written from the dad's perspective, recounts the simple things that are important to his child." SLJ

Making a friend; illustrated by Marc Rosenthal. Atheneum Books for Young Readers 2011 40p il $16.99
Grades: K 1 2   E
   1. Snow -- Fiction 2. Seasons -- Fiction 3. Friendship -- Fiction
   ISBN 978-1-4169-8998-1; 1-4169-8998-6

LC 2010041661

When the snow falls, a young boy makes a snowman that becomes his friend until the seasons change

This is written "in minimal but evocative text. . . . This gentle story offers [an] opportunity to discuss the cycle of love, loss, and emotional renewal. The digitally manipulated pencil illustrations have a retro look.

. . . A simple but deeply nuanced story that should resonate with children." SLJ

Mrs. Watson wants your teeth; story by Alison McGhee; pictures by Harry Bliss. Harcourt 2004 un il $16; pa $6
Grades: K 1 2 3   E
   1. School stories 2. Teeth -- Fiction 3. Teachers -- Fiction
   ISBN 0-15-204931-2; 0-15-206348-X pa

LC 2003-21267

A first grader is frightened on her first day of school after hearing a rumor that her teacher is a 300-year-old alien with a purple tongue who steals baby teeth from her students.

"McGhee has the pulse of this blue-ribbon worrier. . . . Bliss's watercolor and black-ink illustrations feature distinctive, large-eyed classmates and a number of humorous toothy references on the walls in the hall and in the classroom." SLJ

★ **Only** a witch can fly; illustrated by Taeeun Yoo. Feiwel and Friends 2009 un il $16.99
Grades: K 1 2   E
   1. Stories in rhyme 2. Flight -- Fiction 3. Witches -- Fiction
   ISBN 978-0-312-37503-4; 0-312-37503-4

LC 2008-28542

A young girl wants to fly like a witch on a broom, and one special night, through enormous effort and with the help of her brother, her black cat, and an owl, she fulfills her dream.

"Yoo's illustrations are linoleum block prints done in shades of green and brown with black and white details, adding a wonderful simplicity to this beautiful story." Libr Media Connect

So many days; with illustrations by Taeeun Yoo. Atheneum Books for Young Readers 2010 un il $15.99
Grades: PreK K 1   E
   1. Conduct of life -- Fiction 2. Parent-child relationship -- Fiction
   ISBN 978-1-4169-5857-4; 1-4169-5857-6

LC 2008038300

Through rhythmic text, a parent reflects on the options and opportunities possible in a beloved child's future.

"This book seamlessly pairs lyrical text and digitally manipulated linocut illustrations in a philosophical offering that encourages youngsters to face life head on." SLJ

Song of middle C; illustrated by Scott Menchin. Candlewick Press 2009 un il $16.99
Grades: K 1 2 3   E
   1. Fear -- Fiction 2. Pianists -- Fiction
   ISBN 978-0-7636-3013-3; 0-7636-3013-6

"One little girl uses imagination, bravado and her lucky underwear to overcome a colossal case of stage fright. She has practiced 'Dance of the Wood Elves' diligently [on the piano]. . . . When she steps confidently onto the stage, however, she totally forgets everything she rehearsed. . . . The only note she can manage is Middle C, so she plays it in several different ways with gusto, verve and true artistry, earning great applause. McGhee . . . employs a first-person narration to tell the story in direct, vivid, fast-paced colloquial language. Menchin's digitally colored pen-and-ink cartoons are remarkably detailed while appearing deceptively simple and childlike." Kirkus

Tell me a tattoo story; by Alison McGhee; illustrated by Eliza Wheeler. Chronicle Books 2015 32 p. color illustrations (alk. paper) $16.99
Grades: PreK K 1 2   E
   1. Tattooing -- Fiction 2. Father-son relationship -- Fiction 3. Tattooing -- Fiction 4. Fathers and sons -- Fiction 5. Fathers and

sons -- Fiction
ISBN 9781452119373

LC 2015002694

In this children's story, by Alison McGhee, illustrated by Eliza Wheeler, a "father tells his little son the story behind each of his tattoos, and together they go on a beautiful journey through family history. There's a tattoo from a favorite book his mother used to read him, one from something his father used to tell him, and one from the longest trip he ever took." (Publisher's note)

"Wheeler's soft blends of dreamy blues, blushing pinks, and incandescent yellows are central to the memory-based tale, and McGhee's sincere yet sparing text ensures that the illustrations—much like tattoos themselves—remain ever in the foreground. A fresh, contemporary take on the bond between images, the art of storytelling, and, yes, hipster dads." Booklist

A **very** brave witch; [by] Alison McGhee; [illustrated by] Harry Bliss. Simon & Schuster Books for Young Readers 2006 un il lib bdg $12.95

Grades: PreK K 1 2   E

1. Witches -- Fiction 2. Halloween -- Fiction

ISBN 0-689-86730-1

"A friendly young witch describes what she likes most about Halloween. . . . After boarding her broom, she zooms in a circle, becomes dizzy, and crashes near some trick-or-treaters. She soon discovers that a brave witch and a brave human girl dressed as a witch are not so very different. . . . The chatty text appears in dialogue balloons. Done in black ink and watercolor, the cartoon artwork captures the holiday's spirit with crisp fall colors and amusing details." SLJ

McGinley, Phyllis

A **year** without a Santa Claus; illustrated by John Manders. Marshall Cavendish 2010 un il $16.99

Grades: PreK K 1 2   E

1. Christmas -- Fiction 2. Santa Claus -- Fiction

ISBN 978-0-7614-5799-2; 0-7614-5799-2

A newly illustrated edition of the title first published 1957 by Lippincott

"This newly illustrated edition maintains all of the original's read-aloud charm while accentuating its playfulness with Mander's vibrant gouache and pencil illustrations." Horn Book Guide

McGinness, Suzanne

My bear Griz. Frances Lincoln Children's Books 2011 un il $17.95

Grades: PreK K   E

1. Bears -- Fiction 2. Teddy bears -- Fiction

ISBN 978-1-84780-113-5; 1-84780-113-7

Billy has a bear called Griz. A Grizzly Bear. And the two friends have all kinds of wonderful adventures together. Is he a real Grizzly Bear or a teddy bear? Well, that's for every reader to decide.

"A bear of imposing presence provides safety and joy in this visually distinctive debut. . . . Griz is striking, drawn in densely hatched and layered pen lines of browns and blacks, too big to fit on the page yet dominating the space. . . . Backgrounds are abstract, mellow watercolor, balancing the energetic lines of Griz's fur. . . . A winner for read-alouds, whether in groups or one-on-one." Kirkus

McGinty, Alice B.

Eliza's kindergarten pet. Marshall Cavendish 2010 un il $15.99

Grades: K 1 2   E

1. School stories 2. Guinea pigs -- Fiction

ISBN 978-0-7614-5702-2; 0-7614-5702-X

When the kindergarten classroom gets a pet guinea pig Eliza is afraid, but when the guinea pig gets lost, Eliza helps find her.

"This is a heartwarming story, enhanced by bright illustrations, about facing one's fears." SLJ

Eliza's kindergarten surprise; illustrated by Nancy Speir. Marshall Cavendish 2007 un il $14.99

Grades: PreK K   E

1. School stories 2. Mother-daughter relationship -- Fiction

ISBN 978-0-7614-5351-2; 0-7614-5351-2

LC 2006022415

On her first day of school, Eliza fills her pocket with objects—buttons, a pebble, a napkin, and a piece of yarn—that remind her of her mother, whom she misses very much

"McGinty avoids overly sweet clichés with a strong concept and smooth telling, and Speir's cartoonlike illustrations balance scenes showing Eliza's anguish with brightly colored views of a welcoming classroom and pictures of a loving mother and daughter that reinforce the warm, reassuring words." Booklist

Another title about Eliza is:

Eliza's kindergarten pet (2010)

McGowan, Jayme

One bear extraordinaire; by Jayme McGowan. Abrams Books for Young Readers 2015 32 p. color illustrations $16.95

Grades: PreK K 1 2   E

1. Bears -- Fiction 2. Bands (Music) -- Fiction 3. Music -- Fiction 4. Animals -- Fiction

ISBN 1419716549; 9781419716546

LC 2014041316

In this children's book by Jayme McGowan "Bear wakes up one morning with a song in his head, but something is missing. What's a one-bear band to do? He travels the forest in search of his song and meets a few other musicians along the way, but even with their help, his song still feels incomplete. Will Bear find the perfect accompaniment and learn that every song sounds sweeter with friends by his side?" (Publisher's note)

"McGowan's art, three-dimensional illustrations of painted, cut, assembled, and photographed scenes, is a wonder to behold in its ingenuity and animation. Now all this story needs is an audience, and it's sure to drum one up." Kirkus

McGowan, Michael

Sunday is for God; illustrated by Lou Fancher and Steve Johnson. Schwartz & Wade Books 2010 un il $17.99; lib bdg $20.99

Grades: 1 2 3   E

1. Church -- Fiction 2. Family life -- Fiction 3. African Americans -- Fiction

ISBN 978-0-375-84188-0; 0-375-84188-1; 978-0-375-94591-5 lib bdg; 0-375-94591-1 lib bdg

LC 2008-48828

"It's Sunday morning and a young African American boy knows what that means: 'Sunday is for God. That's what Momma says.' . . . McGowan unleashes a wealth of sensory details. . . . Johnson and Fancher's artwork . . . gets a lift from its textured mix of acrylic and collage. . . . A tender reflection of many children's Sunday experience." Booklist

McGrath, Barbara Barbieri

The **little** red elf; illustrated by Rosalinde Bonnet. Charlesbridge 2009 un il lib bdg $14.95

Grades: PreK K 1   E

1. Fairies -- Fiction 2. Christmas -- Fiction 3. North Pole -- Fiction

ISBN 978-1-58089-236-0; 1-58089-236-1

LC 2008-25340

In this version of "The Little Red Hen," set at the North Pole, a penguin and a hare refuse to help an elf plant, grow, and decorate an evergreen tree but nevertheless expect to open the presents found under its branches on Christmas Day.

"The acrylic and ballpoint-pen illustrations are full of childlike humor, depicting cute North Pole characters who look like toys themselves. This is that rare beast—an endearing holiday book without a hint of treacle." SLJ

Teddy bear counting; illustrated by Tim Nihoff. Charlesbridge 2010 il lib bdg $16.95; pa $7.95 **E**
1. Color 2. Shape 3. Counting 4. Stories in rhyme 5. Teddy bears -- Fiction
ISBN 978-1-58089-215-5 lib bdg; 978-1-58089-216-2 pa
LC 2008025339
Teddy bears introduce numbers from one to twelve, as well as colors and shapes.

McGrory, Anik
Quick, slow, mango! Bloomsbury Books for Young Readers 2011 un il $16.99; lib bdg $17.89
Grades: PreK K 1 **E**
1. Speed -- Fiction 2. Africa -- Fiction 3. Monkeys -- Fiction 4. Elephants -- Fiction
ISBN 978-1-59990-242-5; 1-59990-242-7; 978-1-59990-592-1 lib bdg; 1-59990-592-2 lib bdg
LC 2010025975
"The attractive pencil-and-watercolor artwork features bright, soft colors and rounded, smiling animals, while the variety of sizes and layouts match and enhance the pace of this simple, utterly charming story." Kirkus

McGuirk, Leslie
★ **If** rocks could sing. Tricycle Press 2011 un il $15.99; lib bdg $18.89
Grades: PreK K 1 2 **E**
1. Alphabet 2. Rocks -- Fiction
ISBN 1-58246-370-0; 1-58246-395-6 lib bdg; 978-1-58246-370-4; 978-1-58246-395-7 lib bdg
LC 2010019206
"This unique alphabet book features photos of ocean-sculpted rocks lovingly collected over the course of a decade by the author. McGuirk amassed a complete alphabet of letter-shaped rocks, which she pairs with other humorously representational geologic findings. She puts the emphasis on the rocks themselves, employing simple text, solid backgrounds, and spare, yet engaging layouts to showcase her finds. . . . Sure to spark imaginative rock-finding hunts and found-object art projects, this quirky title will earn its place in any picture-book collection." SLJ

McKee, David
★ **Elmer**; by David McKee. Lothrop, Lee & Shepard Books 1989 [31] p. $16.99
Grades: PreK K 1 **E**
1. Laughter -- Fiction 2. Elephants -- Fiction 3. Individuality -- Fiction 4. Elephants -- Fiction
ISBN 0688091717; 0688091725; 9780688091712
LC 89002285
In this picture book, by David McKee, "Elmer the elephant is bright-colored patchwork all over. No wonder the other elephants laugh at him! If he were ordinary elephant color, the others might stop laughing. That would make Elmer feel better, wouldn't it? The . . . conclusion . . . is a celebration of individuality and the power of laughter." (Publisher's note)

"Elmer the elephant is a colorful character. His heady optimism and unbridled sense of humor keep the entire community in a cheery mood... McKee's gentle humor and love of irony are in full force in this celebration of individuality and laughter. Well-designed spreads are washed with stunning color and the use of textured, painted and airbrushed surfaces contributes to the powerful visual impression." (Publishers Weekly)

McKissack, Pat, 1944-2017
The **all**-I'll-ever-want Christmas doll; written by Patricia C. McKissack; illustrated by Jerry Pinkney. Schwartz & Wade Books 2007 1 v. (unpaged) col. ill.
Grades: PreK K 1 2 3 4 5 **E**
1. Dolls -- Fiction 2. Sisters -- Fiction 3. Christmas -- Fiction 4. Sharing -- Fiction 5. African Americans -- Fiction 6. Depressions -- 1929 -- Fiction
ISBN 9780375836152
LC 2006030981
In this children's book, "[i]t's Christmas and Nella is beside herself with excitement! She and her sisters have been given a real gift—a beautiful Baby Betty doll. But it's hard to share something you've waited your whole seven-year-old life for, and Nella grabs the doll for herself. It isn't long before she discovers that a doll can't do the fun things she and her sisters do together. So, as Christmas day fades, Nella shares it with her sisters." (Publisher's note)

★ **Flossie** & the fox; pictures by Rachel Isadora. Dial Bks. for Young Readers 1986 un il $15.99
Grades: K 1 2 3 **E**
1. Foxes -- Fiction 2. African Americans -- Fiction
ISBN 0-8037-0250-7
LC 86-2024
A wily fox notorious for stealing eggs meets his match when he encounters a bold little girl in the woods who insists upon proof that he is a fox before she will be frightened

"The watercolor and ink illustrations, with realistic figures set on impressionistic backgrounds, enliven this humorous and well-structured story which is told in the black language of the rural south." SLJ

★ **Goin'** someplace special; [illustrated by] Jerry Pinkney. Atheneum Bks. for Young Readers 2001 un il $16; pa $6.99
Grades: K 1 2 3 **E**
1. Libraries -- Fiction 2. Tennessee -- Fiction 3. Segregation -- Fiction 4. African Americans -- Fiction
ISBN 0-689-81885-8; 1-4169-2735-2 pa
LC 99-88258
Coretta Scott King Award for illustration
In segregated 1950s Nashville, a young African American girl braves a series of indignities and obstacles to get to one of the few integrated places in town: the public library

"Pinkney's watercolor paintings are lush and sprawling as they evoke southern city streets and sidewalks as well as Tricia Ann's inner glow. . . . This book carries a strong message of pride and self-confidence as well as a pointed history lesson." Booklist

★ **Mirandy** and Brother Wind; illustrated by Jerry Pinkney. Knopf 1988 un il $17; pa $6.99
Grades: K 1 2 3 **E**
1. Dance -- Fiction 2. Winds -- Fiction 3. African Americans -- Fiction
ISBN 978-0-394-88765-4; 0-394-88765-4; 978-0-679-88333-3 pa; 0-679-88333-9 pa
LC 87-349
A Caldecott Medal honor book, 1989
Coretta Scott King Award for illustration

"Ms. McKissack and Mr. Pinkney's ebullient collaboration captures the texture of rural life and culture 40 years after the end of slavery." N Y Times Book Rev

★ **Ol'** Clip-Clop; a ghost story. by Patricia C. McKissack; illustrated by Eric Velasquez. Holiday House 2013 32 p. (hardcover) $16.95

Grades: 1 2 3 4 5   E

1. Ghost stories -- Fiction 2. Historical fiction -- Fiction 3. Ghosts -- Fiction 4. Conduct of life -- Fiction

ISBN 0823422658; 9780823422654

LC 2010029448

In this ghost story, "an 18th-century miser, John Leep, rides on horseback to evict a woman from her residence. But as darkness falls over the forest . . . Leep hears the 'Clip, Clop' of a ghostly rider behind him. After cruelly deceiving his desperate tenant ('You're short. This isn't everything you owe me!'), he journeys home, again pursued by the invisible horseman." (Publishers Weekly)

★ **Precious** and the Boo Hag; [by] Patricia C. McKissack and Onawumi Jean Moss; illustrated by Kyrsten Brooker. Atheneum Books for Young Readers 2004 un il $16.95

Grades: K 1 2 3   E

1. Monsters -- Fiction 2. African Americans -- Fiction

ISBN 0-689-85194-4

LC 2002-1571

Home alone with a stomachache while the family works in the fields, a young girl faces up to the horrifying Boo Hag that her brother warned her about.

"With the grand feel of a folktale, this lively story speaks to choosing right in a world full of temptation and peril. . . . Expressive and fluid, Brooker's mixed-media art, comical yet scary, too, pops from the pages." Booklist

McLaren, Meg

Rabbit magic; Meg McLaren. Clarion Books, Houghton Mifflin Harcourt 2017 40 p. color illustrations (hardcover) $16.99; (ebook) $16.99

Grades: PreK K 1 2   E

1. Rabbits -- Fiction 2. Magicians -- Fiction 3. Magic tricks -- Fiction

ISBN 9780544784697; 9781328686053

LC 2015025199

In this children's book, by Meg McLaren, "when a magic trick goes awry, the magician M. Lapin becomes a sad rabbit while his rabbit assistant, Houdini, becomes the star of the show. After trying increasingly spectacular tricks, Houdini realizes that someone else wants and deserves the spotlight, and in his most amazing trick ever, he restores M. Lapin to his former self." (Publisher's note)

"No page turn goes unrewarded, and readers of any age will rush to see the rabbits' ironic background antics. A study in leporine whimsy with lingering poignance." Kirkus

McLeod, Heather

Kiss me! (I'm a prince!) illustrated by Brooke Kerrigan. Fitzhenry & Whiteside 2011 un il $18.95

Grades: K 1 2   E

1. Fairy tales 2. Frogs -- Fiction 3. Princes -- Fiction

ISBN 978-1-55455-161-3; 1-55455-161-7

"This clever variation on the classic 'Frog Prince' features a modern girl wearing a red ball cap, a striped T-shirt, purple pants, and red sneakers. She is carrying a basketball, ready to shoot hoops, when a little green frog with a crown on his head wants a kiss to become a prince. . . . The uncluttered artwork uses a pastel palette and makes good use

of white space. Whether read independently or shared at storytime, this breezy tale of a frog who comes to value being a boy as much as being a prince will elicit smiles." SLJ

McLerran, Alice, 1933-

Roxaboxen; illustrated by Barbara Cooney. Lothrop, Lee & Shepard Bks. 1991 un il pa $6.99; $16.99

Grades: K 1 2 3   E

1. Imagination -- Fiction

ISBN 0-06-052633-5 pa; 0-688-07592-4

LC 89-8057

A hill covered with rocks and wooden boxes in the desert becomes an imaginary town named Roxaboxen for Marian, her sisters, and their friends

"A celebration of the transforming magic of the imagination, the story was inspired by McLerran's mother's reminiscences of her childhood in Yuma, Arizona. . . . The story, told as though from the memory of a Roxaboxenite, brings their play to life through concrete details and a spare, understated style. Equally vivid, Cooney's full-color artwork evokes the striking variety of colors and moods found in the desert landscape." Booklist

McLimans, David

★ **Gone** wild; an endangered animal alphabet. Walker & Company 2006 un il $16.95; lib bdg $17.85

Grades: 1 2 3 4   E

1. Animals 2. Alphabet 3. Endangered species

ISBN 978-0-8027-9563-2; 978-0-8027-9564-9 lib bdg; 0-8027-9563-3; 0-8027-9564-1 lib bdg

LC 2006-44702

A Caldecott Medal honor book, 2007

"Although organized as a conventional alphabet book, the letters here are far from ordinary. McLimans has created a black-and-white iconic representation of 26 endangered animals, and his art is striking. . . . The arresting graphics and clean design will hold viewers' attention and create interest in the topic." SLJ

Includes bibliographical references

McMillan, Bruce

★ **How** the ladies stopped the wind; illustrated with paintings by Gunnella. Houghton Mifflin 2007 32p il $16

Grades: K 1 2 3   E

1. Sheep -- Fiction 2. Trees -- Fiction 3. Winds -- Fiction 4. Iceland -- Fiction 5. Chickens -- Fiction

ISBN 978-0-618-77330-5; 0-618-77330-4

LC 2007-04207

The women of one village in Iceland decide to plant trees to stop the powerful winds that make it difficult even to go for a walk, but first they must find a ways to prevent sheep from eating all of their saplings, while encouraging chickens to fertilize them.

"The team that made stars of a group of Icelandic ladies in The Problem with Chickens returns for another winning round. . . . Gunnella's flat, deadpan oil portraits of the ladies, their polka-dot aprons and their hapless chickens are inherently funny, and every page contains another visual poke in the ribs." Publ Wkly

★ The **problem** with chickens; illustrated with paintings by Gunnella. Houghton Mifflin 2005 32p il $16

Grades: K 1 2 3   E

1. Iceland -- Fiction 2. Chickens -- Fiction

ISBN 0-618-58581-8

LC 2005-01225

When women in an Icelandic village buy chickens to lay eggs for them to use, the chickens follow them, adopting human ways and forgetting their barnyard roots, until the ladies hatch a clever plan.

"The playful text is both silly and joyous, without a wasted word. Gunnella's enchanting oil paintings are full of childlike humor and saturated with appealing primary colors." SLJ

McMullan, Kate

★ **Bulldog's** big day; pictures by Pascal Lemaitre. Orchard Books 2011 un il $16.99
Grades: PreK K   E
1. Dogs -- Fiction 2. Animals -- Fiction 3. Occupations -- Fiction
ISBN 0-545-17155-5; 978-0-545-17155-7

LC 2010-26235

While looking for a job, Bulldog tries being a firefighter, a window washer, a sign painter, and a bookseller before finding just the right job for himself. "Ages four to seven." (Bull Cent Child Books)

"The illustrations were created in pen and ink, colored in Adobe Photoshop. . . . There are five or six scenes per spread. Everything is outlined in a thin black line and colored in flat hues. There's a lot to look at on each page, and children will enjoy poring over all the details." SLJ

★ **I** stink! [by] Kate & Jim McMullan. HarperCollins Pubs. 2002 un il $15.95; lib bdg $15.89; pa $6.99
Grades: PreK K 1 2   E
1. Refuse and refuse disposal -- Fiction
ISBN 0-06-029848-0; 0-06-029849-9 lib bdg; 0-06-443836-8 pa

LC 00-54229

Boston Globe-Horn Book Award Honor: Picture Book (2002)

A big city garbage truck makes its rounds, consuming everything from apple cores and banana peels to leftover ziti with zucchini

"Kate McMullan creates an automotive beast whose narrative style reeks of personality, and Jim McMullan's renderings are a perfect match, coaxing steely features into flexible, expressive shapes." Bull Cent Child Books

★ **I'm** bad; [by] Kate & Jim McMullan. Joanna Cotler Books 2008 un il $16.99; lib bdg $17.89
Grades: PreK K 1   E
1. Dinosaurs -- Fiction
ISBN 978-0-06-122971-8; 0-06-122971-7; 978-0-06-122972-5 lib bdg; 0-06-122972-5 lib bdg

LC 2007032020

A hungry Tyrannosaurus rex searches for food in the prehistoric forest but is thwarted in its attempts to find something to eat

"The high-energy illustrations and macho narrator's words create a rowdy, crowd-pleasing whole. Children will delight in the dinosaur's wild expressions and the dynamic text, filled with comic-book sound effects." Booklist

★ **I'm** big! [by] Kate & Jim McMullan. Balzer + Bray 2010 un il $16.99; lib bdg $17.89
Grades: PreK K 1   E
1. Dinosaurs -- Fiction
ISBN 978-0-06-122974-9; 0-06-122974-1; 978-0-06-122975-6 lib bdg; 0-06-122975-X lib bdg

A young Sauropod encounters friends and foes while searching for his pack, who left while he was oversleeping.

"This tale of a young dinosaur finding his inner power is told through childlike vernacular with varying type sizes and colors to emphasize mood. The full-color watercolor illustrations feature plenty of action and multiple perspectives. . . . Perfect as a read-aloud or a read-alone." SLJ

I'm cool! Kate McMullan, Jim McMullan; [edited by] Alessandra Balzer. Balzer + Bray 2015 40 p. 32 plates; color illustrations (hardcover) $17.99
Grades: PreK K 1   E
1. Ice 2. Hockey 3. Vehicles
ISBN 0062306294; 9780062306296

LC 2014947373

In this children's book by Kate McMullan, illustrated by Jim McMullan, "when the ice is full of cuts and ruts, only one machine has the GUTS to clean it up. But can this slow-movin' ice fixer smooth the grooves before the next period? Or will he lose his COOL? The timer's ticking!" (Publisher's note)

"Portraying the proud, hardworking Zamboni on the ice, the illustrations personify the machine while showing how it cleans up the rough ice and lays down a smooth surface. Highly recommended for hockey fans as well as truck-lovers." Booklist

★ **I'm** dirty! [by] Kate & Jim McMullan. Joanna Cotler Books 2006 un il $16.99; lib bdg $17.89
Grades: PreK K 1 2   E
1. Cleanliness -- Fiction 2. Construction equipment -- Fiction
ISBN 978-0-06-009293-1; 0-06-009293-9; 978-0-06-009294-8 lib bdg; 0-06-009294-7 lib bdg

LC 2005-17919

A busy backhoe loader describes all the items it hauls off a lot and all the fun it has getting dirty while doing so

"With its saucy tone and dynamic color cartoon illustrations, this picture book exudes energy." SLJ

I'm mighty! [by] Kate & Jim McMullan. Joanna Cotler Bks. 2003 un il $17.99
Grades: PreK K 1 2   E
1. Tugboats -- Fiction
ISBN 0-06-009290-4

LC 2002-7948

A little tugboat shows how he can bring big ships into the harbor even though he is small

"The tugboat that narrates this picture book tells his story with more than a splash of moxie. Strong ink drawings define the harbor setting from a variety of perspectives and show the emotions of the anthropomorphic figures of boats and trucks, while color brightens the scenes and heightens the drama." Booklist

Mama's kisses; Kate McMullan; Illustrated by Tao Nyeu. Dial Books for Young Readers 2017 40 p. (hardcover) $16.99
Grades: PreK K   E
1. Stories in rhyme 2. Jungle animals -- Fiction 3. Bedtime -- Fiction 4. Mother-child relationship -- Fiction
ISBN 9780525428329

LC 2015049504

In this book, by Kate McMullan, Illustrated by Tao Nyeu, "it's bedtime in the jungle, but baby panda, elephant, orangutan, and leopard are nowhere to be found. Their mamas set out to look for their wayward little ones, calling them to bed with a soft lullaby. But look! The baby animals are crawling, creeping, hiding, and giggling, playfully staying just one step ahead of their loving mamas." (Publisher's note)

"McMullan's rhymes are spot on in every way, and despite spiky moments of mischief, the overall impression is comforting and lulling.: Pub Wkly

★ **Pearl** and Wagner: one funny day. Dial Books for Young Readers 2009 40p (Dial easy-to-read) $14.99
Grades: K 1 2   E
1. School stories 2. Mice -- Fiction 3. Animals -- Fiction 4.

Rabbits -- Fiction 5. April Fools' Day -- Fiction
ISBN 978-0-8037-3085-4; 0-8037-3085-3

LC 2008007699

ALA ALSC Geisel Award Honor Book (2010)

April Fools' Day is not a happy one for Wagner the mouse because his best friend, Pearl the rabbit, and other children and adults at school keep tricking him.

"Alley's expressive ink-and-watercolor illustrations portray Wagner's shifting emotions with clarity and finesse." Booklist

Other titles about Pearl and Wagner are:

Pearl and Wagner: two good friends (2003)
Pearl and Wagner: three secrets (2004)
Pearl and Wagner: four eyes (2010)
Pearl and Wagner: five days till summer (2012)

McNamara, Margaret

The **apple** orchard riddle; Margaret McNamara; pictures by G. Brian Karas. Schwartz & Wade 2013 40 p. $15.99

Grades: K 1 2   E
1. Apples -- Fiction 2. Field trips -- Fiction 3. Riddles -- Fiction 4. School field trips -- Fiction
ISBN 0375847448; 9780375847448; 9780375957444

LC 2011008742

This book, by Margaret McNamara and illustrated by G. Brian Karas, is "about a school trip to an apple orchard! The students learn a lot about apples and apple orchards--including how apples are harvested, how cider is made, and what the different varieties of apples are--while trying to solve a riddle. The book also celebrates how some children learn differently than others." (Publisher's note)

How many seeds in a pumpkin? illustrated by G. Brian Karas. Schwartz & Wade Books 2007 un il $14.99

Grades: K 1 2   E
1. School stories 2. Size -- Fiction 3. Pumpkin -- Fiction 4. Counting -- Fiction
ISBN 978-0-375-84014-2; 0-375-84014-1; 978-0-375-94014-9 lib bdg; 0-375-94014-6 lib bdg

LC 2006-16866

Charlie, the smallest child in his first grade class, is amazed to discover that of the three pumpkins his teacher brings to school, the tiniest one has the most seeds.

"Karas's characteristic watercolor illustrations done in a fall palette depict a diverse, modern classroom full of warm and humorous details. . . . This enjoyable story, sprinkled with math and science lessons, should be a first-purchase consideration." SLJ

The **three** little aliens and the big bad robot; written by Margaret McNamara; illustrated by Mark Fearing. Schwartz & Wade Books 2011 un il $16.99; lib bdg $19.99

Grades: PreK K 1 2   E
1. Robots -- Fiction 2. Siblings -- Fiction 3. Extraterrestrial beings -- Fiction 4. Outer space -- Exploration -- Fiction
ISBN 978-0-375-86689-0; 0-375-86689-2; 978-0-375-96689-7 lib bdg; 0-375-96689-7 lib bdg

LC 2010050153

Three aliens set off to find a new planet for themselves but soon Bork and Gork have forgotten all of their mother's good advice and only Nklxwcyz builds a home safe enough to withstand the Big Bad Robot.

"With its broad humor and a knowing wink to folktale conventions, this delightful reworking of 'The Three Little Pigs' has potential to become a crowd-pleasing favorite. . . . Fearing's hand-drawn cartoon illustrations rendered digitally with collage techniques offer bugeyed, green aliens and an enjoyable mix of science and playful details." SLJ

McPhail, David M.

Baby Pig Pig talks; David McPhail. Charlesbridge 2014 14 p. color illustrations (board book) $6.95

Grades: PreK   E
1. Pigs -- Fiction 2. Animals -- Fiction 3. Board books for children 4. Board books 5. Speech -- Fiction
ISBN 1580895972; 9781580895972; 9781607347033

LC 2013020489

In this children's book, "David McPhail takes readers back in time to when Pig Pig, star of the popular picture-book series, was a baby. Baby Pig Pig tries to copy his mother's speech as she points out the animals and objects around them, but nothing he says seems to come out right. What will Baby Pig Pig's first real word be?" (Publisher's note)

"McPhail's picture book hero Pig Pig is back—as a baby. As his mother pushes him around in his stroller, she introduces words for things they see... McPhail's watercolors exude warmth and quiet humor, and the aural sources for many of Baby Pig Pig's words ("Dinga" for tricycle, "Quacka" for duck) hint at how the gears are turning in his young porcine brain. PW

Baby Pig Pig walks; David McPhail. Charlesbridge 2014 14 p. color illustrations (board book) $6.95

Grades: PreK   E
1. Pigs -- Fiction 2. Walking -- Fiction 3. Board books for children 4. Board books
ISBN 1580895964; 9781580895965; 9781607347040

LC 2013020490

In this children's story, by David McPhail, "takes readers back in time to when Pig Pig, star of the popular picture-book series, was a baby. Baby Pig Pig is learning to walk. After a few rough starts, he makes his way out of the playpen and into the kitchen, right into his mother's waiting arms." (Publisher's note)

"A piglet toddler learns to walk. After growing bored, Baby Pig Pig learns to pull himself up, climb out of his playpen and walk out of the living room into the kitchen, all in the course of a day...Phail understands the simplicity required for a story for the youngest toddlers. Clarity and humor carry the day." Kirkus

Bad dog; by David McPhail. Holiday House 2014 32 p. (I like to read) (hardcover) $14.95

Grades: PreK K 1   E
1. Dogs -- Fiction 2. Bad behavior -- Fiction 3. Dogs -- Fiction 4. Bad behavior -- Fiction
ISBN 0823428524; 9780823428526

LC 2012038836

"Forgiveness and love triumph at the end of this . . . easy-to-read story of a family dog who is rarely on his best behavior," written and illustrated by David McPhail, and part of the I Like to Read series. (Publisher's note) The dog "irks the family cat, Kit, who one night escapes. Tom is threatened with eviction from the family but is redeemed when he helps the boy see where Kit is hiding." (Kirkus Reviews)

"Tom is a bad dog; he makes the narrator's mom, dad, and cat Kit mad. Just when "Dad says that Tom must go," Kit goes missing, and it's Tom to the rescue. Simple, repetitive text; mild tension; pen-and-ink and watercolor illustrations with plenty of details for kids to notice; and lots of clean white space make this a good pick for beginning readers." Horn Book

Bella loves Bunny; by David McPhail. Abrams Appleseed 2013 22 p. (alk. paper) $8.95

Grades: PreK   E
1. Toys -- Fiction 2. Picture books for children 3. Toys -- Fiction

4. Friendship -- Fiction
ISBN 1419705431; 9781419705434

LC 2012035411

This children's picture book is David McPhail's "companion title to 'Ben Loves Bear'" and "follows a similar day-in-the-life format." Here, a "young girl enjoys the company of her stuffed rabbit from sunup to sundown. . . . Bella and Bunny do some gardening, enjoy a picnic and play the piano." (Kirkus Reviews)

★ **Ben** loves Bear; by David McPhail. Abrams Appleseed 2013 22 p. $8.95

Grades: PreK E

1. Toys -- Fiction 2. Picture books for children 3. Teddy bears -- Fiction 4. Friendship -- Fiction 5. Teddy bears -- Fiction
ISBN 1419703862; 9781419703867

LC 2012003527

In this children's picture book by David McPhail, "Ben and his favorite stuffed toy are together from morning to night, and they seem to exist contentedly in their own little world. They wake up together and then, 'Ben has cereal. Bear has honey' at the kitchen table. They play hide-and-seek, Ben gets dressed while Bear watches, they play outdoors, Bear waits patiently while Ben bathes, and the clay winds down as the two snuggle up for bedtime, complete with a story." (School Library Journal)

"McPhail, in top form here, has created soft watercolors with rounded lines that adroitly capture Ben's toddler movements. The artist's use of full spreads and smaller visual vignettes spotlighted in hazy, round borders gives the simple, easy-reader-like text rhythm and balance. Already a gifted artist, McPhail proves here that he intrinsically understands what the youngest readers want and need." Kirkus

Big Brown Bear's up and down day; [written and illustrated by] David McPhail. Harcourt 2003 un il $16; pa $6

Grades: PreK K 1 2 E

1. Rats -- Fiction 2. Bears -- Fiction
ISBN 0-15-216407-3; 0-15-205684-X pa

LC 2002-15854

Big Brown Bear is visited by a rat who wants to use one of his slippers for a bed

"A warm and gentle story. . . . Beautiful watercolor and pen-and-ink paintings make the most of the size difference between the characters and help to create real personalities by capturing the emotions they experience." SLJ

Other titles about Big Brown Bear are:
Big Brown Bear goes to town (2006)
Big Brown Bear's birthday surprise (2007)

Big Pig and Little Pig; [by] David McPhail. Harcourt 2003 un il (Green light readers) $11.95; pa $3.95

Grades: PreK K 1 E

1. Pigs -- Fiction
ISBN 978-0-15-204818-1; 0-15-204818-9; 978-0-15-204857-0 pa; 0-15-204857-X pa

A reissue of the title first published 2001

Big Pig and Little Pig enjoy spending time together, though they take different approaches to the same task

"McPhail's signature illustrations fill each page as he once again successfully manages to transfer human emotions to his lovable cartoon pigs. Well-chosen vocabulary and repetition of words make this story a suitable choice for those just learning to read." SLJ

Boy, Bird, and Dog; by David McPhail. Holiday House 2011 il (I like to read picture book) $14.95

Grades: PreK K 1 2 E

1. Dogs -- Fiction 2. Birds -- Fiction 3. Tree houses -- Fiction
ISBN 978-0-8234-2346-0; 0-8234-2346-8

LC 2010029435

In this story for beginning readers, Boy, Bird, and Dog have lots of fun in their tree house.

"The story is told in the sparest of language. . . . It reads smoothly with a clear plot, likable characters and an interesting setting. . . . McPhail's signature watercolor-and-ink illustrations are large scale with soft edges. The action and characters are well defined and appealing." Kirkus

★ **Drawing** lessons from a bear; [by] David McPhail. Little, Brown 2000 un il $14.95

Grades: PreK K 1 E

1. Bears -- Fiction 2. Artists -- Fiction
ISBN 0-316-56345-5

LC 98-54966

A bear explains how he became an artist, first experimenting with simple drawings, then continuing to draw both things around him and things in his imagination. Includes tips for drawing

"This gentle story combines a humorous tone with warm, cozy watercolors to create inspiration for budding artists." SLJ

I promise; David McPhail. Little, Brown & Co 2017 40 p. color illustrations (hardcover) $16.99

Grades: PreK K E

1. Promises -- Fiction 2. Bears -- Fiction 3. Mother-child relationship -- Fiction 4. Bears -- Fiction 5. Mother and child -- Fiction
ISBN 9780316297875

LC 2015028882

In this book, by David McPhail, "when Baby Bear asks Mother Bear this important question, she promises her cub that she will feed him, play with him, and do everything she can to keep him safe. But Baby Bear has more questions: What happens if you break a promise? Can his mother promise that he will always be happy?" (Publisher's note)

Mole music; written and illustrated by David McPhail. Holt & Co. 1999 un il $15.95; pa $7.99

Grades: PreK K 1 2 E

1. Music -- Fiction 2. Violins -- Fiction 3. Moles (Animals) -- Fiction
ISBN 0-8050-2819-6; 0-8050-6766-3 pa

LC 98-21318

Feeling that something is missing in his simple life, Mole acquires a violin and learns to make beautiful, joyful music

"McPhail's delicate watercolor-and-ink illustrations work with the simple text to create a lyrical celebration of music and musicians." Booklist

No! Roaring Brook Press 2009 un il $16.95

Grades: K 1 2 3 E

1. War stories 2. Stories without words 3. Bullies -- Fiction
ISBN 978-1-59643-288-8; 1-59643-288-8

LC 2008054607

"In this dark, nearly wordless allegory, the power of a single word ripples outward, stopping a bully, an army, a war. . . . McPhail's . . . delicately tinted crosshatching gives poignancy to the violence the boy witnesses without minimizing it. The idea of taking effective action without fighting is a powerful one, and children and adults alike will find that McPhail's images linger." Publ Wkly

Pig Pig meets the lion; David McPhail. Charlesbridge 2012 32p.

Grades: PreK K   E
1. Lions -- Fiction 2. Children's stories 3. Picture books for children 4. Lion -- Fiction 5. Pigs -- Fiction 6. Friendship -- Fiction 7. English language -- Prepositions -- Fiction
ISBN 9781580893589

LC 2011009031

This book "starring . . . Pig Pig begins wordlessly on the pre-title page and continues onto the opening pages, as a lion escapes from a zoo and climbs up the tree outside Pig Pig's bedroom window. From there, the friendly lion enters Pig Pig's room, much to the delight of Pig Pig, who jumps '"out" of bed' and runs '"down" the stairs,' followed by the lion. Pig Pig and the lion continue their romp through the house, unbeknownst to his ever-distracted mother, and though Pig Pig longs to keep the lion, it must skedaddle when the zookeepers show up on the doorstep on the book's closing endpapers. There's a manifestly educational bent to this escapade, as prepositions are printed in boldfaced type." (Bulletin of the Center for Children's Books)

Pig Pig returns; [by] David McPhail. Charlesbridge 2011 un il lib bdg $15.95
Grades: PreK K 1   E
1. Pigs -- Fiction 2. Aunts -- Fiction 3. Uncles -- Fiction 4. Vacations -- Fiction 5. Automobile travel -- Fiction
ISBN 978-1-58089-356-5; 1-58089-356-2

LC 2010023528

Initially reluctant to leave his mother and cat, Pig Pig spends his summer vacation road tripping with his Aunt Wilma and Uncle Fred across the country in their teal-green camper.
"The line-and-watercolor art is drawn with sweetness and humor. Many kids (and adults) will see their mixed feelings about travel here." Booklist

★ **Pigs** aplenty, pigs galore! [by] David McPhail. Dutton Children's Bks. 1993 un il hardcover o.p. pa $6.99
Grades: PreK K 1 2   E
1. Stories in rhyme 2. Pigs -- Fiction
ISBN 0-525-45079-3; 0-14-055313-4 pa

LC 92-27986

"The rhyme is bouncy enough, but it's the pictures that will have parents and kids howling. Using deep watercolors set against a black background, McPhail presents a magnificent group of porkers, whose capacity for costumes and capers is truly wondrous." Booklist
Other titles about the pigs are:
Pigs ahoy! (1995)
Those can-do pigs (1996)

★ **Sylvie** & True; [by] David McPhail. Farrar, Straus, & Giroux 2007 31p il lib bdg $15
Grades: PreK K 1 2   E
1. Snakes -- Fiction 2. Rabbits -- Fiction 3. Friendship -- Fiction
ISBN 978-0-374-37364-1 lib bdg; 0-374-37364-7 lib bdg

LC 2006048979

In four vignettes, Sylvie the rabbit and her friend True, a giant water snake, share a small apartment in a big city, cook, go bowling, and have a good time together
The scenarios are "simple . . . occasioning affectionate dialogue and terrific sight gags. . . . [This is a] charmer." Publ Wkly

The **teddy** bear; written and illustrated by David McPhail. Holt & Co. 2002 un il $15.95; pa $7.99
Grades: PreK K 1 2   E
1. Teddy bears -- Fiction 2. Homeless persons -- Fiction
ISBN 0-8050-6414-1; 0-8050-7882-7 pa

LC 2001-1500

"By accident a boy leaves his beloved bear in a diner. A homeless man finds it in the garbage and loves the bear as much as the boy did. Then one day the boy sees the bear on a park bench and joyfully grabs it. But when he recognizes the lonely man's sorrow at losing his friend, the child returns the toy. . . . It works because McPhail's beautiful soft-toned watercolor pictures with detailed ink cross-hatching tell the elemental story of shelter and love through the child's eyes." Booklist

Waddles; by David McPhail. Abrams Books for Young Readers 2011 un il $15.95
Grades: PreK K 1 2   E
1. Ducks -- Fiction 2. Raccoons -- Fiction 3. Friendship -- Fiction
ISBN 0-8109-8415-6; 978-0-8109-8415-8

LC 2010023699

Waddles, a very plump and furry raccoon, helps his best friend Emily, a duck, hatch and raise her ducklings, and discovers what makes him truly happy.
"McPhail's ink-and-watercolor illustrations elevate the familiar story of mismatched, devoted friends, coaxing expertly drawn emotion from his endearing characters." Booklist

Water boy; [by] David McPhail. Abrams Books for Young Readers 2007 un il $15.95
Grades: PreK K 1 2   E
1. Magic -- Fiction 2. Water -- Fiction
ISBN 978-0-8109-1784-2; 0-8109-1784-X

LC 2006013578

Fascinated by the fact that humans are made mostly of water, a boy develops an unusual relationship with it once he stops being afraid.
"Beautifully written, illustrated, and designed, this small gem of a book calls to be opened, touched, and read from its texturally and visually appealing cover . . . to the rich, color-drenched pictures of the real and the fantastic inside." SLJ

Weezer changes the world; [by] David McPhail. Beach Lane Books 2009 un il $15.99
Grades: PreK K 1   E
1. Dogs -- Fiction
ISBN 978-1-4169-9000-0; 1-4169-9000-3

LC 2009005537

After an ordinary puppyhood, Weezer develops extraordinary skills that make him a major influence in the world.
"McPhail's amusing tale will inspire young children to consider how they can make the world a better place, and his droll ink-and-watercolor illustrations reinforce the book's simple but powerful message." Booklist

McQuinn, Anna

★ **Leo** loves baby time; Anna McQuinn; illustrated by Ruth Hearson. 1st U.S. edition Charlesbridge 2014 24 p. (reinforced for library use) $9.95 E
1. Play -- Fiction 2. Infants -- Fiction 3. Play -- Fiction 4. Babies -- Fiction 5. Infants -- Fiction 6. Play groups -- Fiction
ISBN 1580896650; 9781580896658; 9781607346654

LC 2013004292

In this children's picture book, "Leo . . . attends a baby program with his mother. He and his fellow sitting-up babes enjoy singing and playing on their grown-ups' laps, as well as exploring books and toys. The single- and double-page spreads include one or two sentences describing the action written in a bold, black type. . . . The setting of this program is left unclear, but it could easily be a public library or a community center in a very diverse neighborhood." (Kirkus Reviews)

Lola at the library; [by] Anna McQuinn; illustrated by Rosalind Beardshaw. Charlesbridge 2006 un il lib bdg $15.95; pa $6.95
Grades: PreK K 1 2   **E**
1. Libraries -- Fiction 2. Books and reading -- Fiction
ISBN 978-1-58089-113-4 lib bdg; 1-58089-113-6 lib bdg; 978-1-58089-142-4 pa; 1-58089-142-X pa
LC 2005019620
Published in the United Kingdom with title: Layla loves the library
Every Tuesday Lola and her mother visit their local library to return and check out books, attend story readings, and share a special treat
"Simple text and large, bright acrylic illustrations of this engaging African-American child make this selection just right for sharing" SLJ
"Another title about Lola is:
Lola loves stories (2010)

My friend Jamal; by Anna McQuinn; illustrated by Ben Frey. Annick 2008 un il (My friend) lib bdg $17.95; pa $8.95
Grades: K 1 2 3   **E**
1. Friendship -- Fiction 2. Immigrants -- Fiction 3. Africans -- United States -- Fiction
ISBN 978-1-55451-123-5 lib bdg; 1-55451-123-2 lib bdg; 978-1-55451-122-8 pa; 1-55451-122-4 pa
"Joseph describes his friendship with Jamal, a boy whose family immigrated to the United States from Somalia. . . . He discusses their similarities . . . as well as their differences. . . . The lively, brightly colored collages consist of original photographs of the main characters and stock photos of food or objects with thickly painted outlines and accents added. Both text and pictures project an energetic, friendly tone." SLJ

My friend Mei Jing; text by Anna McQuinn; artwork by Ben Frey; photography by Irvin Cheung. Annick Press 2009 un il (My friend) $17.95; pa $8.95
Grades: K 1 2 3   **E**
1. Friendship -- Fiction 2. African Americans -- Fiction 3. Chinese Americans -- Fiction
ISBN 978-1-55451-153-2; 1-55451-153-4; 978-1-55451-152-5 pa; 1-55451-152-6 pa
"In this large, colorful book, a Nigerian-American second-grader tells the story of her best friend from school, who is Chinese-American. The girls share a love of arts and crafts, dressing up, and a desire to become veterinarians. Monifa describes aspects of Mei Jing's culture. . . . The story's authentic voice comes from simple declarative sentences. . . . The brightly colored collages combine photographs of the girls' heads and hands with their cartoon bodies and depict them as they work with clay in arts and crafts at school or walk through an outdoor market with Mei Jing's grandma." SLJ

The **sleep** sheep; [by] Anna McQuinn and [illustrated by] Hannah Shaw. Chicken House 2010 un il $17.99
Grades: PreK K 1   **E**
1. Sheep -- Fiction 2. Sleep -- Fiction 3. Bedtime -- Fiction
ISBN 978-0-545-23145-9; 0-545-23145-0
LC 2009051481
When Sylvie cannot fall asleep and her mother suggests that she try counting sheep, the sheep do not cooperate.
"The cartoon pen-and-ink drawings paint vivid scenes of Sylvie's imagination and are flush with fun details. Readers will linger over each page. . . . The Sleep Sheep moves along at a rapid clip and with enough humor to be successful read-aloud." SLJ

Meade, Holly
★ **If** I never forever endeavor. Candlewick Press 2011 un il $15.99

Grades: PreK K 1 2   **E**
1. Birds -- Fiction 2. Flight -- Fiction
ISBN 978-0-7636-4071-2; 0-7636-4071-9
LC 2010-39182
"To fly or not to fly is the question for a little bird weighing the pros and cons of launching into the unknown. . . . Meade effectively uses rhyme . . . onomatopoeia . . . and repetition to accentuate the fledgling's inner conflict. . . . Stunning collages of textured linoleum block prints and watercolors span double-page spreads. . . . An irresistible invitation to test those wings and fly." Kirkus

Inside, inside, inside; written and illustrated by Holly Meade. Marshall Cavendish 2005 un il $16.95
Grades: PreK K 1 2   **E**
1. Games -- Fiction 2. Siblings -- Fiction
ISBN 0-7614-5125-0
LC 2004-19321
Noah and Jenny play a game in which they place one item inside another, over and over, until they place it all in the shower, then imagine and draw the shower inside the house, inside the neighborhood, and all the way to the solar system
"Meade cheerfully mixes cut-paper collage and watercolor, and sprinkles many homey details into the large and small scenes. . . . The messy game is fun, and the concept draws a useful lesson from creative play." SLJ

John Willy and Freddy McGee. Marshall Cavendish 1998 un il hardcover o.p. pa $5.95
Grades: PreK K 1 2   **E**
1. Guinea pigs -- Fiction
ISBN 0-7614-5033-5; 0-7614-5143-9 pa
LC 97-50362
Two guinea pigs escape from their safe but boring cage and have an adventure in the tunnels of the family's pool table
"Zesty cut-paper collages track all of the details of this funny outing." SLJ

Meadows, Michelle
Hibernation station; illustrated by Kurt Cyrus. Simon and Schuster Books for Young Readers 2010 un il $16.99
Grades: PreK K 1 2   **E**
1. Stories in rhyme 2. Sleep -- Fiction 3. Animals -- Fiction
ISBN 978-1-4169-3788-3; 1-4169-3788-9
LC 2008042141
"The hibernation train, fashioned of hollow logs, is filled with all sorts of animals. . . . On its way to the station, it hits a few snags: crowded conditions, leakage from a stream, and a lack of snacks and pillows. As the snow falls heavier and heavier, the bears in charge manage to get everyone squared away. . . . The enjoyable rhyming text provides the perfect platform for the wonderful illustrations that accompany it. Cyrus blends realistic depictions of the animals with just the right anthropomorphic touches." SLJ

Piggies in pajamas; Michelle Meadows; illustrated by Ard Hoyt. 1st ed. Simon & Schuster Books for Young Readers 2012 32 p. col. ill. (hardcover) $15.99
Grades: PreK K 1   **E**
1. Stories in rhyme 2. Pigs -- Fiction 3. Bedtime -- Fiction 4. Pigs -- Fiction 5. Bedtime -- Fiction
ISBN 1416949828; 9781416949824
LC 2010024472
In this children's story, by Michelle Meadows, illustrated by Ard Hoyt, "after Mama has put her kids to bed, she settles in to make some phone calls. But she keeps hearing things from upstairs. Could her little

piggies be jumping on the bed or playing dress-up instead of sleeping? But every time Mama goes up to check on them, they are all tucked in . . . until the noises begin again!" (Publisher's note)

Piggies in the kitchen; illustrated by Ard Hoyt. Simon & Schuster 2011 un il $14.99

Grades: PreK K 1   E

1. Stories in rhyme 2. Pigs -- Fiction 3. Baking -- Fiction

ISBN 978-1-4169-3787-6; 1-4169-3787-0

LC 97-2156

"Five little porkers and their father wave Mama off one bright, sunny day as she leaves the house. Daddy goes to cut the grass while his children enthusiastically descend upon the kitchen. Rhyming couplets filled with onomatopoeia tell the tale of the frenetic piglets making a mess plus a pleasant surprise for their mother. Pen-and-ink with watercolor illustrations in pastel hues humorously reveal the raucous goings-on." SLJ

Meddaugh, Susan

Cinderella's rat. Houghton Mifflin 1997 32p il $15; pa $5.95

Grades: PreK K 1 2   E

1. Fairy tales 2. Rats -- Fiction

ISBN 0-395-86833-5; 0-618-12540-X pa

LC 97-2156

One of the rats that was turned into a coachman by Cinderella's fairy godmother saves his rat sister's life, but an inept magician turns her into a girl who says "woof."

"The telling is a perfect example of a successful fractured fairy tale, with switched point of view. . . . The buoyant line drawings capture the whimsy." SLJ

★ **Harry** on the rocks. Houghton Mifflin 2003 32p il hardcover o.p. pa $6.95

Grades: PreK K 1 2   E

1. Shipwrecks -- Fiction

ISBN 0-618-27603-3; 0-618-84068-0 pa

LC 2002-9740

Harry and his boat become stranded on an island, where he discovers an egg which hatches into a strange lizard with wings

This is "a well-paced, cleanly wrought piece of storytelling. The cheerful watercolor and colored-pencil art has a sturdy matter-of-factness that makes the fantasy endearingly domestic." Bull Cent Child Books

Hog-eye. Houghton Mifflin 1995 32p il hardcover o.p. pa $5.95

Grades: PreK K 1 2   E

1. Pigs -- Fiction 2. Wolves -- Fiction

ISBN 0-395-74276-5; 0-395-93746-9 pa

LC 95-3951

Meddaugh presents a "story within a story as a piglet tells her family how she was caught by a wolf and nearly made into soup. Seeing that her captor is illiterate . . . she reads him a recipe that sends him on a wild wolf chase." SLJ

★ **Martha** speaks. Houghton Mifflin 1992 un il hardcover o.p. pa $6.99

Grades: PreK K 1 2   E

1. Dogs -- Fiction

ISBN 0-395-63313-3; 0-395-72952-1 pa

LC 91-48455

Problems arise when Martha, the family dog, learns to speak after eating alphabet soup

"Good-natured and amusing, with cheerful illustrations of the delightfully stocky Martha and her amazed family." Horn Book

"Other titles about Martha are:

Martha and Skits (2000) Martha and Skits out West (2011) Martha blah blah (1996) Martha calling (1994) Martha walks the dog (1998) Perfectly Martha (2004)

The **witch's** walking stick. Houghton Mifflin 2005 32p il $16

Grades: K 1 2 3   E

1. Magic -- Fiction 2. Witches -- Fiction

ISBN 0-618-52948-9

LC 2004-17509

When a witch loses her magic walking stick, which has been used over the years to grant hundreds of miserable wishes, she tricks a young girl into finding and returning it, with unexpected results.

"Illustrated with watercolor and ink in a style that will put readers in mind of William Steig, Meddaugh's dry, quirky tale of the little guy triumphing over adversity will have children smiling and cheering." SLJ

Medearis, Angela Shelf

Seven spools of thread; a Kwanzaa story. illustrated by Daniel Minter. Whitman, A. 2001 un il $15.95; pa $6.95

Grades: K 1 2 3   E

1. Ghana -- Fiction 2. Blacks -- Fiction 3. Kwanzaa -- Fiction 4. Brothers -- Fiction

ISBN 0-8075-7315-9; 0-8075-7316-7 pa

LC 00-8101

When they are given the seemingly impossible task of turning thread into gold, the seven Ashanti brothers put aside their differences, learn to get along, and embody the principles of Kwanzaa. Includes information on Kwanzaa, West African cloth weaving, and instructions for making a belt

"Well-paced, the story incorporates the Kwanzaa values without spelling them out too much. Minter's attractively composed, dramatic painted linocuts, with strong community images and lively, silhouetted figures, root the story in a sun-drenched, magical landscape." Booklist

Medina, Juana

1 big salad; A Delicious Counting Book. by Juana Medina. Viking Childrens Books 2016 32 p. color illustrations (hardback) $17.99

Grades: PreK K   E

1. Counting -- Fiction 2. Vegetables -- Fiction

ISBN 9781101999745

LC 2015036841

This book, by Juana Medina, is a "counting book. . . . One avocado deer saunters across the spread, two radish mice scurry by, until finally ten watercress seahorses swim onto the scene - all of the ingredients in one big salad!" (Publisher's note)

"Great for a storytime or one-on-one sharing, this vivacious book will inspire youngsters to explore the fruits and veggies in their own kitchens." SLJ

Medina, Meg

★ **Mango,** Abuela, and me; Meg Medina, Angela Dominguez. Candlewick Press 2015 32 p. color illustrations $15.99

Grades: PreK K 1 2   E

1. Parrots -- Fiction 2. Literacy -- Fiction 3. Grandparent-grandchild relationship -- Fiction 4. Interpersonal communication -- Fiction

ISBN 0763669008; 9780763669003

LC 2014951415

Pura Belpre Illustrator Honor Book (2016)

Pura Belpre Author Honor Book (2016)

In this children's story, by Meg Medina and illustrated by Angela Dominguez, when "Mia tries to share her favorite book with Abuela before they go to sleep and discovers that Abuela can't read the words inside. So while they cook, Mia helps Abuela learn English . . . , and Mia learns some Spanish too, but it's still hard for Abuela. . . . Then Mia sees a parrot in the pet-shop window and has the perfecto idea for how to help them all communicate a little better." (Publisher's note)

"In this tale, Medina blends Spanish and English words together as seamlessly as she blends the stories of two distinct cultures and generations. Dominguez's bright illustrations, done in ink, gouache, and marker, make the characters shine as bright as the rich story they depict. The glowing images of Mango, the parrot, a nearly silent star of the book, will win over audiences of all ages but the real magic is in the heartfelt tale of love." SLJ

Tia Isa wants a car. Candlewick Press 2011 un il $15.99
Grades: K 1 2   E
1. Aunts -- Fiction 2. Money -- Fiction 3. Automobiles -- Fiction 4. Family life -- Fiction 5. Hispanic Americans -- Fiction
ISBN 978-0-7636-4156-6; 0-7636-4156-1

LC 2010040128

"Always true to the child's viewpoint, the story shows how hard it is to be separated from loved ones and how long it can take to reunite, and the lively, unframed illustrations in pencil, watercolor, and ink extend the sense of warmth and longing." Booklist

Meinderts, Koos

On My Street; Koos Meinderts, illustrated by Annette Fienieg. Lemniscaat USA 2013 32 p. ill. (hardcover) $12.95
Grades: PreK K   E
1. Neighbors -- Fiction 2. Neighborhood -- Fiction
ISBN 1935954245; 9781935954248

In this children's book, by Koos Meinderts, illustrated by Annette Fienieg, characters created by the illustrator are presented in one story. "For every child born to one of her friends, Annette Fienieg used to make a colorfully decorated teeshirt, with a character you would fall in love with. Now it is time to introduce those creations--Mrs. McQueen Fifi LaPointe, Johnny Deck, Lightfingers Louie and more--to a wider audience." (Publisher's note)

Meisel, Paul

See me dig; by Paul Meisel. Holiday House 2013 32 p. (I like to read) (hardcover) $14.95
Grades: PreK K 1   E
1. Dogs -- Fiction 2. Pirates -- Fiction 3. Dogs -- Fiction
ISBN 0823427439; 9780823427437

LC 2012016549

This children's story, by Paul Meisel, is part of the "I Like to Read" series. "A crew of happy dogs dig merrily in the dirt. But the groundhogs, mice, and moles don't like it. The animals chase the dogs away to another digging spot. This time the dogs dig up a box--a treasure chest--from which ghostly pirates emerge. The dogs are on the run again!" (Publisher's note)

See me run. Holiday House 2011 un il $14.95
Grades: PreK K 1   E
1. Dogs -- Fiction 2. Parks -- Fiction
ISBN 978-0-8234-2349-1; 0-8234-2349-2

LC 2010029445

"Cartoon drawings done in acrylic ink, pen and colored pencils offer a variety of dog breeds; eyes are wide and tongues hang out in their expressive faces as they frolic through the pale green, grassy park. Formatted in a larger trim than the usual early reader, this imaginary rumpus is just right for beginners to successfully read and reread." Kirkus

Meisel, Peter

Stinky Spike the Pirate Dog; by Peter Meisel, illustrated by Paul Meisel. Bloomsbury USA 2016 80 p. $9.99

Grades: K 1 2   E
1. Dogs -- Fiction 2. Pirates -- Fiction
ISBN 1619637782; 9781619637788

In this book, by Peter Meisel, illustrated by Paul Meisel, "Meet Stinky Spike! . . . When this shipyard pup gets lost at sea, he's rescued by a crew of stinky pirates led by Captain Fishbeard. Spike must prove to the captain he can be a real pirate. Luckily, Stinky Spike has the best nose on the seven seas, and he uses it to sniff out all kinds of treasure. But what happens when Spike's sense of smell leads him to some very strange loot?" (Publisher's note)

"Though episodic rather than eventful, it's sure to entertain young readers transitioning to chapter books." Kirkus

Meister, Cari

Tiny's bath; illustrated by Rich Davis. Viking 1998 un il (Viking easy-to-read) hardcover o.p. pa $3.99
Grades: PreK K 1   E
1. Dogs -- Fiction 2. Baths -- Fiction
ISBN 0-670-87962-2; 0-14-130267-4 pa

LC 98-3844

Tiny is a very big dog who loves to dig, and when it is time for his bath, his owner has trouble finding a place to bathe him

"In this book for the least sophisticated beginning readers, each sentence appears on a single line, and only one sentence appears on a page. Illustrations mirror text, providing clues that support readers as they decipher both words and events. Add Tiny to the roll call of great dogs in children's literature." Horn Book Guide

Other titles about Tiny are:
Tiny goes camping (2006)
Tiny goes to the library (2000)
Tiny on the farm (2008)
Tiny the snow dog (2001)
When Tiny was tiny (1999)

Melanson, Luc

Topsy-Turvy Town. Tundra Books 2010 un il $17.95
Grades: PreK K   E
1. Imagination -- Fiction
ISBN 978-0-88776-920-7; 0-88776-920-9

Original French language edition published 2004 in Canada

A boy lives in a town where it rains broccoli that crunches when it lands on the tops of umbrellas, where police officers march to a very different beat, where you can go fishing in your living room or even juggle a wildcat before bedtime.

"This highly imaginative tale is told in simple text with outstanding illustrations. Round-headed humans and buildings with harlequin faces abound, as well as a menagerie of animals reminiscent of classic wooden toys." SLJ

Melling, David

Don't worry, Douglas! Tiger Tales 2011 il $12.95
Grades: PreK K 1   E
1. Hats -- Fiction 2. Bears -- Fiction 3. Gifts -- Fiction 4. Animals -- Fiction
ISBN 978-1-58925-106-9; 1-58925-106-7

"Douglas the bear loves the fuzzy orange hat that his father gives him, but when the hat snags on a branch, it turns into a 'long string of spaghetti.' Douglas's friends offer suggestions—the sheep try to wind it into a ball, a cow demonstrates how it can still be worn like a wig—but when it starts to rain, Douglas takes Rabbit's advice to tell his father the truth about what happened. Melling's artwork brims with physical comedy as he delivers his message about coming clean with sensitivity and good humor." Publ Wkly

"Another title about Douglas is:

Hugless Douglas (2010)

Hugless Douglas. Tiger Tales 2010 un il $15.95
Grades: PreK K 1　　　　　　　　　　　　　　　　　E
　1. Bears -- Fiction 2. Hugging -- Fiction
　ISBN 978-1-58925-098-7; 1-58925-098-2

"Melling gives new meaning to the phrase, 'a big bear hug' with this tale of a cub who sets off one morning in search of that special feeling he needs. A gigantic boulder is too heavy to hug and a tree trunk is too splintery. Douglas knows that a hug feels comfy, and he is not having an easy time locating one. Colorful illustrations enhance the humor." SLJ

Melmed, Laura Krauss

　Hurry! Hurry! Have you heard? illustrated by Jane Dyer. Chronicle Books 2008 un il $16.99
Grades: PreK K 1 2　　　　　　　　　　　　　　　　　E
　1. Stories in rhyme 2. Birds -- Fiction 3. Animals -- Fiction
　ISBN 978-0-8118-4225-9

　　　　　　　　　　　　　　　　　　　　LC 2007021062

A small bird, her heart filled with love, hurries from her perch above the manger to spread the news to creatures of the field and forest that a child, to whom all are precious, has been born.

"This contemporary-set Nativity story, featuring seasonally clad but otherwise realistic-looking animals, has energy and movement." Horn Book Guide

Meltzer, Lynn

　The **construction** crew; illustrated by Carrie Eko-Burgess. Henry Holt 2011 un il $12.99
Grades: PreK K　　　　　　　　　　　　　　　　　E
　1. Stories in rhyme 2. Tools -- Fiction 3. Trucks -- Fiction 4. Building -- Fiction 5. Construction equipment -- Fiction
　ISBN 978-0-8050-8884-7; 0-8050-8884-9

　　　　　　　　　　　　　　　　　　　　LC 2010039763

A construction crew tears down an old building and builds a new house in its place.

"Truck and construction fans will find an energetic exploration of both in this square-format volume. . . . Crisp, electric digital illustrations spotlight vehicles, construction equipment, and workers who resemble fleshed-out Lego characters. . . . The rhyming text offers variations on the same question ('Tons of dirt/ And lots of muck/ What do we need?/ DUMP TRUCK!'), . . . a narrative device that will have children shouting out the answers in no time." Publ Wkly

Menchin, Scott

　What if everything had legs? Candlewick Press 2010 un il $15.99
Grades: PreK K 1　　　　　　　　　　　　　　　　　E
　1. Imagination -- Fiction
　ISBN 978-0-7636-4220-4; 0-7636-4220-7

　　　　　　　　　　　　　　　　　　　　LC 2010038719

Feeling too tired to walk the rest of the way home, a little girl wonders why the house cannot have legs to come to her and her mother, then imagines what else would change if everything had legs.

"The simple text and wacky, hybrid illustrations of objects sprouting legs (and arms) combine for an entertaining read-aloud that will engage young children and stir up their own creative juices." SLJ

Meng, Cece

　I will not read this book; written by Cece Meng; illustrated by Joy Ang. Clarion Books 2011 32p il $15.99
Grades: K 1 2　　　　　　　　　　　　　　　　　E
　1. Books and reading -- Fiction
　ISBN 978-0-547-04971-7; 0-547-04971-4

　　　　　　　　　　　　　　　　　　　　LC 2010043175

A child adamantly refuses to read a book, regardless of the increasingly outrageous circumstances that might occur.

"Oh, yes, you will read this book. You'll be reeled in by the feisty, angular, frequently exciting digital illustrations, not to mention that confrontational title." Booklist

Merino, Gemma

　The **Cow** Who Climbed a Tree; by Gemma Merino. Albert Whitman & Co 2016 32 p. color illustrations $16.99
Grades: PreK K 1 2　　　　　　　　　　　　　　　　　E
　1. Cattle -- Fiction 2. Sisters -- Fiction
　ISBN 0807512982; 9780807512982

In this children's book, by Gemma Merino, "Tina isn't like the other cows. She believes that the sky is the limit and that everything is possible. But her sisters aren't convinced—and when Tina tells them she has climbed a tree and met a dragon, they decide that her nonsense has gone too far. Off they go into the woods to find her and soon discover a world of surprises!" (Publisher's note)

"An outrageously silly story that celebrates the value of creative thinking and taking chances." Kirkus

Merlin, Christophe

　Under the hood; [by] Merlin. Candlewick Press 2011 il $14.99
Grades: PreK　　　　　　　　　　　　　　　　　E
　1. Animals -- Fiction 2. Automobiles -- Fiction
　ISBN 978-0-7636-5535-8; 0-7636-5535-X

　　　　　　　　　　　　　　　　　　　　LC 2010042743

A mechanic welcomes the reader to his garage where he will try to fix his car, but first needs help in finding his friends, Mouse, Crocodile, and Bird under lift-up flaps and fold-out pages.

"The large, humorous illustrations are done in vivid hues set against cream-colored backgrounds. Children will delight in the mystery of what lies beneath all those flaps." SLJ

Meschenmoser, Sebastian

　Pug Man's 3 Wishes; by Sebastian Meschenmoser. NorthSouth 2016 48 p. color illustrations $16.95
Grades: K 1 2 3 4　　　　　　　　　　　　　　　　　E
　1. Dogs -- Fiction 2. Emotions -- Fiction 3. Humorous fiction -- Fiction
　ISBN 0735842612; 9780735842618

"Sebastian Mechenmoser's Mr. Pug 's 3 Wishes is a hilarious remedy for a bad day! Grumpy Mr. Pug is having a terrible day. But when he's offered 3 wishes by an overly eager fairy, what he wishes for is very surprising and will leave little listeners laughing and cheering for him." (Publisher's note)

"His modest wishes, especially the unexpected and curmudgeonly third one, will delight readers. Rarely has abject misery been so fun." Pub Wkly

　★ **Waiting** for winter. Kane Miller 2009 un il $15.95
Grades: PreK K 1 2　　　　　　　　　　　　　　　　　E
　1. Snow -- Fiction 2. Forest animals -- Fiction
　ISBN 978-1-935279-04-4; 1-935279-04-1

　　　　　　　　　　　　　　　　　　　　LC 2009-922111

Deer has told Squirrel how wonderful snow is. But Squirrel gets bored with the wait. With his friend Hedgehog they pass the time by singing and waking Bear. Soon things are falling from the sky, but they aren't snow. But eventually they find what snow is.

"The illustrations are deftly drawn in colored pencils, complete with sketching lines that give the renderings depth and maturity. . . . This is a beautiful title to share with children on a lap or with a small group." SLJ

Meserve, Jessica

Bedtime without Arthur; illustrated by Jessica Meserve. Andersen Press USA 2009 un il $16.95
Grades: K 1 2   **E**
    1. Fear -- Fiction 2. Bedtime -- Fiction 3. Siblings -- Fiction 4. Teddy bears -- Fiction
    ISBN 978-0-7613-5497-0; 0-7613-5497-2

Arthur, Bella's very special bear, protects her from monsters while she sleeps, but when Arthur goes missing one night, Bella makes an interesting discovery.

Meshon, Aaron

The **best** days are dog days; by Aaron Meshon. Dial Books for Young Readers, an imprint of Penguin Group (USA) 2016 40 p. color illustrations (hardcover : acid-free paper) $16.99
Grades: PreK K   **E**
    1. Dogs -- Fiction 2. Play -- Fiction 3. Girls -- Fiction
    ISBN 9780525428176

            LC 2015008057

This children's story, by Aaron Meshon, follows "a little girl and her pet French bulldog.... When his family sets out to explore the neighborhood, one puppy is eager to join in the fun! He gets to do everything his sister does—with his own added flair, of course. Together they eat ..., bathe ..., and play.... Side by side, they enjoy the same things, each in their own way. And when the long day comes to an end, both settle down for a restful sleep." (Publisher's note)

"With brightly colored images, playful visual clues scattered throughout, large-font sentences embellished with splashes of eye-catching hand-lettering, and a delightful friendship at its heart, this would be a great choice for a group story time." Booklist

★ **Take** me out to the Yakyu; Aaron Meshon. Atheneum Books for Young Readers 2013 40 p. (hardcover) $15.99
Grades: PreK K 1   **E**
    1. Picture books for children 2. Baseball -- Fiction 3. Grandfathers -- Fiction 4. Japan -- Fiction 5. Racially mixed people -- Fiction
    ISBN 1442441771; 9781442441774; 9781442441781

            LC 2011050907

In this children's book by Aaron Meshon readers can "join one little boy and his family for two ballgames--on opposite sides of the world! Come along with one little boy and his grandfathers, one in America and one in Japan, as he learns about baseball and its rich, varying cultural traditions." (Publisher's note)

Tools rule! by Aaron Meshon. Atheneum Books for Young Readers 2014 40 p. (hardcover) $16.99
Grades: PreK K 1 2   **E**
    1. Tools -- Fiction
    ISBN 1442496010; 9781442496019

            LC 2013009361

This children's book, by Aaron Meshon, "features animated tool characters, each with its own individual traits. T Square rounds up a crew of tools to clean up a messy yard and build a tool shed. T Square and Pencil draft plans; Wheelbarrow gathers materials; Saw saws Wood; Drill drills Screws; Level inspects; Glue glues on Roof Tiles, etc. Together, they work hard, and when the project is finished, they go to sleep in an organized toolshed feeling satisfied." (Kirkus Reviews)

"A diligent T-square rallies its fellow tools to get to work building a shed. One helpful illustration shows the tools, strewn about the lawn, but with captionlike arrows to identify what's what. Meshon's lively text is full of tool-centric wordplay; a detailed note describes his process for creating the digitally colored mixed-media illustrations of smiley tools with a can-do attitude." Horn Book

Messer, Claire

★ **Grumpy** pants; words & pictures by Claire Messer. Albert Whitman & Co 2016 32 p. color illustrations (hardback) $16.99
Grades: PreK K 1   **E**
    1. Baths -- Fiction 2. Bedtime -- Fiction 3. Penguins -- Fiction 4. Mood (Psychology) -- Fiction 5. Baths -- Fiction 6. Bedtime -- Fiction 7. Mood (Psychology) -- Fiction
    ISBN 9780807530757

            LC 2016005800

This picture book, by Claire Messer, asks "Have you ever had a grumpy day and not known why? Penguin is having a grumpy day like that. No matter what he does, he just can't shake it! Sometimes the only thing left to do is wash the grumpy day away and start over. The simple text and lively illustrations are the perfect cure for even the grumpiest of days." (Publisher's note)

"Penguin's ability to bring himself to a more content and optimistic place without any outside or parental help offers concrete, empowering ideas for readers who might be wearing their own grumpy outfits." Pub Wkly

Metaxas, Eric

It's time to sleep, my love (a lullabye) illustrated by Nancy Tillman. Feiwel and Friends 2008 un il $16.95; bd bk $7.99
Grades: PreK K   **E**
    1. Lullabies 2. Stories in rhyme 3. Animals -- Fiction 4. Bedtime -- Fiction
    ISBN 978-0-312-38371-8; 0-312-38371-1; 978-0-312-67336-9 bd bk; 0-312-67336-1 bd bk

            LC 2008028550

At bedtime, birds, bees, fishes, and other creatures urge their tired children to go to sleep

"Mextaxas' words set the sleepy-time tone with lulling sounds, repetition, and rhythms in short lines that read like poetry.... Tillman combines vibrantly colored photos and textured paintings in digital collages of the detailed animals." Booklist

Meyer, Susan Lynn

★ **New** shoes; by Susan Lynn Meyer; illustrated by Eric Velasquez. Holiday House 2015 40 p. col. ill. (hardcover) $16.95
Grades: K 1 2 3   **E**
    1. Shoes -- Fiction 2. Picture books for children 3. African Americans -- Segregation -- Fiction 4. Segregation -- Fiction 5. Discrimination -- Fiction
    ISBN 0823425282; 9780823425280

            LC 2012019673

NAACP Image Award Nominee: Outstanding Literary Work- Children (2016)

This history story, by Susan Lynn Meyer and illustrated by Eric Velasquez, is "set in the [American] South during the time of segregation. This lushly illustrated picture book brings the civil rights era to life for contemporary readers as two young girls find an inventive way to foil Jim Crow laws." (Publisher's note)

"The tale stands out from other stories of children overcoming obstacles, emphasizing how resistance and transformation can be found in the smallest of actions. An author's note gives readers background on Jim Crow and the Civil Rights and Voting Rights acts." Kirkus

Meyers, Susan

Bear in the air; illustrated by Amy Bates. Abrams Books for Young Readers 2010 il $15.95
Grades: PreK K 1   **E**
    1. Stories in rhyme 2. Adventure fiction 3. Teddy bears -- Fiction 4. Lost and found possessions -- Fiction
    ISBN 978-0-8109-8398-4; 0-8109-8398-2

When a teddy bear is lost by the child who loves him, the bear begins an adventurous journey to get back home again.

"Words are almost unnecessary as the pencil and watercolor illustrations, in appealing beach tones of blue, brown, and tan, tell the story of the lost, bewildered-looking bear and his surprising journey. . . . A sweet story that will capture the imaginations of young children." SLJ

★ **Everywhere** babies; illustrated by Marla Frazee. Harcourt 2001 un il $16; bd bk $6.95

Grades: PreK K 1   **E**
1. Infants 2. Stories in rhyme
ISBN 0-15-202226-0; 0-15-205315-8 bd bk

LC 99-6288

Describes babies and the things they do from the time they are born until their first birthday

"The rhythmic rhyming text hums along pleasantly. . . . The many moods, expressions, and body movements of babies are faithfully, gracefully rendered in the pencil drawings, and brightened with watercolors in rather muted hues." Booklist

Michalak, Jamie
Joe and Sparky go to school; Jamie Michalak, illustrated by Frank Remkiewicz. Candlewick Press 2013 48 p. (Joe and Sparky) $15.99

Grades: K 1 2 3   **E**
1. School stories 2. Friendship -- Fiction 3. Giraffe -- Fiction 4. Turtles -- Fiction 5. High interest-low vocabulary books
ISBN 076366278X; 9780763662783

LC 2012943657

In this children's book by Jamie Michalak, "Joe Giraffe and Sparky, a turtle, live in Safari Land, 'the famous cageless zoo.' In four chapters they see a school bus and climb on to satisfy their curiosity; end up at school with the 'noisy short people'; try to blend in but the 'magic pond' (the toilet) provides some silliness; and Joe attempts to get a star for good work since Sparky has earned several. The animals experience the ups and downs of friendship." (School Library Journal)

Joe and Sparky, superstars! illustrated by Frank Remkiewicz. Candlewick Press 2011 37p il $15.99

Grades: K 1 2   **E**
1. Turtles -- Fiction 2. Giraffes -- Fiction 3. Friendship -- Fiction
ISBN 978-0-7636-4578-6; 0-7636-4578-8

LC 2009006425

When Joe the giraffe and his friend Sparky, a turtle, see a television talent show, Joe tries to find Sparky's talent so that they can compete.

"The font is large and at times changes in appearance to reflect emotion and sound. Michalak and Remkiewicz have written another enjoyable book about two friends who bring out the best in each other." SLJ

Michelson, Richard
Across the alley; [by] Richard Michelson; illustrated by E. B. Lewis. G. P. Putnam's Sons 2006 un il $16.99

Grades: K 1 2 3   **E**
1. Jews -- Fiction 2. Baseball -- Fiction 3. Friendship -- Fiction 4. Violinists -- Fiction 5. African Americans -- Fiction
ISBN 0-399-23970-7

LC 2005032656

Jewish Abe's grandfather wants him to be a violinist while African-American Wille's father plans for him to be a great baseball pitcher, but it turns out that the two boys are more talented when they switch hobbies.

"The poignancy of two boys who can be friends only at night is revealed brilliantly in both text and rich watercolor art." SLJ

Busing Brewster; illustrated by R. G. Roth. Knopf 2010 un il $16.99

Grades: 1 2 3   **E**
1. School stories 2. African Americans -- Fiction 3. School integration -- Fiction
ISBN 978-0-375-83334-2; 0-375-83334-X; 978-0-375-93334-9 lib bdg; 0-375-93334-4 lib bdg

LC 2009-22626

Bused across town to a school in a white neigborhood of Boston in 1974, a young African American boy named Brewster describes his first day in first grade. Includes historical notes on the court-ordered busing.

"This title will make a good addition for libraries that want to strengthen their picture book collection by adding material on this period in the African-American experience. " Libr Media Connect

Miché, Mary
Nature's patchwork quilt; understanding habitats. by Mary Miché; illustrated by Consie Powell. Dawn Publications 2012 32 p.

Grades: 1 2 3   **E**
1. Nature 2. Habitat (Ecology) 3. Natural history 4. Nature study -- Activity programs
ISBN 1584691697; 9781584691693; 9781584691709

LC 2011048064

This children's book by Mary Miché "presents [natural] habitats while introducing environmental vocabulary: interdependence, niche, food chain, adaptations, biodiversity, deforestation and domestication, among others. . . . [W]atercolor quilts of different patterns dominate Powell's double-page compositions. A large center scene is surrounded by tiny blocks that each house lifelike depictions of the plants and animals that make up a habitat: forest, desert, ocean, rainforest, etc." (Kirkus)

Includes bibliographical references

Micklethwait, Lucy
★ **I** spy: an alphabet in art; devised & selected by Lucy Micklethwait. Greenwillow Bks. 1992 un il $19.99; pa $10.99

Grades: K 1 2 3   **E**
1. Alphabet 2. Art appreciation
ISBN 0-688-11679-5; 0-688-14730-5 pa

LC 91-42212

Presents objects for the letters of the alphabet through paintings by such artists as Magritte, Picasso, Botticelli, and Vermeer

"The author's stated intention of introducing young children to fine art, her choice of paintings, the handsome book design, and the quality of paper and reproduction take this beyond the usual alphabet book." Booklist

Other titles in this series are:
I spy a freight train: transportation in art (1996)
I spy a lion: animals in art (1994)
I spy colors in art (2007)
I spy shapes in art (2004)
I spy two eyes: numbers in art (1993)

Middleton, Julie
Are the dinosaurs dead, Dad? written by Julie Middleton; illustrated by Russell Ayto. Peachtree Publishers 2013 32 p. ill. (reinforced) $16.95

Grades: K 1 2   **E**
1. Museums -- Fiction 2. Dinosaurs -- Fiction 3. Father-child relationship -- Fiction
ISBN 156145690X; 9781561456901

LC 2012025716

"This story follows Dave and his dad to a natural history museum, where dinosaurs on exhibit come alive when Dad's back is turned, winking at Dave, tickling him, and attempting to snag a bite of his burger Dave's dad dismisses questions . . . with the classic parental response

'It's just your imagination.' But when a Tyrannosaurus rex follows the pair out of the exhibit and lets loose with an ear-splitting roar, Dad changes his mind at a dead run." (School Library Journal)

Miéville, China, 1972-

The **worst** breakfast; China Mieville, Zak Smith. Black Sheep/Akashic Books 2016 32 p. color illustrations (hardcover) $16.95
Grades: PreK K 1 2   E
> 1. Disgust -- Fiction 2. Breakfast -- Fiction
ISBN 9781617754869; 9781617755163; 9781617755170
LC 2016935094

In this children's story, by China Mieville, illustrated by Zak Smith, "two sisters sit down one morning and begin describing all of the really gross things that were in the worst breakfast they ever had, until all they can picture is a table piled sky-high with the weirdest, yuckiest, slimiest, slickest, stinkiest breakfast possible. And then they have the best breakfast ever . . . almost." (Publisher's note)

"A brilliant, original, infinitely rereadable book that can sit alongside Sendak and Dahl." Kirkus

Miles, Victoria

Old Mother Bear; by Victoria Miles; illustrated by Molly Bang. Chronicle Books 2007 un il $16.95
Grades: 1 2 3 4   E
> 1. Bears -- Fiction
ISBN 978-0-8118-5033-9; 0-8118-5033-1
LC 2006011651

A twenty-four-year-old grizzly bear gives birth to her last litter of cubs, then spends three years teaching them what they need to know to survive in their southern British Columbia home before they go off on their own. Includes facts about grizzlies and the Khutzeymateen Grizzly Bear Sanctuary.

"The detailed zoology facts are the gripping story in this realistic picture book, which is based on true events and illustrated in beautifully textured, closeup, oil-and-chalk artwork by . . . artist Bang." Booklist

Milgrim, David

Eddie gets ready for school. Cartwheel Books 2011 un il $8.99
Grades: PreK K 1   E
> 1. School stories 2. Mother-son relationship -- Fiction
ISBN 978-0-545-27329-9; 0-545-27329-3
LC 2010016779

As young Eddie goes through his checklist to get ready for school, his mother does not agree with all of his choices.

"Big, bold cartoons make their lighthearted tug-of-war the center of attention, as grinning Eddie sheepishly responds to the amended checklist. . . . Readers accustomed to chasing the bus with one shoe on will relate." Publ Wkly

Go, Otto, go! story and pictures by David Milgrim. Simon Spotlight 2016 32 p. color illustrations (hardcover) $16.99
Grades: PreK K 1   E
> 1. Robots -- Fiction 2. Rockets (Aeronautics) -- Fiction 3. Robots -- Fiction
ISBN 9781481467230; 9781481467247
LC 2015046177
Geisel Honor Book (2017)

In this book, by David Milgrim, "Otto the robot builds a spaceship. . . . See Otto work. Work, work, work on a spaceship to take him home. Since landing on Earth, Otto has made many friends, but what Otto wants most is to visit his family. Will Otto's spaceship take him up, up, up, so he can go, go, go?" (Publisher's note)

"When Otto looks up from the wreckage to see his jubilant friends and realizes he's 'looking at his home' and his found family, readers will

feel the complexity of his emotions. Welcome back, Otto. Glad you're here to stay." Kirkus

Other books about Otto are:
See Pip point (2003)
Swing, Otto, swing (2004)
See Santa nap (2004)

My dog, Buddy. Scholastic 2008 un il pa $3.99
Grades: K 1 2   E
> 1. Dogs -- Fiction 2. Family life -- Fiction
ISBN 978-0-545-03593-4 pa; 0-545-03593-7 pa
LC 2007-22795

Mom, Dad, and brother Pete all try to get Buddy to obey, but only one family member understands how to communicate with the mischievous canine.

"Digitally created art suggests line and watercolor in its smooth planes of color neatly bordered by slightly off-kilter lines. . . . Packed with pithy humor, sly irreverence, and rampant usefulness, this is a beginning reader's best friend." Bull Cent Child Books

★ **Santa** Duck. G.P. Putnam's Sons 2008 un il lib bdg $16.99
Grades: PreK K 1 2   E
> 1. Ducks -- Fiction 2. Animals -- Fiction 3. Christmas -- Fiction 4. Santa Claus -- Fiction
ISBN 978-0-399-25018-7; 0-399-25018-2
LC 2007-43162

When Nicholas Duck, wearing a Santa hat and coat he found on his doorstep, goes looking for Santa to tell him what he wants for Christmas, all the other animals mistake him for Mr. Claus.

"Nicholas's silliness and frustration will appeal to youngsters as will the simple message. Milgrim's charming digital ink and oil pastel illustrations use a successful mix of narrative text and cartoon balloons to move the story along at a brisk pace." SLJ

Another title about Santa Duck is:
Santa Duck and his merry helpers (2010)

Santa Duck and his merry helpers. G.P. Putnam's Sons 2010 un il $12.99
Grades: PreK K 1 2   E
> 1. Ducks -- Fiction 2. Christmas -- Fiction 3. Santa Claus -- Fiction
ISBN 978-0-399-25473-4; 0-399-25473-0

It's Christmastime, so Nicholas Duck puts on his Santa's helper suit and proudly starts gathering wish lists for Santa. But this year, Nicholas's little brothers and sister want to help.

"A multifaceted plot and some succinct lessons are skillfully conveyed in just a few pages, with the funny dialogue contained in speech balloons within the holiday-bright, cartoon-style illustrations." Kirkus

Milich, Zoran

City 1 2 3. Kids Can Press 2005 un il $15.95; pa $6.95
Grades: PreK K 1 2   E
> 1. Counting
ISBN 1-55337-540-8; 1-55453-163-2 pa

Photographs of objects such as skyscrapers, bags of leaves, fire trucks, and taxis illustrate numbers from 1 to 10

"An excellent, well-constructed concept book. . . . The superb pictures feature not only the required number of items, but the corresponding numeral as well." SLJ

City colors. Kids Can Press 2004 un il $14.95; pa $5.95
Grades: PreK K 1 2   E
> 1. Color
ISBN 1-55337-542-4; 1-55337-981-0 pa

This is a collection of color photographs of objects found in cities such as a red bus, a blue warehouse wall, and a yellow highway cone, a green swing, an orange cylindrical curb block, and a purple playground stool.

This is "a dazzling . . . concept book. . . . Precise partial photos inspire speculation on each verso with the recto revealing the complete image." SLJ

Millen, C. M.

The **ink** garden of brother Theophane; illustrated by Andrea Wisnewski. Charlesbridge 2010 un il $17.95

Grades: 1 2 3 4   E
   1. Stories in rhyme 2. Monks -- Fiction 3. Middle Ages -- Fiction 4. Illumination of books and manuscripts -- Fiction
   ISBN 978-1-58089-179-0; 1-58089-179-9

In medieval Ireland, Theophane's boredom with his duties as a scribe distracts the other monks, but when he is sent to the kitchens he discovers that he can make inks of many colors from plants, allowing the others to illustrate their work. Includes facts about the history of monasteries, scriptoriums, and illuminated manuscripts.

"Written in rhythmic, rhyming, and rear-rhyming verse, the simple story unfolds in a satisfying way, accompanied by short poems inspired by the writings of Irish monks. The richly detailed illustrations were created by using a paper-cut design to print bold, black lines and brightening the pictures with watercolors." Booklist

Miller, Pat

★ **Sophie's** squash; Pat Zietlow Miller; [illustrations by] Anne Wilsdorf. Schwartz & Wade 2013 40 p. $16.99

Grades: PreK K 1 2   E
   1. Picture books for children 2. Friendship -- Fiction 3. Squashes -- Fiction
   ISBN 0307978966; 9780307978967; 9780307978974
                         LC 2012006438

In this children's picture book, when "Sophie selects a butternut squash at the farmer's market, her parents assume they will be having it for dinner. Sophie, however, quashes that plan by adopting the vegetable as her new best friend and naming her Bernice . . . . Despite gentle prodding to relinquish Bernice before she rots, Sophie brings her deteriorating pal to the library and somersaults with her in the yard." (Publishers Weekly)

Another book about Sophie is:

Sophie's squash go to school (2016)

Squirrel's New Year's resolution; illustrated by Kathi Ember. Albert Whitman & Co. 2010 un il $16.99

Grades: PreK K 1   E
   1. New Year -- Fiction 2. Squirrels -- Fiction 3. Forest animals -- Fiction
   ISBN 978-0-8075-7591-8; 0-8075-7591-7
                         LC 2009-49305

Squirrel cannot think of a New Year's resolution until she realizes that by helping her friends, she has made one after all.

"The simple dialogue and predictable plot make this a good read-aloud, and the brightly colored, acrylic cartoons are full of fun details and expression, giving the woodland creatures anthropomorphic characteristics." SLJ

Miller, Sara Swan

Three more stories you can read to your dog; illustrated by True Kelley. Houghton Mifflin 2000 un il $14; pa $5.95

Grades: PreK K 1 2   E
   1. Dogs -- Fiction
   ISBN 0-395-92293-3; 0-618-15244-X pa
                         LC 99-39880

Stories addressed to dogs and written from a dog's point of view, featuring such topics as going to the vet, making friends with a rocklike creature, and getting a bath

"The witty, believable portrayal of canine thoughts and behavior will amuse readers. . . . True Kelley's lively ink-and-watercolor illustrations brighten every page." Booklist

Other titles in this series are:
Three more stories you can read to your cat (2002)
Three stories you can read to your cat (1997)
Three stories you can read to your dog (1995)
Three stories you can read to your teddy bear (2004)

Miller, William

★ **Night** golf; illustrated by Cedric Lucas. Lee & Low Bks. 1999 un il hardcover o.p. pa $8.95

Grades: K 1 2 3   E
   1. Golf -- Fiction 2. Prejudices -- Fiction 3. African Americans -- Fiction
   ISBN 1-880000-79-2; 1-58430-056-6 pa
                         LC 98-47168

Despite being told that only whites can play golf, James becomes a caddy and is befriended by an older African American man who teaches him to play on the course at night

"Gentle paste and pencil illustrations support this quietly powerful story." Horn Book Guide

★ **Rent** party jazz; illustrated by Charlotte Riley-Webb. Lee & Low Bks. 2001 un il $16.95; pa $7.95

Grades: K 1 2 3   E
   1. Jazz 2. New Orleans (La.) 3. Jazz music -- Fiction 4. New Orleans (La.) -- Fiction
   ISBN 1-58430-025-6; 1-60060-344-0 pa
                         LC 2001-16449

When Sonny's mother loses her job in New Orleans during the Depression, Smilin' Jack, a jazz musician, tells him how to organize a rent party to raise the money they need

"Miller uses folksy dialogue to tell the story that celebrates both community and the uplifting power of music. Evocative artwork, done in broad, swirling strokes, fills pages with color and motion." Booklist

Millman, Isaac

★ **Moses** goes to school. Farrar, Straus & Giroux 2000 un il $16
Grades: PreK K 1 2   E
   1. School stories 2. Deaf -- Fiction 3. Sign language -- Fiction
   ISBN 0-374-35069-8
                         LC 99-40582

Moses and his friends enjoy the first day of school at their special school for the deaf and hard of hearing, where they use sign language to talk to each other

"Child-friendly cartoon illustrations do a marvelous job of emphasizing the normalcy and charm of these youngsters. . . . The double page layouts nicely accommodate the primary pictorial action along with written text and ASL inserts. . . . [This is a] great contribution to children's education about disabilities that also succeeds as effective storytelling in its own right." SLJ

Other titles about Moses are:
Moses goes to a concert (1998)
Moses goes to the circus (2003)
Moses sees a play (2004)

Mills, Claudia

Gus and Grandpa and the two-wheeled bike; pictures by Catherine Stock. Farrar, Straus & Giroux 1999 47p il hardcover o.p. pa $7.99
Grades: K 1 2 3　　　　　　　　　　　　　　　　　　　　E
　　1. Cycling -- Fiction　2. Grandfathers -- Fiction
　　ISBN 0-374-32821-8; 0-374-42816-6 pa
　　　　　　　　　　　　　　　　　LC 97-44203
Gus doesn't want to give up the training wheels on his bike, even for a new five-speed bicycle, until Grandpa helps him learn how to get along without them

"Mills conveys strong sentiment without a trace of mawkishness, and Stock's illustrations in loose line and watercolor augment the story of this childhood rite of passage expressively." Horn Book Guide

Other titles about Gus and Grandpa are:
Gus and Grandpa (1997)
Gus and Grandpa and show-and-tell (2000)
Gus and Grandpa and the Christmas cookies (1997)
Gus and Grandpa and the Halloween costume (2002)
Gus and Grandpa and the piano lesson (2004)
Gus and Grandpa at basketball (2001)
Gus and Grandpa at the hospital (1998)
Gus and Grandpa go fishing (2003)
Gus and Grandpa ride the train (1998)

Milton, Joyce

Dinosaur days; Joyce Milton; illustrated by Franco Tempesta. Random House Inc 2014 48 p. (Step into reading. Step 3) (pbk.) $3.99
Grades: 1 2 3　　　　　　　　　　　　　　　　　　　　E
　　1. Dinosaurs　2. Readers　3. Dinosaurs
　　ISBN 0385379234; 9780307978707; 9780375973383;
9780385379236
　　　　　　　　　　　　　　　　　LC 2013044052
This book, written by Joyce Milton and illustrated by Franco Tempesta, "highlights or at least names over a dozen dinos, from the diminutive Citipati to the humongous Argentinosaurus. . . . Prehistoric contemporaries that were not dinosaurs also get nods, as do modern paleontology, the great extinction and the continued survival of birds." (Kirkus Reviews)

Milway, Katie Smith

One hen; how one small loan made a big difference. written by Katie Smith Milway; illustrated by Eugenie Fernandes. Kids Can Press 2008 32p il $18.95
Grades: 2 3 4　　　　　　　　　　　　　　　　　　　　E
　　1. Eggs -- Fiction　2. Ghana -- Fiction　3. Loans -- Fiction　4. Chickens -- Fiction
　　ISBN 978-1-55453-028-1; 1-55453-028-8
"In Ghana, young Kojo has a business idea, borrowing a small bit of money from his mother to purchase a hen, intending to sell her extra eggs at the market. Slowly his income grows so that he can not only pay his mother back but he can also buy more hens; eventually, he has enough money to go back to school. . . . [This gains] power from its modeling on a real Ghanian entrepeneur, Kwabena Darko. . . . The beneficial effects of small loans and small projects are thoughtfully and carefully explained in the extensive text. . . . Acrylic illustrations, vivid and lively with an emphasis on sunny hues and warm earthtones, balance out the large blocks of text." Bull Cent Child Books
　　Includes glossary

Minarik, Else Holmelund

★ **Little** Bear; pictures by Maurice Sendak. Harper & Row 1957 63p il (I can read book) $16.95; lib bdg $17.89; pa $3.95

Grades: PreK K 1 2　　　　　　　　　　　　　　　　　　E
　　1. Bears -- Fiction
　　ISBN 0-06-024240-X; 0-06-024241-8 lib bdg; 0-06-444004-4 pa
The pictures "depict all the warmth of feeling and the special companionship that exists between a small child and his mother." Publ Wkly
　　Other titles about Little Bear are:
Father Bear comes home (1959)
A kiss for Little Bear (1968)
Little Bear's friend (1960)
Little Bear's visit (1961)
Little Bear and the Marco Polo (2010)

Little Bear and the Marco Polo; pictures by Dorothy Doubleday. Harper 2010 32p il (I can read) $16.99; pa $3.99
Grades: PreK K 1 2　　　　　　　　　　　　　　　　　　E
　　1. Bears -- Fiction　2. Grandfathers -- Fiction
　　ISBN 978-0-06-085485-0; 0-06-085485-5; 978-0-06-085487-4 pa; 0-06-085487-1 pa
Little Bear hears about his grandfather's exploits as a sea captain when they are cleaning out the attic together.

"Water-washed ink drawings display a series of family vignettes and Little Bear's activities while appropriate simple sentences and childlike questioning keep the pages turning." SLJ

★ **No** fighting, no biting! pictures by Maurice Sendak. Harper & Row 1958 62p il (I can read book) lib bdg $17.89; pa $3.95
Grades: PreK K 1 2　　　　　　　　　　　　　　　　　　E
　　1. Alligators -- Fiction
　　ISBN 0-06-024291-4 lib bdg; 0-06-444015-X pa
"A young lady who is unable to read in peace because of two children squabbling beside her tells them a story about two little alligators whose fighting and biting almost lead to disastrous consequences with a big hungry alligator. Children are sure to accept and enjoy the lesson in this little adventure tale and be amused by the expressive old-fashioned drawings." Booklist

Mineko Mamada

Which is round? Which is bigger? written and illustrated by Mineko Mamada. Kids Can Press 2013 24 p. $16.95
Grades: PreK K　　　　　　　　　　　　　　　　　　　E
　　1. Concept learning　2. Size
　　ISBN 1554539730; 9781554539734
This book by Mineko Mamada is a "concept book [that] prompts the reader to compare pairs of objects and then choose which one has a particular attribute. At first the answer seems obvious until the page is turned to reveal a delightful twist!" (Publisher's note) "Other comparisons include longer and faster. The question 'What do you think?' creates opportunity for discussion. Simple text and color cartoon animals on solid backgrounds allow children to focus on the investigations." (School Library Journal)

Minor, Florence

If you were a panda bear; Wendell and Florence Minor. Katherine Tegen Books, an imprint of HarperCollinsPublishers 2013 32 p. (hardcover bdg.) $17.99
Grades: PreK K 1　　　　　　　　　　　　　　　　　　E
　　1. Stories in rhyme　2. Bears -- Fiction
　　ISBN 0061950904; 9780061950902
　　　　　　　　　　　　　　　　　LC 2012040150
This book, written by Florence Minor and illustrated by Wendell Minor, "introduces different types of bears to young children. Through the poems in this . . . storybook, kids will learn that pandas are shy and eat bamboo, black bears love to climb trees, and grizzly bears can be up to

ten feet tall. A section at the back includes even more . . . animal facts." (Publisher's note)

Includes bibliographical references

Minor, Wendell, 1944-
My farm friends. G.P. Putnam's Sons 2011 un il $16.99
Grades: PreK K   E
1. Stories in rhyme 2. Farm life -- Fiction 3. Domestic animals -- Fiction
ISBN 0399244778; 9780399244773

LC 2010014793

Simple, rhyming text describes the characteristics of different farm animals. Includes 'Farm friends fun facts' and books and websites for further reading.

"Drawing on childhood memories of his family's Illinois farm, Minor celebrates farm animals—furry, feathered, hairy, and woolly—with warm watercolor-and-gouache artwork and cozy, playful rhymes that young children will love to hear many times over." Booklist

Miranda, Anne
★ To market, to market; written by Anne Miranda; illustrated by Janet Stevens. Harcourt Brace & Co. 1997 un il $16; pa $7
Grades: PreK K 1 2   E
1. Stories in rhyme 2. Animals -- Fiction
ISBN 0-15-200035-6; 0-15-216398-0 pa

LC 95-26326

"Patterned, staccato verses tell the zany tale, but it is Stevens's wonderfully wild illustrations that bring it to life." SLJ

Miron, Marie-Charlotte
My Little Handbook of Experiments; Physics, Water and Light, Ecology. by Marie-Charlotte Miron and Melanie Perez; illustrated by Vincent Hubert and Sandrine Lamour; translated by Susan Allen Maurin. Innovative Logistics Llc 2012 144 p. ill. (hardcover) $12.95
Grades: 2 3 4   E
1. Science -- Experiments 2. Science -- Study and teaching
ISBN 2733821474; 9782733821473

This book packs a "collection of science activities into three sections. . . . The unspecified 'Sciences' section is . . . approximately 18 activities including color, electricity and magnets, plus photography, astronomy, meteorology, and more. 'Water and Light' and 'Ecology' are" also included. (School Library Journal)

Mitchell, Margaree King
★ Uncle Jed's barbershop; illustrated by James Ransome. Simon & Schuster Bks. for Young Readers 1993 un il hardcover o.p. pa $6.99
Grades: PreK K 1 2   E
1. Uncles -- Fiction 2. African Americans -- Fiction 3. Barbers and barbershops -- Fiction
ISBN 0-671-76969-3; 0-689-81913-7 pa

LC 91-44148

Despite serious obstacles and setbacks Sarah Jean's Uncle Jed, the only black barber in the county, pursues his dream of saving enough money to open his own barbershop

"The author's convivial depictions of family life are enhanced by Ransome's . . . spirited oil paintings, which set the affectionate intergenerational cast against brightly patterned walls and crisp, leaf-strewn landscapes." Publ Wkly

When grandmama sings; illustrated by James Ransome. HarperCollins/Amistad 2011 un il $16.99
Grades: 2 3 4   E
1. Singers -- Fiction 2. Jazz music -- Fiction 3. Segregation --

Fiction 4. Grandmothers -- Fiction 5. Race relations -- Fiction 6. African Americans -- Fiction
ISBN 978-0-688-17563-4; 0-688-17563-5

"Set in the segregated South of the 1950s, Mitchell's poignant story features eight-year-old Belle and her loving, stalwart African-American family. When Grandmama, who can't read but whose singing voice captures the hearts of all who hear her, joins a jazz band for a tour of the South, Belle pleads to go along. . . . She experiences firsthand the difficulties her people face: hotels marked 'White Only,' diners that refuse them service, police who search their cars and luggage for no reason. . . . Ransome's full-page images, rich in color and feeling, portray the landscapes of the South and the individual emotions of the characters with equal aplomb." SLJ

Mitchell, Stephen
The ugly duckling; retold by Stephen Mitchell; illustrated by Steve Johnson and Lou Fancher. Candlewick Press 2008 un il $16.99
Grades: K 1 2 3   E
1. Authors 2. Novelists 3. Dramatists 4. Fairy tales 5. Swans -- Fiction 6. Children's authors 7. Short story writers
ISBN 978-0-7636-2159-9

LC 2007-34235

An ugly duckling spends an unhappy year ostracized by the other animals before he grows into a beautiful swan.

"Mitchell retells the familiar story, preserving just enough of the character of Andersen's narrative voice to give his adaptation a tart, bracing flavor. . . . Johnson and Fancher's lacy, luminous art, rich with underwaterlike greens, gives [the swan's transformation] all the visual splendor it deserves." Horn Book

Miyakoshi, Akiko
The storm; by Akiko Miyakoshi. Kids Can Press 2016 32 p. illustrations (some color) $16.95
Grades: PreK K 1 2   E
1. Dreams -- Fiction 2. Storms -- Fiction
ISBN 1771385596; 9781771385596

In this picture book, by Akiko Miyakoshi, "a little boy is excited about a trip to the beach with his parents planned for the following day. But a bad storm is coming, and he has started to worry they won't be able to go. He watches as the sky grows darker through the afternoon. . . Then the storm arrives. All through dinner, the rain beats hard against the shutters. . . . [However], to his delight, when he awakens, he finds his dream of clear blue skies has come true." (Publisher's note)

"This simple story, first published in Japan, captures anticipation, disappointment, worry, relief, and joy with subtlety and precision." Horn Book

The Tea Party in the Woods; Akiko Miyakoshi. Kids Can Press 2015 32 p. color illustrations $16.95
Grades: PreK K 1 2 3   E
1. Parties -- Fiction 2. Forests and forestry -- Fiction
ISBN 1771381078; 9781771381079

In this children's book by Akiko Miyakoshi "Kikko chases through the woods after her father with a pie for Grandma. Finding herself outside a different house, she joins a tea party. When her animal hosts hear that her pie had been crushed, they assemble an assorted dessert and parade with her to Grandma's house before disappearing." (School Library Journal)

"With great delicacy and keen draftsmanship, Japanese artist Miyakoshi weaves fairy-tale elements into a dreamy and sometimes haunting story." Pub Wkly

The way home in the night; Akiko Miyakoshi. Kids Can Press 2017 32 p. illustrations (chiefly color) $16.95

Grades: PreK K 1 2   E
1. Night -- Fiction 2. Bedtime -- Fiction 3. Rabbits -- Fiction
ISBN 1771386630; 9781771386630
First published in Japanese as "Yoru no kaerimichi"
"This beautiful picture book captures the magical wonder a child feels at being outside in the night. Award-winning author and illustrator Akiko Miyakoshi's softly focused black-and-white illustrations with just a touch of neutral color have a dreamlike quality, just right for nodding off to sleep with. The book is intriguing in that it contains twice-told stories, once as they are observed and second as the bunny imagines them." (Publisher's note)

Miyares, Daniel
★ **Float**; Daniel Miyares. Simon & Schuster Books for Young Readers 2015 48 p. (hardcover) $17.99
Grades: PreK K 1 2 3   E
1. Rain -- Fiction 2. Boats and boating -- Fiction 3. Toys -- Fiction 4. Stories without words 5. Lost and found possessions -- Fiction
ISBN 1481415247; 9781481415248
LC 2014016404
In this picture book by Daniel Miyares "a boy's small paper boat--and his large imagination--fill the pages . . . that includes endpaper instructions for building a boat of your own. A little boy takes a boat made of newspaper out for a rainy-day adventure. The boy and his boat dance in the downpour and play in the puddles, but when the boy sends his boat floating down a gutter stream, it quickly gets away from him." (Publisher's note)
"The joys, fears, and frustrations of exploration -- as well as the safety, support, and love of home -- are examined in this wordless story. Using inspiration from the newspaper, a boy and his caregiver (the only two characters in the narrative) together fold a paper boat. When the boy takes it outside to play, he pretends to sail the boat around the neighborhood. After a downpour, it floats for real -- first in a puddle and then out of the boy's grasp into a sewer grate...Miyares's strong command of perspective and line produces a comfortable suspense between panels and delivers a visual tale of a small moment made spectacular in the eyes of a child. Endpapers supply directions for readers to make their own paper boats and airplanes." Horn Book

That **neighbor** kid; Daniel Miyares. Simon & Schuster Books for Young Readers 2017 32 p. color illustrations (hardcover) $17.99
Grades: PreK K 1 2   E
1. Neighbors -- Fiction 2. Friendship -- Fiction 3. Tree houses -- Fiction
ISBN 9781481449793
LC 2016014172
In this picture book, by Daniel Miyares, "there's a new boy in the neighborhood, and he's up to something very curious. His next door neighbor, a girl his age with two long braids, . . . watches as he scavenges wood . . . , drags around a hammer and a bucket of nails, and reads a book about living in trees. When she finally works up the courage to say 'hi,' she finds herself invited to help build the private getaway every child has dreamed of: a tree house." (Publisher's note)

Mobin-Uddin, Asma
★ The **best** Eid ever; [by] Asma Mobin-Uddin; illustrated by Laura Jacobsen. Boyds Mills Press 2007 un il $16.95
Grades: K 1 2 3   E
1. Muslims -- Fiction 2. Id al-Adha -- Fiction 3. Grandmothers -- Fiction 4. Pakistani Americans -- Fiction
ISBN 978-1-59078-431-0; 1-59078-431-6
LC 2006037945
Eid is the Islamic holiday that marks the end of Ramadan. In this story, young Aneesa meets two girls at the prayer hall dressed in ill-fitting clothes and discovers they are refugees. Aneesa comes up with a plan to make this the best Eid ever
"This is a heartwarming tale of a child's generosity, and Jacobsen's illustrations flesh out the warmth and tenderness of the characters' interaction." SLJ

A **party** in Ramadan; illustrated by Laura Jacobsen. Boyds Mills Press 2009 un il $16.95
Grades: K 1 2 3   E
1. Muslims -- Fiction 2. Parties -- Fiction 3. Ramadan -- Fiction
ISBN 978-1-59078-604-8; 1-59078-604-1
LC 2008-43890
"With lively pastel-and-pencil artwork, this warm picture book shows and tells the observance and meaning of Ramadan through the viewpoint of a Muslim child. Leena is happy to be invited to her friend's birthday party, although it turns out that the event is on a day during Ramadan when Leena plans to fast with her family.... The blend of the upbeat with challenging moments will spark discussion, and a final note fills in more about the holy month." Booklist

Mochizuki, Ken
★ **Baseball** saved us; written by Ken Mochizuki; illustrated by Dom Lee. Lee & Low Bks. 1993 un il $16.95; pa $6.95
Grades: K 1 2 3   E
1. Baseball -- Fiction 2. Prejudices -- Fiction 3. World War, 1939-1945 -- Fiction 4. Japanese Americans -- Evacuation and relocation, 1942-1945 -- Fiction
ISBN 1-880000-01-6; 1-880000-19-9 pa
LC 92-73215
The narrator, Shorty, interned with his family in a camp for Japanese Americans during World War II, "tells how baseball was used as a diversion from the dire situation in which the camp's inhabitants found themselves.... {In one game}, the usually weak-hitting Shorty catches a glimpse of one of the ever-present guards and channels his anger toward the man into his swing, resulting in a winning home run. After the war and his return home, he continues to play ball while at the same time being subjected to racial taunts, again refocusing his anger to produce positive results on the diamond.... Grades two to four." (SLJ)
"Fences and watchtowers are in the background of many of Lee's moving illustrations, some of which were inspired by Ansel Adams' 1943 photographs of Manzanar.... The baseball action will grab kids—and so will the personal experience of bigotry." Booklist

Heroes; written by Ken Mochizuki; illustrated by Dom Lee. Lee & Low Bks. 1995 un il hardcover o.p. pa $6.95
Grades: K 1 2 3   E
1. Prejudices -- Fiction 2. Japanese Americans -- Fiction
ISBN 1-880000-16-4; 1-880000-50-4 pa
LC 94-26541
"The book is a powerful exploration of the cruelty children can inflict upon one another and of the confusion and pain borne by the target of such unthinking racism." Horn Book

Modarressi, Mitra
Taking care of Mama. G.P. Putnam's Sons 2010 un il $16.99
Grades: PreK K 1 2   E
1. Stories in rhyme 2. Sick -- Fiction 3. Raccoons -- Fiction 4. Family life -- Fiction
ISBN 978-0-399-25216-7; 0-399-25216-9
LC 2009011315
When Mama raccoon gets sick, Papa and the kids wear themselves out doing the cooking and cleaning for the day.
"The watercolor scenes .... capture cozy family chaos, while the smooth text make this a good read-aloud choice." Booklist

Moerbeek, Kees

★ **Count** 1 to 10. Abrams 2011 un il

Grades: K 1 2 3 4   **E**

1. Counting 2. Pop-up books

ISBN 0-8109-9644-8; 978-0-8109-9644-1

LC 2010928779

"A showpiece of popup design features the numbers one through 10 worked into multileveled constructs of dazzling virtuosity. Made from brightly colored digits floating over contrasting monochromatic backgrounds . . . the pop-ups range from a die-cut '1' that rotates into place and a pair of '2's folding out from behind a screen to phalanxes of '9's and '10's floating up as thier spreads open. . . . Every opening provides initial surprises, plenty of angles and spaces to explore and a rich visual experience."

"A showpiece of popup design features the numbers one through 10 worked into multileveled constructs of dazzling virtuosity. Made from brightly colored digits floating over contrasting monochromatic backgrounds . . . the pop-ups range from a die-cut '1' that rotates into place and a pair of '2's folding out from behind a screen to phalanxes of '9's and '10's floating up as thier spreads open. . . . Every opening provides initial surprises, plenty of angles and spaces to explore and a rich visual experience." Kirkus

Mol, Sine van

Meena; illustrated by Carianne Wijffels. Eerdmans Books for Young Readers 2011 un il $17

Grades: 1 2 3   **E**

1. Fear -- Fiction 2. Old age -- Fiction 3. Prejudices -- Fiction 4. Grandmothers -- Fiction

ISBN 978-0-8028-5394-3; 0-8028-5394-3

LC 2010049547

The children of Fly Street fear and taunt their neighbor Meena, thinking she is a witch, but when they meet her granddaughter and taste her red currant pie, they learn the truth.

"Simple sentences and a lot of dialogue will appeal to emerging readers. Wijffels uses childlike line drawings to show the youngsters' fevered imaginings. . . . Collage elements, children's art, and blue line drawings on uncluttered white space give the story unexpected depth." SLJ

Molchadsky, Yael

The **chameleon** that saved Noah's ark; Yael Molchadsky; illustrated by Orit Bergman; translated from Hebrew by Annette Appel. Nancy Paulsen Books 2016 32 p. color illustrations (hardback) $16.99

Grades: PreK K 1 2 3   **E**

1. Chameleons -- Fiction 2. Noah's Ark -- Fiction

ISBN 9781101996768

LC 2015033521

In this children's story, by Yael Molchadsky, illustrated by Orit Bergman, and translated by Annette Appel, is a "tale about the purpose of every creature and the harmony of nature. Noah and his family work hard to keep all the animals on the ark happy and well-fed . . . —except for the two chameleons. These picky eaters won't eat anything! . . . It is not until the ark's food supply is suddenly threatened, that Noah gets a surprising answer." (Publisher's note)

"This delightful narrative balances respect for tradition with inviting, accessible storytelling; a very well-executed debut for children and an appealing addition to family reading time." Kirkus

Mollel, Tololwa M.

★ **My** rows and piles of coins; illustrated by E. B. Lewis. Clarion Bks. 1999 32p il $15

Grades: K 1 2 3   **E**

1. Money -- Fiction 2. Bicycles -- Fiction 3. Tanzania -- Fiction

ISBN 0-395-75186-1

LC 98-21586

A Coretta Scott King honor book for illustration, 2000

A Tanzanian boy saves his coins to buy a bicycle so that he can help his parents carry goods to market, but then he discovers that in spite of all he has saved, he still does not have enough money

"The story is natural and never excessively moralistic. The fluid, light-splashed watercolor illustrations lend a sense of place and authenticity." SLJ

Monari, Manuela

Zero kisses for me! illustrated by Virginie Soumagnac. Tundra Books 2010 un il $12.95

Grades: PreK K   **E**

1. Kissing -- Fiction 2. Parent-child relationship -- Fiction

ISBN 978-1-77049-208-0; 1-77049-208-9

"A little one goes on strike against kisses. . . . Told mostly in a loving dialogue between mother and child, the language and syntax are true to life and utterly believable. Soumagnac's cartoon-style illustrations are a perfect match. . . . This is a sit-on-your-lap, kiss-and-hug read-aloud." Kirkus

Monjo, F. N.

★ The **drinking** gourd; a story of the Underground Railroad. pictures by Fred Brenner. newly il ed.; HarperCollins Pubs. 1993 62p il (I can read book) pa $3.99

Grades: K 1 2 3   **E**

1. Underground railroad -- Fiction

ISBN 0-06-444042-7 pa

LC 92-10823

First published 1970

Set in New England in the decade before the Civil War. For mischievous behavior in church, Tommy is sent home to his room, but wanders instead into the barn. There he discovers that his father is helping runaway slaves escape to Canada

"The simplicity of dialogue and exposition, the level of concepts, and the length of the story [makes] it most suitable for the primary grades reader. The illustrations are deftly representational, the whole a fine addition to the needed body of historical books for the very young." Bull Cent Child Books

Monroe, Chris

Monkey with a tool belt. Carolrhoda 2008 un il lib bdg $16.95

Grades: K 1 2 3   **E**

1. Tools -- Fiction 2. Monkeys -- Fiction

ISBN 978-0-8225-7631-0; 0-8225-7631-7

LC 2007-10020

Clever monkey Chico Bon Bon builds lots of things with his many tools, and when he is captured by an organ grinder, he uses them to help him escape and get back home.

"Slightly edgy, highly detailed comics-style art will have readers poring over the pages. . . . Not only gadget jockeys will enjoy this visually polished tale." Publ Wkly

Other titles about Chico are:

Monkey with a tool belt and the noisy problem (2009)

Monkey with a tool belt and the seaside shenanigans (2011)

Monkey with a tool belt and the maniac muffins (2016)

Monkey with a tool belt and the maniac muffins; by Chris Monroe. Carolrhoda Books 2016 32 p. color illustrations (ebook) $17.99; (lb : alk. paper) $17.99

Grades: PreK K 1 2 3   **E**

1. Tools -- Fiction 2. Cooking -- Fiction 3. Monkeys -- Fiction 4. Animals -- Fiction 5. Elephants -- Fiction

ISBN 9781467795623; 1467721557; 9781467721554

LC 2015037490

In this children's book by Chris Monroe, "Clark's baking project is not going as planned. Now gigantic maniac muffins are on the loose! To stop them, Chico Bon Bon needs a plan . . . and his tool belt, of course. With the right tools and some quick thinking, this crumbly disaster might just have a tasty solution!" (Publisher's note)

"With a plethora of details and powerful humor, this title will be a popular segue into STEM sessions. Expect an explosive storytime." SLJ

Monkey with a tool belt and the seaside shenanigans; written and illustrated by Chris Monroe. Carolrhoda Books 2011 il $16.95; e-book $12.95

Grades: K 1 2 3   **E**

1. Monkeys -- Fiction 2. Resorts -- Fiction 3. Elephants -- Fiction 4. Repairing -- Fiction

ISBN 978-0-7613-5616-5; 0-7613-5616-9; 978-0-7613-7943-0 e-book

LC 2011003013

Chico the clever monkey helps his friend Clark the elephant solve a problem at a seaside resort.

"Monroe's breezy, detailed illustrations match the energy and enthusiasm of her tale." Kirkus

★ **Sneaky** sheep. Carolrhoda Books 2010 un il lib bdg $16.95

Grades: PreK K 1 2   **E**

1. Sheep -- Fiction

ISBN 978-0-7613-5615-8 lib bdg; 0-7613-5615-0 lib bdg

LC 2009040852

Blossom and Rocky, two sneaky and not very bright sheep, keep trying to get away from the rest of the flock, in spite of the dangers they encounter.

"Monroe's pen-and-ink and watercolor illustrations are entertaining; kids will enjoy following Rocky and Blossom's antics both in and out of panels." SLJ

Montes, Marisa

★ **Los** gatos black on Halloween; illustrated by Yuyi Morales. Henry Holt and Company 2006 un il $16.95

Grades: PreK K 1 2   **E**

1. Stories in rhyme 2. Halloween -- Fiction 3. Spanish language -- Vocabulary

ISBN 978-0-8050-7429-1; 0-8050-7429-5

LC 2005-20049

A Pura Belpré Author Award honor book, 2008

Easy to read, rhyming text about Halloween night incorporates Spanish words, from las brujas riding their broomsticks to los monstruos whose monstrous ball is interrupted by a true horror.

"Montes smoothly incorporates Spanish terms into a rhythmic poem. . . . The full-bleed paintings create a creepy mood with curving lines, fluid textures, and dusky hues. . . . The pictures are eerie enough to tingle spines, but the effect is leavened with bits of humor." SLJ

Montijo, Rhode

The **Halloween** Kid. Simon & Schuster 2010 un il $12.99

Grades: PreK K 1 2   **E**

1. Cowhands -- Fiction 2. Halloween -- Fiction

ISBN 978-1-4169-3575-9; 1-4169-3575-4

The brave and trusty Halloween Kid saves trick-or-treaters from a crowd of sweet-stealing Goodie Goblins.

"This rollicking story projects a delightfully retro style and sensibility, aided by black, white, and orange brush-and-ink illustrations. . . . A treat for storytime as well as for independent reading and a must for Halloween picture-book collections." SLJ

Moore, Eva

Lucky Ducklings; by Eva Moore; illustrations by Nancy Carpenter. Orchard Books 2013 32 p. (hardcover : alk. paper) $16.99

Grades: K 1 2 3   **E**

1. Animal rescue 2. Ducks -- Fiction 3. Animal babies -- Fiction 4. Rescues -- Fiction 5. Animals -- Infancy -- Fiction

ISBN 0439448611; 9780439448611

LC 2012002444

Author Eva Moore presents a children's picture book on ducks. "Early one morning, Mama Duck takes her babies for a walk. They follow safely behind her as they leave their pond, waddle through the park, and stop in the little sunlit town's parking lot for yummy breakfast. But one by one, Mama's little ducklings get separated when they disappear into the slats of the town's storm drain." Moore describes "how three firemen and a pickup truck rush to their rescue." (Publisher's note)

Moore, Genevieve

Catherine's story; illustrated by Karin Littlewood. Frances Lincoln Children's 2010 un il $17.95

Grades: 1 2 3   **E**

1. People with disabilities -- Fiction

ISBN 978-1-84507-655-9; 1-84507-655-9

"Catherine, who wears leg braces, has a special walk and a special way of clapping her hands (so quietly, no one ever hears them). Her cousin Frances thinks she can walk like Catherine but when she tries, she falls over. When she says that Catherine can't talk, Catherine's dad says, 'lots and lots of people talk . . . too much . . . Catherine listens—really, really hard.' Catherine is loved and valued. . . . The lovely watercolor illustrations capture joy and optimism. With subtlety and grace, they perfectly depict a child with disabilities." SLJ

Moore, Inga

A **house** in the woods. Candlewick Press 2011 il $16.99

Grades: PreK K 1   **E**

1. Building -- Fiction 2. Friendship -- Fiction 3. Forest animals -- Fiction 4. House construction -- Fiction

ISBN 978-0-7636-5277-7; 0-7636-5277-6

LC 2010050827

Two Little Pigs whose small homes in the woods have been accidentally destroyed by Bear and Moose decide to build a house they can all share, and with the help of Beaver Builders they soon have a fine new home.

"The gentle arc of the story about a warm friendship is perfectly echoed by the large, detailed illustrations. The pencil, pastel, and wash art is full of autumn colors and delicate touches and details that bring the woods and the animals to life." SLJ

Moore, Jodi

When a dragon moves in; written by Jodi Moore; illustrated by Howard McWilliam. Flashlight Press 2011 un il $16.95

Grades: PreK K 1   **E**

1. Beaches -- Fiction 2. Dragons -- Fiction 3. Family life -- Fiction 4. Imagination -- Fiction

ISBN 978-0-979974-67-0; 0-979974-67-4

"While enjoying a day at the beach with his family, a boy builds a perfect sand castle and a dragon promptly moves in toting a well-worn suitcase. The youngster can't believe his luck while the rest of the family can't believe him. Mischief blamed on the dragon eventually gets the child in trouble. . . . While the text is fun, the story is truly told through the comical illustrations. The friendly red dragon's expressions are hilarious. . . . This story of a runaway imagination will make for an entertaining storytime as well as an enjoyable one-on-one read." SLJ

Followed by When a dragon moves in again (2015)

Mora, Pat

Abuelos; story by Pat Mora; pictures by Amelia Lau Carling. Groundwood Books 2008 un il $18.95

Grades: PreK K 1 2   **E**

1. Winter -- Fiction 2. New Mexico -- Fiction 3. Hispanic Americans -- Fiction

ISBN 978-0-88899-716-6; 0-88899-716-7

Mora "introduces the intriguing midwinter New Mexican festival of 'los abuelos' in this playful tale. The narrator, Amelia, is about to experience the spooky-sounding tradition for the first time, and Papá offers reassurances. . . . Played by costumed villagers in scary masks, the abuelos chase the children around bonfires; when one snatches her brother, Amelia grabs the abuelo's mask, only to discover her uncle beneath it. Carling's . . . watercolor and pastel illustrations impart Amelia's apprehension as well as family togetherness." Publ Wkly

★ **Book** fiesta! celebrate Children's Day/Book Day. illustrated by Rafael Lopez. HarperCollins 2009 un il $17.99

Grades: PreK K 1 2 3   **E**

1. Books and reading -- Fiction 2. Bilingual books -- English-Spanish

ISBN 978-0-06-128877-7; 0-06-128877-2

ALA ALSC Belpre Illustrator Medal (2010)

"Mora encourages teachers, parents, and librarians to celebrate Children's Day/Book Day and includes ideas for observing the festivities. Written in English and Spanish, the text shows children reading in a variety of places, going to the library, listening to stories, and enjoying books. López's acrylic illustrations fill the pages with color. His upbeat iconic style shows how much fun this celebration can be." SLJ

★ **Dona** Flor; a tall tale about a giant woman with a great big heart. illustrated by Raul Colón. Knopf 2005 un il $15.99; lib bdg $17.99

Grades: K 1 2 3   **E**

1. Tall tales 2. Pumas -- Fiction 3. Giants -- Fiction

ISBN 0-375-82337-9; 0-375-92337-3 lib bdg

Doña Flor, a giant woman with a big heart, sets off to protect her neighbors from what they think is a dangerous animal, but soon discovers the tiny secret behind the huge noise.

"A charming tall tale. . . Colón uses his signature mix of watercolor washes, etching, and litho pencils for the art. There is great texture and movement on each page in the sunbaked tones of the landscape." SLJ

★ **Gracias**; Thanks. ilustraciones por John Parra; traducción por Adriana Domínguez; illustrations by John Parra; translation by Adriana Dominguez. Lee & Low Books 2009 un il

Grades: PreK K 1 2   **E**

1. Hispanic Americans -- Fiction 2. Racially mixed people -- Fiction 3. Bilingual books -- English-Spanish

ISBN 1600602584; 9781600602580

LC 2009013060

ALA ALSC Belpre Illustrator Medal Honor Book (2010)

In this bilingual picture book, a young boy says thank you for many things in his life. "Primary." (Horn Book)

"From the sun waking him up in the morning to a cricket chirping him to sleep at night, a young boy gives thanks for the many things and people who enrich his life. These blessings are remarkable for their childlike imagination and fresh imagery. . . . The bilingual format features Spanish on the left-hand page and English on the right. . . . Parra's

vivid acrylic illustrations have the feel of folk-art woodcuts and whimsically portray the details of the boy's world." Booklist

Here, kitty, kitty; illustrated by Maribel Suarez. Rayo 2008 un il (My family, mi familia) $14.99; lib bdg $15.89

Grades: PreK K   **E**

1. Cats -- Fiction 2. Bilingual books -- English-Spanish

ISBN 978-0-06-085044-9; 0-06-085044-2; 978-0-06-085045-6 lib bdg; 0-06-085045-0 lib bdg

"This joyful picture book tells a lively story of a young girl who gets a shy new kitten that hides and makes trouble. With English and Spanish text on each double-page spread, the line-and-watercolor pictures show the loving family as the kitten hides under the sofa, under sister's bed, in a flowerpot, until finally the soft friend snuggles up on the girl's lap." Booklist

Tomas and the library lady; illustrated by Raúl Colón. Knopf 1997 un il $17; pa $6.99

Grades: K 1 2 3   **E**

1. Poets 2. Authors 3. Novelists 4. Essayists 5. College teachers 6. Libraries -- Fiction 7. College administrators 8. Migrant labor -- Fiction 9. Books and reading -- Fiction 10. Mexican Americans -- Fiction

ISBN 0-679-80401-3; 0-375-80349-1 pa

LC 89-37490

While helping his family in their work as migrant laborers far from their home, Tomás finds an entire world to explore in the books at the local public library

"Mora's story is based on a true incident in the life of the famous writer Tomás Rivera, the son of migrant workers who became an education leader and university president. . . . Colón's beautiful scratchboard illustrations, in his textured, glowingly colored, rhythmic style, capture the warmth and the dreams that the boy finds in the world of books." Booklist

Uno, dos, tres; one, two, three; illustrated by Barbara Lavallee. Clarion Bks. 1996 43p il hardcover o.p. pa $6.95

Grades: PreK K 1 2   **E**

1. Counting 2. Stories in rhyme 3. Mexico -- Fiction 4. Bilingual books -- English-Spanish

ISBN 0-395-67294-5; 0-618-05468-5 pa

LC 94-15337

"Two girls search a Mexican market for gifts for their mother's birthday in this counting book in both English and Spanish. . . . Cheerful stylized paintings in muted reds, blues, and yellows depict designs from Mexican art and use pattern to highlight the number sequence." Horn Book Guide

Wiggling pockets. Rayo 2009 un il (My family, mi familia) $12.99

Grades: PreK K   **E**

1. Frogs -- Fiction 2. Family life -- Fiction 3. Bilingual books -- English-Spanish

ISBN 978-0-06-085047-0; 0-06-085047-7

"When Danny comes to the table with wiggling pockets, Mom and Dad ask what he has in them. Four frogs jump out and cause minor chaos. The simple text in both English and Spanish and the warm illustrations portray a loving family." Horn Book Guide

Morales, Melita

Jam & honey; illustrations by Laura J. Bryant. Tricycle Press 2011 un il $15.99

Grades: PreK K 1   E

1. Stories in rhyme 2. Bees -- Fiction
ISBN 978-1-58246-299-8; 1-58246-299-2

Tells the story of a young girl and a honeybee who learn to coexist peacefully in the same garden as they go about their respective tasks.

"Simple, bouncing rhymes switch from the child's viewpoint . . . to the bee's voice. . . . The whimsical, uncluttered watercolor-and-pencil illustrations show each character busy at first, then scared of the other, and finally safe and satisfied on their way home." Booklist

Morales, Yuyi

★ **Just** in case; a trickster tale and Spanish alphabet book. Roaring Brook Press 2008 un il $16.95

Grades: 1 2 3   E

1. Ghost stories 2. Gifts -- Fiction 3. Alphabet -- Fiction 4. Birthdays -- Fiction
ISBN 978-1-59643-329-8; 1-59643-329-9

LC 2007-44061

Awarded the Pura Belpre Illustrator Award, 2009

A Pura Belpre Author Award honor book, 2009

As Senor Calavera prepares for Grandma Beetle's birthday he finds an alphabetical assortment of unusual presents, but with the help of Zelmiro the Ghost, he finds the best gift of all.

"Luminous, jewel-tone spreads chronicle the collection of gifts and pay homage to a rich Mexican culture. . . . Part ghost story and part alphabet book, this trickster tale transcends both. Librarians will want to share it for the beautiful language, the spirited artwork, and the rightness of the ending." SLJ

Little Night. Roaring Brook Press 2006 un il $16.95

Grades: PreK K   E

1. Sky -- Fiction 2. Night -- Fiction 3. Bedtime -- Fiction 4. Mother-daughter relationship -- Fiction
ISBN 978-1-59643-088-4; 1-59643-088-5

LC 2006011571

At the end of a long day, Mother Sky helps her playful daughter, Little Night, to get ready for bed

"Morales has created a sumptuous feast of metaphors in her text: a bathtub filled with falling stars, a dress crocheted from clouds. The equally splendid illustrations effectively convey each of the images and heighten the comfort and serenity inspired by the text." Booklist

★ **Niño** wrestles the world; Yuyi Morales. 1st ed. Roaring Brook Press 2013 40 p. ill. (hardcover) $16.99

Grades: PreK K 1 2 3   E

1. Picture books for children 2. Wrestling -- Fiction 3. Monsters -- Fiction 4. Imagination -- Fiction 5. Brothers and sisters -- Fiction
ISBN 1596436042; 9781596436046

LC 2012012989

Pura Belpre Illustrator Award (2014)

In this children's picture book, "playing alone in his room, Niño dons his Lucha Libre mask and lets his imagination take flight. (According to an endnote, Lucha Libre is a dramatic form of professional wrestling followed by fans in Mexico.) The young hero is then ready to take on an eclectic cast of monstrous opponents. Spurred on by chanting crowds, the boy handily defeats the Guanajuato Mummy (La Momia de Guanajuato), Olmec Head (Cabeza Olmeca), and the Weeping Woman (La Llorona)." (School Library Journal)

Rudas; Niño's Horrendous Hermanitas. Yuyi Morales. Roaring Brook Press 2016 40 p. color illustrations (hardback) $17.99

Grades: PreK K 1 2 3   E

1. Wrestling -- Fiction 2. Brothers and sisters -- Fiction
ISBN 1626722404; 9781626722408

LC 2016004882

In this children's story about Mexican wrestling by Yuyi Morales, "no opponent is too big a challenge for the cunning skills of Las Hermanitas, Lucha Queens! Their Poopy Bomb Blowout will knock em' down! Their Tag-Team Teething will gnaw opponents down to a pulp! Their Pampered Plunder Diversion will fell even the most determined competitor! But what happens when Niño comes after them with a move of his own?" (Publisher's note)

"With acrylics and inks Morales depicts the spectacular battle between Niño and his two little sisters in brilliantly colored cartoons, as each page blasts our senses with eye-popping bold-font styles and bubble text and backgrounds of explosive stars. Another hit for award winner Morales!" Booklist

★ **Viva** Frida! Yuyi Morales; photography by Tim O'Meara. Roaring Brook Press 2014 40 p. color illustrations (hardcover) $17.99

Grades: K 1 2 3   E

1. Artists 2. Painters -- Mexico -- Biography
ISBN 1596436034; 9781596436039

LC 2013044236

Caldecott Honor Book (2015)

Pura Belpré (Illustrator) Award (2015)

Written by Yuyi Morales, with photography by Tim O'Meara, this children's book describes how "Frida Kahlo, one of the world's most famous and unusual artists is revered around the world. Her life was filled with laughter, love, and tragedy, all of which influenced what she painted on her canvases." (Publisher's note)

"Morales layers English and Spanish words--never more than four to a page--to depict a Frida who is curious, playful, wise, and inspired. Rather than tell a story, the text captures fragments of Frida's life, like snapshots with bilingual captions." Booklist

Morgan, Sally

Me and my dad; [by] Sally Morgan and Ezekiel Kwaymullina; illustrated by Matt Ottley. Little Hare Books 2011 un il $16.99

Grades: PreK K 1   E

1. Fear -- Fiction 2. Birds -- Fiction 3. Beaches -- Fiction 4. Father-son relationship -- Fiction
ISBN 978-1-921541-81-0; 1-921541-81-4

"During an action-filled day at the beach, a boy recounts everything his father isn't afraid of. . . . Making dynamic use of perspective and scale, Ottley shows the boy's father laughing as a skyscraper-high sandcastle tumbles down on him, flexing his bicep while a surging wave threatens to swallow him up, and confidently swimming amid transparent jellyfish to unhook a fishing line. There's a cartoonish sense of playfulness throughout, right up to the final scene in which the father's sole, improbable fear—seagulls—is revealed, giving the boy a chance to be the brave one." Publ Wkly

Morpurgo, Michael

Mirror. Seven Footer Kids 2010 un il $15.95

Grades: PreK K 1 2   E

1. Mirrors -- Fiction
ISBN 978-1-934734-39-1; 1-934734-39-X

In this wordless book "a small girl sits in the corner of a spread, her isolation and loneliness underscored by her head-down, hunkered-over posture as well as the austere palette . . . and stark white backdrop. Her mood . . . changes to surprise when she catches sight of her likeness in a mirror . . . and eventually transforms into playful exuberance as she makes faces at and dances with her reflected double. . . . A blank spread provides a narrative beat, and when the action resumes, the child's reflection no longer parallels her movements, taking on a life of its own. Enraged, the protagonist seems to push at the mirror, which shatters. . . . Lee's illustrations cut to the core to express deep-seated feelings." SLJ

★ **Wave**. Chronicle Books 2008 un il $15.99

Grades: PreK K   E

1. Stories without words 2. Ocean -- Fiction 3. Beaches -- Fiction

ISBN 978-0-8118-5924-0; 0-8118-5924-X

LC 2007-62026

A wordless picture book that shows a little girl's first experiences at the beach, as she goes from being afraid of the roaring waves to playing on the shore while gulls soar overhead.

"A panoramic trim size beautifully supports the expansiveness of the beach. . . . Loosely rendered charcoal and acrylic images curl and flow like water and reflect playfulness, especially in the facial and bodily expressions of the child and seagulls. . . . A simple, well-crafted story." SLJ

Morris, Jackie

I **am** cat; by Jackie Morris. Frances Lincoln Children's Books 2013 32 p. ill. (hardcover) $17.99

Grades: 1 2 3 4   E

1. Cats -- Poetry 2. Picture books for children

ISBN 1847801358; 9781847801357

In this children's picture book, "Cat, curled tight on a round tasseled pillow, sleeps and dreams. The tabby's poetic musings accompany . . . watercolor paintings of 10 great cats." Among the cats included are the Siberian tiger, the cheetah, and the lynx. "Cat also dreams of the Scottish wildcat on the verge of extinction and the regal Amur leopard, its 'thick coat coloured like leaves in autumn,/ almost the last' of its kind." (School Library Journal)

Morris, Richard T.

Bye-bye, baby! by Richard Morris; illustrated by Larry Day. Walker & Co. 2009 un il $16.99; lib bdg $17.89

Grades: PreK   E

1. Infants -- Fiction 2. Siblings -- Fiction

ISBN 978-0-8027-9772-8; 0-8027-9772-5; 978-0-8027-9773-5 lib bdg; 0-8027-9773-3 lib bdg

LC 2008044318

Felix does not like his new baby sister and thinks his parents should take her back, until a trip to the zoo makes him realize that she might not be as bad as he thought.

"Outstanding illustrations are done in pen, ink, watercolor, and gouache. The characters' expressions and body language could tell this story alone, but wonderfully enhance the strong and simple text." SLJ

This is a moose; by Richard Morris; illustrated by Tom Lichtenheld. Little, Brown & Co. 2014 48 p. $18

Grades: PreK K 1   E

1. Documentary films -- Fiction 2. Humorous stories 3. Moose -- Fiction 4. Animals -- Habits and behavior -- Fiction 5. Documentary films -- Production and direction -- Fiction

ISBN 0316213608; 9780316213608

LC 2013015681

In this children's book, by Richard Morris and illustrated by Tom Lichtenheld, "a movie director tries to capture the life of a moose on film. . . . It turns out the moose has a dream bigger then just being a moose–he wants to be an astronaut and go to the moon. His forest friends step in to help him, and action ensues. Lots of action. Like a lacrosse-playing grandma, a gigantic slingshot into space, and a flying, superhero chipmunk." (Publisher's note)

"This romp chronicles the making of a documentary about a moose. The hapless (and visually absent, until book's end) director grows increasingly frustrated as silly situations ("would someone kindly get the

moose out of the space suit?") and interjections from offstage interrupt filming. Energy and over-the-top hilarity abound, but there are some befuddling plot details. Ever-changing fonts and text formats hamper readability." Horn Book

Morrow, Barbara Olenyik

A **good** night for freedom; illustrated by Leonard Jenkins. Holiday House 2004 un il $16.95

Grades: K 1 2 3   E

1. Abolitionists 2. Slavery -- Fiction 3. Underground railroad -- Fiction

ISBN 0-8234-1709-3

LC 2002-192207

Hallie discovers two runaway slaves hiding in Levi Coffin's home and must decide whether to turn them in or help them escape to freedom. Includes historical notes on the Underground Railroad and abolitionists Levi and Catharine Coffin.

"The well-written text smoothly blends fact and fiction. . . . Jenkins's mixed-media illustrations capture the emotions of the characters as well as the details of pre-Civil War life." SLJ

Includes bibliographical references

Mortensen, Denise Dowling

Bug patrol; by Denise Dowling Mortensen; illustrated by Cece Bell. Clarion Books 2012 32 p. col. ill. (hardcover) $16.99

Grades: PreK K 1 2   E

1. Stories in rhyme 2. Police -- Fiction 3. Insects -- Fiction 4. Police -- Fiction 5. Insects -- Fiction

ISBN 0618790241; 9780618790241

LC 2011041586

In this children's book, by Denise Dowling Mortensen, illustrated by Cece Bell, "bugs are a misbehaving bunch, so Captain Bob, insect cop, has a busy beat. The beetles are using their bug mobiles like bumper cars, the roaches are protesting for better housing . . . , and the crickets are up late, partying. Can Captain Bob keep the peace and maintain law and order?" (Publisher's note)

Mortensen, Lori

Cowpoke Clyde and Dirty Dawg; by Lori Mortensen; illustrated by Michael Allen Austin. Clarion Books 2013 32 p. (hardcover) $16.99

Grades: PreK K 1 2   E

1. Dogs -- Fiction 2. Baths -- Fiction 3. Cowboys -- Fiction 4. Dogs -- Fiction 5. Baths -- Fiction 6. Stories in rhyme 7. Cowboys -- Fiction

ISBN 0547239939; 9780547239934

LC 2011052429

This book, by Lori Mortensen, tells "the tale of a cowboy who likes to keep things clean and tidy. Clyde tries tactic after tactic to catch his dog for a scrub down, each new method adding another layer of mayhem to the scene . . . Finally Clyde takes a bath in the moonlight by himself while singing . . . and that is the winning lure that gets the dirty Dawg into the washtub." (Kirkus)

Another title in this series is:

Cowpoke Clyde Rides the Range (2016)

Mortimer, Anne

Pumpkin cat; written & illustrated by Anne Mortimer. Katherine Tegen Books 2011 un il $14.99; lib bdg $15.89

Grades: PreK K 1   E

1. Cats -- Fiction 2. Mice -- Fiction 3. Pumpkin -- Fiction

ISBN 978-0-06-187485-7; 0-06-187485-X; 978-0-06-187486-4 lib bdg; 0-06-187486-8 lib bdg

"One morning in May, Cat wondered, 'How do pumpkins grow? 'I know,' said Mouse. 'And I will show you how.' Mouse proceeds to guide Cat through the various steps and stages, one phase featured on each spread, until October arrives and they are rewarded with a large orange pumpkin. . . . Mortimer has masterfully captured the texture of her subjects—the softness of the animals' fur, the scratchiness of burlap bags, the silkiness of delicate flower petals, etc. . . . A lovely addition that should be popular in any season." SLJ

Mortiz, Dianne

Hush little beachcomber; illustrated by Holly McGee. Kane Miller 2011 un il $14.99

Grades: PreK K 1   E

1. Stories in rhyme 2. Seashore -- Fiction

ISBN 978-1-935279-81-5; 1-935279-81-5

"'Hush, Little Baby' receives a bright makeover, with seagulls and sand pies replacing mockingbirds and diamond rings. Repetitive phrases may mirror the soothing lullaby's format, but this blissful beach day opens with a more enthusiastic call for action. . . . The cheerful voice remains optimistic throughout. . . . The lilting text naturally progresses through each experience. . . . Pastel spreads flash with smudges of golden color, with their hazy hues dominating each page, the brief rhyming text highlighting each featured activity." Kirkus

Morton, Carlene

The **library** pages; illustrated by Valeria Docampo. UpstartBooks 2010 un il $17.95

Grades: K 1 2 3   E

1. School stories 2. Libraries -- Fiction

ISBN 978-1-60213-045-6; 1-60213-045-0

While Mrs. Heath, the school librarian, is on maternity leave, the library pages put all the thin books together, shelve the books by color, mend them with duct tape, cut pictures out of encyclopedias, shelve every third book with the pages pointing out, and borrow books without checking them out.

"Docampo's colorful combination of manual and digital illustrations sets a perfectly mood for this story. This is an entertaining read-aloud, a humorous joke, and an excellent starter for library orientation." SLJ

Moser, Lisa

Cowboy Boyd and Mighty Calliope; by Lisa Moser; illustrated by Sebastiaan Van Doninck. 1st ed. Random House Inc 2013 40 p. ill. (hardcover) $17.99; (library) $20.99; (ebook) $53.97

Grades: PreK K 1   E

1. Picture books for children 2. Rhinoceros -- Fiction 3. Cowboys -- Fiction 4. Ranch life -- Fiction 5. Rhinoceroses -- Fiction

ISBN 0375870563; 0375970568; 9780375870569; 9780375970566; 9780375980794

LC 2012025379

In this picture book, "Rancher Rose and her hired hands are skeptical when Cowboy Boyd and his unusual mount arrive for a job at the Double R Ranch. As it happens, Calliope is a sensitive and affectionate rhinoceros, though she is not a very good ranch horse. Each task that she attempts ends in failure and, unsurprisingly, the very night that Rancher Rose tells Boyd and Calliope to 'roll on,' a situation arises where only her unique talents can provide a happy ending." (School Library Journal)

Kisses on the wind; illustrated by Kathryn Brown. Candlewick Press 2009 un il $15.99

Grades: K 1 2 3   E

1. Moving -- Fiction 2. West (U.S.) -- Fiction 3. Grandmothers -- Fiction 4. Frontier and pioneer life -- Fiction

ISBN 978-0-7636-3110-9; 0-7636-3110-8

LC 2008-53490

Young Lydia struggles to say goodbye to her grandmother as her parents finish packing their wagon for the long journey to Oregon in the nineteenth century.

"Moser and Brown tell a wise, gentle story about good-byes. . . . The fluid watercolors amplify the story's mood of transition." Booklist

Railroad Hank; by Lisa Moser; illustrations by Benji Davies. Random House Children's Books 2012 40 p. col. ill. (trade) $16.99

Grades: PreK K 1 2   E

1. Farm life -- Fiction 2. Railroads -- Fiction 3. Humorous fiction -- Fiction 4. Humorous stories 5. Railroad trains -- Fiction

ISBN 0375868496; 9780375868498; 9780375968495

LC 2011030231

In this children's story, by Lisa Moser, illustrated by Benji Davies, "Railroad Hank is headed up the mountain in his . . . little train to see Granny Bett. . . . Along the way, he stops to talk to Missy May, Country Carl, Cinnamon Cobbler, and Reel-'Em-In Sam. Each friend offers up something to cheer Granny Bett. . . . By the time he reaches the mountaintop, his train is bursting with crazy cargo! And Granny Bett has a great idea for what to do with it all." (Publisher's note)

"Moser's folksy writing style is paired well with Davies's perky acrylic illustrations... This satisfying, good-humored picture book sends a worthy message about looking after other people." SLJ

Squirrel's world; illustrated by Valeri Gorbachev. Candlewick Press 2007 44p il $14.99; pa $4.99

Grades: 1 2 3   E

1. Animals -- Fiction 2. Squirrels -- Fiction

ISBN 978-0-7636-2929-8; 0-7636-2929-4; 978-0-7636-4088-0 pa; 0-7636-4088-3 pa

LC 2007-60859

Squirrel's well-meaning attempts to help his forest friends do not always turn out as planned.

"Gorbachev's loosely hatched linework provides appealing informal texture to the forest clan, and his illustrations offer plenty of decoding clues for novices. . . . Early independent readers will revel in the abundant repetition." Bull Cent Child Books

Moses, Will

Mary and her little lamb; the true story behind the nursery rhyme. Philomel Books 2011 36p il $17.99

Grades: 1 2 3   E

1. School stories 2. Sheep -- Fiction 3. Farm life -- Fiction 4. Massachusetts -- Fiction

ISBN 978-0-399-25154-2; 0-399-25154-5

LC 2010037445

In 1810s Massachusetts, young Mary Elizabeth Sawyer nurses a sickly lamb back to health and becomes the subject of a famous nursery rhyme. Includes facts about the real Mary, John Roulstone who wrote the rhyme, and Lowell Mason who set it to music.

"Moses's rich oil paintings, rendered in his characteristic folk-art style, beautifully depict rural 19th-century life. They include spreads, framed pictures with images of books and hens in the margins, and vignettes accompanying the lengthy text." SLJ

Moss, Lloyd

★ **Zin!** zin! zin! a violin; illustrated by Marjorie Priceman. Simon & Schuster Bks. for Young Readers 1995 un il $17.95; pa $6.99

Grades: K 1 2 3   E

1. Counting 2. Stories in rhyme 3. Musical instruments

ISBN 0-671-88239-2; 0-689-83524-8 pa

LC 93-37902

A Caldecott Medal honor book, 1996

"Rhyming couplets present 10 instruments and their characteristics. . . . In the process of adding instruments, the book teaches the names of musical groups up to a chamber group of 10 as well as the categories into which the instruments fall: strings, reeds, and brasses. Amazingly, Moss conveys this encyclopedic information while keeping the poem streamlined and peppy. Priceman's sprightly, sunny hued gouache paintings should take a bow, too." Booklist

Moss, Peggy

One of us; illustrated by Penny Weber. Tilbury House 2010 un il $16.95

Grades: 1 2 3   E

1. School stories 2. Moving -- Fiction 3. Friendship -- Fiction 4. Individualism -- Fiction

ISBN 978-0-88448-322-9; 0-88448-322-3

Roberta is welcomed by different groups on her first day at a new school, only to be told she does not fit in with them for some reason, but by the next day, members of each group have begun to see that they do not have to be alike in every way.

"Expressive eyes, happy faces, and rosy cheeks are indicative of the engaging illustrations that complement this winning color picture book. It can be used to supplement guidance lessons, welcome new students, or just as a fun discussion after a read-aloud session." Libr Media Connect

Most, Bernard

ABC T-Rex. Harcourt Brace & Co. 2000 un il $14; pa $6

Grades: PreK K 1   E

1. Alphabet 2. Dinosaurs -- Fiction

ISBN 0-15-202007-1; 0-15-205028-0 pa

LC 98-51128

A young T-Rex loves his ABCs so much that he eats them up, experiencing on each letter a word that begins with that letter

"Heavy black lines define the cartoonlike drawings, brightened with a colorful palette emphasizing shades of green, purple, and orange. Fun for alphabetically inclined preschoolers." Booklist

★ **Whatever** happened to the dinosaurs? written and illustrated by Bernard Most. Harcourt Brace Jovanovich 1984 un il hardcover o.p. pa $4.95

Grades: PreK K 1   E

1. Dinosaurs -- Fiction

ISBN 0-15-295295-0; 0-15-295296-9 pa

LC 84-3779

"A hilarious book, sure to be popular for individual reading or with groups." Child Book Rev Serv

Moulton, Mark Kimball

The **very** best pumpkin; written by Mark Kimball Moulton; illustrated by Karen Hillard Good. Simon & Schuster Books for Young Readers 2010 un il $12.99

Grades: PreK K 1   E

1. Autumn -- Fiction 2. Pumpkin -- Fiction 3. Friendship -- Fiction

ISBN 978-1-4169-8288-3; 1-4169-8288-4

LC 2008046639

While Peter carefully tends a special pumpkin on his grandparents' farm, quiet Meg watches from her new home next door.

"Illustrations, rendered in watercolors mottled by instant coffee and bleach, are full of life and happy moments. The iconic symbols of the season—falling leaves, acorns, ripe apples—help provide an idyllic autumnal setting for the appealing friendship story." Booklist

Moundlic, Charlotte

The **bathing** costume, or, The worst vacation of my life; by Charlotte Moundlic; illustrated by Olivier Tallec; translated by Claudia Zoe Bedrick. Enchanted Lion Books 2013 40 p. ill. (hardcover) $15.95

Grades: K 1 2 3   E

1. Summer -- Fiction 2. Cousins -- Fiction 3. Vacations -- Fiction 4. Grandparents -- Fiction

ISBN 1592701418; 9781592701414

LC 2013011002

Mildred L. Batchelder Honor Book (2014)

In this children's story, by Charlotte Moundlic, illustrated by Olivier Tallec, "this summer, Michel will go away alone . . . to stay with his grandparents while his parents move apartments. To add to the horror, Michel's older boy cousins will be going, too. . . . Between a competition to see who can shower the least, wild bike rides without gear, and a tooth that finally falls out, Michel discovers both independence and real moments of happiness." (Publisher's note)

The **scar**; [illustrations by Olivier Tallec] Candlewick Press 2011 il $14.99

Grades: K 1   E

1. Death -- Fiction 2. Mothers -- Fiction 3. Bereavement -- Fiction

ISBN 978-0-7636-5341-5; 0-7636-5341-1

LC 2010042792

When his mother dies, a little boy is angry at his loss but does everything he can to hold onto the memory of her scent, her voice, and the special things she did for him, even as he tries to help his father and grandmother cope.

"Rendered in pencil and wash in a limited palette of reds and yellows, simple illustrations stress the boy's distress and isolation while powerfully conveying his progression from anger and fear to sadness and acceptance. A sympathetic exploration of the stages of grief through the eyes of one little boy." Kirkus

Mozelle, Shirley

Zack's alligator and the first snow; story by Shirley Mozelle; pictures by James Watts. Harper 2011 32p il (I can read!) $16.99; pa $3.99

Grades: PreK K 1 2   E

1. Snow -- Fiction 2. Alligators -- Fiction

ISBN 978-0-06-147370-8; 0-06-147370-7; 978-0-06-147372-2 pa; 0-06-147372-3 pa

LC 2008034359

Zack and Bridget, his alligator keychain that grows into a fun-loving, full-sized alligator when it gets wet, enjoy the day playing in the snow, ice-fishing, and sledding.

"Watts' softly-colored illustrations reflect the joy and exuberance that snow brings, while Bridget's innocence is charming. . . . Simple sentences and vocabulary and a lively story make this just right for developing readers." Kirkus

Other titles about Zack's alligator are:

Zack's alligator (1989)

Zack's alligator goes to school (1994)

Muldrow, Diane

We planted a tree; illustrated by Bob Staake. Golden Books 2010 un il $17.99; lib bdg $20.99

Grades: PreK K 1 2   E

1. Trees -- Fiction 2. Growth -- Fiction 3. Ecology -- Fiction

ISBN 0-375-86432-6 lib bdg; 978-0-375-86432-2; 978-0-375-96432-9 lib bdg

LC 2009000394

"A family in Brooklyn plants a tree in their small backyard; turn the page and a Kenyan family plants a tree on the bare African savannah

Then in Paris, Tokyo, and more places across the globe, each newly planted tree grows up, as the children in the family do. Muldow weaves some science into the lines. . . . Illustrating the simple poetry are clean-lined digital illustrations that show the botany details and celebrate the connections between plants and people, present and long-term, across time and space." Booklist

Munari, Bruno

Bruno Munari's zoo; [by] Bruno Munari. Chronicle Books 2005 un il $17.95

Grades: PreK K   **E**

1. Zoos 2. Animals

ISBN 0-8118-4830-2

LC 2004-21214

A reissue of the title first published 1963 by World Publishing

Illustrations and brief text introduce more than twenty zoo animals, including a rhinoceros that is always ready to fight and a peacock that struts proudly because he is the peacock.

"A stunning picture book of birds and beasts original in design, brilliant with color, and touched with humor." Booklist

Muncaster, Harriet

I am a witch's cat; by Harriet Muncaster. Harper 2014 32 p. col. ill. (hardcover bdg.) $15.99

Grades: PreK K 1 2   **E**

1. Cats -- Fiction 2. Witches -- Fiction

ISBN 0062229141; 9780062229144

LC 2012022152

In this children's book, by Harriet Muncaster, "a little girl believes her mother is a good witch--and she is a special witch's cat! After all, every good witch needs a black cat. Together, this playful girl and her loving mom are a perfect twosome, whether they are mixing potions, growing magical plants, or dreaming of wild broomstick rides under a full moon." (Publisher's note)

"Muncaster's miniatures create an alluring backdrop for this ode to creative, capable mothers and their adoring familiars... er, children. And the story doesn't shut the door to the possibility of real magic, either. " Pub Wkly

Another title in this series is:

Happy Halloween, Witch's Cat! (2015)

Muntean, Michaela

★ **Do** not open this book! illustrated by Pascal LeMaitre. Scholastic Press 2006 un il $15.99

Grades: PreK K 1 2   **E**

1. Pigs -- Fiction 2. Authorship -- Fiction 3. Books and reading -- Fiction

ISBN 0-439-69839-1

As Pig tries to write a book, he chastises the reader who keeps interrupting him by turning the pages.

"Along with hand lettering Muntean's text, LeMaitre contributes bright, comics-style pictures that clarify the occasionally dizzying concepts. . . . Children will be . . . enraptured by the irreverent, interactive premise and will emerge with a fresh understanding of the powerful qualities of words." Booklist

Murphy, Claire Rudolf

Marching with Aunt Susan; Susan B. Anthony and the fight for women's suffrage. written by Claire Rudolf Murphy; illustrated by Stacey Schuett. Peachtree 2011 un il $16.95

Grades: 1 2 3 4   **E**

1. Suffragists 2. Abolitionists 3. Sex role -- Fiction 4. Women's rights -- Fiction 5. Women -- Suffrage -- Fiction

ISBN 978-1-56145-593-5; 1-56145-593-8

LC 2011002703

Not allowed to go hiking with her father and brothers because she is a girl, Bessie learns about women's rights when she attends a suffrage rally led by Susan B. Anthony.

"Schuett's somewhat impressionistic gouache paintings effectively capture the time and place and convey the emotionally charged tenor of the campaign. The endnotes, accompanied by photographs, provide factual material about the real Bessie Keith Pond, Anthony, and the suffrage movement, especially in California." SLJ

Murphy, Mary

Good night, sleep tight, like this; Mary Murphy. Candlewick Press 2016 32 p. color illustrations (hardcover) $12.99

Grades: PreK K   **E**

1. Bedtime -- Fiction

ISBN 9780763679705; 0763679704

LC 2015933234

This children's story, by Mary Murphy, seeks to be "the perfect soothing bedtime book for little children. The rhythmic text is just right for gently lulling them to sleep while cuddly rabbits, bears, dogs, and even a dragonfly each take turns tucking in their little ones. The gentle pacing and sweet pictures will be sure to elicit lots of oohs, aahs, and . . . zzzzzzs!" (Publisher's note)

"The cutaway pages, used consistently throughout... provid[e] an engaging, interactive experience for readers, as they can transform the illustration from the animal being awake to asleep." SLJ

★ **I** kissed the baby. Candlewick Press 2003 un il hardcover o.p. bd bk $6.99

Grades: PreK K 1   **E**

1. Ducks -- Fiction 2. Animals -- Fiction

ISBN 0-7636-2122-6; 0-7636-2443-8 bd bk

LC 2002-31419

Various animals tell how they saw, fed, sang to, tickled, and kissed the new duckling

"Murphy makes creative use of color on the edges of the black-and-white pages, until the duckling appears in a splash of vibrant yellow, and the text changes to hot pink. This is an ideal book for little eyes and ears, for text, illustrations, and design meld perfectly." SLJ

A **Kiss** like this; Mary Murphy. Candlewick Press 2012 32 p. $12.99

Grades: PreK K   **E**

1. Animals -- Fiction 2. Kissing -- Fiction 3. Parent-child relationship -- Fiction

ISBN 0763661821; 9780763661823

LC 2012942308

In this children's picture book by Mary Murphy, "split-page flaps reveal . . . . a silly series of animal kisses. . . . Each spread features a vibrantly hued child/parent pair of creatures, including giraffes, mice, fish, bees, elephants, owls and bunnies. The black, smudgy hand-lettered text describes the different kinds of kisses. . . . Each phrase ends with an ellipsis prompting readers to flip the half page to reveal 'like this!' and an eyes-closed buss." (Kirkus Reviews)

Say hello like this; Mary Murphy. Candlewick Press 2014 32 p. color illustrations $12.99

Grades: PreK K   **E**

1. Animals 2. Etiquette 3. Animal sounds

ISBN 0763669512; 9780763669515

LC 2013943080

In this children's concept book, written and illustrated by Mary Murphy, "different kinds of animals say hello in their own way. . . . Full of funny adjectives and sound words, this . . . companion to Mary Murphy's 'A Kiss Like This' is a . . . read-aloud for the very youngest of listeners." (Publisher's note)

"Each spread offers just enough detail to pique interest due to some clever bookmaking; when youngsters flip a flap, they will observe that the scene has changed considerably. . . . The repetitive phrasing acts as a prompt, encouraging youngsters to chime in." Booklist

Murphy, Stuart J.

Emma's friendwich. Charlesbridge Pub. 2010 un il (I see I learn) $14.95; pa $6.95

Grades: PreK K   **E**

1. Animals -- Fiction 2. Friendship -- Fiction

ISBN 978-1-58089-450-0; 1-58089-450-X; 978-1-58089-451-7 pa; 1-58089-451-8 pa

LC 2009027784

After moving to a new home, Emma makes friends with the girl next door. Includes questions about the text and notes to parents about visual learning.

"Murphy folds his educational points into a warm stand-alone story, and the cheerful, uncluttered, jellybean-colored spreads clearly illustrate friend-making steps." Booklist

Freda is found. Charlesbridge 2011 un il (I see I learn) $14.95; pa $6.95

Grades: PreK K   **E**

1. School stories 2. Animals -- Fiction 3. Missing children -- Fiction

ISBN 978-1-58089-462-3; 1-58089-462-3; 978-1-58089-463-0 pa; 1-58089-463-1 pa

On a field trip, Freda is separated from her class, but she remembers just what to do. Includes questions about the text and a note to parents about visual learning.

The book has "vibrant, playful illustrations featuring animated characters that reinforce the story [line]. The highlighted text and expanded captions convey the action." SLJ

★ **Leaping** lizards; illustrated by JoAnn Adinolfi. HarperCollins Pubs. 2005 33p il (MathStart) hardcover o.p. pa $4.99

Grades: 1 2 3   **E**

1. Addition 2. Counting 3. Stories in rhyme 4. Lizards -- Fiction

ISBN 0-06-000130-5; 0-06-000132-1 pa

LC 2004-22470

"This book introduces the multiples of five, as lizards of different colors travel through the pages on unicycles, a hot-air balloon, an airplane, and other modes of transport, while a green snake looks on. Finally, the number 50 is reached, and lizards explode in all directions. . . . An intelligent blending of white space and colors make each double-page spread visually stand out. A box on one side of each page helps children keep track of the multiplying lizards, and a closing section offers adults a few more ideas for easy math education." Booklist

Same old horse; illustrated by Steve Björkman. HarperCollins Pubs. 2005 31p il (Mathstart) hardcover o.p. pa $4.99

Grades: K 1 2 3   **E**

1. Horses -- Fiction

ISBN 0-06-055770-2; 0-06-055771-0 pa

Hankie wants to be unpredictable, but the other horses are sure he'll always be the same old Hankie. Someone's in for a surprise in this story about making predictions

This "is a lively story that encourages kids to work with numbers to find out what happens next. Bjorkman's clear, funny ink-and-watercolor

pictures show horses in a barnyard acting just like children on a school playground." Booklist

Write on, Carlos! illustrated by Tim Jones. Charlesbridge 2011 un il $14.95; pa $6.95

Grades: PreK K

1. Literacy -- Fiction 2. Personal names -- Fiction

ISBN 978-1-58089-464-7; 1-58089-464-X; 978-1-58089-465-4 pa; 1-58089-465-8 pa

LC 2010023522

With his mother's help, Carlos learns to write his name, as some of his friends can do.

This book has "vibrant, playful illustrations featuring animated characters that reinforce the story [line]. The highlighted text and expanded captions convey the action." SLJ

Murphy, Yannick

Baby Polar; illustrated by Kristen Balouch. Clarion Books 2009 un il $16   **E**

1. Storms -- Fiction 2. Polar bear -- Fiction 3. Arctic regions -- Fiction 4. Mother-child relationship -- Fiction

ISBN 978-0-618-99850-0; 0-618-99850-0

LC 200801161?

Even though his mother warns him of a coming storm, Baby Polar goes outside to play, but when he cannot see his own paw he realizes that he now faces danger.

"The illustrations are digitally produced and beautifully designed. Stylized white snowflakes and polar bear figures set against a blue gray background convey well the icy coldness of the storm. . . . The book's reassuring conclusion offers a satisfying story for that audience, as well as an introduction to polar bears and their Arctic world." SLJ

Murray, Alison

Apple pie ABC. Disney Hyperion 2011 un il $16.99

Grades: PreK K

1. Alphabet 2. Dogs -- Fiction 3. Pies -- Fiction

ISBN 978-1-4231-3694-1; 1-4231-3694-2

"It all starts with 'A apple pie' in this terse, alphabetically organized story: a towheaded little girl, accompanied by her loyal pooch, bakes that pie, cools it, then dishes out a piece for herself. And that's when her dog develops his obsession: he tries to get at the treat. . . . The illustrations, retro-touched digital art with a strong graphic sensibility and a hearkening back to block prints, take this neat concept and joyously gallop with it." Bull Cent Child Books

Hare and tortoise; Alison Murray. Candlewick Press 2016 32 p color illustrations $16.99

Grades: PreK K 1

1. Aesop's fables

ISBN 9780763687212

LC 201593612?

This book, by Alison Murray, is a "retelling of . . . [an] Aesop's fable with a mischievous twist. Hare (Leapus swifticus) can barely stay still for a minute. He's the fastest on the farm. Tortoise (Slow and steadicus) can stay still for a very long time. She has occasionally been mistaken for a rock. So when they decide to have a race, Hare is certain to win . . . isn't he?" (Publisher's note)

"It's hard to tell a well-known tale in a fresh, new way, but Murray accomplishes that in her version of these famous competitors." Booklist

The **house** that Zack built; Alison Murray. Candlewick Press 2015 32 p. color illustrations (hardcover) $16.99

Grades: PreK K   E
1. Stories in rhyme 2. Farm life -- Fiction
ISBN 9780763678449

LC 2014955413

In this children's story, by Alison Murray, "Zack [and his dog are] . . . enjoying a day on the farm, building an amazing house with his blocks. But nearby, a wandering fly has attracted the attention of an inquisitive and determined feline. Stalking and chasing through stylish illustrations, the cat unintentionally creates havoc." (Publisher's note)

"Perfect for giggling and sharing and right on target for lap-time reading." Kirkus

Little mouse; Alison Murray. 1st U.S. ed. Disney-Hyperion Books 2013 32 p. ill. (reinforced) $16.99
Grades: PreK   E
1. Picture books for children 2. Animals -- Fiction 3. Mother-daughter relationship -- Fiction 4. Nicknames -- Fiction 5. Mother and child -- Fiction
ISBN 1423143302; 9781423143307

LC 2012006147

In this book, "Mommy sometimes calls her daughter little mouse, which amuses the spirited child because her self-perception is that she's strong as an ox and brave as a lion and that she can howl like a wolf. But when bedtime nears and the sprightly child gets sleepy, she is more than happy to curl up in her mother's arms and be that little mouse." (Kirkus)

One two that's my shoe! Alison Murray. Disney-Hyperion Books 2012 32 p.
Grades: PreK   E
1. Counting 2. Stories in rhyme 3. Dogs -- Fiction 4. Picture books for children 5. Animals -- Infancy -- Fiction
ISBN 1423143299; 9781423143291

LC 2011013171

This preschool children's story, written and illustrated by Alison Murray, is a rhyming picture book describing a "mischievous puppy [who] runs off with his owner's shoe, it's a race from one to ten to get it back again!" (Publisher's note) Each page illustrates an exercise of counting household objects, animals, or landscape pieces. "The brief, rhymed text is . . . placed to allow viewers time to count the teddy bears, flowers, etc., along the way." (Kirkus Reviews)

Murray, Diana
City shapes; by Diana Murray; illustrated by Bryan Collier. Little, Brown & Co. 2016 40 p. color illustrations (hardcover) $17.99
Grades: PreK K 1   E
1. Stories in rhyme 2. Shape -- Fiction 3. City and town life -- Fiction 4. Pigeons -- Fiction
ISBN 9780316370929

LC 2015000410

This book, by Diana Murray, illustrated by Bryan Collier, is a "journey through a bustling city. . . . From shimmering skyscrapers to fluttering kites to twinkling stars high in the sky, everyday scenes become extraordinary as a young girl walks through her neighborhood noticing exciting new shapes at every turn." (Publisher's note)

"The rhyming text makes this suitable for story hours, but searching for the less obvious shapes will intrigue one-on-one viewers, as well." Booklist

Murray, Laura
The **gingerbread** man loose in the school; illustrated by Mike Lowery. G. P. Putnam's 2011 il $16.99

Grades: PreK K 1   E
1. School stories 2. Stories in rhyme 3. Cookies -- Fiction
ISBN 978-0-399-25052-1; 0-399-25052-2

LC 2009006642

A gingerbread man searches all over the school for the group of children that made him and then left him behind.

"With a little practice to get the beats just right, the text can be easily read aloud, and youngsters can be invited to chime in on the refrain: 'I'm the Gingerbread Man/and I'm trying to find,/the children who made me,/ but left me behind.' A variety of fonts is used to indicate differences between speakers and the narration. The cartoon illustrations are primitive in style, but suit the story to a tee." SLJ

Other titles in this series are:
The gingerbread man loose on the fire truck (2013)
The gingerbread man loose at Christmas (2015)
The gingerbread man loose at the zoo (2016)

Murray, Marjorie Dennis
Halloween night; by Marjorie Dennis Murray; illustrations by Brandon Dorman. Greenwillow Books 2008 un il $16.99; lib bdg $17.89
Grades: K 1 2 3   E
1. Stories in rhyme 2. Parties -- Fiction 3. Monsters -- Fiction 4. Halloween -- Fiction
ISBN 978-0-06-135186-0; 0-06-135186-5; 978-0-06-135187-7 lib bdg; 0-06-135187-3 lib bdg

LC 2007027686

Loosely based on "The Night Before Christmas," this rhyming story tells of a group of animals, monsters, and witches who prepare such a frightening Halloween party that their expected trick-or-treaters all run away.

"Murray's smooth rhyming text combines well with Dorman's vibrant and extraordinarily detailed digital art, with surprises on every page. This is an energetic romp with a satisfying conclusion that will be a fun read-aloud." SLJ

Murrow, Vita
The **Whale**; by Vita Murrow; illustrated by Ethan Murrow. Candlewick Press 2016 32 p. pencil illustrations $17.99
Grades: K 1 2 3 4   E
1. Whales -- Fiction 2. Stories without words
ISBN 0763679658; 9780763679651

LC 2014952640

This book, by Vita Murrow, illustrated by Ethan Murrow, is a "wordless epic sea adventure. There is a legend that a Great Spotted Whale lives in the ocean, although a sighting fifty years ago was never corroborated. Now two young whale watchers each set out to find the whale, one armed with sound-recording equipment, the other with a camera. When their boats collide, they pool their resources to capture incontrovertible proof that the mythical whale exists." (Publisher's note)

"More astounding is the artist's uncanny ability to reproduce the murky transparency of rippling ocean water, a whale submerged silently just beneath. Wordless, with masterful artwork and an intriguing narrative undertow, this whale's tale will transfix." Kirkus

Muth, Jon J.
Zen ghosts. Scholastic Press 2010 un il $17.99
Grades: K 1 2 3   E
1. Siblings -- Fiction 2. Halloween -- Fiction 3. Giant panda -- Fiction 4. Storytelling -- Fiction 5. Zen Buddhism -- Fiction
ISBN 978-0-439-63430-4; 0-439-63430-X

LC 2009-31236

On Halloween night, Stillwater the giant panda tells Karl, Addy, and Michael a spooky and unusual story. Based on a Zen koan.

"Haunting in multiple senses of the word, this tale should captivate thoughtful readers, as Muth's watercolors convey a world of infinite possibility and gentle enchantment." Publ Wkly

★ **Zen** shorts; illustrated by Jon Muth. Scholastic Press 2005 un il $16.95

Grades: K 1 2 3   E

1. Giant panda -- Fiction 2. Storytelling -- Fiction 3. Zen Buddhism -- Fiction

ISBN 0-439-33911-1

LC 2003-20471

A Caldecott Medal honor book, 2006

When Stillwater the panda moves into the neighborhood, the stories he tells to three siblings teach them to look at the world in new ways.

This "is both an accessible, strikingly illustrated story and a thought-provoking mediation." Booklist

Other titles about Stillwater the panda are:

Zen ties (2008)

Zen ghosts (2010)

Zen socks (2015)

Myers, Christopher

★ **Black** cat. Scholastic Press 1999 un il $16.95

Grades: PreK K 1 2   E

1. Cats -- Fiction 2. City and town life -- Fiction

ISBN 0-590-03375-1

LC 98-28609

A Coretta Scott King honor book for illustration, 2000

A black cat wanders through the streets of a city

"With striking photo-collages enhanced with gouache and ink, this book captures the gritty beauty of the city." Horn Book Guide

My pen; Christopher Myers. Disney-Hyperion 2015 32 p. illustrations hbk $16.99

Grades: K 1 2 3 4 5   E

1. Drawing -- Fiction 2. Imagination -- Fiction 3. Pens -- Fiction

ISBN 1423103718; 9781423103714

LC 2013047312

"Aurelio is a young artist with big eyes, a fedora, and, most importantly, a vivid imagination. In ink renderings on pages that maintain interest by alternating between black on white and the perception of the reverse, the boy contrasts the sense of being small--evoked when he sees rich and famous people--with the power he wields with his pen." (School Library Journal)

"Highly sophisticated concepts and art invite the long and close examination of older readers. Poignant, vulnerable, wise." Kirkus

Wings. Scholastic Press 2000 un il $16.95

Grades: K 1 2 3   E

1. Flight -- Fiction 2. Classical mythology -- Fiction

ISBN 0-590-03377-8

LC 99-87389

"Myers retells the myth of Icarus through the story of Ikarus Jackson, the new boy on the block, who can fly above the rooftops and over the crowd. In this contemporary version, the winged kid nearly falls from the sky . . . because jeering kids in the schoolyard and repressive adults don't like his being different and try to break his soaring spirit. . . . Myers' beautiful cut-paper collages are eloquent and open." Booklist

Myers, Tim

Basho and the river stones; illustrations by Oki S. Han. Marshall Cavendish 2004 un il $16.95

Grades: K 1 2 3   E

1. Poets 2. Authors 3. Foxes -- Fiction 4. Japan -- Fiction 5.

Poetry -- Fiction

ISBN 0-7614-5165-X

LC 2003-26245

Tricked by a fox into giving up his share of cherries, a famous Japanese poet is inspired to write a haiku and the fox, ashamed of his actions, must devise another trick to set things right

"Han's expressive watercolors, with an unusual variety of perspectives, keep the story lively. A clever original fable." Booklist

Another title about Basho by this author and illustrator is:

Basho and the fox (2000)

Myers, Walter Dean, 1937-2014

★ The **blues** of Flats Brown; illustrated by Nina Laden. Holiday House 2000 un il $16.95; pa $6.95

Grades: 1 2 3 4   E

1. Dogs -- Fiction 2. Blues music -- Fiction

ISBN 0-8234-1480-9; 0-8234-1679-8 pa

LC 99-16695

To escape an abusive master, a junkyard dog named Flats runs away and makes a name for himself from Mississippi to New York City playing blues on his guitar

"The narrator's vernacular, rhythmic and easy-rolling, has the feel of a timeless legend, and the vibrant, jewel-toned illustrations, dominated by moody, bittersweet, tonal variations of blue, are filled with rich detail, expressive characters, and fantastic landscapes." Booklist

Looking for the easy life; illustrated by Lee Harper. Harper 2010 un il $16.99

Grades: K 1 2 3   E

1. Work -- Fiction 2. Animals -- Fiction 3. Monkeys -- Fiction 4. Conduct of life -- Fiction

ISBN 978-0-06-054375-4; 0-06-054375-2; 978-0-06-065476-1 lib bdg; 0-06-054376-0 lib bdg

LC 2008-34360

Five monkeys go in search of the easy life, but find that "easy ain't always good" and "a little work ain't always bad."

"Myers . . . offers deft characterizations and quick retorts . . . and Harper's . . . animals grin and flirt engagingly. . . . Myers demonstrates a profound talent for kid-pleasing humor—it's a story-time natural." Publ Wkly

★ **Looking** like me; illustrated by Christopher Myers. Egmont USA 2009 un il

Grades: 1 2 3   E

1. Family life -- Fiction 2. African Americans -- Fiction 3. Harlem (New York, N.Y.) -- Fiction

ISBN 1-60684-001-0; 1-60684-041-X lib bdg; 978-1-60684-001-6; 978-1-60684-041-2 lib bdg

LC 2009-14640

Jeremy sets out to discover all of the different people that make him who he is, including brother, son, writer, and runner. "Grades two to four." (Bull Cent Child Books)

"The innovative art and design represent different identities with colorful silhouettes placed against photos of people, places, and icons. . . . This very contemporary work is encouraging, energetic, and inspired." Booklist

★ **Patrol**; an American soldier in Vietnam. collages by Ann Grifalconi. HarperCollins Pubs. 2002 un il hardcover o.p. lib bdg $16.89; pa $6.99

Grades: 3 4 5 6   E

1. Vietnam War, 1961-1975 -- Fiction 2. African American soldiers

-- Fiction

ISBN 0-06-028363-7; 0-06-028364-5 lib bdg; 0-06-073159-1 pa

LC 00-35009

A frightened American soldier faces combat in the lush forests of Vietnam and sees a young enemy soldier who is as frightened as he is

The story is told "in free verse that is at once ethereal and white-knuckle tense. . . . Grifalconi's intricate paper and photo collages juxtapose snips of explosion smoke, snapshot images of fleeing villagers, and paper constructions of burning huts against a landscape that approaches fantasy in its lush beauty." Bull Cent Child Books

Na, Il Sung

Bird, balloon, Bear; Il Sung Na. Alfred A. Knopf 2017 32 p. color illustrations (hardback) $17.99; (ebook) $53.97

Grades: PreK K   E

1. Bears -- Fiction 2. Birds -- Fiction 3. Friendship -- Fiction 4. Balloons -- Fiction

ISBN 9780399551550; 9780399551567; 9780399551574

LC 2016015829

In this children's book, by Il Sung Na, "Bird is new to the forest, and he's looking for a friend. Bear could use a friend, too. But Bird is too shy to introduce himself. Just as he musters the courage to say hello . . . it's too late! Bear has already found a friend: a bright, shiny red balloon. Has Bird missed his chance?" (Publisher's note)

"Any reader who has suffered on the sidelines will feel instant sympathy for Bird." Pub Wkly

A **book** of babies; by Il Sung Na. Alfred A. Knopf 2014 24 p. (hard cover) $15.99

Grades: PreK   E

1. Ducks -- Fiction 2. Animal babies -- Fiction 3. Birth -- Fiction 4. Animals -- Infancy -- Fiction

ISBN 0385752903; 9780385752909; 9780385752916

LC 2012050490

This picture book, by Il Sung Na, focuses on a "duck [who] leaves his own nest of ducklings to greet new animal babies far and wide. He pops up in . . . locales, observing infant fish, monkeys, zebras, lions, kangaroos, sea horses, polar bears and lizards—all snuggling with mommies and daddies in their habitats." (Kirkus Reviews)

A **book** of sleep. Alfred A. Knopf 2009 un il $15.99; lib bdg $18.99; bd bk $6.99

Grades: PreK K 1   E

1. Owls -- Fiction 2. Sleep -- Fiction 3. Animals -- Fiction

ISBN 978-0-375-86223-6; 0-375-86223-4; 978-0-375-96223-3 lib bdg; 0-375-96223-9 lib bdg; 978-0-375-86618-0 bd bk; 0-375-86618-3 bhd bk

LC 2008-47865

First published 2007 in the United Kingdom with title: Zzzz: a book of sleep

While other animals sleep at night, some quietly and others noisily, some alone and others huddled together, a wide-eyed owl watches.

"Na's textural images recall the lightheartedness and limpid charm of Paul Klee. . . . It's the rare picture book that, upon arrival, feels as though it has been around for years already; Na's belongs to this group." Publ Wkly

★ **Hide** & seek; by Il Sung Na. Alfred A. Knopf 2012 32 p.

Grades: PreK K   E

1. Games -- Fiction 2. Rain forests -- Fiction 3. Picture books for children 4. Rain forest animals -- Fiction 5. Animals -- Fiction 6. Elephants -- Fiction 7. Chameleons -- Fiction 8. Hide-and-seek

-- Fiction

ISBN 0375870784; 9780307974600; 9780375870781; 9780375970788

LC 2011021740

This picture book describes the action when "a group of animals plays a rainforest game of hide-and-seek," as the elephant counts and the flamingo, giraffe, rhino, and others find hiding places. Il Sung Na's artwork depicts a "tie-dyed rainforest awash in reds, yellows, greens and blues" and uses a "fusion of painterly textures, soft patterns and fine outlines . . . with dappled colors that shine like light through a leaf." (Kirkus)

The **opposite** zoo; Il Sung Na. Alfred A. Knopf 2016 24 p. color illustrations (hardcover) $16.99

Grades: PreK   E

1. Zoos -- Fiction 2. Animals -- Fiction 3. Monkeys -- Fiction 4. Opposites -- Fiction 5. Zoo animals -- Fiction 6. Polarity -- Fiction 7. English language -- Antonyms and synonyms -- Fiction

ISBN 9780553511277; 9780553511284

LC 2014043816

In this book, by Il Sung Na, "The sky is dark and the Opposite Zoo is CLOSED. But the monkey's cage is OPEN! Time to explore. . . . Follow the monkey as he visits all the animals in the zoo: fast and slow, big and small, noisy and quiet, soft and prickly! Filled with energetic illustrations, friendly animals, and a clear, simple text, . . . [this book] is a fun and lively introduction to animals and opposites for the youngest picture-book audience." (Publisher's note)

"As opposite books go, this picture book will be visually appealing to both adults and children, and it's a welcome addition to a genre that, for many parents, can often be opposite of interesting." Booklist

★ **Snow** rabbit, spring rabbit; a book of changing seasons. Alfred A. Knopf 2011 un il $15.99; lib bdg $18.99

Grades: PreK K 1   E

1. Winter -- Fiction 2. Animals -- Fiction 3. Rabbits -- Fiction 4. Seasons 5. Animal behavior

ISBN 0-375-86786-4; 0-375-96786-9 lib bdg; 978-0-375-86786-6; 978-0-375-96786-3 lib bdg

LC 2010-09361

First published 2010 in the United Kingdom with title: A book of winter

While other animals migrate, hibernate, or stay busy all winter, a little white rabbit watches.

"Complex and ethereal at the same time, Na's digitally manipulated spreads feature collage, stenciling, and finger painting over thickly daubed backgrounds; the pages teem with interest and texture." Publ Wkly

The **thingamabob**. Alfred A. Knopf 2010 un il $15.99; lib bdg $18.99

Grades: PreK K   E

1. Elephants -- Fiction 2. Umbrellas and parasols -- Fiction

ISBN 978-0-375-86106-2; 0-375-86106-8; 978-0-375-96106-9 lib bdg; 0-375-96106-2 lib bdg

LC 2009003120

First published 2008 in the United Kingdom

An elephant finds a "thingamabob" and experiments until he discovers what to do with it.

"Sumptuous colors and swirling textures turn this slight, silly story into a visual feast, buoyed by a handful of great sight gags and the hands-down adorableness of the animals." Booklist

Welcome home, Bear; a book of animal habitats. by Il Sung Na. Alfred A. Knopf 2015 28 p. color illustrations (hard cover) $16.99

Grades: PreK K 1   E
1. Home -- Fiction 2. Bears -- Fiction 3. Home -- Fiction 4.
Animals -- Habitations -- Fiction
ISBN 0385753756; 9780385753753; 9780385753760
LC 2013047989

In this children's story, by Il Sung Na, "Bear is tired of waking up
every morning in the same green forest, so he decides to search for a new
place to live. He visits the birds in the trees, a mole underground, a camel
in the hot desert sand, puffins in the cold arctic snow . . . only to realize
his own home is the perfect place for him after all." (Publisher's note)

"While successfully capturing the comforts of home, this story's
pleasing visuals feed the wanderlust impulse as well." SLJ

Naberhaus, Sarvinder
Blue sky white stars; Sarvinder Naberhaus; illustrated by Kadir
Nelson. Dial Books for Young Readers 2017 40 p. color illustrations
(hardcover) $17.99
Grades: PreK K 1 2   E
1. Patriotism -- Fiction 2. Flags -- United States 3. United States
-- Fiction 4. Flags -- United States -- Fiction
ISBN 9780803737006
LC 2016024848

This book, by Sarvinder Naberhaus, illustrated by Kadir Nelson, is
"an inspiring and patriotic tribute to the beauty of the American flag, a
symbol of America's history, landscape, and people. . . . Wonderfully
spare, deceptively simple verses pair with richly evocative paintings to
celebrate the iconic imagery of our nation, beginning with the American
flag." (Publisher's note)

Nakagawa, Chihiro
★ **Who** made this cake? text and English translation by Chihiro
Nakagawa; illustrations by Junji Koyose. Front Street 2008 un il
$16.95
Grades: PreK K 1   E
1. Cake -- Fiction 2. Size -- Fiction 3. Baking -- Fiction 4.
Construction equipment -- Fiction
ISBN 978-1-59078-595-9; 1-59078-595-9
LC 2008003070

While a boy and his parents go for an outing, little people invade the
house and use their big construction equipment to bake a cake.

"The understated text is almost unnecessary, as the pictures easily
tell the story and then some. . . . Truck fans will naturally pore over every
busy, action-filled scene." Horn Book

Napoli, Donna Jo
Albert; illustrated by Jim LaMarche. Silver Whistle Bks. 2001 un
il $16; pa $7
Grades: K 1 2 3   E
1. Birds -- Fiction
ISBN 0-15-201572-8; 0-15-205249-6 pa
LC 97-7089

One day when Albert is at his window, two cardinals come to build a
nest in his hand, an event that changes his life

"Napoli has written a pleasing modern fairy tale, transformed into a
picture book by LaMarche's appealing, shaded pencil drawings." Booklist

★ The **crossing**; [illustrated by Jim Madsen] Atheneum Books for
Young Readers 2011 un il $16.99
Grades: K 1 2   E
1. Trappers 2. Fur traders 3. Interpreters 4. Guides (Persons)
5. Native Americans -- Fiction 6. Shoshoni Indians -- Fiction 7.
Overland journeys to the Pacific -- Fiction 8. Lewis and Clark

Expedition (1804-1806) -- Fiction
ISBN 978-1-4169-9474-9; 1-4169-9474-2
LC 2010-08368

In 1805, Sacagawea, a woman of the Shoshoni tribe, helps Meriwether Lewis and William Clark find a passage to the West Coast, in
this story told through the eyes of the baby boy on Sacagawea's back.

"Short, poetic descriptions of the landscape and journey . . . close
with onomatopoetic phrases that refer to the many animals they meet
during the journey. . . . Madsen's . . . full-bleed full and half-spread
digital artwork is rendered in warm, earthy hues, shot through with tiny,
crackling lines that give the images an aura of old oil paintings. . . . A refreshing new angle on a familiar story of American history." Publ Wkly

The **Wishing** Club; a story about fractions. Henry Holt 2007 un
il $16.95
Grades: 1 2 3   E
1. Wishes -- Fiction 2. Siblings -- Fiction 3. Fractions -- Fiction
ISBN 978-0-8050-7665-3; 0-8050-7665-4
LC 2006030767

When four siblings wish on a star, each gets only a fraction of what
he or she wanted, but when they combine their wishes, they just might
get a whole new pet.

"Napoli's story moves smoothly between the magic of wishes granted and the reality of working with fractions. . . . Currey's watercolor-
and-ink illustrations evoke summer nights when barefoot youngsters
lean on porch railings and look at the stars." SLJ

Nargi, Lela
★ The **Honeybee** Man; illustrated by Kyrsten Brooker. Schwartz
& Wade Books 2011 un il $17.99; lib bdg $20.99
Grades: PreK K 1 2   E
1. Bees -- Fiction 2. Beekeeping -- Fiction 3. Brooklyn (New
York, N.Y.) -- Fiction
ISBN 978-0-375-84980-0; 0-375-84980-7; 978-0-375-95695-9
lib bdg; 0-375-95695-6 lib bdg
LC 2009044216

Fred, a beekeeper whose hives are on the roof of his Brooklyn, New
York, apartment building, tends his bees and distributes their honey to
his neighbors. Includes facts about bees and beekeepers.

"Copious details are carefully woven into descriptions of Fred's day-
today activities. . . . In sunny, oil-and-collage compositions, Brooker . .
. captures the bustle of sidewalks and storefronts, as well as the serenity
of Fred's rooftop and a green expanse of park. She also does a fine job
demonstrating the steps of collecting honey. . . . Kids should find this
easygoing blend of fiction and fact fascinating." Publ Wkly

Nascimbeni, Barbara
Animals and their families; Barbara Nascimbeni. Owlkids Books,
Inc. 2012 72 p. ill. (hardcover) $17.95
Grades: K 1 2   E
1. Animal behavior 2. Animals 3. Animal babies
ISBN 1926973321; 9781926973326
LC 2011935958

Parents' Choice Awards - Picture Books: 2012

Author Barbara Nascimbeni's book helps children "explore the animal kingdom . . . . A new creature is introduced in silhouette, while the
facing page shows that same creature in its natural habitat, playing with,
caring for, or teaching its young. All members of the animal family-
-male and female, adult and baby--are illustrated in warm colors and
identified by the proper term. Small bits of text share the sound each
animals makes, where it lives, and what it eats with young readers."
(Publisher's note)

Nazoa, Aquiles

A **small** Nativity; by Aquiles Nazoa; illustrated by Ana Palmero Cáceres; translated by Hugh Hazelton. Groundwood Books 2007 44p il $9.95

Grades: 1 2 3   E

1. Jesus Christ -- Nativity

ISBN 0-88899-839-2

"Venezuelan poet Nazoa's unadorned retelling of the Nativity story offers a homely approach to the familiar tale. . . . Palmero Cáceres illustrates this humble text with devotional pictures inspired by medieval illuminated manuscripts. Her richly colored art successfully combines traditional symbols of Christianity with images of Latin American flora and fauna." Horn Book

Nelson, Kadir

★ **Baby** Bear; words and paintings by Kadir Nelson. Balzer + Bray 2014 40 p. (hardcover bdg.) $17.99

Grades: PreK K 1   E

1. Home -- Fiction 2. Bears -- Fiction 3. Lost children -- Fiction 4. Forest animals -- Fiction

ISBN 0062241729; 9780062241726

LC 2013003083

This children's book, by Kadir Nelson, is "about a lost little bear searching for home." It functions "as the tale of a bear who finds his way home with the help of his animal friends; as a reassuring way to show children how to comfort themselves and find their way in everyday life; . . . as a method of teaching readers that by listening to your heart and trusting yourself, you will always find a true home within yourself." (Publisher's note)

Nelson, Marilyn

★ **Snook** alone; illustrated by Timothy Basil Ering. Candlewick Press 2010 48p il $16.99

Grades: K 1 2 3   E

1. Dogs -- Fiction 2. Monks -- Fiction 3. Islands -- Fiction

ISBN 978-0-7636-2667-9; 0-7636-2667-8

LC 2009-49040

"Snook is a rat terrier who lives with a monk on an island hermitage. . . . He gleefully munches rats while his companion works and prays. This simple, wonderful life is interrupted when a storm strands Snook on a tiny nearby atoll. Nelson writes in delicate stanzas of effortless poetry. . . . Ering's acrylic-and-ink artwork fades from the bright palette of the monk's abode to a nearly two-tone earthiness and creates a style both realistic and emotional. . . . The final reuniting is sudden yet as genuine as everything else about the book." Booklist

Nelson, Vaunda Micheaux

★ The **book** itch; freedom, truth, and Harlem's greatest bookstore. by Vaunda Micheaux Nelson; illustrated by R. Gregory Christie. Carolrhoda Books 2014 32 p. color illustrations (lib. bdg. : alk. paper) $17.99

Grades: 2 3 4 5   E

1. Booksellers and bookselling 2. African Americans -- Harlem (New York, N.Y.) 3. Bookstores 4. National Memorial African Bookstore\ 5. Harlem (New York, N.Y.) -- Intellectual life

ISBN 9780761339434

LC 2013040520

Coretta Scott King Illustrator Honor Book (2016)

This book, by Vaunda Micheaux Nelson, illustrated by R. Gregory Christie, "describes the role of the National Memorial African Bookstore in Harlem, which opened in the 1930s and became a place where all kinds of people came to read, talk, and buy books about African American history. Told from the point of view of Lewis Michaux Jr.—

the bookstore owner's son and the author's relative—this title clearly explains what made this bookstore unique." (School Library Journal)

"This companion to No Crystal Stair (2012) introduces younger readers to Nelson's great-uncle, Lewis Michaux Sr., owner of Harlem's National Memorial African Bookstore. Michaux's young son, Lewis Jr., narrates; he recalls helping his father with the day-to-day operation of the shop; visits from the famous, including Muhammad Ali and Malcolm X; and the devoted community patronage that helped the store thrive for nearly four decades. . . . Appended with generous back matter, including a list of sources, this moving tribute should be a welcome addition to almost any collection." Booklist

Includes bibliographical references

★ **Who** will I be, Lord? illustrated by Sean Qualls. Random House 2009 un il $16.95; lib bdg $19.99

Grades: PreK K 1 2   E

1. Family life -- Fiction 2. Occupations -- Fiction 3. African Americans -- Fiction

ISBN 978-0-375-84342-6; 0-375-84342-6; 978-0-375-94342-3 lib bdg; 0-375-94342-0 lib bdg

LC 2008035186

"An African-American girl looking to the future has a broad range of relatives to emulate—a banjo-playing mailman, a housewife who broke the color barrier, a pool shark, and a burger-flipping aspiring jazzman. Nelson's rhythmic and colloquial first-person narrative introduces the characters not only in terms of the jobs they hold, but also the kind of people they are. . . . Qualls's mixed-media illustrations combine muted and bright elements and feature full-spread renditions of each relative at home or work, followed by a page showing surreal floating heads of the girl and the featured role model as she repeats the title's query. Nelson shows respect for all the ways people live and work." SLJ

Nesbitt, Kenn

More bears! illustrated by Troy Cummings. Sourcebooks/Jabberwocky 2010 un il $12.99

Grades: PreK K 1   E

1. Bears -- Fiction 2. Authors -- Fiction

ISBN 978-1-4022-3835-2; 1-4022-3835-5

When an author starts writing, children yell that they want more bears in the story.

"Cummings's smooth, digitally rendered artwork does the job admirably. There is strong color on every page, and the bears are infused with zaniness and fun. The participatory refrain of 'More Bears' will bring this selection to life at storytimes." SLJ

Ness, Evaline

★ **Sam,** Bangs & Moonshine; written and illustrated by Evaline Ness. Holt & Co. 1966 un il $17.95; pa $6.95

Grades: PreK K 1 2   E

1. Imagination -- Fiction

ISBN 0-8050-0314-2; 0-8050-0315-0 pa

Awarded the Caldecott Medal, 1967

"In this unusually creative story the fantasy in which many, many children indulge is presented in a realistic and sympathetic context. The illustrations in ink and pale color wash (mustard, grayish-aqua) have a touching realism, too. This is an outstanding book." SLJ

Neubecker, Robert

What little boys are made of; by Robert Neubecker. Balzer + Bray 2012 32 p.

Grades: PreK K 1 2   E

1. Boys -- Fiction 2. Play -- Fiction 3. Stories in rhyme 4.

Imagination -- Fiction 5. Picture books for children
ISBN 9780062023551

LC 2011016612

In this children's picture book, the "half-pint hero imagines his way through most boys' obsessions. Astronaut, sports star, knight, dinosaur-tamer--they're all there, presented in action-packed, energetic illustrations. . . . Each verse begins with the boy and his toys in a plain and simple environment. But in resolving the verse ('That's what little boys are made of') . . . visually complex, full spreads are offered, giving readers insight into the boy's rollicking fantasies. . . . The illustrator also pays homage to a certain visual aesthetic for each of the youth's adventures." (Kirkus) "By the end, the text speculates that a boy's makeup consists of sugar and spice or puppy-dogs' tails but decides ultimately on snuggles and love." (School Libr J)

Nevius, Carol

Building with Dad; by Carol Nevius; illustrated by Bill Thomson. Marshall Cavendish 2006 un il $16.99
Grades: PreK K 1 2   E
1. Stories in rhyme 2. Building -- Fiction 3. Construction equipment -- Fiction 4. Father-son relationship -- Fiction
ISBN 978-0-7614-5312-3; 0-7614-5312-1

LC 2005027311

A father and his young child watch the construction of the new school, from the bulldozing of earth and mixing of the concrete for the foundation to the hanging of the new sign.

This is an "energetic picture book with visual punch. . . . The spreads spill down the page vertically, rather than horizontally, for maximum impact. . . . Thomson uses full color, and his photo-realistic paintings bring viewers close up to, sometimes even under, giant machines." Booklist

★ **Karate** hour; illustrated by Bill Thomson. Marshall Cavendish 2004 un il $14.95
Grades: PreK K 1 2   E
1. Stories in rhyme 2. Karate -- Fiction
ISBN 0-7614-5169-2

LC 2003-27122

Rhyming text portrays the exuberance of an hour of karate class. Includes nonfiction information at end

Nevius "deftly captures the excitement and energy of the experience as well as the discipline and commitment required to rise in rank. Thomson's realistic mixed-media artwork is a standout, using light, shadow, and perspective in a variety of interesting ways." SLJ

Soccer hour; illustrated by Bill Thomson. Marshall Cavendish 2010 un il $16.99
Grades: PreK K 1 2   E
1. Stories in rhyme 2. Soccer -- Fiction
ISBN 978-0-7614-5689-6; 0-7614-5689-9

LC 2009014112

Pictures and rhyming text describe the drills and scrimmages of a team at soccer practice.

"This book offers a winning combination of rhyming couplets and striking artwork to describe an hour of practice among boys and girls. While the text reads in bursts of active statements . . . the extraordinary illustrations are the essence of the book. Thomson uses acrylics and colored pencils to create realistic paintings that almost resemble sepia photographs." SLJ

Newberry, Clare Turlay

Marshmallow; story and pictures by Clare Turlay Newberry. rev ed.; HarperCollinsPublishers 2008 un il $16.99; lib bdg $17.89; pa $6.99

Grades: K 1 2   E
1. Cats -- Fiction 2. Rabbits -- Fiction
ISBN 978-0-06-072486-3; 0-06-072486-2; 978-0-06-072487-0 lib bdg; 0-06-072487-0 lib bdg; 978-0-06-072488-7 pa; 0-06-072488-9 pa

LC 2007-30888

First published 1942
A Caldecott Medal honor book, 1943
A cat who is used to being the center of attention learns to share his home with a rabbit

Newbery, Linda

★ **Posy!** illustrated by Catherine Rayner. Atheneum Books for Young Readers 2009 un il $16.99
Grades: PreK K   E
1. Stories in rhyme 2. Cats -- Fiction
ISBN 978-1-4169-7112-2; 1-4169-7112-2

LC 2008-03807

Posy the kitten has lots of adventures catching spiders, swiping crayons, tangling yarn, and cuddling

"Rendered in watercolor pencil crayons, acrylic, and India inks, [Posy] sometimes dominates the broad cream-colored spreads or divides a page into several vignettes with her actions. . . . While grownups, particularly cat lovers, will be charmed by the stylized art, children will notice in the kitten's daily activities much of what interests them." SLJ

Newgarden, Mark

★ **Bow**-Wow bugs a bug; [by] Mark Newgarden and Megan Montague Cash. Harcourt 2007 un il $12.95
Grades: K 1 2 3   E
1. Stories without words 2. Dogs -- Fiction 3. Insects -- Fiction
ISBN 978-0-15-205813-5

LC 2006-11026

A wordless picture book about a persistent terrier who follows a bug through his neighborhood.

"The clever circular plot is funny, quirky, and even suspenseful. . . . The simple, bold, expressive illustrations, outlined with heavy black line, challenge viewers to follow the visual story line and sequences of events." SLJ

Other titles about Bow-Wow are:
Bow-Wow naps by number (2007)
Bow-Wow orders lunch (2007)
Bow-Wow attracts opposites (2008)
Bow-Wow hears things (2008)
Bow-Wow 12 months running (2009)
Bow-Wow's colorful life (2009)

Newman, Jeff

The **boys**; written by Jeff Newman; illustrated by Jeff Newman. Simon & Schuster Books for Young Readers 2009 un il $15.99
Grades: 1 2 3   E
1. Stories without words 2. Old age -- Fiction 3. Shyness -- Fiction 4. Baseball -- Fiction
ISBN 1-4169-5012-5; 978-1-4169-5012-7

LC 2007-47985

A shy boy, seeking the courage to play baseball with the other children in a park, is coaxed out of his shell by some "old-timers" sitting nearby. "Ages six to nine." (Bull Cent Child Books)

"Employing sly visual humor, Newman . . . presents the narrative in sketchy, retro-flavored gouache brushstrokes on a white background. This is a quirky book, but sensitive readers will appreciate the child's shyness and the men's efforts to help him remember what it means to be a kid." Publ Wkly

★ **Hand** book. Simon & Schuster Books for Young Readers 2011 il $15.99

Grades: PreK K 1 2   E

1. Stories in rhyme 2. Hand -- Fiction 3. Growth -- Fiction
ISBN 978-1-4169-5013-4; 1-4169-5013-3

LC 2010007017

Follows a person's journey through life, focusing on the hands and what they do, from babyhood to adulthood when a new pair of hands comes into existence.

"Telegraphic verse and line drawings celebrate the many things hands can do. . . . Newman challenges readers to consider their hands as intricate and capable tools, instruments of emotion, creation, and tenderness; children will almost certainly see them with new respect." Publ Wkly

Newman, Leslea

The **best** cat in the world; written by Lesléa Newman; illustrated by Ronald Himler. Eerdmans Books for Young Readers 2004 un il $16; pa $8

Grades: K 1 2 3   E

1. Cats -- Fiction 2. Death -- Fiction
ISBN 0-8028-5252-1; 0-8028-5294-7 pa

LC 2003-13028

A young boy deals with the loss of his beloved cat Charlie, eventually accepting the arrival of another, very different cat.

"Himler's warm pencil-and-watercolor illustrations generously fill the pages. They portray the casually clad characters with tenderness and contrast the shape of the old and sick animal with that of the young and playful one. . . . For comfort and catharsis, Newman's fine story is the cat's pajamas." SLJ

Daddy, papa, and me; illustrated by Carol Thompson. Tricycle Press 2009 un il bd bk $7.99

Grades: PreK   E

1. Board books for children 2. Homosexuality -- Fiction 3. Father-child relationship -- Fiction
ISBN 978-1-58246-262-2 bd bk; 1-58246-262-3 bd bk
ALA GLBTRT Stonewall Book Award Honor Book (2010)

"A smiling tot describes his role within a nurturing two-dad family. . . . Thompson provides warm, mixed-media illustrations of the happy trio against clean white backgrounds as they play and keep house together. . . . It gives children with single-sex parents validation of their family structures in a healthy, positive way." Kirkus

Donovan's big day. Tricycle Press 2011 un il $15.99; lib bdg $18.99

Grades: PreK K   E

1. Stories in rhyme 2. Lesbians -- Fiction 3. Weddings -- Fiction 4. Mother-son relationship -- Fiction
ISBN 978-1-58246-332-2; 1-58246-332-8; 978-1-58246-392-6 lib bdg; 1-58246-392-1 lib bdg

LC 2009048488

"Plain and poetic, the swiftly flowing free verse perfectly captures the day's excitement, as does Dutton's digitally touched gouache artwork. . . . A welcome addition to the still short shelf of picture books featuring same-sex parents." Booklist

Heather has two mommies; written by Lesléa Newman; illustrated by Laura Cornell. 25th anniv edition Candlewick Press 2015 32 p. color illustrations $16.99

Grades: PreK K 1   E

1. Lesbians -- Fiction 2. Homosexuality -- Fiction 3. Family -- Fiction 4. Lesbian mothers -- Fiction 5. Mothers and daughters

-- Fiction
ISBN 0763666319; 9780763666316

LC 99087285

Originally published 1989

"Heather's favorite number is two. She has two arms, two legs, and two pets. And she also has two mommies. When Heather goes to school for the first time, someone asks her about her daddy, but Heather doesn't have a daddy. Then something interesting happens. When Heather and her classmates all draw pictures of their families, not one drawing is the same." (Publisher's note)

"Newman's picture book about Heather and her mommies first appeared 25 years ago as the product of desktop publishing and a determination to create a story reflecting family diversity. This updated version includes new illustrations by the commercially successful Cornell, which supply humor and avoid lesbian stereotypes that dogged earlier versions." Kirkus

★ **Ketzel,** the cat who composed; Leslea Newman, illustrated by Amy Bates. Candlewick Press 2015 40 p. color illustrations $16.99

Grades: K 1 2 3   E

1. Cats -- Fiction 2. Composers -- United States 3. Pianists -- Fiction 4. Friendship -- Fiction
ISBN 076366555X; 9780763665555

LC 2013957479

This children's book by Leslea Newman, illustrated by Amy June Bates, tells how a "kitten's stroll down a keyboard leads to a celebrated one-minute composition in this charming portrait of a remarkable true friendship. Moshe Cotel was a composer who lived in a noisy building on a noisy street in a noisy city. But Moshe didn't mind. Everything he heard was music to his ears. One day, while out for a walk, he heard a small, sad sound that he'd never heard before. It was a tiny kitten!" (Publisher's note)

"Here's a lovely tale of cross-species affection and creativity, based on a true story (recounted in an afterword). While seeking inspiration in the busy streets of New York City, a composer and pianist named Moshe Cotel finds and adopts a stray kitten, bestowing it with the Yiddish name Ketzel (for "kitten"). Ketzel proves more than a companion: when Moshe needs an entry for a music competition restricted to pieces no longer than one minute, the kitten steps in and composes a piece by walking across the keys (Moshe dubs it "Piece for Piano: Four Paws" and gives her full credit). . . . Bates, working in hues of parchment and gold, produces some wonderfully warm vignettes, pushing the graceful realism of her watercolor, gouache, and pencil drawings just enough to add a glint of magic to a story that's already one of a kind." PW

Miss Tutu's star; illustrated by Carey Armstrong-Ellis. Abrams 2010 un il $16.95

Grades: PreK K 1 2   E

1. Ballet -- Fiction
ISBN 978-0-8109-8396-0; 0-8109-8396-6

Young Selena, who would rather twirl than walk, begins to study ballet and, after years of practice and a great deal of encouragement from Miss Tutu, finally makes her stage debut.

"Armstrong-Ellis's gouache and colored-pencil illustrations add comic touches. . . . The protagonist is a likable character with lots of heart. Many children will recognize themselves in this agreeable offering." SLJ

★ **Mommy,** mama, and me; illustrated by Carol Thompson. Tricycle Press 2009 un il (My family tree) bd bk $7.99

Grades: PreK   E

1. Board books for children 2. Lesbians -- Fiction 3. Mother-child relationship -- Fiction
ISBN 978-1-58246-263-9 bd bk; 1-58246-263-1 bd bk

ALA GLBTRT Stonewall Book Award Honor Book (2010)

"A curly-haired toddler . . . celebrates 'mommy' and 'mama,' and the activities and tender moments they share. . . . The bright colors . . . and pleasing verse offer a simple lesson about love that same-sex parents should embrace." Publ Wkly

Newman, Robin

The **case** of the missing carrot cake; by Robin Newman; illustrated by Deborah Zemke. Creston Books 2015 40 p. (hardback) $15.95

Grades: K 1 2 3 4   **E**

1. Farm life -- Fiction 2. Mystery fiction -- Fiction

ISBN 1939547172; 9781939547170

LC 2015006474

In this children's story, by Robin Newman, illustrated by Deborah Zemke, part of the "Wilcox and Griswold mystery" series, "when Miss Rabbit leaves her carrot cake (with cream-cheese icing) out to cool and returns later to find only a mess of crumbs, she calls Detective Wilcox and Capt. Griswold. Over 100 animals on Ed's farm means there's a lot of suspects." (Kirkus Reviews)

Nichols, Lori

Maple; written and illustrated by Lori Nichols. Nancy Paulsen Books 2014 32 p.

Grades: PreK K 1   **E**

1. Trees -- Fiction 2. Sisters -- Fiction 3. Maple -- Fiction 4. Trees -- Fiction 5. Babies -- Fiction 6. Sisters -- Fiction 7. Friendship -- Fiction

ISBN 9780399160851; 039916085X

LC 2013013715

Other titles in this series are: Maple and Willow Together (2014); Maple and Willow Apart (2015); Maple and Willow's Christmas Tree (2016)

In this book, by Lori Nichols, "when Maple is tiny, her parents plant a maple tree in her honor. She and her tree grow up together, and even though a tree doesn't always make an ideal playmate, it doesn't mind when Maple is in the mood to be loud. Then Maple becomes a big sister, and finds that babies have their loud days, too. Fortunately, Maple and her beloved tree know just what the baby needs." (Publisher's note)

Maple and Willow together; Lori Nichols. Nancy Paulsen Books, an imprint of Penguin Group (USA) 2014 32 p. color illustrations $16.99

Grades: PreK K 1   **E**

1. Sisters -- Fiction 2. Friendship -- Fiction 3. Nature -- Fiction

ISBN 0399162836; 9780399162831

LC 2013043045

Sequel to: Maple (2014)

This children's book by Lori Nichols examines "the dynamics of siblings and their ability to figure things out on their own and find a way to meet halfway. Maple and Willow . . . love playing outside. But it's not always sunshine and rainbows, because sometimes big sisters can be bossy--and sometimes little sisters can be frustrating--and even the best of friends need a break from each other . . . at least until they can no longer bear to be apart." (Publisher's note)

"This paean to sisterhood reintroduces the title character in Maple (2014), whose parents planted a maple tree before she was born. They did the same for Willow, who is a most satisfactory younger sister... Nichols is clever enough to build the sisters' subtle differences, so their breakup comes from somewhere. Children will feel all that the girls do: love, anger, and the happiness that comes with making up." Booklist

Niemann, Christoph

Pet dragon; a story about adventure, friendship, and Chinese characters. by Christoph Niemann. Greenwillow Books 2008 un il $16.99; lib bdg $17.89

Grades: K 1 2 3   **E**

1. Chinese language 2. China -- Fiction 3. Dragons -- Fiction 4. Witches -- Fiction

ISBN 978-0-06-157776-5; 0-06-157776-6; 978-0-06-157777-2 lib bdg; 0-06-157777-4 lib bdg

When Lin's beloved pet dragon disappears, she searches for him far and wide until a witch helps her to reach the dragon's new home. Introduces a different Chinese character on each step of Lin's adventure.

"The book is clever. Its purpose is to introduce the Chinese language, and it succeeds admirably. Each page contains one or more Chinese characters, which appear not only at the bottom with the English translation, but also superimposed on the drawings. . . . The stylized illustrations are jaunty and appealing, and the use of red, a color representing good fortune in China, visually unifies the tale from beginning to end. Playful and humorous." SLJ

The **potato** king; Christoph Niemann. Owlkids Books, Inc. 2015 32 p. (hardcover) $17.95

Grades: K 1 2 3   **E**

1. Potatoes 2. Kings and rulers

ISBN 1771471395; 9781771471398

LC 2014950139

This children's book, illustrated by Christoph Niemann, describes how "once upon a time there was a Prussian King, Frederick, . . . who saw potential in the lowly potato. . . . However, it quickly became clear that his subjects didn't like being told what to eat. Determined to see the potato thrive, Fritz cleverly used reverse psychology to pique his people's curiosity and make the crop popular, and the potato has flourished ever since." (Publisher's note)

★ **Subway**. Greenwillow Books 2010 un il $16.99; lib bdg $17.89

Grades: PreK K 1 2   **E**

1. Stories in rhyme 2. Subways -- Fiction 3. New York (N.Y.) -- Fiction

ISBN 978-0-06-157779-6; 0-06-157779-0; 978-0-06-157780-2 lib bdg; 0-06-157780-4 lib bdg

LC 2009-18756

"This colorful, vivacious, child-centered title began with a post on Niemann's blog, Abstract City, in which he describes a day of riding the subway with his two sons just for fun. The artist uses thick gouache paint to render his characters as standard pictograms, akin to those on city signs, with curved edges for hands and feet, and the technique creates a chalky texture that looks like correction fluid. . . . A sure hit with most youngsters, especially those who are transfixed by trains." SLJ

That's how! Greenwillow Books 2011 un il $16.99

Grades: PreK K 1   **E**

1. Vehicles -- Fiction 2. Imagination -- Fiction

ISBN 978-0-06-201963-9; 0-06-201963-5

LC 2010017210

"A boy entertains his friend with cleverly imagined ideas about how a number of vehicles work. When she asks about a truck, he responds 'Hmmm. . . let me think.' A flip of the page shows a yellow lion pedaling a bicyclelike chain and gears inside a black truck. . . . The freighter is run by an octopus winding a whale's tale, the steamroller by a bird tickling two bears, and so forth. . . . The mixed-media digital illustrations are saturated full-bleed spreads. . . . Boy, girl, animals, and vehicles are all done in bold colors and have a cartoonish, childlike sensibility. The large trim size, popular topic, and brightly colored artwork will work well in storytimes.... A surefire hit." SLJ

Nikola-Lisa, W.

Magic in the margins; a medieval tale of bookmaking. by W. Nikola-Lisa; illustrated by Bonnie Christensen. Houghton Mifflin 2007 un il $17

Grades: 1 2 3 4   E
1. Artists -- Fiction 2. Orphans -- Fiction 3. Apprentices -- Fiction 4. Middle Ages -- Fiction 5. Illumination of books and manuscripts -- Fiction
ISBN 978-0-618-49642-6; 0-618-49642-4

LC 2006017060

At a medieval monastery, orphaned Simon, who is apprenticing in illumination, dreams of the day he can create his own pictures, but finds he must first complete a strange and unusual assignment that Father Anselm has given him.

"Many kids ... will be drawn in by the appealing story of a child's empowerment and the glimpse of the medieval world. Christensen extends the story with strong, clear scenes, bordered by botanical patterns and executed in ink and egg-tempura pigments." Booklist

Setting the turkeys free; written by W. Nikola-Lisa; illustrated by Ken Wilson-Max. Jump at the Sun/Hyperion Books for Children 2004 un il $15.99

Grades: PreK K 1   E
1. Foxes -- Fiction 2. Artists -- Fiction 3. Turkeys -- Fiction
ISBN 0-7868-1952-9

LC 2003-50928

When a sly, hungry fox threatens a flock of turkeys, the young artist who drew the birds must find a way to save them.

"Right at a preschooler's level, the artwork ... has humor as well as momentum.... This clever mixing of art and a spot-on text provides a fun story as well as a surefire craft idea that kids will want to try." Booklist

Nilsson, Ulf

A **Complicated** Case; Ulf Nilsson; illustrated by Gitte Spee. Lerner Pub Group 2016 96 p. color illustrations $16.99

Grades: 1 2 3 4   E
1. Detectives -- Fiction 2. Police -- Fiction 3. Forest animals -- Fiction
ISBN 1776570596; 9781776570591

In this children's book, by Ulf Nilsson and illustrated by Gitte Spee, "there is something going on among the forest animals that's making everyone unhappy. Detective Gordon and police assistant Paddy have a new case to investigate!" (Publisher's note)

"A wonderful choice for independent reading, particularly for kids who become accomplished readers early, the handsome first volume in the Detective Gordon series is a rewarding read-aloud as well." Booklist

Nobisso, Josephine

Francis woke up early; illuminations, Maureen Hyde. Gingerbread House 2011 un il $17.95; pa $9.95

Grades: K 1 2 3   E
1. Saints 2. Italy -- Fiction 3. Saints -- Fiction 4. Wolves -- Fiction 5. Writers on religion 6. Farm life -- Fiction
ISBN 978-0-940112-20-9; 0-940112-20-5; 978-0-940112-22-3 pa; 0-940112-20-5 pa

LC 2011015539

Imagines a moment in the boyhood of Saint Francis of Assisi, in which he befriends a wild she-wolf by sharing with her his breakfast, gathered on his family's farm.

"A beautiful marriage of author, illustrator, and subject.... Hyde's work ... perfectly captures early morning light in 13th-century Assisi. The bordered paintings are filled with tender detail.... This exquisite book will make peaceful family reading." Publ Wkly

Noble, Trinka Hakes

★ The **day** Jimmy's boa ate the wash; pictures by Steven Kellogg. Dial Bks. for Young Readers 1980 un il $16.99; pa $6.99

Grades: PreK K 1 2   E
1. School stories 2. Snakes -- Fiction 3. Farm life -- Fiction
ISBN 0-8037-1723-7; 0-8037-0094-6 pa

LC 80-15098

"The illustrations, which depict disgruntled chickens, expressive pigs, and smiling cats as well as other individualized animal and human characters, show the artist's flair for humorous detail." Horn Book

Other titles about Jimmy's boa are:
Jimmy's boa and the big splash birthday bash (1989)
Jimmy's boa and the bungee jump slam dunk (2003)
Jimmy's boa bounces back (1984)

The **last** brother; a Civil War tale. illustrated by Robert Papp. Sleeping Bear Press 2006 un il $17.95

Grades: 2 3 4 5   E
1. Brothers -- Fiction 2. Gettysburg (Pa.), Battle of, 1863 -- Fiction 3. United States -- History -- 1861-1865, Civil War -- Fiction
ISBN 1-58536-253-0

Eleven-year-old Gabe enlists in the Union Army in Pennsylvania along with his older brother Davy and, as bugler, does his best to protect Davy during the Battle of Gettysburg.

This "story resonates with courage and fear, love and loyalty.... The well-rendered paintings are hauntingly detailed and place readers right in the action." SLJ

Nolan, Dennis

Hunters of the great forest; Dennis Nolan. Roaring Brook Press 2014 40 p. color illustrations (hardcover) $17.99

Grades: PreK K 1 2   E
1. Hunting -- Fiction 2. Stories without words 3. Adventure stories
ISBN 1596438967; 9781596438965

LC 2013044241

In this children's book, by Dennis Nolan, "On a warm night, a band of hunters sets out on a journey. As they travel over hills, through thickets of trees, and around mountains, nothing will keep them from their ultimate goal. What that goal is may surprise you." (Publisher's note)

" Nolan's illustrations are wonderfully detailed and textured, from the jagged roots and tree bark the group climbs to the wings of the dragonfly that soars overhead. His work with shadows is exceptionally impressive ... [h]owever, very young readers may be frightened by the team's antics, as the backyard animals that chase the travelers come across as monsterlike. Overall, this is a good adventure story that's silly and original. Fans of David Wiesner's imaginative works may want to give it a try." SLJ

★ **Sea** of dreams. Roaring Brook Press 2011 il $16.99

Grades: PreK K 1   E
1. Stories without words 2. Beaches -- Fiction
ISBN 978-1-59643-470-7; 1-59643-470-8

LC 2010037815

A wordless picture book featuring a sandcastle that takes on a life of its own.

"Nolan's enchanting artwork creates a gorgeous, wordless nautical fantasy infused with the thrill of life-or-death adventure.... Readers will never look at the beach the same way." Publ Wkly

Nolen, Jerdine

★ **Big** Jabe; illustrations by Kadir Nelson. Lothrop, Lee & Shepard Bks. 2000 un il hardcover o.p. pa $6.99

Grades: K 1 2 3   E

1. Slavery -- Fiction 2. African Americans -- Fiction

ISBN 0-688-13662-1; 0-06-054061-3 pa

LC 99-38001

Momma Mary tells stories about a special young man who does wondrous things, especially for the slaves on the Plenty Plantation

"Nolen recounts her original tale with a light touch and lyrical voices that add depth and resonance to its imagery and serious overtones. The gouache and watercolor illustrations convey both the lush summer and the rigorous life of the slaves. This powerful story will be particularly effective shared aloud." Horn Book Guide

Block party surprise; by Jerdine Nolen, illustrated by Michelle Henninger. Houghton Mifflin Harcourt 2015 48 p. illustrations (The Bradford Street buddies) $3.99

Grades: 1 2 3   E

1. Twins -- Fiction 2. Robots -- Fiction 3. Parties -- Fiction 4. Friendship -- Fiction 5. African Americans -- Fiction 6. Brothers and sisters -- Fiction

ISBN 9780544358638

LC 2014006758

In this book, by Jerdine Nolen, illustrated by Michelle Henninger, "the neighborhood block party is today. Jada and Jamal Perkins are super excited. Their best friends, Carlita Garcia and Josh Cornell, are on their way over. Mr. Perkins promised them a BIG surprise." (Publisher's note)

Another title in this series is:

Backyard camp-out (2015)

Christmas in the time of Billy Lee; illustrated by Barry Moser. Disney/Jump at the Sun Books 2010 un il $16.99

Grades: PreK K 1   E

1. Wishes -- Fiction 2. Christmas -- Fiction 3. Imaginary playmates -- Fiction

ISBN 978-0-7868-1871-6; 0-7868-1871-9

When Ellie makes three wishes and begins to believe in the magic of Christmas, all kinds of miracles occur, from broken tree lights twinkling again, to angel shapes appearing in snow, to the biggest of all: a baby brother arriving soon.

"The acknowledgment of money troubles and other concerns makes the magic feel all the sweeter, as Moser's bucolic winter landscapes and cozy portraits convey a hushed wonderment and warm family bonds." Publ Wkly

Harvey Potter's balloon farm; [illustrated by] Mark Buehner. Lothrop, Lee & Shepard Bks. 1994 un il $16.99; lib bdg $15.93; pa $5.99

Grades: PreK K 1 2   E

1. Tall tales 2. Balloons -- Fiction 3. Farm life -- Fiction

ISBN 0-688-07887-7; 0-688-07888-5 lib bdg; 0-688-15845-5 pa

LC 91-38129

"Harvey Potter's unusual crop is balloons—which grow just like corn on long, sturdy stalks. Harvey Potter himself is not at all unusual, and his friend, a young African-American girl, is determined to uncover the secret of his curious harvest. The story is lively, but of even greater attraction are the vivid, air-brushed illustrations of balloons with expressive faces in every size, color, and shape." Horn Book Guide

★ **Hewitt** Anderson's great big life; illustrated by Kadir Nelson. Simon & Schuster Books for Young Readers 2005 un il $16.95

Grades: PreK K 1 2   E

1. Size -- Fiction 2. Giants -- Fiction

ISBN 0-689-86866-9

LC 98-14039

When tiny Hewitt is born into a family of giants, everyone learns that sometimes small is best of all.

"Nelson's funny, larger-than-life oil paintings warmly depict this African-American family and give readers a real sense of gigantic proportions. . . . Told in colorful language that begs to be read aloud, this humorous, oversize book offers a gentle look at accepting others as they are." SLJ

Pitching in for Eubie; illustrated by E.B. Lewis. Amistad 2007 un il $16.99; lib bdg $17.89

Grades: PreK K 1 2   E

1. Sisters -- Fiction 2. Family life -- Fiction 3. African Americans -- Fiction 4. Money-making projects for children -- Fiction

ISBN 978-0-688-14917-8; 978-0-06-056960-0 lib bdg

LC 2007-06995

Lily tries to find a way to pitch in and help her family make enough money to send her older sister, Eubie, to college

"Imbued with warmth, Nolen's . . . story about a family working together toward a common goal will appeal to many audiences. . . . Each painting helps advance the action and delineate the characters." Publ Wkly

★ **Thunder** Rose; illustrated by Kadir Nelson. Harcourt 2003 un il $16; pa $7

Grades: K 1 2 3   E

1. Tall tales 2. West (U.S.) -- Fiction 3. African Americans -- Fiction

ISBN 0-15-216472-3; 0-15-206006-5 pa

LC 2002-12287

Unusual from the day she is born, Thunder Rose performs all sorts of amazing feats, including building fences, taming a stampeding herd of steers, capturing a gang of rustlers, and turning aside a tornado

"Nolen and Nelson offer up a wonderful tale of joy and love, as robust and vivid as the wide West. The oil, watercolor, and pencil artwork is outstanding." SLJ

Noodleheads see the future; by Tedd Arnold, Martha Hamilton and Mitch Weiss; illustrated by Tedd Arnold. Holiday House 2017 48 p. color illustrations (Noodleheads) (hardcover) $15.95

Grades: K 1 2 3   E

1. Humorous fiction 2. Brothers -- Fiction 3. Fools and jesters -- Fiction 4. Humorous stories 5. Brothers -- Fiction 6. Fools and jesters -- Fiction

ISBN 9780823436736

LC 2016004460

In this book in the Early Chapter series, by Tedd Arnold, Martha Hamilton and Mitch Weiss, "although Mac and Mac are as hollow-headed as, well, noodles, they are certain Mom will bake them a cake if they gather some firewood for her. In the woods, they run into cousin Meatball, who tricks the Noodleheads out of their hard-earned kindling with imaginary clairvoyant powers." (Publisher's note)

Norac, Carl

Swing Cafe; translated from the French by Jacob Homel; illustrated by Rebecca Dautremer. The Sacred Mountain 2010 un il $16.95

Grades: K 1 2 3   E

1. Insects -- Fiction 2. Crickets -- Fiction 3. Jazz music -- Fiction 4. New York (N.Y.) -- Fiction

ISBN 978-2-923163-62-8; 2-923163-62-1

"Norac's story stars a Brazilian jazz-singing cricket named Zaz who dreams of New York City. The death of her butterfly friend Miro releases her; she hops a ride in a flowered hat, befriends a blue fly, and arrives at last at the Swing Cafe. Zaz and the other characters are portrayed as stylish humans with just a trace of their insect nature. . . . Dautremer's visual imagination taps the subconscious brilliantly. . . . Norac's writing is equally arresting. . . . An enclosed CD supplies cherished jazz gems from Ellington, Calloway, Fitzgerald, and more, which accompany a lovely audio recording of the story. Intelligent, poetic, and provocative entertainment." Publ Wkly

Nordqvist, Sven

Tomtes' Christmas porridge; translated by Polly Lawson. Floris 2011 il $17.95

Grades: PreK K 1 2   **E**

1. Sweden -- Fiction 2. Christmas -- Fiction

ISBN 978-0-86315-824-7; 0-86315-824-2

"Nordqvist's amusing watercolor-and-ink illustrations are full of distinct personalities and tiny details in costumes and settings. . . . A charming and sprightly story with the flavor of a traditional tale." Kirkus

Norman, Kimberly

I know a wee piggy; by Kim Norman; pictures by Henry Cole. Dial Books for Young Readers 2014 32 p. col. ill. (hardcover) $16.99

Grades: PreK K 1   **E**

1. Pigs -- Fiction 2. Animals -- Color -- Fiction 3. Stories in rhyme 4. Agricultural exhibitions -- Fiction

ISBN 0803737351; 9780803737358

LC 2011029977

This children's book is the story of a "little piggy [who] has escaped from his owner and is running riot through the county fair, getting covered in gunk, globs, and other stuff representing nine colors: brown from the muddy pig pen, red from the tomato canning display, yellow from the broken yolks in the chicken coop . . . and so forth. By the time the wee piggy proudly wins a blue ribbon," he's very dirty indeed. Author Kimberly E. Norman's text riffs on the folk song "I Know an Old Lady." (Publishers Weekly)

"The star's earnestness is irresistible, and both text and pictures are rich and energetic." (Booklist)

Ten on the sled; by Kim Norman; illustrated by Liza Woodruff. Sterling 2010 un il $14.95

Grades: PreK K 1   **E**

1. Counting 2. Stories in rhyme 3. Animals -- Fiction 4. Sledding -- Fiction

ISBN 978-1-4027-7076-0; 1-4027-7076-6

LC 2009-11501

Animals fall off a speeding sled one by one until only a lonely caribou is left, chasing a giant snowball that has engulfed the falling animals.

"What with animal identification, counting, vocabulary building and print awareness all scaffolded on a can't-lose rhyme, this one's a keeper." Kirkus

North, Sherry

Champ's story; dogs get cancer too! Sylvan Dell 2010 un il $16.95; pa $8.95

Grades: 1 2 3   **E**

1. Dogs -- Fiction 2. Cancer -- Fiction

ISBN 978-1-60718-077-7; 1-60718-077-4; 978-1-60718-088-3 pa; 1-60718-088-X pa

"While practicing for the upcoming agility show, Cody notices a lump on his dog's belly, which turns out to be cancer. The treatment is similar to what a human endures, and Cody is filled with worry for his pet. Champ is able to participate in the show, but it is Cody who

has trouble when he trips and hurts his ankle. Now it's Champ's turn to take care of Cody, and she proves she is a real champion. Children will have empathy for both characters. . . . A sincere, caring story told with a straightforward, honest approach." SLJ

Noullet, Georgette

Bed hog; illustrated by David Slonim. Marshall Cavendish 2011 un il $12.99

Grades: PreK K   **E**

1. Dogs -- Fiction 2. Sleep -- Fiction

ISBN 978-0-7614-5823-4; 0-7614-5823-9

LC 2010008089

"Every night, Bailey, the family dog, travels from room to room trying to find a comfortable place to sleep. Although his owners call him a 'bed hog,' readers will see early on that the pup is not the one taking up all the space. . . . Gentle humor and spare wording with repetitive phrasing will allow pre-readers to retell the simple tale after hearing it once. The colorful cartoonlike illustrations in acrylic and charcoal will put a smile on the face of any family member who frequently finds a dog sleeping in the bed." SLJ

Novak, B. J., 1979-

The **book** with no pictures; B.J. Novak. Dial Books for Young Readers, an imprint of Penguin Group (USA) 2014 48 p. (hardcover) $17.99

Grades: PreK K 1 2 3   **E**

1. Humorous fiction 2. Books and reading -- Fiction

ISBN 0803741715; 9780803741713

LC 2014000725

This children's book, by B. J. Novak, has no pictures. "You might think a book with no pictures seems boring and serious. Except . . . here's how books work. Everything written on the page has to be said by the person reading it aloud. Even if the words say . . . BLORK. Or BLUURF. Even if the words are a preposterous song about eating ants for breakfast, or just a list of astonishingly goofy sounds like BLAGGITY BLAGGITY and GLIBBITY GLOBBITY." (Publisher's note)

"On crisp white pages, in a large black font, listeners and readers are clued in: 'Here is how books work: Everything the words say, the person reading the book has to say.' Listeners will be tickled when adults say ridiculous things and then whine about it, as the text directs. Comic pacing and theatrics ensure a silly trip; visual cues keep (pictureless) pages lively." Horn Book

Novesky, Amy

Georgia in Hawaii; when Georgia O'Keeffe painted what she pleased. written by Amy Novesky; illustrated by Yuyi Morales. Houghton Mifflin Harcourt 2012 40 p.

Grades: K 1 2 3 4   **E**

1. Painting -- Fiction 2. Flowers in art -- Fiction 3. Hawaii -- History -- Fiction 4. Artists -- Fiction 5. Obstinacy -- Fiction 6. Hawaii -- History -- 1900-1959 -- Fiction

ISBN 9780152054205

LC 2010043401

Boston Globe-Horn Book Honor: Nonfiction (2012)

This book tells how in "1939, Georgia O'Keefe was commissioned by the Hawaiian Pineapple Company (later Dole Pineapple) to create two paintings to promote and market pineapple juice. She spent nine weeks traveling around the islands. . . . During that time, she decided she did not want to paint the way the pineapple company wanted her to paint, and they rejected some of the art she created. She discovered and fell in love with the lush greenery and flowers and waterfalls and all the beauty Hawaii had to offer, but she refused to paint a pineapple. . . . After the Hawaiian Pineapple Company airlifted a pineapple plant to her in New York, she agreed to paint what she would call "Pineapple

Bud," which became part of their advertising campaign." (International Reading Association)

★ **Me,** Frida; illustrated by David Diaz. Abrams Books for Young Readers 2010 un il $16.95

Grades: K 1 2 3   E

    1. Artists 2. Painters 3. Artists -- Fiction 4. Women artists -- Fiction 5. San Francisco (Calif.) -- Fiction

    ISBN 978-0-8109-8969-6; 0-8109-8969-7

    Pura Belpré Award honor book (Illustrator), 2011

Artist Frida Kahlo finds her own voice and style when her famous husband, Diego Rivera, is commissioned to paint a mural in San Francisco, California, in the 1930s and she finds herself exploring the city on her own.

"Overflowing with compelling imagery, . . . the story also incorporates the motif of Kahlo as a tiny bird. . . . Vibrant spreads feature backdrops of warm colors dripping into cooler ones (and vice versa). . . . Diaz's . . . overlapping complementary colors add a gorgeous yet slightly unsettling visual element, his intense hues and folk/naive style recalling Kahlo's work." Publ Wkly

Numeroff, Laura Joffe

    Beatrice doesn't want to; illustrated by Lynn Munsinger. Candlewick Press 2004 un il $15.99; pa $6.99

Grades: PreK K 1 2   E

    1. Libraries -- Fiction 2. Books and reading -- Fiction

    ISBN 0-7636-1160-3; 0-7636-3843-9 pa

                           LC 2002-73908

A newly illustrated edition of the title first published 1981 by Watts

On the third afternoon of going to the library with her brother Henry, Beatrice finally finds something she enjoys doing.

"Done in watercolor, ink, and pencil and featuring floppy-eared canine characters, the expressive illustrations perfectly capture the humor of the text." SLJ

    The **Chicken** sisters; by Laura Numeroff; pictures by Sharleen Collicott. HarperCollins Pubs. 1997 un il $15.99; pa $6.95

Grades: PreK K 1 2   E

    1. Wolves -- Fiction 2. Sisters -- Fiction 3. Chickens -- Fiction

    ISBN 0-06-026679-1; 0-06-443520-2 pa

                           LC 96-30297

"Violet, Poppy, and Babs, the chicken sisters, possess talents that annoy the neighbors until a threatening wolf moves into the neighborhood. The illustrations achieve a captivating sense of texture that adds immediacy to the humorous story." Horn Book Guide

    If you give a dog a donut; written by Laura Numeroff; illustrated by Felicia Bond. Balzer + Bray 2011 un il $16.99; lib bdg $17.89

Grades: PreK K 1   E

    1. Dogs -- Fiction

    ISBN 978-0-06-026683-7; 0-06-026683-X; 978-0-06-026684-4 lib bdg; 0-06-026684-8 lib bdg

                           LC 2011016611

Chaos might ensue if you were to give a dog a donut.

"A buoyant, circular story in which a canine's spiraling free association leads to a day's worth of outdoor activities. As usual, Bond's clean, action-filled pictures, set against white backdrops, imbue the title character with abundant personality as he skips and dances his way through the pages." Publ Wkly

    ★ **If** you give a mouse a cookie; by Laura Numeroff; illustrated by Felicia Bond. Harper & Row 1985 un il $15.99; lib bdg $16.89

Grades: PreK K 1   E

    1. Mice -- Fiction

    ISBN 0-06-024586-7; 0-06-024587-5 lib bdg

                           LC 84-48343

Relating the cycle of requests a mouse is likely to make after you give him a cookie takes the reader through a young child's day.

"Children love to indulge in supposition or to ask 'what will happen if . . .?' and here there is a long, satisfying chain of linked and enjoyably nonsensical causes and effects. . . . The illustrations, neatly drawn, spaciously composed, and humorously detailed, extend the story just the way picture book illustrations should." Bull Cent Child Books

Other titles in this series are:

    If you give a cat a cupcake (2008)

    If you give a dog a donut (2011)

    If you give a moose a muffin (1991)

    If you give a mouse a brownie (2016)

    If you give a pig a pancake (1998); If you give a pig a party (2005)

    If you take a mouse to school (2002)

    If you take a mouse to the movies (2000)

    The **Jellybeans** and the big Book Bonanza. Abrams 2010 il $15.95

Grades: PreK K 1 2   E

    1. School stories 2. Animals -- Fiction 3. Friendship -- Fiction 4. Books and reading -- Fiction

    ISBN 978-0-8109-8412-7; 0-8109-8412-1

"Anna and her friends Emily, Nicole, and Bitsy remain, like the candies, 'differenct flavors [that] go well together.' When their class has a Book Bonanza, book-loving Anna is excited, but her friends' expressions suggest they would rather be doing other things. Luckily, the librarian helps each Jellybean find the perfect book. . . . The characters sweetly express friendship dynamics in a group setting." Publ Wkly

    The **Jellybeans** and the big camp kickoff; [by] Laura Numeroff, Nate Evans; illustrated by Lynn Munsinger. Abrams Books for Young Readers 2011 un il $16.95

Grades: PreK K 1 2   E

    1. Camps -- Fiction 2. Animals -- Fiction 3. Friendship -- Fiction

    ISBN 978-0-8109-9765-3; 0-8109-9765-7

                           LC 2010023698

When four friends with different talents and abilities go to summer camp together, they use their strengths to make camp fun for all.

"Though it's a simple story, readers who value their close friendships should appreciate how the girls encourage one another to succeed." Publ Wkly

    Otis & Sydney and the best birthday ever; illustrated by Dan Andreasen. Abrams Books for Young Readers 2010 un il $16.95

Grades: PreK K 1 2   E

    1. Bears -- Fiction 2. Parties -- Fiction 3. Birthdays -- Fiction 4. Friendship -- Fiction

    ISBN 978-0-8109-8959-7; 0-8109-8959-X

                           LC 2009-47199

Otis plans a surprise party for his best friend, Sydney, and although he has put the wrong date on the invitations and no one else comes, the two still have a wonderful time together.

Andreasen's "digitally colored pen and ink art echoes the old-fashioned tenor of Numeroff's . . . story; strong hatching for shading and texture leads the eye and gives the bears' fur a dapper, well-groomed quality. . . . The honeyed story never strays far from its warm and fuzzy core." Publ Wkly

    Ponyella; [by] Laura Numeroff and Nate Evans; pictures by Lynn Munsinger. Disney/Hyperion Books 2011 un il $16.99

Grades: PreK K 1   E
1. Fairy tales 2. Horses -- Fiction
ISBN 978-1-4231-0259-5; 1-4231-0259-2

LC 2010-23406

Ponyella's dream of showing Princess Penelope her tricks at the pony championship comes true with the help of her fairy godmare.

"Cinderella gets a peppy makeover in this pony tale. . . . The frillier moments in Munsinger's pastel-dominated paintings are offset by lightly comedic particulars. . . . A sweet, playful adaptation." Publ Wkly

When sheep sleep; by Laura Numeroff; illustrated by David McPhail. Abrams Books for Young Readers 2006 un il $15.95
Grades: PreK K 1 2   E
1. Counting 2. Stories in rhyme 3. Sleep -- Fiction 4. Animals -- Fiction 5. Bedtime -- Fiction
ISBN 0-8109-5469-9

LC 2005022544

Rhyming text suggests other options when one tries to count sheep but discovers that they are all asleep.

"McPhail's charming watercolor-and-ink illustrations are infused with warmth and are a lovely complement to the gentle, rhyming lullaby." SLJ

Would I trade my parents? by Laura Numeroff; illustrated by James Bernardin. Abrams Books for Young Readers 2009 un il $16.95
Grades: PreK K 1 2   E
1. Parents -- Fiction
ISBN 978-0-8109-0637-2; 0-8109-0637-6

LC 2008030381

A young boy considers what is special about all of his friends' parents, and realizes that his own are the most wonderful of all.

"The illustrations are large and clear, made with acrylics and a digital paint program. They simply illustrate the text. . . This is a straightforward retelling of a common childhood exercise in wishful thinking." SLJ

Nutt, Robert

Amy's light; written and illustrated by Robert Nutt. Dawn 2010 un il (Sharing nature with children) $16.95; pa $8.95
Grades: K 1 2   E
1. Stories in rhyme 2. Fear -- Fiction 3. Fireflies -- Fiction
ISBN 978-1-58469-128-0; 1-58469-128-X; 978-1-58469-129-7 pa; 1-58469-129-8 pa

A young girl discovers a light in nature that helps her overcome her fear of the dark. Includes an author's note about fireflies.

"Told in lyrical poetry, the author has created the magic of lightning bugs. His photo-illustrations capture Amy's fear, delight and joy." Libr Media Connect

Nyeu, Tao

Bunny days. Dial Books for Young Readers 2010 un il $16.99
Grades: PreK K   E
1. Bears -- Fiction 2. Goats -- Fiction 3. Rabbits -- Fiction
ISBN 978-0-8037-3330-5; 0-8037-3330-5

LC 2009-23060

As a pair of busy goats inadvertently cause trouble for six bunnies, their neighbor Bear comes to the rescue.

"Nyeu's illustrations are silk-screened using water-based ink. . . . The simple language and layout of the book make it suitable for beginning readers." SLJ

Squid and Octopus; friends for always. Tao Nyeu. Dial Books for Young Readers 2012 40 p. col. ill. (hardcover) $16.99

Grades: PreK K 1 2   E
1. Squids -- Fiction 2. Octopuses -- Fiction 3. Friendship -- Fiction 4. Best friends -- Fiction
ISBN 0803735650; 9780803735651

LC 2011033194

This children's picture book presents "four stories about the relationship between two eccentric sea creatures. When Squid knits socks for his multiple limbs and Octopus tells him they wear mittens, not socks, the buddies argue. Next, Squid is sad to have lost the X-ray vision bestowed while dreaming--and his status as 'Super Squid.' . . . Octopus then mistakes a cowboy boot for a hat; finally, the duo reads a fortune about everlasting friendship." (Kirkus Reviews)

O Flatharta, Antoine

★ **Hurry** and the monarch; illustrated by Meilo So. Knopf 2005 un il $14.95; pa $7.99
Grades: K 1 2   E
1. Turtles -- Fiction 2. Butterflies -- Fiction
ISBN 0-375-83003-0; 0-385-73719-X pa

LC 2004-15984

Hurry the tortoise befriends a monarch butterfly when she stops in his garden in Wichita Falls, Texas, during her migration from Canada to Mexico. Includes facts about monarch butterflies

"Veined with a tracery of inked details, So's subtle watercolors reference both Asian nature-painting traditions and the limited palette of artwork in the early days of color printing. Together with its informative afterword, this is a particularly attractive, affecting introduction to the wonder of species diversity and the elegant continuum of life." Booklist

O'Brien, Anne Sibley

I'm new here; by Anne Sibley O'Brien. Charlesbridge 2015 32 p. color illustrations (reinforced for library use) $16.95
Grades: K 1 2 3 4 5   E
1. School stories -- Fiction 2. Immigrants -- United States -- Fiction 3. Korean Americans -- Fiction 4. Somali Americans -- Fiction 5. Guatemalan Americans -- Fiction 6. Assimilation (Sociology) -- Fiction 7. Immigrant children -- United States -- Fiction
ISBN 158089612X; 9781580896122

LC 2013049031

In this children's story, written and illustrated by Anne Sibley O'Brien, "Maria is from Guatemala, Jin is from Korea, and Fatima is from Somalia. All three are new to their American elementary school, and each has trouble speaking, writing, and sharing ideas in English. Through self-determination and with encouragement from their peers and teachers, the students learn to feel confident and comfortable in their new school." (Publisher's note)

"The title would be useful in sparking a discussion, and the simple text makes it a good choice for beginning readers." SLJ

O'Connell, Rebecca

The baby goes beep; pictures by Ken Wilson-Max. Albert Whitman 2010 un il bd bk $7.99
Grades: PreK   E
1. Board books for children 2. Sound -- Fiction 3. Infants -- Fiction 4. Parent-child relationship -- Fiction
ISBN 978-0-8075-0508-3 bd bk; 0-8075-0508-0 bd bk

LC 2010002094

First published 2003 by Roaring Book Press

A baby makes various sounds as he explores the world around him.

"Wilson-Max's heavy black outlines and bright, thickly applied colors provide the perfect definition for the images. This pink baby (with a tuft of black hair) is clearly the best thing that ever happened to this set of parents, and this book is one of the best things to happen to those babies lucky enough to encounter it." Kirkus

Danny is done with diapers; a potty ABC. illustrated by Amanda Gulliver. Albert Whitman & Co. 2010 un il $16.99
Grades: PreK   E
1. Alphabet 2. Toilet training -- Fiction
ISBN 978-0-8075-1466-5; 0-8075-1466-7
"This book gently encourages, commends, and celebrates 26 youngsters who are in the process of being toilet trained. It begins 'A is for Accident, Adam had an accident. It's all right Adam.' Sweet, brightly colored acrylic illustrations discreetly show the kids using a potty chair or a toilet, washing hands, and pulling on clothing, with only a few bare bottoms revealed. . . . Written at a young child's level of understanding, this title will be useful in showing toddlers how others have accomplished this feat." SLJ

O'Connor, George

If I had a raptor; George O'Connor. Candlewick Press 2014 32 p. $15.99
Grades: PreK K 1 2   E
1. Pets -- Fiction 2. Dinosaurs -- Fiction 3. Birds of prey -- Fiction
ISBN 0763660124; 9780763660123
LC 2013944012
In this children's picture book, by George O'Connor, an "imaginative little girl dreams of the best pet ever—a fuzzy baby raptor to snuggle. Our heroine can't think of anything better than bringing home a baby raptor. . . . It would cuddle and play, stalk birds and dust bunnies, and curl up on laps. In short, it would be the perfect pet! Readers may notice striking similarities between the raptor's behavior and that of a more common house pet." (Publisher's note)
"This story is a welcome addition to the dinosaur-as-pet genre, in which a girl imagines all of the fun she would have with a dinosaur of her very own...The text is lively and simple enough to make a great read-aloud. O'Connor's charming protagonist is an African American girl, a fact that is not integral to the story but simply wonderful for readers to see. A fun story for any dinosaur fan." SLJ

O'Connor, Jane

Fancy Nancy; pictures by Robin Preiss Glasser. HarperCollins 2006 un il $17.99; lib bdg $17.89
Grades: PreK K   E
1. Family life -- Fiction 2. Clothing and dress -- Fiction
ISBN 0-06-054209-8; 0-06-054210-1 lib bdg
LC 2004-28662
A young girl who loves fancy things helps her family to be fancy for one special night. "Ages four to seven." (N Y Times Book Rev)
"For Nancy, there's no such thing as too, too much; she loves her frilly bedroom, her lace-trimmed socks, and her pen with a plume. Nancy teaches her family how to be fancy, too. . . . Nancy's perky narrative, in short, simple sentences, incorporates some 'fancy' vocabulary for kids to absorb (stupendous, posh), along with a sense of the rewards of a family doing things together. The cheerfully colored art is aptly exuberant, a riotous blending of color and pattern and action." Booklist
Other titles about Fancy Nancy are:
Fancy Nancy and the posh puppy (2007)
Fancy Nancy and the boy from Paris (2008)
Fancy Nancy at the museum (2008)
Fancy Nancy: Bonjour, butterfly (2008)
Fancy Nancy's favorite fancy words (2008)
Fancy Nancy sees stars (2009)
Fancy Nancy: poison ivy expert (2009)
Fancy Nancy: explorer extraordinaire! (2009)
Fancy Nancy tea parties (2009)

Fancy Nancy: the dazzling book report (2009)
Fancy Nancy: splendiferous Christmas (2009)
Fancy Nancy: poet extraordinaire! (2010)
Fancy Nancy: the 100th day of school (2010)
Fancy Nancy: ooh la la! It's beauty day (2010)
Fancy Nancy and the delectable cupcakes (2010)
Fancy Nancy and the fabulous fashion boutique (2010)
Fancy Nancy: aspiring artist (2011)
Fancy Nancy: stellar stargazer (2011)

Fancy Nancy's fabulous fashion boutique; written by Jane O'Connor; illustrated by Robin Preiss Glasser. Harper 2010 un il $17.99; lib bdg $18.89
Grades: PreK K   E
1. Parties -- Fiction 2. Sisters -- Fiction 3. Vocabulary -- Fiction 4. Money-making projects for children -- Fiction
ISBN 978-0-06-123592-4; 0-06-123592-X; 978-0-06-123593-1 lib bdg; 0-06-123593-8 lib bdg
LC 2010007820
Nancy sets up a fabulous fashion boutique to earn money to buy herself a beautiful fuschia fan, and the items she was selling come in handy when her sister's birthday party goes awry.

Fancy Nancy, aspiring artist; written by Jane O'Connor; illustrated by Robin Preiss Glasser. Harper 2011 un il $12.99
Grades: PreK K   E
1. Artists -- Fiction 2. Vocabulary -- Fiction
ISBN 978-0-06-191526-0; 0-06-191526-2
LC 2010040336
Inspired by such art masters as Edgar Degas, Henri Matisse, and Jackson Pollock, Nancy, who likes to use fancy words, dons her beret to create her own fabulous artwork.
"The appealing prima donna, whose energetic body language leaps off the page, encourages kids to explore new subjects and interests." Booklist

Fancy Nancy, stellar stargazer! [by] Jane O'Connor and [illustrated by] Robin Preiss Glasser. Harper 2011 un il $12.99
Grades: PreK K 1   E
1. Stars -- Fiction 2. Sisters -- Fiction 3. Family life -- Fiction
ISBN 978-0-06-191523-9; 0-06-191523-8
Fancy Nancy thinks that everything in the sky is simply stellar, from the sun and the moon to the stars and their constellations (that's a fancy word for the shapes that stars make!). So nothing could make her happier than a special sleepover under the stars with her dad and her little sister, JoJo.

The **perfect** puppy for me; by Jane O'Connor and Jessie Hartland; illustrated by Jessie Hartland. Viking 2003 un il $15.99
Grades: PreK K 1 2   E
1. Dogs -- Fiction
ISBN 0-670-03614-5
LC 2002-15568
While waiting to get his very own puppy, a young boy spends time with various dogs and describes what the different breeds are like
"Each page is jam-packed with good advice, useful information, and bright and cleverly detailed paintings that successfully reflect the pertinent traits of the different canines." SLJ

O'Hair, Margaret

My kitten; illustrated by Tammie Lyon. Marshall Cavendish Childrens 2011 un il $15.99
Grades: PreK   E

1. Stories in rhyme 2. Cats -- Fiction
ISBN 978-0-7614-5811-1; 0-7614-5811-5

LC 2009052902

Brief rhyming text and illustrations show a kitten's activities, from dreaming in the sunlight to playing with a ball of yarn.

This is "toe-tapping and easy to read. . . . The watercolor-and-colored-pencil illustrations are both spot and full-bleed, and they match the action of the text wonderfully. . . . Repeated readings will be required." Kirkus

My pup; by Margaret O'Hair; illustrated by Tammie Lyon. Marshall Cavendish 2008 un il $14.99; bd bk $7.99
Grades: PreK   E

1. Stories in rhyme 2. Dogs -- Fiction
ISBN 978-0-7614-5389-5; 0-7614-5389-X; 978-0-7614-5644-5 bk bk; 0-7614-5644-9 bd bk

LC 2007011719

"Bouncy text and simple rhyming couplets take readers through a day in the life of a little girl and her pet as they play in the mud, enjoy a car ride, get in the way of the cat, go for a walk, and finally cuddle up together in bed. . . . Children will delight in the expressive, brightly colored gouache and pencil spreads of a smiling, round-faced youngster with large, oval animal-print glasses and her pup." SLJ

O'Hora, Zachariah

No fits, Nilson! by Zachariah OHora. Dial Books for Young Readers 2013 32 p. ill. (reinforced) $16.99
Grades: PreK K 1   E

1. Picture books for children 2. Temper tantrums -- Fiction 3. Gorilla -- Fiction 4. Behavior -- Fiction
ISBN 0803738528; 9780803738522

LC 2012021514

In this children's picture book, "Amelia helps a 9-foot blue gorilla named Nilson avoid tantrums by repeatedly reminding him, 'No fits, Nilson!' . . . Illustrations depict age-old meltdown triggers: a toppled block tower, uncooperative sneakers that just (eeergh!) won't get (oof!) on your feet and boring grownup errands." (Kirkus Reviews)

Stop snoring, Bernard. Henry Holt & Co. 2011 un il $16.99
Grades: PreK K 1 2   E

1. Zoos -- Fiction 2. Sleep -- Fiction 3. Otters -- Fiction 4. Animals -- Fiction 5. Snoring -- Fiction
ISBN 978-0-8050-9002-4; 0-8050-9002-9

Bernard the otter snores so loudly that he keeps all of the otters at the zoo awake during naptime and Grumpy Giles tells Bernard to move his snoring somewhere else!

Ohora's "bright, flat paintings, saturated in the limited palette of red, teal, gold, gray, and black, convey depths of emotion in simple strokes and heavy outlines. Jaunty compositions, with animal characters busting out of the frames, make for audacious humor, and hand-painted lettering signifying Bernard's snoring and the animals' admonitions adds visual zing." Booklist

O'Leary, Sara

★ A **family** is a family is a family; by Sara O'Leary, illustrated by Qin Leng. Groundwood Books 2016 32 p. $17.95
Grades: PreK K 1 2   E

1. Family -- Fiction 2. Family life -- Fiction
ISBN 1554987946; 9781554987948

In this picture book by Sara O'Leary, illustrated by Qin Leng, "a teacher asks the children in her class to think about what makes their families special, the answers are all different . . . but the same in the one way that matters most of all. One child is worried that her family is just too different. . . . [As] her classmates describe who they live with and

who loves them, . . . the child realizes that as long as her family is full of caring people, her family is special." (Publisher's note)

"This good-natured but firm response is both empowering and instructive, as is the welcome inclusion of a foster family in this thoughtful, needed book." Kirkus

This is Sadie; Sara O'Leary. Tundra Books of Northern New York 2015 32 p. color illustrations (hardcover) $17.99
Grades: PreK K 1 2   E

1. Storytelling -- Fiction 2. Imagination -- Fiction
ISBN 1770495320; 9781770495326; 9781770495333

LC 2014941840

In this children's book by Sara O'Leary, illustrated by Julie Morstad, "Sadie is a little girl with a big imagination. She has been a girl who lived under the sea and a boy raised by wolves. She has had adventures in wonderland and visited the world of fairytales. She likes to make things -- boats out of boxes and castles out of cushions. But more than anything Sadie likes stories, because you can make them from nothing at all. For Sadie, the world is so full of wonderful possibilities." (Publisher's note)

"Throughout, the warm, understated writing and rich, mixed-media illustrations emphasize that Sadie can be anything or anyone she wants—a snail, the Mad Hatter, a fairy-tale hero—and that, by extension, every reader wields the very same power." Pub Wkly

You are one; Sara O'Leary; illustrated by Karen Klassen. Owlkids Books 2016 24 p. color illustrations (You are) $14.95
Grades: PreK   E

1. Child care 2. Infants -- Care 3. Infants -- Fiction
ISBN 1771470720; 9781771470728

This children's book in the You Are series, by Sara O'Leary, illustrated by Karen Klassen, "is a charming read-aloud that addresses the baby directly. . . . The diverse babies pictured come to life on the page through the realism of the art, and add to the text's warmth, sweetness and broad appeal. . . . [This] is designed as a whimsical gift for new parents who will enjoy reflecting on their baby's first year and expressing how much their little one is loved." (Publisher's note)

Other titles in this series include:
"You are two" and "You are three"

You are two; Sara O'Leary, illustrated by Karen Klassen. Owlkids Books 2016 24 p. color illustrations (hardcover) $14.95
Grades: PreK   E

1. Toddlers 2. Child development
ISBN 1771470739; 9781771470735

LC 2016930938

This second book in the You Are series by Sara O'Leary, illustrated by Karen Klassen, focuses on a baby's second year of life. "Walking, running, understanding more words, speaking their names, and forming first memories are all exciting achievements. . . . Narrated in the second person, [the book] is a charming read-aloud that addresses the baby directly." (Publisher's note)

"Pick up a copy or two for the toddlers and toddler-fans in your life." Kirkus

You are three; Sara O'Leary; illustrated by Karen Klassen. Owlkids Books, Inc. 2017 24 p. color illustrations (You are) $14.95
Grades: PreK   E

1. Child development 2. Picture books for children 3. Parent-child relationship -- Fiction
ISBN 9781771470742

LC 2016946921

This children's book in the You Are series, by Sara O'Leary, illustrated by Karen Klassen, "looks back on each of these memorable achievements and more, inviting little ones to celebrate how much they have grown and discovered. . . . Diverse children pictured add to the text's warmth and broad appeal. . . . [This] is a timely gift for toddlers and their parents, who will enjoy reflecting on the highlights of the third year and expressing how much their child is loved." (Publisher's note)

O'Malley, Kevin

Captain Raptor and the moon mystery; illustrations by Patrick O'Brien. Walker & Co. 2005 un il $16.95; lib bdg $17.85
Grades: PreK K 1 2 3 4   E
1. Graphic novels 2. Science fiction graphic novels 3. Dinosaurs -- Graphic novels
ISBN 0-8027-8935-8; 0-8027-8936-6 lib bdg
LC 2004-53624
When something lands on one of the moons of the planet Jurassica, Captain Raptor and his spaceship crew go to investigate
"An action-packed science-fiction romp starring a cast of dinosaur characters. . . . Presented in comic-book style, this story blends an eye-catching layout with a quick-moving plot, tongue-in-cheek humor, and an imaginative setting." SLJ
Another title about Captain Raptor is:
Captain Raptor and the space pirates (2007)

★ **Gimme** cracked corn and I will share. Walker & Co. 2007 un il $16.95; lib bdg $17.85
Grades: 2 3 4   E
1. Chickens -- Fiction
ISBN 978-0-8027-9684-4; 0-8027-9684-2; 978-0-8027-9685-1 lib bdg; 0-8027-9685-0 lib bdg
LC 2007-03706
Chicken dreams about a treasure and sets off on a dangerous journey to find it
"Fans of corny humor and 'punny yolks' will welcome this tale. . . . The unique illustrations are a combination of pen, ink, and Photoshop." SLJ

Lucky leaf. Walker & Co. 2004 un il hardcover o.p. pa $6.95
Grades: PreK K 1 2   E
1. Leaves -- Fiction
ISBN 0-8027-8924-2; 0-8027-8925-0 lib bdg; 0-8027-9647-8 pa
LC 2003-68868
After his mother tells him to stop playing video games and go outside, a young boy tries to catch the last leaf on a tree, thinking it will bring him luck
"Done in pen and ink and colored in PhotoShop, the illustrations feature crisp, vibrant colors that create a vivid setting. . . . The story is told through spare, but effective, dialogue presented in speech bubbles." SLJ

Once upon a royal superbaby; written and illustrated by Kevin O'Malley; illustrated by Carol Heyer & Scott Goto. Walker & Co. 2010 un il lib bdg $17.89; $16.99
Grades: K 1 2 3   E
1. Infants -- Fiction 2. Authorship -- Fiction 3. Imagination -- Fiction 4. Superheroes -- Fiction 5. Kings and rulers -- Fiction
ISBN 978-0-8027-2165-5 lib bdg; 0-8027-2165-6 lib bdg; 978-0-8027-2164-8; 0-8027-2164-8
LC 2009054216
Cooperatively writing a story for school, a girl imagines a king and queen who have a baby named Sweet Piper who can talk to birds, while a boy names the baby Sweet Viper and gives him super-strength, cool wrestling moves, and a motorcycle and sunglasses.
"The boy and the girl are illustrated by O'Malley. Goto and Heyer's hyperrealistic art functions well to depict the imaginations of the nar-

rators; and children of both genders will relate to the ongoing debate between the boy and girl." SLJ

O'Neill, Alexis

Estela's swap; illustrated by Enrique O. Sanchez. Lee & Low Bks. 2002 un il hardcover o.p. pa $7.95
Grades: K 1 2 3   E
1. Mexican Americans -- Fiction
ISBN 1-58430-044-2; 1-60060-253-3 pa
LC 2001-38785
A young Mexican American girl accompanies her father to a swap meet, where she hopes to sell her music box for money for dancing lessons
"This is a warm, nicely paced story about sharing and bartering that's filled with sensory descriptions of the vibrant open market. The textured acrylics capture the hum and bustle of the stalls." Booklist

O'Neill, Catharine

Annie & Simon; the sneeze and other stories. Catharine O'Neill. 1st ed. Candlewick Press 2013 64 p. col. ill. (reinforced) $15.99
Grades: 1 2   E
1. Pets -- Fiction 2. Siblings -- Fiction 3. Dogs -- Fiction 4. Brothers and sisters -- Fiction
ISBN 076364921X; 9780763649210
LC 2011046618
This story collection is the second in Catharine O'Neill's Annie and Simon series. Here, "Simon's sneeze unleashes a patiently borne flood of little-sister TLC; Annie's efforts to get her dog Hazel to purr end abruptly when she sees the neighbor's cat stroll by with a mouse in his mouth; and the sudden disappearance of a wagonload of horse chestnuts left on the porch sparks a bit of detective work." (Kirkus)

Annie and Simon. Candlewick Press 2008 57p il $15.99
Grades: 1 2   E
1. Dogs -- Fiction 2. Siblings -- Fiction
ISBN 978-0-7636-2688-4; 0-7636-2688-0
LC 2006-47521
Recounts four adventures of Annie, her big brother, Simon, and their dog, Hazel.
"Annie and Simon's four stories collected here will ring true for most newly independent readers. The watercolor illustrations of the two and their bark-full dog Hazel are full of humor and detail. . . . O'Neill's first solo effort in some years is well worth adding to the first-chapter-book collection." Kirkus

O'Neill, Gemma

Monty's magnificent mane; Gemma O'Neill. Templar 2015 40 p. color illustrations $15.99
Grades: PreK K   E
1. Lions -- Fiction 2. Animals -- Fiction 3. Meerkat -- Fiction 4. Crocodiles -- Fiction 5. Friendship -- Fiction
ISBN 0763675938; 9780763675936
LC 2014939340
In this children's book by Gemma O'Neill "Monty the lion loves his long, golden mane, so he's not happy when his meerkat friends mess it up. Stomping off to the waterhole, he's cheered up by the flattery of a new friend . . . a green friend . . . a big, green friend. With a SNAP Monty realizes that his flattering pal is actually a giant crocodile looking for dinner." (Publisher's note)
"A lion named Monty is so proud of his mane that he nearly causes disaster for himself and his little meerkat friends. A charming double-page spread shows Monty relaxing on his back and happily fiddling with a lock of his autumn-hued tresses with one padded paw...The tried-and-

true fable about curbing vanity and appreciating friends enjoys a fresh touch with these ebullient African animals." Kirkus

Oakley, Graham

The **church** mouse. Kane Miller 2010 un il $16.99 **E**
1. Cats -- Fiction 2. Mice -- Fiction 3. Church -- Fiction
ISBN 978-1-935279-69-3; 1-935279-69-6
A reissue of the title first published 1972 by Atheneum

Arthur, a lonely mouse living in a church with only Sampson, a friendly, sleepy cat, for company devises a plan to get all the mice in town to move in with him.

"The cover of this reissue is different from the 1972 original, but inside can be found the same detailed illustrations and child appealing events (e.g., mid-sermon melees, burglars, acrobatics)." Horn Book Guide

Obed, Ellen Bryan

★ **Who** would like a Christmas tree? illustrated by Anne Hunter. Houghton Mifflin Books for Children 2009 un il $16
Grades: 1 2 3 **E**
1. Trees -- Fiction 2. Months -- Fiction 3. Nature -- Fiction 4. Animals -- Fiction 5. Christmas -- Fiction
ISBN 978-0-547-04625-9; 0-547-04625-1
LC 2008052302
Describes the flora and fauna that inhabit a Christmas tree farm throughout the year and use the growing trees for a variety of purposes. Includes section on how the farmer takes care of the farm through the year.

"Though presented as a Christmas book, this informative introduction to the different animals inhabiting a Maine tree plantation can be enjoyed year round.... The charming watercolor and ink illustrations are rendered in naturalistic fashion using nature's hues and cross-hatching techniques for shading and depth.... An excellent resource for getting youngsters enthused about nature." SLJ

Oberman, Sheldon

The **always** prayer shawl; illustrated by Ted Lewin. Boyds Mills Press 1994 un il $15.95; pa $10.95
Grades: 1 2 3 4 **E**
1. Jews -- Fiction 2. Immigrants -- Fiction
ISBN 1-878093-22-3; 1-59078-332-8 pa
This story "tells of the Jewish boy Adam, growing up in a shtetl, whose life drastically changes when famine and chaos in old Russia force his parents to immigrate to America. At parting, Adam's beloved grandfather gives the boy a gift, a prayer shawl . . . which was presented to the grandfather by his grandfather.... The watercolors are abundantly detailed and wonderfully expressive.... The pictures enrich the tranquil telling . . . as it movingly depicts how memory and tradition add texture and richness to our lives." Booklist

Ochiltree, Dianne

Molly, by golly! the legend of Molly Williams, America's first female firefighter. Dianne Ochiltree; illustrated by Kathleen Kemly. Boyds Mills Press 2012 32 p. ill. (reinforced) $16.95
Grades: 2 3 4 **E**
1. Williams, Molly 2. Fire fighting
ISBN 1590787218; 9781590787212
LC 2012933452
This children's book by Diane Ochiltree tells the story of Molly Williams, "The first American female firefighter [and] an African-American cook in the first quarter of the 19th century.... Molly cooked for Mr. Aymar, who was also a volunteer firefighter for the Oceanus Engine Company No. 11. A heavy snowstorm and a wave of influenza laid many of the volunteers low, so Molly . . . put on a leather helmet and

gloves and worked beside the men . . . until finally the blaze was out." (Kirkus Reviews)

Odanaka, Barbara

Crazy day at the Critter Cafe; illustrated by Lee White. Margaret K. McElderry Books 2009 un il $16.99
Grades: K 1 2 **E**
1. Stories in rhyme 2. Animals -- Fiction 3. Restaurants -- Fiction
ISBN 978-1-4169-3914-6; 1-4169-3914-8
A quiet morning in a roadside cafe turns to chaos when a bus breaks down and a managerie of noisy, rude animals enters, demanding to be fed.

"The rhymed text emphasizes the zany sound effects as the mixed-media illustrations comically exaggerate the scenes. Kids will giggle over the heightened food mess the animals leave behind." Booklist

Oelschlager, Vanita

A **tale** of two daddies; illustrated by Kristin Blackwood and Mike Blanc. Vanita 2010 il $15.95
Grades: PreK K 1 2 **E**
1. Homosexuality -- Fiction 2. Father-daughter relationship -- Fiction
ISBN 9780981971452; 0981971458

Ofanansky, Allison

Harvest of light; by Allison Ofanansky; photos by Eliyahu Alpern. Kar-Ben Pub. 2008 un il (Nature in Israel) lib bdg $15.95
Grades: 1 2 3 **E**
1. Jews -- Fiction 2. Israel -- Fiction 3. Olives -- Fiction 4. Hanukkah -- Fiction
ISBN 978-0-8225-7389-0 lib bdg; 0-8225-7389-X lib bdg
LC 2007-43133
"In this wonderfully different Hanukkah book, an Israeli family harvests olives to be processed into the oil. The daughter provides a simple narrative, which is clearly written and accompanied by full-color photographs depicting each step in the process from gathering and sorting the olives to pressing them and using the oil to light the menorah. Resonating with familial warmth and a shared purpose, this is a fine offering." SLJ

The **patchwork** Torah; Allison Ofanansky; illustrated by Elsa Oriol. Kar-Ben Publishing 2014 32 p. (lib. bdg. : alk. paper) $17.95
Grades: K 1 2 3 4 **E**
1. Grandfathers -- Fiction 2. Torah scrolls -- Fiction 3. Jews -- United States -- Fiction
ISBN 1467704261; 9781467704267
LC 2013002194
"Fragments of damaged and rescued Torahs from several periods of history are woven together in this . . . tale of four generations of a Torah scribe and his family," written by Allison Ofanansky and illustrated by Elsa Oriol. (Publisher's note)

"Inspired by tradition, deep faith, and an understanding that to "repair and reuse things" makes the world a better place, a sofer (the Hebrew word for a craftsman-scribe who transcribes sacred documents) takes pieces of four damaged Torah scrolls—ravaged by old age, the Holocaust, fire, and Hurricane Katrina—and creates a wonderful new Torah...Surprisingly inventive and genuinely uplifting, this story beautifully and subtly ties together two key Jewish precepts: l'dor v'dor (generation to generation) and tikkum olam (repair the world)." PW

What's the buzz? honey for a sweet new year. photographed by Eliyahu Alpern. Kar-Ben 2011 il (Nature in Israel) lib bdg $15.95
Grades: K 1 2 3 **E**
1. School stories 2. Bees -- Fiction 3. Honey -- Fiction 4. Israel

-- Fiction 5. Rosh ha-Shanah -- Fiction
ISBN 978-0-7613-5640-0; 0-7613-5640-1

LC 2010026181

A class in Israel tours a farm to learn how honey is made and used to celebrate the Jewish New Year, Rosh Hashanah.

"Ofanansky and Alpern offer a fresh take on Rosh Hashanah. . . . Color photographs and a running narrative combine to produce an easy-to-grasp book that is about science but also about culture." Publ Wkly

Offill, Jenny

11 experiments that failed; written by Jenny Offill; pictures by Nancy Carpenter. 2011 un il $16.99
Grades: PreK K 1 2   E
  1. Science -- Experiments -- Fiction
  ISBN 978-0-375-84762-2; 0-375-84762-6

"The curious and mischief-minded heroine from 17 Things I'm Not Allowed to Do Anymore turns her attention to the scientific method. A typical experiment: 'Question: Do dogs like to be covered in glitter? Hypothesis: Dogs like everything.' Offill's matter-of-fact recounting . . . make for very funny reading and allow Carpenter to go all out with her collages, which create especially lively depictions of the protagonist's misadventures." Publ Wkly

★ 17 things I'm not allowed to do anymore. Schwartz & Wade Books 2006 un il $15.99
Grades: PreK K 1 2   E
  1. Behavior -- Fiction
  ISBN 0-375-83596-2

LC 2005-16414

A young girl lists the sixteen things she is not allowed to do anymore, including not being able to make ice after freezing a fly in one of the cubes.

"Ingenious artwork—a flawless marriage of digital imagery and pen-and-ink—is indisputably the focus of this winning title." SLJ

Another title about this girl is:
11 experiments that failed (2011)

Sparky; by Jenny Offill; illustrated by Chris Appelhans. Schwartz & Wade Books 2013 40 p. $16.99
Grades: PreK K 1   E
  1. Pets -- Fiction 2. Sloths -- Fiction 3. Sloths as pets
  ISBN 0375870237; 9780375870231; 9780375970238

LC 2012047196

In this book, by Jenny Offill, "a young girl desperately wants a pet but has to find one that will meet her mother's low-maintenance stipulations, so she's delighted to discover that a sloth would fill the bill nicely. . . . Know-it-all peer Mary Potts is dismissive of Sparky. . . . The girl, however, doesn't let that ruin her outlook and continues to love Sparky just as he is." (Bulletin of the Center for Children's Books)

"A girl tries to teach her new pet sloth, Sparky, to play hide-and-seek, roll over, fetch: nothing. After a misguided pseudo-talent show, the girl accepts that, while Sparky is no whirling dervish, he is an endearing companion. Appelhans's striking watercolor and pencil illustrations, in a muted color palette of pinks, browns, and green-blues, do much of the story's heavy lifting." Horn Book

While you were napping; Jenny Offill. Schwartz & Wade 2014 40 p. color illustrations $16.99
Grades: K 1 2 3   E
  1. Humorous fiction 2. Sleep -- Fiction 3. Brothers and sisters -- Fiction 4. Humorous stories 5. Naps (Sleep) -- Fiction
  ISBN 0375865721; 9780375865725; 9780375965722

LC 2010048532

This children's book, by Jenny Offill, "featur[es] robots, fire trucks, and pirates, meet an older sister who's more than happy to fill her little brother in on all he missed while he was napping. Since none of the other neighborhood kids had to nap, they came over. Then came the robots, and of course the astronauts. It was tons of fun . . . and luckily for the boy (right?!), he slept through it all!" (Publisher's note)

"A big sister tells her brother everything he missed during his nap: bulldozer-driving, dinosaur fossils, pirates, space travel, and more. That her yarn is based on specific items in her brother's room--toy truck, dinosaur model, pirate book--adds insult to injury. The conversational text gets that teasing big-sisterly tone just right. The illustrations combine child-centered nonsense imagery with wicked humor adults will appreciate." Horn Book

Ogburn, Jacqueline K.

The **bake** shop ghost; illustrated by Marjorie Priceman. Houghton Mifflin 2005 un il $16; pa $6.99
Grades: K 1 2 3   E
  1. Ghost stories 2. Cake -- Fiction 3. Bakers and bakeries -- Fiction
  ISBN 0-618-44557-9; 0-547-07677-0 pa

Miss Cora Lee Meriweather haunts her bake shop after her death, until Annie Washington, the new shop owner, makes a deal with her.

"Priceman's illustrations are charming, with dashes of color and humor and a sense of action in each one. . . . This is a delightful story with a satisfying conclusion." SLJ

The **magic** nesting doll; illustrated by Laurel Long. Dial Bks. 2000 un il $16.99
Grades: K 1 2 3   E
  1. Fairy tales 2. Russia -- Fiction
  ISBN 0-8037-2414-4

LC 98-34397

After her grandmother dies, Katya finds herself in a kingdom where the Tsarvitch has been turned into living ice and she uses the magic nesting dolls her babushka had given her to try to break the curse

"The writings is filled with description and poetic images. . . . Created using oil paints on paper primed with gesso, the illustrations are alive with detail and reminiscent of the miniaturist style used in Russian decorative items." SLJ

Ohi, Debbie Ridpath

Where are my books? Debbie Ridpath Ohi. Simon & Schuster Books for Young Readers 2015 40 p. (hardcover : alk. paper) $17.99
Grades: PreK K 1   E
  1. Squirrels -- Fiction 2. Books and reading -- Fiction 3. Lost and found possessions -- Fiction
  ISBN 144246741X; 9781442467415

LC 2014015990

In this children's book, by Debbie Ridpath Ohi, "Spencer loves to read. He reads a book every night. But one morning his favorite book goes missing, and in its place is a tulip. Spencer searches high and low, but he can't find his book. The next morning another book is missing, a nut in its place. And the morning after that, another book is missing. What is happening to Spencer's books?" (Publisher's note)

Ohi, Ruth

Chicken, pig, cow and the class pet. Annick Press 2011 un il lib bdg $19.95; pa $6.95
Grades: PreK K 1 2   E
  1. School stories 2. Toys -- Fiction 3. Hamsters -- Fiction
  ISBN 1-55451-346-4 pa; 978-1-55451-347-5 lib bdg; 1-55451-347-2 lib bdg; 978-1-55451-346-8 pa

"Three toys take an unexpected field trip. Huddled in close quarters, Cow, Pig and Chicken try to dissect the sounds around them. Readers see that their temporary housing (a makeshift Popsicle-stick barn) confines them to a classroom while their beloved young owner enjoys her day at school. The friends' introduction to the imposing class pet, dubbed Furface by the anxious critters, leads to some wacky interactions. . . . Humorous watercolors splashed against open white backgrounds extend the visual humor, depicting the classroom environment from a toy's-eye point of view." Kirkus

Kenta and the big wave; by Ruth Ohi. Annick Press 2013 32 p. $9.95

Grades: PreK K 1 2
E

1. Japan -- Fiction 2. Tsunamis -- Fiction 3. Evacuation of civilians

ISBN 1554515769; 1554515777; 9781554515769; 9781554515776

In this book by Ruth Ohi, "when tragedy strikes Kenta's small village in Japan, he does all he can to hang on to the things that matter to him most. But amidst the chaos of an emergency evacuation brought on by the tsunami, Kenta and his family must quickly leave their home. Climbing to safer ground, Kenta watches helplessly as his prized soccer ball goes bouncing down a hill and gets swept away by the waves . . . into the hands of a child who takes it upon himself to return the ball to [Kenta]." (Publisher's note)

Ohora, Zachariah

The **not** so quiet library; by Zachariah OHora. Dial Books for Young Readers 2016 40 p. color illustrations (hardback) $17.99

Grades: PreK K 1
E

1. Bears -- Fiction 2. Monsters -- Fiction 3. Libraries -- Fiction 4. Books and reading -- Fiction

ISBN 9780803741409

LC 2015026297

In this book, by Zachariah OHora, "it's Saturday, which means Oskar and Theodore get to go to the library with their dad! It means donuts for breakfast! And it means endless quiet hours lost in stories. But . . . Oskar and Teddy get a rude surprise when they're interrupted by a five-headed, hangry monster! Will Oskar ever get to finish his book in peace? Will Teddy ever get to gorge on his donuts? Or might both of them hold the secret weapons to taming the beast?" (Publisher's note)

"Lively, detailed, endearing, and bold, the images and text create an unforgettable reading experience for book digesters everywhere." Kirkus

Oldland, Nicholas

★ **Big** bear hug. Kids Can Press 2009 un il $16.95

Grades: PreK K
E

1. Bears -- Fiction 2. Trees -- Fiction 3. Hugging -- Fiction

ISBN 978-1-55453-464-7; 1-55453-464-X

A bear who loves to hug everything meets a human who is about to chop down a tree, and the bear must make a decision on how to save his forest.

"Oldland's rustic-styled digital artwork looks like a hip flannel pajama print . . . and his pictures play sly comic foil to the earnest text." Publ Wkly

The **busy** beaver. Kids Can Press 2011 un il

Grades: PreK K 1
E

1. Animals -- Fiction 2. Beavers -- Fiction

ISBN 1554537495; 9781554537495

A "busy but careless beaver spends his days following random impulses, . . . and leaving in his wake a devastated forest filled with stumps, half-nibbled trees and injured, homeless animals. But then one day the beaver finds himself on the wrong side of a falling tree, which as it turns out, is just the thing to knock some sense into him. After reflecting on his behavior, he decides to make some changes. Soon, the now wiser and gentler beaver is getting down to the business of making things right, much to the delighted surprise of his forest friends." (Publisher's note) "Ages three to five." (Quill Quire)

"Beaver's exuberance for his work leads to careless accidents for a bear, moose, and bird's nest, and eventually for himself. . . . Beaver realizes he has a great deal for which to atone. He exercises, reads a how-to book, and practices apologies. His return is greeted by fear until he shows his newfound consideration with gifts and kind deeds. . . . The comic Photoshop illustrations have a stop-action effect and creative attention to detail." SLJ

Making the moose out of life. Kids Can Press 2010 un il $16.95

Grades: PreK K 1 2
E

1. Moose -- Fiction 2. Friendship -- Fiction

ISBN 978-1-55453-580-4; 1-55453-580-8

"Mild-mannered Moose never joins his friends when they go puddle jumping, kite flying, or skiing. . . . When he sets out alone in a sailboat, he . . . is washed away to a deserted island. It's here that he learns how to fend for himself and he meets a new friend, a tortoise named Tuesday. . . . When Moose is rescued by a cruise ship, he embraces shipboard life, taking part in all of the activities. Finally, he returns to his former friends and is now ready to join them and have some fun. . . . The illustrations are in muted outdoorsy colors of brown, green, and blue with a contemporary folk-art look. . . . Charming and simply told." SLJ

Oliver, Lin

★ **Little** Poems for Tiny Ears; by Lin Oliver; illustrated by Tomie dePaola. Nancy Paulsen Books 2013 32 p. $16.99

Grades: PreK
E

1. Children's poetry

ISBN 039916605X; 9780399166051

LC 2013014049

In this children's picture book, "twenty-three short poems written in the first-person viewpoints of infants and toddlers muse on the small discoveries and quietly joyful moments that are part of early childhood. Among them: learning to make new sounds; discovering one's toes, bellybutton, mouth, and nose . . . cozying up to a parent; and making messes." (Publishers Weekly)

"Everything about this book is child friendly, beginning with its charming cover. Oliver has written 23 highly readable poems about almost every familiar aspect of a young child's life, from belly buttons and diapers to noises and the kitchen drawer...Each poem and illustration is framed to highlight chubby babies and toddlers of all ethnic backgrounds at the center of their world, being active and being loved. Pair with Mem Fox's Ten Little Fingers and Ten Little Toes (2008) for another rhyming celebration of babies and their worlds." (Booklist)

Olshan, Matthew

The **mighty** Lalouche; Matthew Olshan; illustrated by Sophie Blackall. Schwartz & Wade Books 2012 40 p. (hardcover) $17.99; (library) $20.99

Grades: PreK K 1 2
E

1. Boxing -- Fiction 2. Letter carriers -- Fiction 3. Paris (France) -- History -- 20th century -- Fiction 4. France -- History -- Third Republic, 1870-1940 -- Fiction

ISBN 0375862250; 9780375862250; 9780375962257

LC 2010031825

This children's story, by Matthew Olshan, illustrated by Sophie Blackall, begins "in Paris, France, [where] there lived a humble postman named Lalouche. He was small, but his hands were nimble, his legs were fast, and his arms were strong. When his job was replaced by an electric car, he turned to boxing to support himself and his pet finch, Genevieve." (Publisher's note)

Olson, Julie

Tickle, tickle! itch, twitch! written and illustrated by Julie Olson. Marshall Cavendish 2010 un il $12.99

Grades: PreK K   E

1. Mice -- Fiction 2. Marmots -- Fiction

ISBN 978-0-7614-5714-5; 0-7614-5714-3

Gus the groundhog desperately needs to scratch his back after a mouse tickles him with a feather, but the stick, bush, and log he tries to scratch against are not what they appear to be.

"Olson has created a book that just begs to be read aloud. . . . This story is simple and repetitive, allowing for audience participation and many different storytelling techniques such as reader's theater or flannel-board retelling. Young children will enjoy the simple and silly humor and the bright, colorful illustrations that fill the pages." SLJ

Omololu, Cynthia Jaynes

When it's six o'clock in San Francisco; a trip through time zones. illustrated by Randy DuBurke. Clarion Books 2009 31p il map $16

Grades: K 1 2 3   E

1. Time -- Fiction

ISBN 978-0-618-76827-1; 0-618-76827-0

LC 2007012721

When Jared wakes up in San Francisco at six o'clock in the morning, children in other parts of the world are doing other things, like going to school in Buenos Aires, Argentina, playing soccer in London, England, and eating dinner in Lahore, Pakistan, because of the difference in time zones around the globe. Includes factual material about telling time and time zones.

"The diversity and connections across the globe are the story, with warm, colorful, individual portraits that move beyond cultural stereotypes. . . . This is a great choice for science classes and for today's international families." Booklist

Onyefulu, Ifeoma

Play; Ifeoma Onyefulu. Frances Lincoln Children's Books 2013 32 p. chiefly color illustrations (Look at this) $17.99

Grades: PreK K 1   E

1. Play 2. Games

ISBN 1847802672; 9781847802675

Author Ifeoma Onyefulu presents this "culturally diverse word book, with lots to look at and talk about. Hopscotch, cat's cradle, the mud game, football, Waly. . . . Many different ways to play, with games that are familiar all over the world as well as some traditional African games." (Publisher's note)

Oppel, Kenneth

★ The **king's** taster; paintings by Steve Johnson & Lou Fancher. HarperCollinsPublishers 2008 un il $17.99; lib bdg $18.89

Grades: K 1 2 3   E

1. Diet -- Fiction 2. Dogs -- Fiction 3. Food -- Fiction 4. Kings and rulers -- Fiction

ISBN 978-0-06-075372-6; 0-06-075372-2; 978-0-06-075373-3 lib bdg; 0-06-075373-0 lib bdg

LC 2008000779

The royal chef takes Max the dog, the royal taster, on several international journeys to find a dish for the land's pickiest king.

"The mixed-media illustrations are deliciously capricious with clever collage details. . . . Kids will relish this comic culinary calamity." Booklist

Oppenheim, Shulamith

Where do I end and you begin? by Shulamith Oppenheim; illustrated by Monique Felix. Creative Editions 2015 32 p. color illustrations (hardcover : alk. paper) $17.99

Grades: K 1 2 3   E

1. Stories in rhyme 2. Nature -- Fiction

ISBN 1568462743; 9781568462745

LC 2014038210

This children's book, by Shulamith Oppenheim, illustrated by Monique Felix, presents a "rhythmic poem [that] employs a thought-provoking refrain to introduce the concept of interconnectedness in life. By exploring the relationships the parts have to the whole, . . . [it] underscores that where things come together represent the strongest points of connection—and that the connections we make with one another bring everything full circle." (Publisher's note)

There's not a single misstep in the lulling language and rhythms of Oppenheim's verse, and Felix (Good Ship Crocodile) matches it with gentle illustrations, creating a parallel magic that captivates from start to finish. Pub Wkly

Orloff, Karen Kaufman

I wanna go home; Karen Kaufman Orloff; illustrated by David Catrow. G. P. Putnam's Sons, an imprint of Penguin Group (USA) 2014 32 p. color illustrations (hardcover) $16.99

Grades: PreK K 1 2   E

1. Humorous fiction 2. Letters -- Fiction 3. Family life -- Fiction 4. Grandparents -- Fiction 5. Humorous stories

ISBN 0399254072; 9780399254079

LC 2013039319

In this children's book, by Karen Kaufman Orloff & illustrated by David Catrow, "Alex is not happy about being sent to his grandparents' retirement community while his parents go on a fabulous vacation. . . . But as the week goes on, Alex's desperate emails to his parents turn into stories about ice cream before dinner and stickball with Grandpa. Before he knows it, Alex has made a surprising discovery: grandparents are way cooler than he thought!" (Publisher's note)

"Orloff skillfully expresses Alex's gradually shifting attitude, while Catrow's comically exaggerated art provides a hyperbolic sense of fun." Pub Wkly

★ **I** wanna iguana; illustrated by David Catrow. Putnam 2004 un il $15.99

Grades: PreK K 1 2   E

1. Pets -- Fiction 2. Iguanas -- Fiction

ISBN 0-399-23717-8

LC 2002-10895

Alex and his mother write notes back and forth in which Alex tries to persuade her to let him have a baby iguana for a pet.

"This funny story is told through an amusing exchange of notes. . . . Featuring his signature cartoon characters, Catrow's illustrations provide a hilarious extension of the text." SLJ

Another title about Alex is:

I wanna new room (2010)

I wanna new room; illustrated by David Catrow. Putnam 2010 un il $16.99

Grades: PreK K 1 2   E

1. Infants -- Fiction 2. Letters -- Fiction 3. Brothers -- Fiction 4. Family life -- Fiction

ISBN 978-0-399-25405-5; 0-399-25405-6

LC 2009040106

Through a series of brief letters to his parents, Alex presents all the reasons why he should not have to share a room with his younger brother

"The slapstick, sibling anger, and crowding issues are all spot-on." Booklist

Ormerod, Jan

101 things to do with baby; Jan Ormerod. Pgw 2014 32 p. col il $16.95

Grades: PreK   E

1. Picture books for children 2. Siblings -- Graphic novels 3. Infants -- Fiction 4. Play 5. Infants 6. Brothers and sisters
ISBN 1554983797; 9781554983797

LC 844401

In this picture book, by Jan Ormerod, "a little girl and her family find 101 things to do with their new baby. . . . What do you do with a new baby? An imaginative older sister and her parents explore this question in this sweet and authentic depiction of a day in the life of a young family." (Publisher's note)

"This charming and innovative sibling story came out in 1984 and is back in hardcover to celebrate its 30th anniversary With homey, pastel-hued illustrations arranged in graphic novel-esque panels, a new big sister demonstrates for readers 101 daily activities that she can do with her baby brother, from sharing her morning egg to helping keep baby entertained while Mom does the wash...The text is minimal; the art tells the deeper story here. One of the very best books for new siblings." SLJ

The **baby** swap; by Jan Ormerod; illustrated by Andrew Joyner. Little Simon 2015 32 p. (hardcover) $16.99

Grades: PreK K 1   E

1. Babies -- Fiction 2. Jealousy -- Fiction 3. Crocodiles -- Fiction 4. Animals -- Infancy -- Fiction 5. Brothers and sisters -- Fiction
ISBN 1481419145; 9781481419147

LC 2013047673

In this book by Jan Ormerod, "Caroline Crocodile is not thrilled with her baby brother. He drools. A lot. But all Mama Crocodile ever says is how GORGEOUS he is! And so Caroline ventures into a baby shop to swap out her brother. Unfortunately, the baby panda is a fussy eater, the giraffe is missing scales, and the piglet isn't green. Turns out, the best younger sibling around might just be her own yellow-eyed, sharp-clawed, drooling baby brother." (Publisher's note)

If you're happy and you know it! [by] Jan Ormerod, Lindsey Gardiner. Star Bright Books 2003 un il $15.95; pa $5.95

Grades: PreK   E

1. Stories in rhyme 2. Animals -- Fiction
ISBN 1-932065-07-5; 1-932065-10-5 pa

LC 2002-13692

A little girl and various animals sing their own versions of this popular rhyme

"Delightful, colorful animal figures cavort through the pages of this book that puts a twist on the familiar song. . . . The action on each spread gives the story a great deal of energy and the backgrounds are washes of color, from dark pink to yellow to blue." SLJ

★ **Lizzie** nonsense; a story of pioneer days. Clarion Books 2005 32p il lib bdg $15

Grades: PreK K 1 2   E

1. Australia -- Fiction 2. Family life -- Fiction 3. Imagination -- Fiction
ISBN 0-618-57493-X lib bdg

LC 2004-26642

First published 2004 in Australia

"Lizzie lives with her mother, father, and baby brother in a small, isolated house in the Australian bush. Her father has taken his sandalwood into town to sell and will be gone for weeks. Lizzie passes the lonely days by indulging in flights of fancy. . . . The text is simple yet evocative . . . while the skillfully rendered watercolors bring the unique setting to life." SLJ

Orr, Wendy

The **princess** and her panther; illustrated by Lauren Stringer. Simon & Schuster 2010 un il $16.99

Grades: K 1 2   E

1. Fear -- Fiction 2. Camping -- Fiction 3. Sisters -- Fiction 4. Panthers -- Fiction 5. Princesses -- Fiction
ISBN 978-1-4169-9780-1; 1-4169-9780-6

LC 2009034359

A brave princess and a panther who tries to be brave cross the desert together and settle into a red silk tent, in which they listen to "leaf-snakes," an "owl-witch," and other frightening creatures until the princess frightens them away.

"Deep-hued, textured acrylics ably reflect the imaginative story's drama and its nighttime setting." Horn Book Guide

Osborne, Mary Pope

★ **New** York's bravest; paintings by Steve Johnson & Lou Fancher. Knopf 2002 un il $15.95; pa $6.99

Grades: PreK K 1 2   E

1. Fire fighters -- Fiction 2. New York (N.Y.) -- Fiction
ISBN 0-375-82196-1; 0-375-83841-4 pa

LC 2002-455

Tells of the heroic deeds of the legendary New York firefighter, Mose Humphreys

"Boldly executed art supports the tall-tale flavor of a story that is both powerful and humane." Booklist

Oskarsson, Bardur

The **flat** rabbit; Bardur Oskarsson, translated by Marita Thomsen. Owlkids Books, Inc. 2014 40 p. color illustrations hardcover $16.95

Grades: K 1 2 3   E

1. Dogs -- Fiction 2. Rats -- Fiction 3. Rabbits -- Fiction
ISBN 9781771470599; 1771470593

LC 2014932277

"When a dog and a rat come upon a rabbit flattened on the road in their neighborhood, they contemplate her situation, wondering what they should do to help her. They decide it can't be much fun to lie there; she should be moved. But how? And to where? Finally, the dog comes up with an inspired and unique idea and they work together through the night to make it happen." (Publisher's note)

"Although they depict a gruesome subject (r oadkill), there's nothing grotesque about the images. . . . Oskarsson offers a pleasing vision of the afterlife, as the dog and rat try to give the rabbit a gift--an experience it didn't have during its lifetime." Kirkus

Otoshi, Kathryn

★ **One**. KO Kids Books 2008 un il $16.95

Grades: PreK K 1   E

1. Counting 2. Color -- Fiction 3. Bullies -- Fiction 4. Courage -- Fiction
ISBN 0972394648; 9780972394642

Blue is a quiet color. Red's a hothead who likes to pick on Blue. Yellow, Orange, Green, and Purple don't like what they see, but what can they do? When no one speaks up, things get out of hand—until One comes along and shows all the colors how to stand up, stand together, and count.

"The use of colors and numbers gives the story a much-needed universality. . . . Otoshi cleverly offers a way to talk to very young children about the subject of bullying, even as she helps put their imaginations to work on solutions." Booklist

Two; by Kathryn Otoshi. Pgw 2014 40 p. color illustrations hbk $18.95

Grades: PreK K 1   E

1. Numbers 2. Friendship

ISBN 0972394664; 9780972394666

In this book by Kathryn Otoshi, "two is best friends with One. Whenever they'd get the chance, they'd dance! She'd sing and snap. He'd tappity-tap. What a pair they made! At the end of each day, they'd always say, 'ONE, TWO, I'll count on you, 'til the end, we'll be best friends.' Until Three jumps in between them . . . Suddenly One only wants to play with Three." (Publisher's note)

"Although the main storyline is simple, students will quickly pick up on the more complex mathematical and social relationships that unfold. This is certain to generate some teachable moments." Lib Med Con

★ **Zero**. Ko Kids Books 2010 un il $17.95

Grades: PreK K 1   E

1. Counting 2. Courage -- Fiction

ISBN 978-0-9723946-3-5; 0-9723946-3-X

Zero, dismayed by her big, empty, roundness, tries to force herself into the shape of the much-admired One, but must finally accept that she can only be Zero.

"What could have been a pedestrian just-be-yourself tale is distinguished by Otoshi's simple and lucid text, judicious use of white space, and a voice that stays sincere without becoming overly moralistic." Publ Wkly

Owen, Karen

I could be, you could be; [text by] Karen Owen; [illustrations by] Barroux. Barefoot Books 2009 un il $16.99

Grades: PreK K 1   E

1. Stories in rhyme 2. Imagination -- Fiction

ISBN 978-1-84686-405-6; 1-84686-405-4

                          LC 2008039825

"A boy and a girl make believe they are everything from astronauts to animals in the jungle. Each spread has a rhyming couplet that begins either with 'I' or 'You.' . . . This simple formula and clear writing make the story accessible for listeners who love to play pretend games as well as for beginning readers. Barroux's eye-catching acrylic and pencil illustrations are filled with vibrant color and evoke a joyful feeling." SLJ

Pace, Anne Marie

Vampirina ballerina; Anne Marie Pace; illustrated by LeUyen Pham. Disney Hyperion Books 2012 40 p. $14.99

Grades: PreK K   E

1. Ballet -- Fiction 2. Vampires -- Fiction 3. Picture books for children 4. Ballet dancing -- Fiction

ISBN 1423157532; 9781423157533

                          LC 2011026660

In this children's picture book, "a pale little vampire with tiny fangs and a black cape enrolls in an evening class at Madame Sang's Dance Studio. . . . Vampirina does her best to fit in" with the other girls. "The aspiring ballerina practices and practices until she is ready for her debut. On the big night, she dons her costume, overcomes stage fright, and takes a well-earned bow after the performance." (School Library Journal)

Pak, Kenard

Goodbye summer, hello autumn; Kenard Pak. Henry Holt and Company 2016 32 p. color illustrations (hardback) $17.99

Grades: PreK K 1 2   E

1. Autumn -- Fiction 2. Nature -- Fiction 3. Summer -- Fiction 4. Seasons -- Fiction

ISBN 9781627794152

                          LC 2015014262

In this children's book by Kenard Pak, as "blue jays head south, and leaves change their colors, everyone knows--autumn is on its way! Join a young girl as she takes a walk through forest and town, greeting all the signs of the coming season. In a series of conversations with every flower and creature and gust of wind, she says goodbye to summer and welcomes autumn." (Publisher's note)

"A gentle, gorgeous welcome to summer's end and fall's beginning, perfect for storytime or one-on-one reading." SLJ

Pak, Soyung

Dear Juno; illustrated by Susan Kathleen Hartung. Viking 1999 un il hardcover o.p. pa $5.99

Grades: PreK K 1 2   E

1. Letters -- Fiction 2. Grandmothers -- Fiction 3. Korean Americans -- Fiction

ISBN 0-670-88252-6; 0-14-230017-9 pa

                          LC 98-43408

Although Juno, a Korean American boy, cannot read the letter he receives from his grandmother in Seoul, he understands what it means from the photograph and dried flower that are enclosed and decides to send a similar letter back to her

"The handsome layout, featuring ample white space and illustrations that cover anywhere from one page to an entire spread, perfectly suit the gentle, understated tone of the text." SLJ

Pal, Erika

Azad's camel. Frances Lincoln Children's Books 2010 un il $17.95

Grades: PreK K 1 2   E

1. Camels -- Fiction 2. Orphans -- Fiction 3. Arabian Peninsula -- Fiction

ISBN 1-84507-982-5; 978-1-84507-982-6

In a big Arabian city, an orphan boy is forced to work as a camel jockey—a dangerous job he doesn't like. But a new friendship and a magical escape into the desert are about to change his life .

"Pal's striking illustrations in watercolor and ink position sharply delineated characters in the foreground against soft, blurry desert backgrounds. Her heart-tugging tale also folds in a succint social-studies lesson, and a brief afterword explains the controversial 'sport' of camel racing." Kirkus

Palatini, Margie

Bad boys get henpecked! illustrated by Henry Cole. Katherine Tegen Books 2009 un il $17.99; lib bdg $18.89

Grades: PreK K 1 2   E

1. Wolves -- Fiction 2. Chickens -- Fiction

ISBN 978-0-06-074433-5; 0-06-074433-2; 978-0-06-074434-2 lib bdg; 0-06-074434-0 lib bdg

                          LC 2008-11771

Bad boy wolves Willy and Wally try to get a chicken dinner by disguising themselves as the Handy-Dandy Lupino Brothers and going to work for a hen in need of household help.

"With its fast-paced language and witty narrative paired with lively alliteration and puns, the Bad Boys' latest tale will entertain and capture youngsters' imaginations. Cole deftly expresses humor and the power of understatement in his pencil and watercolor illustrations. Expressive facial expressions and body language tell all." SLJ

Boo-hoo moo; illustrated by Keith Graves. Katherine Tegen Books 2009 un il $17.99; lib bdg $18.89

Grades: K 1 2   E

1. Cattle -- Fiction 2. Farm life -- Fiction

ISBN 978-0-06-114375-5; 0-06-114375-8; 978-0-06-114376-2 lib bdg; 0-06-114376-6 lib bdg

                          LC 2007024417

When Hilda Mae Heifer's trademark 'moo' starts sounding even worse, the other animals decide she is lonely and hold auditions to find her some singing partners.

"Palatini's prose is poetic, quirky, inventive, and just plain fun. . . . Graves escalates the sophisticated silliness with his wacky, superbly crafted, almost 3D illustrations." SLJ

★ The **cheese**; paintings by Steve Johnson and Lou Fancher. Katherine Tegan Books 2007 un il $16.99; lib bdg $17.89
Grades: K 1 2 3   E
   1. Nursery rhymes -- Fiction
   ISBN 978-0-06-052630-6; 0-06-052630-0; 978-0-06-052631-3 lib bdg; 0-06-052631-9 lib bdg
                  LC 2006-18163

After they all agree to ignore the story of "The Farmer in the Dell," the rat, cat, dog, child, farmer, and his wife have a party featuring the tempting hunk of cheese.

"The folk-art quality of the illustrations is rich with country colors—barn reds, field greens, and earthy yellows, and the cartoon animals are funny and expressive. A smattering of words and music from the song is worked in effectively on most pages, and the full lyrics are printed on the last page." SLJ

Earthquack! illustrated by Barry Moser. Simon & Schuster Bks. for Young Readers 2002 un il $15.95; pa $6.99
Grades: PreK K 1 2   E
   1. Domestic animals -- Fiction
   ISBN 0-689-84280-5; 1-4169-0260-0 pa
                  LC 2001-31302

When Chucky Ducky feels the earth beneath him grumble and rumble, he runs to alert the other barnyard animals to the coming earthquake, but just as a wily weasel is about to take advantage of their fears, the true source of the rumbling is revealed

"Moser captures the essence of Weasel's dark determination as well as the bug-eyed hysteria of the farm animals in his expressive graphite and transparent watercolor illustrations. . . . Palatini's text is funny, with contemporary dialogue, puns, and a fast-paced narrative rich in rhythm and alliteration." SLJ

Goldie and the three hares; illustrated by Jack E. Davis. Katherine Tegen Books 2010 un il $16.99
Grades: K 1 2 3   E
   1. Fairy tales 2. Rabbits -- Fiction
   ISBN 978-0-06-125314-0; 0-06-125314-6
                  LC 2008036910

When Goldilocks, running from the three bears, falls down a rabbit hole and hurts her foot, a family of hares tries to help but she proves to be a very loud, demanding, and tenacious guest.

"The zingy prose begs for full-throttled performance . . . and there are plenty of visual laughs in both the Hares' wide-eyed, innocent dismay and Goldilocks' overweening narcissism." Publ Wkly

Gorgonzola; a very stinkysaurus. by Margie Palatini; illustrated by Tim Bowers. Katherine Tegen Books 2008 un il $16.99; lib bdg $17.89
Grades: PreK K 1 2   E
   1. Birds -- Fiction 2. Smell -- Fiction 3. Dinosaurs -- Fiction 4. Cleanliness -- Fiction
   ISBN 978-0-06-073897-6; 0-06-073897-9; 978-0-06-073898-3 lib bdg; 0-06-073898-7 lib bdg
                  LC 2006002191

When Gorgonzola the dinosaur learns that everyone runs from him to avoid his smell, rather than out of fear, he is grateful to the little bird who shows him how to brush his teeth and wash

"The over-the-top illustrations of the grossed-out dinosaurs . . . will bring belly laughs to children and inspiration to the grownups who have to wrestle them into the bathtub or dentist's chair. Witty dialogue and an effective layout get the personal hygiene message across without being preachy or didactic." SLJ

Hogg, Hogg & Hog. Simon & Schuster Books for Young Readers 2011 un il $15.99
Grades: PreK K 1 2   E
   1. Pigs -- Fiction 2. Fashion -- Fiction 3. Domestic animals -- Fiction 4. City and town life -- Fiction
   ISBN 1-4424-0322-5; 978-1-4424-0322-2
                  LC 2009053646

Three pigs achieve success in the big city by making oinking the ultimate in fashion, but their fresh, new idea captures the attention of some friends from back on the farm.

"Palatini's smart storytelling bustles with all the ringing phones and over-the-top bluster of 'big business' speech. Attentive text design places the emphasis in all the right places, making this a fun read-aloud. . . . Palatini has created a hilariously relatable tale by including all the old barnyard favorites. . . . Quirky illustrations rendered digitally and mainly in pinks, lavenders, and grays suit this unusual story." SLJ

No nap! yes nap! by Margie Palatini; illustrated by Dan Yaccarino. Little, Brown & Co. 2014 32 p. color illustrations (hardcover) $17
Grades: PreK   E
   1. Infants -- Fiction 2. Mother-child relationship -- Fiction 3. Stories in rhyme 4. Babies -- Fiction 5. Naps (Sleep) -- Fiction
   ISBN 0316248215; 9780316248211
                  LC 2013024729

In this children's picture book with illustrator Dan Yaccarino, author "Margie Palatini brings her signature humor to this rollicking sing-song read-along, inviting readers on a fast-paced chase through every room in the house as we follow Mommy on her quest to settle Baby down for nap." (Publisher's note)

"Babies and toddlers will enjoy the rhythm and upbeat tempo of the text, and the oversize font and repetitive phrases will encourage emerging readers to participate. Both children and adults will enjoy the humorous touches in the cartoonlike drawings." Booklist

Piggie pie! illustrated by Howard Fine. Clarion Bks. 1995 un il $15; pa $5.95
Grades: PreK K 1 2   E
   1. Pigs -- Fiction 2. Wolves -- Fiction 3. Witches -- Fiction
   ISBN 0-395-71691-8; 0-395-86618-9 pa
                  LC 94-19726

"Gritch the Witch sets out for Old MacDonald's Farm to get herself a meal of plump piggies. Alerted, however, . . . the swine hastily don sheep, cow, and other barnyard disguises and fool her. . . . The still-hungry Gritch is persuaded to give up by a Big Bad Wolf . . . and the two go off for lunch, each picturing the other made into a sandwich. . . . The exuberant illustrations are colorful and action-filled. Greedy (but not too bright) witch and wolf both get what they deserve in this thoroughly enjoyable romp." SLJ

★ **Three** French hens; a holiday tale. illustrations by Richard Egielski. Hyperion Books for Children 2005 un il $15.99
Grades: PreK K 1 2   E
   1. Foxes -- Fiction 2. Chickens -- Fiction 3. Christmas -- Fiction 4. New York (N.Y.) -- Fiction
   ISBN 0-7868-5167-8

"The three French hens from the familiar Christmas song are sent by a Parisian lady to her boyfriend, Philippe Renard, in New York. Alas, the hens wind up in lost mail, and when they can't find Philippe in the phone book, they think perhaps they should translate his name: Phil Fox. They find Phil Fox, but he's a downtrodden fox living in the Bronx. . . . [This] is so much fun, it's hard to imagine an artist milking more laughs from it than Egielski. . . . Something really fresh for the holiday season." Booklist

The **three** silly billies; illustrated by Barry Moser. Simon & Schuster Books for Young Readers 2005 un il $15.95
Grades: PreK K 1 2   **E**
1. Goats -- Fiction
ISBN 0-689-85862-0

LC 2002-155835

Three billy goats, unable to cross a bridge because they cannot pay the toll, form a car pool with The Three Bears, Little Red Riding Hood, and Jack of beanstalk fame to get past the rude Troll.

"Painted in cheery watercolors, Moser's figures are in contemporary dress and pop out from the white backgrounds. There is plenty of visual humor. . . . Palatini's hip and punny text is fun to read aloud." SLJ

Pallotta, Jerry
Ocean counting; odd numbers. illustrated by Shennen Bersani. Charlesbridge 2004 un il $16.95; pa $6.95
Grades: PreK K 1   **E**
1. Counting 2. Marine animals
ISBN 0-88106-151-4; 0-88106-150-6 pa

LC 98-46035

"Bersani's bright, realistic colored-pencil illustrations will lure readers into perusing the factoid-loaded, simple, conversational text. . . . This book offers a colorful, engaging, and intriguing slant on the technique of counting." SLJ

Panahi, H. L.
Bebop Express; illustrated by Steve Johnson and Lou Fancher. Laura Geringer Books 2005 un il $15.99
Grades: K 1 2 3   **E**
1. Stories in rhyme 2. Railroads -- Fiction 3. Jazz music -- Fiction
ISBN 0-06-057190-X

LC 2003-24244

A rollicking rhythmic express train takes passengers on a jazzy journey that celebrates the United States and its unique musical culture.

"The intricate collages use old photographs and vintage fabrics to obtain a unique look. Teeming with life, the art visually complements the noisy text." Booklist

Panzieri, Lucia
The **kindhearted** crocodile; by Lucia Panzieri; illustrated by AntonGionata Ferrari. Holiday House 2013 24 p. (hardcover) $16.95
Grades: PreK K 1 2   **E**
1. Pets -- Fiction 2. Crocodiles -- Fiction 3. Crocodiles as pets -- Fiction
ISBN 0823427676; 9780823427673

LC 2012025486

This children's story, by Lucia Panzieri, illustrated by Anton Gionata Ferrari, follows "a crocodile with the kindest of hearts that was gentle and sensitive, and dreamed of one day being a beloved pet in a happy family. Through the magic of a picture book and with an irrepressible desire to please, this ferocious-looking crocodile that tidies toys, washes dishes, and even fights monsters in bad dreams makes his own dream come true." (Publisher's note)

Parenteau, Shirley
★ **Bears** on chairs; illustrated by David Walker. Candlewick Press 2009 un il $15.99

Grades: PreK K   **E**
1. Stories in rhyme 2. Bears -- Fiction
ISBN 978-0-7636-3588-6; 0-7636-3588-X

LC 2008-937035

Four bears are happily seated on four chairs until Big Brown Bear shows up and demands a seat.

"Between the unerringly positive approach to a common early-childhood dilemma and the can't miss rhyme, this volume will likely find its place on many a daycare shelf." Kirkus

Parish, Herman
Amelia Bedelia bakes off; pictures by Lynn Sweat. Greenwillow Books 2010 64p il (An I can read book) $17.99
Grades: K 1 2   **E**
1. Cake -- Fiction 2. Baking -- Fiction 3. Contests -- Fiction 4. Household employees -- Fiction
ISBN 978-0-06-084358-8; 0-06-084358-6

Literal-minded housekeeper Amelia Bedelia lends a hand at the bakery and enters a cakemaking contest, with unexpected results.

Amelia Bedelia's first apple pie; pictures by Lynne Avril. Greenwillow Books 2010 un il $16.99; lib bdg $17.89
Grades: PreK K 1   **E**
1. Pies -- Fiction 2. Apples -- Fiction 3. Baking -- Fiction 4. Grandparents -- Fiction
ISBN 978-0-06-196409-1; 0-06-196409-3; 978-0-06-196410-7 lib bdg; 0-06-196410-7 lib bdg

LC 2010009379

While visiting her grandparents, literal-minded Amelia Bedelia finally learns, despite some mishaps, how to bake an apple pie.

"Children will find the humor relevant and funny. The illustrations flow well with the text." SLJ

Other titles about Amelia Bedelia as a child are:
Amelia Bedelia's first day of school (2009)
Amelia Bedelia's first valentine (2009)
Amelia Bedelia's first field trip (2011)

Amelia Bedelia's first field trip; pictures by Lynne Avril. Greenwillow Books 2011 un il $16.99; lib bdg $17.89
Grades: PreK K 1   **E**
1. School stories 2. Farms -- Fiction
ISBN 978-0-06-196413-8; 0-06-196413-1; 978-0-06-196414-5 lib bdg; 0-06-196414-X lib bdg

LC 2010034175

Amelia Bedelia goes with her class to visit a farm, where her literal-mindedness causes confusion along with some laughs.

"Avril's gouache-and-black-pencil illustrations are filled with bright color, personality and, of course, that brand of humor that is all Amelia Bedelia." Kirkus

Amelia Bedelia's first Valentine; illustrated by Lynne Avril. Greenwillow Books 2009 un il $16.99; lib bdg $17.89
Grades: PreK K 1   **E**
1. School stories 2. Family life -- Fiction 3. Valentine's Day -- Fiction
ISBN 978-0-06-154458-3; 0-06-154458-2; 978-0-06-154459-0 lib bdg; 0-06-154459-0 lib bdg

LC 2009009050

In this book by Herman Parish, illustrated by Lynne Arvil, part of the Amelia Bedelia series, "School is always exciting for Amelia Bedelia, and getting her first Valentine's Day card may be the most exciting surprise of all. But what will she do when she forgets her valentines for her classmates on the bus? Luckily, Amelia Bedelia is resourceful, and she doesn't break any hearts." (Publisher's note)

Amelia Bedelia's "ingenuous spirit will continue to capture hearts." Publ Wkly

Go west, Amelia Bedelia! pictures by Lynn Sweat. Greenwillow Books 2011 64p il $17.99; lib bdg $18.89
Grades: K 1 2   E
  1. Ranch life -- Fiction 2. West (U.S.) -- Fiction
ISBN 978-0-06-084361-8; 0-06-084361-6; 978-0-06-084362-5 lib bdg; 0-06-084362-4 lib bdg
                           LC 2010012429
Amelia Bedelia visits her uncle's dude ranch and makes herself at home on the range, getting all tied up (by her own lasso) and stopping a stampede (with only her own two hands)!

Parish, Peggy
  ★ **Amelia** Bedelia; pictures by Fritz Siebel. Newly illustrated I can read ed.; HarperCollins 1992 63p il (I can read book) $16.99; lib bdg $17.89; pa $3.99
Grades: K 1 2   E
  1. Household employees -- Fiction
ISBN 0-06-020186-X; 0-06-020187-8 lib bdg; 0-06-444155-5 pa
                           LC 91010163
A newly illustrated edition of the title first published 1963
A literal-minded housekeeper causes chaos in the Rogers household when she attempts to make sense of some instructions.
Other titles in this series are:
Thank you, Amelia Bedelia (1993)
Good driving, Amelia Bedelia (1995) by Herman Parish
Come back, Amelia Bedelia (1995)
Amelia Bedelia and the surprise shower (1995)
Play ball, Amelia Bedelia (1996)
Bravo, Amelia Bedelia (1997) by Herman Parish
Amelia Bedelia 4 mayor (1999) by Herman Parish
Calling Doctor Amelia Bedelia (2002) by Herman Parish
Amelia Bedelia, bookworm (2003) by Herman Parish
Amelia Bedelia and the Christmas list (2003) by Herman Parish
Amelia Bedelia goes camping (2003) by Herman Parish
Happy haunting, Amelia Bedelia (2004) by Herman Parish
Amelia Bedelia, rocket scientist (2005) by Herman Parish
Be my valentine, Amelia Bedelia (2005) by Herman Parish
Amelia Bedelia under construction (2006) by Herman Parish
Amelia Bedelia's masterpiece (2007) by Herman Parish
Amelia Bedelia and the cat (2008) by Herman Parish
Amelia Bedelia talks turkey (2008) by Herman Parish
An Amelia Bedelia celebration [Contents: Amelia Bedelia
Good work, Amelia Bedelia
Good driving, Amelia Bedelia
Bravo, Amelia Bedelia] (2009)
Amelia Bedelia bakes off (2010) by Herman Parish
Go west, Amelia Bedelia! (2011) by Herman Parish

An **Amelia** Bedelia celebration; four stories tall. [by] Peggy Parish & Herman Parish; [illustrated by] Lynn Sweat & Fritz Siebel. Greenwillow Books 2009 214p il $19.99
Grades: PreK K 1 2   E
  1. Household employees -- Fiction
ISBN 978-0-06-171030-8; 0-06-171030-X
                           LC 2008043826
Four previously published stories featuring the extremely literal-minded Amelia Bedelia, with related activities and recipes. Includes CD.

Park, Frances
  Good-bye, 382 Shin Dang Dong; [by] Frances and Ginger Park; illustrated by Yangsook Choi. National Geographic Soc. 2002 un il $16.95
Grades: K 1 2 3   E
  1. Korea -- Fiction 2. Immigrants -- Fiction
ISBN 0-7922-7985-9
                           LC 2001-2976
Jangmi finds it hard to say goodbye to relatives and friends, plus the food, customs, and beautiful things of her home in Korea, when her family moves to America
"The oil paintings done in a simple, childlike style are formally framed with white space. . . . Children will find the details of cultural differences and the immigrant experience well evoked." SLJ

Park, Linda Sue
  ★ **Bee**-bim bop! illustrated by Ho Baek Lee. Clarion Books 2005 32p il $15; pa $6.99
Grades: PreK K 1 2   E
  1. Stories in rhyme 2. Cooking -- Fiction 3. Korean Americans -- Fiction
ISBN 0-618-26511-2; 0-547-07671-1 pa
                           LC 2003027697
"Playful, cartoonlike drawings portray a round-faced girl helping her mother. . . . The illustrations . . . are very appealing. . . . The rhyme works well. A recipe follows the story." SLJ

  ★ The **firekeeper's** son; illustrated by Julie Downing. Clarion Books 2004 37p il $16; pa $6.99
Grades: 1 2 3 4   E
  1. Korea -- Fiction
ISBN 0-618-13337-2; 0-547-23769-3 pa
                           LC 2002-13917
In eighteenth-century Korea, after Sang-hee's father injures his ankle, Sang-hee attempts to take over the task of lighting the evening fire which signals to the palace that all is well. Includes historical notes.
"Park's command of place, characterization, and language is as capable and compelling in this picture book as it is in her novels. . . . [This offers] lyrical prose and deftly realized watercolors and pastels." SLJ

  ★ The **third** gift. Clarion Books 2011 il $16.99
Grades: K 1 2   E
  1. Magi -- Fiction 2. Father-son relationship -- Fiction
ISBN 978-0-547-20195-5; 0-547-20195-8; 9780547201955; 0547201958
                           LC 2010050819
"The hyperrealistic acryl-gouache illustrations depict the sandy beige hues and nuanced textures of a dry and inhospitable land, contrasting with the smooth skin and rounded cheeks of the young boy and his loving relationship with his father. This gorgeous picture book sheds thoughtful light on a fascinating facet of the Christmas story." SLJ

  Xander's panda party; by Linda Sue Park and illustrated by Matt Phelan. Clarion Books 2013 40 p. (hardcover) $16.99
Grades: PreK K 1   E
  1. Zoos -- Fiction 2. Parties -- Fiction 3. Stories in rhyme 4. Pandas -- Fiction 5. Zoo animals -- Fiction
ISBN 0547558651; 9780547558653
                           LC 2012039662
In this book by Linda Sue Park "the zoo's paucity of pandas doesn't impede Xander's party planning for long. He decides to invite all the bears. But Koala protests. She's not a bear--she's a marsupial! Does that mean she can't come? Xander rethinks his decision to invite only

bears, and 'Calling all bears' evolves into 'Calling all creatures'" (Publisher's note)

Yaks yak; animal word pairs. Linda Sue Park; illustrated by Jennifer Black Reinhardt. Clarion Books, Houghton Mifflin Harcourt 2016 40 p. color illustrations (hardback) $16.99
Grades: PreK K 1 2 3 4 5   E
  1. Animals -- Fiction 2. English language -- Homonyms -- Fiction
  ISBN 9780544391017
                        LC 2015020003

This illustrated children's book, by Linda Sue Park, illustrated by Jennifer Black Reinhardt, "presents animals acting out the verbs made from their names. Illustrations rich in comic details show hogs hogging, slugs slugging, and other spirited creatures demonstrating homographs, words with different meanings that are spelled and pronounced the same." (Publisher's note)

"Succinct definitions are tucked into the illustrations ("to crow = to boast"), and back matter offers etymological notes about the animal names and verbs. Gleeful linguistic fun that kids will wolf down." Pub Wkly

Parker, Danny

Parachute; Danny Parker; Matt Ottley. Little Hare 2014 32 p. color illustrations $16
Grades: PreK K 1 2   E
  1. Parachutes 2. Cats -- Fiction 3. Fear -- Fiction 4. Emotions -- Fiction
  ISBN 9780802854698; 1921894202; 9781921894206
                        LC 2014431956

In this book, by Danny Parker, illustrated by Matt Ottley, "Toby doesn't like heights. That's why he always carries a parachute with him. His parachute makes him feel safe when he has to climb down from his bunk bed or when he's playing on the swings. But one day, Toby's cat gets stuck in a tree, and it's up to Toby to rescue him. With the help of his parachute, Toby reaches his cat and lowers him safely to the ground. But now Toby is stuck in the tree." (Publisher's note)

"Creative and captivating, this story can be appreciated on many levels and by a wide range of ages." Booklist

Parker, Jake

Little Bot and Sparrow; Jake Parker. Roaring Brook Press 2016 40 p. color illustrations (hardback) $17.99
Grades: PreK K 1 2   E
  1. Sparrows -- Fiction 2. Robots -- Fiction 3. Friendship -- Fiction
  ISBN 9781626723672
                        LC 2015034425

This children's book by Jake Parker tells "a story of friendship that can inspire anyone, even robots, to dream. . . . When Little Bot is thrown out with the garbage, he finds himself in a strange new world. Fortunately, Sparrow is there to take him under her wing. Together, they explore the forest, share adventures, and learn what it means to be forever friends." (Publisher's note)

"It's a moment of profundity and emotional ambiguity that may surprise and even sadden readers, but the discussions this story will spark should prove as rewarding as the happiest of endings." Pub Wkly

Parker, Marjorie Blain

A **paddling** of ducks; animals in groups from A to Z. written by Marjorie Blain Parker; illustrated by Joseph Kelly. Kids Can Press 2010 il $16.95
Grades: PreK K 1   E
  1. Animals 2. Alphabet
  ISBN 978-1-55337-682-8; 1-55337-682-X

"This ABC book provides a delightfully offbeat introduction to collective nouns, featuring groups of animals at a Riviera-like resort locale with palm trees and a seaside Ferris wheel. . . . Even better than learning some of the unusual ways to refer to multiple animals is the way Kelly's soft-focus oil and acrylic paintings riff on the terms themselves. . . . The anthropomorphic animals feel anatomically authentic, but with exaggerated joie de vivre to spare." Publ Wkly

Parker, Michael

You are a star! Michael Parker; illustrations by Judith Rossell. Walker 2012 40 p. (hardback) $16.99
Grades: PreK K 1 2 3   E
  1. Fear -- Fiction 2. Stars -- Fiction 3. Bedtime -- Fiction 4. Astronomy -- Fiction 5. Life (Biology) -- Fiction
  ISBN 0802728413; 9780802728418; 9780802728425
                        LC 2011050073

In this children's bedtime story, by Michael Parker, illustrated by Judith Rossell, "readers take a journey through the night sky to the moment a star is born. Starting as a fire in the sky that explodes into millions of pieces, stars eventually become part of Earth with all the living things on it-meaning that everyone has a little bit of stardust inside them." (Publisher's note)

Parnell, Peter

★ **And** Tango makes three; by Justin Richardson and Peter Parnell; illustrated by Henry Cole. Simon & Schuster Bks. for Young Readers 2005 un il $14.95
Grades: PreK K 1 2   E
  1. Penguins -- Fiction 2. Homosexuality -- Fiction
  ISBN 0-689-87845-1

At New York City's Central Park Zoo, two male penguins fall in love and start a family by taking turns sitting on an abandoned egg until it hatches

"Done in soft watercolors, the illustrations set the tone for this uplifting story, and readers will find it hard to resist the penguins' comical expressions. . . . This joyful story about the meaning of family is a must for any library." SLJ

Parot, Annelore

Kimonos. Chronicle Books 2011 un il
Grades: PreK K 1   E
  1. Dolls -- Fiction 2. Japan -- Fiction
  ISBN 145210493X; 9781452104935
                        LC 2011008003

Original French edition 2009

Inspired by traditional Japanese dolls, this story introduces readers to the Kokeshis' kimonos and hair-dos as well as Japanese culture. Contains die-cut pages, flaps and gatefolds.

"Sharp-eyed children will enjoy poring over the pages again and again. Scenes that evoke everyday life in Japan . . . add delightfully authentic cultural texture, while lift-the-flap and die-cut panels enhance the book's interactivity." SLJ

Parr, Todd

The **goodbye** book; Todd Parr. Little, Brown & Co. 2015 32 p. color illustrations (hc) $17
Grades: PreK K   E
  1. Loss (Psychology) -- Fiction 2. Loss (Psychology) -- Fiction
  ISBN 9780316404976
                        LC 2014010658

This children's book is a "poignant and reassuring story about loss. Through the lens of a pet fish who has lost his companion, Todd Parr tells a moving and wholly accessible story about saying goodbye. Touching upon the host of emotions children experience, Todd reminds readers that it's okay not to know all the answers, and that someone will always be there to support them." (Publisher's note)

"The bright, cheerful colors and warm message lighten a serious topic and offer kids helpful tools for dealing with difficult feelings. An approachable, age-appropriate guide to grieving." Booklist

Paschkis, Julie

Mooshka; written and illustrated by Julie Paschkis. Peachtree Publishers 2012 35 p.

Grades: PreK K 1   E

1. Magic -- Fiction 2. Quilts -- Fiction 3. Infants -- Fiction 4. Sisters -- Fiction 5. Picture books for children 6. Babies -- Fiction 7. Sharing -- Fiction

ISBN 9781561456208

LC 2011020463

In this picture book, "Karla loves her quilt, and Mooshka makes Karla feel safe, brightening dark days. Made by Karla's grandmother from scraps of old fabric, Mooshka is unusual because it talks to Karla, telling her the stories behind each piece of the quilt. . . . When Karla's life changes--her mother's bulging belly is a hint of baby Hannah's arrival--Mooshka goes strangely silent. . . . Soon, both children curl up under the quilt with Karla retelling the family stories." (Horn Book Magazine)

"Vivid artwork, a lively, endearing heroine and a warm, loving look at a pivotal experience give this one classic potential." Kirkus

★ **P.** Zonka lays an egg; by Julie Paschkis. Peachtree Publishers 2015 32 p. color illustrations $16.95

Grades: PreK K 1 2   E

1. Eggs -- Fiction 2. Color -- Fiction 3. Chickens -- Fiction

ISBN 1561458198; 9781561458196

LC 2014006507

In this children's story, by Julie Paschkis, the "hen [named] P. Zonka spends her time taking in the beauty around her. . . . The other hens can't understand why she never lays eggs like they do. Finally, P. Zonka gives in and lays an egg. To everyone's delight, she produces a wondrous egg that contains all the colors and designs that she has stored in her creative imagination." (Publisher's note)

"Paschkis's watercolors are filled with repeated patterns and a beautiful use of black outlines. Some pages contain brightly colored backgrounds while on others, colors pop off bright white backgrounds.....P. Zonka's lesson is gently delivered: take time to produce something you will be proud of." Horn Book

Paterson, Katherine

★ **Brother** Sun, Sister Moon; Saint Francis of Assisi's Canticle of the Creatures. retold by Katherine Paterson; illustrated by Pamela Dalton. Chronicle Books 2011 un il

Grades: PreK K 1   E

1. Nature -- Fiction 2. Prayer -- Fiction

ISBN 0-8118-7734-5; 978-0-8118-7734-3

LC 2010035120

Reimagines Francis of Assisi's 1224 prayer of praise in celebration of God's gifts throughout the universe.

"As Paterson expresses thankfulness to God for various forces of creation . . . debut artist Dalton offers delicately detailed, loosely symmetrical cut-paper tableaus, set against black backdrops and framed by birds' nests, willow trees, vines, and branches." Publ Wkly

Patricelli, Leslie

Be quiet, Mike! Candlewick Press 2011 un il $14.99

Grades: PreK K 1 2   E

1. Stories in rhyme 2. Drums -- Fiction 3. Noise -- Fiction 4.

Monkeys -- Fiction 5. Musicians -- Fiction

ISBN 978-0-7636-4477-2; 0-7636-4477-3

LC 2010044814

Monkey Mike is reprimanded for making noise when he taps pencils and clangs trash cans until he sees a drum set in the music store and puts his hands-on talents to work in a most impressive way.

"This rhythmic, rhyming romp about a youngster who must drum is illustrated with bold lines and colors in acrylic that suggest a jazzy ease. The bright, ever-changing background hues keep the focus on Mike and the onomatopoeic words scattered throughout the story." SLJ

The **birthday** box. Candlewick Press 2007 un il $15.99; bd bk $6.99

Grades: PreK   E

1. Boxes -- Fiction 2. Birthdays -- Fiction 3. Imagination -- Fiction

ISBN 978-0-7636-2825-3; 0-7636-2825-5; 978-0-7636-4449-9 bd bk; 0-7636-4449-8 bd bk

LC 2006-49084

"A child wearing only a diaper and a striped party hat gets a present from Grandma. . . . The toddler takes off the wrapping paper . . . and discovers A big brown box! A box is full of possibilities and this child lets imagination reign. . . . Patricelli's simple, first-person narration is refreshing. With bold black outlines, the acrylic paintings are rudimentary but nonetheless expressive and endearing." SLJ

★ **Higher!** higher! Candlewick Press 2009 un il $15.99; bd bk $6.99

Grades: PreK K 1   E

1. Play -- Fiction 2. Imagination -- Fiction

ISBN 978-0-7636-3241-0; 0-7636-3241-4; 978-0-7636-4433-8 bd bk; 0-7636-4433-1 bd bk

Boston Globe-Horn Book Award honor book: Picture Book (2009)

"As an adult pushes a pigtailed girl in a striped sweater and socks on a swing, the child calls out: 'Higher! Higher!' The ride gradually takes her from a giraffe's-eye view, to a mountaintop, to an airplane, and finally high enough to trade high fives with a one-eyed, green alien. . . . The repetitive text is ideal for new readers, and the cartoon paintings, though spare, provide plenty of room for imagination." SLJ

Potty. Candlewick Press 2010 un il $6.99

Grades: PreK   E

1. Board books for children 2. Toilet training -- Fiction

ISBN 978-0-7636-4476-5; 0-7636-4476-5

LC 2009-49045

Baby, a toddler, decides to use the potty for the first time.

This "appealing [book features] simple text, bright acrylic illustrations, and [an] everyday [situation] that [is] certain to engage the very young." SLJ

Tubby. Candlewick Press 2010 un il $6.99

Grades: PreK   E

1. Board books for children 2. Baths -- Fiction 3. Infants -- Fiction

ISBN 978-0-7636-4567-0; 0-7636-4567-2

LC 2009-49046

Baby loves playing during bath time.

This "appealing [book features] simple text, bright acrylic illustrations, and [an] everyday [situations] that [is] certain to engage the very young." SLJ

Pattison, Darcy S.

The **journey** of Oliver K. Woodman; written by Darcy Pattison; illustrated by Joe Cepeda. Harcourt 2003 un il $16; pa $6.99

Grades: K 1 2 3 **E**
1. Travel -- Fiction
ISBN 0-15-202329-1; 0-15-206118-5 pa
LC 2001-5320
Oliver K. Woodman, a man made of wood, takes a remarkable journey across America, as told through the postcards and letters of those he meets along the way

"The boldly colored, textured illustrations were made with oils over an acrylic under-painting on boards. . . . A fresh, unusual tale." SLJ
Another title about Oliver K. Woodman is:
Searching for Oliver K. Woodman (2005)

Paul, Alison
The **Plan**; by Alison Paul; illustrated by Barbara Lehman. Houghton Mifflin Harcourt 2015 32 p. color illustrations $17.99
Grades: PreK K 1 2 **E**
1. Flight -- Fiction 2. Father-daughter relationship -- Fiction
ISBN 0544283333; 9780544283336
In this children's story, by Alison Paul and illustrated by Barbara Lehman, "a child's desire to fly to space turns into a transformative project with her father. . . . The story is nearly wordless, with a single changing word appearing in bold text on some pages. . . . The 20 words help to ground the story as it unfolds, telling why the plane sits in the weeds, who flew it before, how it will get back into the air." (Kirkus Reviews)
"This lovely story blends a sense of rootedness with the spirit of exploration—a rare combination." Pub Wkly

Paul, Ann Whitford
Count on Culebra; go from 1 to 10 in Spanish. Holiday House 2008 un il $16.95
Grades: PreK K 1 **E**
1. Counting 2. Iguanas -- Fiction 3. Rattlesnakes -- Fiction 4. Desert animals -- Fiction 5. Spanish language -- Vocabulary
ISBN 978-0-8234-2124-4; 0-8234-2124-4
LC 2007017303
When Iguana stubs her toe and cannot make her popular candies known as cactus butter dulces, Culebra the rattlesnake finds a cure that introduces the Spanish words for the numbers from one to ten.
"The well-paced story exudes a charming silliness and invites participation. Bright cartoon-style illustrations, rendered in gouache and colored pencil, nicely depict the foolishness and are large enough for group sharing. . . . The introduction of Spanish words and counting concepts along with the appealing art and offbeat story make this a treat." Booklist

Fiesta fiasco; illustrated by Ethan Long. Holiday House 2007 un il $16.95
Grades: PreK K 1 2 3 **E**
1. Gifts -- Fiction 2. Rabbits -- Fiction 3. Desert animals -- Fiction 4. Spanish language -- Vocabulary
ISBN 0-8234-2037-X; 978-0-8234-2037-7
LC 2006-12112
When shopping for Culebra's birthday, Conejo convinces his friends Iguana and Tortuga to buy all the wrong presents. Includes a glossary of Spanish words used.
"A fiery palette enlivens the simple cartoon artwork set in the desert. The scenes are fun to look at." SLJ
Other titles about these characters are:
Mañana Iguana (2004)
Tortuga in trouble (2009)

Snail's good night; by Ann Whitford Paul; illustrated by Rosanne Litzinger. Holiday House 2008 32p il $14.95

Grades: PreK K 1 **E**
1. Snails -- Fiction 2. Bedtime -- Fiction
ISBN 978-0-8234-1912-8; 0-8234-1912-6
LC 2007-614
When Snail realizes that his friends are going to bed, he begins a very long, very slow slide to wish them all good night.
"Created using watercolor, gouache, and colored pencil, the fanciful artwork features mild-mannered animal characters and a benevolent moon shining down on the world. . . . The large type and short sentences make this gently amusing story just right for beginning readers." Booklist

Word builder; illustrated by Kurt Cyrus. Simon & Schuster Books for Young Readers 2009 un il $16.99
Grades: PreK K 1 **E**
1. Authorship -- Fiction
ISBN 978-1-4169-3981-8; 1-4169-3981-4
LC 2007045244
Text explains how putting letters into words, words into sentences, sentences into paragraphs, and paragraphs into chapters ends up creating a book
"This oversize book uses direct language and terrific artwork to show children how literal and figurative construction works. . . . The art, rendered in pencil and digital color, seems almost three-dimensional and will fascinate readers." Booklist

Payne, Emmy
Katy No-Pocket; pictures by H. A. Rey. Houghton Mifflin 1944 un il lib bdg $17; pa $5.95
Grades: PreK K 1 2 **E**
1. Animals -- Fiction 2. Kangaroos -- Fiction
ISBN 0-395-17104-0 lib bdg; 0-395-13717-9 pa
Katy Kangaroo was most unfortunately unprovided with a pocket in which to carry her son Freddy. She asked other animals with no pockets how they carried their children but none of their answers seemed satisfactory. Finally a wise old owl advised her to try to find a pocket in the City, and so off she went and in the City she found just what she and Freddy needed

Pearce, Emily Smith
Slowpoke; illustrated by Scot Ritchie. Boyds Mills Press 2010 39p il $16.95
Grades: K 1 2 3 **E**
1. Speed -- Fiction 2. Family life -- Fiction
ISBN 978-1-59078-705-2; 1-59078-705-6
LC 2009033955
After pokey Fiona attends Speed School, where she learns to wash dishes, brush her teeth, and clean her room at the same time, she decides to demonstrate to her family the value of sometimes doing things more slowly.
"The text is interspersed with black-and-white illustrations that do a stellar job of conveying both leisure and frenzy. A clever early reader with challenging vocabulary and some food for thought to boot." Kirkus

Pearce, Philippa
The **squirrel** wife; illustrated by Wayne Anderson. Candlewick Press 2007 un il $16.99
Grades: K 1 2 3 **E**
1. Fairy tales 2. Fairies -- Fiction 3. Brothers -- Fiction 4. Squirrels -- Fiction 5. Forests and forestry -- Fiction
ISBN 978-0-7636-3551-0; 0-7636-3551-0
LC 2006052454

As a reward for saving the life of one of the feared green people, Jack acquires a beautiful and loving squirrel wife, knowledgeable in the secrets of the forest.

"Anderson's mixed-media illustrations strengthen the story's connections while amplifying the sense of enchantment with images of the elfin, lime-colored folk and the forest scenes, rendered in feathery strokes and an earthy green palette of moss and mushrooms. An intriguing, atmospheric offering." Booklist

Pearle, Ida

A **child's** day; an alphabet of play. Harcourt 2008 un il $12.95
Grades: PreK K   E
1. Alphabet 2. Play -- Fiction
ISBN 978-0-15-206552-2; 0-15-206552-0

LC 2007-33966

"This simple, attractive alphabet of action words and pictures depicts children engaged in play and other activities. . . . The design is particularly effective. Large, colorful cut-paper collages of multiethnic children feature interesting patterns that stand out against solid backgrounds." SLJ

The **moon** is going to Addy's house; by Ida Pearle. Dial Books for Young Readers, an imprint of Penguin Group (USA) Inc. 2015 32 p. color illustrations (hardcover) $17.99
Grades: PreK K 1   E
1. Moon -- Fiction 2. Bedtime -- Fiction
ISBN 0803740549; 9780803740549

LC 2014020048

In this children's bedtime story, by Ida Pearle, "Addy and her sister have been building with blocks at a friend's home in the city. The pale moon is visible through the window and in subsequent compositions. As the family drives home, the girls play hide-and-seek with the orb, searching throughout the bustling neighborhood, under the bridge, and behind the mountains." (School Library Journal)

"Working in collage, Pearle (A Child's Day: An Alphabet of Play) sets delicately cut, classically proportioned human figures onto backdrops of striking colors and patterns. The effect is breathtaking. . . . Pearle captures silky motion, conjures up a sense of warmth without reserve, and celebrates children's intuitive grasp of the natural world." PW

Pearlman, Robb

Groundhog's day off; by Robb Pearlman; illustrated by Brett Helquist. Bloomsbury 2015 40 p. color illustrations (hardcover) $16.99
Grades: K 1 2   E
1. Groundhog Day -- Fiction 2. Humorous stories 3. Woodchuck -- Fiction
ISBN 9781619632899

LC 2014038764

In this children's story, by Robb Pearlman and illustrated by Brett Helquist, "every year, people ask Groundhog the same, boring old question. Is spring around the corner? Or are we doomed to more winter? Sure, they care about his shadow, but what about him and his interests? He's had enough! Groundhog packs his bags and sets out for a much-needed vacation. Now the town is holding auditions to find someone to fill his spot. None of the animals seem right for the job, though." Publisher's note)

"The naturalistic drawings are rendered in acrylic and oil paint on watercolor paper. Groundhog has a cute, toothy grin, and the large pictures make the book easy to use in group settings." SLJ

Pearson, Debora

Sophie's wheels; by Debora Pearson; art by Nora Hilb. Annick Press 2006 un il lib bdg $18.95; pa $6.95

Grades: PreK   E
1. Growth -- Fiction 2. Wheels -- Fiction
ISBN 978-1-55451-038-2 lib bdg; 1-55451-038-4 lib bdg; 978-1-55451-037-5 pa; 1-55451-037-6 pa

"The language is descriptive. . . . The text is accompanied by simple, soft-washed watercolor illustrations. . . . .This [is a] satisfying, peaceful tale." SLJ

Pearson, Susan

How to teach a slug to read; illustrated by David Slonim. Marshall Cavendish Children's 2011 un il $16.99
Grades: PreK K 1 2   E
1. Reading -- Fiction 2. Slugs (Mollusks) -- Fiction
ISBN 978-0-7614-5805-0; 0-7614-5805-0

LC 2010-24289

Provides simple, step-by-step instructions for teaching a slug how to read, including using Mother Slug rhymes, helping your slug sound out words, and making vocabulary lists.

"The two main slug characters are portrayed both affectionately and creatively. The literary references are fast and furious . . . and, fortunately, very accessible to current listeners. . . . Slonim's acrylic-and-charcoal illustrations have a pleasantly informal silliness, with rough, sketchy charcoal lines partnering with the paint." Bull Cent Child Books

We're going on a ghost hunt; by Susan Pearson; illustrated by S.D. Schindler. Marshall Cavendish 2012 32 p. (hardcover) $16.99
Grades: K 1 2 3   E
1. Children's poetry 2. Picture books for children 3. Ghost stories -- Fiction 4. Adventure and adventurers -- Fiction
ISBN 0761463070; 9780761463078; 9780761463085

LC 2011031815

In this children's picture book, the "familiar cadence and words associated with 'We're Going on a Bear Hunt' are giving a seasonal twist by [Susan] Pearson. These kids are heading off on a ghost hunt. . . . But when they reach the graveyard and a ghost appears, their courage wavers and they make a fast trip back home retracting their steps through the woods, across the stream, cornfield and swamp to race into their beds." (Children's Literature)

Pearson, Tracey Campbell

★ **Bob.** Farrar, Straus & Giroux 2002 un il $16; pa $6.95
Grades: PreK K 1 2   E
1. Animals -- Fiction 2. Roosters -- Fiction
ISBN 0-374-39957-3; 0-374-40871-8 pa

LC 2001-40439

While looking for someone to teach him how to crow, a rooster learns to sound like many different animals and finds that his new skills come in handy

"The droll, repetitive text, perfect for reading aloud, is delightfully complemented by bright, lively watercolor illustrations." SLJ

Peet, Bill

Big bad Bruce. Houghton Mifflin 1977 38p il $17; pa $8.95
Grades: PreK K 1 2   E
1. Bears -- Fiction 2. Witches -- Fiction
ISBN 0-395-25150-8; 0-395-32922-1 pa

LC 76-62502

Bruce, a bear bully, never picks on anyone his own size until he is diminished in more ways than one by a small but very independent witch

"The language of the text is almost musical, with lots of words used for the sheer pleasure or appropriateness of their sounds. The illustrations are colorful and amusing." Child Book Rev Serv

Huge Harold; written and illustrated by Bill Peet. Houghton Mifflin 1961 un il hardcover o.p. pa $8.95
Grades: PreK K 1 2   E
   1. Stories in rhyme 2. Rabbits -- Fiction
   ISBN 0-395-18449-5; 0-395-32923-X pa
This story, "told in rhyming couplets and colored drawings, is action filled and laughable." Booklist

The **whingdingdilly**; written and illustrated by Bill Peet. Houghton Mifflin 1970 60p il $17; pa $9.95
Grades: PreK K 1 2   E
   1. Dogs -- Fiction 2. Witches -- Fiction
   ISBN 0-395-24729-2; 0-395-31381-3 pa
"Scamps, the dog, wants to be a horse, but a well-meaning witch turns him into a Whingdingdilly with the hump of a camel, zebra's tail, giraffe's neck, elephant's front legs and ears, rhinoceros' nose, and reindeer's horns." Adventuring With Books. 2d edition

Peete, Holly Robinson
   My brother Charlie; written by Holly Robinson Peete and Ryan Elizabeth Peete with Denene Millner; pictures by Shane W. Evans. Scholastic Press 2010 un il
Grades: 1 2 3 4   E
   1. Twins -- Fiction 2. Autism -- Fiction 3. Siblings -- Fiction
   ISBN 0-545-09466-6; 978-0-545-09466-5
                                LC 2009005589
A girl tells what it is like living with her twin brother who has autism and sometimes finds it hard to communicate with words, but who, in most ways, is just like any other boy. Includes authors' note about autism
"The authors, a mother-daughter team, based this story on personal experience. Evans's bright, mixed-media illustrations skillfully depict the family's warmth and concern." SLJ

Pelham, David
   ★ **Trail**; paper poetry. Little Simon/Simon & Schuster Books for Young Readers 2007 un il $26.99
Grades: 1 2 3 4   E
   1. Pop-up books 2. Snails -- Fiction
   ISBN 978-1-4169-4894-0
In five pop-up spreads a silver line of poetry on white paper follows a small snail through its day, from roots and leaf on the forest floor to a pond at sunset. Pelham lays the verse out on a paper wheel that must be turned to be read in its entirety.

Pelley, Kathleen T.
   Magnus Maximus, a marvelous measurer; [pictures by] S.D. Schindler. Farrar Straus Giroux 2010 un il $16.99
Grades: K 1 2   E
   1. Counting -- Fiction 2. Measurement -- Fiction
   ISBN 978-0-374-34725-3; 0-374-34725-5
                                LC 2006-51714
As the town's official measurer, Magnus Maximus is consumed with measuring and counting everything and everyone, missing out on life's simple pleasures, until one day when he breaks his glasses.
"Children will enjoy the humor in this eccentric's ever-increasing obsession. Fine ink lines and muted watercolors fill the illustrations with small details, add humor, and complete the story. The art firmly places it in the Victorian era, a time of scientific exploration. The style perfectly captures the focus of the marvelous measurer and his scientific obsession." SLJ

   Raj, the bookstore tiger; illustrated by Paige Keiser. Charlesbridge 2011 un il lib bdg $15.95

Grades: K 1 2 3   E
   1. Cats -- Fiction 2. Tigers -- Fiction 3. Books and reading -- Fiction
   ISBN 978-1-58089-230-8; 1-58089-230-2
                                LC 2010007585
When a new manager brings Snowball, a grouchy cat, to the shop where Raj and his owner live and work, Snowball informs Raj that he is not the tiger everyone believes him to be.
"The lively, descriptive narrative will provide an entertaining read-aloud, while the cheery watercolor-and-pencil illustrations feature expressive feline and human characters. . . . A whimsical title with a positive message." Booklist

Pendziwol, Jean
   Marja's skis; [by] Jean E. Pendziwol; pictures by Jirina Marton. Groundwood 2007 un il $17.95
Grades: 1 2 3   E
   1. Canada -- Fiction 2. Skiing -- Fiction 3. Fathers -- Fiction 4. Immigrants -- Fiction 5. Lumber and lumbering -- Fiction
   ISBN 978-0-88899-674-9
"Marja can hardly wait to be big and strong enough to help with Father's horses and attend school. . . . But after her father dies . . . being strong seems too hard. One day . . . Marja sees someone who has fallen through the ice and . . . she finds the courage to help him. . . . Evocative oil-pastels illustrate the text. . . . A simply told, emotionally resonant tale." Booklist

Penn, Audrey
   A **bedtime** kiss for Chester Raccoon; illustrated by Barbara Gibson. Tanglewood 2011 il $7.95
Grades: PreK   E
   1. Stories in rhyme 2. Board books for children 3. Fear -- Fiction 4. Bedtime -- Fiction 5. Raccoons -- Fiction
   ISBN 978-1-933718-52-1; 1-933718-52-8
                                LC 201004671
"As Chester Raccoon nestles into his lair, he begins to imagine frightening creatures in the light that streams across his bedroom. . . . The ink and watercolor illustrations are realistic and reassuringly expressive. . . . Designed for younger children, this board book features rounded corners, rhyming couplets, and a simpler text than the earlier books in the series. It should find an audience in most public libraries." SLJ

   Other titles about Chester Raccoon are:
   Chester Raccoon and the acorn full of memories (2009)
   Chester Raccoon and the big bad bully (2008)
   The kissing hand (2006)

   Chester Raccoon and the acorn full of memories; illustrated by Barbara L. Gibson. Tanglewood 2009 un il $16.95
Grades: K 1 2 3   E
   1. Death -- Fiction 2. Memory -- Fiction 3. Raccoons -- Fiction 4. Bereavement -- Fiction 5. Forest animals -- Fiction 6. Mother-child relationship -- Fiction
   ISBN 978-1-933718-29-3; 1-933718-29-3
                                LC 200901373
After his mother explains why his classmate is not returning to school, she teaches Chester Raccoon how to make a memory.
"Simple, direct dialogue demonstrates the love between this mother and child. Bright, stylized illustrations on high-gloss pages depict the animals with human emotions, convey warmth, and reinforce the text." SLJ

Pennypacker, Sara, 1951-

★ **Meet** the Dullards; Sara Pennypacker; illustrated by Daniel Salmieri. Balzer + Bray 2014 32 p. color illustrations (hardcover) $17.99

Grades: K 1 2 3   E

1. Boredom -- Fiction 2. Family -- Fiction 3. Humorous stories 4. Family life -- Fiction 5. Moving, Household -- Fiction

ISBN 9780062198563; 0062198564

LC 2013037321

This children's book about the Dullard family, written by Sara Pennypacker and illustrated by Daniel Salmieri, describes how "Their home is boring. Their food is plain. Their lives are monotonous. And Mr. and Mrs. Dullard like it that way. But their children--Blanda, Borely, and Little Dud--have other ideas." (Publisher's note)

"This title follows in the quirky tradition of Harry Allard's 'The Stupids' books (Houghton), with clever wordplay and subversive fun that will appeal to children everywhere." SLJ

★ **Sparrow** girl; illustrated by Yoko Tanaka. Hyperion 2009 un il $16.99

Grades: 1 2 3 4   E

1. Birds -- Fiction 2. Sparrows -- Fiction 3. China -- History -- 1949-1976 -- Fiction

ISBN 978-1-4231-1187-0; 1-4231-1187-7

LC 2009-6758

When China's leader declares war on sparrows in 1958, everyone makes loud noise in hopes of chasing the hungry birds from their land except for Ming-Li, a young girl whose compassion and foresight prevent a disaster

"Pennypacker strikes a suitably moralistic tone and tells her story with rich, descriptive detail. Tanaka matches the somber elegance of the text with opaque, folk-inspired paintings in a subdued palette. An author's note explains the difficult facts behind the story." Booklist

Peot, Margaret

Crow made a friend; Margaret Peot. Holiday House 2014 24 p. color illustrations (I like to read) (hardcover) $14.95

Grades: PreK K 1   E

1. Crows -- Fiction 2. Friendship -- Fiction

ISBN 0823432971; 9780823432974

LC 2014024929

This children's book, by Margaret Peot, is part of the "I Like to Read" series. "Crow is all alone. But . . . using autumn leaves for wings, sticks for the body and a crab apple for the head, Crow makes a friend! But winter winds blow in, destroying his creation. Undaunted, Crow fashions another bird friend out of snow but cannot prevent it from melting. . . . Alone again, Crow hears the caw, caw, caw of a real, live bird and finally forms a friendship that will last." (Publisher's note)

"The overall message of the importance of friends and family is sweet but not cloying. A brightly illustrated story perfect for the very beginner reader." Kirkus

Perez, Amada Irma

My diary from here to there; story, Amada Irma Pérez; illustrations, Maya Christina Gonzalez. Children's Bk. Press 2002 un il $16.95

Grades: 2 3 4   E

1. Immigrants -- Fiction 2. Mexican Americans -- Fiction 3. Bilingual books -- English-Spanish

ISBN 0-89239-175-8

LC 2001-58251

A young girl describes her feelings when her father decides to leave their home in Mexico to look for work in the United States

"The diary entries, written in conversational English and Spanish, resonate with the tensions of the experience. . . . The full-page, bright acrylic paintings complement the text, with the blocky primitive forms adding a reassuring note to the whole." SLJ

★ **My** very own room; story by Amada Irma Pérez; illustrations by Maya Christina Gonzalez. Children's Bk. Press 2000 30p il $16.95

Grades: PreK K 1 2   E

1. Family life -- Fiction 2. Mexican Americans -- Fiction 3. Bilingual books -- English-Spanish

ISBN 0-89239-164-2

LC 00-20769

With the help of her family, a resourceful Mexican American girl realizes her dream of having a space of her own to read and to think

"Gonzalez' palette is replete with joyfully exuberant colors; rich magentas, purples, and blues contrast with the warm golds of faces and arms, and the dark eyes and hair offer further contrast with the backgrounds and skin colors. Pérez based this story on her own life . . . and the text . . . exudes a comfortably familiar, accessible voice." Bull Cent Child Books

Perez, L. King

First day in grapes; illustrated by Robert Casilla. Lee & Low Bks. 2002 un il $16.95

Grades: K 1 2 3   E

1. School stories 2. California -- Fiction 3. Migrant labor -- Fiction 4. Mexican Americans -- Fiction

ISBN 1-58430-045-0

LC 2001-38787

When Chico starts the third grade after his migrant worker family moves to begin harvesting California grapes, he finds that self confidence and math skills help him cope with the first day of school

This story "sheds light on the life of migrant children in a poignant, balanced manner. . . . The watercolor, colored-pencil, and pastel illustrations bring warmth and color to this portrait of life in rural California." SLJ

Pericoli, Matteo

Tommaso and the missing line. Alfred A. Knopf 2008 un il $15.99; lib bdg $18.99

Grades: K 1 2 3   E

1. Italy -- Fiction 2. Drawing -- Fiction 3. Lost and found possessions -- Fiction

ISBN 978-0-375-84102-6; 0-375-84102-4; 978-0-375-94102-3 lib bdg; 0-375-94102-9 lib bdg

When Tommaso discovers that a line is missing from his favorite drawing, he goes looking for it all around town and notices many lines he never saw before.

Pericoli "demonstrates remarkable draftsmanship and a vivid eye for detail and perspective; the mostly black-and-white pictures combine the elegant extravagance of architectural engravings with the playfulness and spontaneity of a great doodle. The Italian setting adds to the charm. . . . The design is striking. . . . Facing each illustration, the text drops out from solid orange; the effect is eye-popping." Publ Wkly

The **true** story of Stellina. Knopf 2006 un il $15.95; lib bdg $17.99

Grades: PreK K 1 2   E

1. Finches 2. New York (N.Y.)

ISBN 0-375-83273-4; 0-375-93273-9 lib bdg

The true story of a baby finch rescued and raised by the author and his wife when no zoo would take the abandoned bird fallen from her nest onto a busy street in the middle of New York City.

"A precise linguistic lyricism is at play. . . . The art is sophisticated and spare, but utterly accessible." Booklist

Perkins, Lynne Rae

★ The **cardboard** piano. Greenwillow Books 2008 un il $17.99; lib bdg $18.89

Grades: PreK K 1 2   **E**

1. Pianos -- Fiction 2. Friendship -- Fiction

ISBN 978-0-06-154265-7; 0-06-154265-2; 978-0-06-154266-4 lib bdg; 0-06-154266-0 lib bdg

LC 2007-39194

When Debbie tries to interest Tina in playing the piano by creating a cardboard keyboard, they find not only does it not have the same appeal but also that they do not need to share everything to be best friends.

"Perkins engages her young audience on three levels: the straightforward yet emotionally complex text; conversational asides in word balloons that develop characterization; and intricate pen-and-ink and watercolor illustrations. . . . Perkins presents the delicate nature of friendship without patronizing." Horn Book

★ **Frank** and Lucky get schooled; by Lynne Rae Perkins. Greenwillow Books, an imprint of HarperCollins Publishers 2016 32 p. color illustrations (trade ed.) $17.99

Grades: PreK K 1 2 3   **E**

1. Dogs -- Fiction 2. Humorous fiction 3. Learning and scholarship -- Fiction 4. Humorous stories 5. Learning -- Fiction

ISBN 9780062373458

LC 2015015559

In this book, by Lynne Rae Perkins, "Frank's parents take him to the shelter to get a new dog. That's how Frank finds Lucky, and from that moment on, they're inseparable. As Frank and Lucky venture out into the world around them, they discover they both have a lot to learn. Exploring their neighborhood teaches them about biology. . . . Sharing a bed teaches them about fractions. . . . They even learn different languages." (Publisher's note)

"As Perkins comments on art, history, geography, and more, she brings a warm, conversational tone to the narrative, while her mixed-media pictures play up the story's humor through the use of comics elements, including panel sequences and speech balloons." Pub Wkly

Snow music. Greenwillow Bks. 2003 un il $15.99

Grades: PreK K 1   **E**

1. Snow -- Fiction 2. Sound -- Fiction

ISBN 0-06-623956-7

LC 2002-192758

Boston Globe-Horn Book Award Honor: Picture Book (2004)

When a dog gets loose from the house on a snowy day, his owner searches for him and experiences the sounds of various animals and things in the snow

"With whispery, musical words and detailed, soft-focus images that depict typical winter scenes, this gentle book gives children a sense of what snow is." SLJ

Perl, Erica S.

Dotty; illustrated by Julia Denos. Abrams Books for Young Readers 2010 un il $16.95

Grades: PreK K 1   **E**

1. School stories 2. Imaginary playmates -- Fiction 3. Teacher-student relationship -- Fiction

ISBN 978-0-8109-8962-7; 0-8109-8962-X

Ida's imaginary friend, Dotty, is tied to her with a blue string and when Ida's classmates tease her about Dotty, Ida is surprised to discover that her teacher carries a red string with her wherever she goes.

"Denos's illustrations subtly show the characters and the seasons changing, and the pressures of growing up. The text is best suited for one-on-one reading as the pictures have hidden nuggets of information for those who look carefully. This enjoyable tale of maturing at one's own pace and on one's own terms will resonate with children and parents alike." SLJ

Perlman, Janet

The **delicious** bug. Kids Can Press 2009 un il $16.95

Grades: PreK K 1 2 3   **E**

1. Insects -- Fiction 2. Chameleons -- Fiction

ISBN 978-1-55337-996-6; 1-55337-996-9

"With a flick of the tongue, two hungry chameleons catch the same bumblebug. Neither is willing to let go, and they have a knockdown-dragout fight to claim the snack. Eventually they realize, thanks to some equally hungry crocodiles, how much they need each other. The snappy story . . . is accompanied by cartoony digital illustrations bordered by panel drawings." Horn Book Guide

Perlman, Willa

Good night, world; illustrated by Carolyn Fisher. Beach Lane Books 2011 il $16.99

Grades: PreK K   **E**

1. Stories in rhyme 2. Bedtime -- Fiction

ISBN 978-1-4424-0197-6; 1-4424-0197-4

LC 2009053078

Rhyming text bids goodnight to the world and everything that is in it, including stars, streams, animals, and roads.

"The evocative rhyme scans perfectly. . . . Each verse is grandly illustrted with a large, double-page painting. Fisher's multicolored, textured paintings match the expansive tone of the book with a wide palette of swirling colors and layed details." SLJ

Perlov, Betty Rosenberg

Rifka takes a bow; by Betty Rosenberg Perlov; illustrated by Cosei Kawa. Kar-Ben Publishing 2013 32 p. $7.95

Grades: K 1 2 3   **E**

1. Picture books for children 2. Historical fiction 3. Theater, Yiddish -- Fiction 4. Jews -- United States -- Fiction

ISBN 0761381287; 9780761381273; 9780761381280

LC 2012028985

In this book, "Rifka lives in early 20th-century New York City with her glamorous, devoted parents, who are stars of the Yiddish theater. She marvels at the transformations that they undergo and revels in backstage life, with its dressing rooms filled with makeup, ribbons, and beads; its clever props . . .; and even its rules for how to perform a kiss. . . . When Rifka accidentally ends up on stage during a performance, she blanches only for a minute." (Publishers Weekly)

Perret, Delphine

The **Big** Bad Wolf and me; [by] Delphine Perret. Sterling Pub. 2006 un il $9.95

Grades: K 1 2 3   **E**

1. Wolves -- Fiction

ISBN 978-1-4027-3725-1; 1-4027-3725-4

LC 2005031460

Original French edition 2005

When the Big Bad Wolf is mistaken for a dog, he comes to live in a boy's closet and eat chocolate chip cookies.

"Told in witty, thumbnail-size line drawings accompanied by brief text in very small type. . . . The story's humor, absurdity, and heart will please a wide readership." Booklist

The **Big** Bad Wolf Goes on Vacation; Delphine Perret. Sterling 2013 64 p. (hardcover) $12.95

Grades: K 1 2 3   **E**

1. Picture books for children 2. Summer -- Fiction 3. Voyages and travels -- Fiction 4. Humorous stories 5. Wolves -- Fiction

6. Vacations -- Fiction 7. Grandfathers -- Fiction 8. Characters in literature -- Fiction
ISBN 1402786336; 9781402786334

LC 2012009933

This book is Delphine Perret's sequel to "The Big Bad Wolf and Me" and "again stars Louis and his wolf friend, Bernard." Here, Louis and Bernard go on a summer trip with Louis's Grandpa. "During their travels, the three enjoy lunch in a park when they can't take Bernard into a restaurant, come upon a herd of odiferous cows blocking the roadway, and stop to stretch their legs near woods. Arriving at the seaside, Louis and Bernard partake of plenty of interactive seaside fun." (School Library Journal)

Perrin, Martine

Look who's there! Albert Whitman 2011 un il
Grades: PreK   **E**
1. Stories in rhyme 2. Board books for children 3. Animals -- Fiction
ISBN 080757676X; 9780807576762

LC 2010037841

Original French edition 2005

Text and images on die-cut pages lead the reader to discover the hiding places of a variety of animals in the water and near the shore.

This is a "striking hide-and-seek book. . . . A stylish presentation." Publ Wkly

What do you see? Albert Whitman 2011 un il
Grades: PreK   **E**
1. Board books for children 2. Animals -- Fiction
ISBN 0807567124; 9780807567128

LC 2010037477

Original French editiion 2005

Text and images on die-cut pages lead the reader to discover the hiding places of a variety of small animals.

"Kids will appreciate the objects profiled: boots, buckets, bibs, cribs, and the like." Booklist

Perry, Andrea

The **Bickeys'** birdbath; illustrated by Roberta Angaramo. Atheneum 2010 un il $16.99
Grades: PreK K 1 2   **E**
1. Stories in rhyme
ISBN 978-1-4169-0624-7; 1-4169-0624-X

A cumulative rhyme in the style of "The House That Jack Built," describing the antics that occur when a mailman lands in a birdbath causing it to break.

"This jaunty cumulative tale has a pleasingly playful complexity, both in the wording and in its sense of time. Perry concocts a rhythmic text with unexpected twists and turns, and rather than moving the story forward, it works backward. . . . Sweetly clever." Kirkus

Peterkin, Allan

The **flyaway** blanket; illustrated by Emmeline Pidgen. Magination Press 2011 un il $14.95; pa $9.95
Grades: PreK K 1 2   **E**
1. Blankets -- Fiction 2. Mother-child relationship -- Fiction
ISBN 978-1-4338-1047-3; 1433810476; 978-1-4338-1046-6 pa; 1-4338-1046-8 pa

LC 2011011079

"In a sensitive lullaby, a small boy and his mother hang the laundry to dry on the clothesline, as she sings, 'time to fly, touch the sky, fly up, high up, wave goodbye.' Jake doesn't want to let go of his comforting blue blanket, but his mother assures him that it will soon be dry. As they sit together in the sun, Jake falls asleep, and a gust of wind sends the blanket sailing. . . . Pidgen's cheerful artwork is reassuring, with a bright palette, loose, sweeping lines, and plenty of attention on mother-child tenderness, human and animal alike. The message about attachment, security, and sometimes letting go is conveyed subtly and organically." Publ Wkly

Peters, Lisa Westberg

★ **Cold** little duck, duck, duck; pictures by Sam Williams. Greenwillow Bks. 2000 un il $15.99
Grades: PreK K 1   **E**
1. Stories in rhyme 2. Ducks -- Fiction 3. Spring -- Fiction
ISBN 0-688-16178-2

LC 99-29880

Early one spring a little duck arrives at her pond and finds it still frozen, but not for long

"The poetic text, well served by expressive watercolors, is set in a large black typeface (inviting letter and word recognition); colorful and playful typefaces are used for the rhythmic three-word refrains." Horn Book Guide

Frankie works the night shift; illustrated by Jennifer Taylor. Greenwillow Books 2010 un il $16.99
Grades: PreK K   **E**
1. Counting 2. Cats -- Fiction 3. Night -- Fiction
ISBN 978-0-06-009095-1; 0-06-009095-2

LC 2008012644

In this counting book, Frankie the cat's night prowling causes a ruckus, waking sleeping neighbors who do not share Frankie's love of the "night shift."

"Peters's spare text, full of exclamatory statements in the second half . . . moves the story forward with energy and speed, but Taylor's artwork is the showstopper, creating a surreal environment for Frankie's nocturnal adventures." Publ Wkly

Petersen, David

Snowy Valentine; written and illustrated by David Petersen. Harper 2011 un il $14.99
Grades: PreK K 1   **E**
1. Love -- Fiction 2. Gifts -- Fiction 3. Rabbits -- Fiction 4. Forest animals -- Fiction 5. Valentine's Day -- Fiction
ISBN 978-0-06-146378-5; 0-06-146378-7

LC 2009027197

Jasper Bunny spends a snowy Valentine's Day visiting his forest friends in hopes of finding the perfect gift for his beloved Lilly.

"Petersen's whimsical, full-bleed illustrations with Victorian-pattern details add warmth and gentle humor to the story. . . . The timeless quality of the theme and perfect cast of supporting characters make this valentine story a head (or at least two rabbit ears) above the rest." SLJ

Peterson, Brenda

Seal pup rescue; by Brenda Peterson. Square Fish 2013 32 p. $15.99
Grades: K 1 2   **E**
1. Marine animals 2. Seals (Animals)
ISBN 1250027756; 9781250027757

This book, by Brenda Peterson, presents an "adaptation of the picture book 'Leopard & Silkie' [and is designed] for new readers who love animals. [Noting that] baby seals can swim soon after they are born, but they also need to rest on shore [it asks] how can they stay safe if the beach is full of dogs and people?" (Publisher's note)

Petricic, Dusan, 1946-

My family tree and me; Dusan Petricic. Kids Can Press 2015 24 p. color illustrations $16.95

Grades: PreK K 1 2 3   E
1. Genealogy
ISBN 1771380497; 9781771380492

This picture book, by Dusan Petricic, "provides a beautifully simple introduction to the concept of family ancestry. It uses two stories in one to explore a small boy's family tree: the boy tells the family story of his father's side starting from the front of the book, and that of his mother's side starting from the back of the book. Four previous generations are introduced for each, from his great-great-grandparents to his parents." (Publisher's note)

"Petricic's exaggerated watercolor figures all have happy faces and rosy cheeks, and family resemblances are impossible to miss. Small details link each colorful illustration and hint at historical changes. This lively and easy-to-follow family tree gracefully traces the little boy's vast and varied ancestry." Booklist

Pfeffer, Wendy

★ **Light** is all around us; by Wendy Pfeffer; illustrated by Paul Meisel. First edition Harper, an imprint of HarperCollinsPublishers 2014 40 p. (hardback) $17.99
Grades: K 1 2 3   E
1. Light
ISBN 0060291214; 9780060291211; 9780064409247
                 LC 2013021512

This children's book, by Wendy Pfeffer and illustrated by Paul Meisel, shows children that light "comes in many forms: Light from the sun brightens our day, firelight flickers in the night, electric lights fill our homes--and some animals even make the sea glow! . . . This is a Stage 2 Let's-Read-and-Find-Out, which means the book explores more challenging concepts for children in the primary grades and supports the Common Core Learning Standards and Next Generation Science Standards." (Publisher's note)

"This strong series entry introduces youngsters to light: where it comes from, how fast it travels, and how it enables us to see. The prose is generally lively, but Pfeffer is all business when it comes to scientific explanations. Lighthearted paintings, outlined in pen and ink, add humor but never distract from the text. Three simple experiments are appended." Horn Book

Pfister, Marcus

Questions, questions; [translated by NordSu¿d Verlag; English adaptation by Marcus Pfister and Susan Pearson] NorthSouth 2011 un il $16.95
Grades: PreK K   E
1. Nature 2. Questions and answers
ISBN 978-0-7358-4000-3; 0-7358-4000-8
First published in Switzerland
Questions on nature.

"Pfister has created images as pithy as they are poignant, boldly graphic and dramatically cropped against white backgrounds. A blue-headed songbird is reminiscent of Asian watercolor; a storm cloud looks like it's been fashioned from salt dough; falling leaves seem cut from pieces of thickly tufted carpet. Although each was created using the same painted paper method (explained on the final page), the results are as varied as the questions." Publ Wkly

Snow puppy. North-South 2011 il $16.95
Grades: PreK K 1   E
1. Dogs -- Fiction 2. Snow -- Fiction 3. Christmas -- Fiction
ISBN 978-0-7358-4031-7; 0-7358-4031-8

A puppy is lost in the snowy woods and needs to make his way home.
"Rascal is a big-nosed scamp, full of curiosity and joy. Pfister's scenes are speckled throughout with the falling snow, wintry whites

contrasting with the forest browns. This nicely captures a puppy's (or a child's) distractibility." Kirkus

Pham, LeUyen

★ **All** the things I love about you; written and illustrated by LeUyen Pham. Balzer + Bray 2010 un il $16.99
Grades: PreK K 1 2   E
1. Love -- Fiction 2. Mother-son relationship -- Fiction
ISBN 978-0-06-199029-8; 0-06-199029-9
                 LC 2009054255

A mother relates some of the many things that she loves about her young son.
"In capturing the goofy spontaneity of affection and everyday family life without a whiff of treacle, Pham proves once again that she's among the most natural and gifted illustrators working today." Publ Wkly

Phillipps, Julie C.

★ **Wink**: the ninja who wanted to be noticed. Viking Children's Books 2009 un il $15.99
Grades: K 1 2 3   E
1. School stories 2. Ninja -- Fiction
ISBN 978-0-670-01092-9; 0-670-01092-8
                 LC 2008-23238

Although ninjas should be silent and use stealth, Wink finds his enthusiasm gets him into trouble with his teacher until he finds the perfect way to express both traits.
"The story's oft-told message of acceptance has been invigorated with originality and humor. The collage-style illustrations often appear to have a three-dimensional effect and Wink practically bounds off the pages with barely contained energy." SLJ

Another title about Wink is:
Wink: the ninja who wanted to nap (2011)

Wink: the ninja who wanted to nap; by J.C. Phillipps. Viking 2011 un il $15.99
Grades: K 1 2 3   E
1. Fame -- Fiction 2. Japan -- Fiction 3. Ninja -- Fiction 4. Sleep -- Fiction
ISBN 978-0-670-01192-6; 0-670-01192-4
                 LC 2010025107

Wink loves being the most famous ninja in Japan but when he needs a nap his fans will not leave him alone, and so he seeks guidance from his former teacher, Master Zutsu.
"Phillipps offers wit aplenty in cut-paper compositions that match Wink's boundless energy and bravado. Even when sleepy, her hero demands to be noticed." Publ Wkly

Pichon, Liz

The **three** horrid little pigs; by Liz Pichon. Tiger Tales 2008 un il $15.95
Grades: PreK K 1 2   E
1. Pigs -- Fiction 2. Wolves -- Fiction
ISBN 978-1-58925-077-2; 1-58925-077-X

When their mother sends them packing, three pigs find despicable ways to find new accommodations, but when the big, friendly wolf tries to show them the error of their ways, the pigs respond by huffing and puffing.
"The lively narrative, printed in playfully arranged text of varying size, is well suited for spirited read-alouds, as are the colorful illustrations that add to the hilarity with expressive characters. Children will enjoy the clever twist on a familiar story." Booklist

Pien, Lark

★ **Mr.** Elephanter. Candlewick Press 2010 un il $14.99

Grades: PreK K   E
   1. Nannies -- Fiction 2. Elephants -- Fiction
   ISBN 978-0-7636-4409-3; 0-7636-4409-9

LC 2010-07577

From early morning until sunset, beloved Mr. Elephanter takes care of the rambunctious youngsters of the Elephantery, preparing their breakfast, taking them to the park, tucking them in for naps, and joining them at play.

"The simple story will speak to youngsters, and Pien's clever wording captures the humor in daily life. The sketchy watercolor illustrations portray both movement and story well." SLJ

Pilkey, Dav

The **Hallo**-wiener. Blue Sky Press (NY) 1995 un il $16.95; pa $5.99
Grades: PreK K 1 2   E
   1. Dogs -- Fiction 2. Halloween -- Fiction
   ISBN 0-590-41703-7; 0-439-07946-2 pa

LC 94-40949

All the other dogs make fun of Oscar the dachshund until one Halloween when, dressed as a hot dog, Oscar bravely rescues the others

"Pilkey's bold, colorful illustrations add life to his simple tale of courage and friendship." Horn Book Guide

★ The **paperboy**; story and paintings by Dav Pilkey. Orchard Bks. 1996 un il $16.95; pa $6.99
Grades: PreK K 1 2   E
   1. Newspaper carriers -- Fiction
   ISBN 0-531-09506-1; 0-531-07139-1 pa

LC 95-30641

A Caldecott Medal honor book, 1997

"The palette of the artwork is rich and inviting, and an emphasis is put on balance and geometric form, giving solidity to this celebration of routine. A meditative evocation of the extraordinary aspects of ordinary living." Horn Book Guide

Pinder, Eric

If all the animals came inside; by Eric Pinder; illustrated by Marc Brown. Little, Brown and Company 2012 40 p.
Grades: PreK K 1 2   E
   1. Home -- Fiction 2. Stories in rhyme 3. Animals -- Fiction 4. Picture books for children
   ISBN 0316098833; 9780316098830

LC 2011020100

In this picture book, a "young boy imagines the riot that would ensue if his house were overrun with wild animals. . . . The hodgepodge of animals ranges from forest chipmunks and savanna giraffes to Australian kangaroos and even an octopus. And they all come with mischief in mind. . . . From ruining the furniture and eating all the food to taking up the comfiest places, they would eventually leave no room for the boy and his family, relegating them to sleeping outside. And in fact, the boy wisely decides in the end that, as much fun as all the animals might be, he will be satisfied with just his cat and dog." (Kirkus)

Pinfold, Levi

Black dog; Levi Pinfold. Candlewick Press 2012 32 p. ill. (hardcover) $15.99
Grades: PreK K 1 2   E
   1. Dogs -- Fiction 2. Fear -- Fiction 3. Picture books for children 4. Family life -- Fiction
   ISBN 0763660973; 9780763660970

LC 2011048380

Boston Globe-Horn Book Honor: Picture Book (2013).

This book tells how "when the Hope family wakes up one morning, they're stunned to see 'a black dog the size of an elephant' outside their house. . . . The youngest Hope, known as Small, fearlessly marches out to meet the humongous pooch. Singing a taunting rhyme, she entices him to chase her, darting under the bridge, through the playground slide, and back home through the cat flap in the door. With each obstacle negotiated, the dog shrinks somewhat, until . . . he clearly has become the new house pet." (Bulletin of the Center for Children's Books)

★ The **Django**. Templar Books 2010 un il $16.99
Grades: K 1 2   E
   1. Romanies -- Fiction 2. Imaginary playmates -- Fiction
   ISBN 978-0-7636-4788-9; 0-7636-4788-8

A young Gypsy boy named Jean has an imaginary friend, Django, who keeps getting him in trouble and eventually is "sent away," but whenever Jean plays the banjo he continues to feel close to Django. Inspired by the life of jazz musician Django Reinhardt; includes facts about his life.

"Fish-eyed perspectives and generous detailing almost suck readers' gazes into Pinfold's exotic and pastoral artwork. Once in, children will revel in the bouncy rhythms and nonsense words sprinkled throughout the fun-to-read-and-hear narrative." Booklist

Pinkney, Andrea Davis

★ **Boycott** blues; how Rosa Parks inspired a nation. illustrations by Brian Pinkney. Greenwillow Books 2008 un il $16.99; lib bdg $17.89
Grades: 1 2 3 4   E
   1. Civil rights activists 2. African Americans -- Fiction 3. Montgomery (Ala.) -- Fiction
   ISBN 978-0-06-082118-0; 0-06-082118-3; 978-0-06-082119-7 lib bdg; 0-06-082119-1 lib bdg

LC 2006-38273

Illustrations and rhythmic text recall the December, 1955, bus boycott in Montgomery, Alabama.

"Color and movement are vibrant components in this extraordinary book. . . . Text and illustration work in perfect sync. Andrea Pinkney chose the rhythm of the blues as cadence for the guitar-strumming hound-dog narrator. . . . The evocative text is bolstered by Brian Pinkney's perceptive vision. . . . Against electric blues and greens diffused with streaks of black line, Pinkney's artwork rivets the eye." SLJ

Includes bibliographical references

Peggony-Po; a whale of a tale. illustrated by Brian Pinkney. Jump at the Sun/Hyperion Books for Children 2006 un il $16.99
Grades: K 1 2 3   E
   1. Tall tales 2. Whales -- Fiction 3. Whaling -- Fiction 4. African Americans -- Fiction
   ISBN 0-7868-1958-8

LC 2005047537

Peggony-Po, carved out of wood by his father, a one-legged whaler, determines to catch the huge whale that ate his father's leg.

"Told with humor and verve, this [is a] rollicking tall tale. . . . The illustrations brim with activity and energy." SLJ

Pinkney, J. Brian, 1961-

On the ball; by Brian Pinkney. Disney-Hyperion 2015 40 p. color illustrations $17.99
Grades: PreK K   E
   1. Sports -- Fiction 2. Ability -- Fiction 3. Soccer -- Fiction 4. Balls (Sporting goods) -- Fiction
   ISBN 1484723295; 9781484723296

LC 2014039581

In this children's book by Brian Pinkey "Owen loves playing ball. But it doesn't always 'love' him back. And after a particularly disastrous day on the field, Owen is benched. He is feeling so low that he doesn't even notice the ball rolling through a hole in the fence until it's gotten away. In his effort to get it back, he discovers that he has more skills than he realizes." (Publisher's note)

"Owen is a young boy who loves playing ball, but "playing ball didn't always love Owen." When he is benched at a soccer game, the ball takes on a life of its own. Owen follows it into a fantasy world—a down-the-rabbit-hole adventure—where he becomes a sea creature, a tiger, and a bird before returning back to the field. . . . A joyful selection for all collections." SLJ

Pinkney, Jerry

The **grasshopper** & the ants; Jerry Pinkney. Little, Brown & Co. 2015 40 p. (hardcover) $18

Grades: PreK K 1 2   E

1. Ants 2. Fables 3. Winter 4. Grasshoppers 5. Folklore
ISBN 0316400815; 9780316400817

LC 2013042074

In this fable, by Jerry Pinkney, "a playful grasshopper wonders why the busy ants around him won't join in his merrymaking as the seasons pass by. But when winter arrives, he soon sees the value of his friends' hard work--just as the ants learn the value of sharing what they've worked for." (Publisher's note)

"Moving right up Maslow's hierarchy of needs, Pinkney transforms Aesop's harsh fable about the consequences of improvidence into one celebrating the value of the arts. . . . Pinkney's woodland scenes, in his signature style, teem with recognizable flora, insects, and seasonal activity; once again, there's a wealth of variety in the endpapers plus both jacket and binding art, none of it to be missed. A genial note apologizes for depicting ants and grasshopper in different scale. No need; it's all just right as it is." Horn Book

Grasshopper and the ants

★ The **lion** & the mouse. Little, Brown Books for Young Readers 2009 un il $16.99

Grades: PreK K 1 2   E

1. Fables 2. Authors 3. Folklore 4. Stories without words 5. Storytellers
ISBN 978-0-316-01356-7; 0-316-01356-0

LC 2008-43852

Boston Globe-Horn Book Award honor book: Picture Book (2010)
Awarded the Caldecott Medal (2010)

In this wordless retelling of an Aesop fable, an adventuresome mouse proves that even small creatures are capable of great deeds when he rescues the King of the Jungle.

Young readers will be drawn "into watercolors of . . . detail and splendor. Pinkney's soft, multihued strokes make everything in the jungle seem alive. . . . His luxuriant use of close-ups humanizes his animal characters without idealizing them." Booklist

The **little** match girl; [by] Hans Christian Andersen; adapted and illustrated by Jerry Pinkney. Phyllis Fogelman Books 1999 un il hardcover o.p. pa $6.99

Grades: 1 2 3 4   E

1. Authors 2. Novelists 3. Dramatists 4. Fairy tales 5. Children's authors 6. Short story writers
ISBN 0-8037-2314-8; 0-14-230188-4 pa

LC 99-13814

The wares of the poor little match girl illuminate her cold world, bringing some beauty to her brief, tragic life

"A faithful retelling of a classic tale. . . . The story's haunting death imagery . . . may disturb the very young, but ultimately Pinkney's vision proves as transcendent as Andersen's." Publ Wkly

The **three** billy goats gruff; Jerry Pinkney. Little, Brown & Co. 2017 40 p. color illustrations (hc) $17.99

Grades: PreK K 1 2   E

1. Fairy tales 2. Folklore -- Norway
ISBN 0316341576; 9780316341578

LC 2015036064

In this children's book, by Jerry Pinkney, "when the three billy goats Gruff are hungry, they see bountiful grass to eat across an old bridge. But the bridge is home to a terrible troll, who is peckish himself, and looking for a tasty morsel to gobble up. . . . Pinkney shows there's little good to come from greed--but in the end, redemption for even the most trollish bully is possible. A dramatic gatefold heightens the climax of this brilliant rendition." (Publisher's note)

★ The **tortoise** & the hare; Jerry Pinkney. Little, Brown and Co. 2013 40 p. $18

Grades: PreK K   E

1. Fables 2. Animals -- Fiction 3. Folklore
ISBN 0316183563; 9780316183567

LC 2012048426

In this book, by Jerry Pinkney, "even the slowest tortoise can defeat the quickest hare, and even the proudest hare can learn a timeless lesson from the most humble tortoise: Slow and steady wins the race! Here is a . . . journey from starting line to finish that embodies the bravery, perseverance, and humility we can all find inside ourselves." (Publisher's note)

"Following up on his superb rendition of The Lion & the Mouse (Little, Brown, 2009), Pinkney has created yet another stunning interpretation of a classic tale in this virtually wordless picture book... Tortoise and Hare, each sporting a bandana, are joined by their animal friends at the starting line for the famous race...Pinkney uses watercolor, colored pencil, and pastel paintings to create vibrant characters that are in colorful contrast to the tans and natural browns of the desert... Pinkney takes care to show Tortoise overcoming challenges and Hare demonstrating good sportsmanship and healthy competition. An artist's note explains the creative process and motivation for retelling the well-known tale. This spectacular success is certain to become a classic in its own right." (School Library Journal)

★ **Twinkle,** twinkle, little star. Little, Brown Books for Young Readers 2011 40 p. il $16.99

Grades: PreK   E

1. Nursery rhymes 2. Stars -- Fiction 3. Chipmunks -- Fiction
ISBN 9780316056960; 0316056960

"Pinkney's flora and fauna are exquisite, as is his palette, dominated by rich earth tones and brilliant blues. Soothing and magical, this one should conjure some sweet dreams." Pub Wkly

★ The **ugly** duckling; [by] Hans Christian Andersen; adapted and illustrated by Jerry Pinkney. Morrow Junior Bks. 1999 un il $16.99; lib bdg $17.89

Grades: 1 2 3 4   E

1. Authors 2. Novelists 3. Dramatists 4. Fairy tales 5. Swans -- Fiction 6. Children's authors 7. Short story writers
ISBN 0-688-15932-X; 0-688-15933-8 lib bdg

LC 98-23604

A Caldecott Medal honor book, 2000

An ugly duckling spends an unhappy year ostracized by the other animals before he grows into a beautiful swan

"This is an elegantly accessible retelling, with illustrations full of lively, emotive animals and the kind of vigorous movement that young children are bound to find appealing." Bull Cent Child Books

Pinkwater, Daniel Manus, 1941-

Bear in love; by Daniel Pinkwater; illustrations by Will Hillenbrand. 1st ed. Candlewick Press 2012 40 p. col. ill. (reinforced) $15.99

Grades: PreK K 1 2   **E**

1. Bears -- Fiction 2. Friendship -- Fiction 3. Picture books for children 4. Humorous stories 5. Rabbits -- Fiction

ISBN 0763645699; 9780763645694

LC 2011046620

This picture book is the story of an "impulsive, happy-go-lucky bear [who] keeps finding carrots on a flat rock outside his cave, left by some anonymous well-wisher. After days of this, the bear places honeycomb on the rock as a lure . . . , and pretty soon there's a full-scale war of random acts of kindness going on." (Publishers Weekly)

Another title in this series is:

Bear and Bunny (2015)

★ **Bear's** picture; written by Daniel Pinkwater; illustrated by D. B. Johnson. Houghton Mifflin Company 2008 un il $16

Grades: K 1 2 3   **E**

1. Bears -- Fiction 2. Painting -- Fiction

ISBN 978-0-618-75923-1; 0-618-75923-9

LC 2007-15149

A newly illustrated edition of the title first published 1972 by Holt, Rinehart and Winston

A bear continues to paint what he likes despite criticism from two passing gentlemen.

This is "a quirky, sardonic, and highly entertaining view of what makes art. . . . Johnson . . . provides . . . fabulous mixed-media artwork, including paper sculptures that add both angular dimension and a wry touch to the simple story." Booklist

★ **Beautiful** Yetta; the Yiddish chicken. by Daniel Pinkwater; illustrated by Jill Pinkwater. Feiwel and Friends 2010 un il $16.99

Grades: PreK K 1 2   **E**

1. Parrots -- Fiction 2. Chickens -- Fiction 3. Spanish language -- Vocabulary 4. Yiddish language -- Vocabulary 5. Brooklyn (New York, N.Y.) -- Fiction

ISBN 978-0-312-55824-6; 0-312-55824-4

"With wry humor, this multilingual picture book tells the story of a brave chicken, Yetta. Determined that she will not be soup, she escapes from a delivery crate and runs into the streets of Brooklyn. . . . She saves a little green parrot from a pouncing cat, and the wild parrots who witness the act welcome her and show her how to find food. Yetta speaks Yiddish (gevahlt!), and her speech is printed in both Hebrew and English alphabets with the English translation. The rich language mix does not stop there, though. The parrots speak Spanish, and their dialogue, shown in italics, includes a pronunciation guide. A warm twist on the immigration story that celebrates the richness of urban diversity." Booklist

Beautiful Yetta's Hanukkah Kitten; by Daniel Manus Pinkwater; illustrated by Jill Pinkwater. Feiwel & Friends 2014 32 p. color illustrations $17.99

Grades: PreK K 1 2   **E**

1. Cats -- Fiction 2. Parrots -- Fiction 3. Hanukkah -- Fiction 4. Chickens -- Fiction 5. City and town life -- Fiction

ISBN 0312621345; 9780312621346

In this children's book, by Daniel Pinkwater, illustrated by Jill Pinkwater, "Yetta, beautiful Yetta, manages to escape from the butcher's shop. But now she is lost in Brooklyn - a strange place filled with rude rats and dangerous buses! . . . But then, brave Yetta saves a small green bird from a sneaky cat, and his friends, the wild parrots of Brooklyn, are very grateful. . . . Has beautiful Yetta found her new home?" (Publisher's note)

"In her second book, the Brooklyn-based Jewish-mama hen and her Spanish-speaking parrot pals find a lost kitten during Hanukkah. Yetta knows what to do: "take her to the old grandmother!" Kitten and Bubbie find companionship--and the birds benefit from homemade latkes. The speech-bubble text is in English and Spanish or Yiddish (phonetic pronunciation included). Energetic limited-palette illustrations fly off the pages." Horn Book

I am the dog; by Daniel Pinkwater; illustrated by Jack E. Davis. Harper 2010 un il $16.99

Grades: PreK K 1   **E**

1. Dogs -- Fiction

ISBN 978-0-06-055505-4; 0-06-055505-X

Jacob the boy trades places with Max the dog.

"This amiable and impressive walk for Pinkwater breezily showcases his skill as a comic storyteller. . . . Davis keeps the dry humor right up on the surface, the tone bright . . . but not frantic." Kirkus

Piper, Watty

★ The **little** engine that could; illustrated by Loren Long. Philomel 2005 un il $17.99

Grades: PreK K 1 2   **E**

1. Toys -- Fiction 2. Railroads -- Fiction

ISBN 0-399-24467-0

A newly illustrated edition of the title first published 1930 by Grosset & Dunlap

Although she is not very big, the Little Blue Engine agrees to try to pull a stranded train full of toys over the mountain.

"Grand in scale but cozy in effect, the impressive acrylic paintings use subtle strokes of rich colors to create a series of narrative scenes large enough to be clearly visible back to the last row of storytime or classroom. . . . This edition provides a brilliant new setting that many readers will prefer to the original picture book." Booklist

Pitman, Gayle E.

This day in June; by Gayle E. Pitman; illustrated by Kristyna Litten. Magination Press 2014 32 p. color illustrations (hardcover) $14.95

Grades: PreK K 1 2   **E**

1. LGBT people 2. Stories in rhyme 3. Parades -- Fiction 4. Gay pride parades -- Fiction

ISBN 143381658X; 1433816598; 9781433816581; 9781433816598

LC 2013021623

Stonewall Book Award: Children's & Young Adult Literature (2015)

This children's picture book, by Gayle E. Pitman, illustrated by Kristyna Litten, "welcomes readers to experience a pride celebration and share in a day when we are all united. Also included is a Reading Guide chock-full of facts about LGBT history and culture, as well as a Note to Parents and Caregivers with information on how to talk to children about sexual orientation and gender identity in age-appropriate ways." (Publisher's note)

"Filled with saturated colors and vivid illustrations, this picture book uses rhyming couplets to convey the fun and exuberant feelings associated with a pride parade for lesbian, gay, bisexual, and transgender (LGBT) people and families. . . . The diversity shown at the pride parade is realistic; both homosexual and heterosexual people, young and old, are depicted as well as individuals, couples, and families." SLJ

Piven, Hanoch

My best friend is as sharp as a pencil; and other funny classroom portraits. Schwartz & Wade 2010 un il $17.99

Grades: K 1 2 3   E

1. Portraits -- Fiction

ISBN 0375853383; 9780375853388; 978-0-375-85338-8; 0-375-85338-3

"Vibrant portraits in words and realia-collage illustrations, purportedly created by the child narrator in anticipation of her grandmother's inevitable questions about school, will delight readers. One double-page spread gives each new character's traits, expressed in several verbal metaphors . . . and in photos of objects. . . . On the next spread, a painting incorporating those objects forms an eye-catching, idiosyncratic portrait."

"Vibrant portraits in words and realia-collage illustrations, purportedly created by the child narrator in anticipation of her grandmother's inevitable questions about school, will delight readers. One double-page spread gives each new character's traits, expressed in several verbal metaphors . . . and in photos of objects. . . . On the next spread, a painting incorporating those objects forms an eye-catching, idiosyncratic portrait." Booklist

My dog is as smelly as dirty socks; and other funny family portraits. Schwartz & Wade 2007 un il $16.99; lib bdg $18.99

Grades: PreK K 1 2   E

1. Portraits -- Fiction 2. Family life -- Fiction

ISBN 978-0-375-84052-4; 0-375-84052-4; 978-0-375-94052-1 lib bdg; 0-375-94052-9 lib bdg

LC 2006-21936

A young girl draws a family portrait, then makes it more accurate by adding common objects to show aspects of each member's personality, such as her father's playfulness, her mother's sweetness, and her brother's strength

"Childlike line drawings are paired with the more creative portraits, in which representational objects are glued on gouache-and-watercolor backgrounds to make the figures. Children will get caught up in this playful, fun, creative, and easy-to-do art concept and will want to follow through with their own creations." Booklist

Pizzoli, Greg

Good night Owl; Greg Pizzoli. Disney-Hyperion 2016 48 p. color illustrations $16.99

Grades: PreK K 1   E

1. Owls -- Fiction 2. Noise -- Fiction 3. Bedtime -- Fiction

ISBN 1484712757; 9781484712757

LC 2015011769

Geisel Honor Book (2017)

In this children's picture book, by Greg Pizzoli, "Owl is ready for bed. But as soon as he settles in, he hears a strange noise. He'll never get to sleep unless he can figure out what's going on!" (Publisher's note)

"Well-designed pages and energetic cartoon art in candy colors bring out the story's humor while showing readers what the text does not tell: a small, mischievous mouse is teasing Owl. Frustrated Owl systematically goes on to pull up the floorboards, pry off the roof, and tear down the walls until he completely dismantles his house. After each new effort, he climbs back into bed and wishes himself good night -- only to be disturbed again." Horn Book

★ **Number** one Sam; Greg Pizzoli. Disney-Hyperion 2014 40 p. $16.99

Grades: PreK K   E

1. Dogs -- Fiction 2. Automobile racing -- Fiction 3. Chickens -- Fiction 4. Competition (Psychology) -- Fiction

ISBN 142317111X; 9781423171119

LC 2013021231

In this children's book, by Greg Pizzoli, "Sam is used to winning everything, including car racing, his sport of choice. His wall of trophies and trinkets show off his talent for success until the day the unthinkable happens: the pup loses the big race because he stops for a group of oblivious chickens in the middle of the track. Then his cheering friends and the chickens let him know that he is still number one with them." (Publisher's note)

"Sam is used to winning everything, including car racing, his sport of choice. His wall of trophies and trinkets show off his talent for success until the day the unthinkable happens: the pup loses the big race because he stops for a group of oblivious chickens in the middle of the track . . . Pizzoli's use of four-color art provides an airy, uncluttered vision for his story that will definitely attract children. The simple yet exciting text drives the story forward and will make it a popular choice at storytimes." SLJ

The **watermelon** seed; Greg Pizzoli. 1st ed. Disney Hyperion Books 2013 40 p. ill. (reinforced) $16.99

Grades: PreK K   E

1. Seeds -- Fiction 2. Crocodiles -- Fiction 3. Imagination -- Fiction 4. Watermelons -- Fiction

ISBN 1423171012; 9781423171010

LC 2012020297

Theodor Seuss Geisel Award (2014)

This children's story, written and illustrated by Greg Pizzoli, "introduces us to one funny crocodile who has one big fear: swallowing a watermelon seed. What will he do when his greatest fear is realized? Will vines sprout out his ears? Will his skin turn pink? This crocodile has a wild imagination." (Publisher's note)

Platt, Cynthia

A **little** bit of love; illustrated by Hannah Whitty. Tiger Tales 2011 il $15.95

Grades: PreK K   E

1. Food -- Fiction 2. Love -- Fiction 3. Mice -- Fiction 4. Baking -- Fiction 5. Mother-child relationship -- Fiction

ISBN 978-1-58925-095-6; 1-58925-095-8

"Small Mouse is tired of plain old cheese and crumbs and wants something new and sweet to eat, so her mother takes her on a journey gathering ingredients to make something out of love. . . . Together they make a pie, and the youngster understands how good things are made with a mother's love. This is a sweet story that not only teaches a child how a pie is made, but also how each ingredient comes from nature. . . . The colors in the art are soft but sunny, making this a cozy read. The loving facial expressions between the mice are endearing." SLJ

Player, Micah

Chloe, instead; by Micah Player. Chronicle Books 2012 32 p. (alk. paper) $15.99

Grades: PreK K 1 2   E

1. Picture books for children 2. Sisters -- Fiction 5. Individuality -- Fiction

ISBN 0811878651; 9780811878654

LC 2011012717

This children's book, by Micah Player, follows "Molly[, who] always dreamed of having a sister who is just like her. But she got Chloe instead. These two sisters are nothing alike: Molly loves to color with crayons. Chloe prefers the taste of wax. . . . Molly is frustrated! But then she realizes that maybe sisters aren't the ones next to you on the piano bench, they're the ones dancing to the music you play!" (Publisher's note)

Plourde, Lynn

Field trip day; illustrated by Thor Wickstrom. Dutton Children's Books 2010 un il $16.99

Grades: PreK K 1 2   E

1. School stories 2. Farm life -- Fiction

ISBN 978-0-525-47994-9; 0-525-47994-5

Today is Field Trip Day at school, and everyone in Mrs. Shepherd's class is excited to visit Fandangle's Farm, especially Juan, who loves to explore. But Juan just might be too good at exploring, and Mrs. Shepherd and the chaperones have trouble keeping track of him!

"This good-natured story . . . will appeal to children, especially those who adore farm animals. The watercolor-and-ink cartoons are lively and depict a diverse class that lauds thinking and questioning over strict rule-keeping." SLJ

A **mountain** of mittens; [by] Lynn Plourde; illustrated by Mitch Vane. Charlesbridge 2007 un il $15.95; pa $7.95

Grades: PreK K 1   E

1. Clothing and dress -- Fiction 2. Lost and found possessions -- Fiction

ISBN 978-1-57091-585-7; 978-1-57091-466-9 pa

LC 2006021253

Molly's parents try various methods to help her remember her mittens but nothing seems to work.

"Readers will chuckle as they recognize what a problem mateless mittens can become. Vane's watercolor-and-ink drawings have a jaunty air." Booklist

You're wearing that to school?! by Lynn Plourde; illustrated by Sue Cornelison. Disney-Hyperion Books 2013 32 p. (hardcover) $16.99

Grades: PreK K 1   E

1. Picture books for children 2. Mice -- Fiction 3. Schools -- Fiction 4. Hippopotamus -- Fiction 5. Individuality -- Fiction 6. First day of school -- Fiction

ISBN 1423155106; 9781423155102

LC 2011031614

This children's picture book follows hippo Penelope, who's "excited about starting school. Her retiring friend Tiny, a mouse, is a pessimistic first-grader determined to prevent what he expects would be gaffes on her first day. Penelope plans to wear her favorite outlandish outfit, bring her well-worn stuffed toy for show-and-tell, and pack a picnic lunch. Tiny quashes her cheerful plans, dialing her down to jeans and a T-shirt, a rock, and PB&J. Undeterred, the hippo ignores Tiny." (School Library Journal)

Another title in this series is:

You're doing that in the talent show?! (2016)

Pochocki, Ethel

The **blessing** of the beasts; by Ethel Pochocki; illustrated by Barry Moser. Paraclete Press 2007 39p il $18.95

Grades: K 1 2 3   E

1. Skunks -- Fiction 2. Animals -- Fiction 3. Religion -- Fiction 4. Cockroaches -- Fiction 5. New York (N.Y.) -- Fiction

ISBN 978-1-55725-502-0; 1-55725-502-4

LC 2007002231

Martin the skunk and Francesca the cockroach wend their way across the city to attend the blessing of the animals celebration on the Feast of St. Francis at the Cathedral of St. John the Divine.

This is a "delightful fantasy. . . . Cats and dogs are the usual celebrants at the real service; here they are joined by lions, bears, and falcons. . . . Funny, sly, and noble, the animal pictures range from amusing takeoffs to moving tributes." Booklist

Polacco, Patricia

Babushka's doll. Simon & Schuster Bks. for Young Readers 1990 un il hardcover o.p. pa $6.95

Grades: K 1 2 3   E

1. Dolls -- Fiction

ISBN 0-671-68343-8; 0-689-80255-2 pa

LC 89-6122

"Polacco's distinctive artwork interprets the story with style and verve. Using pencil, marker, and paint, she creates a series of varied compositions, highlighting muted shades with an occasional flare of bright colors and strong patterns. . . . A good, original story, illustrated with panache." Booklist

The **blessing** cup; Patricia Polacco. Simon & Schuster Books for Young Readers 2013 48 p. (hardcover) $17.99

Grades: 1 2 3 4 5   E

1. Picture books for children 2. Heirlooms 3. Jews -- Fiction 4. Family life -- Fiction

ISBN 1442450479; 9781442450479; 9781442450486

LC 2012023596

This book is Patricia Polacco's prequel to "The Keeping Quilt." Here, "readers learn how Polacco's great-grandmother Anna and her parents were forced from their shtetl in Czarist Russia and made their way to America. Among the few treasures the family took with them was a vibrantly painted tea set, a kind of familial talisman . . . , which also served as a reminder that they would always be rich in what matters: resilience and love." (Publishers Weekly)

Bun Bun Button. G. P. Putnam's Sons 2011 il $17.99

Grades: PreK K 1   E

1. Toys -- Fiction 2. Grandmothers -- Fiction 3. Lost and found possessions -- Fiction

ISBN 978-0-399-25472-7; 0-399-25472-2

LC 2010047740

Paige Darling loves the stuffed rabbit her grandmother has made for her, but when she ties a helium-filled balloon to Bun Bun Button the toy gets loose and goes floating away, and it may take some Darling luck to bring her home.

"Brimming with nostalgia, heartfelt sentimentality, and eccentricity, this portrait of a tight-knit intergenerational bond will charm Polacco enthusiasts with its old-fashioned tone and bright illustrations. Even when she is illustrating a picture of a grandmother reading to her granddaughter, Polacco fills the pages with tumbling action, familial warmth, and love." Publ Wkly

The **butterfly**. Philomel Bks. 2000 un il $16.99; pa $7.99

Grades: 2 3 4   E

1. Jews -- Fiction 2. France -- Fiction 3. World War, 1939-1945 -- Fiction

ISBN 0-399-23170-6; 0-14-241306-2 pa

LC 99-30038

During the Nazi occupation of France, Monique's mother hides a Jewish family in her basement and tries to help them escape to freedom

"Polacco's use of color has never been more effective. . . . The bold pattern and heightened color of the insect provides a counterpoint to the equally dynamic black-on-red swastikas. Convincing in its portrayal of both the disturbing and humanitarian forces of the time." SLJ

★ **Chicken** Sunday. Philomel Bks. 1992 un il $16.99; pa $6.99

Grades: K 1 2 3   E

1. Jews -- Fiction 2. Easter -- Fiction 3. Friendship -- Fiction 4. African Americans -- Fiction

ISBN 0-399-22133-6; 0-698-11615-1 pa

LC 91-16030

To thank old Eula for her wonderful Sunday chicken dinners, her two grandsons and their friend, a girl who has "adopted" her since her own "babushka" died, sell decorated eggs and buy her a beautiful Easter hat

"Without being heavy-handed, Polacco's text conveys a tremendous pride of heritage as it brims with rich images from her characters' African American and Russian Jewish cultures. Her vibrant pencil-and-wash illustrations glow—actual family photographs have been worked into several spreads." Publ Wkly

★ **G** is for goat. Philomel Bks. 2003 un il $16.99; pa $6.99; bd bk $6.99

Grades: PreK K 1 2   E

1. Goats 2. Alphabet 3. Stories in rhyme

ISBN 0-399-24018-7; 0-14-240550-7 pa; 0-399-24530-8 bd bk

LC 2002-11551

A rhyming celebration of goats and their antics, from A to Z

"The charming animals will energize any storytime. . . . The pencil-and-watercolor illustrations against white backgrounds steal the spotlight, with charming details." SLJ

★ **Ginger** and Petunia; [by] Patricia Polacco. Philomel Books 2007 un il $16.99

Grades: K 1 2 3   E

1. Pigs -- Fiction

ISBN 978-0-399-24539-8

LC 2006024878

When her beloved Ginger, a piano-playing socialite and very snappy dresser, makes a last-minute trip to London not knowing her housesitter has cancelled, Petunia the pig does more than fend for herself, she becomes Ginger.

"Polacco's comic portrayal of pampered pet and attentive owner is spot-on—and her characteristic watercolor illustrations highlight both characters' sense of fashion and joie de vivre. . . . A delight from start to finish." Booklist

In our mothers' house. Philomel Books 2009 un il $17.99

Grades: 1 2 3 4   E

1. Mothers -- Fiction 2. Adoption -- Fiction 3. Lesbians -- Fiction 4. Family life -- Fiction

ISBN 978-0-399-25076-7; 0-399-25076-X

LC 2008-32615

"The oldest of three adopted children recalls her childhood with mothers Marmee and Meema, as they raised their African American daughter, Asian American son, and Caucasian daughter in a lively, supportive neighborhood. . . . The energetic illustrations in pencil and marker, . . . teem with family activities and neighborhood festivity." Booklist

★ **John** Philip Duck. Philomel Books 2004 un il $16.99

Grades: K 1 2 3   E

1. Ducks -- Fiction 2. Memphis (Tenn.) -- Fiction 3. Hotels and motels -- Fiction

ISBN 0-399-24262-7

During the Depression, a young Memphis boy trains his pet duck to do tricks in the fountain of a grand hotel and ends up becoming the Duck Master of the Peabody Hotel

"This is Polacco at the height of her form in terms of both text and illustration. The story moves smoothly from start to finish and has a refreshing air of innocence. The artwork is simply beautiful as the artist orchestrates a harmonious symphony of color." SLJ

★ The **keeping** quilt; rev format ed; Simon & Schuster Bks. for Young Readers 1998 un il $17.95; pa $6.99

Grades: K 1 2 3

1. Jews -- Fiction 2. Quilts -- Fiction

ISBN 0-689-82090-9; 0-689-84447-6 pa

LC 97-47690

A reissue of the title first published 1988

A homemade quilt ties together the lives of four generations of an immigrant Jewish family, remaining a symbol of their enduring love and faith

"Jewish customs and the way they've shifted through the years are portrayed unobtrusively in the story, which is illustrated in sepia pencil, except for the quilt, which sparks every page with its strong colors." Booklist

★ The **Lemonade** Club; [by] Patricia Polacco. Philomel Books 2007 un il $16.99

Grades: 2 3 4   E

1. School stories 2. Cancer -- Fiction 3. Teachers -- Fiction 4. Friendship -- Fiction

ISBN 978-0-399-24540-4

LC 2007011440

When Marilyn and her teacher, Miss Wichelman, both get cancer, they encourage each other and, aided by medical treatments and support from friends, they get better. Based on a true story.

"Polacco continues to draw from rich family experiences to weave satisfying, inspirations stories. . . . Pencil-and-marker illustrations in Polacco's usual free style gently convey the emotions." Booklist

★ **Mr.** Lincoln's way. Philomel Bks. 2001 un il $16.99

Grades: K 1 2 3   E

1. School stories 2. Prejudices -- Fiction

ISBN 0-399-23754-2

LC 00-66939

When Mr. Lincoln, "the coolest principal in the whole world," discovers that Eugene, the school bully, knows a lot about birds, he uses this interest to help Eugene overcome his intolerance

"The book may be useful to schools in need of a springboard for discussion of the topic and is graced with impressive watercolors." SLJ

Mr. Wayne's masterpiece; Patricia Polacco. G. P. Putnam's Sons 2014 40 p. color illustrations (reinforced) $17.99

Grades: 2 3 4 5   E

1. School stories 2. Theater -- Fiction 3. Schools -- Fiction 4. Teachers -- Fiction 5. Public speaking -- Fiction

ISBN 0399160957; 9780399160950

LC 2013046428

"Speaking in front of an audience terrifies Trisha. Ending up in Mr. Wayne's drama class is the last thing she wants! But Mr. Wayne gives her a backstage role painting scenery for the winter play. As she paints, she listens to the cast rehearse, memorizing their lines without even realizing it." (Publisher's note)

"Early elementary readers will relate to the self-doubt Polacco expresses, and they will also find vicarious comfort through her supportive relationships with teachers, as well as her ultimate triumph over fear." Booklist

Mrs. Katz and Tush. Doubleday Books for Young Readers 1992 un il $16.99; lib bdg $19.99; pa $6.99

Grades: K 1 2 3   E

1. Jews -- Fiction 2. Friendship -- Fiction 3. African Americans -- Fiction

ISBN 0-553-08122-5; 0-385-90650-1 lib bdg; 0-440-40936-5 pa

LC 91-18710

A long-lasting friendship develops between Larnel, a young African-American, and Mrs. Katz, a lonely, Jewish widow, when Larnel presents Mrs. Katz with a scrawny kitten without a tail

"Polacco has used loving details in both words and art work to craft a moving and heartfelt story of a friendship that reaches across racial and generational differences." Horn Book

My rotten redheaded older brother. Simon & Schuster Bks. for Young Readers 1994 un il $17.95; pa $6.99

Grades: PreK K 1 2 3   E
  1. Siblings -- Fiction
ISBN 0-671-72751-6; 0-689-82036-4 pa

LC 93-13980

"Featuring an obnoxious, freckle-faced, bespectacled boy and a comforting, tale-telling grandmother, this autobiographical story is as satisfying as a warm slice of apple pie. Patricia can't quite understand how anyone could possibly like her older brother Richard. Whether picking blackberries or eating raw rhubarb, he always manages to outdo her, rubbing it in with one of his 'extra-rotten, weasel-eyed, greeny-toothed grins.' When their Bubbie teaches Patricia to wish on a falling star, she knows just what to ask for." SLJ

★ **Oh,** look! Philomel Books 2004 un il $16.99

Grades: PreK K 1 2   E
  1. Goats -- Fiction
ISBN 0-399-24223-6

Three goats visit a fair but run home after they seem to encounter a troll.

"In this colorful picture book, the . . . author transfers the rhythms and movement of the traditional bear-hunt chant to safer ground. . . . Polacco's signature pencil-and-watercolor paintings cascade across the ages, creating festive scenes and bright hues." SLJ

★ **Pink** and Say. Philomel Bks. 1994 un il $16.99

Grades: 2 3 4   E
  1. Friendship -- Fiction 2. African American soldiers -- Fiction 3. United States -- History -- 1861-1865, Civil War -- Fiction
ISBN 0-399-22671-0

LC 93-36340

Say Curtis describes his meeting with Pinkus Aylee, a black soldier, during the Civil War, and their capture by Southern troops

"Polacco pulls out all the stops in this heart-wrenching tale . . . which has been passed through several generations of the author's family. . . . Polacco's signature line-and-watercolor paintings epitomize heroism, tenderness, and terror. . . . Unglamorized details of the conventions and atrocities of the Civil War target readers well beyond customary picture book age." Horn Book

★ **Rechenka's** eggs; written and illustrated by Patricia Polacco. Philomel Bks. 1988 un il lib bdg $16.99; pa $6.99

Grades: K 1 2 3   E
  1. Eggs -- Fiction 2. Geese -- Fiction 3. Easter -- Fiction
ISBN 0-399-21501-8 lib bdg; 0-698-11385-3 pa

LC 87-16588

An injured goose rescued by Babushka, having broken the painted eggs intended for the Easter Festival in Moscva, lays thirteen marvelously colored eggs to replace them, then leaves behind one final miracle egg form before returning to her own kind

"Polacco achieves optimal dramatic contrast by using bold shapes against uncluttered white space and by contrasting rich colors and design details with faces in black and white." Bull Cent Child Books

Someone for Mr. Sussman; [by] Patricia Polacco. Philomel Books 2008 un il $16.99

Grades: 2 3 4   E
  1. Grandmothers -- Fiction 2. Jews -- United States -- Fiction 3. Dating (Social customs) -- Fiction
ISBN 978-0-399-25075-0; 0-399-25075-1

LC 2008000660

Although she is the best matchmaker in the neighborhood, Jerome's Bubbie has a hard time finding a match for the fussy Mr. Sussman.

"The author brings in homey, Fiddler on the Roof syntax . . . along with words like 'oy' and 'farklempt,' illustrating the story in her signature style of comfortable caricatures and broad strokes. A good-natured spirit percolates throughout." Publ Wkly

★ **Thank** you, Mr. Falker. Philomel Bks. 1998 un il $16.99

Grades: K 1 2 3   E
  1. Reading -- Fiction 2. Teachers -- Fiction 3. Learning disabilities -- Fiction
ISBN 0-399-23166-8

LC 97-18685

At first, Trisha loves school, but her difficulty learning to read makes her feel dumb, until, in the fifth grade, a new teacher helps her understand and overcome her problem

"Young readers struggling with learning difficulties will identify with Trisha's situation and find reassurance in her success. Polacco's gouache-and-pencil compositions deftly capture the emotional stages—frustration, pain, elation—of Trisha's journey." Publ Wkly

★ The **trees** of the dancing goats. Simon & Schuster Bks. for Young Readers 1996 un il hardcover o.p. pa $6.99

Grades: K 1 2 3   E
  1. Jews -- Fiction 2. Hanukkah -- Fiction 3. Christmas -- Fiction
ISBN 0-689-80862-3; 0-689-83857-3 pa

LC 95-26670

"On the family farm in Michigan, Trisha and Richard watch as Babushka and Grampa prepare for Hanukkah in their native Russian way. . . . When scarlet fever debilitates their neighbors, Trisha's whole family pitches in to make and deliver holiday dinners and Christmas trees." Publ Wkly

When lightning comes in a jar. Philomel Bks. 2002 un il $16.99; pa $6.99

Grades: 2 3 4   E
  1. Family life -- Fiction 2. Grandmothers -- Fiction 3. Family reunions -- Fiction
ISBN 0-399-23164-1; 0-14-240350-4 pa

LC 2001-45925

A young girl describes the family reunion at her grandmother's house, from the food and baseball and photos to the flickering fireflies on the lawn

"The watercolor-and-pencil illustrations, skillfully composed on the pages, expressively sketch the characters. . . . This autobiographical story will convey the joys of family." Booklist

Polhemus, Coleman

The **crocodile** blues; [by] Coleman Polhemus. Candlewick Press 2007 un il $16.99

Grades: PreK K   E
  1. Stories without words 2. Eggs -- Fiction 3. Crocodiles -- Fiction
ISBN 978-0-7636-3543-5; 0-7636-3543-X

LC 2006051848

A wordless tale in which a man and his pet cockatoo discover, much to their dismay, the true nature of the egg they bring home from the store

"Youngsters will laugh at both the story line and the characters depicted in this zany book. The simple royal blue and black silhouettes capture the feeling of the dark night, and the bright yellow of the daylight offers a realistic contrast." SLJ

Politi, Leo

Emmet. Getty Publications 2009 un il $16.95
Grades: PreK K 1 2   E
1. Dogs -- Fiction
ISBN 978-0-89236-992-8; 0-89236-992-2
A reissue of the title first published 1971 by Scribner
Emmet, one of the many stray dogs taken in by old Mr. Winkel, was always the troublemaker of the lot. Mr. Winkel's neighbors are ready to call the dogcatcher when the rascally dog saves the grocer's shop from a fire set by a prowler.

Juanita. Getty Publications 2009 un il $16.95
Grades: K 1 2 3   E
1. Easter -- Fiction 2. Birthdays -- Fiction 3. Mexican Americans -- Fiction 4. Los Angeles (Calif.) -- Fiction
ISBN 978-0-89236-991-1; 0-89236-991-4
A reissue of the title first published 1948 by Scribner
A Caldecott honor book, 1949
Juanita, a Mexican girl of Olvera Street in Los Angeles, brings the dove she received for her birthday to the Blessing of the Animals on the day before Easter.
"The pictures in soft colors have a warmth and tenderness." Horn Book

Pedro, the angel of Olvera Street. Getty Publications 2009 un il $14.96
Grades: K 1 2 3   E
1. Christmas -- Fiction 2. Mexican Americans -- Fiction 3. Los Angeles (Calif.) -- Fiction
ISBN 978-0-89236-990-4; 0-89236-990-6
A reissue of the title first published 1946 by Scribner
A Caldecott Medal honor book, 1947
Little Pedro, who sings like an angel, is allowed to lead the Christmas procession, known as La Posada, through the old Mexican section of downtown Los Angeles.
"Beguiling both in text and in the pictures with their soft, rich colors." Bookmark

Song of the swallows. Getty Publications 2009 un il $16.98
Grades: 2 3 4   E
1. Missions -- Fiction 2. Swallows -- Fiction 3. California -- Fiction
ISBN 978-0-89236-989-8; 0-89236-989-2
A reissue of the title first published 1949 by Scribner
Awarded the Caldecott Medal, 1950
Sad when the swallows leave for the winter, young Juan prepares to welcome them back to the old California Mission at Capistrano on St. Joseph's Day the next spring.
This is a "tender poetic story. . . Lovely pictures in soft colors bring out the charm of the southern California landscape and the melody of the swallow song adds to the feeling of Spring." Horn Book

Pomerantz, Charlotte

The **chalk** doll; pictures by Frané Lessac. Lippincott 1989 30p il hardcover o.p. pa $6.99
Grades: K 1 2 3   E
1. Dolls -- Fiction 2. Jamaica -- Fiction 3. Mother-daughter relationship -- Fiction
ISBN 0-06-443333-1 pa
LC 88-872

"The stylized illustrations by the West Indian artists Frané Lessac are primitive in bright, oscillating colors, evoking poverty in a tropical paradise as well as mother-daughter affection in a well-appointed home." N Y Times Book Rev

Portis, Antoinette

★ **Best** frints in the whole universe; Antoinette Portis. Roaring Brook Press 2016 40 p. color illustrations (hardback) $16.99
Grades: PreK K 1 2   E
1. Humorous stories 2. Friendship -- Fiction 3. Extraterrestrial beings -- Fiction
ISBN 9781626721364
LC 2015024468
In this book, by Antoinette Portis, "Yelfred and Omek have been best frints since they were little blobbies. They play and snack, and sometimes they even fight, all in a language similar to but slightly different from, English. When Omek decides to borrow Yelfred's new spaceship without asking (and then crashes it), it sparks the biggest fight yet. Can these two best frints make up and move on?" (Publisher's note)
"Her dot-matrix layers of retro color add dimension to the simple shapes and close-up images, and her flamboyant misspellings and soundalike words let beginning readers in on the sly jokes while crafting an all-too-knowing portrait of what frintship often looks like." Pub Wkly

Froodle; Antoinette Portis. Roaring Brook Press 2014 32 p. (hardback) $16.99
Grades: PreK K 1 2   E
1. Birds -- Fiction 2. Birdsongs -- Fiction 3. Individuality -- Fiction
ISBN 159643922X; 9781596439221
LC 2013032417
In this book, by Antoinette Portis, "a little brown bird is sick of peeping like she's supposed to and lets out an unexpected 'Froodle.' Her other bird friends are shocked, but soon Cardinal is spouting 'Ickle zickle' instead of 'Chirp,' and Dove sings 'Oobly snoobly' instead of 'Coo.' Crow who is not silly, tries to keep the other birds in line, but they're having too much fun to listen, and Crow flies off. . . . Silliness is contagious though, and Crow can't stay away for long." (Booklist)
"All of the birds say, "caw," "coo," "chip," or "peep," except Little Brown Bird, who wants to try something different. She finds it more enjoyable to say things like, "Froodle sproodle" and "Tiffle biffle./just a little/miffle!" Crow is annoyed, especially when the other birds join in, but who could resist participating in fun like this?...The cadence of the birds' dialogue might take a few read-throughs to get used to, but that will only provide more laughs in the meantime. This book will work in many settings and is certain to prompt giggles from young audiences." SLJ

Kindergarten diary; as told to Antoinette Portis by me, Annalina. Harper 2010 un il $12.99; lib bdg $14.89
Grades: PreK K   E
1. School stories
ISBN 978-0-06-145691-6; 0-06-145691-8; 978-0-06-145692-3 lib bdg; 0-06-145692-6 lib bdg
"Imaginative, spirited Annalina narrates a month of days in her life beginning with the day before she starts kindergarten. . . . Realistic and gorgeously patterned collage items outlined in black are mingled with simple paintings to create an explosion of color, shape, and texture. The narrative and illustrations are gently funny and filled with little detail and jokes." SLJ

★ **Not** a box. HarperCollins 2007 un il $12.99; lib bdg $14.89

Grades: PreK K   **E**

1. Boxes -- Fiction 2. Rabbits -- Fiction 3. Imagination -- Fiction
ISBN 978-0-06-112322-1; 0-06-112322-6; 978-0-06-112323-8 lib bdg; 0-06-112323-4 lib bdg

LC 2006002477

To an imaginative bunny, a box is not always just a box.

"The spare, streamlined design and the visual messages about imagination's power will easily draw young children, who will recognize their own flights of fantasy." Booklist

★ **Not** a stick. HarperCollinsPublishers 2008 un il $12.99; lib bdg $14.89

Grades: PreK K   **E**

1. Pigs -- Fiction 2. Play -- Fiction 3. Imagination -- Fiction
ISBN 978-0-06-112325-2; 0-06-112325-0; 978-0-06-112326-9 lib bdg; 0-06-112326-9 lib bdg

LC 2007-14475

An imaginative young pig shows some of the many things that a stick can be.

"Portis's simple color palette and playful drawings with never a line out of place represent the best in children's illustration." SLJ

★ A **penguin** story. HarperCollins 2009 un il $17.99; lib bdg $18.89

Grades: PreK K 1 2   **E**

1. Color -- Fiction 2. Penguins -- Fiction
ISBN 978-0-06-145688-6; 0-06-145688-8; 978-0-06-145689-3 lib bdg; 0-06-145689-6 lib bdg

LC 2008020210

Edna the penguin tries to find something in her surroundings that is not black, white, or blue.

"This gentle tribute to dreamers crackles with quiet humor, and the art's limited palette both parallels the plot and lends the book a classic feel. Portis's ability to convey emotion and character through the slightest change in Edna's beady eyes and flippers is extraordinary, and the interplay of the text and pictures nears perfection. A delightful story, delightfully told." SLJ

Princess Super Kitty. Harper 2011 il $14.99

Grades: K 1 2   **E**

1. Imagination -- Fiction
ISBN 978-0-06-182725-9; 0-06-182725-8

LC 2010032230

Maggie, a little girl with a huge imagination, becomes a cat, a superhero, a princess, and more in the course of a day.

"This girl is bouncy, delightful and not to be easily typed or contained. Bold lines and solid colors—not overly dominated by pink—surrounded by plenty of empty space keep the focus firmly on the girl and her props. Readers and listeners both bold and retiring will find much to like in this charming depiction of a child with a strong sense of self and confidence in her imaginative makeovers." Kirkus

★ **Wait**; by Antoinette Portis. Roaring Brook Press 2015 32 p. (hardback) $16.99

Grades: PreK K 1   **E**

1. Patience -- Fiction 2. Attention -- Fiction
ISBN 1596439211; 9781596439214

LC 2014027119

In this children's picture book, by Antoinette Portis, "a boy and his mother move quickly through the city [and] they're drawn to different things. The boy sees a dog, a butterfly, and a hungry duck while his mother rushes them toward the departing train. It's push and pull, but in the end, they both find something to stop for." (Publisher's note)

"A harried mother rushes her toddler son through the busy city streets, and he resists, stalling to look at everything they encounter. This fundamental tension plays out in a series of spreads illustrating the same refrain...Observant children will notice slickers, umbrellas, and other clues of things to come throughout the pages (is that a rainbow pop he points to on the ice-cream truck?), adding richness to this sweet story about appreciating life's simple pleasures." Horn Book

Portnoy, Mindy Avra

Tale of two Seders; illustrated by Valeria Cis. Kar-Ben Pub. 2010 32p il lib bdg $17.95; pa $7.95

Grades: PreK K 1 2   **E**

1. Jews -- Fiction 2. Divorce -- Fiction 3. Passover -- Fiction 4. Family life -- Fiction
ISBN 978-0-8225-9907-4; 0-8225-9907-4; 978-0-8225-9931-9 pa; 0-8225-9931-7 pa

LC 2008033570

After her parents' divorce, a young girl experiences a variety of Passover seders. Includes recipes and facts about Passover.

"Cis's delightful acrylic paintings beautifully complement the text. . . . [This is a] realistic, contemporary story." SLJ

Potter, Beatrix

The **story** of Miss Moppet. Warne 2002 32p il $6.99

Grades: PreK K 1 2 3   **E**

1. Cats -- Fiction 2. Mice -- Fiction
ISBN 0-7232-4790-0

First published 1906

Miss Moppet is a kitten who uses her wiles to capture a curious mouse. But her trickery amounts to naught when she herself is outwitted

Other titles about Moppet's brother Tom and sister Mittens are:
The complete adventures of Tom Kitten and his friends (1984)
The roly-poly pudding (1908)
The tale of Tom Kitten (1935)

★ The **tailor** of Gloucester. Warne 2002 56p il $6.99

Grades: PreK K 1 2 3   **E**

1. Mice -- Fiction 2. Christmas -- Fiction 3. Tailoring -- Fiction
ISBN 0-7232-4772-2

First published in 1903

"A read-aloud classic in polished style, perfectly complemented by the author's exquisite watercolor illustrations." Hodges. Books for Elem Sch Libr

★ The **tale** of Jemima Puddle-duck. Warne 2002 56p il $6.99; bd bk $6.99

Grades: PreK K 1 2 3   **E**

1. Ducks -- Fiction
ISBN 0-7232-4778-1; 0-7232-6434-1 bd bk

First published 1908

"Jemima Puddle-duck's obstinate determination to hatch her own eggs, makes a story of suspense and sly humor." Toronto Public Libr. Books for Boys & Girls

★ The **tale** of Mr. Jeremy Fisher. Warne 2002 56p il $6.99

Grades: PreK K 1 2 3   **E**

1. Frogs -- Fiction
ISBN 0-7232-4776-5

First published 1906

A frog fishing from his lilly pad boat doesn't catch any fish, but one catches him

★ The **tale** of Mrs. Tiggy-Winkle. Warne 2002 56p il $6.99

Grades: PreK K 1 2 3   E
1. Hedgehogs -- Fiction
ISBN 0-7232-4775-7
First published 1905
Lucie visits the laundry of Mrs. Tiggy-Winkle, a hedgehog, and finds
her lost handerchiefs

The **tale** of Mrs. Tittlemouse. Warne 2002 56p il $6.99
Grades: PreK K 1 2 3   E
1. Mice -- Fiction
ISBN 0-7232-3470-1
First published 1910
The story of a little mouse's funny house, the visitors she has there,
and how she finally rids herself of the untidy, messy ones

★ The **tale** of Peter Rabbit. Warne 2002 69p il $6.99
Grades: PreK K 1 2 3   E
1. Rabbits -- Fiction
ISBN 0-7232-4770-6
First published 1903
All about the famous rabbit family consisting of Flopsy, Mopsy,
Cotton-tail and especially Peter Rabbit who disobeys Mother Rabbit's
admonishment not to go into Mr. McGregor's garden
"Distinctive writing and a strong appeal to a small child's sense of
justice and his sympathies make this an outstanding story. The water
color illustrations add charm to the narrative by their simplicity of detail
and delicacy of color." Child Books Too Good to Miss
Other titles about Peter Rabbit and his family are:
The tale of Benjamin Bunny (1904)
The tale of Mr. Tod (1912)
The tale of the flopsy bunnies (1909)

★ The **tale** of Pigling Bland. Warne 2002 80p il $6.99
Grades: PreK K 1 2 3   E
1. Pigs -- Fiction
ISBN 0-7232-4784-6
First published 1913
"Pigling's story ends happily with a perfectly lovely little black
Berkshire pig called Pigwig." Toronto Public Libr. Books for Boys &
Girls

★ The **tale** of Squirrel Nutkin. Warne 2002 56p il $6.99
Grades: PreK K 1 2 3   E
1. Squirrels -- Fiction
ISBN 0-7232-4771-4
First published 1903
Each day the squirrels gather nuts, Nutkin propounds a riddle to Mr.
Brown, the owl, until impertinent Nutkin, over-estimating Mr. Brown's
patience, gets his due

The **tale** of the Flopsy Bunnies; Original and authorized ed; Fred-
erick Warne 2002 56p il $6.99
Grades: PreK K 1 2 3   E
1. Rabbits -- Fiction
ISBN 0-7232-4779-X
First published 1909
Benjamin Bunny is now married to his cousin Flopsy, and their six
little bunnies get into all manner of mischief.

★ The **tale** of Timmy Tiptoes. Warne 2002 56p il $6.99
Grades: PreK K 1 2 3   E
1. Squirrels -- Fiction
ISBN 0-7232-4781-1
First published 1911

An innocent squirrel accused of stealing nuts is forced down a hole
in a tree, where he meets a friendly chipmunk

★ The **tale** of two bad mice. Warne 2002 56p il $6.99
Grades: PreK K 1 2 3   E
1. Mice -- Fiction
ISBN 0-7232-4774-9
First published 1904
"Two mischievous little mice pilfer a doll's house to equip their
own. They are caught and finally make amends for what they have done.
Perfectly charming illustrations and a most enticing tale." Adventuring
With Books. 2d edition

Potter, Giselle
★ **This** is my dollhouse; Giselle Potter. Schwartz & Wade Books
2016 40 p. color illustrations (alk. paper) $17.99
Grades: PreK K 1 2   E
1. Dollhouses -- Fiction 2. Imagination -- Fiction
ISBN 9780553521535; 9780553521542
LC 2015005879
In this book, by Giselle Potter, a "little girl proudly walks the reader
through her handmade dollhouse, pointing out the bricks she painted
on the outside, the wallpaper she drew on the inside, the fancy clothes
she made for her dolls, and the little elevator she made out of a paper
cup. She's proud of her house and has lots of fun using her imagination
to play with it—until she discovers her friend Sophie's 'perfect' store-
bought house." (Publisher's note)
"The realization that creative, outside-the-box artistry can be more
inspiring than anything manufactured makes for a wonderful story, one
that may motivate future members of the artisanal economy." Pub Wkly

Pow, Tom
Tell me one thing, Dad; illustrated by Ian Andrew. Candlewick
Press 2004 un il $15.99
Grades: PreK K 1 2 3   E
1. Bedtime -- Fiction 2. Father-daughter relationship -- Fiction
ISBN 0-7636-2474-8
LC 2003-65272
Molly and her father play a bedtime game that shows how much they
love each other
"The sharp yet simple text avoids the obvious, going for interesting
images. . . . The watercolor-and-ink artwork . . . brims with whimsy in
both design and execution." Booklist

Poydar, Nancy
The **biggest** test in the universe. Holiday House 2005 un il
$16.95
Grades: K 1 2 3   E
1. School stories 2. Examinations -- Fiction
ISBN 0-8234-1944-4
Sam and his classmates dread Friday, the day they are to take the
infamous Big Test.
"Enlivened by colorful and humorous illustrations depicting the stu-
dents' worries, this book is fun and cheerful, as well as unique in its
subject." SLJ

No fair science fair. Holiday House 2011 32p il $14.95
Grades: K 1 2   F
1. School stories 2. Birds -- Fiction 3. Science projects -- Fiction
ISBN 978-0-8234-2269-2; 0-8234-2269-0
LC 2010023224
As the judging of his class's science fair approaches, Otis has trouble
even thinking of an idea but once he has built a bird feeder he is deter-
mined to make some good observations, no matter how long it takes.

"A great book for sharing with classes on many levels, this is both a good primer for science fairs and for skills such as being a good friend, appreciating differences and persistence." Kirkus

Prahin, Andrew

Brimsby's hats; Andrew Prahin. Simon & Schuster Books for Young Readers 2013 40 p. col. ill. (hardcover : alk. paper) $15.99

Grades: K 1 2   E

1. Hats -- Fiction 2. Friendship -- Fiction 3. Creative ability -- Fiction

ISBN 1442481471; 9781442481473; 9781442481480

LC 2012024049

In this picture book by Andrew Prahin, "a lonely hat maker uses quirky creativity to make friends. Brimsby is a happy hat maker--until his best friend goes off to find adventure at sea. Now Brimsby is a lonely hat maker, unsure of what to do. But since making hats is what he does best, perhaps his talents can help him find some friends." (Publisher's note)

"There's no dialogue—Prahin narrates the whole story comfortingly in the third person, softening Brimsby's feelings of loss—and much of the humor appears in the stylish spreads. In one, a bison tries on a comically small hat; in another, Brimsby and his friend fantasize in pictorial dialogue balloons about fighting a pirate octopus." Pub Wkly

Prasadam-Halls, Smriti

T-Veg; written by Smriti Prasadam-Halls; illustrated by Katherina Manolessou. Abrams Books for Young Readers 2017 32 p. color illustrations (hardback) $16.95

Grades: PreK K 1 2   E

1. Dinosaurs -- Fiction 2. Individuality -- Fiction 3. Stories in rhyme 4. Vegetarianism -- Fiction 5. Tyrannosaurus rex -- Fiction

ISBN 9781419724947

LC 2016029745

In this children's book, by Smriti Prasadam-Halls, illustrated by Katherina Manolessou, "Reginald's a T. Rex just as fierce and ferocious as the rest: he's got a mighty roar, gnashing teeth, and all the speed a dino could need. But when it comes to mealtime, Reg would rather chow down on broccoli, beans, and greens than the juicy steaks his paleo pals prefer. When Reginald realizes how different he is from the others, he hopes to find a place to fit in among the herbivores." (Publisher's note)

Preller, James

★ A **pirate's** guide to first grade; illustrated by Greg Ruth. Feiwel and Friends 2010 un il $16.99

Grades: PreK K 1   E

1. School stories 2. Pirates -- Fiction 3. Imagination -- Fiction

ISBN 978-0-312-36928-6; 0-312-36928-X

"Throughout his first day of first grade, a young boy describes his everyday actions in briny pirate terms, from breakfasting on grub in the galley to meeting Cap'n Silver (his new teacher) and walking the plank (seesaw) at recess. Each sharply rendered, full-color scene shows a crew of imagined pirates, differentiated in gray-toned drawings, who follow the boy and provide friendly company throughout the day. Young would-be buccaneers facing their own first-day jitters will enjoy this droll title." Booklist

Preston-Gannon, Frann

Pepper & Poe; by Frann Preston-Gannon. Orchard Books 2015 32 p. (hardcover : alk. paper) $16.99

Grades: PreK K   E

1. Cats -- Fiction 2. Kittens -- Fiction

ISBN 0545683572; 9780545683579

LC 2014027393

This children's book, by Frann Preston-Gannon, is the "story about two soon-to-be sibling cats, Pepper & Poe. Pepper is an old cat. He's set in his ways, and used to his normal routine in the house that he rules--or thinks he rules, anyway! Yup, he's got everything down to a science, including how to manipulate the house dog. That is until a new kitty named Poe comes along and starts messing up everything! Can Poe get Pepper to accept him as part of the family?" (Publisher's note)

"Pepper, a gray cat with green eyes, likes Sundays, Mondays, and Tuesdays. However, one Wednesday, something changes: Poe, a tiny white kitten with orange eyes, is introduced to Pepper, who takes one look at that smiling face before thinking, "I don't like it." It's downhill from there, as Thursday is bad, Friday is worse, and Saturday is "nearly impossible." . . . Sweet and silly, this is a good book for learning the days of the week and accepting a new sibling. Pair with Sam Lloyd's Mr. Pusskins and Little Whiskers (2008) for a similar tale of reluctant feline friendship." Booklist

Pepper and Poe

Preus, Margi

The **Peace** Bell; illustrated by Hideko Takahashi. Henry Holt and Co. 2008 un il $16.95

Grades: K 1 2 3   E

1. Bells -- Fiction 2. Japan -- Fiction 3. Peace -- Fiction 4. New Year -- Fiction 5. Friendship -- Fiction 6. Grandmothers -- Fiction

ISBN 978-0-8050-7800-8; 0-8050-7800-2

LC 2007040897

Yoko's grandmother tells about how the bell in their town that would ring on New Year's Eve is given up during the war for scrap metal, finds its way back to their village, and becomes known as the Peace Bell.

"The simple plot is clearly developed with descriptive language, and an author's note provides more historical details. Done in Japanese acrylic paints, the realistic illustrations accurately portray the setting and capture the characters' various emotions." SLJ

Price, Mara

Grandma's chocolate; illustrated by Lisa Fields. Pinata Books 2010 un il $16.95

Grades: PreK K 1 2   E

1. Mayas -- Fiction 2. Grandmothers -- Fiction 3. Mexican Americans -- Fiction 4. Bilingual books -- English-Spanish

ISBN 1-55885-587-4; 978-1-55885-587-8

LC 2009053975

When Sabrina's grandmother visits from Mexico, she brings gifts that make Sabrina feel like a Mayan princess.

"Field's strongest paintings are those of the rosy-cheeked family, which make evident the influence of their cultural roots and the strength of their intergenerational bonds." Publ Wkly

Priceman, Marjorie

★ **Hot** air; the (mostly) true story of the first hot-air balloon ride. Atheneum Books for Young Readers 2005 un il $16.95

Grades: K 1 2 3   E

1. Balloons

ISBN 0-689-82642-7

LC 2004-14743

A Caldecott Medal honor book, 2006

"With vibrant colors and varied use of panels, full-page illustrations, and spreads, Priceman paces the tale perfectly." SLJ

How to make a cherry pie and see the U.S.A. Alfred A. Knopf 2008 un il $16.99; lib bdg $19.99

Grades: PreK K 1 2   E

1. Baking -- Fiction 2. United States -- Fiction 3. Voyages and

travels -- Fiction

ISBN 978-0-375-81255-2; 0-375-81255-5; 978-0-375-91255-9 lib bdg; 0-375-91255-X lib bdg

LC 2007-46064

Since the Cook Shop is closed, the reader is led around the United States to gather coal, cotton, granite, and other natural resources needed to make the utensils for preparing a cherry pie

"The trip is a madcap adventure. . . . The art brims with good cheer and excites with detail." Booklist

★ **How** to make an apple pie and see the world. Knopf 1994 un il $16; pa $6.99

Grades: PreK K 1 2   E

1. Baking -- Fiction 2. Voyages and travels -- Fiction

ISBN 0-679-83705-1; 0-679-88083-6 pa

LC 93-12341

Since the market is closed, the reader is led around the world to gather the ingredients for making an apple pie

"The perfect blend of whimsical illustrations and tongue-in-cheek humor makes this an irresistable offering. The recipe is included." Child Book Rev Serv

Prigger, Mary Skillings

Aunt Minnie McGranahan; illustrated by Betsy Lewin. Clarion Bks. 1999 31p il $15; pa $5.95

Grades: K 1 2 3   E

1. Aunts -- Fiction 2. Orphans -- Fiction

ISBN 0-395-82270-X; 0-618-60488-X pa

LC 98-33501

The townspeople in St. Clere, Kansas, are sure it will never work out when the neat and orderly spinster, Minnie McGranahan, takes her nine orphaned nieces and nephews into her home in 1920

"In a dexterous style, Prigger employs repetitive elements to establish and maintain a spry tempo in clipped, spruce sentences. . . . The black outlines of Lewin's . . . witty, loose watercolors punctuate the pages in a flurry of scribbles, suggesting the kind of bursting-at-the-seams activity." Publ Wkly

Another title about Aunt Minnie is:
Aunt Minnie and the twister (2002)

Primavera, Elise

Louise the big cheese and the back-to-school smarty-pants. Simon & Schuster 2011 il $16.99

Grades: PreK K 1 2   E

1. School stories

ISBN 978-1-4424-0600-1; 1-4424-0600-3

Louise the Big Cheese is determined to make the grade in school this year and that means straight As. But she's stuck with the toughest teacher ever.

"Watercolor and black-line illustrations energetically depict the irrepressible Louise and [a] host of supporting characters." SLJ

Louise the big cheese: divine diva; illustrated by Diane Goode. Simon & Schuster Books for Young Readers 2009 un il $16.99

Grades: PreK K 1 2   E

1. Theater -- Fiction 2. Friendship -- Fiction

ISBN 978-1-4169-7180-1; 1-4169-7180-7

LC 2008-23608

When she learns her class will be doing a play, little Louise Cheese has big dreams of being the star, but when her best friend is given the lead she learns that even the small roles count

"Primavera's breezy story . . . and Goode's distinctive artwork intermingle wonderfully. In both story and art, Louise makes a splash. . . . Goode is at her best here." Booklist

Other titles about Louise are:
Louise the big cheese and the la-di-da shoes (2009)
Louise the big cheese and the back-to-school smarty-pants (2011)

Thumb love. Robin Corey Books 2010 un il $16.99; lib bdg $19.99

Grades: PreK K 1 2   E

1. Thumb sucking -- fiction

ISBN 978-0-375-84481-2; 0-375-84481-3; 978-0-375-95182-4 lib bdg; 0-375-95182-2 lib bdg

"Dedicated to thumb suckers the world over, this story tells of Lulu's addictive relationship with her thumb and how she gave it all up and invented a program with steps to keep her on track and to help others. Although Lulu's habit brings tsk-tsking from adults and taunts from children, her thumb reassures her that thumb sucking is the best thing. After a bad dream in which she is bucktoothed and has impaired speech, Lulu begins to doubt that their intense relationship is such a good thing and so founds a 12-step-like program for thumb suckers." (Booklist)

Primavera, Elise, 1954-

Louise the big cheese and the Ooh-la-la Charm School; Elise Primavera; illustrated by Diane Goode. Simon & Schuster Books for Young Readers 2012 40 p.

Grades: PreK K 1 2   E

1. Etiquette -- Fiction 2. Popularity -- Fiction 3. Picture books for children 4. Female friendship -- Fiction 5. Friendship -- Fiction

ISBN 1442405996; 9781442405998

LC 2009047236

This picture book tells the story of "Louise, the little girl with big ideas about getting noticed. . . . A new kid, Claire Eclaire, takes Louise under her wing and shows her how life is lived in Paris. . . . When it becomes clear that Claire is from Paris, Maine, Louise not only knows she's been duped but regrets her treatment of best-friend Fern." (Booklist)

". . . Louise has high hopes of improving her status that don't quite work out as planned. . . . [T]here's also a villain of sorts who leads her astray: snooty Claire . . . [who] uses the promise of "charm school" lessons to coerce Louise into doing her chores and letting her win at games. In the process, Louise . . . embarrasses herself in front of family and friends as usual." (Kirkus)

Prince, April Jones

★ **Twenty**-one elephants and still standing; written by April Jones Prince; illustrated by Francois Roca. Houghton Mifflin 2005 un il $16

Grades: K 1 2 3 4   E

1. Circus executives 2. Elephants -- Fiction 3. Brooklyn Bridge (New York, N.Y.) -- Fiction

ISBN 0-618-44887-X

LC 2004-05229

Upon completion of the Brooklyn Bridge, P.T. Barnum and his twenty-one elephants parade across to prove to everyone that the bridge is safe.

A "well-researched, handsomely illustrated picture book. . . . The sparse, yet powerful text contains both alliteration and occasional rhyme, making it a pleasure for readers and listeners alike. Roca's masterful paintings capture both the spirit of the times and of the expansive bridge." SLJ

Princesse Camcam, 1982-

Fox's garden; Princesse Camcam. Enchanted Lion Books 2014 32 p. color illustrations (Stories without words) (alk. paper) $14.95

Grades: K 1 2 3   E

1. Foxes -- Fiction 2. Kindness -- Fiction 3. Stories without words

4. Boys 5. Animal Welfare
ISBN 1592701671; 9781592701674

LC 2014934817

In this children's book, by Princesse Camcam, "[o]ne snowy night, a fox loses its way, entering a village. Chased away by the grown ups, Fox takes shelter in a greenhouse. A little boy sees this from his window. Without hesitating, he brings a basket of food to the greenhouse, where he leaves it for the fox. His gift is noticed and the night becomes a garden of new life, nourished by compassion and kindness." (Publisher's note)

"An act of tender compassion is given (and repaid) in secret during an icy winter night in this memorable addition to the Stories Without Words series, the U.S. debut for this French artist, born Camille Garoche. The story concerns a sleek, rust-colored fox seen darting through a gnarled forest of pale lavender trees beneath swirling snowy skies. . . Camcam creates her images by assembling cut-paper dioramas, which are then lit and photographed. The resulting images possess a subtle dimensionality while the story exudes a haunting winter magic and a strong sense of the way a small kindness can make an enormous difference. " Pub Wkly

Pritchett, Dylan

★ The **first** music; as told by Dylan Pritchett; illustrated by Erin Bennett Banks. August House Little Folk 2006 un il $16.95
Grades: PreK K 1 2   E
1. Music -- Fiction 2. Animals -- Fiction
ISBN 0-87483-776-6

A series of accidents in the jungle proves that everyone has something special to add when it comes to making music.

"Fresh and intriguing, this African cumulative tale of the origin of music unfolds in a vibrant storyteller's voice. . . . The message (everyone has something to add to the mix) is subtle, but clear enough for children to understand. However, it's the stylized, earth-toned illustrations, resembling carved wooden figures, that really rock and roll, evoking the synergy of the forest animals." Booklist

Prochovnic, Dawn Babb

Hip hip hooray! it's Family Day! sign language for family. by Dawn Babb Prochovnic; illustrated by Stephanie Bauer. ABDO/Magic Wagon 2012 32 p. col. ill. $28.50
Grades: K 1 2   E
1. Family 2. Counting 3. Sign language 4. Stories in rhyme
ISBN 1616418370; 9781616418373

LC 2011027065

Author Dawn Babb Prochovnic "invites readers to chant along and learn American Sign Language signs for the members of a family including grandma, grandpa, cousins, siblings, and pets. . . . [The] literacy-based, finger-play [teaches signing for children]. . . . [Included are] illustrated handshapes for the alphabet, numbers 1-10, and signs from the stories." (Publisher's note)

"Despite the somewhat bland text, the childlike, cheerful art (including a small demo diagram) and familiar themes (e.g., the alphabet, Halloween, and counting) will make this series welcome in classrooms looking to explore American Sign Language." Horn Book

Includes bibliographical references (p. 32).

Proimos, James

Patricia von Pleasantsquirrel. Dial Books for Young Readers 2009 un il $15.99
Grades: K 1 2   E
1. Princesses -- Fiction
ISBN 978-0-8037-3066-3; 0-8037-3066-7

LC 2008015776

After failing to convince her parents that she is a princess, Patricia von Pleasantsquirrel leaves her moatless house in search of a "princessdom."

"Proimos's story plays 'cheeky homage' to Sendak and Max, but the bold-lined, cartoon-style illustrations and Patricia's postmodern sassiness also owe a debt to James Marshall, calling to mind his bossy Goldilocks." SLJ

Todd's TV. Katherine Tegen Books 2010 un il $15.99
Grades: PreK K 1 2   E
1. Parents -- Fiction 2. Television -- Fiction
ISBN 978-0-06-170985-2; 0-06-170985-9

LC 2009-18507

When Todd's parents are too busy to take care of him, his television steps in to handle the parenting.

"With broad strokes and witty slapdashery, Proimos's light cartoon art and plotline carry some weighty themes. . . . Amusing cartoon drawings in shades of gray, black, and persimmony-red against a white background and a satiric twist at the story's end further enhance this funnyscary cautionary tale." SLJ

Prokofiev, Sergey

Peter and the wolf; translated by Maria Carlson; illustrated by Charles Mikolaycak. Viking 1982 un il hardcover o.p. pa $5.99
Grades: K 1 2 3 4   E
1. Fairy tales 2. Wolves -- Fiction
ISBN 0-14-050633-0 pa

LC 81-70402

This book retells the orchestral fairy tale of the boy who, ignoring his grandfather's warnings, proceeds to capture a wolf

"Prokofiev's classic, designed to teach children the instruments of an orchestra, has been published in picture book form before, but never better illustrated. The translation is smooth. . . . The paintings are rich in color, dramatic in details of costume or architecture, strong in composition, with distinctive individuality in the faces of people and of the wolf." Bull Cent Child Books

Prosek, James

★ **Bird,** butterfly, eel; story and paintings by James Prosek. Simon & Schuster Books for Young Readers 2009 un il map $16.99
Grades: K 1 2 3   E
1. Eels -- Fiction 2. Birds -- Fiction 3. Butterflies -- Fiction
ISBN 978-0-689-86829-0; 0-689-86829-4

LC 2007-15734

Follows a bird, a monarch butterfly, and an eel from summer on a farm until they make their respective fall voyages south, and then later begin to return north again when the weather warms.

"A well-designed and useful resource to pique curiosity about an amazing aspect of the lives of many animals." SLJ

A **good** day's fishing. Simon & Schuster Bks. for Young Readers 2004 un il $15.95
Grades: 1 2 3 4   E
1. Fishing -- Fiction
ISBN 0-689-85327-0

LC 2003-7383

A child searches through the hooks, lures, bobbers, and other paraphernalia in his tacklebox for the one thing he needs to ensure a good day's fishing. Includes a detailed glossary

"A beautifully illustrated, simple story. . . . Young fishing enthusiasts will certainly learn more about which tackle works best to catch particular kinds of fish, while the wonderfully detailed, gentle watercolor illustrations of fish and gear offer a lovely introduction." Booklist

Protopopescu, Orel

★ **Thelonious** Mouse; [by] Orel Protopopescu; pictures by Anne Wilsdorf. Farrar Straus Giroux 2011 un il $16.99

Grades: PreK K 1   E

1. Cats -- Fiction 2. Mice -- Fiction

ISBN 978-0-374-37447-1; 0-374-37447-3

Thelonious is a hipster mouse who cannot keep himself from taunting the cat of the house, but once Thelonious discovers a toy piano, he and the cat make some beautiful music together.

"Plenty of action and droll interior details to spy should capture kids' fancy, while grown-ups trying this as a read-aloud might need to pause to untangle their tongues. . . . Replete with scat-y, cat-and-mouse-y wordplay, this is giggle-worthy fun." Kirkus

Provensen, Alice

★ A **day** in the life of Murphy. Simon & Schuster Bks. for Young Readers 2003 un il $16.95; pa $6.99

Grades: PreK K 1 2 3   E

1. Dogs -- Fiction 2. Farm life -- Fiction

ISBN 0-689-84884-6; 1-4169-1800-0 pa

LC 2002-4309

Murphy, a farm terrier, describes a day in his life as he gets fed in the kitchen, hunts mice, goes to the vet, returns to the house for dinner, investigates a noise outside, and retires to the barn for sleep

"With charming, lively illustrations and peppy, descriptive prose, Provensen portrays the smells, sounds, and activities of a delightful, active pup." Booklist

Provensen, Alice, 1918-

Murphy in the city; Alice Provensen. Simon & Schuster Books for Young Readers 2015 40 p. color illustrations (hardback) $17.99

Grades: PreK K 1 2 3   E

1. Dogs -- Fiction 2. Cities and towns -- Fiction 3. Humorous stories 4. Terriers -- Fiction

ISBN 1442419717; 9781442419711

LC 2015005872

In this illustrated children's book, by Alice Provensen, "a perky pup trades in his country life for some city adventures. [Readers] spend the day with the irresistibly mischievous Murphy as he ventures into the city. Usually a country dog, Murphy experiences the joys and pitfalls of city life." (Publisher's note)

"This delightful pup's-eye view of the world is great for reading aloud and sure to be popular. Everyone will want to take Murphy home, so purchase multiple copies." Booklist

Pullen, Zachary

★ **Friday** my Radio Flyer flew; [by] Zachary Pullen. Simon & Schuster Books for Young Readers 2008 un il $16.99 E

1. Days -- Fiction 2. Flight -- Fiction 3. Imagination -- Fiction 4. Father-son relationship -- Fiction

ISBN 978-1-4169-3983-2; 1-4169-3983-0

LC 2007041852

A father and son find an old Radio Flyer wagon when cleaning out the attic and, through the course of a week, turn it back into a wonderful toy

"Subtle alliteration moves the story through the week. . . . Full-color spreads are oversize and beautifully done in oil paints. . . . The final spread . . . is take-your-breath-away wonderful. This is a strong first purchase, affirming the bond between boys and their fathers as well as the power of imagination." SLJ

Pulver, Robin

Christmas kitten; home at last. illustrated by Layne Johnson. Albert Whitman 2010 un il $16.99

Grades: PreK K 1 2   E

1. Cats -- Fiction 2. Christmas -- Fiction 3. Santa Claus -- Fiction

ISBN 978-0-8075-1157-2; 0-8075-1157-9

When Santa's allergies prevent him from keeping a homeless kitten, he and Mrs. Claus find it a perfect home.

"Johnson's oil paintings are rich with detail and expression, giving life to Cookie and all the North Pole denizens. The artist's careful attention to light and shadow, along with the use of bold primary colors, gives the book a perfect blend of warmth and exuberance. This is a sweet, fun read-aloud." SLJ

Happy endings; a story about suffixes. illustrated by Lynn Rowe Reed. Holiday House 2011 un il $16.95

Grades: 2 3 4   E

1. School stories 2. English language -- Fiction 3. English language

ISBN 978-0-8234-2296-8; 0-8234-2296-8

LC 2010024066

When Mr. Wright makes his students study word endings on the last day of school, even the suffixes rebel.

"Reed's sunny acrylics keep the story light and humorous. . . . Grammar will be a lot less boring with a library of Ms. Pulver's books at hand." Horn Book

Me first! by Robin Pulver; illustrated by Lynn Rowe Reed. Holiday House 2016 32 p. color illustrations (ebook) $16.95; (hardcover) $16.95

Grades: K 1 2 3   E

1. English language -- Suffixes and prefixes -- Fiction 2. Schools -- Fiction

ISBN 9780823437306; 9780823436446

LC 2015040850

In this children's book by Robin Pulver, illustrated by Lynn Rowe Reed, "it's Leadership Day in Mr. Wright's classroom, and the prefixes are IMpatient to take center stage. . . . Prefixes attach to the beginning of words and change what they mean. But they are MIStaken about their role in the day's festivities. . . . Mr. Wright has a lesson on President Abraham Lincoln PREpared. The prefixes are in DISbelief that they could be so carelessly IGnored." (Publisher's note)

Never say boo! Holiday House 2009 un il $16.95

Grades: PreK K 1 2   E

1. Ghost stories 2. School stories

ISBN 978-0-8234-2110-7; 0-8234-2110-4

LC 2008022609

When Gordon, a ghost, moves to a new school, everyone is afraid of him until they learn that he is not as scary as they thought he was.

"In Lucke's creepy and comical gouache illustrations, Gordon's bulging eyes and pasty white skull stand out on the mostly black background and are in contrast to his orange-yellow striped shirt and human classmates. Add in Pulver's straightforward dialogue and you have an amusing read-aloud." SLJ

Nouns and verbs have a field day; illustrated by Lynn Rowe Reed. Holiday House 2006 un il $16.95; pa $6.95

Grades: 2 3 4   E

1. School stories 2. English language -- Fiction

ISBN 0-8234-1982-7; 0-8234-2097-3 pa; 978-0-8234-1982-1; 978-0-8234-2097-1 pa

LC 2005-46207

When the children in Mr. Wright's class have a field day, nouns and verbs in the classroom make their own fun. "Primary." (Horn Book)

"The nouns and verbs decide to have some fun of their own while the kids in Mr. Wright's class are away participating in a field day. The nouns pair up with other nouns and the verbs with other verbs, until they realize they must cooperate. . . . Reed's vividly colored cartoons capture the high-energy activity. . . . Although the emphasis is on silliness, Pulver makes her point about the parts of speech; even the youngest listeners will realize that sentences need both nouns and verbs in order to make sense." Booklist

Punctuation takes a vacation; illustrated by Lynn Rowe Reed. Holiday House 2003 un il $16.95; pa $6.95
Grades: 2 3 4   E
1. School stories 2. Punctuation -- Fiction
ISBN 0-8234-1687-9; 0-8234-1820-0 pa
LC 2002-68915
When all the punctuation marks in Mr. Wright's class decide to take a vacation, the students discover just how difficult life can be without them
"Pulver's clever story moves along at a nice clip and makes its point without belaboring the matter. Reed's acrylics-on-canvas illustrations are rich in color and texture, and add to the amusement of the story." SLJ
Other titles in the author's series about Mr. Wright's class are:
Nouns and verbs have a field day (2006)
Silent letters loud and clear (2008)
Happy endings (2011)

Saturday is Dadurday; by Robin Pulver; illustrated by R.W. Alley. Walker Books For Young Readers Distrib. to the trade by Macmillan Publishers 2013 32 p. (hardcover) $16.99
Grades: PreK K 1 2   E
1. Father-daughter relationship -- Fiction 2. Fathers -- Fiction
ISBN 080278691X; 9780802786098; 9780802786913
LC 2012032293
In this book, written by Robin Pulver and illustrated by R.W. Alley, "the best day of the week [for Mimi] is always Saturday, because she gets to spend it with just her Dad. Every 'Dadurday' begins the same way--Mimi and Dad make silly-shaped pancakes, read the comics section of the newspaper and make lists of fun things to do together. But when Dad gets a new work schedule, 'Dadurday' is ruined. Can Mimi find a way to still make it a special day for her and dad?" (Publisher's note)

Silent letters loud and clear; written by Robin Pulver; illustrated by Lynn Rowe Reed. Holiday House 2008 un il $16.95
Grades: 2 3 4   E
1. School stories 2. English language -- Fiction
ISBN 0-8234-2127-9; 978-0-8234-2127-5
LC 2007016057
When Mr. Wright's students express a dislike for silent letters, the offended letters decide to teach them a lesson by going on strike.
"Mr Wright's uncertain fate (happily resolved) adds a dose of drama to the absurd situation. The playful design points up the silent letters within the text, and the faux-naive mixed-media illustrations give both human and letter characters lots of personality." Horn Book

Thank you, Miss Doover; illustrated by Stephanie Roth Sisson. Holiday House 2010 un il $16.95
Grades: K 1 2 3   E
1. School stories 2. Letters -- Fiction 3. Teachers -- Fiction 4. Authorship -- Fiction
ISBN 978-0-8234-2046-9; 0-8234-2046-9
Jack learns the value of revision as he practices Miss Doover's lesson on how to write a proper thank-you note.
"Pulver's characterization of the elementary schoolers' thought processes and lack of tact is spot-on. Sisson's colored pencil-and-acrylic illustrations go hand-in-hand with the funny text." Kirkus

Purmell, Ann
Apple cider making days; illustrated by Joanne Friar. Millbrook Press 2002 un il lib bdg $21.90
Grades: K 1 2 3   E
1. Apples -- Fiction 2. Farm life -- Fiction
ISBN 0-7613-2364-3
LC 2001-44920
Alex and Abigail join the whole family in processing and selling apples and apple cider at their grandfather's farm
"The comfortable, colorful art brings little ones up close to the process and gives them a good look at the conveyor belts and presses and other machinery involved. . . . A double-page spread, 'Cider Lore,' following the story, provides wonderful tidbits about the cider-making process. An excellent resource for autumn units or to use in preparation for a trip to the orchard." Booklist

Maple syrup season; by Ann Purmell; illustrated by Jill Weber. Holiday House 2008 un il $16.95
Grades: K 1 2 3   E
1. Family life -- Fiction 2. Maple sugar -- Fiction 3. Grandfathers -- Fiction
ISBN 978-0-8234-1891-6; 0-8234-1891-X
LC 2006-03455
Grandpa leads the way as his family works together to tap maple trees, collect sap, and make syrup.
"This gentle story has a straightforward text and folksy, colorful gouache illustrations. . . . A glossary and two pages of maple syrup lore are appended. This book would be a great addition to units on seasons, farms, or plants and trees." SLJ

Puttock, Simon
Little lost cowboy; illustrated by Caroline Jayne Church. Egmont USA 2011 un il $16.99
Grades: PreK K 1 2   E
1. Coyotes -- Fiction 2. West (U.S.) -- Fiction
ISBN 978-1-60684-259-1; 1-60684-259-5
LC 2010050495
A kindly toad helps a "lonesome and lost" young coyote find his mother.
"The repetitive text is accessible and child-friendly, and the desert setting is skillfully evoked with warm, earth-toned illustrations created from beautifully textured handmade paper, finished with bold black lines." SLJ

Qiong, Yu Li
A **New** Year's reunion. Candlewick Press 2011 un il $15.99
Grades: PreK K 1 2   E
1. China -- Fiction 2. Fathers -- Fiction 3. Family life -- Fiction 4. Chinese New Year -- Fiction
ISBN 978-0-7636-5881-6; 0-7636-5881-2
First published 2008 in Taipei
"Two things make this Chinese New Year story remarkable—Zhu's meticulously observed gouaches and the family's poignant backstory." Publ Wkly

Quackenbush, Robert M.
First grade jitters; written by Robert Quackenbush; illustrated by Yan Nascimbene. Harper 2010 un il $16.99
Grades: PreK K   E
1. School stories 2. Worry -- Fiction
ISBN 978-0-06-077632-9; 0-06-077632-3
LC 2009007290
A newly illustrated edition of the title first published 1982

Aidan is about to enter first grade and doesn't know quite what to expect. Will his friends be there? Will he have to know how to read and spell? What if he can't understand anything his teacher says?

"The text and pictures explore this common anxiety effectively and with a touch of humor." SLJ

Quattlebaum, Mary

Jo MacDonald saw a pond; by Mary Quattlebaum; illustrated by Laura J. Bryant. Dawn Publications 2011 il $16.95; pa $8.95

Grades: PreK K 1   E
1. Pond ecology -- Fiction 2. Folk songs -- United States
ISBN 978-1-58469-150-1; 1-58469-150-6; 978-1-58469-151-8 pa; 1-58469-151-4 pa
LC 2011011700

In this version of the classic song 'Old MacDonald Had a Farm,' the farmer's granddaughter discovers the creatures living at a pond. End notes present facts, outdoor activities, and games related to this lively ecosystem.

"The familiar tune starts on page one and never misses a beat, begging kids to participate. . . . Observant readers will notice the clever design of the illustrations that hides the last-mentioned animal and the next one within the spread. Bryant's softly colored watercolor creatures echo Jo's rosy-cheeked childhood innocence and have just a touch of expression in their faces." Kirkus

Includes bibliographical references

Mighty Mole and Super Soil; by Mary Quattlebaum; illustrated by Chad Wallace. Dawn Publications 2015 32 p. (hardback) $16.95

Grades: PreK K 1 2   E
1. Soils 2. Moles (Animals) -- Fiction
ISBN 1584695382; 9781584695387; 9781584695394
LC 2014048927

In this children's book by Mary Quattlebaum, illustrated by Chad Wallace, "Mighty Mole is on the move. Like a swimmer in dirt, she strokes through the soil. Her tunnels are everywhere! She finds food, eludes a predator, has a family, and helps to make Super Soil. Soil is a largely invisible ecosystem and yet is vital to the health of the world. Following the story, two Explore More for Kids pages offer a matching challenge and a review of some of the remarkable traits that make moles 'mighty.'" (Publisher's note)

"Though this is the term used by biologists, it will likely confuse lay readers. There are few books available for young readers about these important soil-improvers, so this fills a niche." Kirkus

Includes bibliographical references

Quay, Emma

Good night, sleep tight; a book about bedtime. [illustrated by] Anna Walker. Board book ed.; Dial books for Young Readers 2011 un il (Hello friends!) bd bk $5.99

Grades: PreK   E
1. Board books for children 2. Owls -- Fiction 3. Sheep -- Fiction 4. Bedtime -- Fiction 5. Camping -- Fiction 6. Giant panda -- Fiction
ISBN 978-0-8037-3581-1; 0-8037-3581-2
LC 2010020620

First published 2010 in Australia

When Panda, Owl, and Sheep go camping, they find that only one has a comfortable sleeping bag.

Rabinowitz, Alan

★ **A** boy and a jaguar; written by Alan Rabinowitz; illustrated by Catia Chien. First edition Houghton Mifflin Books for Children 2013 32 p. color illustrations $16.99

Grades: PreK K 1 2 3   E
1. Human-animal relationship 2. Panthera -- Conservation 3. Wildlife conservationists -- United States
ISBN 054787507X; 9780547875071
LC 2012025531

Schneider Family Book Award (2015)

In this children's book by Alan Rabinowitz, illustrated by Catia Chen, "Alan loves animals, but the great cat house at the Bronx Zoo makes him sad. Why are they all alone in empty cages? Are they being punished? More than anything, he wants to be their champion--their voice--but he stutters uncontrollably. . . . He searches for his voice and fulfills a promise to speak for animals, and people, who cannot speak for themselves." (Publisher's note)

"An unusual picture book autobiography, written by an animal scientist who began his lifelong interest in big cats when he found he could communicate more easily with animals than with people due to his stuttering. Rabinowitz's commitment to petitioning for wildlife conservation has helped him communicate more comfortably. This accessible story, with quietly emotive, impressionistic art, will help children understand both concerns." Horn Book

Raczka, Bob

Fall mixed up; illustrations by Chad Cameron. Carolrhoda Books 2011 un il lib bdg $17.95

Grades: PreK K 1 2   E
1. Stories in rhyme 2. Autumn -- Fiction
ISBN 978-0-7613-4606-7; 0-7613-4606-6
LC 2009038922

The delights of autumn are described in mixed-up verse and illustrations, and the reader is challenged to uncover the errors.

"Silly as the rhyming verses are, they need Cameron's zany illustrations to truly make them come alive. . . . Digital paintings with photo-collage elements draw readers' eye through the scenes. . . . A true celebration of fall certain to be a winner." Kirkus

Niko draws a feeling; by Bob Raczka; illustrated by Simone Shin. Carolrhoda Books 2017 32 p. color illustrations (lb : alk. paper) $17.99

Grades: K 1 2 3   E
1. Drawing -- Fiction 2. Drawing -- Fiction
ISBN 9781467798433
LC 2015044789

In this book, by Bob Raczka, illustrated by Simone Shin, "Niko loves to draw his world: the ring-a-ling of the ice cream truck, the warmth of sun on his face. But no one appreciates his art. Until one day, Niko meets Iris . . . This imaginative and tender story explores the creative process, abstract art, friendship, and the universal desire to feel understood." (Publisher's note)

Snowy, blowy winter; [by] Bob Raczka; illustrated by Judy Stead. Albert Whitman & Co. 2008 un il $16.99

Grades: PreK K 1 2   E
1. Stories in rhyme 2. Snow -- Fiction 3. Winter -- Fiction
ISBN 978-0-8075-7526-0; 0-8075-7526-7
LC 2007052608

Illustrations and simple rhyming text portray winter activities, from snowman-building, sledding, and sitting by a fire to feeding birds

"The text is simple and bouncy, and the cartoon illustrations are bright, clear, and inclusive. The book's quick pace and cheerful pictures make it a perfect choice for seasonal storytimes." SLJ

Spring things; by Bob Raczka; illustrated by Judy Stead. Albert Whitman 2007 un il $16.95

Grades: PreK K 1 2   **E**
   1. Spring -- Fiction
   ISBN 978-0-8075-7596-3

LC 2006023403
Winter melts into spring with the sights and sounds of hopping and skipping, sowing and mowing, and blading and lemonading

"Stead's paintings add an entertaining element and useful clarification to the active text." SLJ

Who loves the fall? by Bob Raczka; illustrated by Judy Stead. Albert Whitman 2007 un il $16.95
Grades: PreK K 1 2   **E**
   1. Stories in rhyme 2. Autumn -- Fiction
   ISBN 978-0-8075-9037-9; 0-8075-9037-1

LC 2007001506
Rhyming text and illustrations portray the sights and sounds of autumn, from "rakers, leapers, and corn crop reapers" to "trickers, treaters, and turkey eaters"

"The brightly colored, well-designed illustrations pulsate with energy, movement, and charm." SLJ

Radunsky, Vladimir

What does peace feel like? by V. Radunsky and children just like you from around the world. Atheneum Books for Young Readers 2004 un il $14.95
Grades: K 1 2 3   **E**
   1. Peace
   ISBN 0-689-86676-3

LC 2003-11506
Simple text and illustrations portray what peace looks, sounds, tastes, feels, and smells like to children around the world.

"As much a celebration of the five senses as an antiwar message, this bright picture book combines Radunsky's playful gouache double-page scenarios with quotes from grade-schoolers at an international school in Rome." Booklist

You? translated from Dog-ese to English by my learned dog, Tsetsa. Harcourt, Inc. 2009 un il $16
Grades: PreK K 1 2   **E**
   1. Dogs -- Fiction
   ISBN 978-0-15-205177-8; 0-15-205177-5

LC 2008-3281
A lonely girl and a stray dog find one another in a park.
"Radunsky makes the most of his canvas. . . . Thin, energetic lines define the forms minimally on gouache blobs of color, all arrayed on a generous expanse of buff-colored handmade paper. . . . The heartfelt, plaintive dialogue will hold readers' interest, and the wait makes the inevitable discovery—'Woof! YOU!'—all the sweeter." Kirkus

Rahaman, Vashanti

Divali rose; [by] Vashanti Rahaman; illustrated by Jamel Akib. Boyds Mills Press 2008 un il $16.95
Grades: 2 3 4   **E**
   1. Divali -- Fiction 2. Trinidad -- Fiction 3. Prejudices -- Fiction 4. East Indians -- Fiction 5. Grandparents -- Fiction
   ISBN 978-1-59078-524-9; 1-59078-524-X

LC 2007049686
As the festival of Divali approaches, Ricki wants to confess that he accidentally broke a rosebud off the bush he and his grandfather planted, but grandfather is busy blaming the neighbors who are newly arrived in Trinidad from India. Includes facts about Divali and the people and language of Trinidad

"This appealing, multilayered story will provoke discussion about resentments between different generations of immigrants. . . . Akib's

impressionistic pastel paintings portray the tropical setting and Ricki's feelings of guilt." SLJ

Ramos, Jorge

I'm just like my mom/I'm just like my dad; illustrated by Akemi Gutierrez. Rayo 2008 un il $16.99
Grades: PreK K   **E**
   1. Bilingual books -- English-Spanish 2. Father-son relationship -- Fiction 3. Mother-daughter relationship -- Fiction
   ISBN 978-0-06-123968-7; 0-06-123968-2
In two stories in English and Spanish, printed back to back, children reflect on how much they resemble their parents.

"This is a comforting celebration of family. . . . Spare illustrations is subtle colors completely fill each double-page spread and feature pleasant figures with enlarged oval heads, giving a happy, open, comfortable feel to the narratives." Booklist

Ramos, Mario

I am so strong; [translated by Jean Anderson] Gecko Press 2011 il
Grades: PreK K 1   **E**
   1. Wolves -- Fiction
   ISBN 0-9582-7877-6; 978-0-9582-7877-5
   Original French edition, 2001

"This offering from Belgian author/illustrator Ramos is a single, drawn-out joke, but achieves keeper status with intelligent dialogue and Gallic sophistication. A megalomaniacal wolf strolls through the forest buttonholing fairy tale creatures and asking them to burnish his ego. . . . Ramos's thickly brushed paintings alternate between woodland scenes suggestive of stage scenery and closer shots of the wolf and other creatures against white backdrops, the better to appreciate the comic tension. . . . The wolf's comeuppance is deeply satisfying; the only disappointment is that the book is over so soon. Better read it again." Publ Wkly

Ramsey, Calvin Alexander

Belle, the last mule at Gee's Bend; [by] Calvin Alexander Ramsey and Bettye Stroud; illustrated by John Holyfield. Candlewick Press 2011 un il $15.99
Grades: PreK K 1 2   **E**
   1. Clergy 2. Mules -- Fiction 3. Alabama -- Fiction 4. Nonfiction writers 5. Civil rights activists 6. Nobel laureates for peace 7. African Americans -- Civil rights
   ISBN 978-0-7636-4058-3; 0-7636-4058-1

LC 2010048132
In Gee's Bend, Alabama, Miz Pettway tells young Alex about the historic role her mule played in the struggle for civil rights led by Dr. Martin Luther King, Jr. Includes factual information about the community of Gee's Bend and Martin Luther King, Jr.

"Holyfield's intense acrylic paintings, in blues, yellows and browns, evoke the heat and the drama. . . . A solid choice for parents and teachers who are introducing the 1960s to young children. An intergenerational story filled with heart and soul." Kirkus

★ **Ruth** and the Green Book; [by] Calvin Alexander Ramsey, with Gwen Strauss; illustrations by Floyd Cooper. Carolrhoda Books 2010 un il
Grades: K 1 2 3   **E**
   1. Segregation -- Fiction 2. Southern States -- Fiction 3. Automobile travel -- Fiction 4. African Americans -- Segregation -- Fiction
   ISBN 0761352554; 9780761352556

LC 2009034284
When Ruth and her parents take a motor trip from Chicago to Alabama to visit her grandmother, they rely on a pamphlet called "The Negro Motorist Green Book" to find places that will serve them. This title

concludes with a historical note on the Green Book itself. "Ages five to nine." (Bull Cent Child Books)

This is a "powerful picture book. . . . Cooper's glowing, unframed, sepia-toned artwork delivers a strong sense of the period from a child's viewpoint. . . . This is a compelling addition to U.S. history offerings." Booklist

Rand, Ann

I know a lot of things; by Ann & Paul Rand. Chronicle Books 2009 un il $16.99

Grades: PreK K 1   E

1. Growth -- Fiction

ISBN 978-0-8118-6615-6

LC 2008020680

A reissue of the title first published 1956

Celebrates the many things young children know about their world, while looking forward to a time when they will know more

This is written "in poetic text. . . . Paul Rand's simply composed, ahead-of-their-time illustrations don't look the least bit dated and perfectly reflect the concepts in the text." Horn Book Guide

Sparkle and spin; a book about words. by Ann & Paul Rand. Chronicle Books 2006 un il $15.95

Grades: PreK K 1   E

1. Communication 2. English language

ISBN 978-0-8118-5003-2; 0-8118-5003-X

LC 2004-23260

A reissue of the title first published 1957 by Harcourt, Brace, and World

Lyrical text explores what words are and how they are used, highlighting such characteristics as that some words are spoken softly, some are shouted, some sound like their meaning, and some evoke certain feelings.

This "is a vibrantly eye-catching collection of visual puns and graphic double-entendres." NY Times Book Rev

Randall, Alison L.

The **wheat** doll; [by] Alison L. Randall; illustrated by Bill Farnsworth. Peachtree Publishers 2008 30p il $16.95

Grades: K 1 2 3   E

1. Dolls -- Fiction 2. Storms -- Fiction 3. Frontier and pioneer life -- Fiction 4. Lost and found possessions -- Fiction

ISBN 978-1-56145-456-3; 1-56145-456-7

LC 2008-4562

On the nineteenth-century Utah frontier, Mary Ann is heartbroken when her doll Betty is lost during a fierce storm and her sadness lasts all winter long, until spring brings a wonderful surprise.

"This is a sweet story of loss and renewal told with empathy and feeling that is never heavy-handed. . . . Farnsworth's realistic oil paintings have a warm, soft quality that matches the tone of the text. . . . This picture book is a great addition." SLJ

Rania

The **sandwich** swap; by Her Majesty Queen Rania; with Kelly DiPucchio; illustrations by Tricia Tusa. Disney-Hyperion Books 2010 un il $16.99

Grades: PreK K 1 2   E

1. School stories 2. Food -- Fiction 3. Friendship -- Fiction 4. Toleration -- Fiction

ISBN 978-1-4231-2484-9; 1-4231-2484-7

LC 2009018673

"The day Lily stops eating her peanut butter and jelly sandwich to tell Salma her hummus and pita sandwich looks yucky—and vice versa—is the day they stop being friends. . . . When the two girls get caught

in the middle of a food fight and called to the principal's office, they decide it's time to make some changes. . . . Soft watercolor cartoon illustrations portray a lively student body and a slightly forbidding principal. This engaging title reminds children that having the courage to try new things can result in positive experiences." SLJ

Rankin, Laura

Ruthie and the (not so) teeny tiny lie; [by] Laura Rankin. Bloomsbury Children's Books 2007 un il $15.95

Grades: PreK K   E

1. School stories 2. Foxes -- Fiction 3. Truthfulness and falsehood -- Fiction

ISBN 978-1-59990-010-0; 1-59990-010-6

LC 2006013192

Ruthie the fox loves tiny things and when she finds a tiny camera on the playground she is very happy, but after she lies and says the camera belongs to her, nothing seems to go right

"Emotionally authentic in text and art, this story gets its message across without preaching." SLJ

Ruthie and the (not so) very busy day; by Laura Rankin; illustrated by Laura Rankin. Bloomsbury 2014 32 p. col. ill. (hardcover) $17.99

Grades: PreK K   E

1. Girls -- Fiction 2. Parent-child relationship -- Fiction 3. Family life -- Fiction 4. Parent and child -- Fiction

ISBN 1599900521; 9781599900520; 9781619631625; 9781619632127

LC 2013034315

"It's Saturday morning--Ruthie's very favorite day. No school. No homework. No practices. Just a day to be with Mom and Dad. And Ruthie has BIG plans with her day off. But they keep getting interrupted. Dad has to go off to help Grandma. Mom has errands to run. Poor Ruthie is suddenly having the worst day ever!" (Publisher's note)

"Endearing illustrations of an anthropomorphized fox family depict both the chaos and pathos that are inevitable with this kind of day. Readers of all ages will easily identify with Ruthie's trying day." -Kirkus

Ransom, Candice F.

The **old** blue pickup truck; written by Candice F. Ransom; illustrated by Jenny Mattheson. Walker & Co. 2009 un il $16.99; lib bdg $17,89

Grades: PreK K 1   E

1. Trucks -- Fiction 2. Father-daughter relationship -- Fiction

ISBN 978-0-8027-9591-5; 0-8027-9591-9; 978-0-8027-9592-2 lib bdg; 0-8027-9592-7 lib bdg

LC 2008-40316

As a girl and her father run errands in their old blue pickup, she discovers how many different ways they can use their truck.

"This enjoyable story is accompanied by oil on primed paper illustrations that have a bright and clean feel." SLJ

Ransome, James

Gunner, football hero; [by] James E. Ransome. Holiday House 2010 un il $16.95

Grades: PreK K 1   E

1. Football -- Fiction

ISBN 978-0-8234-2053-7; 0-8234-2053-1

LC 2008-48487

When short, round Gunner, the third-string quarterback, finally gets to play in a big game, everyone treats him like a hero.

"The simple, economical narrative supposes a fair amount of familiarity with football but certainly conveys the thrill of Gunner's short time on the field. . . . Ransome's watercolor-and-line drawings as well as page layouts are appropriately full of action, and the faces of the players and crowds engagingly expressive and humorous." Kirkus

New red bike! [by] James E. Ransome. Holiday House 2011 un il $16.95

Grades: PreK K 1   E

1. Cycling -- Fiction 2. Bicycles -- Fiction 3. Friendship -- Fiction

ISBN 978-0-8234-2226-5; 0-8234-2226-7

Tom enjoys the thrill of riding his brand new bicycle, and then shares it with a friend.

"Story takes a backseat to a bigger emotional truth: a bike is an awesome thing. Wearing a bright red helmet that matches the bike's frame, Tom is truly at one with his machine, and Ransome . . . provides Zenlike text to match. . . . Each moment of action . . . gets its own watercolor and pencil image and perspective. . . . Newbie bikers should find that this book gives full voice to the joys of having wheels of one's own." Publ Wkly

Rao, Sandhya

My mother's sari; illustrated by Nina Sabnani. North South Books 2006 un il $14.95; pa $6.95

Grades: PreK K 1 2   E

1. India -- Fiction 2. Clothing and dress -- Fiction 3. Mother-daughter relationship -- Fiction

ISBN 0-7358-2101-1; 0-7358-2233-6 pa

First published in India

A little girl is fascinated by her mother's sari and finds many uses for it.

"Subtle backgrounds, lightly decorated with objects from nature, provide a gentle showcase for the children and the saris. Rao [uses] . . . childlike drawings to represent the kids and photographs of the cloths, bringing the fabric designs, colors, and folds up close. A winsome look at a fresh subject." Booklist

Rappaport, Doreen

★ The **secret** seder; illustrated by Emily Arnold McCully. Hyperion Books for Children 2005 un il $16.99

Grades: 2 3 4   E

1. Jews -- Fiction 2. France -- Fiction 3. Passover -- Fiction 4. Holocaust, 1933-1945 -- Fiction

ISBN 0-7868-0777-6

LC 2003-57115

During the Nazi occupation of France, a boy and his father slip out of their village and into the mountains, where they join a group of fellow Jews at a humble seder table

"Rappaport interweaves themes and descriptive text to create a meaningful story in a distinctive setting. An excellent discussion starter." SLJ

Raschka, Chris

★ **Daisy** gets lost; Chris Raschka. Schwartz & Wade Books 2013 32 p. (glb) $20.99

Grades: PreK K   E

1. Stories without words 2. Dogs -- Fiction 4. Lost and found possessions -- Fiction

ISBN 0449817423; 9780449817414; 9780449817421

LC 2012049221

Author Chris Raschka's book will "follow Daisy the dog on her next adventure. . . . Raschka has created a story that explores fear as only he can. Any child who has ever felt lost will relate to Daisy's despair upon finding herself in an unfamiliar part of the park after chasing a squirrel. In a nearly wordless picture book, Daisy encounters the unease of being lost and the joys of being found." (Publisher's note)

"With only Daisy's called-out name and that howl for text, the pictures chart the eventful outing in a mix of full spreads and sequential strips or panels--with a midcourse aerial view that reassuringly reveals that the two are never very far apart. The duckling Daisy in Jane Simmons' Come Along, Daisy! (1998) may be more venturesome, but young children will readily identify with the mix of high spirits and vulnerability this Daisy, literally and figuratively fetching, displays. Endearing." Kirkus

★ **Everyone** can learn to ride a bicycle; Chris Raschka. Schwartz & Wade Books 2013 32 p. (hardcover) $16.99

Grades: PreK K 1 2   E

1. Picture books for children 2. Bicycles -- Fiction 3. Fathers and daughters -- Fiction 4. Bicycles and bicycling -- Fiction

ISBN 0375870075; 9780375870071; 9780375970078

LC 2012009172

In this children's picture book, by Chris Raschka, "a father takes his daughter through all the steps in the process [of riding a bike]--from choosing the perfect bicycle to that triumphant first successful ride. . . . [The] picture book . . . not only shows kids how to learn to ride, but captures what it feels like to fall . . . get up . . . fall again . . . and finally . . . ride a bicycle!" (Publisher's note)

"Rendered in Raschka's signature style of fluid, kinetic brushstrokes, the ink-and-watercolor illustrations beautifully capture the action and emotion in each scene...Deceptively simple and perfectly paced for read-alouds, this latest from the two-time Caldecott medalist captures a child's everyday experience with gentle, joyful sensitivity." Booklist

Hip hop dog; words by Chris Raschka; pictures by Vladimir Radunsky. Harper 2010 un il $16.99; lib bdg $17.89

Grades: PreK K 1 2   E

1. Stories in rhyme 2. Dogs -- Fiction 3. Hip-hop -- Fiction 4. Rap music -- Fiction

ISBN 978-0-06-123963-2; 0-06-123963-1; 978-0-06-123964-9 lib bdg; 0-06-123964-X lib bdg

LC 2008031449

A neglected dog finds his purpose through rapping and rhyming.

"This is great for reading aloud. . . . The well-matched mixed-media illustrations show lively urban scenes. . . . Kids will chant along to the text, which slides and whirls across the pages." Booklist

Raschka, Christopher

★ A **ball** for Daisy; by Chris Raschka. Schwartz & Wade Books 2011 1 v. col. ill. $16.99; lib bdg $19.99

Grades: PreK K 1   E

1. Stories without words 2. Dogs -- Fiction 3. Play -- Fiction

ISBN 978-0-375-85861-1; 0-375-85861-X; 978-0-375-95861-8 lib bdg; 0-375-95861-4 lib bdg

LC 2010024132

Caldecott Medal (2012)

In this wordless picture book, Daisy the dog "loves playing with her ball . . . until the fateful moment that another dog bites too hard on the ball and deflates it. . . . Raschka uses fairly sophisticated comic-book arrangements . . . but masks them with soft watercolor edges instead of sharp corners. The result feels like something made of pure emotion, a pretty close approximation of what it's probably like to be a dog." Booklist

Farmy farm; by Chris Raschka. Orchard Books 2011 il $8.99

Grades: PreK   E

1. Stories in rhyme 2. Sounds -- Fiction 3. Farm life -- Fiction 4. Domestic animals -- Fiction

ISBN 978-0-545-21981-5

LC 2010039061

Rhyming text and touch-and-feel illustrations introduce a variety of farm animals and the sounds they make.

"The book's repeated verse, buoyant palette, and soft texture should find an enthusiastic toddler-aged audience." Publ Wkly

Five for a little one; [by] Chris Raschka. Atheneum Books for Young Readers 2006 un il $16.95
Grades: PreK K　　　　　　　　　　　　E
1. Counting 2. Stories in rhyme 3. Rabbits -- Fiction 4. Senses and sensation -- Fiction
ISBN 978-0-689-84599-4; 0-689-84599-5
LC 2005-08963

"A buoyant bunny, drawn in thick ink outline with a fuzzy body and delightfully mismatched ears (one downy and one plain), introduces readers to the senses, numbering them one through five. The rhyming verses and ebullient artwork convey a child's curiosity and enthusiasm for investigating the world in various ways." SLJ

John Coltrane's Giant steps; remixed by Chris Raschka. Atheneum Bks. for Young Readers 2002 33p il $17
Grades: K 1 2 3　　　　　　　　　　　E
1. Jazz music
ISBN 0-689-84598-7
LC 2001-33755

John Coltrane's musical composition is performed by a box, a snowflake, some raindrops, and a kitten

"Like Coltrane, Raschka is creating something deeply personal here that we don't need to understand fully to appreciate. Instead, he asks us to trust our own understanding of raindrops, snowflakes, kittens, and music to experience the book. Anyone who's still intimidated by jazz after giving this book a chance is probably just trying too hard." Horn Book

★ **Little** black crow; [by] Chris Raschka. Atheneum Books for Young Readers 2010 un il $16.99
Grades: K 1 2 3　　　　　　　　　　　E
1. Stories in rhyme 2. Crows -- Fiction
ISBN 978-0-689-84601-4; 0-689-84601-0
LC 2009032110

A boy thinks about the life of a little black crow that he sees, wondering where it goes in the snow, where it sleeps, and whether or not it worries like he does.

"Impressionistic watercolor landscapes perfectly set the mood and style for these awe-filled inquiries of a curious child." SLJ

New York is English, Chattanooga is Creek; by Chris Raschka. Atheneum Books for Young Readers 2005 un il $16.95
Grades: K 1 2 3　　　　　　　　　　　E
1. Cities and towns -- Fiction 2. Geographic names -- Fiction
ISBN 0-689-84600-2
LC 2004-23188

New York City, though a bit boastful, decides to throw a party to make new friends of other unique cities like Chattanooga and Minneapolis

"This is both a fascinating exploration of the etymology and derivation of American city names and a characteristic Raschka farcical flight-of-fancy.... Raschka's illustrations rendered in ink and watercolor employ his loose, impressionistic, brushy style to perfect effect, giving the book its humor while artfully delivering his message and entertaining information." SLJ

★ **Peter** and the wolf; retold by Chris Raschka. Atheneum Books for Young Readers 2008 un il $17.99

Grades: PreK K 1 2　　　　　　　　　　　E
1. Fairy tales 2. Wolves -- Fiction
ISBN 978-0-689-85652-5; 0-689-85652-0
LC 2008-04472

Retells the orchestral fairy tale in which a boy ignores his grandfather's warnings and captures a wolf with the help of a bird, a duck, and a cat

"Raschka conveys the mounting suspense in lilting words, swerving zigzags and curves.... Raschka's pictures—of characters venturing close to the wolf's bear-trap jaws, of the cat's enormous face looming over a tiny Peter—gain extra energy from geometrically shaped color blocks on the same spreads.... One reading will not be enough to appreciate the artist's keen attention to detail." Publ Wkly

★ **Yo!** Yes? by Chris Raschka. Orchard Bks. 1993 un il $15.95
Grades: PreK K 1 2　　　　　　　　　　　E
1. Friendship -- Fiction 2. Race relations -- Fiction 3. African Americans -- Fiction
ISBN 0-531-05469-1
LC 92-25644

A Caldecott Medal honor book, 1994

Two lonely characters, one black and one white, meet on the street and become friends

"The design and drawing are bold, spare and expressive; the language has the strength and rhythm of a playground chant." Bull Cent Child Books

Another title about these characters is:
Ring! Yo? (2000)

Rathmann, Peggy
★ **10** minutes till bedtime. Putnam 1998 un il $16.99; pa $6.99; bd bk $7.99
Grades: PreK K 1 2　　　　　　　　　　　E
1. Bedtime -- Fiction 2. Hamsters -- Fiction
ISBN 0-399-23103-X; 0-14-240024-6 pa; 0-399-23770-4 bd bk
LC 97-51295

A boy's hamster leads an increasingly large group of hamsters on a tour of the boy's house, while his father counts down the minutes to bedtime

"Children will pore over the comical details and follow closely the antics of the numbered hamsters, each one with a personality of its own." SLJ

★ The **day** the babies crawled away. Putnam 2003 un il $16.99
Grades: PreK K 1 2　　　　　　　　　　　E
1. Stories in rhyme 2. Infants -- Fiction
ISBN 0-399-23196-X
LC 2002-152002

A boy follows fives babies who crawl away from a picnic and saves the day by bringing them back

This is a "rollicking rhyming tale, illustrated in needle-sharp, atmospheric silhouettes against twilight skies." Publ Wkly

★ **Good** night, Gorilla. Putnam 1994 un il
Grades: PreK K 1 2　　　　　　　　　　　E
1. Zoos -- Fiction 2. Animals -- Fiction
ISBN 0-399-22445-9; 0-399-23003-3 bd bk; 0-698-11649-6 pa
LC 92-29020

In this picture book, "a zookeeper makes his final rounds of the day, bidding his charges good night, while unbeknownst to him the gorilla, who has taken his keys, lets each animal out after the keeper has passed. ... {They} follow the zookeeper home to his house and curl up for the night in his room, undiscovered until his wife says 'Good night, dear' and gets more responses than she had bargained for. Mrs. Zookeeper then trudges back to the zoo and returns the would-be guests, but the gorilla and his mouse sidekick sneak back again. . . . Ages two to five." (Bull Cent Child Books)

"In a book economical in text and simple in illustration, the many amusing, small details, as well as the tranquil tone of the story, make this an outstanding picture book." Horn Book Guide

★ **Officer** Buckle and Gloria. Putnam 1995 un il

Grades: PreK K 1 2   E

1. School stories 2. Dogs -- Fiction 3. Safety education -- Fiction
ISBN 0399226168

LC 93-43887

Awarded the Caldecott Medal, 1996

"When rotund, good-natured Officer Buckle visits school assemblies to read off his sensible safety tips, the children listen, bored and polite, dozing off one by one. But when the new police dog, Gloria, stands behind him, secretly miming the dire consequences of acting imprudently, the children suddenly become attentive, laughing uproariously and applauding loudly. The good policeman is first gratified with the response, then deflated to learn that Gloria was stealing the show. Finally, he realizes that he and Gloria make a great team, and they take their show on the road again, adding a new message, 'Always Stick With Your Buddy!'" (Booklist) "Kindergarten to grade three." (SLJ)

"When rotund, good-natured Officer Buckle visits school assemblies to read off his sensible safety tips, the children listen, bored and polite, dozing off one by one. But when the new police dog, Gloria, stands behind him, secretly miming the dire consequences of acting imprudently, the children suddenly become attentive, laughing uproariously and applauding loudly. . . . The deadpan humor of the text and slapstick wit of the illustrations make a terrific combination. Large, expressive line drawings illustrate the characters with finesse, and the Kool-Aid-bright washes add energy and pizzazz." Booklist

Rattigan, Jama Kim

Dumpling soup; illustrated by Lillian Hsu-Flanders. Little, Brown 1993 un il hardcover o.p. pa $6.99

Grades: K 1 2 3   E

1. Hawaii -- Fiction 2. New Year -- Fiction 3. Family life -- Fiction
ISBN 0-316-73445-4; 0-316-73047-5 pa

LC 91-42949

"Marisa, a seven-year-old Asian-American girl who lives in Hawaii, explains the traditions that exist in her family to celebrate the New Year. Her family . . . consists of people who are Japanese, Chinese, Korean, Hawaiian, and haole (Hawaiian for white person). . . . A glossary of English, Hawaiian, Japanese, and Korean words provides pronunciations and definitions for many of the possibly unfamiliar terms that weave in and out of the text. A thoroughly enjoyable celebration of family warmth and diverse traditions, illustrated with cheery watercolors." Horn Book

Rau, Dana Meachen, 1971-

Robot, Go Bot! by Dana Meachen Rau; illustrated by Wook Jin Jung. Random House Inc. 2013 32 p. col. ill. (paperback) $3.99; library) $12.99

Grades: PreK K 1   E

1. Robots -- Fiction 2. Cartoons and comics 3. Robots -- Cartoons and comics
ISBN 0375870830; 9780375870835; 9780375970832

LC 2012027691

In this book for beginning readers, "a girl assembles a robot and then treats it like a slave until it goes on strike. Having put the robot together from a jumble of loose parts, the budding engineer issues an increasingly peremptory series of rhymed orders--'Throw, Bot. / Row, Bot'--that turn from playful activities like chasing bubbles in the yard to tasks like hoe-

ing the garden, mowing the lawn and towing her around in a wagon." (Kirkus Reviews)

Rausch, Molly

My cold went on vacation; [by] Molly Rausch and [illustrated by] Nora Krug. G.P. Putnam's Sons 2011 un il $16.99

Grades: PreK K   E

1. Sick -- Fiction 2. Cold (Disease) -- Fiction
ISBN 978-0-399-25474-1; 0-399-25474-9

A little boy is curious about all the places his cold might go after it leaves him.

"Bold, whimsical art neatly complements the text, adding fantastical details and additional humor. . . . A perfect choice for readers with the sniffles and those who enjoy their stories with a twist." SLJ

Raven, Margot

Circle unbroken; the story of a basket and its people. [by] Margot Theis Raven; pictures by E. B. Lewis. Farrar, Straus and Giroux 2004 un il $16; pa $7.99

Grades: K 1 2 3   E

1. Baskets -- Fiction 2. Gullahs -- Fiction 3. African Americans -- Fiction
ISBN 0-374-31289-3; 0-312-37603-0 pa

LC 2002-24009

A grandmother tells the tale of Gullahs and their beautiful sweetgrass baskets that keep their African heritage alive

"Raven's text masterfully frames several hundred years of African-American history within the picture-book format. Lewis's double-page, watercolor images are poignant and perfectly matched to the text and mood." SLJ

★ **Night** boat to freedom; [by] Margot Theis Raven; pictures by E. B. Lewis. Farrar, Straus and Giroux 2006 un il $16; pa $6.99

Grades: 1 2 3 4   E

1. Quilts -- Fiction 2. Slavery -- Fiction 3. African Americans -- Fiction 4. Underground railroad -- Fiction
ISBN 978-0-374-31266-4; 0-374-31266-4; 978-0-312-55018-9 pa; 0-312-55018-9 pa

At the request of his fellow slave Granny Judith, Christmas John risks his life to take runaways across a river from Kentucky to Ohio.

"The older mentor is as tough as the young boy, and Lewis' beautiful, unframed double-page spreads depict the bond between them. . . . Words and pictures work perfectly together." Booklist

Rawlinson, Julia

★ **Fletcher** and the falling leaves; pictures by Tiphanie Beeke. Greenwillow Books 2006 un il $16.99; pa $6.99

Grades: PreK K 1 2   E

1. Foxes -- Fiction 2. Trees -- Fiction 3. Autumn -- Fiction 4. Leaves -- Fiction
ISBN 978-0-06-113401-2; 0-06-113401-5; 978-0-06-157397-2 pa; 0-06-157397-3 pa

LC 2005-34348

When his favorite tree begins to lose its leaves, Fletcher the fox worries that it is sick, but instead a magical sight is in store for him.

"This potent synthesis of art and prose conveys a child's first awareness of the changing seasons with reverence and wonder. . . . Beeke's resplendent watercolors work beautifully with the book's tone, content, layout, and design." SLJ

Other titles about Fletcher the fox are:

Fletcher and the springtime blossoms (2009)
Fletcher and the snowflake Christmas (2010)

Fletcher and the snowflake Christmas; pictures by Tiphanie Beeke. Greenwillow Books 2010 un il $16.99
Grades: PreK K 1 2   E

1. Snow -- Fiction 2. Foxes -- Fiction 3. Winter -- Fiction 4. Rabbits -- Fiction 5. Christmas -- Fiction

ISBN 978-0-06-199033-5; 0-06-199033-7

At Christmastime, Fletcher the fox and the other forest animals lay a trail of sticks to help Santa find the rabbits' new burrow.

This offers "beautifully distinctive illustrations skillfully integrated with the text. . . . The gentle, simple story is deftly told with just the right amount of suspense and a nice balance of dialogue and exposition. Beeke's glowing pastel illustrations in her irresistible style captivate readers with their unusual hues and textures." Kirkus

Ray, Jane

Ahmed and the feather girl. Frances Lincoln Children's 2010 un il $17.95
Grades: K 1 2 3   E

1. Magic -- Fiction 2. Circus -- Fiction 3. Orphans -- Fiction

ISBN 978-1-84507-988-8; 1-84507-988-4

Ahmed is a poor orphan who lives with a travelling circus and works for cruel Madame Saleem. His life is changed forever when he finds a beautiful egg in the forest and brings it back to the circus. From the egg hatches a little girl called Aurelia, and as she grows she sprouts soft feathers that turn into wings.

"The moving story, layered with magical moments, is truly expressed in Ray's triumphant art. With her signature mix of patterning, collage, and golden flourishes, the spreads have much to look at." Booklist

★ The **apple**-pip princess. Candlewick Press 2008 un il $16.99
Grades: PreK K 1 2   E

1. Fairy tales 2. Seeds -- Fiction 3. Apples -- Fiction 4. Princesses -- Fiction

ISBN 0-7636-3747-5; 978-0-7636-3747-7

LC 2007-34239

In a land that has stood barren, parched by drought and ravaged by frosts since the Queen's death, the King sets his three daughters the task of making the kingdom bloom again, and discovers that sometimes the smallest things can make the biggest difference.

"Ray's rich language and sure pacing create a winning read-aloud, but it's the shining collage artwork that really stands out. Mixing color photos into her typically fine, elaborately decorated illustrations, Ray creates dramatic scenes." Booklist

The **dollhouse** fairy. Candlewick Press 2009 un il $16.99
Grades: PreK K 1 2   E

1. Sick -- Fiction 2. Fairies -- Fiction 3. Dollhouses -- Fiction 4. Father-daughter relationship -- Fiction

ISBN 978-0-7636-4411-6; 0-7636-4411-0

LC 2009-18405

Worried about her father's trip to the hospital, Rosy goes to play with the special dollhouse he built for her and finds Thistle, a very messy and mischievous fairy who needs a place to stay while her injured wing mends.

"The story unfolds with subtlety and sensitivity to the emotional issues at its heart. The book's large format gives plenty of space for the vibrant mixed-media artwork." Booklist

Ray, Mary Lyn

★ **Christmas** farm; illustrated by Barry Root. Harcourt 2008 un il $17

Grades: K 1 2   E

1. Trees -- Fiction 2. Gardening -- Fiction

ISBN 978-0-15-216290-0; 0-15-216290-9

LC 2007-15216

Wilma decides to plant Christmas trees with the help of her young neighbor, Parker.

"Root's appealing watercolor-and-gouache illustrations invite inspection. . . . [This is] a story that lovingly depicts the hard work, cooperation, and patience necessary to grow crops." Booklist

Deer dancer; Mary Lyn Ray; illustrated by Lauren Stringer. Beach Lane Books 2014 40 p. col. ill. (hardcover) $17.99
Grades: PreK K 1 2   E

1. Deer -- Fiction 2. Dance -- Fiction

ISBN 144243421X; 9781442434219; 9781442434226

LC 2012042214

In this picture book, by Mary Lyn Ray and illustrated by Lauren Stringer, "a young ballerina finds dancing inspiration in the natural world. 'There's a place I go that's green and grass, a place I thought that no one knew - until the deer came.'" (Publisher's note)

"Poetic text and soft, sun-dappled acrylic illustrations capture the enchantment of their duet, the hidden clearing, and the girl's love of movement." Horn Book

Goodnight, good dog; written by Mary Lyn Ray and illustrated by Rebecca Malone. Houghton Mifflin Harcourt 2015 32 p. color illustrations (hardback) $16.99
Grades: PreK K 1 2   E

1. Dogs -- Fiction 2. Sleep -- Fiction 3. Bedtime -- Fiction

ISBN 054428612X; 9780544286122

LC 2014049687

In this children's book by Mary Lyn Ray, illustrated by Rebecca Malone, "it's time to say goodnight. But what if a dog isn't sleepy? Intimate and accessible, this young dog story captures how a reluctant pup warms to bedtime in a way that children will recognize immediately--and find as reassuring as their own beds." (Publisher's note)

"Created with acrylics, the artwork features firm black lines defining characters, objects, and settings, while subtly modulated colors shape the forms in a series of shadowy, nighttime scenes. In contrast, a few bright white pages feature just the dog and his bed. A satisfying picture book that's just right for bedtime reading." Booklist

★ **Stars**. Beach Lane Books 2011 un il $16.99
Grades: PreK K 1   E

1. Stars -- Fiction

ISBN 978-1-4424-2249-0; 1-4424-2249-1

LC 2010033253

"A poetic paean to stars both real and metaphorical brings the heavenly down to readers without robbing it of mystery. . . . Frazee excels at illustrating textual details in fresh ways, keeping young children engaged and curious. . . . Her pictures ebb and flow with the text, alternating charming spots of self-possessed, spirited youngsters with ink-black or gloriously blue, starry heavens inviting dreamy meditation." Kirkus

Rayner, Catherine

★ The **bear** who shared. Dial Books for Young Readers 201 un il $16.99
Grades: PreK K 1   E

1. Mice -- Fiction 2. Bears -- Fiction 3. Raccoons -- Fiction 4 Friendship -- Fiction

ISBN 978-0-8037-3576-7; 0-8037-3576-6

LC 2010012142

First published 2010 in the United Kingdom with title: Norris, the bear who shared

Norris the bear has been waiting patiently for the last ripe fruit to fall from the tree, and when it does he decides to share it with his two new friends, Tulip the raccoon and Violet the mouse.

"Rayner's quirky illustrations are the real star of the book; deceptively basic compositions with barely-there watercolor strokes that manage to look simultaneously haphazard and carefully applied. . . . The minimal text is accessible to the very youngest readers." Kirkus

★ **Ernest,** the moose who doesn't fit. Farrar, Straus and Giroux 2010 un il $16.99

Grades: PreK K 1   **E**

1. Size -- Fiction 2. Moose -- Fiction 3. Chipmunks -- Fiction

ISBN 978-0-374-32217-5; 0-374-32217-1

A rather large moose who cannot fit on the page teams up with his little chipmunk friend to find a solution. Final pages form a gatefold.

"The collage illustrations on a background of a softly hued green grid contrast the moose's grand dimensions with that of the tiny chipmunk in a gently humorous fashion. . . . The language is engaging and inventive." Kirkus

Solomon Crocodile. Farrar Straus & Giroux 2011 un il $15.99

Grades: PreK K 1   **E**

1. Play -- Fiction 2. Crocodiles -- Fiction 3. Friendship -- Fiction

ISBN 978-0-374-38064-9; 0-374-38064-3

LC 2010045855

Solomon Crocodile's rough play prevents him from making friends down by the river until a stranger comes stomping through the reeds!

"Rayner's lush illustrations reflect the tension between the puppyish croc and his staider neighbors. . . . Solomon practically vibrates energy. . . The well-paced story has just enough tension to draw in little troublemakers who will cheer for Solomon's eventual triumph." Horn Book

Reagan, Jean

How to babysit a grandma; by Jean Reagan; illustrated by Lee Wildish. Alfred A. Knopf 2014 32 p. (hardcover library binding) $19.99

Grades: PreK K 1 2   **E**

1. Humorous fiction 2. Babysitters -- Fiction 3. Grandmothers -- Fiction

ISBN 0385753853; 9780385753845; 9780385753852

LC 2013019509

In this children's book, written by Jean Reagan and illustrated by Lee Wildish, "a young girl heads over to her grandma's house for a sleepover babysitting session-with the child providing clear and humorous instructions to readers on how to care for a grandma. The to-do list contains many choices for Grandma to select from, including a walk to the park, reading, taking photos, playing dress-up, and adding sugary sprinkles to her meal items." (School Library Journal)

"In this companion to How to Babysit a Grandpa (2012), Reagan offers a fun, relatable story about the qualities of being a good babysitter, told from the perspective of a little girl who is spending quality time with her grandmother . . . Particularly clear in an evening scene as the girl and her grandma observe the stars in the purplish night sky, the mood of kindness, love, and togetherness comes through on every page." Booklist

How to babysit a grandpa; by Jean Reagan; illustrated by Lee Wildish. Alfred A. Knopf 2012 32 p. (hard cover) $16.99

Grades: PreK K 1 2   **E**

1. Humorous fiction 2. Babysitters -- Fiction 3. Grandfathers -- Fiction 4. Humorous stories

ISBN 0375867139; 9780375867132; 9780375967139

LC 2010052507

This children's book, written by Jean Reagan and illustrated by Lee Wildish, is "about a child spending time with his grandpa. Written in a how-to style, the narrator gives important tips for 'babysitting' a grandpa, including what to eat for snack, . . . what to do on a walk, . . . and how to play with a grandpa." (Publisher's note)

"A boy's tips for babysitting a grandpa include hiding when he arrives; fixing snacks such as "anything dipped in ketchup"; looking for "lizards, cool rocks, and dandelion puffs" on walks; and so on...The humorous illustrations include a snoozing grandpa with a meowing cat atop his head to wake him up. Youngsters will recognize some of the sayings they've heard from their own grandparents and will thoroughly enjoy the tongue-in-cheek role reversal." SLJ

Recorvits, Helen

★ **My** name is Yoon; pictures by Gabi Swiatkowska. Frances Foster Bks. 2002 un il $16

Grades: PreK K 1 2   **E**

1. Immigrants -- Fiction 2. Korean Americans -- Fiction

ISBN 0-374-35114-7

LC 00-51395

Disliking her name as written in English, Korean-born Yoon, or "shining wisdom," refers to herself as "cat," "bird," and "cupcake," as a way to feel more comfortable in her new school and new country

"Swiatkowska's stunningly spare, almost surrealistic paintings enhance the story's message. . . . A powerful and inspiring picture book." SLJ

Other titles about Yoon are:

Yoon and the Christmas mitten (2006)

Yoon and the jade bracelet (2008)

Reed, Lynn Rowe

Basil's birds. Marshall Cavendish Children 2010 un il $17.99

Grades: K 1 2   **E**

1. Birds -- Fiction 2. Janitors -- Fiction

ISBN 978-0-7614-5627-8; 0-7614-5627-9

LC 2009007071

While Basil the school janitor is napping, birds build a nest atop his head and when the eggs hatch, he becomes a proud 'dad' to the chicks.

"Brightly painted clay birds and photographs of the nest and worms are scanned into Reed's gouache illustrations. Her childlike paintings are done in flat spring colors, often showing faces in profile and bodies so loose jointed that they hardly seem earthbound." SLJ

Roscoe and the pelican rescue. Holiday House 2011 un il $14.95

Grades: PreK K 1   **E**

1. Pelicans -- Fiction 2. Vacations -- Fiction 3. Oil spills -- Fiction 4. Wildlife conservation -- Fiction 5. Gulf of Mexico oil spill, 2010 -- Fiction

ISBN 978-0-8234-2352-1; 0-8234-2352-2

LC 2010045005

The Gulf Coast oil spill turns Tony's summer vacation into an animal rescue mission.

"Reed's narrative is straightforward, ending happily. . . . Reed's illustrations are deliberately child-like. . . . This . . . should appeal to many young nature lovers." Booklist

Rees, Douglas

Jeannette Claus saves Christmas; illustrated by Olivier Latyk. Margaret K. McElderry Books 2010 un il $16.99

Grades: PreK K 1 2   **E**

1. Reindeer -- Fiction 2. Christmas -- Fiction 3. Santa Claus -- Fiction

ISBN 978-1-4169-2686-3; 1-4169-2686-0

LC 2008023021

When Santa falls sick on Christmas Eve, his feisty daughter Jeannette takes his place in the sleigh and saves the day, despite rebellious reindeer.

"The Photoshop-rendered artwork has a retro cut-paper feel and is filled with implausibly pastel animals and romantic big-city backdrops. With its unlikely antagonists and plucky heroine, this has the potential to be a fan favorite." Booklist

Reibstein, Mark

★ **Wabi** Sabi; art by Ed Young. Little, Brown 2008 un il $16.99

Grades: 2 3 4   E

1. Cats -- Fiction 2. Japan -- Fiction 3. Animals -- Fiction 4. Aesthetics -- Fiction

ISBN 978-0-316-11825-5; 0-316-11825-7

LC 2007-50895

Wabi Sabi, a cat living in the city of Kyoto, learns about the Japanese concept of beauty through simplicity as she asks various animals she meets about the meaning of her name.

"Young's beautiful collages have an almost 3D effect and perfectly complement the spiritual, lyrical text." SLJ

Reich, Susanna

★ **Minette's** feast; the delicious story of Julia Child and her cat. by Susanna Reich; illustrated by Amy Bates. Abrams Books for Young Readers 2012 40 p.

Grades: K 1 2 3   E

1. Cats -- Fiction 2. French cooking -- Fiction 3. Paris (France) -- Fiction 4. Picture books for children 5. France -- Fiction 6. Food habits -- Fiction

ISBN 1419701770; 9781419701771

LC 2011034275

This biographical picture book "introduces the iconic American chef Julia Child to a new audience of young readers through the story of her spirited cat, Minette, whom Julia adopted when living in Paris. While Julia is in the kitchen learning to master delicious French dishes, the only feast Minette is truly interested in is that of fresh mouse!" (Publisher's note)

Includes bibliographical references.

Reid, Alastair

Supposing; illustrated by Bob Gill. New York Review Books 2010 il (New York Review Children's Collection) $15.95

Grades: PreK K 1   E

1. Imagination -- Fiction

ISBN 978-1-59017-369-5; 1-59017-369-4

LC 2010016522

First published 1960 by Little, Brown

A child imagines many silly, impossible, and even naughty things and their possible consequences, from learning unusual languages to building a tiny boat and sailing around the world.

"The scenarios are (often surreal) springboards for readers' imaginations. . . . There's an understated but fitting whimsy in Gill's artwork." Publ Wkly

Reid, Barbara

★ **Perfect** snow. Albert Whitman & Company 2011 un il

Grades: K 1 2   E

1. School stories 2. Snow -- Fiction 3. Friendship -- Fiction

ISBN 0-8075-6492-3; 978-0-8075-6492-9

LC 2010045643

On the first snow of the season, Jim and Scott and their classmates build an enormous snowman fort.

"The boys' personality differences are marked throughout the book, but their rock-solid friendship is at the heart of the understated, but satisfying story. Reid's artwork takes two forms; large, colorful plasticine illustrations, and small ink drawings with sepia-toned, watercolor washes."

In either medium, the figures of children are expressive and pleasing." Booklist

★ **Picture** a tree; Barbara Reid. Albert Whitman 2013 32 p. (hardcover) $16.99

Grades: PreK K 1   E

1. Trees -- Fiction 2. Picture books for children

ISBN 0807565261; 9780807565261

LC 2012019530

In this children's picture book, "viewers are invited to think about how trees can be pictured: as a drawing on the sky, a skeleton, a tunnel, an ocean, a pirate ship, and more. . . . The book is not a guide to learning about trees but rather a lyrical request to explore them in our personal worlds." (School Library Journal)

"The book is not a guide to learning about trees but rather a lyrical request to explore them in our personal worlds... The vibrant pictures will draw in readers, while the text will encourage them to view the world in a different way." SLJ

Reid, Rob

Comin' down to storytime; pictures by Nadine Bernard Westcott. Upstart Books 2009 32p il $17.95

Grades: PreK K 1   E

1. Songs 2. Farm life -- Fiction 3. Libraries -- Fiction 4. Storytelling -- Fiction

ISBN 978-1-60213-039-5; 1-60213-039-6

"Building on the familiar song 'She'll Be Coming 'Round the Mountain,' Reid's animal version begins, 'We'll be comin' down to storytime when we come. Yee ha!' as all the farm animals run excitedly to the barn. It ends with 'We will check out lots of books when we leave. Bye now!' . . . Illustrations fit the rollicking mood perfectly. Westcott imbues each scene with plenty of color and lively action." SLJ

Reidy, Jean

All through my town; by Jean Reidy; illustrated by Leo Timmers. Bloomsbury Childrens 2013 32 p. col. ill. (hardcover) $14.99; (library) $15.89

Grades: PreK   E

1. Stories in rhyme 2. Neighborhoods -- Fiction 3. City and town life -- Fiction

ISBN 9781599907857; 9781619630291

LC 2012023304

Time (out) for monsters! by Jean Reidy; pictures by Robert Neubecker. Disney-Hyperion Books 2012 32 p.

Grades: K 1 2   E

1. Picture books for children 2. Monsters -- Fiction 3. Behavior -- Fiction 4. Imagination -- Fiction

ISBN 1423131274; 9781423131274

LC 2011013049

In this children's book, by Jean Reidy, illustrated by Robert Neubecker, a young boy is dissatisfied with the decor of his "time-out corner. 'Mom says it's fine, but I know better. I spend a LOT of time there.' . . So he conjures up a world of excitement that includes a killer view, a fire brigade, a dump truck full of ice cream, and some kingly accoutrements." (Publishers Weekly)

Too purpley! illustrated by Genevieve Leloup. Bloomsbury Children's Books 2010 un il $11.99; lib bdg $12.89

Grades: PreK K 1 2   E

1. Stories in rhyme 2. Clothing and dress -- Fiction

ISBN 978-1-59990-307-1; 1-59990-307-5; 978-1-59990-437-5 lib bdg; 1-59990-437-3 lib bdg

LC 2009004741

A young girl rejects many outfits before finding the perfect clothes o wear

"This fun book has lots of descriptive words that tickle the ear, great colors and patterns, and a charming protagonist." SLJ

Reinhardt, Jennifer Black

Blue Ethel; written and illustrated by Jennifer Black Reinhardt. Margaret Ferguson Books/Farrar, Straus & Giroux 2017 40 p. color illustrations (hardback) $17.99

Grades: PreK K 1   E

1. Cats -- Fiction 2. Change -- Fiction 3. Self-confidence -- Fiction
ISBN 9780374303822

LC 2016035845

In this picture book, written and illustrated by Jennifer Black Reinhardt, "Ethel is old, she is fat, she is black, and she is white. She is also a cat who is very set in her ways...until the day she turns blue! . . . [The story] show[s] readers that being different can be a good thing." Publisher's note)

Reiser, Lynn

★ **Tortillas** and lullabies. Tortillas y cancioncitas; pictures by Corazones Valientes; coordinated and translated by Rebecca Hart. Greenwillow Bks. 1998 40p il $16.99; pa $6.99

Grades: PreK K 1 2   E

1. Grandmothers -- Fiction 2. Bilingual books -- English-Spanish
3. Mother-daughter relationship -- Fiction
ISBN 0-688-14628-7; 0-06-089185-8 pa

LC 97-7096

Companion volume to Cherry pies and lullabies

In this "picture book, four everyday activities are depicted—making tortillas, gathering flowers, washing clothes, and singing a lullaby—as they are repeated by the women of a family over the last four generations. . . . Six Costa Rican women worked together to produce the striking acrylic folk-art paintings. With deeply saturated, glowing tones and a decidedly Central American style, the pictures enhance and extend the lyrical narrative, which is printed in English and in Spanish." SLJ

Rennert, Laura Joy

Buying, training & caring for your dinosaur; written by Laura Joy Rennert; pictures by Marc Brown. Alfred A. Knopf 2009 un il $16.99; lib bdg $19.99

Grades: PreK K 1 2   E

1. Pets -- Fiction 2. Dinosaurs -- Fiction
ISBN 978-0-375-83679-4; 0-375-83679-9; 978-0-375-93679-1 lib bdg; 0-375-93679-3 lib bdg

LC 2008-50680

Includes instructions for choosing and caring for a pet dinosaur

"This features funny, colorful illustrations. . . . Youngsters will quickly become absorbed in this enjoyable mix of facts, fantasy, and fossils." Booklist

Rex, Adam

Pssst! Harcourt 2007 un il $16

Grades: PreK K 1 2   E

1. Zoos -- Fiction 2. Animals -- Fiction
ISBN 978-0-15-205817-3; 0-15-205817-6

LC 2006-24551

"A zoo-going girl talks to the animals, but the novelty wears off when the pushy beasts send her on errands. . . . Rex packs increasingly crisp conversations into tight six-panel comics, relaxing into airy spreads as the girl meanders along zoo paths. . . . A very funny excursion." Publ Wkly

★ **School's** first day of school; Adam Rex, Christian Robinson. Roaring Brook Press 2016 40 p. (hardback) $17.99

Grades: PreK K 1 2   E

1. School stories -- Fiction 2. Schools -- Fiction 3. Buildings -- Fiction 4. School buildings -- Fiction 5. First day of school -- Fiction
ISBN 9781596439641

LC 2015034414

In this book, by Adam Rex and Christian Robinson, "it's the first day of school at Frederick Douglass Elementary and everyone's just a little bit nervous, especially the school itself. What will the children do once they come? Will they like the school? Will they be nice to him? The school has a rough start, but as the day goes on, he soon recovers when he sees that he's not the only one going through first-day jitters." (Publisher's note)

"Using his signature, simple style, Robinson alternates scenes of the building and its interiors with shots that show the boisterously diverse kids' first day. A unique point of view makes this school book stand out." Kirkus

Rex, Michael

Goodnight goon; a petrifying parody. [by] Michael Rex. G.P. Putnam's Sons 2008 un il $14.99

Grades: K 1 2 3   E

1. Stories in rhyme 2. Bedtime -- Fiction 3. Monsters -- Fiction
ISBN 0-399-24534-0; 978-0-399-24534-3

LC 2007-16585

A young monster says goodnight to the other monsters in his bedroom. "Ages five to eight." (Bull Cent Child Books)

"This book is a hilarious adaptation of the classic bedtime story, Goodnight Moon. . . . This is a delightfully funny and witty story containing adorable illustrations with tons of details. . . . Author and illustrator Michael Rex has created a wonderful page-by-page companion to the original." Libr Media Connect

Truck Duck; [by] Michael Rex. G.P. Putnam's Sons 2004 un il hardcover o.p. bd bk $7.99

Grades: PreK K 1 2   E

1. Stories in rhyme 2. Animals -- Fiction 3. Vehicles -- Fiction
ISBN 0-399-24009-8; 0-399-25092-1 bd bk

LC 2003-707

A variety of animals drive vehicles whose names rhyme with their own

"This is the stuff of toddlers' play, with vrooming action and small characters in charge. The sounds of the words add to the fun, and to little ones' vocabularies. The vehicles are big, bright, and clear." Booklist

A companion to this title is:
Dunk skunk (2005)

Rey, H. A.

★ **Curious** George. Houghton Mifflin 1941 un il $16; pa $6.95

Grades: PreK K 1   E

1. Monkeys -- Fiction
ISBN 0-395-15993-8; 0-395-15023-X pa

Colored picture book, with simple text, describing the adventures of a curious small monkey, and the difficulties he had in getting used to city life, before he went to live in the zoo

"The bright lithographs in red, yellow, and blue, are gay and lighthearted, following the story closely with the same speed and animated humour." Ont Libr Rev

Other titles about Curious George are:
Curious George flies a kite (1958)
Curious George gets a medal (1957)
Curious George goes to the hospital (1966)

Curious George learns the alphabet (1963)
Curious George rides a bike (1952)
Curious George takes a job (1947)

Curious George: Cecily G. and the 9 monkeys; written and illustrated by H. A. Rey; afterword by Louise Borden. Houghton Mifflin Company 2007 un il $16; pa $6.99
Grades: PreK K 1   E
1. Monkeys -- Fiction 2. Giraffes -- Fiction
ISBN 978-0-618-80066-7; 0-618-80066-2; 978-0-618-99794-7 pa; 0-618-99794-6 pa
                                                                                LC 2006-38698
First published 1942
A lonely giraffe teams up with the nine playful monkeys.
"This edition of the first story to feature Curious George includes a new afterword." Horn Book Guide

Reynolds, Aaron
★ **Back** of the bus; illustrated by Floyd Cooper. Philomel Books 2010 un il $16.99
Grades: K 1 2 3   E
1. Civil rights activists 2. Race relations -- Fiction 3. African Americans -- Fiction 4. African Americans -- Civil rights -- Fiction
ISBN 978-0-399-25091-0; 0-399-25091-3
                                                                                LC 2008018109
From the back of the bus, an African American child watches the arrest of Rosa Parks.
Reynolds's "lyrical yet forceful text conveys the narrator's apprehension and Park's calm resolve. . . . Cooper's . . . filmy oil paintings are characterized by a fine mistlike texture, which results in warm, lifelike portraits that convincingly evoke the era, the intense emotional pitch of this incident, and the everyday heroism it embodied." Publ Wkly

Carnivores; by Aaron Reynolds; illustrated by Dan Santat. Chronicle Books 2012 40 p. $16.99
Grades: 1 2 3   E
1. Picture books for children 2. Carnivorous animals -- Fiction 3. Clubs -- Fiction 4. Animals -- Fiction 5. Carnivores -- Fiction 6. Food chains (Ecology) -- Fiction
ISBN 0811866904; 9780811866903
                                                                                LC 2008035029
In this children's book, three carnivores including "a lion . . . , great white shark . . . and timber wolf . . . take up vegetarianism in an effort to fit in and then try donning disguises. When neither strategy butters the biscuit, they turn to a great horned owl as a carnivore consultant," who tells them to own their carnivore status. (Kirkus Reviews)

★ **Creepy** carrots! words Aaron Reynolds; pictures Peter Brown. Simon & Schuster Books for Young Readers 2012 40 p. (hardcover : alk. paper) $16.99
Grades: PreK K 1 2   E
1. Carrots -- Fiction 2. Rabbits -- Fiction 3. Picture books for children 4. Humorous stories
ISBN 1442402970; 9781442402973
                                                                                LC 2010035099
Odyssey Honor Recording (2014)
Caldecott Honor Book (2013)
In this book, "Jasper Rabbit [didn't] think twice about plundering the carrots of Crackenhopper Field 'until they started following him.' Jasper glimpses three jack-o-lantern-jawed carrots behind him in the bathroom mirror (when he turns around it's just a washcloth, shampoo bottle, and rubber duck--or is it?), and he yells for his parents when a carrot shadow looms on his bedroom wall." (Publishers Weekly)

Here comes Destructosaurus! by Aaron Reynolds; illustrated by Jeremy Tankard. Chronicle Books 2014 32 p. (alk. paper) $16.99
Grades: PreK K   E
1. Orderliness 2. Monsters -- Fiction 3. Dinosaurs -- Fiction 4. Children -- Conduct of life -- Fiction 5. Conduct of life -- Fiction
ISBN 145212454X; 9781452124544
                                                                                LC 2013015843
In this children's book, written by Aaron Reynolds and illustrated by Jeremy Tankard, "a baby dinosaur emerges from the sea and goes on a rampage across New York City, tracking seaweed and dead fish all over the tourists and setting fire to every ship in the harbor. His tail the size of a small planet, Destructosaurus is chastised by the narrator for his lack of self-control and for his sassy attitude, much like a mother would speak to a wild child." (School Library Journal)
"Tankard's cartoon-style art is the perfect foil for Reynolds' seemingly rational text. His humorous illustrations feature boldly outlined characters, vivid colors, and rich backgrounds. The compositions are often cluttered (apropos to the mayhem depicted) but Destructosaurus (and the child's perspective) remain clear focal points." Booklist

Metal man; illustrated by Paul Hoppe. Charlesbridge 2008 un il lib bdg $15.95; pa $7.95
Grades: PreK K 1 2   E
1. Metalwork -- Fiction 2. Sculpture -- Fiction 3. African Americans -- Fiction
ISBN 978-1-58089-150-9 lib bdg; 1-58089-150-0 lib bdg; 978-1-58089-151-6 pa; 1-58089-151-9 pa
                                                                                LC 2007-17187
One hot summer day, a man who makes sculpture out of junk helps a boy create what he sees in his mind's eye.
"Beautifully understated, the story is about the capacity of art to empower the artist and to affect how others see the world. The poetic text is visceral. . . . The cartoon illustrations, in rusty browns and shiny blues depict the metal man as tall, strong, gentle, and wise, a larger-than-life hero. . . . A wonderful example of sensory writing and colloquial storytelling." SLJ

Nerdy Birdy; by Aaron Reynolds; illustrated by Matt Davies. Roaring Brook Press 2015 40 p. color illustrations (hardback) $16.99
Grades: PreK K 1 2   E
1. Birds -- Fiction 2. Friendship -- Fiction
ISBN 1626721270; 9781626721272
                                                                                LC 2014044216
In this children's story, by Aaron Reynolds and illustrated by Matt Davies, "Nerdy Birdy likes reading, video games, and reading about video games, which immediately disqualifies him for membership in the cool crowd. . . . When he's at his lowest point, Nerdy Birdy meets a flock just like him. He has friends and discovers that there are far more nerdy birdies than cool birdies in the sky." (Publisher's note)
"The author of Creepy Carrots! (2012) takes a humorous look at avian friendships. The cool birdies (with their abs of steel, superior vision, and sculpted chest muscles) will have nothing to do with bespectacled, tiny-winged, allergic Nerdy Birdy, so he joins the other nerdy birds, who spend their time reading and playing World of Wormcraft. . . . Davies' detailed and slightly satirical illustrations reflect the influence of his years as an editorial cartoonist, especially in the spreads depicting the cool birdies demonstrating their impressive (labeled) attributes. This will work best as a one-on-one so that readers have a chance to fully absorb the illustrative details." Booklist

Superhero School; illustrated by Andy Rash. Bloomsbury Children's Books 2009 un il $16.99; lib bdg $17.89
Grades: K 1 2 3 4   E
1. School stories 2. Mathematics -- Fiction 3. Superheroes -

Fiction
ISBN 978-1-59990-166-4; 1-59990-166-8; 978-1-59990-346-0
lib bdg; 1-59990-346-6 lib bdg

LC 2008031374

When Leonard starts attending Superhero School he is disappointed to find that all they learn is math, but when the ice zombies strike, Leonard and his classmates put their newly-acquired knowledge to good use

"Rash's illustrations in digital collage of gouache and Sharpies create his trademark cartoons that pulsate with energy and engage readers. Reynolds creatively blends the use of math skills in word-problem superhero settings that are playful, smart, and positive." SLJ

Reynolds, Peter
The **dot**; [by] Peter H. Reynolds. Candlewick Press 2003 un il $14
Grades: PreK K 1 2   E
1. School stories 2. Drawing -- Fiction
ISBN 0-7636-1961-2

LC 2002-041113

Vashti believes that she cannot draw, but her art teacher's encouragement leads her to change her mind

"In this engaging, inspiring tale, Reynolds . . . demonstrates the power of a little encouragement. . . . Rendered in watercolor, ink and tea, Reynolds's spare, wispy illustrations exude a fresh, childlike quality pleasingly in sync with his hand-lettered text." Publ Wkly

Happy dreamer; by Peter H. Reynolds. Orchard Books, an imprint of Scholastic Inc. 2017 32 p. color illustrations (hardcover : alk. paper) $17.99
Grades: PreK K 1 2   E
1. Imagination -- Fiction 2. Individuality -- Fiction 3. Creative ability -- Fiction 4. Imagination -- Fiction
ISBN 9780545865012

LC 2016016853

This children's book, by Peter H. Reynolds, "celebrates all those moments in between when the mind and spirit soar and we are free to become our own true dreamer maximus! In Peter's signature voice and style, this empowering picture book reminds children of how much their dreams matter, and while life will have ups and downs, he enlists readers to stay true to who they are, to tap into their most creative inner selves, and to never ever forget to dream big!" (Publisher's note)

"A sweet gift to praise spirited individuality, this choice encourages readers to dream big. Let those sparkles fly!" Kirkus

★ **I'm** here; [by] Peter H. Reynolds. Atheneum Books for Young Readers 2011 il $15.99
Grades: PreK K 1 2   E
1. Parks -- Fiction 2. Friendship -- Fiction
ISBN 978-1-4169-9649-1; 1-4169-9649-4

LC 2010038962

In a crowded park, a boy makes an airplane out of a piece of paper carried to him by a gentle breeze, sends it on its way, and watches a new friend bring it back to him.

"Though back matter explains that the book was written 'to help us all reach out, embrace, and appreciate children in the autism spectrum,' the pared-down prose and artwork, painted in Reynolds's typical loose style, are open to multiple interpretations and may facilitate conversations about reaching out to others who are different—and alone—for many reasons." Publ Wkly

Ish; [by] Peter H. Reynolds. Candlewick Press 2004 un il $14

Grades: PreK K 1 2 3   E
1. Drawing -- Fiction 2. Siblings -- Fiction
ISBN 0-7636-2344-X

LC 2003-66196

Ramon loses confidence in his ability to draw, but his sister gives him a new perspective on things

"The overriding theme about creativity versus exactitude will resonate with many. The line-and-color artwork is simple, but it has great emotion and warmth." Booklist

Rose's garden; [by] Peter H. Reynolds. Candlewick Press 2009 un il $15.99
Grades: K 1 2 3   E
1. Flowers -- Fiction 2. Gardens -- Fiction
ISBN 978-0-7636-4641-7; 0-7636-4641-5

LC 2009-24175

Rose finds a neglected patch of earth in the middle of a bustling city where she can plant the flower seeds collected from her travels in her magical teapot

"This inspiring fable will capture the hearts and imaginations of readers and show them that anything is possible. . . . Reynolds's outstanding illustrations done in watercolor and ink begin in shades of gray and then explode with color and joy as the garden evolves and people come to enjoy it." SLJ

Rice, Eve
Sam who never forgets. Greenwillow Bks. 1977 un il hardcover o.p. pa $5.99
Grades: PreK K   E
1. Zoos -- Fiction 2. Animals -- Fiction
ISBN 0-688-07335-2 pa

LC 76-30370

"A simple, unpretentious story with child appeal that lies in the naive, straightforward telling and elemental emotional interactions of the characters. . . . Rice has forsaken her pen drawings for bright, unlined colored shapes. The figures are pleasantly stylized, the scenes evenly composed." Booklist

Richards, Beah
★ **Keep** climbing, girls; by Beah E. Richards; illustrated by R. Gregory Christie; introduction by LisaGay Hamilton. Simon & Schuster Books for Young Readers 2006 un il $15.95
Grades: PreK K 1 2   E
1. Girls -- Poetry
ISBN 1-4169-0264-3

LC 2004-29153

"In this picture-book rendition of Richards's 1951 poem of the same name, girls are urged to 'keep climbing' no matter what obstacles get in the way. Bold gouache illustrations create a beguiling green-and-gold landscape with an irresistible tree and a determined little girl who climbs it higher and higher with every page turn." SLJ

Richards, Chuck
Critter sitter; [by] Chuck Richards. Walker & Company 2008 un il $16.99; lib bdg $17.89
Grades: 1 2 3 4   E
1. Pets -- Fiction
ISBN 978-0-8027-9595-3; 0-8027-9595-1; 978-0-8027-9596-0 lib bdg; 0-8027-9596-X lib bdg

LC 2008004314

When the Mahoney family hires Henry the Critter Sitter to watch their dog, cat, bird, fish, frog, and snake, he thinks he is up for the challenge since creature control is his game, but the pets have a different idea.

"The storytelling is well paced and amusing, but the artwork is the real grabber here. Created with colored-pencil and watercolor, the illustrations cleverly mix realism with humorous exaggeration." SLJ

Richards, Keith, 1943-

Gus & me; the story of my granddad and my first guitar. Keith Richards, Theodora Richards. Little, Brown & Co. 2014 32 p. color illustrations (hardcover) $18

Grades: PreK K 1 2 3 4   E

1. Musicians 2. Grandfathers 3. Musical instruments 4. Grandparent and child

ISBN 031632065X; 9780316281911; 9780316320634; 9780316320658

LC 2014936772

This children's book is a "look into the childhood of the legendary Keith Richards through this poignant and inspiring story that is lovingly illustrated with Theodora Richards's exquisite pen-and-ink collages. This unique autobiographical picture book honors the special bond between a grandfather and grandson and celebrates the artistic talents of the Richards family." (Publisher's note)

"Rolling Stones guitarist Keith Richards has penned a poignant picture book depicting his close relationship with his grandfather Gus... Loose black-and-white pen-and-ink illustrations, done by Keith's daughter, affectionately depict the title characters, as well as the various objects in their orbit (musical instruments, Big Ben, tea kettles, a double-decker bus), while backgrounds provide rich washes of purples, blues, yellows, and green, emphasizing the beauty and the sense of magic of the music. A gentle story celebrating the importance of family." SLJ

Richardson, Justin

Christian, the hugging lion; [by] Justin Richardson and Peter Parnell; illustrated by Amy Bates. Simon & Schuster Books for Young Readers 2010 un il $16.99

Grades: PreK K 1 2   E

1. Kenya -- Fiction 2. Lions -- Fiction 3. London (England) -- Fiction

ISBN 978-1-4169-8662-1; 1-4169-8662-6

LC 2009002297

When Ace and John find a lion cub for sale at Harrods department store, they buy him, name him Christian, and the three live happily for a year in a London apartment, but eventually Christian grows too big and they must let him go to live the life of a wild cat. Based on a true story; includes an author's note.

"Bates captures the friendship and love between Christian, Ace and John when they go visit him years later. Justin Richardson and Peter Parnell write this story like a fairy tale—whimsical and entertaining." Libr Media Connect

Richardson, Nan

The **pearl**; written by Nan Richardson; illustrations by Alexandra Young. Umbrage Editions, Inc. 2011 il $17

Grades: K 1 2   E

1. Actors 2. Opera -- Fiction 3. Russia -- Fiction 4. Singers -- Fiction

ISBN 978-1-884167-24-9; 1-884167-24-1

Tells the love story of Nicolas Cheremeteff, a wealthy courtier and Praskovia, a serf girl in eighteenth-century Russia.

"Richly illustrated in bold pen-and-ink and watercolor, the story is brought to life in sumptuous detail and precisely placed splashes of color. Readers will relish this unique, Russian Cinderella tale." SLJ

Ries, Lori

★ **Aggie** and Ben; three stories. illustrated by Frank W. Dormer. Charlesbridge 2006 48p il lib bdg $12.95; pa $5.95

Grades: K 1 2   E

1. Dogs -- Fiction

ISBN 978-1-57091-549-9 lib bdg; 1-57091-594-6 lib bdg; 978-1-57091-649-6 pa; 1-57091-649-7 pa

LC 2005-28702

After choosing a new dog, Ben describes what the pet Aggie can do and should not do around the house

"Funky but tender, Dormer's pen-and-ink cartoons with watercolor washes add depth to the simple story and provide that perfect illustration-to-text match that one seeks in successful easy readers." SLJ

Other titles about Aggie and Ben are:

Good dog, Aggie (2009)

Aggie the brave (2010)

Aggie gets lost (2011)

Aggie gets lost; illustrated by Frank Dormer. Charlesbridge 2011 il $12.95

Grades: K 1 2   E

1. Dogs -- Fiction 2. Blind -- Fiction 3. Lost and found possessions -- Fiction

ISBN 978-1-570-91633-5; 1-570-91633-0

LC 2010007533

Ben and Aggie are playing in the park when she chases a ball and does not return, but after looking for her and worrying about her, Ben speaks with his blind friend, Mr. Thomas, who suggests a different approach.

"Art in pen, ink and watercolor shows the characters and their emotions clearly in a faux childlike drawing style. . . . Anyone who has worried about the loss of a special friend will understand the feelings involved with great sympathy and empathy." Kirkus

Riggs, Shannon

Not in Room 204; illustrated by Jaime Zollars. Albert Whitman 2007 un il $15.95

Grades: K 1 2 3   E

1. School stories 2. Child sexual abuse -- Fiction

ISBN 978-0-8075-5764-8

LC 2006023402

"Quiet Regina feels comfortable in her classroom, where Mrs. Salvador runs a tight ship and insists on hard work and fair play. When the teacher starts the annual Stranger Danger unit, she departs from the usual script by saying that most often an adult who touches a child inappropriately is not a stranger but someone known to the child. . . . The next morning, Regina arrives early at Room 204 to confide her secret, which involves her father. . . . This picture book's strength is in the forthrightness of its message and the sensitivity of its presentation. . . The text and digitally enhanced artwork work together well to express the book's message smoothly. . . . This helpful picture book will raise children's awareness of sexual abuse without raising anxiety." Booklist

Riley, Linnea Asplind

Mouse mess; [by] Linnea Riley. Blue Sky Press (NY) 1997 un il $16.95

Grades: PreK K 1   E

1. Stories in rhyme 2. Food -- Fiction 3. Mice -- Fiction

ISBN 0-590-10048-3

LC 96-49499

A hungry mouse leaves a huge mess when it goes in search of a snack

"Cut-paper collages, set against black backgrounds, depict a chubby-cheeked mouse spilling, cutting, and eating a variety of colorful foods . . . . The rhyming text, filled with crunching and munching sounds, is rhythmic and fun to read aloud." SLJ

Rim, Sujean

Birdie's big-girl dress. Little, Brown 2011 il $16.99

Grades: PreK K **E**

1. Parties -- Fiction 2. Birthdays -- Fiction 3. Clothing and dress -- Fiction

ISBN 978-0-316-13287-9; 0-316-13287-X

LC 2010049435

Birdie's excitement over her approaching birthday party fades when she finds that her favorite party dress is too small, and nothing at her mother's favorite boutique is quite right.

"As Birdie shimmies into each potentially restrictive outfit, Rim's illustrations capture each halfhearted shrug and sucked-in breath. Collage and watercolor accents lend a sensory feel to chromatic, textured design . . . [and] canine companion Monster remains a supportive secondary choice, dressed to the nines in his top hat to rave reviews." Kirkus

Birdie's big-girl hair; Sujean Rim. Little, Brown and Co. 2013 40 p. color illustrations $17

Grades: PreK K **E**

1. Hair -- Fiction 2. Fashion -- Fiction 3. Identity -- Fiction 4. Hairstyles -- Fiction 5. Individuality -- Fiction 6. Mothers and daughters -- Fiction

ISBN 0316227919; 9780316227919

LC 2012039921

In this book, by Sujean Rim, "It's time for Birdie's very first haircut, and the miniature fashionista yearns for more than just a simple trim. . . . She looks through pictures . . . to find the best new look, and she and Mommy head to the salon. Her haircut looks fantastic, but begins to sag later on at the playground... because Birdie doesn't just love fashion - she likes to run and jump and play! . . . Mommy reminds her that the most perfect Birdie look is the one that lets her be herself." (Publisher's note)

"Birdie needs a haircut and wants a new look. She spends most of the book agonizing about what look to try; the adorable mixed-media art has Birdie with Betty Draper, Holly Golightly, Princess Leia, and Farrah Fawcett dos. Though this third Birdie vehicle will be relatable and appealing to a fashionista readership, the "be yourself" message feels rather obligatory." Horn Book

Birdie's big-girl shoes. Little, Brown Books for Young Readers 2009 un il $15.99

Grades: PreK K **E**

1. Play -- Fiction 2. Shoes -- Fiction 3. Mother-daughter relationship -- Fiction

ISBN 978-0-316-04470-7; 0-316-04470-9

LC 2008-43799

Five-year-old Birdie loves her mother's shoes, but when she is finally granted permission to wear some for a little while, she discovers that her 'barefoot shoes' are best of all

"The bold, stylized watercolor and collage illustrations, paired with spare, simple text, are set against ample white space and burst with bright, attractive textile patterns. A light confection for the preschool dress-up set." SLJ

Other titles in this series are:

Birdie's big-girl dress (2011)

Birdie plays dress-up (2012)

Birdie's big-girl hair (2014)

Birdie's first day of school (2015)

Rinck, Maranke

I feel a foot! [by] Maranke Rinck & Martijn van der Linden. Lemniscaat 2008 un il $16.95

Grades: PreK K 1 **E**

1. Animals -- Fiction 2. Imagination -- Fiction

ISBN 978-1-59078-638-3; 1-59078-638-6

LC 2008000917

Five animal friends, awakened by a strange noise, discover a creature in the dark that seems to be a giant-sized version of each of them.

"With simple wording, Rinck injects personality into each animal and van der Linden's images interact well with the text. His stark black backgrounds spotlight expressively imagined animals that appear in psychedelic colors and patterns reminiscent of a kaleidoscope." SLJ

Ringgold, Faith

★ **Tar** Beach. Crown 1991 un il $18; lib bdg $18.99; pa $6.99

Grades: PreK K 1 2 **E**

1. Dreams -- Fiction 2. African Americans -- Fiction 3. Harlem (New York, N.Y.) -- Fiction

ISBN 0-517-58030-6; 0-517-58031-4 lib bdg; 0-517-88544-1 pa

LC 90-40410

A Caldecott Medal honor book, 1992

Eight-year-old Cassie dreams of flying above her Harlem home, claiming all she sees for herself and her family. Based on the author's quilt painting of the same name

"Part autobiographical, part fictional, this allegorical tale sparkles with symbolic and historical references central to African-American culture. The spectacular artwork, a combination of primitive naive figures in a flattened perspective against a boldly patterned cityscape, resonates with color and texture." Horn Book

Another title about Cassie is:

Cassie's word quilt (2002)

Ringtved, Glenn

★ **Cry,** Heart, but Never Break; Glenn Ringtved; illustrations by Charlotte Pardi; translated from the Danish by Robert Moulthrop. Enchanted Lion Books 2016 32 p. illustrations hbk $16.95

Grades: PreK K 1 2 **E**

1. Death -- Fiction 2. Grief -- Fiction 3. Children and death -- Fiction

ISBN 1592701876; 9781592701872

LC 2015044306

Originally published in Denmark in 2001 as Græd Blot Hjerte

Mildred L. Batchelder Award (2017)

"Aware their grandmother is gravely ill, four siblings make a pact to keep death from taking her away. But Death does arrive all the same, as it must. He comes gently, naturally. And he comes with enough time to share a story with the children that helps them to realize the value of loss to life and the importance of being able to say goodbye." (Publisher's note)

"Pardi creates a cozy, lived-in ambiance in her pencil and watercolor art; Death's almost grandfatherly persona suggests that there is a time to go gently into that good night." Pub Wkly

Rinker, Sherri Duskey

★ **Goodnight,** goodnight, construction site; illustrated by Tom Lichtenheld. Chronicle Books 2011 un il $16.99

Grades: PreK K 1 **E**

1. Stories in rhyme 2. Trucks -- Fiction 3. Bedtime -- Fiction 4. Construction equipment -- Fiction

ISBN 0-8118-7782-5; 978-0-8118-7782-4

LC 2010025008

At sunset, when their work is done for the day, a crane truck, a cement mixer, and other pieces of construction equipment make their way to their resting places and go to sleep.

"Lichtenheld's detailed and textured illustrations, rendered in wax oil pastels on vellum paper, perfectly complement the fun, rhyming text, cleverly personifying each truck with expressive eyes and amusing details." SLJ

Mighty, mighty construction site; Sherri Duskey Rinker and Tom Lichtenheld. Chronicle Books LLC 2017 40 p. color illustrations (ebook) $15.59; (alk. paper) $16.99
Grades: PreK K 1   **E**
1. Stories in rhyme 2. Trucks -- Fiction 3. Cooperativeness -- Fiction 4. Construction equipment -- Fiction
ISBN 9781452157719; 9781452152165

LC 2016012070

In this book, by Sherri Duskey Rinker, illustrated by Tom Lichtenheld, "all of our favorite trucks are back on the construction site—this time with a focus on team-building, friendship, and working together to make a big task seem small! Down in the big construction site, the crew faces their biggest job yet, and will need the help of new construction friends to get it done. Working as a team, there's nothing they can't do!" (Publisher's note)

"Rinker and Lichtenheld are an equally solid team, and their bouncy rhymes and earth-toned images of cheerfully anthropomorphic vehicles keep the tone upbeat and amicable. Another job well done." Pub Wkly

★ **Steam** train, dream train; by Sherri Duskey Rinker; illustrated by Tom Lichtenheld. Chronicle Books 2013 40 p. ill. (hardcover) $16.99
Grades: PreK K 1   **E**
1. Stories in rhyme 2. Animals -- Fiction 3. Railroad trains -- Fiction
ISBN 1452109206; 9781452109206

LC 2012030942

In this children's story, by Sherri Duskey Rinker, illustrated by Tom Lichtenheld, "the dream train pulls into the station, and one by one the train cars are loaded: polar bears pack the reefer car with ice cream, elephants fill the tanker cars with paints, tortoises stock the auto rack with race cars, bouncy kangaroos stuff the hopper car with balls." (Publisher's note)

"The strength of this book is in the striking spreads in wax oil pastel. ... The beginning and end of the book are filled with expressive and enjoyable railroad sounds, yet the rhyming text loses a bit of steam in the middle, describing but not always enhancing the activity depicted in the illustrations. Still, this is a book that will...be embraced as a nighttime standard, particularly among train lovers everywhere." SLJ

Riphagen, Loes
Animals home alone. Seven Footer Press 2011 il $15.95
Grades: PreK K 1   **E**
1. Stories without words 2. Animals -- Fiction
ISBN 1-93473455-1; 978-193473455-1

This picture book introduces readers to fifteen animals who begin to act in unusual ways when the humans are away,. In wordless pages, each animal finds a unique activity or bit of mischief to get into. At the book's conclusion, readers are asked questions about what the animals have done.

"This wordless picture book is a playful romp. . . . The little dramas will have children (and adults) flipping back and forth for more whimsical and hilarious details." SLJ

Ritchie, Alison
Duck says don't! Alison Ritchie; [illustrated by] Hannah George. Good Books 2012 26 p. col. ill. (hardcover : alk. paper) $16.99
Grades: K 1 2   **E**
1. Picture books for children 2. Animals 3. Friendship -- Fiction 4. Ducks -- Fiction 5. Geese -- Fiction 6. Ponds -- Fiction 7. Bossiness -- Fiction 8. Pond animals -- Fiction
ISBN 9781561487455; 1561487457

LC 2011031770

Author Alison Ritchie presents a children's picture book. "Goose leaves Duck in charge when she leaves her pond, with unhappy results. Power goes immediately to Duck's head. First, he stops the dragonflies from racing, although they point out that flying is what they do . . . Soon he forbids the kingfishers from fishing and the frogs from diving, and . . . signs appear forbidding, well, everything. Then Duck realizes all his friends have gone . . . and [he] welcomes everyone back to do what they do." (Kirkus)

Ritz, Karen
Windows with birds; written and illustrated by Karen Ritz. Boyds Mills Press 2010 un il $16.95
Grades: PreK K 1 2   **E**
1. Cats -- Fiction 2. Moving -- Fiction
ISBN 978-1-59078-656-7; 1-59078-656-4

LC 2009-19504

"This delicate and understated book tells a simple story about a striped cat with green eyes that loves a boy and a house. All of the feline's comforts are in that house, but one day the boy takes it to live in an apartment. The cat sulks and hides, while the boy tries to coax it out. . . . By morning, the cat realizes that the things it loves best—hiding places, windows with birds, and the boy—are in the new environment as well. . . . The realistic, closeup watercolors convey many emotions. . . . This is a beautiful book for cat lovers and for those who are uncomfortable with change." SLJ

Robbins, Jacqui
The new girl . . . and me; story by Jacqui Robbins; with art by Matt Phelan. Atheneum 2006 un il $16.95
Grades: K 1 2   **E**
1. School stories 2. Iguanas -- Fiction 3. Friendship -- Fiction
ISBN 0-689-86468-X

LC 2004-09931

Two girls named Shakeeta and Mia become friends when Shakeeta boasts that she has a pet iguana and Mia learns how to help Shakeeta "feel at home" even when she is in school.

"The characters are realistically and sympathetically portrayed, and the conversations and actions of the children are natural. Phelan's cartoon-style watercolors depict a realistic-looking classroom with a mix of children from a variety of backgrounds." SLJ

Two of a kind; [by] Jacqui Robbins and Matt Phelan. Atheneum Books for Young Readers 2008 un il $16.99
Grades: K 1 2   **E**
1. School stories 2. Friendship -- Fiction
ISBN 978-1-4169-2437-1; 1-4169-2437-X

LC 2006033210

When Anna abandons her best friend, Julisa, to spend time with Kayla and Melanie, whose friendship is considered very special, she soon learns that she has little in common with her new friends.

"Phelan's restrained watercolor-and-pencil illustrations are particularly apt at capturing the emotions at play in the story, while Kayla and Melanie's devilish expressions provide a gentle comic lift. A great introduction to early conversations are character, bullying, and peer pressure." Booklist

Robert, Francois
★ **Find** a face; by Francois and Jean Robert, with Jane Gittings. Chronicle Books 2004 un il $15.95
Grades: PreK K 1 2   **E**
1. Face in art
ISBN 0-8118-4338-6

LC 2003-17593

Presents, with accompanying rhyming text, photographs of everyday objects depicting faces

This is "a fun book that demonstrates that faces can be found anywhere if you look hard enough. . . . The photographs are clear and bright, and set against boldly colored backgrounds. Youngsters will never again look at a light switch in the same way." SLJ

Robert, Na'ima B.

Ramadan moon; by Na'íma B. Robert; illustrated by Shirin Adl. Frances Lincoln Children's Books 2009 un il $17.99
Grades: K 1 2 3   **E**
    1. Muslims -- Fiction 2. Ramadan -- Fiction
    ISBN 1-84507-922-1; 978-1-84507-922-2

This "follows a Muslim family through its observance of the 'Month of Mercy.' . . . This book's poetic words and playful, patterned collage artwork capture both the solemnity and joy of religious practice and, in a series of scenes of worshippers of every type and hue, show the diversity of the Muslim community around the world." Booklist

Robinson, Fiona

What animals really like; a new song composed & conducted by Mr. Herbert Timerteeth. Abrams 2011 un il
Grades: 1 2   **E**
    1. Animals -- Fiction
    ISBN 0-8109-8976-X; 978-0-8109-8976-4

"This amusing story begins when readers open two foldouts to part a pair of red curtains. On stage is a large group of animals ready to give voice to the composer/conductor's new song. Unfortunately, his preconceived notions about the creatures are evident. . . . The pen, ink and marker-pens illustrations show a number of animals dressed in their finest. They become livelier and bolder as their performance goes on. Although Robinson keeps the focus and humor on the well-lit stage, he occasionally pans over to the audience where all readers see are the many colorful eyeballs peering out of the darkness. Sublime silliness." SLJ

Robinson, Michelle

What to do if an elephant stands on your foot; by Michelle Robinson; pictures by Peter H. Reynolds. Dial 2012 32 p. (hardback) $16.99
Grades: PreK K   **E**
    1. Elephants -- Fiction 2. Jungle animals -- Fiction 3. Picture books for children 4. Humorous stories
    ISBN 9780803733985
           LC 2011035450

This children's picture book offers tongue-in-cheek information about "[s]afari etiquette . . . . From what to do if an elephant stands on your foot . . . , to how to escape the attentions of a crocodile . . . , our . . guide leads our unlucky hero on a jungle adventure, barely avoiding tigers, a rhino," and "snakes." (Amazon.com

Rocco, John

★ **Blackout**. Disney/Hyperion Books 2011 un il lib bdg $16.99
Grades: K 1 2 3   **E**
    1. Night -- Fiction 2. Summer -- Fiction 3. Family life -- Fiction 4. City and town life -- Fiction 5. Electric power failures -- Fiction
    ISBN 978-1-4231-2190-9 lib bdg; 1-4231-2190-2 lib bdg

"The plot line, conveyed with just a few sentences, is simple enough, but the dramatic illustrations illuminate the story. . . . Page composition effectively intermingles boxed pages and panels with double-page spreads, generating action. Brilliant designed, with comic bits." Kirkus

Blizzard; by John Rocco. Disney-Hyperion Books 2014 40 p. color illustrations (hardback) $17.99

Grades: PreK K 1 2 3   **E**
    1. Blizzards -- Fiction 2. Heroes and heroines -- Fiction 3. Snow -- Fiction 4. Heroes -- Fiction
    ISBN 1423178653; 9781423178651
           LC 2014003220

This children's book "is based on John Rocco's childhood experience during the now infamous Blizzard of 1978, which brought fifty-three inches of snow to his town in Rhode Island. . . . The book opens with a boy's excitement upon seeing the first snowflake fall outside his classroom window. It ends with the neighborhood's immense relief upon seeing the first snowplow break through on their street." (Publisher's note)

"Young readers will be tickled by a young boy's resourcefulness in this story of how he and his family survive a monumental blizzard. The first flake falls on Monday while the young narrator is at school, and by the time he and his sister make it home after being dismissed early, the snow is over their boots. On Tuesday, the family's door won't open, and the kids climb out the window to play outside (though it's too deep for sledding and even walking). Wednesday, Dad shovels, but the snowplows don't come (though the kids can now build snow tunnels and forts). . . . The Caldecott honoree's pencil, watercolor and digital paint illustrations are reminiscent of Steven Kellogg in their light and line and detail, and readers will pore over the pages as they vicariously live through a blizzard. An author's note explains that the story is based on his own experience in the New England blizzard of 1978. A kid is the hero in this tale of ingenuity and bravery." Kirkus

Moonpowder; story and pictures by John Rocco. Hyperion Books for Children 2008 un il $15.99
Grades: K 1 2   **E**
    1. Dreams -- Fiction 2. Bedtime -- Fiction
    ISBN 978-1-4231-0011-9; 1-4231-0011-5
           LC 2007-042236

Even though Eli is the "Fixer of all things fixable," one thing he cannot fix is his bad dreams, until one night when Mr. Moon appears and asks him to come fix the Moonpowder factory, where sweet dreams are created.

"Steeped in dreamy sepia tones suffused with golden light and brightened by unexpected patches of electric blue, the illustrations are lush and painterly. Using spreads combined with comic-style panels, Rocco creates a hint of a graphic novel for the youngest readers." SLJ

Wolf! wolf! Hyperion Books for Children 2007 un il $15.99
Grades: K 1 2 3   **E**
    1. China -- Fiction 2. Goats -- Fiction 3. Wolves -- Fiction
    ISBN 1-4231-0012-3
           LC 2007-04636

"This twisted treatment of Aesop's fable flips everything readers know about the boy who cried wolf on its head. . . . Ancient China unfolds as the stage and setting for this story. In this variant, children get a little insight into the wolf's point of view. . . . The purposeful use of frames, unusual setting, and visual humor makes this an excellent addition to any collection." SLJ

Rockliff, Mara

The **case** of the July 4th jinx; by Lewis B. Montgomery; illustrated by Amy Wummer. Kane Press 2010 96p il (The Milo & Jazz mysteries) lib bdg $22.60; pa $6.95
Grades: 1 2 3   **E**
    1. Mystery fiction
    ISBN 978-1-57565-315-0 lib bdg; 1-57565-315-X lib bdg; 978-1-57565-308-2 pa; 1-57565-308-7 pa
           LC 2009049886

With the help of ace detective Dash Marlowe, sleuths-in-training Mio and Jazz investigate a so-called jinx at the local Fourth of July fair

"The story is simple, and children will enjoy solving the mystery. Black-and-white spot art appears frequently throughout, creating a text that will not intimidate children just starting to read chapter books." SLJ

Chik Chak Shabbat; by Mara Rockliff, illustrated by Kyrsten Brooker. First edition. Candlewick Press 2014 32 p. color illustrations $15.99

Grades: PreK K 1 2   E

1. Jewish cooking 2. Cooking -- Fiction 3. Neighbors -- Fiction 4. Jewish holidays -- Fiction 5. Dinners and dining 6. children's stories

ISBN 0763655287; 9780763655280

LC 2013953462

In this children's book, by Mara Rockliff and illustrated by Kyrsten Brooker, "Goldie Simcha doesn't joyfully throw open her door to welcome everyone in to her apartment for a meal of her famous cholent.... Little Lali Omar knocks on the door to 5-A, only to learn that Goldie was feeling too sick on Friday to cook, and everyone knows you can't make cholent in a hurry.... But it just isn't Shabbat without cholent. What can her neighbors do to save the day?" (Publisher's note)

"Designed to cook unattended for 12 hours over the Sabbath, when observant Jews cannot perform work, cholent is a fragrant stew. Goldie Simcha, a youngish woman living in a big-city apartment building, 'doesn't celebrate Shabbat exactly as my grandma did,' but she honors her memory (the book's title is a colloquialism for 'hurry up') by inviting her neighbors to feast on cholent every Saturday. The dish (a recipe concludes the book) is such a mainstay of building life that when Goldie gets sick and can't fix cholent, her neighbors bring dishes from their own homelands ... lovely, unassuming story of tradition and multicultural community is smartly paired with Brooker's (The Honeybee Man) oil and collages. At once homespun and stylish, the pictures speak to the possibilities for human connection in a modern, urban setting." Pub Wkly

The **Grudge** Keeper; written by Mara Rockliff; illustrated by Eliza Wheeler. Peachtree Publishers 2014 32 p. $16.95

Grades: K 1 2 3 4   E

1. Children's stories 2. City and town life -- Fiction 3. Forgiveness -- Fiction

ISBN 1561457299; 9781561457298

LC 2012048880

"No one in the town of Bonnyripple ever kept a grudge. No one, that is, except old Cornelius, the Grudge Keeper. Ruffled feathers, petty snits, minor tiffs and major huffs, insults, umbrage, squabbles, dust-ups, and imbroglios-the Grudge Keeper received them all, large and small, tucking each one carefully away in his ramshackle cottage." (Publisher's note)

"Wheeler's strong, witty ink-and-watercolor illustrations combine with the text to humorously demonstrate that 'holding a grudge' is a bad thing. Wordplay and humor provide an effective vehicle for a valuable moral." Kirkus

Me and Momma and Big John; text by Mara Rockliff; illustrations by William Low. Candlewick 2012 32 p. (hardback) $16.99

Grades: PreK K 1 2   E

1. Mothers -- Fiction 2. Cathedrals -- Fiction 3. Picture books for children 4. Building -- Fiction 5. Stonecutters -- Fiction 6. New York (N.Y.) -- Fiction 7. Mothers and sons -- Fiction 8. African Americans -- Fiction 9. Cathedral of St. John the Divine (New York, N.Y.) -- Fiction

ISBN 0763643599; 9780763643591

LC 2011046649

In this story, "our narrator ... greets his mother ... when she returns from work, tired and covered with gray dust. She has been hired to cut stone for the cathedral in the city called Big John." She spends many days on just one stone. "John expects to see his mother's name on the stone .... When the stone is finished, the whole" family goes to see it, and though "her name is not on it, Momma knows that many people will come and see it, high atop the cathedral." (Children's Literature)

Rockwell, Anne F.

Apples and pumpkins; illustrated by Lizzy Rockwell. Simon & Schuster 2011 il $14.99

Grades: PreK   E

1. Apples -- Fiction 2. Autumn -- Fiction 3. Pumpkin -- Fiction

ISBN 978-1-4424-0350-5; 1-4424-0350-0

A reissue of the title first published 1989

A little girl spends a glorious Fall day picking apples and searching for the perfect pumpkin.

This edition "has new cover art that punches up the fall colors, adds a chicken, and features apples and pumpkins in the foreground. The text's typeface has changed, but everything else is kept in its original perfection so that yet another generation of youngsters will celebrate autumn from orchard visits to trick-or-treating." SLJ

At the supermarket. Henry Holt 2010 un il $16.99

Grades: PreK   E

1. Shopping -- Fiction 2. Birthdays -- Fiction 3. Supermarkets -- Fiction

ISBN 0-8050-7662-X; 978-0-8050-7662-2

LC 200900922

A revised and newly illustrated edition of The Supermarket, published 1979 by MacMillan

A boy and his mother fill a cart at the supermarket with everything from grapes to paper towels, finishing off with ingredients for a birthday cake.

"The well-written narration explains their trip from start to finish including how the checkout line works. The brightly colored gouache illustrations on white backgrounds show the child helping to fill the cart and feature such items as produce and a container of ice cream alone on the page, making identification easy. This is a fun, educational read aloud." SLJ

Big wheels; by Anne Rockwell. Walker & Co. 2003 un il $14.95 bd bk $6.95

Grades: PreK K 1   E

1. Vehicles 2. Machinery

ISBN 0-8027-8882-3; 0-8027-8903-X bd bk

LC 2002-34348

A reissue of the title first published 1986 by Dutton Children's Bks

Introduces a number of big-wheeled trucks, such as bulldozers, power shovels, and dump trucks, and explains what they do

"Although the author-artist has supplied a very brief text, she uses active, vivid verbs, such as dig, dump, and chop up, effectively conveying a sense of the machinery in the fewest words necessary. Likewise her illustrations contain exactly the right amount of detail to satisfy but not confuse." Horn Book

First day of school; pictures by Lizzy Rockwell. Harper 2011 un il $16.99

Grades: PreK K 1   E

1. School stories

ISBN 978-0-06-050191-4; 0-06-050191-X

LC 201001016

Mrs. Madoff's students compare notes about getting ready for their first day of school after vacation.

"The uncluttered, brightly colored pictures capture the children's nervousness as they anticipate what's ahead, as well as their excitement as they prepare for their first day. . . . A cheerful, reassuring offering that nicely covers the range of first-day jitters." Booklist

★ **Four** seasons make a year; pictures by Megan Halsey. Walker & Co. 2004 un il $15.95; lib bdg $16.85

Grades: PreK K 1   E

1. Seasons

ISBN 0-8027-8883-1; 0-8027-8885-8 lib bdg

LC 2003-57171

Describes the passing of the seasons through the changes in plants and animals that occur on a farm

"The first-person text is simple and childlike, a tone reflected in the clearly delineated collages. Combining ink drawings with acrylic paintings on torn paper, these illustrations create eye-catching compositions." Booklist

My preschool; [by] Anne Rockwell. Holt 2008 un il $16.95

Grades: PreK   E

1. School stories

ISBN 978-0-8050-7955-5; 0-8050-7955-6

LC 2007002834

Follows a little boy during his day at preschool, from cheerful hellos in circle time, to painting colorful pictures and playing at the water table, to passing out paper cups for snack

In the illustrations Rockwell uses "colorful inks and traditional Japanese woodblock printing. . . . The detail and realistic depiction of the preschool experience will help to calm some newcomers' trepidations about attending school for the first time." SLJ

★ The **toolbox**; by Anne & Harlow Rockwell. Walker & Company 2004 un il hardcover o.p. bd bk $6.95

Grades: PreK K 1   E

1. Tools

ISBN 0-8027-8930-7; 0-8027-9609-5 bd bk

LC 2003-66562

A reissue of the title first published 1971 by Macmillan

An easy-to-read description of the basic tools found in a toolbox

"The brief text is printed in clear, handsome type. . . . [The illustrations] make ingenious use of watercolor to show textures and surfaces of wood and metal." Horn Book

Rodman, Mary Ann

First grade stinks; written by Mary Ann Rodman; illustrated by Beth Spiegel. Peachtree 2006 un il $15.95; pa $8.95

Grades: K 1 2   E

1. School stories

ISBN 1-56145-377-3; 1-56145-462-1 pa

LC 2006-02711

First-grader Haley wishes she were back having fun in kindergarten with her old teacher, until she finds out that first-grade is special, too

"The scratchy, fluid, full-color watercolor-and-ink illustrations feature plenty of white space. Perfect as a read-aloud." SLJ

★ **My** best friend; illustrated by E.B. Lewis. Viking 2005 un il $14.99; pa $5.99

Grades: PreK K 1   E

1. Friendship -- Fiction

ISBN 0-670-05989-7; 0-14-240806-9 pa

LC 2004-22778

Six-year-old Lily has a best friend all picked out for play group day, but unfortunately the differences between first-graders and second-graders are sometimes very large

"Rodman's honest text captures the girl's heartbroken disappointment and makes it real for young readers, and Lewis's shining, sun-drenched illustrations convey both the harshness and warmth of the bright days at the pool." SLJ

★ **Surprise** soup; illustrated by G. Brian Karas. Viking 2009 un il $15.99

Grades: PreK K 1   E

1. Bears -- Fiction 2. Soups -- Fiction 3. Cooking -- Fiction 4. Brothers -- Fiction 5. Family life -- Fiction

ISBN 978-0-670-06274-4; 0-670-06274-X

LC 2008-22548

"Frequent, playful sound effects . . . will make read-alouds fun, and Rodman perfectly captures the rhythm and words of family dialogue. . . . Kara's collage artwork combines thickly lined, expressive figures with patterned details." Booklist

A **tree** for Emmy; written by Mary Ann Rodman; illustrated by Tatjana Mai-Wyss. Peachtree 2009 un il $15.95

Grades: K 1 2   E

1. Trees -- Fiction 2. Birthdays -- Fiction

ISBN 978-1-56145-475-4; 1-56145-475-3

LC 2008036745

Emmy loves the mimosa tree in her grandmother's yard and asks for one for her birthday, only to find that stores do not sell wild trees.

"The repetition of phrases, the cadence of the text, and the understanding of a child's emotions make this picture book a fine choice for reading aloud." Booklist

Rodriguez, Beatrice

★ The **chicken** thief. Enchanted Lion Books 2010 un il $14.95

Grades: PreK K 1   E

1. Stories without words 2. Foxes -- Fiction 3. Chickens -- Fiction

ISBN 1-59270-092-6; 978-1-59270-092-9

"In Rodriguez's wordless debut, a bear and rabbit are enjoying a peaceful lunch in the garden outside their cottage when a fox makes off with one of their hens. The rooster wrings his wings melodramatically, and all three give chase. . . . Rodriguez succeeds in creating a distinctive personality for each of the characters, and her ability to capture the players' emotions via body language is masterful. . . . For readers who love a good chase—and who doesn't?—this one is a delight from beginning to end." Publ Wkly

Other titles in this series are:

Fox and Hen together (2011)

Rooster's revenge (2011)

Rooster's revenge. Enchanted Lion 2011 il $14.95

Grades: PreK K 1   E

1. Stories without words 2. Foxes -- Fiction 3. Chickens -- Fiction

ISBN 978-1-59270-112-4; 1-59270-112-4

"This conclusion to the wordless trilogy that began with The Chicken Thief picks up where that book ended, with Rabbit, Bear, and Rooster departing the happy couple. At sea, a storm dumps them on a mysterious island, where Rooster discovers a glowing, green ball and runs off with it. In action-filled panoramas, Bear and Rabbit pursue Rooster through exceptionally surreal landscapes before returning to their cozy farm, where Rooster gets a big (and heartwarming) surprise after dropping his treasure. Rodriguez remains a master of body language and facial expressions, and the final scene leaves no doubt of a happily-ever-after for all involved." Publ Wkly

Rogers, Gregory

The **hero** of Little Street; Gregory Rogers. Roaring Brook Press 2012 32 p.

Grades: PreK K 1 2 3   **E**

1. Stories without words 2. Picture books for children 3. Art museums -- Fiction 4. Dogs -- Fiction 5. England -- Fiction 6. Painting -- Fiction 7. Time travel -- Fiction 8. London (England) -- Fiction 9. Netherlands -- History -- 17th century -- Fiction 10. Delft (Netherlands) -- History -- 17th century -- Fiction

ISBN 1596437294; 9781596437296

LC 2010042371

This children's book by Gregory Rogers is the final entry in the "Boy, Bear" trilogy. "Narrowly escaping from a gang of bullies, a boy slips into a grand old gallery--the perfect hiding place, full of mystery and treasures. Suddenly, a painting comes to life and the boy finds himself on an adventure led by a mischievous dog that has leapt from the canvas. The two slip into a Vermeer painting and are transported to Little Street, Delft in seventeenth-century Holland, where the boy has to use every ounce of his ingenuity to rescue his new friend from an untimely fate."(Publisher's note)

Rohmann, Eric

★ **Bone** dog. Roaring Brook Press 2011 un il $16.99

Grades: K 1 2   **E**

1. Dogs -- Fiction 2. Death -- Fiction 3. Skeleton -- Fiction 4. Halloween -- Fiction

ISBN 978-1-59643-150-8; 1-59643-150-4

LC 2010045142

Although devastated when his pet dog dies, a young boy goes trick-or-treating and receives a timely visit from an old friend during a scary encounter with graveyard skeletons.

"Rohmann's . . . friendly figures and soft, autumnal colors give this spooky story an overlay of tranquility. . . . It's an offbeat mixture of humor and sadness." Publ Wkly

★ A **kitten** tale. Alfred A. Knopf 2008 un il $15.99; lib bdg $18.99

Grades: PreK   **E**

1. Cats -- Fiction 2. Snow -- Fiction 3. Seasons -- Fiction

ISBN 978-0-517-70915-3; 978-0-517-70916-0 lib bdg

LC 2007-11093

As four kittens who have never seen winter watch the seasons pass, three of them declare the reasons they will dislike snow when it arrives, while the fourth cannot wait to experience it for himself

This is a "marvel of sly simplicity for the very young. . . . [Rohmann's] uncluttered, inventive scenes masterfully echo the repetitive rhythm in the words." Booklist

★ **My** friend Rabbit. Roaring Brook Press 2002 un il $15; pa $6.99

Grades: PreK K 1 2   **E**

1. Mice -- Fiction 2. Rabbits -- Fiction 3. Friendship -- Fiction

ISBN 0-7613-1535-7; 0-312-36752-X pa

LC 2002-17764

Awarded the Caldecott Medal, 2003

Something always seems to go wrong when Rabbit is around, but Mouse lets him play with his toy plane anyway because he is his good friend

"The double-page, hand-colored relief prints with heavy black outlines are magnificent, and children will enjoy the comically expressive pictures of the animals." SLJ

Time flies. Crown 1994 un il $17; lib bdg $17.99; pa $6.99

Grades: PreK K 1 2   **E**

1. Stories without words 2. Birds -- Fiction 3. Dinosaurs -- Fiction

ISBN 0-517-59598-2; 0-517-59599-0 lib bdg; 0-517-88555-7 pa

LC 93-28200

A Caldecott Medal honor book, 1995

A wordless tale in which a bird flying around the dinosaur exhibit in a natural history museum has an unsettling experience when the dinosaur seems to come alive and view the bird as a potential meal

"The handsome, atmospheric paintings heighten the drama as they tell their simple, somewhat mysterious, and quite short story." Booklist

Roode, Daniel

Little Bea. Greenwillow Books 2011 un il $12.99

Grades: PreK   **E**

1. Day -- Fiction 2. Bees -- Fiction 3. Animals -- Fiction 4. Friendship -- Fiction

ISBN 978-0-06-199392-3; 0-06-199392-1

LC 2009053681

From morning to night, Little Bea buzzes through her neighborhood helping friends and having fun.

"Roode's computer-generated images are highly stylized. . . . The text is full of sounds . . . internal rhymes, . . . and the simple pleasures of knock-knock jokes and games of 'duck, duck, goose' and 'peekaboo' . . . There's reassurance and contentment throughout. Friendly, fuzzy creatures abound; the lives of characters who live in a tightly knit community of friends they see and enjoy every day is a satisfying theme." Publ Wkly

Another title about Little Bea is:

Little Bea and the snowy day (2011)

Little Bea and the snowy day. Greenwillow Books 2011 32p il $12.99

Grades: PreK   **E**

1. Bees -- Fiction 2. Snow -- Fiction 3. Animals -- Fiction

ISBN 978-0-06-199395-4; 0-06-199395-6

LC 2010032236

Little Bea and her friends enjoy a day of snow angels, skating, and even making a new snow friend.

"The simplistic text and singsong rhyme are best suited for two-year-olds. . . . Children will delight in the bright, animated digital art and large, two-dimensional perspective." SLJ

Roop, Peter

Down East in the ocean; a Maine counting book. written by Peter and Connie Roop; illustrated by Nicole Fazio. Down East 2011 il $16.95

Grades: PreK K 1   **E**

1. Counting 2. Stories in rhyme 3. Maine -- Fiction 4. Seashore -- Fiction 5. Marine animals -- Fiction

ISBN 978-0-89272-709-4; 0-89272-709-8

"This rhyming counting book features animals associated with the Maine seashore, but that can also be found on many other beaches. Each spread tells a mini story of parent and offspring while introducing the concept of counting. . . . This is an engaging way to learn numbers and a great beach book. Music notations are included at the end to put the verses to song." SLJ

Roosa, Karen

Pippa at the parade; illustrated by Julie Fortenberry. Boyds Mills Press 2009 un il $16.95

Grades: PreK K   **E**

1. Stories in rhyme 2. Parades -- Fiction

ISBN 978-1-59078-567-6; 1-59078-567-3

LC 2008028127

A young child has a fun-filled day with her parents at the big parade

"Bursting with movement, the spirited and free-flowing watercolors capture cartwheeling gymnasts and marching scout troops. . . . The brief rhyming verses . . . include a few onomatopoeic phrases that invite young listeners to join in." Booklist

Root, Phyllis

Big Momma makes the world; written by Phyllis Root; illustrated by Helen Oxenbury. Candlewick Press 2003 un il $16.99; pa $6.99
Grades: PreK K 1 2   E
    1. Creation -- Fiction
    ISBN 0-7636-1132-8; 0-7636-2600-7 pa
                       LC 2002-17498

Boston Globe-Horn Book Award: Picture Book (2003)

Big Momma, with a baby on her hip and laundry piling up, makes the world and everything in it and, at the end of the sixth day, tells the people she has made that they must take care of her creation

"Root's text is strong and sassy, with a down-home cadence that has immediate appeal, and Oxenbury's Big Momma is the perfect embodiment of the story's earth mother." Booklist

Creak! said the bed; illustrated by Regan Dunnick. Candlewick Press 2010 un il $15.99
Grades: PreK K   E
    1. Beds -- Fiction 2. Noise -- Fiction
    ISBN 978-0-7636-2004-2; 0-7636-2004-1

"The increasingly crowded bed . . . is by now a standard picture-book plotline. Fresh takes on the subject are hard to come by, but Root manages to make it feel new by punctuating the story with the sounds of impending disaster. . . . The economy of the story line is paralleled by gouache illustrations . . . that reinforce the bed-centered tale but also pull in and zoom out on its inhabitants for different perspectives. The lantern-jawed, snub-nosed family is cartoon cute, making for a perfect storytime read." Booklist

Flip, flap, fly! illustrated by David Walker. Candlewick 2009 un il $14.99
Grades: PreK   E
    1. Stories in rhyme 2. Animals -- Fiction
    ISBN 978-0-7636-3109-3; 0-7636-3109-4

An "assortment of baby animals flap, wiggle and splash their way through the forest, spotting each other in turn as they play with their mamas. Human babies and toddlers will love guessing which animal comes next as they follow clues from Root's contagious, rhyming text and Walker's bright and warm acrylic illustrations." Kirkus

Kiss the cow; illustrated by Will Hillenbrand. Candlewick Press 2000 un il hardcover o.p. pa $6.99
Grades: K 1 2 3   E
    1. Cattle -- Fiction
    ISBN 0-7636-0298-1; 0-7636-2003-3 pa
                       LC 00-20926

Annalisa, the most curious and stubborn of Mama May's children, disobeys her mother and upsets the family's magic cow by refusing to kiss her in return for the milk she gives

"Elements of folklore echo through the story that reads aloud rhythmically with a satisfying, folksy sound. . . . The well-conceived illustrations, warm in color and graceful in line, depict a variety of scenes with style and panache." Booklist

Paula Bunyan; illustrated by Kevin O'Malley. Farrar, Straus and Giroux 2009 un il $16.95
Grades: K 1 2 3   E
    1. Tall tales 2. Size -- Fiction
    ISBN 978-0-374-35759-7; 0-374-35759-5
                       LC 2007-43728

Recounts the exploits of Paul Bunyan's "little" sister, Paula, who lived in the North Woods, sang three-part harmony with the wolves, and used an angry bear for a foot warmer.

"O'Malley's white-framed, woodcutlike pictures, heavily outlined with intricate line shading, appear throughout this appropriately tall book. Sweeping panoramic views, Paula's thunderous voice depicted in large speech bubbles, bear-carrying mosquitoes, comical animal expressions, and energetic black-and-white drawings add to the fun. The timely environmental message is an added plus." SLJ

Scrawny cat; illustrated by Alison Friend. Candlewick Press 2011 un il $16.99
Grades: PreK K 1 2   E
    1. Cats -- Fiction
    ISBN 978-0-7636-4164-1; 0-7636-4164-2
                       LC 2010047671

A lost, lonely, and scrawny cat, hungry and afraid, unexpectedly meets someone who takes him in and loves him.

"Delicious language and a winsome feline ensure that this new iteration of an oft-told plot will find an appreciative audience. . . . Friend's gouache paintings, including vignettes, single pages and double page spreads, illuminate the straightforward action. . . . She captures the fluctuating reactions of the cat perfectly." Kirkus

Thirsty Thursday; illustrated by Helen Craig. Candlewick Press 2009 un il $9.99
Grades: PreK K   E
    1. Rain -- Fiction 2. Flowers -- Fiction 3. Farm life -- Fiction
    ISBN 978-0-7636-3628-9; 0-7636-3628-2

"It's Thursday on Bonnie Bumble's farm, and everyone is thirsty—especially the flowers. . . . Not a drop of rain is in sight, but luckily Bonnie has an idea. She puts the sheep on top of the cow and the pig on top of the sheep, and she climbs on top of the pig . . . and tickles the cloud with a feather. . . . Short, sweet and unabashedly darling, Root's text employs just the right amount of repetition to get toddlers chiming in by the second reading. Craig's ink, watercolor and pencil illustrations lend Bonnie, animals and flowers expressive personalities." Kirkus

Toot toot zoom! illustrated by Matthew Cordell. Candlewick Press 2009 un il $15.99
Grades: PreK K   E
    1. Animals -- Fiction 2. Friendship -- Fiction 3. Automobiles -- Fiction
    ISBN 978-0-7636-3452-0; 0-7636-3452-2
                       LC 2008-934781

"A simple storyline, great sound effects, a touch of humor, and big, bold illustrations make this a lively choice for storytime." Bull Cent Child Books

Rose, Deborah Lee

All the seasons of the year; illustrated by Kay Choaro. Abrams Books for Young Readers 2010 un il $16.95
Grades: PreK K 1   E
    1. Stories in rhyme 2. Cats -- Fiction 3. Seasons -- Fiction 4. Mother-child relationship -- Fiction
    ISBN 978-0-8109-8395-3; 0-8109-8395-8

"This rhyming story portrays a mother cat's love for her child. . . . With two spreads devoted to each season, the first-person narrative describes some of their favorite activities. Chorao's lush illustrations in gouache, colored pencils, and ink fill the pages with colorful pastel depictions of the momma and her kitten diving into a pile of autumn leaves, sledding down a winter slope, flying kites in the spring, watering summer blossoms, and celebrating the youngster's birthday in the fall." SLJ

Rose, Naomi C.

Tashi and the Tibetan flower cure. Lee & Low Books 2011 il $18.95

Grades: 1 2 3   E

1. Sick -- Fiction 2. Flowers -- Fiction 3. Grandfathers -- Fiction 4. Community life -- Fiction

ISBN 978-1-60060-425-6; 1-60060-425-0

LC 2011010556

"The softly brushed paintings have a naive, self-tutored look, but suit the text's homespun tone. The story, outwardly realistic, turns on two charming ideas: that of a child using ancient wisdom to restore the health of a relative, and that of a sterile American suburb becoming as close-knit as a Tibetan village." Publ Wkly

Rosen, Michael, 1946-

Bear flies high; [illustrated by Adrian Reynolds] Bloomsbury 2009 un il $16.99; lib bdg $17.89

Grades: PreK K 1 2   E

1. Bears -- Fiction 2. Flight -- Fiction

ISBN 978-1-59990-386-6; 1-59990-386-5; 978-1-59990-387-3 lib bdg; 1-59990-387-3 lib bdg

LC 2008-55015

Bear usually spends his days on the beach, singing and watching birds, but when he leaves to visit a carnival, his dream of flying may just come true.

"The lyrical call-and-response and glowing illustrations give the book a cadence that's perfect for afternoon naps or lazy days." Publ Wkly

I'm number one; illustrated by Bob Graham. Candlewick Press 2009 un il $16.99

Grades: PreK K 1 2   E

1. Toys -- Fiction

ISBN 978-0-7636-4535-9; 0-7636-4535-4

LC 2009004246

A wind-up soldier bosses and berates the other toys, making them feel terrible, until they suddenly start to rebel.

"The pen-and-watercolor illustrations are filled with expressive characters and Graham's signature, whimsical details, such as the stuffed pig's snout ring. This simple, affecting story will be welcome anywhere that more than two young kids are gathered together and where laughter, not mean words, is the lingua franca." Booklist

★ **Michael** Rosen's sad book; words by Michael Rosen; pictures by Quentin Blake. Candlewick Press 2005 un il $16.99; pa $6.99

Grades: 3 4 5 6   E

1. Bereavement -- Fiction

ISBN 0-7636-2597-3; 0-7636-4104-9 pa

LC 2004-45787

Boston Globe-Horn Book Honor: Nonfiction (2005)

A man tells about all the emotions that accompany his sadness over the death of his son, and how he tries to cope

"Blake's evocative watercolor-and-ink illustrations use shades of gray for the pictures where sadness has taken hold but brighten with color at the memory of happy times. This story is practical and universal and will be of comfort to those who are working through their bereavement. A brilliant and distinguished collaboration." SLJ

Red Ted and the lost things; illustrated by Joel Stewart. Candlewick Press 2009 40p il

Grades: PreK K 1 2   E

1. Toys -- Fiction 2. Teddy bears -- Fiction 3. Lost and found possessions -- Fiction

ISBN 0-7636-4537-0; 0-7636-4624-5 pa; 978-0-7636-4537-3; 978-0-7636-4624-0 pa

LC 2009-02992

When a teddy bear is accidentally left on the seat of a train, he uses his ingenuity—and some new friends—to search for the little girl who lost him. "Grades two to three." (Bull Cent Child Books)

"Rosen's quirky combination of characters is matched by Stewart's muted colors and deliberately hazy backgrounds, which nicely spotlight the stuffed animals. . . . The plucky and determined Red Ted deserves a place among the many lost-toys books on library shelves." SLJ

Send for a superhero! Michael Rosen, illustrated by Katharine McEwen. Candlewick Press 2014 40 p. color illustrations $16.99

Grades: PreK K 1 2 3   E

1. Bedtime -- Fiction 2. Superheroes -- Fiction 3. Comic books, strips, etc.

ISBN 0763664383; 9780763664381

LC 2013944084

"Comic-book action meets picture-book adventure in this . . . new outing from beloved author Michael Rosen and illustrator Katharine McEwen. Tune in as a father reads his children a bedtime story about the exploits of two villains, Filth and Vacuum, and their wicked plan to suck all the money out of the banks and cover everything with muck and slime." (Publisher's note)

" The comic adventure is laid out in frames with urgent declarations and sound effects, with a printed-on-newsprint effect, whereas the scenes with Elmer and Emily are often on full-bleed pages and pulse with saturated colors. Although this approach has been used before, rarely has it been executed with such hilarious results." - Kirkus

★ Tiny Little Fly; words by Michael Rosen; pictures by Kevin Waldron. Candlewick Press 2010 un il $15.99

Grades: PreK K   E

1. Stories in rhyme 2. Flies -- Fiction 3. Tigers -- Fiction 4. Elephants -- Fiction 5. Hippopotamus -- Fiction

ISBN 978-0-7636-4681-3; 0-7636-4681-4

LC 2010-07549

With a tramp and a roll and a swat, Great Big Elephant, Great Big Hippo, and Great Big Tiger try to capture Tiny Little Fly as he teases each one in turn.

"The consistently patterned, simple rhyming text is accompanied by rustic, large-scale, digitally enhanced pencil-and-gouache art. . . . The words and images create an easily absorbed, enjoyable adventure." Booklist

★ Totally wonderful Miss Plumberry; [by] Michael Rosen; illustrated by Chinlun Lee. Candlewick Press 2006 un il $15.99

Grades: PreK K 1 2   E

1. School stories 2. Teachers -- Fiction

ISBN 0-7636-2744-5

LC 2005045392

Molly's day turns from totally wonderful to totally horrible when her classmates are not interested in the special crystal she has brought to school, until Miss Plumberry steps in to help

"This gentle picture book captures the impact a sensitive teacher has on the lives of her students. . . . The soft watercolor-and-pencil illustrations reveal [Molly's] emotions and expose the fickle attention of children in engaging . . . spreads." SLJ

★ We're going on a bear hunt; anniversary edition of a modern classic. retold by Michael Rosen; illustrated by Helen Oxenbury. Margaret K. McElderry Books 2009 un il $18.99

Grades: PreK K 1 2   **E**
1. Bears -- Fiction 2. Hunting -- Fiction
ISBN 978-1-4169-8711-6; 1-4169-8711-8

LC 2008-53214

First published 1989

Brave bear hunters go through grass, a river, mud, and other obstacles before the inevitable encounter with the bear forces a headlong retreat

"Glorious puddles of watercolor alternate with impish charcoal sketches in this refreshing interpretation of an old hand rhyme in which a man, four children, and a dog stalk the furry beast through mud and muck, high and low. A book with a genuine atmosphere of togetherness and boundless enthusiasm for the hunt." SLJ

Rosen, Michael J.
★ **Chanukah** lights; illustrations by Robert Sabuda. Candlewick Press 2011 un il $34.99
Grades: K 1 2   **E**
1. Counting 2. Pop-up books 3. Jews -- Fiction 4. Hanukkah stories 5. Hanukkah -- Fiction
ISBN 978-0-7636-5533-4; 0-7636-5533-3

LC 2011013664

Counts the candles of a menorah on each night of Hanukkah while recalling images of Jewish life in different places and times, such Herod's temple in Jerusalem, a shtetl in Russia, and a refugee ship bound for the New World.

"This is a gorgeous and fragile holiday book for adults and children to enjoy together." SLJ

Night of the pumpkinheads; illustrations by Hugh McMahon. Dial Books for Young Readers 2011 il $16.99
Grades: K 1 2   **E**
1. Pumpkin -- Fiction 2. Halloween -- Fiction 3. Vegetables -- Fiction
ISBN 978-0-8037-3452-4; 0-8037-3452-2

LC 2010039314

Determined to make Halloween a frightening night of the pumpkinheads, the pumpkins transform themselves into a variety of scary monsters and then head for town hoping to terrify everyone they meet.

"Digitally assembled with photographs of McMahon's work and pencil drawings, the illustrations treat readers to spirited images of spunky pumpkins rising up to take an active part in trick-or-treating instead of remaining parked on porches.... A solid addition to the Halloween shelf, especially for those who have graduated from safer, sweeter stories." Kirkus

Rosenberg, Liz
Tyrannosuarus dad. Roaring Brook Press 2011 il $16.99
Grades: PreK K 1 2   **E**
1. Fathers -- Fiction 2. Dinosaurs -- Fiction
ISBN 9781596435315; 1596435313

Tobias's father is a lot like other fathers—he likes corny jokes, and doing magic tricks, and works really hard at the office. But there the resemblance ends. He has teeth as sharp as steak knives, is forty feet high, and weighs as much as a locomotive. He is, in fact, a tyrannosaurus.

"Rosenberg's well-paced dialogue and succinct descriptions result in a most engaging read. Myers' oil paintings truly amaze." Kirkus

What James said; Liz Rosenberg; illustrated by Matthew Myers. Roaring Brook Press 2015 32 p. color illustrations (hardcover) $16.99
Grades: PreK K 1 2   **E**
1. Gossip -- Fiction 2. Friendship -- Fiction 3. Rumor -- Fiction 4. Best friends -- Fiction
ISBN 1596439084; 9781596439085

LC 2014031488

In this children's book by Liz Roseberg, illustrated by Matthew Myers, "when a little girl thinks that her best friend James has been saying bad things about her behind her back, she takes action in the form of the silent treatment. As they go about their day and James tries harder and harder to get her to talk to him, they both realize that true friendship surpasses any rumor . . . or misunderstanding." (Publisher's note)

"A charming tale of misunderstanding and reconciliation." Booklist

Rosenberg, Madelyn
Happy birthday, Tree; a Tu B'Shevat story. by Madelyn Rosenberg; illustrated by Jana Christy. Albert Whitman & Co. 2012 24 p. (hardcover) $15.99
Grades: PreK K 1 2   **E**
1. Trees -- Fiction 6. Tu bi-Shevat -- Fiction 3. Jews -- Fiction
ISBN 0807531510; 9780807531518

LC 2011034187

In this children's picture book by Madelyn Rosenberg, illustrated by Jana Christy, "Joni strives to create a celebration befitting her old majestic tree . . . on the Jewish holiday of Tu B'Shevat, the birthday of the trees. . . . Determined to find the right gift for her leafy friend, Joni concludes that a new tree planted close by and a promise to continue to nurture her arboreal companions is the best way to observe the holiday." (Kirkus)

The **Schmutzy** Family; by Madelyn Rosenberg; illustrated by Paul Meisel. Holiday House 2012 32 p. (hardcover) $16.95
Grades: PreK K 1   **E**
1. Jews -- Fiction 2. Picture books for children 3. Sabbath -- Fiction 4. Cleanliness -- Fiction 5. Family life -- Fiction
ISBN 0823423719; 9780823423712

LC 2011040341

In this children's picture book, "wading in Feldman Swamp, making mud pies, painting with tomato sauce, and other messy activities are a part of the Schmutzy family activities. Despite how grimy the playing gets, Mama Schmutzy does not mind one bit except on Friday when" they must prepare for the Sabbath. (Children's Literature)

Rosenstock, Barbara
The **littlest** mountain; illustrated by Melanie Hall. Kar-Ben Pub. 2011 un il $17.95; pa $7.95
Grades: PreK K 1 2 3   **E**
1. Jewish legends 2. God -- Fiction 3. Mountains -- Fiction
ISBN 978-0-7613-4495-7; 0-7613-4495-0; 978-0-7613-4497-1 pa; 0-7613-4497-7 pa

LC 2010021249

"This pourquoi story about why God chose Mount Sinai as the location for giving the Ten Commandments has its roots in Jewish legend. Various mountains in the land of Israel list their best qualities and argue over which should be chosen. In the end, God picks humble, faithful Mount Sinai. . . . This is a lovely tale. . . . Kids will get a kick out of the folktale feeling and the talking mountains, caregivers will like the lesson on the value of being humble and faithful, and Jewish educators will be thrilled to have a great read-aloud for the holiday of Shavuot, which commemorates the receiving of the Ten Commandments." SLJ

Rosenthal, Amy Krouse
Al Pha's bet; illustrated by Delphine Durand. G. P. Putnam's Sons 2011 un il $16.99
Grades: PreK K   **E**
1. Alphabet -- Fiction
ISBN 978-0-399-24601-2; 0-399-24601-0

LC 2010028171

Al Pha makes a bet with himself that he can invent the perfect order for the twenty-six letters.

Durand's "loopy acrylic paintings carry the story through a long, long middle section about how Al comes to arrange each of the letters as he does ... populating Al's world with a wacky assortment of proto-trees and flowers, as well as a cast of equally goofy-looking villagers and animals. Pages are well designed and visually lively throughout, the text peppered with spot illustrations.... Fans of dopey puns everywhere, rejoice!" Publ Wkly

Bedtime for Mommy; illustrated by LeUyen Pham. Bloomsbury 2010 un il $16.99; lib bdg $17.89
Grades: PreK K 1 2   **E**
    1. Bedtime -- Fiction 2. Mother-daughter relationship -- Fiction
    ISBN 978-1-59990-341-5; 1-59990-341-5; 978-1-59990-465-8 lib bdg; 1-59990-465-9 lib bdg
                              LC 2009-18205
In a reversal of the classic bedtime story, a child helps her mommy get ready for bed, enduring pleas for one more book, five more minutes of play time, and a glass of water before the lights go out.

"The facial expressions throughout are priceless, and the final illustration showing the parents peeking in at a sleeping daughter round out this tale. This very visual story will appeal to beginning readers as well as parents and librarians looking for a fun bedtime read-aloud." Libr Media Connect

Chopsticks; illustrated by Scott Magoon. Disney/Hyperion 2012 un il $16.99
Grades: PreK K 1 2   **E**
    1. Chopsticks -- Fiction 2. Friendship -- Fiction
    ISBN 978-1-4231-0796-5; 1-4231-0796-9
                              LC 2011010269
This book "outlines the ... activities of a pair of chopsticks who are not only working partners but also BFFs. Then the tip of one chopstick is broken in an unfortunate encounter with an asparagus spear, and after getting medical attention (the glue bottle mends him and wraps the 'wound' with a bandage) the injured chopstick must 'stay off it until it sets.' At first, the non-injured chopstick stays close by his friend's side, but the injured one finally tells him, 'You need to get out ... venture off on your own a bit.' The chopsticks discover that time away from each other can also be a good thing." (Bulletin of the Center for Children's Books)

"The marriage of text, digital art, and design provide plentiful puns and laugh-out-laud humor." Publ Wkly

★ **Cookies**; bite-size life lessons. written by Amy Krouse Rosenthal; illustrated by Jane Dyer. HarperCollins Publishers 2006 un il $12.99; lib bdg $13.89
Grades: PreK K 1 2   **E**
    1. Cookies 2. Conduct of life
    ISBN 978-0-06-058081-0; 0-06-058081-X; 978-0-06-058082-7 lib bdg; 0-06-058082-8 lib bdg
                              LC 2005-15134
"Using the activity of making and eating cookies, the author defines some important concepts for young children, such as respect, trustworthiness, patience, politeness, loyalty, etc.... Lovely pastel watercolor illustrations show appealing children and anthropomorphic animals interacting with one another and the treats.... The utilization of the cookies to explain the concepts is a brilliant idea and works well on a child's level. The text is short and clear, and the book is delightful to look at and browse through." SLJ

Other titles in this series are:
Christmas cookies (2008)
Sugar cookies (2009)
One smart cookie (2010)

★ **Duck!** Rabbit! [illustrated by] Tom Lichtenheld. Chronicle Books 2009 un il $16.99
Grades: PreK K 1 2   **E**
    1. Ducks -- Fiction 2. Rabbits -- Fiction
    ISBN 978-0-8118-6865-5; 0-8118-6865-6
                              LC 2008-28102
This children's book by Amy Krouse Rosenthal, illustrated by Tom Lichtenheld, asks "Is it a duck or a rabbit? Depends on how you look at it . With more than 100,000 copies sold, this classic picture book is now available in a sturdy board book that little ones will love holding in their own two hands." (Publisher's note)

Rosenthal and Lichtenheld play "with perspective and visual trickery, ... using a classic image that looks like either a rabbit (with long ears) or a duck (with a long bill).... Two off-stage speakers, their words appearing on either side of the animal's head, argue their points of view. The snappy dialogue makes for [a] fine read-aloud." Publ Wkly

I scream ice cream! a book of wordles. by Amy Krouse Rosenthal and illustrated by Serge Bloch. Chronicle Books 2013 40 p. (alk. paper) $16.99
Grades: K 1 2   **E**
    1. English language -- Terms and phrases 2. Word games -- Fiction 3. Plays on words -- Fiction
    ISBN 1452100047; 9781452100043
                              LC 2013011487
This book, by Amy Krouse Rosenthal and illustrator Serge Bloch, examines English language words that sound the same. "Amy Krouse Rosenthal unleashes her ... wit in this ... book of wordplay. Complemented by ... illustrations from Serge Bloch, this ... book will have young readers thinking about words in an entirely new way! (Publisher's note)

★ **Little** Hoot; illustrated by Jen Corace. Chronicle Books 2008 un il $12.99
Grades: PreK K   **E**
    1. Owls -- Fiction 2. Bedtime -- Fiction
    ISBN 0-8118-6023-X; 978-0-8118-6023-9
                              LC 2007-24966
Little Hoot wants to go to bed early, like all of his friends do, and he is hopping mad when Mama and Papa Owl insist that he stay up late and play. "Age three and up." (N Y Times Book Rev)

The "owl family ... feels recognizable.... This outing is not to be missed." Publ Wkly

Other titles in the series are:
Little oink (2009)
Little pea (2005)

The **OK** book; [by] Amy Krouse Rosenthal & Tom Lichtenheld. HarperCollins 2007 un il $12.99
Grades: PreK K 1 2   **E**
    1. Ability -- Fiction 2. Self-acceptance -- Fiction
    ISBN 978-0-06-115255-9; 0-06-115255-2
                              LC 2006030432
"The book's hero is a little stick figure whose head is the O of OK and whose arms and legs are the K.... I like to try a lot of different things, the OK figure says. I'm not great at all of them, but I enjoy them all the same.... One day, I'll grow up to be really excellent at something, OK says, while lying in bed.... It can't hurt to remind kids that the pleasure we take in simple activities is what makes life worthwhile." Publ Wkly

★ **This** plus that; life's little equations. Amy + Krouse + Rosenthal = writer; Jen + Corace = artist. Harper 2011 un il $14.99

Grades: PreK K 1 2   E

1. Mathematics -- Fiction 2. Conduct of life -- Fiction 3. Addition
ISBN 978-0-06-172655-2; 0-06-172655-9

LC 2008-34357

"Two pigtailed girls squabble, then reason with each other. The outcome is a simple sum: 'yes + no = maybe.' The same two girls gossip through a tin-can telephone: 'laughter + keeping secrets + sharing = best friend.' Witty observations—'anything + sprinkles = better'—alternate with improving messages as well as nods to the seasons, arts, and kid-friendly activities. . . . Corace's stylized pen and ink vignettes show a world that's safe and secure; the same family members appear throughout. . . . It's the kind of math that children won't have any trouble comprehending." Publ Wkly

Uni the unicorn; by Amy Krouse Rosenthal; illustrated by Brigette Barrager. Random House Inc. 2014 48 p. col. ill. (hardcover) $17.99; (library) $20.99

Grades: PreK K 1   E

1. Girls -- Fiction 2. Unicorns -- Fiction 3. Picture books for children
ISBN 0385375557; 9780385375559; 9780375972065

LC 2013009884

In this story by Amy Krouse Rosenthal, illustrated by Brigette Barrager, "Uni the unicorn is told there's no such thing as little girls! No matter what the grown-up unicorns say, Uni believes that little girls are real. Somewhere there must be a smart, strong, wonderful, magical little girl waiting to be best friends." (Publisher's note)

"The book features Rosenthal's familiar mix of humor and wit, making this book ideal for reading out loud or independently. Barrager's illustrations offer full page spreads of whimsical, dreamlike images that will make every reader want to believe in unicorns (or little girls)." SLJ

Yes Day! [by] Amy Krouse Rosenthal & [illustrated by] Tom Lichtenheld. HarperCollins 2009 un il $14.99; lib bdg $15.89

Grades: PreK K 1   E

1. Day -- Fiction 2. Wishes -- Fiction
ISBN 978-0-06-115259-7; 0-06-115259-5; 978-0-06-115260-3 lib bdg; 0-06-115260-9 lib bdg

LC 2008-20219

A little boy gets everything he asks for on Yes Day, a special day that only comes once a year.

"Lichtenheld's bright and funny cartoons bring the story to life, with character expressions that are right on the mark." SLJ

Rosenthal, Eileen

I must have Bobo! illustrated by Marc Rosenthal. Atheneum Books for Young Readers 2010 un il $14.99

Grades: PreK K 1   E

1. Cats -- Fiction 2. Toys -- Fiction 3. Lost and found possessions -- Fiction
ISBN 978-1-4424-0377-2; 1-4424-0377-2

LC 2010-04963

When Willy wakes up without his favorite toy, he looks everywhere until he finds it.

"Illustrator Marc Rosenthal's . . . ability to capture Earl's feline deviousness—the way Earl cranes his neck to see if Willy is coming, or hides under the covers with Bobo—is one of the book's chief charms. . . . Soft pencil drawings on cream-colored pages add to the generally calm, bedtime atmosphere." Publ Wkly

I'll save you Bobo! Eileen Rosenthal; illustrated by Marc Rosenthal. Atheneum Books for Young Readers 2012 40 p.

Grades: PreK K 1 2 3   E

1. Cats -- Fiction 2. Toys -- Fiction 3. Drawing -- Fiction 4.

Picture books for children 5. Adventure fiction -- Fiction 6. Fear -- Fiction 7. Storytelling -- Fiction
ISBN 1442403780; 9781442403789

LC 2011278288

This picture book tells the story of Willy, the young boy introduced in Eileen Rosenthal's previous book 'I Must Have Bobo!' and his companions, his favorite toy Bobo and Earl the cat. "Willy . . . . here puts down the book he's reading in order to create a more exciting story himself, while his sock monkey Bobo serves as audience for his crayon drawings and narrative about a jungle adventure. . . . The cartoon illustrations create a kind of spotlight for the story: boy, drawing table and crayons, armchair, Bobo and cat." (Kirkus)

I will save you Bobo!

Rosenthal, Marc

Archie and the pirates. Joanna Cotler Books 2009 un il $16.99

Grades: K 1 2 3   E

1. Islands -- Fiction 2. Monkeys -- Fiction 3. Pirates -- Fiction 4. Friendship -- Fiction
ISBN 978-0-06-144164-6; 0-06-144164-3

LC 2008-35251

When Archie the monkey finds himself on a strange island, he makes a multitude of new friends who help him defend their home from intruding pirates.

"Rosenthal relates the adventure in a simple, matter-of-fact way and pairs the narrative to neatly drawn . . . cartoons. . . . Loaded with child appeal." Booklist

Rosner, Jennifer

The **mitten** string; repairing the world, a stitch at a time. by Jennifer Rosner; illustrated by Kristina Swarner. Random House Inc 2014 32 p. color illustrations (jacketed hardcover : alk. paper) $17.99

Grades: 1 2 3   E

1. Jewish legends 2. Deaf -- Fiction 3. Jews -- Fiction 4. People with disabilities -- Fiction 5. Mittens -- Fiction
ISBN 0385371187; 9780375971860; 9780385371186

LC 2013018685

This children's book, by Jennifer Rosner and illustrated by Kristina Swarner, is a "Jewish folktale about a girl who knits, a deaf woman, and a piece of blue yarn. When her family invites a deaf woman and her baby to stay, Ruthie, a talented knitter of mittens, wonders how the mother will know if her child wakes in the night. The surprising answer inspires Ruthie to knit a special gift that offers great comfort to mother and baby--and to Ruthie herself." (Publisher's note)

"The Tobers raise sheep, and young Ruthie loves to knit mittens from their wool for the villagers. When her family befriends a deaf woman whose wagon has broken down and her baby, the child observes how the mother, Bayla, sleeps with a string tied between her own wrist and Aaron's, to alert her if her son wakes up in the night . . . The 'old country' Jewish setting is subtle, giving the story flavor without dominating it. Knitting and sign-language glossaries round out this attractive title. This beautiful story of kindness, acceptance, and resourcefulness will have wide appeal." SLJ

Rosoff, Meg

Jumpy Jack and Googily; [by] Meg Rosoff; illustrated by Sophie Blackall. Henry Holt 2008 un il $16.95

Grades: PreK K 1   E

1. Fear -- Fiction 2. Snails -- Fiction 3. Monsters -- Fiction 4. Friendship -- Fiction
ISBN 978-0-8050-8066-7; 0-8050-8066-X

LC 2007-07227

Jumpy Jack the snail is terrified that there are monsters around every corner despite the reassurances of his best friend, Googily.

"The interplay between the two creates a wonderfully safe space for children to explore their fears.... The text ... employs a formal elevated tone that gently chides Jumpy Jack's childish fears, adding an element of dry humor. The illustrations are filled with whimsical details." SLJ

★ **Meet** wild boars; [written by] Meg Rosoff and [illustrated by] Sophie Blackall. Henry Holt & Co. 2005 un il $15.95; pa $6.99
Grades: PreK K 1 2   E
   1. Boars -- Fiction
   ISBN 0-8050-7488-0; 0-312-37963-3 pa
                               LC 2004-8985

It is very hard to be friends with wild boars because they are dirty and smelly, bad-tempered, and rude

This is "bitingly funny and deeply satisfying.... Blackall's roll-on-the-ground-in-laughter illustrations are incisively rendered in ink and gouache." Booklist

Another title about the wild boars is:
Wild boars cook (2008)

Ross, Fiona
   Chilly Milly Moo. Candlewick Press 2011 il $15.99
Grades: PreK K   E
   1. Milk -- Fiction 2. Cattle -- Fiction 3. Weather -- Fiction
   ISBN 978-0-7636-5693-5; 0-7636-5693-3
                               LC 2010051446

While the other cows are enjoying the sun and making plenty of milk, Milly Moo is too hot to make a drop but when the temperature falls, Milly Moo shows the farmer and the rest of the herd what she can do.

"This is a great addition to read-alouds centered on the theme of individuality (with a snack tie-in built right in). Delightfully different, just like Milly Moo." Kirkus

Ross, Michael Elsohn
   Mama's milk; by Michael Elsohn Ross; illustrated by Ashley Wolff. Tricycle Press 2007 un il $12.95
Grades: PreK K   E
   1. Stories in rhyme 2. Animals -- Fiction 3. Mammals -- Fiction 4. Breast feeding -- Fiction
   ISBN 978-1-58246-181-6; 1-58246-181-3
                               LC 2006020873

"From humans to a variety of aquatic and land animals, Ross's rhyming text describes the different ways that mothers nurse their babies.... The pastel-infused watercolor illustrations tastefully depict the nursing pairs." SLJ

Ross, Pat
   Meet M & M; pictures by Marylin Hafner. Pantheon Bks. 1980 41p il hardcover o.p. pa $4.99
Grades: K 1 2   E
   1. Friendship -- Fiction
   ISBN 0-14-038731-5
                               LC 79-190

"Beginning readers will have no difficulty with the humorously told, very real incidents.... The many black-and-white pencil drawings capture the girls' facial expressions especially well." Horn Book

Other titles about M and M (Mandy and Mimi) are:
M and M and the bad news babies (1983)
M and M and the Halloween monster (1991)
M and M and the haunted house game (1980)
M and M and the mummy mess (1986)

Ross, Tony
   I want a party! written and illustrated by Tony Ross. Andersen Press 2011 un il $16.95
Grades: PreK K 1 2   E
   1. Parties -- Fiction 2. Princesses -- Fiction
   ISBN 978-0-7613-8089-4; 0-7613-8089-2
                               LC 2011001597

Little Princess discovers that she can have a lovely party with just one guest.

"Ross's illustrations are produced in colorful ink and watercolors. The whimsy and simple story line will appeal to young children." SLJ

   I want my light on! Andersen Press USA 2010 un il $16.95
Grades: PreK K   E
   1. Fear -- Fiction 2. Princesses -- Fiction
   ISBN 978-0-7613-6443-6; 0-7613-6443-9

Everyone says there are no such things as ghosts that live under beds, but the Little Princess knows better.

"Clear, expressive watercolors add humor to the simple text, and the Little Princess formula still works well at cleverly addressing common early childhood issues." SLJ

Other titles about the Little Princess are:
I want a party! (2011)
I want to do it myself (2011)
I want two birthdays! (2010)

Rossell, Judith
   Oliver; written and illustrated by Judith Rossell. Harper 2012 32 p.
Grades: PreK K 1 2   E
   1. Boys -- Fiction 2. Imagination -- Fiction 3. Picture books for children 4. Penguins -- Fiction 5. Mothers and sons -- Fiction
   ISBN 0062022105; 9780062022103
                               LC 2011019368

This picture book tells the story of a curious young boy named Oliver, who wonders about where penguins go on vacation and especially about what lives in the drain. His mother won't let him feed a banana to whatever is down there making gurgling noises, "so Oliver builds a submarine and takes it for a ride to see just what the drain is harboring. Here Oliver turns into a kid's drawing ... in watercolor and pencil, with a touch of collage elsewhere; maybe this is all in his head? And what's down the drain? Penguins, of course." (Kirkus)

Rostoker-Gruber, Karen
   ★ **Bandit;** illustrated by Vincent Nguyen. Marshall Cavendish Children's Books 2008 un il $15.99
Grades: PreK K 1 2   E
   1. Cats -- Fiction 2. Moving -- Fiction
   ISBN 978-0-7614-5382-6; 0-7614-5382-2
                               LC 2007011720

When Bandit's family moves to a new house, the cat runs away and returns to the only home he knows, but after he is brought back, he understands that the new house is now home

"By telling the story from the point of view of an extremely territorial pet, Rostoker-Gruber approaches the issue of moving in a fresh way.... Nguyen's mixed-media illustrations have an attractive Pop Art style.... A funny, stylish book." SLJ

Another title about Bandit is:
Bandit's surprise (2010)

   ★ **Ferret** fun; illustrated by Paul Ratz de Tagyos. Marshall Cavendish Children's 2011 un il

Grades: PreK K 1 2   E

  1. Cats -- Fiction 2. Ferrets -- Fiction

  ISBN 0-7614-5817-4; 978-0-7614-5817-3

LC 2010-21301

Two nervous pet ferrets named Fudge and Einstein try to convince a visiting cat that they are not rats. "Grades two to four." (Bull Cent Child Books)

"Rátz de Tagyos's magic-marker-and-ink graphic-novel-style illustrations are the real draw; the bouncy, fanged trio are a terrific balance between Saturday morning cartoon and real animals. Just enough lesson hidden in the fun." Kirkus

Roth, Carol

The **little** school bus; illustrated by Pamela Paparone. North-South Bks. 2002 un il hardcover o.p. pa $6.95

Grades: PreK K   E

  1. Stories in rhyme 2. Buses -- Fiction 3. Animals -- Fiction

  ISBN 0-7358-1646-8; 0-7358-1905-X pa

LC 2002-71417

An assortment of animals, including a goat in a coat, a quick chick, and a hairy bear, ride the bus to and from school

"Paparone's bright, sprightly illustrations feature plenty of cheery mugging out the windows and other amusing side business. . . . This will take children on a verbal and visual ride that they'll want to repeat as often as possible." Booklist

Will you still love me? illustrated by Daniel Howarth. Albert Whitman 2010 un il $15.99

Grades: PreK K   E

  1. Love -- Fiction 2. Animals -- Fiction 3. Siblings -- Fiction 4. Parent-child relationship -- Fiction

  ISBN 978-0-8075-9114-7; 0-8075-9114-9

Young animals and a little boy are reassured that their mothers will still love them after a new baby arrives.

"Howarth's sunny watercolor and ink illustrations match the upbeat tone of the bouncy, rhyming text." SLJ

Rotner, Shelley

Senses at the seashore. Millbrook Press 2006 un il lib bdg $22.60

Grades: PreK K 1 2   E

  1. Seashore 2. Senses and sensation

  ISBN 978-0-7613-2897-1 lib bdg; 0-7613-2897-1 lib bdg

LC 2005-06151

"This picture book tells what children see, hear, smell, touch, and taste at the beach. . . . A few of the clear, colorful photos show adults (fishermen, a lifeguard) at work, but most of the illustrations are closeups of children at play. An inviting, kid-friendly introduction to the senses and the seashore." Booklist

Senses in the city; by Shelley Rotner. Millbrook Press 2008 un il (Shelley Rotner's early childhood library) lib bdg $23.93

Grades: PreK K 1   E

  1. City and town life 2. Senses and sensation

  ISBN 978-0-8225-7502-3 lib bdg; 0-8225-7502-7 lib bdg

"Both an exciting celebration of city life and a show-and-tell about the five senses, this photo-essay will draw even very young children. Clear, direct words and unframed pictures show children in the packed streets of an unnamed city, where they see the skyline and hear trains passing by, go inside tall buildings, and travel in a subway car." Booklist

Shades of people; by Shelley Rotner and Sheila M. Kelly; photographs by Shelley Rotner. Holiday House 2009 un il $16.95

Grades: PreK K 1   E

  1. Race 2. Skin 3. Color

  ISBN 978-0-8234-2191-6; 0-8234-2191-0

LC 2008022574

Explores the many different shades of human skin, and points out that skin is just a covering that does not reveal what someone is like inside.

"Filled with smiles and hugs, the pictures prove an upbeat confirmation of the book's central idea. . . . This will enrich and spark discussions of diversity." Booklist

Rowand, Phyllis

It is night; by Phyllis Rowand; illustrated by Laura Dronzek. Greenwillow Books, an imprint of HarperCollinsPublishers 2014 32 p. (trade ed.) $16.99

Grades: PreK K   E

  1. Toys -- Fiction 2. Animals -- Fiction 3. Bedtime -- Fiction

  ISBN 0062250248; 9780062250247

LC 2013028060

In this children's book, written by Phyllis Rowand and illustrated by Laura Dronzek, "A little girl says good-night and finds the perfect beds for each and every animal, for dolls big and small, and even for a railroad train. . . . In a gentle surprise ending, no matter where their beds should be, each animal or object is a toy. And so they all belong tucked into bed with the little girl because she loves them all." (Publisher's note)

"A series of bedtime questions ("Where does a railroad train go at night?") receive answers in this book first published in 1953 with illustrations by Rowand. The lulling litany is sweetly updated in Dronzek's blanket-soft, moon-drenched art. Some unlikely groupings (tiger and giraffe) presage the satisfying conclusion in which it is shown that the creatures are dolls, toys, and pets." Horn Book

Rubel, David

The **carpenter's** gift; a Christmas tale about the Rockefeller Center tree. illustrated by Jim LaMarche. Random House 2011 un il $17.99; lib bdg $20.99

Grades: K 1 2 3   E

  1. Trees -- Fiction 2. Christmas stories 3. Kindness -- Fiction 4. Christmas -- Fiction 5. Rockefeller Center -- Fiction.

  ISBN 978-0-375-86922-8; 0-375-86922-0; 978-0-375-96922-5 lib bdg; 0-375-96922-5 lib bdg; 978-0-375-98933-9 e-book

LC 2010033203

In Depression-era New York City, construction workers at the Rockefeller Center site help a family in need—a gift that is repaid years later in the donation of an enormous Christmas tree.

"Rubel's story . . . puts the now magnificent symbol in perspective. LaMarche conveys emotional resonance with gauzy, soft-hued paintings of the inspirational proceedings." Publ Wkly

Rubin, Adam

Dragons love tacos; by Adam Rubin; illustrated by Daniel Salmieri. Dial Books for Young Readers 2012 40 p. col. ill $16.99; (hardcover) $16.99

Grades: PreK K 1   E

  1. Tacos -- Fiction 2. Dragons -- Fiction 3. Picture books for children 4. Humorous stories 5. Food habits -- Fiction

  ISBN 0803736800; 9780803736801

LC 2011035699

This children's picture book "starts with an incantatory edge: 'Hey, kid! Did you know that dragons love tacos? They love beef tacos and chicken tacos. They love really big gigantic tacos and tiny little baby tacos as well.' . . . [T]he kicker . . . [is] that dragons hate spicy salsa, which ignites their inner fireworks . . . the kid throws a taco party for the dragons . . . the clearly labeled 'totally mild' salsa comes with spicy jalapenos in the fine print, prompting the dragons to burn down the house, resulting in a barn-raising at which more tacos are served." (Kirkus Reviews)

Another title in this series is:
Dragons Love Tacos 2 (2017)

Those darn squirrels and the cat next door; illustrated by Daniel Salmieri. Clarion Books 2011 32p il $16.99

Grades: K 1 2 3   E
1. Cats -- Fiction 2. Birds -- Fiction 3. Squirrels -- Fiction
ISBN 0-547-42922-3; 978-0-547-42922-9

"Mr. Fookwire, his beloved backyard birds, and his relentlessly clever squirrel frenemies are united against a new neighbor and common enemy: a corpulent, take-no-prisoners cat named Muffins, whose idea of fun is giving the squirrels noogies, wet willies, and wedgies. . . . Rubin's sly ironies and Salmieri's spare but deeply goofy aesthetic is child-friendly urbanity at its best." Publ Wkly

Those darn squirrels! by Adam Rubin; illustrated by Daniel Salmieri. Clarion Books 2008 32p il $16

Grades: K 1 2 3   E
1. Birds -- Fiction 2. Old age -- Fiction 3. Squirrels -- Fiction
ISBN 978-0-547-00703-8; 0-547-00703-5
                                                    LC 2007040110

When grumpy Old Man Fookwire builds feeders to try to keep birds—the only creatures he likes—from leaving for the winter, he finds himself in a battle with clever, crafty squirrels who want a share of the abundant food

"This simple tale has a sneaky, edgy humor that erupts into hilarity. . . . [The] paintings [are] reminiscent of some of the best European children's book illustrations." SLJ

Another title about these characters is:
Those darn squirrels and the cat next door (2011)

Ruddell, Deborah

Who said coo? illustrated by Robin Luebs. Beach Lane Books 2010 un il $16.99

Grades: PreK K 1   E
1. Stories in rhyme 2. Pigs -- Fiction 3. Sounds -- Fiction 4. Animals -- Fiction 5. Bedtime -- Fiction
ISBN 978-1-4169-8510-5; 1-4169-8510-7
                                                    LC 2009000929

"Unbeknownst to Lulu the pig, Pigeon and Owl have shown up on her doorstep at bedtime. . . . Lulu's slumber is interrupted by a loud 'Cooooo' and then a 'Whooooo.' Lulu confronts the likely culprits, but Pigeon and Owl refuse to fess up. . . . Luebs's acrylic paintings feature a luminescent pastel palette, which makes the story's nighttime scenes glow. A few deft strokes convey Lulu's contentedness, exasperation, and anger." Publ Wkly

Ruddra, Anshumani

Dorje's stripes; illustrated by Gwangjo and Jung-a-Park. Kane Miller 2010 un il $15.99

Grades: 1 2 3 4   E
1. Monks -- Fiction 2. Tigers -- Fiction 3. Monasteries -- Fiction 4. Tibet (China) -- Fiction
ISBN 978-1-935279-98-3; 1-935279-98-X

Dorje is a beautiful Royal Bengal tiger but he has no stripes. In a small Buddhist monastery in Tibet, Master Wu explains the reasons behind Dorje's missing stripes, and offers hope for the future.

"This heartwarming story is enhanced by stunning watercolors that add to its peaceful tone and suggest a quiet beauty as well as depict the action and emotions of each character." SLJ

Rueda, Claudia

★ **No**; translated by Elisa Amado. Groundwood Books/House of Anansi Press 2010 un il $18.95

Grades: PreK K   E
1. Snow -- Fiction 2. Bears -- Fiction 3. Winter -- Fiction 4. Hibernation -- Fiction 5. Mother-child relationship -- Fiction
ISBN 978-0-88899-991-7; 0-88899-991-7
Original Spanish edition 2009

"Mother suggests that it is time to hibernate for the winter, but little bear has other ideas. . . . But when a blinding snowstorm practically buries little bear, he realizes mother might have known best. . . . Flat figures in a minimal wintry palette nevertheless burst with personality, abetted by clever compositions." Kirkus

Rumford, James

From the good mountain; how Gutenberg changed the world. James Rumford. 1st ed. Roaring Brook Press 2012 40 p. (reinforced : alk. paper) $17.99

Grades: 3 4 5   E
1. Riddles 2. Book industry 3. Printing -- History 4. Books -- History 5. Printers -- Germany -- Biography 6. Printing -- History -- Origin and antecedents
ISBN 1596435429; 9781596435421
                                                    LC 2011033796

Author James Rumford presents a history on printmaking. "What was made of rags and bones, soot and seeds? What took a mountain to make? For the answer, travel back to the fifteenth century—to a time when books were made by hand and a man named Johannes Gutenberg invented a way to print books with movable type . . . [The book is w]ritten as a series of riddles . . . [with things] to learn about how the very thing you are holding in your hands came to be." (Publisher's note)

Includes bibliographical references and index.

★ **Rain** school; written and illustrated by James Rumford. Houghton Mifflin Books for Children 2010 un il $16.99

Grades: PreK K 1 2   E
1. School stories 2. Chad -- Fiction 3. Rain -- Fiction
ISBN 0-547-24307-3; 978-0-547-24307-8
                                                    LC 2009-49701

Thomas, who lives in Chad in Africa is ready for his first day of school, but "when he arrives at the schoolyard he finds that there is no school. . . . After Thomas and his schoolmates build the school from mud and grass, they're ready for their nine-month school year. . . . Ages five to eight." (Bull Cent Child Books)

"While serving as a Peace Corps volunteer, Rumford was a teacher in Chad, and the authentic details illuminate the spare text and beautiful artwork. . . . The colored-pencil, ink, and pastel images echo the words' elemental rhythms. . . . This moving offering will leave kids thinking about the daily lives of other young people around the world." Booklist

★ **Silent** music; a story of Baghdad. Roaring Brook Press 2008 un il $17.95

Grades: K 1 2 3   E
1. Iraq -- Fiction 2. Calligraphy -- Fiction 3. Baghdad (Iraq) -- Fiction 4. Iraq War, 2003- -- Fiction
ISBN 978-1-59643-276-5; 1-59643-276-4
                                                    LC 2007-23600

As bombs and missiles fall on Baghdad in 2003, a young boy named Ali uses the art of calligraphy to distance himself from the horror of war

"Art sings on the pages of this visual celebration of Arabic calligraphy as Rumford's . . . collages of floral and geometric designs and flowing lines deftly echo Arabic language and patterns. . . . Spreads incorporating stamps, money and postcards reinforce the Baghdad setting and complement representational scenes." Publ Wkly

Tiger and turtle. Roaring Brook 2010 un il $17.99
Grades: 1 2 3   E
1. Tigers -- Fiction 2. Turtles -- Fiction 3. Friendship -- Fiction
ISBN 978-1-59643-416-5; 1-59643-416-3

When a tiger and a turtle both want a flower that has fallen to the ground, they argue over it until a fight breaks out between them.

"The brief text is well paced, with repeated rising and falling action, and the resolution of the most suspenseful moments requires a page turn. Read this tale aloud . . . for a lively storyhour." SLJ

Runton, Andy

Owly and Wormy, friends all aflutter! Atheneum Books for Young Readers 2011 un il $15.99
Grades: PreK K 1 2   E
1. Stories without words 2. Owls -- Fiction 3. Worms -- Fiction 4. Butterflies -- Fiction
ISBN 978-1-4169-5774-4; 1-4169-5774-X
LC 2010-06123

Good friends Owly and Wormy are disappointed when their new plant attracts fat, green, bug-like things, instead of butterflies, until a metamorphosis occurs.

"Even very young children will be able to puzzle out the story's details from the expressions on the characters' faces, and Runton's unvarnished sentimentality creates an atmosphere of absolute security." Publ Wkly

Russo, Marisabina, 1950-

I will come back for you; a family in hiding during World War II. Schwartz & Wade 2011 un il $17.99; lib bdg $20.99
Grades: K 1 2 3   E
1. Italy -- Fiction 2. Bracelets -- Fiction 3. Grandmothers -- Fiction 4. Jews -- Italy -- Fiction 5. World War, 1939-1945 -- Italy -- Fiction
ISBN 978-0-375-86695-1; 0-375-86695-7; 978-0-375-96695-8 lib bdg; 0-375-96695-1 lib bdg
LC 2010044523

A grandmother tells her granddaughter the story of the charm bracelet that represent her own childhood experiences while she and her family tried to evade the Nazis in Italy during World War II.

"Russo bases this book on her own family history. Her writing is direct but always reassuring, and her naif [gouache] illustrations, rendered in saturated autumnal tones, feel very close to the actual family photographs that serve as the book's endpapers. Ingenuity and compassion are recurring themes in this eloquent portrayal of a family's struggle for freedom." Publ Wkly

Little Bird takes a bath; Marisabina Russo. Schwartz & Wade Books 2015 40 p. color illustrations (hc) $16.99; (glb) $19.99
Grades: PreK K 1   E
1. Rain -- Fiction 2. Baths -- Fiction 3. Birds -- Fiction 4. New York (N.Y.) -- Fiction 5. Rain and rainfall -- Fiction 6. City and town life -- New York (State) -- New York -- Fiction
ISBN 0385370156; 9780385370141; 9780385370158
LC 2013018300

In this book by Marisabina Russo, "a little bird in the big city searches for the perfect puddle. . . . He searches far and wide, but some puddles are too big, some are too small, and some are already crowded with bathers. . . . When Little Bird finds a good-looking puddle in a city park, one surprise after another spoils his bath. . . . But soon, Little Bird finds the perfect puddle to call his own." (Publisher's note)

"Without stretching a point too far, the interconnectedness of nature and city, the consequences of action and play, the sounds and sense of an urban environment make for a really nice story whose words and images repay repeated readings." Kirkus

Peter is just a baby; written and illustrated by Marisabina Russo. Eerdmans Books for Young Readers 2011 un il $16
Grades: PreK K 1   E
1. Infants -- Fiction 2. Siblings -- Fiction 3. French language -- Vocabulary
ISBN 978-0-8028-5384-4; 0-8028-5384-6
LC 2011022480

"The title is the favorite refrain of the narrator, an anthropomorphized six-year-old bear and Peter's big sister. . . . Delineating Peter's babyish ways . . . lets her cite all the ways she is more mature and sophisticated. . . . With help from her tutor, the narrator learns to say 'Bon appetit!' before eating and 'Quel dommage!' when disappointed. . . . This worldly-wise and ultimately accepting attitude, combined with the parallel story of learning French . . . gives an otherwise typical tale of sibling rivalry a stylish, refreshing twist. . . . [The book is illustrated with] cheery, naif gouache pictures." Publ Wkly

Ruth, Greg

★ **Coming** Home; by Greg Ruth. Feiwel & Friends 2014 32 p. color illustrations $16.99
Grades: PreK K 1 2 3   E
1. Veterans 2. Soldiers -- Fiction 3. Mothers and Sons -- Fiction 4. Children of military personnel -- Fiction 5. Families of military personnel -- Fiction
ISBN 1250055474; 9781250055477

In this picture book, by Greg Ruth, "readers follow the anxious progress of a young boy in a red T-shirt as he looks through the crowds of returning veterans and their loved ones. Along with him, there's a border collie dashing into its owner's arms, a man tenderly touching the belly of a pregnant woman, tight embraces, and comradely photo shoots." (School Library Journal)

"This affecting picture book is simplicity itself. Nuanced drawings drive the action, with only occasional words appearing every other page or so...This gently reassuring selection will resonate with children who have parents in the military or with anyone who is separated from a family member for any reason..." Booklist

Ruzzier, Sergio, 1966-

This is not a picture book; by Sergio Ruzzier. Chronicle Books Llc 2016 40 p. color illustrations (alk. paper) $16.99
Grades: PreK K 1   E
1. Ducks -- Fiction 2. Books and reading -- Fiction
ISBN 9781452129075
LC 2015038210

This book, by Sergio Ruzzier, is "about the joy and power of reading. Duck learns that even books without pictures can be fun. While he and his friend Bug may struggle at first to decipher their book, they stick with it, and before long they discover that not only can they read it, but it deserves a place on the shelf with all their favorite picture books." (Publisher's note)

"This sweet title effectively demonstrates the magic of reading and the power of imagination. Recommended for all collections." SLJ

★ **Two** mice; Sergio Ruzzier. Clarion Books, Houghton Mifflin Harcourt 2015 32 p. color illustrations (hardcover) $12.99
Grades: PreK K 1 2   E
1. Counting 2. Mice -- Fiction 3. Adventure and adventurers

-- Fiction
ISBN 0544302095; 9780544302099

LC 2014042966

This children's story, written and illustrated by Sergio Ruzzier, features "one house, two mice, three cookies . . . and the adventure begins. . . . [It] takes two mice through their exciting and eventful day. Funny, lively, and easy to follow, the book offers the youngest readers the chance to count from one to three and back again." (Publisher's note)

"The simplicity of the text means that the earliest readers will soon be able to pick it up and will return to it over and over. One story. Two mice. Three cheers. Lots to love." Kirkus

Ryan, Candace

Ribbit rabbit; illustrated by Mike Lowery. Walker Books for Young Readers 2011 un il
Grades: PreK K 1   E
1. Frogs -- Fiction 2. Rabbits -- Fiction 3. Friendship -- Fiction
ISBN 0-8027-2180-X; 0-8027-2181-8 lib bdg; 978-0-8027-2180-8; 978-0-8027-2181-5 lib bdg

LC 2010-08418

Frog and Bunny are the best of friends, even though they sometimes get into fights. "Ages three to five." (Bull Cent Child Books)

"The rhythmic, onomatopoetic text is a pretty music, the kind of song you'd sing in the dark to lift your spirits. Equally joyful and engaging—and that's a tall order—is Lowery's artwork. It has a childlike, elemental tone, with neat planes of color, but it is wonderfully, touchingly emotive." Kirkus

Ryan, Pam Muñoz

★ Tony Baloney; illustrated by Edwin Fotheringham. Scholastic Press 2011 un il $16.99
Grades: PreK K 1   E
1. Penguins -- Fiction 2. Siblings -- Fiction
ISBN 0-545-23135-3; 978-0-545-23135-0

LC 2009-51693

Tony, a macaroni penguin, is a middle child with very exasperating siblings, and although he never looks for trouble, it often finds him.

"Dominated by bold primary colors, Fotheringham's . . . hyperbolic digital illustrations counterbalance the slyly understated narrative, portraying Tony's (and Dandelion's) antics with humor." Publ Wkly

Tony Baloney; buddy trouble. by Pam Muñoz Ryan; illustrated by Edwin Fotheringham. Scholastic Press 2014 40 p. color illustrations (alk. paper) $6.99
Grades: K 1 2 3   E
1. Penguins -- Fiction 2. Brothers and sisters -- Fiction 3. Behavior -- Fiction 4. Helpfulness -- Fiction
ISBN 0545481694; 9780545481694

LC 2012026700

This book, written by Pam Munoz Ryan and illustrated by Edwin Fotheringham, is the author's second early reader featuring the penguin Tony. "Tony Baloney and his best friend, Bob, can't wait for tonight. It's Books and Buddies, the best school event ever! But will a fight with Big Sister ruin everything?" (Publisher's note)

"Fotheringham's macaroni penguins are as delightful as ever, their every facial expression and gesture broadcasting their feelings and personalities." Kirkus

Ryder, Joanne

Dance by the light of the moon; written by Joanne Ryder; illustrated by Guy Francis. Hyperion Books for Children 2007 un il $15.99
Grades: PreK K 1 2   E
1. Dance -- Fiction 2. Animals -- Fiction
ISBN 0-7868-1820-4

"Buffalo Flo gets an invitation to 'come out tonight and dance by the light of the moon' and proceeds to collect her friends Goose, Cat, and Pig for the occasion. . . . The rhymes dance, and so do Francis's paintings. Detailed moonlit landscapes are filled with animal characters that seem to leap from the pages." SLJ

Each living thing; illustrations by Ashley Wolff. Harcourt 2000 un il $16
Grades: K 1 2   E
1. Stories in rhyme 2. Animals -- Fiction
ISBN 0-15-201898-0

LC 98-51832

Celebrates the creatures of the earth, from spiders dangling in their webs to owls hooting and hunting out of sight, and asks that we respect and care for them

"Wolff's intense gouache paintings, outlined in black, are as lyrical as the text, with just the right balance of simplicity and subtle detail." Booklist

My father's hands; illustrated by Mark Graham. Morrow Junior Bks. 1994 un il $16.99
Grades: PreK K 1 2   E
1. Gardening -- Fiction 2. Father-daughter relationship -- Fiction
ISBN 0-688-09189-X

LC 93-27116

"A little girl and her father share the wonders of nature as they examine several small creatures in the garden—a pink worm, a golden beetle, a sliding snail, and a praying mantis. Graham's lovely double-page, impressionistic oil paintings clearly focus on the man and his daughter, with closeups of faces and hands in nearly every illustration. The garden in the background, lush with flowers and vegetable plants, provides a picturesque setting for this simple, straightforward description of a special parent/child outing." SLJ

Rylant, Cynthia

★ All in a day; illustrated by Nikki McClure. Abrams Books for Young Readers 2009 un il $17.95
Grades: PreK K 1 2   E
1. Stories in rhyme 2. Day -- Fiction
ISBN 978-0-8109-8321-2; 0-8109-8321-4

LC 2008030521

Illustrations and rhyming text pay homage to a new day, with promises for the future in its "perfect piece of time."

"Alternating backdrops of color, finch-yellow and a soft, muted blue, allow for a whole new outlook with every page turn. This uplifting picture book succeeds in introducing children to the perennial promise of tomorrow through lithe language and honed imagery." Kirkus

Annie and Snowball and the Book Bugs Club; the ninth book of their adventures. illustrated by Su¿cie Stevenson. Simon Spotlight 2011 40p il (Ready-to-read) $15.99
Grades: K 1 2   E
1. Clubs -- Fiction 2. Summer -- Fiction 3. Books and reading -- Fiction
ISBN 978-1-4169-7199-3; 1-4169-7199-8

LC 2009054121

Annie and Henry join the summer reading club at the library, and vow to be 'Book Bugs' for life.

"Rylant's celebration of the versatility and diversity of reading selections and experiences is nondidactic and gently amusing." Horn Book Guide

Annie and Snowball and the cozy nest. Simon & Schuster 2009 39p il (Ready-to-read) $15.99

Grades: PreK K 1 2 **E**
1. Dogs -- Fiction 2. Birds -- Fiction 3. Cousins -- Fiction 4.
Rabbits -- Fiction
ISBN 978-1-4169-3943-6; 1-4169-3943-1

"Annie, her bunny, her cousin Henry, and his dog Mudge sit on the porch swing and watch as a robin sits on five eggs in her nest. . . . Accessible to preschoolers as well as beginning readers, this gentle story has bits of childlike humor and plenty of good cheer, which arises from the colorful ink-and-wash artwork as well as the simple text." Booklist

★ **Annie** and Snowball and the dress-up birthday; the first book of their adventures. illustrated by Su¿cie Stevenson. Simon & Schuster Books for Young Readers 2007 40p il (Ready-to-read) $15.95; pa $3.99

Grades: K 1 2 **E**
1. Parties -- Fiction 2. Rabbits -- Fiction 3. Birthdays -- Fiction
ISBN 978-1-4169-0938-5; 1-4169-0938-9; 978-1-4169-1459-4 pa; 1-4169-1459-5 pa

LC 2006-02516

Annie and her pet bunny, Snowball, love living next door to Annie's favorite cousin, Henry and his dog, Mudge. Whether it's playing Frisbee or watching old movies, there's no shortage of fun to be had when these four are together.

"Stevenson's lively pen-and-ink and watercolor illustrations depict lots of action in the story's four short chapters, and amplify the characters' warmth, affection, and laughter." SLJ

Other titles about Annie and Snowball are:
Annie and Snowball and the prettiest house (2007)
Annie and Snowball and the pink surprise (2008)
Annie and Snowball and the teacup club (2008)
Annie and Snowball and the cozy nest (2009)
Annie and Snowball and the shining star (2009)
Annie and Snowball and the magical house (2010)
Annie and Snowball and the wintry freeze (2010)
Annie and Snowball and the Book Bugs Club (2011)

Annie and Snowball and the shining star; illustrated by Sucie Stevenson. Aladdin 2009 40p il (Ready-to-read) $15.99

Grades: PreK K 1 2 **E**
1. Dogs -- Fiction 2. Rabbits -- Fiction 3. Theater -- Fiction
ISBN 978-1-4169-3946-7; 1-4169-3946-6

LC 2009011780

Annie's friends Henry and Mudge, and especially her rabbit Snowball, help her get over feeling nervous about being in a school play.

Annie and Snowball and the wintry freeze; the eighth book of their adventures. illustrated by Su¿cie Stevenson. Simon Spotlight 2010 40p il (Ready-to-read) $15.99

Grades: K 1 2 **E**
1. Ice -- Fiction 2. Dogs -- Fiction 3. Winter -- Fiction 4. Cousins -- Fiction
ISBN 978-1-4169-7205-1; 1-4169-7205-6

LC 2009032066

Annie and her cousin Henry, along with Henry's dog Mudge and Annie's rabbit Snowball, enjoy a sparkling, wintry ice storm.

"Accompanying pen-and-ink and watercolors add even more warmth to the scenes." Horn Book Guide

Brownie & Pearl go for a spin; by Cynthia Rylant; pictures by Brian Biggs. Beach Lane Books 2012 24 p.

Grades: PreK K **E**
1. Cats -- Fiction 2. Automobiles -- Fiction 3. Picture books for

children 4. Automobile travel -- Fiction
ISBN 1416986332; 9781416986331

LC 2010018320

This children's book is part of Cynthia Rylant's "Brownie and Pearl" series in which, "Brownie and her cat are taking a spin in the girl's pink convertible. Pearl loves riding in the car and retrieving and delivering mail so much that she doesn't want to get out when they return home. Brownie finds a solution through a delicious 'takeout' meal that they can enjoy together on the grass. With its simple story line, ample white space, and vivid digitally rendered illustrations, this is a welcome addition to a popular series." (School Libr J)

Brownie and Pearl go for a spin

Brownie & Pearl grab a bite; pictures by Brian Biggs. Beach Lane 2011 un il $13.99

Grades: PreK K **E**
1. Cats -- Fiction 2. Food -- Fiction
ISBN 978-1-4169-8634-8; 1-4169-8634-0

Brownie and her cat, Pearl go to the kitchen for stringy cheese, apples, crackers and milk.

"Fans of this perfect preschool fare will once again delight in the series' playful treatment of the everyday activities. . . . Biggs' boldly colored, digital art is presented in clean, clear compositions that make good use of white space." Kirkus

Brownie & Pearl hit the hay; pictures by Brian Biggs. Peach Lane Books 2011 un il $13.99

Grades: PreK K **E**
1. Cats -- Fiction 2. Bedtime -- Fiction
ISBN 978-1-4169-8635-5; 1-4169-8635-9

LC 2010009414

A little girl and her cat enjoy preparing for bed with a bath, snack, and bedtime story.

"The text is written in short sentences suitable for beginner readers and perfect for sharing with toddlers at bedtime. Biggs's digitally rendered illustrations are full of bright colors, clean lines, and great expressions, and have plenty of white space." SLJ

Brownie & Pearl see the sights; illustrated by Brian Biggs. Beach Lane Books 2010 un il $13.99

Grades: PreK K **E**
1. Cats -- Fiction 2. Shopping -- Fiction
ISBN 978-1-4169-8637-9; 1-4169-8637-5

LC 2009012577

After visiting the shoe shop, the hat shop, and the cupcake shop, a weary little girl and her sleepy cat head home for a nap.

"Rylant provides just enough text to develop her characters and her plot, making this a satisfying read-aloud for toddlers and read-alone for beginning readers. Biggs's thick-lined, digital cartoons assume a pleasing muted tone for the outside, snowy scenes while allowing protagonists to pop. Like Brownie and Pearl, this book and its collaborators are very 'smart.'" Kirkus

Brownie & Pearl step out; pictures by Brian Biggs. Beach Lane Books 2010 un il $12.99

Grades: PreK K **E**
1. Cats -- Fiction 2. Parties -- Fiction 3. Birthdays -- Fiction
ISBN 978-1-4169-8632-4; 1-4169-8632-4

LC 2008032804

A little girl named Brownie arrives at a birthday party feeling shy while her cat Pearl confidently enters through the "kitty door."

"Rylant addresses the challenges and rewards of facing new social situations in short, conversational text perfectly suited to its young audience. Biggs' digitally rendered, cartoonlike illustrations . . . make this first title in the Brownie and Pearl series as delicious and appealing as a triple-layered birthday cake." Booklist

Other titles about Brownie & Pearl are:

Brownie & Pearl get dolled up (2010)

Brownie & Pearl see the sights (2010)

Brownie & Pearl take a dip (2011)

Brownie & Pearl grab a bite (2011)

Brownie & Pearl hit the hay (2011)

Brownie & Pearl take a dip; illustrated by Brian Biggs. Beach Lane Books 2011 un il $13.99

Grades: PreK K   E

1. Cats -- Fiction

ISBN 978-1-4169-8638-6; 1-4169-8638-3

"It's a hot day, so Brownie and her cat, Pearl, decide to go for a dip in the little backyard pool. . . . The bright, digitally rendered illustrations are cheerful, and the large, bold letters on white backgrounds suit the easy-reader text." SLJ

★ The **case** of the missing monkey; story by Cynthia Rylant; pictures by G. Brian Karas. Greenwillow Bks. 2000 48p il (High-rise private eyes) pa $3.99

Grades: K 1 2   E

1. Mystery fiction

ISBN 0-06-444306-X

LC 99-16878

While having breakfast at their favorite diner, two detectives, Bunny and Jack, find a missing glass monkey

"The full-color illustrations, rendered in acrylic gouache, and pencil, capture the cartoonlike animals' animated expressions and poses. . . . Children will enjoy searching the pages for the reported clues." SLJ

Other titles in the High-rise private eyes series are:

The case of the baffled bear (2004)

The case of the climbing cate (2000)

The case of the desperate duck (2005)

The case of the fidgety fox (2003)

The case of the puzzling possum (2001)

The case of the sleepy sloth (2002)

The case of the troublesome turtle (2001)

Cat Heaven; written and illustrated by Cynthia Rylant. Blue Sky Press (NY) 1997 40 p. col il $17.99

Grades: PreK K 1 2   E

1. Cats -- Fiction 2. Heaven -- Fiction 3. Stories in rhyme

ISBN 0590100548; 9780590100540

LC 96049501

In this book, "Writing in rhyme, [author and illustrator Cynthia] Rylant assures readers that all cats already know the way to heaven's yellow door, and once past it will never want for laps, toys, or full kitty dishes. Rylant paints in the same extremely naive style of the first book, with large brushes and bright, opaque colors; heaven is a place with trees and clouds to perch on, fields to leap through--and a garden full of tall flowers, where God walks." (Kirkus)

★ **Dog** Heaven; written and illustrated by Cynthia Rylant. Blue Sky Press (NY) 1995 40 p. col il $17.99

Grades: PreK K 1 2   E

1. Heaven -- Fiction 2. Dogs -- Fiction

ISBN 0590417010; 9780590417013

LC 94040950

This picture book by Cynthia Rylant tells of a place called "Dog Heaven, where there are endless fields for running; clear lakes filled with teasing, honking geese; and loving angel children playing everywhere. There are tasty biscuits shaped like cats and fluffy cloud beds for sleep-

ing, memory trips back to favorite spots and people, and cozy homes with petting hands. . . . Preschool to grade two." (SLJ)

★ **Henry** and Mudge; the first book of their adventures. story by Cynthia Rylant; pictures by Suçie Stevenson. Simon & Schuster Books for Young Readers 1996 39p il (Ready-to-read) $15.99; pa $3.99

Grades: K 1 2   E

1. Dogs -- Fiction

ISBN 0-689-81004-0; 0-689-81005-9 pa

First published 1987 by Bradbury Press

Henry, feeling lonely on a street without any other children, finds companionship and love in a big dog named Mudge.

"The stories are lighthearted and affectionate. Backed by line-and-wash cartoon drawings, they celebrate the familiar in a down-to-earth way that will please young readers." Booklist

Other titles about Henry and Mudge are:

Henry and Mudge and a very Merry Christmas (2004)

Henry and Mudge and Annie's good move (1998)

Henry and Mudge and Annie's perfect pet (2000)

Henry and Mudge and Mrs. Hopper's house (2003)

Henry and Mudge and the bedtime thumps (1991)

Henry and Mudge and the best day of all (1995)

Henry and Mudge and the big sleepover (2006)

Henry and Mudge and the careful cousin (1994)

Henry and Mudge and the forever sea (1989)

Henry and Mudge and the funny lunch (2004)

Henry and Mudge and the great grandpas (2005)

Henry and Mudge and the happy cat (1990)

Henry and Mudge and the long weekend (1992)

Henry and Mudge and the sneaky crackers (1998)

Henry and Mudge and the Snowman plan (1999)

Henry and Mudge and the starry night (1998)

Henry and Mudge and the tall tree house (1999)

Henry and Mudge and the tumbling trip (2005)

Henry and Mudge and the wild goose chase (2003)

Henry and Mudge and the wild wind (1993)

Henry and Mudge get the cold shivers (1989)

Henry and Mudge in puddle trouble (1987)

Henry and Mudge in the family trees (1997)

Henry and Mudge in the green time (1987)

Henry and Mudge in the sparkle days (1988)

Henry and Mudge take the big test (1991)

Henry and Mudge under the yellow moon (1987)

Henry and Mudge and a very Merry Christmas; the twenty-fifth book of their adventures. story by Cynthia Rylant; pictures by Suçie Stevenson. Simon & Schuster Books for Young Readers 2004 40p il $14.95; pa $3.99

Grades: K 1 2   E

1. Dogs -- Fiction 2. Christmas -- Fiction

ISBN 0-689-81168-3; 0-689-83448-9 pa

LC 98-20940

At Christmastime Henry and his dog Mudge enjoy baked treats, visits from relatives, lots of presents, and each other.

"Rylant's words and Stevenson's pictures work together to create a charming and funny holiday title that beginning readers and their grown-ups will savor year-round." SLJ

Henry and Mudge and Annie's good move; the eighteenth book of their adventures. story by Cynthia Rylant; pictures by Suçie Stevenson. Simon & Schuster Books for Young Readers 1998 40p il (Ready-to-read) $15.95; pa $3.99

Grades: K 1 2   E

1. Dogs -- Fiction 2. Fear -- Fiction 3. Moving -- Fiction 4

Wishes -- Fiction 5. Cousins -- Fiction
ISBN 0-689-81174-8; 0-689-83284-2 pa

LC 97002723

When Henry's cousin Annie prepares to move in next door he and Mudge help calm her fears.

"The pen-and-ink and watercolor cartoons perfectly express the emotional nuances of the text." SLJ

Henry and Mudge and the bedtime thumps; the ninth book of their adventures. story by Cynthia Rylant; pictures by Su¿cie Stevenson. Simon & Schuster Books for Young Readers 1996 40p il (Ready-to-read) pa $3.99

Grades: K 1 2   E

1. Dogs -- Fiction 2. Grandmothers -- Fiction
ISBN 0-689-80162-9

First published 1991 by Bradbury Press

Henry worries about what will happen to his big dog Mudge during their visit to his grandmother's house in the country.

"The simple text, full of rhythmic poetic repetition, conveys the hesitancies and humor in this common situation. To this are added lively watercolors that amplify characters, emotions, and setting. This is a perfect marriage of pictures and words." SLJ

Henry and Mudge and the best day of all; the fourteenth book of their adventures. story by Cynthia Rylant; pictures by Su¿cie Stevenson. Simon & Schuster Books for Young Readers 1995 40p il (Ready-to-read) hardcover o.p. pa $3.99

Grades: K 1 2   E

1. Dogs -- Fiction 2. Parties -- Fiction 3. Birthdays -- Fiction
ISBN 0-689-81006-7; 0-689-81385-6 pa

Henry and his big dog Mudge celebrate Henry's birthday with a piñata, a lively birthday party, and a cake shaped like a fish tank, making May first the best day ever.

Henry and Mudge and the careful cousin; the thirteenth book of their adventures. story by Cynthia Rylant; pictures by Su¿cie Stevenson. Simon & Schuster Books for Young Readers 1999 47p il $15.99; pa $3.99

Grades: K 1 2   E

1. Dogs -- Fiction 2. Cousins -- Fiction
ISBN 0-689-81007-5; 0-689-81386-4 pa

First published 1994 by Bradbury Press

At first Henry's very neat cousin doesn't like the cookies from under his bed or Mudge's slobbery kisses, but when they all play frisbee, she begins to enjoy her visit.

"Simple and funny, this beginning reader has plenty of appeal. Stevenson's line-and-watercolor illustrations seem slapdash and informal yet manage to catch the right facial expression and body language time and time again." Booklist

Henry and Mudge and the great grandpas; the twenty-third book of their adventures. story by Cynthia Rylant; pictures by Su¿cie Stevenson. Simon & Schuster Books for Young Readers 1999 40p il (Ready-to-read) $14.95; pa $3.99

Grades: K 1 2   E

1. Dogs -- Fiction 2. Old age -- Fiction 3. Grandfathers -- Fiction
ISBN 0-689-81170-5; 0689834470 pa

LC 98-18317

When Henry and his dog Mudge go with Henry's parents to visit Great-Grandpa Bill in the home with lots of other grandpas, they lead them all on a wonderful adventure

"Rylant manages to make things idyllic without being soppy, partly because the mischief is both cozy and farcical; and Stevenson's clear, active line-and-watercolor pictures individualize the grandpas and show

their affectionate bond with Henry and the huge, slobbering mutt." Booklist

Henry and Mudge and the happy cat; the eighth book of their adventures. story by Cynthia Rylant; pictures by Su¿cie Stevenson. Simon & Schuster Books for Young Readers 1996 47p il (Ready-to-read) pa $3.99

Grades: K 1 2   E

1. Cats -- Fiction 2. Dogs -- Fiction
ISBN 0-689-81013-X

First published 1990 by Bradbury Press

Henry's family takes in a stray cat, the ugliest cat they have ever seen, and an amazing relationship blossoms between it and their big dog Mudge

Henry and Mudge and the snowman plan; the nineteenth book of their adventures. story by Cynthia Rylant; pictures by Su¿cie Stevenson. Simon & Schuster Bks. for Young Readers 1999 40p il (Ready-to-read) hardcover o.p. pa $3.99

Grades: K 1 2   E

1. Dogs -- Fiction 2. Snow -- Fiction
ISBN 0-689-81169-1; 0-689-83449-7 pa

LC 98-7042

Henry, his dog Mudge, and his father enter a snowman building contest at the local park and win third place

"Humor, simple sentence structure, and bright, detailed pictures again prove a winning combination." Booklist

Henry and Mudge and the starry night; the seventeenth book of their adventures. pictures by Su¿cie Stevenson. Simon & Schuster Books for Young Readers 1998 40p il (Ready-to-read) hardcover o.p. pa $3.99

Grades: K 1 2   E

1. Dogs -- Fiction 2. Camping -- Fiction
ISBN 0-689-81175-6; 0-689-82586-2 pa

LC 96-44443

Henry, his dog Mudge, and his parents go on a quiet camping trip to Big Bear Lake, enjoying the clean smell of trees and wonderful green dreams

"Stevenson's warm, active illustrations extend the gentle words, the physicalness of the pet story, the sense of connection in a solitary place." Booklist

Henry and Mudge get the cold shivers; the seventh book of their adventures. story by Cynthia Rylant; pictures by Su¿cie Stevenson. Simon & Schuster Books for Young Readers 1994 48p il (Ready-to-read) hardcover o.p. pa $3.99

Grades: K 1 2   E

1. Dogs -- Fiction 2. Sick -- Fiction
ISBN 0-689-81014-8; 0-689-81015-6 pa

First published 1989 by Bradbury Press

When Henry's dog Mudge gets sick unexpectedly, Henry does all he can to make him feel better.

"The bond of caring and special friendship between these two young friends is once again humorously and sensitively delivered." SLJ

Henry and Mudge in the family trees; the fifteenth book of their adventures. story by Cynthia Rylant; pictures by Su¿cie Stevenson. Simon & Schuster Bks. for Young Readers 1997 40p il (Ready-to-read) hardcover o.p. pa $3.99

Grades: K 1 2   E

1. Dogs -- Fiction 2. Family reunions -- Fiction
ISBN 0-689-81179-9; 0-689-82317-7 pa

LC 96-19964

"Henry and his parents are invited to a family reunion at Cousin Annie's house. . . . The boy is excited to go, but worries that his relatives won't understand Mudge and his dog drool. But to the boy's delight, the family is thrilled to see Mudge. . . . Rylant writes in a straightforward, engaging voice, keeping the action simple but interesting. . . . Stevenson's warm pen-and-ink and watercolor illustrations add to the liveliness of the story." SLJ

Henry and Mudge in the green time; the third book of their adventures. pictures by Suçie Stevenson. Simon & Schuster Books for Young Readers 1998 48p il (Ready-to-read) hardcover o.p. pa $3.99
Grades: K 1 2   E
1. Dogs -- Fiction 2. Summer -- Fiction
ISBN 0-689-81000-8; 0-689-81001-6 pa
First published 1988 by Bradbury Press
For Henry and his big dog Mudge, summer means going on a picnic in the park, taking a bath under the garden hose, and going to the top of the big green hill.
"The cheery watercolors shimmer with the brightness of the summertime setting, and Mudge in particular is an engaging fellow." SLJ

Henry and Mudge in the sparkle days; the fifth book of their adventures. story by Cynthia Rylant; pictures by Suçie Stevenson. Simon & Schuster Books for Young Readers 1996 un il $15.95; pa $3.99
Grades: K 1 2   E
1. Dogs -- Fiction
ISBN 0-689-81018-0; 0-689-81019-9 pa
Another title in the author's series about Henry and Mudge
First published 1988 by Bradbury Press
"Rylant's easy-to-read text manages a full repertoire of emotions and activity—brought to buoyant life in Stevenson's cheerful colorful illustrations. The beginning reader couldn't ask for a better pair of companions." Horn Book

Little penguins; by Cynthia Rylant; illustrated by Christian Robinson. Schwartz & Wade Books 2016 40 p. color illustrations (hardcover) $17.99
Grades: PreK K 1   E
1. Winter -- Fiction 2. Penguins -- Fiction
ISBN 9780553507706; 9780553507713
LC 2015036757
In this children's book by Cynthia Rylant, illustrated by Christian Robinson, winter is coming and five "excited penguins pull out scarves, mittens, heavy socks, and boots, and Mama helps them bundle up. But when it's time to go out, one timid penguin decides to stay home. [This book is] filled with waddling baby penguins, playful text, and delightful illustrations." (Publisher's note)
"A very warm and satisfying bedtime book and a paean to penguins and winter delights." Kirkus

Moonlight: the Halloween cat; illustrated by Melissa Sweet. HarperCollins Pubs. 2003 un il $14.99; lib bdg $15.89; pa $6.99
Grades: PreK K 1 2   E
1. Cats -- Fiction 2. Halloween -- Fiction
ISBN 0-06-029711-5; 0-06-029712-3 lib bdg; 0-06-443814-7 pa
LC 2001-39511
Moonlight the cat loves everything about Halloween, from pumpkins to children to candy
"In simple, poetic prose, Rylant tracks the meandering cat's night journey. . . . Sweet's endearingly childlike, color-rich paintings convey an appreciation for the ever-deepening night. . . . A soothing, ghoul-free, utterly noncreepy Halloween picture book for the preschool set." Booklist

Mr. Putter & Tabby clear the decks. Houghton Mifflin Harcourt 2010 un il $15
Grades: K 1 2   E
1. Cats -- Fiction 2. Dogs -- Fiction 3. Boats and boating -- Fiction
ISBN 978-0-15-206715-1; 0-15-206715-9
"Rylant's adorable characters are bored, so Mr. [Putter's] neighbor Mrs. Teaberry suggests an adventure on a sightseeing boat. The Olden Days is the perfect vessel. Mrs. Teaberry's dog, Zeke, loves it so much that he doesn't want to leave and sinks his teeth into the mast, and the captain helps them out. Howard's delightful pictures created with pencil, watercolor, and gouache add humor and panache to the story." SLJ

Mr. Putter & Tabby drop the ball; Cynthia Rylant; illustrated by Arthur Howard. Harcourt Children's Books, Houghton Mifflin Harcourt 2013 44 p. $14.99
Grades: K 1 2   E
1. Cats -- Fiction 2. Baseball -- Fiction 3. Elderly men -- Fiction
ISBN 0152050728; 9780152050726
LC 2012046367
In this picture book, by Cynthia Rylant and illustrated by Arthur Howard, "Mr. Putter and his fine cat, Tabby, love to take naps -- too many naps. What they need is a sport! Luckily Mrs. Teaberry and her good dog, Zeke, know of a baseball team they can join. It's not long before Mr. Putter is ready to play ball, but will his creaky knees cooperate? And can Zeke avoid wreaking havoc on the field?" (Publisher's note)

Mr. Putter & Tabby hit the slope; Cynthia Rylant & Arthur Howard Houghton Mifflin Harcourt 2016 40 p. color illustrations (hardback) $14.99
Grades: K 1 2   E
1. Old age -- Fiction 2. Cats -- Fiction 3. Winter -- Fiction 4. Sledding -- Fiction 5. Friendship -- Fiction
ISBN 0152064273; 9780152064273
LC 2015033309
In this picture book, by Cynthia Rylant, illustrated by Arthur Howard, "Mr. Putter and his fine cat, Tabby, like winter. But when the snow is deep outside and there's nothing to do inside, even a cozy winter day can be a little slow. Not for long! When Mrs. Teaberry and her good dog Zeke, pull two sleds out of the garage, the four friends head for the sledding slope for the wildest ride ever. Maybe winter is not so slow after all!" (Publisher's note)
"Howard's pencil, watercolor, and gouache illustrations both reflect the text and provide contextual cues as well as adding to the subtle humor. Simple words can still surprise with adventure and humor." Kirkus

★ **Mr.** Putter & Tabby pour the tea; illustrated by Arthur Howard Harcourt Brace & Co. 1994 un il $14; pa $5.95
Grades: K 1 2   E
1. Cats -- Fiction 2. Old age -- Fiction
ISBN 0-15-256255-9; 0-15-200901-9 pa
LC 93-21470
"Rylant's charming story of two elderly characters is complemented and enhanced by Howard's delightful illustrations, done in pencil, watercolor, and gouache." SLJ
Other titles about Mr. Putter and Tabby are:
Mr. Putter & Tabby bake the cake (1994)
Mr. Putter & Tabby walk the dog (1994)
Mr. Putter & Tabby pick the pears (1995)
Mr. Putter & Tabby row the boat (1997)
Mr. Putter & Tabby fly the plane (1997)
Mr. Putter & Tabby take the train (1998)
Mr. Putter & Tabby toot the horn (1998)
Mr. Putter & Tabby paint the porch (2000)
Mr. Putter & Tabby feed the fish (2001)

Mr. Putter & Tabby catch the cold (2002)

Mr. Putter & Tabby stir the soup (2003)

Mr. Putter & Tabby write the book (2004)

Mr. Putter & Tabby make a wish (2005)

Mr. Putter & Tabby spin the yarn (2006)

Mr. Putter & Tabby see the stars (2007)

Mr. Putter & Tabby run the race (2008)

Mr. Putter & Tabby spill the beans (2009)

Mr. Putter & Tabby clear the decks (2010)

Mr. Putter & Tabby ring the bell (2011)

Mr. Putter and Tabby dance the dance (2012)

Mr. Putter and Tabby drop the ball (2013)

Mr. Putter and Tabby turn the page (2014)

Mr. Putter and Tabby smell the roses (2015)

Mr. Putter and Tabby hit the slop (2016)

Mr. Putter & Tabby ring the bell; written by Cynthia Rylant; illustrated by Arthur Howard. Houghton Mifflin Harcourt 2011 il $14.99

Grades: K 1 2   E

1. School stories 2. Cats -- Fiction 3. Dogs -- Fiction 4. Autumn -- Fiction 5. Old age -- Fiction

ISBN 0-15-205071-X; 978-0-15-205071-9

LC 2010043403

While enjoying autumn weather and activities, Mr. Putter, realizing how much he misses going to school, takes his cat Tabby, their adventurous neighbor, Mrs. Teaberry, and her cake-loving dog Zeke to "Show and Tell."

"Howard's pencil, watercolor and gouache illustrations charmingly convey Mr. Putter's longings, the mischievousness of his plan and his delight in being back at school. Rylant's ever-fresh text will gracefully coax emergent readers into independence." Kirkus

Mr. Putter & Tabby smell the roses; Cynthia Rylant & Arthur Howard. Houghton Mifflin Harcourt 2015 40 p. $14.99

Grades: K 1 2   E

1. Garden rooms 2. Cats -- Fiction 3. Dogs -- Fiction 4. Birthdays -- Fiction 5. Conservatories -- Fiction

ISBN 9780152060817

LC 2014038080

In this book, by Cynthia Rylant, illustrated by Arthur Howard, "Mr. Putter wants Mrs. Teaberry's birthday to be extra special this year. So how about a trip to the Conservatory to see the beautiful trees and plants and flowers? It will be heavenly. And it is! Mr. Putter and Tabby and Mrs. Teaberry and Zeke sniff the air. They smell the roses. They learn the plant facts. It's the perfect celebration . . . until Zeke finds the banana tree." (Publisher's note)

"There is a nice balance between intriguing text and creative pictures, making this a wonderful choice for developing readers." SLJ

Mr. Putter & Tabby turn the page; Cynthia Rylant; illustrated by Arthur Howard. Houghton Mifflin Harcourt 2014 40 p. chiefly color illustrations $14.99

Grades: K 1 2   E

1. Cats -- Fiction 2. Dogs -- Fiction 3. Libraries -- Fiction 4. Books and reading -- Fiction

ISBN 0152060634; 9780152060633

LC 2013042822

Theodor Seuss Geisel Honor Book (2015)

In this book, by Cynthia Rylant, illustrated by Arthur Howard, "Mr. Putter and his fine cat, Tabby, love reading their favorite books over and over. So when Mr. Putter sees a sign at the library that says "Read Aloud with Your Pet at Story Time," he signs up! But then Mr. Putter's friend and neighbor, Mrs. Teaberry, wants to join. If Mrs. Teaberry brings her

good dog, Zeke, to the library, who knows what will happen?" (Publisher's note)

"The simple story is broken up into five short chapters, and Howard's pencil, watercolor and gouache illustrations successfully reinforce the gentle humor of the story and characterization." Kirkus

★ **Poppleton**; book one. illustrated by Mark Teague. Blue Sky Press (NY) 1997 48p il hardcover o.p. pa $3.99

Grades: K 1 2   E

1. Pigs -- Fiction 2. Friendship -- Fiction

ISBN 0-590-84783-X; 0-590-84782-1 pa

LC 96-3365

"City pig Poppleton adjusts to small-town life in this . . . chapter book. In 'Neighbors,' the polite Poppleton tries to think up a polite way to say 'no thanks' to Cherry Sue, a friendly llama who invites him to breakfast, lunch and dinner every single day. . . . The second vignette, 'The Library,' details Poppleton's reading ritual, which demands solitude. Finally, 'The Pill' introduces Fillmore, a sick goat who refuses to take his pill unless Poppleton hides it in a cake. . . . [Rylant's] concise sentences mimic the characters' good manners and wryly point up the failures of etiquette. Teague contributes fetching watercolor-and-pencil images of the pudgy pig, slender llama and dignified goat." Publ Wkly

Other titles about Poppleton are:

Poppleton and friends (1997)

Poppleton everyday (1998)

Poppleton forever (1998)

Poppleton has fun (2000)

Poppleton in Fall (1999)

Poppleton in Spring (1999)

Poppleton in Winter (2001)

Poppleton through and through (2000)

Puppies and piggies; illustrated by Ivan Bates. Harcourt 2008 32p il $16

Grades: PreK   E

1. Stories in rhyme 2. Animals -- Fiction

ISBN 978-0-15-202321-8; 0-15-202321-6

LC 2004-3136

Rhyming text describes what various animals do and what they love, as well as a baby who loves his bed and his mother.

"Told in reassuring rhyme, the simple upbeat text showcases happy animals doing what comes naturally while Bates's idyllic watercolor and crayon illustrations present a bucolic barnyard teeming with contented critters. . . . Comforting and carefree fare for tiny tots." Kirkus

★ **The relatives came**; story by Cynthia Rylant; illustrated by Stephen Gammell. rev format ed.; Atheneum Books for Young Readers 2001 un il $16.95; pa $6.99

Grades: PreK K 1 2   E

1. Family life -- Fiction

ISBN 0-689-84508-1; 0-689-71738-5 pa

A reformatted edition of the title first published 1985 by Bradbury Press

A Caldecott Medal honor book, 1986

"If there's anything more charming than the tone of voice in this story, it's the drawings that go with it. Stephen Gammell . . . fills the pages with bright, crayony pictures teeming with details that children should enjoy poring over for hours." NY Times Book Rev

★ **Snow**; illustrated by Lauren Stringer. Harcourt 2008 un il $17

Grades: PreK K 1 2   E

1. Snow -- Fiction

ISBN 978-0-15-205303-1; 0-15-205303-4

LC 2006-06171

Celebrates the beauty of a snowfall and its happy effects on children. "Snow is not an uncommon subject in picture books, but few have both the grace and exuberance of this lovely collaboration featuring Rylant's evocative words and Stringer's entrancing paintings." Booklist

When I was young in the mountains; illustrated by Diane Goode. Dutton 1982 un il $15.99; pa $6.99

Grades: K 1 2 3   **E**

1. Appalachian region -- Fiction

ISBN 0-525-42525-X; 0-525-44198-0 pa

LC 81-5359

A Caldecott Medal honor book, 1983

"The people in the story are poor in material things, but rich in family pleasures. The title becomes a pleasing refrain. . . . Illustrations and text are placed on a bed of white space, without borders, which makes them look uncrowded and imparts a great feeling of freedom." SLJ

Saab, Julie

Little Lola; by Julie Saab; pictures by David Gothard. Greenwillow Books, an imprint of HarperCollinsPublishers 2014 32 p. (trade ed.) $16.99

Grades: PreK K 1 2   **E**

1. School stories 2. Cats -- Fiction 3. Schools -- Fiction

ISBN 0062274570; 9780062274571

LC 2013030016

In this children's book, by Julie Saab, "Lola is curious about everything . . . especially school. What is school like? Find out when Lola the cat heads to school herself and gets a paw (or two) into just about everything." (Publisher's note)

"Little Lola, a cat, "has big plans." She dresses herself as a kid, hops on the bus, and goes to school. Lola manages to fit right in...until her show-and-tell mouse gives her away and disrupts everything. Gothard's watercolor art combines a retro look with comic action and brings Lola vividly to life, though her human counterparts appear stiff in comparison." Horn Book

Sabuda, Robert

The **Christmas** alphabet; deluxe anniversary edition; Orchard Books 2004 un il $22.95

Grades: K 1 2 3 4   **E**

1. Alphabet 2. Christmas 3. Pop-up books

ISBN 0-439-67256-2

First published 1994

"Four large flaps per spread—each representing a letter of the alphabet—open to reveal sophisticated 3D images, some with parts that move in uncommonly inventive ways. Many of the pop-ups are obvious Christmas symbols. . . . Others have ambiguous—but resourceful—ties to the holiday. . . . A yuletide gem." Publ Wkly

The **dragon** & the knight; a pop-up misadventure. Robert Sabuda. Simon & Schuster 2014 22 p. $29.99

Grades: K 1 2 3 4   **E**

1. Fairy tales 2. Dragons -- Fiction 3. Knights and knighthood -- Fiction

ISBN 1416960813; 9781416960812

In this children's book by Robert Sabuda "a Dragon and a Knight race through a fairy tale treasury, visiting the worlds of all of your favorite stories--from Rapunzel to Aladdin, to Cinderella, The Three Little Pigs, and more! With characters who literally pop right off the pages, this tour de force will have readers young and old speeding through the book to see just how this chase will end!" (Publisher's note)

The **Little** Mermaid; a pop-up adaptation of the classic fairytale. by Robert Sabuda. 1st ed. Simon & Schuster 2013 12 p. $29.99

Grades: 2 3 4 5   **E**

1. Fairy tales 2. Princes -- Fiction 3. Mermaids -- Fiction 4. Toy and movable books -- Fiction

ISBN 1416960805; 144245086X; 9781416960805; 9781442450868

This pop-up book, by Robert Sabuda, is an "adaptation of the beloved fairy tale 'The Little Mermaid.' . . . Amazing three-dimensional paper structures pop off each page, bringing this classic underwater adventure to life. This [is a] visually stunning tale of adventure, true love, and sacrifice." (Publisher's note)

"Sabuda graces Andersen's dark tale with enormous, elaborate pop-up illustrations. Each of five double-page spreads contains one large construction; sidebars open to additional pop-ups. The paper engineering is more remarkable for its intricacy and atmosphere-building than its role in the storytelling. Children familiar with Disney's version may be surprised at the tragedy in this adaptation, which stays close to Andersen's original." (Horn Books)

★ **Peter** Pan: a classic collectible pop-up. Simon & Schuster Children's Pub. 2008 un il $29.99

Grades: 2 3 4 5 6   **E**

1. Fairy tales 2. Pop-up books

ISBN 978-0-689-85364-7; 0-689-85364-5

"Sabuda enhances the already powerful enchantments of J. M. Barrie's classic 1902 tale with astonishing paper engineering. Illustrations suggest a hybrid of period styles, somewhere between arts and crafts with their rich patterning, and art nouveau, with their Tiffany glass-like outlines and colorations. . . . Not to be missed." Publ Wkly

Sacre, Antonio

A **mango** in the hand; a story told through proverbs. illustrated by Sebastia Serra. Abrams Books for Young Readers 2011 un il $16.95

Grades: K 1 2 3   **E**

1. Cuba -- Fiction 2. Mangoes -- Fiction 3. Proverbs -- Fiction 4. Family life -- Fiction 5. Spanish language -- Vocabulary

ISBN 978-0-8109-9734-9; 0-8109-9734-7

LC 2010024423

Guided by proverbs from his father and other relatives, Francisco makes several attempts to bring ripe mangoes home for dessert on his saint day, and in the process learns lessons in love and generosity. Includes glossary of Spanish terms.

"Sacre's snappy storytelling avoids being overly moralistic, and Serra's digitally colored pencil-and-ink artwork creates a friendly, close-knit neighborhood for Francisco, the kind in which food, conversation—and proverbs—can be found in abundance." Publ Wkly

La Noche Buena; a Christmas story. illustrated by Angela Dominguez. Abrams Books for Young Readers 2010 un il $16.95

Grades: K 1 2 3   **E**

1. Florida -- Fiction 2. Christmas -- Fiction 3. Family life -- Fiction 4. Grandmothers -- Fiction 5. Cuban Americans -- Fiction

ISBN 978-0-8109-8967-2; 0-8109-8967-0

LC 200905220

While spending Christmas with her Cuban American grandmother in Miami, Florida, young Nina misses her usual New England holiday but enjoys learning about the foods and other traditions her father knew as a child.

"Attractive paintings with simple lines and bright, solid colors help tell this warm, loving story in an understated way." Kirkus

Sage, James

Stop feedin' da boids! James Sage; illustrated by Pierre Pratt. Kids Can Press 2017 32 p. color illustrations $16.95

Grades: K 1 2   **E**
1. Pigeons -- Fiction 2. Neighbors -- Fiction 3. City and town life -- Fiction
ISBN 1771386134; 9781771386135

"Author James Sage's funny picture book explores what happens when a nature-loving girl meets city birds. The playful, vibrant artwork by award-winning illustrator Pierre Pratt offers its own comic narrative. Readers are in on the havoc below the bird feeder that Swanda doesn't see." (Publisher's note)

Saint-Lot, Katia Novet

Amadi's snowman; illustrated by Dimitrea Tokunbo. Tilbury House 2008 un il $16.95
Grades: PreK K 1 2   **E**
1. Nigeria -- Fiction 2. Books and reading -- Fiction 3. Igbo (African people) -- Fiction
ISBN 978-0-88448-298-7; 0-88448-298-7

LC 2007043343

As a young Igbo man, Amadi does not understand why his mother insists he learn to read, since he already knows his numbers and will be a businessman one day, but an older boy teaches him the value of learning about the world through books

"Children will enjoy reading about Amadi's life in the village, depicted in the earth-toned, intimate scenes." Booklist

Sakai, Komako

★ **Mad** at Mommy. Arthur A. Levine Books 2010 un il $16.99
Grades: PreK K 1   **E**
1. Anger -- Fiction 2. Rabbits -- Fiction 3. Mother-child relationship -- Fiction
ISBN 978-0-545-21209-0; 0-545-21209-X

Original Japanese edition, 2000

A little rabbit is very angry at his mother, and he tells her the reasons why.

"Sakai's paintings are simply composed and staged, allowing rabbit's expressive poses to shine. . . . A playful story that offers young readers—and their big feelings—a serious voice. Charming, classy and current." Kirkus

★ The **snow** day. Arthur A. Levine Books 2009 un il $16.99
Grades: PreK K   **E**
1. Snow -- Fiction 2. Rabbits -- Fiction
ISBN 978-0-545-01321-5; 0-545-01321-6

LC 2007-49949

Original Japanese edition 2005

A little rabbit enjoys having a day off from kindergarten and spending time with his mother during a snowstorm, but his father's flight home is cancelled until the snow stops falling.

Sakai's "subdued palette and minimalist text suggest the blanketed sound produced by a heavy snowfall. . . . The layers of paint are applied to a black ground with a combination of wet and dry brushes, producing a convincing depth and texture. . . . The sentences are appropriately concise, yet with lovely rhythms and interesting details." SLJ

Salas, Laura Purdie

A **leaf** can be; by Laura Purdie Salas; illustrations by Violeta Dabija. Millbrook Press 2012 32 p. (lib. bdg. : alk. paper) $17.95
Grades: K 1 2 3   **E**
1. Stories in rhyme 2. Leaves -- Fiction
ISBN 0761362037; 9780761362036

LC 2011022227

In this book of poetry, by Laura Purdie Salas, rhyming text explores the many roles a leaf can play, from providing shelter for animals in the rain . . . to housing cocoons, . . . to purifying the air, . . . to providing

autumnal entertainment for children. . . . [The] book offers abundant opportunity for discussion of scientific concepts from photosynthesis ("Sun taker/ Food maker") to camouflage ("Moth matcher" and "Snake concealer"). (Bulletin of the Center for Children's Books)

"In a simple rhyming text, Salas examines the ways that leaves play a part in our world's ecosystem... A lovely observation about nature, suitable for a variety of science units or individual sharing." SLJ

Includes bibliographical references [p. 31]

★ **Water** can be; by Laura Purdie Salas; illustrations by Violeta Dabija. Millbrook Press 2014 32 p. (lib. bdg. : alk. paper) $17.95
Grades: PreK K 1 2 3 4   **E**
1. Water
ISBN 1467705918; 9781467705912

LC 2013017772

"Water can be a thirst quencher, kid drencher, cloud fluffer, fire snuffer. Find out about the many roles water plays in this poetic exploration of water throughout the year," written by Laura Purdie Salas and illustrated by Violeta Dabija. (Publisher's note)

"Calling attention to water helps children appreciate this necessary and ubiquitous resource. In lilting rhymed text, Salas shows readers that water can be 'many things': a 'thirst quencher' and 'kid drencher'; a 'cloud fluffer' and 'fire snuffer.' Each couplet is attractively illustrated, predominantly in various shades of blues and greens. Appended 'More About Water' explanations help extend the text." Honor Book

Salley, Coleen

Epossumondas saves the day; written by Coleen Salley; illustrated by Janet Stevens. Harcourt 2006 un il $16
Grades: K 1 2 3   **E**
1. Turtles -- Fiction 2. Opossums -- Fiction 3. Birthdays -- Fiction
ISBN 0-15-205701-3

LC 2005-27538

In this variation on the folktale, Sody Salyraytus, each of Epossumondas's birthday guests disappears until it is finally up to him to rescue them all and bring home the "sody" for his birthday biscuits.

"Salley's text is alive with the colorful expressions of the South . . . which make the story a delight to read aloud. Stevens's hilarious mixed-media illustrations are a perfect match for the narrative." SLJ

Saltzberg, Barney

Beautiful oops! Workman 2010 un il $11.95
Grades: PreK K 1 2   **E**
1. Errors -- Fiction 2. Creative ability -- Fiction
ISBN 978-0-7611-5728-1; 0-7611-5728-X

"A celebration of creative thinking, Saltzberg's small-format book encourages readers to view mistakes not as failures but opportunities. . . . Various spills and blobs are transformed into animals, a crumpled piece of paper becomes wool for a sheep, and . . . a panel with a hole in the center telescopes outward, accordian-style, to reveal a tiny creature way at the bottom. Inspirational without being saccharine." Publ Wkly

Chengdu could not, would not, fall asleep; written and illustrated by Barney Saltzberg. Disney-Hyperion Books 2014 48 p. (hardback) $16.99
Grades: PreK K   **E**
1. Sleep -- Fiction 2. Bedtime -- Fiction 3. Pandas -- Fiction
ISBN 142316721X; 9781423167211

LC 2013029121

In this children's book, written and illustrated by Barney Saltzberg, "a young panda named Chengdu lies awake, even though everyone around him is quietly sleeping. He tosses and he turns. He scrunches and he squirms, until he finally finds the perfect spot." (Publisher's note)

"All the pandas are sleeping peacefully except for little Chengdu. Saltzberg gives the book an old-fashioned look by limiting the colors to black, white, gray, and the green of the bamboo trees, catching the soft textures of a dark forest at night. Gentle sight gags add humor without breaking the calming mood, making this an ideal nighttime book for the very young." Horn Book

I want a dog! Random House Children's Books 2009 un il $11.99
Grades: PreK K   **E**

1. Pop-up books 2. Dogs -- Fiction
ISBN 978-0-375-85783-6; 0-375-85783-4

"The earnest speaker in this fun story, based on the author's song of the same title, pleads for a dog, promising that it 'will never, ever make a mess' (via a pull tab, she sweeps his 'mess' into a dustpan as she holds her nose). Other animals—a hippo, a pig—won't do (turning a wheel helps the girl feed an endless bucket of slop to a tubby swine). On a final pop-up spread, she embraces a dog, surrounded by blooming, red hearts. Effective interactive elements and simple humor will charm." Publ Wkly

Stanley and the class pet; [by] Barney Saltzberg. Candlewick Press 2008 un il $16.99
Grades: PreK K 1 2   **E**

1. School stories 2. Birds -- Fiction 3. Hamsters -- Fiction
ISBN 978-0-7636-3595-4; 0-7636-3595-2

LC 2007-40541

Stanley is excited about bringing the class pet, a bird, home for the weekend, but when his friend Larry urges him to open the cage and let Figgy out to fly, it is hard to know who is to blame for the ensuing disaster.

"With clearly lined acrylic paintings and a smoothly paced text that avoids a too-heavy message, Saltzberg deftly turns a common classroom scenario into a gentle story about peer pressure and responsibility." Booklist

Other titles about Stanley are:
Crazy hair day (2003)
Star of the week (2006)

Salzano, Tammi

One rainy day; illustrated by Hannah Wood. Tiger Tales 2011 un bd bk $8.95
Grades: PreK   **E**

1. Board books for children 2. Rain -- Fiction 3. Color -- Fiction 4. Ducks -- Fiction
ISBN 978-1-58925-860-0; 1-58925-860-6

"Beneath light showers of foil raindrops, a duckling sporting red boots and an orange umbrella happily encounters a green frog, pink worms, yellow flowers, and other color-linked items. The text in this padded-cover board book runs to just a short phrase per spread, and the fuzzy yellow duck's joie de vivre glows in each simply composed scene." Booklist

Samuels, Barbara

★ The **trucker**. Farrar, Straus and Giroux 2010 un il $16.99
Grades: PreK K 1   **E**

1. Cats -- Fiction 2. Toys -- Fiction 3. Trucks -- Fiction
ISBN 978-0-374-37804-2; 0-374-37804-5

LC 2007029266

A boy who loves trucks is disappointed when he receives a cat named Lola instead of a toy fire truck, but Lola proves to be a "trucker" after all.

"A winner for young children, this offers a real story along with all of the vehicle action. Kids will enjoy the combination of active play and cozy snuggling." Booklist

Sanabria, José

As Time Went By; by José Sanabria. NorthSouth 2016 48 p. color illustrations $18.95
Grades: PreK K 1 2 3   **E**

1. Poverty -- Fiction 2. Boats and boating -- Fiction
ISBN 0735842485; 9780735842489

Mildred L. Batchelder Honor Book (2017)

"A steamship makes a journey across time from luxury and exclusivity, industry and abandonment, to stewardship and inclusion as we see the evolving functions of the ship and the changing faces of the people who cherish it most of all." (Publisher's note)

"This layered allegory of the cyclical nature of life and human behavior is beautifully illustrated in textured watercolors in which the grays, browns, and blues of the landscape dominate the mood. The human figures are tiny when compared to the giant ship, but the color and life they bring to its decks in the final image is transformative." Booklist

Sandall, Ellie

Birdsong. Egmont USA 2011 un il $16.99
Grades: PreK   **E**

1. Birds -- Fiction 2. Birdsongs -- Fiction
ISBN 978-1-60684-193-8; 1-60684-193-9

LC 2010017006

A crowd of birds lands in a tree, sharing their different songs, until one last winged creature proves to be too much.

"The book has rhythm, bird sounds that are great fun to hear and say, and illustrations that depict each cast member as a winged creature of distinction." Horn Book Guide

Sandemose, Iben

Gracie & Grandma & the itsy, bitsy seed; translated from Norwegian by Tonje Vetleseter. MacKenzie Smiles 2009 un il $14.95
Grades: PreK K 1 2   **E**

1. Growth -- Fiction 2. Plants -- Fiction 3. Grandmothers -- Fiction
ISBN 978-0-9790347-5-6; 0-9790347-5-2

"Spunky and imaginative Gracie presents her equally exuberant grandmother with a surprise–an itsy, bitsy seed. But what will it grow into? As the plant gets larger and larger, Grandma incorrectly guesses that it is a banana, lemon, fried mackerel, balloon, jungle, cow, or ghost tree until she spots a large red dot growing at the top and shouts: 'A big tomato!' . . . The simple yet expressive text, in a large, bold typeface, perfectly complements the wacky, exaggerated, dazzlingly bright colored ink and marker cartoon illustrations." SLJ

Other titles in this series are:
Gracie & Grandma (2008)
Gracie & Grandma under water (2008)

Sanders-Wells, Linda

Maggie's monkeys; illustrated by Abby Carter. Candlewick Press 2009 un il $16.99
Grades: K 1 2   **E**

1. Siblings -- Fiction 2. Family life -- Fiction 3. Imagination -- Fiction
ISBN 978-0-7636-3326-4; 0-7636-3326-7

LC 2008-2871

When Maggie reports that pink monkeys have moved into the refrigerator, her mother and father play along and accomodate the invisible visitors, much to the frustration of Maggie's older, reality-obsessed brother

"Sanders-Wells wonderfully encapsulates the difficulties of being a middle child—simultaneously too old and too young. Carter's masterful facial expressions reflects this inner battle. Her gouache artwork is done in a bright, tropical palette that emphasizes the imaginative theme . . . . A humorous tale sure to make siblings smile, even as they inwardly groan." Kirkus

Sanna, Francesca

★ The **Journey**; Francesca Sanna. Flying Eye Books 2016 48 p. color illustrations (hardcover) $17.95

Grades: PreK K 1 2   E

1. Refugees -- Fiction 2. Mother-child relationship -- Fiction 3. Immigration and emigration -- Fiction

ISBN 1909263990; 9781909263994

LC 2016049512

This children's book by Francesca Sanna presents "the story of a widowed mother fleeing a war-torn homeland with her two children. . . . The family members have black hair and pale skin, and the mother takes advice from a friend who wears the hijab, though her own hair is uncovered. They travel by car, by bicycle, hidden in the backs of trucks, and on foot until they reach a wall. . . . After a dangerous sea crossing, the family moves with hope toward a safer place." (Kirkus Reviews)

"Simultaneously heartbreaking, scary, and brightly hopeful, this timely tale with simply captivating artwork will spur little ones to ask questions that lack easy answers." Booklist

Santat, Dan

★ The **adventures** of Beekle; the unimaginary friend. Dan Santat. First edition Little, Brown and Co. 2014 40 p. $17

Grades: PreK K 1 2   E

1. Friendship 2. Friendship -- Fiction 3. Imaginary playmates -- Fiction

ISBN 0316199982; 9780316199988

LC 2013017700

Caldecott Medal (2015)

In this book by Dan Santat, "an imaginary friend . . . longs for the day when a child will 'imagine' him, and thus choose and name him. As the days pass and he remains unchosen, the intrepid fellow goes in search of his intended child, leaving his imaginary home for the real world. . . . Finally a girl named Alice chooses him; once she dubs him 'Beekle' a bond is formed, and the two go on to have adventures, both real and imaginary, together." (Bulletin of the Center for Children's Books)

"Imaginary friend Beekle waits and waits for a child to think him into existence. When it doesn't happen, Beekle sails off to the real world--a city full of boring adults--to find her. Santat's bright digital illustrations capture the vivid land of imagination, the drab adult world, and the giggle-inducing expressions on marshmallow-like Beekle's pudgy white face." Horn Book

Are we there yet? Dan Santat. Little, Brown & Co. 2016 40 p. color illustrations (hardcover) $17.99

Grades: PreK K 1 2   E

1. Time travel -- Fiction 2. Automobile travel -- Fiction 3. Space and time -- Fiction 4. Automobile driving -- Fiction

ISBN 0316199990; 9780316199995

LC 2015011643

In this children's book, by Dan Santat, " a boy feels time slowing down so much that it starts going backward--into the time of pirates! Of princesses! Of dinosaurs! The boy was just trying to get to his grandmother's birthday party, but instead he's traveling through Ancient Egypt and rubbing shoulders with Ben Franklin. When time flies, who knows where--or when--he'll end up." (Publisher's note)

"A multilayered, modern-day parable reminding readers there's no greater gift than the present." Kirkus

Sarah, Linda

Big friends; Linda Sarah; illustrated by Benji Davies. Henry Holt & Co. 2016 32 p. color illustrations (hardcover) $16.99

Grades: PreK K 1 2   E

1. Play -- Fiction 2. Friendship -- Fiction 3. Imagination -- Fiction

4. Best friends -- Fiction

ISBN 9781627793308; 1627793305

LC 2015005998

In this children's book by Linda Sarah, illustrated by Benji Davies, "Birt and Etho are best friends. Together they play outside in big cardboard boxes. Sometimes they're kings, soldiers, astronauts. Sometimes they're pirates sailing wild seas and skies. But always, always they're Big friends. Then one day a new boy arrives, and he wants to join them. Can two become three?" (Publisher's note)

"Charming artwork graces each page, complementing the perfectly paced flow of the story, which is written as a free-verse poem. Whimsical, endearing illustrations make this picture book an even more charming and tender tale." SLJ

Sarcone-Roach, Julia

The **bear** ate your sandwich; by Julia Sarcone-Roach. Alfred A. Knopf 2015 40 p. color illustrations (lib. bdg.) $19.99

Grades: PreK K 1 2   E

1. Bears -- Fiction 2. City and town life 3. Dogs -- Fiction 4. Humorous stories 5. Sandwiches -- Fiction 6. City and town life -- Fiction

ISBN 0375958606; 9780375858604; 9780375958601

LC 2014013199

Written by Julia Sarcone-Roach, this children's book tells the "tale of a bear, lost in the city, who happens upon an unattended sandwich in the park. The bear's journey from forest to city and back home again is full of happy accidents, funny encounters, and sensory delights. The story is so engrossing, it's not until the very end that we begin to suspect this is a TALL tale." (Publisher's note)

"'By now I think you know what happened to your sandwich,' begins the very unreliable narrator in this amusing picture book. His story? A woodland bear fell asleep in the back of a truck and awoke to find himself in the city . . . The city scenes reward attention with intriguing, sometimes comical details. This is a picture book that kids will want to hear again immediately, once they know who is telling the story." Booklist

Subway story. Alfred A. Knopf 2011 un il $16.99; lib bdg $19.99

Grades: PreK K   E

1. Subways -- Fiction 2. New York (N.Y.) -- Fiction

ISBN 978-0-375-85859-8; 0-375-85859-8; 978-0-375-95859-5 lib bdg; 0-375-95859-2 lib bdg

LC 2010045487

Jessie, a subway car 'born' in St. Louis, Missouri, enjoys many years as an important part of the New York City subway system, and after she is replaced by more modern cars she begins another important job.

"The author's acrylics gently anthropomorphize Jessie, giving her headlight-eyes and a winsome smile. Immensely readable and surprisingly touching, this large heft of metal totes a lot of charm." Kirkus

Includes bibliographical references

Sartell, Debra

Time for bed, baby Ted; illustrations by Kay Chorao. Holiday House 2010 un il $16.95

Grades: PreK   E

1. Stories in rhyme 2. Bedtime -- Fiction

ISBN 978-0-8234-1968-5; 0-8234-1968-1

LC 2008-48652

At bedtime, Baby Ted finds many ways to avoid going to bed.

"The various animal sounds and action words in the short text, coupled with Chorao's pleasing illustrations, featuring a mop-topped Ted and his pretend menagerie, make this a fun read-aloud for parent and child and a natural for sharing with a young group of children." Booklist

Sasso, Sandy Eisenberg

The **Shema** in the mezuzah; listening to each other. Sandy Eisenberg Sasso; Illustrations by Joani Keller Rothenberg. Jewish Lights Pub. 2012 30 p. col. ill. $18.99

Grades: K 1 2 3   E

1. Mezuzah -- Fiction 2. Listening -- Fiction 3. Jews -- Fiction 4. Judaism -- Customs and practices -- Fiction

ISBN 1580235069; 9781580235068

LC 2012007709

National Jewish Book Awards: Illustrated Children's Book (2012)

This Jewish children's story, by Rabbi Sandy Eisenberg Sasso, is about "compromise and listening. The townspeople have mezuzahs but cannot agree on how to put them up on their doorways. . . . To end their arguing, they consult the wise rabbi of the town, who advises them to carefully read the Shema in the mezuzah to find the answer. This . . . tale [is] based on a twelfth-century rabbinic debate." (Publisher's note)

Sattler, Jennifer

★ **Pig** kahuna. Bloomsbury Children's Books 2011 un il $14.99; lib bdg $15.89

Grades: PreK K 1 2   E

1. Pigs -- Fiction 2. Surfing -- Fiction

ISBN 978-1-59990-635-5; 1-59990-635-X; 978-1-59990-636-2 lib bdg; 1-59990-636-8 lib bdg

LC 2010035629

Fergus is afraid to go in the water, but he and his baby brother Dink find a surfboard while collecting treasures along the seashore.

"The briskly paced text . . . offers alliteration and deadpan humor. Together words and pictures create an utterly engaging picture-book experience—eye-catching, thought-provoking and just plain fun." Kirkus

Pig kahuna pirates! Jennifer Sattler. Bloomsbury 2014 32 p. (hardback) $16.99

Grades: PreK K 1 2   E

1. Pigs -- Fiction 2. Play -- Fiction 3. Beaches -- Fiction 4. Brothers -- Fiction

ISBN 1619632004; 9781619632004; 9781619632011; 9781619632035

LC 2013028954

In this children's book, by Jennifer Sattler, "Fergus and Dink love playing at the beach. But when Dink wakes up from his nap in a crabby mood, it's up to big brother Fergus to pull him out of it. Does the little fella want to take a swim? Build a sand castle? Have a juice box? Aaargh! Only one thing will tame the tantrum: When Fergus invites Dink to play with his new pirate ship of sand, and gives him the starring role as pirate captain." (Publisher's note)

"Fergus likes swimming in the ocean, but his young brother, Dink, who wakes up from his nap out of sorts, finds it too cold. He's in a horrible mood, and Fergus can't seem to cheer him up...The detail and line of the pigs make them pop to the forefront of the summery seaside scene. The large font and short sentences make this book easy to share with a group, and the subject matter and the single plotline are a great match for a preschool audience." SLJ

Sylvie. Random House 2009 un il $15.99; lib bdg $18.99

Grades: PreK K 1   E

1. Food -- Fiction 2. Color -- Fiction 3. Flamingos -- Fiction

ISBN 978-0-375-85708-9; 0-375-85708-7; 978-0-375-95708-6 lib bdg; 0-375-95708-1 lib bdg

LC 2008-11259

When Sylvie the pink flamingo learns her color comes from the little pink shrimp she eats, she decides to expand her choices, trying everything under the sun and, unfortunately, overdoing it.

"Sattler's art steals the show; the colors are eye-popping and vibrant, right to the swirling bright endpapers. . . . This title is sure to create storytime magic." SLJ

Uh-oh, dodo! Jennifer Sattler. Boyds Mills Press 2013 32 p. (reinforced) $15.95

Grades: PreK K   E

1. Dodo -- Fiction 2. Picture books for children

ISBN 9781590789292; 1590789296

LC 2012947460

In this children's story, written and illustrated by Jennifer Sattler, Dodo "loves an adventure. He is always willing to try new things. He enjoys making new friends. But not everything turns out the way Dodo expects. Even a walk with his Mama turns into a topsy-turvy day of discoveries, challenges, and surprises. Good thing Dodo has a sense of humor!" (Publisher's note)

Saudo, Coralie

My dad at the zoo; Coralie Saudo; illustrated by Kris Di Giacomo; translated from the French by Claudia Bedrick and Kris Di Giacomo. Enchanted Lion Books 2016 32 p. (hardback) $17.95

Grades: PreK K 1 2   E

1. Zoos -- Fiction 2. Fathers -- Fiction

ISBN 9781592701902

LC 2015044310

This book, by Coralie Saudo, illustrated by Kris Di Giacomo, "is another tale of role reversal in which Dad reverts to the unsocialized, wild ways of childhood. Probably tired from all of his wearying antics around bedtime, here Dad heads off to the zoo with his son and goes completely zany." (Publisher's note)

"A tongue-in-cheek masterpiece echoing most parents' outings with small children." Kirkus

Sauer, Tammi

Chicken dance; illustrated by Dan Santat. Sterling 2009 un il $14.95

Grades: PreK K 1   E

1. Chickens -- Fiction 2. Contests -- Fiction 3. Domestic animals -- Fiction

ISBN 978-1-4027-5366-4; 1-4027-5366-7

LC 2008-50578

Determined to win tickets to an Elvis Poultry concert, hens Marge and Lola enter the Barnyard Talent Show, then, while the ducks who usually win the contest jeer, they test out their abilities.

"The zippy narrative features punchy dialogue and witty interactions. . . . Santat's rich ink-and-acrylic designs provide a humorous context through animated expressions. . . . Fly the coop to enjoy this hilarious adventure." Kirkus

Mary had a little glam; Tammi Sauer, illustrated by Vanessa Brantley-Newton. Sterling Pub Co Inc 2016 32 p. color illustrations (hardcover) $14.95

Grades: PreK K 1 2   E

1. Picture books for children 2. Fashion -- Fiction 3. Children -- Fiction

ISBN 1454913932; 9781454913931

In this children's book by Tammi Sauer, illustrated by Vanessa Brantley-Newton, "this little Mary has STYLE! In this fun take on Mother Goose, fashion-forward Mary helps some of childhood's most beloved characters go glam. From the kid who lives in a shoe (and dons some fab footwear, too) to Jack, who breaks his crown but gets a great new one, Mary's school friends look fantastic in their finery. But are they now too well dressed for recess?" (Publisher's note)

"Mary's enthusiasm is catching among her multiethnic classmates, who have a ball in both their sparkles and mud splatters on the playground. An inventive and fun read-aloud for groups or one-on-one." Booklist

Nugget and Fang; friends forever--or snack time? Tammi Sauer; illustrated by Michael Slack. Harcourt Children's Books 2013 40 p. (reinforced) $16.99
Grades: PreK K 1 2   E
1. Humorous stories 2. Fishes -- Fiction 3. Sharks -- Fiction 4. Minnows -- Fiction 5. Friendship -- Fiction 6. Peer pressure -- Fiction
ISBN 0547852851; 9780547852850
LC 2012025329

Your Alien; Tammi Sauer; illustrated by Goro Fujita. Sterling Pub Co Inc. 2015 32 p. color illustrations (hardcover) $14.95
Grades: PreK K 1   E
1. Friendship -- Fiction 2. Human-alien encounters -- Fiction
ISBN 9781454911296; 1454911298

In this children's story, by Tammi Sauer and illustrated by Goro Fujita, "when a little boy meets a stranded alien child, the two instantly strike up a fabulous friendship. They go to school, explore the neighborhood, and have lots of fun. But at bedtime, the alien suddenly grows very, very sad. Can the boy figure out what his new buddy needs most of all?" (Publisher's note)

"At its core, the sentiments of the book are heartwarming—the little boy in the story realizes the importance of home—and the use of you draws readers into the story." SLJ

Savage, Stephen
★ **Little** Tug; Stephen Savage. Roaring Book Press 2012 32 p. (alk. paper) $12.99
Grades: PreK K 1   E
1. Picture books for children 2. Tugboats -- Fiction 3. Boats and boating -- Fiction
ISBN 1596436484; 9781596436480
LC 2011033799

This children's picture book "depicts Little Tug as beloved and helpful from the start. The story has the tempo of a waltz, as readers meet three other ships (a sailboat, a speedboat, and an ocean liner), each of which get into trouble of a sort, and are rescued in turn by Little Tug." (Publishers Weekly)

"Little Tug isn't the tallest, fastest, or biggest boat in the harbor, but he's very helpful when the other boats need a push, a pull, or a guide. Savage's illustrations give the boats distinct personalities and provide punch for the story. Tug's busy day will resonate with children, especially toddlers who also spend their days measuring up, helping out, and thoroughly exhausting themselves." Horn Book

★ **Supertruck**; Stephen Savage. Roaring Brook Press 2015 32 p. color illustrations (hardback) $12.99
Grades: PreK K 1   E
1. Snow -- Fiction 2. Trucks -- Fiction 3. Heroes and heroines -- Fiction 4. Heroes -- Fiction 5. Snow removal -- Fiction 6. Refuse collection vehicles -- Fiction
ISBN 1596438215; 9781596438217
LC 2014009901

Theodor Seuss Geisel Honor Book (2016)

In this children's book, by Stephen Savage, "the city is hit by a colossal snowstorm [and] only one superhero can save the day. But who is this mysterious hero, and why does he disappear once his job is done? Find out in this snowy tale about a little truck with a very big job." Publisher's note)

"Savage exploits shapes and colors to create interesting imagery and atmospheric environments for the truck that show that collecting trash is just as heroic as powerfully plowing through snow." Kirkus

Ten orange pumpkins; by Stephen Savage. Dial Books for Young Readers 2013 48 p. (hardcover) $16.99
Grades: PreK K 1 2   E
1. Pumpkin -- Fiction 2. Counting -- Fiction 3. Halloween -- Fiction 4. Stories in rhyme
ISBN 0803739389; 9780803739383
LC 2012042091

Author Stephen Savage presents a "counting book [that] opens with 10 orange pumpkins on a farm. As the rhyming, rhythmic verses roll along, one pumpkin after another disappears, but observant children will be able to figure out what happens to each." (Publisher's note)

★ **Where's** Walrus? Scholastic Press 2011 un il
Grades: PreK K 1   E
1. Stories without words 2. Zoos -- Fiction 3. Walruses -- Fiction
ISBN 0-439-70049-3; 978-0-439-70049-8
LC 2010-922375

"With the zookeeper on his trail, an escaped walrus hides out in the city. . . . His trick is to blend in to each particular scene. However, he can't help but stand out in a diving competition where he wins a gold medal. . . . The collagelike illustrations in this wordless book were created in Adobe Illustrator. They are large, clear, and simple; the colors are bright, although flat. Young children will take delight in their ability to spot the wandering walrus." SLJ

Where's walrus? and penguin? Stephen Savage. Scholastic Press 2015 32 p. color illustrations (hardcover) $16.99
Grades: PreK K 1   E
1. Animals -- Fiction 2. Hide-and-seek -- Fiction
ISBN 9780545402958; 0545402956
LC 2014953444

In this children's story, by Stephen Savage, "Walrus escapes the zoo with his mischievous pal, Penguin. Will . . . these clever runaways stay one step ahead disguised as subway riders, baseball players, and even grand opera performers? Hiding in plain sight, they elude the clueless zookeeper until a fly ball at a baseball game leads Walrus and Penguin to a chance encounter with surprising results!" (Publisher's note)

"Savage's wordless illustrations continue to be cheeky, bold, and great fun. The modern, digitally created artwork uses heavy, clean lines and predominately primary colors, wherein Savage manages to hide his protagonists seamlessly, making spotting them all the more rewarding." Booklist

Say hello, Sophie; by Rosemary Wells. Viking 2017 32 p. color illustrations (Sophie books) (hardcover) $17.99
Grades: PreK K   E
1. Etiquette -- Fiction 2. Family life -- Fiction 3. Communication -- Fiction
ISBN 9781101999257
LC 2016020349

In this book, author Rosemary Wells again "uses mouse-girl Sophie as a stand-in Everychild, and tackles a problem that afflicts a wide swath of children. The straightforward text is matched by Wells' rather stolid art, leavened by the whimsy of the mouse cast. Give this to shy little ones--or those who just want to speak on their own." (Booklist)

Say, Allen
★ **Allison**. Houghton Mifflin 1997 32p il $17; pa $6.95

Grades: PreK K 1 2   **E**
1. Adoption -- Fiction 2. Japanese Americans -- Fiction
ISBN 0-395-85895-X; 0-618-49537-1 pa

LC 97-7528

When Allison realizes that she looks more like her Japanese doll than like her parents, she comes to terms with this unwelcomed discovery through the help of a stray cat

"A subtle, sensitive probing of interracial adoption, this exquisitely illustrated story will encourage thoughtful adult-child dialogue on a potentially difficult issue." Publ Wkly

The **bicycle** man. Parnassus Press 1982 un il lib bdg $16; pa $5.95
Grades: K 1 2 3   **E**
1. Japan -- Fiction 2. Cycling -- Fiction
ISBN 0-395-32254-5 lib bdg; 0-395-50652-2 pa

LC 82-2980

The amazing tricks two American soldiers do on a borrowed bicycle are a fitting finale for the school sports day festivities in a small village in occupied Japan

"The kindly, openhearted story is beautifully pictured in a profusion of delicate pen-and-ink drawings washed in gentle colors." Horn Book

★ **Boy** in the garden; written and illustrated by Allen Say. Houghton Mifflin Harcourt 2010 un il $17.99
Grades: PreK K 1 2   **E**
1. Japan -- Fiction 2. Dreams -- Fiction 3. Cranes (Birds) -- Fiction
ISBN 978-0-547-21410-8; 0-547-21410-3

After Jiro encounters a life-like garden statue of a tall bird, he falls asleep and dreams of the story his mother once told him about a grateful crane.

"Say is a master of composition. . . . Positions and postures are eloquent. . . . A gently unsettling tale of the power of the imagination." Horn Book

★ **Erika**-san. Houghton Mifflin Books for Children 2009 un il $17
Grades: 2 3 4   **E**
1. Japan -- Fiction 2. Teachers -- Fiction
ISBN 978-0-618-88933-4; 0-618-88933-7

LC 2008-00601

After falling in love with Japan as a little girl, Erika becomes a teacher and fulfills her childhood dream by moving to a remote Japanese island.

"With luminous watercolors and economical text . . . Say . . . tells of an American girl whose ingenuous hopes of reaching 'old Japan' are finally realized." Publ Wkly

The **favorite** daughter; Allen Say. Arthur A. Levine Books 2013 32 p. (hardcover) $17.99
Grades: K 1 2 3   **E**
1. Picture books for children 2. Japanese Americans -- Fiction 3. Fathers and daughters -- Fiction 4. Artists -- Fiction 5. Schools -- Fiction 6. Teasing -- Fiction 7. Japanese Americans -- Fiction 8. San Francisco (Calif.) -- Fiction
ISBN 054517662X; 9780545176620

LC 2012026830

In this children's picture book, by Allen Say, "Yuriko hates her name when the children make fun of it. . . . The teasing makes her want to hide, to retreat even from the art projects she used to love. Fortunately she has a patient, kind father who finds gentle ways of drawing her out and reminding Yuriko of the traditions they share that have always brought her joy." (Publisher's note)

★ **Grandfather's** journey; written and illustrated by Allen Say. Houghton Mifflin 1993 32p il $16.95; pa $7.99
Grades: 1 2 3 4   **E**
1. Japan -- Fiction 2. Grandfathers -- Fiction 3. Japanese Americans -- Fiction 4. Voyages and travels -- Fiction
ISBN 0-395-57035-2; 0-547-07680-0 pa

LC 93-18836

Awarded the Caldecott Medal, 1994

A Japanese American man recounts his grandfather's journey to America which he later also undertakes, and the feelings of being torn by a love for two different countries

"The brief text is simple and unaffected, but the emotions expressed are deeply complex. The paintings are astonishingly still, like the captured moments found in a family photo album. Each translucent watercolor is suffused with light." SLJ

★ **Kamishibai** man; written and illustrated by Allen Say. Houghton Mifflin Co. 2005 32p il $17
Grades: PreK K 1 2 3   **E**
1. Japan -- Fiction 2. Entertainers -- Fiction
ISBN 0-618-47954-6

After many years of retirement, an old Kamishibai man—a Japanese street performer who tells stories and sells candies—decides to make his rounds once more even though such entertainment declined after the advent of television.

"The quietly dramatic, beautifully evocative tale contains a cliffhanger of its own, and its exquisite art, in the style of Kamishibai picture cards, will attract even the most jaded kid away from the TV to enjoy a good, good book." Booklist

★ **Tea** with milk. Houghton Mifflin 1999 32p il $17; pa $6.99
Grades: K 1 2 3 4   **E**
1. Japan -- Fiction 2. Japanese Americans -- Fiction
ISBN 0-395-90495-1; 0-547-23747-2 pa

LC 98-11667

After growing up near San Francisco, Masako (or May) returns with her parents to their native Japan, but she feels foreign and out of place until she finds a job in Osaka and marries a man with a similarly mixed background

"Say's masterfully executed watercolors tell as much of this story . . . as his eloquent prose." Publ Wkly

Tree of cranes; written and illustrated by Allen Say. Houghton Mifflin 1991 32p il $17.95; pa $7.99
Grades: K 1 2 3   **E**
1. Japan -- Fiction 2. Christmas -- Fiction 3. Mother-son relationship -- Fiction
ISBN 0-395-52024-X; 0-547-24830-X pa

LC 91-1410

A Japanese boy learns of Christmas when his mother decorates a pine tree with paper cranes

"The quiet, graciously told picture book is a perfect blend of text and art. Fine-lined and handsome, Say's watercolors not only capture fascinating details of the boy's far away home . . . but also depict, with simple grace, the rich and complex bond between mother and child that underlies the story." Booklist

Sayre, April Pulley
Dig, wait, listen; a desert toad's tale. pictures by Barbara Bash. Greenwillow Bks. 2001 un il $15.95
Grades: PreK K 1 2   **E**
1. Toads -- Fiction 2. Desert animals -- Fiction
ISBN 0-688-16614-8

LC 00-3211

A spadefoot toad waits under the sand for the rain, hears the sounds of other desert animals, and eventually mates and spawns other toads

"Created with pencil, pen and ink, and watercolor, Bash's pictures illustrate the desert scenes with pleasingly varied colors, perspectives, and layouts. Preschool and primary-grade children will find this well-crafted book a wholly satisfying introduction to the spadefoot toad in particular and desert animals and the idea of life cycles in general." Booklist

★ **Eat** like a bear; by April Pulley Sayre; illustrated by Steve Jenkins. Henry Holt and Company 2013 32 p. (hardback) $16.99
Grades: PreK K 1 2 3   E
1. Picture books for children 2. Bears -- Fiction 3. Grizzly bear -- Fiction
ISBN 0805090398; 9780805090390
LC 2013015686
This children's picture book by April Pulley, a "grizzled, lumbering bear wakes up in the springtime. What is there to eat? . . . 'With long, strong claws, / dig in. Dig down. / Paw and claw and pull. / Find . . . // . . . ants! / Chew them, / sour and squirming. / Lick your lips.' As the months go by, bears eat many different types of food." (Kirkus Reviews)

If you're hoppy; pictures by Jackie Urbanovic. Greenwillow Books 2011 un il $16.99
Grades: PreK K 1   E
1. Stories in rhyme 2. Animals -- Fiction
ISBN 978-0-06-156634-9; 0-06-156634-9
LC 2010-04103
In rhyming text reminiscent of the traditional song, "If you're happy and you know it," presents various animals that are hoppy, sloppy, growly, flappy, or slimy, scaly and mean.

"Urbanovic's sprightly watercolor-and-ink cartoons add humor and vivacious energy. . . . Sure to be a storytime staple, with many requests for repeat performances." SLJ

One is a snail, ten is a crab; a counting by feet book. [by] April Pulley Sayre and Jeff Sayre; illustrated by Randy Cecil. Candlewick Press 2003 un il hardcover o.p. pa $6.99
Grades: PreK K 1 2   E
1. Foot 2. Animals 3. Counting
ISBN 0-7636-1406-8; 0-7636-2631-7 pa
LC 2001-52494
A counting book featuring animals with different numbers of feet
"Very simple text in large type is appropriate for group use as well as beginning readers. Uncluttered, black-outlined, oil-on-paper pictures clearly illustrate the concepts, and Cecil's googly-eyed snails, sports-minded crabs, and other animals add a touch of humor." SLJ

Turtle, turtle, watch out! illustrated by Annie Patterson. Charlesbridge 2010 un il lib bdg $17.95; pa $7.95
Grades: K 1 2   E
1. Sea turtles -- Fiction
ISBN 978-1-58089-148-6 lib bdg; 1-58089-148-9 lib bdg; 978-1-58089-149-3 pa; 1-58089-149-7 pa
LC 2008025338
A newly illustrated edition of the title first published 2000 by Orchard Books
From before the time she hatches until she returns to the same beach to lay eggs of her own, a sea turtle is helped to escape from danger many times by different human hands.

"The simple, direct text reads aloud well, drawing readers into the turtles' story without anthropomorphism. Impressive pastel illustrations, including many dramatic double-page spreads, depict with power and beauty the turtles' world of sand and shore." Booklist

Scanlon, Liz Garton

Bob, not Bob! *to be read as though you have the worst cold ever. by Audrey Vernick and Liz Garton Scanlon; illustrated by Matthew Cordell. Disney-Hyperion 2017 40 p. color illustrations (hardcover) $17.99
Grades: PreK K   E
1. Sick -- Fiction 2. Humorous stories 3. Cold (Disease) -- Fiction 4. Mother and child -- Fiction
ISBN 9781484723029
LC 2015033354
In this children's book, by Audrey Vernick and Liz Garton Scanlon, illustrated by Matthew Cordell, "Little Louie is stuck in bed with a bad cold. His nose is clogged, his ears are crackling, and his brain feels full. All he wants is his mom to take care of him, but whenever he calls out for her, his stuffed-up nose summons slobbery dog Bob instead!" (Publisher's note)

"For a book that really comes down to a sick kid yelping for his mother, his nose so clogged it needs dynamite to clear, the story has a lot of adorable acreage." Kirkus

The **Good**-Pie Party; by Liz Garton Scanlon; illustrated by Kady Macdonald Denton. Arthur A. Levine Books, An Imprint of Scholastic Inc. 2014 32 p. color illustrations (hardcover : alk. paper) $17.99
Grades: PreK K 1 2 3   E
1. Baking -- Fiction 2. Moving -- Fiction 3. Female friendship -- Fiction 4. Pies -- Fiction 5. Parties -- Fiction 6. Friendship -- Fiction 7. Moving, Household -- Fiction
ISBN 0545448700; 9780545448703
LC 2013006975
In this children's book, by Liz Garton Scanlon, "Posy, Megan, and Mae have always been the best of friends--but now Posy has to move away. Only their favorite activity can comfort the girls: baking pie! And when they realize they can host a good-pie party instead of a good-bye party, the sad situation becomes a sweet gathering for their entire community." (Publisher's note)

"Posy is feeling the moving blues. Lamenting her near departure, Posy and her two best friends decide to make a pie amidst the packed boxes. Inspired by their 'hot, sweet, good pie' they elect to throw a 'good-pie party' rather than a 'good-bye' one. Soft, emotionally detailed ink and watercolor illustrations lighten up the stressful subject and capture the warmth of childhood friendship." Horn Book

Noodle & Lou. Beach Lane Books 2011 un il $15.99
Grades: PreK K 1   E
1. Birds -- Fiction 2. Worms -- Fiction 3. Friendship -- Fiction
ISBN 978-1-4424-0288-1; 1-4424-0288-1
LC 2009-42950
Noodle and Lou are unlikely friends. One is a worm and one is a bird. When Noodle is having a bad day, Lou knows just what to say to cheer up his wormy friend and help him see what it means to be liked just the way you are.

"Howard's cartoon-style illustrations match the bouncy rhythm of Scanlon's couplets perfectly and keep the tone light. . . . Chirpy, instructive and fun." Kirkus

Schachner, Judith Byron

The **Grannyman**. Dutton Children's Bks. 1999 un il $15.99; pa $6.99
Grades: PreK K 1 2   E
1. Cats -- Fiction 2. Old age -- Fiction
ISBN 0-525-46122-1; 0-14-250062-3 pa
LC 98-52964

Simon the cat is so old that most of his parts have stopped working, but just when he is ready to breathe his last breath, his family brings home a new kitten for him to raise

"Schachner's expressive watercolor-and-mixed-media artwork mirrors the affection, humor, and warmth of her finely crafted text." Booklist

Schachner, Judy

Skippyjon Jones class action; by Judy Schachner. Dutton Children's Books 2011 un il $16.99

Grades: PreK K 1   E

1. School stories 2. Cats -- Fiction 3. Dogs -- Fiction

ISBN 0-525-42228-5; 978-0-525-42228-0

LC 2009053293

Skippyjon Jones, a Siamese cat who would rather be his Chihuahua alter ego, is determined to attend dog obedience school.

"Schachner's style, the book has hilarious songs, wild antics, a smattering of Spanish words, and humor that everyone can appreciate. The zany illustrations add to its exuberant nature. Children will enjoy the amusing details on each page. As with the earlier books, this one makes for a wonderful read-aloud that will have young audiences laughing out loud." SLJ

Schaefer, Carole Lexa

The **children's** garden; growing food in the city. Carole Lexa Schaefer; illustrated by Pierr Morgan. Little Bigfoot, an imprint of Sasquatch Books 2017 32 p. color illustrations $16.99

Grades: PreK K 1 2   E

1. Gardens -- Fiction 2. Community gardens -- Fiction 3. City and town life -- Fiction

ISBN 9781570619847

LC 2016033143

This picture book, by Carole Lexa Schaefer, illustrated by Pierr Morgan, "shows children as urban farmers, exploring the sights, smells, sensations, and tastes of growing their own food in a community garden. The story invites young readers to enjoy summer's bounty and the hands-on experience of tending and harvesting it, while the colorful illustrations depict a multicultural community of children learning about and enjoying a sustainable, local food system." (Publisher's note)

Dragon dancing; illustrated by Pierr Morgan. Viking 2007 un il $16.99

Grades: PreK K 1   E

1. School stories 2. Dragons -- Fiction 3. Birthdays -- Fiction 4. Imagination -- Fiction

ISBN 0-670-06084-9

A group of children pretend that they are a dragon to celebrate their classmate's birthday.

"An excellent choice for storytime, the text features . . . many fun sounds. . . . The color of the gouache-and-marker illustrations increases in brightness as the students transition gradually from the classroom into their imaginative fantasy. . . . Pleasing to the eye and the ear." SLJ

Schaefer, Lola M.

Happy Halloween, Mittens; story by Lola M. Schaefer; pictures by Susan Kathleen Hartung. Harper 2010 23p il (I can read!) $16.99; pa $3.99

Grades: PreK K 1   E

1. Cats -- Fiction 2. Halloween -- Fiction

ISBN 978-0-06-170222-8; 0-06-170222-6; 978-0-06-170221-1 pa; 0-06-170221-8 pa

LC 2008045065

While Nick prepares for Halloween, Mittens the kitten tries her best to help out.

"Mittens's exploits continue to be entertaining and satisfying for the very youngest readers." Horn Book Guide

★ **Loose** tooth; story by Lola M. Schaefer; pictures by Sylvie Wickstrom. HarperCollinsPublishers 2004 31p il (My first I can read book) hardcover o.p. pa $3.99

Grades: PreK K 1 2   E

1. Stories in rhyme 2. Teeth -- Fiction

ISBN 0-06-052776-5; 0-06-052778-1 pa

LC 2003-6322

A young child experiences a loose tooth for the first time and eagerly waits for it to come out

"With a few words, lots of repetition, some rhyme, and good rhythm, this story is perfect for beginning readers. The cartoon illustrations add details to the plot and create interest." SLJ

Mittens; story by Lola M. Schaefer; pictures by Susan Kathleen Hartung. HarperCollinsPublishers 2006 25p il (I can read!) $16.99; lib bdg $15.89; pa $3.99

Grades: PreK K 1 2   E

1. Cats -- Fiction

ISBN 0-06-054659-X; 0-06-054660-3 lib bdg; 0-06-054661-1 pa

Nick helps Mittens the kitten adjust to life in a new home

"The controlled vocabulary in this gentle, unassuming story is made up primarily of one-syllable words, and the sentence structure is very basic. The soft pastel illustrations are simple and uncluttered and enhance the quiet tone of the text." SLJ

Other titles about Mittens are:

Follow me, Mittens (2007)

What's that, Mittens (2008)

Happy Halloween, Mittens (2010)

Mittens, where is Max? (2011)

One busy day; A Story for Big Brothers and Sisters. written by Lola Schaefer; illustrated by Jessica Meserve. First edition Disney-Hyperion Books 2014 40 p. color illustrations $16.99

Grades: PreK K 1   E

1. Play -- Fiction 2. Imagination -- Fiction 3. Brothers and sisters -- Fiction

ISBN 1423171128; 9781423171126

LC 2013000494

In this children's book, written by Lola Schaefer and illustrated by Jessica Meserve, "all Mia wants is for her big brother, Spencer, to play with her. But he's always too busy! So Mia paints, and dances, and explores, and keep busy all by herself. But with a little imagination and a lot of love, Mia might just be able to show Spencer that it's a lot more fun to be busy together." (Publisher's note)

"Schaefer and Meserve depict a growing sibling bond between big brother Spencer and little sister Mia. No longer a baby, Mia longs to play with Spencer. . . . Meserve's art cleverly extends the text to expound upon plucky Mia's imaginative flights of fancy. . . . The pleasing text culminates in a circular ending that showcases the pair as 'busy. Very, very busy—together.' Throughout, Meserve's digitally rendered illustrations employ soft visual texture and bold colors to create a cheery, charming world for the two children to enjoy. Hooray for sibling revelry!" Kirkus

One special day; by Lola Schaefer; illustrated by Jessica Meserve Disney/Hyperion Books 2012 40p. col. ill.

Grades: PreK K 1   E

1. Siblings -- Fiction 2. Picture books for children 3. Babies -- Fiction 4. Behavior -- Fiction 5. Brothers -- Fiction

ISBN 1423137604; 9781423137603

LC 2011015977

In this book, "Spencer . . . [is] fast as a horse, tall as a giraffe, funny as a monkey and more. Yet when his parents come home with a new arrival, Spencer finds a new way to describe himself. He may be like animals in many respects, but now he's gentle, just as a big brother should be. . . .The text allows readers to guess what animal Spencer will come to resemble next, until finally there is only one thing left to be." (Kirkus Reviews)

"With a simple interactive text and thoroughly engaging illustrations, this book is a perfect blending of words and pictures." SLJ

This is the sunflower; pictures by Donald Crews. Greenwillow Bks. 2000 un il $15.99
Grades: PreK K 1 2   E
   1. Stories in rhyme 2. Sunflowers -- Fiction
   ISBN 0-688-16413-7
                                 LC 98-46682

A cumulative verse describing how a sunflower in a garden blossoms and, with the help of the birds, spreads its seeds to create an entire patch of sunflowers

"A beautiful, noteworthy title. The velvety watercolors are clearly defined and saturated with color. . . . This is perfect for story hours; also recommend it to budding ornithologists, who will appreciate the illustrated key identifying the birds pictured in the text." Booklist

Scheer, Julian

Rain makes applesauce; by Julian Scheer & Marvin Bileck. Holiday House 1964 un il $16.95
Grades: PreK K 1 2   E
   ISBN 0-8234-0091-3
A Caldecott Medal honor book, 1965

"A book of original nonsense, illustrated with intricate drawings. Small children live the refrains, 'Rain makes applesauce' and 'You're just talking silly talk,' and enjoy the fantastic details in the pictures." Hodges. Books for Elem Sch Libr

Schertle, Alice

★ **Little** Blue Truck; illustrated by Jill McElmurry. Harcourt Children's Books 2008 un il $16
Grades: PreK K 1 2   E
   1. Trucks -- Fiction 2. Animals -- Fiction 3. Friendship -- Fiction
   ISBN 0-15-205661-0; 978-0-15-205661-2
                               LC 2006-29445

A small blue truck finds his way out of a jam, with a little help from his friends. "Ages three to six." (Bull Cent Child Books)

"Schertle contrasts a huge dump truck, hurtling self-importantly down a country road, with a small pickup that greets each farm animal. . . When the dump truck bogs down in a deep slough, its cries of distress go unanswered. When the pickup gets stuck while trying to help, the animals rush in to lend a hearty push. . . . McElmurry creates crisply drawn rural scenes. . . . Along with being a natural for storytime, this upbeat tale may spark a discussion about friendships and helping one another." Booklist

Another title about Little Blue Truck is:
Little Blue Truck leads the way (2009)

Such a little mouse; [text] Alice Schertle; [illustrations] Stephanie Yue. Orchard Books 2015 32 p. $16.99
Grades: PreK K   E
   1. Mice -- Fiction 4. Seasons -- Fiction
   ISBN 0545649293; 9780545649292
                              LC 2014022920

In this book by Alice Schertle, "every day of each season little mouse pops out of his hole. The friends he meets during his day are a wood pecker, a prickly porcupine, some snails, bees, and many more.

This little mouse is clever and smart. As he enjoys his day, he is always sure to bring home a special treat each evening. Be it a seed, watercress, or an acorn! Winter will be coming and mouse must be prepared." (Children's Literature)

Schiffer, Miriam B.

Stella brings the family; a tale of two dads on Mother's Day. by Miriam Baker Schiffer; illustrations by Holly Clifton Brown. Chronicle Books 2015 36 p. color illustrations (alk. paper) $16.99
Grades: PreK K 1 2 3   E
   1. Families -- Fiction 2. Gay fathers -- Fiction 3. Gay parents -- Fiction 4. Mother's Day -- Fiction
   ISBN 9781452111902
                               LC 2013033259

In this book, by Miriam Baker Schiffer, illustrated by Holly Clifton Brown, "Stella's class is having a Mother's Day celebration, but what's a girl with two daddies to do? It's not that she doesn't have someone who helps her with her homework, or tucks her in at night. Stella has her Papa and Daddy who take care of her, and a whole gaggle of other loved ones who make her feel special and supported every day." (Publisher's note)

Schimel, Lawrence

Let's go see Papa! translated from Spanish by Elisa Amado; illustrated by Alba Marina Rivera. Groundwood Books 2011 un il $18.95
Grades: 1 2 3   E
   1. Spain -- Fiction 2. Immigrants -- Fiction 3. Father-daughter relationship -- Fiction
   ISBN 978-1-55498-106-9; 1-55498-106-9

"A young girl waits by the telephone every Sunday for a call from Papá. He left 'one year, eight months and twenty two days' ago to find work in the United States. . . . When Papá asks her and Mamá to join him, she is thrilled to be reunited, but also sad to leave her abuela and friends. Rivera's pencil, crayon, and watercolor illustrations capture the daily details of a loving extended family. . . . . The feelings of missing a loved one are realistically conveyed and will resonate with children." SLJ

Schlitz, Laura Amy

Princess Cora and the Crocodile; by Laura Amy Schlitz, illustrated by Brian Floca. Candlewick Press 2017 80 p. color illustrations $16.99
Grades: 1 2 3 4   E
   1. Crocodiles -- Fiction 2. Princesses -- Fiction
   ISBN 0763648221; 9780763648220
                               LC 2017009443

In this book, by Laura Amy Schlitz, illustrated by Brian Floca, "Princess Cora is sick of boring lessons. She's sick of running in circles around the dungeon gym. She's sick, sick, sick of taking three baths a day. And her parents won't let her have a dog. But when she writes to her fairy godmother for help, she doesn't expect that help to come in the form of a crocodile—a crocodile who does not behave properly." (Publisher's note)

"With fairly large type, ample white space, and lively, colorful illustrations on almost every page, this early chapter book is beautifully designed for newly independent readers." Booklist

Schmid, Paul

Hugs from Pearl; story and pictures by Paul Schmid. Harper 2011 un il $14.99
Grades: PreK K   E
   1. School stories 2. Hugging -- Fiction 3. Porcupines -- Fiction
   ISBN 978-0-06-180434-2; 0-06-180434-7
                               LC 2010015906

A friendly porcupine figures out how to give hugs without hurting others with her sharp quills.

"With his simple pastel and charcoal illustrations set against pale green and blue pages, Schmid brings just the right touch of sweetness to this charming tale." SLJ

★ **Oliver** and his alligator; Paul Schmid. Disney-Hyperion Books 2013 40 p. $15.99
Grades: PreK K 1   E
     1. Fear -- Fiction 2. School children -- Fiction 3. Alligators -- Fiction 4. Schools -- Fiction 5. First day of school -- Fiction
ISBN 1423174372; 9781423174370
LC 2012020298

This book by Paul Schmid is a "tale about overcoming first day of school jitters. Oliver is nervous about the first day of school, so he picks up an alligator at the swamp, just in case. Whenever anything scares Oliver-be it a teacher, a classmate, or the prospect of learning everything-the alligator makes the problem go away. Quickly, school becomes much simpler . . . and a little lonely. But Oliver knows just what to do!" (Publisher's note)

★ A **pet** for Petunia. Harper 2011 un il $12.99
Grades: PreK K 1   E
     1. Pets -- Fiction 2. Skunks -- Fiction 3. Parent-child relationship -- Fiction
ISBN 978-0-06-196331-5; 0-06-196331-3

Petunia so desperately wants a pet skunk that she refuses to believe her parents when they say skunks stink.

Schmid's "line drawings are simple, fluid, and convey lots of valuable information. . . . Enthusiastic and single-minded, Petunia makes delightful company; kids will recognize themselves and clamor for re-reads." Publ Wkly

Petunia goes wild; by Paul Schmid. HarperCollins 2012 40 p.
Grades: PreK K 1 2   E
     1. Temper tantrums 2. Tigers -- Fiction 3. Temper tantrums -- Fiction 4. Children's costumes -- Fiction 5. Parent-child relationship -- Fiction 6. Humorous stories 7. Behavior -- Fiction 8. Parent and child -- Fiction
ISBN 9780061963346; 9780061963353
LC 2011001888

In this children's book, "Petunia . . . would much rather be an animal than a human girl, a preference that she expresses by wearing a tiger tail, roaring at passersby, and pleading with her parents for a cave in which to live. As a compromise, she offers to be their pet, an offer that provokes a page-long parental lecture: "No, you may NOT! Where did you get such an idea? Of all the crazy things! That is NOT how nice little girls behave." Feeling completely misunderstood, Petunia addresses a packing box to Africa and climbs in, only to have second thoughts when she overhears her mother singing in the kitchen ("Tigers did not sing, thought Petunia. Or tickle at bedtime, neither"), and she decides to stay." (Bulletin of the Center for Children's Books)

Schneider, Josh
Bedtime monsters; Josh Schneider. Clarion Books, Houghton Mifflin Harcourt 2013 32 p. (hardcover) $16.99
Grades: PreK K 1   E
     1. Picture books for children 2. Bedtime -- Fiction 3. Monsters -- Fiction 4. Fear of the dark -- Fiction
ISBN 0544002709; 9780544002708
LC 2012036483

In this book, "Arnold knows he has nothing more to be afraid of at bedtime after the winged fargle, the horrible tooth gnasher, the grozny buzzler, and other monsters with their own fears crawl into his bed.

These colorful figures lurk in the darkest corners of bedrooms, but, as Arnold discovers, the scary creatures have more in common with him than he could have imagined." (School Library Journal)

The **meanest** birthday girl; by Josh Schneider. Clarion Books 2013 48 p. col. ill. (hardcover) $14.99
Grades: 1 2 3   E
     1. Birthdays -- Fiction 2. Elephants -- Fiction 3. Gifts -- Fiction
ISBN 054783814X; 9780547838144
LC 2011041587

In this children's story, by Josh Schneider, "it's Dana's birthday, so she can do what she likes. And what Dana likes to do is pinch. And call people names. And steal her classmates' desserts. You probably know a kid like Dana. What can stop her from being so mean? . . . Sometimes, it takes a little creativity (and possibly a very large pet) to change a mean kid's ways." (Publisher's note)

★ **Princess** Sparkle-Heart gets a makeover; Josh Schneider. Clarion Books, Houghton Mifflin Harcourt 2014 32 p. (hardcover) $16.99
Grades: PreK K 1 2   E
     1. Dogs -- Fiction 2. Dolls -- Fiction 3. Jealousy -- Fiction 4. Dolls -- Repairing -- Fiction
ISBN 0544142284; 9780544142282
LC 2013004355

In this book, by Josh Schneider, "Amelia and her dog are best friends . . . until Princess Sparkle-Heart comes along. Soon, Amelia and Princess Sparkle-Heart are doing everything together: having tea parties, attending royal weddings, keeping each other's secrets. Princess Sparkle-Heart may be an awesome princess doll - but is she any match for a jealous canine?" (Publisher's note)

"Amelia's jealous dog hates Amelia's beloved princess doll. Following 'an accident' (read: the dog destroys the doll), Amelia rebuilds Princess Sparkle-Heart, but readers don't see until book's end that it now resembles a dog-repelling Raggedy Ann like horror-movie creation. Schneider plays it perfectly: Amelia is mellow throughout, and he never tips his hand regarding her sinister side. The droll art is pleasantly sparkle-light." Horn Book

Schnur, Steven
Winter; an alphabet acrostic. illustrated by Leslie Evans. Clarion Bks. 2002 un il $15
Grades: K 1 2 3   E
     1. Winter 2. Alphabet 3. Acrostics
ISBN 0-618-02374-7
LC 2001-17358

"On each page, a winter-related word provides the basis for an acrostic that reads like a short poem. . . . A striking, hand-colored linoleum print illustrates each small, boxed acrostic." Booklist

Schnur, Susan
Tashlich at Turtle Rock; by Susan Schnur and Anna Schnur-Fishman; illustrated by Alex Steele-Morgan. Kar-Ben Pub. 2010 un il lib bdg $17.95; pa $7.95
Grades: K 1 2 3   E
     1. Jews -- Fiction 2. Rosh ha-Shanah -- Fiction
ISBN 978-0-7613-4509-1 lib bdg; 0-7613-4509-4 lib bdg; 978-0-7613-4510-7 pa; 0-7613-4510-8 pa
LC 2009001871

Annie leads her family on a Rosh Hashanah hike to observe tashlich where each person will ask God's forgiveness for the things they regret doing the previous year. Includes facts about this Jewish custom.

"Throughout, the authors emphasize environmental awareness . . . and Steele-Morgan's boldly colored heavily textured illustrations highlight the rich colors of autumn. . . . Handled with a light touch, this is secular enough to make it useful for general as well as religious collections." Booklist

Schoenherr, Ian

★ **Don't** spill the beans! Greenwillow Books 2010 un il $16.99; lib bdg $17.89

Grades: PreK   E

1. Stories in rhyme 2. Bears -- Fiction 3. Animals -- Fiction 4. Birthdays -- Fiction

ISBN 978-0-06-172457-2; 0-06-172457-2; 978-0-06-172458-9 lib bdg; 0-06-172458-0 lib bdg

LC 2008042363

A bear tries hard to keep a birthday surprise a secret.

"The story is told in short rhyming sentences of large, colorful, hand-lettered text. The ink and acrylic paint illustrations depict cheerfully clothed animals with expressive faces." SLJ

★ **Read** it, don't eat it! Greenwillow Books 2009 un il $17.99; lib bdg $18.89

Grades: PreK K   E

1. Stories in rhyme 2. Books and reading -- Fiction

ISBN 978-0-06-172455-8; 0-06-172455-6; 978-0-06-178034-9 lib bdg; 0-06-178034-0 lib bdg

LC 2008027716

Rhyming advice on how to take care of a library book

"One white, hand-lettered sentence per page is set against a bold color, and the ink and acrylic art features endearing animal library users in an expansive white space. The book is simple enough to use with preschool children and funny enough to be appreciated by early readers." SLJ

Schoettler, Joan

Good fortune in a wrapping cloth; illustrated by Jessica Lanan. Shen's Books 2011 il $17.95

Grades: 2 3 4   E

1. Korea -- Fiction 2. Sewing -- Fiction 3. Clothing and dress -- Fiction 4. Mother-daughter relationship -- Fiction

ISBN 978-1-885008-40-4; 1-885008-40-6

LC 2011001702

When Ji-su's mother is chosen by the emperor to be a seamstress in his court, Ji-su vows to learn to sew the beautiful Korean bojagi, or wrapping cloths, just as well so that she will also be summoned to the palace and be reunited with her mother.

"Descriptive language and stunning watercolor paintings show the seasons passing as Ji-su works toward her goal. With a masterful eye for color and skillful use of perspective, Lanan brings the text to life and adds depth to Ji-su's emotions." SLJ

Schofield-Morrison, Connie

I got the rhythm; by Connie Schofield-Morrison; illustrated by Frank Morrison. Bloomsbury 2014 32 p. (hardback) $16.99

Grades: PreK K 1   E

1. Dance -- Fiction 2. Musical meter and rhythm 3. Parks -- Fiction 4. Rhythm -- Fiction

ISBN 1619631784; 9781619631786; 9781619631793; 9781619632103

LC 2013038025

In this children's book, written by Connie Schofield-Morrison and illustrated by Frank Morrison, "the joy of music overtakes a mother and daughter. The little girl hears a rhythm coming from the world around her - from butterflies, to street performers, to ice cream sellers everything is musical! She sniffs, snaps, and shakes her way into the heart of the beat, finally busting out in an impromptu dance, which all the kids join in on!" (Publisher's note)

"Music is everywhere in the city, but a warm summer day in the park makes it downright infectious. A young African American girl leaves the house with her mother, using all her senses to find rhythm everywhere as they walk...With text like "STOMP STOMP" and "BEAT BOP" strewn across the pages, the book begs readers to sing and move along with this little dancer as she "pops and locks, hips and hops" her way through the sunny afternoon." Booklist

Schoonmaker, Elizabeth

Square cat; written and illustrated by Elizabeth Schoonmaker. Aladdin 2011 un il $14.99

Grades: PreK K 1   E

1. Cats -- Fiction 2. Shape -- Fiction 3. Individualism -- Fiction

ISBN 978-1-4424-0619-3; 1-4424-0619-4

Eula the cat is square, and while she longs to be round like other cats, her friends show her the benefits of the shape she has. "Ages four to seven." (Bull Cent Child Books)

"This title gently packs a powerful message about self-acceptance and friendship. . . . Ink and bright watercolor illustrations using basic shapes with simple and engaging facial expressions steal the show." SLJ

Schotter, Roni

★ The **boy** who loved words; pictures by Giselle Potter. Schwartz & Wade Books 2006 un il $16.95; lib bdg $18.99

Grades: K 1 2 3   E

1. English language -- Fiction

ISBN 0-375-83601-2; 0-375-93601-7 lib bdg

LC 2005-10850

Selig, who loves words and copies them on pieces of paper that he carries with him, goes on a trip to discover his purpose.

"Potter's signature naive-style art is light and comical, while Schotter's words are a lovely celebration of the power and the music of language." Booklist

★ **Doo**-Wop Pop; by Roni Schotter; illustrated by Bryan Collier. Amistad/HarperCollins 2008 un il $16.99; lib bdg $17.89

Grades: K 1 2 3   E

1. School stories 2. Stories in rhyme 3. Singing -- Fiction 4. Janitors -- Fiction

ISBN 978-0-06-057968-5; 0-06-057968-4; 978-0-06-057974-6 lib bdg; 0-06-057974-9 lib bdg

LC 2008015212

A school janitor teaches children to sing and have confidence in themselves

"Schotter stacks the prose with rhymes, giving the first-person narrative an authentic, contemporary freestyle flow that begs to be read aloud. Collier's trademark collage paintings, shaded with bursts of yellow and green, hum with the students' energy and pride." Booklist

★ **Mama,** I'll give you the world; by Roni Schotter; illustrated by S. Saelig Gallagher. Schwartz & Wade Books 2006 un il $16.95

Grades: K 1 2 3   E

1. Birthdays -- Fiction 2. Beauty shops -- Fiction 3. Mother-daughter relationship -- Fiction

ISBN 978-0-375-83612-1; 0-375-83612-8

At Walter's World of Beauty, Luisa's secret plans are underway to create a very special birthday celebration for her hardworking, single mother who is employed there as a stylist.

"Gallagher's bright-eyed, smiling, subtly modeled faces light up this loving mother-daughter tale." Booklist

Schroeder, Alan

★ **Satchmo's** blues; illustrated by Floyd Cooper. Doubleday Bks. for Young Readers 1996 un il hardcover o.p. pa $6.99

Grades: 1 2 3 4   **E**
1. Singers 2. Jazz musicians 3. Band leaders 4. Trumpet players 5. New Orleans (La.) -- Fiction 6. African American musicians -- Fiction
ISBN 0-385-32046-9; 0-440-41472-5 pa

LC 93-41082

A fictional recreation of the youth of trumpeter Louis Armstrong in New Orleans

"This book is full of gorgeous writing, accompanied by Cooper's atmospheric paintings." SLJ

Schubert, Ingrid

The **umbrella**; [by] Ingrid & Dieter Schubert. Lemniscaat 2011 il $16.95

Grades: PreK K 1 2   **E**
1. Stories without words 2. Dogs -- Fiction 3. Voyages and travels -- Fiction 4. Umbrellas and parasols -- Fiction
ISBN 978-1-9359-5400-2; 1-9359-5400-8

A little dog finds an umbrella in the garden on a windy day. The moment the dog picks up the umbrella, it catches the wind and pulls the dog skywards. The wind carries the umbrella and the dog all over the world, from the desert to the sea, from the jungle to the north pole.

"The illustrations easily tell the story; there's no need for words. The paintings excel at showing the different landscapes and depicting movement. What a great journey!" SLJ

Schubert, Leda

Feeding the sheep; pictures by Andrea U'Ren. Farrar Straus Giroux 2010 un il $16.99

Grades: PreK K 1 2   **E**
1. Stories in rhyme 2. Wool -- Fiction 3. Sheep -- Fiction 4. Weaving -- Fiction 5. Mother-daughter relationship -- Fiction
ISBN 978-0-374-32296-0; 0-374-32296-1

LC 2007-48843

In pictures and rhythmic text, a mother relates to her daughter all the steps involved in making her a snug, wooly sweater, starting at the very beginning with feeding the sheep

"The physicality of the words, . . . the fascinating facts, and the action-filled, brightly colored illustrations will capture kids' attention, as will the cozy family bond between parent and child." Booklist

★ The **Princess** of Borscht; illustrated by Bonnie Christensen. Roaring Brook Press 2011 un il $17.99

Grades: PreK K 1 2   **E**
1. Sick -- Fiction 2. Soups -- Fiction 3. Cooking -- Fiction 4. Grandmothers -- Fiction
ISBN 978-1-59643-515-5; 1-59643-515-1

LC 2010014520

Ruthie's grandmother, who is in the hospital with pneumonia, says she needs homemade borscht by five o'clock and young Ruthie, with the help of her neighbors, tries to make some even without the secret recipe.

"Of course, it's not just about borscht or even about cooking, though there's a great recipe included. Schubert has concocted a sweet mixture of traditions that bind and give comfort, along with love in many forms. . . . Christensen's heavily outlined, strongly colored illustrations emphasize equally strong personalities. The paintings are filled with details that add interest to the proceedings." Kirkus

Reading to Peanut; illustrated by Amanda Haley. Holiday House 2011 un il $16.95

Grades: PreK K 1 2   **E**
1. Dogs -- Fiction 2. Reading -- Fiction 3. Birthdays -- Fiction 4.

Family life -- Fiction
ISBN 978-0-8234-2339-2; 0-8234-2339-5

LC 2010031412

Lucy works hard to learn to read and write before her dog's birthday.

"Colorful, energetic acrylics show Lucy and her ever-present pup Peanut in motion. . . . The appealing character, lively pictures and mild suspense make for a warm family story that shows the fun of having a pet and provides a strategy for learning to read that youngsters will eagerly embrace." Kirkus

Schuch, Steve

★ A **symphony** of whales; illustrated by Peter Sylvada. Harcourt Brace & Co. 1999 un il hardcover o.p. pa $7

Grades: 1 2 3 4   **E**
1. Music -- Fiction 2. Whales -- Fiction
ISBN 0-15-201670-8; 0-15-216548-7 pa

LC 98-17248

Young Glashka's dream of the singing of whales, accompanied by a special kind of music, leads to the rescue of thousands of whales stranded in a freezing Siberian bay

"This is a quiet, powerful story, beautifully extended by Sylvada's paintings of ghostly whale shapes and glowing, fin-shaped skies." Booklist

Schwartz, Amy, 1954-

100 things that make me happy; by Amy Schwartz. Abrams Appleseed 2014 40 p. color illustrations $16.95

Grades: PreK K 1   **E**
1. Stories in rhyme 2. Happiness -- Fiction
ISBN 1419705180; 9781419705182

LC 2013042633

This children's book, by Amy Schwartz, is "tribute to 100 everyday things worth celebrating. The list, in rhyming couplets, draws directly from a preschooler's world--from slippery floors to dinosaurs, from goldfish to a birthday wish." (Publisher's note) "Each vignette is illustrated with pictures of smiley kids of different ethnicities following their bliss." (Horn Book Magazine)

"Lollipop colors and utterly cheery simplicity make for a rousing read-aloud chant. A multiethnic cast of small children and adults list happy-making small joys in rhyme. . . . The pictures range from multiple small vignettes on a spread to full-page illustrations. . . . Fine line and strong color make each image a joy: There's lots of pattern and movement to every figure, therefore muc h to revel in visually. All 100 things are numbered and reproduced as a poster on the inside of the dust jacket, and the endpapers are striped in every color used. It is a book chock-full of fun—what more could one want?" Kirkus

One hundred things that make me happy

Dee Dee and me; written and illustrated by Amy Schwartz. 1st ed Holiday House 2013 32 p. ill. (reinforced) $16.95

Grades: PreK K 1 2   **E**
1. Picture books for children 2. Sisters -- Fiction
ISBN 082342524X; 9780823425242

LC 201201656

In this children's picture book, "Hannah is an easy target for Dee Dee. She's younger and shorter (Dee Dee says the brains are in the 5 1/ inches of height Hannah's missing), and she longs for her sister's acceptance. But after one too many manipulations, Hannah learns to assert herself--and now she's sure her brains are growing!" (Kirkus Reviews)

★ **What** James likes best. Atheneum Bks. for Young Readers 2003 un il $16.95

Grades: PreK K 1 2   E
1. Transportation -- Fiction
ISBN 0-689-84059-4

LC 2001-22988

James goes with his parents on an express bus to visit twins, in a taxi to visit Grandma, and in a car to see the county fair, then walks next door with his mother for a play date

"Schwartz's pristine illustrations are streamlined and clean; the lucid, transparent colors make her gouache and pen-and-ink illustrations . . . seem almost weightless. This is a terrifically simple, successful way to get readers and listeners to interact with printed text." Bull Cent Child Books

Willie and Uncle Bill; Amy Schwartz. 1st ed. Holiday House 2012 40 p. col. ill. (hardcover) $16.95
Grades: K 1 2   E
1. Picture books for children 2. Uncles -- Fiction 3. Babysitters -- Fiction
ISBN 0823422038; 9780823422036

LC 2011007274

In this picture book, "[e]ach of the three stories . . . begins 'The doorbell rang three times,' and in comes Uncle Bill to babysit. In the first story, as Uncle Bill . . . makes tacos and chocolate pudding for lunch. . . . The second story features a concoction they call 'Icky Stew.' . . . In the third story, the two of them go out at night and ride the subway to go listen to--and play along with--a garage band." (Horn Book Magazine)

Schwartz, Betty Ann
The **splendid** spotted snake. Workman 2011 un il $13.95
Grades: PreK K   E
1. Snakes -- Fiction
ISBN 978-0-7611-6360-2; 0-7611-6360-3

"A yellow snake, made from a ribbon that is woven through slots in the pages, is born with red spots, but as he gets longer, he gains additional spots of different colors. . . . Turning the pages pulls a new section of ribbon through, making the winding snake grow. Schwartz and Wilensky combine a satisfying tactile experience with a lighthearted lesson on size and color recognition, well-suited for preschoolers." Publ Wkly

Schwartz, Corey Rosen
The **three** ninja pigs; Corey Rosen Schwartz; illustrated by Dan Santat. G.P. Putnam's Sons 2012 40 p. (hardcover) $16.99
Grades: PreK K 1 2 3   E
1. Pigs -- Fiction 2. Fractured fairy tales 3. Martial arts -- Fiction 4. Ninja -- Fiction 5. Stories in rhyme
ISBN 0399255141; 9780399255144

LC 2011037111

In this fractured fairy tale for children by Corey Rosen Schwartz, illustrated by Dan Santat, "These three little pigs just aren't going to take it from that bully anymore! The first starts aikido lessons--he'll make mincemeat out of that wolf! His brother learns a little jujitsu--he'll chop that guy to pieces! But when the wolf actually appears, it turns out these two pigs aren't quite ready after all. Good thing their sister has been training every day." (Publisher's note)

"In this fractured fairy tale, three little pigs are portrayed as frustrated siblings fed up with a wolf that loves to huff and puff and blow houses down. In an attempt to protect their homes in their Japanese village, they train at a Ninja school...Youngsters with an interest in martial arts and those seeking strong female characters will relish this picture book." SLJ

Schwartz, Howard
Gathering sparks; illustrated by Kristina Swarner. Roaring Brook Press 2010 un il $16.99

Grades: K 1 2 3   E
1. Jews -- Fiction 2. Love -- Fiction 3. Stars -- Fiction 4. Kindness -- Fiction 5. Grandfathers -- Fiction 6. Conduct of life -- Fiction
ISBN 978-1-59643-280-2; 1-59643-280-2

Based on the Jewish concept of Tikkun olam, "the narration begins when 'you' ask 'your grandfather' about the origin of the stars. He responds that before people were created, God sent ships carrying light sailing across the sky. These fragile vessels broke apart, scattering their precious cargo across the Earth and sky. It is the job of the human race to gather the 'sparks of light' and restore them to their proper place by doing acts of kindness and love. . . . Schwartz's language is simple, personal, and poetic, and his use of the second person adds a sense of intimacy. . . . Swarner's stylized, painterly artwork is soft and gentle and complements the peaceful mood of the text. . . . This is a handsome book with a timeless message." SLJ

Schwartz, Joanne
★ **City** alphabet; words by Joanne Schwartz; photos by Matt Beam. Groundwood Books 2009 un il $18.95; pa $12.95
Grades: K 1 2 3 4   E
1. Alphabet 2. City and town life
ISBN 978-0-88899-928-3; 0-88899-928-3; 978-0-88899-962-7 pa; 0-88899-962-3 pa
"Stark, metallic and urban, these images may encourage children to think about alternate ways of seeing their surroundings." Publ Wkly

★ **Our** corner grocery store; illustrated by Laura Beingessner. Tundra Books 2009 un il $19.95
Grades: K 1 2 3   E
1. Family life -- Fiction 2. Grandparents -- Fiction 3. Retail trade -- Fiction 4. Italian Americans -- Fiction
ISBN 978-0-88776-868-2; 0-88776-868-7
"This sweet story takes readers through young Anna Maria's Saturday as she helps her grandparents in their neighborhood store. The day is special for its simplicity; the book is special for its rich evocation of the delights of a little Italian market and the loving relationships between a girl and her grandparents. Beingessner's folksy illustrations and Schwartz's easy text fit well together and are filled with details." SLJ

Town is by the sea; Joanne Schwartz; illustrated by Sydney Smith. Groundwood Books 2017 52 p. color illustrations $19.95
Grades: 1 2 3 4   E
1. Coal miners -- Fiction 2. Ocean mining -- Fiction 3. Father-son relationship
ISBN 1554988713; 9781554988716
In this book, by Joanne Schwartz, illustrated by Sydney Smith, "a young boy wakes up to the sound of the sea, visits his grandfather's grave after lunch and comes home to a simple family dinner, but all the while his mind strays to his father digging for coal deep down under the sea." (Publisher's note)

Schwartz, Roslyn
Splat! starring the vole brothers. by Roslyn Schwartz. Pgw 2014 32 p. $16.95
Grades: PreK K   E
1. Humorous fiction 2. Pigeons -- Fiction 3. Brothers -- Fiction 4. Adventure and adventurers 5. Humorous stories 6. Voles -- Fiction
ISBN 1771470097; 9781771470094
In this book, by Roslyn Schwartz, "the Vole Brothers, are on their next adventure. . . . In signature cinematic style, one half of the loveable bickering duo finds himself at the mercy of a flying pigeon as it flap, flap, flaps by and then drops in, literally with a splat! . . . Nearly wordless and told entirely through sight-gags and sound effects, this easy-to-read adventure." (Publisher's note)

"This slapstick comedy plays out primarily in spare ink and pencil-crayon illustrations, especially in Schwartz's expressive characters. Two vole brothers look up to see a pigeon flying overhead: "Ooooooo..." But then--"SPLAT!" The clueless pigeon drops a bird-poo bomb on one brother's head. The silliness continues with a banana-peel pratfall and more bird poo--it's a recipe for a rollicking if low-brow storytime." Horn Book

Schwarz, Viviane

Is there a dog in this book? Viviane Schwarz. Candlewick Press 2014 32 p. color illustrations $16.99

Grades: PreK   **E**

1. Cats -- Fiction 2. Dogs -- Fiction 3. Toys and moveable
ISBN 0763669911; 9780763669911

LC 2013955681

This children's story, written and illustrated by Viviane Schwarz, asks "can cats and dogs share the same turf? Revisit the age-old dilemma with a hide-and-seek romp among furry friends. Brimming with humor . . . , here is a lively interactive exploration of the surprising joys of unlikely friendships." (Publisher's note)

"With the uncertainty of There Are Cats in This Book (2008) and There Are No Cats in This Book (2010) behind us, our trio of flighty felines have a new problem: someone drank their milk, chewed their toy, and left behind a peculiar odor. Horrors! It must be a 'snappy and yappy, smelly and noisy, hair and scary' dog. By directly asking the reader for help lifting flaps, the cats go into hiding, first behind a sofa, then a piano, in a closet. . . . With sturdy construction nearly worthy of a board book, this ought to withstand plenty of repeat abuse, which it will get, thanks to Schwarz's gregarious dialogue-only text and her adorably simple pen-and-inks. Let the fur fly." Booklist

There are no cats in this book! Candlewick Press 2010 un il $16.99

Grades: PreK   **E**

1. Pop-up books 2. Cats -- Fiction 3. Books and reading -- Fiction
ISBN 978-0-7636-4954-8; 0-7636-4954-6

LC 2009-51510

Companion volume to: There are cats in this book (2008)

Filled with the spirit of adventure, three cats pack their suitcases and try to escape from their book.

"This explores on the notion that the book—or at least the cats in it—are looking back at the viewers and interacting with them, and the paper-engineering elements such as foldouts and popups add playful entertainment. . . . The illustrations are uncomplicated yet fluid, with saturated watercolor pigments . . . against warm-toned pages, and elements of layered-paper collage adding dimension." Bull Cent Child Books

Scieszka, Jon

★ **Baloney** (Henry P.) received and decoded by Jon Scieszka; visual recreation by Lane Smith. Viking 2001 un il $15.99

Grades: K 1 2 3   **E**

1. Life on other planets -- Fiction
ISBN 0-670-89248-3

LC 00-12041

A transmission received from outer space in a combination of different Earth languages tells of an alien schoolboy's fantastic excuse for being late to school again

"Every Earth kid will immediately recognize a soul mate in this extraterrestrial truth-stretcher and tall-tale teller. . . . Illustrator Smith has been having equal fun stretching the visual truth to create a vision of space that is not only artfully outer but also utterly outre. The result is wacky fun for everyone." Booklist

Battle Bunny; by Jon Scieszka and Mac Barnett and Alex; pictures by Matthew Myers but mostly Alex. Simon & Schuster Books for Young Readers 2013 32 p. (hardcover) $14.99

Grades: K 1 2   **E**

1. Drawing -- Fiction 2. Rabbits -- Fiction 3. Humorous stories 4. Parties -- Fiction 5. Birthdays -- Fiction 6. Supervillains -- Fiction 7. Forest animals -- Fiction
ISBN 1442446730; 9781442446731; 9781442446748

LC 2012025515

In this book, by Jon Scieszka, "Alex has been given a saccharine, sappy, silly-sweet picture book about Birthday Bunny that his grandma found at a garage sale. Alex isn't interested--until he decides to make the book something he'd actually like to read. So he takes out his pencil, sharpens his creativity, and totally transforms the story!" (Publisher's note)

★ The **Frog** Prince continued; story by Jon Scieszka; paintings by Steve Johnson. Viking 1991 un il $15.99; pa $6.99

Grades: 2 3 4 5   **E**

1. Fairy tales 2. Frogs -- Fiction
ISBN 0-670-83421-1; 0-14-054285-X pa

LC 90-26537

After the frog turns into a prince, he and the Princess do not live happily ever after and the Prince decides to look for a witch to help him turn back into a frog

"The dialogue is witty; the plot, as logical as it is offbeat. Steve Johnson's paintings, executed in a rich and somber palette, are like stage settings; his depiction of the various characters is inspired." Horn Book

Pete's party; written by Jon Scieszka; characters and environments developed by the Design Garage: David Gordon, Loren Long, David Shannon. Aladdin 2008 un il (Jon Scieszka's Trucktown: Ready-to-roll) lib bdg $13.89; pa $3.99

Grades: PreK K 1   **E**

1. Trucks -- Fiction 2. Signs and signboards -- Fiction
ISBN 978-1-4169-4149-1 lib bdg; 1-4169-4149-5 lib bdg; 978-1-4169-4138-5 pa; 1-4169-4138-X pa

LC 2007027154

The Trucktown trucks follow the road signs directing them to Pete's party

This title "will draw beginning readers into the zany world of anthropomorphic trucks, whose distinct personalities and endearing facial expressions roll across the colorful pages." SLJ

Other titles in this series are:

Dizzy Izzy (2010)
Kat's mystery (2009)
Melvin's valentine (2009)
Snow trucking! (2008)
Zoom! boom? bully (2008)
The spooky tire (2009)
Uh-oh Max (2009)

★ **Science** verse; illustrated by Lane Smith. Viking 2004 un il $16.99

Grades: 2 3 4 5   **E**

1. Poetry -- Fiction 2. Science -- Fiction
ISBN 0-670-91057-0

LC 2004-1641

Companion volume to Math curse

When the teacher tells his class that they can hear the poetry of science in everything, a student is struck with a curse and begins hearing nothing but science verses that sound very much like some well known poems.

"Children need not be familiar with the works upon which the spoofs are based to enjoy the humor, but this is a perfect opportunity to introduce the originals and to discuss parody as a poetic form. The dynamic cartoons are an absolute delight." SLJ

Scillian, Devin

Pappy's handkerchief; by Devin Scillian; illustrated by Chris Ellison. Sleeping Bear Press 2007 un il (Tales of young Americans) $17.95

Grades: 2 3 4   E

1. Oklahoma -- Fiction 2. Family life -- Fiction 3. African Americans -- Fiction 4. Frontier and pioneer life -- Fiction
ISBN 978-1-58536-316-2

LC 2007006394

In 1889, young Moses and his family sell everything they own and leave their Baltimore, Maryland, home to join many other settlers—black and white—in a race to claim land in the newly-opened territory of Oklahoma.

"This history of a unique and interesting part of the settling of the West is illustrated in beautiful paintings of warm, soft browns, yellows, and blues that complement the narrative, together creating a fascinating look at the past." SLJ

Scott, Ann Herbert

On Mother's lap; illustrated by Glo Coalson. Clarion Bks. 1992 32p il $16; pa $6.95; bd bk $5.95

Grades: PreK K   E

1. Inuit -- Fiction 2. Mother-child relationship -- Fiction
ISBN 0-395-58920-7; 0-395-62976-4 pa; 0-618-05159-7 bd bk

LC 91-17765

A newly illustrated edition of the title first published 1972 by McGraw-Hill

"Sitting on his mother's lap, a young Eskimo boy gathers his belongings until he, some toys, his puppy, and a blanket are all crowded together in the rocking chair. When his baby sister cries, the boy claims there is no room for her, but Mother proves him wrong, and the threesome settle comfortably in the chair. Soft illustrations depict a cozy scene and a loving family." Horn Book

Scotton, Rob

Russell the sheep; by Rob Scotton. HarperCollins 2005 un il $17.99; lib bdg $18.89

Grades: PreK K 1 2   E

1. Sheep -- Fiction 2. Bedtime -- Fiction
ISBN 0-06-059848-4; 0-06-059849-2 lib bdg

LC 2003-24274

Russell the sheep tries all different ways to get to sleep

"Scotton makes a captivating debut with this comical tale. He illustrates it with a witty, engaging, and fluffy character bathed in calming blue hues." SLJ

Other titles about Russell are:
Russell and the lost treasure (2006)
Russell's Christmas magic (2007)

Scaredy-cat, Splat! Harper 2010 un il $16.99; lib bdg $17.89

Grades: K 1 2   E

1. Cats -- Fiction 2. Costume -- Fiction 3. Halloween -- Fiction
ISBN 978-0-06-117760-6; 0-06-117760-1; 978-0-06-117761-3 lib bdg; 0-06-117761-X lib bdg

LC 2009-49483

Splat the cat accidently succeeds in being the scariest cat in the class for Halloween.

"Splat's perma-flustered expression and the eye-popping dramatics of his fellow cats are particularly well suited to the chills of Halloween." Publ Wkly

Splat the cat. HarperCollins 2008 un il $16.99; lib bdg $17.89

Grades: K 1 2   E

1. School stories 2. Cats -- Fiction 3. Friendship -- Fiction
ISBN 978-0-06-083154-7; 0-06-083154-5; 978-0-06-083155-4 lib bdg; 0-06-083155-3 lib bdg

LC 2008-20218

"The fuzzy black feline is worried about his first day of school, and despite determined attempts to avoid the inevitable, he ends up there. . . . This lighthearted story, told with a generous helping of humor and goofy characterizations, will have broad appeal." SLJ

Other titles about Splat are:
Love, Splat (2008)
Merry Christmas, Splat (2009)
Scaredy-cat, Splat! (2010)
Splat the cat sings flat (2011)
Splish, splash, Splat! (2011)

Sebe, Masayuki

Let's count to 100! Kids Can Press 2011 il $16.95

Grades: PreK K 1 2   E

1. Counting
ISBN 978-1-55453-661-0; 1-55453-661-8

"Every spread in this high-energy counting book contains 100 cartoon people, objects, or animals, as Sebe provides enthusiastic prompts. . . . Conversations and interactions between the creatures add to the fun. . . . With much to discover, a wry sense of humor, and a clean aesthetic, it's a lively pick for readers ready for more adventurous counting challenges." Publ Wkly

Seder, Rufus Butler

Gallop! [by] Rufus Butler Seder. Workman Pub. 2007 un il $12.95

Grades: PreK K 1 2   E

1. Stories in rhyme 2. Animals -- Fiction 3. Animal locomotion -- Fiction
ISBN 978-0-7611-4763-3

LC 2007024247

"Readers will gasp with delight when they open this book." Publ Wkly

Swing! Workman Pub. 2008 un il $12.95

Grades: PreK K 1 2   E

1. Sports -- Fiction
ISBN 978-0-7611-5127-2; 0-7611-5127-3

"Open the die-cut cover and see a baseball player swing his bat at a ball, then watch as the ball zooms ever-larger to fit the acetate window showcasing all this action. . . . Colored fonts and multicolored borders offset the severity of the b&w pictures and generate reader participation. . . . On other spreads, child athletes perform soccer drills, run, cartwheel, twirl on ice skates, shoot hoops, swim and lead cheers—it's all jaw-dropping, even if the novelty technology has yet to find its most imaginative application." Publ Wkly

Waddle! Workman Pub. 2009 un il $12.95

Grades: PreK K 1 2   E

1. Animals -- Fiction 2. Animal locomotion -- Fiction
ISBN 978-0-7611-5112-8; 0-7611-5112-5

Text asks if the reader can move like a variety of animals. Striped acetate overlays on board pages give illustrations the illusion of movement.

"The level of detail . . . is striking . . . [and the] readers should find the animations mesmerizing." Publ Wkly

Seeger, Laura Vaccaro

★ **Black?** white! day? night! a book of opposites. Roaring Brook Press 2006 20p il $16.95

Grades: PreK K 1 2   **E**

1. Opposites

ISBN 978-1-59643-185-0; 1-59643-185-7

LC 2005-32378

On the first page of this picture book "a large black flap with a cutout [reveals] a black bat set against a pure white background. The single word black? printed in white, stands out clearly on the page. When kids lift the flap, they'll see the word white! (in white type) and discover that what appeared to be a bat is really the mouth of a ghost. Each of 18 opposites is similarly conveyed using only one word and the lift of a flap. . . . Each flap is a different bold color . . . and the scenes under the flaps are in keeping with the simple yet sophisticated graphic design of the book. Thick, shiny pages add to the sense of richness." Booklist

Bully; by Laura Vaccaro Seeger. 1st ed. Roaring Brook Press 2013 40 p. ill. (reinforced) $16.99

Grades: PreK K 1 2   **E**

1. Bullies -- Fiction 2. Domestic animals -- Fiction

ISBN 1596436301; 9781596436305

LC 2012012991

In this book, author Laura Vaccaro Seeger "uses . . . barnyard animals to tell her story about bullying, casting a bull in the title role. The trouble starts when the young bull is rejected by an older one: 'Go away!' it shouts. The young bull is shaken, but he's learned something--how to hurt others. . . .The more he abuses the others, the larger he grows, his angry bluster feeding his self-importance. At last a goat speaks truth to power: 'Bully!'" (Publishers Weekly)

Dog and Bear; tricks and treats. Laura Vaccaro Seeger. Roaring Brook Press 2014 32 p. color illustrations (hardcover) $14.99

Grades: PreK K 1   **E**

1. Dogs -- Fiction 2. Bears -- Fiction 3. Halloween -- Fiction 4. Friendship -- Fiction 5. Teddy bears -- Fiction

ISBN 1596436328; 9781596436329

LC 2013016658

Boston Globe-Horn Book Award: Picture Book (2007)

In this book, written and illustrated by Laura Vaccaro Seeger, part of the Dog and Bear Series, "Dog and Bear are back in three new Halloween stories that are sure to delight their many fans and win them new ones. Join them as they search for the perfect costume, hand out candy to trick-or-treaters (or not!), and then go trick-or-treating themselves." (Publisher's note)

"The humor strengthens the friendship of the eager and fun-loving characters in an amusing and inclusive way. The acrylic paint and India ink illustrations are painterly with broad brushstrokes and thick black outlines, while the simple white background keeps the spotlight on the action." SLJ

★ **Dog** and Bear: two friends, three stories. Roaring Brook Press 2007 un il $12.95

Grades: PreK K 1   **E**

1. Dogs -- Fiction 2. Bears -- Fiction 3. Friendship -- Fiction

ISBN 978-1-59643-053-2; 1-59643-053-2

LC 2006-11687

"Bear is a multicolored stuffed toy; Dog is a playful, rowdy dachshund. . . . In the first episode, Dog helps timid Bear down from a high stool. In the second, Dog wants to play, but Bear needs some quiet time alone. And in the final story, Dog suffers a small identity crisis, but Bear

helps him recognize that he is just fine as he is. . . . Seeger's minimal text is perfectly paced for new readers, who will love the dose of humor at each story's close. In pictures as spare and charming as the text, Seeger captures preschoolers' expressions and body language." Booklist

Other titles about Dog and Bear are:

Dog and Bear: two's company (2008)

Dog and Bear: three to get ready (2009)

★ **First** the egg. Roaring Brook Press 2007 un il $14.95

Grades: PreK K   **E**

1. Growth

ISBN 978-1-59643-272-7; 1-59643-272-1

LC 2006-32924

A Caldecott Medal honor book, 2008

"Pages are color-saturated and as minimalist as the text. . . . Cleverly conceived and executed cutouts reinforce the book's tactile appeal. . . . The best picture books creat a world in themselves, and this tour de force is one of them." Horn Book

★ **Green**; Laura Vaccaro Seeger. Roaring Brook Press 2012 40 p.

Grades: PreK K 1 2   **E**

1. Plants -- Color 2. Animals -- Color 3. Stories in rhyme 4. Picture books for children 5. Green -- Fiction

ISBN 9781596433977

LC 2011013495

Caldecott Honor Book (2013)

This picture book is an exploration of the color green. "In four simple quatrains, two-word lines each suggest a kind of green, introducing a scene that might show natural, domestic or built elements. . . . [Laura Vaccaro] Seeger's paintings vary in perspective; in their portrayal of animals such as fish, a tiger, and a lizard, trees and flowers, and children. The die-cuts reveal green-related words demonstrated by the vignettes within the paintings." (Kirkus Reviews)

I used to be afraid; Laura Vaccaro Seeger. Roaring Brook Press 2015 40 p. color illustrations (hardcover) $17.99

Grades: PreK K 1 2   **E**

1. Fear -- Fiction

ISBN 159643631X; 9781596436312

LC 2014039510

In this children's story, by Laura Vaccaro Seeger, "there are a lot of things to be afraid of in this world: spiders, the dark, being alone. . . . This simple . . . picture book . . . shows that what seems scary at first, can become magical. It all depends on perspective. Using die-cuts, learn that a scary spider can actually produce an intricate and gorgeous web and that sometimes the dark can transform into a magical night sky." (Publisher's note)

"A short but cleverly designed tale about a little girl who overcomes her fears by looking at scary things from another perspective. Illustrated with Seeger's signature acrylic paint collages with die-cuts, each spread alternates between the phrase "I used to be afraid of [the scary thing in question]" and the cutout of the scary object, and the next spread that shows it transformed into something less threatening with the words "but not anymore." . . . A wonderful story to engender a discussion about being afraid and possibly even inspire its young audience to conquer their own fears." Booklist

★ **Lemons** are not red. Roaring Brook Press 2004 un il $14.95

Grades: PreK K 1 2   **E**

1. Color

ISBN 1-59643-008-7

"The first spread reads, 'Lemons are not/ RED.' The word 'RED' appears on a bright yellow page beneath the die-cut shape of a lemon with a red background showing through. When the page is turned, the die-cut shape falls on the correct yellow background, with the words 'Lemons are YELLOW' underneath. . . . This framework continues throughout the book. . . . Illustrated with richly colored yet simple oil paintings, this offering will delight preschoolers." SLJ

★ **One** boy. Roaring Brook Press 2008 un il $14.95
Grades: PreK K 1 2   E
    1. Counting 2. Painting -- Fiction 3. Vocabulary -- Fiction
ISBN 978-1-59643-274-1; 1-59643-274-8
                                LC 2007-45941
    A Geisel Award honor book, 2009
    A boy creates ten paintings in this counting book that also explores the relationship of words within words.
    Seeger "crafts another nifty peek-a-boo book, counting to 10 and identifying new words by exposing or covering letters with die-cuts. . . . Seeger uses pared-down digital art and flat saturated colors." Publ Wkly

★ **Walter** was worried. Roaring Book Press 2005 un il $15.95
Grades: PreK K 1 2   E
    1. Storms -- Fiction 2. Emotions -- Fiction
ISBN 1-59643-066-8
                             LC 2004-024558
    Children's faces, depicted with letters of the alphabet, react to the onset of a storm and its aftermath in this picture book, accompanied by simple alliterative text.
    "The artwork uses bold colors with wide brush marks as backdrops and primary colors with almost graphic shapes to represent rain, snow flakes, leaves, and branches. With only one sentence per page, there is surprising depth in this wonderful collaboration of art and story." SLJ

★ **What** if? Roaring Brook Press 2010 un il $15.99
Grades: PreK K   E
    1. Beaches -- Fiction 2. Seals (Animals) -- Fiction 3. Choice (Psychology)
ISBN 978-1-59643-398-4; 1-59643-398-1
    This book presents three different scenarios which show what happens when different choices are made. "Ages three to six." (Bull Cent Child Books)
    "What if a boy found a beach ball and kicked it into the ocean? What if two seals found it and began to play? What if a third seal appeared on the beach looking for a friend? In this . . . book, Laura Vaccaro Seeger shows us the same story with three different outcomes, each highlighting the possibility in possibilities." Publisher's note

Seeger, Pete, 1919-2014
    The **deaf** musicians; by Pete Seeger and Paul DuBois Jacobs; illustrations by R. Gregory Christie. Putnam 2006 un il $16.99
Grades: K 1 2 3   E
    1. Deaf -- Fiction 2. Musicians -- Fiction 3. Jazz music -- Fiction
ISBN 0-399-24316-X
                          LC 2005026901
    Lee, a jazz pianist, has to leave his band when he begins losing his hearing, but he meets a deaf saxophone player in a sign language class and together they form a snazzy new band.
    "Christie's snazzy style matches perfectly with the book's vivacity. The expressive faces and bold use of color make the story sing. . . . Both uplifting and inclusive, it is a celebration of music and resilience." SLJ

Segal, John
    Alistair and Kip's great adventure; written and illustrated by John Segal. Margaret K. McElderry Books 2008 un il $15.99
Grades: PreK K 1 2   E
    1. Cats -- Fiction 2. Dogs -- Fiction 3. Whales -- Fiction 4. Boats

and boating -- Fiction
ISBN 978-1-4169-0280-5; 1-4169-0280-5
                           LC 2006019870
    Alistair the cat and Kip the dog build a boat and soon find themselves sailing down the creek to the river to the bay and out to sea where a violent storm threatens to capsize them
    "The quick-paced story is told through both dialogue and simple narrative. Beautifully rendered watercolors in bright hues comically depict the self-confident cat and his smaller canine pal." SLJ

    Carrot soup; written and illustrated by John Segal. Margaret K. McElderry Books 2006 un il $12.95
Grades: PreK K 1 2   E
    1. Carrots -- Fiction 2. Rabbits -- Fiction 3. Gardening -- Fiction
ISBN 0-689-87702-1
                           LC 2004-16963
    After working hard on his garden all spring and summer, Rabbit looks forward to harvest time when he can make soup, but every carrot disappears and Rabbit must find out who has taken them. Includes a recipe for carrot soup
    "The clues are in Segal's stylized pencil and watercolor pictures, and observant children won't have any trouble determining where the carrots went. The delicate springtime greens and browns used in the background contrast nicely with Rabbit's comically expressive face." Booklist

    Far far away. Philomel Books 2009 un il $16.99
Grades: PreK K 1   E
    1. Pigs -- Fiction 2. Runaway children -- Fiction 3. Mother-child relationship -- Fiction
ISBN 978-0-399-25007-1; 0-399-25007-7
                           LC 2008035855
    When an unhappy young pig decides to run away, his mother helps him to see that everything he needs and wants is right there at home.
    "Segal's art, executed in pencil and watercolors, features stylized pigs set against backgrounds that alternate between mottled colors and pure white. The pictures make good use of space and squeeze every bit of humor out of a familiar situation." Booklist

Seibold, J. Otto
    ★ **Olive** the other reindeer; by J. Otto Seibold and Vivian Walsh. Chronicle Bks. 1997 un il $15.99
Grades: PreK K 1 2   E
    1. Dogs -- Fiction 2. Reindeer -- Fiction 3. Christmas -- Fiction 4. Santa Claus -- Fiction
ISBN 0-8118-1807-1
                           LC 97-9876
    Thinking that "all of the other reindeer" she hears people singing about include her, Olive the dog reports to the North Pole to help Santa Claus on Christmas Eve
    "Seibold has developed a signature style with computer digitized art, and his playful skewed lines and warm shades of ochre, pimento and olive green are user-friendly." Publ Wkly

Seki, Sunny
    Yuko-chan and the Daruma doll; the adventures of a blind Japanese girl who saves her village. story and illustrations by Sunny Seki. Tuttle Pub. 2012 32 p.
Grades: 1 2 3   E
    1. Fables 2. Blind -- Fiction 3. Dolls -- Fiction 4. Japan -- Fiction
ISBN 4805311878; 9784805311875
                           LC 2011031332
    In this children's story, by Sunny Seki, "Yuko-chan, an adventurous blind orphan, . . . trips and tumbles down a snowy cliff. She discovers . . . her tea gourd, regardless of how she drops it, always lands right-

side-up. . . . Inspired by this, she creates the famous Daruma doll toy, which rights itself when tipped--a true symbol of resilience. Thanks to Yuko-chan's invention, the villagers are able to earn a living and feed themselves by selling the dolls." (Publisher's note)

Selbert, Kathryn

★ **War** dogs; Churchill and Rufus. Kathryn Selbert. Charlesbridge 2013 48 p. ill. (reinforced) $17.95

Grades: 2 3 4   E

1. Dogs   2. World War, 1939-1945 -- Great Britain   3. Dogs -- Great Britain   4. Great Britain -- History -- George VI, 1936-1952

ISBN 1580894143; 9781580894142

LC 2012000794

This children's book, by Kathryn Selbert, profiles Winston Churchill and his dog. "Churchill, often noted for his tenacious, bulldog-like personality, was one of the greatest wartime leaders of the modern era. But few people know that he was also a devoted poodle owner. The friendship between the British Bulldog and his faithful miniature poodle, Rufus, spans World War II and takes readers through the bombings of London, the invasion of Normandy, and post-war reconstruction." (Publisher's note)

Includes bibliographical references

Sendak, Maurice

★ **Alligators** all around; an alphabet. Harper & Row 1962 un il lib bdg $16.89; pa $5.95

Grades: PreK K 1 2   E

1. Alphabet

ISBN 0-06-025530-7 lib bdg; 0-06-443254-8 pa

Originally published in smaller format as volume one of the ¿Nutshell library¿

An alphabet book of alligators doing dishes, juggling jelly beans, throwing tantrums and wearing wigs, all from A to Z

★ **Bumble**-Ardy. HarperCollins 2011 un il $17.95

Grades: PreK K 1 2   E

1. Counting   2. Stories in rhyme   3. Pigs -- Fiction   4. Parties -- Fiction   5. Birthdays -- Fiction

ISBN 978-0-06-205198-1; 0-06-205198-9

Bumble-Ardy is a mischievous pig who has reached the age of nine without ever having had a birthday party. But all that changes when Bumble throws a party for himself and invites all his friends, leading to a wild masquerade that quickly gets out of hand.

"Savvy readers will notice references to Sendak's previous books and an ebullient cameo; scholars will undoubtedly discover personal iconography in the densely populated watercolors. Familiar themes abound: the quest for home, the capacity children have for navigating their circumstances, the pleasure of cake, the presence of death. . . . Nobody does naughty quite like [Sendak] does." SLJ

★ **Chicken** soup with rice; a book of months. Harper & Row 1962 30p il lib bdg $16.89; pa $5.95

Grades: PreK K 1 2   E

1. Stories in rhyme   2. Seasons -- Fiction

ISBN 0-06-025535-8 lib bdg; 0-06-443253-X pa

Originally published in smaller format as volume two of the ¿Nutshell library¿

Pictures and verse illustrate the delight of eating chicken soup with rice in every season of the year

★ **In** the night kitchen; 25th anniversary ed; HarperCollins Pubs. 1996 un il $17.95; lib bdg $18.89; pa $6.95

Grades: PreK K 1 2 3   E

1. Fantasy fiction

ISBN 0-06-026668-6; 0-06-026669-4 lib bdg; 0-06-443436-2 pa

First published 1970

A Caldecott Medal honor book, 1971

"A perfect midnight fantasy. The feelings, smells, sights, and comforting emotions which young children experience are here in lovely dream colors." Brooklyn. Art Books for Child

★ **Mommy?** [art by Maurice Sendak; scenario by Arthur Yorinks; paper engineering by Matthew Reinhart] Scholastic 2006 un il $24.95

Grades: PreK K 1 2   E

1. Pop-up books   2. Monsters -- Fiction

ISBN 0-439-88050-5

"This pop-up tour de force abounds with humor, vibrant artwork, and visual fireworks." SLJ

★ **One** was Johnny; a counting book. Harper & Row 1962 un il lib bdg $16.89; pa $5.95

Grades: PreK K 1 2   E

1. Counting

ISBN 0-06-025540-4 lib bdg; 0-06-443251-3 pa

Originally published in smaller format as volume three of the ¿Nutshell library¿

Counting from one to ten and back again to one, Johnny, who starts off alone, acquires too many numbered visitors for his own comfort, until they disappear one by one

★ **Outside** over there. Harper & Row 1981 un il $22.95; pa $9.95

Grades: K 1 2 3   E

1. Fairy tales   2. Sisters -- Fiction

ISBN 0-06-025523-4; 0-06-443185-1 pa

LC 79-2682

A Caldecott Medal honor book, 1982

With Papa off to sea and Mama despondent, Ida must go outside over there to rescue her baby sister from goblins who steal her to be a goblin's bride

"A gentle yet powerful story in the romantic tradition. . . . Soft in tones, rich in the use of light and color . . . the pictures are particularly distinctive for the tenderness with which the children's faces are drawn, the classic handling of texture, the imaginative juxtaposition of infant faces and the baroque landscape details that might have come from Renaissance paintings." Bull Cent Child Books

★ **Pierre**; a cautionary tale in five chapters and a prologue. Harper & Row 1962 48p il lib bdg $16.89; pa $5.95

Grades: PreK K 1 2   E

1. Stories in rhyme

ISBN 0-06-025965-5 lib bdg; 0-06-443252-1 pa

Originally published in smaller format as volume four of the ¿Nutshell library¿

A story in verse about a little boy called Pierre who insisted upon saying 'I don't care' until he said it once too often and learned a well needed lesson

★ **Where** the wild things are; story and pictures by Maurice Sendak. Harper & Row 1963 un il $17.95; lib bdg $18.89; pa $8.95

Grades: PreK K 1 2   E

1. Fantasy fiction

ISBN 0-06-025492-0; 0-06-025493-9 lib bdg; 0-06-443178-9 pa

Awarded the Caldecott Medal, 1964

"This vibrant picture book in luminous, understated full color has proved utterly engrossing to children with whom it has been shared. . .

. A sincere, preceptive contribution which bears repeated examination." Horn Book

Senior, Olive

Anna Carries Water; by Olive Senior; illustrated by Laura James. Tradewind Books 2014 40 p. $18.95

Grades: PreK K 1 2   E

1. Water -- Fiction 2. Jamaica -- Fiction 3. Family life -- Fiction 4. Brothers and sisters -- Fiction

ISBN 1896580602; 9781896580609

In this book, by Olive Senior and illustrated by Laura James, "Anna fetches water from the spring every day, but she can't carry it on her head like her older brothers and sisters can. In this charming and poetic family story set in Jamaica, . . . Senior shows young readers the power of determination, as Anna achieves her goal and overcomes her fear." (Publisher's note)

"Anna, the youngest in a large family, desperately wants to carry her coffee can of water on her head. She doesn't yet have this skill that all her siblings have mastered. Why, Karen can even read while she carries a water container on her head, a detail noted in the exuberant paintings accompanying the simple text, ideal for reading aloud...When water easily comes out of a faucet, young readers rarely think about the difficult chore of carrying water, but they will empathize with Anna's desire to reach an important milestone." (Kirkus)

Birthday suit; by Olive Senior; paintings by Eugenie Fernandes. Annick Press 2012 32 p.

Grades: PreK K   E

1. Nudity 2. Picture books for children 3. Children's clothing -- Fiction

ISBN 1554513685; 9781554513680

This book tells the story of "Johnny, [who] likes to run around naked . . . . But now that he's 4, mom insists on clothes at all times. She buys him red trunks for playing in the water. As soon as her back is turned, however, he's out of them and back to the titular birthday suit. . . . It takes a man-to-man talk with dad for Johnny to realize that he really does want to be a big boy. He puts on his overalls and everybody claps. Now he has fun with clothes, zipping and tying and snapping." (Kirkus Reviews)

Senir, Mirik

When I first held you; a lullaby from Israel. [by] Mirik Snir; [illustrated by] Eleyor Snir; translated from the Hebrew by Mary Jane Shubow. Kar-Ben 2009 un il $9.95

Grades: PreK K 1   E

1. Lullabies 2. Stories in rhyme 3. Nature -- Fiction 4. Parent-child relationship -- Fiction

ISBN 978-0-7613-5098-9; 0-7613-5098-5

LC 2008-53741

A parent describes, in rhyming text, the beauty of the world on the day a young child is born

"The unassuming and calming melodious text, fluidly translated by Shubow, will certainly encourage serenity and comfort at the end of each day." Kirkus

Serfozo, Mary

Plumply, dumply pumpkin; written by Mary Serfozo; illustrated by Valeria Petrone. Margaret K. McElderry Bks. 2001 un il hardcover o.p. pa $6.99; bd bk $6.99

Grades: PreK K 1 2   E

1. Stories in rhyme 2. Pumpkin -- Fiction 3. Halloween -- Fiction

ISBN 0-689-83834-4; 0-689-87135-X pa; 0-689-86277-6 bd bk

LC 00-32421

Peter finds the perfect pumpkin so that he and his Dad can make a jack-o-lantern

"Toddlers will relish the bouncy, rhyming stanzas and silly word-play, which help make this a great, nonspooky Halloween storytime choice. The subtly textured computer-generated art has solid child appeal." Booklist

Serrano, Francisco

La Malinche; the princess who helped Cortés conquer the Aztec Empire. Francisco Serrano. Groundwood Books/House of Anansi Press 2012 37 p. $18.95

Grades: 4 5 6   E

1. Picture books for children

ISBN 1554981115; 9781554981113

This is a "picture-book biography about the controversial Mexican figure 'La Malinche.' Malinali, a Nahuatl princess, was sold into slavery and eventually traded to Spanish explorer Hernán Cortés." (School Library Journal) "Presented here as an enigma La Malinche is viewed by some as the mother of a new culture and by others as a traitor who helped Cortes defeat an indigenous people of which she was a part. What is agreed upon is that Cortes . . . may not have had success without her." (Children's Literature)

Seto, Loretta

Mooncakes; Loretta Seto, Renne Benoit. Orca Book Publishers 2013 32 p. (hardcover) $19.95

Grades: PreK K 1 2   E

1. Moon -- Folklore 2. Festivals -- Fiction

ISBN 1459801075; 9781459801073

LC 2012952944

This children's story, by Loretta Seto, illustrated by Renné Benoit, follows "a young girl who shares the special celebration of the Chinese Moon Festival with her parents. As they eat mooncakes, drink tea and watch the night sky together, Mama and Baba tell ancient tales of a magical tree that can never be cut down, the Jade Rabbit who came to live on the moon and one brave woman's journey to eternal life." (Publisher's note)

Seuss, Dr., 1904-1991

The **500** hats of Bartholomew Cubbins. Random House 1990 un il $14.95

Grades: PreK K 1 2 3   E

1. Hats -- Fiction

ISBN 0-394-84484-X

LC 88-38412

A reissue of the title first published 1938 by Vanguard Press

"It is a lovely bit of tomfoolery which keeps up the suspense and surprise until the last page, and of the same ingenious and humorous imagination are the author's black and white illustrations in which a red cap and then an infinite number of red caps titillate the eye." N Y Times Book Rev

★ **And** to think that I saw it on Mulberry Street. Random House 1989 un il $14.95; lib bdg $15.99

Grades: PreK K 1 2   E

1. Stories in rhyme

ISBN 0-394-84494-7; 0-394-94494-1 lib bdg

LC 88-38411

A reissue of the title first published 1937 by Vanguard Press

"A fresh, inspiring picture-story book in bright colors. . . . As convincing to a child as to the psychologist in quest of a book with an appeal to the child's imaginations." Horn Book

Bartholomew and the oobleck; written and illustrated by Dr. Seuss. Random House 1949 un il $14.95; lib bdg $15.99

Grades: PreK K 1 2　　　　　　　　　　　　　　E

　ISBN 0-394-80075-3; 0-394-90075-8 lib bdg

　A Caldecott Medal honor book, 1950

"Bored with the same old kinds of weather, the King of Didd commanded his magicians to stir up something new and different. What they produced was a gooey, gummy green stuff which might have wrecked the kingdom had it not been for Bartholomew Cubbins, the page boy." Booklist

The **Bippolo** Seed and other lost stories; by Dr. Seuss; introduction by Charles D. Cohen. Random House 2011 69p il $15

Grades: K 1 2 3 4　　　　　　　　　　　　　　E

　1. Short stories 2. Stories in rhyme

　ISBN 978-0-375-86435-3; 0-375-86435-0

　　　　　　　　　　　　　　　LC 2009052588

Presents seven Dr. Seuss stories first published in magazines between 1948 and 1959, with an introduction and commentary on each.

"The stories' rhymed couplets are pitch-perfect, the verse's rhythm as snappy as in any of Seuss's better-known works. . . . Fans old and young will deem these 'lost' stories a tremendous find." Publ Wkly

★ The **cat** in the hat; by Dr. Seuss. 50th anniversary ed.; Random House 2007 61p il $8.99 E

　1. Stories in rhyme 2. Cats -- Fiction

　ISBN 978-0-394-80001-1

　A reissue of the title first published 1957

A nonsense story in verse illustrated by the author about an unusual cat and his tricks which he displayed for the children one rainy day

　Another title about The cat in the hat is:

　The cat in the hat comes back (1958)

★ **Green** eggs and ham. Beginner Bks. 1960 62p il $8.99; lib bdg $11.99; pa $9.95

Grades: PreK K 1 2　　　　　　　　　　　　　　E

　1. Stories in rhyme 2. Food -- Fiction

　ISBN 0-394-80016-8; 0-394-90016-2 lib bdg; 0-394-89220-8 pa

"The happy theme of refusal-to-eat changing to relish will be doubly enjoyable to the child who finds many common edibles as nauseating as the title repast. The pacing throughout is magnificent, and the opening five pages, on which the focal character introduces himself with a placard: 'I am Sam,' are unsurpassed in the controlled-vocabulary literature." Saturday Rev

Hooray for Diffendoofer Day! [by] Dr. Seuss with some help from Jack Prelutsky & Lane Smith. Knopf 1998 un il $17; lib bdg $18.99

Grades: PreK K 1 2　　　　　　　　　　　　　　E

　1. School stories 2. Stories in rhyme

　ISBN 0-679-89008-4; 0-679-99008-9 lib bdg

　　　　　　　　　　　　　　　LC 97-39725

The students of Diffendoofer School celebrate their unusual teachers and curriculum, including Miss Fribble who teaches laughing, Miss Bonkers who teaches frogs to dance, and Mr. Katz who builds robotic rats

"Given an unfinished manuscript (some sketches, snippets of verse, and jottings of names—but no plot) retrieved after Seuss's death, Prelutsky and Smith have brought this fragment to fruition in a style that does credit to all three artists." Horn Book Guide

Horton and the Kwuggerbug and more lost stories; by Dr. Seuss; introduction by Charles D. Cohen. Random House Inc 2014 56 p. (trade) $15

Grades: K 1 2 3 4　　　　　　　　　　　　　　E

　1. Stories in rhyme 2. Children's stories 3. Short stories 4.

Children's stories, American

　ISBN 0385382987; 9780375973420; 9780385382984

　　　　　　　　　　　　　　　LC 2014003038

In this children's book by Dr. Seuss, "Seuss fans will learn more about Horton's integrity, Marco's amazing imagination, a narrowly avoided disaster on Mulberry Street, and a devious Grinch." The book features "a color palette enhanced beyond that of the magazines in which the stories originally appeared." (Publisher's note)

"Readers will delight in this book of "lost" stories, told in Seuss's signature inventive rhyme...The introduction, by scholar Charles D. Cohen, is chock-full of background and offers the provenance of these stories collected from a variety of magazines. Dr. Seuss stories are irresistible, and this collection is no exception." SLJ

★ **Horton** hatches the egg. Random House 1940 un il $14.95; lib bdg $15.99

Grades: PreK K 1 2　　　　　　　　　　　　　　E

　1. Stories in rhyme 2. Elephants -- Fiction

　ISBN 0-394-80077-X; 0-394-90077-4 lib bdg

"Horton, the elephant, is faithful one hundred percent as he carries out his promise to watch a bird's egg while she takes a rest. Hilarious illustrations and a surprise ending." Adventuring with Books. 2d edition

★ **Horton** hears a Who! Random House 1954 un il $14.95; lib bdg $16.99

Grades: PreK K 1 2　　　　　　　　　　　　　　E

　1. Stories in rhyme 2. Elephants -- Fiction

　ISBN 0-394-80078-8; 0-394-90078-2 lib bdg

"The verses are full of the usual lively, informal language and amazing rhymes that have delighted such a world-wide audience in the good 'doctor's' other books." N Y Her Trib Books

★ **How** the Grinch stole Christmas. Random House 1957 un il $15; lib bdg $18

Grades: PreK K 1 2　　　　　　　　　　　　　　E

　1. Stories in rhyme 2. Christmas -- Fiction

　ISBN 0-394-80079-6; 0-394-90079-0 lib bdg

"The verse is as lively and the pages are as bright and colorful as anyone could wish." Saturday Rev

★ **If** I ran the circus. Random House 1956 un il $14.95; lib bdg $15.99

Grades: PreK K 1 2　　　　　　　　　　　　　　E

　1. Stories in rhyme 2. Circus -- Fiction

　ISBN 0-394-80080-X; 0-394-90080-4 lib bdg

The author-illustrator "presents the fabulous Circus McGurkus with its highly imaginative young owner, Morris McGurk and its intrepid performer, Sneelock, behind whose store the circus is to be housed. There are the expected number of strange creatures with nonsensical names, but the real humor lies in the situations, and especially those involving Mr. Sneelock. There is fun for the entire family here." Bull Cen Child Books

★ **If** I ran the zoo. Random House 1950 un il $14.95; lib bdg $16.99

Grades: PreK K 1 2　　　　　　　　　　　　　　E

　1. Stories in rhyme 2. Zoos -- Fiction

　ISBN 0-394-80081-8; 0-394-90081-2 lib bdg

　A Caldecott Medal honor book, 1951

"As you turn the pages, the imaginings get wilder and funnier, the rhymes more hilarious. There will be no age limits for this book, because families will be forced to share rereading and quotation, for a long long time." NY Her Trib Books

McElligot's pool; written and illustrated by Dr. Seuss. Random House 1947 un il $14.95; lib bdg $16.99

Grades: PreK K 1 2   **E**

1. Stories in rhyme 2. Fishing -- Fiction
ISBN 0-394-80083-4; 0-394-90083-9 lib bdg

A Caldecott Medal honor book, 1948

"Fine color surrounding a host of strange creatures enlivens this amazing fish story for all ages." Horn Book

Yertle the turtle and other stories; A 50th anniversary retrospective. with 32 pages of rarely seen Seuss images and commentary by Charles D. Cohen. 50th anniversary ed.; Random House 2008 114p il $24.99; lib bdg $27.99

Grades: PreK K 1 2   **E**

1. Stories in rhyme 2. Turtles -- Fiction
ISBN 978-0-375-83850-7; 0-375-83850-3; 978-0-375-93850-4 lib bdg; 0-375-93850-8 lib bdg

LC 2007033486

A reissue of the title first published 1958

Includes three humorous stories in verse, Yertle the Turtle, Gertrude McFuzz, and The Big Brag, followed by commentary and end notes, reproductions of illustrations from other Dr. Seuss books, and two poems, 'The Ruckus' and 'The Kindly Snather'

Includes bibliographical references

Seven, John

Happy punks 1 2 3; A Counting Story. Manic D Press 2013 32 p. $15.95

Grades: PreK K   **E**

1. Counting -- Fiction 2. Punk culture -- Fiction
ISBN 1933149671; 9781933149677

This "counting book . . . takes readers up to 12 as musicians prepare to give a free concert. . . . 'Six happy punks go to the thrift store. . . . Perry buys a funny jacket. Siobhan loves that strange gizmo.' The book doesn't get specific about what punk means, but the diversity of characters (including a second-wave ska fan, anthropomorphic animals and robots, and a jetpack-wearing punk of the steam variety) hint at a be-yourself, anything-goes mentality." (Publishers Weekly)

The **ocean** story; written by John Seven; illustrated by Jana Christy. Picture Window Books 2011 un il

Grades: PreK K 1 2   **E**

1. Ocean -- Fiction 2. Water -- Fiction 3. Oil spills -- Fiction 4. Marine animals -- Fiction 5. Water pollution -- Fiction
ISBN 1-4048-6785-6; 978-1-4048-6785-7

LC 2011006480

Relates the story of the oceans that are home to so many creatures, that are part of the water cycle which produces rain, and that can become very messy if we do not take care of them.

"Endpapers filled with images of ocean life are the auspicious beginning of this beautiful eco-tale. . . . This splendid call to stewardship is gloriously illustrated with paintings, each a gift of color and texture that encourages lingering. . . . This book is a perfect blend of poetry, visual art, and science." SLJ

Shahan, Sherry

Spicy hot colors: colores picantes; illustrated by Paula Barragan. August House 2004 un il $16.95

Grades: PreK K 1 2   **E**

1. Color 2. Bilingual books -- English-Spanish
ISBN 0-87483-741-3

This is an "introduction to the names of nine colors in Spanish. Snappy, image-filled verses bring to life some of the hues and traditions of Latino culture. . . . Vibrant paintings that have both ethnic and fine-art references are appealing and attention grabbing." SLJ

Shange, Ntozake, 1948-

★ **Ellington** was not a street; written by Ntozake Shange; illustrations by Kadir Nelson. Simon & Schuster Bks. for Young Readers 2004 un il $15.95

Grades: K 1 2 3 4   **E**

1. Children's poetry 2. African Americans -- Poetry
ISBN 0-689-82884-5

LC 00-45060

"Shange's poem 'Mood Indigo,' an adult recollection of a childhood spent 'in the company of men/ who changed the world,' receives a . . . treatment through illustrations that follow a demure little girl who nonchalantly interacts with the mid-twentieth-century African-American luminaries who visit her father. . . . Grades three to six." (Bull Cent Child Books)

"Nelson illustrates the noted poet's 'Mood Indigo,' from her collection entitled A Daughter's Geography. . . . In the poem, Shange recalls her childhood when her family entertained many of the . . . 'men/ who changed the world,' including Paul Robeson, W.E.B. DuBois, Ray Barretto, Dizzy Gillespie, 'Sonny Til' Tilghman, Kwame Nkrumah, and Duke Ellington. Both the words and the rich, nostalgic illustrations are a tribute to these visionaries. . . . A biographical sketch of each man appears at the end, along with the poem reprinted on a single page." SLJ

Shannon, David

★ **Alice** the fairy. Blue Sky Press 2004 un il $15.95

Grades: PreK K 1 2   **E**

1. Fairies -- Fiction 2. Imagination -- Fiction
ISBN 0-439-49025-1

LC 2003-23478

Alice, who claims to be a Temporary Fairy, still has a lot to learn, such as how to make her clothes put themselves away in the closet.

"Kids will find most of the humor right at their level, in terms of both wit and imagination. The pictures are richly colored, some almost effervescent in their playfulness." Booklist

★ **Bugs** in My Hair! David Shannon. Blue Sky Press 2013 32 p. (hardcover : alk. paper) $17.99

Grades: K 1 2 3   **E**

1. Hair -- Fiction 2. Lice -- Fiction 3. Humorous stories
ISBN 0545143136; 9780545143134

LC 2012042220

In this children's picture book by David Shannon, "there's a Lice-a-Palooza going on-right on top of the narrator's head. Our hero . . . has head lice. His ever-attentive mother is on the attack, with stinky stuff and a nit comb. Head lice may have taken over the boy's life, but his mom can conquer just about anything. . . . The book imparts . . . information while revealing the humiliation, embarrassment, frustration, and downright itchiness of these little nasties." (School Library Journal)

★ **Duck** on a bike. Blue Sky Press (NY) 2002 un il $15.95

Grades: PreK K 1 2   **E**

1. Ducks -- Fiction 2. Cycling -- Fiction 3. Domestic animals -- Fiction
ISBN 0-439-05023-5

LC 2001-35992

A duck decides to ride a bike and soon influences all the other animals on the farm to ride bikes too

"This delightful story will have youngsters chiming in on the repeated phrases and predicting, in no time, what will happen next, and the many animal sounds provide ample opportunities for role-playing. Shannon's brightly colored spreads are filled with humor." SLJ

★ **Good** boy, Fergus! Blue Sky Press 2006 un il $15.99
Grades: PreK K 1 2   E
1. Dogs -- Fiction
ISBN 0-439-49027-8
LC 2005-08541
Except for his bath, Fergus experiences the perfect doggy day, from chasing cats and motorcycles to being scratched on his favorite tickle spot.
"This book is all about the impressive, oversize visuals—pictures that show the adorable doggie in full canine-caper mode." Booklist

★ **No,** David! Blue Sky Press (NY) 1998 un il $16.99
Grades: PreK K 1 2   E
1. Behavior -- Fiction 2. Mother-son relationship -- Fiction
ISBN 0-590-93002-8
LC 97-35125
A Caldecott Medal honor book, 1999
A young boy is depicted doing a variety of naughty things for which he is repeatedly admonished, but finally he gets a hug. "Preschool to grade two." (SLJ)
"The vigorous and wacky full-color acrylic paintings portray a lively and imaginative boy whose stick-figure body conveys every nuance of anger, exuberance, defiance, and best of all, the reassurance of his mother's love." SLJ
Other titles about David are:
David goes to school (1999)
David gets in trouble (2002)
It's Christmas, David! (2010)

★ The **rain** came down. Blue Sky Press (NY) 2000 un il lib bdg $15.95
Grades: PreK K 1 2   E
1. Quarreling 2. Rain -- Fiction 3. Rain and rainfall
ISBN 0-439-05021-9
LC 99-86363
An unexpected rain shower causes quarreling and confusion among the members of a small community. However, when the sun comes out, everyone feels better. "Ages five to eight." (Bull Cent Child Books)
"This deceptively simple story showcases Shannon's quirky humor and offbeat illustrations." SLJ

★ **Too** many toys. Blue Sky Press 2008 un il $16.99
Grades: PreK K 1 2   E
1. Toys -- Fiction
ISBN 0-439-49029-4; 978-0-439-49029-0
LC 2007-44753
Although he finally agrees that he has too many toys and needs to give them away, there is one toy that Spencer absolutely cannot part with. "Ages six to nine." (Bull Cent Child Books)
"A master at capturing the workings of a young mind, Shannon combines realistic dialogue with his boisterous illustrations to create another surefire hit." SLJ

Shannon, George
★ **One** family; George Shannon; pictures by Blanca Gomez. Farrar, Straus & Giroux 2015 32 p. color illustrations (hardcover) $17.99
Grades: PreK K 1   E
1. Counting 2. Family -- Fiction 3. Families -- Fiction
ISBN 0374300038; 9780374300036
LC 2014040391

This children's book, by George Shannon, "celebrates family and community, while also offering young readers a chance to practice counting. Each spread features an increasing number of people who form a family. From babies in buggies to white-haired elders holding hands, families stretch across generations and races." (School Library Journal)
"A playful counting book also acts as a celebration of family and human diversity. Shannon's text is delivered in spare, rhythmic, lilting verse that begins with one and counts up to 10 as it presents different groupings of things and people in individual families, always emphasizing the unitary nature of each combination. . . . Interracial families are included, as are depictions of men with their arms around each other, and a Sikh man wearing a turban. This inclusive spirit supports the text's culminating assertion that "One is one and everyone. One earth. One world. One family." A visually striking, engaging picture book that sends the message that everyone counts." Kirkus

Tippy-toe chick, go! pictures by Laura Dronzek. Greenwillow Bks. 2003 un il $15.99; lib bdg $16.89
Grades: PreK K 1 2   E
1. Dogs -- Fiction 2. Chickens -- Fiction
ISBN 0-06-029823-5; 0-06-029824-3 lib bdg
LC 2002-17509
When a mean dog blocks the path to the garden where a delicious breakfast awaits, Little Chick shows her family how brave and clever she is
"The narrative has a fresh, buoyant vitality that begs to be read aloud. . . . The bright, uncluttered acrylic illustrations neatly match the spare text." Booklist

★ **Tomorrow's** alphabet; pictures by Donald Crews. Greenwillow Bks. 1996 un il $17; pa $6.99
Grades: PreK K 1 2 3   E
1. Alphabet
ISBN 0-688-13504-8; 0-688-16424-2 pa
LC 94-19484
"In 26 double-page spreads, the letters of the alphabet are used to demonstrate where things come from. 'A is for seed' is followed on the next page with 'tomorrow's APPLE.' 'D is for puppy—tomorrow's DOG.'. . . All of the combinations are clever, well chosen, and well within youngsters' experience. . . . Each two-page spread offers brightly colored, large and realistic depictions of the objects named." SLJ

Turkey Tot; by George Shannon; illustrated by Jennifer K. Mann. Holiday House 2013 32 p. color illustrations (hardcover) $16.95
Grades: PreK K 1   E
1. Turkeys -- Fiction 2. Inventions -- Fiction 3. Picture books for children 4. Animals -- Fiction 5. Determination (Personality trait) -- Fiction
ISBN 0823423794; 9780823423798
LC 2011022103
In this picture book, written by George Shannon and illustrated by Jennifer K. Mann, "Turkey Tot thinks outside the box. He's hopeful, imaginative, and persistent, refusing to let his Debbie Downer friends in the farmyard discourage him. He's determined to retrieve juicy blackberries that hang just out of reach, but he needs a little help to implement the plans he makes to get within range." (School Library Journal)
"Big, comic-style thought balloons show the friends imagining each of the turkey's schemes failing, their round eyes with black dots somehow giving away their thoughts. With its short words and sentences and humorous repetition, this makes a good early reader as well as an entertaining storytime book." Horn Book

A **very** witchy spelling bee; George Shannon; illustrated by Mark Fearing. HMH Books for Young Readers 2013 32 p. $16.99

Grades: 1 2 3 4   **E**

1. Picture books for children 2. Witches -- Fiction 3. Spelling bees -- Fiction 4. English language -- Spelling -- Fiction
ISBN 0152066969; 9780152066963

LC 2012045935

This children's picture book is a "story about a purple-haired witch named Cordelia who loves spelling words and casting spells . . . . After Cordelia enters a spelling bee, the mean-spirited 203-year-old reigning champ, Beulah Divine, vows to defeat the young witch; Cordelia wins by adding the letter R to the word 'F-I-E-N-D,' turning her rival into an ally." (Publishers Weekly)

★ **White** is for blueberry; pictures by Laura Dronzek. Greenwillow Books 2005 un il $17.99; lib bdg $17.89

Grades: PreK K 1 2 3   **E**

1. Color
ISBN 0-06-029275-X; 0-06-029276-8 lib bdg

LC 2004-10147

"The bold, uncluttered scenes, rendered in acrylics, have a sweetness and strength that is quite pleasing to the eye. Easy to read and fun to share, this paean to the wonder of cycles and the rewards of close observation is the perfect prelude to a thoughtful excursion." SLJ

Sharmat, Marjorie Weinman

Gila monsters meet you at the airport; pictures by Byron Barton. Macmillan 1980 un il hardcover o.p. pa $5.99

Grades: PreK K 1 2   **E**

1. Moving -- Fiction 2. West (U.S.) -- Fiction
ISBN 0-02-782450-0; 0-689-71383-5 pa

LC 80-12264

A New York City boy's preconceived ideas of life in the West make him very apprehensive about the family's move there

"The exaggeration is amusing, the style yeasty, with a nice final touch; the illustrations are comic and awkward, but add little that's not inherent in the story." Bull Cent Child Books

★ **Nate** the Great; illustrated by Marc Simont. Delacorte Press 2002 60p il $13.95; pa $4.50

Grades: K 1 2   **E**

1. Mystery fiction
ISBN 978-0-385-73017-4; 0-385-73017-9; 978-0-440-46126-5 pa; 0-440-46126-X pa
A reissue of the title first published 1972 by McCann & Geoghegan
Nate the Great, a junior detective who has found missing balloons, books, slippers, chickens and even a goldfish, is now in search of a painting of a dog by Annie, the girl down the street.

"The illustrations capture the exaggerated, tongue-in-cheek humor of the story." Booklist

Other titles about Nate the Great are:
Nate the Great and me: the case of the fleeing fang (1998)
Nate the Great and the big sniff (2001)
Nate the Great and the boring beach bag (1987)
Nate the Great and the crunchy Christmas (1996)
Nate the Great and the fishy prize (1985)
Nate the Great and the Halloween hunt (1989)
Nate the Great and the hungry book club (2009)
Nate the Great and the lost list (1975)
Nate the Great and the missing key (1981)
Nate the Great and the monster mess (1999)
Nate the Great and the mushy valentine (1994)
Nate the Great and the musical note (1990)
Nate the Great and the phony clue (1977)
Nate the Great and the pillowcase (1993)
Nate the Great and the snowy trail (1982)

Nate the Great and the sticky case (1978)
Nate the Great and the stolen base (1992)
Nate the Great and the tardy tortoise (1995)
Nate the Great goes down in the dumps (1989)
Nate the Great goes undercover (1974)
Nate the Great on the Owl Express (2003)
Nate the Great, San Francisco detective (2000)
Nate the Great saves the King of Sweden (1997)
Nate the Great stalks stupidweed (1986)
Nate the Great talks turkey (2006)

Sharmat, Mitchell

Gregory, the terrible eater; illustrated by Jose Aruego and Ariane Dewey. Four Winds Press 1985 un il $16.95

Grades: PreK K 1 2   **E**

1. Diet -- Fiction 2. Goats -- Fiction
ISBN 0-02-782250-8

LC 85-29290

A reissue of the title first published 1980

"Aruego and Dewey's illustrations are highly amusing, thanks to their goats' dot-eyed facial expressions. . . . There is energy in the pictures; they are beguiling and help to carry the humor." Booklist

Sharratt, Nick

What's in the witch's kitchen? Candlewick Press 2011 un il $12.99

Grades: PreK K   **E**

1. Stories in rhyme 2. Pop-up books 3. Witches -- Fiction 4. Halloween -- Fiction
ISBN 978-0-7636-5224-1; 0-7636-5224-5

LC 2010042323

The contents of the witch's kitchen are hidden by flaps that can be opened either to the left or right to reveal pop-up illustrations of either a delight or a nasty fright.

"Sharratt's digital illustrations are colorful and large. . . . Humorous contrasts, cheery colors, and smiling bats and ghosts make this book a perfect fit for storytimes about homes, rhymes, or surprises." SLJ

Shaskan, Stephen

A **dog** is a dog. Chronicle Books 2011 un il $14.99

Grades: PreK K 1   **E**

1. Stories in rhyme 2. Animals -- Fiction
ISBN 978-0-8118-7896-8; 0-8118-7896-1

LC 2010041949

Using various animals as examples, this rhyming picture book explores what makes them the same and what makes them different.

This "looks simple, but it's in fact a polished and controlled piece of work. . . . There's a chunky, woodcut feel to Shaskan's hip and cheery art, and he gives each of the animals abundant personality. Children attracted to Escher-like paradoxes will appreciate the endless loop of animal costumes and low-key surprises." Publ Wkly

Max speed; Stephen Shaskan. Simon & Schuster Books for Young Readers 2016 32 p. color illustrations (hardcover) $17.99; (ebook) $15.99

Grades: PreK K 1   **E**

1. Imagination -- Fiction 2. House cleaning -- Fiction
ISBN 9781481445900; 9781481445917

LC 2015025636

In this picture book, by Stephen Shaskan, "Max, a tiny speed racer, is off on the adventure of a lifetime. . . . As soon as Max has finished cleaning his room, he's off racing his super-secret car at incredible speeds, soaring over rivers of lava, sky diving, and swimming with sharks." (Publisher's note)

"An additional selection for libraries seeking books on imaginative play." SLJ

Toad on the road; a cautionary tale. by Stephen Shaskan. Harper, an imprint of HarperCollinsPublishers 2017 32 p. color illustrations (hardback) $17.99

Grades: PreK K 1   E
1. Animals -- Fiction 2. Humorous stories 3. Roads -- Fiction 4. Stories in rhyme 5. Toads -- Fiction 6. Safety -- Fiction
ISBN 9780062393470

LC 2016027575

In this book, by Stephen Shaskan, "a little toad carelessly squats in the middle of the road hungrily watching a fly buzz by. . . . Bear and bike end up in a ditch, and the bear yells at the little toad. . . . Unsurprisingly, the little toad does not listen, and soon along comes a top-hatted croc in a car. . .and there's another crash. . . . When, finally, along comes mother toad in a tow truck, readers hear 'Hey, little love, get out of the way! . . . That's no place to play.'" (Kirkus Review)

Shaw, Charles
★ **It** looked like spilt milk. Harper & Row 1947 un il $16.99; lib bdg $18.89; pa $6.99; bd bk $6.99

Grades: PreK K 1   E
ISBN 0-06-025566-8; 0-06-025565-X lib bdg; 0-06-443159-2 pa; 0-694-00491-X bd bk

White silhouettes on a blue background with simple captions: "sometimes it looked like a tree," "Sometimes it looked like a bird," etc. lead to a surprise ending "sometimes it looked like split milk, but what it was was—"

"What one thing could look like all of these? On the last page you are told, and I could no more tell you now than I could spoil an adult mystery by a review that gives away its solution." N Y Her Trib Books

Shaw, Hannah
★ **School** for bandits. Alfred A. Knopf 2011 un il $16.99

Grades: K 1 2   E
1. Raccoons -- Fiction 2. Etiquette -- Fiction
ISBN 978-0-375-86768-2; 0-375-86768-6

LC 2010039516

Ralph Raccoon is too polite so his parents send him to Bandit School to learn to behave like a properly bad raccoon.

"This clever story is packed with childlike humor. The pen-and-ink drawings are in bold colors and are full of action and creative details." SLJ

Shaw, Nancy
★ **Sheep** in a jeep; illustrated by Margot Apple. Houghton Mifflin 1986 32p il lib bdg $15; pa $5.95; bd bk $5.95

Grades: PreK K 1 2   E
1. Stories in rhyme 2. Sheep -- Fiction
ISBN 0-395-41105-X lib bdg; 0-395-47030-7 pa; 0-395-86786-X bd bk

LC 86-3101

"Shaw demonstrates a promising capacity for creating nonsense rhymes. . . . Veteran illustrator Apple's whimsical portraits of the sheep bring the story to life. Pleasing and lighthearted, this has much appeal for young readers." Publ Wkly

Other titles about the sheep are:
Sheep blast off! (2008)
Sheep in a shop (1991)
Sheep on a ship (1989)
Sheep out to eat (1992)
Sheep take a hike (1994)
Sheep trick or treat (1997)

Shea, Bob
Ballet Cat; Dance! dance! underpants! by Bob Shea. Disney-Hyperion 2016 56 p. color illustrations $9.99

Grades: K 1 2   E
1. Encouragement -- Fiction 2. Cats -- Fiction 3. Bears -- Fiction 4. Ballet dancing -- Fiction
ISBN 9781484713792

LC 2014049276

In this picture book, by Bob Shea, "Ballet Cat is getting her friend Butter Bear ready for her big ballet debut. "Leap, Butter, leap!" Ballet Cat prompts. But Butter Bear would prefer to just point her toe. When Ballet Cat keeps pushing, Butter Bear gets hungry, then thirsty, then sleepy . . . The bottom line is that Butter Bear would rather do almost anything to avoid making a big leap. Why? Because her bottom is covered in silly underpants!" (Publisher's note)

"Each page has solid, bright colored backgrounds. The backgrounds help the dialogue bubbles pop, and the bubbles themselves are colored so that readers can identify the speaker and follow the flow of the story." SLJ

★ **Big** plans; [illustrated by] Lane Smith. Hyperion 2008 42p il $17.99

Grades: 1 2 3 4   E
1. School stories 2. Imagination -- Fiction
ISBN 1-4231-1100-1; 978-1-4231-1100-9

LC 2008-00707

A little boy sits in the corner of his classroom dreaming about his big plans for his future.

"Smith is the perfect artist for this illogically logical scenario, with retro tones of gold and avocado predominating in his carefully disorganized oversized compositions. . . .An escapist adventure, a victory over important adults, and a new catch-phrase to triumphantly wield." Bull Cent Child Books

Cheetah can't lose; Bob Shea. Balzer + Bray 2013 40 p. (trade bdg.) $17.99

Grades: K 1 2   E
1. Racing -- Fiction 2. Animal babies -- Fiction 3. Cats -- Fiction 4. Humorous stories 5. Cheetah -- Fiction 6. Winning and losing -- Fiction
ISBN 0061730831; 9780061730832

LC 2012008407

Author Bob Shea presents a children's story about a cheetah. "It's race day, and once and for all, it's time to determine the better feline little cats or big cheetah. Cheetah might be bigger, taller, stronger, faster . . . but the little cats have some tricks up their sleeves, so don't count them out!" Shea presents a "story about the difference between brains and brawn." (Publisher's note)

★ **Dinosaur** vs. bedtime. Hyperion Books for Children 2008 un il $15.99

Grades: PreK K   E
1. Bedtime -- Fiction 2. Dinosaurs -- Fiction
ISBN 978-1-4231-1335-5; 1-4231-1335-7

"Incorporating paper, paint, photo collage and quick strokes of crayon, Shea's freewheeling compositions convey both a beguiling spontaneity and a preschooler's sense of invincibility." Publ Wkly

Other titles about Dinosaur are:
Dinosaur vs. the potty (2010)
Dinosaur vs. the library (2011)
Dinosaur vs. Santa (2012)
Dinosaur vs. school (2014)
Dinosaur vs. Mommy (2015)

The **happiest** book ever! Bob Shea. Disney-Hyperion 2016 40 p. color illustrations (hardback) $16.99

Grades: K 1 2 3   E

1. Frogs -- Fiction 2. Humorous stories 3. Happiness -- Fiction

ISBN 9781484730454

LC 2015049602

In this children's book by Bob Shea, "in a quest to be the happiest book ever, this interactive story has lined up lots of help. Readers supply happy thoughts. All is well, except for the frowny frog. The only solution is to kick the frog out of the book entirely. Now everybody's happy, right? Well, no, not exactly." (School Library Journal)

"A wonderful rethinking of the picture book as its own character. Wacky, zany, and downright fun." Kirkus

I'm a shark! Balzer + Bray 2011 un il $16.99

Grades: PreK K 1   E

1. Fear -- Fiction 2. Sharks -- Fiction 3. Courage -- Fiction

ISBN 978-0-06-199846-1; 0-06-199846-X

LC 2010-21850

A boastful shark is not afraid of anything, which impresses his underwater friends until they ask about spiders.

"Witty banter begs for audience participation. . . . Thick, dark crayon strokes convey both Shark's powerful physique and his endearing vulnerability. . . . Bold, uncluttered mixed-media spreads emphasize this predator's sharp-toothed, goofy grin." Kirkus

Kid sheriff and the terrible Toads; written by Bob Shea; illustrated by Lane Smith. Roaring Brook Press 2014 32 p. color illustrations (hardback) $17.99

Grades: K 1 2 3   E

1. Toads -- Fiction 2. Sheriffs -- Fiction 3. Humorous stories 4. Dinosaurs -- Fiction 5. West (U.S.) -- Fiction 6. Robbers and outlaws -- Fiction

ISBN 1596439750; 9781596439757

LC 2014001767

In this book by Bob Shea, illustrated by Lane Smith, "Sheriff Ryan might only be seven years old, and he might not know much about shooting and roping. But he knows a lot about dinosaurs. Yes, dinosaurs. And it turns out that knowing a thing or two about paleontology can come in handy when it comes to hoodwinking and rounding up a few no-good bandits." (Publisher's note)

"Shea's enjoyably bizarre take on a good old fashioned hoodwinkin' finds a perfect executor in Smith, whose desert-hued illustrations have all the hard corners and sneering lines of a wanted poster." Booklist

★ **Oh,** Daddy! Balzer + Bray 2010 un il $16.99

Grades: PreK K   E

1. Hippopotamus -- Fiction 2. Father-child relationship -- Fiction

ISBN 978-0-06-173080-1; 0-06-173080-7

A young hippopotamus shows his father the right way to do things, such as getting dressed, watering the flowers, and especially giving big hugs.

"The concise text captures the child's voice perfectly. . . . The mixed-media illustrations incorporate collage elements into a spare, cartoonlike world. . . . The gentle humor . . . will keep kids entertained." SLJ

Race you to bed. Katherine Tegen Books 2010 un il $16.99

Grades: PreK K 1   E

1. Stories in rhyme 2. Bedtime -- Fiction 3. Rabbits -- Fiction

ISBN 978-0-06-170417-8; 0-06-170417-2

LC 2008044525

"A fuzzy white rabbit with an oversize head races readers to bed, but he finds many reasons to delay bedtime. Animals, toys, and other objects divert his attention. . . . The singsong rhyme flows as the rabbit cavorts

through the flat colored pages. The backgrounds are all done in soothing pastel colors, with the exuberant youngster cavorting across the pages. Clever details in the art enhance the telling." SLJ

★ **Unicorn** thinks he's pretty great; by Bob Shea. Disney-Hyperion 2013 40 p. $15.99

Grades: PreK K 1 2   E

1. Picture books for children 2. Jealousy -- Fiction 3. Envy -- Fiction 4. Goats -- Fiction 5. Unicorns -- Fiction 6. Friendship -- Fiction

ISBN 1423159527; 9781423159520

LC 2012047987

In this children's book, a goat is jealous of a unicorn. "The goat bakes marsh-mallow squares. The unicorn can make it rain cupcakes! The goat tries a magic trick. The unicorn can turn things into gold! . . . It turns out that the unicorn actually has some goat envy," himself, and the two become friends. (Publishers Weekly)

"Rainbows, smiling cupcakes, and flying unicorns in one picture book can be a recipe for a cutesy-wootsy disaster, but not so in this hilarious friendship story... An ideal choice for fans of silliness." SLJ

Shea, Susan A.

★ **Do** you know which ones will grow? Blue Apple Books 2011 un il $16.99

Grades: PreK K 1   E

1. Life (Biology) 2. Stories in rhyme 3. Growth -- Fiction

ISBN 978-1-60905-062-7; 1-60905-062-2

"Shea's book debut is a clever, rhymed test of kids' notions of living and nonliving things that's great for both lap and group sharing. . . . [The book offers] a terrific interplay of rhyming questions and cunningly designed gatefold illustrations: 'If a calf grows and becomes a cow, / can a shovel grow and become . . . a plow?'. . . . Other rhymes include duck and truck, bear and chair, cat and hat . . . and kangaroo and you. . . . Slaughter's illustrations bring pop art to mind: vivid reds, blues, yellows and greens, few details, simple backgrounds and blocks of color." Kirkus

Shelby, Anne

★ The **man** who lived in a hollow tree; by Anne Shelby and Cor Hazelaar. Atheneum Books for Young Readers 2009 un il $17.99

Grades: K 1 2 3   E

1. Tall tales 2. Trees -- Fiction 3. Ecology -- Fiction 4. Carpentry -- Fiction

ISBN 978-0-689-86169-7; 0-689-86169-9

LC 2008-10369

Carpenter Harlan Burch, who builds everything from cradle to casket, plants two trees for every one he cuts down, and when he is very old his sap begins to rise, he grows young again, and starts a family that still lives all over the mountains.

"The storyteller's voice is vibrant, and the earth-toned acrylics on textured backgrounds of cardboard and linen have a quaint, collage-like feel." Booklist

Sher, Emil

★ **Away;** Emil Sher; illustrated by Qin Leng. Groundwood Books 2017 32 p. color illustrations $18.95

Grades: PreK K 1 2   E

1. Camping -- Fiction 2. Mother-daughter relationship -- Fiction

ISBN 1554984831; 9781554984831

In this picture book, by Emil Sher, illustrated by Qin Leng, "between work and school, homework and housework, a mother and daughter don't always get to spend as much time together as they'd like. Add to that a little girl's fears about leaving home for the first time, and the need to stay close through handwritten notes becomes even more important.

As the camp departure date gets closer, Mom does her best to soothe her daughter's nerves." (Publisher's note)

Sheridan, Sara

I'm me! illustrated by Margaret Chamberlain. Chicken House 2011 un il $15.99

Grades: PreK K 1   **E**

1. Play -- Fiction 2. Aunts -- Fiction 3. Imagination -- Fiction

ISBN 978-0-545-28222-2; 0-545-28222-5

"Imogen's visits to her aunt's house are always an adventure. As the child rushes in, Auntie Sara asks her what she wants to play. 'Can we play pretend?' And the woman replies 'Yes, yes, yes, we can!' A turn of each page reveals a suggestion.... But to each inquiry, Imogen smilingly replies 'No! Today I want to be....' and she reveals she just wants to be herself.... The exuberant, candy-colored illustrations show the pair delighting in each other as they cavort across the spreads. There are few books starring an aunt and her niece, and this playful gem that explores pretending and being oneself will find a welcome place in libraries." SLJ

Sherman, Pat

Ben and the Emancipation Proclamation; written by Pat Sherman; illustrated by Floyd Cooper. Eerdmans Books for Young Readers 2010 un il $16.99

Grades: 3 4 5   **E**

1. Slaves 2. Teachers 3. Slavery -- Fiction 4. African Americans -- Fiction 5. Books and reading -- Fiction 6. Emancipation Proclamation (1863) -- Fiction

ISBN 978-0-8028-5319-6; 0-8028-5319-6

"Based on the life of Benjamin Holmes, a slave who taught himself to read at a young age, this picture book is an inspiring account of overcoming oppression. Sherman's fictionalized telling is stirring, especially when Holmes revels in the discovery of new words.... Sherman's text has a stately simplicity. Cooper's paintings glow with a hopeful, golden warmth.... This is a powerful tale of a bright ray of light in a very dark period in America." SLJ

Includes bibliographical references

Sherry, Kevin

I'm the biggest thing in the ocean. Dial Books for Young Readers 2007 un il $16.99

Grades: PreK   **E**

1. Size -- Fiction 2. Squids -- Fiction 3. Marine animals -- Fiction

ISBN 978-0-8037-3192-9; 0-8037-3192-2

LC 2006-27815

A giant squid brags about being bigger than everything else in the ocean—almost.

"A lighthearted, clever story presented in an oversize, colorful package." SLJ

Another title about the giant squid is:

I'm the best artist in the ocean (2008)

Turtle Island; story and pictures by Kevin Sherry. Dial Books for Young Readers, an imprint of Penguin Group (USA) Inc. 2014 32 p. color illustrations (hardcover) $16.99

Grades: PreK K 1   **E**

1. Family -- Fiction 2. Animals -- Fiction 3. Turtles -- Fiction 4. Islands -- Fiction 5. Friendship -- Fiction 6. Loneliness -- Fiction

ISBN 0803733917; 9780803733916

LC 2013027091

"Turtle is big. But the ocean is bigger. And Turtle is all alone. Until four shipwrecked folks--a bear, an owl, a frog, and a cat--climb to safety on his shell. Before long, they're fast friends, and the sea doesn't seem so vast anymore. But when Frog confides that he misses his family, Turtle doesn't understand. Isn't he their family?" (Publisher's note)

"Sherry uses brilliant, speckled watercolor washes for the ocean and sky, while the creatures are rendered in simple, colorful shapes with thick outlines and cartoonishly big eyes. Lovable Turtle and his happy, friend-filled future will likely strike a chord with little ones feeling lonely." Booklist

Sheth, Kashmira

Monsoon afternoon; written by Kashmira Sheth; illustrated by Yoshiko Jaeggi. Peachtree 2008 un il $16.95

Grades: PreK K 1 2   **E**

1. Rain -- Fiction 2. India -- Fiction 3. Monsoons -- Fiction 4. Grandfathers -- Fiction

ISBN 978-1-56145-455-6; 1-56145-455-9

LC 2008004565

A young boy and his grandfather find much they can do together on a rainy day during monsoon season in India

"Jaeggi's atmospheric watercolors nicely translate the sensory details in the words.... The scenes give a strong sense of everyday life in the boy's Indian community, as well as the sweet bond between grandfather and grandson." Booklist

My Dadima wears a sari; written by Kashmira Sheth; illustrated by Yoshiko Jaeggi. Peachtree 2007 un il $16.95

Grades: K 1 2 3   **E**

1. Grandmothers -- Fiction 2. Clothing and dress -- Fiction 3. East Indians -- United States -- Fiction

ISBN 1-56145-392-7

LC 2006024334

Two young sisters raised in America learn about the beauty and art of wearing a sari from their wise Indian grandmother.

"Soft watercolor paintings capture the magnificent fabrics of Dadima's saris and accentuate the loving story." SLJ

★ **Tiger** in my soup; written by Kashmira Sheth; illustrated by Jeffrey Ebbeler. Peachtree Publishers 2013 32 p. (reinforced) $15.95

Grades: PreK K 1   **E**

1. Siblings -- Fiction 2. Imagination -- Fiction 3. Babysitters -- Fiction 4. Books and reading -- Fiction 5. Brothers and sisters -- Fiction

ISBN 1561456969; 9781561456963

LC 2012025539

In this book by Kashmira Sheth, "[a]n unnamed narrator is left in the care of his older sister.... Although he asks her to read him a book about a tiger, she would rather read her own book. He captures her attention long enough to get her to heat up some alphabet soup, but she ... doesn't even notice when a tiger rises up out of the steaming bowl. The boy uses ... handy utensils to fend off the raging beast until his sister finally ... agrees to read to him." (School Library Journal)

"Ebbeler truly knocks it out of the park, gleefully building on Sheth's prose with dynamic perspectives, a realistically detailed (and menacing) tiger, abundant visual hyperbole, and unexpected delights on nearly every page." Pub Wkly

Shields, Carol Diggory

★ **Baby's** got the blues; Carol Diggory Shields, illustrated by Lauren Tobia. Candlewick Press 2014 32 p. $16.99

Grades: PreK K 1   **E**

1. Infants -- Fiction

ISBN 0763632600; 9780763632601

LC 2013943085

This book, by Carol Diggory Shields, illustrated by Lauren Tobia, is a "tale of soggy diapers, mushy meals, and sleepin' behind bars... . Babies can't talk, can't walk, can't even really chew. It's enough to make the baby in this story blue, blue, blue." The book "gives a tip of the fedora to B.B. King in an ode to babyhood." (Publisher's note)

"Who can blame a baby for singing the blues? Representative lyrics from this soulfully silly book (with more parent- than kid appeal): "I'd like to eat some pizza, / Macaroni, or beef stew, / But I haven't got a single tooth, / So I can't even chew." Happily, the conclusion is pop-song upbeat. Tobia uses spare lines to capture the baby's emotions." (Horn Book)

Shields, Gillian

Library Lily; illustrated by Francesca Chessa. William B. Eerdmans 2011 un il $16

Grades: PreK K 1 2   E

1. Play -- Fiction 2. Libraries -- Fiction 3. Friendship -- Fiction 4. Books and reading -- Fiction

ISBN 978-0-8028-5401-8; 0-8028-5401-X

LC 2010053737

From the day her mother introduces her to the library, Lily wants to spend all of her time reading until she meets Milly, who hates reading but loves adventure.

"The simple text includes some dialogue and quotes from the books that Lily is reading and is placed attractively around the illustrations. Bright, vibrant, cartoon artwork enhances the text and evokes a cheerful feeling." SLJ

When the world is ready for bed. Bloomsbury 2009 un il $14.99; lib bdg $15.89

Grades: PreK K   E

1. Stories in rhyme 2. Bedtime -- Fiction 3. Rabbits -- Fiction

ISBN 978-1-59990-339-2; 1-59990-339-3; 978-1-59990-385-9 lib bdg; 1-59990-385-7 lib bdg

LC 2009002858

"This calming tale follows three brown bunnies as their day draws to a close. They have dinner, tidy up, tell dad about the fun they've had, brush their teeth, and listen to one last story. . . . The gentle singsong text makes for excellent bedtime reading, and the homey watercolors are equally pleasant. The bunnies wear distinctive outfits and have a variety of expressions." SLJ

Another title about this rabbit family is:

When the world was waiting for you (2011)

When the world was waiting for you; illustrated by Anna Currey. Bloomsbury Childrens Books 2011 un il $14.99; lib bdg $15.89

Grades: PreK K   E

1. Stories in rhyme 2. Infants -- Fiction 3. Rabbits -- Fiction

ISBN 978-1-59990-531-0; 1-59990-531-0; 978-1-59990-532-7 lib bdg; 1-59990-532-9 lib bdg

LC 2010029861

Illustrations and simple rhyming text tell the story of a rabbit family anticipating the birth of a baby.

"With just a few rhyming lines of text, this story . . . makes a memorable addition to the welcoming-the-new-baby subgenre. . . . The large-format watercolor illustrations of the rabbits are done in a loose style with delightful details." Kirkus

Shireen, Nadia

Good little wolf. Alfred A. Knopf 2011 il

Grades: K 1 2   E

1. Wolves -- Fiction

ISBN 0-375-86904-2; 0-375-96904-7 lib bdg; 978-0-375-86904-4; 978-0-375-96904-1 lib bdg

LC 2011003517

Rolf is proud when his friend, Mrs. Boggins, calls him a good little wolf, but when the Big Bad Wolf teases him Rolf tries to prove himself by howling at the moon and blowing down Little Pig's house.

"Simple, strikingly colored illustrations, rendered in pencil, ink, and collage with digital enhancements, feature the characters against bare backgrounds, allowing them to pop off the pages. . . . These bold illustrations, as well as the short text, make this a good read-aloud for audiences old enough to understand the tongue-in-cheek humor." Booklist

Shirley, Debra

Best friend on wheels; by Debra Shirley; illustrated by Judy Stead. Albert Whitman & Co. 2008 un il $15.95

Grades: K 1 2 3   E

1. Stories in rhyme 2. Friendship -- Fiction 3. Children with physical disabilities -- Fiction

ISBN 978-0-8075-8868-0; 0-8075-8868-7

LC 2007024252

A young girl relates all the ways she and her best friend, Sarah, are alike, in spite of the fact that Sarah uses a wheelchair.

"The colorful cartoon illustrations delightfully capture [the friends] in their favorite activities. . . . The rhyme moves quickly yet touches on many aspects of life for people in wheelchairs. . . . The artwork conveys the same positive fun as the text. The book's lesson is evident without being didactic." SLJ

Shulevitz, Uri

Dusk; Uri Shulevitz. Farrar, Straus & Giroux (BYR) 2013 32 p. (hardcover) $17.99

Grades: PreK K 1   E

1. Picture books for children 2. Cities and towns -- Fiction 3. Night -- Fiction 4. City and town life -- Fiction

ISBN 0374319030; 9780374319038

LC 2012045967

In this companion to Uri Shulevitz's Caldecott Honor-winning book "Snow," a boy and his dog who are "out for a walk with his 'grandfather with beard,' comes to realize that a city (especially if it's New York City) can come alive in magical ways at dusk. The sidewalks and streets fill with people (and one extraterrestrial) headed home or out for a night's adventure." (Publishers Weekly)

★ **How** I learned geography. Farrar, Straus & Giroux 2008 un il $16.95

Grades: PreK K 1 2   E

1. Maps -- Fiction 2. Refugees -- Fiction 3. Geography -- Fiction 4. Kazakhstan -- Fiction 5. Imagination -- Fiction

ISBN 978-0-374-33499-4; 0-374-33499-4

LC 2007-11889

A Caldecott Medal honor book, 2009

As he spends hours studying his father's world map, a young boy escapes the hunger and misery of refugee life. Based on the author's childhood in Kazakhstan, where he lived as a Polish refugee during World War II.

The "text is clear and straightforward but vivid, and small memorable touches . . . add dimensionality. Watercolor illustrations avoid demonizing the boy's real-life: the town (Turkestan, according to Shulevitz' note) looks like an interesting place. . . . Chunky lines and sweeps of washy watercolor gain additional textures in the map worlds." Bull Cent Child Books

★ **Snow**. Farrar, Straus & Giroux 1998 un il $16; pa $6.99

Grades: PreK K 1 2   E

1. Snow -- Fiction

ISBN 0-374-37092-3; 0-374-46862-1 pa

LC 97-37257

A Caldecott Medal honor book, 1999

As snowflakes slowly come down, one by one, people in the city ignore them, and only a boy and his dog think that the snowfall will amount to anything

"Passersby are caricatured into humorous figures bent into impossible postures, their tall hats, parasols, and funny shoes giving them an almost circus-clown appearance. . . . The elegantly stark text suits the elegant architectural lines of the cityscape." Bull Cent Child Books

★ So sleepy story. Farrar Straus Giroux 2006 un il $16
Grades: PreK K 1 2   E
1. Night -- Fiction 2. Sleep -- Fiction
ISBN 0-374-37031-1
LC 2005-51146

"A sleepy sleepy boy is fast asleep in his sleepy sleepy bed along with everything else in his sleepy sleepy house until music comes drifting in, in ever louder tones. Then the child and his surroundings gradually come alive, dance, and shake to the beat, and drift back to sleep as the notes and instruments depart. The brief repetitive text takes a backseat to the whimsical watercolor-and-ink cartoon illustrations." SLJ

Troto and the trucks; Uri Shulevitz. Margaret Ferguson Books, Farrar, Straus & Giroux 2015 32 p. (hardback) $17.99
Grades: PreK K 1   E
1. Automobiles -- Fiction 2. Automobile racing -- Fiction 3. Size -- Fiction 4. Trucks -- Fiction 5. Teasing -- Fiction
ISBN 0374300801; 9780374300807
LC 2014040549

In this children's story, by Uri Shulevitz, "Troto is a happy little car who likes to go places. One day after a long drive, he arrives in Cactusville, where he meets some big trucks. But when those big trucks laugh at how small Troto is, Troto doesn't feel very happy anymore, so he challenges them to a race to show them just what a little car can do." (Publisher's note)

When I wore my sailor suit. Farrar, Straus & Giroux 2009 un il $16.95
Grades: K 1 2 3   E
1. Adventure fiction 2. Sailors -- Fiction 3. Imagination -- Fiction
ISBN 978-0-374-34749-9; 0-374-34749-2
LC 2008016187

A young child spends the day imagining himself to be a sailor on a grand adventure.

"Shulevitz combines child-size sentences with words that stretch and please. . . . The artist's mastery of the medium produces both warm, dappled interiors and Old Master severity, with convincing fades into the fantastic. . . . This is the work of a wise and wonderful storyteller." SLJ

Shulman, Mark

★ Mom and Dad are palindromes; a dilemma for words . . . and backwards. by Mark Shulman; illustrated by Adam McCauley. Chronicle Books 2006 un il $15.95
Grades: 1 2 3 4   E
1. Palindromes -- Fiction
ISBN 978-0-8118-4328-7; 0-8118-4328-9
LC 2005023614

When Bob realizes that he is surrounded by palindromes, from his mom, dad, and sis Anna to his dog Otto, he discovers a way to deal with the palindrome puzzle

"In all, Shulman cleverly weaves over 101 palindromes into the text. . . . The mixed-media cartoon art amplifies the zany situation." SLJ

Siddals, Mary McKenna

Compost stew; an A to Z recipe for the earth. illustrated by Ashley Wolff. Tricycle Press 2010 un il $15.99; lib bdg $18.99
Grades: PreK K 1 2   E
1. Alphabet 2. Stories in rhyme 3. Compost -- Fiction
ISBN 978-1-58246-316-2; 1-58246-316-6; 978-1-58246-341-4 lib bdg; 1-58246-341-7 lib bdg
LC 2009016300

"With bouncing, rhyming lines, this cheerful title uses the alphabet to introduce children to ingredients that make great compost, from apple cores to zinnias. . . . A short supplementary note about what compost is and why it is beneficial is included. . . . This title . . . provides a light-hearted introduction to an earth- and kid-friendly activity. The brightly patterned collage artwork featuring a cast of multicultural kids working together will easily draw a young audience." Booklist

Shivery Shades of Halloween; by Mary McKenna Siddals; illustrated by Jimmy Pickering. Random House Childrens Books 2014 32 p. color illustrations $12.99
Grades: PreK K 1 2   E
1. Color -- Fiction 2. Halloween -- Fiction
ISBN 0385369999; 9780385369992

This book, by Mary McKenna Siddals, illustrated by Jimmy Pickering, asks "[w]hat color is Halloween? Why, it's as green as an 'eerie glow, evil grin, vile brew, clammy skin,' as white as 'cobwebs clinging, a misty trail, a skull, a spook, a face gone pale . . .' Children will learn their colors as they follow a cute little creature on his adventure through haunted halls, moonlit forests . . . perhaps even a Halloween party!" (Publisher's note)

"Can colors other than orange and black be associated with Halloween? Upbeat rhymes make the case for a multihued holiday...A nice summary of all the colors appears at the end, as if the aforementioned wizard conjured up a spell to make a perfect Halloween. A solid and fun read-aloud." SLJ

Sidman, Joyce

★ Before morning; by Joyce Sidman; illustrated by Beth Krommes. Houghton Mifflin Harcourt 2015 48 p. color illustrations (ebook) $17.99; (hardback) $17.99
Grades: PreK K 1 2   E
1. Stories in rhyme 2. Snow -- Fiction 3. Wishes -- Fiction 4. Snow -- Fiction 5. City and town life -- Fiction
ISBN 9781328686091; 9780547979175
LC 2014048523

In this children's book by Joyce Sidman, illustrated by Beth Krommes, "there are planes to fly and buses to catch, but a child uses the power of words, in the form of an invocation, to persuade fate to bring her family a snow day--a day slow and unhurried enough to spend at home together." (Publisher's note)

"Throughout, Krommes's illustrations do the narrative work, and a series of wordless spreads at book's end provides a sweet balance to the front matter's opening scenes, slowly easing the reader out of this mesmerizing book." Horn Book

★ Red sings from treetops; a year in colors. illustrated by Pamela Zagarenski. Houghton Mifflin Harcourt 2009 un il $16
Grades: PreK K 1   E
1. Color -- Fiction 2. Nature -- Fiction 3. Seasons -- Fiction
ISBN 978-0-547-01494-4; 0-547-01494-5
LC 2008-35947

ALA ALSC Caldecott Medal Honor Book (2010)

Nature displays different colors to announce the seasons of the year.

"Fresh descriptions and inventive artistry are a charming inspiration to notice colors and correlate emotions. Details in the artwork will invite repeated readings and challenge kids to muse about other color icons." Kirkus

Siegel, Mark

★ **Moving** house. Roaring Brook Press 2011 il $16.99
Grades: PreK K 1   E
1. Home -- Fiction 2. Moving -- Fiction
ISBN 978-1-59643-635-0; 1-59643-635-2

LC 2010036602

When Joey and Chloe and their family are getting ready to move, their house decides it wants to go too.

"Siegel's . . . background as an illustrator (and an editor) serve him well; his vignettes and spreads are drafted in clean ink lines, with watercolor washes of blue and red signaling the clean skies above Foggytown. He's crafted a strong story, too." Publ Wkly

Siegel, Randy

Grandma's smile; illustrated by Dyanne DiSalvo. Roaring Brook Press 2010 32p il $15.99
Grades: PreK K 1 2   E
1. Airports -- Fiction 2. Grandmothers -- Fiction
ISBN 978-1-59643-438-7; 1-59643-438-4

DiSalvo's "sketch-style watercolors achieve an authenticity and immediacy that should give even infrequent fliers a shudder of recognition. . . . This is a wry and contemporary reality check on the going-to-Grandma's genre." Publ Wkly

My snake Blake; Randy Siegel; illustrations by Serge Bloch. Roaring Brook Press 2012 32 p. $16.99
Grades: PreK K   E
1. Pets -- Fiction 2. Snakes -- Fiction 3. Picture books for children 4. Snakes as pets -- Fiction 5. Human-animal relationships -- Fiction
ISBN 1596435844; 9781596435841

LC 2011018402

This book "tell[s] the story of a 'super-long, bright green snake' who wows the young narrator by helping him with his homework, eating rejected Brussels sprouts, and fighting bullies. 'He's a perfectly polite, delightful snake,' the boy says." The illustrations show "Blake engaged in a series of charmingly unsnakelike activities: he cooks, finds lost keys, and enjoys cuddling on park benches." (Publishers Weekly)

Sierra, Judy

Ballyhoo Bay; illustrated by Derek Anderson. Simon & Schuster Books for Young Readers 2009 un il $16.99
Grades: K 1 2   E
1. Stories in rhyme 2. Artists -- Fiction 3. Beaches -- Fiction 4. Social action -- Fiction 5. Environmental protection -- Fiction
ISBN 978-1-4169-5888-8; 1-4169-5888-6

LC 2007-49720

Mira Bella mobilizes her art students, from grandmothers to children, crabs to seagulls, to stop a dastardly plan for turning the beach at Ballyhoo Bay into an exclusive resort, and offers an alternative—leave the beach as it is

"Lively, humorous acrylic cartoons have a buoyancy that captures the sparkle of the seaside setting and the exaggerated antics of the characters. This upbeat ecological message is delivered with plenty of panache. Told in rhyming couplets, the story reads aloud well." SLJ

Born to read; story by Judy Sierra; pictures by Marc Brown. Alfred A. Knopf 2008 un il $16.99; lib bdg $19.99

Grades: PreK K 1 2   E
1. Stories in rhyme 2. Reading -- Fiction
ISBN 978-0-375-84687-8; 0-375-84687-5; 978-0-375-94687-5 lib bdg; 0-375-94687-X lib bdg

LC 2007-2306

A little boy named Sam discovers the many unexpected ways in which a love of reading can come in handy, and sometimes even save the day

This is written "in quick, quirky rhymed couplets. . . . Brown's gouache illustrations are cheery, and each page pours into the next through the use of subtly repeated background motifs. . . . This is an easy, obvious choice for events with literacy and early learning as their themes." SLJ

E-I-E-I-O! how Old MacDonald got his farm with a little help from a hen. Judy Sierra, illustrated by Matthew Myers. Candlewick Press 2014 32 p. (hbk.) $16.99
Grades: PreK K 1 2 3   E
1. Farms -- Fiction 2. Gardening -- Fiction 3. Stories in rhyme 4. Domestic animals -- Fiction
ISBN 0763660434; 9780763660437

LC 2013934306

In this book, by Judy Sierra, "Little Red Hen gives old MacDonald some pointers on composting—and a legendary farm is born. . . . Once upon a time, Old MacDonald didn't have a farm. He just had a yard—a yard he didn't want to mow. But under the direction of . . . Little Red Hen, Mac learns to look at the environment in a very different way, and whole new worlds start to bloom with the help of some mud, garbage, horse poop, and worms!" (Publisher's note)

"Most children know about Old MacDonald and his animals, but did they ever wonder how he got that farm? Sierra imagines a rollicking suburban scenario that starts when MacDonald gets tired of mowing the lawn and begins to seek out creative alternatives...This title offers a great way to extend the song into a lesson about the plant cycle and suburban farming. An excellent purchase for general collections as well as curriculum support." (SLJ)

Make way for readers; Judy Sierra; illustrated by G. Brian Karas. Simon & Schuster Books for Young Readers 2015 32 p. color illustrations (hardcover) $17.99
Grades: PreK K 1 2   E
1. Stories in rhyme 2. Toddlers -- Fiction 3. Animals -- Fiction 4. Books and reading -- Fiction
ISBN 9781481418515

LC 2014011224

In this book, by Judy Sierra, illustrated by G. Brian Karas, "in Miss Bingo's classroom there's always time to tell a story! Here are Jiro and Annabelle, Rufus and Rory. They're here to have fun with amazing Miss Bingo, the storytime rhymer, the singing flamingo. She tells them of kittens, and mittens, and mice, Miss Muffet, her tuffet, and sugar, and spice." (Publisher's note)

"Any adult who has ever read to a group of preschoolers will grin with delight over these familiar antics, and regular storytimers will enjoy seeing this favorite activity depicted." Kirkus

Sleepy little alphabet; a bedtime story from Alphabet Town. written by Judy Sierra; illustrated by Melissa Sweet. Alfred A. Knopf 2009 un il $16.99; lib bdg $19.99
Grades: PreK K 1   E
1. Alphabet 2. Stories in rhyme 3. Children's poetry 4. Bedtime -- Fiction
ISBN 0-375-84002-8; 0-375-94002-2 lib bdg; 978-0-375-84002-9; 978-0-375-94002-6 lib bdg

LC 2008-24526

Sleepy letters of the alphabet get ready for bed

"The bounce of Sierra's meter, the time-for-bed theme and Sweet's offhand pencil and watercolor drawings make the story feel fresh. Throughout, Sierra inserts vocabulary items that incorporate the letters . . . while Sweet provides the laughs." Pub Wkly

Tell the truth, B.B. Wolf; written by Judy Sierra; illustrated by J. Otto Seibold. Alfred A. Knopf 2010 un il $16.99; lib bdg $19.99
Grades: PreK K 1 2 3   E
   1. Wolves -- Fiction 2. Honesty -- Fiction
ISBN 978-0-375-85620-4; 0-375-85620-X; 978-0-375-95620-1 lib bdg; 0-375-95620-4 lib bdg
                            LC 2009030778

When Big Bad Wolf, who now lives at the Villain Villa Retirement Residence, is invited to tell his story at the library, he faces the truth about what he did to the three little pigs and decides to make amends.

"This brilliant retelling deserves a place at the head of the fractured-fairy-tale pack. . . . Seibold's vivid computer illustrations, replete with comic touches, are a perfect match for Sierra's zany tale." SLJ

   Another title about B. B. Wolf is:
   Mind your manners, B. B. Wolf (2007)

★ **Thelonius** Monster's sky-high fly pie; illustrations by Edward Koren. Knopf 2006 un il $16.95; lib bdg $18.99
Grades: K 1 2 3   E
   1. Stories in rhyme 2. Pies -- Fiction 3. Flies -- Fiction 4. Monsters -- Fiction
ISBN 0-375-83218-1; 0-375-93218-6 lib bdg
                            LC 2005-16773

A good-natured monster thinks a pie made out of flies would be a good dessert, and invites all his friends and relatives over to try it.

"An incomparable rhymester has teamed up with a master cartoonist to conjure up some haute cuisine on the fly. . . . The words are carefully chosen. . . . A lovable and entertaining work of art." SLJ

★ **Wild** about books; by Judy Sierra; pictures by Marc Brown. Knopf 2004 un il $16.95
Grades: PreK K 1 2   E
   1. Stories in rhyme 2. Animals -- Fiction 3. Libraries -- Fiction 4. Books and reading -- Fiction
ISBN 0-375-82538-X

A librarian named Mavis McGrew introduces the animals in the zoo to the joy of reading when she drives her bookmobile to the zoo by mistake.

"Sierra's text has a wacky verve and enough clever asides and allusions to familiar characters to satisfy bibliophiles of all ages. . . . Brown's cheerful, full-color illustrations stretch his trademark art with ever-so-slightly stylized spreads that are rich in pattern, texture, and nuance." SLJ

Wild about you! Judy Sierra; pictures by Marc Brown. Alfred A. Knopf 2012 40 p. (library binding) $20.99
Grades: PreK K 1   E
   1. Zoos -- Fiction 2. Picture books for children 3. Animal babies -- Fiction 4. Stories in rhyme 5. Zoo animals -- Fiction 6. Animals -- Infancy -- Fiction
ISBN 0375971076; 9780307931788; 9780375971075
                            LC 2011029010

This children's picture book looks at zoo animals. All the animals are "having babies, all except the tree kangaroo and the pandas. Even though some parents say that the babies are bothersome, none of them will give theirs up to the childless ones. When a van from Animal Rescue delivers an endangered egg, all of the birds refuse it, but the tree kangaroo offers her pouch." A baby penguin hatches, and all the animals pitch in to help the kangaroo feed it. (School Library Journal)

★ **ZooZical**; pictures by Marc Brown. Alfred A. Knopf 2011 un il $17.99; lib bdg $20.99
Grades: PreK K 1   E
   1. Stories in rhyme 2. Zoos -- Fiction 3. Animals -- Fiction 4. Theater -- Fiction
ISBN 978-0-375-86847-4; 0-375-86847-X; 978-0-375-96847-1 lib bdg; 0-375-96847-4 lib bdg
                            LC 2010038565

When the winter doldrums arrive at the zoo, a very small hippo and a young kangaroo decide to stage a "ZooZical," a show to display their singing, dancing, acrobatic, and other talents to the people of Springfield.

"With humor and gusto, Brown's richly textured folk art-inspired pictures convey the characters' dramatic shift in moods and imbue them with abundant personality. Meanwhile, Sierra's riffs on familiar tunes guarantee that readings will be very musical affairs, with children enthusiastic participants." Publ Wkly

Silverman, Erica
★ **Cowgirl** Kate and Cocoa; written by Erica Silverman; painted by Betsy Lewin. Harcourt 2005 un il $15
Grades: K 1 2   E
   1. Horses -- Fiction 2. Cowhands -- Fiction
ISBN 0-15-202124-8
                            LC 2004-5739

Cowgirl Kate and her cowhorse Cocoa, who is always hungry, count cows, share a story, and help each other fall asleep.

"Children will . . . recognize the friends' good-natured banter and lively dialogue. . . . Lewin's bold-lined illustrations extend the comedy and the affectionate friendship." Booklist

   Other titles about Kate and Cocoa are:
   Cowgirl Kate and Cocoa: partners (2006)
   Cowgirl Kate and Cocoa: school days (2007)
   Cowgirl Kate and Cocoa: rain or shine (2008)
   Cowgirl Kate and Cocoa: horse in the house (2009)
   Cowgirl Kate and Cocoa: spring babies (2010)

The **Hanukkah** hop; written by Erica Silverman; illustrated by Steven D'Amico. Simon & Schuster 2011 un il $12.99
Grades: PreK K 1   E
   1. Hanukkah stories 2. Parties -- Fiction 3. Hanukkah -- Fiction 4. Jews -- United States -- Fiction
ISBN 978-1-4424-0604-9

Rhymed text and illustrations follow a family's activities as they prepare to celebrate Hanukkah.

"Like the enthusiastic revelers, Silverman's gleeful text has rhythm. D'Amico's angular illustrations, with their circa-1950s flair, keep up the pace. . . . Readers' toes are sure to be tapping throughout this unabashedly joyful Hanukkah romp." Horn Book

Silverstein, Shel, 1930-1999
Who wants a cheap rhinoceros? by Shel Silverstein. 50th anniversary edition Simon & Schuster Books for Young Readers 2014 un illustrations hbk $17.99
Grades: K 1 2 3   E
   1. Pets -- Fiction 2. Rhinoceros -- Fiction
ISBN 9781481415934; 148141593X
   First published 1964

"Silverstein's economical black-line drawings illustrate the joys of owning a rhinoceros. . . . The deadpan text belies the goofiness of the pictures, with the rhinoceros jumping rope, playing pirates, and opening a soda can with his horn." Horn Book Guide

Siminovich, Lorena

★ **Alex** and Lulu: two of a kind. Templar Books 2009 un il $14.99

Grades: PreK K 1   E

  1. Cats -- Fiction 2. Dogs -- Fiction 3. Friendship -- Fiction

  ISBN 978-0-7636-4423-9; 0-7636-4423-4

"Alex, a white dog with a large black spot over one eye, is best friends with a white cat with black markings. One day, Lulu gets her pal thinking about the ways in which they are different. . . . He worries that their relationship is in jeopardy. To reassure him, Lulu offers several examples of true opposites . . . and reminds Alex that they share many interests in common. . . . Siminovich's spare scenes offer patterned backgrounds and an occasional charming detail. . . . With their retro feel and lack of fuss, the artwork is delectable." SLJ

You are my baby; garden. Lorena Siminovich. Chronicle Books 2014 10 p. color illustrations (alk. paper) $8.99

Grades: PreK   E

  1. Animal babies 2. Gardens -- Fiction 3. Board books

  ISBN 1452126496; 9781452126494

                              LC 2013025142

"Two books in one introduce youngsters to garden critters and their babies. An ingenious cutaway design separates the book into two distinct, connected pieces, creating a small book that sits nestled inside a larger one. . . . Each striking double-page spread has a distinct design, making it easy for children to match the baby animals in the smaller book with the adults on the larger pages." Kirkus

You know what I love? by Lorena Siminovich. Dial Books for Young Readers 2013 32 p. (hardcover) $16.99

Grades: PreK K   E

  1. Love -- Fiction 2. Dolls -- Fiction

  ISBN 0803737777; 9780803737778

                              LC 2012035617

This book, by Lorena Siminovich, is "one doll's . . . tribute to her little girl. From playing dress up to finding hidden treasures, these two always have fun because it turns out that what they love most of all is each other." (Publisher's note)

"A doll describes what she loves about her owner. The bland valentine of a narrative hinges on the crisp digital-collage art: "That we always make new friends together" has doll and girl seated before food arranged to look like faces; "Singing songs very loudly while we wait in traffic" spurs a cute image of the doll "riding" in a shoe." (Horn Book)

Simms, Laura

Rotten teeth; illustrated by David Catrow. Houghton Mifflin 1998 un il $16

Grades: K 1 2 3   E

  1. School stories 2. Teeth -- Fiction

  ISBN 0-395-82850-3

                              LC 97-2528

When Melissa takes a big glass bottle of authentic pulled teeth from her father's dental office for a show-and-tell presentation, she becomes a first-grade celebrity

"Catrow's watercolors are a suitably twisted complement to Simms' somewhat warped sense of humor (actually, it's perfect for this audience)." Bull Cent Child Books

Simon, Norma

All kinds of friends; by Norma Simon; illustrated by Cherie Zamazing. Albert Whitman 2013 32 p. (hardcover) $16.99

Grades: PreK K 1 2   E

  1. Friendship

  ISBN 9780807502839

                              LC 2012017376

"Simon . . . offers an unassuming exploration of friendship. The text conveys information in a straightforward, simple way. . . . The illustrations also make the point that friendships can thrive across gender, age and ethnic boundaries, and children are sure to recognize themselves and others they know in the diverse array of characters that populate the pages." Kirkus

Simon, Richard

★ **Oskar** and the eight blessings; written by Richard and Tanya Simon; illustrated by Mark Siegel. Roaring Brook Press 2015 40 p. illistrations color (hardback) $17.99

Grades: PreK K 1 2 3   E

  1. Kindness -- Fiction 2. Christmas -- Fiction 3. Jews -- Fiction 4. Hanukkah -- Fiction 5. Kindness -- Fiction 6. Refugees -- Fiction 7. Holocaust, Jewish (1939-1945) -- Fiction

  ISBN 9781596439498

                              LC 2015005061

In this children's story, written by Richard and Tanya Simon, illustrated by Mark Siegel, "a refugee seeking sanctuary from the horrors of Kristallnacht, Oskar arrives by ship in New York City with only a photograph and an address for an aunt he has never met. It is both the seventh day of Hanukkah and Christmas Eve, 1938. As Oskar walks the length of Manhattan, . . . each [resident]]offers Oskar a small act of kindness." (Publisher's note)

"A wonderful, heartwarming picture book for any library at any time of year." SLJ

Simont, Marc

Nate the Great and the stolen base; illustrations by Marc Simont. Coward-McCann 1992 47p il hardcover o.p. pa $4.50

Grades: K 1 2   E

  1. Mystery fiction

  ISBN 0-698-20708-4; 0-440-40932-2 pa

                              LC 91-26153

Nate the Great investigates the mysterious disappearance of the purple plastic octopus that his baseball team uses for second base

"Sharmat does not condescend to her audience, and readers are provided with enough information to find the answer themselves. Subtle humor sparkles through the young detective's narration." SLJ

★ The **stray** dog; retold and illustrated by Marc Simont from a true story by Reiko Sassa. HarperCollins Pubs. 2001 un il $16.99; lib bdg $18.89

Grades: PreK K 1 2   E

  1. Dogs -- Fiction

  ISBN 0-06-028933-3; 0-06-028934-1 lib bdg

  Boston Globe-Horn Book Award Honor: Picture Book (2001)

"Simont's art and narrative play off each other strategically, together imparting the tale's humor and tenderness." Publ Wkly

Simpson, Lesley

Yuvi's candy tree; illustrated by Janice Lee Porter. Kar-Ben Pub. 2011 un il lib bdg $17.95; pa $7.95

Grades: K 1 2 3   E

  1. Trees -- Fiction 2. Israel -- Fiction 3. Ethiopia -- Fiction 4. Jewish refugees -- Fiction 5. Jews -- Ethiopia -- Fiction

  ISBN 978-0-7613-5651-6; 0-7613-5651-7; 978-0-7613-5652-3 pa; 0-7613-5652-5 pa

                              LC 2010003880

Fleeing famine in her native Ethiopia, five-year-old Yuvi is sure she will have a candy tree when she arrives in Jerusalem.

"Flowing illustrations in browns, blues, and oranges bring this story, based on one woman's experience with Operation Moses, to life." Horn Book Guide

Singer, Marilyn

I'm your bus; pictures by Evan Polenghi. Scholastic Press 2009 un il $16.99

Grades: PreK   E

1. Buses -- Fiction

ISBN 978-0-545-08918-0; 0-545-08918-2

LC 2008017870

In rhyming text, a school bus describes its busy day transporting children to and from school.

"The digitally rendered pictures, composed of bold black outlines and bright colors, create a wholly endearing character. . . . Both energetic and reassuring." Booklist

Tallulah's Nutcracker; by Marilyn Singer; illustrated by Alexandra Boiger. Clarion Books 2013 48 p. (hardcover) $16.99

Grades: PreK K 1 2   E

1. School stories 2. Ballet -- Fiction 3. Christmas -- Fiction 4. Ballet dancing -- Fiction 5. Nutcracker (Choreographic work) -- Fiction

ISBN 054784557X; 9780547845579

LC 2012034744

In this book by Marilyn Singer, "it's Christmastime, and Tallulah finally gets what she's been wishing for--a part in a real ballet, a professional production of The Nutcracker. She's only a mouse, but she works as hard as if she had been cast as the Sugar Plum Fairy. On the night of the show, everything is perfect. But then disaster strikes! Does Tallulah have what it takes to become a real ballerina?" (Publisher's note)

Tallulah's solo; written by Marilyn Singer; illustrated by Alexandra Boiger. Clarion Books 2012 40 p. $16.99

Grades: PreK K 1 2   E

1. School stories 2. Ballet -- Fiction 3. Brothers and sisters -- Fiction

ISBN 0547330049; 9780547330044

LC 2011025729

In this book by Marilyn Singer, "Tallulah is certain she will have a solo in her dance school's upcoming performance of The Frog Prince. After all, she is now an excellent ballerina. And she's proud that her little brother, Beckett, has started taking ballet too. But then Tallulah gets an unexpected surprise . . . and not the good kind. What's a ballerina to do when everything does not go as planned?" (Publisher's note)

Tallulah's tap shoes; Marilyn Singer, illustrations by Alexandra Boiger. Clarion Books, Houghton Mifflin Harcourt 2015 48 p. color illustrations (hardcover) $16.99

Grades: PreK K 1 2   E

1. Ballet -- Fiction 2. Tap dancing -- Fiction 3. Camps -- Fiction 4. Dance -- Fiction 5. Ballet dancing -- Fiction 6. Perseverance (Ethics) -- Fiction

ISBN 0544236874; 9780544236875

LC 2014021786

In this children's story, by Marilyn Singer and Alexandra Boiger, "Tallulah is excited about going to dance camp. . . . She'll have to take tap, too, and she's NOT excited about that. . . . And she's right--tap class is not much fun. Plus there's a girl her same age who's maddeningly good at tap dancing. But that same girl isn't very good at ballet . . . could it be that she and Tallulah have something in common?" (Publisher's note)

"Young readers will learn about the importance of being patient and open-minded when it comes to trying new things. The text is complemented with soft and expressive watercolor illustrations." SLJ

Tallulah's toe shoes; by Marilyn Singer; illustrated by Alexandra Boiger. Clarion Books 2013 48 p. (hardcover) $16.99

Grades: PreK K 1 2   E

1. Shoes -- Fiction 2. Ballet -- Fiction 3. Ballet dancing -- Fiction 4. Ballet slippers -- Fiction

ISBN 054748223X; 9780547482231

LC 2012010869

In this book by Marilyn Singer "Tallulah is back in ballet class and now she wants to go en pointe—to dance up on the tips of her toes in pink satin toe shoes, like a real ballerina. But going en pointe is not good for growing feet, and her ballet teacher says her feet aren't ready yet. Oh, yes, they are, Tallulah thinks. Not only is she ready, she's determined. And nothing stops Tallulah when her mind is made up!" (Publisher's note)

Tallulah's tutu; illustrated by Alexandra Boiger. Clarion Books 2011 un il $16.99

Grades: PreK K 1 2   E

1. Ballet -- Fiction

ISBN 978-0-547-17353-5; 0-547-17353-9

LC 2010-05441

Tallulah takes ballet lessons and eagerly awaits her coveted tutu, which, she learns, she must work hard to earn.

"Even children who don't share Tallulah's ballet dreams may long for such an idyllic world. . . . Boiger's expressive paintings emphasize Tallulah's enthusiasm, grace, and large-eyed innocence." Booklist

What is your dog doing? illustrated by Kathleen Habbley. Atheneum Books for Young Readers 2011 il $12.99

Grades: PreK K 1   E

1. Stories in rhyme 2. Dogs -- Fiction

ISBN 978-1-4169-7931-9; 1-4169-7931-X

LC 2010016351

Illustrations and simple, rhyming text reveal that dogs do much more than sit, stay, and roll over.

"This fun look at canine activities will be a hit with dog people, cat people, and all people at storytime or anytime." SLJ

Sis, Peter

★ **Ballerina!** Greenwillow Bks. 2001 un il $14.95; bd bk $7.99

Grades: PreK K 1   E

1. Color 2. Ballet -- Fiction

ISBN 0-688-17944-4; 0-06-075966-6 bd bk

LC 00-35401

A little girl puts on costumes of different colors and imagines herself dancing on stage

Sis "creates a beautifully realized spot-on view of creative kids at play." Booklist

★ **Dinosaur!** Greenwillow Bks. 2000 un il $15.99; bd bk $7.99

Grades: PreK K 1   E

1. Dinosaurs 2. Stories without words

ISBN 0-688-17049-8; 0-06-075967-4 bd bk

LC 99-32923

While taking a bath, a young boy is joined by all sorts of dinosaurs

"A wordless picture book that takes readers on a wild adventure of the imagination. . . . This imaginative story with wonderful end-papers naming the creatures should appeal to all young dinosaur lovers. Sis's barely fleshed-out, cookie-cutter cartoons tell the story." SLJ

★ **Fire** truck. Greenwillow Bks. 1998 un il $15.99; bd bk $6.99

Grades: PreK K 1   E

1. Fire engines -- Fiction

ISBN 0-688-15878-1; 0-06-056259-5 bd bk

LC 97-29320

Matt, who loves fire trucks, wakes up one morning to find that he has become a fire truck, with one driver, two ladders, three hoses, and ten boots. Features a gate-fold illustration that opens into a three-page spread

"Sis blends simple text with bold pictures to give insight into one boy's vivid imagination." SLJ

★ **Ice** cream summer; by Peter Sis. Scholastic Press 2015 40 p. $17.99

Grades: PreK K 1 2 3 4   E

1. Summer -- Fiction 2. Grandfathers -- Fiction 3. Ice cream, ices, etc. -- Fiction 4. Grandparent-grandchild relationship -- Fiction 5. Letter writing -- Fiction 6. Grandparent and child -- Fiction

ISBN 0545731615; 9780545731614

LC 2014025155

In this book, author and illustrator "Peter Sis's delicious tongue-in-cheek vision of summer dishes up the whole scoop on everyone's favorite frozen treat--and proves that ice cream is every bit as enriching for the mind as it is for the taste buds. Readers everywhere will be begging for seconds and thirds!" (Publisher's note)

"The text is Joe's brief letter to his grandfather detailing his 'delicious' summer. The boy's descriptions of his various activities (reading, writing, practicing math) never mention that each revolves around ice cream. However, Sís's summery-hued illustrations, along with occasional incorporated text, put ice cream into everything Joe does." Horn Book

Komodo! Greenwillow Bks. 1993 un il $17.99

Grades: K 1 2 3   E

1. Indonesia -- Fiction 2. Komodo dragon -- Fiction

ISBN 0-688-11583-7; 0-688-11584-5 lib bdg

LC 92-25811

"Mad about dragons, the boy who narrates this picture book is pleased when his doting parents decide to take him to Indonesia, home of the Komodo dragon (aka monitor lizard). When the family disembarks on the Island of Komodo, the parents join a throng of tourists waiting for the Dragon Show, but the shy lizard never ventures out of its leafy shelter. Their adventuresome son, however, takes the road less traveled through the jungle, where he encounters the dragon of his dreams." (Booklist) "Ages five to eight." (Bull Cent Child Books)

"The story, assisted by the art in its moodily surreal tone, is simply written buy implies worlds." Bull Cent Child Books

Madlenka. Farrar, Straus & Giroux 2000 un il $17

Grades: PreK K 1 2 3   E

1. Teeth -- Fiction 2. New York (N.Y.) -- Fiction

ISBN 0-374-39969-7

LC 99-57730

Madlenka, whose New York City neighbors include the French baker, the Indian news vendor, the Italian ice-cream man, the South American grocer, and the Chinese shopkeeper, goes around the block to show her friends her loose tooth and finds that it is like taking a trip around the world

"The real magic comes in the cleverly cut-away windows in each storefront through which children glimpse complex, global dreamscapes. Madlenka journeys through these mystical places, too, and it is these surreal, wordless stories-within-the-story that will excite a wide range of children, launching them in their own imagined departures." Booklist

Other titles about Madlenka are:

Madlenka's dog (2002)

Madlenka, soccer star (2010)

★ **Trucks,** trucks, trucks. Greenwillow Bks. 1999 un il $16.99; bd bk $7.99

Grades: PreK K   E

1. Trucks -- Fiction

ISBN 0-688-16276-2; 0-06-056258-7 bd bk

LC 98-4482

A little boy cleans up his room using a variety of trucks and gives a one word description of their work such as hauling, plowing, and loading. Features a gate-fold illustration that opens into a three-page spread

"Sis creates a simple, bold look. . . . Gouache paints in yellow, black, and gray are set off by plenty of white space. The single verbs on each page are rendered in shades of blue, purple, green, and orange. This cheery romp is perfect for toddlers." SLJ

Sit, Danny

Tucker; little dog lost and found. Sterling 2011 un il $9.95

Grades: PreK K   E

1. Dogs -- Fiction 2. Beaches -- Fiction 3. Lost and found possessions -- Fiction

ISBN 978-1-4027-5999-4; 1-4027-5999-1

LC 2010031378

Tucker the Jack Russell terrier packs his bags and takes the train to the beach for an adventure, but after a fun day he discovers that he does not know how to get home.

"A strong narrative voice, charming photographs and an utterly appealing little dog protagonist coalesce to create a winning story about a Jack Russell terrier named Tucker. . . . Each page contains only a few sentences, making this a good choice for younger preschoolers and a possible selection for newly independent readers as well. Tucker's charming personality and the quality of the photographic illustrations help this stand out from the pack." Kirkus

Skofield, James

Detective Dinosaur undercover; illustrated by R. W. Alley. HarperCollins 2010 36p il (I can read) $16.99

Grades: K 1 2   E

1. Mystery fiction 2. Dinosaurs -- Fiction

ISBN 978-0-06-623878-4; 0-06-623878-1

In three brief mysteries, Detective Dinosaur learns about doing undercover work, gets chased by strange blobs, and finds rain on a sunny day.

"The dino's genial expressions projected in colorful pen-and-ink and watercolor cartoons follow the action. Conversation and onomatopoeia spice up the text, presented in large font. . . . His innocent confusion creates entertaining problems with simple solutions." SLJ

Other titles in this series are:

Detective Dinosaur (1996)

Detective Dinosaur: lost and found (1998)

Slack, Michael

Elecopter; Michael Slack. Henry Holt and Company 2013 32 p. (hardcover) $15.99

Grades: PreK   E

1. Elephants -- Fiction 2. Heroes and heroines -- Fiction 3. Stories in rhyme 4. Helicopters -- Fiction

ISBN 0805093044; 9780805093049

LC 2012046317

This children's picture book by Michael Slack focuses on "a hybrid elephant/helicopter who patrols the savannah. . . . . In the story's tensest sequence, Elecopter rescues a group of animals from wildfire: 'Flying into danger, she's first on the scene/ to airlift a rhino from a rocky ravine.' She also escorts to safety a cheetah, a passel of baboons, and a giraffe, and, best of all, she works for peanuts." (Publishers Weekly)

Other titles in this series are:

Race Car Count (2015)

Turtle Tug to the Rescue (2017)

Monkey Truck; [by] Michael Slack. Henry Holt & Co. 2011 un il $12.99

Grades: PreK K 1 **E**

1. Stories in rhyme 2. Trucks -- Fiction 3. Jungles -- Fiction 4. Monkeys -- Fiction

ISBN 978-0-8050-8878-6; 0-8050-8878-4

LC 2010011687

Monkey Truck comes racing to the rescue anytime there is trouble in the jungle.

"Slack produces a zippy jungle jaunt with enough action and rhythm for any preschooler in his first solo effort. The bright, blocky and, above all, goofy digitally painted illustrations will grab attention, and Monkey Truck's hooting mug (and tooting bottom) will keep the giggles flowing." Kirkus

Slate, Jenny

Marcel the Shell with shoes on; things about me. by Jenny Slate & Dean Fleischer-Camp; paintings by Amy Lind. Razorbill 2011 un il $18.99

Grades: K 1 2 **E**

1. Fantasy fiction 2. Shells -- Fiction

ISBN 978-1-59514-455-3; 1-59514-455-2

"Like the popular Internet video it's based on, this picture book stars a pink-shod, one-eyed snail shell who is happy to discuss his habits, preferences, and inner life, while revealing a life that's both miniature and writ large. . . . The artwork trades the jerky animation of the original for Lind's thick, luminous oil paintings, which provide a fittingly off-kilter realism." Publ Wkly

Slate, Joseph

★ **I** want to be free; illustrated by E. B. Lewis. G.P. Putnam's Sons 2009 un il $16.99

Grades: 2 3 4 **E**

1. Stories in rhyme 2. Slavery -- Fiction 3. African Americans -- Fiction

ISBN 978-0-399-24342-4; 0-399-24342-9

LC 2007-38356

Based on a sacred Buddhist tale as related in Rudyard Kipling's novel "Kim," tells of an escaped slave who rescues an abandoned baby from slave hunters

"The spare words and pictures never sensationalize the drama or the universal themes of cruelty, courage, and kindness." Booklist

Miss Bindergarten celebrates the 100th day of kindergarten; illustrated by Ashley Wolff. Dutton Children's Bks. 1998 un il $16.99; pa $6.99

Grades: PreK K 1 **E**

1. Stories in rhyme 2. Animals -- Fiction 3. Kindergarten -- Fiction

ISBN 0-525-46000-4; 0-14-250005-4 pa

LC 98-10486

To celebrate one hundred days in Miss Bindergarten's kindergarten class, all her students bring one hundred of something to school, including a one hundred-year-old relative, one hundred candy hearts, and one hundred polka dots

"Wolff's sturdy, genially observed illustrations prove a perfect match for Slate's rhyming text." Publ Wkly

Other titles about Miss Bindergarten are:

Miss Bindergarten celebrates the last day of kindergarten (2006)

Miss Bindergarten gets ready for kindergarten (1996)

Miss Bindergarten has a wild day in kindergarten (2005)

Miss Bindergarten stays home from kindergarten (2000)

Miss Bindergarten takes a field trip with kindergarten (2001)

Miss Bindergarten's craft center (1999)

Slater, Dashka

Baby shoes; by Dashka Slater; pictures by Hiroe Nakata. Bloomsbury Children's Books 2006 un il $15.95

Grades: PreK **E**

1. Stories in rhyme 2. Color -- Fiction 3. Shoes -- Fiction

ISBN 978-1-58234-684-7; 1-58234-684-4

LC 2005053581

After taking a walk with his mother, Baby's new white shoes with the blue stripe are covered with a variety of colors

"In the text, loping lines of rhymed couplets are interspersed with staccato sections, followed by a refrain that reins in the pace. . . . The changing rhythm creates a pleasing pattern and gives listeners places to chime in. Setting a sunny tone for the excursion, Nakata's airy watercolor artwork sympathetically depicts an increasingly scruffy toddler and his tired but resilient mother." Booklist

Slater, David Michael

The **boy** & the book; David Michael Slater; illustrated by Bob Kolar. Charlesbridge 2015 32 p. (reinforced) $16.95

Grades: PreK K **E**

1. Stories without words 2. Libraries -- Fiction 3. Books and reading -- Fiction

ISBN 158089562X; 9781580895620

LC 2013049017

In this story without words, by David Michael Slater, illustrated by Bob Kolar, "a library book tries desperately to evade the destructive clutches of a little boy. What drives the Boy, however, is enthusiasm and love--not malice--and the Book eventually responds in kind, accepting his rough but worthy fate." (Publisher's note)

Boy and the book

Slater, Kate

Magpie's treasure. Andersen 2011 un il $16.99

Grades: PreK K **E**

1. Moon -- Fiction 2. Birds -- Fiction 3. Thieves -- Fiction

ISBN 978-1-84939-008-8; 1-84939-008-8

"Magnus Magpie, a bird with an eye for burglary, steals the shiniest, most dazzling things and stashes them secretly. . . . What he wants most of all, though, is the shining moon. . . . With a sweet final twist, he find that home and a family of his own are what he wants most. . . . The energetic text is well paced for read-alouds, and kids will enjoy picking out the objects in Slater's vibrant, mixed-media collage illustrations." Booklist

Slegers, Liesbet

Bathing. Clavis 2011 un il bd bk $5.95

Grades: PreK **E**

1. Board books for children 2. Baths -- Fiction

ISBN 978-1-60537-092-7; 1-60537-092-4

"A smiling toddler makes bath time seem easy and fun in this warm board book. . . . He uses his orange washcloth, happily lets his mother shampoo his hair, and sails his red boat in the bathwater, finishing up with a cuddly towel. Slegers's characteristically bright, smudgy paintings convey a common experience with a light, appealing touch." Publ Wkly

Katie goes to the doctor. Clavis Pub. 2011 un il $12.95

Grades: PreK   E
   1. Sick -- Fiction 2. Physicians -- Fiction
   ISBN 978-1-60537-076-7; 1-60537-076-2

Katie doesn't feel well—she has a cough, a runny nose, and she feels dizzy. Her mother explains that she has a fever and takes Katie to see the doctor.

This "presents a common childhood experience through a friendly narrator who explains step-by-step what is happening. [It] will guide parents through a discussion of what to expect as they prepare and reassure their children. Large, colorful illustrations support the [text]." SLJ

   Kevin goes to the library. Clavis 2011 un il $12.95
Grades: PreK   E
   1. Libraries -- Fiction 2. Books and reading -- Fiction
   ISBN 978-1-60537-075-0; 1-60537-075-4

Explores the cyclical nature of borrowing library books and emphasizes the many joys of reading as Kevin, a young boy, describes his experiences at the library

"Toddlers should be drawn to this straightforward depiction of a common experience." Publ Wkly

Sloat, Teri
   Berry magic; written by Teri Sloat and Betty Huffmon; illustrated by Teri Sloat. Alaska Northwest Books 2004 un il hardcover o.p. $15.95
Grades: K 1 2 3   E
   1. Inuit -- Fiction 2. Alaska -- Fiction 3. Berries -- Fiction
   ISBN 0-88240-575-6; 0-88240-576-4 pa

                                                    LC 2003-70851
Long ago, the only berries on the tundra were hard, tasteless, little crowberries. When Anana sings, she turns four dolls into little girls who run and tumble over the tundra creating patches of fat, juicy berries: blueberries, cranberries, salmonberries, and raspberries

"Done in a palette of deep, earthy hues, ethereal blues, and bright highlights, Sloat's pictures are vibrant and engaging. . . . The rich language enlightens readers to different elements of the Eskimo culture." SLJ

   There was an old man who painted the sky; illustrated by Stefano Vitale. Henry Holt 2009 32p il $16.95
Grades: PreK K 1 2   E
   1. Songs 2. Prehistoric art -- Fiction 3. Cave drawings and paintings -- Fiction
   ISBN 978-0-8050-6751-4; 0-8050-6751-5

                                                    LC 2008-18340
In this song based on 'The Old Woman Who Swallowed a Fly,' a prehistoric man, contemplating the creation of the world, paints images on the ceiling of a cave, that are later discovered by a young Spanish girl in 1879

"Vitale's vibrant illustrations, in mixed media on board, reference both cave drawings and folk art. Appropriate for a wide audience, this will find its ideal fit with families wishing to impart diverse beliefs about the Earth's beginnings to their children." Booklist

Slobodkina, Esphyr
   ★ **Caps** for sale; a tale of a peddler, some monkeys & their monkey business. told and illustrated by Esphyr Slobodkina. Addison Wesley Longman 1947 un il $17.99; pa $6.99
Grades: PreK K   E
   1. Monkeys -- Fiction 2. Peddlers and peddling -- Fiction
   ISBN 0-201-09147-X; 0-06-443143-6 pa

A picture book story which "provides hilarious confusion. A cap peddler takes a nap under a tree. When he wakes up, his caps have disap-

peared. He looks up in the tree and sees countless monkeys, each wearing a cap and grinning." Parent's Guide To Child Read

Small, David
   George Washington's cows. Farrar, Straus and Giroux 1994 un il hardcover o.p. pa $6.95
Grades: PreK K 1 2   E
   1. Generals 2. Presidents 3. Stories in rhyme 4. Animals -- Fiction
   ISBN 0-374-32535-9; 0-374-42534-5 pa

                                                    LC 93-39989
Humorous rhymes about George Washington's farm where the cows wear dresses, the pigs wear wigs, and the sheep are scholars

"Small's watercolors immeasurably extend his zany poem and make maximum use of the double-page spreads. Cleverly designed and well-executed scenes are filled with silly details that children will love." Booklist

   Imogene's antlers; written and illustrated by David Small. Crown 2000 un il $16.99; pa $6.99
Grades: PreK K 1 2   E
   1. Humorous fiction 2. Metamorphosis -- Fiction
   ISBN 978-0-375-81048-0; 0-375-81048-X; 978-0-517-56242-0 pa; 0-517-56242-1 pa
   First published 1985

One Thursday Imogene wakes up with a pair of antlers growing out of her head and causes a sensation wherever she goes

The author "maximizes the inherent humor of the absurd situation by allowing the imaginative possibilities of Imogene's predicament to run rampant. The brief text is supported by Small's expansive watercolors. They brim with humorous details." SLJ

Smallcomb, Pam
   ★ **I'm** not; not drawn by Pam Smallcomb; not written by Robert Weinstock. Schwartz & Wade Books 2010 un il $15.99; lib bdg $18.99
Grades: PreK K 1   E
   1. Friendship -- Fiction
   ISBN 0-375-86115-7; 0-375-96115-1 lib bdg; 978-0-375-86115-4; 978-0-375-96115-1 lib bdg

                                                    LC 2009-46742
Our shy narrator lists all the things that her best friend, Evelyn, is good at—from jumping on the bed to roller skating really fast. Luckily, Evelyn points out what makes her so special: she's a one-of-a-kind true blue best friend.

"Weinstock captures the friends as rotund, squat reptiles who suggest trash-compacted dragons, and the scenes are confidently laced with absurdity. . . . This offers a nice reminder that good friendships always offer mutual benefits." Bull Cent Child Books

Smallman, Steve
   Poo in the Zoo! Steve Smallman; illustrated by Ada Grey. Tiger Tales 2015 32 p. color illustrations $16.99
Grades: PreK K 1 2 3 4   E
   1. Zookeepers -- Fiction 2. Zoos -- Fiction
   ISBN 1589251970; 9781589251977

In this children's book by Steve Smallman, illustrated by Ada Grey, " Bob McGrew, the head keeper at the zoo, loves his job--except when he has to clean up after the animals! One day, after escaping his cage, the iguana leaves behind something that catches the attention of the entire town -- and a poo museum owner -- that ends up making Bob¿s messy job a lot easier!" (Publisher's note)

"Certain to excite gushes—of hysterical laughter, that is—from lone readers and storytime audiences alike." Kirkus

Smee, Nicola

What's the matter, Bunny Blue? Boxer Books 2010 un il $14.95
Grades: PreK   E
1. Animals -- Fiction 2. Rabbits -- Fiction 3. Grandmothers -- Fiction
ISBN 978-1-906250-91-1; 1-906250-91-X

"A wide-eyed little blue bunny . . . calls, 'Granny! Granny! Where are you?' No sooner does he explain his dilemma to Duck and Bee than the tears begin. A series of animals—a tiger, alligator, bear, and fox—ask the despondent bunny what Granny looks like. . . . All the animals join the ultimately successful search for Granny. The very real, small details of twinkly eyes, a big smile, and soft furry arms are just what matter to children when they experience separation anxiety. The uncluttered pages with lots of white space and sympathetic, childlike animals are perfect for the toddler set." Booklist

Smiley, Jane, 1949-

Twenty Yawns; by Jane Smiley; illustrated by Lauren Castillo. Amazon Childrens Pub 2016 32 p. color illustrations $17.99
Grades: PreK K 1   E
1. Bedtime -- Fiction
ISBN 1477826351; 9781477826355

LC 2014915910

In this book, "As her mom reads a bedtime story, Lucy drifts off. But later, she awakens in a dark, still room, and everything looks mysterious. How will she ever get back to sleep? Pulitzer Prize winner Jane Smiley's first picture book, illustrated by Caldecott Honor artist Lauren Castillo, evokes the splashy fun of the beach and the quietude of a moonlit night, with twenty yawns sprinkled in for children to discover and count." (Publisher's note)

"Castillo's color-saturated illustrations capture every bit of the joy of the family's busy beach day; the shivery strangeness of being the only one awake in the house; and the love and warmth that permeate all the interactions here. And the twenty yawns (yes, you can count them) are pure genius." Horn Book

Smith, Alex T.

Foxy and Egg; a book by Alex T. Smith. Holiday House 2011 un il $17.95
Grades: K 1 2   E
1. Eggs -- Fiction 2. Foxes -- Fiction 3. Alligators -- Fiction
ISBN 978-0-8234-2330-9; 0-8234-2330-1

LC 2010026416

First published 2010 in the United Kingdom

"Foxy DuBois gives Egg shelter for the evening, but as a chicken connoisseur, she plots to fatten up her guest and make a tasty meal out of him. Her plans run afowl—sorry, afoul—when Egg cracks open and reveals a sizable, mustachioed alligator named Alphonso hankering for a taste of fox. Children will have fun poring over the spreads to find silly touches like chicken wallpaper, fork and spoon finials on the guest bed, and, in a neat little turn, the silhouettes of a fox on Alphonso's teacup. Smith's art . . . [mixes] cartoonlike sketches with photographs of patterns and objects." SLJ

Smith, Cynthia Leitich

Jingle dancer; illustrated by Cornelius Van Wright and Ying-Hwa Hu. Morrow Junior Bks. 2000 un il $17.99; lib bdg $18.89
Grades: K 1 2 3   E
1. Creek Indians -- Fiction 2. Native American dance -- Fiction
ISBN 0-688-16241-X; 0-688-16242-8 lib bdg

LC 99-15503

Jenna, a member of the Muscogee, or Creek, Nation, borrows jingles from the dresses of several friends and relatives so that she can perform the jingle dance at the powwow. Includes a note about the jingle dance tradition and its regalia

"The colorful, well-executed watercolor illustrations lend warmth to the story." Booklist

Smith, Danna

The **hawk** of the castle; a story of medieval falconry. Danna Smith; illustrated by Bagram Ibatoulline. Candlewick Press 2017 40 p. color illustrations $16.99
Grades: K 1 2 3   E
1. Picture books for children 2. Falconry -- Fiction
ISBN 0763679925; 9780763679927

In this book, by Danna Smith, illustrated by Bagram Ibatoulline, "join a young girl and her father, the falconer at a medieval castle, as they experience the joys of taking a goshawk out for a training flight. The girl leads readers through all the preparations and equipment needed for the flight--from the hawk's hood and bells to the falconer's gloves--culminating in a dramatic demonstration of the hawk's hunting skill." (Publisher's note)

Contains index

Pirate nap; a book of colors. illustrated by Valeria Petrone. Clarion Books 2011 il $14.99
Grades: PreK K 1   E
1. Color 2. Stories in rhyme 3. Play -- Fiction 4. Pirates -- Fiction 5. Brothers -- Fiction 6. Imagination -- Fiction
ISBN 978-0-547-57531-5; 0-547-57531-9

LC 2010043253

Two brothers use their imaginations to turn their surroundings--from a white bandana and yellow coins to a red blanket and even their baby sister-- into a colorful pirate adventure before naptime.

"Clever rhyming text in 'pirate speak' and colorful, digital gouache illustrations in muted tones create a standout concept book. . . . The eight basic colors are introduced in the humorous text and in the imaginative pictures. . . . Children will pore over the small and large details in the artwork. This title inspires creative play, and is likely to be a treasure for years to come." SLJ

Two at the zoo; illustrated by Valeria Petrone. Clarion 2009 32p il $16
Grades: PreK K   E
1. Stories in rhyme 2. Zoos -- Fiction 3. Animals -- Fiction 4. Grandfathers -- Fiction
ISBN 978-0-547-04982-3; 0-547-04982-X

A grandfather and grandchild go to the zoo, where they count animals from one to ten.

"The digital gouache illustrations have vibrant colors, clean lines, and palpable texture. . . . An engaging read-aloud for storytime and one-on-one sharing." SLJ

Smith, Lane

★ **Abe** Lincoln's dream; written and illustrated by Lane Smith. 1st ed. Roaring Brook Press 2012 32 p. col. ill. (hardcover) $16.99
Grades: 1 2 3   E
1. Ghost stories 2. United States -- Fiction 3. Ghosts -- Fiction 4. White House (Washington, D.C.) -- Fiction
ISBN 1596436085; 9781596436084

LC 2012020110

In this children's picture book by Lane Smith, "when a schoolgirl gets separated from her tour of the White House and finds herself in the Lincoln bedroom, she also discovers the ghost of the great man himself. Together they embark on a journey across the country to answer [Abraham] Lincoln's questions and quiet his concerns about the nation for which he gave his life." (Publisher's note)

★ **Grandpa** Green. Roaring Brook Press 2011 un il $16.99
Grades: K 1 2   E
1. Gardens -- Fiction 2. Old age -- Fiction 3. Grandfathers -- Fiction
ISBN 978-1-59643-607-7; 1-59643-607-7

LC 2010038729

In this children's book, author "Lane Smith explores aging, memory, and the bonds of family history and love. Grandpa Green wasn't always a gardener. He was a farmboy and a kid with chickenpox and a soldier and, most of all, an artist. In this captivating new picture book, readers follow Grandpa Green's great-grandson into a garden he created, a fantastic world where memories are handed down in the fanciful shapes of topiary trees and imagination recreates things forgotten." (Publisher's note)

"The idea of a garden as a lockbox of memories is not a new one, but rarely is it pulled off with this kind of panache. . . . Sketched with a finely lined fairy-tale wispiness and dominated by verdant green, the illustrations are not just creative but poignant. . . . The perfect book to help kids understand old age." Booklist

★ **It's** a book. Roaring Book Press 2010 un il $12.99
Grades: PreK K 1 2   E
1. Animals -- Fiction 2. Electronic books -- Fiction 3. Books and reading -- Fiction
ISBN 978-1-59643-606-0; 1-59643-606-9

"Smith jump-starts the action on the title page where readers meet the characters—a mouse, a jackass, and a monkey. . . . Slapstick humor ensues in an armchair face-off when one character, reared on a diet of Web 2.0 and gaming, cannot fathom what to do with a book and slings a barrage of annoying questions, 'Can you blog with it? How do you scroll down? Can you make the characters fight?' Readers know who is speaking by each animal's unique font type and color, achieving economy and elegance on each page. . . . A clever choice for readers, young and old, who love a good joke and admire the picture book's ability to embody in 32 stills the action of the cinema." SLJ

★ **John,** Paul, George & Ben. Hyperion Books for Children 2006 un il $16.99
Grades: 2 3 4   E
1. Authors 2. Generals 3. Diplomats 4. Governors 5. Inventors 6. Statesmen 7. Architects 8. Presidents 9. Scientists 10. Vice-presidents 11. Artisans 12. Essayists 13. Metalworkers 14. Revolutionaries 15. Colonial leaders 16. Writers on science 17. Members of Congress
ISBN 0-7868-4893-6

LC 2005-52735

This is a humorous look at George Washington, John Hancock, Paul Revere, Benjamin Franklin, and Thomas Jefferson. "Grades three to five." (Bull Cent Child Books)

"Describing each man in turn as either bold, noisy, honest, clever, or independent, and taking many liberties with the truth, Smith relates how the Founding Fathers of the title [John Hancock, Paul Revere, George Washington, Benjamin Franklin]—and [Thomas] Jefferson, too—played a part in securing America's freedom. . . . The pen-and-ink cartoon illustrations, richly textured with various techniques, add to the fun. . . . A true-and-false section in the back separates fact from fiction." SLJ

★ **Madam** President. Hyperion Books for Children 2008 un il lib bdg $16.99

Grades: K 1 2   E
1. Sex role -- Fiction 2. Presidents -- Fiction
ISBN 1-4231-0846-9 lib bdg; 978-1-4231-0846-7 lib bdg

LC 2008-04509

Katy imagines what her day would be like if she were President of the United States. "Ages six to ten." (Bull Cent Child Books)

This is a "sly, witty recitation of a president's responsibilities. . . . The list . . . does grow rather long. But the stretch can be forgiven because it provides more opportunity to enjoy Smith's amazing artwork. Madam President, with her boxy head and triangular body appears against a variety of backgrounds . . . with disparate uses of materials and images that often give the look of collage." Booklist

A **perfect** day; Lane Smith. Roaring Brook Press 2016 32 p. (hardback) $17.99
Grades: PreK K 1 2   E
1. Animals -- Fiction 2. Happiness -- Fiction
ISBN 1626725365; 9781626725362

LC 2016024231

In this children's story, by Lane Smith, "Cat is lounging among the daffodils. Dog is sitting in the wading pool, deep in the cool water. Chickadee is eating fresh seed from the birdfeeder. Squirrel is munching on his very own corncob. Today is a perfect day in Bert's backyard. Until Bear comes along, that is." (Publisher's note)

"This gently humorous book is sure to circulate well in any picture book collection. A perfect way to introduce the concept of point of view." SLJ

Smith, Maggie
Christmas with the Mousekins. Alfred A. Knopf 2010 un il $15.99; lib bdg $18.99
Grades: PreK K 1   E
1. Mice -- Fiction 2. Christmas -- Fiction 3. Family life -- Fiction
ISBN 978-0-375-83330-4; 0-375-83330-7; 978-0-375-93330-1 lib bdg; 0-375-93330-1 lib bdg

LC 2010003878

A mouse family tells stories, bakes cookies, makes crafts, and more as they prepare for Christmas. Includes directions for each of the crafts and recipes for cookies.

"The cheerful text and busy, colorful illustrations combine for a charmingly old-fashioned overall tone." Booklist

Snell, Gordon
The **King** of Quizzical Island; illustrated by David McKee. Candlewick Press 2009 un il
Grades: K 1 2 3   E
1. Stories in rhyme 2. Earth -- Fiction 3. Explorers -- Fiction 4. Kings and rulers -- Fiction 5. Voyages and travels -- Fiction
ISBN 0-7636-3857-9; 978-0-7636-3857-3

LC 2008-26510

When no one can answer his question about what is at the edge of the world, the King of Quizzical Island builds a boat and sets sail to find out for himself, despite the objections of his fearful people. "Ages six to nine." (Bull Cent Child Books)

"The text is a case study in clever rhyme, and the pen-and-ink and watercolor illustrations—in black-and-white except for the king—show readers that curiosity is like a light in the darkness." Horn Book Guide

Snicket, Lemony, 1970-
13 words; [illustrated by] Maira Kalman. HarperCollins 2010 un il

Grades: K 1 2   **E**
1. Vocabulary -- Fiction
ISBN 0061664650; 0061664669 lib bdg; 9780061664656;
9780061664663 lib bdg

LC 2009039671

A dog attempts to cheer up his friend, a despondent bird, in a tale that introduces a series of words from "baby" to "haberdashery."

"Snicket and Kalman are perfectly matched here, both revelers in life's delicious . . . details and things best left unexplained. . . . This charming chef-d'oeuvre sings like a mezzo-soprano." Kirkus

★ The **composer** is dead; written by Lemony Snicket; with music composed by Nathaniel Stookey and illustrations by Carson Ellis. HarperCollinsPublishers 2008 un il $17.99; lib bdg $18.89
Grades: K 1 2 3   **E**
1. Mystery fiction 2. Orchestra -- Fiction 3. Musical instruments -- Fiction
ISBN 978-0-06-123627-3; 0-06-123627-6; 978-0-06-123628-0
lib bdg; 0-06-123628-4 lib bdg

LC 2007-20834

An inspector seeks to solve a murder mystery at the symphony by questioning each of the musical instruments.

This offers "witty wordplay. . . . Ellis . . . brightens the heavily black stage scenes with coral, gold and sepia accents against expansive white backgrounds. . . . The accompanying CD features Snicket narrating and the San Francisco Symphony Orchestra performing Stookey's original score." Publ Wkly

★ The **dark**; by Lemony Snicket; illustrated by Jon Klassen. Little, Brown and Co. 2013 40 p. (reinforced) $16.99
Grades: K 1 2   **E**
1. Fear -- Fiction 2. Picture books for children 3. Fear of the dark -- Fiction
ISBN 0316187488; 9780316187480

LC 2012026498

This children's picture book by Lemony Snicket offers a "suspenseful take on childhood fear. Laszlo, a solemn boy in blue pajamas, is scared of the dark, and it's easy to see why. He lives in a house with 'a creaky roof, smooth, cold windows, and several sets of stairs.' The floors are bare, the halls are empty, and the windows are uncurtained. And the dark in his house is not just any dark--it has a will of its own." (Publishers Weekly)

Goldfish Ghost; Lemony Snicket; illustrated by Lisa Brown. Roaring Brook Press 2017 40 p. color illustrations (hardcover) $17.99
Grades: PreK K 1 2   **E**
1. Fishes -- Fiction 2. Goldfish -- Fiction 3. Future life -- Fiction 4. Ghosts -- Fiction
ISBN 9781626725072

LC 2016035287

In this book, by Lemony Snicket, illustrated by Lisa Brown, "Goldfish Ghost was born on the surface of the water in the bowl on a dresser in a boy's room. The boy's room was pleasant and familiar, but Goldfish Ghost wanted company, so he set out to find a friend. He floats over the neighborhood, past the pier, and let the breeze carry him into town where he discovers that not many people pay attention to goldfish ghosts." (Publisher's note)

★ The **latke** who couldn't stop screaming; a Christmas story. by Lemony Snicket; illustrations by Lisa Brown. McSweeney's Books 2007 43p il $9.95
Grades: K 1 2 3 4   **E**
1. Hanukkah -- Fiction 2. Christmas -- Fiction
ISBN 978-1-932416-87-9

"The miraculous birth here is of a potato pancake, which . . . begins screaming the moment it gets cooked. Leaping out of the frying pan and into the great white spaces of Brown's retro-cool graphics, the latke screams even louder as it tries in vain to explain itself and its role at Hanukkah to flashing colored lights . . . and an equally Christmas-centric candy cane and tree. Embedding the satirical sting in his elegantly cadenced prose, the author . . . up-ends any number of conventions in what may be his funniest book yet." Publ Wkly

Snyder, Laurel
Charlie & Mouse; by Laurel Snyder, illustrated by Emily Hughes. Chronicle Books 2016 48 p. color illustrations (Charlie & Mouse) $14.99
Grades: 1 2 3 4   **E**
1. Brothers -- Fiction 2. Family life -- Fiction 3. Family life -- Fiction 4. Families -- Fiction
ISBN 9781452131535

LC 2014026791

In this book, by Laurel Snyder, illustrated by Emily Hughes, "join Charlie and Mouse as they talk to lumps, take the neighborhood to a party, sell some rocks, and invent the bedtime banana." (Publisher's note)
Charlie and Mouse

The **longest** night; a Passover story. Laurel Snyder; [illustrations by] Catia Chien. Schwartz & Wade Books 2013 40 p. col. ill. (hardcover) $17.99; (library) $20.99
Grades: K 1 2 3 4   **E**
1. Stories in rhyme 2. Picture books for children 3. Passover -- Fiction 4. Slavery -- Fiction 5. Jews -- History -- To 1200 B.C. -- Fiction 6. Bible O.T. -- History of Biblical events -- Fiction 7. Egypt -- History -- Eighteenth dynasty, ca. 1570-1320 B.C. -- Fiction
ISBN 0375869425; 037596942X; 9780375869426; 9780375969423

LC 2011011009

This children's picture book, by Laurel Snyder, illustrated by Catia Chien, offers a Passover story. "This . . . book in verse follows the actual story of the Exodus. Told through the eyes of a young slave girl, [the] author . . . and illustrator . . . skillfully and gently depict the story of Pharoah, Moses, the 10 plagues, and the parting of the Red Sea." (Publisher's note)

Soetoro-NG, Maya
★ **Ladder** to the moon; illustrated by Yuyi Morales. Candlewick Press 2011 un il $16.99
Grades: K 1 2 3   **E**
1. Moon -- Fiction 2. Compassion -- Fiction 3. Grandmothers -- Fiction
ISBN 0-7636-4570-2; 978-0-7636-4570-0

LC 2010039183

Suhaila's wish to know her deceased grandmother is granted when a golden ladder appears at her window and Grandma Annie invites her on a journey to the moon, where they welcome people who are facing tragedy. Includes facts about the painting and woman who inspired the story.

This is "a lush, haunting story. . . . It's hard to imagine a more perfect illustrator for this text than Morales, whose rounded shapes, sunset colors, and softness and strength mirror the words." Booklist

Solheim, James
Born yesterday; the diary of a young journalist. illustrated by Simon James. Philomel Books 2010 un il lib bdg $15.99
Grades: PreK K   **E**
1. Diaries -- Fiction 2. Infants -- Fiction 3. Siblings -- Fiction
ISBN 978-0-399-25155-9 lib bdg; 0-399-25155-3 lib bdg

LC 2009006251

A baby who plans to grow up to be a writer records thoughts and events in a private journal.

"The watercolor and ink illustrations . . . faithfully follow the humorous text. . . . The book is a fresh and amusing slant on sibling adjustment." SLJ

Soltis, Sue

Nothing like a puffin; illustrated by Bob Kolar. Candlewick Press 2011 un il $15.99

Grades: PreK K 1 2   **E**

1. Puffins -- Fiction

ISBN 978-0-7636-3617-3; 0-7636-3617-7

          LC 2010040796

A narrator sets out to prove that there is nothing like a puffin but discovers that many things, including a newspaper and a helicopter, are a little bit like one and that a penguin is very much like a puffin.

"Kolar's . . . bold, cheerful cartoons show the bird causing lighthearted havoc. . . . What's more, his restrained palette reinforces the similarities Soltis so effectively uncovers. . . . Delightful, thought-provoking fun." Publ Wkly

Soman, David

The **amazing** adventures of Bumblebee Boy; by David Soman & Jacky Davis. Dial Books for Young Readers 2011 il $16.99

Grades: PreK K 1   **E**

1. Play -- Fiction 2. Brothers -- Fiction 3. Imagination -- Fiction 4. Superheroes -- Fiction

ISBN 978-0-8037-3418-0; 0-8037-3418-2

          LC 2011004567

As imaginary superhero Bumblebee Boy, Sam rejects his pesky little brother's help in defeating pirates, dragons, and saber-toothed lions, but when Sam comes up against some scary aliens, he discovers the advantage of having a sidekick.

"The contrast between Sam's brawny superhero exploits and the humble domestic scenes from which they derive . . . will charm readers, and so will the cute-as-a-button Owen in his blankie cape and aviator's hat with flaps." Publ Wkly

Ladybug Girl; [by] David Soman and Jacky Davis. Dial Books for Young Readers 2008 un il $16.99

Grades: PreK K   **E**

1. Play -- Fiction 2. Siblings -- Fiction 3. Imagination -- Fiction 4. Superheroes -- Fiction

ISBN 978-0-8037-3195-0

          LC 2007008619

Other titles about Ladybug Girl are:

Ladybug Girl and Bumblebee Boy (2009);

Ladybug Girl at the beach (2010);

Ladybug Girl and the bug squad (2011);

Ladybug Girl and the best every playdate (2015); Ladybug Girl's day out with Grandpa (2017)

After her brother tells her she is too little to play with him, Lulu, dressed as Ladybug Girl, makes her own fun.

"Readers' eyes are inexorably drawn to Lulu's red ladybug costume, which sets off the subdues earth tones. . . . Simple sentences throughout the story usually express just one thought or directive at a time, usually in just one sentence per page. A super book for lapsits and storyhours." SLJ

★ **Three** bears in a boat; by David Soman. Dial Books for Young Readers, an imprint of Penguin Group (USA) Inc. 2014 40 p. (hardcover) $17.99

Grades: PreK K 1   **E**

1. Bears -- Fiction 2. Boats and boating -- Fiction 3. Brothers and sisters -- Fiction 4. Adventure and adventurers -- Fiction

ISBN 0803739931; 9780803739932

          LC 2013017796

In this book, by David Soman, "three bear siblings break their mother's favorite blue seashell, and rather than tell her, they decide to set out in their sailboat to find her a new one. On their quest they encounter salty sailors, strange new islands, huge whales, and vast seas but no blue seashells. When a treacherous storm suddenly blows in, the three bears find themselves tossed about in their little boat, far from Mama." (Publisher's note)

"Breaking a prized blue seashell while their mother is away and knowing they'll be in big trouble, three mischievous bears set out to sea to find a replacement. The plot is simple, yet the bears don't find what they're looking for immediately . . . The gorgeous, bright and detailed illustrations are a perfect fit for the text. A first purchase for all." SLJ

Soto, Gary, 1952-

Too many tamales; illustrated by Ed Martinez. Putnam 1992 un il $16.99; pa $7.99

Grades: PreK K 1 2   **E**

1. Christmas stories 2. Christmas -- Fiction 3. Mexican Americans -- Fiction

ISBN 0-399-22146-8; 0-698-11412-4 pa

          LC 91-19229

Maria tries on her mother's wedding ring while helping make tamales for a Christmas family get together, but panic ensues when hours later, she realizes the ring is missing

This is "a very funny story, full of delicious surprise. The handsome, realistic oil paintings, in rich shades of brown, red, and purple, are filled with light, evoking the togetherness of an extended family." Booklist

Souhami, Jessica

Foxy! written and illustrated by Jessica Souhami. Frances Lincoln Children's Books 2013 32 p. ill. (hardcover) $17.99

Grades: PreK K 1 2   **E**

1. Tricksters -- Folklore 2. Foxes -- Fiction 3. Picture books for children

ISBN 1847802184; 9781847802187

In this children's picture book, a trickster fox "catches a bee in the opening scene and places it in a sack." When he meets a woman with a fine rooster, he "asks the woman to watch after his sack, cautioning her not to look inside. Of course, the woman does just that, and after the rooster chases away the bee, Foxy claims the rooster as recompense. The pattern repeats, with Foxy trading up to gain a pig and then a small boy before he meets his match in a woman who turns the tables on him." (Publishers Weekly)

Spanyol, Jessica

★ **Little** neighbors on Sunnyside Street; [by] Jessica Spanyol. Candlewick Press 2007 un il $16.99

Grades: PreK K   **E**

1. Day -- Fiction 2. Animals -- Fiction

ISBN 978-0-7636-2986-1; 0-7636-2986-3

          LC 2005053641

On Sunnyside Street "the animal and insect residents enjoy doing their own things. . . . [The] peek into their everyday activities is accompanied with boisterous word sounds [and] playful typefaces. . . . Pen-and-gouache illustrations are a melding of . . . simple shapes, flat dimension, and busy pages with plenty of preschool child appeal." SLJ

Sperring, Mark

The **sunflower** sword; illustrated by Miriam Latimer. Andersen 2011 un il $16.95

Grades: PreK K 1 2   **E**

1. Fairy tales 2. Dragons -- Fiction 3. Knights and knighthood -- Fiction

ISBN 0-7613-7486-8; 978-0-7613-7486-2

LC 2010032954

In a land marked by endless fighting between knights and dragons, a mother gives her eager little boy a sunflower rather than the sword he requests, and when he wields it against a real dragon, new understanding begins.

This is a "charming tale. . . . The cheerful patchwork illustrations painted in bright, springtime colors add touches of humor to the story." SLJ

Spiegelman, Art

Jack and the box; a toon book. Raw Junior 2008 32p il (Toon books) $12.95

Grades: K 1   **E**

1. Toys -- Fiction 2. Rabbits -- Fiction

ISBN 978-0-9799238-3-8; 0-9799238-3-2

"Spiegelman has produced a polished and fun story following a young bunny's struggle with his new jack-in-the-box, which proves to be hyperactive and rather argumentative. [This is filled] with plenty of word repetition and age-appropriate humor to keep pre- and early readers engaged and curious." Booklist

Spinelli, Eileen

The best story; [by] Eileen Spinelli; illustrations by Anne Wilsdorf. Dial Books for Young Readers 2008 un il $16.99

Grades: 1 2 3   **E**

1. Authorship -- Fiction

ISBN 978-0-8037-3055-7; 0-8037-3055-1

LC 2007028478

When a contest at the local library offers a prize for the best story, a girl tries to write one using her family's suggestions, but her story does not seem right until she listens to her heart.

"Lively energy and imagination permeate both the watercolor and ink illustrations and the warm text." Horn Book Guide

Buzz; illustrated by Vincent Nguyen. Simon & Schuster Books for Young Readers 2010 un il $15.99

Grades: PreK K 1   **E**

1. Bees -- Fiction 2. Flight -- Fiction 3. Animals -- Fiction

ISBN 978-1-4169-4925-1; 1-4169-4925-9

LC 2008042191

After learning that a bee's body is too chunky for flight, Buzz the bumblebee defies the laws of aerodynamics to save a friend in need.

"Delightful mixed-media illustrations incorporate painted oils and Photoshop to show the pixie-faced Buzz and stage the uncluttered story line with gentle and luminous images." Booklist

Cold snap; by Eileen Spinelli; illustrated by Marjorie Priceman. Alfred A. Knopf 2012 40 p. $17.99

Grades: PreK K 1   **E**

1. Picture books for children 2. Winter -- Fiction 3. City and town life -- Fiction 4. Cold -- Fiction 5. Community life -- Fiction

ISBN 0375857001; 9780375857003; 9780375957000

LC 2011013290

In author Eileen Spinelli's book, "[t]he Toby Mills cold snap begins innocently enough on a Friday, with snow angels, sledding and an icicle on the nose of the statue of the town founder . . . By [next] Friday, the statue's icicle reaches the ground, along with everyone's patience. But the mayor's wife has just the solution—a warm winter surprise

that brings out the best in everyone and makes them forget the cold." (Kirkus)

Do you have a cat? illustrated by Geraldo Valerio. Eerdmans Books for Young Readers 2010 un il $15.99

Grades: PreK K 1 2   **E**

1. Stories in rhyme 2. Cats -- Fiction 3. History -- Fiction 4. Biography -- Fiction

ISBN 978-0-8028-5351-6; 0-8028-5351-X

LC 2010001642

Simple, rhyming text introduces historical figures through the cats each owned. Includes facts about each person.

"Delightful, whimsical paintings contribute to this joyous portrait of pet ownership. The historical figures are as diverse as their feline companions. . . . Animal lovers are sure to enjoy this charming story." SLJ

Do you have a dog? illustrated by Geraldo Valerio. Eerdmans Books for Young Readers 2011 un il $16

Grades: PreK K 1 2   **E**

1. Stories in rhyme 2. Dogs -- Fiction

ISBN 978-0-8028-5387-5; 0-8028-5387-0

LC 2011005650

Rhyming text describes some famous historical figures, from Annie Oakley and Merriwether Lewis to Sigmund Freud and Billie Holiday, and their beloved dogs. Includes facts about the people cited in the book.

"Young readers itching for a furry friend will find only the benefits of dog ownership in Spinelli's buoyant verse and Valério's cheerful acrylics. Endpapers provide further details about the historical figures mentioned within." Publ Wkly

I know it's autumn; illustrated by Nancy Hayashi. HarperCollinsPublishers 2004 un il $15.99; lib bdg $16.89

Grades: PreK K 1 2   **E**

1. Stories in rhyme 2. Autumn -- Fiction

ISBN 0-06-029422-1; 0-06-029423-X lib bdg

LC 2003-4099

A rhyming celebration of the sights, smells, and sounds of autumn, such as pumpkin muffins, turkey stickers on spelling papers, and piles of raked leaves

"Large enough for group sharing and as quiet and comfortable as the text, Hayashi's illustrations feature rounded lines, soft shading, and gentle colors." Booklist

Miss Fox's class goes green; illustrated by Anne Kennedy. Albert Whitman 2009 un il $16.99

Grades: K 1 2   **E**

1. School stories 2. Animals -- Fiction 3. Environmental protection -- Fiction

ISBN 978-0-8075-5166-0; 0-8075-5166-X

LC 2008055693

The students in Miss Fox's class lead their school in making choices to help keep the planet healthy, such as turning off lights when leaving a room, taking shorter showers, and using cloth bags instead of plastic ones

"The best part of this, besides Kennedy's exuberant watercolor pictures, is the way the kids consider their actions." Booklist

Other titles about Miss Fox's class are:

Peace Week in Miss Fox's class (2009)

Miss Fox's class earns a field trip (2010)

Miss Fox's class shapes up (2011)

Night shift daddy; illustrated by Melissa Iwai. Hyperion Bks. for Children 2000 un il $14.99

Grades: PreK K 1 2   E
  1. Stories in rhyme 2. Bedtime -- Fiction 3. Father-daughter relationship -- Fiction
  ISBN 0-7868-0495-5

LC 98-52499

A father shares dinner and bedtime rituals with his daughter before going out to work the night shift

"The rhyming text manages to convey many feelings—love, loneliness, anticipation—in few words; the mood is reinforced beautifully by the rich, detailed illustrations, especially those depicting a child's room at night." Horn Book Guide

Nora's ark; written by Eileen Spinelli; illustrated by Nora Hilb. Zonderkidz 2013 32 p. (hardcover) $14.99
Grades: PreK K 1   E
  1. Noah's ark -- Fiction 2. Play -- Fiction 3. Imagination -- Fiction
  ISBN 0310720060; 9780310720065

LC 2011023551

In this children's book, by Eileen Spinelli, illustrated by Nora Hilb, "the weatherman predicted rain. So Nora built an ark.... Nora's passenger list includes two backyard spiders, a pair of battery-operated monkeys, and a couple of unimpressed cats. Nora also employs her little brother, some dusty wooden boxes, and a sizeable dose of contagious imagination in her distinctive re-creation of the timeless story." (Publisher's note)

★ **Sophie's** masterpiece; a spider's tale. illustrations by Jane Dyer. Simon & Schuster Bks. for Young Readers 2001 un il $16
Grades: PreK K 1 2   E
  1. Spiders -- Fiction
  ISBN 0-689-80112-2

LC 95-44063

Sophie the spider makes wondrous webs, but the residents of Beekman's Boarding House do not appreciate her until at last, old and tired, she weaves her final masterpiece

"The graceful telling glimmers with feeling and occasional humor, while the full-page watercolors and lacy spot art capture the delicate magic of Sophie's webs and enhance the tale's quiet mood." Horn Book Guide

Wanda's monster; written by Eileen Spinelli; illustrated by Nancy Hayashi. Whitman, A. 2002 un il $15.95; pa $6.95
Grades: PreK K 1 2   E
  1. Monsters -- Fiction 2. Grandmothers -- Fiction
  ISBN 0-8075-8656-0; 0-8075-8657-9 pa

LC 2002-1955

When Wanda fears that she has a monster in her closet, she takes her grandmother's advice and begins to look at things from the monster's point of view

"Hayashi's watercolor and colored-pencil illustrations do a great job of melding the real and the imaginary in Spinelli's story, staying true to the child's fearful fantasies and transforming them with warmth and affection." Booklist

When Papa comes home tonight; illustrated by David McPhail. Simon & Schuster Books for Young Readers 2009 un il $16.99
Grades: PreK   E
  1. Stories in rhyme 2. Bedtime -- Fiction 3. Father-child relationship -- Fiction
  ISBN 978-1-4169-1028-2; 1-4169-1028-X

LC 2008008860

A father and child enjoy a range of activities together before bedtime.

"A sweet ode to family life, beautifully illustrated in pencil, pen-and-ink, and watercolor. . . . The rhyming phrases are gentle but not cloying." SLJ

When you are happy; illustrated by Geraldo Valério. Simon & Schuster Books for Young Readers 2006 un il $16.95
Grades: PreK K 1   E
  1. Emotions -- Fiction 2. Family life -- Fiction
  ISBN 0-689-86251-2

"Using a comforting refrain (When you are . . .) , each member of the young girl's family reassures her when she is cold, sick, lonely, tired, grumpy, lost, and happy. . . . Appealingly offbeat, whimsical illustrations characterize the girl's emotions." Booklist

Spinelli, Jerry

I can be anything; illustrated by Jimmy Liao. Little, Brown 2010 un il $16.99
Grades: PreK K   E
  1. Stories in rhyme 2. Occupations -- Fiction
  ISBN 0-316-16226-4; 978-0-316-16226-5

A little boy ponders the many possible jobs in his future, from paper-plane folder and puppy-dog holder to mixing-bowl licker and tin-can kicker.

"Aided by Liao's cleverly integrated full-bleed mixed-media illustrations, which radiate every hue of the rainbow, and dynamic typesetting with words that swoop and dive, the author's perspective on this adult-inspired question yields some refreshingly child-oriented answers. . . . An inspired take on a timeless question." Kirkus

Spinner, Stephanie

It's a miracle! a Hanukkah storybook. written by Stephanie Spinner; illustrated by Jill McElmurry. Atheneum Bks. for Young Readers 2003 un il $16.95
Grades: K 1 2 3   E
  1. Hanukkah -- Fiction 2. Grandmothers -- Fiction
  ISBN 0-689-84493-X

LC 2002-6137

"Owen Block, aged six and a half, has just been named O.C.L.-Official Candle Lighter. Each night, as he performs his duty, he listens to Grandma Karen's cozy stories of family life. . . . A brief retelling of the Hanukkah legend and blessings in Hebrew, English, and transliteration appear at the end of the book. McElmurry's gouache illustrations add a light, humorous touch. Adults will appreciate the lessons gracefully imparted, and children will enjoy the silliness of Grandma's fanciful, zany family stories." SLJ

The **Nutcracker**; retold by Stephanie Spinner; illustrated by Peter Malone; with a fully orchestrated CD of Peter Ilyich Tchaikovsky music. Alfred A. Knopf 2008 un il $16.99; lib bdg $19.99
Grades: K 1 2 3 4   E
  1. Fairy tales 2. Christmas -- Fiction
  ISBN 978-0-375-84464-5; 0-375-84464-3; 978-0-375-94464-2 lib bdg; 0-375-94464-8 lib bdg

LC 2007041524

In this retelling of the original 1816 German story, Godfather Drosselmeier gives young Marie a nutcracker for Christmas, and she finds herself in a magical realm where she saves the nutcracker and sees him change into a handsome prince

"Malone's richly colored, opaque watercolors embellish the dancers' magic. . . . This book, which comes with a CD, provides a good entry-point before attending a performance as well as a chance to relive the experience afterward." Horn Book

Spires, Ashley

The **Most** Magnificent Thing; Ashley Spires. Kids Can Press 2014 32 p. color illustrations $16.95

Grades: PreK K 1 2   **E**

ISBN 1554537045; 9781554537044

2015 ALA Notable Children's Book

This picture book by Ashely Spires is "about an unnamed girl and her very best friend, who happens to be a dog. The girl has a wonderful idea. . . . But making her magnificent thing is anything but easy, and the girl tries and fails, repeatedly. Eventually, the girl gets really, really mad." (Publisher's note)

"he colorful caricatures and creations contrast with the digital black outlines on a white background that depict an urban neighborhood. Intermittent blue-gray panels break up the white expanses on selected pages showing sequential actions. When the first piece doesn't turn out as desired, the protagonist tries again, hoping to achieve magnificence." Kirkus

Spohn, Kate

★ **Turtle** and Snake's day at the beach. Viking 2003 32p il (Viking easy-to-read) hardcover o.p. pa $3.99

Grades: K 1 2   **E**

1. Snakes -- Fiction 2. Beaches -- Fiction 3. Turtles -- Fiction

ISBN 0-670-03628-5; 0-14-240157-9 pa

LC 2002-153376

Turtle and Snake go to the beach, where they and some other animals participate in a sandcastle-making contest

"Brightly colored, simple drawings capture the pleasure of this fun-in-the-sun day at the beach. . . . It's difficult to find easy-to-read books that have charm and a real story, and this one does." SLJ

Other titles about Turtle and Snake are:

Turtle and Snake and the Christmas tree (2000)

Turtle and Snake at work (1999)

Turtle and Snake fix it (2002)

Turtle and Snake go camping (2000)

Turtle and Snake's spooky Halloween (2002)

Turtle and Snake's Valentine's Day (2003)

Springett, Martin

Kate and Pippin; Martin Springett; photos by Isobel Springett. Henry Holt 2012 32 p.

Grades: K 1 2 3   **E**

1. Deer 2. Dogs 3. Friendship 4. Animal babies 5. Picture books for children 6. Great Dane -- Fiction 9. Parental behavior in animals -- Fiction

ISBN 0805094873; 9780805094879

LC 2011033499

In this picture book, "[w]hen Pippin, a fawn abandoned by her mother, cries out for help, she is found by author Isobel Springett. After carrying the tiny fawn back to her home, Isobel places Pippin next to Kate, a Great Dane who has never had puppies of her own. What follows is a remarkable and unlikely friendship. Kate successfully raises Pippin to be an independent deer, and Pippin always returns from the forest to visit her best friend." (Publisher's note)

"Pippin learns to negotiate a milk-bottle nipple and later a set of porch steps. . . . [T]he two plainly enjoy each other's company, and the pictures underscore their closeness at rest or play. . . . [T]he narrative . . . notes that Pippin is a wild animal "but she and Kate remain the best of friends." (Kirkus)

Srinivasan, Divya

Little Owl's day; by Divya Srinivasan. Viking 2014 32 p. chiefly color illustrations (hardcover) $16.99

Grades: PreK K 1   **E**

1. Owls -- Fiction 2. Bedtime -- Fiction 3. Forest animals -- Fiction 4. Forests and forestry -- Fiction

ISBN 0670016500; 9780670016501

LC 2013047053

"A squirrel is chittering. Bees are buzzing. The sun is high in the sky. And Little Owl is supposed to be asleep, but when he wakes up early, he's just too curious to close his eyes again. The forest he knows so well at nighttime is completely different--and exciting--in the day!" (Publisher's note)

"Through carefully controlled application of color washes and linear patterns, Srinivasan conveys the magic of a fantasy world that will delight very young children and their caregivers." Kirkus

★ **Little** Owl's night. Viking Childrens Books 2011 un il $16.99

Grades: PreK K 1   **E**

1. Owls -- Fiction 2. Night -- Fiction 3. Forest animals -- Fiction 4. Forests and forestry -- Fiction

ISBN 978-0-670-01295-4; 0-670-01295-5

LC 2010049513

Little Owl enjoys a lovely night in the forest visiting his friend the raccoon, listening to the frogs croak and the crickets chirp, and watching the fog that hovers overhead.

"The story's chief virtue is its graceful, balletic prose; the [artwork has] crisp edges and cold greens and blacks. . . . It's a provocative inversion of the classic bedtime story, and a solid first outing. Srinavasan's message is that night is a delightful place, and that's useful knowledge for small children." Publ Wkly

Octopus alone; by Divya Srinivasan. Viking 2013 40 p. (hardcover) $16.99

Grades: PreK K   **E**

1. Shyness -- Fiction 2. Octopuses -- Fiction 3. Bashfulness -- Fiction 4. Marine animals -- Fiction

ISBN 0670785156; 9780670785155

LC 2012029678

This children's picture book, by Divya Srinivasan, is "about shy Octopus who lives on a lively reef, and what happens when she finds herself in a new place far from home, wonderfully, peacefully alone." In it the octopus is constantly interrupted by other sea creatures who live in the reef and she learns to appreciate her neighbors. (Publisher's note

Staake, Bob

★ **Bluebird**; Bob Staake. 1st ed. Schwartz & Wade Books 2013 40 p. col. ill. (hardcover) $17.99; (library) $20.99

Grades: PreK K 1 2 3   **E**

1. Stories without words 2. Human-animal relationships -- Fiction 3. Bluebirds -- Fiction 4. Friendship -- Fiction

ISBN 0375870377; 9780375870378; 9780375970382

LC 2012007043

This children's picture book, by Bob Staake, "explores . . . loneliness, bullying, and the importance of friendship. In this emotional picture book, readers will . . . follow the journey of a bluebird as he develops a friendship with a young boy and ultimately risks his life to save the boy from harm." (Publisher's note)

"Color changes, from blue to near black to white to blue again, allow readers to feel every emotion, including the devastating climax and the begs-to-be-discussed ending." Kirkus

The **donut** chef. Random House 2008 un il $14.99; lib bdg $17.99

Grades: PreK K 1 2   E

1. Stories in rhyme 2. Baking -- Fiction

ISBN 978-0-375-84403-4; 0-375-84403-1; 978-0-375-94716-2 lib bdg; 0-375-94716-7 lib bdg

A baker hangs out his shingle on a small street and soon the line for his donuts stretches down the block. But it's not long before the competition arrives and a battle of the bakers ensues.

"The entire book has a retro tone, from its lengthy rhyming text to its Art Deco-style illustrations, which are updated with more modern-looking graphic shapes and a multicolored palette.... The story's lively rhythmic text and colorful artwork should make it a good pick for storytime." SLJ

★ **Look!** A book! a zany seek-and-find adventure. Little, Brown 2011 un il $16.99

Grades: K 1 2   E

1. Picture puzzles 2. Stories in rhyme 3. Books and reading -- Fiction

ISBN 0-316-11862-1; 978-0-316-11862-0

LC 2010001540

Easy-to-read, rhyming text invites the reader to search for items on a different theme on each page, while celebrating the wonder of a picture book.

"With polished typography, minty-fresh layout, and crisp-edged figures, the book stays tidy despite the frenetic action, and the rhymed and metered text is carefully wrought." Publ Wkly

★ **Look!** Another book! Bob Staake. Little, Brown 2012 48 p. $16.99

Grades: PreK   E

1. Paper crafts 2. Picture books for children 3. Picture puzzles 4. Stories in rhyme 5. Books and reading -- Fiction

ISBN 0316204595; 9780316204590

LC 2011053200

This book is the sequel to Bob Staake's "Look! A Book!" The "solid-colored pages are graced with small die cuts that reveal little tidbits of the busy scenes hiding on the following spreads. Sometimes the page turns make the images blend seamlessly into the busy new scene .... The die cuts themselves also seem to disappear with the page turn, leading readers to touch the pages to find the circles and to prove that they are still there." (Kirkus)

The **red** lemon. Golden Books 2006 un il $14.95; lib bdg $16.99

Grades: PreK K 1   E

1. Stories in rhyme 2. Lemons -- Fiction

ISBN 0-375-83593-8; 0-375-93593-2 lib bdg

LC 2005-09854

Farmer McPhee's yellow lemons are ready to be picked and made into lemonade, pies, and muffins, but when a red lemon is found in the crop and discarded, it eventually yields some surprises.

"Bold, enticing illustrations dominate the pages. Staake creates a fun, dynamic world . . . in its sweeping arcs, bright colors, multicolored cartoon people, and effortlessly rhyming text." SLJ

Stangl, Katrin

Strong as a bear; Katrin Stangl. Enchanted Lion Books 2016 40 p. color illustrations $16.95

Grades: PreK K 1   E

1. Stories without words 2. Human-animal relationships -- Fiction 3. Analogy 4. Animals 5. Children

ISBN 1592701981; 9781592701988

LC 2016296364

In this children's book, written and illustrated by Katrin Stangl, "pictures tell a story about the relationships and emotions that run between

and connect humans to other animals. Forceful in language, concept, and color, this book is also big-hearted in how it renders children, animals, their feelings and expressions." (Publisher's note)

"This is a delightful, appealingly crafted way to introduce similes and enhance children's vocabulary. German graphic artist Stangl's striking bold style for this title caused it to be recognized as one of Germany's most beautiful books in 2012, and it is just as likely to impress in the U.S." Booklist

Stanley, Diane

The **Giant** and the beanstalk; written and illustrated by Diane Stanley. HarperCollinsPublishers 2004 un il $17.99; lib bdg $17.89

Grades: K 1 2 3   E

1. Fairy tales

ISBN 0-06-000010-4; 0-06-000011-2 lib bdg

LC 2003-1818

In this version of the traditional tale, a young giant chases Jack down the beanstalk to rescue his beloved hen and meets other Jacks from various nursery rhymes along the way

"Stanley injects her characteristic, understated humor into both text and art, and young ones will take pleasure in identifying the individual elements of the thoroughly mixed-up story." Booklist

Goldie and the three bears. HarperCollins Pubs. 2003 un il $15.99; lib bdg $17.89; pa $6.99

Grades: K 1 2 3   E

1. Bears -- Fiction 2. Friendship -- Fiction

ISBN 0-06-000008-2; 0-06-000009-0 lib bdg; 0-06-113611-5 pa

LC 2002-23843

In this story, loosely based on that of Goldilocks, Goldie, who has yet to find a friend to "love with all her heart," makes an unplanned visit to the house of some bears

"The writing is smooth, concise, and rhythmic. . . . The pictures are marvelous, with fine lines; soft, glowing colors; and winsome, telling details." SLJ

★ **Rumpelstiltskin's** daughter. Morrow Junior Bks. 1997 un il $17.99; lib bdg $16.89; pa $7.99

Grades: K 1 2 3   E

1. Fairy tales

ISBN 0-688-14327-X; 0-688-14328-8 lib bdg; 0-06-441095-1 pa

LC 96-14834

"Rumpelstiltskin's daughter relies on her cleverness instead of magic. When the king orders her to spin straw into gold, she tricks him out of his greedy ways and becomes prime minister of his kingdom. The illustrations provide splendid, detailed palace interiors and endow the characters, especially the king and his minions, with comically exaggerated features." Horn Book Guide

Saving Sweetness; illustrated by G. Brian Karas. Putnam 1996 un il $16.99; pa $5.99

Grades: K 1 2 3   E

1. Orphans -- Fiction 2. West (U.S.) -- Fiction

ISBN 0-399-22645-1; 0-698-11767-0 pa

LC 95-10621

The sheriff of a dusty western town rescues Sweetness, an unusually resourceful orphan, from nasty old Mrs. Sump and her terrible orphanage

"Telling the tale from the sheriff's point of view, Stanley packs this fast-paced adventure full of language that begs to be read aloud. . . . Combining gouache, acrylic, and pencil drawings with cyanotype photographs, Karas's illustrations evoke the arid landscape of the West yet remain wonderfully original." SLJ

Another title about Sweetness is:

Raising Sweetness (1999)

★ The **trouble** with wishes. HarperCollins Pubs. 2007 un il $16.99; lib bdg $17.89

Grades: 1 2 3 4   **E**

1. Wishes -- Fiction 2. Sculpture -- Fiction 3. Classical mythology -- Fiction

ISBN 0-06-055451-7; 0-06-055452-5 lib bdg

Jane wishes she were more like her friend Pyg the sculptor until Pyg's statue of a beautiful goddess comes to life and teaches them both to be careful what they wish for. Based on the Greek myth of Pygmalion

"Stanley's fresh artwork, which mixes the grandeur of old classical forms and the absurdity of the new, is in perfect balance with the parody." Booklist

Stanley, Malaika Rose

Baby Ruby bawled; with illustrations by Ken Wilson-Max. Transworld Publishers 2011 32p il pa $9.99

Grades: PreK   **E**

1. Infants -- Fiction 2. Siblings -- Fiction 3. Family life -- Fiction 4. Racially mixed people -- Fiction

ISBN 978-1-84-853017-1; 1-84-853017-X

"Theo's baby sister cries and cries whenever it is time to go to sleep. Dad tries soothing Ruby with a bath, Mum feeds her, Nana takes her for a ride in the car, Grandad carries her around in the baby backpack, and Uncle Clyde pushes her in the buggy. Nothing works until Theo sings her a lullaby. . . . Bright, bold painterly illustrations, sharply outlined in black, beautifully depict the love, and frustration, of this mixed-race family. Anyone who has ever struggled to get a fussy baby to sleep will relate to this British import, and the ending will give older siblings a sense of pride and empowerment." SLJ

Stanton, Karen

Monday, Wednesday, and Every Other Weekend; by Karen Stanton. 1st ed. Feiwel & Friends 2014 40 p. $16.99

Grades: PreK K 1   **E**

1. Dogs -- Fiction 2. Parent-child relationship -- Fiction 3. Children of divorced parents -- Fiction 4. Divorce -- Fiction

ISBN 1250034892; 9781250034892

In this book, by Karen Stanton, "Henry Cooper and his dog Pomegranate have two houses. On Mondays, Wednesdays, and every other weekend, they live with Mama in her new apartment, but on Tuesdays, Thursdays, and every other weekend, they live with Papa in his new house. Henry knows that sometimes Pomegranate gets confused and just wants to go . . . home. [Stanton presents a] story about dealing with the many changes that come with divorce." (Publisher's note)

Papi's gift; by Karen Stanton; illustrated by Rene King Moreno. Boyds Mills Press 2007 un il $16.95

Grades: K 1 2 3   **E**

1. Droughts -- Fiction 2. Birthdays -- Fiction 3. Latin America -- Fiction 4. Father-daughter relationship -- Fiction

ISBN 978-1-59078-422-8; 1-59078-422-7

LC 2006011569

Graciela's Papi has been working in the United States for so long that she has almost forgotten his face, so when the box he promised for her seventh birthday does not arrive, she is very upset and nearly loses hope that he— and the rain—will someday return

"A few Spanish words and phrases add authenticity to the engaging text. Moreno uses pastels to render soothing, warm illustrations that have a Latin American flavor and elements of folk art." SLJ

Starkoff, Vanina

Along the river; by Vanina Starkoff, translated by Jane Springer. Groundwood Books 2017 32 p. color illustrations $17.95

Grades: PreK K 1 2 3 4 5 6   **E**

1. Rivers -- Fiction 2. Travel -- Fiction 3. Boats and boating -- Fiction

ISBN 1554989779; 9781554989775

Originally published in Portuguese.

In this book, by Vanina Starkoff, translated by Jane Springer, "boats of all shapes and sizes travel on the river, through the seasons, toward the sea. Who will you meet on the river? This vibrant picture book from Brazil depicts the joy of the journey, showing in simple yet detailed illustrations the people you might meet along the way, the sights you might see and the food you might eat." (Publisher's note)

Staub, Leslie

Everybody gets the blues; written by Leslie Staub; pictures by R.G. Roth. Houghton Mifflin Harcourt 2012 un il $16.99 **E**

1. Stories in rhyme 2. Emotions -- Fiction 3. Blues music -- Fiction

ISBN 978-0-15-206300-9; 0-15-206300-5

LC 2010043400

"Writing cheerfully about sadness sounds like an oxymoron, but Staub . . . performs this balancing act with casual grace. . . . Blues Guy, a sweet-faced, bulky gentleman dressed in tweed, sits with the boy, radiating sympathy and asking nothing. They sing together ('I've got the blues so bad,/ I want to cry, cry, cry'), and the strength of their song lifts them into the sky to bring comfort to 'everyone who's feeling low.' . . . Roth's . . . flat, cutout figures have a retro feel, but reflect the present-day world with figures of many ages, colors, and sizes. Staub's verses scan as neatly as an old radio hit." Publ Wkly

Stead, Philip C.

Bear has a story to tell; Philip C. Stead; illustrated by Erin E. Stead. 1st ed. Roaring Brook Press 2012 32 p. ill. (reinforced : alk. paper) $16.99

Grades: PreK K 1   **E**

1. Bears -- Fiction 2. Hibernation -- Fiction 3. Storytelling -- Fiction 4. Picture books for children 5. Animals -- Fiction

ISBN 1596437456; 9781596437456

LC 2011033795

In this children's picture book, "Bear wants to tell a story, but his friends Mouse, Duck, Frog, and Mole are busy preparing for winter. . . . Instead, Bear offers help to his friends." He "raises a great paw to check the wind for Duck and tucks Frog tenderly into his hole. When winter passes, the animals are reunited, but Bear has forgotten his story; now it's his friends' turn to help him." (Publishers Weekly)

Hello, my name is Ruby; Philip C. Stead. 1st ed. Henry Holt & Co 2013 40 p. (hardcover) $16.99

Grades: PreK K 1   **E**

1. Picture books for children 2. Birds -- Fiction 3. Friendship -- Fiction

ISBN 1596438096; 9781596438095

LC 2012046929

In this children's picture book, "Ruby is a diminutive, yellow bird whose frequent introductions are a touch formal: 'I am glad to meet you.' She fearlessly initiates conversation with much bigger birds and is the kind of friend who offers ideas and is willing to try the suggestions of others. In the process, much is gleaned about avian (and human) behavior." (Kirkus Reviews)

A **home** for Bird; Philip C. Stead. Roaring Brook Press 2012 32 p.

Grades: PreK K   **E**

1. Home -- Fiction 2. Birds -- Fiction 3. Toads -- Fiction 4.

Picture books for children 5. Clocks and watches -- Fiction 6.
Cuckoos -- Fiction
ISBN 1596437111; 9781596437111

LC 2011012742

In this picture book for children, "Vernon is both a toad and a forager
for found objects. Ambling along with his latest haul, he chances upon
a creature he seeks to know and then to help. . . . Vernon observes that
'Bird is shy . . . but also a very good listener,' when he introduces Bird to
his friends. He and his pals conclude that Bird is lost and unhappy, so the
thoughtful, resourceful amphibian readies a teacup boat for the journey
to help this quiet stranger return home." (Kirkus Reviews)

Ideas are all around; Philip C. Stead. Roaring Brook Press 2016
48 p. color illustrations (hardback) $18.99
Grades: K 1 2 3 4   E
1. Imagination -- Fiction 2. Neighborhood -- Fiction 3. Creative
thinking -- Fiction 4. Authors -- Fiction 5. Authorship -- Fiction
ISBN 9781626721814

LC 2015013183

In this children's story, by Philip C. Stead, "as an author and his dog,
Wednesday, walk through their neighborhood, they look at sunflowers,
say hi to Frank, a turtle, . . . and watch a train rumble by as they walk
uphill to a big purple house that belongs to their friend Barbara. . . .
Thoughts open up to other thoughts, and ideas are born and carried forward, often transforming into other ideas until he finds that ideas really
are all around." (Publisher's note)

"Stead has given readers a deeply felt, deeply connected story that is
homage to creation—and really quite brilliant." Kirkus

Jonathan and the big blue boat; [by] Philip Christian Stead. Roaring Brook Press 2011 un il $16.99
Grades: K 1 2   E
1. Teddy bears -- Fiction 2. Boats and boating -- Fiction 3. Voyages
and travels -- Fiction
ISBN 978-1-59643-562-9; 1-59643-562-3

LC 2010012952

When Jonathan's parents decide that he has gotten too old to have a
stuffed animal, they trade his favorite bear, Frederick, for a toaster, so he
sets off aboard a boat, looking for Frederick.

"Stead . . . uses squiggly ink lines and washes of warm color against
a background of collaged newsprint, charts, and stamps that underscore
the nautical theme and distance traveled. Frederick shows up at the end
in the nicest possible way, and Jonathan's slow, reflective journey-filled
with pitch-perfect details, sound effects, and vocabulary . . . offers a
lovely, gentle adventure for younger readers." Publ Wkly

★ **Lenny** & Lucy; written by Philip C. Stead; illustrated by Erin E.
Stead. Roaring Brook Press 2015 40 p. (hardback) $17.99
Grades: PreK K 1 2 3   E
1. Moving -- Fiction 2. Friendship -- Fiction 3. Moving, Household
-- Fiction
ISBN 1596439327; 9781596439320

LC 2015001166

In this children's picture book, written by Philip C. Stead and illustrated by Erin E. Stead, "Peter and his father are moving to a new home,
beyond the dark unfriendly woods. When they arrive at their new home,
Peter wants to turn back. Fortunately, he has Harold for company, but
Harold is just a dog and can't help Peter. . . . Together, [they] . . . discover
that this new place isn't so scary after all." (Publisher's note)

"Peter and his dog Harold are unhappy to find themselves on a journey with their dad through the dark woods on their way to a new home.
Peter thinks the move is a terrible idea and if Harold weren't a dog, even
he would do something about it. . . . A wonderfully creative story of
resilience and friendship." SLJ

Lenny and Lucy

Sebastian and the balloon; Philip C. Stead. Roaring Brook Press
2014 40 p. color illustrations (hardcover) $17.99
Grades: PreK K 1 2   E
1. Balloons -- Fiction 2. Voyages and travels -- Fiction 3. Hot air
balloons -- Fiction
ISBN 1596439300; 9781596439306

LC 2013044240

"On a boring day, on a dull street, Sebastian sat high atop his roof-
-something he was never supposed to do. When he launched himself into
the air in his balloon made of Grandma's afghans and patchwork quilts,
his journey took on a life of its own and his boring day turned into the
adventure of a lifetime." (Publisher's note)

"The sophisticated nature of the book requires readers to slow down
and read the pictures as carefully as the text--and both carry equal, impressive weight." Kirkus

★ A **sick** day for Amos McGee; written by Philip C. Stead; il-
lustrated by Erin E. Stead. Roaring Brook Press 2010 un il $16.99
Grades: PreK K 1 2   E
1. Sick -- Fiction 2. Zoos -- Fiction 3. Animals -- Fiction
ISBN 978-1-59643-402-8; 1-59643-402-3
Awarded the Caldecott Medal, 2011

Amos McGee he spends a little bit of time each day with each of his
friends at the zoo, running races with the tortoise, keeping the shy penguin company, and even reading bedtime stories to the owl. But when
Amos is too sick to make it to the zoo, his animal friends decide it's time
they returned the favor.

"The artwork in this quiet tale of good deeds rewarded uses wood-
block-printing techniques, soft flat colors, and occasional bits of red.
Illustrations are positioned on the white space to move the tale along
and underscore the bonds of friendship and loyalty. Whether read individually or shared, this gentle story will resonate with youngsters." SLJ

Special delivery; Philip C. Stead; illustrated by Matthew Cordell.
Roaring Brook Press 2015 40 p. (hardback) $17.99
Grades: PreK K 1 2   E
1. Elephants -- Fiction 2. Transportation -- Fiction 3. Voyages and
travels -- Fiction
ISBN 1596439319; 9781596439313

LC 2014009900

In this children's book by Philip C. Stead, illustrated by Matthew
Cordell, "Sadie is on her way to deliver an elephant to her Great-Aunt
Josephine, who lives completely alone and can really use the company.
She tries everything from mailing the elephant to boarding a plane, a
train, and an alligator to get to her aunt's home. Along the way she meets
an array of interesting characters, including an odd postal worker and a
gang of bandit monkeys." (Publisher's note)

Steggall, Susan
Following the tractor; by Susan Steggall. Frances Lincoln Chil-
dren's Books 2014 32 p. color illustrations $17.99
Grades: PreK K 1   E
1. Farms -- Fiction 2. Tractors -- Fiction 3. Seasons -- Fiction
ISBN 1847804896; 9781847804891

In this children's book, by Susan Steggall, "follow the hard-working
tractor on its journey as it plows, sows, and harvests the fields throughout the course of a year. With a whole host of farm machinery to pore
over . . . this richly illustrated book will be read time and time again."
(Publisher's note)

"Steggall follows a bright red tractor throughout the seasons, introducing children to a variety of farm equipment...The book's large size
and vivid spreads make it an excellent choice for storytimes, and its

clear font and simple rhyming text make it a good early-reader choice. Recommended for all kids who love farms and big vehicles." SLJ

Steig, William

★ The **amazing** bone. Farrar, Straus & Giroux 1976 un il $17.99; pa $7.99

Grades: PreK K 1 2 3   E

1. Pigs -- Fiction 2. Bones -- Fiction

ISBN 0-374-30248-0; 0-374-40358-9 pa

A Caldecott Medal honor book, 1977

On her way home from school, Pearl finds an unusual bone that has unexpected powers

"Steig's marvelously straightfaced telling comes with a panoply of ultra-spring landscapes for pink-dressed Pearl to tiptoe through. And there's no holding back the chortles at the wonderfully expressive faces the artist delights in. This is a tight mesh of witty storytelling and art bound to please any audience." Booklist

★ **Brave** Irene. Farrar, Straus & Giroux 1986 un il

Grades: PreK K 1 2 3   E

1. Courage -- Fiction 2. Blizzards -- Fiction

ISBN 0-374-30947-7; 0-374-40927-7 pa

LC 86-80957

Plucky Irene, a dressmaker's daughter, braves a fierce snowstorm to deliver a new gown to the duchess in time for the ball. "Ages five to nine." (N Y Times Book Rev)

"With sure writing and well-composed, riveting art, Steig keeps readers with Irene every step of the long way. The pictures . . . are done in winter blues, purples, and grays that gradually get darker as Irene trudges on." Booklist

Caleb & Kate. Farrar, Straus & Giroux 1977 un il hardcover o.p. pa $6.95

Grades: PreK K 1 2 3   E

1. Dogs -- Fiction 2. Witches -- Fiction

ISBN 0-374-41038-0 pa

LC 77-4947

"The well-cadenced storytelling has a certain old-fashioned elegance of language, and the humor is emphasized by an atmosphere of mock-pathos." Horn Book

★ **Doctor** De Soto. Farrar, Straus & Giroux 1982 un il $17; pa $7.99

Grades: PreK K 1 2   E

1. Mice -- Fiction 2. Animals -- Fiction 3. Dentists -- Fiction

ISBN 0-374-31803-4; 0-374-41810-1 pa

LC 82-15701

A Newbery Medal honor book, 1983

"The story achieves comic heights partly through the delightful irony of the situation. . . . Watercolor paintings, with the artist's firm line and luscious color, depict with aplomb the eminently dentistlike mouse as he goes about his business." Horn Book

Another title about Doctor De Soto is:

Doctor De Soto goes to Africa (1992)

★ **Pete's** a pizza. HarperCollins Pubs. 1998 un il $16.99; lib bdg $17.89

Grades: PreK K 1 2   E

1. Father-son relationship -- Fiction

ISBN 0-06-205157-1; 0-06-205158-X lib bdg

LC 97-78384

"The watercolor illustrations are executed in a clean palette with precise lines in tightly controlled compositions, the semi-formality of

which only add to the hilarity. . . . This is a jolly, affectionate story." Bull Cent Child Books

Shrek! twentieth anniversary edition; Farrar Straus Giroux 2010 un il $16.99

Grades: K 1 2 3 4   E

1. Monsters -- Fiction

ISBN 978-0-374-36879-1; 0-374-36879-1

A reissue of the title first published 1990

"The pictures are just as nutty as the story, blending with the text so thoroughly, sometimes echoing, sometimes expanding it, that it's hard to imagine one without the other. . . . The fast-forward movement of the story and the inventive challenging language, full of surprises, make this especially fun to read aloud." SLJ

★ **Sylvester** and the magic pebble. Simon & Schuster Books for Young Readers 2005 un il $16.95

Grades: PreK K 1 2 3   E

1. Donkeys -- Fiction

ISBN 1-4169-0206-6

LC 2004-15445

A reissue of the title first published 1969

Awarded the Caldecott Medal, 1970

In a moment of fright, Sylvester the donkey asks his magic pebble to turn him into a rock but then can not hold the pebble to wish himself back to normal again

"A remarkable atmosphere of childlike innocence pervades the book; beautiful pictures in full, natural color show daily and seasonal changes in the lush countryside and greatly extend the kindly humor and the warm, unselfconscious tenderness." Horn Book

When everybody wore a hat. Joanna Cotler Bks. 2003 un il $17.99; pa $8.99

Grades: PreK K 1 2 3   E

ISBN 0-06-009700-0; 0-06-009702-7 pa

LC 2002-6512

"In 1916, Steig was eight years old. This autobiography describes that year of his life. . . . The childlike, watercolor artwork that accompanies the memories features flattened tables, nostrils on the sides of noses, and a sidewalk extending up into the air. Yet the illustrations' naiveté belies their underlying sophistication. With a few spare lines, the artist manages to convey body language, facial expression, and gesture." SLJ

Stein, David Ezra

Cowboy Ned and Andy; [by] David Ezra Stein. Simon & Schuster Books for Young Readers 2006 un il $14.95

Grades: PreK K 1 2   E

1. Horses -- Fiction 2. Cowhands -- Fiction 3. Birthdays -- Fiction 4. West (U.S.) -- Fiction

ISBN 978-1-4169-0041-2; 1-4169-0041-1

LC 2005006969

On a cattle drive in the desert on the night before Cowboy Ned's birthday, his horse Andy goes in search of a birthday cake, which he thinks will make Ned's birthday complete

"Stein's language is simple yet expressive. . . . Done in ink and watercolor, the cartoon illustrations make the most of the Western landscape." SLJ

Another title about Cowboy Ned and Andy is:

Ned's new friend (2007)

Dinosaur kisses; by David Ezra Stein. Candlewick Press 2013 32 p. ill. (reinforced) $15.99

Grades: PreK   E
1. Kissing -- Fiction 2. Dinosaurs -- Fiction
ISBN 076366104X; 9780763661045

LC 2012954335

In this book, written and illustrated by David Ezra Stein, "an energetic young dinosaur figures out her own way to give a kiss. For newly hatched dinosaur Dinah, the world is an exciting place. After a few disastrous attempts, can she figure out how to give someone a kiss without whomping, chomping, or stomping them first?" (Publisher's note)

I'm my own dog; David Ezra Stein. Candlewick Press 2014 32 p. color illustrations $15.99
Grades: PreK K 1   E
1. Dogs -- Fiction 2. Pets -- Fiction
ISBN 0763661392; 9780763661397

LC 2013952833

"Many dogs have human owners. Not this dog. He fetches his own slippers, curls up at his own feet, and gives himself a good scratch. But there is one spot, in the middle of his back, that he just can't reach. So one day, he lets a human scratch it. And the poor little fella follows him home. What can the dog do but get a leash to lead the guy around with?" (Publisher's note)

"The cartoonlike drawings perfectly illuminate the life and attitudes of this canine character, from his contented chewing on a slipper to his joyful, bowlegged run during a game of fetch. Minimal text makes this a great read-aloud for listeners with short attention spans, while the humor will tickle older kids and grown-ups." SLJ

★ **Interrupting** chicken. Candlewick Press 2010 un il $16.99
Grades: PreK K 1 2   E
1. Bedtime -- Fiction 2. Chickens -- Fiction 3. Storytelling -- Fiction 4. Father-daughter relationship -- Fiction
ISBN 978-0-7636-4168-9; 0-7636-4168-5

LC 2009017523

A Caldecott Medal honor book, 2011
Little Red Chicken wants Papa to read her a bedtime story, but interrupts him almost as soon as he begins each tale.

"Stein's droll cartoons use watercolor, crayon, china marker, pen, and tea. The rich colors of the characters perfectly contrast with the sepia pages of the storybooks." SLJ

★ **Leaves.** Putnam 2007 un il $15.99
Grades: PreK K 1 2   E
1. Bears -- Fiction 2. Leaves -- Fiction 3. Seasons -- Fiction
ISBN 978-0-399-24636-4; 0-399-24636-3

LC 2006-24753

A curious bear observes how leaves change throughout the seasons.
"Bamboo pen and earth-toned watercolors are used to great effect. . . . The serene scenes and streamlined story line reflect perfectly the gentle passage of time." SLJ

★ **Love,** Mouserella. Nancy Paulsen Books un il $15.99
Grades: PreK K   E
1. Mice -- Fiction 2. Letters -- Fiction 3. Grandmothers -- Fiction
ISBN 978-0-399-25410-9; 0-399-25410-2
Mouserella misses her grandmouse, so she writes her a letter. At first she can't think of anything to say, but once she starts, the news begins to flow.

"Showing his customary gift for spot-on evocations of childlike voice and sensibility, . . . Stein . . . interweaves Mouserella's loosely connected comments with decorative crayon sketches, relatively more finished vignettes representing pictures in her imagination or scenes she

is describing and painted 'photos' of a pet chrysalis, Dadmouse and other subjects. . . . Sometimes snail mail is just better. Here's proof." Kirkus

★ **Pouch!** G.P. Putnam's Sons 2009 un il $15.99
Grades: PreK K 1   E
1. Growth -- Fiction 2. Kangaroos -- Fiction 3. Mother-child relationship -- Fiction
ISBN 978-0-399-25051-4; 0-399-25051-4

LC 2008-53558

A baby kangaroo takes his first tentative hops outside of his mama's pouch, meeting other creatures and growing bolder each time.

"The short, pithy text tells a story young listeners will immediately understand. . . . Done in marker, watercolor, and crayon, the artwork has a fresh energetic quality that suits the story well." Booklist

Stein, Eric
Granddaddy's turn; Michael Bandy, Eric Stein, illustrated by Jame Ransome. Candlewick Press 2015 32 p. color illustrations $16.99
Grades: K 1 2 3   E
1. African Americans -- Suffrage 2. Grandfathers -- Fiction
ISBN 9780763665937

LC 2014931837

NAACP Image Award Nominee: Outstanding Literary Work: Children (2016)
In this children's book by Michael S. Bandy and Eric Stein, illustrated by James E. Ransome, "for the very first time, Granddaddy is allowed to vote, and he couldn't be more proud. But can Michael be patient when it seems that justice just can't come soon enough? This . . . story shares one boy's perspective of growing up in the segregated South, while . . . illustrations depict the rural setting." (Publisher's note)

Stein, Joel Edward
A **Hanukkah** with Mazel; by Joel Edward Stein; illustrated by Elisa Vavouri. Kar-Ben Publishing, a division of Lerner Publishing Group 2016 32 p. color illustrations (pb : alk. paper) $7.99; (ebook) $6.99
Grades: PreK K 1 2   E
1. Cats -- Fiction 2. Hanukkah -- Fiction 3. Loneliness -- Fiction
ISBN 9781467781718; 9781467781763; 9781512409369

LC 2015040985

In this children's book, by Joel Edward Stein, illustrated by Elisa Vavouri, "Misha, a poor artist, has no one to celebrate Hanukkah with until he discovers a hungry cat in his barn. The lucky little cat, whom Misha names Mazel, inspires Misha to turn each night of Hanukkah into something special. He doesn't have money for Hanukkah candles, but he can use his artistic skills to bring light to his home - as Mazel brings good luck to his life." (Publisher's note)
"A fresh take on a very old holiday." Booklist

Stein, Peter
Cars galore; illustrated by Bob Staake. Candlewick Press 2011 un il $15.99
Grades: PreK K 1 2   E
1. Stories in rhyme 2. Vehicles -- Fiction 3. Automobiles -- Fiction
ISBN 978-0-7636-4743-8; 0-7636-4743-8

LC 2010038923

"Rhythmic verse and lively illustrations showcase autos of every color, size, style, and speed. . . . The illustrator's familiar cartoon style easily matches the text. Crisp, clean lines and bright colors pop against the white background, while black traffic-filled roads crisscross and loop around the pages. Readers will eagerly search for and find every vehicle mentioned." SLJ

Stephens, Helen

The **big** adventure of the Smalls; Helen Stephens. Aladdin 2012
32 p. col. ill. $15.99

Grades: K 1 2   E

1. Adventure fiction 2. Adventure stories 3. Children's stories
ISBN 1442450584; 9781442450585

LC 2011277645

In this children's book by Helen Stephens "it's the night of the Small
Hall Ball, and everyone in the Small family is getting ready for one of
the BIGGEST parties of the year. Everyone, that is, except for Paul and
Sally Small, who are too young to join in the fun. But when Paul's tiny
teddy bear goes missing, he and Sally have no choice but to sneak into
the festivities, and nothing . . . will stop the smallest of the Smalls from
finding Paul's furry little friend." (Publisher's note)

How to hide a lion; Helen Stephens. Henry Holt and Company
2013 32 p. (hardcover) $16.99

Grades: PreK K 1 2   E

1. Picture books for children 3. Lion -- Fiction
ISBN 0805098348; 9780805098341

LC 2013001930

"In this children's picture book, a girl named Iris secretly cares for
a lion she knows to be kind--a lion who eventually saves the town from
burglary. All the lion wants as he strolls into town is to purchase a hat,
but he soon finds himself fleeing from terrified, broom-and-rolling-pin-
armed townspeople. . . . Iris recognizes his gentleness, but it isn't easy to
hide him." (Kirkus Reviews)

Steven, Kenneth

Why dogs have wet noses; Øyvind Torseter, Kenneth Steven. Enchanted Lion Books 2015 40 p. color illustrations (hardcover) $17.95

Grades: K 1 2 3   E

1. Dogs -- Fiction 2. Noah's Ark -- Fiction
ISBN 1592701736; 9781592701735

LC 2016297435

This children's story, by Øyvind Torseter and Kenneth Steven, "is a
secular story of how, not long after the world began, it started to rain. . .
. Wise as he was, a man named Noah decided to build a lifeboat, and he
set about gathering as many kinds of creatures as he could think of . . . ,
[including] a funny looking dog with a big soft nose trudge on board all
by himself. Had he not done so, the Ark, as you may not know, would
definitely have sunk." (Publisher's note)

"It's a nifty combination of a biblical tale and a canine trait, but it's
the humorous details of life aboard the Ark that are most likely to captivate readers." Pub Wkly

Stevens, April

★ **Edwin** speaks up; written by April Stevens; illustrated by Sophie Blackall. Schwartz & Wade Books 2011 un il $16.99; lib bdg
$19.99

Grades: PreK K 1   E

1. Ferrets -- Fiction 2. Infants -- Fiction 3. Shopping -- Fiction 4.
Birthdays -- Fiction 5. Family life -- Fiction
ISBN 978-0-375-85337-1; 0-375-85337-5; 978-0-375-95633-1
lib bdg; 0-375-95633-6 lib bdg

LC 2009-28009

Before his family leaves the grocery store, Baby Edwin (a ferret)
makes sure their grocery cart contains the last ingredient needed to make
his birthday celebration complete.

"Stevens' spot-on story about every mother's nightmare, the group
grocery-store shop, is matched by Blackall's delicious art. . . . This is
a book that's clever in every sense of the word: skillful, original, and
witty." Booklist

Stevens, Janet

★ **Cook-a-doodle-doo!** [by] Janet Stevens and Susan Stevens
Crummel; illustrated by Janet Stevens. Harcourt Brace & Co. 1999 un
il $17; pa $7

Grades: PreK K 1 2   E

1. Animals -- Fiction 2. Cooking -- Fiction
ISBN 0-15-201924-3; 0-15-205658-0 pa

LC 98-8853

With the questionable help of his friends, Big Brown Rooster manages to bake a strawberry shortcake which would have pleased his great-
grandmother, Little Red Hen

"With the main story and each hilarious, mouthwatering double-
page picture of pandemonium, there is a quiet sidebar in small type that
explains what recipes are, what ingredients are, what measuring and
baking means, and how to make a strawberry shortcake, step by step.
The luscious illustrations on hand-made paper are beautifully drawn and
deliciously textured. . . . The full recipe is printed on the last page."
Booklist

★ The **great** fuzz frenzy; written by Janet Stevens and Susan Stevens Crummel; illustrated by Janet Stevens. Harcourt 2005 un il $17

Grades: PreK K 1 2 3   E

1. Prairie dogs -- Fiction
ISBN 0-15-204626-7

When a fuzzy tennis ball lands in a prairie-dog town, the prairie dogs
discover that their newfound frenzy for fuzz creates no end of trouble.

"The marvelously rendered mixed-media illustrations, with vivid
blues, earthy browns, and that luminescent green, capture the true fuzzy
nature and greenish glow of the ball." SLJ

Stevenson, James

No laughing, no smiling, no giggling. Farrar, Straus and Giroux
2004 un il $16

Grades: PreK K 1 2   E

1. Animals -- Fiction
ISBN 0-374-31829-8

LC 2003-45508

Companion volume to Don't make me laugh (1999)

The reader joins Freddy Fafnaffer the pig as he deals with Mr. Frim-
dimpny, a crocodile who never laughs and who decides on the rules for
reading this book.

"Children will enjoy the humorous cartoons and delight in helping
Freddy out of his predicament. The act of inviting readers to actively
participate in the plot has great appeal." SLJ

Stevenson, Robert Louis

Block city; illustrated by Daniel Kirk. Simon & Schuster Books for
Young Readers 2005 un il $14.95

Grades: PreK K 1   E

1. Play -- Fiction
ISBN 0-689-86964-9

A child creates a world of his own which has mountains and sea, a
city and ships, all from toy blocks.

"This colorfully illustrated version of Stevenson's poem is as relevant today as when it was written for A Child's Garden of Verses in
1883. . . . Done in colored pencils and gouache in rich, deep colors, the
large, clear pictures have a retro feel." SLJ

★ The **moon**; [by] Robert Louis Stevenson; pictures by Tracey
Campbell Pearson. Farrar, Straus and Giroux 2006 un il $16

Grades: PreK K 1 2   E

1. Moon -- Poetry
ISBN 0-374-35046-9

LC 2005040067

"Stevenson's famous 12-line poem, which begins 'The moon has a face / like the clock in the hall,' becomes the text of a picture-book depiction of the nighttime outing of a contemporary father and his child. Leaving Mother and Baby behind, they climb into a truck with the dog, the cat, and some provisions; travel to the dock; and take their boat across a cove and back again while they watch the places and creatures illuminated by the moon. The pictured journey creates a vivid, visual counterpoint to the poetry, which flows as magically as an incantation. . . . The luminous ink-and-watercolor illustrations reflect Pearson's creative imagination and her sure sense of what is visually interesting to young children." Booklist

Stewart, Sarah

★ The **friend**; pictures by David Small. Farrar, Straus and Giroux 2004 un il $16
Grades: K 1 2 3   E
  1. Household employees -- Fiction
  ISBN 0-374-32463-8

LC 2003-64352

With Mom too busy and Dad away much of the time, Belle finds companionship with a household employee who after each day's work takes Belle "hand in hand" to the beach

"David Small's elegant, moving illustrations . . . show the twosome touchingly small on the vast beach. . . . In both illustrations and text, Bea is not merely a playmate but her own person." NY Times Book Rev

★ The **gardener**; pictures by David Small. Farrar, Straus & Giroux 1997 un il $16; pa $6.95
Grades: K 1 2 3   E
  1. Letters -- Fiction 2. Gardening -- Fiction 3. Great Depression, 1929-1939 -- Fiction
  ISBN 0-374-32517-0; 0-374-42518-3 pa

LC 96-30894

A Caldecott Medal honor book, 1998

"Stewart's quiet story, relayed in the form of letters written by a little girl, focuses on a child who literally makes joy blossom. Small's illustrations . . . [offer] wonderfully expressive characters, ink-line details, and patches of pastel." Booklist

★ The **journey**; pictures by David Small. Farrar, Straus & Giroux 2001 un il $16; pa $6.95
Grades: K 1 2 3   E
  1. Amish -- Fiction 2. City and town life -- Fiction
  ISBN 0-374-33905-8; 0-374-40010-5 pa

LC 99-31001

A young Amish girl tells her "silent friend," her diary, about all the wonderous experiences she has on her first trip to the city

"This title offers so much: a glimpse into Amish culture and Chicago treasures; a winsome main character and many sensitively depicted supporting personalities; a fresh, authentic voice; and a design perfectly melded to its subtle message." SLJ

The **library**; pictures by David Small. Farrar, Straus & Giroux 1995 un il $16.50; pa $6.95
Grades: K 1 2 3   E
  1. Stories in rhyme 2. Books and reading -- Fiction
  ISBN 0-374-34388-8; 0-374-44394-7 pa

LC 94-30320

Elizabeth Brown loves to read more than anything else, but when her collection of books grows and grows, she must make a change in her life

"Framed watercolors give the book an old-fashioned, scrapbooklike appearance. . . . Small black-ink line drawings decorate the verses below

and often add an additional touch of humor. This is a funny, heartwarming story about a quirky woman with a not-so-peculiar obsession." SLJ

The **quiet** place; Sarah Stewart; pictures by David Small. Margaret Ferguson Books 2012 44 p. $16.99
Grades: K 1 2 3   E
  1. Aunts -- Fiction 2. Letters -- Fiction 3. Immigrants -- Fiction 4. Homesickness -- Fiction 5. Mexican Americans -- Fiction
  ISBN 0374325650; 9780374325657

LC 2011031768

This children's story, by Sarah Stewart, illustrated by David Small, is the winner of the "Kirkus Reviews" Best Children's Book award of 2012. "When Isabel and her family move to the United States, Isabel misses all the things she left behind in Mexico. . . . But she also experiences some wonderful new things. . . . Even better, Papa and her brother Chavo help her turn a big box into her own quiet place, where she keeps her books and toys and writes letters to Aunt Lupita." (Publisher's note)

Stiegemeyer, Julie

Seven little bunnies; pictures by Laura J. Bryant. Marshall Cavendish Children 2010 un il $15.99
Grades: PreK K   E
  1. Counting 2. Stories in rhyme 3. Bedtime -- Fiction 4. Rabbits -- Fiction
  ISBN 978-0-7614-5600-1; 0-7614-5600-7

LC 2009006337

Seven bunnies find many other things to do when it is time for them to go to bed.

"The sounds and action will appeal to young preschoolers in this lively bedtime rhyme that includes a counting exercise. . . . The words are lively . . . and as kids chant along, they'll also follow the subtraction and addition as seamless parts of the story." Booklist

Stier, Catherine

Bugs in my hair?! written by Catherine Stier; illustrated by Tammie Lyon. Albert Whitman & Co. 2008 un il $15.95
Grades: K 1 2 3   E
  1. School stories 2. Lice -- Fiction
  ISBN 0807509086; 9780807509081

LC 2007024250

When immaculately groomed Ellie gets head lice she is terribly upset, but once she learns some facts about the creatures, she calms down and figures out a way to help her classmates.

"Stier has taken a difficult topic and turned it into a charming story that demystifies the fears and false information surrounding lice infestation. The writing . . . comes across simply without sounding didactic. Cartoon illustrations capture Ellie's emotions." SLJ

Today on election day; Catherine Stier; illustrated by David Leonard. A. Whitman & Co. 2012 32 p. (hardcover) $16.99
Grades: 2 3 4   E
  1. Picture books for children 2. Elections -- United States 3. Election Day -- History 4. Elections -- United States -- History
  ISBN 0807580082; 9780807580080

LC 2011035248

This informational picture book about U.S. election day offers children a "salute to the first Tuesday after the first Monday in November." It presents "information . . . [on] political parties, campaigns, Congress, the history of the vote, Constitutional amendments, debates and voting." Author Catherine Stier "situates the activity around the children's school." (Kirkus Reviews)

Stileman, Kali

Roly-poly egg. Tiger Tales 2011 un il $12.95

Grades: PreK K 1   E
1. Eggs -- Fiction 2. Birds -- Fiction 3. Mother-child relationship -- Fiction
ISBN 978-1-58925-852-5; 1-58925-852-5

"Mother love leads to near tragedy in this tale of an egg. Rendered in smears of fiery red paint, Splotch the bird personifies her name. She learns the true testament of a mother's love after she lays a magnificent polka-dotted egg. . . . In her utter joy, she bounces her branch—and the egg falls off into the lush jungle habitat. Met with ambivalence by some and threat from others, the little one is tossed until it's gently returned to her grateful mom. . . . Paint streaks collide with textured papers, creating a bright array of rainbow hues. Spare, crisp sentences describe each action, leaving lots of room for expansion in the bold mixed-media spreads. Vibrant designs breathe life into this mama." Kirkus

Stimpson, Colin

Jack and the baked beanstalk; Colin Stimpson. Candlewick Press 2012 40 p. col. ill. (hardback) $15.99

Grades: K 1 2 3 4   E
1. Fairy tales 2. Restaurants -- Fiction 3. Picture books for children 4. Magic -- Fiction 5. Giants -- Fiction 6. Cooking -- Fiction 7. Characters in literature -- Fiction
ISBN 0763655635; 9780763655631

LC 2011047003

In this children's picture book, "Jack and his mother live and work in a broken-down burger truck parked at the edge of town. When a new overpass diverts traffic away from their location, business dries up. Jack is sent to the store with their last pennies for milk and coffee beans, but instead buys a can of magic baked beans from a mysterious stranger and is tossed out by his angry mother. After the purchase grows into a vine sprouting shiny cans of this delicious staple, the boy climbs up and meets a fearsome-looking giant, but soon discovers that this lonely individual would rather cook for him than eat him." (School Library Journal)

Stock, Catherine

A porc in New York; [by] Catherine Stock. Holiday House 2007 un il $16.95

Grades: PreK K 1 2   E
1. Animals -- Fiction 2. Vacations -- Fiction 3. New York (N.Y.) -- Fiction
ISBN 978-0-8234-1994-4; 0-8234-1994-0

LC 2006002015

Monsieur Monmouton and his dog Cabot fly from France to New York City in pursuit of his farm animals, who are taking a vacation to see such sights as Blooming Dells and MOOMA

"The story is fun, and the expansive, exuberant artwork shows Stock at the top of her game." Booklist

Stoeke, Janet Morgan

★ A hat for Minerva Louise. Dutton Children's Bks. 1994 un il hardcover o.p. pa $5.99

Grades: PreK K 1 2   E
1. Hats -- Fiction 2. Chickens -- Fiction
ISBN 0-525-45328-8; 0-14-055666-4 pa

LC 94-2139

Other titles about Minerva Louise are: A friend for Minerva Louise (1997); Minerva Louise (1988); Minerva Louise and the colorful eggs (2006); Minerva Louise and the red truck (2002); Minerva Louise at school (1996); Minerva Louise at the fair (2000); Minerva Louise on Christmas Eve (2007); Minerva Louise on Halloween (2009);

Minerva Louise, a snow-loving chicken, mistakes a pair of mittens for two hats to keep both ends warm

This "is a rare find: a picture book exactly on target for preschoolers that sacrifices none of the essential elements of plot, character, and

humor. . . . The pictures, in large rectangles of bright primary colors, are easy for preschoolers to 'read' and contain most of the book's considerable humor." Horn Book

★ The Loopy Coop hens. Dutton Children's Books 2011 un il $16.99

Grades: PreK K   E
1. Chickens -- Fiction 2. Roosters -- Fiction
ISBN 0-525-42190-4; 978-0-525-42190-0

LC 2010-13354

Chickens Pip, Midge, and Dot admire Rooster Sam and his ability to fly up to the barn roof, but when they spy on him to see how he does it, they get a big surprise. "Grades one to two." (Bull Cent Child Books)

"The simple text and sentences are ideal for new readers, but it is Stoeke's loose, unfussy artwork that emphasizes the slapstick humor and carries much of the character development. The fowls' body language is especially hilarious in scenes where they attempt to fly and find themselves flat on the ground, or when overconfident Rooster Sam strolls by." Publ Wkly

Stohner, Anu

Brave Charlotte; [illustrated by Henrike Wilson; translated from the German by Alyson Cole] Bloomsbury Children's Bks. 2005 un il $16.95

Grades: PreK K 1 2   E
1. Sheep -- Fiction
ISBN 1-58234-690-9

Charlotte, a headstrong sheep, rescues the flock when their shepherd is injured.

"There is a lot to like in 'Brave Charlotte': the gentle way the story unfolds, and the lovely way the illustrator . . . expresses an inviting dingy fluffiness. . . . Each dreamlike image is suffused with colors that are rich yet subdued." NY Times Book Rev

Another title about Charlotte is:
Brave Charlotte and the wolves (2009)

Stojic, Manya

★ Rain; written and illustrated by Manya Stojic. Crown 2000 un il $15.95

Grades: PreK K 1 2   E
1. Rain -- Fiction 2. Africa -- Fiction 3. Animals -- Fiction
ISBN 0-517-80085-3; 0-517-80086-1 lib bdg

LC 99-35298

The animals of the African savanna use their senses to predict and then enjoy the rain

"The brilliant double-page spreads, the play on the five senses, and a text that invites participation make this one trip to Africa you can't afford to miss!" SLJ

Stone, Kate

One spooky night; a Halloween adventure. Accord Publishing 2011 36p il pa $11.99

Grades: PreK K 1   E
1. Fear -- Fiction 2. Monsters -- Fiction 3. Halloween -- Fiction
ISBN 978-1-4494-0330-0; 1-4494-0330-1

"Cut pages and vellum layers combine to striking effect in this story about a little monster's nocturnal journey. The monster isn't afraid when an owl hoots, and he doesn't cower at grinning jacko'lanterns or ghosts. The transparent layers and stained glass-style cutouts with black, yellow and purple accents create dramatic dimension. When the monster finally arrives at a haunted house, a bright foldout reveals that he is really a boy in costume." Publ Wkly

Stone, Tanya Lee

Who says women can't be doctors? the story of Elizabeth Blackwell. Tanya Lee Stone; illustrated by Marjorie Priceman. 1st ed. Christy Ottaviano Books/Henry Holt and Co. 2013 40 p. (reinforced) $16.99
Grades: K 1 2 3   E
1. Women -- History   2. Women physicians -- United States -- Biography
ISBN 0805090487; 9780805090482
LC 2011043528
This children's book, by Tanya Lee Stone, illustrated by Marjorie Priceman, is a biographical story of Elizabeth Blackwell. "In the 1830s, . . . women were supposed to be wives and mothers. . . . Certainly no women were doctors. But Elizabeth refused to accept the common beliefs that women weren't smart enough to be doctors, or that they were too weak for such hard work. . . . Although she faced much opposition, she worked hard and finally . . . proved her detractors wrong." (Publisher's note)
Includes bibliographical references.

Stoop, Naoko

Sing with me! Action Songs Every Child Should Know. Naoko Stoop. Henry Holt & Co. 2016 32 p. color illustrations (hardback) $16.99
Grades: PreK   E
1. Nursery rhymes 2. Children's songs 3. Songs 4. Children's poetry 5. Children's songs -- Texts
ISBN 9780805099041
LC 2015015549
In this book, by Naoko Stoop, "thirteen favorite nursery songs, including 'Twinkle, Twinkle, Little Star,' 'Itsy, Bitsy Spider,' and 'Pat-a-Cake,' are beautifully brought to life with sweet animal characters and charming scenes." (Publisher's note)
"Brief instructions for the songs' movements accompany the lyrics, and the soft plywood graining and sweetly surreal imagery of Stoop's artwork create a soothing, bedtime-ready atmosphere throughout." Pub Wkly

Stott, Ann

Always; illustrated by Matt Phelan. Candlewick Press 2008 un il $15.99
Grades: PreK   E
1. Love -- Fiction 2. Mother-son relationship -- Fiction
ISBN 978-0-7636-3232-8; 0-7636-3232-5
LC 2007052020
A child is reassured by his mother that she will love him even when he misbehaves.
"A sweet, understated story. . . . Phelan's illustrations bring this quiet text to exuberant life with pastel watercolors." SLJ

I'll be there; [illustration by Matt Phelan] Candlewick Press 2011 un il $14.99
Grades: PreK K 1 2   E
1. Growth -- Fiction 2. Mother-son relationship -- Fiction
ISBN 978-0-7636-4711-7; 0-7636-4711-X
LC 2010039180
A young boy and his mother talk about what she did for him as a baby, what he can do for himself now, and that she will always be there when he needs her.
"Phelan's warm, sketchy watercolors in a restrained palette of blues, greens, and grays with orange accents reinforce the sweet sentiment. While the touching story, with its simple text and accessible images, is easily suitable for story hour, this will doubtless be a favorite for sharing at home, as well." Booklist

Stringer, Lauren

★ **Winter** is the warmest season; by Lauren Stringer. Harcourt 2006 un il $16
Grades: PreK K 1 2   E
1. Winter -- Fiction
ISBN 0-15-204967-3
LC 2005005723
A child describes pleasant ways to stay warm during the winter, from sipping hot chocolate and eating grilled cheese sandwiches to wearing wooly sweaters and sitting near a glowing fireplace.
"It takes special art to accentuate the evocative words, and Stringer . . . provides distinctive pictures for herself. . . . The deeply hued acrylic artwork ranges from friendly to joyous. . . . A special book worthy of many readings, this radiates warmth." Booklist

Yellow time; Lauren Stringer. Beach Lane Books 2016 40 p. color illustrations (ebook) $15.99; (hardcover : alk. paper) $17.99
Grades: PreK K 1 2   E
1. Autumn -- Fiction 2. Leaves -- Fiction
ISBN 9781481431576; 1481431560; 9781481431569
LC 2015029955
This book, by Lauren Stringer, "celebrates the coming of autumn. . . . Children and animals alike excitedly anticipate yellow time, when the trees release their colorful leaves to blanket the earth, crows raise their voices joyfully from the bare branches, and squirrels busy themselves preparing their nests for winter. This lyrical celebration of the beauty and fun of autumn is sure to become a perennial fall favorite." (Publisher's note)
"It's a joyful reminder to make the most of fall when it's here." Pub Wkly

Strom, Kellie

Sadie the air mail pilot. David Fickling Books 2007 un il $17.78
Grades: K 1 2 3   E
1. Cats -- Fiction 2. Air pilots -- Fiction
ISBN 978-0-385-60506-9; 0-385-60506-4
Although her day got off to a bad start, Sadie, a highflying cat, is confident that she can make the air mail run to Knuckle Peak Weather Station, even after the station reports that a storm is headed their way.
"Strom peppers the narrative with memorable rhymes. . . . Children will be fascinated by the courage of this determined pilot. They will pore over the antique-appearing illustrations that glow in an orangish-red palette with rusty browns and golden yellows." SLJ

Stroud, Bettye

The **patchwork** path; a quilt map to freedom. illustrated by Erin Susanne Bennett. Candlewick Press 2005 32p il $15.99
Grades: K 1 2 3   E
1. Quilts -- Fiction 2. Slavery -- Fiction 3. African Americans -- Fiction 4. Underground railroad -- Fiction
ISBN 0-7636-2423-3
LC 2004-45786
While her father leads her toward Canada and away from the plantation where they have been slaves, a young girl thinks of the quilt her mother used to teach her a code that will help guide them to freedom.
"The exciting escape story makes the history immediate, and the fascinating quilt-code messages will have children revisiting the page that shows each symbol and its secret directions. Bennett's bright oil paintings make dramatic use of collage." Booklist

Stubbs, Lisa

Grumpy feet; Lisa Stubbs. Simon & Schuster Books for Young Readers 2017 32 p. (ebook) $15.99; (hardback) $17.99

Grades: PreK K 1   E
1. Bears -- Fiction 2. Friendship -- Fiction 3. Mood (Psychology) -- Fiction 4. Imaginary playmates -- Fiction
ISBN 9781481471688; 9781481471671

LC 2016008277

In this children's book in the Lily and Bear series by Lisa Stubbs, "Lily loves to draw, but today something feels different. Things feel a little frumpy and bumpy, just not so and not quite right. Her pencils are too pointy. Her paints are too sloshy. And her crayons are too stubby. Even her friend Bear can't help, until they realize that Lily has Grumpy Feet! It takes a special friend like Bear to turn Lily's day around!" (Publisher's note)

"Stubbs describes Lily's mood with rhymes and playful made-up words... nicely complementing the bright, effervescent illustrations, packed with jostling, colorful designs and patterns on crisp, white backgrounds." Booklist

Stuchner, Joan Betty

Can hens give milk? illustrated by Joe Weissmann. Orca Book Publishers 2011 un il $19.95
Grades: PreK K 1   E
1. Jews -- Folklore 2. Chickens -- Fiction
ISBN 978-1-55469-319-1; 1-55469-319-5

"On this visit to Chelm, which in Jewish folklore is the hotbed for all things silly, readers meet Shlomo and Rivka, a kindly couple who have 'five children, twelve scrawny hens, one rooster and not much money.' Yearning for a little milk and cheese and unable to afford a cow, Shlomo engages in some magical thinking of the animal husbandry kind. Since cows eat grass, he reasons, '...if we feed grass to our hens, they will still lay eggs, but they will also give us milk.'" Publ Wkly

Sturges, Philemon

I love trains! illustrated by Shari Halpern. HarperCollins Pubs. 2001 un il $12.95; lib bdg $13.89
Grades: PreK K   E
1. Stories in rhyme 2. Railroads -- Fiction
ISBN 0-06-028900-7; 0-06-028901-5 lib bdg

LC 99-86367

A boy expresses his love of trains, describing many kinds of train cars and their special jobs

This offers "clear, bright, double-page pictures with thick black lines and neon colors. . . . Toddlers will enjoy making the hoot, roar, and rumble sounds and identifying the various cars." Booklist

Other titles in this series are:
I love planes! (2003)
I love school! (2004)

Sturgis, Brenda Reeves

Still a Family; A Story About Homelessness. by Brenda Reeves Sturgis, illustrated by Jo-Shin Lee. Albert Whitman & Co. 2017 32 p. color illustrations $16.99
Grades: PreK K 1 2   E
1. Homeless persons -- Fiction
ISBN 0807577073; 9780807577073

LC 2017000583

In this book, by Brenda Reeves Sturgis, illustrated by Jo-Shin Lee, "a little girl and her parents have lost their home and must live in a homeless shelter. Even worse, due to a common shelter policy, her dad must live in a men's shelter, separated from her and her mom. Despite these circumstances, the family still finds time to be together." (Publisher's note)

"A sensitive and necessary picture book to provide comfort and raise awareness and empathy." Kirkus

Stutson, Caroline

★ **By** the light of the Halloween moon; illustrated by Kevin Hawkes. Marshall Cavendish 2009 un il $16.99
Grades: PreK K 1 2   E
1. Stories in rhyme 2. Halloween -- Fiction
ISBN 978-0-7614-5553-0; 0-7614-5553-1

LC 2008022965

A reissue of the title first published 1993 by Lothrop, Lee, & Shepherd Books

In this cumulative tale, a host of Halloween spooks, including a cat, a witch, and a ghoul, are drawn to the tapping of a little girl's toe.

"Not only is the text rhythmically bouncy and appealing, but the illustrations are of the least fearful and most amusing of ghastly creatures, very effectively set against a black and gloomy background. A sure Halloween hit." Horn Book

Cats' night out; illustrated by J. Klassen. Simon & Schuster Books for Young Readers 2010 un il $15.99
Grades: K 1 2 3   E
1. Stories in rhyme 2. Cats -- Fiction 3. Dance -- Fiction 4. City and town life -- Fiction
ISBN 978-1-4169-4005-0; 1-4169-4005-7

LC 2008-52268

Cats dance the night away out on the town, doing the tango, rumba, twist, fox trot, and more

"Klassen's eye-catching digitally rendered urban streetscapes resemble the sets of classic musical theater. . . . The finely detailed illustrations feature a subdued palette of brown, gray, and charcoal enlivened by splashes of color. The subtle charms of this lighter-than-air confection should delight young connoisseurs of dance and style." SLJ

Suen, Anastasia

★ **Subway**; written by Anastasia Suen; illustrated by Karen Katz. Viking 2004 un il $15.99
Grades: PreK K 1 2   E
1. Stories in rhyme 2. Subways -- Fiction
ISBN 0-670-03622-6

LC 2003-14020

"In brief, rhyming verses, an African-American child describes her ride on the subway. . . . The rhythmic language captures the feel of her journey and a repeated refrain invites readers to participate in the telling of the story. The bright, bold artwork depicts each scene in a realistic manner from the child's point of view." SLJ

Sullivan, Mary

Ball; word and pictures by Mary Sullivan. Houghton Mifflin Harcourt 2013 40 p. $12.99
Grades: PreK K 1   E
1. Dogs -- Fiction 2. Picture books for children
ISBN 0547759363; 9780547759364
Theodor Seuss Geisel Honor Book (2014)

This children's picture book is about a ball-obsessed dog. "The dog's curly headed owner is delighted to play with him, but after she leaves for school he's stuck with her meditating mother and a squalling baby. He tries listlessly to amuse himself, then dozes off. His dreams are a parade of mad, creative whimsy. A tiered cake dotted with balls, a monstrous baby, and an interstellar game of chase climax with a journey down the toilet and through a maze of pipes." (Publishers Weekly)

Treat; Mary Sullivan. Houghton Mifflin Harcourt 2016 40 p. color illustrations (hardcover) $14.99
Grades: PreK K 1   E
1. Dogs -- Fiction 2. Picture books for children
ISBN 9780544472709; 0544472705

In this children's story, by Mary Sullivan, "there's a new dog in town and he is focused on finding a treat, no matter the cost. But endless tricks and futile searching (you can't eat Grandma's dentures!) can be pretty exhausting. Just when he's about to give up hope . . . what's this? TREAT!" (Publisher's note)

"Sullivan's digitally colored pencil illustrations are packed with imagination, energy, and humor, and the dog's many emotions are captured particularly well. Kids will eat up this over-the-top ode to snacks." Booklist

Sullivan, Sarah

Once upon a baby brother; pictures by Tricia Tusa. Farrar Straus Giroux 2010 un il $16.99
Grades: PreK K 1 2   E
1. Infants -- Fiction 2. Siblings -- Fiction 3. Authorship -- Fiction 4. Storytelling -- Fiction
ISBN 978-0-374-34635-5; 0-374-34635-6
LC 2008016791

Lizzie, who loves to tell and write stories, is surprised to discover that much of her storytelling inspiration comes from her messy baby brother.

"Sullivan has found an oblique way to write about the ups and downs of a school-age child adjusting to a much younger sibling, and she carries it out with skill. Bringing the story to life, Tusa's strong, quirky line-and-wash drawings define characters and settings, add bits of visual humor, amplify the book's emotional content, and give the jacket its winsome appeal." Booklist

Passing the music down; illustrated by Barry Root. Candlewick Press 2010 un il $16.99
Grades: K 1 2 3   E
1. Folk music -- Fiction 2. Violinists -- Fiction 3. Country life -- Fiction
ISBN 978-0-7636-3753-8; 0-7636-3753-X
LC 2008037104

A boy and his family befriend a country fiddler, who teaches the boy all about playing the old tunes, which the boy promises to help keep alive. Inspired by Melvin Wine and Jake Krack.

"Root's sweet illustrations in watercolor and gouache show the man and boy in an almost grandfather-grandson setting, making pancakes, hunting ginseng, and picking beans, and at the end of their hard day's work, they make music together. . . . Told in free verse, this picture book would be a good accompaniment to music-appreciation lessons focused on American roots music." SLJ

Surgal, Jon

Have you seen my dinosaur? illustrated by Joe Mathieu. Random House Children's Books 2010 un il $8.99
Grades: PreK K 1 2   E
1. Stories in rhyme 2. Dinosaurs -- Fiction 3. Lost and found possessions -- Fiction
ISBN 978-0-375-85639-6; 978-0-375-95639-3 lib bdg
LC 2007043166

A five-year-old boy searches high and low for his missing dinosaur, and the people he asks for help do not believe such a creature actually exists.

"A boy looks for his dinosaur at the zoo, the museum, and other places. No one can help him, but readers will easily see the large green reptile in the illustrations. While the rhyming text strains to tell the story, the generic-looking cartoony illustrations are mildly diverting." Horn Book

Surovec, Yasmine

I see Kitty; Yasmine Surovec. Roaring Brook Press 2013 40 p. hardcover) $15.99
Grades: PreK K 1   E
1. Cats -- Fiction 2. Imagination -- Fiction 3. Animals -- Infancy -- Fiction
ISBN 1596438622; 9781596438620
LC 2012050306

In this children's picture book, " Chloe, a petite preschooler in a polka-dot dress, eyes a 'Pet Adoptions' sign and beams with joy at the sight of an orange-and-white kitten. Her mother says, 'Not today,' but her coy smile does not rule out the possibility of a future pet. 'Now Chloe sees Kitty everywhere she goes,' writes Surovec as Chloe points out cat shapes in a cloud, the auburn bouffant of a woman waiting for the bus, a tower of pink cotton candy, and her bubble bath." (Publishers Weekly)

Sutton, Sally

Construction; Sally Sutton, illustrated by Brian Lovelock. Candlewick Press 2014 34 p. color illustrations $15.99
Grades: PreK K 1   E
1. Construction workers -- Fiction 2. Construction equipment -- Fiction 3. Building -- fiction 4. Building sites -- fiction
ISBN 0763673250; 9780763673253
LC 2013953459

This children's book, by Sally Sutton, illustrated by Brian Lovelock, describes the construction of a library building. "Thonk! Clonk! Clap! The team behind 'Roadwork' and 'Demolition' returns to the construction site, where big machines and busy workers dig, hoist, and hammer away." (Publisher's note)

"The New Zealand duo who created Roadwork (2008) and Demolition (2012, both Candlewick) turn their considerable talents to the building of a library. The foundation is prepared, the holes are filled with concrete, and the building rises. Clad in safety gear, men and women of different ethnic backgrounds cut the planks, raise the roof, fit the doors and windows, lay the pipes, and run the wires. . . . Printed in large, clear letters, the rhythmic text uses basic vocabulary, strong verbs, and onomatopoeia, making it wonderful to read aloud. Artwork is done in ink, acrylic, and colored pencil on full-bleed spreads where pigmented inks and a variety of perspectives are used to great effect. A picture vocabulary at the end identifies excavators, cranes, and trucks on site as well as the safety equipment worn by workers. The simplicity of the telling and the rich details in the spreads make this a must-have for all libraries serving young children." SLJ

Roadwork! [by] Sally Sutton; illustrated by Brian Lovelock. Candlewick Press 2008 32p il $15.99
Grades: PreK   E
1. Stories in rhyme 2. Trucks -- Fiction 3. Construction equipment -- Fiction
ISBN 978-0-7636-3912-9; 0-7636-3912-5

"Kids who love trucks and construction will find an ideal vehicle for their passions in this exuberant book from New Zealand, which uses full-bleed art and rhyming text to show how each of seven machines functions in the building of a road. Sutton's rhythms invite audience participation, as do the sound effects that end each verse . . . Using ink, acrylics and colored pencils, Lovelock conjures artful landscapes with visible brushwork, reserving a speckling effect not unlike concrete for the road." Publ Wkly

Suzuki, David T.

There's a barnyard in my bedroom; [by] David Suzuki; Eugenie Fernandes, illustrator. Greystone Books 2010 un il $12.95
Grades: K 1 2   E
1. Imagination -- Fiction 2. Natural history -- Fiction
ISBN 978-1-55365-532-9; 1-55365-532-X

With the help of their parents and their own imaginations, Jamie and Megan discover that natural magic is all around them, even in their own home. Sheets and pillows, fruits and furniture—they all come from nature. What's more, the air isn't just empty space—it's full of smells, sounds, water, and life-giving gases.

Suzuki "presents a whimsical and beautifully illustrated children's book that speaks to a child's imagination and creativity. . . . The illustrations are lively and boldly colored." Sci Books Films

Swallow, Pamela Curtis

Groundhog gets a say; as told to Pamela Curtis Swallow; illustrated by Denise Brunkus. G.P. Putnam's Sons 2005 un il $15.99

Grades: PreK K 1 2   E

1. Crows -- Fiction 2. Marmots -- Fiction 3. Squirrels -- Fiction

ISBN 0-399-23876-X

A groundhog describes his various characteristics to a skeptical squirrel and crow. Text includes various facts about groundhogs

"The humorous text is completed by Brunkus's finely executed, animated, watercolor-and-colored-pencil drawings." SLJ

Swanson, Susan Marie

★ The **house** in the night; written by Susan Marie Swanson and illustrated by Beth Krommes. Houghton Mifflin Company 2008 un il $16

Grades: PreK K 1   E

1. Light -- Fiction 2. Night -- Fiction 3. Houses -- Fiction

ISBN 978-0-618-86244-3; 0-618-86244-7

LC 2007012921

Awarded the Caldecott Medal, 2009

Illustrations and easy-to-read text explore the light that makes a house in the night a home filled with light.

"Inspired by traditional cumulative poetry, Swanson weaves a soothing song that is as luminescent and soulful as the gorgeous illustrations that accompany her words. . . . Krommes's folk-style black-and-white etchings with touches of yellow-orange make the world of the poem an enchanted place." SLJ

Sweeney, Linda Booth

When the wind blows; Linda Booth Sweeney; illustrated by Jana Christy. G. P. Putnam's Sons 2014 32 p. (hardcover) $16.99

Grades: PreK K 1   E

1. Spring -- Fiction 2. Kites -- Fiction 3. Winds -- Fiction 4. Stories in rhyme 5. Storms -- Fiction 6. Family life -- Fiction

ISBN 0399160159; 9780399160158

LC 2013040049

In this children's book by Linda Booth Sweeney, illustrated by Jana Christy, "when wind chimes start singing and clouds race across the sky, one little guy knows just what to do--grab his kite! But as the kite soars, the wind picks up even more, and soon he and his grandma are chasing the runaway kite into town. As they pass swirling leaves, bobbing boats, and flapping scarves, . . . the sky darkens. Can they squeeze in one more adventure before the downpour?" (Publisher's note)

Sweet, Melissa

Carmine; a little more red. by Melissa Sweet. Houghton Mifflin 2005 un il $16

Grades: PreK K 1 2   E

1. Alphabet 2. Fairy tales 3. Dogs -- Fiction 4. Wolves -- Fiction

ISBN 0-618-38794-3

LC 2004-9212

While a little girl who loves red—and loves to dillydally—stops to paint a picture on the way to visit her grandmother, her dog Rufus meets a wolf and leads him directly to Granny's house.

"A fetching retelling of 'Little Red Riding Hood' that also works as an effective alphabet book. . . . The fresh and imaginative mixed-media art imitates the sketchbook of a child artist." SLJ

★ **Tupelo** rides the rails; written and illustrated by Melissa Sweet. Houghton Mifflin Company 2008 un il $17

Grades: K 1 2 3   E

1. Dogs -- Fiction 2. Stars -- Fiction 3. Tramps -- Fiction 4. Wishes -- Fiction 5. Railroads -- Fiction

ISBN 978-0-618-71714-9; 0-618-71714-5

LC 2007012924

After being left by the side of a road with nothing but her favorite sock toy, Tupelo meets a pack of dogs named the BONEHEADS (The Benevolent Order of Nature's Exalted Hounds Earnest And Doggedly Sublime), led by a hobo named Garbage Pail Tex. Tupelo joins them as they are wishing on Sirius, the Dog Star, for new homes, and as they catch a passing train.

"Sweet's beautifully detailed artwork, in watercolor and mixed-media, is packed with feeling and story." Booklist

Swenson, Jamie A.

Big rig; by Jamie Swenson; illustrated by Ned Young. Disney Hyperion Books 2014 32 p. $16.99

Grades: PreK K   E

1. Traffic accidents 2. Trucks -- Fiction 3. Tractor trailers -- Fiction

ISBN 1423163303; 9781423163305

LC 2013012223

In this book, by Jamie A. Swenson, readers "come along for the ride as Frankie the big rig truck takes us on the job, driving past kiddie cars (school buses) and land yachts (RVs). [After] a blow-out . . . a service truck saves the day so we can get the job done and make a very special delivery." (Publisher's note)

"This bright, colorful look at an eighteen-wheeler surely will be a hit with young audiences...The big and bold cartoon illustrations and the text's use of sound effects and a few unusual phrases should make this a fun read-aloud for toddlers and a good storytime participation book as well. Given the number of books on cars and trucks available, this might not be a necessary purchase, but it will be a popular one." (School Library Journal)

If you were a dog; Jamie Swenson; pictures by Chris Raschka. Farrar, Straus & Giroux 2014 40 p. col. ill. (reinforced) $17.99

Grades: PreK K 1 2 3   E

1. Animals -- Fiction 2. Imagination -- Fiction

ISBN 9780374335304; 0374335303

LC 2011034922

This book by Jamie Swenson and illustrated by Chris Raschka explores the question, "if you could be any kind of animal, what would you be? Would you be a dog . . . ? Or maybe you would be a sharp-toothed dinosaur . . . ! Perhaps you might want to be a hopping frog . . . ? But maybe you would want to be the best kind of animal of all: a child!" (Publisher's note)

"Swenson's rhythmic cadences coupled with Raschka's wry, upbeat illustrations yield a title that's a cheery picker-upper." Kirkus

Swiatkowska, Gabi

Queen on Wednesday; Gabi Swiatkowska. Frances Foster Books Farrar Straus Giroux 2014 40 p. color illustrations (hardcover) $17.99

Grades: K 1 2 3   E

1. Pets -- Fiction 2. Queens -- Fiction 3. Kings, queens, rulers, etc. -- Fiction

ISBN 0374374465; 9780374374464

LC 2013019719

"On Wednesday, Thelma is bored--so she decides to become a queen. She makes the royal announcement on Thursday and chooses the royal pets on Friday. But she needs a castle to keep the pets, and royally qualified trainers to tame them, and of course someone to clean up after the messes. . . . Filled with playful humor and stunning artwork, 'Queen on Wednesday' marks renowned illustrator Gabi Swiatkowska's debut as a picture book author." (Publisher's note)

" The children in her delightfully weird paintings look like they have stepped out of a nineteenth-century painting and into an absurd wonderland full of odd animals and objects that juxtapose amusingly. It's a familiar story of imaginative play, but Swiatkowska's whimsical pictures set it apart." Booklist

Swift, Hildegarde Hoyt

★ The **little** red lighthouse and the great gray bridge; by Hildegarde H. Swift and [illustrated by] Lynd Ward. Harcourt 2002 un il $16

Grades: PreK K 1 2   E
1. Lighthouses -- Fiction 2. George Washington Bridge (N.Y. and N.J.) -- Fiction
ISBN 0-15-204571-6
                                                        LC 2001-7106
A reissue of the title first published 1942
"The story is written with imagination and a gift for bringing alive this little lighthouse and its troubles. . . . [Lynd Ward's] illustrations have some distinction and one in particular, the fog creeping over the river clutching at the river boats, has atmosphere, rhythm and good colour." Ont Libr Rev

Swinburne, Stephen R.

Whose shoes? a shoe for every job. Boyds Mills Press 2010 un il $16.95

Grades: PreK   E
1. Shoes
ISBN 978-1-59078-569-0; 1-59078-569-X
Swinburne "offers a guessing game in which a photo on the right-hand page shows a person below the knees and asks, Whose shoes? A turn of the page gives the answer and a full-length photo of a ballerina (or farmer, Army National Guard soldier, post office worker, clown . . .) on the left. The facing page repeats the question Whose Shoes? with a new photo. . . . The clear, colorful photos provide plenty of talking points, while the short text flows in a conversational way." Booklist

Swope, Sam

Gotta go! Gotta go! pictures by Sue Riddle. Farrar, Straus & Giroux 2000 un il hardcover o.p. pa $5.95

Grades: PreK K 1 2   E
1. Butterflies -- Fiction 2. Caterpillars -- Fiction
ISBN 0-374-32757-2; 0-374-427867-0 pa
                                                        LC 99-28503
Although she does not know why or how, a caterpillar who becomes a monarch butterfly is certain that she must make her way to Mexico
"The rhythm and repetition are infectious; and the pen-and-ink and watercolor illustrations, set against expanses of white space, enlarge the book remarkably." Horn Book Guide

Taback, Simms

★ **I** miss you every day; by Simms Taback. Viking Children's Books 2007 un il $16.99

Grades: PreK K 1 2   E
1. Stories in rhyme 2. Postal service -- Fiction
ISBN 978-0-670-06192-1
                                                        LC 2007008046

A little girl misses someone so much that she wraps herself up like a package and sends herself through the mail.

"Anyone who has ever yearned for an absent loved one will treasure this beautifully simple picture book. . . . Taback's trademark wavy outlines and simple shapes . . . add both whimsy and wide appeal." SLJ

Simms Taback's farm animals. Blue Apple Books 2011 un bd bk $12.99

Grades: PreK   E
1. Board books for children 2. Farm life -- Fiction 3. Domestic animals -- Fiction
ISBN 978-1-60905-078-8; 1-60905-078-9
                                                        LC 2011019081
The reader is invited to guess which farm animal is hiding beneath fold-outs that reveal a succession of clues.

"The simple, boldly outlined and brightly colored illustrations portray each animal standing against a monochromatic sky ranging in color from yellow to blue to purple. The pages are constructed of sturdy card stock, allowing small fingers to practice unfolding and re-folding the flaps. An amusing and instructive story." SLJ

Tafolla, Carmen

★ **Fiesta** babies; illustrated by Amy Cordova. Tricycle Press 2010 un il $12.99

Grades: PreK K   E
1. Stories in rhyme 2. Infants -- Fiction 3. Mexican Americans -- Fiction
ISBN 978-1-5824-6319-3; 1-5824-6319-0
                                                        LC 2009016301
Pura Belpré Award honor book (Illustrator), 2011
"Short lines of bouncy, rhyming text describe how several adorable, chubby babies and toddlers participate in their local Hispanic celebration. . . . The length and rhythm of the text make this book an excellent choice for toddler and preschool storytimes. Córdova once again demonstrates how her award-winning style brilliantly brings an author's words to life. Her bold acrylic colors and brisk brushstrokes capture the fiesta's energy and good cheer." SLJ

What can you do with a paleta? by Carmen Tafolla; illustrations by Magaly Morales. Tricycle Press 2009 un il $14.99

Grades: PreK K 1 2 3   E
1. Mexican Americans -- Fiction 2. City and town life -- Fiction
ISBN 978-1-58246-221-9; 1-58246-221-6
                                                        LC 2008-21051
A young Mexican American girl celebrates the paleta, an icy fruit popsicle, and the many roles it plays in her lively barrio.

What can you do with a rebozo? by Carmen Tafolla; illustrations by Amy Cordova. Tricycle Press 2007 un il $14.95

Grades: PreK K 1   E
1. Stories in rhyme 2. Mexican Americans -- Fiction 3. Clothing and dress -- Fiction
ISBN 978-1-58246-220-2; 1-58246-220-8
                                                        LC 2006-39624
A Pura Belpre Illustrator Award honor book, 2009
A spunky, young Mexican American girl explains the many uses of her mother's red rebozo, or long scarf.

"Bright, textured acrylic illustrations with a strong sense of line decorate this celebration of cultural heritage. An author's note gives more information about the rebozo as well as asking readers what they might do with one." Horn Book Guide

Tafuri, Nancy

All kinds of kisses. Little, Brown 2012 un il $16.99

Grades: PreK   **E**

1. Bedtime -- Fiction 2. Kissing -- Fiction 3. Domestic animals
-- Fiction

ISBN 978-0-316-12235-1; 0-316-12235-1

LC 2010049433

Each barnyard animal has its favorite kind of kiss, but the best of all
is a mother's goodnight kiss.

"Using her distinctively recognizable artwork rendered in watercolor and colored pencil, Tafuri has created another loving book for toddlers." SLJ

The **big** storm; a very soggy counting book. Simon & Schuster
Books for Young Readers 2009 un il $15.99

Grades: PreK K   **E**

1. Counting 2. Storms -- Fiction 3. Animals -- Fiction

ISBN 978-1-4169-6795-8; 1-4169-6795-8

LC 2007047989

Ten animals find shelter in a hill hollow one by one, but when the
storm is over, a rumbling tells them there is still danger afoot.

"This title accomplishes much with simplicity. Repetitive words . . .
add tension to the plot. Dramatic poses picture the animals' wariness of
the storm ahead. . . . An autumn-colored palette with orange-and-yellow
leaves swirling across a spread is rendered in watercolor and watercolor
pencils." SLJ

★ **Blue** Goose. Simon & Schuster Books for Young Readers 2008
un il $15.99

Grades: PreK K   **E**

1. Color -- Fiction 2. Animals -- Fiction 3. Farm life -- Fiction

ISBN 978-1-4169-2834-8; 1-4169-2834-0

LC 2006-38368

When Farmer Gray goes away for the day, Blue Goose, Red Hen,
Yellow Chick, and White Duck get together and paint their black and
white farm.

"The scenes have the bold, graphic punch of murals. . . . [The] generously sized animals and pithy text extend a warm welcome to readers."
Publ Wkly

★ **Five** little chicks. Simon & Schuster Books for Young Readers
2006 un il $14.95

Grades: PreK K   **E**

1. Chickens -- Fiction

ISBN 0-689-87342-5

Five chicks and their mother peck in the corn patch in search
of breakfast.

"Created with brush pen, watercolor pencils, and ink, the gorgeous
double-page spreads, in warm shades of red, yellow, and brown, manage
to be both clear and fuzzy, simple and rich." Booklist

★ **Have** you seen my duckling? Greenwillow Bks. 1984 un il
$16.99; lib bdg $17.89; pa $6.99; bd bk $6.99

Grades: PreK K   **E**

1. Ducks -- Fiction

ISBN 0-688-02797-0; 0-688-02798-9 lib bdg; 0-688-10994-2 pa;
0-688-14899-9 bd bk

LC 83-17196

A Caldecott Medal honor book, 1985

"Tafuri's artwork . . . features clean lines, generous figures, and clear,
cool colors. She also adds nice detail—feathers, for instance, that you
can almost feel under your hands." Booklist

★ **This** is the farmer. Greenwillow Bks. 1994 un il $16.99

Grades: PreK K 1 2   **E**

1. Farm life -- Fiction

ISBN 0-688-09468-6

LC 92-30082

A farmer's kiss causes an amusing chain of events on the farm

"The well-defined, watercolor-and-ink double-spread illustrations
are . . . of the highest quality. The brief story is rhythmic, predictable,
and printed in extra-large type." SLJ

Whose chick are you? Greenwillow Books 2007 un il $16.99;
lib bdg $17.89

Grades: PreK K   **E**

1. Birds -- Fiction 2. Swans -- Fiction

ISBN 0-06-082514-6; 0-06-082515-4 lib bdg

Goose, Duck, Hen, Bird and the little chick, itself, cannot tell to
whom a new hatchling belongs, but its mother knows.

"The artwork's close-up perspective and the combination of large
type, onomatopoeia, and the clues to Little Chick's parents scattered
through the pictures will draw children into the scenes." Booklist

Tallec, Olivier

Louis I, King of the Sheep; Oliver Tallec. Enchanted Lion Books
2015 40 p. color illustrations $17.95

Grades: K 1 2 3   **E**

1. Sheep -- Fiction 2. Imagination -- Fiction 3. Kings and rulers
-- Fiction

ISBN 159270185X; 9781592701858

In this children's book by Olivier Tallec "readers will delight in
Louis¿s increasingly elaborate fantasy of what comes with being a
supreme ruler: the pleasures, the responsibilities, the capriciousness."
(Publisher's note)

"The story's droll humor is on full display in Tallec's painted illustrations, which mix double-page vistas in country colors with spot illustrations that demonstrate Louis' escalating circumstance. While little
ones won't understand the full effect of Louis' actions, they will enjoy
the inherent absurdity of the story and likely recognize the behavior of
a bully." Booklist

Waterloo & trafalgar; Olivier Tallec. Enchanted Lion Books 2012
64 p. (alk. paper) $17.95

Grades: 1 2 3 4 5   **E**

1. War stories 2. Soldiers

ISBN 1592701272; 9781592701278

LC 201293756

This children's picture book by Olivier Tallec "portrays two characters, separated only by narrow walls, who watch each other ceaselessly
through the seasons. Moving between day and night . . . they fight their
cold war, full of suspicion, never daring to bridge the gap between them.
As time passes, a snail shows up, and then a bird, and one day, to their
utter surprise, they come face-to-face in a different way, and they discover that their differences don't make them enemies."(Publisher's note)

Tan, Shaun

★ **Rules** of summer; Shaun Tan. Arthur A. Levine Books 2014 48
p. (hardcover : alk. paper) $18.99

Grades: 3 4 5 6 7 8 9   **E**

1. Summer -- Fiction 2. Conduct of life -- Fiction 3. Picture books
for children 4. Friendship -- Fiction

ISBN 0545639123; 9780545639125

LC 2013040915

Boston Globe-Horn Book Honor: Picture Book (2014)

In this picture book, written and illustrated by Shaun Tan, "one summer, two brothers live by mysteriously dire rules laid down by the older
of the pair. The little one lists what he learned. . . . What if you break

a rule? You risk facing monstrous red rabbits, crow armies, teetering robots, lumbering metal dinosaurs, large lizards, overgrown fungus and more." (Publisher's note)

"On left-hand pages the narrator enumerates a series of 'rules' ('Never eat the last olive at a party'). The right-hand pages depict, in thickly textured paintings, a young boy (presumably the narrator) and an older boy (perhaps his brother) in a variety of enigmatically surreal situations. The book delivers superb artwork that elicits both a cerebral and emotional response." Horn Book

Taro Miura

The **tiny** king; Taro Miura. Candlewick Press 2013 32 p. $14.99
Grades: PreK K 1 2   E
   1. Happiness -- Fiction 2. Family life -- Fiction 3. Kings and rulers -- Fiction
   ISBN 0763666874; 9780763666873

LC 2012955151

In this children's picture book by Taro Miura "the Tiny King lives all alone in his big castle with too much space, accompanied only by an army. When he falls in love with a big princess, they soon have 10 children who share his massive table, ride in a carriage pulled by his giant white horse, splash in the gigantic bathtub, and fill up the once-empty bed. The king is so happy that he sends his army marching home for a holiday." (School Library Journal)

Tarpley, Natasha

Bippity Bop barbershop; by Natasha Anastasia Tarpley; illustrated by E.B. Lewis. Little, Brown 2002 un il $15.95
Grades: PreK K 1 2   E
   1. African Americans -- Fiction 2. Barbers and barbershops -- Fiction
   ISBN 0-316-52284-8

LC 00-30188

A story celebrating a young African-American boy's first trip to the barbershop

"Expressive watercolors showcase [the child's] curiosity, fear, and satisfaction, as well as a close father-son relationship." Horn Book Guide

Tarpley, Todd

Beep, beep, go to sleep; by Todd Tarpley. Little, Brown & Co. 2014 40 p. color illustrations (hardcover) $17
Grades: PreK K   E
   1. Stories in rhyme 2. Robots -- Fiction 3. Bedtime -- Fiction 4. Toys -- Fiction
   ISBN 0316254436; 9780316254434

LC 2013023723

In this children's bedtime story, by Todd Tarpley and illustrated by John Rocco, "as nighttime approaches, a little boy gathers his three little robots to take them to bed. He guides them through his pre-bedtime routine of tooth-brushing, toilet use, and bathing, and then they stroll toward the bedroom. . . . [There] the boy tries mightily to find new ways to make his three little robots fall asleep." (Kirkus Reviews)

"This anthropomorphic animal book introduces readers to a variety of patient moms and their "beastly," mischievous children. The babies' playfulness is reflected in both the rollicking rhyming text and mixed-media illustrations, both of which have plenty of funny details (e.g., as the little elephants butt into Mom's back: "there goes Mama's noontime nap!"). An ideal read-aloud for similarly active little ones." Horn Book

Tavares, Matt

Mudball; [by] Matt Tavares. Candlewick Press 2005 un il $15.99

Grades: K 1 2 3   E
   1. Baseball -- Fiction
   ISBN 0-7636-2387-3

LC 2004-40671

During a rainy Minneapolis Millers baseball game in 1903, Little Andy Oyler has the chance to become a hero by hitting the shortest and muddiest home run in history

"The large-scale, softly shaded pencil drawings have plenty of motion, just right for a sports story. . . . An attractive book for baseball fans who enjoy watching small heroes triumph and don't mind a bit of nostalgia." Booklist

Taxali, Gary

This is silly! Scholastic Press 2010 un il $17.99
Grades: PreK K   E
   1. Stories in rhyme
   ISBN 978-0-439-71836-3; 0-439-71836-8

Billy, Willy, Dilly, and Lilly take turns being silly.

"The rhyming text is not plot-driven but revels in phonemic silliness, with lots of action and playful turns of phrase. . . . The combination of vibrant illustrations with rollicking rhymes will engage young readers and art buffs alike." SLJ

Taylor, Debbie A.

Sweet music in Harlem; illustrated by Frank Morrison. Lee & Low Books 2004 un il $16.95
Grades: K 1 2 3   E
   1. Jazz musicians -- Fiction 2. African Americans -- Fiction 3. Harlem (New York, N.Y.) -- Fiction
   ISBN 1-58430-165-1

LC 2003-8994

C.J., who aspires to be as great a jazz musician as his uncle, searches for Uncle Click's hat in preparation for an important photograph and inadvertently gathers some of the greatest musicians of 1950s Harlem to join in on the picture

"This dazzling tale is filled with energy, rhythm, and style from its attention-grabbing cover to its satisfying ending. . . . The acrylic illustrations make the text come alive." SLJ

Taylor, Sean

Hoot owl, master of disguise; Sean Taylor, illustrated by Jean Jullien. Candlewick Press 2015 48 p. color illustrations reinforced $15.99
Grades: PreK K 1 2   E
   1. Owls -- Fiction 2. Humorous fiction 3. Disguise -- Fiction
   ISBN 0763675784; 9780763675783

LC 2013957281

In this story by Sean Taylor, illustrated by Jean Jullien, "Hoot Owl is no ordinary owl. He is a master of disguise! In the blackness of night, he's preparing to swoop on his prey before it can realize his dastardly tricks. Look there--a tasty rabbit for him to eat! Hoot Owl readies his costume, disguising himself as . . . a carrot!" (Publisher's note)

"Smart pacing, easy-to-read spreads, and complete confidence that no animals will be hurt in the reading of this book make it a winner." Pub Wkly

Huck runs amuck! story by Sean Taylor; art by Peter H. Reynolds. Dial Books for Young Readers 2011 un il $16.99
Grades: PreK K 1 2   E
   1. Goats -- Fiction
   ISBN 0-8037-3261-9; 978-0-8037-3261-2

"Huck is a goat with an eclectic appetite. . . . His all-time favorite tasty treats are flowers. . . . Even flower patterns on clothing or table linens call to him. Huck tries, but each attempt to reach those elusive flowers leads to disaster. . . . Taylor employs simple, conversational language in a fast-paced, almost breathless, easy-breezy cadence that draws readers right into Huck's adventures. Double-page spreads of Reynolds' detailed, cartoon-like, watercolor, ink and tea illustrations on a bright, white background surround the large-print text. . . . [Huck's] expressions are wildly enthusiastic, goofy and totally demented. Hilarious, laugh-out-loud fun." Kirkus

The **world** champion of staying awake; [illustrations by] Jimmy Liao. Candlewick Press 2011 il $15.99
Grades: PreK K 1   E
  1. Toys -- Fiction 2. Bedtime -- Fiction
  ISBN 978-0-7636-4957-9; 0-7636-4957-0
                            LC 2009051511
At bedtime, Stella must find a way to make her toys fall asleep before she can go to sleep.

"In contrast to the spot illustrations of the main story, which are set against white backgrounds, the characters' imagined expeditions are rich, full-bleed watercolor scenes, accompanied by rhymed couplets that balance the rowdiness of the bedtime preparations with cozy imagery and soothing rhythms. It's just the thing for testing the mettle of those who would lay claim to the titular honorific." Publ Wkly

Teague, David
The **red** hat; by David Teague; illustrated by Antoinette Portis. Disney-Hyperion Books 2014 40 p. color illustrations (hardback) $16.99
Grades: PreK K 1   E
  1. Winds -- Fiction 2. Friendship -- Fiction 3. Skyscrapers -- Fiction 4. Neighbors -- Fiction 5. Perseverance (Ethics) -- Fiction
  ISBN 9781423134114
                            LC 2014005679
In this book, author David Teague narrates that "Once upon a time, high atop the world, there lived a boy named Billy Hightower and the wind. When a new neighbour appears--a girl in a red hat--Billy Hightower can hardly wait to meet her and introduce himself. But the wind has other ideas."(Publisher's note)

"A simply told, graphically arresting tale." Kirkus

Teague, Mark
Dear Mrs. LaRue; letters from obedience school. written and illustrated by Mark Teague. Scholastic Press 2002 un il $15.95
Grades: PreK K 1 2 3   E
  1. Dogs -- Fiction
  ISBN 0-439-20663-4
                            LC 2001-43479
Gertrude LaRue receives typewritten and paw-written letters from her dog Ike, entreating her to let him leave the Igor Brotweiler Canine Academy and come back home

"The humorous acrylic illustrations are, at times, a howl and the over-sized format is well-suited to storytelling." SLJ

Other titles about Mrs. LaRue and her dog Ike are:
Detective LaRue (2004)
LaRue for mayor (2008)
LaRue across America: postcards from the vacation (2011)

Funny Farm. Orchard Books 2009 un il $16.99
Grades: PreK K   E
  1. Dogs -- Fiction 2. Animals -- Fiction 3. Farm life -- Fiction
  ISBN 978-0-439-91499-4; 0-439-91499-X
                            LC 2008-02477
"When Edward, a city-slicker dog, arrives at his canine relatives' farm for a visit, Teague provides the perfect setup for this goofily sweet fish-out-of-water tale. . . . The narrative nature of the crisp oil illustra-

tions reveals a much more entertaining version of the story than does the straightforward text. . . . Young readers will find plenty to revisit in the humorous bucolic scenes of barnyard creatures at work and play." Publ Wkly

Another title about Edward is:
Firehouse! (2010)

Pigsty. Scholastic 1994 un il hardcover o.p. pa $6.99
Grades: PreK K 1 2 3   E
  1. Pigs -- Fiction 2. Cleanliness -- Fiction
  ISBN 0-590-45915-5; 0-439-59843-5 pa
                            LC 93-21179
When Wendell doesn't clean up his room, a whole herd of pigs comes to live with him

"Much of the tale's fun resides in Teague's quirky acrylic art. . . . Whether Wendell and his friends are jumping on the bed or playing Monopoly on the rug, their antics are rendered in the bold palette of a gleefully inventive imagination. Highly recommended for neat-freaks and mess-makers alike." Publ Wkly

Teckentrup, Britta
Little wolf's song. Boxer Books 2010 un il $16.95
Grades: PreK K 1   E
  1. Wolves -- Fiction
  ISBN 978-1-907152-33-7; 1-907152-33-4
Even though Little Wolf's mom, dad, sister, and brothers all have their own special song, he can only manage a poor, pitiful squeak. But one snowy day, Little Wolf finds himself lost and alone in the woods and he discovers his own special, beautiful voice.

"This effective picture book touches on many issues that children experience. . . . Created using digital collage of hand-printed paper, the large-scale illustrations feature clean lines, simple forms, and restrained use of color." Booklist

Tegen, Katherine
The **story** of the Jack O'Lantern; illustrated by Brandon Dorman. Harper 2010 un il $12.99; lib bdg $14.89
Grades: K 1 2 3   E
  1. Devil -- Fiction 2. Pumpkin -- Fiction 3. Halloween -- Fiction
  ISBN 978-0-06-143088-6; 0-06-143088-9; 978-0-06-143090-9 lib bdg; 0-06-143090-0 lib bdg
                            LC 2008046150
On Halloween night, Jack—a stingy and mean man—makes a deal with the devil for a free dinner, only to regret his choice many years later when the devil comes to collect.

"Lavish, carefully composed, full-page illustrations with the look of oil paintings clearly depict the actions of the despicable characters against pleasingly detailed backgrounds. . . . Well suited for use in a pumpkin-decorating program—or any Halloween program." Booklist

The **story** of the leprechaun; illustrated by Sally Anne Lambert. Harper 2011 un il $12.99; lib bdg $14.89
Grades: PreK K 1 2   E
  1. Magic -- Fiction 2. Wishes -- Fiction 3. Fairies -- Fiction 4. Leprechauns -- Fiction
  ISBN 978-0-06-143086-2; 0-06-143086-2; 978-0-06-143085-5 lib bdg; 0-06-143085-4 lib bdg
                            LC 2008034358
A clever leprechaun who has amassed a pot of gold by making beautiful shoes for people decides to hide his money at the end of a rainbow knowing that no one will find it there.

"The descriptive, entertaining narrative is well paced and read-aloud-friendly, and enchanting color illustrations, with soft textures and patterns, portray characters, settings, and events in both small vignettes and page-filling spreads." Booklist

Tekavec, Heather

Storm is coming! pictures by Margaret Spengler. Dial Bks. for Young Readers 2002 un il $14.99

Grades: PreK K 1 2   E

  1. Storms -- Fiction 2. Domestic animals -- Fiction

  ISBN 0-8037-2626-0

                LC 00-34622

The animals misunderstand the farmer's "Storm" warning and expect someone scary and mean

"Children will giggle over the animals' confusion and enjoy the well-paced buildup of suspense. Inviting pastel illustrations feature round, cartoonlike animals and dramatic use of perspective." Horn Book Guide

Tenzing Norbu

Secret of the snow leopard; [by] Tenzing Norbu, Lama with Stéphane Frattini. Douglas & McIntyre 2004 un il $16.95

Grades: 1 2 3 4   E

  1. Nepal -- Fiction 2. Himalaya Mountains -- Fiction

  ISBN 0-88899-544-X

Tsering, a boy from a small Nepali village, and "his stepfather accompany the village healer, who is gravely ill, on a journey to the monastery where he will seek a cure. . . . On the way home, Tsering . . . asserts his independence by climbing the dangerous pass where his father . . . lost his life. . . . Handsome earth-tone paintings, stylized and carefully composed, portray the people and animals that belong to this stark landscape. . . . The quiet authority of the artwork and the drama of the story will engage children emotionally." SLJ

Another title about Tsering is:

Himalaya (2002)

Thayer, Jane

The **popcorn** dragon; written by Jane Thayer; illustrated by Lisa McCue. Morrow Junior Bks. 1989 un il $17.99

Grades: PreK K 1 2   E

  1. Dragons -- Fiction

  ISBN 0-688-08340-4

                LC 88-39855

A newly illustrated edition of the title first published 1953

Though his hot breath is the envy of all the other animals, a young dragon learns that showing off does not make friends

"McCue's new full-color illustrations capture the whimsical mood of the fable. The animals, although too coy, have appealing humanlike expressions which convey their envy and contempt." SLJ

The **puppy** who wanted a boy; illustrated by Lisa McCue. HarperCollins Pubs. 2003 un il $14.99; lib bdg $15.89

Grades: PreK K 1 2   E

  1. Dogs -- Fiction 2. Christmas -- Fiction

  ISBN 0-06-052696-3; 0-06-052697-1 lib bdg

A reissue of the edition published 1986 by Morrow; story first published 1958 with different illustrations

When Petey the puppy decides that he wants a boy for Christmas, he discovers that he must go out and find one on his own

"It is the same, somewhat sentimental but certainly appealing tale that Thayer fashioned in 1958, when this was originally published; however, McCue's affectionately drawn, warmly colored illustrations go a long way toward perking up the story." Booklist

Thisdale, François, 1964-

Nini. Tundra Books 2011 un il $15.95

Grades: PreK K 1   E

  1. Adoption -- Fiction

  ISBN 978-1-77049-270-7; 1-77049-270-4

  Original French edition published 2009 in Canada

Long before Nini was born, she was in a safe place where a familiar voice promised her a loving home. But once she was born, that soft voice was replaced by the words of care givers in an orphanage. Then, one day, a man and a woman on the other side of the world learned that their dreams were about to come true. They would finally have a baby to love.

This is a "heart-warming poetic story of adoption. . . . Thisdale's imaginative use of traditional drawing and painting, digitally manipulated, produces double pages that suggest rather than stipulate the images." SLJ

Thomas, Jan

Can you make a scary face? Beach Lane Books 2009 un il $12.99

Grades: PreK K 1   E

  1. Frogs -- Fiction 2. Ladybugs -- Fiction 3. Imagination -- Fiction

  ISBN 978-1-4169-8581-5; 1-4169-8581-6

                LC 2008-38288

A ladybug invites the reader to play a game of "let's pretend."

"This book will have youngsters jumping, wiggling, dancing, pretending, and laughing. . . . The expressive ladybug is outlined in broad black lines and seems only inches away from readers. Adults will enjoy using this title to encourage lively activity and imaginative games. Children will love everything about it—especially the surprise ending." SLJ

The **doghouse**. Harcourt 2008 un il $12.95

Grades: PreK K   E

  1. Dogs -- Fiction 2. Fear -- Fiction 3. Animals -- Fiction

  ISBN 978-0-15-206533-1; 0-15-206533-4

                LC 2007038355

Cow, Pig, Duck, and Mouse are afraid to retrieve their ball when it goes into the dog's house, but when they do go in they are pleasantly surprised.

"The simple cartoon characters, scenery, and dialogue balloons are outlined in thick, bold lines. Colors are smooth and flat, with backgrounds done in bright blues, purple, and lime green. The pictures are large and distinct, and will work well with a group." SLJ

Another title about Cow, Pig, Duck, and Mouse is:

A birthday for Cow! (2008)

Pumpkin trouble (2011)

Is everyone ready for fun? Beach Lane Books 2011 un il $12.99

Grades: PreK K 1   E

  1. Cattle -- Fiction 2. Chickens -- Fiction

  ISBN 978-1-4424-2364-0; 1-4424-2364-1

                LC 2011005212

Chicken's cow visitors try to jump, dance, and wiggle on his couch, which is much too tiny for such exuberant activities.

"Thomas's illustrations energetically emphasize the cows' frenetic energy and the chicken's frustration, which are sure to draw giggles." Publ Wkly

Pumpkin trouble. Harper 2011 un il $9.99; lib bdg $12.99

Grades: PreK K   E

  1. Mice -- Fiction 2. Pigs -- Fiction 3. Ducks -- Fiction 4. Pumpkin -- Fiction

  ISBN 978-0-06-169284-0; 0-06-169284-0; 978-0-06-169285-7 lib bdg; 0-06-169285-9 lib bdg

                LC 2010007029

When Duck decides to make a jack-o-lantern, he and his friends Pig and Mouse are in for a scary adventure.

"With well-paced, slapstick action and opportunities for children to practice making predictions, this story features characters who can hold their own. . . . A terrific Halloween read-aloud." Booklist

★ **Rhyming** dust bunnies. Atheneum Books for Young Readers 2009 un il $12.99

Grades: K 1 2   E

1. Dust -- Fiction 2. Rhyme -- Fiction

ISBN 978-1-4169-7976-0; 1-4169-7976-X

LC 2008-28779

As three dust bunnies, Ed, Ned, and Ted, are demonstrating how much they love to rhyme, a fourth, Bob, is trying to warn them of approaching danger.

"The simple text and rhyming game-playing make this a natural as an early reader while also offering entertaining opportunities for readers-aloud. Digitally rendered art offers coloring-book strength and simplicity." Bull Cent Child Books

Another title about the dust bunnies is:

Here comes the big, mean dust bunny! (2009)

What will Fat Cat sit on? Harcourt 2007 un il $12.95

Grades: PreK K   E

1. Cats -- Fiction 2. Animals -- Fiction

ISBN 978-0-15-206051-0; 0-15-206051-0

LC 2006-24558

A group of animals is terrified at the prospect of being sat upon by the imposing Fat Cat, until the mouse comes up with a solution that satisfies everyone.

"Thomas . . . makes this book a laugh-out-loud pas de deux between Dick-and-Jane-get-stylish typography . . . and the supremely silly visual evocation of high anxiety. . . . She renders her barnyard characters in super-saturated colors and thick, bold outlines." Publ Wkly

Thomas, Patricia

Red sled; [by] Patricia Thomas; illustrated by Chris L. Demarest. Boyds Mills Press 2008 un il $16.95

Grades: PreK K 1   E

1. Stories in rhyme 2. Sledding -- Fiction 3. Father-son relationship -- Fiction

ISBN 978-1-59078-559-1; 1-59078-559-2

LC 2007-50838

A boy and his father lift one another's spirits by going sledding on a winter's night.

"The brief text consists of easy-to-read words in rhyming pairs. . . . Bright watercolor pictures capture perfectly the downcast faces of the characters when they are stuck inside during a snowstorm, . . . their expressions of happiness and excitement during their nocturnal adventure on the red sled." SLJ

Thomas, Shelley Moore

A **Good** Knight's rest; pictures by Jennifer Plecas. Dutton Children's Books 2011 un il (Dutton easy reader) $16.99

Grades: PreK K 1 2   E

1. Dragons -- Fiction 2. Vacations -- Fiction 3. Friendship -- Fiction 4. Knights and knighthood -- Fiction

ISBN 978-0-525-42195-5; 0-525-42195-5

LC 2010037564

The Good Knight's hard work has earned him a vacation, but his three little dragon friends come along and make the trip anything but relaxing.

"The cartoon-style illustrations are done in watercolors and ink, perfectly capturing the weariness of the Good Knight and the antics of his

friends. . . . This well-told tale is a good choice for listeners and early readers." SLJ

★ **Good** night, Good Knight; pictures by Jennifer Plecas. Dutton Children's Bks. 2000 47p il (Dutton easy reader) $13.99

Grades: PreK K 1 2   E

1. Bedtime -- Fiction 2. Dragons -- Fiction 3. Knights and knighthood -- Fiction

ISBN 0-525-46326-7

LC 99-28415

A Good Knight helps three little dragons who are having trouble getting to sleep.

"The short, simple, repetitive phrases are sure to capture the imaginations of young children. . . . With a palette dominated by the blues, grays, and purples of the nightime setting, Plecas's illustrations are a wonderful complement to this endearing tale." SLJ

Other titles about the Good Knight are:

A cold winter's Good Knight (2008)

Get well, Good Knight (2002)

Happy birthday, Good Knight (2006)

Take care Good Knight (2006)

A Good Knight's rest (2011)

Thomassie, Tynia

Feliciana Feyra LeRoux; a Cajun tall tale. illustrated by Cat Bowman Smith. Pelican 2005 un il $15.95

Grades: K 1 2 3   E

1. Cajuns -- Fiction 2. Louisiana -- Fiction 3. Alligators -- Fiction

ISBN 1-58980-286-1

A reissue of the title first published 1995 by Little, Brown

This "combines breezy watercolors and a swinging text that's perfect for reading aloud. A note on Cajun culture, a glossary, and a pronunciation guide are included." Booklist

Another title about Feliciana is:

Feliciana meets d'Loup Garou (1998)

Thompson, Carol

I like you the best. Holiday House 2011 un il

Grades: PreK K 1   E

1. Pigs -- Fiction 2. Rabbits -- Fiction 3. Friendship -- Fiction 4. Meditation -- Fiction

ISBN 0823423417; 9780823423415

LC 201003074

Dolly the pig and Jack Rabbit are best friends, even after they have a fight. "Ages five to seven." (Bull Cent Child Books)

"Dolly and Jack overcome their feelings, thanks to some basic meditative skills. . . . Thompson's drawings, mostly spot images, are gems. Smudgy and rough-edged, they have a sketchbooklike immediacy and eloquently articulate two personalities who like to turn the emotional dial up to 11." Publ Wkly

Thompson, Emma, 1959-

The **Further** Tale of Peter Rabbit. Penguin Group USA 2012 7p. $20.00

Grades: PreK K   E

1. Rabbits -- Fiction 2. Scotland -- Fiction 3. Voyages and travel -- Fiction

ISBN 0723269106; 9780723269106

This book is a "new adventure of the mischievous bunny who first appeared 110 years ago in Beatrix Potter's original tale. . . . Peter (again) wriggles under Mr. McGregor's gate, this time into an 'interesting basket smelling of onions.' After eating the picnic lunch within, he nods off, awakened later by the jostling of a horse-drawn cart he's been loaded onto, which is en route to, of all places, Scotland," where he meets his cousin and has an adventure in the Highland Games. (Publishers Weekly)

Thompson, Lauren

★ The **apple** pie that Papa baked; illustrated by Jonathan Bean. Simon & Schuster Books for Young Readers 2007 un il $15.99
Grades: PreK K 1   E
1. Pies -- Fiction 2. Trees -- Fiction 3. Apples -- Fiction
ISBN 1-4169-1240-1; 978-1-4169-1240-8
"A pigtailed girl introduces the apple pie 'warm and sweet that Papa baked.' Then moving backward, the girl runs . . . out to the tree 'crooked and strong,' where shiny red apples are waiting to be picked. The roots 'deep and fine,' feed the tree. . . . Rain waters the roots, clouds drop the rain, the sky carries the clouds, the sun lights the sky. . . . The text is clear, and it's well matched by delightful illustrations . . . The intricately detailed art is reminiscent of the time when picture books were rarely full color." Booklist

The **Christmas** magic; illustrated by Jon J. Muth. Scholastic Press 2009 un il $16.99
Grades: K 1 2 3   E
1. Magic -- Fiction 2. Christmas -- Fiction 3. Santa Claus -- Fiction
ISBN 978-0-439-77497-0; 0-439-77497-7
                           LC 2008-43308
As Santa prepares for the upcoming holiday season, it is the Christmas magic that truly makes everything happen.
"Muth's haunting watercolor and pastel illustrations bring the simple story to magical life. . . . This gentle and lovely book is sheer enchantment." SLJ

★ **Leap** back home to me; illustrated by Matthew Cordell. Margaret K. McElderry Books 2011 un il $15.99
Grades: PreK K   E
1. Stories in rhyme 2. Frogs -- Fiction 3. Mother-child relationship -- Fiction
ISBN 978-1-4169-0664-3; 1-4169-0664-9
                           LC 2009-53708
A little frog makes increasingly bold leaps out into the world, and then comes back to his mother after each excursion.
"Sweet and simple, lively and expressive, this picture book provides a loving template for parents who want to encourage their children to explore an ever-widening world without losing their connection to home and family." Publ Wkly

Little Quack; pictures by Derek Anderson. Simon & Schuster Bks. for Young Readers 2003 un il $14.95
Grades: PreK K   E
1. Counting 2. Ducks -- Fiction
ISBN 0-689-84723-8
                           LC 2002-5567
One by one, four ducklings find the courage to jump into the pond and paddle with Mama Duck, until only Little Quack is left in the nest, trying to be brave
"Here's a familiar story kicked up a notch by a counting element and irresistible art. The story is reassuring and utterly straightforward. . . . The charm is in Anderson's comical, eye-commanding acrylics." Booklist
Other titles about Little Quack are:
Little Quack's bedtime (2005)
Little Quack's hide and seek (2004)
Little Quack's new friend (2006)

★ **One** starry night; illustrated by Jonathan Bean. Margaret K. McElderry Books 2011 un il $16.99

Grades: PreK K 1   E
1. Stories in rhyme 2. Christmas stories 3. Animals -- Fiction 4. Christmas -- Fiction
ISBN 978-0-689-82851-5; 0-689-82851-9
                           LC 2011008776
One starry night, as all sorts of animals watch over their young, Mary and Joseph watch over their baby boy, Jesus, in Bethlehem.
"This tender, poetic retelling of the age-old story takes the form of a whispered prayer as it highlights the nurturing given to babies of many species. The art and the words strike just the right tone of reverence and delight. A lovely offering." SLJ

Polar bear night; illustrated by Stephen Savage. Scholastic Press 2004 un il $15.95
Grades: PreK K 1 2   E
1. Night -- Fiction 2. Polar bear -- Fiction
ISBN 0-439-49524-5
                           LC 2003-27538
After wandering out at night to watch a magical star shower, a polar bear cub returns home to snuggle with her mother in their warm den.
"With comforting, carefully chosen words and soft pastels shading linocut prints, this book has all the elements to make it a bedtime favorite." SLJ
Another title in this series is:
Polar bear morning (2013)

Wee little chick; by Lauren Thompson; illustrated by John Butler. Simon & Schuster Books for Young Readers 2008 un il $14.99
Grades: PreK   E
1. Size -- Fiction 2. Animals -- Fiction 3. Chickens -- Fiction
ISBN 978-1-4169-3468-4; 1-4169-3468-5
                           LC 2007016411
When the other barnyard animals comment on how tiny the littlest chick is, the proud little one peeps louder, stands taller, and runs faster than any of them
"Thompson's simple, rhythmic text moves the action along at a brisk, even pace. Butler's bright acrylic and pencil illustrations artistically portray the story's springtime mood and warmhearted tone." SLJ
Other titles in this series are:
Wee little lamb (2009)
Wee little bunny (2010)

Thomson, Bill

★ **Chalk**. Marshall Cavendish Children 2010 un il $15.99
Grades: PreK K 1 2   E
1. Stories without words 2. Drawing -- Fiction
ISBN 978-0-7614-5526-4; 0-7614-5526-4
                           LC 2009014141
A wordless picture book about three children who go to a park on a rainy day, find some chalk, and draw pictures that come to life.
"With eye-catching, realistic illustrations, clever details, and some dramatic suspense, this wordless picture book offers a fresh take on the drawings-come-to-life theme. . . . Vibrant acrylic and colored-pencil illustrations, rendered with intricate precision, nearly leap off the page." Booklist

The **Typewriter**; by Bill Thomson. Amazon Childrens Pub 2016 34 p. chiefly color illustrations $17.99
Grades: PreK K 1 2 3   E
1. Fantasy fiction -- Fiction 2. Adventure fiction -- Fiction
ISBN 1477849750; 9781477849750
This book, by Bill Thomson, "takes readers on another unforgettable journey. When three children discover a typewriter on a carousel, they are transported on an adventure of their own creation—complete with a

giant beach ball and a threatening crab. Stunning, richly colored artwork is paired with limited text so children can tell their own version of the story." (Publisher's note)

"Words rule in this intriguing, impressive, imaginative, nearly wordless narrative drama." Kirkus

Thomson, Sarah L.

Cub's big world; Sarah L. Thomson; illustrated by Joe Cepeda. Harcourt Children's Books, Houghton Mifflin Harcourt 2013 32 p. $16.99

Grades: PreK K   E

1. Arctic regions -- Fiction 2. Bears -- Fiction 3. Polar bear -- Fiction 4. Mother and child -- Fiction 5. Animals -- Infancy -- Fiction

ISBN 0544057392; 9780544057395

LC 2012045056

In this picture book, by Sarah L. Thomson, "Cub knows all about the familiar world in the snow den where she was born. When she follows Mom out of their den, tumbling into the Arctic wilderness, she finds that the world under the wide blue sky is big, big, BIG! It's easy to be curious when there's so much to explore—and when Mom is nearby. But when she thinks she's all alone, can Cub be brave?" (Publisher's note)

Imagine a night; paintings by Rob Gonsalves; text by Sarah L. Thomson. Atheneum Books for Young Readers 2003 un il $16.95

Grades: 2 3 4 5 6   E

1. Night -- Fiction 2. Imagination -- Fiction

ISBN 0-689-85218-5

LC 2002-10718

Presents a night when imagination takes over and gravity does not work quite as expected.

"Magical realism permeates Gonsalves's large acrylic paintings, and they are essential to the lyrical text. . . . This is a fascinating foray into the imagination and a fine discussion starter for older children." SLJ

Other titles in this series are:

Imagine a day (2005)

Imagine a place (2008)

Pirates, ho! by Sarah L. Thomson; illustrated by Stephen Gilpin. Marshall Cavendish 2008 un il $14.99

Grades: K 1 2   E

1. Stories in rhyme 2. Pirates -- Fiction

ISBN 978-0-7614-5435-9; 0-7614-5435-7

LC 2007-29792

Pirates Peg-Leg Tom, Angus Black, Dreadful Nell, and One-Eyed Jack chase ships on the high seas, tell ghost stories, and fall asleep counting gold instead of sheep.

"Gilpin's wacky cartoons have a retro, take-no-prisoners abandon. . . . This funny, fabulously illustrated rhyme is certainly worth adding." SLJ

Thong, Roseanne Greenfield

Dia De Los Muertos; by Roseanne Greenfield Thong; illustrated by Carles Ballesteros. Albert Whitman & Co. 2015 32 p. color illustrations $16.99

Grades: PreK K 1 2   E

1. Holidays 2. Day of the Dead 3. Mexico -- Social life and customs

ISBN 0807515663; 9780807515662

In this book, by Roseanne Greenfield Thong, illustrated by Carles Ballesteros, it's "Dia de Los Muertos (Day of the Dead) and children throughout the pueblo, or town, are getting ready to celebrate! They decorate with colored streamers, calaveras, or sugar skulls, and pan de muertos, or bread of the dead. There are altars draped in cloth and cov-

ered in marigolds and twinkling candles. . . . Join the fun and festivities [and] learn about a different cultural tradition." (Publisher's note)

"A festive and colorful celebration of the Mexican and Latin American holiday. Thong's rhyming narrative introduces the traditions practiced during El Día de los Muertos or the Day of the Dead, from the sugary, skull-shaped candies (calaveras) and altars built in remembrance of the dearly departed to decorating tombstones and picnics at the cemetery. Spanish words are sprinkled throughout, sometimes defined through their context or otherwise included in the helpful glossary. . . . A jovial primer on the Latin American holiday for the uninitiated and a fiesta for those who already partake." SLJ

Fly free! illustrated by Eujin Kim Neilan. Boyds Mills Press 2010 un il $17.95

Grades: 3 4 5   E

1. Vietnam -- Fiction 2. Buddhism -- Fiction 3. Kindness -- Fiction 4. Conduct of life -- Fiction

ISBN 978-1-59078-550-8; 1-59078-550-9

LC 2009020248

When Mai feeds the caged birds at a Buddhist temple in Vietnam, her simple act of kindness starts a chain of thoughtful acts that ultimately comes back to her. Includes author's note explaining the Buddhist concepts of karma and samsara, or the wheel of life.

"The lesson of this simple story, that helping others is helpful to you, is universal. The muted and warm watercolor-on-board illustrations glow with gold, orange, red, and brown tones." SLJ

★ Green is a chile pepper; a book of colors. by Roseanne Greenfield Thong; illustrated by John Parra. Chronicle Books 2014 40 p. color illustrations (alk. paper) $16.99

Grades: PreK K 1 2   E

1. Color -- Fiction 2. Latin America -- Civilization 3. Stories in rhyme 4. Hispanic American children 5. Hispanic Americans -- Fiction

ISBN 1452102031; 9781452102030

LC 2013021561

Pura Belpré (Illustrator) Honor Book (2015)

In this children's book by Roseanne Greenfield Thong, illustrated by John Parra, "children discover a world of colors all around them: red is spices and swirling skirts, yellow is masa, tortillas, and sweet corn cake. Many of the featured objects are Latino in origin, and all are universal in appeal." (Publisher's note)

"Each double-page spread introduces a color in rhyming, explanatory verse; attractive art; and a colored bubble with the word in English and Spanish." Booklist

One is a drummer; written by Roseanne Thong; illustrated by Grace Lin. Chronicle Books 2004 un il $14.95; pa $6.99

Grades: PreK K 1 2   E

1. Counting 2. Stories in rhyme 3. Chinese Americans -- Fiction

ISBN 0-8118-3772-6; 0-8118-6482-4 pa

LC 2003-10810

A young girl numbers her discoveries in the world around her, from one dragon boat to four mahjong players to ten bamboo stalks

"The rhymes provide a pleasing framework for the book, and Lin's striking artwork gives it great visual appeal. . . . An appealing counting book, particularly for Chinese American children who want to learn a little about their heritage." Booklist

Red is a dragon; a book of colors. written by Roseanne Thong; illustrated by Grace Lin. Chronicle Bks. 2001 un il hardcover o.p. pa $6.99

Grades: PreK K 1 2   E

1. Color 2. Stories in rhyme 3. Asian Americans 4. Chinese

Americans -- Fiction
ISBN 0-8118-3177-9; 0-8118-6481-2 pa

LC 2001-93

A Chinese American girl provides rhyming descriptions of the great variety of colors she sees around her, from the red of a dragon, firecrackers, and lychees to the brown of her teddy bear

"Lin's simply drawn gouache illustrations, outlined in black, fairly explode with color. . . . This is a must-have for libraries serving Chinese American populations, and it will be a welcome addition to preschool story hours for children of all backgrounds." Booklist

Round is a mooncake; a book of shapes. written by Roseanne Thong; illustrated by Grace Lin. Chronicle Books 2000 un il $15.99
Grades: PreK K 1 2   E
1. Shape 2. Stories in rhyme 3. Chinese Americans -- Fiction
ISBN 0-8118-2676-7

LC 99-50852

As a little girl discovers things round, square, and rectangular in her urban neighborhood, she is reminded of her Chinese American culture

"Lin's gouache paintings are bright and arresting, presenting scenes that have an interest beyond shape identification." Booklist

★ **Round** is a tortilla; by Roseanne Greenfield Thong; illustrated by John Parra. Chronicle Books 2013 40 p. col. ill. (reinforced) $16.99
Grades: PreK K 1 2   E
1. Stories in rhyme 2. Hispanic Americans -- Fiction 3. Shape -- Fiction 4. Form perception -- Fiction
ISBN 9781452106168 (alk. paper); 1452106169

LC 2012013341

In this children's picture book, by Roseanne Greenfield Thong, illustrated by John Parra, "children discover a world of shapes all around them: rectangles are ice-cream carts and stone metates, triangles are slices of watermelon and quesadillas. Many of the featured objects are Latino in origin, and all are universal in appeal." (Publisher's note)

Thornhill, Jan
The **wildlife** 1 2 3; a nature counting book. by Jan Thornhill. Owlkids Books 2012 32 p. $14.95; $7.95
Grades: PreK K   E
1. Counting 2. Animals
ISBN 0671679260; 1926973461; 9781926973463

LC 89005970

This book, by Jan Thornhill, "communicates simple information through colorful illustrations and classic design; every page [is designed to engage] young readers' interest and imagination. At the end of the book, 'Nature Notes' provide additional information on each of the featured animals and their habitats." (Publisher's note)

Thurber, James
★ **Many** moons; illustrated by Louis Slobodkin. Harcourt Brace Jovanovich 1943 un il $17; pa $7
Grades: 1 2 3 4   E
1. Fairy tales 2. Moon -- Fiction 3. Princesses -- Fiction
ISBN 0-15-251873-8; 0-15-656980-9 pa
Awarded the Caldecott Medal, 1944

"Louis Slobodkin's pictures float on the pages in four colors: black and white cannot represent them. They are the substance of dreams . . . the long thoughts little children, and some adults wise as they, have about life." N Y Her Trib Books

The **Tiger** Who Would Be King; by James Thurber; illustrated by JooHee Yoon. Enchanted Lion Books 2015 40 p. color illustrations $18.95

Grades: K 1 2 3 4   E
1. Tigers -- Folklore
ISBN 1592701825; 9781592701827

This children's book is a retelling of a James Thurber classic fable by artist JooHee Moon. It "is as entertaining as it is wise, as wry as it is passionate. Yoon's humorous images support this beautifully written text with wit and insight. Her final portrait of the tiger in a sea of silence will stay with the reader for a long, long time." (Publisher's note)

"A picture book that will be embraced due to its successful handling of difficult themes." Kirkus

Thurlby, Paul
★ **Paul** Thurlby's alphabet. Candlewick Press 2011 un il $16.99
Grades: PreK K   E
1. Alphabet
ISBN 978-0-7636-5565-5; 0-7636-5565-1

LC 2010045400

"From a cover that features a boy's head and arms on a body shaped like the letter A to Z for zipper, the illustrator explains that he 'pursues the challenge of fusing the object of the word with the shape of the letter.' His approach succeeds in a fascinating way. The lower and uppercase letter is centered on the verso pages against textured, vividly colored papers, while the letter designs appear on the recto and have a posterlike quality. . . . The digital-media artwork has a distinctive look that will be best appreciated by young ones who already know the ABCs. Skillfully constructed and cleverly composed, it's an awesome alphabet book." Kirkus

Tibo, Gilles
My diary; the totally true story of me! illustrations by Josee Bisaillon. Magination Press 2011 un il pa $12.95
Grades: K 1 2   E
1. Diaries -- Fiction
ISBN 978-1-4338-095-83; 1-4338-0958-3

LC 2011007778

A young girl shares many things, including thoughts on becoming a big sister, freedom, joy, death, peace, and hope, through secrets, lists, poems, and inventions recorded in her diary.

"This well-crafted book would be useful as an example for a writing workshop. Others may find it equally as helpful as a means to begin discussions about emotions." SLJ

Tierney, Fiona
Lion's lunch? illustrated by Margaret Chamberlain. Chicken House 2010 un il $17.99
Grades: K 1 2 3   E
1. Lions -- Fiction 2. Animals -- Fiction 3. Drawing -- Fiction
ISBN 978-0-545-17691-0; 0-545-17691-3

LC 2009-08267

When Lion comes upon Sarah walking in the jungle, he threatens to eat her unless she shows that she can do something none of the other animals can do.

"Vibrant, brightly colored illustrations of the lively animals and cheerful child fill every bit of space on the spreads and are sure to engage readers. This clever tale of courage and confidence teaches an important life lesson in a fun way." SLJ

Tillman, Nancy
On the night you were born. Feiwel & Friends 2006 un il $16.95
Grades: K 1 2   E
1. Stories in rhyme 2. Nature -- Fiction 3. Childbirth -- Fiction
ISBN 0-312-34606-9
First published 2005 by Darling Press

The moon, wind, rain, and a variety of animals celebrate the special occasion that is the birth of a child.

Tillman's "writing has the authenticity of whispered conversation. . . . The pictures subtly radiate golden glints of moonlight, and her almost sculptural rendering style gives her characters a hefty physicality that counterbalances the ethereal sentiments being expressed." Publ Wkly

The **spirit** of Christmas. Feiwel and Friends 2009 un il $16.99
Grades: PreK K 1 2   E
    1. Stories in rhyme 2. Christmas -- Fiction
    ISBN 978-0-312-54965-7; 0-312-54965-2
                       LC 2008-48139

Despite the arrival of the Spirit of Christmas, who brings all sorts of trimmings and reminders of seasonal joys, something is still lacking.

"Realism and fantasy are satisfyingly paired to bring the mixed-media illustrations of treasured holiday scenes to life. . . . A beautiful and timeless book." SLJ

Timberlake, Amy

The **dirty** cowboy; pictures by Adam Rex. Farrar, Straus & Giroux 2003 un il $16
Grades: K 1 2 3   E
    1. Dogs -- Fiction 2. Cowhands -- Fiction
    ISBN 0-374-31791-7
                       LC 2001-53224

Telling his faithful dog to make sure nobody touches his clothes but him, a cowboy jumps into a New Mexico river for a bath, not realizing just how much the scrubbing will change his scent

"Told in descriptive language that rolls off the tongue, this story makes the most of a humorous situation. . . . The paintings have a gritty, sinewy look that matches the earthy tone of the tale." SLJ

Tinkham, Kelly

Hair for Mama; [by] Kelly A. Tinkham; illustrated by Amy June Bates. Dial Books for Young Readers 2007 un il $16.99
Grades: K 1 2 3   E
    1. Hair -- Fiction 2. Cancer -- Fiction 3. African Americans -- Fiction 4. Mother-son relationship -- Fiction
    ISBN 0-8037-2955-3; 978-0-8037-2955-1
                       LC 2005-10621

When Marcus's mother has chemotherapy for her cancer and loses her hair, he tries to find new hair for her to make her well again.

"This is a beautifully written story about an African-American family dealing with cancer. . . . The lovely watercolor illustrations fit the text well, using gold, brown, orange, and green tones to show a family going through tough times together." SLJ

Titcomb, Gordon

The **last** train; paintings by Wendall Minor. Roaring Brook Press 2010 un il $16.99
Grades: PreK K 1 2   E
    1. Railroads -- Fiction
    ISBN 978-1-59643-164-5; 1-59643-164-4

"Based on musician Titcomb's 2005 song, this stunning book both celebrates and eulogizes the golden era of railway travel. Minor's luminous, occasionally almost photographic, paintings portray the adult narrator as a boy, surrounded by a ghostly haze as he walks along the tracks." Publ Wkly

Titherington, Jeanne

Pumpkin, pumpkin. Greenwillow Bks. 1986 23p il $16.99; pa $6.99

Grades: PreK K 1 2   E
    1. Pumpkin -- Fiction 2. Gardening -- Fiction
    ISBN 0-688-05695-4; 0-688-09930-0 pa
                       LC 84-25334

Jamie "plants a seed, then grows and harvests a pumpkin from which he saves seeds for next year. The large, detailed drawings capture Jamie's anticipation and pleasure just right. . . . Nonreaders can easily follow the story in pictures alone. Very large, clear print on facing pages makes the simple narrative inviting for beginning readers, too." SLJ

Tobin, Jim

The **very** inappropriate word; Jim Tobin; illustrated by Dave Coverly. Christy Ottaviano Books 2013 40 p. (hardcover) $16.99
Grades: K 1 2 3 4   E
    1. Picture books for children 2. Vocabulary – Fiction 3. Schools -- Fiction 4. Swearing -- Fiction
    ISBN 0805094741; 9780805094749
                       LC 2012021084

In this children's picture book, "Michael is a budding logophile: 'He picked up new words at practice and downtown and even in school, where Mrs. Dixon gave the kids one new spelling word every day.' But when Michael picks up an 'inappropriate' word (albeit one that grownups use with impunity) on the school bus, he can't resist helping it go viral ('Michael could see there was some thing kind of bad about it. But there was also something about it that he kind of liked')." (Publishers Weekly)

Tolman, Marije

The **tree** house; [by] Marije Tolman & Ronald Tolman. Lemniscaat un il $17.95
Grades: PreK K 1   E
    1. Stories without words 2. Animals -- Fiction
    ISBN 978-1-59078-806-6; 1-59078-806-0
    Original Dutch edition 2009

"A wordless picture book about an elaborate wooden structure in the tree. Three stories tall, it soaks up the water surrounding its base as animals inhabit its various nooks and crannies. Bears, peacocks, and owls, and a hippo all find different ways to amuse themselves while up so high. . . . Soft pastel spreads allow readers to see all the activity in and around the tree. . . . Children will gaze in wonder at this tree house. . . . This oversize picture book celebrates acceptance of others and the splendor of nature." SLJ

Tomoko Ohmura

The **long,** long line; Tomoko Ohmura. Owlkids Books 2013 40 p. $16.95
Grades: PreK K 1 2   E
    1. Picture books for children 2. Amusement parks -- Fiction 3. Animals -- Fiction
    ISBN 1926973925; 9781926973920
                       LC 2013930499

The story of this children's picture book "starts opposite the title page with a small frog looking up at a sign that requests 'Please line up in single file.' Turn the page, and animals stand politely, clearly wondering what's at the front of the line. As the numbers decrease, the size of the animals increases: #4 is hippo. Turn the page after #1, elephant, to a gatefold sign: JUMBO COASTER," which turns out to be a whale giving rides. (Kirkus Reviews)

"In this Japanese import, fifty animals stand in a line, roughly in size order, waiting for...what? Readers wait alongside and guess at what lies ahead as small dramas unfold. The illustrations are simple and bright, rendered in saturated colors and outlined with thick black brushstrokes against ample white space. The wealth of storytelling detail on each double-page spread rewards repeat viewing." (Horn Book)

Tompert, Ann

Little Fox goes to the end of the world; illustrated by Laura J. Bryant. Marshall Cavendish 2010 un il $16.99

Grades: PreK K 1 2   **E**

1. Foxes -- Fiction 2. Mother-child relationship -- Fiction

ISBN 978-0-7614-5703-9; 0-7614-5703-8

A newly illustrated edition of the title first published 1976 by Crown

"Capturing a young child's yearning for independence, Tompert describes the story of Little Fox, who tells her mother, 'Some day . . . I'm going to travel to the end of the world.' Her mother's wise reply encourages Little Fox's imagination and conversation by asking appropriate questions such as, 'What will you see?' 'Won't you be scared?' Bryant's dramatic watercolor artwork frequently fills the spreads." SLJ

Tonatiuh, Duncan

★ **Dear** Primo; a letter to my cousin. Abrams 2010 un il $15.95

Grades: 1 2 3   **E**

1. Mexico -- Fiction 2. Cousins -- Fiction 3. Country life -- Fiction 4. Mexican Americans -- Fiction 5. City and town life -- Fiction

ISBN 978-0-81093-872-4; 0-81093-872-3

Pura Belpré Award honor book (Illustrator), 2011

Two cousins, one in Mexico and one in New York City, write to each other and learn that even though their daily lives differ, at heart the boys are very similar.

"The digitally enhanced collage illustrations are based on traditional Mixtec art, and show the characters posed in profile in simply composed scenes. This useful method of comparing and contrasting can serve as a fine general introduction to contemporary rural life in Mexico, while it also demonstrates the fun of having a pen pal and reinforces the sense that kids around the world are more alike than different." Booklist

★ **Pancho** Rabbit and the coyote; a migrant's tale. by Duncan Tonatiuh. Abrams Books for Young Readers 2013 32 p. ill. (reinforced) $16.95

Grades: K 1 2   **E**

1. Allegories 2. Coyote -- Fiction 3. Rabbits -- Fiction 4. Migrant labor -- Fiction 5. Voyages and travels -- Fiction

ISBN 1419705830; 9781419705830

LC 2012022573

Pura Belpre Author Honor Book (2014)

Pura Belpre Illustrator Honor Book (2014)

"In this allegorical picture book, [by Duncan Tonatiuh,] a young rabbit named Pancho eagerly awaits his papa's return. Papa Rabbit traveled north two years ago to find work in the great carrot and lettuce fields. . . . When Papa does not return, Pancho sets out to find him. . . . He meets a coyote, who offers to help Pancho in exchange for some of Papa's food. They travel together until the food is gone and the coyote decides he is still hungry . . . for Pancho!" (Publisher's note)

Torres, Jennifer

Finding the music; by Jennifer Torres; illustrated by Renato Alarcao; Spanish translation by Alexis Romay = En pos de la música / por Jennifer Torres; ilustrado por Renato Alarcão; traducción al español por Alexis Romay. Children's Book Press, an imprint of Lee & Low Books Inc. 2015 40 p. color illustrations (hardcover : alk. paper) $18.95

Grades: 1 2 3 4   **E**

1. Guitars -- Fiction 2. Grandfathers -- Fiction 3. Hispanic Americans -- Fiction 4. Mariachi -- Fiction 5. Musicians -- Fiction 6. Spanish language materials -- Bilingual

ISBN 9780892392919

LC 2013041044

In this book, by Jennifer Torres, illustrated by Renato Alarcao, "when Reyna accidentally breaks Abuelito's vihuela a small guitar-like instrument she ventures out into the neighborhood determined to find

someone who can help her repair it. No one can fix the vihuela, but along the way Reyna gathers stories and mementos of Abuelito and his music. Still determined, Reyna visits the music store." (Publisher's note)

Busca de la música

Torrey, Richard

Ally-Saurus & the First Day of School; Richard Torrey. Sterling Pub Co Inc 2015 32 p. illustrations $14.95

Grades: 3 4 5 6   **E**

1. Dinosaurs -- Fiction 2. School stories -- Fiction 3. First day of school -- Fiction

ISBN 1454911794; 9781454911791

LC 2015296576

In this children's story, written and illustrated by Richard Torrey, "when Ally roars off to her first day at school, she hopes she'll meet lots of other dinosaur-mad kids in class. Instead, she's the only one chomping her food with fierce dino teeth and drawing dinosaurs on her nameplate. Even worse, a group of would-be 'princesses' snubs her! Will Ally ever make new friends?" (Publisher's note)

"It's the first day of school, and Ally—or Ally-saurus as she likes to be called—wonders if there will be "other dinosaurs" in her grade? She is one of many spirited children in her class, and while Ally is obsessed with dinosaurs, each child has his or her own passion. . . . This book can easily be used in classrooms in September to relieve the anxiety that children might feel at the beginning of the school year." SLJ

Almost. HarperCollinsPublishers 2009 un il $17.99; lib bdg $18.89

Grades: PreK K   **E**

1. Growth -- Fiction

ISBN 978-0-06-156166-5; 0-06-156166-5; 978-0-06-156167-2 lib bdg; 0-06-156167-3 lib bdg

LC 2008011724

Almost six-year-old Jack lists all the ways in which he is almost a grown-up.

"The large, cartoonlike spreads have plenty of pleasing color and detail, and expand on the simple text. . . . This simple story addresses both the desire of children to be older and sibling rivalry. It's sure to be a hit at storytime." SLJ

Other titles about Jack are:

Why? (2010)

Because (2011)

Because; [by] Richard Torrey. Harper 2011 un il $16.99

Grades: PreK K   **E**

1. Brothers -- Fiction 2. Family life -- Fiction

ISBN 978-0-06-156173-3; 0-06-156173-8

LC 2010010510

"Young Jack promises to show examples of why 'because' is a 'real answer.' Amusing drawings and the boy's single-sentence clarifications for questionable behavior justify why cereal is spread across the floor, why the dog is in timeout, and why boy and dog are covered in strawberry icing. . . . The story will allow youngsters to recall fondly their own 'because' moments." SLJ

My dog, Bob; Richard Torrey. Holiday House 2015 32 p. color illustrations (hardcover : alk. paper) $16.95

Grades: PreK K 1 2   **E**

1. Dogs -- Fiction 2. Pets -- Training -- Fiction 3. Humorous stories

ISBN 0823433862; 9780823433865

LC 2014036926

In this children's book by Richard Torrey "like all dogs, Bob likes breakfast, riding in the family car, and digging for bones. But unlike other dogs, Bob cooks breakfast for himself and his family, drives the family car and digs for dinosaur bones with a paleontologist. When the girl next door challenges Bob's owner to a contest to see whose dog is best, Bob doesn't sit, fetch or speak on command. Bob loses. But to make up for his deficiencies, Bob makes pizza for the family." (Publisher's note)

"Simply drawn in oil pencil and brightened with watercolors, Torrey's expressive, cartoonlike illustrations contribute greatly to the book's tone, combining wit with affection. Whether Bob's feats are seen as real or imagined, this charmer of a picture book, reminiscent of Norman Bridwell's original Clifford the Big Red Dog (1973), is great fun for reading aloud." Booklist

Why? [by] Richard Torrey. Balzer & Bray 2010 un il $16.99
Grades: PreK K   E
1. Brothers -- Fiction
ISBN 978-0-06-156170-2; 0-06-156170-3
LC 2009-11749

Jack asks a lot of questions, including 'Why does everyone think I ask too many questions?'

"Torrey's affecting portrait of a small boy is made up almost entirely of questions, all of which begin with 'Why?' Torrey . . . paints Jack's world with gentle colors and softly brushed forms. . . . Jack isn't just cute or just annoying; he's doing his best to understand the world, and Torrey's sensitivity brings Jack's feelings home to readers." Publ Wkly

Toscano, Charles
Papa's pastries; illustrated by Sonja Lamut. Zonderkidz 2010 un il $15.99
Grades: PreK K 1 2   E
1. Baking -- Fiction 2. Poverty -- Fiction 3. Kindness -- Fiction
ISBN 978-0-310-71602-0; 0-310-71602-0

Miguel sees the results of his father's faith and generosity when, although his own family is facing the oncoming winter with threadbare clothing, a leaky roof, and no firewood, Papa gives away the pastries he has baked.

"Effective use of repetition and a pleasing rhythm invigorate . . . Toscano's predictable but touching tale. . . . The illustrations . . . effectively convey communal warmth and industry against a backdrop of poverty and looming fear." Publ Wkly

Tougas, Chris
Art's supplies; by Chris Tougas. Orca Book Publishers 2008 un il $19.95
Grades: 1 2 3   E
1. Art -- Fiction
ISBN 978-1-55143-920-4; 1-55143-920-4

"Bright colors, heavy doses of humor, and puns to make readers groan fill the pages as a boy's art supplies prepare for a personality-plus party. . . . Art's endearing, off-centered features combine with google-eyed markers, crayons, boxes, brushes, tapes, scissors, and glue. . . . This lively title is sure to be a favorite of youngsters learning to appreciate both subtle humor and engaging cartoon art." SLJ

Tourville, Jacqueline
Albie's first word; a tale inspired by Albert Einstein's childhood. Jacqueline Tourville; illustrated by Wynne Evans. Schwartz & Wade books 2014 40 p. color illustrations (glb) $20.99
Grades: PreK K 1 2   E
1. Speech 2. Children 3. Speech -- Fiction
ISBN 030797894X; 9780307978936; 9780307978943
LC 2013007891

This book, by Jacqueline Tourville, is a "historical fiction picture book that provides a rare glimpse into the early childhood of Albert Einstein. . . . Three-year-old Albie has never said a single word. When his worried mother and father consult a doctor, he advises them to expose little Albie to new things: a trip to the orchestra, an astronomy lecture, a toy boat race in the park. But though Albie dances with excitement at each new experience, he remains silent." (Publisher's note)

"Spun from a remark of Albert Einstein's that he took several years to begin talking, this mostly extrapolated tale takes a silent yet expressive lad through a series of experiences: family outings, concerts, a science lecture, and a model boat race . . . An extended note introduces Einstein in greater detail and explains that while many of the story's specifics are invented, its core, his parents' fear he might never learn, is true. A reassuring episode for late bloomers, and their parents, too." Booklist

Trapani, Iza
Haunted party. Charlesbridge 2009 un il lib bdg $15.95; pa $7.95
Grades: PreK K 1 2   E
1. Counting 2. Ghost stories 3. Stories in rhyme 4. Parties -- Fiction 5. Halloween -- Fiction 6. Supernatural -- Fiction
ISBN 978-1-58089-246-9 lib bdg; 1-58089-246-9 lib bdg; 978-1-58089-247-6 pa; 1-58089-247-7 pa
LC 2008025330

In this counting book that introduces the numbers from one to ten, a ghost and his supernatural friends have a party on Halloween night.

This is a "rollicking Halloween tale. . . . Rhyming stanzas build steadily then shrink to single lines, adding to the guests' speedy departure. Humor abounds . . . in the watercolor, colored-pencil, and ink illustrations." Horn Book Guide

Tresselt, Alvin R.
Hide and seek fog; by Alvin Tresselt; illustrated by Roger Duvoisin. Lothrop, Lee & Shepard Bks. 1965 un il lib bdg $18.89; pa $6.99
Grades: PreK K 1   E
1. Fog
ISBN 0-688-51169-4 lib bdg; 0-688-07813-3 pa
A Caldecott Medal honor book, 1966

"This is . . . a mood picture book . . . describing a fog which rolls in from the sea to veil an Atlantic seacoast village for three days. The beautiful paintings . . . and the brief, poetic text sensitively and effectively evoke the atmosphere of the 'worst fog in twenty years' and depict the reactions of children and grown-ups to it." Booklist

★ **White** snow, bright snow; by Alvin Tresselt; illustrated by Roger Duvoisin. Lothrop, Lee & Shepard Bks. 1988 un il $17.99; lib bdg $18.89; pa $6.99
Grades: PreK K 1   E
1. Snow -- Fiction
ISBN 0-688-41161-4; 0-688-51161-9 lib bdg; 0-688-08294-7 pa
LC 88-10018

A reissue of the title first published 1947
Awarded the Caldecott Medal, 1948
When it begins to look, feel, and smell like snow, everyone prepares for a winter blizzard

Trewin, Trudie
I lost my kisses; [by] Trudie Trewin; illustrations by Nick Bland. Scholastic 2008 32p il $14.99
Grades: PreK K   E
1. Kissing -- Fiction 2. Lost and found possessions -- Fiction
ISBN 0-545-05557-1; 978-0-545-05557-4

Matilda Rose loves to kiss hello, goodbye, good morning, and goodnight, but on the day her father is to return from a trip, she cannot find her kisses anywhere, despite knowing how they feel, taste, and sound.

"Bland's striking black-and-white pencil illustrations have splashes of watercolor highlighting the wide-eyed cow's polka-dotted tights as she searches high and low. . . . Matilda Rose has a whimsical charm." SLJ

Trottier, Maxine

★ **Migrant**; pictures by Isabelle Arsenault. Groundwood Books/ House of Anansi Press 2011 un il $18.95
Grades: K 1 2 3   E
  1. Mennonites -- Fiction 2. Migrant agricultural laborers -- Fiction
  ISBN 978-0-88899-975-7; 0-88899-975-5

"Each spring Anna leaves her home in Mexico and travels north with her family where they will work on farms harvesting fruits and vegetables. Sometimes she feels like a bird, flying north in the spring and south in the fall. Sometimes she feels like a jack rabbit living in an abandoned burrow, as her family moves into an empty house near the fields. But most of all she wonders what it would be like to stay in one place. The Low German-speaking Mennonites from Mexico are a unique group of migrants who moved from Canada to Mexico in the 1920s and became an important part of the farming community there. But it has become increasingly difficult for them to earn a livelihood, and so they come back to Canada each year as migrant workers in order to survive." (Publisher's note) "Ages four to seven." (Quill Quire)

"Trottier frames the outlook of a child in a family of migrant workers within a series of metaphors and similes. Anna sees herself as part of a flock that travels its seasonal round from Mexico to Canada like migratory geese. . . . Arsenault's mixed-media images of doll-like figures in overalls and long print dresses, hats and headscarves effectively capture both Anna's sense of isolation and the close family ties that keep her immediate family and larger community together. [Anna] . . . belongs to a group of Low German-speaking Mennonite farmers who emigrated to Mexico in the early 20th century but kept their Canadian citizenship and still travel northward each summer. . . . [This] is a moving, inventive and thoughtful look at a way of life many people share" Kirkus

The **paint** box; [illustrations by] Stella East. Fitzhenry & Whiteside 2003 32p il $16.95; pa $8.95
Grades: 2 3 4   E
  1. Painters 2. Artists -- Fiction 3. Venice (Italy) -- Fiction
  ISBN 1-55041-801-7; 1-55041-808-4 pa

LC 2003-464840

"'Long ago in Venice there was a girl named Marietta who loved to paint. She was the daughter of the great artist Tintoretto.' With her father's help, she disguises herself as a boy in order to explore the art world of Venice. . . . Marietta befriends an enslaved cabin boy and they spend their days sketching and exploring the city, and telling one another about their lives. When it is time for Piero's owner to leave the city, Marietta helps him escape and return to his family. This poignant tale has its roots in historical fact. . . . Trottier's fictional story about Marietta and her friend seems plausible, due in part to her descriptive and expressive writing style. East's painterly illustrations are magnificent. Each spread captures the feeling of Renaissance Venice and supports the accompanying text." SLJ

Tryon, Leslie

Albert's birthday; written and illustrated by Leslie Tryon. Atheneum Bks. for Young Readers 1999 un il $16; pa $6.99
Grades: PreK K 1 2   E
  1. Animals -- Fiction 2. Birthdays -- Fiction
  ISBN 0-689-82296-0; 0-689-85251-7 pa

LC 98-36621

Patsy Pig plans a surprise birthday party for her friend Albert, giving careful instructions to all their friends, but she forgets to invite the guest of honor

"The prose is personable and engaging, and colorful, exquisitely detailed illustrations portray the animal cast in such familiar human settings as a classroom and a town." Booklist
  Other titles about Albert are:
  Albert's alphabet (1991)
  Albert's ballgame (1996)
  Albert's Christmas (1997)
  Albert's field trip (1993)
  Albert's Halloween (1998)
  Albert's play (1992)
  Albert's Thanksgiving (1994)

Ts'o, Pauline, 1961-

Whispers of the wolf; written and illustrated by Pauline Ts'o; foreword by Rosemary Lonewolf; preface, Vivian Arviso Deloria. Wisdom Tales 2015 40 p. color illustrations (hardcover : alk. paper) $16.95
Grades: PreK K 1 2 3   E
  1. Wolves -- Fiction 2. Pueblo Indians -- Fiction 3. Wildlife conservation -- Fiction 4. Human-animal relationship -- Fiction 5. Wildlife rescue -- Fiction 6. Human-animal relationships -- Fiction 7. Pueblo Indians -- Southwest, New -- Fiction 8. Indians of North America -- Southwest, New -- Fiction
  ISBN 9781937786458

LC 2015022016

This book, written and illustrated by Pauline Ts'o, "is a beautiful picture book set around 500 years ago among the Pueblo Indians of the desert Southwest. A heartwarming piece of historical fiction, it weaves together themes of community, tradition, self-esteem, and respect for all life, creating a realistic portrait of a culture that continues to exert a vibrant, living influence today." (Publisher's note)

"Ts'o has written a rare and beautiful book about Native Americans that is free of clichés and stereotypes and belongs in every library collection." Booklist
  Includes bibliographical references

Tsiang, Sarah

A **flock** of shoes; story by Sarah Tsiang; art by Qin Leng. Annick Press 2010 un il lib bdg $19.95; pa $8.95
Grades: PreK K 1 2   E
  1. Shoes -- Fiction 2. Seasons -- Fiction
  ISBN 978-1-55451-249-2 lib bdg; 1-55451-249-2 lib bdg; 978-1-55451-248-5 pa; 1-55451-248-4 pa

"At the end of summer, Abby refuses to give up her sandals despite all her mother's reasons for letting them go. But while Abby's playing at the park . . . her flip-flops slip off her feet and fly away, joining other sandals headed southward in a V formation. At first, she grudgingly puts on boots and wears them all winter, though she imagines her sandals vacationing at the beach and sending her fond postcards. . . . Tsiang expresses childlike emotions and thoughts in a simple text that reads aloud well. Washed with cheerful colors, Leng's cartoon-style drawings interpret the story with originality and wit." Booklist

Tuck, Justin

Home-field advantage; illustrated by Leonardo Rodriguez. Simon & Schuster 2011 il $16.99
Grades: PreK K 1   E
  1. Football players 2. Hair -- Fiction 3. Twins -- Fiction 4. Football -- Fiction 5. Siblings -- Fiction 6. Family life -- Fiction
  ISBN 978-1-4424-0369-7; 1-4424-0369-1

LC 2010043733

New York Giants defensive end Justin Tuck observes that growing up with five sisters helped make him tough, and tells of when twins Christale and Tiffany gave him an unforgettable haircut.

"The plot is realistic and believable. Rodriguez's comical watercolor illustrations match well with the text." SLJ

Tucker, Kathy

The **seven** Chinese sisters; written by Kathy Tucker; illustrated by Grace Lin. Whitman, A. 2003 un il $15.95; pa $6.99

Grades: K 1 2 3   E

1. China -- Fiction 2. Dragons -- Fiction 3. Sisters -- Fiction
ISBN 0-8075-7309-4; 0-8075-7310-5 pa

LC 2002-11330

When a dragon snatches the youngest of seven talented Chinese sisters, the other six come to her rescue

Lin "expertly captures the drama and humor of the story with delightful paintings that reveal lovely Chinese landscapes and a quirky, not-too-scary dragon. A wonderful read-aloud." Booklist

Tucker, Lindy

Porkelia; a pig's tale. written and illustrated by Lindy Tucker. Mackinac Island Press, Inc. 2011 il $9.95

Grades: PreK K 1 2   E

1. Stories in rhyme 2. Pigs -- Fiction 3. Dancers -- Fiction
ISBN 978-1-934133-28-6; 1-934133-28-0

Porkelia has always wanted to be a dancer, but not just any dancer—a Rockette! But Porkelia is a pig. Everyone laughs and makes fun of her, but she sets out on her own to be discovered and become famous.

"Tucker tells this appealing sty-to-Broadway fame story with an appealingly silly, rhyming text. . . . The spare pictures, rendered in clean black lines and pink accents, extend the fun." Booklist

Tudor, Tasha

1 is one. Simon & Schuster Bks. for Young Readers 2000 un il $16

Grades: PreK K 1 2   E

1. Counting
ISBN 0-689-82843-8

LC 99-31290

A reissue of the title first published 1956 by Oxford University Press
A Caldecott Medal honor book, 1957

"The author-artist has with characteristic charming quaintness written and illustrated a counting book. Delicately tinted, decoratively bordered pictures and rhyming lines of text count from one to twenty." Booklist

Corgiville fair; by Tasha Tudor. Little, Brown & Company 1998 1v. (unpg) col. ill. $12.23; pa $6.95

Grades: PreK K 1 2   E

1. Fairs -- Fiction 2. Animals -- Fiction 3. Picture books for children 4. Cats -- Fiction 5. Dogs -- Fiction
ISBN 0-316-85312-7; 0-316-85329-1 pa; 9780316853125

LC 97029665

This picture book takes place in the "village of Corgiville, 'west of New Hampshire and east of Vermont,' the population of cats, rabbits, corgis ('enchanted' small dogs the color of foxes), and boggarts (toy-like 'trolls') turn out for the annual country fair. The plan of young Caleb Brown, a corgi, to ride his goat Josephine in the Grand Race, is almost foiled by rival Edgar Tomcat who feeds Caleb a soporific hot dog and stuffs Josephine with mince pies and cigars. But Caleb's resourceful buddy Merton Boggart gets the groaning Josephine going by feeding her the rockets for his fireworks display. . . . Caleb wins the race, leads the grand parade, starts off the Virginia Reel with Miss Corgiville, . . . and applauds Merton's closing fireworks display." (Kirkus)

Tullet, Hervé

10 times 10; Herve Tullet. Abrams 2014 128 p. illustrations $15.95

Grades: 1 2   E

1. Counting -- Fiction
ISBN 1849762473; 9781849762472

LC 2013949412

In this children's book, author Herve Tullet asks "[h]ow many ways can you count to 10? With numbers, fingers, paints? How about with racing cars or with a fairy tale? In fact, you can do it almost any way you like!" (Publisher's note) "A wordless retelling of the Genesis creation story adds elements of nature through to Adam, Eve, and the serpent. Cubist-inspired art is achieved by adding multiple body parts to a giant pink head." (Bulletin of the Center for Children's Books)

"Tullet counts to 10 in 10 wildly eccentric ways, channeling the energy of a messy preschool art room... A riff on the Biblical story of creation and a fairy tale about two princes, three princesses, four witches, and so on are just a couple of the ways Tullet takes something as simple as counting to 10 and uses it as a springboard for loopy, creative experimentation." PW

The **book** with a hole. Abrams 2011 un il pa $14.50

Grades: PreK K 1 2   E

1. Imagination -- Fiction
ISBN 978-1-85437-946-7; 1-85437-946-1

"As the title suggests, this oversize book has a die-cut hole—a large semicircle is cut out of the book's spine, which becomes a full circle in the center of the book when opened, serving different interactive functions in a series of spare b&w scenes. . . . Tullet's simple innovation allows readers to become active participants in the experience of reading." Publ Wkly

The **game** of finger worms. Phaedon Press 2011 un il bd bk $8.95

Grades: PreK K   E

1. Games 2. Board books for children
ISBN 978-0-7148-6071-8; 0-7148-6071-9

LC 201128905

Invites the reader to complete the illustrations by drawing eyes and a mouth on one's finger and inserting it through the die-cut hole in each page as a "finger worm."

The book has "whimsical art done in bold watercolors. The [book is] appropriate for hands-on learning in early education settings or one-on-one with an adult to help youngsters develop finger dexterity and fine motor skills." SLJ

The **game** of let's go! Phaedon Press 2011 un il bd bk $8.95

Grades: PreK K   E

1. Games 2. Board books for children
ISBN 978-0-7148-6075-6; 0-7148-6075-1

LC 201128905C

Invites the reader to close one's eyes and follow a felt line through the book with one's finger, around and through various die-cut holes imagining where the journey leads.

The book has "whimsical art done in bold watercolors. The [book is] appropriate for hands-on learning in early education settings or one-on-one with an adult to help youngsters develop finger dexterity and fine motor skills." SLJ

The **game** of light. Phaidon 2011 un il bd bk $8.95

Grades: PreK K   E

1. Games 2. Board books for children
ISBN 978-0-7148-6189-0; 0-7148-6189-8

This board book "makes for a fun nighttime activity as simple cutout shapes on each page can be illuminated with a flashlight. . . .The [book has] whimsical art done in bold watercolors. The [book is] appropriate for hands-on learning in early education settings or one-on-one with an adult to help youngsters develop finger dexterity and fine motor skills." SLJ

The game of mix and match. Phaidon 2011 un il bd bk $8.95
Grades: PreK K   **E**
   1. Games   2. Board books for children
   ISBN 978-0-7148-6073-2; 0-7148-6073-5

In this board book, "each page contains four flaps that children can mix and match to create more than 50 pictures among familiar objects such as hearts, stars, and the sun. . . .The [book has] whimsical art done in bold watercolors. The [book is] appropriate for hands-on learning in early education settings or one-on-one with an adult to help youngsters develop finger dexterity and fine motor skills." SLJ

The game of mix-up art. Phaidon 2011 un il bd bk $8.95
Grades: PreK K   **E**
   1. Games   2. Board books for children
   ISBN 978-0-7148-6188-3; 0-7148-6188-X

This board book "contains colorful shapes and obscure patterns among zigzagged cut-page flaps that create new artwork and designs as different flaps are turned. . . . The [book has] whimsical art done in bold watercolors. The [book is] appropriate for hands-on learning in early education settings or one-on-one with an adult to help youngsters develop finger dexterity and fine motor skills." SLJ

The game of patterns. Phaidon 2011 un il bd bk $8.95
Grades: PreK K   **E**
   1. Games   2. Board books for children
   ISBN 978-0-7148-6187-6; 0-7148-6187-1

This board book "provides the opportunity to point out as many patterns and similarities children can find on each spread. They increase in difficulty as the book progresses. The [book has] whimsical art done in bold watercolors. The [book is] appropriate for hands-on learning in early education settings or one-on-one with an adult to help youngsters develop finger dexterity and fine motor skills." SLJ

★ **I** Am Blop! Hervé Tullet. Phaidon Inc Ltd 2013 110 p. col. ill. (hardcover) $19.95
Grades: PreK K   **E**
   1. Color   2. Shape
   ISBN 0714865338; 9780714865331

LC 2012285660

This children's story, by Hervé Tullet, explores "the world of Blop! A Blop is a simple shape, somewhere between a flower and a butterfly, a sponge and a drawing of a little man -- above all Blop is whatever you want it to be . . . explor[ing] many concepts encountered for the first time by young children, including up and down, single and plural, individual and family, city and countryside etc." (Publisher's note)

"The latest in a series of offbeat, imaginative creations by renowned French artist Tullet will intrigue children and encourage them to think outside the blop... Any child bored with standard activity-book fare will love using this open-ended, imaginative tool for creating their own universe...[T]aps directly into the heart of a child's natural creativity by avoiding the didactic explanatory tone of similar books." Kirkus

Mix it up! Hervé Tullet; translated by Christopher Franceschelli. Chronicle Books 2014 56 p. color illustrations (reinforced) $15.99

Grades: PreK K 1   **E**
   1. Art   2. Color   3. Imagination -- Fiction
   ISBN 9781452137353; 1452137358

LC 2014006665

In this book by Hervé Tullet, readers will "follow the artist's simple instructions, and suddenly colors appear, mix, splatter, and vanish in a world powered only by the reader's imagination." It "sets readers on an extraordinary interactive journey all within the printed page." (Publisher's note)

"Franceschelli is a talented translator, and the book's conversational tone is an important part of its charm. It's an effective presentation of basic color mixing, and great fun for paint lovers in places where paints can't be used." Pub Wkly

★ **Press** here; [translated by Christopher Franceschelli] Chronicle Books 2011 un il
Grades: PreK K 1 2   **E**
   1. Toy and movable books   2. Imagination -- Fiction
   ISBN 0-8118-7954-2; 978-0-8118-7954-5

LC 2010035579

Original French edition 2010

Instructs the reader on how to interact with the illustrations to create imaginative images.

"Tullet's brilliant creation proves that books need not lose out to electronic wizardry. . . . The fun continues as the dots proliferate, travel around the page, grow and shrink in response to commands to clap, shake, and tilt the book, etc." Publ Wkly

Turk, Evan

★ The **storyteller**; Evan Turk. Atheneum Books for Young Readers 2016 48 p. color illustrations (hardcover) $18.99
Grades: 1 2 3 4 5 6   **E**
   1. Morocco -- Fiction   2. Droughts -- Fiction   3. Storytelling -- Fiction   4. Jinn -- Fiction   5. Storytellers -- Fiction   6. Droughts -- Morocco -- Fiction
   ISBN 1481435183; 9781481435185

LC 2014044090

In this children's story, by Evan Turk, "long, long ago, like a pearl around a grain of sand, the Kingdom of Morocco formed at the edge of the great, dry Sahara. . . . But as the kingdom grew, the people forgot the dangers of the desert, and they forgot about the storytellers, too. All but one young boy, who came to the Great Square for a drink and found something that quenched his thirst even better: wonderful stories." (Publisher's note)

"Turk's layered ode to storytelling's magic begs to be shared aloud with a group, though the detailed art merits close inspection. A concluding author's note on storytelling traditions contextualizes this beautiful, original folktale." Booklist

Includes bibliographical references.

Turnbull, Victoria

Kings of the Castle; by Victoria Turnbull. Candlewick Press 2017 44 p. color illustrations $16.99
   Grades: PreK K 1   **E**
   1. Friendship -- Fiction   2. Imagination -- Fiction
   ISBN 0763692956; 9780763692957

In this picture book, by Victoria Turnbull, "George didn't want to waste the night moon bathing. He wanted to build a sand castle that would turn any monster green with envy! But when George meets the strangest creature he has ever seen, the night takes an unexpected turn." (Publisher's note)

Turnbull, Victoria

  Pandora; Victoria Turnbull. Clarion Books, Houghton Mifflin Harcourt 2017 32 p. color illustrations (hardcover) $16.99

  Grades: PreK K 1 2   E

  1. Birds -- Fiction 2. Foxes -- Fiction 3. Nature -- Fiction 4. Loneliness -- Fiction

  ISBN 9780544947337

LC 2016016163

  In this children's book, by Victoria Turnbull, "Pandora lives alone, in a world of broken things. She makes herself a handsome home, but no one ever comes to visit. Then one day something falls from the sky . . . a bird with a broken wing. Little by little, Pandora helps the bird grow stronger. . . . The bird begins to fly again, and always comes back--bringing seeds and flowers and other small gifts. But then one day, it flies away and doesn't return." (Publisher's note)

Turner, Ann Warren

  ★ **Dust** for dinner; story by Ann Turner; pictures by Robert Barrett. HarperCollins Pubs. 1995 64p il (I can read book) hardcover o.p. pa $3.99

  Grades: K 1 2 3   E

  1. Farm life -- Fiction 2. Family life -- Fiction 3. Great Depression, 1929-1939 -- Fiction

  ISBN 0-06-023377-X lib bdg; 0-06-444225-X pa

LC 93-34634

  Jake narrates the story of his family's life in the Oklahoma dust bowl and the journey from their ravaged farm to California during the Great Depression

  "Turner takes a sad episode in history and fashions it into a story that has some depth as well as some drama. . . . Realistic, nicely executed illustrations decorate every page." Booklist

Turner, Pamela S.

  ★ **Hachiko**; written by Pamela S. Turner; illustrated by Yan Nascimbene. Houghton Mifflin 2004 un il $15

  Grades: K 1 2 3   E

  1. Dogs -- Fiction 2. Japan -- Fiction

  ISBN 0-618-14094-8

LC 2002-155546

  This "picture book pays tribute to one of the world's lesser-known animal heroes: Hachiko, a dog who kept vigil for nearly 10 years at a Tokyo train station, waiting for his deceased master to return from work. Turner unfolds this poignant true story in the natural, unaffected voice of Kentaro, a fictional little boy, who wonders at the dog's unswerving devotion. Unobtrusive details evoke a sense of place . . . as does Nascimbene's spare line-and-watercolor artwork, reminiscent of Japanese woodblock prints. . . . This will resonate with any child who has loved a dog and been loved in return." Booklist

Tusa, Tricia

  ★ **Follow** me; written and illustrated by Tricia Tusa. Harcourt Children's Books 2011 un il $16.99

  Grades: PreK K 1 2   E

  1. Color -- Fiction 2. Imagination -- Fiction

  ISBN 978-0-547-27201-6; 0-547-27201-4

LC 2010009061

  A girl travels through an imaginative world of colors by way of a swing.

  "The beautiful etchings are rich in color and alive with vibrant line. . . . A glorious visual meditation on light, color and home for even the smallest child and artist." Kirkus

Twohy, Mike

  Mouse & Hippo; Mike Twohy. Simon & Schuster 2017 32 p. color illustrations (ebook) $15.99; (hardback) $17.99

  Grades: PreK K 1 2   E

  1. Mice -- Fiction 2. Painting -- Fiction 3. Friendship -- Fiction 4. Hippopotamus -- Fiction

  ISBN 9781481451253; 9781481451246

LC 2016010821

  In this picture book, by Mike Twohy, "Mouse offers to paint a portrait of his new friend Hippo, but Hippo doesn't quite fit on Mouse's canvas. Still Hippo is delighted. In return, Hippo returns the favor for his new friend in the best way he knows how. In a surprising story sure to cause giggles, picture book readers will ask for this book over and over again!" (Publisher's note)

  "While there are plenty of picture books that feature unlikely friendships, young listeners will be pleased to make the acquaintance of these two cheerful creatures and, quite possibly, inspired to view the world in engaging new ways." Kirkus

  Oops, Pounce, Quick, Run! An Alphabet Caper. Mike Twohy. Balzer + Bray 2016 32 p. color illustrations $17.99

  Grades: K 1 2 3 4   E

  1. Alphabet 2. Dogs -- Fiction 3. Mice -- Fiction

  ISBN 0062377000; 9780062377005

  Geisel Honor Book (2017)

  This children's book, by Mike Twohy, is "an alphabetical romp that tells what happens when Dog accidentally rolls his ball into Mouse's house. Dog is irritated about the missing ball and winds up chasing Mouse out of his den and all through the house. The story resolves with Mouse wrapping the ball up and giving it to Dog." (Publisher's note)

  "The crisp, uncluttered design and playful story line make letter identification plenty of fun." Booklist

  ★ **Poindexter** makes a friend. Simon & Schuster Books for Young Readers 2011 un il $15.99

  Grades: K 1 2   E

  1. Pigs -- Fiction 2. Shyness -- Fiction 3. Turtles -- Fiction 4. Libraries -- Fiction 5. Friendship -- Fiction 6. Books and reading -- Fiction

  ISBN 978-1-4424-0965-1; 1-4424-0965-7

LC 2010018489

  Poindexter is a very shy pig who, while helping out at the library meets a turtle who is also shy, and together they read a book about making a friend in four easy steps.

  "The watercolor illustrations in this gentle story are done in a cartoon style. Humorous details . . . will bring smiles. The pals' pleasure in sharing books with a dim-eyed mole and each other is palpable. . . . This reassuring story will envelop youngsters like a warm, cozy blanket." SLJ

Uchida, Yoshiko

  The **bracelet**; story by Yoshiko Uchida; illustrated by Joanna Yardley. Philomel Bks. 1993 un il $17.99; pa $6.99

  Grades: K 1 2 3   E

  1. Friendship -- Fiction 2. World War, 1939-1945 -- Fiction 3. Japanese Americans -- Evacuation and relocation, 1942-1945 -- Fiction

  ISBN 0-399-22503-X; 0-698-11390-X pa

LC 92-2619[6]

  Emi, a Japanese American in the second grade, is sent with her family to an internment camp during World War II, but the loss of the bracelet her best friend has given her proves that she does not need a physical reminder of that friendship

This "is a gentle, honest introduction to the treatment of the Japanese-Americans during the war, and Yardley's delicate pencil-and-watercolor paintings are cleanly drawn and richly colored." Bull Cent Child Books

Udry, Janice May

The **moon** jumpers; Pictures by Maurice Sendak. Harper 1959 31 p. ill. (hardcover) $17.95

Grades: PreK K 1 2   E

1. Night -- Fiction

ISBN 0060284609; 9780060284602

LC 58007757

"A full moon on a summer night turns an ordinary landscape into a world of mystery and the uninhibited caperings of children into a joyous dance. There are black-and-white drawings and brief text in between double-page spreads in full ... color." (Horn Bk)

★ A **tree** is nice; pictures by Marc Simont, Harper & Row 1956 un il $17.99; lib bdg $18.89; pa $6.99

Grades: PreK K 1 2   E

1. Trees -- Fiction

ISBN 0-06-026155-2; 0-06-026156-0 lib bdg; 0-06-443147-9 pa

Awarded the Caldecott Medal, 1957

"In childlike terms and in enticing pictures, colored and black and white, author and artist set forth reasons why trees are nice to have around—trees fill up the sky, they make everything beautiful, cats get away from dogs in them, leaves come down and can be played in, and trees are nice to climb in, to hang a swing in, or to plant. A picture book sure to please young children." Booklist

Uegaki, Chieri

Rosie and Buttercup; written by Chieri Uegaki; illustrated by Stéphane Jorisch. Kids Can Press 2008 un il $17.95

Grades: PreK K 1 2   E

1. Sisters -- Fiction

ISBN 978-1-55337-997-3

"At first Rosie's perfect life seems even more perfect when little sister Buttercup arrives. . . . In time, Rosie becomes disenchanted and gives Buttercup away—to her sitter, Oxford. . . . Predictably, she is soon sorry. . . . Uegaki's assured text assumes an intelligent reader. . . . Jorisch's watercolor illustrations, uncluttered but dense with patterns, are crisp against generous fields of white space." Publ Wkly

Suki's kimono; written by Chieri Uegaki; illustrated by Stephane Jorisch. Kids Can Press 2003 un il hardcover o.p. pa $7.95

Grades: PreK K 1 2   E

1. Japanese -- Fiction

ISBN 1-55337-752-4 pa; 1-55337-084-8

LC 2003-495264

"On her first day of first grade [Suki] chooses to wear her beloved Japanese kimono to school, despite the objections of her older sisters and the initial laughter of other children on the playground. . . . Her day ends in triumph, with her teacher and classmates won over by her impromptu dance performance. . . . This is an appealing story of courage and independence. Delicate, playful watercolor-and-ink illustrations perfectly capture the child's neighborhood and the characters' facial expressions." SLJ

Uhlberg, Myron

Dad, Jackie, and me; illustrated by Colin Bootman. Peachtree Publishers 2005 un il $16.95

Grades: K 1 2 3   E

1. Baseball players 2. Army officers 3. Deaf -- Fiction 4. Baseball -- Fiction 5. Father-son relationship -- Fiction 6. Brooklyn (New

York, N.Y.) -- Fiction

ISBN 1-56145-329-3

LC 2004-16711

In Brooklyn, New York, in 1947, a boy learns about discrimination and tolerance as he and his deaf father share their enthusiasm over baseball and the Dodgers' first baseman, Jackie Robinson.

"Bootman's lovely watercolor paintings add detail and wistful nostalgia. . . . [Readers] will appreciate the story's insightful treatment of deafness as viewed through the eyes of a child." SLJ

The **sound** of all things; by Myron Uhlberg; illustrated by Ted Papoulas. Peachtree Publishers 2016 36 p. color illustrations $17.95

Grades: 1 2 3 4   E

1. Deaf -- Fiction 2. Parents -- Fiction 3. Brooklyn (New York, N.Y.) -- Fiction 4. Coney Island (New York, N.Y.) -- Fiction 5. Sounds, Words for -- Fiction 6. Brooklyn (New York, N.Y.) -- History -- 20th century -- Fiction 7. Coney Island (New York, N.Y.) -- History -- 20th century -- Fiction

ISBN 1561458333; 9781561458332

LC 2015030683

This book, by Myron Uhlberg, illustrated by Ted Papoulas, presents a "day in the life of a young hearing boy and his deaf parents. The Brooklyn family takes an outing to Coney Island, where they enjoy the rides, the food, and the sights. The father longs to know about how everything sounds, and his son does his best to interpret the noisy surroundings through sign language but finds it difficult." (Publisher's note)

"The narrator deftly and respectfully describes his conflicting feelings of love and resentment, sometimes envying other children who don't have to interpret for their fathers, but love wins out... A tender demonstration of how familial love is like translation—inexact, difficult, and beautiful." Kirkus

★ A **storm** called Katrina; written by Myron Uhlberg; illustrated by Colin Bootman. Peachtree 2010 un il $17.95

Grades: 1 2 3 4   E

1. Floods -- Fiction 2. African Americans -- Fiction 3. New Orleans (La.) -- Fiction 4. Hurricane Katrina, 2005 -- Fiction

ISBN 978-1-56145-591-1; 1-56145-591-1

LC 2009024518

When flood waters submerge their New Orleans neighborhood in the aftermath of Hurricane Katrina, a young cornet player and his parents evacuate their home and struggle to survive and stay together.

"Bootman's dramatic oil paintings and the boy's first-person narration provide realistic immediacy. . . . Readers are in for a deeply personal and sometimes uncomfortable look at a disaster whose ramifications are still being felt." Publ Wkly

Uman, Jennifer

Jemmy button; Jennifer Uman, Valerio Vidali. Candlewick Press 2013 48 p. (reinforced) $16.99

Grades: K 1 2 3   E

ISBN 9780763664879

LC 2012942662

"Exchanged for the single mother-of-pearl button that gave him his nickname, an indigenous Tierra del Fuegan boy named Orundellico spent many years in England in the early 1800s as part of a failed experiment in forced civilization. Less a biography than an attempt to represent this alienating experience from Jemmy's point of view, it is distinguished by lyrical prose-poetry...and intensely creative and beautifully conceived paintings." Publ Wkly

Underwood, Deborah

★ **Bad** bye, good bye; written by Deborah Underwood; illustrated by Jonathan Bean. Houghton Mifflin Books for Children, Houghton Mifflin Harcourt 2014 32 p. $16.99

Grades: PreK K 1 2   E

1. Stories in rhyme 2. Moving -- Fiction 3. Moving, Household -- Fiction

ISBN 0547928521; 9780547928524

                LC 2013017616

In this children's book, written by Deborah Underwood and illustrated by Jonathan Bean, "a boy and his family are packing up their old home, and the morning feels scary and sad. But when he arrives at his new home, an evening of good byes awaits: bye to new friends, bye to glowing fireflies, bye to climbing trees." (Publisher's note)

"An upset little boy sees nothing good about his family's move: "Bad truck / Bad guy / Bad wave / Bad bye." But the journey to and exploration of his new house are full of good experiences, including making a friend. Bean's dynamic ink and Prismacolor-tone illustrations creatively highlight the passage of time, and Underwood's simple rhymes skillfully address common emotions about moving." Horn Book

A **balloon** for Isabel; illustrations by Laura Rankin. Greenwillow Books 2010 un il $16.99

Grades: K 1 2   E

1. School stories 2. Candy -- Fiction 3. Balloons -- Fiction 4. Porcupines -- Fiction

ISBN 978-0-06-177987-9; 0-06-177987-3

                LC 2009018759

As graduation day approaches, Isabel tries to convince her teacher that she and Walter, both porcupines, should receive balloons on the big day just like the other children.

"Illustrations full of color and personality add to the story's depth and appeal. Authentic dialogue, a touch of humor, and Isabel's ingenious invention make this title of desire and determination a keeper." SLJ

The **Christmas** quiet book; by Deborah Underwood; illustrated by Renata Liwska. Houghton Mifflin Books for Children 2012 32 p. $12.99

Grades: PreK K 1   E

1. Christmas 2. Quietude -- Fiction 3. Sound -- Fiction 4. Animals -- Fiction 5. Christmas -- Fiction

ISBN 0547558635; 9780547558639

                LC 2011040920

In this children's book by Deborah Underwood, illustrated by Renata Liwska, "the holidays are filled with joyful noise. But Christmas is sometimes wrapped in quiet: 'Searching for presents quiet,' 'Getting caught quiet,' and 'Hoping for a snow day quiet.'. . . The book features "soft colored pencil illustrations of bunnies, bears, and more." (Publisher's note)

Here comes Santa Cat; by Deborah Underwood; pictures by Claudia Rueda. Dial Books for Young Readers, an imprint of Penguin Group (USA) Inc. 2014 88 p. color illustrations (hardcover) $16.99

Grades: PreK K 1 2   E

1. Cats -- Fiction 2. Gifts -- Fiction 3. Humorous fiction 4. Santa Claus -- Fiction 5. Conduct of life -- Fiction 6. Humorous stories

ISBN 0803741006; 9780803741003

                LC 2013035538

In this children's book, by Deborah Underwood, "Cat has a hunch he's not on Santa's 'nice' list. Which means? No presents for Cat. So he tries to be good, but children, it seems, aren't wild for his brand of gift-giving. Still, Cat might surprise himself, and best of all, he may just get to meet the man in the red suit himself--and receive a holiday surprise of his own." (Publisher's note)

"Naughty Cat (Here Comes the Easter Cat) figures that if he dresses up as Santa Claus, he can give himself a present. But he quickly abandons the idea when he realizes Santa's job entails not only getting sooty but also delivering gifts to others. Underwood and Rueda's spot-on use of comedic timing, page turns, and layout creates another holiday winner." Horn Book

★ **Here** comes the Easter Cat! by Deborah Underwood; pictures by Claudia Rueda. Dial Books for Young Readers 2014 80 p. (hardcover) $16.99

Grades: PreK K 1 2   E

1. Cats 2. Easter bunny 3. Humorous fiction 4. Cats -- Fiction 5. Humorous stories 6. Easter Bunny -- Fiction

ISBN 0803739397; 9780803739390

                LC 2012038134

This book, by Deborah Underwood and illustrated by Claudia Rueda, tells the story of a cat that attempts to deliver eggs on Easter. "He dons his sparkly suit, jumps on his Harley, and roars off into the night. But it turns out delivering Easter eggs is hard work. And it doesn't leave much time for naps (of which Cat has taken five--no, seven). So when a pooped-out Easter Bunny shows up, and with a treat for Cat, what will Cat do?" (Publisher's note)

"In this witty offering, Cat is unhappy about the Easter Bunny's arrival. The text addresses jealous Cat directly, and he responds using placards, humorous expressions, and body language. Rueda expertly uses white space and page turns to focus attention on Cat and the repartee. Underwood's knowledgeable authorial voice and Rueda's loosely sketched, textured ink and colored-pencil illustrations make this an entertaining tale." Horn Book

Other titles about Cat are:

Here comes Santa Cat (2014)
Here comes the Tooth Fairy Cat (2015)
Here comes Valentine Cat (2016)
Here comes Teacher Cat (2017)

Here comes the Tooth Fairy Cat; by Deborah Underwood; illustrated by Claudia Rueda. Dial Books 2015 96 p. (hardcover) $16.99

Grades: PreK K 1 2   E

1. Cats -- Fiction 2. Mice -- Fiction 3. Humorous stories 4. Tooth fairy -- Fiction

ISBN 0525427740; 9780525427742

                LC 2014025751

In this children's book by Deborah Underwood, illustrated by Claudia Rueda, "when Cat loses a tooth, the Tooth Fairy delivers a wholly unwanted sidekick: a mouse. Together, Cat and Mouse are tasked with running a few Tooth Fairy-related errands—a challenge, since Mouse is just as competitive and mischievous and hilariously self-involved as Cat. The stakes rise and so does the deadpan humor, culminating in a satisfying surprise." (Publisher's note)

Here comes Valentine Cat; Deborah Underwood' illustrated by Claudia Rueda. Dial Books for Young Readers 2016 88 p. color illustrations (hardcover) $16.99

Grades: PreK K 1 2   E

1. Cats -- Fiction 2. Dogs -- Fiction 3. Humorous stories 4. Valentine's Day -- Fiction

ISBN 0525429158; 9780525429159

                LC 2014048401

In this children's book by Deborah Underwood, illustrated by Claudia Rueda, "Cat does NOT like Valentine's Day. No way is he making anyone a valentine--especially not . . . Dog. Dog refuses to respect the fence: He keeps tossing over old bones and hitting Cat in the head! But just as Cat's about to send Dog an angry "valentine" telling him exactly what he can do with his bones, Dog throws a ball over the fence. Cat is in for a . . . surprise in this story about being perhaps too quick to judge." (Publisher's note)

"The humorous ink and color pencil illustrations of the stout, sand-colored kitty will endear Cat to young readers, and they will appreciate the lesson Cat learns."

Interstellar Cinderella; Deborah Underwood; illustrated by Meg Hunt. Chronicle Books LLC 2015 32 p. color illustrations (alk. paper) $16.99
Grades: PreK K   E
1. Interplanetary voyages -- Fiction 2. Fairy tales 3. Stories in rhyme 4. Sex role -- Fiction 5. Mechanics -- Fiction 6. Outer space -- Fiction 7. Cinderella (Legendary character) -- Fiction
ISBN 1452125325; 9781452125329
LC 2014001505
Author Deborah Underwood and illustrator Meg Hunt present "this galactic retelling of the beloved children's story. With the help of her sidekick, a robotic mouse named Murgatroyd, she tinkers with her step-mother's household appliances, but dreams of repairing spaceships. When the royal ship has engine trouble, Interstellar Cinderella comes to the rescue. The grateful prince whisks her away to the Gravity Free Ball." (School Library Journal)

"Like Cinder for the picture-book crowd, this futuristic take on Cinderella recasts the heroine as a skilled mechanic, one who studies rocket-ship repair late into the night. With her wide eyes, pink hair, and work goggles, Hunt's Cinderella looks like she's stepped out of a contemporary indie webcomic, and her extraterrestrial world hints at mid-century illustration influences. . . . Cinderella and the prince bond after she repairs his ship (their budding friendship isn't just interplanetary but interracial, too), and when he asks her to be his bride, "She thought this over carefully./ Her family watched in panic./ 'I'm far too young for marriage,/ but I'll be your chief mechanic!'?" It's another strong showing from Underwood, and a notable debut for Hunt." PW

★ The **loud** book! illustrated by Renata Liwska. Houghton Mifflin Harcourt 2011 un il $12.99
Grades: PreK K   E
1. Day -- Fiction 2. Noise -- Fiction
ISBN 978-0-547-39008-6; 0-547-39008-4
LC 2010006784
From the blare of an alarm clock in the morning to snores and crickets in the evening, simple text explores the many loud noises one might hear during the course of a day.

"Fortified with the same charm and humor as the first book, this has enough activity and drama to elicit interesting observations and reactions from young audiences." Booklist

★ The **quiet** book; illustrated by Renata Liwska. Houghton Mifflin Books for Children 2010 un il $12.95
Grades: PreK K   E
1. Noise -- Fiction 2. Animals -- Fiction
ISBN 978-0-547-21567-9; 0-547-21567-3
From the quiet of being the first one awake in the morning to "sweet dreams quiet" when the last light is turned off, simple text explores the many kinds of quiet that can exist during the day.

"The soft, matte feel of the illustrations, created with pencil, are digitally enhanced, and are priceless. The animals' facial expressions and body language are endearing. . . . All of the scenarios are child-centric and realistic." SLJ

Ungerer, Tomi
Adelaide; the flying kangaroo. Phaidon Press 2011 un il $14.95
Grades: K 1 2   E
1. Flight -- Fiction 2. Kangaroos -- Fiction 3. Paris (France)

-- Fiction
ISBN 978-0-7148-6083-1; 0-7148-6083-2
First published 1959 by Harper
Adelaide is a little bit different to most kangaroos because most kangaroos don't have wings.

"Ungerer remains a master of suggestion: with marvelous skill, his agile pen embellishes the straightforward visual narrative, arrayed on spacious white, with a wealth of comical details of posture and countenance." Horn Book

★ **Crictor**. Harper & Row 1958 32p il $17.99; pa $6.99
Grades: PreK K 1 2   E
1. Snakes -- Fiction
ISBN 0-06-026180-3; 0-06-443044-8 pa
A story "about the boa constrictor that was sent to Madame Bodot, who lived and taught school in a little French town. . . . The boys used him for a slide and the girls for a jump-rope. When Crictor captured a burglar by coiling around him until the police came, he was awarded impressive tokens of esteem and affection of the townspeople. Engaging line drawings echo the restrained and elegant absurdities of the text." Bull Cent Child Books

★ **Otto**; the autobiography of a teddy bear. Phaidon Press 2010 un il $16.95
Grades: 1 2 3   E
1. Jews -- Fiction 2. Soldiers -- Fiction 3. Friendship -- Fiction 4. Teddy bears -- Fiction 5. Holocaust, 1933-1945 -- Fiction 6. World War, 1939-1945 -- Fiction
ISBN 978-0-7148-5766-4; 0-7148-5766-1
First published 1999 by Robert Rinehard
Otto the teddy bear belongs to David, a Jewish boy in Germany. When David and his parents are taken away by the Nazis, David gives Otto to his friend Oskar, whose father goes to war. After a bombing raid, Otto is found by an American soldier. Years later Oskar rediscovers Otto in antique store in the U.S. and David finds them too.

"Ungerer's illustrations—expressive, carefully worked paintings . . . —present some potentially scary images; parents and teachers should prepare for questions. But Otto's tranquil voice allows Ungerer to tell his story at a safe remove, and his unvarnished honesty makes this a vital account." Publ Wkly

Urban, Linda
Little Red Henry; Linda Urban, illustrated by Madeline Valentine. Candlewick Press 2015 40 p. $16.99
Grades: PreK K 1 2 3   E
1. Growth -- Fiction 2. Family life -- Fiction 3. Brothers and sisters -- Fiction
ISBN 0763661767; 9780763661762
LC 2014939355
In this children's book, written by Linda Urban and illustrated by Madeline Valentine, "Little redheaded Henry's family treats him like a baby. They dress him. They feed him. They brush his 'widdle toofers.' But he's not a baby anymore. He's a little boy who wants to do things for himself. So with his family watching anxiously from the wings, Henry sets out on a glorious day of independence." (Publisher's note)

Mouse was mad; illustrated by Henry Cole. Harcourt Children's Books 2009 un il $16
Grades: PreK K 1 2   E
1. Mice -- Fiction 2. Anger -- Fiction 3. Animals -- Fiction
ISBN 978-0-15-205337-6; 0-15-205337-9
LC 2007045081

Mouse struggles to find the right way to express his anger, modeling the behavior of Hare, Bear, Hedgehog, and Bobcat, only to discover that his own way may be the best way of all.

"Through playful language and expressive watercolors with colored pencil and ink, this story about anger management proves to be both entertaining and therapeutic." SLJ

Urbanovic, Jackie

Duck at the door. HarperCollins 2007 un il $16.99; lib bdg $17.89

Grades: PreK K 1 2   E

1. Ducks -- Fiction 2. Winter -- Fiction 3. Animals -- Fiction
ISBN 0-06-121438-8; 0-06-121439-6 lib bdg

When Max the duck decides to stay behind when his flock flies south, Irene invites him to stay with her for the winter.

"Urbanovic's animals, with their expressive, engaging facial features, take center stage in the open, cheery illustrations. . . . Great fun for storyhours." SLJ

Other titles about Max the duck are:

Duck soup (2008)

Duck and cover (2009)

Sitting duck (2010)

Urdahl, Catherine

Polka-dot fixes kindergarten; illustrated by Mai S. Kemble. Charlesbridge 2011 un il $16.95; pa $7.95; e-book $6.99

Grades: PreK K   E

1. School stories 2. Kindergarten -- Fiction
ISBN 978-1-57091-737-0; 1-57091-737-X; 978-1-57091-738-7 pa; 1-57091-738-8 pa; 978-1-60734-312-7 e-book

On the first day of kindergarten, Polka-dot uses the fix-it kit her grandpa has prepared for her to help her make a friend.

"The colorful watercolor illustrations support the text well. Kemble does a particularly good job of rendering facial expressions to mirror the children's emotions: worry, anger, hopefulness, shame, discomfort, and ultimately, kindness. Character education is becoming increasingly important in schools, and this book will make a solid addition to the resource shelf." SLJ

Usher, Sam

Rain; Sam Usher. Candlewick Press 2017 32 p. color illustrations $16.99

Grades: PreK K 1   E

1. Rain -- Fiction 2. Patience -- Fiction 3. Grandparent-grandchild relationship -- Fiction
ISBN 0763692964; 9780763692964

In this children's book, by Sam Usher, "Sam wants to go out, but it's pouring rain, so Granddad says they need to stay inside until the rain stops. Sam drinks hot chocolate and reads his books and dreams of adventures while Granddad does some paperwork. When Granddad needs to mail his letter, it's time to go out--despite the rain and floods--and Sam and Granddad have a magical adventure." (Publisher's note)

Vail, Rachel

Sometimes I'm Bombaloo; illustrated by Yumi Heo. Scholastic Press 2001 un il $15.95

Grades: PreK K 1 2   E

1. Anger -- Fiction
ISBN 0-439-08755-4

LC 99-58709

When Katie Honors feels angry and out of control, her mother helps her to be herself again

"Vail captures the intensity of emotion that children (and many adults) feel when they are angry, and then distills it with laughter. Heo

uses lots of stripes and splotches of color to match Katie's emotions. . . . Kudos to Vail and Heo for making a scary subject manageable." Booklist

Vainio, Pirkko

Who hid the Easter eggs? NorthSouth Books 2011 un il $16.95

Grades: PreK K   E

1. Eggs -- Fiction 2. Birds -- Fiction 3. Easter -- Fiction 4. Squirrels -- Fiction 5. Grandmothers -- Fiction
ISBN 978-0-7358-2304-4; 0-7358-2304-9

"A loving grandmother . . . hides her beautiful, hand-painted Easter eggs for her five grandchildren to find. The story focuses on a charming squirrel named Harry who lives in the grandmother's backyard. He is horrified to discover that a jackdaw (a European bird like a crow) has stolen all the eggs and hidden them in his nest. . . . The simple story is predictable and sweet, but the large-format watercolor illustrations . . . elevate this effort beyond the usual Easter Bunny adventure. . . . The Easter eggs are painted in traditional Ukrainian style, with tiny geometric prints and patterns that add a special touch to this story." Kirkus

Valdivia, Paloma

Up above and down below; Paloma Valdivia. Owlkids Books, Inc. 2012 32 p. col. ill., maps $15.95

Grades: PreK K   E

1. Earth 2. Geography 3. Picture books for children
ISBN 1926973399; 9781926973395

LC 2011943194

This children's picture book "highlights the notion that although different kinds of people live in different places around the world, we share many things in common. The title subtly references the Earth's northern and southern hemispheres, launching readers into a picture book with spreads characterized by a line bisecting each page into upper and lower halves." (Kirkus)

Vamos, Samantha R.

★ The **cazuela** that the farm maiden stirred. Charlesbridge 2011 un il lib bdg $17.95

Grades: PreK K 1 2   E

1. Cooking -- Fiction 2. Domestic animals -- Fiction 3. Spanish language -- Vocabulary
ISBN 978-1-58089-242-1; 1-58089-242-6

LC 2010007547

"Inspired by 'The House that Jack Built,' Vamos offers a fresh, new twist, playfully introducing Spanish into this cumulative tale. . . . Lopez's artwork, with its desert palette punctuated by brilliant primary colors and its graphic, hard edges, suggestive of folk art, is a perfect match. . . . A wonderful read-aloud, filled with merriment and conviviality." Kirkus

Van Allsburg, Chris, 1949-

★ **Ben's** dream; story and pictures by Chris Van Allsburg. Houghton Mifflin 1982 31p il lib bdg $16.95

Grades: K 1 2 3 4   E

1. Dreams -- Fiction
ISBN 0-395-32084-4

LC 81-20029

"When rain spoils Ben's ball game with Margaret, he returns to an empty house, falls asleep in his father's chair, and embarks on a dream. In a marvelous series of double-page black-and-white pictures meticulously textured with hatching, one shares Ben's voyage past such sights as the Statue of Liberty, the Sphinx, and the Mount Rushmore presidents, all with flood waters lapping about their respective chins and waists. . . . A visual tour de force." Horn Book

The **garden** of Abdul Gasazi; written and illustrated by Chris Van Allsburg. Houghton Mifflin 1979 un il lib bdg $18.95

Grades: 1 2 3 4   **E**

1. Dogs -- Fiction 2. Magic -- Fiction
ISBN 0-395-27804-X

A Caldecott Medal honor book, 1980

When the dog he is caring for runs away from Alan into the forbidden garden of a retired dog-hating magician, a spell seems to be cast over the contrary dog

The full page "lithographlike drawings are astonishing—eerie, monumental, surreal and witty all at once—and the effect of the whole is original and unforgettable." Books of the Times

★ **Jumanji**; written and illustrated by Chris Van Allsburg. 30th anniversary edition Houghton Mifflin Books for Children 2011 1 v. (unpaged) ill. (book and CD) $18.99

Grades: K 1 2 3 4   **E**

1. Play -- Fiction 2. Games -- Fiction
ISBN 9780547608389

LC 2011456885

Originally published 1981
Caldecott Medal (1982)

Left on their own for an afternoon, two bored and restless children find more excitement than they bargained for in a mysterious and mystical jungle adventure board game.

"Through the masterly use of light and shadow, the interplay of design elements, and audacious changes in perspective and composition, the artist conveys an impression of color without losing the dramatic contrast of black and white." Horn Book

The **mysteries** of Harris Burdick. Houghton Mifflin 1984 un il lib bdg $18.95

Grades: 1 2 3 4   **E**

1. Imagination -- Fiction 2. Storytelling -- Fiction
ISBN 0-395-35393-9

LC 84-9006

Presents a series of loosely related drawings each accompanied by a title and a caption which the reader may use to make up his or her own story

Rendered in the author's "signature velvet black and white . . . the pictures are nothing short of spectacular. . . . While some may find this just an excuse for handsome artwork, others will see its great potential for stretching a child's imagination. Although the book could be used in countless ways, primarily it will make storytellers of children." Booklist

★ The **Polar** Express; written and illustrated by Chris Van Allsburg. Twentieth anniversary ed.; Houghton Mifflin 2005 un il $35

Grades: PreK K 1 2 3   **E**

1. Christmas -- Fiction 2. North Pole -- Fiction 3. Santa Claus -- Fiction
ISBN 978-0-618-61169-0; 0-618-61169-X

LC 2005281613

A reissue of the title first published 1985
Awarded the Caldecott Medal, 1986

A magical train ride on Christmas Eve takes a boy to the North Pole to receive a special gift from Santa Claus.

This offers "stunning paintings in which Van Allsburg uses dark, rich colors and misty shapes in contrast with touches of bright white-gold light to create scenes, interior and exterior, that have a quality of mystery that imbues the strong composition to achieve a soft, evocative mood." Bull Cent Child Books

The **stranger**. Houghton Mifflin 1986 un il lib bdg $18.95

Grades: 1 2 3 4   **E**

1. Seasons -- Fiction
ISBN 0-395-42331-7

LC 86-15235

The enigmatic origins of the stranger Farmer Bailey hits with his truck and brings home to recuperate seem to have a mysterious relation to the weather.

"The full-color illustrations, framed in white, evoke an old-fashioned New England landscape at the end of summer; some are remarkably peaceful in tone, others slightly spooky by virtue of brooding colors, unexpected perspectives, or the stranger's peculiar expressions." Bull Cent Child Books

The **widow's** broom. Houghton Mifflin 1992 un il $18.95

Grades: 1 2 3 4   **E**

1. Magic -- Fiction 2. Witchcraft -- Fiction
ISBN 0-395-64051-2

LC 92-7110

A witch's worn-out broom serves a widow well, until her neighbors decide the thing is wicked and dangerous

"In addition to being a neatly understated piece of storytelling, this fuels Van Allsburg's best kind of illustration—darkly rounded, speckle-textured art with eerie effects." Bull Cent Child Books

The **wreck** of the Zephyr; Chris Van Allsburg. 30th anniversary edition Houghton Mifflin Harcourt 2013 un color illustrations hbk $18.99

Grades: 1 2 3 4   **E**

1. Fantasy fiction 2. Imagination -- Fiction 3. Boats and boating -- Fiction
ISBN 9780544050051; 0544050053
First published 1983

A boy's ambition to be the greatest sailor in the world brings him to ruin when he misuses his new ability to sail his boat in the air.

This "displays recognizable hallmarks of the artist's work: beauty of composition, striking contrasts of light and shadow, and especially the fascinating ambiguity of illusion and reality." Horn Book

Van Camp, Katie

Cookiebot! a Harry and Horsie adventure. [by] Katie Van Camp and [illustrated by] Lincoln Agnew. Balzer + Bray 2011 un il $16.99

Grades: PreK K 1 2   **E**

1. Robots -- Fiction 2. Cookies -- Fiction 3. Imagination -- Fiction
ISBN 978-0-06-197445-8; 0-06-197445-5

LC 2010017684

When Harry and his best friend Horsie build a robot that can reach the cookie jar for them, it goes out of control and wreaks havoc around the city.

"Iconic splash pages capture the scope of Harry's spirited imagination, while detailed illustrations offer clever, hidden humor. Once again, friendship rules for Harry and Horsie; and for Van Camp and Agnew, their seemingly seamless collaboration perfectly tells the story." Kirkus

Harry and Horsie; illustrated by Lincoln Agnew. Balzer & Bray 2009 un il $16.99

Grades: PreK K 1 2   **E**

1. Imagination -- Fiction
ISBN 978-0-06-175598-9; 0-06-175598-2

When a boy named Harry sneaks out of bed one night with his best friend, Horsie, to play with his Super Duper Bubble Blooper—an out-of-this-world adventure begins!

"Agnew's art uses an effectively limited color palette, faded dot patterns, and crisp lines to create a retro-cartoon feel. . . . With dashing visuals that capture Harry's deep-space adventure with verve to spare, and a comforting resolution, this has potential to be a bedtime favorite." Booklist

Another title about Harry and Horsie is:

Cookiebot! A Harry and Horsie adventure (2011)

Van Camp, Richard, 1971-

★ **Little** you; Richard Van Camp, Julie Flett. Orca Book Publishers 2013 24 p. (hardcover) $9.95

Grades: PreK   E

1. Infants -- Fiction 2. Parent-child relationship -- Fiction

ISBN 1459802489; 9781459802483; 9781459802490

LC 2012952954

In this book, by Richard Van Camp and illustrated by Julie Flett, "a mother and father profess their love for their little one. With Van Camp's spare second-person verse on the left-hand page and Flett's graphic art in various shades of red, orange, tan, gray, black and orange against a white background on the facing page, the spreads . . . depict a young child growing from infancy to toddlerhood." (Kirkus Reviews)

Van de Vendel, Edward, 1964-

The **dog** that Nino didn't have; by Edward Van De Vendel; illustrated by Anton Van Hertbruggen. Eerdmans Books for Young Readers 2015 34 p. color illustrations $17

Grades: K 1 2 3   E

1. Dogs -- Fiction 2. Pets -- Fiction 3. Imagination -- Fiction

ISBN 9780802854513

LC 2014048102

In this book, by Edward Van De Vendel, illustrated by Anton Van Hertbruggen, "Nino doesn't have a dog, but he likes to imagine that he does. His imaginary dog chases squirrels and plays in the lake with him. His imaginary dog licks the tears off Nino's face and helps Nino feel less lonely while his dad is traveling. But when Nino gets a real dog, it's not quite what he expected." (Publisher's note)

"With such gaze-worthy art, it's hard not to pore over each scene, and given the depth of detail, those long looks are rewarding. More rewarding still is the gentle, subtle, and nonjudgmental presentation of tricky feelings that will be familiar to many young readers, as well as the jubilant discovery of the joyful, comforting power of imagination." Booklist

Van Dusen, Chris

The **circus** ship. Candlewick Press 2009 un il $16.99

Grades: PreK K 1 2 3   E

1. Stories in rhyme 2. Circus -- Fiction 3. Animals -- Fiction 4. Shipwrecks -- Fiction

ISBN 978-0-7636-3090-4; 0-7636-3090-X

LC 2008938402

Van Dusen "uses an actual 1836 shipwreck as the seed for this charming and humorous picture book. . . . The rhyming text provides the structure for the story; however, the vividly colored, meticulously drawn illustrations articulate the story so well that they could practically stand on their own." Booklist

King Hugo's huge ego. Candlewick Press 2011 il

Grades: PreK K 1   E

1. Stories in rhyme 2. Kings and rulers -- Fiction

ISBN 0-7636-5004-8; 978-0-7636-5004-9

LC 2010040458

When haughty King Hugo tangles with a sorceress, she causes him to see himself in a more realistic light.

"A life lesson and true love tie up the loose ends, but not before readers are treated to a terrific mélange of satire, slapstick, and caricature, all served up with expert comic timing." Publ Wkly

Learning to ski with Mr. Magee. Chronicle Books 2010 un il $15.99

Grades: PreK K 1   E

1. Stories in rhyme 2. Dogs -- Fiction 3. Skiing -- Fiction

ISBN 978-0-8118-7495-3; 0-8118-7495-8

An encounter with a moose while they are learning to ski provides Mr. Magee and his dog with some unexpected excitement.

"The gouache illustrations are clean, crisp, and colorful. Various shades of blue, green, and purple nicely show the chill of the winter day. The rhyming text, with occasional bolded words, scans easily. Fans of Mr. Magee will feel at home with this one." SLJ

Other titles about Mr. Magee are:

A camping spree with Mr. Magee (2003)

Down to the sea with Mr. Magee (2000)

Van Fleet, Matthew

Heads. Simon & Schuster 2010 un il $17.99

Grades: PreK K   E

1. Pop-up books 2. Animals -- Fiction

ISBN 978-1-4424-0379-6; 1-4424-0379-9

"Children begin the safari that celebrates the traits of diverse animals by pulling a tab that allows a giraffe, elephant, rhino, tiger, and alligator to assemble jumbled letters to create the title. On each busy page, more tabs open a platypus egg, enlarge a frog's throat, and wiggle an elephant's ears. Watercolor cartoon critters rock the pages with greedy grins, loving licks, and astonished yelps. . . . This fun board book is designed to entertain toddlers time and again." SLJ

Moo; photos by Brian Stanton. Simon & Schuster 2011 il $16.99

Grades: PreK   E

1. Board books for children 2. Domestic animals -- Fiction

ISBN 978-1-4424-3503-2; 1-4424-3503-8

"Van Fleet's interactive board book identifies farm animals using simple, playful rhymes. . . . Textures—a woolly sheep, a duck's downy chest feathers—provide a touch-and-feel aspect, while flaps and pop-ups make this a playful excursion." Publ Wkly

Van Hout, Mies

Happy; Mies van Hout. Lemniscaat 2012 52 p.

Grades: PreK K 1 2 3   E

1. Fishes -- Fiction 2. Emotions -- Fiction 3. Vocabulary -- Fiction 4. Animals -- Pictorial works 5. Picture books for children

ISBN 1935954148; 9781935954149

In this picture book, "vibrant fish--although not ones found in nature--illustrate emotions in this art piece for children and for adults translated from the Dutch. Each double-page spread is constructed with an image of a fish on one side, in what looks like a chalk drawing on a blackboard. Opposite is a single hand-lettered word, also drawn in chalk or crown, on a jewel-toned, textured sheet. 'Brave' is a very small pale fish with a tentative smile, isolated in the lower corner of the black page. . . . The 'content' green fish aligns itself in the precise middle of the page; one can almost see it wriggling in its satisfaction. The "shocked" square-ish fish is shocking pink and purple and prickly, with open mouth and round eyes." (Kirkus)

Playground; by Mies van Hout. Lemniscaat USA 2016 32 p. color illustrations $17.95

Grades: PreK K   E

1. Playgrounds -- Fiction

ISBN 1935954512; 9781935954514

In this book, by Mies van Hout, "Two friends take a fun, fantastical trip to the playground. . . . Climb through the trees, find the way across the crocodile-infested river, and bushwhack through the blackberries, feel your way through the dark cave, escape from the monster, and slide into safety on your way to the jungle gym. Note a special treat: a new creature joins the children from each landscape." (Publisher's note)

"Beautifully produced, with a humorous detail at every turn of the mazes, this book will give endless hours of point-and-trace fun to young children and their caregivers." Kirkus

Van Laan, Nancy

When winter comes; illustrated by Susan Gaber. Atheneum Bks. for Young Readers 2000 un il $16

Grades: PreK K 1 2   E

1. Stories in rhyme 2. Winter -- Fiction 3. Animals -- Fiction

ISBN 0-689-81778-9

LC 97-32914

Rhyming text asks what happens to different animals and plants "when winter comes and the cold wind blows"

"The rhyming answers use simple and accessible language. Gaber's exuberant acrylic paintings show a child, mother, father, and dog taking a walk through the woods during a snowfall." SLJ

Van Leeuwen, Jean

★ **Amanda** Pig and the awful, scary monster; pictures by Ann Schweninger. Phyllis Fogelman Bks. 2003 48p il (PJF easy-to-read) hardcover o.p. pa $3.99

Grades: K 1 2   E

1. Pigs -- Fiction 2. Bedtime -- Fiction 3. Monsters -- Fiction

ISBN 0-8037-2766-6; 0-14-240203-6 pa

LC 2001-33519

Amanda pig sees monsters at night, but her parents and her brother find different ways to convince her that there are no monsters

"Van Leeuwen captures childhood emotions perfectly and includes just the right amount of humor. With bright illustrations done in carbon pencil, colored pencils, and watercolor washes on every page, this book will delight the piglet's many fans." SLJ

Other titles about Amanda Pig are:

Amanda Pig and her big brother Oliver (1982)

Tales of Amanda Pig (1983)

More tales of Amanda Pig (1985)

Oliver, Amanda, and Grandmother Pig (1987)

Oliver and Amanda's Christmas (1989)

Oliver and Amanda's Halloween (1992)

Oliver and Amanda and the big snow (1995)

Amanda Pig, school girl (1997)

Amanda Pig and her best friend Lollipop (1998)

Amanda Pig and the really hot day (2005)

Amanda Pig, first grader (2007)

Amanda Pig and the wiggly tooth (2008)

Chicken soup; by Jean Van Leeuwen; illustrated by David Gavril. Abrams Books for Young Readers 2009 un il $16.95

Grades: PreK K 1   E

1. Chickens -- Fiction 2. Farm life -- Fiction

ISBN 978-0-8109-8326-7; 0-8109-8326-5

LC 2008030824

When they hear that Mrs. Farmer is making soup, all the frightened chickens run for their lives, but Mr. Farmer finds Little Chickie, who has a bad cold, and he takes her to the kitchen for some nice hot vegetable soup.

"This simple, just-scary-enough story will appeal to preschoolers with its repetition and bright, childlike pen and watercolor illustrations." SLJ

Van Lieshout, Maria

Bloom! a little book about finding love. written and illustrated by Maria van Lieshout. Feiwel and Friends 2008 un il $12.95

Grades: PreK K 1   E

1. Love -- Fiction 2. Pigs -- Fiction 3. Friendship -- Fiction 4. Butterflies -- Fiction

ISBN 978-0-312-36913-2; 0-312-36913-1

LC 2007-33411

Bloom, a pig who prefers flowers to mud puddles, falls in love with a flying flower," but when the butterfly leaves she is brokenhearted until a friend gives her a reason to smile again.

"Van Lieshout's loosely drawn pen and ink illustrations, mostly on stark white pages, wring Oscar-winning expressions from the slenderest curves and squiggles. The minimalist text begins before the title page, when Bloom's faithful friend urges her to join him playing in a puddle. . . . This paper-overboard book's stylish design and small square format designate it as a natural for Valentine's Day." Publ Wkly

Bye-bye binky; Maria van Lieshout. Chronicle Books 2016 24 p. color illustrations (alk. paper) $9.99

Grades: PreK K   E

1. Infants 2. Life change events 3. Pacifiers (Infant care) 4. Growth -- Fiction 5. Toddlers -- Fiction

ISBN 1452135363; 9781452135366

LC 2015021995

In this children's book, by Maria van Lieshout, "a smiling toddler narrates her transition from a crying baby comforted only by her binky to a girl who can ask for what she needs. She marks her transition to 'big kid' by passing her binky along to another baby. The digital illustrations match the simple text and mainly feature the central character, rendered in thick black lines and positioned against a solid background." (Publisher's note)

"Simple and engaging, these titles will work for even the shortest attention spans." SLJ

Flight 1-2-3; by Maria van Lieshout. Chronicle Books 2013 40 p. (hardcover) $14.99

Grades: PreK K 1   E

1. Picture books for children 2. Airports -- Fiction 3. Counting -- Fiction 4. Airplanes -- Fiction

ISBN 1452116628; 9781452116624

LC 2012033606

This children's counting story, by Maria van Lieshout, follows a boy on a airplane. "What can you see when you go on an airplane journey? 1 airplane, 2 luggage carts, 3 check-in counters, and so much more! Using familiar airport signs, this . . . book introduces little ones not only to numbers, but to the world around them." (Publisher's note)

Hopper and Wilson. Philomel Books 2011 un il $16.99

Grades: PreK K 1   E

1. Mice -- Fiction 2. Sailing -- Fiction 3. Elephants -- Fiction

ISBN 978-0-399-25184-9; 0-399-25184-7

LC 2010-19396

An elephant and a mouse embark on a journey to discover what it looks like at the end of the world.

Van Lieshout "plays up the suspense of the separation with lots of space in the spreads and long waits. . . . [The] story is filled with adventure, emotion, and imagery that supplies lots of effervescent warmth." Publ Wkly

Tumble; a little book about having it all. written and illustrated by Maria van Lieshout; designed by Molly Leach. Feiwel & Friends 2010 un il $12.99

Grades: PreK K 1   E
1. Polar bear -- Fiction
ISBN 978-0-312-54859-9; 0-312-54859-1

When three little bears find a red toy to play with and Tumble claims it for his own, this proves to be not such a good idea.

"This title gently reminds youngsters about the rewards of sharing. . . . The pencil, ink, and watercolor artwork is digitally enhanced and done in van Lieshout's expressive trademark style. . . . A perfect choice for a wintertime storyhour or one-on-one sharing." SLJ

Van Slyke, Rebecca
Lexie, the word wrangler; Rebecca Van Slyke; illustrated by Jessie Hartland. Nancy Paulsen Books 2017 40 p. color illustrations $17.99
Grades: PreK K 1 2   E
1. Picture books for children 2. Cowhands -- Fiction 3. Vocabulary -- Fiction 4. Cowgirls -- Fiction
ISBN 9780399169571

LC 2016003364

In this picture book, by Rebecca Van Slyke, illustrated by Jessie Hartland, "Lexie is the best wrangler west of the Mississippi--word wrangler, that is. She watches over baby letters while they grow into words and ties shorter words together into longer ones; she herds words into sentences, hitches sentences together, and pens them all in to tell a story. But lately, something seems off at the ranch." (Publisher's note)

Van Steenwyk, Elizabeth
Prairie Christmas; written by Elizabeth Van Steenwyk; illustrated by Ronald Himler. Eerdmans 2006 un il $17
Grades: 1 2 3 4   E
1. Midwives -- Fiction 2. Nebraska -- Fiction 3. Christmas -- Fiction 4. Mother-daughter relationship -- Fiction
ISBN 0-8028-5280-7

On the Nebraska prairie in 1880, eleven-year-old Emma finds a way to celebrate the spirit of Christmas while her mother, a midwife, delivers a baby on Christmas Eve.

"This memorable tale is beautifully told in clear and simple prose, which is complemented perfectly by the uncluttered, colored-pencil and watercolor drawings." SLJ

Van, Muon
In a village by the sea; by Muon Van; illustrated by April Chu. Creston Books 2015 32 p. illustrations (hardback) $16.95
Grades: PreK K 1 2   E
1. Vietnam -- Fiction 2. Homesickness -- Fiction 3. Seafaring life -- Fiction
ISBN 1939547156; 9781939547156

LC 2015006486

This children's story, by Muon Van, illustrated by April Chu, "set[s] human and animal characters into seascapes and interior scenes in an almost timeless Vietnam and extend the story far beyond the words. A wife and a baby are in their traditional kitchen anxiously awaiting the fisherman-husband's return. He is in his boat, fearfully viewing the dark waves and black clouds but also looking at family photos (a hint of modernity)." (Kirkus Reviews)

The **little** tree; by Muon Van; illustrations by JoAnn Adinolfi. Creston Books 2015 32 p. color illustrations (hardback) $16.95
Grades: PreK K 1 2 3   E
1. Trees -- Fiction 2. Mother-child relationship -- Fiction
ISBN 9781939547194

LC 2015017748

In this children's book, by Muon Van, with illustrations by JoAnn Adinolfi, "[w]hen the Little Tree sees the world around her narrowing, she worries about what life will be like for her Little Seed. She decides to take the biggest risk of all, and let Little Seed find a richer life on her own." (Publisher's note)

"Full of gentle rhythm and repetition, this deceptively simple, layered poetic tale will charm its way into readers' hearts and begs to be read over and over again." Kirkus

Vander Zee, Ruth
Always with you; written by Ruth Vander Zee; illustrated by Ronald Himler. Eerdmans Books for Young Readers 2008 un il $17
Grades: 2 3 4   E
1. Orphans -- Fiction 2. Vietnam -- Fiction 3. Mother-daughter relationship -- Fiction
ISBN 978-0-8028-5295-3

LC 2007009354

Orphaned at the age of four when her village in Vietnam is bombed, Kim is rescued by soldiers and raised in an orphanage, always finding comfort in her mother's last words "Don't be afraid. I will always be with you."

Mississippi morning; written by Ruth Vander Zee; illustrated by Floyd Cooper. Eerdmans Books for Young Readers 2004 un il $16
Grades: 1 2 3 4   E
1. Mississippi -- Fiction 2. Ku Klux Klan -- Fiction 3. Race relations -- Fiction 4. Father-son relationship -- Fiction
ISBN 0-8028-5211-4

LC 2002-151212

Amidst the economic depression and the racial tension of the 1930s, a boy discovers a horrible secret of his father's involvement in the Ku Klux Klan.

"Cooper's large, warm oil paintings create the perfect sense of time, place, and atmosphere. . . . A sad and poignant story." SLJ

Vanderwater, Amy Ludwig
Forest has a song; poems. by Amy Ludwig VanDerwater; illustrations by Robbin Gourley. Clarion Books 2013 40 p. col. ill. (reinforced) $16.99
Grades: 2 3 4   E
1. Seasons -- Poetry 2. Picture books for children
ISBN 0618843493; 9780618843497

LC 2011052433

In this children's picture book, moving "through the seasons. newcomer [Amy Ludwig] VanDerwater shares a girl's experience of what the forest has to offer. On a chilly spring day, she 'stop[s] to read/ the Forest News! in mud or fallen snow./ Articles are printed/ by critters on the go.'" She encounters the forest in summer, autumn, and winter as well. (Publishers Weekly)

VanHecke, Susan
An apple pie for dinner; retold by Susan VanHecke; illustrated by Carol Baicker-McKee. Marshall Cavendish Children 2009 un il $17.99
Grades: K 1 2 3   E
1. Apples -- Fiction 2. Baking -- Fiction 3. Barter -- Fiction
ISBN 978-0-7614-5452-6; 0-7614-5452-7

LC 2008003664

Wishing to bake an apple pie, Old Granny Smith sets out with a full basket, trading its contents for a series of objects until she gets the apples she needs.

"The bas-relief illustrations, made from baked clay and mixed-media of found objects, create a 3-D, Claymation effect. . . . The fascinating tactile details will have young and old poring over the pages. . . . Complete with a pie recipe and notes from both the author and illustrator that cite the origin of the tale (the English folktale 'An Apple Dumpling' and directions on how to make bas-reliefs, the book is a delicious treat to be shared anytime." Booklist

Velasquez, Eric

★ **Grandma's** gift. Walker 2010 un il $16.99; lib bdg $17.89
Grades: K 1 2 3   E
1. Gifts -- Fiction 2. Artists -- Fiction 3. Christmas -- Fiction 4. Grandmothers -- Fiction 5. Puerto Ricans -- Fiction 6. New York (N.Y.) -- Fiction 7. African Americans -- Fiction 8. Metropolitan Museum of Art (New York, N.Y.) -- Fiction
ISBN 978-0-8027-2082-5; 0-8027-2082-X; 978-0-8027-2083-2 lib bdg; 0-8027-2083-8 lib bdg
LC 2010005326

Prequel to: Grandma's records (2004)
Pura Belpré Award for illustration, 2011

The author describes Christmas at his grandmother's apartment in Spanish Harlem the year she introduced him to the Metropolitan Museum of Art and Diego Velazquez's portrait of Juan de Pareja, which has had a profound and lasting effect on him.

"The realistic oil paintings reveal a strong and stylish grandmother of great character and a polite child. . . . The sweetly understated story has Spanish words and sentences skillfully woven into the text throughout with translations provided in parenthesis." Kirkus

Looking for Bongo; Eric Velasquez. Holiday House 2016 32 p. color illustrations (hardcover) $16.95
Grades: PreK K   E
1. Toys -- Fiction 2. Hispanic Americans -- Fiction 3. Lost and found possessions -- Fiction
ISBN 9780823435654
LC 2015022330

In this children's story, by Eric Velasquez, "a boy's beloved stuffed toy, Bongo, is missing. . . . When he asks his abuela where Bongo is, she answers, Yo no se. . . . Mom and Dad haven't seen Bongo either. Gato just says Meow, and runs away. When Bongo finally turns up behind Dad's drum, the problem of Bongo's whereabouts is resolved . . . but it doesn't answer how Bongo got there!" (Publisher's note)

"The illustrations of the narrator's quest are active, consisting of many gestures and close-up facial expressions, and the colors are warm creams, blues, and oranges. Home life is multigenerational and loving." Booklist

Veldkamp, Tjibbe

Tom the tamer; illustrated by Philip Hopman. Lemniscaat USA 2011 32p il
Grades: PreK K   E
1. Fear -- Fiction 2. Animals -- Fiction 3. Father-son relationship -- Fiction
ISBN 1-9359-5405-9; 978-1-9359-5405-7

"This tender, loopy, and unconventional work . . . . stars a boy who wants to lure his phobic father away from his model railway and into the backyard so that the father can meet the animals he's frightened of face-to-face. . . . Tom purchases a polar bear from the local pet store and discovers that the bear can do an uncanny imitation of an armchair. . . . This success sets the stage for a full-scale animal-furniture renovation. . . . The episodes recall gentler moments from Roald Dahl or Russell Hoban. Similarly, Hopman's illustrations are first cousin to Quentin Blake's, full of fanciful color and a jumble of imagined detail."

Verburg, Bonnie

The **kiss** box; illustrated by Henry Cole. Orchard Books 2011 un l lib bdg $16.99
Grades: PreK   E
1. Love -- Fiction 2. Bears -- Fiction 3. Kissing -- Fiction 4.

Mother-child relationship -- Fiction
ISBN 978-0-545-11284-0; 0-545-11284-2
LC 2009012102

As they prepare for a short separation, Mama Bear and Little Bear find a way to reassure each other while they are apart.

"Cole's charming and cheery watercolor and colored-pencil illustrations of Mama Bear and Little Bear enjoying the day before she leaves do much to make this title appealing." SLJ

Verde, Susan

I am yoga; by Susan Verde; illustrated by Peter H. Reynolds. Abrams Books for Young Readers 2015 32 p. color illustrations $14.95
Grades: PreK K 1 2 3   E
1. Individualism 2. Creative ability 3. Yoga -- Fiction 4. Imagination -- Fiction
ISBN 1419716646; 9781419716645
LC 2014040993

For this book "illustrator Peter H. Reynolds and author and certified yoga instructor Susan Verde team up again . . . about creativity and the power of self-expression. 'I Am Yoga' encourages children to explore the world of yoga and make room in their hearts for the world beyond it. A kid-friendly guide to 16 yoga poses is included." (Publisher's note)

"Although an appended author's note lacks discussion of possible age or physical considerations, or precautions for yoga beginners, children's yoga teacher Verde highlights yoga concepts and potential benefits for kids and adults and provides the names, descriptions, and instructions for the 16 poses featured in this book." Booklist

The **museum**; written by Susan Verde; art by Peter H. Reynolds. Abrams Books for Young Readers 2013 32 p. (reinforced) $16.95
Grades: PreK K 1 2   E
1. Picture books for children 2. Stories in rhyme 3. Museums -- Fiction 4. Art museums -- Fiction 5. Art appreciation -- Fiction
ISBN 1419705946; 9781419705946
LC 2012022518

This children's picture book focuses on a girl's experience at an art museum. "A girl in pigtails embodies the emotions elicited by the paintings she sees, leaping, twirling, giggling, and—inspired by the famous Munch work—even shrieking, as she tours a museum gallery filled with European and American masterpieces." (Publishers Weekly)

The **water** princess; written by Susan Verde; illustrated by Peter H. Reynolds. G.P. Putnam's Sons, an imprint of Penguin Group (USA) 2016 40 p. color ill., color photographs (hardcover) $17.99; (ebook) $53.97
Grades: K 1 2 3   E
1. Africa -- Fiction 2. Water supply -- Fiction 3. Blacks -- Africa -- Fiction
ISBN 9780399172588; 9780698181618
LC 2014046250

In this book, by Susan Verde, illustrated by Peter H. Reynolds, "Princess Gie Gie's kingdom is a beautiful land. But clean drinking water is scarce in her small African village. And try as she might, Gie Gie cannot bring the water closer; she cannot make it run clearer. Every morning, she rises before the sun to make the long journey to the well. Instead of a crown, she wears a heavy pot on her head to collect the water." (Publisher's note)

"A lovely picture book, filled with messages of perseverance and hope." SLJ

Verdick, Elizabeth

Mealtime; illustrated by Marieka Heinlen. Free Spirit Pub. 2011 un il bd bk $7.95

Grades: PreK   E
1. Food 2. Etiquette 3. Nutrition 4. Board books for children
ISBN 978-1-57542-366-1; 1-57542-366-9

LC 2010045051

"Pretty much every main lesson adults try to impart about mealtime is covered here: washing hands, using utensils, displaying manners, trying new food, sitting still, and cleaning up. This . . . list of demands is relayed via a group of four beaming multicultural children wearing wild color and set before even more wildly colored backdrops." Booklist

Vere, Ed
Banana! Henry Holt & Co. 2010 un il $12.99
Grades: PreK K 1   E
1. Banana -- Fiction 2. Monkeys -- Fiction
ISBN 978-0-8050-9214-1; 0-8050-9214-5

LC 2009-936514

"Especially noteworthy are the bold graphic illustrations: the digitally scrawled figures are oversized, and in each spread they're set against a different field of solid color. . . . [The monkeys'] faces are remarkably expressive, showing a range of emotions from frustration to desperation to fury. . . . This would be a lively title to share in a toddler storytime, but its simplicity and illustratively conveyed plot make it an enjoyable work for youngsters to pore over solo." Bull Cent Child Books

Max the Brave; Ed Vere. Sourcebooks Inc. 2015 32 p. color illustrations (hardcover) $16.99
Grades: PreK K 1   E
1. Cats -- Fiction 2. Courage -- Fiction 3. Mice -- Fiction
ISBN 1492616516; 9781492616511

In this children's picture book, by Ed Vere, "Max is a fearless kitten. Max is a brave kitten. Max is a kitten who chases mice. There's only one problem--Max doesn't know what a mouse looks like! With a little bit of bad advice, Max finds himself facing a much bigger challenge. Maybe Max doesn't have to be Max the Brave all the time." (Publisher's note)

"It's a simple formula but one that works because of the understated humor and attractive layout. Max should find himself chasing Mouse into storytimes again and again." Booklist

Another title about Max is:
Max at Night (2016)

Vernick, Audrey
First grade dropout; Audrey Vernick; illustrated by Matthew Cordell. Clarion Books, Houghton Mifflin Harcourt 2015 32 p. color illustrations (hardcover) $16.99
Grades: K 1 2 3 4   E
1. Self-consciousness 2. School children -- Fiction 3. School stories -- Fiction 4. Humorous stories 5. Schools -- Fiction 6. Embarrassment -- Fiction
ISBN 0544129857; 9780544129856

LC 2014021780

In this children's book by Audrey Vernick, illustrated by Matthew Cordell, "the first grade narrator of this book has been lots of things: Hungry. Four years old. Crazy bored. Soaking wet. Pretty regular kid . . . until he makes a mistake so big that he's sure he will never be able to go back to Lakeview Elementary School. All readers . . . will find the narrator's feelings familiar, and discover that even though embarrassing things happen, they're usually not as bad as they seem." (Publisher's note)

Another title in this series is:
Second grade holdout (2017)

Is your buffalo ready for kindergarten? illustrated by Daniel Jennewein. Balzer + Bray 2010 un il $16.99

Grades: PreK K   E
1. School stories 2. Bison -- Fiction
ISBN 978-0-06-176275-8; 0-06-176275-X

LC 2009-11841

"This is a silly book about the first day of kindergarten with one's own buffalo. . . . The story prompts readers to remind the buffalo that finger painting is fun and it's okay to get messy; those hooves could create a masterpiece. Buffaloes (and children) learn how to get along without using their horns. . . . This wacky picture book, with its bold cartoonlike illustrations of a buffalo that snorts, dances, and makes faces, may help apprehensive youngsters to be more at ease about going to school." SLJ

Another title about the buffalo is:
Teach your buffalo to play drums (2011)

Verplancke, Klaas
Applesauce; Klaas Verplancke, Helen Mixter. Groundwood Books/ House of Anansi Press 2012 40 p. $18.95
Grades: PreK K 1   E
1. Anger -- Fiction 2. Picture books for children 3. Fathers -- Fiction 4. Father-son relationship -- Fiction
ISBN 1554981867; 9781554981861

This children's book by Klaas Verplancke is about a father-son relationship. "Johnny's daddy has smooth cheeks, an apple in his throat and sounds like a mom when he sings in the bath. . . . Other times his hands are cold and flash like lightning, and he becomes a thunder-daddy. When this happens Johnny wants to find a new daddy, but he eventually realizes that thunder-daddies don't last forever. And that there's nothing like the comfort that comes from those we love." (Publisher's note)

Vestergaard, Hope
Potty animals; what to know when you've gotta go! illustrated by Valeria Petrone. Sterling Pub. 2010 un il $14.95
Grades: PreK   E
1. Stories in rhyme 2. Animals -- Fiction 3. Toilet training -- Fiction
ISBN 978-1-4027-5996-3; 1-4027-5996-7

"Petrone's cheery digital characters and Vestergaard's decorous yet humorous rhymes invite readers to help civilize the bathroom habits of some uncouth preschool-age animals. . . . Petrone's wide-eyed cartoon animals capture a broad spectrum of toddler emotions." Publ Wkly

Villnave, Erica Pelton
Sophie's lovely locks. Marshall Cavendish 2011 un il $16.99
Grades: PreK K 1 2   E
1. Hair -- Fiction
ISBN 978-0-7614-5820-3; 0-7614-5820-4

LC 2010010055

Sophie loves her long hair, but when it becomes too hard to manage and she decides to get it cut, she finds something generous to do with it. Includes list of organizations that make wigs from donated hair.

"Soft lines in the watercolor illustrations show [the hair's] movement and [Sophie's] delight in it as she twirls and swirls. . . . The playful main character presents the obvious message in a joyous, engaging way." SLJ

Viorst, Judith
★ **Alexander** and the terrible, horrible, no good, very bad day; illustrated by Ray Cruz; with a new preface by Judith Viorst and Ray Cruz. Special limited ed.; Atheneum Books for Young Readers 2009 un il $17.99
Grades: PreK K 1 2   E
1. Day -- Fiction
ISBN 978-1-4169-8595-2; 1-4169-8595-6

LC 2008049478

A reissue of the title first published 1972

On a day when everything goes wrong for him, Alexander is consoled by the thought that other people have bad days too.

"Small listeners can enjoy the litany of disaster, and perhaps be stimulated to discuss the possibility that one contributes by expectation. The illustrations capture the grumpy dolor of the story, ruefully funny." Sutherland. The Best In Child Books

Other titles about Alexander are:

Alexander, who is not (do you hear me?) going (I mean it) to move (1995)

Alexander, who used to be rich last Sunday (1978)

And two boys booed; Judith Viorst; pictures by Sophie Blackall. Margaret Ferguson Books, Farrar Straus Giroux 2014 32 p. (hardcover) $16.99

Grades: PreK K 1 2   E

1. Anxiety -- Fiction 2. Talent shows -- Fiction 3. Fear -- Fiction 4. Stage fright -- Fiction

ISBN 0374303029; 9780374303020

LC 2013007871

In this children's book by Judith Viorst, illustrated by Sophie Blackall, "on the day of the talent show, a boy is ready to sing his song, and he isn't one bit scared because he has practiced a billion times, plus he's wearing his lucky blue boots and his pants with all ten pockets. But as all of the other kids perform before him, he gets more and more nervous." (Publisher's note)

"It's the day of the class talent show, and our little-boy protagonist is ready. He's last to go, though, and the nerves sneak up. He freezes, "... and two boys booed." Viorst uses repetition to create a cumulative pattern that she then breaks as the protagonist's confidence falters. Blackall's art masterfully captures the boy's ambivalence. Occasional lift-the-flaps pace the story and offer unexpected visual treats." Horn Book

Earrings! illustrated by Nola Langner Malone. Atheneum Books for Young Readers 2010 un il $16.99

Grades: 1 2 3   E

1. Earrings -- Fiction

ISBN 978-1-4442-1281-1; 1-4442-1281-X

LC 2010502964

A reissue of the title first published 1990

A young girl uses various arguments to convince her parents to let her have her ears pierced.

"Viorst homes in on minor childhood crises with the perfect blend of humor and insight, and Malone's expressive and comic figures are miniature character studies in themselves." Horn Book

Just in case; written by Judith Viorst; illustrated by Diana Cain Bluthenthal. Atheneum Books for Young Readers 2006 un il $15.95

Grades: PreK K 1 2   E

1. Worry -- Fiction

ISBN 0-689-87164-3

LC 2003-26068

Charlie likes to be ready for anything, imagining that his house could be flooded or a mermaid might kidnap him, but he learns that it is sometimes good to be unprepared

"Blumenthal's colorful, mixed-media illustrations add some good cheer, sly wit, ... and a companionable canine to the catalog of Charlie's hypothetical 'just in case' concerns." Booklist

The **tenth** good thing about Barney; illustrated by Erik Blegvad. Atheneum Pubs. 1971 25p il $15.95; pa $5.99

Grades: PreK K 1 2   E

1. Cats -- Fiction 2. Death -- Fiction

ISBN 0-689-20688-7; 0-689-71203-0 pa

"The author succinctly and honestly handles both the emotions stemming from the loss of a beloved pet and the questions about the finality of death . . . An unusually good book that handles a difficult subject straightforwardly." Horn Book

Viva, Frank

★ **Along** a long road. Little, Brown 2011 un il $16.99

Grades: PreK K 1 2   E

1. Cycling -- Fiction

ISBN 978-0-316-12925-1; 0-316-12925-9

LC 2010019751

Illustrations and brief text evoke a bicycle ride, with its ups and downs, sweeping turns, and vivid views.

"Viva's artwork combines supple curves, big areas of soft black background, light blue for water and shading, and the occasional brick-red accent; it's simultaneously stylish and restrained. Simple, lilting text reproduces the smooth, rhythmic pace of cycling and the meditative state of mind it induces. . . . It's the kind of book that creates a mood rather than telling a story, evoking the freedom of traveling, the joy of movement, and the exhilaration of being outside." Publ Wkly

★ **A long** way away; Frank Viva. Little, Brown Books for Young Readers 2013 40 p. (hardback) $16.99

Grades: PreK K 1   E

1. Outer space -- Fiction 2. Voyages and travels -- Fiction 3. Ocean -- Fiction 4. Upside-down books 5. Interplanetary voyages -- Fiction

ISBN 0316221961; 9780316221962

LC 2012028757

This children's picture book follows an alien family's journey. "Their alien child starts a downward slide along a yellow path past celestial bodies (and a shoe), through the Earth's atmosphere, past a whale and school of dapper fish, and into the blackest ocean depths. 'Deep asleep,' the final page reads, as the alien lodges on an underwater cliff. The return trip shows the creature rising up through the ocean and back through deep space . . . before being reunited with his family." (Publishers Weekly)

Outstanding in the rain; Frank Viva. Little, Brown & Co. 2015 32 p. color illustrations (hardcover) $18

Grades: 1 2 3   E

1. Coney Island (New York, N.Y.) -- Fiction 2. Stories in rhyme 3. Birthdays -- Fiction 4. English language -- Homonyms

ISBN 9780316366274

LC 2013039335

This children's book, by Frank Viva, "finds a boy and his mother celebrating his fourth birthday at Coney Island, a locale that provides plenty of illustrative opportunity for Viva to display his . . . retro graphic style. Strategically placed die-cut holes . . . create new words and images with every page turn." (Publisher's note)

"A must have because of the originality of the concept, the unusual palette, and the thrill of the reading experience." Booklist

Vogel, Amos

★ **How** little Lori visited Times Square; pictures by Maurice Sendak. HarperCollins Pubs. 2001 un il $14.95

Grades: PreK K 1 2   E

1. New York (N.Y.) -- Fiction

ISBN 0-06-028462-5

A reissue of the title first published 1963

This "tells the story of Lori's many misadventures trying to get to Times Square on various modes of transportation, with a slow-moving turtle finally bearing him off." Horn Book Guide

Vries, Anke de

Raf; [illustrated by] Charlotte Dematons. Lemniscaat 2009 un il $16.95

Grades: PreK K   E

1. Toys -- Fiction 2. Africa -- Fiction 3. Voyages and travels -- Fiction

ISBN 978-1-59078-749-6

Original Dutch edition, 2008

This "follows a toy giraffe that spontaneously disappears from his child's room to travel through Africa. . . . In postcards sent to his owner/pal, Ben . . . Raf tells of encounters with camels, flamingos, elephants, monkeys, and giraffes. . . . Just in time for Ben's birthday, the toy arrives in the mail, dressed in kente cloth and colored beads. . . . In addition to being a great success with preschool fans of toy tales, this story could also be shared with primary-grade children in conjunction with units on biome study or continents." SLJ

Waber, Bernard, 1921-2013

Ask me; by Bernard Waber; illustrated by Suzy Lee. Houghton Mifflin Harcourt 2015 40 p. $16.99

Grades: PreK K 1 2   E

1. Questions and answers 2. Parent-child relationship 3. Parent and child -- Fiction 4. Questions and answers -- Fiction

ISBN 0547733941; 9780547733944

LC 2014009668

In this children's story, by Bernard Waber and illustrated by Suzy Lee, "a father and daughter walk through their neighborhood, brimming with questions as they explore their world. With so many things to enjoy, and so many ways to ask--and talk--about them, it's a snapshot of an ordinary day in a world that's anything but." (Publisher's note)

The **house** on East 88th Street. Houghton Mifflin 1962 48p il lib bdg $16.95; pa $6.95

Grades: PreK K 1 2   E

1. Crocodiles -- Fiction 2. New York (N.Y.) -- Fiction

ISBN 0-395-18157-7; 0-395-19970-0 pa

LC 62-8144

"In an amusing fantasy, Mr. and Mrs. Joseph F. Primm and their young son Joshua move into a new home in New York City and discover a crocodile [named Lyle] in the bathtub. The illustrations detail the wrought iron railings, the graceful doorway with its fanlight, the sweeping staircase, elaborate fireplaces, and ornate chandeliers, characteristic of a comfortable old brownstone dwelling."

"Illustrations have verve and are a perfect complement to the story. Highly recommended." SLJ

★ **Ira** sleeps over. Houghton Mifflin 1972 48p il lib bdg $16; pa $6.95

Grades: PreK K 1 2   E

1. Friendship -- Fiction 2. Teddy bears -- Fiction

ISBN 0-395-13893-0 lib bdg; 0-395-20503-4 pa

Ira is excited at the prospect of spending the night at his friend's house but worries how he'll get along without his teddy bear

"An appealing picture book which depicts common childhood qualms with empathy and humor in brief text and colorful illustrations." Booklist

Another title about Ira is:

Ira says goodbye (1988)

★ **Lyle,** Lyle, crocodile. Houghton Mifflin 1965 48p il $16; pa $6.95

Grades: PreK K 1 2   E

1. Crocodiles -- Fiction 2. New York (N.Y.) -- Fiction

ISBN 0-395-16995-X; 0-395-13720-9 pa

"The illustrations are cartoon-like, lively, and colorful. . . . The situation is nicely exploited with a bland daffiness." Bull Cent Child Books

Other titles about Lyle are:

Funny, funny Lyle (1987)

The house on East 88th Street (1962)

Lovable Lyle (1969)

Lyle and the birthday party (1966)

Lyle at Christmas (1998)

Lyle at the office (1994)

Lyle finds his mother (1974)

Lyle walks the dogs (2010)

Waddell, Martin

Can't you sleep, Little Bear? illustrated by Barbara Firth. special anniversary edition; Candlewick Press 2002 un il $15.99

Grades: PreK   E

1. Bears -- Fiction 2. Bedtime -- Fiction

ISBN 978-0-76361-929-9; 0-76361-929-9

First published 1988 in the United Kingdom

When bedtime comes Little Bear is afraid of the dark, until Big Bear brings him lights and love.

"Firth's brightly lit watercolor and soft pencil illustrations, framed in the dark blue of the night, capture the cozy, physical affection of the story, the playfulness of Little Bear, . . . the shadowy mystery of the moonlit landscape, and the huge comforting presence of a parent who is always there when you call." Booklist

Other titles about Little Bear are:

Good job, Little Bear! (1999)

Let's go home, Little Bear (1993)

Little Bear's baby book (2000)

Sleep tight Little Bear (2005)

Well done, Little Bear (1999)

You and me, Little Bear (1996)

★ **Captain** Small Pig; illustrated by Susan Varley. Peachtree Pubs. 2009 un il $15.95

Grades: PreK K   E

1. Pigs -- Fiction 2. Goats -- Fiction 3. Turkeys -- Fiction 4. Boats and boating -- Fiction

ISBN 978-1-56145-519-5; 1-56145-519-9

Small Pig persuades Old Goat and Turkey to go out on Blue Lake in a row boat with him and fish for whales

"This book pleases at every level. The simplicity of its concept, the ease of its words, and the ink-and-watercolor art's subtle mix of wit and whimsy combine in a comfortable way." Booklist

★ **Farmer** duck; illustrated by Helen Oxenbury. Candlewick Press 1992 un il hardcover o.p. pa $5.99; bd bk $6.99

Grades: PreK K 1 2   E

1. Ducks -- Fiction 2. Farm life -- Fiction

ISBN 1-56402-009-6; 1-56402-596-9 pa; 0-7636-2167-6 bd bk

LC 91-71855

First published 1991 in the United Kingdom

When a kind and hardworking duck nearly collapses from overwork, while taking care of a farm because the owner is too lazy to do so, the rest of the animals get together and chase the farmer out of town

"Hilarious art masterfully captures the expressions of the put-upon duck, the supportive cast, and the slovenly ergophobic who reads the newspaper and chomps on bonbons in bed. . . . With its lilting, large-print text and satisfying resolution, it's as perfect for beginning readers as it is for story hours." SLJ

★ **Owl** babies; illustrated by Patrick Benson. Candlewick Press 1992 un il hardcover o.p. pa $6.99; bd bk $6.99

Grades: PreK K 1 2   E
   1. Owls -- Fiction
   ISBN 1-56402-101-7; 0-7636-1710-5 pa; 1-56402-965-4 bd bk
              LC 91-58750
   Three owl babies whose mother has gone out in the night try to stay calm while she is gone
   "The illustrations, executed in black ink and watercolor, capture in every feather and expression the little owls' worry and watchfulness as well as their complete joy when Owl Mother returns." Horn Book

   ★ **Tiny's** big adventure; illustrated by John Lawrence. Candlewick Press 2004 un il $15.99; pa $6.99
Grades: PreK K   E
   1. Mice -- Fiction 2. Siblings -- Fiction 3. Country life -- Fiction
   ISBN 0-7636-2170-6; 0-7636-3819-6 pa
              LC 2002-35004
   Katy Mouse teaches her younger brother, Tiny, the names of some of the things they see, including a boot, a snail, and a pheasant, when they go to the cornfield to play games
   "The rich mixture of vinyl engravings, watercolor washes, and printed wood textures gives a timeless flavor to the adventure, as do Waddell's sweet story line and clear sentences." Booklist

Wadham, Tim

   ★ The **Queen** of France; illustrated by Kady MacDonald Denton. Candlewick Press 2011 un il $16.99
Grades: PreK K 1   E
   1. Imagination -- Fiction 2. Kings and rulers -- Fiction 3. Parent-child relationship -- Fiction
   ISBN 978-0-7636-4102-3; 0-7636-4102-2
              LC 2010039185
   Rose wakes up one morning feeling royal and, donning jewels and a crown, she seeks her parents who behave as her royal subjects, causing Rose to wonder what they would think if the queen traded places with their daughter
   Wadham's "rhythmic prose and comic pacing feel elegant and effortless. . . . Denton . . . wonderfully conveys the story's impishness, emotional subtleties, and familial affections." Publ Wkly

Wadsworth, Ginger

   Yosemite's songster; one coyote's story. Ginger Wadsworth, Daniel San Souci. Yosemite Conservancy 2013 32 p. $15.95
Grades: PreK K 1 2   E
   1. Picture books for children 2. Yosemite National Park (Calif.)
   ISBN 1930238347; 9781930238343
              LC 2012952115
   In this children's picture book, Ginger Wadsworth follows "a coyote that has been separated from her mate. A rock slide divides the pair, and Coyote dashes away, first taking refuge underneath a canvas cabin in Curry Village, and then exploring further. Coyote's travels give Wadsworth many opportunities to point out the park's highlights and show how visitors are enjoying it." (Publishers Weekly)

Wadsworth, Olive A.

   ★ **Over** in the meadow; a counting rhyme. illustrated by Anna Wojtech. North-South Bks. 2002 un il $15.95
Grades: PreK K 1 2   E
   1. Counting 2. Nursery rhymes
   ISBN 0-7358-1596-8; 0-7358-1597-6 lib bdg
              LC 2001-51434
   An old nursery poem introduces animals and their young and the number one through ten

   "Although many versions of the verse, both traditional and nontraditional, are available, this is an accessible rendition that children will enjoy in storytime and on their own." SLJ

Waechter, Philip

   Bravo! illustrated by Moni Port; [translated from German by Sally-Ann Spencer] Gecko Press 2011 un il $17.95
Grades: PreK K 1   E
   1. Cats -- Fiction 2. Noise -- Fiction 3. Trumpet -- Fiction 4. Listening -- Fiction 5. Family life -- Fiction 6. Father-daughter relationship -- Fiction
   ISBN 978-1-8774-6771-4; 1-8774-6771-5
   "Helena, a trumpet-playing kitten who lives with her mother, father, and little brother, has almost a perfect life, except for one thing. Her father is a shouter who comes from a long line of shouters. She dislikes his yelling so much that she leaves home to find another person with whom to live. . . . The muted, full-color art is delicate and sketchy. The illustrations feature plenty of white space and large vistas that focus the action on the family. Children will respond to Helena." SLJ

Wahl, Jan

   The **art** collector; illustrated by Rosalinde Bonnet. Charlesbridge 2011 un il $15.95
Grades: K 1 2 3   E
   1. Art appreciation -- Fiction 2. Collectors and collecting -- Fiction
   ISBN 978-1-58089-270-4; 1-58089-270-1
              LC 2010022760
   Oscar is not pleased with his own artistic efforts but treasures his great-grandmother's drawing goes on to collect art throughout his life.
   "Created with acrylic paint, pencil, and collage, the precisely drawn illustrations offer pleasing views of Oscar's world. An unusual, potentially eye-opening picture book." Booklist

   ★ **Candy** shop; illustrated by Nicole Wong. Charlesbridge 2004 un il lib bdg $15.95
Grades: K 1 2 3   E
   1. Toleration -- Fiction 2. African Americans -- Fiction 3. Taiwanese Americans -- Fiction
   ISBN 1-57091-508-3
              LC 2003-3695
   When a boy and his aunt find that a bigot has written hurtful words on the sidewalk just outside the candy shop owned by "Miz Chu," a new immigrant from Taiwan, they set out to comfort her
   "The clean hues and supple lines of the pictures support Wahl's gentle message of comfort and tolerance." Booklist

   The **golden** Christmas tree; illustrated by Leonard Weisgard. Golden Book 2010 un il $8.99; lib bdg $11.99
Grades: PreK K 1   E
   1. Trees -- Fiction 2. Animals -- Fiction 3. Christmas -- Fiction
   ISBN 978-0-375-82747-1; 0-375-82747-1; 978-0-375-92747-8 lib bdg; 0-375-92747-6 lib bdg
   A reissue of the title first published 1988 by Western Pub.
   "Animals gather to decorate a fir tree and celebrate Christmas together. Wahl's quiet, reverent text is extended by Weisgard's art in which the lines of the animals' fur connect them visually with the fir tree's needles, unifying the pages." Horn Book Guide

Wahl, Phoebe

   ★ **Sonya's** chickens; Phoebe Wahl. Tundra Books of Northern New York 2015 32 p. color illustrations (hardcover) $17.99

Grades: PreK K 1 2   E

1. Loss (Psychology) 2. Chickens -- Fiction 3. Nature

ISBN 1770497897; 9781770497894; 9781770497917

LC 2014951815

In this children's book by Phoebe Wahl, "Sonya raises her three chickens from the time they are tiny chicks. She feeds them, shelters them and loves them. One night, Sonya hears noises coming from the chicken coop and discovers that one of her hens has disappeared. Where did the hen go? When Sonya discovers the answers, she learns some important truths about the interconnectedness of nature and the true joys and sorrows of caring for another creature." (Publisher's note)

"Papa soothes Sonya's sadness, explaining that a fox has taken the hen to feed his family of kits, and does so in a way that makes an upsetting situation more understandable. . . . The brilliantly colored artwork, produced in watercolor, collage, and colored pencil, is stunning." Booklist

Wahman, Wendy

A **cat** like that. Henry Holt 2011 il

Grades: PreK K 1   E

1. Cats -- Fiction 2. Friendship -- Fiction

ISBN 0-8050-8942-X; 978-0-8050-8942-4

LC 2010026952

A cat presents the characteristics of a perfect human friend.

"Executed with the Photoshop lasso tool, the graphic elements here are standouts. . . . An attractive primer for kids who love cats—or may some day." Booklist

Waldron, Kevin

Mr. Peek and the misunderstanding at the zoo. Candlewick Press 2010 il $15.99

Grades: PreK K 1 2   E

1. Zoos -- Fiction 2. Worry -- Fiction 3. Animals -- Fiction

ISBN 978-0-7636-4549-6; 0-7636-4549-4

LC 2009015137

First published 2008 in the United Kingdom

"Poor Mr. Peek thinks he has suddenly gained a tremendous amount of weight when he puts on his zookeeper jacket and a button pops off. As he makes his morning rounds, he complains to himself about how fat and wrinkled he is. . . . He does not notice that the zoo animals are worried because they think he is talking to them. Luckily, he returns home to discover that he had inadvertently switched jackets with his son. . . . Waldron's digital-media illustrations humorously convey the alarmed expressions of the animals while the quirky font and creative text placement reinforce Mr. Peek's stream-of-consciousness muttering." SLJ

Walker, Anna

I love Christmas. Simon & Schuster Books for Young Readers 2009 un il $9.99

Grades: PreK K 1   E

1. Stories in rhyme 2. Dogs -- Fiction 3. Zebras -- Fiction 4. Christmas -- Fiction

ISBN 978-1-4169-8317-0; 1-4169-8317-1

"A zebra named Ollie runs down some of his favorite holiday activities. Sweet, soft watercolors show Ollie and his dog decorating the Christmas tree, baking holiday treats with Nanna, and waiting for Santa, creating a cozy, merry accompaniment to the simple rhyming text. This is a great choice for a lap-sit and also as a read-alone for beginning readers." SLJ

Other titles about Ollie are:

I love to dance (2009)

I love to sing (2009)

I love my dad (2010)

I love my mom (2010)

I love birthdays (2010)

I love vacations (2011)

Peggy; a brave chicken on a big adventure. by Anna Walker. Clarion Books, Houghton Mifflin Harcourt 2014 32 p. (hardback) $16.99

Grades: PreK K 1 2   E

1. Chickens -- Fiction 2. City and town life -- Fiction 3. Adventure and adventurers -- Fiction

ISBN 0544259009; 9780544259003

LC 2013034562

In this book, by Anna Walker, "Peggy the hen is contented with her quiet existence and daily routine. When a powerful gust of wind sweeps her up and deposits her in the midst of a busy city, she explores her new surroundings, makes new friends, and cleverly figures out how to get home—with a newly kindled appetite for adventure." (Publisher's note)

"After a gust of wind transports her to the big city, suburban chicken Peggy explores her new surroundings. Walker's ink and photo-collage art is full of clever details that add levity to the story. The subtle color palette remains constant, regardless of Peggy's surroundings, exuding a calm throughout that is emulated by the varied illustration formats, the text, and Peggy herself." Horn Book

Walker, Rob D.

★ **Mama** says; a book of love for mothers and sons. by Rob D. Walker; illustrations by Leo & Diane Dillon. The Blue Sky Press 2008 un il $16.99

Grades: K 1 2 3   E

1. Faith 2. Stories in rhyme 3. Conduct of life -- Fiction 4. Mother-son relationship -- Fiction

ISBN 978-0-439-93208-0; 0-439-93208-4

LC 2007029821

"This elegantly designed book pairs a series of poems with stunning illustrations to celebrate the bond between mothers and sons. . . . The poems appear in English as well as another language (among them Cherokee, Danish, Hebrew, and Inuktitut). . . . The illustrations . . . are well-researched and lavish, showing mothers in traditional dress lovingly engaged with their sons. . . . The Dillons' breathtaking painting and the quiet dignity of the poems merit a wide audience." Publ Wkly

Walker, Sally M.

Druscilla's Halloween; illustrations by Lee White. Carolrhoda Books 2009 un il lib bdg $16.95

Grades: PreK K   E

1. Old age -- Fiction 2. Witches -- Fiction 3. Halloween -- Fiction

ISBN 978-0-8225-8941-9 lib bdg; 0-8225-8941-9 lib bdg

LC 2008-41162

In the time when witches tiptoe about to have their Halloween fun, ancient Druscilla knows her creaking knees will prevent her from being sneaky and sets out to find a silent conveyance for herself, her cat, and her jack-o-lantern

"Walker shows her lighter side in this witty picture book. White's expressive paintings, wonderfully varied in size and approach but unified by style, capture both the comedy and the pathos of Druscilla's predicament." Booklist

★ **Freedom** song; the story of Henry 'Box' Brown. by Sally M. Walker; illlustrated by Sean Qualls. 1st ed. Harper 2012 40 p. col. il (hardcover) $17.99

Grades: 2 3 4   E

1. Slaves -- Fiction 2. Gospel music -- Fiction 3. Historical fiction -- Fiction 4. Slaves 5. Magicians 6. Abolitionists 7. Singing -- Fiction 8. Slavery -- Fiction 9. Virginia -- Fiction 10. African

Americans -- Fiction 11. Underground railroad -- Fiction
ISBN 006058310X; 9780060583101

LC 2010024448

In this book, author Sally M. Walker discusses the "rhythm and song sustained [Henry] Brown throughout his years of enslaved labor and inspired him to seek his freedom when his wife and children were sold away from Virginia. [She looks at Brown, a slave who shipped himself to New York, and how he] sang for many years in a church choir." (Bulletin of the Center for Children's Books)

The **Vowel** family; a tale of lost letters. by Sally M. Walker; illustrated by Kevin Luthardt. Carolrhoda Books 2008 un il lib bdg $16.95

Grades: 1 2 3   E

1. English language -- Fiction
ISBN 978-0-8225-7982-3 lib bdg; 0-8225-7982-0 lib bdg

LC 2007-9952

The members of the Vowel family have a hard time talking until their children, Alan, Ellen, Iris, Otto, and Ursula, are born, and when one of them gets lost one day, it takes their Aunt Cyndy to fix the problem

"Luthardt's bright illustrations, featuring people with cartoonish balloon heads, ably echo the story's silliness. This clever approach to learning vowels will prove far more fun than just the basic recitation that's commonly taught." Booklist

Wallace, Carol

★ **Turkeys** together; illustrated by Jacqueline Rogers. Holiday House 2005 38p il (Holiday house reader) $15.95

Grades: K 1 2   E

1. Dogs -- Fiction 2. Eggs -- Fiction 3. Turkeys -- Fiction
ISBN 0-8234-1895-2

LC 2004-52392

A pointer dog puppy helps a mother turkey figure out how to protect her eggs from being stolen.

"A sweet tale about cooperation and friendship, with a satisfying conclusion. . . . Soft watercolor illustrations add meaning to the text and provide clues for some of the more difficult words. . . . The expressive animal faces are charming and realistic." SLJ

Wallace, Nancy Elizabeth

Pond walk; written and illustrated by Nancy Elizabeth Wallace. Marshall Cavendish Children's 2011 un il $17.99

Grades: PreK K 1 2   E

1. Ponds -- Fiction 2. Animals -- Fiction 3. Pond ecology -- Fiction
ISBN 978-0-7614-5816-6; 0-7614-5816-6

LC 2010025281

One summer day, Buddy Bear and his mother take a walk around a pond and observe the animals and insects that live there.

"Interspersed in the sequential text are Buddy's love of food and his sense of humor in the form of some nature jokes and puns. Wallace's familiar mixed-media collage illustrations (cut paper, photographs, and colored pencil) make this a visually appealing and informative look at limnology." SLJ

Pumpkin day! written and illustrated by Nancy Elizabeth Wallace. Marshall Cavendish 2002 un il $16.95

Grades: PreK K 1 2   E

1. Pumpkin -- Fiction 2. Rabbits -- Fiction
ISBN 0-7614-5128-5

LC 2002-834

Companion volume to Apples, apples, apples (2000)

A bunny family picks pumpkins at a local farm and learns pumpkin facts in the process

"Although there are many other books on the topic, this one stands apart because of its simple, yet dynamic collage artwork and the quality and quantity of information that is tucked into the text in all sorts of interesting ways." Booklist

Ready! Set! 100th day! written and illustrated by Nancy Elizabeth Wallace. Marshall Cavendish Children 2011 il $17.99

Grades: K 1   E

1. School stories 2. Rabbits -- Fiction 3. Set theory -- Fiction 4. Family life -- Fiction
ISBN 978-0-7614-5956-9; 0-7614-5956-1; 978-0-7614-6070-1 e-book

LC 2011001128

Minna's family pitches in to help her come up with the perfect project for the hundredth day of school, from twenty sets of five sticks to two sets of fifty pieces of pasta.

"This is definitely a book that will appeal to children. All of the characters are anthropomorphic brown rabbits done in large, colorful collages. The concepts are shown in a straightforward way that will be useful for introducing and reinforcing the number sets." SLJ

Recycle every day! written and illustrated by Nancy Elizabeth Wallace. Marshall Cavendish 2003 un il $16.95

Grades: PreK K 1 2   E

1. Rabbits -- Fiction 2. Recycling -- Fiction
ISBN 0-7614-5149-8

LC 2001-26050

When Minna has a school assignment to make a poster about recycling, her entire rabbit family spends the week practicing various kinds of recycling and suggesting ideas for her poster

"Using found materials to create the lovely art, the author/illustrator practices what she preaches and invites readers to search for the recycled materials. An activity and a game are appended. While the book's message is obvious, there is enough of a story to keep youngsters interested." SLJ

Other titles about Minna are:
The kindness quilt (2006)
Stars! Stars! Stars! (2009)

Seeds! Seeds! Seeds! written and illustrated by Nancy Elizabeth Wallace. Marshall Cavendish 2004 un il hardcover o.p. pa $5.99

Grades: PreK K 1 2   E

1. Bears -- Fiction 2. Seeds -- Fiction
ISBN 0-7614-5159-5; 0-7614-5366-0 pa

LC 2003-9318

Buddy Bear learns about different kinds of seeds and their uses when he opens a package sent by his grandfather

"The artwork consists of cut-paper collages with shadowing and life-sized photos of real seeds that look as though they can be picked right off the pages. The story is entertaining and educational." SLJ

Walsh, Barbara

★ **Sammy** in the sky; paintings by Jamie Wyeth. Candlewick Press 2011 un il $16.99

Grades: PreK K 1 2   E

1. Dogs -- Fiction 2. Death -- Fiction
ISBN 978-0-7636-4927-2; 0-7636-4927-9

LC 2010040744

A little girl tells about her special pet, Sammy, "the best hound dog in the whole world," and how, after he becomes sick and dies, she comes to know the truth of her mother's words, that Sammy's spirit is everywhere.

"This timeless story, told in straightforward prose, is brought to life in textured, soft-edged watercolor paintings in a predominant palette of blue, green, and gold. The feelings of the protagonist and the playful personality of the dog are palpably rendered in their facial expressions and body language." SLJ

Walsh, Ellen Stoll

Balancing act. Beach Lane 2010 un $16.99

Grades: PreK K   E

1. Mice -- Fiction 2. Animals -- Fiction 3. Balance -- Fiction
ISBN 978-1-4424-0757-2; 1-4424-0757-3

"This deceptively simple and creative book is loaded with fun. Two adorable mice create a teeter-totter using a stick balanced on a rock. A salamander joins one side, creating an imbalance, but then another one of equal weight joins the other mouse, and all is in order—until it happens again with a frog and a bird.... Observant children will want to converse about animal and color identification, as well as why the actions and reactions of the animals are creating balances/imbalances on the teeter-totter. The delightful illustrations were done using cut-paper collage and then splattered with acrylic paints...." This book is full of wonder and can be used at storytime or one-on-one." SLJ

Hop Jump. HMH Books for Young Readers 1996 32 p. $6.99 E
1. Dance -- Fiction 2. Frogs -- Fiction
ISBN 015201375X; 9780152013752

LC 9221037

Author Ellen Stoll Walsh's book focuses on a frog named Betsy. "Tired of hopping and jumping, Betsy the frog sees the leaves float down from the trees and is inspired to leap and twirl--she calls it dancing. At first the other frogs tell her there is no room for dancing. But she eventually teaches everyone that there is room for hopping, jumping, and dancing." (Publisher's note)

★ **Mouse** shapes. Harcourt 2007 un il $16

Grades: PreK K   E

1. Mice -- Fiction 2. Shape -- Fiction
ISBN 978-0-15-206091-6

LC 2006-13695

Three mice make a variety of things out of different shapes as they hide from a scary cat

"The collage technique works well for distinguishing the brightly colored shapes, and the simple story is pitched perfectly for sharing with the youngest of listeners." SLJ

Other titles about the mice are:

Mouse paint (1989)
Mouse count (1991)

Where is Jumper? Ellen Stoll Walsh. Beach Lane Books 2015 32 p. color illustrations (hardback) $17.99

Grades: PreK K 1 2   E

1. English language -- Grammar 2. Mice -- Fiction 3. Hide-and-seek -- Fiction 4. English language -- Prepositions -- Fiction
ISBN 1481445081; 9781481445085

LC 2015005164

In Ellen Stoll Walsh's children's book, readers learn about "prepositions while searching for a missing mouse. The mice can't find their friend Jumper! They look over branches and under leaves. They look between the weeds and down into Mole's tunnel. But still no Jumper. Where, oh where, could their sneaky pal be?" (Publisher's note)

"Walsh has a knack for creating illustrations and text that seem ever so simple yet have plenty of acumen, emotion, and pure fun. More mice, please." Kirkus

Walsh, Joanna

The **biggest** kiss; illustrated by Judi Abbot. Simon & Schuster Books for Young Readers 2011 il $12.99 E

1. Stories in rhyme 2. Kissing -- Fiction
ISBN 978-1-4424-2769-3; 1-4424-2769-8

LC 2011019442

A celebratioin of kisses from the sleepy goodnight kiss and the splishy splashy fish kiss to the sticky lipstick kiss and finally the best kiss of all.

"The engaging rhymes are perfectly complemented by the colorful, whimsical illustrations. A wonderful cuddle-up-and-read choice." SLJ

Walsh, Liam Francis

Fish; by Liam Francis Walsh. Henry Holt & Co. 2016 32 p. chiefly color illustrations $17.99

Grades: PreK K 1 2 3   E

1. Fishing -- Fiction 2. Letters -- Fiction
ISBN 1626723338; 9781626723337

LC 2015951000

In this book, by Liam Francis Walsh, a "boy and his dog embark on a fishing journey. Their first catch of the day: a big fat letter F. Their second? A slippery I. After an epic journey beneath the lake's surface, they find what they came for-- a FISH, along with some unanticipated menace from a few other letters." (Publisher's note)

"A full-bodied story with an economy of style, this will be particularly rewarding for emerging readers." Kirkus

Walsh, Melanie

Living with mom and living with dad; Melanie Walsh. Candlewick Press 2012 40 p.

Grades: PreK K   E

1. Toy and movable books 2. Parent-child relationship -- Fiction 3. Children of divorced parents -- Fiction 4. Divorce -- Fiction
ISBN 0763658693; 9780763658694

LC 2011047029

This children's picture book follows a little girl whose parents are divorced. "Sometimes she lives with her mom, and sometimes with her dad.... [A] lift-the-flap design juxtaposes how things are in one home versus the other. On her birthday, the girl's mother makes a cake, and the flap lifts to show her dad taking her bowling.... Other pages show joint activities--both parents attend a school play, and both are included in a photo album that the girl can look at if she misses one of them." (Kirkus Reviews)

Walter, Mildred Pitts

Alec's primer; illustrated by Larry Johnson. Vermont Folklife Center 2004 un il (Vermont Folklife Center children's book series) $15.95

Grades: K 1 2 3   E

1. Reading -- Fiction 2. Slavery -- Fiction 3. African Americans -- Fiction
ISBN 0-916718-20-4

LC 2003-27716

A young slave's journey to freedom begins when a plantation owner's granddaughter teaches him how to read. Based on the childhood of Alec Turner (1845-1923) who escaped from slavery by joining the Union Army during the Civil War and later became a landowner in Vermont

"Walter's spare, dramatic words and Johnson's stirring double-page paintings present a glimpse of the history in a brutal world." Booklist

Walters, Eric

My name is Blessing; Eric Walters. Tundra Books of Northern New York 2013 32 p. (hardcover) $17.95

Grades: PreK K 1 2   E

1. Picture books for children 2. People with disabilities -- Fiction
ISBN 1770493018; 9781770493018; 9781770493971

LC 2012955581

In this book, "physically disabled child Baraka and eight cousins
ve with their grandmother. She gives them boundless love, but there is
ever enough money or food, and life is hard-love doesn't feed hungry
tomachs or clothe growing bodies, or school keen minds. Baraka is
oo young, and, with his disability, needs too much, and she is too old.
A difficult choice must be made, and grandmother and grandchild set
ff on a journey to see if there is a place at the orphanage for Baraka."
Publisher's note)

Today is the day; Eric Walters. Tundra Books of Northern New
ork 2015 32 p. color illustrations (hardcover) $16.99
Grades: PreK K 1 2   E

1. Birthdays -- Fiction 2. Orphanages -- Fiction
ISBN 1770496483; 9781770496484; 9781770496507

LC 2014951814

In this children's story, by Eric Walters, illustrated by Eugenie Fer-
andes, "Mutanu is excited. . . . For today is no ordinary day at the
rphanage she lives in. Every year, the orphanage honors its newest ar-
ivals by creating a birthday day especially for them. From that mo-
nent forward, the orphans have a day that they know is theirs--a day
o celebrate, a day to enjoy, a day to remember. And today is the day!"
Publisher's note)

"Endnotes ground the story in its inspiration from a real orphanage
n Kenya while also explaining to more privileged Western children how
omeone might not know his or her birthday. Both deeply important and
urely joyful." Kirkus

Walters, Virginia

Are we there yet, Daddy? illustrated by S.D. Schindler. Viking
999 un il hardcover o.p. pa $6.99
Grades: PreK K 1 2   E

1. Stories in rhyme 2. Maps -- Fiction 3. Automobile travel --
Fiction
ISBN 0-670-87402-7; 0-14-230013-6 pa

LC 97-18220

A young boy describes the trip he and his father make to Grandma's
ouse, measuring how many miles are left at various points on the trip

"This unique picture book combines maps and counting skills with
a bouncy refrain that invites kids to join in. . . . The flat, pastel pictures
dd enlivening details to the repetitive text." SLJ

Wang Xiaohong

One year in Beijing; written by Xiaohong Wang; illustrated by
Grace Lin. ChinaSprout 2006 un il map $16.95
Grades: PreK K 1 2   E

1. China -- Fiction
ISBN 0-97473-025-4; 978-0-97473-025-7

In this introduction to China and Chinese culture, an eight-year-old
girl named "Ling Ling points out famous places as well as some of her
favorite spots, describes foods eaten during special occasions, and explains traditions associated with particular celebrations throughout the
year. . . . Grace Lin's bright, colorful illustrations and accompanying
cartoonlike ink sketches accentuate the narrative's informality and make
this engaging personal tour an excellent supplement to classroom textbooks." Booklist

Warburton, Tom

1000 times no; as told by Mr. Warburton. Laura Geringer Books
2009 un il $17.99

Grades: PreK K 1   E

1. Polyglot materials
ISBN 978-0-06-154263-3; 0-06-154263-6

LC 2007044270

When Noah's mother tells him that it is time to go, he finds more
than a few ways to refuse.

"Gouache cartoon scenes visually reinforce Noah's multilingual ve-
toes, from a full-page sphinx and hieroglyphics to a small square panel
with a text message. Endpapers provide identification of the languages,
pronunciations, and cultures that the precocious youngster employs. Delightful fun in its theme and delivery, this story will be asked for again
and again." SLJ

Ward, Helen, 1962-

★ The **town** mouse and the country mouse; an Aesop fable. Helen
Ward. Candlewick Press 2012 48 p. $16.99
Grades: PreK K 1 2   E

1. Fables 2. Mice -- Fiction 3. City and town life -- Fiction
ISBN 0763660981; 9780763660987

LC 2012942271

This children's fable, retold by Helen Ward, is "set in a 1930s-era
city at Christmastime. . . . Beguiled by his cousin's amazing tales, the
country mouse visits the electric city. Unfortunately the town mouse
forgot to mention that the city has a lot of noise, tall buildings . . . and
dangerous dogs! . . . In the end the reader understands both why the town
mouse loves his exciting life and why the country mouse is content with
his peaceful home." (Publisher's note)

Ward, Jennifer

What will hatch? by Jennifer ward; illustrated by Susie Ghahremani. 1st ed. Walker & Company 2013 40 p. col. ill. (hardcover)
$12.99; (library) $13.89
Grades: 1 2 3   E

1. Eggs 2. Animal reproduction 3. Eggs -- Incubation
ISBN 080272311X; 9780802723116; 9780802723123

LC 2011046330

In this children's picture book, "[Jennifer] Ward introduces seven
animals that hatch from eggs-sea turtle, penguin, tadpole, crocodile,
robin, caterpillar, and platypus. The first spread includes a two to three
word 'clue,' and the question, 'What Will Hatch?' On the second spread,
the clue's rhyme is completed and the answer is provided in words and
illustration (e.g., 'SANDY ball./WHAT will HATCH?/PADDLE and
CRAWL-/SEA TURTLE.')." (School Library Journal)

Ward, Lindsay

Henry finds his word; by Lindsay Ward. Dial Books for Young
Readers 2014 32 p. (hardcover) $16.99
Grades: PreK K 1   E

1. Speech -- Fiction 2. Infants -- Fiction 3. Babies -- Fiction
ISBN 0803739907; 9780803739901

LC 2013035183

In this children's story, by Lindsay Ward, "Baby Henry is under a lot
of pressure to say his first word. His parents are all excited about what
it will be, but Henry doesn't see what the big deal is. He says things all
the time like 'bbbghsh' and 'boop,' but no one seems to understand what
he means. So, Henry decides that he better start searching for a word.
Luckily, just when he needs it most, his first word comes looking for
him." (Publisher's note)

"Seeing that baby talk isn't working as well as he'd like, Henry decides to find his first word. Inaugural-word picture books remain perennial favorites, and this one distinguishes itself by committing whole-
heartedly to little Henry's perspective . . . Here's exactly how a baby
decodes and interprets the world around him, which can be a scary place
when mama isn't in sight! Suddenly seemingly alone, Henry's first word

bursts forth: 'MAMA.' And from there, as all mothers know, it never stops. Let this be the first first-word book to pull from the shelf." Kirkus

Ward, Lynd Kendall

The **biggest** bear; by Lynd Ward. Houghton Mifflin 1988 84p il lib bdg $16; pa $6.95

Grades: PreK K 1 2   E

1. Bears -- Fiction

ISBN 0-395-14806-5 lib bdg; 0-395-15024-8 pa

LC 88-176366

A reissue of the title first published 1952

Awarded the Caldecott Medal, 1953

"Johnny Orchard never did acquire the bearskin for which he boldly went hunting. Instead, he brought home a cuddly bear cub, which grew in size and appetite to mammoth proportions and worried his family and neighbors half to death." Child Books Too Good to Miss

Wardlaw, Lee

Red, white, and boom! Lee Wardlaw; illustrated by Huy Voun Lee. Henry Holt 2012 32 p. col. ill. (hc : reinforced binding) $16.99

Grades: PreK K 1   E

1. Fourth of July -- Fiction 2. Holidays -- United States 3. Picture books for children 4. Stories in rhyme

ISBN 0805090657; 9780805090659

LC 2011018541

In this children's picture book from author Lee Wardlaw, "[i]t's the Fourth of July! [Readers can] [t]ravel across the country for a city parade, a beach picnic, and fireworks in the park in this . . . celebration of the many cultures and traditions that make America's birthday BOOM!" (Amazon.com)

★ **Won** Ton; a cat tale told in haiku. illustrated by Eugene Yelchin. Henry Holt & Co. 2011 40 p. color illustrations $16.99

Grades: PreK K 1 2 3   E

1. Haiku 2. Children's poetry 3. Cats -- Fiction 4. Animal shelters -- Fiction

ISBN 0805089950; 9780805089950

LC 2009029414

A cat arrives at a shelter, arranges to go home with a good family, and settles in with them, all the while letting them know who is boss and, finally, sharing his real name.

"Wardlaw . . . has a fine understanding of the feline mind, and each 17-syllable poem packs a big impact—especially in the first section, which imagines the emotional life of a cat in a shelter. . . . The Japanese haiku theme . . . is carried through with elements and backgrounds lifted from old woodblock prints. The final page, a delicate painting of the boy nuzzling the cat, is a fitting reward for the boy's patience and Won Ton's resilience. A surprisingly powerful story in verse." Publ Wkly

Warhola, James

Uncle Andy's. Putnam 2003 un il $16.99

Grades: K 1 2 3   E

1. Artists 2. Artists -- United States 3. Motion picture directors

ISBN 0-399-23869-7

LC 2002-7766

The author describes a trip to see his uncle, the soon-to-be-famous artist Andy Warhol, and the fun that he and his family had on the visit

"This catches the excitement that the creative process can engender, both for the established artist and for the dreamer." Booklist

Another title about Uncle Andy is:

Uncle Andy's cats (2009)

Waring, Geoffrey

Oscar and the bat; a book about sound. [by] Geoff Waring. Candlewick Press 2008 27p il (Start with science) $14.99

Grades: PreK K 1 2   E

1. Bats -- Fiction 2. Cats -- Fiction 3. Sound -- Fiction

ISBN 978-0-7636-4025-5; 0-7636-4025-5

LC 2007052195

First published 2006 in the United Kingdom

Bat teaches Oscar the kitten to hear and identify the sounds around him, whether they are made by animals and birds or by a passing thunderstorm

This is "clear and immediate. . . . Spacious digital color illustrations show Oscar the Cat in a meadow with his friend, Bat, who answers Oscar's questions with fascinating scientific detail." Booklist

Other titles about Oscar are:

Oscar and the bird (2009)

Oscar and the cricket (2008)

Oscar and the frog (2007)

Oscar and the moth (2007)

Oscar and the snail (2009)

Warnes, Tim

Daddy hug; by Tim Warnes; illustrated by Jane Chapman. HarperCollins 2008 un il $16.99; lib bdg $17.89

Grades: PreK K   E

1. Stories in rhyme 2. Animals -- Fiction 3. Fathers -- Fiction

ISBN 978-0-06-058950-9; 0-06-058950-7; 978-0-06-058951-6 lib bdg; 0-06-058951-5 lib bdg

LC 2005017867

"In a jolly, rhyming text, this book describes various animal fathers. . . . The vibrant, painterly illustrations, featuring fathers interacting with their offspring, are filled with action and color. . . . The simple text and warm-hued artwork create a feeling of security that will appeal to children." SLJ

Washington, Donna L.

★ **Li'l** Rabbit's Kwanzaa; illustrated by Shane W. Evans. Katherine Tegen Books 2010 un il $12.99

Grades: PreK K 1   E

1. Gifts -- Fiction 2. Kwanzaa -- Fiction 3. Rabbits -- Fiction 4. Grandmothers -- Fiction

ISBN 978-0-06-072816-8; 0-06-072816-7

L'il Rabbit searches for a gift for his grandmother when she is sick during Kwanzaa, and surprises her with the best gift of all. Includes 'The Nguzo Saba' The Seven Principles of Kwanzaa.

"The yellow undertones . . . add warmth to the cartoon artwork. Sweetly capturing the spirit of the season, the story comes in handy as a lovely supplement to resources that provide straightforward facts about Kwanzaa." SLJ

Watkins, Rowboat, 1967-

Rude cakes; cooked up by Rowboat Watkins. Chronicle Books LLC 2015 32 p. color illustrations (alk. paper) $16.99

Grades: PreK K 1   E

1. Cake -- Fiction 2. Courtesy -- Fiction 3. Etiquette -- Fiction 4. Conduct of life -- Fiction

ISBN 1452138516; 9781452138510

LC 2014026316

In this children's story, by Rowboat Watkins, "a not-so-sweet cake--who never says please or thank you or listens to its parents--gets its just desserts. Mixing hilarious text and pictures, . . . [this story] can also be served up as a delectable discussion starter about manners or bullying, as it sweetly reminds us all that even the rudest cake can learn to change its ways." (Publisher's note)

"Using humor and tasty snacks, Watkins demonstrates the importance of good manners without being preachy, sneaking in the lesson like zucchini in a muffin." Booklist

Watson, Renee

A **place** where hurricanes happen; illustrated by Shadra Strickland. Random House 2010 un il lib bdg $20.99

Grades: 1 2 3 4   E

1. New Orleans (La.) -- Fiction 2. Hurricane Katrina, 2005 -- Fiction

ISBN 978-0-375-85609-9; 0-375-85609-9; 978-0-375-95609-6 lib bdg; 0-375-95609-3 lib bdg

LC 2009017826

Told in alternating voices, four friends from the same New Orleans neighborhood describe what happens to them and their community when they are separated, then reunited, as a result of Hurricane Katrina.

"The text is lyrical and realistically portrays a child's point of view, deftly describing in a few words how the children are affected. . . . The evocative watercolor-and-ink illustrations in soft pastels and grays limn the devastation but also the good times of the neighborhood to great effect." SLJ

Watson, Wendy

★ **Bedtime** bunnies; story and pictures by Wendy Watson. Clarion Books 2010 un il $16

Grades: PreK K   E

1. Bedtime -- Fiction 2. Rabbits -- Fiction

ISBN 978-0-547-22312-4; 0-547-22312-9

Bunnies scamper, scurry, splash, zip, and snuggle as they get ready for bed.

"Rendered in pencil, watercolor, and acrylic paint, Watson's buoyant, gauzy pictures reveal several 'oops' moments: one bunny spills juice down the front of his overalls, and another drops a bar of soap while taking a bath. . . . At once soothing and spirited, this is a charmingly crafted bedtime tale for cold winter nights." Publ Wkly

Watt, Mélanie, 1975-

Chester; written and illustrated by Melanie Watt. Kids Can Press 2007 un il $16.95

Grades: PreK K 1 2   E

1. Cats -- Fiction 2. Authorship -- Fiction

ISBN 1-55453-140-3; 978-1-55453-140-0

"Watt presents audiences with the story of a mouse—or she tries to, but her cat Chester has a red marker and his own idea about the subject of the story: himself. . . . Grades two to four." (Bull Cent Child Books)

"Watt presents audiences with the story of a mouse—or she tries to, but her cat Chester has a red marker and his own idea about the subject of the story: himself. . . . The notion is entertaining and its execution . . . is frequently hilarious. . . . This entertains both as a cat story and as an entry-level metatextual narrative." Bull Cent Child Books

Other titles about Chester are:

Chester's back! (2008)

Chester's masterpiece (2010)

Have I got a book for you! Kids Can Press 2009 un il $16.95

Grades: PreK K 1 2   E

1. Selling -- Fiction 2. Books and reading -- Fiction

ISBN 978-1-55453-289-6; 1-55453-289-2

Mr. Al Foxword is one persistent salesman! He will do just about anything to sell you this book. Al tries every trick of the trade. But just when you're ready to close the book on him, he comes up with a clever tactic you simply can't refuse!

"Charcoal pencil illustrations are digitally assembled and feature bright orange, yellow, and green. Foxword's clever sales techniques make this book funny to the hilt." SLJ

Scaredy Squirrel. Kids Can Press 2006 un il $14.95

Grades: PreK K 1 2   E

1. Fear -- Fiction 2. Squirrels -- Fiction

ISBN 1-55337-959-4

Scaredy Squirrel never leaves his nut tree because he's afraid of the unknown "out there." But then, something unexpected happens that may just change his outlook.

"With his iconic nervous grin and over-the-top punctiliousness, Scaredy Squirrel is an endearing character. Thick-lined cartoons with bold patches of color, quirky charts and graphs, and clever asides provide humor that will appeal to children." SLJ

Other titles about Scaredy Squirrel are:

Scaredy Squirrel makes a friend (2007)

Scaredy Squirrel at the beach (2008)

Scaredy Squirrel at night (2009)

Scaredy Squirrel has a birthday party (2011)

Scaredy Squirrel prepares for Christmas (2012)

Scaredy Squirrel goes camping (2013)

Scaredy Squirrel prepares for Halloween (2013)

Scaredy Squirrel Prepares for Halloween; A Safety Guide for Scaredies. Mélanie Watt. Kids Can Press 2013 64 p. $17.95

Grades: PreK K 1 2   E

1. Picture books for children 2. Halloween -- Fiction

ISBN 1894786874; 9781894786874

This book looks at celebrating Halloween. In eight chapters, Scaredy Squirrel "explains how best to carve pumpkins (don't use an ax or chainsaw, and 'always go with a friendly look'), decorate one's home (stick to 'unscary' black and orange items like top hats and popsicles), pick a costume, and host a party ('Pipe organ music makes a great soundtrack for dancing. The very gloomy tempo will slow festivities down.')." (Publishers Weekly)

Watts, Bernadette

The **Smallest** Snowflake. North-South 2009 un il $16.95

Grades: PreK K 1 2   E

1. Snow -- Fiction 2. Spring -- Fiction 3. Winter -- Fiction

ISBN 978-0-7358-2258-0; 0-7358-2258-1

"Smallest Snowflake, longing for 'someplace special,' drifts along through the air until she lands in the window box of a little cottage. . . . Finally, green shoots push up through the dirt and snowdrop flowers open on the stalks. . . . Watts writes a tale as sturdy yet delicate as her artwork. . . . This quiet yet involving picture book is highly recommended for reading aloud as winter turns to spring." Booklist

The **ugly** duckling; by Hans Christian Andersen; adapted and illustrated by Bernadette Watts. North-South Bks. 2000 un il $15.95; lib bdg $16.95

Grades: K 1 2 3 4   E

1. Authors 2. Novelists 3. Dramatists 4. Fairy tales 5. Swans -- Fiction 6. Children's authors 7. Short story writers

ISBN 0-7358-1388-4; 0-7358-1389-2 lib bdg

LC 00-35125

An ugly duckling spends an unhappy year ostracized by the other animals before he grows into a beautiful swan

The "detailed double-paged spreads are beautiful. . . . Watts' active pastoral landscapes, filled with light and movement, capture the changing seasons and the sturdy, unwanted outsider's search for home." Booklist

Watts, Jeri

A **Piece** of Home; by Jeri Watts; illustrated by Hyewon Yum. Candlewick Press 2016 32 p. color illustrations $16.99

Grades: K 1 2 3   E

1. West Virginia -- Fiction 2. Friendship -- Fiction 3. Immigrants -- United States -- Fiction

ISBN 0763669717; 9780763669713

In this book, by Jeri Watts, illustrated by Hyewon Yum, "Hee Jun's family moves from Korea to West Virginia. . . . His eyes are not big and round like his classmates', and he can't understand anything the teacher says, even when she speaks s-l-o-w-l-y and loudly at him. As he lies in bed at night, the sky seems smaller and darker. But little by little Hee Jun begins to learn English words and make friends on the playground." (Publisher's note)

"The lengthy text paints a realistic picture of difficulties faced by a family striving to make a new start, and the positive resolution is quietly satisfying. A solid addition for most collections." SLJ

Wayland, April Halprin

New Year at the pier; a Rosh Hashanah story. illustrated by Stephane Jorisch. Dial Books for Young Readers 2009 un il $16.99

Grades: K 1 2 3   E

1. Jews -- Fiction 2. Rosh ha-Shanah -- Fiction

ISBN 978-0-8037-3279-7; 0-8037-3279-1

LC 2007039812

On Rosh Hashanah, Izzy and his family make lists of the wrongs they have committed over the past year, and after they have apologized, they throw pieces of bread into the water to 'clean their hearts' in a ceremony called tashlich.

"The empathetic, low-key prose makes important points about personal responsibility without pummeling readers, while the stylish, keenly observed watercolors convey both Izzy's sheepish chagrin and the joys of communal tradition." Publ Wkly

Weatherford, Carole Boston, 1956-

★ **Freedom** in Congo Square; by Carole Boston Weatherford; illustrated by R. Gregory Christie. Simon & Schuster 2016 40 p. color illustrations (hardcover) $17.99

Grades: K 1 2 3 4   E

1. Slavery -- United States -- History 2. Louisiana -- History -- 19th century

ISBN 1499801033; 9781499801033

LC 2015039042

Caldecott Honor Book (2017)

Coretta Scott King (Illustrator) Honor Book (2017)

This book, by Carole Boston Weatherford and illustrated by R. Gregory Christie, tells of how slaves "in 19th century Louisiana . . . were briefly able to congregate in Congo Square in New Orleans. . . . They were free to forget their cares, their struggles, and their oppression. This story chronicles slaves' duties each day . . . and builds to the freedom of Sundays and the special experience of an afternoon spent in Congo Square." (Publisher's note)

"Christie . . . takes readers on a visual journey, moving from searing naïf scenes of plantation life to exuberantly expressionistic and abstract images filled with joyous, soaring curvilinear figures. An introduction and afterword provide further historic detail." Pub Wkly

★ **Freedom** on the menu; the Greensboro sit-ins. paintings by Jerome Lagarrigue. Dial Books for Young Readers 2005 un il $16.99

Grades: K 1 2 3   E

1. North Carolina -- Fiction 2. Race relations -- Fiction 3. African Americans -- Fiction 4. Civil rights demonstrations -- Fiction

ISBN 0-8037-2860-3

LC 2002-13226

The 1960 civil rights sit-ins at the Woolworth's lunch counter in Greensboro, North Carolina, are seen through the eyes of a young Southern black girl.

"Simple and straightforward, the first-person narrative relates events within the context of one close-knit family. . . . The well-composed painterly illustrations show up well from a distance. A handsome book." Booklist

Sugar Hill; Harlem's historic neighborhood. Carole Boston Weatherford; illustrated by R. Gregory Christie. Albert Whitman & Company 2014 32 p. color illustrations (hardback) $16.99

Grades: 2 3 4   E

1. Harlem (New York, N.Y.) -- Fiction 2. African Americans -- Harlem (New York, N.Y.) 3. Stories in rhyme 4. African Americans -- Fiction 5. New York (N.Y.) -- History -- 1898-1951 -- Fiction 6. African Americans -- New York (State) -- New York -- Fiction 7. Harlem (New York, N.Y.) -- History -- 20th century -- Fiction

ISBN 0807576506; 9780807576502

LC 2013030748

In this book, by Carole Boston Weatherford, "take a walk through Harlem's Sugar Hill and meet all the . . . people who made this neighborhood legendary. . . . Includes brief biographies of jazz [musicians] Duke Ellington, Count Basie, Sonny Rollins, and Miles Davis; artists Aaron Douglas and Faith Ringgold; entertainers Lena Horne and the Nicholas Brothers; writer Zora Neale Hurston; civil rights leader W. E. B. DuBois and lawyer Thurgood Marshall." (Publisher's note)

"Weatherford's poetic, swinging textual rhythms meet Christie's artistic razzmatazz to create one hot picture book. A historic and cultural tour of Harlem's famous neighborhood, the book drops names aplenty: Miles Davis, Lena Horne, Zora Neale Hurston, Thurgood Marshall and W.E.B. Du Bois, among others . . . Sparsely detailed but action-packed Christie's illustrations echo the lives of the star-studded cast of characters. . . . The backmatter offers biographical blurbs that emphasize the longitudinal impact this neighborhood has had on Harlem and on the nation; birthdates begin in 1868 (Du Bois) and end in the present . . . A fine tribute to the local color of Sugar Hill, who have made America a better and more interesting country for almost a century." Kirkus

Weaver, Tess

Cat jumped in! by Tess Weaver; illustrated by Emily Arnold McCully. Clarion Books 2007 32p il $16

Grades: PreK K 1 2   E

1. Cats -- Fiction

ISBN 978-0-618-61488-2

LC 2006039217

An inquisitive feline walks through the rooms of a house, jumping into one mess after another, before landing in the loving arms of its owner.

"Some 26 different verbs describe the cat's movements, infusing the story with plenty of action, and the bright watercolors seem quickly, carefully rendered." Booklist

Weber, Elka

One little chicken; illustrations by Elisa Kleven. Tricycle Press 2011 un il $16.99

Grades: K 1 2 3   E

1. Jews -- Fiction 2. Goats -- Fiction 3. Chickens -- Fiction 4. Conduct of life -- Fiction 5. Lost and found possessions -- Fiction

ISBN 1-58246-374-3; 978-1-58246-374-2

LC 2010000891

Retells a story in the Talmud about a family that cares for a lost chicken, turning its eggs into a profit which they later give to its owner.

"Kleven's engaging mixed-media folk-art collages brim with detail like a border of cakes and pies, or a coy goat offering a bouquet to Leora

The colors are rich; the textures and patterns beg to be touched, and the ending is likely to leave readers pondering this story." SLJ

Webster, Sheryl

Noodle's knitting; [illustrated by] Caroline Pedler. Good Books 2010 un il $16.99
Grades: PreK K 1   E
    1. Mice -- Fiction 2. Animals -- Fiction 3. Knitting -- Fiction
    ISBN 978-1-56148-694-6; 1-56148-694-9
                LC 2010004920
A mouse named Noodle finds a ball of wool and decides to knit a scarf, which grows so big that she is trapped inside her house.
  "Webster's prose makes for a fluid read-aloud, and Pedler's full and double-page paintings are playful, warm, and cozy." SLJ

Weeks, Sarah

Drip, drop; story by Sarah Weeks; pictures by Jane Manning. HarperCollins Pubs. 2000 32p il (I can read book) hardcover o.p. pa $3.99
Grades: PreK K 1 2   E
    1. Stories in rhyme 2. Mice -- Fiction 3. Rain -- Fiction
    ISBN 0-06-028523-0; 0-06-028524-9 lib bdg; 0-06-443597-0 pa
                LC 00-21652
Pip Squeak the mouse is kept awake all night by the drips from his leaky roof
  "Short, simple sentences keep the action moving along while a single problem focuses readers' attention. The snappy narrative is coupled with expressive, silly illustrations." SLJ
  Another title about Pip Squeak is:
  Pip Squeak (2007)

Ella, of course! written by Sarah Weeks; illustrated by Doug Cushman. Harcourt 2007 un il $16
Grades: PreK K   E
    1. Pigs -- Fiction 2. Dance -- Fiction
    ISBN 978-0-15-204943-0; 0-15-204943-6
                LC 2005-25910
When Ella the pig is banned from bringing her umbrella to the dance recital, she comes up with an ingenious solution to the problem
  "Weeks' short text includes lots of repetitive phrases and sound effects that will easily encourage participation. Cushman adds slapstick humor with double-page scenes." Booklist

Mac and Cheese; illustrated by Jane Manning. Laura Geringer Books 2010 32p il $16.99; pa $3.99
Grades: K 1 2   E
    1. Stories in rhyme 2. Cats -- Fiction 3. Friendship -- Fiction
    ISBN 978-0-06-117079-9; 0-06-117079-8; 978-0-06-117081-2 pa; 0-06-117081-X pa
                LC 2008014199
Two cats that are as different as night and day are nevertheless best friends.
  "The simple sentences with ample white space suit the brief snippets of rhyming dialogue between the two characters, and brightly colored watercolor illustrations of the feline alley friends reveal expressions ranging from Mac's sheer glee to Cheese's exasperated disgust. Simplicity of text, action illustrated to lead readers in turning the page, and satisfying conclusion makes this easy reader a solid selection for all libraries." SLJ

★ Sophie Peterman tells the truth! illustrated by Robert Neubecker. Beach Lane Books 2009 un il $16.99

Grades: PreK K 1 2   E
    1. Infants -- Fiction 2. Siblings -- Fiction
    ISBN 978-1-4169-8686-7; 1-4169-8686-3
                LC 2008-51058
A disgruntled big sister reveals unpleasant facts about babies.
  This offers "thick-lined cartoon illustrations in bright colors and clear bold type that gets bigger and bigger. . . . The details of messy daily life and the honest, unsentimental expressions of rage and bonding are just right for young children to recognize and laugh about together." Booklist

Two eggs, please; written by Sarah Weeks; illustrated by Betsy Lewin. Atheneum Bks. for Young Readers 2003 un il $15.95
Grades: PreK K 1 2   E
    1. Eggs -- Fiction 2. Animals -- Fiction 3. Restaurants -- Fiction
    ISBN 0-689-83196-X
                LC 2002-5291
  "An all-night diner attracts a wide variety of customers in the middle of the night, including a rhino cab driver, two wolf police officers, and a crocodile street performer and his snake. One by one, they take stools at the counter and order the same thing, 'Two eggs, please,' but each order is different: soft-boiled, hard-boiled, poached, raw (for the snake). The premise is as basic as fried eggs, and handled with a light touch, but Lewin's inviting watercolor and ink illustrations add flavor and expand the story to involve young listeners and readers." Horn Book

★ Woof; a love story. illustrated by Holly Berry. Laura Geringer Books 2009 un il $16.99
Grades: PreK K 1 2   E
    1. Stories in rhyme 2. Cats -- Fiction 3. Dogs -- Fiction 4. Love -- Fiction 5. Communication -- Fiction
    ISBN 978-0-06-025007-2; 0-06-025007-0
                LC 2006022295
Despite a language barrier, a dog and cat fall in love with the help of a buried trombone.
  "This affectionate and funny story is told almost musically, in rhythmic . . . verse by expert storyteller Weeks. Berry's exuberant collage illustrations spill over the pages, gorgeously chaotic and filled with heart." SLJ

Weiss, Ellen

Playtime for twins; by Ellen Weiss; illustrated by Sam Williams. Little Simon 2012 30 p. col. ill. (board bk) $7.99
Grades: PreK   E
    1. Twins -- Fiction 2. Imagination -- Fiction 3. Board books 4. Play -- Fiction
    ISBN 1442430273; 9781442430273
                LC 2011287842
In this children's book by Ellen Weiss, "the twins are ready for some fun! Laugh along as these cheerful siblings make some noise, read about rocket ships, seesaw, and more before they wave good-bye to the sun as it sets and head for home. Pitch-perfect rhyming text from . . . Weiss and soft, engaging images from bestselling illustrator Sam Williams showcase the twins' appealing personalities." (Publisher's note)
  "Although the illustrations and text are intentionally vague, the twins in question are likely a fraternal pair of undefined gender. The duo engages in traditional toddler play: block building, pot banging, pulling every book off the shelf, swinging and sand play." Kirkus

Porky and Bess; by Ellen Weiss and Mel Friedman; illustrated by Marsha Winborn. Random House 2010 il $12.99
Grades: K 1 2 3   E
    1. Cats -- Fiction 2. Pigs -- Fiction 3. Poetry -- Fiction 4.

Friendship -- Fiction
ISBN 9780375854583; 9780375961137 lib bdg; 9780375861130 pa

LC 2009013384

Despite their differences, Porky the messy pig and Bess the fussy cat are best friends and support each other in all their endeavors, from poetry writing to cake baking.

"In between outings with his best friend Bess (a meticulous cat, mother of three kittens), Porky (a messy, disorganized, bachelor pig) is trying to write a special poem for Poem-Reading Day. By book s end, Porky has found the perfect words to celebrate their friendship. Gently humorous and expressive pictures illustrate this odd-couple pair." Horn Book

The **taming** of Lola; a shrew story; a picture book in five acts. illustrated by Jerry Smath. Abrams Books for Young Readers 2010 un il $15.95
Grades: PreK K 1 2   E
1. Shrews -- Fiction 2. Cousins -- Fiction 3. Grandmothers -- Fiction
ISBN 978-0-8109-4066-6; 0-8109-4066-3

LC 2009-00617

Lola, a shrew, is famous all over West Meadow for her temper tantrums, but when her cousin Lester comes for a visit and gets special treatment just because he demands it, Lola begins to rethink her behavior.

"Screwball dialogue and banter, . . . asides from the narrator, and details about the shrew diet . . . combine to keep action and laughs coming. The pacing is even, the goody-goody peacemaking is leavened by the wisecracks, and there's even a surprise ending." Publ Wkly

Weitzman, Jacqueline Preiss
Superhero Joe; written by Jacqueline Preiss; drawn by Ron Barrett. Simon & Schuster Books for Young Readers 2011 un il $16.99
Grades: K 1 2   E
1. Fear -- Fiction 2. Imagination -- Fiction 3. Superheroes -- Fiction
ISBN 978-1-4169-9157-1; 1-4169-9157-3

LC 2009034390

Five-year-old Joey uses his super powers to help his parents out of a sticky situation.

"Barrett's line drawings are rendered in ink and colored digitally. The crisp text is hand lettered. The graphic-novel format and retro atmosphere mimic the comic books whose heroes Joe emulates. Weitzman acknowledges the boy's feelings and provides imaginative solutions followed by more practical ones. An upbeat, humorous selection." SLJ
Another title in this series is:
Superhero Joe and the creature next door (2013)

★ **You** can't take a balloon into the Metropolitan Museum; story by Jacqueline Preiss Weitzman; pictures by Robin Preiss Glasser. Dial Bks. for Young Readers 1998 37p il hardcover o.p. pa $7.99
Grades: K 1 2 3   E
1. Stories without words 2. New York (N.Y.) -- Fiction 3. Metropolitan Museum of Art (New York, N.Y.) -- Fiction
ISBN 0-8037-2301-6; 0-14-056816-6 pa

LC 97-31629

In this wordless story, a young girl and her grandmother view works inside the Metropolitan Museum of Art, while the balloon she has been forced to leave outside floats around New York City causing a series of mishaps that mirror scenes in the museum's artworks

"Lively, squiggly ink sketches with characters picked out in watercolor and gouache for accent, along with reproductions of art from the Met . . . tell a vivid, happy tale." Booklist
Other titles in this series are:

You can't take a balloon into the Museum of Fine Arts (2002)
You can't take a balloon into the National Gallery (2000)

Wellington, Monica
Apple farmer Annie. Dutton Children's Bks. 2001 un il $14.99
Grades: PreK K 1 2   E
1. Apples -- Fiction
ISBN 0-525-46727-0

LC 00-46203

Annie the apple farmer saves her most beautiful apples to sell fresh at the farmers' market

"Charming and cheery, [this] story makes a great read-aloud. The illustrations seem to step right out of a coloring book with simple shapes objects, and bright, crayon-box colors." SLJ

★ **Mr.** Cookie Baker; [by] Monica Wellington. rev ed.; Dutton Children's Books 2006 un il $15.99
Grades: PreK   E
1. Baking -- Fiction 2. Cookies -- Fiction
ISBN 0-525-47763-2
First published 1992
After a day of making and selling cookies, Mr. Baker gets to enjoy one himself. Includes cookie recipes.

"Done in gouache and colored pencil, the artwork features clean lines and flat colors that are as cheery as the cookies' sugar sprinkles." Booklist

Pizza at Sally's; [by] Monica Wellington. Dutton Children's Books 2006 un il $14.99
Grades: PreK K 1 2   E
1. Pizza -- Fiction 2. Cooking -- Fiction 3. Restaurants -- Fiction
ISBN 978-0-525-47715-0; 0-525-47715-2

LC 2005026493

With vegetables from her own garden and other fresh ingredients Sally mixes and bakes hot and bubbly pizzas for her customers to take home or eat in her pizzeria

"Cheerful, precisely composed gouache paintings accented with photo collages of fresh ingredients add warmth and humor to the story." SLJ

Riki's birdhouse. Dutton Children's Books 2009 un il $15.99
Grades: PreK K 1 2   E
1. Birds -- Fiction 2. Birdhouses -- Fiction
ISBN 978-0-525-42079-8; 0-525-42079-7

LC 2008013890

Riki, who loves to watch, feed, and listen to the birds that come to his garden, decides to build a birdhouse

"Riki's passion for birds is evident, and likely to be contagious. . . . The bold colors, simple shapes and clean lines of the gouache illustrations are in sharp contrast to the details found in the photographic elements cut out and glued onto the artwork. . . . Backmatter include instructions for building and installing a birdhouse, a recipe for bird food cupcakes and information about birdbaths, feeders and bluebirds. Kirkus

Truck driver Tom; [by] Monica Wellington. Dutton Children's Books 2007 un il $15.99
Grades: PreK K   E
1. Trucks -- Fiction
ISBN 978-0-525-47831-7

LC 2006035917

The driver of a tractor-trailer picks up a load of fresh fruits and vegetables, then drives through the countryside, past small towns, and int the big city, passing farms, construction sites, and many other vehicles, then delivers the produce and relaxes with other drivers

"The simple text is printed in a large block font that is just right for beginning readers. . . . Clearly drawn gouache paintings are enhanced with meticulously cut photos to add texture and character to the scene." SLJ

Wells, Rosemary

★ **Emily's** first 100 days of school. Hyperion Bks. for Children 2000 un il hardcover o.p. pa $7.99
Grades: PreK K   E
   1. Counting 2. School stories 3. Rabbits -- Fiction
ISBN 0-7868-0507-2; 0-7868-1354-7 pa
                     LC 99-27021

Starting with number one for the first day of school, Emily the rabbit learns the numbers to one hundred in many different ways

"Wells manages to find fresh, engaging presentations for that many numbers. Alive with color and thematically relevant decoration, the oversized pages are sometimes divided into several panels, but never feel too busy." Horn Book Guide

Another title about Emily and her school is:
My kindergarten (2004)

Hands off, Harry! Katherine Tegen Books 2011 un il (Kindergarters) $14.99
Grades: K 1 2   E
   1. School stories 2. Alligators -- Fiction 3. Kindergarten -- Fiction
ISBN 978-0-06-192112-4; 0-06-192112-2
                   LC 2010016046

Harry has trouble keeping his hands off his classmates until Tina thinks of the perfect piece of gym equipment to teach him about personal space.

Wells "builds a sense of drama while showing that she knows kindergarten inside and out. Kids will appreciate her faith in their inventiveness and sense of community—and they'll also enjoy the genial, neatly framed collaged images, which use textured materials to convey the alligators' bumpy skin and vibrant wardrobe." Publ Wkly

★ **Love** waves. Candlewick Press 2011 un il $15.99
Grades: PreK K   E
   1. Stories in rhyme 2. Love -- Fiction 3. Parent-child relationship -- Fiction
ISBN 978-0-7636-4989-0; 0-7636-4989-9
                   LC 2010040460

While they are at work a mother and father send powerful "love waves" to their child at home, offering reassurance and comfort in their absence.

"With cozy pastel scenes and gentle verse, Wells makes tangible the powerful emotional connection between parent and child, reminding children that longing and, more importantly, love are both two-way streets." Publ Wkly

Max & Ruby's treasure hunt; by Rosemary Wells. Viking 2012 32 p. (hardcover) $17.99
Grades: PreK K   E
   1. Treasure hunt (game) -- Fiction 2. Rabbits -- Fiction 3. Grandmothers -- Fiction 4. Brothers and sisters -- Fiction 5. Treasure hunt (Game) -- Fiction
ISBN 0670063177; 9780670063178
                   LC 2011048535

This children's book by Rosemary Wells presents a "return adventure for Max and Ruby. . . . When a thunderstorm ruins Ruby's tea party, Grandma suggests the four bunnies have a treasure hunt. . . . The final treasure box has five gold coins filled with chocolate -- but wait, there

are only four bunnies! They decide to give the fifth to Lily's doll, Dagmar, but where is she? . . . [T]he bunnies retrace their steps and clues to find the doll." (Kirkus)

★ **Morris's** disappearing bag. Viking 1999 un il hardcover o.p. pa $6.99
Grades: PreK K 1 2   E
   1. Rabbits -- Fiction 2. Christmas -- Fiction
ISBN 0-670-88721-8; 0-14-230004-7 pa
                   LC 00-267633

First published 1975 by Dial Bks. for Young Readers
Morris is so disappointed with his Christmas present that he invents a disappearing bag, which gives him a chance to share his brother's and sister's gifts

In this version "Morris re-appears in a full-color, full-size edition of the Christmas day story." Horn Book Guide

★ **Noisy** Nora; with all new illustrations [by] Rosemary Wells. Dial Bks. for Young Readers 1997 un il $15.99; pa $6.99
Grades: PreK K 1 2   E
   1. Stories in rhyme 2. Mice -- Fiction
ISBN 0-670-88722-6; 0-14-056728-3 pa
A newly illustrated edition of the title first published 1973
Little Nora, tired of being ignored, tries to gain her family's attention by being noisy. When this doesn't work Nora disappears but returns when she is sure she has been missed

"All new illustrations infuse this much-loved picture book . . . with energy. Vibrant colors and a larger format make the characters seem to jump out at readers." SLJ

Otto runs for President. Scholastic Press 2008 un il $15.99
Grades: K 1 2   E
   1. School stories 2. Dogs -- Fiction 3. Politics -- Fiction
ISBN 978-0-545-03722-8; 0-545-03722-0
                   LC 2007024816

While the popular Tiffany and athletic Charles make increasingly outrageous promises in their campaigns for President of Canine Country Day School, Otto quietly enters the race, vowing only to try to do what students really want.

"Wells' canine coterie . . . is satisfyingly personable and appealing, and kids will find the knowledge they accrue from the book very useful." Booklist

Read to your bunny. Scholastic 1998 un il $7.95; pa $3.99
Grades: PreK K   E
   1. Stories in rhyme 2. Rabbits -- Fiction 3. Books and reading -- Fiction
ISBN 0-590-30284-1; 0-439-08717-1 pa
                   LC 97-17704

Brief rhyming text and colorful illustrations tell what happens when parents and children share twenty minutes a day reading

"Each line of text gets one of Wells' delightful bordered pictures of parents and children at all sorts of activities, from bathing to skating, but always with a book in hand." Booklist

★ **Ruby's** beauty shop. Viking 2002 un il $16.99; pa $6.99
Grades: PreK K 1 2   E
   1. Rabbits -- Fiction 2. Siblings -- Fiction 3. Beauty shops -- Fiction
ISBN 0-670-03553-X; 0-14-240194-3 pa
                   LC 2001-7730

Louise and Ruby use Louise's "Deluxe Beauty Kit" to give Max a make-over, but when Grandma calls to schedule her own make-over, she makes an appointment with Max

"Wells is in top form. . . . The author's affinity for kid-based glee is playfully evident." Bull Cent Child Books

Other titles about Max and Ruby are:
Bunny cakes (1997)
Bunny mail (2004)
Bunny money (1997)
Bunny party (2001)
Max and Ruby at the Warthogs' wedding (2014)
Max and Ruby's bedtime book (2010)
Max and Ruby's first Greek myth: Pandora's box (1993)
Max and Ruby's Midas: another Greek myth (1995)
Max and Ruby's preschool pranks (2016)
Max and Ruby's treasure hunt (2012)
Max cleans up (2000)
Max counts his chickens (2007)
Max's ABC (2006)
Max's bath (1985)
Max's bedtime (1985)
Max's birthday (1985)
Max's breakfast (1985)
Max's bunny business (2008)
Max's chocolate chicken (1989)
Max's Christmas (1986)
Max's dragon shirt (1991)
Max's first word (1979)
Max's new suit (1979)
Max's ride (1979)
Max's toys (1979)

Shy Charles; [by] Rosemary Wells. Viking 2001 un il hardcover o.p. pa $5.99
Grades: PreK K 1 2   E
1. Stories in rhyme 2. Mice -- Fiction
ISBN 0-670-88729-3; 0-14-056843-3 pa
LC 2001-271649
A reissue of the title first published 1988 by Dial Books for Young Readers

"Wells' illustrations . . . show the plump, large-eared cast to be full of charm and cleverness. Facial expressions, posture, and background details substantially extend the humor of the story. The simple rhythm of the rhyming text is subtle and playful." SLJ

Stella's starliner; Rosemary Wells. Candlewick Press 2014 32 p. color illustrations $15.99
Grades: PreK K 1 2 3   E
1. Mobile homes 2. Bullies -- Fiction 3. Family life -- Fiction
ISBN 0763614955; 9780763614959
LC 2013943104
In this children's book, by Rosemary Wells, "Stella lives in a sparkling home on wheels. . . . Her home is called the Starliner, and it has everything Stella and her mama and daddy need to be happy. Until, that is, some big weasels pop up along the road, saying mean things about the Starliner. Mama comes to soothe away the hurt, and Daddy hitches their home to a truck and drives it away to a brand-new place, where Stella meets friends who are as enchanted as she is with her shiny home." (Publisher's note)

"A little fox lives contentedly with her family in Airstream-style trailer, a small but ingenious living space . . . Stella's sense of security evaporates when a gang of weasels mocks the Starliner . . . but when Stella's Daddy hitches the trailer to his pickup truck and moves the family to a place where there are palm trees and shimmering water, Stella makes new friends who think her life in the Starliner is worthy of 'A squillionaire!' Curiously, Wells never clarifies the reason behind the relocation, and so a story that draws so much power from its sense of emo-

tional truth concludes with an ending that seems almost too magical. . . . as income inequality takes it toll on more and more children, this story and its heroine are an important reminder of just how resilient families can and must be." Pub Wkly

★ **Time**-out for Sophie; by Rosemary Wells. Viking Childrens books 2013 32 p. (hardcover) $15.99
Grades: PreK K 1   E
1. Mice -- Fiction 2. Picture books for children 3. Bad behavior -- Fiction 4. Behavior -- Fiction 5. Family life -- Fiction
ISBN 0670785113; 9780670785117
LC 2012015263
In this children's book, "after getting sent to time-out for unnecessary roughness during dinner with Mama . . . and upsetting the laundry Daddy has folded . . . , Sophie comes up against a master: Granny. Instead of giving Sophie a time-out for repeated eyeglasses-snatching, Granny gives herself one, moving from the sofa to the rocking chair, where she sits implacably, arms folded." (Publishers Weekly)

"Like-minded preschoolers will find an ally in this spirited mousechild, who revels in her gleeful transgressions. As always, Wells portrays her character's developmentally appropriate behavior with genuine respect and affection." Horn Book

Other books about Sophie are:
Sophie's Terrible Twos (2014)
Use Your Words, Sophie (2015)
Ten Kisses for Sophie (2016)
Say hello, Sophie (2017)

★ **Yoko**. Hyperion Bks. for Children 1998 un il $14.95; pa $6.99
Grades: PreK K 1 2   E
1. School stories 2. Cats -- Fiction 3. Food -- Fiction 4. Japanese Americans -- Fiction
ISBN 0-7868-0395-9; 1-4231-1983-5 pa
LC 98-12342
When Yoko the cat brings sushi to school for lunch, her classmates make fun of what she eats—until one of them tries it for himself

"Wells sets the story in an active preschool classroom, and her clean ink-and-watercolor pictures have never been more expressive and tender, with a range of animal characters that are endearingly human in body language and expression." Booklist

Other titles about Yoko are:
Yoko's paper cranes (2001)
Yoko's world of kindness (2005)
Yoko writes her name (2008)
Yoko's show and tell (2010)
Yoko learns to read (2012)
Yoko finds her way (2013)

Wentworth, Marjory
Shackles; by Marjory Heath Wentworth; illustration by Leslie Darwin Pratt-Thomas. Legacy 2009 un il $16.99
Grades: 2 3 4 5   E
1. Slavery -- Fiction 2. South Carolina -- Fiction 3. African Americans -- Fiction
ISBN 978-0-93310-106-7; 0-93310-106-6
"Hunter, 11, watches his pesky little brothers dig for buried treasure in their backyard on Sullivan's Island, South Carolina. When they dig up 'an armful of mud and metal,' their neighbor . . . explains to them that what they have found are shackles used on slaves to prevent their escape. . . . Based on a true story, this compelling picture book speaks in clear, lyrical prose, true to Hunter's perspective, with beautiful oil paintings." Booklist

Wenzel, Brendan

★ **They** all saw a cat; Brendan Wenzel. Chronicle Books, LLC 2016 44 p. color illustrations (ebook) $14.29; (alk. paper) $16.99

Grades: K 1 2 3   **E**

1. Cats -- Fiction 2. Identity (Psychology) -- Fiction 3. Identity -- Fiction

ISBN 9781452150482; 1452150133; 9781452150130

LC 2015045046

Caldecott Honor Book (2017)

This book, by Brendan Wenzel, is a "celebration of observation, curiosity, and imagination. . . . Wenzel shows us the many lives of one cat, and how perspective shapes what we see. When you see a cat, what do you see?" (Publisher's note)

"Along with inviting more reflective viewers to ruminate about perception and subjectivity, the cat's perambulations offer elemental visual delights in the art's extreme and sudden shifts in color, texture, and mood from one page or page turn to the next." Kirkus

Wewer, Iris

My wild sister and me. North-South 2011 un il $16.95

Grades: PreK K 1 2   **E**

1. Siblings -- Fiction

ISBN 978-0-7358-4003-4; 0-7358-4003-2

Having a wild big sister—who can be a giraffe one day, a giant bear the next, and a racing rabbit the day after that—is just about the very best thing that can happen to little brother.

"With great sensitivity and sweetness, German writer Wewer probes the never-quite-settled nature of sibling relationships. . . . Wewer doesn't promise an end to the hostilities, but her honesty will touch siblings on both sides of the age divide." Publ Wkly

Whatley, Bruce

Clinton Gregory's secret; [by] Bruce Whatley. Abrams Books for Young Readers 2008 un il $15.95

Grades: K 1 2   **E**

1. Dreams -- Fiction

ISBN 978-0-8109-9364-8; 0-8109-9364-3

LC 2007012760

Clinton Gregory has fantastic adventures every night, from fighting dragons to flying around the world with his friends, and he keeps each one a secret.

"Everything is big in Whatley's colorful and fantastical spreads, which include details sure to appeal to children. . . . An entertaining addition to help wind down the day." SLJ

Wait! No paint! written and illustrated by Bruce Whatley. HarperCollins Pubs. 2001 31p il hardcover o.p. pa $6.99

Grades: PreK K 1 2   **E**

1. Pigs -- Fiction 2. Wolves -- Fiction 3. Illustrators -- Fiction

ISBN 0-06-028270-3; 0-06-028271-1 lib bdg; 0-06-443546-6 pa

LC 00-61351

The three little pigs are in their usual trouble with the big bad wolf, until a mysterious Voice gets involved and mixes things up

"The 'Voice' is the careless illustrator of the story, and . . . he's run out of red paint! . . . A quirky retelling of a perennial favorite, this may appeal most to early-elementary-age children, who will delight in the picture's conceptual surprises." Booklist

Wheeler, Lisa

★ **Boogie** knights; words by Lisa Wheeler; pictures by Mark Siegel. Atheneum Books for Young Readers 2008 un il $16.99

Grades: PreK K 1   **E**

1. Stories in rhyme 2. Parties -- Fiction 3. Monsters -- Fiction 4.

Knights and knighthood -- Fiction

ISBN 978-0-689-87639-4; 0-689-87639-4

LC 2007-24158

When the knights of the castle are awakened by the noise from the Madcap Monster Ball, they decide to join the party.

"Wheeler's rhythmic text is filled with taut rhymes, alliteration, and vivid images. . . . Done in charcoal, pencil, and Photoshop, Siegel's sophisticated, graphic-novel-style artwork . . . demands a second look. . . . Sepia tones, splashes of color, silhouettes, and outline sketches cleverly underscore the plot elements and keep the pages interesting." SLJ

Bubble gum, bubble gum; illustrated by Laura Huliska-Beith. Little, Brown and Co. 2004 un il $15.99

Grades: PreK K 1 2   **E**

1. Stories in rhyme 2. Animals -- Fiction

ISBN 0-316-98894-4

LC 2002-16268

After a variety of animals get stuck one by one in bubble gum melting in the road, they must survive encounters with a big blue truck and a burly black bear.

"A fast-paced, rhyming story with vibrant, bouncing illustrations." SLJ

★ **Jazz** baby; illustrations by R. Gregory Christie. Harcourt 2007 un il $16

Grades: PreK K 1   **E**

1. Stories in rhyme 2. Infants -- Fiction 3. Jazz music -- Fiction 4. Family life -- Fiction

ISBN 0-15-202522-7; 978-0-15-202522-9

LC 2006-09236

Baby and the family make music. "Ages one to three." (Bull Cent Child Books)

"The percussive text scans like a musical dream, a nearly flawless scat on music, dance, and the contagious joy of jazz. Christie's gouache illustrations—in a sixties palette of olive, gold, and brick—feature characters with fluid bodies and mobile faces that fill the images with movement and energy." Booklist

★ **Old** Cricket; illustrations by Ponder Goembel. Atheneum Bks. for Young Readers 2003 un il $16.95

Grades: PreK K 1 2   **E**

1. Crickets -- Fiction

ISBN 0-689-84510-3

LC 2002-2199

Old Cricket doesn't feel like helping his wife and neighbors to prepare for winter and so he pretends to have all sorts of ailments that require the doctor's care, but hungry Old Crow has other ideas

"Wheeler invests her delightful tale with all the characteristics of a good fable, and Goembel's sharp, highly detailed acrylic artwork gives a clever, humorous bug's-eye view of the world." Booklist

The **pet** project; cute and cuddly vicious verses. by Lisa Wheeler; illustrated by Zachariah OHora. Atheneum Books for Young Readers 2013 40 p. col. ill. (hardcover) $16.99

Grades: K 1 2 3 4 5   **E**

1. Stories in rhyme 2. Pets -- Fiction 3. Animals -- Fiction

ISBN 1416975950; 9781416975953

LC 2011029647

This children's book, by Lisa Wheeler, illustrated by Zachariah O'Hora, presents a series of poems focused on animals and pets. "If you think you'd like a cute and cuddly pet, you may need to do some research. . . . Join one budding young scientist as she catalogs the pros and pitfalls of potential pet ownership in this assortment of zany . . . poems that will change the way you look at cuddly animals--and give you the giggles." (Publisher's note)

Ugly Pie; illustrated by Heather Solomon. Harcourt 2010 un il $16

Grades: PreK K 1   E

1. Pies -- Fiction 2. Bears -- Fiction
ISBN 978-0-15-216754-7; 0-15-216754-4

LC 2008-4535

After baking a scrumptious Ugly Pie, made from ingredients donated by his neighbors, Ol' Bear invites everyone over for a slice. Includes pie recipe.

"Large, bright watercolors, acrylics, and collage trace the bear's search as he goes from house to house. . . . This humorous tale should appeal greatly to little cubs everywhere." SLJ

Whelan, Gloria

The **listeners**; written by Gloria Whelan; illustrated by Mike Benny. Sleeping Bear Press 2009 un il $17.95

Grades: 1 2 3   E

1. Slavery -- Fiction 2. African Americans -- Fiction
ISBN 978-1-58536-419-0; 1-58536-419-3

LC 2009005436

After a day of picking cotton in late 1860, Ella May, a young slave, joins her friends Bobby and Sue at their second job of listening outside the windows of their master's house for useful information

This is "a spare, lyrical narrative. . . . Benny's unframed, dusk-toned, double-page paintings emphasize the stark contrast between slave shacks and plantation mansion." Booklist

★ **Queen** Victoria's Bathing Machine; by Gloria Whelan; illustrated by Nancy Carpenter. Simon & Schuster 2014 40 p. $17.99

Grades: K 1 2 3   E

1. Swimming 2. Swimming
ISBN 1416927530; 9781416927532

In this picture book, by Gloria Whelan, "Prince Albert comes up with a royally creative solution to Queen Victoria's modesty. . . . She loves to swim, but can't quite figure out how to get to the water without her devoted subjects glimpsing her swimming suit. (Because, of course, such a sight would compromise her regal dignity.) Fortunately for the water-loving monarch, it's Prince Albert to the rescue with an invention fit for a queen!" (Publisher's note)

"Modesty decreed that Queen Victoria mustn't be seen in her bathing costume. It's Prince Albert to the rescue with a queen-sized bathing machine. This entertaining story nicely encapsulates a curious bit of social history, with a jaunty tall-tale tone governing a rhymed text. The stifling frills of Victorian dress; the loving couple's delight in each other--Carpenter renders each in comical detail." Horn Book

Waiting for the owl's call; [illustrated by] Pascal Milelli. Sleeping Bear Press 2009 un il (Tales of the world) $17.95

Grades: 2 3 4 5   E

1. Weaving -- Fiction 2. Afghanistan -- Fiction 3. Child labor -- Fiction 4. Rugs and carpets -- Fiction
ISBN 1-58536-418-5; 978-1-58536-418-3

LC 2009005437

For generations the women of Zulviya's family have earned their living by weaving rugs by hand. During one work day, Zulviya will tie thousands of knots. As she sits at her work, Zulviya weaves not one but two patterns. The pattern on the loom will become a fine rug. She weaves a second pattern in her mind.

"Impressionistic paintings in muted colors accompany Zulviya's lyrical description of her Afghan homeland and her yearning to escape

'the shadow of the loom.' An author's note provides details about illegal child labor in the Afghani rug-making industry." Horn Book Guide

Yuki and the one thousand carriers; written by Gloria Whelan; illustrated by Yan Nascimbene. Sleeping Bear Press 2008 un il (Tales of the world) $17.95

Grades: 1 2 3   E

1. Haiku -- Fiction 2. Japan -- Fiction 3. Voyages and travels -- Fiction
ISBN 978-1-58536-352-0; 1-58536-352-9

LC 2007046318

In Japan, as a provincial governor, his wife, and daughter Yuki, followed by 1,000 attendants, travel the historic Tokaido Road to the Shogun's palace in Edo, Yuki keeps up with her lessons by writing poems describing the journey

"Nascimbene stays true to Yuki's childish perspective. . . . Accompanying the simple prose narrative, are haiku . . . that express intense feelings in clear, casual words." Booklist

Whitaker, Zai

Kali and the rat snake; story by Zai Whitaker; illustrations by Srividya Natarajan. Kane/Miller 2006 un il $15.95

Grades: 1 2 3   E

1. School stories 2. India -- Fiction 3. Snakes -- Fiction 4. Prejudices -- Fiction
ISBN 1-933605-10-3

First published 2000 in India

"Kali has always been proud of his father, who is the best snake catcher in their Indian village. But when he attends school, the children make fun of his Irula ways. . . . But one day the classroom is visited by a six-foot-long rat snake. . . . Kali grabs it and becomes the class hero. The text is smoothly written, with lots of cultural details. . . . Natarajan's stylized illustrations are a mixture of smaller pencil drawings and luscious larger paintings that seem to be done on silk." SLJ

White, Dianne

★ **Blue** on blue; Dianne White; illustrated by Beth Krommes. Beach Lane Books 2014 48 p. (hardcover) $17.99

Grades: PreK K 1 2   E

1. Stories in rhyme 2. Rain -- Fiction 3. Storms -- Fiction 4. Rain and rainfall -- Fiction
ISBN 1442412674; 9781442412675; 9781442456877

LC 201201423

In this children's book by Dianne White, illustrating by Beth Krommes, readers will "Join a farming family as they experience the full range of a thrilling seaside thunderstorm--from the wild wind and the very first drops; to the pouring, pouring rain; to the wonderful messy mud after the sun returns!" (Publisher's note)

"A beautiful sunny day darkens as clouds gather and rain arrives. From morning till bedtime, the story follows a young family on their farm. Rhyming, spare text augments the striking scratchboard and watercolor illustrations...The combination of limited, strong text; rich illustrations; and child-centric perspective make this a strong choice for storytimes and one-on-one sharing." SLJ

White, Linda

Too many turkeys; illustrated by Megan Lloyd. Holiday House 2010 un il $16.95

Grades: K 1 2 3   E

1. Turkeys -- Fiction 2. Farm life -- Fiction
ISBN 978-0-8234-2084-1; 0-8234-2084-1

LC 200804921

Chaos ensues when Farmer Fred's wife fertilizes her beautiful garden with an secret ingredient that attracts turkeys from miles around.

"Bright watercolors wash over detailed illustrations. . . . Text moves readers forward with italicized first-person ruminations and the occasional 'but then . . .' encouragement to turn the page. An engaging story, . . this book is a welcome addition for all libraries." SLJ

Whiting, Sue

The **firefighters**; [by] Sue Whiting; illustrated by Donna Rawlins. Candlewick Press 2008 un il $15.99

Grades: PreK K 1 2   E

1. School stories 2. Imagination -- Fiction 3. Fire fighters -- Fiction

ISBN 978-0-7636-4019-4; 0-7636-4019-0

LC 2007051895

After dressing up as fire fighters, building a fire truck out of a cardboard box, and extinguishing imaginary fires on the playground, Mrs. Iverson's students are surprised by the arrival of a real fire engine with real fire fighters on board

"Rawlins's acrylic illustrations feature bright, primary colors that stand out against the clean, white backgrounds. . . . A great choice for introducing not only fire safety, but also creative play." SLJ

Whitman, Walt

When I heard the learn'd astronomer; words by Walt Whitman; pictures by Loren Long. Simon & Schuster Books for Young Readers 2004 un il $16.95

Grades: 1 2 3 4   E

1. Astronomy -- Poetry

ISBN 0-689-86397-7

LC 2004-7538

"A little boy obsessed with outer space has been dragged to an astronomy lecture. . . . The fidgety youngster takes his toy rocket ship outside, where he marvels at the 'perfect silence of the stars, casting a decisive vote for creative speculation over chilly analysis.' The painterly artwork . . . gets its own injection of childlike wonder through playful doodles contributed by Long's two children." Booklist

★ Whoo goes there? illustrated by Bert Kitchen. Roaring Brook Press 2009 un il $17.99

Grades: K 1 2 3   E

1. Owls -- Fiction 2. Night -- Fiction 3. Animals -- Fiction

ISBN 978-1-59643-371-7; 1-59643-371-X

"With every sound Owl hears in the night--a rustle, a thump, a splash--he imagines he's about to catch a different tasty animal for his dinner. However, he keeps guessing wrong. Readers will enjoy turning the pages to find out which animal, painted with meticulous detail, is actually making the nighttime noise." Horn Book

Whybrow, Ian

The **noisy** way to bed; illustrated by Tiphanie Beeke. Arthur A. Levine Books 2004 un il $15.95

Grades: PreK K 1 2   E

1. Stories in rhyme 2. Animals -- Fiction 3. Bedtime -- Fiction

ISBN 0-439-55689-9

LC 2003-2785

As a sleepy boy decides it is bedtime and sets out across the farm toward home, he meets several animals who, in their noisy way, express the same idea

"This engaging bedtime story begs for participation from children. . . [Beeke's] full-page, mixed-media pictures are captivating, providing an eye-pleasing blend of colors, textures, and facial expressions." SLJ

Wiesner, David

★ **Art** & Max. Clarion Books 2010 un il $17.99

Grades: K 1 2 3   E

1. Artists -- Fiction 2. Lizards -- Fiction 3. Painting -- Fiction 4. Artists' materials -- Fiction

ISBN 978-0-618-75663-6; 0-618-75663-9

LC 2010005205

Max the lizard wants to be an artist like Arthur, but his first attempt at using a paintbrush sends the two friends on a whirlwind trip through various media, with unexpected consequences.

"This small-scale and surprisingly comedic story takes place against a placid backdrop of pale desert colors, which recedes to keep the focus squarely on the dynamic between the two lizards and the wide range of emotions that Wiesner masterfully evokes." Publ Wkly

★ **Flotsam**. Clarion Books 2006 un il $17

Grades: K 1 2 3 4   E

1. Stories without words 2. Beaches -- Fiction 3. Cameras -- Fiction

ISBN 0-618-19457-6

Awarded the Caldecott Medal, 2007

"A wave deposits an old-fashioned contraption at the feet of an inquisitive young beachcomber. It's a Melville underwater camera, and the excited boy quickly develops the film he finds inside. The photos are amazing. . . . This wordless books vivid watercolor paintings have a crisp realism that anchors the elements of fantasy. . . . Filled with inventive details and delightful twists, each snapshot is a tale waiting to be told." SLJ

Free fall. Lothrop, Lee & Shepard Bks. 1988 un il lib bdg $18.89; pa $6.99

Grades: K 1 2 3 4   E

1. Stories without words 2. Dreams -- Fiction

ISBN 0-688-05584-2 lib bdg; 0-688-10990-X pa

LC 87-22834

A Caldecott Medal honor book, 1989

A young boy dreams of daring adventures in the company of imaginary creatures inspired by the things surrounding his bed

"Technical virtuosity is the trademark of the double-page watercolor spreads. Especially notable is the solidity of forms and architectural details." SLJ

Hurricane. Clarion Bks. 1990 un il $16; pa $6.95

Grades: K 1 2 3   E

1. Brothers -- Fiction 2. Hurricanes -- Fiction

ISBN 0-395-54382-7; 0-395-62974-8 pa

LC 90-30070

"A family weathers a hurricane; the next day, in the post-hurricane yard, the two boys in the family play on a great fallen elm, imagining it to be a jungle, a pirate ship, and a space ship. A handsome book, affording opportunities for sharing fears and dreams of adventure." Horn Book Guide

June 29, 1999. Clarion Bks. 1992 un il $16; pa $5.95

Grades: K 1 2 3 4   E

1. Vegetables -- Fiction

ISBN 0-395-59762-5; 0-395-72767-7 pa

LC 91-34854

"Here an understated, fairly straightforward text is a perfect foil for the outrageous scenes of vegetables run amok. Realistic watercolors reveal red peppers that need to be roped down, beans with bemused Arizona sheep clambering over them, and gargantuan peas floating down the Mississippi like logs to the sawmill. Fans of Wiesner's offbeat sense of humor will be delighted." Horn Book

★ **Mr.** Wuffles! by David Wiesner. Clarion Books, Houghton Mifflin Harcourt 2013 32 p ill. (hardcover) $17.99
Grades: PreK K 1 2 3   E
1. Cats -- Fiction 2. Picture books for children 3. Toys -- Fiction 4. Extraterrestrial beings -- Fiction
ISBN 0618756612; 9780618756612

LC 2012046025

Caldecott Honor Book (2014)

In this children's picture book, a housecat is battling some tiny aliens. The aliens' "initial celebration at landing turns to mayhem as their craft is buffeted by Mr. Wuffles. The aliens assess a smoldering engine part and disembark for help. . . . A ladybug and several ants assist them, and the repair's successfully made by harvesting cross sections of detritus: pencil eraser, M&M, marble and metal screw." (Kirkus Reviews)

★ **Sector** 7. Clarion Bks. 1999 un il $16
Grades: K 1 2 3 4   E
1. Stories without words 2. Clouds -- Fiction 3. Empire State Building (New York, N.Y.) -- Fiction
ISBN 0-395-74656-6

LC 96-40343

A Caldecott Medal honor book, 2000

While on a school trip to the Empire State Building, a boy is taken by a friendly cloud to visit Sector 7, where he discovers how clouds are shaped and channeled throughout the country

"Wiesner's lofty watercolors render words superfluous as he transforms the sky into magical scenes of marine life, reminding children of the innate power of their own imagination." Publ Wkly

★ The **three** pigs. Clarion Bks. 2001 un il $16
Grades: K 1 2 3 4   E
1. Pigs 2. Pigs -- Fiction 3. Characters in literature
ISBN 0618007016

LC 00-57016

Awarded the Caldecott Medal, 2002

The three pigs escape the wolf by going into another world where they meet the cat and the fiddle, the cow that jumped over the moon, and a dragon. "Ages four to eight." (NY Times Book Rev)

"Wiesner's brilliant use of white space and perspective evokes a feeling that the characters can navigate endless possibilities—and that the range of story itself is limitless." Publ Wkly

★ **Tuesday.** Clarion Bks. 1991 un il $17; pa $6.95
Grades: K 1 2 3 4   E
1. Frogs -- Fiction
ISBN 0-395-55113-7; 0-395-87082-8 pa

LC 90-39358

Awarded the Caldecott Medal, 1992

Frogs rise on their lily pads, float through the air, and explore the nearby houses while their inhabitants sleep

"Wiesner offers a fantasy watercolor journey accomplished with soft-edged realism. Studded with bits of humor, the narrative artwork tells a simple, pleasant story with a consistency and authenticity that makes the fantasy convincing." Booklist

Wigger, J. Bradley, 1958-
Thank you, God; by J. Bradley Wigger; illustrated by Jago. Eerdmans Books for Young Readers 2014 26 p $16
Grades: PreK K 1 2   E
1. Gratitude 2. Children -- Religious life 3. Gratitude -- Prayers and devotions 4. Christian children -- Prayers and devotions
ISBN 0802854249; 9780802854247

LC 2013044346

A children's book written by J. Bradley Wigger and illustrated by Jago "'Thank You, God' is a celebration of family and friends, of homes and food to share, and of the wonder of creation from the first light of day to the calm, peaceful night." It "offers readers of all ages and backgrounds the perfect chance to reflect on all the things that they have to be grateful for." (Publisher's note)

"Created with digital paints and photographic textures, this religious picture book is elegant and enjoyable... The diversity is refreshing and reflective of many families, a pleasure to see in children's books. This book would be a great tool for devotions in the home, classroom, or church." SLJ

Wild, Margaret
★ **Harry** & Hopper. Feiwel & Friends 2011 un il $16.99
Grades: PreK K   E
1. Dogs -- Fiction 2. Pets -- Fiction 3. Bereavement -- Fiction
ISBN 978-0-312-64261-7; 0-312-64261-X

"Redheaded Harry and his spotted dog, Hopper, are constant companions, accomplices . . . and bedmates. The dog's sudden death (an accident that happens while Harry is at school), leaves the boy devastated. . . . Wild's . . . understated, empathic prose offers both a voice for a child unable to articulate his grief and the reassurance that those we love never really disappear. Blackwood's . . . predominantly charcoal drawings are equally eloquent, particularly in her use of texture to capture the emotional essence of good and sad times." Publ Wkly

Itsy-bitsy babies; illustrated by Jan Ormerod. Little Hare Books 2010 un il $15.99
Grades: PreK   E
1. Stories in rhyme 2. Infants -- Fiction
ISBN 978-1-9215413-6-0; 1-9215413-9-X

"This picture book introduces a multicultural cast of babies and toddlers engaged in everyday activities. . . . Short and precise, Wild's rhyming couplets offer plenty of chances for children to chime in with the end words. . . . Ormerod's clean, crayonlike drawings illustrate one or more babies with a few props . . . and create a sense of changing settings with flat, toned color above and below the horizon line in each picture." Booklist

Kiss kiss! [by] Margaret Wild & Bridget Strevens-Marzo. Simon & Schuster Books for Young Readers 2004 un il $12.95
Grades: PreK K   E
1. Hippopotamus -- Fiction 2. Mother-child relationship -- Fiction
ISBN 0-689-86279-2

LC 2002-154516

First published 2003 in Australia

Baby Hippo is in such a rush to play one morning he forgets to kiss his mama, but strangely all the jungle noises seem to remind him

"This is a story filled with movement and physical affection. The lap-sit audience will love the squishy, lumpy sounds and the repetition of the text as they point to the animals in the clear, bright pictures." Booklist

★ **Our** granny; story by Margaret Wild; pictures by Julie Vivas. Ticknor & Fields 1994 un il $17; pa $6.95
Grades: PreK K 1 2   E
1. Grandmothers -- Fiction
ISBN 0-395-67023-3; 0-395-88395-4 pa

LC 93-11950

First published 1993 in Australia

"Two young children present a catalog of all the varying sizes, shapes, and types of grandmothers, interspersed with loving comments about their own granny, who has 'a wobbly bottom' and wears a funny bathing suit. . . . Vivas's lively illustrations capture the grandmothers in their most comic moments." Horn Book Guide

★ **Piglet** and Mama; illustrated by Stephen Michael King. Harry N. Abrams 2005 un il $14.95
Grades: PreK K   E
1. Pigs -- Fiction 2. Mothers -- Fiction 3. Farm life -- Fiction
ISBN 0-8109-5869-4

LC 2004-19497

When Piglet cannot find her mother, all of the barnyard animals try to make her feel better, but Piglet wants nothing but Mama.

"The text is reassuring and rhythmic. . . . The cheery watercolor cartoons depict farm life on a bright, sunny day, and the gentle pastel color scheme matches the tender tone of the text." SLJ

Other titles about Piglet are:
Piglet and Papa (2007)
Piglet and Granny (2009)

The **treasure** box; by Margaret Wild; illustrated by Freya Blackwood. Candlewick Press 2017 40 p. color illustrations $16.99
Grades: 1 2 3 4   E
1. War casualties -- Fiction 2. Children -- Books and reading -- Fiction
ISBN 0763690848; 9780763690847

This picture book, by Margaret Wild, illustrated by Freya Blackwood, "looks at what we hold most dear--and carry with us--when we are forced to flee our homes because of war. . . . As war rages around them, Peter and his father, alongside so many refugees, flee their home, taking with them a treasure box that holds something rarer than rubies and more precious than gold. . . . As the years go by, Peter never forgets the treasure box, and one day he returns to find it." (Publisher's note)

Wildsmith, Brian

Brian Wildsmith's ABC. Star Bright Bks. 1995 un bd bk $6.95
Grades: PreK K   E
1. Alphabet 2. Board books for children
ISBN 978-1-88773-402-8 bd bk; 1-88773-402-3 bd bk

LC 95-31730

First published 1962 in the United Kingdom; first U.S. edition 1963 by Watts

"From A/apple to Z/zebra, Wildsmith's 26 playful renderings of objects and animals are highlighted with an eye-catching, colorful design; kaleidoscopic animals constructed from bold circles, triangles and squares add an unexpected geometric element to the counting book." Publ Wkly

Brian Wildsmith's Amazing animal alphabet. Star Bright Books 2009 un $17.95; pa $7.95
Grades: PreK K   E
1. Animals 2. Alphabet
ISBN 978-1-59572-104-4; 1-59572-104-5; 978-1-59572-185-3 pa; 1-59572-185-1 pa

LC 2007033811

"Wildsmith's distinctive, detailed animals pop against brightly colored backgrounds as they illustrate each letter of the alphabet. Preschoolers will easily recognize most of the creatures, with a few refreshingly unusual exceptions (quetzel for Q, vole for V, xenops for X). Four pages of 'Amazing Animal Facts' conclude the animal parade." Horn Book Guide

Jungle party. Star Bright Books 2006 un il $16.95; pa $6.95

Grades: PreK K 1 2   E
1. Animals -- Fiction 2. Parties -- Fiction 3. Pythons -- Fiction
ISBN 978-1-59572-052-8; 1-59572-052-9; 978-1-59572-053-5 pa; 1-59572-053-7 pa

First published 1974 by Oxford University Press with title: Python's party

Although he is hungry, Python tries to prove his goodwill by throwing a party for all the jungle animals

"Wildsmith excels at bold, brightly colored illustrations of animals, and this cautionary tale is a visual delight." Horn Book Guide

Wiles, Deborah

Freedom Summer; illustrated by Jerome Lagarrigue. Atheneum Bks. for Young Readers 2001 un il $16
Grades: K 1 2 3   E
1. Friendship -- Fiction 2. Race relations -- Fiction 3. African Americans -- Fiction
ISBN 0-689-87829-X

LC 98-52805

In 1964, Joe is pleased that a new law will allow his best friend John Henry, who is colored, to share the town pool and other public places with him, but he is dismayed to find that prejudice still exists

"The text, though concise, is full of nuance, and the oil paintings shimmer with the heat of the South in summer." Horn Book Guide

Willems, Mo

★ A **big** guy took my ball! text and illustrations by Mo Willems. Hyperion Books for Children 2013 64 p. ill. (reinforced) $8.99
Grades: K 1 2 3   E
1. Picture books for children 2. Bullies -- Fiction 3. Pigs -- Fiction 4. Play -- Fiction 5. Whales -- Fiction 6. Animals -- Fiction 7. Elephants -- Fiction 8. Friendship -- Fiction
ISBN 1423174917; 9781423174912

LC 2012010899

Theodor Seuss Geisel Honor Book (2014)

In this book, author and illustrator Mo "Willems observes truths about human behavior through the eyes of Gerald, an elephant, and Piggie. The premise this time is that Piggie's recently acquired ball has been snatched by some unknown creature, one so big that Piggie begs Gerald to intervene. But Gerald's perceived power and genuine desire to help his smaller friend cannot provide him with sufficient courage once he sees that he'll have to confront an enormous whale." (School Library Journal)

"This morality play in false assumptions and relativity unfurls with Willems' customary command of visual pacing; gags are spaced just right to keep the pages turning and readers giggling." Kirkus

★ **Cat** the Cat, who is that? Balzer & Bray 2010 un il $12.99; lib bdg $14.89
Grades: PreK K 1   E
1. Cats -- Fiction 2. Animals -- Fiction 3. Friendship -- Fiction
ISBN 978-0-06-172840-2; 0-06-172840-3; 978-0-06-172841-9 lib bdg; 0-06-172841-1 lib bdg

LC 2008-46187

An exuberant cat introduces readers to her friends.

"Willems provides just enough humor and surprise to entertain youngest audiences and . . . Cat could become another favorite; her personality sparkles in expansive gestures and gleeful interactions." Publ Wkly

Other titles about Cat the Cat and her friends are:
Let's say hi to friends who fly! (2010)
What's your sound, Hound the Hound ?(2010)
Time to sleep, Sheep the Sheep! (2010)

★ **City** Dog, Country Frog; words, Mo Willems; pictures, Jon J. Muth. Hyperion Books for Children 2010 un il
Grades: PreK K 1 2   E
1. Dogs -- Fiction 2. Frogs -- Fiction 3. Seasons -- Fiction 4. Friendship -- Fiction
ISBN 1423103009; 9781423103004

City Dog and Country Frog play together in the spring and summer and fall, but in winter Country Frog is gone. Then when spring comes again City Dog makes a new friend.

Willems "is gracefully spare here, making every word count. That leaves room for Muth's watercolors, richly seasonal, which fill every page. The pictures are imbued with hope and happiness, leaving and longing. This wonderful collaboration makes a significant impact with subtlety and wit." Booklist

★ **Don't** let the pigeon drive the bus! words and pictures by Mo Willems. Hyperion Bks. for Children 2003 un il $12.99
Grades: PreK K 1 2   E
1. Buses -- Fiction 2. Pigeons -- Fiction
ISBN 0-7868-1988-X
A Caldecott Medal honor book, 2004

"When a bus driver goes on break, he asks the audience to keep an eye on his vehicle and the daft, bug-eyed pigeon who desperately wants to drive it. The pigeon then relentlessly begs readers for some time behind the wheel." Publ Wkly

"An unflinching and hilarious look at a child's potential for mischief. In a plain palette, with childishly elemental line drawings, Willems has captured the essence of unreasonableness in the very young." SLJ

Other titles about the pigeon are:
The pigeon finds a hot dog! (2004)
Don't let the pigeon stay up late (2006)
The pigeon wants a puppy (2008)
The pigeon needs a bath! (2014)

The **duckling** gets a cookie!? words and picture by Mo Willems. Hyperion Books for Children 2012 40 p.
Grades: PreK K 1 2   E
1. Ducks -- Fiction 2. Cookies -- Fiction 3. Pigeons -- Fiction 4. Etiquette -- Fiction 5. Temper tantrums -- Fiction 6. Humorous stories
ISBN 9781423151289

LC 2011012304

As this book "opens, the yellow Duckling requests a cookie, receives one immediately, and graciously thanks the unseen provider with a "flappy flip flap!" The Pigeon, whom the Duckling cajoled into sharing a hot dog in the earlier book, soon arrives to express astonishment. Multipanel spreads and emphatic voice balloons reveal his outrage as The Pigeon throws a colossal tantrum ("I ask for things all the time!/ I ask to drive the bus! . . . I've asked for a walrus! . . . But do I get what I ask for? Nooooool"). In an unexpected turn, the Duckling gives the Pigeon the entire cookie, shocking the bird." (Publishers Weekly)

★ **Goldilocks** and the three dinosaurs; as retold by Mo Willems. Balzer + Bray 2012 40 p. $17.99
Grades: PreK K 1 2 3   E
1. Dinosaurs -- Fiction 2. Fairy tales -- Fiction 3. Picture books for children
ISBN 0062104187; 9780062104182

In this book, Goldilocks "ventures into the home of three diabolical dinosaurs. Having cooked up three bowls of chocolate pudding and arranged their house 'just so,' the two olive-green T. rexes and smaller brown dino lick their lips. . . . Goldilocks doesn't hesitate to enter the dinos' house or stick her whole head in their food . . . and she wises

up just in time to give herself, if not the dinosaurs, a happy ending." (Publishers Weekly)

★ **Hooray** for Amanda & her alligator! words and pictures by Mo Willems. Balzer + Bray 2011 68p $17.99
Grades: PreK K 1 2   E
1. Toys -- Fiction 2. Alligators -- Fiction 3. Friendship -- Fiction
ISBN 978-0-06-200400-0; 0-06-200400-X; 006200400X; 9780062004000

LC 2010009633

Amanda and her alligator have lots of fun together, but when Amanda's grandfather buys her a panda, Alligator must learn to make new friends.

"With the book's minimal backgrounds and roomy page design, the focus falls squarely on Willems' cleanly styled characters, whose facial expressions are carried in the simplest of just-so lines. Willems may not have the market cornered on best friends, but few do them better." Booklist

I broke my trunk! Hyperion Books for Children 2011 57p il $8.99
Grades: PreK K 1 2   E
1. Pigs -- Fiction 2. Elephants -- Fiction 3. Storytelling -- Fiction
ISBN 978-1-4231-3309-4; 1-4231-3309-9

LC 2010035528

"Willems' use of pastel colors and vast white backdrops work minimalist wonders." Booklist

★ **Knuffle** Bunny; a cautionary tale. Hyperion Books for Children 2004 un il $15.99
Grades: PreK K 1 2   E
1. Lost and found possessions -- Fiction
ISBN 0-7868-1870-0
A Caldecott Medal honor book, 2005

After Trixie and daddy leave the laundromat, something very important turns up missing.

A "concise, deftly told narrative. . . . Printed on olive-green backdrops, the illustrations are a combination of muted, sepia-toned photographs upon which bright cartoon drawings of people have been superimposed. . . . A seamless and supremely satisfying presentation of art and text." SLJ

Other titles about Knuffle Bunny are:
Knuffle Bunny too (2007)
Knuffle Bunny free (2010)

Knuffle Bunny free; an unexpected diversion. Balzer + Bray 2010 un il $17.99; lib bdg $18.89
Grades: PreK K 1 2   E
1. Toys -- Fiction 2. Growth -- Fiction 3. Airplanes -- Fiction 4. Netherlands -- Fiction 5. Grandparents -- Fiction 6. Lost and found possessions -- Fiction
ISBN 978-0-06-192957-1; 0-06-192957-3; 978-0-06-192958-8 lib bdg; 0-06-192958-1 lib bdg

When Trixie travels to Holland to visit her grandparents, her beloved toy Knuffle Bunny is accidentally left on the airplane bound for China.

This is a "droll, observant, and seriously heartbreaking ode to growing up. . . . A gorgeous four-page foldout dream of Knuffle Bunny's life in the wider world puts Trixie at ease. The denouement is enough to give you goose bumps, and young children may be wiping tears from their parents' cheeks." Booklist

★ **Leonardo,** the terrible monster. Hyperion 2005 un il $16.99
Grades: PreK K 1 2   E
1. Monsters -- Fiction
ISBN 0-7868-5294-1

Leonardo is a terrible monster he can't seem to frighten anyone. When he discovers the perfect nervous little boy, will he scare the lunch out of him? Or will he think of something better?

"Willems's familiar cartoon drawings work hand in glove with the brief text to tell this perfectly paced story." SLJ

Let's go for a drive! by Mo Willems. Hyperion Books for Children 2012 57 p. (hardback) $8.99
Grades: PreK K 1 2   E
1. Pigs -- Fiction 2. Humorous stories 3. Elephants -- Fiction 4. Automobile travel -- Fiction
ISBN 1423164822; 9781423164821
LC 2011053285

Theodor Seuss Geisel Honor Book (2013)

In this children's picture book, "Gerald the elephant and Piggie decide to go for a drive, [but] they find that all the planning in the world can't replace one crucial ingredient. . . . Gerald, a touch on the OCD side, insists on a plan that includes a number of items: map, sunglasses, umbrellas, bags and, as there will be 'a lot of driving on [their] drive,' a car. Oops. Piggie doesn't have one; '[a] pig with a car would be silly.' Neither does Gerald. Whatever will they do?" (Kirkus)

★ **Naked** Mole Rat gets dressed; words and pictures by Mo Willems. Hyperion Books for Children 2009 un il $16.99
Grades: PreK K 1 2   E
1. Naked mole rat -- Fiction
ISBN 978-1-4231-1437-6; 1-4231-1437-X
LC 2008-48251

Willems "informs readers that 'for this story' they need only know three things about naked mole rats: '1. They are a little bit rat. 2. They are a little bit mole. 3. They are all naked.' The exception to point number three, however, is Wilbur, who revels in a wardrobe that ranges from a turtleneck and beret to an astronaut suit—infuriating his brethren. . . . [Willems'] legion of emotive, square-headed rodents . . . are paired successfully with droll prose." Publ Wkly

Nanette's baguette; by Mo Willems. Hyperion Books for Children, an imprint of Disney Book Group 2016 40 p. (hardcover) $17.99
Grades: PreK K 1   E
1. Stories in rhyme 2. Frogs -- Fiction 3. Family life -- Fiction
ISBN 9781484722862
LC 2015045460

This picture book written and illustrated by Mo Willems, "follows [Nanette] . . . on her first big solo trip to the bakery. But . . . will Nanette get the baguette from baker Juliette? Or will Nanette soon be beset with regret? Set in a meticulously handcrafted-paper-modeled French village, . . . get set to krack into an irresistible tale you won't soon forget!" (Publisher's note)

The **thank** you book; by Mo Willems. Hyperion Books for Children, an imprint of Disney Book Group 2016 57 p. color illustrations $9.99
Grades: PreK K 1 2   E
1. Pigs -- Fiction 2. Animals -- Fiction 3. Elephants -- Fiction 4. Gratitude -- Fiction 5. Friendship -- Fiction
ISBN 1423178289; 9781423178286
LC 2015001585

In this book, by Mo Willems, "Gerald is careful. Piggie is not. Piggie cannot help smiling. Gerald can. Gerald worries so that Piggie does not have to. Gerald and Piggie are best friends. In [this book], Piggie wants to thank EVERYONE. But Gerald is worried Piggie will forget someone . . . someone important." (Publisher's note)

"The 25th installment in the winning series is a must-have for every collection and will lead kids to go back and revisit the earlier titles again and again." SLJ

★ **That** is not a good idea! Mo Willems. Balzer + Bray 2013 48 p. ill. $17.99
Grades: PreK K 1 2   E
1. Motion pictures -- Fiction 2. Foxes -- Fiction 3. Geese -- Fiction 4. Humorous stories 5. Dinners and dining -- Fiction
ISBN 0062203096; 9780062203090
LC 2012277475

This children's story, by Mo Willems, "presents itself as a movie in book form, observed not only by readers, but by a gaggle of excitable goslings. The action begins when a dapper fox and a plump goose meet . . . as the wide-eyed goose follows the fox from the city to his home in the woods. The goslings' antics grow progressively frantic . . . as their warnings increase in intensity. The climax proves that appearances can be deceiving." (Kirkus Reviews)

"This charmer is lovingly composed as an homage to silent movies and the concept of picture books as the "theater of the lap." Readers will become totally involved as they watch, along with several chicks, a drama unfolding, certain to end in tragedy... Children and adults will relish being taken for such a thrilling, suspenseful ride again and again." SLJ

There is a bird on your head! Hyperion Books for Children 2007 57p il $8.99
Grades: PreK K 1 2   E
1. Pigs -- Fiction 2. Birds -- Fiction 3. Elephants -- Fiction 4. Friendship -- Fiction
ISBN 978-1-4231-0686-9; 1-4231-0686-5
Geisel Award (2008)

Gerald the elephant discovers that there is something worse than a bird on your head two birds on your head! Piggie will try to help her best friend.

"The conversation between the friends flows smoothly and allows beginning readers to practice expression as they read. [This] appealing [title] will tickle the funny bones of children." SLJ

★ **Today** I will fly! Hyperion Books for Children 2007 57p il $8.99
Grades: PreK K 1 2   E
1. Pigs -- Fiction 2. Elephants -- Fiction 3. Friendship -- Fiction
ISBN 978-14231-0295-3; 1-4231-0295-9
LC 2006-49621

While Piggie is determined to fly, Elephant is skeptical, but when Piggie gets a little help from others, amazing things happen.

"Characters zip in and out of white space, proffer speech-bubble remarks, and express emotion through spot-on body language. . . . Accessible, appealing, and full of authentic emotions." Booklist

Other titles in this series are:
My friend is sad (2007)
I am invited to a party! (2007)
There is a bird on your head (2007)
I love my new toy! (2008)
I will surprise my friend! (2008)
Are you ready to play outside? (2008)
Elephants cannot dance! (2009)
Pigs make me sneeze! (2009)
Watch me throw the ball! (2009)
I am going! (2010)
Can I play too? (2010)
We are in a book! (2010)
I broke my trunk! (2011)
Should I share my ice cream? (2011)

Happy Pig Day! (2011)

Listen to my trumpet! (2012)

Let's go for a drive! (2012)

A big guy took my ball! (2013)

I'm a frog! (2013)

My new friend is so fun! (2014)

Waiting is not easy! (2014)

I will take a nap! (2015)

I really like slop! (2015)

The thank you book (2016)

Waiting is not easy! by Mo Willems. First edition Hyperion Books for Children 2014 57 p. color illustrations (Elephant and Piggie) hc $8.99

Grades: PreK K 1 2   E

1. Pigs -- Fiction 2. Elephants -- Fiction 3. Humorous stories 4. Patience -- Fiction

ISBN 142319957X; 9781423199571

LC 2014007802

Theodor Seuss Geisel Honor Book (2015)

In this book, part of Mo Willems' "Elephant and Piggie" series, "Gerald loses patience with Piggie when he is told that a surprise is in store but that he must wait for it. His reactions include producing several loud GROANS and reminding Piggie repeatedly that waiting is NOT easy. Piggie knows that the surprise is worth the wait, but she has to keep Gerald there to see it." (School Library Journal)

"A lesson that never grows old, enacted with verve by two favorite friends." Kirkus

★ **We** are growing! A Mo Willems' Elephant & Piggie Like Reading! Book. by Laurie Keller. Hyperion Books for Children, an imprint of Disney Book Group 2016 64 p. color illustrations (hardback) $9.99

Grades: K 1 2 3   E

1. Humorous stories 2. Growth -- Fiction 3. Grasses -- Fiction

ISBN 9781484726358

LC 2015042555

Theodor Seuss Geisel Award (2017)

"Walt and his friends are growing up fast! Everyone is the something-est. But . . . what about Walt? He is not the tallest, or the curliest, or the silliest. He is not the anything-est! As a BIG surprise inches closer, Walt discovers something special of his own!" (Publisher's note)

"Keller's googly-eyed grasses brim with personality, her emphatic cartooning creates some wonderful slapstick moments, and raucous sound effects make the action of grass growing sound more like a five-car pileup. The underlying ideas--to stick to your strengths even when life (or a power mower) cuts you down, and that 'We are all the something-est!'--are winners, much like the book itself." Pub Wkly

We are in a book! Hyperion Books for Children 2010 57p il (Elephant & Piggie book) $8.99

Grades: PreK K 1 2   E

1. Pigs -- Fiction 2. Elephants -- Fiction 3. Friendship -- Fiction 4. Books and reading -- Fiction

ISBN 978-1-4231-3308-7; 1-4231-3308-0

"Stalwart friends Piggie and Gerald the elephant push the metafictive envelope in a big way when they realize that 'someone is looking at us.' . . . Emergent readers just beginning to grapple one-on-one with the rules of the printed codex will find the friends' antics both funny and provocative. . . . Willems displays his customary control of both body language and pacing even as he challenges his readers to engage with his characters and the physicality of their book." Kirkus

Willey, Margaret

A **Clever** Beatrice Christmas; illustrated by Heather M. Solomon. Atheneum Books for Young Readers 2006 un il $16.95

Grades: K 1 2 3   E

1. Christmas -- Fiction 2. Santa Claus -- Fiction

ISBN 0-689-87017-5

LC 2005-10281

As Christmas approaches, Clever Beatrice sets out to prove the existence of Père Noël to three questioning children

This is "a pleasing, seasonal picture book. Solomon's appealing artwork combines elements of acrylic and oil painting with fluid watercolors and collage elements that add unexpected textures to the illustrations." Booklist

Williams, Barbara

Albert's impossible toothache; illustrated by Doug Cushman. Candlewick Press 2003 un il $15.99

Grades: PreK K 1 2   E

1. Turtles -- Fiction

ISBN 0-7636-1723-7

LC 2002-67059

A newly illustrated edition of Albert's toothache, published 1974 by Dutton

When Albert the turtle complains of a toothache, no one in his family believes him, until his grandmother takes the time to really listen to him

"This title is a worthwhile addition to any picture-book collection." SLJ

Another title about Albert is:

Albert's gift for grandmother (2006)

Williams, Brenda

Lin Yi's lantern; a Moon Festival tale. [text by] Brenda Williams; [illustrations by] Benjamin Lacombe. Barefoot Books 2009 un il $16.99

Grades: K 1 2 3   E

1. China -- Fiction 2. Shopping -- Fiction 3. Festivals -- Fiction

ISBN 978-1-84686-147-5; 1-84686-147-0

LC 2008043900

When his mother sends him to the market to buy necessities for the upcoming festival, Lin Yi is certain his bargaining skills will get him the best prices and he will have money left over for his coveted red rabbit lantern

"Handsome, stylized gouache illustrations portray the Chinese characters and scenes from a variety of perspectives. . . . The length of the narrative and accompanying cultural information make this an excellent supplement for primary multicultural units." Booklist

Williams, C. K.

A **not** scary story about big scary things; illustrated by Gabi Swiatkowska. Harcourt Children's Books 2010 un il $16.99

Grades: PreK K 1 2   E

1. Fear -- Fiction 2. Monsters -- Fiction

ISBN 978-0-15-205466-3; 0-15-205466-9

A little boy walking through an ordinary forest encounters an extraordinary monster.

"Sharing a surreal sense of logic and elegance, Williams and Swiatkowska convey a mood that's both dreamy and reassuringly matter-of-fact. Swiatkowska . . . is in particularly fine form, with wry drawings that range from florid to schematic, and clever collages that underscore the silliness of conventional wisdom." Publ Wkly

Williams, Emma

The **story** of Hurry; Emma Williams, Ibrahim Quraishi. Seven Stories Press 2014 36 p. illustrations $16.95

Grades: K 1 2 3 4   E
1. Zoos 2. Israel-Arab conflicts 3. Zoos -- Fiction 4. Donkeys -- Fiction 5. Poverty -- Fiction 6. Gaza Strip -- Fiction 7. Arab-Israeli conflict -- Fiction
ISBN 1609805895; 9781609805890

LC 2014005764

This children's story, by Emma Williams, illustrated by Ibrahim Quraishi, recounts how "after a major invasion of the Gaza Strip in late 2008, twenty-year-old Mahmoud Barghout decided to become a zookeeper. . . . But the war made feeding and caring for the animals impossible. . . . So Mr. Barghout came up with a solution for at least one animal: he dyed two local white donkeys with dark stripes, to create zebras, which visiting children could touch and even ride." (Publisher's note)

"Williams, a physician and journalist who witnessed the second Palestinian intifada while living in Jerusalem, bases this haunting, hopeful, and relevant story on an incident that took place in the Gaza Strip in 2008 . . . An assemblage of photos, stark silhouettes, and abstract flourishes, the pictures mesh comforting and disturbing images—Hurry himself appears as a wooden toy, a striking symbol of innocence in a story built around children forced to grow up quickly." PW

Williams, Karen Lynn

★ A **beach** tail; illustrated by Floyd Cooper. Boyds Mills Press 2010 un il $17.95
Grades: PreK K 1 2   E
1. Beaches -- Fiction 2. African Americans -- Fiction 3. Father-son relationship -- Fiction
ISBN 978-1-59078-712-0; 1-59078-712-9

"At the beach with his father, Greg strays from his beach umbrella, but stays calm and remembers the two things Dad told him: 'Don't go in the water, and don't leave Sandy.' Sandy is a lion Greg has drawn in the sand, and because Greg hasn't lifted the stick with which he has drawn Sandy's long, long tail . . . he's able to retrace his steps to find his father. . . . Cooper . . . draws a startlingly real Greg in a series of tight closeups. . . . Grainy pastel and washed-out color evoke the seashore's bleached palette. . . . Williams's . . . even pacing and soothing text reassure children without losing momentum." Publ Wkly

Four feet, two sandals; written by Karen Lynn Williams and Khadra Mohammed; illustrated by Doug Chayka. Eerdmans Books for Young Readers 2007 un il $17
Grades: 2 3 4   E
1. Shoes -- Fiction 2. Pakistan -- Fiction 3. Refugees -- Fiction 4. Friendship -- Fiction 5. Afghanistan -- Fiction
ISBN 978-0-8028-5296-0

LC 2006002635

Two young Afghani girls living in a refugee camp in Pakistan share a precious pair of sandals brought by relief workers

"The thickly brushed, double-page paintings show the long lines of desperate refugees and then close-ups of the two Muslim girls. . . . This is a personal drama behind the daily news." Booklist

Galimoto; illustrated by Catherine Stock. Lothrop, Lee & Shepard Bks. 1990 un il $16.95; pa $6.99
Grades: PreK K 1 2   E
1. Toys -- Fiction 2. Malawi -- Fiction
ISBN 0-688-08789-2; 0-688-10991-8 pa

LC 89-2258

"In Malawi, Africa, according to the author's note, galimoto are intricate and popular push toys crafted by children. Williams tells the story of seven-year-old Kondi's quest to find ample scrap material to fashion his own toy pickup truck. . . . Kondi's perseverance and the pleasure he takes in his accomplishment are just two of the delights of this appealing story. Stock's graceful watercolors portray life in a bustling village

and include enough detail . . . to give readers the flavor of a day in this southern African nation." Horn Book

My name is Sangoel; written by Karen Lynn Williams and Khadra Mohammed; illustrated by Catherine Stock. Eerdmans Books for Young Readers 2009 un il $17
Grades: 1 2 3   E
1. Refugees -- Fiction 2. Immigrants -- Fiction 3. Personal names -- Fiction 4. Sudanese Americans -- Fiction
ISBN 978-0-8028-5307-3; 0-8028-5307-2

LC 2008-31735

As a refugee from Sudan to the United States, Sangoel is frustrated that no one can pronounce his name correctly until he finds a clever way to solve the problem.

"Stock's bright watercolor scenarios, accentuated with thick black lines, express the wrenching leave-taking and then the combination of exciting new things, . . . as well as disorienting ones. . . . [This is a] moving story." Booklist

Painted dreams; pictures by Catherine Stock. Lothrop, Lee & Shepard Bks. 1998 un il hardcover o.p. lib bdg $15.93
Grades: PreK K 1 2   E
1. Haiti -- Fiction 2. Artists -- Fiction
ISBN 0-688-13901-9; 0-688-13902-7 lib bdg

LC 97-32920

Because her Haitian family is too poor to be able to buy paints for her, eight-year-old Ti Marie finds her own way to create pictures that make the heart sing

"Beautifully composed and full of life, Stock's watercolors suggest the personalities of the characters through their expressions and gestures." Booklist

Williams, Laura E.

The **Can** Man; illustrated by Craig Orback. Lee & Low 2010 un il $18.95
Grades: K 1 2 3   E
1. Homeless persons -- Fiction
ISBN 1-60060-266-5; 978-1-60060-266-5

"Tim wants a skateboard badly, but money is tight. Watching a homeless man every calls the Can Man . . . collect cans to redeem for cash, Tim decides to do the same to bankroll his skateboard. . . . Orback's . . . realistic oil paintings on canvas bring the tale's urban setting into clear focus in warmly lit scenes that illuminate the characters' feelings." Publ Wkly

Williams, Linda

★ The **little** old lady who was not afraid of anything; illustrated by Megan Lloyd. Crowell 1986 un il
Grades: PreK K 1 2   E
1. Fear -- Fiction
ISBN 0-06-443183-5 pa; 0-690-04584-0; 0-690-04586-7 lib bdg

LC 85-48250

Coming home late to her cabin by the woods, a fearless little old lady "sees two big shoes in her path. . . . She tells them to get out of the way, but they follow her, going 'CLOMP, CLOMP.' Shoes are followed by pants, 'WIGGLE, WIGGLE'; shirt, 'SHAKE, SHAKE'; gloves, 'CLAP, CLAP'; hat, 'NOD, NOD'; and, finally, a scary pumpkin, 'BOO, BOO.' Even the intrepid little old lady is a little shaken by this, and she runs home. She finally helps them all . . . by suggesting they become a scarecrow." (Horn Book) "Preschool to grade two." (SLJ)

"A delightful picture book, perfect for both independent reading pleasure and for telling aloud." SLJ

Williams, Sherley Anne

Working cotton; written by Sherley Anne Williams; illustrated by Carole Byard. Harcourt Brace Jovanovich 1992 un il hardcover o.p. pa $7

Grades: PreK K 1 2   E

1. Cotton -- Fiction 2. Migrant labor -- Fiction 3. African Americans -- Fiction

ISBN 0-15-299624-9; 0-15-201482-9 pa

LC 91-21586

A Caldecott Medal honor book, 1993

A young black girl relates the daily events of her family's migrant life in the cotton fields of central California

"Byard's acrylic paintings contribute weight and emotion to Williams's spare text. The fields and family members fill each full-page spread, drawing the reader very close to the action of the story. The mural-like paintings glow with blue and brown tones, recreating the textures and hues of the cotton fields. Williams's text, based on her poems, has a lyrical, rhythmic quality." Horn Book

Williams, Sue

Let's go visiting; written by Sue Williams; illustrated by Julie Vivas. Harcourt Brace & Co. 1998 un il hardcover o.p. pa $7; bd bk $6.95

Grades: PreK K   E

1. Counting 2. Stories in rhyme 3. Domestic animals -- Fiction

ISBN 0-15-201823-9; 0-15-202410-7 pa; 0-15-204638-0 bd bk

LC 97-34398

A counting story in which a boy visits his farmyard friends, from one brown foal to six yellow puppies

"The bold illustrations, simple yet full of motion, combine with a lively text to make this perfect for toddler story hours." Booklist

Williams, Suzanne

Library Lil; illustrated by Steven Kellogg. Dial Bks. for Young Readers 1997 un il $16.99; pa $6.99

Grades: PreK K 1 2 3   E

1. Tall tales 2. Librarians -- Fiction 3. Books and reading -- Fiction

ISBN 0-8037-1698-2; 0-14-056837-9 pa

LC 95-23490

A formidable librarian makes readers not only out of the once resistant residents of her small town, but out of a tough-talking, television-watching motorcycle gang as well

"The silliness of both story and pictures are perfectly matched. Kellogg's distinctive toothy kids and laughing cats crowd the pages, fitting right in with the baby-faced biker banditos." SLJ

Williams, Vera B.

A **chair** for my mother; by Vera B. Williams. Greenwillow Bks. 1982 un il lib bdg $16.89; pa $6.99; hbk $15.99

Grades: PreK K 1 2 3   E

1. Chairs -- Fiction 2. Family life -- Fiction 3. Saving and investment -- Fiction

ISBN 0-688-00914-X; 0-688-00915-8 lib bdg; 0-688-04074-8 pa; 9780688009144

LC 81-7010

Caldecott Honor Book (1983)

Rosa, her waitress mother, and her grandmother save dimes to buy a comfortable armchair after all their furniture is lost in a fire

"The cheerful paintings take up the full left-hand page and face, in most cases, a small chunk of the text set against a modulated wash of a complementing color; a border containing a pertinent motif surrounds the two pages, further unifying the design. The result is a superbly conceived picture book expressing the joyful spirit of a loving family." Horn Book

Other titles about Rosa and her family are:

Music, music for everyone (1984)

Something special for me (1983)

A chair for always (2009)

★ **Cherries** and cherry pits. Greenwillow Bks. 1986 un il hardcover o.p. $17.99; pa $6.99

Grades: PreK K 1 2 3   E

1. Drawing -- Fiction 2. African Americans -- Fiction

ISBN 0-688-05145-6; 0-688-05146-4 lib bdg; 0-688-10478-9 pa

LC 85-17156

"Williams' portraits of Bidemmi drawing are done in watercolor; the drawings Bidemmi makes are done with bright markers, some being simple sketches, others filling the page with color, looking like naive, but glorious icons. The interior stories are well integrated with each other, and the whole adds up to a study of child as artist that is fresh, vibrant, and exciting." Bull Cent Child Books

Lucky song. Greenwillow Bks. 1997 un il $16.99

Grades: PreK K 1   E

1. Day -- Fiction 2. Kites -- Fiction 3. Songs -- Fiction

ISBN 0-688-14459-4

LC 96-7151

"Evie flies the kite made by her grandfather until it's time to go home for supper all tired and ready for bed. This patterned story, showing a little girl surrounded by a loving family, ends by circling back to the beginning. It is illustrated using brilliantly colored watercolors." Child Book Rev Serv

★ **More** more more said the baby; 3 love stories. Greenwillow Bks. 1990 un il $17.99; lib bdg $18.89; pa $6.99; bd bk $7.99

Grades: PreK K 1   E

1. Infants -- Fiction 2. Family life -- Fiction

ISBN 0-688-09173-3; 0-688-09174-1 lib bdg; 0-688-814736-4 pa; 0-688-15634-7 bd bk

LC 89-2023

A Caldecott Medal honor book, 1991

Three babies are caught up in the air and given loving attention by a father, grandmother, and mother

"The pages reverberate with bright colors and vigorous forms, and the rhythmic language begs to be read aloud." Horn Book Guide

★ **Stringbean's** trip to the shining sea; greetings from Vera B. Williams, story and pictures; and Jennifer Williams, more pictures. Greenwillow Bks. 1987 un il hardcover o.p. $18.99; pa $7.99

Grades: K 1 2 3   E

1. West (U.S.) -- Fiction 2. Automobile travel -- Fiction

ISBN 0-688-07161-9; 0-688-07162-7 lib bdg; 0-688-16701-2 pa

LC 86-29502

"The use of mixed media—watercolors, Magic Markers, and colored pencils—is as aesthetically pleasing as it is skillful. Nothing has been forgotten; nothing more needs to be added. Not for the usual picture-book set, this travelogue storybook will appeal to slightly older audiences." Horn Book

Three days on a river in a red canoe. Greenwillow Bks. 1984 un il hardcover o.p. pa $6.99

Grades: K 1 2 3   E

1. Camping -- Fiction 2. Canoes and canoeing -- Fiction

ISBN 0-688-84307-7 lib bdg; 0-688-04072-1 pa

LC 80-23893

In this book, a "canoe trip for two children and two adults is recorded with all its interesting detail in a spontaneous first-person account and engaging full-color drawings on carefully designed pages. Driving to a river site, making camp, paddling the craft, negotiating a waterfall, swimming, fishing, dealing with a sudden storm, and even rescuing one overboard child are all described as important incidents in a summertime adventure." Horn Book

Willis, Jeanne

★ The **bog** baby; written by Jeanne Willis; illustrated by Gwen Millward. Schwartz & Wade Books 2009 un il $16.99; lib bdg $19.99

Grades: K 1 2 3   **E**

1. Magic -- Fiction 2. Sisters -- Fiction

ISBN 978-0-375-86176-5; 0-375-86176-9; 978-0-375-96176-2 lib bdg; 0-375-96176-3 lib bdg

LC 2008-47635

First published 2008 in the United Kingdom

When two sisters go fishing in a magic pond, they find a winged blue bog baby and take it home with them.

"The glorious illustrations reveal a lush dreamscape of a backyard flush with tendrils, bluebells, Queen Anne's lace, birch trees, cherry trees, dragonflies, ladybugs, and more, all delicately and minutely drawn, and painted in watercolors. The child-voiced, economical narrative transports readers into the squelches and squeaks of tromping through the mud and spring plants." SLJ

Gorilla! Gorilla! [by] Jeanne Willis and [illustrated by] Tony Ross. Simon & Schuster 2006 un il $15.95

Grades: PreK K 1 2   **E**

1. Mice -- Fiction 2. Gorillas -- Fiction

ISBN 978-1-4169-1490-7; 1-4169-1490-0

"While searching for her lost baby, a mouse is chased by a great, big, hairy, scary ape! . . . Young readers will guess what the mother mouse, in her terror, can't see—that the seemingly fierce gorilla is simply trying to return her baby to her. The brief, lively text and the melodramatic refrain make for a humorous and boisterous read-aloud. Ross's bright pastel illustrations capture the mouse's fear and the gorilla's determination with verve." SLJ

★ **Susan** laughs; illustrated by Tony Ross. Holt & Co. 2000 un il $15

Grades: PreK K 1   **E**

1. Stories in rhyme 2. Play -- Fiction 3. People with physical disabilities -- Fiction

ISBN 0-8050-6501-6

LC 99-59560

Rhyming couplets describe a wide range of common emotions and activities experienced by a little girl who uses a wheelchair

"Without being condescending or preachy, the words, pictures, and design of this very simple picture book show that a physically disabled child is 'just like me, just like you.' Only on the very last page do we discover that Susan uses a wheelchair." Booklist

Wilson, Karma

★ **Bear** snores on; illustrations by Jane Chapman. Margaret K. McElderry Bks. 2002 un il $16; bd bk $7.99

Grades: PreK K 1   **E**

1. Stories in rhyme 2. Bears -- Fiction 3. Animals -- Fiction 4. Parties -- Fiction

ISBN 0-689-83187-0; 1-4169-0272-4 bd bk

LC 00-28371

On a cold winter night many animals gather to party in the cave of a sleeping bear, who then awakes and protests that he has missed the food and the fun

"The characters are infused with warmth and humor. . . . The warm, soft tones of these acrylic illustrations perfectly capture the coziness of Bear's lair and capture the action." SLJ

Other titles in this series are:

Bear feels scared (2008)

Bear feels sick (2007)

Bear stays up for Christmas (2004)

Bear wants more (2003)

Bear's loose tooth (2011)

Bear's new friend (2006)

The **cow** loves cookies; illustrated by Marcellus Hall. Margaret K. McElderry Books 2010 un il $16.99

Grades: PreK K 1 2   **E**

1. Stories in rhyme 2. Cattle -- Fiction 3. Cookies -- Fiction 4. Farmers -- Fiction 5. Domestic animals -- Fiction

ISBN 978-1-4169-4206-1; 1-4169-4206-8

LC 2009-00742

While all the other animals on the farm enjoy eating their regular food, the cow chooses to eat the one thing that she loves best.

"The big, clear watercolor pictures with thick ink lines leave lots of white space, and the simple rhyming lines, with descriptive words and messy action, will encourage preschoolers to join in." Booklist

A **frog** in the bog; [illustrated by] Joan Rankin. Margaret K. McElderry Bks. 2003 un il $16.95

Grades: PreK K 1   **E**

1. Counting 2. Stories in rhyme 3. Frogs -- Fiction 4. Insects -- Fiction

ISBN 0-689-84081-0

LC 2002-5903

A frog in the bog grows larger and larger as he eats more and more bugs, until he attracts the attention of an alligator who puts an end to his eating

"This gastronomic adventure is told in catchy rhyming verse, complemented by soft, dreamy watercolors that perfectly recreate the bog. The illustrations are enhanced by humorous details." SLJ

Hogwash; illustrated by Jim McMullan. Little, Brown 2011 un il $16.99

Grades: PreK K   **E**

1. Stories in rhyme 2. Pigs -- Fiction 3. Baths -- Fiction 4. Farmers -- Fiction 5. Cleanliness -- Fiction

ISBN 978-0-316-98840-7; 0-316-98840-5

LC 2010019754

When his stubborn pigs refuse a sudsy cleaning, a determined farmer learns that mud baths can be just as fun.

"Kids will be plenty entertained by the lanky, bespectacled Farmer's many disguises (and escalating frustration), but the crafty, confident, and expressive pigs hog the spotlight in every scene. It's a highly satisfying story." Publ Wkly

How to bake an American pie; illustrated by Raul Colón. Simon & Schuster 2007 un il $16.99

Grades: K 1 2 3   **E**

1. Stories in rhyme 2. Patriotism -- Fiction

ISBN 0-689-86506-6; 978-0-689-86506-0

Rhyming text and illustrations present a recipe for how to bake a pie from all the things that make America great.

"In these watercolor-and-ink paintings, the action rolls across the spreads in all sorts of fantastical ways. Purple mountain majesties grow out of teacups, and the cooks pull rainbows out of a sky studded with stars and stripes. . . . [This is a] wild, wonderful celebration." Booklist

Mama, why? illustrations by Simon Mendez. Margaret K. McElderry Books 2011 un il $16.99

Grades: PreK K 1   E

1. Stories in rhyme 2. Sky -- Fiction 3. Night -- Fiction 4. Bedtime -- Fiction 5. Polar bear -- Fiction 6. Mother-child relationship -- Fiction

ISBN 978-1-4169-4205-4; 1-4169-4205-X

A sleepy polar bear cub asks his mother questions about the night sky as he gets ready to go to sleep.

"Wilson's conversational style beautifully captures a homespun imagination and the feel of a mother's end-of-day murmurs to her 'dearest one.' There's genuine magic in Mendez's soft-focus arctic scenes, particularly the way his lighting conveys the warm glow of the moon, the glittering night, and the glacial air." Publ Wkly

Where is home, Little Pip? [by] Karma Wilson; illustrated by Jane Chapman. Margaret K. McElderry Books 2008 un il $16.99

Grades: PreK K 1   E

1. Animals -- Fiction 2. Penguins -- Fiction 3. Antarctica -- Fiction

ISBN 978-0-689-85983-0; 0-689-85983-X

LC 2006019094

After Little Pip the penguin gets lost she meets a whale, a kelp gull, and sled dogs who cannot help her, but with the aid of her family's song, home finds her

"Well-structured text, genuine emotions, and beautiful full-bleed illustrations in a palette that ranges from cool whites and blues to warm pinks, corals, and tans combine to produce a wonderful story of a loving family separated and then reunited." SLJ

Other titles about Little Pip are:

Don't be afraid, Little Pip (2009)

What's in the egg, Little Pip? (2010)

Whopper cake; [by] Karma Wilson; [illustrated by] Will Hillenbrand. Margaret K. McElderry Books 2007 un il $16.99

Grades: PreK K 1 2   E

1. Tall tales 2. Stories in rhyme 3. Cake -- Fiction 4. Birthdays -- Fiction

ISBN 0-689-83844-1

LC 00058742

Grandad bakes Grandma a whopper of a birthday cake. Includes recipe and directions for chocolate cake

"Rendered in ink and egg tempera, Hillenbrand's illustrations spill off the spreads." SLJ

Wimmer, Sonja

The **word** collector. Cuento de Luz 36 p. $15.95

Grades: 1 2 3   E

1. New words 2. Picture books for children

ISBN 8415241348; 9788415241348

This children's picture book tells of Luna, who lives in the sky and collects words. "But one day the words stop coming. Luna learns that the people have become too busy to remember the importance of words. With her collection, she travels across the land. Where Luna finds darkness and despair she plants words of compassion and love. When her words run out, people begin to create—and generously share—new words." (Kirkus)

Wing, Natasha

Go to bed, monster! written by Natasha Wing; illustrated by Sylvie Kantorovitz. Harcourt 2007 un il $16

Grades: PreK K 1   E

1. Bedtime -- Fiction 2. Monsters -- Fiction

ISBN 978-0-15-205775-6

LC 2006010849

Trying to avoid bedtime, Lucy uses her imagination and some crayons to draw a monster to play with.

"Kantorovitz's whimsical ink-and-watercolor pictures on open white backgrounds . . . are perfectly paired to Wing's engaging and breezy text and characters." SLJ

Winstanley, Nicola

Cinnamon baby; [text by] Nicola Winstanley; [illustrations by] Janice Nadeau. Kids Can Press 2011 un il $16.95

Grades: PreK K 1 2   E

1. Baking -- Fiction 2. Infants -- Fiction 3. Racially mixed people -- Fiction

ISBN 1-55337-821-0; 978-1-55337-821-1

Miriam the baker marries Sebastian and they have a baby who won't stop crying, until the smell of Miriam's cinnamon bread calms it.

"Both the words and pictures engage the senses in a heady, tangled mix. . . . Miriam is paper white, Sebastian is cocoa brown, and their cinammon-colored child gives the title a sly double meaning. A charming offering infused with warmth, romantic whimsy, and love." Booklist

The **pirate's** bed; Nicola Winstanley. Tundra Books of Northern New York 2015 32 p. color illustrations (hardcover) $17.99

Grades: PreK K 1 2   E

1. Bedtime -- Fiction 2. Pirates -- Fiction

ISBN 1770496165; 9781770496163; 9781770496187

LC 2014941836

In this children's story, by Nicola Winstanley, illustrated by Matt James, "a pirate is sleeping snug in his bed, dreaming pirate dreams, when a great storm comes up at sea. The pirate sleeps on, but his bed is awake and scared of the thunder and the angry waves. Tossed this way and that, the ship finally crashes, sending the pirate to a tropical island and his bed off to sea." (Publisher's note)

A pirate snoozes through a great storm while his frightened bed is buffeted about. The storm pitches the sleeping pirate and his crew overboard then to an island where they live "in peace for the rest of their days, eating sweet fruit and teaching parrots to talk." . . . This is a treasure of a book." SLJ

Winstead, Rosie, 1977-

Sprout helps out; Rosie Winstead. Dial Books for Young Readers, an imprint of Penguin Group (USA) Inc. 2013 32 p. color illustrations (hardcover) $16.99

Grades: PreK K   E

1. Helping behavior -- Fiction 2. Mother-daughter relationship -- Fiction 3. Helpfulness -- Fiction

ISBN 0803730721; 9780803730724

LC 2013008765

This children's book, by Rosie Winstead, is "about helping Mom and making a sweet, sweet mess of it. . . . Sprout's small, but she's good at helping. She makes the bed (with Mom still in it), cooks (if cooking is overflowing the cereal bowl), vacuums (up the cat--almost), and looks after her baby sister Bea (like a champ). Sure, sometimes Sprout's plans backfire, but good intentions go a long way--and make life interesting." (Publisher's note)

"Ironic narration, primly positive and perky, allows playful pictures to reveal how much (or little) Sprout really helps around her house. She brushes her teeth without being reminded and then takes care of the forgetful dog's teeth, for instance—with her mother's toothbrush. She conscientiously does the laundry after getting dirty—but her baby sister needs to rescue the cat from the washing machine! Simple sentences imbued with wide-eyed innocence work alongside illustrations showing Sprout's misguided household management to winning comedic effect. Winstead's breezy pencil, gouache and watercolor illustrations suit Sprout's comfortable household, with its charming wallpapers, art supplies and scattered toys. . . . High, sly entertainment for troublemakers and helpers alike." Kirkus

Winston, Sam

A **child** of books; Oliver Jeffers, Sam Winston. Candlewick Press 2016 40 p. illustrations (chiefly color) $17.99

Grades: 1 2 3 4 5   E

1. Picture books for children 2. Adventure travel 3. Creative activities 4. Children -- Books and reading

ISBN 9780763690779

LC 2016943940

In this picture book for children by Oliver Jeffers and Sam Winston, "a little girl sails her raft across a sea of words, arriving at the house of a small boy and calling him away on an adventure. Through forests of fairy tales and across mountains of make-believe, the two travel together on a fantastical journey that unlocks the boy's imagination. Now a lifetime of magic and adventure lies ahead of him . . . but who will be next?" (Publisher's note)

"A gorgeous, innovative musing on the power of storytelling." SLJ

Winter, Jeanette

★ **Biblioburro**; a true story from Colombia. Beach Lane Books 2010 un il

Grades: PreK K 1 2   E

1. Libraries 2. Books and reading 3. Colombia 4. Reading teachers 5. Elementary school teachers

ISBN 1416997784; 9781416997788

"After amassing piles of books, Luis, a voracious reader, dreams up a way to share his collection with 'faraway villages.' He starts with two burros—one for himself, one for books—and heads off. Tough terrain and menacing bandits challenge him along the way, but at last he reaches a remote town, where he holds a story hour and loans titles to eager kids before returning home to his wife and reading late into the night. Winter's captivating paintings evoke a South American feel in their brilliant palette and dense, green tropical scenes teeming with creatures, including large, orange-winged butterflies on every page. . . . Winter's text is spare and streamlined, as usual, and here it has a particularly engaging, repetitive rhythm that builds into a lulling bedtime beat." Booklist

★ **Calavera** abecedario; a Day of the Dead alphabet. Harcourt 2004 un il $16

Grades: PreK K 1 2   E

1. Alphabet 2. All Souls' Day -- Fiction 3. Spanish language -- Vocabulary 4. Mexico -- Social life and customs

ISBN 0-15-205110-4

LC 2004-1554

Every year Don Pedro makes papier-mache skeletons, or calaveras, for Mexico's Day of the Dead fiesta. From Angel to Unicornio, each letter of the alphabet has its own special calavera. Spanish words illustrate each letter of the alphabet.

This "features jaunty illustrations inspired by Mexican folk art. . . This is a lovely book that approaches the Day of the Dead from an unusual angle." SLJ

★ **Follow** the drinking gourd; story and pictures by Jeanette Winter. Alfred A. Knopf 2008 un il hardcover o.p. pa $7.99

Grades: K 1 2 3   E

1. Slavery -- Fiction 2. African Americans -- Fiction 3. Underground railroad -- Fiction

ISBN 978-0-394-89694-6; 978-0-679-81997-4 pa

A reissue of the title first published 1988

By following directions in a song, taught them by an old sailor, runaway slaves journey north along the Underground Railroad to freedom in Canada.

"Complementing the few lines of text per page are dark-hued illustrations horizontally framed with a fine black line and plenty of white space. . . . The art carries the weight of introducing children to a riveting piece of U.S. history, and the music included at the end of the book will fix it in their minds." Bull Cent Child Books

Kali's song; Jeanette Winter. Schwartz & Wade Books 2012 40 p.

Grades: PreK K 1 2   E

1. Music -- Fiction 2. Mammoths -- Fiction 3. Bow and arrow -- Fiction 4. Picture books for children 5. Prehistoric peoples -- Fiction 6. Hunting -- Fiction 7. Cave dwellers -- Fiction

ISBN 9780375870224; 9780375970221

LC 2011009357

In this illustrated children's book, "[w]hen young Kali . . . is given a bow to practice hunting, he discovers that if he puts it to his mouth and plucks the string he can make music. . . . [W]hen the big hunt occurs, Kali stuns everyone by playing his bow so musically that even the herd of mammoths is entranced. The people decide that Kali is a shaman . . . and he lives out his days healing and guiding his community." (Bulletin of the Center for Children's Books)

Mama; a true story in which a baby hippo loses his mama during a tsunami, but finds a new home, and a new mama. Harcourt 2006 un il $16

Grades: PreK K 1 2   E

1. Turtles 2. Hippopotamus 3. Indian Ocean earthquake and tsunami, 2004

ISBN 978-0-15-205495-3; 0-15-205495-2

LC 2005-20905

Boston Globe-Horn Book Honor: Picture Book (2006)

Set against the backdrop of the devastating 2004 tsunami, this book reveals the true story of a rescued baby hippo who adopts a new "mother"—a 130-year-old male tortoise

"This visually poetic book's subtitle is longer than its entire text. . . . Winter reassuringly portrays how friendship can ease a devastating loss." Publ Wkly

Nanuk the ice bear; Jeanette Winter. Beach Lane Books 2015 48 p. color illustrations (hardback) $17.99

Grades: PreK K 1 2 3   E

1. Bears -- Fiction 2. Polar bear -- Fiction 3. Arctic regions -- Fiction

ISBN 9781481446679

LC 2015005169

This book, by Jeanette Winter, is "about a loving polar bear family. . . . At the top of the world, Nanuk the ice bear hunts for food, meets a mate, and hibernates through the winter with her newborn cubs. When spring arrives, Nanuk teaches her beloved cubs how to hunt and swim and survive in the arctic." (Publisher's note)

"As in other books by the author, big issues are presented in an accessible manner and subtly enough that adults can guide children to an age-appropriate understanding of them." Kirkus

Winter, Jonah

★ **The fabulous** feud of Gilbert & Sullivan; illustrated by Richard Egielski. Arthur A. Levine Books 2009 un il hardcover o.p. $16.99

Grades: K 1 2 3   E

1. Authors 2. Composers 3. Dramatists 4. Librettists 5. Authors -- Fiction 6. Operetta -- Fiction 7. Composers -- Fiction 8. Theatrical directors 9. Great Britain -- History -- 19th century -- Fiction

ISBN 978-0-439-93050-5; 0-439-93050-2; 978-0-439-93051-2 pa; 0-439-93051-0 pa

LC 2008-27027

In the late nineteenth century, Mr. Gilbert and Mr. Sullivan, who write operas together for a theater called Topsy-Turvydom, have a falling-out when Mr. Sullivan refuses to write music for another ridiculous story that is like all the others.

"The clearly written story comes alive in a series of distinctive ink-and-watercolor illustrations that are full of intriguing details and show great skill in the use of color, shading, and composition." Booklist

★ **Here** comes the garbage barge! written by Jonah Winter; illustrated by Red Nose Studio. Schwartz & Wade Books 2010 un il $17.99; lib bdg $20.99

Grades: K 1 2   E

1. Long Island (N.Y.) -- Fiction 2. Voyages and travels -- Fiction 3. Refuse and refuse disposal -- Fiction

ISBN 978-0-375-85218-3; 0-375-85218-2; 978-0-375-95218-0 lib bdg; 0-375-95218-7 lib bdg

LC 2008-40709

In the spring of 1987, the town of Islip, New York, with no place for its 3,168 tons of garbage, loads it on a barge that sets out on a 162-day journey along the east coast, around the Gulf of Mexico, down to Belize, and back again, in search of a place willing to accept and dispose of its very smelly cargo

"A fictionalized account of real events. . . . The illustrations are photographs of objects made from garbage. The people, full of personality and expression, were made from polymer clay, and wire, wood scraps, and leftover materials of all kinds were used for the tugboat and barge. The inside of the paper jacket explains how the art was done. This title should be a part of every elementary school ecology unit." SLJ

★ **Lillian's** right to vote; a celebration of the Voting Rights Act of 1965. Jonah Winter; illustrator Shane W. Evans. Schwartz & Wade Books 2015 40 p. color illustrations (alk. paper) $17.99

Grades: K 1 2 3 4   E

1. African Americans -- Suffrage 2. Voting -- Fiction 3. African Americans -- History -- Fiction

ISBN 0385390289; 9780385390286; 9780385390293

LC 2014010937

In this book, by Jonah Winter, illustrated by Shane W. Evans, as "Lillian, a one-hundred-year-old African American woman, makes a 'long haul up a steep hill' to her polling place, she sees more than trees and sky—she sees her family's history. She sees the passage of the Fifteenth Amendment and her great-grandfather voting for the first time. She sees her parents trying to register to vote. And she sees herself marching in a protest from Selma to Montgomery." (Publisher's note)

"Lillian may be old, but it's Voting Day, and she's going to vote. As she climbs the hill (both metaphorical and literal) to the courthouse, she sees her family's history and the history of the fight for voting rights unfold before her, from her great-great-grandparents being sold as slaves to the three marches across Selma's famous bridge. . . . A powerful historical picture book." SLJ

★ **Steel** Town; illustrated by Terry Widener. Atheneum Books for Young Readers 2008 un il $16.99

Grades: 2 3 4   E

1. Factories -- Fiction 2. Steel industry -- Fiction 3. Cities and towns -- Fiction

ISBN 978-1-4169-4081-4; 1-4169-4081-2

LC 2006-29284

In Steel Town, it's always raining, freight trains come and go, the big furnace roars, and the steel mill never sleeps.

"The acrylic artwork creates an atmosphere of gloom with fiery furnaces and gray skies. Against this backdrop is the rhythmic, repetitious language detailing a day in the life of Steel Town. . . . Both informa-

tive and visually stunning, . . . beautifully written and powerfully illustrated." SLJ

Winters, Kari-Lynn

Bad Pirate; Kari-Lynn Winters, illustrated by Dean Griffiths. Pajama Press 2015 32 p. colour illustrations $17.95

Grades: PreK K 1 2   E

1. Pirates -- Fiction 2. Conduct of life -- Fiction 3. Fathers and daughters -- Fiction

ISBN 1927485711; 9781927485712

"Barnacle Garrick is bold and saucy and selfish. And for a pirate captain, that's good, very good. And his crew are all scurvy sea dogs-selfish down to the last fleabitten scuttle-butt. And that's good too. But Augusta Garrick is shy, polite, and selfless. For a pirate, that's bad, very bad. Despite her father's horrible example, the sea pup can't stop helping out." (Publisher's note)

"This seagoing tale with its endearing heroine will be a sure hit with youngsters." SLJ

Another title in this series is:

Good Pirate (2016)

Winters, Kay

My teacher for President; illustrated by Denise Brunkus. Dutton Children's Books 2004 un il $14.99

Grades: PreK K 1 2   E

1. Teachers -- Fiction 2. Presidents -- Fiction

ISBN 0-525-47186-3

LC 2003-19222

A second-grader writes a television station with reasons why his teacher would make a good president, but only if she can continue teaching till the end of the year

"Brunkus' cheerful illustrations show a gray-haired woman in large, round glasses. . . . The humorous tone brings lofty ideals about desirable presidential qualities down to an everyday, accessible level." Booklist

This school year will be the best! illustrated by Renée Andriani. Dutton Children's Books 2010 un il $16.99

Grades: K 1 2   E

1. School stories

ISBN 978-0-525-42275-4; 0-525-42275-7

When a teacher asks her students on the first day of school what they wish for in the coming year, the answers range from having a good school picture to receiving a perfect report card.

"The short text leaves plenty of space for Andriani to work in, and she uses it imaginatively, creating upbeat and sometimes comical ink-and-wash illustrations. A good discussion starter for the beginning of the school year." Booklist

Winthrop, Elizabeth

Shoes; illustrated by William Joyce. Harper & Row 1986 19p il lib bdg $16.89; pa $6.99

Grades: PreK K   E

1. Stories in rhyme 2. Shoes -- Fiction

ISBN 0-06-026592-2 lib bdg; 0-06-443171-1 pa

LC 85-45841

"This lilting rhyme about shoes and feet easily pleases, . . . Backing the verses are full-color drawings of children busily involved with one kind of shoe or another. Joyce's pictures are animated, energetic, and warmly colored." Booklist

Wiseman, Bernard

Morris and Boris at the circus; by B. Wiseman. Harper & Row 1988 64p il (I can read book) hardcover o.p. pa $3.99

Grades: PreK K 1 2   **E**
1. Bears -- Fiction 2. Moose -- Fiction 3. Circus -- Fiction
ISBN 0-06-026478-0 lib bdg; 0-06-444143-1 pa

LC 87-45682

"The cartoon illustrations with bold colors provide ample context clues for beginning readers. This delightful combination of text and illustrations will entice children to read and re-read this book." SLJ

Wishinsky, Frieda

Maggie can't wait; illustrated by Dean Griffiths. Fitzhenry & Whiteside 2009 un il $17.95
Grades: PreK K 1   **E**
1. Cats -- Fiction 2. Infants -- Fiction 3. Sisters -- Fiction 4. Adoption -- Fiction
ISBN 978-1-55455-103-3; 1-55455-103-X

Maggie the cat "is excited about the arrival of her newly adopted baby sister. But when she takes a picture of Rose to school, a mean-spirited nemesis dubs the baby ugly. . . . The drama of a cruel comment is fully realized in a manner and tone that children will identify with; Maggie's mortification is as believable as her triumph." SLJ

Another title about Maggie is:

Give Maggie a chance (2002)

Please, Louise! [by] Frieda Wishinsky; illustrated by Marie-Louise Gay. Groundwood Books 2007 un il $17.95
Grades: PreK K 1 2   **E**
1. Dogs -- Fiction 2. Siblings -- Fiction
ISBN 0-88899-796-5; 978-0-88899-796-8

Jake is annoyed that his little sister Louise won't leave him alone. He wishes Louise were a dog. Suddenly Louise is gone and a little dog appears to be in her place. Jake is worried that his wish may have come true.

"Deft pencil drawings, brightened with watercolor washes and collage elements, capture every nuance of the characters' emotions. . . . [The] story . . . unfolds with surprise and wit." Booklist

You're mean, Lily Jean! illustrated by Kady MacDonald Denton. Albert Whitman 2011 un il $16.99
Grades: PreK K 1 2   **E**
1. Play -- Fiction 2. Sisters -- Fiction 3. Friendship -- Fiction
ISBN 0-8075-9476-8; 978-0-8075-9476-6

LC 2010027028

Sisters Carly and Sandy have always played together, but when Lily moves in next door she only wants to play with Sandy, and insists that if Carly joins them she must be a baby, or a cow, or a dog.

"Wishinsky re-creates a common childhood experience through realistic dialogue and actions that convery every emotional shift. Just as engaging, Denton's watercolor illustrations capture the girls' attitudes with gestures and facial expressions that speak volumes. Well paced and fine for reading aloud." Booklist

Witte, Anna

★ **Lola's** fandango; written by Anna Witte; illustrated by Micha Archer. Barefoot Books 2010 un il $16.99
Grades: K 1 2 3   **E**
1. Dance -- Fiction 2. Flamenco -- Fiction 3. Hispanic Americans -- Fiction
ISBN 978-1-84686-174-1; 1-84686-174-8

LC 2008028143

After learning how to dance a style of flamenco known as the fandango, Lola plans a surprise for her mother's birthday.

"Witte and Archer hit all the right notes here. The text dances across the pages, with 'tacs' and 'tocs' and 'ticas' beating out the rhythm. The action, both external and internal, is visualized in the charming collage-

style artwork. . . . A CD is included, and a Spanish-language version is also available." Booklist

The **parrot** Tico Tango; written and illustrated by Anna Witte. Barefoot Books 2004 un il $15.99; pa $6.99
Grades: PreK K 1 2   **E**
1. Stories in rhyme 2. Parrots -- Fiction 3. Rain forest animals -- Fiction
ISBN 1-84148-243-9; 1-84148-890-9 pa

LC 2004-17922

A cumulative rhyme in which a greedy parrot keeps taking fruit from the other creatures of the rainforest until he can hold no more.

"The rhymes are unusually taut and rhythmic, and the mixed-media art, which features fabric swatches, amounts to a feast of tropical colors." Horn Book Guide

Wittenstein, Barry

Waiting for Pumpsie; Barry Wittenstein; illustrated by London Ladd. Charlesbridge 2017 32 p. color illustrations (reinforced for library use) $16.99
Grades: K 1 2 3 4   **E**
1. Discrimination -- Fiction 2. African American baseball players -- Fiction 3. Baseball -- Fiction 4. Boston Red Sox (Baseball team) -- Fiction 5. African American families -- Fiction 6. Boston (Mass.) -- History -- 20th century -- Fiction 7. Baseball -- United States -- History -- Fiction 8. Boston (Mass.) -- History -- 20th century -- Fiction 9. Boston Red Sox (Baseball team) -- History -- Fiction 10. Discrimination in sports -- United States -- History -- Fiction
ISBN 9781580895453

LC 2016013776

This book, by Barry Wittenstein, illustrated by London Ladd, "captures the true story of baseball player Pumpsie Green's rise to the major leagues. The story is a snapshot of the Civil Rights Movement and a great discussion starter about the state of race relations in the United States today." (Publisher's note)

Includes bibliographical references

Wiviott, Meg

★ **Benno** and the Night of Broken Glass; illustrated by Josee Bisallion. Kar-Ben Pub. 2010 un il lib bdg $17.95; pa $7.95
Grades: 2 3 4 5   **E**
1. Cats -- Fiction 2. Jews -- Germany -- Fiction 3. Kristallnacht, 1938 -- Fiction 4. Holocaust, 1933-1945 -- Fiction 5. Germany -- History -- 1933-1945 -- Fiction
ISBN 978-0-8225-9929-6 lib bdg; 0-8225-9929-5 lib bdg; 978-0-8225-9975-3 pa; 0-8225-9975-9 pa

LC 2008033482

In 1938 Berlin, Germany, a cat sees Rosenstrasse change from a peaceful neighborhood of Jews and Gentiles to an unfriendly place where, one November night, men in brown shirts destroy Jewish-owned businesses and arrest or kill Jewish people. Includes facts about Kristallnacht and a list of related books and web resources.

"The straightforward text describes events without sentimentality. . . . But what truly distinguishes this book is the striking multimedia artwork composed of paper, fabric, and drawn images in hues of olive, brown, and red. Interesting angles, textures, and patterns add to the visual effect throughout. . . . The message of terror and sadness that marks the beginning of the Holocaust is transmitted in a way that is both meaningful and comprehensible." SLJ

Includes bibliographical references

Wohl, Lauren L.

The **eighth** menorah; by Lauren L. Wohl and illustrated by Laura Hughes. Albert Whitman & Company 2013 32 p.

Grades: PreK K 1   **E**

1. Jews -- Fiction 2. Hanukkah -- Fiction 3. Jewish holidays -- Fiction 4. Menorah -- Fiction 5. Jews -- United States -- Fiction

ISBN 9780807518922

LC 2013005188

In this book, by Lauren L. Wohl, "Hanukkah is a few weeks away, and Sam can't wait to celebrate with his family, especially his grandma. At Sunday school, everyone in his class is busy making clay menorahs to give as Hanukkah gifts! Sam likes how his menorah is turning out, but he's worried--his family already has seven menorahs! His teacher reassures him that his parents will love it, but Sam is determined to solve this problem on his own and find the perfect home for his menorah." (Publisher's note)

Wojciechowski, Susan

The **Christmas** miracle of Jonathan Toomey; illustrated by P. J. Lynch. Candlewick Press 2004 un il $12.99

Grades: 1 2 3 4   **E**

1. Christmas -- Fiction 2. Friendship -- Fiction 3. Wood carving -- Fiction

ISBN 0-7636-2621-X

A reissue of the title first published 1995

The widow McDowell and her seven-year-old son Thomas ask the gruff Jonathan Toomey, the best woodcarver in the valley, to carve the figures for a Christmas creche

"The story verges on the sentimental, but it's told with feeling and lyricism. . . . Lynch's sweeping illustrations, in shades of wood grain, are both realistic and gloriously romantic, focusing on faces and hands at work before the fire and in the lamplight." Booklist

A **fine** St. Patrick's day; illustrated by Tom Curry. Random House 2004 un il hardcover o.p. pa $6.99

Grades: K 1 2 3   **E**

1. Ireland -- Fiction 2. Saint Patrick's Day -- Fiction

ISBN 0-375-82386-7; 978-0-385-73640-4 pa; 0-385-73640-1 pa

LC 2002-11684

Two towns, Tralee and Tralah, compete in an annual St. Patrick's Day decorating contest which Tralah boastfully always wins, but when their hearts are put to the test by a little man with pointed ears, Tralee wins with no effort at all

"Wojciechowski's charming tale is beautifully complemented by Curry's stylized depictions of green rolling hills and thatched-roof houses. Both text and art convey a sturdy feeling about community and charity, brushed with touch of whimsy." Booklist

Wolf, Sallie

Truck stuck; illustrated by Andy Robert Davies. Charlesbridge 2008 un il $14.95

Grades: PreK K 1   **E**

1. Stories in rhyme 2. Trucks -- Fiction 3. Vehicles -- Fiction

ISBN 978-1-58089-119-6; 1-58089-119-5

"A red 18-wheeler gets stuck under a viaduct and causes a huge traffic jam. Nearby, two children who have a lemonade stand observe the incident and try to keep everyone cool by selling their wares. . . . Eventually, a huge tow truck arrives and, after the air has been let out of the semi's tires, the road is cleared for traffic to resume just in time, because the children are out of lemonade. The bright, flat, cartoon art brings the minimal rhyming text to life and really tells the story." SLJ

Wolff, Ashley, 1956-

Baby Bear sees blue; Ashley Wolff. Beach Lane Books 2012 40 p.

Grades: PreK K 1   **E**

1. Bears -- Fiction 2. Color -- Fiction 3. Nature -- Fiction 4.

Picture books for children 5. Mother-child relationship -- Fiction

ISBN 1442413069; 9781442413061

LC 2010005992

This picture book about a "mother bear and cub . . . introduces colors and images from the natural world. Between awakening in the den and cuddling down for the night, Baby Bear's day is full of new experiences and prescient questions. 'A glow creeps in. / 'Who is warming me, Mama?'/ asks Baby Bear. / 'That is the sun,' Mama says. / Page turns . . . deliver the color lessons: Silhouetted against the golden light of dawn, 'Baby Bear sees yellow.' The cub sees green oak leaves waving, smells fragrant red strawberries, and hears the growl of thunder against a stormy gray sky. [Ashley] Wolff's . . . compositions feature inked linoleum block prints that render those bears a strikingly deep, matte black. . . . [W]atercolors illuminate the scenes--colors in the downpour's puddles reflect a rainbow." (Kirkus)

Wolff, Ferida

It is the wind; illustrated by James Ransome. HarperCollins 2005 un il $14.99; lib bdg $15.89

Grades: PreK K 1 2   **E**

1. Sound -- Fiction 2. Bedtime -- Fiction

ISBN 0-06-028191-X; 0-06-028192-8 lib bdg

LC 00-63197

"In his room at night, a boy looks outside and tries to imagine what is making the noise he hears. . . . The mesmerizing effect of the verse makes this a good bedtime story. . . . Ransome makes the most of the simple story with graceful scenes of the African American boy and the rural night scenes he sees and imagines." Booklist

The **story** blanket; [written by Ferida Wolff and Harriet May Savitz; illustrated by Elena Odriozola] Peachtree 2008 un il $16.95

Grades: K 1 2 3   **E**

1. Gifts -- Fiction 2. Blankets -- Fiction 3. Storytelling -- Fiction

ISBN 978-1-56145-466-2; 1-56145-466-4

LC 2008-08627

With no wool to be found in the village, Babba Zarrah, the storyteller, starts unraveling her story blanket bit by bit, to secretly supply the needs of the community, and when the villagers realize what is happening they return the favor.

"Colorful illustrations accompany this story of generosity and ingenuity. Rosy-cheeked children and the bright folk art quilt suggest a timelessness to the story as well as the underlying message." Libr Media Connect

Won, Brian

Hooray for hat! Brian Won. Harcourt Children's Books, Houghton Mifflin Harcourt 2014 40 p. $16.99

Grades: PreK K 1 2   **E**

1. Hats -- Fiction 2. Elephants -- Fiction 3. Mood (Psychology) -- Fiction

ISBN 0544159039; 9780544159037

LC 2013020189

In this children's book, by Brian Won, "Elephant wakes up grumpy - until ding, dong! What's in the surprise box at the front door? A hat! HOORAY FOR HAT! Elephant marches off to show Zebra, but Zebra is having a grumpy day, too -until Elephant shares his new hat and cheers up his friend. Off they march to show Turtle! The parade continues as every animal brightens the day of a grumpy friend. An irresistible celebration of friendship, sharing, and fabulous hats." (Publisher's note)

"As everyone well knows, there's nothing so cheering as a good fashion accessory . . . HOORAY FOR FRIENDS! Won's expressively posed animal figures and the spare narrative are placed on white backgrounds that both brighten the colors and give each scene a clean, spacious look. Moreover, the repeated chorus endows the episode with storytime-friendly rhythm and predictability. A tip of the hat to this buoyant debut." Booklist

Hooray for today! Brian Won. Houghton Mifflin Harcourt 2016 40 p. color illustrations (ebook) $16.99; (hardback) $16.99
Grades: PreK K 1 2   E
    1. Owls -- Fiction 2. Play -- Fiction 3. Animals -- Fiction 4. Bedtime -- Fiction 5. Friendship -- Fiction 6. Nocturnal animals -- Fiction
    ISBN 9781328661517; 0544748034; 9780544748033
LC 2015033308

In this children's book by Brian Won, "when the moon is up, Owl is wide awake and ready for fun: 'Hooray for today! Would you like to play?' But everyone says, 'Not now! I'm sleepy!' Owl's play day gets lonely fast as each friend turns her away—until sunrise, when Owl discovers a friendly surprise. . . . [This book] celebrates playtime, sharing, and friendship." (Publisher's note)

"Buoyant and funny, this second outing cleverly works within the structure of Won's debut, but he allows himself more freedom to riff and, in doing so, hits all the right notes." Kirkus

Wondriska, William
A **long** piece of string. Chronicle Books 2010 un il $15.99
Grades: PreK K 1   E
    1. Alphabet 2. String figures -- Fiction
    ISBN 978-0-8118-7493-9; 0-8118-7493-1
    First published 1963 by Holt
Follows a piece of string through images that correspond to the letters of the alphabet.

"The string's journey is a page-turning visual narrative that subtly reveals the connections among the various objects throughout the book." Horn Book Guide

Wong, Janet S.
Apple pie 4th of July; pictures by Margaret Chodos-Irvine. Harcourt 2002 un il $16
Grades: PreK K 1 2   E
    1. Fourth of July -- Fiction 2. Chinese Americans -- Fiction
    ISBN 0-15-202543-X
LC 2001-1313

A Chinese American girl fears that the food her parents are preparing to sell on the Fourth of July will not be eaten

"An appealing story with believable characters and emotions, written in the girl's spare, lyrical voice. Chodos-Irvine . . . captures the story's uncluttered, elemental qualities in opaque prints that resemble paper cutouts." Booklist

Homegrown house; illustrated by E.B. Lewis. Margaret K. McElderry Books 2009 un il $16.99
Grades: K 1 2 3   E
    1. Home -- Fiction 2. Moving -- Fiction 3. Grandmothers -- Fiction
    ISBN 978-0-689-84718-9; 0-689-84718-1
LC 2006038599

A young girl describes her grandmother's comfortable, long-time home, and wishes that she and her parents could stay in the same house instead of moving so often.

"Wong's poignant poem nicely captures a child's sense of powerlessness and disorientation. With his usual mastery and sensitivity, Lewis creates a true story from the words in sensitive scenes." Booklist

This next New Year; pictures by Yangsook Choi. Foster Bks. 2000 un il $16

Grades: PreK K 1 2
    1. Chinese New Year -- Fiction
    ISBN 0-374-35503-7
LC 99-22377

"A Chinese-Korean boy reflects on what Chinese New Year means to him. By sweeping last year's mistakes and bad luck out of the house, he hopes to make room for 'a fresh start, my second chance.'" Horn Book Guide

"Choi's smooth, brightly colored paintings . . . ably illustrate the optimistic activity and the yearning in the accessible, rhythmic text." Booklist

Wood, Audrey
Blue sky; Audrey Wood. The Blue Sky Press 2012 32p
Grades: PreK K 1 2 3   E
    1. Sky 2. Children's stories 3. Picture books for children 4. Sky -- Fiction 5. Nature -- Fiction
    ISBN 9780545316101
LC 2011010374

In this children's picture book, "a child and his family experience the fun of a sunny-sky day at the beach, then the electricity of a thunderstorm sky, and finally the magical delight of a rainbow sky. . . . Using only two words per page -- 'Blue Sky,' 'Cloud Sky,' 'Storm Sky' . . . [the book] will encourage young readers to make up their own simple descriptions of the sky above." (Publisher's note) Other illustrations depict "Wish Sky/ Sleep Sky/ Dream Sky." The illustrations were created with "pastel paper in deep colors for the backgrounds . . . [and] gouache highlights and colored pencils." (Kirkus)

Elbert's bad word; illustrated by Audrey and Don Wood. Harcourt Brace Jovanovich 1988 un il hardcover o.p. pa $7
Grades: K 1 2 3 4   E
    1. Parties -- Fiction
    ISBN 0-15-225320-3; 0-15-201367-9 pa
LC 86-7557

"A bad word, spoken by a small boy at a fashionable garden party, creates havoc, and the child, Elbert, gets his mouth scrubbed out with soap. The bad word, in the shape of a long-tailed furry monster, will not go away until a wizard-gardener cooks up some really delicious, super-long words that everyone at the party applauds. This single-idea cautionary tale has lively, absurdist pictures of tiara-crowned, formally dressed adults recoiling in horror or cavorting with glee when Elbert, the only child at the party, speaks a word." SLJ

★ **Heckedy** Peg; illustrated by Don Wood. Harcourt Brace Jovanovich 1987 un il lib bdg $17; pa $7
Grades: K 1 2 3 4   E
    1. Fairy tales 2. Witches -- Fiction
    ISBN 0-15-233678-8 lib bdg; 0-15-233679-6 pa
LC 86-33639

"The poor mother of seven children, each named for a day of the week, goes off to market promising to return with individual gifts that each child has requested and admonishing them to lock the door to strangers and not to touch the fire. The gullible children are tricked into disobeying their mother by the witch, Heckedy Peg, who turns them all into various kinds of food. The mother can rescue her children only by guessing which child is the fish, the roast rib, the bread. . . . This story, deep and rich with folk wisdom, is stunningly illustrated with Don Wood's luminous paintings. . . . With variety of color and line he enhances every nuance of the text." SLJ

★ **King** Bidgood's in the bathtub; written by Audrey Wood; illustrated by Don Wood. Harcourt Brace Jovanovich 1985 un il lib bdg $17

Grades: K 1 2 3 4 **E**

1. Baths -- Fiction 2. Kings and rulers -- Fiction

ISBN 0-15-242730-9

LC 85-5472

A Caldecott Medal honor book, 1986

Despite pleas from his court, a fun-loving king refuses to get out of his bathtub to rule his kingdom

"The few simple words of text per large, well-designed page invite story-telling—but keep the group very small, so the children can be close enough to pore over the brilliant, robust illustrations." SLJ

★ The **napping** house. Harcourt Children's Books 2009 un il $17.99

Grades: K 1 2 3 **E**

1. Sleep -- Fiction

ISBN 978-0-15-256708-8; 0-15-256708-9

A reissue, with new audio CD, of the title first published 1984

"The cool blues and greens are superseded by warm colors and bursts of action as each sleeper wakes, ending in an eruption of color and energy as naptime ends. A deft matching of text and pictures adds to the appeal of cumulation, and to the silliness of the mound of sleepers—just the right kind of humor for the lap audience." Bull Cent Child Books

Another book about these characters is:

The full moon at the napping house (2015)

★ **Piggies**; written by Don and Audrey Wood; illustrated by Don Wood. Harcourt Brace Jovanovich 1991 un il $17; pa $8; bd bk $5.95

Grades: PreK K 1 2 **E**

1. Pigs -- Fiction 2. Bedtime -- Fiction

ISBN 0-15-256341-5; 0-15-200217-0 pa; 0-15-202638-X bd bk

LC 89-24598

Ten little piggies dance on a young child's fingers and toes before finally going to sleep

"A happy text and luxuriant, witty pictures make this a book to pore over again and again." Booklist

Wood, Douglas

Miss Little's gift; illustrated by Jim Burke. Candlewick Press 2009 un il $16.99

Grades: 1 2 3 **E**

1. Reading 2. Teachers 3. Hyperactive children 4. Attention deficit disorder

ISBN 978-0-7636-1686-1; 0-7636-1686-9

LC 2008-17915

"This autobiographical picture book chronicles the author's struggles in second grade. Smaller than everyone else, new in town, and speaking with an unfamiliar Southern accent, Wood also found reading to be a chore. . . . The story works as a tribute to those unsung teacher heroes whose dedication to their craft and native intuition about children have changed lives. . . . Burke's large, realistic oils, with their rich greens and blues, complement the story nicely." SLJ

What dads can't do; pictures by Doug Cushman. Simon & Schuster Bks. for Young Readers 2000 un il $14

Grades: PreK K **E**

1. Fathers -- Fiction

ISBN 0-689-82620-6

LC 98-41773

"This amusing picture book will tickle youngsters' funny bones and make every parent and child smile with recognition. . . . Cushman's large, delightful, pen-and-ink and watercolor cartoons . . . capture perfectly the father-and-son interactions." SLJ

Other titles in this series are:

What grandmas can't do (2005)

What moms can't do (2000)

What Santa can't do (2003)

What teachers can't do (2000)

When a dad says "I love you" Douglas Wood; illustrated by Jennifer A. Bell. 1st ed. Simon & Schuster Books for Young Readers 2013 32 p. col. ill. (hardcover) $16.99

Grades: PreK K **E**

1. Father-child relationship -- Fiction 3. Love -- Fiction 4. Fathers -- Fiction 5. Father and child -- Fiction

ISBN 0689875320; 9780689875328

LC 2012013268

This children's picture book, by Douglas Wood, illustrated by Jennifer A. Bell, shows how "dads know how to do everything. They can help with homework and carry you on their shoulders. They can make pancakes and teach you how to sing songs. These loving actions are just some of the ways dads show how much they care." (Publisher's note)

Where the sunrise begins; words by Douglas Wood; art by Wendy Popp. Simon & Schuster Books for Young Readers 2010 un il $16.99

Grades: PreK K 1 **E**

1. Sun -- Fiction 2. Nature -- Fiction

ISBN 978-0-689-86172-7; 0-689-86172-9

Reveals the part that each of us plays in the beginning of every day.

"Science is in full view as the author searches for the place where the sunrise begins. The beautiful watercolor drawings complement the simple but rich text. Not only are different cultures revealed, but geography is also put on display as the author, a naturalist, explores the world trying to find exactly where the sunrise begins. What the book unveils will amaze and delight the reader." Libr Media Connect

Woodruff, Elvira

The **memory** coat; story by Elvira Woodruff; illustrations by Michael Dooling. Scholastic Press 1999 un il $17.99

Grades: K 1 2 3 **E**

1. Jews -- Fiction 2. Immigrants -- Fiction 3. Ellis Island Immigration Station -- Fiction

ISBN 0-590-67717-9

LC 95-30048

In the early 1900s, cousins Rachel and Grisha leave their Russian shtetl with the rest of their family to come to America, hopeful that they will all pass the dreaded inspection at Ellis Island

This offers "warm, realistic period paintings, some in color, some in sepia shades. . . . In a long, interesting author's note, Woodruff discusses the shtetl and immigrant history." Booklist

Woodson, Jacqueline

★ **Coming** on home soon; illustrated by E.B. Lewis. Putnam's 2004 un il $16.99

Grades: K 1 2 3 **E**

1. Grandmothers -- Fiction 2. African Americans -- Fiction 3. World War, 1939-1945 -- Fiction 4. Mother-child relationship -- Fiction

ISBN 0-399-23748-8

LC 2003-21949

A Caldecott Medal honor book, 2005

After Mama takes a job in Chicago during World War II, Ada Ruth stays with Grandma but misses her mother who loves her more than rain and snow.

"Woodson and Lewis tell a moving historical story of longing and separation. . . . Lewis' beautiful watercolors establish the setting. . . . Period and place are wonderfully specific." Booklist

★ **Each** kindness; Jacqueline Woodson; illustrated by E.B. Lewis. Nancy Paulsen Books 2012 32 p. $16.99

Grades: 1 2 3 4   E

1. Bullies -- Fiction 2. Schools -- Fiction 3. Kindness -- Fiction 4. Friendship -- Fiction

ISBN 0399246525; 9780399246524

LC 2011046800

Coretta Scott King Author Honor Book (2013)

Charlotte Zolotow Award (2012)

In this book, "Chloe, Kendra, and Sophie are a tight trio, and when new girl Maya arrives, with her shabby clothes and obvious desperation, they resist her overtures of friendship. . . . When their teacher leads an exercise about kindness and its effects, Chloe realizes she can't think of any kind act she's ever done, and when Maya leaves her classroom never to return, Chloe realizes that she'll never be able to rectify her rejection." (Bulletin of the Center for Children's Books)

★ The **other** side; illustrations by E. B. Lewis. Putnam 2001 un il $16.99

Grades: K 1 2 3   E

1. Summer 2. Friendship -- Fiction 3. Race relations -- Fiction 6. African Americans -- Fiction

ISBN 0-399-23116-1; 978-0-399-23116-2

LC 99-42055

Two girls, one white and one black, gradually get to know each other as they sit on the fence that divides their town. "Ages six to nine." (Bull Cent Child Books)

"Lewis' watercolors provide a telling backdrop to the action. . . . This is an emotionally intricate tale presented simply and intimately." Bull Cent Child Books

★ **Pecan** pie baby; illustrated by Sophie Blackall. G.P. Putnam's Sons 2010 un il

Grades: PreK K 1   E

1. Infants -- Fiction 2. Siblings -- Fiction 3. Pregnancy -- Fiction 4. African Americans -- Fiction 5. Mother-daughter relationship -- Fiction

ISBN 0-399-23987-1; 978-0-399-23987-8

When Mama's pregnancy draws attention away from Gia, she worries that the special bond they share will disappear forever once the baby is born. "Preschool, primary." (Horn Book)

"Blackall's apt watercolor-and-ink pictures capture the grounded serenity of a multiracial family (and community) with its priorities on straight. . . . Fresh and wise." Kirkus

★ **Show** way; illustrated by Hudson Talbott. G. P. Putnam's Sons 2005 un il $16.99

Grades: K 1 2 3   E

1. Quilts -- Fiction 2. Slavery -- Fiction 3. African Americans -- Fiction

ISBN 0-399-23749-6

LC 2004-28093

A Newbery Medal honor book, 2006

The making of "Show ways," or quilts which once served as secret maps for freedom-seeking slaves, is a tradition passed from mother to daughter in the author's family.

"The gorgeous, multimedia art includes chalk, watercolors, and muslin. An outstanding tribute, perfectly executed in terms of text, design, and illustration." SLJ

Visiting day; illustrated by James E. Ransome. Scholastic Press 2002 un il $15.95

Grades: K 1 2 3   E

1. Fathers -- Fiction 2. Prisoners -- Fiction 3. African Americans

-- Fiction

ISBN 0-590-40005-3

LC 00-35772

A young girl and her grandmother visit the girl's father in prison

"The text is spare, gentle, and reassuring. . . . Ransome's vibrant acrylic paintings fill each page at home with intense pinks, yellows, greens, and blues in contrast to the monotone hue of the prison walls. Both author and illustrator provide notes that relate this story to their own personal experiences." SLJ

Wortche, Allison

Rosie Sprout's time to shine; story by Allison Wortche; pictures by Patrice Barton. Alfred A. Knopf 2011 il $17.99; lib bdg $20.99

Grades: K 1 2 3   E

1. School stories 2. Plants -- Fiction

ISBN 978-0-375-86721-7; 978-0-375-96721-4 lib bdg; 978-0-375-98459-4 e-book

LC 2011004092

Rosie's rival, Violet, outdoes her in everything until the class plants seeds for a unit on gardening.

"Wortche possesses both a refreshing directness and a willingness to trust her readers. She also has the courage to conclude not with reconciliation, but with a bittersweet and profoundly wise acknowledgment that it takes all kinds. This impressive new author is well served by Barton . . . whose digital classroom sketches convey a tumult of emotion and have just the right amounts of energy and vulnerability." Publ Wkly

Wright, Maureen

★ **Sleep,** Big Bear, sleep! illustrated by Will Hillenbrand. Marshall Cavendish Children 2009 un il $16.99

Grades: PreK K 1   E

1. Stories in rhyme 2. Bears -- Fiction 3. Winter -- Fiction 4. Hibernation -- Fiction

ISBN 978-0-7614-5560-8; 0-7614-5560-4

LC 2008029402

As winter comes and Big Bear prepares to hibernate, he keeps thinking he hears Old Man Winter giving him exhausting orders that prevent him from sleeping.

"The text moves at a steady clip, and the refrain will encourage child participation. . . . The story reads aloud well, and the limited text and oversize illustrations will be effective in storytime. The artwork is the real star here, though. Hillenbrand imbues his characters with motion and personality." SLJ

Another title about Big Bear is:

Sneeze, Big Bear, Sneeze (2011)

Sneeze, Big Bear, sneeze! illustrated by Will Hillenbrand. Marshall Cavendish Children 2011 un il $16.99

Grades: PreK K 1   E

1. Stories in rhyme 2. Bears -- Fiction 3. Winds -- Fiction 4. Autumn -- Fiction 5. Sneezing -- Fiction

ISBN 978-0-7614-59590; 0-7614-5959-6; 978-0-7614-6074-9 e-book

LC 2011001125

Big Bear thinks that his tremendous sneezes are causing the leaves and apples to fall off the trees and the geese to fly away, but when the wind finally convinces him otherwise, he knows what to do.

"Hillenbrand's sweeping mixed-media spreads should stir up anticipation for apple-picking season." Publ Wkly

Wright, Michael

Jake goes peanuts. Feiwel and Friends 2010 un il $16.99

Grades: PreK K   E

1. Stories in rhyme 2. Peanuts -- Fiction

ISBN 978-0-312-54967-1; 0-312-54967-9

In an effort to get Jake to eat something other than peanut butter, his parents declare it "Peanut Butter Week" and create such dishes as peanut butter soup, peanut butter pot roast, and even peanut butter dog food for their pet.

"Wright's crisp rhymes and droll cartoons should make picky eaters smile, and perhaps consider a little diversity in their own diets." Publ Wkly

Another title about Jake is:

Jake starts school (2008)

Wyatt, Valerie

Boy meets dog; a word-game adventure. Kids Can Press 2013 32 p. $16.95

Grades: K 1 2   E

1. Word games

ISBN 1554538246; 9781554538249

In this children's picture book, author "[Valerie] Wyatt introduces kids to word ladders, in which a starting word leads step by step, by the substitution of one letter at a time, to a final word. . . . The artwork . . . borrows from conventions of animation to provide two-page scenes that carry readers on each word journey, and there is a little narrative twist at the end, about whether or not a character is real or just a toy (boy into toy)." (Kirkus Reviews)

Wynne Pechter, Lesley

Alligator, bear, crab; a baby's ABC. Orca Book Publishers 2011 un il bd bk $9.95

Grades: PreK   E

1. Alphabet 2. Board books for children 3. Animals -- Fiction

ISBN 978-1-55469-360-3; 1-55469-360-8

LC 2010-941967

"Endearing animals introduce the ABCs in an inviting board book. Pechter's organic paintings feature soft lines, kindly faces, and a soothing palette of creamy sunset colors and sky blues. . . . Uncommon additions like an urchin and a vole broaden the menagerie. . . . With care paid to each image, this is a charming, distinctive primer." Publ Wkly

Xinran

★ **Motherbridge** of love; text provided by Mother Bridge of Love; illustrated by Josee Masse. Barefoot 2007 un il $16.99

Grades: PreK K 1 2   E

1. Mothers -- Fiction 2. Adoption -- Fiction

ISBN 978-1-84686-047-8

Celebrates the bond between parent and child as the adoptive parent of a little Chinese girl speaks about her love for her adopted daughter.

"Simple, lyrical language and gorgeous art make this more than just another adoption story. . . . The sentiment is exactly right—loving, caring, and thoughtful—and the stylized acrylic illustrations, in thick brush strokes and swirling shapes, evoke the lyrical tone with grace and elegance." Booklist

Yaccarino, Dan

★ **Doug** unplugged! Dan Yaccarino. Alfred A. Knopf 2013 40 p. (trade) $16.99

Grades: K 1 2 3 4   E

1. Robots -- Fiction 2. City and town life -- Fiction

ISBN 0375866434; 9780375866432; 9780375966439

LC 2011047496

This children's book, by Dan Yaccarino, follows a robot named Doug. "His parents want him to be smart, so each morning they plug him in and start the information download. After a morning spent learn-

ing facts about the city, Doug suspects he could learn even more about the city by going outside and exploring it. And so Doug . . . unplugs. What follows is an exciting day of adventure and discovery." (Publisher's note)

Lawn to lawn. Alfred A. Knopf 2010 un il $17.99; lib bdg $20.99

Grades: K 1 2 3   E

1. Adventure fiction 2. Gardens -- Fiction 3. Voyages and travels -- Fiction

ISBN 0-375-85574-2; 0-375-95574-7 lib bdg; 978-0-375-85574-0; 978-0-375-95574-7 lib bdg

LC 2009002303

When their family moves away and leaves them behind, a group of lawn ornaments sets out on a dangerous trek across the country to try to find them.

"Yaccarino's clean, bright illustrations have an appealing retro look, and the trek through suburbs, swamps, fields, and city is a visual treat." Booklist

Yamasaki, Katie

Fish for Jimmy; based on one family's experience in a Japanese American internment camp. Katie Yamasaki. Holiday House 2013 40 p. (reinforced) $16.95

Grades: 1 2 3 4 5   E

1. Historical fiction 2. Picture books for children 3. Brothers -- Fiction 4. Japanese Americans -- Evacuation and relocation, 1942-1945 -- Fiction

ISBN 0823423751; 9780823423750

LC 2012006584

In this children's picture book, "following the bombing of Pearl Harbor, Taro's father is taken away for questioning by the FBI, and Taro, his younger brother, and their mother are transported to an internment camp. Jimmy refuses to eat and becomes withdrawn and listless. Taro finds a way to slip outside the camp fences to obtain fresh fish to entice his brother to eat." (School Library Journal)

Yamashita, Haruo

Seven little mice go to school; illustrated by Kazuo Iwamura. NorthSouth 2011 un il $16.95

Grades: PreK K 1 2   E

1. School stories 2. Mice -- Fiction

ISBN 978-0-7358-4012-6; 0-7358-4012-1

Original Japanese edition 1981

"Mama Mouse has seven little mice who are about to start school . . . The septuplets are reluctant to go. Clever Mama gets an idea. . . . She takes two blue balls of yarn and makes a path through the forest all the way to school. The next morning she announces, 'All aboard! The train for school is leaving now!.' . . . The children eagerly pick up on the game and follow along. . . . The pen-and-ink and watercolor illustrations perfectly complement the story. The mice are individualized with gently humorous details. . . . This clever take on the afraid-to-go-to-school theme should have broad appeal." SLJ

Another title about the seven little mice is:

Seven little mice have fun on the ice (2011)

Yang, Belle

Hannah is my name. Candlewick Press 2004 un il $16.99

Grades: K 1 2 3   E

1. Immigrants -- Fiction 2. Chinese Americans -- Fiction 3. San Francisco (Calif.) -- Fiction

ISBN 0-7636-2223-0

LC 2003-6967

A young Chinese girl and her parents emigrate to the United States and try their best to assimilate into their San Francisco neighborhood while anxiously awaiting the arrival of their green cards.

"The bright gouache pictures of San Francisco draw strongly on Chinese and American traditions. . . . The struggle with documentation and the celebration when the green cards finally arrive in the mail is a drama many immigrant families will recognize." Booklist

Yankovic, Al

When I grow up; illustrations by Wes Hargis. Harper 2011 un il $17.99
Grades: PreK K 1 2   E
  1. School stories 2. Stories in rhyme 3. Occupations -- Fiction
ISBN 978-0-06-192691-4; 0-06-192691-4

                        LC 2010021966

An exuberant eight-year-old details for his teacher and classmates the astonishing variety of inventive careers he is thinking of pursuing when he grows up.

"As the boy's fantasies about his future get wilder and wilder, Hargis' hilarious, detailed illustrations in clear line and watercolor extend the uproarious nonsense. . . . Along with the imaginative play, the farce and parody make this a rare book with appeal to both kids and adults." Booklist

Yarrow, Peter

Puff the magic dragon pop-up book; [by] Peter Yarrow, Lenny Lipton; with paintings by Eric Puybaret and paper engineering by Bruce Foster. Sterling 2011 un il $26.95
Grades: PreK K 1 2   E
  1. Pop-up books 2. Dragons -- Fiction
ISBN 978-1-4027-8711-9; 1-4027-8711-1

"Puybaret's capricious paintings combine elegantly with pop-up engineering by Bruce Foster in a condensed, interactive version of this bestselling 2007 picture book. The story unfolds in six graceful pop-up scenes, some of which have side panels that conceal additional pop-up effects. . . . Includes a four-song CD recording." Publ Wkly

Yates, Louise

★ **Dog** loves books. Alfred A. Knopf 2010 un il $16.99; lib bdg $19.99
Grades: PreK K 1 2   E
  1. Dogs -- Fiction 2. Books and reading -- Fiction
ISBN 978-0-375-86449-0; 0-375-86449-0; 978-0-375-96449-7 lib bdg; 0-375-96449-5 lib bdg

                        LC 2009-11097

Dog loves books so much that he decides to open a book store.

"The simple story is accompanied by soft pastel pencil and watercolor drawings that give the book a whimsical, dreamy quality. Dog is surrounded by nonthreatening dinosaurs, space aliens, and other creatures when he is reading about them. Young children can enjoy the book by themselves by following the charming illustrations." SLJ

Dog loves drawing; Louise Yates. Alfred A. Knopf 2012 32 p. (trade) $16.99; $16.99
Grades: PreK K 1 2   E
  1. Dogs -- Fiction 2. Drawing -- Fiction 3. Picture books for children 4. Animals -- Fiction
ISBN 9780307974495; 9780375870675; 9780375970672; 0375870679

                        LC 2011032353

In "this follow-up to the . . . 'Dog Loves Books' . . . the pup receives blank book as a gift. He quickly realizes that it's a sketchbook, and though initially struck by artist's block, he soon uses his pencils and pens to draw himself some friends, a boat and a train to ride, and food

for them to feast on, all of which magically come to life on the page. When one of Dog's new friends draws a monster, though, Dog must quickly use his skills to contain it and create an escape route." (School Library Journal)

Yee, Wong Herbert, 1953-

Mouse and Mole, secret valentine; Wong Herbert Yee. Houghton Mifflin Books for Children 2014 48 p. $15.99
Grades: K 1 2 3   E
  1. Moles (Animals) -- Fiction 2. Mice -- Fiction 3. Friendship -- Fiction 4. Best friends -- Fiction 5. Valentine's Day -- Fiction
ISBN 0547887191; 9780547887197

                        LC 2012041660

In this picture book, by Wong Herbert Yee, "Mouse and Mole are best friends, but with Valentine's Day coming soon, each has a peculiar feeling of butterflies in the stomach when thinking of the other. . . . As Valentine's Day nears, Mouse and Mole get together to decorate cards. Mouse is good at making a list of friends and writing the words, while Mole's specialty is cutting out paper hearts and sprinkling glitter over glue to create a sparkly message." (Kirkus Review)

  Secret valentine

My autumn book; Wong Herbert Yee. Henry Holt & Co. 2015 32 p. color illustrations (hardback) $14.99
Grades: PreK K 1   E
  1. Stories in rhyme 2. Autumn -- Fiction 3. Nature study -- Fiction
ISBN 0805099220; 9780805099225

                        LC 2014041426

In this children's book, written and illustrated by Wong Herbert Yee, "a little girl senses the coming of autumn from changes in the air and sky, and proceeds to investigate, collect, and record details about the new season. She uses a camera and notebook to capture an array of natural images. . . . The girl ultimately creates an Autumn Book, with photographs and decorated pages." (School Library Journal)

"A girl celebrates autumn in Yee's fourth in a quartet of books about the seasons (Tracks in the Snow, rev. 11/03; Who Likes Rain?, rev. 3/07; Summer Days and Nights, rev. 7/12). The young narrator continues her fascination with animals, insects, and, here, trees. Roaming her yard with backpack and camera in hand, she identifies several types of specimens (cicada, woodpecker, chipmunk, dogwood, and more), takes pictures, collects acorns and leaves, then gathers everything into a scrapbook." Horn Book

Summer days and nights; Wong Herbert Yee. Henry Holt 2012 32 p. (hc) $14.99
Grades: PreK K 1   E
  1. Stories in rhyme 2. Summer -- Fiction 3. Day -- Fiction 4. Night -- Fiction
ISBN 0805090789; 9780805090789

                        LC 2011028598

In this children's picture book by Wong Herbert Lee, "a little girl finds ways to entertain herself and stay cool. She catches a butterfly, sips lemonade, jumps in a pool, and goes on a picnic. At night, she sees an owl in a tree and a frog in a pond, and hears leaves rustling. Before long, she's fast asleep, dreaming about more summer days and summer nights." (Publisher's note)

Tracks in the snow. H. Holt 2003 un il $15.95
Grades: PreK K 1 2   E
  1. Stories in rhyme 2. Snow -- Fiction 3. Animal tracks -- Fiction
ISBN 0-8050-6771-X

                        LC 2002-10854

A little girl investigates tracks in the snow, trying to determine what could have made them.

"The gentle, rhyming text makes an ideal read-aloud, and young listeners will chime in on the repeated phrases. The soft-focus, colored-pencil illustrations portray a small Asian girl exploring her safe world, but a world transformed by the fresh snowfall." SLJ

Upstairs Mouse, downstairs Mole. Houghton Mifflin Co. 2005 un il $15

Grades: K 1 2 3   **E**

1. Mice -- Fiction 2. Friendship -- Fiction 3. Moles (Animals) -- Fiction

ISBN 0-618-47313-0

LC 2004-5238

Mouse and her downstairs neighbor, Mole, discover that when they help each other, housecleaning and other daily tasks are much easier

"The expressive bamboo-pen and watercolor with colored-pencil illustrations capture the humor of the situations as well as the emotions of the characters. . . . A real winner." SLJ

Other titles about Mouse and Mole are:

Abracadabra! Magic with Mouse and Mole (2007)

A brand-new day with Mouse and Mole (2008)

Mouse and Mole: fine feathered friends (2009)

Mouse and Mole: a winter wonderland (2010)

Mouse and Mole: a perfect Halloween (2011)

Who likes rain? Holt & Co. 2007 un il $14.95

Grades: PreK K 1   **E**

1. Rain -- Fiction

ISBN 978-0-8050-7734-6; 0-8050-7734-0

LC 2006-03429

As a young girl splashes in the rain, she plays a guessing game with the reader about other living things that enjoy a cloudburst.

"The rhyming text tells the story as naturally as if the rhythm and rhyme just fell into place. . . . Fine strokes of color softly define the shapes of characters and settings." Booklist

Yep, Laurence, 1948-

Auntie Tiger; pictures by Insu Lee. HarperCollinsPublishers 2009 un il $17.99; lib bdg $18.89

Grades: K 1 2 3   **E**

1. Fairy tales 2. China -- Fiction 3. Tigers -- Fiction 4. Sisters -- Fiction

ISBN 978-0-06-029551-6; 0-06-029551-1; 978-0-06-029552-3 lib bdg; 0-06-029552-X lib bdg

LC 2006-28649

In this version of Red Riding Hood set in China, Big Sister sets aside her differences with Little Sister to rescue her from a tiger in disguise.

"Bright, energetic illustrations done in jewel tones bring this story to life. The cunning tiger with his large head, bulging eyes, and small pointy teeth is scarcely contained in three of the spreads." SLJ

Yin

Coolies; illustrated by Chris K. Soentpiet. Philomel Bks. 2001 un il $16.99

Grades: 2 3 4   **E**

1. Brothers -- Fiction 2. Chinese Americans -- Fiction 3. Central Pacific Railroad -- Fiction

ISBN 0-399-23227-3

LC 98-40403

A young boy hears the story of his great-great-great-grandfather and his brother who came to the United States to make a better life for themselves helping to build the transcontinental railroad

"Soentpiet's strong, realistic watercolor paintings, in shades of blue and gold, show the bond between the brothers. . . . The American history

is powerful. Yin provides notes and a bibliography for readers who want to know more." Booklist

Yolen, Jane

★ **Baby** Bear's books; written by Jane Yolen; illustrated by Melissa Sweet. Harcourt 2006 un il $16

Grades: PreK K   **E**

1. Stories in rhyme 2. Bears -- Fiction 3. Books and reading -- Fiction

ISBN 0-15-205290-9

LC 2005019203

Throughout the day, Baby Bear finds a book to fit every special moment.

"Mixed-media and collage illustrations create a warm and comfortable world. . . . The charming double-page pictures are large enough to share with groups, and the rhymes will engage listeners." SLJ

Other titles about Baby Bear are:

Baby Bear's chairs (2005)

Baby Bear's big dreams (2007)

Come to the fairies' ball; illustrated by Gary Lippincott. Wordsong 2009 un il $17.95

Grades: 1 2 3 4   **E**

1. Stories in rhyme 2. Fairies -- Fiction

ISBN 978-1-59078-464-8; 1-59078-464-2

LC 2009018247

All the fairies are excited to be invited to the King's ball, except for one young fairy whose only party dress is in tatters.

"An enchanting picture book full of whimsy and magic. . . . Lippincott's paintings take the forefront in this book, while Yolen's clever verse adds to the unfolding pictorial drama." SLJ

Commander Toad and the voyage home; pictures by Bruce Degen Putnam 1998 64p il hardcover o.p. pa $5.99

Grades: 1 2 3 4   **E**

1. Science fiction 2. Toads -- Fiction

ISBN 0-399-23122-6; 0-698-11602-X pa

LC 96-21730

Commander Toad leads the lean green space machine "Star Warts" to find new worlds but runs into trouble when he sets course for home

"Yolen captures the high drama of space fiction in a delightful story that never loses sight of developing readers, who will be old enough to get the jokes but still young enough to relish the goofiness." Booklist

Other titles about Commander Toad are:

Commander Toad and the big black hole (1996)

Commander Toad and the dis-asteroid (1996)

Commander Toad and the intergalactic spy (1997)

Commander Toad and the Planet of the Grapes (1996)

Commander Toad and the space pirates (1997)

Commander Toad in space (1996)

Creepy monsters, sleepy monsters; a lullaby. illustrated by Kelly Murphy. Candlewick Press 2011 32p il $14.99

Grades: PreK K 1   **E**

1. Stories in rhyme 2. Bedtime -- Fiction 3. Monsters -- Fiction

ISBN 978-0-7636-4201-3; 0-7636-4201-0

LC 2010040341

Two rambunctious monsters creep, gurgle, crawl, and tumble before falling asleep.

This is a "whimsical, warmhearted rhyme, which turns bumps in the night into the sweetest sounds of all. . . . Murphy's oil, acrylic, and gel illustrations instantly grab attention with their unusual points of view. . . Bedtime fare you can count on." Booklist

★ The **day** Tiger Rose said goodbye; illustrations by Jim La-Marche. Random House 2011 un il
Grades: PreK K 1 2   **E**
    1. Cats -- Fiction 2. Death -- Fiction 3. Country life -- Fiction
    ISBN 0-375-86663-9; 0-375-96663-3 lib bdg; 978-0-375-86663-0; 978-0-375-96663-7 lib bdg

LC 2010013548

A cat whose kitten days are far behind her says goodbye to her human family, and the animals and places that have made her life special, before leaving this life behind.

"The calm tone of the text is just right: matter-of-fact but compassionate. Reflecting the delicate beauty of the writing, LaMarche's mixed-media illustrations show equal finesse in line, color, texture, and composition." Booklist

★ **Elsie's** bird; illustrated by David Small. Philomel Books 2010 un il $17.99
Grades: K 1 2 3   **E**
    1. Canaries -- Fiction 2. Nebraska -- Fiction 3. Frontier and pioneer life -- Fiction
    ISBN 978-0-399-25292-1; 0-399-25292-4

Young Elsie must find a way to adapt to her new home on the Nebraska prairie after she and her father leave their comfortable city life in Boston.

"Yolen's evocative story, full of wonder and warmth, rolls smoothly along on carefully worded phrases, capturing the child's emotions as well as the flavor of the time and setting in a simple yet heartfelt way. Small's delivery, completely in sync with the author's, brings Elsie deftly to life. The illustrations, rendered in brush and ink with watercolor and pastel, realize both the streets of Boston and the grasslands of Nebraska with equal ease and aplomb." SLJ

How do dinosaurs act when they're mad? Jane Yolen; illustrated by Mark Teague. The Blue Sky Press 2013 40 p. (hardcover : alk. paper) $16.99
Grades: PreK K   **E**
    1. Picture books for children 2. Dinosaurs -- Fiction 3. Anger -- Fiction 4. Stories in rhyme 5. Behavior -- Fiction 6. Emotions -- Fiction
    ISBN 0545143152; 9780545143158

LC 2012040941

This children's picture book "features angry dinosaurs acting out and, with the help of human parents, learning how to cope with this powerful emotion. A different dino is featured in each rhyming scenario. . . After he is told to take a time-out, the Afrovenator counts to 10 and breathes calmly. The Sauropelta proceeds to clean up the mess he made; Beipiaosaurus apologizes to his mom and gives her a hug." (School Library Journal)

★ **How** do dinosaurs say goodnight? illustrated by Mark Teague. Blue Sky Press (NY) 2000 un il $15.95
Grades: PreK K 1   **E**
    1. Stories in rhyme 2. Bedtime -- Fiction 3. Dinosaurs -- Fiction
    ISBN 0-590-31681-8

LC 98-56134

Mother and child ponder the different ways a dinosaur can say goodnight, from slamming his tail and pouting to giving a big hug and kiss

"The text is sweet and simple—just right for the wonderful pictures that really make this picture book special. . . . Endpapers introduce the critter cast in all their gorgeous glory: tyrannosaurus rex, dimetrodon, and more, in vivid, yet still earthbound colors." Booklist

Other titles in this series are:

How do dinosaurs clean their rooms? (2004)
How do dinosaurs count to ten? (2004)

How do dinosaurs eat cookies? (2012)
How do dinosaurs eat their food? (2005)
How do dinosaurs get well soon? (2003)
How do dinosaurs go to school? (2007)
How do dinosaurs go up and down? (2011)
How do dinosaurs laugh out loud? (2010)
How do dinosaurs learn their colors? (2006)
How do dinosaurs learn to read? (2003)
How do dinosaurs love their cats? (2010)
How do dinosaurs love their dogs? (2010)
How do dinosaurs play all day? (2011)
How do dinosaurs play with their friends? (2006)
How do dinosaurs say happy birthday? (2011)
How do dinosaurs say Happy Chanukah? (2012)
How do dinosaurs say I love you? (2009)
How do dinosaurs say I'm mad? (2013)
How do dinosaurs say Merry Christmas? (2012)
How do dinosaurs stay safe (2015)

My father knows the names of things; illustrated by Stephane Jorisch. Simon & Schuster Books for Young Readers 2010 un il $15.99
Grades: PreK K 1   **E**
    1. Stories in rhyme 2. Father-child relationship -- Fiction
    ISBN 978-1-4169-4895-7; 1-4169-4895-3

LC 2007-41840

Rhyming text depicts a father sharing with his child such things as seven words that all mean blue and the name of every kind of cloud.

"Yolen's easeful rhymes and Jorisch's warm illustrations craft a bighearted tribute to fathers' seemingly infinite capacities for information—and their willingness to share it." Publ Wkly

Naming Liberty; by Jane Yolen; illustrated by Jim Burke. Philomel Books 2008 un il $16.99
Grades: 1 2 3   **E**
    1. Artists 2. Sculptors 3. Jews -- Fiction 4. Immigrants -- Fiction 5. Statue of Liberty (New York, N.Y.) -- Fiction 6. United States -- History -- 1865-1898 -- Fiction
    ISBN 978-0-399-24250-2; 0-399-24250-3

In parallel stories, a Ukrainian Jewish family prepares to emigrate to the United States in the late 1800s, and Frederic Auguste Bartholdi designs, raises funds for, and builds the Statue of Liberty in honor of the United States' centennial.

"Burke's luminous paintings, designed on burnt sienna oil-washed boards, convey the landscapes and details of nineteenth-century Europe and New York. . . . An ideal choice for introducing the concepts of immigration and liberty to young listeners." Booklist

Not all princesses dress in pink; [by] Jane Yolen and Heidi Stemple Yolen; illustrated by Anne-Sophie Lanquetin. Simon & Schuster Books for Young Readers 2010 un il $15.99
Grades: PreK K 1   **E**
    1. Stories in rhyme 2. Girls -- Fiction 3. Sex role -- Fiction 4. Princesses -- Fiction
    ISBN 978-1-4169-8018-6; 1-4169-8018-0

LC 2008-38122

Rhyming text affirms that girls can pursue their many interests, from playing sports to planting flowers in the dirt, without giving up their tiaras.

"The snappy, upbeat illustrations and blithely confident characters are plenty of fun." Publ Wkly

On Bird Hill; Jane Yolen, illustrated by Bob Marstall. Cornell Lab Publishing Group 2016 32 p. color illustrations (hardcover) $15.95

Grades: PreK K 1   **E**

  1. Nursery rhymes 2. Stories in rhyme 3. Birds

  ISBN 1943645027; 9781943645022

This children's story, by Jane Yolen, illustrated by Bob Marstall, is "loosely based on the old cumulative nursery rhyme/song 'The Green Grass Grew All Around,' a nursery rhyme first published as a song in 1912 with words by William Jerome and melody by Harry Von Tilzer. But in this version, it's a boy and his dog who find the bird in a nest on a hill in a strange valley." (Publisher's note)

"Carefully crafted rhyming couplets beg to be read aloud again and again. An imaginative and original depiction of one of life's everyday miracles." Kirkus

★ **Owl** moon; illustrated by John Schoenherr. 20th anniversary edition; Philomel 2007 un il $16.99

Grades: PreK K 1 2   **E**

  1. Owls -- Fiction 2. Father-daughter relationship -- Fiction

  ISBN 978-0-399-24799-6; 0-399-24799-8

A reissue of the title first published 1987

Awarded the Caldecott Medal, 1988

On a winter's night under a full moon, a father and daughter trek into the woods to see the great horned owl

This book "conveys the scary majesty of winter woods at night in language that seldom overreaches either character or subject. . . . This book has a magic that is extremely rare in books for any age." NY Times Book Rev

Pretty princess pig; by Jane Yolen and Heidi E. Y. Stemple; illustrated by Sam Williams. Little Simon 2011 un il $9.99

Grades: PreK K 1   **E**

  1. Stories in rhyme 2. Pigs -- Fiction 3. Parties -- Fiction

  ISBN 978-1-4424-0833-3; 1-4424-0833-2

Follows Pretty Princess Pig as she gets ready to throw a party by painting the dining room, baking, and digging up flowers.

"With their pastel palette and nimble linework, Williams's watercolors match this princess's verve." Publ Wkly

Sing a season song; by Jane Yolen; illustrated by Lisel Jane Ashlock. Creative Editions 2015 32 p. color illustrations (hardcover : alk. paper) $18.99

Grades: PreK K 1 2 3   **E**

  1. Stories in rhyme 2. Seasons -- Fiction

  ISBN 1568462557; 9781568462554

                                LC 2014022593

In this children's book, by Jane Yolen, illustrated by Lisel Jane Ashlock, "Each season is celebrated for many different reasons, but one never fails to roll right into the next. Jane Yolen's lilting verses and Lisel Jane Ashlock's sensitive portraits convey the cyclical nature of the seasons in this poetic tribute to the characteristics of the four periods of the year." (Publisher's note)

"The well-designed book has notably thick, richly printed pages and exceptionally pleasing proportions. While many nature books for children are anthropomorphic or didactic, this one celebrates nature and its ability to inspire awe and appreciation. This lovely book introduces young readers to the poetry of words, art, and nature—it's a welcome addition." Kirkus

Sleep, black bear, sleep; by Jane Yolen and Heidi E. Y. Stemple; illustrated by Brooke Dyer. HarperCollins 2007 un il $15.99; lib bdg $16.89

Grades: PreK K 1   **E**

  1. Stories in rhyme 2. Winter -- Fiction 3. Animals -- Fiction 4.

Bedtime -- Fiction 5. Hibernation -- Fiction

  ISBN 978-0-06-081560-8; 0-06-081560-4; 978-0-06-081561-5 lib bdg; 0-06-081561-2 lib bdg

                                LC 2006000344

As winter's chill spreads, different animals settle into their cozy homes for a long sleep

"The rhyme scheme is as lilting as a lullaby, and Dyer's ineffably sweet watercolor illustrations enrich this bedtime story." Booklist

Yolleck, Joan

  ★ **Paris** in the spring with Picasso; illustrated by Marjorie Priceman. Schwartz & Wade Books 2010 un il $17.99; lib bdg $20.99

Grades: K 1 2 3   **E**

  1. Poets 2. Artists 3. Authors 4. Painters 5. Novelists 6. Dramatists 7. Essayists 8. Memoirists 9. Art critics 10. Literary critics 11. Private secretaries 12. Paris (France) -- Fiction

  ISBN 978-0-375-83756-2; 0-375-83756-6; 978-0-375-93756-9 lib bdg; 0-375-93756-0 lib bdg

                                LC 2008-05867

Describes how some of Paris's famous artists and writers, such as Pablo Picasso, Max Jacob, and Guillaume Apollinaire, spend their day before preparing to attend a party at Gertrude Stein's apartment.

"Priceman's brightly colored illustrations exhibit energy, creativity, and general joie de vivre. . . . This whirlwind tour flows easily thanks to clear writing and carefully chosen details." SLJ

Yoo, Paula

  Want to play? Paula Yoo; illustrated by Shirley Ng-Benitez. Lee & Low Books 2016 32 p. color illustrations (Dive into reading) (hardcover : alk. paper) $14.95

Grades: K 1 2   **E**

  1. Friendship -- Fiction 2. Play -- Fiction 3. Hispanic Americans -- Fiction

  ISBN 9781620142509; 9781620142592

                                LC 2015029155

In this picture book, "it's a warm, sunny day, and the gang heads to the neighborhood playground to play. What should they play? Henry wants to play basketball, and Padma wants to play Follow the Leader. Finally Pablo comes up with a great idea: to play pretend. It s a game that everyone can do easily. They can pretend to be archaeologists, astronauts, and explorers. There s no limit to what they imagine they can be!" (Publisher's note)

Other titles in this series are:

Lilly's new home (2016)

Yoon, Salina

  Found; by Salina Yoon; illustrated by Salina Yoon. Walker & Co 2014 40 p. color illustrations (hardback) $14.99

Grades: PreK K 1   **E**

  1. Toys -- Fiction 2. Bears -- Fiction 3. Moose -- Fiction 4. Lost and found possessions -- Fiction

  ISBN 0802735592; 9780802735591; 9780802735607

                                LC 201302920

"When Bear finds a lost stuffed toy bunny in the forest, he begins to worry. After all, the stuffed bunny must feel lonely and want to return safely to its owner and home! But as Bear diligently searches for the bunny's owner, posting notices high and low, he begins to grow attached to his newfound friend. What will happen when the bunny's owner finally comes forward?" (Publisher's note)

"Wishing he could keep the found bunny for himself, Bear searches high and low for the stuffed animal's original owner. When grown-up Moose recognizes his old toy, he also recognizes the opportunity to pass it on to someone younger who will love it like he did. Simple, colorful bold-lined digital illustrations evoke the complex and conflicting feelings about letting something go." Horn Book

Other books about Bear and Bunny are:

Stormy night (2015)

Bear's big day (2016)

One, two, buckle my shoe; a counting nursery rhyme. Robin Corey Books 2011 un il bd bk $6.99

Grades: PreK   E

1. Counting 2. Board books for children 3. Circus -- Fiction

ISBN 978-0-375-86479-7; 0-375-86479-2

"Square die-cut windows offer clues about what comes next in this Big Top twist on the classic nursery rhyme. The opening spread places one purple square opposite a die-cut that frames two yellow circles. Turning the page reveals a polka-dotted clown's shoe, with the purple square becoming the buckle.... Watching abstract images turn into concrete shapes should please toddlers, and the inclusion of the words and numerals for each number cements the concept." Publ Wkly

Opposnakes; a lift-the-flap book about opposites. Little Simon 2009 un il $9.99

Grades: PreK K   E

1. Opposites 2. Snakes -- Fiction

ISBN 978-1-4169-7875-6; 1-4169-7875-5

"Yoon introduces opposites via friendly snakes. The spare text focuses on simple concepts: 'Cold snake/Hot snake,' 'Skinny snake/Plump snake,' 'One snake/Many snakes!' Brightly colored, cartoonlike reptiles stretch across the double-foldout spreads and are set against a white background. They are full of amusing details.... A book that entertains as it informs." SLJ

Penguin and Pinecone; a friendship story. Salina Yoon. Walker & Co. 2012 40 p. $12.99

Grades: PreK K 1   E

1. Trees -- Fiction 2. Penguins -- Fiction 3. Friendship -- Fiction 4. Pine cones -- Fiction

ISBN 080272843X; 9780802728432; 9780802728449

LC 2011037221

In this children's book, by Salina Yoon, "when Penguin finds a lost pinecone one day, an unlikely friendship blooms. But Grandpa reminds Penguin that pinecones can't live in the snow--they belong in the warm forest far away. Though he will miss his friend, Penguin returns Pinecone to his home, dreaming of the day they can reunite. And when he finally returns to the forest to check on his friend, Penguin discovers that love only grows over time-and so do little pinecones!" (Publisher's note)

Other titles in this series are:

Penguin on Vacation (2013)

Penguin in Love (2013)

Penguin and Pumpkin (2014)

Penguin's Christmas Wish (2016)

Who do I see? Robin Corey Books 2011 un il bd bk $6.99

Grades: PreK   E

1. Color 2. Animals 3. Board books for children

ISBN 978-0-375-87309-6; 0-375-87309-0

"This guess-the-animal book contains circular die-cut windows that offer a peek at bright animal prints adorned with shimmery holographic foil. Prompts encourage readers to guess what animal appears on the next page.... Friendly-looking naïf animals and an eye-catching design make this a gentle introduction to colors and patterns." Publ Wkly

Yorinks, Arthur

Flappy and Scrappy; story by Arthur Yorinks; pictures by Aleksey and Olga Ivanov. HarperCollinsPublishers 2011 42p il (I can read!) $16.99

Grades: K 1 2   E

1. Dogs -- Fiction 2. Play -- Fiction 3. Parties -- Fiction 4. Birthdays -- Fiction

ISBN 978-0-06-205117-2; 0-06-205117-2

LC 2008027467

After canine friends Scrappy and Flappy play an unusual game of catch, Scrappy complains that everyone has forgotten his birthday, but Flappy surprises him.

"Emerging readers will enjoy the Ivanovs' cheerful, expressive illustrations, which are thoughtfully placed with the text in spot or full-spread layouts. Beginning readers in the city, suburbs, or country will enjoy these engaging animals and the very simple text." SLJ

★ **Happy** bees; by Arthur Yorinks; illustrated by Carey Armstrong-Ellis. Harry N. Abrams 2005 un il $15.95

Grades: PreK K 1 2   E

1. Bees -- Fiction

ISBN 0-8109-5866-X

LC 2004-15454

Rhythmic text describes the carefree life of bees as they sting knees, munch on Swiss cheese, and laugh in the breeze.

"The nonsensical text doubles as the lyrics of the first tune on the accompanying CD.... The happy-go-lucky insects have loads of personality.... Listeners will enjoy the romp, whether spoken or sung, and can discover more bee-guiling silliness in the other selections on the CD." SLJ

★ **Hey,** Al; story by Arthur Yorinks; pictures by Richard Egielski. Farrar, Straus & Giroux 1986 un il $17; pa $7.99

Grades: PreK K 1 2 3   E

1. Fantasy fiction 2. Birds -- Fiction

ISBN 0-374-33060-3; 0-374-42985-5 pa

LC 86-80955

Awarded the Caldecott Medal, 1987

"Egielski's solid naturalism provides just the visual foil needed to establish the surreal character of this fantasy.... Text and pictures work together to challenge readers' concept of reality." SLJ

Homework; illustrations by Richard Egielski. Walker & Co. 2009 un il $16.99; lib bdg $17.89

Grades: K 1 2   E

1. Homework -- Fiction 2. Writing -- Materials and instruments -- Fiction

ISBN 978-0-8027-9585-4; 0-8027-9585-4; 978-0-8027-9586-1 lib bdg; 0-8027-9586-2 lib bdg

LC 2008-28011

When Tony's pens, along with his pencil and eraser, come to life, the squabbling set of writing tools tries to complete Tony's neglected homework

"Yorinks has devised a pleasing homage to the creative process and uses a light touch to show how inspiration can derive from the unlikeliest of places.... A simple but amusing winner." Booklist

★ The **invisible** man; illustrated by Doug Cushman. Harper 2011 un il $16.99

Grades: PreK K 1 2   E

1. Fruit -- Fiction 2. Supernatural -- Fiction

ISBN 978-0-06-156148-1; 0-06-156148-7

LC 2009-1404

Sy Kravitz, a Brooklyn fruit seller, explains why becoming invisible should never happen to you.

"Yorinks employs a narrative tone that's a cross between an old Jewish comedian and The Twilight Zone's Rod Serling, which adds to the deadpan humor, while Cushman's splendid watercolor art becomes ever more clever the closer you look. A fine bit of funnery." Booklist

The **witch's** child; by Arthur Yorinks; illustrated by Jos. A. Smith. Abrams Books for Young Readers 2007 un il $16.95

Grades: K 1 2 3   E

1. Fairy tales 2. Witches -- Fiction

ISBN 978-0-8109-9349-5

LC 2006031980

Desiring a child of her own, Rosina the witch fashions one out of straw and scraps, but when she cannot bring the rag child to life she becomes enraged and turns the village children into shrubs, where they stay until a kind girl discovers the discarded doll and saves her.

"Yorinks's flowing language is evocative, and the plot builds steadily to an exciting climax. Smith's detailed paintings depict Rosina with jet-black standing-on-end hair and exaggerated facial features that vividly—and frighteningly—express her emotions." SLJ

★ **You** read to me & I'll read to you; 20th-century stories to share. selected by Janet Schulman. Knopf 2001 250p il $34.95

Grades: PreK K 1 2   E

1. Short stories

ISBN 0-375-81083-8

LC 2001-29211

Companion volume to The 20th century children's book treasury (1998)

This is a collection of 26 picture books and selections from early chapter books by such authors as Maurice Sendak, William Steig, Dr. Seuss, and Florence Parry Heide

"A great choice for family or classroom sharing." SLJ

Young, Amy

Belinda, the ballerina. Viking 2002 un il $15.99

Grades: PreK K 1 2   E

1. Ballet -- Fiction

ISBN 0-670-03549-1

LC 2001-8395

When Belinda auditions for the Spring Ballet Recital and the judges tell her she can not be a ballerina because her feet are too big, she tries to forget about dancing

This offers "spirited gouache paintings that capture the sadness, the humor and the triumph of Belinda's story. . . . The story puts physical defects into perspective and offers something to laugh about at the same time." Booklist

Other titles about Belinda are:

Belinda and the glass slipper (2006)

Belinda begins ballet (2008)

Belinda in Paris (2005)

Young, Cybèle

A **few** bites; by Cybele Young. Groundwood Books/House of Anansi Press 2012 48 p. col. ill. (hardcover) $18.95

Grades: K 1 2   E

1. Siblings -- Fiction 2. Vegetables -- Fiction 3. Imagination -- Fiction

ISBN 1554982952; 9781554982950

Author Cybele Young tells a story of a sister who tries to entice her brother to eat his lunch by making up stories about the food. "Viola has made lunch for her little brother Ferdie: broccoli, carrot sticks, ravioli . . . Ferdie does not want this lunch . . . [so] Viola launches into a brilliant saga of dinosaurs [and] . . . aliens and their Orange Power Sticks." (Kirkus)

★ A **few** blocks. Groundwood Books 2011 un il $18.95

Grades: K 1 2   E

1. Siblings -- Fiction 2. Imagination -- Fiction

ISBN 978-0-88899-995-5; 0-88899-995-X

"It's time for school, but Viola's younger brother, Ferdie, isn't interested. . . . Resourceful and creative, Viola uses Ferdie's jacket, a leaf, and a piece of cardboard to turn their short walk into three heroic adventures, as they become superheroes, seek buried treasure, and prepare to battle a dragon. . . . Young's collages cast shadows on the white background below, with silhouettes of curling waves, sea creatures, and blobby monsters painted in pale blues, greens, and reds and filled in with crisp imagery of the duo's urban neighborhood. With empathy and respect for both characters' emotions, Young presents a loving story of sibling camaraderie." Publ Wkly

★ **Nancy** knows; Cybele Young. Tundra Books of Northern New York 2014 40 p. (hardcover) $17.99

Grades: PreK K 1 2 3 4   E

1. Memory -- Fiction 2. Elephants -- Fiction

ISBN 1770494820; 9781770494824; 9781770494831

LC 2013943888

In this children's book by Cybele Young, "Nancy knows she's forgotten something. Something important. When she tries to remember she thinks of all kinds of other things instead. She remembers things she knows and things she doesn't quite know. She remembers things one way, then another. . . . Nancy Knows is the . . . story of an elephant who remember lots of things, except the very thing she is trying to remember." (Publisher's note)

"Nancy, an elephant, knows that she has forgotten something important, but she can't for the life of her think what it is...Her elephantine shape is filled with colorful Japanese paper sculptures that reflect what's on her mind. For example, when she thinks of things with wheels, her shape is filled with a paper bicycles, a scooter, a wheelbarrow, a unicycle, and a shopping cart. Nancy is a charming protagonist with a memory like an elephant. She won't be soon forgotten." SLJ

★ **Some** Things I've Lost. Groundwood Books 2015 32 p. color illustrations $19.95

Grades: K 1 2 3 4 5   ▮

1. Change 2. Lost and found possessions 3. Picture books for children 4. Japanese paper -- Pictorial works

ISBN 1554983398; 9781554983391

"An introduction describing the frustration we feel when we lose something is followed by a catalogue of misplaced objects. Each item is shown first in its original form and then, through a series of gatefold spreads, is shown in the process of transforming into a marvelous and mysterious sea creature. At the very end of the book, we see these transformed objects in their new, watery habitat, a conclusion which will leave readers astonished by the distance they like the lost objects themselves have travelled." (Publisher's note)

"Young, a paper sculptor and author of The Queen's Shadow (Kids Can, 2015), Nancy Knows (Tundra, 2014), and Out the Window (Groundwood, 2014), among other titles, displays her brilliant artistry in a book replete with fantastic imagery and surprising gatefolds. . . . Purchase for its artistry and as an introduction to paper crafting." SLJ

★ **Ten** birds. Kids Can Press 2011 un il $18.95

Grades: 1 2 3 4   ▮

1. Counting 2. Birds -- Fiction 3. Problem solving -- Fiction

ISBN 978-1-55453-568-2; 1-55453-568-9

"Ten birds are trying to figure out how to get to the other side of the river. The bird they call 'Brilliant' devises a pair of stilts. The bird they call 'Highly Satisfactory' engineers a raft. One by one, nine resourceful birds make the crossing until a single bird is left behind—the one they call 'Needs Improvement.' This bird's solution proves surprising—and absurdly simple." (Publisher's note) "Primary." (Horn Book)

"Ten small birds . . . need to get across a river and have only a deserted lot full of discarded odds and ends—and their own ingenuity—to help them. . . . The straightforward text provides structure and clarity, while the striking and intricate pen-and-ink illustrations perfectly capture the stillness of a night full of wintry snow, show the birds' innovative and slightly mystical solutions to the problem at hand and seamlessly depict the decreasing numbers that represent the birds who have yet to cross. . . . This quietly dazzling selection is a subtle celebration of individuality and creativity." Kirkus

Young, Ed

The **cat** from Hunger Mountain; Ed Young. Philomel Books 2016 32 p. color illustrations $17.99

Grades: K 1 2 3   E

1. Cats -- Fiction 2. Wealth -- Fiction 3. Droughts -- Fiction 4. Conduct of life -- Fiction

ISBN 9780399172786

LC 2015050281

In this book, by Ed Young, "in a place called Hunger Mountain there lives a lord who has everything imaginable yet never has enough. To satisfy his every desire, he hires builders to design the tallest pagoda; a world-famous tailor to make his clothing from silk and gold threads; and a renowned chef to cook him lavish meals with rice from the lord's own fields. What more could he possibly want?" (Publisher's note)

"A compelling fable that is crucial for humanity and will spark meaningful classroom conversations." SLJ

Young, Jessica

My blue is happy; Jessica Young, illustrated by Catia Chien. Candlewick Press 2013 32 p. $15.99

Grades: PreK K 1   E

1. Color -- Fiction 2. Emotions -- Fiction

ISBN 0763651257; 9780763651251

LC 2012950616

In this children's picture book by Jessica Young, "a little girl realizes that not everyone feels the same about colors. Her sister sees blue as sad and associates it with lonely songs. But the protagonist sees it as happy because it reminds her of her favorite jeans and the pool on a hot day. Dad says brown is ordinary like a paper bag but chocolate syrup is the association that the child makes." (School Library Journal)

Young, Judy Dockrey

A **pet** for Miss Wright; written by Judy Young; illustrated by Andrea Wesson. Sleeping Bear Press 2011 un il $15.95

Grades: PreK K 1   E

1. Pets -- Fiction 2. Authorship -- Fiction

ISBN 978-1-58536-509-8; 1-58536-509-2

LC 2010034399

A lonely writer searches for the perfect pet to keep her company in her solitary work.

"Both the story and the illustrations have a light, charming flavor, with understated humor and a sophisticated air that assumes that intelligent children will enjoy this story." Kirkus

Young, Rebecca

Teacup; Rebecca Young; illustrated by Matt Ottley. Dial Books for Young Readers 2016 40 p. color illustrations (hardback) $17.99

Grades: PreK K 1 2   E

1. Self-reliance -- Fiction 2. Voyages and travels -- Fiction 3. Immigration and emigration -- Fiction 4. Emigration and immigration -- Fiction

ISBN 9780735227774

LC 2016001607

In this book, by Rebecca Young, illustrated by Matt Ottley, "a boy must leave his home and find another. He brings with him a teacup full of earth from the place where he grew up, and sets off to sea. Some days, the journey is peaceful, and the skies are cloudless and bright. Some days, storms threaten to overturn his boat. And some days, the smallest amount of hope grows into something glorious." (Publisher's note)

"The delightful results of his determination to hold onto his soil-filled teacup and an unexpectedly sweet ending add to that message the notion that those who strive and dream will eventually thrive. Enchanting, beautiful, and full of hope." Kirkus

Yuly, Toni

Cat Nap; Toni Yuly. Feiwel & Friends 2016 40 p. illustrations (chiefly color) $16.99

Grades: PreK   E

1. Cats -- Fiction 2. Sleep -- Fiction 3. Opposites -- Fiction

ISBN 1250054583; 9781250054586

In this children's book by Toni Yuly "it's naptime, and Cat is ready for Kitten to settle down. But Kitten has other ideas! In this book filled with opposites (big and little, black and white, sleepy and awake) . . . Yuly [shows] that simple concepts come alive for the youngest readers through bold art and charming language." (Publisher's note)

"Facial expressions add depth and humor to the story line, allowing text to be sparse—perfect for the intended audience. As an extra bonus, slightly older readers will enjoy finding the little mouse hidden on each page." SLJ

★ **Early** Bird; by Toni Yuly. First edition Feiwel & Friends 2014 40 p. $15.99

Grades: PreK   E

1. Birds

ISBN 1250043271; 9781250043276

This children's book, by Toni Yuly, tells the "story of an early-rising red bird, which also introduces a handful of directional prepositions. . . .After awakening, she stretches, 'takes a deep breath of fresh morning air and then Early Bird gets going!' The bird's rambles take her 'across the grass/through the flowerbed/ under the spiderweb/up the path' and beyond." (Publishers Weekly)

"A little red bird wakes early and goes on a preposition-laden journey: "Across...through...under...up...and over" until she finds the Early Worm. Readers may think they know the little worm's fate, but Early Bird gets the worm--and shares a strawberry breakfast. The large-size type plays around, under, and over the bold shapes and colors in this simple, pleasing story." Horn Book

Night owl; Toni Yuly. Feiwel & Friends 2015 40 p. color illustrations (hardback) $15.99; (board book) $7.99

Grades: PreK   E

1. Owls -- Fiction 2. Sound -- Fiction 3. Board books for children 4. Animals -- Infancy -- Fiction

ISBN 1250054575; 9781250054579; 9781250072917

LC 2014045970

In this children's book by Toni Yuly, "little Night Owl happily greets the night. But where is his mother? In a series of onomatopoeic moments, the owlet hears different sounds and wonders if it's his mother's. Alas, each one reveals a cricket, a train, a toad or other source of the sound-- but no mother. When a storm crashes in, the owlet wings bravely home to his tree where his mother soon joins him." (School Library Journal)

"Although Night Owl is portrayed as independent, curious, and brave, toddlers and preschoolers will understand that he really wants his mother during the storm. . . . With its question-and-response text, this is a satisfying choice for reading aloud." Booklist

Zagarenski, Pamela

Henry and Leo; written and illustrated by Pamela Zagarenski. Houghton Mifflin Harcourt 2016 40 p. color illustrations (ebook) $17.99; (hardback) $17.99
Grades: PreK K 1 2   E
1. Toys -- Fiction 2. Picture books for children 3. Friendship -- Fiction 4. Lost and found possessions -- Fiction
ISBN 9781328661876; 9780544648111

                         LC 2015032158

In this children's book by Pamela Zagarenski, "Leo isn't just a stuffed toy, he is Henry's best friend and brother. He is as real as a tree, a cloud, the sun, the moon, the stars, and the wind. But when the two are accidentally separated, no one in Henry's family believes Leo is real enough to find his way home." (Publisher's note)

"The interplay between what is real and what is imaginary -- and Henry's thoughts on the subject -- will make this a fertile book for children and adults to discuss." Horn Book

The **whisper**; written and illustrated by Pamela Zagarenski. Houghton Mifflin Harcourt 2015 40 p. color illustrations (hardback) $17.99
Grades: PreK K 1 2 3   E
1. Magic -- Fiction 2. Imagination -- Fiction 3. Books and reading -- Fiction
ISBN 0544416864; 9780544416864

                         LC 2014048551

In this children's book, by Pamela Zagarenski, a "sweet-faced girl in a red hood borrows a special book from her teacher. As she runs home, oblivious to what is happening, the words escape. . . . At home, the child is disappointed, thinking the book lacks a story. Then she hears the whisper: 'You can imagine the words¿the stories¿.There are never any rules¿imagining just is.'" (School Library Journal)

"This tribute to the imagination shows young readers the magic of creating stories, in addition to reading them, and that is a powerful thing." Booklist

Zalben, Jane Breskin

★ **Baby** shower. Roaring Brook Press 2010 un il $16.99
Grades: PreK K 1 2   E
1. Dogs -- Fiction 2. Pets -- Fiction 3. Aunts -- Fiction 4. Animals -- Fiction
ISBN 978-1-5964-3465-3; 1-5964-3465-1

"Zoe wants a pet. . . . To get her mind off dogs . . . and cats . . . Mama suggests that Zoe help with her aunt's baby shower. That night in bed Zoe . . . [dreams] about a baby shower—of puppies, kittens, and even piglets and ducklings. . . . Much of the charm comes from Zalben's sweet and funny ink-and-watercolor pictures, filled with delicious detail in both the homey scenes and windswept expanses of tumbling babies." Booklist

Mousterpiece; Jane Breskin Zalben. Roaring Brook Press 2012 30 p. $16.99
Grades: PreK K 1 2   E
1. Mice -- Fiction 2. Painting -- Fiction 3. Picture books for children 4. Artists -- Fiction 5. Museums -- Fiction 6. Art museums -- Fiction
ISBN 1596435496; 9781596435490

                         LC 2011021755

In this book, "Janson the mouse lives in an art museum . . . . When she happens upon the modern wing, she is mesmerized. Paintings by Picasso and Matisse, Munch and Pollack, Van Gogh and Warhol spark her creative talents and she emulates them all. When the wing is closed for renovation, Janson is bereft. . . . Rather than leave the space empty, she paints . . . until the room is once again filled with art. The museum director happens upon her work and mounts a show for her." (School Library Journal)

Zeltser, David

Ninja baby; by David Zeltser; illustrated by Diane Goode. Chronicle Books LLC 2015 32 p. color illustrations $16.99
Grades: PreK K 1   E
1. Ninja -- Fiction 2. Infants -- Fiction 3. Siblings -- Fiction 4. Humorous stories 5. Toddlers -- Fiction 6. Brothers and sisters -- Fiction
ISBN 1452135428; 9781452135427

                         LC 2014021775

In this children's book by David Zeltser, illustrated by Diane Goode, "from the day she was born, Nina was a ninja baby. She obliterated her applesauce. She concealed herself at bath time. And she was training herself in advanced infiltration (of movie night). Nina wants to do everything by herself, until the day her parents bring home a Kung Fu Master (a baby brother). Now with a sibling, Nina will face the one thing she cannot do alone: be part of a family." (Publisher's note)

"This spirited and stealthy new sibling story is one in which young readers can enjoy the exaggerated premise while their grown-ups can possibly glean some comfort." SLJ

Zia, F.

Hot, hot roti for Dada-ji; art by Ken Min. Lee & Low Books 2011 il $17.95
Grades: K 1 2   E
1. Grandfathers -- Fiction 2. East Indian Americans -- Fiction
ISBN 978-1-60060-443-0; 1-60060-443-9

                         LC 2010034694

Aneel and his grandfather, Dada-ji, tell stories, use their imaginations, and make delicious roti, a traditional Indian flatbread.

"Min echoes the narrative's exuberance with bright, blocky acrylic scenes of an Indian family in Western surroundings, dressed in a mix of contemporary and traditional styles and headlined by the lad and his elder. . . . A natural for reading aloud, laced with great tastes, infectious sound effects and happy feelings." Kirkus

Includes glossary

Ziefert, Harriet

Bunny's lessons; paintings by Barroux. Blue Apple 2011 un il $16.99
Grades: PreK K 1 2   E
1. Toys -- Fiction 2. Rabbits -- Fiction
ISBN 978-1-60905-028-3; 1-60905-028-2

                         LC 2010046645

A stuffed rabbit learns much from Charlie, his constant companion, including the meaning of the words "loud," "ouch," and "messy," but also about saying you are sorry and knowing you are loved.

"With simple lines, Barroux creates emotions of surprise, anger, joy, and sadness in his childlike paintings. Thick paper and a matte finish give the book a sturdy, solid feel that complements the sturdy, solid message of friendship." Booklist

Lucy rescued; Harriet Ziefert; paintings by Barroux. Blue Apple Books 2012 40 p. (hardback) $16.99
Grades: PreK K 1 2   E
1. Dogs -- Fiction 2. Toys -- Fiction 3. Picture books for children

4. Animals -- Infancy -- Fiction
ISBN 1609051874; 9781609051877

LC 2011039015

In this children's picture book, a family adopts a puppy named Lucy from the pound. "Out of nowhere that evening Lucy begins to howl a horrific howl. Morning, noon and night the howling went on and on. The little girl and her parents tried everything to stop it. . . . One night the little girl presented Lucy with a simple toy for her to snuggle with and the howling stopped. . . . But when one of Lucy's favorite toys comes up missing, the howling begins again." (Children's Literature)

My dog thinks I'm a genius; illustrated by Barroux. Blue Apple Books 2011 il $16.99
Grades: PreK K   E
1. Dogs -- Fiction 2. Painting -- Fiction
ISBN 978-1-60905-059-7; 1-60905-059-2

LC 2011018936

A budding artist goes to school after painting a picture with input from his dog Louie, and returns home to find that the dog has some talent, as well.

"Both the text and illustrations are true to the voice of an eight-year-old boy. . . . The colors in the illustrations are perfectly suited to the story. . . . Share this book as an introduction to art, or simply as a sweet dog story." SLJ

Zimmerman, Andrea Griffing

★ **Dig!** [by] Andrea Zimmerman and David Clemesha; illustrated by Marc Rosenthal. Harcourt 2004 un il $16
Grades: PreK K   E
1. Dogs -- Fiction 2. Construction workers -- Fiction 3. Excavating machinery -- Fiction
ISBN 0-15-216785-4

LC 2003-4373

Follows Mr. Rally and his dog, Lightning, as they travel the town on a big yellow digging machine, taking care of five important jobs

"Earth-tone illustrations are created with watercolor and Prismacolor pencil. . . . The pace, repetition, and word choices make the book appropriate for beginning readers. The uncluttered art, catchy refrain, and focus on heavy machinery make it a natural for storytimes." SLJ

★ **Digger** man; [by] Andrea Zimmerman & David Clemesha. Holt & Co. 2003 un il $15.95
Grades: PreK K 1 2   E
1. Brothers -- Fiction 2. Steam-shovels -- Fiction
ISBN 0-8050-6628-4

LC 2002-10856

A young boy imagines how he will use his digger to make a park where he and his little brother can play

"The joyful acrylic illustrations and the sparse, confident text will delight other digger-wannabes." Booklist

Another book about these characters is:
Fire engine man (2007)

★ **Trashy** town; [by] Andrea Zimmerman and David Clemesha; illustrated by Dan Yaccarino. HarperCollins Pubs. 1999 un il $17.99
Grades: PreK K   E
1. Refuse and refuse disposal -- Fiction
ISBN 0-06-027139-6

LC 98-27495

Little by little, can by can, Mr. Gillie, the trash man, cleans up his town

"Short energetic sentences propel the tale. . . . Employing primary colors dominated by bold blues, Yaccarino's vibrant art has a retro look." Booklist

Zion, Gene

★ **Harry** the dirty dog; pictures by Margaret Bloy Graham. Harper & Row 1956 un il $17.99; lib bdg $17.89; pa $6.99; bd bk $7.99
Grades: PreK K   E
1. Dogs -- Fiction
ISBN 0-06-026865-4; 0-06-026866-2 lib bdg; 0-06-443009-X pa; 0-06-084244-X bd bk

"A runaway dog becomes so dirty his family almost doesn't recognize him. Harry's flight from scrubbing brush and bath water takes him on a tour of the city." Moorachian. What is a City?
Other titles about Harry are:
Harry and the lady next door (1960)
Harry by the sea (1965)
No roses for Harry! (1958)

Zoehfeld, Kathleen Weidner

★ **Secrets** of the seasons; orbiting the sun in our backyard. Kathleen Weidner Zoehfeld; illustrated by Priscilla Lamont. First edition Alfred A. Knopf 2014 40 p. (trade) $16.99
Grades: K 1 2 3   E
1. Sun -- Fiction 2. Earth -- Fiction 3. Seasons -- Fiction
ISBN 0517709945; 9780517709948; 9780517709955

LC 2013021351

This book, written by Kathleen Weidner Zoehfeld and illustrated by Priscilla Lamont, is "about backyard science that explains why the seasons change. Alice and her friend Zack explore the reasons for the seasons. Alice's narrative is all about noticing the changes as fall turns into winter, spring, and then summer. She explains how the earth's yearlong journey around the sun, combined with the tilt in the earth's axis, makes the seasons happen." (Publisher's note)

"Alice and friends from Secrets of the Garden return to enjoy her nature-filled backyard. This time, she learns to notice and welcome differences in weather, plants, and animal life in each of the four seasons of the temperate northern hemisphere. Throughout, airy pen and watercolor illustrations make the appeal of nature accessible to even the youngest readers." Horn Book

Zolotow, Charlotte

Mr. Rabbit and the lovely present; pictures by Maurice Sendak. Harper & Row 1962 un il $16.99; pa $5.99
Grades: PreK K 1 2   E
1. Color -- Fiction 2. Rabbits -- Fiction 3. Birthdays -- Fiction
ISBN 0-06-026945-6; 0-06-443020-0 pa
A Caldecott Medal honor book, 1963

"A serious little girl and a tall, other-worldly white rabbit converse about a present for her mother. 'But what?' said the little girl. 'Yes, what?' said Mr. Rabbit. It requires a day of searching—for red, yellow, green, and blue, all things the mother likes, to make a basket of fruit for the present." Horn Book

"The quiet story, told in dialogue, is illustrated in richly colored pictures which exactly fit the fanciful mood." Hodges. Books for Elem Sch Libr

When the wind stops; illustrated by Stefano Vitale. rev and newly illustrated ed; HarperCollins Pubs. 1995 un il hardcover o.p. pa $6.99
Grades: PreK K   E
1. Nature -- Fiction
ISBN 0-06-025425-4; 0-06-443472-9 pa

LC 94-14477

A revised and newly illustrated edition of the title first published 1962 by Abelard-Schuman

This is a revised edition of Zolotow's 1962 title, with a new illustrator. "A little boy feels sorry when the day is over, but his mother

explains that day is beginning somewhere else, and that 'Nothing ends
. . . It begins in another place or in a different way.'" (Bull Cent Child
Books) "Ages four to eight." (Booklist)

"The full-color scenes, painted on wood, gloriously depict heaven
and earth and give concrete meaning to abstract concepts. Not only wonderful for lap sharing, this beautiful book will also be a rich supplement
for a science unit on the elements or the seasons." Booklist

★ **William's** doll; pictures by William Pène Du Bois. Harper &
Row 1972 30p il $16.99; pa $6.99
Grades: PreK K 1 2   E
1. Dolls -- Fiction 2. Sex role -- Fiction
ISBN 0-06-027047-0; 0-06-027048-9 lib bdg; 0-06-443067-7 pa
When little William asks for a doll, the other boys scorn him and his
father tries to interest him in conventional boys' playthings such as a
basketball and a train. His sympathetic grandmother buys him the doll,
explaining his need to have it to love and care for so that he can practice
being a father

"Very, very special. The strong, yet delicate pictures . . . convey a
gentleness of spirit and longing most effectively, as William pantomimes
his craving." N Y Times Book Rev

Zommer, Yuval
One Hundred Bones; by Yuval Zommer. Candlewick Press 2016
32 p. color illustrations $16.99
Grades: PreK K 1 2   E
1. Bones -- Fiction 2. Dogs -- Fiction
ISBN 0763681830; 9780763681838
LC 2015938141
In this picture book, by Yuval Zommer, "Scruff the dog is a stray
who just loves to dig. It doesn't make him the most popular dog in town.
But when he sniffs out a pile of old bones, he gets all the neighborhood
dogs to help him. They uncover not one, not two, not three . . . but
100 bones and make the most exciting dinosaur discovery of all time!
Scruff's find wins him new friends and a new home." (Publisher's note)

"The dynamic digital illustrations are varied in composition and in
point of view, showing an amusing dog's-eye view of people (legs only)
in the park scenes, and an intriguing, cut-away underground view of the
dig site full of bones. The volume's large format showcases Zommer's
strong, engaging artwork and makes this lively picture book as rewarding for reading aloud to groups as to individuals." Booklist

Another title in this series is:
One Hundred Sausages (2017)

Zuckerman, Andrew
★ **Creature** ABC. Chronicle Books 2009 un il $19.99
Grades: PreK K 1 2   E
1. Animals 2. Alphabet
ISBN 978-0-8118-6978-2; 0-8118-6978-4
LC 2009-04365
"This is a first choice for libraries." Bull Cent Child Books
Includes glossary

Zuffi, Stefano
Art 123; count from 1 to 12 with great works of art. Abrams Books
for Young Readers 2011 32p $12.95
Grades: K 1 2   E
1. Counting 2. Art appreciation
ISBN 978-1-4197-0100-9; 1-4197-0100-2
LC 2011009728
"From Caravaggio to Lichtenstein, this enriching counting book
features a different work of Western art for numbers one through 12, ac-
companied by a brief, descriptive rhyme. . . . In addition to introducing

numbers and counting, the book works well as a basic primer on viewing
(and thinking about) art." SLJ

Zuill, Andrea
Wolf camp; Andrea Zuill. Schwartz & Wade Books 2016 40 p.
color illustrations (hardback) $16.99
Grades: PreK K 1 2   E
1. Dogs -- Fiction 2. Camps -- Fiction 3. Wolves -- Fiction
ISBN 9780553509120; 9780553509137
LC 2015018906
This children's story, written and illustrated by Andrea Zuill, follows
"Homer . . . , a dog . . . [who] also secretly fancies himself part wolf.
So when an invitation to attend WOLF CAMP . . . falls out of his kibble
bag one morning, he's determined to go. After his people finally agree,
Homer boards the bus bound for Wolf Camp, along with fellow campers
Trixie and Rex." (Publisher's note)

"Full-page illustrations, packed with details and funny asides, show
Homer and other dogs as they slowly improve their wilderness skills.
Kids with camp jitters of their own will laugh out loud at Homer's antics
as he overcomes his nervousness in pursuit of his dream, and they'll
enjoy watching his transition from plain old Homer to honorary wolf."
Booklist

Zullo, Germano
Little bird; Germano Zullo; illustrated by Albertine. Enchanted
Lion Books 2012 72 p.
Grades: PreK K 1 2   E
1. Birds -- Fiction 2. Flight -- Fiction 3. Friendship -- Fiction 4.
Picture books for children
ISBN 1592701183; 9781592701186
LC 2011052462
This picture book, a French Caldecott Medal winner, tells the story
of a man who frees a group of birds from his truck so that they can fly
away. When one small bird remains, he keeps it company and tries to
show it how to fly. The little bird returns later with the entire flock, lifting up the man and flying with him. The story "suggests that little things
can change lives--and perhaps even the world. Placing small, uncomplicated shapes against large fields of uniform color . . . [illustrator] Albertine provides a visual plot for [Germano] Zullo's meditative abstractions
. . . the characters express fear, friendship, yearning and delight through
glances, posture and other cues." (Kirkus)

Zuravicky, Oril
★ **C** is for city; an alphabet book. illustrated by Giuseppe Castel-
lano. Little Simon 2011 il $7.99
Grades: PreK K   E
1. Alphabet 2. Stories in rhyme 3. Board books for children
ISBN 978-1-4424-2049-6; 1-4424-2049-9
"Mister Doodle may be a simple stick figure, but he lives in a vibrant
photo-collage world. In this alphabet book, he and his dog, Sketch, share
a new noun for every letter of the alphabet. . . . Mister Doodle's adventures unfold in bouncy, playful rhymes. . . . A great little introduction to
the alphabet, this lively outing . . . should inspire kids to notice details."
Publ Wkly

Fic FICTION

50 Cent, 1975-
Playground; with Aura Moser. Razorbill 2011 314p $17.99
Grades: 7 8 9 10   Fic
1. Young adult literature 2. Bullies -- Fiction
ISBN 978-1-59514-434-8; 1-59514-434-X

Thirteen-year-old Butterball doesn't have much going for him. He's teased about his weight. He hates the Long Island suburb his mom moved them to so she could go to nursing school and start her life over. He wishes he still lived with his dad in New York City where there's always something happening, even if his dad doesn't have much time for him. Still, that's not why he beat up Maurice on the playground.

"Readers who were ever confused about having a gay parent, or being overweight, or going through a parental breakup, or just wanting to fit in and be accepted by their peers, will relate to Butterball. 50 Cent's debut young adult novel is a quick read that will be great for discussions on a variety of important and timely topics." VOYA

Abbott, Tony
Firegirl. Little, Brown 2006 145p $15.99; pa $5.99
Grades: 5 6 7 8   **Fic**
1. School stories 2. Burns and scalds -- Fiction
ISBN 978-0-316-01171-6; 0-316-01171-1; 978-0-316-01170-9 pa; 0-316-01170-3 pa
LC 2005-07964

A middle school boy's life is changed when Jessica, a girl disfigured by burns, starts attending his Catholic school while receiving treatment at a local hospital.

"Through realistic settings and dialogue, and believable characters, readers will be able to relate to the social dynamics of these adolescents who are trying to handle a difficult situation." SLJ

The **forbidden** stone; by Tony Abbott. Katherine Tegen Books, an imprint of HarperCollinsPublishers 2014 432 p. (The Copernicus legacy) (hardback) $16.99
Grades: 4 5 6 7   **Fic**
1. Antiquities -- Fiction 2. Secret societies -- Fiction 3. Voyages and travels -- Fiction 4. Adventure and adventurers -- Fiction
ISBN 006219447X; 9780062194473
LC 2013038560

"Four precocious preteens and a distracted astrophysicist travel to Europe to unravel a mystery that has already claimed several lives... Filled with riddles and ciphers, this first of 12 installments will keep readers intellectually stimulated as well as entertained. The stepbrothers' bond, a budding crush and a mystery that plays off of real historical figures and facts make this more than a pedestrian whodunit. With engaging characters, a globe-trotting plot and dangerous villains, it is hard to find something not to like. Equal parts edge-of-your-seat suspense and heartfelt coming-of-age." (Kirkus)

Kringle; illustrated by Greg Call. Scholastic Press 2005 324p il $14.99
Grades: 5 6 7 8   **Fic**
1. Fantasy fiction 2. Orphans -- Fiction 3. Santa Claus -- Fiction
ISBN 0-439-74942-5
LC 2005-12697

In the fifth century A.D., as order retreats from Britain with the departing Roman Army, orphaned, twelve-year-old Kringle determines to rescue his beloved guardian from the evil goblins who terrorize the countryside by kidnapping and enslaving humans and, in the process, with the help of elves and others along the way, discovers his true destiny.

"The enticing premise, appealing young hero, and nonstop action will appeal to many fantasy lovers." Booklist

The **serpent's** curse; Tony Abbott, Bill Perkins; [edited by] Claudia Gabel. HarperCollins 2014 496 p. illustrations (The copernicus legacy) (hardcover) $16.99
Grades: 4 5 6 7   **Fic**
1. Curses -- Fiction 2. Relics -- Fiction 3. Kidnapping -- Fiction 4. Adventure and adventurers 5. Adventure stories 6. Antiquities

-- Fiction 7. Secret societies -- Fiction 8. Voyages and travels -- Fiction
ISBN 0062194461; 9780062194466
LC 2014937634

Sequel to: The Forbidden Stone (2014)

This book, by Tony Abbott, is "a globe-trotting adventure packed with more riddles, puzzles, and secret histories. The hunt for Copernicus's first relic sent Wade, Darrell, Lily, and Becca to the far reaches of the world and put them in serious danger. But they never imagined Sara Kaplan - Darrell and Wade's mother - would be kidnapped by the conniving Galina Krause. Now they must race the evil Teutonic Order to find the Serpens relic and rescue Sara before it's too late." (Publisher's note)

"Still reeling from their last adventure in The Forbidden Stone (HarperCollins, 2014) which ended only hours before, Wade, Darrell, Becca, and Lily are nearly killed by Galina and the evil Order...Readers learn a bit more about each of the four young heroes in this second installment, but those wishing for more character development will want to read the novellas. Fans of the series will eagerly await the next entry."

Wade and the scorpion's claw; by Tony Abbott. Katherine Tegen Books/HarperCollins 2014 224 p. illustrations (The Copernicus archives) (paperback) $3.99
Grades: 4 5 6 7   **Fic**
1. Adventure fiction 2. Relics -- Fiction 3. Antiquities -- Fiction 4. Secret societies -- Fiction 5. Voyages and travels -- Fiction 6. Adventure and adventurers -- Fiction
ISBN 0062314726; 9780062314727
LC 2014010026

"'Wade and the Scorpion's Claw' picks up right where 'The Copernicus Legacy: The Forbidden Stone' left off, with the Kaplan family seeking the next Copernicus relic. Now Wade, the curious, analytical, yet starry-eyed member of the group, leads the chase for another relic through the busy streets of San Francisco while on the run from one of Galina Krause's most treacherous henchmen." (Publisher's note)

"This first in a string of novellas is intended to link each of the six full-length novels in the Copernicus Legacy series. . . . This fast-paced adventure features vivid settings, difficult brainteasers and likable characters." Kirkus

Another title in this series is:
Becca and the prisoner's curse (2015)

Abdel-Fattah, Randa
★ **Where** the streets had a name; Randa Abdel-Fattah. Scholastic Press 2010 313p (reinforced binding) $17.99
Grades: 5 6 7 8   **Fic**
1. Jerusalem -- Fiction 2. Voyages and travels -- Fiction 3. Jewish-Arab relations -- Fiction 4. Israel -- Fiction 5. Muslims -- Fiction 6. West Bank -- Fiction 7. Family life -- Fiction 8. Palestinian Arabs -- Fiction
ISBN 0545172926; 9780545172929; 978-0-545-17292-9; 0-545-17292-6
LC 2009043122

This book tells the story of 13-year-old Hayaat, who "lives behind the Israeli-built Separation Wall in the West Bank City of Bethlehem. When her beloved grandmother falls ill . . . . [she] decides to make her way to Jerusalem to fill an empty hummus jar with soil from the land of her grandmother's ancestral home. She is certain that this will mend her heart. Unfortunately, although Jerusalem is merely minutes away, curfews, checkpoints, and an identity card that doesn't allow her to cross the border mean that Hayaat and her soccer-loving, troublemaker friend Samy face a perilous journey." (School Lib J)

"At the many checkpoints, the friends encounter soldiers, both brutal and kind, and also an Israeli peacenik couple who helps the kids get past the towering barriers." (Booklist)

"Hayaat chronicles this life-altering journey in the first-person, present tense, giving readers an intimate glimpse into the life of her warm, eccentric Muslim family, who survive despite the volatile political environment. A refreshing and hopeful teen perspective on the Israeli-Palestinian dilemma." Kirkus

Abdul-Jabbar, Kareem, 1947-
Sasquatch in the paint; by Kareem Abdul-Jabbar and Raymond Obstfeld. Disney-Hyperion Books 2013 272 p. (hardback) $16.99
Grades: 4 5 6 7   **Fic**
1. Clubs -- Fiction 2. Basketball -- Fiction 3. School sports -- Fiction 4. Schools -- Fiction 5. Science clubs -- Fiction 6. Middle schools -- Fiction 7. African Americans -- Fiction 8. Mystery and detective stories 9. Jews -- United States -- Fiction 10. Interpersonal relations -- Fiction
ISBN 142317870X; 9781423178705
LC 2013007147
In this book by Kareem Abdul-Jabbar and Raymond Obstfeld "Theo Rollins' . . . new height is making everyone expect more from him. Coach Mandrake wants to transform him from . . . science geek into star basketball player, even though Theo has little experience. Training is starting to hurt his science club's chances of winning the "Aca-lympics," the school's trivia competition. Theo . . . [is] accused of stealing. Can he find the real thief before he is kicked off the basketball and science club teams?' (Publisher's note)

Abela, Deborah
The ghosts of Gribblesea Pier. Farrar Straus Giroux 2011 232p $16.99
Grades: 4 5 6   **Fic**
1. Ghost stories 2. Circus -- Fiction 3. Family life -- Fiction 4. Great Britain -- Fiction 5. Swindlers and swindling -- Fiction 6. Eccentrics and eccentricities -- Fiction
ISBN 978-0-374-36239-3; 0-374-36239-4
LC 2010022517
Aurelie Bonhoffen, who has grown up in the circus, discovers a remarkable family secret on her twelfth birthday that may help in dealing with a sinister man who wants to take over her family's pier.

This is a "charmer of a ghostly adventure tale. . . . This fast-paced, engaging, and charming story has echoes of Jeanne Birdsall's 'Penderwicks' . . . and some Dickensian elements, but in the end this is just a finely executed story of family and friendship and the ties that bind a community." SLJ

Abouet, Marguerite
Akissi; feline invasion. by Marguerite Abouet; illustrated by Mathiew Sapin. Flying Eye Books 2013 48 p. ill. (hbk.) $14.95
Grades: 2 3 4 5   **Fic**
1. Siblings -- Fiction 2. Conduct of life -- Fiction
ISBN 190926301X; 9781909263017
This book, by Marguerite Abouet, presents "African vignettes aimed at a younger audience. All seven episodes feature young Akissi and her brother Fofana or her friends getting into trouble for less-than-exemplary . . . behavior. In 'Good Mums,' . . . she borrows a neighbor's baby and tenderly feeds it a stew concocted from discarded scraps found in the market. 'Home Cinema' has her playing lookout while Fofana sells spots in front of the television set to neighborhood children." (Kirkus Reviews)

Abraham, Susan Gonzales
Cecilia's year; by Susan Gonzales Abraham & Denise Gonzales Abraham. Cinco Puntos Press 2004 210p il $16.95; pa $11.95

Grades: 4 5 6 7   **Fic**
1. Poverty -- Fiction 2. Sex role -- Fiction 3. New Mexico -- Fiction 4. Hispanic Americans -- Fiction
ISBN 978-0-938317-87-6; 0-938317-87-3; 978-1-933693-02-6 pa; 1-933693-02-9 pa
LC 2004-13374
Nearly fourteen and poor, Cecilia Gonzales wants desperately to go to high school and become a teacher until her mother's old-fashioned ideas about a woman's place threaten her dreams

"The cultural details are vivid and integrated into the story, providing a rich context and a snapshot of an entire community. . . . This fictionalized biography succeeds on several levels." SLJ

Another title about Cecilia is:
Surprising Cecilia (2005)

Acampora, Paul
Rachel Spinelli punched me in the face. Roaring Brook Press 2011 168p $15.99
Grades: 5 6 7 8   **Fic**
1. Moving -- Fiction 2. Trumpet -- Fiction 3. Musicians -- Fiction 4. Friendship -- Fiction 5. Connecticut -- Fiction 6. Family life -- Fiction 7. Single parent family -- Fiction
ISBN 978-1-59643-548-3; 1-59643-548-8
LC 2010027436
When fourteen-year-old Zachary and his father move to Falls, Connecticut, he spends a summer falling in love, coming to terms with his mother's absence, and forming eclectic friendships.

"Realistic dialogue and poignantly amusing situations . . . all come together to gently flesh out a few months in the lives of people readers will savor getting to know. . . . An outstanding, humane coming-of-age tale of loss, yearning and forgiveness." Kirkus

Achebe, Chinua
How the leopard got his claws; [by] Chinua Achebe and John Iroaganachi; illustrated by Mary Grandpre. Candlewick Press 2011 il $16.99
Grades: 4 5 6   **Fic**
1. Allegories 2. Jungles -- Fiction 3. Leopards -- Fiction
ISBN 978-0-7636-4805-3; 0-7636-4805-1
LC 2010040344
Recounts how the leopard got his claws and teeth and why he rules the forest with terror.

"First published in the 1970s, this political fable still makes provocative reading. Grand Pré's new Lion King-style illustrations both capture the tale's intensity and provide a needed contemporary look. . . . The stately prose will make a profound impression on readers, as will the large, dimly lit closeups of snarling jaws and strong animal bodies." Booklist

Ada, Alma Flor, 1938-
Dancing home; [by] Alma Flor Ada and Gabriel M. Zubizarreta Atheneum Books for Young Readers 2011 147p $14.99
Grades: 3 4 5 6   **Fic**
1. Cousins -- Fiction 2. California -- Fiction 3. Family life -- Fiction 4. Mexican Americans -- Fiction 5. Father-daughter relationship -- Fiction
ISBN 978-1-4169-0088-7; 1-4169-0088-8
LC 2010013229
When Margie's cousin Lupe comes from Mexico to live in California with Margie's family, Lupe must adapt to America, while Margie, who thought it would be fun to have her cousin there, finds that she is embarrassed by her in school and jealous of her at home.

"This story will assist readers in embracing their own heritage and developing an appreciation for their classmates' backgrounds. It's an enjoyable offering (and a great read-aloud) that will capture readers' attention." SLJ

Adams, Richard

★ **Watership** Down; Scribner classics ed.; Scribner 1996 429p $30; pa $15

Grades: 6 7 8 9 10   **Fic**

1. Allegories 2. Young adult literature 3. Rabbits -- Fiction

ISBN 0-684-83605-X; 0-7432-7770-8 pa

First published 1972 in the United Kingdom; first United States edition 1974 by Macmillan

"Faced with the annihilation of its warren, a small group of male rabbits sets out across the English downs in search of a new home. Internal struggles for power surface in this intricately woven, realistically told adult adventure when the protagonists must coordinate tactics in order to defeat an enemy rabbit fortress. It is clear that the author has done research on rabbit behavior, for this tale is truly authentic." Shapiro Fic for Youth. 3d edition

Adderson, Caroline

Jasper John Dooley; Not in Love. by Caroline Adderson; illustrated by Ben Clanton. Kids Can Pr 2014 132 p.

Grades: 1 2 3   **Fic**

1. Crushes -- Fiction 2. Love -- Fiction 3. Trampolines and trampolining -- Fiction 4. Humorous stories 5. Schools -- Fiction 6. Only child -- Fiction

ISBN 1554538033; 9781554538034

In this book, by Caroline Adderson, "Jasper struggles to deal with the excessive attentions of his classmate Isabel, who just won't leave him alone. . . . After school, she invites him over for a playdate! When Jasper complains to his parents that he's too sick to go to her house. . . . However, once he arrives, Jasper is thrilled to discover Isabel has a trampoline. . . . Can Jasper find a way to keep using her trampoline and get her to stop being in love with him?" (Publisher's note)

"All Jasper wants to do is play knights and dragons, but his friend Isabel insists on playing babies and planning their wedding. Yuck! At least she has a cool trampoline in her backyard. Like the previous two installments, this third book features short chapters, ample white space, and periodic black-and-white illustrations." SLJ

Adler, David A.

Cam Jansen and the mystery at the haunted house; illustrated by Susanna Natti. Viking 1992 58p il lib bdg $11

Grades: 2 3 4   **Fic**

1. Mystery fiction

ISBN 0-670-83419-X

LC 91-28863

Cam and her friend Eric chase the thief of Aunt Katie's wallet through an amusement park and find themselves involved in another case requiring their special detective skills

★ **Cam** Jansen and the mystery of the stolen diamonds; illustrated by Susanna Natti. Viking 1980 58p il hardcover o.p. $13.99

Grades: 2 3 4   **Fic**

1. Mystery fiction

ISBN 0-670-20039-5; 0-14-034670-8 pa

LC 79-20695

Cam Jansen, a fifth-grader with a photographic memory, and her friend Eric help solve the mystery of the stolen diamonds

This is a "fast-action uncomplicated adventure . . . [with] a touch of humor, a breezy writing style, and some very enjoyable pen-and-ink drawings." Booklist

Other titles about Cam Jansen are:

Cam Jansen and the barking treasure mystery (1999)

Cam Jansen and the birthday mystery (2000)

Cam Jansen and the catnapping mystery (1998)

Cam Jansen and the chocolate fudge mystery (1993)

Cam Jansen and the first day of school mystery (2002)

Cam Jansen and the ghostly mystery (1996)

Cam Jansen and the mystery at the haunted house (1992)

Cam Jansen and the mystery at the monkey house (1985)

Cam Jansen and the mystery of Flight 54 (1989)

Cam Jansen and the mystery of the Babe Ruth baseball (1982)

Cam Jansen and the mystery of the carnival prize (1984)

Cam Jansen and the mystery of the circus clown (1983)

Cam Jansen and the mystery of the dinosaur bones (1981)

Cam Jansen and the mystery of the gold coins (1982)

Cam Jansen and the mystery of the monster movie (1984)

Cam Jansen and the mystery of the stolen corn popper (1986)

Cam Jansen and the mystery of the television dog (1981)

Cam Jansen and the mystery of the UFO (1980)

Cam Jansen and the scary snake mystery (1997)

Cam Jansen and the school play mystery (2001)

Cam Jansen and the Secret Service mystery (2006)

Cam Jansen and the snowy day mystery (2004)

Cam Jansen and the Sports Day mysteries (2009)

Cam Jansen and the summer camp mysteries (2007)

Cam Jansen and the tennis trophy mystery (2003)

Cam Jansen and the Triceratops Pops mystery (1995)

Cam Jansen and the Valentine baby mystery (2005)

Cam Jansen and the wedding cake mystery (2011)

Cam Jansen and the Secret Service mystery; by David A. Adler; illustrated by Susanna Natti. Viking 2006 57p il $13.99

Grades: 2 3 4   **Fic**

1. Mystery fiction

ISBN 0-670-06092-5

LC 2005033490

Cam and her friend Danny help solve the mystery of a stolen pearl necklace when the governor comes to visit their school for the dedication of the new library.

"Readers can depend on this beginning chapter-book series for a clever story illustrated with plenty of black-and-white illustrations." Booklist

Cam Jansen and the snowy day mystery; illustrated by Susanna Natti. Viking 2004 57p il $13.99

Grades: 2 3 4   **Fic**

1. Mystery fiction

ISBN 0-670-05922-6

LC 2004-1643

Using her photographic memory Cam Jansen joins Eric in solving the mystery of how some of the school computers were stolen.

Cam Jansen and the Sports Day mysteries; a super special. by David A. Adler; illustrated by Joy Allen. Puffin Books 2009 118p il $14.99; pa $5.99

Grades: 2 3 4   **Fic**

1. School stories 2. Mystery fiction 3. Sports -- Fiction

ISBN 978-0-670-01163-6; 0-670-01163-0; 978-0-14-241225-1 pa; 0-14-241225-2 pa

LC 2008029568

Supersleuth Cam Jansen solves three mysteries during her class's Sports and Good Nutrition Day: The Backwards Race Mystery, The Soccer Game Mystery, and The Baseball Glove Mystery.

Cam Jansen and the summer camp mysteries; a super special. [by] David A. Adler; illustrated by Joy Allen. Viking 2007 117p il $14.99; pa $4.99

Grades: 2 3 4 **Fic**

1. Mystery fiction 2. Camps -- Fiction

ISBN 978-0-670-06218-8; 978-0-14-240742-4 pa

LC 2006014998

A collection of three Cam Jansen summer camp mysteries in which Cam Jansen and her best friend are spending three weeks at Camp Eagle Lake, where they play sports, do crafts, and solve three mysteries.

Cam Jansen and the Valentine baby mystery; illustrated by Susanna Natti. Viking 2005 80p il $13.99; pa $3.99

Grades: 2 3 4 **Fic**

1. Mystery fiction 2. Infants -- Fiction 3. Hospitals -- Fiction 4. Valentine's Day -- Fiction

ISBN 978-0-670-06009-2; 0-670-06009-7; 978-0-14-240694-6 pa; 0-14-240694-5 pa

Using her photographic memory Cam Jansen joins Eric in solving the mystery of a Valentine's day robbery in a hospital waiting room.

This "offers familiar characters in a new situation, foreshadows events with simple clues, and follows through with a satisfying ending." Booklist

Cam Jansen and the wedding cake mystery; illustrated by Joy Allen. Viking 2010 57p il $14.99

Grades: 2 3 4 **Fic**

1. Mystery fiction 2. Theft -- Fiction

ISBN 978-0-670-06295-9; 0-670-06295-2

LC 2009048129

When Cam and her father go to a talent show at the local senior center, Cam's help is needed to find out who stole a wedding cake from the delivery truck.

"Energetic dialogue and clear black-and-white drawings will engage readers as the caper unfolds." Horn Book Guide

Cam Jansen, the mystery of the dinosaur bones; illustrated by Susanna Natti. Puffin Books 2004 56p il pa $3.99

Grades: 2 3 4 **Fic**

1. Mystery fiction 2. Fossils -- Fiction 3. Dinosaurs -- Fiction

ISBN 978-0-14-240012-8; 0-14-240012-2

LC 2004557388

First published 1981

When she notices some bones missing from a dinosaur skeleton exhibited in the museum, Cam uses her photographic memory to try and discover who has been taking them and why.

"An uncluttered plot, a clever heroine, clear language, and a dash of humor make for a zestful mystery." SLJ

Cam Jansen, the mystery at the monkey house; illustrated by Susanna Natti. Puffin Books 2004 56p il pa $3.99

Grades: 2 3 4 **Fic**

1. Mystery fiction 2. Zoos -- Fiction 3. Monkeys -- Fiction

ISBN 978-0-14-240019-7; 0-14-240019-X

First published 1985

Fifth-grade sleuth Cam Jansen uses her photographic memory to solve a monkey-smuggling mystery at the city zoo.

Cam Jansen, the mystery of the Babe Ruth baseball; illustrated by Susanna Natti. Puffin Books 2004 57p il pa $3.99

Grades: 2 3 4 **Fic**

1. Mystery fiction 2. Baseball -- Fiction

ISBN 978-0-14-240015-9; 0-14-240015-7

LC 2004557391

First published 1982

Cam uses her photographic memory to identify the person who stole a valuable autographed baseball.

Cam Jansen, the mystery of the carnival prize; illustrated by Susanna Natti. Puffin Books 2004 57p il pa $3.99

Grades: 2 3 4 **Fic**

1. School stories 2. Mystery fiction

ISBN 978-0-14-240018-0; 0-14-240018-1

LC 2004557394

First published 1984

When fifth-grader Cam notices that the prizes for the most difficult game at the school carnival are rapidly disappearing, she uses her amazing photographic memory to investigate.

Cam Jansen, the mystery of the circus clown; illustrated by Susanna Natti. Puffin Books 2004 57p il pa $3.99

Grades: 2 3 4 **Fic**

1. Mystery fiction 2. Circus -- Fiction

ISBN 978-0-14-240016-6; 0-14-240016-5

LC 2004557392

First published 1983

Fifth-grader Cam Jansen uses her photographic memory to help find a pickpocket at the circus.

Cam Jansen, the mystery of the gold coins; illustrated by Susanna Natti. Puffin Books 2004 57p il pa $3.99

Grades: 2 3 4 **Fic**

1. Mystery fiction

ISBN 978-0-14-240014-2; 0-14-240014-9

LC 2004557390

First published 1982

While using her photographic memory to find her missing science fair project, Cam accidently locates two valuable gold coins.

Cam Jansen, the mystery of the monster movie; illustrated by Susanna Natti. Puffin Books 2004 57p il pa $3.99

Grades: 2 3 4 **Fic**

1. Mystery fiction

ISBN 978-0-14-240017-3; 0-14-240017-3

LC 2004557393

First published 1984

A fifth-grader uses her photographic memory, her mother, and her friend Eric to find a missing reel of a monster film they go to see.

Cam Jansen, the mystery of the stolen corn popper; illustrated by Susanna Natti. Puffin Books 2004 58p il pa $3.99

Grades: 2 3 4 **Fic**

1. Mystery fiction

ISBN 978-0-14-240178-1; 0-14-240178-1

LC 2005270166

First published 1986

Fifth-grade sleuth Cam Jansen uses her photographic memory to catch a thief during a department store sale.

This is "another quickly paced, easy-to-read mystery. . . . The story will hold readers' attention." SLJ

Cam Jansen, the mystery of the U.F.O. illustrated by Susanna Natti. Puffin Books 2004 58p il pa $3.99

Grades: 2 3 4 **Fic**

1. Mystery fiction

ISBN 978-0-14-240011-1; 0-14-240011-4

LC 2004557387

First published 1980

Ten-year-old Cam, possessor of a photographic memory, and her friend Eric investigate what seems to be a brief appearance of U.F.O.s.

Cam Jansen, the Triceratops Pops mystery; illustrated by Susanna Natti. Puffin Books 2004 56p il pa $3.99

Grades: 2 3 4   **Fic**

1. Mystery fiction

ISBN 978-0-14-240206-1; 0-14-240206-0

LC 2005270161

When Cam Jansen and her friend Eric go the music store at the mall for the latest CD by the Triceratops Pops band, Cam uses her photographic memory to foil a crime.

"The contemporary setting, light humor, and mild mystery will appeal to Cam's fans." Booklist

Agell, Charlotte

The **accidental** adventures of India McAllister. Henry Holt 2010 151p il $16.99

Grades: 3 4 5   **Fic**

1. Maine -- Fiction 2. Divorce -- Fiction 3. Friendship -- Fiction 4. Homosexuality -- Fiction 5. Chinese Americans -- Fiction

ISBN 978-0-8050-8902-8; 0-8050-8902-0

LC 2009-18907

India, an unusual nine-and-a-half-year-old living in small-town Maine, has a series of adventures which bring her closer to her artist-mother, strengthen her friendship with a neighbor boy, and help her to accept the man for whom her father moved away.

"The word "adventures" could mislead some readers, but those looking for a realistic new character to love won't be disappointed in nine-year-old India McCallister, who could step right out of the lifestyles section of any contemporary newspaper...An adventure for India is an early-morning walk with her dog; her worst day is when her best (boy) friend walks home from school with her archenemy. Sketchy line drawings, accompanied by India's commentary, provide appealing additional diary-like detail. A delightful addition to the middle-grade canon." PW

Aiken, Joan

The **wolves** of Willoughby Chase; illustrated by Pat Marriott. Delacorte Press 2000 181p il hardcover o.p. pa $6.99

Grades: 5 6 7 8   **Fic**

1. Great Britain -- Fiction

ISBN 0-385-32790-0; 0-440-49603-9 pa

First published 1962 in the United Kingdom; first United States edition 1963 by Doubleday

"Plot, characterization, and background blend perfectly into an amazing whole. . . . Highly recommended." SLJ

Other titles in this series are:

Black hearts in Battersea (1964)

Cold Shoulder Road (1996)

The cuckoo tree (1971)

Dangerous games (1999)

Is underground (1993)

Midwinter nightingale (2003)

Nightbirds on Nantucket (1966)

The stolen lake (1981)

The witch of Clatteringshaws (2005)

Ain, Beth

Starring Jules (in drama-rama) Beth Ain; illustrated by Anne Keenan Higgins. Scholastic Press 2013 176 p. (Starring Jules) (alk. paper) $14.99

Grades: 2 3 4 5   **Fic**

1. Child actors -- Fiction 2. School stories -- Fiction 3. Acting -- Fiction 4. Schools -- Fiction 5. Auditions -- Fiction 6. Friendship

-- Fiction 7. Best friends -- Fiction 8. New York (N.Y.) -- Fiction 9. Elementary schools -- Fiction

ISBN 0545443547; 9780545443548

LC 2012041838

This is the second of Beth Ain's Jules Bloom books. Here, "Jules has been asked to audition for a TV show about a New York City family; she would be the youngest of three siblings. . . . Jules skitters from problem to problem like a city cab, balancing her audition with another project: cheering up her new friend Elinor, who is from London. Things are busy at school, too: Her ex-best friend Charlotte continues to steal the limelight there, receiving the plum role in the end-of-the-year play." (Kirkus Reviews)

Al-Mansour, Haifaa, 1974-

The **green** bicycle; Haifaa Al Mansour. Chronicle Books LLC 2015 352 p. (hardback) $16.99

Grades: 5 6 7 8   **Fic**

1. Girls -- Fiction 2. Bicycles -- Fiction 3. Saudi Arabia -- Fiction 4. Coming of age -- Fiction

ISBN 0525428062; 9780525428060

LC 2015014551

This children's story, by Haifaa Al Mansour, is a "Middle Eastern coming-of-age story is told with warmth, spirit, and a mischievous sense of humor. Spunky eleven-year-old Wadjda lives in Riyadh, Saudi Arabia with her parents. She desperately wants a bicycle so that she can race her friend Abdullah, even though it is considered improper for girls to ride bikes. . . . With the bicycle so closely in her sights, she will stop at nothing to get what she wants." (Publisher's note)

"Young readers will easily sympathize with Wadjda's wish for a bike, and they will come away with a deeper understanding of a faraway culture." Booklist

Albarn, Jessica

The **boy** in the oak; [text & illustrations by] Jessica Albarn. Simply Read Books 2010 un il $17.95

Grades: 4 5 6 7   **Fic**

1. Fantasy fiction 2. Magic -- Fiction 3. Trees -- Fiction 4. Fairies -- Fiction

ISBN 978-1-897476-52-9; 1-897476-52-3

"A spare, lightly haunting narrative tells a fairy-tale-like story of a lonely boy whose play in the woods was 'insensitive and cruel. He trampled the flowers. He tore limbs off trees and carved his initials into their trunks.' A group of fairies . . . trap him inside an ancient 'Druidic Oak,' where the boy watches the seasons pass until a young girl arrives. . . . Pages of prose alternate with wordless spreads featuring spindly artwork and semitranslucent sheets imprinted with close-up photos of nature textures. . . . The book draws the most lasting power from its harmonious layers of imagery and sophisticated bookmaking." Booklist

Alber, Merryl

And the tide comes in; exploring a Georgia salt marsh. by Merryl Alber; illustrated by Joyce Mihran Turley. Taylor Trade Pub. 2012 32 p. ill. (hardcover) $15.95

Grades: 1 2 3   **Fic**

1. Marshes 2. Picture books for children 3. Ecology

ISBN 0981770053; 9780981770055

In this children's picture book, a "child in Georgia takes her Colorado cousin on daily visits to a nearby salt marsh. Ginger discovers the cyclical nature of this habitat as she observes and asks about this ecosystem. Alongside the description of the activities of the two girls is an explanation of an aspect of the marsh. Representational animals such as fiddler crabs, blue crabs, and shrimp and the importance of a marsh to their survival are described." (School Library Journal)

Alcott, Louisa May

Little women; illustrated by Scott McKowen. Sterling Pub. 2004
525p il $9.95

Grades: 5 6 7 8   **Fic**

1. Sisters -- Fiction 2. Family life -- Fiction 3. New England
-- Fiction

ISBN 978-1-4027-1458-0; 1-4027-1458-0

LC 2004-15669

First published 1868

Chronicles the joys and sorrows of the four March sisters as they
grow into young women in mid-nineteenth-century New England.

Other titles about members of the March family are:

Eight cousins (1875)

Jo's boys (1886)

Little men (1871)

Rose in bloom (1876)

Alexander, Kwame, 1968-

★ **Booked**; Kwame Alexander. Houghton Mifflin Harcourt 2016
320 p. (hardback) $16.99

Grades: 5 6 7 8 9   **Fic**

1. Soccer -- Fiction 2. Friendship -- Fiction 3. Books and reading
-- Fiction

ISBN 9780544570986; 0544570987

LC 2015033312

National Book Award Longlist: Young People's Literature (2016)

In this novel by Kwame Alexander "soccer, family, love, and friendship, take center stage as twelve-year-old Nick learns the power of
words as he wrestles with problems at home, stands up to a bully, and
tries to impress the girl of his dreams. Helping him along are his best
friend and sometimes teammate Coby, and The Mac, a rapping librarian
who gives Nick inspiring books to read." (Publisher's note)

"Alexander scores again with this sports-themed verse novel, a companion to his Newbery Medal-winning The Crossover. Eighth grader
Nick, a devoted soccer player and fan, enjoys some friendly competition
with his best friend, Coby. What Nick doesn't like is words—neither
the ones in the dictionary that his linguistics professor father wrote (and
is making him read) nor the ones he learns in his honors English class.
But the school's quirky rapping librarian, Mr. Mac, helps Nick discover
both a love of reading and a way to connect with the girl of his dreams.
. . . Emotionally resonant and with a pace like a player on a breakaway,
Nick's story will have readers agreeing: "The poems/ were cool./ The
best ones were/ like bombs,/ and when all the right words/ came to-
gether/ it was like an explosion./ So good, I/ didn't want it to end." PW

★ The **crossover**; by Kwame Alexander. Houghton Mifflin Harcourt 2014 240 p. hc $16.99

Grades: 6 7 8 9 10   **Fic**

1. Rap music 2. Brothers -- Fiction 3. Basketball -- Fiction 4.
Young adult literature 5. Novels in verse 6. Twins -- Fiction 7.
Fathers and sons -- Fiction 8. African Americans -- Fiction

ISBN 0544107713; 9780544107717

LC 2013013810

Coretta Scott King Author Award Honor Book (2015)

Newbery Medal (2015)

In this novel, by Kwame Alexander, "12-year old Josh Bell . . . and
his twin brother Jordan are awesome on the court. But Josh has more
than basketball in his blood, he's got mad beats, too, that tell his family's
story in verse. . . . Josh and Jordan must come to grips with growing up
on and off the court to realize breaking the rules comes at a terrible price,
as their story's . . . climax proves a game-changer for the entire family."
(Publisher's note)

"Twins Josh and Jordan are junior high basketball stars, thanks in
large part to the coaching of their dad, a former professional baller who

was forced to quit playing for health reasons, and the firm, but loving
support of their assistant-principal mom...Despite his immaturity, Josh
is a likable, funny, and authentic character. Underscoring the sports and
the fraternal tension is a portrait of a family that truly loves and supports
one another. Alexander has crafted a story that vibrates with energy and
heart and begs to be read aloud. A slam dunk." SLJ

Alexander, Lloyd

The **Black** Cauldron; [by] Lloyd Alexander. rev. ed.; H. Holt
1999 182p (Chronicles of Prydain) $19.95

Grades: 5 6 7 8   **Fic**

1. Fantasy fiction

ISBN 0-8050-6131-2; 978-08050-6131-4

LC 98040896

First published 1965

Taran, Assistant Pig-Keeper of Prydain, faces even more dangers as
he seeks the magical black cauldron, the chief implement of the evil
powers of Arawn, lord of the Land of Death.

★ The **book** of three; rev ed.; Holt & Co. 1999 190p (Chronicles
of Prydain) $19.95; pa $6.99

Grades: 5 6 7 8   **Fic**

1. Fantasy fiction 2. Fantasy

ISBN 0-8050-6132-0; 0-8050-8048-1 pa; 978-0-8050-6132-1;
978-0-8050-8048-3 pa

LC 98-40901

First published 1964

"Related in a simple, direct style, this fast-paced tale of high adventure has a well-balanced blend of fantasy, realism, and humor." SLJ

Other titles about the mythical land of Prydain are:

The black cauldron (1965)

The castle of Llyr (1966)

The foundling and other tales of Prydain (1999)

The high king (1968)

Taran Wanderer (1967)

The **castle** of Llyr; [by] Lloyd Alexander. rev.ed.; H. Holt 1999
172p (Chronicles of Prydain) $19.95

Grades: 5 6 7 8   **Fic**

1. Fantasy fiction

ISBN 0-8050-6133-9

LC 98040897

First published 1966

When Princess Eilonwy is sent to the Isle of Mona for training, she
is bewitched by the evil enchantress Achren, so Taran and other friends
must try to rescue her.

The **golden** dream of Carlo Chuchio. Henry Holt & Co. 2007
306p il $16.95

Grades: 5 6 7 8 9   **Fic**

1. Fantasy fiction 2. Middle East -- Fiction 3. Buried treasure --
Fiction 4. Voyages and travels -- Fiction

ISBN 978-0-8050-8333-0; 0-8050-8333-2

LC 2006-49710

Naive and bumbling Carlo, his shady camel-puller Baksheesh, and
Shira, a girl determined to return home, follow a treasure map through
the deserts and cities of the infamous Golden Road, as mysterious
strangers try in vain to point them toward real treasures

This "is an exuberant and compassionate tale of adventure."
Publ Wkly

The **high** king; rev ed; Holt & Co. 1999 253p (Chronicles of
Prydain) $19.95

Grades: 5 6 7 8   **Fic**
1. Fantasy fiction
ISBN 0-8050-6135-5

LC 98-40900

Concluding title in the chronicles of Prydain which include: The book of three, The black cauldron, The castle of Llyr, and Taran Wanderer
First published 1968
Awarded The Newbery Medal, 1969
"The fantasy has the depth and richness of a medieval tapestry, infinitely detailed and imaginative." Saturday Rev

The **remarkable** journey of Prince Jen. Dutton Children's Bks. 1991 273p hardcover o.p. pa $6.99
Grades: 5 6 7 8   **Fic**
1. Adventure fiction 2. China -- Fiction
ISBN 0-14-240225-7 pa

LC 91-13720

Bearing six unusual gifts, young Prince Jen in Tang Dynasty China embarks on a perilous quest and emerges triumphantly into manhood
"Alexander satisfies the taste for excitement, but his vivid characters and the food for thought he offers will nourish long after the last page is turned." SLJ

Taran Wanderer; [by] Lloyd Alexander. rev ed.; H. Holt 1999 222p (Chronicles of Prydain) $19.95
Grades: 5 6 7 8   **Fic**
1. Fantasy fiction
ISBN 0-8050-6134-7

LC 98040904

The fourth book of the Prydain cycle tells of the adventures that befell Taran when he went in search of his birthright and the truth about himself.

Alexander, William
Ambassador; William Alexander. Margaret K. McElderry Books 2014 240 p. (hardcover) $16.99
Grades: 5 6 7 8   **Fic**
1. Science fiction 2. Human-alien encounters -- Fiction 3. Ambassadors -- Fiction 4. Illegal aliens -- Fiction 5. Mexican Americans -- Fiction
ISBN 1442497645; 9781442497641; 9781442497658

LC 2013037333

In this middle grade book by William Alexander, "Gabe Fuentes is reading under the covers one summer night when he is interrupted by a creature who looks like a purple sock puppet. The sock puppet introduces himself as the Envoy and asks if Gabe wants to be Earth's ambassador to the galaxy. What sane eleven-year-old could refuse?" Publisher's note)
"A shape-shifting creature called 'the Envoy' informs eleven-year-old Gabe that it has appointed him Earth's ambassador to 'everyone else.' Gabe travels across space (while he's asleep) to the Embassy. When he wakes up back home, he discovers his father is to be deported to Mexico the next day--and one of the other ambassadors is trying to kill Gabe. A meaty and entertaining novel." Horn Book
Another title in this series is:
Nomad (2015)

Nomad. Simon & Schuster 2015 272 p. $16.99
Grades: 5 6 7 8   **Fic**
1. Space warfare -- Fiction 2. Human-alien encounters -- Fiction
ISBN 144249767X; 9781442497672

"Gabe Fuentes is in a race against time—and aliens—in this intergalactic sequel to Ambassador, which Booklist called 'an exciting sci-fi

adventure, perceptively exploring what it means to be alien,' from National Book Award winner William Alexander.

When we last left Earth's Ambassador, Gabe Fuentes, he was stranded on the moon. And when he's rescued by Kaen, another Ambassador, things don't get better: It turns out that the Outlast—a race of aliens that has been systematically wiping out all other creatures—are coming. And they've set their sights on Earth.

Enter Nadia. She was Earth's Ambassador before Gabe, but left her post in order to stop the Outlast. Nadia has discovered that the Outlast can conquer worlds by travelling fast through lanes created by the mysterious Machinae. No one has communicated with the Machinae in centuries, but Nadia is determined to try, and Gabe and Kaen want to help her. But the three Ambassadors don't know that the Outlast have discovered what they are doing, and have sent assassins to track them down.

As Nadia heads deeper into space to find the Machinae, Gabe and Kaen return to Earth, where Gabe is trying to find another type of alien—his father, who was deported to Mexico, and who Gabe is desperate to bring home. From a detention center in the center of the Arizona desert to the Embassy in the center of the galaxy, the three Ambassadors race against time to save their worlds in this exciting, funny, mind-bending adventure." Publisher's Note
"'Alexander is clearly passionate about science, space exploration, and social justice, but he never allows that passion to shortchange the crackerjack adventure." Kirkus

Allen, Crystal
Spirit week showdown; Crystal Allen. Balzer + Bray 2016 240 p. illustrations (hardback) $16.99
Grades: 4 5 6   **Fic**
1. School stories 2. Female friendship -- Fiction 3. Schools -- Fiction 4. Promises -- Fiction 5. Friendship -- Fiction
ISBN 9780062342331

LC 2015015384

"Nine-year-old Mya Tibbs is boot-scootin' excited for . . . SPIRIT WEEK! She and her megapopular best friend, Naomi Jackson, even made a pinky promise to be Spirit Week partners so they can win the big prize. . . . But when the partner picking goes horribly wrong, Mya gets paired with Mean Connie Tate—the biggest bully in school. And she can't get out of it." (Publisher's note)

Allison, Jennifer
★ **Gilda** Joyce, psychic investigator. Sleuth/Dutton 2005 321p pa $6.99; $13.99
Grades: 5 6 7 8   **Fic**
1. Mystery fiction 2. Cousins -- Fiction
ISBN 0-14-240698-8 pa; 0-525-47375-0; 978-0-14-240698-4 pa; 978-0-525-47375-6

LC 2004-10834

During the summer before ninth grade, intrepid Gilda Joyce invites herself to the San Francisco mansion of distant cousin Lester Splinter and his thirteen-year-old daughter, where she uses her purported psychic abilities and detective skills to solve the mystery of the mansion's boarded-up tower.
"Allison pulls off something special here. She not only offers a credible mystery . . . but also . . . provides particularly strong characterizations." Booklist
Other titles about Gilda Joyce are:
Gilda Joyce: the Ladies of the Lake (2006)
Gilda Joyce: the ghost sonata (2007)
Gilda Joyce: the dead drop (2009)
Gilda Joyce: the bones of the holy (2011)

Almond, David

The **boy** who climbed into the moon; illustrated by Polly Dunbar. Candlewick Press 2010 117p il $15.99

Grades: 3 4 5 **Fic**

1. Adventure fiction 2. Moon -- Fiction 3. Great Britain -- Fiction

ISBN 978-0-7636-4217-4; 0-7636-4217-7

LC 2009-11158

Helped by a very long ladder, some unusual acquaintances, two rather worried parents, and a great deal of community spirit, a young English boy makes an astonishing discovery when he embarks on a mission to prove that the moon is nothing but a big hole in the sky

"Almond employs all manners of amusements . . . while never losing sight of some refreshing realities: Paul's parents are a real presence, and the city feels appropriately dense. . . . Dunbar's full-color illustrations . . . nimbly dodge the prose." Booklist

The **Boy** who swam with piranhas; David Almond, illustrated by Oliver Jeffers. Candlewick Press 2013 256 p. $15.99

Grades: 4 5 6 7 **Fic**

1. Orphans -- Fiction 2. Carnivals -- Fiction 3. Runaway children -- Fiction

ISBN 0763661694; 9780763661694

LC 2012947721

"Stanley Potts's uncle Ernie has developed an over-the-top fascination with canning fish in the house, and life at 69 Fish Quay Lane has turned barmy. But there's darkness in the madness, and when Uncle Ernie's obsession takes an unexpectedly cruel turn, Stan has no choice but to leave. As he journeys away from the life he's always known, he mingles with a carnival full of eccentric characters and meets the legendary Pancho Pirelli, the man who swims in a tank full of perilous piranhas." (Publisher's note)

"After his parents' deaths, Stanley Potts runs away with a carnival. He meets Pancho Pirelli, who performs the death-defying act of swimming with piranhas. Pirelli takes Stan under his wing, grooming him to become his sidekick and successor. Almond offers up some lighthearted fare, complete with old-fashioned intrusive narrator and numerous spot illustrations. The silliness is tempered by unsentimental, clear-eyed wisdom." Horn Book

Heaven Eyes. Delacorte Press 2001 233p hardcover o.p. pa $5.50

Grades: 5 6 7 8 **Fic**

1. Adventure fiction 2. Orphans 3. Orphans -- Fiction 4. Adventure and adventurers

ISBN 0-385-32770-6; 0-440-22910-3 pa

LC 00-31798

First published 2000 in the United Kingdom

Having escaped from their orphanage on a raft, Erin, January, and Mouse float down into another world of abandoned warehouses and factories, meeting a strange old man and an even stranger girl with webbed fingers and toes named Heaven Eyes. "Intermediate, middle school." (Horn Book)

"The ambiguous and surreal setting and the lyricism of the metaphor-laden prose make this a compelling and original novel." SLJ

Mouse bird snake wolf; David Almond, illustrated by David McKean. Candlewick Press 2013 80 p. (reinforced) $17.99

Grades: 4 5 6 7 **Fic**

1. Animals -- Fiction 2. Fantasy fiction -- Fiction

ISBN 0763659126; 9780763659127

LC 2012950556

In this book, "Harry, Sue, and Little Ben live in a world whose lazy gods have made creatures like whales and camels but have given up their work, leaving blank spaces . . . . The children discover that they can create animals themselves, using sticks, leaves, and clay; Little Ben makes a mouse; Sue, a bird; and Harry, a snake. But Harry and Sue aren't satisfied. They create a terrifying wolf that turns on them and eats them, and Little Ben must summon the courage to save them." (Publishers Weekly

My dad's a birdman; illustrated by Polly Dunbar. Candlewick Press 2008 115p il $15.99

Grades: 4 5 6 **Fic**

1. Flight -- Fiction 2. Fathers -- Fiction

ISBN 978-0-7636-3667-8; 0-7636-3667-3

In a rainy town in the north of England, there are strange goings-on Dad is building a pair of wings, eating flies, and feathering his nest Lizzie is missing her Mom and looking after Dad by letting him follow his newfound whimsy. What's behind it all? It's the great human bird competition.

"Handsomely produced, the book is printed in varying size typeface and enhanced by Dunbar's pencil, watercolor, and collage illustration interspersed throughout the text. Casual yet evocative, they perfectly interpret Almond's broadly sketched characters. A fine read-aloud." SLJ

★ **My** name is Mina. Delacorte Press 2011 300p $15.99; lib bdg $18.99

Grades: 5 6 7 8 **Fic**

1. Authorship -- Fiction

ISBN 978-0-385-74073-9; 0-385-74073-5; 978-0-375-98964-3 lib bdg; 0-375-98964-1 lib bdg; 978-0-375-98965-0 e-book

LC 201004014.

"This intimate prequel to Skellig is built around Mina McKee, the curious and brilliant home-schooled child who eventually befriends that book's protagonist, Michael. Mina, a budding writer, reveals her love o words in her journal; most of the book unfolds in a handwritten-looking font, with Mina's more emphatic entries exploding onto the pages i massive display type. Her lyrical, nonlinear prose records her reflections on her past, existential musings . . . and self-directed writing exercises. . . Almond gives readers a vivid picture of the joyfully freeform working of Mina's mind and her mixed emotions about being an isolated child Her gradual emergence from the protective shell of home is beautifully portrayed. . . . This novel will inspire children to let their imaginations soar." Publ Wkly

★ **Skellig**; 10th anniversary ed.; Delacorte Press 2009 182 $16.99; pa $6.99

Grades: 5 6 7 8 9 10 **Fic**

1. Fantasy fiction 2. Young adult literature

ISBN 978-0-385-32653-7; 0-385-32653-X; 978-0-440-41602-9 pa; 0-440-41602-7 pa

First published 1998 in the United Kingdom; first United State edition 1999

Michael L. Printz Award honor book

Unhappy about his baby sister's illness and the chaos of moving into a dilapidated old house, Michael retreats to the garage and finds a mysterious stranger who is something like a bird and something like an angel

"The plot is beautifully paced and the characters are drawn with graceful, careful hand. . . . A lovingly done, thought-provoking novel. SLJ

Slog's dad; illustrated by Dave McKean. Candlewick Press 201 52p il $15.99

Grades: 5 6 7 8 **Fic**

1. Death -- Fiction 2. Future life -- Fiction 3. Great Britain - Fiction 4. Father-son relationship -- Fiction

ISBN 978-0-7636-4940-1; 0-7636-4940-6

LC 2010-3870

When Slog's father died he promised to return for one last visit in the spring, but when Slog spots a scruffy man on a bench outside the butcher shop and identifies him as his father, his best friend Davie is skeptical.

"This grief-strafed wonder tale is brilliantly matched by some of McKean's most moving artwork yet. Text pages, featuring a voice steeped on Northern English flavor, are counterpoised against wordless illustration sequences that move readers from heaven to earth and back again, beginning with a celestial descent from the sky to a park bench by a man trailing clouds of watercolor glory." Bull Cent Child Books

Alvarez, Julia

★ **How** Tia Lola came to visit/stay. Knopf 2001 147p $15.95; pa $5.50

Grades: 4 5 6 7 **Fic**

1. Aunts -- Fiction 2. Divorce -- Fiction 3. Vermont -- Fiction 4. Dominican Americans -- Fiction

ISBN 0-375-80215-0; 0-440-41870-4 pa

LC 00-62932

Although ten-year-old Miguel is at first embarrassed by his colorful aunt, Tia Lola, when she comes to Vermont from the Dominican Republic to stay with his mother, his sister, and him after his parents' divorce, he learns to love her.

"Readers will enjoy the funny situations, identify with the developing relationships and conflicting feelings of the characters, and will get a spicy taste of Caribbean culture in the bargain." SLJ

Other titles about Tia Lola are:

How Tia Lola learned to teach (2010)

How Tia Lola saved the summer (2011)

How Tia Lola ended up starting over (2011)

★ **Return** to sender. Alfred A. Knopf 2009 325p $16.99; lib bdg $19.99

Grades: 4 5 6 7 **Fic**

1. Vermont -- Fiction 2. Farm life -- Fiction 3. Friendship -- Fiction 4. Migrant labor -- Fiction 5. Illegal aliens -- Fiction

ISBN 978-0-375-85838-3; 0-375-85838-5; 978-0-375-95838-0 lib bdg; 0-375-95838-X lib bdg

LC 2008-23520

Awarded the Belpre Author Medal (2010)

After his family hires migrant Mexican workers to help save their Vermont farm from foreclosure, eleven-year-old Tyler befriends the oldest daughter, but when he discovers they may not be in the country legally, he realizes that real friendship knows no borders.

"Readers will be moved by small moments. . . . A tender, well-constructed book." Publ Wkly

Amato, Mary

Edgar Allan's official crime investigation notebook. Holiday House 2010 140p

Grades: 3 4 5 **Fic**

1. School stories 2. Mystery fiction 3. Poetry -- Fiction 4. Teachers -- Fiction 5. Lost and found possessions -- Fiction

ISBN 0-8234-2271-2; 978-0-8234-2271-5

LC 2010-11604

When someone takes a pet goldfish, then other items from Ms. Herchel's classroom, each time leaving a clue in the form of a poem, student Edgar Allan competes with a classmate to be the first to solve the mystery. "Grades three to five." (Bull Cent Child Books)

"While there is enough of a mystery plot here to satisfy genre fans, this is ultimately a story about friendship, and Amato is particularly adept at developing strong characterizations of a diverse group of kids without delving into stereotypes." Bull Cent Child Books

Snarf attack, underfoodle, and the secret of life; the Riot brothers tell all. by Mary Amato; illustrated by Ethan Long. Holiday House 2004 151p il (The Riot Brothers) $16.95; pa $6.95

Grades: 2 3 4 **Fic**

1. School stories 2. Brothers -- Fiction

ISBN 0-8234-1750-6; 0-8234-2062-0 pa

Orville and Wilbur Riot have no shortage of daily adventures. Sometimes they are undercover detectives. Other times they challenge each other to see who can get the most underwear on his head in exactly thirty seconds.

"Young readers will appreciate the Riot brothers' attempts to make something exciting happen every day. Long's playful cartoon illustrations extend the fun." Booklist

Anaya, Rudolfo A.

The **first** tortilla; a bilingual story. [by] Rudolfo Anaya; illustrated by Amy Cordova; translated into Spanish by Enrique R. Lamadrid. University of New Mexico 2007 un il $16.95

Grades: 2 3 4 **Fic**

1. Mexico -- Fiction 2. Bilingual books -- English-Spanish

ISBN 978-0-8263-4214-0

Guided by a blue hummingbird, Jade brings an offering to the Mountain Spirit who lives near her village in Mexico, and asks if he will send rain to end the drought that threatens the people.

"Anaya has retold a Mexican legend and made it his own with his spiritual prose. . . . Córdova's rich acrylic paintings lend a traditional feel to the setting while maintaining the tale's mystical elements. A beautifully written and illustrated title." SLJ

Andersen, Hans Christian

The **little** match girl; illustrated by Rachel Isadora. Putnam 1987 30p il $16.99

Grades: 3 4 5 **Fic**

ISBN 0-399-21336-8

LC 85-30082

The wares of the poor little match girl illuminate her cold world, bringing some beauty to her brief, tragic life

"Isadora follows Andersen's lead, neither sensationalizing nor apologizing for the tale's potentially sentimental plot. . . . A moving, original picture-book interpretation of the classic tale." Booklist

The **princess** and the pea; illustrated by Dorothée Duntze. North-South Bks. 1985 un il $16.95; pa $7.95

Grades: K 1 2 3 **Fic**

1. Fairy tales

ISBN 1-55858-034-4; 1-55858-381-5 pa

LC 85-7199

A young girl feels a pea through twenty mattresses and twenty featherbeds and proves she is a real princess

"This classic Andersen fairy tale is presented in simple text and with elaborate illustrations. . . . Duntze appears to set the story during the Renaissance, and her illustrations are precise, intricate and detailed." SLJ

Anderson, Jodi Lynn

May Bird among the stars; book two. [by] Jodi Lynn Anderson. 1st ed.; Atheneum Books for Young Readers 2006 260p $16.95

Grades: 5 6 7 8 **Fic**

1. Fantasy fiction

ISBN 978-0-689-86924-2; 0-689-86924-X

LC 2005028832

Sequel to May Bird and The Ever After (2005)

Still trapped in The Ever After, ten-year-old May Bird struggles to decide whether to save the world of her ghostly friends from the evil Bo Cleevil or to return to her West Virginia home.

"Anderson has clearly had a great deal of fun creating a world not so different from our own where spirits go after death, and readers will love her humorous jabs at popular culture." SLJ

Followed by May Bird, warrior princess (2007)

May Bird, warrior princess; book three. [by] Jodi Lynn Anderson. Atheneum Books for Young Readers 2007 244p $16.99

Grades: 5 6 7 8   **Fic**

1. Fantasy fiction

ISBN 0-689-86925-8; 978-0-689-86925-9

LC 2007002944

Three years after her return from the Ever After, May Bird, now thirteen, draws her scattered friends—Pumpkin, Fabbio, Beatrice, and Lucius—out of hiding to take a final stand against Evil Bo Cleevil, as May herself makes ready to live up to the prophecy that placed the fate of the Ever After, and her own world, in her hands.

"The novel . . . will not disappoint fans. A reading of the previous two titles is recommended." SLJ

My diary from the edge of the world; by Jodi Lynn Anderson. Aladdin 2015 432 p. $16.99

Grades: 4 5 6 7   **Fic**

1. Magic -- Fiction 2. Adventure fiction 3. Death -- Fiction 4. Diaries -- Fiction 5. Family life -- Fiction 6. Supernatural -- Fiction 7. Animals, Mythical -- Fiction 8. Automobile travel -- Fiction

ISBN 1442483873; 9781442483873; 9781442483880

LC 2014039910

In this novel by Jodi Lynn Anderson "Gracie Lockwood has lived in Cliffden, Maine, her whole life. She's a typical girl in an atypical world: one where sasquatches helped to win the Civil War, where dragons glide over Route 1 on their way south for the winter . . . and where Dark Clouds come for people when they die. A Cloud comes looking for her little brother Sam. Her parents pack the family into a used Winnebago and set out on an epic search for a safe place that most people say doesn't exist: The Extraordinary World." (Publishers' note)

"An endearing narrator, a beguiling world that accommodates both mermaids and Pixy Stix, and a genuinely moving family story propel this adventure for readers who don't look too hard at the details." Kirkus

Anderson, John David

Minion; John David Anderson. Walden Pond Press, an imprint of HarperCollins 2014 288 p. (hardback) $16.99

Grades: 4 5 6 7   **Fic**

1. Adoption -- Fiction 2. Criminals -- Fiction 3. Superheroes -- Fiction 4. Good and evil -- Fiction 5. Supervillains -- Fiction

ISBN 006213311X; 9780062133113

LC 2013043188

In this book, by John David Anderson, "Michael Morn might be a villain, but he's really not a bad guy. When you live in New Liberty, known across the country as the City without a Super, there are only two kinds of people, after all: those who turn to crime and those who suffer. Michael and his adoptive father spend their days building boxes-special devices with mysterious abilities. . . . But then a Super comes to town, and Michael's world is thrown into disarray." (Publisher's note)

"The author of Sidekicked (2013) continues to scuff up the line between heroism and villainy. Spirited from the orphanage when he was nine, Michael Marion Magdalene Morn (named by the nuns) has spent four years in hiding with kind but closemouthed Professor Edson - an eccentric inventor of small black boxes capable of all sorts of shady exploit...Michael's musing that "sometimes it's just hard to know what's right and what's best and why there even has to be a difference" provides both a specific theme for this outing and an overall one for all of the author's thought-provoking work to date." (Booklist)

Ms. Bixby's Last Day; by John David Anderson. Harpercollins Childrens Books 2016 320 p. $16.99

Grades: 4 5 6 7   **Fic**

1. Teachers -- Fiction

ISBN 006233817X; 9780062338174

LC 2015947628

In this book, by John David Anderson, "Ms. Bixby is . . . the sort of teacher who makes you feel like school is somehow worthwhile. Who recognizes something in you that sometimes you don't even see in yourself. . . . Topher, Brand, and Steve know this better than anyone. And so when Ms. Bixby unexpectedly announces that she won't be able to finish the school year, they come up with a risky plan—more of a quest really—to give Ms. Bixby the last day she deserves." (Publisher's note)

"Through their individual, interwoven narratives, these well-developed characters become the most intriguing elements of the story. A smart, funny, ultimately moving novel." Booklist

★ **Posted;** by John David Anderson. Harpercollins Childrens Books 2017 384 p. $16.99

Grades: 5 6 7 8   **Fic**

1. Bullies -- Fiction 2. Middle schools -- Fiction 3. Written communication -- Fiction

ISBN 006233820X; 9780062338204

This book, by John David Anderson, is "story about bullying, broken friendships, and the failures of communication between kids. . . . When cell phones are banned at Branton Middle School, Frost and his friends Deedee, Wolf, and Bench come up with a new way to communicate: leaving sticky notes for each other all around the school. It catches on, and soon all the kids in school are leaving notes—though for every kind and friendly one, there is a cutting and cruel one as well." (Publisher's note)

★ **Sidekicked**; John David Anderson. Walden Pond Press, an imprint of HarperCollinsPublishers 2013 384 p. (hardback) $16.99

Grades: 4 5 6 7   **Fic**

1. Adolescence -- Fiction 2. Superheroes -- Fiction 3. Humorous stories 4. Ability -- Fiction 5. Schools -- Fiction 6. Identity -- Fiction 7. Middle schools -- Fiction 8. Self-confidence -- Fiction

ISBN 0062133144; 9780062133144

LC 2012025495

In this book, "the main character is a sidekick named Andrew Bean. Like the best superheroes, he's down on his luck, always forgetting his utility belt when he needs it. Andrew is part of a school environmental club, H.E.R.O., that . . . doubles as a training program for sidekicks (motto: 'WE KEEP THE TRASH OFF THE STREETS'). Andrew's mentor is the Titan, an aging hero who'd rather go out drinking than fight crime." (Kirkus Reviews)

Anderson, Laurie Halse, 1961-

★ **Chains**; seeds of America. Simon & Schuster Books for Young Readers 2008 316p $17.99

Grades: 6 7 8 9 10   **Fic**

1. Young adult literature 2. Spies -- Fiction 3. Slavery -- Fiction 4. New York (N.Y.) -- Fiction 5. African Americans -- Fiction 6. United States -- History -- 1775-1783, Revolution -- Fiction

ISBN 1-4169-0585-5; 1-4169-0586-3 pa; 978-1-4169-0585-1; 978-1-4169-0586-8 pa

LC 2007-52139

National Book Award Finalist: Young People's Literature (2008)

After being sold to a cruel couple in New York City, a slave named Isabel spies for the rebels during the Revolutionary War. "Grades seven to ten." (Bull Cent Child Books)

"This gripping novel offers readers a startlingly provocative view of the Revolutionary War. . . . [Anderson's] solidly researched exploration of British and Patriot treatment of slaves during a war for freedom is nuanced and evenhanded, presented in service of a fast-moving, emotionally involving plot." Publ Wkly

Followed by: Forge (2010)

Fever, 1793. Simon & Schuster Bks. for Young Readers 2000 251p $17.99; pa $6.99

Grades: 5 6 7 8 9 **Fic**

1. Young adult literature 2. Epidemics 3. Philadelphia (Pa.) 4. Epidemics -- Fiction 5. Yellow fever -- Fiction 6. Philadelphia (Pa.) -- Fiction 7. Pennsylvania -- History -- 1775-1865 8. Yellow fever -- Pennsylvania -- Philadelphia

ISBN 0689838581; 0689848919 pa; 9780689838583; 9780689848919 pa

LC 00-32238

ALA YALSA Margaret A. Edwards Award (2009)

In 1793 Philadelphia, sixteen-year-old Matilda Cook, separated from her sick mother, learns about perseverance and self-reliance when she is forced to cope with the horrors of a yellow fever epidemic. "Age ten and up." (N Y Times Book Rev)

"A vivid work, rich with well-drawn and believable characters. Unexpected events pepper the top-flight novel that combines accurate historical detail with a spellbinding story line." Voice Youth Advocates

★ **Forge**. Atheneum Books for Young Readers 2010 297p (Seeds of America) $16.99

Grades: 6 7 8 9 10 **Fic**

1. Young adult literature 2. Slavery -- Fiction 3. Soldiers -- Fiction 4. Pennsylvania -- Fiction 5. African Americans -- Fiction 6. United States -- History -- 1775-1783, Revolution -- Fiction

ISBN 978-1-4169-6144-4; 1-4169-6144-5

LC 2010-15971

Sequel to: Chains (2008)

Separated from his friend Isabel after their daring escape from slavery, fifteen-year-old Curzon serves as a free man in the Continental Army at Valley Forge until he and Isabel are thrown together again, as slaves once more.

"Weaving a huge amount of historical detail seamlessly into the story, Anderson creates a vivid setting, believable characters both good and despicable and a clear portrayal of the moral ambiguity of the Revolutionary age. Not only can this sequel stand alone, for many readers it will be one of the best novels they have ever read." Kirkus

Anderson, M. T., 1968-

The **chamber** in the sky. Scholastic Press 2012 282 p. (hardcover) $17.99

Grades: 5 6 7 8 **Fic**

1. American satire 2. Fantasy fiction 3. Human-alien encounters -- Fiction

ISBN 0545334934; 9780545334938

This novel, by National Book Award and Printz Honor winner M. T. Anderson, is book four of "The Norumbegan Quartet" series. "Brian and Gregory have . . . . gone to investigate intergalactic suburban sprawl that was infringing on the Vermont forests, and landed in the empire of New Norumbega inside the huge body of an alien. They've escaped certain death . . . and wreaked small amounts of havoc of their own. And finally, they're going to make sense of all their travels and adventures." (Publisher's note)

The **empire** of gut and bone. Scholastic 2011 324p (The Norumbegan quartet) $17.99

Grades: 5 6 7 8 **Fic**

1. Games -- Fiction 2. Supernatural -- Fiction

ISBN 978-0-545-13884-0; 0-545-13884-1

Sequel to: Suburb beyond the stars (2010)

"Bent on tracking down the elven Norumbegans in order to save Vermont from an invasion of dream-sucking Thusser, Brian, Gregory and the mechanical troll Kalgrash pass through an interdimensional curtain—to find themselves inside an organic alien body. . . . Returning fans will find the unapologetically intellectual looniness uncannily, happily familiar." Kirkus

The **Game** of Sunken Places; [by] M. T. Anderson. Scholastic Press 2004 260p (The Norumbegan quartet) $16.95; pa $5.99

Grades: 5 6 7 8 **Fic**

1. Games -- Fiction 2. Vermont -- Fiction

ISBN 0-439-41660-4; 0-439-41661-2 pa

LC 2003-20055

When two boys stay with an eccentric relative at his mansion in rural Vermont, they discover an old-fashioned board game that draws them into a mysterious adventure.

"Deliciously scary, often funny, and crowned by a pair of deeply satisfying surprises, this tour de force leaves one marveling at Anderson's ability to slip between genres as fluidly as his middle-grade heroes straddle worlds." Booklist

Other titles in this series are:

The suburb beyond the stars (2010)

The empire of gut and bone (2011)

He laughed with his other mouths; M.T. Anderson; illustrations by Kurt Cyrus. First edition Beach Lane Books 2014 304 p. illustrations (Pals in peril) (hardcover) $17.99

Grades: 4 5 6 7 **Fic**

1. Adventure fiction 2. Outer space -- Fiction 3. Humorous stories 4. Extraterrestrial beings -- Fiction 5. Adventure and adventurers -- Fiction

ISBN 1442451106; 9781442451100; 9781442451117

LC 2013034710

"In this action-packed conclusion to the celebrated Pals in Peril series, Jasper Dash soars to unprecedented heights--as in, intergalactic, out-of-this-world dimensions--in order to locate the father he's never known." (Publisher's note)

"The novel doesn't transcend the wacky sci-fi of old that inspired it but rather embraces it and dissects it, celebrating it and exploring why so many people fell in love with these silly worlds and gee-whiz heroes in the first place." Kirkus

The **suburb** beyond the stars. Scholastic Press 2010 223p (The Norumbegan quartet) $17.99

Grades: 5 6 7 8 **Fic**

1. Games -- Fiction 2. Vermont -- Fiction 3. Supernatural -- Fiction

ISBN 978-0-545-13882-6; 0-545-13882-5

LC 2009051836

Sequel to: The Game of Sunken Places (2004)

Friends Brian and Gregory have survived the Game of Sunken Places, but are once again drawn back to cousin Prudence's house in Vermont, where they discover that something has gone very wrong with time, people have disappeared, and danger is lurking everywhere.

"This is a fun and gripping read, with action, suspense, and creepy monsters." SLJ

Followed by: The empire of gut and bone (2011)

★ **Whales** on stilts; illustrations by Kurt Cyrus. Harcourt 2005 188p il (Pals in peril) $15; pa $5.95

Grades: 4 5 6 7 **Fic**

1. Science fiction

ISBN 0-15-205340-9; 0-15-205394-8 pa

LC 2004-17754

Racing against the clock, shy middle-school student Lily and her best friends, Katie and Jasper, must foil the plot of her father's conniving boss to conquer the world using an army of whales.

"A story written with the author's tongue shoved firmly into his cheek. . . . It's full of witty pokes at other series novels and Jasper's nutty inventions." SLJ

Other titles in this series are:

The clue of the linoleum lederhosen (2006)

Jasper Dash and the Flame-pits of Delaware (2009)

Agent Q., or the smell of danger! (2010)

Zombie mommy (2011)

He laughed with his other mouths (2012)

Anderson, R. J.

A **pocket** full of murder; R.J. Anderson. Atheneum Books for Young Readers 2015 352 p. (hardcover) $16.99

Grades: 5 6 7 8 **Fic**

1. Fantasy fiction 2. Mystery fiction 3. Magic -- Fiction 4. Murder -- Fiction 5. Social classes -- Fiction 6. Fantasy 7. Mystery and detective stories

ISBN 1481437712; 9781481437714; 9781481437721

LC 2014040718

In this book, by R.J. Anderson, a "young girl joins forces with an adventure-loving street boy to solve a magical murder mystery. . . . In the spell-powered city of Tarreton, the wealthy have all the magic they desire while the working class can barely afford a simple spell to heat their homes. Twelve-year-old Isaveth is poor, but she¿s also brave, loyal, and zealous in the pursuit of justice -- which is lucky, because her father has just been wrongfully arrested for murder." (Publisher's note)

"An appealing novel for readers who like fast-paced fantasy with a dash of mystery and a political angle. . . . Fantasy readers who also enjoy a bit of mystery will appreciate the story, cast of characters, and layers." SLJ

Angleberger, Tom

Darth Paper strikes back; an Origami Yoda book. Tom Angleberger. Amulet Books 2011 159p il $12.95

Grades: 4 5 6 7 **Fic**

1. School stories 2. Origami -- Fiction 3. Puppets and puppet plays -- Fiction 4. Eccentrics and eccentricities -- Fiction

ISBN 978-1-4197-0027-9; 1-4197-0027-8

LC 2011010388

Harvey, upset when his Darth Paper finger puppet brings humiliation, gets Dwight suspended, but Origami Yoda asks Tommy and Kellan, now in seventh grade, to make a new casefile to persuade the School Board to reinstate Dwight.

This is "a satisfying tale of friendship and just resistance to authority. Pitch-perfect middle-school milieu and enough Star Wars references (and laughs) to satisfy fans and win new ones." Kirkus

Emperor Pickletine rides the bus; Tom Angleberger. Amulet Books 2014 205 p. illustrations (hardback) $13.95

Grades: 4 5 6 7 **Fic**

1. School stories 2. Origami -- Fiction 3. Humorous stories 4. Bus travel -- Fiction 5. Finger puppets -- Fiction 6. Washington (D.C.) -- Fiction 7. School field trips -- Fiction 8. Interpersonal relations -- Fiction 9. Eccentrics and eccentricities -- Fiction

ISBN 141970933X; 9781419709333

LC 2014012574

Origami Yoda

This middle grade novel by Tom Angleberger is "the final Origami Yoda case file from the kids at McQuarrie Middle School! After successfully fighting to save their field trip in 'Princess Labelmaker to the Rescue!,' Tommy and the gang prepare for a well-earned day of fun and adventure in Washington, DC . . . but of course it won't be that easy! This trip to the nation's capital will be full of shifting alliances and betrayals, carsickness and sugar rushes." (Publisher's note)

"The seventh grade of McQuarrie Middle School hits Washington, D.C., in this final installment of the popular Origami Yoda series. Exciting as a field trip is, the Rebel Alliance is reeling because Principal Rabbski has banned origami for the entire trip! . . . Origami Yoda has an earth-shattering revelation or two to impart before the book's end, making for a fitting series conclusion." Booklist

Fake mustache; or, how Jodie O'Rodeo and her wonder horse (and some nerdy guy) saved the U.S. Presidential election from a mad genius criminal mastermind. Tom Angleberger; illustrated by Jen Wang. Amulet Books 2012 196 p. ill. (hardback) $13.95

Grades: 2 3 4 5 6 **Fic**

1. Humorous stories 2. Disguise -- Fiction 3. Criminals -- Fiction 4. Hypnotism -- Fiction 5. Mustaches -- Fiction 6. Politics, Practical -- Fiction

ISBN 1419701940; 9781419701948

LC 2012000556

Edgar Award: Best Juvenile Shortlist (2013)

In this book, "[w]hen twelve-year-old Lenny . . . lends his best friend, Casper, ten dollars to purchase . . . [a] fake mustache at a local gag shop, he has no idea he's just become an accomplice in Casper's plot for world domination. In the days following, a mysterious man with some impressive facial hair . . . steamrolls his way into the governor's seat, takes over the . . . nation's leading manufacturer of voting booths and launches a presidential campaign." (Bulletin of the Center for Children's Books)

Horton Halfpott; or, The fiendish mystery of Smugwick Manor, or, The loosening of M'Lady Luggertuck's corset. Tom Angleberger with illustrations by the author. Amulet Books 2011 206p il $14.95

Grades: 4 5 6 7 **Fic**

1. Mystery fiction 2. Social classes -- Fiction 3. Household employees -- Fiction 4. Eccentrics and eccentricities -- Fiction 5. Great Britain -- History -- 19th century -- Fiction

ISBN 978-0-8109-9715-8; 0-8109-9715-0

LC 2010-38096

Horton, an upstanding kitchen boy in a castle in nineteenth-century England, becomes embroiled in a mystery surrounding a series of thefts "Grades four to six." (Bull Cent Child Books)

"Readers will enjoy Angleberger's . . . penchant for the absurd as well as his many droll asides. . . . The ending satisfies, and with Angleberger's many eclectic characters, his wild-and-witty storytelling, and a lighthearted but perplexing mystery . . . readers are in for a treat." Publ Wkly

Inspector Flytrap; by Tom Angleberger; illustrated by Cece Bell. Amulet Books 2016 112 p. color illustrations (hardcover) $14.95

Grades: 1 2 3 4 **Fic**

1. Goats -- Fiction 2. Plants -- Fiction 3. Mystery fiction -- Fiction 4. Humorous stories 5. Animals -- Fiction 6. Venus's flytrap -- Fiction 7. Mystery and detective stories

ISBN 9781419709487

LC 2015016400

This illustrated chapter-book by Tom Angleberger and illustrated by Cece Bell focuses on "a mystery-solving Venus flytrap. . . . Celebrating the disabled yet enabled, the character of Inspector Flytrap is wheeled everywhere (on a skateboard, of course) by his goat sidekick as this mystery-solving duo works on cases such as 'The Big Deal Mystery of the Stinky Cookies' and 'The Big Deal Mystery of the Missing Rose.'" (Publisher's note)

"Abundant punning and absurdity, Bell's equally raucous cartoon-ing, and the trail of destruction that Nina and the inspector leave in their wake make this series opener a 'big deal' winner. " Pub Wkly

Another title in this series is:

The President's Mane is Missing (2016)

Inspector Flytrap in The Goat Who Chewed Too Much (2017)

Inspector Flytrap in The goat who chewed too much; by Tom An-gleberger; illustrated by Cece Bell. Amulet Books 2017 100 p. color illustrations (Inspector Flytrap) (hardback) $14.95; (ebook) $5.95
Grades: 1 2 3 4 **Fic**
1. Goats -- Fiction 2. Humorous stories 3. Animals -- Fiction 4. Venus's flytrap -- Fiction 5. Mystery and detective stories
ISBN 1419709569; 9781419709562; 9781613120170
LC 2016032056

In this children's book, by Tom Angleberger, illustrated by Cece Bell, "when his goat assistant is arrested for stealing the golden pickle paperweight, a mystery-solving Venus flytrap is determined to find the real thief." (Publisher's note)

"The relationship between the animated inspector and the deadpan, ever-nibbling Nina develops in touching ways, and many familiar char-acters return to enrich this witty, wacky romp of a mystery." Booklist

Princess Labelmaker to the rescue! an Origami Yoda book. by Tom Angleberger. Harry N. Abrams Inc. 2014 208 p. $13.95
Grades: 4 5 6 7 **Fic**
1. School stories 2. Star Wars films 3. Origami -- Fiction 4. Schools -- Fiction 5. Finger puppets -- Fiction 6. Interpersonal relations -- Fiction 7. Eccentrics and eccentricities -- Fiction
ISBN 1419710524; 9781419710520
LC 2013047291

In this book, part of the Origami Yoda series, by Tom Angleberger, "At McQuarrie Middle School, the war against the FunTime Menace--aka test prep--wages on. . . . To defeat the Dark Standardized Testing forces they're going to need an even bigger, even more surprising ally: Principal Rabbski. But with great forces--aka the school board--pushing her from above, will the gang's former enemy don a finger puppet and join the Rebellion--or will her transformation to Empress Rabbski, Dark Lord of the Sith, be complete?" (Publisher's note)

"The FunTime Menace (a deadly boring test prep program) is still wreaking havoc at McQuarrie Middle School in the sixth book in the se-ries. The only way to abolish FunTime is to get Principal Rabbski on the side of the Rebellion, but the Origami Rebel Alliance will have to risk everything to win her over. Angleberger continues to develop authentic and engaging voices in these "case files."" Horn Book

Other titles include:

The surprise attack of Jabba the Puppett

Darth Paper strikes back

The strange case of Origami Yoda

Emperor Pickletine rides the bus

The secret of the Fortune Wookiee

Rocket and Groot; Stranded on Planet Stripmall! Tom Angleberg-er. Disney Press 2016 224 p. chiefly color illustrations $13.99
Grades: 5 6 7 8 **Fic**
1. Superheroes -- Fiction 2. Shopping centers and malls -- Fiction
ISBN 1484714520; 9781484714522

In this children's novel, by Tom Angleberger, "after battling deadly space piranhas in Sector 7 of the Cosmos, Rocket and Groot crash-land on a planet made up of strip malls, maniacal robots bent on customer service, and killer toilets. Told through the eyes of Rocket, the 'Adven-tures of Rocket and Groo't will feature simple black-and-white drawing

throughout . . . while Veronica, their space recording companion, lays out the adventure in text!" (Publisher's note)

The **secret** of the Fortune Wookiee; an Origami Yoda book. Tom Angleberger. Amulet Books 2012 190 p. ill. (hardcover) $12.95
Grades: 4 5 6 **Fic**
1. Middle schools -- Fiction 2. Origami -- Fiction 3. Schools -- Fiction 4. Finger puppets -- Fiction 5. Interpersonal relations -- Fiction 6. Eccentrics and eccentricities -- Fiction
ISBN 1419703927; 9781419703928
LC 2012010027

In this book by Tom Angleberger "the kids of McQuarrie Middle School are on their own -- no Origami Yoda to give advice and help them navigate the treacherous waters of middle school. Then Sara gets a gift. . . . It's a Fortune Wookiee, and it seems to give advice that's just as good as Yoda's . . . In the meantime, Dwight is fitting in a little too well at Tip-pett [Academy]. . . . It's up to his old friends . . . to remind their kooky friend that it's in his weirdness that his greatness lies." (Publisher's note)

The **strange** case of Origami Yoda; Tom Angleberger. Amulet Books 2010 141p il $12.95
Grades: 4 5 6 7 **Fic**
1. School stories 2. Origami -- Fiction 3. Puppets and puppet plays -- Fiction
ISBN 978-0-8109-8425-7; 0-8109-8425-3
LC 2009-39748

Tommy and his friends describe their experiences with a paper pup-pet of Yoda, made by their sixth-grade classmate Dwight, as they try to decide whether or not the puppet can really predict the future. "Grades four to seven." (Bull Cent Child Books)

"The situations that Yoda has a hand in are pretty authentic, and the setting is broad enough to be any school. The plot is age-old but with the twist of being presented on crumpled pages with cartoon sketches, supposed hand printing, and varying typefaces. Kids should love it." SLJ

The **surprise** attack of Jabba the Puppett; an Origami Yoda book. by Tom Angleberger. Harry N. Abrams 2013 224 p. $12.95
Grades: 4 5 6 **Fic**
1. Middle schools -- Fiction 2. Educational tests and measurements 3. Puppets and puppet plays -- Fiction 4. Origami -- Fiction 5. Schools -- Fiction 6. Finger puppets -- Fiction 7. Interpersonal relations -- Fiction 8. Eccentrics and eccentricities -- Fiction
ISBN 1419708589; 9781419708589
LC 2013020765

In this book by Tom Angleberger "dark times have fallen on Mc-Quarrie Middle School. Dwight's back . . . as the gang faces the FunTime Menace: a new educational program. When Principal Rabbski cancels the students' field trip . . . to make time for FunTime, the students turn to Origami Yoda for help. United, can they defeat the FunTime Menace and . . . a surprise attack from Jabba the Puppett?" (Publisher's note)

Angus, Jennifer

In search of Goliathus hercules; by Jennifer Angus. Albert Whit-man 2012 350 p. (hardcover) $17.99
Grades: 3 4 5 6 7 **Fic**
1. Fantasy fiction 2. Insects -- Fiction 3. Human-animal communication -- Fiction 4. Metamorphosis -- Fiction
ISBN 0807529907; 9780807529904
LC 2011037135

In this novel, by Jennifer Angus, "Henri Bell, . . . in 1890 . . . strikes up a conversation with a friendly fly on the windowsill and discovers he possesses the astounding ability to speak with insects. Thus commences an epic journey for Henri as he manages a flea circus, commands an army of beetles, and ultimately sets out to British Malaya to find the mythical giant insect known as Goliathus Hercules." (Publisher's note)

Appelfeld, Aharon

★ **Adam** and Thomas; by Aharon Appelfeld; translated from Hebrew by Jeffrey Green; illustrated by Philippe Dumas. Seven Stories Press 2015 160 p. color illustrations (hardback) $18.95

Grades: 4 5 6 7 8   **Fic**

1. Jews -- Fiction 2. Survival skills -- Fiction 3. Holocaust, 1939-1945 -- Fiction 4. World War, 1939-1945 -- Fiction 5. Refugees -- Fiction 6. Survival -- Fiction 7. Holocaust, Jewish (1939-1945) -- Fiction 8. World War, 1939-1945 -- Fiction

ISBN 1609806344; 9781609806347

LC 2015010371

Mildred L. Batchelder Honor Book (2016)

This book, by Aharon Appelfeld, "is the story of two nine-year-old Jewish boys who survive World War II by banding together in the forest. They are alone, visited only furtively, every few days by Mina, a mercurial girl who herself has found refuge from the war by living with a peasant family. She makes secret journeys and brings the boys parcels of food at her own risk." (Publisher's note)

"Translated from the original Hebrew text and accompanied by Dumas' moving illustrations, the story is one of quiet perseverance and growing friendship between two very different boys experiencing the world together in a horrific time and place." Booklist

Appelt, Kathi, 1954-

★ **Keeper**; illustrations by August Hall. Atheneum Books for Young Readers 2010 399p il $16.99

Grades: 5 6 7 8   **Fic**

1. Ocean -- Fiction 2. Sailing -- Fiction 3. Mermaids and mermen -- Fiction 4. Mother-daughter relationship -- Fiction

ISBN 978-1-4169-5060-8; 1-4169-5060-5

LC 2010000795

On the night of the blue moon when mermaids are said to gather on a sandbar in the Gulf of Mexico, ten-year-old Keeper sets out in a small boat, with her dog BD and a seagull named Captain, determined to find her mother, a mermaid, as Keeper has always believed, who left long ago to return to the sea.

"Deftly spinning together mermaid lore, local legend and natural history, this stunning tale proves 'every landscape has its magical beings,' and the most unlikely ones can form a perfect family. Hall's black-and-white illustrations lend perspective and immediacy. Beautiful and evocative—an absolute 'keeper.'" Kirkus

Maybe a Fox; Kathi Appelt and Alison McGhee. Simon & Schuster 2016 272 p. (hardback) $16.99

Grades: 4 5 6 7 8   **Fic**

1. Foxes -- Fiction 2. Grief -- Fiction

ISBN 9781442482432; 9781442482425; 1442482427

LC 2015033463

In this juvenile novel, by Kathi Appelt and Alison McGhee, "a fox kit born with a deep spiritual connection to a rural Vermont legend has a special bond with 11-year-old Jules. . . . In the opening chapters, impulsive Sylvie makes a dash to throw a wishing rock into the Slip, . . . it is Jules who discovers that Sylvie tripped on a tree root, sliding in March snow to her death. Meanwhile, Jules' kind friend Sam . . . and aches for his war-veteran brother, who mourns Zeke, who didn't return from Afghanistan." (Kirkus Reviews)

"A good cry can be cathartic, and this book about nourishing one's soul during times of great sadness does the trick." Horn Book

★ The **true** blue scouts of Sugarman Swamp; by Kathi Appelt 1st ed. Atheneum Books for Young Readers 2013 336 p. (hardcover) $16.99

Grades: 5 6 7 8   **Fic**

1. Swamps -- Fiction 2. Raccoons -- Fiction 3. Humorous stories 4. Swamp animals -- Fiction 5. Land developers -- Fiction 6. Scouting (Youth activity) -- Fiction

ISBN 1442421053; 9781442421059; 9781442481213

LC 2012023723

National Book Award Finalist: Young People's Literature (2013)

This book is "told from the perspectives of animals and humans. . . .The main concern of Bingo and Jeremiah, two raccoon Swamp Scouts is the approaching brood of feral hogs, which could destroy the precious canebrake sugar used to make fried pies at the local Paradise Pies cafe. Meanwhile, 12-year-old Chap Brayburn, the cafe proprietor's son is worried about rich, horrible Sonny Boy Beaucoup, who wants to turn the swamp into the 'Gator World Wrestling Arena and Theme Park.'" (Publishers Weekly)

★ The **underneath**; illustrated by David Small. Atheneum Books for Young Readers 2008 313p il $16.99; pa $7.99

Grades: 3 4 5 6   **Fic**

1. Cats -- Fiction 2. Dogs -- Fiction

ISBN 978-1-4169-5058-5; 1-4169-5058-3; 978-1-4169-5059-2 pa; 1-4169-5059-1 pa

LC 2007031969

National Book Award Finalist: Young People's Literature (2008)

A Newbery Medal honor book, 2009

An abandoned "calico cat, about to have kittens, hears the lonely howl of [Ranger], a chained-up hound deep in the backwaters of the bayou. . . . Ranger urges the cat to hide underneath the porch, to raise her kittens there because Gar-Face, the man living inside the house, will surely use them as alligator bait should he find them." (Publisher's note) "Intemediate." (Horn Book)

"Well realized in Small's excellent full-page drawings, this fine book is most of all distinguished by the originality of the story and the fresh beauty of its author's voice." Horn Book

Applegate, Katherine

★ **Crenshaw**; Katherine Applegate. Feiwel & Friends 2015 256 p. $16.99

Grades: 3 4 5 6   **Fic**

1. Imaginary playmates 2. Cats -- Fiction 3. Magic -- Fiction

ISBN 1250043239; 9781250043238

LC 2015017957

In this children's book by Katherine Applegate "Jackson and his family have fallen on hard times. There's no more money for rent. And not much for food, either. His parents, his little sister, and their dog may have to live in their minivan. Crenshaw is a cat. He's large, he's outspoken, and he's imaginary. He has come back into Jackson's life to help him. But is an imaginary friend enough to save this family from losing everything?" (Publisher's note)

"Though the story is weighty, it is a quick read that encourages people of all ages to be honest with one another and value family and friends (real and imaginary!)." Booklist

Home of the brave. Feiwel & Friends 2007 249p $16.95

Grades: 5 6 7 8   **Fic**

1. Novels in verse 2. Cattle -- Fiction 3. Africans -- Fiction 4. Refugees -- Fiction 5. Minnesota -- Fiction 6. Immigrants -- Fiction

ISBN 0-312-36765-1; 978-0-312-36765-7

LC 2006-3205

Kek, an African refugee, is confronted by many strange things at the Minneapolis home of his aunt and cousin, as well as in his fifth grad classroom, and longs for his missing mother, but finds comfort in the company of a cow and her owner.

"This beautiful story of hope and resilience is written in free verse." Voice Youth Advocates

★ The **one** and only Ivan; illustrated by Patricia Castelao. Harper 2012 il $16.99

Grades: 3 4 5 6   **Fic**

1. Gorillas -- Fiction 2. Elephants -- Fiction 3. Animal welfare -- Fiction

ISBN 978-0-06-199225-4; 0-06-199225-9

LC 2011010034

John Newbery Medal (2013)

When Ivan, a gorilla who has lived for years in a down-and-out circus-themed mall, meets Ruby, a baby elephant that has been added to the mall, he decides that he must find her a better life.

"Ivan narrates his tale in short, image-rich sentences and acute, sometimes humorous, observations that are all the more heartbreaking for their simple delivery. . . . Spot art captures poignant moments throughout. Utterly believable, this bittersweet story, complete with an author's note identifying the real Ivan, will inspire a new generation of advocates." Kirkus

Arbuthnott, Gill

The **Keepers'** tattoo. Chicken House 2010 425p $17.99

Grades: 6 7 8 9   **Fic**

1. Fantasy fiction 2. Young adult literature 3. Dreams -- Fiction 4. Uncles -- Fiction 5. Tattooing -- Fiction 6. Identity (Psychology) -- Fiction

ISBN 978-0-545-17166-3; 0-545-17166-0

LC 2009-26327

Months before her fifteenth birthday, Nyssa learns that she is a special member of a legendary clan, the Keepers of Knowledge, as she and her uncle try to escape from Alaric, the White Wolf, who wants to use lines tattooed on her to destroy the rest of her people.

Arbuthnott "writes with restraint and thoughtfulness, never condescending to her readers. Nyssa is a convincing mixture of ignorance, courage, and resourcefulness." Publ Wkly

Armstrong, Alan

Looking for Marco Polo; illustrated by Tim Jessell. Random House 2009 286p $16.99

Grades: 4 5 6 7   **Fic**

1. Travelers 2. Travel writers 3. Venice (Italy) -- Fiction 4. Missing persons -- Fiction

ISBN 978-0-375-83321-2; 0-375-83321-8

When they lose touch with his father's Gobi Desert expedition, eleven-year-old Mark accompanies his mother to Venice, Italy, and there, while waiting for news of his father, learns about the legendary Marco Polo and his adventures in the Far East.

"Armstrong ably conjures up the atmosphere of damp, foggy Venice in late December while blowing some dust off of the accounts of Marco Polo's travels with his lively storytelling. . . . Whether or not readers know the specifics of Marco Polo's voyages, they will enjoy this entertaining blend of contemporary and historical adventure." Booklist

Racing the moon; by Alan Armstrong; illustrated by Tim Jessell. Random House 2012 214 p. (hc : alk. paper) $16.99

Grades: 5 6 7 8   **Fic**

1. Adventure fiction 2. Historical fiction 3. Siblings -- Fiction 4. Aeronautics -- Fiction 5. Space flight -- Fiction 6. Brothers and sisters -- Fiction 7. Rockets (Aeronautics) -- Fiction 8. Adventure

and adventurers -- Fiction

ISBN 037585889X; 9780375858895; 9780375858901; 9780375893094

LC 2012016261

In this children's book by Alan Armstrong "Twelve-year-old Alex hangs out with her reckless 17-year-old brother Chuck, who's always getting them in trouble. . . . Alex wants to be another Amelia Earhart [and][m]eeting her new neighbor, Captain Ebbs, Alex finds a mentor. . . . She arranges for Alex to meet pioneer rocket scientist Wernher von Braun, organizes a sailing trip to a Chesapeake Bay island near a rocket launch and provides needed direction for the risk-taking duo." (Kirkus)

Raleigh's page; illustrated by Tim Jessell. Random House 2007 328p il $16.99; lib bdg $19.99

Grades: 4 5 6 7   **Fic**

1. Poets 2. Authors 3. Explorers 4. Historians 5. Adventure fiction 6. Courtiers 7. Travel writers 8. Virginia -- Fiction 9. Native Americans -- Fiction 10. Great Britain -- History -- 1485-1603, Tudors -- Fiction

ISBN 978-0-375-83319-9; 978-0-375-93319-6 lib bdg

LC 2006-08434

In the late 16th century, fifteen-year-old Andrew leaves school in England and must prove himself as a page to Sir Walter Raleigh before embarking for Virginia, where he helps to establish relations with the Indians.

Armstrong "weaves a richly detailed historical narrative. . . . Historical figures such as Raleigh, Thomas Harriot, and Manteo mix with fictional characters in an adventure that makes for compelling reading. Illustrated with expressive pencil drawings." Booklist

★ **Whittington**; illustrated by S. D. Schindler. Random House 2005 191p il $14.95; lib bdg $16.99; pa $6.50

Grades: 4 5 6   **Fic**

1. Cats -- Fiction 2. Domestic animals -- Fiction

ISBN 0-375-82864-8; 0-375-92864-2 lib bdg; 0-375-82865-6 pa

LC 2004-05789

A Newbery Medal honor book, 2006

"A battered cat who calls himself Whittington takes up residence in a shabby barn already inhabited by a variety of scruffy livestock, owned by Bernie. . . . Bernie offers refuge not only to his animals but also to his parentless grandchildren, Abby and Ben, who carry burdens of their own. The children [can] communicate . . . with the animals, so Abby and Ben join the audience when Whittington the cat retells the story of Dick Whittington and his cat." (Bull Cent Child Books) "Intermediate, middle school." (Horn Book)

"The story works beautifully, both as historical fiction about medieval street life and commerce and as a witty, engaging tale of barnyard camaraderie and survival." Booklist

Armstrong, William Howard

★ **Sounder**; [by] William H. Armstrong; illustrations by James Barkley. Harper & Row 1969 116p il $15.99; pa $5.99

Grades: 5 6 7 8   **Fic**

1. Young adult literature 2. Dogs -- Fiction 3. Family life -- Fiction 4. African Americans -- Fiction

ISBN 0-06-020143-6; 0-06-440020-4 pa

Awarded the Newbery Medal, 1970

"Set in the South in the era of sharecropping and segregation, this succinctly told tale poignantly describes the courage of a father who steals a ham in order to feed his undernourished family; the determination of the eldest son, who searches for his father despite the apathy of prison authorities; and the devotion of a coon dog named Sounder." Shapiro. Fic for Youth. 3d edition

Arnold, Elana K.

A **boy** called bat; Elana K. Arnold; illustrated by Charles Santoso; edited by Jordan Brown. Walden Pond Press 2017 208 p. illustrations (hardcover) $16.99; (ebook) $15.99

Grades: 2 3 4 5 **Fic**

1. Skunks -- Fiction 2. Veterinarians -- Fiction 3. Autistic children -- Fiction

ISBN 9780062445827; 9780062445841

LC 2016932066

In this book, by Elana K. Arnold, illustrated by Charles Santoso, and edited by Jordan Brown, "Bixby Alexander Tam, or Bat, has autism. . . . [One day,] his mother, a vet, . . . tells him about the baby skunk she has brought home. The mother skunk did not survive a car accident, but Bat's mom was able to save the kit, and they will raise him at home for a month. . . . Bat tries to find a way to convince his mother to keep the kit as a pet." (Publisher's note)

"The challenges faced by kids like Bat are often underrepresented in children's literature; this is a refreshing depiction. Readers will appreciate this funny and thoughtful novel." SLJ

Far from fair; Elana K. Arnold. Houghton Mifflin Harcourt 2016 240 p. (hardcover) $16.99

Grades: 5 6 7 **Fic**

1. Dogs -- Fiction 2. Anger -- Fiction 3. Family life -- Fiction 4. Family problems -- Fiction 5. Moving, Household -- Fiction 6. Recreational vehicles -- Fiction

ISBN 9780544602274

LC 2015013893

In this children's novel, by Elana K. Arnold, "Odette Zyskoski's life is being ruined by her parents' decision to sell their house and head north in an RV they've dubbed the Coach. . . . By using a third-person narration that keeps Odette at a slight remove from her family, Arnold captures the loneliness of a young teenager's inability to express the emotions that accompany life's upheavals." (Kirkus Reviews)

Arnold "deals with the many bumps in the road honestly, yet maintains an onward-and-upward outlook on life." Booklist

The **question** of miracles; by Elana K. Arnold. Houghton Mifflin Harcourt 2015 240 p. (hardback) $16.99

Grades: 4 5 6 7 **Fic**

1. Miracles -- Fiction 2. Friendship -- Fiction 3. Grief -- Fiction 4. Corvallis (Or.) -- Fiction 5. Moving, Household -- Fiction

ISBN 0544334647; 9780544334649

LC 2014000738

In this novel by Elana K. Arnold "Iris is starting sixth grade in a new school in Oregon-new house, new people, new life. Her parents want to distract her from the recent death of her best friend in California. . . . She turns away from potential friends, seeking instead someone she can barely tolerate--so that she must only endure minimal interaction. His name is Boris, and while he is obviously an outcast, Iris prefers to be on the outskirts." (School Library Journal)

"Sixth-grader Iris hates her new home in rainy Corvallis, Oregon. The move from Southern California was ostensibly because of her mother's new job...She asks the questions that many children would ask in this circumstance, and the book puts a smart circle of caring adults to help her find answers. But it is her realistic relationship with the matter-of-fact Boris, a most unlikely miracle, that will catch readers and help pull them toward seeking answers of their own for the story's very large questions." Booklist

Arnosky, Jim

The **pirates** of Crocodile Swamp. G. P. Putnam's Sons 2009 230p il $15.99

Grades: 3 4 5 6 **Fic**

1. Adventure fiction 2. Florida -- Fiction 3. Brothers -- Fiction 4. Wetlands -- Fiction 5. Runaway children -- Fiction

ISBN 978-0-399-25068-2; 0-399-25068-9

Kidnapped by their father, two boys escape into the mangrove swamps of Key Largo, Florida, where they learn to live on their own among the wildlife.

This "is an exciting story, with plenty of Arnosky's trademark insight into the delights and dangers of the natural (and human) world. The prose is direct and gripping, the characterization strong, and the story includes just enough of the author's illustrations to enrich the fast-moving tale." SLJ

Arnston, Steven

★ The **Wikkeling**; illustrated by Daniela Jaglenka Terrazzini. Running Press Kids 2011 256p il $18

Grades: 4 5 6 **Fic**

1. Science fiction

ISBN 978-0-7624-3903-4; 0-7624-3903-3

"In Henrietta's world, every part of life is monitored and regulated by computers. House cats are considered wild and dangerous animals. Old houses and old books can make children sick. The girl's orderly and safe life is disrupted the day she discovers a secret attic above her bedroom. . . . Soon after this discovery, she starts seeing the Wikkeling, a menacing yellow creature that gives children headaches with the touch of a finger. . . . Arntson has created a detailed and fascinating dystopian world that seems eerily similar to our own, and Terrazzini's illustrations strike just the right note." SLJ

Aronson, Sarah

Beyond lucky. Dial Books for Young Readers 2011 250p $16.99

Grades: 4 5 6 7 **Fic**

1. Mystery fiction 2. Chance -- Fiction 3. Soccer -- Fiction 4. Brothers -- Fiction

ISBN 978-0-8037-3520-0; 0-8037-3520-0

LC 2010-28800

Twelve-year-old Ari Fish is sure that the rare trading card he found has changed his luck and that of his soccer team, but after the card is stolen he comes to know that we make our own luck, and that heroes can be fallible.

"Aronson skillfully dodges the predictability of sports-themed books by creating multilayered characters and an intriguing whodunit. . . . Aronson . . . includes a lot of fun on-field action, but the off-field story is just as interesting. . . . Aronson's graceful storytelling will keep even nonsoccer buffs turning pages." Publ Wkly

Asch, Frank

Gravity buster; journal #2 of a cardboard genius. Kids Can Press 2007 143p il $14.95; pa $5.95

Grades: 3 4 5 **Fic**

1. Brothers -- Fiction 2. Inventors -- Fiction 3. Space vehicles -- Fiction

ISBN 978-1-55453-068-7; 1-55453-068-7; 978-1-55453-069-4 pa; 1-55453-069-5 pa

Followed by Time twister (2008)

"The young inventor featured in Star Jumper (Kids Can, 2006) returns in a second novel full of amazing contraptions and humorous escapades. This time, the self-proclaimed 'Boy Supergenius' perfects his spaceship and develops several other handy gadgets along the way. . . . Numerous black-and-white drawings contribute to the premise that the book is a scientist's journal and also match the text's whimsical tone. The combination of imaginative science and family humor should have strong appeal to children." SLJ

Star jumper; journal of a cardboard genius. Kids Can Press 2006 128p $14.95; pa $5.95

Grades: 3 4 5   **Fic**

1. Brothers -- Fiction 2. Inventors -- Fiction 3. Space vehicles -- Fiction

ISBN 978-1-55337-886-0; 1-55337-886-5; 978-1-55337-887-7 pa; 1-55337-887-3 pa

"Using his astounding scientific ability . . . Alex designs the Star Jumper. This advanced cardboard spacecraft will take him across the galaxy to a brother-free planet—if only he can keep the first grader out of the way until liftoff. The first-person narration is lively and realistic." SLJ

Other titles about Alex and his brother are:

Gravity buster (2007)

Time twister (2008)

Time twister; journal #3 of a cardboard genius. by Frank Asch. Kids Can Press 2008 144p il $14.95; pa $5.95

Grades: 3 4 5   **Fic**

1. Brothers -- Fiction 2. Inventors -- Fiction 3. Space flight -- Fiction 4. Space and time -- Fiction

ISBN 978-1-55453-230-8; 1-55453-230-2; 978-155453-231-5 pa; 1-55453-231-0 pa

Alex's "intergalactic spaceship, Star Jumper, is ready for deep space travel, but his copilot Zoe Breen finds a glitch: when Star Jumper returns from her voyage, more than fifty years will have passed on earth! It's time for Alex to invent a time machine." Publisher's note

Ashley, Bernard

Ronnie's war. Frances Lincoln Children's Books 2011 190p $16.95

Grades: 3 4 5   **Fic**

1. London (England) -- Fiction 2. World War, 1939-1945 -- Fiction 3. Mother-son relationship -- Fiction

ISBN 978-1-84780-162-3; 1-84780-162-5

Eleven-year-old Ronnie and his mother struggle through hardships and joys caused by World War II in England.

"Ashley makes a clear, straightforward narrative that accommodates a surprising amount of information about England during the war, and he does it with a strong story lucid and true enough to engage younger readers. . . . A moving snapshot of a time that still resonates." Kirkus

Atinuke (Author)

★ **Anna** Hibiscus; illustrated by Lauren Tobia. Kane/Miller 2010 109p il

Grades: 1 2 3 4   **Fic**

1. Africa -- Fiction 2. Family life -- Fiction

ISBN 1-935279-73-4 pa; 978-1-935279-73-0 pa

Boston Globe-Horn Book Award Honor: Fiction (2011)

"Linked short stories star Anna Hibiscus, who lives in a large house in a compound in 'amazing Africa' with baby brothers Double and Triple, parents and extended family. . . . The family goes on vacation, an auntie visits from America, Anna learns what it is to do hard work and she gets an invitation to visit her Canadian grandmother. . . . These stories celebrate the extended family and the combination of traditional ways with conveniences of the modern world; they contrast Anna's relatively privileged life with that of others in her country. . . . Tobia's sketches, pen-and-ink with a gray wash, will help early readers visualize the family, unfamiliar customs and clothing and Anna's community."

"Linked short stories star Anna Hibiscus, who lives in a large house in a compound in 'amazing Africa' with baby brothers Double and Triple, parents and extended family. . . . The family goes on vacation, an auntie visits from America, Anna learns what it is to do hard work and she gets an invitation to visit her Canadian grandmother. . . . These stories celebrate the extended family and the combination of traditional ways with conveniences of the modern world; they contrast Anna's relatively privileged life with that of others in her country. . . . Tobia's sketches, pen-and-ink with a gray wash, will help early readers visualize the family, unfamiliar customs and clothing and Anna's community." Kirkus

Other titles about Anna Hibiscus are:

Hooray for Anna Hibiscus! (2011)

Good luck, Anna Hibiscus! (2011)

Have fun, Anna Hibiscus! (2011)

Anna Hibiscus' song; [illustrated by] Lauren Tobia. Kane/Miller 2011 un il $15.99

Grades: PreK K   **Fic**

1. Africa -- Fiction 2. Happiness -- Fiction 3. Family life -- Fiction

ISBN 978-1-61067-040-1; 1-61067-040-X

"In amazing Africa, Anna Hibiscus discovers her own special way to show her happiness after trying out what other family members do. . . . Tobia illustrated the Anna Hibiscus chapter books with gray scale drawings, but here she presents Anna in full color. . . . Young readers and listeners will surely embrace her as enthusiastically as chapter-book readers already have." Kirkus Reviews

Good luck, Anna Hibiscus! illustrated by Lauren Tobia. Kane/Miller 2011 110p il pa $5.99

Grades: 1 2 3 4   **Fic**

1. Africa -- Fiction 2. Family life -- Fiction

ISBN 1-61067-007-8 pa; 978-1-61067-007-4 pa

Anna Hibiscus, who lives in Africa, is looking forward to visiting her grandmother in Canada, where she will see snow for the first time! But before she goes, she must find suitable clothes to keep her warm in the cold winter weather, and say goodbye to the family she loves.

"These gentle stories are illustrated on nearly every page with Tobia's gray-scale sketches. Accurate cultural details will appeal to readers curious about life in an unfamiliar world. . . . The third-person narration moves briskly, with plenty of dialogue." Kirkus

Have fun, Anna Hibiscus! illustrated by Lauren Tobia. Kane/Miller 2011 110p il pa $5.99

Grades: 1 2 3 4   **Fic**

1. Snow -- Fiction 2. Canada -- Fiction 3. Africans -- Fiction 4. Christmas -- Fiction 5. Family life -- Fiction

ISBN 978-1-61067-008-1; 1-61067-008-6

Anna Hibiscus has never been away from her home in Africa, surrounded by her parents and baby brothers, as well as all of her aunts and uncles and cousins. But now she is going to Canada to visit her grandmother for Christmas. She has never met Granny Canada and she can't wait to see snow!

"The Nigerian-born author has drawn on her own childhood travel to make this experience real for young readers today. On every spread, Tobia's sketches, black and white with gray fill, add interest and appeal. A welcome addition to the sparse collection of stories for young readers about modern Africa." Kirkus

Hooray for Anna Hibiscus! illustrated by Lauren Tobia. Kane/Miller 2010 108p il pa $5.99

Grades: 1 2 3 4   **Fic**

1. Africa -- Fiction 2. Family life -- Fiction

ISBN 978-1-935279-74-7 pa; 1-935279-74-2 pa

First published 2008 in the United Kingdom

Anna Hibiscus lives in Africa with her family in a house in a beautiful garden in a big city. Anna sings for the president, gets in a terrible tangle with her hair and visits the other side of the city.

The **no.** 1 car spotter; illustrated by Warwick Johnson Cadwell. Kane/Miller 2011 il pa $5.99
Grades: 1 2 3 **Fic**
1. Africa -- Fiction 2. Travel -- Fiction 3. Automobiles -- Fiction
ISBN 978-1-61067-051-7; 1-61067-051-5

"Oluwalase Babatunde Benson, otherwise known as No. 1, is not only the best car-spotter in his African village, his electric ideas improve village life." Kirkus Reviews

Atkinson, Cale

Maxwell the monkey barber; by Cale Atkinson. Owlkids Books 2016 32 p. color illustrations $16.95
Grades: PreK K 1 **Fic**
1. Monkeys -- Fiction 2. Elephants -- Fiction 3. Barbers and barbershops -- Fiction
ISBN 1771471034; 9781771471039
LC 2015956792

In this children's book, by Cale Atkinson, "Maxwell the monkey operates a barbershop, where he offers everything from a trim to a chop. He excels at helping his fellow animals look shipshape and feel their best, no matter how unruly their locks. . . . All's well until Elephant comes in, feeling sad because he has no hair. Can Maxwell help? Of course! After some careful thinking, he devises a solution to help even Elephant feel his best." (Publisher's note)

"Atkinson's jungle denizens will easily charm one and all." Kirkus

Atkinson, E. J.

★ **I,** Emma Freke; [by] Elizabeth Atkinson. Carolrhoda Books 2010 234p $16.95
Grades: 4 5 6 7 **Fic**
1. Wisconsin -- Fiction 2. Family life -- Fiction 3. Massachusetts -- Fiction 4. Family reunions -- Fiction 5. Single parent family -- Fiction 6. Eccentrics and eccentricities -- Fiction
ISBN 978-0-7613-5604-2; 0-7613-5604-5
LC 2009-38923

Growing up near Boston with her free-spirited mother and old-world grandfather, twelve-year-old Emma has always felt out of place but when she attends the family reunion her father's family holds annually in Wisconsin, she is in for some surprises.

"This rich story of self-acceptance offers readers much to think about. . . . The first-person narrative moves along briskly, with believable dialogue and plenty of humor." Booklist

Atwater, Richard Tupper

★ **Mr.** Popper's penguins; [by] Richard and Florence Atwater; illustrated by Robert Lawson. Little, Brown 1988 138p il $18.99; pa $6.99
Grades: 3 4 5 **Fic**
1. Penguins -- Fiction
ISBN 0-316-05842-4; 0-316-05843-2 pa

Reissue first published in 1938

A Newbery Medal honor book, 1939

When Mr. Popper, a mild little painter and decorator with a taste for books and movies on polar explorations, was presented with a penguin, he named it Captain Cook. From that moment on life was changed for the Popper family

"To the depiction of the penguins in all conceivable moods Robert Lawson [the] artist has brought not only his skill but his individual humor, and his portrayal of the wistful Mr. Popper is memorable." N Y Times Book Rev

Auch, Mary Jane

A **dog** on his own. Holiday House 2008 153p $16.95; pa $6.95

Grades: 3 4 5 **Fic**
1. Dogs -- Fiction
ISBN 978-0-8234-2088-9; 0-8234-2088-4; 978-0-8234-2243-2 pa; 0-8234-2243-7 pa
LC 2008-15963

After a daring escape from the animal shelter, Pearl, Peppy, and K-10—so named because he is one step above all the other canines—explore the outside world while moving from one adventure to another.

"This is a compelling, affectionate story of opening not just one's home, but also one's heart." Booklist

I was a third grade science project; illustrated by Herm Auch. Holiday House 1998 96p il $16.95; pa $5.50
Grades: 2 3 4 **Fic**
1. School stories 2. Hypnotism -- Fiction
ISBN 0-8234-1357-8; 0-440-41606-X
LC 97-41996

While trying to hypnotize his dog for the third grade science fair, Brian accidentally makes his best friend Josh think he's a cat

"Auch's wisecracking third-graders and superb comic timing will have readers rolling on the floor." Booklist

Other titles about Brian are:

I was a third grade bodyguard (2003)

I was a third grade spy (2001)

Journey to nowhere. Holt & Co. 1997 202p hardcover o.p. pa $4.99
Grades: 4 5 6 7 **Fic**
1. New York (State) -- Fiction 2. Frontier and pioneer life -- Fiction
ISBN 0-440-41491-1 pa
LC 96-42249

This is the first title in the Genesee trilogy. In 1815, while traveling by covered wagon to settle in the wilderness of western New York, eleven-year-old Mem experiences a flood and separation from her family

"A well-written, realistic, and thoroughly researched novel." Booklist

Other titles in the Genesee trilogy are

Frozen summer (1998)

The road to home (2000)

One-handed catch; [by] MJ Auch. Henry Holt and Co. 2006 248p $16.95; pa $6.99
Grades: 4 5 6 **Fic**
1. Family life -- Fiction 2. People with disabilities -- fiction
ISBN 978-0-8050-7900-5; 0-8050-7900-9; 978-0-312-53575-9 pa; 0-312-53575-9 pa
LC 2006-00370

After losing his hand in an accident in his father's butcher shop in 1946, sixth-grader Norman uses hard work and humor to learn to live with his disability and to succeed at baseball, art, and other activities.

"Loosely based on childhood experiences of the author's husband, this story offers both inspiration and useful information, deftly wrapped in an engaging narrative." Booklist

Wing nut; [by] MJ Auch. Henry Holt & Co. 2005 231p $16.95
Grades: 4 5 6 **Fic**
1. Birds -- Fiction 2. Moving -- Fiction 3. Old age -- Fiction
ISBN 0-8050-7531-3
LC 2004-54046

When twelve-year-old Grady and his mother relocate yet again, they find work taking care of an elderly man, who teaches Grady about cars, birds, and what it means to have a home

"Auch's story . . . is engaging. . . . What will attract readers . . . is the author's careful integration of bird lore and the unusual challenges of creating and maintaining a purple martin colony." Booklist

Auxier, Jonathan

★ The **Night** Gardener; by Jonathan Auxier. Amulet Books 2014 368 p. (hardback) $16.95

Grades: 4 5 6 7   **Fic**

1. Ghost stories 2. Young adult literature 3. Horror stories 4. Ghosts -- Fiction 5. Orphans -- Fiction 6. Dwellings -- Fiction 7. Storytelling -- Fiction 8. Household employees -- Fiction 9. Blessing and cursing -- Fiction 10. Brothers and sisters -- Fiction

ISBN 141971144X; 9781419711442

LC 2013047655

"'The Night Gardener' follows two abandoned Irish siblings who travel to work as servants at a creepy, crumbling English manor house. But the house and its family are not quite what they seem. Soon the children are confronted by a mysterious spectre and an ancient curse that threatens their very lives." (Publisher's note)

"Molly's whimsical tales illustrate life's essential lessons even as they entertain. As the characters face the unhealthy pull of the tree's allurements, they grow and change, revealing unexpected personality traits. Storytelling as a force to cope with life's challenges is subtly expressed and adds complexity to the fast-paced plot." SLJ

Peter Nimble and his fantastic eyes; a story. Amulet Books 2011 381p il $16.95

Grades: 4 5 6 7   **Fic**

1. Eye -- Fiction 2. Blind -- Fiction 3. Magic -- Fiction 4. Orphans -- Fiction 5. Thieves -- Fiction

ISBN 978-1-4197-0025-5; 1-4197-0025-1

LC 2010048692

Raised to be a thief, blind orphan Peter Nimble, age ten, steals from a mysterious stranger three pairs of magical eyes, that lead him to a hidden island where he must decide to become a hero or resume his life of crime.

"The fast-paced, episodic story, accompanied by Auxier's occasional pen-and-ink drawings, is inventive, unpredictable, and—like its hero—nimble." Publ Wkly

★ **Sophie** Quire and the last Storyguard; by Jonathan Auxier. Amulet Books 2016 464 p. illustrations (hardback) $18.95

Grades: 4 5 6 7   **Fic**

1. Fantasy fiction -- Fiction 2. Magic -- Fiction 3. Books and reading -- Fiction 4. Adventure and adventurers -- Fiction

ISBN 9781419717475

LC 2015039272

Sequel to: Peter Nimble and His Fantastic Eyes (2011)

In this children's story, by Jonathan Auxier, part of the "Peter Nimble Adventure" series, "Sophie knows little beyond the four walls of her father's bookshop, where she repairs old books and dreams of escaping the confines of her dull life. But when a strange boy and his talking cat/horse companion show up with a rare and mysterious book, she finds herself pulled into an adventure beyond anything she has ever read." (Publisher's note)

"Twelve-year-old Sophie Quire is a gifted bookmender, like her mother, who mysteriously died when Sophie was young. She also loves reading, finding joy and escape in the stories filling her father's bookshop. But storybooks may disappear altogether in Bustleburgh after Inquisitor Prigg decides they are "nonsense" and is determined to destroy them all in a mass book burning. Then gifted, cocky thief Peter Nimble arrives with an intriguing, magical book needing repair. The book, it seems, is one of a set, and when Professor Cake charges the trio with collecting them, it begins a perilous quest full of events and beings and unexpected revelations. . . . Ultimately, this affecting, compelling story stands on its own, embodying and highlighting the power and impact of tales well told—and why they endure." Booklist

Avi

A **beginning,** a muddle, and an end; the right way to write writing. with illustrations by Tricia Tusa. Harcourt 2008 164p il $14.95

Grades: 3 4 5   **Fic**

1. Ants -- Fiction 2. Snails -- Fiction 3. Animals -- Fiction 4. Authorship -- Fiction

ISBN 978-0-15-205555-4; 0-15-205555-X

LC 2007-16580

Avon the snail decides to become a writer with the help of his friend Edward the ant, which leads them into a series of adventures involving close encounters with an anteater, a crow, a tree frog, and a hungry fish.

"Clever prose provides thought-provoking scenes full of wit and charm, and well-placed sketches add insightful visuals into the mood of the characters." SLJ

The **Book** Without Words; a fable of medieval magic. Hyperion Books for Children 2005 203p hardcover o.p. pa $5.99

Grades: 5 6 7 8   **Fic**

1. Magic -- Fiction 2. Middle Ages -- Fiction 3. Supernatural -- Fiction 4. Great Britain -- History -- 0-1066 -- Fiction

ISBN 0-7868-0829-2; 0-7868-1659-7 pa

"At the dawning of the Middle Ages, Thorston, an old alchemist, works feverishly to create gold and to dose himself with a concoction that will enable him to live forever. The key to his success lies in a mysterious book with blank pages that can only be read by desperate, green-eyed people. . . . Avi's compelling language creates a dreary foreboding. . . . Clearly this is a story with a message, a true fable. Thoughtful readers will devour its absorbing plot and humorous elements, and learn a 'useful truth' along the way." SLJ

Crispin at the edge of the world. Hyperion Books for Children 2006 234p $16.99

Grades: 5 6 7 8   **Fic**

1. Orphans -- Fiction 2. Middle Ages -- Fiction 3. Great Britain -- History -- 1154-1399, Plantagenets -- Fiction

ISBN 0-7868-5152-X

LC 2006-41111

Sequel to Crispin: the cross of lead (2002)

Branded as traitors by the king's authorities, Crispin and his guardian, Bear, flee to coastal towns in fourteenth-century England, where they perform a musical juggling act and bond as a family after befriending a disfigured girl.

"Along with plenty of action and adventure, this displays a solid emotional base." Booklist

Followed by Crispin: the end of time (2010)

★ **Crispin**: the cross of lead. Hyperion Bks. for Children 2002 $15.99; pa $6.99

Grades: 5 6 7 8   **Fic**

1. Young adult literature 2. Orphans -- Fiction 3. Middle Ages -- Fiction 4. Great Britain -- History -- 1154-1399, Plantagenets -- Fiction

ISBN 0-7868-0828-4; 0-7868-1658-9 pa

LC 2001-51829

Awarded the Newbery Medal, 2001

Falsely accused of theft and murder, an orphaned peasant boy in fourteenth-century England flees his village and meets a larger-than-life juggler who holds a dangerous secret

This "book is a page-turner from beginning to end. . . . A meticulously crafted story, full of adventure, mystery, and action." SLJ

Other titles in this series are:

Crispin at the edge of the world (2006)

Crispin: the end of time (2010)

The **end** of the beginning; being the adventures of a small snail (and an even smaller ant) with illustrations by Tricia Tusa. Harcourt 2004 143p il $14.95; pa $6.95

Grades: 3 4 5   Fic

1. Ants -- Fiction 2. Snails -- Fiction

ISBN 0-15-204968-1; 0-15-205532-0 pa

LC 2004-2696

Avon the snail and Edward, a take-charge ant, set off together on a journey to an undetermined destination in search of unspecified adventures.

"Whimsical pen-and-ink sketches add much to this wise little book. It's perfect for reading and discussing." SLJ

Another title about Avon the snail and Edward the ant is:

A beginning, a muddle, and an end (2008)

Ereth's birthday; illustrated by Brian Floca. HarperCollins Pubs. 2000 180p il (Dimwood Forest tales) pa $5.99

Grades: 3 4 5   Fic

1. Foxes -- Fiction 2. Animals -- Fiction 3. Porcupines -- Fiction

ISBN 0-380-97734-6; 0-380-80490-5 pa

LC 99-46481

Feeling neglected on his birthday, Ereth, the cantankerous old porcupine, sets out looking for his favorite treat and instead finds himself acting as "mother" to three young fox kits.

"Avi delivers another crackling good read, one shot through with memorable descriptions . . . and crisp, credible dialogue." Publ Wkly

The **fighting** ground. Lippincott 1984 157p hardcover o.p. lib bdg $16.89; pa $5.99; rpt $5.99

Grades: 5 6 7 8   Fic

1. United States -- History -- 1775-1783, Revolution -- Fiction

ISBN 0-397-32073-6; 0-397-32074-4 lib bdg; 0-06-440185-5 pa; 9780064401852 rpt

LC 82-47719

"It's April 1776, and the fighting ground is both the farm country of Pennsylvania and the heart of a boy which is 'wonderful ripe for war.' Twenty-four hours transform Jonathan from a cocky 13-year-old, eager to take on the British, into a young man who now knows the horror, the pathos, the ambiguities of war." Voice Youth Advocates

Iron thunder; the battle between the Monitor and the Merrimac, a civil war novel. Hyperion 2007 205p il $15.99; pa $5.99

Grades: 4 5 6   Fic

1. Ships -- Fiction 2. Brooklyn (New York, N.Y.) -- Fiction 3. United States -- History -- 1861-1865, Civil War -- Fiction

ISBN 978-1-4231-0446-9; 1-4231-0446-3; 978-1-4231-0518-3 pa; 1-4231-0518-4 pa

LC 2004-2696

"This fascinating adventure taken from U.S. history begins in Brooklyn in 1862, when Tom Carroll, 13, is hired at the Iron Works in Greenpoint for a secret project, derisively known around the borough as Ericsson's Folly. John Ericsson, a Swedish inventor, is trying to build an ironclad ship that can battle the Merrimac, a Confederate ship being outfitted with metal plates in Virginia. . . . Illustrated with period engravings, this is gripping historical fiction from a keenly imagined perspective." Publ Wkly

Midnight magic. Scholastic Press 1999 249p hardcover o.p. pa $5.99

Grades: 5 6 7 8   Fic

1. Italy -- Fiction 2. Magicians -- Fiction 3. Renaissance -- Fiction

ISBN 0-590-36035-3; 0-439-24219-3 pa

LC 98-50192

In Italy in 1491, Mangus the magician and his apprentice are summoned to the castle of Duke Claudio to determine if his daughter is indeed being haunted by a ghost.

An "entertaining tale of mystery and intrigue." SLJ

Another title about Mangus and Fabrizio is:

Murder at midnight (2009)

★ **Poppy**; [by] Avi; illustrated by Brian Floca. Revised Harper Trophy ed.; HarperTrophy 2005 156p il pa $5.99

Grades: 3 4 5   Fic

1. Mice -- Fiction 2. Owls -- Fiction 3. Animals -- Fiction

ISBN 978-0-380-72769-8 pa; 0-380-72769-2 pa

LC 2005281589

First published 1995 by Orchard Books

Poppy the deer mouse urges her family to move next to a field of corn big enough to feed them all forever, but Mr. Ocax, a terrifying owl, has other ideas

"This exciting story is richly visual, subtly humorous, and skillfully laden with natural-history lessons. The anthropomorphism is believable and the characters are memorable." SLJ

Other titles in this series are:

Poppy and Rye (1998)

Ragweed (1999)

Ereth's birthday (2000)

Poppy's return (2005)

Poppy and Ereth (2009)

Poppy and Ereth; illustrated by Brian Floca. HarperCollinsPublishers 2009 208p il $15.99; $16.89

Grades: 3 4 5   Fic

1. Bats -- Fiction 2. Mice -- Fiction 3. Friendship -- Fiction 4. Porcupines -- Fiction

ISBN 978-0-06-111969-9; 0-06-111969-5; 978-0-06-111970-5 lib bdg; 0-06-111970-9 lib bdg

LC 2008019662

After a long, hard winter in Dimwood forest, Poppy the deer mouse finds new adventure thrust upon her while rescuing Ereth the porcupine from the mud.

"Series fans will enjoy spending time with these endearing characters." Booklist

Poppy and Rye; illustrated by Brian Floca. Avon Bks. 1998 182p il $14

Grades: 3 4 5   Fic

1. Animals -- Fiction

ISBN 0-380-97638-2

LC 97-31000

When their home next to a brook is destroyed by beavers, a large family of golden mice is aided by Poppy the deer mouse and her grumpy porcupine friend, who in the process forges a relationship with the son he had abandoned

"Accompanied once again by Brian Floca's witty yet pastoral pencil drawings, this is a sequel worthy of its predecessor." Horn Book

Poppy's return; illustrated by Brian Floca. HarperCollins Publishers 2005 223p il (Dimwood Forest tales) hardcover o.p. pa $5.99

Grades: 3 4 5   Fic

1. Mice -- Fiction 2. Skunks -- Fiction 3. Animals -- Fiction 4.

Porcupines -- Fiction
ISBN 0-06-000012-0; 0-06-000013-9 lib bdg; 0-06-000014-7 pa
LC 2004-30054

Poppy, accompanied by her troublesome son Junior, his skunk friend, and Uncle Ereth the porcupine, responds to a summons to return to her ancestral home, Gray House, to save the mice there from destruction by a bulldozer.

Ragweed; illustrated by Brian Floca. Avon Bks. 1999 178p il $17.99; pa $5.99
Grades: 3 4 5 **Fic**
1. Mice -- Fiction
ISBN 0-380-97690-0; 0-380-80167-1 pa
LC 98-55160
Prequel to: Poppy (1995) and Poppy and Rye (1998)

Ragweed, a young country mouse, leaves his family and travels to the big city, where he finds excitement and danger and sees cats for the first time

"Consummate storyteller Avi outdoes himself . . . with a crackerjack tale that's pure delight from start to finish." Publ Wkly

Traitor's gate. Atheneum Books for Young Readers 2007 351p $17.99
Grades: 5 6 7 8 **Fic**
1. Young adult literature 2. Spies -- Fiction 3. Poverty -- Fiction 4. Family life -- Fiction 5. London (England) -- Fiction
ISBN 0-689-85335-1

When his father is arrested as a debtor in 1849 London, fourteen-year-old John Huffman must take on unexpected responsibilities, from asking a distant relative for help to determining why people are spying on him and his family.

"With plenty of period detail, this action-packed narrative of twists, turns, and treachery is another winner from a master craftsman." SLJ

★ The **true** confessions of Charlotte Doyle; decorations by Ruth E. Murray. Orchard Bks. 1990 215p $16.95; pa $5.99; rpt $16.99
Grades: 5 6 7 **Fic**
1. Sea stories
ISBN 0-531-05893-X; 0-380-72885-0 pa; 9780545477116 rpt
LC 90-30624
A Newbery Medal honor book, 1991

"Charlotte Doyle, thirteen, returning from school in England to join her family in Rhode Island, is deposited on a seedy ship with a ruthless, mad captain and a mutinous crew. Refusing to heed warnings about Captain Jaggery's brutality, Charlotte seeks his guidance and approval only to become his victim." (SLJ)

The author has "fashioned an intriguing, suspenseful, carefully crafted tale, with nonstop action on the high seas." Booklist

The **unexpected** life of Oliver Cromwell Pitts; being an absolutely accurate autobiographical account of my follies, fortune & fate. Avi. Algonquin Young Readers 2017 314 p. $16.95
Grades: 4 5 6 7 **Fic**
1. Runaways -- Fiction 2. Criminals -- Fiction 3. Voyages and travels -- Fiction 4. Great Britain -- History -- George I, 1714-1727 -- Fiction
ISBN 9781616205645
LC 2016042923

In this novel, by Avi, "in the seaside town of Melcombe Regis, England, 1724, Oliver Cromwell Pitts wakes to find his father missing and his house flooded by a recent storm. . . . Oliver's father has left, . . . he's gone to London, where Oliver's sister, Charity, is in trouble. . . . Oliver flees, following the trail of his father and sister. The journey is full of thieves, adventurers, and treachery--and London might be the most dangerous place of all." (Publisher's note)

"An ingeniously plotted Dickensian story filled with suspense, surprises, and ultimately satisfaction." Booklist.

Avi, 1937-
Catch you later, traitor; a novel. by Avi. Algonquin Young Readers 2015 304 p. hbk $16.95
Grades: 4 5 6 7 **Fic**
1. Mystery fiction 2. Communism -- Fiction 3. Families -- Fiction 4. Brooklyn (New York, N.Y.) -- History -- 20th century -- Fiction
ISBN 1616203595; 9781616203597
LC 2014031983

This novel by Avi is set in 1951 Brooklyn, New York. "Pete Collison is a regular kid who loves Sam Spade detective books and radio crime dramas, but when an FBI agent shows up at Pete's doorstep accusing his father of being a Communist, Pete finds himself caught in a real-life mystery. Could there really be Commies in Pete's family? As Pete follows the quickly accumulating clues, he begins to wonder if the truth could put his family's livelihood--and even their freedom--at risk." (Publisher's note)

"Avi's tale of one Brooklyn family living in a time of intolerance effectively explores the natures of suspicion, loyalty, and freedom, following a young protagonist who comes to learn the importance of freedom of speech and 'staying true to your own thoughts.'" Horn Book

Includes bibliographical references

★ **City** of orphans; with illustrations by Greg Ruth. Atheneum Books for Young Readers 2011 350p il $16.99
Grades: 5 6 7 8 **Fic**
1. Mystery fiction 2. Young adult literature 3. Gangs -- Fiction 4. Immigrants -- Fiction 5. Family life -- Fiction 6. New York (N.Y.) -- Fiction 7. Homeless persons -- Fiction 8. Waldorf-Astoria Hotel (New York, N.Y.) -- Fiction.
ISBN 978-1-4169-7102-3; 1-4169-7102-5
LC 2010049229

In 1893 New York, thirteen-year-old Maks, a newsboy, teams up with Willa, a homeless girl, to clear his older sister, Emma, from charges that she stole from the brand new Waldorf Hotel, where she works. Includes historical notes.

"Avi's vivid recreation of the sights and sounds of that time and place is spot on, masterfully weaving accurate historical details with Maks' experiences." Kirkus

Includes bibliographical references

The **Most** Important Thing; Stories About Sons, Fathers, and Grandfathers. by Avi. Candlewick Press 2016 224 p. $16.99
Grades: 5 6 7 8 **Fic**
1. Short stories -- Collections 2. Father-son relationship -- Fiction
ISBN 0763681113; 9780763681111
LC 2015941423

This book, by Avi, "presents seven short stories exploring the vital ties between fathers and sons. Luke sees the ghost of his father but can't figure out what Dad wants him to do. Paul takes a camping trip with the grandfather he's just met and discovers what lies behind the man's erratic behavior. Ryan has some surprising questions when he interviews his prospective stepfather for the job." (Publisher's note)

"Avi's deft incorporation of humor, heartache, and the occasional touch of the supernatural will draw readers in as they ponder how family ties bind in both positive and negative ways." Pub Wkly

★ **Sophia's** war; a tale of the Revolution. Avi. Beach Lane Books 2012 302 p. (hardcover) $16.99

Grades: 5 6 7 8 **Fic**

1. Traitors -- Fiction 2. Women spies -- Fiction 3. United States -- History -- 1775-1783, Revolution -- Fiction 4. Spies -- Fiction 5. United States -- History -- Revolution, 1775-1783 -- Fiction 6. New York (N.Y.) -- History -- Revolution, 1775-1783 -- Fiction 7. New York (N.Y.) -- History -- Revolution, 1775-1783 -- Fiction 8. United States -- History -- Revolution, 1775-1783 -- Prisoners and prisons -- Fiction

ISBN 1442414413; 9781442414419; 9781442414426; 9781442414433

LC 2012007962

In this novel by Avi "Sophia Calderwood witnesses the execution of Nathan Hale in New York City, which is newly occupied by the British army . . . in 1776. . . . Recruited as a spy, . . . she becomes aware that someone in the American army might be switching sides, and she uncovers a plot that will grievously damage the Americans if it succeeds. But the identity of the would-be traitor is so shocking that no one believes her, and so Sophia decides to stop the treacherous plot herself." (Publisher's note)

Includes bibliographical references

Axelrod, Amy

Your friend in fashion, Abby Shapiro. Holiday House 2011 261p il $17.95

Grades: 4 5 6 **Fic**

1. Editors 2. Socialites 3. Letters -- Fiction 4. Spouses of presidents 5. Family life -- Fiction 6. Massachusetts -- Fiction 7. Fashion designers -- Fiction

ISBN 978-0-8234-2340-8; 0-8234-2340-9

LC 2010-24185

Beginning in 1959, Abby, nearly eleven, writes a series of letters to Jackie Kennedy, each with sketches of outfits she has designed, as she faces family problems, concerns about neighbors, and her own desperate desire for both her first bra and a Barbie doll.

"Abby is an especially memorable protagonist, but all [Axelrod's] characters vibrate with life. . . . Funny, lively, sensitive—a real winner." Kirkus

Babbitt, Natalie

The **eyes** of the Amaryllis. Farrar, Straus & Giroux 1977 127p hardcover o.p. pa $6.99

Grades: 5 6 7 8 **Fic**

1. Sea stories 2. Grandmothers -- Fiction

ISBN 0-312-37008-3 pa

LC 77-11862

"The book succeeds as a well-wrought narrative in which a complex philosophic theme is developed through the balanced, subtle use of symbol and imagery. It is a rare story." Horn Book

Jack Plank tells tales. Scholastic 128p il $15.95

Grades: 3 4 5 6 **Fic**

1. Pirates -- Fiction 2. Storytelling -- Fiction

ISBN 978-0-5450-0496-1; 0-5450-0496-9

Jack Plank, a former pirate, tells stories at the boarding house where he lives explaining why he is not well suited to jobs such as farmer, baker, and fisherman.

"Written in a straightforward manner with touches of wry wit, Jack's stories unfold with the economy and assurance that readers expect of Babbitt." Booklist

Kneeknock Rise; story and pictures by Natalie Babbitt. Farrar, Straus & Giroux 1970 117p il hardcover o.p. pa $6.99

Grades: 4 5 6 **Fic**

1. Allegories 2. Superstition -- Fiction

ISBN 0-312-37009-1 pa

A Newbery Medal honor book, 1971

"An enchanting tale imbued with a folk flavor, enlivened with piquant imagery and satiric wit." Booklist

The **search** for delicious. Farrar, Straus & Giroux 1969 167p il hardcover o.p. pa $6.99

Grades: 5 6 7 8 **Fic**

1. Fantasy fiction

ISBN 0-374-36534-2; 0-312-36982-4 pa

The Prime Minister is compiling a dictionary and when no one at court can agree on the meaning of delicious, the King sends his twelve-year-old messenger to poll the country

"The theme, foolish arguments can lead to great conflict, may not be clear to all children who will enjoy this fantasy." Best Sellers

★ **Tuck** everlasting. Farrar, Straus & Giroux 1975 139p $16 pa $6.99

Grades: 5 6 7 8 **Fic**

1. Fantasy fiction

ISBN 0-374-37848-7; 0-312-36981-6 pa

The Tuck family is confronted with an agonizing situation when they discover that a ten-year-old girl and a malicious stranger now share their secret about a spring whose water prevents one from ever growing any older

"The story is macabre and moral, exciting and excellently written." N Y Times Book Rev

Babbitt, Natalie, 1932-2016

The **moon** over High Street; Natalie Babbitt. Scholastic 2012 148 p. (alk. paper) $15.95

Grades: 3 4 5 6 7 **Fic**

1. Family -- Fiction 2. Friendship -- Fiction 3. Decision making -- Fiction 4. Adopted children -- Fiction

ISBN 054537636X; 9780545376365

LC 2011926880

This children's novel by Natalie Babbitt "presents 12-year-old Joe . . . Orphaned shortly after his birth, Joe, who loves the moon, has been raised by his Gran, but after she breaks a hip, he's sent to spend some of the summer with his father's cousin. . . . In nearly idyllic Midville, . . . he inadvertently comes to the attention of the very wealthy factory owner Mr. Boulderwall . . . who decides that he will adopt Joe and raise him to take over his company." (Kirkus)

Baccalario, Pierdomenico

The **long**-lost map; [text by Pierdomenico Baccalario; original cover and illustrations by Iacopo Bruno; graphics by Iacopo Bruno and Laura Zuccotti; translation by Leah Janeczko] Scholastic 2006 261p il (Ulysses Moore) $12.99

Grades: 4 5 6 **Fic**

1. Mystery fiction 2. Adventure fiction 3. Twins -- Fiction

ISBN 0-439-77439-X

LC 200503212

Eleven-year-old twins Jason and Julia, along with their friend Rick, find themselves in ancient Egypt in search of an important map after going through a magical door in their old English mansion.

"The characters are clearly delineated, but adventure is prime here. The illustrations (including handsome pencil drawings) at the beginnings of chapters have a three-dimensional quality in keeping with the book's pretense that readers are looking at the recovered manuscripts of the mysterious Ulysses Moore." Booklist

Baker, Deirdre F.

Becca at sea. Groundwood 2007 165p $16.95

Grades: 4 5 6 **Fic**

1. Islands -- Fiction 2. Family life -- Fiction 3. Grandmothers -- Fiction 4. British Columbia -- Fiction

ISBN 978-0-88899-737-1

After Becca's mom becomes pregnant, Becca visits her grandmother at her rustic cabin by the sea alone, and although she dreads it at first, she finds adventures and friendship and returns to the island again and again.

"Each episode enriches the portrait of Becca's memorable extended family with delightfully preposterous, yet insightful detail. . . . This funny, endearing book should find a wide audience." Horn Book

Baker, Matthew

If you find this; by Matthew Baker. Little, Brown & Co. 2015 368 p. illustrations (hardcover) $17

Grades: 4 5 6 7 **Fic**

1. Old age -- Fiction 2. Heirlooms -- Fiction 3. Friendship -- Fiction 4. Grandfathers -- Fiction 5. Lost and found possessions -- Fiction

ISBN 0316240087; 9780316240086

LC 2013044749

In this book, by Matthew Baker, "Nicholas is a math and music genius with no friends and a huge problem: His father has lost his job, and they'll have to sell their house, which holds the only memory Nicholas has of his younger brother. Just in time, Nicholas's senile grandfather arrives, filled with tales of priceless treasure he has hidden somewhere in town--but where?" (Publisher's note)

"The vivid setting, complex characters, and original writing style result in a story with lasting impact. Reminiscent of Louis Sachar's Holes (1998), this is a rich, captivating tale about family and redemption that redefines the meaning of treasure." Booklist

Baker-Smith, Grahame

Farther; Grahame Baker-Smith. Templar Publishing 2010 32 p. (reinforced) $17.99

Grades: K 1 2 **Fic**

1. Flight -- Fiction 2. Picture books for children 3. Father-son relationship -- Fiction

ISBN 0763663700; 9780763663704

LC 2011431018

In this Kate Greenaway Medal children's picture book, by Grahame Baker-Smith, "a boy lovingly remembers . . . [how] his father worked ceaselessly to fashion a flying machine. . . . That dream is never to be realized, as the day comes when the father dons a uniform and leaves for great war, never to return. Years later, the son, now grown, resumes work on the machine, succeeds and then shares the vision with his own son." (Kirkus Reviews)

Balliett, Blue

The **Calder** game; illustrated by Brett Helquist. Scholastic Press 2008 379p il $17.99

Grades: 5 6 7 8 **Fic**

1. Artists 2. Sculptors 3. Mystery fiction 4. Sculpture -- Fiction 5. Great Britain -- Fiction 6. Missing persons -- Fiction

ISBN 978-0-439-85207-4; 0-439-85207-2

LC 2007031385

When seventh-grader Calder Pillay disappears from a remote English village—along with an Alexander Calder sculpture to which he has felt strangely drawn—his friends Petra and Tommy fly from Chicago to help his father find him.

Balliett "outdoes herself with this ambitious novel. . . . The mystery crafted more solidly than in either of Balliett's previous titles, and the setting . . . proves completely enticing. And once again Helquist encodes his b&w illustrations with puzzle pieces." Publ Wkly

★ **Chasing** Vermeer; illustrated by Brett Helquist. Scholastic Press 2004 254p il $16.95

Grades: 5 6 7 8 **Fic**

1. Artists 2. Painters 3. Mystery fiction 4. Art -- Fiction

ISBN 0-439-37294-1

LC 2002-152106

When seemingly unrelated and strange events start to happen and a precious Vermeer painting disappears, eleven-year-olds Petra and Calder combine their talents to solve an international art scandal.

Balliett's purpose "seems to be to get children to think—about relationships, connections, coincidences, and the subtle language of artwork. . . . [This is] a book that offers children something new upon each reading. . . . Helquist . . . outdoes himself here, providing an interactive mystery in his pictures." Booklist

Other titles about Petra and Calder are:

The Wright 3 (2006)

The Calder game (2008)

The **Danger** Box. Scholastic Press 2010 306p $16.99

Grades: 5 6 7 8 **Fic**

1. Naturalists 2. Travel writers 3. Diaries -- Fiction 4. Writers on science 5. Antiques -- Fiction 6. Michigan -- Fiction 7. Family life -- Fiction 8. Grandparents -- Fiction

ISBN 978-0-439-85209-8; 0-439-85209-9

LC 2010-16622

In small-town Michigan, twelve-year-old Zoomy and his new friend Lorrol investigate the journal found inside a mysterious box and find family secrets and a more valuable treasure, while a dangerous stranger watches and waits.

"This highly satisfying story will enlighten readers even as it inspires them to think about their own danger boxes." SLJ

Hold fast; by Blue Balliett. Scholastic Press 2013 288 p. (jacketed hardcover) $17.99

Grades: 3 4 5 6 **Fic**

1. Theft -- Fiction 2. Mystery fiction -- Fiction 3. Smuggling -- Fiction 4. Kidnapping -- Fiction 5. Chicago (Ill.) -- Fiction 6. Missing persons -- Fiction 7. Homeless persons -- Fiction 8. Mystery and detective stories 9. Fathers and daughters -- Fiction

ISBN 0545299888; 9780545299886

LC 2012041035

This book focuses on "the Pearl family: Dash, Summer, 11-year-old Early, and the little Jubie. Do they have a lot? Well, yes, they have Dash's love of words, their devotion to each other, and their dream: to have a home. Trying to help that dream along, Dash, a page at the Chicago Public Library, makes extra money inventorying a private collection of old books. One . . . day, Dash disappears, and the family must move to a shelter after an odd robbery sees their . . . apartment destroyed." (Booklist)

Pieces and players; Blue Balliett; [edited by] David Levithan. Scholastic Press 2015 320 p. illustrations $17.99

Grades: 5 6 7 8 **Fic**

1. Mystery fiction 2. Art thefts -- Fiction 3. Art museums -- Fiction

ISBN 054529990X; 9780545299909

LC 2014947736

In this children's book, by Blue Balliett, "thirteen extremely valuable pieces of art have been stolen from one of the most secretive museums in the world. A Vermeer has vanished. A Manet is missing. And nobody has any idea where they and the other eleven artworks might be . . . or who might have stolen them. . . . Calder, Petra, and Tommy are no strangers to heists and puzzles. Now they've been matched with two new sleuths -- Zoomy . . . and Early." (Publisher's note)

"This time it's a small family museum and 13 missing pieces of art providing the mystery that brings back characters met in previous titles. Tommy, Petra, and Calder are joined by Early Pearl and Zoomy Chamberlain. With all five kids led by their teacher Mrs. Hussey, each of the detective's special skills add to their understanding and help them arrive at the solution. Fans of the previous books will be delighted as these characters continue with their familiar predilections such as Calder's pentominoes clacking in his pockets. . . . Fun and engaging; a fitting addition for readers addicted to these art mysteries." SLJ

The **Wright** 3; illustrated by Brett Helquist. Scholastic Press 2006 318p il $16.99
Grades: 5 6 7 8   Fic
1. Architects 2. School stories 3. Mystery fiction 4. Nonfiction writers
ISBN 0-439-69367-5
                                                    LC 2005-19608
In the midst of a series of unexplained accidents and mysterious coincidences, sixth-graders Calder, Petra, and Tommy lead their classmates in an attempt to keep Frank Lloyd Wright's famous Robie House from being demolished.

"The mystery itself and the perfectly realized setting make this an essential purchase." SLJ

Banerjee, Anjali
★ **Looking** for Bapu. Wendy Lamb Books 2006 162p hardcover o.p. pa $6.50
Grades: 4 5 6 7   Fic
1. Hindus -- Fiction 2. Bereavement -- Fiction 3. Grandfathers -- Fiction 4. East Indians -- United States -- Fiction
ISBN 978-0-385-74657-1; 0-385-90894-6; 978-0-553-49425-9 pa; 0-553-49425-2 pa
                                                    LC 2006-02021
When his beloved grandfather dies, eight-year-old Anu feels that his spirit is near and will stop at nothing to bring him back, including trying to become a Hindu holy man.

"With episodes that ring true to a boy's perspective, Banerjee's novel provides discussable issues and multicultural insights as well as humor and emotion. An excellent read aloud." Booklist

Seaglass summer. Wendy Lamb Books 2010 163p il $15.99; lib bdg $18.99
Grades: 4 5 6   Fic
1. Uncles -- Fiction 2. Veterinarians -- Fiction 3. Washington (State) -- Fiction 4. East Indian Americans -- Fiction
ISBN 978-0-385-73567-4; 0-385-73567-7; 978-0-385-90555-8 lib bdg; 0-385-90555-6 lib bdg
                                                    LC 2009-25468
"Eleven-year-old Poppy wants to be a veterinarian like her uncle Sanjay. So while her parents are in India visiting relatives, she spends several weeks with him on Nisqually Island, Washington, helping out at his Furry Friends Animal Clinic. Episodic chapters focus on the people and animals that Poppy meets, [and] her efforts to do a good job. . . . There are many moving events here. . . . Sometimes amusing, sometimes gross, and always true to itself, this should find a wide readership. Pencil illustrations enliven the chapter headings." Booklist

Banks, Angelica
Blueberry pancakes forever; Angelica Banks; with illustrations by Stevie Lewis. Henry Holt & Co. 2017 320 p. illustrations (ebook) $60; (hardcover) $16.99

Grades: 4 5 6
1. Authors -- Fiction 2. Adventure fiction -- Fiction 3. Books and reading -- Fiction
ISBN 9781250109477; 9781627791564
                                                    LC 2016020537
In this book in the Tuesday McGillycuddy Adventures series, by Angelica Banks, illustrated by Stevie Lewis, "after an unthinkable loss, time seems to freeze for Tuesday and her mother, the famous author Serendipity Smith. In the land of story, Vivienne Small's world is frozen too—a perpetual winter has fallen. When a terrible villain takes Vivienne hostage, it's up to Tuesday to save her friend—and herself." (Publisher's note)

"Richly complex and nourishing." Kirkus

Finding Serendipity; Angelica Banks; illustrations by Stevie Lewis. Henry Holt & Co. 2015 281 p. illustrations (hardcover) $16.99
Grades: 4 5 6   Fic
1. Magic -- Fiction 2. Adventure fiction 3. Books and reading -- Fiction 4. Authors -- Fiction 5. Authorship -- Fiction 6. Adventure and adventurers -- Fiction
ISBN 162779154X; 9781627791540
                                                    LC 2014037083
In this book, "when Tuesday McGillicuddy goes to check on her author mother's progress, Serendipity has disappeared, with only a mysterious box containing the words 'The End' offering a clue to her whereabouts. Tuesday types her own story in hopes that it will bring her to her mother at The End, and her words take on the form of silver thread encircling Tuesday and her loyal dog, Baxterr, and pulling them out the window into the night." (Bulletin of the Center for Children's Books)

"Spunky characters; spot-on pacing, providing perfectly timed plot revelations; and fully imagined worlds make this a charming winner for curling up with a good book or classroom read-alouds." Booklist

A **week** without Tuesday; Angelica Banks; illustrated by Stevie Lewis. Henry Holt & Co. 2016 384 p. illustrations (hardback) $16.99
Grades: 4 5 6   Fic
1. Magic -- Fiction 2. Adventure fiction 3. Books and reading -- Fiction 4. Adventure and adventurers -- Fiction
ISBN 9781627791557
                                                    LC 201501199
Sequel to: Finding serendipity

In this book, by Angelica Banks, illustrated by Stevie Lewis, "something is broken in the land of story. Real and imaginary worlds are colliding—putting everything and everyone in grave peril. Tuesday and Baxterr, at the request of the Librarian, and with the help of Vivienne Small, venture to find the Gardener—the one person who can stop this catastrophe. On their way, they'll meet friends and foes, and discover strengths they didn't know they had." (Publisher's note)

"A stimulating read that validates and encourages the creative impulse—highly recommended." Kirkus

Banks, Kate
Dillon Dillon. Foster Bks. 2002 150p hardcover o.p. pa $5.95
Grades: 4 5 6 7   Fic
1. Loons -- Fiction 2. Adoption -- Fiction 3. Family life -- Fiction 4. New Hampshire -- Fiction
ISBN 0-374-31786-0; 0-374-41715-6 pa
                                                    LC 2001-3320
During the summer that he turns ten years old, Dillon Dillon learns the surprising story behind his name and develops a relationship with three loons, living on the lake near his family's New Hampshire cabin that help him make sense of his life

This "succeeds as an emotionally intricate, quietly well-observed symbolically charged novel." Horn Book

Bar-el, Dan

Audrey (cow) an oral account of a most daring escape, based more or less on a true story. Dan Bar-el. Tundra Books of Northern New York 2014 240 p. illustrations (hardcover) $19.99

Grades: 4 5 6 **Fic**

1. Farms -- Fiction 2. Cattle -- Fiction 3. cows -- fiction 4. animals -- fiction 5. escapes -- fiction

ISBN 1770496025; 9781770496026

LC 2013953683

In this children's book, by Dan Bar-El, "Audrey is a cow with poetry in her blood, who yearns for the greener pastures beyond Bittersweet Farms. But when Roy the horse tells this bovine dreamer that she is headed for Abbot's War, the slaughter house, Audrey knows that she must leave her home and friends sooner than she ever imagined. With the help of a whole crew of animals and humans alike, Audrey attempts to escape the farm she lives on--and certain death." (Publisher's note)

"In a multiple-perspective, documentary-like format, each animal tells its part of the story with terrific humor and personality. . . . Part Great Escape, part Hatchet, part Charlotte's Web, all wonderful." Kirkus

Barden, Stephanie

★ **Cinderella** Smith; illustrations by Diane Goode. Harper 2011 48p il

Grades: 3 4 5 **Fic**

1. School stories 2. Friendship -- Fiction 3. Family life -- Fiction 4. Stepsisters -- Fiction 5. Tap dancing -- Fiction 6. Seattle (Wash.) -- Fiction

ISBN 0-06-196423-9; 978-0-06-196423-7

LC 2010015980

Cast off by her old friends, Cinderella agrees to help a new student deal with the stepsisters she will soon have, and meantime, a former friend tries to prevent Cinderella from dancing the lead in their tap recital.

"Line illustrations by the gifted Goode enhance the lightheartedness and fun of the story. . . . The awkwardness Cinderella feels with her former friends is palpable yet not overly serious, and her inclusive enjoyment of life is contagious. The resolution to the stepsister problem is especially satisfying." Booklist

The **super** secret mystery; by Stephanie Barden; illustrations by Diane Goode. Harpercollins Childrens Books 2013 144 p. (Cinderella Smith) (hardcover bdgs) $16.99

Grades: 3 4 5 **Fic**

1. Report writing 2. Mystery fiction 3. Libraries -- Fiction 4. Schools -- Fiction 5. Endangered species -- Fiction 6. Mystery and detective stories

ISBN 0062004433; 9780062004437

LC 2012050667

In this book by Stephanie Barden, "third in the Cinderella Smith chapter-book series, Cinderella is excited to write a report on an endangered species. She can't wait to investigate this important environmental issue. But every book she needs to do her research has disappeared from the library! That won't stop Cinderella. She won't be stopped by the mean-girl bullies and will follow every clue until she solves the mystery." (Publisher's note)

Barker, M. P.

A **difficult** boy. Holiday House 2008 298p $16.95; pa $7.95

Grades: 5 6 7 8 **Fic**

1. Massachusetts -- Fiction 2. Contract labor -- Fiction 3. Irish Americans -- Fiction 4. Swindlers and swindling -- Fiction

ISBN 978-0-8234-2086-5; 0-8234-2086-8; 978-0-8234-2244-9 pa; 0-8234-2244-5 pa

LC 2007-37059

In Farmington, Massachusetts, in 1839, nine-year-old Ethan experiences hardships as an indentured servant of the wealthy Lyman family alongside Daniel, a boy scorned simply for being Irish, and the boys bond as they try to right a terrible wrong.

"A memorable tale of friendship and a fascinating glimpse into mid-19th-century Massachusetts." SLJ

Mending horses; by M.P. Barker. Holiday House 2014 309 p. (hardcover) $17.95

Grades: 5 6 7 8 **Fic**

1. Orphans -- Fiction 2. Prejudices -- Fiction 3. Child abuse -- Fiction 4. Irish Americans -- Fiction 5. Peddlars -- Fiction 6. Sex role -- Fiction 7. New England -- History -- 1775-1865 -- Fiction

ISBN 0823429482; 9780823429486

LC 2013019208

In this book, by M.P. Barker, "Daniel Linnehan is an indentured servant no more. He has his papers, his beloved horse, Ivy, and a new direction in life. But an Irish teenager, wearing fine clothes and riding an even finer horse, is asking for trouble. After a terrible misunderstanding leaves Daniel beaten, the peddler Jonathan Stocking takes Daniel under his wing. But Billy, another Irish youngster traveling with Mr. Stocking, is not thrilled that the two must work together." (Publisher's note)

Barnett, Mac

★ The **case** of the case of mistaken identity; illustrations by Adam Rex. Simon & Schuster Books for Young Readers 2009 179p il (The Brixton Brothers) $14.99

Grades: 4 5 6 **Fic**

1. Mystery fiction 2. Police -- Fiction 3. Quilts -- Fiction 4. Librarians -- Fiction 5. Books and reading -- Fiction

ISBN 978-1-4169-7815-2; 1-4169-7815-1

LC 2008-43305

When twelve-year-old Steve Brixton, a fan of Bailey Brothers detective novels, is mistaken for a real detective, he must elude librarians, police, and the mysterious Mr. E as he seeks a missing quilt containing coded information.

The book provides "action and adventure but adds a level of humor that will sometimes have readers laughing out loud. Similarly, Rex's illustrations have a mid-twentieth-century look, and in an accomplished, deadpan manner, offer one of the book's funniest moments." Booklist

Other titles in this series are:

The ghostwriter secret (2010)

It happened on a train (2011)

The **ghostwriter** secret; illustrated by Adam Rex. Simon & Schuster Books for Young Readers 2010 226p il (Brixton Brothers) $14.99

Grades: 4 5 6 **Fic**

1. Mystery fiction 2. Crime -- Fiction 3. Authors -- Fiction

ISBN 978-1-4169-7817-6; 1-4169-7817-8

LC 2009052021

Twelve-year-old Steve Brixton is investigating a diamond heist but the case suddenly changes when the author of the Bailey Brothers detective novels writes him a letter to say that he fears for his life.

"Shot through with moments of goofiness and dotted with Rex's black-and-white illustrations, this is sure to please existing fans and win new ones." Kirkus

It **happened** on a train; illustrations by Adam Rex. Simon & Schuster Books for Young Readers 2011 il (The Brixton Brothers) $15.99

Grades: 4 5 6 **Fic**

1. Mystery fiction 2. Thieves -- Fiction 3. Railroads -- Fiction 4.

California -- Fiction
ISBN 978-1-4169-7819-0; 1-4169-7819-4; 978-1-4424-2313-8
e-book

LC 2011009114

Seventh-grader Steve Brixton finds himself pulled back into sleuthing when, during a train trip down the California coast, he uncovers a mystery involving a fleet of priceless automobiles, an assassin, and a private rail car.

This "chugs along with plenty of laughs and enough honest-to-gosh mystery to please any lover of boy detective fiction. Rex's black-and-white pencils . . . are still a fine match for the goofiness." Kirkus

Barnhill, Kelly

★ The **girl** who drank the moon; Kelly Barnhill. Algonquin Young Readers 2016 400 p. $16.95

Grades: 5 6 7 8   **Fic**
1. Magic -- Fiction 2. Witches -- Fiction 3. Friendship -- Fiction
4. Friendship -- Fiction
ISBN 9781616205676; 1616205679

LC 2016006542

Newbery Medal (2017)

In this book, by Kelly Barnhill, "every year, the people of the Protectorate leave a baby as an offering to the witch who lives in the forest. They hope this sacrifice will keep her from terrorizing their town. But the witch in the Forest, Xan, is kind. She shares her home with a wise Swamp Monster and a Perfectly Tiny Dragon. Xan rescues the children and delivers them to welcoming families on the other side of the forest, nourishing the babies with starlight on the journey." (Publisher's note)

"The swiftly paced, highly imaginative plot draws a myriad of threads together to form a web of characters, magic, and integrated lives. Spiritual overtones encompass much of the storytelling with love as the glue that holds it all together." SLJ

★ The **mostly** true story of Jack; by Kelly Barnhill. Little, Brown 2011 323p il $16.99

Grades: 5 6 7 8   **Fic**
1. Iowa -- Fiction 2. Magic -- Fiction 3. Friendship -- Fiction 4.
Family life -- Fiction
ISBN 978-0-316-05670-0; 0-316-05670-7

LC 2010044934

Jack is practically invisible at home, but when his parents send him to Hazelwood, Iowa, to spend a summer with his odd aunt and uncle, he suddenly makes friends, is beaten up by the town bully, and is plotted against by the richest man in town.

"A truly splendid amalgamation of mystery, magic and creeping horror will spellbind the middle-grade set. . . . The mystery deepens with each chapter, revealing exactly the right amount with each step. Answers are doled out so meticulously that readers will be continually intrigued rather than frustrated. The result is the ultime page-turner." Kirkus

★ The **witch's** boy; Kelly Barnhill. Algonquin Young Readers 2014 384 p. $16.95

Grades: 5 6 7 8   **Fic**
1. Fantasy 2. Magic -- Fiction 3. Twins -- Fiction 4. Witches --
Fiction 5. Brothers -- Fiction 6. Friendship -- Fiction 7. Robbers
and outlaws -- Fiction
ISBN 9781616203511

LC 2014014704

In this juvenile fantasy novel, by Kelly Regan Barnhill, "when Ned and his identical twin brother tumble from their raft into a raging river, only Ned survives. Villagers are convinced the wrong boy lived. But when a Bandit King comes to steal the magic Ned's mother, a witch, is meant to protect, it's Ned who safeguards the magic and summons the strength to protect his family and community." (Publisher's note)

"The writing is beautiful and lyrical, but keeps pace with an action packed story. Powerful themes of grief, redemption, forgiveness, sacrifice, and generosity are all present." VOYA

Barnholdt, Lauren

Girl meets ghost; by Lauren Barnholdt. Aladdin 2013 224 p. (alk paper) $15.99

Grades: 4 5 6 7   **Fic**
1. Ghost stories -- Fiction 2. School stories -- Fiction 3. Mystery
fiction -- Fiction 4. Dead -- Fiction 5. Ghosts -- Fiction 6. School
-- Fiction 7. Middle schools -- Fiction 8. Psychic ability -- Fiction
9. Mystery and detective stories
ISBN 1442442468; 9781442442467

LC 201203223

In this children's story, by Lauren Barnholt, "a tween girl becomes reluctant medium. . . . There's an old saying that 'dead men tell no tales' -but that saying is definitely not true. Just ask twelve-year-old Kendall Williams, who can't get dead people to stop talking to her. . . . It's pretty frustrating being able to hear and see people that no one else can. . . . But Kendall is going to have to learn how to deal, because the only way to quiet the dead is to help them." (Publisher's note)

Barrett, Tracy

The **100**-year-old secret. Henry Holt and Co. 2008 157p (The Sherlock files) $15.95

Grades: 4 5 6 7   **Fic**
1. Mystery fiction 2. Siblings -- Fiction 3. Great Britain -- Fiction
ISBN 978-0-8050-8340-8; 0-8050-8340-5

LC 200703400

Xena and Xander Holmes, an American brother and sister living in London for a year, discover that Sherlock Holmes was their great-great-great grandfather when they are inducted into the Society for the Preservation of Famous Detectives and given his unsolved casebook, from which they attempt to solve the case of a famous missing painting

"The main characters are observant, bright, and gifted with power of deduction." SLJ

Other titles in this series are:
The beast of Blackslope (2009)
The case that time forgot (2010)
The missing heir (2011)

The **Beast** of Blackslope. Henry Holt 2009 174p $15.99

Grades: 4 5 6 7   **Fic**
1. Mystery fiction 2. Siblings -- Fiction 3. Great Britain -- Fiction
ISBN 978-0-8050-8341-5; 0-8050-8341-3

LC 200803694

Xena and Xander Holmes, an American brother and sister spending year in England, use clues in their ancestor Sherlock Holmes' casebook as they try to solve the mystery of a monster threatening a peaceful country village where a documentary film is being made.

"Xena's methodical and calm rationality balances with Xander's intuitive imaginativeness so that they complement one another." SLJ

Barrie, J. M.

Peter Pan and Wendy; illustrated by Robert Ingpen; foreword by David Barrie. Centenary edition; Sterling 2010 216p il $19.95

Grades: 3 4 5 6   **F**
1. Fairy tales
ISBN 978-1-4027-2868-6; 1-4027-2868-9

First published 1911 by Scribner with title: Peter and Wendy; a reissue of the 2004 edition published by Orchard Books

The adventures of the three Darling children in Neverland with Peter Pan, the boy who would not grow up.

This "edition is notable for its painterly illustrations, which reflect touches of Sendak, Wyeth, the pre-Raphaelites, and others. The overall effect of the art is impressionistic, and the book itself is handsome." Horn Book Guide

Barron, T. A.

The **book** of magic; illustrated by August Hall. Philomel Books 2011 il (Merlin) $17.99 **Fic**
1. Fantasy fiction 2. Magic -- Fiction 3. Merlin (Legendary character) -- Fiction
ISBN 978-0-399-24741-5; 0-399-24741-6

LC 2011013552

A compendium of maps, character descriptions, magical terms, timelines, and other tidbits from the author's Merlin saga.

"Guides to long-running series have two important jobs. They should remind fans of all the things they particularly love about the books, and they should whet the appetites of newcomers, thus creating more fans. Barron's guide to his 12-book saga about Merlin succeeds in both objectives." SLJ

The **fires** of Merlin. Philomel Bks. 1998 261p $20.99; pa $5.99
Grades: 5 6 7 8 **Fic**
1. Fantasy fiction 2. Merlin (Legendary character) -- Fiction
ISBN 0-399-23020-3; 0-441-00957-3 pa

LC 97-49561

Sequel to: The seven songs of Merlin (1997)

This is the third volume in the trilogy about Merlin's youth. Having voyaged to the Otherworld in his quest to find himself, the young wizard Merlin must face fire in many different forms and deal with the possibility of losing his own magical power

This "saga just keeps getting richer in characterization, ambience, and Celtic lore." Booklist

Followed by: the mirror of Merlin (1999)

★ The **lost** years of Merlin. Philomel Bks. 1996 326p pa $7.99; $19.99
Grades: 5 6 7 8 **Fic**
1. Fantasy fiction 2. Young adult literature 3. Merlin (Legendary character) -- Fiction
ISBN 9780441006687 pa; 9780399230189

LC 96-33920

"A boy, hurled on the rocks by the sea, regains consciousness unable to remember anything—not his parents, not his own name. He is sure that the secretive Branwen is not his mother, despite her claims, and that Emrys is not his real name. The two soon find themselves feared because of Branwen's healing abilities and Emrys' growing powers. . . . Barron has created not only a magical land populated by remarkable beings but also a completely magical tale, filled with ancient Celtic and Druidic lore, that will enchant readers." Booklist

Other titles in this series are:
The seven songs of Merlin (1997)
The fires of Merlin (1998)
The mirror of Merlin (1999)
The wings of Merlin (2000)

The **mirror** of Merlin. Philomel Bks. 1999 245p il $20.99; pa $7.99
Grades: 5 6 7 8 **Fic**
1. Fantasy fiction 2. Merlin (Legendary character)
ISBN 0-399-23455-1; 0-441-00846-1 pa

LC 99-13043

Sequel to: The fires of Merlin (1998)

This is the fourth volume in the author's series about Merlin's youth. Through adventures involving a haunted marsh, talking trees, and the creature called the ballymag, the young wizard Merlin continues to experience both his growing powers and his essential humanity

"With lots of surprises and some laugh-out-loud humor to leaven the palpable feeling of doom, this should be eagerly devoured by the saga's fans." Booklist

Followed by: The wings of Merlin (2000)

The **seven** songs of Merlin. Philomel Bks. 1997 306p $19.99; pa $7.99
Grades: 5 6 7 8 **Fic**
1. Fantasy fiction 2. Merlin (Legendary character) -- Fiction
ISBN 0-399-23019-X; 0-441-00701-5 pa

LC 97-9619

Sequel to: The lost years of Merlin (1996)

This is the second volume in the author's series about Merlin's youth. Having stumbled upon his hidden powers, the young wizard Merlin voyages to the Otherworld in his quest to find himself and the way to the realm of the spirit

"The tale is spellbinding (pun intended), and readers will relish not only the action and the well-crafted setting but also Merlin's growth from a callow youth to a wiser, more caring wizard-in-training." Booklist

Followed by: The fires of Merlin (1998)

The **wings** of Merlin. Philomel Books 2000 352p $21.99; pa $7.99
Grades: 5 6 7 8 **Fic**
1. Fantasy fiction 2. Merlin (Legendary character) -- Fiction
ISBN 0-399-23456-X; 0-441-00988-3 pa

LC 00-27553

Sequel to: The mirror of Merlin (1999)

Merlin's fragile home on the isle of Fincayra is threatened by the attack of a mysterious warrior with swords for arms and by the escape of Stangmar from his imprisonment, as Merlin continues to move toward his ultimate destiny.

"Barron brings his Lost Years of Merlin saga to a resounding, satisfying close with this fifth volume." Booklist

Barrow, Randi G.

Saving Zasha; by Randi Barrow. Scholastic Press 2011 229p $16.99
Grades: 4 5 6 7 **Fic**
1. Dogs -- Fiction 2. Russia -- Fiction 3. Journalists -- Fiction 4. Single parent family -- Fiction 5. World War, 1939-1945 -- Fiction
ISBN 978-0-545-20632-7; 0-545-20632-4

LC 2010-16899

In 1945 Russia, those who own German shepherds are considered traitors, but thirteen-year-old Mikhail and his family are determined to keep the dog a dying man brought them, while his classmate Katia strives to learn his secret.

"Mikhail's sense of humor, concern for his family, and love of Zasha are all readily apparent in his narration, which smoothly incorporates background information for readers unfamiliar with 20th-century Russian life and history. . . . Barrow's novel is quick reading yet weighty, and captures the prejudices and aftereffects of war." Publ Wkly

Barrows, Annie

★ **Ivy** + Bean; written by Annie Barrows; illustrated by Sophie Blackall. Chronicle Books 2006 113p il $14.95; pa $5.99
Grades: 1 2 3 **Fic**
1. Friendship -- Fiction
ISBN 978-0-8118-4903-6; 0-8118-4903-1; 978-0-8118-4909-8 pa; 0-8118-4909-0 pa

LC 2005023944

When seven-year-old Bean plays a mean trick on her sister, she finds unexpected support for her antics from Ivy, the new neighbor, who is less boring than Bean first suspected.

"The deliciousness here is in the details, with both girls drawn distinctly and with flair. . . . Even with all the text's strong points, what takes the book to a higher level is Blackall's artwork, which captures the girls' spirit." Booklist

Other titles about Ivy and Bean are:
Ivy + Bean and the ghost that had to go (2006)
Ivy + Bean break the fossil record (2007)
Ivy + Bean take care of the babysitter (2008)
Ivy + Bean: bound to be bad (2009)
Ivy + Bean: doomed to dance (2009)
Ivy + Bean: what's the big idea? (2010)

Ivy + Bean and the ghost that had to go; written by Annie Barrows; illustrated by Sophie Blackall. Chronicle 2006 125p il $14.95
Grades: 1 2 3   Fic
1. Ghost stories 2. School stories 3. Friendship -- Fiction
ISBN 0-8118-4910-4
Second-graders Ivy and Bean set out to expel the ghost who is living in the girls' bathroom at their school.

"As before, the series' strong suits are humor and the spot-on take on relationships." Booklist

Ivy + Bean bound to be bad; [written by] Annie Barrows; [illustrated by] Sophie Blackall. Chronicle Books 2009 120p il $14.99
Grades: 1 2 3   Fic
1. Friendship -- Fiction 2. Family life -- Fiction
ISBN 978-0-8118-6265-3; 0-8118-6265-8
                                                    LC 2008005280
Best friends Ivy and Bean learn that being very good, or very bad, can be a real challenge when they set out to become like a man Ivy heard about who was so pure of heart that birds and animals followed him.

This is "plenty fun, especially for the duo's many fans. As always, Blackall's delightful illustrations add smiles and substance." Booklist

Ivy + Bean break the fossil record; written by Annie Barrows; illustrated by Sophie Blackall. Chronicle Books 2007 114p il $14.95
Grades: 1 2 3   Fic
1. Fossils -- Fiction 2. Friendship -- Fiction
ISBN 978-0-8118-5683-6; 0-8118-5683-6
                                                    LC 2007001471
Everyone in second grade seems set on breaking a world record and friends Ivy and Bean are no exception, deciding to become the youngest people ever to discover a dinosaur skeleton.

"Barrows' dynamic duo is as appealing here as in the first two books, and emergent readers will identify with their outrageous antics." Booklist

Ivy + Bean take care of the babysitter; by Annie Barrows; illustrated by Sophie Blackall. Chronicle Books 2008 122p il $14.99; pa $5.99
Grades: 1 2 3   Fic
1. Sisters -- Fiction 2. Babysitters -- Fiction
ISBN 978-0-8118-5685-0; 0-8118-5685-2; 978-0-8118-6584-5 pa; 0-8118-6584-3 pa
                                                    LC 2007028224
When Bean's parents leave her in the care of her older sister Nancy for the afternoon, she enlists her neighbor and best friend Ivy to come over and teach Nancy how to be a really good babysitter.

"The frequent black-and-white Chinese ink illustrations capture the mood and carefree attitude of the story well. Early chapter-book readers will enjoy this installment in this light-hearted series." SLJ

Ivy + Bean: doomed to dance; written by Annie Barrows; illustrated by Sophie Blackall. Chronicle Books 2009 129p il (Ivy + Bean) $14.99
Grades: 1 2 3   Fic
1. Ballet -- Fiction 2. Friendship -- Fiction
ISBN 978-0-8118-6266-0; 0-8118-6266-6
                                                    LC 2009004367
Second-grade best friends Ivy and Bean beg for ballet lessons, then, when they are cast as squids in their first recital, scheme to find a way out of what seems to be boring, hard, and potentially embarrassing.

"The story is solidly written, and the expressive black-and-white illustrations, some full page, add to the humor. Early chapter-book readers will appreciate and relate to the friends' dilemma." SLJ

Ivy + Bean: what's the big idea? written by Annie Barrows; illustrated by Sophie Blackall. Chronicle Books 2010 131p il (Ivy + Bean) $14.99
Grades: 1 2 3   Fic
1. School stories 2. Science projects -- Fiction
ISBN 978-0-8118-6692-7; 0-8118-6692-0
                                                    LC 2010008258
When all the second grade students must enter the science fair, which has global warming as its theme, best friends Ivy and Bean team up to create an unusual project.

"Barrows and Blackall deserve kudos for keeping this seventh book in the series original and fun." Horn Book

The **magic** half. Bloomsbury Children's Books 2008 211p $15.95; pa $6.99
Grades: 3 4 5   Fic
1. Twins -- Fiction 2. Sisters -- Fiction
ISBN 978-1-59990-132-9; 1-59990-132-3; 978-1-59990-358-3 pa; 1-59990-358-X pa
                                                    LC 2007-23551
Eleven-year-old Miri Gill feels left out in her family, which has two sets of twins and her, until she travels back in time to 1935 and discovers Molly, her own lost twin, and brings her back to the present day.

"Readers will savor the author's lively observations . . . while the heroine's adaptability and independent thinking endow her with the appeal of a Ramona Quimby or a Clementine." Publ Wkly

Barry, Dave
Peter & the shadow thieves; by Dave Barry and Ridley Pearson; illustrations by Greg Call. Disney Editions/Hyperion Books for Children 2006 556p il $18.99
Grades: 5 6 7   Fic
1. Fairy tales 2. Adventure fiction
ISBN 0-7868-3787-X
                                                    LC 2005-56033
Sequel to Peter and the starcatchers (2004)
Realizing that Molly and the other Starcatchers are in danger when the sinister being Lord Ombra visits the island and seems to control people through their shadows, Peter and Tinker Bell travel to England to help save the stardust. "Age ten and up." (N Y Times Book Rev)

This "is filled with enough rollicking, death-defying adventure to satisfy anyone." SLJ

Followed by Peter and the secret of Rundoon (2007)

Peter and the secret of Rundoon; by Dave Barry and Ridley Pearson; illustrations by Greg Call. Disney Editions/Hyperion Books for Children 2007 482p il $18.99

Grades: 5 6 7   **Fic**

1. Fairy tales 2. Adventure fiction
ISBN 0-7868-3788-8; 978-0-7868-3788-5

LC 2007006306

Sequel to Peter and the shadow thieves (2006)

Fearing that the sinister Lord Ombra was not destroyed, Peter and Molly travel to the land of Rundoon, which is ruled by the evil King Zarboff.

"This is a fun, intense, and totally worthwhile adventure." SLJ

Followed by Peter and the Sword of Mercy (2009)

Peter and the starcatchers; by Dave Barry and Ridley Pearson; illustrations by Greg Call. Hyperion 2004 451p il $17.99; pa $7.99

Grades: 5 6 7   **Fic**

1. Fairy tales 2. Adventure fiction 3. Pirates -- Fiction
ISBN 0-7868-5445-6; 0-7868-4907-X pa

LC 2004-55275

Soon after Peter, an orphan, sets sail from England on the ship Never Land, he befriends Molly, a young Starcatcher, whose mission is to guard a trunk of magical stardust from a greedy pirate and the native inhabitants of a remote island. "Age ten and up." (N Y Times Book Rev)

"The authors plait multiple story lines together in short, fast-moving chapters. . . . Capitalizing on familiar material, this adventure is carefully crafted to set the stage for Peter's later exploits. This smoothly written page-turner just might send readers back to the original." SLJ

Peter and the Sword of Mercy; by Dave Barry and Ridley Pearson; illustrations by Greg Call. Disney/Hyperion Books 2009 515p il $18.99

Grades: 5 6 7   **Fic**

1. Fairy tales 2. Adventure fiction
ISBN 978-1-4231-2134-3; 1-4231-2134-1

Sequel to: Peter and the secret of Rundoon (2007)

James, one of Peter's original Lost Boys, is now working for Scotland Yard and suspects that the heir to England's throne, Prince Albert Edward, is under the influence of shadow creatures who are after starstuff hidden in an underground vault which has only one key: the Sword of Mercy.

"This adventure is fast and intense, and readers will feel compelled to find out what happens next." VOYA

Followed by: The bridge to Never Land (2011)

The **worst** class trip ever; Dave Barry. First edition Disney-Hyperion Books 2015 214 p. illustrations, map $13.99

Grades: 5 6 7   **Fic**

1. Field trips -- Fiction 2. Terrorism -- Prevention -- Fiction 3. Washington (D.C.) -- Description and travel 4. Humorous stories 5. Terrorism -- Fiction 6. Conduct of life -- Fiction 7. Washington (D.C.) -- Fiction 8. School field trips -- Fiction
ISBN 1484708490; 9781484708491

LC 2014013171

"On a class trip to Washington, DC, eighth grader Wyatt Palmer and his best friend Matt believe that they have uncovered a terrorist plot. During a scuffle with these passengers, Matt removes an odd device from one man's backpack. This event gets Matt and Wyatt into trouble with their teacher. For the rest of their trip, Wyatt, Matt, and a few more of their classmates . . . avoid bad guys, sneak away from the rest of their class, and conceal the whole situation from their chaperones." (Publisher's note)

"With its wacky humor and mildly suspenseful scenarios, this appealing book will be a good fit for most libraries." SLJ

Another title in this series is:
The worst night ever (2016)

Barshaw, Ruth McNally

Ellie McDoodle: best friends fur-ever. Bloomsbury 2010 171p $12.99

Grades: 2 3 4 5   **Fic**

1. School stories 2. Pets -- Fiction 3. Drawing -- Fiction 4. Parrots -- Fiction 5. Family life -- Fiction
ISBN 978-1-59990-426-9; 1-59990-426-8

Ellie pet-sits for her neighbor's African grey parrot Alix, about whom she is writing a report, while her family argues over whether to get a cat or a dog, and her little brother accidentally lets Alix out of his cage, all of which is chronicled in Ellie's ever-present sketchbook.

"Interspersed in this story are instructions for games, yoga breathing, and crafts that add to the fun. . . . Exuberant black-and-white sketches and dialogue balloons enliven the pages." SLJ

Ellie McDoodle: have pen, will travel; written and illustrated by Ruth McNally Barshaw. Bloomsbury Children's Books 2007 170p il $11.95; pa $5.99

Grades: 2 3 4 5   **Fic**

1. Camping -- Fiction 2. Cousins -- Fiction
ISBN 978-1-58234-745-5; 1-58234-745-X; 978-1-59990-276-0 pa; 1-59990-276-1 pa

LC 2006-28424

Eleven-year-old Ellie McDoodle illustrates her sketchbook with chronicles of her adventures and mishaps while camping with her cousins, aunt, and uncle.

"The engaging text reflects a contemporary preadolescent sensibility and is chock-full of clean, distinguished line drawings on each spread." SLJ

Other titles about Ellie McDoodle are:
Ellie McDoodle: new kid in school (2008)
Ellie McDoodle: best friends fur-ever (2010)

Ellie McDoodle: new kid in school; written and illustrated by Ruth McNally Barshaw. Children's Books 2008 188p il $12.99

Grades: 2 3 4 5   **Fic**

1. School stories 2. Moving -- Fiction 3. Family life -- Fiction
ISBN 978-1-59990-238-8; 1-59990-238-9

LC 2007050833

Ellie writes and doodles in a journal of her family's move to a new home and her struggle to make friends, which gets a lot easier as she leads a nonviolent protest about long lunch lines at school.

This is "a humorous and realistic look at moving. . . . [Ellie's] story is told through a notebook, which is a combination of handwritten text and line drawings. The pictures, comic frames, and dialogue balloons serve to further the story. Reluctant and struggling readers and young fans of graphic novels are sure to find this title appealing." SLJ

Bartoletti, Susan Campbell

★ The **boy** who dared. Scholastic Press 2008 202p $16.99

Grades: 5 6 7 8   **Fic**

1. Young adult literature 2. Courage -- Fiction 3. Underground leaders 4. National socialism -- Fiction 5. Germany -- History -- 1933-1945 -- Fiction
ISBN 0-439-68013-1; 978-0-439-68013-4

LC 2007014166

In October, 1942, seventeen-year-old Helmuth Hübener, imprisoned for distributing anti-Nazi leaflets, recalls his past life and how he came to dedicate himself to bringing the truth about Hitler and the war to the German people.

Bartoletti "does and excellent job of conveying the political climate surrounding Hitler's ascent to power, seamlessly integrating a complex range of socioeconomic conditions into her absorbing drama." Publ Wkly

Base, Graeme

Enigma; a magical mystery. [by] Graeme Base. Abrams Books for Young Readers 2008 36p il $19.95

Grades: 3 4 5   **Fic**

1. Picture puzzles 2. Stories in rhyme 3. Badgers -- Fiction 4. Ciphers -- Fiction 5. Rabbits -- Fiction 6. Magicians -- Fiction 7. Grandfathers -- Fiction

ISBN 978-0-8109-7245-2; 0-8109-7245-X

LC 2007042397

When Bertie the badger visits his grandfather at a retirement home for magicians, he learns that his grandfather's rabbit, Enigma, has disappeared along with everyone's magical things, and the reader is invited to help break a code to find the items hidden throughout the book. Includes a built-in decoder.

"Readers could simply hunt for the missing objects, which Base conceals within elaborately detailed paintings, but then they would miss out on the tricky fun of mastering several codes also embedded in the book. . . . A set of bonus challenges will keep kids (and older siblings) poring closely over the pages for weeks, enthralled." Publ Wkly

Baskin, Nora Raleigh

The **truth** about my Bat Mitzvah. Simon & Schuster Books for Young Readers 2008 138p $15.99; pa $5.99

Grades: 5 6 7 8   **Fic**

1. Jews -- Fiction 2. Bat mitzvah -- Fiction 3. Grandmothers -- Fiction

ISBN 978-1-4169-3558-2; 1-4169-3558-4; 978-1-4169-7469-7 pa; 1-4169-7469-5 pa

LC 2007-01248

After her beloved grandmother, Nana, dies, non-religious twelve-year-old Caroline becomes curious about her mother's Jewish ancestry.

"Readers will identify with Caroline and her preoccupations. . . . This quick read will be a hit with preteens contemplating their own identities." Booklist

Baskin, Nora Raleigh, 1961-

★ **Anything** but typical. Simon & Schuster Books for Young Readers 2009 195p il $15.99

Grades: 4 5 6 7   **Fic**

1. School stories 2. Autism -- Fiction 3. Authorship -- Fiction 4. Family life -- Fiction

ISBN 1416963782; 9781416963783

LC 2008-20994

ALA Schneider Family Book Award Honor Book (2010)

Jason, a twelve-year-old who wants to become a writer, relates what life is like as he tries to make sense of his world. "Grades six to nine." (Bull Cent Child Books)

"This is an enormously difficult subject, but Baskin, without dramatics or sentimentality, makes it universal." Booklist

Nine, ten; a September 11 story. Nora Raleigh Baskin. Atheneum Books for Young Readers 2016 208 p. (hardcover) $16.99

Grades: 4 5 6 7 8   **Fic**

1. Middle schools -- Fiction 2. September 11 terrorist attacks, 2001 -- Fiction

ISBN 9781442485068; 9781442485075

LC 2015011934

This book, by Nora Raleigh Baskin, presents a "look at the days leading up to the tragic events of September 11, 2001, and how that day

impacted the lives of four middle schoolers. . . . Sergio . . . is struggling to come to terms with the absentee father he hates. . . . Will's father is gone, too, killed in a car accident. . . . Naheed has never before felt uncomfortable about being Muslim. . . . Aimee is starting a new school in a new city and missing her mom." (Publisher's note)

"Adults may be chilled by key names and places and what they portend, but children may gain a small sense of the magnitude of the changes that day wrought on our world. Tense, disturbing, and thought-provoking." Kirkus

Ruby on the outside; Nora Raleigh Baskin. First edition Simon & Schuster Books for Young Readers 2015 176 p. (hardcover) $16.99

Grades: 4 5 6 7 8   **Fic**

1. Friendship -- Fiction 2. Children of prisoners -- Fiction 3. Mother-daughter relationship -- Fiction 4. Aunts -- Fiction 5. Friendship -- Fiction 6. Best friends -- Fiction 7. Prisoners' families -- Fiction 8. Mothers and daughters -- Fiction

ISBN 1442485035; 9781442485037; 9781442485044

LC 2014018268

In this novel, by Nora Raleigh Baskin, "Ruby's mom is in prison, and to tell anyone the truth is to risk true friendship. . . . Eleven-year-old Ruby Danes is about to start middle school, and only her aunt knows her deepest, darkest, most secret secret: her mother is in prison. Then Margalit Tipps moves into Ruby's condo complex, and the two immediately hit it off. Ruby thinks she's found her first true-blue friend--but can she tell Margalit the truth about her mom?" (Publisher's note)

"This lyrical novel explores multiple aspects of the effects of incarceration on family—guilt, fear, anger, loneliness, and heavy responsibility. Baskin's plot structure, which flows from the present to periodic flashbacks, keeps the story from being unbearably dark. Margalit may be too good to be true, but she is just what the doctor ordered for Ruby's healing." Booklist

Runt; Nora Raleigh Baskin. Simon & Schuster Books for Young Readers 2013 208 p. (hardback) $15.99

Grades: 5 6 7 8   **Fic**

1. School stories -- Fiction 2. Female friendship -- Fiction 3. Dogs -- Fiction 4. Schools -- Fiction 5. Bullying -- Fiction 6. Popularity -- Fiction 7. Middle schools -- Fiction 8. Online social networks -- Fiction

ISBN 1442458070; 9781442458079; 9781442458086

LC 2012049461

This book shows "the day-to-day torments of students in a sixth-grade class. In a series of brief vignettes, [Nora Raleigh Baskin] moves between classmates including 'Smelly-Girl' Elizabeth, who can't shake the lingering scent (or shed hair) of her mother's dog-sitting business, Elizabeth's nemesis, Maggie, who . . . hasn't been able to repair her fallout with her artistically talented former best friend Freida; and Stewart and Matthew, two athletes whose rivalry leads to a fight." (Publishers Weekly)

Bateman, Colin

Running with the Reservoir Pups; [by] Colin Bateman. Delacorte Press 2005 263p (Eddie & the gang with no name) hardcover o.p. lib bdg $17.99

Grades: 5 6 7 8   **Fic**

1. Gangs -- Fiction 2. Divorce -- Fiction 3. Northern Ireland -- Fiction

ISBN 0-385-73244-9; 0-385-90268-9 lib bdg

LC 2004-43912

First published 2003 in the United Kingdom

When his parents divorce and his mother moves with him to Belfast, Northern Ireland, twelve-year-old Eddie contends with the Reservoir Pups, a gang of children who rule his neighborhood.

This "author's hilarious, dark Northern Irish wit, penchant for action-packed mayhem, sense of irony, and snappy dialogue are all evident n this [book]." SLJ

Another title about Eddie is:

Bring me the head of Oliver Plunkett (2005)

Bateson, Catherine

Being Bee. Holiday House 2007 126p il $16.95; pa $7.95
Grades: 4 5 6   **Fic**
1. Australia -- Fiction 2. Family life -- Fiction 3. Guinea pigs -- Fiction 4. Father-daughter relationship -- Fiction
ISBN 978-0-8234-2104-6; 0-8234-2104-X; 978-0-8234-2208-1 pa; 0-8234-2208-9 pa

LC 2006-101561

Bee faces friction at home and at school when her widowed father egins seriously dating Jazzi, who seems to take over the house and their ives, but as shared secrets and common interests finally begin to draw hem together, Jazzi accidentally makes a terrible mistake.

"Bee's emotions are perspectives are honest and clearly presented. . . She is a likable, believable character." SLJ

Magenta McPhee. Holiday House 2010 170p $16.95
Grades: 4 5 6 7   **Fic**
1. Australia -- Fiction 2. Authorship -- Fiction 3. Single parent family -- Fiction 4. Dating (Social customs) -- Fiction 5. Father-daughter relationship -- Fiction
ISBN 978-0-8234-2253-1; 0-8234-2253-4

LC 2009-10854

First published 2009 in Australia

Thinking her father needs a new interest in his life after he is laid-off of work, teenaged Magenta, who envisions herself as a future fantasy author, decides to dabble in matchmaking which brings unexpected results.

"With a personality as colorful as her name, Bateson's . . . eponymous heroine has a narrative voice that is smart, wry, and down-to-earth. . . This [is a] real and ultimately reassuring story." Publ Wkly

Baucom, Ian

Through the skylight; a Venice tale. Ian Baucom. 1st ed. Atheneum Books for Young Readers 2013 400 p. ill. (hardcover) $17.99
Grades: 5 6 7 8   **Fic**
1. Fantasy fiction 2. Time travel -- Fiction 3. Venice (Italy) -- Fiction 4. Italy -- Fiction 5. Magic -- Fiction 6. Americans -- Italy -- Fiction 7. Mystery and detective stories 8. Brothers and sisters -- Fiction
ISBN 1416917772; 9781416917779

LC 2012010642

In this juvenile novel, by Ian Baucom, illustrated by Justin Gerard, when Jared, Shireen, and Miranda are each given one glittering gift rom an old Venetian shopkeeper, they never fathom the powers they are low able to unleash. . . . For in another time, centuries earlier, another rio . . . have been kidnapped and, along with hundreds of other children, vill be sold into child slavery. Unless, that is, they can find some way to ave them all." (Publisher's note)

"Frequent black-and-white illustrations support the narrative. Baucom's familiarity with the setting and use of Italian words heighten the tmosphere. . . . The mix of protagonists' genders, historical details, and nteresting magic creates a story with broad appeal and a message about he power of words. . ." SLJ

Bauer, A. C. E.

★ **Come** Fall. Random House 2010 231p $15.99; lib bdg $18.99
Grades: 4 5 6 7   **Fic**
1. School stories 2. Crows -- Fiction 3. Fairies -- Fiction 4.

Friendship -- Fiction 5. Foster home care -- Fiction
ISBN 978-0-375-85825-3; 0-375-85825-3; 978-0-375-95855-7 lib bdg; 0-375-95855-X lib bdg

LC 2009-32419

Drawn together by a mentoring program and an unusual crow, middle school misfits Salman, Lu, and Blos form a strong friendship despite teasing by fellow students and the maneuverings of fairies Oberon, Titania, and Puck.

"Weaving in magic, dreams, doubles, contrasts, and other elements from the original play, Bauer spins an enticing variant." Booklist

★ **No** castles here. Random House 2007 270p $15.99; lib bdg $18.99
Grades: 4 5 6 7   **Fic**
1. Magic -- Fiction 2. New Jersey -- Fiction 3. Choirs (Music) -- Fiction 4. Books and reading -- Fiction 5. City and town life -- Fiction
ISBN 978-0-375-83921-4; 978-0-375-93921-1 lib bdg

LC 2006023601

Eleven-year-old Augie Boretski dreams of escaping his rundown Camden, New Jersey, neighborhood, but things start to turn around with help from a Big Brother, a music teacher, and a mysterious bookstore owner, so when his school is in trouble, he pulls the community together to save it

This is a "heartwarming novel." Booklist

Bauer, Joan

Almost home; by Joan Bauer. Viking 2012 264 p. (hardcover) $16.99
Grades: 5 6 7 8   **Fic**
1. Pets -- Fiction 2. Homeless persons -- Fiction 3. Mother-daughter relationship -- Fiction 4. Mothers and daughters -- Fiction
ISBN 0670012890; 9780670012893

LC 2011050483

In this book by Joan Bauer, "when twelve-year-old Sugar's grandfather dies and her gambling father takes off yet again, Sugar and her mother . . . head to Chicago for a fresh start, only to discover that fresh starts aren't so easy to come by for the homeless. . . .With the help of a rescue dog . . . a foster family . . . and her own grace and good humor, Sugar comes to understand that while she can't control the hand life deals her, she can control how she responds." (Publisher's note)

Close to famous. Viking 2011 250p $16.99
Grades: 5 6 7 8   **Fic**
1. Baking -- Fiction 2. Literacy -- Fiction 3. Country life -- Fiction 4. West Virginia -- Fiction 5. Single parent family -- Fiction
ISBN 0-670-01282-3; 978-0-670-01282-4

LC 2010030022

Twelve-year-old Foster McFee and her mother escape from her mother's abusive boyfriend and end up in the small town of Culpepper, West Virginia, where they use their strengths and challenge themselves to build a new life, with the help of the friends they make there.

"Bauer skillfully brings readers to the heart of Culpepper with rich depictions of contemporary small town and its residents and rhythms." Publ Wkly

Soar; Joan Bauer. Viking 2016 304 p. (hardcover) $16.99
Grades: 5 6 7 8   **Fic**
1. Baseball -- Coaching 2. Moving, Household -- Fiction 3. Adoption -- Fiction 4. Baseball -- Fiction 5. Teamwork (Sports) -- Fiction 6. Coaches (Athletics) -- Fiction 7. Heart -- Transplantation -- Fiction
ISBN 9780451470348; 0451470346

LC 2015013293

In this novel, by Joan Bauer, when Jeremiah is "told he can't play baseball following an operation on his heart, Jeremiah decides he'll do the next best thing and become a coach. Hillcrest, where Jeremiah and his father Walt have just moved, is a town known for its championship baseball team. But Jeremiah finds the town caught up in a scandal and about ready to give up on baseball. It's up to Jeremiah and his can-do spirit to get the town—and the team—back in the game." (Publisher's note)

"An outstanding, tender exploration of courage and the true nature of heroism and, for good measure, a fine homage to America's game, as well." Kirkus

Bauer, Marion Dane

A **bear** named Trouble. Clarion Books 2005 120p $15
Grades: 3 4 5 6   **Fic**

1. Zoos -- Fiction 2. Bears -- Fiction 3. Alaska -- Fiction
ISBN 0-618-51738-3

LC 2004-21259

In Anchorage, Alaska, two lonely boys make a connection—a brown bear injured just after his mother sends him out on his own, and a human whose father is a new keeper at the Alaska Zoo and whose mother and sister are still in Minnesota.

"With a strong plot, well-developed characters, and an engaging writing format, this book is a great choice for young readers." SLJ

★ The **blue** ghost; illustrated by Suling Wang. Random House 2005 85p il $11.95; lib bdg $13.99; pa $3.99
Grades: 2 3 4   **Fic**

1. Ghost stories
ISBN 0-375-83179-7; 0-375-93179-1 lib bdg; 0-375-83339-0 pa

At her grandmother's log cabin, nine-year-old Liz is led to make contact with children she believes may be her ancestors.

"This gentle ghost story, written in simple prose, blends mild suspense with a look at how the past connects to and influences the present. Mystery fans will enjoy the spooky premise, and Wang's softly rendered black-and-white drawings increase the ghostly atmosphere." Booklist

Other titles in this series are:
The green ghost (2008)
The red ghost (2008)
The golden ghost (2011)

Little cat's luck; a novel. Marion Dane Bauer; illustrated by Jennifer A. Bell. Simon & Schuster Books for Young Readers 2016 224 p. illustrations (hardcover) $16.99
Grades: 3 4 5   **Fic**

1. Cats -- Fiction 2. Dogs -- Fiction 3. Novels in verse 4. Animals -- Infancy -- Fiction 5. Adventure and adventurers -- Fiction
ISBN 9781481424882; 9781481424899

LC 2014037635

In this book, by Marion Dane Bauer, illustrated by Jennifer A. Bell, "When an indoor calico cat named Patches spots a golden autumn leaf fluttering past her window, she can't help but venture outside to chase it. But soon, Patches feels something tugging at her, telling her to find a special place." (Publisher's note)

"Newbery Honor Book author Bauer (On My Honor, 1987) has written a poetic and charming tale for young readers, bolstered by Bell's adorable, breezy illustrations. Animal lovers will want to take this home pronto." Booklist

Little dog, lost; Marion Dane Bauer; with illustrations by Jennifer Bell. Atheneum Books for Young Readers 2012 197 p. ill. (hardcover) $14.99
Grades: 4 5 6 7   **Fic**

1. Dogs -- Fiction 2. Picture books for children 3. Interpersonal relations -- Fiction 4. Novels in verse 5. Parks -- Fiction 6. Loneliness -- Fiction 7. City and town life -- Fiction
ISBN 1442434236; 9781442434233; 9781442434257

LC 2011034024

This book tells the tale of "three needy creatures." Buddy the dog is "re-homed with a clueless though kind woman" after her family moves; Mark "feels his life is empty without the dog he desperately needs but his mother won't permit"; and "Charles Larue, the aging caretaker of a nearby mansion . . . spends his lonely days waiting for something—anything—to bring meaning to his life." The story is written in "[l]ong, thin lines of free-verse text." Additionally, "black-and-white illustrations are included. (Kirkus)

★ **On** my honor. Clarion Bks. 1986 90p $15
Grades: 4 5 6 7   **Fic**

1. Accidents -- Fiction
ISBN 0-89919-439-7

LC 86-267

A Newbery Medal honor book, 1987

When his best friend drowns while they are both swimming in a treacherous river that they had promised never to go near, Joel is devastated and terrified at having to tell both sets of parents the terrible consequences of their disobedience

"Bauer's association of Joel's guilt with the smell of the polluted river on his skin is particularly noteworthy. Its miasma almost rises off the pages. Descriptions are vivid, characterization and dialogue natural and the style taut but unforced. A powerful, moving book." SLJ

Bauer, Marion Dane, 1938-

Bauer, Michael Gerard

Just a dog; Michael Gerard Bauer. Scholastic Press 2012 144 p (hc) $15.99
Grades: 4 5 6   **Fic**

1. Dogs -- Fiction 2. Family life -- Fiction 3. Dalmatians -- Fiction
ISBN 0545374529; 9780545374521; 9780545374538

LC 201201442

This children's book, by Michael Gerard Bauer, is about a family's pet dog. "Sometimes a dog isn't just a dog--sometimes he's the glue that holds a whole family together. Mr. Mosely is a special dog. . . . He's special because he seems to know exactly what everyone in Corey's family needs, even when they don't know themselves. This is the story of Mr. Mosely, from his puppyhood to the last time he curls up on the back porch." (Publisher's note)

Baum, L. Frank

The **Wizard** of Oz; illustrated by Charles Santore; with an introduction by Michael Patrick Hearn. Sterling 2009 96p il $16.95
Grades: 3 4 5   **Fic**

1. Fantasy fiction
ISBN 978-1-4027-6625-1; 1-4027-6625-4

LC 200804686

A reissue of the edition first published 1991 by Random House

After a cyclone transports her to the land of Oz, Dorothy must seek out the great Wizard in order to return to Kansas

"This edition has been skillfully condensed for those not ready for the longer original work. Santore's many paintings, including spot art and full- and double-page spreads, add a successful dose of drama to the classic fantasy." Horn Book Guide

★ The **wonderful** Wizard of Oz; with pictures by W. W. Denslow. 100th anniversary ed.; HarperCollins Publishers 2000 267p $24.99

Grades: 3 4 5 6   **Fic**
1. Fantasy fiction
ISBN 0-06-029323-3

LC 2001-265945

First published 1900

After a cyclone transports her to the land of Oz, Dorothy must seek out the great wizard in order to return to Kansas.

"For those who want the look and feel of the 1900 publication, this fills the bill. It's a very handsome facsimile, printed on high-quality paper and containing all of W. W. Denslow's 24 original colorplates and 130 two-color drawings." Booklist

Beard, Darleen Bailey

Annie Glover is not a tree lover; pictures by Heather Maione. Farrar Straus Giroux 2009 120p il $15.99

Grades: 3 4 5   **Fic**
1. Trees -- Fiction 2. Grandmothers -- Fiction 3. Environmental protection -- Fiction
ISBN 978-0-374-30351-8; 0-374-30351-7

LC 2008043418

When her grandmother chains herself to the tree across from the school to save it from being cut down, fourth-grader Annie wants to die of humiliation, but when she dicovers the town's history, her attitude changes.

"Light fun, with a save-the-planet message, Beard's fast-paced plot accompanied by Maione's comic illustrations will have plenty of fans, including reluctant readers." SLJ

Operation Clean Sweep; [by] Darleen Bailey Beard. Farrar Straus Giroux 2004 151p $16

Grades: 3 4 5 6   **Fic**
1. Oregon -- Fiction 2. Elections -- Fiction 3. Women -- Suffrage -- Fiction
ISBN 0-374-38034-1

LC 2003-49430

In 1916, just four years after getting the right to vote, the women of Umatilla, Oregon band together to throw the mayor and other city officials out of office, replacing them with women

"Beard's story, based on real events, features believable characters, strong local color, and a plot that gently makes its point without offending anyone." Booklist

Bearn, Emily

★ **Tumtum** & Nutmeg: adventures beyond Nutmouse Hall. Little, Brown Books for Young Readers 2009 504p $16.99

Grades: 4 5 6   **Fic**
1. Mice -- Fiction 2. Siblings -- Fiction
ISBN 978-0-316-02703-8; 0-316-02703-0

LC 2008-45294

Wealthy, married mice Tumtum and Nutmeg find adventure when they secretly try to help two human siblings who live in a tumbledown cottage with their absent-minded inventor father.

"The stories are filled with descriptions of good food, cheering fires and warm beds. Price's black-and-white line drawings have a scratchy, comic air that brings a welcome edge to the gentle storytelling. . . . The sympathetic characters, enchanting setting and quickly paced plots will hold readers' interest." Publ Wkly

Another title in this series is:
Tumtum & Nutmeg: The Rose Cottage tales (2010)

Tumtum & Nutmeg: the Rose Cottage tales. Little, Brown 2010 398p $16.99

Grades: 4 5 6   **Fic**
1. Mice -- Fiction 2. Seashore -- Fiction 3. Siblings -- Fiction 4.

Birthdays -- Fiction 5. Christmas -- Fiction
ISBN 0-316-08599-5; 978-0-316-08599-1

LC 2010032962

Wealthy, married mice Tumtum and Nutmeg have a series of adventures as they try to help the impoverished human children, Arthur and Lucy Mildew, to have a good Christmas, enjoy a seaside holiday, and celebrate Arthur's birthday.

This book includes "three rousing adventures. . . . Even when [Tumtun & Nutmeg's] world gets exciting, though, it's still a cozy read." Kirkus

Beasley, Cassie

★ **Circus** Mirandus; by Cassie Beasley. Dial Books for Young Readers, an imprint of Penguin Group (USA) Inc. 2015 304 p. (hardcover) $17.99

Grades: 4 5 6   **Fic**
1. Magic -- Fiction 2. Circus -- Fiction 3. Grandfathers -- Fiction 4. Sick -- Fiction 5. Orphans -- Fiction 6. Friendship -- Fiction 7. Great aunts -- Fiction
ISBN 0525428437; 9780525428435

LC 2014031463

In this novel by Cassie Beasley "even though his awful Great-Aunt Gertrudis doesn't approve, Micah believes in the stories his dying Grandpa Ephraim tells him of the magical Circus Mirandus: the invisible tiger guarding the gates . . . and the magician . . . the Man Who Bends Light. Finally, Grandpa Ephraim offers proof. The Circus is real. And the Lightbender owes Ephraim a miracle. Micah sets out to find the Circus and the man he believes will save his grandfather." (Publisher's note)

Beatty, Robert

Serafina and the Twisted Staff; Robert Beatty. Disney-Hyperion 2016 384 p. (hardback) $16.99

Grades: 5 6 7   **Fic**
1. Good and evil -- Fiction 2. Mystery fiction -- Fiction 3. Paranormal fiction -- Fiction 4. Horror stories 5. Identity -- Fiction 6. Supernatural -- Fiction 7. Shapeshifting -- Fiction 8. Biltmore Estate (Asheville, N.C.) -- Fiction
ISBN 9781484775035

LC 2016006654

Sequel to: Serafina and the black cloak

In this novel in the Serafina series by Robert Beatty, "Serafina finds herself caught between two worlds: she's too wild for Biltmore Estate's beautifully dressed ladies and formal customs, and too human to fully join her forest kin. Late one night, she encounters a strange and terrifying figure, and then she's attacked by the vicious wolfhounds under his control. . . . She's convinced that the stranger is not alone, that he has sent his accomplice into Biltmore in disguise." (Publisher's note)

"Even better than its predecessor, a sequel that delivers nonstop thrills from beginning to end." Kirkus

Beaty, Andrea

Attack of the fluffy bunnies; illustrated by Dan Santat. Amulet Books 2010 184p il $12.95

Grades: 3 4 5   **Fic**
1. Camps -- Fiction 2. Twins -- Fiction 3. Siblings -- Fiction 4. Extraterrestrial beings -- Fiction
ISBN 978-0-8109-8416-5; 0-8109-8416-4

At Camp Whatsitooya, twins Joules and Kevin and new friend Nelson face off against large, rabbitlike creatures from the Mallow Galaxy who thrive on sugar, but are not above hypnotizing and eating human campers.

"Beaty's tale of high silliness is sure to please, and it's dotted with Santat's mini-comics and spot illustrations, which move the story along.

If at times the reach for a larff is a bit of a stretch, it's all in fun. The hint at a possible sequel will have humorous-adventure lovers asking." Kirkus

Cicada summer. Amulet Books 2008 167p $15.95

Grades: 4 5 6 7   **Fic**

1. Illinois -- Fiction 2. Siblings -- Fiction 3. Bereavement -- Fiction

ISBN 978-0-8109-9472-0; 0-8109-9472-0

LC 2007-22266

Twelve-year-old Lily mourns her brother, and has not spoken since the accident she feels she could of prevented but the summer Tinny comes to town she is the only one who realizes Lily's secret.

"This is compelling fiction that will be a hit with young readers. . . . Rich and thought-provoking and yet . . . accessible." Horn Book

Dorko the magnificent; by Andrea Beaty. Amulet Books 2013 213 p. (hardcover) $16.95

Grades: 3 4 5 6   **Fic**

1. Magicians -- Fiction 2. Grandmothers -- Fiction 3. Humorous stories 4. Family life -- Fiction 5. Magic tricks -- Fiction

ISBN 1419706381; 9781419706387

LC 2012045674

In this book by Andrea Beaty "Robbie loves magic and he's good at it—sort of. When Grandma Melvyn moves in and takes over his room, Robbie discovers that she was once an internationally renowned magician and learns about the heartache that turned her into a bitter woman. Against all odds, Robbie and Grandma Melvyn form an uneasy alliance to show the world—or at least the kids of Hobson Elementary School— that he is a true magician." (Publisher's note)

Becker, Bonny

Holbrook; a lizard's tale. by Bonny Becker; illustrated by Abby Carter. Clarion Books 2006 150p il $15

Grades: 3 4 5   **Fic**

1. Artists -- Fiction 2. Lizards -- Fiction 3. City and town life -- Fiction

ISBN 978-0-618-71458-2; 0-618-71458-8

LC 2006-03962

Holbrook the lizard has an artist's soul, but when his paintings are ridiculed by the owls, geckoes, and other creatures in his desert town, he decides to seek his fortune in the big city, unaware of the dangers of urban life.

"The story moves along quickly, enlivened by dramatic situations, dry wit, and dynamic full-page illustrations. An enjoyable romp." Booklist

The **magical** Ms. Plum; illustrated by Amy Portnoy. Alfred A. Knopf 2009 104p il $12.99; lib bdg $15.99

Grades: 2 3 4   **Fic**

1. School stories 2. Magic -- Fiction 3. Teachers -- Fiction

ISBN 978-0-375-85637-2; 0-375-85637-4; 978-0-375-95637-9 lib bdg; 0-375-95637-9 lib bdg

LC 2008-42682

The students in Ms Plum's third grade class soon learn that there is something very special about their teacher and her classroom's mysterious supply closet.

"Readers will relate to the youngsters' problems and enjoy their magical resolutions. Illustrated with delightful black-and-white drawings and filled with clever and short vignettes, this fast-paced story is a good choice for struggling readers." SLJ

Beckhorn, Susan Williams

The **wolf's** boy; by Susan Williams Beckhorn. Disney-Hyperion 2016 240 p. $16.99

Grades: 4 5 6 7   **Fic**

1. Wolves -- Fiction 2. Prehistoric peoples -- Fiction 3. Wilderness survival -- Fiction 4. Survival -- Fiction

ISBN 9781484725535

LC 2015016834

In this book, by Susan Williams Beckhorn, "Kai burns to become a hunter and to earn a rightful place among his people. But that can never be. He was born with a clubfoot. It is forbidden for him to use or even touch a hunter's sacred weapons. Shunned by the other boys, Kai turns to his true friends, the yellow wolves, for companionship. They have not forgotten the young human they nurtured as an abandoned infant." (Publisher's note)

"The bond between boy and canine—even one that's just learning to be a dog—is timeless, and animal-lovers in particular will be touched by this telling." Booklist

Behar, Ruth

Lucky broken girl; Ruth Behar. Nancy Paulsen Books 2017 256 p. illustrations (hardback) $16.99

Grades: 5 6 7 8   **Fic**

1. Neighbors -- Fiction 2. Immigrants -- Fiction 3. Cuban Americans -- Fiction 4. Fractures -- Fiction 5. Family life -- New York (State) -- New York -- Fiction 6. Queens (New York, N.Y.) -- History -- 20th century -- Fiction

ISBN 9780399546440

LC 2016022378

This novel, by Ruth Behar, is an "unforgettable multicultural coming-of-age narrative--based on the author's childhood in the 1960s--a young Cuban-Jewish immigrant girl is adjusting to her new life in New York City when her American dream is suddenly derailed. Ruthie's plight will intrigue readers, and her powerful story of strength and resilience, full of color, light, and poignancy, will stay with them for a long time." (Publisher's note)

Behrens, Andy

The **fast** and the furriest. Alfred A. Knopf 2010 247p $15.99; lib bdg $18.99

Grades: 4 5 6 7   **Fic**

1. Dogs -- Fiction 2. Obesity -- Fiction 3. Football -- Fiction

ISBN 978-0-375-85922-9; 0-375-85922-5; 978-0-375-95922-6 lib bdg; 0-375-95922-X lib bdg

LC 2009018365

The overweight and unathletic son of a famous former football star discovers that his equally fat and lazy dog is unexpectedly—and obsessively—interested in competing in dog agility contests.

"Behrens's engaging style will appeal to children. Students will relate to likable Kevin's self-deprecating humor, and Cromwell's perseverance gives anyone with an unrealized dream a glimmer of hope." SLJ

Beil, Michael

The **Red** Blazer Girls: the mistaken masterpiece. Alfred A. Knopf 2011 309p $16.99; lib bdg $19.99

Grades: 5 6 7 8   **Fic**

1. School stories 2. Mystery fiction 3. Puzzles -- Fiction 4. Art thefts -- Fiction

ISBN 978-0-375-86740-8; 0-375-86740-6; 978-0-375-96740-5 lib bdg; 0-375-96740-0 lib bdg

LC 2010030006

Sophie and her friends, who call themselves The Red Blazer Girls, embark on solving a case involving mistaken identities, switched paintings, and some priceless family heirlooms.

"Sophie narrates with humor and self-effacing aplomb. Visual evidence inserted in the text invites reader participation." Kirkus

Beil, Michael D.

★ The **Red** Blazer Girls: the ring of Rocamadour. Alfred A. Knopf 2009 299p $15.99; lib bdg $18.99

Grades: 5 6 7 8   **Fic**

1. School stories 2. Mystery fiction 3. Puzzles -- Fiction 4. Friendship -- Fiction

ISBN 978-0-375-84814-8; 0-375-84814-2; 978-0-375-94814-5 lib bdg; 0-375-94814-7 lib bdg

LC 2008-25254

Catholic-schooled seventh-graders Sophie, Margaret, Rebecca, and Leigh Ann help an elderly neighbor solve a puzzle her father left for her estranged daughter twenty years ago.

"The dialogue is fast and funny, the clues are often solvable." Booklist

Other titles about the Red Blazer Girls are:

The Red Blazer Girls: the vanishing violin (2010)

The Red Blazer Girls: the mistaken masterpiece (2011)

The **Red** Blazer Girls: The vanishing violin. Alfred A. Knopf 2010 329p $16.99; lib bdg $19.99

Grades: 5 6 7 8   **Fic**

1. Mystery fiction 2. Violins -- Fiction

ISBN 978-0-375-86103-1; 0-375-86103-3; 978-0-375-96103-8 lib bdg; 0-375-96103-8 lib bdg

"Sophie, Margaret, Rebecca, and Leigh Ann . . . find themselves in the midst of several interlocking mysteries, mostly involving violins. . . Beil has lost none of his edge when it comes to setting up sleuthing scenarios and offering kids codes and clues that will intrigue (or drive them crazy). Smartly plotted, smartly played." Booklist

Bell, Jennifer

The **crooked** sixpence; by Jennifer Bell; illustrated by Brett Helquist. Crown Books for Young Readers 2016 320 p. illustrations (Uncommoners) (ebook) $50.97; (hc) $16.99

Grades: 4 5 6   **Fic**

1. Fantasy fiction 2. Magic -- Fiction 3. Family secrets -- Fiction 4. Brothers and sisters -- Fiction 5. Fantasy

ISBN 9780553498455; 9780553498431; 9780553498448

LC 2015035036

In this book, by Jennifer Bell, illustrated by Brett Helquist, "when their grandmother Sylvie is rushed to the hospital, Ivy Sparrow and her annoying big brother Seb cannot imagine what adventure lies in store. Soon their house is ransacked by unknown intruders, and a very strange policeman turns up on the scene, determined to apprehend them . . . with a toilet brush." (Publisher's note)

"There's plenty of exposition and back story to support the adventure promised to continue in subsequent volumes of this trilogy. An auspicious trilogy opener." Kirkus

Bellairs, John

The **house** with a clock in its walls; pictures by Edward Gorey. Dial Bks. for Young Readers 1973 179p il pa $5.99

Grades: 5 6 7 8   **Fic**

1. Witchcraft -- Fiction

ISBN 0-14-240257-5

In 1948, Lewis, a ten-year-old orphan, goes to New Zebedee, Michigan with his warlock Uncle Jonathan, who lives in a big mysterious house and practices white magic. Together with their neighbor, Mrs. Zimmerman, a witch, they search to find a clock that is programmed to end the world and has been hidden in the walls of the house by the evil Isaac Izard

"Bellairs's story and Edward Gorey's pictures are satisfyingly frightening." Publ Wkly

Other titles about Lewis are:

The doom of the haunted opera (1995)

The figure in the shadows (1975)

The ghost in the mirror (1993)

The letter, the witch, and the ring (1976)

The vengeance of the witch-finder (1993)

Benjamin, Ali

★ The **thing** about jellyfish; by Ali Benjamin. Little, Brown & Co. 2015 352 p. (hardcover) $17

Grades: 4 5 6 7 8 9   **Fic**

1. Grief -- Fiction 2. Jellyfishes -- Fiction 3. Friendship -- Fiction 4. Best friends -- Fiction

ISBN 0316380865; 9780316380867

LC 2014044025

National Book Award Finalist: Young People's Literature (2015)

In this novel by Ali Benjamin "after her best friend dies in a drowning accident, Suzy is convinced that the true cause of the tragedy was a rare jellyfish sting. Retreating into a silent world of imagination, she crafts a plan to prove her theory--even if it means traveling the globe, alone. Suzy's achingly heartfelt journey explores life, death, the astonishing wonder of the universe...and the potential for love and hope right next door." (Publisher's note)

"Benjamin's inverse approach to tragedy, placing the death at the beginning of the novel and storytelling through the grieving process, transcends the trope, as the story triumphs in the affecting realities of emotional response and resilience." SLJ

Berk, Josh

Strike three, you're dead; Josh Berk. Knopf Books for Young Readers 2013 256 p. (hardback) $16.99

Grades: 3 4 5 6 7   **Fic**

1. Mystery fiction 2. Baseball -- Fiction 3. Friendship -- Fiction 4. Murder -- Fiction 5. Best friends -- Fiction 6. Philadelphia Phillies (Baseball team) -- Fiction

ISBN 0375870083; 9780375870088; 9780375970085; 9780375987366

LC 2012023892

Edgar Award Finalist: Best Juvenile (2014)

In this mystery, by Josh Berk, twelve-year-old "Lenny, with the help of his buddies Mike and Other Mike, enters and wins a contest to guest-announce a Philadelphia Phillies game. When the hot rookie pitcher drops dead, the kids suspect that it's more than a previously undetected heart condition. They join another local sports fan and begin investigating the crime . . . while meeting their hero, flashy catcher Ramon Famosa, and other players in the process." (Publishers Weekly)

"Baseball aficionados will appreciate all the trivia Berk works into the story, with references to famous players and Phillies history scattered throughout. The wisecracking interplay between the boys is a strong point, though the solution to the mystery is really never in doubt." Pub Wkly

Berkeley, Jon

The **hidden** boy. Katherine Tegen Books 2010 262p (Bell Hoot fables) $16.99

Grades: 3 4 5 6   **Fic**

1. Adventure fiction 2. Siblings -- Fiction 3. Missing children -- Fiction

ISBN 978-0-06-168758-7; 0-06-168758-8; 978-0-06-168759-4 lib bdg; 0-06-168759-6 lib bdg

LC 2009-12272

When Bea and her family are transported aboard an underwater bus to a strange land, her younger brother Theo is lost during the voyage, and somehow it falls to Bea to find out what has become of him.

"Berkeley's arch writing and his characters' hilarious, pathos-inspiring tempers and abilities make this magical stew both compelling and delightful." Booklist

Berlin, Eric

The **potato** chip puzzles; Eric Berlin; [drawings by Katrina Damkoehler] G.P. Putnam's Sons 2009 244p il $16.99; pa $7.99
Grades: 4 5 6 7   **Fic**
1. Mystery fiction 2. Puzzles -- Fiction 3. Contests -- Fiction
ISBN 978-0-399-25198-6; 0-399-25198-7; 978-0-14-241637-2 pa; 0-14-241637-1 pa

LC 2008-33698

Sequel to: The puzzling world of Winston Breen (2007)

Winston and his friends enter an all-day puzzle contest to win fifty-thousand dollars for their school, but they must also figure out who is trying to keep them from winning. Puzzles for the reader to solve are included throughout the text.

"The pace is suspenseful but allows for pauses for problem-solving. The joy for both contestants and readers of this brain-teasing mystery will be in the process." Kirkus

★ The **puzzling** world of Winston Breen; the secret in the box. Putnam 2007 215p il $16.99; pa $7.99
Grades: 4 5 6 7   **Fic**
1. Mystery fiction 2. Puzzles -- Fiction 3. Siblings -- Fiction
ISBN 978-0-399-24693-7; 0-399-24693-2; 978-0-14-241388-3 pa; 0-14-241388-7 pa

LC 2006-20531

Puzzle-crazy, twelve-year-old Winston and his ten-year-old sister Katie find themselves involved in a dangerous mystery involving a hidden ring. Puzzles for the reader to solve are included throughout the text

"A delightfully clever mystery. . . . There is plenty of suspense to engage readers." SLJ

Followed by: The potato chip puzzles (2009)

Berner, Rotraut Susanne

Hound and hare; translated by Shelley Tanaka. Groundwood Books 2011 75p il $18.99
Grades: K 1 2   **Fic**
1. Dogs -- Fiction 2. Rabbits -- Fiction
ISBN 978-0-88899-987-0; 0-88899-987-9

"The illustrations are done in colored pencil and ink, each creature and picture frame defined by soft blue lines. Hounds and hares emerge as regular Hatfields and McCoys and overtly harass each other with wickedly humorous, singsong taunts. Although classmates Harley Hare and Hugo Hound share interests, they've absorbed their families' prejudices and shun each other. . . . The happily-ever-after ending delivers a satisfying resolution to a story about tolerance that successfully uses humor and engaging artwork to avoid didacticism." Kirkus

Betancourt, Jeanne

Ava Tree and the wishes three. Feiwel and Friends 2009 130p il $14.99
Grades: 2 3 4   **Fic**
1. Wishes -- Fiction 2. Orphans -- Fiction 3. Parties -- Fiction 4. Siblings -- Fiction 5. Birthdays -- Fiction
ISBN 978-0-312-37760-1; 0-312-37760-6

LC 2008015265

"Waking up on her eighth birthday, Ava tears up thinking about her parents, who died in a car accident. . . . She now lives with her 22-year-old brother, Jack. . . . Struggling to clean her pet rabbit's litter box, Ava

wishes it 'would use the toilet like a person' and when it suddenly does, Ava and Jack wonder if it could be a birthday gift from their mother, who had been a magician. Ava's 'wishing power' seems to continue, though some of her wishes—that her parents weren't dead—go unanswered. . . . Kids will embrace this bighearted novel and its thoughtful, resilient narrator." Publ Wkly

Bianco, Margery Williams

★ The **velveteen** rabbit; or, How toys become real. by Margery Williams; with illustrations by William Nicholson. Doubleday 1991 33p il $13.95
Grades: 2 3 4   **Fic**
1. Fairy tales 2. Toys -- Fiction 3. Rabbits -- Fiction
ISBN 0-385-07725-4

LC 90-25339

First published 1922 by Doran

By the time the velveteen rabbit is dirty, worn out, and about to be burned, he has almost given up hope of ever finding the magic called Real.

"Quiet, graceful illustrations accentuate the classic tale's nostalgic tone." Publ Wkly

Billingsley, Franny

The **Folk** Keeper. Atheneum Bks. for Young Readers 1999 162p hardcover o.p. pa $4.99; pa $5.99
Grades: 5 6 7 8   **Fic**
1. Fantasy fiction
ISBN 0-689-82876-4; 0-689-84461-1 pa; 9780689844614 pa

LC 98-48778

Boston Globe Horn Book Winner (2000)

Orphaned Corinna disguises herself as a boy to pose as a Folk Keeper, one who keeps the supernatural Folk underground at bay. She discovers her heritage as a seal maiden when she is summoned to become the Folk Keeper for a wealthy family in their manor by the sea. "Ages ten to fourteen." (N Y Times Book Rev)

"The intricate plot, vibrant characters, dangerous intrigue, and fantastical elements combine into a truly remarkable novel steeped in atmosphere." Horn Book

Binding, Tim

★ **Sylvie** and the songman; with illustrations by Angela Barrett. Random House 2009 339p il $15.99; lib bdg $18.99
Grades: 5 6 7 8   **Fic**
1. Fantasy fiction
ISBN 978-0-385-75157-5; 0-385-75159-1; 978-0-385-75159-9 lib bdg; 0-385-75159-1 lib bdg

"Sylvie's composer father . . . goes missing and that's the first odd thing that interrupts her happy routine. Next, the animals seem to have lost their voices. The third is the arrival of the eerie, malevolent Woodpecker Man. . . . The dense narrative is packed with surreal imagery. . . . It's a testament to Binding's assured writing that the abstractions become visceral thrills, like a dream you just can't shake. . . . An unforgettable tale." Booklist

Birdsall, Jeanne

★ The **Penderwicks**; a summer tale of four sisters, two rabbits, and a very interesting boy. Knopf 2005 262p (The Penderwicks) $15.95; lib bdg $17.77; pa $6.99
Grades: 3 4 5 6   **Fic**
1. Sisters -- Fiction 2. Single parent family -- Fiction
ISBN 0-375-83143-6; 0-375-93143-0 lib bdg; 0-440-42047-4 pa

LC 2004-20364

National Book Award: Young People's Literature (2005)

"Four sisters—Rosalind, Skye, Jane, and Batty—spend a few weeks with their father and dog at a cottage on the grounds of a stately home in the Berkshires, where they complicate the lives of a handsome gardener, a lonely boy, and the boy's officious mother. . . . Grades four to seven." Bull Cent Child Books)

"This comforting family story . . . [offers] . . . four marvelously appealing sisters, true childhood behavior . . ., and a writing style that will draw readers close." Booklist

The **Penderwicks** at Point Mouette. Alfred A. Knopf 2011 295p (The Penderwicks) $16.99
Grades: 4 5 6 7   **Fic**
1. Maine -- Fiction 2. Summer -- Fiction 3. Vacations -- Fiction 4. Family life -- Fiction
ISBN 978-0-375-85851-2; 0-375-85851-2

This is the third book about the Penderwick family, who appeared previously in The Penderwicks (2005) and The Penderwicks on Gardam Street (2008). "When summer comes around, it's off to the beach for Rosalind . . . and off to Maine with Aunt Claire for the rest of the Penderwick girls, as well as their old friend, Jeffrey. That leaves Skye as OAP (oldest available Penderwick). . . . Things look good as they settle into their cozy cottage. . . . But can Skye hold it together long enough to figure out Rosalind's directions about not letting Batty explode? Will Jane's Love Survey come to a tragic conclusion after she meets the alluring Dominic? . . . And will Jeffrey be able to keep peace between the girls?" (Publisher's note) "Intermediate." (Horn Book)

"Balancing the novel's comedy is an affecting, neatly crafted subplot that builds up to the emotionally charged revelation involving Jeffrey. From start to finish, this is a summer holiday to savor." Publ Wkly

The **Penderwicks** in spring; Jeanne Birdsall. Knopf Books for Young Readers 2015 352 p. (The Penderwicks) (hardback) $16.99; (lib. bdg.) $19.99
Grades: 4 5 6 7   **Fic**
1. Birthdays -- Fiction 2. Family life -- Fiction 3. Massachusetts -- Fiction 4. Money-making projects for children -- Fiction 5. Singing -- Fiction 6. Surprise -- Fiction 7. Moneymaking projects -- Fiction 8. Single-parent families -- Fiction 9. Family life -- Massachusetts -- Fiction
ISBN 0375870776; 9780375870774; 9780375970771
LC 2014023537

Sequel to: The Penderwicks at Point Mouette (2011)

In this book, by Jeanne Birdsall, "springtime is finally arriving on Gardam Street, and there are surprises in store for each member of the family. Some surprises are just wonderful, like neighbor Nick Geiger coming home from war. And some are ridiculous, like Batty's new dog-walking business. Batty is saving up her dog-walking money for an extra-special surprise for her family, which she plans to present on her upcoming birthday." (Publisher's note)

"[T]he compelling story line examines the guilt that Batty feels over both the death of her mother and her inability to keep the family dog, Hound, alive--and it does so in touching ways. Batty is the narrator most of the time, but younger Ben takes over on occasion, and 2-year-old Lydia is an eccentric presence." Booklist

The **Penderwicks** on Gardam Street; [illustrations by David Frankland] Alfred A. Knopf 2008 307p il $15.99; lib bdg $18.99
Grades: 3 4 5 6 7   **Fic**
1. Sisters -- Fiction 2. Family life -- Fiction 3. Massachusetts -- Fiction 4. Dating (Social customs) -- Fiction
ISBN 978-0-3758-4090-6; 978-0-375-94090-3 lib bdg
LC 2007-49232

Sequel to: The Penderwicks (2005)

The four Penderwick sisters are faced with the unimaginable prospect of their widowed father dating, and they hatch a plot to stop him.

"Laugh-out-loud moments abound and the humor comes naturally from the characters and situations. . . . This is a book to cherish." SLJ

Birdseye, Tom
Storm Mountain. Holiday House 2010 135p $16.95
Grades: 4 5 6 7   **Fic**
1. Adventure fiction 2. Cousins -- Fiction 3. Blizzards -- Fiction 4. Mountaineering -- Fiction 5. Washington (State) -- Fiction 6. Wilderness survival -- Fiction
ISBN 978-0-8234-2130-5; 0-8234-2130-9
LC 2010005768

Two thirteen-year-old cousins Cat and Ty are trapped in a blizzard on the same treacherous mountain in the Cascades that claimed the lives of their world-famous, mountain-climber, twin fathers exactly two years earlier.

"Birdseye's prose, full of careening action, melodrama and overwrought similes, reflects Ty's bulldozing personality. Add believable characters, the author's mountain-climbing expertise and a tear-jerking conclusion, and there's plenty here for young adventure enthusiasts." Kirkus

Birney, Betty G.
Adventure according to Humphrey; [by] Betty G. Birney. G.P. Putnam's Sons 2009 120p $14.99
Grades: 2 3 4   **Fic**
1. School stories 2. Hamsters -- Fiction
ISBN 978-0-399-24731-6; 0-399-24731-9
LC 2008002347

Humphrey the classroom hamster has adventures going to the library, learning about the ocean, and sailing across a pond on a sailboat.

Friendship according to Humphrey; [by] Betty G. Birney. G.P. Putnam's Sons 2005 150p $14.99; pa $5.99
Grades: 2 3 4   **Fic**
1. School stories 2. Frogs -- Fiction 3. Hamsters -- Fiction 4. Friendship -- Fiction
ISBN 0-399-24264-3; 978-0-399-24264-9; 0-14-240633-3 pa; 978-0-14-240633-5 pa
LC 2004009538

When Humphrey the hamster returns to Mrs. Brisbane's class after the winter break, a new class pet and some other surprises give him an opportunity to reflect on the meaning of friendship.

"The theme of friendship is as pervasive as the title implies, making this chapter book a charming read-aloud." SLJ

The **seven** wonders of Sassafras Springs; written by Betty Birney; illustrated by Matt Phelan. Atheneum Books for Young Readers 2005 210p il $16.95; pa $6.99
Grades: 3 4 5 6   **Fic**
1. Family life -- Fiction 2. Country life -- Fiction
ISBN 0-689-87136-8; 1-4169-3489-8 pa
LC 2004-11399

Eben McAllister searches his small town to see if he can find anything comparable to the real Seven Wonders of the World

"Black-and-white sketches enhance the text and its folksy character. Perfect for reading aloud." SLJ

Summer according to Humphrey. G.P. Putnam's Sons 2010 167p $14.99

Grades: 2 3 4 **Fic**

1. Camps -- Fiction 2. Hamsters -- Fiction

ISBN 978-0-399-24732-3; 0-399-24732-7

LC 2009008532

When summer arrives, Humphrey, the pet hamster of Longfellow School's Room 26, is surprised and pleased to learn that he will be going to Camp Happy Hollow.

Surprises according to Humphrey; [by] Betty G. Birney. G. P. Putnam's Sons 2008 136p $14.99

Grades: 2 3 4 **Fic**

1. School stories 2. Hamsters -- Fiction

ISBN 978-0-399-24730-9; 0-399-24730-0

LC 2007007457

While continuing to help his classmates solve their problems, Humphrey, pet hamster of Longfellow School's Room 26, faces many surprises, like rolling in a hamster ball, a substitute janitor who might be an alien, and the possibility of Mrs. Brisbane retiring.

"Humphrey is a witty, fun, and lovable character with great kid appeal." SLJ

Trouble according to Humphrey; [by] Betty. G. Birney. Putnam 2007 167p $14.99; pa $5.99

Grades: 2 3 4 **Fic**

1. School stories 2. Hamsters -- Fiction

ISBN 978-0-399-24505-3; 0-399-24505-7; 978-0-14-241089-9 pa; 0-14-241089-6 pa

LC 2006003604

Humphrey, the pet hamster of Longfellow School's Room 26, relates the ups and downs experienced by his human classmates as they begin a project to create a model town complete with houses and community services.

"Humphrey's escapes . . . are related in a lively, first-person narrative, laced with humor, heart, and hamster facts." Booklist

The **world** according to Humphrey. G. P. Putnam's Sons 2004 124p $14.99; pa $5.99

Grades: 2 3 4 **Fic**

1. School stories 2. Hamsters -- Fiction

ISBN 978-0-399-24198-7; 0-399-24198-1; 978-0-14-240352-5 pa; 0-14-240352-0 pa

LC 2003-5974

Humphrey, pet hamster at Longfellow School, learns that he has an important role to play in helping his classmates and teacher.

The "lively, first-person narrative, filled with witty commentary on human and hamster behavior, makes for an engaging, entertaining read." Booklist

Other titles about Humphrey are:

Friendship according to Humphrey (2005)

Trouble according to Humphrey (2007)

Surprises according to Humphrey (2008)

Adventure according to Humphrey (2009)

Summer according to Humphrey (2010)

Björk, Christina

★ **Linnea** in Monet's garden; text, Christina Björk; drawings, Lena Anderson. Sourcebooks Jabberwocky 2012 46 p. il $16.99

Grades: 2 3 4 5 **Fic**

1. Artists 2. Painters 3. Paris (France) -- Fiction 4. Art 5. Gardens 6. Painters -- France -- Biography

ISBN 9781402277290; 1402277296

LC 8745163

Original Swedish edition, 1985

Linnea, a young Swedish garden enthusiast, and her elderly neighbor, Mr. Bloom, "travel to Paris, visit Monet's home in Giverny, picni in the artist's garden, and admire the waterlilies and the Japanese bridg which he often painted. In Paris, the two companions stop at a museum to see Impressionist paintings, view the sunlight over the Seine, an chatter about the life and times of the artist. The book ends with a pag of information about things to do and see in Paris." (SLJ)

"This twenty-fifth anniversary edition (in a revised format) intro duces a new generation of readers to artist Claude Monet and the Im pressionism movement through art- and flower-lover Linnea's exuberan description of a trip to Paris. The book's engaging mix of photographs watercolor illustrations, and reproductions of Monet's paintings pul readers into the story, which smoothly incorporates facts and informa tion." Horn Book

Blabey, Aaron

The **Bad** Guys; Aaron Blabey. Scholastic Press 2016 144 p. il lustrations (ebook) $5.99; $5.99

Grades: 2 3 4 5 **Fi**

1. Humorous stories 2. Heroes -- Fiction 3. Animals -- Fiction 4 Rescues -- Fiction

ISBN 9780545917148; 9780545912402

LC 201503784

In this children's book in the Bad Guys series, by Aaron Blabey "they sound like bad guys, . . . but Mr. Wolf, Mr. Piranha, Mr. Snake, an Mr. Shark are about to change all of that... Mr. Wolf has a daring plan fo the Bad Guys' first good mission. They are going to break two hundre dogs out of the Maximum Security City Dog Pound. Will Operation Do Pound go smoothly? Will the Bad Guys become the Good Guys? An will Mr. Snake please stop swallowing Mr. Piranha?!" (Publisher's note

"With illustrations that startle in their manic comedy and deadpa direct address and with a narrative that follows four endearingly sar donic characters trying to push past (sometimes successfully) their fear causing natures, this book instantly joins the classic ranks of Captai Underpants and The Stinky Cheese Man. We challenge anyone to rea this and keep a straight face." Kirkus

The **Bad** Guys in mission unpluckable; Aaron Blabey. Scholasti Press 2016 144 p. illustrations (The Bad Guys) (ebook) $5.99; (pb $5.99

Grades: 2 3 4 5 **Fi**

1. Heroes & heroines 2. Humorous stories 3. Heroes -- Fiction 4 Animals -- Fiction 5. Rescues -- Fiction

ISBN 9780545917162; 9780545912419

LC 201601378

In this book, in The Bad Guys series, by Aaron Blabey, "the Ba Guys next mission, [is to] rescue 10,000 chickens from a high-tech cag farm. But they are up against sizzling lasers, one feisty tarantula, an their very own Mr. Snake . . . who's also known as 'The Chicken Swa lower.' What could possibly go wrong? Get ready to laugh up your lunc with the baddest bunch of do-gooders in town!" (Publisher's note)

"The narrative has lost no comic momentum from first to secon book, juxtaposing classic riffs on Mission Impossible and new visua gags unique to these delightfully wry characters. Another uproariou romp that explores what it is to be good as well as do good." Kirkus

Mission unpluckable

Black, Holly, 1971-

The **copper** gauntlet; Holly Black and Cassandra Clare; with il lustrations by Scott Fischer. Scholastic Press 2015 272 p. illustration (Magisterium) (jacketed hardcover) $17.99

Grades: 5 6 7 8 **Fi**

1. Adventure fiction 2. Magic -- Fiction 3. Wolves -- Fiction 4

Secrets -- Fiction 5. Adventure and adventurers -- Fiction
ISBN 0545522285; 9780545522281

LC 2015015713

In this book, Holly Black and Cassandra Clare, "Callum Hunt's summer break isn't like other kids'. His closest companion is a Chaos-ridden wolf, Havoc. His father suspects him of being secretly evil. And, of course, most kids aren't heading back to the magical world of the Magisterium in the fall. It's not easy for Call . . . and it gets even harder after he checks out his basement and discovers that his dad might be trying to destroy both him and Havoc." (publisher's note)

"The third-person narration, filtered through Callum's delightfully insecure-and-overcompensating-with-snarky-bravado perspective, carries a tone that will likely have readers chortling in recognition. A promising beginning to a complex exploration of good and evil, as well as friendship's loyalty." Kirkus

Sequel to "The Iron Trial"

★ **Doll** bones; Holly Black. 1st ed. Margaret K. McElderry Books 2013 256 p. (hardcover) $16.99
Grades: 5 6 7 8 **Fic**
1. Ghost stories 2. Dolls -- Fiction 3. Adventure fiction 4. Ghosts -- Fiction 5. Friendship -- Fiction 6. Family problems -- Fiction 7. Adventure and adventurers -- Fiction
ISBN 1416963987; 9781416963981; 9781442474871

LC 2012018299

Newberry Honor Book (2104)

In this book, by Holly Black, illustrated by Eliza Wheeler, "a doll that may be haunted leads three friends on a thrilling adventure. . . . Zach, Poppy, and Alice have been . . . playing one continuous, ever-changing game. . . . Ruling over all is the Great Queen, . . . cursing those who displease her. . . . Zach and Alice and Poppy set off on one last adventure to lay the Queen's ghost to rest. But nothing goes according to plan, and . . . creepy things begin to happen." (Publisher's note)

"Veteran Black packs both heft and depth into a deceptively simple and convincingly uncanny) narrative. . . . A few rich metaphors . . . are woven throughout the story, as every encounter redraws the blurry lines between childishness and maturity, truth and lies, secrecy and honesty, magic and madness. Spooky, melancholy, elegiac and ultimately hopeful; a small gem." Kirkus

The **iron** trial; Holly Black, Cassandra Clare. First edition Scholastic Press 2014 304 p. illustrations (Magisterium) (hardcover) $17.99
Grades: 4 5 6 7 8 **Fic**
1. Fantasy fiction 2. Magic -- Fiction
ISBN 0545522250; 9780545522250

LC 2014937300

In this fantasy novel by Holly Black and Cassandra Clare, part of the Magisterium series, "most kids would do anything to pass the Iron Trial. Not Callum Hunt. He wants to fail. All his life, Call has been warned by his father to stay away from magic. If he succeeds at the Iron Trial and is admitted into the Magisterium, he is sure it can only mean bad things for him." (Publisher's note)

"The third-person narration, filtered through Callum's delightfully insecure-and-overcompensating-with-snarky-bravado perspective, carries a tone that will likely have readers chortling in recognition. A promising beginning to a complex exploration of good and evil, as well as friendship's loyalty." Kirkus

Other titles in this series are:
The copper gauntlet (2015)
The bronze key (2016)

Black, Peter Jay
Urban outlaws; Peter Jay Black. Bloomsbury USA Childrens 2014 288 p. illustration (hardback) $16.99
Grades: 5 6 7 8 **Fic**
1. Science fiction 2. Ability -- Fiction 3. Orphans -- Fiction 4. Criminals -- Fiction 5. Adventure and adventurers 6. Computers -- Fiction 7. Adventure and adventurers -- Fiction
ISBN 1619634007; 9781619634008

LC 2014005604

In this middle-grades book, by Peter Jay Black, "deep beneath the city live five extraordinary kids: world-famous hacker Jack, gadget geek Charlie, free runner Slink, communications chief Obi, and decoy expert Wren. Orphans bonded over their shared sense of justice, the kids have formed the Urban Outlaws, a group dedicated to outsmarting criminals and handing out their stolen money through Random Acts of Kindness (R.A.K.s)." (Publisher's note)

"Five orphans—Jack, Charlie, Wren, Obi, and Slink—have made a home for themselves in a WWII bunker under the London subway. They are skilled in various ways—technological savvy, surveillance, and physical prowess in particular—and work together as the Urban Outlaws, using their knowledge to play Robin Hood against local criminals and sharing the benefits of their activities with those less fortunate than themselves...The characters are warm and well developed and will appeal to reluctant readers across middle school. This new series will be an excellent choice for younger fans of Alex Rider." Booklist

Other titles in the series are:
Blackout (2015)

Blackwood, Gary
Curiosity; by Gary Blackwood. Dial Books for Young Readers, an imprint of Penguin Group (USA) Inc. 2014 320 p. (hardcover) $16.99
Grades: 5 6 7 8 **Fic**
1. Chess -- Fiction 2. Robots -- Fiction 3. Historical fiction 4. Poverty -- Fiction 5. Apprentices -- Fiction 6. Philadelphia (Pa.) -- History -- 19th century -- Fiction
ISBN 0803739249; 9780803739246

LC 2013013438

This novel, by Gary Blackwood, begins in "Philadelphia, PA, 1835. Rufus, a twelve-year-old chess prodigy, is recruited by a shady showman named Maelzel to secretly operate a mechanical chess player called the Turk. . . . But Rufus's job working the automaton must be kept secret, and he fears he may never be able to escape his unscrupulous master. And what has happened to the previous operators of the Turk, who seem to disappear as soon as Maelzel no longer needs them?" (Publisher's note)

"Blackwood excels in writing historical fiction that is as informative as it is entertaining." Horn Book

Second sight; [by] Gary Blackwood. Dutton 2005 279p hardcover o.p. pa $6.99
Grades: 5 6 7 8 **Fic**
1. Lawyers 2. Presidents 3. State legislators 4. Members of Congress 5. Clairvoyance -- Fiction 6. Washington (D.C.) -- Fiction 7. United States -- History -- 1861-1865, Civil War -- Fiction
ISBN 0-525-47481-1; 0-14-240747-X pa
In Washington, D.C., during the last days of the Civil War, a teen-age boy who performs in a mind reading act befriends a clairvoyant girl whose frightening visions foreshadow an assassination plot.

"This is a well-researched, engrossing story grounded in historical detail." SLJ

★ The **Shakespeare** stealer; [by] Gary Blackwood. Dutton Children's Bks. 1998 216p $15.99; pa $5.99
Grades: 5 6 7 8 **Fic**
1. Poets 2. Authors 3. Dramatists 4. Orphans -- Fiction 5.

Theater -- Fiction 6. Great Britain -- History -- 1485-1603, Tudors -- Fiction

ISBN 0-525-45863-8; 0-14-130595-9 pa

LC 97-42987

A young orphan boy is ordered by his master to infiltrate Shakespeare's acting troupe in order to steal the script of "Hamlet," but he discovers instead the meaning of friendship and loyalty

"Wry humor, cliffhanger chapter endings, and a plucky protagonist make this a fitting introduction to Shakespeare's world." Horn Book

Other titles in this series are:

Shakespeare's scribe (2000)

Shakespeare's spy (2003)

Shakespeare's scribe; [by] Gary Blackwood. Dutton Children's Bks. 2000 265p hardcover o.p. pa $6.99

Grades: 5 6 7 8   **Fic**

1. Poets 2. Authors 3. Dramatists 4. Orphans -- Fiction 5. Theater -- Fiction 6. Great Britain -- History -- 1485-1603, Tudors -- Fiction

ISBN 0-525-46444-1; 978-0-14-230066-4 pa; 0-14-230066-7 pa

LC 00-34603

In plague-ridden 1602 England, Widge, a fifteen-year-old orphan boy, who has become an apprentice actor, goes on the road with Shakespeare's troupe, and finds out more about his parents along the way

"The story is extremely well structured, with several interesting subplots. . . . The characters are well developed, with Widge being particularly memorable. The dialogue is realistic, and the humorous plays on words add another level of interest." SLJ

Followed by: Shakespeare's spy (2003)

Shakespeare's spy; [by] Gary Blackwood. Dutton Children's Bks. 2003 281p $16.99; pa $6.99

Grades: 5 6 7 8   **Fic**

1. Orphans -- Fiction 2. Theater -- Fiction 3. Great Britain -- History -- 1485-1603, Tudors -- Fiction

ISBN 0-525-47145-6; 0-14-240311-3 pa

LC 2003-61659

The winter of 1602 brings many changes for Widge, a young apprentice at London's Globe Theatre, as he becomes infatuated with Shakespeare's daughter Judith, attempts to write a play, learns more about his past, endangers himself to help a friend, acquires a new identity, and finds a new purpose in life

"Blackwood's well-integrated plot and intriguing subplots ensure a fast-paced tale of Elizabethan England that fans of the earlier novels will love." SLJ

Blackwood, Sage

★ Jinx; Sage Blackwood. Harper 2013 368 p. (Jinx) (trade bdg.) $16.99

Grades: 4 5 6 7   **Fic**

1. Fantasy fiction 2. Magic -- Fiction 3. Voyages and travels -- Fiction 4. Fantasy

ISBN 0062129902; 9780062129901

LC 2012005249

This fantasy book is set "in the Urwald, an enormous, sentient forest where humans exist on sufferance . . . . After Jinx's brutal stepfather decides to abandon him in the forest, the boy is saved by a crusty, morally ambiguous wizard named Simon, who takes him in as a servant, eventually teaching him some magic. Years later, a 12-year-old Jinx and two new friends set off to find another wizard, the monstrous Bonemaster, in hopes he can help them overcome their respective magical troubles." (Publishers Weekly)

Jinx's fire; Sage Blackwood. Katherine Tegen Books, an imprint of HarperCollinsPublishers 2015 400 p. map (hardback) $16.99

Grades: 4 5 6 7   **Fic**

1. Fantasy fiction 2. Wizards -- Fiction 3. Forests and forestry -- Fiction 4. Fantasy 5. Magic -- Fiction 6. Orphans -- Fiction

ISBN 0062129961; 9780062129963

LC 2014022688

Sequel to: Jinx's magic

In this novel by Sage Blackwood, "the young wizard Jinx concludes his suspenseful and dryly humorous adventures in the magical forest of the Urwald with this third installment in the series. . . . The forest is under attack and its magic is fading. Can Jinx summon enough of his magic . . . to rescue Simon, defeat the Bonemaster, unite the Urwald, and fight off the invaders?" (Publisher's note)

"In this concluding volume of Blackwood's critically acclaimed series, Jinx is nearly 15, and he finally rescues his mentor, Simon, from the fate the evil Bonemaster wrought in Jinx's Magic (2014). . . . Series fans will be elated to have another outing with the sweetly sardonic hero whose conscience is almost as troublesome as his grasp of spells. Fans of Cornelia Funke should add this to their stacks." Booklist

Jinx's magic; Sage Blackwood. Katherine Tegen Books 2014 400 p. (hardcover) $16.99

Grades: 4 5 6 7   **Fic**

1. Fantasy 2. Magic -- Fiction 3. Wizards -- Fiction 4. Orphans -- Fiction 5. Forests and forestry -- Fiction

ISBN 9780062129932; 0062129937

LC 2013010171

Sequel to: Jinx

"Jinx knows he can do magic. But he doesn't know why he's being stalked by a werewolf with a notebook, why the trees are starting to take back the only safe paths through the Urwald, or why the elves think Jinx and the evil Bonemaster are somehow connected." (Publisher's note)

"The plot is a little convoluted, wrapping up loose ends from the first volume and setting up elements for the next before finally establishing its own internal tension, but the unique setting, smart pace, likable characters, and sprightly voice hold the narrative together." Horn Book

Miss Ellicott's school for the magically minded; Sage Blackwood edited by Melissa Miller. Katherine Tegen Books 2017 368 p. illustrations (ebook) $15.99; (hardcover) $16.99

Grades: 4 5 6 7 8   **Fic**

1. Magic -- Fiction 2. Missing persons -- Fiction 3. Private school -- Fiction

ISBN 9780062402653; 9780062402639

LC 2016935939

In this book, by Sage Blackwood, edited by Melissa Miller, "Chantel would much rather focus on her magic than on curtsying, which is why she often finds herself in trouble at Miss Ellicott's School for Magical Maidens. But when Miss Ellicott mysteriously disappears along with all the other sorceresses in the city, Chantel's behavior becomes the least of her problems. Without any magic protecting the city, it is up to Chantel and her friends to save the Kingdom." (Publisher's note)

"This clever fantasy is a strong purchase for most middle grade collections." SLJ

Blakemore, Megan Frazer

The **spy** catchers of Maple Hill; by Megan Frazer Blakemore Bloomsbury 2014 320 p. (hardback) $16.99

Grades: 4 5 6 7   **Fic**

1. Mystery fiction 2. Vermont -- Fiction 3. Country life -- Fiction 4. Spies -- Fiction 5. Cold War -- Fiction 6. Friendship -- Fiction 7. City and town life -- Vermont -- Fiction 8. Vermont -- History

-- 20th century -- Fiction
ISBN 1619633485; 9781619633483

LC 2013039857

In this children's novel by Megan Frazer Blakemore, "Hazel Kaplansky is a firm believer in the pursuit of knowledge and truth--and she also happens to love a good mystery. When suspicions swirl that a Russian spy has infiltrated her small town of Maple Hill, Vermont, amidst the fervor of Cold War era McCarthyism, Hazel knows it's up to her to find a suspect starting with Mr. Jones, the quietly suspicious grave digger." (Publisher's note)

"The book does a wonderful job of displaying the way in which the fear inherent in the McCarthy era turned neighbor against neighbor. While the heart of the story lies within the issues of trust and truth, the writing is never preachy, using Hazel's innate humor to deflect moments that veer close to saccarine or preachy. A strong work of historical fiction for mystery fans." SLJ Reviews

The **Water** Castle; by Megan Frazer Blakemore. Walker 2013 352 p. (hardback) $16.99

Grades: 3 4 5 6 7   **Fic**
1. Magic -- Fiction 2. Castles -- Fiction 3. Family secrets -- Fiction 4. Maine -- Fiction 5. Families -- Fiction 6. Dwellings -- Fiction 7. Moving, Household -- Fiction 8. Discoveries in science -- Fiction
ISBN 0802728391; 9780802728395

LC 2012016442

In this novel by Megan Frazer Blakemore "Ephraim Appledore-Smith is an ordinary boy, and up until his father's stroke he lived an ordinary life. But all that changes when his family moves to the Water Castle. . . . Mallory Green's family has always been the caretakers of the Water Castle. . . . She has been raised to protect the legendary Fountain of Youth, hidden on the estate grounds. When Ephraim learns of the Fountain, he's sure finding it can cure his dad." (Publisher's note)

Block, Francesca Lia
★ **House** of dolls; illustrated by Barbara McClintock. Harper 2010 61p il $15.99

Grades: 3 4 5 6   **Fic**
1. Fantasy fiction 2. Dolls -- Fiction
ISBN 978-0-06-113094-6; 0-06-113094-X

"Young Madison is growing tired of her dollhouse and its residents. . . Increasingly abandoned by her mother, Madison begins exercising a capacious cruelty [to the dolls]. . . . The reality/unreality of any of this is a tightrope Block toes with precision. . . . What at first seems to be about the perennial war between familial generations is expanded into a message about the global forces of pride and avarice that plunge innocents into devastation. This is powerful, haunting, and—just when you don't think it's possible—inspiring too." Booklist

Blom, Jen K.
Possum summer. Holiday House 2011 155p $17.95

Grades: 3 4 5   **Fic**
1. Dogs -- Fiction 2. Oklahoma -- Fiction 3. Opossums -- Fiction 4. Ranch life -- Fiction 5. Father-daughter relationship -- Fiction
ISBN 978-0-8234-2331-6; 0-8234-2331-X

LC 2010023476

While her father is away at war, eleven-year-old Princess ignores his warning that pet ownership leads to pain when she raises an orphaned possum on their Oklahoma ranch, then tries to send it back to the wild.

"Animal-loving readers will sympathize with P throughout this well-paced coming-of-age story." Horn Book Guide

Blos, Joan W.
★ A **gathering** of days: a New England girl's journal, 1830-32; a novel. Scribner 1979 144p $16.95; pa $4.99

Grades: 6 7 8 9   **Fic**
1. New Hampshire -- Fiction
ISBN 0-684-16340-3; 0-689-71419-X pa

LC 79-16898

Awarded the Newbery Medal, 1980

The journal of a 14-year-old girl, kept the last year she lived on the family farm, records daily events in her small New Hampshire town, her father's remarriage, and the death of her best friend

"The 'simple' life on the farm is not facilely idealized, the larger issues of the day are felt . . . but it is the small moments between parent and child, friend and friend that are at the fore, and the core, of this low-key, intense, and reflective book." SLJ

Letters from the corrugated castle; a novel of gold rush California, 1850-1852. Atheneum Books for Young Readers 2007 310p $17.99; pa $5.99

Grades: 5 6 7 8   **Fic**
1. California -- Fiction 2. Mexican Americans -- Fiction 3. Gold mines and mining -- Fiction 4. Frontier and pioneer life -- Fiction 5. Mother-daughter relationship -- Fiction
ISBN 978-0-689-87077-4; 0-689-87077-9; 978-0-689-87078-1 pa; 0-689-87078-7 pa

LC 2007-02673

A series of letters and newspaper articles reveals life in California in the 1850s, especially for thirteen-year-old Eldora, who was raised in Massachusetts as an orphan only to meet her influential mother in San Francisco, and Luke, who hopes to find a fortune in gold.

"It is Blos' sturdy characters, whose experiences reveal the complexity of human relationships and wisdom about 'the salt and the sweet of life,' who will make this last." Booklist

Blume, Judy
★ **Are** you there God?, it's me, Margaret; rev format ed.; Atheneum 2001 149p hc $17.99

Grades: 4 5 6 7   **Fic**
1. Bildungsromans 2. Puberty -- Fiction 3. Religion -- Fiction
ISBN 0-689-84158-2; 9781481413978

A reissue of the title first published 1970 by Bradbury Press

A "story about the emotional, physical, and spiritual ups and downs experienced by 12-year-old Margaret, child of a Jewish-Protestant union." Natl Counc of Teach of Engl. Adventuring with Books. 2d edition

BFF* * best friends forever; two novels. Delacorte Press 496p $18.99 **Fic**
1. Friendship -- Fiction. 2. Family problems -- Fiction. 3. Gifted children -- Fiction. 4. Brothers and sisters -- Fiction. 5. Interpersonal relations -- Fiction.
ISBN 978-0-385-73407-3

A compilation of two previously published novels: Just as long and we're together (1987) and Here's to you Rachel Robinson (1993)

Cool zone with the Pain and the Great One; [illustrated by] James Stevenson. Delacorte Press 2008 109p il $12.99; lib bdg $19.99

Grades: 1 2 3   **Fic**
1. School stories 2. Siblings -- Fiction 3. Family life -- Fiction
ISBN 978-0-385-73306-9; 0-385-73306-2; 978-0-385-90325-7 lib bdg; 0-385-90325-1 lib bdg

LC 2007-17126

More adventures at school and at home with Jake, a first-grader, and his older sister Abigail, known to each other as the Pain and the Great One.

"Recently independent readers will find this just the book to push their skills forward. Stevenson's gray-washed line illustrations add to the fun." Booklist

Double Fudge. Dutton Children's Bks. 2002 213p $15.99; pa $5.99

Grades: 3 4 5 6   Fic

1. Brothers -- Fiction 2. Family life -- Fiction
ISBN 0-525-46926-5; 0-14-240878-6 pa
LC 2002-67774

His younger brother Fudge's obsession with money and the discovery of long-lost cousins Flora and Fauna provide many embarrassing moments for twelve-year-old Peter

"This is a snappy, humorous title that lends itself to being read aloud, and Fudge fans in need of a fix will find that it hits the spot." Bull Cent Child Books

Freckle juice; illustrated by Sonia O. Lisker. Four Winds Press 1971 40p il hc $16.99

Grades: 2 3 4   Fic

1. Humorous fiction 2. School stories -- Fiction 3. Self-perception -- Fiction 4. Freckles -- Fiction
ISBN 9781481411035

"A gullible second-grader pays 50¢ for a recipe to grow freckles." Best Books for Child

"Spontaneous humor, sure to appeal to the youngest reader." Horn Book

Friend or fiend? with the Pain & the Great One; illustrations by James Stevenson. Delacorte Press 2009 108p il $12.99; lib bdg $16.99

Grades: 1 2 3   Fic

1. School stories 2. Siblings -- Fiction 3. Family life -- Fiction
ISBN 978-0-385-73308-3; 0-385-73308-9; 978-0-385-90327-1 lib bdg; 0-385-90327-8 lib bdg
LC 2008030780

First-grader Jake "The Pain" and his sister, third-grader Abigail "The Great One" have more adventures, including visiting their cousins in New York and celebrating their cat Fluzzy's birthday.

"Blume's singular ability to portray the minutiae of a child's everyday life with humor is perfectly complemented by Stevenson's occasional line drawings that extend the story's charm and fully shaped characters." Booklist

Fudge-a-mania. Dutton Children's Bks. 1990 147p hardcover o.p. pa $5.99

Grades: 3 4 5 6   Fic

1. Brothers -- Fiction 2. Vacations -- Fiction
ISBN 0-525-44672-9 lib bdg; 0-425-19382-9 pa
LC 90-39627

Pete describes the family vacation in Maine with the Tubmans, highlighted by the antics of his younger brother Fudge

"The story is filled with humor, and the upbeat mood is sustained at a hectic pace from first page to last." SLJ

Going, going, gone! with the Pain and the Great One; [by] Judy Blume; illustrations by James Stevenson. Delacorte Press 2008 109p il $12.99; lib bdg $16.99

Grades: 1 2 3   Fic

1. School stories 2. Siblings -- Fiction 3. Family life -- Fiction
ISBN 978-0-385-73307-6; 0-385-73307-0; 978-0-385-90326-4 lib bdg; 0-385-90326-X lib bdg

Further adventures of first-grader Jake "the Pain" and his sister third-grader Abigail "the Great One," include a trip to the beach with Grandma, to a county fair with Aunt Diana, and to a mall with Dad.

The "stories beautifully capture the experiences of siblings who love one another but who don't always get along. . . . Stevenson's drawing perfectly complement the tales." SLJ

Otherwise known as Sheila the Great. Dutton Children's Book 2002 138p $16.99; pa $5.99

Grades: 4 5 6   Fi

1. Fear -- Fiction 2. Vacations -- Fiction
ISBN 978-0-525-46928-5; 0-525-46928-1; 978-0-14-240879-7 pa; 0-14-240879-4 pa
A reissue of the title first published 1972

A summer in Tarrytown, N.Y., is a lot of fun for ten-year-old Sheil even though her friends make her face up to some self-truths she doesn' want to admit.

"An unusual and merry treatment of the fears of a young girl. . . . This is a truly appealing book in which the author makes her point without a single preachy word." Publ Wkly

Soupy Saturdays with The Pain and The Great One; illustration by James Stevenson. Delacorte Press 2007 108p il $12.99; lib bd $16.99

Grades: 1 2 3   Fi

1. Siblings -- Fiction
ISBN 978-0-385-73305-2; 0-385-73305-4; 978-0-385-90324-0 lib bdg; 0-385-90324-3 lib bdg
LC 2006-2689

"Third-grader Abigail calls her little brother 'The Pain' because he causes so much trouble. Jake is in first grade and calls his older siste 'The Great One' because she thinks so highly of herself. The book . . . is a series of vignettes in which the children continually clash and the reconcile. . . . The stories are sweet and accurately depict the growing pains of childhood. Stevenson's black-and-white ink illustrations are en tertaining." SLJ

Other titles about the The Pain and The Great One are:
Cool zone with The Pain and The Great One (2008)
Going, going, gone! with The Pain and The Great One (2008)
Friend or fiend? with The Pain and The Great One (2009)

Starring Sally J. Freedman as herself; by Judy Blume. Atheneum Books for Young Readers 2014 376 p. (hardback) $17.99

Grades: 4 5 6   Fi

1. Moving -- Fiction 2. Family life -- Fiction 3. Imagination - Fiction 4. Miami Beach (Fla.) -- Fiction 5. Jews -- United States -- Fiction 6. Moving, Household -- Fiction 7. Family life -- Florida -- Fiction 8. Miami Beach (Fla.) -- History -- 20th century -- Fiction
ISBN 1481414372; 9781481413558; 9781481414371
LC 2013049265

In this middle grade book by Judy Blume, "Sally J. Freedman was ten when she made herself a movie star. She would have been happy to reach stardom in New Jersey, but in 1947 her older brother Douglas became ill, so the Freedman family traveled south to spend eight months in the sunshine of Florida. That's where Sally met her friends Andrea Barbara, Shelby, Peter, and Georgia Blue Eyes—and her unsuspecting enemy, Adolf Hitler." (Publisher's note)

Superfudge. Dutton Children's Books 2002 178p $15.99; pa $5.99

Grades: 3 4 5 6   Fi

1. Brothers -- Fiction 2. Family life -- Fiction
ISBN 0-525-46930-3; 0-14-240880-8 pa
LC 2004270849

Sequel to Tales of a fourth grade nothing

A reissue of the title first published 1980

Peter describes the highs and lows of life with his younger brother, Fudge

"A genuinely funny story." NY Times Book Rev

★ **Tales** of a fourth grade nothing. Dutton Children's Books 2002 120p $15.99; pa $5.99

Grades: 3 4 5 6 **Fic**

1. Brothers -- Fiction 2. Family life -- Fiction

ISBN 0-525-46931-1; 0-14-240881-6 pa

A reissue of the title first published 1972

This story describes the trials and tribulations of nine-year-old Peter Hatcher who is saddled with a pesky two-year-old brother named Fudge who is constantly creating trouble, messing things up, and monopolizing their parents' attention. Things come to a climax when Fudge gets at Peter's pet turtle

"The episode structure makes the book a good choice for reading aloud." Saturday Rev

Other titles about Peter and Fudge are:

Double Fudge (2002)

Fudge-a-mania (1990)

Superfudge (1980)

Blume, Lesley M. M.

The **rising** star of Rusty Nail; [by] Lesley M.M. Blume. Alfred A. Knopf 2007 270p $15.99; lib bdg $18.99; pa $6.50

Grades: 4 5 6 **Fic**

1. Pianists -- Fiction 2. Minnesota -- Fiction 3. Musicians -- Fiction 4. Russian Americans -- Fiction

ISBN 978-0-375-83524-7; 978-0-375-93524-4 lib bdg; 978-0-440-42111-5 pa

LC 2006024252

In the small town of Rusty Nail, Minnesota, in the early 1950s, musically talented ten-year-old Franny wants to take advanced piano lessons from newcomer Olga Malenkov, a famous Russian musician suspected of being a communist spy by gossipy members of the community

"Blume has skillfully combined humor, history, and music to create an enjoyable novel that builds to a surprising crescendo." SLJ

Blundell, Judy

A **city** tossed and broken; the diary of Minnie Bonner. Judy Blundell. Scholastic Inc. 2013 224 p. (paper over board) $12.99

Grades: 4 5 6 7 **Fic**

1. Historical fiction 2. Household employees -- Fiction 3. San Francisco (Calif.) -- History -- Fiction 4. Diaries -- Fiction 5. Earthquakes -- Fiction 6. Family life -- California -- Fiction 7. San Francisco Earthquake and Fire, Calif., 1906 -- Fiction

ISBN 0545310229; 9780545310222

LC 2012014742

This novel, by Judy Blundell, presents the diary of the girl Minnie Bonner during the San Francisco, California earthquake of 1906 as part of the "Dear America" series. A "wealthy gentleman . . . offers Minnie chance to work as a lady's maid. . . . But when a powerful earthquake strikes, Minnie finds herself the sole survivor among them. . . . Minnie as turned into an heiress overnight . . . and she is soon wrapped up in deception that leads her down a dangerous path." (Publisher's note)

"The author deftly incorporates true events, circumstances and key historical figures into the rapidly unfolding fictional plot... Exciting, suspenseful, absorbing and informative." Kirkus

Bode, N. E.

The **slippery** map; by N.E. Bode; illustrated by Brandon Dorman. HarperCollinsPublishers 2007 273p il $16.99; lib bdg $17.89

Grades: 4 5 6 **Fic**

1. Adventure fiction 2. Parents -- Fiction 3. Convents -- Fiction 4. Imagination -- Fiction 5. Baltimore (Md.) -- Fiction

ISBN 978-0-06-079108-7; 0-06-079108-X; 978-0-06-079109-4 lib bdg; 0-06-079109-8 lib bdg

LC 2007010900

Oyster R. Motel, a lonely boy raised as a foundling in a Baltimore nunnery, travels through a portal to the imaginary world of his parents, where he heroically confronts the villainous Dark Mouth

The author "effortlessly renders an expansive, entertainingly quirky cast of creatures benign and malevolent. Her snappy prose makes the case for the story's explicit messages about the value of unbridled imagination." Publ Wkly

Bodeen, S. A.

Shipwreck Island; by S. A. Bodeen. Feiwel & Friends 2014 192 p. hc $16.99

Grades: 5 6 7 8 **Fic**

1. Islands -- Fiction 2. Shipwrecks -- Fiction 3. Family life -- Fiction 4. Stepmothers -- Fiction

ISBN 9781250027771; 1250027772

In this book, by S. A. Bodeen, "Sarah is not happy that her dad has married again, forcing her to deal with a new stepmom and two new brothers. To help them bond, Sarah's dad and stepmom decide to take everyone on a vacation to Tahiti, rent a yacht, and cruise to their own private island. They sail right into a terrible storm, the captain is swept overboard, and the yacht runs aground on a deserted island.." (Library Media Connection)

"These very human protagonists respond in believable ways to their new family situation while encountering freakish animals, bizarrely dangerous weather, and a creepy, empty house." SLJ

Boelts, Maribeth

Happy like soccer; illustrated by Lauren Castillo. 1st ed. Candlewick Press 2012 32 p. col. ill. (reinforced trade) $15.99

Grades: 2 3 4 **Fic**

1. Soccer teams 2. Soccer -- Fiction 3. Family life -- Fiction 4. Aunts -- Fiction 5. Social classes -- Fiction 6. Problem solving -- Fiction

ISBN 0763646164; 9780763646165

LC 2011018624

In this children's book by Maribeth Boelts, "Sierra struggles with conflicting emotions about her new soccer team. Traveling out of the city, Sierra now plays on . . . fields unlike the one near the apartment where she lives with her aunt, which is exciting. However, being on this new team has some drawbacks. . . . Sierra is sad to be the only player without family members to cheer for her during games. Yet, with a little ingenuity, Sierra discovers a solution to her dilemma." (Kirkus Reviews)

★ The **PS** brothers. Harcourt 2010 137p $15

Grades: 3 4 5 **Fic**

1. Dogs -- Fiction 2. Uncles -- Fiction 3. Bullies -- Fiction 4. Money-making projects for children -- Fiction

ISBN 978-0-547-34249-8; 0-547-34249-7

LC 2009-49975

Sixth-graders Russell and Shawn, poor and picked on, work together scooping dog droppings to earn money for a Rottweiler puppy to protect them from bullies, but when they learn the puppies' owner is running an illegal dog-fighting ring, they are torn about how to respond.

This is "a genuinely touching look at a boy who doesn't believe that there's anybody of consequence on his side. . . . There is humor in Russell and Shawn's business, but the kids are admirably industrious as well; the ethical quandary they encounter . . . is one that will hit kids right in their dog-loving and impoverished guts." Bull Cent Child Books

Boie, Kirsten

The **princess** plot; translated by David Henry Wilson. Scholastic 2009 378p $17.99

Grades: 5 6 7 8   **Fic**

1. Princesses -- Fiction 2. Conspiracies -- Fiction

ISBN 978-0-545-03220-9; 0-545-03220-2

LC 2008-24403

Original German edition, 2005

Believing that she is on a film set after auditioning and winning the role of a princess, fourteen-year-old Jenna becomes the unsuspecting pawn in a royal conspiracy

"This novel takes simple, straightforward writing and layers it with kidnappings, political intrigue, and an abundance of secret plots. Readers will enjoy leisurely uncovering the mystery of Jenna's heritage, right along with Jenna herself." Booklist

Another title about Jenna is:

The princess trap (2010)

The **princess** trap; translated by David Henry Wilson. Chicken House/Scholastic 2010 405p $17.99

Grades: 5 6 7 8   **Fic**

1. School stories 2. Princesses -- Fiction

ISBN 978-0-545-22261-7; 0-545-22261-3

LC 2010010072

Sequel to: The princess plot (2009)

Original German edition, 2007

Palace rules, boarding school, and paparazzi have Jenna, princess of the newly unified kingdom of Scandia, longing for her former anonymity, but when she runs away she finds herself in grave danger—and in a position to prevent the outbreak of civil war.

Bolden, Tonya

★ **Finding** family. Bloomsbury 2010 181p il $15.99

Grades: 4 5 6 7   **Fic**

1. Aunts -- Fiction 2. Family life -- Fiction 3. Grandfathers -- Fiction 4. West Virginia -- Fiction 5. African Americans -- Fiction

ISBN 978-1-59990-318-7; 1-59990-318-0

LC 2010-00535

Raised in Charleston, West Virginia, at the turn of the twentieth century by her grandfather and aunt on off-putting tales of family members she has never met, twelve-year-old Delana is shocked when, after Aunt Tilley dies, she learns the truth about her parents and some of her other relatives.

"This richly lyrical and historically persuasive coming-of-age story explores the ties that bind, break and renew an affluent African-American family. . . . Period photographic portraits from Bolden's personal collection illustrate the book. Each carefully posed subject is a fascinating enigma." Kirkus

Boles, Philana Marie

Little divas. Amistad 2006 164p $15.99; lib bdg $16.89; pa $5.99

Grades: 5 6 7 8   **Fic**

1. Cousins -- Fiction 2. Divorce -- Fiction 3. African Americans -- Fiction 4. Father-daughter relationship -- Fiction

ISBN 0-06-073299-7; 0-06-073300-4 lib bdg; 0-06-073301-2 pa

The summer before seventh grade, Cassidy Carter must come to terms with living with her father, practically a stranger, as well as her relationships with her cousins, all amidst the overall confusion of adolescence.

"Boles portrays this variable age well, and readers will feel for Cassidy's trials." SLJ

Boling, Katharine

January 1905. Harcourt 2004 170p $16; pa $5.95

Grades: 4 5 6 7   **Fi**

1. Twins -- Fiction 2. Sisters -- Fiction 3. Child labor -- Fiction

ISBN 0-15-205119-8; 0-15-205121-X pa

LC 2003-2447

In a 1905 mill town, eleven-year-old twin sisters, Pauline, wh goes to work with the rest of the family, and Arlene, whose cripple foot keeps her home doing the cooking, cleaning, and washing, are con vinced that the other sister has an easier life until a series of incident helps them see each other in a new light.

"This vivid account will draw readers into the period." Hor Book Guide

Bond, Michael

★ A **bear** called Paddington; with drawings by Peggy Fortnum Houghton Mifflin 1998 128p il $15; pa $4.95

Grades: 2 3 4 5   **Fi**

1. Bears -- Fiction 2. Great Britain -- Fiction

ISBN 0-395-92951-2; 0-618-15071-4 pa

First published 1958 in the United Kingdom; first United State edition 1960

"Mr. and Mrs. Brown first met Paddington on a railway platform i London. Noticing the sign on his neck reading 'Please look after thi bear. Thank you,' they decided to do just that. From there on home wa never the same though the Brown children were delighted." Publ Wkly

Other titles about Paddington Bear are:

More about Paddington

Paddington abroad

Paddington at large

Paddington at work

Paddington goes to town

Paddington here and now

Paddington helps out

Paddington marches on

Paddington on screen

Paddington on stage

Paddington on top

Paddington takes the air

Paddington takes the test

Paddington takes to TV

Paddington treasury

Bond, Nancy

A **string** in the harp. Atheneum Pubs. 1976 370p il $19.95; p $6.99

Grades: 6 7 8 9   **Fi**

1. Fantasy fiction 2. Wales -- Fiction

ISBN 0-689-50036-X; 1-4169-2771-9 pa

LC 75-2818

A Newbery Medal honor book, 1977

"Present-day realism and the fantasy world of sixth-century Taliesi meet in an absorbing novel set in Wales. The story centers around th Morgans—Jen, Peter, Becky, and their father—their adjustment to an other country, their mother's death, and especially, Peter's bitter despai which threatens them all." LC. Child Books, 1976

Bond, Victoria

Zora and me; the song of Ivory. [by] Victoria Bond and T. R. S mon. Candlewick Press 2010 170p $16.99; pa $6.99

Grades: 4 5 6 7   **Fi**

1. Authors 2. Novelists 3. Dramatists 4. Memoirists 5 Folklorists 6. Short story writers 7. Race relations -- Fiction 8

African Americans -- Fiction
ISBN 978-0-7636-4300-3; 0-7636-4300-9; 978-0-7636-5814-4
pa; 0-7636-5814-6 pa

LC 2009-47410

Coretta Scott King/John Steptoe New Talent Award (Author), 2011

This is a fictionalized account of Zora Neale Hurston's childhood
~~w~~ith her best friend Carrie, in Eatonville, Florida. Annotated bibliogra-
~~p~~hy. "Grades four to seven." (Bull Cent Child Books)

"The brilliance of this novel is its rendering of African-American
~~ch~~ild life during the Jim Crow era as a time of wonder and imagina-
~~ti~~on, while also attending to its harsh realities. Absolutely outstanding."
~~K~~irkus

~~B~~ondoux, Anne-Laure

A **time** of miracles; translated from the French by Y. Maudet.
~~D~~elacorte Press 2010 180p map $17.99; lib bdg $20.99

~~G~~rades: 6 7 8 9   **Fic**

1. War stories 2. Europe -- Fiction 3. Refugees -- Fiction
ISBN 978-0-385-73922-1; 0-385-73922-2; 978-0-385-90777-4
lib bdg; 0-385-90777-X lib bdg

LC 2010008539

Mildred L. Batchelder Award, 2011

"Readers will find themselves mesmerized not only by the eloquent
~~la~~nguage but by a plot every bit as harrowing and surprising as Kou-
~~m~~ail's cherished bedtime story." Horn Book

~~B~~oniface, William

The **hero** revealed; [by] William Boniface; illustrations by Stephen
~~G~~ilpin. HarperCollins Pub. 2006 294p il (The extraordinary adven-
~~t~~ures of Ordinary Boy) $15.99; lib bdg $16.89; pa $6.99

~~G~~rades: 4 5 6 7   **Fic**

1. Superheroes -- Fiction
ISBN 978-0-06-077464-6; 0-06-077464-9; 978-0-06-077465-3
lib bdg; 0-06-077465-7 lib bdg; 978-0-06-077466-0 pa; 0-06-
077466-5 pa

LC 2005018676

Ordinary Boy, the only resident of Superopolis without a superpow-
~~e~~r, uncovers and foils a sinister plot to destroy the town

"This first book in a new series is great fun. . . . Boniface wields a
~~c~~ynical, but definitely kid-friendly, sense of humor, and Gilpin's illustra-
~~ti~~ons are sharp and witty." SLJ

Other titles in this series are:
The return of Meteor Boy? (2007)
The great powers outage (2008)

~~B~~onk, John J.

Madhattan mystery; by John J. Bonk. Walker Pub. 2012 292 p.
~~h~~ardback) $16.99

~~G~~rades: 4 5 6 7 8   **Fic**

1. Mystery fiction 2. Theft -- Fiction 3. Siblings -- Fiction 4.
Friendship -- Fiction 5. New York (N.Y.) -- Fiction 6. Aunts --
Fiction 7. Camps -- Fiction 8. Mystery and detective stories 9.
Robbers and outlaws -- Fiction 10. Brothers and sisters -- Fiction
11. New York (N.Y.) -- New York -- Fiction
ISBN 0802723497; 9780802723499

LC 2011034590

In this children's book, "set to spend their summer in New York City
~~w~~ith their aunt while their father is honeymooning with his new wife,
~~L~~exi and her younger brother Kevin's snoozy summer plans turn into
~~h~~igh-stakes adventure when Lexi overhears a plot to steal Cleopatra's
~~f~~amous jewels from the Metropolitan Museum of Art. Joining forces
~~w~~ith budding investigative journalist Kim Ling Levine, they ditch day
~~c~~amp to track down the thieves and rake in the reward money. Can Lexi,

Kevin, and Kim find out who's behind the jewel heist without getting
into too much trouble themselves?" (Publisher's note)

"Would-be journalist Kim Ling is bright, caustic, and knows how
to toss in a Yiddish word when appropriate; Kevin is the quintessential
10-year-old; and Lexi's dynamic first-person narrative shows her evolu-
tion--to readers and herself." Booklist

Booraem, Ellen

★ **Small** persons with wings. Dial Books for Young Readers 2011
302p $16.99

Grades: 4 5 6 7   **Fic**

1. Fantasy fiction 2. Magic -- Fiction 3. Fairies -- Fiction 4.
Grandfathers -- Fiction
ISBN 978-0-8037-3471-5; 0-8037-3471-9

LC 2010008400

When Mellie Turpin's grandfather dies and leaves her family his
run-down inn and bar, she learns that for generations her family members have been fairy guardians. "Grades five to eight." (Bull Cent
Child Books)

"In a fairy story that's wistful, humorous, and clever, Booraem . . .
suggests that the real world—with its disappointments and failings—is
still better than living with illusions. . . . The theme of making progress, rather than ignoring problems, is a strong one, gently presented."
Publ Wkly

Texting the underworld; by Ellen Booraem. Dial Books for Young
Readers 2013 319 p. (hardcover) $16.99

Grades: 5 6 7 8   **Fic**

1. Banshees -- Fiction 2. School stories -- Fiction 3. Fantasy fiction
-- Fiction 4. Death -- Fiction 5. Humorous stories 6. Schools --
Fiction 7. Supernatural -- Fiction 8. Middle schools -- Fiction
ISBN 0803737041; 9780803737044

LC 2012032488

In this book by Ellen Booraem, "Conor O'Neill is a smart but timid
seventh-grader. . . . When a banshee straight out of his Irish-born grandfather's stories appears in Conor's room, he's terrified that someone he
loves is going to die soon. The banshee, Ashling, is new at her job, and
. . . she's curious about the present day, [so] she masquerades as a new
student at Conor's school." (Publishers Weekly)

Booth, Coe

Kinda like brothers; Coe Booth. Scholastic Press 2014 256 p.
(hardcover) $17.99

Grades: 4 5 6 7 8   **Fic**

1. Brothers -- Fiction 2. Foster home care -- Fiction 3. Foster home
care 4. African Americans 5. Interpersonal relations
ISBN 0545224969; 9780545224963

LC 2014937301

This book by Coe Booth "introduces an African-American family
in Newark who open their home to foster children. By the time Kevon,
12, and his two-year-old sister, Treasure, arrive in the middle of the
night, 11-year-old Jarrett has had enough of his mother's charity. Jarrett
is forced to share a room with Kevon, who acts distant and ungrateful,
and he's also annoyed to be attending summer school, with the threat of
having to repeat the sixth grade." (Publishers Weekly)

Borden, Louise

Across the blue Pacific; a World War II story. illustrated by Robert
Andrew Parker. Houghton Mifflin 2006 un il $17

Grades: 2 3 4 5   **Fic**

1. World War, 1939-1945 -- Fiction
ISBN 0-618-33922-1

LC 2004-9206

A woman reminisces about her neighbor's son who was the object of a letter writing campaign by some fourth-graders when he went away to war in 1943.

"Beautifully written in an understated tone, the story offers a believable picture of life during the war. . . . Restrained yet expressive, the artwork conveys moods and mindsets as well as a strong sense of the time and place." Booklist

The **greatest** skating race; a World War II story from the Netherlands. illustrated by Niki Daly. Margaret K. McElderry Books 2004 44p il $18.95

Grades: 2 3 4 5   **Fic**
    1. Ice skating -- Fiction 2. Netherlands -- Fiction 3. World War, 1939-1945 -- Fiction
    ISBN 0-689-84502-2
                                                        LC 2002-12040

During World War II in the Netherlands, a ten-year-old boy's dream of skating in a famous race allows him to help two children escape to Belgium by ice skating past German soldiers and other enemies.

"Told with immediacy and suspense. . . . The gorgeously detailed watercolor illustrations capture a sense of the time. The subdued, winter hues of brown and smoky gray are those often found in the oil paintings of Dutch and Flemish masters and match the quiet tone of the text." SLJ

The **last** day of school; written by Louise Borden; illustrated by Adam Gustavson. Margaret K. McElderry Books 2005 un il $15.95

Grades: 2 3 4   **Fic**
    1. School stories 2. Gifts -- Fiction
    ISBN 0-689-86869-3
                                                        LC 2003025124

Matthew Perez, the official timekeeper of Mrs. Mallory's third-grade class, has a special goodbye gift for her

"Varied sizes of colorful oil illustrations accompany the tale of Matts patient delivery of the perfect gift. True to a childs remembrance of final school days, each page recalls memorable moments for students and teachers." SLJ

The **lost**-and-found tooth; [by] Louise Borden; illustrated by Adam Gustavson. Margaret K. McElderry Books 2008 un il $16.99

Grades: K 1 2   **Fic**
    1. School stories 2. Teeth -- Fiction 3. Lost and found possessions -- Fiction
    ISBN 978-1-4169-1814-1; 1-4169-1814-0
                                                        LC 2006028761

A special calendar hangs in Mr. Reilly's second grade classroom, and Lucy Webb impatiently awaits the day when she can add her name for losing a tooth, but when her time arrives something unexpected happens

"The low-key story is nicely illustrated with watercolors and is well suited to either independent reading or classroom sharing." Booklist

Bosch, Pseudonymous

If you're reading this, it's too late; illustrations by Gilbert Ford. Little, Brown 2008 385p il $16.99

Grades: 4 5 6   **Fic**
    1. Adventure fiction 2. Magic tricks -- Fiction
    ISBN 978-0-316-11367-0; 0-316-11367-0
                                                        LC 2008012405

Sequel to: The name of this book is secret (2007)

Cass and Max-Ernest discover the Museum of Magic, unscramble more coded messages, and solve new mysteries in their attempt to thwart the Terces Society's ambitions of discovering immortality.

This "combines mystery, adventure, and fantasy. . . . The numerous parenthetical comments and footnotes are often laugh-out-loud funny. .

. . The dark illustrations, descending chapter numbers, and playful fonts will catch readers' attention." SLJ

Followed by: This book is not good for you (2009)

The **name** of this book is secret; by Pseudonymous Bosch; illustrations by Gilbert Ford. Little, Brown & Co. 2007 360p il $16.99; pa $5.99

Grades: 4 5 6   **Fic**
    1. Adventure fiction 2. Immortality -- Fiction
    ISBN 978-0-316-11366-3; 0-316-11366-2; 978-0-316-11369-4 pa; 0-316-11369-7 pa
                                                        LC 2007021909

Two eleven-year-old misfits try to solve the mystery of a dead magician and stop the evil Dr. L and Ms. Mauvais, who are searching for the secret of immortality

This "is equal parts supernatural whodunit, suspense-filled adventure and evocative coming-of-age tale." Publ Wkly

Other titles in this series are:
If you're reading this, it's too late (2008)
This book is not good for you (2009)
This isn't what it looks like (2010)

This book is not good for you; chef de cuisine, Pseudonymous Bosch; illustrations by Gilbert Ford. Little, Brown 2009 394p $16.99

Grades: 4 5 6   **Fic**
    1. Adventure fiction 2. Desserts -- Fiction 3. Immortality -- Fiction
    ISBN 978-0-316-04086-0; 0-316-04086-X

Sequel to: If you're reading this, it's too late (2008)

As an evil dessert chef concocts a recipe for disaster in the form of a tempting chocolate bar, Cass and Max-Ernest attempt to stop an evil organization from carrying out its plot to gain immortality and wreak havoc on the world.

"Twists and turns in the ordering of the chapters give the author time for commentary and a choose-your-own adventure for readers who will still be on the edges of their seats at the end for the Secret to be revealed." Voice Youth Advocates

Followed by: This isn't what it looks like (2010)

This isn't what it looks like; illustrations by Gilbert Ford. Little, Brown 2010 423p il $16.99

Grades: 4 5 6   **Fic**
    1. Adventure fiction 2. Magic -- Fiction 3. Chocolate -- Fiction 4. Immortality -- Fiction 5. Time travel -- Fiction
    ISBN 978-0-316-07625-8; 0-316-07625-2
                                                        LC 2010010519

Sequel to: This book is not good for you (2009)

Cass finds herself alone and disoriented in a dream-like world, while back at home she is in the hospital in a coma with Max-Ernest desperately searching for a way to awaken her.

"The book's blend of mystery, fantasy, puzzles, puns, and puckish sometimes snarky sense of humor will keep readers engaged." Horn Book Guide

Bouwman, H. M.

The **remarkable** and very true story of Lucy and Snowcap; [by] H.M. Bouwman. Marshall Cavendish 2008 270p $16.99

Grades: 5 6 7 8   **Fic**
    1. Adventure fiction 2. Magic -- Fiction 3. Infants -- Fiction 4. Islands -- Fiction
    ISBN 978-0-7614-5441-0; 0-7614-5441-1
                                                        LC 2008003180

In 1788, thirteen years after English convicts are shipwrecked on the magical islands of Tathenland, two twelve-year-old girls, one a native

Colay, the other the child-governor of the English, set out on a journey to stop the treachery from which both peoples are suffering

"The page-turning adventure fronts for a subtle moral tale about loyalty, perseverance, and the power of finding one's own particular gifts. . . . The combination of historical and fantasy elements gives Lucy and Snowcap's quest folkloric as well as dramatic appeal." Bull Cent Child Books

Boyne, John

The **Terrible** Thing That Happened to Barnaby Brocket; John Boyne; illustrated by Oliver Jeffers. Knopf Books for Young Readers 2013 288 p. ill. $16.99

Grades: 2 3 4 5   **Fic**

1. Runaway children -- Fiction 2. Adventure fiction -- Fiction
ISBN 0307977625; 9780307977625; 9780307977632

LC 2012277133

In this novel, by John Boyne and illustrated by Oliver Jeffers, "Barnaby Brocket is an ordinary 8-year-old boy in most ways, but he was born different in one important way: he floats. Unlike everyone else, Barnaby does not obey the law of gravity. . . . And when the unthinkable happens, Barnaby finds himself on a journey that takes him all over the world. From Brazil to New York, . . . and . . . meets all sorts of different people- -and discovers who he really is along the way." (Publisher's note)

Bradford, Chris

Young samurai: the way of the sword. Disney-Hyperion Books 2010 422p $16.99

Grades: 4 5 6 7   **Fic**

1. Adventure fiction 2. Japan -- Fiction 3. Ninja -- Fiction 4. Orphans -- Fiction 5. Samurai -- Fiction 6. Martial arts -- Fiction
ISBN 978-1-4231-2025-4; 1-4231-2025-6

LC 2009008309

Sequel to: Young samurai: the way of the warrior (2009)

In 1611 Japan, English orphan Jack Fletcher continues his difficult training at Niten Ichi Ryu Samurai School, while also trying to get back the rutter, his father's navigational logbook, that an evil ninja wants to possess.

"With straightforward prose, [Bradford] has managed to pen lively and exciting fight sequences and is slowly beginning to develop a keen edge to his cast of characters, laying significant groundwork for future installments." Booklist

★ **Young** samurai: the way of the warrior. Hyperion Books for Children 2009 359p $16.99

Grades: 4 5 6 7   **Fic**

1. Adventure fiction 2. Japan -- Fiction 3. Samurai -- Fiction 4. Martial arts -- Fiction
ISBN 978-1-4231-1871-8; 1-4231-1871-5

LC 2008-46180

First published 2008 in the United Kingdom

Orphaned by a ninja pirate attack off the coast of Japan in 1611, twelve-year-old English lad Jack Fletcher is determined to prove himself, despite the bullying of fellow students, when the legendary sword master who rescued him begins training him as a samurai warrior.

"Jack's story alone makes for a page-turner, but coupling it with intriguing bits of Japanese history and culture, Bradford produces an adventure novel to rank among the genre's best." Publ Wkly

Includes bibliographical references

Followed by: Young samurai: the way of the sword (2010)

Bradley, Kimberly Brubaker

★ **Jefferson's** sons; a founding father's secret children. Dial Books for Young Readers 2011 368p $17.99

Grades: 5 6 7 8   **Fic**

1. Slaves 2. Architects 3. Presidents 4. Vice-presidents 5. Essayists 6. Mistresses 7. Slavery -- Fiction 8. Virginia -- Fiction 9. African Americans -- Fiction
ISBN 978-0-8037-3499-9; 0-8037-3499-9

LC 2010049650

"The characters spring to life. . . . [This is a] fascinating story of an American family that represents so many of the contradictions of our history. The afterword is as fascinating as the novel." Kirkus

★ The **war** that saved my life; by Kimberly Brubaker Bradley. Dial Books for Young Readers, an imprint of Penguin Group (USA) Inc. 2015 320 p. (hardcover) $16.99

Grades: 4 5 6 7   **Fic**

1. Brothers and sisters -- Fiction 2. People with disabilities -- Fiction 3. Great Britain -- History -- 20th century -- Fiction 4. World War, 1939-1945 -- Evacuation of civilians -- Fiction 5. Great Britain -- History -- George VI, 1936-1952 -- Fiction
ISBN 0803740816; 9780803740815

LC 2014002168

Odyssey Award (2015)

Newbery Honor Book (2016)

Schneider Family Book Award, Middle School (2016)

In this book, by Kimberly Brubaker Bradley, "[n]ine-year-old Ada has never left her one-room apartment. Her mother is too humiliated by Ada's twisted foot to let her outside. So when her little brother Jamie is shipped out of London to escape the war, Ada doesn't waste a minute - she sneaks out to join him. So begins a new adventure of Ada, and for Susan Smith, the woman who is forced to take the two kids in." (Publisher's note)

"When word starts to spread about Germans bombing London, Ada's mother decides to send her little brother, Jamie, to the country. Not 11-year-old Ada, though—she was born with a crippling clubfoot, and her cruel mother treats her like a slave...The home-front realities of WWII, as well as Ada's realistic anger and fear, come to life in Bradley's affecting and austerely told story, and readers will cheer for steadfast Ada as she triumphs over despair." Booklist

Branford, Anna

Violet Mackerel's brilliant plot; by Anna Branford; illustrated by Elanna Allen. Reprint Atheneum Books for Young Readers 2012 102 p. ill. (reinforced) $14.99; (paperback) $5.99

Grades: 1 2 3   **Fic**

1. Flea markets -- Fiction 2. Imagination -- Fiction 3. Individuality -- Fiction 4. Moneymaking projects -- Fiction
ISBN 1442435852; 9781442435858; 9781442435865

LC 2011022584

In this book by Anna Branford, "young Violet accompanies her older siblings and her mother to the flea market . . . where Violet looks longingly at a blue china bird for sale in one of the stalls. She decides to hatch a plot to obtain the bird for her own, but her many efforts fail; a simple act of generosity on her part, though, gains the attention of Vincent, the stall owner, and he eventually gives Violet the very thing she wanted all along." (Bulletin of the Center for Children's Books)

★ **Violet** Mackerel's natural habitat; by Anna Branford and illustrated by Elanna Allen. Atheneum Books for Young Readers 2013 112 p. (hardcover : alk. paper) $15.99

Grades: 1 2 3   **Fic**

1. Ladybugs -- Fiction 2. Family life -- Fiction 3. Habitat (Ecology) -- Fiction
ISBN 1442435941; 9781442435940; 9781442435957; 9781442435964

LC 2012015000

In this book, by Anna Branford, "Violet is the smallest in her family, and has a special affinity for Small Things everywhere. So when she finds a tiny ladybug in the garden, she expects she knows how it feels. Violet wants to help the ladybug, so she names her Small Gloria, puts her in a jar, and feeds her. Violet wakes up to a horrible surprise. But thankfully, even as Violet learns a hard lesson about natural habitats, she realizes how nice it is to share her own habitat with a big sister." (Publisher's note)

Violet Mackerel's personal space; Anna Branford; illustrated by Elanna Allen. Atheneum Books for Young Readers 2013 128 p. (Violet Mackerel) (pbk.) $5.99

Grades: 2 3 4   **Fic**

1. Moving -- Fiction 2. Weddings -- Fiction 3. Remarriage -- Fiction 4. Family life -- Fiction 5. Moving, Household -- Fiction
ISBN 1442435925; 9781442435919; 9781442435926
LC 2012025783

In this children's book, by Anna Branford, "Violet Mackerel believes that wherever you leave something small, a tiny part of you gets to stay too - like how the little piece of green sea glass under the mattress at the beach house means that a little piece of Violet gets to stay on summer holiday. Violet's theory is put to the test when Mama and Vincent announce some very special news: They are going to get married. And they are all going to move." (Publisher's note)

"Mama and her boyfriend, Vincent, are getting married. Planning for the wedding is fun, but looking for a new house is divisive...With its gentle wisdom and sincerity, this series has made a space for itself among early chapter books, and hopefully there are more Violet Mackerel books to come."

Other titles in the series include:
Violet Mackerel's Brilliant Plot (2012)
Violet Mackerel's Natural Habitat (2013)
Violet Mackerel's Pocket Protest (2014)
Violet Mackerel's Possible Friend (2014)
Violet Mackerel's Remarkable Recovery (2011)

Violet Mackerel's pocket protest; Anna Branford; illustrated by Elanna Allen. Atheneum Books for Young Readers 2014 128 p. (hardcover) $16.99

Grades: 2 3 4   **Fic**

1. Social action -- Fiction 2. Oak -- Fiction 3. Trees -- Fiction 4. Protest movements -- Fiction 5. Environmental protection -- Fiction
ISBN 1442494581; 9781442494589; 9781442494596
LC 2013035382

In this children's book by Anna Branford, illustrated by Elanna Allen, part of the Violet Mackerel series, "Violet and Rose start a very small protest to make a very big impact. . . . when Johnson's Tree Services stomps in and posts a sign that says PUBLIC NOTICE-TREE REMOVAL, they know that they must do something to stop them. When their first protest washes away in the rain, Violet and Rose feel discouraged." (Publisher's note)

"Sweet and likable Violet and best friend Rose band together to protect their beloved oak tree, which is in danger of being demolished. The latest entry in this charming, Australia-set chapter book series will inspire readers to find their voices and advocate for their own causes, big or small." SLJ

Other titles in the series include:
Violet Mackerel's Brilliant Plot (2012)
Violet Mackerel's Natural Habitat (2013)
Violet Mackerel's Personal Space (2014)
Violet Mackerel's Possible Friend (2014)
Violet Mackerel's Remarkable Recovery (2011)

Violet Mackerel's possible friend; Anna Branford; illustrated by Elanna Allen. Atheneum Books for Young Readers 2014 128 p. (hardcover) $15.99

Grades: 2 3 4   **Fic**

1. Worry -- Fiction 2. Moving -- Fiction 3. Friendship -- Fiction 4. Family life -- Fiction 5. Moving, Household -- Fiction
ISBN 1442494557; 9781442494558; 9781442494565
LC 2013013568

In this book, by Anna Branford, "Violet Mackerel hopes . . . that her new next door neighbor, Rose, might turn out to be a very good friend. But even after a nice morning at Rose's house, Violet still has quite a few worrying thoughts. Is she too messy for Rose's tidy family? Will Rose be disappointed that the ice in Violet's house comes from a plastic tray instead of a special box with fancy tongs? Will Violet wear the wrong sort of costume to Rose's flower-themed birthday party?" (Publisher's note)

"Violet and her family are settling into their new home with all the joys and uncertainties relocation brings . . . This is a gentle story of kindred spirits recognizing each other, and a happy addition to this continually excellent series." Booklist

Other titles in the series include:
Violet Mackerel's Brilliant Plot (2012)
Violet Mackerel's Natural Habitat (2013)
Violet Mackerel's Pocket Protest (2014)
Violet Mackerel's Personal Space (2013)
Violet Mackerel's Remarkable Recovery (2011)

Violet Mackerel's remarkable recovery; Anna Branford; illustrated by Elanna Allen. 1st ed. Atheneum Books for Young Readers 2012 128 p. ill. (hardcover) $15.99; (paperback) $5.99

Grades: 1 2 3 4   **Fic**

1. Gifts -- Fiction 2. Tonsillectomy -- Fiction 3. Sick -- Fiction 4. Friendship -- Fiction
ISBN 1442435887; 9781442435889; 9781442435896
LC 2011023703

In this children's story, by Anna Branford, "seven-year-old Violet Mackerel has a new theory: If someone has a problem and you give them something small, . . . that small thing might have a strange and special way of helping them. Violet gets the chance to put 'The Theory of Giving Small Things' to the test when a bad case of tonsillitis requires the removal of her tonsils, and she suspects that the purple lozenge from Doctor Singh may help her in quite an extraordinary way.' (Publisher's note)

Branford, Henrietta
Fire, bed, & bone. Candlewick Press 1998 122p hardcover o.p pa $5.99

Grades: 5 6 7 8   **Fic**

1. Dogs -- Fiction 2. Middle Ages -- Fiction 3. Great Britain -- History -- 1154-1399, Plantagenets -- Fiction
ISBN 0-7636-0338-4; 0-7636-2992-8 pa
LC 97-17491

In 1381 in England, a hunting dog recounts what happens to his beloved master Rufus and his family when they are arrested on suspicion of being part of the peasants' rebellion led by Wat Tyler and the preacher John Ball

"The dog's observant eye, sympathetic personality, and courageous acts hook the reader into what is both irresistible adventure and educational historical fiction." Booklist

Bransford, Nathan
Jacob Wonderbar and the cosmic space kapow. Dial Books for Young Readers 2011 281p il $14.99

Grades: 4 5 6   **Fic**
1. Adventure fiction 2. Fathers -- Fiction 3. Teachers -- Fiction 4. Interplanetary voyages -- Fiction
ISBN 978-0-8037-3537-8; 0-8037-3537-5

LC 2010-38152

When sixth-grade classroom terror Jacob Wonderbar and his friends Sarah and Dexter find a spaceship crashed in the woods near their suburban neighborhood, their discovery leads them to a series of adventures including space travel, substitute teachers, kidnapping, and more.

"Readers will appreciate Bransford's unique view of the universe. . . Jacob's ongoing search for his father . . . promises to keep this series moving through at least two forthcoming sequels." Booklist

Brawer, Michael

Archie takes flight; by Wendy Mass and Michael Brawer; illustrated by Elise Gravel. Little, Brown & Co. 2014 112 p. V1 illustrations (hardcover) $15
Grades: 2 3 4   **Fic**
1. Science fiction 2. Outer space -- Fiction 3. Extraterrestrial beings -- Fiction 4. Father-son relationship -- Fiction 5. Fathers and sons -- Fiction 6. Interplanetary voyages -- Fiction 7. Adventure and adventurers -- Fiction
ISBN 0316243191; 9780316243193

LC 2013021622

In this book, the first in a series by Wendy Mass and Michael Brawer, "Archie Morningstar is finally old enough to join his dad on the midnight taxi shift for 'Take Your Kid to Work Day.' When they blast out of orbit, it quickly becomes clear that his dad has an unusual job and that his vehicle is no ordinary taxi. Archie is now privy to the secret family business: driving aliens around the galaxy in a high-tech space vehicle." School Library Journal)

"Archie Morningstar has been waiting for 'eight years, eight months, and eight days' to ride along with his taxicab-driving father. But when the night finally arrives, the experience proves to be out of this world. Archie had been looking forward to seeing more of the city, but his father is no ordinary cabbie. He drives a space taxi, with fares all over the known universe. Archie serves as his father's co-pilot for the night, helping him navigate wormholes, avoid asteroid fields and work the taxi's thrusters. . . . Zany adventures, a wacky plot and plenty of slapstick humor make this a quick, enjoyable read. Simple illustrations and trio of scientific definitions add to the narrative. A solid start to a new chapter-book series." Kirkus

Water planet rescue; by Wendy Mass and Michael Brawer; illustrations by Elise Gravel. Little, Brown & Co. 2014 128 p. illustrations (Space taxi) (hardcover) $15
Grades: 2 3 4   **Fic**
1. Interplanetary voyages -- Fiction 2. Father-son relationship -- Fiction 3. Fathers and sons -- Fiction 4. Adventure and adventurers -- Fiction
ISBN 031624323X; 9780316243230

LC 2013044221

In this children's book, by Wendy Mass and Michael Brawer, "Archie Morningstar's dad drives a taxi through outer space! And with the help of a talking cat named Pockets, Archie and his dad help fight crime across the universe. In the second book in this series, Archie, his dad, and Pockets fly to a planet in peril: someone is stealing the water from his underwater world!" (Publisher's note)

"The second installment of the Space Taxi series find eight-year-old Archie Morningstar, navigator of his father's space taxi and newly appointed deputy of the Intergalactic Security Force, setting out on a mission to the watery planet Nautilus...This rollicking adventure, full of goofy antics and subtle lessons in acceptance, is complemented by

simple line drawings and concludes with a trio of fun space facts "to impress your friends and teachers." Booklist

Breathed, Berke

Flawed dogs; the shocking raid on Westminster. written and illustrated by Berkeley Breathed. Philomel Books 2009 216p il $16.99
Grades: 4 5 6   **Fic**
1. Dogs -- Fiction
ISBN 978-0-399-25218-1; 0-399-25218-5

LC 2009-2638

After being framed by a jealous poodle, a dachshund is left for dead, but comes back with a group of mutts from the National Last Ditch Dog Depository to disrupt the prestigious Westminster Kennel Club dog show and exact revenge on Cassius the poodle.

"Dramatically lit and featuring comically exaggerated characters (human and canine alike), Berkeley's b&w artwork augments the story's drama and humor. A moving tale about the beauty of imperfections and the capacity for love." Publ Wkly

Bredsdorff, Bodil

The **Crow**-girl; translated from the Danish by Faith Ingwersen. Farrar Straus Giroux 2004 155p map (The children of Crow Cove) $16
Grades: 4 5 6   **Fic**
1. Denmark -- Fiction 2. Orphans -- Fiction 3. Grandmothers -- Fiction
ISBN 0-374-31247-8

LC 2003-49310

Original Danish editon, 1993

After the death of her grandmother, a young orphaned girl leaves her house by the cove and begins a journey which leads her to people and experiences that exemplify the wisdom her grandmother had shared with her

"Touching on universal themes, this quiet adventure story has the depth and flavor of a tale from long ago and far away." SLJ

Other titles in this series are:
Eidi (2009)
Tink (2011)

★ **Eidi**; translated from the Danish by Kathryn Mahaffy. Farrar Straus Giroux 2009 138p (The children of Crow Cove series) $16.99
Grades: 4 5 6   **Fic**
1. Denmark -- Fiction 2. Orphans -- Fiction
ISBN 978-0-374-31267-1; 0-374-31267-2

LC 2008-26052

Sequel to: The Crow-girl (2004)
Batchelder Award honor book (2010)

Eidi leaves her mother and stepfather in Crow Cove to live in a nearby village, where she meets the much younger Tink and rescues him from the abusive man he has been living with

"This unassuming yet compelling story is notable for the simplicity and power of the storytelling, the clarity of description and characterization, and the humanity of the ideas at the novel's heart." Booklist

Followed by: Tink (2011)

Tink; translated from the Danish by Elisabeth Kallick Dyssegaard. Farrar Straus & Giroux 2011 138p (The children of Crow Cove) $16.99
Grades: 4 5 6   **Fic**
1. Denmark -- Fiction 2. Orphans -- Fiction 3. Alcoholism -- Fiction
ISBN 978-0-374-31268-8; 0-374-31268-0

LC 2009051967

Sequel to: Eidi (2009)

Feeling as though he does not belong there, Tink leaves Crow Cove, only to return with the drunken Burd, who teaches Tink to fish and to have confidence in himself and his place in the community.

Brewster, Hugh

Carnation, Lily, Lily, Rose; the story of a painting. by Hugh Brewster; with paintings by John Singer Sargent. Kids Can Press 2007 48p il $17.95

Grades: 3 4 5   Fic

1. Artists 2. Painters 3. Artists -- Fiction
ISBN 978-1-55453-137-0; 1-55453-137-3

This volume "introduces a true episode from nineteenth-century art history, delivering facts about John Singer Sargent and his luminous masterwork, Carnation, Lily, Lily, Rose, through the imagined words of a child present during its creation. . . . Widely accessible are the profuse visuals, including some of Sargent's sketchbook doodles and real photos of the featured family." Booklist

Brezenoff, Steve

The **burglar** who bit the Big Apple; illustrated by C. B. Canga. Stone Arch Books 2010 81p il (Field trip mysteries) lib bdg $23.99; pa $5.95

Grades: 2 3 4   Fic

1. School stories 2. Mystery fiction 3. New York (N.Y.) -- Fiction
ISBN 978-1-4342-2139-1 lib bdg; 1-4342-2139-3 lib bdg; 978-1-4342-2771-3 pa; 1-4342-2771-5 pa

"Cat, Sam, Egg, and Gum are sixth-grade pals with a penchant for solving mysteries. . . . In [this book], they arrive in New York City just as a lunch box has been lifted from the Ralph Kramden statue in the Port Authority Bus Terminal. Later there is more vandalism at the Museum of Natural History and the Bronx Zoo, setting these kids on the trail of a suspicious girl who just happens to know their itinerary. . . . [This] compact chapter [book] offers leading characters of both genders, some full-page, full-color illustrations, a 'detective's dictionary' (aka glossary), a useful model of a school report on the featured city, and evidence-based discussion questions. [This title is an] excellent [introduction] to the mystery genre; the graphics and short chapters make [it] accessible to struggling or reluctant readers." SLJ

The **zombie** who visited New Orleans; illustrated by C. B. Canga. Stone Arch Books 2010 80p il (Field trip mysteries) lib bdg $23.99; pa $5.95

Grades: 2 3 4   Fic

1. School stories 2. Mystery fiction 3. Zombies -- Fiction 4. New Orleans (La.) -- Fiction
ISBN 978-1-4342-2141-4 lib bdg; 1-4342-2141-5 lib bdg; 978-1-4342-2773-7 pa; 1-4342-2773-1 pa

LC 2010022580

"Cat, Sam, Egg, and Gum are sixth-grade pals with a penchant for solving mysteries. . . . In New Orleans, the friends witness acts of voodoo at every tourist attraction and wonder if certain people might be zombies in disguise. . . . [This] compact chapter [book] offers leading characters of both genders, some full-page, full-color illustrations, a 'detective's dictionary' (aka glossary), a useful model of a school report on the featured city, and evidence-based discussion questions. [This title is an] excellent [introduction] to the mystery genre; the graphics and short chapters make [it] accessible to struggling or reluctant readers." SLJ

Brezenoff, Steven

The **painting** that wasn't there; illustrated by C.B. Canga. Stone Arch Books 2010 $17.99

Grades: 3 4 5 6   Fic

1. School stories 2. Mystery fiction
ISBN 9781434216083

LC 2009002572

"This title...marries the always high-interest topic of an art heist with a breezy, straightforward story just right for reluctant readers." Booklist

Brink, Carol Ryrie

★ **Caddie** Woodlawn; illustrated by Trina Schart Hyman. Macmillan 1973 275p il $17.95; pa $6.99

Grades: 4 5 6   Fic

1. Wisconsin -- Fiction 2. Frontier and pioneer life -- Fiction
ISBN 0-02-713670-1; 1-4169-4028-6 pa

A newly illustrated edition of the title first published 1935

Awarded the Newbery Medal, 1936

Caddie Woodlawn was eleven in 1864. Because she was frail, she had been allowed to grow up a tomboy. Her capacity for adventure was practically limitless, and there was plenty of adventure on the Wisconsin frontier in those days. The story covers one year of life on the pioneer farm, closing with the news that Mr. Woodlawn had inherited an estate in England, and the unanimous decision of the family to stay in Wisconsin

Based upon the reminiscences of the author's grandmother

The typeface "is eminently clear and readable, and the illustrations in black and white . . . are attractive and expressive." Wis Libr Bull

Britt, Fanny

Jane, the fox & me; [written by] Fanny Britt; [illustrated by] Isabelle Arsenault; translated by Christine Morelli and Susan Ouriou. Pgw 2013 101 p. $19.95

Grades: 5 6 7 8 9   Fic

1. Teenage girls -- Fiction 2. Alienation (Social psychology) -- Fiction
ISBN 1554983606; 9781554983605

Written by Fanny Britt, illustrated by Isabelle Arsentault, and translated by Christine Morelli and Susan Ouriou, this "graphic novel reveals the casual brutality of which children are capable, but also assures readers that redemption can be found through connecting with another whether the other is a friend, a fictional character or even, amazingly, a fox." (Publisher's note) It "centers on Hélène, ostracized by her former friends and now a loner at school." (Horn Book Magazine)

"Britt's well-constructed narrative is achieved sensitively through Arsenault's impressionistic artwork. . . . An elegant and accessible approach to an important topic." Booklist

Brittain, Bill

The **wish** giver; three tales of Coven Tree. drawings by Andrew Glass. Harper & Row 1983 181p il $16.89; pa $5.99

Grades: 5 6 7 8   Fic

1. Magic -- Fiction 2. Wishes -- Fiction
ISBN 0-06-020687-X; 0-06-440168-5 pa

LC 82-4826

A Newbery Medal honor book, 1984

"Captivating, fresh, and infused with homespun humor." Horn Book

Other titles about Coven Tree are:

Dr. Dredd's wagon of wonders (1987)

Professor Popkin's prodigious polish (1990)

Broach, Elise

James to the rescue; Elise Broach; illustrated by Kelly Murphy. Henry Holt & Co. 2015 112 p. color illustrations (The masterpiece adventures) (hardback) $15.99

Grades: 1 2 3   Fic

1. Beetles -- Fiction 2. Rescues -- Fiction 3. Friendship -- Fiction 4. Collectors and collecting -- Fiction 5. Human-animal

relationships -- Fiction
ISBN 162779316X; 9781627793162

LC 2014042196

In this children's book by Elise Broach and illustrated by Kelly Murphy "Marvin the beetle is going collecting with his family. All is good and well until Uncle Albert gets hurt. Marvin needs James's help to save Uncle Albert before it's too late." (Publisher's note)

The characters have distinct personalities, the story is well-paced, and the focus on unlikely alliances and mutual trust suffuses the tale with warmth. Full of drama and heart, this is the kind of series that can show newly independent readers the power of a good story." Kirkus

Sequel to "The Miniature World of Marvin and James"

Masterpiece; illustrated by Kelly Murphy. Henry Holt & Co. 2008 292p il $16.95

Grades: 4 5 6 7 **Fic**

1. Mystery fiction 2. Artists -- Fiction 3. Beetles -- Fiction 4. New York (N.Y.) -- Fiction

ISBN 978-0-8050-8270-8; 0-8050-8270-0

After Marvin, a beetle, makes a miniature drawing as an eleventh birthday gift for James, a human with whom he shares a house, the two new friends work together to help recover a Durer drawing stolen from the Metropolitan Museum of Art.

Broach "packs this fast-moving story with perennially seductive themes: hidden lives and secret friendships, miniature worlds lost to disbelievers. . . . Loosely implying rather than imitating the Old Masters they reference, the finely hatched drawings depict the settings realistically and the characters, especially the beetles, with joyful comic license." Publ Wkly

The **miniature** world of Marvin & James; Elise Broach; illustrated by Kelly Murphy. Henry Holt and Co. 2014 112 p. illustrations (The masterpiece adventures) (hardback) $15.99

Grades: 1 2 3 **Fic**

1. Beetles -- Fiction 2. Insects -- Fiction 3. Vacations -- Poetry 4. Friendship -- Fiction 5. Human-animal relationships -- Fiction

ISBN 0805091904; 9780805091908

LC 2013036081

In this book, by Elise Broach and illustrated by Kelly Murphy, James is going on vacation for a week. His best friend, Marvin the beetle, has to stay at home. Without James to keep him company, Marvin has to play with his annoying cousin, Elaine. Marvin and Elaine quickly find themselves getting into all sorts of trouble, even getting trapped inside a pencil sharpener! Marvin misses James and starts to worry about their friendship." (Publisher's note)

"A new early chapter book series follows the friendship of beetle Marvin and human James (Masterpiece) for a younger audience. The sentences are shorter and the illustrations more prominent, but the amiable tone and relatable characters are the same. New readers will be rewarded by this page-turning adventure, written throughout with emotional authenticity and ending with a satisfying conclusion." Horn Book

Another title in this series is:
James to the rescue (2015)

★ **Missing** on Superstition Mountain; [illustrated by Antonio Javier Caparo] Henry Holt 2011 262p il $15.99

Grades: 3 4 5 **Fic**

1. Mystery fiction 2. Arizona -- Fiction 3. Brothers -- Fiction 4. Mountains -- Fiction

ISBN 978-0-8050-9047-5; 0-8050-9047-9

LC 2010-49007

When brothers Simon, Henry, and Jack move with their parents to Arizona, they are irresistibly drawn to explore the aptly named Superstition Mountain, in spite of warnings that it is not safe.

"Caparo's skillful grayscale illustrations add a spooky element: three skulls mark each new chapter, and images like a black cat sitting on a crooked gravestone inspire chills. Classic horror and thriller elements combine with modern touches in Broach's page-turner." Publ Wkly

Revenge of Superstition Mountain; Elise Broach; illustrated by Aleksey and Olga Ivanov. Christy Ottaviano Books 2014 294 p. illustrations (hardback) $16.99

Grades: 3 4 5 **Fic**

1. Mystery fiction 2. Arizona -- Fiction 3. Brothers -- Fiction 4. Mountains -- Fiction 5. Mystery and detective stories 6. Superstition Mountains (Ariz.) -- Fiction

ISBN 0805089098; 9780805089097; 9781250056863

LC 2014005283

In this book, by Elise Broach, illustrated by Aleksey and Olga Ivanov, "the Barker brothers and their good friend Delilah secretly climb up to Superstition Mountain one last time. There are still mysteries to solve--is the creepy librarian really the ghost of Julia Thomas from a century before? What was their uncle Hank's role in discovering the gold mine? . . . And, most of all, who is trying to kill them?" (Publisher's note)

"The Barker brothers and Delilah are back on Superstition Mountain for one last secret climb, determined to solve its mysteries and get back into the gold mine that was covered by the avalanche in book two. A satisfying end to a fun and creepy series." SLJ

Other titles in the series include:
Missing on Superstition Mountain (2011)
Treasure on Superstition Mountain (2012)

Shakespeare's secret; [by] Elise Broach. Henry Holt 2005 250p il $16.95; pa $5.99

Grades: 5 6 7 8 **Fic**

1. Mystery fiction

ISBN 0-8050-7387-6; 0-312-37132-2 pa

LC 2004-54020

Named after a character in a Shakespeare play, misfit sixth-grader Hero becomes interested in exploring this unusual connection because of a valuable diamond supposedly hidden in her new house, an intriguing neighbor, and the unexpected attention of the most popular boy in school.

"The mystery alone will engage readers. . . . The main characters are all well developed, and the dialogue is both realistic and well planned." SLJ

Treasure on Superstition Mountain; Elise Broach; illustrated by Antonio Javier Caparo. Henry Holt 2012 224 p. (hardcover) $15.99

Grades: 3 4 5 **Fic**

1. Adventure fiction 2. Buried treasure -- Fiction 3. Arizona -- Fiction 4. Brothers -- Fiction 5. Mountains -- Fiction 6. Mystery and detective stories 7. Gold mines and mining -- Fiction 8. Superstition Mountains (Ariz.) -- Fiction

ISBN 0805077634; 9780805077636; 9780805096408

LC 2012006475

Sequel to: Missing on Superstition Mountain

This is the second installment of Elise Broach's Superstition Mountain series. Here, "two weeks after the children's . . . escape from Arizona's Superstition Mountain, during which they unearthed a treasure map and a gold nugget, the young adventurers—undeterred by Delilah's broken leg, their parents' admonishments, and anonymous warnings—are more determined than ever both to find a hidden gold mine and discover who is trying to stop them." (Publishers Weekly)

The **wolf** keepers; Elise Broach; with illustrations by Alice Ratterree. Henry Holt & Co. 2016 352 p. illustrations, maps (ebook) $60; (hardback) $16.99

Grades: 4 5 6 7 8   **Fic**

1. Zoos -- Fiction 2. Wolves -- Fiction 3. Runaways -- Fiction 4. Friendship -- Fiction 5. Mystery and detective stories

ISBN 9781250113047; 0805098992; 9780805098990

LC 2015049899

In this children's novel by Elise Broach, illustrated by Alice Ratterree, "Lizzie Durango and her dad have always had a zoo to call their home. . . . One afternoon . . . she finds Tyler Briggs, a runaway who has secretly made the zoo his makeshift home. The two become friends and . . . stumble into a covert investigation involving the zoo wolves who are suddenly dying. . . . This mystery will draw them into a high-stakes historical adventure involving the legend of John Muir." (Publisher's note)

"Tyler's wry comments about his race add further dimensions to a thoughtful, well-told tale, as do the pencil drawings. John Muir's spirit hums along under a well-developed plot with likable characters." Kirkus

Brodien-Jones, Christine

The **glass** puzzle; Christine Brodien-Jones. Delacorte Press 2013 336 p. (hc) $16.99

Grades: 4 5 6 7   **Fic**

1. Horror fiction -- Fiction 2. Fantasy fiction -- Fiction 3. Wales -- Fiction 4. Cousins -- Fiction 5. Time travel -- Fiction 6. Supernatural -- Fiction 7. Tenby (Wales) -- Fiction 8. Adventure and adventurers -- Fiction 9. Wales -- History -- 1063-1284 -- Fiction

ISBN 0385742975; 9780307979933; 9780375990878; 9780385742979; 9780385742986

LC 2012015999

In this book, Zoé Badger and her cousin find an antique glass puzzle and unwittingly release Scravens—evil creatures with a craterous third eye and massive wings—into Tenby. The cousins, in turn, are magically transported to Wythernsea, an island long submerged underwater, whence the Scravens come. There they learn that Scravens are taking over the bodies of Tenby inhabitants—as well as terrorizing Wythernsea—and that they must save both towns from the creatures." (Kirkus Reviews)

Bromley, Anne C.

The **lunch** thief; [by] Anne C. Bromley; illustrated by Robert Casilla. Tilbury House Publishers 2010 un il

Grades: 4 5 6   **Fic**

1. School stories 2. Theft -- Fiction 3. Homeless persons -- Fiction

ISBN 0-88448-311-8; 978-0-88448-311-3

LC 2008045822

Rafael is angry that a new student is stealing lunches, but he takes time to learn what the real problem is before acting.

"Full-color illustrations realistically portray the cast of characters and the boys' multicultural school. With a few well-placed remarks by Rafael's hardworking mother and no preachy overtones, this entirely credible story of how a thoughtful boy elects to 'light one candle' in response to the larger problem of homelessness and hunger would make an excellent touchstone for class discussion." SLJ

Brooks, Bruce

Everywhere. Harper & Row 1990 70p lib bdg $16.89

Grades: 4 5 6 7   **Fic**

1. Death -- Fiction 2. Grandfathers -- Fiction

ISBN 0-06-020729-9

LC 90-4073

Afraid that his beloved grandfather will die after suffering a heart attack, a nine-year-old boy agrees to join ten-year-old Dooley in performing a mysterious ritual called soul switching

"Echoes of the great Southern writers with their themes of loneliness and faith can be heard in this masterly novella. . . . Brooks's precise use of language is a tour de force." Horn Book

Brown, Gavin

Josh Baxter levels up; by Gavin Brown. Scholastic Press 2016 192 p. illustrations $12.99

Grades: 4 5 6 7 8   **Fic**

1. Moving, Household -- Fiction 2. Schools -- Fiction 3. Bullying -- Fiction 4. Family life -- Fiction 5. Video games -- Fiction 6. Middle schools -- Fiction

ISBN 9780545772945

LC 2015016236

In this book, by author Gavin Brown, "Josh Baxter is sick and tired of hitting the reset button. It's not easy being the new kid for the third time in two years. . . . Josh knows that his best bet is to keep his head down and stay under the radar. . . . But when Josh's mom sees his terrible grades and takes away his video games, it's clear his strategy has failed. Josh needs a new plan, or he'll never make it to the next level, let alone the next grade." (Publisher's note)

"Smartly paced and emotionally engaging, a book even those who have never held a controller will enjoy." Kirkus

Brown, Peter, 1979-

★ The **wild** robot; by Peter Brown. Little, Brown & Co. 2016 288 p. illustrations (hardback) $16.99

Grades: 3 4 5   **Fic**

1. Robots -- Fiction 2. Animals -- Fiction 3. Islands -- Fiction 4. Survival -- Fiction 5. Friendship -- Fiction

ISBN 9780316381994

LC 2015021094

In this middle grade novel, by Peter Brown, "when robot Roz opens her eyes for the first time, she discovers that she is alone on a remote wild island. Why is she there? Where did she come from? And, most important, how will she survive in her harsh surroundings? Roz's only hope is to learn from the island's hostile animal inhabitants. . . . Until one day, the robot's mysterious past comes back to haunt her." (Publisher's note)

Brown, Susan Taylor

Hugging the rock; [by] Susan Taylor Brown; [cover illustration by] Michael Morgenstern] Tricycle Press 2006 170p $14.95; pa $6.95

Grades: 5 6 7 8   **Fic**

1. Divorce -- Fiction 2. Father-daughter relationship -- Fiction 3. Mother-daughter relationship -- Fiction

ISBN 978-1-58246-180-9; 1-58246-180-5; 978-1-58246-236-3 pa; 1-58246-236-4 pa

LC 2006005735

Through a series of poems, Rachel expresses her feelings about her parents' divorce, living without her mother, and her changing attitude towards her father

"This is a poignant character study of a dysfunctional family. . . . Written in straightforward language, the text clearly reveals Rachel's emotions, describing moments both painful and reassuring." SLJ

Brown, Tami Lewis

The **map** of me. Farrar Straus Giroux 2011 152p $16.99

Grades: 4 5 6   **Fic**

1. Sisters -- Fiction 2. Kentucky -- Fiction 3. Family life -- Fiction 4. Automobile travel -- Fiction

ISBN 978-0-374-35655-2; 0-374-35655-6

LC 201002926

Twelve-year-old Margie finds her sister, Peep, intolerable since the youngster skipped from third grade to sixth, but when their mother eaves home, Margie packs Peep into their father's car and starts driving across Kentucky to find her.

This novel "combines pathos and humor for an emotionally resonant story." Publ Wkly

Bruchac, Joseph

The **arrow** over the door; pictures by James Watling. Dial Bks. for Young Readers 1998 89p il hardcover o.p. pa $4.99

Grades: 4 5 6 **Fic**

1. Native Americans -- Fiction 2. Society of Friends -- Fiction 3. United States -- History -- 1775-1783, Revolution -- Fiction

ISBN 0-8037-2078-5; 0-14-130571-1 pa

LC 96-36701

"Bruchac's elegant and powerful writing fills in much of the fascinating detail of this serendipitous wartime friendship. . . . Watling's rugged, textured pen-and-ink drawings provide an atmospheric backdrop." Publ Wkly

Bearwalker; [by] Joseph Bruchac; illustrations by Sally Wern Comport. HarperCollinsPublishers 2007 208p il $15.99; lib bdg $16.89; pa $5.99

Grades: 5 6 7 8 **Fic**

1. Bears -- Fiction 2. Camping -- Fiction 3. Mohawk Indians -- Fiction 4. Adirondack Mountains (N.Y.) -- Fiction

ISBN 978-0-06-112309-2; 0-06-112309-9; 978-0-06-112311-5 lib bdg; 0-06-112311-0 lib bdg; 978-0-06-112315-3 pa; 0-06-112315-3 pa

LC 2006-30420

Although the littlest student in his class, thirteen-year-old Baron Braun calls upon the strength and wisdom of his Mohawk ancestors to face both man and beast when he tries to get help for his classmates, who are being terrorized during a school field trip in the Adirondacks.

"This exciting horror story, illustrated with b/w drawings, is based on Native American folklore." Kliatt

★ The **dark** pond; illustrations by Sally Wern Comport. HarperCollins 2004 142p il hardcover o.p. pa $6.99

Grades: 5 6 7 8 **Fic**

1. Ponds -- Fiction 2. Monsters -- Fiction 3. Shawnee Indians -- Fiction

ISBN 0-06-052995-4; 0-06-052998-9 pa

LC 2003-22212

After he feels a mysterious pull drawing him toward a dark, shadowy pond in the woods, Armie looks to old Native American tales for guidance about the dangerous monster lurking in the water.

"Effectively illustrated by Comport, this eerie story skillfully entwines Native American lore, suspense, and the realization that people and things are not always what they seem to be on the surface. . . . A perfect choice for reluctant readers." SLJ

Dragon castle. Dial Books for Young Readers 2011 346p $16.99

Grades: 4 5 6 7 **Fic**

1. Fairy tales 2. Dragons -- Fiction 3. Princes -- Fiction 4. Kings and rulers -- Fiction

ISBN 978-0-8037-3376-3; 0-8037-3376-3

LC 2010028798

Young prince Rashko, aided by wise old Georgi, must channel the power of his ancestor, Pavol the great, and harness a magical dragon to face the evil Baron Temny after the foolish King and Queen go missing.

Bruchac "spins a good-natured and humorous fairy tale. . . . With its subtle focus on peaceful resistance and use of classic folk-tale elements, this story exudes a gentle sense of fun." Publ Wkly

Night wings; illustrations by Sally Wern Comport. HarperCollins 2009 194p $15.99; lib bdg $16.89

Grades: 5 6 7 8 **Fic**

1. Monsters -- Fiction 2. New Hampshire -- Fiction 3. Abnaki Indians -- Fiction

ISBN 978-0-06-112318-4; 0-06-112318-8; 978-0-06-112319-1 lib bdg; 0-06-112319-6 lib bdg

LC 2008032096

After being taken captive by a band of treasure seekers, thirteen-year-old Paul and his Abenaki grandfather must face a legendary Native American monster at the top of Mount Washington.

"The intriguing Native American lore, the realistic teen narrative, and cliff-hanger sentences that build suspense at the end of each chapter are signature Bruchac and will captivate readers." SLJ

★ **Skeleton** man. HarperCollins Pubs. 2001 114p il $15.99; pa $4.99

Grades: 4 5 6 7 **Fic**

1. Kidnapping -- Fiction 2. Mohawk Indians -- Fiction

ISBN 0-06-029075-7; 0-06-440888-4 pa

LC 00-54345

After her parents disappear and she is turned over to the care of a strange "great-uncle," Molly must rely on her dreams about an old Mohawk story for her safety and maybe even for her life

"The mix of traditional and contemporary cultural references adds to the story's haunting appeal, and the quick pace and suspense . . . will likely hold the interest of young readers." Publ Wkly

Another title about Skeleton man is:

The return of Skeleton man (2006)

Squanto's journey; the story of the first Thanksgiving. Joseph Bruchac; illustrated by Greg Shed. Silver Whistle 2000 32 p. col. ill. (paperback) $6.99; (prebind) $15.99; (reinforced) $17

Grades: 2 3 4 5 **Fic**

1. Wampanoag Indians 2. Pilgrims (New England colonists) -- Fiction 3. Indians of North America -- Massachusetts -- Fiction

ISBN 9780152060442; 9781442073890; 0152018174; 9780152018177

LC 99012012

This illustrated children's book, by Joseph Bruchac, illustrated by Greg Shed, tells the story of the 17th century Native American Squanto. "In 1620 an English ship called the Mayflower landed on the shores inhabited by the Pokanoket people, and it was Squanto who welcomed the newcomers and taught them how to survive in the rugged land they called Plymouth." (Publisher's note)

Talking leaves; by Joseph Bruchac. Dial Books for Young Readers 2016 256 p. illustrations (hardback) $16.99

Grades: 4 5 6 7 8 **Fic**

1. Cherokee Indians -- Fiction 2. Native Americans -- Fiction 3. Language and languages -- Fiction 4. Indians of North America -- Fiction

ISBN 9780803735088

LC 2015035887

In this book, by Joseph Bruchac, "thirteen-year-old Uwohali has not seen his father, Sequoyah, for many years. So when Sequoyah returns to the village, Uwohali is eager to reconnect. But Sequoyah's new obsession with making strange markings causes friends and neighbors in their tribe to wonder whether he is crazy, or worse—practicing witchcraft. What they don't know, and what Uwohali discovers, is that Sequoyah is a genius and his strange markings are actually an alphabet." (Publisher's note)

"An illuminating read for middle graders; purchase anywhere historical fiction is in demand." SLJ

Walking two worlds; Joseph Bruchac; illustrated by David Fadden. 7th Generation 2015 120 p. (pbk.) $9.95

Grades: 5 6 7 8 9   **Fic**

1. Racism -- Fiction 2. Education -- Fiction 3. Seneca Indians -- Fiction 4. Native Americans -- Fiction
ISBN 9781939053107; 9781939053138

LC 2014046212

This book, by Joseph Bruchac, illustrated by David Fadden, and part of the Pathfinders series, is the "story of the early education of a famous Native American who gained greatness in the white man's world while staying true to his Seneca people. Hasanoanda was his Indian name. But in mission school he became Ely. He encountered racism and deceit but, against all odds, did not give up on his quest to walk between two worlds." (Publisher's note)

"Though the book lacks formal resources and references, and the time frame of events, including Ely's birth date, is occasionally unclear, Ely's challenges and successes are supportively portrayed, and may inspire readers to learn more about his life and times. An afterword provides some information on his later years." Booklist

Bruel, Nick

Bad Kitty; Drawn to Trouble. Nick Bruel. Roaring Brook Press 2013 128 p. (hardcover) $13.99

Grades: 2 3 4   **Fic**

1. Cartooning 2. Cats -- Fiction 3. Humorous stories 4. Authorship -- Fiction 5. Illustration of books -- Fiction
ISBN 1596436719; 9781596436718

LC 2013001633

In this book by Nick Bruel, "Kitty encounters what may be her most formidable foe yet: her creator! Kitty soon learns that feline manipulation works both ways--especially when you're at the wrong end of your author's pencil. Along the way, Nick shows kids how a book is created, despite the frequent interruptions." (Publisher's note)

"Bad Kitty makes her tenth appearance in this humorous (and partly nonfiction!) introduction to writing stories. Bruel teaches readers how to draw Bad Kitty and write stories of their own by introducing key story components (plot, conflict, character, etc.) and demonstrating them with good old Bad Kitty, who proves an unwilling model...Fun Facts and a glossary are included to help readers grasp the fundamentals of composition. Bruel's sky's-the-limit attitude will encourage boys and girls to use their imaginations and get writing." (Booklist)

Bad Kitty gets a bath. Roaring Brook Press 2008 125p il $12.95

Grades: 2 3 4   **Fic**

1. Cats -- Fiction 2. Baths -- Fiction
ISBN 978-1-59643-341-0; 1-59643-341-8

LC 2008-20296

Takes a humorous look at the normal way cats bathe, why it is inappropriate for humans to bathe that way, and the challenges of trying to give a cat a real bath with soap and water. Includes fun facts, glossary, and other information.

This "pairs Bruel's witty asides and spastic, tongue-in-cheek commentaries with more high-energy cartoon illustrations. . . . Young and reluctant readers will get plenty of laughs from this comic and informative chapter book." Booklist

Bad Kitty meets the baby. Roaring Brook Press 2011 143p il $13.99

Grades: 2 3 4   **Fic**

1. Cats -- Fiction 2. Infants -- Fiction 3. Adoption -- Fiction
ISBN 978-1-59643-597-1; 1-59643-597-6

LC 201003569

Bad kitty is not pleased when a baby joins her family. Includes fun facts and tips for training a cat to perform tricks.

Bruel "offers his trademark spastic black-and-white illustration in full-bleed and spots with plenty of baby and cat sounds in dialogue bubbles (translated into English where necessary). . . . Further proof that Bad Kitty can be good . . . especially in the eyes of her many fans." Kirkus

Bad Kitty vs. Uncle Murray; the uproar at the front door. Roaring Brook Press 2010 157p il $13.99

Grades: 2 3 4   **Fic**

1. Cats -- Fiction
ISBN 978-1-59643-596-4; 1-59643-596-8

Uncle Murray "is here to 'pet sit' Bad Kitty and Poor Puppy. The feline is not happy with this arrangement and gives Uncle Murray a horrible time. . . . Different fonts and huge scrawling words appear throughout, and the black-and-white cartoons on every page often show Bad Kitty and Murray with exaggerated gestures. The style gives the book fast pace and adds to the comedic atmosphere." SLJ

Happy birthday Bad Kitty. Roaring Brook Press 2009 159p il $13.99

Grades: 2 3 4   **Fic**

1. Cats -- Fiction 2. Birthdays -- Fiction
ISBN 978-1-59643-342-7; 1-59643-342-6

"Bad Kitty's day starts off with a special alphabetical "Birthday Breakfast" that includes Aardvark Bagels, Clam Doughnuts and Egg Fritters. Each chapter focuses on a different part of the day's festivities . . . The story becomes a whodunit when Bad Kitty's presents vanish and the prime suspect ends up being the lovable slow-wit, Puppy. . . . Bruel has fun with the format, using footnotes, different font sizes, comedic/informative interludes about cat behavior. . . . As usual, it's Bad Kitty's unapologetic, curmudgeon nature that delivers the laugh-out-loud funny." SLJ

Bruton, Catherine

Pop! Catherine Bruton. Egmont Books 2012 496 p. (pbk.) $10.99

Grades: 4 5 6 7   **Fic**

1. Fame -- Fiction 2. Reality television programs -- Fiction
ISBN 1405261331; 9781405261333

This novel, by Catherine Bruton, "mixes social issues with the absurdity of reality TV. The first round of auditions was a bit crazy. All these wannabe popstars sitting around trying to look wacky/soulful/tragic (delete as appropriate) to catch the attention of the TV cameras. A story of [the narrator], Agnes, Jimmy, and baby Alfie too; the tears, the tragedy, the broken homes and feuding families, the star-crossed lovers And only some of it was made up." (Publisher's note)

Buckley, Michael

The **Everafter** War; pictures by Peter Ferguson. Amulet Books 2009 306p il (The Sisters Grimm) $14.95; pa $6.95

Grades: 4 5 6   **Fic**

1. War stories 2. Mystery fiction 3. Magic -- Fiction 4. Sisters -- Fiction
ISBN 978-0-8109-8355-7; 0-8109-8355-9; 978-0-8109-8429-5 pa; 0-8109-8429-6 pa

LC 2008045921

After their parents awake from a sleeping spell, Daphne and Sabrina become caught in the middle of a war between the Scarlet Hand and

Prince Charming's Everafter army and learn a shocking secret about a deadly enemy.

The **fairy**-tale detectives; pictures by Peter Ferguson. Amulet Books 2005 284p il (The sisters Grimm) $15.95
Grades: 4 5 6   **Fic**
1. Fairy tales 2. Orphans -- Fiction 3. Sisters -- Fiction 4. Monsters -- Fiction 5. Grandmothers -- Fiction
ISBN 0-8109-5925-9

LC 2005011784

"After the mysterious disappearance of their parents, Sabrina and Daphne Grimm spend a year and a half as victims of New York's foster care system until a woman claiming to be their long-dead grandmother comes to claim them. . . . Granny reveals to the girls that they are descendants of the Brothers Grimm, and the fairy tales that the brothers wrote are actually a history of the magical people known as 'Everafters.' . . . Sabrina and Daphne are intrepid heroines, and the modern interpretations of familiar fairy-tale characters are often truly hilarious." Voice of Youth Advocates

Other titles in this series are:
The usual suspects (2005)
The problem child (2006)
Once upon a crime (2007)
Magic and other misdemeanors (2007)
Tales from the hood (2008)
The Everafter War (2009)
The inside story (2010)

The **inside** story; pictures by Peter Ferguson. Amulet Books 2010 (The Sisters Grimm) $15.95
Grades: 4 5 6   **Fic**
1. Mystery fiction 2. Magic -- Fiction 3. Sisters -- Fiction
ISBN 978-0-8109-8430-1; 0-8109-8430-X

LC 2009052207

As the fairytale detectives race through the Book of Everafter searching for their baby brother, they encounter various characters including the Editor and his army of Revisers, who threaten the children with dire consequences if they continue to change the stories.

Magic and other misdemeanors; pictures by Peter Ferguson. Amulet Books 2007 283p il (The Sisters Grimm) $14.95; pa $6.95
Grades: 4 5 6   **Fic**
1. Mystery fiction 2. Magic -- Fiction 3. Sisters -- Fiction 4. Grandmothers -- Fiction
ISBN 978-0-8109-9358-7; 0-8109-9358-9; 978-0-8109-7263-6 pa; 0-8109-7263-8 pa

LC 2007029429

Fairy-tale detectives Sabrina and Daphne Grimm face their first case without Granny Relda's help when the future gets mixed up with the past in Ferryport Landing, and because some of the future does not look right, Puck helps them try to make some changes.

Once upon a crime; pictures by Peter Ferguson. Amulet Books 2007 271p (The Sisters Grimm) $14.95; pa $6.95
Grades: 4 5 6   **Fic**
1. Mystery fiction 2. Sisters -- Fiction 3. Grandmothers -- Fiction 4. New York (N.Y.) -- Fiction
ISBN 978-0-8109-1610-4; 0-8109-1610-X; 978-0-8109-9549-9 pa; 0-8109-9549-2 pa

LC 2006033516

When the fairy-tale detectives rush to New York City hoping to find an Everafter who can cure Puck, they trigger a chain of events that includes a murder mystery, and learn many new things about their mother who, along with their father, is still in an enchanted sleep.

The **problem** child; pictures by Peter Ferguson. Abrams 2006 292p (The Sisters Grimm) $15.95; pa $6.95
Grades: 4 5 6   **Fic**
1. Mystery fiction 2. Orphans -- Fiction 3. Sisters -- Fiction 4. Grandmothers -- Fiction
ISBN 0-8109-4914-8; 0-8109-9359-7 pa

With the help of a long lost relative, and a little magic, Sabrina Grimm and her sister Daphne try to find out who has kidnapped their parents and rescue them.

"Recommend this to anyone who is craving a bit of dark humor rolled up with whimsy and adventure." SLJ

Tales from the hood; pictures by Peter Ferguson. Amulet Books 2009 274p il (The Sisters Grimm) $14.95
Grades: 4 5 6   **Fic**
1. Mystery fiction 2. Magic -- Fiction 3. Trials -- Fiction 4. Sisters -- Fiction
ISBN 978-0-8109-9478-2; 0-8109-9478-X

LC 2008000962

When a kangaroo court of Everafters, led by Judge Mad Hatter, tries Mr. Canis for his past crimes as the Big Bad Wolf, the Grimms seek evidence to save their friend, although Sabrina questions whether he should be saved.

The **unusual** suspects; illustrated by Peter Ferguson. Amulet Books 2005 290p (The Sisters Grimm) $14.95; pa $6.95
Grades: 4 5 6   **Fic**
1. Mystery fiction 2. Orphans -- Fiction 3. Sisters -- Fiction 4. Monsters -- Fiction 5. Grandmothers -- Fiction
ISBN 978-0-8109-5926-2; 0-8109-5926-7; 978-0-8109-9323-5 pa; 0-8109-9323-6 pa

LC 2005024149

"In this second book in the series, Sabrina and Daphne continue their family's fairy-tale detective work in the Hudson River town of Ferryport Landing. . . . Here, the sisters start attending the local elementary school where the principal just happens to be the Pied Piper of Hamelin and Snow White is a most beloved teacher. Almost instantly, one of their teachers is found dead in his classroom. . . . The story is fast paced and the main characters are sympathetic and appealing." SLJ

Burg, Ann E.

Serafina's promise; by Ann E. Burg. Scholastic Press 2013 304 p. (alk. paper) $16.99
Grades: 5 6 7 8   **Fic**
1. Girls -- Fiction 2. Floods -- Fiction 3. Haiti -- Social conditions 4. Novels in verse 5. Haiti -- Fiction 6. Earthquakes -- Fiction 7. Brothers and sisters -- Fiction 8. Family life -- Haiti -- Fiction 9. Port-au-Prince (Haiti) -- Fiction
ISBN 0545535646; 9780545535649

LC 2012045609

Parents' Choice: Gold Medal Fiction (2013)

In this book, by Ann E. Burg, "Serafina is an 11-year-old Haitian struggling to keep her dream of becoming a doctor alive. Living in a desolate mountain village, Serafina toils at her daily chores while planning to attend school . Serafina has a warm family . . . who all come to support her vision. Then a flood washes away the family home, and the roaring stampede of an earthquake devastates the city of Port-au-Prince, where Serafina's father works." (Publisher's note)

Burgis, Stephanie

The dragon with a chocolate heart; Stephanie Burgis. Bloomsbury 2017 256 p. (hardback) $16.99

Grades: 4 5 6 7   Fic

1. Magic -- Fiction 2. Dragons -- Fiction 3. Chocolate -- Fiction
ISBN 9781681193434

LC 2016037694

In this book, by Stephanie Burgis, "Aventurine is a brave young dragon ready to explore the world outside of her family's mountain cave . . . if only they'd let her leave it. Her family thinks she's too young to fly on her own, but she's determined to prove them wrong by capturing the most dangerous prey of all: a human." (Publisher's note)

Burnett, Frances Hodgson

A little princess; illustrated by Tasha Tudor. HarperCollins 1999 245p il (Illustrated junior library) $17.99; pa $6.99

Grades: 4 5 6   Fic

1. School stories 2. Great Britain -- Fiction
ISBN 978-0-3973-0693-0; 0-3973-06938; 978-0-06-440187-6 pa; 0-06-440187-1 pa

First American edition published 1892 by Scribner in shorter form with title: Sara Crewe

The story of Sara Crewe, a girl who is sent from India to a boarding school in London, left in poverty by her father's death, and rescued by a mysterious benefactor

"The story is inevitably adorned with sentimental curlicues but the reader will hardly notice them since the story itself is such a satisfying one. Tasha Tudor's gentle, appropriate illustrations make this a lovely edition." Publ Wkly

The secret garden; illustrated by Inga Moore. Candlewick Press 2008 278p il $21.99

Grades: 3 4 5 6   Fic

1. Gardens -- Fiction 2. Orphans -- Fiction 3. Great Britain -- Fiction
ISBN 0-7636-3161-2; 978-0-7636-3161-1

LC 2006051838

First published 1911

A ten-year-old orphan comes to live in a lonely house on the Yorkshire moors where she discovers an invalid cousin and the mysteries of a locked garden.

"Burnett's tale . . . is presented in an elegant, oversize volume and handsomely illustrated with Moore's detailed ink and watercolor paintings. Cleanly laid-out text pages are balanced by artwork ranging from delicate spot images to full-page renderings." SLJ

Burns, Khephra

Mansa Musa; the lion of Mali. illustrated by Leo & Diane Dillon. Harcourt 2001 un il $18

Grades: 4 5 6 7   Fic

1. Kings 2. Mali -- Fiction
ISBN 0-15-200375-4

LC 97-50559

A fictional account of the nomadic wanderings of the boy who grew up to become Mali's great fourteenth-century leader, Mansa Musa

This is "part coming-of-age tale, part cautionary tale, and part fairy tale. . . . Burn's story moves in a languid magical atmosphere beautifully supported by the Dillons' jewel-like illustrations and stylized text ornaments, which, together with parchment-colored pages, give the impression of an illuminated manuscript." Horn Book

Busby, Cylin

The nine lives of Jacob Tibbs; Cylin Busby; illustrated by Gerald Kelley. Alfred A. Knopf 2016 272 p. illustrations (hardback) $16.99

Grades: 4 5 6   Fic

1. Cats -- Fiction 2. Seafaring life -- Fiction 3. Adventure and adventurers -- Fiction
ISBN 9780553511239; 9780553511246

LC 2015012040

In this children's story, by Cylin Busby and illustrated by Gerald Kelley, "Captain Natick does not want to take a kitten on board his ship when it sets sail in 1837, but his daughter convinces him that the scrawny yellow cat will bring good luck. Onto the ship the kitten goes, and so begins the adventurous, cliff-hanging, lucky life of Jacob Tibbs." (Publisher's note)

"An absorbing historical coming-of-age adventure supported by deeper themes of grief, despair, and determination." Kirkus

Butler, Dori Hillestad

The case of the fire alarm; pictures by Jeremy Tugeau. Albert Whitman & Co. 2010 132p il (The Buddy files) $14.99

Grades: 1 2 3   Fic

1. School stories 2. Mystery fiction 3. Dogs -- Fiction
ISBN 978-0-8075-0913-5; 0-8075-0913-2

LC 2010004320

When Buddy goes to school to become a therapy dog, he ends up helping figure out who pulled the fire alarm instead.

"Tugeau's sweet line drawings bring Buddy and friends to life, while Butler keeps the story entertaining and sometimes suspenseful." Kirkus

The case of the library monster; pictures by Jeremy Tugeau and Dan Crisp. Albert Whitman 2011 134p il (The Buddy files) $14.99

Grades: 1 2 3   Fic

1. School stories 2. Mystery fiction 3. Dogs -- Fiction 4. Libraries -- Fiction
ISBN 978-0-8075-0914-2; 0-8075-0914-0

LC 201003330

Buddy the dog discovers a strange, blue-tongued creature in the school library, and investigates what it is and how it got there.

"The breezy text, friendly illustrations, and, above all, likable dog hero continue to make this series a solid choice for readers new to chapter books." Horn Book Guide

The case of the lost boy; pictures by Jeremy Tugeau. Albert Whitman 2010 123p il (The Buddy files) $14.99

Grades: 1 2 3   Fic

1. Mystery fiction 2. Dogs -- Fiction 3. Missing children -- Fiction
ISBN 978-0-8075-0910-4; 0-8075-0910-8

LC 2009-2376

While searching for his mysteriously lost human family, King the dog detective is adoped by another family, who names him Buddy.

"The type is large, the text is easy, and the occasional black-and-white illustrations complement the text well. The clues are unique and true to the fact that a dog is telling the story." SLJ

Other titles in this series are:

The case of the mixed up mutts (2010)

The case of the fire alarm (2010)

The case of the missing family (2010)

The case of the library monster (2011)

The case of the missing family; pictures by Jeremy Tugeau. Albert Whitman & Co. 2010 131p il (The Buddy files) $14.99

Grades: 1 2 3   Fic

1. Mystery fiction 2. Dogs -- Fiction 3. Missing persons -- Fiction
ISBN 978-0-8075-0912-8; 0-8075-0912-4

Buddy the dog risks everything when he leaves his new family to investigate what happened to his beloved Kayla and her father, his beloved former owners, by slipping into a van her uncle Marty is using to empty her house in the middle of the night.

"Effective twists and turns, humor, and the possibilities of becoming a school therapy dog and learning to read ease the bittersweet conclusion." SLJ

The **case** of the mixed-up mutts; pictures by Jeremy Tugeau. Albert Whitman 2010 128p il (The Buddy files) $14.99
Grades: 1 2 3   **Fic**
1. Mystery fiction 2. Dogs -- Fiction
ISBN 978-0-8075-0911-1; 0-8075-0911-6

While attending obedience class with his new humans, Buddy the dog helps solve a mystery involving two Pomeranians that were switched at the dog park.

The **truth** about Truman School; by Dori Hillestad Butler. Albert Whitman 2008 170p $15.95; pa $7.99
Grades: 5 6 7 8   **Fic**
1. School stories 2. Bullies -- Fiction 3. Journalism -- Fiction 4. Newspapers -- Fiction
ISBN 978-0-8075-8095-0; 0-8075-8095-3; 978-0-8075-8096-7 pa; 0-8075-8096-1 pa

LC 2007-29977

Tired of being told what to write by the school newspaper's advisor, Zibby and her friend Amr start an underground newspaper online where everyone is free to post anything, but things spiral out of control when a cyberbully starts using the site to harrass one popular girl.

"The story moves at a good pace and the timely subject of cyberbullying will be relevant to readers. The language is accessible and the students' voices ring true." SLJ

Butterworth, Oliver
★ The **enormous** egg; illustrated by Louis Darling. Little, Brown 1956 187p il hardcover o.p. pa $6.99
Grades: 4 5 6 7   **Fic**
1. Dinosaurs -- Fiction
ISBN 0-316-11920-2 pa

This story is "great fun. . . . And if you have any trouble visualizing a Triceratops moving placidly through the twentieth-century world you need only turn to Louis Darling's illustrations to believe." NY Times Book Rev

Buyea, Rob
★ **Because** of Mr. Terupt. Delacorte Press 2010 269p $16.99; lib bdg $19.99
Grades: 4 5 6   **Fic**
1. School stories 2. Teachers -- Fiction 3. Connecticut -- Fiction 4. Family life -- Fiction
ISBN 0-385-73882-X; 0-385-90749-4 lib bdg; 978-0-385-73882-8; 978-0-385-90749-1 lib bdg

LC 2010-03414

Seven fifth-graders at Snow Hill School in Connecticut relate how their lives are changed for the better by "rookie teacher" Mr. Terupt. "Grades four to six." (Bull Cent Child Books)

"Introducing characters and conflicts that will be familiar to any middle-school student, this powerful and emotional story is likely to spur discussion." Publ Wkly

Mr. Terupt falls again; Rob Buyea. Delacorte Press 2012 356 p. (hc) $16.99
Grades: 4 5 6   **Fic**
1. School stories 2. Romance fiction 3. Teacher-student relationship -- Fiction 4. Summer -- Fiction 5. Classrooms --

Fiction 6. Moving, Household -- Fiction
ISBN 0385742053; 9780375989100; 9780375990380; 9780385742054

LC 2012010897

This book is a follow-up to Rob Buyea's "Because of Mr. Terupt." Here, "looping with his students into sixth grade, Mr. Terupt continues to surprise them with challenging projects and perfect reading suggestions." For the seven students who narrate the story, "family worries go along with lingering questions about the health of their teacher. Sixth-grade relationships and a grown-up romance" are also explored. (Kirkus)

Saving Mr. Terupt; Rob Buyea. Delacorte Press 2015 384 p. (hc) $16.99
Grades: 4 5 6 7   **Fic**
1. School stories 2. Teacher-student relationship -- Fiction 3. Schools -- Fiction 4. Teachers -- Fiction 5. Interpersonal relations -- Fiction
ISBN 9780375991202; 9780385743556

LC 2014031776

In this young adult novel, by Rob Buyea, "the kids from Mr. Terupt's fifth- and sixth-grade classes are entering their first year of junior high school. . . . Everyone is missing Mr. Terupt. When a fight threatens to break up the group forever, they think their favorite teacher is the only one who can help them. But the kids soon find out that it's Mr. Terupt who needs saving." (Publisher's note)

"Necessary background is deftly woven in, making this third in the series as easy for new readers to pick up as it is for returning fans. A warmly gracious invitation to a convincing middle school world." Kirkus

Saving Mister Terupt

Byars, Betsy Cromer
The **dark** stairs; a Herculeah Jones mystery. by Betsy Byars. Viking 1994 130p hardcover o.p. pa $5.99
Grades: 4 5 6   **Fic**
1. Mystery fiction
ISBN 0-670-85487-5; 0-14-240592-2 pa

LC 94-14012

The intrepid Herculeah Jones helps her mother, a private investigator, solve a puzzling and frightening case

"There is plenty to laugh at in this book, including classic chapter headings guaranteed to cause shivers for the uninitiated; practiced mystery readers may feel that they are in on a bit of a joke and appreciate the hint of parody. This is a page-turner that is sure to entice the most reluctant readers." SLJ

Other titles about Herculeah Jones are:
Tarot says beware (1995)
Dead letter (1996)
Death's door (1997)
Disappearing acts (1998)
The black tower (2006)
King of murder (2006)

The **keeper** of the doves; by Betsy Byars. Viking 2002 121p $14.99; pa $5.99
Grades: 4 5 6 7   **Fic**
1. Sisters -- Fiction 2. Kentucky -- Fiction 3. Family life -- Fiction
ISBN 0-670-03576-9; 0-14-240063-7 pa

LC 2002-9283

In the late 1800s in Kentucky, Amie McBee and her four sisters both fear and torment the reclusive and seemingly sinister Mr. Tominski, but their father continues to provide for his needs

"This is Byars at her best—witty, appealing, thought-provoking." Horn Book

Little Horse; [by] Betsy Byars; illustrated by David McPhail. Holt & Co. 2001 45p il $15.95

Grades: 1 2 3 **Fic**

1. Horses -- Fiction

ISBN 0-8050-6413-3

LC 00-40983

Little Horse falls into the stream and is swept away into a dangerous adventure and a new life

"Byars deftly combines crisp action with a lyrically evoked setting. Language is simple, but not simplistic; uncommon terms are clearly defined in the text and the soft black-and-white art." Horn Book Guide

Another title about Little Horse is:

Little Horse on his own (2004)

★ The **pinballs**; [by] Betsy Byars. Harper & Row 1977 136p lib bdg $16.89; pa $5.99

Grades: 5 6 7 8 **Fic**

1. Friendship -- Fiction 2. Foster home care -- Fiction

ISBN 0-06-020918-6 lib bdg; 0-06-440198-7 pa

"A deceptively simple, eloquent story, its pain and acrimony constantly mitigated by the author's light, offhand style and by Carlie's wryly comic view of life." Horn Book

The **SOS** file; [by] Betsy Byars, Betsy Duffey, Laurie Myers; illustrated by Arthur Howard. Henry Holt 2004 71p il $15.95

Grades: 3 4 5 **Fic**

1. School stories

ISBN 0-8050-6888-0

LC 2003-18240

The students in Mr. Magro's class submit stories for the SOS file about their biggest emergencies, and then they read them aloud for extra credit

"Some tales are poignant, others are humorous; all are as credible as the characters sketched. . . . Lighthearted sketches enhance characterization. . . . [An] engaging, plausible, and highly readable collection of anecdotes." SLJ

★ **Tornado**; by Betsy Byars; illustrations by Doron Ben-Ami. HarperCollins Pubs. 1996 49p il lib bdg $15.89; pa $4.99

Grades: 2 3 4 **Fic**

1. Dogs -- Fiction 2. Tornadoes -- Fiction

ISBN 0-06-026452-7 lib bdg; 0-06-442063-9 pa

LC 95-41584

As they wait out a tornado in their storm cellar, a family listens to their farmhand tell stories about the dog that was blown into his life by another tornado when he was a boy

"The handsome illustrations by Doron Ben-Ami give the volume a more distinguished, less juvenile look than the typical chapter book and convey the story's drama, warmth, and occasional humor. Parents and teachers will find this an excellent book to read aloud, and dog lovers of any age will find it irresistible." Booklist

Cabot, Meg

Allie Finkle's rules for girls: book two; The new girl; [by] Meg Cabot. 1st ed.; Scholastic Press 2008 222p (Allie Finkle's rules for girls) $15.99

Grades: 3 4 5 **Fic**

1. School stories 2. Moving -- Fiction 3. Bullies -- Fiction 4. Friendship -- Fiction 5. Family life -- Fiction 6. Grandmothers

-- Fiction

ISBN 978-0-545-04049-5; 0-545-04049-3

LC 2007050719

Guided by her rules, nine-year-old Allie works to get past being just the new girl at school, eagerly awaits the arrival of her kitten, and faces turmoil when her grandmother visits while the family is still settling into their new home.

Best friends and drama queens. Scholastic Press 2009 202p (Allie Finkle's rules for girls) $15.99

Grades: 3 4 5 **Fic**

1. School stories 2. Friendship -- Fiction

ISBN 978-0-545-04043-3; 0-545-04043-4

LC 2008032678

Nine-year-old Allie Finkle's list of rules helps her navigate a tricky situation with a new girl at school.

This "sympathetically portrays the broad emotional range of fourth-graders." Booklist

Blast from the past. Scholastic Press 2010 224p (Allie Finkle's rules for girls) $15.99

Grades: 3 4 5 **Fic**

1. School stories 2. Friendship -- Fiction

ISBN 978-0-545-04048-8; 0-545-04048-5

LC 2010014160

Fourth-grader Allie establishes a new set of rules after she is forced to pair up with ex-best friend Mary Kay on a class trip to a historic one-room schoolhouse.

"Sometimes wryly amusing, this first-person chapter book . . . . captures the day-to-day thoughts of this well-intentioned narrator." Booklist

From the notebooks of a middle school princess; written & illustrated by Meg Cabot. First edition Feiwel & Friends 2015 192 p illustrations (hardback) $16.99

Grades: 4 5 6 7 **Fic**

1. Orphans -- Fiction 2. Princesses -- Fiction 3. School stories -- Fiction 4. Diaries -- Fiction 5. Schools -- Fiction 6. Families -- Fiction 7. Middle schools -- Fiction

ISBN 1250066026; 9781250066022

LC 2014043847

In this children's novel by Meg Cabot "Olivia Grace Clarisse Mignonette Harrison is a completely average twelve-year-old. The only things about her that aren't average are her name . . . and the fact that she is a half-orphan who has never met her father. Then one completely average day . . . a limo containing Princess Mia Thermopolis of Genovia pulls up to invite her to New York to finally meet her father, who promptly invites her to come live with him." (Publisher's note)

"Cabot manages to combine wit and lavish details to positive effect, as evidenced by a royal grandmother who manages to be both familiar and surprising. While readers who already know the Princess Diaries might find this fairy tale a bit too retold, young newcomers to the Cabot magic will be charmed. A sweet fantasy, both funny and highly satisfying." Kirkus

Glitter girls and the great fake out. Scholastic Press 194p (Allie Finkle's rules for girls) $15.99

Grades: 3 4 5 **Fic**

1. Friendship -- Fiction 2. Truthfulness and falsehood -- Fiction

ISBN 978-0-545-04047-1; 0-545-04047-7

While trying to spare Erica's feelings so she could go to Brittany's birthday party, Allie disobeys one of her own rules and lies.

"Fine-tuned to the nuances of human relations and self-justification, Cabot creates another eminently readable, first-person narrative." Booklist

Moving day. Scholastic Press 2008 228p (Allie Finkle's rules for girls) $15.99; pa $5.99
Grades: 3 4 5 **Fic**
1. School stories 2. Moving -- Fiction 3. Friendship -- Fiction 4. Family life -- Fiction
ISBN 978-0-545-03947-5; 0-545-03947-9; 978-0-545-04041-9 pa; 0-545-04041-8 pa

LC 2007-27836

Nine-year-old Allie Finkle has rules for everything and is even writing her own rule book, but her world is turned upside-down when she learns that her family is moving across town, which will mean a new house, school, best friend, and plenty of new rules.

Cabot's "trademark frank humor makes for compulsive reading—as always. . . . Allie is funny, believable and plucky . . . but most of all, and most interestingly, Allie is ambivalent." Publ Wkly

Other titles in this series are:
The new girl (2008)
Best friends and drama queens (2009)
Stage fright (2009)
Glitter girls and the great fake out (2010)
Blast from the past (2010)

Stage fright. Scholastic Press 2009 216p (Allie Finkle's rules for girls) $15.99
Grades: 3 4 5 **Fic**
1. School stories 2. Theater -- Fiction 3. Friendship -- Fiction 4. Family life -- Fiction
ISBN 978-0-545-04045-7; 0-545-04045-0

LC 2009005422

Allie's theatrical hopes are crushed when, instead of being cast as the princess, she is given the role of the evil queen in the fourth-grade class play.

"Written in a convincingly childlike voice, Allie's appealing first-person narrative features wry observations of the foibles, actions, emotions, and relationships of both the children and the adults in her life." Booklist

Cadenhead, Mackenzie
Sally's bones; illustrated by T. S. Spookytooth. Sourcebook Jabberwocky 2011 il pa $6.99
Grades: 4 5 6 **Fic**
1. Mystery fiction 2. Dogs -- Fiction 3. Skeleton -- Fiction
ISBN 978-1-4022-5943-2; 1-4022-5943-3

2 Months, 28 Days, 9 Hours, and 12 minutes earlier Sally Simplemith's life changed forever. She came face-to-face with death a delightful, dearly departed little dog she lovingly calls Bones. But when the cadaverous canine is accused of a crime he didn't commit, Sally decides to solve the case herself!

"Writing a novel that tackles tough issues like grief and loss while maintaining a measure of levity is no easy feat, but that is exactly what Cadenhead accomplishes here. . . . Spooky without being scary, dark without being morbid, this is a winning tale about loyalty in the face of loss." Booklist

Caldwell, Charlotte
Kirby's journal; backyard butterfly magic. Charlotte Caldwell. University of South Carolina Press 2015 56 p. color illustrations (pbk. alk. paper) $17.95
Grades: 4 5 6 **Fic**
1. Diaries -- Fiction 2. Butterflies -- Fiction 3. Photography --

Fiction 4 Grandparents -- Fiction 5. Charleston (S.C.) -- Fiction
ISBN 9781611175530

LC 2015012342

In this juvenile book, by Charlotte Caldwell, "eleven-year-old Kirby, Grandma, and Grandpa plant a butterfly garden, and Kirby documents the wondrous adventures in learning that follow. Their observations, excitement, and curiosity are vividly captured through Kirby's journal and newly acquired hobby of photography as together they discover an abundance of life just outside their own backdoor." (Publisher's note)

"The photographs will attract browsers, especially images depicting the fascinating, minute-by-minute views of a monarch butterfly cracking its way out of its chrysalis. Kirby is a personable and likable character whose diary will appeal to kids." SLJ

Includes bibliographical references and index

Calkhoven, Laurie
Daniel at the Siege of Boston, 1776. Dutton Children's Books 2010 195p (Boys of wartime) $16.99
Grades: 4 5 6 7 **Fic**
1. Spies -- Fiction 2. Patriotism -- Fiction 3. Family life -- Fiction 4. Boston (Mass.) -- Fiction 5. United States -- History -- 1775-1783, Revolution -- Fiction
ISBN 978-0-525-42144-3; 0-525-42144-0

LC 2009012125

In 1776 Boston, twelve-year-old Daniel Prescott enjoys assuming his father's role in taking care of his mother and sister, as well as his work as a spy and messenger for the American revolutionaries, but the pleasure ends when he witnesses the horrors of war firsthand, and learns that a trusted patriot is actually a British spy.

"This historical novel weaves actual people, places, and events of the Siege of Boston into an engaging fictional narrative." Booklist

Michael at the invasion of France, 1943; by Laurie Calkhoven. Dial Books for Young Readers 2012 231 p. (hardcover) $16.99
Grades: 4 5 6 7 **Fic**
1. Children and war -- Fiction 2. Holocaust, 1939-1945 -- Fiction 3. France -- History -- 1940-1945, German occupation -- Fiction 4. World War, 1939-1945 -- Underground movements -- France -- Fiction 5. France -- History -- German occupation, 1940-1945 -- Fiction
ISBN 0803737246; 9780803737242

LC 2011021634

In this young adult novel, a "young Parisian joins the French Resistance in this Boys of Wartime series entry. . . . Michael joins a friend in distributing taunting leaflets. His involvement in Resistance activities soon escalates into helping captured British and American airmen make their way to Spain. At first he acts only as a courier of forged identity documents, but later he helps first to slip a Jewish neighbor's child out of the city, then hides an ailing American. . . . Meanwhile, he serves as a witness to . . . wartime life under the Nazis, while seeing friends, neighbors and his own older brother taken away and ultimately earning sufficient self-esteem to lose his dependence on his father's regard." (Kirkus

Includes bibliographical references

Will at the Battle of Gettysburg, 1863. Dutton Children's Books 2011 230p (Boys of wartime) $16.99
Grades: 4 5 6 7 **Fic**
1. Gettysburg (Pa.), Battle of, 1863 -- Fiction 2. United States -- History -- 1861-1865, Civil War -- Fiction
ISBN 978-0-525-42145-0; 0-525-42145-9

LC 2010013307

In 1863, twelve-year-old Will, who longs to be a drummer in the Union army, is stuck in his sleepy hometown of Gettysburg, Pennsylvania, but when the Union and Confederate armies meet right there in his town, he and his family are caught up in the fight. Includes historical notes, glossary, and a timeline of events.

"This solid piece of fiction will appeal to history buffs and reluctant readers alike." SLJ

Includes glossary and bibliographical references

Cameron, Ann

Colibri. Farrar, Straus & Giroux 2003 227p $17; pa $5.99

Grades: 5 6 7 8   **Fic**

1. Mayas -- Fiction 2. Kidnapping -- Fiction

ISBN 0-374-31519-1; 0-440-42052-0 pa

LC 2002-192542

Kidnapped when she was very young by an unscrupulous man who has forced her to lie and beg to get money, a twelve-year-old Mayan girl endures an abusive life, always wishing she could return to the parents she can hardly remember

"The taut, chilling suspense and search for riches will keep readers flying through the pages. But it's Cameron's beautiful language and Rosa's larger identity quest that make this novel extraordinary." Booklist

Gloria's way; pictures by Lis Toft. Farrar, Straus & Giroux 2000 96p il hardcover o.p. pa $4.99

Grades: 2 3 4   **Fic**

1. Friendship -- Fiction 2. Family life -- Fiction 3. African Americans -- Fiction

ISBN 0-374-32670-3; 0-14-230023-3 pa

LC 99-12104

This companion volume to the series featuring Julian and Huey centers on their friend Gloria. Gloria shares special times with her mother and father and with her friends

"Lis Toft's shaded pencil drawings portray these African American characters and their predicaments with warmth and humor." Booklist

Another title about Gloria is:

Gloria rising (2002)

★ **Spunky** tells all; pictures by Lauren Castillo. Farrar Straus Giroux 2011 105p il $15.99

Grades: 2 3 4   **Fic**

1. Cats -- Fiction 2. Dogs -- Fiction

ISBN 978-0-374-38000-7; 0-374-38000-7

LC 2010019815

Called a troublemaker by his human family, a reflective dog defends himself and then relates the family's adoption of an aristocratic but incompetent cat, who gives him a life purpose and and new way of looking at his world.

"Readers ready for chapter books will delight in seeing the world through Spunky's eyes and powerful nose." Kirkus

★ The **stories** Julian tells; illustrated by Ann Strugnell. Pantheon Bks. 1981 71p il hardcover o.p. pa $4.99

Grades: 2 3 4   **Fic**

1. Family life -- Fiction 2. African Americans -- Fiction

ISBN 0-394-82892-5 pa

LC 80-18023

"Strugnell's delightful drawings depict Julian, his little brother Huey and their parents as black, but they could be members of any family with a stern but loving and understanding father." Publ Wkly

Other titles about Julian and his family are:

Julian, dream doctor (1990)

Julian, secret agent (1988)

Julian's glorious summer (1987)

More stories Huey tells (1997)

More stories Julian tells (1986)

The stories Huey tells (1995)

Cameron, Anne

The **lightning** catcher; by Anne Cameron. Greenwillow Books an imprint of HarperCollinsPublishers 2013 432 p. (trade ed.) $16.99

Grades: 4 5 6   **Fic**

1. Storms -- Fiction 2. Fantasy fiction 3. Weather -- Fiction 4. Adventure and adventurers -- Fiction

ISBN 9780062112767; 0062112767

LC 2012042848

The young adult fantasy book, "The Lightning Catcher," is the first in a four-book series by Anne Cameron. Here, 11-year-old Angus Mc Fangus, a "trainee at the Perilous Exploratorium for Violent Weather and Vicious Storms on the Isle of Imbur, tries to find his missing parents and prevent the unleashing of an eternal storm." The adventure story features themes including world domination. (Kirkus Reviews)

Cammuso, Frank

The **Misadventures** of Salem Hyde; 1 Spelling Trouble. by Frank Cammuso. Harry N Abrams Inc 2013 96 p. chiefly color illustration $14.95

Grades: 2 3 4   **Fic**

1. Occult fiction -- Fiction 2. School stories -- Fiction

ISBN 1419708031; 9781419708039

This is the first book in Frank Cammuso's Salem Hyde series. Here, "Salem Hyde just wants a friend. After a misguided attempt to use her magic lands her in the principal's office, Salem's family decides she needs an animal companion. One well-placed call later, she meets knowledgeable and talkative feline Percival J. Whamsford III, otherwise known as Whammy. Whammy isn't just a chatty kitty; he is a Magical Animal Companion and will help Salem learn how to use her magic properly." (Kirkus Reviews)

Other titles in this series are:

Big birthday bash (2014)

Cookie camp catastrophe (2014)

Dinosaur dilemma (2015)

Frozen fiasco (2016)

Cao Wenxuan

Bronze and sunflower; by Cao Wenxuan, illustrated by Meilo So, translated by Helen Wang. Candlewick Press 2017 400 p. illustration (ebook) $16.99; $16.99

Grades: 4 5 6 7 8   **Fic**

1. Domestic fiction 2. Adoption -- Fiction 3. Friendship -- Fiction

ISBN 9780763693688; 0763688169; 9780763688165

LC 2017005320

In this book, by Cao Wenxuan, illustrated by Meilo So, and translated by Helen Wang, "Sunflower is an only child, and when . . . her father tragically drowns, Sunflower is taken in by the poorest family in . . . [a rural] village, a family with a son named Bronze. . . . [Bronze hasn't spoken a word since he was traumatized by a terrible fire. Bronze and Sunflower become inseparable, understanding each other as only the closest friends can." (Publisher's note)

"Readers of all ages should be prepared to laugh, cry, and sigh with satisfaction." Kirkus

Carbone, Elisa Lynn

Blood on the river; James Town 1607. [by] Elisa Carbone. Viking 2006 237p $16.99; pa $6.99

Grades: 5 6 7 8   **Fic**

1. Powhatan Indians -- Fiction 2. Jamestown (Va.) -- History -- Fiction 3. United States -- History -- 1600-1775, Colonial period -- Fiction

ISBN 0-670-06060-7; 0-14-240932-4 pa

LC 2005023640

Traveling to the New World in 1606 as the page to Captain John Smith, twelve-year-old orphan Samuel Collier settles in the new colony of James Town, where he must quickly learn to distinguish between friend and foe.

"A strong, visceral story of the hardship and peril settlers faced, as well as the brutal realities of colonial conquest." Booklist

Storm warriors; [by] Elisa Carbone. Knopf 2001 168p hardcover o.p. pa $6.50

Grades: 4 5 6 7   **Fic**

1. North Carolina -- Fiction 2. African Americans -- Fiction 3. United States -- Life-Saving Service -- Fiction

ISBN 0-375-80664-4; 0-440-41879-8 pa

LC 00-59924

In 1895, after his mother's death, twelve-year-old Nathan moves with his father and grandfather to Pea Island off the coast of North Carolina, where he hopes to join the all-black crew at the nearby lifesaving station, despite his father's objections

"This thoughtfully crafted first-person narrative combines historical figures with created characters in the best traditions of the historical novel." Horn Book Guide

Carey, Benedict

Poison most vial; a mystery. by Benedict Carey. Amulet Books 2012 215 p. (hardcover) $16.95

Grades: 5 6 7 8   **Fic**

1. Mystery fiction 2. Forensic sciences -- Fiction 3. Murder -- Fiction 4. Neighbors -- Fiction 5. Mystery and detective stories 6. Fathers and daughters -- Fiction

ISBN 1419700316; 9781419700316

LC 2011038222

In this novel by Benedict Carey "Ruby's janitor father becomes the prime suspect in a murder . . . [of] [f]orensics expert Dr. Ramachandran . . . [and] the eighth grader decides it's up to her to clear his name. . . . [She] enlists the aid of her large, Jamaican buddy, Rex, and reclusive, retired toxicologist Clara Whitmore, who lives in Ruby's building. What with hacking into computers, evading gangs and like spy-jinx, the mystery demands a lot of brain work." (Kirkus)

Carlson, Natalie Savage

The **family** under the bridge; pictures by Garth Williams. Harper & Row 1958 99p il lib bdg $16.89; pa $5.99

Grades: 3 4 5   **Fic**

1. Tramps -- Fiction 2. Christmas -- Fiction 3. Paris (France) -- Fiction

ISBN 0-06-020991-7 lib bdg; 0-06-440250-9 pa

A Newbery Medal honor book, 1959

"Garth Williams' illustrations are perfect for this thoroughly delightful story of humor and sentiment." Libr J

Carman, Patrick

The **field** of wacky inventions; Patrick Carman. Scholastic Press 2013 224 p. (jacketed hardcover) $16.99

Grades: 3 4 5 6   **Fic**

1. Fantasy fiction 2. Voyages and travels -- Fiction 3. Adventure stories 4. Puzzles -- Fiction 5. Hotels, motels, etc. -- Fiction 6. Adventure and adventurers -- Fiction

ISBN 054525521X; 9780545255219

LC 2013006690

This is the final book in Patrick Carman's hotel trilogy. "With their parents away on their honeymoon and Merganzer D. Whippet looking after them, stepbrothers Leo and Remi are poised for adventure. . . . The boys have just spent a week or so knocking about learning its secrets. They have missed a rather big one though, which becomes evident when

the entire top floor lifts off of the building. They travel a vast, mysterious distance." (Children's Literature)

Floors. Scholastic Press 2011 261p $16.99

Grades: 3 4 5 6   **Fic**

1. Puzzles -- Fiction 2. Hotels and motels -- Fiction 3. Eccentrics and eccentricities -- Fiction

ISBN 978-0-545-25519-6; 0-545-25519-8

LC 2011032516

Ten-year-old Leo's future and the fate of the extraordinary Whippet Hotel, where his father is the maintenance man, are at stake when a series of cryptic boxes leads Leo to hidden floors, strange puzzles, and unexpected alliances.

"The author is a fine storyteller; he rides the mystery right up to the edge invests his characters with quirks that aren't merely cute but essential to the person's identity." Kirkus

Carmichael, Clay

★ **Wild** things; [written and illustrated by Clay Carmichael] Front Street 2009 248p il $18.95

Grades: 5 6 7 8   **Fic**

1. Cats -- Fiction 2. Uncles -- Fiction 3. Artists -- Fiction 4. Orphans -- Fiction 5. Family life -- Fiction

ISBN 978-1-59078-627-7; 1-59078-627-0

LC 2007-49911

Stubborn, self-reliant, eleven-year-old Zoe, recently orphaned, moves to the country to live with her prickly half-uncle, a famous doctor and sculptor, and together they learn about trust and the strength of family

"Carmichael gives a familiar plot a fresh new life in this touching story with a finely crafted sense of place." Booklist

Carris, Joan

Welcome to the Bed & Biscuit; [by] Joan Carris; illustrated by Noah Jones. Candlewick Press 2006 116p il $15.99; pa $5.99

Grades: 2 3 4   **Fic**

1. Animals -- Fiction 2. Veterinarians -- Fiction

ISBN 0-7636-2151-X; 0-7636-4621-0 pa

LC 2004062857

The family animals at the Bed & Biscuit begin to feel slighted when Dr. Bender returns from a fire with something that occupies the time usually reserved for them.

"This is a small, remarkably sweet beginning chapter book with more than its fair share of amusing illustrations and gentle humor." SLJ

Another title about the Bed & Biscuit is:

Wild times at the Bed & Biscuit (2009)

Wild times at the Bed & Biscuit; [by] Joan Carris; illustrated by Noah Z. Jones. Candlewick Press 2009 124p il $15.99; pa $5.99

Grades: 2 3 4   **Fic**

1. Animals -- Fiction 2. Veterinarians -- Fiction

ISBN 978-0-7636-3705-7; 0-7636-3705-X; 978-0-7636-5294-4 pa; 0-7636-5294-6 pa

LC 2008-938398

Ever since Grampa Bender opened his doors (and veterinary skills) to a despondent Canada goose, a cranky muskrat, and two tiny but rebellious fox kits, his animal boarding house has been turned upside down.

This "would make a great read-aloud for the primary grades and is sure to be a hit with competent easy-chapter-book readers." SLJ

Carroll, Lewis, 1832-1898

Alice's adventures in Wonderland; illustrated by Alison Jay. Dial Books for Young Readers 2006 203p il $25.99

Grades: 4 5 6 7 **Fic**
1. Fantasy fiction
ISBN 0-8037-2940-5
Alice falls down a rabbit hole and discovers a world of nonsensical and amusing characters.

"Heavy white pages and spacious book design showcase Jay's distinctive paintings. Combining elegance with innocence, the artwork features rounded forms of people, trees, and animals that are each a little apart from the others, isolated in a splendid but strange dream world. . . . The paintings glow with color under the crackle-glaze textured varnish." Booklist

Lewis Carroll's Alice in Wonderland; illustrated by Rodney Matthews. Candlewick Press 2009 95p il $24.99
Grades: 4 5 6 7 **Fic**
1. Fantasy fiction
ISBN 978-0-7636-4568-7; 0-7636-4568-0
On a hot summer day, a little girl sitting by her sister on the bank, having nothing to do, begins to let her imagination grow. Her curiosity and hatred of logic cause her to dream of a nonsensical world filled with amusing characters

Matthews' illustrations "have an imagination-stretching, other-worldly veneer. . . . The cartoon artwork portrays Alice with a somewhat angular face and straight blond hair. The depictions of the other characters are fresh and creative. . . . The small-size type, which may demand more accomplished or patient readers, and the sophisticated visual tone make this volume appropriate for older Alice fans." SLJ

Carroll, Michael
Hunter; a Super human clash. Michael Carroll. Philomel Books, an imprint of Penguin Group (USA) 2014 360 p. hbk $16.99
Grades: 5 6 7 8 9 **Fic**
1. Superheroes -- Fiction 2. Supervillains -- Fiction
ISBN 0399163670; 9780399163678
LC 2013024006
"The defeat of the near-invincible villain Krodin has left a void in the superhuman hierarchy, a void that two opposing factors are trying to fill. The powerful telepath Max Dalton believes that the human race must be controlled and shepherded to a safe future, while his rival Casey Duval believes that strength can only be achieved through conflict." (Publisher's note)

"After parting ways with the superhumans, Lance relies on his persuasive skills to make his way in the world and evade mind-controlling Max Dalton. This fourth book follows Lance's journey over the years, from working in a traveling circus to running his own global organization. Series followers will appreciate con-man Lance's character development and the implications of the story's surprising conclusion." Horn Book
Other titles in this series are:
Super Human (2010)
The Ascension (2011)
Stronger (2012)

Stronger; a Super human clash. Michael Carroll. Philomel Books 2012 378 p. ill. hbk $16.99
Grades: 5 6 7 8 9 **Fic**
1. Science fiction 2. Prisoners -- Fiction 3. Superheroes -- Fiction 4. Adventure and adventurers -- Fiction
ISBN 0399257616; 9780399257612
LC 2011022436
In this book, "Gethin Rao is a 12-year-old choir boy who suffers a sudden inexplicable transformation during church service one Sunday, becoming a blue-skinned giant who is almost impervious. Twenty-seven years into the future, he is a prisoner known as 'Brawn,' made to mine

platinum with others like him in a secure domed facility in an unknown location. . . . The novel switches back and forth between these two time periods." (School Library Journal)

"A thoughtful narrative about individual choices and their consequences connects with plenty of wham-bang action sequences for an engaging superhero adventure. " Booklist
Other titles in the series include:
Super Human (2010)
The Ascension (2011)
Hunter (2014)

Super human; Michael Carroll. Philomel Books 2010 325 p. ill. (hardcover) $16.99; (paperback) $8.99
Grades: 5 6 7 8 9 **Fic**
1. Young adult literature 2. Superheroes -- Fiction 3. Good and evil -- Fiction
ISBN 9780399252976; 9780142419052; 0142419052; 0399252975
LC 2009-29965
A group of teenage superheroes tackle a powerful warrior who has been brought back from 4,000 years in the past to enslave the modern world. (Bull Cent Child Books)

"There is enough fighting in this book to appeal to middle school boys, and the telekinetic Roz, with a controlling superhero big brother, will appeal to girls. This title is a fast read with tension, suspense, and likeable characters." Libr Media Connect
Followed by: The ascension: a super human clash (2011)

Casanova, Mary
The **epic** fail of Arturo Zamora; Pablo Cartaya. Penguin Group USA 2017 256 p. $16.99
Grades: 5 6 7 **Fic**
1. Community life -- Fiction 2. Latinos (U.S.) -- Fiction 3. Cities and towns -- Fiction
ISBN 1101997230; 9781101997239
In this book, by Pablo Cartaya, "for Arturo, summertime in Miami means playing basketball until dark, sipping mango smoothies, and keeping cool under banyan trees. And maybe a few shifts as junior lunchtime dishwasher at Abuela's restaurant. Maybe. But this summer also includes Carmen, a cute poetry enthusiast who moves into Arturo's apartment complex and turns his stomach into a deep fryer." (Publisher's note)

The **klipfish** code; by Mary Casanova. Houghton Mifflin Company 2007 227p map $16
Grades: 4 5 6 7 **Fic**
1. Norway -- Fiction 2. Family life -- Fiction 3. World War, 1939-1945 -- Norway -- Fiction 4. World War, 1939-1945 -- Underground movements -- Fiction
ISBN 978-0-618-88393-6; 0-618-88393-2
LC 2007012752
Sent with her younger brother to Godøy Island to live with her aunt and grandfather after Germans bomb Norway in 1940, ten-year-old Marit longs to join her parents in the Resistance and when her aunt, a teacher, is taken away two years later, she resents even more the Nazis' presence and her grandfather's refusal to oppose them.

"Casanova spins an adventure-filled and harrowing story." SLJ
Includes glossary and bibliographical references

Cassidy, Cathy
Indigo Blue. Viking 2005 215p hardcover o.p. pa $6.99
Grades: 5 6 7 8 **Fic**
1. Moving -- Fiction 2. Abused women -- Fiction 3. Great Britain

-- Fiction

ISBN 0-670-05927-7; 0-14-240703-8 pa

Eleven-year-old Indigo, her mother, and her toddler sister have to
move out of their apartment because of troubles with Mum's boyfriend,
while Indie is also having best friend problems at school, leaving her
stressed, confused, and lonely.

"This British story of domestic abuse is firmly child-centered, and
Indigo's confusion and fear . . . are sensitively portrayed. . . . The hopeful
ending rings true." Booklist

Cassidy, Sara

A **boy** named Queen; Sara Cassidy. Groundwood Books 2016 96
$14.95; (ebook) $12.95

Grades: 4 5 6   **Fic**

1. Friendship -- Fiction 2. Self-esteem -- Fiction 3. Peer pressure
-- Fiction

ISBN 1554989051; 9781554989058; 9781554989065

In this children's book by Sara Cassidy, "Evelyn is an only child
with a strict routine and an even stricter mother. And yet in her quiet
way she notices things. She takes particular notice of this boy named
Queen. The way the bullies don't seem to faze him. . . . Evelyn and
Queen become friends, almost against Evelyn's better judgment. . . .
her visit to Queen's house opens Evelyn's eyes to a whole new world."
(Publisher's note)

"The contrast between Evelyn and Queen serves as a meaningful
background to the friendship that forms naturally between them. A
small, eloquent book with a powerful message." Kirkus

Catalanotto, Peter

No more pumpkins; [by] Peter Catalanotto and Pamela Schembri.
Henry Holt 2007 62p (2nd-grade friends) $15.95

Grades: 1 2 3   **Fic**

1. School stories 2. Pumpkin -- Fiction 3. Friendship -- Fiction

ISBN 978-0-8050-7839-8; 0-8050-7839-8

LC 2006035464

Second-grader Emily is tired of pumpkins being at the center of every lesson in school, but she is not prepared when a jealous friend damages the jacko-lantern portrait Emily made for Open House

"The black-and-white illustrations are well done and expressive.
Fans of Barbara Park's 'Junie B. Jones' series and Patricia Reilly Giff's
'Polk Street School' books . . . will enjoy this beginning chapter book."
SLJ

Other titles in this series are:

The secret lunch special (2006)

The Veteran's Day visitor (2008)

The **secret** lunch special; [by] Peter Catalanotto and Pamela
Schembri. Henry Holt and Company 2006 56p il (2nd-grade friends)
$15.95

Grades: 1 2 3   **Fic**

1. School stories

ISBN 0-8050-7838-X; 978-0-8050-7838-1

LC 2006-02374

"The text provides a solid bridge from beginning readers to chapter
books. Like the black-and-white illustrations, this gentle read is warm
and smooth around the edges." SLJ

The **Veteran's** Day visitor; [by] Peter Catalanotto and Pamela
Schembri. Henry Holt 2008 63p il (2nd-grade friends) $15.95

Grades: 1 2 3   **Fic**

1. Veterans -- Fiction 2. Narcolepsy -- Fiction 3. Grandfathers
-- Fiction 4. Veterans Day -- Fiction

ISBN 978-0-8050-7840-4; 0-8050-7840-1

LC 2007-40938

"Frequent black-and-white illustrations keep the reader involved and
move the story to its brisk resolution." Horn Book

Catanese, P. W.

Dragon games. Aladdin 2010 373p il (The books of Umber)
$16.99

Grades: 5 6 7 8   **Fic**

1. Fantasy fiction 2. Adventure fiction

ISBN 1-4169-7521-7; 978-1-4169-7521-2

LC 2009018743

Sequel to: Happenstance found (2009)

This is a sequel to Happenstance Found (2009). Having learned
more about his mysterious past, Happenstance accompanies Lord Umber on a journey that could affect the future of Kuraharen. "Grades seven
to ten." (Bull Cent Child Books)

"The fast-paced and high-energy action of this video-game-like
quest will please fantasy adventure fans." Kirkus

The **End** of Time; The Books of Umber, Book 3. Aladdin 2011
(The Books of Umber) $16.99

Grades: 5 6 7 8   **Fic**

ISBN 9781416975205; 1416975209

"As Happenstance struggles to master his unusual abilities, he realizes that time is running out--because Umber's rivals threaten to undo all
the good he has achieved, while an unexpected new enemy with terrible
destructive power approaches the kingdom." (Publisher's note)

Happenstance found. Aladdin 2009 342p il (The books of Umber) $16.99

Grades: 5 6 7 8   **Fic**

1. Fantasy fiction 2. Adventure fiction 3. Magic -- Fiction

ISBN 978-1-4169-7519-9; 1-4169-7519-5

LC 2008-45966

A boy awakens, blindfolded, with no memory of even his name,
but soon meets Lord Umber, an adventurer and inventor, who calls him
Happenstance and tells him that he has a very important destiny—and
a powerful enemy.

"Catanese packs a lot into the book: rich characterizations, . . . well-
choreographed action sequences and genuinely surprising twists at the
end." Publ Wkly

Followed by: Dragon games (2010)

Catmull, Katherine

Summer and Bird; by Katherine Catmull. Dutton Children's
Books 2012 344 p. (hardback) $16.99

Grades: 5 6 7 8   **Fic**

1. Fairy tales 2. Sisters -- Fiction 3. Fantasy 4. Birds -- Fiction
5. Sisters -- Fiction 6. Puppeteers -- Fiction 7. Adventure and
adventurers -- Fiction

ISBN 0525953469; 9780525953463

LC 2012015587

This children's book, by Katherine Catmull, is "an enchanting--and
twisted--tale of two sisters' quest to find their parents. When their parents disappear in the middle of the night, young sisters Summer and
Bird set off on a quest to find them. A cryptic picture message from their
mother leads them to a familiar gate in the woods, but comfortable sights
quickly give way to a new world entirely--Down--one inhabited by talking birds and the evil Puppeteer queen." (Publisher's note)

Cavanaugh, Nancy J.

★ **This** journal belongs to Ratchet; by Nancy J. Cavanaugh.
Sourcebooks Jabberwocky 2013 320 p. (hardcover) $12.99

Grades: 4 5 6 7   **Fic**

1. Diaries -- Fiction 2. Home schooling -- Fiction 3. Father-

daughter relationship -- Fiction 4. Self-acceptance -- Fiction 5. Fathers and daughters -- Fiction 6. Environmental protection -- Fiction

ISBN 1402281064; 9781402281068

LC 2012041339

This juvenile novel, by Nancy Cavanaugh, begins on "the first day of school for all the kids in the neighborhood. But not for me. I'm home-schooled. . . . The best I've got is this notebook. I'm supposed to use it for my writing assignments, but my dad never checks. Here's what I'm really going to use it for: Ratchet's Top Secret Plan . . . : turn my old, recycled, freakish, friendless, motherless life into something shiny and new." (Publisher's note)

"At first it seems artificial, with observations that are too on-the-nose. But as the novel's unexpectedly multifaceted plot comes together, it becomes increasingly compelling, suspenseful and moving. Triumphant enough to make readers cheer; touching enough to make them cry." Kirkus

Cazet, Denys

Minnie and Moo, hooves of fire; by Denys Cazet. Creston Books 2014 208 p. (hardcover) $15.95

Grades: 2 3 4 5   **Fic**

1. Humorous fiction 2. Farm life -- Fiction 3. Fund raising -- Fiction 4. Talent shows -- Fiction 5. Cows -- Fiction 6. Humorous stories 7. Domestic animals -- Fiction

ISBN 1939547083; 9781939547088

LC 2013038846

In this children's book, by Denys Cazet, "it's a perfect day for the First Annual Hoot, Holler, and Moo Talent Festival. . . . Mr. and Mrs. Farmer are away on vacation, Minnie and Moo are dressed in their togas, Elvis has his bagpipe, the hyenas their jokes, the fox his magic tricks, the sheep a protest poem, and the cash box is stuffed with money from ticket sales. A perfect day. Wait a minute . . . Where is the cash box?" (Publisher's note)

"When the farmer and his wife take a vacation, cows Minnie and Moo seize the opportunity to put on a show. There's no shortage of local talent and wannabe stars...The second entry in the chapter book series is a good bet for kids who discovered the characters when they began reading and are ready for longer books. With amusing dialogue, expressive black-and-white drawings, and a chapter called "Race of the Port-A-Potties," fans won't be disappointed." Booklist

Other titles in this series include:

Minnie & Moo and the Seven Wonders of the World (2003)

Cecil, Randy

Lucy; by Randy Cecil. Candlewick Press 2016 144 p. illustrations $19.99

Grades: 1 2 3 4   **Fic**

1. Dogs -- Fiction 2. Family life -- Fiction 3. City and town life -- Fiction

ISBN 0763668087; 9780763668082

LC 2015934395

In this children's book by Randy Cecil, "a tiny dog, a kindhearted girl, and a nervous juggler converge in a cinematic book in four acts. . . .Lucy is a small dog without a home. She had one once, but she remembers it only in her dreams. Eleanor is a little girl who looks forward to feeding the stray dog that appears faithfully beneath her window each day. Eleanor's father is a juggler with stage fright." (Publisher's note)

"The conclusion unfolds naturally, while Cecil's understated writing and careful pacing contribute substantially to this sweetly satisfying story." Pub Wkly

Cerra, Kerry O'Malley

Just a drop of water; Kerry O'Malley Cerra. Skyhorse Publishing Inc. 2014 320 p. (hardback) $14.95

Grades: 5 6 7 8 9   **F**

1. School stories 2. Friendship -- Fiction 3. September 11 terror attacks, 2001 -- Fiction 4. Muslims -- Fiction 5. Best friends Fiction 6. Arab Americans -- Fiction 7. Family life -- Florida Fiction 8. September 11 Terrorist Attacks, 2001 -- Fiction

ISBN 1629146137; 9781629146133

LC 20140159

In this novel by Kerry O'Malley Cerra's "historical novel takes place in . . . the days leading up to and after September 11, 2001. Jake Green struggles with the knowledge that one of the hijackers was living in h town prior to the attacks. His best friend and neighbor, Sam Medina, Arab Muslim, is targeted by boys in their class. [When] Sam's father taken into FBI custody after the discovery that he serviced the hijack at the bank he worked . . . Jake soon finds himself at odds with his in mediate family." (School Library Journal)

"The tragedy of 9/11 forces a 13-year-old Florida boy who has a ways lived with a comfortable, straightforward code of conduct to e plore the issues of loyalty, patriotism and fair play... Cerra does a go job of re-creating the combination of fear, confusion, patriotism, pre dice and community spirit the attack engendered, and readers shou identify with Jake's plight. A perceptive exploration of an event its au ence already sees as history." Kirkus

Cervantes, Angela

Allie, first at last; by Angela Cervantes. Scholastic Press 2016 2 p. (hardcover) $16.99

Grades: 4 5 6   **F**

1. Contests -- Fiction 2. Self-confidence -- Fiction 3. Fema friendship -- Fiction 4. Schools -- Fiction 5. Family life -- Ficti 6. Best friends -- Fiction 7. Great-grandfathers -- Fiction Hispanic Americans -- Fiction

ISBN 9780545812238

LC 20150313

In this middle grade novel, by Angela Cervantes, "Allie . . . [is] d termined to add a shiny medal, blue ribbon, or beautiful trophy to h family's award shelf. When a prestigious school contest is announce Allie has the perfect opportunity to take first--at last. There's just o small snag . . . her biggest competition is also her ex-best friend, Sa Can Allie take top prize and win back a friend--or is she destined to lo it all?" (Publisher's note)

"Throughout the clearly written, first-person narrative, the viv scenes of fifth-grade conflicts, old and new friendships, and affectiona family life make this an accessible, appealing chapter book." Booklis

Gaby, Lost and Found. Scholastic Inc. 2013 224 p. $16.99

Grades: 5 6 7   **F**

1. Bullies -- Fiction 2. Immigrants -- Fiction

ISBN 0545489458; 9780545489454

In this book, Gaby's mother is deported to Honduras, "Though sh lives with her dad, Gaby basically parents herself with the help of h friend Alma's family. Her physical and emotional needs are barely m at home. Gaby's world brightens when her class begins a long-term vo unteer project at the Furry Friends animal shelter. Like her mom, Gaby an animal lover, and she develops her writing talent by crafting adopti profiles for the cats and dogs." (Kirkus Reviews)

Cervantes, Jennifer

Tortilla sun. Chronicle Books 2010 224p $16.99

Grades: 5 6 7 8   **F**

1. New Mexico -- Fiction 2. Grandmothers -- Fiction 3. Fathe

daughter relationship -- Fiction

ISBN 0-8118-7015-4; 978-0-8118-7015-3

While spending a summer in New Mexico with her grandmother, twelve-year-old Izzy makes new friends, learns to cook, and for the first time hears stories about her father, who died before she was born.

"Cervantes evokes the beauty of the setting and develops a memorable cast of characters, brought to life through Izzy's heartfelt narration. A beautiful and engaging debut novel." Kirkus

Chari, Sheela

Vanished. Disney/Hyperion Books 2011 240p $16.99

Grades: 5 6 7 8   **Fic**

1. Mystery fiction 2. East Indian Americans -- Fiction 3. Lost and found possessions -- Fiction

ISBN 978-1-4231-3163-2; 1-4231-3163-0

LC 2010019660

Eleven-year-old Neela must solve the mystery when her beautiful, but cursed, veena, a classical Indian musical instrument, goes missing.

"Well-paced and with moments of family humor . . . the novel offers a strong cast of characters and richly-described settings; both the legend and the contemporary come alive for readers. . . . Chari . . . strikes the right note with this engaging, intricate story that spans generations and two countries." Kirkus

Includes bibliographical references

Chatterton, Martin

The **Brain** finds a leg. Peachtree Publishers 2009 212p $16.95

Grades: 4 5 6   **Fic**

1. School stories 2. Mystery fiction 3. Animals -- Fiction 4. Australia -- Fiction 5. Intellect -- Fiction 6. Inventions -- Fiction

ISBN 978-1-56145-503-4; 1-56145-503-2

LC 2009-00304

First published 2007 in Australia

In Farrago Bay, Australia, thirteen-year-old Sheldon is recruited by a new student, Theo Brain, to help investigate a murder, which is tied not only to bizzare animal behavior but also to a diabolical plot to alter human intelligence.

"Several deaths in the story war against the comedy but the laughs win. Readers shouldn't expect anything remotely realistic and instead surrender themselves to the industrial-strength zaniness." Kirkus

Another title about The Brain is:

The Brain full of holes (2010)

The **Brain** full of holes. Peachtree 2010 250p $16.95

Grades: 4 5 6   **Fic**

1. Mystery fiction 2. Inventions -- Fiction 3. Switzerland -- Fiction

ISBN 978-1-56145-527-0; 1-56145-527-X

"Kid detective The Brain and his Watson are called in on a missing-person case. Their search takes them to Switzerland, home of the new super-particle accelerator, but their real adventure occurs in an alternate universe filled with zaniness. Chatterton explores speculations about physics throughout in amusing ways. . . . Those who like laughs along with a sf-influenced mystery will enjoy this." Booklist

Cheaney, J. B.

My friend, the enemy. Knopf 2005 266p hardcover o.p. pa $6.50

Grades: 5 6 7 8   **Fic**

1. Friendship -- Fiction 2. Japanese Americans -- Fiction 3. World War, 1939-1945 -- Fiction

ISBN 0-375-81432-9; 0-440-42102-0 pa

LC 2004-26927

During World War II, a twelve-year-old girl becomes friends with a young Japanese-American boy she discovers being sheltered and hidden by her neighbor.

"Written in first person, this novel offers quiet but finely tuned portrayal of the stresses that changed life on the home front and one child's attempts to cope with it all." Booklist

Chen, Pauline

Peiling and the chicken-fried Christmas; [by] Pauline Chen. Bloomsbury Children's Books 2007 133p $15.95

Grades: 4 5 6   **Fic**

1. Christmas -- Fiction 2. Taiwanese Americans -- Fiction

ISBN 978-1-59990-122-0; 1-59990-122-6

LC 2006102095

Fifth-grader Peiling Wang wants to celebrate "a real American Christmas," much to the displeasure of her traditional, Taiwanese-born father

"Peiling makes an appealingly levelheaded protagonist, and . . . [Chen] doesn't miss much in this often-amusing picture of the Wang family working at fitting its new and old cultures together." Booklist

Cheng, Andrea

Brushing Mom's hair; illustrations by Nicole Wong. Wordsong 2009 59p il $17.95

Grades: 4 5 6 7 8   **Fic**

1. Novels in verse 2. Young adult literature 3. Sick -- Fiction 4. Cancer -- Fiction 5. Mother-daughter relationship -- Fiction

ISBN 978-1-59078-599-7; 1-59078-599-1

LC 2009021965

A fourteen-year-old girl, whose mother's breast cancer diagnosis and treatment have affected every aspect of their lives, finds release in ballet and art classes.

"With one or two words on each line, the poems are a fast read, but the chatty voice packs in emotion. . . . Wong's small black-and-white pencil drawings on every page extend the poetry through the characters' body language." Booklist

Honeysuckle house. Front Street 2004 136p $16.95; pa $10.95

Grades: 3 4 5   **Fic**

1. Friendship -- Fiction 2. Immigrants -- Fiction 3. Chinese Americans -- Fiction

ISBN 1-886910-99-5; 1-59078-632-7 pa

An all-American girl with Chinese ancestors and a new immigrant from China find little in common when they meet in their fourth grade classroom, but they are both missing their best friends and soon discover other connections

"Told in first person in alternating chapters, the narratives balance well between large issues . . . and more intimate ones. . . . With a smoothly drawn and interesting plot, strong characters, and graceful writing, the story has more immediacy than much realistic contemporary fiction." SLJ

The **lace** dowry. Front Street 2005 113p $16.95

Grades: 4 5 6 7   **Fic**

1. Hungary -- Fiction 2. Sex role -- Fiction 3. Friendship -- Fiction

ISBN 1-932425-20-9

LC 2004-21186

In Hungary in 1933, a twelve-year-old from Budapest befriends the Halas village family of lacemakers hired to stitch her dowry.

"Cheng tells a familiar story of children discovering empathy across class and cultural divides, enriching the theme with a vivid historical setting and Juli's strong narration, which is written in spare language and a believable voice." Booklist

Only one year; illustrations by Nicole Wong. Lee & Low Books 2010 97p il $16.95

Grades: 2 3 4   **Fic**
1. Siblings -- Fiction 2. Family life -- Fiction 3. Chinese Americans -- Fiction
ISBN 978-1-60060-252-8; 1-60060-252-5

         LC 201044

"Although she sometimes finds him troublesome, fourth-grader Sharon can't bear the idea that her two-year-old brother, Di Di, will spend a whole school year with relatives in China while she and her first-grade sister, Mary, go to school and her parents work. . . . Supportive black-and-white illustrations and a glossary/pronunciation guide for the occasional Chinese words and phrases complete the appealing package of this gentle family story." Booklist

Shanghai messenger; illustrated by Ed Young. Lee & Low 2005 un il $18.95
Grades: 3 4 5 6   **Fic**
1. Novels in verse 2. China -- Fiction 3. Chinese Americans -- Fiction
ISBN 1-58430-238-0

         LC 2004-4025934

A free-verse novel about eleven-year-old Xiao Mei's visit with her extended family in China, where the Chinese-American girl finds many differences but also the similarities that bind a family together.

"Cheng does an admirable job of capturing this experience from the perspective of a child, and each free-verse chapter is brief but satisfying. . . . Young's illustrations delicately intertwine with the text, gently supporting each vignette. This is a superb book." SLJ

Where do you stay? Boyds Mills Press 2011 134p $17.95
Grades: 4 5 6 7   **Fic**
1. Aunts -- Fiction 2. Cousins -- Fiction 3. Pianists -- Fiction 4. Bereavement -- Fiction 5. Homeless persons -- Fiction
ISBN 1-59078-707-2; 978-1-59078-707-6

Jerome is staying with his Aunt Geneva and her family, now that his mother has passed away. Aunt Geneva tries to make Jerome feel welcome, but his cousins are not happy about the new "member" of their family. Though Jerome has a place to stay, he doesn't feel he has a home, until he meets Mr. Willie, who lives in a ramshackle carriage house.

"In short chapters of lyrical prose, Cheng . . . provides a moving tribute to a multigenerational community's ability to sustain and recreate itself in times of change through resilience, hard work, and a commitment to beauty and kindness." Publ Wkly

Where the steps were. Front Street 2008 143p il $16.95
Grades: 3 4 5 6   **Fic**
1. School stories 2. Novels in verse 3. Teachers -- Fiction 4. Friendship -- Fiction
ISBN 978-1-932425-88-8; 1-932425-88-8

         LC 2007-18787

Verse from the perspectives of five students in Miss D.'s third grade class details the children's last year together before their inner city school is to be torn down

This is "a spare, eloquent novel in verse illustrated in [the author's] own bold block prints." Publ Wkly

The **year** of the book; by Andrea Cheng; illustrated by Abigail Halpin. Houghton Mifflin 2012 146 p. $15.99
Grades: 2 3 4 5   **Fic**
1. School stories 2. Friendship -- Fiction 3. Chinese Americans -- Fiction 4. Best friends -- Fiction
ISBN 0547684630; 9780547684635

         LC 2011036331

In this children's book, by Andrea Cheng, "narrator Anna Wang . . . always has her head stuck in a book. Nine-year-old Anna reads for all the

right reasons, . . . but she also uses reading as a shield against social exclusion . . . and her own lack of confidence. . . . At school, Anna's friend from last year . . . now hangs out with the popular girls. . . . Sometimes a book helps illuminate Anna's own life, . . . sometimes a book is part of the external plot." (Horn Book Magazine)

"A slim but solid novel about friends and family issues, Cheng's latest follows an Asian American girl through most of fourth grade. . . . Halpin's illustrations offer sweet scenes and images of Anna's life including her growing interest in Chinese characters." Booklist

Other titles in this series are:
The year of the baby (2013)
The year of the fortune cookie (2014)
The year of the three sisters (2015)
The year of the garden (2017)

Cheng, Jack
     See you in the Cosmos; by Jack Cheng. Dial Books 2017 320 p. (ebook) $50.97; (hardback) $16.99
Grades: 5 6 7 8   **Fic**
1. Friendship -- Fiction 2. Family life -- Fiction 3. Rockets (Aeronautics) -- Fiction 4. Resilience (Personality trait) -- Fiction
ISBN 9780399186394; 9780399186370

         LC 2016032255

In this novel, by Jack Cheng, "Alex Petroski loves space and rockets . . . All he wants is to launch his golden iPod into space the way [astronomer] Carl Sagan . . . launched his Golden Record on the Voyager spacecraft in 1977. From Colorado to New Mexico, Las Vegas to L.A., Alex records a journey on his iPod. . . . But his destination keeps changing And the . . . remarkable people he meets along the way can only partially prepare him for the secrets he'll uncover." (Publisher's note)

"Riveting, inspiring, and sometimes hilarious." Kirkus

Cheshire, Simon
     The **curse** of the ancient mask and other case files; pictures by R W. Alley. Roaring Book Press 2009 169p il (Saxby Smart, private detective) $13.95
Grades: 3 4 5   **Fic**
1. Mystery fiction 2. Lost and found possessions -- Fiction
ISBN 978-1-59643-474-5; 1-59643-474-0
First published 2007 in the United Kingdom

"Saxby Doyle Christie Chandler Ellin Allan Smart wants to be a detective as good as the greats. . . . In the first of three 'case files,' . . . Saxby . . . discovers that [an ancient] mask's real curse is a case of competitive sabotage. [In the] second case file . . . Saxby uncovers the secret behind the appearance of purple goo on his classmates' projects. In the third mystery, Saxby sets out to find the thief of a valuable coat clasp. . . . The stories are liberally illustrated with Alley's homey sketches plus representations of Saxby's notebooks. While each short mystery is involving, the distinguishing aspect of this series opener is Saxby's enthusiastic invitations to readers to participate in the sleuthing." Kirkus

Other titles in this series are:
The treasure of Dead Man's Lane and other case files (2010)
The pirate's blood and other case files (2011)

The **pirate's** blood and other case files; pictures by R. W. Alley. Roaring Brook Press 2011 224p il (Saxby Smart, private detective) $15.99
Grades: 3 4 5   **Fic**
1. School stories 2. Mystery fiction 3. Theft -- Fiction 4. Pirates -- Fiction
ISBN 978-1-59643-476-9; 1-59643-476-7

         LC 2010029240

Saxby Smart, schoolboy private detective, invites the reader to follow the clues as he investigates three cases involving hidden treasure, a tring of break-ins where nothing is stolen, and a rare comic book taken rom an undamaged safe.

The **treasure** of Dead Man's Lane and other case files; pictures by R. W. Alley. Roaring Brook Press 2010 195p il (Saxby Smart, private detective) $15.99

Grades: 3 4 5 **Fic**

1. Mystery fiction

ISBN 978-1-59643-475-2; 1-59643-475-9

"In the first case, Saxby must find a rare comic book that's gone missing from a locked safe, and he uncovers lots of interesting comic-book trivia in the process of discovering the motive-old-fashioned greed—and the perp. The middle is the most engrossing of the three stories, involving an historic mansion with a dark past where Saxby's friend finds a scroll hidden in the wall. . . . Last, Saxby must unravel the enigma of six students who all have two things in common: home intruders and an anti-stress class. . . . Generously dappled with Alley's breezy line drawings, the cases are timely and twisting enough to keep the light bulb bright in the young sleuth's mind." Kirkus

Chick, Bryan

The **secret** zoo. Greenwillow Books 2010 295p $16.99

Grades: 4 5 6 **Fic**

1. Fantasy fiction 2. Mystery fiction 3. Zoos -- Fiction 4. Animals -- Fiction 5. Siblings -- Fiction

ISBN 978-0-06-198750-2; 0-06-198750-6

First published 2007 by Second Wish Press

Noah and his friends follow a trail of mysterious clues to uncover a secret behind the walls of the Clarksville City Zoo—a secret that must be protected at all costs.

"Chick debuts with an action-packed and breathless story about teamwork. . . . The story should appeal both to animal-lovers and a broader audience. While many threads are resolved, Chick lays the groundwork for later books." Publ Wkly

Other titles in this series are:

The secret zoo: secrets and shadows (2011)

The secret zoo: riddles and danger (2011)

The **secret** zoo: riddles and danger. Greenwillow Books 2011 284p $16.99

Grades: 4 5 6 **Fic**

1. Zoos -- Fiction 2. Magic -- Fiction 3. Friendship -- Fiction 4. Secret societies -- Fiction

ISBN 978-0-06-198927-8; 0-06-198927-4

LC 2011005930

Sequel to: The secret zoo: secrets and shadows (2011)

Having discovered a magical society beneath the exhibits at the Clarksville City Zoo where animals and humans live harmoniously together as equals, Noah and his friends must protect the secret zoo at all costs.

The **secret** zoo: secrets and shadows. Greenwillow Books 2011 266p $16.99

Grades: 4 5 6 **Fic**

1. Mystery fiction 2. Zoos -- Fiction 3. Sasquatch -- Fiction 4. Friendship -- Fiction

ISBN 978-0-06-198925-4; 0-06-198925-8

LC 2010017221

Sequel to: The secret zoo (2010)

Noah and his friends in the Secret Society join forces with four teens known as the Descenders to try to protect the Secret Zoo hidden below the Clarksville City Zoo from monstrous sasquatches and the evil Shadow Master.

"The four friends are well developed characters. . . . Descriptions are delightful. . . . Fans of fantasy, animal fiction, and adventure will enjoy this fast-moving story." SLJ

Child, Lauren

Clarice Bean spells trouble; [by] Lauren Child. Candlewick Press 2005 189p il $15.99; pa $5.99

Grades: 3 4 5 **Fic**

1. Authorship -- Fiction 2. Friendship -- Fiction

ISBN 0-7636-2813-1; 0-7636-2903-0 pa

Clarice Bean, aspiring actress and author, unsuccessfully tries to avoid getting into trouble as she attempts to help a friend in need by following the rules of the fictional spy, Ruby Redfort.

This is written "with fresh, childlike turns of phrase and a hyper-awareness of words. . . . With a sprinkling of small, childlike line drawings, a few other illustrations, and some creative typography, this entertaining chapter book will please readers." Booklist

Other titles about Clarice Bean are:

Clarice Bean, don't look now (2007)

Utterly me, Clarice Bean (2003)

Clarice Bean, don't look now; [by] Lauren Child. Candlewick Press 2007 252p il $15.99

Grades: 3 4 5 **Fic**

1. School stories 2. Friendship -- Fiction 3. Family life -- Fiction

ISBN 978-0-7636-3536-7

"Clarice is codifying her fears into a list of worst worries when the kitchen ceiling comes crashing down after her older sister floods the bathroom. . . . Troubles continue at school when her best friend, Betty, annouces that she is moving to San Francisco, and a strange new student from Sweden arrives. . . . The story is told in Child's familiar stream-of-consciousness style and punctuated with creative vocabulary." SLJ

Utterly me, Clarice Bean. Candlewick Press 2003 190p il hardcover o.p. pa $5.99

Grades: 3 4 5 **Fic**

1. School stories

ISBN 0-7636-2186-2; 0-7636-2788-7 pa

LC 2002-41528

When someone steals the winner's trophy for the school book project, Clarice emulates her favorite book heroine, Ruby Redfort the detective

"Clarice is an exceptionally strong character, and her story, delivered in deadpan, forthright prose, perfectly captures a child's voice in a way that will elicit laughter even from the grumpy." Booklist

Chilton, Andrew S.

The **goblin's** puzzle; the adventures of a boy with no name and two girls called Alice. by Andrew S. Chilton; illustrations by Jensine Eckwall. Alfred A. Knopf 2016 288 p. illustrations (hardback) $16.99

Grades: 4 5 6 7 8 **Fic**

1. Fantasy fiction 2. Humorous fiction

ISBN 9780553520705; 9780553520712

LC 2015013261

In this juvenile fantasy novel, by Andrew S. Chilton, with illustrations by Jensine Eckwall, "a nameless slave on a mission to uncover his true destiny . . . , [a] goblin . . . too tricky to be trusted . . . , a bookish peasant girl . . . and Princess Alice . . . are tangled up in a sinister plot to take over the kingdom, and together they must face kind monsters, a cruel magician, and dozens of deathly boring palace bureaucrats." (Publisher's note)

"An emphasis on questioning fate, societal rules, and traditions as well as the importance of wit and logic rather than brawn renders this lighthearted adventure fresh." Kirkus

Choldenko, Gennifer

Al Capone does my homework; by Gennifer Choldenko. Dial Books for Young Readers 2013 224 p. (Al Capone Trilogy) (hardcover) $17.99

Grades: 5 6 7 8   **Fic**
1. Mystery fiction 2. Historical fiction 3. Fires -- Fiction 4. Autism -- Fiction 5. Brothers and sisters -- Fiction 6. Swindlers and swindling -- Fiction 7. Alcatraz Island (Calif.) -- History -- 20th century -- Fiction 8. United States Penitentiary, Alcatraz Island, California -- Fiction

ISBN 0803734727; 9780803734722

LC 2012039138

Sequel to: Al Capone shines my shoes

This book, set on Alcatraz Island in the 1930s, is the third in Gennifer Choldenko's Al Capone trilogy. Moose lives with his parents and autistic sister on the island. "When Moose's dad gets promoted to Associate Warden, . . . it's a big deal. But the cons have a point system for targeting prison employees, and his dad is now in serious danger. After a fire starts in the Flanagan's apartment, Natalie is blamed, and Moose bands with the other kids to track down the possible arsonist." (Publisher's note)

Includes bibliographical references

★ **Al** Capone does my shirts. G.P. Putnam's Sons 2004 225p il $15.99; pa $6.99

Grades: 5 6 7 8   **Fic**
1. Autism -- Fiction 2. Siblings -- Fiction 3. Alcatraz Island (Calif.) -- Fiction

ISBN 0-399-23861-1; 0-14-240370-9 pa

LC 2002-31766

A Newbery Medal honor book, 2005

A twelve-year-old boy named Moose moves to Alcatraz Island in 1935 when guards' families were housed there, and has to contend with his extraordinary new environment in addition to life with his autistic sister.

"With its unique setting and well-developed characters, this warm, engaging coming-of-age story has plenty of appeal, and Choldenko offers some fascinating historical background on Alcatraz Island in an afterword." Booklist

Followed by: Al Capone shines my shoes (2009)

Al Capone shines my shoes. Dial Books for Young Readers 2009 274p $16.99

Grades: 5 6 7 8   **Fic**
1. Autism -- Fiction 2. Siblings -- Fiction 3. Alcatraz Island (Calif.) -- Fiction

ISBN 978-0-8037-3460-9; 0-8037-3460-3

LC 2009-04157

Sequel to: Al Capone does my shirts (2004)

Moose Flanagan, who lives on Alcatraz along with his family and the families of the other prison guards, is frightened when he discovers that noted gangster Al Capone, a prisoner there, wants a favor in return for the help that he secretly gave Moose.

"Effortless period dialogue, fully developed secondary characters and a perfectly paced plot combine to create a solid-gold sequel that will not disappoint." Kirkus

Includes bibliographical references

Chasing secrets; Gennifer Choldenko. Wendy Lamb Books, an imprint of Random House Children's Books 2015 288 p. (trade) $16.99

Grades: 5 6 7 8   **Fic**
1. San Francisco (Calif.) -- Fiction 2. Historical fiction 3. Father-daughter relationship -- Fiction 4. Plague -- Fiction 5. Friendship -- Fiction 6. Quarantine -- Fiction 7. Chinese Americans -- Fiction 8.

Fathers and daughters -- Fiction 9. San Francisco (Calif.) -- History -- 20th century -- Fiction

ISBN 0385742533; 9780375990632; 9780385742535; 9780385742542

LC 201404032

This novel, by Gennifer Choldenko, is set in "San Francisco, 1900. . . . A fantastic time to be alive for lots of people . . . but not thirteen-year old Lizzie Kennedy. . . . Lizzie's secret passion is science, an unsuitable subject for finishing-school girls. Lizzie lives to go on house calls with her physician father. On those visits to his patients, she discovers a hidden dark side of the city--a side that¿s full of secrets, rats, and rumors o the plague." (Publisher's note)

"Thirteen-year-old Lizzie is a smart, scientifically-minded girl, ou of place in a San Francisco finishing school in 1900. Applying the scien tific method to rumors of the bubonic plague in Chinatown, Lizzie faces the power of the media and racist political schemes as she attempts to rescue her Chinese housekeeper from quarantine. Appealing, convinc ing characters and a detail-rich setting keep the light mystery afloat." Horn Book

No passengers beyond this point. Dial Books for Young Reader 2011 244p $16.99

Grades: 5 6 7 8   **Fic**
1. Fantasy fiction 2. Siblings -- Fiction 3. Space and time -- Fiction

ISBN 978-0-8037-3534-7; 0-8037-3534-0

LC 2009-5166

With their house in foreclosure, sisters India and Mouse and brother Finn are sent to stay with an uncle in Colorado until their mother can join them, but when the plane lands, the children are welcomed by cheering crowds to a strange place where each of them has a perfect house and a clock that is ticking down the time.

"Choldenko keeps the plot moving rapidly and constantly shifts the point of view, with each chapter narrated by one of the three siblings, se that both readers and characters feel discombobulated—everything i both concrete yet dreamlike. . . . No one can write a hormonal teenag girl at war with her family like Choldenko, but in the end the family relationships and the determination each sibling has to protect the other is what saves them all." Horn Book

Notes from a liar and her dog. Putnam 2001 216p hardcover o.p pa $5.99

Grades: 5 6 7 8   **Fic**
1. Family life -- Fiction 2. Truthfulness and falsehood -- Fiction

ISBN 0-399-23591-4; 0-14-250068-2 pa

LC 00-5535

Eleven-year-old Ant, stuck in a family that she does not like, cope by pretending that her "real" parents are coming to rescue her, by loving her dog Pistachio, by volunteering at the zoo, and by bending the truth and telling lies

"Choldenko's writing is snappy and tender, depicting both Ant's bravado and her isolation with sympathy." Bull Cent Child Books

Christopher, John

The **City** of gold and lead; 35th anniversary ed.; Simon & Schuste Books for Young Readers 2003 180p hardcover o.p. pa $5.99

Grades: 5 6 7 8   **Fic**
1. Science fiction

ISBN 0-689-85505-2; 0-689-85666-0 pa

LC 2002026670

Sequel to: The White Mountains

A reissue of the title first published 1967

Three boys set out on a secret mission to penetrate the City of the Tripods and learn more about these strange beings that rule the earth.

Followed by: The pool of fire

The **pool** of fire; 35th anniversary ed.; Simon & Schuster Books for Young Readers 2003 176p hardcover o.p. pa $5.99
Grades: 5 6 7 8   **Fic**
1. Science fiction
ISBN 0-689-85506-0; 0-689-85669-5 pa
                                            LC 2002026883
Sequel to: City of gold and lead
A reissue of the title first published 1968
Will and a small group of free people plan to destroy the three great cities of the Tripods before the arrival of a space ship destined to loom humanity.

When the Tripods came. Dutton 1988 151p hardcover o.p. pa $5.99
Grades: 5 6 7 8   **Fic**
1. Science fiction
ISBN 0-525-44397-5; 978-0-689-85762-1 pa; 0-689-85762-4 pa
                                            LC 88-478
"A prequel to the author's well-known White Mountains trilogy . . . this relates how the Tripods came to Earth and imposed a new subserient order on its population. The protagonist is Laurie Corday, who, with his friend Andy, witnesses the first arrival of these towering metallic creatures. . . . The story's scenario exudes a chill; Laurie lives in the present, not some futuristic world, and the Tripods' insidious rise to power seems quite reasonable in the context of the story." Booklist

The **White** Mountains; 35th anniversary ed; Simon & Schuster Bks. for Young Readers 2003 164p hardcover o.p. pa $5.99
Grades: 5 6 7 8   **Fic**
1. Science fiction
ISBN 0-689-85504-4; 0-689-85672-5 pa
                                            LC 2002-70808
A reissue of the title first published 1967 by Macmillan
Young Will Parker and his companions make a perilous journey toward an outpost of freedom where they hope to escape from the ruling Tripods, who capture mature human beings and make them docile, obedient servants
This "remarkable story . . . belongs to the school of science-fiction which puts philosophy before technology and is not afraid of telling an exciting story." Times Lit Suppl
Other titles about the Tripods are:
The city of gold and lead (2003 c1967)
The pool of fire (2003 c1968)
When the Tripods came (2003 c1988)

Christopher, Lucy
Flyaway; Lucy Christopher. Chicken House 2011 314p $16.99
Grades: 5 6 7 8   **Fic**
1. Sick -- Fiction 2. Swans -- Fiction 3. Hospitals -- Fiction 4. Wildlife conservation -- Fiction 5. Family life -- Fiction 6. Father-daughter relationship -- Fiction
ISBN 0545317711; 9780545317719
                                            LC 2010051425
In this young adult novel, "when newly constructed power lines ruin the annual return of the whooping swans Isla and her father rise early to witness, the death of several of the wild creatures and her father's sudden and severe illness both confound Isla and emphasize her loneliness. At the hospital where her father awaits a heart operation, Harry, waiting there for a bone-marrow transplant, befriends Isla and points out the young swan he can see from his bed. . . . News broadcasts . . . about deadly outbreaks of bird flu contrast with the small unfolding of Isla's widowed grandfather's stiff grief as he helps her construct an art

project--a harness and wings from an ancient stuffed swan--and innocent romance flutters between Isla and Harry even as the young swan regains flight and her father begins to recover." (Kirkus)
Christopher offers "readers a quiet but compelling story with several well-realized, idiosyncratic characters. She skillfully develops the novel's varied elements and weaves them into a unified narrative. . . . This sensitive novel will resonate with many readers." Booklist

Christopher, Neil
On the Shoulder of a Giant; An Inuit Folktale. Neil Christopher; illustrated by James Nelson. Inhabit Media 2015 40 p. color illustrations $16.95
Grades: K 1 2 3   **Fic**
1. Giants -- Fiction 2. Inuit -- Folklore
ISBN 1772270024; 9781772270020
In this children's book by Neil Christopher, illustrated by James Nelson, "Inukpak was big, even for a giant. He loved to walk across the tundra, striding over the widest rivers and wading through the deepest lakes. But being so big, and traveling so far, Inukpak was often alone. Until one day when he came across a little hunter on the tundra, Inukpak decided to adopt him. And so, from the shoulder of one of the biggest giants to ever roam the Arctic, this hunter experiences Inukpak's world." (Publisher's note)
"Rendered in a milky palette that captures the vast seas and skies of the Arctic setting, Nelson's richly developed artwork playfully emphasizes the hunter's plight while making it clear that the giant is friendly and caring, despite his goofs. A good pick for readers eager to learn about giants beyond Paul Bunyan and Goliath." Pub Wkly

Clark, Clara Gillow
Secrets of Greymoor. Candlewick Press 2009 166p $15.99
Grades: 4 5 6 7   **Fic**
1. School stories 2. Wealth -- Fiction 3. Grandmothers -- Fiction 4. New York (State) -- Fiction
ISBN 978-0-7636-3249-6; 0-7636-3249-X
                                            LC 2008019063
As her grandmother's financial situation worsens, Hattie is forced to attend a "common school," in late nineteenth-century Kingston, New York, where she stands up to a show-off, shares embellished stories about life as a rich girl, and tries to recover her family's wealth.
"Even readers new to Hattie's story will cheer. . . . [This is an] accessible first-person narrative." Booklist

Clarke, Cat
The **Pants** Project; Cat Clarke. Sourcebooks Jabberwocky 2017 272 p. (hardcover : alk. paper) $16.99
Grades: 4 5 6 7   **Fic**
1. Middle schools -- Fiction 2. Transgender people -- Fiction 3. Schools -- Fiction 4. Uniforms -- Fiction 5. Family life -- Fiction 6. Gay parents -- Fiction 7. Middle schools -- Fiction 8. Lesbian mothers -- Fiction
ISBN 9781492638094
                                            LC 2016028642
This book, by Cat Clarke, tells the efforts of 11-year-old transgender Liv "to convince the school's new principal that students should have some choice in clothing. . . . His coming-out to friend Jacob is realistically brief and an enormous relief. Liv's two moms add further dimension to a tale that unabashedly affirms the importance of accepting and celebrating differences." (Kirkus Review)

Clayton, Emma
The **roar**. Chicken House/Scholastic Inc. 2009 481p $17.99

Grades: 5 6 7 8　　　　　**Fic**

1. Science fiction 2. Twins -- Fiction

ISBN 978-0-439-92593-8; 0-439-92593-2

LC 2008-8311

"Mika and Ellie live in a future behind a wall: Solid concrete topped with high-voltage razor wire and guarded by a battalion of Ghengis Borgs, it was built to keep out the animals, because animals carry the plague. At least that's what Ellie, who was kidnapped as a child, has always been taught. But when she comes to suspect the truth behind her captivity, she's ready to risk exposure to the elements and answer the call of the wild." (Publisher's note) "Grades six to nine." (Bull Cent Child Books)

"This is an unusually gripping adventure that targets a younger audience than most young adult sci-fi." Bull Cent Child Books

Cleary, Beverly

Beezus and Ramona; illustrated by Louis Darling. Avon Books 1990 159p il pa $5.99

Grades: 3 4 5　　　　　**Fic**

1. Sisters -- Fiction

ISBN 0-380-70918-X

A reissue of the title first published 1955

Beezus' biggest problem is her 4-year-old sister Ramona. Even though Beezus knows sisters are supposed to love each other, with a sister like Ramona, it seems impossible.

★ **Dear** Mr. Henshaw; illustrated by Paul O. Zelinsky. Morrow 1983 133p il $15.99; lib bdg $16.89; pa $5.99

Grades: 4 5 6 7　　　　　**Fic**

1. School stories 2. Divorce -- Fiction 3. Parent-child relationship -- Fiction

ISBN 0-688-02405-X; 0-688-02406-8 lib bdg; 0-380-70958-9 pa

LC 83-5372

Awarded the Newbery Medal, 1984

"Leigh Botts lives with his recently divorced mother and writes to his favorite author, Boyd Henshaw. When Henshaw answers his letters and encourages him to keep a journal, he does so, and in the process solves the mystery of who is stealing food from his lunchbox, tries to write a novel, and in the end, writes a prize-winning short story about an experience with his father. . . , Grades four to seven." (SLJ)

"Leigh Botts started writing letters to his favorite author, Boyd Henshaw, in the second grade. Now, Leigh is in the sixth grade, in a new school, and his parents are recently divorced. This year he writes many letters to Mr. Henshaw, and also keeps a journal. Through these the reader learns how Leigh adjusts to new situations, and of his triumphs." Child Book Rev Serv

Followed by: Strider (1991)

Henry and Beezus; illustrated by Louis Darling. Avon Books 2001 192p il pa $5.99

Grades: 3 4 5　　　　　**Fic**

1. Bicycles -- Fiction 2. Friendship -- Fiction 3. Money-making projects for children -- Fiction

ISBN 0-380-70914-7

LC 2001271522

A reissue of the title first published 1952

All Henry Huggins can think about is owning a bicycle, and he and his friend Beezus come up with various ideas to make money.

Henry and Ribsy; illustrated by Louis Darling. Avon 1990 192p il pa $5.99

Grades: 3 4 5　　　　　**Fic**

1. Dogs -- Fiction 2. Father-son relationship -- Fiction

ISBN 0-380-70917-1

A reissue of the title first published 1954

Henry Huggins makes a deal with his father—if Henry can keep his dog Ribsy out of trouble for a month, he can go fishing with his father Ribsy does his best to make Henry lose the deal.

"Genuinely funny." Booklist

Henry Huggins; illustrated by Louis Darling. HarperCollins Pubs 2000 155p il $15.99; pa $5.99

Grades: 3 4 5　　　　　**Fic**

1. School stories 2. Family life -- Fiction

ISBN 0-688-21385-5; 0-380-70912-0 pa

LC 00-2756

A reissue of the title first published 1950 by Morrow

"Henry Huggins is a typical small boy who, quite innocently, get himself into all sorts of predicaments—often with the very apt thought 'Won't Mom be surprised.' There is not a dull moment but some hi lariously funny ones in the telling of Henry's adventures at home and a school." Booklist

Other titles about Henry Huggins are:

Henry and Beezus (1952)

Henry and Ribsy (1954)

Henry and the clubhouse (1962)

Henry and the paper route (1957)

Ribsy (1964)

The **mouse** and the motorcycle; illustrated by Louis Darling. Mor row 1965 158p il $16; pa $5.99

Grades: 3 4 5　　　　　**Fi**

1. Mice -- Fiction

ISBN 0-688-21698-6; 0-380-70924-4 pa

"The author shows much insight into the thoughts of children. Sh carries the reader into an imaginative world that contains many realisti emotions." Wis Libr Bull

Other titles about Ralph are:

Ralph S. Mouse (1982)

Runaway Ralph (1970)

★ **Muggie** Maggie; illustrated by Kay Life. Morrow Junior Bks 1990 70p il $15.99; pa $5.99

Grades: 2 3 4　　　　　**Fi**

1. School stories 2. Handwriting -- Fiction

ISBN 0-688-08553-9; 0-380-71087-0 pa

LC 89-3895

Maggie resists learning cursive writing in the third grade, until sh discovers that knowing how to read and write cursive promises to ope up an entirely new world of knowledge for her

"This deceptively simple story is accessible to primary-grade reader able to read longhand, as some of the text is in script. . . . Everythin in this book rings true, and Cleary has created a likable, funny heroin about whom readers will want to know more." SLJ

Ralph S. Mouse; illustrated by Paul O. Zelinsky. Harper Troph 2000 160p il pa $5.99

Grades: 3 4 5　　　　　**Fi**

1. Mice -- Fiction

ISBN 0-380-70957-0

LC 200127865

A reissue of the title first published 1982

Presents the further adventures of a motorcycle-riding mouse wh goes to school and becomes the instigator of an investigation of roden and the peacemaker for two lonely boys.

Ramona and her father; illustrated by Alan Tiegreen. Morro 1977 186p il lib bdg $16.99; pa $5.99

Grades: 3 4 5 **Fic**
1. Family life -- Fiction 2. Father-daughter relationship -- Fiction
ISBN 0-688-22114-9; 0-380-70916-3 pa
LC 77-1614
A Newbery Medal honor book, 1978
The family routine is upset during Ramona's year in second grade when her father unexpectedly loses his job.

Ramona and her mother; illustrated by Alan Tiegreen. HarperTrophy 2002 207p il pa $5.99
Grades: 3 4 5 **Fic**
1. Family life -- Fiction 2. Mother-daughter relationship -- Fiction
ISBN 0-380-70952-X
A reissue of the title first published 1979
Ramona at 7 1/2 sometimes feels discriminated against by being the youngest in the family.

Ramona forever; illustrated by Alan Tiegreen. HarperTrophy 2002 182p il pa $5.99
Grades: 3 4 5 **Fic**
1. School stories 2. Family life -- Fiction
ISBN 0-380-70960-0
A reissue of the title first published 1984
Ramona's year in third grade is highlighted by the arrival of Howie's rich uncle, a change in her afterschool situation, a surprise wedding, a death and a new arrival in the family, and her father's getting a job.

Ramona Quimby, age 8; illustrated by Alan Tiegreen. Morrow 1981 190p il $16.99; pa $5.99
Grades: 3 4 5 **Fic**
1. School stories 2. Family life -- Fiction
ISBN 0-688-00477-6; 0-380-70956-2 pa
LC 80028425
A Newbery Medal honor book, 1982
The further adventures of the Quimby family as Ramona enters the third grade.

Ramona the brave; illustrated by Tracy Dockray. HarperTrophy 2006 176p il pa $5.99
Grades: 3 4 5 **Fic**
1. School stories 2. Family life -- Fiction
ISBN 978-0-380-70959-5; 0-380-70959-7
A reissue of the title first published 1975
Six-year-old Ramona tries to cope with an unsympathetic first-grade teacher.

★ **Ramona** the pest; illustrated by Louis Darling. Morrow 1968 192p il $16.99; pa $5.99
Grades: 3 4 5 **Fic**
1. School stories 2. Kindergarten -- Fiction
ISBN 0-688-21721-4; 0-380-70954-6 pa
"Ramona Quimby comes into her own. Beezus keeps telling her to stop acting like a pest, but Ramona is five now, and she is convinced that she is 'not' a pest; she feels very mature, having entered kindergarten, and she immediately becomes enamoured of her teacher. Ramona's insistence on having just the right kind of boots, her matter-of-fact interest in how Mike Mulligan got to a bathroom, her determination to kiss one of the boys in her class, and her refusal to go back to kindergarten because Miss Binney didn't love her any more—all of these incidents or situations are completely believable and are told in a light, humorous, zesty style." Bull Cent Child Books
Other titles about Ramona are:
Beezus and Ramona (1955)
Ramona and her father (1977)

Ramona and her mother (1979)
Ramona, forever (1984)
Ramona Quimby, age 8 (1981)
Ramona the brave (1975)
Ramona's world (1999)

Ramona's world; illustrated by Alan Tiegreen. Morrow Junior Bks. 1999 192p il $15; lib bdg $14.93; pa $5.99
Grades: 3 4 5 **Fic**
1. School stories 2. Family life -- Fiction
ISBN 0-688-16816-7; 0-688-16818-3 lib bdg; 0-380-73272-6 pa
LC 99-19038
Follows the adventures of nine-year-old Ramona at home with big sister Beezus and baby sister Roberta and at school in Mrs. Meacham's class

Runaway Ralph; illustrated by Louis Darling. HarperTrophy 2000 175p il pa $5.99
Grades: 3 4 5 **Fic**
1. Mice -- Fiction 2. Camps -- Fiction
ISBN 0-380-70953-8
LC 2001278668
A reissue of the title first published 1970
Ralph the mouse runs away looking for freedom but winds up a prisoner at a summer camp.

Socks; illustrated by Beatrice Darwin. Morrow 1973 156p il $16.99; pa $5.99
Grades: 3 4 5 **Fic**
1. Cats -- Fiction 2. Infants -- Fiction
ISBN 0-688-20067-2; 0-380-70926-0 pa
"Not being child-centered, this may have a smaller audience than earlier Cleary books, but it is written with the same easy grace, the same felicitous humor and sharply observant eye." Bull Cent Child Books

Strider; illustrated by Paul O. Zelinsky. Morrow Junior Bks. 1991 179p il hardcover o.p. lib bdg $16.89; pa $5.99
Grades: 4 5 6 7 **Fic**
1. Dogs -- Fiction 2. Divorce -- Fiction
ISBN 0-688-09900-9; 0-688-09901-7 lib bdg; 0-380-71236-9 pa
LC 90-6608
Sequel to Dear Mr. Henshaw
In a series of diary entries, Leigh tells how he comes to terms with his parents' divorce, acquires joint custody of an abandoned dog, and joins the track team at school
"The development of the narrative is vintage Beverly Cleary, an inimitable blend of comic and poignant moments." Horn Book

Clements, Andrew
About average; Andrew Clements; illustrations by Mark Elliott. Simon & Schuster 2012 120 p. (hardback) $16.99
Grades: 3 4 5 6 **Fic**
1. Natural disasters -- Fiction 2. Personal appearance -- Fiction 3. Heroes -- Fiction 4. Ability -- Fiction 5. Schools -- Fiction 6. Tornadoes -- Fiction 7. Individuality -- Fiction
ISBN 1416997245; 9781416997245; 9781416997269
LC 2012015106
In author Andrew Clements's book, protagonist "Jordan Johnston is average. Not short, not tall. Not plump, not slim. Not blond, not brunette. Not gifted, not flunking out. Even her shoe size is average. She's ordinary for her school, for her town, for even the whole wide world, it seems. . . . Jordan feels doomed to a life of wallowing in the vast, soggy

middle. So she makes a goal: By the end of the year, she will discover her great talent." (Publisher's note)

★ **Extra** credit; illustrations by Mark Elliott. Atheneum Books for Young Readers 2009 183p il $16.99
Grades: 4 5 6 **Fic**
1. Letters -- Fiction 2. Illinois -- Fiction 3. Afghanistan -- Fiction 4. Family life -- Fiction
ISBN 978-1-4169-4929-9; 1-4169-4929-1
LC 2008-42877

"Unless [Abby] wants to repeat the sixth grade, she'll have to meet some specific conditions, including taking on an extra-credit project: find a pen pal in a foreign country. Simple enough (even for a girl who hates homework). Abby's first letter arrives at a small school in Afghanistan, and Sadeed Bayat is chosen to be her pen pal.... Well, kind of. He is the best writer, but he is also a boy, and in his village it is not appropriate for a boy to correspond with a girl. So his younger sister dictates and signs the letter. Until Sadeed decides what his sister is telling Abby isn't what he'd like Abby to know." (Publisher's note) "Grades four to seven." (Bull Cent Child Books)

Clements "successfully bridges two cultures in this timely and insightful dual-perspective story." Publ Wkly

Fear itself; illustrated by Adam Stower. Atheneum Books for Young Readers 2010 204p il (Benjamin Pratt & the Keepers of the School) $14.99; pa $5.99
Grades: 4 5 6 **Fic**
1. School stories 2. Mystery fiction 3. Riddles -- Fiction
ISBN 978-1-4169-3887-3; 1-4169-3887-7; 978-1-4169-3908-5 pa; 1-4169-3908-3 pa
LC 2010015876

As the new Keepers of the School, sixth-graders Ben and Jill must decipher a handful of clues written as maritime riddles to save their school from demolition by a greedy company.

"Expressive pen-and-ink illustrations add detail and excitement to the adventure, including the clues and coins found. Solid writing, likable characters, danger, a seaside setting, and now treasure will make readers eager for the third installment." SLJ

★ **Frindle**; [by] Andrew Clements; pictures of Brian Selznick. Simon & Schuster Books for Young Readers 2006 105p il $15.95
Grades: 4 5 6 **Fic**
1. School stories
ISBN 978-0-689-80669-8; 0-689-80669-8

A reissue of the title first published 1996

When he decides to turn his fifth grade teacher's love of the dictionary around on her, clever Nick Allen invents a new word and begins a chain of events that quickly moves beyond his control.

"Sure to be popular with a wide range of readers, this will make a great read-aloud as well." Booklist

Lost and found; illustrations by Mark Elliott. Atheneum Books for Young Readers 2008 161p il $16.99
Grades: 4 5 6 **Fic**
1. School stories 2. Ohio -- Fiction 3. Twins -- Fiction 4. Moving -- Fiction 5. Brothers -- Fiction
ISBN 978-1-4169-0985-9; 1-4169-0985-0
LC 2008-07018

Twelve-year-old identical twins Jay and Ray have long resented that everyone treats them as one person, and so they hatch a plot to take advantage of a clerical error at their new school and pretend they are just one.

"This slim story has all the elements readers have come to expect from Clements . . . : a school setting, likable secondary characters, sup-

portive adults and a challenge to the audience to see things from a different perspective." Publ Wkly

Lunch money; illustrations by Brian Selznick. Simon & Schuster Books for Young Readers 2005 222p il $15.95; pa $5.99
Grades: 4 5 6 **Fic**
1. School stories 2. Cartoons and comics -- Fiction 3. Money-making projects for children -- Fiction
ISBN 0-689-86683-6; 0-689-86685-2 pa
LC 2005-0006

Twelve-year-old Greg, who has always been good at moneymaking projects, is surprised to find himself teaming up with his lifelong rival Maura, to create a series of comic books to sell at school.

"The characters are rich with interesting quirks and motivations. . . . Along with providing a fast-paced and humorous story line, the author examines concepts of true wealth, teamwork, community mindedness and the value of creative expression. Selznick's pencil sketches add comic touches throughout." SLJ

★ **No** talking; illustrations by Mark Elliott. Simon & Schuster Books for Young Readers 2007 146p il $15.99; pa $5.99
Grades: 3 4 5 6 **Fic**
1. School stories
ISBN 1-4169-0983-4; 1-4169-0984-2 pa; 978-1-4169-0983-5; 978-1-4169-0984-2 pa
LC 2006-31883

The noisy fifth grade boys of Laketon Elementary School challenge the equally loud fifth grade girls to a "no talking" contest. "Ages eight to twelve." (N Y Times Book Rev)

"This is an interesting and thought-provoking book. . . . The plot quickly draws readers in and keeps them turning pages. . . . The black and-white pencil drawings add immediacy to the story." SLJ

The **report** card. Simon & Schuster Books for Young Reader 2004 173p
Grades: 4 5 6 **Fic**
1. School stories
ISBN 0689845154; 0689845243
LC 2003-738

Fifth-grader Nora Rowley has always hidden the fact that she is a genius from everyone because all she wants is to be normal, but when she comes up with a plan to prove that grades are not important, things begin to get out of control. "Ages eight to twelve." (N Y Times Book Rev)

"Clements has . . . built a solid story around a complex issue for which there is no easy answer, and to his credit, he never tries to offer one. . . . A novel sure to generate strong feelings and discussion." Booklist

Room one; a mystery or two. illustrations by Chris Blair. Simon & Schuster Books for Young Readers 2006 162p il $15.95; pa $5.99
Grades: 3 4 5 **Fic**
1. School stories 2. Mystery fiction 3. Nebraska -- Fiction 4. Homeless persons -- Fiction
ISBN 0-689-86686-9; 0-689-86687-9 pa

Ted Hammond, the only sixth grader in his small Nebraska town's one-room schoolhouse, searches for clues to the disappearance of a homeless family.

"There is a good balance of seriousness and humor with brisk, realistic dialogue and observations. Small black-and-white illustrations emphasize key points in the plot. Clements's usual excellent sense of character is evident." SLJ

Troublemaker; Andrew Clements; illustrated by Mark Elliott. Atheneum Books for Young Readers 2011 p. cm. $16.99

Grades: 4 5 6 7 **Fic**

1. Schools -- Fiction 2. Behavior -- Fiction 3. Brothers -- Fiction
ISBN 978-1-4169-4930-5; 1-4169-4930-5; 1416949305; 9781416949305

LC 2010045018

When his older brother gets in serious trouble, sixth-grader Clay decides to change his own mischief-making ways, but he cannot seem to shake his reputation as a troublemaker.

"Clements here enters into provocative territory and pulls it off like the pro he is. Kids will easily relate to Clay, and the secondary characters come alive as well." Kirkus

We the children; illustrated by Adam Stower. Atheneum Books for Young Readers 2010 142p il (Benjamin Pratt and the Keepers of the school) $14.99

Grades: 4 5 6 **Fic**

1. School stories 2. Mystery fiction 3. Adventure fiction 4. Massachusetts -- Fiction
ISBN 978-1-4169-3886-6; 1-4169-3886-9

LC 2009-36428

"Sixth-grader Ben Pratt is thrust into a mystery-adventure when his school's janitor shoves a gold coin in his hand, passing on the responsibility to save Oakes School from developers. Captain Oakes gave the school to the community back in 1783; its original building overlooks the Massachusetts town's harbor. But the land has been sold, and buildings will be razed to make way for a theme park. . . . Clements ably sets up his planned six-volume series with topical problems, convincing, likable characters and intriguing extra details." Kirkus

Another title in this series is Fear itself (2010)

Clifton, Lutricia

Freaky Fast Frankie Joe; Lutricia Clifton. Holiday House 2012 248 p. (hardcover) $16.95

Grades: 4 5 6 **Fic**

1. Boys -- Fiction 2. Family -- Fiction 3. Brothers -- Fiction 4. Illinois -- Fiction 5. Stepfamilies -- Fiction 6. Mothers and sons -- Fiction 7. Delivery of goods -- Fiction 8. Family life -- Illinois -- Fiction 9. Community life -- Illinois -- Fiction
ISBN 0823423670; 9780823423675

LC 2011019976

This is the story of Frankie Joe. While "his mom is in jail, Frankie Joe tries to adjust to living with his newly surfaced father, FJ, his stepmother and 'the four legitimate Huckaby sons.' The brothers tease Frankie Joe because, academically, he is 'freaky slow,' which is at odds with how fast he is when he runs or bikes. . . . Frankie Joe . . . launches Frankie Joe's Freaky Fast Delivery Service. With his income, he plans his escape back home from Illinois to Texas. But with each day Frankie Joe becomes more integrated into—and essential to—the town and the family, starting with his friendship with another town oddball, elderly Miss Peachcott. She tells Frankie Joe his family history." (Kirkus)

Coatsworth, Elizabeth Jane

The **cat** who went to heaven; [by] Elizabeth Coatsworth; illustrated by Lynd Ward. Macmillan 1958 62p il $17.95; pa $4.99

Grades: 4 5 6 7 **Fic**

1. Cats -- Fiction 2. Japan -- Fiction
ISBN 0-02-719710-7; 1-4169-4973-9 pa

LC 58-10917

First published 1930. The 1958 edition is a reprint with new illustrations of the book which won the Newbery Medal award in 1931

"Into this lovely and imaginative story the author has put something of the serenity and beauty of the East and of the gentleness of a religion that has a place even for the humblest of living creatures." N Y Times Book Rev

Cody, Matthew

Powerless. Alfred A. Knopf 2009 279p $15.99; lib bdg $18.99

Grades: 5 6 7 8 **Fic**

1. School stories 2. Moving -- Fiction 3. Bullies -- Fiction 4. Family life -- Fiction 5. Superheroes -- Fiction 6. Pennsylvania -- Fiction 7. Supernatural -- Fiction
ISBN 978-0-375-85595-5; 0-375-85595-5; 978-0-375-95595-2 lib bdg; 0-375-95595-X lib bdg

LC 2008-40885

Soon after moving to Noble's Green, Pennsylvania, twelve-year-old Daniel learns that his new friends have super powers that they will lose when they turn thirteen, unless he can use his brain power to protect them.

"This first novel has an intriguing premise, appealing characters, and a straightforward narrative arc with plenty of action as well as some serious moments." Booklist

Super; Matthew Cody. Alfred A. Knopf 2012 298 p. (Sequel to Powerless) (trade) $16.99; (lib. bdg.) $19.99

Grades: 5 6 7 8 **Fic**

1. Adventure fiction 2. Superheroes -- Fiction 3. Pennsylvania -- Fiction 4 Supernatural -- Fiction 5. Supervillains -- Fiction
ISBN 0375968946; 9780375868948; 9780375899799; 9780375968945

LC 2012008220

In this children's novel, by Matthew Cody, "Daniel Corrigan is as regular as can be, especially when compared to the Supers: kids in his new hometown with actual powers like flight and super strength. But . . . only he was able to stop the Shroud, a supervillian bent on stealing his newfound friends' powers. . . . Now Daniel himself is starting to display powers, while . . . his friends are losing theirs. . . . Daniel worries there may be something . . . sinister at work." (Publisher's note)

Coggin, Linda

The **dog**, Ray; Linda Coggin. Candlewick Press 2016 208 p. $15.99

Grades: 4 5 6 7 **Fic**

1. Dogs -- Fiction 2. Death -- Fiction 3. Reincarnation -- Fiction
ISBN 9780763679385

LC 2016947247

In this book, by Linda Coggin, "Daisy, age twelve, has died in a car accident. She finds herself in the afterworld, which resembles nothing more than a job center. Her soul is being returned to Earth, but not as a human being—she's returning as a dog. A dog who retains Daisy's thoughts and pluck and is determined to get back to her parents and to get back home." (Publisher's note)

"A tender and heartfelt tale that is sure to delight dog-loving readers or anyone who likes their happy endings to be hard-earned." SLJ

Cohagan, Carolyn

The **lost** children. Aladdin 2010 313p $16.99

Grades: 4 5 6 **Fic**

1. Friendship -- Fiction 2. Time travel -- Fiction 3. Voyages and travels -- Fiction
ISBN 978-1-4169-8616-4; 1-4169-8616-2

LC 2009-16608

When twelve-year-old Josephine falls through a worm-hole in her garden shed into another time and place, she realizes the troubles she has at home are minor compared to what she has to tackle now in the world where she has landed.

"The main characters are well developed, particularly the spunky and plain-spoken Ida, the laconic but loyal Fargus, and Josephine." Booklist

Cohen, Barbara

Thank you, Jackie Robinson; drawings by Richard Cuffari. Lothrop, Lee & Shepard Bks. 1974 125p il hardcover o.p. pa $4.99

Grades: 4 5 6   **Fic**

1. Baseball -- Fiction 2. Friendship -- Fiction 3. African Americans -- Fiction

ISBN 0-688-15293-7 pa

"Cohen's characters have unusual depth and her story succeeds as a warm, understanding consideration of friendship and, finally, death." Booklist

Cohen, Marina

The **Inn** Between; by Marina Cohen; illustrations by Sarah Watts. Roaring Brook Press 2016 208 p. (hardcover) $16.99

Grades: 5 6 7 8   **Fic**

1. Ghost stories 2. Horror fiction 3. Friendship -- Fiction 4. Hotels and motels -- Fiction 5. Horror tales 6. Horror stories 7. Ghosts -- Fiction 8. Best friends -- Fiction 9. Haunted places -- Fiction

ISBN 9781626722026

LC 2015004042

In this book, by Marina Cohen, "Quinn's best friend Kara has to move away [and] she goes on one last trip with Kara and her family. They stop over at the first hotel they see, a Victorian inn that instantly gives Quinn the creeps, and she begins to notice strange things happening around them. When Kara's parents and then brother disappear without a trace, the girls are stranded." (Publisher's note)

"Readers looking for a mystery with heart, humor, and hairy moments will be captivated" Kirkus

Cohn, Rachel

Two steps forward. Simon & Schuster for Young Readers 2006 227p $15.95

Grades: 5 6 7 8   **Fic**

1. Family life -- Fiction 2. Stepfamilies -- Fiction 3. Los Angeles (Calif.) -- Fiction

ISBN 0-689-86614-3

Sequel to The steps (2003)

Fourteen-year-old Annabel's extended family gathers in Los Angeles for several weeks over the summer where she must contend with step and half sisters and brothers and her own mother's failing second marriage.

"With the four blended families converging, tensions and humor run high. Chapters are told from alternating viewpoints. . . . This blended narrative offers a lighthearted glimpse into weighty matters." SLJ

Cole, Henry

★ A **nest** for Celeste; a story about art, inspiration, and the meaning of home. [written and illustrated by] Henry Cole. Katherine Tegen Books 2010 342p il $16.99; lib bdg $17.89

Grades: 4 5 6   **Fic**

1. Artists 2. Painters 3. Illustrators 4. Ornithologists 5. Home -- Fiction 6. Mice -- Fiction 7. Artists -- Fiction 8. Writers on science 9. New Orleans (La.) -- Fiction

ISBN 978-0-06-170410-9; 0-06-170410-5; 978-0-06-170411-6 lib bdg; 0-06-170411-3 lib bdg

LC 2009-11813

Celeste, a mouse longing for a real home, becomes a source of inspiration to teenaged Joseph, assistant to the artist and naturalist John James Audubon, at a New Orleans, Louisiana, plantation in 1821

"Evocative illustrations, compelling characters, and thoughtful reflections on the nature of home combine to powerful effect." Publ Wkly

Colfer, Eoin

Airman; [by] Eoin Colfer. Hyperion Books for Children 200❚ 412p $17.99; pa $7.99

Grades: 5 6 7 8 9   **Fi❚**

1. Adventure fiction 2. Young adult literature 3. Ireland -- Fictio❚ 4. Airplanes -- Fiction 5. Inventors -- Fiction 6. Prisoners - Fiction

ISBN 978-1-4231-0750-7; 1-4231-0750-0; 978-1-4231-0751-4 pa; 1-4231-0751-9 pa

LC 2007-3841

In the late nineteenth century, when Conor Broekhart discovers ❚ conspiracy to overthrow the king, he is branded a traitor, imprisoned and forced to mine for diamonds under brutal conditions while he plan❚ a daring escape from Little Saltee prison by way of a flying machine tha❚ he must design, build, and, hardest of all, trust to carry him to safety.

This is "polished, sophisticated storytelling. . . . A tour de force." Publ Wkly

★ **Artemis** Fowl. Hyperion Bks. for Children 2001 277p $16.95 pa $7.99

Grades: 5 6 7 8   **Fi❚**

1. Fantasy fiction 2. Fairies -- Fiction

ISBN 0-7868-0801-2; 1-4231-2452-9 pa

LC 2001-1663❚

When a twelve-year-old evil genius tries to restore his family fortun❚ by capturing a fairy and demanding a ransom in gold, the fairies figh❚ back with magic, technology, and a particularly nasty troll

"Colfer's antihero, techno fantasy is cleverly written and filled to th❚ brim with action, suspense, and humor." SLJ

Other titles in this series are:

Artemis Fowl: the Arctic incident (2002)
Artemis Fowl: the Eternity code (2003)
Artemis Fowl: the Opal deception (2005)
Artemis Fowl: the lost colony (2006)
Artemis Fowl: the time paradox (2008)
Artemis Fowl: the Atlantis complex (2010)

Artemis Fowl: the Arctic incident. Hyperion Books for Childre❚ 2002 277p $16.95

Grades: 5 6 7 8   **Fi❚**

1. Fantasy fiction 2. Fairies -- Fiction

ISBN 0-7868-0855-1

When Artemis learns that his father has been kidnapped by the Ru❚ sian mob, he races to the Arctic Circle to make a daring rescue where h❚ finds an old acquaintance, Captain Holly Short, who is investigating ❚ plot of the goblin mob.

"Colfer's finger is firmly on the pulse of his target market, and alon❚ with extra helpings of sly humor." Publ Wkly

Artemis Fowl: The Atlantis complex. Disney/Hyperion Book❚ 2010 357p $17.99

Grades: 5 6 7 8   **Fi❚**

1. Fantasy fiction 2. Magic -- Fiction 3. Fairies -- Fiction 4. Spac❚ and time -- Fiction

ISBN 978-1-4231-2819-9; 1-4231-2819-2

LC 201001715❚

Teenaged criminal mastermind Artemis Fowl must save the unde❚ water fairy metropolis of Atlantis from danger, while battling a psych❚ logical affliction known as the Atlantis Complex.

"Colfer keeps the action moving with laughs and gadgetry." Bookli❚

Artemis Fowl: the Eternity code. Miramax Books\Hyperion Boo❚ for Children 2003 309p $16.95; pa $5.99

Grades: 5 6 7 8 **Fic**
1. Fantasy fiction 2. Fairies -- Fiction
ISBN 0-7868-1914-6; 978-0-7868-5628-2 pa; 0-7868-5628-9 pa
LC 2003-46431

After Artemis uses stolen fairy technology to create a powerful microcomputer and it is snatched by a dangerous American businessman, Artemis, Juliet, Mulch, and the fairies join forces to try to retrieve it

This "features Colfer's trademark broad humor, engaging . . . characters, and high-speed action, not to mention the unlikely mix of magic and technology." Voice Youth Advocates

Artemis Fowl; The last guardian. Eoin Colfer. 1st U.S. ed. Disney Hyperion Books 2012 328 p. (hardcover) $18.99
Grades: 4 5 6 7 8 9 **Fic**
1. Fantasy fiction 2. Magic -- Fiction 3. Fairies -- Fiction 4. Spirits -- Fiction 5. Genius -- Fiction 6. Space and time -- Fiction
ISBN 1423161610; 9781423161615
LC 2012009997
Odyssey Honor Audiobook (2013)
This book by Eoin Colfer is the eighth installment of the Artemis Fowl series. "This time his arch rival has reanimated dead fairy warriors who were buried in the grounds of Fowl Manor. . . . The warriors don't seem to realize that the battle they were fighting when they died is long over. Artemis has until sunrise to get the spirits to vacate his brothers and go back into the earth where they belong." (Publisher's note)

Artemis Fowl: the lost colony; [by] Eoin Colfer. Hyperion Books for Children 2006 385p $16.95
Grades: 5 6 7 8 **Fic**
1. Fantasy fiction 2. Fairies -- Fiction
ISBN 0-7868-4956-8

Once again, Artemis will have to pair up with his old comrade, Captain Holly Short, to track down the missing demon and rescue him before the time spell dissolves and the lost demon colony returns violently to Earth.

"Colfer delivers not only continuous action but also witty wordplay and dialogue, understated humor, and plenty of magical technology and gadgetry." Booklist

Artemis Fowl: The opal deception. Miramax Books/Hyperion Books for Children 2005 342p $16.95; pa $7.99
Grades: 5 6 7 8 **Fic**
1. Fantasy fiction 2. Fairies -- Fiction
ISBN 0-7868-5289-5; 0-7868-5290-9 pa
LC 2006271670

After his last run-in with the fairies, Artemis Fowl's mind was wiped of memories of the world belowground and any goodness grudgingly learned is now gone with the young genius reverting to his criminal lifestyle.

Colfer "uses many different British accents and dialects to make both the human and the supernatural characters come alive, and his pacing is faultless throughout the dialogue and the narrative." SLJ

Artemis Fowl: the time paradox; [by] Eoin Colfer. Hyperion Books for Children 2008 391p $17.99
Grades: 4 5 6 7 8 **Fic**
1. Magic -- Fiction 2. Fairies -- Fiction 3. Space and time -- Fiction
ISBN 978-1-4231-0836-8; 1-4231-0836-1

Artemis's mother has contracted a deadly disease and the only cure lies in the brain fluid of African lemurs. Unfortunately, Artemis himself was responsible for making the lemurs extinct five years ago. Now he must enlist the aid of his fairy friends to travel back in time and save them. Not only that, but he must face his deadliest foe yet his younger self.

"The story flows with quick-witted humor and action-packed scenes, and Colfer's love of science shines through in the story's inventions and clever use of engineering. . . . The author once again offers an exhilarating ride through the fantastical world of Artemis Fowl." SLJ

The **forever** man; Eoin Colfer. Hyperion 2015 339 p. (W.A.R.P.) (hardback) $17.99
Grades: 5 6 7 8 **Fic**
1. Magic -- Fiction 2. Orphans -- Fiction 3. Time travel -- Fiction 4. Science fiction 5. Assassins -- Fiction 6. London (England) -- History -- 19th century -- Fiction 9. Great Britain -- History -- Victoria, 1837-1901 -- Fiction
ISBN 9781484726037
LC 2015015538
In this book in the W.A.R.P. series, by Eoin Colfer, "Riley, an orphan boy living in Victorian London, has achieved his dream of becoming a renowned magician, the Great Savano. He owes . . . his success to Chevie, [an] . . . FBI agent who traveled from the future in a time pod and helped him defeat his murderous master, Albert Garrick. But it is difficult for Riley to enjoy his new life, for he has always believed that Garrick will . . . return to seek vengeance." (Publisher's note)

The **hangman's** revolution; Eoin Colfer. Hyperion 2014 384 p. (W.A.R.P.) (hardback) $17.99
Grades: 5 6 7 8 **Fic**
1. Science fiction 2. Assassins -- Fiction 3. Time travel -- Fiction 4. London (England) -- Fiction 5. Great Britain -- History -- Fiction
ISBN 9781423161639; 1423161637
LC 2014001938
Sequel to: The Reluctant Assassin (2013)
In this book, "young FBI agent Chevie Savano arrives back in modern-day London after a time-trip to the Victorian age, to find the present very different from the one she left. Europe is being run by a Fascist movement known as the Boxites. . . . Chevie's memories come back to her in fragments, and just as she is learning about the WARP program from Professor Charles Smart, inventor of the time machine, he is killed by secret service police." (Publisher's note)

"Returning from her jaunt to Victorian London in The Reluctant Assassin, Chevie Savano finds that fellow time-traveler Colonel Box must have succeeded in his conquest, since she's now a cadet in the repressive Boxite Empire's military academy. Going back to the past, Chevie reunites with magician and good friend Riley to change history in this funny, high-octane adventure with thought-provoking time-travel insights." Horn Book

Iron man; Eoin Colfer. Marvel Press 2016 288 p. (hardcover) $16.99; (ebook) $16.99
Grades: 4 5 6 7 **Fic**
ISBN 9781484741603; 9781484744321
LC 2016943368
In this book, by Eoin Colfer, illustrated by Owen Richardson, "Tony Stark is known throughout the world as many things: billionaire, inventor, Avenger. But mainly for being the Invincible Iron Man. Just when Tony is about to add his pizzazz to an international eco-summit in Ireland, someone close to him forces him to question his role in making the world a more dangerous place with his high-tech weaponry. But Stark doesn't have much time to reflect before an old enemy presents him with an even greater challenge." (Publisher's note)

"Best of all, the author successfully captures the vulnerability and infuriatingly seductive arrogance of Stark, who polices the world to atone for his father's sins. Ideal for readers who are breathlessly awaiting the next film in the Marvel superhero franchise." Kirkus

The **reluctant** assassin; Eoin Colfer. Hyperion Book CH 2013 352 p. (W.A.R.P.) (hardcover) $17.99

Grades: 5 6 7 8 **Fic**

1. Science fiction 2. Assassins -- Fiction 3. Time travel -- Fiction 4. London (England) -- History -- 19th century -- Fiction 5. Great Britain -- History -- Victoria, 1837-1901 -- Fiction

ISBN 1423161629; 9781423161622

LC 2012048160

This is the first book in the time-travel W.A.R.R. series from Eoin Colfer. "After a bungled mission, [FBI agent] Chevie has been sent to London where she is 'babysitting a metal capsule,' which she learns is one end of a wormhole to the year 1898, when [young assassin] Riley (and a corpse) materialize, direct from the Victorian era." (Publishers Weekly)

Collier, James Lincoln

★ **My** brother Sam is dead; by James Lincoln Collier and Christopher Collier. Four Winds Press 1985 216p $17.95

Grades: 6 7 8 9 **Fic**

1. United States -- History -- 1775-1783, Revolution -- Fiction

ISBN 0-02-722980-7

LC 84-28787

A reissue of the title first published 1974

A Newbery Medal honor book, 1975

"In 1775 the Meeker family lived in Redding, Connecticut, a Tory community. Sam, the eldest son, allied himself with the Patriots. The youngest son, Tim, watched a rift in the family grow because of his brother's decision. Before the war was over the Meeker family had suffered at the hands of both the British and the Patriots." Shapiro. Fic for Youth. 3d edition

War comes to Willy Freeman; [by] James Lincoln Collier, Christopher Collier. Delacorte Press 1983 178p hardcover o.p. pa $5.99

Grades: 6 7 8 9 **Fic**

1. Slavery -- Fiction 2. African Americans -- Fiction 3. United States -- History -- 1775-1783, Revolution -- Fiction

ISBN 0-440-49504-0 pa

LC 82-70317

This deals with events prior to those in Jump ship to freedom, and involves members of the same family. "Willy is thirteen when she begins her story, which takes place during the last two years of the Revolutionary War; her father, a free man, has been killed fighting against the British, her mother has disappeared. Willy makes her danger-fraught way to Fraunces Tavern in New York, her uncle, Jack Arabus, having told her that Mr. Fraunces may be able to help her. She works at the tavern until the war is over, goes to the Arabus home to find her mother dying, and participates in the trial (historically accurate save for the fictional addition of Willy) in which her uncle sues for his freedom and wins." Bull Cent Child Books

Collins, Pat Lowery

Daughter of winter. Candlewick Press 2010 272p $16.99

Grades: 4 5 6 7 **Fic**

1. Winter -- Fiction 2. Massachusetts -- Fiction 3. Wampanoag Indians -- Fiction 4. Wilderness survival -- Fiction

ISBN 978-0-7636-4500-7; 0-7636-4500-1

LC 2009049099

In the mid-nineteenth-century shipbuilding town of Essex, Massachusetts, twelve-year-old Addie learns a startling secret about her past when she escapes servitude by running away to live in the snowy woods and meets an elderly Wampanoag woman.

"Collins' sense of place, incorporation of cultural and historical details, and the richly evoked winter setting make for a vividly imagined novel. An engaging survival story intertwined with a search for identity." Booklist

Collins, Suzanne

Gregor and the Code of Claw. Scholastic Press 2007 412p (Underland chronicles) $17.99

Grades: 4 5 6 7 **Fic**

1. Fantasy fiction

ISBN 978-0-439-79143-4; 0-439-79143-X

LC 2006028839

When twelve-year-old Gregor finally learns the ancient prophecy, which foretells his death, he must gather his courage to defend Regalia from the army of rats, take his mother and sister home safely, and fight his own dark side.

Gregor and the curse of the warmbloods; by Suzanne Collins. 1st ed; Scholastic 2005 358p (Underland chronicles) $16.95

Grades: 4 5 6 7 **Fic**

1. Fantasy fiction

ISBN 0-439-65623-0

LC 2004-59010

Sequel to Gregor and the prophecy of bane (2004)

Eleven-year-old Gregor and his younger sister, Boots, return to the Underworld beneath New York City to find the cure for a terrible plague that threatens the life of their mother, as well as the lives of the people, bats, and rats who populate the underworld.

This is a "fast-paced, suspenseful story." Booklist

Gregor and the marks of secret. Scholastic Press 2006 343p (Underland chronicles) $16.99

Grades: 4 5 6 7 **Fic**

1. Fantasy fiction

ISBN 0-439-79145-6

LC 2005-27969

Twelve-year-old Gregor returns to the world beneath New York City, where he joins forces with Princess Lexa and Ripred the rat to defend the Underlanders and the Nibblers from the army led by the adolescent rat king, the Bane.

Gregor and the prophecy of Bane. Scholastic Press 2004 312p (Underland chronicles) $16.95

Grades: 4 5 6 7 **Fic**

1. Fantasy fiction

ISBN 0-439-65075-5

Sequel to Gregor the Overlander

In his second adventure, eleven-year-old Gregor returns to the world beneath New York City to rescue his kidnapped sister, Boots, and fulfill a prophecy that will restore peace to the people, bats, rats, cockroaches, and spiders who populate the underworld.

"Fans will not be disappointed with this exciting, action-packed sequel, whose ending suggests more adventures to come." Booklist

★ **Gregor** the Overlander. Scholastic Press 2003 311p (Underland chronicles) $16.95; pa $5.99

Grades: 4 5 6 7 **Fic**

1. Fantasy fiction

ISBN 0-439-43536-6; 0-439-67813-7 pa

LC 2002-155865

When eleven-year-old Gregor and his two-year-old sister are pulled into a strange underground world, they trigger an epic battle involving men, bats, rats, cockroaches, and spiders while on a quest foretold by ancient prophecy

"Collins creates a fascinating, vivid, highly original world and a superb story to go along with it." Booklist

Other titles in this series are:
Gregor and the prophecy of Bane (2004)
Gregor and the curse of the warmbloods (2005)
Gregor and the marks of secret (2006)
Gregor and the code of claw (2007)

Collodi, Carlo

★ The **adventures** of Pinocchio; [by] Carlo Collodi; illustrated by Roberto Innocenti; designed by Rita Marshall. Creative Editions 2005 191p il $24.95

Grades: 3 4 5 6   **Fic**
1. Fairy tales 2. Puppets and puppet plays -- Fiction
ISBN 1-56846-190-9

LC 2003-62740

A wooden puppet full of tricks and mischief, with a talent for getting into and out of trouble, wants more than anything else to become a real boy

Innocenti's illustrations have a "19th-century European setting, and the careful composition, use of perspective, and dark earth tones are an apt visual expression of this complex moral tale." SLJ

★ **Pinocchio**; illustrated by Quentin Greban; translated by Claude Sartirano and Juanita Havill. North-South Books 2010 80p il $19.95
Grades: 3 4 5 6   **Fic**
1. Fantasy fiction 2. Puppets and puppet plays -- Fiction
ISBN 978-0-7358-2324-2; 0-7358-2324-3

A wooden puppet full of tricks and mischief, with a talent for getting into and out of trouble, wants more than anything else to become a real boy.

"This edition of the Italian classic Pinocchio strikes a good balance between nineteenth-century writing conventions and modern readers' tastes. Translated and somewhat abridged, the text offers a story that is true to the original in spirit and detail. . . . Gréban . . . creates distinctive illustrations with notable clarity of line, drama of composition, and subtlety of watercolor washes. Even libraries with several editions of Pinocchio should consider adding this one, for the clarity and grace of its writing as well as the luminous beauty of its illustrations." Booklist

Columbus, Chris, 1958-

Battle of the beasts; Chris Columbus, Ned Vizzini, Greg Call; [edited by] Alessandra Balzer. Balzer + Bray 2014 480 p. (House of secrets) (hardcover) $17.99

Grades: 5 6 7 8   **Fic**
1. Fantasy fiction 2. Adventure fiction 3. Witches -- Fiction 4. Brothers and sisters -- Fiction
ISBN 0062192493; 9780062192493

LC 2013956357

This book, by Chris Columbus and Ned Vizzini, is the sequel to "House of Secrets." "Since the siblings' last adventure, life in the Walker household is much improved the family is rich and the Wind Witch is banished. But no Walker will be safe until she is found, and summoning her to San Francisco brings all the danger that comes with her and puts the Walkers in the crosshairs of a mysterious journey through Denver Kristoff's books." (Publisher's note)

"An exorcism is just the beginning; the siblings also battle gladiators in ancient Rome, outwit cyborg Nazis, and face Yeti-like monsters in a Tibetan monastery in another imaginative, fast-paced adventure that is sure to please fans. Vizzini's older readers will miss his elegant and often eloquent, wry tone. Here's hoping another writer steps in to finish the planned trilogy." Booklist

Clash of the Worlds; Chris Columbus, Ned Vizzini, and Chris Rylander. Harpercollins Childrens Books 2016 528 p. illustrations (House of secrets) $17.99

Grades: 5 6 7 8   **Fic**
1. Books -- Fiction 2. Magic -- Fiction 3. Imaginary creatures -- Fiction
ISBN 0062192515; 9780062192516

In this novel, by Chris Colubus, Ned Vizzini, and Chris Rylander, "with the police closing in, the Walkers must figure out how to save their giant friend. When a frost beast is spotted in Santa Rosa—and more mystical creatures start appearing all over America—it's soon clear that the characters from Denver Kristoff's works are invading the real world. It's up to Brendan, Eleanor, and Cordelia to reenter the book world one last time to keep the worlds from colliding, causing mass destruction." (Publisher's note)

"The action is nonstop, and likable side characters find themselves paying high prices as the kids skip through Western, science-fiction, fantasy, and other worlds. The children have to work hard for their happy ending. Generally, an enjoyable book with high stakes and a solid ending..." Kirkus

House of secrets; Chris Columbus; Ned Vizzini. 1st ed. Balzer + Bray 2013 496 p. (hardcover) $17.99

Grades: 5 6 7 8   **Fic**
1. Haunted houses -- Fiction 2. Fantasy fiction 3. Adventure fiction 4. Fantasy 5. Dwellings -- Fiction 6. Supernatural -- Fiction 7. Books and reading -- Fiction 8. Brothers and sisters -- Fiction
ISBN 0062192469; 9780062192462

LC 2012051815

In this juvenile fantasy story, by Chris Columbus and Ned Vizzini, three siblings "relocate to an old Victorian house that used to be the home of occult novelist Denver Kristoff. . . . By the time the Walkers realize that one of their neighbors has sinister plans for them, they're banished to a primeval forest way off the grid. . . . Bloodthirsty medieval warriors patrol the woods around them, supernatural pirates roam the neighboring seas, and a power-hungry queen rules the land." (Publisher's note)

Coman, Carolyn

★ The **Memory** Bank; [by] Carolyn Coman & Rob Shepperson. Arthur A. Levine Books 2010 263p il $16.99

Grades: 3 4 5 6   **Fic**
1. Dreams -- Fiction 2. Memory -- Fiction 3. Sisters -- Fiction 4. Sabotage -- Fiction 5. Banks and banking -- Fiction
ISBN 978-0-545-21066-9; 0-545-21066-6

When Hope learns that, while her memory account is seriously low, she is a champion dreamer, she stays at the World Wide Memory Bank trying to locate her sister Honey, whom their parents abandoned and told Hope to forget.

"Energetic Quentin Blake-like pencil illustrations tell the tale of Hope's beloved Honey as she falls in with a rebel lot of lost children who threaten to overthrow the WWMB. Brilliantly crafted, thoroughly enjoyable and, though so very like Dahl, unique as a fascinating new way to ponder dreams and memories." Kirkus

Sneaking suspicions; [by] Carolyn Coman; drawings by Rob Shepperson. 1st ed.; Front Street 2007 245p il $16.95

Grades: 3 4 5 6   **Fic**
1. Siblings -- Fiction 2. Family life -- Fiction 3. Everglades (Fla.) -- Fiction 4. Swindlers and swindling -- Fiction
ISBN 978-1-59078-491-4; 1-59078-491-X

LC 2006101610

Sequel to The big house (2004)

Ivy and Ray accompany their parents on a trip to the Florida Everglades in order to find their only living relative, a distant cousin who, according to their great-grandfather's memoirs, absconded with a valuable, if unspecified, item.

"The children are believable characters. . . . Shepperson's black-and-white illustrations sprinkled liberally throughout masterfully capture the emotions of the Fitts family." SLJ

Comerford, Lynda B.

Rissa Bartholomew's declaration of independence. Scholastic Press 2009 250p $16.99

Grades: 4 5 6 7   **Fic**

1. School stories 2. Illinois -- Fiction 3. Friendship -- Fiction
ISBN 978-0-545-05058-6; 0-545-05058-8

LC 2008-26618

Having told off all of her old friends at her eleventh birthday party, Rissa starts middle school determined to make new friends while being herself, not simply being part of a herd.

"Rissa's troubles are ones that many middle-schoolers will identify with: new schools, shifting allegiances, new feelings, and changing bodies. First-time novelist Comerford gives her readers an appealing heroine who, despite her flaws and quirks, finds herself along the way." Booklist

Compestine, Ying Chang

Crouching tiger; illustrated by Yan Nascimbene. Candlewick Press 2011 il $16.99

Grades: 2 3 4   **Fic**

1. Grandfathers -- Fiction 2. Martial arts -- Fiction 3. Chinese Americans -- Fiction 4. Racially mixed people -- Fiction 5. Chinese -- United States -- Fiction
ISBN 978-0-7636-4642-4; 0-7636-4642-3

LC 2010048133

When Ming Da's Chinese grandpa comes to visit, he overcomes his initial embarrassment at his grandfather's traditions and begins to appreciate him.

"Compestine creates a simple portrait of a familiar cultural bridge, conveying Vinson's awe, shyness and embarrassment about his serious grandfather. Nascimbene captures both the compact energy of the small boy and the graceful, composed grace of the adult. His contained, quiet style with warm colors nicely matches the low-key narrative. . . . A celebration of family and Chinese New Year along with a simple introduction to Wudang martial arts, especially tai chi-and to the idea that strength can be gentle." Kirkus

Condie, Ally

Summerlost; a novel. Ally Condie. Dutton Children's Books 2016 272 p. (hardback) $17.99

Grades: 5 6 7 8   **Fic**

1. Summer theater 2. Mystery fiction 3. Loss (Psychology) -- Fiction
ISBN 9780399187193; 0399187197

LC 2015028569

In this young adult novel, by Ally Condie, "it's the first real summer since the devastating accident that killed Cedar's father and younger brother. But now Cedar and what's left of her family are returning to the town of Iron Creek for the summer. Cedar follows [Leo] to the renowned Summerlost theatre festival. Soon, she not only has a new friend in Leo [but] finds herself surrounded by mystery. The mystery of the tragic, too-short life of the Hollywood actress who haunts the halls of Summerlost." (Publisher's note)

"There's no monumental grief breakthrough, nor should there be: this is the realistic going on, day by day, after bereavement. Honest, lovely, and sad." Kirkus

Conford, Ellen

Annabel the actress starring in Gorilla my dreams; illustrated by Renée Williams-Andriani. Simon & Schuster Bks. for Young Readers 1999 64p il hardcover o.p. pa $3.99

Grades: 2 3 4   **Fic**

1. Actors -- Fiction 2. Parties -- Fiction
ISBN 0-689-81404-6; 0-689-83883-2 pa

LC 97-39449

Though a little disappointed that her first acting part is to be a gorilla at a birthday party, Annabel determines to really get into the role

"The vocabulary is appropriate for those graduating from easy-readers, but the language is never stilted. Amusing pen-and-ink illustrations appear on almost every page." SLJ

Other titles about Annabel are:
Annabel the actress starring in ¿Hound of the Barkervilles¿ (2002)
Annabel the actress, starring in ¿Camping it up¿ (2004)
Annabel the actress, starring in ¿Just a little extra¿ (2000)

★ A **case** for Jenny Archer; illustrated by Diane Palmisciano. Little, Brown 1988 61p il (Springboard books) hardcover o.p. pa $4.99

Grades: 2 3 4   **Fic**

1. Mystery fiction
ISBN 0-316-01486-9 pa

LC 88-14169

After reading three mysteries in a row, Jenny becomes convinced that the neighbors across the street are up to no good and decides to investigate

"This lots-of-fun advanced easy reader contains eight chapters, all about three pages long, with large, clear print, and lots of white space. . . The children here are lively, the adults funny, wise, and supportive." SLJ

Other titles about Jenny Archer are:
Can do, Jenny Archer (1991)
Get the picture, Jenny Archer (1994)
Jenny Archer, author (1989)
Jenny Archer to the rescue (1990)
A job for Jenny Archer (1988)
Nibble, nibble, Jenny Archer (1993)
What's cooking, Jenny Archer (1989)

Conkling, Winifred

Sylvia and Aki. Tricycle Press 2011 151p $16.99; lib bdg $19.99

Grades: 3 4 5 6   **Fic**

1. Farm life -- Fiction 2. Race relations -- Fiction 3. Mexican Americans -- Fiction 4. Segregation in education -- Fiction 5. Poston Relocation Center (Ariz.) -- Fiction 6. Japanese Americans -- Evacuation and relocation, 1942-1945 -- Fiction
ISBN 978-1-58246-337-7; 1-58246-337-9; 978-1-58246-397-1 lib bdg; 1-58246-397-2 lib bdg

LC 2010024182

At the start of World War II, Japanese-American third-grader Aki and her family are sent to an internment camp in Poston, Arizona, while Mexican-American third-grader Sylvia's family leases their Orange County, California, farm and begins a fight to stop school segregation.

"Told in alternating chapters from the girls' points of view, this story about institutional racism will enlighten readers to events in recent history. From the court case of Mendez v. Westminster to the conditions at Poston, readers will be moved by this novel based on true events." SLJ

Conly, Jane Leslie

Crazy lady! HarperCollins Pubs. 1993 180p lib bdg $18.89; pa $5.99

Grades: 5 6 7 8   **Fic**

1. Death -- Fiction 2. Alcoholism -- Fiction 3. Prejudices -- Fiction 4. People with physical disabilities -- Fiction
ISBN 0-06-021360-4 lib bdg; 0-06-440571-0 pa

LC 92-18348

A Newbery Medal honor book, 1994

As he tries to come to terms with his mother's death, Vernon finds solace in his growing relationship with the neighborhood outcasts, an alcoholic and her retarded son

The narration "is fast and blunt, and the conversations are lively and true." Bull Cent Child Books

★ **Murder** afloat. Hyperion Books for Children 2010 164p $17.99

Grades: 5 6 7 8   **Fic**
1. Adventure fiction 2. Kidnapping -- Fiction 3. Seafaring life -- Fiction

ISBN 978-1-4231-0416-2; 1-4231-0416-1

Benjamin Franklin Orville is caught up in a scuffle, kidnapped with a group of immigrants and forced to work aboard the Ella Dawn—one of the most ill-reputed oystering vessels in Baltimore.

"With compelling characters and details of the little-known process of oystering woven throughout, Conly's tale touches on the hardships of many German immigrants to the U.S., whose desperate plights offer parallels to contemporary immigration issues. Short chapters and suspenseful plot twists will keep readers turning the pages in this engaging historical adventure." Booklist

Connor, Leslie
All Rise for the Honorable Perry T. Cook; Leslie Connor. Harpercollins Childrens Books 2016 400 p. (hardcover) $16.99

Grades: 4 5 6 7 8   **Fic**
1. Children of prisoners -- Fiction 2. Mother-son relationship -- Fiction

ISBN 0062333461; 9780062333469

LC 2015940765

In this middle-grade novel, by Leslie Connor, "Eleven-year-old Perry was born and raised by his mom at the Blue River Co-ed Correctional Facility in tiny Surprise, Nebraska. His mom is a resident on Cell Block C.... That is, until a new district attorney discovers the truth—and Perry is removed from the facility and forced into a foster home.... Desperate to be reunited with his mom, Perry goes on a quest for answers about her past crime." (Publisher's note)

"With complex, memorable characters, a situation that demands sympathy, and a story that's shown, not just told, this is fresh and affecting. Well-crafted, warm, and wonderful." Kirkus

★ **Crunch**. Katherine Tegen Books 2010 330p $16.99; lib bdg $17.89

Grades: 5 6 7 8   **Fic**
1. Bicycles -- Fiction 2. Siblings -- Fiction 3. Family life -- Fiction 4. New England -- Fiction 5. Energy conservation -- Fiction 6. Business enterprises -- Fiction

ISBN 0-06-169229-8; 0-06-169233-6 lib bdg; 978-0-06-169229-1; 978-0-06-169233-8 lib bdg

LC 2009-24339

Dewey Marriss "never guessed that the gas pumps would run dry the same week he promised to manage the family's bicycle-repair business. Suddenly everyone needs a bike. And nobody wants to wait. Meanwhile, the crunch has stranded Dewey's parents far up north with an empty fuel tank and no way home. It's up to Dewey and his sister, Lil, to look after their younger siblings and run the bike shop on their own.... Age ten and up." (Publisher's note)

This novel concerns "the trials and tribulations of 14-year-old Dewey Mariss and his family. His parents are away from home, unable to return because of a gasoline shortage. Running their small family business, the Bike Barn, with his younger brother and helping older sister Lil look after the five-year-old twins keeps Dewey plenty busy.... Characters are colorful but believable, dialogue crisp and amusing. The New

England setting is attractively realized, and the underlying energy crisis treated seriously but not sensationally." Kirkus

★ **Waiting** for normal. Katherine Tegen Books 2008 290p $16.99; lib bdg $17.89

Grades: 5 6 7 8   **Fic**
1. Mothers -- Fiction 2. Family life -- Fiction 3. New York (State) -- Fiction

ISBN 978-0-06-089088-9; 0-06-089088-6; 978-0-06-089089-6 lib bdg; 0-06-089089-4 lib bdg

LC 2007-06881

Twelve-year-old Addie tries to cope with her mother's erratic behavior and being separated from her beloved stepfather and half-sisters when she and her mother go to live in a small trailer by the railroad tracks on the outskirts of Schenectady, New York.

"Connor . . . treats the subject of child neglect with honesty and grace in this poignant story.... Characters as persuasively optimistic as Addie are rare, and readers will gravitate to her." Publ Wkly

Conrad, Pam
★ **My** Daniel. Harper & Row 1989 137p pa $5.99

Grades: 5 6 7 8   **Fic**
1. Nebraska -- Fiction

ISBN 0-06-440309-2 pa

LC 88-19850

"Rendering scenes from both the past and the present with equal skill, Conrad is at the peak of her storytelling powers." Publ Wkly

Cook, Kacy
Nuts. Marshall Cavendish 2010 155p $16.99

Grades: 4 5 6   **Fic**
1. Ohio -- Fiction 2. Pets -- Fiction 3. Squirrels -- Fiction 4. Family life -- Fiction

ISBN 978-0-7614-5652-0; 0-7614-5652-X

LC 2009-04354

When eleven-year-old Nell finds a tiny baby squirrel on the ground in her yard, she begs her parents to let her raise it as a pet, even after the research she does shows that this is not a good idea.

"Cook does a nice job of taking a seemingly innocent plot and almost sneaking in (a little like pureed vegetables) much weightier themes of love, honesty and death.... The straightforward, upbeat prose consistently engages readers, and her characters are dead on. There's more here than meets the eye." Kirkus

Coombs, Kate
The **runaway** dragon. Farrar, Straus and Giroux 2009 292p $16.99

Grades: 5 6 7 8   **Fic**
1. Fairy tales 2. Dragons -- Fiction 3. Princesses -- Fiction

ISBN 978-0-374-36361-1; 0-374-36361-7

LC 2008034362

Sequel to: The runaway princess (2006)

When her beloved dragon Laddy runs away from the castle, Princess Meg and some of her friends embark on a quest to find him and bring him home.

"Funny, lighthearted.... Enchanted forests, rampant transmogrification, evil sorceresses and giants are all fine fodder for Coombs's inventive twists on traditional fairy tales." Kirkus

The **runaway** princess. Farrar, Straus and Giroux 2006 279p $17

Grades: 5 6 7 8   **Fic**
1. Fairy tales 2. Dragons -- Fiction 3. Princesses -- Fiction

ISBN 0-374-35546-0

LC 2005-51225

Fifteen-year-old Princess Meg uses magic and her wits to rescue a baby dragon and escape the unwanted attentions of princes hoping to gain her hand in marriage through a contest arranged by her father, the king.

"This witty, humorous tale will be popular with fantasy buffs who enjoy takeoffs on fairy tales." Booklist

Another title about Princess Meg is:
The runaway dragon (2009)

Cooper, Abby

Sticks & stones; Abby Cooper. Farrar, Straus & Giroux 2016 288 p. (hardback) $16.99
Grades: 4 5 6 7 8 **Fic**
1. School stories 2. Self-acceptance -- Fiction 3. Schools -- Fiction 4. Diseases -- Fiction 5. Friendship -- Fiction 6. Middle schools -- Fiction
ISBN 0374302871; 9780374302870
LC 2015039454

In this juvenile novel, by Abby Cooper, "Elyse . . . has to deal with cognadjivisibilitis, or CAV: a disease that causes words to appear all over her body whenever they're spoken aloud. . . . As if that's not embarrassing enough, Elyse has just discovered that anything she thinks about herself (positive or negative) shows up, too. Now somebody at her school is sending her secret notes, claiming to want to help her with her predicament." (School Library Journal)

"Without being heavy-handed or sad, the book encourages resilience and addresses the pervasive self-esteem issues that plague so many young people today." Booklist

Cooper, Ilene

Lucy on the ball; illustrated by David Merrell. Random House 2011 102p il (Absolutely Lucy) lib bdg $12.99; pa $4.99
Grades: 2 3 4 **Fic**
1. Dogs -- Fiction 2. Soccer -- Fiction
ISBN 978-0-375-95559-4 lib bdg; 0-375-95559-3 lib bdg; 978-0-375-85559-7 pa; 0-375-85559-9 pa; 978-0-375-89820-4 e-book
LC 2010005183

Lucy the beagle does not mind her humans very well until third-grader Bobby joins a soccer team, Lucy becomes the mascot, and the coach gives Lucy obedience training.

Lucy on the loose; illustrated by Amanda Harvey. Golden Books 2000 76p il (Absolutely Lucy) hardcover o.p. pa $4.99
Grades: 2 3 4 **Fic**
1. Cats -- Fiction 2. Dogs -- Fiction 3. Shyness -- Fiction 4. Lost and found possessions -- Fiction
ISBN 0-307-46508-X; 0-307-26508-0 pa
LC 00021432

When his beagle Lucy runs off chasing a big orange cat, Bobby must overcome his shyness in order to find them again.

Cooper, Susan

★ The **Boggart**. Margaret K. McElderry Bks. 1993 196p hardcover o.p. pa $5.99
Grades: 4 5 6 7 **Fic**
1. Canada -- Fiction 2. Scotland -- Fiction 3. Supernatural -- Fiction
ISBN 0-689-50576-0; 0-689-86930-4 pa
LC 92-15527

After visiting the castle in Scotland which her family has inherited and returning home to Canada, twelve-year-old Emily finds that she has accidentally brought back with her a boggart, an invisible and mischievous spirit with a fondness for practical jokes

"Using both electronics and theater as metaphors for magic, Cooper has extended the world of high fantasy into contemporary children's lives through scenes superimposing the ordinary and the extraordinary." Bull Cent Child Books

Another title about the Boggart is:
The Boggart and the monster (1997)

The **Boggart** and the monster. Margaret K. McElderry Bks. 1997 185p $17.99; pa $5.99 **Fic**
1. Supernatural -- Fiction
ISBN 0-689-81330-9; 0-689-86931-2 pa
LC 96-42389

The Boggart, the invisible and mischievous spirit living in the Scottish Castle Keep, sets out to help save Nessie the Loch Ness Monster one of its few remaining cousins

"Cooper adroitly incorporates ancient lore into a contemporary setting while producing an imaginative and compelling tale." Publ Wkly

The **dark** is rising. Simon Pulse 2007 244p il pa $8.99
Grades: 4 5 6 7 **Fic**
1. Fantasy fiction 2. Good and evil -- Fiction 3. Great Britain -- Fiction
ISBN 978-1-416-94965-7; 1-416-94965-8
Sequel to: Over sea, under stone
A reissue of the title first published 1973
On his eleventh birthday, Will Stanton discovers that he is the last of the Old Ones, destined to seek the six magical Signs that will enable the Old Ones to triumph over the evil forces of the Dark.

★ **Ghost** Hawk; by Susan Cooper. 1st ed. Margaret K. McElderry Books 2013 328 p. map (hardcover) $16.99
Grades: 5 6 7 8 **Fic**
1. Friendship -- Fiction 2. Native Americans -- North America 3. Native Americans -- Relations with early settlers 4. Ghosts -- Fiction 5. Survival -- Fiction 6. Coming of age -- Fiction 7. Wampanoag Indians -- Fiction 8. Massachusetts -- History -- New Plymouth, 1620-1691 -- Fiction
ISBN 1442481412; 9781442481411; 9781442481435
LC 201203989.

Parents' Choice: Gold Medal Fiction (2013)

This novel is "a story of adventure and friendship between a young Native American and a colonial New England settler. Little Hawk is sent into the woods alone [and] if [he] survives three moons by himself, he will be a man. John Wakely is only ten when his father dies. . . . John sees how quickly the relationships between settlers and natives are deteriorating. His friendship with Little Hawk will put both boys in grave danger." (Publisher's note)

Greenwitch. Simon Pulse 2007 147p pa $8.99
Grades: 4 5 6 7 **Fic**
1. Fantasy fiction 2. Good and evil -- Fiction 3. Great Britain -- Fiction
ISBN 978-1-416-94966-4; 1-416-94966-6
Sequel to: The dark is rising
A reissue of the title first published 1974
Jane's invitation to witness the making of the Greenwitch begins a series of sinister events in which she and her two brothers help the Old Ones recover the grail stolen by the Dark.

★ The **grey king**; illustrated by Michael Heslop. Atheneum Pubs 1975 208p il $19.99; pa $8.99
Grades: 5 6 7 8 **Fic**
1. Fantasy fiction 2. Wales -- Fiction 3. Good and evil -- Fiction
ISBN 0-689-50029-7; 1-4169-4967-4 pa

Awarded the Newbery Medal, 1976

"So well-crafted that it stands as an entity in itself, the novel . . . is nevertheless strengthened by its relationship to the preceding volumes—as the individual legends within the Arthurian cycles take on deeper significance in the context of the whole. A spellbinding tour de force." Horn Book

★ **King** of shadows. Margaret K. McElderry Bks. 1999 186p $16; pa $4.99; pa $6.99
Grades: 5 6 7 8   **Fic**
1. Poets 2. Authors 3. Dramatists 4. Actors -- Fiction 5. Globe Theatre (London, England) -- Fiction
ISBN 0-689-82817-9; 0-689-84445-X pa; 9780689844454 pa
LC 98-51127
Boston Globe Horn Book Honor Book (2000)

"Nat Field is thrilled when theater director Richard Babbage chooses him to become a player in the Company of Boys, an American summer drama troupe that will appear in Shakespeare's A Midsummer Night's Dream at the new replica of the Globe Theater in London. Shortly after his arrival in England, though, Nat feels ill and falls into a troubled sleep. To the doctor's astonishment, he seems to be suffering from the effects of the bubonic plague. He awakens in 1599 as another Nat Field, a child actor from St. Paul's School who is about to go to the Globe to rehearse A Midsummer Night's Dream in the role of Puck." (Booklist) "Grades six to nine." (Bull Cent Child Books)

"Cleverly explicating old and new acting and performance techniques, Susan Cooper entertains her contemporary readers while giving them a first-rate theatrical education." N Y Times Book Rev

The **magician's** boy; illustrated by Serena Riglietti. Margaret K. McElderry Bks. 2005 100p il $15.95; pa $7.95
Grades: 2 3 4   **Fic**
1. Fairy tales 2. Magicians -- Fiction
ISBN 0-689-87622-X; 1-4169-1555-9 pa
A boy who works for a magician meets familiar fairy tale characters when he is transported to the Land of Story in search of a missing puppet
"Fanciful and mildly amusing, the dreamlike story flows along smoothly through a strange yet vaguely familiar wonderland. Riglietti contributes a series of expressive, stylized illustrations." Booklist

★ **Over** sea, under stone; illustrated by Margery Gill. Harcourt Brace Jovanovich 1966 252p il $19; pa $5.99
Grades: 5 6 7 8   **Fic**
1. Fantasy fiction 2. Young adult literature 3. Good and evil -- Fiction 4. Great Britain -- Fiction
ISBN 0-15-259034-X; 0-689-84035-7 pa
First published 1965 in the United Kingdom
Three children on a holiday in Cornwall find an ancient manuscript which sends them on a dangerous quest for a grail that would reveal the true story of King Arthur and that entraps them in the eternal battle between the forces of the Light and the forces of the Dark.
"The air of mysticism and the allegorical quality of the continual contest between good and evil add much value to a fine plot, setting, and characterization." Horn Book
Other titles in this series are:
The dark is rising (1973)
Greenwitch (1974)
The grey king (1975)
Silver on the tree (1977)

Silver on the tree. Atheneum Pubs. 1977 ix, 269p $19.99; pa $8.99

Grades: 5 6 7 8   **Fic**
1. Fantasy fiction 2. Wales -- Fiction
ISBN 0-689-50088-2; 978-1-416-94968-8 pa
LC 77-5361
In this conclusion of the tale begun in "Over Sea, Under Stone," Will Stanton, the Welsh boy Bran, and the Drew children try to locate the crystal sword that alone can vanquish the strong forces of Dark

Victory. Margaret K. McElderry Books 2006 196p il $16.95; pa $6.99
Grades: 5 6 7 8   **Fic**
1. Admirals 2. Sea stories 3. Great Britain -- Fiction
ISBN 1-4169-1477-3; 1-4169-1478-1 pa
LC 2005-16747
Alternating chapters follow the mysterious connection between a homesick English girl living in present-day America and an eleven-year-old boy serving in the British Royal Navy in 1803, aboard the H.M.S. Victory, commanded by Admiral Horatio Nelson.
"Seamlessly weaving details of period seamanship into the narrative, Cooper offers a vivid historical tale within the framework of a compelling modern story." Booklist

Cornwell, Betsy
Mechanica; Betsy Cornwell. Houghton Mifflin Harcourt 2016 320 p. $8.99
Grades: 5 6 7 8 9 10   **Fic**
1. Inventors -- Fiction 2. Fractured fairy tales 3. Fairy tales 4. Magic -- Fiction 5. Inventions -- Fiction
ISBN 0544668685; 9780544668683
LC 2015001336
This young adult novel, by Betsy Cornwell, is a retelling of the story of Cinderella. "Nicolette's awful stepsisters call her 'Mechanica.' . . . When she discovers a secret workshop in the cellar on her sixteenth birthday¿and befriends Jules, a tiny magical metal horse¿Nicolette starts to imagine a new life for herself. . . . Determined to invent her own happily-ever-after, Mechanica seeks to wow the prince and eager entrepreneurs alike." (Publisher's note)
"Though the premise will beg comparisons to Marissa Meyer's Cinder (2011), Nick and her friends travel a very different journey, sidestepping typical romantic structures to find their own way. A smart, refreshing alternative to stale genre tropes." Kirkus

Cornwell, Nicki
Christophe's story; [by] Nicki Cornwell; illustrated by Karin Littlewood. Frances Lincoln Children's 2007 74p il $14.95; pa $7.95
Grades: 2 3 4   **Fic**
1. School stories 2. Rwanda -- Fiction 3. Refugees -- Fiction 4. Immigrants -- Fiction
ISBN 978-1-84507-765-5; 1-84507-765-2; 978-1-84507-521-7 pa; 1-84507-521-8 pa
Coping with a new country, a new school and a new language, Christophe wants to tell everyone why he had to leave Rwanda.
"The book succeeds, giving insight into the refugee experience and a glimpse of the horrors in Rwanda that will not overwhelm young readers." Booklist

Correa, Shan
Gaff; written by Shan Correa. Peachtree 2010 212p $15.95
Grades: 4 5 6 7   **Fic**
1. Hawaii -- Fiction 2. Roosters -- Fiction 3. Animal welfare -- Fiction
ISBN 978-1-56145-526-3; 1-56145-526-1
In Hawaii, thirteen-year-old Paul Silva is determined to find a way to get his family out of the illegal cockfighting business.

"Correa's debut evokes the lush melange of sights, sounds and smells in 13-year-old Paulie's multicultural neighborhood in Hawaii. . . . Also woven into this ethical debate, rooted in economics and traditions, is Hawaiian pidgin English, which may challenge even experienced readers. . . . A fascinating look at the United States most mainlanders have never seen." Kirkus

Cotler, Steve

Cheesie Mack is cool in a duel; Steve Cotler; illustrated by Adam McCauley. Random House 2012 229 p. (hardcover library binding) $18.99

Grades: 4 5 6　　　　　　　　　　　　　　　　**Fic**
1. Camps -- Fiction 2. Siblings -- Fiction 3. Interpersonal relations -- Fiction 4. Maine -- Fiction 5. Contests -- Fiction
ISBN 9780375864384; 9780375895715; 9780375964381
LC 2011016921

This book is the second in the Cheesie Mack series. "Ronald 'Cheesie' Mack and his best friend Georgie secured the funds to go to summer camp on Bufflehead Lake in Maine. Days later, the duo climbs aboard a bus and head off to Camp Windward. Unfortunately Cheesie's older sister, June . . . will be none too far away at Camp Leeward. . . . T late registration results in both boys being stuck in a cabin with the older guys… including Kevin, [June's] boyfriend. When Kevin gives Cheesie a hard time once too often, Cheesie suggests a Cool Duel. Each night the boys in the cabin will vote on who did the coolest thing; in a week, the loser will have to embarrass himself in front of the whole camp by bowing to the winner. Can Cheesie prevail and still have fun at the camp he worked so hard to attend?" (Kirkus Reviews)

Cheesie Mack is not a genius or anything; illustrated by Adam Mc-Cauley. Random House 2011 229p il $15.99; lib bdg $18.99
Grades: 4 5 6　　　　　　　　　　　　　　　　**Fic**
1. Mystery fiction 2. Summer -- Fiction 3. Friendship -- Fiction
ISBN 978-0-375-86437-7; 0-375-86437-7; 978-0-375-96437-4
lib bdg; 0-375-96437-1 lib bdg; 978-0-375-89570-8 e-book
LC 2009-33329

Ronald, aka Cheesie, Mack and his best friend Georgie find opportunies for summertime mischief "when Georgie finds a nearly century-old letter containing a worn penny and a locket, a mystery that eventually leads the pals to the Haunted Toad, a local rundown mansion. . . . Cheesie's . . . easygoing, accessible voice will certainly appeal to middle-grade readers. . . . The action . . . is all fun and games. . . . A light-hearted and fast-moving read for kids looking for middle-school shenanigans." Bull Cent Child Books

Cheesie Mack is running like crazy! by Steve Cotler; illustrated by Douglas Holgate. 1st ed. Random House Inc. 2013 256 p. ill. (hardcover) $15.99; (library) $18.99; (ebook) $47.97; (paperback) $6.99
Grades: 4 5 6　　　　　　　　　　　　　　　　**Fic**
1. Elections -- Fiction 2. Schools -- Fiction 3. Friendship -- Fiction 4. Best friends -- Fiction 5. Middle schools -- Fiction 6. Track and field -- Fiction 7. Brothers and sisters -- Fiction
ISBN 0307977145; 9780307977137; 9780307977144;
9780307977151; 9780307977168
LC 2012017978

In this book by Steve Colter, "Cheesie and his best friend, Georgie, are off to the middle school, where there will be lots of new kids and new teachers. Cheesie has a terrific idea--what better way to meet all the new kids than to run for class president? Plus, if he wins, it'll drive his evil older sister nuts! Then Cheesie gets bad news. One of his friends from his old school is also running for president." (Publisher's note

Cottrell Boyce, Frank

The **astounding** broccoli boy; Frank Cottrell Boyce. Walden Pond Press, an imprint of HarperCollinsPublishers 2015 384 p. (hardback) $16.99

Grades: 4 5 6　　　　　　　　　　　　　　　　**Fic**
1. School stories 2. Bullies -- Fiction 3. Superheroes -- Fiction 4. Humorous stories 5. Heroes -- Fiction 6. Bullying -- Fiction 7. Imagination -- Fiction 8. Virus diseases -- Fiction 9. Adventure and adventurers -- Fiction
ISBN 0062400177; 9780062400178
LC 2015005996

In this children's novel by Frank Cottrell Boyce "when Rory Rooney . . . suddenly turns green on a class trip, he is blamed and ridiculed before a helicopter whisks him to a London hospital. Rory is dismayed to learn he is stuck in quarantine . . . with the only other known sufferer of the mysterious green affliction his arch nemesis, Grim (real name Tommy-Lee). Hoping their greenness means they are secretly superheroes, Rory and Tommy-Lee become convinced they have acquired superpowers." (Publisher's note)

"Humorous and fast-paced, this distinctive tale with well-developed characters will appeal to those readers who have ever searched for their own superpowers." SLJ

★ **Cosmic**. Walden Pond Press 2010 311p $16.99; lib bdg $17.89
Grades: 4 5 6 7　　　　　　　　　　　　　　　**Fic**
1. Size -- Fiction 2. Outer space -- Exploration -- Fiction
ISBN 978-0-06-183683-1; 0-06-183683-4; 978-0-06-183686-2
lib bdg; 0-06-183686-9 lib bdg
LC 2008277816

Boyce "knows how to tell a compellingly good story. But in his latest extravagantly imaginative and marvelously good-natured novel he has also written one that is bound to win readers' hearts." Booklist

The **unforgotten** coat; photographs by Carl Hunter and Clare Heney. Candlewick Press 2011 112p il $15.99
Grades: 3 4 5 6　　　　　　　　　　　　　　　**Fic**
1. Mongols -- Fiction 2. Brothers -- Fiction 3. Refugees -- Fiction 4. Friendship -- Fiction 5. Immigrants -- Fiction 6. Great Britain -- Fiction
ISBN 978-0-7636-5729-1; 0-7636-5729-8
LC 2010048224

This is "a tight, powerful story—brimming with humor, mystery, and pathos—about illegal immigration and the price it exacts on children." Publ Wkly

Couloumbis, Audrey

★ **Getting** near to baby. Putnam 1999 211p $17.99; pa $5.99
Grades: 5 6 7 8　　　　　　　　　　　　　　　**Fic**
1. Aunts -- Fiction 2. Death -- Fiction 3. Sisters -- Fiction
ISBN 0-399-23389-X; 0-698-11892-8 pa
LC 99-18191

A Newbery Medal honor book, 2000

Although thirteen-year-old Willa Jo and her Aunt Patty seem to be constantly at odds, staying with her and Uncle Hob helps Willa Jo and her younger sister come to terms with the death of their family's baby

"Couloumbis's writing is strong; she captures wonderfully the Southern voices of her characters and conveys with great depth powerful emotions. . . . A compelling novel." SLJ

Jake. Random House 2010 162p $15.99; lib bdg $18.99
Grades: 3 4 5　　　　　　　　　　　　　　　　**Fic**
1. Accidents -- Fiction 2. Christmas -- Fiction 3. Hospitals --

Fiction 4. Grandfathers -- Fiction 5. Baltimore (Md.) -- Fiction
ISBN 978-0-375-85630-3; 0-375-85630-7; 978-0-375-95630-0
lib bdg; 0-375-95630-1 lib bdg

LC 2009-29383

When ten-year-old Jake's widowed mother breaks her leg just before Christmas while her sister and best friend are both away, a grandfather Jake barely remembers must come to Baltimore, Maryland, to help a neighbor take care of him.

"Never message heavy, the drama about the meaning of family will touch readers." Booklist

★ **Lexie**; illustrated by Julia Denos. Random House 2011 199p
il $15.99; lib bdg $18.99

Grades: 3 4 5 6   **Fic**
1. Beaches -- Fiction 2. Divorce -- Fiction 3. Vacations -- Fiction
4. Remarriage -- Fiction 5. Father-daughter relationship -- Fiction
ISBN 978-0-375-85632-7; 0-375-85632-3; 978-0-375-95632-4
lib bdg; 0-375-95632-8 lib bdg

LC 2010-20751

When ten-year-old Lexie goes with her father to the beach for a week, she is surprised to find that he has invited his girlfriend and her two sons to join them for the entire week.

"Couloumbis demonstrates her skill at writing with quiet understanding and unstudied polish for younger readers. Her ability to walk through complicated emotional dynamics in kid-accessible language . . . is impressive." Bull Cent Child Books

Maude March on the run! or, Trouble is her middle name. Random House 2007 309p $15.99; lib bdg $17.99

Grades: 4 5 6 7   **Fic**
1. Adventure fiction 2. Orphans -- Fiction 3. Frontier and pioneer life -- Fiction
ISBN 978-0-375-83246-8; 978-0-375-93246-5 lib bdg; 978-0-375-83248-2 pa

LC 2005036133

Due to a misunderstanding over her involvement in a botched robbery, Maude, with younger sister Sallie, hides out at the home of an uncle, but when she is discovered and arrested, the orphaned sisters flee, trying to clear Maude's name.

"The excitement of the Wild West comes to life in this action-packed sequel to The Misadventures of Maude March." SLJ

★ The **misadventures** of Maude March; or, Trouble rides a fast horse. [by] Audrey Couloumbis. Random House 2005 295p hardcover o.p. lib bdg $17.99; pa $7.50

Grades: 4 5 6 7   **Fic**
1. Adventure fiction 2. Orphans -- Fiction 3. Frontier and pioneer life -- Fiction
ISBN 0-375-83245-9; 0-375-93245-3 lib bdg; 0-375-83247-5 pa

LC 2004-16464

After the death of the stern aunt who raised them since they were orphaned, eleven-year-old Sallie and her fifteen-year-old sister escape their self-serving guardians and begin an adventure resembling those in the dime novels Sallie loves to read. "Grades six to ten." (Bull Cent Child Books)

"Sallie's narration is delightful, with understatements that are laugh-out-loud hilarious. . . . Hard to put down, and a fun read-aloud." SLJ

★ **War** games; a novel based on a true story. [by] Audrey Couloumbis & Akila Couloumbis. Random House Children's Books 2009 232p $16.99; lib bdg $19.99

Grades: 5 6 7 8   **Fic**
1. Greece -- Fiction 2. Cousins -- Fiction 3. Brothers -- Fiction 4.

World War, 1939-1945 -- Underground movements -- Fiction
ISBN 978-0-375-85628-0; 0-375-85628-5; 978-0-375-95628-7
lib bdg; 0-375-95628-X lib bdg

LC 2008-46784

"For 12-year-old Petros, World War II feels unreal and far away. . . . But when the Germans invade Greece, the war suddenly comes impossibly close. Overnight, neighbors become enemies. People begin to keep secrets (Petros's family most of all). And for the first time, Petros has the chance to show Zola that he's not just a little brother but that he can truly be counted on." (Publisher's note) "Grades six to nine." (Bull Cent Child Books)

"The climactic violence is believable, and the resolution—though it takes place offstage—is deeply satisfying. Memorable." SLJ

Coville, Bruce

Amber Brown is tickled pink; written by Bruce Coville and Elizabeth Levy; illustrated by Tony Ross. G.P. Putnam's Sons 2013 154 p. (hardcover) $14.99

Grades: 2 3 4 5   **Fic**
1. Children of divorced parents -- Fiction 2. Weddings -- Fiction
3. Remarriage -- Fiction
ISBN 0399256563; 9780399256561

LC 2011039493

In this book by Bruce Coville and Elizabeth Levy, "Amber can't wait to be Best Child when her mom and Max get married, but planning a wedding comes with lots of headaches. Amber can't find the right dress, her dad keeps making mean cracks about Max, and Mom and Max have very different ideas about how much this wedding should cost. Her mother even suggests they go to city hall and skip the party altogether!" (Publisher's note)

Cursed; Bruce Coville; illustrations by Paul Kidby. Yearling, an imprint of Random House Children's Books, a division of Penguin Random House LLC 2016 241 p. illustrations (pbk.) $6.99

Grades: 3 4 5 6   **Fic**
1. Magic -- Fiction 2. Diaries -- Fiction 3. Orderliness -- Fiction
4. Imaginary creatures -- Fiction 5. Blessing and cursing -- Fiction
6. Humorous stories 7. Family life -- Fiction
ISBN 0385392508; 9780385392501

LC 2016007817

In this book, by Bruce Coville, with illustrations by Paul Kidby, "Angus is a brownie. No, not the kind you eat! He's a tiny magical creature that loves to do chores. Angus has just "inherited" a new human girl, Alex. To say that Alex is messy would be an understatement. She's a total hurricane-like disaster—and she likes it that way, thankyouverymuch! Living with each other isn't easy but Angus and Alex soon learn there is a curse that binds them." (Publisher's note)

Diary of a mad brownie; Bruce Coville. Random House Inc. 2015 256 p. illustrations (hardback) $16.99

Grades: 3 4 5 6   **Fic**
1. Orderliness 2. Magic -- Fiction 3. Imaginary creatures -- Fiction
4. Humorous stories 5. Diaries -- Fiction 6. Family life -- Fiction
9. Blessing and cursing -- Fiction 10. Adventure and adventurers -- Fiction
ISBN 0385392478; 9780385392471; 9780385392488

LC 2014026335

In this children's novel by Bruce Coville "Angus is . . . a tiny magical creature that loves to do chores. Angus has just 'inherited' a new human girl, Alex. To say that Alex is messy would be an understatement. Living with each other isn't easy but Angus and Alex soon learn there is a curse that binds them. What's worse, it threatens Alex's family! Working together, Angus and Alex will set out to break the curse." (Publisher's note)

" Bound by a family curse, Angus the brownie must leave Scotland for America to serve young Alex Carhart, the great-great-great-niece of his recently deceased mistress. . . . The story moves quickly, energized by Angus' engaging voice and the use of shifting perspectives. Largely made up of the brownie's diary entries, the narrative also includes passages from Alex's journal as well as letters, text messages, news articles, poems, and other documents. Kidby's madcap jacket art and many black-and-white illustrations will draw young readers to the book. The first volume of the Enchanted Files series is smart, amusing, and a lot of fun." Booklist

Jennifer Murdley's toad; a magic shop book. illustrated by Gary A. Lippincott. Harcourt 2002 159p il $17; pa $5.95
Grades: 4 5 6   **Fic**
1. Fantasy fiction 2. Toads -- Fiction
ISBN 0-15-204613-5; 0-15-206246-7 pa
                                              LC 2002-24107
A reissue of the title first published 1992
When an ordinary-looking fifth grader purchases a talking toad, she embarks on a series of extraordinary adventures
"This light, fast-paced fantasy has touches of humor (at times low comedy), an implicit moral, and a hint that Jennifer may be in for more adventures." Booklist

★ **Jeremy** Thatcher, dragon hatcher; a magic shop book. illustrated by Gary A. Lippincott. Harcourt 2002 151p il $17; pa $5.95
Grades: 4 5 6   **Fic**
1. Fantasy fiction 2. Dragons -- Fiction
ISBN 0-15-204614-3; 0-15-206252-1 pa
                                              LC 2002-68714
A reissue of the title first published 1991
Small for his age but artistically talented, twelve-year-old Jeremy Thatcher unknowingly buys a dragon's egg
This is "right on target. Not only is the story involving but the reader can really get a feeling for Jeremy as a person. Coville's technique of combining the real world with a fantasy one works well in this story." Voice Youth Advocates

Juliet Dove, Queen of Love; a magic shop book. Harcourt 2003 190p $17; pa $5.95
Grades: 4 5 6   **Fic**
1. Magic -- Fiction 2. Classical mythology -- Fiction
ISBN 0-15-204561-9; 0-15-205217-8 pa
                                              LC 2003-11846
A shy twelve-year-old girl must solve a puzzle involving characters from Greek mythology to free herself from a spell which makes her irresistible to boys
"Although humorous, the story has surprising depth. . . . Coville capably interweaves mythological characters with realistic modern ones, keeping readers truly absorbed." SLJ

The **skull** of truth; a magic shop book. illustrated by Gary A. Lippincott. Harcourt 2002 194p il $17
Grades: 4 5 6   **Fic**
1. Fantasy fiction 2. Truthfulness and falsehood -- Fiction
ISBN 0-15-204612-7
                                              LC 2002-24244
A reissue of the title first published 1997
Charlie, a sixth-grader with a compulsion to tell lies, acquires a mysterious skull that forces its owner to tell only the truth, causing some awkward moments before he understands its power
"Coville has structured the story very carefully, with a great deal of sensitivity to children's thought processes and emotions. The mood

shifts from scary to funny to serious are fused with understandable language and sentence structures." SLJ

Thor's wedding day; by Thialfi, the goat boy. as told to and translated by Bruce Coville; illustrations by Matthew Cogswell. Harcourt 2005 137p il $15; pa $5.95
Grades: 4 5 6 7   **Fic**
1. Giants -- Fiction 2. Norse mythology -- Fiction
ISBN 0-15-201455-1; 0-15-205872-9 pa
                                              LC 2004-29580
Thialfi, the Norse thunder god's goat boy, tells how he inadvertently helped the giant Thrym to steal Thor's magic hammer, the lengths to which Thor must go to retrieve it, and his own assistance along the way.
"Coville takes a Norse poem called the Thrymskvitha and turns it into a delightful prose romp. . . . Throughout, he injects a modern sensibility while keeping the feel of the original myth." Booklist

Cowley, Joy
Snake and Lizard; [written by] Joy Cowley; [illustrated by] Gavin Bishop. Kane Miller Pub. 2008 85p il $14.95
Grades: 2 3 4   **Fic**
1. Snakes -- Fiction 2. Lizards -- Fiction 3. Friendship -- Fiction
ISBN 978-1-933605-83-8; 1-933605-83-9
"Snake and Lizard were born to squabble. . . . Each argument begins in misunderstanding and ends in companionable accord; yet their disagreements spring so obviously from their natures, and their repartee is so comical—snappy, ludicrous yet logical—that the salutary message is absorbed with delight. . . . Bishop's art (apparently pen-and-ink, with cheery watercolor added) enlivens almost every spread of this attractive small volume, capturing each interaction with wit and affection." Horn Book

Cox, Judy
Butterfly buddies; illustrated by Blanche Sims. Holiday House 2001 86p il $15.95
Grades: 2 3 4   **Fic**
1. School stories 2. Friendship -- Fiction 3. Butterflies -- Fiction
ISBN 0-8234-1654-2
                                              LC 2001-16720
Third grader Robin has a series of mishaps and learns the value of honesty as she tries to become best friends with Zoey, her partner for a class project on raising butterflies. Includes butterfly care tips
"Written in simple, highly descriptive language that brings settings and characters alive, and sprinkled with lively drawings, this warmhearted friendship story is a good choice for readers transitioning to chapter books." Booklist

Nora and the Texas terror; illustrated by Amanda Haley. Holiday House 2010 87p il $15.95
Grades: 2 3 4   **Fic**
1. School stories 2. Oregon -- Fiction 3. Cousins -- Fiction 4. Family life -- Fiction
ISBN 978-0-8234-2283-8; 0-8234-2283-6
                                              LC 2010-14329
When Nora's uncle loses his job and house in Texas, he and his family come to stay with Nora's family in Portland, Oregon, and Nora must try very hard to adjust to her cousin Ellie, who is loud, stubborn, and a tease.
"This is an entertaining and original early chapter book; the dynamic between Nora and Ellie is realistically portrayed, and the simple plot is well developed. . . . Monochromatic line-and-watercolor illustrations . . . add further entertainment value." Bull Cent Child Books

Puppy power; illustrated by Steve Björkman. Holiday House 2008 91p il $15.95; pa $6.95
Grades: 2 3 4 **Fic**
1. School stories 2. Dogs -- Fiction
ISBN 978-0-8234-2073-5; 0-8234-2073-6; 978-0-8234-2210-4 pa; 0-8234-2210-0 pa
LC 2007-28395
Boisterous third-grader Fran has trouble controlling herself, but learning how to train her gigantic Newfoundland puppy helps her gain enough self-control to win the part of princess in the class play. Includes instructions on puppy training.
This is an "entertaining novel full of believable kids with recognizable problems. . . . With a brisk plot, short chapters, and frequent pen-and-ink illustrations, this story is a choice selection." Booklist

Ukulele Hayley; by Judy Cox; illustrated by Amanda Haley. Holiday House 2013 82 p. (hardcover) $16.95
Grades: 2 3 4 **Fic**
1. School stories -- Fiction 2. Music -- Study and teaching -- Fiction 3. Music -- Fiction 4. Schools -- Fiction 5. Ukulele -- Fiction
ISBN 082342863X; 9780823428632
LC 2012045825
In this book, by Judy Cox, "Hayley has finally found her talent: playing ukulele like her great-great aunt Ruby, who traveled all over with her band, the Ragtime Rascals. She's so enthusiastic that she gets a ukulele band started at school with the new music teacher. Just as the band is getting popular, horrible news comes: the music program and the teacher are being cut." (Publisher's note)
"This cheerful story about a third grader who finds her talent, and then uses it to organize a band (and save the school's music program), will appeal to independent readers who like everyday, undemanding school stories with a peppy heroine. The happy ending ties everything up in a neat bow. Black-and-white wash illustrations break up the chapters. Ukelele-playing tips are appended." (Horn Book)

Coy, John
Eyes on the goal. Feiwel and Friends 2010 164p (4 for 4) $16.99
Grades: 3 4 5 6 **Fic**
1. Soccer -- Fiction 2. Friendship -- Fiction
ISBN 978-0-312-37330-6; 0-312-37330-9
This "finds the quartet of Jackson, Gig, Isaac, and Diego readying for a trip to soccer camp, even though except for Diego, they're more taken by sports that don't bafflingly forbid the use of hands. Like before, Coy includes some issues for character depth, from Gig's father being sent to Afghanistan to Jackson maybe having to move in with his mom's new boyfriend, but these take a firm backseat to the action on the field, which Coy describes with straightforward, articulate prose. Light, enjoyable reading." Booklist

Love of the game. Feiwel and Friends 2011 182p $16.99
Grades: 4 5 6 7 **Fic**
1. School stories 2. Football -- Fiction 3. Family life -- Fiction
ISBN 978-0-312-37331-3; 0-312-37331-7
LC 2010050897
Sixth-grader Jackson has a rough start in middle school, with bullies on the bus, few classes with his friends, and changes at home but some good teachers, meeting a girl, joining a club, and playing football soon turn things around.
"Realistic characters, believable dialogue and a genuine feel for the rhythms and issues of middle-schoolers make this a satisfying addition to a solid middle-grade set." Kirkus

Top of the order. Feiwel and Friends 2009 182p $16.99

Grades: 3 4 5 6 **Fic**
1. School stories 2. Divorce -- Fiction 3. Baseball -- Fiction 4. Sex role -- Fiction 5. Friendship -- Fiction 6. Family life -- Fiction
ISBN 978-0-312-37329-0; 0-312-37329-5
LC 2008-28551
Ten-year-old Jackson lives for baseball, but becomes distracted by the approach of middle school, his mother's latest boyfriend, and the presence of a girl—his good friend's sister—on his team.
"Coy effortlessly captures the voices of boys on the verge of adolescence. Jackson and his friends are fully developed. . . . Gripping play-by-play and a fast-moving plot will appeal to sports enthusiasts and reluctant readers." SLJ
Another title about Jackson is:
Eyes on the goal (2010)

Creech, Sharon
★ **Absolutely** normal chaos. HarperCollins Pubs. 1995 230p $16.99; pa $5.99
Grades: 5 6 7 8 **Fic**
1. Family life -- Fiction
ISBN 0-06-026989-8; 0-06-440632-6 pa
LC 95-22448
First published 1990 in the United Kingdom
"Those in search of a light, humorous read will find it; those in search of something a little deeper will also be rewarded." SLJ

★ **Bloomability**. HarperCollins Pubs. 1998 273p hardcover o.p. pa $5.99
Grades: 5 6 7 8 **Fic**
1. School stories 2. Switzerland -- Fiction
ISBN 0-06-026993-6; 0-06-440823-X pa
LC 98-14601
When her aunt and uncle take her from New Mexico to Lugano, Switzerland, to attend an international school, thirteen-year-old Dinnie discovers her world expanding
"As if fresh, smart characters in a picturesque setting weren't engaging enough, Creech also poses an array of knotty questions, both personal and philosophical. . . . A story to stimulate both head and heart." Booklist

Chasing Redbird. HarperCollins Pubs. 1997 261p hardcover o.p. pa $5.99
Grades: 5 6 7 8 **Fic**
1. Kentucky -- Fiction 2. Family life -- Fiction
ISBN 0-06-026987-1; 0-06-440696-2 pa
LC 96-44128
Thirteen-year-old Zinnia Taylor uncovers family secrets and self truths while clearing a mysterious settler trail that begins on her family's farm in Kentucky
"With frequent flashbacks, the narrative makes clear the complexities of the story, while the unsolved puzzles lead the reader on to the end. The writing is laced with figurative language and folksy comments that intensify both atmosphere and emotion." Horn Book Guide

Granny Torrelli makes soup; drawings by Chris Raschka. HarperCollins Pubs. 2003 141p il $15.99; lib bdg $16.89; pa $5.99
Grades: 4 5 6 **Fic**
1. Grandmothers -- Fiction
ISBN 0-06-029290-3; 0-06-029291-1 lib bdg; 0-06-440960-0 pa
LC 2002-152662
With the help of her wise old grandmother, twelve-year-old Rosie manages to work out some problems in her relationship with her best friend, Bailey, the boy next door who is blind

"This gets high marks for its unique voice (make that voices) and for the way the subtleties that are woven into the story." Booklist

The **great** unexpected; Sharon Creech; edited by Alyson Day. HarperCollins 2012 240 p. (lib. bdg.) $17.89

Grades: 4 5 6 7   **Fic**

1. Ireland -- Fiction 2. Orphans -- Fiction 3. Friendship -- Fiction
ISBN 0061892335; 9780061892325; 9780061892332

LC 2012942431

In this book by Sharon Creech, "best friends and orphans Naomi Deane and Lizzie Scatterding are surprised when a strange boy falls out of a tree in their little town of Blackbird Tree, USA. His name is Finn, and Naomi falls immediately under his spell. . . . Meanwhile, in Ireland, an old woman and her companion talk of murder and revenge." (Horn Book Magazine)

Hate that cat. Joanna Cotler Books 2008 153p $15.99; lib bdg $16.89

Grades: 4 5 6 7   **Fic**

1. School stories 2. Novels in verse 3. Poetry -- Fiction
ISBN 978-0-06-143092-3; 978-0-06-143093-0 lib bdg

LC 2007044182

Jack is studying poetry again in school, and he continues to write poems reflecting his understanding of famous poems and how they relate to his life.

"Creech employs sensitivity and spare verse to carve an indelible portrait of a boy who discovers the power of self-expression." Booklist

★ **Love** that dog. HarperCollins Pubs. 2001 86p $15.99; lib bdg $14.89; pa $5.99

Grades: 4 5 6 7   **Fic**

1. School stories 2. Poetry 3. Poetry -- Fiction
ISBN 0-06-029287-3; 0-06-029289-X lib bdg; 0-06-440959-7 pa
LC 00-54233

"Jack thinks that boys don't write poetry. . . . The trouble is that his teacher, Ms. Stretchberry, keeps insisting that he read more and more poetry. Worse, she keeps insisting that he write poems, as well! . . . This book comes to us in the form of journal entries in Jack's own freeverse." (Christ Sci Monit) "Ages eight to twelve." (N Y Times Book Rev)

"Creech has created a poignant, funny picture of a child's encounter with the power of poetry. . . . This book is a tiny treasure." SLJ

Another title about Jack is:

Hate that cat (2008)

★ **Moo**; A Novel. Sharon Creech. Harpercollins Childrens Books 2016 288 p. (hardcover) $16.99

Grades: 4 5 6 7   **Fic**

1. Country life -- Fiction 2. Domestic animals -- Fiction
ISBN 9780062415240; 0062415247

This novel by Sharon Creech follows "one family's . . . move from the city to rural [country]. . . . When Reena, her little brother, Luke, and their parents first move to Maine, Reena doesn't know what to expect. She's ready for beaches, blueberries, and all the lobster she can eat. Instead, her parents 'volunteer' Reena and Luke to work for an eccentric neighbor named Mrs. Falala, who has a pig named Paulie, a cat named China, a snake named Edna—and that stubborn cow, Zora." (Publisher's note)

"A heartfelt tale that will be embraced by Creech's fans, work well as a classroom read-aloud, and find a spot in book groups." SLJ

★ **Ruby** Holler. HarperCollins Pubs. 2002 310p hardcover o.p. pa $5.99

Grades: 4 5 6 7   **Fic**

1. Twins -- Fiction 2. Orphans -- Fiction 3. Country life -- Fiction
ISBN 0-06-027732-7; 0-06-056015-0 pa

LC 00-6637

Thirteen-year-old fraternal twins Dallas and Florida have grown up in a terrible orphanage but their lives change forever when an eccentric but sweet older couple invites them each on an adventure, beginning in an almost magical place called Ruby Holler

"This poignant story evokes a feeling as welcoming as fresh-baked bread. . . . The novel celebrates the healing effects of love and compassion." Publ Wkly

The **unfinished** angel. Joanna Cotler Books 2009 164p

Grades: 4 5 6   **Fic**

1. Angels -- Fiction 2. Orphans -- Fiction 3. Villages -- Fiction 4. Switzerland -- Fiction
ISBN 0-06-143095-1; 0-06-143096-X lib bdg; 0-06-143097-8 pa; 978-0-06-143095-4; 978-0-06-143096-1 lib bdg; 978-0-06-143097-8 pa

LC 2009-0279

In a tiny village in the Swiss Alps, an angel meets an American girl named Zola who has come with her father to open a school, and together Zola and the angel rescue a group of homeless orphans. "Ages eight to twelve." (Publisher's note)

"Some books are absolute magic, and this is one of them. . . . Creech's protagonist is hugely likable. . . . Creech's offering deserves to be read out loud and more than once to truly enjoy the angel's hilarious malapropisms and outright invented words, and to appreciate the book's tender, comical celebration of the human spirit." SLJ

★ **Walk** two moons. HarperCollins Pubs. 1994 280p $16.99; lib bdg $17.89; pa $6.99

Grades: 6 7 8 9   **Fic**

1. Death -- Fiction 2. Friendship -- Fiction 3. Family life -- Fiction 4. Grandparents -- Fiction
ISBN 0-06-023334-6; 0-06-023337-0 lib bdg; 0-06-440517-6 pa
LC 93-31277

Awarded the Newbery Medal, 1995

After her mother leaves home suddenly, thirteen-year-old Sal and her grandparents take a car trip retracing her mother's route. Along the way, Sal recounts the story of her friend Phoebe, whose mother also left

"An engaging story of love and loss, told with humor and suspense . . . A richly layered novel about real and metaphorical journeys." SLJ

Cronin, Doreen

The **legend** of Diamond Lil; a J.J. Tully mystery. Doreen Cronin; illustrated by Kevin Cornell. Balzer + Bray 2012 125 p. illustrations $15.89

Grades: 2 3 4   **Fic**

1. Mystery fiction 2. Children's stories 3. Dogs -- Fiction 4. Chickens -- Fiction 5. Humorous fiction -- Fiction 6. Mystery and detective stories
ISBN 0061985783; 9780061779961; 9780061985782

LC 2011945710

In this children's book, by Doreen Cronin, illustrated by Kevin Cornell, "all search-and-rescue dog J.J. Tully wants is to enjoy his retirement. But mama chick Moosh and chicks Dirt and Sugar are acting strange. A possum keeps finding its way into the chicken coop. And J.J. has questions about Diamond Lil, the fancy new dog next door. He'll have to track down the clues and sniff out the evidence to save the day." (Publisher's note)

"The eye-catching illustrations do a great job of drawing readers' attention to important story details. Children who like a little bit of everything mixed into their reading, particularly mystery, adventure, and animals, will enjoy this book." - SLJ

The **trouble** with chickens; a J. J. Tully mystery. illustrated by Kevin Cornell. Balzer + Bray 2011 119p il $14.99; lib bdg $15.89
Grades: 2 3 4 **Fic**
1. Mystery fiction 2. Dogs -- Fiction 3. Chickens -- Fiction
ISBN 978-0-06-121532-2; 0-06-121532-5; 978-0-06-121533-9
lib bdg; 0-06-121533-3 lib bdg
LC 2009-31213
A hard-bitten former search-and-rescue dog helps solve a complicated missing chicken case.

"Fast-paced and funny, with interesting vocabulary and a well-constructed plot, this is terrific fare for readers who are ready to move beyond picture books, but are intimidated by longer works. Cornell's pencil drawings have a mix of energy and humor that adds to the fun." Publ Wkly

Crossan, Sarah
★ The **Weight** of Water; by Sarah Crossan. Bloomsbury USA 2013 224 p. $16.99
Grades: 5 6 7 8 **Fic**
1. Immigrants -- Fiction 2. School stories -- Fiction 3. Novels in verse 4. England -- Fiction 5. Swimming -- Fiction 6. Race relations -- Fiction 7. Coventry (England) -- Fiction 8. Mothers and daughters -- Fiction 9. Alienation (Social psychology) -- Fiction
ISBN 1599909677; 9781599909677
LC 2012038645
In this book, "12-year-old Kasienka moves with Mama from Gdansk, Poland, to Coventry, England, to find Tata, her father. The adjustment is difficult. At school, Kasienka is ostracized. At home, she questions why they are searching for a man who ran from them. When Kasienka complains, Mama questions her love. Kasienka feels powerful only when she swims at the pool—something Tata taught her to do. That is also where William, a schoolmate, first notices her." (Kirkus Reviews)

Crowder, Melanie
★ A **nearer** moon; Melanie Crowder. Atheneum Books for Young Readers 2015 160 p. (hardcover) $16.99
Grades: 4 5 6 7 8 **Fic**
1. Magic -- Fiction 2. Rivers -- Fiction 3. Sisters -- Fiction 4. Family life -- Fiction 5. Water spirits -- Fiction
ISBN 1481441485; 9781481441483
LC 2014043590
In this book, by Melanie Crowder, "[a]long a lively river, in a village raised on stilts, lives a girl named Luna. All her life she has heard tales of the time before the dam appeared, when sprites danced in the currents and no one got the mysterious wasting illness from a mouthful of river water. . . . [W]hen Luna's little sister falls ill with the river sickness, . . . Luna is determined to find a cure for her beloved sister, no matter what it takes.." (Publisher's note)

"Luna's brave journey to save her sister takes her to places her mother told her never to go and to the very heart of the dark magic. Told in alternating chapters of the past fairy time and Luna's present, this lyrical tale highlights the power of sisterly love in a truly enchanting way. VERDICT The book is an easy read and will appeal to lower level/higher interest readers but its charming narrative will be sure to captivate everyone.Luna's brave journey to save her sister takes her to places her mother told her never to go and to the very heart of the dark magic. Told in alternating chapters of the past fairy time and Luna's present, this lyrical tale highlights the power of sisterly love in a truly enchanting way. VERDICT The book is an easy read and will appeal to lower level/

higher interest readers but its charming narrative will be sure to captivate everyone." SLJ

Three pennies; Melanie Crowder. Atheneum Books for Young Readers 2017 192 p. (hardcover) $16.99
Grades: 4 5 6 **Fic**
1. Foster children -- Fiction 2. Foster home care -- Fiction 3. Interpersonal relations -- Fiction
ISBN 9781481471879; 9781481471886
LC 2016041975
In this book, by Melanie Crowder, "a girl in foster care tries to find her birth mother. . . . For a kid bouncing from foster home to foster home, The Book of Changes is the perfect companion. That's why Marin carries three pennies and a pocket-sized I Ching with her everywhere she goes. Yet when everything in her life suddenly starts changing--when Marin lands in a foster home that feels like somewhere she could stay, maybe forever--the pennies don't have any answers for her." (Publisher's note)

Crowley, James
Starfish; illustrations by Jim Madsen. Disney/Hyperion Books 2010 310p il $16.99
Grades: 4 5 6 7 **Fic**
1. Adventure fiction 2. Montana -- Fiction 3. Siblings -- Fiction 4. Siksika Indians -- Fiction 5. Runaway children -- Fiction
ISBN 978-1-4231-2588-4; 1-4231-2588-6
In the early part of the 1900s, Beatrice and Lionel, two Blackfeet Indian children, escape from the Chalk Bluff Indian Boarding School in Montana to find their grandfather, and must elude their pursuers and make a life for themselves in the wilderness.

"This is a fast-paced and interesting novel that will maintain reader interest. Readers will be drawn into the plight of Native Americans trying to survive brutal conditions." Libr Media Connect

Cuevas, Michelle
The **masterwork** of a painting elephant; pictures by Ed Young. Frances Foster Books/Farrar Straus Giroux 2011 136p il $15.99
Grades: 3 4 5 6 **Fic**
1. Love -- Fiction 2. Artists -- Fiction 3. Orphans -- Fiction 4. Elephants -- Fiction 5. Voyages and travels -- Fiction
ISBN 978-0-374-34854-0; 0-374-34854-5
LC 2010033108
Pigeon Jones, abandoned as a baby, is found and raised by Birch, a white, former circus elephant who paints beautiful pictures, and through their travels and adventures they discover the meanings of love and family.

"Pigeon's first-person voice traces the story's meanderings with a natural poetry, while Young's spare ink drawings ground the procedings, conveying remarkable emotional weight in a few gestures. The unlikely combination of zany story arc, resonant illustrations, and graceful telling come together in a memorable and original offering." Booklist

Cuffe-Perez, Mary
Skylar; a story. illustrated by Renata Liwska. Philomel Books 2008 138p il $14.99
Grades: 3 4 5 **Fic**
1. Geese -- Fiction 2. Birds -- Migration -- Fiction
ISBN 978-0-399-24543-5; 0-399-24543-X
LC 2007-20437
Skylar, who claims he was once wild, leads four pond geese in their first attempt at migration when an injured heron asks their help in reaching Lost Pond, where the annual Before the Migration Convention is about to be held.

"Nature imagery and extensive information on the migratory habits of Canada geese infuse a text, punctuated by occasional soft, black-and-white full-page illustrations. . . . The pace quickens when the geese talk with each other, their near constant bickering adding a dose of humor." Booklist

Cullen, Lynn

Dear Mr. Washington; by Lynn Cullen; pictures by Nancy Carpenter. Dial Books for Young Readers 2013 32 p. color illustrations (hardcover) $16.99

Grades: K 1 2 3 4 **Fic**

1. Portraits -- Fiction 2. Letters -- Fiction 3. Behavior -- Fiction 4. Etiquette -- Fiction 5. Brothers and sisters -- Fiction

ISBN 0803730381; 9780803730380

LC 2012001098

In this children's book by Lynn Cullen, illustrated by Nancy Carpenter, "Charlotte, James, and baby John have promised to be on their very best behavior for when George Washington comes to have his portrait painted by their father, Gilbert Stuart. But, it seems like every time George Washington comes to visit, Charlotte has to write another apology letter, even when they try to follow George Washington's Rules of Good Behavior." (Publisher's note)

"When President George Washington visits the home of the prominent painter Gilbert Stuart to have his portrait painted, Stuart's children, Charlotte, James, and baby John, try really hard to be good. But, try as they will, it's one disaster after another...The artwork, created using a combination of pen on paper, acrylic paint on canvas, and digital media, is hilarious and bright, with clever attention to detail. A fabulous addition to picture book collections." SLJ

Curry, Jane Louise

The **Black** Canary. Margaret K. McElderry Books 2005 279p $16.95

Grades: 5 6 7 8 **Fic**

1. Generals 2. Courtiers 3. Conspirators 4. Royal favorites 5. Singers -- Fiction 6. London (England) -- Fiction 7. Racially mixed people -- Fiction 8. Great Britain -- History -- 1485-1603, Tudors -- Fiction

ISBN 0-689-86478-7

LC 2003-26150

As the child of two musicians, twelve-year-old James has no interest in music until he discovers a portal to seventeenth-century London in his uncle's basement, and finds himself in a situation where his beautiful voice and the fact that he is biracial might serve him well.

"A genuinely good story that conveys a sense of darkness and mystery in the textured backdrop of a storied time and place." Booklist

Curtis, Christopher Paul

★ **Bud,** not Buddy. Delacorte Press 1999 245p $16.95; pa $6.50

Grades: 4 5 6 7 **Fic**

1. Orphans -- Fiction 2. African Americans -- Fiction 3. Great Depression, 1929-1939 -- Fiction

ISBN 0-385-32306-9; 0-440-41328-1 pa

LC 99-10614

Awarded the Newbery Medal, 2000

Coretta Scott King Award for text

Ten-year-old Bud, a motherless boy living in Flint, Michigan, during the Great Depression, escapes a bad foster home and sets out in search of the man he believes to be his father—the renowned bandleader, H. E. Calloway of Grand Rapids

"Curtis says in a afterword that some of the characters are based on real people, including his own grandfathers, so it's not surprising that

the rich blend of tall tale, slapstick, sorrow, and sweetness has the wry, teasing warmth of family folklore." Booklist

★ **Elijah** of Buxton. Scholastic 2007 341p $16.99; pa $7.99

Grades: 5 6 7 8 **Fic**

1. Canada -- Fiction 2. Slavery -- Fiction

ISBN 0-439-02344-0; 978-0-439-02344-3; 0-439-02345-9 pa; 978-0-439-02345-0 pa

LC 2007-05181

A Newbery Medal honor book, 2008

In 1859, eleven-year-old Elijah Freeman, the first freeborn child in Buxton, Canada, which is a haven for slaves fleeing the American south, uses his wits and skills to try to bring to justice the lying preacher who has stolen money that was to be used to buy a family's freedom.

"Many readers drawn to the book by humor will find themselves at times on the edges of their seats in suspense and, at other moments, moved to tears." Booklist

The **madman** of Piney Woods; Christopher Paul Curtis. Scholastic Press 2014 384 p. $16.99

Grades: 4 5 6 7 **Fic**

1. Adventure fiction 2. n 3. Freedmen -- Fiction 4. Veterans -- Fiction 5. Immigrants -- Fiction 6. Irish -- Canada -- Fiction 7. Blacks -- Canada -- Fiction 8. Canada -- History -- 1867-1914 -- Fiction 9. Post-traumatic stress disorder -- Fiction 10. Chatham (Ont.) -- History -- 20th century -- Fiction 11. North Buxton (Ont.) -- History -- 20th century -- Fiction

ISBN 0545156645; 9780545156646; 9780545156653; 9780545633765

LC 2014003493

"Benji and Red couldn't be more different. They aren't friends. They don't even live in the same town. But their fates are entwined. A chance meeting leads the boys to discover that they have more in common than meets the eye. Both of them have encountered a strange presence in the forest, watching them, tracking them. Could the Madman of Piney Woods be real?" (Publisher's note)

The **mighty** Miss Malone; Christopher Paul Curtis. Wendy Lamb Books 2012 307 p.

Grades: 4 5 6 **Fic**

1. Girls -- Fiction 2. African Americans -- Fiction 3. Great Depression, 1929-1939 -- Fiction 4. Poverty -- Fiction 5. Family life -- Fiction 6. Depressions -- 1929 -- Fiction 7. Gary (Ind.) -- History -- 20th century -- Fiction 8. Flint (Mich.) -- History -- 20th century -- Fiction

ISBN 9780375897368; 9780385734912; 9780385904872; 9780440422143

LC 2011036317

This book tells the story of "Deza Malone, who shares dishwashing duties with Bud Caldwell during his brief stay at a Hooverville in Flint, Mich. . . . It's 1936 in Gary, Ind., and the Great Depression has put 12-year-old Deza's father out of work. After a near-death experience trying to catch fish for dinner, Roscoe Malone leaves for Flint, hoping he'll find work. But Deza's mother loses her job shortly after, putting all the Malones out on the street. . . . [Author Christopher Paul] Curtis threads . . . bits of African-American history throughout the narrative, using the Joe Louis-Max Schmeling fight to expose the racism prevalent even among people like the librarian who tells Deza that Louis is 'such a credit to your race.'" (Publishers Weekly)

★ The **Watsons** go to Birmingham--1963; a novel. Delacorte Press 1995 210p $16.95; pa $6.50

Grades: 4 5 6 7 **Fic**

1. Prejudices -- Fiction 2. Family life -- Fiction 3. African

Americans -- Fiction
ISBN 0-385-32175-9; 0-440-41412-1 pa

LC 95-7091

A Newbery Medal honor book, 1996

The ordinary interactions and everyday routines of the Watsons, an African American family living in Flint, Michigan, are drastically changed after they go to visit Grandma in Alabama in the summer of 1963

"Curtis's ability to switch from fun and funky to pinpoint-accurate psychological imagery works unusually well. . . . Ribald humor, sly sibling digs, and a totally believable child's view of the world will make this book an instant hit." SLJ

Cushman, Karen

★ **Alchemy** and Meggy Swann. Clarion Books 2010 167p $16
Grades: 5 6 7 8   Fic
1. Alchemy -- Fiction 2. Poverty -- Fiction 3. London (England) -- Fiction 4. People with Disabilities -- Fiction 5. Father-daughter relationship -- Fiction 6. Great Britain -- History -- 1485-1603, Tudors -- Fiction
ISBN 978-0-547-23184-6; 0-547-23184-9

LC 2009-16387

In 1573, the crippled, scorned, and destitute Meggy Swann goes to London, where she meets her father, an impoverished alchemist, and eventually discovers that although her legs are bent and weak, she has many other strengths.

"Writing with admirable economy and a lively ability to recreate the past believably, Cushman creates a memorable portrayal of a troubled, rather mulish girl who begins to use her strong will in positive ways." Booklist

The **ballad** of Lucy Whipple. Clarion Bks. 1996 195p $15; $16.00
Grades: 5 6 7 8   Fic
1. Family life -- Fiction 2. Frontier and pioneer life -- Fiction 3. California -- Gold discoveries -- Fiction
ISBN 0-395-72806-1; 9780395728062

LC 95-45257

"Twelve-year-old Lucy is taken by her mother from their comfortable 19th-century home in Massachusetts to the rough-and-tumble California goldfields. Lucy's younger siblings don't object to this new life, but Lucy dislikes the dirt, hard work, and lack of civilization—especially reading material. When not helping Mama run Mr. Scatter's boarding house for miners, Lucy spends her time complaining or scheming a return to her beloved Massachusetts. Despite the losses she suffers in the makeshift town of Lucky Diggins, Lucy makes some surprising discoveries about herself and what she's gained in the West." (Christ Sci Monit) "Grades five to eight." (Booklist)

"Cushman's heroine is a delightful character, and the historical setting is authentically portrayed." SLJ

★ **Catherine,** called Birdy. Clarion Bks. 1994 169p $16
Grades: 6 7 8 9   Fic
1. Middle Ages -- Fiction 2. Great Britain -- Fiction
ISBN 0-395-68186-3

LC 93-23333

A Newbery Medal honor book, 1995

The fourteen-year-old daughter of an English country knight keeps a journal in which she records the events of her life, particularly her longing for adventures beyond the usual role of women and her efforts to avoid being married off

"In the process of telling the routines of her young life, Birdy lays before readers a feast of details about medieval England. . . . Superb historical fiction." SLJ

Matilda Bone. Clarion Bks. 2000 167p $15; pa $5.99
Grades: 5 6 7 8   Fic
1. Physicians -- Fiction 2. Middle Ages -- Fiction 3. Great Britain -- Fiction
ISBN 0-395-88156-0; 0-440-41822-4 pa

LC 00-24032

Fourteen-year-old Matilda, an apprentice bonesetter and practitioner of medicine in a village in medieval England, tries to reconcile the various aspects of her life, both spiritual and practical

"A fascinating glimpse into the colorful life and times of the 14th century. . . . Cushman's character descriptions are spare, with each word carefully chosen to paint wonderful pictures." SLJ

Includes bibliographical references

★ The **midwife's** apprentice. Clarion Bks. 1995 122p $12; pa $5.99
Grades: 6 7 8 9   Fic
1. Midwives -- Fiction 2. Middle Ages -- Fiction 3. Great Britain -- Fiction
ISBN 0-395-69229-6; 0-06-440630-X pa

LC 94-13792

Awarded the Newbery Medal, 1996

In medieval England, a nameless, homeless girl is taken in by a sharp-tempered midwife, and in spite of obstacles and hardship, eventually gains the three things she most wants: a full belly, a contented heart, and a place in this world

"Earthy humor, the foibles of humans both high and low, and a fascinating mix of superstition and genuinely helpful herbal remedies attached to childbirth make this a truly delightful introduction to a world seldom seen in children's literature." SLJ

Rodzina. Clarion Bks. 2003 215p $16; pa $6.50
Grades: 5 6 7 8   Fic
1. Orphans -- Fiction 2. Polish Americans -- Fiction
ISBN 0-618-13351-8; 0-440-41993-X pa

LC 2002-15976

A twelve-year-old Polish American girl is boarded onto an orphan train in Chicago with fears about traveling to the West and a life of unpaid slavery

"The story features engaging characters, a vivid setting, and a prickly but endearing heroine. . . . Rodzina's musings and observations provide poignancy, humor, and a keen sense of the human and topographical landscape." SLJ

Includes bibliographical references

★ **Will** Sparrow's road; Karen Cushman. Clarion Books 2012 216 p. (hardback) $16.99
Grades: 5 6 7 8   Fic
1. Historical fiction 2. Runaway children -- Fiction 3. Swindlers and swindling -- Fiction 4. Runaways -- Fiction 5. Freak shows -- Fiction 6. Conduct of life -- Fiction 7. Great Britain -- History -- Elizabeth, 1558-1603 -- Fiction
ISBN 0547739621; 9780547739625

LC 2011045898

In this book by Karen Cushman, set in Elizabethan England, "Will Sparrow, liar and thief, becomes a runaway. On the road, he encounters a series of con artists . . . and learns that others are more adept than he at lying and thieving. Then he reluctantly joins a traveling troupe of 'oddities,' including a dwarf and a cat-faced girl. . . . At last Will is forced to understand that appearances are misleading and that he has been his own worst deceiver." (Publisher's note)

Includes bibliographical references.

Cutler, Jane

Leap, frog; pictures by Tracey Campbell Pearson. Farrar, Straus & Giroux 2002 197p il $16

Grades: 3 4 5   **Fic**

1. Frogs -- Fiction 2. Contests -- Fiction

ISBN 0-374-34362-4

LC 2001-54456

Edward and his new friend Charley prepare for the First Annual Mark Twain Memorial Jumping Frog Contest

There's "plenty for fans of the series to enjoy: humorous dialogue that doesn't strain too hard for laughs, eccentric secondary characters . . . and, in Edward, an appealing third-grade protagonist." Horn Book

Rats! pictures by Tracey Campbell Pearson. Farrar, Straus & Giroux 1996 114p il hardcover o.p. pa $5.95

Grades: 3 4 5   **Fic**

1. Brothers -- Fiction 2. Family life -- Fiction

ISBN 0-374-36181-9; 0-374-46203-8 pa

LC 95-22953

Fourth-grader Jason and his younger brother Edward shop for school clothes, get ready for Halloween, acquire a couple of pet rats, and deal with not-birthday presents from Aunt Bea

"The brothers, alternately squabbling and supporting each other, are convincing in this lighthearted episodic novel." Horn Book Guide

Other titles about Jason and Edward are:

'Gator aid (1999)

Leap, frog (2002)

No dogs allowed (1992)

D'Adamo, Francesco

Iqbal; a novel. written by Francesco D'Adamo; translated by Ann Leonori. Atheneum Bks. for Young Readers 2003 120p $15.95; pa $4.99

Grades: 5 6 7 8   **Fic**

1. Murder victims 2. Factory workers 3. Pakistan -- Fiction 4. Child labor -- Fiction 5. Children's rights advocates

ISBN 0-689-85445-5; 1-4169-0329-1 pa

LC 2002-153498

Original Italian edition, 2001

A fictionalized account of the Pakistani child who escaped from bondage in a carpet factory and went on to help liberate other children like him before being gunned down at the age of thirteen

"The situation and setting are made clear in this novel. Readers cannot help but be moved by the plight of these youngsters. . . . This readable book will certainly add breadth to most collections." SLJ

D'Lacey, Chris

Gauge; illustrated by Adam Stower. Orchard Books 105p il (The dragons of Wayward Crescent) $9.99

Grades: 2 3 4   **Fic**

1. Fantasy fiction 2. Dragons -- Fiction 3. Great Britain -- Fiction 4. Clocks and watches -- Fiction

ISBN 978-0-545-16831-1; 0-545-16831-7

When the town council decides to demolish the old library clock and replace it with a fancy modern one, Lucy and her mother try to save the historic timepiece—with the help of a dragon.

Gruffen; illustrated by Adam Stower. Orchard Books 2009 104p il (The dragons of Wayward Crescent) $9.99

Grades: 2 3 4   **Fic**

1. Fantasy fiction 2. Dragons -- Fiction 3. Great Britain -- Fiction

ISBN 978-0-545-16815-1; 0-545-16815-5

LC 2009011824

Lucy thinks there is a monster lurking outside her bedroom window, so her mother makes a dragon out of clay to protect her while she sleeps.

"This is a cozy and safe tale with bits of humor sprinkled throughout. Line drawings add visual interest; their cartoon style also enforces the light, upbeat mood." SLJ

Another title in this series is:

Gauge (2009)

Dahl, Michael

Guardian of Earth; written by Michael Dahl; illustrated by Dan Schoening. Stone Arch Books 2011 48p il (DC super heroes: Green Lantern) lib bdg $25.32; pa $5.95

Grades: 2 3 4   **Fic**

1. Superheroes -- Fiction 2. Extraterrestrial beings -- Fiction

ISBN 978-1-4342-2611-2 lib bdg; 1-4342-2611-5 lib bdg; 978-1-4342-3081-2 pa; 1-4342-3081-3 pa

LC 2010025600

Ace pilot Hal Jordan has a too-close-for-comfort encounter with a UFO. His jet takes a nosedive, but a gigantic green hand appears, grabs the aircraft, and prevents the crash. Hal's alien rescuer offers him an amazing green ring of untold power and announces that the human pilot is now the new Guardian of Earth.

This "chapter-book [adaptation] of [a] popular comic [superhero has] great, full-page illustrations and . . . onomatopoeia. . . . [The cover is a] 3-D [hologram] that will attract kids. . . . [This is] action-packed." SLJ

Includes glossary and bibliographical references

The **man** behind the mask; written by Michael Dahl; illustrated by Dan Schoening; Batman created by Bob Kane. Stone Arch Books 2010 48p il (DC super heroes. Batman) lib bdg $25.32; pa $5.95

Grades: 3 4 5   **Fic**

1. Superheroes -- Fiction 2. Batman (Fictional character)

ISBN 978-1-4342-1563-5 lib bdg; 1-4342-1563-6 lib bdg; 978-1-4342-1730-1 pa; 1-4342-1730-2 pa

LC 2009006303

This "full-color chapter [book is] fast moving and entertaining. . . . The story serves as a nice starting point for readers unfamiliar with the character. . . . The retro comic-book illustrations . . . appear every few pages, adding a vibrant visual element to the proceedings. Sound effects are displayed in large, expressive fonts and colors, capturing the feel of comics." SLJ

Dahl, Roald

The **BFG;** pictures by Quentin Blake. Farrar, Straus & Giroux 1982 219p il $18

Grades: 4 5 6   **Fic**

1. Giants -- Fiction 2. Orphans -- Fiction

ISBN 0-374-30469-6

LC 82-15548

Kidsnatched from her orphanage by a BFG (Big Friendly Giant), who spends his life blowing happy dreams to children, Sophie concocts with him a plan to save the world from nine other man-gobbling cannybull giants

This "is a book not all adults will like, but most kids will. . . . Highly unusual, often hilarious, and occasionally vulgar, even grisly." Booklist

★ **Charlie** and the chocolate factory; illustrated by Quentin Blake. rev ed.; Knopf 2001 162p il $15.95; lib bdg $17.99

Grades: 4 5 6 7   **Fic**
1. Conduct of life -- Fiction
ISBN 0-375-81526-0; 0-375-91526-5 lib bdg

LC 2001-29461

A newly illustrated edition of the title first published 1964

Each of five children lucky enough to discover an entry ticket into Mr. Willy Wonka's mysterious chocolate factory takes advantage of the situation in his own way

"Blake's energetic black-and-white illustrations enliven and update Dahl's cautionary rags-to-riches story. . . . The slapdash effect of the whimsical drawings matches Wonka's hyperactive speech and the generally frenetic narrative." Horn Book Guide

The **enormous** crocodile; illustrated by Quentin Blake. Knopf 2000 un il hardcover o.p. pa $7.99
Grades: 2 3 4   **Fic**
1. Animals -- Fiction 2. Crocodiles -- Fiction
ISBN 0-14-241453-0 pa

A reissue of the title first published 1978

"Mr. Dahl's gift for sonorous and inventive language carries the story along merrily . . . and Quentin Blake's squidgy jungle and scaly villain, colorful crowds and righteous elephant couldn't be improved upon." N Y Times Book Rev

★ **James** and the giant peach; a children's story. illustrated by Lane Smith. Knopf 1996 126p il $16; lib bdg $17.99
Grades: 4 5 6   **Fic**
1. Fantasy fiction
ISBN 0-679-88090-9; 0-679-98090-3 lib bdg

LC 91-33489

A newly illustrated edition of the title first published 1961

After the death of his parents, little James is forced to live with Aunt Sponge and Aunt Spike, two cruel old harpies. A magic potion causes the growing of a giant-sized peach on a puny peach tree. James sneaks inside the peach and finds a new world of insects. With his new family, James heads for many adventures

"A 'juicy' fantasy, 'dripping' with humor and imagination." Commonweal

The **magic** finger; illustrated by Quentin Blake. Viking 1995 62p hardcover o.p. pa $5.99
Grades: 2 3 4   **Fic**
1. Magic -- Fiction 2. Hunting -- Fiction
ISBN 0-670-85252-X; 0-14-241385-2 pa

LC 92-31443

A newly illustrated edition of the title first published 1966 by Harper & Row

Angered by a neighboring family's sport hunting, an eight-year-old girl turns her magic finger on them

This is an "original and intriguing fantasy." Booklist

Matilda; illustrations by Quentin Blake. Viking Kestrel 1988 240p $16.99; pa $6.99
Grades: 4 5 6   **Fic**
1. School stories
ISBN 0-670-82439-9; 0-14-241037-3 pa

LC 88-40312

Odyssey Honor Recording (2014)

"Dahl has written another fun and funny book with a child's perspective on an adult world. As usual, Blake's comical sketches are the perfect complement to the satirical humor." SLJ

Dakin, Glenn
The **Society** of Dread. Egmont USA 2010 318p (Candle Man) $15.99
Grades: 5 6 7 8   **Fic**
1. Adventure fiction 2. Superheroes -- Fiction
ISBN 978-1-60684-019-1; 1-60684-019-3

LC 2010023104

Sequel to: The Society of Unrelenting Vigilance (2009)

Now head of the Society of Good Works, teenaged Theo must reluctantly use his mysterious ability to melt evil when he ventures underground to face villains of old.

"This appealing contemporary fantasy has a fast-paced plot and enough inventive monsters and villains to captivate even the most reluctant readers." SLJ

The **Society** of Unrelenting Vigilance; [illustrations by Greg Swearingen] Egmont 2009 300p il (Candle Man) $15.99; lib bdg $18.99
Grades: 4 5 6 7   **Fic**
1. Adventure fiction 2. Superheroes -- Fiction
ISBN 978-1-60684-015-3; 1-60684-015-0; 978-1-60684-047-4 lib bdg; 1-60684-047-9 lib bdg

LC 2009-14035

Thirteen-year-old Theo, who has lived in seclusion his entire life, discovers he is the descendant of the Candle Man, a Victorian vigilante with the ability to melt criminals with a single touch.

This is a "lighthearted, action-driven adventure. . . . With the help of a cast of appealing characters, the nonstop action rolls to a satisfying conclusion." SLJ

Followed by: The Society of Dread (2010)

Dale, Anna
Magical mischief. Bloomsbury Children's Books 2011 300p $16.99; pa $7.99
Grades: 4 5 6   **Fic**
1. Magic -- Fiction 2. Booksellers and bookselling -- Fiction
ISBN 1-59990-629-5; 1-59990-630-9 pa; 978-1-59990-629-4; 978-1-59990-630-0 pa

LC 2010035627

Mr. Hardbattle, aided by his friends Miss Quint and resourceful thirteen-year-old Arthur, seeks a new place for all of the magic that has gone out of control and taken over his bookshop and home.

"Many charming details create their own sort of magic in this unusual story. . . . This chapter book should appeal to young readers who like their fantasy on the cozy side." Booklist

Daley, Michael J.
Space station rat; by Michael J. Daley. Holiday House 2005 181p $15.95; pa $6.99
Grades: 4 5 6   **Fic**
1. Science fiction 2. Rats -- Fiction 3. Space stations -- Fiction
ISBN 0-8234-1866-9; 0-8234-2151-1 pa

LC 2004-40534

A lavender rat that has escaped from a laboratory, and Jeff, a lonely boy whose parents are scientists, meet on an orbiting space station, communicate by email, and ultimately find themselves in need of each other's help and friendship

"The point of view shifts between Jeff and Rat. . . . The developing interspecies communication raises interesting questions about the nature of intelligence and individuality. A thoughtful and satisfying adventure." SLJ

Another title about Jeff and Rat is:
Rat trap (2008)

Daly, Niki

★ **Bettina** Valentino and the Picasso Club. Farrar, Straus and Giroux 2009 103p il $16

Grades: 4 5 6   **Fic**

1. School stories 2. Art -- Fiction 3. Teachers -- Fiction
ISBN 978-0-374-30753-0; 0-374-30753-9

LC 2008-03827

A controversial new teacher at Bayside Preparatory School introduces the exciting world of art to aspiring artist Bettina Valentino and her fifth-grade classmates, encouraging them to see everyday life in a different way.

"If the story's execution wasn't delightful enough (it is), Daly provides wonderful ink-and-wash drawings . . . that up the amusing ante. Not only are the cast's eccentricities on display, but Daly sometimes draws on the styles of famous artists." Booklist

Daneshvari, Gitty

Class is not dismissed! [illustrations by Carrie Gifford] Little, Brown and Company 2010 307p il $16.99

Grades: 4 5 6   **Fic**

1. School stories 2. Phobias -- Fiction
ISBN 978-0-316-03328-2; 0-316-03328-6

LC 2010006889

Sequel to: School of Fear (2009)

Thirteen-year-olds Madeleine, Theo, and Lulu, fourteen-year-old Garrison, and ten-year-old new "contestant" Hyacinth, must face their phobias and join forces to learn who is stealing wigs and pageant trophies from the School of Fear.

"Filled with an eclectic, and often eccentric, cast of characters, this sequel uses the wry humor and outrageous situations that characterized the first book and makes for an entertaining read." SLJ

The **League** of Unexceptional Children; when average calls. by Gitty Daneshvari. Little, Brown & Co. 2015 240 p. illustrations (hardcover : alk. paper) $17

Grades: 4 5 6   **Fic**

1. Humorous fiction 2. Spies -- Fiction 3. Popularity -- Fiction 4. Humorous stories 5. Kidnapping -- Fiction 6. Vice-Presidents -- Fiction
ISBN 0316405701; 9780316405706

LC 2014045518

This juvenile story, by Gitty Daneshvari, is the "first book in a . . . new adventure series. . . . The League of Unexceptional Children is a covert network that uses the nation's most average, normal, and utterly unexceptional children as spies. Why the average kids? Why not the brainiacs? Or the beauty queens? Or the jocks? It's simple: People remember them. But not the unexceptionals. They are the forgotten ones." (Publisher's note)

"This humorous new series is sure to appeal to fans of Daneshvari and other lovers of the ludicrous." Kirkus

School of Fear; illustrated by Carrie Gifford. Little, Brown Books for Young Readers 2009 339p il $15.99

Grades: 4 5 6   **Fic**

1. School stories 2. Phobias -- Fiction
ISBN 978-0-316-03326-8; 0-316-03326-X

LC 2008051309

Twelve-year-olds Madeleine, Theo, and Lulu, and thirteen-year-old Garrison, are sent to a remote Massachusetts school to overcome their phobias, but tragedy strikes and the quartet must work together—with no adult assistance—to face their fears.

This is "tautly paced, spine-tingling and quite funny." Publ Wkly

Followed by: Class is not dismissed! (2010)

Danneberg, Julie

Family reminders; illustrated by John Shelley. Charlesbridge 2009 105p il $14.95

Grades: 3 4 5   **Fic**

1. Colorado -- Fiction 2. Family life -- Fiction 3. Frontier and pioneer life -- Fiction
ISBN 978-1-58089-320-6; 1-58089-320-1

In 1890s Cripple Creek, Colorado, when young Mary McHugh's father loses his leg in a mining accident, she tries to help, both by earning money and by encouraging her father to go back to carving wooden figurines and playing piano.

"Shelley's India ink and pen illustrations add to the historical feel of this gentle, yet gripping story. This is a heartwarming novel about overcoming hardship." SLJ

Danziger, Paula

Amber Brown goes fourth; illustrated by Tony Ross. Putnam 1995 101p il $16.99

Grades: 2 3 4   **Fic**

1. Divorce -- Fiction 2. Friendship -- Fiction
ISBN 0-399-22849-7

LC 94-41935

Entering fourth grade, Amber faces some changes in her life as her best friend moves away and her parents divorce

"Reluctant and beginning readers will be drawn in by Danziger's present-tense, staccato style and by the short chapters. Kids coping with problems similar to Amber's will find encouragement, sympathy, and an upbeat way of taking responsibility for solving them. Entertaining and satisfying." SLJ

Amber Brown is feeling blue; illustrated by Tony Ross. Putnam 1998 130p il $16.99

Grades: 2 3 4   **Fic**

1. Divorce -- Fiction
ISBN 0-399-23179-X

LC 98-11233

Nine-year-old Amber Brown faces further complications because of her parents' divorce when her father plans to move back from Paris and she must decide which parent she will be with on Thanksgiving

"A likable nine year old with much common sense, she is willing to talk about her feelings openly and honestly and her first-person narration allows readers to be privy to these thoughts and emotions. Another winner in an appealing contemporary series." SLJ

Amber Brown is green with envy; illustrated by Tony Ross. Putnam 2003 151p il $16.99

Grades: 2 3 4   **Fic**

1. Divorce -- Fiction 2. Family life -- Fiction
ISBN 0-399-23181-1

LC 2003-127

Fourth-grader Amber Brown must make some important decisions when her mother and Max move their wedding date up and prepare to buy a house together, while her father makes some bad choices of his own

"The first-person narrative is fresh, articulate, and occasionally funny, though Danziger delivers more than light entertainment here. . . . Ross contributes lively, expressive ink drawings." Booklist

★ **Amber** Brown is not a crayon; illustrated by Tony Ross. Putnam 1994 80p il $15.99; pa $4.99

Grades: 2 3 4   **Fic**

1. School stories 2. Moving -- Fiction 3. Friendship -- Fiction
ISBN 0-399-22509-9; 0-14-240619-8 pa

LC 92-34673

The year she is in the third grade is a sad time for Amber because her best friend Justin is getting ready to move to a distant state

"Ross's black-and-white sketches throughout add humor and keep the pages turning swiftly. Danziger reaches out to a younger audience in this funny, touching slice of third-grade life, told in the voice of a feisty, lovable heroine." SLJ

Other titles about Amber Brown are:
Amber Brown goes fourth (1995)
Amber Brown is feeling blue (1998)
Amber Brown is green with envy (2003)
Amber Brown sees red (1997)
Amber Brown wants extra credit (1996)
Forever Amber Brown (1996)
I, Amber Brown (1999)
You can't eat your chicken pox, Amber Brown (1995)

Amber Brown sees red; illustrated by Tony Ross. Putnam 1997 116p il $15.99
Grades: 2 3 4   **Fic**
1. School stories 2. Divorce -- Fiction
ISBN 0-399-22901-9

LC 96-41227
The year that she is in the fourth grade is a difficult one for Amber, as she tries to deal with escalating telephone fights between her divorced parents and her father's impending return to take joint custody of her

"Ross's black-and-white cartoons help convey the character's feelings. Real emotion is mixed with comic relief, creating colorful characters in a lively story." SLJ

Amber Brown wants extra credit; illustrated by Tony Ross. Putnam 1996 120p il $16.99
Grades: 2 3 4   **Fic**
1. School stories 2. Divorce -- Fiction
ISBN 0-399-22900-0

LC 95-586
Unhappy over her parents' divorce and her mother's boyfriend Max, nine-year-old Amber finds her schoolwork suffering

"Danziger skillfully weaves the emotional threads into the fabric of a fourth-grader's everyday life. From the colorful jacket to the drawings throughout the book, Tony Ross' expressive and sometimes comical illustrations capture the spirit of the story." Booklist

Forever Amber Brown; illustrated by Tony Ross. Putnam 1996 101p il $15.99
Grades: 2 3 4   **Fic**
1. Family life -- Fiction
ISBN 0-399-22932-9

LC 96-19343
Amber's life has changed dramatically: her parents are divorced, her father lives in France, her best friend has moved to another state, and now her mother must decide whether to remarry.

"Through all the chaos, irrepressible Amber, buoyed by her loving relationship with her mother as well as her lively imagination and wonderful sense of humor, develops a growing understanding of herself and the people around her. Danziger's characterizations ring true." SLJ

I, Amber Brown; illustrated by Tony Ross. Putnam 1999 140p il $14.99
Grades: 2 3 4   **Fic**
1. Divorce -- Fiction
ISBN 0-399-23180-3

LC 98-52884

Because her divorced parents share joint custody of her, nine-year-old Amber suffers from lack of self-esteem and feels that she is a piece of jointly-owned property

"Full of Amber's puns and laugh-out-loud situational humor, this is also a deft handling of a very difficult yet common childhood dilemma." Booklist

You can't eat your chicken pox, Amber Brown; illustrated by Tony Ross. Putnam 1995 100p il $15.99
Grades: 2 3 4   **Fic**
1. Sick -- Fiction 2. Aunts -- Fiction 3. Divorce -- Fiction 4. Chickenpox -- Fiction
ISBN 0-399-22702-4

LC 93-37761
At the end of third grade, Amber is excited about her trip with her aunt to London and Paris, where she will see her father again, but her plans change when she comes down with chicken pox

"Danziger deftly balances the serious with the lighthearted, as Amber's chatty, first-person narration is also filled with humorous reflections and observations." Publ Wkly

Davies, Jacqueline
The **bell** bandit; by Jacqueline Davies. Houghton Mifflin 2012 174 p. ill. (The lemonade war series) $15.99
Grades: 3 4 5   **Fic**
1. Mystery fiction 2. Grandmothers -- Fiction 3. Mystery and detective stories 4. Brothers and sisters -- Fiction
ISBN 0547567375; 9780547567372

LC 2011039906
"When siblings Jessie and Evan (The Lemonade War, 2007, and The Lemonade Crime, 2011) accompany their mother on the time-honored midwinter holiday visit to their grandmother's home in the mountains, the changes are alarming. Fire damage to the house and Grandma's inability to recognize Evan are as disquieting as the disappearance of the iron bell, hung long ago by their grandmother on Lowell Hill and traditionally rung at the New Year." (Kirkus)

"Difficult issues are dealt with, including Maxwell's apparent autism-spectrum disorder and Grandma's dementia. Jessie's drawings are scattered throughout the book, adding both clarity and amusement. Though this is the third book of the Lemonade Wars series, it stands well on its own, and is a fine choice for young fans of mysteries or family stories." Library Review

Candy smash; by Jacqueline Davies. Houghton Mifflin Harcourt 2013 240 p. illustrations (The lemonade war series) $15.99
Grades: 3 4 5   **Fic**
1. School stories 2. Secrets -- Fiction 3. Love -- Fiction 4. Poetry -- Fiction 5. Schools -- Fiction 6. Brothers and sisters -- Fiction
ISBN 0544022084; 9780544022089

LC 2012033305
"As Valentine's Day approaches, Evan suffers through hearts-and-flowers crafts in school while wrestling with his secret crush on a classmate and discovering that he loves reading and writing poetry. Meanwhile, his precocious younger sister, Jessie (an aspiring journalist and also a classmate, having skipped a grade), prepares to reveal all in the latest edition of her newspaper." (Booklist)

"The Lemonade War series' fourth book captures the nuances of elementary-school drama and sibling dynamics. School-newspaper excerpts, poetry terms, and famous poems are appended." Horn Book

The **lemonade** crime. Houghton Mifflin Harcourt 2011 152p $15.99

Grades: 3 4 5   **Fic**
1. School stories 2. Trials -- Fiction 3. Siblings -- Fiction
ISBN 978-0-547-27967-1; 0-547-27967-1
LC 2010015231
Sequel to: The lemonade war (2007)
When money disappears from fourth-grader Evan's pocket and
everyone thinks that his annoying classmate Scott stole it, Evan's
younger sister stages a trial involving the entire class, trying to prove
what happened.
"The realistic depiction of the children's emotions and ways of expressing them will resonate with readers. Great for discussion, this involving and, at times, riveting chapter book has something to say and a
deceptively simple way of saying it." Booklist

The **lemonade** war. Houghton Mifflin Company 2007 173p $16;
pa $6.99
Grades: 3 4 5   **Fic**
1. Siblings -- Fiction 2. Money-making projects for children --
Fiction
ISBN 978-0-618-75043-6; 0-618-75043-6; 978-0-547-23765-7
pa; 0-547-23765-0 pa
LC 2006026076
Evan and his younger sister, Jesse, react very differently to the news
that they will be in the same class for fourth grade and as the end of summer approaches, they battle it out through lemonade stands, each trying
to be the first to earn 100 dollars. Includes mathematical calculations and
tips for running a successful lemonade stand.
The author "does a good job of showing the siblings' strengths,
flaws, and points of view in this engaging chapter book." Booklist
Followed by: The lemonade crime (2011)

The **magic** trap; Book 5. by Jacqueline Davies. Houghton Mifflin
Harcourt 2014 272 p. illustrations (The lemonade war series) (hardback) $15.99
Grades: 3 4 5   **Fic**
1. Children's stories 2. Magic tricks -- Fiction 3. Fathers -- Fiction
4. Brothers and sisters -- Fiction
ISBN 0544052897; 9780544052895
LC 2013024154
In this children's story by Jacqueline Davies, part of The Lemonade War Series, "Jessie and Evan Treski have waged a lemonade war,
sought justice in a class trial, unmasked a bell thief, and stood at opposite ends over . . . secrets. Now they are creating a magic show--a
professional magic show, in their own backyard! They practice, they
study, and they practice some more. And who shows up? Their father,
who has done such a good job of disappearing over the past few years."
(Publisher's note)
"One of the pleasures of reading the Lemonade War series...is watching the gradual development of the two main characters and the subtle
shifts in their relationship, never more apparent than in this story....
Readers intrigued by the magic theme will also appreciate the appended
instructions for a card trick. The series' many fans won't want to miss
this one." Booklist

Davies, Katie
The **great** dog disaster; Katie Davies; illustrated by Hannah Shaw.
Beach Lane Books 2013 208 p. (hardback) $12.99
Grades: 3 4 5 6 7   **Fic**
1. Dogs -- Fiction 2. Pets -- Fiction 3. Humorous stories 4.
England -- Fiction 5. Newfoundland dog -- Fiction 6. Brothers and
sisters -- Fiction 7. Family life -- England -- Fiction
ISBN 1442445173; 9781442445178; 9781442445185;
9781442445192
LC 2012041868

This book is the final book in the Great Critter Capers series by Katie Davies. Here, Suzanne is "thrilled to inherit Aunt Deidra's Beatrice,
an ancient, smelly, incontinent Newfoundland who remains stubbornly
inert until" Suzanne and her friend Anna realize: "Beatrice is depressed!
To boost her spirits, the girls bathe her in Suzanne's baby brother's
bath." But "a huge vet bill with the promise of more to come has Suzanne's parents murmuring that Beatrice would be better off elsewhere."
(Kirkus Reviews)

The **great** hamster massacre; illustrated by Hannah Shaw. Beach
Lane 2011 177p il (Great critter capers) $12.99
Grades: 2 3 4   **Fic**
1. Mystery fiction 2. Hamsters -- Fiction 3. Friendship -- Fiction
ISBN 978-1-4424-2062-5; 1-4424-2062-6
LC 2011-02046
Best friends and next-door neighbors Anna and Suzanne try to solve
the mystery of the death of Anna's two pet hamsters.
"Inspired use of simple words, straightforward syntax and effective
repetition make this a top pick for slow or reluctant readers. . . . Under
the plot's frothy surface lie serious depths. . . . An auspicious debut."
Kirkus
"Another title about Anna and Suzanne is:
The great rabbit rescue (2011)

The **great** rabbit rescue; illustrated by Hannah Shaw. Beach Lane
Books 2012 il (Great critter capers) $12.99
Grades: 2 3 4   **Fic**
1. Sick -- Fiction 2. Rabbits -- Fiction 3. Friendship -- Fiction
ISBN 978-1-4424-2064-9; 1-4424-2064-2
LC 201100832C
When Joe goes to live with his father across town and must leave
behind his beloved pet rabbit, his friends Anna and Suzanne try to take
care of it for him, but when the rabbit becomes ill and then Joe follows
suit, the girls are certain that both will die unless they are reunited.
This "showcases Davies' laconic style and deadpan humor, so well
matched to the chapter-book format. Neatly complementing the text,
Shaw's sly, witty illustrations, pie charts and graphics are a treat." Kirkus

Davies, Nicola, 1958-
The **Lion** who stole my arm; Nicola Davies, illustrated by Annabel
Wright. Candlewick Press 2014 96 p. illustrations $14.99
Grades: 2 3 4 5   **Fic**
1. Lions -- Fiction 2. Courage -- Fiction 3. Revenge -- Fiction 4
Wildlife conservation -- Fiction
ISBN 0763666203; 9780763666200
LC 201394308
This book, by Nicola Davies, is an "illustrated novel for young readers that proves you don't need two arms to be strong. Pedru has always
wanted to be a great hunter like his father, but after a lion takes his arm
he worries that he'll always be the crippled boy instead. Pedru longs to
kill the lion that mauled him and strengthens himself to be ready for the
hunt. But when the opportunity arises, will Pedru have the strength to
turn his back on revenge?" (Publisher's note)
"The terrifying title should attract readers with strong stomachs. Pedru, son of the best local hunter, lives in a village in East Africa. His
senses are attuned to the local animals, but one night, while checking his
snares at dusk, a lion attacks him. Pedru courageously fights, but he loses
his right arm. His life is entirely changed by this event, as the boy meets
scientists who are studying lions. He and his father become involved in
this project, and his father is later hired when a tourist lodge that allows
the lions to be seen but not hunted is built nearby. Pedru goes to college
and becomes a scientist himself. The pen-and-wash illustrations provide
details on the people, animals and village life in this part of Africa. An
afterword gives information about lion-conservation projects and how

they protect people while allowing the large cats to live. . . . Though on the purposive side, the tale both provides adventure and fills a cultural niche for chapter-book readers ." Kirkus.

The **Promise**; Nicola Davies, illustrated by Laura Carlin. Candlewick Press 2014 40 p. $16.99

Grades: K 1 2 3 4   **Fic**
1. Girls -- Fiction 2. Life change events -- Fiction 3. Acorns -- Fiction 4. Promises -- Fiction
ISBN 0763666335; 9780763666330

LC 2013934311

In this children's book by Nicola Davies, illustrated by Laura Carlin, "on a mean street in a mean, broken city, a young girl tries to snatch an old woman's bag. But the frail old woman, holding on with the strength of heroes, says the thief can't have it without giving something in return: the promise. It is the beginning of a journey that will change the thieving girl's life--and a chance to change the world, for good." (Publisher's note)

"A girl, with no name and of no particular age, describes a place as gritty as its people are hard: When I was young, I lived in a city that was mean and hard and ugly. She lives by stealing, and one day, she wrestles with an old woman for her bag, which the lady finally lets go of, with a condition: If you promise to plant them...Bright hues and plenty of greenery enliven the pages and lift the spirits. Lots to look at, think about, and discuss here." Booklist

Davis, Aubrey

A **hen** for Izzy Pippik. Kids Can 2012 32 p.

Grades: K 1 2   **Fic**
1. Folklore 2. Poverty -- Fiction 3. Cooperation -- Fiction 4. Picture books for children 5. Chickens -- Fiction
ISBN 9781554532438

This picture book depicts the adventures of a girl named Shaina, who "discovers an unusual hen . . . and strives to find its rightful owner -- a man called Izzy Pippik. Despite Shaina's insistence that he take back the hen, Pippik allows the hen, Yevka, and her flock of chicks to remain in their poor town. . . . Author Aubrey Davis has drawn upon Talmudic and Islamic folklore." (Kirkus Reviews)

Davis, Tony

Roland Wright: brand-new page; illustrated by Gregory Rogers. Delacorte Press 2010 133p il $12.99

Grades: 2 3 4   **Fic**
1. Castles -- Fiction 2. Middle Ages -- Fiction 3. Knights and knighthood -- Fiction
ISBN 978-0-385-73802-6; 0-385-73802-1
Sequel to: Roland Wright, future knight (2009)
First published 2008 in Australia

In 1409, aspiring knight Roland Wright joins the royal household at Twofold Castle as a new page, but his plan to impress King John and his knights quickly backfires.

"Goofy cartoon illustrations keep the mood light. . . . A solid choice for children who are ready to make the leap to chapter books." SLJ

Roland Wright: future knight. Delacorte Press 2009 129p il $12.99; lib bdg $15.99

Grades: 2 3 4   **Fic**
1. Middle Ages -- Fiction 2. Knights and knighthood -- Fiction
ISBN 978-0-385-73800-2; 0-385-73800-5; 978-0-385-90706-4 lib bdg; 0-385-90706-0 lib bdg

LC 2008053074

First published 2007 in the United Kingdom

In 1409, skinny, clumsy Roland, the ten-year-old son of a black-smith, pursues his dream of becoming a knight.

"This engaging book, the first in a series, has accurate details about the Middle Ages and a feisty, persevering hero. . . . Rogers's charming pen-and-ink illustrations enhance the story and may also make it more appealing to reluctant readers." SLJ

Another title about Roland Wright is:
Roland Wright: brand-new page (2010)

De Angeli, Marguerite Lofft

The **door** in the wall; by Marguerite de Angeli. Doubleday 1989 120p il hardcover o.p. pa $4.99

Grades: 4 5 6   **Fic**
1. Middle Ages -- Fiction 2. Great Britain -- Fiction 3. Children with physical disabilities -- Fiction
ISBN 0-385-07283-X; 0-440-22779-8 pa
First published 1949
Awarded the Newbery Medal, 1950

Robin, a crippled boy in fourteenth-century England, proves his courage and earns recognition from the King

"An enthralling and inspiring tale of triumph over handicap. Unusually beautiful illustrations, full of authentic detail, combine with the text to make life in England during the Middle Ages come alive." N Y Times Book Rev

Thee, Hannah! written and illustrated by Marguerite de Angeli. Herald Press 2000 99p il pa $15.99

Grades: 3 4 5   **Fic**
1. Philadelphia (Pa.) -- Fiction 2. Society of Friends -- Fiction
ISBN 0-8361-9106-4

LC 99-52422

A reissue of the title first published 1940 by Doubleday

Nine-year-old Hannah, a Quaker living in Philadelphia just before the Civil War, longs to have some fashionable dresses like other girls but comes to appreciate her heritage and its plain dressing when her family saves the life of a runaway slave

"Hannah and the other children are very real and, in addition to the [author's] lovely pictures that follow the story, the street cries of old Philadelphia are effectively introduced and illustrated at the beginning of each chapter." Libr J

De Fombelle, Timothée, 1973-

Toby alone; translated by Sarah Ardizzone; illustrated by François Place. Candlewick Press 2009 384p il $17.99; pa $8.99

Grades: 5 6 7 8   **Fic**
1. Fantasy fiction 2. Trees -- Fiction
ISBN 0-7636-4181-2; 0-7636-4815-9 pa; 978-0-7636-4181-8; 978-0-7636-4815-2 pa
Original French edition 2006

Toby is just one and a half millimeters tall, and he's the most wanted person in his world of the great oak Tree. When Toby's father discovers that the Tree is alive, he realizes that exploiting it could do damage to their world. Refusing to reveal the secret to an enraged community, Toby's parents have been imprisoned. Only Toby has managed to escape, but for how long?

"The impressive debut novel from French playwright de Fombelle deftly weaves mature political commentary, broad humor and some subtle satire into a thoroughly enjoyable adventure." Publ Wkly

De Goldi, Kate

The **ACB** with Honora Lee; by Kate De Goldi; drawings by Gregory O'Brien. Longacre 2012 124 p. ill. (chiefly col.) (hardcover) $17.99

Grades: 4 5 6 7   **Fic**
1. Patience 2. Alphabet -- Fiction 3. Grandparent-grandchild relationship 4. Rest homes -- Fiction 5. Grandparent and child

-- Fiction
ISBN 1770497226; 9781869799892; 9781770497221
LC 2012515235

In this juvenile book, by Kate De Goldi, illustrated by Gregory O'Brien, "Perry's mother and father are busy people . . . they're impatient, they're tired, they get cross easily. And they think that only children, like Perry, should be kept busy. . . . Perry . . . discovers her Gran has an unconventional interest in the alphabet, so Perry decides to make an alphabet book. . . . Soon everyone is interested in Perry's book project." (Publisher's note)

"Nine-year-old Perry, an only child, spends Thursday afternoons with her grandmother, Honora Lee, who lives at the Santa Lucia nursing home and suffers from dementia. With Honora Lee's help, Perry writes and illustrates an alphabet book about the residents. Fans of middle grade novels with quirky female protagonists will enjoy this story and its stylish color illustrations, which suit the mood of the text." Horn Book

De Guzman, Michael

Henrietta Hornbuckle's circus of life. Farrar, Straus and Giroux 2010 152p $16.99

Grades: 4 5 6 **Fic**

1. Death -- Fiction 2. Circus -- Fiction 3. Clowns -- Fiction 4. Bereavement -- Fiction 5. Family life -- Fiction
ISBN 978-0-374-33513-7; 0-374-33513-3
LC 2009-13602

Twelve-year-old Henrietta Hornbuckle and her parents perform as clowns in a tiny, ramshackle traveling circus until a family tragedy jeopardizes Henrietta's whole offbeat world

"The writing is worthy of a tall tale, but the details are all realistic. A simple and satisfying story with a likable, unusual star." Booklist

De Lint, Charles, 1951-

The **cats** of Tanglewood Forest; written by Charles de Lint; illustrated by Charles Vess. Little, Brown 2013 304 p. $17.99

Grades: 4 5 6 **Fic**

1. Cats -- Fiction 2. Trees -- Fiction 3. Fantasy fiction 4. Magic -- Fiction 5. Orphans -- Fiction 6. Snakebites -- Fiction
ISBN 0316053570; 9780316053570
LC 2011042982

Expanded version of A Circle of Cats (2003)

In this children's story, by Charles de Lint, illustrated by Charles Vess, "Lillian Kindred spends her days exploring the Tanglewood Forest, a magical, rolling wilderness. . . . Until the day the cats of the forest save her life by transforming her into a kitten. Now Lillian must set out on a perilous adventure that will lead her through untamed lands of fabled creatures--from Old Mother Possum to the fearsome Bear People--to find a way to make things right." (Publisher's note)

Seven wild sisters; A Modern Fairy Tale. written by Charles de Lint; illustrated by Charles Vess. Little, Brown and Co. 2013 272 p. color illustrations $18

Grades: 4 5 6 **Fic**

1. Magic -- Fiction 2. Fairies -- Fiction 3. Sisters -- Fiction 4. Kidnapping -- Fiction 5. Adventure and adventurers -- Fiction
ISBN 0316053562; 9780316053563
LC 2012045328

This book, by Charles de Lint, is a "companion novel to 'The Cats of Tanglewood Forest.' . . . When it comes to fairies, Sarah Jane Dillard must be careful what she wishes for. . . . When Sarah Jane discovers a tiny man wounded by a cluster of miniature poison arrows, she brings him to the reclusive Aunt Lillian for help. But the two quickly find themselves ensnared in a longtime war between rival fairy clans, and Sarah Jane's six sisters have been kidnapped to use as ransom." (Publisher's note)

"Beautiful bookmaking, lovely storytelling and wondrous illustrations make for a splendid sequel-of-sorts to The Cats of Tanglewood Forest (2013). The little girl of the earlier tale is now 'Aunt' Lillian, a woman in her 80s who lives alone and who fascinates young Sarah Jane Dillard, the middle of seven red-haired sisters. . . . The language is as pretty on the page as it is in the speaking, with rich echoes of fantasy tropes. The story and the art are reworked from a limited edition of some time ago, described by Vess in an artist's note. There is a promise of more stories at the ever-so-satisfying end, which comes with the tiniest hint of romance past and future-readers will be enchanted." Kirkus

De Quidt, Jeremy

The **toymaker**; with illustrations by Gary Blythe. David Fickling Books 2010 356p il $16.99; lib bdg $19.99

Grades: 5 6 7 8 **Fic**

1. Adventure fiction 2. Young adult literature 3. Toys -- Fiction
ISBN 978-0-385-75180-3; 0-385-75180-X; 978-0-385-75181-0 lib bdg; 0-385-75181-8 lib bdg

"Mathias . . . upon the death of his conjurer grandfather, is spirited away from the decrepit carnival they called home. His unknown new guardian appears to be after the secret contained on an inherited piece of paper, which is now in Mathias' possession. . . . Moving briskly across an atmospheric Germanic setting, the characters are chased by howling wolves, a dangerous dwarf, and unforgiving cold in a bloody, mysterious, and darkly thrilling quest." Booklist

Deedy, Carmen Agra

★ The **Cheshire** Cheese cat; a Dickens of a tale. [by] Carmen Agra Deedy & Randall Wright; drawings by Barry Moser. Peachtree Publishers 2011 228p il $16.95

Grades: 5 6 7 8 **Fic**

1. Young adult literature 2. Cats -- Fiction 3. Mice -- Fiction 4. London (England) -- Fiction 5. Great Britain -- History -- 19th century -- Fiction
ISBN 978-1-56145-595-9; 1-56145-595-4
LC 2010052275

"The vagaries of tavern life in 19th-century London come alive in this delightful tale. . . . The fast-moving plot is a masterwork of intricate detail that will keep readers enthralled, and the characters are well rounded and believable. Language is a highlight of the novel; words both elegant and colorful fill the pages. . . . Combined with Moser's precise pencil sketches of personality-filled characters, the book is a success in every way." SLJ

The **yellow** star; the legend of King Christian X of Denmark. illustrated by Henri Sørensen. Peachtree Pubs. 2000 un il $16.95

Grades: 3 4 5 **Fic**

1. Kings 2. Denmark -- Fiction 3. Holocaust, 1933-1945 -- Fiction 4. World War, 1939-1945 -- Fiction
ISBN 1-56145-208-4
LC 00-20602

Retells the story of King Christian X and the Danish resistance to the Nazis during World War II

"Deedy's language is simple and rhythmic. . . . This is an interesting and thought-provoking piece of work." SLJ

DeFelice, Cynthia C.

Bringing Ezra back. Farrar, Straus & Giroux 2006 147p $16

Grades: 4 5 6 7 **Fic**

1. Voyages and travels -- Fiction 2. Frontier and pioneer life -- Fiction
ISBN 0-374-39939-5
LC 2005-4976

In the mid-1800s, twelve-year-old Nathan journeys from his farm on the Ohio frontier to Western Pennsylvania to rescue a friend held captive by the owners of a freak show.

"Told in Nathan's voice, this adventure treats readers to a double-dip cliff-hanging plot and heart-searing maturation." SLJ

Sequel to Weasel (1990)

Fort; Cynthia DeFelice. Farrar, Straus & Giroux 2015 208 p. (hardback) $16.99

Grades: 4 5 6 7 **Fic**

1. Summer -- Fiction 2. Bullies -- Fiction 3. Friendship -- Fiction 4. Bullying -- Fiction 5. Great-aunts -- Fiction 6. Best friends -- Fiction 7. Great-uncles -- Fiction

ISBN 0374324271; 9780374324278

LC 2014040167

This book by Cynthia DeFelice "is told as a flashback in the 'What I Did on My Summer Vacation' essay that" narrator Wyatt "has no intention of showing to a teacher." (Booklist) "When older boys tear apart the fort where they have been enjoying a wonderful summer, Wyatt and Augie team up with another bullied kid to exact revenge, with unexpected consequences." (Publisher's note)

"Stuffed full of clever pranks and summertime nostalgia, this is a story of kindness and adventure, and a rare breed in the middle-grade canon that doesn't rely on cheap humor to hold attention. A boisterous and poignant coming-of-age tale." Booklist

The **ghost** and Mrs. Hobbs; [by] Cynthia DeFelice. Farrar, Straus & Giroux 2001 180p $16; pa $5.99

Grades: 4 5 6 **Fic**

1. Ghost stories

ISBN 0-374-38046-5; 0-06-001172-6 pa

LC 00-52827

Hindered by a fight with her friend Dub and a series of mysterious fires, eleven-year-old Allie investigates the fire seventeen years earlier which claimed the lives of the husband and infant son of a school cafeteria worker, as well as the handsome young man whose ghost asks Allie for help

"This is a diverting and suspenseful ghost story offering a likable protagonist and a thrilling romantic spark." Horn Book

The **ghost** of Cutler Creek; [by] Cynthia DeFelice. 1st ed; Farrar, Straus and Giroux 2004 181p $16; pa $5.95

Grades: 4 5 6 **Fic**

1. Ghost stories 2. Mystery fiction 3. Dogs -- Fiction

ISBN 0-374-38058-9; 0-374-40004-0 pa

LC 2003-49051

When Allie is contacted by the ghost of a dog, she and Dub investigate the surly new boy at school and his father, who may be running a puppy mill, to see if they are involved.

"DeFelice has created a suspenseful tale that will leave readers rapidly turning pages." SLJ

★ The **ghost** of Fossil Glen; by Cynthia DeFelice. Farrar, Straus & Giroux 1998 167p (Ghost Mysteries) $16; pa $7.99

Grades: 4 5 6 **Fic**

1. Ghost stories

ISBN 0-374-31787-9; 9780312602130 pa

LC 97-33230

"Strange events begin when a calm, unknown voice prevents Allie from panicking and falling from a dangerous cliff while fossil hunting. Then, an old journal mysteriously appears in her mailbox. Allie often feels a presence nearby and dreams of a girl falling from the cliff. She then discovers the grave marker of an 11-year-old girl who was missing and presumed dead in 1994. Because of her reputation for telling

stories, Allie cannot convince anyone to believe her except her longtime friend and fellow fossil hunter, Dub. Driven to pursue the mystery, Allie finds an old diary that provides her with facts about the girl's death. Foolishly, she reveals what she knows and endangers her own life. . . . Grades four to six." (SLJ)

"Sixth-grader Allie Nichols encounters the ghost of Lucy Stiles and becomes involved with Lucy's unsolved death, eventually finding proof that Lucy was murdered." Horn Book Guide

The **ghost** of Poplar Point; [by] Cynthia DeFelice. 1st ed.; Farrar, Straus and Giroux 2007 183p $16

Grades: 4 5 6 7 **Fic**

1. Ghost stories 2. Seneca Indians -- Fiction 3. New York (State) -- Fiction

ISBN 0-374-32540-5; 978-0-374-32540-4

LC 2006047329

Prompted by the ghost of a young Seneca Indian girl, twelve-year-old Allie and her friend Dub are determined, despite the opposition of an unscrupulous property developer, that the historical pageant celebrating the founding of their town tells the truth about the fate of the Seneca people who lived there during the Revolutionary War.

"This engaging book moves along quickly to a satisfying conclusion." Booklist

The **missing** manatee; [by] Cynthia DeFelice. Farrar, Straus and Giroux 2005 181p $16; pa $6.95

Grades: 5 6 7 8 **Fic**

1. Mystery fiction 2. Fishing -- Fiction 3. Florida -- Fiction

ISBN 0-374-31257-5; 0-374-40020-2 pa

LC 2004-50633

While coping with his parents' separation, eleven-year-old Skeet spends most of Spring Break in his skiff on a Florida river, where he finds a manatee shot to death and begins looking for the killer

"DeFelice offers a realistic adventure story that is fast paced and full of drama. . . . The characters are multifaceted and well developed, and the story should prompt readers to think about cause and effect." SLJ

★ **Signal**. Farrar, Straus and Giroux 2009 151p $16.99

Grades: 5 6 7 8 **Fic**

1. Moving -- Fiction 2. Friendship -- Fiction 3. Loneliness -- Fiction 4. Child abuse -- Fiction 5. Country life -- Fiction

ISBN 978-0-374-39915-3; 0-374-39915-8

LC 2008-09278

After moving with his emotionally distant father to the Finger Lakes region of upstate New York, twelve-year-old Owen faces a lonely summer until he meets an abused girl who may be a space alien.

"Well-drawn secondary characters create a threatening backdrop to the developing mystery, while Owen's poignant relationship with his work-driven father elicits sympathy. The tension builds on several fronts to a gripping climax and satisfying conclusion. Owen's likable voice, the plot's quick pace and the science fiction overtones make this a winner." Publ Wkly

Weasel; [by] Cynthia DeFelice. Avon Books 1990 119p pa $4.99

Grades: 4 5 6 7 **Fic**

1. Ohio -- Fiction 2. Frontier and pioneer life -- Fiction

ISBN 978-0-380-71358-5 pa; 0-380-71358-6 pa

First published 1990 by Macmillan

Alone in the frontier wilderness in the winter of 1839 while his father is recovering from an injury, eleven-year-old Nathan runs afoul of the renegade killer known as the weasel and makes a surprising discovery about the concept of revenge

"A masterfully told, riveting tale sure to inspire strong discussion about moral choices." SLJ

Wild life; by Cynthia DeFelice. Farrar, Straus and Giroux 2011 177p $16.99

Grades: 4 5 6   **Fic**

1. Dogs -- Fiction 2. Hunting -- Fiction 3. Grandparents -- Fiction 4. North Dakota -- Fiction 5. Runaway children -- Fiction 6. Wilderness survival -- Fiction

ISBN 978-0-374-38001-4; 0-374-38001-5

When twelve-year-old Eric's parents are deployed to Iraq, he goes to live with grandparents he hardly knows in small-town North Dakota, but his grandfather's hostility and the threat of losing the dog he has rescued are too much and Eric runs away.

"Themes of accepting change and learning to let go are woven into this winning tale of boy and dog." SLJ

DeGross, Monalisa

Donavan's double trouble; [by] Monalisa DeGross; illustrated by Amy Bates. Amistad 2008 180p il $15.99; lib bdg $17.89

Grades: 2 3 4   **Fic**

1. School stories 2. Uncles -- Fiction 3. Amputees -- Fiction 4. African Americans -- Fiction

ISBN 978-0-06-077293-2; 978-0-06-077294-9 lib bdg

LC 2007011244

Fourth-grader Donavan is sensitive about the problems he has understanding math, and then when his favorite uncle, a former high school basketball star, returns from National Guard duty an amputee, Donavan's problems get even worse as he struggles to accept this "new" Uncle Vic.

"The fast, funny dialogue between friends and the warm family relationships will draw readers to the realistic story." Booklist

Another title about Donavan is:

Donavan's word jar (1994)

DeJong, Meindert

The **wheel** on the school; pictures by Maurice Sendak. Harper & Row 1954 298p il $18.95; pa $6.95

Grades: 4 5 6   **Fic**

1. School stories 2. Storks -- Fiction 3. Netherlands -- Fiction

ISBN 0-06-021585-2; 0-06-021586-0 lib bdg; 0-06-440021-2 pa

Awarded the Newbery Medal, 1955

"This author goes deeply into the heart of childhood and has written a moving story, filled with suspense and distinguished for the quality of its writing." Child Books Too Good To Miss

DeKeyser, Stacy

The **Brixen** Witch; Stacy DeKeyser. Margaret K. McElderry Books 2012 208 p. (hardcover) $15.99

Grades: 4 5 6 7 8   **Fic**

1. Horror fiction 2. Paranormal fiction 3. Witches -- Fiction 4. Rats -- Fiction 5. Magic -- Fiction 6. Witchcraft -- Fiction 7. Community life -- Fiction

ISBN 9781442433281; 9781442433304

LC 2011033680

In this book, "12-year-old Rudi Bauer thinks he's found a treasure, [but] no good can come from taking something that belongs to the Brixen Witch. His sleep is plagued by nightmares, but when they stop there's no relief--the village is infested with rats. . . . As his Oma points out, young Rudi, the one child left behind after the children disappear and the one who precipitated the crisis, is the one to make things right." (Kirkus Reviews)

DeLaCroix, Alice

The **best** horse ever; illustrated by Ronald Himler. Holiday House 2010 74p il $15.95

Grades: 3 4 5   **Fic**

1. Horses -- Fiction 2. Friendship -- Fiction

ISBN 978-0-8234-2254-8; 0-8234-2254-2

LC 2009-2554

"Abby gets her heart's desire: her parents purchase Griffin, the gentle horse she has grown to love during her riding lessons. But when her best friend, Devon, can't get past her fear of the horse to share Abby' excitement, they quarrel. . . . Although girls who love horses are the obvious audience, other readers will also enjoy this appealing chapter book with its simple plot and subtly drawn characters. . . . Himler contributes shaded pencil drawings that capture the actions and emotions of the characters." Booklist

Delaney, Joseph, 1945-

The **ghost** prison; Joseph Delaney. Sourcebooks Fire 2013 11. p. (hc : alk. paper) $12.99

Grades: 4 5 6 7 8   **Fic**

1. Horror fiction 2. Prisons -- Fiction 3. Horror stories 4. Ghost -- Fiction 5. Orphans -- Fiction 6. Supernatural -- Fiction

ISBN 1402293186; 9781402293184

LC 201301789

This novella is set in the same universe as Joseph Delaney's Last Apprentice series. The story "is narrated by orphan Billy Calder, who is apprehensive about the new job he has landed: helping guard an infamously haunted prison on the night shift. The ghosts and dangers turn out to be all too real, as Billy learns about the prison's bloody history and has life-altering encounter one night while on the job." (Publishers Weekly)

★ **Revenge** of the witch; illustrations by Patrick Arrasmith. Greenwillow Bks. 2005 344p il (The last apprentice) $14.99; lib bdg $15.89; pa $7.99

Grades: 5 6 7 8   **Fic**

1. Witches -- Fiction 2. Supernatural -- Fiction

ISBN 0-06-076618-2; 0-06-076619-0 lib bdg; 0-06-076620-4 pa

LC 2004-5400

Young Tom, the seventh son of a seventh son, starts work as an apprentice for the village spook, whose job is to protect ordinary folk from "ghouls, boggarts, and all manner of wicked beasties"

"Delaney grabs readers by the throat and gives them a good shake in a smartly crafted story. . . . This is a gristly thriller. . . . Yet the twisted horror is amply buffered by an exquisitely normal young hero, matter-of-fact prose, and a workaday normalcy." Booklist

Other titles in this series are:

Curse of the bane (2006)

Night of the soul-stealer (2007)

Attack of the fiend (2008)

Wrath of the Bloodeye (2008)

Clash of the demons (2009)

Rise of the huntress (2010)

Rage of the fallen (2011)

Grimalkin, the witch assassin (2012)

Lure of the dead (2012)

Slither (2013)

I am Alice (2013)

Fury of the seventh son (2014)

Dellinger, Paul

Fuzzy; by Tom Angleberger and Paul Dellinger. Amulet Books 2016 272 p. (hardback) $14.95

Grades: 4 5 6 7   **Fic**

1. Robots -- Fiction 2. Schools -- Fiction 3. Secrets -- Fiction

Middle schools -- Fiction
ISBN 9781419721229

LC 2016012399

In this book by Tom Angleberger and Paul Dellinger "when Max—Maxine Zelaster—befriends her new robot classmate Fuzzy, part of Vanguard One Middle School's new Robot Integration Program, she helps him learn everything he needs to know about surviving middle school—the good, the bad, and the really, really, ugly. Little do they know that surviving seventh grade is going to become a true matter of life and death, because Vanguard has an evil presence at its heart." (Publisher's note)

"The result is a smart, sci-fi page-turner that will grab kids' imagination and appeal to their conscience and sense of humor." Booklist

DeMatteis, J. M.

Imaginalis. Katherine Tegen Books 2010 248p $16.99

Grades: 5 6 7 8   **Fic**

1. Fantasy fiction 2. Magic -- Fiction 3. Imagination -- Fiction 4. Books and reading -- Fiction

ISBN 978-0-06-173286-7; 0-06-173286-9

Devastated that her favorite fantasy book series will not be completed, twelve-year-old Mehera discovers that only her belief, imagination, and courage will save the land of Imaginalis and its inhabitants from being lost forever.

This is "a sure-footed fantasy. . . . The well-drawn characters, abundant action and humor, and hopeful message about the power of reading and belief keep it afloat." Publ Wkly

Derby, Sally

Kyle's island. Charlesbridge 2010 191p $16.95

Grades: 5 6 7 8   **Fic**

1. Lakes -- Fiction 2. Islands -- Fiction 3. Michigan -- Fiction 4. Siblings -- Fiction 5. Family life -- Fiction

ISBN 978-1-58089-316-9; 1-58089-316-3

LC 2009-17581

Kile, almost thirteen, spends much of the summer yearning to explore a nearby island, striving to be a good brother, fishing with an elderly neighbor, and fuming at his parents over their separation that is forcing his mother to sell the family's cabin on a Michigan lake.

"Derby writes a subtle coming-of-age novel that is engaging from start to finish. Kyle's character is so well developed that many readers will be able to understand the realistic emotions and situations taking place." Libr Media Connect

Deriso, Christine Hurley

The **Right**-Under Club; [by] Christine Hurley Deriso. Delacorte Press 2007 195p $15.99; lib bdg $18.99

Grades: 5 6 7 8   **Fic**

1. Friendship -- Fiction 2. Stepfamilies -- Fiction

ISBN 978-0-385-73334-2; 978-0-385-90351-6 lib bdg

LC 2006019768

Over the summer, five middle school girls form a club based on the fact that they all feel neglected and misunderstood by their blended families

"In this timely novel, Deriso introduces solid characters. . . . The changing voices are easy to navigate and lend charm to the narrative." SLJ

DeStefano, Lauren

A **curious** tale of the in-between; by Lauren DeStefano. Bloomsbury 2015 240 p. (hardcover) $16.99

Grades: 4 5 6 7   **Fic**

1. Ghost stories 2. Aunts -- Fiction 3. Orphans -- Fiction 4. Friendship -- Fiction 5. Loss (Psychology) -- Fiction 6. Ghosts

-- Fiction 7. Psychic ability -- Fiction
ISBN 161963600X; 9781619636002

LC 2014035767

In this book, by Lauren DeStefano, "Pram Bellamy is special--she can talk to ghosts. She doesn't have too many friends amongst the living, but that's all right. . . . Then Pram meets Clarence, a boy from school who has also lost a parent and is looking for answers. Together they arrive at the door of the mysterious Lady Savant, who promises to help. But this spiritualist knows the true nature of Pram's power, and what she has planned is more terrifying than any ghost. " (Publisher's note)

"Pram's pregnant mother committed suicide, but the doctors managed to save the baby. Eleven years later, eccentric Pram talks to the dead, and her best friend is ghostly Felix. When she enters the memories of the dead, Pram learns more about her own past, and Felix's, than she bargained for. Fans of Holly Black's Doll Bones may well enjoy this creepy, character-based tale." Horn Book

The **peculiar** night of the blue heart; by Lauren DeStefano. Bloomsbury 2016 208 p. (hardback) $16.99

Grades: 4 5 6 7   **Fic**

1. Orphans -- Fiction 2. Spirits -- Fiction 3. Friendship -- Fiction 4. Best friends -- Fiction 5. Spirit possession -- Fiction

ISBN 9781619636453; 1619636433; 9781619636439

LC 2015046636

In this book, by Lauren DeStefano, "Lionel is a wild boy, who doesn't much like to be around other people. . . . Marybeth is a nice girl . . . and she's kind to everyone at the orphanage . . . Lionel most of all. Different though they are, Lionel and Marybeth are best friends in a world that has forgotten about them. So when a mysterious blue spirit possesses Marybeth--and starts to take control--they know they must stop it before the real Marybeth fades away forever." (Publisher's note)

"As the mystery unravels, she incorporates difficult subjects that include murder, abuse, and grief, handling them in a straightforward manner that readers will appreciate." Pub Wkly

Diamand, Emily

Flood and fire. Chicken House/Scholastic 2011 351p il (Raiders' ransom) $17.99

Grades: 4 5 6 7   **Fic**

1. Science fiction 2. Adventure fiction 3. Cats -- Fiction 4. Robots -- Fiction 5. Computers -- Fiction 6. Terrorism -- Fiction 7. Great Britain -- Fiction

ISBN 978-0-545-24268-4; 0-545-24268-1

LC 2010023544

Sequel to: Raiders' ransom (2009)

In 22nd-century Cambridge, England, thirteen-year-old Lilly Melkun must try to stop the strange, uncontrollable robots that were activated when a sinister-looking chip in her hand-held computer triggered a false anti-terrorist alert.

"The rare combination of action at breakneck speed and significant, believable character development makes this just about impossible to put down." Kirkus

★ **Raiders'** ransom. Chicken House/Scholastic 2009 334p map $17.99

Grades: 4 5 6 7   **Fic**

1. Science fiction 2. Adventure fiction 3. Pirates -- Fiction 4. Kidnapping -- Fiction 5. Great Britain -- Fiction 6. Environmental degradation -- Fiction

ISBN 978-0-545-14297-7; 0-545-14297-0

LC 2008-43692

It's the 22nd century and, because of climate change, much of England is underwater. Poor Lilly is out fishing with her trusty sea-cat when greedy raiders pillage the town—and kidnap the prime minister's daughter. Her village blamed, Lilly decides to find the girl.

This is a "captivating story. . . . A well-drawn world, plot twists galore and spunky characters make this one a true page-turner." Kirkus

Folllowed by: Flood and fire (2011)

Diaz, Alexandra

The **only** road; Alexandra Diaz. Simon & Schuster Books for Young Readers 2016 320 p. (hardback) $16.99

Grades: 4 5 6   **Fic**

1. Bildungsromans 2. Refugees -- Fiction 3. Organized crime -- Fiction 4. Guatemalan Americans -- Fiction 5. Emigration and immigration -- Fiction

ISBN 1481457500; 9781481457507

LC 2015046179

Pura Belpre Author Honor Book (2017)

In this novel, by Alexandra Diaz, "everyone in Jaime's small town in Guatemala knows someone who has been killed by the Alphas, a powerful gang that's known for violence and drug trafficking. Anyone who refuses to work for them is hurt or killed—like Miguel. With Miguel gone, Jaime fears that he is next. There's only one choice: accompanied by his cousin Ángela, Jaime must flee his home to live with his older brother in New Mexico." (Publisher's note)

"Readers will find themselves immersed in the fast-paced narrative as the cousins struggle to find a moment of safety on a dangerous route to an uncertain future. Diaz, herself a child of immigrants, laces Jaime and Ángela's tale with plenty of Spanish words, and a glossary offers definitions, as well as pronunciation tips, for non-Spanish speakers." Booklist

DiCamillo, Kate

★ **Because** of Winn-Dixie. Candlewick Press 2000 182p $15.99; pa $6.99

Grades: 4 5 6 7   **Fic**

1. Dogs -- Fiction 2. Florida -- Fiction

ISBN 978-0-7636-0776-0; 0-7636-0776-2; 978-0-7636-4432-1 pa; 0-7636-4432-3 pa

LC 99-34260

A Newbery honor book, 2001

Ten-year-old India Opal Buloni describes her first summer in the town of Naomi, Florida, and all the good things that happen to her because of her big ugly dog Winn-Dixie

"This well-crafted, realistic, and heartwarming story will be read and reread as a new favorite deserving a long-term place on library shelves." SLJ

★ **Bink** & Gollie; [by] Kate DiCamillo and Alison McGhee; illustrated by Tony Fucile. Candlewick Press 2010 81p il $15.99

Grades: 1 2 3   **Fic**

1. Friendship -- Fiction

ISBN 0-7636-3266-X; 978-0-7636-3266-3

LC 2009-49100

Two roller-skating best friends share adventures involving bright socks, a trek to the Andes, and an unlikely companion. "Ages six to eight." (N Y Times Book Rev)

"In the first tale, Bink's outrageous socks offend Gollie's sartorial eye, but the two compromise for friendship's sake. The second story sends Gollie on an imagined climb up the Andes, shutting Bink out of the house until she arrives at the door with a sandwich. . . . In the final episode, Gollie is jealous of Bink's new pet fish until Bink reassures her that no one can take her place. All three stories . . . offer delightful portrayals of two headstrong characters who, despite their differences and idiosyncratic quirks, know the importance of true friendship. The

delightful digitalized cartoon illustrations . . . . reinforce the humor of the text." SLJ

Another title about Bink & Gollie is:

Two for one (2012)

★ **Flora** and Ulysses; The Illuminated Adventures. by Kate Di-Camillo; illustrated by K. G. Campbell. Candlewick Press 2013 240 p. ill. (reinforced) $17.99

Grades: 3 4 5 6   **Fic**

1. Fantasy fiction 2. Adventure fiction 3. Girls -- Fiction 4. Squirrels -- Fiction 5. Superheroes -- Fiction

ISBN 076366040X; 9780763660406

LC 2012947748

Newberry Medal (2014)

National Book Awards: Young People's Literature Long List (2013)

Parents' Choice Awards: Gold Medal Fiction (2013)

In this book by Kate DiCamillo, "bitter about her parents' divorce. Flora Buckman has withdrawn into her favorite comic book The Amazing Incandesto! and memorized the advisories in its ongoing bonus feature, Terrible Things Can Happen to You! She puts those life-saving tips into action when a squirrel is swallowed whole by a neighbor's new vacuum cleaner. . . . Flora resuscitates the squirrel," who now has superpowers. (Publishers Weekly)

Francine Poulet meets the ghost raccoon; Kate DiCamillo. Candlewick Press 2015 112 p. illustrations (Tales from Deckawoo Drive) $12.99

Grades: 1 2 3 4   **Fic**

1. Fear -- Fiction 2. Humorous fiction 3. Raccoons -- Fiction 4. Animal welfare -- Fiction

ISBN 0763668869; 9780763668860

LC 2014951801

In this book, by Kate DiCamillo, illustrated by Chris Van Dusen, "Francine Poulet is the greatest animal control officer in Gizzford County. . . . She is never scared--until, that is, she's faced with a screaming raccoon that may or may not be a ghost. Maybe Francine isn't cut out to be an animal control officer after all! But the raccoon is still on the loose, and the folks on Deckawoo Drive need Francine back. Can she face her fears?" (Publisher's note)

"No one offers early readers better quality prose than DiCamillo, who never allows the constrictions of this format to deter her from excellent writing." Booklist

★ **Leroy** Ninker saddles up; tales from Deckawoo Drive, volume one. Kate DiCamillo. Candlewick Press 2014 96 p. (Tales from Deckawoo Drive) $12.99

Grades: 1 2 3 4   **Fic**

1. Romance fiction 2. Cowboys -- Fiction 3. Horses -- Fiction

ISBN 0763663395; 9780763663391

LC 2013953473

In this children's book by Kate DiCamillo, illustrated by Chris Van Dusen and part of the Tales from Deckawoo Drive series, "Leroy Ninker has a hat, a lasso, and boots. What he doesn't have is a horse--until he meets Maybelline, that is, and then it's love at first sight. Maybelline loves spaghetti and sweet nothings, and she loves Leroy, too. But when Leroy forgets the third and final rule of caring for Maybelline, disaster ensues." (Publisher's note)

"DiCamillo's use of inventive and colorful language and Van Dusen's stylized gouache illustrations make this story click." Booklist

Other titles in this series are:

Francine Poulet meets the ghost raccoon (2015)

Where are you going, Baby Lincoln? (2016)

★ The **magician's** elephant; illustrated by Yoko Tanaka. Candlewick Press 2009 201p il $16.99

Grades: 4 5 6 7   **Fic**

1. Adventure fiction 2. Orphans -- Fiction 3. Siblings -- Fiction 4. Elephants -- Fiction 5. Missing children -- Fiction

ISBN 978-0-7636-4410-9; 0-7636-4410-2

LC 2009-07359

When ten-year-old orphan Peter Augustus Duchene encounters a fortune teller in the marketplace one day and she tells him that his sister, who is presumed dead, is in fact alive, he embarks on a remarkable series of adventures as he desperately tries to find her.

"The profound and deeply affecting emotions at work in the story are bouyed up by the tale's succinct, lyrical text; gentle touches of humor; and uplifting message." Booklist

Mercy Watson fights crime; [by] Kate DiCamillo; illustrated by Chris Van Dusen. 1st ed.; Candlewick Press 2006 70p il $12.99

Grades: PreK K 1 2   **Fic**

1. Pigs -- Fiction

ISBN 0-7636-2590-6

LC 2005053639

Mercy the pig's love of buttered toast leads to the capture of a small thief who would rather be a cowboy.

"The shiny, retro pictures still amuse. Even beginning readers will wish for more." Booklist

Mercy Watson goes for a ride; [by] Kate DiCamillo; illustrated by Chris Van Dusen. 1st ed.; Candlewick Press 2006 72p il $12.99

Grades: K 1 2 3   **Fic**

1. Pigs -- Fiction

ISBN 0-7636-2332-6; 978-0-7636-2332-6

LC 2004051832

After Mercy the pig snuggles to sleep with the Watsons, all three awaken with the bed teetering on the edge of a big hole in the floor.

"Van Dusen's larger-than-life characters and retro sensibility extend the dry humor of the situation, and his shiny, rainbow-bright gouache art shoots the energy . . . right off the page. Great for emergent readers." Booklist

Mercy Watson thinks like a pig; [by] Kate DiCamillo; illustrated by Chris Van Dusen. 1st ed.; Candlewick Press 2008 70p il $12.99

Grades: K 1 2 3   **Fic**

1. Pigs -- Fiction 2. Flowers -- Fiction

ISBN 978-0-7636-3265-6; 0-7636-3265-1

LC 2007040623

After Mercy Watson follows the delightful scent and delicious taste of the pansies her thoughtful neighbors plant to beautify their yard, Animal Control Officer Francine Poulet is called out to handle the case, which brings unexpected results.

"As usual, Van Dusen's shiny, stylized artwork captures all the fun of Mercy's capers." Booklist

★ **Mercy** Watson to the rescue; illustrated by Chris Van Dusen. Candlewick Press 2005 68p il $12.99

Grades: K 1 2 3   **Fic**

1. Pigs -- Fiction

ISBN 0-7636-2270-2

LC 2004-51896

After Mercy the pig snuggles to sleep with the Watsons, all three awaken with the bed teetering on the edge of a big hole in the floor.

"Appropriate as both a picture book and a beginning reader, this joyful story combines familiar elements . . . with a raucous telling that lets readers in on the joke. . . . The gouache illustrations are polished to a sheen and have plenty of heft." Booklist

Other titles about Mercy Watson are:
Mercy Watson fights crime (2006)
Mercy Watson goes for a ride (2006)
Mercy Watson: princess in disguise (2007)
Mercy Watson thinks like a pig (2008)
Mercy Watson: something wonky this way comes (2009)

Mercy Watson: princess in disguise; [by] Kate DiCamillo; illustrated by Chris Van Dusen. 1st ed.; Candlewick Press 2007 70p il $12.99

Grades: 1 2 3   **Fic**

1. Pigs -- Fiction 2. Halloween -- Fiction

ISBN 978-0-7636-3014-0; 0-7636-3014-4

LC 2006051827

Persuaded by the word "treating" to dress up as a princess for Halloween, Mercy the pig's trick-or-treat outing has some very unexpected results.

"This installment has the same bright appeal as the previous books, and the pictures are priceless." Booklist

Mercy Watson: something wonky this way comes. Candlewick Press 2009 86p il $12.99

Grades: K 1 2 3   **Fic**

1. Pigs -- Fiction 2. Motion pictures -- Fiction

ISBN 978-0-7636-3644-9; 0-7636-3644-4

Mr. and Mrs. Watson take their pig, Mercy, to a drive-in movie.

"Illustrations are done in gouache using a bright, retro palette of glossy colors, bringing the text vibrantly to life. All of the elements of the earlier stories are here—jovial characters, good-humored mayhem, and effortless repetition that moves the story forward." SLJ

★ The **miraculous** journey of Edward Tulane; illustrated by Bagram Ibatoulline. Candlewick Press 2006 198p il $18.99; pa $6.99

Grades: 3 4 5 6   **Fic**

1. Toys -- Fiction 2. Rabbits -- Fiction

ISBN 0-7636-2589-2; 0-7636-4367-X pa

LC 2004-56129

Boston Globe-Horn Book Award: Fiction and Poetry(2006)

Edward Tulane, a coldhearted and proud toy rabbit, loves only himself until he is separated from the little girl who adores him and travels across the country, acquiring new owners and listening to their hopes, dreams, and histories.

"This achingly beautiful story shows a true master of writing at her very best. . . . Ibatoulline's lovely sepia-toned gouache illustrations and beautifully rendered color plates are exquisite." SLJ

★ **Raymie** Nightingale; by Kate DiCamillo. Candlewick Press 2016 272 p. hbk $16.99

Grades: 4 5 6 7 8   **Fic**

1. Emotions -- Fiction 2. Female friendship -- Fiction 3. Competition (Psychology) -- Fiction 4. Father-daughter relationship -- Fiction 5. Beauty contests -- Fiction 6. Family problems -- Fiction

ISBN 9780763681173; 9780763687083; 0763681172

National Book Award Finalist: Young People's Literature (2016)

In this book, by Kate DiCamillo, "Raymie Clarke has come to realize that everything . . . depends on her. . . . If Raymie can win the Little Miss Central Florida Tire competition, then her father, who left town two days ago . . . will see Raymie's picture in the paper and come home. . . . She also has to contend with the wispy, frequently fainting Louisiana Elefante, who has a show-business background, and the fiery, stubborn Beverly Tapinski, who's determined to sabotage the contest." (Publisher's note)

"The limited third-person narration gives Raymie her distinctive voice and spot-on pre-adolescent perspective of a young girl trying to make sense of the world around her. Here DiCamillo returns--triumphantly--to her Winn-Dixie roots." Horn Book

★ The **tale** of Despereaux; being the story of a mouse, a princess, some soup, and a spool of thread. illustrated by Timothy Basil Ering. Candlewick Press 2003 267p il $17.99; pa $7.99

Grades: 3 4 5 6   **Fic**
   1. Fairy tales 2. Mice -- Fiction
ISBN 0-7636-1722-9; 0-7636-2529-9 pa
                             LC 2002-34760
Awarded the Newbery Medal, 2004
   The adventures of Despereaux Tilling, a small mouse of unusual talents, the princess that he loves, the servant girl who longs to be a princess, and a devious rat determined to bring them all to ruin
   "Forgiveness, light, love, and soup. These essential ingredients combine into a tale that is as soul stirring as it is delicious. . . . Ering's soft pencil illustrations reflect the story's charm." Booklist

Where are you going, Baby Lincoln? Kate DiCamillo, Chris Van Dusen. Candlewick Press 2016 112 p. illustrations (Tales from Deckawoo Drive) $14.99

Grades: 1 2 3 4   **Fic**
   1. Sisters -- Fiction 2. Runaway children -- Fiction
ISBN 9780763673116
                           LC 2016940244
   In this book, by Kate DiCamillo, illustrated by Chris Van Dusen, "Baby Lincoln's older sister, Eugenia, is very fond of telling Baby what to do. . . . But one day Baby has had enough. She decides to depart on a Necessary Journey, even though she has never gone anywhere without Eugenia telling her what to take and where to go. And in fact Baby doesn't knowwhere she is headed." (Publisher's note)
   "These stories -- with their portrait of timeless small-town America; their use of adult characters as kid stand-ins; their celebration of mild ironies; and their pleasure in language... are a welcome addition to a time-honored tradition of children's writing." Horn Book

Dickens, Charles
   ★ A **Christmas** carol; [by] Charles Dickens; [illustrated by] Brett Helquist; [abridged by Josh Greenhut] HarperCollins 2009 un il $17.99; lib bdg $18.89

Grades: 3 4 5 6   **Fic**
   1. Ghost stories 2. Christmas -- Fiction 3. Great Britain -- History -- 19th century -- Fiction
ISBN 978-0-06-165099-4; 0-06-165099-4; 978-0-06-165100-7 lib bdg; 0-06-165100-1 lib bdg
                           LC 2008044031
   A miser learns the true meaning of Christmas when three ghostly visitors review his past and foretell his future.
   "Sacrificing none of Dickens's rich language, this retelling reads beautifully. The artist uses watercolor, pencil, and pastel to create cinematic artwork that contains amusing details; additionally, there are a number of pen-and-ink vignettes that help set the scenes. A winning combination of sparkling prose and exciting art." SLJ

Dionne, Erin
   Ollie and the science of treasure hunting; a 14 day mystery. by Erin Dionne. Dial Books for Young Readers, an imprint of Penguin Group (USA) Inc. 2014 288 p. (hardcover) $16.99

Grades: 5 6 7 8   **Fic**
   1. Mystery fiction 2. Camps -- Fiction 3. Adventure fiction 4. Buried treasure -- Fiction 5. Mystery and detective stories 6. Vietnamese Americans -- Fiction 7. Racially mixed people --

Fiction 8. Boston Harbor Islands (Mass.) -- Fiction
ISBN 9780803738720; 0803738722
                           LC 2013031211
   "While at Wilderness camp on the Boston Harbor Islands, Ollie must navigate new friends, new enemies, and a high-stakes game of tag, so the last thing he needs is a mystery. But then Ollie meets Grey, an elusive girl with knowledge of the island's secrets, including the legend of a lost pirate treasure, which may not be a legend after all." (Publisher's note)
   "A cast of likable campers, each with his or her own quirks --midnight swimmer, sensitive to sun, cartography genius--drive this fast-paced adventure led by a camp ranger with a gambling problem. Nothing should surprise readers in this thoroughly satisfying tale of friendship, intrigue, and Boston Harbor Island topography." Booklist
   Includes bibliographical references
   Companion to:
   Moxie and the Art of Rule Breaking (2013)

DiSalvo, DyAnne
   The **sloppy** copy slipup; [by] DyAnne DiSalvo. Holiday House 2006 103p il $16.95; pa $6.95

Grades: 2 3 4   **Fic**
   1. School stories 2. Authorship -- Fiction
ISBN 0-8234-1947-9; 0-8234-2189-9 pa
   Fourth-grader Brian Higman worries about how his teacher Miss Fromme—nicknamed The General—will react when he fails to hand in a writing assignment, but he ends up being able to tell his story, after all
   "DiSalvo combines spot-on humor, vivid classroom scenes, and tension that builds from the first page, and Brian's story . . . will keep children eagerly engaged." Booklist

DiTerlizzi, Tony
   The **battle** for WondLa; Tony DiTerlizzi; with illustrations by the author. 1st edition Simon & Schuster Books for Young Readers 2014 480 p. col. ill., col. map (The search for WondLa) (hardcover) $17.99

Grades: 2 3 4 5   **Fic**
   1. Fantasy fiction 2. Extraterrestrial beings -- Fiction 3. War -- Fiction 4. Science fiction 5. Human-alien encounters -- Fiction
ISBN 1416983147; 9781416983149
                           LC 2013035219
   "All hope for a peaceful coexistence between humankind and aliens seems lost in the third installment of the WondLa trilogy. Eva Nine has gone into hiding for fear of luring the wicked Loroc to her companions. However, news of the city Solas being captured by the human leader, Cadmus Pryde, forces Eva into action once again." (Publisher's note)
   "Of particular interest is Eva's development into a young woman of unwavering compassion and courage, even in the face of betrayal, loss, and injury. DiTerlizzi's beautiful illustrations are worth the price of admission, as usual, and they do much to help the reader distinguish among the plethora of strange creatures." Booklist

   A **hero** for WondLa; by Tony DiTerlizzi; with illustrations by the author. Simon & Schuster Books for Young Readers 2012 445 p. (hardcover) $17.99

Grades: 5 6 7 8   **Fic**
   1. Science fiction 2. Rescue work -- Fiction 3. Life on other planets -- Fiction 4. Identity -- Fiction 5. Human-alien encounters -- Fiction
ISBN 1416983120; 9781416983125; 9781442450844
                           LC 2011037031
   Author Tony DiTerlizzi tells a science fiction story. "Eva Nine had never seen another human, but after a human boy named Hailey rescues her along with her companions, she couldn't be happier. Eva thinks she has everything she's ever dreamed of, especially when Hailey brings her and her friends to the colony of New Attica, where humans of all shapes

and sizes live in apparent peace and harmony. But all is not idyllic in New Attica, and Eva Nine soon realizes that something sinister is going on . . . [that] could mean the end of everything and everyone on planet Orbona." (Publisher's note)

Kenny & the dragon; [by] Tony DiTerlizzi. Simon & Schuster Books for Young Readers 2008 151p $15.99

Grades: 4 5 6 7 **Fic**

1. Dragons -- Fiction 2. Rabbits -- Fiction 3. Knights and knighthood -- Fiction

ISBN 978-1-4169-3977-1; 1-4169-3977-6

LC 2008-7309

Book-loving Kenny the rabbit has few friends in his farming community, so when one, bookstore owner George, is sent to kill another, gentle dragon Grahame, Kenny must find a way to prevent their battle while satisfying the dragon-crazed townspeople.

"DiTerlizzi's novel is lighthearted and his informal pencil sketches enhance the creative interpretation of what would otherwise be a simple animal story." Publ Wkly

★ The **search** for WondLa; with illustrations by the author. Simon & Schuster Books for Young Readers 2010 477p il $17.99

Grades: 5 6 7 8 **Fic**

1. Science fiction 2. Extraterrestrial beings -- Fiction

ISBN 978-1-4169-8310-1; 1-4169-8310-4

LC 2010-01326

Living in isolation with a robot on what appears to be an alien world populated with bizarre life forms, a twelve-year-old human girl called Eva Nine sets out on a journey to find others like her.

"The abundant illustrations, drawn in a flat, two-tone style, are lush and enhance readers' understanding of this unique universe. . . . DiTerlizzi is pushing the envelope in his latest work, nearly creating a new format that combines a traditional novel with a graphic novel and with the interactivity of the computer. Yet, beneath this impressive package lies a theme readers will easily relate to: the need to belong, to connect, to figure out one's place in the world. The novel's ending is a stunning shocker that will leave kids frantically awaiting the next installment." SLJ

Divakaruni, Chitra Banerjee

The **conch** bearer. Roaring Brook Press 2003 265p (Brotherhood of the conch) $16.95; lib bdg $23.90

Grades: 5 6 7 8 **Fic**

1. India -- Fiction 2. Magic -- Fiction

ISBN 978-0-7613-1935-1; 0-7613-1935-2; 978-0-7613-2793-6 lib bdg; 0-7613-2793-2 lib bdg

LC 2003-8578

In India, a healer invites twelve-year-old Anand to join him on a quest to return a magical conch to its safe and rightful home, high in the Himalayan mountains

"Divakaruni keeps her tale fresh and riveting." Publ Wkly

Other titles in this series are:

The mirror of fire and dreaming (2005)

Shadowland (2009)

Dolan, Elys

The **Mystery** of the Haunted Farm; by Elys Dolan. Nosy Crow, an imprint of Candlewick Press 2016 unpaged color illustrations $17.99

Grades: K 1 2 3 4 **Fic**

1. Pigs -- Fiction 2. Farms -- Fiction

ISBN 0763686581; 9780763686581

In this book, by Elys Dolan, "strange and spooky things are happening down on the farm, and Farmer Greg knows exactly who to call —Ghost-hunters! A specialist team of three little ghost-hunting pigs

equipped with the latest gadgets seem to be the perfect guys for the job. There's certainly something suspicious about the mysterious chicken coop up on the hill, but . . . the pigs realize that perhaps all is not quite as it seems." (Publisher's note)

Donoghue, Emma

The **Lotterys** plus one; Emma Donoghue, illustrated by Caroline Hadilaksono. Arthur A. Levine Books, an imprint of Scholastic Inc. 2017 320 p. illustrations (ebook) $17.99; (hardcover : alk. paper) $17.99

Grades: 4 5 6 7 **Fic**

1. Domestic fiction 2. Siblings -- Fiction 3. Canada -- Fiction 4. Family life -- Fiction 5. Grandfathers -- Fiction 6. Toronto (Ont.) -- Fiction 7. Brothers and sisters -- Fiction 8. Brothers and sisters -- Fiction 9. Families -- Ontario -- Toronto -- Fiction

ISBN 9780545925822; 9780545925815

LC 2016008863

In this book, by Emma Donoghue, illustrated by Caroline Hadilaksono, "Sumac Lottery is . . . the self-proclaimed 'good girl' of her (VERY) large, . . . unruly family . . . [with] four parents, children both adopted and biological, and a menagerie of pets, all living . . . together in a sprawling house called Camelottery. Then one day, the news breaks that one of their grandfathers is suffering from dementia and will be coming to live with them." (Publisher's note)

"Full of clever names and wordplay, this engaging tale is moving without veering into sentimentality." Kirkus

Donovan, Gail

In loving memory of Gorfman T. Frog; [illustrated by Janet Pedersen] Dutton Children's Books 2009 180p il $15.99

Grades: 3 4 5 **Fic**

1. School stories 2. Frogs -- Fiction 3. Family life -- Fiction

ISBN 978-0-525-42085-9; 0-525-42085-1

LC 2008-13897

When irrepressible fifth-grader Josh finds a five-legged frog in his backyard pond, it leads to him learning a lot about amphibians—and himself.

"Pedersen's full-page illustrations ramp up the comedy and action, and Donovan ably shows how the school world of kids is separate and little understood by adults." Booklist

Doodler, Todd H.

Super Fly! the world's smallest superhero. by Todd H. Doodler. Bloomsbury 2015 128 p. (hardcover) $14.99

Grades: 2 3 4 **Fic**

1. Flies -- Fiction 2. Insects -- Fiction 3. Bullying -- Fiction 4. Superheroes -- Fiction

ISBN 1619633795; 9781619633780; 9781619633797

LC 2014029077

This story, by Todd H. Doodler, "is the story of Eugene Flystein, a small and nerdy, mild-mannered housefly, who also happens to be the world's smallest superhero and humanity's greatest crime fighter. . . . Can this four-eyed little bugger, along with his trusty sidekick Fantastic Flea, take on Crazy Cockroach and his army of insect baddies? It's housefly vs. cockroach in this epic battle of good vs. evil." (Publisher's note)

Another title in this series is:

Revenge of the Roach! (2016)

Dooley, Sarah

Free verse; Sarah Dooley. Penguin Group USA 2016 352 p. (hardback) $16.99

Grades: 5 6 7 8 **Fic**

1. Poetry -- Fiction 2. Bereavement -- Fiction 3. Family life

-- Fiction
ISBN 9780399165030; 0399165037

LC 2015038249

This novel, by Sarah Dooley, is "set in a West Virginia coal-mining town. When her brother dies in a fire, Sasha Harless has no one left. . . . But then Sasha discovers family she didn't know she had. . . . Sasha even makes her first friend at school, and is slowly learning to cope with her brother's death through writing poetry, finding a new way to express herself when spoken words just won't do." (Publisher's note)

"Dooley winningly combines engaging plot twists and rich character development with the introspective and thematic power of poetry: not to be missed." Kirkus

Dorris, Michael

Morning Girl. Hyperion Bks. for Children 1992 74p hardcover o.p. pa $4.99

Grades: 4 5 6 7   **Fic**

1. Taino Indians -- Fiction 2. America -- Exploration -- Fiction
ISBN 0-7868-1358-X pa

LC 92-52989

Twelve year old Morning Girl, a Taino Indian who loves the day, and her younger brother Star Boy, who loves the night, take turns describing their life on a Bahamian island in 1492; in Morning Girl's last narrative, she witnesses the arrival of the first Europeans to her world

"The author uses a lyrical, yet easy-to-follow, style to place these compelling characters in historical context. . . . Dorris does a superb job of showing that family dynamics are complicated, regardless of time and place. . . . A touching glimpse into the humanity that connects us all." Horn Book

Sees Behind Trees. Hyperion Bks. for Children 1996 104p hardcover o.p. pa $4.99

Grades: 4 5 6 7   **Fic**

1. Native Americans -- Fiction 2. Vision disorders -- Fiction
ISBN 0-7868-1357-1 pa

LC 96-15859

"For the partially sighted Walnut, it is impossible to prove his right to a grown-up name by hitting a target with his bow and arrow. With his highly developed senses, however, he demonstrates that he can do something even better: he can see 'what cannot be seen' which earns him the name Sees Behind Trees. . . . Set in sixteenth-century America, this richly imagined and gorgeously written rite-of-passage story has the gravity of legend. Moreover, it has buoyant humor and the immediacy of a compelling story that is peopled with multidimensional characters." Booklist

Dowd, Siobhan

★ The **London** Eye mystery. David Fickling Books 2008 322p $15.99; lib bdg $18.99; pa $7.50

Grades: 5 6 7 8   **Fic**

1. Mystery fiction 2. Cousins -- Fiction 3. Siblings -- Fiction 4. London (England) -- Fiction 5. Missing children -- Fiction 6. Asperger's syndrome -- Fiction
ISBN 978-0-375-84976-3; 0-375-84976-9; 978-0-375-94976-0 lib bdg; 0-375-84976-3 lib bdg; 978-0-385-75184-1 pa; 0-385-75184-2 pa

LC 2007-15119

First published 2007 in the United Kingdom

When Ted and Kat's cousin Salim disappears from the London Eye ferris wheel, the two siblings must work together—Ted with his brain that is "wired differently" and impatient Kat—to try to solve the mystery of what happened to Salim.

"Everything rings true here, the family relationships, the quirky connections of Ted's mental circuitry, and . . . the mystery. . . . A page turner with heft." Booklist

Dowell, Frances O'Roark

★ **Chicken** boy. Atheneum Books for Young Readers 2005 201p $15.95; pa $5.99

Grades: 4 5 6 7   **Fic**

1. Chickens -- Fiction 2. Friendship -- Fiction 3. Family life -- Fiction
ISBN 0-689-85816-7; 1-4169-3482-0 pa

LC 2004-10928

Since the death of his mother, Tobin's family life and school life have been in disarray, but after he starts raising chickens with his seventh-grade classmate, Henry, everything starts to fall into place. "Intermediate, middle school." (Horn Book)

"There is no glib resolution, here. But the strong narration and the child's struggle with forgiveness make for poignant, aching drama." Booklist

★ **Dovey** Coe. Atheneum Bks. for Young Readers 2000 181p $16; pa $5.99

Grades: 5 6 7 8   **Fic**

1. Mountain life -- Fiction 2. North Carolina -- Fiction
ISBN 0-689-83174-9; 0-689-84667-3 pa

LC 99-46870

When accused of murder in her North Carolina mountain town in 1928, Dovey Coe, a stronged-willed twelve-year-old girl, comes to a new understanding of others, including her deaf brother

"Dowell has created a memorable character in Dovey, quick-witted and honest to a fault. . . . This is a delightful book, thoughtful and full of substance." Booklist

★ **Falling** in. Atheneum Books for Young Readers 2010 245p il $16.99

Grades: 4 5 6 7   **Fic**

1. Fantasy fiction
ISBN 978-1-4169-5032-5; 1-4169-5032-X

LC 2009-10412

Middle-schooler Isabelle Bean follows a mouse's squeak into a closet and falls into a parallel universe where the children believe she is the witch they have feared for years, finally come to devour them.

"This perfectly paced story has enough realistic elements to appeal even to nonfantasy readers." Booklist

The **kind** of friends we used to be. Atheneum Books for Young Readers 2009 234p $16.99

Grades: 5 6 7 8   **Fic**

1. School stories 2. Friendship -- Fiction
ISBN 978-1-4169-5031-8; 1-4169-5031-1

LC 2008-22245

Sequel to: The secret language of girls (2004)

Twelve-year-olds Kate and Marylin, friends since preschool, draw further apart as Marylin becomes involved in student government and cheerleading, while Kate wants to play guitar and write songs, and both develop unlikely friendships with other girls and boys.

"Dowell gets middle-school dynamics exactly right, and while her empathetic portraits of Kate and Marylin are genuine and heartfelt, even secondary characters are memorable. A realistic and humorous look at the trials and tribulations of growing up and growing independent." SL

Phineas L. MacGuire . . . blasts off! illustrated by Preston McDaniels. Atheneum Books for Young Readers 2008 188p il (From the highly scientific notebooks of Phineas L. MacGuire) $16.99

Grades: 2 3 4   **Fic**

  1. School stories 2. Science -- Experiments -- Fiction

  ISBN 978-1-416-92689-4; 1-416-92689-5

                                LC 2007-030162

Hoping to earn money to attend Space Camp, fourth-grade science whiz Phineas MacGuire gets a job as a dog walker, then enlists the aid of his friends Ben and Aretha to help with experiments using the dog's 'slobber.'

"Amusing black-and-white illustrations add to the fun, and readers will enjoy trying the Mars-related experiments added as back matter. A welcome addition to a solid series for middle-grade readers." Horn Book

Phineas L. MacGuire . . . gets slimed! illustrated by Preston L. McDaniels. Atheneum Books for Young Readers 2007 190p il (From the highly scientific notebooks of Phineas L. MacGuire) $16.99

Grades: 2 3 4   **Fic**

  1. School stories 2. Science -- Experiments -- Fiction

  ISBN 978-1-4169-0196-9; 1-4169-0196-5

                                  LC 2006-14193

When his new best friend, Ben, decides to run for class president, fourth-grade science whiz Phineas MacGuire reluctantly agrees to be his campaign manager in exchange for help with his latest experiment—cultivating exhibits for a mold museum.

"Full of amusing faux-scientific observations . . . as well as actual scientific facts, this lighthearted, illustrated chapter book should appeal to any young reader who can stand a little mold." Booklist

Phineas L. Macguire erupts! the first experiment. Atheneum Books for Young Readers 2006 167p il (From the highly scientific notebooks of Phineas L. MacGuire) $15.95; pa $4.99

Grades: 2 3 4   **Fic**

  1. School stories 2. Science -- Experiments -- Fiction

  ISBN 978-1-4169-0195-2; 1-4169-0195-7; 978-1-4169-4734-9 pa; 1-4169-4734-5 pa

                                  LC 2005-12605

Fourth-grade science whiz Phineas MacGuire is forced to team up with the new boy in class on a science fair project, but the boy's quirky personality causes Phineas to wonder if they have any chance of winning.

"The type is large and well spaced, and black-and-white art playfully captures the characters. . . . Budding scientists will find instructions for their own experiments at the end of the book." Booklist

  Other titles in this series are:

  Phineas L. MacGuire . . . gets slimed! (2007)

  Phineas L. MacGuire . . . blasts off! (2008)

Sam the man and the chicken plan; Frances O'Roark Dowell. Atheneum Books for Young Readers 2016 128 p. illustrations (hc : alk. paper) $15.99; (ebook) $15.99

Grades: 1 2 3 4   **Fic**

  1. Chickens -- Fiction 2. Family life -- Fiction 3. Families -- Fiction 4. Moneymaking projects -- Fiction

  ISBN 9781481440660; 9781481440677; 9781481440684

                                  LC 2015007119

In this children's book by Frances O'Roark Dowell and illustrated by Amy June Bates, "Sam the Man needs a job. Sam decides to ask his next door neighbor if she needs help doing other chores. . . . When Mrs. Kerner, another neighbor, asks if Sam would like to watch her chickens, Sam jumps on the task. Visiting the chickens is the one thing that can coax Mr. Stockfish out of the house! But what does a seven-year-old do with all the money he's earning?" (Publisher's note)

"Well-structured, shaded pencil drawings illustrate characters and scenes with energy, perception, and gentle humor." Booklist

  Another title in this series is:

Sam the man and the rutabaga plan (2017)

★ The **second** life of Abigail Walker; Frances O'Roark Dowell. Atheneum Books for Young Readers 2012 228 p. (hardcover) $16.99

Grades: 4 5 6 7   **Fic**

  1. Self-confidence -- Fiction 2. Friendship -- Fiction 3. Middle schools -- Fiction 4. Overweight persons -- Fiction 5. Human-animal relationships -- Fiction

  ISBN 1442405937; 9781442405936

                                  LC 2012010646

This novel, by Frances O'Roark Dowell, follows a youth struggling with popularity. "Seventeen pounds. That's the difference between . . . chubby and slim, between teased and taunting. Abby is fine with her body, . . . so she speaks out against Kristen and her groupies--and becomes officially unpopular. Embracing her new status, Abby heads to an abandoned lot across the street and crosses an unfamiliar stream that leads her to a boy who's as different as they come." (Publisher's note)

The **secret** language of girls. Atheneum Books for Young Readers 2004 247p $15.95; pa $5.99

Grades: 5 6 7 8   **Fic**

  1. School stories 2. Friendship -- Fiction

  ISBN 0-689-84421-2; 978-1-4169-0717-6 pa

                                  LC 2003-12026

Marylin and Kate have been friends since nursery school, but when Marylin becomes a middle school cheerleader and Kate begins to develop other interests, their relationship is put to the test.

"Excellent characterization, an accurate portrayal of the painful and often cruel machinations of preteens, and evocative dialogue will make this tale resonate with most readers." SLJ

  Followed by: The kind of friends we used to be (2009)

★ **Shooting** the moon. Atheneum Books for Young Readers 2008 163p $16.99; pa $5.99

Grades: 4 5 6 7   **Fic**

  1. Soldiers -- Fiction 2. Family life -- Fiction 3. Vietnam War, 1961-1975 -- Fiction

  ISBN 978-1-4169-2690-0; 1-4169-2690-9; 978-1-4169-7986-9 pa; 1-4169-7986-7 pa

                                  LC 2006-100347

Boston Globe-Horn Book Award honor book: Fiction and Poetry (2008)

When her brother is sent to fight in Vietnam, twelve-year-old Jamie begins to reconsider the army world that she has grown up in.

"The clear, well-paced first-person prose is perfectly matched to this novel's spare setting and restrained plot. . . . This [is a] thoughtful and satisfying story. . . . Readers will find beauty in its resolution, and will leave this eloquent heroine reluctantly." SLJ

The **sound** of your voice, only really far away; by Frances O'Roark Dowell. Atheneum Books for Young Readers 2013 192 p. (hardcover) $16.99

Grades: 5 6 7 8   **Fic**

  1. Friendship -- Fiction 2. High school students -- Fiction 3. Interpersonal relations -- Fiction 4. Schools -- Fiction 5. Popularity -- Fiction 6. Best friends -- Fiction 7. Middle schools -- Fiction

  ISBN 1442432896; 9781442432895; 9781442432918

                                  LC 2012030308

  Sequel to: The kind of friends we used to be

In this novel by Frances O'Roark Dowell "Marylin and Kate find that boys can be just as complicated as friendship. As a middle school cheerleader . . . Marylin [learns] there are also rules about whom she's allowed to like—and Benjamin, the student body president, is . . . unacceptable. She'll pretend that she's using him to get new cheerleading uniforms. When Matthew tells Kate that the school's Audio Lab needs funding . . ., she decides to . . . help him get it. There isn't enough money to go around, and it soon becomes clear that only one of the two girls can get her way." (Publisher's note)

Downer, Ann

The **dragon** of Never-Was. Atheneum Books for Young Readers 2006 305p il hardcover o.p. pa $5.99
Grades: 4 5 6 7   **Fic**
1. Magic -- Fiction 2. Dragons -- Fiction 3. Scotland -- Fiction
ISBN 978-0-689-85571-9; 0-689-85571-0; 978-1-4169-5453-8 pa; 1-4169-5453-8 pa

LC 2005017727

Sequel to Hatching magic (2003)

With the help of a bottle of blue fire and a magical brooch, Theodora searches for a dragon on an island off the coast of Scotland before it causes any harm.

"Smart, observant, and self-aware, Theodora makes a sympathetic character, convincing even in the most supernatural circumstances." Booklist

★ **Hatching** magic. Atheneum Bks. for Young Readers 2003 242p $16.95; pa $5.99
Grades: 4 5 6 7   **Fic**
1. Magic -- Fiction 2. Dragons -- Fiction
ISBN 0-689-83400-4; 0-689-87057-4 pa

LC 00-56570

When a thirteenth-century wizard confronts twenty-first century Boston while seeking his pet dragon, he is followed by a rival wizard and a very unhappy demon, but eleven-year-old Theodora Oglethorpe may hold the secret to setting everything right

"With likable characters, and laced with plenty of humor and adventure, Downer's fantasy will have solid appeal for young genre fans." Booklist

Another title about Theodora is:
The dragon of never-was (2006)

Downey, Jen Swann

The **ninja** librarians; the accidental keyhand. Jen Swann Downey. Sourcebooks Jabberwocky 2014 384 p. (hc : alk. paper) $16.99
Grades: 4 5 6 7   **Fic**
1. Adventure fiction 2. Libraries -- Fiction 3. Librarians -- Fiction 4. Censorship -- Fiction 5. Space and time -- Fiction 6. Secret societies -- Fiction
ISBN 1402287704; 9781402287701

LC 2013049956

In this adventure story by Jen Swann Downey, "when Dorrie and her brother Marcus chase Moe--an unusually foul-tempered mongoose--into the janitor's closet of their local library, they make an astonishing discovery: the headquarters of a secret society of ninja librarians. Their mission: protect those whose words get them into trouble, anywhere in the world and at any time in history." (Publisher's note)

"Delightfully funny from the first page, where Dorrie laments having never been bitten by anything more bloodthirsty than her little sister, this middle-grade time-travel adventure is surprisingly full of fun and action (and a madcap mongoose). Downey's hilarious debut is perfect for any library-loving reader as well as those who never considered librarians to be cool." Booklist

Drago, Ty

The **Undertakers**: rise of the Corpses. Sourcebooks Jabberwocky 2011 465p pa $10.99

Grades: 4 5 6 7   **Fic**
1. Horror fiction 2. Zombies -- Fiction
ISBN 978-1-4022-4785-9; 1-4022-4785-0

"Whatever you do, do not call them zombies! These are Corpses 'reanimated bodies that have been possessed,' and they are everywhere, although they are only visible to a select few, including 12-year-old Will Ritter. After realizing suddenly that he is able to see, Will is taken in by the Undertakers, a rogue group that rescues other, similarly targeted teens and fights to defeat the Corpses' evil plans to conquer Philadelphia and, ultimately, the world. . . . Calling into action a cast of distinctive characters with authentic voices and behaviors, . . . Will's breathless adventures . . . are thoughtful and exciting, and the descriptions of decaying flesh will likely both disgust and delight readers." Booklist

Drake, Salamanda

★ **Dragonsdale**; illustrations by Gilly Marklew. Chicken House/Scholastic 2007 269p il (Dragonsdale) $16.99
Grades: 3 4 5   **Fic**
1. Fantasy fiction 2. Dragons -- Fiction
ISBN 978-0-439-87173-0; 0-439-87173-5

LC 2006-32890

Cara yearns to ride her beloved Skydancer, a rare Goldenbrow dragon, but her father refuses to permit her to fly and she must be content with mucking out stalls and helping raise young dragons at the famed stud and training farm known as Dragonsdale.

"This will delight precisely the audience it's meant to—young girls who find tame dragons captivating." Booklist

Followed by: Riding the storm (2008)

Draper, Sharon M.

The **birthday** storm. Scholastic Press 2009 108p (Sassy) $14.99
Grades: 3 4 5   **Fic**
1. Florida -- Fiction 2. Birthdays -- Fiction 3. Hurricanes -- Fiction 4. Family life -- Fiction 5. Sea turtles -- Fiction 6. Grandparents -- Fiction 7. African Americans -- Fiction
ISBN 978-0-545-07152-9; 0-545-07152-6

LC 2009007170

While in Florida to celebrate her Grammy's birthday, nine-and-a-half-year-old Sassy worries that an approaching hurricane will ruin not only the party, but a nest of sea turtle eggs, as well. Includes facts about hurricanes and sea turtles.

"Told in Sassy's first-person, present-tense voice, the mix of family love and friction and the elemental nature facts will grab even newcomers to the series." Booklist

The **dazzle** disaster dinner party. Scholastic Press 2010 123p (Sassy) $15.99
Grades: 3 4 5   **Fic**
1. School stories 2. Cooking -- Fiction
ISBN 978-0-545-07154-3; 0-545-07154-2

Sassy wants to cook a fancy meal and it turns out to be a disaster. The recipe goes wrong. The cooking is a mess. And—the dog eats the cake.

"Draper has whipped up another delicious tale sure to please followers of Sassy and anyone looking for a fun chapter book." SLJ

Little Sister is not my name. Scholastic Press 2009 102p (Sassy) $14.99
Grades: 3 4 5   **Fic**
1. Size -- Fiction 2. Family life -- Fiction 3. African Americans -- Fiction
ISBN 978-0-545-07151-2; 0-545-07151-8

LC 2008-15634

Fashion-savy Sassy does not like being the smallest student in her fourth-grade class, until a family emergency calls for a pint-sized hero.

"Draper hits her middle-grade target in this cheerful yet reflective novel about feeling appreciated and finding one's place. . . . Filled with energy and opinion, Sassy more than lives up to her name." Publ Wkly

Other titles in this series are:

The birthday storm (2009)

The silver secret (2010)

The dazzle disaster dinner party (2010)

★ **Out** of my mind. Atheneum 2010 295p $16.99

Grades: 5 6 7 8   **Fic**

1. Cerebral palsy -- Fiction

ISBN 978-1-4169-7170-2; 1-4169-7170-X

LC 2009-18404

Josette Frank Award for Fiction, 2011

"Fifth-grader Melody has cerebral palsy, a condition that affects her body but not her mind. Although she is unable to walk, talk, or feed or care for herself, she can read, think, and feel. A brilliant person is trapped inside her body, determined to make her mark in the world despite her physical limitations. . . . Told in Melody's voice, this highly readable, compelling novel quickly establishes her determination and intelligence and the almost insurmountable challenges she faces. . . . Uplifting and upsetting." Booklist

The **silver** secret. Scholastic Press 2010 126p (Sassy) $15.99

Grades: 3 4 5   **Fic**

1. Piccolo -- Fiction 2. Concerts -- Fiction 3. Family life -- Fiction 4. African Americans -- Fiction

ISBN 978-0-545-07153-6; 0-545-07153-4

LC 2009052427

Because she has a terrible singing voice, fourth-grader Sassy must use a different talent to be part of her school's musical performance on the importance of saving our planet. Includes "Fifteen ways that you can help save our earth."

★ **Stella** by starlight; Sharon Draper. Atheneum Books for Young Readers 2015 336 p. (hardcover) $16.99

Grades: 4 5 6 7 8   **Fic**

1. Ku Klux Klan 2. Segregation -- Fiction 3. Southern States -- Fiction 4. Prejudices -- Fiction 5. Civil rights -- Fiction 6. African Americans -- Fiction 7. Ku Klux Klan (1915-) -- Fiction 8. North Carolina -- History -- 20th century -- Fiction

ISBN 1442494972; 9781442494978; 9781442494985

LC 2014038728

NAACP Image Award Nominee: Outstanding Literary Work- Youth/ Teens (2016)

In this novel by Sharon M. Draper "when the Ku Klux Klan's unwelcome reappearance rattles Stella's segregated southern town, bravery battles prejudice in this Depression-era tour de force. As Stella's community--her world--is upended, she decides to fight fire with fire. And she learns that ashes don't necessarily signify an end." (Publisher's note)

"Coretta Scott King Award winner Draper draws inspiration from her grandmother's journal to tell the absorbing story of a young girl growing up in Depression-era, segregated North Carolina...This is an engrossing historical fiction novel with an amiable and humble heroine who does not recognize her own bravery or the power of her words. She provides inspiration not only to her fellow characters but also to readers who will relate to her and her situation. Storytelling at its finest." SLJ

Du Bois, William Pene

The **twenty**-one balloons; written and illustrated by William Pène Du Bois. Viking 1947 179p il $16.99; pa $5.99

Grades: 5 6 7 8   **Fic**

1. Balloons -- Fiction

ISBN 0-670-73441-1; 0-14-032097-0 pa

Awarded the Newbery Medal, 1948

"Professor Sherman set off on a flight across the Pacific in a giant balloon, but three weeks later the headlines read 'Professor Sherman in wrong ocean with too many balloons.' This book is concerned with the professor's explanation of this phenomenon. His account of his one stopover on the island of Krakatoa which blew up with barely a minute to spare to allow time for his escape, is the highlight of this hilarious narrative." Ont Libr Rev

Dudley, David L.

The **bicycle** man. Clarion Books 2005 249p $16

Grades: 4 5 6   **Fic**

1. Georgia -- Fiction 2. Country life -- Fiction 3. African Americans -- Fiction

ISBN 0-618-54233-7

LC 2005-06409

In poor, rural Georgia in 1927, twelve-year-old Carrisa and her suspicious mama take in an elderly drifter with a shiny bicycle, never expecting how profoundly his wise and patient ways will affect them.

Readers "will find complex characters and rich themes. . . . There is much here to digest and a wealth of material for book discussions." SLJ

Duey, Kathleen

Following magic; illustrated by Sandara Tang. Aladdin 2010 115p il (Faeries' promise) $15.99; pa $4.99

Grades: 3 4 5   **Fic**

1. Magic -- Fiction 2. Fairies -- Fiction

ISBN 978-1-4169-8458-0; 1-4169-8458-5; 978-1-4169-8459-7 pa; 1-4169-8459-3 pa; 978-1-4424-0980-4 e-book

LC 2009045801

Sequel to: Silence and stone (2010)

Having escaped from the tower where she was trapped, the faerie Alida and her human helper Gavin try to elude capture by Lord Dunraven's men while they search for Alida's family.

This "is sweet without being too cloying." Horn Book Guide

Followed by: The full moon (2011)

The **full** moon; illustrated by Sandara Tang. Aladdin 2011 115p il (Faeries' promise) $15.99; pa $4.99

Grades: 3 4 5   **Fic**

1. Magic -- Fiction 2. Fairies -- Fiction

ISBN 978-1-4169-8462-7; 1-4169-8462-3; 978-1-4169-8463-4 pa; 1-4169-8463-1 pa

LC 2010019165

Sequel to: Following magic (2010)

After many trials and much adversity, the faeries have returned to their meadow home, but Lord Dunraven vows that they must not remain.

Lara and the gray mare; by Kathleen Duey. Dutton Children's Books 2005 140p (Hoofbeats) hardcover o.p. pa $4.99

Grades: 4 5 6   **Fic**

1. Horses -- Fiction 2. Ireland -- Fiction

ISBN 0-525-47332-7; 0-14-240230-3 pa

LC 2004-53521

While her father is away fighting the Normans and other Irish clans, nine-year-old Lara works hard to help harvest food and also cares for the pregnant gray mare that she loves

"Writing with a keen appreciation for everyday goings-on in thirteenth-century Ireland and an unusual ability to bring the past to life, Duey creates a convincing setting, a thoroughly likable heroine, and a strong narrative." Booklist

Other titles in the Hoofbeats series are:

Lara and the Moon-colored filly (book two) (2005)

Lara at Athnery Castle (book three) (2005)

Lara at the silent place (book four) (2005)
Silence and Lily (2007)

Silence and stone; illustrated by Sandara Tang. Aladdin 2010
109p il (The faeries' promise) $15.99; pa $4.99
Grades: 3 4 5   **Fic**
1. Magic -- Fiction 2. Fairies -- Fiction
ISBN 978-1-4169-8456-6; 1-4169-8456-9; 978-1-4169-8457-3
pa; 1-4169-8457-7 pa
             LC 2009-42542
Kidnapped and confined to a room in a castle before she can de-
velop her flying and magical skills, Alida the faerie patiently plans her
escape—with the help of a human boy.
"With its magical tone, sturdy characters, and predictable yet satisfy-
ing plot, this simple fantasy will engage young readers and leave them
eager to read the next book." SLJ
Other titles in this series are:
Following magic (2010)
The full moon (2011)
Wishes and wings (2011)

Wishes and wings; illustrated by Sandara Tang. Aladdin 2011
113p il (Faeries' promise) $15.99; pa $4.99
Grades: 3 4 5   **Fic**
1. Magic -- Fiction 2. Fairies -- Fiction
ISBN 978-1-4169-8460-3; 1-4169-8460-7; 978-1-4169-8461-0
pa; 1-4169-8461-5 pa
             LC 2010001080
The human and faerie worlds intersect as the faeries return to their
meadow home near Lord Dunraven's castle.
"The story line and illustrations are engaging and uncluttered." Horn
Book Guide

Dumas, Firoozeh

It ain't so awful, falafel; by Firoozeh Dumas. Clarion Books/
Houghton Mifflin Harcourt 2016 384 p. (hardback) $16.99
Grades: 4 5 6 7   **Fic**
1. Moving -- Fiction 2. Iranian Americans -- Fiction 3. Nineteen
seventies -- Fiction 4. Immigrants -- United States -- Fiction
ISBN 9780544612310; 0544612310
             LC 2015034779
In this book, by Firoozeh Dumas, "Zomorod (Cindy) Yousefzadeh is
the new kid on the block . . . for the fourth time. California's Newport
Beach is her family's latest perch, and she's determined to shuck her
brainy loner persona and start afresh with a new Brady Bunch name-
-Cindy. It's the late 1970s, and fitting in becomes more difficult as Iran
makes U.S. headlines with protests, revolution, and finally the taking of
American hostages." (Publisher's note)
"On her own journey to maturity, Cindy deftly guides young readers
through Iran's complicated realities in this fresh take on the immigrant
experience---authentic, funny, and moving from beginning to end."
Kirkus

Dunrea, Olivier

Hanne's quest; [by] Olivier Dunrea. Philomel Books 2005 95p
il $16.99
Grades: 3 4 5   **Fic**
1. Fairy tales 2. Chickens -- Fiction 3. Scotland -- Fiction
ISBN 0-399-24216-3
             LC 2004-9091
On an island off the coast of Scotland, a young hen must prove her-
self pure, wise, and brave in a quest to help her beloved owner, Mem
Pocket, from losing her family's farm.

"Beautifully composed and often darkly atmospheric, the handsome
full-page paintings rival . . . those in the best picture books. This handsome, well-written book will find a rapt audience among children who
prefer sturdy, homespun fairy tales." Booklist

DuPrau, Jeanne

The **city** of Ember. Random House 2003 270p (Books of Ember)
$15.95; lib bdg $17.99; pa $6.99
Grades: 5 6 7 8   **Fic**
1. Science fiction
ISBN 0-375-82273-9; 0-375-92274-1 lib bdg; 0-385-73628-2 pa
             LC 2002-10239
"The writing and storytelling are agreeably spare and remarkably
suspenseful." Horn Book
Other titles in this series are:
The people of Sparks (2004)
The prophet of Yonwood (2006)
The diamond of Darkhold (2008)

The **diamond** of Darkhold. Random House 2008 285p (Books of
Ember) $16.99; lib bdg $19.99
Grades: 5 6 7 8   **Fic**
1. Fantasy fiction
ISBN 978-0-375-85571-9; 0-375-85571-8; 978-0-375-95571-6
lib bdg; 0-375-95571-2 lib bdg; 978-0-375-85572-6 pa; 0-375-
85572-6 pa
             LC 2007-47929
When a roamer trades them an ancient book with only a few pages
remaining, Lina and Doon return to Ember to seek the machine the book
seems to describe in hopes that it will get their new community, Sparks,
through the winter.
"A solid and satisfying conclusion to the 'Ember Saga,' set in a post-
disaster future." SLJ

The **people** of Sparks. Random House 2004 338p (Books of
Ember) $15.95; lib bdg $17.99
Grades: 5 6 7 8   **Fic**
1. Science fiction
ISBN 0-375-82824-9; 0-375-92824-3 lib bdg
             LC 2003-20760
Sequel to The City of Ember
"DuPrau continues the adventures of Lina and Doon, who have led
the 400 residents from the underground city of Ember to the unfamiliar
world above. The refugees are tentatively welcomed, housed, and fed
by the people of Sparks, located near the wasteland left by the long-ago
Disaster that destroyed most of civilization. Conflicts arise between the
two groups. . . . DuPrau clearly explores themes of nonviolence and
when to stand up for oneself. The text smoothly involves new readers
and fans of the first story, creating a range of three-dimensional characters." Booklist

The **prophet** of Yonwood. Random House 2006 289p (Books of
Ember) $15.95; lib bdg $17.99; pa $6.99
Grades: 5 6 7 8   **Fic**
1. Science fiction
ISBN 0-375-87526-3; 0-375-97526-8 lib bdg; 0-440-42124-1 pa
             LC 2005-22423
Prequel to The city of Ember (2003) and The people of Sparks (2004)
While visiting the small town of Yonwood, North Carolina, eleven-
year-old Nickie makes some decisions about how to identify both good
and evil when she witnesses the townspeople's reactions to the apoca-
lyptic visions of one of their neighbors

"This novel has a great deal of immediacy in light of current world events. It sharply brings home the idea of people blindly following a belief without questioning it." SLJ

Durand, Hallie

Dessert first; illustrations by Christine Davenier. Atheneum Books for Young Readers 2009 153p il $14.99
Grades: 3 4 5   **Fic**
1. School stories 2. Family life -- Fiction 3. Restaurants -- Fiction
ISBN 978-1-4169-6385-1; 1-4169-6385-5
LC 2008-11390
Third-grader Dessert's love of treats leads to a change in her large family's dinner routine, then an awful mistake, and later a true sacrifice after her teacher, Mrs. Howdy Doody, urges students to march to the beat of their own drums

"Experiences are delightfully imagined through Dessert's realistic, child-centered perspective. Short chapters interspersed with Davenier's pen-and-ink washes add immediacy to the text." Kirkus

Other titles about Dessert are:
Just desserts (2010)
No room for Dessert (2011)

Just Desserts; illustrated by Christine Davenier. Atheneum Books for Young Readers 2010 190p il $15.99
Grades: 3 4 5   **Fic**
1. School stories 2. Clubs -- Fiction 3. Siblings -- Fiction 4. Family life -- Fiction 5. Restaurants -- Fiction
ISBN 978-1-4169-6387-5; 1-4169-6387-1
LC 2009018400
Third-grader Dessert, inspired by Mrs. Howdy Doody's lessons about the American Revolution, decides she and her friends should fight back against annoying siblings, but the club she starts only makes matters worse.

"The real-life application of taxation without representation is clever, providing an entertaining 'aha' as it develops. Pen-and-ink wash illustrations are scattered throughout." SLJ

No room for Dessert; illustrated by Christine Davenier. Atheneum Books for Young Readers 2011 177p il $14.99
Grades: 3 4 5   **Fic**
1. School stories 2. Siblings -- Fiction 3. Inventions -- Fiction 4. Family life -- Fiction 5. Restaurants -- Fiction
ISBN 978-1-4424-0360-4; 1-4424-0360-8
LC 2010022039
Eight-year-old Donahue 'Dessert' Schneider is feeling completely ignored and unloved at home, but she is certain that will change when her invention wins the Thomas Edison Contest at school.

"Davenier's sparkling line drawings help young readers visualize the action. Another romp full of zesty, true-life fun." Kirkus

Durango, Julia

The **walls** of Cartagena; by Julia Durango; illustrated by Tom Pohrt. Simon & Schuster Books for Young Readers 2008 152p il $15.99
Grades: 5 6 7 8   **Fic**
1. Leprosy -- Fiction 2. Slavery -- Fiction 3. Colombia -- Fiction 4. Catholic Church -- Fiction
ISBN 978-1-4169-4102-6; 1-4169-4102-9
LC 2007041861
Thirteen-year-old Calepino, an African slave in the seventeenth-century Caribbean city of Cartagena, works as a translator for a Jesuit priest who tends to newly-arrived slaves and, after working for a Jewish doctor in a leper colony and helping an Angolan boy and his mother escape, he realizes his true calling

"Illustrated with occasional small ink sketches, the ultimate rescue adventure is gripping, but more compelling is the authentic history of people desperate and brave." Booklist

Durham, Paul

Fork-tongue charmers; Paul Durham; illustrations by Petur Antonsson. Harper, an imprint of HarperCollinsPublishers 2015 416 p. illustrations, maps (The Luck Uglies) (hardcover) $16.99
Grades: 4 5 6 7 8   **Fic**
1. Magic -- Fiction 2. Criminals -- Fiction 3. Fantasy 4. Monsters -- Fiction 5. Secret societies -- Fiction 6. Adventure and adventurers -- Fiction
ISBN 0062271539; 9780062271532
LC 2014038648
Sequel to: The Luck Uglies (2014)
In this novel by Paul Durham, illustrated by Petur Antonsson, "Rye O'Chanter was shocked to discover that her father was the leader . . . of outlaws known as the Luck Uglies. Now she too has been declared a criminal . . . and she must flee to the strange and remote Isle of Pest while her father faces off against . . . the Fork-Tongue Charmers, on the mainland. When the battle moves to the shores of Pest . . . Rye must . . . lead the charge in defending the island." (Publisher's note)

"There is not a single dull moment in this story, which packs in as many clever twists and fully fleshed characters as the first book. And the writing remains a total delight: witty, richly layered, and capable of creating a world as real as this one. A bittersweet ending assures the reader that Rye's adventures are not over yet." Booklist

The **luck** uglies; Paul Durham; illustrations by Petur Antonsson. Harper, an imprint of HarperCollinsPublishers 2014 400 p. (hardback) $16.99
Grades: 4 5 6 7 8   **Fic**
1. Fantasy fiction 2. Secret societies -- Fiction 3. Monsters -- Fiction 4. Adventure and adventurers -- Fiction
ISBN 0062271504; 9780062271501
LC 2013047720
In this book, by Paul Durham, "a terrifying encounter has eleven-year-old Rye O'Chanter convinced that the monstrous, supposedly extinct Bog Noblins have returned. Now Rye's only hope is an exiled secret society so notorious its name can't be spoken aloud: the Luck Uglies. As Rye dives into Village Drowning's maze of secrets, rules, and lies, she'll discover the truth behind the village's legends of outlaws and beasts . . . and that it may take a villain to save them from the monsters." (Publisher's note)

"Rye O'Chanter and her friends Quinn and Folly live in Drowning, which is ruled by the tyrannical Earl Longchance, who bans women from reading. When the earl does nothing to protect the villagers from marauding monsters, Drowning's only hope is the Luck Uglies, a notorious outlaw gang--that may or may not exist. Durham's fast-paced narrative and clever characters enhance this humorous and engaging tale." Horn Book

Durst, Sarah Beth

The **girl** who could not dream; by Sarah Beth Durst. Clarion Books, Houghton Mifflin Harcourt 2015 384 p. (hardback) $16.99
Grades: 4 5 6 7   **Fic**
1. Dreams -- Fiction 2. Monsters -- Fiction 3. Family life -- Fiction 4. Adventure and adventurers -- Fiction 5. Families -- Fiction
ISBN 0544464974; 9780544464971
LC 2015001324
In this book, by Sarah Beth Durst, "Sophie loves the hidden shop below her parents' bookstore, where dreams are secretly bought and sold. When the dream shop is robbed and her parents go missing, Sophie must unravel the truth to save them. Together with her best friend, a wise-

cracking and fanatically loyal monster named Monster, she must decide whom to trust with her family's carefully guarded secrets. Who will help them, and who will betray them?" (Publisher's note)

"Sophie's parents run a secret shop beneath their bookstore selling dreams. One night Sophie, who can't dream, steals one and discovers that she has the dangerous power to bring dream-creatures into the waking world. Sophie's dream-friends Monster and the delightfully arrogant unicorn Glitterhoof keep the story merry with their precocious quips, but the adventure does take some turns through dark and perilous territory." Horn Book

Dutton, Sandra

Mary Mae and the gospel truth. Houghton Mifflin Books for Children 2010 134p $15

Grades: 4 5 6 **Fic**

1. School stories 2. Ohio -- Fiction 3. Family -- Fiction 4. Creationism -- Fiction 5. Christian life -- Fiction 6. Mother-daughter relationship -- Fiction

ISBN 978-0-547-24966-7; 0-547-24966-7

LC 2009-49706

Ten-year-old Mary Mae, living with her parents in fossil-rich southern Ohio, tries to reconcile, despite her mother's strong disapproval, her family's Creationist beliefs with the prehistoric fossils she studies in school.

"Very few books for this age group tackle religious subjects as this one does, in a way that shows respect for all sides. Dutton allows Mary Mae to retain both her questions and her faith; instead of a definitive answer, she shows evolutionists and creationists working to find a small, shared piece of middle ground. Mary Mae is a memorable character— spunky but not defiant—whose search for truth drives the narrative." Kirkus

Dyer, Heather

Ibby's magic weekend; illustrated by Peter Bailey. Chicken House 2008 140p il $16.99

Grades: 2 3 4 5 **Fic**

1. Magic -- Fiction 2. Cousins -- Fiction 3. Magicians -- Fiction

ISBN 0-545-03209-1; 978-0-545-03209-4

While visiting her two troublemaking cousins, Ibby learns about a magic box the boys found in the attic in their country home. She soon stumbles upon the strange tale of Uncle Godfrey, a professional magician who mysteriously vanished many years ago.

"This action-filled story is just right for beginning chapter book readers, who will be fascinated with the magic as well as the personalities. Bailey's black-and-white line drawings help make the book accessible to reluctant readers." SLJ

Eager, Edward

★ **Half** magic; illustrated by N.M. Bodecker; introduction by Jack Gantos. 50th anniversary ed.; Harcourt 2004 217p il $18.95

Grades: 4 5 6 **Fic**

1. Fantasy fiction

ISBN 0-15-205302-6

A reissue with a new introduction of the title first published 1954

Faced with a dull summer in the city, Jane, Mark, Katharine, and Martha suddenly find themselves involved in a series of extraordinary adventures after Jane discovers an ordinary-looking coin that seems to grant wishes

"Entertaining and suspenseful fare for readers of make-believe." Booklist

Other titles in this series are:

Knight's castle (1956)
Magic by the lake (1957)
The time garden (1958)

Eames, Brian

The dagger Quick. Simon & Schuster Books for Young Readers 2011 320p $15.99

Grades: 4 5 6 7 **Fic**

1. Sea stories 2. Adventure fiction 3. People with disabilities -- Fiction 4. Pirates -- Fiction

ISBN 978-1-4424-2311-4; 1-4424-2311-0

LC 2011-04405

Twelve-year-old Christopher "Kitto" Wheale, a clubfooted boy seemingly doomed to follow in the boring footsteps of his father as a cooper in seventeenth-century England, finds himself on a dangerous seafaring adventure with his newly discovered uncle, the infamous pirate William Quick.

"Thoroughly researched, fast-paced, and tense, this coming-of-age adventure doesn't sugarcoat the dangers of the era, even as it embraces the mythical glamour of a pirate's life." Publ Wkly

Followed by The dagger X (2013)

Easton, Kelly

The outlandish adventures of Liberty Aimes; illustrated by Greg Swearingen. Wendy Lamb Books 2009 214p il $15.99; lib bdg $18.99

Grades: 3 4 5 6 **Fic**

1. Adventure fiction 2. Inventors -- Fiction 3. Family life -- Fiction 4. Runaway children -- Fiction

ISBN 978-0-375-83771-5; 0-375-83771-X; 978-0-375-93771-2 lib bdg; 0-375-93771-4 lib bdg

LC 2008-22119

Ten-year-old Libby Aimes escapes her prison-like home by using a strange concoction of her father's, then tries to make her way to the boarding school of her dreams, aided by various people and animals.

"The understated humor and friendly, imperturbable tone of the narration bring to mind the fantasies of Eva Ibbotson. The charming illustrations sprinkled throughout add immense appeal to this warm, delightfully odd fantasy." SLJ

Eckert, Allan W.

Incident at Hawk's Hill; with illustrations by John Schoenherr. Little, Brown 1998 173p il hardcover o.p. pa $5.95

Grades: 6 7 8 9 **Fic**

1. Badgers -- Fiction 2. Saskatchewan -- Fiction 3. Wilderness survival -- Fiction

ISBN 0-316-21905-3; 0-316-20948-1 pa

First published 1971

A Newbery Medal honor book, 1972

This account of an actual incident in Saskatchewan at the turn of the century tells of six-year-old Ben Macdonald, more attuned to animals than to people, who gets lost on the prairie and is nurtured by a female badger for two months before being found. Although a strange bond continues between the boy and the badger, the parents' understanding of their son and his communication with them improve as a result of the bizarre experience

"A very deeply moving, well written book." Jr Bookshelf

Followed by Return to Hawk's Hill (1998)

Edgar, Elsbeth

The Visconti house. Candlewick Press 2011 287p $16.99

Grades: 4 5 6 7 **Fic**

1. Houses -- Fiction 2. Australia -- Fiction 3. Family life -- Fiction

ISBN 0-7636-5019-6; 978-0-7636-5019-3

LC 2010-39172

Laura Horton has always been an outsider, more interested in writing, drawing, or spending time with her free-spirited family than in her fellow teens, but she is drawn to Leon, a new student, as together they explore the mysteries of her eccentric old house.

"Convincing dialogue and well-drawn characters, both major and minor, bring energy to the story. . . . A fine, sensitive first novel." Booklist

Edge, Christopher

Twelve minutes to midnight; Christopher Edge; illustrations by Eric Orchard. Albert Whitman & Company 2014 256 p. $16.99
Grades: 4 5 6 7   **Fic**
1. Orphans -- Fiction 2. Supernatural -- Fiction 3. Psychiatric hospitals -- Fiction 4. Great Britain -- History -- Victoria, 1837-1901 -- Fiction 5. Authorship -- Fiction 6. Mystery and detective stories 7. Publishers and publishing -- Fiction 8. London (England) -- History -- 19th century -- Fiction
ISBN 080758133X; 9780807581339
    LC 2013029481

In this book, by Christopher Edge, "Penelope Tredwell is the . . . orphan heiress of Victorian Britain's bestselling magazine, the Penny Dreadful. Her . . . tales–concealed under the pen name Montgomery Finch–are gripping the public. One day she receives a letter from the governor of the Bedlam madhouse requesting Finch's help to investigate the asylum's strange goings-on. Every night at precisely twelve minutes to midnight, the inmates all begin feverishly writing-incoherent ramblings." (Publisher's note)

"An atmospheric and spine-tingling series for middle graders who love old-fashioned mysteries." SLJ

Ehrlich, Amy

★ The **Snow** Queen; [by] Hans Christian Andersen; retold by Amy Ehrlich; [illustrated by] Susan Jeffers. Dutton Children's Books 2006 40p il $16.99
Grades: 2 3 4   **Fic**
1. Authors 2. Novelists 3. Dramatists 4. Fairy tales 5. Children's authors 6. Short story writers
ISBN 0-525-47694-6
    LC 2006004415

A revised reissue of the edition published 1982 by Dial Books
The strength of a little girl's love enables her to overcome many obstacles and free a boy from the Snow Queen's spell

Elfman, Eric

Tesla's attic; by Neal Shusterman and Eric Elfman. Disney-Hyperion Books 2014 256 p. (Accelerati trilogy) $16.99
Grades: 5 6 7 8   **Fic**
1. Houses -- Fiction 2. Tesla, Nikola, 1856-1943 3. Science fiction 4. Inventions -- Fiction 5. Colorado Springs (Colo.) -- Fiction
ISBN 1423148037; 9781423148036
    LC 2012039773

This children's novel, by Eric Elfman and Neal Shusterman, is the first book of "The Accelerati Trilogy." "After getting rid of . . . odd antiques in a garage sale, Nick befriends some local kids . . . and they discover that all of the objects have extraordinary properties. What's more, Nick figures out that the attic is a strange magnetic vortex, which attracts all sorts of trouble. It's as if the attic itself has an intelligence . . . and a purpose." (Publisher's note)

"Lively, intelligent prose elevates this story of teenagers versus mad scientists, the third-person point of view offering a stage to various players in their play of galactic consequence." Kirkus

Other titles in this series are:
Edison's alley (2015)
Hawking's hallway (2016)

Elish, Dan

The **attack** of the frozen woodchucks; by Dan Elish; illustrations by Greg Call. Laura Geringer Books 2008 247p il $16.99; lib bdg $17.89; pa $6.99
Grades: 4 5 6   **Fic**
1. Science fiction 2. Marmots -- Fiction 3. New York (N.Y.) -- Fiction 4. Extraterrestrial beings -- Fiction
ISBN 978-0-06-113870-6; 0-06-113870-3; 978-0-06-113871-3 lib bdg; 0-06-113871-1 lib bdg; 978-0-06-113872-0 pa; 0-06-113872-X pa
    LC 2006-102962

When extraterrestrial woodchucks attack, ten-year-old Jimmy, his two-and-a-half-year-old sister, friend William, and an eccentric classmate who has built a flying saucer in her Manhattan brownstone, join forces to save the universe.

"This is ridiculous, over-the-top fun all the way. . . . Science fiction fans who welcome absurdity as much as planet-hopping in their reads will find this an ideal balance of both." Bull Cent Child Books

The **family** Hitchcock; story by Jennifer Flackett and Mark Levin; written by Dan Elish. HarperChildren's 2011 288p $16.99
Grades: 4 5 6   **Fic**
1. Adventure fiction 2. Family life -- Fiction 3. Paris (France) -- Fiction
ISBN 978-0-06-189394-0; 0-06-189394-3
    LC 2011016610

When they agree to a summertime house swap with an unknown family in Paris, the four members of the Hitchcock family inadvertently get mixed up in a ring of international espionage.

"The plot-driven story is preposterous fun with genuine touches of emotion about family dynamics." SLJ

The **School** for the Insanely Gifted. Harper 2011 289p $15.99
Grades: 3 4 5 6   **Fic**
1. School stories 2. Genius -- Fiction 3. Missing persons -- Fiction 4. Voyages and travels -- Fiction
ISBN 978-0-06-113873-7; 0-06-113873-8
    LC 2010-21962

Eleven-year-old musical genius Daphna Whispers embarks on a global journey to find her missing mother, only to uncover a shocking secret about the Blatt School for the Insanely Gifted where she is a student.

"Elish has created a school story with genius students and a likable main character. . . . This lively adventure parades enough gadgets to capture readers' imaginations" SLJ

Elliott, Laura

Give me liberty; [by] L. M. Elliott. Katherine Tegen Books 2006 376p $16.99; lib bdg $17.89; pa $7.99
Grades: 5 6 7 8   **Fic**
1. Virginia -- Fiction 2. United States -- History -- 1775-1783, Revolution -- Fiction
ISBN 0-06-074421-9; 0-06-074422-7 lib bdg; 0-06-074423-5 pa
Follows the life of thirteen-year-old Nathaniel Dunn, from May 1774 to December 1775, as he serves his indentureship with a music teacher in Williamsburg, Virginia, and witnesses the growing rift between patriots and loyalists, culminating in the American Revolution.

"Elliott packs a great deal of historical detail into a novel already filled with action, well-drawn characters, and a sympathetic understanding of many points of view." Booklist

Ellis, Deborah

I am a taxi. Groundwood Books/House of Anansi Press 2006 205p (The cocalero novels) $16.95; pa $9.95

Grades: 5 6 7 8   **Fic**
1. Bolivia -- Fiction 2. Cocaine -- Fiction
ISBN 978-0-88899-735-7; 0-88899-735-3; 978-0-88899-736-4
pa; 0-88899-736-1 pa

"Diego, 12, lives in prison in the city of Cochabamba, Bolivia, stuck there with his parents, who have been falsely arrested for smuggling drugs. He attends school and works as a 'taxi,' running errands for the inmates in the great street market. Then his friend, Mando, persuades him to make big money, and the boys find themselves stomping coca leaves in cocaine pits in the jungle.... Readers will be caught up by the nonstop action in the prison, and also in the jungle survival adventure." Booklist

Followed by Sacred leaf (2007)

★ **No** ordinary day. Groundwood Books 2011 160p $16.95
Grades: 5 6 7   **Fic**
1. India -- Fiction 2. Leprosy -- Fiction 3. Orphans -- Fiction 4. Poverty -- Fiction 5. Homeless persons -- Fiction
ISBN 978-1-55498-134-2; 1-55498-134-4

"Valli, about 10, lives in the poverty-stricken town of Jharia, India, where she is a coal picker. When she makes a shocking discovery about her family, she runs away and, after a series of harrowing events, reaches the bustling city of Kolkata.... While begging for change one day, she is befriended by a kind doctor who recognizes Valli's symptoms of leprosy.... With the help of the doctor and other leprosy patients, Valli gets treatment and education, learns tolerance for people different from herself, and simultaneously realizes her own self-worth. Although many important lessons are presented in this even-paced, clearly written story, it is never heavyhanded or didactic. Valli is a well-developed, realistic, and engaging narrator.... An important, inspiring tale." SLJ

Sacred leaf. Groundwood Books/House of Anansi Press 2007 206p (The cocalero novels) $16.95; pa $9.95
Grades: 5 6 7 8   **Fic**
1. Bolivia -- Fiction 2. Cocaine -- Fiction
ISBN 978-0-88899-751-7; 978-0-88899-808-8 pa
Sequel to: I am a taxi (2006)
Twelve year old Diego escapes from slavery at an illegal cocaine operation and is taken in by the Ricardos, coca farmers.

"An easy read that touches on issues seldom addressed for young teens." SLJ

Ellis, Sarah
Outside in; by Sarah Ellis. Pgw 2014 206 p. $16.95
Grades: 5 6 7 8   **Fic**
1. Canada -- Fiction 2. Teenage girls -- Fiction 3. Mother-daughter relationship -- Fiction 4. Eccentrics and eccentricities -- Fiction 5. Friendship -- Fiction 6. Homeless girls -- Fiction
ISBN 1554983673; 9781554983674

In this book, by Sarah Ellis, "Lynn is a typical 13-year-old Canadian, navigating through life.... Things start to fall apart when her mom wrecks her relationship with the only man who has ever stuck around and Lynn's passport doesn't come in time for her to take the choir trip with the rest of her friends, who leave for Portland..... Then a mysterious girl named Blossom is thrust into her life and introduces her to a wonderful world within their city called the Underland." (Publisher's note)

"With the exception of her quirky, unmarried mother, Lynn is a typical 13-year-old Canadian, navigating through life filled with choir practice, projects, best friends, and school...Lynn's difficult relationship with her mother and her strong bonds with friends make this story very relatable. A thoughtful, exciting read that makes everything ordinary suddenly have the possibility to be extraordinary." (SLJ)

The **several** lives of Orphan Jack; pictures by Bruno St-Aubin. Douglas & McIntyre 2003 84p il hardcover o.p. pa $7.95
Grades: 3 4 5 6   **Fic**
1. Adventure fiction 2. Orphans -- Fiction
ISBN 0-88899-529-6; 0-88899-618-7 pa

When, at the age of twelve, he is sent out from the Opportunities School for Orphans and Foundlings to be a bookkeeper's apprentice, Jack finds his heretofore predictable life full of unusual adventures.

"Ellis has created a small gem here, with messages about following your heart tucked into the sentences, phrases, thoughts, and ideas that she seamlessly weaves together." Booklist

Emerson, Kevin
Last day on mars; Kevin Emerson; [edited by] Jordan Brown. HarperCollins 2017 336 p. (Book one of the Chronicle of the dark star) (hardcover) $16.99
Grades: 4 5 6 7 8   **Fic**
1. Science fiction 2. Mars (Planet) -- Fiction
ISBN 9780062306715
                                                           LC 2016938987

In this book, by Kevin Emerson, "it is Earth year 2213--but, of course there is no Earth anymore.... The human race has fled to Mars, .. Liam Saunders-Chang is one of the last humans left on Mars. The son of two scientists who have been racing against time to create technology vital to humanity's survival, Liam, along with his friend Phoebe, will be on the last starliner to depart before Mars, like Earth before it, is destroyed." (Publisher's note)

"While much of the novel serves to set up the next books, it's a satisfying, if unsettling, beginning." Pub Wkly

Enderle, Dotti
Crosswire. Calkins Creek 2010 143p $17.95
Grades: 5 6 7 8   **Fic**
1. Texas -- Fiction 2. Brothers -- Fiction 3. Droughts -- Fiction 4. Ranch life -- Fiction 5. Father-son relationship -- Fiction
ISBN 978-1-59078-751-9; 1-59078-751-X
                                                           LC 2010-07522

When an 1883 drought drives free-range cattlemen to shred Texas ranchers' barbed wire fences and steal water, thirteen-year-old Jesse works hard to help while dealing with his father and brother's falling out and his own fear of guns.

"Enderle writes with restraint, her research neatly woven into the story, her characters carefully drawn. A small gem of a story." Kirkus
Includes bibliographical references

Engle, Margarita
Silver people; voices from the Panama Canal. Margarita Engle. Houghton Mifflin Harcourt 2014 272 p. (hardback) $17.99
Grades: 5 6 7 8   **Fic**
1. Panama Canal 2. Novels in verse 3. Young adult literature 4. Rain forests -- Fiction 5. Migrant labor -- Fiction 6. Racism -- Fiction 7. Segregation -- Fiction 8. Panama Canal (Panama) -- History -- Fiction
ISBN 0544109414; 9780544109414
                                                           LC 201303748

This children's book, by Margarita Engle, is an "exploration of the construction of the Panama Canal.... Mateo, a 14-year-old Cuban lured by promises of wealth, journeys to Panama only to discover the recruiters' lies and a life of harsh labor. However, through his relationship with Anita, an 'herb girl,' Henry, a black Jamaican worker, and Augusto, a Puerto Rican geologist, Mateo is able to find a place in his new land." (Kirkus Reviews)

"In melodic verses, Engle offers the voices of the dark-skinned workers (known as the 'silver people'), whose backbreaking labor helped build the Panama Canal, along with the perspective of a local girl. Interspersed are occasional echoes from flora and fauna as well as cameo appearances by historical figures. Together, they provide an illuminating picture of the project's ecological sacrifices and human costs." Horn Book

Includes bibliographical references

The **wild** book; Margarita Engle. Harcourt Children's Books 2012 133p $16.99

Grades: 5 6 7 8 **Fic**

1. Novels in verse 2. Children's stories 3. Dyslexia -- Fiction 4. Cuba -- History -- 1909-1933 -- Fiction

ISBN 9780547581316

LC 2011027320

This book tells the story of "Josefa 'Fefa' de la Caridad Uría Peña. . . . Diagnosed with 'word blindness' (a misnomer for dyslexia), Fefa struggles at school. . . . Discounting a doctor's opinion . . . her mother gives her a blank diary: 'Let the words sprout / like seedlings, / then relax and watch / as your wild diary / grows.' . . . Her reading difficulties are heightened when bandits begin roving the countryside, kidnapping local children for ransom." (Kirkus Reviews)

English, Karen

Francie. Farrar, Straus & Giroux 1999 199p hardcover o.p. $17

Grades: 5 6 7 8 **Fic**

1. Alabama -- Fiction 2. Race relations -- Fiction 3. African Americans -- Fiction

ISBN 0-374-32456-5; 0-374-42459-4 pa

LC 98-53047

Coretta Scott King honor book for text, 2000

"The best student in her small, all-black school in preintegration Alabama, 12-year-old Francie hopes for a better life. . . . When Jessie, an older school friend who is without family, is forced on the run by a racist employer, Francie leaves her mother's labeled canned food for him in the woods. Only when the sheriff begins searching their woods . . . does she realize the depth of the danger she may have brought to her family. Francie's smooth-flowing, well-paced narration is gently assisted by just the right touch of the vernacular. Characterization is evenhanded and believable, while place and time envelop readers." SLJ

Nikki & Deja; wedding drama. by Karen English; illustrated by Laura Freeman. Clarion Books 2012 108 p.

Grades: 1 2 3 **Fic**

1. Weddings -- Fiction 2. Friendship -- Fiction 3. Women teachers -- Fiction 4. African American children -- Fiction 5. Teacher-student relationship -- Fiction 6. Schools -- Fiction 7. Teachers -- Fiction 8. Best friends -- Fiction 9. African Americans -- Fiction

ISBN 0547615647; 9780547615646

LC 2011027484

In this book, part of the "Nikki & Deja" series from author Karen English, main characters Niki and Deja find out that "[t]heir beloved teacher, Ms. Shelby, is getting married. The excitement reaches a new high when she announces two last-minute guest cancellations and says she would like two students to attend. She draws names out of a hat, and Nikki and Deja are chosen "fair and square." The rest of the class is jealous but soon moves on to invent a classroom contest to see which team can create the best imaginary wedding. Meanwhile, Nikki and her mother revel in finding a dress and the perfect panini maker, while Deja worries about Auntie Dee's new jobless status and fears what a homemade dress might look like." (Kirkus)

Nikki and Deja, wedding drama

Wedding drama

Nikki & Deja: birthday blues; illustrated by Laura Freeman. Clarion Books 2009 92p il $15

Grades: 2 3 4 **Fic**

1. School stories 2. Aunts -- Fiction 3. Parties -- Fiction 4. Birthdays -- Fiction 5. Friendship -- Fiction 6. African Americans -- Fiction

ISBN 978-0-618-97787-1; 0-618-97787-2

LC 2007-50189

As her eighth birthday approaches, Deja's biggest concern is whether her father will attend her party, until her aunt is called away on business and a classmate schedules a "just because party" on the same afternoon.

"Early chapter-book readers will relate to the protagonist's authentic emotions as English acknowledges the challenges and complexities of classroom life." SLJ

Companion volume to:

Nikki & Deja (2007)

Nikki & Deja: the newsy news newsletter. Clarion Books 2010 91p $15

Grades: 2 3 4 **Fic**

1. School stories 2. Friendship -- Fiction 3. Newspapers -- Fiction

ISBN 978-0-547-22247-9; 0-547-22247-5

LC 2009015845

When Nikki and her best friend, Deja, start a newsletter about what is happening on their street and in their school, they focus more on writing exciting stories than on finding the truth.

"English writes with wit, feeling, and a spot-on voice that acknowledges the realistic friendship and problems of the protagonists. Freeman's cartoon illustrations enhance the story." SLJ

Nikki and Deja: election madness; illustrated by Laura Freeman. Clarion Books 2011 108p il $14.99

Grades: 2 3 4 **Fic**

1. School stories 2. Elections -- Fiction 3. Friendship -- Fiction 4. African Americans -- Fiction

ISBN 978-0-547-43558-9; 0-547-43558-4

LC 2011008151

When Carver Elementary holds school-wide elections for the first time, third-grader Deja puts all her efforts into running for school president, ignoring her best friend Nikki's problems.

"Freeman's occasional black-and-white illustrations capture the dramatic tension between the girls." Kirkus

Skateboard party; by Karen English; illustrated by Laura Freeman. Clarion Books, Houghton Mifflin Harcourt 2014 128 p. illustrations (The Carver chronicles) (hardback) $14.99

Grades: 2 3 4 **Fic**

1. School stories 2. Parties -- Fiction 3. Skateboarding -- Fiction 4. Schools -- Fiction 5. African Americans -- Fiction

ISBN 0544283066; 9780544283060

LC 2013048934

In this children's book, part of Karen English's Carver Chronicles series, "Richard can't wait to show off his flat-ground Ollies at a friend's birthday party at the skate park, but a note home from his teacher threatens to ruin his plans. He really meant to finish his assignment on howler monkeys, but he just got . . . distracted. Can Richard manage to put off getting the note signed (and facing the consequences) until after the party, or will the deception make things even worse?" (Publisher's note)

"Kids will recognize themselves in this series entry (including the occasional black-and-white illustrations) starring a realistic, likable boy of color." Horn Book

Epstein, Adam Jay

The **familiars**; [by] Adam Jay Epstein [and] Andrew Jacobson; art by Peter Chan & Kei Acedera. Harper 2010 360p il $16.99

Grades: 4 5 6   **Fic**

1. Adventure fiction 2. Cats -- Fiction 3. Magic -- Fiction
ISBN 978-0-06-196108-3; 0-06-196108-6

LC 2010-13686

When a scrappy alley cat named Aldwyn passes himself off as a magical animal companion to Jack, a young wizard in training, Aldwyn and his fellow "familiars," a know-it-all blue jay and bumbling tree frog, must save the kingdom after the evil queen of Vastia kidnaps Jack and two other wizards.

"The consistently suspenseful narrative moves quickly and is full of twists and turns. . . . This winning combination of action and humor will keep readers turning pages right up to the ending." SLJ

Followed by: Secrets of the crown (2011)

Secrets of the crown; [by] Adam Jay Epstein, Andrew Jacobson; art by Peter Chan & Kei Acedera. Harper 2011 374p il (The familiars) $16.99

Grades: 4 5 6   **Fic**

1. Fantasy fiction 2. Magic -- Fiction 3. Animals -- Fiction
ISBN 978-0-06-196111-3; 0-06-196111-6

LC 2011002086

Sequel to: The familiars (2010)

When human magic is destroyed, familiars Aldwyn the cat, Skylar the blue jay, and Gilbert the tree frog set out without their wizards to seek the Crown of the Snow Leopard, the only object that can save the kingdom of Vastia from the evil hare Paksahara.

"The familiars' adventures are exciting, and the revelations about Aldwyn's long-lost parents are touching. Fans of the first book will be pleased." SLJ

Erdrich, Louise, 1954-

★ The **birchbark** house. Hyperion Bks. for Children 1999 244p il hardcover o.p. pa $6.99

Grades: 5 6 7 8   **Fic**

1. Ojibwa Indians -- Fiction
ISBN 0-7868-0300-2; 0-7868-1454-3 pa

LC 98-46366

Omakayas, a seven-year-old Native American girl of the Ojibwa tribe, lives through the joys of summer and the perils of winter on an island in Lake Superior in 1847.

"Erdrich crafts images of tender beauty while weaving Ojibwa words seamlessly into the text. Her gentle spot art throughout complements this first of several projected stories that will 'attempt to retrace [her] own family's history.'" Horn Book Guide

Followed by: The game of silence (2004)

★ **Chickadee**; Louise Erdrich. Harper 2012 256p. (trade bdg.) $16.99

Grades: 5 6 7 8   **Fic**

1. Brothers -- Fiction 2. Ojibwe Indians -- Fiction 3. Voyages and travels -- Fiction 4. Kidnapping -- Fiction 5. Family life -- Fiction 6. Métis -- Fiction 7. Ojibwa Indians -- Fiction 8. Great Plains -- History -- 19th century -- Fiction 9. Superior, Lake, Region -- History -- 19th century -- Fiction
ISBN 9780060577902; 9780060577919

LC 2012006565

Sequel to: The porcupine year.
Scott O'Dell Award for Historical Fiction (2013)

This book is the "fourth book of The Birchbark House Series. Omakayas is now a young mother with lively 8-year-old twins named Chickadee and Makoons." Makoons plays a trick on the tribe's bully, resulting

in the bully's sons kidnapping Chickadee. He escapes, then "runs into his Uncle Quill driving an ox cart of furs to sell in St. Paul. Quill and Chickadee travel with fellow traders on the Red River ox cart trail, arriving in Pembina to find Makoons seriously ill." (Kirkus)

★ The **game** of silence; [by] Louise Erdrich. HarperCollins 2004 256p $15.99; lib bdg $16.89; pa $5.99

Grades: 5 6 7 8   **Fic**

1. Ojibwa Indians -- Fiction
ISBN 0-06-029789-1; 0-06-029790-5 lib bdg; 0-06-441029-3 pa

LC 2004-6018

Sequel to: The birchbark house (1999)

Nine-year-old Omakayas, of the Ojibwa tribe, moves west with her family in 1849

"Erdrich's captivating tale of four seasons portrays a deep appreciation of our environment, our history, and our Native American sisters and brothers." SLJ

Followed by: The porcupine year (2008)

Makoons; by Louise Erdrich. Harpercollins Childrens Books 2016 176 p. $16.99

Grades: 5 6 7 8   **Fic**

1. Ojibwe Indians -- Fiction
ISBN 0060577932; 9780060577933

In this book, author and illustrator Louise Erdrich "continues her award-winning Birchbark House series. . . . Named for the Ojibwe word for little bear, Makoons and his twin, Chickadee, have traveled with their family to the Great Plains of Dakota Territory. There they must learn to become buffalo hunters and once again help their people make a home in a new land. But Makoons has had a vision that foretells great challenges—challenges that his family may not be able to overcome." (Publisher's note)

"Erdrich's simple text and delicate pencil illustrations provide a detailed, honest portrait of Plains life through the antics and experiences of two Ojibwe boys. A warm and welcome addition to the unfolding saga of a 19th-century Ojibwe family." Kirkus

★ The **porcupine** year. HarperCollinsPublishers 2008 193p $15.99; lib bdg $16.89

Grades: 5 6 7 8   **Fic**

1. Family life -- Fiction 2. Ojibwa Indians -- Fiction 3. Voyages and travels -- Fiction
ISBN 978-0-06-029787-9; 0-06-029787-5; 978-0-06-029788-6 lib bdg; 0-06-029788-3 lib bdg

LC 2008000757

Sequel to: The game of silence (2004)

In 1852, forced by the United States government to leave their beloved Island of the Golden Breasted Woodpecker, fourteen-year-old Omokayas and her Ojibwe family travel in search of a new home.

"Based on Erdrich's own family history, this celebration of life will move readers with its mischief, its anger, and its sadness. What is left unspoken is as powerful as the story told." Booklist

Erskine, Kathryn

The **absolute** value of Mike. Philomel Books 2011 247p $16.99

Grades: 5 6 7 8   **Fic**

1. Pennsylvania -- Fiction 2. Business enterprises -- Fiction 3. Father-son relationship -- Fiction
ISBN 978-0-399-25505-2; 0-399-25505-2

LC 2010-1333

Fourteen-year-old Mike, whose father is a brilliant mathematician but who has no math aptitude himself, spends the summer in rural Pennsylvania with his elderly and eccentric relatives Moo and Poppy, helping the townspeople raise money to adopt a Romanian orphan.

"Erskine weaves together a large but entertaining cast of characters. . . . Despite many laugh-out-loud moments, the heart of the book is essentially serious." Horn Book

The **badger** knight; Kathryn Erskine. Scholastic Press 2014 352 p. illustrations $17.99

Grades: 5 6 7 8   **Fic**

1. Paganism 2. War stories 3. Medieval civilization 4. Adventure stories 5. Archers -- Fiction 6. Runaways -- Fiction 7. Friendship -- Fiction 8. Albinos and albinism -- Fiction 9. Great Britain -- History -- Edward III, 1327-1377 -- Fiction

ISBN 0545464420; 9780545464420; 9780545464437; 9780545662932

LC 2013042527

In this book by Kathryn Erskine, "13-year-old Adrian--small, asthmatic, and an albino--dreams of becoming a soldier and fighting the 'pagan Scots' that threaten 1346 England. Perceived as weak and touched by the devil, the self-dubbed 'Badger' is a skilled archer and has the rare ability to read and write. When his amiable friend Hugh joins the English army, Adrian runs away to follow him." (Publishers Weekly)

"Erskine hits the bull's-eye in her retelling of the hero's journey through the eyes of a young, medieval archer determined to prove his worth through battle... Erskine excels at combining action, historical tidbits (Badger hides in an ancient Roman latrine and muses on the soldiers who came before him), and thoroughly likable characters with modern sensibilities. Much like Karen Cushman's notable books, Erskine's latest deserves a place in most middle school libraries." SLJ

★ **Mockingbird**. Philomel Books 2010 235p

Grades: 4 5 6   **Fic**

1. School stories 2. Siblings -- Fiction 3. Bereavement -- Fiction 4. Asperger's syndrome -- Fiction

ISBN 0-399-25264-9; 978-0-399-25264-8

LC 2009-06741

National Book Award, 2010

Ten-year-old Caitlin, who has Asperger's Syndrome, struggles to understand emotions, show empathy, and make friends at school, while at home she seeks closure by working on a project with her father. "Age ten and up." (Publisher's note)

"The sharp insights into Caitlyn's behavior enhance this fine addition to the recent group of books with narrators with autism and Aspergers." Booklist

Seeing red; by Kathryn Erskine. Scholastic Press 2013 352 p. $16.99

Grades: 5 6 7 8   **Fic**

1. Family -- Fiction 2. Friendship -- Fiction 3. Race relations -- Fiction 4. Grief -- Fiction 5. Bereavement -- Fiction 6. Family life -- Virginia -- Fiction

ISBN 0545464404; 9780545464406; 9780545464413; 9780545576451

LC 2013004261

Author Kathryn Erskin presents a "story of family, friendship, and race relations in the South. Red's daddy, his idol, has just died, leaving Red and Mama with some hard decisions and a whole lot of doubt. Should they sell the Porter family business? When Red discovers the injustices that have been happening in Rocky Gap since before he was born, he's faced with unsettling questions about his family's legacy." (Publisher's note)

Estes, Eleanor

Ginger Pye; with illustrations by the author. Harcourt 2000 306p $17; pa $6

Grades: 4 5 6   **Fic**

1. Dogs -- Fiction

ISBN 0-15-202499-9; 0-15-202505-7 pa

LC 00-26700

A reissue of the title first published 1951

Awarded the Newbery Medal, 1952

The disappearance of a new puppy named Ginger and the appearance of a mysterious man in a mustard yellow hat bring excitement into the lives of the Pye children

Estes' drawings are "vivid, amusing sketches that point up and confirm the atmosphere of the story. It is a book to read and reread." Saturday Rev

Another title about the Pye family is:
Pinky Pye (1958)

★ The **hundred** dresses; illustrated by Louis Slobodkin. New ed; Harcourt 2004 80p il $16; pa $7

Grades: 4 5 6   **Fic**

1. Friendship -- Fiction 2. Polish Americans -- Fiction

ISBN 0-15-205170-8; 0-15-205260-7 pa

LC 2003-57037

A reissue of the title first published 1944

A Newbery honor book, 1945

"The 100 dresses are just dream dresses, pictures Wanda Petronski has drawn, but she describes them in self-defense as she appears daily in the same faded blue dress. Not until Wanda, snubbed and unhappy, moves away leaving her pictures at school for an art contest, do her classmates realize their cruelty." Books for Deaf Child

Etchemendy, Nancy

The **power** of Un. Front St./Cricket Bks. 2000 148p $16.95; pa $4.99

Grades: 4 5 6 7   **Fic**

1. Fantasy fiction

ISBN 0-8126-2850-0; 0-439-31331-7 pa

LC 99-58281

When he is given a device that will allow him to "undo" what has happened in the past, Gib Finney is not sure what event from the worst day in his life he should change in order to keep his sister from being hit by a truck

The author has a "knack for writing hilarious dialogue that perfectly paints the funny, poignant, and altogether unpredictable world of eleven and twelve year olds. . . . A unique, thought-provoking book." Voice Youth Advocates

Eulberg, Elizabeth

The **great** Shelby Holmes; by Elizabeth Eulberg. Bloomsbury 2016 256 p. illustrations (hardcover) $16.99

Grades: 4 5 6   **Fic**

1. Mystery fiction 2. Friendship -- Fiction 3. Harlem (New York, N.Y.) -- Fiction 4. Mystery and detective stories

ISBN 9781681190518

LC 2015040010

In this children's novel, by Elizabeth Eulberg, "Shelby Holmes is not your average sixth grader. She's nine years old, barely four feet tall, and the best detective her Harlem neighborhood has ever seen. . . . When eleven-year-old John Watson moves downstairs, Shelby finds something that's eluded her up till now: a friend. The easy-going John isn't sure of what to make of Shelby, but he soon finds himself her most-trusted (read: only) partner in a dog-napping case." (Publisher's note)

"Readers will delight in Shelby's ability to read clues in this well-plotted mystery and sympathize with Watson who, along with the rest of the supporting cast, is generally two steps behind Shelby." Pub Wkly

Evans, Lissa

Horten's incredible illusions; magic, mystery & another very strange adventure. by Lissa Evans. Sterling Children's Books 2012 349 p. $14.95

Grades: 3 4 5 6 7   **Fic**

1. Adventure fiction 2. Magic -- Fiction 3. Magicians

ISBN 1402798709; 9781402798702

In this sequel to "Horten's Miraculous Mechanisms" by Lissa Evans, "10-year-old Stuart Horten is catapulted on yet another adventure left to him by his Great-Uncle Tony. . . . It is up to Stuart to follow clues to locate the great magician's will. He and his friend April soon discover, however, that Tony's Tricks are truly magic: each one transports them to another time or place, where a puzzle must be solved." (School Library Journal)

Horten's miraculous mechanisms; magic, mystery & a very strange adventure. by Lissa Evans. Sterling 2012 270 p. $14.95

Grades: 3 4 5 6 7   **Fic**

1. Mystery fiction 2. Adventure fiction 3. Children's stories 4. Inventors -- Fiction 5. Magicians -- Fiction

ISBN 9781402798061

In this book, author Lissa "Evans borrows several classic tropes and themes--magic, riddles, a quest, and even a night at a museum--for the . . . story of 10-year-old Stuart Horten . . . who stumbles into a family mystery when he and his parents move to the small British town of Beeton. There, Stuart discovers that his Great-Uncle Tony Horten, who disappeared years ago without a trace, was both an inventor of mechanical devices and a magician. A chance phone call in a broken phone booth is the first step in a journey that leads Stuart around town, as he unearths his great-uncle's legacy and secrets. Stuart also draws the attention of April, May, and June (the journalistically inclined triplets next door), as well as Beeton residents with more sinister intentions." (Publishers Weekly)

Evans, Nate

Meet the beast; [by] Nate Evans and [illustrated by] Vince Evans. Soucebooks Jabberwocky 2010 111p il (Beast friends forever) pa $4.99

Grades: 2 3 4   **Fic**

1. Monsters -- Fiction 2. Siblings -- Fiction

ISBN 978-1-4022-4050-8 pa; 1-4022-4050-3 pa

"This well-plotted and fanciful opener promises a series that early chapter-book readers will appreciate. . . . Bouncy cartoon illustrations and a few passages in comic-strip format punctuate the brief chapters, but the narrative is seamless despite these multiple storytelling approaches." Booklist

Fagan, Cary

Banjo of destiny; pictures by Sel¿cuk Demirel. Groundwood Books/House of Anansi Press 2011 127p il $14.95

Grades: 4 5 6   **Fic**

1. Banjos -- Fiction 2. Wealth -- Fiction

ISBN 978-1-55498-085-7; 1-55498-085-2; 978-1-55498-086-4 pa

"Jeremiah's nouveau riche parents want only the best for their gawky son—private school plus lessons in etiquette, dancing, art, and piano. When Jeremiah hears a banjo playing he becomes obsessed with following his true destiny. Fagan's straightforward, nondidactic narrative hints at the fact that individualism has its own rewards." Horn Book Guide

The big swim. Groundwood Books 2010 128p $14.95

Grades: 4 5 6   **Fic**

1. Camps -- Fiction 2. Summer -- Fiction 3. Friendship -- Fiction

ISBN 978-0-88899-969-6; 0-88899-969-0

"Ethan works hard to integrate himself into summer-camp routine. Much to his surprise, he makes friends easily and succeeds at not being the worst at any activity. Everything changes, though, when Zachary arrives, shrouded in a bad attitude and a mysterious past. . . . The setting is rich and the characters are interesting and fresh." SLJ

Fagan, Deva

Fortune's folly. Henry Holt 2009 260p $17.95

Grades: 5 6 7 8   **Fic**

1. Fairy tales 2. Adventure fiction 3. Prophecies -- Fiction

ISBN 978-0-8050-8742-0; 0-8050-8742-7

LC 2008-36780

Ever since her mother died and her father lost his shoemaking skills, Fortunata has survived by pretending to tell fortunes, but when she is tricked into telling the fortune of a prince, she is faced with the impossible task of fulfilling her wild prophecy to save her father's life.

"Fagan's language evokes images of fairy tales and legends, and the protagonist's first-person narrative sparkles with humor. In this book, words are powerful, impressive, mystical, and, sometimes, downright silly." SLJ

Fairlie, Emily

The lost treasure of Tuckernuck; Emily Fairlie. Katherine Tegen Books 2012 283 p. (hardback) $16.99

Grades: 4 5 6 7 8   **Fic**

1. Mystery fiction 2. Buried treasure -- Fiction 3. Historic buildings -- Fiction 4. Schools -- Fiction

ISBN 0062118900; 9780062118905

LC 2012025279

This book by Emily Fairlie "tells the story of Bud and Laurie's quest to find the infamous Tutweiler Treasure. They're hot (or at least lukewarm) on the trail of clues, but time is running out -- the school board wants to tear down Tuckernuck Hall. Can Bud and Laurie find the treasure before it's lost forever?" (Publisher's note)

The magician's bird; a Tuckernuck mystery. Emily Fairlie; Illustrated by Antonio Javier Caparo. Katherine Tegen Books, an imprint of HarperCollinsPublishers 2013 288 p. (hardcover bdg.) $16.99

Grades: 4 5 6   **Fic**

1. Schools -- Fiction 2. Magicians 3. Treasure hunt (Game) -- Fiction 4. Historic buildings -- Fiction 6. Mystery and detective stories

ISBN 0062118935; 9780062118936

LC 2012051733

In this book, by Emily Fairlie, "the mystery Bud and Laurie must solve is much more serious than a treasure hunt—their beloved school founder, Maria Tutweiler, has been accused of murdering Marchetti the Magician! Can Bud and Laurie—with the help of enthusiastic Misti and evil but useful Calliope—prove Maria Tutweiler's innocence? Or will Tuckernuck Hall be closed down for good?" (Publisher's note)

Falls, Kat

Dark life. Scholastic Press 2010 297p $16.99; pa $6.99

Grades: 4 5 6 7   **Fic**

1. Science fiction 2. Ocean -- Fiction

ISBN 978-0-545-17814-3; 0-545-17814-2; 978-0-545-17815-0 pa; 0-545-17815-0 pa

LC 2009-2490

"Ty has lived subsea his entire life. His family members moved below the water to make a better life for themselves. In this future, the climate changes on Earth have been so drastic that hardly any solid ground exits anymore. . . . This book will appeal to middle grade readers, who will enjoy the novel's mystery and suspense. It is a definite must-read for SF fans." Voice Youth Advocates

Followed by: Rip tide (2011)

Rip tide. Scholastic Press 2011 320p $16.99

Grades: 4 5 6 7 **Fic**

1. Science fiction 2. Ocean -- Fiction

ISBN 0-545-17843-6; 978-0-545-17843-3

Sequel to: Dark life (2010)

"While preparing to sell the season's seaweed crop, Ty stumbles across an abandoned township, its doors chained shut and its residents murdered. Soon after, the colonists' deal with another township goes bad, and Ty's parents are kidnapped. As Ty and Gemma try to track down those responsible and save their loved ones, they're forced to join up with the notorious Seablite Gang, infiltrate the rough-and-tumble town of Rip Tide, fight for their lives against sea monsters and human predators, and discover who's killing entire townships—and why.... There's no shortage of action, intrigue, or daring exploits in this aquatic thriller. Atmospheric and tense, built around an expertly used postapocalyptic meets Wild West setting, this story's a whole lot of fun." Publ Wkly

Fantaskey, Beth

Isabel Feeney; Star Reporter. Beth Fantaskey. Houghton Mifflin Harcourt 2016 352 p. $17.99

Grades: 4 5 6 **Fic**

1. Gangs 2. Criminal investigation 3. Journalists -- Fiction 4. Gangsters -- Fiction 5. Newspapers -- Fiction 6. Mystery and detective stories 7. Reporters and reporting -- Fiction 8. Chicago (Ill.) -- HIstory -- 20th century -- Fiction

ISBN 9780544582491; 0544582497

LC 2014048445

This children's novel, by Beth Fantaskey, is set in "1920s Chicago--the guns-and-gangster era of Al Capone. Ten-year-old Isabel Feeney is ... unusually obsessed with being a news reporter. She can't believe her luck when she stumbles not only into a real-live murder scene, but also into her hero, the famous journalist Maude Collier. The story [is] of how the smart, curious, loyal Isabel fights to defend the honor of her accused friend and latches on to the murder case." (Publisher's note)

"It's a story chockfull of colorful historical information with a heroine who is impetuous, flawed, and very easy to root for." Pub Wkly

Farber, E. S.

Seagulls don't eat pickles; by Erica Farber; illustrated by Jason Beene. Chronicle Books 2013 184 p. (Fish Finelli) (alk. paper) $15.99

Grades: 4 5 6 7 **Fic**

1. Pirates -- Fiction 2. Adventure fiction 3. Librarians -- Fiction 4. Historic sites -- Fiction 5. Buried treasure -- Fiction 6. Mystery and detective stories 7. Treasure troves -- Fiction 8. Historic sites -- Conservation and restoration -- Fiction

ISBN 145210820X; 9781452108209

LC 2012027739

This is the first book in E.S. Farber's Fish Finelli series. "Fish Finelli wants nothing more . . . than to fix up his boat with a supercharged Seagull motor and win Whooping Hollow's annual Captain Kidd Classic boat race," but has only saved half the necessary funds, "When local bully Bryce Billings baits Fish into a bet that he and his friends Roger and T.J. can't find Captain Kidd's fabled lost treasure, . . . Fish finds himself knee-deep in a mysterious pirate adventure." (School Library Journal)

Other titles in this series are:

Operation fireball (2014)

Ghosts don't wear glasses (2015)

Farley, Walter

The **Black** Stallion; by Walter Farley; illustrated by Keith Ward. Random House 2008 275p il $15.99; lib bdg $18.99

Grades: 4 5 6 7 **Fic**

1. Horses -- Fiction

ISBN 978-0-375-85582-5; 0-375-85582-3; 978-0-375-95578-5 lib bdg; 0-375-95578-X lib bdg

A reissue of the title first published 1941

Young Alec Ramsay is shipwrecked on a desert island with a horse destined to play an important part in his life. Following their rescue their adventure continues in America.

Other titles in this series are:

The Black Stallion and Flame (1960)

The Black Stallion and the shape-shifter (2008) by Steven Farley

The Black Stallion returns (1945)

The Black Stallion's ghost (1969)

The Black Stallion's shadow (1996) by Steven Farley

The Black Stallion's steeplechaser (1997) by Steven Farley

Son of the Black Stallion (1947)

The young Black Stallion (1989)

Farmer, Nancy

★ The **Ear,** the Eye, and the Arm; a novel. Puffin Books 1995 311p pa $6.99

Grades: 6 7 8 9 10 **Fic**

1. Science fiction 2. Young adult literature 3. Zimbabwe -- Fiction

ISBN 978-0-14-131109-8; 0-14-131109-6

LC 95019982

First published 1994 by Orchard Books

A Newbery Medal honor book, 1995

In 2194 in Zimbabwe, General Matsika's three children are kidnapped and put to work in a plastic mine while three mutant detectives use their special powers to search for them

"Throughout the story, it's the thrilling adventure that will grab readers, who will also like the comic, tender characterizations." Booklist

★ A **girl** named Disaster. Orchard Bks. 1996 309p $19.95; pa $7.99

Grades: 6 7 8 9 **Fic**

1. Adventure fiction 2. Young adult literature 3. Zimbabwe -- Fiction 4. Mozambique -- Fiction 5. Supernatural -- Fiction

ISBN 0-531-09539-8; 0-14-038635-1 pa

LC 96-15141

A Newbery Medal honor book, 1997

While journeying from Mozambique to Zimbabwe to escape an arranged marriage, eleven-year-old Nhamo struggles to escape drowning and starvation and in so doing comes close to the luminous world of the African spirits

"This story is humorous and heartwrenching, complex and multilayered." SLJ

The **Islands** of the Blessed. Atheneum Books for Young Readers 2009 479p (Sea of Trolls) $18.99

Grades: 5 6 7 8 9 **Fic**

1. Fantasy fiction 2. Norse mythology -- Fiction 3. Druids and Druidism -- Fiction

ISBN 978-1-4169-0737-4; 1-4169-0737-8

LC 2008045415

Sequel to: Land of the Silver Apples (2007)

Two years after their adventures in The Land of the Silver Apples, the apprentice bard Jack and his Viking companion Thorgil confront the malevolent spirit of a vengeful mermaid and begin a quest that casts them among the fin folk of Notland.

This is an "exciting story, which contains a cast of lively, multifaceted characters." Booklist

Includes bibliographical references

The **Land** of the Silver Apples. Atheneum Books for Young Readers 2007 496p il $18.99; pa $9.99

Grades: 5 6 7 8 9   **Fic**

1. Fantasy fiction 2. Vikings -- Fiction 3. Norse mythology -- Fiction 4. Druids and Druidism -- Fiction

ISBN 978-1-4169-0735-0; 1-4169-0735-1; 978-1-4169-0736-7 pa; 1-4169-0736-x pa

LC 2006-31433

Sequel to: The Sea of Trolls (2004)

After escaping from the Sea of Trolls, the apprentice bard Jack plunges into a new series of adventures, traveling underground to Elfland and uncovering the truth about his little sister Lucy.

"Farmer beautifully balances pell-mell action and quieter thematic points. . . . This hearty adventure, as personal as it is epic, will cradle readers in the 'hollow it its hand.'" Booklist

Followed by: The Islands of the Blessed (2009)

★ The **Sea** of Trolls. Atheneum Books for Young Readers 2004 459p $17.95; pa $9.99

Grades: 5 6 7 8 9   **Fic**

1. Fantasy fiction 2. Vikings -- Fiction 3. Norse mythology -- Fiction 4. Druids and Druidism -- Fiction

ISBN 0-689-86744-1; 0-689-86746-8 pa

LC 2003-19091

After Jack becomes apprenticed to a Druid bard, he and his little sister Lucy are captured by Viking Berserkers and taken to the home of King Ivar the Boneless and his half-troll queen, leading Jack to undertake a vital quest to Jotunheim, home of the trolls.

"This exciting and original fantasy will capture the hearts and imaginations of readers." SLJ

Includes bibliographical references

Other titles in this series are:

The Land of the Silver Apples (2007)

The Islands of the Blessed (2009)

Farrant, Natasha

After Iris; by Natasha Farrant. Dial Books for Young Readers 2013 272 p. (hardcover) $16.99

Grades: 5 6 7 8   **Fic**

1. Grief -- Fiction 2. Babysitters -- Fiction 3. Twins -- Fiction 4. Diaries -- Fiction 5. Au pairs -- Fiction 6. Brothers and sisters -- Fiction 7. Family life -- England -- London -- Fiction 8. Video recordings -- Production and direction -- Fiction

ISBN 0803739826; 9780803739826

LC 2012039136

In this book, 12-year-old "Bluebell Gadsby's family has been collapsing ever since Blue's twin sister, Iris, died three years ago. Blue's father is working on the other side of the country, and their mother is traveling overseas, which leaves new au pair Zoran in charge. Between Blue's older sister Flora's rebelliousness, her two younger siblings' antics, and the family's pet rats, which live in the garden of their London home, Zoran has his hands full." (Publishers Weekly)

Farrey, Brian

The **Grimjinx** rebellion; Brian Farrey. HarperCollins 2014 432 p. illustrations (hardcover) $16.99

Grades: 4 5 6 7   **Fic**

1. Fantasy fiction 2. Magic -- Fiction 3. Brothers and sisters -- Fiction 4. Swindlers and swindling -- Fiction 5. Fantasy

ISBN 0062049348; 9780062049346

LC 2013043194

In this book, by Brian Farrey, "Jaxter Grimjinx and his family haven't had much time for thieving. Through no fault of their own, they've been too busy saving the day. But the danger in the Five Provinces is only just

beginning. The Palatinate Mages are almost ready to unveil their master plan, and legendary monsters will soon roam the land once more. Then Jaxter's sister, Aubrin, is kidnapped by the Mages." (Publisher's note)

"When mage sentinels carry off Jaxter Grimjinx's little sister Aubrin to be their new augur, the family's quest to get her back leads to the opening elements of a prophecy in which Jaxter will save the Five Provinces from a deadly scourge but die doing so. The twisted but coherent puzzle plot unfolds swiftly, speeded along by irreverent Grimjinx humor." Horn Book

Other titles in the series include:

The Vengekeep Prophecies (2012)

The Shadowhand Covenant (2013)

The **secret** of Dreadwillow Carse; Brian Farrey. Algonquin Young Readers 2016 240 p. $16.95

Grades: 4 5 6 7 8   **Fic**

1. Fairy tales 2. Friendship -- Fiction 3. Princesses -- Fiction 4. Kings and rulers -- Fiction 5. Depression (Psychology) -- Fiction 6. Depression, Mental -- Fiction 7. Kings, queens, rulers, etc. -- Fiction

ISBN 9781616205058

LC 2015031467

In this book, by Brian Farrey, a "princess and a peasant girl embark on a dangerous quest. . . . In the center of the verdant Monarchy lies Dreadwillow Carse, a desolate bog the people of the land do their best to ignore. Little is known about it except an ominous warning: If any monarch enters Dreadwillow Carse, then the Monarchy will fall. Twelve-year-old Princess Jeniah yearns to know what the marsh could conceal that might topple her family's thousand-year reign." (Publisher's note)

"Part fairy tale, part seemingly utopian society with a dark underbelly, this is a gripping, compelling story that will leave readers mulling over the ethical questions raised." Booklist

The **Shadowhand** Covenant; by Brian Farrey and illustrated by Brett Helquist. HarperCollins 2013 384 p. (hardback) $16.99

Grades: 4 5 6 7 8   **Fic**

1. Thieves -- Fiction 2. Conspiracies -- Fiction 3. Secret societies -- Fiction 4. Fantasy

ISBN 0062049313; 9780062049315

LC 2013021825

Sequel to: The Vengekeep prophecies

In this book by Brian Farrey, "trouble is brewing in the Five Provinces. Mysterious magical artifacts have gone missing from the royal vaults. Master thieves from a secret society known as the Shadowhands are disappearing. And without explanation, the High Laird has begun imprisoning the peaceful Sarosan people. Jaxter Grimjinx and his parents receive a summons from the Shadowhands—a summons that they would be foolish to ignore—and Jaxter is thrust into the heart of the conspiracy." (Publisher's note)

The **Vengekeep** prophecies; Brian Farrey; illustrated by Brett Helquist. Harper 2012 390 p. (hardback) $16.99

Grades: 4 5 6 7   **Fic**

1. Magic -- Fiction 2. Prophecies -- Fiction 3. Swindlers and swindling -- Fiction 4. Fantasy 5. Monsters -- Fiction

ISBN 0062049283; 9780062049285

LC 2012025282

In this book by Brian Farrey, "12-year-old Jaxter Grimjinx is anxious to prove himself at the family business: thievery. Jaxter's first attempt at burglary ends with . . . his family being jailed, but his parents have . . . replaced the prophetic tapestry that predicts the year ahead . . . with one that shows the Grimjinx family as heroes. The family quickly discovers, however, that the fake tapestry is actually enchanted, and every disaster it depicts is coming true." (Publishers Weekly)

Faruqi, Reem

Lailah's lunchbox; A Ramadan Story. by Reem Faruqi; illustrated by Lea Lyon. Tilbury House Publishers 2015 32 p. color illustrations (hardcover) $16.95 **Fic**

1. Islamic holidays 2. Muslims -- Fiction 3. Ramadan -- Fiction 4. Schools -- Fiction 5. Middle Eastern Americans -- Fiction 6. Fasts and feasts -- Islam -- Fiction 7. Islam -- Customs and practices -- Fiction

ISBN 9780884484318

LC 2014042485

"Lailah is in a new school in a new country, thousands of miles from her old home, and missing her old friends. When Ramadan begins, she is excited that she is finally old enough to participate in the fasting but worried that her classmates won't understand why she doesn't join them in the lunchroom. Lailah solves her problem with help from the school librarian and her teacher." (Publisher's note)

Federle, Tim

★ **Better** Nate than ever; Tim Federle. Simon & Schuster Books for Young Readers 2013 288 p. (hardcover) $16.99
Grades: 5 6 7 8 **Fic**

1. Theater -- Fiction 2. Musicals -- Fiction 3. New York (N.Y.) -- Fiction 4. Auditions -- Fiction 5. New York (N.Y.) -- Fiction 6. Broadway (New York, N.Y.) -- Fiction

ISBN 1442446897; 9781442446892; 9781442446908

LC 2011050388

Odyssey Honor Recording (2014)

Rainbow List (2014)

Lambda Literary Awards Finalist (2014)

Stonewall Honor Book: Children and Young Adult (2014)

In author Tim Federle's book, "Nate Foster has big dreams. His whole life, he's wanted to star in a Broadway show. (Heck, he'd settle for seeing a Broadway show.) But how is Nate supposed to make his dreams come true when he's stuck in Jankburg, Pennsylvania . . . ? With Libby's help, Nate plans a daring overnight escape to New York. There's an open casting call for 'E.T.: The Musical,' and Nate knows this could be the difference between small-town blues and big-time stardom." (Publisher's note)

Five, six, seven, Nate! by Tim Federle. Simon & Schuster Books for Young Readers 2014 304 p. (hardcover) $16.99
Grades: 5 6 7 8 **Fic**

1. Theater 2. Actors -- Fiction 3. Theater -- Fiction 4. Musicals -- Fiction 5. Friendship -- Fiction 6. Best friends -- Fiction 7. New York (N.Y.) -- Fiction 8. Broadway (New York, N.Y.) -- Fiction

ISBN 1442446935; 9781442446939

LC 2012051239

Sequel to: Better Nate than ever

In this book, by Tim Federle, "Nate is off to start rehearsals for 'E.T.: The Broadway Musical.' It's everything he ever practiced his autograph for! But as thrilling as Broadway is, rehearsals are nothing like Nate expects: full of intimidating child stars, cut-throat understudies, and a director who can't even remember Nate's name." (Publisher's note)

"Nate successfully auditioned for Broadway's E.T.: The Musical in Better Nate Than Ever. Of course, he's actually only an understudy's understudy, his chorus part keeps diminishing, and rehearsals are going poorly, but good-humored Nate takes it all in stride. Federle addresses his likable character's burgeoning interest in boys in a laudably straightforward way, making this entertaining backstage pass especially rewarding." (Horn Book)

Feiffer, Kate

The **problem** with the Puddles; illustrated by Tricia Tusa. Simon & Schuster Books for Young Readers 2009 193p il $16.99

Grades: 3 4 5 **Fic**

1. Dogs -- Fiction 2. Family life -- Fiction 3. Lost and found possessions -- Fiction

ISBN 978-1-4169-4961-9; 1-4169-4961-5

LC 20080-51388

The Puddle parents cannot seem to agree about anything, but when their dogs go missing the whole family embarks on an unlikely quest that eventually answers many unasked questions.

"The kid-friendly humor . . . the full cast of eccentric characters and Tusa's . . . lively b&w spot art should readily win fans for the Puddle family." Publ Wkly

Fenner, Carol

Snowed in with Grandmother Silk; illustrated by Amanda Harvey. Dial Books for Young Readers 2003 75p il hardcover o.p. pa $6.99

Grades: 2 3 4 **Fic**

1. Snow -- Fiction 2. Grandmothers -- Fiction

ISBN 0-8037-2857-3; 0-14-240472-1 pa

LC 2002-152296

Ruddy is disappointed when his parents go on a cruise and he must stay with his fussy grandmother for a whole week, but an unexpected snowstorm reveals a surprising side of Grandmother Silk

"Harvey's pencil-and-watercolor artwork extends the warmth and gentle humor in this chapter book, which will be a good choice for beginning readers as well as for reading aloud." Booklist

Yolonda's genius. Margaret K. McElderry Bks. 1995 211p $18.95; pa $5.99

Grades: 4 5 6 **Fic**

1. Siblings -- Fiction 2. Musicians -- Fiction 3. African Americans -- Fiction

ISBN 0-689-80001-0; 0-689-81327-9 pa

LC 94-46962

A Newbery Medal honor book, 1996

After moving from Chicago to Grand River, Michigan, fifth grader Yolonda, big and strong for her age, determines to prove that her younger brother is not a slow learner but a true musical genius

"In this brisk and appealing narrative, readers are introduced to a close-knit, middle-class African-American family. . . . [This novel] is suffused with humor and spirit." Horn Book

Fergus, Maureen

Ortega. Kids Can Press 2010 224p $16.95

Grades: 5 6 7 8 **Fic**

1. Science fiction 2. Gorillas -- Fiction

ISBN 978-1-55453-474-6; 1-55453-474-7

Eleven years ago, an infant lowland gorilla was acquired by a privately funded laboratory. An elite surgical team undertook a series of radical procedures designed to make it physically possible for the infant gorilla to acquire speech.

"The story's excitement and suspense as well as the emotional drama will ensnare readers. This interesting, affecting novel will definitely find an audience." SLJ

Ferraiolo, Jack D.

The **big** splash; by Jack D. Ferraiolo. Amulet Books 2008 277p $15.95

Grades: 4 5 6 7 **Fic**

1. School stories 2. Mystery fiction

ISBN 978-0-8109-7067-0; 0-8109-7067-8

LC 2007-49978

Matt Stevens, an average middle schooler with a glib tongue and a knack for solving crimes, uncovers a mystery while working with "the organization," a mafia-like syndicate run by seventh-grader Vincent "Mr. Biggs" Biggio, specializing in forged hall passes, test-copying rings, black market candy selling, and taking out hits with water guns.

This "novel delivers plenty of laughs, especially in the opening chapters, and fans of private-eye spoofs will enjoy this entertaining read." Booklist

Ferrari, Michael

Born to fly. Delacorte Press 2009 212p $15.99; lib bdg $18.99

Grades: 4 5 6   **Fic**

1. Sex role -- Fiction 2. Air pilots -- Fiction 3. Friendship -- Fiction 4. Family life -- Fiction 5. Rhode Island -- Fiction 6. World War, 1939-1945 -- Fiction

ISBN 0-385-73715-7; 0-385-90649-8 lib bdg; 978-0-385-73715-9; 978-0-385-90649-4 lib bdg

LC 2008035664

This novel takes place at the start of World War II. Eleven-year-old Bird has always loved flying with her mechanic dad, but now he has enlisted. She makes friends with newcomer Kenji, the son of Japanese parents who have been interned. "Intermediate." (Horn Book)

"Ferrari's fast-paced plot and well-developed characters will keep readers engaged until the last page." Booklist

Ferris, Jean

Much ado about Grubstake. Harcourt 2006 265p $17

Grades: 5 6 7 8   **Fic**

1. Orphans -- Fiction 2. Colorado -- Fiction 3. City and town life -- Fiction 4. Gold mines and mining -- Fiction

ISBN 0-15-205706-4

When two city folks arrive in the depressed mining town of Grubstake, Colorado in 1888, sixteen-year-old orphaned Arley tries to discover why they want to buy the supposedly worthless mines in the area

"Ferris combines adventure, love, and off-the-wall characters in a page-turning story full of good laughs and common sense messages." Voice Youth Advocates

Once upon a Marigold; by Jean Ferris. Harcourt 2002 266 p. $17

Grades: 5 6 7 8   **Fic**

1. Love -- Fiction 2. Princesses -- Fiction 3. Triangles (Interpersonal relations) -- Fiction 4. Fairy tales 5. Princesses/Fiction

ISBN 0152050841; 0152167919; 9780152167912

LC 2002000311

Marigold series

This novel by Jean Ferris focuses on Christian, who did not know "love could be so amazing. He was clueless when he started spying on the royal family. He lives in a cave with a troll for a dad. If his dad had only warned him about all that mind-boggling love stuff, maybe things wouldn't be such a mess. But then, maybe, Princess Marigold would be dead. And now that he's fallen for the princess, it's up to him to untwist an odd love triangle . . . and foil a scheming queen." (Publisher's note)

"This complex, fast-paced plot, a mixture of fantasy, romance, comedy, and coming-of-age novel, succeeds because these characters are compelling, well developed, and sympathetic." SLJ

Followed by: Twice upon a Marigold (2008)

Field, Rachel

Hitty: her first hundred years; [by] Rachel Field; with illustrations by Dorothy P. Lathrop. Macmillan 1929 207p il $19.99; pa $6.99

Grades: 4 5 6 7   **Fic**

1. Dolls -- Fiction

ISBN 0-02-734840-7; 0-689-82284-7 pa

Awarded the Newbery Medal, 1930

"Hitty, a doll of real character carved from a block of mountain ash, writes a story of her eventful life from the security of an antique-shop window which she shares with Theobold, a rather over-bearing cat. . . .

The illustrations by Dorothy P. Lathrop are the happiest extension of the text." Cleveland Public Libr

Fine, Anne

The **diary** of a killer cat; [by] Anne Fine; pictures by Steve Cox. Farrar, Straus and Giroux 2006 58p il $15

Grades: 2 3 4   **Fic**

1. Cats -- Fiction

ISBN 0-374-31779-8

LC 2004-56212

First published 2001 in the United Kingdom

Tuffy the pet cat tries to defend himself against accusations of terrifying other animals and murdering the neighbor's rabbit

"The book is funny throughout. . . . The black-and-white sketches, some full page, bring movement and personality to the characters." SLJ

Another title about the killer cat is:

The return of the killer cat (2007)

Jamie and Angus together; illustrated by Penny Dale. Candlewick Press 2007 102p il $15.99

Grades: PreK K 1 2   **Fic**

1. Play -- Fiction 2. Toys -- Fiction 3. Friendship -- Fiction

ISBN 978-0-7636-3374-5; 0-7636-3374-7

LC 2007-25166

Best friends Jamie and his toy Highland bull Angus tackle a lively playmate, become muddled by a pretend game, and discover that playing is not fun unless they are doing it together.

"Fine renders another pitch-perfect transitional chapter book. . . . Spare yet vivid language captures Jamie's perspective while supplying humor for adult readers. . . . Soft pencil illustrations . . . capture Jamie's loving family and convey his deep friendship with Angus." Booklist

Another title about Jamie and Angus is:

The Jamie and Angus stories (2002)

Fireside, Bryna J.

Private Joel and the Sewell Mountain seder; by Bryna J. Fireside; illustrations by Shawn Costello. Kar-Ben Pub. 2008 47p il lib bdg $16.95; pa $6.95

Grades: 2 3 4   **Fic**

1. Passover -- Fiction 2. Jews -- United States -- Fiction 3. United States -- History -- 1861-1865, Civil War -- Fiction

ISBN 978-0-8225-7240-4 lib bdg; 0-8225-7240-0 lib bdg; 978-0-8225-9050-7 pa; 0-8225-9050-6 pa

LC 2007005275

A group of Jewish soldiers, and three freed slaves, have a Passover seder in 1862 on the battlefields of the Civil War

The book is based "on a true story. . . . Costello's impressionistic artwork seems well suited to this nostalgic story. Although respectful in tone, the illustrations also pick up on occasional humor." Booklist

Fitzgerald, John D.

★ The **Great** Brain; illustrated by Mercer Mayer. Dial Bks. for Young Readers 1967 175p il $17.99; pa $5.99

Grades: 4 5 6 7   **Fic**

1. Utah -- Fiction

ISBN 0-8037-2590-6; 0-14-240058-0 pa

"The Great Brain was Tom Dennis ('T.D.') Fitzgerald, age ten, of Adenville, Utah; the time, 1896. . . . This autobiographical yarn is spun by his brother John Dennis ('J.D.'), age seven . . . who can tell stories about himself and his family with enough tall-tale exaggeration to catch the imagination." Horn Book

Other titles about the Great Brain are:

The Great Brain at the academy (1972)

The Great Brain does it again (1975)

The Great Brain is back (1995)
The Great Brain reforms (1973)
Me and my little brain (1971)
More adventures of the Great Brain (1969)
The return of the Great Brain (1974)

The **Great** Brain is back; illustrated by Diane DeGroat. Dial Bks. for Young Readers 1995 121p il $16.99

Grades: 4 5 6 7   **Fic**

1. Utah -- Fiction
ISBN 0-8037-1346-0

LC 94-17433

"The year is 1899, and J.D. narrates this episodic novel.... It is J.D. on the defense as he describes his big brother Tom's conniving ways from the first chapter, in which Tom sells J.D. a wagonload of soap, through the last, in which J.D. claims that Tom is finally outswindled— by his own mother. DeGroat's full-page pencil drawings, one per chapter, capture the era well and portray the characters sympathetically, but the book's gentle humor finds expression mainly through the writing." Booklist

Fitzgerald, Laura Marx

The **gallery**; Laura Marx Fitzgerald. Dial Books for Young Readers 2016 336 p. (hardback) $16.99

Grades: 4 5 6 7   **Fic**

1. Art -- Fiction 2. Mystery fiction 3. Irish Americans -- Fiction 4. New York (N.Y.) -- Fiction 5. Household employees -- Fiction 6. Mystery and detective stories 7. New York (N.Y.) -- History -- 1898-1951 -- Fiction
ISBN 9780525428657

LC 2015029009

In this book, by Laura Marx Fitzgerald, "Martha has no choice but to work as a maid in the New York City mansion of the wealthy Sewell family. But, despite the Gatsby-like parties and trimmings of success, she suspects something might be deeply wrong in the household--specifically with Rose Sewell, the formerly vivacious lady of the house who now refuses to leave her room. The other servants say Rose is crazy, but scrappy, strong-willed Martha thinks there's more to the story." (Publisher's note)

"Fitzgerald balances mystery and history in a feminist narrative that invites readers to find out more." Kirkus

Under the egg; by Laura Marx Fitzgerald. Dial Books for Young Readers 2014 256 p. (hardcover) $16.99

Grades: 4 5 6 7   **Fic**

1. Mystery fiction 2. Art -- Fiction 3. New York (N.Y.) -- Fiction 4. Holocaust, 1939-1945 -- Fiction 5. Recluses -- Fiction 6. Friendship -- Fiction 7. Neighborhoods -- Fiction 8. Mystery and detective stories 9. Greenwich Village (New York N.Y.) -- Fiction
ISBN 0803740018; 9780803740013

LC 2013017790

In this book, by Laura Marx Fitzgerald, "Theodora Tenpenny spills a bottle of rubbing alcohol on her late grandfather's painting [and] discovers . . . an old Renaissance masterpiece underneath. That's great news for Theo, who's struggling to hang onto her family's . . . townhouse and support her unstable mother. . . . There's just one problem: Theo's grandfather was a security guard at the Metropolitan Museum of Art, and she worries the painting may be stolen." (Publisher's note)

"Theo's household is vividly portrayed, from her grandfather's creative ingenuity to her mother's tenuous hold on reality. Smart and determined, down-to-earth and insightful, Theo makes an engaging narrator as she follows a winding trail of discovery." Booklist

Fitzgerald, Sarah Moore

The **apple** tart of hope; by Sarah Moore Fitzgerald. Holiday House 2016 160 p. (hardcover) $16.95

Grades: 5 6 7 8   **Fic**

1. Hope -- Fiction 2. Friendship -- Fiction 3. Missing children -- Fiction
ISBN 9780823435616

LC 2015022313

In this book, by Sarah Moore Fitzgerald, "fourteen-year-old Oscar Dunleavy is missing, presumed dead. His bike was found at sea, out past the end of the pier, and everyone in town seems to have accepted this as a teenage tragedy. But Oscar's best friend Meg knows he isn't dead. Oscar is an optimistic and kind boy who bakes the world s best apple tarts; he would never kill himself, and Meg is going to prove it." (Publisher's note)

" Fully developed secondary characters—such as Oscar's disabled younger brother and Paloma, who tries to take Meg's place—add richness and depth to this lyrically written tale, which explores themes of manipulation, self-discovery, hope, and love... This touching novel is one to savor." Booklist

Fitzhugh, Louise

★ **Harriet,** the spy; written and illustrated by Louise Fitzhugh. Delacorte Press 2000 300p il $15.95

Grades: 4 5 6 7   **Fic**

1. School stories
ISBN 0-385-32783-8

LC 00712298

A reissue of the title first published 1964 by Harper & Row

Eleven-year-old Harriet keeps notes on her classmates and neighbors in a secret notebook, but when some of the students read the notebook, they seek revenge.

"A very, very funny and a very, very affective story; the characterizations are marvelously shrewd, the pictures of urban life and of the power structure of the sixth grade class are realistic." Bull Cent Child Books

Another title about Harriet is:
The long secret (1965)

Fitzmaurice, Kathryn

A **diamond** in the desert; Kathryn Fitzmaurice. Viking 2012 258 p. (hardcover) $16.99

Grades: 5 6 7 8   **Fic**

1. Baseball -- Fiction 2. Father-son relationship -- Fiction 3. World War, 1939-1945 -- United States -- Fiction 4. Japanese Americans -- Evacuation and relocation, 1942-1945 -- Fiction 5. Guilt -- Fiction 6. Gila River Relocation Center -- Fiction
ISBN 0670012920; 9780670012923

LC 2011012041

In this book, "Tetsu is twelve when he and his mother and sister are relocated by World War II's infamous Executive Order 9066, which justified the internment of Japanese-Americans, to the camp at Gila River. His father, a leader in the Japanese-American community, is detained separately in another location, and Tetsu generally takes his responsibility as the oldest male in the immediate family very seriously. He's particularly solicitous of his younger sister, Kimi, who is . . . traumatized by the lack of privacy in the camp.... Kimi . . . wanders out into the desert, where she nearly dies. Guilt-stricken, Tetsu withdraws from baseball and from his friends, until his father arrives at Gila River and rekindles his son's interest in life." (Bulletin of the Center for Children's Books)

Includes bibliographical references (p. 255)

The **year** the swallows came early. Bowen Press 2009 277p $16.99; lib bdg $17.89

Grades: 4 5 6 **Fic**

1. Prisoners -- Fiction 2. Father-daughter relationship -- Fiction
ISBN 978-0-06-162497-1; 0-06-162497-7; 978-0-06-162499-5
lib bdg; 0-06-162499-3 lib bdg

LC 2008-20156

After her father is sent to jail, eleven-year-old Groovy Robinson must decide if she can forgive the failings of someone she loves.

This "novel is peopled with three-dimensional characters whose imperfections make them believable and interesting. . . . The well-structured plot is underscored by clear writing and authentic dialogue." SLJ

Fixmer, Elizabeth

Saint training. Zonderkidz 2010 239p $14.99

Grades: 5 6 7 8 **Fic**

1. School stories 2. Catholics -- Fiction 3. Family life -- Fiction
4. Christian life -- Fiction
ISBN 978-0-310-72018-8; 0-310-72018-4

LC 2010010831

During the turbulent 1960s, sixth-grader Mary Clare makes a deal with God: she will try to become a saint if He provides for her large, cash-strapped family.

"The politically fervent period of the late 1960s, with its dramatic upheavals in family, gender, social, and religious conventions, comes to life with pathos and humor in this powerful debut." Publ Wkly

Flake, Sharon G.

★ The **broken** bike boy and the Queen of 33rd Street. Jump at the Sun/Hyperion Books for Children 2007 132p il $15.99; pa $5.99

Grades: 4 5 6 7 **Fic**

1. School stories 2. Friendship -- Fiction 3. African Americans -- Fiction
ISBN 978-1-4231-0032-4; 1-4231-0032-8; 978-1-4231-0035-5
pa; 1-4231-0035-2 pa

LC 2006-35590

Ten-year-old Queen, a spoiled and conceited African American girl who is disliked by most of her classmates, learns a lesson about friendship from an unlikely "knight in shining armor."

"Complex intergenerational characters and a rich urban setting defy stereotyping. . . . Infrequent detailed pencil illustrations . . . add a welcome dimension." Horn Book

Flanagan, John

The **battle** for Skandia; [by] John Flanagan. 1st American ed.; Philomel Books 2008 294p (Ranger's apprentice) $16.99; pa $7.99

Grades: 5 6 7 8 **Fic**

1. Fantasy fiction
ISBN 978-0-399-24457-5; 0-399-24457-3; 978-0-14-241340-1
pa; 0-14-241340-2 pa

LC 2007023646

Sequel to The icebound land (2007)

After Ranger's apprentice Will battles Temujai warriors to rescue Evanlyn, Will's kingdom of Skandia joins forces with rival kingdom Araluen to defeat a common enemy.

"Even readers drawn to the series for its deftly drawn characters and setting may find themselves caught up in the action." Booklist

The **burning** bridge. Philomel Books 2006 262p (Ranger's apprentice) $16.99

Grades: 5 6 7 8 **Fic**

1. Fantasy fiction
ISBN 0-399-24455-7

Sequel to The ruins of Gorlan (2005)

Will is forced to overcome his fear of Wargals, the foot soldiers of rebel warlord Morgarath, as Araluen's army prepares to battle Morgarath's forces.

"The pace is swift, and action is often at the forefront, but elements of humor and nuances of emotion are apparent as well." Booklist

Followed by The icebound land (2007)

The **emperor** of Nihon-Ja. Philomel Books 2011 438p (Ranger's apprentice) $17.99

Grades: 5 6 7 8 **Fic**

1. Fantasy fiction 2. Kings and rulers -- Fiction
ISBN 978-0-399-25500-7; 0-399-25500-1

LC 2010025784

Sequel to: Halt's peril (2010)

In a faraway land, a young warrior must protect an emperor from an uprising and train an inexperienced army, with assistance from his Ranger friends.

Erak's ransom. Philomel Books 2010 373p (Ranger's apprentice) $17.99

Grades: 5 6 7 8 **Fic**

1. War stories 2. Fantasy fiction 3. Deserts -- Fiction 4. Apprentices -- Fiction
ISBN 978-0-399-25205-1; 0-399-25205-3

LC 2009011665

Sequel to: The siege of Macindaw (2009)

First published 2007 in Australia

On a mission to pay the ransom of a new ally, apprentice Will and his friends find themselves in a desert wasteland awash with enemies.

"Bringing together many favorite characters for a grand adventure, this book delivers both excitement and quiet good times." Booklist

Followed by: The kings of Clonmel (2010)

Halt's peril. Philomel Books 2010 386p (Ranger's apprentice) $17.99

Grades: 5 6 7 8 **Fic**

1. Fantasy fiction 2. Cults -- Fiction
ISBN 978-0-399-25207-5; 0-399-25207-X

Sequel to: The kings of Clonmel (2010)

Tennyson, the false prophet of the Outsider cult, has escaped and Halt is determined to stop him before he crosses the border into Araluen, but Genovesan assassins put Will and Halt's extraordinary archery skills to the test.

"Series fans will enjoy the dialogue and camaraderie as much as the action." Booklist

Followed by: The Emperor of Nihon-Ja (2011)

The **hunters**; John Flanagan. Philomel 2012 403 p. (hardback) $18.99

Grades: 5 6 7 8 **Fic**

1. Pirates -- Fiction 2. Friendship -- Fiction 3. Adventure and adventurers -- Fiction 4. Fantasy 5. Courage -- Fiction 6. Seafaring life -- Fiction 9.
ISBN 0399256210; 9780399256219

LC 2012020986

This book by John Flanagan is part of the Brotherband Chronicles series. "Hal and his brotherband crew are hot on the trail of the pirate Zavac and they have one thing only on their minds: Stopping the bloodthirsty thief before he can do more damage. Of course, they also know Zavac has the Andomal, the priceless Skandian artifact stolen when the brotherband let down their guard. The chase leads down mighty rivers, terrifying rapids, to the lawless fortress of Ragusa." (Publisher's note)

The **icebound** land; [by] John Flanagan. 1st American ed.; Philomel Books 2007 260p (Ranger's apprentice) $16.99
Grades: 5 6 7 8   Fic
1. Fantasy fiction
ISBN 978-0-399-24456-8
LC 2006034561
Sequel to The burning bridge (2006)

Chasing the Skandian slave-traders who kidnapped Will and Evanlyn, Ranger Halt and warrior student Horace find themselves in the frozen northern islands, where they battle a ruthless black-clad knight as they attempt to rescue their friends.

"Flanagan's deft character portrayals and well-paced story will engage readers." Booklist

Followed by The battle for Skandia (2008)

The **invaders**; John Flanagan. Philomel Books 2012 429 p. (The Brotherband chronicles) (hardback) $18.99
Grades: 5 6 7 8   Fic
1. Pirates -- Fiction 2. Friendship -- Fiction 3. Adventure fiction 4. Fantasy 5. Courage -- Fiction
ISBN 0399256202; 9780399256202
LC 2012000424

This book by John Flanagan is part of the Brotherband Chronicles series. "Hal and the Herons have done the impossible. This group of outsiders has beaten out the strongest, most skilled young warriors in all of Skandia to win the Brotherband competition. But their celebration comes to an abrupt end when the Skandians' most sacred artifact, the Andomal, is stolen--and the Herons are to blame." (Publisher's note)

The **kings** of Clonmel. Philomel Books 2010 358p (Ranger's apprentice) $17.99
Grades: 5 6 7 8   Fic
1. War stories 2. Fantasy fiction 3. Cults -- Fiction
ISBN 978-0-399-25206-8; 0-399-25206-1
Sequel to: Erak's ransom (2010)

Hair, Will, and Horace set out for Hiberia, where a quasi-religious group, the Outsiders, is sowing confusion and sedition, and they find that secrets from Halt's past may hold the key to restoring order before the last kingdom is undermined.

"There's wit as well as action here, and the revelation of Halt's backstory adds a new dimension to the saga." Booklist

Followed by: Halt's peril (2010)

★ The **outcasts**. Philomel Books 2011 434p (Brotherband chronicles) $18.99
Grades: 5 6 7 8   Fic
1. Fantasy fiction 2. Adventure fiction 3. Friendship -- Fiction
ISBN 978-0-399-25619-6; 0-399-25619-9

Hal, who does not fit into Skandian society, ends up in a brotherband, a group of boys learning the skills that they need to become warriors, with other outcasts, and they compete with other brotherbands in a series of challenges.

"This enjoyable, old-fashioned tale should have easy appeal for Flanagan's many fans, who are already invested in the world he's created." Publ Wkly

★ The **royal** ranger; John Flanagan. Philomel Books, an imprint of Penguin Group (USA) Inc. 2013 464 p.
Grades: 5 6 7 8   Fic
1. Apprentices -- Fiction 2. Fantasy fiction 3. Adventure and adventurers -- Fiction 4. Fantasy
ISBN 9780399163609
LC 2013015910

In this book, by John Flanagan, "Will Treaty has come a long way from the small boy with dreams of knighthood. Life had other plans for him, and as an apprentice Ranger under Halt, he grew into a legend. . . . The time has come to take on an apprentice of his own, and it's the last person he ever would have expected. Fighting his personal demons, Will has to win the trust and respect of his difficult new companion—a task that at times seems almost impossible." (Publisher's note)

"Taking place at least 16 years after the original 10 volumes of the Ranger's Apprentice series, this sequel sees Will training 15-year-old Maddie, the first girl to become a ranger's apprentice... Series fans will hang on every word of this adventure; Maddie emerges as a strong character and could easily develop a following among readers who enjoy Tamora Pierce's books about Alanna, another resourceful, independent-minded heroine." (Booklist)

★ The **ruins** of Gorlan. Philomel Books 2005 249p (Ranger's apprentice) $15.99; pa $7.99
Grades: 5 6 7 8   Fic
1. Fantasy fiction
ISBN 0-399-24454-9; 0-14-240663-5 pa

When fifteen-year-old Will is rejected by battleschool, he becomes the reluctant apprentice to the mysterious Ranger Halt, and winds up protecting the kingdom from danger.

"Flanagan concentrates on character, offering readers a young protagonist they will care about and relationships that develop believably over time." Booklist

Other titles in this series are:
The burning bridge (2006)
The icebound land (2007)
The battle for Skandia (2008)
The sorcerer of the north (2008)
The siege of Macindaw (2009)
Erak's ransom (2010)
The kings of Clonmel (2010)
Halt's peril (2010)
The Emperor of Nihon-Ja (2011)

The **siege** of Macindaw. Philomel Books 2009 293p (Ranger's apprentice) $17.99; pa $7.99
Grades: 5 6 7 8   Fic
1. War stories 2. Fantasy fiction
ISBN 978-0-399-25033-0; 0-399-25033-6; 978-0-14-241524-5 pa; 0-14-241524-3 pa
LC 2008032630
Sequel to: The sorcerer of the north (2008)

Now a full-fledged Ranger, Will must rescue his friend Alyss from a rogue knight and uncover vital information needed to ward off a Scotti invasion.

"Series fans will relish the familiar details of warfare and comradeship as well as the surprising fireworks in both war and love." Booklist

Followed by: Erak's Ransom (2010)

The **sorcerer** of the north; [by] John Flanagan. Philomel Books 2008 288p (Ranger's apprentice) $16.99
Grades: 5 6 7 8   Fic
1. Fantasy fiction
ISBN 978-0-399-25032-3; 0-399-25032-8
LC 2008-16528
Sequel to: The battle for Skandia (2008)

Now a full-fledged Ranger responsible for a sleepy fief, Will finds a new adventure seeking the traitors who poisoned the king, investigating rumors of sorcery, and trying to rescue his friend Alyss, who is taken hostage.

"Flanagan is to be complimented for creating a fantasy world that relies on character and action rather than magic." Voice Youth Advocates

Fleischman, Paul

Bull Run; woodcuts by David Frampton. HarperCollins Pubs. 1993 104p il pa $4.99

Grades: 6 7 8 9   **Fic**

1. Bull Run, 1st Battle of, 1861 -- Fiction 2. United States -- History -- 1861-1865, Civil War -- Fiction

ISBN 0-06-440588-5 pa

LC 92-14745

"Abandoning the conventions of narrative fiction, Fleischman tells a vivid, many-sided story in this original and moving book. An excellent choice for readers' theater in the classroom or on stage." Booklist

The **dunderheads**; illustrated by David Roberts. Candlewick Press 2009 54p il

Grades: 2 3 4 5   **Fic**

1. School stories 2. Teachers -- Fiction

ISBN 0-7636-2498-5; 978-0-7636-2498-9; 978-0-7636-5239-5 pa

When Miss Breakbone confiscates Junkyard's crucial find, Wheels, Pencil, Spider, and the rest of the Dunderheads plot to teach her a lesson.

"Roberts's quirky watercolor and ink interpretations of Fleischman's deadpan humor and impeccable pacing produce hilarious results." SLJ

Followed by: The Dunderheads behind bars (2012)

★ The **Half**-a-Moon Inn; illustrated by Kathy Jacobi. Harper & Row 1980 88p il hardcover o.p. pa $4.99

Grades: 4 5 6   **Fic**

1. Kidnapping -- Fiction 2. Hotels and motels -- Fiction 3. Children with physical disabilities -- Fiction

ISBN 0-06-440364-5 pa

LC 79-2010

"Despite the grimness of Aaron's predicament, accentuated by dark scratch drawings of figures in grotesque proportion, the story's tone is hopeful and its style concrete and brisk. Elements of folklore exist in the story's characterization, structure, and narration." SLJ

Fleischman, Sid

The **13th** floor; a ghost story. illustrations by Peter Sís. Greenwillow Bks. 1995 134p il $15.99; pa $5.99

Grades: 4 5 6   **Fic**

1. Fantasy fiction 2. Pirates -- Fiction

ISBN 0-688-14216-8; 0-06-134503-2 pa

LC 94-42806

When his older sister disappears, twelve-year-old Buddy Stebbins follows her back in time and finds himself aboard a seventeenth-century pirate ship captained by a distant relative

"Liberally laced with dry wit and thoroughly satisfying. . . . Readers could hardly ask for more." Publ Wkly

★ **By** the Great Horn Spoon! illustrated by Eric von Schmidt. Little, Brown 1963 193p il hardcover o.p. pa $6.99

Grades: 4 5 6   **Fic**

1. California -- Gold discoveries -- Fiction

ISBN 0-316-28577-3; 0-316-28612-5 pa

"Jack and his aunt's butler, Praiseworthy, stow away on a ship bound for California. Here are their adventures aboard ship and in the Gold Rush of '49." Publ Wkly

★ The **dream** stealer; pictures by Peter Sís. Greenwillow Books 2009 89p il $16.99; lib bdg $17.89 **Fic**

1. Dreams -- Fiction 2. Mexico -- Fiction 3. Mythical animals

-- Fiction

ISBN 978-0-06-175563-7; 0-06-175563-X; 978-0-06-175564-4 lib bdg; 0-06-175564-8 lib bdg

LC 2008-47694

A plucky Mexican girl tries to recover her dream from the Dream Stealer who takes her to his castle where countless dreams and even more adventures await

"The range of imaginative inventions . . . will delight children, as will the narrator's expertly modulated storyteller's cadence." Booklist

Here comes McBroom! three more tall tales. illustrated by Quentin Blake. Greenwillow Bks. 1992 79p il hardcover o.p. pa $4.95

Grades: 3 4 5   **Fic**

1. Tall tales 2. Farm life -- Fiction

ISBN 0-688-16364-5 pa

LC 91-32689

The stories were originally published separately by Grosset and Dunlap

The tall tale adventures of a farm family

Fleischman's "humor is still as fresh as ever, and Quentin Blake's illustrations continue to delight." Booklist

Other titles about McBroom are:

McBroom tells a lie (1976)

McBroom tells the truth (1981)

McBroom's wonderful one-acre farm: three tall tales (1992)

McBroom's wonderful one-acre farm; three tall tales. illustrated by Quentin Blake. Greenwillow Bks. 1992 63p il hardcover o.p. pa $6.99

Grades: 3 4 5   **Fic**

1. Tall tales 2. Farms -- Fiction

ISBN 0-688-11159-9; 978-0-688-15595-7 pa

LC 91-31906

Three humorous tall tales on McBroom's wonderful one-acre prairie farm

★ The **whipping** boy; illustrations by Peter Sís. Greenwillow Bks. 1986 90p il $16.99; pa $5.99

Grades: 5 6 7 8   **Fic**

1. Adventure fiction 2. Thieves -- Fiction

ISBN 0-688-06216-4; 0-06-052122-8 pa

LC 85-17555

Awarded the Newbery Medal, 1987

"A round tale of adventure and humor, this follows the fortunes of Prince Roland (better known as Prince Brat) and his whipping boy, Jemmy, who has received all the hard knocks for the prince's mischief. . . . There's not a moment's lag in pace, and the stock characters, from Hold-Your-Nose Billy to Betsy's dancing bear Petunia, have enough inventive twists to project a lively air to it all." Bull Cent Child Books

★ The **white** elephant; [illustrated by] Robert McGuire. Greenwillow Books 2006 95p il $15.99; lib bdg $16.89

Grades: 3 4 5   **Fic**

1. Thailand -- Fiction 2. Elephants -- Fiction

ISBN 978-0-06-113136-3; 0-06-113136-9; 978-0-06-113137-0 lib bdg; 0-06-113137-7 lib bdg

LC 2005-46793

In old Siam, young elephant trainer Run-Run and his old charge, Walking Mountain, must deal with the curse of a sacred white elephant.

"Fleischman successfully immerses readers in this ancient culture, creating clever and believable plot twists that bring the story to a satisfying but open-ended conclusion." SLJ

Fleming, Candace

The **fabled** fifth graders of Aesop Elementary School. Schwartz & Wade Books 2010 170p $15.99; lib bdg $18.99

Grades: 3 4 5   **Fic**

1. School stories

ISBN 978-0-375-86334-9; 0-375-86334-6; 978-0-375-96334-6 lib bdg; 0-375-96334-0 lib bdg

Throughout their fifth-grade year, a group of rambunctious students learns fable-like lessons from extraordinary activities, singing hamsters, and eccentric teachers, led by the inimitable Mr. Jupiter.

"A rare adventure—one that many teachers and students will take to heart." Horn Book

Lowji discovers America. Atheneum Books for Young Readers 2005 152p $15.95; pa $5.99

Grades: 3 4 5   **Fic**

1. Moving -- Fiction 2. Immigrants -- Fiction 3. East Indians -- United States -- Fiction

ISBN 0-689-86299-7; 1-4169-5832-0 pa

LC 2004-6899

A nine-year-old East Indian boy tries to adjust to his new life in suburban America

"Fleming tells a gentle, effective story about the loneliness and bewilderment that come with moving, and her brisk, lively sentences make this a good choice for readers gaining confidence with chapter books." Booklist

Fleming, David

★ The **Saturday** boy; by David Fleming. Viking Children's 2013 240 p. (hardcover) $16.99

Grades: 5 6 7 8   **Fic**

1. School stories -- Fiction 2. Families of soldiers -- Fiction 3. Bullies -- Fiction 4. Schools -- Fiction 5. Behavior -- Fiction 6. Family life -- Fiction 7. Families of military personnel -- Fiction

ISBN 0670785512; 9780670785513

LC 2012029680

In this book, Derek is the son of "a soldier who flies Apache helicopters and is stationed in Afghanistan for another tour. . . . Derek is a good-hearted kid who just naturally attracts trouble--he doesn't mean to, but he's always in the wrong place at the wrong time and often the victim. He's also impulsive and has a hard time staying focused, which adds to his problems." Then one day, "he sees his dad on the news and his world falls apart." (School Library Journal)

Fletcher, Charlie

Ironhand. Hyperion Books for Children 2008 400p (Stoneheart trilogy) lib bdg $16.99

Grades: 5 6 7 8   **Fic**

1. Fantasy fiction

ISBN 978-1-4231-0177-2 lib bdg; 1-4231-0177-4 lib bdg

LC 2007-42073

Sequel to: Stoneheart (2007)

Having upset the balance between the warring statues of London, twelve-year-old George is confronted with new challenges as he tries to free his captured friends Edie and The Gunner from the formidable Walker and deal with the three strange veins of marble, bronze, and stone that have begun to grow out of his hand.

"Cliff-hanger chapters . . . will leave readers breathless. George's story is particularly vivid." Booklist

Followed by: Silvertongue (2009)

Silvertongue. Hyperion Books for Children 2009 (Stoneheart trilogy) $16.99

Grades: 5 6 7 8   **Fic**

1. Fantasy fiction

ISBN 978-1-4231-0179-6; 1-4231-0179-0

Sequel to: Ironhand (2008)

The battle between the statues and gargoyles of London rages on- and 12-year-old George Chapman and his friend Edie are caught in the middle. With the Walker intent on forcing his evil designs on the city and the world, George realizes that his destiny is inextricably tied to the Walker's destruction.

"George and Edie's action-packed experiences are told in alternate chapters. . . . The book does not stand on its own, but those familiar with the earlier titles will be satisfied." SLJ

Fletcher, Ralph

★ **Flying** solo. Clarion Bks. 1998 138p $15; pa $5.99

Grades: 5 6 7 8   **Fic**

1. School stories 2. Death -- Fiction

ISBN 0-395-87323-1; 0-547-07652-5 pa

LC 98-10775

Rachel, having chosen to be mute following the sudden death of a classmate, shares responsibility with the other sixth-graders who decide not to report that the substitute teacher failed to show up

"Fletcher expertly balances a wide variety of emotions, giving readers a story that is by turns sad, poignant, and funny." Booklist

Fletcher, Susan

Shadow spinner. Atheneum Bks. for Young Readers 1998 219p hardcover o.p. pa $4.99

Grades: 6 7 8 9   **Fic**

1. Iran -- Fiction 2. Storytelling -- Fiction 3. People with disabilities 4. People with disabilities -- Fiction

ISBN 0-689-81852-1; 0-689-83051-3 pa

LC 97-37346

When Marjan, a thirteen-year-old crippled girl, joins the Sultan's harem in ancient Persia, she gathers for Shahrazad the stories which will save the queen's life

"An elegantly written novel that will delight and entertain even as it teaches." SLJ

Flint, Shamini

Ten; a soccer story. Shamini Flint. Clarion Books, Houghton Mifflin Harcourt 2017 176 p. (hardback) $16.99

Grades: 4 5 6   **Fic**

1. Soccer -- Fiction 2. Divorce -- Fiction 3. Malaysia -- Fiction 4. Gender role -- Fiction 5. Racially mixed people -- Fiction 6. Sex role -- Fiction 7. Malaysia -- History -- 20th century -- Fiction

ISBN 0544850017; 9780544850019

LC 2016016164

"First published in Singapore in 2009 by Sunbear Publishing Pte. Ltd."--Copyright page.

In this book, by Shamini Flint, "Maya is a passionate soccer fan eager to start playing soccer herself. This is extra challenging because soccer is considered a 'boys' game' in Malaysia in 1986. She teaches herself basic soccer skills with only her mother and a potted rosebush as training partners, then gradually persuades enough girls to join her to form a team, all the while trying to keep her unpredictable biracial family together." (Publisher's note)

Flores-Gabis, Enrique

★ **90** miles to Havana. Roaring Brook Press 2010 292p $17.99

Grades: 5 6 7 8   **Fic**

1. Cuba -- Fiction 2. Florida -- Fiction 3. Cuban refugees -- Fiction

ISBN 978-1-59643-168-3; 1-59643-168-7

"Drawing on his own experience as a child refugee from Cuba, Flores-Galbis offers a gripping historical novel about children who were evacuated from Cuba to the U.S. during Operation Pedro Pan in 1961. Julian, a young Cuban boy, experiences the violent revolution and watches mobs throw out his family's furniture and move into their home. For his safety, his parents send him to a refugee camp in Miami. . . . This is a seldom-told refugee story that will move readers with the first-person, present-tense rescue narrative, filled with betrayal, kindness, and waiting for what may never come." Booklist

Flying lessons & other stories; edited by Ellen Oh. Crown Books for Young Readers 2017 240 p. (hardback) $16.99
Grades: 4 5 6 7 **Fic**
1. Children's stories 2. Short stories -- Collections
ISBN 9781101934616; 9781101934593; 9781101934609; 9781101934623
LC 2016016160

This anthology, edited by Ellen Oh, "celebrates the uniqueness and universality in all of us. In a partnership with We Need Diverse Books, industry giants Kwame Alexander, Soman Chainani, Matt de la Peña, Tim Federle, Grace Lin, Meg Medina, Walter Dean Myers, Tim Tingle, and Jacqueline Woodson join newcomer Kelly J. Baptist in a story collection that is as humorous as it is heartfelt." (Publisher's note)

"A natural for middle school classrooms and libraries, this strong collection should find eager readers." Kirkus

Foley, Lizzie K.
Remarkable; a novel. by Lizzie K. Foley. Dial Books for Young Readers 2012 325 p. (hardcover) $16.99
Grades: 3 4 5 6 7 **Fic**
1. Fantasy fiction 2. Humorous fiction 3. Ability -- Fiction 4. Young adult literature 5. Community life -- Fiction 6. Humorous stories 7. Pirates -- Fiction 8. Secrets -- Fiction 9. Eccentrics and eccentricities -- Fiction
ISBN 9780803737068
LC 2011021641

This book presents the story of an average girl named Jane Doe who lives in "the town of Remarkable, so named for its abundance of talented citizens, everyone lives up to its reputation. . . . Jane should be just as remarkable. Instead, this average 10-year-old girl is usually overlooked. . . . Mix in a rival town's dispute over jelly, hints of a Loch Ness Monster-like creature and a psychic pizzeria owner who sees the future in her reflective pizza pans. . . . With the help of her quiet Grandpa John, who's also forgotten most of the time, Jane learns to be true to herself and celebrate the ordinary in life." (Kirkus)

Fombelle, Timothee de
Toby and the secrets of the tree; illustrated by Fran¿cois Place; translated by Sarah Ardizzone. Candlewick Press 2010 414p il $16.99
Grades: 5 6 7 8 **Fic**
1. Fantasy fiction 2. Trees -- Fiction
ISBN 978-0-7636-4655-4; 0-7636-4655-5
LC 2009014833

Sequel to: Toby alone (2009)

Thirteen-year-old Toby's tiny world is under greater threat than ever as Leo Blue holds Elisha prisoner while hunting the Grass People and anyone who stands in the way of his devastating plans for the oak Tree in which they all live, but this time Toby is not alone.

"Place's pen-and-ink illustrations are scattered generously throughout and enhance the overall quirkiness. . . . This interesting piece of eco-fantasy provides a satisfying conclusion for those who enjoyed the first book." SLJ

Forbes, Esther
Johnny Tremain; a novel for old & young. with illustrations by Lynd Ward. Houghton Mifflin Books for Children 1943 256p il $17; pa $6.99
Grades: 5 6 7 8 **Fic**
1. United States -- History -- 1775-1783, Revolution -- Fiction
ISBN 978-0-395-06766-6; 0-395-06766-9; 978-0-440-44250-9 pa; 0-440-44250-8 pa
Awarded the Newbery Medal, 1944

"Johnny, an orphan, works as a favored apprentice to an aging silversmith until he burns his hand severely while working on an important project. During the Revolutionary War he serves as a dispatch rider for the Committee on Public Safety, meeting such men as Paul Revere and John Hancock. An outcast for a time, he finally learns on the battlefield of Lexington that his crippled hand can be put to use." Shapiro. Fic for Youth. 3d edition

Forester, Victoria
★ The **girl** who could fly. Feiwel and Friends 2008 329p $16.95
Grades: 4 5 6 7 **Fic**
1. School stories 2. Science fiction 3. Flight -- Fiction
ISBN 978-0-312-37462-4; 0-312-37462-3
LC 2008-06882

When homeschooled farm girl Piper McCloud reveals her ability to fly, she is quickly taken to a secret government facility to be trained with other exceptional children, but she soon realizes that something is very wrong and begins working with brilliant and wealthy Conrad to escape.

"The story soars, just like Piper, with enough loop-de-loops to keep kids uncertain about what will come next. . . . Best of all are the book's strong, lightly wrapped messages about friendship and authenticity and the difference between doing well and doing good." Booklist

Forever, or a long, long time; Caela Carter; [edited by] Karen Chaplin. HarperCollins 2017 320 p. (ebook) $15.99; (hardcover) $16.99
Grades: 5 6 7 **Fic**
1. Adoption -- Fiction 2. Foster children -- Fiction 3. Brothers and sisters -- Fiction
ISBN 9780062385703; 9780062385680
LC 2016949993

This book, by Caela Carter, is a "story about two foster children who want desperately to believe that they've found their forever home. . . . Flora and her brother, Julian, . . . can't remember where they came from. And even now that they've been adopted, Flora still struggles to believe in forever. So along with their new mother, Flora and Julian begin a journey to go back and discover their past—for only then can they really begin to build their future." (Publisher's note)

"Poetic and meditative, this emotionally enthralling novel undresses assumptions with purpose and hope." Kirkus

Fox, Helen
★ **Eager**. Wendy Lamb Books 2004 280p hardcover o.p. pa $6.50
Grades: 5 6 7 8 **Fic**
1. Science fiction 2. Robots -- Fiction
ISBN 0-385-74672-5; 0-553-48795-7 pa
LC 2003-19489

Unlike Grumps, their old-fashioned robot, the Bell family's new robot, Eager, is programmed to not merely obey but to question, reason, and exercise free will.

"There is a lot of warmth and humor in this engaging . . . novel. . . . The characters are well developed and the action moves quickly. The author also raises thought-provoking questions about what it means to be human, the dangers of technology, and the concept of free will." SLJ

Another title about Eager is:

Eager's nephew (2006)

Fox, Paula

★ The **slave** dancer. Atheneum 2001 176p $18.99; pa $6.99
Grades: 5 6 7 8   **Fic**
1. Sea stories 2. Slave trade -- Fiction
ISBN 978-0-689-84505-5; 0-689-84505-7; 978-1-4169-7139-9
pa; 1-4169-7139-4 pa
A reissue of the title first published 1973 by Bradbury Press
Awarded the Newbery Medal, 1974
"Thirteen-year-old Jessie Bollier is kidnapped from New Orleans
and taken aboard a slave ship. Cruelly tyrannized by the ship's captain,
Jessie is made to play his fife for the slaves during the exercise period
into which they are forced in order to keep them fit for sale. When a
hurricane destroys the ship, Jessie and Ras, a young slave, survive. They
are helped by an old black man who finds them, spirits Ras north to freedom, and assists Jessie to return to his family." Shapiro. Fic for Youth.
3d edition

The **stone**-faced boy. Front Street 2005 83p pa $8.95
Grades: 4 5 6   **Fic**
1. Dogs -- Fiction 2. Siblings -- Fiction 3. Family life -- Fiction
ISBN 978-1-932425-42-0 pa; 1-932425-42-X pa
                                              LC 2005-12056
First published 1968 by Bradbury Press
Only his strange great-aunt seems to understand the thoughts behind
a young boy's expressionless face as he returns on an eerie, snowy night
from rescuing a dog that dislikes him

Foxlee, Karen

★ **Ophelia** and the marvelous boy; by Karen Foxlee. Alfred A.
Knopf 2014 240 p. $16.99
Grades: 4 5 6 7 8   **Fic**
1. Snow -- Fiction 2. Museums -- Fiction 3. Prisoners -- Fiction
4. Magic -- Fiction 5. Heroes -- Fiction 6. Wizards -- Fiction 7.
Kings, queens, rulers, etc. -- Fiction
ISBN 0385753543; 9780385753548; 9780385753555
                                              LC 2013012236
In this book, by Karen Foxlee, "Ophelia Jane Worthington-Whittard
. . . and her sister Alice are still grieving for their dead mother when
their father takes a job in a strange museum in a city where it always
snows. On her very first day in the museum Ophelia discovers a boy
locked away in a long forgotten room. He is a prisoner of Her Majesty
the Snow Queen. As Ophelia embarks on an incredible journey to rescue
the boy everything that she believes will be tested." (Publisher's note)
"Loosely based on Hans Christian Andersen's The Snow Queen, this
clever story-within-a-story reads easily yet offers deep lessons about
trust, responsibility, and friendship." Booklist

Frank, Steven B.

Armstrong & Charlie; written by Steven B. Frank. Houghton Mif-
flin Harcourt 2017 298 p. (hardcover) $16.99
Grades: 5 6 7 8   **Fic**
1. School stories 2. Jews -- Fiction 3. Friendship -- Fiction 4.
Race relations -- Fiction 5. African Americans -- Fiction 6. School
integration -- Fiction 7. Los Angeles (Calif.) -- Fiction 8. Schools
-- Fiction 9. Best friends -- Fiction 10. Jews -- United States --
Fiction
ISBN 9780544826083
                                              LC 2016014199
In this book, written by Steven B. Frank, "Charlie isn't looking for-
ward to sixth grade. If he starts sixth grade, chances are he'll finish it.
And when he does, he'll grow older than the brother he recently lost.
Armstrong isn't looking forward to sixth grade, either. . . . When these

two land at the same desk, it's the Rules Boy next to the Rebel, a boy
who lost a brother elbow-to-elbow with a boy who longs for one." (Publisher's note)

Fraustino, Lisa Rowe

The **Hole** in the Wall. Milkweed Editions 2010 214p $16.95
Grades: 4 5 6   **Fic**
1. Twins -- Fiction 2. Siblings -- Fiction 3. Family life -- Fiction 4.
Supernatural -- Fiction 5. Coal mines and mining -- Fiction
ISBN 978-1-57131-696-7; 1-57131-696-5
                                              LC 2010017732
An imaginative eleven-year-old named Sebby discovers that the
strange things he has been seeing are real, and connected somehow with
the strip-mining operation that has destroyed his town, but getting help
from his bickering family seems unlikely.
"More than the science-fiction elements, it's the urgent details of
conservation that will pull readers, and when the issues reach right to
Sebby's home, the questions increase. . . . . This title will capture young
environmentalists." Boolist

Frazier, Angie

The **mastermind** plot; by Angie Frazier. Scholastic Press 2012
231 p. (Suzanna Snow mysteries) (hardcover : alk. paper) $16.99
Grades: 4 5 6 7   **Fic**
1. Mystery fiction 2. Adventure fiction 3. Children's stories 4.
Arson -- Fiction 5. Uncles -- Fiction 6. Schools -- Fiction 7.
Grandmothers -- Fiction 8. Mystery and detective stories 9. Family
life -- Massachusetts -- Boston -- Fiction 10. Boston (Mass.) --
History -- 20th century -- Fiction
ISBN 0545208645; 9780545208642
                                              LC 2011003770
Sequel to: The midnight tunnel
This children's mystery by Angie Frazier continues the adventures
of Suzanna Snow. "She's just arrived in Boston, the city she's wanted to
visit for as long as she can remember. . . . Her grandmother and cousin,
Will, welcome her warmly, but her famous detective uncle, Bruce Snow,
seems anything but pleased. He doesn't want [her] meddling in his current case involving a string of mysterious warehouse fires along the harbor front. But Zanna can't help herself. Is someone setting the fires? Just
when she thinks she's on to something, a strange man starts following
her. Is he a threat? Zanna needs to solve the case before she has the
chance to find out." (Publisher's note)

The **midnight** tunnel; a Suzanna Snow mystery. Scholastic Press
2011 283p $16.99
Grades: 4 5 6 7   **Fic**
1. Mystery fiction 2. Canada -- Fiction 3. Uncles -- Fiction 4.
Missing children -- Fiction 5. Hotels and motels -- Fiction
ISBN 978-0-545-20862-8; 0-545-20862-9
                                              LC 2010-26770
In 1905, Suzanna is in training to be a well-mannered hostess at a
Loch Harbor, New Brunswick, hotel, but her dream of being a detective
gets a boost when a seven-year-old guest goes missing and Suzanna's
uncle, a famous detective, comes to solve the case.
"What Zanna lacks in grace and composure, she makes up for in
pluck, persistence and cleverness, emerging a likely and likable Edward-
ian Nancy Drew." Kirkus

Frazier, Sundee T.

Cleo Edison Oliver, playground millionaire; Sundee T. Frazier; illustrations by Jennifer L. Meyer. Arthur A. Levine Books, an imprint of
Scholastic Inc. 2016 224 p. (hardcover : alk. paper) $16.99
Grades: 4 5 6   **Fic**
1. Friendship -- Fiction 2. Business enterprises -- Fiction 3. Money-

making projects for children 4. African Americans -- Fiction 5. Adoption -- Fiction 6. California -- Fiction 7. Friendship -- Fiction
ISBN 9780545822350; 9780545822367

LC 2015015763

In this book, by Sundee T. Frazier, illustrated by Jennifer L. Meyer, "Cleopatra Edison Oliver has always been an entrepreneur, just like her inspiration, successful businesswoman Fortune A. Davies. So when Cleo's fifth-grade teacher assigns her class a 'Passion Project,' Cleo comes up with her best business idea yet: the finest 'tooth-pulling' company in town." (Publisher's note)

"Frazier offers a rare, clear-eyed view of adoption, understanding that even the best are founded on loss as well as love and that assimilating this bittersweet, difficult truth is a lifelong journey. A funny, compassionate tale." Kirkus

Frazier, Sundee Tucker

★ The **other** half of my heart; [by] Sundee T. Frazier. Delacorte Press 2010 296p $16.99

Grades: 5 6 7 8 **Fic**

1. Twins -- Fiction 2. Sisters -- Fiction 3. Prejudices -- Fiction 4. Grandmothers -- Fiction 5. Beauty contests -- Fiction 6. African Americans -- Fiction 7. Racially mixed people -- Fiction
ISBN 978-0-385-73440-0; 0-385-73440-9

LC 2009013209

Twin daughters of interracial parents, eleven-year-olds Keira and Minna have very different skin tones and personalities, but it is not until their African American grandmother enters them in the Miss Black Pearl Pre-Teen competition in North Carolina that red-haired and pale-skinned Minna realizes what life in their small town in the Pacific Northwest has been like for her more outgoing, darker-skinned sister.

"Frazier addresses issues faced by mixed-race children with a grace and humor that keep her from being pedantic. The story is enjoyable in its own right, and will also encourage readers to rethink racial boundries and what it means to be black or white in America." SLJ

Freedman, Paula J.

★ **My** basmati bat mitzvah; by Paula J. Freedman. Harry N. Abrams 2013 256 p. (alk. paper) $16.95

Grades: 4 5 6 **Fic**

1. Bat mitzvah -- Fiction 2. Jewish children -- Fiction 3. Judaism -- Fiction 4. East Indian Americans -- Fiction 5. Jews -- United States -- Fiction
ISBN 1419708066; 9781419708060

LC 2013005791

In this book, by Paula J. Freedman, "during the fall leading up to her bat mitzvah, Tara Feinstein has a lot more than her Torah portion on her mind. Between Hebrew school and study sessions with the rabbi, there doesn't seem to be enough time to hang out with her best friend Ben-O--who might also be her boyfriend--and her other best friend, Rebecca. Amid all this drama, Tara considers how to balance her Indian and Jewish identities and what it means to have a bat mitzvah while questioning her faith." (Publisher's note)

"How could Tara let know-it-all Sheila Rosenberg get away with saying, "You're not even Jewish," when Tara's Indian-born mother converted "way before I was even born"? With her bat mitzvah on the horizon, Tara secretly wonders: "Was I about to become more Jewish, or less Indian?" A light, warm, humorous story about cultural identity, inner harmony, and ordinary middle-school trials and tribulations. Glos." (Horn Book)

Freeman, Martha

The **trouble** with cats; illustrated by Cat Bowman Smith. Holiday House 2000 77p il $15.95

Grades: 2 3 4 **Fic**

1. School stories 2. Cats -- Fiction 3. Stepfathers -- Fiction 4. San Francisco (Calif.) -- Fiction
ISBN 0-8234-1479-5

LC 99-29291

After a difficult first week of third grade, Holly begins to adjust to her new school and living in her new stepfather's tiny apartment with his four cats

"Bowman contributes pen-and-ink drawings with lines that quiver with energy. . . . Freeman has a knack for wholesome, undemanding fiction . . . with enough action and humor to carry the plot." Bull Cent Child Books

Other titles about Holly are:
The trouble with babies (2002)
The trouble with twins (2007)

Who is stealing the 12 days of Christmas? by Martha Freeman. Holiday House 2003 200 p. (Chickadee Court mysteries) $16.95

Grades: 4 5 6 **Fic**

1. Mystery fiction 2. Christmas -- Fiction
ISBN 0823417883; 9780823417889

LC 2002191920

In this book, by Martha Freeman, "every Christmas since Alex can remember, his family and neighbors have filled their front yards with decorations from each of the twelve days mentioned in the song 'The Twelve Days of Christmas.' But this year someone is stealing them one by one. Alex is determined to solve this caper, but will he be able to do it in time to save the twelve days of Christmas?" (Publisher's note)

"There's a ""Christmas crime wave"" on nine-year-old Alex's street, which features a popular ""Twelve Days of Christmas"" display every year. The police are writing it off as a kids' prank, so it's up to Alex, his best friend, Yasmeen, and his ""ace detective"" cat, Luau, to track down clues, conduct interviews, and try to piece together the evidence. The amiable mystery is entertaining and moves at a brisk pace." (Horn Book)

Who stole Grandma's million-dollar pumpkin pie? Holiday House 2009 209p (The Chickadee Court mysteries) $16.95

Grades: 4 5 6 **Fic**

1. Mystery fiction 2. Pies -- Fiction 3. Thanksgiving Day -- Fiction
ISBN 978-0-8234-2215-9; 0-8234-2215-1

LC 2008048486

When the recipe for his grandmother's famous pumpkin pie is suddenly missing just before Thanksgiving Day, Alex and his friend Yasmeen try to solve the mystery of its disappearance.

"Engaging text with a lot of humor. . . . Children who like fast-paced whodunits with a touch of humor will enjoy the story." SLJ

Who stole Halloween? Holiday House 2005 232p il (The Chickadee Court mysteries) $16.95; pa $7.95

Grades: 4 5 6 **Fic**

1. Mystery fiction 2. Cats -- Fiction 3. Halloween -- Fiction
ISBN 0-8234-1962-2; 0-8234-2170-8 pa

When nine-year-old Alex and his friend Yasmeen investigate the disappearance of cats in their neighborhood, they stumble onto a larger mystery involving a haunted house and a ghostly cat.

"The story unfolds to a satisfying resolution . . . Characters are well drawn, and the book will entice even reluctant readers with its action and humor." SLJ

Other titles about Alex and Yasmeen are:
Who is stealing the 12 days of Christmas (2003)
Who stole Uncle Sam? (2008)
Who stole Grandma's million-dollar pumpkin pie? (2009)

Who stole New Year's Eve? by Martha Freeman and illustrated by Eric Brace. Holiday House 2013 224 p. (A Chickadee Court mystery) (hardcover) $16.95

Grades: 4 5 6 **Fic**

1. Mystery fiction 2. Sculpture -- Fiction 3. Friendship -- Fiction 4. Carnivals -- Fiction 5. Ice carving -- Fiction 6. Pennsylvania -- Fiction

ISBN 0823427501; 9780823427505

LC 2012019674

In this book by Martha Freeman, part of the "Chickadee Court Mystery" series, "twelve-year-old sleuths, Yasmeen and Alex, are having friendship issues. Yasmeen thinks that she's being replaced by a new girl who has come to Chickadee Court. Then, the whole gang comes together to solve the frosty mystery [of stolen ice sculptures]. The clues lead to a fracking operation and the laboratory of a professor who is racing to invent a new alternative fuel before his competitors do." (Publisher's note)

"When all the ice sculptures intended for the town's annual Ice Carnival are stolen, eleven-year-old Alex Parakeet and his sleuth friends follow clues (water containing volatile chemicals; a dog that doesn't bark) to solve the case. This fifth series mystery is solid and satisfying, set against a background of holiday celebrations and enhanced with much humor and intrigue." (Horn Book)

Who stole Uncle Sam? by Martha Freeman. 1st ed.; Holiday House 2008 250 p. (Chickadee Court mysteries) $16.95

Grades: 4 5 6 **Fic**

1. Mystery fiction 2. Missing persons -- Fiction 3. School stories -- Fiction 4. Mystery -- fiction 5. Baseball -- fiction 6. Family life -- fiction 7. Pennsylvania -- Fiction

ISBN 0823420914; 9780823420919

LC 2007043054

In this book by Martha Freeman "two eleven-year-old sleuths crack a case about the disappearance of a baseball coach. Alex and Yasmeen made a pact to stop solving mysteries. However, when Alex's baseball coach, a patriotic war veteran nicknamed Uncle Sam, goes missing, it's hard for the young detectives to resist. Soon the two are tracking down clues involving porta-potties, lawn care chemicals, and secret baseball scouts." (Publisher's note)

"Coach Banner steps inside a Porta Potty to change into his Uncle Sam costume before the annual Memorial Day race--then seemingly vanishes. Freeman takes her time building up to his mysterious disappearance, and she lobs a lot of balls into the air here (Vietnam War, lawn-care chemicals, baseball), but her super-sleuths Alex and Yasmeen, lively and likable as ever, keep readers hooked." (Horn Book)

Freymann-Weyr, Garret

★ **French** ducks in Venice; illustrated by Erin McGuire. Candlewick Press 2011 il $16.99

Grades: 2 3 4 **Fic**

1. Ducks -- Fiction 2. Canals -- Fiction 3. California -- Fiction

ISBN 978-0-7636-4173-3; 0-7636-4173-1

LC 2010047672

When Polina Panova's "prince" moves out of their Venice, California, house, two ducks that live on the canals but believe themselves to be French try to help Polina, a designer of magical dresses of thread, silk, velvet, grass, and pieces of night sky, by giving her something to make her stop being sad.

"Freymann-Weyr's mannered narrative voice keeps emotions firmly in check . . . and her storytelling gifts are unmistakable. . . . There's virtue in presenting a portrait of loss with a spoonful of sugar; readers learn how to talk about hurt . . . while McGuire's cinematically lit pictures recall classic Disney images of winsome animals consoling star-crossed heroines." Publ Wkly

Friedman, Laurie B.

Back to school, Mallory; by Laurie Friedman; illustrations by Tamara Schmitz. Lerner Pub. Group 2004 175p il lib bdg $15.95; pa $5.95

Grades: 2 3 4 **Fic**

1. School stories 2. Moving -- Fiction 3. Family life -- Fiction

ISBN 1-575-05658-5 lib bdg; 978-1-575-05658-6 lib bdg; 1-575-05865-0 pa; 978-1-575-05865-8 pa

LC 2003-18043

After moving, eight-year-old Mallory struggles with being new at school, especially because her mother is now the music teacher and director of the third grade play.

"A dynamic design, complete with handwritten notes and cartoon drawings, contributes to the chapter book's friendly feel." Horn Book Guide

Campfire Mallory; by Laurie Friedman; illustrations by Jennifer Kalis. Carolrhoda Books 2008 175p il lib bdg $15.95; pa $5.95

Grades: 2 3 4 **Fic**

1. Camps -- Fiction 2. Friendship -- Fiction

ISBN 978-0-8225-7657-0 lib bdg; 0-8225-7657-0 lib bdg; 978-1-58013-841-3 pa; 1-58013-841-1 pa

LC 2007022218

Nine-and-a-half-year-old Mallory's trepidation about going to sleep-away camp is multiplied when she and her best friend are assigned to different cabins, and a new "friend" seems determined to get Mallory in trouble

"The plot is believable, and the language is well suited to the intended audience. Mallory's diary entries and black-and-white cartoons appear throughout. The action is well paced. . . . A lighthearted, enjoyable read." SLJ

Other titles about Mallory are:
Back to school Mallory (2004)
Mallory on the move (2004)
Mallory vs. Max (2005)
Happy birthday, Mallory (2005)
In business with Mallory (2006)
Heart-to-heart with Mallory (2006)
Mallory on board (2007)
Honestly, Mallory (2007)
Step fourth, Mallory (2008)
Happy New Year, Mallory (2009)
Red, white & true blue Mallory (2009)
Mallory goes green (2010)
Mallory in the spotlight (2010)
Mallory's super sleepover (2011)
Mallory's guide to boys, brothers, dads, and dogs (2011)

Happy birthday, Mallory! by Laurie Friedman; illustrations by Tamara Schmitz. Carolrhoda Books 2005 159p il lib bdg $15.95; pa $5.95

Grades: 2 3 4 **Fic**

1. Birthdays -- Fiction

ISBN 1-575-05823-5 lib bdg; 978-1-575-05823-8 lib bdg; 0-8225-6502-1 pa; 978-0-8225-6502-4 pa

LC 2004031080

After a difficult year, Mallory plans a month-long celebration of her ninth birthday in hopes that her next year will be wonderful.

"Mallory's enthusiasm is infectious. . . . Cartoonlike drawings and large print make the story accessible to early chapter-book readers." SLJ

Happy New Year, Mallory! by Laurie Friedman; illustrations by Jennifer Kalis. Carolrhoda Books, Inc. 2009 $15.95

Grades: 2 3 4   **Fic**
1. Sick -- Fiction 2. New Year -- Fiction 3. Friendship -- Fiction
4. Family life -- Fiction
ISBN 978-0-8225-8883-2; 0-8225-8883-8

LC 2008041164

When a bad stomachache sends Mallory to the hospital during a winter reunion with neighbor Mary Ann and their summer camp bunkmates, she is sad that her friends seem to be having great fun without her.

"This offers a very readable story and expressive black-and-white illustrations." Booklist

Heart-to-heart with Mallory; by Laurie Friedman; illustrations by Barbara Pollak. Carolrhoda Books 2006 159p il lib bdg $15.95; pa $5.95

Grades: 2 3 4   **Fic**
1. Friendship -- Fiction 2. Remarriage -- Fiction 3. Valentine's Day -- Fiction
ISBN 978-1-575-05932-7 lib bdg; 1-575-05932-0 lib bdg;
0-8225-7133-1 pa; 978-0-8225-7133-9

LC 2005034106

Nine-year-old Mallory turns to her diary to sort through her emotions when she finds out she has a secret admirer and her two best friends' parents may be getting engaged.

"Pencil cartoons and a font that resembles a child's handwriting lend appeal. Friedman finds a true voice for her likable . . . character." SLJ

Honestly, Mallory! by Laurie Friedman; illustrations by Barbara Pollak. Carolrhoda Books 2007 159p il lib bdg $15.95; pa $5.95

Grades: 2 3 4   **Fic**
1. School stories 2. Honesty -- Fiction
ISBN 978-0-8225-6193-4 lib bdg; 0-8225-6193-X lib bdg; 978-1-580-13840-6 pa; 1-580-13840-3 pa

LC 2006101328

When Mallory cannot decide what to be on Career Day, it makes her feel like she is not good at anything and she ends up telling a lie that quickly gets out of control.

Mallory "faces the internal turmoil that comes with knowing you've done something wrong, and young readers will empathize with her. . . . Pollak's simple cartoon pictures appear throughout." SLJ

In business with Mallory; by Laurie Friedman; illustrations by Barbara Pollak. Carolrhoda Books 2006 159p il lib bdg $15.95; pa $5.95

Grades: 2 3 4   **Fic**
1. Money-making projects for children -- Fiction
ISBN 978-1-575-05925-9 lib bdg; 1-575-05925-8 lib bdg; 978-0-8225-6561-1 pa; 0-8225-6561-7 pa

LC 2005020620

When Mallory's mother refuses to buy her a purse, Mallory tries a series of businesses in order to make money and buy it herself.

"The illustrations are dark and bold, and interesting to look at. From the characterizations to the visuals, this chapter book is a winner." SLJ

Mallory goes green; by Laurie Friedman; illustrations by Jennifer Kalis. Carolrhoda Books 2010 159p il $15.95

Grades: 2 3 4   **Fic**
1. School stories 2. Environmental protection -- Fiction
ISBN 978-0-8225-8885-6; 0-8225-8885-4

LC 2009014503

When Mallory is appointed to the Fern Falls Elementary School Environmental Committee, which is deciding on class projects for the upcoming Green Fair, she rapidly succeeds in alienating her classmates, friends, and family by her overzealous efforts to save the planet.

"This features large type, widely spaced lines, and stylized illustrations. Good chapter-book fare." Booklist

Mallory in the spotlight; by Laurie Friedman; illustrations by Jennifer Kalis. Darby Creek 2010 158p il $14.99

Grades: 3 4 5   **Fic**
1. School stories 2. Theater -- Fiction 3. Friendship -- Fiction
ISBN 978-0-8225-8884-9; 0-8225-8884-6

LC 2009045341

When Mallory gets the lead in the school play, she cannot understand why her best friend Mary Ann is not just as excited as she is, but eventually she finds out—and learns who her real friends are.

This "is a fast-moving chapter book. . . . Bold drawings add visual appeal." Booklist

Mallory on board; by Laurie Friedman; illustrations by Barbara Pollak. Carolrhoda Books 2007 175p il lib bdg $15.95; pa $5.95

Grades: 2 3 4   **Fic**
1. Friendship -- Fiction 2. Remarriage -- Fiction 3. Family life -- Fiction 4. Ocean travel -- Fiction
ISBN 978-0-8225-6194-1 lib bdg; 0-8225-6194-8 lib bdg; 978-0-8225-9023-1 pa; 0-8225-9023-9 pa

LC 2006013841

Despite her fears of being a "third wheel," Mallory goes on a cruise for the wedding of the mother and father of her two best friends.

Mallory on the move; by Laurie B. Friedman; illustrations by Tamara Schmitz. Carolrhoda Books 2004 158p il lib bdg $15.95; pa $5.95

Grades: 2 3 4   **Fic**
1. Moving -- Fiction 2. Friendship -- Fiction 3. Family life -- Fiction
ISBN 1-575-05538-4 lib bdg; 978-1-575-05538-1 lib bdg; 1-575-05831-6 pa; 978-1-575-05831-3 pa

LC 2003-8937

After moving to a new town, eight-year-old Mallory keeps throwing stones in the "Wishing Pond" but things will not go back to the way they were before, and she remains torn between old and new best friends.

"Black-and-white drawings and the lively text reveal some very contemporary kids." Horn Book Guide

Mallory vs. Max. Carolrhoda 159p il lib bdg $15.95; pa $5.95

Grades: 2 3 4   **Fic**
1. Dogs -- Fiction 2. Siblings -- Fiction 3. Family life -- Fiction
ISBN 1-57505-795-6 lib bdg; 978-1-57505-795-8 lib bdg; 1-575-05863-4 pa; 978-1-575-05863-4 pa

Eight-year-old Mallory feels left out when her older brother, Max gets a dog that becomes the center of attention.

"Schmitz's expressive cartoon illustrations and the large typeface make the book appealing to beginning chapter-book readers." SLJ

Mallory's guide to boys, brothers, dads, and dogs; illustrations by Jennifer Kalis. Darby Creek 2011 159p il $15.95

Grades: 2 3 4   **Fic**
1. School stories 2. Dogs -- Fiction 3. Family life -- Fiction
ISBN 978-0-8225-8886-3; 0-8225-8886-2

LC 201002222

Ten-year-old Mallory's crush on J.T., a boy in her older brother's class, gets her in trouble with her teacher, her family, and her friends but no matter what she does, J.T. does not seem interested in her.

"The book's dynamic design, including numerous line drawings, emails, and journal entry style pages, help enliven the story." Horn Book Guide

Mallory's super sleepover; by Laurie Friedman; illustrations by Jennifer Kalis. Carolrhoda Books 2011 il $15.95
Grades: 2 3 4   **Fic**
1. Parties -- Fiction 2. Birthdays -- Fiction 3. Sleepovers -- Fiction
ISBN 978-0-8225-8887-0; 0-8225-8887-0

LC 2010044418

When Mallory plans a sleepover to celebrate her tenth birthday, she has a hard time pleasing both her friends and her parents.

Play it again, Mallory; by Laurie B. Friedman; illustrations by Jennifer Kalis. Darby Creek 2013 159 p. (Mallory) (trade hard cover : alk. paper) $15.95
Grades: 2 3 4   **Fic**
1. School stories 2. Bands (Music) -- Fiction 3. Musical instruments -- Fiction 4. Music -- Fiction 5. Schools -- Fiction
ISBN 0761360751; 9780761360759

LC 2012048866

In this book by Laurie B. Friedman "Mallory is excited about the six-week arts electives program at Fern Falls Elementary—until she gets stuck in her last-choice class, band. To make matters worse, she is assigned to the tuba. But with some good guidance from her mom and her band teacher, Mallory learns the meaning of 'practice makes perfect' and that, in fact, making music can be lots of fun." (Publisher's note)

Red, white, and true blue Mallory; by Laurie Friedman; illustrations by Jennifer Kalis. Carolrhoda Books 2009 183p il $15.95
Grades: 2 3 4   **Fic**
1. School stories 2. Friendship -- Fiction 3. Washington (D.C.) -- Fiction
ISBN 978-0-8225-8882-5; 0-8225-8882-X

LC 2008016035

Mallory's journal of her fourth-grade trip to Washington D.C. reveals how much fun she has, despite a loose tooth, being upset with her best friend Mary Ann and getting separated from her class in a museum.

"Pencil drawings, supposedly by Mallory, illustrate the journal effectively. . . . Fans of the Mallory series and young visitors to the nation's capital may enjoy her take on Washington D.C. sightseeing." Booklist

Step fourth, Mallory! by Laurie Friedman; illustrations by Jennifer Kalis. Carolrhoda Books 2008 175p il lib bdg $15.95
Grades: 2 3 4   **Fic**
1. School stories 2. Friendship -- Fiction
ISBN 978-0-8225-8881-8 lib bdg; 0-8225-8881-1 lib bdg

LC 2007034771

Mallory enters fourth grade with high hopes for her best year ever, but instead she starts by breaking the teacher's rules and then feels left out when her best friend likes the same boy she does.

"Mallory's first-person narrative . . . convincingly portrays both her high hopes and her low spirits as she tries to find her way. Illustrated with fresh, childlike drawings." Booklist

Too good to be true; by Laurie Friedman. Darby Creek 2014 158 p. (The mostly miserable life of April Sinclair) (trade hard cover : alk. paper) $17.95
Grades: 5 6 7 8   **Fic**
1. Diaries -- Fiction 2. Friendship -- Fiction 3. Dating (Social customs) -- Fiction 4. Interpersonal relations -- Fiction
ISBN 1467709263; 9781467709262

LC 2013026434

In this book, by Laurie Friedman, "eighth grade is off to a surprisingly promising start for April Sinclair. . . Making the dance team is the icing on the cake. But with one unexpected move from her hot neighbor, Matt Parker, April's life starts to spin out of control. In the blink of an eye, her best friend is furious, her boyfriend dumps her, and the girls on

the dance team don't want anything to do with her. How could things go so wrong so fast?" (Publisher's note)

"April (Can You Say Catastrophe?) begins eighth grade with great news: she's selected for a highly coveted spot on the high school dance team. The team's grueling schedule, however, leads to hard feelings between April and her boyfriend, and her best friend. Readers will relate to April's struggle to maintain old friendships while forging new ones, and cheer for her as she navigates the aftermath of a bad romantic decision." Horn Book

Friend, Catherine

Barn boot blues. Marshall Cavendish 2011 142p $16.99
Grades: 5 6 7 8   **Fic**
1. Moving -- Fiction 2. Farm life -- Fiction 3. Minnesota -- Fiction
ISBN 978-0-7614-5827-2; 0-7614-5827-1

LC 2011001909

When her parents swap urban life in Minneapolis for rural life on a farm 100 miles away, twelve-year-old Taylor feels as if she is living on another planet.

"In this refreshingly compact novel, readers learn interesting, authentic details about everything from spinning wool to collecting eggs to in a kind-of-gross, kind-of-wonderful climax birthing lambs. In Taylor, Friend has created a plucky, lightly sarcastic protagonist whose frustration at her situation is palpable but who never comes off as unlikable or bratty." Horn Book

Friesen, Jonathan

The last Martin. Zonderkidz 2011 266p $14.99
Grades: 4 5 6 7   **Fic**
1. Family life -- Fiction
ISBN 978-0-310-72080-5; 0-310-72080-X

LC 2010-48275

Thirteen-year-old Martin Boyle struggles to break a family curse after discovering that he has twelve weeks to live.

"Spiced with plenty of slapstick, the yarn speeds its protagonist through a succession of highs, lows and improbable triumphs on the way to a hilariously melodramatic finish." Kirkus

Frost, Helen

Applesauce weather; by Helen Frost; illustrated by Amy June Bates. Candlewick Press 2016 112 p. illustrations $14.99
Grades: 3 4 5 6   **Fic**
1. Family -- Fiction 2. Uncles -- Fiction 3. Family life -- Fiction 4. Family traditions -- Fiction 5. Loss (Psychology) -- Fiction
ISBN 9780763675769; 0763675768

LC 2016940426

In this book by Helen Frost, illustrated by Amy June Bates, "when the first apple falls from the tree, Faith and Peter know that it's applesauce weather. . . . It also means Uncle Arthur should be here to tell his stories, . . . tales about how he came to have a missing finger. But this is the first year without Aunt Lucy, and when Uncle Arthur arrives, there's no . . . stories waiting to be told." (Publisher's note)

★ **Salt;** by Helen Frost. Farrar, Straus, and Giroux 2013 160 p. (hardcover) $17.99
Grades: 5 6 7 8   **Fic**
1. War stories 2. Native Americans 3. Historical fiction 4. War of 1812 -- Fiction 5. Novels in verse. 6. Friendship -- Fiction 7. Miami Indians -- Fiction 8. Trading posts -- Fiction 9. Frontier and pioneer life -- Indiana -- Fiction 10. United States -- History -- War of 1812 -- Fiction 11. Fort Wayne (Ind.) -- History -- 19th century -- Fiction
ISBN 0374363870; 9780374363871

LC 2012029521

This book, by Helen Frost, "set during the War of 1812 . . . is the story of the friendship between Anikwa, a Miami Indian boy, and James, the son of a trader. As both British and American armies advance on the area, other Native American peoples arrive hoping to fight with the British against the Americans. The plan fails, and Anikwa's peaceful people must flee. Will they have to abandon their traditional home, and will the friendship between the boys be sundered?" (Publisher's note)

Spinning through the universe; a novel in poems from room 214. Farrar, Straus and Giroux 2004 93p $16

Grades: 4 5 6 7   **Fic**

1. Poetry 2. School stories
ISBN 0-374-37159-8

LC 2003-48056

A collection of poems written in the voices of Mrs. Williams of room 214, her students, and a custodian about their interactions with each other, their families, and the world around them. Includes notes on the poetic forms represented

"Interwoven dramatic stories and interesting poetic patterns give this book extra appeal. A boon for poetry classes." SLJ

Fry, Michael

The **Odd** Squad; Bully Bait. by Michael Fry. Disney Hyperion 2013 224 p. (hardcover) $12.99

Grades: 4 5 6 7   **Fic**

1. Bullies -- Fiction 2. Friendship -- Fiction 3. School stories -- Fiction 4. Schools -- Fiction 5. Middle schools -- Fiction 6. Interpersonal relations -- Fiction
ISBN 1423169247; 9781423169246

LC 2012014286

This children's story, by Michael Fry, is part of the "Odd Squad" series. "Nick is the shortest seventh-grader in the history of the world . . ., doesn't fit in . . ., and spends more time inside than outside his locker. . . . When a well-intentioned guidance counselor forces Nick to join the school's lamest club . . .', what starts off as a reluctant band of hopeless oddballs morphs into an effective and empowered team ready to face whatever middle school throws at them." (Publisher's note)

"Cartoonist Fry humorously mines the world of middle school as seen through the eyes of bullied Nick to answer the question: Can three oddballs team together to take down the school bully? ...Abundant cartoon-style illustrations enhance the book's silly yet sensitive portrayal of bullying and unlikely friendships." Kirkus

Other titles in this series are:
Zero Tolerance (2013)
King Karl (2014)

Funke, Cornelia Caroline

Dragon rider; [by] Cornelia Funke; translated by Anthea Bell. Scholastic 2004 523p il $12.95

Grades: 5 6 7 8   **Fic**

1. Fantasy fiction 2. Dragons -- Fiction
ISBN 0-439-45695-9

LC 2004-45419

Original German edition 1997

After learning that humans are headed toward his hidden home, Firedrake, a silver dragon, is joined by a brownie and an orphan boy in a quest to find the legendary valley known as the Rim of Heaven, encountering friendly and unfriendly creatures along the way, and struggling to evade the relentless pursuit of an old enemy.

"Funke proves she knows how to tickle the imaginations of younger readers. . . . This is a good, old-fashioned ensemble-cast quest." Booklist

Inkdeath; [by] Cornelia Funke; translated from the German by Anthea Bell. Scholastic 2008 683p il map $24.99

Grades: 5 6 7 8   **Fic**

1. Fantasy fiction 2. Kidnapping -- Fiction 3. Books and reading -- Fiction
ISBN 978-0-439-86628-6; 0-439-86628-6

LC 2008-19922

Sequel to: Inkspell (2005)

As Bluejay—Mo's fictitious double—tries to keep the Book of Immortality from unraveling, Adderhead kidnaps all the children in the kingdom, asking for Bluejay's surrender or the children will be doomed to slavery in the silver mines.

"The assortment of villains is vivid and frightening. . . . The finale includes a thoroughly engrossing climax." SLJ

★ **Inkheart**; [by] Cornelia Funke; translated from the German by Anthea Bell. Scholastic 2003 534p $19.95; pa $9.99

Grades: 5 6 7 8   **Fic**

1. Fantasy fiction 2. Books and reading -- Fiction
ISBN 0-439-53164-0; 0-439-70910-5 pa

LC 2003-45844

Twelve-year-old Meggie learns that her father, who repairs and binds books for a living, can "read" fictional characters to life when one of those characters abducts them and tries to force him into service.

The author "proves the power of her imagination; readers will be captivated by the chilling and thrilling world she has created here." Publ Wkly

Other titles in this series are:
Inkspell (2005)
Inkdeath (2008)

Funny Girl; Funniest. Stories. Ever. edited by Betsy Bird. Penguin Group USA 2017 240 p. illustrations $16.99

Grades: 4 5 6 7 8   **Fic**

1. Humorous fiction 2. American fiction -- Women authors
ISBN 0451477316; 9780451477316

This book, by Betsy Bird, "is a collection of uproarious stories, rollicking comics, rib-tickling wit, and more, from 25 of today's funniest female writers for kids. . . . With clever contributions from award-winning and bestselling authors including Cece Bell, Sophie Blackall, Libba Bray, Shannon Hale, Lisa Graff, and Raina Telgemeier, this anthology of funny girls will make you laugh until you cry. Or cry until you laugh. Or maybe you won't cry at all. Either way, you'll definitely laugh." (Publisher's note)

"Hilarious and heartfelt, this won't only appeal to funny girls and boys, it'll inspire them." Booklist

Fusco, Kimberly Newton

★ The **wonder** of Charlie Anne. Alfred A. Knopf 2010 272p $16.99; lib bdg $19.99

Grades: 5 6 7 8   **Fic**

1. Farm life -- Fiction 2. Friendship -- Fiction 3. Massachusetts -- Fiction 4. Race relations -- Fiction 5. African Americans -- Fiction 6. Great Depression, 1929-1939 -- Fiction
ISBN 978-0-375-86104-8; 0-375-86104-1; 978-0-375-96104-5 lib bdg; 0-375-96104-6 lib bdg

LC 2009-3883

In a 1930s Massachusetts farm town torn by the Depression, racial tension, and other hardships, Charlie Anne and her black next-door neighbor Phoebe form a friendship that begins to transform their community.

"Good humor, kindness and courage triumph in this warm, richly nuanced novel that cheers the heart like a song sweetly sung." Kirkus

Gaiman, Neil

★ **Coraline**; [by] Neil Gaiman; with illustrations by Dave McKean. HarperCollins Pubs. 2002 162p il pa $6.99; $16.99

Grades: 5 6 7 8   **Fic**
1. Horror fiction 2. Supernatural -- Fiction
ISBN 0-380-80734-3 pa; 0-380-97778-8

LC 2002-18937

Looking for excitement, Coraline ventures through a mysterious door into a world that is similar, yet disturbingly different from her own, where she must challenge a gruesome entity in order to save herself, her parents, and the souls of three others

"Gaiman twines his taut tale with a menacing tone and crisp prose fraught with memorable imagery . . . yet keeps the narrative just this side of terrifying." Publ Wkly

★ **Fortunately,** the milk; by Neil Gaiman; illustrated by Skottie Young. Harper, an imprint of HarperCollinsPublishers 2013 128 p. (hardcover bdgs) $14.99
Grades: 4 5 6 7   **Fic**
1. Fathers -- Fiction 2. Humorous stories 3. Space and time -- Fiction 4. Adventure and adventurers -- Fiction
ISBN 0062224077; 9780062224071

LC 2012050670

This children's picture book by Neil Gaiman is "about a father who has taken an excessively long time to return from the corner store with milk for his children's breakfast." He "is abducted by aliens, made to walk the plank by pirates, and rescued by a stegosaurus in a balloon, among other outrageous escapades." (Publishers Weekly)

★ The **graveyard** book; with illustrations by Dave McKean. HarperCollins 2008 312p il $17.99; lib bdg $18.89
Grades: 5 6 7 8 9 10   **Fic**
1. Death -- Fiction 2. Cemeteries -- Fiction 3. Supernatural -- Fiction
ISBN 0-06-053092-8; 0-06-053093-6 lib bdg; 978-0-06-053092-1; 978-0-06-053093-8 lib bdg

LC 2008-13860

Awarded the Newbery Medal (2009)

Nobody Owens, nicknamed Bod, is a normal boy, except that he has been raised by in a graveyard by ghosts. "Grades five to nine." (Bull Cent Child Books)

"Gaiman writes with charm and humor, and again he has a real winner." Voice Youth Advocates

Odd and the Frost Giants; illustrated by Brett Helquist. HarperCollinsPublishers 2009 117p il $14.99
Grades: 3 4 5 6   **Fic**
1. Norse mythology -- Fiction
ISBN 978-0-06-167173-9; 0-06-167173-8

LC 2009014574

An unlucky twelve-year-old Norwegian boy named Odd leads the Norse gods Loki, Thor, and Odin in an attempt to outwit evil Frost Giants who have taken over Asgard.

"Along with Gaiman's deft humor, lively prose, and agile imagination, a few unexpected themes—the double-edged allure of beauty, the value of family—sneak into this slim tale with particular appeal to kids drawn to Norse mythology, but suitable for any readers of light fantasy." Booklist

Galante, Cecilia

Willowood. Simon & Schuster 2010 265p $16.99
Grades: 4 5 6 7   **Fic**
1. Geckos -- Fiction 2. Moving -- Fiction 3. Friendship -- Fiction 4. Single parent family -- Fiction
ISBN 978-1-4169-8022-3; 1-4169-8022-9

Eleven-year-old Lily has trouble leaving her best friend behind and moving to the city when her mother changes jobs, but she makes some very unlikely friends that soon become like family members.

"The characters . . . are fully realized individuals. . . . [This book has a] finely tuned plot and poetic language. . . . Children will enjoy the story of Lily's first few months in the big city." SLJ

Gale, Eric Kahn

The **Bully** Book; Eric Kahn Gale. Harpercollins Childrens Books 2012 240 p. $16.99
Grades: 4 5 6 7 8   **Fic**
1. School stories 2. Bullies -- Fiction 3. Friendship -- Fiction 4. Middle schools -- Fiction 5. Diaries -- Fiction
ISBN 0062125117; 9780062125118

LC 2012050677

Originally published in a different format as an ebook by the author

"When the author was eleven, he was bullied. This book is loosely based on incidents that happened to him in sixth grade. Eric Haskins, the new sixth-grade bully target, is searching for answers. And unlike many of us who experienced something awful growing up, he finds them. Though they may not be what he expected." (Publisher's note)

"The juxtaposition of Eric's journal against the Bully Book allows readers to see both the bullies' methodology and Eric's unwitting complicity. . . . A compelling and unusual look at a complex and intractable problem that succeeds admirably as story as well." Kirkus

The **Zoo** at the Edge of the World; by Eric Kahn Gale; illustrations by Matthew Howley. Balzer + Bray, an imprint of HarperCollinsPublishers 2014 240 p. illustrations (hardback) $16.99
Grades: 4 5 6 7   **Fic**
1. Zoos -- Fiction 2. Stuttering -- Fiction 3. Jungle animals -- Fiction 4. Human-animal communication -- Fiction
ISBN 0062125168; 9780062125163

LC 2014002144

In this book, by Eric Kahn Gale, "Marlin is not slow, or mute; what he is is a stutterer, and that makes it impossible for him to convince people otherwise. What he is also is a Rackham: the youngest son of the world-famous explorer Roland Rackham, who is the owner and proprietor of the Zoo at the Edge of the World, a resort where the well-to-do from all over the world can come to experience the last bit of the wild left in the world at the end of the nineteenth century." (Publisher's note)

"A secondary plot concerning Marlin's relationships with his father and brother is equally nuanced and powerful, making the book a formidable read on two fronts. The romantic setting and striking prose are icing on the cake, creating an intoxicatingly charming book. Beautiful and fully absorbing." Kirkus

Gannon, Nicholas

The **Doldrums**; written and illustrated by Nicholas Gannon. Greenwillow Books, an Imprint of HarperCollins Publishers 2015 368 p. color illustrations (hardback) $17.99
Grades: 3 4 5 6   **Fic**
1. Explorers 2. Friendship -- Fiction 3. Imagination -- Fiction 4. Humorous stories 5. Museums -- Fiction 6. Explorers -- Fiction 7. Family life -- Fiction 8. Eccentrics and eccentricities -- Fiction
ISBN 0062320947; 9780062320940

LC 2014045372

In this novel by Nicholas Gannon "Archer B. Helmsley wants an adventure. His grandparents were famous explorers . . . until they got stuck on an iceberg. Now Archer's mother barely lets him out of the house. As if that would stop a true Helmsley. Archer enlists Adelaide--the girl who, according to rumor, lost her leg to a crocodile--and Oliver--the boy next door--to help him rescue his grandparents." (Publisher's note)

"This whimsical coming-of-age story has a touch of mystery that will endear it to fans of Roald Dahl." SLJ

Gantos, Jack

★ **Dead** end in Norvelt; Jack Gantos. Farrar Straus Giroux 2011 341p. $15.99

Grades: 4 5 6 7   **Fic**

1. Old age -- Fiction 2. Pennsylvania -- Fiction

ISBN 978-0-374-37993-3; 0-374-37993-9

LC 2010054009

Newbery Medal (2012)

Scott O'Dell Historical Fiction Award (2012)

In the historic town of Norvelt, Pennsylvania, twelve-year-old Jack Gantos spends the summer of 1962 grounded for various offenses until he is assigned to help an elderly neighbor with a most unusual chore involving the newly dead, molten wax, twisted promises, Girl Scout cookies, underage driving, lessons from history, typewriting, and countless bloody noses.

This is a "wildly entertaining meld of truth and fiction. . . . Memorable in every way." Publ Wkly

★ **From** Norvelt to nowhere; Jack Gantos. Farrar, Straus and Giroux 2013 288 p. (hardback) $16.99

Grades: 4 5 6 7   **Fic**

1. Old age -- Fiction 2. Friendship -- Fiction 3. Humorous stories 4. Mystery and detective stories 5. Norvelt (Pa.) -- History -- 20th century -- Fiction

ISBN 0374379947; 9780374379940

LC 2013022251

Sequel to: Dead end in Norvelt

National Book Awards: Young People's Literature Long List (2013)

Author Jack Gantos' book "opens deep in the shadow of the Cuban missile crisis. But . . . other kinds of trouble are raining down on young Jack Gantos. . . . After an explosion, a new crime by an old murderer, and the sad passing of the town's founder, twelve-year-old Jack will soon find himself launched on a mission that takes him hundreds of miles away, escorting his slightly mental elderly mentor, Miss Volker, on her relentless pursuit of the oddest of outlaws." (Publisher's note)

★ **Heads** or tails; stories from the sixth grade. Farrar, Straus Giroux 1994 151p il $16; pa $4.95

Grades: 5 6 7 8   **Fic**

1. School stories 2. Diaries -- Fiction 3. Family life -- Fiction

ISBN 0-374-32909-5; 0-374-42923-5 pa

LC 93-43117

"Jack is trying to survive his sixth-grade year, and he narrates, through a series of short-stories-cum-chapters, his difficulties in dodging the obstacles life throws in his path. . . . The writing is zingy and specific, with snappily authentic dialogue and a vivid sense of juvenile experience. . . . Jack and his family have a recognizably thorny relationship. This is a distinctive and lively sequence of everyday-life stories." Bull Cent Child Books

Other titles about Jack are:

Jack adrift (2003)

Jack on the tracks (1999)

Jack's black book (1997)

Jack's new power (1995)

I am not Joey Pigza. Farrar, Straus and Giroux 2007 215p $16

Grades: 5 6 7 8   **Fic**

1. Fathers -- Fiction 2. Restaurants -- Fiction 3. Attention deficit disorder -- Fiction

ISBN 978-0-374-39941-2; 0-374-39941-7

LC 2006-38681

Joey's father returns, calling himself Charles Heinz and apologizing for his past bad behavior, and he swears that once Joey and his mother change their names and help him fix up the old diner he has bought, their lives will change for the better

"The plot doesn't move so much as careen from one over-the-top event to the next, the achievement being that every one of them feels entirely plausible." Publ Wkly

Jack Adrift; fourth grade without a clue. Farrar, Straus & Giroux 2003 197p $16.99; pa $7.99

Grades: 4 5 6 7   **Fic**

1. School stories 2. Family life -- Fiction

ISBN 0-374-39987-5; 0-374-43718-1 pa

LC 2002-192880

When his father rejoins the Navy and moves the family to Cape Hatteras, North Carolina, ten-year-old Jack becomes confused by a crush on his teacher, contradictory advice from his parents, and a very strange neighbor

"Gantos' wonderful writing . . . is witty, smart, and unafraid to tackle tough topics." Booklist

Jack on the tracks; four seasons of fifth grade. Farrar, Straus & Giroux 1999 182p il $16; pa $5.95

Grades: 5 6 7 8   **Fic**

1. School stories 2. Family life -- Fiction 3. Miami (Fla.) -- Fiction

ISBN 0-374-33665-2; 0-374-43717-3 pa

LC 99-27897

Moving with his unbearable sister to Miami, Florida, Jack tries to break some of his bad habits but finds himself irresistibly drawn to things disgusting, gross, and weird

"Jack is a likable and appealing fifth grader. His first-person preadolescent musings and worries are poignant, funny, and real." SLJ

Other titles in this series are:

Heads or tails (1994)

Jack's black book (1997)

Jack's new power (1995)

Jack's black book. Farrar, Straus & Giroux 1997 165p hardcover o.p. pa $7.99

Grades: 5 6 7 8   **Fic**

1. Authorship -- Fiction

ISBN 0-374-33662-8; 0-374-43716-5 pa

LC 96-5310

"Back in Florida, Jack decides that becoming a writer will allow him to turn his worst experiences, and he has many, into money. He flubs his IQ test, nearly flunks wood shop, almost gets a date with a beautiful girl, visits a fortune teller, digs up his dead dog not once but twice, and copes with members of an off-kilter family who constantly remind him of his stupidity. . . . The narrative sparkles with wit and, although exaggerated, rings with the authenticity of adolescent humor, embarrassment, and fascination with the absolutely gross." SLJ

Jack's new power; stories from a Caribbean year. Farrar, Straus & Giroux 1995 214p hardcover o.p. pa $8.99

Grades: 5 6 7 8   **Fic**

1. Barbados -- Fiction 2. Family life -- Fiction

ISBN 0-374-33657-1; 978-0-374-43715-2 pa

LC 94-4444

"Gantos achieves an intriguing balance of the bitter and the sweet in this account; young readers whose lives are similarly mixed will appreciate Jack's narrative." Bull Cent Child Books

Joey Pigza loses control. Farrar, Straus & Giroux 2000 195p $1

Grades: 5 6 7 8   **Fic**

1. Father-son relationship -- Fiction 2. Attention deficit disorder -- Fiction

ISBN 0-374-39989-1

LC 00-20098

A Newbery Medal honor book, 2001

Joey, who is still taking medication to keep him from getting too wired, goes to spend the summer with the hard-drinking father he has never known and tries to help the baseball team he coaches win the championship

"This high-voltage, honest novel mixes humor, pain, fear and courage with deceptive ease." Publ Wkly

★ **Joey** Pigza swallowed the key. Farrar, Straus & Giroux 1998 153p $16.99

Grades: 5 6 7 8   **Fic**

1. School stories 2. Schools -- Fiction 3. Single-parent families -- Fiction 4. Attention deficit disorder -- Fiction 5. Attention-deficit hyperactivity disorder -- Fiction

ISBN 0-374-33664-4

LC 98-24264

To the constant disappointment of his mother and his teachers, Joey has trouble paying attention or controlling his mood swings when his prescription meds wear off and he starts getting worked up and acting wired

This "frenetic narrative pulls at heartstrings and tickles funny bones." SLJ

Other titles about Joey Pigza are:

Joey Pigza loses control (2000)

What would Joey do? (2002)

I am not Joey Pigza (2007)

The key that swallowed Joey Pigza (2014)

★ The **key** that swallowed Joey Pigza; Jack Gantos. Fararr, Straus & Giroux 2014 160 p. (hardback) $16.99

Grades: 4 5 6 7   **Fic**

1. Boys -- Fiction 2. Family life -- Fiction 3. Babies -- Fiction 4. Brothers -- Fiction 5. Single-parent families -- Fiction 6. Attention-deficit hyperactivity disorder -- Fiction

ISBN 0374300836; 9780374300838

LC 2014023370

First edition

This book by Jack Gantos is "the fifth and final book in the groundbreaking Joey Pigza series. . . . With his dad MIA in the wake of appearance-altering plastic surgery, Joey must give up school to look after his new baby brother and fill in for his mom, who hospitalizes herself to deal with a bad case of postpartum blues." (Publisher's note)

"Joey's indomitable spirit, grounded in his fierce, tender devotion to baby Carter and expressed through Gantos' inimitable comic tone, shows the fragile adults around him just what it looks like to be the man of the house." Booklist

What would Joey do? Farrar, Straus & Giroux 2002 229p $16.99; pa $5.99

Grades: 5 6 7 8   **Fic**

1. Grandmothers -- Fiction 2. Attention deficit disorder -- Fiction

ISBN 0-374-39986-7; 0-06-054403-1 pa

LC 2002-22823

Joey tries to keep his life from degenerating into total chaos when his mother sends him to be home-schooled with a hostile blind girl, his divorced parents cannot stop fighting, and his grandmother is dying of emphysema

"The boy's first-person narration is as frenetically fun as it was in the first two books." SLJ

Gardiner, John Reynolds

Stone Fox; illustrated by Marcia Sewall. Crowell 1980 81p il $15.99; lib bdg $16.89; pa $5.50

Grades: 2 3 4 5   **Fic**

1. Dogs -- Fiction 2. Sled dog racing -- Fiction

ISBN 0-690-03983-2; 0-690-03984-0 lib bdg; 0-06-440132-4 pa

LC 79-7895

This story "is rooted in a Rocky Mountain legend, a locale faithfully represented in Sewall's wonderful drawings. . . . In Gardiner's bardic chronicle, the tension is teeth rattling, with the tale flying to a conclusion that is almost unbearably moving, one readers won't soon forget." Publ Wkly

Gardner, Lyn

★ **Into** the woods; pictures by Mini Grey. David Fickling Books 2007 427p il $16.99; lib bdg $19.99; pa $7.50

Grades: 4 5 6 7 8   **Fic**

1. Fantasy fiction 2. Sisters -- Fiction

ISBN 978-0-385-75115-5; 0-385-75115-X; 978-0-385-75116-2 lib bdg; 0-385-75116-8 lib bdg; 978-0-440-42223-5 pa; 0-440-42223-X pa

LC 2006-24350

Pursued by the sinister Dr. DeWilde and his ravenous wolves, three sisters—Storm, the inheritor of a special musical pipe, the elder Aurora, and the baby Any—flee into the woods and begin a journey filled with danger as they try to find a way to defeat their pursuer and keep him from taking the pipe and control of the entire land. "Grades five to eight." (Bull Cent Child Books)

"Gardner's fast-paced fantasy-adventure cleverly borrows from well-known fairy tales, and astute readers will enjoy identifying the many folkloric references. . . . Grey's appealing black-and-white illustrations add humor and detail to the story." Booklist

Followed by: Out of the woods (2010)

Out of the woods; pictures by Mini Grey. David Fickling Books 2010 348p il $17.99; lib bdg $20.99

Grades: 4 5 6 7 8   **Fic**

1. Fantasy fiction 2. Sisters -- Fiction

ISBN 978-0-385-75154-4; 0-385-75154-0; 978-0-385-75156-8 lib bdg; 0-385-75156-7 lib bdg

Sequel to: Into the woods (2007)

This is a sequel to Into the Woods (2007). The Eden sisters "are being lured into a wicked witch's lair. . . . Belladonna wants Aurora's heart and Storm's all-powerful musical pipe, and she will stop at nothing to get them." (Publisher's note) "Grades five to eight." (Bull Cent Child Books)

"Aurora, Storm, and Any Eden thought their troubles were over when Storm tossed the Pied Piper's powerful, seductive pipe . . . into the sea and defeated the pipe's erstwhile owner, the villainous Dr. DeWilde. . . . But it seems their troubles have only begun. . . . A missing prince, a cowardly lion, a marauding dragon, seven dwarfs, and even the Grimm brothers all make appearances, and while the fractured fairy-tale stew is considerably more haphazard than that of the sisters' first outing, it's a well-conceived and entertaining mash-up nonetheless." Horn Book

Gardner, Sally

Three Pickled Herrings 2; Sally Gardner; illustrated by David Roberts. Orion Paperbacks 2013 192 p. $12.99

Grades: 2 3 4 5   **Fic**

1. Theft -- Fiction 2. Detectives -- Fiction 3. School children -- Fiction

ISBN 080509914X; 1444003739; 9780805099140; 9781444003734

In this children's book by Sally Gardner, illustrated by David Roberts, "at the Wings & Co. Fairy Detective Agency, Emily Vole and her friends are beginning to worry. They haven't had a single case! Then local landowner Sir Walter Cross dies in sudden and mysterious circumstances. And soon the detectives hear more baffling news: Mr. Rollo the tailor has mysteriously lost everything, and Pan Smith's wedding plans have been ruined. Now Wings & Co. has not one, but three pickled herrings to solve!" (Publisher's note)

Garland, Sarah

Azzi in Between; by Sarah Garland. Frances Lincoln Children's Books 2013 40 p. $17.99

Grades: 1 2 3 4 **Fic**

1. Refugees -- Fiction 2. Immigrants -- Fiction
ISBN 1847802613; 9781847802613

In this book, illustrated by Sarah Garland, "Azzi and her parents . . . have to leave their home and escape to another country. . . In the new country they must learn to speak a new language, find a new home and Azzi must start a new school. . . . Azzi begins to learn English and understand that she is not the only one who has had to flee her home. . . . But Grandma has been left behind and Azzi misses her more than anything. Will Azzi ever see her grandma again?" (Publisher's note)

"[T]his sensitive tale of a young war refugee slowly adapting to a new life will strike chords of sympathy and recognition almost anywhere." Kirkus

Garlick, Nick

Aunt Severe and the dragons; illustrated by Nick Maland. Andersen 2010 120p il pa $7.99

Grades: 2 3 4 **Fic**

1. Aunts -- Fiction 2. Dragons -- Fiction
ISBN 978-1-8493-9055-2; 1-8493-9055-X

LC 2011290327

"Eight years old when his explorer parents disappear, Daniel goes to live with the relative he secretly names Aunt Severe. She packs away his books, feeds him cold spinach sandwiches, and forces him to help her collect rubbish from the gutters. Daniel's life brightens considerably when he befriends four young runaway dragons, who are hiding in his aunt's garden. . . . Garlick . . . infuses this appealing, eventful story with a childlike sense of imagination, humor, and justice. Well designed for readers new to chapter books, this attractive paperback features short chapters, a good-size type, and many engaging, crosshatched ink drawings." Booklist

Garretson, Dee

Wildfire run. Harper 2010 261p $16.99; pa $6.99

Grades: 5 6 7 8 **Fic**

1. Adventure fiction 2. Fires -- Fiction 3. Presidents -- Fiction 4. Earthquakes -- Fiction 5. Wilderness survival -- Fiction
ISBN 978-0-06-195347-7; 0-06-195347-4; 978-0-06-195350-7 pa; 0-06-195350-4 pa

LC 2009049482

A relaxing retreat to Camp David turns deadly after a faraway earthquake sets off a chain of disastrous events that traps the president's twelve-year-old son, Luke, and his two friends within the compound.

"Along with a breathlessly paced plot, Garretson crafts a preteen protagonist who grows out of being a whiny, moody sort and, with his companions, displays generous measures of courage and ingenuity in rising to the occasion." Booklist

Garza, Xavier

★ Lucha libre: the Man in the Silver Mask; a bilingual cuento. written & illustrated by Xavier Garza. Cinco Puntos Press 2005 un il $17.95

Grades: 2 3 4 5 **Fic**

1. Mexico -- Fiction 2. Uncles -- Fiction 3. Wrestling -- Fiction 4. Bilingual books -- English-Spanish
ISBN 0-938317-92-X

LC 2004-29756

When Carlitos attends a wrestling match in Mexico City with his father, his favorite masked-wrestler has eyes that are strangely familiar.

"Smoothly integrated information in fluid colloquial English and Spanish combines with grainy graphic-novel-style illustrations executed in acrylic to create an oddly compelling and sophisticated package. An informative endnote, in English only, presents a brief but engrossing history of lucha libre." SLJ

Maximilian and the mystery of the Guardian Angel; a bilingual lucha libre thriller. written and illustrated by Xavier Garza. 1st ed. Cinco Puntos Press 2011 207 p. ill. (paperback) $12.95

Grades: 3 4 5 6 **Fic**

1. Wrestling -- Fiction 2. Adventure fiction -- Fiction 3. Texas -- Fiction 4. Heroes -- Fiction 5. Uncles -- Fiction 6. Mexican Americans -- Fiction 7. Family life -- Texas -- Fiction 8. Spanish language materials -- Bilingual
ISBN 1933693983; 9781933693989

LC 2010037400

In this book, "eleven-year-old Max is fascinated with the world of Lucha Libre and the great wrestler known as the Guardian Angel. . . . Max lives in Texas, where it has become tremendously popular. Much to his great joy, he is given the opportunity to attend a match . . . where his hero will be challenging the ruthless Red Devil. In all the emotion of attending the event, Max falls into the ring and thus into the Guardian Angel's path," discovering a familial connection with him. (School Library Journal)

Other titles in this series are:
Maximillian and the Bingo Rematch (2011)
Maximillian and the Lucha Libre Club (2016)

Gassman, Julie

You can't spike your serves; illustrated by Jorge Santillan. Stone Arch Books 2011 49p il (Sports Illustrated kids) lib bdg $25.32; pa $5.95

Grades: 1 2 3 4 **Fic**

1. Volleyball -- Fiction
ISBN 978-1-4342-2231-2 lib bdg; 1-4342-2231-4 lib bdg; 978-1-4342-3080-5 pa; 1-4342-3080-5 pa

LC 2010048182

"Alicia wants to help her pen pal, Jenny, earn money to purchase new pom-poms, and when an Olympic volleyball player comes to school to teach the fourth graders her sport, Alicia comes up with the idea of a tournament to raise the needed funds. . . . She discovers how hard serving is without being able to jump, but Reese suggests the perfect technique for her. Manga-style graphics give this book a cutting-edge look and enhance understanding of the text. Short chapters, colorful cartoon illustrations, and engaging subject matter make this title appropriate for those new to chapter books as well as older readers." SLJ

Includes glossary and bibliographical references

Gates, Doris

Blue willow; illustrated by Paul Lantz. Viking 1940 172p il hardcover o.p. pa $5.99

Grades: 4 5 6 7 **Fic**

1. California -- Fiction 2. Migrant labor -- Fiction
ISBN 0-14-030924-1 pa

"Having to move from one migrant camp to another intensifies Janey Larkin's desire for a permanent home, friends, and school. The only beautiful possession the family has is a blue willow plate handed down from generation to generation. It is a reminder of happier days in Texas and represents dreams and promises for a better future. Reading about this itinerant family's ways of life, often filled with despair and yet always hopeful, leaves little room for the reader's indifference." Read Ladders for Hum Relat. 6th edition

Gauch, Patricia Lee

★ **This** time, Tempe Wick? illustrated by Margot Tomes. Boyds Mills Press 2003 43p il hardcover o.p. $16.95

Grades: 3 4 5   **Fic**

1. United States -- History -- 1775-1783, Revolution -- Fiction
ISBN 1-59078-179-1; 1-59078-185-6 pa

A reissue of the title first published 1974 by Coward, McCann & Geoghegan

Everyone knows Tempe Wick is a most surprising girl, but she exceeds even her own reputation when two mutinous Revolutionary soldiers try to steal her beloved horse.

"The writing is the perfect vehicle for the illustrations—in the artist's inimitable style—which capture the down-to-earth, unpretentious, and humorous quality of the storytelling." Horn Book

Gayton, Sam

Hercufleas; by Sam Gayton. Clarion Books 2016 272 p. (hardback) $16.99; (ebook) $16.99

Grades: 4 5 6 7   **Fic**

1. Fleas -- Fiction 2. Humorous fiction 3. Heroes and heroines -- Fiction
ISBN 9780544636200; 9780544635340

LC 2015034636

This novel by Sam Gayton is "a story about family, friendship and loss, and the power of hope and unity. . . . To protect her village from a giant, Greta recruits a champion: Hercufleas! He may be tiny, but this young flea is certain he's destined for greatness. Being a hero is harder than it seems, though, and Hercufleas and Greta face unexpected choices--and consequences--in their desperate attempts to save the village, and each other." (Publisher's note)

"Twists and turns, reversals, and chance meetings prove several times over that hope and determination are the most reliable weapons—and armor—no matter the size or situation of the hero." Kirkus

Gemeinhart, Dan

Some Kind of Courage; Dan Gemeinhart. Scholastic 2016 240 p. (hardcover) $16.99

Grades: 4 5 6 7   **Fic**

1. Theft -- Fiction 2. Courage -- Fiction 3. Western stories -- Fiction
ISBN 0545665779; 9780545665773

LC 2015047293

In this juvenile western novel, by Dan Gemeinhart, "Joseph Johnson has lost just about everyone he's ever loved. . . . And now, he's lost his pony-fast, fierce, beautiful Sarah. . . . Joseph can sure enough get her back, though. The odds are stacked against him, but he isn't about to give up. He will face down deadly animals, dangerous men, and the fury of nature itself on his quest to be reunited with the only family he has left." (Publisher's note)

"Gemeinhart's riveting tale of grit and grief is equally tragic and triumphant." SLJ

George, Jean Craighead

Charlie's raven; written and illustrated by Jean Craighead George. Dutton Children's Books 2004 190p il hardcover o.p. pa $6.99

Grades: 5 6 7 8   **Fic**

1. Ravens -- Fiction 2. Naturalists -- Fiction 3. Grandfathers -- Fiction
ISBN 0-525-47219-3; 0-14-240547-7 pa

Charlie's friend, Singing Bird, a Teton Sioux, tells him that ravens have curing powers, so Charlie steals a baby bird from its nest, hoping to heal his ailing Granddad, a retired naturalist.

"The story is technically accurate and offers a vivid sense of place and a window into Native American beliefs through storytelling." SLJ

★ **My** side of the mountain trilogy; written and illustrated by Jean Craighead George. Dutton Children's Books 2000 177, 170, 258p il $24.99

Grades: 5 6 7 8   **Fic**

1. Falcons -- Fiction 2. New York (State) -- Fiction 3. Wilderness survival -- Fiction
ISBN 0-525-46269-4

LC 00-712305

Originally published as three separate volumes, 1959, 1990, and 1999 respectively

My side of the mountain was a Newbery honor book, 1960

In My Side of the Mountain Sam Gribley tells of his year in the wilderness of the Catskill Mountains. In On the Far Side of the Mountain Sam's peaceful existence in his wilderness home is disrupted when his sister runs away and his pet falcon is confiscated by a conservation officer. In Frightful's Mountain Sam's pet falcon must learn to live as a wild bird

There's an owl in the shower; illustrated by Christine Herman Merrill. HarperCollins Pubs. 1995 133p il hardcover o.p. pa $5.99

Grades: 3 4 5   **Fic**

1. Owls -- Fiction 2. Endangered species -- Fiction
ISBN 0-06-024891-2; 0-06-440682-2 pa

LC 94-38893

Because protecting spotted owls has cost Borden's father his job as a logger in the old growth forest of northern California, Borden intends to kill any spotted owl he sees, until he and his father find themselves taking care of a young owlet

"George's writing skill and knowledge of animal behavior turn what could have been nothing but a message into an absorbing story that shows both sides of the controversy. . . . Merrill's drawings perfectly capture the engaging bird and the family's affection for it." SLJ

George, Jessica Day

Dragon flight; [by] Jessica Day George. 1st U.S. ed.; Bloomsbury Children's Books 2008 262p $16.95

Grades: 5 6 7 8   **Fic**

1. Fantasy fiction 2. Dragons -- Fiction
ISBN 978-1-59990-110-7; 1-59990-110-2

LC 2007050762

Sequel to: Dragon slippers (2007)

Young seamstress Creel finds herself strategizing with the dragon king Shardas once again when a renegade dragon in a distant country launches a war against their country, bringing an entire army of dragons into the mix.

"Fans of the first book will find the same strengths here: the imaginatively detailed scenes; the thrilling, spell-fueled action; the possibility of romance with a prince; and the appealing, brave heroine." Booklist

Dragon slippers. Bloomsbury Children's Books 2007 324p $16.95; pa $7.99

Grades: 5 6 7 8   **Fic**

1. Fantasy fiction 2. Dragons -- Fiction 3. Orphans -- Fiction
ISBN 978-1-59990-057-5; 1-59990-057-2; 978-1-59990-275-3 pa; 1-59990-275-3 pa

LC 2006-21142

Orphaned after a fever epidemic, Creel befriends a dragon and unknowingly inherits an object that can either save or destroy her kingdom.

"The plot is fast paced with all the right touches of romance and adventure. . . . The characters are wonderfully drawn." Voice Youth Advocates

Followed by: Dragon flight (2008)

Dragon spear; Jessica Day George. Bloomsbury 2009 248 p. $16.99

Grades: 5 6 7 8 **Fic**

1. Fantasy fiction 2. Dragons -- Fiction 3. Fantasy 4. Kings, queens, rulers, etc. -- Fiction

ISBN 1599903695; 9781599903699

LC 2008044414

Sequel to: Dragon flight

In this book, by Jessica Day George, "with peace established between the humans and the dragons, young couple Creel and Luka are planning their wedding. But then the dragon queen, Velika, is kidnapped by a band of rogue dragons in need of a ruler. When Creel and Luka rush to help, they discover that Luka's father has plans to take back the Far Islands from the dragons. Creel's happily ever after just might be postponed . . . again." (Publisher's note)

"As in the previous series titles, George creates richly satisfying fantasy realms, from opulent palaces to forest lairs, while the tender romances, genuine friendships, rapid dialogue, and thrilling adventures will continue to delight readers." Booklist

Tuesdays at the castle. Bloomsbury 2011 (Castle Glower) $16.99

Grades: 3 4 5 6 **Fic**

1. Fairy tales 2. Castles -- Fiction 3. Princesses -- Fiction 4. Kings and rulers -- Fiction

ISBN 978-1-59990-644-7; 1-59990-644-9

LC 2011016739

"Tuesdays at Castle Glower are Princess Celi's favorite days. That's because on Tuesdays the castle adds a new room, a turret, or sometimes even an entire wing. No one ever knows what the castle will do next, and no on--other than Celie, that is--takes the time to map out the new additions. But when King and Queen Glower are ambushed and their fate is unknown, it's up to Celie, with her secret knowledge of the castle's never-ending twists and turns, to protect their home and save their kingdom." (Publisher's note)

"Castle Glower is the true star of this charming story of court intrigue and magic. A satisfying mix of Hogwarts and Howl's Moving Castle, . . . Castle Glower helps its true citizens, but never at the expense of plot or character development." SLJ

Other titles in this series are:

Wednesdays in the tower (2013)

Thursdays with the crown (2014)

Fridays with the wizards (2016)

Saturdays at sea (2017)

Gephart, Donna

★ **How** to survive middle school. Delacorte Press 2010 247p $15.99; lib bdg $18.99

Grades: 5 6 7 8 **Fic**

1. School stories 2. Family life -- Fiction

ISBN 978-0-385-73793-7; 0-385-73793-9; 978-0-385-90701-9 lib bdg; 0-385-90701-X lib bdg

LC 2009-21809

When thirteen-year-old David Greenberg's best friend makes the start of middle school even worse than he feared it could be, David becomes friends with Penny, who shares his love of television shows and posts one of their skits on YouTube, making them wildly popular—online, at least.

"Gephart crafts for her likable protagonist an engaging, feel-good transition into adolescence that's well stocked with tears and laughter." Booklist

Olivia Bean, trivia queen; Donna Gephart. Delacorte Press 2012 278 p. $16.99

Grades: 3 4 5 6 7 **Fic**

1. Game shows -- Fiction 2. Children of divorced parents -- Fiction 3. Father-daughter relationship -- Fiction 4. Divorce -- Fiction 5. Fathers -- Fiction 6. Curiosities and wonders -- Fiction 7. Jeopardy (Television program) -- Fiction

ISBN 0385740522; 9780385740524

LC 2011006023

In this book, "Olivia Bean has watched 'Jeopardy!' every evening since she was a little girl, but the nightly tradition just hasn't been the same since her father . . . took off for California two years ago. When the show announces auditions for Kids Week, Olivia is intent on making the cut, not only to compete but, more importantly, to get a plane ticket out to the show's taping in L.A. with the hopes of meeting up with her estranged dad." (Bulletin of the Center for Children's Books).

Gewirtz, Adina Rishe

Zebra forest; Adina Rishe Gewirtz. Candlewick Press 2013 208 p. (reinforced) $15.99

Grades: 5 6 7 8 **Fic**

1. Hostages -- Fiction 2. Siblings -- Fiction

ISBN 0763660418; 9780763660413

LC 2012947251

In this novel, by Adina Rishe Gewirtz, "an escaped fugitive upends everything two siblings think they know about their family, their past, and themselves. . . . A rattling at the back door, an escapee from the prison holding them hostage in their own home, four lives that will never be the same. . . . [The book] portrays an unfolding standoff of truth against family secrets." (Publisher's note)

"Debut author Gewirtz successfully conveys the terror and tedium of being trapped. . . While the situation may frighten some readers, the matter-of-fact way [the protagonists] make the best of difficult circumstances . . . may be comforting to those whose families don't match the ideal. An emotionally honest family story with an ending that's hopeful without being implausibly upbeat." Pub Wkly

Gibbs, Stuart

Belly up. Simon & Schuster Books for Young Readers 2010 294p $15.99; pa $6.99

Grades: 4 5 6 7 **Fic**

1. Mystery fiction 2. Zoos -- Fiction 3. Hippopotamus -- Fiction

ISBN 1-4169-8731-2; 1-4169-8732-0 pa; 978-1-4169-8731-4; 978-1-4169-8732-1 pa

LC 2009-34860

Twelve-year-old Teddy investigates when a popular Texas zoo's star attraction, Henry the hippopotamus, is murdered.

"The characters are well-developed and believable, making this book appealing to reluctant readers and those who enjoy animal stories and mysteries." Libr Media Connect

Big game; Stuart Gibbs. Simon & Schuster Books for Young Readers 2015 342 p. (hardcover) $16.99

Grades: 4 5 6 7 **Fic**

1. Mystery fiction 2. Zoos -- Fiction 3. Poaching -- Fiction 4. Rhinoceros -- Fiction 5. Endangered species -- Fiction 6. Zoo animals -- Fiction 7. Rhinoceroses -- Fiction 8. Mystery and detective stories

ISBN 1481423339; 9781481423335; 9781481423342

LC 2014042145

Sequel to: Poached

In this book, by Stuart Gibbs, "When someone takes aim at Rhonda Rhino, FunJungle's pregnant (and endangered) Asian greater one-horned rhinoceros, the zoo steps up security measures in order to protect this rare animal and her baby. But the extra security isn't enough—someone is still getting too close for comfort. Teddy and company start to suspect that whoever is after Rhonda is really after her horn, which is worth a lot of money on the black market." (Publisher's note)

"Monkey business included, this adventure strikes a neat balance between shenanigans and gravitas to inspire young conservationists." Kirkus

The last musketeer. Harper 2011 244p $16.99

Grades: 5 6 7 8   **Fic**

1. Cardinals 2. Statesmen 3. Adventure fiction 4. Time travel -- Fiction 5. France -- History -- 1589-1789, Bourbons -- Fiction

ISBN 978-0-06-204838-7; 0-06-204838-4

LC 2011019376

In Paris with his parents to sell family heirlooms, fourteen-year-old Greg Rich suddenly finds himself four hundred years in the past, and is aided by boys who will one day be known as 'The Three Musketeers.'

"From the gripping first sentence . . . the excitement never flags in this newly imagined Musketeer adventure. . . . Using Alexandre Dumas' stories as a jumping-off point, Gibbs mixes fact, fantasy and thrills to create a galloping swashbuckler." Kirkus

Panda-monium; Stuart Gibbs. Simon & Schuster Books for Young Readers 2017 352 p. (FunJungle) (hardcover) $16.99

Grades: 4 5 6 7   **Fic**

1. Zoos -- Fiction 2. Pandas -- Fiction 3. Mystery fiction 4. Mystery and detective stories

ISBN 9781481445672; 9781481445689

LC 2016002113

Sequel to: Big game

In this book in the FunJungle series, by Stuart Gibbs, "FunJungle is frenzied, awaiting the arrival of its most thrilling animal yet--Li Ping--a rare and very expensive giant panda that the zoo went to enormous lengths to secure. But when the truck transporting Li Ping shows up, its precious cargo has vanished into thin air. The FBI steps in to investigate, and Teddy is happy to leave the job in their (supposedly) capable hands." (Publisher's note)

Poached; Stuart Gibbs. Simon & Schuster Books for Young Readers 2014 329 pages (hardcover) $15.99

Grades: 4 5 6 7   **Fic**

1. Mystery fiction 2. Zoos -- Fiction 3. Koalas -- Fiction 4. Bullies -- Fiction 5. Texas -- Fiction 6. Zoo animals -- Fiction 7. Mystery and detective stories 8. Family life -- Texas -- Fiction

ISBN 1442467770; 9781442467774

LC 2013000539

In this sequel to "Belly Up," by Stuart Gibbs, "12-year-old trouble-magnet Teddy is still living at FunJungle, a massive zoo and amusement park, with his primatologist mother and wildlife photographer father. . . . When the school bully, Vance, forces Teddy to throw a fake arm into the shark tank . . . [it] has a large-scale snowball effect that positions Teddy as the key suspect in the theft of Kazoo, a koala on loan from Australia." (Kirkus Reviews)

"Gibbs weaves interesting trivia (newborn koalas are jellybean-size) and plenty of humor (a poop-throwing chimp helps ID an industrial spy/saboteur) into his action-packed mystery." Horn Book

Space case; Stuart Gibbs. First edition Simon & Schuster Books for Young Readers 2014 352 p. (hardcover) $16.99

Grades: 4 5 6 7   **Fic**

1. Mystery fiction 2. Space colonies -- Fiction 3. Moon -- Fiction 4. Science fiction 5. Mystery and detective stories 6. Human-alien encounters -- Fiction

ISBN 1442494867; 9781442494862; 9781442494879

LC 2013033587

"Like his fellow lunarnauts--otherwise known as Moonies--living on Moon Base Alpha, twelve-year-old Dashiell Gibson is famous the world over for being one of the first humans to live on the moon. . . . Then Moon Base Alpha's top scientist turns up dead. Dash senses there's foul play afoot, but no one believes him." (Publisher's note)

"Closed quarters and techno–mumbo-jumbo add delightful color to the proceedings. Thankfully, the author doesn't let the high-concept setting overshadow the novel's mystery. The whodunit is smartly paced and intricately plotted." Kirkus

Another title in this series is:

Spaced out (2016)

Spy camp; Stuart Gibbs. 1st ed. Simon & Schuster Books for Young Readers 2013 336 p. (hardcover) $17.99

Grades: 4 5 6 7   **Fic**

1. Spies -- Fiction 2. Camping -- Fiction 3. Camps -- Fiction 4. Survival -- Fiction

ISBN 1442457538; 9781442457539

LC 2012019416

Sequel to: Spy school

In this story by Stuart Gibbs, "Ben Ripley is a middle-schooler . . . [who] spent the last year training to be a top-level spy and dodging all sorts of associated danger. So now that summer's finally here, Ben's ready to have some fun and relax. Except . . . a spy-in-training's work is never done, and the threats from SPYDER, an enemy spy organization, are as unavoidable as the summer heat. Will Ben be able to keep his cover--and his cool?" (Publisher's note)

"After escaping assassination by the top-secret organization SPYDER, Ben Ripley (Spy School) is looking forward to chilling out this summer. But SPYDER is turning up the heat, insisting that Ben come to work for them. Gorgeous fellow-spy-in-training Erica is ready to help, and her legendary grandfather also appears on the scene. Clever descriptions and plot twists make this a top-notch summer read." Horn Book

Spy ski school; Stuart Gibbs. Simon & Schuster Books for Young Readers 2016 368 p. (A Spy school novel) (hardcover) $16.99; (ebook) $15.99

Grades: 4 5 6 7   **Fic**

1. Spies -- Fiction 2. Skiing -- Fiction 3. Schools -- Fiction 4. Friendship -- Fiction

ISBN 1481445626; 9781481445627; 9781481445634; 9781481445658

LC 2015037993

In this middle grade novel in the Spy School series by Stuart Gibbs, "Ben Ripley is not exactly the best student spy school has ever seen--he keeps flunking Advanced Self Preservation. But outside of class, Ben is pretty great at staying alive. . . . After all . . . [his] unexpected success, the CIA has decided to activate Ben for real. The Mission: Become friends with Jessica Shang, the daughter of a suspected Chinese crime boss, and find out all of her father's secrets." (Publisher's note)

"Readers will be glad they strapped on their boots and went along for the ride." Kirkus

Giblin, James

The boy who saved Cleveland; based on a true story. [by] James Cross Giblin; illustrated by Michael Dooling. Henry Holt and Company 2006 64p il $15.95

Grades: 3 4 5   **Fic**
1. Ohio -- Fiction 2. Malaria -- Fiction 3. Epidemics -- Fiction 4.
Frontier and pioneer life -- Fiction
ISBN 0-8050-7355-8; 978-0-8050-7355-3

LC 2005021695

During a malaria epidemic in late eighteenth-century Cleveland,
Ohio, ten-year-old Seth Doan surprises his family, his neighbors,
and himself by having the strength to carry and grind enough corn to
feed everyone.

"Young readers will enjoy the clear writing and plot-driven pace.
Dooling's full-page pencil-on-paper illustrations convey the time period
as well as the emotional tone. A solid choice for those seeking pioneer
fiction and strong characters." Booklist

Gibson, Julia Mary

Copper magic; Julia Mary Gibson. Starscape 2014 336 p. map
(hardback) $16.99
Grades: 4 5 6 7 8   **Fic**
1. Magic -- Fiction 2. Historical fiction 3. Great Lakes region
-- Fiction 4. Talismans -- Fiction 5. Teenage girls -- Fiction 6.
United States -- History -- 20th century -- Fiction
ISBN 0765332116; 9780765332110

LC 2014014660

"The year is 1906, and on the shores of Lake Michigan twelve-year-
old Violet Blake unearths an ancient talisman--a copper hand. Violet's
touch warms the copper hand and it begins to reveal glimpses of another
time." (Publisher's note)

"The summer of 1906 promises to be an exciting one for twelve-
year-old Violet Blake: she gets her first job as an assistant for a visiting
photographer; she meets a new friend; and best of all, she discovers an
ancient copper talisman in the shape of a hand buried near the creek
where her mother used to harvest medicinal herbs. . . . The presence of
magic is subtle in the story, but in the end, it matters little whether the
copper hand has magical power or not. Instead it is Violet's growth from
a self-centered child to one who carefully considers the feelings and
needs of those around her that give this story weight." VOYA

Gidwitz, Adam

The **Grimm** conclusion; by Adam Gidwitz and illustrated by Hugh
D'Andrade. Dutton Children's Books 2013 368 p. (hardcover) $16.99
Grades: 4 5 6   **Fic**
1. Fairy tales 2. Horror fiction 3. Humorous stories 4. Brothers
and sisters -- Fiction 5. Characters in literature -- Fiction 6.
Adventure and adventurers -- Fiction
ISBN 0525426159; 9780525426158

LC 2013021686

In this book by Adam Gidwitz and illustrated by Hugh D'Andrade,
"two children venture through forests, flee kingdoms, face ogres and
demons and monsters, and, ultimately, find their way home. Oh yes, and
they may die. Just once or twice." (Publisher's note) "An omniscient
narrator comments throughout, offering warnings, consolation, and explanations." (Horn Book Magazine)

In a glass Grimmly; Adam Gidwitz. Dutton Juvenile 2012 314 p.
(hardback) $16.99
Grades: 4 5 6 7 8   **Fic**
1. Horror fiction 2. Paranormal fiction 3. Fractured fairy tales 4.
Fairy tales 5. Frogs -- Fiction 6. Humorous stories 7. Cousins
-- Fiction 8. Characters in literature -- Fiction 9. Adventure and
adventurers -- Fiction
ISBN 0525425810; 9780525425816

LC 2012015515

This book is Adam Gidwitz's second collection of reimagined fairy
tales. "The protagonists in this installment are Jack, Jill, and a talking

frog, whose adventures begin separately in reworkings of 'The Frog
Prince' and 'The Emperor's New Clothes,' before the three join forces in
'Jack and the Bean-stalk.'" (Publishers Weekly)

★ The **Inquisitor's** Tale; Or, The Three Magical Children and
Their Holy Dog. Adam Gidwitz, illustrated by Hatem Aly. Penguin
Group USA 2016 384 p. illustrations $17.99
Grades: 5 6 7 8 9   **Fic**
1. France -- Fiction 2. Fairy tales -- Fiction 3. Adventure fiction
-- Fiction
ISBN 9781101612606; 0525426167; 9780525426165

LC 2016024174

Newbery Honor Book (2017)

In this book, by Adam Gidwitz, illustrated by Hatem Aly, it is "1242.
On a dark night, travelers from across France cross paths at an inn and
begin to tell stories of three children. Their adventures take them on a
chase through France: they are taken captive by knights, sit alongside
a king, and save the land from a farting dragon. On the run to escape
prejudice and persecution and save precious and holy texts from being
burned." (Publisher's note)

"A masterpiece of storytelling that is addictive and engrossing."
Kirkus

Includes bibliographical references (pages 355-363).

★ A **tale** dark & Grimm. Dutton 2010 256p il $16.99
Grades: 5 6 7 8   **Fic**
1. Fairy tales 2. Siblings -- Fiction
ISBN 978-0-525-42334-8; 0-525-42334-6; 9780525425816

LC 2009-53289

This book follows Hansel and Gretel as they walk out of their own
story and into eight more tales. "Age ten and up." (N Y Times Book Rev)

"An audacious debut that's wicked smart and wicked funny."
Publ Wkly

Giff, Patricia Reilly

Eleven. Wendy Lamb Books 2008 164p $15.99; lib bdg $18.99;
pa $6.50
Grades: 4 5 6 7   **Fic**
1. Woodwork -- Fiction 2. Friendship -- Fiction 3. Kidnapping
-- Fiction 4. Learning disabilities -- Fiction
ISBN 978-0-385-73069-3; 978-0-385-90098-0 lib bdg; 978-0-
440-23802-7 pa

LC 2007-12638

When Sam, who can barely read, discovers an old newspaper clipping just before his eleventh birthday, it brings forth memories from
his past, and, with the help of a new friend at school and the castle they
are building for a school project, his questions are eventually answered.

This is an "exquisitely rendered story of self-discovery." Publ Wkly

Flying feet; illustrated by Alasdair Bright. Wendy Lamb Books
2011 71p il (Zigzag kids) $11.99; lib bdg $14.99; pa $4.99
Grades: 2 3 4   **Fic**
1. School stories 2. Inventors -- Fiction
ISBN 978-0-385-73887-3; 0-385-73887-0; 978-0-385-90754-5
lib bdg; 0-385-90754-0 lib bdg; 978-0-375-89637-8 e-book;
978-0-375-85911-3 pa; 0-375-85911-X pa

LC 2010022645

Charlie often thinks of inventions that seldom work, but his latest
idea just might be able to help Jake the Sweeper get rid of a big pile of
trash and save "Come as a Character" day, too.

"The cheerful drawings offer levity to the spare, straightforward
prose laid out in one- or two-sentence paragraphs. The tension builds
mildly, exploring the concept of individuality and the expanding pres-

sures of growing up, demonstrating Giff's keen understanding of chapter-book readers." Kirkus

Lily's crossing. Delacorte Press 1997 180p $15.95; pa $6.50; $15.95

Grades: 4 5 6 7   **Fic**

1. Friendship -- Fiction 2. World War, 1939-1945 -- Fiction

ISBN 0-385-32142-2; 0-440-41453-9 pa; 9780385321426

      LC 96-23021

A Newbery Medal honor book, 1998

"Set during World War II, this . . . story tells of the war's impact on two children, one an American and one a Hungarian refugee. Lily Mollahan, a spirited, sensitive youngster being raised by her grandmother and Poppy, her widower father, has a comfortable routine that includes the family's annual summer migration to Gram's beach house in Rockaway, NY. Lily looks forward to summer's freedom and fishing outings with Poppy. She meets Albert, a Hungarian boy who is staying at a neighbor's house. . . . Eventually the two become good friends. The war interferes directly with Lily's life when Poppy, an engineer, is sent to Europe to help with clean-up operations." (SLJ) "Grades five to eight." (Booklist)

"Gentle elements of danger and suspense . . . keep the plot moving forward, while the delicate balance of characters and setting gently coalesces into an emotional whole that is fully satisfying." Bull Cent Child Books

Maggie's door. Wendy Lamb Bks. 2003 158p pa $6.50

Grades: 5 6 7 8   **Fic**

1. Ireland -- Fiction 2. Immigrants -- Fiction

ISBN 0-385-32658-0; 0-385-90095-3 lib bdg; 0-440-41581-0 pa

      LC 2003-2415

Sequel to: Nory Ryan's song (2000)

In the mid-1800s, Nory and her neighbor and friend, Sean, set out separately on a dangerous journey from famine-plagued Ireland, hoping to reach a better life in America

"Giff uses vivid language and precisely detailed observation to convey both experience and emotion." Horn Book

Nory Ryan's song. Delacorte Press 2000 148p hardcover o.p. pa $5.99

Grades: 5 6 7 8   **Fic**

1. Famines -- Fiction 2. Ireland -- Fiction

ISBN 0-385-32141-4; 0-440-41829-1 pa

      LC 00-27690

When a terrible blight attacks Ireland's potato crop in 1845, twelve-year-old Nory Ryan's courage and ingenuity help her family and neighbors survive

"Giff brings the landscape and the cultural particulars of the era vividly to life and creates in Nory a heroine to cheer for. A beautiful, heart-wrenching novel that makes a devastating event understandable." Booklist

Another title about Nory is:

Maggie's door (2003)

Pictures of Hollis Woods. Wendy Lamb Bks. 2002 166p $15.95; pa $6.50

Grades: 5 6 7 8   **Fic**

1. Artists -- Fiction 2. Old age -- Fiction 3. Foster home care -- Fiction

ISBN 0-385-32655-6; 0-440-41578-0 pa

      LC 2002-426

A Newbery Medal honor book, 2003

"She was named for the place where she was found as an abandoned baby. Twelve-year-old Hollis Woods has been through many foster homes—and she runs away, every time. In her latest placement, with an artist named Josie, the tightly wound Hollis begins to relax ever so slightly. . . . But Josie is slowly slipping into dementia, and Hollis knows that she'll be taken away from her if Josie is found out. . . . Giff has a sure hand with language, and the narrative is taut and absorbing." Booklist

Storyteller. Wendy Lamb Books 2010 166p $15.99; lib bdg $18.99

Grades: 5 6 7 8   **Fic**

1. Aunts -- Fiction 2. Family life -- Fiction 3. New York (State) -- Fiction 4. Father-daughter relationship -- Fiction 5. United States -- History -- 1775-1783, Revolution -- Fiction

ISBN 978-0-375-83888-0; 0-375-83888-0; 978-0-375-93888-7 lib bdg; 0-375-93888-5 lib bdg

      LC 2009-48130

Forced to spend months at an aunt's house, Elizabeth feel a connection to her ancestor Zee, whose picture hangs on the wall, and who reveals her story of hardships during the Revolutionary War as Elizabeth comes to terms with her own troubles

"As she brings these characters and history alive, Giff again demostrates her own gift for storytelling." Publ Wkly

Water Street. Wendy Lamb Books 2006 164p $15.95; lib bdg $17.99; pa $6.50

Grades: 5 6 7 8   **Fic**

1. Family life -- Fiction 2. Irish Americans -- Fiction 3. Brooklyn (New York, N.Y.) -- Fiction

ISBN 978-0-385-90097-3; 0-385-73068-3; 978-0-385-90097-3 lib bdg; 0-385-90097-X lib bdg; 978-0-440-41921-1 pa; 0-440-41921-2 pa

      LC 2006-02024

In the shadow of the construction of the Brooklyn Bridge, eighth-graders and new neighbors Bird Mallon and Thomas Neary make some decisions about what they want to do with their lives.

"Continuing the Irish American immigration story begun in Nory Ryan's Song (2000) and Maggie's Door (2003), [this] novel, set in 1875, is about the next generation. . . . A poignant immigration story of friendship, work, and the meaning of home." Booklist

Giff, Patricia Reilly, 1935-

R my name is Rachel. Wendy Lamb Books 2011 166p $15.99; lib bdg $18.99; e-book $10.99

Grades: 4 5 6 7   **Fic**

1. Moving -- Fiction 2. Siblings -- Fiction 3. Farm life -- Fiction 4. Great Depression, 1929-1939 -- Fiction

ISBN 978-0-375-83889-7; 0-375-83889-9; 978-0-375-93889-4 lib bdg; 0-375-93889-3; 978-0-375-98389-4 e-book

      LC 2011004303

Three city siblings, now living on a farm during the Great Depression, must survive on their own when their father takes a construction job miles away.

"Rachel's searing, present-tense narrative exposes her fears, determination, and hopefulness in the face of wrenching challenges. Recurring motifs—color, flowers, and drawings by a neighbor that Rachel discovers in unlikely places—add lyricism to this story of family solidarity." Publ Wkly

Winter sky; by Patricia Reilly Giff. Wendy Lamb Books, an imprint of Random House Children's Books 2014 160 p. illustrations (hardback) $15.99

Grades: 4 5 6 7   **Fic**

1. Courage -- Fiction 2. Friendship -- Fiction 3. Family life --

Fiction 4. Fire fighters -- Fiction

ISBN 0375838929; 9780375838927; 9780385371926

LC 2013022399

In this book, by Patricia Reilly Giff, "Siria's dad is a firefighter who doesn't know that someone special watches out for him; each time his daughter hears a siren, she sneaks out of her apartment building to chase his fire truck and make sure he is safe. During one such nightly pursuit, Siria discovers evidence of what she believes to be arson. Who could be purposely setting fires? When clues point to someone close to home, Siria must find the strength to unravel the mystery." (School Library Journal)

"Worried about her firefighter father's safety, every time a siren wails eleven-year-old Siria sneaks out and chases the truck, watching to make sure he escapes harm. Over Christmas break, Siria notices small fires being set all over town and decides to investigate on her own. Unadorned but engaging prose and Giff's well-drawn characters add depth to a simple story about courage and friendship." Horn Book

Giles, Stephen M.

The **body** thief. Sourcebooks Jabberwocky 2010 221p il (The death (and further adventures) of Silas Winterbottom) $12.99

Grades: 3 4 5 6   **Fic**

1. Mystery fiction 2. Uncles -- Fiction 3. Cousins -- Fiction 4. Australia -- Fiction 5. Immortality -- Fiction 6. Inheritance and succession -- Fiction

ISBN 978-1-4022-4090-4; 1-4022-4090-2

LC 2010-14380

First published 2009 in Australia

Lured to their sick Uncle Silas's home under the pretense of becoming heirs to his vast fortune, cousins Adele, Isabella, and Milo soon learn that the old man has a diabolical plan to prevent his own death.

"Giles delivers even the macabre twists of the tale with a light touch, giving readers plenty of incentive to stick with the series." Publ Wkly

Gilman, Laura Anne

Grail quest: the Camelot spell; book one. HarperCollins 2006 291p $10.99; lib bdg $14.89

Grades: 5 6 7 8   **Fic**

1. Kings 2. Magic -- Fiction 3. Middle Ages -- Fiction 4. Knights and knighthood -- Fiction

ISBN 0-06-077279-4; 0-06-077280-8 lib bdg

Three teenagers living in Camelot are forced to undertake a dangerous mission when King Arthur's court falls under a mysterious enchantment on the eve of the quest for the Holy Grail.

"The believable dialogue, succinct plot, and uncomplicated references to court life will appeal to middle graders who are beginning to explore Aurthurian legend." Voice Youth Advocates

Other titles in this series are:

Grail quest: Morgain's revenge (2006)

Grail quest: The shadow companion (2006)

Gilson, Jamie

Bug in a rug; illustrated by Diane deGroat. Clarion Books 1998 69p il hardcover o.p. $15

Grades: 2 3 4   **Fic**

1. School stories 2. Uncles -- Fiction 3. Clothing and dress -- Fiction

ISBN 0-395-86616-2; 0-618-31670-1

LC 97-16437

Seven-year-old Richard is self-conscious when he receives a pair of purple pants from his aunt and uncle and has to wear them to school, but he is even more worried when his uncle shows up for a visit to his classroom

"Gilson captures the thoughts and fears of second graders through authentic dialogue and solid characterization." SLJ

Other titles about Richard are:

Chess! I love it, I love it, I love it! (2008)

Gotcha! (2006)

It goes Eeeeeeeeeeeee! (1994)

Itchy Richard (1991)

Chess! I love it, I love it, I love it! illustrated by Amy Wummer. Clarion Books 2008 82p il $15

Grades: 2 3 4   **Fic**

1. School stories 2. Chess -- Fiction

ISBN 978-0-6189-7790-1; 0-6189-7790-2

When second-grader Richard and three other members of the Sumac School Chess Club compete in their first tournament, they each learn something about luck, concentration, and teamwork.

"Gilson shows a sound knowlege of grade-school psychology in this entertaining chapter book." Booklist

Gino, Alex

★ **George**; Alex Gino. Scholastic Press 2015 240 p. (jacketed hardcover) $16.99

Grades: 4 5 6 7   **Fic**

1. School stories 2. Identity (Psychology) 3. Gender role -- Fiction 4. Transgender people -- Fiction

ISBN 0545812542; 9780545812542

LC 2014957885

Lambda Literary Awards: LGBT Children's/Young Adult (2016)

Stonewall Book Award, Children's (2016)

In this novel by Alex Gino, "when people look at George, they think they see a boy. But she knows she's not a boy. She knows she's a girl. Then her teacher announces that their class play is going to be Charlotte's Web. George really, really, REALLY wants to play Charlotte. But the teacher says she can't even try out for the part. With the help of her best friend, Kelly, George comes up with a plan. Not just so she can be Charlotte -- but so everyone can know who she is, once and for all." (Publisher's note)

"George, a fourth-grader who knows she is a girl, despite appearances, begins to tell her secret. The word 'transgender' is used midway through, but far more work is done by the simple choice to tell George's story using third-person narration and the pronouns 'she' and 'her'. . . A coda to the Charlotte's Web story, in which George presents herself as a girl for the first time, is deeply moving in its simplicity and joy. Warm, funny, and inspiring." Kirkus

Gipson, Frederick Benjamin

Old Yeller; [by] Fred Gipson; drawings by Carl Burger. Harper & Row 1956 158p il $23; pa $5.99

Grades: 6 7 8 9   **Fic**

1. Dogs -- Fiction 2. Texas -- Fiction 3. Frontier and pioneer life -- Fiction

ISBN 0-06-011545-9; 0-06-440382-3 pa

LC 56-8780

A Newbery Medal honor book, 1957

"Travis at fourteen was the man of the family during the hard summer of 1860 when his father drove his herd of cattle from Texas to the Kansas market. It was the summer when an old yellow dog attached himself to the family and won Travis' reluctant friendship. Before the summer was over, Old Yeller proved more than a match for thieving raccoons, fighting bulls, grizzly bears, and mad wolves. This is a skillful tale of a boy's love for a dog as well as a description of a pioneer boyhood and it can't miss with any dog lover." Horn Book

Glaser, Linda

Bridge to America; based on a true story. Houghton Mifflin Co. 2005 200p $16

Grades: 4 5 6 **Fic**

1. Jews -- Fiction 2. Immigrants -- Fiction

ISBN 0-618-56301-6

Eight-year-old Fivel narrates the story of his family's Atlantic Ocean crossing to reunite with their father in the United States, from its desperate beginning in a shtetl in Poland in 1920 to his stirrings of identity as an American boy.

"Even reluctant readers will enjoy this riveting account and sensitive portrayal of what it means to be an immigrant." SLJ

Glatstein, Jacob

Emil and Karl; by Yankev Glatshteyn; translated by Jeffrey Shandler. Roaring Brook Press 2006 194p $17.95; pa $6.99

Grades: 5 6 7 8 **Fic**

1. Jews -- Fiction 2. Friendship -- Fiction 3. Vienna (Austria) -- Fiction 4. Holocaust, 1933-1945 -- Fiction

ISBN 1-59643-119-9; 0-312-37387-2 pa

LC 2005-26800

Original Yiddish edition 1940

A story about the dilemma faced by two young boys—one Jewish, the other not—when they suddenly find themselves without homes or families in Vienna on the eve of World War II.

"The fast-moving prose is stark and immediate. Glatshteyn was, of course, writing about what was happening to children in his time. . . . The translation, 65 years after the novel's original publication, is nothing short of haunting." Booklist

Glatt, Lisa

Abigail Iris: the one and only. Walker & Co. 2009 148p $14.99

Grades: 2 3 4 **Fic**

1. Siblings -- Fiction 2. Friendship -- Fiction 3. Family life -- Fiction

ISBN 978-0-8027-9782-7; 0-8027-9782-2

LC 2008007391

Abigail Iris thinks she would rather be an only child but after going on vacation with her best friend, who is an "Only," she realizes there are benefits of being one of many.

"Told in the first person from Abigail Iris' point of view, this chapter book comes to life through her ingenuous voice and reflections. Appealing black-and-white drawings show the characters' personalities, attitudes, and emotions." Booklist

Another title about Abigail Iris is:

Abigail Iris: the pet project (2010)

Abigail Iris: the pet project; [by] Lisa Glatt and Suzanne Greenberg; illustrated by Joy Allen. Walker 2010 164p il $14.99; pa $6.99

Grades: 2 3 4 **Fic**

1. Cats -- Fiction 2. Family life -- Fiction

ISBN 978-0-8027-8657-9; 0-8027-8657-X; 978-0-8027-2235-5 pa; 0-8027-2235-0 pa

When Abigail Iris finally gets the new kitten she has been wanting, she learns about the responsibilities that come with pet ownership, as well as the impact a kitten can have on a large family like hers.

"Fast-paced conversation, coupled with realistic events, creates a fun read while full-page black-and-white illustrations add interest." SLJ

Gliori, Debi

Witch Baby and me. Corgi 2010 246p il pa $7.99

Grades: 4 5 6 **Fic**

1. Magic -- Fiction 2. Infants -- Fiction 3. Sisters -- Fiction 4.

Witches -- Fiction 5. Scotland -- Fiction

ISBN 978-0-552-55676-7; 0-552-55676-9

"Three witches from Ben Screeeiiighe, a wildly remote area of Scotland, are searching for a baby. Their plan, at first, is to cast a spell on an infant, allow the human parents to raise her, then take over her witchy education when she becomes older. . . . But the witches do not foresee that Baby Daisy MacRae's sister [Lily] . . . can see their magic, and knows that her sister is a witch even if no one believes her. . . . Readers will laugh at Lily's imagination and her attempts to keep people from finding out that her sister is really a spell-casting witch-in-training. Entertaining line drawings complement the [text]." SLJ

Other titles in this series are:

Witch Baby and me after dark (2010)

Witch Baby and me at school (2009)

Witch Baby and me on stage (2011)

Witch Baby and me after dark. IPG 2010 291p il pa $7.99

Grades: 4 5 6 **Fic**

1. Sisters -- Fiction 2. Witches -- Fiction

ISBN 978-0-552-55678-1; 0-552-55678-5

Nine-year-old Lily has her hands full trying to protect baby sister Daisy from being exposed as a witch.

"Readers will laugh at Lily's imagination and her attempts to keep people from finding out that her sister is really a spell-casting witch-in-training. Entertaining line drawings complement the [text]." SLJ

Witch Baby and me on stage. Corgi 2011 il pa $7.99

Grades: 4 5 6 **Fic**

1. Magic -- Fiction 2. Sisters -- Fiction 3. Witches -- Fiction 4. Scotland -- Fiction

ISBN 978-0-552-55679-8; 0-552-55679-3

This "finds Lily preparing to play the bagpipes for a school concert, toddler-sibling Daisy (aka Witch Baby) continuing to experiment with spells and nocturnal neighborhood flights, and the Sisters of Hiss (Nose, Chin, and Toad) unexpectedly yearning for motherhood. . . . Gliori's upbeat style, comical black-line drawings, footnoted asides, and much diaper humor are sure to please series fans." Booklist

Godden, Rumer

The **doll's** house; illustrated by Tasha Tudor. Viking 1962 136p il hardcover o.p. pa $5.99

Grades: 2 3 4 **Fic**

1. Dolls -- Fiction 2. Dollhouses -- Fiction

ISBN 0-14-030942-X pa

First published 1947 in the United Kingdom; first United States edition illustrated by Dana Saintsbury published 1948

Adventures of a brave little hundred-year-old Dutch farthing doll, her family, their Victorian dollhouse home and the two little English girls to whom they all belonged. Tottie's great adventure was when she went to the exhibition, Dolls through the ages, and was singled out for notice by the Queen who opened the exhibition

"Each doll has a firmly drawn, recognizably true character; the children think and behave convincingly. . . . The story is enthralling, and complete in every detail." Spectator

Godwin, Laura

The **Doll** people set sail; by Ann M. Martin and Laura Godwin; with pictures by Brett Helquist. Disney-Hyperion Books 2014 304 p. (The Doll people) $17.99

Grades: 3 4 5 **Fic**

1. Sea stories 2. Dolls -- Fiction

ISBN 1423136837; 9781423136835

LC 2013041937

In this fourth installment of the Doll People series, by Ann M. Martin and Laura Godwin, "Annabelle Doll, Tiffany Funcraft, and their families are whisked out to sea when the Palmers accidentally place them in a box destined for charity donation. And it turns out they're not alone-there are plenty of other doll people on the ship, too. After traveling thousands of miles, will they be able to find their way home?" (Publisher's note)

"Surprisingly, these doll characters continue to mature; Annabelle becomes braver and Tiffany more restrained. [Brett] Helquist, taking over for Brian Selznick, illustrates in keeping with Selznick's tone." Booklist

Other titles in the series include:

The Doll People (2000)

The Meanest Doll in the World (2003)

The Runaway Dolls (2008)

Going, K. L.

The **garden** of Eve. Harcourt 2007 234p $17; pa $6.99
Grades: 4 5 6 7   **Fic**
1. Death -- Fiction 2. Magic -- Fiction 3. Bereavement -- Fiction 4. New York (State) -- Fiction
ISBN 978-0-15-205986-6; 0-15-205986-5; 978-0-15-206614-7 pa; 0-15-206614-4 pa
                                                   LC 2007-05074

Eve gave up her belief in stories and magic after her mother's death, but a mysterious seed given to her as an eleventh-birthday gift by someone she has never met takes her and a boy who claims to be a ghost on a strange journey, to where their supposedly cursed town of Beaumont, New York, flourishes.

"Believably and with delicacy, Going paints a suspenseful story suffused with the poignant questions of what it means to be alive, and what might await on the other side." Horn Book

Goldblatt, Mark

Finding the worm; Mark Goldblatt. Random House Inc 2015 352 p. (lib. bdg.) $19.99
Grades: 5 6 7 8   **Fic**
1. School discipline 2. Teenagers -- Fiction 3. Vandalism -- Fiction 4. Friendship -- Fiction 5. Bar mitzvah -- Fiction 6. Conduct of life -- Fiction 7. Jews -- United States -- Fiction 8. Queens (New York, N.Y.) -- History -- 20th century -- Fiction
ISBN 0385391099; 9780385391085; 9780385391092
                                                   LC 2014004052
Sequel to: Twerp

In this novel by Mark Goldblatt "trouble always seems to find thirteen-year-old Julian Twerski. He's been accused of vandalizing a painting. The principal doesn't want to suspend him again, so instead, he asks Julian to write a 200-word essay on good citizenship. Being falsely accused is bad enough, but outside of school, Julian's dealing with even bigger issues. His friend Quentin has been really sick. How can life be fair when the nicest guy in your group has cancer?" (Publishers' note)

"Julian Twerski and the gang from Twerp (Random, 2013) are now in seventh grade, and it seems like they're dealing with an even bigger set of challenges than last year. . . . Goldblatt takes advantage of Julian's newfound love of writing, adding an honest and forthright tone to the boy's journal entries. A wide variety of readers will relate to Julian's questions about fairness, faith, and friendship.." SLJ

Twerp; Mark Goldblatt. Random House Inc 2013 288 p. $16.99
Grades: 6 7 8   **Fic**
1. School stories 2. Diaries -- Fiction 3. Friendship -- Fiction 4. Conduct of life -- Fiction 5. Self-realization -- Fiction 6. Interpersonal relations -- Fiction 7. Queens (New York, N.Y.) -- Fiction 8. Schools -- Fiction 9. Queens (New York, N.Y.) --

History -- 20th century -- Fiction
ISBN 0375971424; 9780375971426
                                                   LC 2012005033

In this book, by Mark Goldblatt, "Julian Twerski isn't a bully. He's just made a big mistake. So when he returns to school after a weeklong suspension, his English teacher offers him a deal: if he keeps a journal and writes about the terrible incident that got him and his friends suspended, he can get out of writing a report on Shakespeare. Julian jumps at the chance. And so begins his account of life in sixth grade." (Publisher's note)

Gonzalez, Christina Diaz, 1969-

Moving target; Christina Diaz Gonzalez. Scholastic Press 2015 248 p. illustrations (ebook) $6.99; (hardcover) $17.99
Grades: 4 5 6 7 8   **Fic**
1. Murder -- Fiction 2. Rome (Italy) -- Fiction 3. Mystery fiction -- Fiction 4. Secret societies -- Fiction 5. Italy -- Fiction 6. Holy Lance -- Fiction 7. Americans -- Italy -- Fiction 8. Mystery and detective stories
ISBN 9780545773201; 0545773180; 9780545773188
                                                   LC 2014038851

In this middle grade novel by Christina Diaz Gonzalez, "Cassie Arroyo, an American studying in Rome, has her world ripped apart when someone tries to kill her father, an art history professor. . . . [Cassie learns] that she is a member of an ancient bloodline that enables her to use the Spear of Destiny--a legendary object that can alter the future. . . . Cassie must--with the help of some friends--decipher the clues that will lead her to the Spear." (Publisher's note)

"An adventure that will keep readers engaged until the cliffhanger ending and leave them waiting for the next book." Kirkus

Goscinny

Nicholas; [by] Rene Goscinny & [illustrated by] Jean-Jacques Sempe; translated by Anthea Bell. Phaidon 2005 126p il $19.95
Grades: 4 5 6   **Fic**
1. School stories
ISBN 0-7148-4529-9

"This classic book about a mischievous schoolboy and his friends, originally published in French in 1959, is now available in English. The expertly translated text is enlivened by artwork by a New Yorker cartoonist to create the unforgettable milieu of Nicholas and his rowdy friends. A collection of 19 escapades, the stories introduce the protagonist and his cohorts as they wreak havoc out of simple, everyday situations at school, on the playground, and at home." SLJ

Other titles about Nicholas are:

Nicholas again (2006)

Nicholas on vacation (2007)

Grabenstein, Chris

Beach party surf monkey; by Chris Grabenstein; illustrations by Brooke Allen. Random House 2017 320 p. illustrations (Welcome to Wonderland) (hardcover) $13.99
Grades: 4 5 6   **Fic**
1. Florida -- Fiction 2. Hotels and motels -- Fiction 3. Motion pictures -- Production and direction -- Fiction 4. Hotels, motels, etc. -- Fiction
ISBN 9780553536102; 9780553536119; 9780553536133
                                                   LC 2016014007

In this book, by Chris Grabenstein, illustrated by Brooke Allen "there's always something wacky happening when you live in a motel and P.T. . . . has grown up at the world's wackiest! When word gets out that the hottest teen idols in Hollywood (plus current YouTube sensation Kevin the Monkey!) will be filming their next movie—Beach Party Surf Monkey—right in St. Pete's Beach, Florida, P.T. and his frien

Gloria know that the Wonderland would be the perfect location." (Publisher's note)

The **black** heart crypt; a haunted mystery. Random House 2011 328p (Haunted places mystery) $16.99; lib bdg $19.99; e-book $16.99
Grades: 5 6 7 8   **Fic**
1. Ghost stories 2. Mystery fiction 3. Demonology -- Fiction
ISBN 978-0-375-86900-6; 0-375-86900-X; 978-0-375-96900-3 lib bdg; 0-375-96900-4 lib bdg; 978-0-375-89987-4 e-book
LC 2011001939

A 200-year-old ghost inhabits a living ancestor in order to take revenge on eleven-year-old Zack and his family.

"The pace never flags. Through flurries of ultrashort chapters, events spiral to a suspenseful climax, and the mix of corpses and comedy add up to a faintly macabre tone that isn't dispelled even by the end's just deserts and happy outcomes." Kirkus

The **crossroads**. Random House 2008 325p (Haunted places mystery) $16.99; lib bdg $19.99; pa $6.99
Grades: 5 6 7 8   **Fic**
1. Ghost stories 2. Connecticut -- Fiction 3. Stepmothers -- Fiction
ISBN 978-0-375-84697-7; 0-375-84697-2; 978-0-375-94697-4 lib bdg; 0-375-94697-7 lib bdg; 978-0-375-84698-4 pa; 0-375-84698-0 pa
LC 2007024803

When eleven-year-old Zack Jennings moves to Connecticut with his father and new stepmother, they must deal with the ghosts left behind by a terrible accident, as well as another kind of ghost from Zack's past

"An absorbing psychological thriller . . . as well as a rip-roaring ghost story, this switches points of view among humans, trees, and ghosts with astonishing élan." Booklist

Other titles in this series are:
The Hanging Hill (2009)
The smoky corridor (2010)
The Black Heart Crypt (2011)

Escape from Mr. Lemoncello's library; Chris Grabenstein. 1st ed. Random House Inc. 2013 304 p. (hardcover) $16.99; (library) $19.99
Grades: 5 6 7   **Fic**
1. Contests -- Fiction 2. Libraries -- Fiction 3. Games -- Fiction 4. Books and reading -- Fiction
ISBN 037587089X; 9780375870897; 9780375970894
LC 2012048122

In this book, twelve "seventh-graders win a chance to spend an overnight lock-in previewing their town's new public library," which was conceived by Luigi Lemoncello, the . . . founder of Mr. Lemoncello's Imagination Factory, which is a source for every kind of game imaginable. During the lock-in the winners . . . are offered a further challenge: 'Find your way out of the library using only what's in the library.' The winner will become spokesperson for the Imagination Factory." Publishers Weekly)

The **Hanging** Hill. Random House 2009 322p (Haunted places mystery) $16.99; lib bdg $19.99
Grades: 5 6 7 8   **Fic**
1. Ghost stories 2. Theater -- Fiction 3. Criminals -- Fiction 4. Connecticut -- Fiction 5. Stepmothers -- Fiction
ISBN 978-0-375-84699-1; 0-375-84699-9; 978-0-375-94699-8 lib bdg; 978-0-375-84700-4 pa
LC 2008027274

While working at a summer stock theater, eleven-year-old Zack and his stepmother encounter the ghost of one of Connecticut's most notorious criminals.

"The story line is hauntingly delicious as the fully fleshed-out creepiness comes tempered with humor." SLJ

Home sweet motel; Chris Grabenstein; illustrated by Brooke Allen. Random House Inc. 2016 304 p. illustrations (Welcome to Wonderland) (ebook) $41.97; (hardcover) $13.99
Grades: 4 5 6   **Fic**
1. Mystery fiction -- Fiction 2. Hotels and motels -- Fiction 3. Mystery and detective stories
ISBN 9780553536041; 0553536028; 9780553536027; 9780553536034
LC 2015030808

In this first book in the Welcome to Wonderland series by Chris Grabenstein, illustrated by Brooke Allen, "P. T. Wilkie may be the greatest storyteller alive. But he knows one thing for a fact: the Wonderland Motel is the best place a kid could ever live! . . . There's only one thing the Wonderland doesn't have, though-customers. And if the Wonderland doesn't get them soon, P.T. and his friend Gloria may have to say goodbye to their beloved motel forever." (Publisher's note)

"A funny and promising start to a new series." Kirkus

House of robots; James Patterson and Chris Grabenstein; illustrated by Juliana Neufeld. Little, Brown & Co. 2014 352 p. illustrations
Grades: 4 5 6 7 8   **Fic**
1. School stories 2. Robots -- Fiction 3. Humorous stories 4. Schools -- Fiction 5. Inventors -- Fiction 6. Family life -- Fiction 7. Middle schools -- Fiction
ISBN 9780316405911
LC 2013041672

In this book by James Patterson and Chris Grabbenstein, "an extraordinary robot signs up for an ordinary fifth grade class. It was never easy for Sammy Hayes-Rodriguez to fit in, so he's dreading the day when his genius mom insists he bring her newest invention to school: a walking, talking robot he calls E--for 'Error.' Sammy's no stranger to robots--his house is full of a colorful cast of them. But this one not only thinks it's Sammy's brother... it's actually even nerdier than Sammy." (Publisher's note)

"A fast-moving plot, lots of jokes, and a host of weird robots will draw readers in." SLJ

Mr. Lemoncello's Library Olympics; Chris Grabenstein. Random House Inc 2016 288 p. (hardcover) $16.99
Grades: 5 6 7   **Fic**
1. Libraries -- Fiction 2. Contests -- Fiction 3. Censorship -- Fiction 4. Books and reading -- Fiction 5. Eccentrics and eccentricities -- Fiction
ISBN 9780553510409; 9780553510416; 055351041X
LC 2015024473

In this children's novel, by Chris Grabenstein, "the world-famous game maker, Luigi Lemoncello . . . has invited teams from all across America to compete in the first ever LIBRARY OLYMPICS. But something suspicious is going on . . . books are missing from Mr. Lemoncello's library. Is someone trying to CENSOR what the kids are reading?! In between figuring out mind-boggling challenges, the kids will have to band together to get to the bottom of this mystery." (Publisher's note)

"This is a successful blend of mystery, adventure, and suspense, with a sizable cast of characters, in a wholly satisfying sequel that easily stands alone." SLJ

Word of mouse; James Patterson and Chris Grabenstein; illustrated by Joe Sutphin. Little, Brown & Co. 2016 304 p. $13.99
Grades: 3 4 5 6   **Fic**
1. Mice -- Fiction 2. Friendship -- Fiction 3. Adventure and

adventurers -- Fiction
ISBN 9780316349567

LC 2016001773

This middle grades book, by James Patterson and Chris Grabenstein, illustrated by Joe Sutphin, "follows the illuminating journey of a very special mouse, and the unexpected friendships that he makes along the way. . . . Isaiah can read, and write. He can also talk to humans...if any of them are willing to listen! After a dramatic escape from a mysterious laboratory, Isaiah is separated from his . . . family, and has to use his special skills to survive." (Publisher's note)

"With smart witticisms to launch each quick-paced chapter, Isaiah is truly a mouse that roars." Kirkus

Grabien, Deborah

Dark's tale. Egmont USA 2010 300p $15.99

Grades: 4 5 6   **Fic**

1. Cats -- Fiction 2. Parks -- Fiction 3. Animals -- Fiction 4. San Francisco (Calif.) -- Fiction

ISBN 978-1-60684-037-5; 1-60684-037-1

"Dark, a house cat abandoned in San Francisco's Golden Gate Park, must learn to survive in her new habitat. Befriended by a raccoon, she learns to recognize park inhabitants she must fear, like the 'crazybad' people, and those she can trust, including a wise owl named Memorie and a magical woman in rags who calls herself Streetwise Sal. . . . Written in first person from Dark's point of view, the novel creates a believable natural world, where predators hunt smaller animals and a cat must rely on her senses, her skills, and her friends for survival." Booklist

Graff, Lisa

★ **Absolutely** almost; Lisa Graff. Philomel Books, an imprint of Penguin Group (USA) 2014 304 p. $16.99

Grades: 4 5 6 7   **Fic**

1. Self-esteem -- Fiction 2. Ability -- Fiction 3. Schools -- Fiction 4. Babysitters -- Fiction 5. Racially mixed people -- Fiction 6. Family life -- New York (State) -- New York -- Fiction

ISBN 0399164057; 9780399164057

LC 2013023620

In this book, by Lisa Graff, "Albie has never been the smartest kid in his class. He has never been the tallest. Or the best at gym. Or the greatest artist. Or the most musical. In fact, Albie has a long list of the things he's not very good at. But then Albie gets a new babysitter, Calista, who helps him figure out all of the things he is good at and how he can take pride in himself." (Publisher's note)

"Ten-year-old New Yorker Albie is a middle-of-the-road (at best) student. He's buoyed by small successes in math club and on spelling tests, and by his new babysitter's low-key approach to confidence-boosting. Albie is a sweet, vulnerable kid who just needs a little extra help and to whom readers may well relate. Short chapters add to the story's accessibility and keep the pace moving." (Horn Book)

★ **Lost** in the sun; Lisa Graff. Philomel Books, an imprint of Penguin Group (USA) 2015 304 p. $16.99

Grades: 4 5 6 7 8 9   **Fic**

1. Guilt -- Fiction 2. Brothers -- Fiction 3. Friendship -- Fiction 4. Remarriage -- Fiction 5. Tricks -- Fiction

ISBN 0399164065; 9780399164064

LC 2014027868

In this book by Lisa Graff, "Trent knows nothing could be worse than the year he had in fifth grade, when a freak accident on Cedar Lake left one kid dead, and Trent with a brain full of terrible thoughts he can't get rid of. Trent's pretty positive the entire disaster was his fault. . . . It isn't until Trent gets caught up in the whirlwind that is Fallon Little--the girl with the mysterious scar across her face--that things begin to change." (Publisher's note)

"Trent Zimmerman is consumed by rage. The universe has been manifestly unfair to him and he doesn't know how to handle it. Seven months ago, he struck a hockey puck at a bad angle, sending it like a missile into the chest of a boy with a previously undiagnosed heart ailment. That boy died and Trent feels responsible...Weighty matters deftly handled with humor and grace will give this book wide appeal." SLJ

Sophie Simon solves them all; pictures by Jason Beene. Farrar, Straus & Giroux 2010 103p il $14.99

Grades: 2 3 4   **Fic**

1. School stories 2. Friendship -- Fiction

ISBN 978-0-374-37125-8; 0-374-37125-3

Sophie Simon, a third-grade genius, wants a graphing calculator so she can continue to study calculus while she rides the bus to school, but her parents are more concerned that she does not have any friends.

"Sometimes exaggerated for comic effect and occasionally poignant, the black-and-white illustrations capture the story's sense of humor as well as its sense of style. A fresh, funny chapter book for young readers." Booklist

A **tangle** of knots; Lisa Graff. Philomel Books 2013 240 p. $16.99

Grades: 3 4 5 6   **Fic**

1. Baking -- Fiction 2. Orphans -- Fiction 3. Ability -- Fiction 4. Identity -- Fiction 5. Poughkeepsie (N.Y.) -- Fiction 6. Family life -- New York -- Fiction

ISBN 0399255176; 9780399255175

LC 2012009573

Parents' Choice: Gold Medal Fiction (2013)

This novel is set "in a slightly magical world where everyone has a Talent. . . . Eleven-year-old Cady is an orphan with a phenomenal Talent for cake baking. . . . And her destiny leads her to a mysterious address that houses a lost luggage emporium, an old recipe, a family of children searching for their own Talents, and a Talent Thief who will alter her life forever. However, these encounters hold the key to Cady's past and how she became an orphan." (Publisher's note)

Followed by: A clatter of jars (2016)

The **thing** about Georgie; a novel. by Lisa Graff. Laura Geringer Books 2006 220p $15.99; lib bdg $16.89; pa $5.99

Grades: 3 4 5 6   **Fic**

1. School stories 2. Dwarfism -- Fiction 3. Friendship -- Fiction 4. Family life -- Fiction

ISBN 978-0-06-087589-3; 0-06-087589-5; 978-0-06-087590-9 lib bdg; 0-06-087590-9 lib bdg; 978-0-06-087591-6 pa; 0-06-087591-7 pa

LC 2006000392

Georgie's dwarfism causes problems, but he could always rely on his parents, his best friend, and classmate Jeanie the Meanie's teasing until a surprising announcement, a new boy in school, and a class project shake things up

"An upbeat and sensitive look at what it's like to be different, this novel will spark discussion." Booklist

Umbrella summer. Laura Geringer Books 2009 235p $15.99

Grades: 4 5 6   **Fic**

1. Death -- Fiction 2. Worry -- Fiction 3. Bereavement -- Fiction

ISBN 978-0-06-143187-6; 0-06-143187-7

LC 2008-2601

After her brother Jared dies, ten-year-old Annie worries about the hidden dangers of everything, from bug bites to bicycle riding, until she is befriended by a new neighbor who is grieving her own loss.

"Annie's story deals with death with sensitivity, love, and understanding." SLJ

Grahame, Kenneth, 1859-1932

★ The **reluctant** dragon; by Kenneth Grahame; illustrated by Ernest H. Shepard. Holiday House 2013 64 p. (hardcover) $16.95
Grades: 3 4 5   Fic
1. Dragons -- Fiction 2. Villages -- Fiction
ISBN 0823428206; 9780823428205; 9780823428212
LC 2012030238
In this book, by Kenneth Grahame and illustrated by Ernest H. Shepard, "a young boy befriends a poetry-loving dragon living in the Downs above his home. When the town-folk send for St. George to slay the dragon, the boy needs to come up with a clever plan to save his friend and convince the townsfolk to accept him." (Publisher's note)

The **wind** in the willows. Palazzo 2008 224p col. ill. $19.95
Grades: 3 4 5 6   Fic
1. Animals -- Fiction
ISBN 978-0-9553046-3-7; 0-9553046-3-6
LC 2008425442
First published 1908
"This handsomely illustrated, unabridged edition celebrates the 100th anniversary of Grahame's classic animal fantasy. Ingpen's detailed paintings blend earthy tones with firelit highlights to create a warm mood.... Both the woodland scenes and animal abodes are charmingly depicted, and the characters, costumed in 19th-century garb, have loads of personality." SLJ

Grant, Holly

The **dastardly** deed; Holly Grant; illustrated by Josie Portillo. Random House 2015 368 p. illustrations (hardcover library binding) $19.99
Grades: 4 5 6 7   Fic
1. Family secrets -- Fiction 2. Adventure fiction -- Fiction 3. Humorous stories 4. Orphans -- Fiction 5. Secrets -- Fiction 6. Kidnapping -- Fiction 7. Princesses -- Fiction
ISBN 9780385370257; 9780385370264
LC 2015009492
In this middle-grade novel, by Holly Grant, illustrated by Josie Portillo, book 2 in "The League of Beastly Dreadfuls" series, "after their narrow escape from a NEFARIOUS kidnapping ring, Anastasia, Ollie, and Quentin (a.k.a. The League of Beastly Dreadfuls!) are looking forward to a relaxing vacation.... [But] Anastasia makes the SHOCKING discovery that her family is at the heart of a centuries-old scandal ... [and] the Dreadfuls have another MYSTERY to solve." (Publisher's note)
"With its strong characterization, especially of the most despicable figures, and Lemony Snicket appeal, this adventure will keep fans hooked and eager for the next installment." Booklist

The **league** of beastly dreadfuls; book 1 Holly Grant. Random House Inc 2015 294 p. illustrations (hardcover library binding) $19.99
Grades: 4 5 6 7   Fic
1. Aunts -- Fiction 2. Institutional care 3. Orphans -- Fiction 4. Humorous stories 5. Shadows -- Fiction 6. Kidnapping -- Fiction
ISBN 0385370083; 9780385370073; 9780385370080
LC 2013050800
Other titles in this series: The dastardly deed
In this children's novel by Holly Grant "Anastasia is a completely average almost-eleven-year-old. That is, UNTIL her parents die in a tragic vacuum-cleaner accident. UNTIL she's rescued by two long-lost great-aunties.... Anastasia soon begins to suspect that her aunties are not who they say they are. So when she meets ... two mysterious brothers, the three join together to plot their great escape!" (Publisher's note)
"With just the right mix of humor, magic, maliciousness, and suspense, Grant leaves readers waiting for Anastasia's next adventure." Booklist

Grant, Katy

Hide and seek. Peachtree 2010 230p $15.95
Grades: 5 6 7 8   Fic
1. Arizona -- Fiction 2. Divorce -- Fiction 3. Kidnapping -- Fiction 4. Family life -- Fiction 5. Wilderness survival -- Fiction
ISBN 978-1-56145-542-3; 1-56145-542-3
LC 2009040519
In the remote mountains of Arizona where he lives with his mother, stepfather, and two sisters, fourteen-year-old Chase discovers two kidnapped boys and gets caught up in a dangerous adventure when he comes up with a plan to get them to safety.
"Mystery and adventure propel this readable survival story that will hit the spot with Gary Paulsen's fans and may also entice reluctant readers." SLJ

Grant, Michael, 1954-

★ The **call**; Michael Grant. 1st ed. Katherine Tegen Books 2010 243 p. ill. (hardcover) $16.99
Grades: 4 5 6   Fic
1. Fantasy fiction 2. Adventure fiction 3. Fantasy 4. Humorous stories 5. Good and evil -- Fiction 6. Adventure and adventurers -- Fiction
ISBN 0061833665; 9780061833663
LC 2009044815
A seemingly average twelve-year-old learns that he is destined to gather a team of similarly gifted children to try to save the world from a nameless evil, which is threatening to reappear after an absence of three thousand years. "Age ten and up." (Publisher's note)
"The author keeps the story moving at a brisk pace with suspenseful action and laugh-out-loud humor." Kirkus
Followed by: The trap (2011)

The **trap**. Katherine Tegen Books 2011 294p (The Magnificent 12) $16.99
Grades: 4 5 6   Fic
1. Fantasy fiction 2. Adventure fiction 3. Good and evil -- Fiction
ISBN 0-06-183368-1; 978-0-06-183368-7
LC 2010040580
Sequel to: The call (2010)
Mack MacAvoy, an average-seeming twelve-year-old boy who happens to have special powers, travels to China in an effort to assemble an elite team of his peers to help him thwart the evil Pale Queen.

Gratz, Alan

The **Brooklyn** nine; a novel in nine innings. Dial Books 2009 299p $16.99
Grades: 5 6 7 8 9   Fic
1. Baseball -- Fiction 2. Family life -- Fiction 3. German Americans -- Fiction 4. United States -- History -- Fiction 5. Brooklyn (New York, N.Y.) -- Fiction
ISBN 978-0-8037-3224-7; 0-8037-3224-4
LC 2008-21263
This novel follows the fortunes of a German immigrant family through nine generations, beginning in 1845, as they experience American life and play baseball. "Grades five to nine." (Bull Cent Child Books)
Gratz "builds this novel upon a clever ... conceit ... and executes it with polish and precision." Booklist

The **League** of Seven; Alan Gratz; illustrated by Brett Helquist. Starscape 2014 352 p. map (hardback) $16.99
Grades: 5 6 7 8   Fic
1. Steampunk fiction 2. United States -- History -- Fiction 3. Science fiction 4. Monsters -- Fiction 5. Secret societies -- Fiction

6. Adventure and adventurers -- Fiction
ISBN 076533822X; 9780765338228

LC 2014015435

"'The League of Seven' is the first book in [a] steampunk series by the acclaimed author of 'Samurai Shortstop,' Alan Gratz. In an alternate 1875 America electricity is forbidden, Native Americans and Yankees are united, and eldritch evil lurks in the shadows. Young Archie Dent knows there really are monsters in the world. His parents are members of the Septemberist Society, whose job it is to protect humanity from hideous giants called the Mangleborn." (Publisher's note)

"This hybrid of steampunk and alternate American history features a hell-raising girl's school, Atlantis, and three highly likable leads in a yarn rip-roaring from start to finish. . . . Moments of humor and pathos enliven the history and fantasy." Booklist

Projekt 1065; A Novel of World War II. Alan Gratz. Scholastic Press 2016 320 p. (hardcover) $16.99; (ebook) $16.99
Grades: 5 6 7 8   **Fic**
1. Spy stories -- Fiction 2. World War, 1939-1945 -- Fiction 3. Spies -- Fiction 4. Jet planes -- Fiction 5. Hitler Youth -- Fiction 6. Irish -- Germany -- Fiction 6. Germany -- History -- 1933-1945 -- Fiction 7. Berlin (Germany) -- History -- 1918-1945 -- Fiction 8. Diplomatic and consular service, Irish -- Germany
ISBN 9780545880169; 9780545880176

LC 2016016960

In this children's novel by Alan Gratz, "Michael O'Shaunessey, originally from Ireland, now lives in Nazi Germany with his parents. Like the other boys in his school, Michael is a member of the Hitler Youth, but . . . he and his parents are spies. . . . When Michael learns about Projekt 1065, a secret Nazi war mission, things get even more complicated. He must prove his loyalty to the Hitler Youth at all costs -- even if it means risking everything he cares about." (Publisher's note)

"A rare insider's glimpse into the Hitler Youth: animated, well-researched, and thought-provoking." Kirkus

Includes bibliographical references

Graves, Keith
The **orphan** of Awkward Falls. Chronicle Books 2011 337p $16.99
Grades: 4 5 6 7   **Fic**
1. Mystery fiction 2. Orphans -- Fiction 3. Homicide -- Fiction 4. Inventors -- Fiction 5. Mentally ill -- Fiction 6. Science -- Experiments -- Fiction
ISBN 978-0-8118-7814-2; 0-8118-7814-7

LC 2011008008

Josephine Cravitz, the new girl in Awkward Falls, and her neighbor Thaddeus Hibble, a reclusive and orphaned boy inventor, become the targets of a mad cannibal from the local asylum for the criminally insane.

"Graves crafts a quick-moving plot composed of macabre twists. . . . Wordless opening and closing sequences, plus a handful of interior illustrations, both fill in background detail and intensify the overall macabre atmosphere." Kirkus

Green, Tim
Baseball great. HarperCollinsPublishers 2009 250p $16.99; lib bdg $17.89
Grades: 5 6 7 8   **Fic**
1. School stories 2. Baseball -- Fiction 3. Father-son relationship -- Fiction
ISBN 978-0-06-162686-9; 0-06-162686-4; 978-0-06-162687-6 lib bdg; 0-06-162687-2 lib bdg

LC 2008051778

All twelve-year-old Josh wants to do is play baseball but when his father, a minor league pitcher, signs him up for a youth champion-

ship team, Josh finds himself embroiled in a situation with potentially illegal consequences.

"Issues of peer and family pressure are well handled, and the short, punchy chapters and crisp dialogue are likely to hold the attention of young baseball fans." SLJ

Other titles in this series are:
Rivals (2010)
Best of the best (2011)
Home run (2016)

Best of the best; a baseball great novel. Harper 2011 262p $16.99; lib bdg $17.89
Grades: 5 6 7 8   **Fic**
1. Divorce -- Fiction 2. Baseball -- Fiction
ISBN 978-0-06-168622-1; 0-06-168622-0; 978-0-06-168623-8 lib bdg; 0-06-168623-9 lib bdg

LC 2010022976

Sequel to: Rivals (2010)

Determined to play in the Little League World Series, twelve-year-old Josh struggles to concentrate on his game and be the team's leader while also trying to cope with his parents' impending divorce.

"Ethics in sports lifts this above the usual sports saga." Kirkus

The **big** time; a Football genius novel. Harper 2010 277p (Football genius) $16.99; lib bdg $17.89
Grades: 5 6 7 8   **Fic**
1. Football -- Fiction 2. Criminals -- Fiction 3. Atlanta (Ga.) -- Fiction 4. Father-son relationship -- Fiction
ISBN 978-0-06-168619-1; 0-06-168619-0; 978-0-06-168620-7 lib bdg; 0-06-168620-4 lib bdg

LC 2010009398

Twelve-year-old Troy always dreamed of meeting his father, but when the man finally appears his mother's anger, his father's shady business dealings, and Troy's own feelings make the reunion difficult and confusing.

"The story moves along at a brisk clip, the language is straightforward and accessible, and the issues raised are likely to engage readers." SLJ

Deep zone. Harper Collins 2011 265p (Football genius) $15.99
Grades: 5 6 7 8   **Fic**
1. Football -- Fiction
ISBN 978-0-06-201244-9; 0-06-201244-4

Twelve-year-old football stars Troy White and Ty Lewis are eager to face each other in a seven-on-seven tournament being held at the Super Bowl in Miami, unaware that bad choices made by members of their families will put both boys in danger.

"The football insights are the best part, as both professional games and seven-on-seven play are described in satisfying detail." Kirkus

Football champ. HarperCollins Children's Books 2009 280p $16.99; lib bdg $17.89
Grades: 5 6 7 8   **Fic**
1. Football -- Fiction 2. Journalists -- Fiction 3. Atlanta (Ga.) -- Fiction 4. Atlanta Falcons (Football team) -- Fiction.
ISBN 978-0-06-162689-0; 0-06-162689-9; 978-0-06-162690-6 lib bdg; 0-06-162690-2 lib bdg

LC 2008-5177?

Sequel to: Football genius (2007)

Twelve-year-old Troy's uncanny gift for predicting football plays proves a powerful secret weapon for the Atlanta Falcons, but a seedy reporter with a vendetta suspects something is going on and sets out to shred the reputations of Troy and star linebacker Seth Halloway.

"The characters are engaging and the game action is exciting. Short cliffhanger chapters make this a good bet for reluctant readers." SLJ

Football genius. HarperCollinsPublishers 2007 244p $16.99; lib bdg $17.89; pa $6.99

Grades: 5 6 7 8   **Fic**

1. Football -- Fiction 2. Atlanta (Ga.) -- Fiction
ISBN 978-0-06-112270-5; 0-06-112270-X; 978-0-06-112272-9 lib bdg; 0-06-112272-6 lib bdg; 978-0-06-112273-6 pa; 0-06-112273-4 pa

LC 2006-29470

Troy, a sixth-grader with an unusual gift for predicting football plays before they occur, attempts to use his ability to help his favorite team, the Atlanta Falcons, but he must first prove himself to the coach and players.

The author "imparts many insider details that football fans will love. Green makes Troy a winning hero, and he ties everything together with a fast-moving plot." Booklist

Other titles in this series are:
Football champ (2009)
The big time (2010)
Deep zone (2011)

Football hero. HarperCollinsPublishers 2008 297p $16.99; lib bdg $17.89; pa $6.99

Grades: 5 6 7 8   **Fic**

1. Mafia -- Fiction 2. Football -- Fiction 3. New Jersey -- Fiction
ISBN 978-0-06-112274-3; 0-06-112274-2; 978-0-06-112275-0 lib bdg; 0-06-112275-0 lib bdg; 978-0-06-112276-7 pa; 0-06-112276-9 pa

LC 2007-24184

When twelve-year-old Ty's brother Thane is recruited out of college to play for the New York Jets, their Uncle Gus uses Ty to get insider information for his gambling ring, landing Ty and Thane in trouble with the Mafia.

"The novel is briskly paced and undemanding, and might be a good bet for sports-minded reluctant readers." SLJ

Force out; Tim Green. 1st ed. Harper 2013 288 p. (hardcover) $16.99

Grades: 4 5 6   **Fic**

1. Baseball -- Fiction 2. Friendship -- Fiction 3. Best friends -- Fiction
ISBN 0062089595; 9780062089595

LC 2012026752

In this juvenile novel, by Tim Green, "Joey and Zach have always been best friends. They're also two of the best baseball players in their league, and shoo-ins for the all-star team at the end of the season. Their dream is to play together on the Center State select team, and they will do anything to help each other get there. . . . Then the unthinkable happens: The boys learn there's only one open spot on the select team." Publisher's note)

"Though Green is no stylist, he does a better job of avoiding the sports fantasy and sticking to real life than usual. There's plenty of play-by-play for those who want the sports to be the focus, but the interactions off the field are never shortchanged. . . . A slice of life for middle school readers who know that their sport is a microcosm of the larger world." Kirkus

Home Run; Tim Green. Harpercollins Childrens Books 2016 352 p. (Baseball Great Novel) (hardcover) $16.99

Grades: 5 6 7 8   **Fic**

1. Baseball -- Fiction 2. Family life -- Fiction
ISBN 0062317113; 9780062317117

In this juvenile novel, by Tim Green, part of the "Baseball Great" series, "Josh's life has just fallen apart. . . . But then Benji tells Josh of a home-run derby in which the winner gets a brand-new house. All Josh has to do to qualify is hit twenty home runs during his travel-team season. With Benji and Jaden's help, Josh is hoping to hit it out of the park and save his family, because if he strikes out, he may just lose everything." (Publisher's note)

"Any sports fiction fan who wants plenty of play-by-play will find it here, along with some coaching tips and an exploration of the influence of big business on kids' sports." Kirkus

New kid; Tim Green. HarperCollins 2014 320 p. (hardback) $16.99

Grades: 4 5 6 7 8   **Fic**

1. School stories 2. Moving -- Fiction 3. Baseball players -- Fiction 4. Schools -- Fiction 5. Baseball -- Fiction 6. Fathers and sons -- Fiction 7. Moving, Household -- Fiction 8. Interpersonal relations -- Fiction
ISBN 0062208721; 9780062208729

LC 2013032816

In this "baseball novel," by Tim Green, "Tommy's the new kid in town--who now goes by the name Brock--and he's having a hard time fitting in. Thanks to a prank gone wrong, he may be able to settle in on the baseball team. But can he prove himself before he becomes a new kid . . . again?" (Publisher's note)

"A teenage baseball star struggles not only with game-day stress, but also with the ever-present fear that his world is about to end. . . . His dad's job is mysterious and dangerous, and it requires them to stay on the run. Moving abruptly has only gotten harder as Brock gets older, and when he finds a great baseball coach and a good friend—and a potential girlfriend—the thought of leaving it all behind terrifies him even more. Best-selling author and former NFL defensive end Green delivers a riveting book about the complexities of being a teenager caught in unusual circumstances beyond his control. His writing is both compelling and intelligent, and even the implausible scenes—like a visit from a baseball great—still maintain a feel of authenticity. Even readers who aren't sports fans will find plenty of familiar drama and entertainment in this book. Exciting, romantic and thought-provoking, this book scores a home run." Kirkus

Rivals. Harper 2010 261p $16.99

Grades: 5 6 7 8   **Fic**

1. Baseball -- Fiction
ISBN 978-0-06-162692-0; 0-06-162692-9

Sequel to: Baseball great (2009)

"12-year-old Josh LeBlanc has his hands full as he tries to lead his team to victory in the Hall of Fame National Championship Tournament. . . . He uncovers a plot on the part of a former major leaguer to fix the games. . . . Everything is handled with a light, deft touch. . . . Enjoyable, unpretentious escapism for youngsters, especially reluctant readers." SLJ

Followed by: Best of the best (2011)

Greene, Bette

Philip Hall likes me, I reckon maybe; pictures by Charles Lilly. Dial Bks. for Young Readers 1974 135p il hardcover o.p. pa $5.99

Grades: 4 5 6   **Fic**

1. Arkansas -- Fiction 2. Friendship -- Fiction 3. African Americans -- Fiction
ISBN 0-14-130312-3 pa

A Newbery Medal honor book, 1975

Eleven-year-old Beth, an African American girl from Arkansas, thinks that Philip Hall likes her, but their on-again, off-again relationship sometimes makes her wonder

"The action is sustained; . . . the illustrations are excellent black-and-white pencil sketches." Read Teach

Other titles about Beth and Philip Hall are:

Get out of here, Philip Hall (1981)

I've already forgotten your name, Philip Hall (2004)

Greene, Jacqueline Dembar

★ The **secret** shofar of Barcelona; illustrated by Doug Chayka. Kar-Ben 2009 un il lib bdg $17.95

Grades: 2 3 4 5   **Fic**

1. Spain -- Fiction 2. Musicians -- Fiction 3. Jews -- Spain -- Fiction 4. Rosh ha-Shanah -- Fiction

ISBN 978-0-8225-9915-9 lib bdg; 0-8225-9915-5 lib bdg

LC 2008031197

In the late 1500s, while the conductor of the Royal Orchestra of Barcelona prepares for a concert to celebrate Spain's colonies in the New World, his son secretly practices playing the Shofar to help Jews, who must hide their faith from the Inquisition, to celebrate Rosh Hashanah. Includes historical facts and glossary

"Based on a legend, this intriguing slice of converso life offers a thoughtful hero and a suspenseful plot. The warm opaque paintings are expressive and create a strong sense of place." SLJ

Greene, Stephanie

Happy birthday, Sophie Hartley. Clarion Books 2010 127p $16

Grades: 3 4 5   **Fic**

1. Siblings -- Fiction 2. Birthdays -- Fiction 3. Family life -- Fiction

ISBN 978-0-547-25128-8; 0-547-25128-9

A girl in a large family is looking forward to her first "double digit" birthday, but soon discovers that growing up brings some unwanted changes.

"All the plot strands merge in a satisfying denouement that's tidy but not in the least predictable. Greene explores her themes of identity, ambivalence about growing up, and friendship with an unusual naturalness and depth, yet the themes never trump story or character." Horn Book

★ **Owen** Foote, frontiersman; illustrated by Martha Weston. Clarion Bks. 1999 88p il $14; pa $4.95

Grades: 2 3 4   **Fic**

1. Outdoor life -- Fiction

ISBN 0-395-61578-X; 0-618-24620-7 pa

LC 98-44843

Second grader Owen Foote is looking forward to spending time with his friend Joseph in their tree fort, until some bullies visiting his neighbor, Mrs. Gold, threaten to wreck the fort

"Real-boy characters with an appealingly loyal friendship, a good balance of narrative and dialogue, and an honestly childlike sense of the way the world works." Horn Book

Other titles about Owen Foote are:

Owen Foote, mighty scientist (2004)

Owen Foote, money man (2000)

Owen Foote, second grade strongman (1997)

Owen Foote, super spy (2001)

Owen Foote, soccer star (1998)

Owen Foote, mighty scientist; illustrated by Catherine Bowman Smith. Clarion Books 2004 90p il $15

Grades: 2 3 4   **Fic**

1. School stories 2. Science projects -- Fiction

ISBN 0-618-43016-4

LC 2003-27072

Third grade best friends Owen and Joseph struggle to come up with a great science fair project that they will both enjoy doing, then something goes wrong and they have to change their plans two days before the fair.

"This is a great title to spark discussion in science classes, not just for the physical facts and issues related to testing hypotheses but also for the realistic account of failure and learning from mistakes at home and in the classroom." Booklist

Owen Foote, money man; illustrated by Martha Weston. Clarion Books 2000 96p $15; pa $5.99

Grades: 2 3 4   **Fic**

1. Work -- Fiction 2. Family life -- Fiction 3. Money-making projects for children -- Fiction

ISBN 0-618-02369-0; 0-618-37837-5 pa

LC 00-27716

Ingenious eight-year-old Owen wants to make money for the things he absolutely needs, such as plastic vomit, but he tries to come up with some alternatives to earning an allowance, which sounds like too much work.

"Kid-friendly humor, good characterization, and a believable and fast-moving plot distinguish this book." SLJ

Princess Posey and the first grade parade; illustrated by Stephanie Roth Sisson. G.P. Putnam's Sons 2010 83p il $12.99

Grades: K 1 2   **Fic**

1. School stories 2. Fear -- Fiction

ISBN 978-0-399-25167-2; 0-399-25167-7

LC 2009-12471

Posey's fear of starting first grade is alleviated when her teacher invites the students to wear their most comfortable clothes to school on the first day.

"Emergent readers can be anxious as they make the transition from easy readers to early chapter books and, like Posey, can be overwhelmed by new challenges. Short sentences, a generous font, ample white space and Sisson's charming, expressive black-and-white illustrations make this sweet story just right for them." Kirkus

Other titles about Princess Posey are:

Princess Posey and the perfect present (2011)

Princess Posey and the next-door dog (2011)

Princess Posey and the perfect present; illustrated by Stephanie Roth Sisson. G. P. Putnam's Sons 2011 85p il

Grades: K 1 2   **Fic**

1. School stories 2. Teachers -- Fiction 3. Friendship -- Fiction

ISBN 0-399-25462-5; 978-0-399-25462-8

LC 201000147 6

For first-grader Posey, every school day is great until her teacher's birthday, when her best friend's gift of an enormous bouquet puts Posey's few, home-grown roses to shame.

"Very short chapters, generous font, lots of eye-saving white space on each page and frequent black-and-white illustrations make this longish early chapter book accessible to the very earliest reader. Posey is flawed in a way that is absolutely perfect." Kirkus

The **show**-off; by Stephanie Greene; illustrated by Joe Mathieu. 1st ed.; Marshall Cavendish 2007 50p il $14.99

Grades: 1 2 3   **Fic**

1. Pigs -- Fiction 2. Moose -- Fiction 3. Friendship -- Fiction

ISBN 978-0-7614-5374-1

LC 200700025 2

Hildy looks forward to a visit from her cousin, Winston, but when he arrives he bores her and annoys all of her friends by declaring his superior intelligence and expertise on every subject, until Moose convinces him to try something different.

"This beginning chapter book is full of gentle humor. The pencil-and-gray-wash illustrations work well with the story." SLJ

Sophie Hartley and the facts of life; by Stephanie Greene. Clarion Books, Houghton Mifflin Harcourt 2013 144 p. (hardcover) $16.99
Grades: 3 4 5   **Fic**
    1. Puberty -- Fiction 2. Family -- Fiction 3. Family life -- Fiction 4. Maturation (Psychology) -- Fiction
    ISBN 0547976526; 9780547976525

    LC 2012041489

In this book, by Stephanie Greene, "Sophie Hartley, age ten, does not want to be a teenager. She vows she'll never be like her older sister, Nora, who has tantrums about her hair and almost everything else.... Next year Sophie's class will see the movie about body changes, and her classmates are already buzzing about it. Sophie doesn't want to know about that embarrassing stuff yet. Does that mean she's immature? How can she prove otherwise?" (Publisher's note)

"Upbeat middle child Sophie, ten, has no interest in puberty or the teenage obsessions of older siblings Thad and Nora. But her fellow fourth graders accuse her of being immature. Meanwhile, her mother goes on a business trip, leaving Mr. Hartley with the bickering kids. The messages in this fourth book are somewhat overt but nevertheless useful, and Sophie remains an engaging character." (the Horn Book)

Sophie Hartley, on strike. Clarion Books 2006 152p $15
Grades: 3 4 5   **Fic**
    1. Family life -- Fiction
    ISBN 978-0-618-71960-0; 0-618-71960-1

    LC 2006-08375

After their mother sets up a new list of household chores for them to do, Sophie and her siblings argue about housekeeping and finally go on strike.

"Readers will empathize with this spunky youngster and her true-to-life problems." SLJ

Greenfield, Eloise
  ★ The **friendly** four; illustrations by Jan Spivey Gilchrist. HarperCollins/Amistad 2006 47p il $16.99; lib bdg $17.89
Grades: 2 3 4   **Fic**
    1. Summer -- Fiction 2. Friendship -- Fiction 3. African Americans -- Fiction
    ISBN 978-0-06-000759-1; 0-06-000759-1; 978-0-06-000760-7 lib bdg; 0-06-000760-5 lib bdg

    LC 2005-18588

"Free-verse poems tell the story of a group of children who find each other during one otherwise lonely summer.... The African-American friends all bond, play, and build and paint an elaborate cardboard town they call Goodsummer. The simple watercolors work well at setting scenes of tidy streets lined with homes and lots of backyards and parks. Gilchrist's talent shows in her use of color, splashed with light.... For a younger audience than most novels-in-verse, this accessible and well-written book has a nostalgic tone." SLJ

Sister; drawings by Moneta Barnett. Crowell 1974 83p il hardcover o.p. pa $4.99
Grades: 4 5 6 7   **Fic**
    1. Sisters -- Fiction 2. African Americans -- Fiction 3. Single parent family -- Fiction
    ISBN 0-690-00497-4; 0-06-440199-5 pa

A 13-year-old black girl whose father is dead watches her 16-year-old sister drifting away from her and her mother and fears she may fall into the same self-destructive behavior herself. While waiting for her sister's return home, she leafs through her diary, reliving both happy and unhappy experiences while gradually recognizing her own individuality

"The book is strong . . . strong in perception, in its sensitivity, in its realism." Bull Cent Child Books

Greenwald, Lisa
  My life in pink and green. Amulet Books 2010 288 p. (hbk.) $16.95
Grades: 4 5 6 7   **Fic**
    1. Cosmetics -- Fiction 2. Environmental protection -- Fiction 3. Mother-daughter relationship -- Fiction
    ISBN 0810983524; 0810989840 pa; 9780810983526; 9780810989849

    LC 2008025577

When the family's drugstore is failing, seventh-grader Lucy uses her problem solving talents to come up with solution that might resuscitate the business, along with helping the environment.

"Greenwald deftly blends eco-facts and makeup tips, friendship dynamics, and spot-on middle-school politics into a warm, uplifting story." Booklist

Welcome to Dog Beach; Lisa Greenwald. Amulet Books 2014 272 p. (Seagate summers) $15.95
Grades: 5 6 7 8   **Fic**
    1. Dogs -- Fiction 2. Summer -- Fiction 3. Beaches -- Fiction 4. Friendship -- Fiction 5. Vacations -- Fiction 6. Dog walking -- Fiction
    ISBN 9781419710186; 1419710184

    LC 2013023282

"Eleven-year-old Remy loves Seagate, the island where her grandmother had a house and where her family spends every summer vacation. But this year's different. Remy misses her dog, Danish, who recently passed away. The usual Seagate traditions don't feel the same--and neither does her relationship with her two best friends, Micayla and Bennett.... Remy takes comfort in the company of Dog Beach." (Publisher's note)

"Greenwald's gentle read is tailor-made for those on the cusp of friendship misunderstandings, burgeoning popularity awareness, awkward crushes, and the wobbly feeling that can come from deviating from comfortable routine." Booklist

Greenwald, Tommy
  ★ **Charlie** Joe Jackson's guide to not reading. Roaring Brook Press 2011 220p il $14.99
Grades: 4 5 6 7   **Fic**
    1. School stories 2. Books and reading -- Fiction
    ISBN 978-1-59643-691-6; 1-59643-691-3

    LC 2010-24079

Middle schooler Charlie Joe is proud of his success at avoiding reading, but eventually his schemes go too far.

"With its subversive humor and contemporary details drawn straight from kids' worlds, this clever title should attract a wide following." Booklist

Charlie Joe Jackson's guide to summer vacation; by Tommy Greenwald; illustrated by J. P. Coovert. 1st ed. Roaring Brook Press 2013 231 p. ill. (hardcover) $14.99
Grades: 4 5 6 7   **Fic**
    1. Camps -- Fiction 2. Reading -- Fiction 3. Vacations -- Fiction 4. Humorous stories 5. Interpersonal relations -- Fiction
    ISBN 159643757X; 9781596437579; 9781596438804

    LC 2012034249

In this graphic novel by Tommy Greenwald "Charlie Joe Jackson finds himself in a terrible dream he can't wake up from: Camp Rituhbukkee ... a place filled with grammar workshops, Read-a-Ramas, and kids who actually like reading. But Charlie Joe is determined to convince the entire camp to hate reading and writing—one genius at a time. Tommy Greenwald's 'Charlie Joe Jackson's Guide to Summer Vacation' is another . . . installment in the life of a reluctant reader." (Publisher's note)

Griffin, Paul

When friendship followed me home; by Paul Griffin. Dial Books for Young Readers 2016 256 p. illustrations (hardcover) $16.99

Grades: 5 6 7 8   **Fic**

1. Dogs -- Fiction 2. Cancer -- Fiction 3. Schools -- Fiction 4. Adoption -- Fiction 5. Friendship -- Fiction 6. Middle schools -- Fiction

ISBN 9780803738164

LC 2015032638

In this juvenile novel, by Paul Griffin, "twelve-year-old Ben, a science fiction fan with low self-esteem after years of foster care, meets a stray dog outside the Coney Island Public Library. Flip . . . in turn helps Ben get to know a girl who is fighting cancer, and her family. When Ben's life gets turned upside down again, Flip remains. This is a 'kitchen sink' book; it has bullying, adoption, homelessness, death, abuse, and cancer." (School Library Journal)

"Griffin's characters are unique and charmingly multidimensional. Readers looking for a deep read will take to this story as quickly as Flip takes to Ben." Booklist

Griffin, Peni R.

The **ghost** sitter. Dutton Children's Bks. 2001 131p $14.99; pa $5.99

Grades: 4 5 6 7   **Fic**

1. Ghost stories

ISBN 0-525-46676-2; 0-14-230216-3 pa

LC 00-65859

When she realizes that her new house is haunted by the ghost of a ten-year-old girl who used to live there, Charlotte tries to help her find peace

"Griffin's book has several strong appeals: new best friends solving a mystery together, a just-scary-enough ghost girl, and a deathless bond between sisters that provides the book with its resoundingly satisfying conclusion and bang-up last sentence." Horn Book

Griffiths, Andy

The **13**-story Treehouse; Any Griffiths; illustrated by Terry Denton. Feiwel & Friends 2013 256 p. ill. (hardcover) $13.99

Grades: 3 4 5   **Fic**

1. Graphic novels 2. Treehouses -- Graphic novels

ISBN 1250026903; 9781250026903

In this children's graphic novel, "Andy and Terry live in a treehouse. In addition to the normal rooms found in a house, it has a theater and library, a bowling alley, and a games room. The boys write and illustrate books, and are far behind on their deadline for their publisher, Mr. Big Nose. They bicker and procrastinate and experience many adventures and misadventures." (School Library Journal)

The **26**-story treehouse; Andy Griffiths; illustrated by Terry Denton. 1st US edition Feiwel & Friends 2014 352 p. illustrations $13.99

Grades: 3 4 5   **Fic**

1. Imagination -- Fiction 2. Tree houses -- Fiction

ISBN 9781250073273; 1250026911; 9781250026910

LC 2014430138

Sequel to: The 13-Story Treehouse (2013)

In this children's story, by Andy Griffiths, illustrated by Terry Denton, "Andy and Terry live in a 26-story treehouse. (It used to be 13 stories, but they've expanded.) It has a bumper car rink, a skate ramp, an antigravity chamber, an ice cream parlor with 78 flavors, and the Maze of Doom--a maze so complicated that nobody who has gone in has ever come out again. Well, not yet, anyway." (Publisher's note)

"Griffiths and Denton follow the uproarious The 13-Story Treehouse with another cartoon-laden carnival of slapstick and self-referential humor--this time, with pirates. . . . Denton's furiously scrawled line drawings milk the silly, gross-out gags for everything they're worth." Pub Wkly

Grimes, Nikki

Almost zero; a Dyamonde Daniel book. illustrated by R. Gregory Christie. G. P. Putnam's Sons 2010 112p il $10

Grades: 2 3 4   **Fic**

1. School stories 2. Volunteer work -- Fiction 3. African Americans -- Fiction

ISBN 978-0-399-25177-1; 0-399-25177-4

LC 2010002282

Dyamonde is angry at her mother for not buying her the shoes she wants, but when she finds out that a classmate is in a worse situation, she is determined to help.

"This chapter book continues to introduce interesting secondary characters to keep Dyamonde's young fans engaged. Christie's modern black-and-white illustrations are perfect for the urban setting." Kirkus

Chasing freedom; the life journeys of Harriet Tubman and Susan B. Anthony, inspired by historical facts. Nikki Grimes; [illustrations by] Michele Wood. Orchard Books, an imprint of Scholastic Inc. 2015 5[] p. color illustrations $18.99

Grades: 3 4 5 6   **Fic**

1. Slavery -- Fiction 2. Women's rights -- Fiction 3. African Americans -- Fiction 4. Women -- Suffrage -- Fiction 5. Underground Railroad -- Fiction

ISBN 0439793386; 9780439793384

LC 201401483[]

NAACP Image Award Nominee: Outstanding Literary Work- Children (2016)

This juvenile biographical book, by Nikki Grimes, illustrated by Michele Wood, "offers a glimpse into the inspiring lives of Susan B. Anthony and Harriet Tubman. . . . [It] richly imagines the experiences of Tubman and Anthony, set against the backdrop of the Underground Railroad, the Civil War, and the Women's Suffrage Movement. Additional back matter invites curious young readers to further explore this period in history--and the larger-than-life figures who lived it." (Publisher's note)

"Two iconic women recount their stories. In New York state in 1904, a suffragist convention is about to begin, and Susan B. Anthony is scheduled to introduce Harriet Tubman. But first the two women meet at Anthony's home for tea and talk. Grimes artfully creates an afternoon of conversation and reminiscence in carefully constructed, fact-based vignettes that allow each to recount her life, accomplishments and continuing dreams...A tremendous opportunity for children to understand what these women worked so hard to accomplish—one succeeding and one coming close. (capsule biographies, additional notes, bibliography author's note) ." Kirkus

Includes bibliographical references

Garvey's choice; Nikki Grimes. WordSong 2016 120 p. $16.95

Grades: 4 5 6   **Fic**

1. Boys -- Fiction 2. Choirs (Music) -- Fiction 3. Choice (Psychology) -- Fiction 4. Father-son relationship -- Fiction

ISBN 9781629797403

LC 201693215

In this children's novel in verse by Nikki Grimes, "Garvey's father has always wanted Garvey to be athletic, but Garvey is interested in astronomy, science fiction, reading—anything but sports. . . . Whe his only friend encourages him to join the school chorus, Garvey's life changes. . . . Through chorus, Garvey finds a way to accept himself, and a way to finally reach his distant father—by speaking the language of music instead of the language of sports." (Publisher's note)

"A short, sweet, satisfying novel in verse that educators and readers alike will love." SLJ

Make way for Dyamonde Daniel; illustrated by R. Gregory Christie. G.P. Putnam's Sons 2009 74p il $10.99

Grades: 2 3 4 **Fic**

1. Moving -- Fiction 2. Friendship -- Fiction 3. African Americans -- Fiction

ISBN 978-0-399-25175-7; 0-399-25175-8

LC 2008-26788

Spunky third-grader Dyamonde Daniel misses her old neighborhood, but when she befriends a boy named Free, another new student at school, she finally starts to feel at home.

"Dyamonde . . . is a memorable main character. . . . Her actions and feelings ring true. Christie's illustrations flesh out the characters, and along with patterned page borders, contribute child appeal." SLJ

Other titles about Dyamonde Daniel are:
Rich (2009)
Almost zero (2010)

★ **Planet** Middle School. Bloomsbury Childrens 2011 154p $15.99

Grades: 4 5 6 7 **Fic**

1. School stories 2. Novels in verse 3. Basketball -- Fiction 4. Friendship -- Fiction 5. Family life -- Fiction

ISBN 978-1-59990-284-5; 1-59990-284-2

LC 2010050744

A series of poems describes all the baffling changes at home and at school in twelve-year-old Joylin's transition from tomboy basketball player to not-quite-girly girl.

"In freeflowing free-verse poems, multi–awardwinning author and poet Grimes . . . explores the riot of hormones and expected gender roles that can make negotiating the preteen years such a challenge. . . . A work that should help adolescent readers find the courage and humor to grow into the individuals they already are." Kirkus

Poems in the attic; by Nikki Grimes; illustrations by Elizabeth Zunon. Lee & Low Books Inc. 2014 48 p. color illustrations (hardcover : alk. paper) $19.95

Grades: 1 2 3 4 5 6 **Fic**

1. Poetry 2. Military bases -- Fiction 3. Moving, Household -- Fiction 4. Mothers and daughters -- Fiction

ISBN 1620140276; 9781620140277

LC 2014010354

In this children's story, by Nikki Grimes and illustrations by Elizabeth Zunon, "during a visit to her grandma's house, a young girl discovers a box of poems in the attic, poems written by her mother when she was growing up. Her mother's family often moved around the United States and the world because her father was in the Air Force. Over the years, her mother used poetry to record her experiences in the many places the family lived." (Publisher's note)

"On a visit to her grandmother's house, a little girl finds her mother's stash of childhood poems in the attic. The poems written by the mom in this story are tanka poems, an ancient Japanese form made up of five lines each and with strict syllable requirements. The daughter is a poet, too, and her poems about the experience of finding and reading her mother's work appear in free verse on left-hand pages (the mother's poems are on the right, italicized). . . . The final spread is a celebration of love and poetry as the girl is reunited with her mother. Young poets (and their parents and grandparents) will be inspired to write poems for future generations; the author's note and notes on the poetic forms will help them get started." Horn Book

Rich; a Dyamonde Daniel book. illustrated by R. Gregory Christie. G.P. Putnam's Sons 2009 95p il $10.99

Grades: 2 3 4 **Fic**

1. Poetry 2. Friendship -- Fiction 3. Homeless persons -- Fiction 4. African Americans -- Fiction

ISBN 978-0-399-25176-4; 0-399-25176-6

LC 2009001033

Free is excited about a local poetry contest because of its cash prize, but when he and Dyamonde befriend a classmate who is homeless and living in a shelter, they rethink what it means to be rich or poor.

This "volume looks at the sensitive issues of poverty and homelessness from different angles and in a reassuringly matter-of-fact way. Expressive ink drawings illustrate this fine beginning chapter book." Booklist

The **road** to Paris. G. P. Putnam's Sons 2006 153p $15.99; pa $6.99

Grades: 4 5 6 7 **Fic**

1. Siblings -- Fiction 2. Foster home care -- Fiction 3. Racially mixed people -- Fiction

ISBN 0-399-24537-5; 978-0-399-24537-4; 978-0-14-241082-0 pa; 0-14-241082-9 pa

LC 2005-28920

Inconsolable at being separated from her older brother, eight-year-old Paris is apprehensive about her new foster family but just as she learns to trust them, she faces a life-changing decision.

"In clear, short chapters, Grimes tells a beautiful story of family, friendship, and faith from the viewpoint of a child in search of home in a harsh world." Booklist

★ **Words** With Wings; by Nikki Grimes. Boyds Mills Press 2013 96 p. $15.95

Grades: 2 3 4 **Fic**

1. Child authors -- Fiction 2. Dreams -- Fiction 3. Imagination -- Fiction

ISBN 1590789857; 9781590789858

Coretta Scott King Honor Book: Author (2014)

In this book, by Nikki Grimes, "Gabby . . . is a daydreamer, and words fire her imagination, creating new worlds for her to inhabit. After her parents separate and Gabby must go to a different school, her daydreams become increasingly vivid, intruding on the realities of the classroom and schoolwork. To Gabby's occasional puzzlement, her mother worries . . . but her wonderful new teacher is more patient, wisely helping her capture her daydreams on paper and inspiring a new dream to become an author." (Booklist)

Grisham, John

Theodore Boone: the abduction. Dutton Children's Books 2011 217p $16.99

Grades: 4 5 6 7 **Fic**

1. Lawyers -- Fiction 2. Kidnapping -- Fiction

ISBN 978-0-525-42557-1; 0-525-42557-8

LC 2011006060

When his best friend disappears from her bedroom in the middle of the night, thirteen-year-old Theo uses his legal knowledge and investigative skills to chase down the truth and save April.

"The book is smoothly written, and there's a mild tutorial on the criminal justice system." Publ Wkly

Theodore Boone: kid lawyer. Dutton Children's Books 2010 263p $16.99

Grades: 4 5 6 7 **Fic**

1. Mystery fiction 2. Lawyers -- Fiction

ISBN 0-525-42384-2; 978-0-525-42384-3

With two attorneys for parents, thirteen-year-old Theodore Boone knows more about the law than most lawyers do. But when a high profile murder trial comes to his small town and Theo gets pulled into it, it's up to this amateur attorney to save the day.

"Grisham serves up a dandy legal adventure that moves along quickly. Without intruding on the story's trajectory, he gives plenty of background about the legal process and explores various ethical questions." Horn Book Guide

Gunderson, Jessica

Stranger on the silk road; a story of ancient China. by Jessica Gunderson; illustrated by Caroline Hu. Picture Window Books 2009 64p il (Read-it! chapter books: historical tales) lib bdg $21.26

Grades: 2 3 4 **Fic**

1. Silk -- Fiction 2. China -- Fiction

ISBN 978-1-4048-4736-1 lib bdg; 1-4048-4736-7 lib bdg

LC 2008006308

Song Sun likes to talk but never listens. After talking too much to a stranger, Song Sun accidentally gives away the Chinese secret of silk making

"Sassy, graphic-novel-style illustrations give [this] great little first chapter [book] extra appeal. . . . [This is a] wonderful [introduction] to historical fiction." SLJ

Guo Yue

★ **Little** Leap Forward; a boy in Beijing. by Guo Yue and Clare Farrow; illustrated by Helen Cann. Barefoot Books 2008 126p il $16.99

Grades: 3 4 5 6 **Fic**

1. Communism -- Fiction 2. Friendship -- Fiction 3. Family life -- Fiction 4. China -- History -- 1949-1976 -- Fiction

ISBN 978-1-84686-114-7; 1-84686-114-4

LC 2007-42676

In Communist China in 1966, eight-year-old Leap Forward learns about freedom while flying kites with his best friend, by trying to get a caged wild bird to sing, and through the music he is learning to play on a bamboo flute. Includes author's notes on his childhood in Beijing, life under Mao Zedong, and the Cultural Revolution.

"The simple prose is quiet and physical. . . . The beautifully detailed, clear illustrations in ink and brilliant watercolors combine realistic group scenes with spare, individual portraits." Booklist

Gutman, Dan

Abner & me; a baseball card adventure. HarperCollins 2005 166p (Baseball card adventure) $16.99; lib bdg $17.89; pa $5.99

Grades: 4 5 6 7 **Fic**

1. Baseball -- Fiction 2. Gettysburg (Pa.), Battle of, 1863 -- Fiction 3. United States -- History -- 1861-1865, Civil War -- Fiction

ISBN 0-06-053443-5; 0-06-053444-3 lib bdg; 0-06-053445-1 pa

LC 2004-6315

With his ability to travel through time using baseball cards and photographs, thirteen-year-old Joe and his mother go back to 1863 to ask Abner Doubleday whether he invented baseball, but instead find themselves in the middle of the Battle of Gettysburg.

Babe & me; a baseball card adventure. Avon Bks. 2000 161p il (Baseball card adventure) $15.99

Grades: 4 5 6 7 **Fic**

1. Baseball players 2. Baseball -- Fiction

ISBN 0-380-97739-7

LC 99-36778

With their ability to travel through time using vintage baseball cards, Joe and his father have the opportunity to find out whether Babe Ruth really did call his shot when he hit that homerun in the third game of the 1932 World Series against the Chicago Cubs

"Readers will enjoy the action, the rich baseball lore, and the sense of adventure." Booklist

The **Christmas** genie; illustrated by Dan Santat. Simon & Schuster Books for Young Readers 2009 150p il $15.99

Grades: 3 4 5 **Fic**

1. School stories 2. Wishes -- Fiction 3. Christmas -- Fiction 4. Meteorites -- Fiction

ISBN 978-1-4169-9001-7; 1-4169-9001-1

LC 2009017765

When a meteorite crashes into a fifth-grade classroom at Lincoln School in Oak Park, Illinois, the genie inside agrees to grant the class a Christmas wish—if they can agree on one within an hour.

This is "lively, thought-provoking, and hilarious. . . . Gutman packs plenty of history, science, and ethics lessons in this fun, well-paced fantasy." SLJ

The **homework** machine. Simon & Schuster Books for Young Readers 2006 146p $15.95; pa $5.99

Grades: 4 5 6 **Fic**

1. School stories

ISBN 0-689-87678-5; 0-689-87679-3 pa

LC 2005-19785

Four fifth-grade students—a geek, a class clown, a teacher's pet, and a slacker—as well as their teacher and mothers, each relate events surrounding a computer programmed to complete homework assignments.

"This fast-paced, entertaining book has something for everyone: convincing characters deftly portrayed . . .; points of discussion on ethics and student computer use; and every child's dream machine." Booklist

Followed by: Return of the homework machine (2009)

Honus & me; a baseball card adventure. Avon Bks. 1997 140p il (Baseball card adventure) $16.99; pa $5.99

Grades: 4 5 6 7 **Fic**

1. Baseball players 2. Baseball coaches 3. Baseball managers 4. Baseball -- Fiction

ISBN 0-380-97350-2; 0-380-78878-0 pa

LC 96-31439

Joey, who loves baseball but is not very good at it, finds a valuable 1909 Honus Wagner card and travels back in time to meet Honus

"This clever adventure will capture the hearts of anyone who has ever held a baseball bat in his or her hands. Gutman's voice rings true from start to finish." SLJ

Jackie & me; a baseball card adventure. Avon Bks. 1999 145p il (Baseball card adventure) $15.99; pa $5.99

Grades: 4 5 6 7 **Fic**

1. Baseball players 2. Army officers 3. Baseball -- Fiction

ISBN 0-380-97685-4; 0-380-80084-5 pa

LC 98-53347

With his ability to travel through time by using baseball cards, Joe goes back to 1947 to meet Jackie Robinson, turning into a black boy in the process

"Full of action, this title will spark history discussions and be a good choice for book reports and leisure reading." SLJ

Jim & me; a baseball card adventure. HarperCollins Publishers 2008 195p (Baseball card adventure) $15.99; lib bdg $16.89

Grades: 4 5 6 7 **Fic**

1. Decathletes 2. Pentathletes 3. Olympic athletes 4. Baseball

-- Fiction
ISBN 978-0-06-059494-7; 978-0-06-059495-4 lib bdg

LC 2007030703

Joe and his longtime enemy, Bobby Fuller, use a vintage baseball card to travel in time, hoping to stop Jim Thorpe from participating in the 1912 Olympics and losing his medals, but instead they watch Thorpe struggle during his first season with the New York Giants.

The **Lincoln** Project; Dan Gutman. Harper, an imprint of HarperCollinsPublishers 2016 240 p. illustrations, map (Flashback Four) (hardback) $16.99

Grades: 3 4 5   **Fic**
1. Time travel -- Fiction 2. Photography -- Fiction 3. Adventure and adventurers -- Fiction
ISBN 9780062374417

LC 2015015557

In this juvenile novel, by Dan Gutman, part of the "Flashback Four" series, "four very different kids are picked by a mysterious billionaire to travel through time and photograph some of history's most important events. This time, the four friends are headed to 1863 to catch Abraham Lincoln delivering his famous Gettysburg Address. They'll have to work together to ask the right questions, meet the right people, and capture the right moment. And most important—not get caught!" (Publisher's note)

"Breezy, good-natured fun and a fair amount of history, too." Kirkus
Another title in this series is:
The Titanic Mission (2017)

Mickey & me; a baseball card adventure. HarperCollins Pubs. 2003 152p il (Baseball card adventure) $15.99; pa $5.99

Grades: 4 5 6 7   **Fic**
1. Baseball players 2. Baseball -- Fiction
ISBN 0-06-029247-4; 0-06-029248-2 lib bdg; 0-06-447258-2 pa

LC 2002-5641

When Joe travels back in time to 1944, he meets the Milwaukee Chicks, one of the only all-female professional baseball teams in the history of the game

"Like the other books in the series, this one delivers a fast-moving plot, lots of action, and colorful depictions of famous sports heroes of the past." Booklist

Mission unstoppable. Harper 2011 293p (The genius files) $16.99; lib bdg $17.89

Grades: 5 6 7 8   **Fic**
1. Adventure fiction 2. Twins -- Fiction 3. Genius -- Fiction 4. Siblings -- Fiction 5. Family life -- Fiction
ISBN 0-06-182764-9; 0-06-182765-7 lib bdg; 978-0-06-182764-8; 978-0-06-182765-5 lib bdg

LC 2010-09390

On a cross-country vacation with their parents, twins Coke and Pepsi, soon to be thirteen, fend off strange assassins as they try to come to terms with their being part of a top-secret government organization known as The Genius Files.

"Gutman's novel offers a quirky look at Americana that will engage curious minds. . . . Those looking for a fun and suspenseful read . . . will not be disappointed." Booklist

Another title in this series is:
Never say genius (2012)

Never say genius. Harper 2012 (Genius files) $16.99; lib bdg $17.89

Grades: 5 6 7 8   **Fic**
1. Adventure fiction 2. Twins -- Fiction 3. Genius -- Fiction 4.

Siblings -- Fiction 5. Family life -- Fiction
ISBN 978-0-06-182767-9; 0-0-6182767-3; 978-0-06-182768-6 lib bdg; 0-06-182768-1 lib bdg

LC 2011019363

As their cross-country journey with their parents continues through the midwest, twins Coke and Pepsi, now thirteen, again face strange assassins at such places as the first McDonald's restaurant and Cedar Point amusement park.

"The author brings his confused but resourceful youngsters to an explosive climax and a shocking revelation that guarantees further adventures on the road back to the left coast." Kirkus

Ray & me; a baseball card adventure. HarperCollinsPublishers 2009 173p (Baseball card adventure) $15.99

Grades: 4 5 6 7   **Fic**
1. Baseball players 2. Baseball -- Fiction
ISBN 978-0-06-123481-1; 0-06-123481-8; 978-0-06-123482-8 lib bdg

LC 2008019645

After recovering from being hit in the head during a baseball game, Stosh travels back in time to try to save Ray Chapman, a batter who was killed by a pitch in New York in 1920.

The **return** of the homework machine. Simon & Schuster Books for Young Readers 2009 162p $15.99

Grades: 4 5 6   **Fic**
1. School stories 2. Arizona -- Fiction 3. Grand Canyon (Ariz.) -- Fiction
ISBN 978-1-4169-5416-3; 1-4169-5416-3

LC 2008029543

Sequel to: The homework machine (2006)

After discarding their infamous homework machine, four friends, now in sixth grade, find themselves once again at the police station, this time giving testimony about an incident involving a powerful computer chip, a Grand Canyon treasure, and a dead body.

Roberto & me; a baseball card adventure. Harper 2010 180p (Baseball card adventure) $15.99; lib bdg $16.89

Grades: 4 5 6 7   **Fic**
1. Baseball players 2. Baseball -- Fiction
ISBN 978-0-06-123484-2; 0-06-123484-2; 978-0-06-123485-9 lib bdg; 0-06-123485-0 lib bdg

LC 2009014267

Stosh travels back to 1969 to try to prevent the untimely death of Roberto Clemente, a legendary baseball player and humanitarian, but upon his return to the present, he meets his own great-grandson who takes him into the future, and what he finds there is more shocking than anything he has encountered in his travels to the past.

"This series entry is both amusing and informative." Booklist

Satch & me; a baseball card adventure. HarperCollins 2006 175p (Baseball card adventures) $15.99; lib bdg $16.89

Grades: 4 5 6 7   **Fic**
1. Baseball players 2. Baseball -- Fiction
ISBN 978-0-06-059491-6; 0-06-059491-8; 978-0-06-059492-3 lib bdg; 0-06-059492-6 lib bdg

LC 2005005717

With his ability to travel through time using vintage baseball cards, Joe takes Flip with him to find out whether Satchel Paige really was the fastest pitcher ever.

"Enhancing the action-driven story are plenty of well-written baseball scenes, black-and-white photos, and the appearance of Negro League players Josh Gibson, Cool Papa Bell, and Buck ONeil." SLJ

Shoeless Joe & me; a baseball card adventure. HarperCollins Pubs. 2002 163p (Baseball card adventures) hardcover o.p. lib bdg $17.89; pa $5.99

Grades: 4 5 6 7 **Fic**

1. Baseball players 2. Baseball -- Fiction

ISBN 0-06-029253-9; 0-06-029254-7 lib bdg; 0-06-447259-0 pa

LC 2001-24638

Joe Stoshack travels back to 1919, where he meets Shoeless Joe Jackson and tries to prevent the fixing of the World Series in which Jackson was wrongly implicated

"Shoeless Joe is compelling, and Joe's adventures are exciting." Voice Youth Advocates

Other titles in the Baseball card adventures series are:

Abner & me (2005)
Babe & me (2000)
Honus & me (1997)
Jackie & me (1999)
Jim & me (2008)
Mickey & me (2003)
Ray & me (2009)
Roberto & me (2010)
Satch & me (2006)

Haas, Jessie

Bramble and Maggie; horse meets girl. Jessie Haas; illustrated by Alison Friend. Candlewick Press 2012 51 p. $3.99

Grades: 1 2 3 **Fic**

1. Horses -- Fiction 2. Human-animal relationship -- Fiction

ISBN 0763662518; 9780763649555; 9780763662516

LC 2011018625

In this children's story, by Jessie Haas and illustrated by Alison Friend, "Maggie wants a pony to ride and take care of, and to prepare she's been reading a big book on horse care. Meanwhile, Bramble is bored with giving riding lessons and walking in circles. She's looking for just the right person to take her away from her routine. Is it a perfect match?" (Publisher's note)

"aggie and her horse, Bramble, are back in another beginning chapter book. With a slightly mischievous, frisky attitude in the cooler fall weather, Bramble takes risks and pretends to be fearful, while Maggie introduces her to the sights and sounds of autumn...Dialogue, Maggie's occasional reflections, and a bit of onomatopoeia allow the narrative text to flow nicely as a trusting relationship develops between horse and rider. A solid addition for general purchase." SLJ

Other titles include:

Give and Take (2013)
Spooky Season (2014)
Horse meets girl

Bramble and Maggie give and take; give and take. Jessie Haas, Alison Friend. Candlewick Press 2013 56 p. col. ill. (Bramble and Maggie.) $14.99

Grades: 1 2 3 **Fic**

1. Horses -- Fiction 2. Horsemanship -- Fiction 3. Human-animal relationship -- Fiction 4. Friendship -- Fiction 5. Human-animal relationships -- Fiction

ISBN 0763650218; 9780763650216

LC 2012942618

In this book, by Jessie Haas, "Bramble, an opinionated mare, isn't about to be taken advantage of. For instance, she knows all about rides: 'The rider sat in the saddle. The horse did all the hard work.' Young Maggie, as always, has Bramble's number, and with a little judicious bribery (give-and-take, thinks Bramble), they are soon having adventures together, Maggie in the saddle, Bramble content." (Kirkus Reviews)

"When Maggie attempts to saddle and bridle her horse, Bramble, she finds her uncooperative until they reach a solution she sees as give-and-take...Portraying human and animal characters empathetically, the narrative features moments of humor as well as insight. Expressive watercolor artwork will draw horse lovers to this highly satisfying book for beginning readers." Booklist

Other titles in the series include:

Horse meets Girl (2012)
Spooky Season (2014)
Give and take

Bramble and maggie spooky season; spooky season. Jessie Haas, illustrated by Alison Friend. First edition 2014 Candlewick Press 2014 56 p. colour illustrations $14.99

Grades: 1 2 3 **Fic**

1. Autumn -- Fiction 2. Horses -- Fiction 3. Halloween -- Fiction 4. Horsemanship -- Fiction 5. Children's stories 6. Human-animal relationships

ISBN 0763664502; 9780763664503

LC 2013952844

In this book, by Jessie Haas, "Bramble and Maggie explore a new season together—fall! Leaves crunch underfoot. Acorns ping off rooftops. It all makes Bramble feel wonderfully spooky. But Bramble's frisky-pretend-scary gait makes Maggie jumpy, and soon Bramble really is nervous. . . . When Maggie takes a fall, will she want to get back in the saddle? And when Halloween comes, can Maggie trust Bramble to brave the tricks and lead them both safely to the treats?" (Publisher's note)

"Clear, lively prose and soft, expressive gouache illustrations combine for a Halloween friendship story." Horn Book

Haddix, Margaret Peterson, 1964-

Caught; Book 5 Margaret Peterson Haddix. Simon & Schuster Books for Young Readers 2012 343 p. (The Missing) (hardcover : alk. paper) $16.99

Grades: 5 6 7 8 **Fic**

1. Science fiction 2. Time travel -- Fiction 3. Einstein, Albert, 1879-1955 -- Fiction 4. Space and time -- Fiction 5. Serbia -- History -- 1804-1918 -- Fiction 6. Switzerland -- History -- 20th century -- Fiction

ISBN 141698982X; 9781416989820; 9781442422889

LC 2011018654

In this fifth installment of Margaret Peterson Haddix's "Missing" series, "Jonah and Katherine are accustomed to traveling through time, but when learn they next have to return Albert Einstein's daughter to history, they think it's a joke -- they've only heard of his sons. But it turns out that Albert Einstein really did have a daughter, Lieserl, whose 1902 birth and subsequent disappearance was shrouded in mystery." (Publisher's note)

Children of exile; Margaret Peterson Haddix. Simon & Schuster Books for Young Readers 2016 304 p. (ebook) $15.99; (hardcover) $17.99

Grades: 5 6 7 8 9 **Fic**

1. Science fiction 2. Parent-child relationship -- Fiction 3. Parent and child -- Fiction

ISBN 9781442450059; 9781442450035; 9781442450042

LC 2015031239

In this novel by Margaret Peterson Haddix, "Rosi must decide what she's willing to risk to save her family—and maybe even all of humanity. . . . For the past twelve years, adults called 'Freds' have raised Rosi, her younger brother Bobo, and the other children of their town, saying it is too dangerous for them to stay with their parents, but now they are all being sent back. . . . Will Rosi and the other kids be able to adjust to their new reality?" (Publisher's note)

"Haddix gives readers lots to mull over regarding conflict, justice, and prejudice." Pub Wkly

★ **Found**. Simon & Schuster Books for Young Readers 2008 314p (The missing) $15.99; pa $6.99

Grades: 5 6 7 8 9   **Fic**
1. Science fiction 2. Adoption -- Fiction
ISBN 978-1-4169-5417-0; 1-4169-5417-1; 978-1-4169-5421-7 pa; 1-4169-5421-X pa

LC 2007-23614

When thirteen-year-olds Jonah and Chip, who are both adopted, learn they were discovered on a plane that appeared out of nowhere, full of babies with no adults on board, they realize that they have uncovered a mystery involving time travel and two opposing forces, each trying to repair the fabric of time.

This is "a tantalizing opener to a new series. . . . Readers will be hard-pressed to wait for the next installment." Publ Wkly

Other titles in this series are:
Sent (2009)
Sabotaged (2010)
Torn (2011)

Risked; Margaret Peterson Haddix. Simon & Schuster Books for Young Readers 2013 320 p. (The missing) (hardcover : alk. paper) $16.99

Grades: 5 6 7 8 9   **Fic**
1. Time travel -- Fiction 2. Soviet Union -- History -- 1917-1921, Revolution -- Fiction 3. Science fiction
ISBN 1416989846; 9781416989844; 9781442426474

LC 2012006770

In this book, by Margaret Peterson Haddix, "When Jonah and Katherine find themselves on a mission to return Alexei and Anastasia Romanov to history and then save them from the Russian Revolution, they are at a loss. Because in their own time, the bones of Alexei and Anastasia have been positively identified through DNA testing. What hope do they have of saving Alexis and Anastasia's lives when the twenty-first century has proof of their deaths?" (Publisher's note)

Sabotaged. Simon & Schuster Books for Young Readers 2010 377p (The missing) $16.99

Grades: 5 6 7 8 9   **Fic**
1. Science fiction 2. Colonists 3. Roanoke Island (N.C.) -- History -- Fiction
ISBN 978-1-4169-5424-8; 1-4169-5424-4

Sequel to: Sent (2009)

Time-travelers Jonah and Katherine are summoned to help another missing child from history, this time Virginia Dare from the Roanoke Colony, but their journey is sabotaged and goes dangerously awry, leaving them in the wrong time period. Includes author's note about the history of Roanoke Colony and Virginia Dare.

Sent. Simon & Schuster Books for Young Readers 2009 313p (The missing) $15.99; pa $6.99

Grades: 5 6 7 8 9   **Fic**
1. Science fiction 2. Kings 3. Time travel -- Fiction 4. Great Britain -- Fiction
ISBN 978-1-4169-5422-4; 1-4169-5422-8; 978-1-4169-5423-1 pa; 1-4169-5423-6 pa

LC 2008-11552

Sequel to: Found (2008)

Jonah, Katherine, Chip, and Alex suddenly find themselves in 1483 at the Tower of London, where they discover that Chip and Alex are Prince Edward V and Richard of Shrewsbury, imprisoned by their uncle, King Richard III, but trying to repair history without knowing what is supposed to happen proves challenging. Author's note includes historical facts about the princes and king

"Haddix conveys quite a bit of real history painlessly to her target audience and even mixes in some physics. . . . Valuable fun for tweens." Kirkus

Followed by: Sabotaged (2010)

Torn. Simon & Schuster Books for Young Readers 2011 345p (The missing) $15.99

Grades: 5 6 7 8   **Fic**
1. Explorers 2. Science fiction 3. Time travel -- Fiction 4. Voyages and travels -- Fiction
ISBN 978-1-4169-8980-6; 1-4169-8980-3

LC 2010019645

Time travelers Jonah and Katherine arrive in 1611 to rescue missing child John Hudson, son of the explorer Henry Hudson, but just as the mutiny on the Discovery is supposed to start, Jonah and Katherine's knowledge of history is tested once again, and they fear that more is at stake than just one boy's life. Author's note includes facts about Henry Hudson's explorations.

"Hudson's ill-fated explorations provide an excellent opportunity for readers to learn about sailing ships, survival, and mutiny. Plenty of action and an extended author's note sustain this fourth entry in the Missing series." Booklist

Under their skin; Margaret Peterson Haddix. Simon & Schuster Books for Young Readers 2016 320 p. (hardcover) $16.99

Grades: 4 5 6 7   **Fic**
1. Family secrets -- Fiction 2. Science fiction 5. Twins -- Fiction 6. Robots -- Fiction 7. Secrets -- Fiction 8. Human beings -- Fiction 9. Brothers and sisters -- Fiction 10. Extinction (Biology) -- Fiction
ISBN 9781481417587; 9781481417594

LC 2014036962

This juvenile novel, by Margaret Peterson Haddix, is "the first book in a brand-new thrilling series about twins who are on a quest to discover the secrets being kept by their new family. Nick and Eryn's mom is getting remarried, and the twelve-year-old twins are skeptical when . . . Mom tells them . . . they won't ever have to meet their stepsiblings. . . . So the twins set out on a mission to find out who these kids are—and why they're being kept hidden." (Publisher's note)

"Haddix offers a gripping blend of science fiction, suspense, and mystery, taking middle graders and teens on a fast-paced ride that will interest even the most reluctant reader." SLJ

Another title in this series is:
In over their heads (2017)

Haddon, Mark

Boom! (or 70,000 light years) David Fickling Books 2010 194p $15.99; lib bdg $18.99

Grades: 4 5 6 7   **Fic**
1. Science fiction 2. Great Britain -- Fiction 3. Interplanetary voyages -- Fiction 4. Extraterrestrial beings -- Fiction
ISBN 978-0-385-75187-2; 0-385-75187-7; 978-0-385-75188-9 lib bdg; 0-385-75188-5 lib bdg

First published 1992 in the United Kingdom with title: Gridzbi spudvetch

When Jim and Charlie overhear two of their teachers talking in a secret language and the two friends set out to solve the mystery, they do not expect the dire consequences of their actions.

"Adventure and quirky humor keep the pages turning, and readers will connect to Jimbo with little difficulty. If they can overcome some of the cultural differences, they will appreciate the simple and engaging tale." SLJ

Hagen, George

★ **Gabriel** Finley and the raven's riddle; George Hagen. Schwartz & Wade Books 2014 384 p. illustrations, maps (lib bdg) $19.99
Grades: 5 6 7 8　　　　　　　　　　　　　　　**Fic**
1. Fantasy fiction 2. Ravens -- Fiction 3. Magic -- Fiction 4. Missing persons -- Fiction 5. Voyages and travels -- Fiction 6. Adventure and adventurers -- Fiction
ISBN 9780385371049; 0385371047; 9780385371032
　　　　　　　　　　　　　　　　　　LC 2013032533
This fantasy by George Hagen follows the "twelve-year-old Gabriel [trying to] find his missing father, who seems to have vanished without a trace. . . . With the help of Paladin--a young raven with whom he has a magical bond that enables them to become one creature--he flies to the foreboding land of Aviopolis, where he must face a series of difficult challenges and unanswerable riddles that could lead to his . . . or to his death." (Publisher's note)
"Hagen's first children's book, flavored with Norse mythology, is brimful of antic energy and inventive flair, like the best middle-grade fantasies." Kirkus
Gabriel Finley and the raven's riddle

Hahn, Mary Downing

All the lovely bad ones; a ghost story. Clarion Books 2008 182p $16; pa $5.99
Grades: 4 5 6 7　　　　　　　　　　　　　　　**Fic**
1. Ghost stories 2. Vermont -- Fiction 3. Siblings -- Fiction 4. Hotels and motels -- Fiction
ISBN 978-0-618-85467-7; 978-0-547-24878-3 pa
　　　　　　　　　　　　　　　　　　LC 2007-37932
While spending the summer at their grandmother's Vermont inn, two prankster siblings awaken young ghosts from the inn's distant past who refuse to "rest in peace."
"In addition to crafting some genuinely spine-chilling moments, the author takes a unique approach to a well-traversed genre." Publ Wkly

★ The **ghost** of Crutchfield Hall. Clarion Books 2010 153p $17
Grades: 5 6 7 8　　　　　　　　　　　　　　　**Fic**
1. Ghost stories 2. Cousins -- Fiction 3. Orphans -- Fiction 4. Great Britain -- History -- 19th century -- Fiction
ISBN 978-0-547-38560-0; 0-547-38560-9
In the nineteenth century, ten-year-old Florence Crutchfield leaves a London orphanage to live with her great-uncle, great-aunt, and sickly cousin James, but she soon realizes the home has another resident, who means to do her and James harm.
"A deliciously spine-tingling tale that even the most reluctant readers will enjoy." SLJ

★ **Hear** the wind blow. Clarion Bks. 2003 212p $15
Grades: 5 6 7 8　　　　　　　　　　　　　　　**Fic**
1. Siblings -- Fiction 2. United States -- History -- 1861-1865, Civil War -- Fiction
ISBN 0-618-18190-3
　　　　　　　　　　　　　　　　　　LC 2002-15977
With their mother dead and their home burned, a thirteen-year-old boy and his little sister set out across Virginia in search of relatives during the final days of the Civil War
The author "gives readers an entertaining and thought-provoking combination: a strong adventure inextricably bound to a specific time and place, but one that resonates with universal themes." Horn Book

★ **Wait** till Helen comes; a ghost story. Clarion Bks. 1986 184p $15; pa $5.95; pa $6.99

Grades: 4 5 6　　　　　　　　　　　　　　　**Fic**
1. Ghost stories 2. Stepchildren -- Fiction
ISBN 0-89919-453-2; 0-547-02864-4 pa; 9780380704422 pa
　　　　　　　　　　　　　　　　　　LC 86-2648
"Molly, the 12-year-old narrator, and her brother Michael dislike their bratty 5-year-old stepsister Heather and resent the family move to an isolated converted church in the country. The adjourning graveyard frightens Molly, but Heather seems drawn to it. Molly discovers that the ghost of a child (Helen) who died in a fire a century ago wants to lure Heather to her doom. Molly determines to save her stepsister. In so doing, she learns that Heather's strange behavior stems from her feelings of guilt at having accidentally caused her mother's death by playing near a stove and starting a fire. Eventually, Molly wrests Heather from Helen's arms as the ghost attempts to drown them. The girls discover the skeletons of Helen's parents, and their burial finally puts to rest Helen's spirit. . . . Grades four to seven." (SLJ)
"Intertwined with the ghost story is the question of Molly's moral imperative to save a child she truly dislikes. Though the emotional turnaround may be a bit quick for some, this still scores as a first-rate thriller." Booklist

★ **Witch** catcher. Clarion Books 2006 236p $16
Grades: 3 4 5 6　　　　　　　　　　　　　　　**Fic**
1. Fairies -- Fiction 2. Witches -- Fiction 3. West Virginia -- Fiction 4. Father-daughter relationship -- Fiction
ISBN 0-618-50457-5
　　　　　　　　　　　　　　　　　　LC 2005-24795
Having just moved into the West Virginia home they inherited from a distant relative, twelve-year-old Jen is surprised that her father is already dating a local antiques dealer, but more surprised by what the spooky woman really wants.
"A fast-paced, suspenseful fantasy in which an appealing heroine stands against forces seemingly beyond her control." Booklist

Haig, Matt

A **boy** called Christmas; Matt Haig; with illustrations by Chris Mould. Alfred A. Knopf 2016 240 p. illustrations (hardback) $16.99
Grades: 2 3 4 5 6　　　　　　　　　　　　　　　**Fic**
1. Christmas -- Fiction 2. Santa Claus -- Fiction
ISBN 0399552650; 9780399552656; 9780399552663
　　　　　　　　　　　　　　　　　　LC 2015043442
In this book, by Matt Haig, with illustrations by Chris Mould, "eleven-year-old Nikolas—nicknamed 'Christmas'—has received only one toy in his life: a doll carved out of a turnip. But he's happy with his turnip doll, because it came from his parents, who love him. Then one day his father goes missing, and Nikolas must travel to the North Pole to save him. Along the way, Nikolas befriends a surly reindeer, bests a troublesome troll, and discovers a hidden world of enchantment." (Publisher's note)
"The clever story is powdered with puckish illustrations and reminds humans and elves alike that goodness and kindness are a kind of magic. Like stockings hung by the fire, this spellbinding opus may well become a yuletide tradition." Kirkus

Hale, Dean

The **princess** in black takes a vacation; Shannon Hale, Dean Hale, LeUyen Pham. Candlewick Press 2016 96 p. color illustrations (Princess in Black) (hardcover) $14.99
Grades: K 1 2 3　　　　　　　　　　　　　　　**Fic**
1. Monsters -- Fiction 2. Princesses -- Fiction
ISBN 9780763694517; 9780763665128
　　　　　　　　　　　　　　　　　　LC 2016947248
In this children's story, by Shannon Hale and Dean Hale, illustrated by LeUyen Pham, "after battling monsters all night, a sleepy Princess

in Black decides that she needs a vacation. After all, the Goat Avenger, a new hero who looks oddly familiar, has offered to protect the goats while she takes a much needed break. . . . But just as Princess Magnolia is about to take a nap on her hammock, she hears a 'ROAR!' Seriously? A monster?" (Publisher's note)

"As always, hilarious; perhaps the strongest Princess in Black outing since the first." Kirkus

Hale, Shannon

★ **Princess** Academy; Shannon Hale. Bloomsbury Children's Books 2005 314 p. (hc) $17.99

Grades: 5 6 7 8   **Fic**
   1. Telepathy -- Fiction 2. Princesses -- Fiction 3. Schools -- Fiction
   ISBN 1582349932; 9781582349930

           LC 2004065958
   Newbery Honor Book (2006)

While attending a strict academy for potential princesses with the other girls from her mountain village, fourteen-year-old Miri discovers unexpected talents and connections to her homeland.

"Hale weaves an intricate, multilayered story about families, relationships, education, and the place we call home." SLJ

The **Princess** in Black; Shannon Hale, Dean Hale, illustrated by LeUyen Pham. Candlewick Press 2014 96 p. col. ill. $14.99

Grades: K 1 2 3   **Fic**
   1. Monsters -- Fiction 2. Princesses -- Fiction 3. Superheroes -- Fiction
   ISBN 076366510X; 9780763665104

           LC 2013955700

In this book, by Shannon Hale and Dean Hale, "Princess Magnolia is having hot chocolate and scones with Duchess Wigtower when . . . Brring! Brring! The monster alarm! A big blue monster is threatening the goats! Stopping monsters is no job for dainty Princess Magnolia. But luckily Princess Magnolia has a secret—she's also the Princess in Black, and stopping monsters is the perfect job for her!" (Publisher's note)

"With her cherubic face, gold curls, sparkly tiara, glass slippers, and meringuelike pink-on-pink ensemble, Princess Magnolia seems the epitome of a 'prim and perfect' princess. But she has a secret life, one that involves donning a stylish black costume and defeating monsters (who are more goofy than scary, truth be told) that threaten her kingdom. . . . Pham (A Piece of Cake) offers little jolts of energy and wit on every page, with full-page and spot illustrations that have the vivaciousness and irreverence of contemporary animation." Pub Wkly

   Another title in this series is:
   The Princess in Black and the Perfect Princess Party (2015)
   The Princess in Black and the Hungry Bunny Horde (2016)

The **princess** in black and the perfect princess party; Shannon and Dean Hale, LeUyen Pham. Candlewick Press 2015 96 p. color illustrations (Princess in black) $14.99

Grades: K 1 2 3   **Fic**
   1. Princesses -- Fiction 2. Superheroes -- Fiction
   ISBN 0763665118; 9780763665111

           LC 2014949932

In this children's story, by Shannon and Dean Hale, illustrated by LeUyen Pham, "today is Princess Magnolia's birthday party, and she wants everything to be perfect. But just as her guests are arriving . . . Brring! Brring! The monster alarm! Princess Magnolia runs to the broom closet, ditches her frilly clothes, and becomes the Princess in Black! She rushes to the goat pasture, defeats the monster, and returns to the castle before her guests discover her secret." (Publisher's note)

"A chuckle-inducing, entirely worthy stand-alone follow-up to the terrific The Princess in Black (2014)." Kirkus

The **storybook** of legends; by Shannon Hale. Little Brown & Co 2013 320 p. (Ever After High) (hardback) $14.99

Grades: 4 5 6 7   **Fic**
   1. Fairy tales 2. School stories 3. Schools -- Fiction 4. Friendship -- Fiction 5. Fairy tales -- Fiction 6. Boarding schools -- Fiction 7. Fate and fatalism -- Fiction 8. Characters in literature -- Fiction
   ISBN 0316401226; 9780316401227

           LC 2013024496

"At Ever After High, an enchanting boarding school, the children of fairytale legends prepare themselves to fulfill their destinies as the next generation of Snow Whites, Prince Charmings and Evil Queens . . . whether they want to or not. Each year on Legacy Day, students sign the Storybook of Legends to seal their scripted fates." (Publisher's note)

"Raven Queen and Apple White, the daughters of famous fairy-tale characters, begin their much-anticipated Legacy Year at Ever After High. They investigate the mystery of a lost story, and Raven realizes that being evil might not be her only path. Fans of the Inkheart and Sisters Grimm series will enjoy the 'hexellent' fairy-tale-infused lingo and lively characters." Horn Book

   Other titles in this series are:
   The unfairest of them all (2014)
   A Wonderlandiful world (2014)

Hamilton, Virginia

Drylongso; illustrated by Jerry Pinkney. Harcourt Brace Jovanovich 1992 54p il hardcover o.p. pa $10

Grades: 3 4 5   **Fic**
   1. Droughts -- Fiction 2. Farm life -- Fiction 3. African Americans -- Fiction
   ISBN 0-15-201587-6 pa

           LC 91-25575

As a great wall of dust moves across their drought-stricken farm, a family's distress is relieved by a young man called Drylongso, who literally blows into their lives with the storm

"In an understand story of drought and hard times and longing for rain, a great writer and a great artists have pared down their rich, exuberant styles to something quieter but no less intense." Booklist

★ The **house** of Dies Drear; illustrated by Eros Keith. Macmillan 1968 246p il hardcover o.p. pa $5.99

Grades: 5 6 7 8   **Fic**
   1. Mystery fiction 2. Ohio -- Fiction 3. African Americans -- Fiction
   ISBN 0-02-742500-2; 1-4169-1405-6 pa

"The answer to the mystery comes in a startling dramatic dénouement that is pure theater. This is gifted writing; the characterization is unforgettable, the plot imbued with mounting tension." Saturday Rev

   Followed by The mystery of Drear House (1987)

★ **M.C.** Higgins, the great; 25th anniversary ed; Simon & Schuster 1999 232p $18; pa $5.99

Grades: 5 6 7 8   **Fic**
   1. Family life -- Fiction 2. African Americans -- Fiction 3. Appalachian region -- Fiction
   ISBN 0-689-83074-2; 1-4169-1407-2 pa

           LC 99014288
   Awarded the Newbery Medal, 1975

As a slag heap, the result of strip mining, creeps closer to his house in the Ohio hills, fifteen-year-old M.C. is torn between trying to get his family away and fighting for the home they love

"This is a deeply involving story possessing a folklorish quality." Child Book Rev Serv

Han, Jenny

★ **Clara** Lee and the apple pie dream; with pictures by Julia Kuo. Little, Brown and Company 2011 149p il $14.99

Grades: 2 3 4   **Fic**

1. School stories 2. Family life -- Fiction 3. Korean Americans -- Fiction

ISBN 978-0-316-07038-6; 0-316-07038-6

LC 2010-06900

Korean American fourth-grader Clara Lee longs to be Little Miss Apple Pie, and when her luck seems suddenly to change for the better, she overcomes her fear of public speaking and enters the competition.

Han "captures an 8-year-old's perspective perfectly.... The message shines through but doesn't overwhelm this engaging chapter book that will be welcomed by middle-grade fans of Clementine." Kirkus

Hanlon, Abby

Dory Dory black sheep; by Abby Hanlon. Dial Books for Young Readers, an imprint of Penguin Random House, LLC 2017 160 p. illustrations (Dory fantasmagory) (hardback) $14.99; (ebook) $44.97

Grades: 1 2 3   **Fic**

1. Imagination -- Fiction 2. Books and reading -- Fiction 3. Imaginary playmates -- Fiction

ISBN 1101994266; 9781101994269; 9781101994283

LC 2016011714

In this third book in the Dory Fantasmagory series by Abby Hanlon, "ever since Dory met Rosabelle, ... school has been pretty good. But now the class is learning to read, and it's proving to be a challenge for Dory. While Rosabelle can read chapter books in her head, Dory is stuck with baby books about a happy little farm. Dory wishes for a potion to turn her into a reader but things don't go as planned." (Publisher's note)

"With amusing situations and expressive, childlike drawings, the third entry in the Dory Fantasmagory series will satisfy the many young chapter-book readers who like their books served with a generous helping of fun." Booklist

★ **Dory** Fantasmagory; by Abby Hanlon. Dial Books for Young Readers, an imprint of Penguin Group (USA) Inc. 2014 160 p. illustrations (hardcover) $14.99

Grades: 1 2 3   **Fic**

1. Family life -- Fiction 2. Imagination -- Fiction 3. Imaginary playmates -- Fiction 4. Brothers and sisters -- Fiction

ISBN 0803740883; 9780803740884

LC 2013034996

In this book by Abby Hanlon, "Dory really wants attention, and more than anything she wants her brother and sister to play with her. But she's too much of a baby for them, so she's left to her own devices.... Her siblings may roll their eyes at her childish games, but Dory has lots of things to do: outsmarting the monsters all over the house, escaping from prison (aka time-out), and exacting revenge on her sister's favorite doll." (Publisher's note)

"The frequent kidlike illustrations integrate seamlessly with the text, adding another layer of madcap humor. Try this as a lively group read-aloud." Horn Book

Other title about Dory:

Dory and the Real Friend (2015)

Hannigan, Kate

The **detective's** assistant; by Kate Hannigan. Little, Brown & Co. 2015 368 p. (hardcover) $17

Grades: 4 5 6 7   **Fic**

1. Mystery fiction 2. Aunts -- Fiction 3. Orphans -- Fiction 4. Chicago (Ill.) -- Fiction 5. Women detectives -- Fiction 6. Sex

role -- Fiction

ISBN 0316403512; 9780316403511

LC 2014015131

In this book, by Kate Hannigan, "Nell Warne arrives on her aunt's doorstep. . . . If her Aunt Kate rejects her, it's the miserable Home for the Friendless. Luckily, canny Nell makes herself indispensable to Aunt Kate...and not just by helping out with household chores. For Kate Warne is the first-ever female detective employed by the legendary Pinkerton Detective Agency. And Nell has a knack for the kind of close listening and bold action that made Pinkerton detectives famous." (Publisher's note)

"Nell Warne, eleven, is all alone in the world. Aunt Kitty might provide a home, but she's busy being Pinkerton's first female detective. Nell must prove herself an able assistant by going undercover and maybe even saving the president-to-be. Set against the backdrop of the looming Civil War, Nell's spirited first-person narration is juxtaposed with letters to her African American friend Jemma." Horn Book

Hannigan, Katherine

★ **Emmaline** and the bunny. Greenwillow Books 2009 94p il $14.99

Grades: 1 2 3   **Fic**

1. Rabbits -- Fiction 2. Loneliness -- Fiction 3. Cleanliness -- Fiction

ISBN 978-0-06-162654-8; 0-06-162654-6

LC 2008012639

Everyone and everything in the town of Neatasapin is tidy, except Emmaline who likes to dig dirt and jump in puddles, and wants to adopt an untidy bunny.

"Told in very short chapters and using language in unusual ways, this is a small delight, cunningly illustrated by Hannigan's own sweet watercolors." Booklist

True (. . . sort of) Greenwillow Books 2011 360p $16.99; lib bdg $17.89

Grades: 4 5 6   **Fic**

1. School stories 2. Siblings -- Fiction 3. Friendship -- Fiction 4. Family life -- Fiction

ISBN 978-0-06-196873-0; 0-06-196873-0; 978-0-06-196874-7 lib bdg; 0-06-196874-9 lib bdg

For most of her eleven years, Delly has been in trouble without knowing why, until her little brother, R. B., and a strange, silent new friend, Ferris, help her find a way to be good—and happy—again.

"Told in carefully crafted language that begs to be read aloud, the story runs the gamut from laugh-out-loud funny to emotionally wrenching." SLJ

Hansen, Joyce

Home is with our family; [illustrated by] E. B. Lewis. Hyperion 2010 272p il (Black pioneers) $16.99

Grades: 4 5 6 7   **Fic**

1. Abolitionists -- Fiction 2. African Americans -- Fiction

ISBN 978-0-7868-5217-8; 0-7868-5217-8

Maria Peterson is looking forward to turning 13. She envisions new adult prestige and responsibility, like attending abolitionist meetings and listening to inspiring speakers like Sojourner Truth. However, she doesn't bank on all the unexpected changes that her 13th year brings.

"The plot flows quickly and has enough action to hold a reader's attention. Teachers can use this book to provide their students with a deeper understanding of the Fugitive Slave Act." Libr Media Connect

Haptie, Charlotte

Otto and the flying twins; the first book of the Karmidee. [by] Charlotte Haptie. Holiday House 2004 304p il $17.95

Grades: 4 5 6 7   **Fic**
1. Fantasy fiction 2. Magic -- Fiction
ISBN 0-8234-1826-X

LC 2003-57135

First published 2002 in the United Kingdom

Young Otto comes to the rescue when he discovers that his family and city are the last remnants of an ancient magical world now under threat from the Normal Police

"The amazing oddities and quirks of this world and its residents are described with delicious nonchalance. . . . The characters are equally surprising and unpredictable. . . . The writing is as fresh and invigorating as the setting." SLJ

Another title about Otto is:
Otto and the bird charmers (2005)

Hardinge, Frances
Fly by night. HarperCollinsPublishers 2006 487p hardcover o.p. lib bdg $17.89; pa $7.99
Grades: 5 6 7 8   **Fic**
1. Fantasy fiction
ISBN 978-0-06-087627-2; 0-06-087627-1; 978-0-06-087629-6 lib bdg; 0-06-087629-8 lib bdg; 978-0-06-087630-2 pa; 0-06-087630-1 pa

LC 2005-20598

Mosca Mye and her homicidal goose, Saracen, travel to the city of Mandelion on the heels of smooth-talking con-man, Eponymous Clent.

"Through rich, colorful language and a sure sense of plot and pacing, Hardinge has created a distinctly imaginative world full of engaging characters, robust humor, and true suspense." SLJ

Followed by: Fly trap (2011)

Fly trap; Frances Hardinge. HarperCollins 2011 592 p. hbk $16.99
Grades: 5 6 7 8   **Fic**
1. Fantasy fiction 2. Geese -- Fiction 3. Orphans -- Fiction
ISBN 0060880449; 9780060880446

LC 2010027755

Sequel to: Fly by night (2006)

"Having barely escaped the revolution they had a huge (if accidental) part in causing, sharp-eyed orphan Mosca Mye; her guard goose, Saracen; and their sometimes-loyal companion, the con man Eponymous Clent, must start anew.

All too quickly, they find themselves embroiled in fresh schemes and twisting politics as they are trapped in Toll, an odd town that changes its entire personality as day turns to night. Mosca and her friends attempt to fend off devious new foes, subvert old enemies, prevent the kidnapping of the mayor's daughter, steal the town's Luck, and somehow manage to escape with their lives--and hopefully a little money in their pockets." (Publisher's note)

Crammed with eccentric, Dickensian characters, unexpected plot turns, and numerous very niche gods and goddesses . . . , Hardinge's world is rich enough to fuel two or three fantasy novels. It's a beautifully written tale, by turns humorous and heartbreaking and a sheer pleasure to read. Publ Wkly

Hardy, Janice
Blue fire. Balzer + Bray 2010 373p (The Healing Wars) $16.99
Grades: 5 6 7 8   **Fic**
1. War stories 2. Fantasy fiction 3. Orphans -- Fiction 4. Sisters -- Fiction
ISBN 978-0-06-174741-0; 0-06-174741-6

LC 2009053446

Sequel to: The shifter (2009)

While trying to lead the Takers out of Geveg, fifteen-year-old Nya is captured by bounty-hunters and taken to Baseer, where she escapes and soon finds herself helping the Baseeri.

"The climax . . . yields much narrative tension but doesn't resolve the driving issues of the story. For that, readers will have to wait for book three in this thrilling, complex saga." Horn Book

Darkfall. Balzer + Bray 2011 418p (The healing wars) $16.99
Grades: 5 6 7 8   **Fic**
1. Fantasy fiction 2. Orphans -- Fiction 3. Sisters -- Fiction
ISBN 978-0-06-174750-2; 0-06-174750-5

LC 2011001946

With the rebellion in full swing, fifteen year-old Nya's loyaltie are put to the ultimate test.and she is forced to choose between leading an army against the Duke or abandoning her people to save her sister.

"The finale offers suspense, resolution of prior wrongs, the sweetness of first love and a battle-tested heroine who fights with her head and heart." Kirkus

Harkrader, Lisa
The **adventures** of Beanboy; written and illustrated by Lisa Harkrader. Houghton Mifflin Harcourt 2012 234p. ill.
Grades: 4 5 6 7 8   **Fic**
1. Family -- Fiction 2. Domestic relations 3. Superhero comic books, strips, etc. 4. Comic books, strips, etc. -- Fiction 5. Schools -- Fiction 6. Contests -- Fiction 7. Middle schools -- Fiction 8. Family problems -- Fiction
ISBN 9780547550787

LC 2011012161

In this book, "Tucker MacBean is a collector and aspiring creator of comic books, a preoccupation that he realizes doesn't rank high 'on the sliding scale of middle-school coolness.' He enters a contest to create a sidekick for his favorite superhero, convinced that a win will jump-start his popularity; he plans to give the prize--a college scholarship--to his overextended single mother, who's juggling classes and work. Tucker joins the art club to prepare his entry, and Sam (a classmate who Tucker sees as 'arch nemesis to the world') is hired to babysit his special-needs brother after school. . . . Tucker displays his own heroism when he reaches out to Sam after discovering why she is so belligerent and defensive." (Publishers Weekly)

Harper, Charise Mericle
Alien encounter; Charise Mericle Harper. First edition Christy Ottaviano Books, Henry Holt & Company 2014 208 p. illustrations (Sasquatch and aliens) (hardback) $12.99
Grades: 3 4 5 6   **Fic**
1. Yeti -- Fiction 2. Friendship -- Fiction 3. Family life -- Fiction 4. Extraterrestrial beings -- Fiction 5. Humorous stories 6. Family life -- Northwest, Pacific -- Fiction
ISBN 0805096213; 9780805096217

LC 2013039906

This book, the first in Charise Mericle Harper's "Sasquatch and Aliens" series, "introduces a pair of nine-year-old boys who are propelled into an adventure that may or may not involve otherworldly creatures. Anxiety-prone Morgan first meets new kid Lewis as Lewis is hanging from a tree by his underwear. After Morgan reluctantly rescues Lewis (whose family just bought a creepy motel), a tentative friendship is born." (Publishers Weekly)

"With an authentic, zany splash of fourth-grade humor, perspective, and imagination, this inaugural series title targets boys and will captivate elementary readers. . . . Morgan is a spunky, verbal, resourceful protagonist whose nonstop adventures resonate with self-discovery, family relationships, friendships, and creative problem-solving." SLJ

Dreamer, wisher, liar; by Charise Mericle Harper. Balzer + Bray, an imprint of HarperCollinsPublishers 2014 352 p. (hardcover bdg.) $16.99

Grades: 4 5 6   **Fic**

1. Babysitters -- Fiction 2. Magic tricks -- Fiction 3. Female friendship -- Fiction 4. Mother-daughter relationship -- Fiction 5. Magic -- Fiction 6. Wishes -- Fiction 7. Babysitter -- Fiction 8. Mothers and daughters -- Fiction

ISBN 0062026755; 9780062026750

LC 2013008222

This book is a "story about one girl's transformative summer full of friendship, secret magic, and family. . . . When her best friend is moving away and her mom has arranged for some strange little girl to come and stay with them, Ash . . . is expecting the worst summer of her life. Then seven-year-old Claire shows up. Armed with a love of thrift-store clothes and an altogether too-sunny disposition, Claire proceeds to turn Ash's carefully constructed life upside down." (Publisher's note)

"When a best friend is leaving you, what can you do? Ashley dreads the upcoming summer and her last few weeks at camp with her best friend, Lucy, who is moving away...Through Harper's skillful combination of fantastical and wholly realistic situations, readers are presented with gently larger-than-life characters, who are magnified through Ash's eyes and take on the roles she needs them to as she steps into her coming-of-age journey. As sweet and tart as a strawberry lemonade, readers will want to sip slowly and savor every page." Booklist

Just Grace. Houghton Mifflin 2007 138p il $15; pa $4.99

Grades: 2 3 4   **Fic**

1. School stories

ISBN 978-0-618-64642-5; 0-618-64642-6; 978-0-547-01440-1 pa; 0-547-01440-6 pa

LC 2006-17062

Misnamed by her teacher, seven-year-old Just Grace prides herself on being empathetic, but when she tries to help a neighbor feel better, her good intentions backfire.

"Grace is a funny, mischievous protagonist who should easily find a place in the pantheon of precocious third graders." SLJ

Other titles about Just Grace are:

Still Just Grace (2007)

Just Grace walks the dog (2008)

Just Grace goes green (2009)

Just Grace and the snack attack (2009)

Just Grace and the Terrible Tutu (2011)

Just Grace and the double surprise (2011)

Just Grace and the double surprise; written and illustrated by Charise Mericle Harper. Houghton Mifflin Books for Children 2011 167p il $14.99

Grades: 2 3 4   **Fic**

1. School stories 2. Dogs -- Fiction 3. Adoption -- Fiction 4. Siblings -- Fiction 5. Friendship -- Fiction

ISBN 0-547-37026-1; 978-0-547-37026-2

LC 2011015929

While Grace and her best friend Mimi are waiting for the arrival of the baby sister Mimi's family plans to adopt, Grace gets a big surprise.

"Readers unfamiliar with adoption will appreciate Grace's humorous, informative primer. . . . Harper's humorous black-and-white cartoons . . . help break up the text into manageable chunks ideal for new chapter-book readers. These simple but charming drawings evoke a typical young girl's notebook or journal doodles. . . . Harper has crafted an engaging story, the book's strength lies in its protagonist's strong, distinctive voice." SLJ

Just Grace and the snack attack; written and illustrated by Charise Mericle Harper. Houghton Mifflin Books for Children 2009 164p il $15

Grades: 2 3 4   **Fic**

1. School stories 2. Family life -- Fiction

ISBN 978-0-547-15223-3; 0-547-15223-X

LC 2009-32048

As Grace and her classmates study foods from other cultures, she has the opportunity to ponder such mysteries as whether Owen 1 is really bad or not, why she feels jealous when her father helps her best friend with her hot dog report, and how Augustine Dupre, her family's French boarder, can be so wise.

"Once again Grace's cartoon drawings . . . help make reading a breeze, and Harper's knowledge of third graders' concerns is right on target." Horn Book

Just Grace and the super sleepover; written and illustrated by Charise Mericle Harper. Houghton Mifflin Books for Children, Houghton Mifflin Harcourt 2014 208 p. $15.99

Grades: 2 3 4   **Fic**

1. Fear -- Fiction 2. Camping -- Fiction 3. Honesty -- Fiction 4. Schools -- Fiction 5. Birthdays -- Fiction 6. Friendship -- Fiction 7. Sleepovers -- Fiction

ISBN 054404584X; 9780544045842

LC 2013004813

In this children's book, by Charise Mericle Harper, book eleven of the Just Grace series, "it's time for Just Grace to go to a super sleepover! Birthdays and sleepovers are always super fun, but there's just one thing that keeps Just Grace from getting super excited about this sleepover." (Publisher's note)

"Third grader Grace does not want to sleep in a tent at Grace F.'s birthday party, but keeping her fears a secret leads to small lies that snowball. When help arrives from an unexpected source, Grace is able to come clean. As always, the illustrations (including Grace's own comics) add lots of humor to the story, which will appeal to fans and newcomers alike." Horn Book.

Just Grace and the Terrible Tutu; written and illustrated by Charise Mericle Harper. Houghton Mifflin Harcourt 2011 166p il $15

Grades: 2 3 4   **Fic**

1. Sisters -- Fiction 2. Friendship -- Fiction

ISBN 978-0-547-15224-0; 0-547-15224-8

LC 2010006768

Eight-year-old Grace is excited to learn that her best friend, Mimi, is going to become an older sister, but when both try to be "mother's helpers" for a family renting a house on their street, little Lily likes Grace best, causing Mimi to doubt herself and Grace to form a plan to fix things.

"Grace's dilemma is easy for readers to relate to, and her voice is consistently funny, frank and believable." Horn Book

Just Grace and the trouble with cupcakes; written and illustrated by Charise Mericle Harper. Houghton Mifflin Harcourt 2013 208 p. (hardcover) $15.99

Grades: 2 3 4   **Fic**

1. School stories -- Fiction 2. Female friendship -- Fiction 3. Fairs -- Fiction 4. Schools -- Fiction 5. Cupcakes -- Fiction

ISBN 0547877447; 9780547877440

LC 2012033824

This is the tenth installment of Charise Mericle Harper's Just Grace series. Here, "Just Grace is still in third grade, her best friend, Mimi, lives next door, and she loves to romp with her dog, Mr. Scruffers. The plot centers on a visit from Grace's grandmother, her excellent cupcake recipe . . . and the annual school fair. When Grace accidentally suggests cupcakes for the fair theme, she breaks a pinky-swear promise with Mimi: to support Mimi's idea that candy should be the theme." (Kirkus)

Just Grace gets crafty; by Charise Mericle Harper. Houghton Mifflin Harcourt 2014 192 p. (hardback) $15.99

Grades: 2 3 4 **Fic**

1. Friendship -- Fiction 2. Handicraft -- Fiction 3. Best friends -- Fiction

ISBN 0544080238; 9780544080232

LC 2013038995

Written and illustrated by Charise Mericle Harper and part of the Just Grace Series, this children's book describes how "There's a new crossing guard in town named Marie who needs a bit of help making friends, a fun substitute teacher for Miss Lois, and most exciting, Grace and Mimi are going to have their own table at the craft fair! They are going to make lots of crafts to sell--and hopefully save up enough money to go to the county fair." (Publisher's note)

"The frank and hilarious Grace and her best friend Mimi have entered the school craft fair. Peppered with Grace's comics, this charmingly depicts school and family strife with the beloved third grader's witty flair." SLJ

Just Grace goes green; written and illustrated by Charise Mericle Harper. Houghton Mifflin Books for Children 2009 178p il $15

Grades: 2 3 4 **Fic**

1. Recycling -- Fiction 2. Friendship -- Fiction

ISBN 978-0-618-95957-0; 0-618-95957-2

Grace can do a lot of things . . . but can she save the planet? Or at the very least, can she help her best friend Mimi get her favorite stuffed animal back?

"The facts about conservation will enthrall readers as much as the friends' fun and mischief. . . . [This book has] short, snappy sentences and lots of small black-and-white cartoons." Booklist

Just Grace walks the dog; written and illustrated by Charise Mericle Harper. Houghton Mifflin 2008 163p $15

Grades: 2 3 4 **Fic**

1. School stories 2. Dogs -- Fiction 3. Friendship -- Fiction

ISBN 978-0-618-95973-0; 0-618-95973-4

LC 2007041169

Eight-year-old Just Grace and her best friend Mimi embark on a campaign to convince Grace's parents that they are responsible and dependable enough to get a dog.

"Perfect for beginning chapter book readers, the text is broken up by headings, cartoons (drawn by Grace), lists, charts, and journal entries. It flows smoothly and easily." SLJ

Still Just Grace; written and illustrated by Charise Mericle Harper. Houghton Mifflin Company 2007 152p $15

Grades: 2 3 4 **Fic**

1. School stories 2. Friendship -- Fiction

ISBN 978-0-618-64643-2; 0-618-64643-4

LC 2007012746

When a struggling student teacher assigns a group project, seven-year-old Just Grace gets so involved in working with Grace W. and Grace F. that she fails to understand why she and her best friend, Mimi, are drifting apart.

"Dealing with the problems of friendship and change in a lively way, this book is a good addition to the middle-grade shelves." SLJ

Harper, Jessica

★ **Uh-oh**, Cleo; illustrated by Jon Berkeley. G. P. Putnam's Sons 2008 58p il $14.99

Grades: K 1 2 3 **Fic**

1. Twins -- Fiction 2. Illinois -- Fiction 3. Siblings -- Fiction 4. Family life -- Fiction 5. Medical care -- Fiction 6. Wounds and injuries -- Fiction

ISBN 978-0-399-24671-5; 0-399-24671-1

LC 2007027507

What starts out as a perfectly ordinary day in the Small house turns into Stiches Saturday when Cleo gets a cut on the head after her twin brother, Jack, accidentally pulls down their "Toy House."

This is an "engaging early chapter book. . . . The story is studded with observations, incidents, and conversations that reflect true-to-life sibling relationships and realistic individual foibles. . . . Large type, spacious design, and appealing drawings add to the accessiblity." Booklist

Other titles about Cleo re:

Underpants on my head (2009)

I barfed on Mrs. Kenly (2010)

Underpants on my head; illustrated by Jon Berkeley. G.P. Putnam's Sons 2009 60p il (Uh-oh Cleo) $14.99

Grades: K 1 2 3 **Fic**

1. Hiking -- Fiction 2. Vacations -- Fiction 3. Family life -- Fiction

ISBN 978-0-399-24672-2; 0-399-24672-X

LC 2007-39268

When Cleo and her family go on vacation, they experience a freak August snow storm while hiking on Mt. Baldy.

"Cleo's chatty narration and Berkeley's warm black-and-white illustrations will appeal to early chapter-book readers." SLJ

Harper, Suzanne

A **gaggle** of goblins. Greenwillow Books 2011 300p (The unseen world of Poppy Malone) $16.99

Grades: 4 5 6 **Fic**

1. Texas -- Fiction 2. Goblins -- Fiction 3. Family life -- Fiction

ISBN 0-06-199607-6; 978-0-06-199607-8

LC 2010025558

Eleven-year-old Poppy's parents are paranormal investigators who have never actually found anything, but that may change when they move to Austin, Texas, and Poppy meets a goblin in the attic of their new house.

"The book shines through the consistently amusing dynamics and dialogue among the Malones; Harper has abundant fun with the Malone parents' eccentricities, and kids will too. Readers will want more from this family." Publ Wkly

Harrell, Rob

Troll overboard; by Rob Harrell. Dial Books for Young Readers, an imprint of Penguin Random House, LLC 2016 265 p. illustrations (Life of Zarf) (hardcover) $15.99; (ebook) $23.97

Grades: 4 5 6 7 **Fic**

1. Trolls -- Fiction 2. Humorous fiction -- Fiction 3. Adventure and adventurers -- Fiction 4. Humorous stories

ISBN 0803741057; 9780803741058; 9780698145757

LC 2015049505

Sequel to: Troll who cried wolf

In this third book in the Life of Zarf series by Rob Harrell, the troll Zarf "is already at the bottom of the food chain when it comes to popularity at Cotswin Middle School. So when his Gramps shows up at career day, Zarf is sure his cool factor will hit an all-time low. What he doesn't expect is for the super-obnoxious Prince Roquefort to take an interest in Gramps's nautical know-how. Zarf is sure the prince is up to something."(Publisher's note)

"Interspersed with bratty illustrations, this ought to find a sweet spot at the nexus between fans of humor and fans of fractured fantasies." Booklist

Harrington, Janice N.

Catching a storyfish; Janice N. Harrington. WordSong 2016 224 p. $17.95

Grades: 4 5 6 7 **Fic**

1. Moving -- Fiction 2. Listening -- Fiction 3. Friendship -- Fiction 4. Grandfathers -- Fiction

ISBN 1629794295; 9781629794297; 9781629797434

LC 2016936167

In this book, by Janice N. Harrington, "Keet knows the only good thing about moving away from her Alabama home is that she'll live near her beloved grandfather. When Keet starts school, it's even worse than she expected, as the kids tease her about her southern accent. Now Keet, who can 'talk the whiskers off a catfish,' doesn't want to open her mouth. Slowly, though, while fishing with her grandfather, she learns the art of listening." (Publisher's note)

"A gentle-spirited book about a black girl who almost gives up her gift but for love and friendship." Kirkus

Harrington, Karen

Courage for beginners; by Karen Harrington. Little, Brown and Co. 2014 304 p. (hardcover) $17

Grades: 4 5 6 7 8 **Fic**

1. Texas -- Fiction 2. Friendship -- Fiction 3. Schools -- Fiction 4. Agoraphobia -- Fiction 5. Middle schools -- Fiction 6. Family problems -- Fiction

ISBN 031621048X; 9780316210485

LC 2013021596

Sequel to: Sure Signs of Crazy (2013)

"Twelve-year-old Mysti Murphy wishes she were a character in a book. If her life were fictional, she'd magically know how to deal with the fact that her best friend, Anibal Gomez, has abandoned her in favor of being a 'hipster.' She'd be able to take care of everyone when her dad has to spend time in the hospital. And she'd certainly be able to change her family's secret." (Publisher's note)

"Mysti's curatorial narration--as if she were describing paintings or book characters--works on multiple levels, showing off her snark and emphasizing her mother's sheltered influence. Her mother is flawed but sympathetic; she knows her fears are disproportionate, but their debilitating effect is real. With gallows humor and believable small victories, this unusual novel is a window into making friends and facing fears." Kirkus

Sure signs of crazy; by Karen Harrington. 1st ed. Little Brown & Co 2013 288 p. (hardcover) $17

Grades: 4 5 6 7 8 **Fic**

1. Adolescence -- Fiction 2. Parent-child relationship -- Fiction 3. Texas -- Fiction 4. Coming of age -- Fiction 5. Mental illness -- Fiction 6. Family problems -- Fiction

ISBN 0316210587; 9780316210584

LC 2012030683

Parents' Choice: Silver Medal Fiction (2013)

In this book, "worried that she will grow up to be crazy like her mother or alcoholic like her father, rising seventh-grader Sarah Nelson takes courage from Harper Lee's 'To Kill a Mockingbird,' writing letters to Atticus Finch and discovering her own strengths. . . . She describes the events of the summer she turns 12, gets her period, develops a crush on a neighbor and fellow word lover, and comes to terms with her parents' failings." (Kirkus Reviews)

Harris, Lewis

A **taste** for red. Clarion Books 2009 169p $16

Grades: 4 5 6 **Fic**

1. Vampires -- Fiction 2. Friendship -- Fiction 3. Missing children -- Fiction

ISBN 978-0-547-14462-7; 0-547-14462-8

LC 2008-25318

When some of her classmates disappear, sixth-grader Svetlana along with her new friends go in search of the missing students using her newfound ability as an Olfactive, one who has heightened smell, hearing, and the ability to detect vampires.

"Svetlana comes across as a strong character. . . . Her first-person narrative is fast-paced and witty, and her mild scorn for everything she encounters at school will appeal to angst-ridden tweens. Sure to be a crowd-pleaser." SLJ

Harris, Teresa E.

The **perfect** place; Teresa E. Harris. Clarion Books 2014 272 p. (hardcover) $16.99

Grades: 5 6 7 8 **Fic**

1. Aunts -- Fiction 2. Family life -- Fiction 3. African Americans -- Fiction 4. Home -- Fiction 5. Virginia -- Fiction 6. Great-aunts -- Fiction 7. Segregation -- Fiction 8. Moving, Household -- Fiction 9. Family life -- Virginia -- Fiction

ISBN 0547255195; 9780547255194

LC 2013036214

In this book, "12-year-old Treasure is tired of moving from place to place every time her unreliable father leaves the family. At the opening of the novel, Treasure's father is gone and her mother leaves her and her younger sister, Tiffany, with their Great-Aunt Grace in the small town of Black Lake, Virginia. Treasure does not want to be there, and her introduction to her no-nonsense relative only strengthens her resolve to stay detached during her mother's absence." (School Library Journal)

"Two months after 12-year-old Treasure's dad left without further word, her mom decides to search for him, and she takes Treasure and her younger sister to stay with their cantankerous Great-Aunt Grace in Black Lake, Virginia... Readers will find sly humor here as well as the pleasure of seeing justice done on several levels. A satisfying first novel with a realistic but heartening ending." Booklist

Harrison, Michelle

13 curses. Little, Brown 2011 486p (13 Treasures Trilogy) $15.99; pa $6.99

Grades: 5 6 7 8 **Fic**

1. Magic -- Fiction 2. Fairies -- Fiction 3. Orphans -- Fiction 4. Kidnapping -- Fiction

ISBN 978-0-316-04150-8; 0-316-04150-5; 978-0316041492 pa

Sequel to: 13 treasures (2010)

When fairies steal her brother, thirteen-year-old Rowan Fox promises that in exchange for his return she will find the thirteen charms that the fairies have enchanted and hidden in the human world.

"The sure-handed storytelling creates a completely credible setting—by turns violent and tender, sinister and poignant. . . . Contrasts between human emotion and commitment and the cold, often cruel magic and mischief of the fairy realm create terrific tension and afford opportunities for heroism for the young protagonists." Kirkus

13 secrets; Michelle Harrison; [interior illustrations by Kelly Louise Judd] Little, Brown & Co. 2012 421 p. illustrations (The 13 treasures trilogy) $16.99

Grades: 5 6 7 8 **Fic**

1. Fantasy fiction 2. Fairies -- Fiction 3. Secrets -- Fiction 4. Changelings -- Fiction

ISBN 0316185639; 9780316185639

LC 2011033368

In this book, by Michelle Harrison, with illustrations by Kelly Louise Judd, "happy with life at Elvesden Manor, Rowan is doing her best to put the past behind her. But it's tough to forget the past when fairy messengers won't leave her be, no matter how many magical boundaries are put in place to keep them away. When Tanya arrives to spend the summer at the manor, she notices that Rowan is acting strangely and becomes determined to find out what she's hiding." (Publisher's note)

★ **13** treasures. Little, Brown Books for Young Readers 2010 355p il $15.99

Grades: 5 6 7 8 **Fic**

1. Mystery fiction 2. Fairies -- Fiction 3. Grandmothers -- Fiction 4. Great Britain -- Fiction

ISBN 978-0-316-04148-5; 0-316-04148-3

LC 2008-45511

Bedeviled by evil fairies that only she can see, thirteen-year-old Tanya is sent to stay with her cold and distant grandmother at Elvesden Manor, where she and the caretaker's son solve a disturbing mystery that leads them to the discovery that Tanya's life is in danger.

"Harrison writes with great assuredness, creating a seductive setting and memorable, fully developed characters. . . . It's an excellent choice for fans of the Spiderwick Chronicles and other modern-day fairy tales." Publ Wkly

Followed by: 13 curses (2011)

Harrold, A. F.

The **imaginary**; by A.F. Harrold; illustrations by Emily Gravett. Bloomsbury 2015 224 p. illustrations (some color) (hardcover) $16.99

Grades: 4 5 6 7 8 **Fic**

1. Friendship -- Fiction 2. Supernatural -- Fiction 3. Adventure and adventurers 4. Imaginary playmates -- Fiction 5. Mother-daughter relationship -- Fiction 6. Best friends -- Fiction 7. Mothers and daughters -- Fiction 8. Adventure and adventurers -- Fiction

ISBN 0802738117; 9780802738110; 9781619636965

LC 2014016677

"Rudger is Amanda Shuffleup's imaginary friend. Nobody else can see Rudger-until the evil Mr. Bunting arrives at Amanda's door. Mr. Bunting hunts imaginaries. Rumor has it that he even eats them. And now he's found Rudger. Soon Rudger is alone, and running for his imaginary life. He needs to find Amanda before Mr. Bunting catches him-and before Amanda forgets him and he fades away to nothing." (Publisher's note)

"This inventive mix of humor and suspense starts with the amusing appearance of Amanda's imaginary friend, Rudger. Their summer of make-believe adventures quickly darkens, though, when Mr. Bunting shows up. He's a grown-up who can not only see "Imaginaries" like Rudger, but also eats them to prolong his own life. . . . A great choice for readers who like fantastic tales with a dose of true scariness." SLJ

Hartnett, Sonya, 1968-

★ The **children** of the King; Sonya Hartnett. 1st U.S. edition Penguin Books (Australia) 2012 265 p. ill. $16.99

Grades: 5 6 7 8 **Fic**

1. Historical fiction 2. Friendship -- Fiction 3. World War, 1939-1945 -- Great Britain -- Fiction 4. World War, 1939-1945 -- Evacuation of civilians -- Fiction 5. England -- Fiction 6. World War, 1939-1945 -- Children -- Great Britain -- Fiction 7. World War, 1939-1945 -- Evacuation of civilians -- England -- Fiction

ISBN 0763667358; 9780670076130; 9780763667351

LC 2013414845

This book, by Sonya Hartnett, "takes place in England during World War II. . . . Siblings Cecily and Jeremy, along with their mother Heloise, are sent to the northern countryside to live with Heloise's brother, Peregrine Lockwood, in mysterious Heron Hall. . . . The family winds up taking in May Bright, a 10-year-old refugee from London. The two girls become fast friends and . . . come across two boys in the ruins of a nearby castle." (School Library Journal)

"Twelve-year-old Cecily, her older brother Jeremy, and their mother flee WWII London for the safety of Uncle Peregrine's country manor. Once there, Cecily discovers two boys hiding in some nearby ruins. Hartnett's gift for language deftly conveys both the sublime and the mundane in life. She grounds the book's fantasy elements with a heartfelt examination of the hardships endured by civilians in wartime." Horn Book

Sadie and Ratz; Sonya Hartnett; illustrated by Ann James. 1st U.S. ed. Candlewick Press 2012 59 p. ill. (reinforced) $14.99

Grades: K 1 2 3 **Fic**

1. Hand -- Fiction 2. Imagination -- Fiction 3. Sibling rivalry -- Fiction

ISBN 0763653152; 9780763653156

LC 2011045899

"Sadie and Ratz are the names of Hannah's hands. . . . They're always after four-year-old Baby Boy (whom Sadie wishes were a dog). . . . Baby Boy knows how to turn the tables, though, and when he spills milk on the carpet, he tells Grandma that Sadie and Ratz pushed him. But when Baby Boy goes too far, Hannah may have to send Sadie and Ratz on vacation to prove their innocence." (Publisher's note)

★ The **silver** donkey; illustrated by Don T. Powers. Candlewick Press 2006 266p il $15.99; pa $7.99

Grades: 5 6 7 8 **Fic**

1. France -- Fiction 2. Soldiers -- Fiction 3. World War, 1914-1918 -- Fiction

ISBN 978-0-7636-2937-3; 0-7636-2937-5; 978-0-7636-3681-4 pa; 0-7636-3681-9 pa

LC 2006-42582

First published 2004 in Australia

In France during World War I, four French children learn about honesty, loyalty, and courage from an English army deserter who tells them a series of stories related to his small, silver donkey charm

"Occasional full-page black-and-white art deftly suggests setting and mood without intruding on readers' imaginations. Provocative, timely, and elegantly honed." Horn Book

Hartry, Nancy

Watching Jimmy. Tundra Books 2009 152p $16.95

Grades: 5 6 7 8 **Fic**

1. Child abuse -- Fiction 2. Brain -- Wounds and injuries -- Fiction

ISBN 0-88776-871-7; 978-0-88776-871-2

This story takes place in Canadia in 1958. Eleven-year-old Carolyn walks an emotional tightrope knowing what really happened to her best friend, Jimmy, the day his Uncle Ted chose to teach him a lesson that left Jimmy brain-damaged. But when Uncle Ted threatens his beleaguered family with even more abuse and the loss of their home, Carolyn must find the courage to match wits with him and to speak out, using the truth as her only weapon. "Age nine and up." (Quill Quire)

"Like a steady beat that pulses louder and louder, the story unfolds against a backdrop of postwar social and political concerns and Remembrance Day. Carolyn is a passionate and feisty character, delineated with love and precision, and readers will be drawn to her. A compelling and satisfying novel." SLJ

Harvey, Matthea

Cecil the pet glacier; Matthea Harvey; illustrated by Giselle Potter. Schwartz & Wade Books 2012 40 p. $17.99

Grades: PreK K 1 2 **Fic**

1. Pets -- Fiction 2. Glaciers -- Fiction 3. Picture books for children 4. Norway -- Fiction 5. Eccentrics and eccentricities -- Fiction

ISBN 9780375867736; 9780375967733

LC 2011018657

This book is "[Matthea] Harvey's . . . . tale of a misunderstood child and her equally misunderstood glacier. Lonely Ruby has flamboyantly eccentric parents who run a topiary and tiara business. . . . A family trip to Norway nets Ruby a pet, a pint-size glacier named Cecil who follows her everywhere; Ruby--who wanted a dog--scorns him." It isn't until "Cecil . . . performs a daring rescue. . . that Ruby realizes how wrong she's been." (Publishers Weekly)

Hashimi, Nadia

One half from the east; Nadia Hashimi. HarperCollins 2016 272 p. (ebook) $15.99; (hardcover) $16.99

Grades: 4 5 6 7 8   **Fic**

1. Bombings -- Fiction 2. Impersonation -- Fiction 3. Gender identity -- Fiction 4. Female friendship -- Fiction 5. Children of parents with disabilities -- Fiction 6. Girls -- Afghanistan -- Social conditions -- Fiction

ISBN 9780062421920; 0062421905; 9780062421906

LC 2016938972

In this middle grade novel by Nadia Hashimi that is set in Afghanistan, "Obayda's family is in need of some good fortune, and her aunt has an idea to bring the family luck—dress Obayda, the youngest of four sisters, as a boy, a bacha posh. . . . Once Obayda meets another bacha posh, everything changes. Their transformation won't last forever, though—unless the two best friends can figure out a way to make it stick and make their newfound freedoms endure." (Publisher's note)

"Well-told through appealing characters, this tale sheds light from a unique cultural perspective on the link between vastly different, rigidly enforced roles for boys and girls and gender-identity issues." Kirkus

Haskell, Merrie

The princess curse. Harper 2011 325p $16.99

Grades: 4 5 6 7   **Fic**

1. Fairy tales 2. Magic -- Fiction 3. Princesses -- Fiction

ISBN 978-0-06-200813-8; 0-06-200813-7

LC 2010040424

"Author Haskell has her way with the story of 'The Twelve Dancing Princesses,' incorporating references to other myths and legends and adding many twists of her own, not least of which is making the royals' attempted rescuer a strong-willed, 13-year-old apprentice herbalist, Reveka. . . . When Vasile offers the hand of any of his daughters in marriage to anyone who banishes the curse (or a 'fabulous dowry' if the curse-breaker is female), Reveka is determined to win the reward. . . . With a good sense of humor, an able and empowered protagonist, and a highly original take on this tale, Haskell's story gives readers much to enjoy." Publ Wkly

Hattemer, Kate

The vigilante poets of Selwyn Academy; Kate Hattemer. Alfred A. Knopf 2014 336 p. $16.99

Grades: 8 9 10 11 12   **Fic**

1. School stories 2. Poetry -- Fiction 3. Young adult literature 4. Arts -- Fiction 5. Schools -- Fiction 6. Minnesota -- Fiction 7. Friendship -- Fiction 8. Creative ability -- Fiction 9. Family life -- Minnesota -- Fiction 10. Reality television programs -- Fiction

ISBN 0385753780; 9780385753784; 9780385753791

LC 2013014325

"Witty, sarcastic Ethan and his three friends decide to take down the reality TV show, 'For Art's Sake,' that is being filmed at their high school, the esteemed Selwyn Arts Academy, where each student is more talented than the next. While studying Ezra Pound in English class, the friends are inspired to write a vigilante long poem and distribute it to the student body, detailing the evils of 'For Art's Sake.'" (Publisher's note)

"Relying on the passion and ideals that drive adolescence, this has a vibrancy and authenticity that will resonate with anyone who has fought for their beliefs--or who has loved a hamster." Booklist

Hawkins, Aaron R.

The year money grew on trees; written and illustrated by Aaron R. Hawkins. Houghton Mifflin 2010 293p il $16

Grades: 5 6 7 8   **Fic**

1. Apples -- Fiction 2. Cousins -- Fiction 3. Siblings -- Fiction 4. Farm life -- Fiction 5. New Mexico -- Fiction 6. Money-making projects for children -- Fiction

ISBN 978-0-547-27977-0; 0-547-27977-9

In early 1980s New Mexico, thirteen-year-old Jackson Jones recruits his cousins and sisters to help tend an elderly neighbor's neglected apple orchard for the chance to make big money and, perhaps, to own the orchard.

"Hawkins's children's book debut is rich with details that feel drawn from memory, . . . and Jackson's narration sparkles. His hard work, setbacks, and motivations make this a highly relatable adventure in entrepreneurship." Publ Wkly

Haydu, Corey Ann

The someday suitcase; by Corey Ann Haydu. Katherine Tegen Books 2017 304 p. (hardcover) $16.99

Grades: 5 6 7 8   **Fic**

1. Sick -- Fiction 2. Magic -- Fiction 3. Best friends -- Fiction

ISBN 9780062352750

LC 2016949691

In this book, by Corey Ann Haydu, "Clover and Danny are the kind of best friends who make each other even better. . . . But when Danny comes down with a mysterious illness that won't go away, the doctors can't figure out what's wrong with him. So Clover decides to take matters into her own hands. . . . Will science be able to save Danny, or is this the one time when magic can overcome the unthinkable?" (Publisher's note)

Hayes, Christine

Mothman's curse; Christine Hayes; illustrated by James Hindle. Roaring Brook Press 2015 320 p. illustrations (hardback) $15.99

Grades: 4 5 6 7   **Fic**

1. Horror fiction 2. Blessing and cursing -- Fiction 3. Brothers and sisters -- Fiction 4. Horror stories 5. Ohio -- Fiction 6. Mothman -- Fiction 7. Supernatural -- Fiction 8. Single-parent families -- Fiction

ISBN 1626720274; 9781626720275

LC 2014047412

In this juvenile novel, by Christine Hayes, illustrated by James Hindle, "Josie . . . live[s] in the most haunted town in America. . . . When she and her brothers discover a Polaroid camera that prints pictures of the ghost of local recluse John Goodrich, they are drawn into a mystery dating back over a hundred years." (Publisher's note)

"Josie Fletcher and her brothers, Fox and Mason, have grown up helping out at their family's auction house. They know which trinkets are actually worth money and which ones are straight-up junk. The siblings aren't allowed to buy stuff once it's on the auction floor, but sometimes they borrow objects to play with and return them before the auction. . . . Scary enough to appeal to readers who are growing out of R.L. Stine titles, this may also tempt fans of realistic fiction." SLJ

Hayles, Marsha

Breathing room; Marsha Hayles. Henry Holt and Co. 2012 244 p. (hc) $17.99

Grades: 5 6 7 8   **Fic**

1. Bildungsromans 2. Historical fiction 3. Teenagers -- Fiction 4

Tuberculosis -- Fiction 5. Sick -- Fiction 6. Hospitals -- Fiction 7. Coming of age -- Fiction 8. Minnesota -- History -- 20th century -- Fiction

ISBN 0805089616; 9780805089615

LC 2011034055

Author Marsha Hayles' book is "set in 1940 at a sanitarium in Loon Lake, Minn. . . . Thirteen-year-old Evvy Hoffmeister has tuberculosis and feels abandoned by her family when she's sent to the sanitarium to be cured. The cold nurses, strict rules, mind-numbing routines, and endless bed rest are dispiriting for Evvy and her roommates: kind Beverly, glamorous Pearl, and defensive Dena. . . . Nonetheless, the girls find strength in each other and discover creative ways to bring cheer." (Publishers Weekly)

Hazen, Lynn E.

The **amazing** trail of Seymour Snail; illustrated by Doug Cushman. Henry Holt and Co. 2009 64p il $16.95

Grades: 1 2 3   **Fic**

1. Snails -- Fiction 2. Artists -- Fiction 3. New York (N.Y.) -- Fiction

ISBN 978-0-8050-8698-0; 0-8050-8698-6

LC 2008036939

Hoping to become a famous artist one day, Seymour Snail takes a job in a New York City art gallery, where everyone is buzzing about a "magnificent mystery artist."

"With only a few sentences and at least one illustration per page, this title is perfect for students transitioning to chapter books. . . . Cushman's black-and-white cartoons delineate the characters and add humor and perspective." SLJ

Cinder Rabbit; [by] Lynn E. Hazen; illustrated by Elyse Pastel. Henry Holt & Co. 2008 64p il $15.95

Grades: K 1 2   **Fic**

1. School stories 2. Rabbits -- Fiction 3. Theater -- Fiction

ISBN 978-0-8050-8194-7; 0-8050-8194-1

LC 2007027318

Zoe is chosen for the role of Cinder Rabbit in her school play and is also supposed to lead the class in the Bunny Hop at the end, but ever since wicked Winifred laughed at her for landing in a mud puddle, Zoe has forgotten how to hop

"This simple, sweet beginning chapter book contains the right amount of story for children just starting to read longer books; and the charming black-and-white illustrations, decorating every page, will engage kids." Booklist

Healy, Christopher

The **Hero's** Guide to Being an Outlaw; Christopher Healy, illustrated by Todd Harris. Harpercollins Childrens Books 2014 528 p. illustrations (The Hero's guide; book 3) $16.99

Grades: 4 5 6 7   **Fic**

1. Fantasy fiction 2. Princes -- Fiction

ISBN 006211848X; 9780062118486

LC 2014018251

"The League of Princes returns in the hilariously epic conclusion to the hit series that began with Christopher Healy's 'The Hero's Guide to Saving Your Kingdom.' . . . Posters plastered across the thirteen kingdoms are saying that Briar Rose has been murdered--and the four Princes Charming are the prime suspects. Now they're on the run in a desperate attempt to clear their names." (Publisher's note)

"Throughout the heroes' and heroines' travels, the antiprince conspiracy is revealed in each kingdom--it's directly related to loose ends from The Hero's Guide to Storming the Castle (2013). Side characters make comedic final appearances, and a surprise villain team-up provides

closure to the trilogy. Part screwball comedy, part sly wit and all fun." Kirkus

The **hero's** guide to saving your kingdom; written by Christopher Healy; with drawings by Todd Harris. Walden Pond Press 2012 438 p. ill., map $16.99

Grades: 4 5 6 7   **Fic**

1. Princes -- Fiction 2. Fairy tales -- Fiction 3. Heroes and heroines -- Fiction 4. Fairy tales 5. Humorous stories 6. Witches -- Fiction

ISBN 0062117432; 9780062117434

LC 2011053347

In this book, "four Princes . . . must team up on a . . . quest to save their kingdoms. . . . Cinderella wants adventure more than sheltered Prince Frederic does. Prince Gustav's pride is still badly damaged from having needed Rapunzel's teary-eyed rescue. Through Sleeping Beauty, Prince Liam learns kissing someone out of enchanted sleep doesn't guarantee compatibility. . . . Although she loves wacky Prince Duncan, Snow White needs some solitude." (Kirkus Reviews)

The **hero's** guide to storming the castle; by Christopher Healy; with drawings by Todd Harris. Walden Pond Press, an imprint of HarperCollinsPublishers 2013 496 p. (Hero's Guide) (hardcover) $16.99

Grades: 4 5 6 7   **Fic**

1. Fractured fairy tales 2. Humorous fiction 3. Fairy tales 4. Humorous stories 5. Heroes -- Fiction 6. Princes -- Fiction 7. Characters in literature -- Fiction

ISBN 0062118455; 9780062118455

LC 2012050668

Sequel to: The hero's guide to saving your kingdom

In this humorous, middle-grade fantasy story, by Christopher Healy, illustrated by Todd Harris, "the charming princes from the fairy tales of Cinderella, Rapunzel, Snow White, and Briar Rose, saved the countryside from an evil witch in 'The Hero's Guide to Saving Your Kingdom.' And now, they have to save the day again, by keeping a magical object from falling into the hands of power-mad warlords who would use it for evil." (Publisher's note)

Heide, Florence Parry

Dillweed's revenge; a deadly dose of magic. [by] Florence Parry Heide, with Roxanne Heide Pierce, David Fisher Parry, and Jeanne McReynolds Parry; illustrated by Carson Ellis. Harcourt Children's Books 2010 un il $16.99

Grades: 2 3 4 5   **Fic**

1. Monsters -- Fiction

ISBN 978-0-15-206394-8; 0-15-206394-3

LC 2009-27599

An adventure-deprived young boy's neglectful parents and abusive servants receive their just desserts.

"Terse sentences and repeated refrains inject humor while leaving room for the playful ink and gouache illustrations, which recall Edward Gorey's work, to fill in the details. . . . The mixture of humor and gruesomeness may offend some, but for fans of Roald Dahl, Lemony Snicket, or Hilaire Belloc, it's right on target." SLJ

The **shrinking** of Treehorn; drawings by Edward Gorey. Holiday House 1971 un il lib bdg $16.95; pa $6.95

Grades: 2 3 4 5   **Fic**

ISBN 0-8234-0189-8 lib bdg; 0-8234-0975-9 pa

Treehorn spends an unhappy day and night shrinking. Yet when he tells his mother, father, teacher and principal of his problem they're all too busy to do anything about it. To Treehorn's great relief he finally discovers a magical game that restores him to his natural size, but then he starts turning green!

This "is an imaginative little whimsy, whose sly humor and macabre touches are perfectly matched in Edward Gorey's illustrations." Book World

Heinz, Brian

★ **Mocha** Dick; the legend and fury. by Brian Heinz; illustrated by Randall Enos. Creative Editions 2014 32 p. (hardcover : alk. paper) $18.99

Grades: 2 3 4 5 **Fic**
1. Whales 2. Whaling -- History 3. Whales -- Fiction 4. Whaling -- Fiction 5. Sperm whale -- Fiction
ISBN 1568462425; 9781568462424

LC 2013040661

"Believed to have been active from 1810 to 1859, Mocha Dick was infamous for the ferocity of his retaliations. . . . From the first recorded encounter near the South American island of Mocha till the fatal harpoon blow, Mocha Dick was a legend in his own time. In language befitting a sea lore, author Brain Heinz describes characteristic episodes of the great whale's life, as illustrator Randall Enos animates the tale in a textured style evocative of scrimshaw." (Publisher's note)

" For almost 50 years, a huge albino sperm whale spotted off Isla Mocha (whence the name Mocha Dick) antagonized whalers by aggressively attacking and evading their ships, and tales of this legendary leviathan went on to inspire Herman Melville to write Moby Dick. Heinz and Enos dramatize a few accounts of Mocha Dick's activity in this beautifully designed picture book...The whale appears both vicious and mischievous, adding an extra dose of drama to Heinz's descriptive lines. While a list of sources or further reading would have been useful, most kiddos will be utterly entranced by the folk art–style illustrations, which seem to tell the story enough on their own." Booklist

Helgerson, Joseph

Crows & cards; a novel. written with diligence by Mr. Joseph Helgerson; to which are added fine illustrations by Mr. Peter Desève; also included is Dictionarium Americannicum; being the words herein most arcane and alien and their definitions. Houghton Mifflin Harcourt 2009 344p il $16; pa $5.99

Grades: 4 5 6 7 **Fic**
1. Slavery -- Fiction 2. Gambling -- Fiction 3. Apprentices -- Fiction 4. Native Americans -- Fiction 5. Saint Louis (Mo.) -- Fiction
ISBN 978-0-618-88395-0; 0-618-88395-9; 978-0-547-33909-2 pa; 0-547-33909-7 pa

LC 2008013308

In 1849, Zeb's parents ship him off to St. Louis to become an apprentice tanner, but the naive twelve-year-old rebels, casting his lot with a cheating riverboat gambler, while a slave and an Indian medicine man try to get Zeb back on the right path. Includes historical notes, glossary, and bibliographical references

"Helgerson surrounds Zeb with a lively cast. . . . A solid choice for fans of high-spun yarns and not-too-tall tales." Booklist

★ **Horns** & wrinkles. Houghton Mifflin 2006 357p il $16; pa $4.95

Grades: 4 5 6 7 **Fic**
1. Magic -- Fiction 2. Trolls -- Fiction 3. Bullies -- Fiction 4. Mississippi River -- Fiction
ISBN 0-618-61679-9; 0-618-98178-0 pa

LC 2005025448

Along a magic-saturated stretch of the Mississippi River near Blue Wing, Minnesota, twelve-year-old Claire and her bullying cousin Duke are drawn into an adventure involving Bodacious Deepthink the Great Rock Troll, a helpful fairy, and a group of trolls searching for their fathers.

"Tongue-in-cheek humor brings a delightful zing to the playfully inventive storytelling and fast-paced plot. Enchanting sketches foreshadow each chapter, adding to the wonder." SLJ

Helget, Nicole

★ The **end** of the wild; Nicole Helget. Little, Brown & Co. 2017 272 p. (hardback) $16.99

Grades: 3 4 5 6 **Fic**
1. Poverty -- Fiction 2. Schools -- Fiction 3. Family life -- Fiction 4. Stepfathers -- Fiction 5. Social action -- Fiction 6. Science projects -- Fiction 7. Forests and forestry -- Fiction 8. Environmental protection -- Fiction
ISBN 9780316245111

LC 2016031990

This book, by Nicole Heglet, "weaves themes of poverty, parenting, appreciation for the natural world, and forgiveness through a balanced presentation of the complicated contemporary issue of energy supplies. Life has not been easy for Fern, a white girl who is sore-pressed to keep her family. . . . The author demonstrates the poverty of Fern's family and friends (including a Muslim family from Somalia) with telling detail, and the tension and action arise naturally." (Kirkus Review)

Hemingway, Edith Morris

Road to Tater Hill; [by] Edith M. Hemingway. Delacorte Press 2009 213p map $16.99; lib bdg $19.99

Grades: 5 6 7 8 **Fic**
1. Friendship -- Fiction 2. Bereavement -- Fiction 3. Grandparents -- Fiction 4. Mountain life -- Fiction 5. North Carolina -- Fiction 6. Depression (Psychology) -- Fiction
ISBN 978-0-385-73677-0; 0-385-73677-0; 978-0-385-90627-2 lib bdg; 0-385-90627-7 lib bdg

LC 2008-24906

At her grandparents' North Carolina mountain home during the summer of 1963, eleven-year-old Annie Winters, grief-stricken by the death of her newborn sister and isolated by her mother's deepening depression, finds comfort in holding an oblong stone 'rock baby' and in the friendship of a neighbor boy and a reclusive mountain woman with a devastating secret

"Drawing on the author's childhood roots, the heart of this first novel is the sense of place, described in simple lyrical words. . . . True to Annie's viewpoint, the particulars tell a universal drama of childhood grief, complete in all its sadness, anger, loneliness, and healing." Booklist

Hemphill, Helen

The **adventurous** deeds of Deadwood Jones. Front Street 2008 228p $16.95

Grades: 5 6 7 8 **Fic**
1. Cousins -- Fiction 2. Cowhands -- Fiction 3. West (U.S.) -- Fiction 4. Race relations -- Fiction 5. African Americans -- Fiction
ISBN 978-1-59078-637-6; 1-59078-637-8

LC 2008005422

Thirteen-year-old Prometheus Jones and his eleven-year-old cousin Omer flee Tennessee and join a cattle drive that will eventually take them to Texas, where Prometheus hopes his father lives, and they find adventure and face challenges as African Americans in a land still recovering from the Civil War.

"Prometheus is an always sympathetic and engaging character, and the dangers and misadventures he encounters . . . make for compelling reading." Booklist

Hemphill, Michael

Stonewall Hinkleman and the Battle of Bull Run; [by] Michael Hemphill and Sam Riddleburger. Dial Books for Young Readers 2009 168p $16.99

Grades: 4 5 6 **Fic**
1. Time travel -- Fiction 2. Bull Run, 1st Battle of, 1861 -- Fiction
3. United States -- History -- 1861-1865, Civil War -- Fiction
ISBN 978-0-8037-3179-0; 0-8037-3179-5

LC 2008-15795

While participating in a reenactment of the Battle of Bull Run,
twelve-year-old Stonewall Hinkleman is transported back to the actual
Civil War battle by means of a magic bugle.

This is a "well-paced time-travel novel. . . . Stonewall is a likable
character whose attitude changes for the better in the story. . . . A good
choice for historical fiction fans." SLJ

Henham, R. D.
The **red** dragon codex. Mirrorstone 2008 244p il map (Dragon
condices) pa $9.95
Grades: 4 5 6 **Fic**
1. Fantasy fiction 2. Dragons -- Fiction
ISBN 978-0-7869-4925-0 pa; 0-7869-4925-2 pa

LC 2007014679

Mudd must seek a silver dragon's help to rescue Shemnara, an
old woman who is practically his mother, when she is kidnapped by a
red dragon.

"Inventive details, dimensional characterizations, and fast-paced action make this a good introduction to the fantasy genre." Booklist

Henkes, Kevin
★ **Bird** Lake moon. Greenwillow Books 2008 179p $15.99; lib
bdg $16.89; pa $5.99
Grades: 4 5 6 7 **Fic**
1. Lakes -- Fiction 2. Divorce -- Fiction 3. Wisconsin -- Fiction
4. Friendship -- Fiction 5. Bereavement -- Fiction 6. Family life
-- Fiction
ISBN 978-0-06-147076-9; 0-06-147076-7; 978-0-06-147078-3
lib bdg; 0-06-147078-3 lib bdg; 978-0-06-147079-0 pa; 0-06-
147079-1 pa

LC 2007-36564

Twelve-year-old Mitch and his mother are spending the summer
with his grandparents at Bird Lake after his parents separate, and ten-
year-old Spencer and his family have returned to the lake where Spencer's little brother drowned long ago, and as the boys become friends
and spend time together, each of them begins to heal

"Characters are gently and believably developed as the story weaves
in and around the beautiful Wisconsin setting. The superbly crafted plot
moves smoothly and unhurriedly, mirroring a slow summer pace." SLJ

The **birthday** room. Greenwillow Bks. 1999 152p $15.99; pa
$5.99
Grades: 5 6 7 8 **Fic**
1. Uncles -- Fiction 2. Family life -- Fiction
ISBN 0-688-16733-0; 0-06-443828-7 pa

LC 98-39887

"Told in spare, unobtrusive prose, a story that helps us see our own
chances for benefiting from mutual tolerance, creative conflict resolution, and other forms of good will." Horn Book

★ **Olive's** ocean. Greenwillow Bks. 2003 217p $15.99; pa $6.99
Grades: 5 6 7 8 **Fic**
1. Family life -- Fiction 2. Grandmothers -- Fiction
ISBN 0-06-053543-1; 0-06-053545-8 pa

LC 2002-29782

A Newbery Medal honor book, 2004

On a summer visit to her grandmother's cottage by the ocean,
twelve-year-old Martha gains perspective on the death of a classmate,

on her relationship with her grandmother, on her feelings for an older
boy, and on her plans to be a writer.

"Rich characterizations move this compelling novel to its satisfying
and emotionally authentic conclusion." SLJ

★ **Sun** & Spoon. Greenwillow Bks. 1997 135p $15.99; pa $5.99
Grades: 4 5 6 7 **Fic**
1. Death -- Fiction 2. Grandmothers -- Fiction
ISBN 0-688-15232-5; 0-06-128875-6 pa

LC 96-46259

"Sensitively placed metaphors enrich the narrative, embuing its
perceptive depictions of grief with a powerful message of affirmation."
Publ Wkly

Words of stone. Greenwillow Bks. 1992 152p $18.99; pa $6.99
Grades: 5 6 7 8 **Fic**
1. Friendship -- Fiction
ISBN 0-688-11356-7; 0-06-078230-7 pa

LC 91-28543

Busy trying to deal with his many fears and his troubled feelings for
his dead mother, ten-year-old Blaze has his life changed when he meets
the boisterous and irresistible Joselle

"A story rich in characterization, dramatic subplots, and some very
creepy moments." SLJ

★ The **year** of Billy Miller; by Kevin Henkes. 1st ed. Harpercollins Childrens Books 2013 240 p. (hardcover) $16.99; (library)
$17.89
Grades: 2 3 4 5 **Fic**
1. Siblings -- Fiction 2. School stories -- Fiction 3. Parent-child
relationship -- Fiction 4. Humorous stories 5. Schools -- Fiction 6.
Wisconsin -- Fiction 7. Family life -- Wisconsin -- Fiction
ISBN 0062268120; 9780062268129; 9780062268136

LC 2012050373

Newberry Honor Book (2014)

This book follows second-grader Billy Miller. It's the "year of several dilemmas for the boy, including the fear he might 'start forgetting
things' due to bumping his head while on vacation over the summer.
Then there's the habitat diorama that Billy is assigned--the bat cave he
creates doesn't turn out quite like he'd hoped." His relationships with
his teacher, father, mother, and sister are examined. (Publishers Weekly)

Henry, Marguerite
Brighty of the Grand Canyon; illustrated by Wesley Dennis. Mac-
millan 1991 222p il hardcover o.p. pa $3.95
Grades: 4 5 6 7 **Fic**
1. Donkeys -- Fiction 2. Grand Canyon (Ariz.) -- Fiction
ISBN 0-02-743664-0; 0-689-71485-8 pa

LC 90-28636

First published 1953 by Rand McNally

"Only those who are unfamiliar with the West would say it is too
packed with drama to be true. And the author's understanding warmth
for all of God's creatures still shines through her superb ability as a story
teller making this a vivid tale." Christ Sci Monit

★ **King** of the wind; illustrated by Wesley Dennis. Macmillan
1991 172p il $18.95; pa $5.99
Grades: 4 5 6 7 **Fic**
1. Horses -- Fiction
ISBN 0-02-743629-2; 0-689-71486-6 pa

LC 91-13474

A reissue of the title first published 1948 by Rand McNally
Awarded the Newbery Medal, 1949

"A beautiful, sympathetic story of the famous [ancestor of a line of great thoroughbred horses] . . . and the little mute Arabian stable boy who accompanies him on his journey across the seas to France and England [in the eighteenth century]. The lad's fierce devotion to his horse and his great faith and loyalty are skillfully woven into an enthralling tale which children will long remember. The moving quality of the writing is reflected in the handsome illustrations." Wis Libr Bull

★ **Misty** of Chincoteague; illustrated by Wesley Dennis. Macmillan 1991 173p il hardcover o.p. pa $5.99

Grades: 4 5 6 7　　　　　　　　　　　　　　　　　　**Fic**

　　1. Horses -- Fiction 2. Chincoteague Island (Va.) -- Fiction

　　ISBN 0-02-743622-5; 1-4169-2783-2 pa

　　　　　　　　　　　　　　　　　　　　　LC 90-27237

First published 1947 by Rand McNally

A Newbery Medal honor book, 1948

"The beauty and pride of the wild horses is the highpoint in the story, and skillful drawings of them reveal their grace and swiftness." Ont Libr Rev

　　Other titles about the ponies of Chincoteague Island are:

　　Sea star, orphan of Chincoteague (1949)

　　Stormy, Misty's foal (1963)

Herlong, M.H.

　　Buddy; by M. H. Herlong. Viking Childrens Books 2012 p. cm.

Grades: 4 5 6　　　　　　　　　　　　　　　　　　**Fic**

　　1. Dogs -- Fiction 2. Pets -- Fiction 3. Hurricane Katrina, 2005 -- Fiction 4. 5. African Americans -- Fiction 6. New Orleans (La.) -- Fiction 7. Family life -- Louisiana -- Fiction 8. Lost and found possessions -- Fiction

　　ISBN 9780670014033

　　　　　　　　　　　　　　　　　　　　LC 2011042854

This book tells the story of Li'l T Roberts, who "meets Buddy when his family's car accidentally hits the stray dog. . . . Buddy turns out to be the dog Li'l T's always wished for--until Hurricane Katrina comes to New Orleans and he must leave Buddy behind. . . . But Li'l T refuses to give up his quest to find his best friend." (Publisher's Note)

Hermes, Patricia

　　Emma Dilemma and the camping nanny. Marshall Cavendish Children 2009 137p $15.99

Grades: 2 3 4　　　　　　　　　　　　　　　　　　**Fic**

　　1. Camping -- Fiction 2. Friendship -- Fiction 3. Family life -- Fiction

　　ISBN 978-0-7614-5534-9; 0-7614-5534-5

　　　　　　　　　　　　　　　　　　　　LC 2008038809

Nine-year-old Emma O'Fallon finds herself in increasing difficulties at home and at school as her determined efforts to break up the growing attachment between Irish nanny Annie and her boyfriend Bo cause chaos on a family camping trip and Emma's relationship with her best friend Luisa seems to be going from bad to worse.

　　"Filled with the challenge of managing everyday emotions, this reassuring read makes another strong entry in the series." Booklist

　　Emma Dilemma and the new nanny. Marshall Cavendish 2006 106p il $15.95

Grades: 2 3 4　　　　　　　　　　　　　　　　　　**Fic**

　　1. Family life -- Fiction

　　ISBN 0-7614-5286-9; 978-0-7614-5286-7

　　　　　　　　　　　　　　　　　　　　LC 2005024668

Emma tries to help her parents understand that, although their beloved new nanny has made a few mistakes, no one can behave perfectly responsibly all the time

"The tumult in a family with five preteen children, several pets, and two working parents provides a lively setting, and the author lightly but effectively conveys the ideas that adults aren't perfect and that admitting mistakes is often the first step toward solutions that leave everyone pleased." Booklist

　　Other titles about Emma are:

　　Emma Dilemma and the two nannies (2007)

　　Emma Dilemma and the soccer nanny (2008)

　　Emma Dilemma and the camping nanny (2009)

　　Emma Dilemma, the nanny, and the secret ferret (2010)

　　Emma Dilemma, the nanny, and the best horse ever (2011)

　　Emma Dilemma and the soccer nanny; by Patricia Hermes. 1st ed. Marshall Cavendish 2008 120p $15.99

Grades: 2 3 4　　　　　　　　　　　　　　　　　　**Fic**

　　1. Pets -- Fiction 2. Soccer -- Fiction 3. Strikes -- Fiction 4. Family life -- Fiction

　　ISBN 978-0-7614-5301-7; 0-7614-5301-6

　　　　　　　　　　　　　　　　　　　　LC 2007034990

When Emma and her brothers and sisters want to get a kitten and another ferret, and Emma wants their nanny to be the chaperone on her soccer team trip instead of her mother, the children decide to go on strike to try to force their parents to meet their demands.

　　Emma Dilemma and the two nannies; by Patricia Hermes. 1st ed. Marshall Cavendish 2007 117p $15.99

Grades: 2 3 4　　　　　　　　　　　　　　　　　　**Fic**

　　1. Family life -- Fiction

　　ISBN 978-0-7614-5353-6

　　　　　　　　　　　　　　　　　　　　LC 2006026563

Emma and her siblings plot to keep their beloved nanny Annie from going on a three-week vacation and leaving them in the care of the totally uncool, animal-hating Mrs. Potts.

　　"This simply told, easy chapter book is the second title about Emma but it can stand alone." SLJ

　　Emma Dilemma, the nanny, and the best horse ever. Marshall Cavendish 2011 137p $15.99

Grades: 2 3 4　　　　　　　　　　　　　　　　　　**Fic**

　　1. Horses -- Fiction 2. Moving -- Fiction 3. Nannies -- Fiction 4. Friendship -- Fiction 5. Family life -- Fiction

　　ISBN 978-0-7614-5905-7; 0-7614-5905-7

　　　　　　　　　　　　　　　　　　　　LC 2010042121

Emma's happy summer of soccer camp with best friend Luisa and visits to Rooney, the beloved old horse at the nearby stables where Annie the nanny helps out, changes when she discovers that Rooney is being sold and Luisa has some unhappy news.

　　"Hermes' latest installment in her winning series provides the right amount of humor, suspense and pathos as her young protagonist reaches a new level of emotional growth." Kirkus

　　Emma Dilemma, the nanny, and the secret ferret. Marshall Cavendish Children 2010 137p $15.99

Grades: 2 3 4　　　　　　　　　　　　　　　　　　**Fic**

　　1. Ferrets -- Fiction 2. Vacations -- Fiction 3. Family life -- Fiction

　　ISBN 978-0-7614-5650-6; 0-7614-5650-3

Emma struggles with finding the perfect time to confess to her parents that she brought her pet ferret on vacation to Maine, and trying to save her favorite tree that a new neighbor wants to cut down.

　　"This addition to the series has a surprisingly sweet ending and should please fans." SLJ

Herrera, Robin

Hope is a ferris wheel; Robin Herrera. Amulet Books 2014 272 p. (alk. paper) $16.95

Grades: 4 5 6 7   **Fic**

1. Clubs -- Fiction 2. Moving -- Fiction 3. Poetry -- Fiction 4. Trailer parks -- Fiction 5. Trailer camps -- Fiction

ISBN 1419710397; 9781419710391

LC 2013026392

In this book, by Robin Herrera, "ten-year-old Star Mackie lives in a trailer park with her flaky mom and her melancholy older sister. . . . Moving to a new town has made it difficult for Star to make friends, when her classmates tease her because of where she lives and because of her layered blue hair. But when Star starts a poetry club, she develops a love of Emily Dickinson and . . . learns some important lessons about herself and comes to terms with her hopes for the future." (Publisher's note)

"Herrera has created a delightful narrator with a memorable voice and surrounded her with a unique supporting cast." Booklist

Herrick, Steven

Naked bunyip dancing; pictures by Beth Norling. Front Street 2008 201p il $16.95

Grades: 3 4 5 6   **Fic**

1. School stories 2. Novels in verse 3. Teachers -- Fiction 4. Australia -- Fiction

ISBN 978-1-59078-499-0

LC 2007-18353

First published 2005 in Australia

This novel in verse follows the school year of Australian students in classroom 6C, as their unconventional teacher encourages them to discover their own strengths and talents and perform in a memorable concert.

"The novel captures the humor and unpredictability of 11 and 12-year-olds. . . . The terse free verse, in short clear lines, is easily accessible. Funny, with some touches of poignancy. . . . The childlike, black-and-white illustrations are reminiscent of the drawings of Shel Silverstein and complement the narrative." SLJ

Hesse, Karen

★ **Brooklyn** Bridge; a novel. Feiwel and Friends 2008 229p il map $17.95

Grades: 5 6 7 8 9 10   **Fic**

1. Immigrants -- Fiction 2. Family life -- Fiction 3. Social classes -- Fiction 4. Homeless persons -- Fiction 5. Russian Americans -- Fiction 6. Brooklyn (New York, N.Y.) -- Fiction

ISBN 978-0-312-37886-8; 0-312-37886-6

LC 2008-05624

In 1903 Brooklyn, fourteen-year-old Joseph Michtom's life changes for the worse when his parents, Russian immigrants, invent the teddy bear and turn their apartment into a factory, while nearby the glitter of Coney Island contrasts with the dismal lives of children dwelling under the Brooklyn Bridge.

Hesse "applies her gift for narrative voice to this memorable story. . . . The novel explodes with dark drama before its eerie but moving resolution." Publ Wkly

★ **Letters** from Rifka. Holt & Co. 1992 148p $16.95; pa $6.99

Grades: 5 6 7 8   **Fic**

1. Jews -- Fiction 2. Letters -- Fiction 3. Immigrants -- Fiction

ISBN 0-8050-1964-2; 0-312-53561-9 pa

LC 91-48007

In letters to her cousin, Rifka, a young Jewish girl, chronicles her family's flight from Russia in 1919 and her own experiences when she must be left in Belgium for a while when the others emigrate to America

"Based on the true story of the author's great-aunt, the moving account of a brave young girl's story brings to life the day-to-day trials and horrors experienced by many immigrants as well as the resourcefulness and strength they found within themselves." Horn Book

★ **Out** of the dust. Scholastic 1997 227p $16.95; pa $6.99

Grades: 5 6 7 8   **Fic**

1. Novels in verse 2. Oklahoma -- Fiction 3. Farm life -- Fiction 4. Dust storms -- Fiction 5. Great Depression, 1929-1939 -- Fiction

ISBN 0-590-36080-9; 0-590-37125-8 pa

LC 96-40344

Awarded the Newbery Medal, 1998

"Hesse's writing transcends the gloom and transforms it into a powerfully compelling tale of a girl with enormous strength, courage, and love. The entire novel is written in very readable blank verse." Booklist

★ **Witness**. Scholastic Press 2001 161p $16.95; pa $5.99

Grades: 6 7 8 9   **Fic**

1. Novels in verse 2. Vermont -- Fiction 3. Prejudices -- Fiction 4. Ku Klux Klan -- Fiction

ISBN 0-439-27199-1; 0-439-27200-9 pa

LC 00-54139

A series of poems express the views of eleven people in a small Vermont town, including a young black girl and a young Jewish girl, during the early 1920s when the Ku Klux Klan is trying to infiltrate the town

"The story is divided into five acts, and would lend itself beautifully to performance. The plot unfolds smoothly, and the author creates multidimensional characters." SLJ

Hest, Amy

★ **Remembering** Mrs. Rossi; [illustrated by] Heather Maione. Candlewick Press 2007 184p il $14.99; pa $6.99

Grades: 3 4 5   **Fic**

1. Death -- Fiction 2. Mothers -- Fiction 3. Teachers -- Fiction 4. New York (N.Y.) -- Fiction 5. Father-daughter relationship -- Fiction

ISBN 978-0-7636-2163-6; 0-7636-2163-3; 978-0-7636-4089-7 pa

LC 2006-41649

Although she loves her father, their home in New York City, and third-grade teacher Miss Meadows, Annie misses her mother who died recently

"Hest imbues her characters with warmth, humor, and realistic imperfections. . . . Maione's ink sketches highlight the tender affections." Booklist

Followed by: Letters to Leo (2012)

Hiaasen, Carl

★ **Flush**. Knopf 2005 263p $16.95; lib bdg $18.99; pa $8.99

Grades: 5 6 7 8   **Fic**

1. Florida -- Fiction 2. Boats and boating -- Fiction 3. Environmental protection -- Fiction

ISBN 0-375-82182-1; 0-375-92182-6 lib bdg; 0-375-84185-7 pa

LC 2005-05259

With their father jailed for sinking a river boat, Noah Underwood and his younger sister, Abbey, must gather evidence that the owner of this floating casino is emptying his bilge tanks into the protected waters around their Florida Keys home

"This quick-reading, fun, family adventure harkens back to the Hardy Boys in its simplicity and quirky characters." SLJ

★ **Hoot**. Knopf 2002 292p $15.95; pa $8.95

Grades: 5 6 7 8   **Fic**

1. Owls -- Fiction 2. Florida -- Fiction 3. Environmental protection

-- Fiction
ISBN 0-375-82181-3; 0-375-82916-4 pa

LC 2002-25478

A Newbery Medal honor book, 2003

Roy, who is new to his small Florida community, becomes involved in another boy's attempt to save a colony of burrowing owls from a proposed construction site. "Grades six to nine." (Bull Cent Child Books)

"The story is full of offbeat humor, buffoonish yet charming supporting characters, and genuinely touching scenes of children enjoying the wildness of nature." Booklist

★ **Scat**. Knopf 2009 371p $16.99; pa $8.99; lib bdg $19.99
Grades: 5 6 7 8   **Fic**
1. Florida -- Fiction 2. Teachers -- Fiction 3. Missing persons -- Fiction 4. Wildlife conservation -- Fiction
ISBN 0-375-83486-9; 0-375-83487-7 pa; 0-375-93486-3 lib bdg; 978-0-375-83486-8; 978-0-375-83487-5 pa; 978-0-375-93486-5 lib bdg

LC 2008-28266

Nick and his friend Marta investigate when a mysterious fire starts near a Florida wildlife preserve and biology teacher Mrs. Starch goes missing. "Grades six to nine." (Bull Cent Child Books)

"Once again, Hiaasen has written an edge-of-the-seat eco-thriller. . . . From the first sentence, readers will be hooked. . . . This well-written and smoothly plotted story, with fully realized characters, will certainly appeal to mystery lovers." SLJ

Hicks, Betty
Basketball Bats; illustrated by Adam McCauley. Roaring Brook Press 2008 55p il (Gym shorts) $15.95
Grades: 2 3 4   **Fic**
1. Basketball -- Fiction
ISBN 978-1-59643-243-7; 1-59643-243-8

LC 2007-019501

Henry and his basketball teammates, the Bats, take on the Tigers, and Henry learns a lesson about working as a team.

"Hicks finds just the right balance between story line, play-by-play action, and wry humor. . . . Nearly every double-page spread includes a droll illustration by McCauley, the illustrator of Scieszka's Time Warp Trio series." Booklist

Other titles in this series are:
Goof-off goalie (2008)
Swimming with sharks (2008)
Scaredy-cat catcher (2009)
Track attack (2009)
Doubles troubles (2010)

Doubles troubles; illustrated by Simon Gane. Roaring Brook Press 55p il (Gym shorts) $15.99
Grades: 2 3 4   **Fic**
1. Tennis -- Fiction 2. Friendship -- Fiction
ISBN 978-1-5964-3489-9; 1-5964-3489-9

"This offers useful life lessons within a story in which . . . friends share a love of sports and a bond of friendship that weathers some realistic trials. Attractive line drawings enhance the appeal of this beginning chapter book." Booklist

Out of order. Roaring Brook Press 2005 169p $15.95; pa $6.99
Grades: 4 5 6   **Fic**
1. Stepfamilies -- Fiction
ISBN 1-59643-061-3; 0-312-37355-4 pa

LC 2004-30107

Four youngsters, ages nine to fifteen, narrate one side of the story of their newly blended family's adjustment, interwoven with grief and loss.

"Hicks provides readers with a fresh look at blended families, offering much food for thought and several multilayered characters." SLJ

Scaredy-cat catcher; illustrated by Adam McCauley. Roaring Brook Press 2009 55p il (Gym shorts) $16.95
Grades: 2 3 4   **Fic**
1. Fear -- Fiction 2. Baseball -- Fiction
ISBN 978-1-59643-246-8; 1-59643-246-2

When Rocky, a talented catcher who was injured during the previous baseball season by an out-of-control runner, develops a reflex that keeps him from tagging the runner out, Rocky's friends—and his dog Chops—help him overcome his fear.

"The fast-moving plot, straightforward writing style, and illustrations on every spread make this selection ideal for students new to chapter books and for reluctant readers, as well as fans of the previous titles in the series." SLJ

Swimming with Sharks; illustrated by Adam McCauley. Roaring Brook Press 2008 55p il (Gym shorts) $15.95
Grades: 2 3 4   **Fic**
1. Swimming -- Fiction 2. Friendship -- Fiction
ISBN 978-1-59643-245-1; 1-59643-245-4

LC 2008-11126

Rita tries to improve her times and flip turns as she struggles to decide whether to remain the best swimmer on the Dolphins team or the worst on the Sharks team, where she could be with her friends.

"Lively black-and-white illustrations . . . add humor and provide ample visual cues on each spread, helping the new reader gain confidence with chapter books." Horn Book

Other titles in this series are:
Goof-off goalie (2008)
Scaredy-cat catcher (2009)

Track attack. Roaring Brook Press 2009 55p il (Gym shorts) $15.99
Grades: 2 3 4   **Fic**
1. Track athletics -- Fiction 2. Father-daughter relationship -- Fiction
ISBN 978-1-59643-488-2; 1-59643-488-0

Jazz loves running sprints on her track team. Her dad loves that she's on the team too, but his enthusiasm is taking all the fun out of running.

"Many expressive black-and-white pictures illustrate this solid addition to the Gym Shorts series." Booklist

The **worm** whisperer; Betty Hicks; illustrated by Ben Hatke. Roaring Brook Press 2012 192 p. (hardcover) $16.99
Grades: 4 5 6   **Fic**
1. Picture books for children 2. Caterpillars -- Fiction 3. Human-animal communication -- Fiction 4. Worms -- Fiction 5. Racing -- Fiction 6. Insects -- Fiction
ISBN 1596434902; 9781596434905; 9781596438460

LC 2012013790

In this children's book by Betty Hicks, illustrated by Ben Hatke, "Ellis Coffey loves animals. He spends so much time outdoors that sometimes he thinks he can talk with them. When he discovers a caterpillar that seems to follow his directions, he knows he has a chance to win the annual Woolly Worm race. The prize money is $1,000--exactly the amount of the deductible for his dad's back surgery." (Publisher's note)

Higgins, F. E.
The **Black** Book of Secrets. Feiwel and Friends 2007 273p $14.95

Grades: 4 5 6 7 **Fic**
1. Apprentices -- Fiction 2. Pawnbrokers -- Fiction
ISBN 978-0-312-36844-9; 0-312-36844-5

LC 2007-32559

When Ludlow Fitch runs away from his thieving parents in the City, he meets up with the mysterious Joe Zabbidou, who calls himself a secret pawnbroker, and who takes Ludlow as an apprentice to record the confessions of the townspeople of Pagus Parvus, where resentments are many and trust is scarce.

This is "an intriguing blend of adventure and historical fiction spiced with a light touch of the fantastic." Voice Youth Advocates

The **bone** magician. Feiwel and Friends 2008 272p $14.95
Grades: 4 5 6 7 **Fic**
1. Mystery fiction 2. Magicians -- Fiction 3. Undertakers and undertaking -- Fiction
ISBN 978-0-312-36845-6; 0-312-36845-3

LC 2008-6777

With his father, a fugitive, falsely accused of multiple murders and the real serial killer stalking the wretched streets of Urbs Umida, Pin Carpue, a young undertaker's assistant, investigates and soon discovers that all of the victims may have attended the performance of a stage magician who claims to be able to raise corpses and make the dead speak.

This offers "no end of picaresque charms, creepy turns, and beguiling cast members." Booklist

Higgins, Simon
Moonshadow; rise of the ninja. Little Brown & Co. 2010 325p il $15.99
Grades: 4 5 6 7 **Fic**
1. Japan -- Fiction 2. Ninja -- Fiction 3. Spies -- Fiction 4. Secret societies -- Fiction
ISBN 978-0-316-05531-4; 0-316-05531-X

First published 2008 in Australia with title: Moonshadow: eye of the beast

It's the dawn of an age of peace in medieval Japan. But a power-hungry warlord is plotting to plunge the national into a deadly civil war. Enter Moonshadow, the newest agent for the Grey Light Order, a secret brotherhood of ninja spy warriors. Can Moonshadow defeat the evil warlord or will his first mission be his last?

"The swordplay is fast and furious, and Japanese terms and places are integrated in a manner that reluctant readers will find accessible. This adventure is part spy novel, part magic, and all fun." SLJ

Followed by: The nightmare ninja (2011)

The **nightmare** ninja. Little, Brown 2011 368p (Moonshadow) $15.99
Grades: 4 5 6 7 **Fic**
1. Japan -- Fiction 2. Ninja -- Fiction 3. Orphans -- Fiction 4. Supernatural -- Fiction
ISBN 978-0-316-05533-8; 0-316-05533-6

LC 2010043177

Sequel to: Moonshadow: rise of the ninja (2010)

Battling a power-hungry warlord in medieval Japan, teenaged Moonshadow, an orphaned ninja in the shogun's secret service with the ability to see through the eyes of animals, encounters a weaponless assassin who enters the mind of his victims during their sleep.

"Higgins effectively uses this work to set the stage for a compelling third installment." Kirkus

Hill, Kirkpatrick
Bo at Ballard Creek; Kirkpatrick Hill; illustrated by LeUyen Pham. Henry Holt and Co. 2013 288 p. (hardcover) $15.99

Grades: 3 4 5 6 **Fic**
1. Historical fiction 2. Adopted children -- Fiction 3. Eskimos -- Fiction 4. Fathers -- Fiction 5. Adoption -- Fiction 6. Alaska -- History -- 1867-1959 -- Fiction 7. Alaska -- History -- 1867-1959 -- Fiction
ISBN 0805093516; 9780805093513

LC 2012046055

Scott O'Dell Award for Historical Fiction (2014)

In this historical novel, "Bo, a 5-year-old girl, was adopted as a newborn by two gruff but tenderhearted blacksmiths who've toiled in the mining camps of the Yukon for years. These unlikely fathers smoke a bit and swear a bit, but they love Bo with all their hearts. Theirs is an extraordinarily generous, solicitous, close-knit community, comprised of indigenous neighbors and workers from around the world." (Kirkus)

The **year** of Miss Agnes. Margaret K. McElderry Bks. 2000 115p $16; pa $5.99
Grades: 3 4 5 **Fic**
1. School stories 2. Alaska -- Fiction 3. Teachers -- Fiction 4. Athapascan Indians -- Fiction
ISBN 0-689-82933-7; 0-689-85124-3 pa

LC 99-46912

Ten-year-old Fred (short for Frederika) narrates the story of school and village life among the Athapascans in Alaska during 1948 when Miss Agnes arrived as the new teacher

"Hill has created more than just an appealing cast of characters; she introduces readers to a whole community and makes a long-ago and faraway place seem real and very much alive. This is an inspirational story." SLJ

Hilmo, Tess
Skies like these; Tess Hilmo. Margaret Ferguson Books, Farrar Straus Giroux 2014 240 p. (hardback) $16.99
Grades: 4 5 6 7 **Fic**
1. Western stories 2. Friendship -- Fiction 3. Aunts -- Fiction 4. Wyoming -- Fiction 5. Eccentrics and eccentricities -- Fiction
ISBN 0374369984; 9780374369989

LC 2013033675

"Twelve-year-old Jade's perfect summers have always been spent reading and watching TV reruns, so she's not happy when her parents send her off to Wyoming to her aunt's house. She meets a boy who calls himself Roy Parker--just like the real name of the legendary rebel cowboy Butch Cassidy. . . . Jade wants to be a good friend, but she's not so sure about Roy's schemes." (Publisher's note)

"In Hilmo's second middle-grade novel, a 12-year-old city girl spends a month in Wyoming and finds big skies, a boy who idolizes Butch Cassidy, and her own sense of adventure. . . . But rest assured, if there's a sequel, their future big plans will likely center around climbing Grand Teton rather than robbing banks." Booklist

★ **With** a name like Love. Margaret Ferguson Books/Farrar Straus Giroux 2011 249p $16.99
Grades: 5 6 7 8 **Fic**
1. Mystery fiction 2. Arkansas -- Fiction 3. Country life -- Fiction 4. Christian life -- Fiction 5. Conduct of life -- Fiction
ISBN 978-0-374-38465-4; 0-374-38465-7

LC 2010036314

Thirteen-year-old Olivene Love gets tangled up in a murder mystery when her itinerant preaching family arrives in the small town of Binder, Arkansas in 1957.

"Hilmo creates a family, town and a mystery that readers won't soon forget." Kirkus

Hilton, Marilyn

Full cicada moon; by Marilyn Hilton. Dial Books, an imprint of Penguin Group (USA) Inc. 2015 400 p. (hardcover) $17.99

Grades: 4 5 6 7   **Fic**

1. Novels in verse 2. Vermont -- Fiction 3. Astronauts -- Fiction 4. Gender role -- Fiction 5. Racially mixed people -- Fiction 6. Sex role -- Fiction

ISBN 0525428755; 9780525428756

LC 2014044894

This book, by Marilyn Hilton, is a "novel-in-verse about fitting in. . . . It's 1969, and the Apollo 11 mission is getting ready to go to the moon. But for half-black, half-Japanese Mimi, moving to a predominantly white Vermont town is enough to make her feel alien. . . . She struggles to fit in with her classmates. . . . And even though teachers and neighbors balk at her mixed-race family and her refusals to conform, Mimi¿s dreams of becoming an astronaut never fade." (Publisher's note)

"Mimi Yoshiko Oliver and her family just moved from Berkeley, California, to Hillsborough, Vermont, where she immediately encounters barrier after barrier to overcome. Mimi's goal is to become an astronaut; however, it's 1969, a time when young girls are encouraged to become mothers, secretaries, teachers, or nurses. . . . Mimi's voice as narrator is clear and focused: she must figure out who she is, instead of answering the question, "What are you?" Out of respect for her parents, the decisions she makes pull from both halves to make a whole. Perfect for readers who straddle societies, feel they don't fit in, or need that confirmation of self-celebration." Booklist

Himmelman, John, 1959-

Tales of Bunjitsu Bunny; written and illustrated by John Himmelman. Henry Holt & Co. 2014 128 p. color illustrations (hardcover) $13.99

Grades: 1 2 3   **Fic**

1. Rabbits -- Fiction 2. Martial arts -- Fiction 3. Animals -- Fiction

ISBN 0805099700; 9780805099706

LC 2013048431

In this children's book, author John Himmelman is "introducing Isabel, aka Bunjitsu Bunny! She is the BEST bunjitsu artist in her school, and she can throw farther, kick higher, and hit harder than anyone else! But she never hurts another creature . . . unless she has to. This series of brief stories about Isabel's adventures are a beguiling combination of child-friendly scenarios and Eastern wisdom perfect for the youngest readers." (Publisher's note)

"Himmelman (Duck to the Rescue) draws on his own experience as a martial arts instructor in 12 brief tales about a rabbit named Isabel, "the best bunjitsu artist in her school."... Spare ink illustrations appear on every page, skillfully balancing humor, bunjitsu action, and understated grace. Like Isabel herself, this one's a winner in unexpected ways." PW

Hirsch, Jeff

The **39** clues: Breakaway; unstoppable: breakaway. Jeff Hirsch. Scholastic 2014 192 p. (The 39 clues: unstoppable) (paper over board) $12.99

Grades: 4 5 6 7   **Fic**

1. Betrayal 2. Adventure stories 3. Brothers and sisters -- Fiction

ISBN 0545521424; 9780545521420

LC 2013942298

In this 39 Clues series book by Jeff Hirsch, "Dan and Amy are facing their greatest threat yet, an enemy who has found a way to use the source of the Cahill family power against them. To stop him, Dan and Amy must set out on a desperate mission that will take them from one of the world's hottest regions all the way to the frozen blast of the Arctic Circle. But with the enemy closing in, Dan finds himself facing the one terror he never imagined--being betrayed by his own sister." (Publisher's note)

Hirsch, Odo

Darius Bell and the glitter pool. Kane/Miller 2010 214p $15.99

Grades: 4 5 6 7   **Fic**

1. Gifts -- Fiction 2. Poverty -- Fiction

ISBN 978-1-935279-65-5; 1-935279-65-3

First published 2009 in Australia

The Bell family's ancestors were showered with honours, gifts and grants of land. In exchange, they have bestowed a Gift, once every 25 years, on the town. Now it's Darius's father's turn and there is no money for an impressive gift. When an earthquake reveals a glorious cave, with the most beautiful minerals lining the walls, he thinks he's found the answer.

"With an inventive cast of characters and a surprise twist at the end, this gentle, appealing story would make a terrific read-aloud for a young audience." Booklist

Hitchcock, Shannon

The **ballad** of Jessie Pearl; Shannon Hitchcock. 1st ed. Namelos llc 2012 131 p. ill. (hardcover) $18.95

Grades: 5 6 7 8   **Fic**

1. Romance fiction 2. Historical fiction 3. Tuberculosis -- Fiction

ISBN 160898141X; 9781608981410; 9781608981427

LC 2012936706

In this novel, by Shannon Hitchcock, "it's 1922, and Jessie has big plans for her future, but that's before tuberculosis strikes. Though she has no talent for cooking, cleaning, or nursing, Jessie puts her dreams on hold to help her family. She falls in love for the first time ever, and suddenly what she wants is not so simple anymore." (Publisher's note)

Hobbs, Valerie

Defiance. Farrar, Straus and Giroux 2005 116p $16; pa $7.99

Grades: 5 6 7 8   **Fic**

1. Death -- Fiction 2. Cancer -- Fiction 3. Country life -- Fiction

ISBN 0-374-30847-0; 0-312-53581-3 pa

LC 2004-61524

While vacationing in the country, eleven-year-old Toby, a cancer patient, learns some important lessons about living and dying from an elderly poet and her cow.

"Spare, graceful writing, with just enough detail to bring the characters and setting to life, skillfully paces the action and keeps the focus on Toby's conflicted feelings. . . . A quiet, yet resonant story." SLJ

★ The **last** best days of summer. Frances Foster Books 2010 197p $16.99

Grades: 5 6 7 8   **Fic**

1. Artists -- Fiction 2. Old age -- Fiction 3. Popularity -- Fiction 4. Grandmothers -- Fiction 5. Down syndrome -- Fiction

ISBN 978-0-374-34670-6; 0-374-34670-4

LC 2008-47145

During a summer visit, twelve-year-old Lucy must come to terms with both her grandmother's failing memory and how her mentally-challenged neighbor will impact her popularity when both enter the same middle school in the fall.

"The story's finely tuned realism is refreshing, particularly in Lucy's yearning for social acceptance and in the fully drawn and wholly memorable characters." Booklist

Maggie and Oliver, or, A bone of one's own; art by Jennifer Thermes. Henry Holt and Company 2011 181p il $15.99

Grades: 4 5 6   **Fic**

1. Dogs -- Fiction 2. Orphans -- Fiction 3. Poverty -- Fiction 4. Boston (Mass.) -- Fiction 5. Homeless persons -- Fiction

ISBN 978-0-8050-9294-3; 0-8050-9294-3

LC 2011005791

A dog whose beloved owner has died and an orphaned ten-year-old girl find each other while enduring poverty and homelessness in early-twentieth-century Boston.

"Thermes' black-and-white illustrations quietly match both tone and period. A touching and emotionally satisfying foundling tale." Kirkus

Hobbs, Will

Crossing the wire. HarperCollins 2006 216p $15.99; lib bdg $16.89; pa $5.99

Grades: 5 6 7 8 **Fic**

1. Young adult literature 2. Mexicans -- Fiction 3. Illegal aliens -- Fiction

ISBN 978-0-06-074138-9; 0-06-074138-4; 978-0-06-074139-6 lib bdg; 0-06-074139-2 lib bdg; 978-0-06-074140-2 pa; 0-06-074140-6 pa

LC 2005-19697

Fifteen-year-old Victor Flores journeys north in a desperate attempt to cross the Arizona border and find work in the United States to support his family in central Mexico.

This is "an exciting story in a vital contemporary setting." Voice of Youth Advocates

★ **Jason's** gold. Morrow Junior Bks. 1999 221p $16.99; pa $5.99

Grades: 5 6 7 8 **Fic**

1. Orphans -- Fiction 2. Voyages and travels -- Fiction 3. Klondike River Valley (Yukon) -- Gold discoveries -- Fiction

ISBN 0-688-15093-4; 0-380-72914-8 pa

LC 99-17973

When news of the discovery of gold in Canada's Yukon Territory in 1897 reaches fifteen-year-old Jason, he embarks on a 10,000-mile journey to strike it rich

"The successful presentation of a fascinating era, coupled with plenty of action, makes this a good historical fiction choice." SLJ

Followed by Down the Yukon (2001)

Never say die; by Will Hobbs. HarperCollins Children's Books 2012 224 p. (trade bdg.) $16.99

Grades: 4 5 6 7 **Fic**

1. Canada -- Fiction 2. Wilderness survival -- Fiction 3. Adventure fiction 4. Bears -- Fiction 5. Caribou -- Fiction 6. Eskimos -- Fiction 7. Brothers -- Fiction 8. Inuit -- Canada -- Fiction 9. Photojournalism -- Fiction 10. Aklavik (N.W.T.) -- Fiction 11. Climatic changes -- Fiction 12. Adventure and adventurers -- Fiction

ISBN 006170878X; 9780061708787; 9780061708794

LC 2011053289

This juvenile adventure novel, by Will Hobbs, is set "in Canada's Arctic, [where] Nick Thrasher is an accomplished Inuit hunter at fifteen. . . . Ryan Powers . . . invites Nick to come along and help him find the caribou. Barely down the river, disaster strikes. . . . With nothing but the clothes on his back and the knife on his hip, Nick is up against it in a world of wolves, caribou, and grizzlies. All the while, the monstrous polar bear stalks the land." (Publisher's note)

Take me to the river. HarperCollins 2011 184p $15.99; lib bdg $16.89

Grades: 5 6 7 8 **Fic**

1. Young adult literature 2. Texas -- Fiction 3. Cousins -- Fiction 4. Canoes and canoeing -- Fiction

ISBN 978-0-06-074144-0; 0-06-074144-9; 978-0-06-074145-7 lib bdg; 0-06-074145-7 lib bdg

LC 2010003147

When North Carolina fourteen-year-old Dylan Sands joins his fifteen-year-old cousin Rio in running the Rio Grande River, they face a tropical storm and a fugitive kidnapper.

"The story unfolds in a disarming manner. The pace is quick, and the challenges are relentless, but the writing is so grounded in physical details and emotional realism that every turn of events seems convincing within the context of the story." Booklist

Hof, Marjolijn

Against the odds; translated by Johanna H. Prins and Johanna W. Prins. Groundwood Books/House of Anansi Press 2009 125p $17.95

Grades: 3 4 5 **Fic**

1. War stories 2. Worry -- Fiction 3. Fathers -- Fiction 4. Physicians -- Fiction

ISBN 978-0-88899-935-1; 0-88899-935-6; 978-0-88899-950-4 pa

"Kiki's father is traveling to a war zone as a doctor, and the child and her mother worry that he won't return. As soon as he leaves, Kiki starts planning to increase the odds that he will be safe. . . . The language and writing style are a bit old-fashioned, yet comforting. The story is engaging and gives readers a chance to develop empathy." SLJ

Mother number zero. Groundwood Books 2011 179p $16.95

Grades: 4 5 6 7 **Fic**

1. Adoption -- Fiction 2. Siblings -- Fiction 3. Family life -- Fiction 4. Netherlands -- Fiction

ISBN 978-1-55498-078-9; 1-55498-078-X

Fay "and his older sister An Bing Wa were both adopted; she was an abandoned baby in China, and he was born to a mother traumatized in the Bosnian conflict. A new girl in the neighborhood, Maud, takes a keen interest in Fay's story and urges him to find his birth mother. . . . Hof . . . writes Fay's narration with a calm, matter-of-fact voice that possesses a literalness and simplicity in keeping with his youth. . . . The story nonetheless treats the characters with quiet percipience. . . . Younger fans of domestic novels who like a tale with more gravitas if not reading difficulty will appreciate this thoughtful family story." Bull Cent Child Books

Hoffmann, E. T. A.

Nutcracker; pictures by Maurice Sendak; translated by Ralph Manheim. Crown 1984 102p il $40

Grades: 4 5 6 7 **Fic**

1. Fairy tales 2. Christmas -- Fiction

ISBN 0-609-61049-X

LC 83-25266

"The smooth, elegant, new translation re-creates the flavor of the period and does justice to the story. . . . The occasional quirkiness of the pictures . . . eerily reflect the mysterious story. Altogether a magnificent, splendid combination of talents." Horn Book

Holczer, Tracy

The **secret** hum of a daisy; Tracy Holczer. G.P. Putnam's Sons, an imprint of Penguin Group (USA) 2014 320 p. (hardback) $16.99

Grades: 5 6 7 8 **Fic**

1. Home -- Fiction 2. Death -- Fiction 3. Moving -- Fiction 4. Grandmothers -- Fiction 5. Treasure hunt (Game) -- Fiction 6. Moving, Household -- Fiction

ISBN 039916393X; 9780399163937

LC 2013039962

In this book, by Tracy Holczer, "twelve-year-old Grace and her mother . . . [travel] from place to place like gypsies. But Grace wants to finally have a home all their own. Just when she thinks she's found it her mother says it's time to move again. Grace summons the courage to tell her mother how she really feels and will always regret that her last words to her were angry ones. After her mother's sudden death, Grace is forced to live with a grandmother she's never met." (Publisher's note)

"Grace is a multifaceted, relatable protagonist: she's pensive, stubborn, lonely, and caring--much like Grandma, which is why they are able to help heal each other's grief. Their relationship evolves in an honest and tender way in this heartfelt debut about loss and love." Horn Book

Holling, Holling C.

Paddle-to-the-sea; written and illustrated by Holling Clancy Holling. Houghton Mifflin 1941 un il lib bdg $20; pa $11.95
Grades: 4 5 6   Fic
  1. Great Lakes region -- Fiction
  ISBN 0-395-15082-5 lib bdg; 0-395-29203-4 pa
A Caldecott Medal honor book, 1942
A toy canoe with a seated Indian figure is launched in Lake Nipigon by the Indian boy who carved it and in four years travels through all the Great Lakes and the St. Lawrence River to the Atlantic. An interesting picture of the shore life of the lakes and the river with striking full page pictures in bright colors and marginal pencil drawings

"The canoe's journey is used to show the flow of currents and of traffic, and each occurrence is made to seem plausible. . . . There are also diagrams of a sawmill, a freighter, the canal locks at the Soo, and Niagara Falls." Libr J

Holm, Jennifer L.

★ The **fourteenth** goldfish; Jennifer L. Holm. Random House Inc 2014 208 p. (hardcover) $16.99; (library binding) $19.99
Grades: 4 5 6 7   Fic
  1. Scientists -- Fiction 2. Grandfathers -- Fiction 3. Aging -- Fiction 4. Family life -- Fiction
  ISBN 0375870644; 9780375870644; 9780375970641
                      LC 2013035052
"Eleven-year-old Ellie has never liked change. She misses fifth grade. She misses her old best friend. She even misses her dearly departed goldfish. Then one day a strange boy shows up. He's bossy. He's cranky. And weirdly enough . . . he looks a lot like Ellie's grandfather, a scientist who's always been slightly obsessed with immortality." (Publisher's note)

"With humor and heart, Holm has crafted a story about life, family, and finding one's passion that will appeal to readers willing to imagine the possible." SLJ
Includes bibliographical references

★ **Full** of Beans; Jennifer L. Holm. Random House Inc. 2016 208 p. (hardback) $16.99
Grades: 3 4 5   Fic
  1. Florida -- Fiction 2. Depressions -- 1929 -- Fiction 3. Gangs -- Fiction 4. Moneymaking projects -- Fiction 5. Key West (Fla.) -- History -- 20th century -- Fiction
  ISBN 9780553510362; 9780553510379
                      LC 2015041078
In this book, by Jennifer L. Holm, "grown-ups lie. That's one truth Beans knows for sure. He and his gang know how to spot a whopper a mile away, because they are the savviest bunch of barefoot conchs (that means 'locals') in all of Key West. Not that Beans really minds; it's 1934, the middle of the Great Depression. With no jobs on the island, and no money anywhere, who can really blame the grown-ups for telling a few tales?" (Publisher's note)

"Filled with humor, heart, and warmth; readers can only hope to hear more about the Curry clan." Kirkus

★ **Middle** school is worse than meatloaf; a year told through stuff. by Jennifer L. Holm; pictures by Elicia Castaldi. Atheneum Books for Young Readers 2007 un il $12.99

Grades: 5 6 7 8   Fic
  1. School stories 2. Family life -- Fiction
  ISBN 0-689-85281-9
"Ginny Davis begins seventh grade with a list of items to accomplish. This list, along with lots of other 'stuff'—including diary entries, refrigerator notes, cards from Grandpa, and IM screen messages—convey a year full of ups and downs. Digitally rendered collage illustrations realistically depict the various means of communication, and the story flows easily from one colorful page to the next. . . . The story combines honesty and humor to create a believable and appealing voice." SLJ

★ **Our** only May Amelia. HarperCollins Pubs. 1999 253p il hardcover o.p. pa $5.99
Grades: 5 6 7 8   Fic
  1. Family life -- Fiction 2. Finnish Americans -- Fiction 3. Washington (State) -- Fiction 4. Frontier and pioneer life -- Fiction
  ISBN 0-06-027822-6; 0-06-440856-6 pa
                      LC 98-47504
A Newbery Medal honor book, 2000
As the only girl in a Finnish American family of seven brothers, May Amelia Jackson resents being expected to act like a lady while growing up in Washington State in 1899

"The voice of the colloquial first-person narrative rings true and provides a vivid picture of frontier and pioneer life. . . . An afterword discusses Holm's research into her own family's history and that of other Finnish immigrants." Horn Book Guide
Followed by: The trouble with May Amelia (2011)

★ **Penny** from heaven. Random House 2006 274p il $15.95; lib bdg $17.99; pa $6.99
Grades: 5 6 7 8   Fic
  1. New Jersey -- Fiction 2. Family life -- Fiction 3. Italian Americans -- Fiction
  ISBN 0-375-83687-X; 0-375-93687-4 lib bdg; 0-375-83689-6 pa
                      LC 2005-13890
A Newbery Medal honor book, 2007
As she turns twelve during the summer of 1953, Penny gains new insights into herself and her family while also learning a secret about her father's death.

"Holm impressively wraps pathos with comedy in this coming-of-age story, populated by a cast of vivid characters." Booklist

The **trouble** with May Amelia; illustrated by Adam Gustavson. Atheneum Books for Young Readers 2011 204p il $15.99
Grades: 5 6 7 8   Fic
  1. Sex role -- Fiction 2. Siblings -- Fiction 3. Finnish American -- Fiction 4. Washington (State) -- Fiction 5. Frontier and pioneer life -- Fiction
  ISBN 1-4169-1373-4; 978-1-4169-1373-3
                      LC 2010042092
Sequel to: Our only May Amelia (1999)
Living with seven brothers and her father, who thinks girls are useless, a thirteen-year-old Finnish American farm girl is determined to prove her worth when a enterprising gentleman tries to purchase their cash-strapped family settlement in Washington State in 1900.

"Holm gets her heroine just right. Narrating events in dryly witty, plainspoken first-person, this indomitable teen draws readers in with her account, through which her world comes alive." Kirkus

★ **Turtle** in paradise. Random House 2010 191p $16.99; lib bdg $19.99
Grades: 3 4 5   Fic
  1. Adventure fiction 2. Cousins -- Fiction 3. Florida -- Fiction 4.

Family life -- Fiction
ISBN 978-0-375-83688-6; 0-375-83688-8; 978-0-375-93688-3
lib bdg; 0-375-93688-2 lib bdg

LC 2009-19077

A Newbery Medal honor book, 2011

In 1935, when her mother gets a job housekeeping for a woman who does not like children, eleven-year-old Turtle is sent to stay with relatives she has never met in far away Key West, Florida.

"Holm's voice for Turtle is winning and authentic—that of a practical, clear-eyed observer—and her nimble way with dialogue creates laugh-out-loud moments. Sweet, funny and superb." Kirkus

Holmes, Sara Lewis

★ **Operation** Yes. Arthur A. Levine Books 2009 234p $16.99
Grades: 5 6 7 8   Fic
1. School stories 2. Acting -- Fiction 3. Cousins -- Fiction 4. Teachers -- Fiction 5. Military bases -- Fiction
ISBN 978-0-545-10795-2; 0-545-10795-4; 978-0-545-10796-9 pa; 0-545-10796-2 pa

LC 2008053732

In her first ever teaching job, Miss Loupe uses improvisational acting exercises with her sixth-grade students at an Air Force base school, and when she experiences a family tragedy, her previously skeptical class members use what they have learned to help her, her brother, and other wounded soldiers

"Quick, funny, sad, full of heart, and irresistibly absorbing." Booklist

Holt, Kimberly Willis

★ **Dancing** in Cadillac light. Putnam 2001 167p hardcover o.p.
pa $5.99
Grades: 5 6 7 8   Fic
1. Texas -- Fiction 2. Old age -- Fiction 3. Grandfathers -- Fiction
ISBN 0-399-23402-0; 0-698-11970-3 pa

LC 00-40267

In 1968, eleven-year-old Jaynell's life in the town of Moon, Texas, is enlivened when her eccentric Grandpap comes to live with her family

"This nostalgic parable about loss and redemption is at once gritty and poetic, stark and sentimental, howlingly funny and depressingly sad, but it is a solid page-turner." SLJ

Piper Reed gets a job; illustrated by Christine Davenier. Henry Holt and Co. 2009 149p il $14.99
Grades: 3 4 5   Fic
1. Florida -- Fiction 2. Parties -- Fiction 3. Birthdays -- Fiction 4. Family life -- Fiction 5. Business enterprises -- Fiction 6. United States. -- Navy -- Fiction.
ISBN 978-0-8050-8199-2; 0-8050-8199-2

LC 2008-50267

When she discovers the price of the coveted clubhouse, ten-year-old Piper and her fellow Gypsy Club members try to earn the money by creating a birthday-party-planning business.

"Occasional black-and-white line drawings capture the girls' expressions and antics. This book is a good addition to the series and is also a natural for fans of Clementine or Judy Moody, as well as readers ready to step beyond Junie B. Jones." SLJ

Piper Reed, campfire girl; illustrated by Christine Davenier. Henry Holt 2010 148p il $15.99
Grades: 3 4 5   Fic
1. Clubs -- Fiction 2. Camping -- Fiction 3. Halloween -- Fiction 4. Family life -- Fiction
ISBN 978-0-8050-9006-2; 0-8050-9006-1

LC 2009050765

Fifth-grader Piper and her sisters are thrilled about their first-ever camping trip until they learn it will be at Halloween, but other Navy families join them, including an annoying new member of the Gypsy Club.

"The fresh, inviting look of Davenier's drawings works well with Holt's amusing and perceptive first-person narrative. A realistic family story with a satisfying conclusion." Booklist

Piper Reed, Navy brat. Henry Holt 2007 146p il $14.95; pa $6.99
Grades: 3 4 5   Fic
1. Moving -- Fiction 2. Florida -- Fiction 3. Family life -- Fiction
ISBN 978-0-8050-8197-8; 0-8050-8197-6; 978-0-312-38020-5 pa; 0-312-38020-8 pa

LC 2006-35467

Piper is sad about leaving her home and friends behind when her father, a Navy aircraft mechanic, is transferred yet again, but with help from her often-annoying sisters and a surprise from their parents, she finds happiness in their new home in Pensacola, Florida.

"Holt tells a lively family story. . . . Davenier's occasional black-and-white pictures capture the daily family dramas." Booklist

Other titles about Piper Reed are:
Piper Reed, the great gypsy (2008)
Piper Reed gets a job (2009)
Piper Reed, campfire girl (2011)

Piper Reed, the great gypsy; illustrated by Christine Davenier. Henry Holt and Co. 2008 152p il $14.95
Grades: 3 4 5   Fic
1. School stories 2. Florida -- Fiction 3. Sisters -- Fiction 4. Family life -- Fiction 5. United States. -- Navy -- Fiction.
ISBN 978-0-8050-8198-5; 0-8050-8198-4

LC 2007-46941

While her father, a Navy Chief, is on ship duty for six months, nine-year-old Piper stays busy with new neighbors, Christmas at a spaceship beach house, a trip to New Orleans, and especially the upcoming Gypsy Club pet show.

"Piper's first-person narration will win over many readers with its accessible depiction of a family's ups and downs. . . . Davenier's line-and-wash drawings illustrate the episodic story with wry humor." Booklist

★ **When** Zachary Beaver came to town. Holt & Co. 1999 227p $17.99
Grades: 5 6 7 8   Fic
1. Texas -- Fiction 2. Obesity -- Fiction 3. Friendship -- Fiction
ISBN 0-8050-6116-9

LC 99-27998

During the summer of 1971 in a small Texas town, thirteen-year-old Toby and his best friend Cal meet the star of a sideshow act, 600-pound Zachary, the fattest boy in the world

"Holt writes with a subtle sense of humor and sensitivity, and reading her work is a delightful experience." Voice Youth Advocates

Holub, Joan

Bed, bats, and beyond; by Joan Holub; illustrated by Mernie Gallagher-Cole. Darby Creek Pub. 2008 64p il $14.95
Grades: 1 2 3   Fic
1. Bats -- Fiction 2. Bedtime -- Fiction 3. Storytelling -- Fiction
ISBN 978-1-58196-077-8; 1-58196-077-8

It's dawn and time for bats to go to bed, but Fang's brother Fink can't sleep. Soon the whole family tries different bedtime stories to lull Fink to sleep

"The narrative as a whole feels satisfying. . . . Gallagher-Cole's illustrations add humorous details. . . . With no more than 15 lines per page and illustrations on every spread, the story is ideal for students who have just graduated to chapter books. Charming and full of humor." SLJ

Holyoke, Polly

The **Neptune** Project; Polly Holyoke. 1st ed. Disney-Hyperion Books 2013 352 p. (reinforced) $16.99

Grades: 4 5 6 7   **Fic**

1. Science fiction 2. Ocean -- Fiction 3. Genetic engineering -- Fiction 4. Survival -- Fiction 5. Undersea colonies -- Fiction 6. Environmental degradation -- Fiction

ISBN 1423157567; 9781423157564

LC 2013000353

In this novel, by Polly Holyoke, "Nere . . . is one of a group of kids who . . . have been genetically altered to survive in the ocean. . . . In order to reach the safe haven of the Neptune colony, Nere and her fellow mutates must swim through hundreds of miles of dangerous waters, relying only on their wits, dolphins, and each other to evade terrifying undersea creatures and a government that will stop at nothing to capture the Neptune kids." (Publisher's note)

Followed by The Neptune Challenge (2015)

Hoover, P. J.

Tut; My Epic Battle to Save the World. P.J. Hoover. St. Martin's Press 2017 336 p. (ebook) $40; $16.99

Grades: 5 6 7 8   **Fic**

1. Tutankhamen, King of Egypt

ISBN 0765390825; 9781466814752; 9780765390820

LC 2017006334

In this book, by P.J. Hoover, "Meet Tut! He used to rule Egypt. Now he's stuck in middle school. Having defeated his evil uncle and the Cult of Set, who tried to send him to the afterlife, the perpetually fourteen-year-old King Tut is looking forward to a relaxing summer vacation. But then Tut discovers that his brother Gilgamesh has been captured by the Egyptian god Apep, Lord of Chaos. Gil helped to vanquish Apep thousands of years ago, and now Apep is back for vengeance." (Publisher's note)

"A sequel that doesn't disappoint; purchase where there are fans of the first book, or buy the series for readers looking for history and adventure." SLJ

Hopkins, Karen Leigh

Labracadabra; [by Jessie Nelson & Karen Leigh Hopkins; illustrated by Deborah Melmon] Viking 2011 36p il $14.99

Grades: 1 2 3   **Fic**

1. Dogs -- Fiction 2. Magic -- Fiction

ISBN 978-0-670-01251-0; 0-670-01251-3

LC 2010-25109

Zach always wanted a dog but Larry, the full-grown mongrel his parents choose, is not it, however, he soon discovers that there is something very special—even magical—about Larry's tail.

"This early chapter book is a beaut of brevity and pacing. . . . With plenty of illustrations and white space, this five-chapter romp flies along. . . . Transitioning independent readers will enjoy getting to know the unnamed narrator and watching his attitude progress as Larry changes from a 'used dog' to 'my dog.'" Kirkus

Hopkinson, Deborah

A **bandit's** tale; the muddled misadventures of a pickpocket. Deborah Hopkinson. Alfred A. Knopf 2016 304 p. illustrations (hardcover) $16.99

Grades: 4 5 6 7 8   **Fic**

1. Thieves -- Fiction 2. New York (N.Y.) -- History -- Fiction 3. Immigrants -- United States -- Fiction 4. Immigrants -- Fiction 5. Child abuse -- Fiction 6. Child labor -- Fiction 7. Conduct of life

-- Fiction 8. Animals -- Treatment -- Fiction 9. Italians -- New York (State) -- New York -- Fiction 10. New York (N.Y.) -- History -- 19th century -- Fiction

ISBN 9780385754996; 9780385755009; 038575499X

LC 2015004491

"Eleven-year-old Rocco is an Italian immigrant who finds himself alone in New York City after he's sold to a padrone by his poverty-stricken parents. While working as a street musician, he meets the boys of the infamous Bandits' Roost, who teach him the art of pickpocketing. Rocco embraces his new life of crime. But when he meets Meddlin' Mary, a strong-hearted Irish girl who's determined to help the horses of New York City, things begin to change." (Publisher's note)

"Rocco's conversational voice resounds with humor, compassion, and an inspiring energy for change. A dynamic historical novel ideal for both classroom studies and pleasure reading." Kirkus

Birdie's lighthouse; written by Deborah Hopkinson; illustrated by Kimberly Bulcken Root. Atheneum Bks. for Young Readers 1997 un il hardcover o.p. pa $6.99

Grades: 1 2 3   **Fic**

1. Maine -- Fiction 2. Lighthouses -- Fiction

ISBN 0-689-81052-0; 0-689-83529-9 pa

LC 94-24097

"With an exemplary assemblage of genre paintings perfectly attuned to the flow of the text, the whole is restrained yet charged with emotion." Horn Book

A **boy** called Dickens; Deborah Hopkinson; illustrations by John Hendrix. 1st ed. Schwartz & Wade Books 2012 40 p. col. ill. (hardcover) $17.99; (lib. bdg.) $20.99; (ebook) $17.99

Grades: 4 5 6   **Fic**

1. Authors 2. Child labor 3. Novelists 4. Authors -- Fiction 5. London (England) -- Fiction 6. Great Britain -- History -- 19th century -- Fiction

ISBN 037596732X; 9780375867323; 9780375967320; 9780375987403

LC 2010048531

This book presents an "account of Charles Dickens' boyhood, specifically his tenure wrapping and labeling bottles of boot blacking while his father and family languish in debtors' prison. Here young Charles passes the ten-hour days by regaling a fellow worker with made-up stories, elements of which would later appear in his best-known novels. . . . A closing note comments more fully on autobiographic references in Dicken's work." (Bulletin of the Center for Children's Books)

The **Great** Trouble; a mystery of London, the blue death, and a boy called Eel. by Deborah Hopkinson. Alfred A. Knopf 2013 256 p. (hard cover) $16.99

Grades: 4 5 6 7 8   **Fic**

1. Cholera 2. Orphans -- Fiction 3. London (England) -- Fiction 4. Cholera -- Fiction 5. Epidemics -- Fiction 6. London (England) -- History -- 19th century -- Fiction 7. Great Britain -- History -- Victoria, 1837-1901 -- Fiction

ISBN 0375848185; 9780375848186; 9780375948183

LC 2012032799

Author Deborah Hopkinson's book, "equal parts medical mystery, historical novel, and survival story about the 1854 London cholera outbreak, . . . introduces Eel, a boy trying to make ends meet on Broad Street. When he visits one of his regular employers, he learns the man has fallen ill. Eel enlists the help of Dr. Snow, and together they work to solve the mystery of what exactly is causing the spread of cholera and how they can prevent it." (Booklist)

Includes bibliographical references (p. 245-247)

Into the firestorm; a novel of San Francisco, 1906. Alfred A. Knopf 2006 200p hardcover o.p. pa $5.99
Grades: 5 6 7 8   **Fic**
1. Orphans -- Fiction 2. Earthquakes -- Fiction 3. San Francisco (Calif.) -- Fiction
ISBN 0-375-83652-7; 0-440-42129-2 pa

LC 2005-37189

Days after arriving in San Francisco from Texas, eleven-year-old orphan Nicholas Dray tries to help his new neighbors survive the 1906 San Francisco earthquake and the subsequent fires.

"The terror of the 1906 disaster is brought powerfully alive in this fast-paced tale. . . . Nick is a thoroughly developed protagonist, as are the supporting characters." SLJ

Includes bibliographical references

Horowitz, Anthony

The **Falcon's** Malteser; a Diamond brothers mystery. [by] Anthony Horowitz. 1st American ed; Philomel Books 2004 191p $16.99
Grades: 5 6 7 8   **Fic**
1. Mystery fiction
ISBN 0-399-24153-1

LC 2004-48322

After his older brother, a fledgling private detective, agrees to safeguard a package for a dwarf who does not live long, thirteen-year-old Nick scampers to solve the mystery while also trying to stay one step ahead of an assortment of thugs.

"The Diamond Brothers stories are invariably funny and full of excitement. Mystery readers with a sense of humor will enjoy [this tale]." Voice Youth Advocates

The **Greek** who stole Christmas; a Diamond Brothers mystery. [by] Anthony Horowitz. Puffin Books 2008 105p pa $6.99
Grades: 5 6 7 8   **Fic**
1. Mystery fiction
ISBN 978-0-14-240375-4 pa; 0-14-240375-X pa

LC 2008025944

Fourteen-year-old Nick and his brother, an ineffectual private detective, try to prevent the threatened murder of an international pop star in London at Christmas time.

"The witty banter between the characters keeps this short novel moving at breakneck speed." SLJ

★ **Public** enemy number two; a Diamond brothers mystery. Philomel Books 2004 190p $16.99; pa $5.99
Grades: 5 6 7 8   **Fic**
1. Mystery fiction
ISBN 0-399-24154-X; 0-14-240218-4 pa

LC 2004-10418

When thirteen-year-old Nick is framed for a jewel robbery, he and his brother, the bumbling detective Tim Diamond, attempt to clear his name by capturing the master criminal known as the Fence.

"Horowitz has a knack for puns and humor, and he successfully combines it with a nonstop action mystery that has everything from hydraulically controlled buses to secret caverns. A readable and exciting adventure." SLJ

Other titles in the Diamond Brothers Mystery series are:
The falcon's Maltester (2004)
South by southeast (2005)
Three of Diamonds (2005)
The Greek who stole Christmas (2008)

South by southeast; a Diamond brothers mystery. [by] Anthony Horowitz. Philomel Bks. 2005 148p $16.99; pa $5.99

Grades: 5 6 7 8   **Fic**
1. Mystery fiction
ISBN 0-399-24155-8; 0-14-240374-1 pa

LC 2005043169

First published 1997 in the United Kingdom
Fourteen-year-old Nick and his bumbling detective brother Tim Diamond investigate a mystery involving international spies and assassins.

"Horowitz has created another well-written, well-paced spy melodrama." SLJ

★ **Stormbreaker**. Philomel Books 2001 192p (An Alex Rider adventure) $17.99; pa $7.99
Grades: 5 6 7 8   **Fic**
1. Adventure fiction 2. Young adult literature 3. Spies -- Fiction 4. Orphans -- Fiction 5. Terrorism -- Fiction 6. Great Britain -- Fiction
ISBN 0-399-23620-1; 0-14-240611-2 pa

LC 00-63683

First published 2000 in the United Kingdom
After the death of the uncle who had been his guardian, fourteen-year-old Alex Rider is coerced to continue his uncle's dangerous work for Britain's intelligence agency, MI6

"Horowitz thoughtfully balances Alex's super-spy finesse with typical teen insecurities to create a likable hero living a fantasy come true. An entertaining, nicely layered novel." Booklist

Other titles about Alex Rider are:
Point blank (2002)
Skeleton key (2003)
Eagle strike (2004)
Scorpia (2005)
Ark angel (2006)
Snakehead (2007)
Crocodile tears (2009)
Scorpia rising (2011)
Russian roulette (2013)

The **switch**; [by] Anthony Horowitz. Philomel Books 2009 162p $16.99
Grades: 5 6 7 8   **Fic**
1. Wealth -- Fiction 2. Criminals -- Fiction 3. Supernatural -- Fiction 4. Great Britain -- Fiction
ISBN 978-0-399-25062-0; 0-399-25062-X

LC 2008-32380

When wealthy, spoiled, thirteen-year-old Tad Spencer wishes he were someone else, he awakens as Bob Snarby, the uncouth, impoverished son of carnival workers, and as he is drawn into a life of crime he begins to discover truths about himself and his family.

"A fun, tongue-in-cheek read that will captivate children who like adventure and mystery." SLJ

Three of diamonds; three Diamonds Brothers mysteries. [by] Anthony Horowitz. Philomel Books 2005 214p $16.99
Grades: 5 6 7 8   **Fic**
1. Mystery fiction
ISBN 0-399-24157-4

LC 2005276176

A collection of three Diamond Brothers mysteries in which Tim and Nick bungle their way through a search for a missing philanthropist, find themselves in a Parisian prison, and are stranded on a Scottish island with a murderer.

"Nick is a realistic character with a voice that is sarcastic and fresh, while Tim's lack of intelligence makes even the most dangerous situations laughable. Plenty of plays on words add to the humor." SLJ

Horvath, Polly

Everything on a waffle. Farrar, Straus & Giroux 2001 149p hardcover o.p. $16
Grades: 4 5 6 7 **Fic**
1. Uncles -- Fiction 2. British Columbia -- Fiction
ISBN 0-374-32236-8; 0-374-42208-7 pa
LC 00-35399
Boston Globe-Horn Book Award Honor: Fiction (2001)
Eleven-year-old Primrose living in a small fishing village in British Columbia recounts her experiences and all that she learns about human nature and the unpredictability of life in the months after her parents are lost at sea
"The story is full of subtle humor and wisdom, presented through the eyes of a uniquely appealing young protagonist." SLJ

Lord and Lady Bunny -- almost royalty! by Mr. & Mrs. Bunny; translated from the Rabbit by Polly Horvath; illustrated by Sophie Blackall. Schwartz & Wade books 2014 304 p. illustrations $16.99
Grades: 3 4 5 6 **Fic**
1. Rabbits -- Fiction 2. Kings and rulers -- Fiction 3. England -- Fiction 4. Hippies -- Fiction 5. Voyages and travels -- Fiction 6. Human-animal communication -- Fiction
ISBN 0307980650; 9780307980656; 9780307980663; 9780307980670
LC 2012027442
Sequel to Mr. and Mrs. Bunny--Detectives Extraordinaire! (2012)
"Madeleine wants nothing more than to save money for college, but her impractical, ex-hippie parents are broke. When the family unexpectedly inherits a sweet shoppe in England that has the potential to earn serious profit, they see an answer to all their problems." (Publisher's note)
"The plot is unapologetically preposterous, but the truly witty banter, near-constant conflict and palpable love between Mr. and Mrs. Bunny are both genuinely affecting and uproariously funny. Blackall's elegant, expressive black-and-white illustrations add whimsy to an already effervescent adventure." Kirkus

★ **Mr.** and Mrs. Bunny-- detectives extraordinaire! by Mrs. Bunny; translated from the Rabbit by Polly Horvath; illustrated by Sophie Blackall. Schwartz & Wade Books 2011 248 p.
Grades: 3 4 5 6 **Fic**
1. Mystery fiction 2. Children's stories 3. Ciphers -- Fiction 4. Rabbits -- Fiction 5. Kidnapping -- Fiction 6. Foxes -- Fiction 7. Hippies -- Fiction 8. Marmots -- Fiction 9. Mystery and detective stories 10. Human-animal communication -- Fiction 11. Hornby Island (B.C. : Island) -- Fiction
ISBN 9780375867552; 9780375898273; 9780375967559
LC 2010024133
In this book, "middle-schooler Madeline has learned to be resourceful, a skill upon which she calls when her [hippie] parents are kidnapped by foxes who want a bunch of coded recipes . . . decoded by Madeline's . . . uncle Runyon, a code-savvy spy. Madeline first seeks out Runyon herself, but he suddenly falls into a coma, so she turns for help to a pair of fedora-wearing rabbits, taking them for detectives. Mr. and Mrs. Bunny are only too happy to assist." (Bulletin of the Center for Children's Books)

★ **My** one hundred adventures. Schwartz & Wade Books 2008 260p $16.99; lib bdg $19.99; pa $7.99
Grades: 4 5 6 7 **Fic**
1. Summer -- Fiction 2. Beaches -- Fiction 3. Siblings -- Fiction 4.

Babysitters -- Fiction 5. Single parent family -- Fiction
ISBN 978-0-375-84582-6; 0-375-84582-8; 978-0-375-95582-2 lib bdg; 0-375-95582-8 lib bdg; 978-0-375-85526-9 pa; 0-375-85526-2 pa
LC 2008-02243
Twelve-year-old Jane, who lives at the beach in a run-down old house with her mother, two brothers, and sister, has an eventful summer accompanying her pastor on bible deliveries, meeting former boyfriends of her mother's, and being coerced into babysitting for a family of ill-mannered children.
With writing as foamy as waves, as gritty as sand, or as deep as the sea, this book may startle readers with the freedom given the heroine. . . . Unconventionality is Horvath's stock and trade, but here the high quirkiness quotient rests easily against Jane's inner story with its honest, childlike core. Booklist
Followed by: Northward to the Moon (2010)

The **Pepins** and their problems; pictures by Marylin Hafner. Farrar Straus Giroux 2004 179p il $16; pa $6.99
Grades: 3 4 5 6 **Fic**
1. Family life -- Fiction
ISBN 0-374-35817-6; 0-312-37751-7 pa
LC 2003-60196
The reader is invited to help solve the Pepin family's unusual problems, which include having a cow who creates lemonade rather than milk and having to cope with a competitive neighbor
"Horvath spins a delightful yarn. . . . Absurd characters and situations and witty repartee are Horvath's strengths, and . . . the wordplay is a great argument for reading this aloud." Booklist

House, Silas
★ **Eli** the Good. Candlewick Press 2009 295p $16.99
Grades: 5 6 7 8 **Fic**
1. Aunts -- Fiction 2. Veterans -- Fiction 3. Friendship -- Fiction 4. Family life -- Fiction 5. Post-traumatic stress disorder -- Fiction
ISBN 978-0-7636-4341-6; 0-7636-4341-6
LC 2009004589
In the summer of 1976, ten-year-old Eli Book's excitement over Bicentennial celebrations is tempered by his father's flashbacks to the Vietnam War and other family problems, as well as concern about his tough but troubled best friend, Edie.
"House writes beautifully, with a gentle tone. He lays out Eli's world in exquisite detail. . . . The story flows along as steadily as a stream. . . . Eli is good company and children will enjoy accompanying him on his journey." SLJ

Howard, Ellen
The **crimson** cap. Holiday House 2009 177p $16.95
Grades: 5 6 7 8 **Fic**
1. Explorers 2. Texas -- Fiction 3. Explorers -- Fiction 4. Native Americans -- Fiction 5. America -- Exploration -- Fiction
ISBN 978-0-8234-2152-7; 0-8234-2152-X
LC 2009-25551
In 1684, wearing his father's faded cap, eleven-year-old Pierre Talon joins explorer Rene-Robert Cavelier on an ill-fated expedition to seek the Mississippi River, but after the expedition falls apart Pierre, deathly ill, is taken in by Hasinai Indians. Includes historical facts.
"A riveting adventure that will prove to be hard to put down. Howard's fast-paced writing brings the story to life. This solid coming-of-age story is based on real events and historical figures." SLJ

Howe, Deborah

★ **Bunnicula**; a rabbit-tale of mystery. by Deborah and James Howe; illustrated by Alan Daniel. 25th anniversary edition; Atheneum Books for Young Readers 2004 92p il $16.95

Grades: 4 5 6   **Fic**

1. Mystery fiction 2. Animals -- Fiction

ISBN 0-689-86775-1

A reissue of the title first published 1979

Though scoffed at by Harold the dog, Chester the cat tries to warn his human family that their foundling baby bunny must be a vampire

This book is "blithe, sophisticated, and distinguished for the wit and humor of the dialogue." Bull Cent Child Books

Howe, James, 1946-

★ **Addie** on the inside; James Howe. Atheneum Books for Young Readers 2011 206 p. $16.99

Grades: 5 6 7 8   **Fic**

1. School stories 2. Novels in verse 3. Self-acceptance -- Fiction 4. Interpersonal relations -- Fiction 5. Grandmothers -- Fiction 6. Identity (Psychology) -- Fiction

ISBN 141691384X; 9781416913849

LC 2010024497

This book, by James Howe, "follows 13-year-old Addie's struggles to define herself according to her own terms. Through her poems, Addie reflects on her life and life in general: her first boyfriend, what it means to be accepted and her endeavors to promote equality. Addie is at her most fragile when she examines her relationship with her boyfriend and the cruel behavior of her former best friend. Her forthright observations address serious topics with a maturity beyond her age." (Kirkus Reviews)

"Howe's artfully crafted lines show Addie's intelligence and wit, and his imagery evokes the aura of sadness surrounding 'this purgatory of/ the middle school years/ when so many things/ that never mattered before/ and will never matter again/ matter.' Readers will empathize with Addie's anguish and admire her courage to keep fighting." Publ Wkly

Dew drop dead; a Sebastian Barth mystery. Atheneum Pubs. 1990 156p hardcover o.p. pa $4.99

Grades: 4 5 6   **Fic**

1. Mystery fiction 2. Homeless persons -- Fiction

ISBN 0-689-31425-6; 0-689-80760-0 pa

LC 89-34697

"The story is well crafted and has substance beyond escapist fare as a result of Howe's inclusion of secondary storylines involving the homeless and Sebastian's own worries about his father's pending job loss." Booklist

Other titles about Sebastian Barth are:

Eat your poison, dear (1986)

Stage fright (1986)

What Eric knew (1985)

★ **Totally** Joe; James Howe. Atheneum Books for Young Readers 2005 189 p. $17.99

Grades: 5 6 7 8 9   **Fic**

1. School stories 2. Friendship -- Fiction 3. Adolescence -- Fiction 4. Homosexuality -- Fiction

ISBN 068983957X; 9780689839573

LC 2004022242

In this book, by James Howe, "Joe's teacher asks his seventh-grade class to write an alphabiography throughout the year, presenting themselves and their lives in entries from A to Z. Joe's essays begin and end with friends, from Addie, a long-time pal and confidant, to Zachary, a new student who, like Joe, has a unique approach to life. . . . Joe demonstrates that he truly is a one-of-a-kind kid, mostly comfortable with

himself but still struggling with common adolescent issues." (School Library Journal)

"Joe, one of the characters in The Misfits (2001), has his say, in a voice uniquely his own. Twelve-year-old Joe knows he is gay. He played with Barbies as a young child, prefers cooking to sports, and has a crush on a male classmate...Joe himself often comes off as a cross between Niles Crane and Harvey Fierstein. But he also reacts like a kid, and readers in his situation will wish for the love and support he receives from friends and family, as well as the happy life he so clearly envisions." Booklist

Howe, Peter

Waggit's tale; drawings by Omar Rayyan. HarperCollinsPublishers 2008 288p il $16.99; lib bdg $17.89; pa $6.99

Grades: 5 6 7   **Fic**

1. Dogs -- Fiction

ISBN 978-0-06-124261-8; 0-06-124261-6; 978-0-06-124262-5 lib bdg; 0-06-124262-4 lib bdg; 978-0-06-124263-2 pa; 0-06-124263-2 pa

LC 2007020878

When Waggit is abandoned by his owner as a puppy, he meets a pack of wild dogs who become his friends and teach him to survive in the city park, but when he has a chance to go home with a kind woman who wants to adopt him, he takes it

"The novel celebrates the wild freedom of the feral dog pack, while also emphasizing the many hazards of urban life for homeless companion animals." Voice Youth Advocates

Other titles in this series are:

Waggit again (2009)

Waggit forever (2009)

Warriors of the black shroud. Harper 2012 $16.99

Grades: 3 4 5   **Fic**

1. Fantasy fiction

ISBN 978-0-06-172987-4; 0-06-172987-6

LC 2011026147

A shy, bookish boy is pulled into an underground land called Nebula and asked to lead a kingdom in its fight against darkness.

This is a "fast-paced fantasy novel. . . . The climax and resolution have just enough surprise to satisfy readers. This attractive world (warriors ride unicorns!) and likable characters—boy heroes with a strong girl sidekick—will give fledgling readers of fantasy a treat." Kirkus

Howell, Troy

The **dragon** of Cripple Creek; a novel. Amulet Books 2011 385p $19.95

Grades: 5 6 7 8   **Fic**

1. Fantasy fiction 2. Adventure fiction 3. Gold -- Fiction 4. Dragons -- Fiction 5. Colorado -- Fiction

ISBN 978-0-8109-9713-4; 0-8109-9713-4

LC 2010-34362

When Kat, her father, and brother visit an old gold mine that has been turned into an amusement park, she falls down a shaft and meets an ancient dragon, the last of his kind, and inadvertently triggers a twenty-first century gold rush.

"Writing in Kat's first person narrative, which is wry and funny, clipped and eloquent, Howell, best known as an illustrator, mixes fantasy adventure with a moving conservation story in a debut that blends sadness, secrecy, and pure fantasy." Booklist

Howland, Leila

The **forget**-me-not summer; Leila Howland. First edition Harpercollins 2015 352 p. illustrations (hardcover) $16.99

Grades: 4 5 6 7 **Fic**
1. Summer -- Fiction 2. Sisters -- Fiction 3. Vacations -- Fiction 4. Great aunts -- Fiction 5. Cape Cod (Mass.) -- Fiction 6. Actors and actresses -- Fiction 7. Interpersonal relations -- Fiction
ISBN 0062318691; 9780062318695

LC 2014027413

"Though Marigold, Zinnia, and Lily Silver couldn't be more different, they're all excited about their various plans for summer vacation. But any expectation of summer fun comes crashing down when the sisters' parents send them to Cape Cod to visit their aunt Sunny. Small-town life is not what these L.A. girls had in mind. They must adjust, however, to things like sharing a room and living without a TV." (Publisher's note)

"An old-fashioned story well-told, with engaging characters--a beach read for preteens that is as comfortable as the old tennis shoes worn on the Massachusetts shore." Kirkus

Hughes, Shirley, 1927-
★ **Hero** on a bicycle; Shirley Hughes. Candlewick Press 2013 224 p. $15.99
Grades: 5 6 7 **Fic**
1. Historical fiction 2. World War, 1939-1945 -- Fiction
ISBN 076366037X; 9780763660376

LC 2012943650

This book is set in Italy during World War II. "The narrative focuses on a city under German occupation, events being perceived principally through the eyes of three members of the Crivelli family: teenager Paolo, his older sister Constanza and Rosemary, their English-born mother. . . . When an opportunity arises for Paolo, Constanza and Rosemary to lend their practical support to the Partisan cause Paolo, in particular, seizes it enthusiastically." (School Librarian)

Hughes, Ted, 1930-1998
The **iron** giant; illustrated by Laura Carlin. Knopf 2011 104p il $19.99
Grades: 4 5 6 **Fic**
1. Science fiction
ISBN 978-0-375-87149-8; 0-375-87149-7

A newly illustrated edition of the title first published 1968 by Harper & Row; published in the United Kingdom with title: The iron man

The fearsome iron giant becomes a hero when he challenges a huge space monster.

"Hughes's 1968 story of unexpected friendships and redemptions returns with new artwork from Carlin in a polished and well-designed edition that uses occasional gatefolds and die-cuts to amplify key moments. Carlin's mixed-media artwork emphasizes the giant's innate otherness. . . . It's an elegant and thoughtful treatment of a story that, with its hopeful message of global unity, feels as important and timely as ever." Publ Wkly

Hulme, John
The **split** second; by John Hulme and Michael Wexler; illustrations by Gideon Kendall. 1st U.S. ed.; Bloomsbury Children's Books 2008 301p il (The Seems) $16.99
Grades: 5 6 7 8 **Fic**
1. Science fiction 2. Terrorism -- Fiction
ISBN 978-1-599-90130-5; 1-599-90130-7

LC 2008012241

Sequel to: The glitch in sleep (2007)

Now thirteen-years-old and still a Fixer in the parallel universe called the Seems, Becker Drane is called upon to repair the damage caused by an enormous bomb planted in the Department of Time, an act of terrorism perpetrated by the evil members of the Tide, a group that is trying to destroy the World.

"This sequel continues to develop a truly ingenious setting while proving every bit as much of a nail-biter as the first." Booklist

Hunt, Irene
Across five Aprils. Berkley Jam Books 2002 212p pa $5.99
Grades: 5 6 7 8 **Fic**
1. Illinois -- Fiction 2. Farm life -- Fiction 3. United States -- History -- 1861-1865, Civil War -- Fiction
ISBN 978-0-425-18278-9; 0-425-18278-9

First published 1964 by Follett

A Newbery Medal honor book, 1965

Young Jethro Creighton grows from a boy to a man when he is left to take care of the family farm in Illinois during the difficult years of the Civil War.

"Authentic background, a feeling for the people of that time, and a story that never loses the reader's interest." Wilson Libr Bull

Hunt, Lynda Mullaly
★ **Fish** in a tree; Lynda Mullaly Hunt. Nancy Paulsen Books an imprint of Penguin Group (USA) 2015 276 p. (hardback) $16.99
Grades: 4 5 6 **Fic**
1. School stories 2. Dyslexia -- Fiction 3. Reading -- Fiction 4. Schools -- Fiction 5. Behavior -- Fiction
ISBN 0399162593; 9780399162596

LC 2014019910

Schneider Family Book Award, Middle School (2016)

In this novel by Lynda Mullaly Hunt, "Ally has been smart enough to fool a lot of smart people. Every time she lands in a new school, she is able to hide her inability to read by creating clever yet disruptive distractions. . . . However, her newest teacher Mr. Daniels sees the bright creative kid underneath the trouble maker. With his help, Ally learns not to be so hard on herself and that dyslexia is nothing to be ashamed of." (Publisher's note)

"When her teacher goes on maternity leave, sixth grader Ally humiliates herself by giving Mrs. Hall a sympathy card. No one had discovered--until now--that Ally cannot read. When substitute teacher Mr. Daniels arrives, things begin to change. Well-developed secondary characters (mean girls, a new BFF who sticks up for herself and others, the heroic teacher) add richness to the story and help Ally grow." Horn Book

One for the Murphys; Lynda Mullaly Hunt. Nancy Paulsen Books 2012 224 p. (hardback) $16.99
Grades: 5 6 7 8 **Fic**
1. Girls -- Fiction 2. Family -- Fiction 3. Foster children -- Fiction 4. Connecticut -- Fiction 5. Stepfathers -- Fiction 6. Family problems -- Fiction 7. Foster home care -- Fiction 8. Mothers and daughters -- Fiction 9. Family life -- Connecticut -- Fiction
ISBN 0399256156; 9780399256158

LC 2011046703

This book by Lynda Mullaly Hunt follows "eighth-grader Carley Connors [as she] learns about a different kind of family life, first resisting and then resisting having to leave the loving, loyal Murphys. . . . She's torn between her love for her mother and her memory of the fight that sent her to the hospital, when her mother caught and held her for her stepfather. Slowly won over at home . . . Carley also finds a friend at school in the prickly, Wicked-obsessed Toni." (Kirkus Reviews)

Hurd, Thacher
Bongo fishing. Henry Holt 2011 233p il $16.99
Grades: 3 4 5 **Fic**
1. Science fiction 2. California -- Fiction 3. Family life -- Fiction 4. Space flight -- Fiction 5. Extraterrestrial beings -- Fiction
ISBN 978-0-8050-9100-7; 0-8050-9100-9

LC 2010-1169

Berkeley, California, middle-schooler Jason Jameson has a close encounter of the fun kind when Sam, a bluish alien from the Pleiades, arrives in a 1960 Dodge Dart spaceship and invites Jason to go fishing.

"The funniest moments come through twists of Earth conventions. . . . Intriguing gadgets and amusing descriptions of alien technology add to the fun, as do the lively illustrations. . . . Sam and his wife are delightfully atypical aliens . . . and the moments of humor are consistently strong throughout." SLJ

Hurst, Carol Otis

You come to Yokum; with illustrations by Kay Life. Houghton Mifflin Co. 2005 137p il $15

Grades: 3 4 5 **Fic**

1. Feminism -- Fiction 2. Family life -- Fiction 3. Massachusetts -- Fiction 4. Women -- Suffrage -- Fiction

ISBN 0-618-55122-0

Twelve-year-old Frank witnesses his mother's struggles to muster support for women's right to vote even as the family's life is transformed by a year running a lodge in western Massachusetts in the early 1920s.

"With mostly short chapters and charming black-and-white illustrations, this is a satisfying read." SLJ

Hurwitz, Johanna

★ The **adventures** of Ali Baba Bernstein; illustrated by Gail Owens. Morrow 1985 82p il hardcover o.p. pa $5.99

Grades: 2 3 4 **Fic**

1. Personal names -- Fiction

ISBN 0-688-04161-2; 0-380-72349-2 pa

LC 84-27387

"Hurwitz' characters, as always, are believable, the situations realistic and the plot well developed." SLJ

Another title about Ali Baba Bernstein is:

Hurray for Ali Baba Bernstein (1989)

★ **Baseball** fever; illustrated by Ray Cruz. Morrow 1981 128p il hardcover o.p. pa $4.99

Grades: 3 4 5 **Fic**

1. Baseball -- Fiction 2. Father-son relationship -- Fiction

ISBN 0-380-73255-6 pa

LC 81-5633

"A brisk, breezy story about a believable family is told with warmth and humor." Bull Cent Child Books

Fourth-grade fuss; illustrated by Andy Hammond. HarperCollins 2004 132p $15.99; lib bdg $16.89

Grades: 2 3 4 **Fic**

1. School stories

ISBN 0-06-052343-3; 0-06-052344-1 lib bdg

LC 2003-22216

A yard sale, ice skating, class pictures, and a surprise party are a few of the things that make fourth grade fun for Julio and his friends, but they must get serious about studying as the statewide end-of-year test approaches.

"Fans of this series as well as young test takers everywhere are sure to appreciate the humorous, reassuring story." Booklist

Mighty Monty; illustrated by Anik McGrory. Candlewick Press 2008 106p il $15.99

Grades: 1 2 3 **Fic**

1. School stories 2. Asthma -- Fiction

ISBN 978-0-7636-2977-9; 0-7636-2977-4

Monty, a quiet first-grader continues to come into his own—playing the part of a tree in a comically miscued school play, sharing his enthusiasm for ants at an outdoor birthday party, and even signing up for karate class despite his asthma.

"Even readers who do not have to deal with asthma or an overprotective parent will see something of themselves in Monty." Booklist

Mostly Monty. Candlewick Press 2007 86p il $15.99; pa $5.99

Grades: 1 2 3 **Fic**

1. Asthma -- Fiction 2. Friendship -- Fiction

ISBN 978-0-7636-2831-4; 0-7636-2831-X; 978-0-7636-4062-0 pa; 0-7636-4062-X pa

LC 2006-49024

Because he suffers from asthma, six-year-old Monty is nervous about starting first grade but he soon learns to cope with his illness and use his special talents to make friends.

"Watercolor illustrations . . . appear every few pages, breaking up the text with pictures of cheerful button-nose children. More reserved children . . . will appreciate seeing themselves reflected in this gently funny story about learning to like oneself." Booklist

Other titles about Monty are:

Mighty Monty (2008)

Magical Monty (2012)

Hurwitz, Michele Weber

Calli be gold. Wendy Lamb Books 2011 198p $15.99; lib bdg $18.99

Grades: 4 5 6 **Fic**

1. School stories 2. Family life -- Fiction

ISBN 978-0-385-73970-2; 0-385-73970-2; 978-0-385-90802-3 lib bdg; 0-385-90802-4 lib bdg

LC 2010-13157

Eleven-year-old Calli, the third child in a family of busy high-achievers, likes to take her time and observe rather than rush around, and when she meets an awkward, insecure second-grader named Noah and is paired with him in the Peer Helper Program, she finds satisfaction and strength in working with him.

"Callie's often-insightful first-person narration provides a thoughtful, child-eyed view look at how adults too often try to find success through their children's achievements. The sometimes over-the-top depiction of stage parents pokes gentle but oh-so-true fun at them, adding to the appeal of this amusing debut." Kirkus

The **summer** I saved the world-- in 65 days; by Michele Weber Hurwitz. Wendy Lamb Books, an imprint of Random House Children's Books 2014 272 p. (trade) $16.99

Grades: 5 6 7 8 **Fic**

1. Summer -- Fiction 2. Neighbors -- Fiction 3. Family life -- Fiction 4. Helping behavior -- Fiction 5. Illinois -- Fiction 6. Friendship -- Fiction 7. Helpfulness -- Fiction 8. Conduct of life -- Fiction 9. Family life -- Illinois -- Fiction

ISBN 0385371063; 9780385371063; 9780385371070; 9780385371094

LC 2013016843

In this book, by Michele Weber Hurwitz, "thirteen-year-old Nina Ross is feeling kind of lost. . . . This summer, Nina decides to change things. She hatches a plan. There are sixty-five days of summer. Every day, she'll anonymously do one small but remarkable good thing for someone in her neighborhood, and find out: does doing good actually make a difference? Along the way, she discovers that her neighborhood, and her family, are full of surprises and secrets." (Publisher's note)

"Insightful writing, realistic dialogue infused with humor, and a sweet romantic element add depth to the story." Booklist

Hyde, Natalie

I owe you one. Orca 2011 125p (Orca young readers) pa $7.95

Grades: 3 4 5   **Fic**
1. Canada -- Fiction 2. Friendship -- Fiction
ISBN 978-1-55469-414-3; 1-55469-414-0

"After old Mrs. Minton saves him from drowning, Wes strikes up an unexpected friendship with her. His friend says that he owes Mrs. Minton a 'life debt,' and Wes worries how he could ever repay it. His chance comes when the town's aspiring pyrotechnic blows up the television tower. . . . The plot moves quickly from one humorous situation to another. Quirky but believable characters populate the small Canadian town. . . . With its slim length, fast pace, and humor, this title will appeal to a wide range of readers." Booklist

★ **Saving** ARM PIT. Fitzhenry & Whiteside 2011
Grades: 3 4 5 6   **Fic**
1. Letters -- Fiction 2. Baseball -- Fiction 3. Postal service -- Fiction
ISBN 1-55455-151-X; 978-1-55455-151-4

The Harmony Point baseball team hasn't won a game in two seasons, and vandals have deleted letters on the the town sign so that it says "arm Pit." A new postmaster becomes the new ball coach, but it takes a letter-writing campaign to save the coach's job and the baseball team.

"This book would be a terrific read-aloud for students to learn about citizenship, community service, and collaboration. Sportsmanship and hard work, respect for coaches are also valuable lessons within the story." SLJ

Ibbotson, Eva
The **beasts** of Clawstone Castle; illustrated by Kevin Hawkes. Dutton Children's Books 2006 243p il hardcover o.p. $16.99
Grades: 4 5 6   **Fic**
1. Ghost stories 2. Cattle -- Fiction 3. Castles -- Fiction 4. Great Britain -- Fiction
ISBN 0-14-240931-6 pa; 0-525-47719-5
                                                     LC 2005-29188
While spending the summer with elderly relatives at Clawstone Castle in northern England, Madlyn and her brother Rollo, with the help of several ghosts, attempt to save the rare cattle that live on the castle grounds. "Grades four to seven." (Bull Cent Child Books)

"Ibbotson's charismatic ghosts are great. . .—as human as they are horrific—and there's plenty of quirky humor in this energetic, diverting read, loaded with charm." Booklist

Dial-a-ghost. Dutton Children's Bks. 2001 195p hardcover o.p. pa $5.99
Grades: 4 5 6   **Fic**
1. Ghost stories 2. Orphans -- Fiction 3. Great Britain -- Fiction
ISBN 0-525-46693-2; 0-14-250018-6 pa
                                                     LC 00-52287
A family of nice ghosts protects a British orphan from the diabolical plans of his evil guardians

"The book is filled with a large and delightful cast of characters. . . . The black-and-white illustrations have an eerie charm." SLJ

Another title about the nice ghosts is:
The great ghost rescue (2002)

★ The **dragonfly** pool; illustrated by Kevin Hawkes. Dutton Children's Books 2008 377p il $17.99; pa $7.99
Grades: 5 6 7 8   **Fic**
1. School stories 2. World War, 1939-1945 -- Fiction
ISBN 978-0-525-42064-4; 0-525-42064-9; 978-0-14-241486-6 pa; 0-14-241486-7 pa

"Ibbotson's trademark eccentric characters and strongly contrasted principles of right and wrong brighten and broaden this uplifting tale." Booklist

★ The **Ogre** of Oglefort; [illustrations by Lisa K. Weber] Dutton Children's Books 2011 246p il $16.99
Grades: 4 5 6   **Fic**
1. Fairy tales 2. Magic -- Fiction 3. Orphans -- Fiction 4. Princesses -- Fiction
ISBN 978-0-525-42382-9; 0-525-42382-6
                                                     LC 2010038137
When the Hag of Dribble, an orphan boy, and a troll called Ulf are sent to rescue a princess from an ogre, it turns out to be far from the routine magical mission they expect.

"Magical creatures abound in this effervescent fairy tale that effectively merges classic tropes with modern sensibilities." Bull Cent Child Books

One dog and his boy; by Eva Ibbotson. Scholastic Press 2012 271 p. $16.99
Grades: 3 4 5 6   **Fic**
1. Children's stories 2. Dogs -- Fiction 3. Pets -- Fiction 4. Wealth -- Fiction 5. England -- Fiction 6. London (England) -- Fiction 7. Voyages and travels -- Fiction 8. Human-animal relationships -- Fiction 9. Family life -- England -- London -- Fiction
ISBN 0545351960; 9780545351966
                                                     LC 2011003773
In this book, by Eva Ibbotson, "[all] Hal has ever wanted is a dog. His busy parents, hoping that he'll tire of the idea, rent a dog from Easy Pets, run by the heartless Mr. and Mrs. Carker. Hal and Fleck, the dog he chooses, bond immediately, and they are both heartbroken when Hal's mother, realizing that Hal's interest isn't waning, sneaks the dog back to Easy Pets. Hal decides to get Fleck back and run away to his grandparents." (Bulletin of the Center for Children's Books)

★ The **secret** of platform 13; illustrated by Sue Porter. Dutton Children's Bks. 1998 231p il hardcover o.p. pa $5.99
Grades: 5 6 7 8   **Fic**
1. Fantasy fiction
ISBN 0-525-45929-4; 0-14-130286-0 pa
                                                     LC 97-44601
First published 1994 in the United Kingdom
Odge Gribble, a young hag, accompanies an old wizard, a gentle fey, and a giant ogre on their mission through a magical tunnel from their Island to London to rescue their King and Queen's son who had been stolen as an infant

"Lively, funny fantasy with a case of mistaken identity and a cast of eccentric characters." SLJ

★ The **star** of Kazan; illustrated by Kevin Hawkes. Dutton 2004 405p il $16.99; pa $7.99
Grades: 5 6 7 8   **Fic**
1. Mystery fiction 2. Germany -- Fiction 3. Vienna (Austria) -- Fiction
ISBN 0-525-47347-5; 0-14-240582-5 pa
                                                     LC 2004-45455
After twelve-year-old Annika, a foundling living in late nineteenth-century Vienna, inherits a trunk of costume jewelry, a woman claiming to be her aristocratic mother arrives and takes her to live in a strangely decrepit mansion in Germany

"This is a rich saga . . . full of stalwart friends, sly villains, a brave heroine, and good triumphing over evil. . . . An intensely satisfying read." SLJ

Iggulden, Conn

★ **Tollins**; explosive tales for children. illustrated by Lizzy Duncan. Harper 2009 172p il $16.99

Grades: 3 4 5 6   Fic

1. Fantasy fiction

ISBN 978-0-06-173098-6; 0-06-173098-X

"Tollins are tiny, nectar-eating woodland creatures with elf ears and wings but bigger than the fairies they casually use as handkerchiefs. They enjoy an idyllic existance until a fireworks factory is built in the village of Chorleywood. . . . The men of the village hunt the Tollins down to use as fodder for their fireworks. . . . Duncan's full-color illustrations and maps bring the world to witty life. A note at the end likens the Tollin's fate to child labor during the Industrial Revolution. There is much to think about and love in this beautifully realized world." Booklist

Ignatow, Amy

The **long**-distance dispatch between Lydia Goldblatt and Julie Graham-Chang. Amulet Books 2011 205p il (The popularity papers) $15.95

Grades: 3 4 5 6   Fic

1. School stories 2. Friendship -- Fiction 3. Popularity -- Fiction

ISBN 978-0-8109-9724-0; 0-8109-9724-X

Sequel to: The popularity papers: research for the social improvement and general betterment of Lydia Goldblatt & Julie Graham-Chang (2010)

After spending all of fifth grade studying popularity together, Julie and Lydia are finally ready to put their hard-earned lessons to use in junior high. But before they can, tragedy strikes: Lydia's mom gets a job in London for six whole months! Meanwhile Julie's stuck navigating the cliques of American junior high on her own, where she is adopted by a group of troublemaking eighth graders known as the Bichons.

"The girls' feelings are authentic, and their fun is contagious." Booklist

★ The **popularity** papers; research for the social improvement and general betterment of Lydia Goldblatt & Julie Graham-Chang. Amulet Books 204p il $15.95

Grades: 3 4 5 6   Fic

1. School stories 2. Popularity -- Fiction

ISBN 978-0-8109-8421-9; 0-8109-8421-0

LC 2009-39741

"Before they leave elementary school behind, two fifth-grade best friends are determined to uncover the secrets of popularity by observing, recording, discussing, and replicating the behaviors of the cool girls. . . . In a notebook format, this heavily illustrated title shows their research in dramatic, alternating, handwritten entries and colorful, hilarious drawings. . . . Ignatow offers a quick, fun, well-developed story that invites repeated readings." Booklist

Other titles about Lydia and Julie are:

The long distance dispatch between Lydia Goldblatt and Julie Graham-Chang (2011)

Words of (questionable) wisdom from Lydia Goldblatt & Julie Graham-Chang (2011)

Words of (questionable) wisdom from Lydia Goldblatt & Julie Graham-Chang. Amulet Books 2011 204p (The popularity papers) $15.95

Grades: 3 4 5 6   Fic

1. School stories 2. Friendship -- Fiction 3. Popularity -- Fiction 4. Scrapbooks -- Fiction

ISBN 978-1-4197-0063-7; 1-4197-0063-4

LC 2011285303

Twelve-year-old best friends Julie and Lydia are reunited after six months apart, but the news that their friend Sukie's mother has died after

a long illness causes them to reevaluate their goals and focus on being supportive of the friends they already have.

Irving, Washington

The **Legend** of Sleepy Hollow; illustrated by Gris Grimly. Atheneum Books for Young Readers 2007 un il $16.99

Grades: 4 5 6   Fic

1. Ghost stories 2. New York (State) -- Fiction

ISBN 1-4169-0625-8; 978-1-4169-0625-4

LC 2005-27502

A superstitious schoolmaster, in love with a wealthy farmer's daughter, has a terrifying encounter with a headless horseman.

"The tale, . . . slightly condensed but with language and ambiguities intact, is reimagined here with humor, vigor, [and] clarity. . . . Irving's language is challenging . . . but Grimly's numerous Halloween-hued panel and spot illustrations . . . parse it into comprehensible tidbits. The comically amplified emotions and warm yellow and orange tones balance the horror aspects of the text." Horn Book

Washington Irving's Rip van Winkle; illustrated by Arthur Rackham. Dover Publications 2005 19p pa $12.95

Grades: 5 6 7 8   Fic

1. Catskill Mountains (N.Y.) -- Fiction

ISBN 0-486-44242-X

LC 2004063543

A reissue of the edition first published 1905 by Doubleday

Rip Van Winkle "is based on a folk tale. Henpecked Rip and his dog Wolf wander into the Catskill mountains before the Revolutionary War. There they meet a dwarf, whom Rip helps to carry a keg. They join a group of dwarfs playing ninepins. When Rip drinks from the keg, he falls asleep and wakes 20 years later, an old man. Returning to his town, he discovers his termagant wife dead, his daughter married, and the portrait of King George replaced by one of George Washington. Irving uses the folk tale to present the contrast between the new and old societies." Reader's Ency. 3d edition

Iserles, Inbali

The **Taken**; by Inbali Iserles. Scholastic Press 2015 272 p. illustrations, map (Foxcraft) $16.99

Grades: 4 5 6 7   Fic

1. Fantasy fiction 2. Foxes -- Fiction 3. Magic -- Fiction

ISBN 0545690811; 9780545690812

In this book, by Inbali Iserles, "Isla and her brother are two young foxes living just outside the lands of the furless -- humans. The life of a fox is filled with dangers, but Isla has begun to learn mysterious skills meant to help her survive. Then the unthinkable happens. Returning to her den, Isla finds it set ablaze and surrounded by strange foxes, and her family is nowhere in sight. Forced to flee, she escapes into the cold, gray world of the furless." (Publisher's note)

"Vivid details, intriguing characters, and a riveting plot are smoothly executed in this exciting new series from one of the authors who write under the pseudonym of Erin Hunter. Beautifully rendered and magical." Kirkus

Iwasa, Megumi

★ **Yours** sincerely, Giraffe; Megumi Iwasa; illustrated by Jun Takabatake. Gecko Press 2017 102 p. illustrations $16.99

Grades: 1 2 3   Fic

1. Animals -- Fiction 2. Letters -- Fiction 3. Friendship -- Fiction

ISBN 1927271886; 9781927271889

Originally published in Japanese as Boku wa Afurika ni sumu kirin to iimasu

In this children's book, by Megumi Iwasa, illustrated by Jun Takabatake, "Giraffe is bored, as usual. He'd love a friend to share things with. So he writes a letter and sends it as far as possible across the other side of the horizon. There he finds a pen pal Penguin." (Publisher's note)

Jackson, Alison

★ Eggs over Evie; illustrated by Tuesday Mourning. Henry Holt 2010 215p il $16.99

Grades: 4 5 6   **Fic**

1. Pets -- Fiction 2. Cooking -- Fiction 3. Divorce -- Fiction 4. Stepfamilies -- Fiction

ISBN 978-0-8050-8294-4; 0-8050-8294-8

LC 2009-50762

Evie feels unsettled and sad after her parents divorce, her father remarries and takes the family dog, and his new wife becomes pregnant, but a cooking class and helping the elderly lady next door with her cat give Evie a way to cope with the changes in her life. Includes recipes.

"Evie tells her story with a pinch of humor and a dash of vulnerability, sifting together the people in her life and blending them into a surprising new family. . . . Sweet and savory." Kirkus

Includes bibliographical references

Rainmaker. Boyds Mills Press 2005 192p $16.95

Grades: 5 6 7 8   **Fic**

1. Florida -- Fiction 2. Droughts -- Fiction 3. Great Depression, 1929-1939 -- Fiction

ISBN 1-59078-309-3

"For 13-year-old Pidge Martin, the summer of 1939 brings changes and challenges. Her town, Frostfree, Florida, faces its longest drought in 40 years, and if it doesn't rain soon, area families . . . may lose their farms. A miracle is in order, and Pidge's father hopes a rainmaker can provide one. . . . Pidge is a well-characterized, sympathetic protagonist that readers will connect with." Booklist

Jacobson, Andrew

Palace of dreams; Adam Jay Epstein & Andrew Jacobson. Harper, an imprint of HarperCollinsPublishers 2013 336 p. illustrations (The familiars) (hardback) $16.99

Grades: 4 5 6   **Fic**

1. Fantasy fiction 2. Magic -- Fiction 3. Animals -- Fiction 4. Blessing and cursing -- Fiction

ISBN 0062120298; 9780062120298

LC 2013032810

In this book, by Adam Jay Epstein & Andrew Jacobson, "their reputation as heroes is short-lived for the Prophesized Three-cat Aldwyn, blue jay Skylar, and tree frog Gilbert-when they are suspected of poisoning Queen Loranella and promptly sent to the dungeon. After a daring escape, the familiars quickly go from being Vastia's most celebrated to its most wanted. Intent on clearing their names and saving Loranella's life, the three embark on an adventuresome journey to find a magical spell." (School Library Journal)

"The signature mixture of dry humor and gripping action makes this a worthy addition to the series." Horn Book

Jacobson, Jennifer

Andy Shane and the barn sale mystery; [by] Jennifer Richard Jacobson; illustrated by Abby Carter. Candlewick Press 2009 un il $14.99

Grades: 1 2 3   **Fic**

1. Mystery fiction 2. Friendship -- Fiction 3. Lost and found possessions -- Fiction

ISBN 978-0-7636-3599-2; 0-7636-3599-5

LC 2008017974

After Andy hosts a barn sale to raise money for a case for Granny Webb's binoculars, he realizes that they accidentally were sold, so with Dolores's help they try to track down the missing binoculars.

"The illustrations move the story along and provide important contextual clues. This satisfying title will appeal to early chapter-book readers." SLJ

Andy Shane and the pumpkin trick; [by] Jennifer Richard Jacobson; illustrated by Abby Carter. 1st ed; Candlewick Press 2006 58p il $13.99; pa $4.99

Grades: 1 2 3   **Fic**

1. Pumpkin -- Fiction 2. Halloween -- Fiction 3. Grandmothers -- Fiction

ISBN 0-7636-2605-8; 0-7636-3306-2 pa

LC 2004-62872

Andy Shane, with help from Grandma Webb and some marbles, tricks the people who keep stealing his friend Dolores Starbuckle's Halloween pumpkin.

"Attractive pen-and-ink illustrations help move the story along. An entertaining, easy chapter book for holiday collections." SLJ

Andy Shane and the Queen of Egypt; [by] Jennifer Jacobson; illustrated by Abby Carter. 1st ed.; Candlewick Press 2008 56p il $13.99

Grades: 1 2 3   **Fic**

1. School stories 2. Friendship -- Fiction

ISBN 978-0-7636-3211-3; 0-7636-3211-2

LC 2007032003

Andy Shane selects Egypt as the topic of his first-ever Culture Fair project, but the very bossy Dolores Starbuckle declares that she is the Queen of Egypt and does not give him a moment's peace until he agrees to let her work with him.

This is "sensitively written and expressively illustrated in pencil with black watercolor wash." Booklist

Andy Shane and the very bossy Dolores Starbuckle; [by] Jennifer Richard Jacobson; illustrated by Abby Carter. Candlewick Press 2005 56p il $13.99; pa $4.99

Grades: 1 2 3   **Fic**

1. School stories 2. Grandmothers -- Fiction

ISBN 0-7636-1940-X; 0-7636-3044-6 pa

LC 2004-57040

Andy Shane hates school, mainly because of a tattletale know-it-all named Dolores Starbuckle, but Granny Webb, who has taken care of him all his life, joins him in class one day and helps him solve the problem

"The characters are complex and realistic. . . . The narrative voice is fresh and whimsical. . . . The pen-and-ink illustrations effectively depict Andy's frustration, Dolores's temper, and Granny's zany self-assuredness." SLJ

Other titles about Andy Shane are:

Andy Shane and the pumpkin trick (2006)

Andy Shane and the Queen of Egypt (2008)

Andy Shane is NOT in love (2008)

Andy Shane and the barn sale mystery (2009)

Andy Shane, hero at last (2010)

Andy Shane is NOT in love; [by] Jennifer Richard Jacobson; illustrated by Abby Carter. Candlewick Press 2008 58p il

Grades: 1 2 3   **Fic**

1. Dogs -- Fiction 2. Friendship -- Fiction

ISBN 9780763632120

LC 2007052880

When Andy Shane befriends the new girl in town, everyone thinks he must be in love with her, but the reason he is spending so much time with her is because her dog just had puppies.

"Issues are handled naturally and without platitudes in this strong entry in a satisfying series for early chapter book readers." Horn Book Guide

Jacobson, Jennifer Richard, 1958-

Andy Shane, hero at last; illustrated by Abby Carter. Candlewick Press 2010 58p il $14.99; pa $6.99

Grades: 1 2 3   **Fic**

1. Parades -- Fiction 2. Contests -- Fiction 3. Heroes and heroines -- Fiction

ISBN 0-7636-3600-2; 0-7636-5293-8 pa; 978-0-7636-3600-5; 978-0-7636-5293-7 pa

"There are two things Andy Shane wants more than anything—to win the contest for best-decorated bike in the parade, and . . . to be a hero. He has a great idea for the bike part. . . . But the second goal has Andy stumped, until the parade is in motion and his eagle eyes catch the reason why the drum corps has suddenly thrown the marchers out of whack." (Publisher's note) "Primary." (Horn Book)

"Jacobson's light touch and respect for her audience make the ordinary happenings of a little boy in a small town universal." Horn Book

★ **Small** as an elephant; [by] Jennifer Richard Jacobson. Candlewick Press 2011 275p $15.99

Grades: 5 6 7 8   **Fic**

1. Adventure fiction 2. New England -- Fiction 3. Abandoned children -- Fiction

ISBN 0-7636-4155-3; 978-0-7636-4155-9

LC 2010039175

When his mother disappears from an Acadia National Park campground, Jack tries to make his way back home to Boston, with only a small toy elephant for company. "Intermediate, middle school." (Horn Book)

"Jacobson masterfully puts readers into Jack's mind—he loves and understands his mother, but sometimes his judgments are not always good, and readers understand. . . . Jack's journey to a new kind of family is inspiring and never sappy." Kirkus

Jacques, Brian

The **Bellmaker**; illustrated by Allan Curless. Philomel Bks. 1994 336p il pa $7.99

Grades: 5 6 7 8 9   **Fic**

1. Fantasy fiction 2. Animals -- Fiction

ISBN 0-399-22805-5; 978-0-441-00315-0 pa; 0-441-00315-X pa

LC 94-9730

Worried about his daughter Mariel, Joseph the Bellmaker is led by a dream from Redwall Abbey to Southsward, where he is caught up in the battle between Squirrelking Gael and the vicious Foxwolf Nagru

Mariel of Redwall; illustrated by Gary Chalk. Philomel Bks. 1992 387p il $24.99; pa $7.99

Grades: 5 6 7 8 9   **Fic**

1. Fantasy fiction 2. Mice -- Fiction 3. Animals -- Fiction

ISBN 978-0-399-22144-6; 0-399-22144-1; 978-0-441-00694-6 pa; 0-441-00694-9 pa

LC 91-17157

"Jacques' characters are fully developed and true to their natures; his dialectal dialog resounds with wit; the plot is filled with action, drama, and larger-than-life violence; and good conquers all. A satisfying tale with wide appeal that extends beyond its intended audience." Booklist

Martin the Warrior; illustrated by Gary Chalk. Philomel Bks. 1994 376p il pa $8.99

Grades: 5 6 7 8 9   **Fic**

1. Fantasy fiction 2. Mice -- Fiction 3. Animals -- Fiction

ISBN 0-399-22670-2; 978-0-14-240055-5 pa; 0-14-240055-6 pa

LC 93-26434

Captured and enslaved by the corsair stoat Badrang, young mouse warrior Martin vows to end the evil beast's plundering and killing

"Studded with vibrant and distinct animal characters, Jacques's classically inspired . . . plot-weaving achieves virtuosity as moments of sensitivity shake his fierce heroes off their warrior paths." Publ Wkly

Mattimeo; illustrated by Gary Chalk. Philomel Bks. 1990 446p il hardcover o.p. pa $8.99

Grades: 5 6 7 8 9   **Fic**

1. Mice -- Fiction 2. Animals -- Fiction

ISBN 0-399-21741-X; 978-0-14-230240-8 pa; 0-14-230240-6 pa

LC 89-37005

Mattimeo, the son of the warrior mouse Matthias, learns to take up the sword and joins the other animal inhabitants of Redwall Abbey in resisting Slagar the fox and his band of marauders

This is "truly thrilling. . . . Jacques's realistically drawn characters are full of personality. . . . The fierceness with which the Redwallers fight back to save their young lends the story credibility within the realm of the animal kingdom, while at the same time taking wonderful liberties with the imagination." Publ Wkly

Mossflower; illustrated by Gary Chalk. Philomel Bks. 1988 431p il $24.99; pa $8.99

Grades: 5 6 7 8 9   **Fic**

1. Fantasy fiction 2. Mice -- Fiction 3. Animals -- Fiction

ISBN 978-0-399-21549-0; 0-399-21549-2; 978-0-14-230238-5 pa; 0-14-230238-4 pa

LC 88-17921

Martin the warrior mouse and Gonff the mousethief set out to find the missing ruler of Mossflower, while the other animal inhabitants of the woodland prepare to rebel against the evil wildcat who has seized power

"The writing is smooth and swift-paced." SLJ

Pearls of Lutra; illustrated by Allan Curless. Philomel Bks. 1997 408p il $23.99; pa $7.99

Grades: 5 6 7 8 9   **Fic**

1. Fantasy fiction 2. Animals -- Fiction

ISBN 978-0-399-22946-6; 0-399-22946-9; 978-0-441-00508-6 pa; 0-441-00508-X pa

LC 96-18444

Tansy, a young hedgehog living at Redwall Abbey, attempts to solve the riddle of the missing pearls while at the same time the evil marten, Mad Eyes, desires them for himself

Rakkety Tam; illustrated by David Elliot. Philomel Books 2004 372p il $7.99

Grades: 5 6 7 8 9   **Fic**

1. Fantasy fiction 2. Animals -- Fiction

ISBN 0-399-23725-9; 0-441-01318-X pa

LC 2003-66449

Two warrior squirrels lead the battle against Gulo, a bloodthirsty wolverine who will stop at nothing to recover the Walking Stone that will give him the authority to rule the lands of ice beyond the Great Sea.

"The colorful writing style, the strong cast of characters, and twisting plot will continue to delight fans of the series." SLJ

★ **Redwall**; illustrated by Gary Chalk. 20th anniversary ed.; Philomel 2007 351p il $23.99; pa $7.99

Grades: 5 6 7 8 9   **Fic**

1. Fantasy fiction 2. Mice -- Fiction 3. Animals -- Fiction

ISBN 978-0-399-24794-1; 0-399-24794-7; 978-0-441-00548-2 pa; 0-441-00548-9 pa

First published 1986

"Thoroughly engrossing, this novel captivates despite its length. . . . The theme will linger long after the story is finished." Booklist

Other titles in this series are:

The Bellmaker (1995)
Doomwyte (2008)
Eulalia! (2007)
High Rhulain (2005)
The legend of Luke (2000)
Loamhedge (2003)
The long patrol (1998)
Lord Brocktree (2000)
Mariel of Redwall (1992)
Marlfox (1998)
Martin the Warrior (1994)
Mattimeo (1990)
Mossflower (1998)
The outcast of Redwall (1996)
Pearls of Lutra (1997)
Rakkety Tam (2004)
The Rogue Crew (2011)
Sable Quean (2009)
Salamandastron (1993)
Taggerung (2001)
Triss (2002)

Salamandastron; illustrated by Gary Chalk. Philomel Bks. 1993
391p il $24.99; pa $8.99
Grades: 5 6 7 8 9   **Fic**
1. Fantasy fiction 2. Animals -- Fiction
ISBN 978-0-399-21992-4; 0-399-21992-7; 978-0-14-250152-8
pa; 0-14-250152-2 pa
                                                    LC 91-46423
Urthstripe the Strong, a wise old badger, leads the animals of the
great fortress of Salamandastron and Redwall Abbey against the weasel
Ferahgo the Assassin and his corps of vermin
  "The reader feels included in the Abbey's history as it is being written, and Jacques encourages that empathy by creating animal characters
that respond to extraordinary circumstances with compellingly humanlike humility and strength. Chalk's black-and-white illustrations above
each chapter number are small marvels of nuance and personality."
Publ Wkly

James, Helen Foster
  Paper son; Lee's journey to America. written by Helen Foster
James and Virginia Shin-Mui Loh; illustrated by Wilson Ong. Sleeping
Bear Press 2013 32 p. ill. (reinforced) $16.99
Grades: 5 6 7 8   **Fic**
1. Chinese Americans -- Fiction 2. Historical fiction 3. Immigrants
-- United States -- Fiction 4. Orphans -- Fiction 5. Immigrants
-- Fiction 6. Chinese Americans -- Fiction 7. Emigration and
immigration -- Fiction 8. Angel Island Immigration Station (Calif.)
-- Fiction 9. Angel Island (Calif.) -- History -- 20th century -- Fiction
ISBN 1585368334; 9781585368334
                                                    LC 2012033691
  This historical novel, by Helen Foster James, Virginia Shin-Mui Loh,
and illustrated by Wilson Ong, is part of the "Tales of Young Americans"
series. "In 1926, 12-year-old Fu Lee['s] . . . parents . . . spent all of their
money buying a 'paper son slot' for Lee to go to America. Being a 'paper
son' means pretending to be the son of a family already in America. . . .
But first he must pass the test at Angel Island Immigration Station in San
Francisco." (Publisher's note)

Janisch, Heinz
  Fantastic adventures of Baron Munchausen; traditional and newly
discovered tales of Karl Friedrich Hieronymus von Munchausen. with
illustrations by Aljoscha Blau; translated by Belinda Cooper. Enchanted
Lion Books 2010 30p il $17.95

Grades: 1 2 3   **Fic**
1. Soldiers 2. Tall tales 3. Voyages and travels -- Fiction
ISBN 978-1-59270-091-2; 1-59270-091-8
                                                    LC 2010001115
  Retells Baron Munchausen's boastful account of some of his incredible adventures around the world, including riding a cannonball during
a spy mission and entering a whale's mouth to hear a musical concert.
  "In his retellings of the Baron's tall tales, Janisch . . . combines the
bravura of Paul Bunyan with the elegance of Voltaire's Candide. Each
story appears on the left, accompanied by a painting on the right of the
beak-nosed Baron. . . . Children with a romantic streak will be taken
both with the Baron and his courtly fictions and by Blau's misty, stately
portraits." Publ Wkly

Jaramillo, Ann
  La linea. Roaring Brook Press 2006 131p $16.95; pa $7.99
Grades: 5 6 7 8   **Fic**
1. Young adult literature 2. Mexicans -- Fiction 3. Siblings --
Fiction 4. Immigrants -- Fiction
ISBN 1-59643-154-7; 0-312-37354-6 pa
                                                    LC 2005-20133
  When fifteen-year-old Miguel's time finally comes to leave his
poor Mexican village, cross the border illegally, and join his parents in
California, his younger sister's determination to join him soon imperils
them both.
  "A gripping contemporary survival adventure, this spare first novel
is also a heart-wrenching family story of courage, betrayal, and love."
Booklist

Jarrell, Randall
  ★ The **animal** family; decorations by Maurice Sendak. Harper-
Collins Pubs. 1996 179p il $16.99; pa $8.95
Grades: 4 5 6 7   **Fic**
1. Fantasy fiction 2. Animals -- Fiction
ISBN 0-06-205088-5; 0-06-205904-1 pa
                                                    LC 94-76270
  A reissue of the title first published 1965 by Pantheon Bks.
  A lonely hunter living in the wilderness beside the sea gains a family
made up of a mermaid, a bear, a lynx, and a boy
  This story is "sensitively related with touches of humor and wisdom.
A delight for the imaginative reader." Booklist

  The **bat**-poet; pictures by Maurice Sendak. HarperCollins Pubs.
1996 42p il $15.95; pa $7.95
Grades: 2 3 4   **Fic**
1. Bats -- Fiction 2. Poetry -- Fiction
ISBN 0-06-205084-2; 0-06-205905-X pa
                                                    LC 94-76271
  A reissue of the title first published 1964 by MacMillan
  A bat who can't sleep days makes up poems about the woodland
creatures he now perceives for the first time
  "A lovely book, perfectly illustrated—one well worth a child's atten-
tion and affection." Publ Wkly

Jeffrey, Mark
  Max Quick: the pocket and the pendant. Harper 2011 294p $15.99
Grades: 4 5 6 7   **Fic**
1. Science fiction 2. Time -- Fiction 3. Voyages and travels --
Fiction 4. Identity (Psychology) -- Fiction
ISBN 978-0-06-198892-9; 0-06-198892-8
                                                    LC 2010-4266.
  First released 2005 as a podcast audiobook
  Young Max, a troubled boy with a mysterious past, joins two other
youths unaffected when the rest of the world was frozen in time on a

journey across America—and time itself—seeking the source of the "Time-stop."

"This fast-paced adventure . . . will keep readers turning pages." SLJ

Jenkins, Emily

Invisible Inkling; illustrations by Harry Bliss. Balzer + Bray 2011 154p il

Grades: 3 4 5 **Fic**

1. Bullies -- Fiction 2. Imaginary playmates -- Fiction 3. Brooklyn (New York, N.Y.) -- Fiction

ISBN 0-06-180220-4; 978-0-06-180220-1

LC 2010-46238

When Hank Wolowitz runs into trouble in the form a of lunch-stealing bully, he finds an unlikely ally in an invisible refugee pumpkin-loving bandapat named Inkling.

"Jenkins' possible series starter . . . is a gently humorous and nicely realistic . . . tale about coping with the loss of a lifelong best friend. . . . Anyone who has ever had an imaginary friend will appreciate sassy Inkling (who's invisible—not imaginary)." Kirkus

Toy dance party; being the further adventures of a bossyboots Stingray, a courageous Buffalo, and a hopeful round someone called Plastic. [by] Emily Jenkins; illustrated by Paul O. Zelinsky. Schwartz & Wade Books 2008 159p il $16.99; lib bdg $19.99

Grades: 1 2 3 **Fic**

1. Toys -- Fiction 2. Friendship -- Fiction

ISBN 978-0-375-83935-1; 0-375-83935-6; 978-0-375-93935-8 lib bdg; 0-375-93935-0 lib bdg

Six stories relate further adventures of three best friends, who happen to be toys, as they encounter a fearsome (possible) shark, enjoy a dance party, and deal with rejection by The Girl, who is growing up.

"These toys have distinct, well-developed characters and behave as children do. . . . Dialogue and song help move the narrative along. . . . Chapter-book readers will welcome these gently humorous tales." Booklist

Toys come home; being the early experiences of an intelligent stingray, a brave buffalo, and a brand-new someone called Plastic. illustrated by Paul O. Zelinsky. Schwartz & Wade Books 2011 132p il $16.99; lib bdg $19.99

Grades: 1 2 3 **Fic**

1. Toys -- Fiction 2. Friendship -- Fiction

ISBN 0-375-86200-5; 0-375-96200-X lib bdg; 978-0-375-86200-7; 978-0-375-96200-4 lib bdg

LC 2010005896

Prequel to: Toys go out (2006) and Toy dance party (2008)

When a little girl gets a plush stingray for her birthday, it makes friends with some of her other toys as they all try to navigate in the world of real people.

"Character-driven episodes unfold in six fully realized chapters; Zelinsky's softly shaded pencil drawings showcase pivital moments, revealing each individual idiosyncrasy." Kirkus

★ **Toys** go out; being the adventures of a knowledgeable Stingray, a toughy little Buffalo, and someone called Plastic. illustrated by Paul O. Zelinsky. Schwartz & Wade Bks. 2006 116p il $16.95; lib bdg $18.99; pa $5.99

Grades: 1 2 3 **Fic**

1. Toys -- Fiction 2. Friendship -- Fiction

ISBN 0-375-83604-7; 0-375-93604-1 lib bdg; 0-385-73661-4 pa

"For beginning chapter-book readers, this . . . relates the experiences of three engaging toy best friends: Lumphy the buffalo, plush StingRay, and Plastic. . . . The simple prose is clever and often hilarious, incorporating dialogue and musings that ring kid-perspective true, and

Zelinsky's charming black-and-white illustrations, wonderfully detailed and textured, expressively portray character situations and feelings." Booklist

Other titles about Lumphy, StingRay, and Plastic are:

Toy dance party (2008)

Toys come home (2011)

Jennings, Patrick

Guinea dog. Egmont USA 2010 135p $15.99; lib bdg $18.99

Grades: 3 4 5 **Fic**

1. School stories 2. Family life -- Fiction 3. Guinea pigs -- Fiction

ISBN 1-60684-053-3; 1-60684-069-X lib bdg; 978-1-60684-053-5; 978-1-60684-069-6 lib bdg

LC 2009-25117

When his mother brings home a guinea pig instead of the dog he has always wanted, fifth-grader Rufus is not happy—until the rodent starts acting exactly like a dog. "Grades three to five." (Bull Cent Child Books)

"Children will have no problem accepting the absurdity of the situation. Early chapter-book readers will enjoy this humorous tale." SLJ

Guinea dog 2; by Patrick Jennings. Egmont USA 2013 164 p. (hardback) $15.99

Grades: 3 4 5 **Fic**

1. Pets -- Fiction 2. Guinea pigs -- Fiction 3. Schools -- Fiction 4. Family life -- Fiction

ISBN 1606844520; 9781606844526

LC 2013000979

In this book by Patrick Jennings, "when his classmates learn about Fido, the guinea pig that acts like a dog, they all want a piece of Rufus, her owner. But Rufus hates the attention. So he decides to make Fido learn how to be an actual guinea pig. But when she goes missing, he feels terrible. Was she lost, 'dognapped,' or did she run away, because he no longer liked her just the way she was?" (Publisher's note)

Odd, weird, and little; Patrick Jennings. Egmont USA 2014 160 p. (hardcover) $15.99

Grades: 4 5 6 7 **Fic**

1. Owls -- Fiction 2. Bullies -- Fiction 3. Schools -- Fiction 4. Friendship -- Fiction 5. Middle schools -- Fiction 6. Eccentrics and eccentricities -- Fiction

ISBN 1606843745; 9781606843741

LC 2013018248

In this book, by Patrick Jennings, "Woodrow and his classmates are surprised at the old-fashioned clothing and the tiny, delicate appearance of Toulouse, a newly arrived student from Canada. . . . Woodrow risks regaining his place as top [bullying] victim as he decides to befriend and protect Toulouse. . . . Readers also learn about the psychology behind bullying and about self-empowerment." (Kirkus Reviews)

Out standing in my field. Scholastic Press 2005 165p hardcover o.p. pa $5.99

Grades: 4 5 6 **Fic**

1. Baseball -- Fiction 2. Father-son relationship -- Fiction

ISBN 0-439-46581-8; 0-439-48749-8 pa

LC 2004-41619

Although fifth-grader Ty Cutter is named after baseball great Ty Cobb, he is the worst player on the Brewer's team—which happens to be coached by his overly-competitive father

"The book is funny, poignant, and deeper than one might think at first glance." SLJ

Jennings, Richard W.

★ **Orwell's** luck; [by] Richard Jennings. Houghton Mifflin 2000 146p $15; pa $6.95

Grades: 5 6 7 8   **Fic**

1. Magic -- Fiction 2. Rabbits -- Fiction
ISBN 0-618-03628-8; 0-618-69335-1 pa

LC 99-33501

While caring for an injured rabbit which becomes her confidant, horoscope writer, and source of good luck, a thoughtful seventh grade girl learns to see things in more than one way

"This absolutely captivating tale is about everyday magic . . . . filled with quiet humor and seamless invention. The characters . . . are the sort that readers fall in love with." Booklist

Jensen, Marion

Almost super; by Marion Jensen. Harper, an imprint of HarperCollinsPublishers 2014 256 p. (hardback) $14.99

Grades: 4 5 6   **Fic**

1. Brothers -- Fiction 2. Superheroes -- Fiction 3. Families -- Fiction 4. Supervillains -- Fiction
ISBN 0062209612; 9780062209610

LC 2013032145

This book, by Marion Jensen, is an "adventure about two brothers in a family of superheroes who must find a way to be heroic despite receiving powers that are total duds. Along with Rafter's algebra class nemesis, Juanita Johnson, Rafter and Benny realize that what they thought they knew about superheroes and supervillains may be all wrong. And it's up to the three of them to put asides their differences and make things right." (Publisher's note)

"In a family where your dad can fly and your great-aunt can breath fire, finding out that your superpower is worthless is, well, devastating. Such is the misfortune of Rafter and Benny Bailey...Packed with action and humor, this is a superhero tale in the spirit of The Incredibles. Jensen's wit and light tone give the story a playful quality while still managing to incorporate a healthy dose of suspense. Family dynamics and teamwork drive a plot that has, above all, a super amount of heart. " (Booklist)

Jinks, Catherine

★ **How** to catch a bogle; by Catherine Jinks; illustrated by Sarah Watts. Harcourt Children's Books 2013 320 p. ill. (hardcover) $16.99

Grades: 5 6 7 8   **Fic**

1. Fantasy fiction 2. Alternative histories 3. Orphans -- Fiction 4. Monsters -- Fiction 5. Apprentices -- Fiction 6. Supernatural -- Fiction 7. London (England) -- History -- 19th century -- Fiction 8. Great Britain -- History -- Victoria, 1837-1901 -- Fiction
ISBN 0544087089; 9780544087088

LC 2012045936

This is the first in a historical fantasy trilogy from Catherine Jinks. Here, "child-eating bogles infest Victorian London, providing work aplenty for 'Go-Devil Man' Alfred Bunce and his intrepid young apprentice, Birdie." Birdie is kidnapped by "would-be warlock Roswell Morton, out to capture one of the monsters for his own evil uses." She also must deal with the unwanted "attentions of Miss Edith Eames," who wants "to see Birdie cleaned up and educated in the social graces." (Kirkus Reviews)

The last bogler; Catherine Jinks; illustrated by Sarah Watts. Houghton Mifflin Harcourt 2016 336 p. illustrations, map (hardback) $16.99

Grades: 5 6 7 8   **Fic**

1. Monsters -- Fiction 2. Apprentices -- Fiction 3. Great Britain -- History -- Victoria, 1837-1901 -- Fiction 4. Orphans -- Fiction 5. Apprentices -- Fiction 6. Supernatural -- Fiction 7. London (England) -- History -- 19th century -- Fiction
ISBN 9780544086968

LC 2015002204

In this juvenile fantasy adventure novel, by Catherine Jinks, illustrated by Sarah Watts, "in Victorian London . . . , bogle hunter Alfred Bunce needs all the help he can get. So Ned Roach becomes a bogler's apprentice, luring child-eating monsters from their lairs just like his friends Jem and Birdie. . . . Yet . . . in London . . . as the machine age emerges, the very existence of bogles is questioned, and the future of bogling is in jeopardy." (Publisher's note)

"A highly satisfying conclusion to this wonderfully crafted fantasy series." SLJ

Saving Thanehaven; by Catherine Jinks. Egmont USA 2013 384 p. (hardcover) $17.99

Grades: 4 5 6 7   **Fic**

1. Computer games -- Fiction 2. Fantasy fiction 3. Science fiction 4. Virtual reality -- Fiction 5. Knights and knighthood -- Fiction
ISBN 1606842749; 9781606842744

LC 2012046190

In this book, "Noble is just an earnest knight in the computer game 'Thanehaven Slayer' when he encounters young Rufus, who strongly suggests that he may be doomed if he doesn't drop all the heroics and start thinking for himself. With Rufus' mantra 'you don't have to do this' ringing in his ears, Noble sets out to change his computer world." (Kirkus Reviews)

Jobling, Curtis

The rise of the wolf. Viking Childrens Books 2011 412p (Wereworld) $16.99

Grades: 4 5 6 7   **Fic**

1. Fantasy fiction 2. Adventure fiction 3. Werewolves -- Fiction
ISBN 978-0-670-01330-2; 0-670-01330-7

LC 2010049517

When a vicious beast invades his father's farm and sixteen-year-old Drew suddenly transforms into a werewolf, he runs away from his family, seeking refuge in the most out of the way parts of Lyssia, only to be captured by Lord Bergan's men and forced to battle numerous werecreatures while trying to prove that he is not the enemy.

"Jobling's characterizations are solid, his world-building is complex and fascinating, and the combat scenes are suitably exciting. The book's themes are familiar—lost prince in exile, voyage of self-discovery, young heroes rebelling against injustice and evil—but Jobling uses them to tell a thoroughly enjoyable adventure that makes particularly inventive use of its shapeshifter elements and mythology." Publ Wkly

John, Jory

The terrible two; by Mac Barnett & Jory John; illustrated by Kevin Cornell. Harry N. Abrams 2015 224 p. illustrations (The terrible two) (hardback) $13.95

Grades: 4 5 6 7 8   **Fic**

1. School stories 2. Practical jokes 3. Humorous stories 4. Tricks -- Fiction 5. Schools -- Fiction 6. Practical jokes -- Fiction 7. Moving, Household -- Fiction
ISBN 1419714910; 9781419714917

LC 201402750

"Miles Murphy is not happy to be moving. In his old school, every one knew him as the town's best prankster, but Miles quickly discover that Yawnee Valley already has a prankster, and a great one. If Miles i going to take the title from this mystery kid, he is going to have to rais his game. It's prankster against prankster in an epic war of trickery, unti the two finally decide to join forces and pull off the biggest prank eve seen." (Publisher's note)

"Cornell's (The Chicken Squad) b&w cartoons layer on the laughs especially when portraying the megalomaniacal Principal Barkin, an

Barnett and John's deadpan writing lets Yawnee Valley's absurdity shine." Pub Wkly

The **terrible** two get worse; Mac Barnett, Jory John; illustrated by Kevin Cornell. Amulet Books 2016 224 p. illustrations (hardback) $13.95

Grades: 4 5 6 7 8   **Fic**

1. Humorous fiction 2. Friendship -- Fiction 3. Practical jokes -- Fiction 4. School superintendants and principals -- Fiction 5. Humorous stories 6. Tricks -- Fiction 7. Schools -- Fiction 8. School principals -- Fiction

ISBN 9781419716805

LC 2015011114

Sequel to: The terrible two

In this book, by Mac Barnett and Jory John, illustrated by Kevin Cornell, "On their own, pranksters Miles and Niles were pretty devious. Now that they've formed a pranking duo, they're terrible! But their powers will be tested when their favorite nemesis, Principal Barkin, is replaced by his stern and cunning father, Former Principal Barkin. Now Miles and Niles will do just about anything to get their old antagonist back --including pranking alongside him." (Publisher's note)

"This humorous sequel makes for engaging, fast-paced reading that again highlights the meaning of friendship, and animated, amusing cartoon illustrations enhance and extend the story." Booklist

Johnson, Angela

★ A **cool** moonlight. Dial Bks. 2003 133p hardcover o.p. pa $6.99

Grades: 4 5 6   **Fic**

1. Skin -- Diseases -- Fiction

ISBN 0-8037-2846-8; 0-14-240284-2 pa

LC 2002-31521

Nine-year-old Lila, born with xeroderma pigmentosum, a skin disease that make her sensitive to sunlight, makes secret plans to feel the sun's rays on her tenth birthday

"The book's real magic resides in the spell cast by Johnson's spare, lucid, lyrical prose. Using simple words and vivid sensory images, she creates Lila's inner world as a place of quiet intensity." Booklist

Johnson, Jaleigh

★ The **mark** of the dragonfly; Jaleigh Johnson. First edition Delacorte Press 2014 400 p. map (glb) $19.99; (hc) $16.99

Grades: 5 6 7 8   **Fic**

1. Magic -- Fiction 2. Fantasy fiction -- Fiction 3. Adventure and adventurers -- Fiction 4. Fantasy

ISBN 0385376456; 9780385376457; 9780385376150

LC 2013019716

This book, by Jaleigh Johnson, is an "adventure story about a mysterious girl and a fearless boy, set in a magical world. . . . Piper has never seen the Mark of the Dragonfly until she finds the girl amid the wreckage of a caravan in the Meteor Fields. The girl doesn't remember a thing about her life, but the intricate tattoo on her arm is proof that she's from the Dragonfly Territories and that she's protected by the king. Which means a reward for Piper if she can get the girl home." (Publisher's note)

"Heart, brains and courage find a home in a steampunk fantasy worthy of a nod from Baum. . . . A well-imagined world of veritable adventure." Kirkus

Other titles in this series are:

The secrets of Solace (2016)

The quest to the Uncharted Lands (2017)

Johnson, Peter

The **amazing** adventures of John Smith, Jr., aka Houdini; by Peter Johnson. HarperCollins Children's Books 2012 168p.

Grades: 4 5 6   **Fic**

1. Domestic relations 2. Teenagers -- Fiction 3. Child authors -- Fiction 4. Authorship -- Fiction 5. Neighborliness -- Fiction 6. Providence (R.I.) -- Fiction 7. Moneymaking projects -- Fiction 8. Interpersonal relations -- Fiction 9. Family life -- Rhode Island -- Fiction

ISBN 9780061988905

LC 2011019387

In this book, "thirteen-year-old John Smith, Jr., also known as Houdini, meets the author of a children's book . . . [and] decides to try . . . writing a novel. . . . [Peter] Johnson offers this title as Houdini's own work, wherein he shares stories about . . . his rough and tumble neighborhood in Providence, Rhode Island; his older brother who is fighting in Iraq; Angel Dimitri, the local bully; and Jackson, the neighborhood crazy/Vietnam vet." (Bulletin of the Center for Children's Books)

Includes bibliographical references

Johnson, Terry Lynn

Ice dogs; by Terry Lynn Johnson. Houghton Mifflin, Houghton Mifflin Harcourt 2013 288 p. $16.99

Grades: 5 6 7 8 9   **Fic**

1. Sled dogs -- Fiction 2. Wilderness survival -- Fiction 3. Sled dog racing -- Fiction 4. Dogs -- Fiction 5. Alaska -- Fiction 6. Survival -- Fiction 7. Dogsledding -- Fiction 8. Wilderness areas -- Fiction

ISBN 0547899262; 9780547899268

LC 2012045061

In this book, by Terry Lynn Johnson, "Victoria Secord, a fourteen-year-old Alaskan dogsled racer, loses her way on a routine outing with her dogs. With food gone and temperatures dropping, her survival and that of her dogs and the mysterious boy she meets in the woods is entirely up to her." (Publisher's note)

Johnson, Varian

★ The **great** Greene heist; by Varian Johnson. Arthur A. Levine Books 2014 240 p. (hardcover) $16.99

Grades: 5 6 7 8   **Fic**

1. School stories 2. Schools -- Fiction 3. Elections -- Fiction 4. Friendship -- Fiction 5. Best friends -- Fiction 6. Middle schools -- Fiction 7. Practical jokes -- Fiction

ISBN 0545525527; 9780545525534; 0545525535; 9780545525527

LC 2013029145

"Jackson Greene has reformed. No, really he has. He was once the best con artist at Maplewood Middle School, and everyone still talks about his Blitz at the Fitz.... But after Principal Kelsey caught him in his office, Jackson swore off scheming for good. Then Keith Sinclair--loser of the Blitz--announces he's running for school president, against Jackson's former almost-girlfriend Gaby de la Cruz." (Publisher's note)

"This fast-paced caper reads like Ocean's 11 for the middle-school set, and that's no coincidence: Johnson (Saving Maddie, 2010) openly credits the film as inspiration, and he has pretty much pulled it off, right down to the dizzying plot twists, incredulous access to the latest tech, and unflappable swagger." Booklist

To catch a cheat; A Jackson Greene Novel. by Varian Johnson. Arthur A. Levine Books, an imprint of Scholastic Inc. 2016 256 p. (hardcover : alk. paper) $16.99

Grades: 5 6 7 8   **Fic**

1. School stories 2. Extortion -- Fiction 3. Friendship -- Fiction 4. African Americans -- Fiction 5. Cheating (Education) -- Fiction 6. Schools -- Fiction 7. Cheating -- Fiction 8. Best friends -- Fiction

9. Middle schools -- Fiction

ISBN 9780545722391; 9780545722407

LC 2015025232

Sequel to: The Great Greene Heist

In this book, by Varian Johnson, "Jackson Greene . . . is officially retired from conning, so Principal Kelsey is (mostly) off his back. His friends have great new projects of their own. . . . Then Jackson receives a link to a faked security video that seems to show him and the rest of Gang Greene flooding the school gym. The jerks behind the video threaten to pass it to the principal -- unless Jackson steals an advance copy of the school's toughest exam." (Publisher's note)

"Fast-paced antics, clever writing, and a diverse cast of characters give this ample broad appeal." Booklist

Johnson-Shelton, Nils

The **Invisible** Tower. HarperCollins 2011 335p (Otherworld chronicles) $16.99

Grades: 4 5 6 7 **Fic**

1. Adventure fiction 2. Kings

ISBN 978-0-06-207086-9; 0-06-207086-X

LC 2011022928

A twelve-year-old boy learns that he is actually King Arthur brought back to life in the twenty-first century—and that the fate of the universe rests in his hands.

"This new take on the Arthurian legends, told in third-person, pits wisecracking contemporary teens with their contemporary banter. . . . against all manner of obstacles. . . . It's always high-spirited and fun. Gives new life to Arthurian legends and may just send readers back to more traditional tellings." Kirkus

The **seven** swords; Nils Johnson-Shelton. HarperCollins 2013 368 p. (Otherworld chronicles) (hardback) $16.99

Grades: 4 5 6 7 **Fic**

1. Arthurian romances -- Adaptations 2. Fantasy fiction 3. Adventure fiction

ISBN 0062070940; 9780062070944

LC 2012019088

This juvenile adventure fantasy, by Nils Johnson-Shelton, second in the "Otherworld Chronicles," follows "Artie Kingfisher, the new King Arthur. On a quest to recover seven magical swords of the Dark Ages, Artie and Kay gather 'New Knights of the Round Table' and try to unite two worlds. Standing in their way is Lordess Morgaine. . . . Artie and his band travel from Ohio via crossover points between worlds in search of swords in Sweden, France and Japan." (Kirkus Reviews)

Johnston, Julie

A **very** fine line. Tundra Books 2006 198p $18.95; pa $10.95

Grades: 5 6 7 8 **Fic**

1. Canada -- Fiction 2. Clairvoyance -- Fiction

ISBN 978-0-88776-746-3; 0-88776-746-X; 978-0-88776-829-3 pa; 0-88776-829-6 pa

Then thirteen-year-old Rosalind's "aunt informs her that as the seventh daughter of a seventh daughter, she can . . . see glimpses of the future, she balks. . . . The story begins in Kepston, Ontario, in 1941. . . . Readers who come to the book intrigued by the idea of clairvoyance will fine much more: several vivid characters, a well-realized setting, and a sensitively nuanced resolution." Booklist

Jonell, Lynne

★ **Emmy** and the incredible shrinking rat. Henry Holt 2007 346p il $16.95; pa $6.99

Grades: 3 4 5 6 **Fi**

1. Rats -- Fiction

ISBN 978-0-8050-8150-3; 0-8050-8150-X; 978-0-312-38460-9 pa; 0-312-38460-2 pa

LC 2006-3546

When Emmy discovers that she and her formerly loving parents are being drugged by their evil nanny with rodent potions that can change people in frightening ways, she and some new friends must try every thing possible to return things to normal.

"This tale turns smoothly on its fanciful premise and fabulous characters." Booklist

Other titles about Emmy are:

Emmy and the Home for Troubled Girls (2008)

Emmy and the rats in the Belfry (2011)

Emmy and the rats in the Belfry; art by Jonathan Bean. Henry Holt and Company 2011 372p il $17.99

Grades: 3 4 5 6 **Fi**

1. Rats -- Fiction

ISBN 978-0-8050-9183-0; 0-8050-9183-1

LC 201004750

Ten-year-old Emmy and her rodent friends must fend off the evil former nanny, Miss Barmy, as they search for Ratty's missing mother.

"This worthy addition to the series is busy and full of surprises." Booklist

★ The **secret** of zoom. Henry Holt 2009 291p $16.99

Grades: 4 5 6 **Fi**

1. Adventure fiction 2. Orphans -- Fiction 3. Energy resources -- Fiction

ISBN 978-0-8050-8856-4; 0-8050-8856-3

LC 2008-5027

Ten-year-old Christina lives a sheltered life until she discovers a secret tunnel, an evil plot to enslave orphans, and a mysterious source of energy known as zoom.

"This exciting tale, with just a touch of fantasy and humor, is a winner. . . . Complete with a cast of clearly drawn characters, the adventure proceeds at a breakneck pace until all is resolved and a happy ending completes the picture." SLJ

Jones, Diana Wynne

★ **Castle** in the air. Greenwillow Bks. 1991 199p hardcover o.p; pa $6.99

Grades: 6 7 8 9 **Fi**

1. Fantasy fiction

ISBN 0-688-09686-7; 0-06-447345-7 pa

LC 90-3026

In this "follow-up to Howl'sMoving Castle . . . the protagonist is a young carpet merchant called Abdullah, who spends much of his time creating a richly developed daydream in which he is the long-lost son of a great prince, kidnapped as a child by a villainous bandit. . . . Feisty Sophie and the Wizard Howl (from Howl's Moving Castle do not become apparent till late in the story, but their fortunes do link up with those of Abdullah and his love. Jones maintains both suspense and wit throughout, demonstrating once again that frequently nothing is what seems to be." Booklist

Earwig and the witch; illustrator, Paul O. Zelinsky. Greenwillow Books 2012 140p il

Grades: 2 3 4 **Fi**

1. Orphans -- Fiction 2. Witches -- Fiction

ISBN 0-06-207511-X; 978-0-06-207511-6

LC 201004899

This book tells the story of Earwig, who "rules the roost at St. Morwald's Home for Children until she is adopted by a witchy woman named Bella Yaga with 'one brown eye and one blue one, and a raggety, ribby look to her face.' Earwig hopes to learn magic from Bella Yaga, but is trapped in the woman's decrepit house, sharing it with the Mandrake, an impossibly tall and grouchy being. Powerful and evil, Bella Yaga uses Earwig as a second pair of hands for grinding up disgusting things in bowls ('The only thing wrong with magic is that it smells so awful,' Earwig quips)." (Publishers Weekly)

"Earwig, illustrated with marvelous vitality by Zelinsky, is not to be trifled with. There's just the right level of grotesquerie and scariness . . . in this utterly charming chapter book." Kirkus

House of many ways. Greenwillow Books 2008 404p $17.99; lib bdg $18.89; pa $8.99

Grades: 5 6 7 8   **Fic**

1. Fantasy fiction 2. Magic -- Fiction 3. Houses -- Fiction 4. Uncles -- Fiction

ISBN 978-0-06-147795-9; 0-06-147795-8; 978-0-06-147796-6 lib bdg; 0-06-147796-6 lib bdg; 978-0-06-147797-3 pa; 0-06-147797-4 pa

LC 2007036147

Sequel to: Howl's moving castle (1986)

When Charmain is asked to housesit for Great Uncle William, the Royal Wizard of Norland, she is ecstatic to get away from her parents, but finds that his house is much more than it seems.

This is "a buoyantly entertaining read. . . . [Jones'] comic pacing and wit are amply evident." Horn Book

★ **Howl's** moving castle. Greenwillow Books 1986 212p hardcover o.p. pa $6.99

Grades: 5 6 7 8   **Fic**

1. Fantasy fiction

ISBN 0-06-147878-4 pa; 0-688-06233-4; 978-0-06-147878-9 pa

LC 85-21981

Sophie "resigns herself to making a living as a hatter and helping her younger sisters prepare to make their fortunes. But adventure seeks her out in the shop where she sits alone dreaming over her hats. The Wicked Witch of the Waste, angered by 'competition' in the area, turns her into an old woman, so she seeks refuge inside the strange moving castle of the wizard Howl. Howl, advertised by his apprentice as an eater of souls, lives a mad, frantic life trying to escape the curse the Witch has placed on him, find the perfect girl of his dreams and end the contract he and his fire demon have entered. Sophie, against her best instincts and at first unaware of her own powers, falls in love. . . . Grade six and up." (SLJ)

"Satisfyingly, Sophie meets a fate far exceeding her dreary expectations. This novel is an exciting, multi-faceted puzzle, peopled with vibrant, captivating characters. A generous sprinkling of humor adds potency to this skillful author's spell." Voice Youth Advocates

Followed by: House of many ways (2008)

Jones, Kelly

Unusual chickens for the exceptional poultry farmer; by Kelly Jones; Illustrated by Katie Kath. Alfred A. Knopf 2015 224 p. illustrations (trade) $16.99

Grades: 4 5 6   **Fic**

1. Chickens -- Fiction 2. Farm life -- Fiction 3. California -- Fiction 4. Supernatural -- Fiction 5. Letters -- Fiction 6. Racially mixed people -- Fiction 7. Farm life -- California -- Fiction

ISBN 038575552X; 9780385755528; 9780385755535

LC 2013050736

In this book, by Kelly Jones, "Sophie Brown feels like a fish out of water when she and her parents move from Los Angeles to the farm

they've inherited from a great-uncle. But farm life gets more interesting when a cranky chicken appears and Sophie discovers the hen can move objects with the power of her little chicken brain." (Publisher's note)

"The epistolary format consists mostly of letters in Sophie's earnest voice; often the addressee is either her late abuelita or her great-uncle Jim in various iterations of the afterlife. . . . Sophie's unique way of figuring life out on her own makes her easy to root for and provides entertainment beyond the inherent humor of chickens." Horn Book

Jones, Rob Lloyd

Wild boy; Rob Lloyd Jones. Candlewick Press 2013 304 p. $16.99

Grades: 5 6 7 8   **Fic**

1. Mystery fiction 2. Steampunk fiction

ISBN 0763662526; 9780763662523

LC 2013931467

In this book, "Wild Boy's head-to-toe fur has garnered him scorn and abuse from commoners, but his extraordinary intellectual gifts eventually win him a future with a powerful, elite group called the Gentlemen. . . . When Wild Boy is about to be hanged by the unseemly circus crew for a murder he did not commit, teen acrobat Clarissa helps him escape. Together, they follow clues through sewers and back alleys, learning about an extraordinary electrical device linked to the murder." (Kirkus Reviews)

Wild boy and the black terror; Rob Lloyd Jones. Candlewick Press 2015 336 p. illustrations, map $16.99

Grades: 5 6 7 8   **Fic**

1. Serial killers -- Fiction 2. Circus performers -- Fiction 3. Great Britain -- History -- Victoria, 1837-1901 -- Fiction 4. Children's stories 5. Murderers--England--London 6. Detective and mystery stories

ISBN 0763662534; 9780763662530

LC 2014945722

This novel by Rob Lloyd Jones is set in "London, 1842. Wild Boy, master detective and former freak-show performer, and Clarissa, circus acrobat and troublemaker, are the secret last hope of a city beset by horror. A poisoner stalks the streets, leaving victims mad with terror--and then dead. Can the Black Terror be traced to a demon called Malphas? Can Wild Boy and Clarissa uncover a cure in time to save the queen and the city?" (Publisher's note)

"Adventure, conspiracy and adrenaline intermingle with dark deeds, devil worship and blood diamonds in this sequel to Wild Boy (2013). . . . The queen and the Gentlemen need them to unearth the cause of a mysterious sickness that blackens veins and sends victims into a stupor of madness before tragic death. . . . Can the duo save all of London from a hellbent killer? Diamonds are a Wild Boy's worst enemy in this steampunk romp not intended for the faint—or black—of heart." Kirkus

Jones, Traci L.

★ **Silhouetted** by the blue. Farrar, Straus & Giroux 2011 200p $16.99

Grades: 5 6 7 8   **Fic**

1. School stories 2. Theater -- Fiction 3. Bereavement -- Fiction 4. African Americans -- Fiction

ISBN 978-0-374-36914-9; 0-374-36914-3

LC 2010008419

After the death of her mother in an automobile accident, seventh-grader Serena, who has gotten the lead in her middle school play, is left to handle the day-to-day challenges of caring for herself and her younger brother when their father cannot pull himself out of his depression.

"Jones has written another winner with this beautiful, haunting tale rich in story and characterization." Booklist

Jones, Ursula

The **islands** of Chaldea; by Diana Wynne Jones; completed by Ursula Jones. Greenwillow Books, an imprint of HarperCollinsPublishers 2013 368 p. (trade ed.) $17.99

Grades: 4 5 6 7 8   **Fic**

1. Cats -- Fiction 2. Fantasy fiction 3. Aunts -- Fiction 4. Magic -- Fiction 5. Fantasy 6. Self-confidence -- Fiction 7. Voyages and travels -- Fiction

ISBN 0062295071; 9780062295071

LC 2013036422

In this book, by Diana Wynne Jones and Ursula Jones, "Aileen comes from a long line of magic makers, and her Aunt Beck is the most powerful magician on Skarr. But even though she is old enough, Aileen's magic has yet to reveal itself. When Aileen is sent over the sea on a mission for the King, she worries that she'll be useless and in the way. A powerful (but mostly invisible) cat changes all of that—and with every obstacle Aileen faces, she becomes stronger and more confident and her magic blooms." (Publisher's note)

"Diana Wynne Jones's humor, insight, and brisk, inventive style shine in this posthumously published novel. Aileen is embarrassed when she fails her Wise Woman initiation. She discovers her own "very vigorous" powers on a quest with her Wise Aunt Beck, a prince, and his attendant through the islands of Chaldea. Jones's imaginative vigor is unabated in this last, picaresque novel." Horn Book

Jordan, Rosa

The **goatnappers**; [by] Rosa Jordan. 1st ed.; Peachtree 2007 209p $14.95

Grades: 5 6 7 8   **Fic**

1. School stories 2. Goats -- Fiction 3. Florida -- Fiction 4. Family life -- Fiction

ISBN 978-1-56145-400-6; 1-56145-400-1

LC 2006030173

Sequel to: Lost Goat Lane (2004)

Justin's place as the first high school freshman in twenty years to make the varsity baseball team is at risk when his math grade plummets while he is trying to cope with the abuse of a young billy goat he sold and a visit from his estranged father to Lost Goat Lane.

"Justin's family is beautifully drawn. . . . The animal cruelty issues will draw readers, and so will the friendships across race, gender, and age that show the meaning of community." Booklist

Followed by: The last wild place (2008)

Lost Goat Lane. Peachtree Publisher 2004 197p $14.95

Grades: 5 6 7 8   **Fic**

1. Goats -- Fiction 2. Florida -- Fiction 3. Race relations -- Fiction 4. African Americans -- Fiction

ISBN 1-56145-325-0

LC 2004-5343

Two families—one white, one black—living near one another in rural Florida overcome their suspicions of each other and find ways to work together, with the help of their children and a few goats

"The fully realized characters and the warmth of the story make up for the small sermons. A tender, satisfying offering." SLJ

Other titles in this series are:

The goatnappers (2007)

The last wild place (2008)

Jung, Mike

Geeks, girls, and secret identities; by Mike Jung; with illustrations by Mike Maihack. Arthur A. Levine Books 2012 307 p. (hardcover : alk. paper) $16.99

Grades: 3 4 5 6 7   **Fic**

1. Boys' clubs 2. Secrecy -- Fiction 3. Friendship -- Fiction 4.

Science fiction 5. Clubs -- Fiction 6. Humorous stories 7. Robots -- Fiction 8. Schools -- Fiction 9. Superheroes -- Fiction 10. Middle schools -- Fiction

ISBN 0545335485; 9780545335485; 9780545335492; 9780545392518

LC 2011042543

In author Mike Jung's book, "Vincent Wu is Captain Stupendous's No. 1 Fan, but even he has to admit that Captain Stupendous has been a little off lately. During Professor Mayhem's latest attack, Captain Stupendous barely made it out alive, although he did manage to save Vincent from a giant monster robot. It's Vincent's dream come true . . . until he finds out Captain Stupendous's secret identity: It's Polly Winnicott-Lee, the girl Vincent happens to have a crush on." (Publisher's note)

Juster, Norton

★ The **phantom** tollbooth; illustrated by Jules Feiffer. Random House 1961 255p il $19.95; pa $6.50

Grades: 5 6 7 8   **Fic**

1. Fantasy fiction

ISBN 0-394-81500-9; 0-394-82037-1 pa

"It's all very clever. The author plays most ingeniously on words and phrases . . . and on concepts of averages and infinity and such . . . while the pictures are even more diverting than the text, for they add interesting details." N Y Her Trib Books

Kadohata, Cynthia

★ **Cracker!** the best dog in Vietnam. Atheneum Books for Young Readers 2007 312p $16.99; pa $7.99

Grades: 5 6 7 8   **Fic**

1. Dogs -- Fiction 2. Vietnam War, 1961-1975 -- Fiction

ISBN 978-1-4169-0637-7; 1-4169-0637-1; 978-1-4169-0638-4 pa; 1-4169-0638-X pa

LC 2006-2202

The author "tells a stirring, realistic story of America's war in Vietnam, using the alternating viewpoints of an army dog named Cracker and her 17-year-old handler, Rick Hanski. . . . The heartfelt tale explores the close bond of the scout-dog team." Booklist

★ **Kira**-Kira. Atheneum Bks. for Young Readers 2004 244p $15.95; pa $6.99

Grades: 5 6 7 8   **Fic**

1. Death -- Fiction 2. Georgia -- Fiction 3. Sisters -- Fiction 4. Japanese Americans -- Fiction

ISBN 0-689-85639-3; 0-689-85640-7 pa

Awarded the Newbery Medal, 2005

Chronicles the close friendship between two Japanese-American sisters growing up in rural Georgia during the late 1950s and early 1960s and the despair when one sister becomes terminally ill.

"This beautifully written story tells of a girl struggling to find her own way in a family torn by illness and horrendous work conditions. . . . All of the characters are believable and well developed." SLJ

★ A **million** shades of gray. Atheneum Books for Young Readers 2010 216p $16.99

Grades: 5 6 7 8   **Fic**

1. Vietnam -- Fiction 2. Elephants -- Fiction 3. Wilderness survival -- Fiction

ISBN 1-4169-1883-3; 978-1-4169-1883-7

LC 2009-3330

In 1975 after American troops pull out of Vietnam, a thirteen-year-old boy and his beloved elephant escape into the jungle when the Viet Cong attack his village. "Grades five to eight." (Bull Cent Child Books)

"Kadohata delves deep into the soul of her protagonist while making a faraway place and stark consequences of war seem very near." Publ Wkly

Outside beauty. Atheneum Books for Young Readers 2008 265p $16.99; pa $8.99

Grades: 5 6 7 8   **Fic**

1. Sisters -- Fiction 2. Japanese Americans -- Fiction 3. Father-daughter relationship -- Fiction 4. Mother-daughter relationship -- Fiction

ISBN 978-0-689-86575-6; 0-689-86575-9; 978-1-4169-9818-1 pa; 1-4169-9818-7 pa

LC 2007-39711

Thirteen-year-old Shelby and her three sisters must go to live with their respective fathers while their mother, who has trained them to rely on their looks, recovers from a car accident that scarred her face

Kadohata's "gifts for creating and containing drama and for careful definition of character prove as powerful as ever in this wise, tender and compelling novel." Publ Wkly

★ The **thing** about luck; Cynthia Kadohata; illustrated by Julia Kuo. 1st ed. Atheneum Books for Young Readers 2013 288 p. (hardcover) $16.99

Grades: 5 6 7 8   **Fic**

1. Luck -- Fiction 2. Japanese Americans -- Fiction 3. Brothers and sisters -- Fiction 4. Kansas -- Fiction 5. Grandparents -- Fiction 6. Farm life -- Kansas -- Fiction

ISBN 1416918825; 9781416918820; 9781442474673

LC 2012021287

Parents' Choice: Silver Medal Fiction (2013)

National Book Award Winner (2013)

Asian/Pacific American Awards for Literature: Children's Literature Winner (2014)

In this novel, by Newbery Medalist Cynthia Kadohata, "Summer knows that kouun means 'good luck' in Japanese, and this year her family has none of it. Just when she thinks nothing else can possibly go wrong, an emergency whisks her parents away to Japan--right before harvest season. Summer and her little brother, Jaz, are left in the care of their grandparents, who come out of retirement in order to harvest wheat and help pay the bills." (Publisher's note)

"Kadohata expertly captures the uncertainties of the tween years as Summer navigates the balance of childlike concerns with the onset of increasingly grown-up responsibilities." (SLJ)

★ **Weedflower**. Atheneum Books for Young Readers 2006 260p $16.95; pa $5.99

Grades: 5 6 7 8   **Fic**

1. Arizona -- Fiction 2. World War, 1939-1945 -- Fiction 3. Japanese Americans -- Evacuation and relocation, 1942-1945 -- Fiction

ISBN 0-689-86574-0; 1-4169-7566-7 pa

LC 2004-24912

After twelve-year-old Sumiko and her Japanese-American family are relocated from their flower farm in southern California to an internment camp on a Mojave Indian reservation in Arizona, she helps her family and neighbors, becomes friends with a local Indian boy, and tries to hold on to her dream of owning a flower shop.

Sumiko "is a sympathetic heroine, surrounded by well-crafted, fascinating people. The concise yet lyrical prose conveys her story in a compelling narrative." SLJ

Kang, Hildi

Chengli and the Silk Road caravan. Tanglewood 2011 178p $14.95

Grades: 5 6 7 8   **Fic**

1. China -- Fiction 2. Fathers -- Fiction 3. Princesses -- Fiction 4. Trade routes -- Fiction

ISBN 978-1-933718-54-5; 1-933718-54-4

LC 2010047359

Called to follow the wind and search for information about his father who disappeared many years ago, thirteen-year-old Chengli, carrying a piece of jade with strange writing that had belonged to his father, joins a caravan charged with giving safe passage to the Emperor's daughter as it navigates the constant dangers of the Silk Road in 630 A.D.

"This fast-paced adventure is filled with friendship, historical detail, changing scenery, and action. It will appeal to a wide range of readers." SLJ

Keating, Jess

How to outfox your friends when you don't have a clue; Jess Keating. Sourcebooks Jabberwocky 2015 304 p. (alk. paper) $7.99

Grades: 5 6 7 8   **Fic**

1. Zoos -- Fiction 2. Friendship -- Fiction 3. Best friends -- Fiction 4. Documentary films -- Production and direction -- Fiction

ISBN 1492617946; 9781492617945

LC 2015016025

In this children's novel by Jess Keating "Ana's long distance BFF is finally coming back to visit. But with her purple hair and new attitude, Liv is barely the girl Ana remembers. This new Liv probably thinks a birthday party at the zoo is lame. Maybe if Ana has a super-secret sleepover instead, she'd never have to introduce Liv to Ashley, former enemy and now Ana's best-ish friend. What could go wrong?" (Publisher's note)

"A sweet reminder that being a middle school girl is about far more than boys and makeup." Kirkus

Kehret, Peg

The **ghost's** grave. Dutton Children's Books 2005 210p $16.99; pa $5.99

Grades: 5 6 7 8   **Fic**

1. Ghost stories 2. Coal miners -- Fiction 3. Washington (State) -- Fiction

ISBN 0-525-46162-0; 0-14-240819-0 pa

LC 2004022064

Apprehensive about spending the summer in Washington State with his Aunt Ethel when his parents get an overseas job, twelve-year-old Josh soon finds adventure when he meets the ghost of a coal miner.

"This fast-paced and engaging book should be a hit with fans of ghost stories. Josh is a rich character to whom readers can relate." SLJ

Keith, Harold

Rifles for Watie. Crowell 1957 332p lib bdg $16.89; pa $5.99

Grades: 6 7 8 9   **Fic**

1. Generals 2. Indian leaders 3. United States -- History -- 1861-1865, Civil War -- Fiction

ISBN 0-690-04907-2 lib bdg; 0-06-447030-X pa

Awarded the Newbery Medal, 1958

"Young Jeff Bussey longs for the life of a Union soldier during the Civil War, but before long he realizes the cruelty and savagery of some men in the army situation. The war loses its glamor as he sees his very young friends die. When he is made a scout, his duties take him into the ranks of Stand Watie, leader of the rebel troops of the Cherokee Indian Nation, as a spy." Stensland. Lit By & About the Am Indian

Keller, Laurie

Invasion of the Ufonuts; Laurie Keller. Henry Holt and Company 2014 126 p. (hardback) $12.99

Grades: 2 3 4 5　　　　　　　　　　　　　　　**Fic**

1. Humorous fiction 2. Doughnuts -- Fiction 3. Extraterrestrial beings -- Fiction 4. Humorous stories 5. Alien abduction -- Fiction

ISBN 0805090754; 9780805090758

LC 2013042139

In this book, by Laurie Keller, "Arnie finds himself in trouble when his neighbor, Loretta Schmoretta, begins telling news reporters that she was the victim of an alien abduction. And not just any aliens—alien doughnuts from outer spastry, who will continue the abductions until people stop eating doughnuts! Although Arnie thinks this is a ridiculous story, he notices that everyone is treating him differently, as if he is an alien doughnut rather than just a doughnut-dog." (Publisher's note)

"Arnie the Doughnut narrates his second adventure with caretaker Mr. Bing and friend Peezo (a pizza slice), in which Earth is threatened by a bizarre invasion. When wacky puns, eccentric characters, and doughnuts from outer space mix together with Keller's recognizable illustrations, it's a recipe for a deliciously zany story. Keller even works in a secret alien-doughnut language (think Pig Latin)." Horn Book

Other titles in this series include:

Bowling Alley Bandit (2013)

Kelley, Jane

The **girl** behind the glass; [by] Jane Kelley. Random House 2011 183p $16.99; lib bdg $19.99; e-book $16.99

Grades: 4 5 6 7　　　　　　　　　　　　　　**Fic**

1. Ghost stories 2. Twins -- Fiction 3. Moving -- Fiction 4. Sisters -- Fiction 5. Family life -- Fiction

ISBN 978-0-375-86220-5; 0-375-86220-X; 978-0-375-96220-2 lib bdg; 0-375-96220-4 lib bdg; 978-0-375-88996-7 e-book

LC 2010-43568

Moving from Brooklyn to a rental house in the country strains the relationship between eleven-year-old identical twins Hannah and Anna Zimmer, a situation made worse by the ghost of a girl who is trapped in the house because of problems with her own sister eighty years before.

"Both chilling and lyrical. . . . The tensions within the Zimmer family are especially well-observed, and Kelley . . . conveys an impressive amount of emotion with few words. The ethereal tone and steady parceling out of warning, clues, and bits of information . . . maintain the novel's intrigue and will keep readers invested in the unfolding mystery." Publ Wkly

Kelly, David A.

The **Fenway** foul-up; illustrated by Mark Meyers. Random House 2011 101p il (Ballpark mysteries) lib bdg $12.99; pa $4.99

Grades: 2 3 4　　　　　　　　　　　　　　　**Fic**

1. Mystery fiction 2. Cousins -- Fiction 3. Baseball -- Fiction 4. Fenway Park (Boston, Mass.)

ISBN 978-0-375-96703-0 lib bdg; 0-375-96703-6 lib bdg; 978-0-375-86703-3 pa; 0-375-86703-1 pa; 978-0-375-89816-7 e-book

LC 2010-08521

"Two nine-year-old sleuths bring sharp powers of observation and deduction into play when a Red Sox slugger's favorite bat disappears. Cousins Mike and Kate are thrilled when Kate's sports-reporter mom brings them to a game, and they are up to the challenge when star player Big D's bat goes missing after batting practice. Folding information about Fenway Park and its colorful history into the tale, Kelly also artfully slips in simple red herrings along with real clues to the thief's identity and the bat's whereabouts. . . . This book should draw baseball fans as well as budding whodunit aficionados." Booklist

Other titles in this series are:

The pinstripe ghost (2011)

The L.A. Dodger (2011)

The **L.A.** Dodger; illustrated by Mark Meyers. Random House 2011 105p il (Ballpark mysteries) lib bdg $12.99; pa $5.99

Grades: 2 3 4　　　　　　　　　　　　　　　**Fic**

1. Mystery fiction 2. Theft -- Fiction 3. Cousins -- Fiction 4. Baseball -- Fiction 5. Los Angeles (Calif.) -- Fiction 6. Dodger Stadium (Los Angeles, Calif.) -- Fiction.

ISBN 978-0-375-96885-3 lib bdg; 0-375-96885-7 lib bdg; 978-0-375-86885-6 pa; 0-375-86885-2 pa; 978-0-375-89968-3 ebook; 0-375-89968-5 ebook

LC 2010038728

Cousins Kate and Mike visit Kate's father, a baseball scout for the Dodgers, in Los Angeles just as a series of suspicious events lead him to think that someone is trying to steal his scouting reports.

The **pinstripe** ghost; illustrated by Mark Meyers. Random House 2011 105p il (Ballpark mysteries) lib bdg $12.99; pa $4.99

Grades: 2 3 4　　　　　　　　　　　　　　　**Fic**

1. Ghost stories 2. Mystery fiction 3. Baseball players 4. Baseball -- Fiction 5. Yankee Stadium (New York, N.Y.)

ISBN 978-0-375-96704-7 lib bdg; 0-375-96704-4 lib bdg; 978-0-375-86704-0 pa; 0-375-86704-X pa; 978-0-375-89817-4 ebook

LC 2010016545

While visiting New York's Yankee Stadium with Kate's mother, cousins Mike and Kate decide to investigate the rumor that the ghost of Babe Ruth is haunting the stadium.

"The baseball lore makes for entertaining reading." Horn Book Guide

Kelly, Erin Entrada

Blackbird fly; by Erin Entrada Kelly. Greenwillow Books, an imprint of HarperCollinsPublishers 2015 304 p. (hardback) $16.99

Grades: 4 5 6 7 8　　　　　　　　　　　　　**Fic**

1. School stories 2. Music -- Fiction 3. Bullies -- Fiction 4. Guitar -- Fiction 5. Middle schools -- Fiction 6. Filipino Americans -- Fiction

ISBN 0062238612; 9780062238610

LC 2014029444

"Apple has always felt a little different from her classmates. . . . It becomes unbearable in middle school, when the boys . . . in Apple's class put her name on the Dog Log, the list of the most unpopular girls in school. When Apple's friends turn on her and everything about her life starts to seem weird and embarrassing, Apple turns to music." (Publisher's note)

"Debut author Kelly skillfully weaves together the story of misfit Apple, her love of music, and a budding romance with a new boy at school, while never losing focus on the central issue of what it is like to be the 'other. . .'" Booklist

★ **Hello** universe; Erin Entrada Kelly, illustrated by Isabel Roxas. Greenwillow Books, an imprint of HarperCollins Publishers 2017 320 p. illustrations (hardback) $16.99; (ebook) $15.99

Grades: 4 5 6 7　　　　　　　　　　　　　　**Fic**

1. Bullies -- Fiction 2. Sisters -- Fiction 3. Friendship -- Fiction 4. Psychic ability -- Fiction 5. Hearing impaired -- Fiction 6. Missing children -- Fiction 7. Bullying -- Fiction

ISBN 9780062414151; 9780062414175

LC 2016022723

This book, by Erin Entrada Kelly, illustrated by Isabel Roxas, "is a funny and poignant neighborhood story about unexpected friendships. Told from four intertwining points of view—two boys and two girls—the novel celebrates bravery, being different, and finding your inner bayani (hero)." (Publisher's note)

"An original and resonant exploration of interconnectedness and friendship." Kirkus

The **land** of forgotten girls; by Erin Entrada Kelly. Greenwillow Books, an imprint of HarperCollinsPublishers 2016 304 p. (hardback) $16.99

Grades: 3 4 5 6 **Fic**

1. Sisters -- Fiction 2. Louisiana -- Fiction 3. Stepmothers -- Fiction 4. Family problems -- Fiction 5. Filipino Americans -- Fiction 6. Immigrants -- Louisiana -- Fiction

ISBN 9780062238641

LC 2015019330

In this children's story, by Erin Entrada Kelly, "Soledad and Ming, two sisters from the Philippines, live in Louisiana with their evil stepmother, Vea. All Sol and Ming have is each other and their stories . . . about [their magical aunt] Jove, who traveled around the world. . . . [But] Sol worries for her younger sister as Ming begins to believe Auntie Jove is a reality, blurring the lines between fact and fiction." (School Library Journal)

"Readers will become engrossed in the enchanting plot propelled by delightful narration. This book will appeal to a broad array of readers, as it has a little bit of everything—fantasy, realism, sisterhood, friendship, suspense, and humor." SLJ

Kelly, Jacqueline

Counting sheep; Jacqueline Kelly; illustrated by Teagan White. Henry Holt & Co. 2017 112 p. (hardback) $15.99

Grades: 2 3 4 **Fic**

1. Gender role -- Fiction 2. Naturalists -- Fiction 3. Veterinarians -- Fiction 4. Sex role -- Fiction 5. Family life -- Texas -- Fiction 6. Texas -- History -- 1846-1950 -- Fiction

ISBN 9781627798709

LC 2016002104

In this second book in the Calpurnia Tate, Girl Vet series, by Jacqueline Kelly, illustrated by Teagan White, "Callie takes a hands-on approach to animal doctoring. When Callie and Granddaddy go exploring by the river, Callie discovers a leaf covered with spots. Those spots, it turns out, are eggs, and those eggs become butterflies. One of her newly hatched butterflies has a problem, though—its wing is broken. Can Callie find a way to help this butterfly fly?" (Publisher's note)

"Her free-spirited personality, her rule-bending ways, and her determination to follow her passion for science, regardless of her mother's misgivings, make her a lively, endearing character." Booklist

★ The **curious** world of Calpurnia Tate; Jacqueline Kelly. Henry Holt & Co. 2015 320 p. (hardcover) $16.99

Grades: 4 5 6 **Fic**

1. Girls -- Fiction 2. Gender role -- Fiction 3. Sex role -- Fiction 4. Veterinarians -- Fiction 5. Family life -- Texas -- Fiction 6. Texas -- History -- 1846-1950 -- Fiction

ISBN 9780805097443; 0805097449

LC 2015000920

Sequel to: The evolution of Calpurnia Tate

In this children's story, by Jacqueline Kelly, "thirteen-year-old Callie Vee returns in this . . . sequel to . . . 'The Evolution of Calpurnia Tate.' . . . Callie's thirst for scientific discovery remains strong, as does her parents' disregard for any[thing but] . . . debutante balls and marrying a well-respected gentleman. In between recording questions and observations in her journal, Callie and brother Travis attempt to make pets of an armadillo, a blue jay, and a coyote mix, to mostly disastrous results." (School Library Journal)

"Recommended for fans of the original novel and strong readers who enjoy character-driven narratives." SLJ

★ The **evolution** of Calpurnia Tate. Henry Holt and Co. 2009 340p $16.99

Grades: 4 5 6 7 **Fic**

1. Texas -- Fiction 2. Nature -- Fiction 3. Family life -- Fiction 4. Naturalists -- Fiction 5. Grandfathers -- Fiction

ISBN 0-8050-8841-5; 978-0-8050-8841-0

LC 2008-40595

A Newbery Medal honor book (2010)

In central Texas in 1899, eleven-year-old Callie Vee Tate is instructed to be a lady by her mother, learns about love from the older three of her six brothers, and studies the natural world with her grandfather. "Grades five to eight." (Bull Cent Child Books)

"Callie is a charming, inquisitive protagonist; a joyous, bright, and thoughtful creation. . . . Several scenes . . . mix gentle humor and pathos to great effect." SLJ

Skunked: Calpurnia Tate, girl vet; Jacqueline Kelly. Henry Holt & Co. 2016 112 p. illustrations (hardback) $15.99; (ebook) $60

Grades: 2 3 4 **Fic**

1. Skunks -- Fiction 2. Naturalists -- Fiction 3. Veterinarians -- Fiction 4. Skunks -- Infancy -- Fiction 5. Family life -- Texas -- Fiction 6. Texas -- History -- 1846-1950 -- Fiction

ISBN 9781627798686; 9781627798693

LC 2015041958

In this book, by Jacqueline Kelly, "when soft-hearted Travis discovers an abandoned baby skunk, he can't help but bring him home and take care of him. Stinky, as Travis names him, settles in pretty well. But when Travis discovers Stinky's litter-mate, Winky, who is in need of some help, things get complicated around the Tate house. One skunk is a piece of cake; two is just asking for trouble." (Publisher's note)

"Delicate leafy branches decorate the top of each page, subtly underscoring Callie's scientific interests." Horn Book

Kelly, Katy

Lucy Rose, big on plans; by Katy Kelly; illustrated by Adam Rex. Delacorte Press 2005 163p il $12.95; lib bdg $14.99; pa $5.50

Grades: 2 3 4 **Fic**

1. Summer -- Fiction 2. Divorce -- Fiction 3. Family life -- Fiction 4. Washington (D.C.) -- Fiction

ISBN 0-385-73204-X; 0-385-90235-2 lib bdg; 0-440-42027-X pa

LC 2004015279

Lucy Rose records in her diary her special summer plans—to make a keychain for her mother, to help decorate the living room, to prevent her parents' divorce, to vanquish some squirrels, and to enjoy a ninth birthday adventure with her father.

"The book's language is rich and the characters are likeable." SLJ

Lucy Rose, busy like you can't believe; by Katy Kelly; illustrated by Adam Rex. Delacorte Press 2006 155p il $12.95

Grades: 2 3 4 **Fic**

1. Divorce -- Fiction 2. Family life -- Fiction 3. Washington (D.C.) -- Fiction

ISBN 0-385-73319-4; 0-385-90338-3 lib bdg

LC 2005023593

Now in fourth grade, palindrome-enthusiast Lucy Rose learns about the perils of eavesdropping while also confiding in her diary her worries that her recently divorced mother is beginning to date

"The uncomplicated text contains hilarious episodes. . . . Rex's occasional full-page illustrations add humor and verve." SLJ

Lucy Rose, here's the thing about me; illustrated by Adam Rex. Delacorte Press 2004 137p il hardcover o.p. pa $5.99

Grades: 2 3 4 **Fic**

1. School stories 2. Moving -- Fiction 3. Family life -- Fiction 4.

Washington (D.C.) -- Fiction
ISBN 0-385-73203-1; 0-440-42026-1 pa

LC 2003-20754

Eight-year-old Lucy Rose keeps a diary of her first year in Washington, D.C., her home since her parents separation, where she spends time with her grandparents, makes new friends, and longs to convince her teacher to let her take care of the class pet during a holiday

"There's something especially endearing about Lucy Rose, and her interactions with her parents, grandparents, teacher, and friends seem believable and comfortable." Booklist

Other titles about Lucy Rose are:

Lucy Rose, big on plans (2005)
Lucy Rose, busy like you can't believe (2006)
Lucy Rose, working myself to pieces and bits (2007)

Lucy Rose, working myself to pieces and bits; [by] Katy Kelly; illustrated by Peter Ferguson. 1st ed.; Delacorte Press 2007 182p il $12.99; lib bdg $15.99
Grades: 2 3 4   **Fic**
1. Family life -- Fiction 2. Washington (D.C.) -- Fiction
ISBN 978-0-385-73408-0; 978-0-385-90425-4 lib bdg

LC 2006028701

In her diary fourth grader Lucy Rose, lover of palindromes and big words, records her adventures with friends Jonique and Melonhead, including their unorthodox ways of raising money for the McBees to remodel their bakery.

"Kelly's use of diction and phrasing usually results in a voice that sounds authentic. . . . Kelly gives a more nuanced and realistic picture of bullies than one normally sees in fiction for this audience." SLJ

Melonhead; illustrated by Gillian Johnson. Delacorte Press 2009 209p il $12.99; lib bdg $15.99
Grades: 3 4 5   **Fic**
1. Inventors -- Fiction 2. Washington (D.C.) -- Fiction
ISBN 978-0-385-73409-7; 0-385-73409-3; 978-0-385-90426-1 lib bdg; 0-385-90426-6 lib bdg

LC 2007-46076

In the Washington, D.C. neighborhood of Capitol Hill, Lucy Rose's friend Adam "Melonhead" Melon, a budding inventor with a knack for getting into trouble, enters a science contest that challenges students to recycle an older invention into a new invention.

This is "laugh-out-loud funny. . . . The capital setting and a unique cast of characters round out this strong chapter-book offering." SLJ

Other titles about Melonhead are:

Melonhead and the big stink (2010)
Melonhead and the undercover operation (2011)

Melonhead and the big stink; illustrated by Gillian Johnson. Delacorte Press 2010 216p il $14.99
Grades: 3 4 5   **Fic**
1. Summer -- Fiction 2. Washington (D.C.) -- Fiction
ISBN 978-0-385-73658-9; 0-385-73658-4

During the summer between fourth and fifth grade, Adam "Melonhead" Melon, who lives in the Washington D.C. neighborhood of Capital Hill, tries to stay out of trouble to earn a trip to New York City to see the giant "stink flower."

"The clever dialogue sparkles, and Johnson's blithe sketches add to the cheerful mood. A breezy and humorous middle-grade tale that illuminates the value of intergenerational relationships." Kirkus

Melonhead and the undercover operation; illustrated by Gillian Johnson. Delacorte Press 2011 243p il (Another title in the author's series about Melonhead) $12.99; lib bdg $15.99; ebook $12.99

Grades: 3 4 5   **Fic**
1. Humorous fiction 2. Spies -- Fiction 3. Family life -- Fiction 4. Washington (D.C.) -- Fiction
ISBN 978-0-385-73659-6; 0-385-73659-2; 978-0-385-90618-0 lib bdg; 0-385-90618-8 lib bdg; 978-0-375-98292-7 ebook; 0-375-98292-2 ebook

LC 2010039057

Ten-year-old Adam 'Melonhead' Melon and his fellow Junior Special Agent, Sam, investigate a fellow resident of Washington D.C.'s Capitol Hill neighborhood, believing that she is one of the FBI's Ten Most Wanted.

"Combined with appearances from neighborhood favorites met in earlier volumes and Johnson's snappy sketches, Melonhead's pure, kid-centric, fun-loving perspective is hard to resist." Kirkus

Kelly, Lynne
Chained; Lynne Kelly. Farrar Straus Giroux 2012 248 p. (hardcover) $16.99
Grades: 4 5 6   **Fic**
1. Debt 2. Circus performers -- Fiction 3. Human-animal relationships -- Fiction 4. India -- Fiction 5. Circus -- Fiction 6. Elephants -- Fiction 7. Child labor -- Fiction 8. Conduct of life -- Fiction 9. Animals -- Treatment -- Fiction
ISBN 0374312370; 9780374312374; 9780374312503

LC 2011031767

In author Lynne Kelly's book, "after ten-year-old Hastin's family borrows money to pay for his sister's hospital bill, he leaves his village in northern India to take a job as an elephant keeper and work off the debt. . . . The crowds that come to the circus see a lively animal . . but Hastin sees Nandita, a sweet elephant and his best friend, who is chained when she's not performing and hurt with a hook until she learns tricks perfectly. Hastin protects Nandita as best as he can, knowing that the only way they will both survive is if he can find a way for them to escape." (Publisher's note)

Kelly, Mark E., 1964-
Astrotwins; project blastoff. Mark Kelly with Martha Freeman. Simon & Schuster Books for Young Readers 2014 224 p. (Astrotwins) (hardback) $16.99
Grades: 4 5 6   **Fic**
1. Twins -- Fiction 2. Brothers -- Fiction 3. Grandfathers -- Fiction 4. Rockets (Aeronautics) -- Fiction
ISBN 148141545X; 9781481415453

LC 201401240?

This middle grade book is "based on the childhoods of real-life astronauts Mark Kelly and his twin brother Scott. It's a long, hot summer and Scott and Mark are in big trouble for taking apart (aka destroying) their dad's calculator. As a punishment, they're sent to their grandfather's house. . . . 'What if you built a go-kart or something?' Grandpa suggests. But it's not a go-kart the twins are interested in. They want to build a rocket." (Publisher's note)

Another Astrotwins book is:

Project rescue (2016)

Kelsey, Marybeth
A **recipe** 4 robbery. Greenwillow Books 2009 282p $16.99; lib bdg $17.89
Grades: 4 5 6   **Fic**
1. Mystery fiction
ISBN 978-0-06-128843-2; 0-06-128843-8; 978-0-06-128845-6 lib bdg; 0-06-128845-4 lib bdg

LC 2008-2914?

An unsupervised goose, missing family heirlooms, and some suspicious characters turn the annual cucumber festival into a robbery investigation for three sixth-grade friends.

"The novel is full of likable characters and fun twists and turns. The plot moves quickly, and Kelsey writes with wit and verve." SLJ

Kennedy, Emma

Wilma Tenderfoot: the case of the frozen hearts. Dial Books for Young Readers 2011 335p $16.99

Grades: 4 5 6   **Fic**

1. Mystery fiction 2. Orphans -- Fiction 3. Great Britain -- Fiction

ISBN 978-0-8037-3540-8; 0-8037-3540-5

LC 2009040050

Wilma Tenderfoot, a ten-year-old orphan who lives at Cooper Island's Lowside Institute for Woeful Children, dreams of escape and of becoming the apprentice of the world-famous detective Theodore P. Goodman, whose every case she follows devotedly in the newspaper.

"Wilma is an appealing character, ever-hopeful that Goodman will take her on as an apprentice and help her find out more about her origins. The fast-paced plot twists and turns, but the conflict between good and evil is clear." Kirkus

Another title in this series is:

Wilma Tenderfoot: the case if the putrid poison (2011)

Wilma Tenderfoot: the case of the putrid poison. Dial Books for Young Readers 2011 314p $16.99

Grades: 4 5 6   **Fic**

1. Mystery fiction 2. Actors -- Fiction 3. Orphans -- Fiction 4. Theater -- Fiction 5. Great Britain -- Fiction 6. Missing persons -- Fiction 7. Poisons and poisoning -- Fiction

ISBN 978-0-8037-3541-5; 0-8037-3541-3

LC 2011001165

Companion volume to: Wilma Tenderfoot: the case of the frozen hearts (2001)

"The writing is straightforward, but Kennedy includes language that may challenge younger readers, irresistible new words like 'irascible,' 'wafting,' 'sordid' and 'maniacally.' A couple of pages of summary of the events of the first book will bring newcomers into the long-term story, but this title stands on its own. Both familiar and fresh, this English import is likely to appeal to American readers as well." Kirkus

Kennedy, Marlane

The **dog** days of Charlotte Hayes. Greenwillow Books 2009 233p $15.99; lib bdg $16.89

Grades: 4 5 6   **Fic**

1. Dogs -- Fiction 2. Old age -- Fiction 3. Family life -- Fiction 4. West Virginia -- Fiction

ISBN 978-0-06-145241-3; 0-06-145241-6; 978-0-06-145242-0 lib bdg; 0-06-145242-4 lib bdg

LC 2008-07507

Eleven-year-old Charlotte is not a dog person but does not like that the rest of her family neglects their Saint Bernard puppy, and so with a lot of determination and a little sneakiness, she works on finding a good home for the gentle giant.

This is a "gentle, appealing story. . . . The familiar family and friendship issues and satisfying resolution make this an agreeable read." Booklist

Kerrin, Jessica Scott

Martin Bridge blazing ahead! written by Jessica Scott Kerrin; illustrated by Joseph Kelly. Kids Can Press 2006 109p il $15.95; pa $6.95

Grades: 2 3 4   **Fic**

1. Camping -- Fiction 2. Friendship -- Fiction 3. Father-son relationship -- Fiction

ISBN 1-55337-961-6; 1-55337-962-4 pa

In the first chapter, Martin "is on an overnight camping trip with the Junior Badgers, including his prankster friend, Alex. In the second chapter, Martin has to help his Dad fix the lawn mower during his favorite show. However, he discovers this time spent with his father has fostered a closer bond and has taught him mechanical skills that he can share with his friends. . . . Kelly's expressive, quirky drawings in graphite and charcoal with digital shading complement the text. The [book offers] delightful characters and engaging stories." SLJ

Martin Bridge in high gear! written by Jessica Scott Kerrin; illustrated by Joseph Kelly. Kids Can Press 2008 111p il $14.95; pa $5.95

Grades: 2 3 4   **Fic**

1. School stories 2. Friendship -- Fiction

ISBN 978-1-5545-3156-1; 1-5545-3156-X; 978-1-5545-3157-8 pa; 1-5545-3157-8 pa

"At least one illustration appears on every double-page spread. . . . A satisfying entry in an accessible, realistic chapter-book series." Booklist

Martin Bridge on the lookout! written by Jessica Scott Kerrin; illustrated by Joseph Kelly. Kids Can Press 2005 142p il $16.95; pa $6.95

Grades: 2 3 4   **Fic**

1. School stories 2. Friendship -- Fiction

ISBN 1-55337-689-7; 1-55337-773-7 pa

"In the first story, Laila Moffatt shows up for Martin's birthday party a day late. . . . In the second story, Martin forgets his permission slip for a class trip and must spend the day with last year's teacher and his class. The last story features Martin, Alex, and Stuart inadvertently letting the class parakeet escape. . . . Kelly's full-page and spot cartoon illustrations, drawn with graphite and charcoal and shaded digitally, will support newly independent readers." SLJ

Martin Bridge out of orbit! written by Jessica Scott Kerrin; illustrated by Joseph Kelly. Kids Can Press 2007 111p il $14.95; pa $4.95

Grades: 2 3 4   **Fic**

1. Parades -- Fiction 2. Friendship -- Fiction 3. Illustrators -- Fiction

ISBN 978-1-55453-148-6; 1-55453-148-9; 978-1-55453-149-3 pa; 1-55543-149-7 pa

Three more stories of Martin's plans unravelling. This time, his school is having a parade, the illustrator of his favorite comic book will be visiting his classroom, and will show him and his classmates how to draw Zip Rideout.

"The frequent charcoal illustrations will help early-chapter-book readers make sense of the text, and the quality of the storytelling makes this title a good read aloud." SLJ

Martin Bridge sound the alarm! written by Jessica Scott Kerrin; illustrated by Joseph Kelly. Kids Can Press 2007 110p il $14.95; pa $4.95

Grades: 2 3 4   **Fic**

1. Friendship -- Fiction

ISBN 978-1-55337-976-8; 1-55337-976-4; 978-1-55337-977-5 pa; 1-55337-977-2 pa

Martin's back in two more stories. He gets a new babysitter and learns that dancing isn't all bad. In the second story, Martin his friend Stuart find themselves locked in a toy store with no way out.

"Martin is a likable character. . . . Kelly's charcoal sketches support the text and will help youngsters comprehend the story." SLJ

Martin Bridge: onwards and upwards! written by Jessica Scott Kerrin; illustrated Joseph Kelly. Kids Can Press 2009 111p il $16.95; pa $6.95

Grades: 2 3 4   **Fic**

1. Clubs -- Fiction 2. Courage -- Fiction 3. Toleration -- Fiction

ISBN 978-1-55453-160-8; 1-55453-160-8; 978-1-55453-161-5 pa; 1-55453-161-6 pa

In two stories, Martin must endure his mother's practice on a keyboard she bought at a garage sale and deal with his classmate, Laila Moffatt, who joins the Junior Badges and who is willing to do everything she can to fit in and be accepted.

★ **Martin** Bridge: ready for takeoff! written by Jessica Scott Kerrin; illustrated by Joseph Kelly. Kids Can Press 2005 120p il $14.95; pa $4.95

Grades: 2 3 4   **Fic**

ISBN 1-55337-688-9; 1-55337-772-9 pa

"Martin Bridge usually has a scheme or project under way. In the three school and home stories presented in this beginning chapter book, he sees how a happy surprise intended for one person makes a positive difference for another, figures out what to say to a little girl whose hamster has died, and suffers the consequences of jealousy. . . . [Martin's] responses are on target for a third grader. Kerrin relates the episodes in a straightforward way that incorporates rich language. Kelly's full-page illustrations and spot art follow the narrative closely enough to support the newly independent readers for whom this book is written." SLJ

Other titles about Martin Bridge are:

Martin Bridge on the lookout! (2005)

Martin Bridge blazing ahead! (2006)

Martin Bridge out of orbit! (2007)

Martin Bridge sound the alarm (2007)

Martin Bridge in high gear! (2008)

Martin Bridge: the sky's the limit (2008)

Martin Bridge: onwards and upwards! (2009)

Martin Bridge: the sky's the limit; written by Jessica Scott Kerrin; illustrated by Joseph Kelly. Kids Can Press 2008 110p il $16.95; pa $6.95

Grades: 2 3 4   **Fic**

1. School stories 2. Cousins -- Fiction

ISBN 978-1-55453-158-5; 1-55453-158-6; 978-1-55453-159-2 pa; 1-55453-159-4 pa

"Martin Bridge and the rest of the Junior Badgers can't wait for the fireworks show on the weekend. When Martin's cousin Fletcher arrives to stay at his house, his guest is not so excited about fireworks, or about Martin's space hero Zip Rideout. . . . In the second story, Martin is struggling to contain his excitement. He's sure he's due to receive his prize for the Zip Rideout Trivia Contest Zip's Space Race Game, deluxe edition." Publisher's note

Kerz, Anna

Better than weird. Orca Book Publishers 2011 218p pa $9.95

Grades: 4 5 6 7   **Fic**

1. School stories 2. Autism -- Fiction 3. Bullies -- Fiction 4. Father-son relationship -- Fiction

ISBN 978-1-55469-362-7 pa; 1-55469-362-4 pa

When Aaron's long-absent father returns, Aaron must cope with bullying at school, his grandmother's illness and his father's pregnant new wife.

"Yet another in a long line of recent books about kids with autism, Kerz's effort nevertheless shines. . . . A heartwarming read for fans of realistic fiction." Booklist

The **gnome's** eye. Orca Book Publishers 2010 210p pa $12.95

Grades: 4 5 6 7   **Fic**

1. Fear -- Fiction 2. Canada -- Fiction 3. Immigrants -- Fiction

ISBN 978-1-55469-195-1 pa; 1-55469-195-8 pa

When Theresa and her family immigrate to Canada after World War II, she confronts her many fears with the help of a talisman given to her by a friend in Austria.

"Both laughter and genuine concern will be evident through Theresa's imaginative storytelling and descriptive narrative." SLJ

Ketchum, Liza

Where the great hawk flies. Clarion Books 2005 264p $16

Grades: 5 6 7 8   **Fic**

1. Vermont -- Fiction 2. Prejudices -- Fiction 3. Pequot Indians -- Fiction

ISBN 0-618-40085-0

LC 2004-29832

Years after a violent New England raid by the Redcoats and their Revolutionary War Indian allies, two families, one that suffered during that raid and one with an Indian mother and Patriot father, become neighbors and must deal with past trauma and prejudices before they can help each other in the present. Based on the author's family history. Includes historical notes and notes on the Pequot Indians.

The author writes "in prose as sturdy and well crafted as a cedar-frame wigwam or hand-pegged pine barn." Booklist

Key, Watt

Alabama moon. Farrar, Straus & Giroux 2006 294p $16; pa $6.99

Grades: 5 6 7 8   **Fic**

1. Alabama -- Fiction 2. Orphans -- Fiction 3. Wilderness survival -- Fiction

ISBN 0-374-30184-0; 0-312-38428-9 pa

LC 2005-40165

After the death of his father, ten-year-old Moon leaves their forest shelter home and is sent to an Alabama institution, becoming entangled in the outside world he has never known and making good friends, a relentless enemy, and finally a new life

"The book is well written with a flowing style, plenty of dialogue, and lots of action. The characters are well drawn and three-dimensional." SLJ

Followed by: Dirt road home (2010)

Khan, Amina

★ **Amina's** voice; Hena Khan. Salaam Reads / Simon & Schuster Books for Young Readers 2017 208 p. (hardcover) $16.99

Grades: 4 5 6 7 8   **Fic**

1. Muslims -- Fiction 2. Friendship -- Fiction 3. Pakistani Americans -- Fiction

ISBN 9781481492065; 9781481492072

LC 2016024621

In this middle grade novel by Hena Khan, "A Pakistani-American Muslim girl struggles to stay true to her family's vibrant culture while simultaneously blending in at school after tragedy strikes her community . . . Amina has never been comfortable in the spotlight. She is happy just hanging out with her best friend, Soojin. Except now that she's in middle school everything feels different." (Publisher's note)

Kidd, Ronald

Night on Fire; Ronald Kidd. Albert Whitman & Co 2015 288 p. $16.99

Grades: 4 5 6 7 8   **Fic**

1. Racism -- Fiction 2. Segregation -- Fiction 3. Civil rights

-- Fiction
ISBN 0807570249; 9780807570241

LC 2015025153

In this novel by Ronald Kidd "thirteen-year-old Billie Simms doesn't think her hometown of Anniston, Alabama, should be segregated, but few . . . share her opinion. So when Billie learns that the Freedom Riders, a group of peace activists . . . will be traveling through Anniston on their way to Montgomery, she thinks that maybe change is finally coming. But what starts as a series of angry grumbles soon turns to brutality as Anniston residents show just how deep their racism runs." (Publisher's note)

"Beautifully written and earnestly delivered, the novel rolls to an inexorable, stunning conclusion readers won't soon forget." Kirkus

Kilworth, Garry

Attica. Little, Brown 2009 334p pa $11.95

Grades: 5 6 7 8   **Fic**

1. Fantasy fiction 2. Stepfamilies -- Fiction
ISBN 978-1-904233-56-5 pa; 1-904233-56-2 pa

"The children have distinct personalities and react to Attica in realistic ways, finding their own strengths in this exhilarating, unpredictable environment. This book is a rare find." Booklist

Kimmel, Elizabeth Cody

★ The **reinvention** of Moxie Roosevelt. Dial Books for Young Readers 2010 256p $16.99

Grades: 4 5 6 7   **Fic**

1. School stories
ISBN 978-0-8037-3303-9; 0-8037-3303-8

LC 2009-37939

On her first day of boarding school, a thirteen-year-old girl who feels boring and invisible decides to change her personality to match her unusual name.

"Kimmel's sharply observed novel reflects a keen understanding of the agony of self-definition that is adolescence. Readers will cheer for Moxie as she charts her path toward self-acceptance." Kirkus

Scaredy Kat. Little, Brown 2009 250p (Suddenly supernatural) $10.99

Grades: 5 6 7 8   **Fic**

1. Ghost stories 2. Friendship -- Fiction 3. Clairvoyance -- Fiction 4. Supernatural -- Fiction 5. Mother-daughter relationship -- Fiction
ISBN 978-0-316-06685-3; 0-316-06685-0

LC 2008005025

Thirteen-year-old Kat, still not comfortable in her role as a medium, and her friend Jac, undergoing a serious crisis about the role of music in her life, try to find a way to help the unhappy spirit of a young boy in the abandoned house next door.

School spirit. Little, Brown and Co. 2008 316p (Suddenly supernatural) $15.99

Grades: 5 6 7 8   **Fic**

1. Ghost stories 2. School stories 3. Popularity -- Fiction 4. Clairvoyance -- Fiction 5. Mother-daughter relationship -- Fiction
ISBN 978-0-316-06683-9; 0-316-06683-4

LC 2007-031542

Like her mother, a professional medium, Kat has been able to see dead people since turning thirteen, and although they would prefer to be normal, Kat and her best friend come to terms with their own talents while helping free the spirit of a girl trapped at their middle school.

"This delightfully fun and well-written story is a fast, clean read. . . . Its nice blend of supernatural and reality will attract fantasy and non-fantasy readers alike." Voice Youth Advocates

Other titles in this series are:

Scaredy Kat (2009)
Unhappy medium (2009)

Unhappy medium; by Elizabeth Cody Kimmel. 1st ed.; Little Brown 2009 277p (Suddenly supernatural) $10.99

Grades: 5 6 7 8   **Fic**

1. Ghost stories 2. Friendship -- Fiction 3. Clairvoyance -- Fiction 4. Supernatural -- Fiction 5. Hotels and motels -- Fiction 6. Mother-daughter relationship -- Fiction
ISBN 978-0-316-06687-7; 0-316-06687-7

LC 2008045021

Kat accompanies her best friend Jac to a musicians' conference at the Whispering Pines Mountain House, where she works to free the spirit of a dead medium and helps Jac resolve a serious conflict.

Kinard, Kami

The **boy** prediction; (notes and observations of Tabitha Reddy) Kami Kinard. Scholastic Press 2014 272 p. illustrations $12.99

Grades: 6 7 8 9   **Fic**

1. Girls -- Fiction 2. Middle schools -- Fiction 3. Humorous stories 4. Schools -- Fiction 5. Friendship -- Fiction 6. Best friends -- Fiction 7. Dating (Social customs) -- Fiction
ISBN 0545575869; 9780545575867

LC 2013025996

"Full of asides about classmates and the kind of detailed gossip only 11 to 13-year-olds can truly follow, this giddy, giggly book reads like a diary and is aimed at tween girls who like their literature frothy. Tabbi, short for Tabitha, is a middle-school student looking for the right guy, a crush who will elevate her status and help her put aside the feeling that she is just a third wheel when she hangs out with her bestie Kara and Kara's boyfriend, Chip. But how is she going to find the guy of her dreams? Tabbi is sure that everything, from the cheese that slid off her pizza and formed the shape of a male face (well, kind of) to a Magic 8 Ball, will predict her future." (Booklist)

" the girls struggle to make their fundraising goal, they learn about handling competition, working in partnership and even a little something about cyberbullying. For any spirited, entrepreneurial teen that's ever had a crush, this sweet read is sprinkled with lessons on life, love and business." - Kirkus

King, Caro

Seven sorcerers; Caro King. Aladdin 2011 324 p. (hbk.) $15.99

Grades: 5 6 7 8   **Fic**

1. Fantasy 2. Missing children -- Fiction 3. Brothers and sisters -- Fiction 4. Adventure and adventurers -- Fiction
ISBN 1442420421; 9781442420427

LC 2011001432

Sequel: Shadow spell
First published 2009 in the United Kingdom

"Nineveh 'Nin' Redstone is 11 years old and resolutely ordinary. Her four-year-old brother is nothing but a nuisance until the awful Wednesday when she wakes up and he's gone. Worse, no one but Nin remembers he exists. It's left to her to reclaim him from Skerridge (a bogeyman) and the Terrible House of Strood." (Publishers Weekly)

A "complex, intelligent fantasy that is at turns funny and terrifying." Booklist

King, Thomas

A **Coyote** solstice tale; pictures by Gary Clement. Groundwood Books 2009 un il $14.95

Grades: 1 2 3 4   **Fic**

1. Stories in rhyme 2. Animals -- Fiction 3. Coyotes -- Fiction 4. Shopping -- Fiction 5. Winter solstice -- Fiction
ISBN 978-0-88899-929-0; 0-88899-929-1

ALA America Indian Library Association American Indian Youth Literature Award (2010)

"Coyote is expecting Beaver, Bear, Otter, and Moose for a solstice dinner at his small house in the woods but a little girl in a reindeer costume shows up first. When the friends follow her tracks to discover where she came from, they discover a huge and frenzied mall just beyond the woods, where Coyote goes wild shopping until he discovers that he has to pay for the stuff. The humor is dry and affectionate, the rhyming text delights with sly turns of phrase, the watercolor cartoons are whimsical, and the small size of the book (a bit bigger than a DVD case) adds to the charm." SLJ

King-Smith, Dick

★ **Babe**; the gallant pig. illustrated by Maggie Kneen. Twentieth anniversary edition; Knopf 2005 130p il $16.95

Grades: 3 4 5   **Fic**

1. Pigs -- Fiction

ISBN 0-375-82970-9

LC 2004-5832

First published 1983 in the United Kingdom with title: The sheeppig; first United States edition 1985 by Crown

A piglet destined for eventual butchering arrives at the farmyard, is adopted by an old sheep dog, and discovers a special secret to success

"Mary Rayner's engaging black-and-white drawings capture the essence of Babe and the skittishness of sheep and enhance this splendid book-which should once and for all establish the intelligence and nobility of pigs." Horn Book

Dinosaur trouble; [by] Dick King-Smith; illustrated by Nick Bruel. Roaring Brook Press 2008 118p il $14.95

Grades: 2 3 4   **Fic**

1. Dinosaurs -- Fiction

ISBN 978-1-59643-324-3; 1-59643-324-8

Young dinosaurs Nosy, a pterodactyl, and Banty, an apatosaurus, become friends, despite their parents' prejudices

"Much of the book's humor relies on wordplay and the juxtaposition of the clever mothers next to their dim-witted husbands. Frequent black-and-white cartoon illustrations . . . enliven the text and add a light comic touch." Booklist

The **mouse** family Robinson; [by] Dick King-Smith; illustrated by Nick Bruel. Roaring Brook Press 2008 71p il $15.95

Grades: 3 4 5   **Fic**

1. Mice -- Fiction 2. Family life -- Fiction

ISBN 978-1-59643-326-7; 1-59643-326-4

LC 2008011139

After a close call with the cat who stalks the hallways, a family of wild mice, including adventurous, young Beaumont and elderly Uncle Brown, emigrates to a more mouse-friendly house down the block

"The lively, often droll narrative, divided into short chapters, and the many captivating illustrations . . . provide an accessible, engaging read filled with everyday details of imagined mouse life and appealing characters." Booklist

Kingfisher, Rupert

Madame Pamplemousse and her incredible edibles; [by] Rupert Kingfisher; illustrated by Sue Hellard. Bloomsbury Children's Books 2008 138p il $15.99

Grades: 2 3 4   **Fic**

1. Food -- Fiction 2. Restaurants -- Fiction 3. Paris (France) -- Fiction

ISBN 978-1-59990-306-4; 1-59990-306-7

LC 2008-10409

Forced to work in her unpleasant uncle's horrible restaurant, a Parisian girl finds comfort and companionship in a shop nearby that sells otherworldly foods prepared by a mysterious cook and her cat

"Kingfisher writes in whimsical, humorous prose, creating vivid scenarios and intriguing characters. . . . This droll title is sprinkled with fanciful line drawings and topped with a moral about the magical power and rewards of following one's heart." Booklist

Kinney, Jeff

★ **Diary** of a wimpy kid: Greg Heffley's journal. Amulet Books 2007 217p pa $14.95

Grades: 5 6 7 8   **Fic**

1. School stories 2. Friendship -- Fiction

ISBN 978-0-8109-9313-6 pa; 0-8109-9313-9 pa

LC 2006-31847

Greg records his sixth grade experiences in a middle school where he and his best friend, Rowley, undersized weaklings amid boys who need to shave twice daily, hope just to survive, but when Rowley grows more popular, Greg must take drastic measures to save their friendship

"Kinney's background as a cartoonist is apparent in this hybrid book that falls somewhere between traditional prose and graphic novel. . . . The pace moves quickly. The first of three installments, it is an excellent choice for reluctant readers, but more experienced readers will also find much to enjoy and relate to." SLJ

Other titles in this series are:

Rodrick rules (2008)

The last straw (2009)

Dog days (2009)

The ugly truth (2010)

Cabin fever (2011)

The third wheel (2012)

Hard luck (2013)

The long haul (2014)

Old school (2015)

Double down (2016)

Diary of a wimpy kid; hard luck. by Jeff Kinney. Harry N Abrams Inc 2013 217 p. (hardback) $13.95

Grades: 5 6 7 8   **Fic**

1. School stories 2. Chance -- Fiction 3. Friendship -- Fiction 4. Luck -- Fiction 5. Humorous stories 6. Diaries -- Fiction 7. Schools -- Fiction 8. Middle schools -- Fiction

ISBN 1419711326; 9781419711329

LC 2013033173

In this book by Jeff Kinney, "Greg Heffley's on a losing streak. His best friend, Rowley Jefferson, has ditched him, and finding new friends in middle school is proving to be a tough task. To change his fortunes, Greg decides to take a leap of faith and turn his decisions over to chance. Will a roll of the dice turn things around, or is Greg's life destined to be just another hard-luck story?" (Publisher's note)

"Greg Heffley's eighth adventure (but who's counting?) centers on his relationship with his best friend, Rowley—more specifically, the demise of that relationship when Rowley gets a girlfriend... As ever, Kinney strikes his comic target in the bull's-eye, exaggerating the trials of adolescence just enough to make them real while deftly exposing the insecurities behind Greg's bravado with his super, simple drawings. Will Greg and Rowley make up? Either way, devotees need not worry; there is plenty more angst in store." (Booklist)

Hard luck

Diary of a wimpy kid: dog days. Amulet Books 2009 224p

Grades: 5 6 7 8   **Fic**

1. Summer -- Fiction 2. Vacations -- Fiction
ISBN 0810983915; 9780810983915

LC 2009024953

In the of middle-schooler Greg Heffley, he records his attempts to spend his summer vacation sensibly indoors playing video games and watching television, despite his mother's other ideas.

"Kinney's gift for telling, pitch-perfect details in both his writing and art remains." Publ Wkly

Diary of a wimpy kid: Rodrick rules. Amulet Books 2008 216p il $12.95

Grades: 5 6 7 8   **Fic**

1. School stories 2. Family life -- Fiction
ISBN 978-0-8109-9473-7; 0-8109-9473-9

LC 2007-32296

Companion volume to: Diary of a wimpy kid: Greg Heffley's journal (2007)

Greg Heffley tells about his summer vacation and his attempts to steer clear of trouble when he returns to middle school and tries to keep his older brother Rodrick from telling everyone about Greg's most humiliating experience of the summer.

"Once again diarist Greg chronicles a hilarious litany of problems. . . . As before, he peppers his journal entries with his own cartoons. . . . He comes across as a real kid, and his story is one that will appeal to all those real kids who feel just like him." Booklist

Diary of a wimpy kid: the last straw. Amulet Books 2009 217p il $12.95

Grades: 5 6 7 8   **Fic**

1. School stories 2. Family life -- Fiction
ISBN 978-0-8109-7068-7; 0-8109-7068-6

LC 2008060022

Middle-schooler Greg Heffley nimbly sidesteps his father's attempts to change Greg's wimpy ways until his father threatens to send him to military school.

"Kinney's spot-on humor and winning formula of deadpan text set against cartoons are back in full force." Publ Wkly

The **third** wheel; Jeff Kinney. Amulet Books 2012 217 p. (Diary of a wimpy kid) $13.95; $13.95

Grades: 5 6 7 8   **Fic**

1. Dance -- Fiction 2. School stories -- Fiction 3. Humorous fiction -- Fiction
ISBN 1419705849; 9781419705847

This children's story, by Jeff Kinney, is book 7 in the "Diary of a Wimpy Kid" series. "A dance at Greg's middle school has everyone scrambling to find a partner, and Greg is determined not to be left by the wayside. So he concocts a desperate plan to find someone . . . to go with on the big night. But Greg's schemes go hilariously awry, and his only option is to attend the dance with his best friend, Rowley Jefferson, and a female classmate as a 'group of friends.'" (Publisher's note)

Kinsey-Warnock, Natalie

True colors; by Natalie Kinsey-Warnock. Alfred A. Knopf Books for Young Readers 2012 242 p. (hard cover) $15.99

Grades: 4 5 6 7   **Fic**

1. Absent mothers -- Fiction 2. Orphans -- Fiction 3. Abandoned children -- Fiction 4. Identity (Psychology) -- Fiction 5. Identity -- Fiction 6. Foundlings -- Fiction 7. Farm life -- Vermont -- Fiction 8. People with mental disabilities -- Fiction 9. Vermont -- History

-- 20th century -- Fiction
ISBN 0375860991; 9780375854538; 9780375860997; 9780375897061; 9780375960994

LC 2011037863

This book by Natalie Kinsey-Warnock "tells the story of one girl's journey to find the mother she never had, set against the period backdrop of a small farming town in 1950s Vermont. For her entire life, 10-year-old Blue has never known her mother. . . . Over the course of one summer, she resolves to finally find out who she is. . . . Her search leads her down a road of self-discovery that will change her life forever." (Publisher's note)

Kirby, Matthew J.

★ The **clockwork** three. Scholastic Press 2010 391p $17.99

Grades: 5 6 7 8   **Fic**

1. Fantasy fiction 2. Friendship -- Fiction 3. Clocks and watches -- Fiction
ISBN 978-0-545-20337-1; 0-545-20337-6

LC 2009-37879

As mysterious circumstances bring Giuseppe, Frederick, and Hannah together, their lives soon interlock like the turning gears in a clock and they realize that each one holds a key to solving the others' mysteries

This is a "riveting historical fantasy. . . . Kirby has assembled all the ingredients for a rousing adventure, which he delivers with rich, transporting prose." Publ Wkly

Icefall. Scholastic Press 2011 325p $17.99

Grades: 5 6 7 8   **Fic**

1. Fantasy fiction 2. Ice -- Fiction 3. Winter -- Fiction 4. Storytelling -- Fiction
ISBN 978-0-545-27424-1; 0-545-27424-9

LC 2011000890

"Kirby turns in a claustrophobic, thought-provoking coming-of-age adventure that shows a young woman growing into her own, while demonstrating the power of myth and legend. Kirby's attention to detail and stark descriptions make this an effective mood piece." Publ Wkly

Klages, Ellen

★ The **green** glass sea. Viking 2006 321p $16.99; pa $7.99

Grades: 5 6 7 8   **Fic**

1. New Mexico -- Fiction 2. Scientists -- Fiction 3. Atomic bomb -- Fiction 4. World War, 1939-1945 -- Fiction
ISBN 0-670-06134-4; 0-14-241149-3 pa

It is 1943, and 11-year-old Dewey Kerrigan is traveling west on a train to live with her scientist father—but no one will tell her exactly where he is. When she reaches Los Alamos, New Mexico, she learns why: he's working on a top secret government program.

"Many readers will know as little about the true nature of the project as the girls do, so the gradual revelation of facts is especially effective, while those who already know about Los Alamos's historical significance will experience the story in a different, but equally powerful, way." SLJ

Followed by: White sands, red menace (2008)

White sands, red menace. Viking 2008 337p $16.99

Grades: 5 6 7 8   **Fic**

1. Cold war -- Fiction 2. New Mexico -- Fiction 3. Scientists -- Fiction 4. Atomic bomb -- Fiction
ISBN 978-0-670-06235-5; 0-670-06235-9

Sequel to: The green glass sea (2006)

"The groundbreaking science is part of daily life for the smart techno-teens, and the adult characters are as compelling as the kids. . . . Along with . . . global issues, Klages' compelling story explores personal relationships and what it means to be a family." Booklist

Klass, David

★ **Stuck** on Earth. Farrar Straus & Giroux 2010 227p $16.99
Grades: 4 5 6 7 **Fic**

1. Science fiction 2. Bullies -- Fiction 3. Extraterrestrial beings -- Fiction

ISBN 978-0-374-39951-1; 0-374-39951-4

LC 2008--48133

On a secret mission to evaluate whether the human race should be annihilated, a space alien inhabits the body of a bullied fourteen-year-old boy.

"Klass's . . . thoughtful, often wrenching book offers plenty to think about, from what's really going on in Tom's head to questions about human responsibility to the planet and each other. It takes 'alienation' to a whole new level." Publ Wkly

Klimo, Kate

The **dragon** in the driveway; with illustrations by John Shroades. Random House Childrens Books 2009 169p (Dragon keepers) $14.99; lib bdg $17.99
Grades: 3 4 5 **Fic**

1. Magic -- Fiction 2. Cousins -- Fiction 3. Dragons -- Fiction
ISBN 978-0-375-85589-4; 0-375-85589-0; 978-0-375-95589-1 lib bdg; 0-375-95589-5 lib bdg

LC 2008034050

Cousins Jesse and Daisy, along with their pet dragon, continue their battle against the evil scientist who has plans to destroy the forest in order to find the magical golden ax that is buried there.

The "plot develops at a fast pace that involves rescuing another of the saint's victims, the hobgoblin queen, by finding the Golden Pickax. Enticing headings and black-and-white illustrations introduce each of the 10 chapters." SLJ

The **dragon** in the library; with illustrations by John Shroades. Random House 2010 218p il (Dragon keepers) $15.99
Grades: 3 4 5 **Fic**

1. Magic -- Fiction 2. Cousins -- Fiction 3. Dragons -- Fiction 4. Libraries -- Fiction
ISBN 978-0-375-85591-7; 0-375-85591-2

LC 2009016592

Dragon Keepers Jesse and Daisy, along with their dragon, Emmy, must save their friend Professor Andersson from an evil witch, who happens to be St. George the Dragon Slayer's girlfriend.

"Incorporating suspense, magic, and humor, the trio's continuing adventures will surely entertain series readers." Booklist

The **dragon** in the sock drawer; with illustrations by John Schroades. Random House Childrens Books 2008 159p il (Dragon keepers) $14.99; lib bdg $17.99
Grades: 3 4 5 **Fic**

1. Eggs -- Fiction 2. Cousins -- Fiction 3. Dragons -- Fiction
ISBN 978-0-375-85587-0; 0-375-85587-4; 978-0-375-95587-7 lib bdg; 0-375-95587-9 lib bdg

LC 2007-42306

Cousins Jesse and Daisy always knew they would have a magical adventure, but they are not prepared when the "thunder egg" Jesse has found turns out to be a dragon egg that is about to hatch

"Illustrated with small black-and-white drawings to introduce each of the 11 chapters, this novel, with its unique and modern twists, is a great addition to the dragon genre for younger readers." SLJ

Other titles in this series are:

The dragon in the driveway (2009)
The dragon in the library (2010)
The dragon in the volcano (2011)

The **dragon** in the volcano; with illustrations by John Shroades. Random House 2011 231p il (Dragon keepers) $15.99; lib bdg $18.99
Grades: 3 4 5 **Fic**

1. Magic -- Fiction 2. Cousins -- Fiction 3. Dragons -- Fiction 4. Volcanoes -- Fiction 5. Lost and found possessions -- Fiction
ISBN 978-0-375-86692-0; 0-375-86692-2; 978-0-375-96692-7 lib bdg; 0-375-96692-7 lib bdg; 978-0-375-89723-8 e-book

LC 2010014970

Emmy the dragon is maturing and growing too large—and bored—for her quarters, but when she disappears her Keepers, cousins Jesse and Daisy, follow her trail to the Fiery Realm in hopes of bringing her home.

Kline, Suzy

★ **Horrible** Harry in room 2B; pictures by Frank Remkiewicz. Viking Kestrel 1988 56p il hardcover o.p. pa $3.99
Grades: 2 3 4 **Fic**

1. School stories
ISBN 0-14-038552-5 pa

LC 88-14204

Harry "is the devilish second grader who plays pranks and gets into mischief but can still end up a good friend. In a series of brief scenes, children meet Harry as he shows a garter snake to Song Lee and later ends up being a snake himself for Halloween. His trick to make scary people out of pencil stubs backfires when no one is scared, and his budding romance with Song Lee goes nowhere on the trip to the aquarium. . . . This story should prove to be popular with those just starting chapter books." SLJ

Other titles about Horrible Harry and Song Lee are:

Horrible Harry and the ant invasion (1989)
Horrible Harry and the Christmas surprise (1991)
Horrible Harry and the dragon war (2002)
Horrible Harry and the Drop of Doom (1998)
Horrible Harry and the dungeon (1996)
Horrible Harry and the goog (2005)
Horrible Harry and the green slime (1989)
Horrible Harry and the holidaze (2003)
Horrible Harry and the June box (2011)
Horrible Harry and the kickball wedding (1992)
Horrible Harry and the locked closet (2004)
Horrible Harry and the missing diamond (2013)
Horrible Harry and the mud gremlins (2003)
Horrible Harry and the purple people (1997)
Horrible Harry and the scarlet scissors (2012)
Horrible Harry and the secret treasure (2011)
Horrible Harry and the stolen cookie (2013)
Horrible Harry and the triple revenge (2006)
Horrible Harry at Halloween (2000)
Horrible Harry bugs the three bears (2008)
Horrible Harry goes to the moon (2000)
Horrible Harry moves up to third grade (1998)
Horrible Harry takes the cake (2006)
Horrible Harry's secret (1990)
Song Lee and Leech Man (1995)
Song Lee and the hamster hunt (1994)
Song Lee and the ¿I hate you¿ notes (1999)
Song Lee in room 2B (1993)

Song Lee and the I hate you notes; pictures by Frank Remkiewicz. Viking 1999 50p il hardcover o.p. pa $3.99
Grades: 2 3 4 **Fic**

1. School stories
ISBN 0-670-87887-1; 0-14-130303-4 pa

LC 98-41376

Song Lee is upset when she receives hateful notes in class, but she finds an appropriate and positive way to deal with them

"Kline has her finger on the pulse of third graders, and realistically portrays their social interactions and problem-solving skills. The language and perceptions of Doug, the narrator, are right on target. Remkiewicz's black-and-white drawings accentuate the full range of the characters emotions." SLJ

Song Lee and the Leech Man; pictures by Frank Remkiewicz. Viking 1995 53p il hardcover o.p. pa $3.99
Grades: 2 3 4   **Fic**
   1. School stories 2. Korean Americans -- Fiction
   ISBN 0-670-85848-X; 0-14-037255-5 pa
                      LC 94-39231

Harry plots revenge against Sidney, the class tattletale, when Miss Mackle's second graders go on a field trip to the pond

"Frank Remkiewicz's cartoonlike black-ink sketches are well suited to the comic story. . . . Independent readers will enjoy this chapter book, which is written in short, simple, chatty sentences." Booklist

Song Lee in Room 2B; pictures by Frank Remkiewicz. Viking 1993 56p il hardcover o.p. pa $3.99
Grades: 2 3 4   **Fic**
   1. School stories 2. Korean Americans -- Fiction
   ISBN 0-670-84772-0; 0-14-130408-1 pa
                      LC 92-41523

Spring becomes a memorable time for Miss Mackle's second-grade classroom because of the antics of Horrible Harry and the special insights of shy Song Lee

"The school setting has great appeal, and the familiar 2B kids deliver lots of funny moments." Booklist

Klise, Kate

Dying to meet you; illustrated by M. Sarah Klise. Harcourt 2009 147p il (43 Old Cemetery Road) $15
Grades: 3 4 5 6   **Fic**
   1. Ghost stories 2. Authors -- Fiction 3. Letters -- Fiction
   ISBN 978-0-15-205727-5; 0-15-205727-7
                      LC 2007-28534

In this story told mostly through letters, children's book author, I. B. Grumply, gets more than he bargained for when he rents a quiet place to write for the summer

"This first title in a new series will appeal to readers, especially reluctant ones, as it moves quickly and leaves its audience eager for book two, which is announced in this ghastly and fun tale." SLJ

Other titles in this series are:
Over my dead body (2009)
Till death do us bark (2011)

The **Greatest** Star on Earth; Kate Klise; illustrated by M. Sarah Klise. Algonquin Young Readers 2014 144 p. (Three-ring rascals) $15.95
Grades: 2 3 4 5   **Fic**
   1. Mice -- Fiction 2. Circus -- Fiction 3. Contests -- Fiction 4. Authorship -- Fiction
   ISBN 1616202459; 9781616202453
                      LC 2013044900

Written by Kate Klise and illustrated by M. Sarah Klise, this children's book, part of the Three-Ring Rascals series, describes how "Everyone knows Sir Sidney's Circus is the best in the world. But who's the star of the show? The Circus Times is having a contest to find out. Just thinking about it gives Sir Sidney a worrywart, and it's quickly clear why. Soon after he goes off to rest, the performers start thinking too

much about winning the trophy and not enough about putting on a good show." (Publisher's note)

"The performers in Sir Sidney's Circus are thrown off their game when a newspaper proposes a contest to determine the best performer. Pun- and gag-filled narration, gentle messaging about teamwork and kindness, and frequent expressive spot art enrich the quirky, accessible story. Characters' struggles to live up to Sir Sidney's expectations are understatedly complex and will resonate with readers." Horn Book

★ **Grounded**. Feiwel and Friends 2010 196p $16.99
Grades: 4 5 6 7   **Fic**
   1. Death -- Fiction 2. Missouri -- Fiction 3. Bereavement -- Fiction 4. Swindlers and swindling -- Fiction
   ISBN 978-0-312-57039-2; 0-312-57039-2
                      LC 2010013008

After her father, brother, and sister are killed in a plane crash, twelve-year-old Daralynn's life in tiny Digginsville, Missouri, proceeds as her mother turns angry and embittered, her grandmother becomes senile, and her flamboyant aunt continues to run the Summer Sunset Retirement Home for Distinguished Gentlemen, while being courted by the owner of the town's new crematorium.

"Dark humor melds with genuine pathos in Klise's moving novel. . . . This quiet story illuminates and celebrates the human need for connection beyond the grave." Booklist

Homesick; Kate Klise. 1st ed. Feiwel and Friends 2012 192 p. (hardcover) $16.99
Grades: 4 5 6 7 8   **Fic**
   1. Divorce -- Fiction 2. Family life -- Fiction
   ISBN 1250008425; 9781250008428

In this book by Kate Klise, "Benny's parents are splitting up. . . . Benny's dad has always liked clutter, but now, he begins hoarding everything. . . . As his house grows more cluttered and his father grows more distant, Benny tries to sort out whether he can change anything at all. Meanwhile, a local teacher enters their quiet Missouri town in America's Most Charming Small Town contest, and the pressure is on to clean up the area, especially Benny's ramshackle of a house." (Publisher's note)

Over my dead body; illustrated by M. Sarah Klise. Harcourt 2009 116p il (43 Old Cemetery Road) $15
Grades: 3 4 5 6   **Fic**
   1. Ghost stories 2. Authors -- Fiction 3. Letters -- Fiction 4. Halloween -- Fiction 5. Books and reading -- Fiction
   ISBN 978-0-15-205734-3; 0-15-205734-X
                      LC 2009007979

In this story told mostly through letters, busybody Dick Tater tries to ban Halloween and ghost stories, as well as to break up the popular writing team of I. B. Grumply, ghost Olive C. Spence, and eleven-year-old illustrator Seymour Hope.

"The short, graphic-heavy text and broad humor will appeal to middle grade readers." SLJ

Regarding the bathrooms; a privy to the past. illustrated by M. Sarah Klise. Harcourt 2006 140p il $15
Grades: 4 5 6 7   **Fic**
   1. School stories
   ISBN 978-0-15-205164-8; 0-15-205164-3
                      LC 2005016813

In this novel told through letters, newspaper articles, and police reports, a middle school principal's bathroom renovation project leads to the discovery of stolen Roman antiquities.

"Puns abound, and there are a few bathroom jokes, though nothing really crass enough to compromise an entertaining novel that celebrates community and history." Booklist

Regarding the bees; a lesson, in letters, on honey, dating, and other sticky subjects. [by] Kate Klise; illustrated by M. Sarah Klise. Harcourt 2007 122p $15

Grades: 4 5 6 7   Fic
    1. School stories
    ISBN 978-0-15-205711-4

                                                    LC 2006017716
While corresponding with their globetrotting substitute teacher, the seventh graders at Geyser Creek Middle School nervously prepare for an important standardized test, navigate the tricky waters of first crushes, and try to bring their bee mascot to a local spelling competition.

"Fans of the series will appreciate this installment, reluctant readers will be drawn to the format, and more advanced readers will appreciate the wordplay and puns sprinkled throughout." SLJ

Regarding the fountain; illustrations by M. Sarah Klise. Avon Bks. 1998 138p $16.99; pa $5.99

Grades: 4 5 6 7   Fic
    1. School stories
    ISBN 0-380-97538-6; 978-0-380-97538-9; 0-380-79347-4 pa; 978-0-380-79347-1 pa

                                                       LC 97-18205
When the principal asks a fifth-grader to write a letter regarding the purchase of a new drinking fountain for Geyser Creek Middle School, he finds that all sorts of chaos results

"Fresh, funny, and a delight to read." SLJ

Regarding the sink; where, oh where, did Waters go? illustrated by M. Sarah Klise. Harcourt 2004 127p il $15

Grades: 4 5 6 7   Fic
    1. School stories
    ISBN 0-15-205019-1

                                                    LC 2003-26560
A series of letters reveals the selection of the famous fountain designer, Florence Waters, to design a new sink for the Geyser Creek Middle School cafeteria, her subsequent disappearance, and the efforts of a class of sixth-graders to find her

"Piecing the story and clues together is satisfying. Introduce this book to savvy readers who are ready for the jump to a clever, unconventional reading experience." SLJ

Other titles in this series are:

Regarding the bathrooms (2006)
Regarding the bees (2007)
Regarding the fountain (1998)
Regarding the trees (2005)

Regarding the trees; a splintered saga rooted in secrets. illustrated by M. Sarah Klise. Harcourt 2005 143p il $15

Grades: 4 5 6 7   Fic
    1. School stories 2. Trees -- Fiction
    ISBN 0-15-205163-5

In this story told primarily through letters, Principal Russ wants the Geyser Creek Middle School trees to be trimmed before his administrative evaluation, but the project is interrupted by a town gender war, dueling chefs, student tree protests, and a surprise wedding.

The **show** must go on! Kate Klise; illustrated by M. Sarah Klise. Algonquin Young Readers 2013 160 p. (Three-ring rascals) $15.95

Grades: 2 3 4 5   Fic
    1. Animals -- Fiction 2. Circus -- Fiction
    ISBN 1616202440; 9781616202446

                                                    LC 2013008940
In this book, "elderly Sir Sidney loves his circus, and he pampers his animals and performers, as well as the two mice and crow who are part of its extended family. When he decides to take some time off, he hires brash Barnabas Brambles, who promises to care for the circus with the same doting attention as Sir Sidney. As soon as the kindhearted owner leaves, though, Barnabas" turns out to be greedy and self-serving. "Things look grim, but the circus folk hold onto their humor." (Publishers Weekly)

Till death do us bark; written by Kate Klise; illustrated by M. Sarah Klise. Harcourt Children's Books 2011 144p il (43 Old Cemetery Road) $15.99

Grades: 3 4 5 6   Fic
    1. Ghost stories 2. Dogs -- Fiction 3. Coins -- Fiction 4. Authors -- Fiction 5. Letters -- Fiction 6. Inheritance and succession -- Fiction
    ISBN 978-0-547-40036-5; 0-547-40036-5

                                                    LC 2010009065
In this story told mostly through letters, Noah Breth's feuding children come to Ghastly, Illinois, to follow a trail of limericks to their inheritance, while Seymour tries to convince Iggy and Olive to let him keep Mr. Breth's dog.

"A heavily illustrated, comedic/ghostly mystery revealed in a series of letters and documents by a quirky cast whose pun-filled names are truly groanworthy." Booklist

Kluger, Jeffrey
    ★ **Freedom** stone. Philomel Books 2011 316p $16.99

Grades: 4 5 6   Fic
    1. Magic -- Fiction 2. Slavery -- Fiction 3. African Americans -- Fiction 4. United States -- History -- 1861-1865, Civil War -- Fiction
    ISBN 978-0-399-25214-3; 0-399-25214-2

                                                    LC 2010-06028
With the help of a magical stone from Africa, a thirteen-year-old slave travels to the battle of Vicksburg to clear her father's name and free her family from bondage.

Kluger "adeptly mixes drama, fantasy, romance, and history, while creating characters so determined to survive that readers can't help being drawn into their plights. In a climax that breaks with reality but that will keep readers hungry to learn the outcome, Kluger proves his storytelling prowess." Publ Wkly

Knight, Joan
    Charlotte in Giverny; by Joan MacPhail Knight; watercolor illustrations by Melissa Sweet. Chronicle Bks. 2000 un il $16.95; pa $6.95

Grades: 3 4 5   Fic
    1. France -- Fiction 2. Artists -- Fiction
    ISBN 0-8118-2383-0; 0-8118-5803-0 pa

                                                       LC 99-6878
While living in France in 1892, Charlotte, a young American girl, writes a journal of her experiences including those among the Impressionist painters at the artist colony of Giverny. Includes profiles of artists who appear in the journal and a glossary of French words

"The profuse illustrations , a mix of 1890s postcards and other memorabilia, reproductions of (mostly) impressionistic paintings by the mentioned artists, and Melissa Sweet's delicately drawn vignettes of vegetables and other items, lay an air of sunny, well-bred tranquility over the scene." Booklist

Other titles in this series are:
Charlotte in New York (2006)
Charlotte in Paris (2003)
Charlotte in London (2009)

Charlotte in London; by Joan MacPhail Knight; illustrations by Melissa Sweet. Chronicle Books 2008 un il $16.99

Grades: 3 4 5   Fic

1. Artists -- Fiction 2. Painting -- Fiction 3. London (England) -- Fiction

ISBN 978-0-8118-5635-5; 0-8118-5635-6

LC 2007024961

Charlotte, a young American girl, keeps a journal as her family leaves the artist colony of Giverny, France, in 1895 and travels to London, England, where they meet famous writers and artists and learn of the city's history.

"The text highlights both French and British culture; French phrases and historical facts are smoothly integrated within the text. Diary entries, watercolor paintings, and museum reproductions combine to create a detailed background. Featured artists' biographical information provides added depth to the period. There's much to explore in the mixed-media and watercolor art." SLJ

Charlotte in New York; by Joan MacPhail Knight; illustrated by Melissa Sweet. Chronicle Books 2006 un il $16.95

Grades: 3 4 5   Fic

1. Artists -- Fiction 2. New York (N.Y.) -- Fiction

ISBN 978-0-8118-5005-6; 0-8118-5005-6

LC 2005019613

In 1894, Charlotte records in a journal her impressions of a family trip from Giverney, France to New York, where her father's paintings will be featured in an exhibition. Includes biographical sketches of painters and reproductions of artworks.

Charlotte in Paris; by Joan MacPhail Knight; illustrations by Melissa Sweet. Chronicle Books 2003 un il $16.95

Grades: 3 4 5   Fic

1. Artists -- Fiction 2. Paris (France) -- Fiction 3. Impressionism (Art) -- Fiction

ISBN 0-8118-3766-1

LC 2002-12654

The young daughter of American artists living in Giverny, France, in 1893, records in her journal her exciting trip to Paris to attend an Impressionist art exhibition. Includes biographical sketches of the artists featured in the story.

"Reproductions of paintings, small watercolors, collages of objects Charlotte has saved, and a certain amount of French vocabulary adorn the utterly engaging text." Booklist

Knudsen, Michelle

The **dragon** of Trelian. Candlewick Press 2009 407p $16.99

Grades: 4 5 6 7   Fic

1. Fantasy fiction 2. Magic -- Fiction 3. Dragons -- Fiction 4. Princesses -- Fiction

ISBN 978-0-7636-3455-1; 0-7636-3455-7

LC 2008025378

A mage's apprentice, a princess, and a dragon combine their strength and magic to bring down a traitor and restore peace to the kingdom of Trelian.

"Knudsen does a fantastic job of creating sympathetic and realistic characters that really drive the story. The tale is adventurous and exciting with many twists and turns along the way." SLJ

Followed by: The princess of Trelian (2012)

The **princess** of Trelian; Michelle Knudsen. Candlewick Press 2012 437 p. (reinforced) $16.99

Grades: 4 5 6 7   Fic

1. Fantasy 2. Magic -- Fiction 3. Dragons -- Fiction 4. Princesses -- Fiction

ISBN 0763650625; 9780763650629

LC 2011047174

Sequel to: The dragon of Trelian (2009)

In this juvenile fantasy novel, by Michelle Knudsen, a "sequel to 'The Dragon of Trelian,' . . . Princess Meg is now heir to the throne, but her subjects are uneasy about her . . . dragon, and it only becomes worse when a neighboring king accuses the dragon of ravaging the countryside. . . . Meanwhile, Meg's best friend Calen has earned his mage's mark, but a mysterious, magical attack occurs. . . . [T]he deposed villain from the previous book is behind all the mischief." (Horn Book Magazine)

Knudson, Mike

Raymond & Graham: bases loaded; illustrated by Stacy Curtis. Viking 2010 155p il $14.99

Grades: 2 3 4   Fic

1. School stories 2. Baseball -- Fiction 3. Friendship -- Fiction 4. Mother-son relationship -- Fiction

ISBN 978-0-670-01205-3; 0-670-01205-X

LC 2009015199

Fourth grade best friends Ray and Graham try to avoid the class bully, have fun with a substitute teacher, and get the attention of the girls they like while concentrating on winning the Little League Championships.

"Filled with tame humor, a few family high jinks, and baseball plays aplenty, this story will likely appeal to young baseball fans and anyone who enjoyed Raymond and Graham Rule the School." SLJ

Raymond & Graham: cool campers; illustrated by Stacy Curtis. Viking 2010 156p $14.99

Grades: 2 3 4   Fic

1. Camps -- Fiction 2. Friendship -- Fiction

ISBN 978-0-670-01206-0; 0-670-01206-8

Best friends Raymond and Graham are determined to be the coolest kids at Camp Grizzly this summer. But soon they find themselves in a war between their patrol and a rival cabin!

Raymond and Graham rule the school; by Mike Knudson and Steve Wilkinson; illustrated by Stacy Curtis. Viking Childrens Books 2008 136p il $14.99; pa $6.99

Grades: 2 3 4   Fic

1. School stories 2. Theater -- Fiction 3. Friendship -- Fiction

ISBN 978-0-670-01101-8; 0-670-01101-0; 978-0-14-241426-2 pa; 0-14-241426-3 pa

LC 2007033350

Best friends Raymond and Graham have looked forward to being the "oldest, coolest, toughest" boys at East Millcreek Elementary School, but from the start of fourth grade everything goes wrong, from getting the scary teacher to not getting the lead in the school play

"This story is filled with nonstop action and kid-friendly humor. Done in an exaggerated cartoon style, Curtis's occasional black-and-white illustrations perfectly suit the tone of the text." SLJ

Other titles about Raymond and Graham are:
Raymond and Graham, dancing dudes (2008)
Raymond and Graham: bases loaded (2010)
Raymond and Graham: cool campers (2010)

Raymond and Graham, dancing dudes; by Mike Knudson; illustrated by Stacy Curtis. Viking 2008 136p il $14.99

Grades: 3 4 5   Fic

1. School stories 2. Friendship -- Fiction 3. Valentine's Day --

Fiction
ISBN 978-0-670-01102-5; 0-670-01102-9

LC 2008-8383

First published 2007 by Banjo Books

Fourth-grade best friends Raymond and Graham write Valentine poems, perform in a hoedown, and learn how to be men.

"Told in bright, breezy, appropriately kidlike language, and with a good number of black-and-white cartoon illustrations, [this book offers] the post-chapter book set enjoyable fare." Horn Book Guide

Another title about Raymond and Graham is:

Raymond and Graham rule the school (2008)

Konigsburg, E. L.

★ **From** the mixed-up files of Mrs. Basil E. Frankweiler. Atheneum Pubs. 1967 162p il $16; pa $9.99

Grades: 4 5 6　　　　　**Fic**

1. Metropolitan Museum of Art (New York, N.Y.) -- Fiction

ISBN 0-689-20586-4; 1-4169-4975-5 pa

Awarded the Newbery Medal, 1968

"Claudia, feeling misunderstood at home, takes her younger brother and runs away to New York where she sets up housekeeping in the Metropolitan Museum of Art, making ingenious arrangements for sleeping, bathing, and laundering. She and James also look for clues to the authenticity of an alleged Michelangelo statue, the true story of which is locked in the files of Mrs. Frankweiler, its former owner. Claudia's progress toward maturity is also a unique introduction to the Metropolitan Museum." Moorachian. What is a City?

Jennifer, Hecate, Macbeth, William McKinley, and me, Elizabeth. Atheneum Pubs. 1967 117p il $16; pa $5.99

Grades: 4 5 6　　　　　**Fic**

1. Friendship -- Fiction 2. Witchcraft -- Fiction 3. African Americans -- Fiction

ISBN 0-689-30007-7; 1-4169-3396-4 pa

A Newbery Medal honor book, 1968

"Two fifth grade girls, one of whom is the first black child in a middle-income suburb, play at being apprentice witches in this amusing and perceptive story." NY Public Libr. Black Exper in Child Books

The **mysterious** edge of the heroic world. Atheneum Books for Young Readers 2007 244p $16.99; pa $5.99

Grades: 5 6 7 8　　　　　**Fic**

1. Florida -- Fiction 2. Friendship -- Fiction 3. Art museums -- Fiction

ISBN 978-1-4169-4972-5; 1-4169-4972-0; 978-1-4169-5353-1 pa; 1-4169-5353-1 pa

"This humorous, poignant, tragic, and mysterious story has intertwining plots that peel away like the layers of an onion." SLJ

A **proud** taste for scarlet and miniver. Atheneum Pubs. 1973 201p il $18.95; pa $5.99

Grades: 5 6 7 8　　　　　**Fic**

1. Queens

ISBN 0-689-30111-1; 0-689-84624-X pa

This is an historical novel about the 12th century queen, Eleanor of Aquitaine, wife of kings of France and England and mother of King Richard the Lion Hearted and King John. Impatiently awaiting the arrival of her second husband, King Henry II, in heaven, she recalls her life with the aid of some contemporaries

The author "has succeeded in making history amusing as well as interesting. . . . The characterization is superb. . . . The black-and-white drawings are skillfully as well as appropriately modeled upon medi-

eval manuscript illuminations and add their share of joy to the book." Horn Book

Up from Jericho Tel. Atheneum Pubs. 1986 178p hardcover o.p. pa $4.99

Grades: 5 6 7 8　　　　　**Fic**

1. Mystery fiction 2. Actors -- Fiction

ISBN 0-689-31194-X; 0-689-82332-0 pa

LC 85-20061

"Konigsburg always provides fresh ideas, tart wit and humor, and memorable characters. As for style, she is a natural and gifted storyteller. . . . This is a lively, clever, and very funny book." Bull Cent Child Books

★ The **view** from Saturday. Atheneum Bks. for Young Readers 1996 163p $16.95; pa $5.99

Grades: 4 5 6 7　　　　　**Fic**

1. School stories 2. Friendship -- Fiction 3. People with physical disabilities -- Fiction

ISBN 0-689-80993-X; 0-689-81721-5 pa

LC 95-52624

Awarded the Newbery Medal, 1997

Four students, with their own individual stories, develop a special bond and attract the attention of their teacher, a paraplegic, who choses them to represent their sixth-grade class in the Academic Bowl competition

"Glowing with humor and dusted with magic. . . . Wrought with deep compassion and a keen sense of balance." Publ Wkly

Koppe, Susanne

The **Nutcracker**; [by] E. T. A. Hoffmann; illustrated by Lisbeth Zwerger; retold by Susanne Koppe; translated from the German by Anthea Bell; North-South Books 2004 un il $15.95; lib bdg $16.50

Grades: 3 4 5　　　　　**Fic**

1. Fairy tales 2. Christmas -- Fiction

ISBN 0-7358-1733-2; 0-7358-1734-0 lib bdg

In this retelling of the original 1816 German story, Godfather Drosselmeier gives young Marie a nutcracker for Christmas, and she finds herself in a magical realm where she saves a boy from an evil curse

"This version features somewhat surreal, almost theatrically presented tableaux, delicately and darkly rendered in pen and ink and watercolor. . . . Koppe's retelling is . . . accessible and detailed." SLJ

Korman, Gordon

Framed. Scholastic Press 2011 234p $16.99

Grades: 3 4 5 6　　　　　**Fic**

1. School stories 2. Adventure fiction 3. Theft -- Fiction 4. Friendship -- Fiction

ISBN 978-0-545-17849-5; 0-545-17849-5

LC 2010002583

Sequel to: Zoobreak (2009)

Griffin Bing is in big trouble when a Super Bowl ring disappears from his middle school's display case, replaced by Griffin's retainer, and the more he and his friends investigate, the worse his situation becomes.

"This mystery will draw readers in with its quickly developing plot that combines unconventional characters and situations with believable dialogue and plot twists." SLJ

Masterminds; Gordon Korman. Balzer + Bray 2015 336 p. (hardback) $16.99

Grades: 4 5 6　　　　　**Fic**

1. Criminals -- Fiction 2. Cloning -- Fiction 3. Experiments -- Fiction

ISBN 0062299964; 9780062299963

LC 2014026839

In this book by Gordon Korman, "when 13-year-old Eli Frieden attempts to bike past the town limits for the first time, he is struck with paralyzing nausea and pain that makes him wonder if Serenity is less of a paradise and more of a prison." He and his friends "decide to investigate. They find that Serenity, which holds honesty and integrity above all else, is built on a lie." (Kirkus Reviews)

"Tiny Serenity, New Mexico, is idyllic as it gets—everyone has a job and a home, the kids are well behaved, and the genial community spirit is intoxicating. Sure, it's boring, and it's suspicious that a town of 185 people has its own helicopter-equipped security force, but 13-year-old Eli is content... The compelling, twisty mystery has a truly gratifying payoff, and the emotional depth of the characters, not to mention the steadily building pace, will keep readers engaged to the final page, which happily lays the groundwork for a sequel. " Booklist

Other titles in this series are:
Criminal destiny (2016)
Payback (2017)

No more dead dogs. Hyperion Bks. for Children 2000 180p $15.99; pa $5.99
Grades: 5 6 7 8　　　　　　　　　　　　　　　**Fic**
  1. School stories 2. Theater -- Fiction
  ISBN 0-7868-0531-5; 0-7868-1601-5 pa
　　　　　　　　　　　　　　　　　　LC 00-24313
"Humor abounds here, but underlying is the true angst of the middle school student." Voice Youth Advocates

Swindle; Gordan Korman. Scholastic Press 2008 252p (Swindle)
Grades: 4 5 6　　　　　　　　　　　　　　　**Fic**
  1. Baseball cards -- Fiction 2. Swindlers and swindling -- Fiction
  ISBN 0-439-90344-0; 0-439-90345-9 pa; 978-0-439-90344-8; 978-0-439-90345-5 pa
　　　　　　　　　　　　　　　　　LC 2007-17225
After unscrupulous collector S. Wendell Palomino cons him out of a valuable baseball card, sixth-grader Griffin Bing puts together a band of misfits to break into Palomino's store and steal the card back, planning to use the money to finance his father's failing invention, the SmartPick fruit picker. "Grades four to six." (Bull Cent Child Books)

"The plot is the main attraction, and its clever intricacies—silly, deceptively predictable, and seasoned with the occasional unexpected twist—do not disappoint." Booklist

Other titles in this series are:
Zoobreak (2009)
Framed (2010)
Showoff (2012)
Hideout (2013)
Jackpot (2014)
Unleashed (2015)
Jingle (2016)

Zoobreak. Scholastic Press 2009 230p $16.99; pa $6.99
Grades: 3 4 5 6　　　　　　　　　　　　　　**Fic**
  1. Adventure fiction 2. Zoos -- Fiction 3. Theft -- Fiction 4. Long Island (N.Y.) -- Fiction 5. Lost and found possessions -- Fiction
  ISBN 978-0-545-12499-7; 0-545-12499-9; 978-0-545-12500-0 pa; 0-545-12500-6 pa
　　　　　　　　　　　　　　　　　LC 2009015456
Sequel to: Swindle (2008)
After a class trip to a floating zoo where animals are mistreated and Savannah's missing pet monkey is found in a cage, Long Island sixth-grader Griffin Bing and his band of misfits plan a rescue.

"Both children and adults will find the story fast moving and enjoyable. The often-unpredictable plot is interesting, full of humor, and good fun." Voice Youth Advocates

Kornblatt, Marc
Izzy's place. Margaret K. McElderry Bks. 2003 118p $16.95
Grades: 4 5 6　　　　　　　　　　　　　　　**Fic**
  1. Death -- Fiction
  ISBN 0-689-84639-8
　　　　　　　　　　　　　　　　　LC 2002-6185
While spending the summer at his grandmother's Indiana home, ten-year-old Henry Stone gets help from a new friend in coping with the recent death of his grandfather and the possibility of his parents getting divorced

"In straightforward language, Kornblatt writes a realistic, affecting account of the challenges of coming to terms with grief and family difficulties and the process of acceptance and healing." Booklist

Krensky, Stephen
Dangerous crossing; the revolutionary voyage of John Quincy Adams. by Stephen Krensky; illustrated by Greg Harlin. Dutton Children's Books 2005 un il $16.99
Grades: 2 3 4　　　　　　　　　　　　　　　**Fic**
  1. Presidents 2. Vice-presidents 3. Senators 4. Members of Congress 5. Secretaries of state 6. Voyages and travels -- Fiction 7. United States -- History -- 1775-1783, Revolution -- Fiction
  ISBN 0-525-46966-4
　　　　　　　　　　　　　　　　　LC 2003-40852
In 1778, ten-year-old Johnny Adams and his father make a dangerous midwinter voyage from Massachusetts to Paris in hopes of gaining support for the colonies during the American Revolution

"Harlin's richly atmospheric paintings dramatize scene after scene with subtle hues and lighting effects. . . . The story offers a stirring account of life aboard ship, spiced with details from the voyage. An appended author's note comments on the story's source and the illustrious careers of the two Adamses." Booklist

Kress, Adrienne
The **door** in the alley; Adrienne Kress; illustrated by Matthew C. Rockefeller. Delacorte Press 2017 320 p. illustrations (Explorers) (hc) $16.99
Grades: 4 5 6　　　　　　　　　　　　　　**Fic**
  1. Boys -- Fiction 2. Secret societies -- Fiction 3. Adventure and adventurers -- Fiction
  ISBN 9781101940051; 9781101940068
　　　　　　　　　　　　　　　　　LC 2016013950
This first book in The Explorers series, by Adrienne Kress, "starts when a very uninquisitive boy stumbles upon a very mysterious society. After that, there is danger and adventure; there are missing persons, hired thugs, a hidden box, a lost map, and famous explorers; and there is a girl looking for help that only uninquisitive boys can offer." (Publisher's note)

Krieg, Jim
★ **Griff** Carver, hallway patrol. Razorbill 2010 224p $15.99
Grades: 4 5 6 7　　　　　　　　　　　　　　**Fic**
  1. School stories 2. Counterfeits and counterfeiting -- Fiction
  ISBN 978-1-59514-276-4; 1-59514-276-2
　　　　　　　　　　　　　　　　　LC 2009-32553
Legendary Griff Carver joins the Rampart Middle School Hallway Patrol and, with the help of his friend Tommy, Griff solves the case of counterfeit hall passes.

"With comically over-the-top cop lingo . . . Griff and Tommy tell their stories through incident reports and interviews, adding drama and humor to the most mundane aspects of school. . . . Krieg will keep readers chuckling through the hilarious but action-packed showdown." Publ Wkly

Krishnaswami, Uma

The **Girl** of the Wish Garden; A Thumbelina Story. Pgw 2013 32 p. (hardcover) $17.95

Grades: K 1 2   **Fic**

1. Fairy tales 2. Picture books for children

ISBN 155498324X; 9781554983247

In this picture book, the "thumb-size Lina begins her journey when she is captured by a giant frog and then the story loosely follows the path of the original [Hans Christian Andersen] tale. She is swept along at the mercy of the winds and follows the tunes of the birds, and each new encounter is foreshadowed by her sung cries for help." (School Library Journal)

★ The **grand** plan to fix everything; [illustrations by Abigail Halpin] Atheneum Books for Young Readers 2011 224p il $16.99

Grades: 4 5 6 7   **Fic**

1. India -- Fiction 2. Actors -- Fiction 3. Moving -- Fiction 4. Friendship -- Fiction 5. East Indian Americans -- Fiction

ISBN 978-1-4169-9589-0; 1-4169-9589-7

LC 2010035145

Eleven-year-old Dini loves movies, and so when she learns that her family is moving to India for two years, her devastation over leaving her best friend in Maryland is tempered by the possibility of meeting her favorite actress, Dolly Singh.

"An out-of-the-ordinary setting, a distinctive middle-grade character with an unusual passion, and the pace of a lively Bollywood 'fillum' make this novel a delight." Publ Wkly

Krull, Kathleen

Fartiste; [by] Kathleen Krull and Paul Brewer; illustrated by Boris Kulikov. Simon & Schuster Books for Young Readers 2008 un il $16.99

Grades: 3 4 5   **Fic**

1. Entertainers 2. Stories in rhyme 3. Entertainers -- Fiction 4. Paris (France) -- Fiction

ISBN 978-1-4169-2828-7; 1-4169-2828-6

LC 2007-37526

In nineteenth-century France, Joseph Pujol, a little boy who can control his farts, grows up to become Le Petomaine, making audiences laugh at the Moulin Rouge in Paris with his animal noises, songs, and other sounds. Includes facts about Joseph Pujol and life in turn-of-the-century Paris.

"Written in well-rhymed couplets, this gleefully tasteless tale reads easily. Kulikov's illustrations allude to the age of vaudevillian stage performance, painted playbills, and fire-hazard footlights that bronzed everything nearest them in golden warmth." SLJ

Krumgold, Joseph

Onion John; illustrated by Symeon Shimin. Crowell 1959 248p il lib bdg $15.89; pa $5.95

Grades: 5 6 7 8   **Fic**

1. Friendship -- Fiction

ISBN 0-690-04698-7 lib bdg; 0-06-440144-8 pa

Awarded the Newbery Medal, 1960

"The writing has dignity and strength. There is conflict, drama, and excellent character portrayal." SLJ

Kuhlman, Evan

Great ball of light; Evan Kuhlman; illustrated by Jeremy Holmes. Atheneum Books for Young Readers 2015 293 p. (hardcover) $16.99

Grades: 4 5 6   **Fic**

1. Family life -- Fiction 2. Dead -- Fiction 3. Twins -- Fiction 4.

Brothers and sisters -- Fiction

ISBN 1416964614; 9781416964612; 9781416964629

LC 2013049286

In this juvenile story, by Evan Kuhlman and illustrated by Jeremy Holmes, "when twin brother and sister Fenton and Fiona find a ball of light in their backyard, things get . . . weird. Especially when Fenton figures out it can bring things back to life. . . . Namely, their grandfather. Because they really do miss him. . . . But be warned: bringing back things from the dead gets a little more complicated when they stick around." (Publisher's note)

"What if you had the power to bring plants, animals, even humans back to life? Thirteen-year-old Fiona North and her twin brother Fenton are forced to confront this question when they discover a great ball of light during a storm . . . The descriptions of the undead are gross and humorous, rather than scary, making this a fun book for the younger zombie-loving set. Recommended for general purchase." SLJ

The **last** invisible boy; written by Evan Kuhlman; illustrated by J P. Coovert. Atheneum Books for Young Readers 2008 233p il $16.99 pa $5.99

Grades: 4 5 6 7   **Fic**

1. School stories 2. Ohio -- Fiction 3. Bereavement -- Fiction 4. Family life -- Fiction 5. Father-son relationship -- Fiction

ISBN 978-1-4169-5797-3; 1-4169-5797-9; 978-1-4169-6089-8 pa; 1-4169-6089-9 pa

LC 2007-40258

In the wake of his father's sudden death, twelve-year-old Finn feels he is becoming invisible as his hair and skin become whiter by the day and so he writes and illustrates a book to try to understand what is happening and to hold on to himself and his father

"Vivid details . . . add depth to the characterizations and grow in meaning as the story progresses. . . . Finn's distinct narrative voice, and the sweet precision with which the story unfolds, give this title a touching resonance." Booklist

Kuhlmann, Torben

Lindbergh; The Tale of a Flying Mouse. by Torben Kuhlmann; translated by Suzanne Levesque. NorthSouth 2014 96 p. color illustrations $19.95

Grades: 2 3 4 5 6   **Fic**

1. Mice -- Fiction 2. Aeronautics -- Fiction

ISBN 0735841675; 9780735841673

In this children's book by Torben Kuhlmann, translated by Suzanne Levesque, "these are dark times . . . for a small mouse. A new invention -the mechanical mousetrap--has caused all the mice but one to flee to America, the land of the free. But with cats guarding the steamships trans-Atlantic crossings are no longer safe. In the bleakest of places . . the one remaining mouse has a brilliant idea. He must learn to fly!" (Publisher's note)

"So strong is the visual narrative that the text is almost superfluous this book can be enjoyed wordlessly. Back matter that includes a short history of aviation rounds out this rich offering." SLJ

Kuijer, Guus

The **book** of everything; a novel. translated by John Nieuwenhuizen. Arthur A. Levine Books 2006 101p hardcover o.p. $16.99

Grades: 5 6 7 8   **Fic**

1. Family life -- Fiction 2. Netherlands -- Fiction 3. Christian life -- Fiction

ISBN 0-439-74918-2; 0-439-74919-0 pa

LC 2005-18717

Nine-year-old Thomas receives encouragement from many sources including candid talks with Jesus, to help him tolerate the strict family life dictated by his deeply-religious father.

"Set in Amsterdam in 1951, this slender Dutch novel is filled with quirky characters, frightening family confrontations, and laugh-out-loud moments. Dark humor and a wry, ironic tone . . . give the story a sharp edge." Booklist

Kurtz, Chris

The **adventures** of a South Pole pig; a novel of snow and courage. Chris Kurtz; illustrations by Jennifer Black Reinhardt. Harcourt Children's Books, Houghton Mifflin Harcourt 2013 288 p. $16.99

Grades: 4 5 6 7   **Fic**

1. Pigs -- Fiction 2. Antarctica -- Fiction 3. Sled dog racing -- Fiction 4. Adventure fiction -- Fiction 5. Dogs -- Fiction 6. Pigs -- Fiction 7. Sled dogs -- Fiction 8. Antarctica -- Fiction 9. Dogsledding -- Fiction 10. Adventure and adventurers -- Fiction

ISBN 0547634552; 9780547634555

LC 2012027226

In this children's story, by Chris Kurtz, illustrated by Jennifer Black Reinhardt, "the day Flora spots a team of sled dogs is the day she sets her heart on becoming a sled pig. Before she knows it, she's on board a ship to Antarctica for the most exhilarating--and dangerous--adventure of her life." (Publisher's note)

The **pup** who cried wolf; illustrations by Guy Francis. Bloomsbury 2010 132p il (Animal tales) $15.99; pa $5.99

Grades: 2 3 4   **Fic**

1. Dogs -- Fiction 2. Wolves -- Fiction

ISBN 978-1-59990-497-9; 1-59990-497-7; 978-1-59990-492-4 pa; 1-59990-492-6 pa

Lobo, a Chihuahua from New York City who feels he is truly a wolf in an undersized body, goes to Yellowstone National Park with his mistress and dreams of running wild with his wolf brothers.

"Children will love this humorous story and empathize with feisty, misguided Lobo. . . . A few black-and-white illustrations, some full page, are scattered throughout. This story will appeal to beginning chapter book and reluctant readers alike." SLJ

Kurtz, Jane

The **storyteller's** beads. Harcourt Brace & Co. 1998 154p $15

Grades: 5 6 7 8   **Fic**

1. Blind -- Fiction 2. Ethiopia -- Fiction 3. Friendship -- Fiction 4. Prejudices -- Fiction

ISBN 0-15-201074-2

LC 97-42312

During the political strife and famine of the 1980's, two Ethiopian girls, one Christian and the other Jewish and blind, struggle to overcome many difficulties, including their prejudices about each other, as they make the dangerous journey out of Ethiopia

"The novel presents an involving portrait of Ethiopian culture through the eyes of two well-defined characters." Horn Book Guide

Kushner, Ellen

The **golden** dreydl; [by] Ellen Kushner; illustrations by Ilene Winn-Lederer. Charlesbridge 2007 126p il $15.95

Grades: 3 4 5   **Fic**

1. Jews -- Fiction 2. Magic -- Fiction 3. Hanukkah -- Fiction

ISBN 978-1-58089-135-6

LC 2006021257

After receiving a magic dreydl at Aunt Leah's Chanukah party, Sara is catapulted into an alternate world of demons, fools, sorcerers, and sages

"The chatty storytelling is fast, furious, and sometimes funny, . . . and scattered throughout are delicate black-and-white illustrations that capture the magical realism." Booklist

L'Engle, Madeleine

Meet the Austins. Farrar, Straus & Giroux 1997 216p hardcover o.p. pa $6.99

Grades: 5 6 7 8   **Fic**

1. Orphans -- Fiction 2. Family life -- Fiction

ISBN 0-374-34929-0; 0-312-37931-5 pa

LC 96-27655

A revised edition of the title first published 1960 by Vanguard Press

ALA YALSA Margaret A. Edwards Award (1998)

A "story of the family of a country doctor, told by the twelve-year-old daughter, during a year in which a spoiled young orphan, Maggy, comes to live with them. . . . [This is an] account of the family's adjustment to Maggy and hers to them." Horn Book

Other titles about the Austins are:

The moon by night (1963)

A ring of endless light (1980)

Troubling a star (1994)

A **swiftly** tilting planet. Farrar, Straus & Giroux 1978 278p $18; pa $6.99

Grades: 5 6 7 8 9 10   **Fic**

1. Fantasy fiction

ISBN 978-0-374-37362-7; 0-374-37362-0; 978-0-312-36856-2 pa; 0-312-36856-9 pa

LC 78-9648

Sequel to: A wind in the door (1973)

ALA YALSA Margaret A. Edwards Award (1998)

The youngest of the Murry children must travel through time and space in a battle against an evil dictator who would destroy the entire universe

A **wind** in the door. Farrar, Straus & Giroux 1973 211p $17.99; pa $6.99

Grades: 5 6 7 8 9 10   **Fic**

1. Fantasy fiction

ISBN 0-374-38443-6; 0-312-36854-2 pa

LC 73-751176

Sequel to: A wrinkle in time (1962)

This episode about the Murrys begins "when Charles Wallace has difficulty adjusting to school. Meg tries to straighten things out, but her help only leads to another adventure in space involving alien creatures." Roman. Sequences

Followed by: A swiftly tilting planet (1978)

★ A **wrinkle** in time. Farrar, Straus & Giroux 1962 211p $17; pa $7.99

Grades: 5 6 7 8 9 10   **Fic**

1. Fantasy fiction 2. Young adult literature

ISBN 0-374-38613-7; 0-312-36754-6 pa

ALA YALSA Margaret A. Edwards Award (1998)

Awarded The Newbery Medal, 1963

This book "makes unusual demands on the imagination and consequently gives great rewards." Horn Book

Other titles in this series are:

A wind in the door (1973)

A swiftly tilting planet (1978)

Many waters (1986)

An acceptable time (1989)

La Fevers, R. L.

Theodosia and the eyes of Horus; [illustrated by Yoko Tanaka] Houghton Mifflin Harcourt 2010 375p il $16

Grades: 4 5 6 7   **Fic**

1. Adventure fiction 2. Magic -- Fiction 3. Museums -- Fiction 4.

Family life -- Fiction 5. London (England) -- Fiction
ISBN 978-0-547-22592-0; 0-547-22592-X

Eleven-year-old Theodosia's ability to detect black magic raises her suspicions about a magician known as the Great Awi Bubu, while Henry, home for the spring holidays, discovers an artifact at the Museum of Legends and Antiquities that is coveted by every black-cloaked occultist in London.

"Once again, supernaturally talented Theodosia navigates around her etiquette-obsessed grandmother and absentminded parents in a suspenseful, satisfying fantasy that's filled with the specifics of magical ritual sure to delight readers." Booklist

Theodosia and the last pharaoh; illustrated by Yoko Tanaka. Houghton Mifflin Harcourt 2011 394p il $16.99
Grades: 4 5 6 7 **Fic**
1. Adventure fiction 2. Egypt -- Fiction 3. Magic -- Fiction 4. Museums -- Fiction 5. Family life -- Fiction
ISBN 978-0-547-39018-5; 0-547-39018-1

LC 2010032224

When eleven-year-old Theodosia and her cat, Isis, travel to Egypt to return the Orb of Ra and the Emerald Tablet, she hopes to learn more about her origins but finds, instead, the Serpents of Chaos and a precious treasure that suddenly appears and disappears.

"Tanaka's drawings nicely extend the action." Booklist

Theodosia and the Serpents of Chaos; illustrated by Yoko Tanaka. Houghton Mifflin 2007 343p il $16; pa $6.99
Grades: 4 5 6 7 **Fic**
1. Adventure fiction 2. Egypt -- Fiction 3. Magic -- Fiction 4. Museums -- Fiction 5. London (England) -- Fiction
ISBN 978-0-618-75638-4; 0-618-75638-8; 978-0-618-99976-7 pa; 0-618-99976-0 pa

LC 2006-34284

Set in 1906 London and Cairo, this mystery adventure introduces an intrepid heroine—Theodosia Throckmorton, who is thrust into the heart of a mystery when she learns an ancient Egyptian amulet carries a curse that threatens to crumble the British Empire

"It's the delicious, precise, and atmospheric details (nicely extended in Tanaka's few, stylized illustrations) that will capture and hold readers." Booklist

Other titles about Theodosia are:
Theodosia and the Staff of Osiris (2008)
Theodosia and the Eyes of Horus (2010)
Theodosia and the last Pharoah (2011)

Theodosia and the Staff of Osiris; [by] R.L. LaFevers; illustrated by Yoko Tanaka. Houghton Mifflin Co. 2008 387p il $16
Grades: 4 5 6 7 **Fic**
1. Adventure fiction 2. Magic -- Fiction 3. Mummies -- Fiction 4. Museums -- Fiction 5. Family life -- Fiction 6. London (England) -- Fiction
ISBN 978-0-618-92764-7; 0-618-92764-6

LC 2008007277

When mummies go missing all over London, eleven-year-old Theodosia puts aside her fight against the Serpents of Chaos to save her father, who is suspected in the thefts, all the while avoiding a string of new governesses.

"Clever and exciting just like the previous book, this also features a layered relationship between Theodosia and her grandmother." Booklist

The **unicorn's** tale; by R.L. LaFevers; illustrated by Kelly Murphy. Houghton Mifflin Books for Children 2011 153p il (Nathaniel Fludd, Beastologist) $14.99

Grades: 3 4 5 **Fic**
1. Adventure fiction 2. Aunts -- Fiction 3. France -- Fiction 4. Unicorns -- Fiction 5. Mythical animals -- Fiction
ISBN 978-0-547-48277-4; 0-547-48277-9

LC 2010025118

Beastologist-in-training Nathaniel Fludd and his Aunt Phil nurse a mysteriously ill unicorn, try to stop Obediah from taking the unicorn's horn, and finally get a solid lead on the whereabouts of Nathaniel's parents.

La Valley, Josanne
The **Vine** basket; by Josanne La Valley. Clarion Books 2013 252 p. (hardcover) $16.99
Grades: 4 5 6 7 8 **Fic**
1. China -- Fiction 2. Farm life -- Fiction 3. Basket making -- Fiction 4. Ethnic relations -- Fiction 5. Farm life -- China -- Fiction 6. Fathers and daughters -- Fiction 7. Uighur (Turkic people) -- Fiction
ISBN 0547848013; 9780547848013

LC 2012021007

Asian/Pacific American Awards for Literature: Children's Literature Honor (2014)

In this novel, by Josanne La Valley, "things aren't looking good for fourteen-year-old Mehrigul. She yearns to be in school, but she's needed on the family farm. . . . Her only hope is an American woman who buys one of her decorative vine baskets for a staggering sum and says she will return in three weeks for more. Mehrigul must brave terrible storms, torn-up hands from working the fields, and her father's scorn to get the baskets done." (Publisher's note)

"The vivid and authentic sense of place, custom, and politics serves as an effective vehicle for the skillfully characterized, emotionally charged story. . . . The realistic and satisfying resolution will resonate with readers . . . An absorbing read and an excellent choice for expanding global understanding." SLJ

Lacey, Josh
Island of Thieves; Josh Lacey. Houghton Mifflin 2012 228 p.
Grades: 4 5 6 7 8 **Fic**
1. Peru -- Fiction 2. Adventure fiction 3. Uncles -- Fiction 4. Pirates -- Fiction 5. Buried treasure -- Fiction 6. Islands -- Fiction 7. Mystery and detective stories 8. Adventure and adventurers -- Fiction
ISBN 0547763271; 9780547763279

LC 2011033893

In this children's novel, a boy takes part in "swashbuckling adventures in faraway places, freed from the strictures of parents, school, siblings and caregivers. . . . Tom nearly ruins his parents' vacation by accidentally burning down the shed in his backyard. . . . Harvey welcomes Tom . . . but as soon as Tom's parents leave, he starts packing for Peru. . . . When he tells Tom it's because he has an opportunity to hunt for pirate treasure, Tom blackmails his uncle into taking him along." (Kirkus)

LaFaye, A.
Water steps. Milkweed Editions 2009 175p $16.95; pa $6.95
Grades: 4 5 6 7 **Fic**
1. Water -- Fiction 2. Phobias -- Fiction 3. Irish Americans -- Fiction
ISBN 978-1-57131-687-5; 1-57131-687-6; 978-1-57131-686-8 pa; 1-57131-686-8 pa

LC 2008011684

Eleven-year-old Kyna, terrified of water since her family drowned in a storm that nearly took her life as well, works to overcome her phobia when her adoptive parents, Irish immigrants with a mysterious past, rent a cabin on Lake Champlain for the summer.

"The language is almost poetic with its use of sensory detail, alliteration, and precise word choices. A satisfying story of overcoming one's fears and discovering secrets." SLJ

Worth. Simon & Schuster Books for Young Readers 2004 144p $15.95; pa $5.99

Grades: 5 6 7 8   **Fic**

1. Orphans -- Fiction 2. Nebraska -- Fiction 3. Frontier and pioneer life -- Fiction

ISBN 0-689-85730-6; 1-4169-1624-5 pa

LC 2003-8101

After breaking his leg, eleven-year-old Nate feels useless because he cannot work on the family farm in nineteenth-century Nebraska, so when his father brings home an orphan boy to help with the chores, Nate feels even worse.

"This short tale has a quietly epic sweep." Horn Book Guide

LaFleur, Suzanne

Beautiful blue world; Suzanne LaFleur. Wendy Lamb Books 2016 224 p. illustrations (hardback) $16.99

Grades: 5 6 7 8   **Fic**

1. Child soldiers -- Fiction 2. Children and war -- Fiction 3. Female friendship -- Fiction 4. War -- Fiction 5. Survival -- Fiction 6. Best friends -- Fiction

ISBN 9780307980328; 9780375990892; 9780385743006

LC 2015046201

In this children's book by Suzanne LaFleur, "Sofarende is at war. For twelve-year-old Mathilde, it means food shortages, feuding neighbors, and bombings. Even so, as long as she and her best friend, Megs, are together, they'll be all right. But the army is recruiting children, and paying families well for their service. If Megs takes the test, Mathilde knows she will pass. Megs hopes the army is the way to save her family. Mathilde fears it might separate them forever." (Publisher's note)

"Deeply emotional, compelling, and brilliant." Kirkus

Eight keys; by Suzanne LaFleur. Wendy Lamb Books 2011 216p $16.99; lib bdg $19.99

Grades: 3 4 5 6   **Fic**

1. School stories 2. Orphans -- Fiction 3. Friendship -- Fiction 4. Family life -- Fiction

ISBN 978-0-385-74030-2; 0-385-74030-1; 978-0-385-90833-7 lib bdg; 978-0-375-89905-8 e-book

LC 2010040137

When twelve-year-old Elise, orphaned since age nine, becomes disheartened by middle school, with its bullies, changing relationships, and higher expectations, keys to long-locked rooms and messages from her late father help her cope.

LaFleur "writes with uncommon sensitivity to the fraught period between childhood and the teenage years, when friendships balance on a razor's edge and nothing feels certain. The heart of the story lies in the layered relationships and characters that give the novel its powerful sense of realism." Publ Wkly

★ **Listening** for Lucca; by Suzanne LaFleur. Wendy Lamb Books 2013 240 p. (trade) $16.99

Grades: 4 5 6 7   **Fic**

1. Diaries -- Fiction 2. Mute persons -- Fiction 3. Supernatural -- Fiction 4. Maine -- Fiction 5. Visions -- Fiction 6. Selective mutism -- Fiction 7. Moving, Household -- Fiction 8. Brothers and sisters -- Fiction 9. Family life -- Maine -- Fiction 10. Maine -- History -- 20th century -- Fiction

ISBN 0385742991; 9780307980304; 9780307980311; 9780375990885; 9780385742993

LC 2012030911

In this novel by Suzanne LaFleur Sienna's "two-year-old brother Lucca stopped talking. Now Mom and Dad are moving the family from Brooklyn to Maine hoping that it will mean a whole new start for Lucca and Siena. When Siena writes in her diary with an old pen she found . . . the pen writes its own story, of Sarah and Joshua, a brother and sister who lived in the same house during World War II. Siena senses that Sarah and Joshua's story might contain the key to unlocking Lucca's voice." (Publisher's note)

★ **Love,** Aubrey. Wendy Lamb Books 2009 262p $15.99; lib bdg $18.99

Grades: 5 6 7 8   **Fic**

1. School stories 2. Letters -- Fiction 3. Vermont -- Fiction 4. Friendship -- Fiction 5. Bereavement -- Fiction 6. Grandmothers -- Fiction 7. Abandoned children -- Fiction 8. Depression (Psychology) -- Fiction

ISBN 978-0-385-73774-6; 0-385-73774-2; 978-0-385-90686-9 lib bdg; 0-385-90686-2 lib bdg

LC 2008-31742

While living with her Gram in Vermont, eleven-year-old Aubrey writes letters as a way of dealing with losing her father and sister in a car accident, and then being abandoned by her grief-stricken mother.

Aubrey's "detailed progression from denial to acceptance makes her both brave and credible in this honest and realistic portrayal of grief." Kirkus

Lagercrantz, Rose

My Happy Life; written by Rose Lagercrantz; illustrated by Eva Eriksson; [translated by Julia Marshall] Lerner Pub Group 2013 136 p. ill. (hardcover) $16.95

Grades: 1 2 3   **Fic**

1. Friendship -- Fiction

ISBN 1877579351; 9781877579356

In this book, "even at a young age, Dani has seen more than her share of heartache: the best friend she meets in chapter four moves away by chapter eight . . . , a departure that prompts the sad revelation that Dani's mother died sometime earlier." But "Dani does indeed have much to be happy about. She has a loving father and extended family, an unflappable teacher . . . , and--above all--an openness to reflection and new possibilities, big and small." (Publishers Weekly)

Other titles in this series are:

My Heart Is Laughing (2014)

When I Am Happiest (2015)

Life According to Dani (2016)

Lai, Thanhha

★ **Inside** out and back again. Harper 2011 262p $15.99

Grades: 4 5 6 7   **Fic**

1. Novels in verse 2. Alabama -- Fiction 3. Vietnam -- Fiction 4. Immigrants -- Fiction 5. Vietnamese Americans -- Fiction

ISBN 978-0-06-196278-3; 0-06-196278-3

LC 2010007855

"For all the ten years of her life, Hà has only known Saigon: the thrills of its markets, the joy of its traditions, and the warmth of her friends close by. But now the Vietnam War has reached her home. Hà and her family are forced to flee as Saigon falls, and they board a ship headed toward hope. In America, Hà discovers the foreign world of Alabama: the coldness of its strangers, the dullness of its food . . . and the strength of her very own family." (Publisher's note)

"Based on Lai's personal experience, this first novel captures a child-refugee's struggle with rare honesty. Written in accessible, short free-verse poems." Booklist

★ **Listen,** Slowly; Thanhha Lai. Harpercollins Childrens Books 2015 272 p. illustration $16.99

Grades: 4 5 6 7 8   **Fic**

1. Culture 2. Family -- Fiction 3. Vietnam -- Fiction 4. Families -- Fiction 5. Grandmothers -- Fiction 6. Vietnam War, 1961-1975 -- Missing in action -- Fiction

ISBN 0062229184; 9780062229182

"A California girl born and raised, Mai . . . has to travel to Vietnam with her grandmother, who is going back to find out what really happened to her husband during the Vietnam War. Mai's parents think this trip will be a great opportunity for their out-of-touch daughter to learn more about her culture. But to Mai, those are their roots, not her own. To survive her trip, Mai must find a balance between her two completely different worlds." (Publisher's note)

"Gracefully written and enriched by apposite figures of speech, Listen, Slowly is a superb, sometimes humorous, always thought-provoking coming-of-age story." Booklist

Lairamore, Dawn

Ivy and the meanstalk. Holiday House 2011 227p $16.95

Grades: 4 5 6 7   **Fic**

1. Fairy tales 2. Giants -- Fiction 3. Dragons -- Fiction 4. Princesses -- Fiction

ISBN 978-0-8234-2392-7; 0-8234-2392-1

LC 2010048627

Sequel to: Ivy's ever after (2010)

Fourteen-year-old Princess Ivy wants nothing more than to have a little fun in the company of her dragon friend, Elridge, but unless she can recover the magical harp snatched by a thieving youth named Jack long ago, her entire kingdom will suffer an unspeakable fate.

This is "delightful and humorous. . . . Lairamore's well-developed characters are excellent riffs on fairy-tale traditions. . . . Various settings are depicted in rich detail while never detracting from the narrative. The plot is filled with action-packed scenes." SLJ

★ **Ivy's** ever after. Holiday House 2010 311p $16.95

Grades: 4 5 6 7   **Fic**

1. Fairy tales 2. Dragons -- Fiction 3. Princesses -- Fiction

ISBN 978-0-8234-2261-6; 0-8234-2261-5

LC 2009-43288

Fourteen-year-old Ivy, a most unroyal princess, befriends Elridge, the dragon sent to keep her in a tower, and together they set out on a perilous quest to find Ivy's fairy godmother, who may be able to save both from their dire fates.

"Ivy is an engaging alternative to the standard damsel-in-distress figure, and with a lushly vivid setting, witty dialogue, and lots of adventure, this well-plotted first novel will appeal to fans of Vivian Vande Velde's A Hidden Magic (1985) and A Well-Timed Enchantment (1990)." Booklist

Followed by: Ivy and the meanstalk (2011)

Landy, Derek

The **Faceless** Ones. Bowen Press 2009 422p (Skulduggery Pleasant) $16.99

Grades: 4 5 6 7   **Fic**

1. Fantasy fiction 2. Magic -- Fiction

ISBN 978-0-06-124091-1; 0-06-124091-5

LC 2008051714

Sequel to: Playing with fire (2008)

Fourteen-year-old Valkyrie and the skeleton mage, Skulduggery Pleasant, try to foil a plot set in motion fifty years before to find and open the gate that will allow the Faceless Ones to return to this reality.

"A gifted storyteller, the author will hook readers on the first page and leave them on the last as wrung out as he leaves his teenage pro-

tagonist—who pays a high price indeed for killing a god or two. Rattling good fun." Kirkus

Playing with fire; by Derek Landy. HarperCollins Pub. 2008 389p $16.99; pa $7.99

Grades: 4 5 6 7   **Fic**

1. Fantasy fiction 2. Magic -- Fiction

ISBN 978-0-06-124088-1; 0-06-124088-5; 978-0-06-124090-4 pa; 0-06-124090-7 pa

Sequel to: Skulduggery Pleasant (2007)

Skulduggery Pleasant, the living-dead wizard-detective, and his apprentice, Valkyrie Cain (once known as twelve-year-old Stephanie Edgley), try to prevent Baron Vengeous from bringing the monster Grotesquery to life and to save the world from the Faceless Ones.

The "style is cinematic, and the action nonstop. Skulduggery's subtle humorous asides . . . lighten the mood, and magical details, such as Valkyrie's ability to throw fireballs, add to the fun." Booklist

Followed by: The faceless ones (2009)

★ **Skulduggery** Pleasant. HarperCollinsPublishers 2007 392p $17.99; lib bdg $18.89; pa $7.99

Grades: 4 5 6 7   **Fic**

1. Fantasy fiction 2. Magic -- Fiction

ISBN 978-0-06-123115-5; 0-06-123115-0; 978-0-06-123116-2 lib bdg; 0-06-123116-9 lib bdg; 978-0-06-123117-9 pa; 0-06-123117-7 pa

LC 2006-29403

When twelve-year-old Stephanie inherits her weird uncle's estate, she must join forces with Skulduggery Pleasant, a skeleton mage, to save the world from the Faceless Ones

This "is a rich fantasy that is as engaging in its creative protagonists and villains as it is in the lightning-paced plot and sharp humor." Bulletin Cent Child Books

Other titles in this series are:

Playing with fire (2008)

The faceless ones (2009)

Lane, Andrew

Black ice; Andrew Lane. Farrar Straus Giroux 2013 288 p. (Sherlock Holmes. The legend begins) (hardcover) $17.99

Grades: 5 6 7 8   **Fic**

1. Mystery fiction 2. Young adult literature 3. Murder -- Fiction 4. Mystery and detective stories 5. Moscow (Russia) -- History -- 19th century -- Fiction 6. Russia -- History -- Alexander II, 1855-1881 -- Fiction 7. Great Britain -- History -- Victoria, 1837-1901 -- Fiction

ISBN 0374387699; 9780374387693

LC 2012004996

This novel, by Andrew Lane, is the third book of the "Sherlock Holmes: The Legend Begins" series. "When Sherlock and Amyus Crowe, his American tutor, visit Sherlock's brother, Mycroft, in London all they are expecting is lunch and some polite conversation. What they find shocks both of them to the core: a locked room, a dead body, and Mycroft holding a knife. . . . Threatened with the gallows, Mycroft needs Sherlock to save him." (Publisher's note)

Rebel fire; Andrew Lane. Farrar Straus Giroux 2012 343 p (Sherlock Holmes. The legend begins) $16.99

Grades: 5 6 7 8   **Fic**

1. Mystery fiction 2. Young adult literature 3. Mystery and detective stories 4. Great Britain -- History -- Victoria, 1837-1901 -- Fiction

ISBN 0374387680; 9780374387686

LC 2011000124

This novel, by Andrew Lane, is part of the "Sherlock Holmes: The Legend Begins" series. "Fourteen-year-old Sherlock Holmes knows that Amyus Crowe, his mysterious American tutor, has some dark secrets. But he didn't expect to find John Wilkes Booth, the notorious assassin, apparently alive and well in England--and Crowe somehow mixed up in it. . . . And so begins an adventure that will take Sherlock across the Atlantic, to the center of a deadly web." (Publisher's note)

Includes bibliographical references

Lane, Kathleen

The **best** worst thing; by Kathleen Lane. Little, Brown & Co. 2016 208 p. (hardcover) $16.99

Grades: 4 5 6   **Fic**

1. Bullies -- Fiction 2. Middle schools -- Fiction 3. Brothers and sisters -- Fiction 4. Safety -- Fiction

ISBN 0316257818; 9780316257817

          LC 2015012906

In this book, by Kathleen Lane, "Maggie is worried. Ever since she started middle school, she sees injustice and danger everywhere--on the news, in her textbooks, in her own neighborhood. Even her best friend seems to be changing. Maggie believes it is up to her, and only her, to make everything all right. Can she come up with a plan to keep everyone safe?" (Publisher's note)

"Lane crafts a powerful portrait of a girl wrangling with deeply relatable concerns, which will easily resonate with readers confronting a complex and uncertain world." Pub Wkly

Lane, Mike

The **incredible** twisting arm; Kate Egan and Mike Lane, illustrated by Eric Wight. Feiwel & Friends 2014 150 p. $14.99

Grades: 3 4 5   **Fic**

1. Magic -- Fiction 2. Magicians -- Fiction 3. Responsibility -- Fiction

ISBN 1250029155; 9781250029157

In this children's book by Kate Egan and Mike Lane, illustrated by Eric Wight, "Life is a little easier for Mike now that he's found The White Rabbit magic shop. But after missing a special show from a visiting magician, Mike realizes he needs a way to get to the shop by himself. Unfortunately, he's exhausted after only a week of being a model student, and Nora, his magician assistant and expert on good behavior, is distracted by a new friendship." (Publisher's note)

"After finding the magic shop in The Vanishing Coin (Feiwel & Friends, 2014), Mike decides he wants to ride his bike downtown to the shop by himself. But convincing his parents that he is mature enough to ride alone may take quite a bit of magic. Includes ample black-and-white illustrations and instructions on how to do several fun magic tricks." SLJ

Other titles in the series include:

Great Escape (2014)
Vanishing Coin (2014)

The **Vanishing** Coin; by Kate Egan and Mike Lane; illustrated by Eric Wight. Feiwel & Friends 2014 160 p. $14.99

Grades: 3 4 5   **Fic**

1. Magicians -- Fiction 2. Friendship -- Fiction 3. Magic tricks -- Fiction 4. Attention deficit disorder -- Fiction

ISBN 1250029147; 9781250029140

In this book, by Kate Egan and Mike Lane, "fourth grade was supposed to be a fresh start, but Mike's already back in the principal's office. . . . And now, his parents won't let him play soccer anymore; instead he has to hang out with his new neighbor Nora. . . . Mike and Nora discover the White Rabbit. It's an odd shop - with a special secret inside. Its owner, Mr. Zerlin, is a magician, and, amazingly, he believes Mike could be a magician, too." (Publisher's note)

"Fourth-grader Mike Weiss can't get the hang of math, forgets his homework, and has trouble sitting still in school. And as if getting sent to the principal's office the first week of school wasn't bad enough, classmate Jackson ('Mike's enemy since birth') won't lay off him, and he's spending his after-school hours with Nora, the gifted new girl next door. . . Mike is left wondering whether magic might be real, something likely to be explored in subsequent books, including The Incredible Twisting Arm, available simultaneously." PW

Other titles include:

Great Escape (2014)
The Incredible Twisting Arm (2014)

Langton, Jane

The **fledgling**. Harper & Row 1980 182p il lib bdg $15.89; pa $5.95

Grades: 5 6 7 8   **Fic**

1. Fantasy fiction 2. Geese -- Fiction

ISBN 0-06-023679-5 lib bdg; 0-06-440121-9 pa

          LC 79-2008

A Newbery Medal honor book, 1981

"The writing is alternately solemn and funny, elevated and colloquial. It is mythic, almost sacred, in passages involving Georgie and the goose; it is satiric, almost irreverent, when it relates to Mr. Preek and Miss Prawn." Horn Book

Larson, Kirby

Audacity Jones; Kirby Larson. Scholastic Press 2016 224 p. (jacketed hardcover) $16.99

Grades: 4 5 6 7   **Fic**

1. Adventure fiction 2. Orphans -- Fiction 3. Kidnapping -- Fiction 4. Adventure stories 5. Conspiracies -- Fiction 6. Adventure and adventurers -- Fiction 7. Washington (D.C.) -- History -- 20th century -- Fiction

ISBN 0545840562; 9780545840569

          LC 2015015919

In this children's novel by Kirby Larson "Audacity Jones is an eleven-year-old orphan who aches for adventure, a challenge to break up the monotony of her life at Miss Maisie's School for Wayward Girls. So when the mysterious Commodore Crutchfield visits the school and whisks Audie off to Washington, DC, she knows she's in for the journey of a lifetime. But soon, it becomes clear that the Commodore has unsavory plans for Audie -- plans that involve the president of the United States and a sinister kidnapping plot." (Publisher's note)

"Larson's entertaining narration shifts attention among multiple characters amid the unfolding mystery of what, exactly, the Commodore is planning. First in a series, Larson's thriller deftly mixes humor, heart-pounding moments, and a strongly evoked historical setting—it's truly a story with something for everyone." Pub Wkly

Dash; Kirby Larson. Scholastic Press 2014 256 p. (hardcover) $16.99

Grades: 4 5 6 7   **Fic**

1. Dogs -- Fiction 2. Japanese Americans -- Evacuation and relocation, 1942-1945 3. World War, 1939-1945 -- Fiction 4. Japanese American children -- Fiction 5. Puyallup Assembly Center (Puyallup, Wash.) -- Fiction 6. Japanese Americans -- Evacuation and relocation, 1942-1945 -- Fiction

ISBN 0545416353; 9780545416351

          LC 2013042525

"Although Mitsi Kashino and her family are swept up in the wave of anti-Japanese sentiment following the attack on Pearl Harbor, Mitsi never expects to lose her home--or her beloved dog, Dash. But, as World War II rages and people of Japanese descent are forced into incarceration camps, Mitsi is separated from Dash, her classmates, and life as she knows it." (Publisher's note)

"Spot-on dialogue, careful cultural details and the inclusion of specific historical characters such as artist Eddie Sato make this an educational read as well as a heartwarming one. An author's note adds further authenticity.This emotionally satisfying and thought-provoking book will have readers pulling for Mitsi and Dash." Kirkus

Duke; Kirby Larson. Scholastic Press 2013 240 p. (jacketed hardcover) $16.99

Grades: 4 5 6 7   **Fic**

1. Dogs -- War use -- Fiction 2. World War, 1939-1945 -- United States -- Fiction 3. Dogs -- Fiction 4. German shepherd dog -- Fiction 5. Human-animal relationships -- Fiction

ISBN 054541637X; 9780545416375

LC 2012046636

In this World War II story by Kirby Larson, "when fifth-grader Hobie Hanson's father leaves his fishing boat in Seattle to pilot a B-24 in Europe, he tells Hobie 'to step up and do what needs to be done.' Whether it is buying war bonds, collecting rubber or simply making due with less, Hobie is giving all he can to the war effort. But when he begins to feel the pressure to lend his beloved German shepherd, Duke, to the Army, Hobie realizes he still has more to give." (Kirkus Reviews)

Liberty; Kirby Larson. Scholastic Press 2016 221 p. (ebook) $16.99; $16.99

Grades: 4 5 6 7   **Fic**

1. Dogs -- Fiction 2. Friendship -- Fiction 3. Race relations -- Fiction 4. African Americans -- Fiction 5. New Orleans (La.) -- Fiction 6. World War, 1939-1945 -- Fiction 7. Prisoners of war -- Fiction 8. People with disabilities -- Fiction

ISBN 9780545840736; 0545840716; 9780545840712

LC 2015048827

In this book, by Kirby Larson, "Fish has a knack for inventing. His annoying neighbor, Olympia, has a knack for messing things up. But when his latest invention leads Fish to Liberty, a beautiful stray dog who needs a home, he and Olympia work together to rescue her. However, a friendship that crosses racial lines is not the norm in 1940s New Orleans." (Publisher's note)

"Larson once again creates an engaging story that is rich in historical details. She purposefully captures both the fear and the hope in a world torn by war as well as the simple love of a boy for his dog. Practically perfect." Kirkus

Larson, M. A.

Pennyroyal Academy; M. A. Larson. G. P. Putnam's Sons, an imprint of Penguin Group (USA) 2014 304 p. maps (hardback) $16.99

Grades: 5 6 7 8   **Fic**

1. Schools 2. Princesses -- Fiction 3. Knights and knighthood -- Fiction 4. Fantasy 5. Dragons -- Fiction 6. Schools -- Fiction 7. Witches -- Fiction 8. Military education -- Fiction 9. Adventure and adventurers -- Fiction

ISBN 0399163247; 9780399163241

LC 2014014516

In this novel by M.A. Larson, "a girl from the forest arrives in a bustling kingdom with no name and no idea why she is there, only to find herself at the center of a world at war. She enlists at Pennyroyal Academy, where princesses and knights are trained to battle the two great menaces of the day: witches and dragons. As Evie learns what it truly means to be a princess, she realizes surprising things about herself and her family." (Publisher's note)

"Forget the notion of traditional princesses. At Pennyroyal Academy, princesses are trained to fight witches and save kingdoms, and, yes, knights learn to slay dragons...the focus and detailed character develop-

ment is on the young women, their hopes and dreams (sometimes dreadfully scary), their real fears, and their disappointments in themselves, their friends, and the adults around them. Since the book ends with some of the princesses and knights selected to return for another school year, Larson has left the door open for a welcome second year at Pennyroyal with Evie and her friends." Booklist

Larwood, Kieran

Freaks; Kieran Larwood. Chicken House/Scholastic 2013 256 p. $16.99

Grades: 5 6 7 8   **Fic**

1. Mystery fiction 2. Circus performers -- Fiction 3. Freak shows -- Fiction 4. Mystery and detective stories 5. Abnormalities, Human -- Fiction 6. London (England) -- History -- 19th century -- Fiction 7. Great Britain -- History -- Victoria, 1837-1901 -- Fiction

ISBN 0545474248; 9780545474245; 9780545474252

LC 2012002639

In this book, 10-year-old "Sheba, better known as the Wolfgirl for her layer of fur and ability to sprout fangs and claws, is an orphan who ends up as part of Plumpscuttle's Peculiars, a freak show that also stars a teenage ninja, a trash-talking monkey boy, a romance-writing strongman, and a woman who talks to rats. This gang of unlikely heroes gets caught up in a mystery involving missing street urchins, steampunk monstrosities, and a fiendish set of villains." (Publishers Weekly)

Lasky, Kathryn

The **escape**; Kathryn Lasky. Scholastic Press 2014 240 p. illustrations (Horses of the dawn) (hardcover) $16.99

Grades: 4 5 6 7 8   **Fic**

1. Horses -- Fiction 2. Mother-daughter relationship -- Fiction 3. Responsibility -- Fiction 4. North America -- History -- Fiction

ISBN 9780545397162; 0545397162

LC 2013037215

This book "reimagines the history of the reintroduction of horses to North America by Spanish conquistadors through the eyes of the horses they brought with them. Estrella, a plucky foal unexpectedly born on board a Spanish ship bound for the New World, is strong, brave, and wise beyond her years. She, along with three others, survives being tossed overboard into shark-infested waters by swimming to the Yucatan Peninsula. Thus begins her quest to find the land of the sweet grass only she can smell." (Booklist)

"Lasky successfully fuses fantasy and fact as she gives her equine characters credible emotional depth and underscores the tensions and disparity between Old and New World sensibilities." Pub Wkly

Other titles in this series are:

Star rise (2015)

Wild blood (2016)

Felix takes the stage; illustrated by Stephen Gilpin. Scholastic Press 2010 142p il (The Deadlies) $15.99

Grades: 3 4 5   **Fic**

1. Moving -- Fiction 2. Spiders -- Fiction

ISBN 978-0-545-11681-7; 0-545-11681-3

Having been discovered, a family of poisonous but friendly brown recluse spiders must flee their cozy home in a symphony hall and go searching for a new place to live.

"Humor and action seamlessly blend as these arachnids struggle for survival against the scary E-Men who threaten them with extermination. Vivid characters, from the theatrical godspider Fat Cat to the pompous orb weaver Oliphant Uxbridge, make up the clever supporting cast. Genuinely funny dialogue helps move the brief chapters along, and Gilpin's lively black-and-white drawings provide an animated accompaniment." Kirkus

Hawksmaid; the untold story of Robin Hood and Maid Marian. Harper 2010 292p $16.99

Grades: 5 6 7 8 **Fic**

1. Young adult literature 2. Falconry -- Fiction 3. Robin Hood (Legendary character) -- Fiction 4. Maid Marian (Legendary character) -- Fiction 5. Great Britain -- History -- 1154-1399, Plantagenets -- Fiction

ISBN 978-0-06-000071-4; 0-06-000071-6

In twelfth-century England, Matty grows up to be a master falconer, able to communicate with the devoted birds who later help her and Fynn, also known as Robin Hood, to foil Prince John's plot to steal the crown.

"Lasky nicely weaves details of 12th-century life into this suspenseful adventure whose fantasy ending may surprise but will certainly please readers." SLJ

Spiders on the case; illustrated by Stephen Gilpin. Scholastic Press 2011 171p il (The Deadlies) $15.99

Grades: 3 4 5 **Fic**

1. Mystery fiction 2. Spiders -- Fiction 3. Libraries -- Fiction 4. Boston (Mass.) -- Fiction 5. Books and reading -- Fiction 6. Boston Public Library -- Fiction

ISBN 978-0-545-11682-4; 0-545-11682-1

LC 2010047587

Buster, a walnut orb weaving spider, enlists the help of Jo Beth, one of a family of poisonous but friendly brown recluse spiders, to help stop humans who are stealing from the rare books room of the Boston Public Library, where the spiders live.

"Young readers will relate to the family drama and rivalry between Jo Bell and her siblings. There are moments of good humor. The spiders in the illustrations are full of expression, and the drawings help move the story along." SLJ

Latham, Irene

Leaving Gee's Bend. G.P. Putnam's Sons 2010 230p $16.99

Grades: 5 6 7 8 **Fic**

1. Quilts -- Fiction 2. Alabama -- Fiction 3. African Americans -- Fiction

ISBN 978-0-399-25179-5; 0-399-25179-0

LC 2009-08732

Ludelphia Bennett, a determined, ten-year-old African American girl in 1932 Gee's Bend, Alabama, leaves home in an effort to find medical help for her sick mother, and she recounts her ensuing adventures in a quilt she is making.

"Ludelphia's voice is authentic and memorable, and Latham captures the tension of her dangerous journey and the racism she encounters." Booklist

Lauren, Ruth

Prisoner of ice and snow; by Ruth Lauren. Bloomsbury 2017 288 p. (hardback) $16.99

Grades: 4 5 6 7 **Fic**

1. Fantasy fiction 2. Fantasy 3. Prisons -- Fiction 4. Sisters -- Fiction

ISBN 9781681191317

LC 2016025579

In this middle grade novel, by Ruth Lauren, "when thirteen-year-old Valor is sent to jail, she couldn't be happier. Demidova's prison for criminal children is exactly where she wants to be. Valor's twin sister, Sasha, is serving a life sentence for stealing from the royal family, and Valor is going to help her escape.... If Valor's plan is to succeed, she'll need to make some unlikely allies. And if the plan fails, she and Sasha could end up with fates worse than prison." (Publisher's note)

"Anyone who likes adventure, survival stories, folktales, or novels with strong female protagonists will not be able to put this down." SLJ

Law, Ingrid

★ **Savvy**. Dial Books for Young Readers 2008 342p $16.99

Grades: 4 5 6 7 **Fic**

1. Magic -- Fiction 2. Family life -- Fiction 3. Voyages and travels -- Fiction

ISBN 978-0-8037-3306-0; 0-8037-3306-2

LC 2007-39814

A Newbery Medal honor book, 2009

Boston Globe-Horn Book Award honor book: Fiction and Poetry (2008)

Recounts the adventures of Mississippi (Mibs) Beaumont, whose thirteenth birthday has revealed her "savvy"—a magical power unique to each member of her family—just as her father is injured in a terrible accident.

"Short chapters and cliffhangers keep the pace quick, while the mix of traditional language and vernacular helps the story feel both fresh and timeless. . . . [This is] a vibrant and cinematic novel that readers are going to love." Publ Wkly

Other titles in this series are:

Scrumble (2010)

Switch (2015)

★ **Scumble**. Dial Books for Young Readers 2010 400p il $16.99

Grades: 4 5 6 7 **Fic**

1. Magic -- Fiction 2. Wyoming -- Fiction 3. Ranch life -- Fiction

ISBN 978-0-8037-3307-7; 0-8037-3307-0

LC 2010-02444

Mibs's cousin Ledge is disappointed to discover that his "savvy" — the magical power unique to each member of their family—is to make things fall apart, which endangers his uncle Autry's ranch and reveals the family secret to future reporter Sarah.

This provides a "satisfying plot, delightful characters, alliterative language, and rich imagery." Booklist

Switch; by Ingrid Law. Dial Books for Young Readers 2015 368 p. (hardback) $16.99

Grades: 4 5 6 7 **Fic**

1. Magic -- Fiction 2. Family -- Fiction 3. Grandmothers -- Fiction 4. Alzheimer's disease -- Fiction 5. Families -- Fiction

ISBN 0803738625; 9780803738621

LC 2015006965

In this book, by Ingrid Law, "Gypsy Beaumont has always been a whirly-twirly free spirit, so as her thirteenth birthday approaches, she hopes to get a magical ability that will let her fly, or dance up to the stars. Instead, she wakes up on her birthday with blurry vision. . . . But when Momma and Poppa announce that her very un-magical, downright mean Grandma Pat has Alzheimer's and is going to move in with them, Gypsy's savvy . . . suddenly becomes its opposite." (Publisher's note)

"Law tenderly handles the challenges of having a grandparent with Alzheimer's, highlighting the power of familial love. Though no explanation for the switch is given, readers will be caught up in this snowy, magical adventure and the characters' efforts to balance their true, sparkly selves with growing up." Booklist

The "second sequel" to Savvy.

Lawlor, Laurie

He will go fearless; [by] Laurie Lawlor. Simon & Schuster Books for Young Readers 2006 210p $15.95

Grades: 5 6 7 8 **Fic**

1. Young adult literature 2. Father-son relationship -- Fiction 3. Overland journeys to the Pacific -- Fiction 4. United States -- History -- 1865-1898 -- Fiction

ISBN 0-689-86579-1

LC 2005-06129

With the Civil War ended and Reconstruction begun, fifteen-year-old Billy resolves to make the dangerous and challenging journey West in search of real fortune – his true father.

"Danger, adventure, and survival combine to make this a richly detailed story." SLJ

The **school** at Crooked Creek; illustrated by Ronald Himler. Holiday House 2004 83p il map $15.95

Grades: 3 4 5　　　　　　　　　　　　　　　　　　　　**Fic**

1. School stories 2. Indiana -- Fiction 3. Frontier and pioneer life -- Fiction

ISBN 0-8234-1812-X

　　　　　　　　　　　　　　　　　　　　　LC 2003-56759

Living on the nineteenth-century Indiana frontier with his parents and irritable older sister Louise, six-year-old Beansie dreads his first day of school, but his resilience surprises even his sister.

"The book is rich with colloquial language, superstitions, and information about the lifestyle of this pioneer family. Nicely done shaded, pencil drawings help set the tone." SLJ

Lawrence, Caroline

★ The **case** of the deadly desperados; Caroline Lawrence. G.P. Putnam's Sons 2011 279 p. (Western mysteries) $16.99

Grades: 4 5 6 7 8　　　　　　　　　　　　　　　　　　**Fic**

1. Mystery fiction 2. Western stories 3. Children's stories 4. Orphans -- Fiction 5. Racially mixed people -- Fiction 6. Disguise -- Fiction 7. Mystery and detective stories 8. Nevada -- History -- 19th century -- Fiction

ISBN 9780399256332

　　　　　　　　　　　　　　　　　　　　　LC 2011013305

In this book, Caroline "Lawrence shifts her sleuthing . . . [to] Virginia City, Montana in the 1860s. . . . Whittlin' Walt . . . has just scalped and slain the foster parents of twelve-year-old P. K. (Pinky) Pinkerton, . . . who holds a coveted deed to an entire region of silver mines. Pinky hightails it to Virginia City . . . to register his claim, . . . [then] to Chicago, where he wants to join the detective whom he believes to be his father." (Bulletin of the Center for Children's Books)

★ **P.K.** Pinkerton and the petrified man; Caroline Lawrence. G.P. Putnam's Sons 2013 320 p. (hardcover) $16.99

Grades: 4 5 6 7 8　　　　　　　　　　　　　　　　　　**Fic**

1. Mystery fiction 2. Western stories 3. Orphans -- Fiction 4. Disguise -- Fiction 5. Mystery and detective stories 6. Racially mixed people -- Fiction 7. Nevada -- History -- 19th century -- Fiction

ISBN 0399256342; 9780399256349

　　　　　　　　　　　　　　　　　　　　　LC 2012026737

This western mystery adventure novel, by Caroline Lawrence, is "starring Master-of-Disguise, P.K. Pinkerton. After vanquishing three notorious Desperados, twelve-year-old P.K. Pinkerton opens a private-eye business in Virginia City. P.K.'s skills are quickly put to the test: When a maid named Martha witnesses a murder, she hires the young detective to track the killer before he finds her too." (Publisher's note)

★ **P.K.** Pinkerton and the pistol-packing widows; Caroline Lawrence. G.P. Putnam's Sons, an imprint of Penguin Group (USA) Inc. 2014 304 p. maps (hardcover) $16.99

Grades: 4 5 6 7 8　　　　　　　　　　　　　　　　　　**Fic**

1. Mystery fiction 2. Nevada -- Fiction 3. Disguise -- Fiction 4. Detectives -- Fiction 5. Orphans -- Fiction 6. Mystery and detective stories 7. Racially mixed people -- Fiction 8. Nevada -- History -- 19th century -- Fiction

ISBN 0399256350; 9780399256356

　　　　　　　　　　　　　　　　　　　　　LC 2013000211

In this book, by Caroline Lawrence, "P.K. Pinkerton's detective agency is thriving in Virginia City--until the evening P.K. is abruptly stuffed into a turnip sack and tossed into the back of a wagon! Surfacing in Chinatown, P.K. is forced into taking a job trailing the abductor's fiancé in Carson City. Danger lurks at every turn. P.K. must battle quicksand, escape the despicable former Deputy Marshall, Jack Williams, and save Poker Face Jace from certain death." (Publisher's note)

"The young detective's dryly hilarious first-person accounts keep the story at a gallop. No disguise can mask P.K. Pinkerton's stout heart and steely resolve in Lawrence's third (and mighty fine) Wild West adventure." Kirkus

Lawrence, Iain

The **buccaneers**. Delacorte Press 2001 244p hardcover o.p. pa $6.50

Grades: 5 6 7 8　　　　　　　　　　　　　　　　　　　**Fic**

1. Adventure fiction 2. Pirates -- Fiction 3. Seafaring life -- Fiction

ISBN 0-385-32736-6; 0-440-41671-X pa

　　　　　　　　　　　　　　　　　　　　　LC 00-6028

Sequel to: The smugglers (1999)

In the eighteenth century sixteen-year-old John Spencer sails from England in his schooner, the Dragon, to the Caribbean, where he and the crew encounter pirates, fierce storms, fever, and a strange man who some fear may be cursed.

"This high-seas tale set in the 19th century offers plenty of full-blooded salty characters, cunning dialogue, surprises around every corner and a classic battle between good and evil. The author's firsthand knowledge of sailing and skill at building suspense will keep reader riveted from first page to last." Publ Wkly

The **giant**-slayer. Delacorte Press 2009 292p $16.99

Grades: 5 6 7 8　　　　　　　　　　　　　　　　　　　**Fic**

1. Imagination -- Fiction 2. Medical care -- Fiction 3. Storytelling -- Fiction 4. Poliomyelitis -- Fiction 5. Father-daughter relationship -- Fiction

ISBN 978-0-385-73376-2; 0-385-73376-3

　　　　　　　　　　　　　　　　　　　　　LC 2008-35400

When her eight-year-old neighbor is stricken with polio in 1955 eleven-year-old Laurie discovers that there is power in her imagination as she weaves a story during her visits with him and other patients confined to iron lung machines.

This is "compelling. . . . This effectively shows how children face life-changing challenges with incredible determination." Booklist

The **smugglers**. Delacorte Press 1999 183p $15.95; pa $6.50

Grades: 5 6 7 8　　　　　　　　　　　　　　　　　　　**Fic**

1. Adventure fiction 2. Smuggling -- Fiction 3. Great Britain -- History -- 1714-1837 -- Fiction

ISBN 0-385-32663-7; 0-440-41596-9 pa

　　　　　　　　　　　　　　　　　　　　　LC 98-4158.

Sequel to: The wreckers (1998)

As the nineteenth century begins, sixteen-year-old John Spencer sets out to sail his father's schooner, The Dragon, from Kent to London and becomes involved in smuggling and danger

"The book's nonstop action, fast-paced plot, and picturesque characters make for a real page-turner." SLJ

Followed by: The buccaneers (2001)

★ The **wreckers**. Delacorte Press 1998 196p hardcover o.p. pa $5.99

Grades: 5 6 7 8　　　　　　　　　　　　　　　　　　　**Fic**

1. Adventure fiction 2. Shipwrecks -- Fiction 3. Great Britain -

History -- 1714-1837 -- Fiction
ISBN 0-385-32535-5; 0-440-41545-4 pa

LC 97-31625

"In 1799 fourteen-year-old John Spencer survives a shipwreck on the coast of Cornwall. To his horror, he soon learns that the villagers are not rescuers, but pirates who lure ships ashore in order to plunder their cargoes. . . . Lawrence creates an edge-of-the-chair survival/mystery story. Fast-moving, mesmerizing." Horn Book Guide

Other titles in this series are:

The smugglers (1999)

The buccaneers (2001)

Lawson, Jessica

The **actual** & truthful adventures of Becky Thatcher; Jessica Lawson. Simon & Schuster Books for Young Readers 2014 224 p. (hardcover) $16.99

Grades: 4 5 6 7   Fic

1. Girls -- Fiction 2. Adventure fiction 3. Behavior -- Fiction 4. Mississippi River -- Fiction 5. Family life -- Missouri -- Fiction 6. Adventure and adventurers -- Fiction 7. Missouri -- History -- 19th century -- Fiction

ISBN 1481401505; 9781481401500; 9781481401531

LC 2013020560

This middle grades novel by Jessica Lawson, illustrated by Iacopo Bruno, describes how "In 1860, eleven-year-old Becky Thatcher is the new girl in town, determined to have adventures like she promised her brother Jon before he died. With her Mama frozen in grief and her Daddy busy as town judge, Becky spends much of her time on her own, getting into mischief. Before long, she joins the boys at school in a bet to steal from the Widow Douglas." (Publisher's note)

"As a more politically correct retelling of The Adventures of Tom Sawyer, Lawson's novel turns several ideas in Mark Twain's original story on their heads. Tom the tattletale lurks in the backdrop of 1860 St. Petersburg, MO, but the focus is on the adventures that Becky plans with her friend Amy Lawrence . . . Nevertheless, readers not familiar with Twain's work will find an enjoyable adventure story with glimmers of mystery. Fans of historical fiction will enjoy the charming heroine and fitting affirmations of family, friendship, and remembrance." SLJ

Actual and truthful adventures of Becky Thatcher

★ **Nooks** & crannies; by Jessica Lawson (Author); Natalie Andrewson (Illustrator) First edition Simon & Schuster Books for Young Readers 2015 336 p. illustrations (hardcover) $16.99

Grades: 3 4 5 6 7   Fic

1. Aristocracy -- Fiction 2. Mystery fiction 3. Inheritance and succession -- Fiction 4. Identity -- Fiction 5. Mystery and detective stories 6. Great Britain -- History -- Edward VII, 1901-1910 -- Fiction

ISBN 1481419218; 9781481419215; 9781481419222

LC 2014023223

In this children's mystery story, by Jessica Lawson and illustrated by Natalie Andrewson, "Tabitha Crum . . . receives one of six invitations to the country estate of wealthy Countess Camilla DeMoss. . . . Then the children beginning disappearing, one by one. So Tabitha takes a cue from her favorite detective novels and, with [her pet mouse] Pemberley by her side, attempts to solve the case and rescue the other children." (Publisher's note)

"Lawson offers a compelling puzzle, vividly drawn characters, and a clever and capable young detective, who bravely sniffs out clues before the final secrets are revealed--with everyone together in the parlor, naturally." Booklist

Nooks and crannies

Waiting for Augusta; Jessica Lawson. Simon & Schuster Books for Young Readers 2016 336 p. (hardback) $16.99

Grades: 4 5 6   Fic

1. Golf -- Fiction 2. Grief -- Fiction 3. Fathers -- Fiction 4. Southern States -- Fiction 5. Runaway children -- Fiction 6. Runaways -- Fiction 7. Southern States -- History -- 20th century -- Fiction

ISBN 9781481448390; 9781481448406

LC 2015026346

In this book, by Jessica Lawson, "Eleven-year-old Benjamin Putter has a lump in his throat, and he's certain it's a golf ball. He knows it sounds crazy, but everything's been topsy-turvy since his father died last month. . . . Then, one day, something starts tugging at Ben, telling him to hurry to Augusta, Georgia—home of the most famous golf course in the world. Ben might be going a little crazy, but escaping Hilltop, Alabama, sounds like a darn good idea." (Publisher's note)

"A whimsical, heartwarming, multilayered story about finding grace enough to accept the flaws in those we love and courage enough to act from our most deeply held beliefs." Kirkus

Lawson, Robert

Ben and me; a new and astonishing life of Benjamin Franklin, as written by his good mouse Amos. lately discovered, edited and illustrated by Robert Lawson. Little, Brown 1939 113p il hardcover o.p. pa $5.95

Grades: 5 6 7 8   Fic

1. Authors 2. Diplomats 3. Inventors 4. Statesmen 5. Scientists 6. Mice -- Fiction 7. Writers on science 8. Members of Congress

ISBN 0-316-51732-1; 0-316-51730-5 pa

"The sophisticated and clever story is illustrated by even more sophisticated and clever line drawings." Roundabout of Books

Mr. Revere and I; set down and embellished with numerous drawings by Robert Lawson. Little, Brown 1953 152p il hardcover o.p. pa $5.95

Grades: 5 6 7 8   Fic

1. Artisans 2. Metalworkers 3. Revolutionaries 4. Horses -- Fiction 5. United States -- History -- 1775-1783, Revolution -- Fiction

ISBN 0-316-51729-1 pa

"A delightful tale which is perfect for reading aloud to the whole family. The make-up is excellent, illustrations are wonderful, and the reader will get a very interesting picture of the American Revolution." Libr J

Rabbit Hill. Viking 1944 127p il lib bdg $16.99; pa $5.99

Grades: 3 4 5 6   Fic

1. Animals -- Fiction 2. Rabbits -- Fiction

ISBN 0-670-58675-7 lib bdg; 0-14-240796-8 pa

Awarded the Newbery Medal, 1945

"Robert Lawson, because he loves the Connecticut country and the little animals of field and wood and looks at them with the eye of an artist, a poet and a child, has created for the boy and girl, indeed for the sensitive reader of any age, a whole, fresh, lively, amusing world." N Y Times Book Rev

Followed by The tough winter (1954)

Le Guin, Ursula K.

Gifts. Harcourt 2004 274p $17; $17; pa $7.95

Grades: 7 8 9 10   Fic

1. Fantasy fiction 2. Young adult literature

ISBN 9780152051235; 0-15-205123-6; 0-15-205124-4 pa

LC 2003-21449

"Brantors, or chiefs, of the various clans of the Uplands have powers passed down through generations, powers to call animals to the hunt, start fires, cast a wasting disease, or undo the very essence of a life or thing. The clans live isolated from the inhabitants of the Lowland cities in an uneasy truce, where each people's ambitions are kept at bay by fear of the other's vengeance. Two Upland teenagers, Gry and Orrec, have grown from childhood friendship into romance and also into a repudiation of their hereditary powers. . . . Rejecting traditions that bind them to roles unwanted and undesired, Gry and Orrec decide to leave their homes and seek a freer if less privileged life in the Lowlands. . . . Grades seven to twelve." (Bull Cent Child Books)

"Although intriguing as a coming-of-age allegory, Orrec's story is also rich in . . . earthy magic and intelligent plot twists." Booklist

Leach, Sara

Count me in. Orca Book Publishers 2011 pa $9.95
Grades: 4 5 6 7   **Fic**
1. Hiking -- Fiction 2. Cousins -- Fiction
ISBN 978-1-55469-404-4; 1-55469-404-3

"The characters and their motivations are well developed. The plot is simple, but entertaining, and the survival aspects of the story are realistic and suspenseful. Chapter transitions are smooth and easy to follow." SLJ

Jake Reynolds: chicken or eagle? Orca Book Publishers 2009 101p (Orca young readers) pa $7.95
Grades: 3 4 5   **Fic**
1. Fear -- Fiction 2. Wolves -- Fiction 3. Courage -- Fiction 4. Islands -- Fiction
ISBN 978-1-55469-145-6 pa; 1-55469-145-1 pa

Jake dreams of being a superhero, but he's not exactly brave, especially when it comes to wolves living on the island where he and his family are staying

"The theme of confronting fear is made vivid in this chapter book. . . . [The book offers] a heart-pounding climax and a very satisfying resolution." Booklist

Leal, Ann Haywood

A **finders**-keepers place. Henry Holt 2010 259p $16.99
Grades: 5 6 7   **Fic**
1. School stories 2. Sisters -- Fiction 3. Mental illness -- Fiction 4. Missing persons -- Fiction 5. Single parent family -- Fiction 6. Manic-depressive illness -- Fiction
ISBN 978-0-8050-8882-3; 0-8050-8882-2

LC 2009-50771

As their mother's manic-depression grows worse, eleven-year-old Esther and her sister Ruth visit various churches hoping to find their father, a preacher named Ezekiel who left them seven years before in 1966.

"Leal excels in pithy characterization, mainly through spot-on dialogue, yielding sympathetic characters, a gripping plot, and no shortage of heartbreaking moments." Publ Wkly

Lean, Sarah

★ A **dog** called Homeless; Sarah Lean. Katherine Tegen Books 2012 202 p. (trade bdg) $16.99
Grades: 3 4 5 6 7   **Fic**
1. Dogs -- Fiction 2. Grief -- Fiction 3. People with disabilities -- Fiction 4. Blind -- Fiction 5. Hearing impaired -- Fiction 6. Selective mutism -- Fiction 7. Single-parent families -- Fiction
ISBN 0062122207; 9780062122209

LC 2011044628

Schneider Family Book Award (2013)

In this book by Sarah Lean, "a girl grieving for her dead mother gives up talking when she becomes convinced that what she says doesn't matter. . . . Cally begins to see her mother . . . dressed in a red raincoat

and sometimes accompanied by a very large dog. . . . Cally also meets Mrs. Cooper, a neighbor in their new apartment building who lovingly cares for her blind, nearly deaf 11-year-old son, Sam." (Kirkus Reviews)

A **hundred** horses; Sarah Lean. Katherine Tegen Books, an imprint of HarperCollinsPublishers 2014 224 p. (hardcover bdg.) $16.99
Grades: 5 6 7 8   **Fic**
1. Farms 2. Female friendship 3. Horses -- Fiction 4. England -- Fiction 5. Runaways -- Fiction 6. Conduct of life -- Fiction 7. Farm life -- England -- Fiction 8. Family life -- England -- Fiction
ISBN 0062122290; 9780062122292

LC 2013008060

In this book by Sarah Lean, "Nell isn't happy about spending her vacation on a farm, but when she meets a half-wild and mysterious girl named Angel, the two girls are tied in an adventure that may help Nell discover something special about herself--and the most special of a hundred horses." (Publisher's note)

"-Eleven-year-old Nell Green is unhappy about having to spend her school vacation on a farm with her aunt and two younger cousins whom she hardly knows...he author intertwines the characters and story line with finesse, keeping readers guessing about Angel's identity and the appearance of the hundredth horse until the end of the evenly paced plot. A touch of magic delivers a satisfying and positive conclusion." (School Library Journal)

Leck, James

★ The **adventures** of Jack Lime; written by James Leck. Kids Can Press 2010 126p $16.95; pa $8.95
Grades: 5 6 7 8   **Fic**
1. Mystery fiction 2. Narcolepsy -- Fiction
ISBN 978-1-55453-364-0; 1-55453-364-3; 978-1-55453-365-7 pa; 1-55453-365-1 pa

"Jack Lime is the guy you come to if you've got a problem. . . . He'll find out what needs finding out. . . . This slim volume contains three cases. In the first, Jack susses out the whereabouts of a missing bike. In the second, he shakes down a hamster-napping and blackmail scheme. And in the final, he recounts his first case on the job. . . . All the touchstones that make for great noir are translated for kids. . . . The lingo that makes hard-boiled reading so much fun is here, but never schticky, and Leck knows that a great hero needs a debilitating flaw: for Jack, it's his narcolepsy." Booklist

Lee, Jenny

Elvis and the underdogs; by Jenny Lee; illustrations by Kelly Light. Balzer + Bray 2013 304 p. ill. (Elvis and the Underdogs) (hardcover bdg) $16.99
Grades: 4 5 6   **Fic**
1. Pet therapy 2. Service dogs 3. Sick -- Fiction 4. Dogs -- Fiction 5. Bullies -- Fiction 6. Schools -- Fiction 7. Family life -- Fiction 8. Human-animal communication -- Fiction
ISBN 0062235540; 9780062235541

LC 2012028329

This book, by Jenny Lee, "is about a sickly boy whose life is turned upside down when he gets a therapy dog who can talk. Elvis brings out the dog lover in the most surprising people and shows Benji that making new friends may not be as scary as he once thought." (Publisher's note)

Lee, Milly

Landed; [by] Milly Lee; pictures by Yangsook Choi. Farrar, Straus & Giroux 2006 un il $16 **Fic**
1. Immigrants -- Fiction 2. Chinese Americans -- Fiction 3. San Francisco (Calif.) -- Fiction
ISBN 0-374-34314-4

LC 2004-47216

After leaving his village in southeastern China, twelve-year-old Sun is held at Angel Island, San Francisco, before being released to join his father, a merchant living in the area. Includes historical notes

"The story is told with quiet restraint. . . . Choi's beautiful, full-page oil paintings, in sepia tones and shades of green, are quiet and packed with feeling." Booklist

Leeds, Constance

The **unfortunate** son; by Constance Leeds. Viking Childrens Books 2012 302 p. (hardcover) $16.99

Grades: 4 5 6 7   **Fic**

1. Bildungsromans 2. Historical fiction 3. Pirates -- Fiction 4. Kidnapping -- Fiction 5. Luck -- Fiction 6. Fishing -- Fiction 7. Slavery -- Fiction 8. Identity -- Fiction 9. Abnormalities, Human -- Fiction 10. Africa -- History -- To 1498 -- Fiction 11. France -- History -- 15th century -- Fiction

ISBN 0670013986; 9780670013982

LC 2011027530

This book is the story of Luc, whose "father hates him, seemingly without reason, so" the boy runs away "to apprentice with a local fisherman. . . . Living with the fisherman's family he grows close to their ward, the beautiful Beatrice, and things seem to be looking up . . . until he's kidnapped by pirates and sold to a Tunisian in North Africa. While Luc receives an education from his learned master, Beatrice" attempts to unravel Luc's past. (Kirkus Reviews)

Legrand, Claire

Some kind of happiness; Claire Legrand. Simon & Schuster Books for Young Readers 2016 384 p. (hardback) $16.99

Grades: 4 5 6 7   **Fic**

1. Fantasy fiction 2. Cousins -- Fiction 3. Secrets -- Fiction 4. Family life -- Fiction 5. Forests and forestry -- Fiction

ISBN 9781442466012

LC 2015033782

In this book, by Claire Legrand, "Finley Hart doesn't want to talk about . . . when life feels overwhelming, and it's hard to keep her head up. . . . Finley's only retreat is the Everwood, a forest kingdom that exists in the pages of her notebook. Until she discovers the endless woods behind her grandparents' house and realizes the Everwood is real. . . . With the help of her cousins, Finley sets out on a mission to save the dying Everwood and uncover its secrets." (Publisher's note)

"A quiet magic is at work in Legrand's novel, in which she adeptly interweaves Fin's imaginative writing with the real-life narrative, underpinning all with an appeal to honesty and self-acceptance. This beautiful and reflective tale carries echoes of Katherine Patterson's The Bridge to Terabithia (1977) and will resonate with thoughtful readers who enjoy pondering life's bigger questions." Booklist

Lendroth, Susan

Calico Dorsey; mail dog of the mining camps. illustrations by Adam Gustavson. Tricycle Press 2010 un il $16.99; lib bdg $19.99

Grades: 2 3 4 5   **Fic**

1. Dogs -- Fiction 2. California -- Fiction 3. Postal service -- Fiction 4. Silver mines and mining -- Fiction

ISBN 978-1-58246-318-6; 1-58246-318-2; 978-1-58246-367-4 lib bdg; 1-58246-367-0 lib bdg

A Border Collie named Dorsey works with Al to deliver the mail and carry supplies to the miners living in Calico, California, during the nineteenth century, but on the morning that Al decides to postpone his duties Dorsey has other plans.

"Gustavson's paintings are intergrated into the text, flowing from page through the centerfold to page, making this obscure story larger than life. The vitality of the characters is enhanced by the artist's accu-

rate, yet expressive details that add humor and sweetness to the faces of both the people and Dorsey." SLJ

Leonard, M. G.

Beetle boy; by M.G. Leonard. Chicken House/Scholastic Inc. 2016 270 p. (hbk.) $16.99

Grades: 4 5 6 7 8   **Fic**

1. Beetles -- Fiction 2. Friendship -- Fiction 3. Best friends -- Fiction 4. Missing persons -- Fiction 5. Uncles -- Fiction 6. Fathers and sons -- Fiction 7. Mystery and detective stories

ISBN 054585346X; 9780545853460

LC 2015028492

In this juvenile novel, by by M. G. Leonard, "Darkus Cuttle's dad mysteriously goes missing . . . so Darkus moves in with his eccentric Uncle Max and next door to . . . two lunatic cousins with an enormous beetle infestation. Darkus soon discovers that the beetles are anything but ordinary. . . . It's up to Darkus and his friends to save the beetles. But they're up against an even more terrifying villain -- mad scientist of fashion, haute couture villainess Lucretia Cutter." (Publisher's note)

"Overall, a charming and (at times) affecting romp through beetle land." Kirkus

Includes bibliographical references

Lerangis, Peter

The **colossus** rises; Peter Lerangis. Harper 2013 348 p. (Seven wonders) (hardcover bdg.) $17.99; (pbk.) $6.99

Grades: 4 5 6 7 8 9   **Fic**

1. Fantasy fiction 2. Adventure fiction 3. Atlantis (Legendary place) 4. Science fiction 5. Ability -- Fiction 6. Friendship -- Fiction 7. Adventure and adventurers -- Fiction

ISBN 0062070401; 006207041X; 9780062070401; 9780062070418

LC 2012025334

This children's fantasy story, by Peter Lerangis, illustrated by Torstein Norstrand and Mike Reagan, is the first of the "Seven Wonders" series. "13-year-old Jack McKinley will die unless he can locate the magic Loculi containing the ancient powers of Atlantis. . . . The problem is that . . . Atlantis was . . . divided into seven containers and hidden in the Seven Wonders of the Ancient World. Finding the powers will not only save Jack's life, but also give him superpowers." (Kirkus Reviews)

Teens Jack, Marco, Aly, and Cass begin a quest to find seven pieces of Atlantis' power that were hidden long ago and that will, if returned to Atlantis, save them from certain death due to the genetic abnormality that also gives them superior abilities.

Lost in babylon; by Peter Lerangis and translated by Torstein Norstrand. HarperCollins 2013 384 p. (Seven wonders) (hardcover bdg.) $17.99

Grades: 4 5 6 7 8 9   **Fic**

1. Occult fiction 2. Adventure fiction 3. Seven Wonders of the World -- Fiction

ISBN 0062070436; 9780062070432

LC 2013942765

This book, by Peter Lerangis, "chronicles Jack McKinley and his friends as they carry on their mission to save their lives—and the world—by locating seven magic orbs called Loculi, which are hidden in the Seven Wonders of the Ancient World. After defeating the Colossus of Rhodes and capturing the first of the Loculi, their friend Marco has disappeared. With no leads, no clues, and no one else to turn to, the kids have no choice but to trust Professor Bhegad and the Karai Institute again as they head off to Babylon." (Publisher's note)

Tomb of shadows; Peter Lerangis, Torstein Norstrand; [edited by] David Linker. HarperCollins 2014 352 p. (Seven wonders) (hardcover) $17.99

Grades: 4 5 6 7 8 9 **Fic**

1. Fantasy fiction 2. Seven Wonders of the World -- Fiction 3. Adventure stories 4. Betrayal -- Fiction

ISBN 0062070460; 9780062070463

LC 2014931071

This middle grades fantasy novel by Peter Lerangis, illustrated by Torstein Norstrand, part of the Seven Wonders series, "chronicles the adventures of Jack McKinley and his friends in a life-or-death race to the Mausoleum at Halicarnassus. In the rubble of this Wonder of the Ancient World, they have to face down their own demons and engage in an epic battle with foes long gone." (Publisher's note)

"Jack, Ally, and Cass continue their quest to save the world—even as their friend Marco joins the enemy's side. Epic battles and fast-moving chapters will keep fans of this "Percy Jackson"-like series engaged." SLJ

Other titles in the series include:

The Colossus Rises (2013)
Lost in Bablyon (2013)

Lester, Julius

★ The **old** African; illustrated by Jerry Pinkney. Dial Bks. 2005 79p il $19.99

Grades: 3 4 5 6 **Fic**

1. Slavery -- Fiction 2. African Americans -- Fiction 3. Extrasensory perception -- Fiction

ISBN 0-8037-2564-7

LC 2003-15671

An elderly slave uses the power of his mind to ease the suffering of his fellow slaves and eventually lead them back to Africa.

"The stirring illustrations, glowing with color and swirling with action, beautifully depict the dramatic escape fantasy (which is based on legend), but they never deny the horror." Booklist

Lettrick, Robert

The **murk**; by Robert Lettrick. Disney-Hyperion 2015 320 p. (hardback) $16.99

Grades: 4 5 6 7 **Fic**

1. Horror fiction 2. Adventure fiction 3. Plants -- Fiction 4. Monsters -- Fiction 5. Friendship -- Fiction 6. Brothers and sisters -- Fiction 7. Horror stories 8. Sick -- Fiction 9. Adventure and adventurers -- Fiction 10. Okefenokee Swamp (Ga. and Fla.) -- Fiction

ISBN 9781423186953

LC 2014031438

In this book, by Robert Lettrick, "the Okefenokee Swamp grows a rare and beautiful flower with a power unlike any other. Many have tried to claim it-no one has come out alive. But fourteen-year-old Piper Canfield is desperate, and this flower may be her only chance to keep a promise she made a long time ago. Accompanied by her little brother, Creeper, her friend Tad, and two local guides, Piper embarks on the quest of a lifetime." (Publisher's note)

"The plot moves fast enough to keep pages turning while leaving just enough room to develop character." SLJ

Levine, Gail Carson

Ella enchanted. HarperCollins Pubs. 1997 232p $16.99; lib bdg $17.89; pa $6.50

Grades: 5 6 7 8 **Fic**

1. Fantasy fiction 2. Young adult literature

ISBN 0-06-027510-3; 0-06-027511-1 lib bdg; 0-06-440705-5 pa

LC 96-30734

A Newbery Medal honor book, 1998

"Ella is blessed by a fairy at birth with the gift of obedience. But the blessing is a horror for Ella, who must literally do what everyone tells her, from sweeping the floor to giving up a beloved heirloom necklace. After her mother dies, and her covetous, caustic father leaves on a trading trip, Ella's world is turned upside down. She battles both ogres and wicked stepsisters, makes friends and loses them, and must deny her love for her prince, Charmont, to save his life and his realm. In making this ultimate sacrifice, she breaks the curse." (Booklist) "Grades five to eight." (Bull Cent Child Books)

"As finely designed as a tapestry, Ella's story both neatly incorporates elements of the original tale and mightily expands them." Booklist

★ **Ever**. HarperCollinsPublishers 2008 256p $16.99; lib bdg $17.89; pa $6.99

Grades: 5 6 7 8 **Fic**

1. Young adult literature 2. Winds -- Fiction 3. Immortality -- Fiction 4. Fate and fatalism -- Fiction 5. Gods and goddesses -- Fiction

ISBN 978-0-06-122962-6; 0-06-122962-8; 978-0-06-122963-3 lib bdg; 0-06-122963-6 lib bdg; 978-0-06-122964-0 pa; 0-06-122964-4 pa

LC 2007-32289

Fourteen-year-old Kezi and Olus, Akkan god of the winds, fall in love and together try to change her fate—to be sacrificed to a Hyte god because of a rash promise her father made—through a series of quests that might make her immortal.

"Levine conducts a riveting journey, offering passion and profound pondering along the way." Publ Wkly

★ A **tale** of Two Castles. Harper 2011 328p $16.99; lib bdg $17.89

Grades: 4 5 6 **Fic**

1. Fantasy fiction 2. Mystery fiction 3. Dragons -- Fiction 4. Apprentices -- Fiction 5. Kings and rulers -- Fiction

ISBN 978-0-06-122965-7; 0-06-122965-2; 978-0-06-122966-4 lib bdg; 0-06-122966-0 lib bdg

LC 2010027756

"Hoping to apprentice as an actor, Elodie travels from her rural home to the city of Two Castles. . . . When she's robbed and then rejected as an actor, she apprentices herself to crafty dragon Meenore as a detective. Shape-shifting Count Jonty Um, a kindly ogre, is their first client. . . . But who is to be trusted and who isn't? . . . Intermediate, middle school." (Horn Book)

"Readers are certain to be pulled, like Elodie herself, right into the midst of the rich and swirling life of Two Castles." SLJ

The **two** princesses of Bamarre. HarperCollins Pubs. 2001 241p $15.99; pa $5.99

Grades: 5 6 7 8 **Fic**

1. Fantasy fiction 2. Sisters -- Fiction 3. Princesses -- Fiction

ISBN 0-06-029315-2; 0-06-440966-X pa

LC 00-47953

With her adventurous sister, Meryl, suffering from the Gray Death, meek and timid Princess Addie sets out to find a cure

"A lively tale with vivid characters and an exciting plot." Book Rep

Levine, Kristin

★ The **best** bad luck I ever had. Putnam 2009 266p $16.99

Grades: 6 7 8 9 **Fic**

1. Young adult literature 2. Alabama -- Fiction 3. Friendship -- Fiction 4. Prejudices -- Fiction 5. Family life -- Fiction 6. Country

life -- Fiction 7. Race relations -- Fiction
ISBN 978-0-399-25090-3; 0-399-25090-5

LC 2008-11570

In Moundville, Alabama, in 1917, twelve-year-old Dit hopes the new postmaster will have a son his age, but instead he meets Emma, who is black, and their friendship challenges accepted ways of thinking and leads them to save the life of a condemned man.

"Tension builds just below the surface of this energetic, seamlessly narrated . . . novel. . . . Levine handles the setting with grace and nuance." Publ Wkly

★ The **lions** of Little Rock; Kristin Levine. G. P. Putnam's Sons 2012 298p.
Grades: 5 6 7 8   **Fic**
1. School stories 2. African Americans -- Fiction 3. School integration -- Fiction 4. Schools -- Fiction 5. Friendship -- Fiction 6. Bashfulness -- Fiction 7. Middle schools -- Fiction 8. Race relations -- Fiction 9. Family life -- Arkansas -- Fiction 10. Little Rock (Ark.) -- History -- 20th century -- Fiction
ISBN 9780399256448

LC 2011031835

This book presents a "portrait of 1958 Little Rock, Ark., the tumultuous year when the governor refused integration by closing local high schools. The story is told through the . . . voice of painfully quiet 12-year-old Marlee Nisbett, who makes a rare friend in Liz, a new student at her middle school. Liz instills some much-needed confidence in Marlee, but when it's revealed that Liz is 'passing' as a white student, Liz must leave school abruptly, putting their friendship to the test. The girls meet in secret, and Marlee joins an antisegregationist organization, both actions inviting serious risk amid escalating racist threats." (Publishers Weekly)

Levitin, Sonia
Journey to America; illustrated by Charles Robinson. Atheneum Pubs. 1993 150p il hardcover o.p. pa $4.99
Grades: 4 5 6 7   **Fic**
1. Family life -- Fiction 2. Jewish refugees -- Fiction 3. World War, 1939-1945 -- Fiction
ISBN 0-689-71130-1 pa

LC 93-163980

A reissue of the title first published 1970

"In a strong immigration story, Lisa Platt, the middle daughter, tells how her family is forced to leave Nazi Germany and make a new life in the United States. First their father leaves, then the others escape to Switzerland, where they endure harsh conditions. After months of separation, the family is reunited in New York." Rochman. Against borders

Followed by Silver days (1989) and Annie's promise (1993)

Levy, Dana Alison
The **family** Fletcher takes Rock Island; Dana Alison Levy. Delacorte Press 2016 272 p. (hc) $16.99
Grades: 4 5 6 7   **Fic**
1. Humorous fiction 2. Summer -- Fiction 3. Neighbors -- Fiction 4. Family life -- Fiction 5. Lighthouses -- Fiction 6. Humorous stories 7. Gay fathers -- Fiction
ISBN 9780553521306; 9780553521313

LC 2015014134

In this book, by Dana Alison Levy, the "Fletchers are back on Rock Island, home of all their best summer memories. But from their first day on vacation, it's clear that this year, things have changed. . . . Over the course of the summer, the Fletchers will learn that sometimes, even in a place where time stands still, the wildest, weirdest, and most wonderful surprises await." (Publisher's note)

"There is constant action and delightful humor, but there are also realistic present-day problems and happy solutions. An old-fashioned summer adventure set in a very modern world, this lively family tale will leave readers impatient for more." Kirkus

The **misadventures** of the family Fletcher; Dana Levy. Delacorte Press 2014 272 p. (glb) $18.99
Grades: 4 5 6 7   **Fic**
1. Interracial adoption 2. Children of gay parents -- Fiction 3. Humorous stories 4. Schools -- Fiction 5. Adoption -- Fiction 6. Brothers -- Fiction 7. Neighbors -- Fiction 8. Family life -- Fiction
ISBN 0385376545; 9780385376525; 9780385376549

LC 2013026320

In this middle grades book by Dana Alison Levy, "With four brothers, a dog, a cat, school projects, soccer matches, and a grumpy neighbor, the Fletchers are your typical American family . . . with two dads, and siblings who are adopted kids from various ethnic backgrounds. While 12-year-old Sam ponders . . . trying out for the school play . . . , 10-year-old Jax negotiates changing friendships and a veteran project that involves talking to the unfriendly Vietnam vet next door." (School Library Journal)

"Four adopted (and racially diverse) brothers and two dads star in this Penderwicks-esque chronicle of a year in their lives. Focusing each chapter on one boy while still keeping the whole family in the picture, Levy provides a compelling, compassionate, and frequently hilarious look at their daily concerns. Readers will want to be part of (or at least friends with) this delightful family." Horn Book

This would make a good story someday; Dana Alison Levy. Delacorte Press 2017 320 p. (hardback) $16.99
Grades: 4 5 6 7 8   **Fic**
1. Family life -- Fiction 2. Railroad travel -- Fiction 3. Authorship -- Fiction 4. Family life -- Fiction 5. Gay parents -- Fiction 6. Lesbian mothers -- Fiction 7.
ISBN 9781101938171; 9781101938188

LC 2016032310

In this book, by Dana Alison Levy, "Sara Johnston-Fischer loves her family, of course. But that doesn't mean she's thrilled when her summer plans are upended for a surprise cross-country train trip with her two moms, Mimi and Carol; her younger sister, Ladybug; her older sister, Laurel; and Laurel's poncho-wearing activist boyfriend, Root. And to make matters worse, one of her moms is writing a tell-all book about the trip." (Publisher's note)

Lewis, C. S. (Clive Staples), 1898-1963
The **horse** and his boy; illustrated by Pauline Baynes. HarperCollins 1994 224p il (The chronicles of Narnia) lib bdg $17; pa $6.99
Grades: 4 5 6 7   **Fic**
1. Fantasy fiction
ISBN 0-06-023489-X lib bdg; 0-06-447106-3 pa

LC 93014300

Sequel to: The silver chair

A reissue of the title first published 1954

A boy and a talking horse share an adventurous and dangerous journey to Narnia to warn of invading barbarians.

Followed by: The magician's nephew

The **last** battle; illustrated by Pauline Baynes. HarperCollins 1994 211p il (The chronicles of Narnia) pa $6.99
Grades: 4 5 6 7   **Fic**
1. Fantasy fiction
ISBN 0-06-023494-6 lib bdg; 0-06-447108-X pa

LC 93014302

Sequel to: The magician's nephew

A reissue of the title first published 1956

When evil comes to Narnia, Jill and Eustace help fight the great last battle and Aslan leads his people to a glorious new paradise.

★ The **lion,** the witch, and the wardrobe; illustrated by Pauline Baynes. HarperCollins Pubs. 1994 189p il (The chronicles of Narnia) $17.99; lib bdg $18.89; pa $7.99

Grades: 4 5 6 7 **Fic**

1. Fantasy fiction

ISBN 0-06-023481-4; 0-06-023482-2 lib bdg; 0-06-440499-4 pa

LC 93-8889

A reissue of the title first published 1950 by Macmillan

Four English schoolchildren find their way through the back of a wardrobe into the magic land of Narnia and assist Aslan, the golden lion, to triumph over the White Witch, who has cursed the land with eternal winter

This begins "the 'Narnia' stories, outstanding modern fairy tales with an underlying theme of good overcoming evil." Child Books Too Good to Miss

Other titles in this series are:

Prince Caspian (1951)

The voyage of the Dawn Treader (1952)

The silver chair (1953)

The horse and his boy (1954)

The magician's nephew (1956)

The last battle (1956)

The **magician's** nephew; illustrated by Pauline Baynes. Harper-Collins 1994 202p il (The chronicles of Narnia) lib bdg $18.89; pa $7.99

Grades: 4 5 6 7 **Fic**

1. Fantasy fiction

ISBN 0-06-023498-9 lib bdg; 0-06-440505-2 pa

LC 93014301

Sequel to: The horse and his boy

A reissue of the title first published 1956

When Digory and Polly try to return the wicked witch Jadis to her own world, the magic gets mixed up and they all land in Narnia where they witness Aslan blessing the animals with human speech.

Followed by: The last battle

Prince Caspian; the return to Narnia. illustrated by Pauline Baynes. HarperCollins 1994 223p il (The chronicles of Narnia) lib bdg $18.89; pa $6.99

Grades: 4 5 6 7 **Fic**

1. Fantasy fiction

ISBN 0-06-023484-9 lib bdg; 0-06-447105-5 pa

LC 93011514

Sequel to: The lion, the witch, and the wardrobe

A reissue of the title first published 1951

Four children help Prince Caspian and his army of Talking Beasts to free Narnia from evil.

Followed by: The voyage of the Dawn Treader

The **silver** chair; illustrated by Pauline Baynes. HarperCollins 1994 243p il (The chronicles of Narnia) lib bdg $18.89; pa $6.99

Grades: 4 5 6 7 **Fic**

1. Fantasy fiction

ISBN 0-06-023496-2 lib bdg; 0-06-447109-8 pa

LC 93014299

Sequel to: The voyage of the Dawn Treader

A reissue of the title first published 1953

Two English children undergo hair-raising adventures as they go on a search and rescue mission for the missing Prince Rilian, who is held captive in the underground kingdom of the Emerald Witch.

Followed by: The horse and his boy

The **voyage** of the Dawn Treader; illustrated by Pauline Baynes. HarperCollins 1994 248p il (The chronicles of Narnia) lib bdg $17.99; pa $6.99

Grades: 4 5 6 7 **Fic**

1. Fantasy fiction

ISBN 0-06-023487-3 lib bdg; 0-06-447107-1 pa

LC 93011515

Sequel to: Prince Caspian

A reissue of the title first published 1952

Lucy and Edmund, accompanied by their peevish cousin Eustace, sail to the land of Narnia where Eustace is temporarily transformed into a green dragon because of his selfish behavior and skepticism.

Followed by: The silver chair

Lewis, Elizabeth Foreman

Young Fu of the upper Yangtze; [by] Elizabeth Foreman Lewis; illustrations by William Low. 75th anniversary ed.; Henry Holt 2007 302p il $17.95; pa $7.99

Grades: 4 5 6 **Fic**

1. China -- Fiction 2. City and town life -- Fiction

ISBN 978-0-8050-8113-8; 0-8050-8113-5; 978-0-312-38007-6 pa; 0-312-38007-0 pa

LC 2006049633

A newly illustrated edition of the title first published 1932 by The John C. Winston Company

Awarded the Newbery Medal, 1933

In the 1920's, a Chinese youth from the country comes to Chungking with his mother where the bustling city offers adventure and his apprenticeship to a coppersmith brings good fortune

This edition "features a foreword by Katherine Paterson, extensive end-notes comparing China then and now, and new, atmospheric black-and-white illustrations." Horn Book Guide

Lewis, Gill

Moon bear; Gill Lewis; illustrated by Alessandro Gottardo. Atheneum Books for Young Readers 2015 384 p. illustrations (hardcover) $16.99

Grades: 4 5 6 7 8 **Fic**

1. Laos -- Fiction 2. Bears -- Fiction 3. Asiatic black bear -- Fiction 4. Animals -- Treatment -- Fiction

ISBN 1481400940; 9781481400947; 9781481400954

LC 2013049285

In this book, by Gill Lewis, "[t]welve-year-old Tam, on a dare, ventures into a moon bear den in the mountains of Northern Laos. His goal is to steal the cub and sell it, making a fortune for his family. But the mother bear's unexpected return upends Tam's plan, and he barely escapes with his life. And then his life implodes anyway. . . . Tam is forced to work hundreds of miles away in the city, at a moon bear farm where bile from bear gall bladders is used for medicine." (Publisher's note)

"Through Tam's selfless quest to get the bear back to the wild, and his protection of the cub at the expense of his own well-being, readers witness the depths of his bravery, compassion, and strong moral compass." Pub Wkly

★ **Wild** wings; illustrated by Yuta Onoda. Atheneum Books for Young Readers 2011 287p il $15.99

Grades: 4 5 6 7 **Fic**

1. Gambia -- Fiction 2. Ospreys -- Fiction 3. Scotland -- Fiction

4. Farm life -- Fiction 5. Friendship -- Fiction
ISBN 1-4424-1445-6; 978-1-4424-1445-7

LC 2010-49228

Callum becomes friends with Iona, a practically feral classmate who has discovered an osprey, thought to be gone from Scotland, on Callum's family farm, and they eventually share the secret with others, including Jeneba who encounters the same bird at her home in Gambia.

This is a "rich, moving tale. . . . The suspenseful story line is surrounded with precise details. . . . Short chapters, some with cliffhanging endings, will read-aloud well. . . . A powerfully memorable story." Kirkus

Lewis, J. Patrick

★ **And** the soldiers sang; [written by] J. Patrick Lewis & [illustrations by] Gary Kelley. Creative Editions 2011 31p il $17.99
Grades: 2 3 4 5 6   **Fic**
1. Soldiers -- Fiction 2. Christmas -- Fiction 3. World War, 1914-1918 -- Fiction
ISBN 978-1-5684-6220-2; 1-5684-6220-4

LC 2010028644

A young Welsh soldier fights along the Western Front during World War I, experiencing the horrors of trench warfare before participating in the famed Christmas Truce of 1914.

This offers "a terse yet lyrical text and stark, dramatic illustrations. . . . Kelley's compelling artwork features mostly dark shades and strong, angular compositions. . . . Grim, upsetting and utterly beautiful, this is both a strong antiwar statement and a fascinating glimpse of a little-known historical event." Kirkus

Lewis, Maggie

★ **Morgy** makes his move; illustrated by Michael Chesworth. Houghton Mifflin 1999 74p il $15; pa $4.95
Grades: 2 3 4   **Fic**
1. School stories 2. Moving -- Fiction 3. Massachusetts -- Fiction
ISBN 0-395-92284-4; 0-618-19680-3 pa

LC 98-43245

When third-grader Morgy MacDougal-MacDuff moves from California to Massachusetts with his parents, he has a lot of new things to get used to before he feels comfortable

"Heavy issues are handled lightly; language is simple and straightforward; Michael Chesworth's illustrations are funny and exaggerated." Booklist

Other titles about Morgy are:
Morgy coast to coast (2005)
Morgy's musical summer (2008)

Morgy's musical summer; by Maggie Lewis; illustrated by Michael Chesworth. Houghton Mifflin Co. 2008 100p il $15
Grades: 2 3 4   **Fic**
1. Camps -- Fiction 2. Musicians -- Fiction
ISBN 978-0-618-77707-5; 0-618-77707-5

LC 2007025780

To encourage his talent for playing the trumpet, Morgy is sent to a music camp over the summer, where he has the displeasure of meeting Damian, an advanced student who likes to tease "promising beginners."

"Illustrated with a dozen full-page drawings with gray washes, the story moves along quickly. . . . [This is an] enjoyable chapter book." Booklist

Lin, Grace

Dumpling days. Little, Brown 2012 $15.99
Grades: 3 4 5   **Fic**
1. Taiwan -- Fiction 2. Birthdays -- Fiction 3. Family life -- Fiction

4. Grandmothers -- Fiction 5. Taiwanese Americans -- Fiction
ISBN 978-0-316-12590-1; 0-316-12590-3

LC 2010048036

When Pacy, her two sisters, and their parents go to Taiwan to celebrate Grandma's sixtieth birthday, the girls learn a great deal about their heritage.

"Deftly weaving together historical anecdotes and simple line illustrations, Lin once again touches the heart of growing up in a multicultural family." Kirkus

★ **Starry** River of the Sky; by Grace Lin. Little, Brown 2012 288 p. col. ill. $17.99
Grades: 3 4 5 6   **Fic**
1. Fairy tales 2. Moon -- Fiction 3. Villages -- Fiction 4. Storytelling -- Fiction
ISBN 0316125954; 9780316125956

LC 2012012651

In this novel by Grace Lin, "the moon is missing from the remote Village of Clear Sky, but only a young boy named Rendi seems to notice! Rendi has run away from home and is now working as a chore boy at the village inn. He can't help but notice the village's peculiar inhabitants and their problems . . . but one day, a mysterious lady arrives at the Inn with the gift of storytelling, and slowly transforms the villagers and Rendi himself." (Publisher's note)

Includes bibliographical references.

★ **When** the sea turned to silver; Grace Lin. Little, Brown Books for Young Readers 2016 384 p. color illustrations (ebook) $57; (hardback) $18.99
Grades: 4 5 6 7   **Fic**
1. Adventure fiction 2. Kidnapping -- Fiction 3. Grandmothers -- Fiction 4. Storytelling -- Fiction 5. China -- History -- Fiction 6. Fairy tales 7. Storytellers -- Fiction 8. Adventure and adventurers -- Fiction
ISBN 9780316396387; 9780316125925

LC 2015041876

National Book Award Finalist: Young People's Literature (2016)

In this book, by Grace Lin, "Pinmei's gentle, loving grandmother always has the most exciting tales for her granddaughter and the other villagers. However, the peace is shattered one night when soldiers of the Emperor arrive and kidnap the storyteller. Everyone knows that the Emperor wants something called the Luminous Stone That Lights the Night. Determined to have her grandmother returned, Pinmei embarks on a journey to find the Luminous Stone alongside her friend Yishan." (Publisher's note)

"A stunning addition to a deservedly beloved set of novels" SLJ
Includes bibliographical references

★ **Where** the mountain meets the moon. Little, Brown and Co. 2009 278p il $16.99
Grades: 4 5 6 7   **Fic**
1. Fairy tales 2. Moon -- Fiction 3. Dragons -- Fiction
ISBN 978-0-316-11427-1; 0-316-11427-8

LC 2008-32818

A Newbery Medal honor book, 2010

Minli, an adventurous girl from a poor village, buys a magical goldfish, and then joins a dragon who cannot fly on a quest to find the Old Man of the Moon in hopes of bringing life to Fruitless Mountain and freshness to Jade River

"With beautiful language, Lin creates a strong, memorable heroine and a mystical land. . . . Children will embrace this accessible, timeless story about the evil of greed and the joy of gratitude." Booklist

★ The **Year** of the Dog; a novel. Little, Brown 2006 134p il $14.99; pa $5.99

Grades: 3 4 5   **Fic**

1. Chinese New Year -- Fiction 2. Taiwanese Americans -- Fiction

ISBN 0-316-06000-3; 0-316-06002-X pa

LC 2005-02586

Frustrated at her seeming lack of talent for anything, Pacy, a young Taiwanese American girl, sets out to apply the lessons of the Chinese Year of the Dog, those of making best friends and finding oneself, to her own life.

"The story . . . is entertaining and often illuminating. Appealing, childlike decorative drawings add a delightful flavor to a gentle tale full of humor." Horn Book

Other titles about Pacy are:

The Year of the Rat (2008)

Dumpling days (2011)

The **Year** of the Rat; a novel. Little, Brown 2007 182p il $14.99

Grades: 3 4 5   **Fic**

1. School stories 2. Family life -- Fiction 3. Chinese New Year -- Fiction 4. New York (State) -- Fiction 5. Taiwanese Americans -- Fiction

ISBN 978-0-316-11426-4; 0-316-11426-X

LC 2007-12327

In the Chinese Year of the Rat, Pacy, a young Taiwanese American girl, faces many challenges: her best friend moves to California and a new boy comes to her school, she must find the courage to forge ahead with her dream of becoming a writer and illustrator, and she must learn to find the beauty in change.

"Young readers will find this episodic, character-driven short novel appealing and relate to its authentically childlike Pacy. . . . Lin's plentiful detailed line drawings add to the story's appeal." SLJ

Lindgren, Astrid

★ **Pippi** Longstocking; [by] Astrid Lindgren; translated by Tiina Nunnally; illustrated by Lauren Child. Viking Children's Books 2007 207p il $25

Grades: 3 4 5 6   **Fic**

1. Sweden -- Fiction

ISBN 978-0-670-06276-8

Original Swedish edition, 1945; first English language edition 1950

Escapades of a lucky little girl who lives with a horse and a monkey—but without any parents—at the edge of a Swedish village

"This oversize edition of the classic story has much to offer a new generation of readers. It has full-color illustrations . . . and a new translation. . . . Nunnally's language flows naturally and gives a fresh, modern feel to the line drawings, filled with color and pattern." SLJ

Other titles about Pippi Longstocking are:

Pippi goes on board (1957)

Pippi in the South Seas (1959)

Lindo, Elvira

Manolito Four-Eyes; illustrated by Emilio Urberuaga; translated by Joanne Moriarity. Marshall Cavendish Children 2008 144p il (Manolito Four-Eyes) $15.99

Grades: 4 5 6   **Fic**

1. School stories 2. Spain -- Fiction 3. Family life -- Fiction 4. Grandfathers -- Fiction

ISBN 978-0-7614-5303-1; 0-7614-5303-2

Original Spanish edition 2003

Recounts the exploits of the irrepressible Manolito as he navigates the world of his small Madrid neighborhood, along with his grandpa, his little brother, and his school friends.

"The protagonist is a wild, spunky, dramatic, comical sort of character sure to be popular with children, who will probably find him, in Manolito's own inimitable words, a 'whole lotta cool.' Lively cartoon illustrations are scattered throughout." SLJ

Other titles about Manolito are:

Manolito Four-Eyes: the 2nd volume of the great encyclopedia of my life (2009)

Manolito Four-Eyes: the 3rd volume of the great encyclopedia of my life (2010)

Manolito Four-Eyes: the 2nd volume of the great encyclopedia of my life. Marshall Cavendish 2009 148p (Manolito Four-Eyes) $15.99

Grades: 4 5 6   **Fic**

1. School stories 2. Spain -- Fiction 3. Grandfathers -- Fiction

ISBN 978-0-7614-5470-0; 0-7614-5470-5

LC 2008-6481

Eight-year-old Manolito recounts further exploits in his small Madrid neighborhood with his grandfather, his little brother Bozo, and his school friends, including a shoplifting prank, recycled art, and the Filthy Feet Gang.

"Kids will both relate to and root for the lovable and spunky protagonist and enjoy the humorous cartoons that accompany his escapades." SLJ

Manolito Four-Eyes: the 3rd volume of the great encyclopedia of my life. Marshall Cavendish Children 2010 126p (Manolito Four-Eyes) $15.99

Grades: 4 5 6   **Fic**

1. Spain -- Fiction 2. Friendship -- Fiction 3. Family life -- Fiction

ISBN 978-0-7614-5651-3; 0-7614-5651-1

LC 2009004350

Original Spanish edition 1996

Recounts the further adventures of the resourceful Manolito and his friends while on summer vacation in the Madrid neighborhood where they all live.

"The lively line drawings underscore the story's comedy, which ranges from bathroom humor of the most literal sort to a backspin of sly wit in seemingly straightforward observations of friends and kin." Booklist

Lipsyte, Robert

The **twinning** project; by Robert Lipsyte. Clarion Books 2012 269 p. (hardback) $16.99

Grades: 4 5 6 7   **Fic**

1. Science fiction 2. Twins -- Fiction 3. Parallel universes -- Fiction 4. Schools -- Fiction 5. Middle schools -- Fiction 6. Space and time -- Fiction

ISBN 0547645716; 9780547645711

LC 2011050252

This book by Robert Lipsyte follows protagonist Tom, who has been "expelled from school after school for fighting bullies. . . . The boy's only comfort comes from talking through his problems with his imaginary twin, Eddie, a jock who lives on a version of Earth 50 years behind Tom's. . . . When the boys' 'grandfather' on both Earths reveals that the twin planets were created by alien scientists, the boys switch places to fight for the survival of both Earths." (Publishers Weekly)

Lisle, Holly

The **Ruby** Key. Orchard Books 2008 361p (Moon & sun) $16.99; pa $7.99

Grades: 5 6 7 8 **Fic**

1. Fantasy fiction 2. Siblings -- Fiction
ISBN 978-0-545-00012-3; 0-545-00012-2; 978-0-545-00013-0
pa; 0-545-00013-0 pa

LC 2007-30217

In a world where an uneasy peace binds Humans and Nightlings, fourteen-year-old Genna and her twelve-year-old brother Dan learn of their uncle's plot to gain immortality in exchange for human lives, and the two strike their own bargain with the Nightling lord, which sets them on a dangerous journey along the Moonroads in search of a key.

"Lisle's fertile imagination provides the nightworlds with monsters . . . but it is her clever plotting in this . . . fantasy, leading up to a thrilling finish . . . That will bewitch her audience." Horn Book

Followed by: The silver door (2009)

The **silver** door. Orchard Books 2009 366p (Moon & sun) $17.99
Grades: 5 6 7 8 **Fic**

1. War stories 2. Fantasy fiction
ISBN 978-0-545-00014-7; 0-545-00014-9

LC 2008-40153

When Genna is chosen as the Sunrider of prophecy, her destiny is to unite the magic of the sun and the moon for the good of both Nightlings and humans.

"This second book of the Moon & Sun series has jarring stop-start feel, but the complexities of the interlaced human and nightling societies continue to unfold in fascinating way, creating a multi-hued, fully realized world for readers to explore." Horn Book

Lisle, Janet Taylor

Afternoon of the elves. Orchard Bks. 1989 122p hardcover o.p.
pa $6.99
Grades: 4 5 6 **Fic**

1. Friendship -- Fiction 2. Mentally ill -- Fiction
ISBN 0-531-05837-9; 0-698-11806-5 pa

LC 88-35099

A Newbery Medal honor book, 1990

"'Afternoon of the elves' is a distinctive portrayal of the way children figure out ways to inhabit the world when there aren't any adults around." N Y Times Book Rev

★ The **art** of keeping cool. Atheneum Bks. for Young Readers 2000 207p hardcover o.p.
Grades: 5 6 7 8 **Fic**

1. Artists 2. Cousins 3. Grandparents 4. Rhode Island 5. Family problems 6. Rhode Island -- Fiction 7. World War, 1939-1945 -- Fiction 8. World War, 1939-1945 -- United States 9. World War, 1939-1945 -- Rhode Island -- Fiction
ISBN 0689837879; 0689837887

LC 00-32778

In 1942, Robert and his cousin Elliot uncover long-hidden family secrets while staying in their grandparents' Rhode Island town. They also become involved with a German artist who is suspected of being a spy. "Ages ten to fourteen." (N Y Times Book Rev)

"Lisle develops an unforgettable cast of characters placed against a fully realized setting. Engrossing, challenging, and well paced." Horn Book

Quicksand Pond; Janet Taylor Lisle. Atheneum Books for Young Readers 2017 256 p. illustrations, map (hardcover) $16.99
Grades: 5 6 7 8 **Fic**

1. Ponds -- Fiction 2. Homicide -- Fiction 3. Friendship -- Fiction 4. Murder -- Fiction
ISBN 9781481472227; 9781481472234

LC 2016009707

In this book, author Janet Taylor Lisle "crafts a stirring story that raises crucial questions about the assumptions we make, the distances we keep, and the vulnerable voices we often fail to hear. As Lisle details Terri's determination to cease a vicious cycle, Henrietta's resolve to remedy an unjust past, and Jessie's aching ambivalence between the cautionary advice of others and her own hard-won revelations, readers are sure to listen." (Booklist)

"A strong purchase for fans of layered, realistic mysteries and drama." School Library Journal.

Little, Kimberley Griffiths

★ **Circle** of secrets. Scholastic Press 2011 326p $17.99
Grades: 5 6 7 8 **Fic**

1. Ghost stories 2. Guilt -- Fiction 3. Louisiana -- Fiction 4. Mother-daughter relationship -- Fiction
ISBN 978-0-545-16561-7; 0-545-16561-X

LC 2011000889

A year after her mother has deserted the family, eleven-year-old Shelby goes to stay with her, deep in the Louisiana bayou, where they both confront old hurts and regrets.

"The gently spooky ghost angle is handled nicely with some religious overtones. A very dramatic climax leads to a sweet, satisfying ending with some surprising twists and with reconciliation occurring for several characters." Kirkus

The **healing** spell. Scholastic Press 2010 354p $17.99
Grades: 5 6 7 8 **Fic**

1. Coma -- Fiction 2. Guilt -- Fiction 3. Mother-daughter relationship -- Fiction
ISBN 978-0-545-16559-4; 0-545-16559-8

LC 2009-28016

Twelve-year-old Livie is living with a secret and it's crushing her. She knows she is responsible for her mother's coma, but she can't tell anyone. It's up to her to find a way to wake her momma up.

"Little explores the extremes of childhood guilt and its consequences in this harsh yet well-crafted story about fully drawn people. The bayou, with its rich culture, is an atmospheric character that overlays the story with mystery and dread." Booklist

The **time** of the fireflies; Kimberley Griffiths Little. Scholastic Press 2014 368 p. (jacketed hardcover) $18.99
Grades: 5 6 7 8 **Fic**

1. Mystery fiction 2. Family secrets -- Fiction 3. Secrets -- Fiction 4. Fireflies -- Fiction 5. Louisiana -- Fiction 6. Family life -- Fiction 7. Time travel -- Fiction 8. Family problems -- Fiction
ISBN 0545165636; 9780545165631

LC 2013027396

In this middle grades book by Kimberley Griffiths Little, "When Larissa Renaud starts receiving eerie phone calls on a disconnected old phone in her family's antique shop, she knows she's in for a strange summer. A series of clues leads her to the muddy river banks. . . . It soon becomes clear that it is up to Larissa to prevent history from repeating itself and a fatal tragedy from striking the people she loves." (Publisher's note)

"Twelve-year-old Larissa's parents own Bayou Bridge Antiques, which features a wall of old phones. When one of the phones begins ringing, Larissa hesitantly picks it up. The female voice on the other end begs Larissa to find the fireflies. . . . [F]ans of Mary Downing Hahn's books will appreciate the spooky porcelain dolls and family curse." Booklist

Llewellyn, Sam

Darksolstice. Orchard Books 2010 365p map (Lyonesse) $17.99

Grades: 5 6 7 8   **Fic**
1. Fantasy fiction 2. Kings
ISBN 978-0-439-93471-8; 0-439-93471-0

LC 2009006283

Sequel to: The well between the worlds (2009)

While Idris Limpet, Rightful King of the Land of Lyonesse, is making the treacherous journey to the distant land of Aegypt to rescue his dear friend and sister, Morgan, he meets a company of friends who shall become his Knights of the Round Table and lead armies to battle the evil regent, Fisheagle.

The **well** between the worlds. Orchard Books 2009 339p (Lyonesse) $17.99
Grades: 5 6 7 8   **Fic**
1. Fantasy fiction 2. Kings
ISBN 978-0-439-93469-5; 0-439-93469-9

LC 2008-20075

Eleven-year-old Idris Limpet, living with his family in the once noble but now evil and corrupt island country of Lyonesse, finds his life taking a dramatic turn when, after a near-drowning incident, he is accused of being allied to the feared sea monsters and is rescued from a death sentence by a mysterious and fearsome stranger.

"Seldom does one find a new fantasy that is so richly textured, so original in concept, and with such a wonderfully interesting story. . . . Fantasy lovers will be impatient to find out where their paths take them." Voice Youth Advocates

Followed by: Darksolstice (2010)

Lloyd, Alison
Year of the tiger. Holiday House 2010 194p $16.95
Grades: 5 6 7 8   **Fic**
1. Adventure fiction 2. China -- Fiction 3. Archery -- Fiction 4. Social classes -- Fiction
ISBN 978-0-8234-2277-7; 0-8234-2277-1

LC 2009033651

First published 2008 in Australia

In ancient China, Hu and Ren forge an unlikely alliance in an effort to become expert archers and, ultimately, to save their city from invading barbarians.

"Brimming with details of daily life in the Han Dynasty, this fast-paced story alternates in the third person between Hu and Ren." Kirkus

Lloyd, Natalie
★ A **snicker** of magic; by Natalie Lloyd. Scholastic Press 2014 320 p. hbk $16.99
Grades: 4 5 6 7   **Fic**
1. Magic -- Fiction 2. Curses -- Fiction 3. Tennessee -- Fiction 4. Friendship -- Fiction 5. Family life -- Fiction 6. Mothers and daughters -- Fiction
ISBN 9780545552707; 0545552702

LC 2013027779

"Midnight Gulch used to be a magical place, a town where people could sing up thunderstorms and dance up sunflowers. But that was long ago, before a curse drove the magic away. Twelve-year-old Felicity knows all about things like that; her nomadic mother is cursed with a wandering heart. . . . But when she arrives in Midnight Gulch, Felicity thinks her luck's about to change." (Publisher's note)

"The unusual language, showing a tinge of Tennessee mountain dialect, spins a web around the story that touches on helping others, budding friendships, and strength of family." Booklist

Lobel, Arnold
★ **Fables**; written and illustrated by Arnold Lobel. Harper & Row 1980 40p il $16.99; lib bdg $18.89; pa $6.99

Grades: 3 4 5   **Fic**
1. Animals -- Fiction
ISBN 0-06-023973-5; 0-06-023974-3 lib bdg; 0-06-443046-4 pa

LC 79-2004

Awarded the Caldecott Medal, 1981

"Short, original fables, complete with moral, poke subtle fun at human foibles through the antics of 20 memorable animal characters. . . . Despite the large picture-book format, the best audience will be older readers who can understand the innuendos and underlying messages. Children of all ages, however, will appreciate and be intrigued by the artist's fine, full-color illustrations. Tones are deftly blended to luminescent shadings, and the pictorial simplicity of ideas, droll expressions, and caricature of behavior work in many instances as complete and humorous stories in themselves." Booklist

Lodding, Linda Ravin
A **gift** for Mama; by Linda Ravin Lodding; illustrated by Alison Jay. Alfred A. Knopf 2014 32 p. (hard cover) $17.99
Grades: PreK K 1 2   **Fic**
1. Gifts -- Fiction 2. Secondhand trade 3. Mother-child relationship -- Fiction 4. Barter -- Fiction 5. Austria -- History -- 1867-1918 -- Fiction 6. Viennna (Austria) -- History -- 19th century -- Fiction
ISBN 0385753314; 9780385753319; 9780385753326

LC 2013006071

"In this lovely, circular story set in 19th-century Vienna, Oskar searches for the perfect gift for his mother, armed with a single coin. Each time he acquires a gift, starting with a perfect yellow rose, he meets someone who convinces him to trade it for something else. Finally, the day is over, and he is back where he started. In the concluding paragraph, Lodding states that most of the people Oskar meets are important figures from Viennese history-Gustav Klimt, Felix Salten, Johann Strauss II, and Empress Sisi-and that this is Vienna's story as well as Oskar's." (School Library Journal)

Loftin, Nikki
Nightingale's nest; Nikki Loftin. Razorbill 2014 256 p. 22 cm (hardcover) $16.99
Grades: 4 5 6 7   **Fic**
1. Boys -- Fiction 2. Friendship -- Fiction 3. Birds -- Fiction 4. Magic -- Fiction 5. Singing -- Fiction 6. Family problems -- Fiction 7. Foster home care -- Fiction 8. Dysfunctional families -- fiction
ISBN 159514546X; 9781595145468

LC 2013047556

"Twelve-year-old John Fischer Jr. . . . is spending his summer helping his father with his tree removal business, clearing brush for Mr. King, the wealthy owner of a chain of Texas dollar stores, when he hears a beautiful song that transfixes him. Inspired by a Hans Christian Andersen story, 'Nightingale's Nest' is a . . . novel about a boy with the weight of the world on his shoulders and a girl with the gift of healing in her voice." (Publisher's note)

"John narrates his story in fluid, lyrical prose, Loftin blending the raw realism of a boy who makes the wrong choice with the fairy-tale magic of a girl with a nightingale voice. Unusual, finely crafted story of loss, betrayal and healing." Kirkus

Wish girl; Nikki Loftin. Razorbill 2015 256 p. (hardcover) $16.99
Grades: 4 5 6 7   **Fic**
1. Friendship -- Fiction 2. Cancer patients -- Fiction 3. Runaway children -- Fiction 4. Texas -- Fiction 5. Cancer -- Fiction 6. Best friends -- Fiction 7. Individuality -- Fiction 8. Family problems -- Fiction 9. Family life -- Texas -- Fiction
ISBN 1595146865; 9781595146861

LC 2014031004

In this children's novel by Nikki Loftin, "when his family moves to the Texas Hill Country, . . . Peter finds a tranquil, natural valley where he can, at last, hear himself think. There, he meets a girl his age: Annie Blythe . . . a 'Make-A-Wish Girl.' And in two weeks she will begin a dangerous treatment to try and stop her cancer from spreading. Annie and Peter hatch a plan to escape into the valley. But the pair soon discovers that the valley--and life--may have other plans for them." (Publisher's note)

"This thoughtful entry into realistic fiction for young teens explores family dysfunction and discord, the depression and emotional issues that plague young people trying to find their way, the importance of mentors, the unfortunate effects of bullying, and last but not least, cancer's impact on children and their families." VOYA

Companion to:

Nightingale's Nest (2014)

Lofting, Hugh

The **voyages** of Doctor Dolittle; told by Hugh Lofting; illustrated by Michael Hague; edited with a foreword by Patricia C. McKissack and Fredrick L. McKissack; afterword by Peter Glassman. HarperCollins Pubs. 2001 355p il $22.95

Grades: 4 5 6 7   Fic

1. Fantasy fiction 2. Animals -- Fiction

ISBN 0-688-14002-5

A newly illustrated and revised edition of the title first published 1922 by Stokes

Awarded the Newbery Medal, 1923

When his colleague Long Arrow disappears, Dr. Dolittle sets off with his assistant, Tommy Stubbins, his dog, Jip, and Polynesia the parrot on an adventurous voyage over tropical seas to floating Spidermonkey Island

Loizeaux, William

Clarence Cochran, a human boy; pictures by Anne Wilsdorf. Farrar, Straus and Giroux 2009 152p il $16

Grades: 4 5 6   Fic

1. Toleration -- Fiction 2. Cockroaches -- Fiction 3. Environmental protection -- Fiction

ISBN 978-0-374-31323-4; 0-374-31323-7

LC 2007-35358

With the threat of extermination looming, a cockroach who has been transformed into a tiny human learns to communicate with his human hosts, leading to an agreement both sides can live with, and a friendship between Clarence and ten-year-old Mimi, a human environmentalist.

"There's a serious message here about environmentalism and the power of words, and the action and suspense make this a good read-aloud or classroom-discussion choice." SLJ

Lombard, Jenny

★ **Drita,** my homegirl. G. P. Putnam's Sons 2006 135p $15.99; pa $5.99

Grades: 3 4 5   Fic

1. Refugees -- Fiction 2. Albanians -- Fiction 3. Friendship -- Fiction 4. New York (N.Y.) -- Fiction 5. African Americans -- Fiction

ISBN 0-399-24380-1; 0-14-240905-7 pa

LC 2005-13501

When ten-year-old Drita and her family, refugees from Kosovo, move to New York, Drita is teased about not speaking English well, but after a popular student named Maxine is forced to learn about Kosovo as a punishment for teasing Drita, the two girls soon bond.

"Maxie's attempts to help Drita understand American ways are touching, and Drita's understanding of her friend's loss is a testament to the emotional intelligence of children." SLJ

London, Alex

Proxy; Alex London. Philomel 2013 379 p. $17.99

Grades: 7 8 9 10   Fic

1. Science fiction 2. Dystopian fiction 3. Gays -- Fiction 4. Social classes -- Fiction

ISBN 0399257764; 9780399257766

LC 2012039704

In this book, "Knox is a 'patron,' a privileged and wealthy citizen of Mountain City. His only concerns are hacking, scoring with girls, and causing trouble while angering his bigwig dad. His proxy, a person who is contractually obligated to serve out Knox's punishments, is a gay teen. In exchange for working as a proxy, Syd is able to pay off his debts. When Knox accidentally kills a girl, 16 years at the Old Sterling Work Colony is too great a punishment for Syd to bear, so he escapes." (School Library Journal)

London, C. Alexander

We are not eaten by yaks; with art by Jonny Duddle. Philomel Books 2011 355p il (An accidental adventure) $12.99

Grades: 3 4 5 6   Fic

1. Adventure fiction 2. Twins -- Fiction 3. Parents -- Fiction 4. Siblings -- Fiction 5. Explorers -- Fiction 6. Television -- Fiction

ISBN 978-0-399-25487-1; 0-399-25487-0

LC 2010-06020

As the children of two world-famous explorers, eleven-year-old twins Celia and Oliver prefer television-watching to adventure-seeking until their father takes them to Tibet to help search for their long-lost mother.

"This text will appeal to reluctant readers who appreciate magic, humor, and predicatble parental behaviors that will cause any tween to roll their eyes. The improbable connection between ubiquitous television shows, poison witches, talking yaks, and reluctant heroes works to make this a light yet intriguing read." Libr Media Connect

Another title in this series is:

We dine with cannibals (2011)

We dine with cannibals. Philomel Books 2011 il (An accidental adventure) $12.99

Grades: 3 4 5 6   Fic

1. Adventure fiction 2. Twins -- Fiction 3. Siblings -- Fiction 4. Explorers -- Fiction 5. Television -- Fiction 6. Rain forests -- Fiction 7. Amazon River valley -- Fiction

ISBN 978-0-399-25488-8; 0-399-25488-9

LC 2010041993

All eleven-year-old twins Oliver and Celia Navel want to do is watch television, but their explorer father takes them in search of El Dorado, the Lost City of Gold, and their long-lost mother.

"London's second in the Accidental Adventure series has more thrills and more mystery (and naturally more complaining and more laughs) than the first." Kirkus

Look, Lenore

Alvin Ho; allergic to babies, burglars, and other bumps in the night. by Lenore Look; pictures by LeUyen Pham. 1st ed. Schwartz & Wade Books 2013 192 p. (hardcover) $15.99; (library) $18.99; (ebook) $47.97

Grades: 2 3 4 5   Fic

1. Siblings -- Fiction 2. Pregnancy -- Fiction 3. Fear -- Fiction 4. Schools -- Fiction 5. Concord (Mass.) -- Fiction 6. Chinese Americans -- Fiction 7. Interpersonal relations -- Fiction

ISBN 0375870334; 9780375870330; 9780375970337; 9780375988899

LC 2012011455

This is the fifth installment in Lenore Look's Alvin Ho series. Here, "though his mom assures a dubious Alvin that she told him months ago about her pregnancy, his new sibling's imminent arrival introduces a whole new set of worries for nerve-wracked Alvin. Paramount among them is his misunderstanding that the 'simply pathetic' (read: sympathetic) pregnancy his mother suggests he's experiencing will result in him actually giving birth." (Kirkus)

Alvin Ho: allergic to camping, hiking, and other natural disasters; pictures by LeUyen Pham. Schwartz & Wade Books 2009 170p il $15.99; lib bdg $18.99

Grades: 2 3 4 5 **Fic**
1. Fear -- Fiction 2. Camping -- Fiction 3. Friendship -- Fiction 4. Massachusetts -- Fiction 5. Chinese Americans -- Fiction
ISBN 978-0-375-85705-8; 0-375-85393-6; 978-0-375-95705-5 lib bdg; 0-375-95705-7 lib bdg

LC 2008-45845

When Alvin's father takes him camping to instill a love of nature, like that of their home-town hero Henry David Thoreau, Alvin makes a new friend and learns that he can be brave despite his fear of everything.

"Alvin's adventures . . . are charmingly genuine and fun to read. Look's pitch-perfect descriptions and phrasing add to the overall humor and heart of the story. . . . Whimsical illustrations pop up mid-page; Pham's expressive characters capture the essence of the story." SLJ

Alvin Ho: allergic to dead bodies, funerals, and other fatal circumstances; illustrations by LeUyen Pham. Schwartz & Wade 2011 197p $15.99; lib bdg $18.99

Grades: 2 3 4 5 **Fic**
1. Fear -- Fiction 2. Death -- Fiction 3. Grandfathers -- Fiction 4. Massachusetts -- Fiction 5. Chinese Americans -- Fiction
ISBN 978-0-375-86831-3; 0-375-86831-3; 978-0-375-96831-0 lib bdg; 978-0-375-96831-0 lib bdg

LC 2010046968

A fearful second grader in Concord, Massachusetts, learns about death when his grandfather's best friend passes away and he offers to accompany his grandfather to the funeral.

"The copious illustrations capture moments both silly and sad as the author again tackles real-kid worries in a truly funny story." Horn Book

★ **Alvin** Ho: allergic to girls, school, and other scary things; pictures by LeUyen Pham. Schwartz & Wade Books 2008 170p il $15.99; lib bdg $18.99

Grades: 2 3 4 5 **Fic**
1. Fear -- Fiction 2. Massachusetts -- Fiction 3. Chinese Americans -- Fiction
ISBN 978-0-375-83914-6; 0-375-83914-3; 978-0-375-93914-3 lib bdg; 0-375-93914-8 lib bdg

LC 2007-029456

Alvin Ho, a young boy in Concord, Massachusetts, who loves superheroes and comes from a long line of brave Chinese farmer-warriors, wants to make friends, but first he must overcome his fear of everything.

Look's "intuitive grasp of children's emotions is rivaled only by her flair for comic exaggeration." Publ Wkly

Other titles about Alvin Ho are:
Alvin Ho: allergic to camping, hiking, and other natural disasters (2009)
Alvin Ho: allergic to birthday parties, science projects, and other man-made catastrophies (2010)
Alvin Ho
allergic to dead bodies, funerals, and other fatal circumstances (2011)

★ **Ruby** Lu, brave and true; illustrated by Anne Wilsdorf. Atheneum Books for Young Readers 2004 105p il $15.95; pa $3.99

Grades: 1 2 3 **Fic**
1. Chinese Americans -- Fiction
ISBN 0-689-84907-9; 1-4169-1389-0 pa

LC 2003-3605

"Almost-eight-year-old" Ruby Lu spends time with her baby brother, goes to Chinese school, performs magic tricks and learns to drive, and has adventures with both old and new friends.

This is a "funny and charming chapter book. . . . [It offers] generous font, ample white space, and animated and active illustrations rendered in India ink." SLJ

Other titles about Ruby Lu are:
Ruby Lu, empress of everything (2006)
Ruby Lu, star of the show (2011)

Ruby Lu, empress of everything; illustrated by Anne Wilsdorf. Atheneum Books for Young Readers 2006 164p il $15.95; pa $4.99

Grades: 1 2 3 **Fic**
1. Deaf -- Fiction 2. Cousins -- Fiction 3. Chinese Americans -- Fiction
ISBN 978-0-689-86460-5; 0-689-86460-4; 1-4169-5003-6 pa

LC 2005014097

After Ruby Lu's deaf cousin, Flying Duck, and her parents come from China to live with her, Ruby finds life challenging as she adjusts to her new family, tries to mend her rocky relationship with her friend Emma, and faces various adventures in summer school

"Simple sentence structure, clear but varied word choice, and attention-grabbing transitions create a smooth chapter book that is suitable for early and reluctant readers. Black-and-white cartoon drawings add emotion, characterization, and humor." SLJ

Ruby Lu, star of the show; illustrated by Stef Choi. Atheneum Books for Young Readers 2011 136p il $15.99

Grades: 1 2 3 **Fic**
1. School stories 2. Dogs -- Fiction 3. Family life -- Fiction 4. Unemployment -- Fiction 5. Chinese Americans -- Fiction
ISBN 978-1-4169-1775-5; 1-4169-1775-6

LC 2010-09927

Ruby Lu's father loses his job on her first day of third grade, which causes many things in her life to change, and she is willing to do a lot to help out but giving up some things seems impossible.

"The cartoon-style sketches add humor to the story's more difficult aspects. . . . Ruby is as effervescent and charming as ever." Booklist

Lopez, Diana

Ask my mood ring how I feel; by Diana Lopez. 1st ed. Little Brown and Co. 2013 324 p. (hardcover) $17

Grades: 4 5 6 7 **Fic**
1. Breast cancer -- Fiction 2. Children of cancer patients -- Fiction 3. Cancer -- Fiction 4. Promises -- Fiction 5. Friendship -- Fiction 6. Fund-raising -- Fiction 7. Christian life -- Fiction 8. Hispanic Americans -- Fiction 9. San Antonio (Tex.) -- Fiction 10. Family life -- Texas -- Fiction
ISBN 0316209961; 9780316209960

LC 201202985

In this book, Chia "mother is diagnosed with breast cancer, which spurs . . . changes throughout their family. . . . After visiting the Basilica of Our Lady of San Juan del Valle in southern Texas, Chia dedicates herself to a promesa, vowing to secure 500 sponsors for a Walk for the Cure in exchange (she hopes) for her mother's recovery." (Publishers Weekly

Confetti girl. Little, Brown and Company 2009 198p $15.99

Grades: 4 5 6 7 **Fic**
1. School stories 2. Texas -- Fiction 3. Friendship -- Fiction 4. Bereavement -- Fiction 5. Mexican Americans -- Fiction 6. Father

daughter relationship -- Fiction
ISBN 978-0-316-02955-1; 0-316-02955-6

LC 2008032819

After the death of her mother, Texas sixth-grader Lina's grades and mood drop as she watches her father lose himself more and more in books, while her best friend uses Lina as an excuse to secretly meet her boyfriend.

"Lopez effectively portrays the Texas setting and the characters' Latino heritage. . . . This . . . novel puts at its center a likable girl facing realistic problems on her own terms." Booklist

Lord, Bette Bao

In the Year of the Boar and Jackie Robinson; illustrations by Marc Simont. Harper & Row 1984 169p il lib bdg $15.89; pa $4.95
Grades: 4 5 6 **Fic**
1. School stories 2. Chinese Americans -- Fiction
ISBN 0-06-024004-0 lib bdg; 0-06-440175-8 pa

LC 83-48440

"Warm-hearted, fresh, and dappled with humor, the episodic book, which successfully encompasses both Chinese dragons and the Brooklyn Dodgers, stands out in the bevy of contemporary problem novels. And the unusual flavor of the text infiltrates the striking illustrations picturing the pert, pigtailed heroine making her way in 'Mei Guo'—her new 'Beautiful Country.'" Horn Book

Lord, Cynthia

Half a chance; Cynthia Lord. Scholastic Press 2014 224 p. (hc) $16.99
Grades: 4 5 6 7 **Fic**
1. Photography -- Fiction 2. Father-daughter relationship -- Fiction 3. Friendship -- Fiction 4. New Hampshire -- Fiction
ISBN 0545035333; 9780545035330

LC 2013013431

"When Lucy's family moves to an old house on a lake, Lucy tries to see her new home through her camera's lens, as her father has taught her--he's a famous photographer, away on a shoot. . . . When she discovers that he's judging a photo contest, Lucy decides to enter anonymously. She wants to find out if her eye for photography is really special--or only good enough." (Publisher's note)

"The story is moving, and readers will find themselves caught up in sensitive Lucy's honest and thoughtful narration." Horn Book

Jelly Bean; Cynthia Lord. Scholastic Press 2014 128 p. (alk. paper) $16.99
Grades: 1 2 3 **Fic**
1. Volunteer work -- Fiction 2. Animal shelters -- Fiction 3. Pets -- Fiction 4. Guinea pigs -- Fiction 5. Voluntarism -- Fiction 6. Responsibility -- Fiction
ISBN 0545635969; 9780545635967

LC 2014005097

In this children's book by Cynthia Lord, illustrated by Erin McGuire, part of the "Shelter Pet Squad" series, "Suzannah's always wanted a pet of her own, but she lives in an apartment where there are absolutely no pets allowed. What she CAN do is volunteer at a local pet shelter. There, although she's the youngest, Suzannah quickly finds herself making friends with the kids and bonding with the animals. She makes toys and treats for the animals." (Publisher's note)

"Second-grader Suzannah wants a live pet, but apartment-building rules won't allow any type of animal. Her mother, however, reads about a new program at the local animal shelter and thinks this might be the answer: the Shelter Pet Squad, where children volunteer to make toys and treats for homeless animals . . . Easy vocabulary, uncomplicated

sentences, generous dialogue, large font, and friendly illustrations make the book accessible." Booklist

★ Touch blue. Scholastic Press 2010 186p $16.99
Grades: 4 5 6 7 **Fic**
1. Maine -- Fiction 2. Islands -- Fiction 3. Foster home care -- Fiction
ISBN 0-545-03531-7; 978-0-545-03531-6

LC 2009042306

When the state of Maine threatens to shut down their island's one-room schoolhouse, 11-year-old Tess and her family take in foster child Aaron in order to increase the school's population. "Intermediate." (Horn Book)

"Aaron's relationship with his foster family . . . develops believably. The tight-knit community and lobster-catching details make for a warm, colorful environment. This is a feel-good story." Booklist

Lorenzi, Natalie Dias

A long pitch home; by Natalie Dias Lorenzi. Charlesbridge 2016 256 p. (reinforced for library use) $16.95
Grades: 3 4 5 6 **Fic**
1. Baseball -- Fiction 2. Culture conflict -- Fiction 3. Pakistani Americans -- Fiction 4. Father-son relationship -- Fiction 5. Cousins -- Fiction 6. Muslims -- Fiction 7. Family life -- Fiction 8. Pakistanis -- United States -- Fiction
ISBN 9781607348702; 9781580897136

LC 2015026830

In this children's book by Natalie Dias Lorenzi, "ten-year-old Bilal liked his life back home in Pakistan. . . . But when his father suddenly sends the family to live with their aunt and uncle in America, nothing is familiar. While Bilal tries to keep up with his cousin Jalaal by joining a baseball league . . . , he wonders when his father will join the family in Virginia. Maybe if Bilal can prove himself on the pitcher's mound, his father will make it to see him play." (Publisher's note)

"A warm, sensitive, realistic portrait of a Muslim boy adjusting to contemporary America." Kirkus

Lottridge, Celia Barker

The listening tree. Fitzhenry & Whiteside 2011 172p $11.95
Grades: 4 5 6 7 **Fic**
1. Canada -- Fiction 2. Courage -- Fiction 3. Great Depression, 1929-1939 -- Fiction
ISBN 978-1-55455-052-4; 1-55455-052-1

It's 1935, and Ellen and her mother must leave their dried-up Saskatchewan farm to board with Aunt Gladys in Toronto. Intimidated by her new surroundings, Ellen chooses to hide in the branches of the large leafy tree outside her window and watch the neighbourhood children playing, rather than joining in their games. But when Ellen overhears a plan to evict the family-next-door from their home, she must overcome her fears and help her neighbours.

"Lottridge provides a wealth of well-developed, believable characters, especially Ellen. The story is a deftly-written, heartbreaking, and heartwarming tale of friendship and the perseverance to withstand hardships. This is a great book to introduce young readers to the impact of the Great Depression." Voice Youth Advocates

Love, D. Anne

Semiprecious. Margaret K. McElderry Books 2006 293p $16.95; pa $6.99
Grades: 5 6 7 8 **Fic**
1. Oklahoma -- Fiction 2. Family life -- Fiction
ISBN 978-0-689-85638-9; 0-689-85638-5; 978-0-689-87389-8 pa; 0-689-87389-1 pa

LC 2005-14906

Uprooted and living with an aunt in 1960s Oklahoma, thirteen-year-old Garnet and her older sister Opal brave their mother's desertion and their father's recovery from an accident, learning that "the best home of all is the one you make inside yourself"

"An involving novel of hurt, healing, and adjustment." Booklist

Lovelace, Maud Hart

Betsy-Tacy; illustrated by Lois Lenski. HarperCollins Pubs. 1994 112p il hardcover o.p. pa $5.99

Grades: 2 3 4   Fic
1. Minnesota -- Fiction 2. Friendship -- Fiction
ISBN 0-06-024415-1; 0-06-440096-4 pa

A reissue of the title first published 1940 by Crowell

Betsy and Tacy (short for Anastacia) were two little five-year-olds, such inseparable friends that they were regarded almost as one person. This is the story of their friendship in a little Minnesota town in the early 1900's

The author "has written a story of real literary merit as well as one with good story interest." Libr J

Other titles about Betsy through adolescence and young womanhood with reading levels to grade 5 and up are:

Betsy and Joe (1948)
Betsy and Tacy go downtown (1943)
Betsy and Tacy go over the big hill (1942)
Betsy and the great world (1952)
Betsy in spite of herself (1946)
Betsy, Tacy and Tib (1941)
Betsy was a junior (1947)
Betsy's wedding (1955)
Heavens to Betsy (1945)

Lövestam, Sara

Wonderful Feels Like This; Sara Lövestam; translated from the Swedish by Laura A. Wideburg. St. Martin's Press 2017 320 p. $17.99

Grades: 7 8 9 10 11 12   Fic
1. Teenagers -- Fiction 2. Self-realization -- Fiction 3. Identity (Psychology) -- Fiction
ISBN 1250095239; 9781250095237

In this book, by Sara Lövestam, "for Steffi, going to school everyday is an exercise in survival. She's never fit in with any of the groups at school, and she's viciously teased by the other girls in her class. The only way she escapes is through her music--especially jazz music. . . . Steffi comes to realize that she won't always be stuck and lonely in her town. She can go to music school in Stockholm. She can be a real musician." (Publisher's note)

Lowry, Lois

★ Anastasia Krupnik. Houghton Mifflin 1979 113p $17; pa $5.99

Grades: 4 5 6   Fic
1. Family life -- Fiction
ISBN 0-395-28629-8; 0-440-40852-0 pa

Anastasia's 10th year has some good things like falling in love and really getting to know her grandmother and some bad things like finding out about an impending baby brother

"Anastasia's father and mother—an English professor and an artist—are among the most humorous, sensible, and understanding parents to be found in . . . children's fiction, and Anastasia herself is an amusing and engaging heroine." Horn Book

Other titles about Anastasia Krupnik are:

Anastasia again! (1981)
Anastasia at your service (1982)
Anastasia, ask your analyst (1984)
Anastasia on her own (1985)

Anastasia has the answers (1986)
Anastasia's chosen career (1987)
Anastasia at this address (1991)
Anastasia, absolutely (1995)

★ Autumn Street. Houghton Mifflin 1980 188p $17; $16

Grades: 4 5 6 7   Fic
1. Friendship -- Fiction 2. World War, 1939-1945 -- Fiction
ISBN 9780395278123; 0-395-27812-0

                                  LC 80-376

"Elizabeth, the teller of the story, feels danger around her when her father goes to fight in World War II. She, her older sister, and her pregnant mother go to live with her grandparents on Autumn Street. Tatie, the black cook-housekeeper, and her street-wise grandson Charley love Elizabeth and reassure her during this difficult time." Child Book Rev Serv

★ The birthday ball; illustrations by Jules Feiffer. Houghton Mifflin Harcourt 2010 186p il $16

Grades: 3 4 5   Fic
1. School stories 2. Birthdays -- Fiction 3. Princesses -- Fiction
ISBN 978-0-547-23869-2; 0-547-23869-X

                              LC 2009-32966

Princess Patricia Priscilla is bored with life as a royal life and the preparations for her 16th birthday ball. "Disguised as a peasant, she attends the village school . . . and attracts friends and the attention of the handsome school master. . . . What began as a cure for boredom, becomes a chance for [the princess] to break the rules and marry the man she loves." (Publisher's note) "Intermediate." (Horn Book)

"Lowry uses her knack for cleverly turning familiar stories on their heads . . . in this tale about a princess who's utterly bored with privileged palace life. . . . Feiffer's wiry ink illustrations paint the characters in offhand caricatures, adding to the merriment. Employing elements from the 'Prince and the Pauper' as well as ample doses of humor and slapstick Lowry sets the stage for a rowdy denouement." Publ Wkly

Bless this mouse; illustrated by Eric Rohmann. Houghton Mifflin Books for Children 2011 151p il $15.99

Grades: 4 5 6   Fic
1. Mice -- Fiction
ISBN 978-0-547-39009-3; 0-547-39009-2

                              LC 2010-0733

Mouse Mistress Hildegarde musters all her ingenuity to keep a large colony of church mice safe from the exterminator and to see that they make it through the dangerous Blessing of the Animals. "Grades three to five." (Bull Cent Child Books)

"The book is an impeccably constructed, good-humored adventure filled with master plans, near disasters, and brave rescues, all gently frightening for readers even younger than the target audience. . . . Fun and lighthearted." Publ Wkly

★ The giver. Houghton Mifflin 1993 180p pa $8.95; $17

Grades: 6 7 8 9 10   Fic
1. Science fiction
ISBN 0-385-73255-4 pa; 0-395-64566-2

                              LC 92-15034

Awarded the Newbery Medal, 1994

This novel is set in a future society "without conflict, poverty, unemployment, divorce, injustice, or inequality. . . . December is the time of the annual Ceremony at which each twelve-year-old receives a life assignment determined by the Elders. . . . Jonas has been chosen for something special. When his selection leads him to an unnamed man—the man called only the Giver—he begins to sense the dark secrets that underlie the fragile perfection of his world." (Publisher's note) "Grades five to eight." (Bull Cent Child Books)

"A riveting, chilling story that inspires a new appreciation for diversity, love, and even pain. Truly memorable." SLJ

Gooney Bird and all her charms; by Lois Lowry and illustrated by Middy Thomas. Houghton Mifflin Harcourt 2014 160 p. $16.99
Grades: 2 3 4   **Fic**
1. Anatomy 2. Skeleton 3. School stories 4. Schools -- Fiction 5. Skeleton -- Fiction 6. Human anatomy -- Fiction 7. Charm bracelets -- Fiction
ISBN 0544113543; 9780544113541
LC 2012041887

In this book, by Lois Lowry, "Gooney Bird and her second-grade classmates are studying the human body. The students are in for a surprise when her uncle, Dr. Walter Oglethorpe, an anatomy professor, loans them a skeleton to help them with their research. The skeleton, on display outside the school to show the location of the respiratory system, goes missing, and Gooney Bird becomes head detective, leading her class on an investigation to solve the mystery." (Publisher's note)

"In her sixth book, bossy but good-natured Gooney Bird Greene livens up the class human body unit with a real skeleton, on loan from her great-uncle, Dr. Oglethorpe. A parent's objection brings tension to the plot laden with amusingly precocious observations of second graders; ultimately, Gooney's charm bracelet helps the kids present their new anatomy knowledge. Simple line drawings illustrate the chapters." (Horn Book)

Gooney Bird and the room mother; illustrated by Middy Thomas. Houghton Mifflin 2005 80p il $15; pa $5.50
Grades: 2 3 4   **Fic**
1. School stories 2. Thanksgiving Day -- Fiction
ISBN 0-618-53230-7; 0440421330 pa
LC 2004-15511

Gooney Bird Greene, an entertaining second grader who introduces challenging vocabulary words and tells "absolutely true" stories, finds a surprise room mother to bring cupcakes for the Thanksgiving pageant.

"This is a fast-paced read, with Thomas's black-and-white drawings highlighting key moments." SLJ

Gooney Bird Greene; illustrated by Middy Thomas. Houghton Mifflin 2002 88p il $15
Grades: 2 3 4   **Fic**
1. School stories 2. Storytelling -- Fiction
ISBN 0-618-23848-4
LC 2002-1478

A most unusual new student who loves to be the center of attention entertains her teacher and fellow second graders by telling absolutely true stories about herself, including how she got her name

"Lowry's masterful writing style reaches directly into her audience, managing both to appeal to young listeners and to engage older readers." Bull Cent Child Books

Other titles about Gooney Bird are:
Gooney Bird and the room mother (2005)
Gooney Bird is so absurd (2009)
Gooney Bird on the map (2011)
Gooney the fabulous (2007)

Gooney Bird is so absurd; illustrated by Middy Thomas. Houghton Mifflin Harcourt 2009 105p il $15
Grades: 2 3 4   **Fic**
1. School stories 2. Poetry -- Fiction
ISBN 978-0-547-11967-0; 0-547-11967-4
LC 2007047738

Mrs. Pidgeon's second grade class studies poetry and her students write haiku, couplets, free verse, and finally, a tribute to Mrs. Pidgeon's mother organized by the irrepressible Gooney Bird Greene.

"A full-page drawing in each chapter reflects the action and the tone of the text. Few beginning chapter books have the range of this one, from hilarity to sadness, from outrage to compassion, and few writers could manage it with such finesse." Booklist

Gooney Bird on the map. Houghton Mifflin Books for Children 2011 $15.99
Grades: 2 3 4   **Fic**
1. School stories 2. Maps -- Fiction
ISBN 978-0-547-55622-2; 0-547-55622-5
LC 2011012160

When her second-grade classmates are envious of the three students who are going away on winter vacation, the creative and ingenious Gooney Bird Greene thinks of a geography activity to cheer them all up.

"Occasional black-and-white illustrations add to the accessibility of this short chapter book. A sure hit for Gooney Bird fans." SLJ

Gooney the fabulous; [by] Lois Lowry; illustrated by Middy Thomas. Houghton Mifflin 2007 94p il $15
Grades: 2 3 4   **Fic**
1. School stories 2. Authorship -- Fiction
ISBN 978-0-618-76691-8; 0-618-76691-X
LC 2006035594

Gooney Bird Greene takes charge of a class project as she and her fellow students in Mrs. Pidgeon's second grade class learn about fables by each making up their own based on an animal that begins with the same letter as their first name.

"Lowry nicely individualizes her characters and gets readers interested in their problems." Booklist

★ **Number** the Stars; Lois Lowry. 25th Anniversary Edition Houghton Mifflin Harcourt 2014 137 p. $17.99
Grades: 4 5 6 7   **Fic**
1. Jews -- Fiction 2. Denmark -- Fiction 3. Friendship -- Fiction 4. World War, 1939-1945 -- Fiction
ISBN 0544340000; 9780544340008
LC 8837134

First published 1989
Newbery Medal (1990)

"As the German troops begin their campaign to 'relocate' all the Jews of Denmark, Annemarie Johansen's family takes in Annemarie's best friend, Ellen Rosen, and conceals her as part of the family. Through the eyes of ten-year-old Annemarie, we watch as the Danish Resistance smuggles almost the entire Jewish population of Denmark, nearly seven thousand people, across the sea to Sweden." (Publisher's note)

"The appendix details the historical incidents upon which Lowry bases her plot. . . . The whole work is seamless, compelling, and memorable." Horn Book

Son; by Lois Lowry. Houghton Mifflin 2012 393 p. $17.99
Grades: 6 7 8 9 10 11 12   **Fic**
1. Science fiction 2. Dystopian fiction 3. Amnesia -- Fiction 4. Mothers -- Fiction 5. Secrecy -- Fiction 6. Identity -- Fiction 7. Young adult literature 8. Mother-child relationship -- Fiction 9. Mother and child -- Fiction 10. Separation (Psychology) -- Fiction
ISBN 0547887205; 9780547887203
LC 2012014034

Author Lois Lowry tells the story of "14-year-old Claire, [who] has no contact with her baby Gabe until she surreptitiously bonds with him in the community Nurturing Center. . . . After living for years with Alys, a childless healer, Claire's memory returns. Intent on finding Gabe, she

. . . encounters the sinister Trademaster and exchanges her youth for his help in finding her child, now living in the same village as middle-aged Jonas and his wife Kira. Elderly and failing, Claire reveals her identity to Gabe, who must use his unique talent to save the village." (Kirkus Reviews)

Stay! Keeper's story. Houghton Mifflin 1997 127p il $15
Grades: 5 6 7 8   Fic
1. Dogs -- Fiction
ISBN 0-395-87048-8

LC 97-1569

"The author proves she is as well versed in animal behavior as in human sensibilities. Her warm sense of humor and vivid imagination . . . accentuate Keeper's unorthodox perceptions of the world." Publ Wkly

A **summer** to die; illustrated by Jenni Oliver. Houghton Mifflin 1977 154p il $16
Grades: 5 6 7 8   Fic
1. Death -- Fiction 2. Sisters -- Fiction
ISBN 0-395-25338-1

LC 77-83

"As told by Meg, the chronicle of this experience is a sensitive exploration of the complex emotions underlying the adolescent's first confrontation with human mortality; the author suggests nuances of contemporary conversation and situations without sacrificing the finesse with which she limns her characters." Horn Book

Lunn, Janet Louise Swoboda

Laura Secord: a story of courage; [by] Janet Lunn; illustrated by Maxwell Newhouse. Tundra Bks. 2001 un il maps $16.95
Grades: 3 4 5   Fic
1. Pioneers 2. War of 1812 -- Fiction
ISBN 0-88776-538-6
"The folkloric rhythm of the tale is underscored in the dramatically colored, naively rendered illustrations." Horn Book Guide

Luper, Eric

Jeremy Bender vs. the Cupcake Cadets. Balzer + Bray 2011 235p $15.99
Grades: 4 5 6   Fic
1. Contests -- Fiction 2. Sex role -- Fiction 3. Boats and boating -- Fiction
ISBN 978-0-06-201512-9; 0-06-201512-5

LC 2010-40808

When sixth-grader Jeremy Bender damages his father's prized boat and needs to come up with a lot of money to get it repaired, he and his best friend dress up as girls and infiltrate the Cupcake Cadet troop in an attempt to win the Windjammer Whirl model sailboat contest, and the prize money that comes with it.
"A not-so-lightweight tale rises above drag jokes to reveal surprising profundity." Kirkus

Lupica, Mike

The **batboy.** Philomel Books 2010 247p $17.99
Grades: 5 6 7 8   Fic
1. Young adult literature 2. Baseball -- Fiction 3. Detroit (Mich.) -- Fiction 4. Mother-son relationship -- Fiction 5. Detroit Tigers (Baseball team) -- Fiction
ISBN 978-0-399-25000-2; 0-399-25000-X

LC 2009015067

Even though his mother feels baseball ruined her marriage to his father, she allows fourteen-year-old Brian to become a bat boy for the Detroit Tigers, who have just drafted his favorite player back onto the team.

Lupica gives "his readers a behind-the-scenes look at major league sports. In this novel, he adds genuine insights into family dynamics and the emotional state of his hero." Booklist

Fantasy league; Mike Lupica. Philomel, an imprint of Penguin Group (USA) 2014 304 p. (hardback) $17.99
Grades: 5 6 7 8   Fic
1. Football -- Fiction 2. Football teams -- fiction 3. Fantasy football -- fiction
ISBN 0399256075; 9780399256073

LC 2014007442

In this book, by Mike Lupica, "12-year-old Charlie is a fantasy football guru. He may be just a bench warmer for his school's football team, but when it comes to knowing and loving the game, he's first-string. He even becomes a celebrity when his podcast gets noticed by a sports radio host, who plays Charlie's fantasy picks for all of Los Angeles to hear. Soon Charlie befriends the elderly owner of the L.A. Bulldogs . . . and convinces him to take a chance on an aging quarterback." (Publisher's note)

"Usually a football book is about whether or not the kid makes the team and the problems that follow. So it's refreshing that those issues are only a part of 12-year-old Charlie Gains' story. See, Charlie is known as the Brain, because he is a football stats genius. He understands which players should be playing where and why. . . . There's a lot of football here: pro and fantasy teams and Charlie's own Pop Warner career. Veteran sportswriter Lupica handles it all very well. However, it's the heart and depth he adds to the story depicting Charlie's relationships with a sterling cast of characters that make this unique. This Moneyball story with kids is on the money." Booklist

Heat. Philomel Books 2006 220p $16.99
Grades: 5 6 7 8   Fic
1. Cubans -- Fiction 2. Orphans -- Fiction 3. Baseball -- Fiction 4. Illegal aliens -- Fiction
ISBN 0-14-240757-7 pa; 0-399-24301-1

LC 2005013521

Pitching prodigy Michael Arroyo is on the run from social services after being banned from playing Little League baseball because rival coaches doubt he is only twelve years old and he has no parents to offer them proof. "Grades five to eight." (Bull Cent Child Books)

"The dialogue crackles, and the rich cast of supporting characters' . . . nearly steals the show. Topnotch entertainment." Booklist

Heavy hitters; Mike Lupica. Scholastic 2014 219 p. hbk $16.99
Grades: 3 4 5 6 7   Fic
1. Baseball -- Fiction 2. Children of divorced parents -- Fiction 3. Fear -- Fiction 4. Friendship -- Fiction 5. Baseball players -- Fiction 6. Dysfunctional families -- Fiction
ISBN 0545381843; 9780545381840

LC 2014430128

In this middle grade book by Mike Lupica, part of the Game Changers series, "Ben and his friends, the Core Four Plus One, are so excited to play in their town's All-Star Baseball league. But in the first game of the season Ben gets hit by a pitch. It's never happened to him before and it shakes him up. . . . Ben discovers that Justin's parents are getting a divorce and Justin is thinking about quitting the team." (Publisher's note)

"Charismatic Ben McBain joins his favorite sidekicks . . . for another sports season, this time All-Star baseball. Conflict comes quickly when Ben slumps after being hit by a pitch and Justin struggles with his parent's divorce. By trying to help one another, the friends also help themselves. Lupica's captivating play-by-play details pull the reader into the games, right alongside these sports-loving characters." Horn Book

Other titles in this series are:
Game changers (2012)

Play makers (2013)

Hot hand; [by] Mike Lupica. Philomel Books 2007 165p (Comeback kids) $9.99; pa $6.99
Grades: 3 4 5   **Fic**
1. Bullies -- Fiction 2. Basketball -- Fiction 3. Father-son relationship -- Fiction
ISBN 978-0-399-24714-9; 978-0-14-241441-5 pa
                                                          LC 2006034562
In the wake of his parents' separation, ten-year-old Billy seems to have continual conflicts with his father, who is also his basketball coach, but his quiet, younger brother Ben, a piano prodigy, is having even more trouble adjusting, and only Billy seems to notice.
"The characters . . . are always sympathetic . . . and the adults have complexity and depth. . . . The strongest point . . . is the quality of the sports play-by-play; Lupica portrays the action clearly and vividly." SLJ
Other titles in this series are:
Two-minute drill (2007)
Safe at home (2008)
Long shot (2008)
Shoot-out (2010)

Long shot. Philomel Books 2008 182p (Comeback kids) $9.99; pa $6.99
Grades: 3 4 5   **Fic**
1. School stories 2. Basketball -- Fiction 3. Mexican Americans -- Fiction
ISBN 978-0-399-24717-0; 0-399-24717-3; 978-0-14-241520-7 pa; 0-14-241520-0 pa
                                                          LC 2008001385
Pedro, an avid basketball player, decides to run for class president, challenging a teammate who is also one of the most popular boys in school.

The **only** game; Mike Lupica. Simon & Schuster Books for Young Readers 2015 320 p. (hardcover) $16.99
Grades: 4 5 6 7   **Fic**
1. Baseball -- Fiction 2. Brothers -- Fiction 3. Friendship -- Fiction 4. Grief -- Fiction 5. Bullies -- Fiction
ISBN 1481409956; 9781481409957; 9781481409964
                                                          LC 2014015989
"Jack Callahan is the star of his baseball team and sixth grade is supposed to be his year. That is, until he up and quits. Jack's brother has passed away, and though [everyone] thinks baseball is just the thing he needs to move on, Jack feels it's anything but. Time spent with . . . new friends unlocks something within Jack, and with their help . . . Jack discovers sometimes it's more than just the love of the game that keeps us moving." (Publisher's note)
"Although the story is sports related, this is more than a baseball book and will appeal to a wide variety of readers. A must-buy." SLJ

Play Makers; Mike Lupica. Scholastic 2013 224 p. (hardcover) $16.99
Grades: 3 4 5 6 7   **Fic**
1. School stories 2. Basketball -- Fiction 3. Competition (Psychology) -- Fiction
ISBN 0545381835; 9780545381833
This novel, by Mike Lupica, is the book 2 of the "Game Changers" series. "Ben McBain and his crew must now prepare for basketball season. . . . But there is a new kid in town, Chase Braggs, a point guard like Ben who seems to be better, stronger, and faster. . . . Ben's rivalry with Chase seems to take the fun out of playing ball with his best friends.

Will Ben be able to pull it together for his team and for himself?" (Publisher's note)

Safe at home. Philomel Books 2008 175p (Comeback kids) $9.99; pa $6.99
Grades: 3 4 5   **Fic**
1. School stories 2. Orphans -- Fiction 3. Adoption -- Fiction 4. Baseball -- Fiction
ISBN 978-0-399-24716-3; 0-399-24716-5; 978-0-14-241460-6 pa; 0-14-241460-3 pa
                                                          LC 2007042100
Playing baseball was the one thing that made twelve-year-old Nick Crandall feel at home until he found acceptance with adoptive parents, but he faces a new struggle to fit in when he becomes the first seventh-grader ever to make the varsity baseball team.

Shoot-out. Philomel Books 2009 165p (Comeback kids) $10.99
Grades: 3 4 5   **Fic**
1. Moving -- Fiction 2. Soccer -- Fiction
ISBN 978-0-399-24718-7; 0-399-24718-1
                                                          LC 2008021588
Twelve-year-old Jake must leave his championship soccer team to play on a team with a losing record when his family moves to a neighboring town.
"An enjoyable sports story with lots of action." Booklist

Two-minute drill; [by] Mike Lupica. Philomel Books 2007 165p (Comeback kids) $9.99
Grades: 3 4 5   **Fic**
1. School stories 2. Dyslexia -- Fiction 3. Football -- Fiction 4. Friendship -- Fiction
ISBN 978-0-399-24715-6; 0-399-24715-7
                                                          LC 2007011745
Brainy Scott, a great kicker who otherwise struggles with football, and star quarterback Chris, who has dyslexia, team up to help each other succeed in both football and school.
"The characters . . . are always sympathetic . . . and the adults have complexity and depth. . . . The strongest point . . . is the quality of the sports play-by-play; Lupica portrays the action clearly and vividly." SLJ

Lyga, Barry
Archvillain. Scholastic Press 2010 180p $16.99
Grades: 4 5 6 7   **Fic**
1. Science fiction 2. Superheroes -- Fiction 3. Good and evil -- Fiction 4. Extraterrestrial beings -- Fiction
ISBN 978-0-545-19649-9; 0-545-19649-3
                                                          LC 2010-05291
Twelve-year-old Kyle Camden develops greater mental agility and superpowers during a plasma storm that also brings Mighty Mike, an alien, to the town of Bouring, but while each does what he thinks is best, Kyle is labeled a villain and Mike a hero.
"Comic book fans in particular will appreciate this clever origin story, first in a new series. . . . Lyga . . . laces his story with ample humor. . . . Readers will find plenty to ponder." Publ Wkly
Other titles in this series are:
The Mad Mask (2012)
Yesterday Again (2013)

Lynch, Chris, 1962-
The **right** fight; Chris Lynch. Scholastic Press 2014 192 p.
Grades: 5 6 7 8   **Fic**
1. War stories 2. War -- Fiction 3. Soldiers -- Fiction 4. World War, 1939-1945 -- Fiction 5. Tanks (Military science) -- Fiction 6. World War, 1939-1945 -- Tank warfare 7. Africa, North -- History

-- 20th century -- Fiction 8. World War, 1939-1945 -- Campaigns -- Africa, North -- Fiction
ISBN 9780545522946

LC 2013014034

In this book, by Chris Lynch, "there are few things Roman loves as much as baseball, but his country is at the top of the list. So when it looks like the United States will be swept up into World War II, he turns his back on baseball and joins the US Army. . . . As it turns out, he is far more talented with a tank than he ever was with a baseball. And he is eager to drive his tank right into the field of battle, where the Army is up against the . . . Nazis of the Afrika Korps." (Publisher's note)

"Roman loves playing semi-professional baseball. Unfortunately, he's not very good. When war breaks out, he volunteers for the army and finds something he can do better than anyone: drive a tank. Here's WWII lite, with fast-paced battle scenes in Northern Africa recalling video-game action. By book's end, however, Lynch has built a lucid, realistic setting for his powerful new war series." (Horn Book)

Lyons, Mary E.

★ **Letters** from a slave girl; the story of Harriet Jacobs. Scribner 1992 146p il hardcover o.p. pa $5.99; pa $5.99

Grades: 6 7 8 9　　　　　　　　　　　　　　　　　　**Fic**

1. Slaves 2. Authors 3. Young adult literature 4. Domestics 5. Memoirists 6. Letters -- Fiction 7. Slavery -- Fiction 8. African Americans -- Fiction
ISBN 0-684-19446-5; 1-4169-3637-8 pa; 9781416936374 pa

LC 91-45778

This is a fictionalized version of the life of Harriet Jacobs, told in the form of letters that she might have written during her slavery in North Carolina and as she prepared for escape to the North in 1842. Glossary. Bibliography. "Age twelve and up." (Horn Book)

This "is historical fiction at its best. . . . Mary Lyons has remained faithful to Jacobs's actual autobiography throughout her readable, compelling novel. . . . Her observations of the horrors of slavery are concise and lucid. The letters are written in dialect, based on Jacobs's own writing and on other slave narrations of the period." Horn Book

Maberry, Jonathan

The **orphan** army; Jonathan Maberry. Simon & Schuster Books for Young Readers 2015 400 p. (The Nightsiders) (hardcover) $16.99

Grades: 5 6 7 8　　　　　　　　　　　　　　　　　　**Fic**

1. Science fiction 2. Monsters -- Fiction 3. Heroes and heroines -- Fiction 4. Magic -- Fiction 5. Heroes -- Fiction 6. Supernatural -- Fiction 7. Extraterrestrial beings -- Fiction
ISBN 1481415751; 9781481415750

LC 2014014576

In this juvenile novel, by Jonathan Maberry, part of "The Nightsiders" series, set "in a slightly futuristic world, where ruthless insectlike monsters are exterminating humans and the Earth itself, Milo discovers secrets that change the tides of war in a serious way. The Nightsiders are a group of mystical beasts leading the fight to defend Earth and its inhabitants from the maleficent Bugs." (School Library Journal)

"Maberry's prowess in fiction as well as comic books is evident in his well-crafted story, which balances over-the-top battle scenes with the quiet moments between characters that give substance to what could be a heartless thriller. This first book in an explosive new series is the perfect mix of science fiction and magic." Kirkus

Vault of shadows; Jonathan Maberry. Simon & Schuster Books for Young Readers 2016 464 p. (Nightsiders) (hardback) $16.99

Grades: 5 6 7 8　　　　　　　　　　　　　　　　　　**Fic**

1. Science fiction 2. Magic -- Fiction 3. Monsters -- Fiction 4. Supernatural -- Fiction 5. Heroes and heroines -- Fiction 6.

Extraterrestrial beings -- Fiction 7. Heroes -- Fiction
ISBN 9781481415781; 9781481415798; 9781481415804

LC 201502766

In this book, by Jonathan Maberry, "after joining forces with the magical Nightsiders and surviving a trip to the enemy Bugs' Hive ship, Milo Silk still has a lot to fear. The Huntsman has pledged a revenge worse than death on Milo, a group of nefarious fairies are bent on taking back Earth, and zombie-like holo-men are trapping humans for the Bugs to take. Even more unsettling is that the Witch of the World has disappeared and a mysterious boy is haunting Milo's dreams in her stead." (Publisher's note)

"With dramatic, humorous, and occasionally dark, edgy touches this offers another engrossing blend of action-adventure, dystopian elements, magic, and retro sci-fi with some classic lit allusions, and it appealing, diversely drawn cast together face dangers and dilemma with courage and ingenuity while trying to save Earth and beyond from obliteration." Booklist

MacDonald, Amy

Too much flapdoodle! [illustrations by Cat Bowman Smith] Farrar Straus Giroux 2008 182p il $16.95

Grades: 3 4 5 6　　　　　　　　　　　　　　　　　　**Fi**

1. Aunts -- Fiction 2. Uncles -- Fiction 3. Farm life -- Fiction 4. Country life -- Fiction
ISBN 978-0-374-37671-0; 0-374-37671-9

LC 200703327

Twelve-year-old Parker reluctantly goes to spend the summer with his eccentric great-aunt and great-uncle on their dilapidated farm, where he discovers that there is more to life than the latest game system and the coolest cell phone

"Hilarious antics ensue as the boy matures and realizes that there i more to life than the latest video game. Black-and-white line drawing enhance the lighthearted text." SLJ

Other titles about these characters are:

No more nice (1996)
No more nasty (2001)

MacDonald, Bailey

The **secret** of the sealed room; a mystery of young Benjamin Franklin. Aladdin 2010 208p $16.99

Grades: 4 5 6 7　　　　　　　　　　　　　　　　　　**Fi**

1. Authors 2. Diplomats 3. Inventors 4. Statesmen 5. Scientist 6. Mystery fiction 7. Writers on science 8. Members of Congress 9. Boston (Mass.) -- Fiction
ISBN 978-1-4169-9760-3; 1-4169-9760-1

When she runs away after her master dies, indentured servant Patience Martin is accused of stealing and needs the help of a young Benjamin Franklin to prove her innocence.

"MacDonald creates a series of events that could very well be factual and leaves the reader curious to know more. Replete with historical fact without being blatant, the well-developed plot will keep mystery lovers guessing until the very last chapter." Booklist

Wicked Will. Aladdin 2009 201p $16.99

Grades: 5 6 7　　　　　　　　　　　　　　　　　　**Fi**

1. Poets 2. Authors 3. Dramatists 4. Mystery fiction 5. Orphans -- Fiction 6. Theater -- Fiction 7. Great Britain -- History -- 1485-1603, Tudors -- Fiction
ISBN 1-4169-8660-X; 978-1-4169-8660-7

LC 2008-5081

Performing in the English town of Stratford-on-Avon in 1576, Viola a young actress (disguised as a boy) and a local lad named Will Shakespeare uncover a murder mystery.

"The chapters themselves logically reveal the twists and turns of the plot in concise, readable prose. The realistic details put flesh on the bones of not only the primary characters, but also of the secondary personages as well." SLJ

MacDonald, Betty

Nancy and Plum; illustrated by Mary Grandpre; with an introduction by Jeanne Birdsall. Alfred A. Knopf 2010 222p il $15.99; lib bdg $18.99

Grades: 3 4 5   Fic

1. Orphans -- Fiction 2. Sisters -- Fiction
ISBN 978-0-375-86685-2; 0-375-86685-X; 978-0-375-96685-9 lib bdg; 0-375-96685-4 lib bdg

A reissue of the title first published 1952

"Orphans Nancy and Plum lead deprived lives at cruel Mrs. Monday's boarding school. . . . The sisters manage to escape her clutches, find wonderful new guardians, redeem their neglectful uncle, and even improve the lot of the other orphans. . . . Their dialogue is full of humorous teasing, and they pull no punches with their feelings about the villainous Mrs. Monday and her dreadful niece. . . . GrandPré's pencil and wash illustrations strike just the right note: old-fashioned yet cheeky." Horn Book

MacDonald, George

The **light** princess; with pictures by Maurice Sendak. Farrar, Straus & Giroux 1969 110p il hardcover o.p. pa $5.95

Grades: 3 4 5 6   Fic

1. Fairy tales
ISBN 0-374-44458-7 pa

This fairy story originally appeared 1864 in the author's novel Adela Cathcart and was reprinted in his 1867 story collection Dealings with the fairies

"The problems of the princess who had been deprived, as an infant, of her gravity and whose life hung in the balance when she grew up are amusing as ever and the sweet capitulation to love that brings her (literally) to her feet, just as touching. All of the best of Macdonald is reflected in the Sendak illustrations: the humor and wit, the sweetness and tenderness, and the sophistication—and they are beautiful." Sutherland. The Best in Child Books

MacFarlane, John

Stormstruck! John Macfarlane. Holiday House 2015 160 p. map (hardcover) $16.95

Grades: 4 5 6 7   Fic

1. Dogs -- Fiction 2. Children and death 3. Sea stories 4. Storms -- Fiction 5. Survival -- Fiction 6. Labrador retriever -- Fiction 7. Islands of the Atlantic -- Fiction 8. Adventure and adventurers -- Fiction
ISBN 0823433943; 9780823433940

LC 2014046751

In this children's novel by John MacFarlane "when twelve-year-old Sam overhears his parents talking about their elderly and infirm Labrador retriever, Pogo, he's convinced they plan to have the dog put down. To save Pogo, Sam sets sail with the dog in a fourteen foot boat for an island off the coast of Maine. The elements conspire against them as they move from one danger to another. As he battles nature's fury, Sam is finally able to come to terms with . . . his brother's death in Afghanistan." (Publisher's note)

"A gripping adventure with weighty themes that will enthrall middle grade readers." SLJ

MacHale, D. J.

SYLO; by D.J. MacHale. Penguin Group USA 2013 416 p. (hardcover) $17.99

Grades: 5 6 7 8 9   Fic

1. Dystopian fiction 3. Adventure fiction
ISBN 1595146652; 9781595146656

This is the first book in a proposed trilogy from D.J. MacHale. Here, Tucker Pierce has a small but satisfying life on a small island. But when the island is quarantined by the U.S. Navy, things start to fall apart. . . . People start dying. The girl he wants to get to know a whole lot better, Tori, is captured along with Tucker and imprisoned behind barbed wire." They must escape to the mainland and try to figure out what this SYLO organization that is imprisoning them is. (Kirkus Reviews)

Mack, Tracy

The **fall** of the Amazing Zalindas; casebook no. 1. by Tracy Mack and Michael Citrin; illustrations by Greg Ruth. Orchard Books 2006 259p il (Sherlock Holmes and the Baker Street irregulars) $16.99; pa $6.99

Grades: 4 5 6 7   Fic

1. Mystery fiction 2. Circus -- Fiction 3. Great Britain -- Fiction
ISBN 0-439-82836-8; 0-545-06939-4 pa

LC 2005-34000

The ragamuffin boys known as the Baker Street Irregulars help Sherlock Holmes solve the mysterious deaths of a family of circus tightrope walkers.

"Colorful, well-defined characters . . . and plenty of historical detail, Cockney slang . . . and Sherlockian references bring Victorian England to life. Vintage-style design elements and evocative black-and-white illustrations further the effect." Booklist

The **mystery** of the conjured man; [by] Tracy Mack & Michael Citrin; [illustrations by Greg Ruth] Orchard Books 2009 il (Sherlock Holmes and the Baker Street Irregulars) hardcover o.p.

Grades: 4 5 6   Fic

1. Mystery fiction 2. Spiritualism -- Fiction 3. Great Britain -- Fiction 4. Swindlers and swindling -- Fiction
ISBN 978-0-439-83667-8 pa

LC 2006035701

The ragtag group of orphan boys known as the Baker Street Irregulars faces shady characters and seemingly real ghosts when they assist the famous detective, Sherlock Holmes, in investigating the mysterious death of Greta Berlinger during a seance.

"A great addition to an entertaining series." SLJ

Mackey, Heather

Dreamwood; Heather Mackey. G.P. Putnam's Sons 2014 336 p. (hardback) $16.99

Grades: 4 5 6 7 8   Fic

1. Supernatural -- Fiction 2. Missing persons -- Fiction 3. Runaway children -- Fiction 4. Forests and forestry -- Fiction 5. Runaways -- Fiction 6. Adventure and adventurers -- Fiction 7. Northwest, Pacific -- History -- 19th century -- Fiction
ISBN 0399250670; 9780399250675

LC 2013039402

In this book, by Heather Mackey, "Lucy Darrington has no choice but to run away from boarding school. Her father, an expert on the supernatural, has been away for too long while doing research in Saarthe, a remote territory in the Pacific Northwest populated by towering redwoods, timber barons, and the Lupine people. But upon arriving, she learns her father is missing: Rumor has it he's gone in search of dreamwood, a rare tree with magical properties." (Publisher's note)

"Dialogue and perilous situations nudge the story along at a steady clip, with the second half a breathless page turner. Dreamwood will please character-focused readers." SLJ

MacLachlan, Patricia, 1938-

The **facts** and fictions of Minna Pratt. Harper & Row 1988 136p
pa $4.95

Grades: 4 5 6 7   **Fic**

1. Musicians -- Fiction
ISBN 0-06-440265-7

                         LC 85-45388

"Ms. MacLachlan's skillful handling of her subject, and above all
her vivid characterization . . . place her story in the ranks of outstanding
middle-grade fiction." N Y Times Book Rev

Fly away; Patricia MacLachlan. Margaret K. McElderry Books
2014 108 p. (hardcover : alk. paper) $15.99

Grades: 3 4 5   **Fic**

1. Floods -- Fiction 2. Siblings -- Fiction 3. Cows -- Fiction 4.
Poets -- Fiction 5. Family life -- Fiction 6. Brothers and sisters
-- Fiction
ISBN 1442460083; 9781442460089; 9781442460102

                      LC 2012040995

This children's story, by Patricia MacLachlan, is "a story about one
brave girl who saves her family from losing everything. Everyone in
Lucy's family sings. . . . Everyone, except Lucy. . . . Just like singing,
helping Aunt Frankie prepare for flooding season is a family tradition.
. . . And this year, when the flood arrives, danger finds its way into the
heart of Lucy's family, and Lucy will need to find her voice to save her
brother." (Publisher's note)

"Lucy and her family make their annual trip to visit Aunt Frankie in
North Dakota just as floodwaters rise, threatening her home. Meanwhile,
Lucy shares a secret with her little brother, Teddy: though the rest of the
family thinks that he can't talk yet, she knows that he can...The appealing jacket art, large type, and wide-spaced lines of text make this volume
an inviting choice for readers who are beginning to read longer chapter
books." Booklist

Kindred souls; Patricia MacLachlan. HarperCollins 2012 119 p.
(trade bdg.) $16.99

Grades: 4 5 6   **Fic**

1. Bereavement -- Fiction 2. Family life -- Fiction 3. Family farms
-- Fiction 4. Grandfathers -- Fiction 5. Houses -- Remodeling
-- Fiction 6. Dogs -- Fiction 7. Old age -- Fiction 8. Prairies --
Fiction 9. Farm life -- Fiction 10. Sod houses -- Fiction
ISBN 9780060522971; 9780060522988

                      LC 2011016617

This book follows narrator Jake and his 88-year-old grandfather
Billy, the eponymous kindred souls of the story's title. The pair "live
on a farm that their family has owned for generations; in fact, Billy was
born in a sod house he remembers fondly, the ruins of which still exist on the property." To comfort their dying grandfather, "Jake and his
siblings undertake a remarkably ambitious project: They rebuild the sod
house; Billy moves into it, and he eventually passes away there." The
"first-person account of a boy coping with his grandfather's death . . .
portrays . . . the opportunity to grieve for a loved one even while he is
still alive." (Kirkus)

★ **Sarah,** plain and tall. Harper & Row 58p $14.99; lib bdg
$15.89; pa $4.99

Grades: 3 4 5   **Fic**

1. Stepmothers -- Fiction 2. Frontier and pioneer life -- Fiction
ISBN 0-06-024101-2; 0-06-024102-0 lib bdg; 0-06-440205-3 pa

                      LC 83-49481

Awarded the Newbery Medal, 1986

When their father invites a mail-order bride to come live with them
in their prairie home, Caleb and Anna are captivated by their new mother
and hope that she will stay

"It is the simplest of love stories expressed in the simplest of prose
Embedded in these unadorned declarative sentences about ordinary
people, actions, animals, facts, objects and colors are evocations of the
deepest feelings of loss and fear, love and hope." N Y Times Book Rev

Other titles in this series are:

Caleb's story (2001)

Grandfather's dance (2006)

More perfect than the moon (2004)

Skylark (1994)

★ **Snowflakes** fall; by Patricia MacLachlan; illustrated by Steven
Kellogg. Random House 2013 32 p. (library binding) $20.99

Grades: PreK K 1 2 3   **Fic**

1. Snow 2. Life cycles (Biology) 3. Snow -- Fiction
ISBN 0375973281; 9780375973284; 9780385376938

                      LC 2013008622

This book, by Patricia MacLachlan and illustrated by Steven Kellogg "portray[s] life's natural cycle: its beauty, its joy, and its sorrow
Together, the words and pictures offer the promise of renewal that car
be found in our lives--snowflakes fall, and return again as raindrops so
that flowers can grow." (Publisher's note)

The **truth** of me; about a boy, his grandmother, and a very good
dog. Patricia MacLachlan. Katherine Tegen Books, an imprint of HarperCollinsPublishers 2013 128 p. (hardcover bdg.) $16.99

Grades: 3 4 5   **Fic**

1. Dogs -- Fiction 2. Grandmothers -- Fiction 3. Parent and child
-- Fiction
ISBN 0061998591; 9780061998591; 9780061998607

                      LC 2012040151

In this book, "Robbie is looking forward to spending the summer
with his grandmother, Maddy. He likes her eccentric stories, he likes
that wild animals come right up to her, and he likes how Maddy makes
his parents nervous. Robbie often feels that his parents, accomplished
professional musicians, love their instruments more than him. Over the
course of the summer, Maddy helps him realize that he can be brave
enough to express his feelings openly." (School Library Journal)

★ **Waiting** for the magic; illustrated by Amy June Bates. Atheneum Books for Young Readers 2011 143p il $15.99

Grades: 3 4 5 6   **Fic**

1. Cats -- Fiction 2. Dogs -- Fiction 3. Family life -- Fiction
ISBN 978-1-4169-2745-7; 1-4169-2745-X

                      LC 2010019668

When Papa goes away for a little while, his family tries to cope with
the separation by adopting four dogs and a cat.

"MacLachlan tackles the familiar yet always heart-wrenching subject of parental separation in her venerable spare and moving style. . .
The characters are individualistic, believable, and likable." Publ Wkly

White fur flying; Patricia MacLachlan. 1st ed. Margaret K
McElderry Books 2013 128 p. (hardcover) $15.99

Grades: 2 3 4 5   **Fic**

1. Dogs -- Fiction 2. Rescue dogs -- Fiction 3. Family problems
-- Fiction 4. Human-animal relationships -- Fiction
ISBN 1442421711; 9781442421714

                      LC 2011046123

In this children's book, by Newbery Medalist Patricia MacLachlan
"A young boy tries to find his voice with the help of some four-legged
friends. . . . Zoe's family rescues dogs in need. . . . But the house across
the street is always silent these days. A new family has moved in and
Phillip, the boy, has stopped speaking. He doesn't even want to try. Zoe

knows that saving dogs and saving boys are different jobs, but she learns that some parts are the same." (Publisher's note)

★ **Word** after word after word. HarperCollins 2010 128p $14.99; lib bdg $15.89

Grades: 2 3 4 5   **Fic**

1. School stories 2. Cancer -- Fiction 3. Poetry -- Fiction 4. Authorship -- Fiction 5. Mother-daughter relationship -- Fiction

ISBN 978-0-06-027971-4; 0-06-027971-0; 978-0-06-027972-1 lib bdg; 0-06-027972-9 lib bdg

"Mrs. Mirabel, a visiting poet, works with a fourth-grade class over several weeks as they first discuss why people write poetry and then attempt to express themselves in verse. . . . Narrator Lucy, whose mother is recovering from cancer treatments, often meets her friends to talk about their hopes, their fears, their families, and their charismatic mentor. . . . Showing great respect for both her readers and her craft, . . . MacLachlan makes every word count in Lucy's smooth-flowing economical narrative." Booklist

Maclear, Kyo, 1970-

Virginia Wolf; Kyo Maclear; [illustrated by] Isabelle Arsenault. Kids Can Press 2012 32 p.

Grades: K 1 2   **Fic**

1. Wolves -- Fiction 2. Painting -- Fiction 3. Picture books for children 4. Depression (Psychology) -- Fiction

ISBN 9781554536498; 1554536499

This picture book tells the story of a girl named Virginia whose bad mood turns her into a wolf. Her sister Vanessa, the narrator, tries to help by painting pictures for her. "The wolf--previously a black near-silhouette with snout and tail, wearing a dress--morphs back into a girl. Wolf ears, silhouetted from behind, become a hair bow. Ink, pencil and paint . . . divide color from black-and-white as emotional symbolism." Kyo Maclear combines the real-life story of writer Virginia Woolf and her sister, painter Vanessa Bell, with "a bad-day/bad-mood or animal-transformation tale" that presents "literal and metaphorical glimpses of real depression." (Kirkus)

Madden, Kerry

Gentle's Holler. Viking 2005 237p $16.99; pa $6.99

Grades: 5 6 7 8   **Fic**

1. Poverty -- Fiction 2. Family life -- Fiction 3. North Carolina -- Fiction

ISBN 0-670-05998-6; 0-14-240751-8 pa

LC 2004-18424

In the early 1960s, twelve-year-old songwriter Livy Two Weems dreams of seeing the world beyond the Maggie Valley, North Carolina, holler where she lives in poverty with her parents and eight brothers and sisters, but understands that she must put family first.

"Livy's narration rings true and is wonderfully voiced, and Madden's message about the importance of forgiveness will be well received." SLJ

Other titles in this series are:

Louisiana's song (2007)

Jessie's mountain (2008)

Madison, Alan

100 days and 99 nights; illustrated by Julia Denos. Little, Brown 2008 137p il $14.99; pa $5.99

Grades: 3 4 5   **Fic**

1. Toys -- Fiction 2. Soldiers -- Fiction 3. Virginia -- Fiction 4. Imagination -- Fiction 5. Father-daughter relationship -- Fiction

ISBN 978-0-316-11354-0; 0-316-11354-9; 978-0-316-11798-2 pa; 0-316-11798-6 pa

As Esme introduces her stuffed animal collection that is alphabetically arranged from Alvin the aardvark to Zelda the zebra she also relates her family's military life and her father's deployment

"In this moving debut novel, wordplay is part of every chapter. . . . This is a mix of hilarious language and one child's terror that there could be bad news." Booklist

Mafi, Tahereh

Furthermore; by Tahereh Mafi. Dutton Children's Books, an imprint of Penguin Random House 2016 416 p. illustrations (hardback) $17.99

Grades: 4 5 6 7 8   **Fic**

1. Fantasy fiction 2. Magic -- Fiction 3. Adventure fiction 4. Missing persons -- Fiction 5. Fantasy 6. Adventure and adventurers -- Fiction

ISBN 9781101994764

LC 2015044898

In this book, by Tahereh Mafi, "there are only three things that matter to twelve-year-old Alice Alexis Queensmeadow: Mother, who wouldn't miss her; magic and color, which seem to elude her; and Father, who always loved her. The day Father disappears from Ferenwood he takes nothing but a ruler with him. But it's been almost three years since then, and Alice is determined to find him." (Publisher's note)

"While Oliver and Alice start off at odds, their friendship, forged in adversity, is the best part of a fast-paced, funny, and richly imaginative story that embraces and celebrates individuality." Pub Wkly

Magaziner, Lauren

The **only** thing worse than witches; Lauren Magaziner. Dial Books for Young Readers, an imprint of Penguin Group (USA) LLC 2014 272 p. (hardcover) $16.99

Grades: 4 5 6   **Fic**

1. Witches -- Fiction 2. Friendship -- Fiction 3. Magic -- Fiction 4. Witchcraft -- Fiction 5. Apprentices -- Fiction 6. Best friends -- Fiction 7. Mothers and sons -- Fiction

ISBN 0803739184; 9780803739185

LC 2013034310

In this middle grades book by Lauren Magaziner, "Rupert Campbell is fascinated by the witches who live nearby. He dreams of broomstick tours and souvenir potions, but Rupert's mother forbids him from even looking at that part of town. The closest he can get to a witchy experience is sitting in class with his awful teacher Mrs. Frabbleknacker, who smells like bellybutton lint and forbids Rupert's classmates from talking to each other before, during, and after class." (Publisher's note)

"Rupert Campbell is a fifth grader in Mrs. Frabbleknacker's class. She's the meanest teacher in school; she discourages her students from becoming friends and forces them to participate in gross projects . . . A solid choice for libraries looking to bolster their collection of lower-reading-level, middle-grade fiction." SLJ

Magnin, Joyce

Carrying Mason; [by] Joyce Magnin. Zonderkidz 2011 153p $14.99

Grades: 5 6 7 8   **Fic**

1. Young adult literature 2. People with mental disabilities -- Fiction 3. Family life -- Fiction 4. Country life -- Fiction 5. Pennsylvania -- Fiction

ISBN 978-0-310-72681-4; 0-310-72681-6

LC 2011014462

In rural Pennsylvania in 1958, when thirteen-year-old Luna's best friend Mason dies, she decides to move in with his mentally disabled mother and care for her as Mason did.

"Gently, deliberately paced, Luna's first-person tale provides a fresh look at mental disabilities and the additional burden of negative attitudes. While Ruby's disability is apparent, this effort also celebrates her capabilities. Although the primary focus is Luna, her quirky father, supportive mother and boy-crazy older sister are also sufficiently developed to provide additional depth. A quiet coming-of-age tale with heart offers a fresh look at mentally disabled adults." Kirkus

Magoon, Kekla

Camo girl. Aladdin 2010 218p $16.99

Grades: 5 6 7 8 **Fic**

1. Young adult literature 2. Friendship -- Fiction 3. Prejudices -- Fiction 4. Racially mixed people -- Fiction

ISBN 978-1-4169-7804-6; 1-4169-7804-6

A novel about a biracial girl living in the suburbs of Las Vegas examines the friendships that grow out of, and despite, her race.

"Magoon . . . offers a sensitive and articulate portrayal of a pair of middle-school outsiders. . . . This poetic and nuanced story addresses the courage it takes to truly know and support someone, as well as the difficult choices that come with growing up." Publ Wkly

Mahy, Margaret

Maddigan's Fantasia. Margaret K. McElderry Books 2007 499p $15.99

Grades: 4 5 6 7 **Fic**

1. Fantasy fiction 2. Magic -- Fiction 3. Circus -- Fiction

ISBN 1-4169-1812-4; 978-1-4169-1817-7

LC 2006-15512

In a world made uncertain by "the Chaos," two time-traveling boys, fifteen-year-old Timon and eleven-year-old Eden, seek to protect a magic talisman, aided by twelve-year-old Garland, a member of a traveling circus known as Maddigan's Fantasia.

"A well-drawn character, Garland resembles other Mahy protagonists—cranky, assertive and filled with self-doubt—and her adventures are invariably exciting." Publ Wkly

Mahy, Margaret, 1936-2012

Mister Whistler; Margaret Mahy. Lerner Pub Group 2013 32 p. $17.95

Grades: PreK K **Fic**

1. Dance -- Fiction 2. Humorous fiction -- Fiction 3. Lost and found possessions -- Fiction

ISBN 187746791X; 9781877467912

In this humorous picture book for children, by Margaret Mahy, illustrated by Gavin Bishop, "Mister Whistler always has a song in his head and a dance in his legs. But when he has to catch the train, he is so distracted he loses his ticket--and has to dance his way out of his clothes to find it!" (Publisher's note)

Malaspina, Ann

Yasmin's hammer; illustrated by Doug Chayka. Lee & Low Books 2010 un il $18.95

Grades: 2 3 4 5 **Fic**

1. Bangladesh -- Fiction 2. Child labor -- Fiction

ISBN 978-1-60060-359-4; 1-60060-359-9

"Swinging a hammer all day as she and her little sister break bricks in the city heat of Dhaka, Bangladesh, Yasmin dreams of going to school. In a moving voice true to her viewpoint, Yasmin speaks in smooth free verse about her longing. . . . Stirring oil paintings bring the setting to a close with images of the sisters in the brickyard and their father pedaling a rickshaw through the crowded streets. The back matter includes a clear map, a glossary, and a bibliography with online sites about how to help children like Yasmin." Booklist

Includes glossary and bibliographical references

Manivong, Laura

Escaping the tiger. Harper 2010 216p il $15.99

Grades: 6 7 8 9 **Fic**

1. Young adult literature 2. Laos -- Fiction 3. Refugees -- Fiction 4. Thailand -- Fiction 5. Family life -- Fiction

ISBN 978-0-06-166177-8; 0-06-166177-5

LC 2009-24095

In 1982, twelve-year-old Vonlai, his parents, and sister, Dalah, escape from Laos to a Thai refugee camp, where they spend four long years struggling to survive in hopes on one day reaching America.

"This compelling novel offers significant historical background. This is certainly a book to prompt purposeful discussion to increase historical and multicultural awareness." SLJ

Manley, Candace

Skeeter's dream; a novel. La Frontera Pub. 2010 183p pa $14.95

Grades: 4 5 6 **Fic**

1. Adventure fiction 2. Texas -- Fiction 3. Arkansas -- Fiction 4. Family life -- Fiction 5. Stepfamilies -- Fiction 6. Runaway children -- Fiction 7. Frontier and pioneer life -- Fiction

ISBN 978-0-9785634-8-6; 0-9785634-8-4

LC 2010027719

When thirteen-year-old Robert "Skeeter" Tates, fed up with his Yankee stepfather and stepbrothers, leaves his Arkansas home for Texas in 1867, he meets up with unexpected traveling companions as well as outlaws and the lawmen tracking them.

"This is a well-written story with believable characters and an intriguing plot. The dialog is authentic and the action is fast-paced. Give this book to fans of historical fiction or to boys looking for a thrilling adventure story." Libr Media Connect

Manushkin, Fran

Pedro, first grade hero; Fran Manushkin; illustrated by Tammie Lyon. Capstone Press 2017 96 p. color illustrations (Pedro) (pbk.) $4.95

Grades: 1 2 3 **Fic**

1. Friendship -- Fiction 2. Latinos (U.S.) -- Fiction 3. Elementary schools -- Fiction 4. Schools -- Fiction 5. Hispanic Americans -- Fiction

ISBN 9781515801122

LC 2016002727

In this children's book in the Pedro series, by Fran Manushkin, illustrated by Tammie Lyon, "spend some time with Pedro, Katie Woo's fun-loving friend. From a buggy disaster to a run for class president, Pedro has what it takes to be the hero of first-grade. No matter what he's doing, Pedro is always good for some laughs and adventure." (Publisher's note)

Marciano, John Bemelmans

The 9 lives of Alexander Baddenfield; by John Bemelmans Marciano. Viking Published by Penguin Group 2013 144 p. (hardcover) $16.99

Grades: 4 5 6 7 8 **Fic**

1. Death -- Fiction 2. Cats -- Fiction 3. Humorous stories 4. Wealth -- Fiction 5. Orphans -- Fiction 6. Reincarnation -- Fiction 7. Conduct of life -- Fiction

ISBN 0670014060; 9780670014064

LC 2012048448

In this book, "Alexander Baddenfield is a horrible boy . . . who is the last in a long line of lying, thieving scoundrels. One day, Alexander has an astonishing idea. Why not transplant the nine lives from his cat into himself? Suddenly, Alexander has lives to spare, and goes about using them up, attempting the most outrageous feats he can imagine. Only when his lives start running out, and he is left with only one just ike everyone else, does he realize how reckless he has been." (Publisher's note)

Marentette, Meghan

The **stowaways**; by Meghan Marentette; illustrated by Dean Griffiths. Orca Book Pub 2014 240 p. $19.95

Grades: 3 4 5   **Fic**

1. Mice -- Fiction 2. Family -- Fiction 3. Secrets -- Fiction 4. Adventure stories

ISBN 1927485339; 9781927485330

In this book, by Meghan Marentette and illustrated by Dean Griffiths, the Stowaways aren't like the other Weedle mice. They are inventive and curious, they go on adventures, and they are much too clever for their own good. In fact, everyone knows that Grampa Stowaway was killed in a trap on one of his adventures. . . . There's something else about the Stowaways. They keep secrets." (Publisher's note)

"Rory Stowaway comes from a long line of adventuring mice. He does not understand why his own papa is so against going out into the world beyond their cozy little home on Biggle's farm . . . . Themes of courage, family, friendship, and accepting differences permeate the story. Intermittent and well-placed black-and-white illustrations lend a vintage feel to the overall design of the book. A fine debut that deserves a place alongside Cynthia Voight's Young Fredle (Knopf) and Richard Peck's Secrets at Sea (Dial, both 2011)." SLJ

Margolis, Leslie

Everybody bugs out. Bloomsbury Children's Books 2011 195p $15.99

Grades: 4 5 6   **Fic**

1. School stories 2. California -- Fiction 3. Friendship -- Fiction 4. Family life -- Fiction

ISBN 1-59990-526-4; 978-1-59990-526-6

     LC 2010035628

Sixth-grader Annabelle realizes that she has a crush on Oliver, with whom she is doing a science fair project, just before the Valentine's Day dance—and just before her friend Claire announces her crush on him.

"Margolis' breezy tone nicely conveys the peaks and valleys of middle-school life." Kirkus

Girl's best friend. Bloomsbury USA Childrens Books 2010 261p $14.99

Grades: 4 5 6 7   **Fic**

1. School stories 2. Mystery fiction 3. Dogs -- Fiction 4. Twins -- Fiction 5. Siblings -- Fiction 6. Family life -- Fiction 7. Brooklyn (New York, N.Y.) -- Fiction

ISBN 978-1-59990-525-9; 1-59990-525-6

     LC 2010000562

In Brooklyn, New York, twelve-year-old dog-walker Maggie, aided by her twin brother Finn and best friend Lucy, investigates someone she believes is stealing pets.

"Characters are well-developed, typical preteens. Readers will easily identify with these seventh graders, and they will love the eccentric landlady who adds a bit of humor. Mystery fans will enjoy this light-hearted whodunit." SLJ

Girls acting catty. Bloomsbury 2009 179p $15.99

Grades: 4 5 6   **Fic**

1. School stories 2. California -- Fiction 3. Remarriage -- Fiction 4. Family life -- Fiction

ISBN 978-1-59990-237-1; 1-59990-237-0

     LC 2009002144

Sequel to: Boys are dogs (2008)

Sixth-grader Annabelle spends autumn coping with competing groups of friends at school, her mother's pre-wedding stress, learning to get along with a cute stepbrother-to-be, and such momentous events as wearing her first bra and learning to shave her legs.

"Margolis handles Annabelle's minor crises with sensitivity and humor." SLJ

Marino, Nan

★ **Neil** Armstrong is my uncle; & other lies Muscle Man McGinty told me. Roaring Brook Press 2009 154p $16.95

Grades: 3 4 5 6   **Fic**

1. Bullies -- Fiction 2. Friendship -- Fiction 3. Foster home care -- Fiction 4. Long Island (N.Y.) -- Fiction

ISBN 978-1-59643-499-8; 1-59643-499-6

"It's the summer of 1969, when astronauts land on the moon, and Tamara Ann Simpson is not having a good time. Foster child and best friend Kebsie has suddenly moved away and now Douglas McGinty is in her spot with Mrs. Kutchner. Tammy dubs him 'Muscle Man' after one outrageous lie. . . . Fierce and plaintive, Tammy's voice crackles with originality and yet is completely childlike. The '60s setting comes to life with sharply honed details. . . . The authenticity of the time and the voice combine with a poignant plot to reveal a depth unusual in such a straightforward first-person narrative." Kirkus

Marr, Melissa, 1972-

Loki's wolves; by K.L. Armstrong and M.A. Marr. 1st ed. Little, Brown and Co. 2013 368 p. ill. (The Blackwell pages) (hardcover) $16.99

Grades: 4 5 6 7 8   **Fic**

1. Norse mythology -- Fiction 2. Adventure fiction 3. Gods -- Fiction 4. Monsters -- Fiction 5. Supernatural -- Fiction 6. Shapeshifting -- Fiction 7. Adventure and adventurers -- Fiction

ISBN 031620496X; 9780316204965

     LC 2012029851

This juvenile fantasy novel, by K. L. Armstrong and M. A. Marr, is the first book in the "Blackwell Pages" series. "Matt hears the words, but he can't believe them. He's Thor's representative? Destined to fight trolls, monstrous wolves and giant serpents . . . or the world ends? He's only thirteen. . . . But now Ragnarok is coming, and it's up to the champions to fight in the place of the long-dead gods." (Publisher's note)

"It is so methodically constructed that readers will welcome the action Ragnarök will offer. . . . Norse mythology brought to life with engaging contemporary characters and future volumes that promise explosive action; ideal for Percy Jackson fans who want to branch out." Kirkus

Odin's ravens; K.L. Armstrong; M.A. Marr. First edition Little, Brown and Co. 2014 352 p. illustrations (The Blackwell pages) (hardcover) $17

Grades: 4 5 6 7 8   **Fic**

1. Adventure fiction 2. Supernatural -- Fiction 3. Norse mythology -- Fiction 4. Gods and goddesses -- Fiction 5. Gods -- Fiction 6. Monsters -- Fiction 7. Valhalla -- Fiction 8. Shapeshifting -- Fiction 9. Mythology, Norse -- Fiction 10. Adventure and adventurers -- Fiction

ISBN 0316204986; 9780316204989

     LC 2013018519

In this sequel to "Loki's Wolves," by K.L. Armstrong and M.A. Marr, "when thirteen-year-old Matt Thorsen, a modern day descendant of the Norse god Thor, was chosen to represent Thor in an epic battle to prevent the apocalypse he thought he knew how things would play out. Gather the descendants standing in for gods like Loki and Odin, defeat a giant serpent, and save the world. No problem, right?" (Publisher's note)

"This sequel stands by itself, as essential details of the first are neatly woven throughout. Intense action, well-crafted scenes and humor-laced dialogue add up to a sure winner. Just enough black-and-white illustrations add a visual dimension to the vivid text." Kirkus

Marsden, Carolyn, 1950-

★ The **gold**-threaded dress. Candlewick Press 2002 73p hardcover o.p. pa $5.99

Grades: 3 4 5　　　　　**Fic**

1. Friendship 2. Prejudices 3. School stories 4. Thai Americans 5. Identity 6. Moving, Household 7. Prejudices -- Fiction 8. Thai Americans -- Fiction

ISBN 0-7636-1569-2; 0-7636-2993-6 pa

LC 2001-25132

When Oy and her Thai American family move to a new neighborhood, her third-grade classmates tease and exclude her because she is different

"Marsden writes with keen observation and finesse about the social dynamics of the classroom and with simplicity reveals the layers of emotion experienced by Oy." Booklist

Another title about Oy is:

The Quail Club (2006)

★ **Silk** umbrellas; [by] Carolyn Marsden. Candlewick Press 2004 134p $15.99; pa $5.99

Grades: 3 4 5 6　　　　　**Fic**

1. Artists -- Fiction 2. Thailand -- Fiction 3. Family life -- Fiction

ISBN 0-7636-2257-5; 0-7636-3376-3 pa

LC 2003-55323

Eleven-year-old Noi worries that she will have to stop painting the silk umbrellas her family sells at the market near their Thai village and be forced to join her older sister in difficult work at a local factory instead.

"In simple, lucid prose, Marsden tells a story that is foreign in detail and texture but universal in appeal. . . . This gracefully told story will resonate with many young readers." Booklist

★ **Take** me with you. Candlewick Press 2010 160p $14.99

Grades: 4 5 6 7　　　　　**Fic**

1. Italy -- Fiction 2. Orphans -- Fiction 3. Friendship -- Fiction 4. Racially mixed people -- Fiction

ISBN 978-0-7636-3739-2; 0-7636-3739-4

LC 2009-38053

This story is set in "Italy after World War II. Pina and Susanna have lived at their Naples orphanage since they were babies. . . . Pina, pretty and blonde, . . . is sure the nuns tell prospective parents she is bad. Susanna is the daughter of an Italian woman and a black American solider. . .; no one looks like her. Then two very different parents come into the girls' lives. . . . Both satisfy the girls' dreams in unexpected ways. Marsden often puts crafts like sewing or crocheting into her stories, and in many ways she is like a master craftsman, using words instead of stitches for her deceptively simple design." Booklist

When heaven fell. Candlewick Press 2007 183p $15.99; pa $8.99

Grades: 4 5 6　　　　　**Fic**

1. Aunts -- Fiction 2. Vietnam -- Fiction 3. Family life -- Fiction

ISBN 978-0-7636-3175-8; 0-7636-3175-2; 978-0-7636-4381-2 pa; 0-7636-4381-5 pa

LC 2006-51712

When her grandmother reveals that the daughter that she had given up for adoption is coming from America to visit their Vietnamese family, nine-year-old Binh is convinced that her newly-discovered aunt is wealthy and will take care of all the family's needs.

"Marsden sensitively portrays expectations and disappointments on both sides. . . . An unusually accessible introduction to the culture of modern Vietnam." Booklist

Marsh, Katherine

The **door** by the staircase; Katherine Marsh; Kelly Murphy (cover design) Disney-Hyperion 2015 288 p. (ebook) $7.99; $16.99

Grades: 4 5 6　　　　　**Fic**

1. Orphans -- Fiction 2. Witches -- Fiction 3. Adoption -- Fiction 4. Baba Yaga (Legendary character) -- Fiction

ISBN 9781484720103; 1423134990; 9781423134992

LC 2014049851

In this book, by Katherine Marsh, illustrated by Kelly Murphy, "twelve-year-old Mary Hayes can't stand her orphanage for another night. But when an attempted escape through the stove pipe doesn't go quite as well as she'd hoped, Mary fears she'll be stuck in the Buffalo Asylum for Young Ladies forever. The very next day, a mysterious woman named Madame Z appears at the orphanage requesting to adopt Mary, and the matron's all too happy to get the girl off her hands." (Publisher's note)

"Well-drawn characters, an original setting, and a satisfying resolution are the ingredients that make this carefully crafted middle-grade adventure a highly rewarding read." Kirkus

Marshall, Joseph M.

In the footsteps of Crazy Horse; Joseph Marshall; illustrated by Jim Yellowhawk. Amulet Books 2015 176 p. illustrations, maps (hardback) $16.95

Grades: 4 5 6　　　　　**Fic**

1. Family life -- Fiction 2. Grandfathers -- Fiction 3. Great Plains -- Fiction 4. Lakota Indians -- Fiction 5. Self-confidence -- Fiction 6. Great Plains -- History -- 19th century -- Fiction 7. Indians of North America -- Great Plains -- Fiction

ISBN 9781419707858

LC 2015002042

In this juvenile novel, by Joseph Marshall and illustrated by Jim Yellowhawk, "Jimmy McClean is a Lakota boy . . . When he embarks on a journey with his grandfather, Nyles High Eagle, he learns more and more about his Lakota heritage—in particular, the story of Crazy Horse, one of the most important figures in Lakota and American history." (Publisher's note)

"This powerful introduction to a great warrior and leader invites readers to ponder the meaning of 'hero'." Kirkus

Includes bibliographical references

Martin, Ann M.

★ **Belle** Teal. Scholastic Press 2001 214p hardcover o.p. pa $5.99

Grades: 4 5 6 7　　　　　**Fic**

1. School stories 2. Race relations -- Fiction

ISBN 0-439-09823-8; 0-439-09824-6 pa

LC 00-13629

Belle Teal Harper is from a poor family in the country, and beginning fifth-grade is a challenge as her grandmother's memory is slipping away, her brother and father are fighting again, and she becomes involved with the two new African American children in her class.

"This is a solid piece of work with an absorbing plot." SLJ

Better to wish; Ann M. Martin. 1st ed. Scholastic 2013 240 p (Family tree) (hardcover) $16.99

Grades: 3 4 5 6 7　　　　　**Fic**

1. Discrimination -- Fiction 2. Historical fiction 3. Depression -- 1929 -- Fiction 4. Family life -- Maine -- Fiction 5. Maine -- History -- 20th century -- Fiction

ISBN 0545359422; 9780545359429

LC 201204794

This is the first book in Ann M. Martin's Family Tree series. "Growing up in Maine, eight-year-old Abby Nichols is the oldest daughter o an ambitious carpenter eager to realize the American Dream. But his prejudices are strong, too: he won't let Abby associate with her Irish Catholic neighbor, Orrin. . . . As Abby's father gains success, she enjoys more privileges, . . . but the family's newfound prosperity doesn't ease her outrage over her father's mistreatment of the less fortunate." (Publishers Weekly)

★ A **corner** of the universe. Scholastic Press 2002 189p $15.95; pa $5.99

Grades: 5 6 7 8 **Fic**

1. Uncles -- Fiction 2. Friendship -- Fiction 3. People with mental disabilities -- Fiction

ISBN 0-439-38880-5; 0-439-38881-3 pa

LC 2001-57611

A Newbery Medal honor book, 2003

The summer that Hattie turns twelve, she meets the childlike uncle she never knew and becomes friends with a girl who works at the carnival that comes to Hattie's small town

"Martin delivers wonderfully real characters and an engrossing plot through the viewpoint of a girl who tries so earnestly to connect with those around her." SLJ

The **doll** people; by Ann M. Martin and Laura Godwin; with pictures by Brian Selznick. Hyperion Bks. for Children 2000 256p il $15.99; pa $6.99

Grades: 3 4 5 **Fic**

1. Dolls -- Fiction

ISBN 0-7868-0361-4; 0-7868-1240-0 pa

LC 98-12344

A family of porcelain dolls that has lived in the same house for one hundred years is taken aback when a new family of plastic dolls arrives and doesn't follow The Doll Code of Honor

"Superbly nuanced drawings echo the action that breathes life into these extraordinary playthings." SLJ

Other titles about the doll family are:

The meanest doll in the world (2003)

The runaway dolls (2008)

★ **Rain** Reign; Ann M. Martin. Feiwel & Friends 2014 240 p. $16.99

Grades: 4 5 6 7 **Fic**

1. Dogs -- Fiction 2. English language -- Homonyms 3. Lost items -- Fiction 4. Asperger's syndrome -- Fiction

ISBN 0312643004; 9780312643003

Schneider Family Book Award (Ages 11 - 13) (2015)

In this middle grades novel by Ann M. Martin, "Rose Howard is obsessed with homonyms. She's thrilled that her own name is a homonym, and she purposely gave her dog Rain a name with two homonyms (Reign, Rein), which, according to Rose's rules of homonyms, is very special. . . . When a storm hits their rural town, rivers overflow, the roads are flooded, and Rain goes missing. . . . Now Rose has to find her dog, even if it means leaving her routines and safe places to search." (Publisher's note)

"Rose, a fifth-grader who has been diagnosed with Asperger syndrome, is often teased at school about her obsession with homonyms and her steadfast conviction that everyone should follow the rules at all times. Rose lives with her harsh, troubled father, but it's Uncle Weldon who cares for her in the ways that matter most. Still, her father did give her Rain, a stray dog that comforts and protects Rose. After Rain is lost in a storm and recovered, Rose learns that her dog has an identification microchip...Rose is driven by the unwavering belief that she must follow the rules, find Rain's former owners, and give the dog back to them... Readers will be moved by the raw portrayal of Rose's difficult home life, her separation from other kids at school, and her loss of the dog that has

loved her and provided a buffer from painful experiences. A strong story told in a nuanced, highly accessible way." (Booklist)

★ **Ten** rules for living with my sister. Feiwel & Friends 2011 228p $16.99

Grades: 3 4 5 6 **Fic**

1. Sisters -- Fiction 2. Family life -- Fiction 3. Grandfathers -- Fiction 4. New York (N.Y.) -- Fiction 5. Apartment houses -- Fiction

ISBN 978-0-312-36766-4; 0-312-36766-X

LC 2011009166

Nine-year-old Pearl and her popular, thirteen-year-old sister, Lexie, do not get along very well, but when their grandfather moves in and the girls have to share a room, they must find common ground.

"Credible characterizations, on-the-nail humor, and well-observed family dynamics add up to another hit from . . . author Martin." Publ Wkly

Martin, Laura

The **ark** plan; Laura Martin; illustrated by Eric Deschamps; [edited by] Tara Weikum. HarperCollins 2016 368 p. illustrations, map (Edge of extinction) (hardcover) $16.99

Grades: 4 5 6 7 8 **Fic**

1. Dinosaurs -- Fiction 2. Friendship -- Fiction 3. Adventure fiction -- Fiction

ISBN 9780062416223

LC 2015946556

This book in the Edge of Extinction series, by Laura Martin, illustrated by Eric Deschamps, and edited by Tara Weikum, is a "clever take on Michael Crichton's Jurassic Park, [with] the tale . . . reimagined on a worldwide scale. Nonstop action, marauding dinosaurs, and kids on the run: What's not to like? This is a great buy for the sci-fi adventure-loving crowd." (School Library Journal)

Another title in this series is:

Code name flood (2017)

Martinez, Arturo O.

Pedrito's world. Texas Tech University Press 2007 131p il pa $16.95

Grades: 4 5 6 **Fic**

1. Texas -- Fiction 2. Farm life -- Fiction 3. Mexican Americans -- Fiction

ISBN 978-0-89672-600-0 pa; 0-89672-600-2 pa

LC 2006-21628

In southern Texas in 1941, six-year-old Pedrito holds onto his hope for a better future as he helps to grow watermelons on his parents' farm and sell them in San Antonio, and attends school five miles from home.

"Readers will be moved . . . through clean writing and well-chosen details that breathe life into the characters and give heft to the setting." Booklist

Mason, Simon

Moon pie. David Fickling Books 2011 327p $16.99

Grades: 3 4 5 6 **Fic**

1. Fathers -- Fiction 2. Alcoholism -- Fiction

ISBN 978-0-385-75235-0; 0-385-75235-0

LC 2010051354

Eleven-year-old Martha tries to keep her family together after her mother's death as her father struggles with alcoholism.

"Mason has conjured a rarity indeed—a tremendously charming, unflinching account of a parent's downward spiral. . . . While the dialogue is realistic and rat-a-tat-tat quick, lyrical prose wends its way throughout. . . . Love conquers all in this bighearted and heartbreaking story." Kirkus

Mason, Timothy

The **last** synapsid. Delacorte Press 2009 311p il $16.99; lib bdg $19.99

Grades: 5 6 7 8   **Fic**

1. Colorado -- Fiction 2. Time travel -- Fiction 3. Space and time -- Fiction 4. Prehistoric animals -- Fiction

ISBN 978-0-385-73581-0; 0-385-73581-2; 978-0-385-90567-1 lib bdg; 0-385-90567-X lib bdg

LC 2008-35678

On a mountain near their tiny town of Faith, Colorado, best friends Rob and Phoebe discover a squat, drooly creature from thirty million years before the dinosaurs, that needs their help in tracking down a violent carnivore that must be returned to its proper place in time, or humans will never evolve.

"Mason has written a highly engaging fantasy that includes something for all readers. . . . Readers will find it difficult to put this book down until they have reached the last page." Libr Media Connect

Mass, Wendy

11 birthdays. Scholastic Press 2009 267p $16.99; pa $6.99

Grades: 4 5 6   **Fic**

1. Time -- Fiction 2. Birthdays -- Fiction 3. Friendship -- Fiction

ISBN 0-545-05239-4; 0-545-05240-8 pa; 978-0-545-05239-9; 978-0-545-05240-5 pa

LC 2008-09784

After celebrating their first nine same-day birthdays together, Amanda and Leo, having fallen out on their tenth and not speaking to each other for the last year, prepare to celebrate their eleventh birthday separately but peculiar things begin to happen as the day of their birthday begins to repeat itself over and over again.

"From the double-entendre title to the solid character portrayals to the clarity and wit of the writing, this novel offers a fresh twist on the familiar themes of middle-grade family and school dynamics." Booklist

Other titles in this series are:

Finally (2010)

13 gifts (2011)

The **candymakers**. Little, Brown 2010 453p $16.99

Grades: 3 4 5 6   **Fic**

1. Candy -- Fiction 2. Contests -- Fiction 3. Friendship -- Fiction

ISBN 0-316-00258-5; 978-0-316-00258-5

LC 2010008621

When four twelve-year-olds, including Logan, who has grown up never leaving his parents' Life Is Sweet candy factory, compete in the Confectionary Association's annual contest, they unexpectedly become friends and uncover secrets about themselves during the process.

"Mass has crafted a solid mystery dipped in sweet candymaking details. Character development moves a lengthy story forward in smooth increments. As each child's story emerges, the mystery becomes one bit clearer, making this a real page-turner. The characters are intricate, flawed heroes with whom readers will identify." SLJ

Another title in this series is:

The candymakers and the great chocolate chase (2016)

★ **Every** soul a star; a novel. Little, Brown and Co. 2008 322p $15.99; pa $6.99

Grades: 5 6 7 8   **Fic**

1. Friendship -- Fiction 2. Solar eclipses -- Fiction

ISBN 978-0-316-00256-1; 0-316-00256-9; 978-0-316-00257-8 pa; 0-316-00257-7 pa

LC 2008009259

Ally, Bree, and Jack meet at the one place the Great Eclipse can be seen in totality, each carrying the burden of different personal problems,

which become dim when compared to the task they embark upon and the friendship they find.

Mass "combines astronomy and storytelling for a well-balanced look at friendships and the role they play in shaping identity. . . . Information about solar eclipses and astronomy is carefully woven into the plot to build drama and will almost certainly intrigue readers." Publ Wkly

Includes bibliographical references

Jeremy Fink and the meaning of life. Little, Brown 2006 289p $15.99; pa $6.99

Grades: 5 6 7 8   **Fic**

1. Conduct of life -- Fiction 2. Father-son relationship -- Fiction

ISBN 978-0-316-05829-2; 0-316-05829-7; 978-0-316-05849-0 pa; 0-316-05849-1 pa

LC 2005037291

Just before his thirteenth birthday, Jeremy Fink receives a keyless locked box—set aside by his father before his death five years earlier—that purportedly contains the meaning of life.

"Mass fashions an adventure in which both journey and destination are worth the trip." Horn Book

The **last** present; Wendy Mass. Scholastic Press 2013 256 p. (hardcover) $16.99

Grades: 4 5 6   **Fic**

1. Birthdays -- Fiction 2. Time travel -- Fiction 3. Paranormal fiction 4. Friendship -- Fiction 5. Best friends -- Fiction 6. Supernatural -- Fiction 7. Blessing and cursing -- Fiction

ISBN 0545310164; 9780545310161

LC 2013014736

In this book, by Wendy Mass, "Amanda and Leo have a history with birthdays. Now their friend's little sister, Grace, has fallen into a strange frozen state on her birthday, and Amanda and Leo must travel in time in order to fix whatever's wrong. As they journey back to each of Grace's birthdays, they start seeing all sorts of patterns . . . which raise all sorts of questions." (Publisher's note)

"Amanda and Leo (11 Birthdays) travel back in time to help their friend's little sister, Grace, who's become mysteriously catatonic after her tenth birthday. The answer lies in Grace's past birthday parties, and Amanda and Leo--with help from Rory (Finally) and Tara (13 Gifts)--must break the curse. Action, magic, and interesting twists will keep readers entranced until the end." (Horn Book)

Pi in the sky; Wendy Mass. 1st ed. Little, Brown and Co. 2013 256 p. (hardcover) $17

Grades: 3 4 5 6 7   **Fic**

1. Creation -- Fiction 2. Science fiction 3. Earth -- Fiction 4. Universe -- Fiction

ISBN 0316089168; 9780316089166

LC 2012030638

In this humorous children's novel, by Wendy Mass, "Joss is the seventh son of the Supreme Overlord of the Universe, and all he gets to do is deliver pies. . . . But when Earth suddenly disappears, Joss is tasked with the not-so-simple job of bringing it back. With the help of an outspoken girl from Earth named Annika, Joss embarks on the adventure of a lifetime and learns that the universe is an even stranger place than he'd imagined." (Publisher's note)

Matti, Truus

★ **Departure** time; translated from the Dutch by Nancy Forest-Flier. Namelos 2010 214p $18.95; pa $9.95

Grades: 5 6 7 8   **Fic**

1. Memory -- Fiction 2. Father-daughter relationship -- Fiction

ISBN 978-1-60898-087-1; 1-60898-087-1; 978-1-60898-009-3 pa; 1-60898-009-X pa

Original Dutch edition 2009

"A 10-year-old girl is lost in a surrealistic landscape—a red-earth desert threatened by an approaching storm. Nothing looks familiar. She can't remember how she got to this place. Alternating with this classic bad-dream setting, which is narrated in the third person, is a first-person, furious tirade by a girl who feels abandoned by her father and neglected by her mother. Readers will be intrigued by the way Matti interweaves these stories and tantalizes with the possible connections between them. . . . Remarkable and arresting and wholly original, this novel lingers in the mind long after the last page has been read." SLJ

★ **Mister** Orange; Truus Matti; translated from the Dutch by Laura Watkinson. Enchanted Lion Books 2013 156 p. (hardcover) $16.95

Grades: 5 6 7 8   **Fic**

1. Historical fiction 2. Friendship -- Fiction 3. Child-adult relationship -- Fiction 4. Artists -- Fiction 5. World War, 1939-1945 -- Fiction 6. New York (N.Y.) -- History -- 1898-1951 -- Fiction 7. Family life -- New York (State) -- New York -- Fiction

ISBN 159270123X; 9781592701230

LC 2012051313

Mildred L. Batchelder Award (2014)

This children's story, by Truus Matti, translated by Laura Watkinson, is set in Manhattan in "1943. . . . Linus Muller works at the family grocery store in the east 70s. . . . One of his customers . . . arranges to have a crate of oranges delivered every other week. Over the course of these deliveries, an intimacy develops between Linus and . . . Mister Orange. In the peacefulness of Mister Orange's spare kitchen, they discuss the war, the future, freedom and imagination." (Publisher's note)

Mayer, Mercer

What a good kitty; Mercer Mayer; edited by Mary-Kate Gaudet. HarperCollins 2012 32 p. (trade bdg.) $3.99

Grades: K 1 2 3   **Fic**

1. Cats -- Fiction 2. Pets -- Fiction

ISBN 0060835656; 9780060835651; 9780060835668

LC 2011941958

In this children's book by Mercer Mayer, "Little Critter loves his kitty, despite the cat's multiple naughty deeds. Wreaking havoc with Dad's newspaper, Mom's knitting, and Little Sister's dolls . . . the cat even disturbs the family dog and pet fish. She is exiled to the yard, and the fire department must come when she and Dad get stuck in a tree. But . . . when a mean dog scares Little Sister, Kitty successfully chases him away." (School Library Journal)

McCall Smith, Alexander, 1948-

The **great** cake mystery; Precious Ramotswe's very first case. Alexander McCall Smith; illustrations by Iain McIntosh. Anchor Books 2012 73 p.

Grades: 2 3 4 5   **Fic**

1. School stories 2. Mystery fiction 3. Children's stories 4. Botswana -- Fiction 5. Blacks -- Botswana -- Fiction 6. Mystery and detective stories

ISBN 0307743896; 9780307743893

LC 2011026494

This children's book by Alexander McCall Smith is part of the "Number 1 Ladies' Detective Agency" series and tells the story of an eight-year-old African school girl in Botswana who wants to become a detective. "Her name is Precious. When a piece of cake goes missing from her classroom . . . Precious . . . sets out to find the real thief. Along the way she learns that your first guess isn't always right. She also learns how to be a detective." (Publisher's note)

The **Mystery** of Meerkat Hill; A Precious Ramotswe Mystery for Young Readers. by Alexander Smith; illustrated by Iain McIntosh. Random House Inc 2013 112 p. $12.99

Grades: 2 3 4 5   **Fic**

1. Meerkats -- Fiction 2. Mystery fiction -- Fiction 3. Botswana -- Fiction 4. Mystery and detective stories 5. Lost and found possessions -- Fiction 6. Ramotswe, Precious (Fictitious character) -- Fiction

ISBN 0345804589; 9780345804587

LC 2013363878

In this book, by Alexander Smith and illustrated by Iain McIntosh, "Precious wants to be a detective when she grows up. She is always practicing at being a detective by asking questions and finding out about other people's lives. There are two new students in her class, a girl called Teb and a boy called Pontsho. She learns that they are brother and sister, and—even more exciting—that Pontsho has a clever pet meerkat named Kosi." (Publisher's note)

"Kind, clever, and compassionate Precious Ramotswe is always eager to hone her budding detective skills. When newcomers Pontsho and Teb can't find their much-needed cow, she uses her quick wit and clue-finding skills to come to their aid...The block-print style illustrations, done in black, gray, and white with lots of touches of red, create interest and intrigue, yet artfully allow readers the luxury of using their imaginations to develop the plot and characters fully. This book will enhance all library collections, especially those eager to include fiction that gives a slice of life in another country. Perfect as a read-aloud or for beginning chapter readers." (School Library Journal)

The **mystery** of the missing lion; a Precious Ramotswe mystery for young readers. by Alexander McCall Smith; illustrations by Iain McIntosh. Anchor Books, a division of Random House LLC 2014 112 p. color illustrations (hardcover) $12.99

Grades: 2 3 4 5   **Fic**

1. Mystery fiction 2. Lions -- Fiction 3. Lions -- Fiction 4. Jungles -- Fiction 5. Botswana -- Fiction 6. Mystery and detective stories

ISBN 1101872020; 9780804173278; 9781101872024

LC 2014021479

In this book by Alexander McCall Smith, "young Precious gets . . . a trip to visit her Aunty Bee at a safari camp. While there she makes a new friend, a boy named Khumo, and meets an actor-lion named Teddy, who is starring in a film. When Teddy disappears, Khumo and Precious will brave hippos and crocodiles as they search for the missing lion." (Publisher's note)

"This is an attractive package, with a compact but entertaining mystery full of fascinating details bolstered by McIntosh's intriguing graphic illustrations." Booklist

McCaughrean, Geraldine

★ The **death**-defying Pepper Roux. Harper 2010 328p $16.99; lib bdg $17.89

Grades: 5 6 7 8   **Fic**

1. Adventure fiction 2. Young adult literature 3. France -- Fiction 4. Fate and fatalism -- Fiction

ISBN 978-0-06-183665-7; 0-06-183665-6; 978-0-06-183666-4 lib bdg; 0-06-183666-4 lib bdg

LC 2009-39665

Having been raised believing he will die before he reaches the age of fourteen, Pepper Roux runs away on his fourteenth birthday in an attempt to elude his fate, assumes another identity, and continues to try to outrun death, no matter the consequences.

"McCaughrean's exuberant prose and whirling humor animate an unforgettable cast of characters." Booklist

★ The **glorious** adventures of the Sunshine Queen. Harper 2011 325p $16.99

Grades: 5 6 7 8 **Fic**

1. Adventure fiction 2. Young adult literature 3. Theater -- Fiction 4. Missouri River -- Fiction

ISBN 978-0-06-200806-0; 0-06-200806-4

LC 2010021958

Sequel to: Stop the train! (2003)

When a diphtheria outbreak forces twelve-year-old Cissy to leave her Oklahoma hometown in the 1890s, she and her two classmates embark on a wild adventure down the Missouri River with a team of traveling actors who are living on a dilapidated paddle steamer.

"McCaughrean invests her characters with humanity and shows a farcical sense for dialogue, while her arch narrative voice, includes the theatrical and clever turns of phrase." Booklist

The **kite** rider; a novel. HarperCollins Pubs. 2002 272p maps hardcover o.p. pa $6.99

Grades: 6 7 8 9 **Fic**

1. Kings 2. China -- Fiction 3. Kites -- Fiction

ISBN 0-06-623874-9; 0-06-441091-9 pa

LC 2001-39522

In thirteenth-century China, after trying to save his widowed mother from a horrendous second marriage, twelve-year-old Haoyou has life-changing adventures when he takes to the sky as a circus kite rider and ends up meeting the great Mongol ruler Kublai Khan

"The story is a genuine page-turner. . . . McCaughrean fully immerses her memorable characters in the culture and lore of the ancient Chinese and Mongols, which make this not only a solid adventure story but also a window to a fascinating time and place." Booklist

Peter Pan in scarlet; by Geraldine McCaughrean; illustrations by Scott M. Fischer. Margaret K. McElderry Books 2006 309p il $17.99; pa $6.99

Grades: 4 5 6 7 **Fic**

1. Fairy tales

ISBN 978-1-4169-1808-0; 1-4169-1808-6; 978-1-4169-1809-7 pa; 1-4169-1809-4 pa

In the 1930s, all is not well. Nightmares are leaking out of Neverland. Fearing for Peter Pan's life, Wendy and the Lost Boys go back to Neverland with the help of the fairy Fireflyer only to discover their worst nightmares coming true!

"McCaughrean's story, with its picaresque descriptions, faithfully rekindled characters and an ending that leaves room for sequels, will keep the pages turning." Publ Wkly

McCloskey, Robert

Centerburg tales. Viking 1951 190p il $17.99; pa $6.99

Grades: 4 5 6 **Fic**

ISBN 0-670-20977-5; 0-14-031072-X pa

LC 51-10675

Sequel to: Homer Price

"Pictures and story show a real, live American boy with a knack for getting into hilarious adventures that make perfect reading aloud." Horn Book

★ **Homer** Price. Viking 1943 149p il $16.99; pa $5.99

Grades: 4 5 6 **Fic**

ISBN 0-670-37729-5; 0-14-240415-2 pa

"Text and pictures are pure Americana, hilarious and convincing in their portrayal of midwestern small-town life." Child Books Too Good to Miss

Another title about Homer Price is:
Centerburg tales (1951)

McCrite, K. D.

In front of God and everybody. Thomas Nelson 2011 298p (Confessions of April Grace) pa $9.99

Grades: 4 5 6 7 **Fic**

1. Arkansas -- Fiction 2. Farm life -- Fiction 3. Christian life -- Fiction 4. Swindlers and swindling -- Fiction

ISBN 978-1-4003-1722-6; 1-4003-1722-3

LC 2011005583

In the summer of 1986, eleven-year-old April Grace, who lives on a rural Arkansas farm with her family, across a field from her grandmother, has her sense of Christian charity tested when a snooty couple from San Francisco moves into a dilapidated house down the road and her grandmother takes up with a loud, obnoxious, and suspicious-acting Texan.

"With keen eyes and good humor, April Grace notes the quirks, presumptions, and motivations of family and neighbors; she has plenty of fodder—the characters' personalities are dialed up to 11." Publ Wkly

McCulloch, Michael

The **other** Felix. Roaring Brook Press 2011 $16.99

Grades: 3 4 5 6 **Fic**

1. School stories 2. Fear -- Fiction 3. Dreams -- Fiction 4. Bullies -- Fiction

ISBN 978-1-5964-3655-8; 1-5964-3655-7

LC 2010050605

Worrying about his father losing his job and the bully at school, fourth-grader Felix has terrifying dreams of the same monster-filled place every night until he meets someone there who looks and sounds strangely familiar.

"The story has a beautifully crafted innocence. . . . This is a satisfying tale in and of itself, as well as a helpful and sensitive guide for those children who are just learning to confront life's sticky challenges. The ending is exquisite." SLJ

McDonald, Megan

Cloudy with a chance of boys. Candlewick Press 2011 260p il (The Sisters Club) $15.99; pa $5.99

Grades: 3 4 5 6 **Fic**

1. Clubs -- Fiction 2. Acting -- Fiction 3. Oregon -- Fiction 4. Sisters -- Fiction 5. Family life -- Fiction 6. Dating (Social customs) -- Fiction

ISBN 978-0-7636-4615-8; 0-7636-4615-6; 978-0-7636-5577-8 pa

LC 2010-39179

While older sister Alex is trying to orchestrate a perfect first kiss with her heartthrob and younger sister Joey prefers frogs to boys, Stevie Reel wonders if she is ready for a boyfriend while being pursued by a new boy in her class.

"The sisters are solidly developed, each with a distinctive narrative style made clear by formatting. . . . Breezy and light-hearted, this makes a nice recommendation for young readers looking for girl power." Bull Cent Child Books

Other titles in this series are:
The Sisters Club (2003)
Rule of three (2009)

★ **Judy** Moody; illustrated by Peter Reynolds. Candlewick Press 2000 160p il $15.99; pa $5.99

Grades: 2 3 4 **Fic**

1. School stories

ISBN 0-7636-0685-5; 0-7636-1231-6 pa

LC 99-13464

Other titles about Judy Moody are: Judy Moody & Stink: the holly joliday (2007); Judy Moody and the bad luck charm (2012); Judy Moody and the bucket list (2016); Judy Moody and the not bummer summer (2012); Judy Moody: around the world in 8 1/2 days (2006)

Judy Moody declares independence (2005); Judy Moody gets famous (2001); Judy Moody, girl detective (2010); Judy Moody goes to college (2008); Judy Moody M.D., the doctor is in (2004); Judy Moody predicts the future (2003); Judy Moody saves the world (2002);

Third grader Judy Moody is in a first day of school bad mood until she gets an assignment to create a collage all about herself and begins creating her masterpiece, the Me collage.

"This beginning chapter book features large type; simple, expressive prose and dialogue; and plenty of child-appealing humor." Booklist

Judy moody and stink and the big bad blackout; Megan McDonald, illustrated by Peter H. Reynolds. Candlewick Press 2014 144 p. color illustrations (Judy Moody and Stink) $14.99
Grades: 2 3 4   **Fic**
1. Adventure fiction 2. Hurricanes -- Fiction 3. Imagination -- Fiction 4. Electric power failures -- Fiction
ISBN 0763665207; 9780763665203
     LC 2013943995

"Judy and Stink and the whole Moody family hunker down with beans and batteries, ready to wait out the storm. But along with massive rain and strong winds, Hurricane Elmer throws down ghosts, squirrels, and aliens. Spooky! Just when things couldn't possibly get any freaker—flicker, flicker, gulp!—the lights go O-U-T out. The Moodys are smack-dab in the middle of a big bad blackout!" (Publisher's note)

"Readers of this fine series will enjoy the full-color illustrations and the little rain clouds above the page numbers. New fans can join in the fun—no need to have read the earlier books to enjoy this newest one. A cozy, comfortable book for a rainy night." Kirkus

Judy Moody and the bucket list; Megan McDonald, Peter H. Reynolds. Candlewick Press 2016 156 p. illustrations (Judy Moody) (ebook) $15.99; $15.99
Grades: 2 3 4   **Fic**
1. Grandmothers -- Fiction 2. Humorous fiction -- Fiction 3. Intergenerational relations -- Fiction
ISBN 9780763691868; 076367995X; 9780763679958
     LC 2015940257

In this book, by Megan McDonald, illustrated by Peter H. Reynolds, Judy is visiting Grandma Lou one day when she accidentally finds an uber-mysterious list of activities—a Bucket List! Which gives Judy an idea: How rare would it be if she made her own way-official bucket list of all the things she wants to do—before she starts fourth grade? Pretty soon Judy is off and running trying to cross off all her items." Publisher's note)

"This latest installment has the heart and humor that readers have come to expect from Judy and will please fans and newcomers alike." SLJ

Judy Moody, Mood Martian; Megan McDonald, illustrated by Peter H. Reynolds. Candlewick Press 2014 208 p. (Judy Moody) $15.99
Grades: 2 3 4   **Fic**
1. Humorous fiction 2. Emotions -- Fiction 3. Friendship -- Fiction 4. Mood (Psychology) -- Fiction 5. Moody, Judy (Fictitious character)
ISBN 076366698X; 9780763666989
     LC 2013953453

In this children's book by Megan McDonald, illustrated by Peter H. Reynolds, part of the Judy Moody series, "It's Backwards Day, so Judy Moody double-dares herself to become Queen of the Good Mood for one whole week. . . . In fact, Judy becomes a NOT moody, cool-as-a-cucumber neat freak for one whole entire day. But when her combed hair, matching outfits, and good moods hang around for days after, her friends begin to worry." (Publisher's note)

"In the 12th book of the popular series, Judy dares herself to try out a new mood. It's Backwards Day, so she spreads good cheer, smiles at everyone, and is nice to her stinky little brother." SLJ

Part of the recommended "Judy Moody" series.

Judy Moody & Stink: the mad, mad, mad, mad treasure hunt. Candlewick Press 2009 114p $14.99
Grades: 2 3 4   **Fic**
1. Pirates -- Fiction 2. Siblings -- Fiction 3. North Carolina -- Fiction
ISBN 978-0-7636-3962-4; 0-7636-3962-1
     LC 2008021533

During a weekend trip to Ocracoke Island, siblings Judy and Stink Moody take part in a pirate treasure-hunting game, in which various clues lead them to silver coins, or 'pieces of eight,' hidden across the island.

"With a mix of pirate slang, silly jokes, Morse code, and tantalizing puzzles, enlivened with full-color cartoons throughout, this book is a humorous summer read." SLJ

Judy Moody, girl detective; illustrated by Peter H. Reynolds. Candlewick Press 2010 170p il $15.99
Grades: 2 3 4   **Fic**
1. Mystery fiction 2. Dogs -- Fiction 3. Lost and found possessions -- Fiction
ISBN 978-0-7636-3450-6; 0-7636-3450-6

When a puppy who is being trained as a police dog goes missing, third-grader Judy forms a detective agency to solve the mystery, imitating her literary heroine, Nancy Drew.

"Judy is an endearing mix of precocious and familiar with just the right amount of exaggeration. The same could be said of the story. Watercolor-and-ink drawings break up the text." SLJ

The **rule** of three. Candlewick Press 2009 234p il (The Sisters Club) $15.99; pa $5.99
Grades: 3 4 5 6   **Fic**
1. Clubs -- Fiction 2. Acting -- Fiction 3. Baking -- Fiction 4. Oregon -- Fiction 5. Sisters -- Fiction 6. Theater -- Fiction 7. Family life -- Fiction
ISBN 978-0-7636-4153-5; 0-7636-4153-7; 978-0-7636-4830-5 pa; 0-7636-4830-2 pa
     LC 2008028859

In Acton, Oregon, sisters Alex, Stevie, and Joey take turns telling about their lives, including auditioning for the same part in the school musical, baking contest-worthy cupcakes, and becoming obsessed with Little Women.

"The story is believable, as are the sisters' interactions. The different styles add to the fun and help move the plot along quickly." SLJ

Stink and the ultimate thumb-wrestling smackdown; illustrated by Peter H. Reynolds. Candlewick Press 2011 128p il $12.99
Grades: 2 3 4   **Fic**
1. Karate -- Fiction
ISBN 978-0-7636-4346-1; 0-7636-4346-7

"Stink is proud of his report card with all the Os for Outstanding, but there is one U for Unsatisfactory; he flunked Phys. Ed. So he looks for a sport he likes and tries thumb wrestling, but it is the karate class that's the best fit. As always, the wordplay is part of the fun in this series . . . and so are the comic-style graphics. Readers will enjoy the karate details, both the action and the calming meditation." Booklist

Stink and the Midnight Zombie Walk; Megan McDonald; illustrated by Peter H. Reynolds. Candlewick Press 2012 144 p.

Grades: K 1 2 3 **Fic**

1. Zombies -- Fiction 2. Books and reading -- Fiction 3. Moneymaking projects -- Fiction

ISBN 0763656925; 9780763656928

LC 2011018620

This children's story by Megan McDonald follows the friends Stink and Webster, who are waiting for "the new book in the Nightmare on Zombie Street series [to come out.] Of corpse Stink will be first in line at the Blue Frog Bookstore to buy his copy and join the town's Midnight Zombie Walk! Until then, Stink and his friends keep busy making ketch-up-stained zombie costumes, trying to raise money to buy the book, and racking up points for Virginia Dare School's race to one million minutes of reading." (Publisher's note)

★ **Stink**: the incredible shrinking kid; illustrated by Peter H. Reynolds. Candlewick Press 2005 102p il $12.99

Grades: 2 3 4 **Fic**

1. School stories

ISBN 0-7636-2025-4

LC 2003-65246

The shortest kid in the second grade, James Moody, also known as Stink, learns all about the shortest president of the United States, James Madison, when they celebrate Presidents' Day at school

"Delightful full-page and spot-art cartoons and playful language in large type bring the child's adventures to life." SLJ

Other titles about Stink are:

Judy Moody & Stink: the holly joliday (2007)

Stink and the great Guinea Pig Express (2008)

Stink and the incredible super-galactic jawbreaker (2006)

Stink and the world's worst super-stinky sneakers (2007)

Stink: solar system superhero (2010)

Stink and the ultimate thumb-wrestling smackdown (2011)

Stink and the shark sleepover; Megan McDonald, illustrated by Peter H. Reynolds. Candlewick Press 2014 176 p. $12.99

Grades: 2 3 4 **Fic**

1. Aquariums 2. Fear -- Fiction 3. Sleepovers -- Fiction 4. Squids -- Fiction 5. Treasure hunt (Game) -- Fiction

ISBN 076366474X; 9780763664749

LC 2013943081

In this children's story, by Megan McDonald, illustrated by Peter H. Reynolds, "when Stink's parents win tickets for the whole family to sleep over at the aquarium (along with Stink's two best friends), it sounds like a science freak's dream come true.... But after some spooky stories around the virtual campfire, can he manage to fall asleep thinking about the eating habits of the vampire squid? Especially Bloody Mary, the mutant, glowing Frankensquid that's supposed to be on the prowl?" (Publisher's note)

"When Stink goes to a sleepover at the aquarium, he's very excited (he loves sharks) but also nervous (he's a bit afraid of sleepovers). Although the children are constantly cracking each other up with silly second-grade jokes, readers will also glean lots of factual information about sea creatures. Reynolds ably illustrates both the wondrous animals and the comical antics." Horn Book

McDonough, Yona Zeldis

The **bicycle** spy; Yona Zeldis McDonough. Scholastic Press 2016 208 p. (ebook) $16.99; $16.99

Grades: 4 5 6 **Fic**

1. Adventure fiction 2. Secrets -- Fiction 3. Bicycles -- Fiction 4. Family life -- Fiction 5. Jews -- France -- Fiction 6. World War, 1939-1945 -- Underground movements -- France -- Fiction 7. War

stories 8. Adventure stories

ISBN 9780545851824; 9780545850957

LC 20160137

In this book, by Yona Zeldis McDonough, "Marcel loves riding his bicycle, whether he's racing through the streets of his small town France or making bread deliveries for his parents' bakery. He dreams of someday competing in the Tour de France, the greatest bicycle race. But ever since Germany's occupation of France began two years ago, 1940, the race has been canceled. Now there are soldiers everywhere interrupting Marcel's rides with checkpoints and questioning." (Publisher's note)

"A fine story of war, friendship, and taking a stand against injustice." Kirkus

Includes bibliographical references

The **cats** in the doll shop; illustrated by Heather Maione. Viking 2011 il $14.99

Grades: 2 3 4 5 **F**

1. Cats -- Fiction 2. Dolls -- Fiction 3. Cousins -- Fiction 4. Immigrants -- Fiction 5. New York (N.Y.) -- Fiction 6. Jews -- United States -- Fiction

ISBN 978-0-670-01279-4; 0-670-01279-3

LC 20110093

With World War I raging in Europe, eleven-year-old Anna is thrilled to learn that her cousin Tania is coming from Russia to stay with Anna's family on the lower East Side of New York, and although Tania is shy and withdrawn when she arrives, her love of cats helps her adjust to her new family.

"Filled with references to Jewish traditions and the rich history of tenement life in New York City, these fully realized characters could be best friends with the girls from Sydney Taylor's All-of-a-Kind Family. A quiet treasure." Kirkus

The **doll** shop downstairs; illustrated by Heather Maione. Viking 2009 118p il $14.99

Grades: 2 3 4 5 **F**

1. Dolls -- Fiction 2. Immigrants -- Fiction 3. Family life -- Fiction 4. New York (N.Y.) -- Fiction 5. World War, 1914-1918 -- Fiction 6. Jews -- United States -- Fiction

ISBN 978-0-670-01091-2; 0-670-01091-X

LC 2009-0193

When World War I breaks out, nine-year-old Anna thinks of a way to save her family's beloved New York City doll repair shop. Includes brief author's note about the history of the Madame Alexander doll, glossary, and timeline.

"Anna's first person narrative creates convincing portrayals of her sisters and parents as well as her personal ups and downs.... Pleasant black-and-white pictures illustrate the action while helping children to visualize the period setting." Booklist

Another title about Anna and the doll shop is:

The cats in the doll shop (2011)

★ The **doll** with the yellow star; illustrated by Kimberly Bulcken Root. Henry Holt and Co. 2005 90p il $16.95

Grades: 3 4 5 **Fi**

1. Jews -- Fiction 2. Dolls -- Fiction 3. Holocaust, 1933-194 -- Fiction

ISBN 0-8050-6337-4

LC 2002-2755

When France falls to Germany at the start of World War II, nine-year-old Claudine must leave her beloved parents and friends to stay with relatives in America, accompanied by her doll, Violette

"This fiction book is informative, enjoyable, and passionately written." Libr Media Connect

McDowell, Marilyn Taylor

★ **Carolina** Harmony. Delacorte 2009 288p $16.99; lib bdg $19.99

Grades: 4 5 6 7   **Fic**

1. Orphans -- Fiction 2. Farm life -- Fiction 3. Blue Ridge Mountains region -- Fiction

ISBN 978-0-385-73590-2; 0-385-73590-1; 978-0-385-90575-6 lib bdg; 0-385-90575-0 lib bdg

"After Carolina's beloved Auntie Shen suffers a stroke, Carolina escapes from an unpleasant foster placement. The orphaned 10-year-old finds love at Harmony Farm, but the web of lies she spins almost leads to losing that home too. . . . This third-person narrative unwinds leisurely, with plenty of backtracking to fill in details of Carolina's life and the glories of her world in the Blue Ridge Mountains. . . . McDowell reveals her love for this part of the world, savoring the language, the environment, and the traditions of mountain culture." Booklist

McElligott, Matthew

Benjamin Franklinstein lives! [by] Matthew McElligott & Larry Tuxbury; illustrated by Matthew McElligott. G. P. Putnam's Sons 2010 121p il $12.99

Grades: 4 5 6 7   **Fic**

1. Authors 2. Diplomats 3. Inventors 4. Statesmen 5. Scientists 6. Science fiction 7. Writers on science 8. Zombies -- Fiction 9. Members of Congress

ISBN 978-0-399-25229-7; 0-399-25229-0

While working on a science fair project, a Philadelphia school boy discovers both a secret laboratory in his basement and Benjamin Franklin, who comes to life after receiving a jolt of electricity.

"It's a light fun read, and McElligott's many diagrams, graphs, and drawings are a nice addition." Booklist

Followed by: Benjamin Franklinstein meets the fright brothers (2011)

Benjamin Franklinstein meets the Fright brothers; by Matthew McElligott and Larry Tuxbury; [illustrated by Matthew McElligott] G. P. Putnam's Sons 2011 147p il $16.99

Grades: 4 5 6 7   **Fic**

1. Authors 2. Diplomats 3. Inventors 4. Statesmen 5. Scientists 6. Writers on science 7. Members of Congress 8. Scientists -- Fiction 9. Secret societies -- Fiction

ISBN 978-0-399-25480-2; 0-399-25480-3

LC 2010040431

Sequel to: Benjamin Franklinstein lives! (2010)

Victor and his friends, aided by Benjamin Franklin, uncover an evil scheme involving giant bats and two mysterious brothers, and learn more about the secretive Modern Order of Prometheus.

"Enhanced by frequent charts, diagrams, lists and other visual aids, a spirit of rational (if often reckless) scientific inquiry pervades the tale, as Ben and his allies translate coded messages, analyze evidence, get a lesson in meteorology and conduct experiments using both real and science-fictional gear on the way to a literally electrifying climax. . . . The authors have way too much fun taking the opener's premise and evil conspiracy to the next level. Readers will too." Kirkus

McGhee, Alison

Bink and Gollie; best friends forever. Kate DiCamillo, Alison McGheeq, Tony Fucile. Candlewick Press 2013 96 p. (Bink and Gollie) (reinforced) $15.99

Grades: 1 2 3 4   **Fic**

1. Girls -- Fiction 2. Friendship -- Fiction

ISBN 0763634972; 9780763634971

LC 2012942669

In this children's story, by Kate DiCamillo and Alison McGhee, illustrated by Tony Fucile, "Gollie is quite sure she has royal blood in her veins, but can Bink survive her friend's queenly airs . . . ? Bink wonders what it would be like to be as tall as her friend, but how far will she stretch her luck to find out? And when Bink and Gollie long to get their picture into a book of record holders, where will they find the kudos they seek?" (Publisher's note)

Firefly Hollow; Alison McGhee; illustrated by Christopher Denise. Atheneum Books for Young Readers 2014 304 p. (hardcover) $16.99

Grades: 2 3 4 5 6   **Fic**

1. Animals -- Fiction 2. Friendship -- Fiction 3. Grief -- Fiction 4. Voles -- Fiction 5. Crickets -- Fiction 6. Fireflies -- Fiction

ISBN 1442423366; 9781442423367

LC 2013004705

In this children's book by Alison McGhee, illustrated by Christopher Denise, "Firefly doesn't merely want to fly, she wants to touch the moon. Cricket doesn't merely want to sing about baseball, he wants to catch. When these two little creatures with big dreams wander out of Firefly Hollow . . . they find themselves face-to-face with . . . a giant. But Peter is a Miniature Giant. He is overwhelmed with sadness, and a summer with his new unlikely friends Firefly and Cricket might be just what he needs." (Publisher's note)

"The denizens of Firefly Hollow deal with loss, maturation, and friendship in this gentle novel. Firefly wants to fly to the moon. Cricket wants most to be the catcher in a baseball game like his hero, Yogi Berra. The miniature giant Peter (a human child) wants his best friend back. . . . Denise's illustrations are lovely, adding tremendously to the charm of the book. VERDICT Fans of Kate DiCamillo and E.B. White will enjoy this charming tale of unlikely inter-species friendships." SLJ

Two for one; by Kate DiCamillo & Alison McGhee; illustrated by Tony Fucile. 1st ed. Candlewick Press 2012 75 p. ill. (some col.) (Bink & Gollie) (reinforced) $15.99; (prebind) $15.99; (paperback) $6.99

Grades: 2 3 4   **Fic**

1. Humorous fiction 2. Fairs -- Fiction 3. Friendship -- Fiction

ISBN 0763633615; 9780763633615; 9781451740134; 9780763664459

LC 2011046625

This children's story by Kate DiCamillo and Alison McGhee, illustrated by Tony Fucile, continues the Theodor Seuss Geisel Award-winning "Bink and Gollie" series. "The state fair is in town, and now Bink and Gollie . . . must use teamwork and their gray matter while navigating its many wonders. . . . As the undaunted duo steps into the mysterious tent of fortune-teller Madame Prunely, one prediction is crystal clear: this unlikely pair will always be the closest of pals." (Publisher's note)

McGraw, Eloise Jarvis

The **moorchild**; [by] Eloise McGraw. Margaret K. McElderry Bks. 1996 241p $17; pa $5.99

Grades: 4 5 6 7   **Fic**

1. Fantasy fiction 2. Fairies -- Fiction

ISBN 0-689-80654-X; 1-4169-2768-9 pa

LC 95-34107

A Newbery Medal honor book, 1997

"Incorporating some classic fantasy motifs and icons, McGraw . . . conjures up an appreciably familiar world that, as evidence of her storytelling power, still strikes an original chord." Publ Wkly

McKay, Hilary, 1959-

★ **Binny** for short; by Hilary McKay and illustrated by Micah Player. Margaret K. McElderry Books 2013 291 p. (hardcover) $16.99

Grades: 4 5 6 7　　　　　　　　　　　　　　　**Fic**
1. Aunts -- Fiction　2. Family -- Fiction　3. Ghosts -- Juvenile
literature　4. Loss (Psychology) -- Fiction　5. Moving, Household
-- Fiction
ISBN 1442482753; 9781442482753
　　　　　　　　　　　　　　　　　　　LC 2013000053

In this book, by Hilary McKay and illustrated by Micah Player,
"Aunty Violet has died, and left Binny and her family an old house in
a seaside town. Binny is faced with a new crush, a new frenemy, and a
ghost. It seems Aunty Violet may not have completely departed. [For
Binny] it's odd being haunted by her aunt, but there is also the warmth
of a busy and loving mother, a musical older sister, and a hilarious little
brother, who is busy with his experiments." (Publisher's note)

Other titles in this series are:
Binny in secret (2015)
Binny bewitched (2017)

Binny in secret; Hilary McKay; with illustrations by Micah Player.
Margaret K. McElderry Books 2015 288 p. illustrations (hardcover)
$16.99
Grades: 4 5 6 7　　　　　　　　　　　　　　　**Fic**
1. School stories　2. Moving -- Fiction　3. Lynx -- Fiction　4.
Schools -- Fiction　5. Bullying -- Fiction　6. Family life -- Fiction
ISBN 1442482788; 9781442482784; 9781442482791
　　　　　　　　　　　　　　　　　　　LC 2014033545
Sequel to: Binny for short

In this book by Hilary McKay, illustrated by Micah Player, "Binny's
blissful summer is over and school is beginning. Binny hates everything
about school and the kids who torment her. When . . . Binny and her
family must move to a rental home out in the country. Binny, . . . sister
Clem, and . . . brother James (and his chickens) begin adjusting to a
new household. Then one of James's beloved chickens vanishes. What
kind of creature is lurking in the undergrowth? And does it need Binny's
protection?" (Publisher's note)

"Binny is wonderful to spend time with, and putting down the book
is like leaving a wonderfully comforting, very British setting filled with
good friends." SLJ

Lulu and the dog from the sea; by Hilary McKay; illustrated by
Priscilla Lamont. Albert Whitman 2013 112 p. (reinforced) $13.99
Grades: 2 3 4　　　　　　　　　　　　　　　**Fic**
1. Dogs -- Fiction　2. Vacations -- Fiction　3. Beaches -- Fiction
ISBN 0807548200; 9780807548202
　　　　　　　　　　　　　　　　　　　LC 2012013697

This children's story, by Hilary McKay, illustrated by Priscilla
Lamont, is the second volume in the "Lulu" series. "Lulu loves animals.
When Lulu goes on vacation, she finds there's a stray dog living on the
beach. Everyone in the town thinks the dog is trouble. But Lulu is sure
he just needs a friend. And that he's been waiting for someone just like
her." (Publisher's note)

Lulu and the duck in the park; by Hilary McKay; illustrated by
Priscilla Lamont. Albert Whitman 2012 104 p. $13.99
Grades: 2 3 4 5　　　　　　　　　　　　　　**Fic**
1. School stories　2. Pets -- Fiction　3. Ducks -- Fiction　4. Humorous
stories　5. Animals -- Fiction　6. Schools -- Fiction
ISBN 0807548081; 9780807548080
　　　　　　　　　　　　　　　　　　　LC 2012008229

This book introduces Lulu, a "girl with a penchant acquiring pets.
. . . The crux of the novel is Lulu's rescue of a duck egg she finds after dogs storm the park during a class outing. She sneaks the egg into
school and, in one" scene "quacks to the egg so 'it doesn't get lonely.'"
(Publishers Weekly)

"McKay shows a rare ability to capture a younger audience in this
involving chapter book for transitional readers." Booklist

Lulu and the hedgehog in the rain; Hilary McKay; illustrated by
Priscilla Lamont. Albert Whitman & Company 2014 104 p. illustra-
tions (hardback) $13.99
Grades: 2 3 4　　　　　　　　　　　　　　　**Fic**
1. Cousins -- Fiction　2. Hedgehogs -- Fiction　3. Animal rescue
-- Fiction　4. Wildlife rescue -- Fiction
ISBN 080754812X; 9780807548127
　　　　　　　　　　　　　　　　　　　LC 2014013381

In this children's book, by Hilary McKay, illustrated by Priscilla
Lamont, "Lulu loves animals. She knows that the hedgehog she rescued
isn't really a pet, but Lulu does want to make sure she's all right. And
so the Hedgehog Club is born. Everyone on the street agrees to keep an
eye on the little hedgehog and keep it away from the road. But come
wintertime the hedgehog disappears! Where could she have gone?"
(Publisher's note)

"After sneaking outdoors during a rainstorm, Lulu rescues a half-
drowned hedgehog and makes a home for it in her family's garden. .
From the Bossy Man to the New Old Lady, the people in Lulu's multicultural neighborhood are well-drawn, distinctive characters. Lamont's
sensitive gray-wash illustrations are as lively as the appealing story in
this early chapter book from the celebrated Lulu series." Booklist

Other titles in the series include:
Lulu and the Rabbit Next Door (2012)
Lulu and the Duck in the Park (2012)
Lulu and the Cat in the Bag (2013)
Lulu and the Dog from the Sea (2013)
Lulu and the Hamster in the night (2015)

★ **Saffy's** angel. Margaret K. McElderry Bks. 2002 152p $16
pa $4.99
Grades: 5 6 7 8　　　　　　　　　　　　　　**Fic**
1. Adoption -- Fiction　2. Family life -- Fiction　3. Great Britain
-- Fiction
ISBN 0-689-84933-8; 0-689-84934-6 pa
　　　　　　　　　　　　　　　　　　　LC 2001-44110
First published 2001 in the United Kingdom
Boston Globe-Horn Book Award Honor: Fiction (2002)

After learning that she was adopted, thirteen-year-old Saffron's relationship with her eccentric, artistic family changes, until they help her go
back to Italy where she was born to find a special momento of her past

"Like the Casson household itself, the plot is a chaotic whirl that careens off in several directions simultaneously. But McKay always skillfully draws each clearly defined character back into the story with witty
well-edited details; rapid dialogue; and fine pacing." Booklist

Other titles in this series are:
Indigo's star (2004)
Permanent Rose (2005)
Caddy ever after (2006)
Forever Rose (2008)

Wishing for tomorrow; the sequel to A little princess. illustrated
by Nick Maland. Margaret K. McElderry Books 2010 273p il $16.99
Grades: 4 5 6　　　　　　　　　　　　　　　**Fic**
1. School stories　2. Friendship -- Fiction　3. London (England)
-- Fiction
ISBN 978-1-4424-0169-3; 1-4424-0169-9
　　　　　　　　　　　　　　　　　　　LC 2009-24868

Relates what becomes of Ermengarde and the other girls left behind
at Miss Minchin's School after Sara Crewe leaves to live with her guardian, the Indian gentleman.

"Enhanced by Maland's period illustrations, the novel convincingly evokes the Victorian era, even as McKay interjects a contemporary sensibility. A surprising, dramatic denouement caps this droll and heartwarming tale, a very worthy follow-up to a well-loved classic." Publ Wkly

McKinlay, Meg

Below; Meg McKinlay. Candlewick Press 2013 224 p. (reinforced) $15.99

Grades: 4 5 6 7   **Fic**

1. Reservoirs -- Fiction 2. Extinct cities -- Fiction

ISBN 0763661260; 9780763661267

LC 2012943652

In this book by Meg McKinlay, "Cassie was . . . the first baby born in the Australian town of New Lower Grange, which was established after the intentional flooding of the previous town to accommodate a dam. . . . [S]he feels the pull of the forbidden lake above Old Lower Grange. There, she is joined by Liam, a classmate whose life was altered in a tragic accident, and together they search for the truth about the town's past as its centenary celebration approaches." (Publishers Weekly)

"Although the author does a masterful job of making sure all the pieces fit at the end, the central mystery is hard to buy. This is mitigated by a reasonably suspenseful climax, an earned family solidarity message and the lesson: that to find the truth, one must delve below the surface. A quietly intriguing meditation on history and truth." Kirkus

Duck for a day; illustrated by Leila Rudge. Candlewick Press 2012 89 p. $12.99

Grades: 1 2 3   **Fic**

1. Children and animals 2. Pets -- Fiction 3. Friendship -- Fiction 4. School stories 5. Ducks -- Fiction 6. Lost and found possessions -- Fiction

ISBN 0763657840; 9780763657840

LC 2011018608

In author Meg McKinlay's book, "class pet is a duck named Max, and pet-deprived Abby longs to earn the privilege of taking him home overnight. Active and involving right from the first, . . . the plot unfolds . . . to include a contest to build Max the ideal 'aquatic environment,' a well-deserved visit to Abby's house, and an exciting chase to find Max after he escapes from her backyard." (Horn Book Magazine)

McKinnon, Hannah Roberts

★ **Franny** Parker. Farrar Straus Giroux 2009 149p $16

Grades: 5 6 7 8   **Fic**

1. Droughts -- Fiction 2. Oklahoma -- Fiction 3. Violence -- Fiction 4. Family life -- Fiction

ISBN 978-0-374-32469-8; 0-374-32469-7

LC 2008-01702

Through a hot, dry Oklahoma summer, twelve-year-old Franny tends wild animals brought by her neighbors, hears gossip during a weekly quilting bee, befriends a new neighbor who has some big secrets, and learns to hope.

"Franny is a relatable and consistent narrator, the homey rural setting is throughtfully rendered and the easy prose should appeal to reluctant readers." Publ Wkly

The **properties** of water. Farrar, Straus, and Giroux 2010 166p $16.99

Grades: 5 6 7 8   **Fic**

1. Sisters -- Fiction 2. Accidents -- Fiction

ISBN 978-0-374-36145-7; 0-374-36145-2

When her older sister, Marni, is paralyzed jumping off the cliffs into the lake near their house, twelve-year-old Lace feels responsible for the accident and struggles to find a way to help heal her family.

McKinnon "has created a cast of believably imperfect characters, and Lace's emotions ring true." Publ Wkly

McKissack, Pat, 1944-2017

Abby takes a stand; illustrated [by] Gordon C. James. Viking 2005 104p il (Scraps of time) $14.99; pa $4.99

Grades: 2 3 4   **Fic**

1. Tennessee -- Fiction 2. African Americans -- Fiction 3. Civil rights demonstrations -- Fiction

ISBN 0-670-06011-9; 0-14-240687-2 pa

LC 2004-21641

Gee recalls for her grandchildren what happened in 1960 in Nashville, Tennessee, when she, aged ten, passed out flyers while her cousin and other adults held sit-ins at restaurants and lunch counters to protest segregation.

"Although short and simply told, the book gives readers a kid's-eye view of important happenings and reminds them that history is something that is always in the making. Fine black-and-white art adds to the ambience of the time." Booklist

Other titles in this series are:

Away west (2006)

A song for Harlem (2007)

The homerun king (2008)

The **clone** codes; [by] Patricia C. McKissack, Fredrick L. McKissack [and] John McKissack. Scholastic 2010 173p $16.99

Grades: 4 5 6 7   **Fic**

1. Science fiction 2. Cloning -- Fiction 3. Segregation -- Fiction 4. Identity (Psychology) -- Fiction

ISBN 978-0-439-92983-7; 0-439-92983-0

LC 2009-24076

On the run from a bounty hunter who arrested her mother for being part of a secret society devoted to freeing clones, thirteen-year-old Leanna learns amazing truths about herself and her family as she is forced to consider the value of freedom and what it really means to be human in 2170 America.

"The story is tight and fast-paced, yet makes room for historical parallels that are vivid without being preachy. An intriguing start to a planned trilogy." Publ Wkly

Followed by: Cyborg (2011)

Cyborg; a Clone codes novel. [by] Patricia C. McKissack, Fredrick L. McKissack, John P. McKissack. Scholastic Press 2011 107p $16.99

Grades: 4 5 6 7   **Fic**

1. Science fiction 2. Civil rights -- Fiction 3. Artificial intelligence -- Fiction

ISBN 978-0-439-92985-1; 0-439-92985-7

LC 2010016075

Sequel to: Clone codes (2010)

Seventeen-year-old Houston, a cyborg since the age of seven, and a fugitive living on the Moon, joins with other cyborgs all over the world in non-violent protest marches to challenge the Cyborg Act 2130 and hopefully secure increased civil liberties.

"The McKissacks continue to successfully draw parallels between a futuristic world that tries to control those considered different and historic racial struggles. . . . The worldbuilding is intriguing, there is plenty of action and ethnic diversity in a science-fiction tale is welcome." Kirkus

★ **Let** my people go; Bible stories told by a freeman of color to his daughter, Charlotte, in Charleston, South Carolina, 1806-16. by Patricia and Fredrick McKissack; illustrated by James Ransome. Atheneum Bks. for Young Readers 1998 134p il $20

Grades: 4 5 6 7   **Fic**

1. Bible stories 2. Slavery -- Fiction 3. African Americans --

Fiction
ISBN 0-689-80856-9

LC 97-19983

Charlotte, the daughter of a free black man who worked as a black-smith in Charleston, South Carolina, in the early 1800s recalls the stories from the Bible that her father shared with her, relating them to the experiences of African Americans

"The poignant juxtaposition of the Biblical characters and Charlotte's personal narrative is authentic and moving. . . . The occasional illustrations are powerful oil paintings in rich colors, emotional and evocative." SLJ

Includes bibliographical references

★ **Never** forgotten. Schwartz & Wade Books 2011 un il $18.99; lib bdg $21.99

Grades: 3 4 5 6 **Fic**

1. Novels in verse 2. Slavery -- Fiction 3. African Americans -- Fiction

ISBN 978-0-375-84384-6; 0-375-84384-1; 978-0-375-94453-6 lib bdg; 0-375-94453-2 lib bdg

LC 2010024789

McKissack's "story about a Malian boy abducted and sold into slavery has frightening moments, but carries dignity and even triumph away from them. . . . The willingness to turn the dark history of the past into literature takes not just talent but courage. McKissack has both." Publ Wkly

A **song** for Harlem; by Patricia C. McKissack; illustrated by Gordon C. James. Viking 2007 108p il (Scraps of time) $14.99; pa $4.99

Grades: 2 3 4 **Fic**

1. Authors 2. Novelists 3. Dramatists 4. Memoirists 5. Folklorists 6. Short story writers 7. Authorship -- Fiction 8. African Americans -- Fiction 9. Harlem Renaissance -- Fiction

ISBN 978-0-670-06209-6; 978-0-14-241238-1 pa

LC 2007015331

In the summer of 1928, Lilly Belle Turner of Smyrna, Tennessee, participates in a young author's writing program, taught by Zora Neale Hurston and hosted by A'Lelia Walker in her Harlem teahouse at the height of the Harlem Renaissance

"Full-page drawings are scattered throughout. This easy-to-read novel has succinct chapters and sentences that, while simple, convey a feel for the characters and the time, and a vivid sense of place." SLJ

Stitchin' and pullin' a Gee's Bend quilt. illustrated by Cozbi A. Cabrera. Random House 2008 un il $17.99; lib bdg $20.99

Grades: 2 3 4 5 **Fic**

1. Novels in verse 2. Quilts -- Fiction 3. Alabama -- Fiction 4. Family life -- Fiction 5. African Americans -- Fiction

ISBN 978-0-375-83163-8; 0-375-83163-0; 978-0-375-93163-5 lib bdg; 0-375-93163-5 lib bdg

LC 2007011066

As a young African American girl pieces her first quilt together, the history of her family, community, and the struggle for justice and freedom in Gee's Bend, Alabama unfolds.

"Rich naif-style paintings in a warm, deep palette bring the poems to life and reflect their tone and spirit. . . . . It's marvelously clear that McKissack understands the creative pulse of the quilter and artist." Horn Book

★ **Tippy** Lemmey; illustrated by Susan Keeter. Simon & Schuster 2003 59p il (Ready-for-chapters) pa $3.99

Grades: 2 3 4 **Fic**

1. Dogs -- Fiction 2. Tennessee -- Fiction 3. African Americans

-- Fiction
ISBN 0-689-85019-0

"In 1951, in Templeton, TN, Leanne Martin and her friends Paul and Jeannie are at war with Tippy Lemmey, a dog that frightens them . . . The kids learn that Tippy is simply a puppy who wants to play, and that his owner is fighting in Korea. Leanne remains unconvinced about the dog's good intentions, but when the friends see thieves stealing him and other neighborhood dogs to sell across state, they rescue the animals and are rewarded when Tippy gets them out of a dangerous situation. . . This charming and humorous story moves along at a fast pace, making it perfect for readers just venturing into chapter-book territory." SLJ

McMullan, Kate

School! adventures at the Harvey N. Trouble Elementary School written by Kate McMullan; inspired and illustrated by George Booth Feiwel and Friends 2010 149p il $12.99

Grades: 1 2 3 4 **Fic**

1. School stories
ISBN 978-0-312-37592-8; 0-312-37592-1

LC 2008-15263

"The story takes readers into Ron's week, from Hotsy-Totsy Monday to Hunky-Dory Thursday, at his outlandish school, where, through extreme silliness, little life lessons are learned. . . . The characters all have giggle-worthy names that relate to their personalities or attributes. . . Booth's great cartoon illustrations add whimsy and pure fun to every page, a quality that, when paired with McMullan's simple, quirky story may well draw in reluctant readers." SLJ

McMullan, Margaret

How I found the Strong; a Civil War story. Houghton Mifflin 2004 136p $15

Grades: 5 6 7 8 **Fic**

1. Slavery -- Fiction 2. Mississippi -- Fiction 3. United States -- History -- 1861-1865, Civil War -- Fiction

ISBN 0-618-35008-X

LC 2003-12294

Frank Russell, known as Shanks, wishes he could have gone with his father and brother to fight for Mississippi and the Confederacy, but his experiences with the war and his changing relationship with the family slave, Buck, change his thinking.

"The crisply written narrative is full of regional speech and detail, creating a vivid portrait." Voice Youth Advocates

When I crossed No-Bob. Houghton Mifflin Company 2007 209p $16

Grades: 5 6 7 8 **Fic**

1. Farm life -- Fiction 2. Mississippi -- Fiction 3. Race relations -- Fiction 4. Abandoned children -- Fiction 5. Reconstruction (1865-1876) -- Fiction

ISBN 978-0-618-71715-6; 0-618-71715-3

LC 2007-12753

Ten years after the Civil War's end, twelve-year-old Addy, abandoned by her parents, is taken from the horrid town of No-Bob by schoolteacher Frank Russell and his bride, but when her father returns to claim her she must find another way to leave her O'Donnell past behind

"The simple prose can be pure poetry. . . . Readers will be drawn by the history close-up and by the elemental moral choice." Booklist

McNamara, Margaret

A **poem** in your pocket; by Margaret McNamara; illustrated by G Brian Karas. Schwartz & Wade Books 2015 40 p. color illustrations (Mr. Tiffin's Classroom Series) (glb) $19.99

Grades: K 1 2 3 **Fic**

1. School stories 2. Poetry -- Fiction 3. Authorship -- Fiction 4

Schools -- Fiction 5. Self-confidence -- Fiction

ISBN 0307979482; 9780307979476; 9780307979483

LC 2014005745

In this children's story, by Margaret McNamara, illustrated by G. Brian Karas, set "in the classroom, . . . poetry - from metaphors to acrostics to haiku - is the name of the game. The focus here is on Elinor, whose confidence falters as she tries to write something 'perfect' for Poem in Your Pocket Day and impress a visiting poet." (Publisher's note)

"Examples of poetry the kids come up with . . . may inspire young readers to attempt their own writing, especially since Karas's gouache, acrylic, and pencil pictures make the diverse group of classmates look like they are having fun." Horn Book

McNamee, Eoin

The **Ring** of Five. Wendy Lamb Books 2010 345p $16.99; lib bdg $19.99

Grades: 5 6 7 8   **Fic**

1. School stories 2. Fantasy fiction 3. Spies -- Fiction

ISBN 978-0-385-73731-9; 0-385-73731-9; 978-0-385-90658-6 lib bdg; 0-385-90658-7 lib bdg

LC 2009-33345

Kidnapped on his way to boarding school, Danny Caulfield, who has one blue eye and one brown eye, ends up at a mysterious academy of spies, where he is to be trained in the art of espionage in an effort to keep the Upper and Lower worlds from colliding.

McQuerry, Maureen Doyle

★ **Beyond** the door; Maureen Doyle McQuerry. Amulet Books 2014 384 p. (Time out of time) $16.95

Grades: 4 5 6 7 8   **Fic**

1. Adventure fiction 2. Magic -- Fiction 3. Celtic mythology -- Fiction 4. Brothers and sisters -- Fiction 5. Space and time -- Fiction 6. Animals, Mythical -- Fiction 7. Mythology, Celtic -- Fiction 8. Adventure and adventurers -- Fiction

ISBN 1419710168; 9781419710162

LC 2013025513

This book, by Maureen Doyle McQuerry, "weaves a . . . coming-of-age story with fantasy and mythology. With his love of learning and the game of Scrabble, Timothy James feels like the only person who understands him is his older sister, Sarah. . . . One night, while his parents and sister are away, the door opens, and mythical creatures appear in his own living room! Soon, a mystery of unparalleled proportions begins to unfold, revealing an age-old battle of Light against Dark." Publisher's note)

"Scrabble-loving loner Timothy and his older sister Sarah access an ancient mythological prophecy when Timothy saves his school tormentor Jessica from being hunted on Beltane, the Gaelic May Day festival. Heavy reliance on Celtic mythology and symbolism doesn't help an awkwardly disjointed plot, though the strong good/evil dichotomy will attract fans to the new series. A code in Ogham script runs along each page." Horn Book

McSwigan, Marie

★ **Snow** treasure; [by] Marie McSwigan; illustrated by Mary Reardon. Dutton's Children's Books 2005 196p il $10.99; pa $5.99

Grades: 3 4 5 6   **Fic**

1. Norway -- Fiction 2. World War, 1939-1945 -- Fiction

ISBN 0-525-47626-1; 0-14-240224-9 pa

LC 2005042108

A reissue of the title first published 1942

In 1940, when the Nazi invasion of Norway reaches their village in the far north, twelve-year-old Peter and his friends use their sleds to transport nine million dollars worth of gold bullion past the German

soldiers to the secret harbor where Peter's uncle keeps his ship ready to take the gold for safekeeping in the United States.

"A dramatic reconstruction of an actual happening. . . . Well written." Booklist

McVoy, Terra Elan

This Is All Your Fault, Cassie Parker; by Terra Elan McVoy. Harpercollins Childrens Books 2016 272 p. $16.99

Grades: 4 5 6 7 8   **Fic**

1. School stories 2. Diaries -- Fiction 3. Popularity -- Fiction 4. Female friendship -- Fiction

ISBN 0062414496; 9780062414496

In this book, by Terra Elan McVoy, "twelve-year-old Fiona Coppleton is living a middle schooler's worst nightmare: her diary was made public and her best friend is partly to blame. Fiona and Cassie are supposed to be best friends forever. No one else listens, . . . and that meant everything when Fiona's parents were divorcing. . . . [A]nd even though Cassie cares a little too much about being popular, Fiona can't imagine life without her." (Publisher's note)

"A smart, heartwarming novel about the ups and downs of family and friendship." Kirkus

Mead, Alice

★ **Junebug**. Farrar, Straus & Giroux 1995 101p hardcover o.p. pa $6.99

Grades: 3 4 5   **Fic**

1. Sailing -- Fiction 2. African Americans -- Fiction

ISBN 0-374-33964-3; 0-312-56126-1 pa

LC 95-5421

"Junebug approaches his tenth birthday with fear because he knows he'll be forced by the older boys in his housing project to join a gang. On his birthday, with luck and persistence, Junebug realizes his secret dream of one day sailing a boat. The novel contains vivid descriptions of the grim realities of inner-city life but also demonstrates that strong convictions and warm hearts can bring about change." Horn Book Guide

Other titles about Junebug are:

Junebug and the Reverend (1998)

Junebug in trouble (2003)

Junebug in trouble. Farrar, Straus & Giroux 2002 135p hardcover o.p. pa $5.50

Grades: 3 4 5   **Fic**

1. African Americans -- Fiction 2. Juvenile delinquency -- Fiction

ISBN 0-374-33969-4; 0-440-41937-9 pa

LC 2001-33268

Sequel to: Junebug and the Reverend

Despite having moved out of the rough housing project where he grew up, ten-year-old Junebug continues to encounter crime, gangs, and violence

"Mead walks a delicate line between problem novel and everyday-life story, and does so with grace. . . . Although the themes are predominantly serious . . . there is warmth in the relationships, some humor in the dialogue, and complete simplicity in the writing style." Horn Book

Medina, Juana

★ **Juana** and Lucas; Juana Medina. Candlewick Press 2016 96 p. color illustrations $14.99

Grades: 2 3 4   **Fic**

1. Girls -- Fiction 2. Human-animal relationships -- Fiction 3. English as a second language -- Fiction

ISBN 0763672084; 9780763672089

Pura Belpre Author Award (2017)

In this children's book by Juana Medina, "Juana loves many things--drawing, eating Brussels sprouts, living in Bogotá, Colombia, and especially her dog, Lucas. . . . She does not love wearing her itchy school uniform, solving math problems, or going to dance class. And she especially does not love learning the English . . . until Juana's abuelos tell her about a special trip they are planning--one that Juana will need to speak English to go on." (Publisher's note)

"An essential selection that creates multicultural awareness, has distinguished and appealing design elements, and has a text that is the stuff of true literature." SLJ

Meloy, Colin

Under Wildwood; Colin Meloy; illustrated by Carson Ellis. Balzer + Bray 2012 559 p. (hardback) $17.99

Grades: 5 6 7 8   Fic

1. Fantasy fiction 2. Adventure fiction 3. Fantasy 4. Animals -- Fiction 5. Portland (Or.) -- Fiction
ISBN 006202471X; 9780062024718

LC 2012019040

Sequel to: Wildwood

This children's picture book is a sequel to "Wildwood." Here, bookish "Prue and bandit-in-training Curtis team up once again to fight a nefarious governess and evil science teacher in this fast-paced fantasy set in Oregon. . . . In this strange land, it can be difficult to tell friend from foe, making for deliciously suspenseful adventures with a rat named Septimus and a circus bear with hooks instead of paws." (Children's Literature)

★ **Wildwood**; illustrations by Carson Ellis. Balzer + Bray 2011 541p il $16.99

Grades: 5 6 7 8   Fic

1. Fantasy fiction 2. Animals -- Fiction 3. Siblings -- Fiction 4. Portland (Or.) -- Fiction 5. Missing persons -- Fiction
ISBN 978-0-06-202468-8; 0-06-202468-X

LC 2011010072

When her baby brother is kidnapped by crows, seventh-grader Prue McKeel ventures into the forbidden Impassable Wilderness—a dangerous and magical forest in the middle of Portland, Oregon—and soon finds herself involved in a war among the various inhabitants.

"Illustrations by Ellis . . . bring forest and inhabitants to gently whimsical life. A satisfying blend of fantasy, adventure story, eco-fable and political satire with broad appeal." Kirkus

Wildwood imperium; Colin Meloy; illustrations by Carson Ellis. Balzer + Bray 2014 592 p. ill (some col.), maps (Wildwood chronicles) (hardcover) $17.99

Grades: 5 6 7 8   Fic

1. Fairy tales 2. Fantasy fiction 3. Orphans -- Fiction 4. Friendship -- Fiction
ISBN 0062024744; 9780062024749

LC 2013953784

This fairy tale, by Colin Meloy, is the third book in the fantasy "Wildwood" series. "A young girl's midnight séance awakens a long-slumbering malevolent spirit. . . . A band of runaway orphans allies with an underground collective of saboteurs and plans a daring rescue of their friends, imprisoned in . . . an industrial wasteland. . . . Two old friends draw closer to their goal of bringing together a pair of exiled toy makers in order to reanimate a mechanical boy prince." (Publisher's note)

"Dramatic shifts in tone and mood--by turns politically astute and subversively witty, elegiac, droll and philosophical--are par for the course, while narrative style ranges from intimate to intergalactically distant." Kirkus

Merrill, Jean

★ The **pushcart** war; by Jean Merrill; with illustrations by Ronni Solbert. Bantam Doubleday Dell Books for Young Readers 1987 222 il pa $6.50

Grades: 5 6 7 8   Fic

1. Trucks -- Fiction 2. New York (N.Y.) -- Fiction
ISBN 0-440-47147-8

A reissue of the title first published 1964 by W. R. Scott

The outbreak of a war between truck drivers and pushcart peddler brings the mounting problems of traffic to the attention of both the city of New York and the world.

"A book that is both humorous and downright funny. . . . Such lively book will need little introducing." Horn Book

The **toothpaste** millionaire; by Jean Merrill; prepared by the Ban Street College of Education. 35th anniversary ed.; Houghton Mifflin 2006 129p il $16; pa $5.95

Grades: 4 5 6   Fic

1. Mathematics -- Fiction 2. Cleveland (Ohio) -- Fiction 3. Business enterprises -- Fiction
ISBN 978-0-618-75924-8; 0-618-75924-7; 978-0-618-75925-5 pa; 0-618-75925-5 pa

A reissue of the title first published 1972

A young girl describes how her school friend made over a million dollars by creating and marketing a cheaper and better toothpaste.

"The illustrations are engaging, the style is light, the project interesting (with more than a few swipes taken at advertising and business practices in our society) and Rufus a believable genius." Bull Cen Child Books

Messer, Stephen

The **death** of Yorik Mortwell; illustrated by Gris Grimly. Random House Children's Books 2011 173p il $15.99; lib bdg $18.99; e book $15.95

Grades: 5 6 7 8   Fic

1. Ghost stories 2. Fantasy fiction 3. Magic -- Fiction 4. Sibling -- Fiction 5. Demonology -- Fiction 6. Good and evil -- Fiction 7 Social classes -- Fiction
ISBN 978-0-375-86858-0; 978-0-375-96858-7 lib bdg; 978-0-375-89928-7 e-book

LC 201001425

Following his death at the hands of fellow twelve-year-old, Lor Thomas, Yorik returns as a ghost to protect his sister from a similar fate but soon learns of ancient magical beings, both good and evil, who are vying for power at the Estate.

"Full-page, macabre illustrations appear throughout. Lemony Snicket, Harry Potter, and Neil Gaiman enthusiasts will appreciate this engaging, eccentric adventure." SLJ

★ **Windblowne**. Random House 2010 304p $16.99

Grades: 4 5 6 7   Fic

1. Fantasy fiction 2. Kites -- Fiction 3. Uncles -- Fiction 4. Space and time -- Fiction
ISBN 978-0-375-86195-6; 0-375-86195-5

LC 2008-4377

Hapless Oliver, who lives in the trees in the town of Windblowne seeks his eccentric great-uncle Gilbert's help in creating a kite for the all-important kite festival, but when Gilbert suddenly disappears, Olive is guided by one of Gilbert's kites in a quest through different world to find him.

"Messer constructs a tale that moves along at a powerful, steady pace to a climactic faceoff, and Oliver's realization that the gateway to worlds is open for those who can truly listen to the wind's voices spark a memorable sea change in his self-image." Kirkus

Messner, Kate

Marty McGuire; illustrated by Brian Floca. Scholastic Press 2011 129p il $15.99; pa $5.99

Grades: 2 3 4   **Fic**

1. School stories 2. Theater -- Fiction

ISBN 978-0-545-14244-1; 0-545-14244-X; 978-0-545-14246-5 pa; 0-545-14246-6 pa

LC 2010-31291

When tomboy Marty is cast as the princess in the third-grade play, she learns about improvisation, which helps her become more adaptable.

"Messner gets all the details of third grade right. . . . Floca's black-and-white sketches are filled with movement and emotion and are frequent enough to help new chapter-book readers keep up with this longer text. [The book features] believable and endearing characters in a realistic elementary-school setting." Kirkus

Followed by: Marty McGuire digs worms! (2012)

Marty McGuire digs worms! by Kate Messner; illustrated by Brian Floca. Scholastic Press 2012 161 p.

Grades: K 1 2 3   **Fic**

1. Worms -- Fiction 2. Compost -- Fiction 3. Recycling -- Fiction 4. School children -- Fiction 5. Environmental protection -- Fiction 6. Schools -- Fiction 7. Grandmothers -- Fiction 8. Recycling (Waste) -- Fiction

ISBN 0545142458; 9780545142458; 9780545142472

LC 2011016291

In this book, "Marty McGuire's third-grade class has a special assignment: Save the Earth! Even more exciting, the best project wins a special award. Marty's pretty sure her classmates' ideas won't stand a chance against her plan to turn the garbage from the school cafeteria into fertilizer. All she needs is a little help from her teammate and best friend, Annie—and the worms in her grandma's garden. . . . [W]hen the critters escape, the whole class starts grumbling. Can Marty save the Earth without losing her friends?" (Publisher's note)

Marty McGuire has too many pets! by Kate Messner; illustrated by Brian Floca. Scholastic Press 2014 168 p. illustrations (hc) $15.99

Grades: 2 3 4   **Fic**

1. Pets -- Fiction 2. Chimpanzees -- Fiction 3. Animal sanctuaries -- Fiction 4. Pet sitting -- Fiction 5. Money-making projects -- Fiction

ISBN 054553559X; 9780545535595; 9780545535601

LC 2013010371

"Marty McGuire really has her hands full this time. . . . After visiting a sanctuary for retired lab chimpanzees, Marty wants to follow in the footsteps of her idol Jane Goodall and help with their care. But 'adopting a chimp' is expensive, so Marty and her third-grade pals hatch a plan to raise money by holding a talent show at school and opening a pet-sitting business in Marty's basement." (Publisher's note)

"Messner makes the most of Marty's story with a nicely differentiated cast of empathetic characters and plenty of dramatic range. The line-and-gray-wash illustrations by Caldecott Medal-winning artist Floca capture moments of anxiety, despair, and happiness with equal grace." (Booklist)

The **seventh** wish; by Kate Messner. Bloomsbury 2016 240 p. (hardback) $16.99

Grades: 4 5 6 7   **Fic**

1. Magic -- Fiction 2. Wishes -- Fiction 3. Family life -- Fiction 4. Schools -- Fiction

ISBN 9781619633773; 9781619633766

LC 2015036430

In this book, by Kate Messner, "Charlie feels like she's always coming in last. From her Mom's new job to her sister's life away at college,

everything else always seems to be more important than Charlie's upcoming dance competition or science project. Unsure of how to get her family's attention, Charlie comes across the surprise of her life one day while ice-fishing . . . in the form of a floppy, scaly fish offering to grant her a wish in exchange for its freedom." (Publisher's note)

"Hopeful, empathetic, and unusually enlightening." Kirkus

Sugar and ice. Walker & Co. 2010 275p $16.99

Grades: 4 5 6 7   **Fic**

1. Ice skating -- Fiction 2. New York (State) -- Fiction

ISBN 978-0-8027-2081-8; 0-8027-2081-1

LC 2009-54217

When Russian skating coach Andrei Grosheva offers farm girl Claire a scholarship to train with the elite in Lake Placid, she encounters a world of mean girls on ice, where competition is everything

"The dialogue between classmates and siblings is realistic, and the intergenerational or extended family relationships are interesting. The author shows the intensity of the world of competitive skating without dwelling on its rough edges, making it accessible not only to tween readers, but also to those who might have Olympic aspirations." SLJ

Meyer, Susan

Black radishes; [by] Susan Lynn Meyer. Delacorte Press 2010 228p map $16.99; lib bdg $19.99

Grades: 5 6 7 8   **Fic**

1. France -- Fiction 2. Jews -- France -- Fiction 3. Paris (France) -- Fiction 4. Holocaust, 1933-1945 -- Fiction

ISBN 978-0-385-73881-1; 0-385-73881-1; 978-0-385-90748-4 lib bdg; 0-385-90748-6 lib bdg

LC 2009-47613

"Set in France during World War II, this historical novel follows eleven-year-old Gustave as his family escapes Paris for safer quarters in the small, provincial town of Saint-Georges. . . . Not long after Gustave's family arrives in Saint-Georges, the Nazis invade and occupy Paris and establish a demarcation line between occupied northern France and unoccupied Vichy France in the south. . . . The episodic narrative offers abundant detail, and the wartime dangers, especially Gustave's father's illicit travel between occupied and unoccupied zones, adds considerable suspense. Gustave's growth over the course of the novel is both realistic and relatable, making this an appealing topical entry for the upper elementary/middle school set." Bull Cent Child Books

Another title in this series is:

Skating with the Statue of Liberty (2016)

Miles, Miska

Annie and the Old One; illustrated by Peter Parnall. Little, Brown 1971 44p il lib bdg $16.95; pa $7.95

Grades: 1 2 3 4   **Fic**

1. Death -- Fiction 2. Navajo Indians -- Fiction

ISBN 0-316-57117-2 lib bdg; 0-316-57120-2 pa

A Newbery Medal honor book, 1972

This is "a poignant, understated, rather brave story of a very real child, set against a background of Navajo traditions and contemporary Indian life. Fine expressive drawings match the simplicity of the story." Horn Book

Milford, Kate

★ The **Boneshaker**; [illustrations by Andrea Offermann] Clarion Books 2010 372p il $17

Grades: 5 6 7 8 9   **Fic**

1. Bicycles -- Fiction 2. Missouri -- Fiction 3. Demonology -- Fiction 4. Supernatural -- Fiction

ISBN 978-0-547-24187-6; 0-547-24187-9

LC 2009-45350

When Jake Limberleg brings his traveling medicine show to a small Missouri town in 1913, thirteen-year-old Natalie senses that something is wrong and, after investigating, learns that her love of automata and other machines make her the only one who can set things right.

"Natalie is a well-drawn protagonist with sturdy supporting characters around her. The tension built into the solidly constructed plot is complemented by themes that explore the literal and metaphorical role of crossroads and that thin line between good and evil." Kirkus

The **Broken** Lands; by Kate Milford; with illustrations by Andrea Offermann. Clarion Books 2012 455 p. ill. (hardback) $16.99

Grades: 5 6 7 8 9 10   **Fic**

1. Bridges -- Fiction 2. Supernatural -- Fiction 3. New York (N.Y.) -- Fiction 4. Orphans -- Fiction 5. Demonology -- Fiction 6. Good and evil -- Fiction 7. New York (N.Y.) -- History -- 1865-1898 -- Fiction 8. Coney Island (New York, N.Y.) -- History -- 19th century -- Fiction

ISBN 0547739664; 9780547739663

LC 2011049466

This book, a prequel to "Kate Milford's 'The Boneshaker,' [is] set in . . . nineteenth-century Coney Island and New York City. Few crossroads compare to the one being formed by the Brooklyn Bridge and the East River, and as the bridge's construction progresses, forces of unimaginable evil seek to bend that power to their advantage. . . . Can the teenagers Sam, a card sharp, and Jin, a fireworks expert, stop them before it's too late?" (Publisher's note)

Greenglass House; by Kate Milford; with illustrations by Jaime Zollars. Clarion Books, Houghton Mifflin Harcourt 2014 384 p. (hardback) $17.99

Grades: 5 6 7 8   **Fic**

1. Mystery fiction 2. Hotels and motels -- Fiction 3. Magic -- Fiction 4. Adoption -- Fiction 5. Mystery and detective stories 6. Hotels, motels, etc. -- Fiction

ISBN 0544052706; 9780544052703

LC 2013036212

National Book Award Long List: Young People's Literature (2014)

Edgar Award: Best Juvenile (2015)

In this middle grade book by Kate Milford, illustrated by Jaime Zollars, "it's wintertime at Greenglass House. The creaky smuggler's inn is always quiet during this season, and twelve-year-old Milo, the innkeepers' adopted son, plans to spend his holidays relaxing. . . . As objects go missing and tempers flare, Milo and Meddy, the cook's daughter, must decipher clues and untangle the web of deepening mysteries to discover the truth about Greenglass House--and themselves." (Publisher's note)

The **Left**-Handed Fate; Kate Milford; illustrated by Eliza Wheeler. Henry Holt & Co. 2016 384 p. illustrations (hardback) $16.99

Grades: 5 6 7 8   **Fic**

1. Sea stories 2. Magic -- Fiction 3. War of 1812 -- Fiction 4. United States -- History -- War of 1812 -- Fiction

ISBN 9780805098006

LC 2015033437

In this book, by Kate Milford, illustrated by Eliza Wheeler, "Lucy Bluecrowne and Maxwell Ault are on a mission: find the three pieces of a strange and arcane engine they believe can stop the endless war raging between their home country of England and Napoleon Bonaparte's France. During the search, however, their ship, the famous privateer the Left-Handed Fate, is taken by the Americans, who have just declared war on England, too." (Publisher's note)

"Rich and strange of place and premise; suspenseful and thought-provoking." Kirkus

Millard, Glenda

Layla, Queen of hearts; illustrated by Patrice Barton. Farrar Straus Giroux 2010 119p il $16.99

Grades: 3 4 5   **Fic**

1. Old age -- Fiction 2. Australia -- Fiction 3. Friendship -- Fiction 4. Family life -- Fiction

ISBN 0-374-34360-8; 978-0-374-34360-6

LC 2008-38748

Sequel to: The naming of Tishkin Silk (2009)

First published 2006 in Australia

Even though she loves the family of her best friend, Griffin Silk, especially grandmother Nell, Layla Elliott, who no longer has a grandmother, determines, despite many difficulties, to find an old person of her own to bring to the school's Senior Citizens' Day.

"Barton's illustrations gently convey the bonds of affection among the author's eccentric, engaging characters." Kirkus

The **naming** of Tishkin Silk; illustrated by Patrice Barton. Farrar, Straus and Giroux 2009 101p il $15.99

Grades: 3 4 5   **Fic**

1. Death -- Fiction 2. Australia -- Fiction 3. Friendship -- Fiction 4. Family life -- Fiction 5. Personal names -- Fiction

ISBN 0-374-35481-2; 978-0-374-35481-7

LC 2008-16796

First published 2003 in Australia

Griffin Silk feels responsible for the absence of his mother and baby sister, but he and his new friend Layla find the perfect way to make everyone feel a little bit better. "Grades two to four." (Bull Cent Child Books)

"Illustrated with softly rendered black-and-white drawings, the gentle, descriptive narrative [is] touched with droll humor . . . and features a likable protagonist and other appealing, diverse characters." Booklist

Followed by: Layla, Queen of Hearts (2010)

Miller, Kirsten

Kiki Strike; the darkness dwellers. by Kirsten Miller. Bloomsbury 2013 416 p. (hardback) $17.99

Grades: 5 6 7 8   **Fic**

1. Girls -- Fiction 2. Adventure fiction 3. Teenagers -- Fiction 4. Crime -- Fiction 5. France -- Fiction 6. Identity -- Fiction 7. Paris (France) -- Fiction 8. New York (N.Y.) -- Fiction

ISBN 1599907364; 9781599907369

LC 2012023303

This teen adventure novel, by Kirsten Miller, is part of the "Kiki Strike" series. "First they ventured deep under New York to save the city itself. Then things got personal as the Irregulars ventured into a haunted mansion in Chinatown to uncover an evil twin. Now, . . . this . . . group of delinquent geniuses jump feet first into a[n] . . . international pursuit, going underground in Paris to pursue a pair of treacherous royals who have killed Kiki's parents." (Publisher's note)

Millet, Lydia

The **fires** beneath the sea. Big Mouth House 2011 256p (The dissenters) $16.95

Grades: 4 5 6 7   **Fic**

1. Otters -- Fiction 2. Mothers -- Fiction 3. Supernatural -- Fiction 4. Cape Cod (Mass.) -- Fiction

ISBN 978-1-931520-71-3; 1-931520-71-2

"Mom vanished two months ago, and summer's ending. While swimming in the ocean, Cara spots a sea otter—but sea otters don't belong on Atlantic beaches. Cara reaches out her fingertips, and the otter streams words into Cara's mind. . . . Millet's prose is lyrically evocative. . . . A lush and intelligent opener for a topical eco-fantasy series." Kirkus

Mills, Claudia

★ 7 x 9; pictures by G. Brian Karas. Farrar, Straus & Giroux 2002 103p il $15; pa $6.95

Grades: 2 3 4 **Fic**

1. School stories 2. Mathematics -- Fiction

ISBN 0-374-36746-9; 0-374-46452-9 pa

LC 2001-16028

Third-grader Wilson struggles with his times-tables in order to beat the class deadline

"Mills' sympathetic and detailed treatment of Wilson's travails makes this both a suspenseful and satisfying beginning chapter book." Bull Cent Child Books

Followed by: Fractions = trouble! (2011)

Basketball disasters. Alfred A. Knopf Books for Young Readers 2012 (Mason Dixon) $12.99; lib bdg $15.99; ebook $9.99

Grades: 3 4 5 **Fic**

1. School stories 2. Dogs -- Fiction 3. Basketball -- Fiction

ISBN 978-0-375-86875-7; 0-375-86875-5; 978-0-375-96875-4 lib bdg; 0-375-96875-X lib bdg; 978-0-375-89960-7 ebook

LC 2011014249

Fourth-grader Mason struggles to enjoy playing basketball after his best friend persuades him to join a team, and learns that the dog-hating lady next door is not so bad after all.

"Mason encounters believable situations enhanced by a fast-paced third-person narration that effectively captures his grade-school perspective." Kirkus

Being Teddy Roosevelt; pictures by R.W. Alley. Farrar, Straus and Giroux 2007 89p il $16

Grades: 2 3 4 **Fic**

1. School stories

ISBN 978-0-374-30657-1; 0-374-30657-51

LC 2006-48978

When he is assigned Teddy Roosevelt as his biography project in school, fourth-grader Riley finds himself inspired by Roosevelt's tenacity and perseverance and resolves to find a way to get what he most wants—a saxophone and music lessons

"Lots of funny lines and comical situations enliven the simple story, which is also enriched by its portrait of grade-school friendships and goofy classroom happenings, depicted in Alley's appealing spot drawings." Booklist

Cody Harmon, king of pets; Claudia Mills; pictures by Rob Shepperson. Farrar, Straus & Giroux 2016 144 p. illustrations (Franklin School friends) (hardback) $15.99

Grades: 2 3 4 **Fic**

1. Pets -- Fiction 2. Schools -- Fiction 3. Pet shows -- Fiction 4. Friendship -- Fiction

ISBN 9780374302238

LC 2015017955

In this book, by Claudia Mills, "Cody Harmon doesn't love reading, math, spelling, or really any of the subjects that Miss Molina teaches in her third-grade class. But he lives on a farm and he loves animals--he even has nine pets--so when the school holds a pet-show fund-raiser, it should be his time to shine. There's a ten-dollar entrance fee per pet, though, and Cody can't pay it for all nine pets. He'd love to take his pig, but what about the others?" (Publisher's note)

"Shepperson's illustrations add verve and joy to the book, capturing the ups and downs of third-grade life. A wonderful read for youngsters navigating chapter books." Booklist

Fractions; [pictures by G. Brian Karas] Farrar Straus Giroux 2011 113p il $15.99

Grades: 2 3 4 **Fic**

1. School stories 2. Fractions -- Fiction 3. Science projects -- Fiction

ISBN 978-0-374-36716-9; 0-374-36716-7

LC 2010-08395

Sequel to: 7 x 9 = trouble! (2002)

While trying to decide on a science fair project, third-grader Wilson struggles with with fractions and, much to his embarrassment, his parents sign him up to work with a math tutor.

"Familiar school concerns, nicely resolved, make this another excellent selection for early chapter-book readers." Kirkus

★ **How** Oliver Olson changed the world; pictures by Heather Maione. Farrar, Straus and Giroux 2009 103p il $15.95

Grades: 2 3 4 **Fic**

1. School stories 2. Colorado -- Fiction 3. Solar system -- Fiction 4. Science projects -- Fiction

ISBN 0-374-33487-0; 978-0-374-33487-1

LC 2007-48846

Afraid he will always be an outsider like ex-planet Pluto, nine-year-old Oliver finally shows his extremely overprotective parents that he is capable of doing great things without their help while his class is studying the solar system.

"An engaging and thought-provoking chapter book." Booklist

Kelsey Green, reading queen; Claudia Mills; illustrated by Rob Shepperson. Farrar, Straus & Giroux 2013 128 p. ill (Franklin School Friends) (hbk.) $15.99

Grades: 2 3 4 **Fic**

1. School stories 2. Contests -- Fiction 3. Reading -- Fiction 4. Schools -- Fiction 5. Books and reading -- Fiction

ISBN 0374374856; 9780374374853; 9780374374884

LC 2011027870

In this children's book by Claudia Mills, illustrated by Rob Shepperson, "Kelsey Green is the best reader in the third grade. When the principal . . . announces a school-wide reading contest . . . she knows she's just the person to lead Mrs. Molina's third graders to victory. But how can they win when her classmate Cody Harmon doesn't want to read anything, and even Kelsey's best friends Annika and Izzy don't live up to her expectations?" (Publisher's note)

"Single-minded and a tad selfish, Kelsey isn't always the most pleasant of third-graders--but she's 100% realistic. And although Kelsey's excitement about the reading contest skews her priorities, she redeems herself (and shares her love of books) when she helps out a classmate who struggles with reading." (Pub Wkly)

Other titles in this series are:

Annika Riz, math whiz (2014)

Izzy Barr, running star (2015)

Simon Ellis, spelling bee champ (2015)

Cody Harmon, king of pets (2016)

One square inch. Farrar, Straus and Giroux 2010 168p $16.99

Grades: 4 5 6 7 **Fic**

1. Mothers -- Fiction 2. Siblings -- Fiction 3. Imagination -- Fiction 4. Manic-depressive illness -- Fiction

ISBN 978-0-374-35652-1; 0-374-35652-1

When their mother's behavior changes and she starts to neglect her children, seventh-grader Cooper and his little sister take refuge in Inchland, an imaginary country inspired by deeds to one square inch of land that their grandfather gave them.

Mills "delivers a compassionate story about life with a bipolar parent. . . . The twist of [Cooper's] emotions and depth of his concern for his mother and sister are believable and deeply moving." Publ Wkly

Pet disasters. Alfred A. Knopf 2011 154p (Mason Dixon) $12.99; lib bdg $15.99

Grades: 3 4 5   **Fic**

1. Dogs -- Fiction 2. Pets -- Fiction 3. Friendship -- Fiction

ISBN 978-0-375-86873-3; 0-375-86873-9; 978-0-375-96873-0 lib bdg; 0-375-96873-3 lib bdg

LC 2010029724

Nine-year-old Mason's parents keep trying to get him a pet, but until he and his best friend Brody adopt a three-legged dog, he's not interested.

"Mills's account of this quirky kid and his trials and tribulations is both funny and touching. . . . An enjoyable read with cartoon-style pen-and-ink illustrations scattered throughout." SLJ

Other titles about Mason Dixon are:

Fourth grade disasters (2011)

Basketball disasters (2012)

The **totally** made-up Civil War diary of Amanda MacLeish. Farrar, Straus and Giroux 2008 197p $16

Grades: 3 4 5   **Fic**

1. School stories 2. Maryland -- Fiction 3. Family life -- Fiction 4. United States -- History -- 1861-1865, Civil War -- Fiction

ISBN 978-0-374-37696-3; 0-374-37696-4

LC 2007-09162

While dealing with her parents' separation and her best friend's distance, Amanda is able to work out some of her anxiety through her fifth-grade project—writing a diary from the point of view of a ten-year-old girl whose brothers fight on opposite sides in the Civil War.

"Mills handles the MacLeish family's separation realistically. . . . Subplots provide the novel's lighter moments. . . . This makes a good choice for Mills' many fans, as well as for children in search of a satisfying family story." Booklist

The **trouble** with ants; Claudia Mills; Illustrated by Katie Kath Boyd. Alfred A. Knopf 2015 176 p. illustrations (The Nora notebooks) (hardback) $14.99

Grades: 2 3 4 5   **Fic**

1. School stories 2. Ants -- Fiction 3. Science -- Fiction 4. Friendship -- Fiction

ISBN 0385391617; 9780385391610; 9780385391627

LC 2015007380

"Science-obsessed fourth grader Nora has ants all figured out--now she just has to try to understand her fellow humans! . . . [After] their teacher Coach Joe has given them [an assignment] to write a persuasive speech and change people's minds about something . . . , will Nora convince her friends that ants are as interesting as she thinks they are?" (Publisher's note)

"In this series starter, bright and charming Nora displays independent thought, vision, and passion, while letting the reader know--through her journal and her assigned persuasive speech--that science is unassailably cool." Booklist

Another title about Nora is:

The trouble with babies (2016)

The **trouble** with babies; by Claudia Mills; illustrated by Katie Kath. Random House Childrens Books 2016 179 p. illustrations (The Nora notebooks) (ebook) $38.97; $12.99

Grades: 3 4 5 6   **Fic**

1. Aunts -- Fiction 2. Infants -- Fiction 3. Friendship -- Fiction

ISBN 9780385391689; 038539165X; 9780385391658

LC 2016031583

In this book, by Claudia Mills, illustrated by Katie Kath, "Nora Alpers has just become a ten-year-old aunt. To prepare for the new arrival, Nora has been writing down baby-related facts in her special notebook, just like she does with her favorite subject: ants. She likes the idea that

someone who studies the A-N-T is also an A-U-N-T, even though she doesn't know anything about taking care of babies." (Publisher's note)

"This charming second title in the Nora Notebooks series is a fine place for middle-grade readers to be introduced to Nora's engaging curiosity about the world." Kirkus

Mills, Rob

Charlie's key. Orca Book Publishers 2011 254p pa $9.99

Grades: 5 6 7 8 9   **Fic**

1. Mystery fiction 2. Orphans -- Fiction

ISBN 978-1-55469-872-1; 1-55469-872-3

A young orphan struggles to unlock the significance of an old key left by his dying father.

"A fast-paced, often riveting mystery with a plausible, thrilling climax." Kirkus

Milne, A. A.

★ The **House** at Pooh Corner; with decorations by Ernest H. Shepard. Dutton 1985 180p il $9.95; pa $4.99

Grades: 1 2 3 4   **Fic**

1. Toys -- Fiction 2. Bears -- Fiction 3. Animals -- Fiction

ISBN 0-525-32302-3; 0-14-036122-7 pa

First published 1928

"It is hard to tell what Pooh Bear and his friends would have been without the able assistance of Ernest H. Shepard to see them and picture them so cleverly. . . . They are, and should be, classics." N Y Times Book Rev

★ **Winnie**-the-Pooh; illustrated by Ernest H. Shepard, colored by Hilda Scott. Dutton 1974 161p il $10.99; pa $4.99

Grades: 1 2 3 4   **Fic**

1. Toys -- Fiction 2. Bears -- Fiction 3. Animals -- Fiction

ISBN 0-525-44443-2; 0-14-036121-9 pa

First published 1926

"The kindly, lovable Pooh is one of an imaginative cast of animal characters which includes Eeyore, the wistfully gloomy donkey, Tigger, Piglet, Kanga, and Roo, all living in a fantasy world presided over by Milne's young son, Christopher Robin. Many of the animals are drawn from figures in Milne's life, though each emerges as a universally recognizable type." Reader's Ency

Milway, Katie Smith

The **good** garden; how one family went from hunger to having enough. written by Katie Smith Milway; illustrated by Sylvie Daigneault. Kids Can Press 2010 30p il (CitizenKid) $18.95

Grades: 3 4 5   **Fic**

1. Honduras -- Fiction 2. Vegetable gardening -- Fiction 3. Sustainable agriculture -- Fiction

ISBN 978-1-55453-488-3; 1-55453-488-7

"When María Luz's Papa makes the tough decision to leave their hillside home in Honduras to seek employment elsewhere, he puts the girl in charge of planting and tending their winter garden. . . . A new teacher has arrived at her school with fresh ideas for how to feed and restore the soil. . . . [Maria] also learns that they need not rely on the unscrupulous 'coyotes' who have historically acted as loan sharks and middlemen. . . . Taken at a literal level, this is a story of how sustainable farming practices can nourish families and the earth simultaneously. On a deeper level, it is about social justice and self-sustaining economies. . . . The stylized colored-pencil artwork is appropriately lush and idealized." SLJ

Mimi's Village; And How Basic Health Care Transformed It. Katie Smith Milway. Kids Can Press 2012 32 p. $18.95

Grades: 1 2 3 4   **Fic**
1. Public health 2. Kenya -- Fiction 3. Malaria -- Fiction
ISBN 1554537223; 9781554537228

Author Katie Smith Milway presents a story on public health care in Kenya. "Mimi Malaho and her family help bring basic health care to their community. By making small changes like sleeping under mosquito nets and big ones like building a clinic with outside help, the Malahos and their neighbors transform their Kenyan village from one afraid of illness to a thriving community." (Publisher's note)

Mitchell, Stephen

The **nightingale**; [by] Hans Christian Andersen; retold by Stephen Mitchell; illustrated by Bagram Ibatoulline. Candlewick Press 2002 un il hardcover o.p. pa $6.95
Grades: 2 3 4   **Fic**
1. Authors 2. Novelists 3. Dramatists 4. Fairy tales 5. Children's authors 6. Short story writers 7. Nightingales -- Fiction
ISBN 0-7636-1521-8; 0-7636-2406-3 pa

LC 2001-25144

Though the emperor banishes the nightingale in preference of a jeweled mechanical imitation, the little bird remains faithful and returns years later when the emperor is near death and no one else can help him

"This is an elegant piece of bookmaking. Mixed-media illustrations (ink, gouache, watercolor) based on Chinese art and costume are rendered in a ceremonial, fairy-tale style." Bull Cent Child Books

The **tinderbox**; [by] Hans Christian Andersen; retold by Stephen Mitchell; illustrated by Bagram Ibatoulline. Candlewick Press 2007 un il $17.99
Grades: 2 3 4 5   **Fic**
1. Authors 2. Novelists 3. Dramatists 4. Fairy tales 5. Children's authors 6. Short story writers
ISBN 978-0-7636-2078-3; 0-7636-2078-5

LC 2006-47554

With the help of a magic tinderbox, a soldier finds a fortune and pursues a princess imprisoned in a castle.

"The soldier may be handsome and the princess lovely, but the old witch and the three giant dogs along with the beautifully developed settings really create the superb fairy-tale ambience of this robust telling of Andersen's tale. Ibatoulline's finely hatched pen drawings, washed in muted tones, resemble lithographs." SLJ

Mobley, Jeannie

★ **Katerina's** wish; Jeannie Mobley. Margaret K. McElderry Books 2012 256 p. (hardcover) $15.99
Grades: 4 5 6 7   **Fic**
1. Wishes -- Fiction 2. Historical fiction 3. Immigrants -- Fiction 4. Czech Americans -- Fiction 5. Coal mines and mining -- Fiction 6. Family life -- Colorado -- Fiction 7. Colorado -- History -- 1876-1950 -- Fiction
ISBN 1442433434; 9781442433434; 9781442433458

LC 2011044392

In this young adult novel, Katerina and her family have immigrated from Bohemia and "settled in a coal mining camp, [where] they are till buried in work and trapped by debt. Then Trina sees a fish that reminds her of a fairy tale about a magic carp; soon after, her two younger sisters' frivolous wishes are granted. Initially skeptical, Trina eventually makes her wish: for a farm that will make her family happy." Publishers Weekly)

Modugno, Maria

★ **Santa** Claus and the Three Bears; by Maria Modugno and illustrated by Jane Dyer and Brooke Dyer. Harpercollins Childrens Books 2013 40 p. $17.99

Grades: PreK K 1 2   **Fic**
1. Bears -- Fiction 2. Santa Claus -- Fiction
ISBN 0061700231; 9780061700231

In this book, "author Maria Modugno teams up with award-winning artists Jane and Brooke Dyer to deliver a festive twist on Goldilocks and the Three Bears, with Santa Claus stepping in as the cheerful intruder. Papa Bear, Mama Bear, and Baby Bear weren't expecting any company when they went for a walk on Christmas Eve, but that's exactly what they got!" (Publisher's note)

Moloney, James

The **Book** of Lies. HarperCollinsPublishers 2007 360p $16.99; lib bdg $17.89
Grades: 5 6 7 8   **Fic**
1. Fantasy fiction 2. Magic -- Fiction 3. Orphans -- Fiction
ISBN 978-0-06-057842-8; 0-06-057842-4; 978-0-06-057843-5 lib bdg; 0-06-057843-2 lib bdg

LC 2006-29874

On the night he was brought to an orphanage, Marcel's memories were taken by a sorceror and replaced with new ones by his Book of Lies, but Bea, a girl with the ability to make herself invisible, was watching and is determined to help him discover his true identity.

"Readers who enjoy the mixture of mystery, riddles, action, and camaraderie will be pleased that the open-ended conclusion leads to a planned sequel." Booklist

Mone, Gregory

Fish. Scholastic Press 2010 241p $16.99
Grades: 4 5 6 7   **Fic**
1. Adventure fiction 2. Ciphers -- Fiction 3. Pirates -- Fiction 4. Buried treasure -- Fiction
ISBN 978-0-545-11632-9; 0-545-11632-5

Eleven-year-old Fish, seeking a way to help his family financially, becomes a reluctant cabin boy on a pirate ship, where he soon makes friends—and enemies—and is asked to help decipher clues that might lead to a legendary treasure.

"Mone seamlessly integrates factual information into his tale of friendship, loyalty, and exploration. . . . Fish makes a splashing good addition to adventure fiction." SLJ

Montgomery, Lewis B.

The **case** of the stinky socks; by Lewis B. Montgomery; illustrated by Amy Wummer. Kane Press 2009 94p il (Milo & Jazz mysteries) pa $6.95; $22.60
Grades: 1 2 3 4   **Fic**
1. Mystery fiction 2. Baseball -- Fiction 3. Clothing and dress -- Fiction
ISBN 1-57565-285-4 pa; 1-57565-288-9; 978-1-57565-285-6 pa; 978-1-57565-288-7

LC 2008027536

Detectives-in-training Milo and Jazz join forces to tackle their first big case—finding out who stole the lucky socks from the high school baseball team's star pitcher.

This book "gets it just right: a fun, easy-to-solve mystery, readily identifiable young detectives, and some extras readers will enjoy. . . . The short chapters, written in a large typeface, are punctuated by pen-and-ink illustrations of better quality than those often seen in series books." Booklist

Other titles in this series are:
The case of the poisoned pig (2009)
The case of the haunted haunted house (2009)
The case of the Amazing Zelda (2009)
The case of the July 4th jinx (2010)
The case of the missing moose (2011)

Montijo, Rhode

Chews your destiny; Rhode Montijo. 1st ed. Disney-Hyperion Books 2013 128 p. (The gumazing Gum Girl!) (alk. paper) $14.99

Grades: 2 3 4   **Fic**

1. Chewing gum -- Fiction 2. Superheroes -- Fiction 3. Bubble gum -- Fiction 4. Hispanic Americans -- Fiction

ISBN 1423157400; 9781423157403

LC 2012036706

In this book by Rhode Montijo, "Gabby Gomez loves to chew bubble gum even though her mother has warned her against it. It's not like she will turn into gum . . . except, that's exactly what happens! With her new, stretch-tastic powers Gabby can help save the day, but she will have to keep her gummy alter-ego a secret from her mother or else she'll find herself in a really sticky situation." (Publisher's note)

Moodie, Craig

Into the trap. Roaring Brook Press 2011 199p $15.99

Grades: 5 6 7 8   **Fic**

1. Adventure fiction 2. Islands -- Fiction 3. Thieves -- Fiction 4. Lobsters -- Fiction

ISBN 978-1-59643-585-8; 1-59643-585-2

LC 2010029238

Twelve-year-old Eddie Atwell accidentally learns who has been stealing lobsters from Fog Island lobstermen and enlists thirteen-year-old Briggs Fairfield, a summer visitor, to help foil their plans.

"Set over a single, tense day, the novel's chapter titles track the hours and give the book an immediate, real-time pace. An exciting drama." Booklist

Moranville, Sharelle Byars

27 magic words; Sharelle Byars Moranville. Holiday House 2016 199 p. (hardcover) $16.95; (ebook) $16.95

Grades: 5 6 7 8   **Fic**

1. Grief -- Fiction 2. Self-perception -- Fiction 3. Children and death -- Fiction 4. Truthfulness and falsehood -- Fiction

ISBN 0823436578; 9780823436576; 9780823437061

LC 2015049142

In this children's novel about facing the future, by Sharelle Byars Moranville, "although Kobi's parents sailed into a storm at sea five years ago, she knows they are alive. If she says Avanti she can see them. Now that her life is being turned upside down again, she will need the magic words her mother left behind more than ever. . . . [But] she must confront not only the untruths she has told others but the stories she has made herself believe." (Publisher's note)

"Distinctive, well-drawn characters drive the plot and provide their own magical contributions to Kobi's widening world. Both tragic and uplifting, this winsome tale perfectly depicts some of the many aspects of magic." Kirkus

Morey, Walt

Gentle Ben; illustrated by John Schoenherr. Dutton 1965 191p il hardcover o.p. pa $6.99

Grades: 5 6 7 8   **Fic**

1. Bears -- Fiction 2. Alaska -- Fiction

ISBN 0-14-240551-5 pa

Set in Alaska before statehood, this is the story of 13-year-old Mark Anderson who befriends a huge brown bear which has been chained in a shed since it was a cub. Finally Mark's father buys the bear, but Orca City's inhabitants eventually insist that the animal, named Ben, be shipped to an uninhabited island. However, the friendship of Mark and Ben endures

The author "has written a vivid chronicle of Alaska, its people and places, challenges and beauties. Told with a simplicity and dignity which befits its characters, human and animal, [it] is a memorable reading experience." SLJ

Morgenstern, Susie Hoch

★ A book of coupons; by Susie Morgenstern; illustrated by Serge Bloch; translated by Gill Rosner. Viking 2001 62p il $12.99

Grades: 3 4 5   **Fic**

1. School stories 2. Teachers -- Fiction

ISBN 0-670-89970-4

LC 00-11940

Original French edition, 1999

Elderly Monsieur Noel, the very unconventional new teacher, gives coupon books for such things as dancing in class and sleeping late, which are bound to get him in trouble with the military discipline of Principal Incarnation Perez

"Morgenstern's witty and poignant tribute to great teachers everywhere proclaims what education should be about. Her message may be pointed, but no reader will be unmoved." Horn Book Guide

Moriarty, Chris

The inquisitor's apprentice; illustrations by Mark Edward Geyer. Harcourt Children's Books 2011 345p il $16.99

Grades: 4 5 6 7   **Fic**

1. Inventors 2. Gangs -- Fiction 3. Magic -- Fiction 4. Witches -- Fiction 5. Apprentices -- Fiction 6. New York (N.Y.) -- Fiction 7. Jews -- United States -- Fiction

ISBN 978-0-547-58135-4; 0-547-58135-1

In this novel, by Chris Moriarty, "being an Inquisitor is no job for a nice Jewish boy. But when the police learn that Sacha Kessler can see witches, he's apprenticed to the department's star Inquisitor, Maximilian Wolf. Their mission is to stop magical crime. And New York at the beginning of the twentieth century is a magical melting pot where each ethnic group has its own brand of homegrown witchcraft, and magical gangs rule the streets from Hell's Kitchen to Chinatown." (Publisher's note)

"Sacha, Lily and Inspector Wolf are all fully developed and multilayered characters, as are the many other distinctive personalities that appear in the tale. The author employs rich language and syntax that please the ear and touch the senses, making it all come alive." Kirkus

The watcher in the shadows; Chris Moriarty; [illustrated by] Mark Edward Geyer. Harcourt Children's Books 2013 336 p. (hardcover) $16.99

Grades: 4 5 6 7   **Fic**

1. Fantasy fiction 2. Jews -- Fiction 3. Mystery fiction

ISBN 0547466323; 9780547466323

LC 2013003919

This juvenile novel, by Chris Moriarty, is part of the "Inquisitor's Apprentice" series. "New York's Bowery District becomes the scene of a terrible murder when the Klezmer King gets fried to a crisp by his Electric Tuxedo--on stage! The Inquisitor's apprentice, thirteen-year-old Sacha Kessler, tries to help find the killer, but the closer he gets to solving the crime, the more it sounds as if the creature that haunted him in his first adventure is back." (Publisher's note)

"Rich language, colorful syntax, vivid description and a brilliant cast of characters beckon readers right into both the adventure and the heartfelt emotional landscape. Exciting, action-packed and absolutely marvelous." Kirkus

Morpurgo, Michael

★ Kensuke's kingdom. Scholastic Press 2003 164p hardcover o.p. pa $5.99

Grades: 4 5 6 7   **Fic**

1. Survival after airplane accidents, shipwrecks, etc. -- Fiction
ISBN 0-439-38202-5; 0-439-59181-3 pa

LC 2002-9078

First published 1999 in the United Kingdom

When Michael is swept off his family's yacht, he washes up on a desert island, where he struggles to survive—until he finds he is not alone

This is "highly readable. . . . The end is bittersweet but believable, and the epilogue is a sad commentary on the long-lasting effects of war." Booklist

★ **On** angel wings; illustrated by Quentin Blake. Candlewick Press 2007 un il $8.99

Grades: 3 4 5   **Fic**

1. Angels -- Fiction 2. Shepherds -- Fiction
ISBN 978-0-7636-3466-7; 0-7636-3466-2

"Morpurgo's tone blends reverence with wit, a combination matched in Blake's pen-and-ink and watercolor cartoons." Publ Wkly

Waiting for Anya. Viking 1991 172p hardcover o.p. pa $4.99

Grades: 5 6 7 8   **Fic**

1. Jews -- Fiction 2. France -- Fiction 3. World War, 1939-1945 -- Fiction
ISBN 0-670-83735-0; 0-14-038431-6 pa

LC 90-50560

First published 1990 in the United Kingdom

"A World War II adventure story set in Vichy, France, this centers on a young shepherd, Jo, who becomes involved in smuggling Jewish children across the border from his mountain village to Spain. Morpurgo has injected the basic conventions of heroism and villainy with some complexities of character. . . . Independent readers will appreciate the simple, clear style and fast-paced plot of the book, which will also hold up well in group read-alouds, commanding attention to ethics as well as action." Bull Cent Child Books

Morris, Gerald

The **adventures** of Sir Lancelot the Great; illustrated by Aaron Renier. Houghton Mifflin Company 2008 92p il (The knights' tales) $15; pa $4.99

Grades: 3 4 5 6   **Fic**

1. Kings 2. Knights and knighthood -- Fiction 3. Lancelot (Legendary character) -- Fiction 4. Great Britain -- History -- 0-1066 -- Fiction
ISBN 978-0-618-77714-3; 0-618-77714-8; 978-0-547-23756-5 pa; 0-547-23756-1 pa

LC 2007-41167

This novel relates the story of Sir Lancelot, the bravest knight in King Arthur's court.

"This trim novel, with simple vocabulary and brief, witty chapters, is an ideal fit for early readers. . . . Fans of the legendary characters may find particular delight in this irreverent and unabashedly silly exploration of Arthur's court and his most influential knight. . . . Frequent black-and-white illustrations supplement the text, highlighting (and in most cases, exaggerating) elements from humorous passages." Bull Cent Child Books

Other titles in this series are:
The adventures of Sir Givret the Short (2008)
The adventures of Sir Gawain the True (2011)

Morris, Jackie

East of the Sun, West of the Moon; Jackie Morris. Pgw 2013 176 p. (hardcover) $14.99

Grades: 6 7 8 9   **Fic**

1. Bears -- Fiction 2. Girls -- Fiction 3. Fantasy fiction -- Fiction
ISBN 184780294X; 9781847802941

This book, by Jackie Morris, describes a friendship between a girl and a bear. The girl goes "first to the bear's secret palace in faraway mountains, where she is treated so courteously, but where she experiences the bear's unfathomable sadness, and a deep mystery. . . As the bear's secret unravels, another journey unfolds . . . that takes the girl to the homes of the four Winds and beyond, to the castle east of the sun, west of the moon." (Publisher's note)

Morrison, Megan

Disenchanted; the trials of Cinderella. Megan Morrison. Arthur A. Levine Books, an imprint of Scholastic Inc. 2016 416 p. illustrations, maps (Tyme) (hardcover : alk. paper) $17.99; (ebook) $17.99

Grades: 5 6 7 8   **Fic**

1. Magic -- Fiction 2. Princes -- Fiction 3. Blessing and cursing -- Fiction 4. Fairy tales 5. Cinderella (Legendary character) -- Fiction
ISBN 054564271X; 9780545642712; 9780545642736

LC 2016008854

In this middle grade novel in the Tyme series by Megan Morrison, "Ella Coach has one wish: revolution. Her mother died working in a sweatshop, and Ella wants every laborer in the Blue Kingdom to receive fairer treatment. . . . Prince Dash Charming has one wish: evolution. . . . Serge can grant any wish -- and has. . . . This is a story about three people who want something better and who together find the faith to change their worlds." (Publisher's note)

"Morrison's magical descriptions illuminate more of the wide magical world that she's created in Tyme. Engrossing and delightful reading—a can't-miss choice for middle-graders." Booklist

Grounded; the tale of Rapunzel. Megan Morrison. Arthur A. Levine Books, an imprint of Scholastic Inc. 2015 384 p. (Tyme) (alk. paper) $17.99

Grades: 5 6 7 8   **Fic**

1. Fractured fairy tales 2. Thieves -- Fiction 3. Fairy tales 4. Magic -- Fiction 5. Fairies -- Fiction 6. Witches -- Fiction 7. Robbers and outlaws -- Fiction 8. Characters in literature -- Fiction 9. Adventure and adventurers -- Fiction
ISBN 0545638267; 9780545638265; 9780545642699; 9780545642705; 9780545754682

LC 2014027138

This story by Megan Morrison, is a retelling of the Rapunzel legend. "In all of Tyme, . . . no one is as lucky as Rapunzel. . . . And she knows this because Witch tells her so--her beloved Witch. . . . [Then] Rapunzel descends to the ground for the first time, and finds a world filled with more peril than Witch promised . . . and more beauty, wonder, and adventure than she could have dreamed." (Publisher's note)

Morse, Scott

Magic Pickle and the garden of evil. Graphix 2009 136p il pa $5.99

Grades: 2 3 4 5   **Fic**

1. Vegetables -- Fiction 2. Superheroes -- Fiction
ISBN 978-0-545-13580-1; 0-545-13580-X

LC 2008037614

Magic Pickle, a fearless, dill superhero, comes to the rescue when Jo Jo's class garden yields a monstrous lettuce plant bent on world domination.

"One of a series of illustrated chapter books coming on the heels of Morse's graphic novel. . . . The spot illustrations are lively, with crackling energy dots and a constant sense of action and movement. . . . The comic segments, typography sound effects, and the like are cues wtih which struggling readers can propel themselves along." SLJ

Moses, Shelia P.

★ **Sallie** Gal and the Wall-a-kee man; illustrated by Niki Daly. Scholastic 2007 152p il $15.99

Grades: 3 4 5 **Fic**

1. Family life -- Fiction 2. North Carolina -- Fiction 3. African Americans -- Fiction

ISBN 978-0-439-90890-0; 0-439-90890-6

LC 2006033171

More than anything, Sallie Gal wants pretty ribbons to wear in her hair, but she knows that they cannot afford them and Momma has too much dignity to accept charity.

"Appealing black-and-white illustrations in various sizes embellish the text. Moses takes a fond look at strong family ties and the values of honesty and hard work. Short paragraphs and peppy dialogue make this easy chapter book a candidate for reading aloud." SLJ

Moss, Marissa

Alien Eraser to the rescue. Candlewick Press 2009 52p il (Max Disaster) $16.99; pa $6.99

Grades: 3 4 5 **Fic**

1. Extraterrestrial beings -- Fiction

ISBN 978-0-7636-3577-0; 0-7636-3577-4; 978-0-7636-4407-9 pa; 0-7636-4407-2 pa

Welcome to Max's book of inventions, experiments, comic strips, and random thoughts about school, pimply older brothers, mutant marshmallows, erasers and good parents who get into bad fights.

"Moss is a master at verbalizing kids' anxieties and channeling their astute observations of family life—both as it breaks apart and begins to mend." Publ Wkly

Other titles in the Max Disaster series are:

Alien Eraser unravels the mystery of the pyramids (2009)

Alien Eraser reveals the secrets of evolution (2009)

Amelia writes again. Simon & Schuster Books for Young Readers 2006 un il $9.95

Grades: 3 4 5 **Fic**

1. School stories 2. Diaries -- Fiction 3. Family life -- Fiction

ISBN 978-1-416-90904-0; 1-416-90904-4

LC 2005051669

A reissue of the title first published 1996 by Tricycle Press

"Ten years old at last, Amelia finds that she has plenty to write about as she discusses the expressiveness of hands, the time she and her sister stuck marshmallows to the ceiling, her reactions to an arson fire at her school, and her discomfort when a friend wants to read her journal. Finally, she and the friend jointly write a story in the notebook. Naive ink-and-watercolor illustrations brighten the blue-lined, hand-printed pages. Many labels and side comments add to the fun." Booklist

★ **Amelia's** 6th-grade notebook. Simon & Schuster Books for Young Readers 2005 un il $9.95

Grades: 3 4 5 6 **Fic**

1. School stories

ISBN 0-689-87040-X

LC 2004-45309

Problems arise for Amelia when she starts sixth grade at the same middle school where her older sister Cleo is an eighth-grader, and she gets the school's meanest teacher for three of her classes

"Both insightful and entertaining, Amelia's first-person narrative rings true.... [This] features a handwritten format; colorful, cartoonlike illustrations; and charming doodles with descriptive asides." Booklist

Other titles about Amelia are:

The all-new Amelia (1999)

Amelia lends a hand (2002)

Amelia works it out (2000)

Amelia writes again (1996)

Amelia's are-we-there-yet longest ever car trip (1997)

Amelia's BFF (2011)

Amelia's book of notes & note passing (2006)

Amelia's boredom survival guide (1999)

Amelia's bully survival guide (1998)

Amelia's family ties (2000)

Amelia's 5th-grade notebook (2003)

Amelia's guide to gossip (2006)

Amelia's itchy-twitchy, lovey-dovey summer at Camp Mosquito (2008)

Amelia's longest, biggest, most-fights-ever family reunion (2006)

Amelia's most unforgettable embarrassing moments (2005)

Amelia's must-keep resolutions for the best year ever! (2007)

Amelia's notebook (1995)

Amelia's school survival guide (2002)

Amelia's science fair disaster (2009)

Luv, Amelia luv, Nadia (1999)

Oh boy, Amelia! (2001)

Vote 4 Amelia (2007)

Amelia's notebook. Simon & Schuster Books for Young Readers 2006 un il $9.95

Grades: 3 4 5 **Fic**

1. School stories 2. Moving -- Fiction 3. Diaries -- Fiction 4. Sisters -- Fiction 5. Friendship -- Fiction

ISBN 978-1-416-90905-7; 1-416-90905-2

LC 2005047750

A reissue of the title first published 1995 by Tricycle Press

The hand-lettered contents of a nine-year-old girl's notebook, in which she records her thoughts and feelings about moving, starting school, and dealing with her older sister, as well as keeping her old best friend and making a new one.

"Both the language and the art style are on target for the age group- Amelia is droll and funny and not too sophisticated for her years; she's also poignant and real." Booklist

Mira's Diary; Lost in Paris. Marissa Moss. Sourcebooks Inc 2012 224 p. $12.99

Grades: 4 5 6 **Fic**

1. Time travel -- Fiction 2. Missing persons -- Fiction

ISBN 1402266065; 9781402266065

In this children's story, by Marissa Moss, "when Mira receives a cryptic postcard from her missing mother, she sets off with her father and brother to find her in Paris. . . . With an innocent touch to a gargoyle sculpture on the roof of Notre Dame, Mira is whisked into the past. There she learns her mother isn't just avoiding the family, she's in serious trouble. Following her mother's clues, Mira travels through time to help change history and bring her mother home." (Publisher's note)

Mould, Chris

★ The **wooden** mile. Roaring Brook Press 2008 176p il (Something wickedly weird) $9.95

Grades: 3 4 5 6 **Fic**

1. Pirates -- Fiction 2. Werewolves -- Fiction 3. Supernatural -- Fiction

ISBN 978-1-59643-383-0; 1-59643-383-3

LC 2008011258

First published 2007 in the United Kingdom

Eleven-year-old Stanley Buggle, happily anticipating a long summer vacation in the house he inherits from his great-uncle, discovers soon after arriving in the seemingly peaceful village of Crampton Rock, that along with the house he has also inherited some sinister neighbors, a talking stuffed fish, and a host of mysteries surrounding his great-uncle's death.

"With its fairly easy text, many black-and-white illustrations, and a dramatic scene silhouetted on the cover, this chapter book will appeal to young readers who like their fiction fast-paced and a bit scary. Mould's richly atmospheric ink drawings capture the rather macabre tone of the story." Booklist

Other titles in this series are:

The icy hand (2008)

The darkling curse (2009)

Smugglers' mine (2010)

Moulton, Erin E.

Flutter; the story of four sisters and an incredible journey. Philomel Books 2011

Grades: 4 5 6 **Fic**

1. Adventure fiction 2. Nature -- Fiction 3. Sisters -- Fiction 4. Vermont -- Fiction 5. Poaching -- Fiction 6. Family life -- Fiction

ISBN 0-399-25515-X; 978-0-399-25515-1

LC 2010014507

Nine-and-a-half-year-old Maple and her older sister, Dawn, must work together to face treacherous terrain, wild animals, and poachers as they trek through Vermont's Green Mountains seeking a miracle for their prematurely-born sister.

"Moulton describes the girls' journey—and their motivation—in vivid, heart-wrenching prose." Horn Book Guide

Mourlevat, Jean-Claude

★ The **pull** of the ocean; [by] Jean-Claude Mourlevat; translated from the French by Y. Maudet. Delacorte Press 2006 190p hardcover o.p. lib bdg $17.99; pa $6.50

Grades: 5 6 7 **Fic**

1. Size -- Fiction 2. Twins -- Fiction 3. France -- Fiction 4. Brothers -- Fiction

ISBN 978-0-385-73348-9; 0-385-73348-8; 978-0-385-90364-6 lib bdg; 0-385-90364-2 lib bdg; 978-0-385-73666-4 pa; 0-385-73666-5 pa

LC 2006001802

Loosely based on Charles Perrault's "Tom Thumb," seven brothers in modern-day France flee their poor parents' farm, led by the youngest who, although mute and unusually small, is exceptionally wise.

This "is a memorable novel that readers will find engaging and intellectually satisfying." SLJ

Mull, Brandon

Rogue Knight; by Brandon Mull. Aladdin 2014 480 p. (Five kingdoms) (hardback) $17.99

Grades: 4 5 6 7 **Fic**

1. Fantasy fiction 2. Knights and knighthood -- Fiction 3. Adventure and adventurers -- Fiction

ISBN 1442497033; 9781442497030; 9781442497047

LC 2014025800

Sequel to: Sky Raiders (2014)

In this novel, by Brandon Mull, book two of the "Five Kingdoms" series, "young Cole enters the second of five kingdoms in the otherworldly Outskirts, is exposed to a second culture and a second flavor of magic, and battles a second monster made of stolen magic as he continues the search for his fellow earthly kidnappees." (Kirkus Reviews)

"Cole is a relatable and brave Everykid hero, and his friends bring different perspectives to this ongoing tale. Mull's latest series continues to be excellent, and it should easily find a home among fans of middle-grade fantasy stories." Booklist

Sky Raiders; by Brandon Mull. Aladdin 2014 432 p. (Five kingdoms) (hardback) $16.99

Grades: 4 5 6 7 **Fic**

1. Fantasy fiction 2. Adventure fiction

ISBN 1442497009; 9781442497009

LC 2013032734

"Cole Randolph was just trying to have a fun time with his friends on Halloween (and maybe get to know Jenna Hunt a little better). But when a spooky haunted house turns out to be a portal to something much creepier, Cole finds himself on an adventure on a whole different level." (Publisher's note)

"Although Mull packs quite a bit into this initial installment, he skillfully mixes the capricious logic of dreams with high stakes and constant danger. The intriguing premise, strong world-building, and numerous twists make this a real page-turner." Pub Wkly

Other titles in this series are:

Rogue Night (2014)

Crystal Keepers (2015)

Death Weaver (2016)

Spirit animals; 1 wild born. Brandon Mull. Scholastic Press 2013 224 p. (Spirit animals) $12.99

Grades: 4 5 6 7 **Fic**

1. Spirits -- Fiction 2. Children and animals 3. Magic -- Fiction

ISBN 0545522439; 9780545522434

LC 2013932302

This book, by Brandon Mull, is set in "the world of Erdas, where every child who comes of age must discover if they have a spirit animal, a rare bond between human and beast that bestows great powers to both. A dark force has risen from distant and long-forgotten lands, and has begun an onslaught that will ravage the world. Now the fate of Erdas has fallen on the shoulders of four young strangers." (Publisher's note)

Other titles in this series are:

Hunted (2013)

Blood Ties (2014)

Fire and Ice (2014)

Against the Tide (2014)

Rise and Fall (2014)

The Evertree (2015)

★ A **world** without heroes. Aladdin 2011 454p (Beyonders) $19.99

Grades: 4 5 6 7 **Fic**

1. Fantasy fiction 2. Magic -- Fiction 3. Space and time -- Fiction 4. Heroes and heroines -- Fiction

ISBN 978-1-4169-9792-4; 1-4169-9792-X

LC 2010-23437

Fourteen-year-old Jason Walker is transported to a strange world called Lyrian, where he joins Rachel, who was also drawn there from our world, and a few rebels, to piece together the Word that can destroy the malicious wizard emperor, Surroth.

"Mull moves his story at a brisk pace, preventing the tragedies from overwhelming the adventure, while offering ample action and feisty dialogue to keep fantasy lovers entertained." Publ Wkly

Murphy, Jill

Dear hound. Walker Books for Young Readers 2010 175p

Grades: 2 3 4 **Fic**

1. Dogs -- Fiction 2. Foxes -- Fiction

ISBN 0-8027-2190-7; 978-0-8027-2190-7

LC 2010006833

When Alfie, a timid deerhound puppy, gets lost in the woods, he will do almost anything—including befriending a pair of foxes—to find his way home to his beloved boy, Charlie, who refuses to believe Alfie is gone for good.

"Murphy deftly conveys the dog's angst with occasional all-caps dialogue. Her charming black-and-white line illustrations appear on every spread, extending the simple text and making this an excellent choice for readers recently transitioned to chapter books." Kirkus

Murphy, Jim

Desperate journey. Scholastic Press 2006 278p il map $16.99

Grades: 5 6 7 8   **Fic**

1. Family life -- Fiction 2. Erie Canal (N.Y.) -- Fiction

ISBN 0-439-07806-7

LC 2006-02526

In the mid-1800s, with both her father and her uncle in jail on an assault charge, Maggie, her brother, and her ailing mother rush their barge along the Erie Canal to deliver their heavy cargo or lose everything.

This is a "gripping novel." Booklist

Murphy, Rita

Bird. Delacorte Press 2008 151p $15.99; lib bdg $18.99

Grades: 5 6 7 8   **Fic**

1. Kites -- Fiction 2. Flight -- Fiction 3. Houses -- Fiction 4. Vermont -- Fiction 5. Supernatural -- Fiction

ISBN 978-0-385-73018-1; 0-385-73018-7; 978-0-385-90557-2 lib bdg; 0-385-90557-2 lib bdg

LC 2008-04690

Miranda, a small, delicate girl easily carried off by the wind, lands at Bourne Manor on the coast of Lake Champlain and is raised by the dour Wysteria Barrows, but she begins to believe rumors that the Manor is cursed and, aided by a new friend and kites secreted in an attic, seeks to escape.

"This enchanting novel is well written with lyrical text and beautiful descriptions. . . . Good for middle school students, this book will make a nice addition to school and public libraries alike." Libr Media Connect

Murphy, Sally

★ **Pearl** verses the world; [illustrations by Heather Potter] Candlewick Press 2011 73p il $14.99

Grades: 3 4 5   **Fic**

1. School stories 2. Novels in verse 3. Death -- Fiction 4. Poetry -- Fiction 5. Loneliness -- Fiction 6. Bereavement -- Fiction 7. Family life -- Fiction 8. Grandmothers -- Fiction

ISBN 0-7636-4821-3; 978-0-7636-4821-3

LC 2010040149

Pearl feels like an island in school, isolated and alone, but at home she feels loved and secure until her grandmother's illness changes the way Pearl views her world.

This is a "poignantly illustrated novella in free verse. . . . Potter's evocative pencil-and-wash drawings, with their excellent renderings of facial expressions and mood, wonderfully complement Murphy's thoughtful narrative." Kirkus

Murray, Kirsty

The **Four** Seasons of Lucy McKenzie; by Kirsty Murray. Allen & Unwin 2014 216 p. illustrations $9.99

Grades: 4 5 6 7   **Fic**

1. Magic -- Fiction 2. Adventure fiction 3. Friendship -- Fiction 4. Children's stories

ISBN 1743317026; 9781743317020

This book, by Kirsty Murray, is a "timeslip adventure set in a hidden valley where an 11-year-old girl travels across the river of time to fight fires, battle floodwaters, and discover the meaning of true friendship. . . . Lucy is horrified to find that she is to spend Christmas, and the summer holidays, with Great-Auntie Big in her isolated country house. . . . She

discovers she can enter the magical floor-to-ceiling paintings of the four seasons that cover the dining room walls." (Publisher's note)

"Murray links past and present with sophisticated plotting and a wonderfully descriptive setting; the Australian bush comes alive in all its beauty and harshness, and the river that flows through both the past and present valley is an expressive metaphor for the flow of time." Kirkus

Musgrove, Marianne

Lucy the good; illustrated by Cheryl Orsini. Henry Holt 2010 137p il $16.99

Grades: 2 3 4   **Fic**

1. School stories 2. Australia -- Fiction 3. Family life -- Fiction

ISBN 978-0-8050-9051-2; 0-8050-9051-7

LC 2009050766

When Lucy's great-aunt Bep comes from Holland to Adelaide, Australia, to visit, she is shocked by some of Lucy's behavior, and Lucy begins to wonder about herself. Includes a glossary of Dutch words and a recipe.

"The dichotomy between what Lucy says and thinks adds ample humor to this heartfelt novel. . . . With humor of their own, Orsini's b&w spot illustrations portray Lucy's behavior." Publ Wkly

Myers, Christopher

H.O.R.S.E. a game of basketball and imagination. Christopher Myers. Egmont USA 2012 1 p. (hardback) $18.99

Grades: 1 2 3   **Fic**

1. Games -- Fiction 2. Sports -- Fiction 3. Friendship -- Fiction 4. Basketball -- Fiction

ISBN 1606842188; 9781606842188

LC 2012003793

Coretta Scott King Illustrator Honor Book (2013)

Author Christopher Myers' book presents a children's story. "One day at the basketball court, two kids, a familiar challenge--H.O.R.S.E. But this isn't your grandmother's game of hoops. Not when a layup from the other side of the court standing on one foot with your eyes closed is just the warm-up. Around the neighborhood, around the world, off Saturn's rings, the pair goes back and forth. The game is as much about skill as it is about imagination." (Publisher's note)

Myers, Laurie

Escape by night; a Civil War adventure. illustrated by Amy June Bates. Henry Holt 2011 120p il $14.99

Grades: 3 4 5   **Fic**

1. Christian life -- Fiction 2. United States -- History -- 1861-1865, Civil War -- Fiction

ISBN 978-0-8050-8825-0; 0-8050-8825-3

LC 2010-30117

Tommy, the son of a Presbyterian minister in Augusta, Georgia, during the Civil War, must search his conscience to decide whether he should help a Yankee soldier escape and return home. Inspired by the early life of Woodrow Wilson.

"Sporadic full-page, black-and-white illustrations by Bates bring the characters . . . to life. This quick and exciting chapter book isn't shy about advancing a moral message but does so with a light touch." Booklist

★ **Lewis** and Clark and me; a dog's tale. illustrations by Michael Dooling. Holt & Co. 2002 64p il $16.95

Grades: 3 4 5 6   **Fic**

1. Explorers 2. Dogs -- Fiction 3. Territorial governors 4. Lewis and Clark Expedition (1804-1806) -- Fiction

ISBN 0-8050-6368-4

LC 00-47298

Seaman, Meriwether Lewis's Newfoundland dog, describes Lewis and Clark's expedition, which he accompanied from St. Louis to the Pacific Ocean

"Myers is a dog lover, and that respect comes through in the dignified portrayal of Seaman. Attractive, realistic paintings illustrate the book, giving a feel for the period and, most importantly, a visual personality to Seaman." SLJ

Includes bibliographical references

Myklusch, Matt

Jack Blank and the Imagine Nation. Aladdin 2010 480p $16.99
Grades: 4 5 6 7   **Fic**
1. Fantasy fiction 2. Science fiction 3. Orphans -- Fiction 4. Superheroes -- Fiction
ISBN 978-1-4169-9561-6; 1-4169-9561-7

Twelve-year-old Jack, freed from a dismal orphanage, makes his way to the elusive and impossible Imagine Nation, where a mentor saves him from dissection and trains him to use his superpower, despite the virus he carries that makes him a threat.

This creates "a richly imagined world with strong appeal to fans of comics. The island is populated by a fun cast of heroes and villains. . . . Brisk narration captures the superhero world with a mixture of fast-paced action, wry humor, and occasional heartfelt speeches about courage and friendship." SLJ

Followed by: Jack Blank and the secret war (2011)

Myracle, Lauren

Eleven. Dutton Children's Books 2004 201p (The Winnie years) $16.99; pa $6.99
Grades: 4 5 6 7   **Fic**
1. Friendship -- Fiction 2. Family life -- Fiction
ISBN 0-525-47165-0; 0-14-240346-6 pa
LC 2003-49076

The year between turning eleven and turning twelve bring many changes for Winnie and her friends

"The inclusion of details about the everyday lives of these girls . . . will make this novel enjoyable, even for reluctant readers. However, it's the book's occasional revelation of harder truths that lifts it out of the ordinary." SLJ

Other titles in this series are:
Twelve (2007)
Thirteen (2008)
Thirteen plus one (2010)
Ten (2011)

★ **Luv** ya bunches. Amulet Books 2009 335p $15.95
Grades: 4 5 6   **Fic**
1. School stories 2. Friendship -- Fiction
ISBN 978-0-8109-4211-0; 0-8109-4211-9
LC 2009012585

Four friends—each named after a flower—navigate the ups and downs of fifth grade. Told through text messages, blog posts, screenplay, and straight narrative

Myracle "displays a shining awareness of and sensitivity to the highly textured society of tween girls. . . . This is a fun, challenging, and gently edifying story." Booklist

Another title about these characters is:
Violet in bloom (2010)

Ten. Dutton Childrens Books 2011 208, 21p $16.99
Grades: 4 5 6   **Fic**
1. School stories 2. Friendship -- Fiction 3. Family life -- Fiction

4. Atlanta (Ga.) -- Fiction
ISBN 978-0-525-42356-0; 0-525-42356-7
LC 2011005186

Winnie's celebrates her unique style through her first year with a double-digit age as she has many new experiences, from the high of spending time in New York City with her aunt and big sister, to the low of her two best friends suddenly becoming interested in boys.

Winnie "is simply the quintessential girl-next-door to whom young readers can comfortably relate. A solid addition to winning series." Kirkus

Violet in bloom; a flower power book. Amulet Books 2010 366p $15.95
Grades: 4 5 6   **Fic**
1. School stories 2. Food -- Fiction 3. California -- Fiction 4. Friendship -- Fiction
ISBN 978-0-8109-8983-2; 0-8109-8983-2
LC 2010-24319

Fifth-graders Katie-Rose, Violet, Milla, and Yasaman seem to have little in common except their flower-related names, but they nurture their new friendship through a social-networking site and a campaign to have healthier snacks served at school.

This is "a realistic, easy-to-relate-to riot of pre-adolescent exuberance. A triumph." Kirkus

Wishing Day; by Lauren Myracle; illustrated by Julie McLaughlin. Harpercollins Childrens Books 2016 336 p. $16.99
Grades: 4 5 6   **Fic**
1. Magic -- Fiction 2. Wishes -- Fiction 3. Sisters -- Fiction
ISBN 0062342061; 9780062342065
LC 2015038865

In this book, by Lauren Myracle, illustrated by Julie McLaughlin, "Natasha is the oldest child in a family steeped in magic, though she's not sure she believes in it. She's full to bursting with wishes, however. She misses her mother, who disappeared nearly eight long years ago. She has a crush on one of the cutest boys in her class. . . . And amid the chaos of a house full of sisters, aunts, and a father lost in grief, she aches to simply be . . . . noticed." (Publisher's note)

"Portraying characters in ways that make them immediately easy to differentiate and ultimately memorable, Myracle lets the reader decide whether magic is really coming into play. The touch of fantasy seems more believable because the story is so firmly grounded in realistic details of setting, character, and plot." Booklist

Naftali, Joel

The **rendering**; [by] Joel Naftali. Egmont USA 2011 275p $15.99
Grades: 5 6 7 8   **Fic**
1. Science fiction 2. Adventure fiction 3. Weblogs -- Fiction
ISBN 978-1-60684-118-1; 1-60684-118-1
LC 2010-36640

Thirteen-year-old Doug relates in a series of blog posts the story of how he saved the world but was falsely branded a terrorist and murderer, forced to fight the evil Dr. Roach and his armored biodroid army with an electronics-destroying superpower of his own.

"Naftali balances tragedy and absurd humor with aplomb, not an easy task when dealing with horrific explosions and giant wisecracking skunks. Readers seeking a fast-paced, action-packed adventure will find this eminently suitable." Bull Cent Child Books

Nagda, Ann Whitehead

The **perfect** cat-sitter; illustrated by Stephanie Roth. Holiday House 2007 104p il $15.95

Grades: 2 3 4　　　　　　　　　　　　　　　　**Fic**

1. School stories 2. Cats -- Fiction
ISBN 978-0-8234-2112-1; 0-8234-2112-0

LC 2007-18301

When her friend Rana goes to India, Susan volunteers to take care of her cat and her sister's fish, but the job turns out to be much more difficult than she expected.

"Humor infuses the story. . . . Classroom dynamics and school friendships are well rendered, as are all sides of Susan's perfectionism. . . . Soft black-and-white illustrations capture Susan's emotions throughout her escapades." Booklist

Naidoo, Beverley

★ **Journey** to Jo'burg; a South African story. illustrations by Eric Velasquez. Lippincott 1986 80p il hardcover o.p. pa $4.99
Grades: 5 6 7 8　　　　　　　　　　　　　　　**Fic**

1. South Africa -- Race relations -- Fiction
ISBN 0-06-440237-1 pa

LC 85-45508

"This touching novel graphically depicts the plight of Africans living in the horror of South Africa. Thirteen-year-old Maledi and her 9-year-old brother leave their small village, take the perilous journey to the city, and encounter, firsthand, the painful struggle for justice, freedom, and dignity in the 'City of Gold.' A provocative story with a message readers will long remember." Soc Educ

Followed by Chain of fire (1990)

Nannestad, Katrina

When mischief came to town; by Katrina Nannestad. Houghton Mifflin Harcourt 2015 192 p. $16.99
Grades: 4 5 6　　　　　　　　　　　　　　　　**Fic**

1. Grief -- Fiction 2. Denmark -- Fiction 3. Orphans -- Fiction 4. Grandmothers -- Fiction 5. Conduct of life -- Fiction 6. Behavior -- Fiction 7. Denmark -- History -- 20th century -- Fiction 8. Bornholm (Denmark) -- History -- 20th century -- Fiction
ISBN 0544534328; 9780544534322

LC 2014028513

This book, by Katrina Nannestad, is "about love, family, grief, joy and the power of laughter and imagination. When Inge Maria arrives on the tiny island of Bornholm in Denmark to live with her grandmother, she's not sure what to expect. Her grandmother is stern, the people on the island are strange, and children are supposed to be seen and not heard. But no matter how hard Inge tries to be good, mischief has a way of finding her." (Publisher's note)

Napoli, Donna Jo

Lights on the Nile. HarperCollins 2011 278p $16.99; lib bdg $17.89
Grades: 4 5 6 7　　　　　　　　　　　　　　　**Fic**

1. Baboons -- Fiction 2. Fairies -- Fiction 3. Kidnapping -- Fiction 4. Egypt -- History -- Fiction
ISBN 978-0-06-166793-0; 0-06-166793-5; 978-0-06-166794-7 lib bdg; 0-06-166794-3 lib bdg

LC 2011010179

Ten-year-old Kepi, a young girl in ancient Egypt, embarks on a journey to save her family when she is unexpectedly taken captive, along with the baby baboon she has rescued from a crocodile.

Napoli "crafts a mystical coming-of-age tale and a love letter of sorts to Egypt, saturated with proverbs, intriguing details of everyday life at the time, and rich descriptions of the places Kepi visits. . . . Kepi's survival skills and perspective are challenged in this absorbing adventure." Publ Wkly

The **prince** of the pond; otherwise known as De Fawg Pin. illustrated by Judy Schachner. Dutton Children's Bks. 1992 151p hardcover o.p. pa $4.99
Grades: 4 5 6　　　　　　　　　　　　　　　　**Fic**

1. Frogs -- Fiction
ISBN 0-525-44976-0; 0-14-037151-6 pa

LC 91-40340

"An animal fantasy that fairy tale readers will relish. . . . Schachner's numerous ink-and-wash drawings go far in supporting the characterization." Bull Cent Child Books

Sly the Sleuth and the pet mysteries; by Donna Jo Napoli and Robert Furrow; illustrated by Heather Maione. Dial Books for Young Readers 2005 96p il $15.99
Grades: 2 3 4　　　　　　　　　　　　　　　　**Fic**

1. Mystery fiction 2. Pets -- Fiction
ISBN 0-8037-2993-6

LC 2003-24090

Sly the Sleuth, also known as Sylvia, solves three mysteries for her friends and neighbors, all involving pets, through her detective agency Sleuth for Hire.

"The stories are easy to read and engaging, the pen-and-ink illustrations convey the light tone of the adventures, and Sly's first-person narration is convincing." Horn Book Guide

Other titles about Sly the Sleuth are:
Sly the Sleuth and the sports mysteries (2006)
Sly the Sleuth and the food mysteries (2007)
Sly the Sleuth and the code mysteries (2009)

Stones in water. Dutton Children's Bks. 1997 209p hardcover o.p. pa $5.99
Grades: 5 6 7 8　　　　　　　　　　　　　　　**Fic**

1. World War, 1939-1945 -- Fiction
ISBN 0-525-45842-5; 0-14-130600-9 pa

LC 97-14253

After being taken by German soldiers from a local movie theater along with other Italian boys including his Jewish friend, Roberto is forced to work in Germany, escapes into the Ukrainian winter, before desperately trying to make his way back home to Venice

This is a "gripping, meticulously researched story (loosely based on the life of an actual survivor)." Publ Wkly

Naylor, Phyllis Reynolds

Alice in rapture, sort of. Atheneum Pubs. 1989 166p hardcover o.p. pa $5.99
Grades: 5 6 7 8　　　　　　　　　　　　　　　**Fic**

1. Family life -- Fiction
ISBN 0-689-31466-3; 1-442-42362-5 pa

LC 88-8174

The summer before she enters the seventh grade becomes the summer of Alice's first boyfriend, and she discovers that love is about the most mixed-up thing that can possibly happen to you, especially since she has no mother to go to for advice

"A book that is wise, perceptive, and hilarious." SLJ

Alice in-between. Atheneum Pubs. 1994 144p pa $5.99
Grades: 4 5 6 7　　　　　　　　　　　　　　　**Fic**

1. Family life -- Fiction
ISBN 0-689-31890-1; 1-416-96770-2 pa

LC 93-816

When motherless Alice turns thirteen she feels in-between, no longer a child but not yet a woman, and discovers that growing up can be both frustrating and wonderful

"This is bound to reassure the many adolescent fans who can identify with the 'in-between blues.'" SLJ

Alice the brave. Atheneum Bks. for Young Readers 1995 130p pa $7.99
Grades: 5 6 7 8   **Fic**
1. Fear -- Fiction 2. Family life -- Fiction
ISBN 0-689-80095-9; 1-416-97542-X pa

LC 94-32340
The summer before eighth grade, Alice tries to confront her fears, not the least of which is a fear of deep water.
"Alice's wry, funny, vulnerable voice expresses every girl's fears about what is 'normal' in an imperfect world." Booklist

All but Alice. Atheneum Pubs. 1992 151p hardcover o.p. pa $5.99
Grades: 5 6 7 8   **Fic**
1. School stories 2. Clubs -- Fiction
ISBN 0-689-31773-5; 1-442-42756-6 pa

LC 91-28722
Seventh grader Alice decides that the only way to stave off personal and social disasters is to be part of the crowd, especially the "in" crowd, no matter how boring and, potentially, difficult
"Naylor's light, but deft touch with important thematic concerns is most appealing." SLJ

★ **Emily's** fortune; illustrated by Ross Collins. Delacorte Press 2010 147p il $14.99
Grades: 3 4 5 6   **Fic**
1. Uncles -- Fiction 2. Orphans -- Fiction 3. West (U.S.) -- Fiction 4. Voyages and travels -- Fiction 5. Inheritance and succession -- Fiction
ISBN 978-0-385-73616-9; 0-385-73616-9

LC 2009013096
While traveling to her aunt's home in Redbud by train and stage-coach, quiet young Emily and her turtle, Rufus, team up with Jackson, fellow orphan and troublemaker extraordinaire, to outsmart mean Uncle Victor, who is after Emily's inheritance.
"The local vernacular is lively and fun and the characters are well developed. Cliff-hangers between chapters are written in large boldface to keep readers hooked. . . . Simple, black-and-white illustrations complement the unfolding story. A rip-roaring good time." SLJ

Faith, hope, and Ivy June. Delacorte Press 2009 280p $16.99; lib bdg $19.99
Grades: 5 6 7 8   **Fic**
1. School stories 2. Kentucky -- Fiction 3. Appalachian region -- Fiction
ISBN 978-0-385-73615-2; 0-385-73615-0; 978-0-385-90588-6 lib bdg; 0-385-90588-2 lib bdg

LC 2008-19625
During a student exchange program, seventh-graders Ivy June and Catherine share their lives, homes, and communities, and find that although their lifestyles are total opposites they have a lot in common.
"This finely crafted novel . . . depicts a deep friendship growing slowly through understanding. As both girls wait out tragedies at the book's end, they cling to hope—and each other—in a thoroughly real and unaffected way. Naylor depicts Appalachia with sympathetic realism." Kirkus

Outrageously Alice. Atheneum Bks. for Young Readers 1997 133p $16.99; pa $5.99

Grades: 5 6 7 8   **Fic**
1. School stories 2. Family life -- Fiction
ISBN 0-689-80354-0; 0-689-80596-9 pa

LC 96-7744
"Alice is, as always, likable, humorous, and true to life." SLJ

★ **Roxie** and the Hooligans; with illustrations by Alexandra Boiger. Atheneum Books for Young Readers 2006 115p il $15.95; pa $4.99
Grades: 3 4 5   **Fic**
1. Adventure fiction
ISBN 1-4169-0243-0; 1-4169-0244-9 pa

LC 2004-24645
Roxie Warbler, the niece of a famous explorer, follows Uncle Dangerfoot's advice on how to survive any crisis when she becomes stranded on an island with a gang of school bullies and a pair of murderous bank robbers.
This "mixes fantasy, absurdity, and reality in a way that never diminishes or overwhelms the story's heart. Boiger's black-and-white illustrations catch the energy of Naylor's over-the-top yet sympathetically portrayed characters." Booklist

★ **Shiloh.** Atheneum Pubs. 1991 144p $16.95; pa $6.99
Grades: 4 5 6   **Fic**
1. Dogs -- Fiction 2. West Virginia -- Fiction
ISBN 0-689-31614-3; 0-689-83582-5 pa

LC 90-603
Awarded the Newbery Medal, 1992
When he finds a lost beagle in the hills behind his West Virginia home, Marty tries to hide it from his family and the dog's real owner, a mean-spirited man known to shoot deer out of season and to mistreat his dogs
"A credible plot and characters, a well-drawn setting, and nicely paced narration combine in a story that leaves the reader feeling good." Horn Book
Other titles about Shiloh are:
Shiloh season (1996)
Saving Shiloh (1997)
A Shiloh Christmas (2015)

A **Shiloh** Christmas; Phyllis Reynolds Naylor. Atheneum Books for Young Readers 2015 256 p. (hardcover) $17.99
Grades: 4 5 6   **Fic**
1. Christmas -- Fiction 2. Dogs -- Fiction 3. Prejudices -- Fiction 4. Clergy -- Fiction 5. West Virginia -- Fiction 6. Family life -- West Virginia -- Fiction
ISBN 1481441515; 9781481441513; 9781481441537

LC 2014040082
In this children's novel, by Phyllis Reynolds Naylor, "a rescued beagle and his boy owner seek love and understanding for their troubled small town in this holiday companion to the Newbery Medal-winning 'Shiloh.' . . . It's been a year since Marty Preston rescued Shiloh from Judd Travers . . . But just as townsfolk grow more accepting of Judd, a fire in the woods destroys many homes, including Judd's, and Judd's newly formed reputation." (Publisher's note)
"This is a Christmas story, but first Marty, Shiloh, and their family must get through a new-school routine, Halloween, and Thanksgiving--and a drought and subsequent wildfire. As in the three previous books centered on now-iconic dog Shiloh, the rural West Virginia setting and the relationships among its inhabitants are warmly but unsentimentally drawn. The conclusion provides the best kind of heartwarming: earned." Horn Book

★ **Starting** with Alice. Atheneum Bks. for Young Readers 2002 181p hardcover o.p. pa $4.99

Grades: 3 4 5 6 **Fic**
1. School stories 2. Friendship -- Fiction 3. Family life -- Fiction
ISBN 0-689-84395-X; 0-689-84396-8 pa

LC 2001-53610

This, the first of three prequels to the series about Alice, is written for younger readers. After she, her older brother, and their father move from Chicago to Maryland, Alice has trouble fitting into her new third grade class, but with the help of some new friends and her own unique outlook, she survives

"New characters and realistic third-grade situations are explored, but young Alice's humor and earnestness are refreshingly the same." Horn Book

Other prequels to the Alice series are:
Alice in Blunderland (2003)
Lovingly Alice (2004)

Nelson, Nina

Bringing the boy home; by N.A. Nelson. HarperCollinsPublishers 2008 211p $15.99; lib bdg $16.89
Grades: 5 6 7 8 **Fic**
1. Rain forests -- Fiction 2. Amazon River valley -- Fiction 3. Senses and sensation -- Fiction 4. Extrasensory perception -- Fiction
ISBN 978-0-06-088698-1; 0-06-088698-6; 978-0-06-088699-8 lib bdg; 0-06-088699-4 lib bdg

LC 2007-31702

As two Takunami youths approach their thirteenth birthdays, Luka reaches the culmination of his mother's training for the tribe's manhood test while Tirio, raised in Miami, Florida, by his adoptive mother, feels called to begin preparations to prove himself during his upcoming visit to the Amazon rain forest where he was born.

"The vivid setting, imagined cultural particulars . . . and magical realism will captivate readers." Booklist

Nelson, S. D.

Digging a hole to heaven; a story about the coal mine boys. by S.D. Nelson. Abrams Books for Young Children 2014 64 p. color illustrations $19.95
Grades: 3 4 5 6 **Fic**
1. Child labor -- Fiction 2. Coal mines and mining -- Fiction 3. Coal mines and mining -- Accidents 4. Child labor -- United States -- History -- 19th century 5. Coal miners -- United States -- History -- 19th century 6. Coal mines and mining -- United States -- History -- 19th century
ISBN 1419707302; 9781419707308

LC 2013035246

In this book by S.D. Nelson "at 12 years old, Conall has already worked in the coal mines of West Virginia for two years. He spends his days deep underground with his faithful mule, Angel, carting loads of coal. One day a tunnel collapses, and his brother is trapped with others on the wrong side! How can Conall and Angel help to save them?" (Publisher's note)

"In this picture book for older readers, historical photographs and sidebars support a fictional tale about two brothers who work in a nineteenth-century Pennsylvania coal mine. Both elements squarely address mining's dangers but also the intense bonds that developed among the boys, men, and beasts who labored deep underground. Nelson's acrylics capture the sooty, lamp-lit atmosphere. An extensive author's note is appended. Timeline. Bib., ind." Horn Book

Includes bibliographical references

Neri, Greg

Chess rumble; by G. Neri; art by Jesse Joshua Watson. Lee & Low Books 2007 64p il $18.95

Grades: 5 6 7 8 **Fic**
1. Chess -- Fiction 2. African Americans -- Fiction
ISBN 978-1-58430-279-7

LC 2007010772

Branded a troublemaker due to his anger over everything from being bullied to his sister's death a year before, Marcus begins to control himself and cope with his problems at home and at his inner-city school when an unlikely mentor teaches him to play chess

"Neri expertly captures Marcus's voice and delicately teases out his alternating vulnerability and rage. The cadence and emotion of the verse are masterfully echoed through Watson's expressive acrylic illustrations." SLJ

Ghetto cowboy; [by] G. Neri; illustrated by Jesse Joshua Watson. Candlewick Press 2011 218p il $15.99
Grades: 4 5 6 7 **Fic**
1. Horses -- Fiction 2. Moving -- Fiction 3. African Americans -- Fiction 4. City and town life -- Fiction 5. Philadelphia (Pa.) -- Fiction 6. Father-son relationship -- Fiction
ISBN 978-0-7636-4922-7; 0-7636-4922-8

LC 2010007565

Twelve-year-old Cole's behavior causes his mother to drive him from Detroit to Philadelphia to live with a father he has never known, but who soon has Cole involved with a group of African-American "cowboys" who rescue horses and use them to steer youths away from drugs and gangs.

"This well-written book is based on a true story of urban cowboys in Philadelphia and New York. Cole's spot-on emotional insight is conveyed through believable dialogue. . . . Watson's illustrations punctuate the intriguing aspects of the story and make the novel more appealing." SLJ

Nesbet, Anne

Cloud and Wallfish; Anne Nesbet. Candlewick Press 2016 400 p. (ebook) $16.99; $16.99
Grades: 5 6 7 8 **Fic**
1. Family secrets -- Fiction 2. Berlin Wall (1961-1989) -- Fiction
ISBN 9780763691806; 9780763688035

LC 2016946908

In this book, by Anne Nesbet, "Noah Keller has a pretty normal life, until one wild afternoon when his parents pick him up from school and head straight for the airport, telling him on the ride that his name isn't really Noah. . . . As Noah—now 'Jonah Brown'—and his parents head behind the Iron Curtain into East Berlin, the rules and secrets begin to pile up so quickly that he can hardly keep track of the questions bubbling up inside him." (Publisher's note)

"Noah's friendship with his neighbor Claudia is genuinely touching, and some truly tense scenes unfold as secrets are revealed and readers witness events leading to the fall of the Berlin Wall." Booklist

Nesbit, E.

★ The **enchanted** castle; illustrated by Paul O. Zelinsky; afterword by Peter Glassman. Morrow Junior Bks. 1992 292p il lib bdg $22.95
Grades: 4 5 6 **Fic**
1. Fantasy fiction 2. Great Britain -- Fiction
ISBN 0-688-05435-8

LC 91-46267

First published 1907 in the United Kingdom; first United States edition 1908 by Harper & Brothers

Four English children find a wonderful world of magic through an enchanted wishing ring

"With fine, cross-hatched lines tinted in luminous colors, Zelinsky's artwork is as lively as the story and very much of the period." Booklist

★ **Five** children and it; illustrated by H.R. Millar; with an introduction by Laurel Snyder. Random House 2010 255p il (Looking Glass library) $9.99; lib bdg $12.99

Grades: 4 5 6   **Fic**

1. Wishes -- Fiction 2. Fairies -- Fiction 3. Siblings -- Fiction 4. Great Britain -- Fiction

ISBN 978-0-375-86336-3; 0-375-86336-2; 978-0-375-96336-0 lib bdg; 0-375-96336-7 lib bdg

LC 2008-54569

First published 1902 in the United Kingdom; first United States edition 1905 by Dodd, Mead & Co.

When four brothers and sisters discover a Psammead, or sand-fairy, in the gravel pit near the country house where they are staying, they have no way of knowing all the adventures its wish-granting will bring them

Other titles in this series are:

The Phoenix and the carpet (1904)

The story of the amulet (1907)

Nesbø, Jo

Doctor Proctor's fart powder; illustrated by Mike Lowery. Aladdin 2010 265p il $14.99

Grades: 4 5 6   **Fic**

1. Norway -- Fiction 2. Bullies -- Fiction 3. Inventors -- Fiction 4. Friendship -- Fiction

ISBN 1-4169-7972-7; 978-1-4169-7972-2

LC 2009-27204

New friends Nilly and Lisa help eccentric professor Doctor Proctor to develop his latest invention, a powder that makes one fart, making them very popular at school, but someone is planning to steal the industrial-strength formula for evil purposes.

"Nesbo tells his fantastical story in a matter-of-fact, deadpan style, and Lowery's simple illustrations match the dry, comedic tone well." Booklist

Follwed by: Bubble in the bathtub (2011)

Neumeier, Rachel

The **Floating** Islands. Alfred A. Knopf 2011 388p map $16.99; lib bdg $19.99

Grades: 5 6 7   **Fic**

1. Fantasy fiction 2. Magic -- Fiction 3. Flight -- Fiction 4. Cousins -- Fiction

ISBN 0-375-84705-7; 0-375-94705-1 lib bdg; 978-0-375-84705-9; 978-0-375-94705-6 lib bdg

LC 2010-12772

The adventures of two teenaged cousins who live in a place called The Floating Islands, one of whom is studying to become a mage and the other one of the legendary island flyers.

"The author delineates complex characters, geographies and societies alike with a dab hand, deftly weaves them all—along with dragons of several sorts, mouthwatering kitchen talk, flashes of humor and a late-blooming romance—into a suspenseful plot and delivers and outstanding tale that is self-contained but full of promise for sequels." Kirkus

Neville, Emily Cheney

It's like this, Cat; [by] Emily Neville; illustrated by Emil Weiss. Harper & Row 1963 180p il $16.99; lib bdg $17.89; pa $5.99

Grades: 5 6 7 8   **Fic**

1. Cats -- Fiction 2. New York (N.Y.) -- Fiction

ISBN 0-06-024390-2; 0-06-024391-0 lib bdg; 0-06-440073-5 pa

Awarded the Newbery Medal, 1964

"A story told with a great amount of insight into human relationships. . . . This all provides a wonderfully real picture of a city boy's outlets and of one likable adolescent's inner feelings. An exceedingly fresh, honest, and well-rounded piece of writing." Horn Book

Newbery, Linda

Lost boy. David Fickling Books 2008 194p $15.99; lib bdg $18.99

Grades: 4 5 6 7   **Fic**

1. Ghost stories 2. Mystery fiction 3. Wales -- Fiction 4. Traffic accidents -- Fiction

ISBN 978-0-375-84574-1; 978-0-375-93617-3 lib bdg

LC 2007-15041

First published 2005 in the United Kingdom

After Matt moves to Hay-on-Wye in Wales, a boy his age who bears the same initials and was killed in a car accident many years earlier, appears to Matt.

"With its imaginative melding of present-day concerns, good storytelling, lush descriptions of the landscape and even a faithful dog, this novel will ensnare readers." Publ Wkly

Lucy and the green man; illustrated by Pam Smy. David Fickling Books 2010 217p il $16.99; lib bdg $19.99

Grades: 3 4 5   **Fic**

1. Gardening -- Fiction 2. Bereavement -- Fiction 3. Grandfathers -- Fiction 4. Great Britain -- Fiction 5. London (England) -- Fiction

ISBN 978-0-385-75204-6; 0-385-75204-0; 978-0-385-75207-7 lib bdg; 0-385-75207-5 lib bdg

LC 2010-13653

Lucy and her grandfather are special because only they can see Lob, the magical 'green man' who helps in the garden, but then something terrible happens and Lucy fears she will never see Lob again

"Black-and-white line spot art and occasional spreads capture the flavor of the story. . . . This gentle fantasy has an old-fashioned quality that will appeal to families and young sensitive readers." SLJ

Newbound, Andrew

Ghoul strike! Chicken House 2010 309p $16.99

Grades: 4 5 6 7   **Fic**

1. Angels -- Fiction 2. Monsters -- Fiction 3. Supernatural -- Fiction

ISBN 978-0-545-22938-8; 0-545-22938-3

LC 2010013580

When twelve-year-old, psychic ghost hunter Alannah Malarra faces demons from another dimension, rather than the treasure-hoarding ghosts she is used to, she needs the help of protectors from the Attack-ready Network of Global Evanescent Law-enforcers (A.N.G.E.L.) police force to help her quell the dangerous uprising

"Alannah is a great female hero. . . . The other main characters are also multidimensional, and descriptions of the various creatures are detailed and entertaining. Readers will enjoy the fast-paced plot and the friendship between Alannah and Wortley." SLJ

Newman, John

Mimi. Candlewick Press 2011 186p $15.99

Grades: 2 3 4 5   **Fic**

1. Bereavement -- Fiction 2. Family life -- Fiction 3. Great Britain -- Fiction

ISBN 978-0-7636-5415-3; 0-7636-5415-9

LC 2010040147

Mimi is determined not to give up on anyone or anything, but since Mammy died, her father never smiles, her sister Sally is in a bad mood, brother Conor keeps to himself, and even Sparkler the dog does not want to go for walks.

Newman "will win readers' hearts through the conversational tone and openhearted observations of . . . narrator Mimi. . . . Newman ably conveys a family hanging together by a thread; that Mimi, who is Chinese, is adopted is nearly incidental to the plot—until a climactic scene in which she stands up to a school bully." Publ Wkly

Newman, Leslea

★ **Hachiko** waits; illustrated by Machiyo Kodaira. Henry Holt and Co. 2004 96p il $15.95; pa $6.99

Grades: 3 4 5   **Fic**

1. Dogs -- Fiction 2. Japan -- Fiction

ISBN 0-8050-7336-1; 0-312-55806-6 pa

LC 2003-68589

Professor Ueno's loyal Akita, Hachiko, waits for him at the train station every afternoon, and even after the professor has a fatal heart attack while at work, Hachiko faithfully continues to await his return until the day the dog dies. Based on a true story

"Yasuo brings a childhood focus to the poignant story . . . and Kodaira's soft, black-and-white sketches help to break up the chapters for younger readers and add interest to the story." Booklist

Nicholls, Sally

★ **Season** of secrets. Arthur A. Levine Books 2011 225p $16.99

Grades: 4 5 6   **Fic**

1. Sisters -- Fiction 2. Bereavement -- Fiction 3. Family life -- Fiction 4. Great Britain -- Fiction

ISBN 978-0-545-21825-2; 0-545-21825-X

LC 2010017070

Sent by their father to live in the country with their grandparents after the sudden death of their mother, Molly's older sister Hannah expresses her grief in a raging rebellion while imaginative Molly finds herself increasingly distracted by visions, that seemingly only she can see, of a strange hunt in the nearby forest.

"Written in gently flowing prose, the plot appropriately transitions from autumn into summer as Molly emerges from grief to acceptance and hope. A poignant story of healing tinged with mystery." Kirkus

★ **Ways** to live forever; [by] Sally Nicholls. Arthur A. Levine Books 2008 212p il $16.99

Grades: 4 5 6 7   **Fic**

1. Death -- Fiction 2. Leukemia -- Fiction 3. Authorship -- Fiction 4. Family life -- Fiction

ISBN 978-0-545-06948-9; 0-545-06948-3

LC 2007047341

Eleven-year-old Sam McQueen, who has leukemia, writes a book during the last three months of his life, in which he tells about what he would like to accomplish, how he feels, and things that have happened to him.

This "skirts easy sentiment to confront the hard questions head-on, intelligently and realistically and with an enormous range of feeling." Publ Wkly

Nielsen, Jennifer A.

Elliot and the goblin war; illustrated by Gideon Kendall. Sourcebooks Jabberwocky 2010 181p il (Underworld chronicles) $14.99

Grades: 4 5 6 7   **Fic**

1. Fantasy fiction 2. Boys -- Fiction 3. Goblins -- Fiction

ISBN 978-1-4022-4019-5; 1-4022-4019-8

This "begins Halloween night, when unsuspecting reluctant hero Elliot happens to save a real Brownie named Patches from a trio of real Goblins. Elliot's good deed results in his acclamation as King of the Brownies, and these spunky but weak creatures truly need a king to help them end a three-year-long war with the evil Goblins. Nielsen ably draws readers into a tale chock-full of light adventure and humor, as

each chapter details the somewhat over-the-top yet entertaining dilemmas Patches and Elliot face. . . . Recommended for those who avoid dark and serious fantasies, as it's sure to evoke more giggles than gasps, despite the introductory admonitions." Kirkus

Other titles in this series are:

Elliot and the pixie plot (2011)

Elliot and the Yeti threat (2011)

Elliot and the pixie plot; illustrated by Gideon Kendall. Sourcebooks Jabberwocky 2011 192p il (Underworld chronicles) $12.99

Grades: 4 5 6 7   **Fic**

1. Fantasy fiction

ISBN 978-1-4022-4020-1; 1-4022-4020-1

"Elliot, King of the Brownies, struggles to balance working with hypercompetitive science-project partner Cami and hosting former nemesis Tubs Lawless, 'his least favorite former bully' for a sleepover. . . . Nielsen cleverly keeps the action and humor flowing from one silly obstacle to the next as Elliot tries to meet the demands of the angry Pixies. This quickly addictive page-turner also entices readers with many sensory details, such as tenacious Gripping Mud, surprisingly tasty turnip juice and a tingly invisibility potion gone wrong. . . . Definitely a series to invest in for those who prefer their fantasy a bit light." Kirkus

Elliot and the Yeti threat; illustrated by Gideon Kendall. Sourcebooks Jabberwocky 2012 il $12.99

Grades: 4 5 6 7   **Fic**

1. Fantasy fiction 2. Yeti -- Fiction

ISBN 978-1-4022-4021-8; 1-4022-4021-X

Being King of the Brownies is no easy job! Elliot outsmarted the Goblins and foiled the Pixie Plot, but now he's being threatened by a giant Yeti. Oh, and there's a mermaid hiding in his bathtub. Elliot might be able to survive some unusual self-defense lessons and a kingnapping plot, but can he withstand the friendship of the neighbor girl—his arch—nemesis–Cami Wortson?

The **false** prince; by Jennifer A. Nielsen. Scholastic Press 2012 342 p. (The ascendance trilogy) hbk $17.99

Grades: 4 5 6 7 8   **Fic**

1. Fantasy fiction 2. Adventure fiction 3. Impersonation -- Fiction 4. Orphans -- Fiction 5. Princes -- Fiction 6. Secrets -- Fiction 7. Courts and courtiers -- Fiction

ISBN 9780545284134

LC 2011006692

This fantasy book depicts the adventures of Sage, a "brazen 15-year-old orphan living in the imaginary kingdom of Carthya [who] becomes embroiled in a treasonous power-play to install a false prince on the vacant throne." He is selected with three other boys from the orphanage by Bevin Connor to compete to impersonate the missing Prince Jaron and act as Connor's pawn on the throne. "Sage's disdain, defiance and reckless arrogance mark him for failure, but his boldness, instinct and innate decency indicate there's more than meets the eye. Could Sage become Prince Jaron?" Jennifer A. Nielsen's story features "ruthless ambition, fierce action and plotting . . . and lots of sword play and hidden passages." (Kirkus)

Mark of the thief; by Jennifer A. Nielsen. Scholastic Press 2015 352 p. (Praetor war) (jacketed hardcover) $17.99

Grades: 5 6 7 8 9   **Fic**

1. Rome -- Fiction 2. Magic -- Fiction 3. Slaves -- Fiction 4. Amulets -- Fiction 5. Slavery -- Fiction 6. Insurgency -- Fiction 7. Rome -- Antiquities -- Fiction 8. Rome -- History -- Empire, 30 B.C.-476 A.D. -- Fiction

ISBN 054556154X; 9780545561549

LC 2014017068

Sequel: Rise of the Wolf (2015)

In this novel by Jennifer A. Nielsen, "when Nic, a slave in the mines outside of Rome, is forced to enter a sealed cavern containing the lost treasures of Julius Caesar, he finds much more than gold and gemstones: He discovers an ancient bulla, an amulet that belonged to the great Caesar and is filled with a magic once reserved for the Gods. He finds himself at the center of a ruthless conspiracy to overthrow the emperor and spark the Praetor War." (Publisher's note)

"This genre mash-up of history, fantasy, and action/adventure is fast-paced and explores themes such as class struggles, familial ties, and the immorality of slavery. Readers will have lots to digest as they quickly flip through the pages to see how Nic will escape his enemies to become a free man." SLJ

The **runaway** king; Jennifer A. Nielsen. Scholastic Press 2013 352 p. (The ascendance trilogy) (hardcover) $17.99
Grades: 4 5 6 7 8 **Fic**
1. Fantasy fiction 2. Kings and rulers -- Fiction 3. Princesses -- Fiction 4. Conspiracies -- Fiction
ISBN 0545284155; 9780545284158
LC 2012035290

"Just weeks after Jaron has taken the throne, an assassination attempt forces him into a deadly situation. Rumors of a coming war are winding their way between the castle walls, and Jaron feels the pressure quietly mounting within Carthya. Soon, it becomes clear that deserting the kingdom may be his only hope of saving it." (Publisher's note)

The **shadow** throne; Jennifer A. Nielsen. First edition Scholastic Press 2014 336 p. (Ascendance trilogy) (hardcover) $17.99
Grades: 4 5 6 7 8 **Fic**
1. Kings and rulers 2. Adventure fiction 3. Battles -- Fiction 4. Adventure stories 5. Rescues -- Fiction 6. Adventure and adventurers -- Fiction
ISBN 9780545284172; 0545284171
LC 2013021841

This book, by Jennifer A. Nielsen, is the "finale of the Ascendance Trilogy. . . . Jaron learns than King Vargan of Avenia and allies from Gelyn and Mendenwal have invaded Carthya and captured Jaron's friend Imogen. Determined to save Imogen, Jaron attempts a rescue and fails, leaving him a prisoner and Imogen presumed dead. As he tries to cope with Imogen's death, captive Jaron discovers how much he loved her." (Kirkus Reviews)

"There's enough adventure, mystery, and romance in this concluding volume to please a variety of genre readers." Horn Book

Nielsen, Susin

Dear George Clooney; please marry my mom. Tundra Books 2010 229p $15.95
Grades: 5 6 7 8 **Fic**
1. Divorce -- Fiction 2. Letters -- Fiction
ISBN 978-0-88776-977-1; 0-88776-977-2

"Smarting from her parent's divorce—her director father left her mother to marry an actress—Violet is fed up with all the 'losers' her mother has since dated. . . . She pens a letter to George Clooney . . . explaining that she's trying to find a suitable suitor for her parent. . . . Nielsen skillfully balances her story's keen humor . . . with poignancy." Publ Wkly

★ **Word** nerd. Tundra Books 2008 248p $18.95; pa $12.95
Grades: 5 6 7 8 **Fic**
1. Friendship -- Fiction 2. Scrabble (Game) -- Fiction 3. Mother-son relationship -- Fiction
ISBN 0-88776-875-X; 0-88776-990-X pa; 978-0-88776-875-0; 978-0-88776-990-0 pa

Twelve-year old Ambrose is "home-schooled. Alone in the evenings when [his mother] Irene goes to work, Ambrose pesters Cosmo, the twenty-five-year-old son of the Greek landlords who live upstairs. Cosmo has just been released from jail for breaking and entering to support a drug habit. Quite by accident, Ambrose discovers that they share a love of Scrabble and coerces Cosmo into taking him to the West Side Scrabble Club, where Cosmo falls for Amanda, the club director. . . . Cosmo, Amanda, and Ambrose soon form an unlikely alliance and, for the first time in his life, Ambrose blossoms." (Publisher's note) "Grades six to nine." (Bull Cent Child Books)

"Twelve-year-old Ambrose Bukowski and his widowed, overprotective mother . . . move frequently. When he almost dies after he bites into a peanut that bullies put in his sandwich, just to see if he is really allergic, Irene . . . decides to homeschool him. . . . Ambrose gets to know 25-year-old-Cosmo, recently released from jail and the son of the Bukowskis' . . . landlords. . . . Ambrose . . . talks Cosmo into taking him to a Scrabble Club. . . . This is a tender, often funny story with some really interesting characters. It will appeal to word nerds, but even more to anyone who has ever longed for acceptance or had to fight unreasonable parental restrictions." SLJ

Nilsson, Ulf

A **Case** in Any Case; by Ulf Nilsson, illustrated by Gitte Spee. Gecko Press 2017 108 p. color illustrations (Detective Gordon) $16.99
Grades: 1 2 3 4 **Fic**
1. Detectives -- Fiction 2. Mystery fiction
ISBN 1776571088; 9781776571086

In this book, by Ulf Nilsson, illustrated by Gitte Spee, "Gordon is on vacation, and Buffy is the sole detective at the small police station in the forest. It is not easy for a police officer to be alone. Especially when there are strange noises outside the station at night. Buffy decides to seek out Gordon in his little cottage by the lake to ask for help. After all, two police think twice as well as one. Two police are twice as brave!" (Publisher's note)

Detective Gordon; The First Case. by Ulf Nilsson (Author), Gitte Spee (illustrator) Lerner Pub Group 2015 96 p. (hardcover) $16.99
Grades: 1 2 3 4 **Fic**
1. Toads -- Fiction 2. Mystery fiction
ISBN 1927271495; 9781927271506; 9781927271490

In this illustrated children's story, by Ulf Nilsson and illustrated by Gitte Spee, "someone's stealing nuts from the forest, and it's up to Detective Gordon to catch the thief! Unfortunately, solving this crime means standing in the snow and waiting for a long time. . . . If only he had an assistant--someone small, fast, and clever--to help solve this terrible case." (Publisher's note)

Nimmo, Jenny

Charlie Bone and the Red Knight. Orchard Books 2010 467p (Children of the Red King) $12.99
Grades: 5 6 7 8 **Fic**
1. School stories 2. Magic -- Fiction 3. Great Britain -- Fiction
ISBN 978-0-439-84672-1; 0-439-84672-2
LC 2009019628

Charlie and the Children of the Red King must call upon all of their strength to defeat the darkness and finally learn the fate of Charlie's family, the evil intentions of the Bloors, what has become of Septimus Bloor's will, and the destiny of the Red King's heirs.

Charlie Bone and the shadow; [by] Jenny Nimmo. 1st Scholastic ed.; Orchard Books 2008 429p $12.99
Grades: 5 6 7 8 **Fic**
1. School stories 2. Magic -- Fiction 3. Castles -- Fiction 4.

Orphans -- Fiction 5. Great Britain -- Fiction
ISBN 978-0-439-84669-1; 0-439-84669-2

LC 2008017739

Magically-gifted Charlie Bone, accompanied by his best friend's
dog, Runner Bean, comes to the rescue when the enchanter Count Har-
ken takes revenge on the Red King's heirs by kidnapping and imprisoning Charlie's ancestors in the dark, forbidding land of Badlock.

Charlie Bone and the time twister. Orchard Books 2003 402p
(Children of the Red King) $10.99
Grades: 5 6 7 8   Fic
    1. School stories 2. Magic -- Fiction 3. Great Britain -- Fiction
ISBN 0-439-49687-X; 978-0-439-49687-2

While at Bloor's Academy, Charlie Bone gets a surprise when
Henry Yewbeam arrives from the year 1916 and needs Charlie's help
to stay alive.

"Through unique characters who stand apart from inimitable comparisons to counterparts in Harry Potter books, Nimmo skillfully creates
an exemplary series that stands on its own." Voice Youth Advocates

Leopards' gold; Jenny Nimmo. Scholastic Press 2013 336 p.
(Chronicles of the Red King) (jacketed hardcover) $16.99
Grades: 4 5 6   Fic
    1. Magic -- Fiction 2. Castles -- Fiction 3. Kings and rulers --
Fiction 4. Brothers and sisters
ISBN 0545251850; 9780545251853

LC 2012043508

This book, by Jenny Nimmo, is the "final installment in the . . . Red
King series. . . . we now meet King Timoken's children, who, with their
own magical endowments, stand divided between the forces of good and
bad. Young Petrello and Tolomeo must fight to protect their siblings and
their kingdom as an evil force invades the once-peaceful Red Castle."
(Publisher's note)

Midnight for Charlie Bone. Orchard Bks. 2003 401p (Children
of the Red King) $12.99
Grades: 5 6 7 8   Fic
    1. School stories 2. Magic -- Fiction 3. Great Britain -- Fiction
ISBN 978-0-439-47429-0; 0-439-47429-9

LC 2002-30738

First published 2002 in the United Kingdom
Charlie Bone's life with his widowed mother and two grandmothers
undergoes a dramatic change when he discovers that he can hear people
in photographs talking.

"This marvelous fantasy is able to stand on its own despite inevitable
comparisons to the students of Hogwarts." Voice Youth Advocates

Other titles in this series are:
Charlie Bone and the time twister (2003)
Charlie Bone and the invisible boy (2004)
Charlie Bone and the castle of mirrors (2005)
Charlie Bone and the hidden king (2006)
Charlie Bone and the beast (2007)
Charlie Bone and the shadow (2008)
Charlie Bone and the Red Knight (2010)

The secret kingdom. Scholastic Press 2011 207p (Chronicles of
the red king) $16.99
Grades: 4 5 6   Fic
    1. Magic -- Fiction 2. Camels -- Fiction 3. Siblings -- Fiction 4.
Voyages and travels -- Fiction
ISBN 978-0-439-84673-8; 0-439-84673-0

LC 2010035710

Timoken and his sister, Zobayda, under the protection of a forest jin-
ni but pursued by evil virideed, straddle the world of men and the world

of enchantments, seeking a home while remaining young by drinking a
potion called Alixir.

"The narrative voice is direct and matter-of-fact, conveying the fantastic as well as the mundane facts of Timoken's incredible life accessibly; new readers will have no difficulty making this an introduction to
Nimmo's work. . . . Timoken is a highly appealing young hero, and his
panoply of human and magical friends provide just the right amount of
help without stealing the show." Publ Wkly

★ The **snow** spider; [by] Jenny Nimmo. Orchard Books 2006
146p (Magician trilogy) $9.99
Grades: 4 5 6 7   Fic
    1. Magic -- Fiction 2. Wales -- Fiction 3. Father-son relationship
-- Fiction
ISBN 978-0-439-84675-2; 0-439-84675-7

LC 2006009445

A reissue of the title first published 1987 by Dutton
Gifts from Gwyn's grandmother on his ninth birthday open up a
whole new world to him, as he discovers he has magical powers that
help him heal the breach with his father that has existed ever since his
sister's mysterious disappearance four years before

"The narration is paced well and builds in excitement along with
the tale." SLJ

Other titles in this series are:
Emlyn's moon (2007)
Chestnut solider (2007)

Nix, Garth, 1963-
    Troubletwisters; [by] Garth Nix and Sean Williams. Scholastic
Press 2011 293p $16.99
Grades: 5 6 7 8   Fic
    1. Fantasy fiction 2. Magic -- Fiction 3. Twins -- Fiction 4.
Siblings -- Fiction 5. Grandmothers -- Fiction
ISBN 978-0-545-25897-5; 0-545-25897-9

LC 2011015765

When their house mysteriously explodes and they are sent to live
with an unknown relative named Grandma X, twelve-year-old twins
Jaide and Jack Shield learn that they are troubletwisters, young Wardens
just coming into their powers, who must protect humanity from The Evil
trying to break into Earth's dimension.

"Full of adventure and the unexpected, . . . [this] is delightfully twisted. The pacing is perfect, the setting is eerily dark, the faceless Evil rings
true, and the resolution is satisfying." Booklist

Noe, Katherine Schlick
    Something to hold. Clarion 2011 $16.99
Grades: 4 5 6   Fic
    1. School stories 2. Oregon -- Fiction 3. Prejudices -- Fiction 4.
Native Americans -- Fiction
ISBN 978-0-547-55813-4; 0-547-55813-9

This book follows 'Kitty,' [who] is so used to moving with each of
her father's job reassignments that making friends in each new location is usually not much of an issue. The Warm Springs Reservation in
central Oregon is, however, a new experience, since she and her brothers
are among the handful of white students in their new school. The brothers easily bond with Wasco, Warm Springs, and Paiute boys through
common enthusiasm for baseball, but Kitty is intimidated by a pair of
her classmates—dour, bullying Raymond and his snappish, aloof sister
Jewel. . . . Raymond and Jewel are often at the mercy of their abusive
white stepfather, and . . . the reservation police and their municipal police are so gridlocked by jurisdictional mandates and prejudice that the
children feel they have no legal recourse. . . Kitty's gradual involvement
with Raymond and Jewel forms the backbone of the novel. (Bulletin of
the Center for Children's Books).

"Kitty Schlick is apprehensive about starting sixth grade on Oregon's Warm Springs Indian Reservation, home to Paiute, Warm Springs and Wasco people, where her father's job has taken the family in 1962. . . . One of the school's few white students, she feels isolated until she's befriended by Pinky, a Wasco classmate whose mother, like Kitty's dad, staffs a fire lookout. As Kitty finds her footing, she's troubled by the preferential treatment teachers give white students and the casual racism of the white girls attending her church. . . . Noe . . . resists didacticism. Kitty's discoveries and ethical dilemmas are age and era-appropriate, the characters affectionately portrayed, rounded individuals." Kirkus

Noel, Alyson

Dreamland; a novel. Square Fish 2011 210p

Grades: 5 6 7 8   Fic

1. Ghost stories 2. Dreams -- Fiction
ISBN 9780312563752

LC 2011024183

Sequel to: Shimmer (2011)

Eager to contact her sister Ever, ghost Riley goes in search of the place where dreams are made, where she finds a renegade ghost boy who has been flouting the rules of Dreamland for decades.

Radiance. Square Fish 2010 183p pa $7.99

Grades: 5 6 7 8   Fic

1. Ghost stories 2. Dead -- Fiction 3. Future life -- Fiction
ISBN 978-0-312-62917-5; 0-312-62917-6

LC 2010015840

After crossing the bridge into the afterlife, a place called Here where the time is always Now, Riley's existence continues in much the same way as when she was alive until she is given the job of Soul Catcher and, together with her teacher Bodhi, returns to earth for her first assignment, a ghost called the Radiant Boy who has been haunting an English castle for centuries and resisted all previous attempts to get him across the bridge.

"Narrating in a contemporary voice with an honest and comfortable cadence, Riley is imperfect, but always likable. . . . In the midst of this wildly fanciful setting, Noël is able to capture with nail-on-the-head accuracy common worries and concerns of today's tweens." SLJ

Other titles in this series are:
Dreamland (2011)
Simmer (2011)

Shimmer; a novel. Square Fish 2011 196p pa $7.99

Grades: 5 6 7 8   Fic

1. Ghost stories 2. Dead -- Fiction 3. Slavery -- Fiction 4. Future life -- Fiction
ISBN 978-0-312-64825-1; 0-312-64825-1

LC 2010048534

Sequel to: Radiance (2010)

Riley, dead at age twelve and now a Soul Catcher, works with her teacher Bodhi to help Rebecca, the daughter of a former plantation owner who, furious about being murdered during a 1733 slave revolt, is keeping those who died with her from crossing over.

"The author's sharp contemporary wit in concert with her fascinating fantasy setting and important historical connections will draw readers through this enjoyable novel." SLJ

Followed by: Dreamland (2011)

Nolan, Lucy A.

★ **On** the road; by Lucy Nolan; illustrated by Mike Reed. Marshall Cavendish 2005 54p il (Down Girl and Sit) $14.95

Grades: 1 2 3   Fic

1. Dogs -- Fiction
ISBN 0-7614-5234-6; 978-0-7614-5234-8

LC 2004-27511

A dog who thinks her name is Down Girl goes on a car ride to the beach, goes camping in the woods, and reluctantly pays a visit to the vet with her master, Rruff.

"Narrated from a dog's point of view, this easy chapter book covers the hilarious antics of two canine friends. . . . A small black-and-white illustration appears on almost every page, supporting the text's humor." SLJ

Other titles in this series are:
Smarter than squirrels (2005)
Bad to the bone (2008)
Home on the range (2010)

Nolen, Jerdine

Calico Girl; Jerdine Nolen. Simon & Schuster Books for Young Readers 2017 192 p. (ebook) $15.99; (hardcover) $16.99

Grades: 4 5 6   Fic

1. Slavery -- Fiction 2. Race relations -- Fiction 3. African Americans -- Fiction 4. Family life -- Virginia -- Fiction 5. Virginia -- History -- 1775-1865 -- Fiction 6. United States -- History -- Civil War, 1861-1865 -- Fiction
ISBN 9781481459839; 9781481459815

LC 2016020651

In this book, by Jerdine Nolen, "Callie Wilcomb and her family are slaves, and the Civil War gives them hope that freedom may be on the horizon. . . . In Virginia, a window was opened where the laws of the land no longer applied. Because of the Contraband Law, slaves no longer had to be returned to their owners, granting them a measure of protection and safety. . . . Callie is eager to learn and become educated and hopes to teach others one day." (Publisher's note)

"At once heartbreaking and uplifting, a gentle, lyrical story of a determined black girl's journey toward freedom during the Civil War." Kirkus

Eliza's freedom road; an Underground Railroad diary. Simon & Schuster Books for Young Readers 2011 139p il map $14.99

Grades: 4 5 6 7   Fic

1. Diaries -- Fiction 2. Slavery -- Fiction 3. African Americans -- Fiction 4. Underground railroad -- Fiction
ISBN 1-4169-5814-2; 978-1-4169-5814-7

LC 2010-20931

A twelve-year-old slave girl begins writing in a journal where she documents her journey via the Underground Railroad from Alexandria, Virginia, to freedom in St. Catharines, Canada.

"Nolen reveals some of the traumas and tragedies of slavery but keeps her focus on those things that allow Eliza the power to escape: literacy, her mother's legacy, a bit of luck and a great deal of courage." Kirkus

Includes bibliographical references

Norcliffe, James

The **boy** who could fly. Egmont USA 2010 312p $15.99

Grades: 5 6 7 8   Fic

1. Fantasy fiction 2. Flight -- Fiction 3. Siblings -- Fiction 4. Abandoned children -- Fiction
ISBN 978-1-60684-084-9; 1-60684-084-3

LC 2009-41167

First published 2009 in New Zealand with title: The loblolly boy

Having grown up in a miserable home for abandoned children, a young boy jumps at the chance to exchange places with the mysterious, flying "loblolly boy," but once he takes on this new identity, he discovers what a harsh price he must pay.

"Norcliffe has written an imaginative and richly atmospheric fantasy with sympathetic characters. . . . This is . . . a haunting tale that will capture most readers' imaginations." Booklist

Northrop, Michael

Plunked; Michael Northrop. Scholastic Press 2012 247 p. (jacketed hardcover) $16.99

Grades: 4 5 6 7 8   **Fic**

1. Fear -- Fiction 2. Ethics -- Fiction 3. Baseball -- Fiction 4. Perseverance (Ethics) -- Fiction

ISBN 0545297141; 9780545297141

LC 2011032737

This children's story by Michael Northrop centers on the "Sixth grader Jack Mogens [who] has it all figured out: He's got his batting routine down, and his outfielding earns him a starting spot alongside his best friend Andy on their Little League team, the Tall Pines Braves. He even manages to have a not-totally-embarrassing conversation with Katie, the team's killer shortstop. But in the first game of the season, a powerful stray pitch brings everything Jack's worked so hard for crashing down around his ears. . . ." Jack then has to face his fears and anxieties and return to the game. (Publisher's note)

Noyce, Pendred

Lost in Lexicon; an adventure in words and numbers. by Pendred Noyce; illustrations by Joan Charles. Scarletta Press 2011 il

Grades: 5 6 7 8   **Fic**

1. Fantasy fiction 2. Cousins -- Fiction 3. Mathematics -- Fiction 4. English language -- Fiction

ISBN 9780983021926 pa; 0983021929 pa; 9780983021933 e-book; 0983021937 e-book

LC 2011013583

When Aunt Adelaide sends thirteen-year-old cousins Ivan and Daphne on a treasure hunt in the rain, they never expect to stumble into a whole new world where words and numbers run wild.

Nye, Naomi Shihab, 1952-

The **turtle** of Oman; a novel. by Naomi Shihab Nye. Greenwillow Books, an imprint of HarperCollinsPublishers 2014 320 p. illustrations (hardback) $16.99

Grades: 4 5 6   **Fic**

1. Oman 2. Moving -- Fiction 3. Immigrants -- Fiction 4. Oman -- Fiction 5. Grandfathers -- Fiction 6. Moving, Household -- Fiction 7. Emigration and immigration -- Fiction

ISBN 0062019724; 9780062019721

LC 2014018263

Written by Naomi Shihab Nye, this middle grades novel "explores themes of moving, family, nature, and immigration. It tells the story of Aref Al-Amri, who must say good-bye to everything and everyone he loves in his hometown of Muscat, Oman, as his family prepares to move to Ann Arbor, Michigan. . . . His mother is desperate for him to pack his suitcase, but he refuses. . . . But rather than pack, Aref and Siddi go on a series of adventures." (Publisher's note)

"In the last week before his family leaves Oman for a three-year stint in Michigan, Aref has a hard time saying good-bye to his beloved home, particularly his grandfather, Sidi. Readers are never told Aref's exact age; he is clearly articulate, yet excerpts from his notebook show his writing has not transitioned to cursive...The omniscient narration thus brings a larger context than Aref alone could share. Simply told, yet richly rewarding." SLJ

Nylund, Eric S.

The **Resisters**; [by] Eric Nylund. Random House 2011 210p $16.99; lib bdg $19.99

Grades: 5 6 7 8   **Fic**

1. Science fiction 2. Brainwashing -- Fiction 3. Extraterrestrial beings -- Fiction

ISBN 978-0-375-86856-6; 0-375-86856-9; 978-0-375-96856-3 lib bdg; 0-375-96856-3 lib bdg

LC 2010-19230

When twelve-year-olds Madison and Felix kidnap him, Ethan learns that the Earth has been taken over by aliens and that all the adults in the world are under mind control.

"Ethan, Felix, and Madison are multidimensional characters with authentic emotions and realistic attitudes and motives. This book mixes considerable background exposition with fast-moving action. While the immediate plot issues are resolved, there are plenty of threads left dangling. Middle school boys will enjoy the high-tech battle action and will look forward to the next installment." SLJ

O'Brien, Annemarie

Lara's gift; by Annemarie O'Brien. Alfred A. Knopf 2013 176 p. (hardcover) $16.99; (ebook) $50.97; (library binding) 19.99

Grades: 5 6 7 8 9   **Fic**

1. Historical fiction 2. Dogs -- Breeding 3. Dogs -- Fiction 4. Borzoi -- Fiction 5. Visions -- Fiction 6. Sex role -- Fiction 7. Family life -- Russia -- Fiction 8. Fathers and daughters -- Fiction 9. Russia -- History -- 1904-1914 -- Fiction

ISBN 0307931749; 9780307931740; 9780307975485; 9780375971051

LC 2012034070

In this book, on "a remote estate in 1910s Russia, Lara must prove herself capable of following in her father's footsteps as the head of a prestigious borzoi breeding kennel. There are so many things between her and the realization of her dream. That she is female is the biggest obstacle, but she must also hide the fact that she has visions of future occurrences that involve the dogs and the dangerous wolves that populate the estate." (Kirkus Reviews)

O'Brien, Robert C.

★ **Mrs.** Frisby and the rats of NIMH; [by] Robert C. O'Brien; illustrated by Zena Bernstein. Atheneum Books for Young Readers 2006 233p il $18; pa $6.99

Grades: 4 5 6 7   **Fic**

1. Mice -- Fiction 2. Rats -- Fiction

ISBN 978-0-689-20651-1; 0-689-20651-8; 978-0-689-71068-1 pa; 0-689-71068-2 pa

A reissue of the title first published 1971

Awarded the Newbery Medal, 1972

Having no one to help her with her problems, a widowed mouse visits the rats whose former imprisonment in a laboratory made them wise and long lived.

"The story is fresh and ingenious, the style witty, and the plot both hilarious and convincing." Saturday Rev

O'Connor, Barbara

★ **Fame** and glory in Freedom, Georgia. Farrar, Straus & Giroux 2003 104p $16; pa $6.95

Grades: 4 5 6 7   **Fic**

1. School stories 2. Contests -- Fiction

ISBN 0-374-32258-9; 0-374-40018-0 pa

LC 2002-190212

Unpopular sixth-grader Burdette Bird Weaver persuades the new boy at school, whom everyone thinks is mean and dumb, to be her partner for a spelling bee that might win her everything she's ever wanted

"An idiosyncratic group of characters play out this touching and well-paced story about friendship, family, and connection." Horn Books

★ The **fantastic** secret of Owen Jester. Farrar Straus Giroux 2010 168p $15.99

Grades: 3 4 5   **Fic**
1. Adventure fiction 2. Frogs -- Fiction 3. Georgia -- Fiction 4. Family life -- Fiction 5. Submersibles -- Fiction
ISBN 978-0-374-36850-0; 0-374-36850-3

After Owen captures an enormous bullfrog, names it Tooley Graham, then has to release it, he and two friends try to use a small submarine that fell from a passing train to search for Tooley in the Carter, Georgia, pond it came from, while avoiding nosy neighbor Viola.

"O'Connor has spun a lovely read that perfectly captures the schemes and plans of school-age kids in the long days of summer." Kirkus

★ **How** to steal a dog; a novel. Farrar, Straus & Giroux 2007 170p pa $6.99; $16

Grades: 4 5 6   **Fic**
1. Dogs -- Fiction 2. Siblings -- Fiction 3. Homeless persons -- Fiction
ISBN 0-312-56112-1 pa; 0-374-33497-8; 978-0-312-56112-3 pa; 978-0-374-33497-0

LC 2005-40166

Living in the family car in their small North Carolina town, Georgina persuades her younger brother to help her in an elaborate scheme to get money by stealing a dog and then claiming the reward that the owners are bound to offer

This is told "in stripped-down, unsentimental prose. . . . The myriad effects of homelessness and the realistic picture of a moral quandary will surely generate discussion." Booklist

On the road to Mr. Mineo's; Barbara O'Connor. Frances Foster Books 2012 181 p. (hardcover) $16.99

Grades: 5 6   **Fic**
1. Pigeons -- Fiction 2. Homing pigeons -- Fiction 3. South Carolina -- Fiction
ISBN 0374380023; 9780374380021

LC 2011049679

In this novel by Barbara O'Conner, "Sherman the one-legged pigeon flies into . . . Meadville, South Carolina . . . and causes a ruckus. First Stella, who's been begging for a dog, spots him on top of a garage roof and decides she wants him for a pet. Then there's Ethel and Amos, an old couple who sees the pigeon in their barn keeping company with a little brown dog that barks all night. Meanwhile, across town, Mr. Mineo has one less homing pigeon than he used to." (Publisher's note)

★ The **small** adventure of Popeye and Elvis. Frances Foster Books 2009 149p $16.99

Grades: 3 4 5 6   **Fic**
1. Adventure fiction 2. Dogs -- Fiction 3. Friendship -- Fiction 4. Grandmothers -- Fiction 5. South Carolina -- Fiction
ISBN 978-0-374-37055-8; 0-374-37055-9

LC 2008-24145

In Fayette, South Carolina, the highlight of Popeye's summer is learning vocabulary words with his grandmother until a motor home gets stuck nearby and Elvis, the oldest boy living inside, joins Popeye in finding the source of strange boats floating down the creek.

"Elvis and Popeye's journey reminds readers to look for and enjoy the small treasures in their lives. Save a spot on your shelves for this small adventure with a grand heart." SLJ

Wish; Barbara O'Connor. Farrar, Straus & Giroux 2016 240 p. (hardback) $16.99

Grades: 4 5 6   **Fic**
1. Dogs -- Fiction 2. Conduct of life -- Fiction 3. Human-animal relationships -- Fiction
ISBN 9780374302733

LC 2015034459

In this book, by Barbara O'Connor, "eleven-year-old Charlie Reese has been making the same secret wish every day since fourth grade. . . . But when she is sent to the Blue Ridge Mountains of North Carolina to live with family she barely knows, it seems unlikely that her wish will ever come true. That is until she meets Wishbone, a skinny stray dog who captures her heart, and Howard, a neighbor boy who proves surprising in lots of ways." (Publisher's note)

"A warm, real, and heartfelt tale." Kirkus

O'Connor, Sheila

★ **Sparrow** Road. G. P. Putnam's Sons 2011 247p $16.99

Grades: 5 6 7 8   **Fic**
1. Artists -- Fiction
ISBN 978-0-399-25458-1; 0-399-25458-7

LC 2010-28290

Twelve-year-old Raine spends the summer at a mysterious artists colony and discovers a secret about her past.

This is a "beautifully written novel. . . . Readers finding themselves in this quiet world will find plenty of space to imagine and dream for themselves." Kirkus

O'Dell, Kathleen

The **aviary**. Alfred A. Knopf 2011 339p $15.99; lib bdg $18.99

Grades: 3 4 5   **Fic**
1. Birds -- Fiction 2. Magic -- Fiction 3. Maine -- Fiction 4. Friendship -- Fiction 5. Family life -- Fiction 6. Inheritance and succession -- Fiction
ISBN 978-0-375-85605-1; 0-375-85605-6; 978-0-375-95605-8 lib bdg; 0-375-95605-0 lib bdg

LC 2010045778

In late nineteenth-century Maine, isolated, eleven-year-old Clara Dooley gains a friend and uncovers a magical secret that changes her life when she learns to care for the once-feared birds in the aviary attached to the Glendoveer mansion where she lives.

"The honeycreeper's encouragement leads to discovery after discovery in a well-paced, high-tension mystery that draws not only on Burnett, but also C.S. Lewis, Zilpha Keatley Snyder, and Neil Gaiman, joining a rich heritage of stories about children with a secret 'room of their own.'" Publ Wkly

O'Dell, Scott

★ **Island** of the Blue Dolphins; illustrated by Ted Lewin. 50th anniversary ed.; Houghton Mifflin Books for Children 2010 177p il $22

Grades: 5 6 7 8   **Fic**
1. Native Americans -- Fiction 2. Wilderness survival -- Fiction 3. San Nicolas Island (Calif.) -- Fiction
ISBN 978-0-547-42483-5; 0-547-42483-3

A reissue of the newly illustrated edition published 1990; first published 1960

Awarded the Newbery Medal, 1961

Left alone on a beautiful but isolated island off the coast of California, a young Indian girl spends eighteen years, not only merely surviving through her enormous courage and self-reliance, but also finding a measure of happiness in her solitary life.

The edition illustrated by Ted Lewin "features twelve full-page, full-color watercolors in purple and blue hues that are appropriate to the island setting. This handsome gift-edition version includes a new introduction by Lois Lowry to commemorate the book's fiftieth anniversary." Horn Book Guide

Sing down the moon. Houghton Mifflin 1970 137p hardcover o.p. pa $6.99

Grades: 5 6 7 8   **Fic**
1. Navajo Indians -- Fiction
ISBN 0-395-10919-1; 978-0-547-40632-9 pa; 0-547-40632-0 pa
A Newbery Medal honor book, 1971

"There is a poetic sonority of style, a sense of identification, and a note of indomitable courage and stoicism that is touching and impressive." Saturday Rev

Streams to the river, river to the sea; a novel of Sacagawea. Houghton Mifflin 1986 191p hardcover o.p. pa $6.99

Grades: 5 6 7 8   **Fic**
1. Interpreters 2. Guides (Persons) 3. Native Americans -- Fiction 4. Lewis and Clark Expedition (1804-1806) -- Fiction
ISBN 0-395-40430-4; 0-618-96642-0 pa

LC 86-936

"An informative and involving choice for American history students and pioneer-adventure readers." Bull Cent Child Books

Obed, Ellen Bryan

★ **Twelve** kinds of ice; by Ellen Bryan Obed; illustrated by Barbara McClintock. Houghton Mifflin Books for Children 2012 64 p. (hardback) $16.99

Grades: 1 2 3 4   **Fic**
1. Ice -- Fiction 2. Winter -- Fiction 3. Family life -- Fiction 4. Ice skating -- Fiction
ISBN 0618891293; 9780618891290

LC 2011046417

This book presents a "memoir of [Ellen Bryan] Obed's dreamy childhood in Maine, built around the 12 kinds of ice that served as successive signposts of the advancing season." (New York Times Book Review) "This homage to rural winter celebrates the gradual freezing of barn buckets and fields, the happy heights of ice-skating season, and the inevitable spring thaw." (Publishers Weekly)

Obstfeld, Raymond

Stealing the game; Kareem Abdul-Jabbar and Raymond Obstfeld. Disney-Hyperion Books 2015 304 p. (Streetball crew) hc $16.99

Grades: 4 5 6 7   **Fic**
1. Brothers -- Fiction 2. Basketball -- Fiction 3. Schools -- Fiction 4. Middle schools -- Fiction 5. African Americans -- Fiction 6. Mystery and detective stories 7. Robbers and outlaws -- Fiction 8. Criminal investigation -- Fiction
ISBN 9781423178712; 1423178718

LC 2013046413

In this book, part of the Streetball Crew series by Kareem Abdul-Jabbar, "Jax asks Chris to recruit his best middle school teammates for a pick-up basketball game. Chris doesn't think much of it until the wrong team wins and Jax goes ballistic. It turns out that Jax bet on the game, hoping to earn enough money to repay a debt. While Chris tries to walk a thin tightrope between helping his brother and staying out of trouble, his friend Theo [tries] to learn what Jax has been up to." (Publisher's note)

"The shifting structure of the story and a clever series of blind alleys keep readers on tenterhooks. A deft, understated sports thriller with a solid moral compass." Kirkus

Odyssey, Shawn Thomas

The **Wizard** of Dark Street; an Oona Crate mystery. Egmont USA 2011 352p $16.99

Grades: 5 6 7   **Fic**
1. Mystery fiction 2. Magic -- Fiction 3. Uncles -- Fiction 4. Orphans -- Fiction 5. Witchcraft -- Fiction 6. Apprentices -- Fiction
ISBN 978-1-60684-143-3; 1-60684-143-2

LC 2011-02496

In 1877, in an enchantment shop on the last of the Faerie roads linking New York City to the Land of the Fey, just after twelve-year-old Oona opts to relinquish her apprenticeship to her uncle, the Wizard, and become a detective, her uncle is stabbed, testing her skills.

"Upbeat in tone, this delight is an excellent blend of fantasy and mystery with a variety of suspicious characters and enough red herrings to keep the reader guessing all the way to the end." Booklist

Oertel, Andreas

The **Archaeolojesters**. Lobster Press 2010 192p pa $10.95

Grades: 4 5 6   **Fic**
1. Antiquities -- Fiction
ISBN 978-1-897550-83-0 pa

There is a drought in Sultana, Manitoba, and "life is getting more dismal by the minute. . . . There aren't even enough tourists to keep the local restaurant busy, and if Cody's best friend's mom loses her job there, the family will have to move away. . . . [Then] Cody, his best friend Eric, and Eric's twin sister, Rachel, concoct an elaborate hoax. . . . An "ancient Egyptian" tablet is discovered in Sultana, and suddenly archaeologists, reporters, and tourists are rushing over. . . . The kids are convinced that their plan has succeeded ... until one suspicious stranger starts trailing every move that Cody and his friends make." (Publisher's note) "Ages nine to twelve." (Quill Quire)

Followed by: Pillars of time (2010)

Okimoto, Jean Davies

Maya and the cotton candy boy. Endicott and Hugh 2011 $16.99; pa $9.99

Grades: 4 5 6 7   **Fic**
1. School stories 2. Siblings -- Fiction 3. Immigrants -- Fiction
ISBN 978-0-9823167-4-0; 0-9823167-4-7; 978-0-9823167-5-7 pa; 0-9823167-5-5 pa

Newly arrived from Kazakhstan, twelve-year-old Maya Alazova resents the way her mother babies her brother, but when she leaves her English Language Learner program for mainstream classes and has to deal with a boy, a bully, and conflict at home, she finds her brother can help with their new culture in ways their parents can't.

"Maya tells her story well, and observant readers will come away with a better understanding of the sacrifices made by similar families." SLJ

Oliver, Lauren

★ **Liesl** & Po; illustrated by Kei Acedera. Harper 2011 307p il $16.99

Grades: 4 5 6 7   **Fic**
1. Ghost stories 2. Fantasy fiction 3. Magic -- Fiction 4. Bereavement -- Fiction
ISBN 978-0-06-201451-1; 0-06-201451-X

Liesl lives in a tiny attic bedroom, locked away by her cruel stepmother. Her only friends are the shadows and the mice—until one night a ghost appears from the darkness. It is Po, who comes from the Other Side. That same night, an alchemist's apprentice, Will, accidentally bungles an important delivery. He switches a box containing the most powerful magic in the world with one containing something decidedly less remarkable.

This is a "charming, insightful fantasy. . . . This original fairy tale, told by a wise and humorous omniscient narrator and peopled with broadly drawn but instantly recognizable characters, avoids sentimentality to show the magic of accepting loss without letting go and finding joy in the lives left behind." Booklist

★ The **spindlers**; Lauren Oliver; illustrated by Iacopo Bruno. 1st ed. Harper 2012 246 p. ill. (hardcover) $16.99

Grades: 4 5 6   **Fic**

1. Monsters -- Fiction 2. Fantasy 3. Brothers and sisters -- Fiction

ISBN 0061978086; 9780061978081

LC 2012009698

This children's fantasy novel, by Lauren Oliver, is about a young girl who travels to a fantasy realm to rescue her younger brother from monsters. "When Liza's brother, Patrick, changes overnight, Liza knows exactly what has happened: The spindlers have gotten to him and stolen his soul. . . . To rescue Patrick, Liza must go Below, armed with little more than her wits and a broom. There, she uncovers a vast world populated with . . . terrible dangers." (Publisher's note)

Oppel, Kenneth

★ The **Boundless**; Kenneth Oppel. First edition Simon & Schuster Books for Young Readers 2014 332 p. illustrations (hardcover : alk. paper) $16.99

Grades: 4 5 6 7 8   **Fic**

1. Adventure fiction 2. Circus -- Fiction 3. Railroads -- Fiction 4. Canada -- History -- Fiction 5. Railroad trains -- Fiction 6. Canada -- History -- 1867-1914 -- Fiction

ISBN 144247288X; 9781442472884; 9781442472891

LC 2013009879

In this book, by Kenneth Oppel, "The Boundless . . . is on its maiden voyage across the country, and first-class passenger Will Everett is about to embark on the adventure of his life! When Will ends up in possession of the key to a train car containing priceless treasures, he becomes the target of sinister figures from his past. In order to survive, Will must join a traveling circus, enlisting the aid of Mr. Dorian, the ringmaster and leader of the troupe." (Publisher's note)

"Will's father is driving the Boundless, the longest train ever, on her maiden voyage. After a series of adventures (involving a sasquatch and a murder), Will finds himself stranded in the caboose, where, with the help of a cute tightrope walker, he dodges a nefarious villain. The third-person present-tense narrative creates suspense as the well-drawn characters travel through an alternate-universe Canadian wilderness." Horn Book)

★ The **nest**; by Kenneth Oppel; illustrated by Jon Klassen. Simon & Schuster Books for Young Readers 2015 256 p. illustrations (hardcover) $16.99

Grades: 4 5 6 7   **Fic**

1. Wasps -- Fiction 2. Brothers -- Fiction 3. Babies -- Fiction 4. Supernatural -- Fiction 5. Horror stories -- Fiction

ISBN 148143232X; 9781481432320; 9781481432337

LC 2014038101

In this juvenile novel, by Kenneth Oppel, "Steve, an older brother struggling with anxiety and his family's distress after his newborn brother, Theodore, is diagnosed with a rare congenital disorder. After a curious gray and white wasp from the hive above their house stings Steve, he develops the ability to speak to the hive's queen, who promises to replace the ailing baby with a new one." (Publishers Weekly)

"Klassen's eerie, atmospheric illustrations, all shadowy corners and half-concealed shapes, contribute to the spooky mood. With subtle, spine-chilling horror at its heart, this tale of triumph over monsters--both outside and in--is outstanding."

Silverwing. Simon & Schuster Bks. for Young Readers 1997 217p hardcover o.p. pa $6.99

Grades: 5 6 7 8   **Fic**

1. Bats -- Fiction

ISBN 0-689-81529-8; 1-4169-4998-4 pa

LC 97-10977

When a newborn bat named Shade but sometimes called "Runt" becomes separated from his colony during migration, he grows in ways that prepare him for even greater journeys

"Oppel's bats are fully developed characters who, if not quite cuddly, will certainly earn readers' sympathy and respect. In Silverwing the author has created an intriguing microcosm of rival species, factions, and religions." Horn Book

Other titles in this series are:

Sunwing (2000)

Firewing (2003)

Darkwing (2007)

Orlev, Uri

The **man** from the other side; translated from the Hebrew by Hillel Halkin. Puffin Books 1995 186p pa $6.99

Grades: 5 6 7 8   **Fic**

1. Jews -- Poland -- Fiction 2. Holocaust, 1933-1945 -- Fiction 3. World War, 1939-1945 -- Fiction

ISBN 0-14-037088-9; 978-0-14-037088-1

LC 94-30189

Living on the outskirts of the Warsaw Ghetto during World War II, fourteen-year-old Marek and his grandparents shelter a Jewish man in the days before the Jewish uprising

"This is a story of individual bravery and national shame that highlights just how hopeless was the fate of the Warsaw Jews as they fought alone and heroically against the Nazi war machine." SLJ

★ The **song** of the whales; translated by Hillel Halkin. Houghton Mifflin Books for Children 2010 108p $16

Grades: 5 6 7 8   **Fic**

1. Jews -- Fiction 2. Dreams -- Fiction 3. Israel -- Fiction 4. Old age -- Fiction 5. Jerusalem -- Fiction 6. Family life -- Fiction 7. Grandfathers -- Fiction

ISBN 978-0-547-25752-5; 0-547-25752-X

LC 2009-49720

At age eight, Mikha'el knows he is different from other boys, but over the course of three years as he helps his parents care for his elderly grandfather in Jerusalem, Grandpa teaches Mikha'el to use the gift they share of making other people's dreams sweeter.

This is "the sort of story that operates on many different levels. . . . With a clean sense that less is more, Orlev has crafted a sweetly mysterious and quietly moving read." Booklist

Orr, Wendy

Lost! A dog called Bear; illustrations by Susan Boase. Henry Holt 2011 103p il (Rainbow Street Shelter) $15.99

Grades: 2 3 4   **Fic**

1. Dogs -- Fiction 2. Moving -- Fiction 3. Divorce -- Fiction 4. Lost and found possessions -- Fiction

ISBN 978-0-8050-8931-8; 0-8050-8931-4

LC 2010029886

When Logan's dog runs away as he and his mother are moving to a new home after his parents separate, a girl named Hannah, who longs for a dog of her own, finds him.

"The book is well designed for readers moving up to chapter books, with its short sentences, well-spaced lines of type, and attractive illustrations. Expressing emotions through subtle physical cues, Boase's shaded pencil drawings depict both people and dogs with grace and sensitivity." Booklist

Missing! A cat called Buster; illustrations by Susan Boase. Henry Holt and Company 2011 116p il (Rainbow Street Shelter) $15.99; pa $5.99

Grades: 2 3 4 **Fic**

1. Cats -- Fiction 2. Pets -- Fiction 3. Loss (Psychology) -- Fiction 4. Lost and found possessions -- Fiction

ISBN 978-0-8050-8932-5; 0-8050-8932-2; 978-0-8050-9382-7 pa; 0-8050-9382-6 pa

LC 2010044786

After his pet rabbit dies, Josh feels sad and does not want to own another pet until an elderly neighbor's cat goes missing.

"This effort sympathetically, if briefly, deals with some complex issues, including the responsibilities of pet ownership, death and aging, but always within the framework of an optimistic, childlike perspective appropriate for the target audience. . . . Attractive black-and-white full and half-page sketches, one or two per chapter, offer some visual interest as well. This early chapter book with plenty of heart and a bit of suspense will appeal to young pet lovers." Kirkus

Mokie & Bik; [by] Wendy Orr; illustrations by Jonathan Bean. Henry Holt 2007 72p il $15.95

Grades: 2 3 4 **Fic**

1. Twins -- Fiction 2. Siblings -- Fiction 3. Boats and boating -- Fiction

ISBN 978-0-8050-7979-1; 0-8050-7979-3

LC 2006011150

For two rambunctious twins, living on a boat means always being underfoot or overboard

"Orr's colorful use of language brings energy to the story. The many crosshatch drawings . . . are often graceful and always appealing." Booklist

Another title about Mokie & Bik is:

Mokie & Bik go to sea (2008)

Mokie & Bik go to sea; illustrations by Jonathan Bean. Henry Holt and Company 2010 75p il $16.95

Grades: 2 3 4 **Fic**

1. Twins -- Fiction 2. Siblings -- Fiction 3. Boats and boating -- Fiction

ISBN 978-0-8050-8174-9; 0-8050-8174-7

LC 2007027590

With their father home from the sea, the rambunctious twins Mokie and Bik make the Bullfrog shipshape for a voyage out to sea, where they make friends with a scaredy-seal, save a runaway boat, and keep track of Waggles.

"Written in a whimsical style that borders on poetry. . . . Frequent black-and-white illustrations add to the zaniness of the fast-paced story." SLJ

Oswald, Nancy

Nothing here but stones; a Jewish pioneer story. [by] Nancy Oswald. Henry Holt 2004 215p $16.95

Grades: 5 6 7 8 **Fic**

1. Jews -- Fiction 2. Colorado -- Fiction 3. Immigrants -- Fiction 4. Frontier and pioneer life -- Fiction

ISBN 0-8050-7465-1

LC 2003-56969

In 1882, ten-year-old Emma and her family, along with other Russian Jewish immigrants, arrive in Cotopaxi, Colorado, where they face inhospitable conditions as they attempt to start an agricultural colony, and lonely Emma is comforted by the horse whose life she saved

"This well-paced, vivid account should capture readers' attention." SLJ

Oz, Amos, 1939-

★ **Suddenly** in the depths of the forest; translated from the Hebrew by Sondra Silverston. Harcourt 2011 134p $15.99

Grades: 4 5 6 7 **Fic**

1. Fables 2. Animals -- Fiction

ISBN 978-0-547-55153-1; 0-547-55153-3

LC 2011-08664

In a gray and gloomy village, all of the animals—from dogs and cats to fish and snails—disappeared years before. No one talks about it and no one knows why, though everyone agrees that the village has been cursed. But when two children see a fish—a tiny one and just for a second—they become determined to unravel the mystery of where the animals have gone.

"In this swiftly moving fable . . . Oz creates palpable tension with a repetitive, almost hypnotic rhythm and lyrical language that twists a discussion-provoking morality tale into something much more enchanting." Booklist

Pakkala, Christine

Last-but-not-least Lola and the wild chicken; Christine Pakkala. Boyds Mills Press 2014 216 p. illustrations (Last-but-not-least Lola) (reinforced) $15.95

Grades: 2 3 4 5 **Fic**

1. Chickens -- Fiction 2. Friendship -- Fiction

ISBN 9781590789834; 1590789830

LC 2014935273

"Spirited, smart, and strong-willed Lola Zuckerman, who is always last but never least, returns for a second adventure. Still struggling with friendships, Lola doesn't want to share her on-again, off-again best friend Amanda with Jessie (who seems to be around all the time) and new girl Savannah." (Publisher's note)

"Pakkala perfectly captures the competitive jealousy that sparks among little girls as they claim best friends, as well as the supportive tone of a good teacher caring for well-intentioned but accident-causing pupils. Hoppe's smart cartoon spot illustrations suit the fast-paced, emotionally resonant, and sometimes silly story." Booklist

Other titles in this series are:

Going Green (2013)

Last-But-Not Least Lola and the Cupcake Queens (2015)

Last-But-Not-Least Lola and a Knot the Size of Texas (2016)

Palacio, R. J.

Auggie & me; three Wonder stories. by R.J. Palacio. Alfred A Knopf 2015 303 p. illustrations $16.99

Grades: 3 4 5 6 **Fic**

1. School stories 2. Friendship -- Fiction 3. Birth defects -- Fiction 4. Middle schools -- Fiction 5. Schools -- Fiction 6. Abnormalities, Human -- Fiction

ISBN 9781101934852; 9781101934869

LC 2015015220

This book, by R.J. Palacio, focuses on "Auggie Pullman, an ordinary boy with an extraordinary face. . . . These stories are an extra peek at Auggie before he started at Beecher Prep and during his first year there. Readers get to see him through the eyes of Julian, the bully; Christopher, Auggie's oldest friend; and Charlotte, Auggie's new friend at school." (Publisher's note)

"Julian's story is the most didactic, but it will have classroom use as an "anatomy of a bully" lesson, suggesting that readers look behind a mean-spirited act to understand what drives it. Readers also spend time with Christopher, Auggie's best friend until his family moved to Connecticut, and Charlotte, a classmate chosen to help Auggie transition from homeschooling to fifth grade. Readers who wanted more about Auggie will flock to this. Ages 8-12." Pub Wkly

Auggie and me

★ **Wonder**; by R.J. Palacio. Alfred A. Knopf 2012 315 p. (hardcover) $15.99
Grades: 3 4 5 6　　　　　　　　　　　　　　　　　　Fic
1. Middle schools 2. Interpersonal relations 3. Birth defects --
Fiction 4. Schools -- Fiction 5. Middle schools -- Fiction 6. Self-
acceptance -- Fiction 7. Abnormalities, Human -- Fiction
ISBN 9780375869020; 9780375899881; 9780375969027
LC 2011027133

In this book, "[a]fter being homeschooled for years, Auggie Pullman
is about to start fifth grade, but he's worried: How will he fit into middle-
school life when he looks so different from everyone else? Auggie has
had 27 surgeries to correct facial anomalies he was born with, but he still
has a face that has earned him such cruel nicknames as Freak, Freddy
Krueger, Gross-out and Lizard face. . . . Palacio divides the novel into
eight parts, interspersing Auggie's first-person narrative with the voices
of family members and classmates, . . . expanding the story beyond
Auggie's viewpoint and demonstrating that Auggie's arrival at school
doesn't test only him, it affects everyone in the community." (Kirkus)

Palatini, Margie
Geek Chic; the Zoey zone. Katherine Tegen Books 2008 184p
$10.99; lib bdg $14.89
Grades: 3 4 5　　　　　　　　　　　　　　　　　　Fic
1. School stories
ISBN 978-0-06-113898-0; 0-06-113898-3; 978-0-06-113899-7 lib
bdg; 0-06-113899-1 lib bdg
A contemporary Cinderella story about Zoey, 10, who desperately
needs a fairy godmother to give her a makeover and teach her about
style if she is ever going to make it into the cool crowd in the lunchroom.
"This amalgamation of graphic novel and chapter book cleverly integrates wrinkled-looking notes, varied typefaces, wacky line drawings,
and movie countdowns with straightforward prose to tell the funny if
farfetched tale." SLJ

Paley, Jane
Hooper finds a family; a Hurricane Katrina dog's survival tale.
Harper 2011 137p il $15.99
Grades: 4 5 6　　　　　　　　　　　　　　　　　　Fic
1. Dogs -- Fiction 2. New York (N.Y.) -- Fiction 3. Hurricane
Katrina, 2005 -- Fiction
ISBN 978-0-06-201103-9; 0-06-201103-0
LC 2011002088

Jimmy, a yellow Labrador puppy, is separated from his Lake Charles,
Louisiana, family and survives the horrors of Hurricane Katrina on his
own before being rescued and taken to New York City, where he tries
to fit in with a new family and the many neighborhood dogs, and accept
his new name.
"A harsh but ultimately heartwarming story about moving forward
after trauma and loss by making space for new loves ones and new possibilities." Kirkus

Paratore, Coleen
Sunny Holiday; [by] Coleen Murtagh Paratore. Scholastic Press
2009 160p $15.99; pa $5.99
Grades: 2 3 4　　　　　　　　　　　　　　　　　　Fic
1. African Americans -- Fiction 2. Mother-daughter relationship
-- Fiction
ISBN 978-0-545-07579-4; 0-545-07579-3; 978-0-545-07588-6
pa; 0-545-07588-2 pa
LC 2008009786

Spunky third-grader Sunny Holiday tries to make the best out of every situation, and even though her father is in prison, she and her mother
count their blessings and manage to find joy in every day
"Difficult situations are handled gently, but realistically. . . . The text
is not difficult and includes some fun images for abstract ideas." SLJ
Followed by: Sweet and sunny (2010)

Park, Barbara
Junie B. Jones and a little monkey business; illustrated by Denise
Brunkus. Random House 1993 68p il lib bdg $11.99; pa $4.99
Grades: 1 2 3　　　　　　　　　　　　　　　　　　Fic
1. School stories 2. Infants -- Fiction 3. Siblings -- Fiction
ISBN 0-679-93886-9 lib bdg; 0-679-838864 pa
LC 92056706

Through a misunderstanding, Junie B. thinks that her new baby
brother is really a baby monkey, and her report of this news creates excitement and trouble in her kindergarten class.

Junie B. Jones and her big fat mouth; illustrated by Denise Brunkus.
Random House 1993 69p il lib bdg $11.99; pa $4.99
Grades: 1 2 3　　　　　　　　　　　　　　　　　　Fic
1. School stories
ISBN 0-679-94407-9 lib bdg; 0-679-84407-4 pa
LC 92-50957

When her kindergarten class has Job Day, Junie B. goes through
much confusion and excitement before deciding on the "bestest" job
of all
"Brunkus' energetic drawings pick up the slapstick action and the
spunky comic hero." Booklist
Other titles about Junie B. Jones are:
Junie B., first grader: Aloha-ha-ha (2006)
Junie B., first grader (at last!) (2001)
Junie B., first grader: boo . . . and I mean it! (2003)
Junie B., first grader: boss of lunch (2002)
Junie B., first grader: cheater pants (2003)
Junie B., first grader: dumb bunny (2007)
Junie B., first grader: jingle bells, Batman smells! (p.s. so does May)
(2005)
Junie B., first grader: one-man band (2003)
Junie B., first grader: shipwrecked (2003)
Junie B., first grader: toothless wonder (2002)
Junie B. Jones and a little monkey business (1993)
Junie B. Jones and some sneaky peeky spying (1994)
Junie B. Jones and that meanie Jim's birthday (1996)
Junie B. Jones and the mushy gushy valentine (1999)
Junie B. Jones and the stupid smelly bus (1992)
Junie B. Jones and the yucky blucky fruitcake (1995)
Junie B. Jones has a monster under her bed (1997)
Junie B. Jones has a peep in her pocket (2000)
Junie B. Jones is a beauty shop guy (1998)
Junie B. Jones is a graduation girl (2001)
Junie B. Jones is a party animal (1997)
Junie B. Jones is (almost) a flower girl (1999)
Junie B. Jones is Captain Field Day (2000)
Junie B. Jones is not a crook (1997)
Junie B. Jones loves handsome Warren (1996)
Junie B. Jones smells something fishy (1998)

Junie B. Jones has a peep in her pocket; illustrated by Denise
Brunkus. Random House 2000 67p il $11.99; pa $4.99
Grades: 1 2 3　　　　　　　　　　　　　　　　　　Fic
1. School stories 2. Fear -- Fiction 3. Farms -- Fiction
ISBN 0-375-90040-3; 0-375-80040-9 pa
LC 00-29067

When Junie B. learns that her kindergarten class is going on a field trip to a farm, she worries about being attacked by a rooster

Junie B. Jones is a graduation girl; illustrated by Denise Brunkus. Random House 2001 69p il $11.95; pa $4.99
Grades: 1 2 3   **Fic**
1. School stories
ISBN 0-375-90292-9; 0-375-80292-4 pa
                                                        LC 00-45975
Junie B. Jones has just turned six and is looking forward to her kindergarten graduation, but when grape juice stains the white gown she could not resist trying on, she is afraid graduation is ruined

Junie B., first grader (at last!) illustrated by Denise Brunkus. Random House 2001 76p il $11.95; lib bdg $13.99
Grades: 1 2 3   **Fic**
1. School stories 2. Friendship -- Fiction
ISBN 0-375-80293-2; 0-375-90293-7 lib bdg
                                                    LC 2001-19076
Junie B. thinks first grade is a flop when her kindergarten friend Lucille prefers the company of twins Camille and Chenille and Junie B. needs glasses
"Just as fresh and funny as the previous books in the series." Booklist

Junie B., first grader: boo and I mean it! illustrated by Denise Brunkus. Random House 2004 86p il $11.95; lib bdg $13.99; pa $4.99
Grades: 1 2 3   **Fic**
1. Fear -- Fiction 2. Halloween -- Fiction
ISBN 978-0-375-82806-5; 978-0-375-92806-2 lib bdg; 978-0-375-82807-2 pa
                                                    LC 2004000362
With Halloween approaching, Junie B. needs to find a costume that will scare off the real witches and ghosts that she believes will be out on the holiday.

Junie B., first grader: boss of lunch; illustrated by Denise Brunkus. Random House 2002 77p il lib bdg $13.99; pa $4.99
Grades: 1 2 3   **Fic**
1. School stories
ISBN 0-375-81517-1; 0-375-91517-6 lib bdg; 0-375-80294-0 pa
                                                    LC 2001-48983
Junie, an outspoken, sometimes exasperating, first grader is thrilled when she is told she can help out in the school cafeteria

Junie B., first grader: toothless wonder; illustrated by Denise Brunkus. Random House 2002 80p il $11.95; lib bdg $13.99; pa $4.99
Grades: 1 2 3   **Fic**
1. School stories 2. Teeth -- Fiction
ISBN 0-375-80295-9; 0-375-90295-3 lib bdg; 0-375-82223-2 pa
                                                    LC 2002-4161
Junie B. Jones learns some interesting things about the Tooth Fairy when she becomes the first student in Room One to lose an upper tooth
"This is an ideal read-aloud to first graders and a choice that they will enjoy reading independently as they move into chapter books. Humorous black-and-white drawings show Junie B. as she interacts with her classmates and family." SLJ

Park, Linda Sue
Cavern of secrets; Linda Sue Park, James Madsen; [edited by] Abby Ranger. HarperCollins 2017 320 p. illustrations (Wing & claw) (ebook) $15.99; (hardcover) $16.99

Grades: 4 5 6 7   **Fic**
1. Magic -- Fiction 2. Adventure fiction -- Fiction
ISBN 9780062327437; 0062327410; 9780062327413
                                                    LC 2016935902
In this book, by Linda Sue Park, illustrated by James Madsen, "Raffa Santana has spent all winter hiding in the harsh wilderness of the Sudden Mountains, and now it's time to return home. Home, where his parents will help him fight back against the vile Chancellor who has captured and altered the wild creatures of the Forest of Wonders. Home, where Raffa's beloved companion, Echo the bat, will recover from his mysterious sickness." (Publisher's note)
"The nail-biting adventure, relevant moral dilemmas, and complex characters will leave readers eager for the final installment." Kirkus

Forest of wonders; Linda Sue Park; Jim Madsen (illustrator) Harpercollins Childrens Books 2016 352 p. illustrations, map (Wing & Claw) (hardcover) $16.99
Grades: 4 5 6 7   **Fic**
1. Forest animals -- Fiction 2. Fantasy fiction -- Fiction
ISBN 9780062327383; 0062327380
                                                    LC 2015940700
In this juvenile fantasy adventure novel, by Linda Sue Park and illustrated Jim Madsen, part one of the "Wing and Claw" trilogy, "after discovering a vine with powerful properties in the protected Forest of Wonders, 12-year-old Raffa journeys to Obsidia's capital, where he uncovers a sinister government plan to use botanicals to endanger and enslave animals." (Kirkus Reviews)
"With its engaging hero, talking animals, arcane magic, moral issues, and unresolved plot, this first of a proposed trilogy promises more exciting forest wonders." Kirkus

Project Mulberry; a novel. Clarion 2005 225p $16; pa $6.99
Grades: 5 6 7 8   **Fic**
1. Korean Americans -- Fiction
ISBN 0-618-47786-1; 0-440-42163-2 pa
                                                    LC 2004-18159
While working on a project for an afterschool club, Julia, a Korean American girl, and her friend Patrick learn not just about silkworms, but also about tolerance, prejudice, friendship, patience, and more. Between the chapters are short dialogues between the author and main character about the writing of the book
"The unforgettable family and friendship story, the quiet, almost unspoken racism, and the excitement of the science make this a great cross-curriculum title." Booklist

★ A **single** shard. Clarion Bks. 2001 152p $15; pa $6.99
Grades: 5 6 7 8   **Fic**
1. Korea -- Fiction 2. Pottery -- Fiction
ISBN 0-395-97827-0; 0-440-41851-8 pa
                                                    LC 00-43102
Awarded the Newbery Medal, 2002
Tree-ear, a thirteen-year-old orphan in medieval Korea, lives under a bridge in a potters' village, and longs to learn how to throw the delicate celadon ceramics himself
"This quiet, but involving, story draws readers into a very different time and place. . . . A well-crafted novel with an unusual setting." Booklist

Storm warning. Scholastic 2010 190p (The 39 clues) $12.99
Grades: 4 5 6 7   **Fic**
1. Ciphers -- Fiction
ISBN 978-0-545-06049-3; 0-545-06049-4
Sequel to: The emperor's code by Gordon Korman (2010)

Amy and Dan hit the high seas as they follow the trail of some infamous ancestors to track down a long lost treasure. However, the real prize isn't hidden in a chest. It's the discovery of the Madrigals' most dangerous secret and, even more shockingly, the true identity of the mysterious man in black.

Followed by: Into the gauntlet by Margaret Peterson Haddix (2010)

Trust no one; Linda Sue Park. 1st ed. Scholastic Press 2013 190 p. (reinforced) $12.99

Grades: 4 5 6 7   **Fic**
1. Spy stories -- Fiction 2. Mystery fiction -- Fiction
ISBN 0545298431; 9780545298438

LC 2012939109

This is the fifth installment of Linda Sue Park's Cahills vs. Vespers series. Here, "Amy and Dan discover that one of their friends is a spy for the Vespers, a group of evil agents who kidnapped seven of their family members. But which friend is it? The shocking secrets continue when the Cahill siblings finally figure out the Vespers' real plan, and it's much worse than they originally thought." (Owl Magazine)

★ **When** my name was Keoko. Clarion Bks. 2002 199p $16; pa $6.99

Grades: 5 6 7 8   **Fic**
1. Korea -- Fiction 2. World War, 1939-1945 -- Fiction
ISBN 0-618-13335-6; 0-440-41944-1 pa

LC 2001-32487

With national pride and occasional fear, a brother and sister face the increasingly oppressive occupation of Korea by Japan during World War II, which threatens to suppress Korean culture entirely

"Park is a masterful prose stylist, and her characters are developed beautifully. She excels at making traditional Korean culture accessible to Western readers." Voice Youth Advocates

Includes bibliographical references

Parker, Marjorie Hodgson

David and the Mighty Eighth; a British boy and a Texas airman in World War II. by Marjorie Hodgson Parker; illustrated by Mark Postlethwaite. Bright Sky Press 2007 176p il $17.95

Grades: 4 5 6 7   **Fic**
1. Great Britain -- Fiction 2. World War, 1939-1945 -- Fiction
ISBN 978-1-931721-93-6; 1-931721-93-9

LC 2007025999

When, during the London Blitz, he and his older sister are evacuated to go live on their grandparents' East Anglia farm, a young English boy finds it difficult to adjust to his new life until the arrival of the pilots and crews of the U.S. Eight Air Force at nearby airfields brings excitement, friendship, and hope for the future.

This is an "exciting novel, based on a true story. . . . The story is framed by extensive historical notes. . . . Spacious type, thick paper, and an occasional black-and-white drawings make this an appealing package all around." Booklist

Parkinson, Siobhan

Blue like Friday. Roaring Brook Press 2008 160p $16.95

Grades: 4 5 6 7   **Fic**
1. Ireland -- Fiction 2. Family life -- Fiction 3. Synesthesia -- Fiction 4. Missing persons -- Fiction
ISBN 978-1-59643-340-3; 1-59643-340-X

When Olivia helps her quirky friend Hal, whose synesthesia causes him to experience everything in colors, with a prank intended to get rid of Hal's potential stepfather, there are unexpected consequences, including the disappearance of Hal's mother.

"Parkinson creates a warm, moving story of real families facing real problems. . . . The economy of her prose is admirable; all the characters are well drawn." Booklist

Parnell, Robyn

The **mighty** Quinn; by Robyn Parnell; illustrated by Aaron and Katie DeYoe. 1st ed. Scarletta Press 2013 263 p. ill. (paperback) $10.95

Grades: 4 5 6 7   **Fic**
1. Bullies -- Fiction 2. Friendship -- Fiction 3. School stories -- Fiction 4. Oregon -- Fiction
ISBN 1938063104; 9781938063107

LC 2012031518

In this story, by Robyn Parnell, "Quinn Andrews-Lee . . . faces a dismal school year. His little sister outshines him . . . , he yearns for a service award his peers disdain, and charismatic bigot Matt Barker's goal in life is to torment Quinn. . . . When Quinn reports an act of vandalism, he is accused of injuring Matt. . . . A free-spirited new kid in Quinn's class, helps Quinn deduce who hurt Matt, but Matt would probably die . . . before admitting the truth." (Publisher's note)

Parr, Maria

Adventures with Waffles; Maria Parr; illustrated by Kate Forrester. Candlewick Press 2015 240 p. $15.99

Grades: 2 3 4   **Fic**
1. Grief -- Fiction 2. Friendship -- Fiction 3. Secrecy -- Fiction
ISBN 0763672815; 9780763672812

LC 2014939361

In this middle grades book by Maria Parr, illustrated by Kate Forrester, translated by Guy Puzey, "Trille loves to share everything with Lena, even Auntie Granny's waffles. But when Lena has to move away and Auntie Granny leaves the world, it sometimes seems like nothing will ever be right again. The warmth of friendship and the support of family suffuse this lightly illustrated novel, proving that when times are tough, a little taste of sweetness can make all the difference." (Publisher's note)

"In this delightful Norwegian import, two friends, a boy nicknamed Trille and his best friend, Lena, get into some hair-raising, frequently hilarious, and, sometimes, injury-inducing escapades over the course of a year. . . . Recommended for public and school libraries, this will be useful as supplementary material in units about day-to-day life in another country." SLJ

Parry, Rosanne

The **turn** of the tide; Rosanne Parry. Random House 2016 304 p. illustrations (hardcover : alk. paper) $16.99

Grades: 4 5 6   **Fic**
1. Oregon -- Fiction 2. Cousins -- Fiction 3. Sailing -- Fiction 4. Friendship -- Fiction 5. Japanese Americans -- Fiction 6. Racially mixed people -- Fiction
ISBN 9780375869723; 9780375969720

LC 2014047701

This book, by Rosanne Parry, is a "story about two cousins. . . . In Japan, you're always prepared for an earthquake. That's why Kai knows just what to do when the first rumbles shake the earth. And then he does the exact opposite of what you're supposed to do: He runs. And then the tsunami hits. Meanwhile, on the other side of the Pacific, Kai's cousin Jet sets sail off the coast of Astoria, Oregon. She knows she should have checked the tide. . . . Except this time she didn't." (Publisher's note)

"Thematically rich, by turns exciting and reflective, this affectionate homage to the mariner life celebrates human commonality and difference in an increasingly interconnected world." Kirkus

Partridge, Elizabeth

★ **Dogtag** summer. Bloomsbury Books for Young Readers 2011 226p $16.99

Grades: 4 5 6 7   **Fic**

1. Hippies -- Fiction 2. Adoption -- Fiction 3. California -- Fiction 4. Family life -- Fiction 5. Vietnamese Americans -- Fiction 6. Racially mixed people -- Fiction 7. Vietnam War, 1961-1975 -- Fiction

ISBN 978-1-59990-183-1; 1-59990-183-8

LC 2010-25515

In the summer of 1980 before she starts junior high school in Santa Rosa, California, Tracy, who was adopted from Vietnam when she was six years old, finds an old ammo box with a dog tag and picture that bring up painful memories for both her Vietnam-veteran father and her.

"This gripping yet tender coming-of-age story reveals multiple nuanced perspectives of the Vietnam War and its aftermath. . . . Powerful historical fiction." Publ Wkly

Pastis, Stephan

Timmy failure; mistakes were made. Stephan Pastis. Candlewick Press 2013 304 p. (reinforced) $14.99

Grades: 4 5 6 7   **Fic**

1. Mystery graphic novels 2. Picture books for children

ISBN 0763660507; 9780763660505

LC 2012942409

This children's graphic novel focuses on Timmy and his detective agency Total Failure Inc. Questions abound: "Who stole the Halloween candy of Timmy's classmate Gabe? Who is the mysterious girl Timmy refuses to discuss? Why is no one fazed that Timmy has a pet polar bear named Total?" (Publishers Weekly)

Other titles about Timmy are:

Now look what you've done (2014)

We meet again (2014)

Sanitized for your protection (2015)

The book you're not supposed to have (2016)

Timmy failure : now look what you've done; Now Look What You've Done. Stephan Pastis. Candlewick Press 2014 288 p. illustrations $14.99

Grades: 4 5 6 7   **Fic**

1. Detectives -- Fiction 2. Polar bear -- Fiction 3. Problem solving -- Fiction 4. Self-confidence -- Fiction 5. Globes 6. Schools 7. Contests 8. Humorous stories 9. Detective and mystery stories

ISBN 0763660515; 9780763660512

LC 2013944145

In this book, by Stephan Pastis, "the too-smart-for-his-own-good kid detective is back for a second zany installment, along with his 1500-pound polar/bear business partner, Total. Timmy has big dreams for his crime-solving empire, fueled by his complete self-confidence, delusions of grandeur, and his assured win in a competition to find a stolen globe worth $500. But first, shenanigans are afoot and must be thwarted." (School Library Journal)

"Great-aunt Coriander and her own wacky aspirations add a new layer to the winning combination of sardonically humorous text and pen-and-ink cartoons that has won Timmy many fans." Horn Book

Paterson, John

★ The **Flint** Heart; a fairy story. freely abriged from Eden Phillpott's 1910 fantasy; by Katherine and John Paterson; illustrated by John Rocco. Candlewick Press 2011 288p il $19.99

Grades: 3 4 5 6   **Fic**

1. Fairy tales

ISBN 978-0-7636-4712-4; 0-7636-4712-8

LC 2010048225

An ambitious Stone Age man demands a talisman that will harden his heart, allowing him to take control of his tribe. Against his better judgment, the tribe's magic man creates the Flint Heart, but the cruelty of it causes the destruction of the tribe. Thousands of years later, the talisman reemerges to corrupt a kindly farmer, an innocent fairy creature, and a familial badger.

"The tale will make an excellent read-aloud. . . . The Patersons have done a lovely job updating and abridging this tale for today's readers. . . . Rocco's fantastic illustrations alone make this edition worth purchasing." SLJ

Paterson, Katherine

★ **Bread** and roses, too. Clarion Books 2006 275p $16; pa $6.99

Grades: 5 6 7 8   **Fic**

1. Strikes -- Fiction 2. Immigrants -- Fiction 3. Lawrence (Mass.) -- Fiction 4. United States -- History -- 1898-1919 -- Fiction

ISBN 978-0-618-65479-6; 0-618-65479-8; 978-0-547-07651-5 pa; 0-547-07651-7 pa

LC 2005-31702

Jake and Rosa, two children, form an unlikely friendship as they try to survive and understand the 1912 Bread and Roses strike of mill workers in Lawrence, Massachusetts.

"Paterson has skillfully woven true events and real historical figures into the fictional story and created vivid settings, clearly drawn characters, and a strong sense of the hardship and injustice faced by the mostly immigrant mill workers." SLJ

★ **Bridge** to Terabithia; illustrated by Donna Diamond. Crowell 1977 128p il $15.99; lib bdg $16.89; pa $5.99

Grades: 4 5 6 7   **Fic**

1. Death -- Fiction 2. Virginia -- Fiction 3. Friendship -- Fiction

ISBN 0-690-01359-0; 0-690-04635-9 lib bdg; 0-06-440184-7 pa

LC 77-2221

Awarded the Newbery Medal, 1978

The life of Jess, a ten-year-old boy in rural Virginia expands when he becomes friends with a newcomer who subsequently meets an untimely death trying to reach their hideaway, Terabithia, during a storm

"Jess and his family are magnificently characterized; the book abounds in descriptive vignettes, humorous sidelights on the clash of cultures, and realistic depictions of rural school life." Horn Book

★ The **great** Gilly Hopkins. Crowell 1978 148p $15.99; lib bdg $16.89; pa $5.99

Grades: 5 6 7 8   **Fic**

1. Foster home care -- Fiction

ISBN 0-690-03837-2; 0-690-03838-0 lib bdg; 0-06-440201-0 pa

LC 77-27075

A Newbery Medal honor book, 1979

"A well-structured story, [this] has vitality of writing style, natural dialogue, deep insight in characterization, and a keen sense of the fluid dynamics in human relationships." Bull Cent Child Books

★ **Lyddie.** Lodestar Bks. 1991 182p $17.99; pa $6.99

Grades: 5 6 7 8 9   **Fic**

1. Factories -- Fiction 2. Massachusetts -- Fiction 3. United States -- History -- 1815-1861 -- Fiction

ISBN 0-525-67338-5; 0-14-240254-0 pa

LC 90-42944

Impoverished Vermont farm girl Lyddie Worthen is determined to gain her independence by becoming a factory worker in Lowell, Massachusetts, in the 1840s

"Not only does the book contain a riveting plot, engaging characters, and a splendid setting, but the language—graceful, evocative, and rhythmic—incorporates the rural speech patterns of Lyddie's folk, the simple Quaker expressions of the farm neighbors, and the lilt of fellow mill girl Bridget's Irish brogue. . . . A superb story of grit, determination, and personal growth." Horn Book

★ **Park's** quest. Lodestar Bks. 1988 148p hardcover o.p. pa $5.99

Grades: 5 6 7 8   **Fic**

1. Farm life -- Fiction 2. Vietnamese Americans -- Fiction
ISBN 0-14-034262-1 pa

LC 87-32422

Eleven-year-old Park makes some startling discoveries when he travels to his grandfather's farm in Virginia to learn about his father who died in the Vietnam War and meets a Vietnamese-American girl named Thanh

The author "confronts the complexity, the ambiguity, of the war and the emotions of those it involved with an honesty that young readers are sure to recognize and appreciate." N Y Times Book Rev

The **same** stuff as stars. Clarion Bks. 2002 242p $15

Grades: 5 6 7 8   **Fic**

1. Brothers and sisters -- Fiction
ISBN 0-618-24744-0

LC 2002-3967

When Angel's self-absorbed mother leaves her and her younger brother Bernie with their poor great-grandmother, the eleven-year-old girl worries not only about her mother and brother, her imprisoned father, the frail old woman, but also about a mysterious man who begins sharing with her the wonder of the stars. "Intermediate." (Horn Book)

"Paterson's deft hand at characterization, her insight into the human soul, and her glorious prose make this book one to rejoice over." Voice Youth Advocates

Patrick, Denise Lewis

Finding someplace; Denise Lewis Patrick. Henry Holt & Co. 2015 224 p. (hardback) $16.99

Grades: 4 5 6   **Fic**

1. New Orleans (La.) -- Fiction 2. Hurricane Katrina, 2005 -- Fiction 3. African Americans -- Fiction 4. New Orleans (La.) -- Fiction 5. Family life -- Louisiana -- New Orleans -- Fiction
ISBN 0805047166; 9780805047165

LC 2015000561

In this juvenile novel, by Denise Lewis Patrick, "Reesie Boone just knows that thirteen is going to be her best year yet. . . . But on Reesie's birthday, everything changes. Hurricane Katrina hits her city. Stranded at home alone, Reesie takes refuge with her elderly neighbor, Miss Martine. The waters rise. They escape in a boat. And soon Reesie is reunited with her family. But her journey back home has only begun." (Publisher's note)

"Reesie Boone's been looking forward to her 13th birthday for a long time. As her big day approaches, people are focused on a hurricane warning, and everyone's leaving New Orleans. Reesie's family is staying put despite evacuation warnings; her father is a policeman and can't miss work. Hurricane Katrina hits while Reesie is at the neighbor's house picking up her birthday cake. . . . A powerful read for middle grade readers already familiar with the hurricane or those learning about it for the first time." SLJ

Patron, Susan

Behind the masks; the diary of Angeline Reddy. Susan Patron. Scholastic 2012 293 p. ill., map (paper-over-board) $12.99

Grades: 5 6 7 8   **Fic**

1. Mystery fiction 2. Diaries -- Fiction 3. Thieves -- Fiction 4. Gold mines and mining -- Fiction 5. Frontier and pioneer life -- California -- Fiction 6. Lawyers -- Fiction 7. Mystery and detective stories 8. Robbers and outlaws -- Fiction 9. California -- History

-- 19th century -- Fiction
ISBN 9780545304375

LC 2011023826

"[T]his Dear America series title [is] set in Bodie, California, in 1880. Fourteen-year-old diarist and would-be dramatist Angeline Reddy does not believe her father, criminal lawyer Patrick Reddy, has been murdered. Convinced his disappearance is purposeful, Angie investigates his 'demise' and tries to bring him back to their rough-and-tumble mining community. Assisted by friends, a dashing young Wells Fargo clerk, and the members of a local theater troupe, . . ., Angie offers a revealing look at frontier life "especially preoccupations with thespian entertainments, racial and social prejudices, and vigilante justice."(Booklist)

★ The **higher** power of Lucky; with illustrations by Matt Phelan. Atheneum Books for Young Readers 2006 134p il $16.95; pa $6.99

Grades: 4 5 6   **Fic**

1. Runaway children -- Fiction
ISBN 978-1-4169-0194-5; 1-4169-0194-9; 978-1-4169-7557-1 pa; 1-4169-7557-8 pa

LC 2005-21767

Awarded the Newbery Medal, 2007

Fearing that her legal guardian plans to abandon her to return to France, ten-year-old aspiring scientist Lucky Trimble determines to run away while also continuing to seek the Higher Power that will bring stability to her life

"Patron's plotting is as tight as her characters are endearing. Lucky is a true heroine." Booklist

Other books about Lucky are:
Lucky breaks (2009)
Lucky for good (2011)

Maybe yes, maybe no, maybe maybe; illustrated by Abigail Halpin. Aladdin Paperbacks 2009 107p il pa $5.99

Grades: 3 4 5   **Fic**

1. Moving -- Fiction 2. Sisters -- Fiction
ISBN 978-1-4169-6176-5 pa; 1-4169-6176-3 pa
First published 1993 by Orchard Books

When her hardworking mother decides to move, eight-year-old PK uses her imagination and storytelling to help her older and younger sisters adjust

Patt, Beverly

★ **Best** friends forever; a World War II scrapbook. with illustrations by Shula Klinger. Marshall Cavendish 2010 92p il $17.99

Grades: 5 6 7 8   **Fic**

1. Friendship -- Fiction 2. Washington (State) -- Fiction 3. World War, 1939-1945 -- Fiction 4. Puyallup Assembly Center (Wash.) -- Fiction 5. Japanese Americans -- Evacuation and relocation, 1942-1945 -- Fiction
ISBN 978-0-7614-5577-6; 0-7614-5577-9

LC 2008-20875

Fourteen-year-old Louise keeps a scrapbook detailing the events in her life after her best friend, Dottie, a Japanese-American girl, and her family are sent to a relocation camp during World War II.

"If the drama of the girls separation isn't enough, a romantic subplot and the antics of Dottie's goofy dog (living with Louise in her absence) will surely keep young readers interested. This heartwarming tale of steadfast friendship makes a wonderful access point for learning more about World War II and Japanese internment." SLJ

Includes bibliographical references

Patten, E. J.

Return to Exile; illustrated by John Rocco. Simon & Schuster 2011 512p (The Hunter chronicles) $16.99

Grades: 5 6 7 8   **Fic**
   1. Fantasy fiction 2. Uncles -- Fiction 3. Monsters -- Fiction
   ISBN 978-1-4424-2032-8; 1-4424-2032-4; 978-1-4169-8259-3
e-book
                         LC 2010053480
   "Sky's twelfth birthday is a mix. His mother's delicious homemade
goulash cannot overshadow the disappearance of his beloved uncle,
Phineas, or the family's return to the small town of Exile. Sky has grown
up reading about the Hunters of Legend, but he never dreamed that they
were real until monsters appear in Exile and make Sky their target. . . .
Patten's first novel excels at world building and pacing; the monsters .
. . . are fully formed and vividly drawn. . . . Interspersed with humor to
keep an otherwise dark story from becoming overbearing, the balance is
just right." Booklist

Patterson, James, 1947-
   ★ **Middle** school, the worst years of my life; [by] James Patterson
and Chris Tebbetts; illustrated by Laura Park. Little, Brown 2011 281p
il $15.99
Grades: 4 5 6 7   **Fic**
   1. School stories 2. Bereavement -- Fiction 3. Family life --
Fiction
   ISBN 0-316-10187-7; 978-0-316-10187-5
                         LC 2010022852
   When Rafe Kane enters middle school, he teams up with his best
friend, "Leo the Silent," to create a game to make school more fun by
trying to break every rule in the school's code of conduct.
   "The book's ultrashort chapters, dynamic artwork, and message that
'normal is boring' should go a long way toward assuring kids who don't
fit the mold that there's a place for them, too." Publ Wkly

Patterson, Nancy Ruth
   Ellie ever; pictures by Patty Weise. Farrar, Straus & Giroux 2010
117p il $15.99
Grades: 3 4 5   **Fic**
   1. School stories 2. Horses -- Fiction 3. Moving -- Fiction 4.
Virginia -- Fiction 5. Bereavement -- Fiction
   ISBN 978-0-374-32108-6; 0-374-32108-6
                         LC 2009013604
   After losing her father and all their possessions in a hurricane, nine-
year-old Ellie and her mother move to a small apartment on a horse farm
in Virginia, where her new classmates think that she lives in a mansion
and is a princess.
   "Horses and animals . . . will initially attract readers, but it's the
straightforward story of the little family, rebounding from terrible tragedy with bravery, honesty, and character, that is the heart of this book's
appeal." Horn Book

Paulsen, Gary, 1939-
   Crush; the theory, practice, and destructive properties of love. Gary
Paulsen. Wendy Lamb Books 2012 136 p.
Grades: 5 6 7 8   **Fic**
   1. Love -- Fiction 2. Humorous fiction 3. Crushes -- Fiction 4.
High school students -- Fiction 5. Dating (Social customs) -- Fiction
6. Humorous stories 7. Interpersonal relations -- Fiction
   ISBN 0385742304; 9780307974532; 9780375990540;
9780385742306; 9780385742313
                         LC 2011028915
   In this book, "Tina, aka the most beautiful girl he's ever seen, has
stolen Kevin's heart, although she's blissfully oblivious to the effect she
has on him. . . . Rather than reveal his ardor outright, Kevin decides
it's safer to first make a scientific study of just how love works by setting up romantic opportunities for his victims (otherwise known as study

subjects). He starts by trying to create a candlelit dinner for his parents,
although he accidentally causes a fire." (Kirkus Reviews)

   Flat broke. Wendy Lamb Books 2011 118p $12.99; lib bdg
$15.99
Grades: 4 5 6   **Fic**
   1. Friendship -- Fiction 2. Family life -- Fiction 3. Business
enterprises -- Fiction 4. Money-making projects for children --
Fiction
   ISBN 978-0-385-74002-9; 0-385-74002-6; 978-0-385-90818-4
lib bdg; 0-385-90818-0 lib bdg
                         LC 2010049415
   Sequel to: Liar, liar (2011)
   Fourteen-year-old Kevin is a hard worker, so when his income is
cut off he begins a series of businesses, from poker games to selling
snacks, earning money to take a girl to a dance, but his partners soon
tire of his methods.
   "A jocular, fast-paced voyage into the sometimes simple but never
quiet mind of an ambitious eighth grader." Kirkus

   ★ **Lawn** Boy. Wendy Lamb Books 2007 88p $12.99; lib bdg
$15.99; pa $6.50
Grades: 4 5 6 7   **Fic**
   1. Summer employment -- Fiction 2. Business enterprises -- Fiction
   ISBN 978-0-385-74686-1; 978-0-385-90923-5 lib bdg; 978-0-
553-49465-5 pa
                         LC 2006-39731
   Things get out of hand for a twelve-year-old boy when a neighbor
convinces him to expand his summer lawn mowing business
   "This rags-to-riches success story has colorful characters, a villain,
and enough tongue-in-cheek humor to make it an enjoyable selection for
the whole family." SLJ
   Followed by: Lawn Boy returns (2010)

   ★ The **legend** of Bass Reeves; being the true and fictional account
of the most valiant marshal in the West. Wendy Lamb Books 2006
137p $15.95; pa $6.50
Grades: 5 6 7 8   **Fic**
   1. Sheriffs 2. Slavery -- Fiction 3. West (U.S.) -- Fiction 4.
African Americans -- Fiction
   ISBN 0-385-74661-X; 0-553-49429-5 pa
                         LC 2006-11492
   "This engrossingly told tale fills in the unrecorded youth of an unjustly obscure historical figure who was born a slave, became a successful rancher, then later in his long life went on to play an integral role
in taming the rough-hewn Oklahoma Territory. . . . A stirring tale of
adventure." Booklist

   Liar, liar; the theory, practice, and destructive properties of deception. Wendy Lamb Books 2011 120p $12.99; lib bdg $15.99
Grades: 4 5 6   **Fic**
   1. School stories 2. Family life -- Fiction 3. Truthfulness and
falsehood -- Fiction
   ISBN 0-385-74001-8; 0-385-90817-2 lib bdg; 978-0-385-74001-
2; 978-0-385-90817-7 lib bdg
                         LC 2010-28356
   Fourteen-year-old Kevin is very good at lying and doing so makes
life easier, until he finds himself in big trouble with his friends, family,
and teachers. "Ages eight to twelve." (Publisher's note)
   "Kevin's grappling with family troubles adds . . . emotional dimension to Paulsen's novel." Publ Wkly
   Followed by: Flat broke (2011)

Masters of disaster. Wendy Lamb Books 2010 102p $12.95; lib bdg $15.99

Grades: 3 4 5 6   **Fic**

1. Friendship -- Fiction

ISBN 978-0-385-73997-9; 0-385-73997-4; 978-0-385-90816-0 lib bdg; 0-385-90816-4 lib bdg

LC 2010013180

"Henry convinces his best friends, Riley and Reed, that the three 12-year-olds should prove their manhood by undertaking a series a daring exploits. . . . Readers willing to suspend disbelief and follow the boys' over-the-top exploits will enjoy plenty of laughs along the way." Booklist

Mudshark. Wendy Lamb Books 2009 83p

Grades: 3 4 5 6   **Fic**

1. School stories 2. Lost and found possessions -- Fiction

ISBN 0-385-74685-7; 0-385-90922-5 lib bdg; 978-0-385-74685-4; 978-0-385-90922-8 lib bdg

LC 2008033271

Principal Wagner confidently deals with a faculty washroom crisis, a psychic parrot, and a terrorizing gerbil, but when sixty-five erasers go missing, he enlists the help of the school's best problem solver and locator of lost items, twelve-year-old Lyle Williams, aka Mudshark.

"Diversions . . . keep this compact story quick and light. Yet . . . Paulsen . . . delves deeper, shaping Mudshark as a credible and compassionate protagonist." Publ Wkly

Notes from the dog. Wendy Lamb Books 2009 133p $15.99; lib bdg $18.99

Grades: 5 6 7 8   **Fic**

1. Cancer -- Fiction 2. Gardening -- Fiction

ISBN 0-385-73845-5; 0-385-90730-3 lib bdg; 978-0-385-73845-3; 978-0-385-90730-9 lib bdg

LC 2009-13300

When Johanna shows up at the beginning of summer to house-sit next door to Finn, he has no idea of the profound effect she will have on his life by the time summer vacation is over.

"The plot is straightforward, but Paulsen's thoughtful characters are compelling and their interactions realistic. This emotional, coming-of-age journey about taking responsibilty for one's own happiness and making personal connections will not disappoint." Publ Wkly

Road trip; by Jim and Gary Paulsen. Wendy Lamb Books 2013 128 p. (trade) $12.99

Grades: 5 6 7 8   **Fic**

1. Dogs -- Fiction 2. Automobile travel -- Fiction 3. Father-child relationship -- Fiction 4. Border collie -- Fiction 5. Animal shelters -- Fiction 6. Fathers and sons -- Fiction

ISBN 038574191X; 9780307930866; 9780375988578; 9780375990311; 9780385741910

LC 2012014284

In this book, by Gary Paulsen and Jim Paulsen, "Dad and Ben haven't been getting along recently and Dad hopes a road trip to rescue a border collie will help them reconnect. But Ben is on to Dad's plan and invites Ben's thuggish buddy, Theo. The family dog, Atticus, comes along too and the story is told by Ben and Atticus. . . . Only sharp-eyed Atticus realizes that Theo is on the run--and someone is following them." (Publisher's note)

Vote; the theory, practice, and destructive properties of politics. Gary Paulsen. 1st ed. Wendy Lamb Books 2013 144 p. (hardcover) $12.99; (ebook) $38.97; (hardcover) $12.99

Grades: 5 6 7 8   **Fic**

1. School stories 2. Humorous fiction 3. Elections -- Fiction 4. Humorous stories 5. Schools -- Fiction 6. Middle schools -- Fiction 7. Politics, Practical -- Fiction 8. Interpersonal relations -- Fiction

ISBN 0385742282; 9780307974525; 9780375990533; 9780385742283 trade; 9780385742290

LC 2012023059

In this humorous children's novel, by Gary Paulsen, the author's lead character from previous stories is reprised when he runs for school office. "Kevin Spencer . . . has a knack for tackling big ideas and goofing up, so what's next? Politics, of course! He's running for office, and his campaign is truly unique." (Publisher's note)

"Those who started this four-book series at the beginning may sense that our protagonist is maturing a wee bit, but not so much as to dampen the humor for fans or newcomers. . . . Fast-paced action and Kevin's penchant for getting into ridiculous situations make this the perfect book bait for not-so-eager readers." BookList

★ The **winter** room. Orchard Bks. 1989 103p $16.95; pa $5.99

Grades: 5 6 7 8   **Fic**

1. Farm life -- Fiction 2. Minnesota -- Fiction

ISBN 0-531-05839-5; 0-545-08534-9 pa

LC 89-42541

A Newbery Medal honor book, 1990

A young boy growing up on a northern Minnesota farm describes the scenes around him and recounts his old Norwegian uncle's tales of an almost mythological logging past

"While this seems at first to be a collection of anecdotes organized around the progression of the farm calendar, Paulsen subtly builds a conflict that becomes apparent in the last brief chapters, forceful and well-prepared. . . . Lyrical and only occasionally sentimental, the prose is clean, clear, and deceptively simple." Bull Cent Child Books

Paver, Michelle

    Ghost hunter. Katherine Tegen Books 2010 285p (Chronicles of ancient darkness) $16.99; pa $6.99

Grades: 5 6 7 8   **Fic**

1. Fantasy fiction 2. Demoniac possession -- Fiction 3. Prehistoric peoples -- Fiction

ISBN 978-0-06-072840-3; 0-06-072840-X; 978-0-06-072842-7 pa; 0-06-072842-6 pa

Sequel to: Oath breaker (2009)

To fulfill his destiny, Torak must defy demons and tokoroths, navigate through the Gorge of Hidden People, and battle the evil Eagle Owl Mage.

Wolf brother. HarperCollins 2005 295p (Chronicles of ancient darkness) $16.99; lib bdg $17.89; pa $6.99

Grades: 5 6 7 8   **Fic**

1. Bears -- Fiction 2. Wolves -- Fiction 3. Demoniac possession -- Fiction 4. Prehistoric peoples -- Fiction

ISBN 0-06-072825-6; 0-06-072826-4 lib bdg; 0-06-072827-2 pa

LC 2004-8857

First published 2004 in the United Kingdom

6,000 years in the past, twelve-year-old Tarak and his guide, a wolf cub, set out on a dangerous journey to fulfill an oath the boy made to his dying father—to travel to the Mountain of the World Spirit seeking a way to destroy a demon-possessed bear that threatens all the clans

"Paver's depth of research into the spiritual world of primitive peoples makes this impressive British import, slated to be the first in a six-book series, intriguing and believable." SLJ

Other titles in this series are:

Spirit walker (2006)

Soul eater (2007)

Outcast (2008)

Oath breaker (2009)

Ghost hunter (2010)

Payne, C. C.

Something to sing about; written by C. C. Payne. Eerdmans Books for Young Readers 2008 167p pa $8.50

Grades: 4 5 6 **Fic**

1. Bees -- Fiction 2. Fear -- Fiction 3. Singing -- Fiction 4. Kentucky -- Fiction 5. Family life -- Fiction 6. Choirs (Music) -- Fiction 7. Christian life -- Fiction

ISBN 978-0-8028-5344-8 pa; 0-8028-5344-7 pa

LC 2008006100

Ten-year-old Jamie Jo's fear of bees keeps her inside most of the time, but a series of events that begins when her mother is excluded from the church choir brings about many changes, including new friendships and greater trust in God

"The word wholesome sometimes gets a bad rap, but here it's leavened by gentle humor and considerable insight, and it fits this book just fine." Booklist

Peacock, Carol Antoinette

Red thread sisters; by Carol Antoinette Peacock. Viking 2012 236 p. (hardcover) $15.99

Grades: 4 5 6 7 8 **Fic**

1. Adoptees -- Fiction 2. Friendship -- Fiction 3. Chinese Americans -- Fiction 4. Adoption -- Fiction 5. Family life -- Fiction 6. Interracial adoption -- Fiction 7. Intercountry adoption -- Fiction

ISBN 0670013862; 9780670013869

LC 2012019511

This novel, by Carol Antoinette Peacock, offers a "story of friendship, family, and love. Wen has spent the first eleven years of her life at an orphanage in rural China . . . [with] her best friend, Shu Ling. When Wen is adopted by an American couple, she struggles . . . knowing that Shu Ling remains back at the orphanage, alone. Wen knows that her best friend deserves a family and a future, too. But finding a home for Shu Ling isn't easy, and time is running out." (Publisher's note)

Pearce, Emily Smith

Isabel and the miracle baby; [by] Emily Smith Pearce. Front Street 2007 125p $15.95

Grades: 2 3 4 5 **Fic**

1. Cancer -- Fiction 2. Infants -- Fiction 3. Family life -- Fiction 4. Mother-daughter relationship -- Fiction

ISBN 978-1-932425-44-4

LC 2006101750

Eight-year-old Isabel feels her mother no longer cares about her because she has no time or energy even to listen when Isa tries to share her sadness about being unpopular, her jealousy over her new baby sister, and, most importantly, her fear that her mother's cancer will come back

"Pearce gets into the mind and soul of a child. . . . [The child's] struggle is what sets this book apart from the dozens of others with the new-sibling theme." SLJ

Pearce, Philippa

A finder's magic; illustrated by Helen Craig. Candlewick Press 2009 119p il $15.99

Grades: 3 4 5 **Fic**

1. Magic -- Fiction 2. Lost and found possessions -- Fiction

ISBN 978-0-7636-4072-9; 0-7636-4072-7

After a mysterious stranger offers to help Till find his dog, they embark on a magical quest, interviewing various witnesses including a heron, a mole, a riddling cat, and Miss Mousey, whose sketch of a peaceful riverbank offers a vital clue.

"The posthumous publication by classic author Pearce envinces her usual gift for blending reality and fantasy in plain and approach-

able style. . . . Younger readers who crave gentle shivers without terrors will appreciate this cozy fantasy quest to find a lost pet." Bull Cent Child Books

Pearsall, Shelley

All of the above; a novel. illustrations by Javaka Steptoe. Little, Brown 2006 234p il hardcover o.p. pa $5.99

Grades: 5 6 7 8 **Fic**

1. School stories 2. City and town life -- Fiction

ISBN 0-316-11524-X; 978-0-316-11524-7; 978-0-316-11526-1 pa; 0-316-11526-6 pa

LC 2005-33109

Five urban middle school students, their teacher, and other community members relate how a school project to build the world's largest tetrahedron affects the lives of everyone involved.

"Pearsall's novel, based on a real event in 2002—is a delightful story about the power of a vision and the importance of a goal. The authentic voices of the students and the well-intentioned, supportive adults surrounding them illustrate all that is good about schools, family, friendship, and community." Booklist

The seventh most important thing; Shelley Pearsall. Knopf Books for Young Readers 2015 288 p. illustrations (hardback) $16.99

Grades: 5 6 7 8 **Fic**

1. Artists -- Fiction 2. Punishment -- Fiction 3. African Americans -- Fiction 4. Juvenile delinquency -- Fiction 5. Folk art -- Fiction 6. Community service (Punishment) -- Fiction 7. Hampton, James, 1909-1964 -- Fiction

ISBN 0553497286; 9780553497281; 9780553497298

LC 2014047761

This book, by Shelley Pearsall, is a "story of anger and art, loss and redemption. . . . It was a bitterly cold day when Arthur T. Owens grabbed a brick and hurled it at the trash picker. Arthur had his reasons, and the brick hit the Junk Man in the arm, not the head. But none of that matters to the judge - he is ready to send Arthur to juvie for the foreseeable future. Amazingly, it's the Junk Man himself who offers an alternative: 120 hours of community service . . . working for him." (Publisher's note)

"A middle school student learns the meaning of redemption in this excellent coming-of-age story. For the rest of the country, it was the year President Kennedy was assassinated. For Arthur Owens, it would always be the year his Dad died." SLJ

Peck, Richard, 1934-

★ **The best** man; Richard Peck. Penguin Group USA 2017 256 p. (pbk.) $8.99; (hbk.) $16.99

Grades: 4 5 6 7 **Fic**

1. School stories 2. Weddings -- Fiction 3. Family life -- Fiction 4. Gays -- Fiction 5. Schools -- Fiction 6. Role models -- Fiction

ISBN 0803738390; 9780147515797; 9780803738393; 0147515793

LC 2015049803

In this book, by Richard Peck, "Archer Magill has spent a lively five years of grade school with one eye out in search of grown-up role models. Three of the best are his grandpa, the great architect; his dad, the great vintage car customizer; and his uncle Paul, who is just plain great. These are the three he wants to be. Along the way he finds a fourth—Mr. McLeod, a teacher. In fact, the first male teacher in the history of the school." (Publisher's note)

"It's an indelible portrait of what it looks like to grow up in an age of viral videos and media frenzies, undergirded by the same powerful sense of family that characterizes so much of Peck's work." Pub Wkly

Here lies the librarian. Dial Books 2006 145p $16.99; pa $6.99

Grades: 4 5 6 **Fic**
1. Indiana -- Fiction 2. Librarians -- Fiction 3. Automobiles --
Fiction 4. Country life -- Fiction
ISBN 0-8037-3080-2; 0-14-240908-1 pa

LC 2005-20279
Fourteen-year-old Eleanor "Peewee" McGrath, a tomboy and automobile enthusiast, discovers new possibilities for her future after the
1914 arrival in her small Indiana town of four young librarians.
"Another gem from Peck, with his signature combination of quirky
characters, poignancy, and outrageous farce." SLJ

★ **A long** way from Chicago; a novel in stories. Dial Bks. for
Young Readers 1998 148p pa $5.99; $15.99
Grades: 5 6 7 8 **Fic**
1. Illinois -- Fiction 2. Grandmothers -- Fiction 3. Depressions
-- 1929 -- Fiction 4. Country life -- Illinois -- Fiction 5. Great
Depression, 1929-1939 -- Fiction
ISBN 0-14-240110-2 pa; 0-8037-2290-7

LC 98-10953
A Newbery Medal honor book, 1999
Joe recounts his annual summer trips to rural Illinois with his sister
during the Great Depression to visit their larger-than-life grandmother
"The novel reveals a strong sense of place, a depth of characteriza-
tion, and a rich sense of humor." Horn Book
Followed by: A year down yonder (2000)

The **mouse** with the question mark tail; a novel. by Richard Peck;
illustrated by Kelly Murphy. Dial Books for Young Readers 2013 240
p. ill. (hardcover) $16.99
Grades: 3 4 5 6 **Fic**
1. Mice -- Fiction 2. Identity -- Fiction 3. Social classes -- Fiction
4. Adventure and adventurers -- Fiction 5. Kings, queens, rulers,
etc. -- Fiction 6. Buckingham Palace (London, England) -- Fiction
7. Great Britain -- History -- Victoria, 1837-1901 -- Fiction
ISBN 0803738382; 9780803738386

LC 2012027992
In this children's story, by Richard Peck, illustrated by Kelly Murphy, "the smallest mouse in London's Royal Mews is such a little mystery that he hasn't even a name.... His Aunt Marigold, Head Needle-
mouse, sews him a uniform and sends him off to be educated at the
Royal Mews Mouse Academy.... Soon he's running for his life, looking
high and low through the grand precincts of Buckingham Palace to find
out who he is and who he might become." (Publisher's note)

★ **On** the wings of heroes. Dial Books 2007 148p $16.99; pa
$6.99
Grades: 4 5 6 7 **Fic**
1. Illinois -- Fiction 2. World War, 1939-1945 -- Fiction
ISBN 0-8037-3081-0; 0-14-241204-X pa

LC 2006011906
A boy in Illinois remembers the homefront years of World War II,
especially his two heroes, his brother in the Air Force and his father, who
fought in the previous war.
"Peck's masterful, detail-rich prose describes wartime in the United
States.... Peck's characters are memorable.... This book is an absolute
delight." SLJ

★ **A season** of gifts. Dial Books for Young Readers 2009 156p
$16.99
Grades: 5 6 7 8 **Fic**
1. Moving -- Fiction 2. Illinois -- Fiction
ISBN 978-0-8037-3082-3; 0-8037-3082-9

LC 2008-48050

Relates the surprising gifts bestowed on twelve-year-old Bob Barn-
hart and his family, who have recently moved to a small Illinois town in
1958, by their larger-than-life neighbor, Mrs. Dowdel.
"The type of down-home humor and vibrant characterizations
Peck fans have come to adore re-emerge in full as Peck resurrects Mrs.
Dowdel, the irrepressible, self-sufficient grandmother featured in A Year
Down Yonder and A Long Way from Chicago." Publ Wkly

★ **Secrets** at sea; illustrations by Kelly Murphy. Dial Books for
Young Readers 2011 238p il $16.99
Grades: 3 4 5 6 **Fic**
1. Adventure fiction 2. Mice -- Fiction 3. Siblings -- Fiction 4.
Ocean travel -- Fiction 5. Social classes -- Fiction
ISBN 978-0-8037-3455-5; 0-8037-3455-7

LC 2011001162
In 1887, the social-climbing Cranstons voyage from New York to
London, where they hope to find a husband for their awkward older
daughter, secretly accompanied by Helena and her mouse siblings, for
whom the journey is both terrifying and wondrous as they meet an array
of titled humans despite their best efforts at remaining hidden.
This is a "rollicking comedy of manners that begs to be read aloud....
. Peck's droll take on human and mouse society is exquisite.... Helena's
meticulous observations .... [are] enhanced by hilariously upended
clichés ... and by Murphy's dandy and detailed pencil illustrations that
add just the right air of royalty." Horn Book

★ **A year** down yonder. Dial Bks. for Young Readers 2000 130p
$16.99; pa $5.99
Grades: 5 6 7 8 **Fic**
1. Grandmothers -- Fiction 2. Great Depression, 1929-1939 --
Fiction
ISBN 0-8037-2518-3; 0-14-230070-5 pa

LC 99-43159
Awarded the Newbery Medal, 2001
"Peck has created a delightful, insightful tale that resounds with a
storyteller's wit, humor, and vivid description." SLJ

Peet, Mal
★ **Cloud** Tea monkeys; by Mal Peet & Elspeth Graham; illustrated
by Juan Wijngaard. Candlewick Press 2010 un il lib bdg $15.99
Grades: 1 2 3 4 **Fic**
1. Tea -- Fiction 2. Monkeys -- Fiction 3. Mother-daughter
relationship -- Fiction
ISBN 978-0-7636-4453-6 lib bdg; 0-7636-4453-6 lib bdg

LC 2009-11868
When her mother becomes too ill to harvest tea on the nearby plantation, Shenaz is too small to fill in, but when she tells the monkeys she
has befriended why she is sad, they bring her a basket filled with rare
and valuable wild tea.
"The tale has the feel of a time-honed fable—simple, elegant, and
moving—which is especially well complemented by Wijngaard's sumptuous illustrations." Booklist

Mysterious traveler; Mal Peet, Elspeth Graham, illustrated by P. J.
Lynch. Candlewick Press 2013 48 p. $15.99
Grades: 3 4 5 **Fic**
1. Sahara Desert -- Fiction 2. Picture books for children
ISBN 0763662321; 9780763662325

LC 2012947823
This children's picture book was "inspired by the guides who navigate the Sahara in Mali." An old man named Issa rescues a baby wearing
a valuable necklace and "raises the infant as his granddaughter, relying
more and more on young Mariama once his eyesight begins to fail....
After a trio of arrogant visitors rejects Issa's guidance, he and Mariama

rescue them just as a potentially deadly sandstorm swirls up." One of the boys turns out to be Mariama's brother. (School Library Journal)

Night sky dragons; Mal Peet, Elspeth Graham, illustrated by Patrick Benson. Candlewick Press 2014 64 p. color illustrations $15.99
Grades: 1 2 3 4 **Fic**
1. Silk Road 2. Kites -- Fiction 3. Grandfathers -- Fiction 4. Father-son relationship -- Fiction
ISBN 0763661449; 9780763661441

LC 2013955686

In this children's book, by Mal Peet, "Yazul loves making kites with his grandfather, but all he truly desires is the approval of his father. Yazul's father, lord of a han along the Silk Road, is a man made stern by loneliness, and Yazul's love of kite-making only seems to elicit disappointment. . . . But when the han is attacked by bandits, Yazul has an idea. With the help of his grandfather, he might just be able to use his kite-making skills to scare the bandits away." (Publisher's note)

"The uniqueness of the story and its setting make it a wonderful offering for readers looking for a far-flung, adventure-filled story." SLJ

Peirce, Lincoln

★ **Big** Nate; in a class by himself. Harper 2010 214p $12.99
Grades: 3 4 5 **Fic**
1. School stories
ISBN 978-0-06-194434-5; 0-06-194434-3; 978-0-06-194435-2 lib bdg; 0-06-194435-1 lib bdg

LC 2009-39668

The author "uses a mix of prose and cartoons to tell a quick story about a day in the life of an extroverted, impish kid. . . . Nate, has been the star of a long-running daily comic strip. . . . He wakes up feeling fine, sweats a bit about an upcoming test, then opens a fortune cookie at school that reads, 'Today you will surpass all others.' . . . The cartoons provide plenty of gags at the expense of various adults and classmates, and Nate's persistent good cheer and moxie make him a likable new proxy for young misfits." Booklist

Other titles in this series are:
Big Nate strikes again (2010)
Big Nate on a roll (2011)

Big Nate on a roll. Harper 2011 216p il $12.99; lib bdg $14.89
Grades: 3 4 5 **Fic**
1. School stories 2. Contests -- Fiction
ISBN 978-0-06-194438-3; 0-06-194438-6; 978-0-06-194439-0 lib bdg; 0-06-194439-4 lib bdg

LC 2011016548

Middle-schooler Nate Wright vies against his rival, the 'perfect' Artur, to win the grand prize of a customized skateboard in their scout troop contest.

This "is the slickest of this series of hybrid comics-and-text chapter books. Nate's an artistic, realistic, funny narrator." Kirkus

Big Nate strikes again. Harper 2010 216p il $12.99; lib bdg $14.89
Grades: 3 4 5 **Fic**
1. School stories 2. Humorous fiction 3. Sports -- Fiction
ISBN 978-0-06-194436-9; 0-06-194436-X; 978-0-06-194437-6 lib bdg; 0-06-194437-8 lib bdg

LC 2010024449

Sequel to: Big Nate: in a class by himself (2010)

Sixth-grader and self-proclaimed genius Nate Wright faces his all-time enemy, Gina, when they are paired to work on a research paper together and she also gets a position on his intramural team.

"Peirce gets all the details of a sixth-grade boy just right: the humiliation of first love and first hate, the monotony of school, the importance of sports, the relentlessness of bullies, and the goofiness of best friends. . . . Even the most jaded middle-schoolers will find much to laugh about here." Horn Book

Pennypacker, Sara, 1951-

★ **Clementine**; [illustrated by] Marla Frazee. Hyperion Books for Children 2006 144p il $14.99; pa $4.99
Grades: 2 3 4 **Fic**
1. School stories 2. Friendship -- Fiction 3. Family life -- Fiction
ISBN 0-7868-3882-5; 0-7868-3883-3 pa

LC 2005-50458

Boston Globe-Horn Book Honor: Fiction (2007)

While sorting through difficulties in her friendship with her neighbor Margaret, eight-year-old Clementine gains several unique hairstyles while also helping her father in his efforts to banish pigeons from the front of their apartment building.

"Humorous scenarios tumble together, blending picturesque dialogue with a fresh perspective. . . . Frazee's engaging pen-and-ink drawings capture the energy and fresh-faced expressions of the irrepressible heroine." SLJ

Other titles about Clementine are:
The talented Clementine (2007)
Clementine's letter (2008)
Clementine, Friend of the Week (2010)
Clementine and the family meeting (2011)

Clementine and the spring trip; Sara Pennypacker; pictures by Marla Frazee. Disney-Hyperion Books 2013 150 p. ill. (Clementine) $14.99
Grades: 2 3 4 **Fic**
1. Field trips 2. School stories 3. Spring -- Fiction 4. Family life -- Massachusetts -- Fiction
ISBN 1423123573; 9781423123576

LC 2011052991

In this book by Sara Pennypacker, "changes continue for Clementine: her mother's belly is growing bigger, the fourth graders continue their reign of terror over the lunchroom (no crunching of any food!), neighbor Margaret's mother is getting married again, the third grade is going to Plimoth Plantation (and has to eat with the fourth graders!), and new girl Olive is stealing some of our heroine's thunder." (Horn Book Magazine)

"Clementine learns important life lessons about growing up, becoming independent, and making choices. She's reminiscent of Ramona, Junie B. Jones, and Judy Moody with her own style and personality that listeners will easily relate to." SLJ

★ **Pax**; Sara Pennypacker; iillustrated by Jon Klassen. Balzer + Bray 2016 288 p. illustrations (hardback) $16.99
Grades: 4 5 6 7 **Fic**
1. Foxes -- Fiction 2. Human-animal relationships -- Fiction 3. Foxes as pets -- Fiction
ISBN 9780062377012; 0062377019

LC 2015015400

This children's novel, by Sara Pennypacker and illustrated by Jon Klassen, is "about the powerful relationship between a boy and his fox. Pax and Peter have been inseparable ever since Peter rescued him as a kit. But one day . . . Peter's dad enlists in the military and makes him return the fox to the wild. At his grandfather's house, three hundred miles away from home, Peter . . . strikes out on his own despite the encroaching war, spurred by love, loyalty, and grief, to be reunited with his fox." (Publisher's note)

"Every moment in the graceful, fluid narrative is believable. Klassen's cover art has a sense of contained, powerful stillness. (Interior illustrations not seen.) Moving and poetic." Kirkus

★ The **summer** of the gypsy moths; Sara Pennypacker. Balzer + Bray 2012 275 p. (tr. bdg.) $15.99

Grades: 4 5 6   **Fic**

1. Siblings -- Fiction 2. Family life -- Fiction 3. Foster children -- Fiction 4. Death -- Fiction 5. Secrets -- Fiction 6. Great aunts -- Fiction 7. Cape Cod (Mass.) -- Fiction 8. Loss (Psychology) -- Fiction

ISBN 0061964204; 9780061964206

LC 2011026095

This middle reader story by Sara Pennypacker follows "Stella[, who] loves living with Great-aunt Louise in her big old house near the water on Cape Cod . . . since her mom is . . . unreliable. So while Mom 'finds herself,' Stella fantasizes that someday she'll come back to the Cape and settle down. The only obstacle to her plan? Angel, the foster kid Louise has taken in. . . . [T]he girls hardly speak to each other. But when tragedy unexpectedly strikes, Stella and Angel are forced to rely on each other to survive." (Publisher's note)

★ **Waylon!** one awesome thing. Sara Pennypacker; pictures by Marla Frazee. Disney-Hyperion 2016 208 p. illustrations (hardcover) $15.99

Grades: 2 3 4   **Fic**

1. School stories 2. Change -- Fiction 3. Genius -- Fiction 4. Schools -- Fiction 5. Brothers and sisters -- Fiction

ISBN 9781484701522

LC 2015009023

In this juvenile novel, by Sara Pennypacker and illustrated by Marla Frazee, "Waylon has lots of ideas for making life more awesome through science, like teleportation, human gills, and attracting cupcakes by controlling gravity. But it's impossible for him to concentrate on his inventions when he's experiencing his own personal Big Bang. Arlo Brody is dividing the fourth grade boys into two groups. Waylon would rather be friends with everyone." (Publisher's note)

"An upbeat celebration of lively imagination, friendship, family, community, and the exuberance of childhood." Kirkus

Perkins, Lynne Rae

★ **Criss** cross. Greenwillow Books 2005 337p $16.99; lib bdg $17.89; pa $6.99

Grades: 6 7 8 9   **Fic**

1. Nineteen sixties -- Fiction 2. Identity (Psychology) -- Fiction

ISBN 0-06-009272-6; 0-06-009273-4 lib bdg; 0-06-009274-2 pa

LC 2004-54023

Awarded the Newbery Medal, 2006

Teenagers in a small town in the 1960s experience new thoughts and feelings, question their identities, connect, and disconnect as they search for the meaning of life and love. "Grades five to eight." (Bull Cent Child Books)

"Debbie . . . and Hector . . . narrate most of the novel. Both are 14 years old. Hector is a fabulous character with a wry humor and an appealing sense of self-awareness. . . . The descriptive, measured writing includes poems, prose, haiku, and question-and-answer formats. There is a great deal of humor in this gentle story." SLJ

Perkins, Mitali

★ **Bamboo** people. Charlesbridge 2010 272p $16.95

Grades: 5 6 7 8   **Fic**

1. Myanmar -- Fiction 2. Wilderness survival -- Fiction

ISBN 978-1-58089-328-2; 1-58089-328-7

LC 2009005495

Two Burmese boys, one a Karenni refugee and the other the son of an imprisoned Burmese doctor, meet in the jungle and in order to survive they must learn to trust each other.

"Perkins seamlessly blends cultural, political, religious, and philosophical context into her story, which is distinguished by humor, astute insights into human nature, and memorable characters." Publ Wkly

★ **Rickshaw** girl; illustrated by Jamie Hogan. Charlesbridge 2007 91p il lib bdg $13.95

Grades: 3 4 5   **Fic**

1. Painting -- Fiction 2. Sex role -- Fiction 3. Bangladesh -- Fiction

ISBN 978-1-58089-308-4

LC 2006-09031

In her Bangladesh village, ten-year-old Naimi excels at painting designs called alpanas, but to help her impoverished family financially she would have to be a boy—or disguise herself as one

"This short chapter book tells a realistic story with surprises that continue until the end. Hogan's bold black-and-white sketches show the brave girl, the beautiful traditional alpana painting and rickshaw art, and the contemporary changes in the girl's rural home." Booklist

Tiger boy; Mitali Perkins; illustrated by Jamie Hogan. Charlesbridge 2015 144 p. (reinforced for library use) $14.95

Grades: 3 4 5 6   **Fic**

1. Tigers -- Fiction 2. Bangladesh -- Fiction 3. Family life -- Fiction 4. Animal rescue -- Fiction 5. Wildlife rescue -- Fiction

ISBN 158089660X; 9781580896603; 9781607345435; 9781607346647

LC 2013049028

"When a tiger cub goes missing from the reserve, Neel is determined to find her before the greedy Gupta gets his hands on her to kill her and sell her body parts on the black market. Neel's parents, however, are counting on him to study hard and win a prestigious scholarship to study in Kolkata. Neel doesn't want to leave his family or his island home and he struggles with his familial duty." (Publisher's note)

Perl, Erica S.

Aces wild; Erica S. Perl. Alfred A. Knopf 2013 224 p. $15.99

Grades: 4 5 6   **Fic**

1. Dogs -- Fiction 2. Family life -- Fiction 3. Grandfathers -- Fiction 4. Vermont -- Fiction 5. Sleepovers -- Fiction 6. Dogs -- Training -- Fiction 7. Jews -- United States -- Fiction 8. Family life -- Vermont -- Fiction

ISBN 0307931722; 9780307931726; 9780307975478; 9780375971044

LC 2012023335

Written by Erica S. Perl, this book describes how "Zelly Fried has finally convinced her parents to let her get a dog, with the help of her grandfather Ace. Unfortunately, said dog (also named Ace) is a shoe-chewing, mud-tracking, floor-peeing kind of dog. . . . Also wild is the other Ace in Zelly's life. Grandpa Ace has decided to begin dating again and is dining and dancing every night, against his doctor's orders." (Publisher's note)

"Zelly (When Life Gives You O.J.) finally has the dog she has always wanted. Now she hopes to host a sleepover at her house in order to help her fit in at her new school. First she has to be able to control Ace, her dog--and Ace, her grandpa. Zelly tries to navigate obedience classes, school, and family in this entertaining sequel." Horn Book

The **capybara** conspiracy; A Novel in Three Acts. Erica S. Perl. Alfred A. Knopf Books for Young Readers 2016 192 p. (ebook) $50.97; (hardback) $16.99

Grades: 5 6 7 8   **Fic**

1. Humorous fiction 2. Mascots -- Fiction 3. Theater -- Fiction

4. Friendship -- Fiction 5. Schools -- Fiction 6. Middle schools
-- Fiction
ISBN 9780399551734; 0399551719; 9780399551710;
9780399551727

LC 2015047497

In this children's book by Erica S. Perl, "seventh-grade playwright
Olive Henry is frustrated by her middle school's lack of appreciation for
anything but sports. . . . So Olive and her best friend, Reynaldo, hatch
a plan to kidnap the school's capybara mascot, planning to return it,
heroically, just in time for the school's pep rally and claim a reward .
. . and, hopefully, some overdue respect for the school's non-athletes."
(Publisher's note)

"Staged over three acts, Perl's novel zips along thanks to all the
back-and-forth dialogue, and is well suited to be performed. An unexpected ending and comprehensive notes on how to stage the play round
out an amusing tale." Pub Wkly

When life gives you O.J. Alfred A. Knopf 2011 198p $15.99; lib
bdg $18.99
Grades: 3 4 5   **Fic**
1. Dogs -- Fiction 2. Vermont -- Fiction 3. Family life -- Fiction 4.
Grandfathers -- Fiction 5. Jews -- United States -- Fiction
ISBN 978-0-375-85924-3; 0-375-85924-1; 978-0-375-95924-0
lib bdg; 0-375-95924-6 lib bdg

LC 2010023844

Zelly Fried wants a dog more than anything, so at the urging of her
grandfather, during the summer before sixth grade she takes care of a
"practice dog" made out of an orange juice jug to show her parents that
she is ready for the responsibility, even though she is sometimes not
entirely sure about the idea.

"Zelly is a sympathetic, believably flawed character. . . . [This is a]
funny, often wise novel." Booklist

Perl, Lila

Isabel's War; Lila Perl. Lizzie Skurnick Books 2014 224 p.
$12.95
Grades: 5 6 7 8   **Fic**
1. Historical fiction 2. World War, 1939-1945 -- Refugees -- Fiction
3. Refugees -- Fiction 4. Holocaust, Jewish (1939-1945) -- Fiction
5. Kindertransports (Rescue operations) -- Fiction
ISBN 1939601274; 1939601363; 9781939601278;
9781939601360
Sydney Taylor Book Awards Honor Book (2013)

In this novel, by Lila Perl, "introduces us to Isabel Brandt, . . .
twelve-year-old New Yorker who's more interested in boys and bobbing
her nose than the distant war across the Pacific. . . . Things change when
Helga . . . comes to live with Isabel and her family. Helga is everything
Isabel's not--cool, blonde, and vaguely aloof. She's also a German war
refugee, with a past that gives a growing Isabel something more important to think about than boys and her own looks." (Publisher's note)

"Isabel Brandt is a typical 12-year-girl who dreams of Frank Sinatra,
boys, and being popular in school. But it is 1942, and the war in Europe
and the Pacific becomes very significant for this Jewish girl from the
Bronx. As her family begins their summer vacation in the Catskills, Isabel meets Helga, her new roommate...As Isabel learns about the war and
the treatment of Jews by Nazis, her relationship with Helga and her outlook on life radically changes. Readers will identify with the protagonist
as she discovers what things are truly important." SLJ

Perro, Bryan

The **key** of Braha; Bryan Perro; translated from the French by Y.
Maudet. Delacorte Press 2012 184 p. (hc) $16.99
Grades: 4 5 6 7   **Fic**
1. Fantasy fiction 2. Adventure fiction 3. Dead -- Fiction 4.

Mythology -- Fiction 5. Fantasy 6. Good and evil -- Fiction 7.
Adventure and adventurers -- Fiction
ISBN 0385907672; 9780375896941; 9780385739047;
9780385907675

LC 2011026173

This book is the second in Bryan Perro's 'Amos Daragon' young
adult fantasy series, translated from French, in which a 12-year-old sorcerer named Amos, "unwittingly takes on a hazardous mission: He's
killed so he can pass into and fix a netherworld crowded with dead souls
who aren't being permitted to pass on to their appointed fates. . . . Once
there Amos receives aid against numerous enemies from a varied cast of
. . . characters, many of whom are figures from mythology (explained in
a lexicon)." (Kirkus)

The **mask** wearer; translated from the French by Y. Maudet. Delacorte Press 2011 167p (Amos Paragon) $16.99; lib bdg $19.99
Grades: 4 5 6 7   **Fic**
1. Fantasy fiction 2. Adventure fiction 3. Good and evil -- Fiction
ISBN 0-385-73903-6; 0-385-90766-4 lib bdg; 978-0-385-73903-
0; 978-0-385-90766-8 lib bdg

LC 2010023725

To defeat the forces of evil which threaten his world, young Amos
Daragon, aided by mythical animal friends, sets out on a journey to find
four masks that harness the forces of nature and sixteen powerful stones
that give the masks their magic.

"Amos's journey of self-discovery and his quick thinking are sure
to keep readers turning the pages to discover the truth behind the never-
ending chaos." SLJ

Peterfreund, Diana

Omega City; by Diana Peterfreund. Harpercollins Childrens
Books 2015 336 p. $16.99
Grades: 4 5 6 7   **Fic**
1. Adventure fiction 2. Cold war -- Fiction 3. Scientists -- Fiction
4. Conspiracies -- Fiction
ISBN 0062310852; 9780062310859

LC 2014952614

In this middle grades book, by Diana Peterfreund, "Gillian Seagret
doesn't listen to people who say her father's a crackpot. His conspiracy
theories about the lost technology of Cold War-era rocket scientist Dr.
Aloysius Underberg may have cost him his job and forced them to move
to the middle of nowhere, but Gillian knows he's right and plans to prove
it. . . . Gillian sets off on a journey into the ruins of Omega City, a vast
doomsday bunker deep inside the earth." (Publisher's note)

Petersen, P. J.

Wild river. Delacorte Press 2009 120p $14.99; lib bdg $17.99
Grades: 4 5 6 7   **Fic**
1. Brothers -- Fiction 2. Kayaks and kayaking -- Fiction 3.
Wilderness survival -- Fiction
ISBN 978-0-385-73724-1; 0-385-73724-6; 978-0-385-90656-2
lib bdg; 0-385-90656-0 lib bdg

LC 2008-24921

Considered lazy and unathletic, twelve-year-old Ryan discovers a
heroic side of himself when a kayak trip with his older brother goes
horribly awry.

"The compelling first-person narration sets this apart from other adventure stories. . . . With sharp pacing, short sentences, and an unintimi-
dating length, this is a strong, accessible choice for younger readers."
Booklist

Peterson, Lois J.

The **ballad** of Knuckles McGraw; written by Lois Peterson. Orca
Book Publishers 2010 105p (Orca young readers) pa $7.95

Grades: 3 4 5 **Fic**
1. Grandparents -- Fiction 2. Foster home care -- Fiction 3. Abandoned children -- Fiction
ISBN 978-1-55469-203-3 pa; 1-55469-203-2 pa

After Kevin's mother abandons him, he takes refuge in his fantasy of becoming a cowboy, but his reality is a foster home and grandparents he doesn't know.

"The author understands how kids think, a fact that will allow kids in your library to thoroughly enjoy this book." Libr Media Connect

Petti, Erin

The **Peculiar** Haunting of Thelma Bee; by Erin Petti; illustrated by Kris Aro McLeod. Mighty Media Junior Readers 2016 216 p. illustrations $16.99
Grades: 4 5 6 **Fic**
1. Ghost stories 2. Adventure fiction 3. Fathers -- Fiction 4. Kidnapping -- Fiction
ISBN 9781938063732; 1938063724; 9781938063725
LC 2016009393

In this book, by Erin Petti, illustrated by Kris Aro McLeod, "eleven-year-old budding scientist Thelma Bee has adventure in her blood. But she gets more than she bargained for when a ghost kidnaps her father. Now her only clues are a strange jewelry box and the word "Return," whispered to her by the ghost. It's up to Thelma to get her dad back, and it might be more dangerous than she thought—there's someone wielding dark magic, and they're coming after her next." (Publisher's note)

"The worlds she creates, especially the ones inside the box, are imaginative and fresh. It is rewarding to read about a scientifically minded female protagonist, and that should help attract an audience." SLJ

Philbrick, Nathaniel

Ben's Revolution; Nathaniel Philbrick; illustrations by Wendell Minor. Nancy Paulsen Books 2017 64 p. color illustrations, color map (hardback) $17.99
Grades: 2 3 4 **Fic**
1. Boston (Mass.) -- Fiction 2. United States -- History -- 1775-1783, Revolution -- Fiction 3. Bunker Hill, Battle of, Boston, Mass., 1775 -- Fiction 4. United States -- History -- Revolution, 1775-1783 -- Fiction 5. Boston (Mass.) -- History -- Revolution, 1775-1783 -- Fiction 6. Bunker Hill, Battle of, Boston, Mass., 1775 -- Fiction 7. Boston (Mass.) -- History -- Revolution, 1775-1783 -- Fiction
ISBN 9780399166747
LC 2016025722

In this book, by Nathaniel Philbrick, illustrated by Wendell Minor, "Ben knew this day was coming; after all, tensions had been mounting between the colonists and the British troops ever since the Boston Tea Party. And now they have finally reached the breaking point. Ben and his friends . . . follow the throngs of redcoats marching out of Boston toward Concord. Much to Ben's surprise, Boston is sealed off later that day—leaving the boys stuck outside the city, in the middle of a war." (Publisher's note)

Philbrick, Rodman, 1951-

★ The **mostly** true adventures of Homer P. Figg; [by] Rodman Philbrick. Blue Sky Press 2009 224p $16.99
Grades: 5 6 7 8 **Fic**
1. Adventure fiction 2. Orphans -- Fiction 3. Brothers -- Fiction 4. United States -- History -- 1861-1865, Civil War -- Fiction
ISBN 978-0-439-66818-7; 0-439-66818-2
LC 2008-16925

A Newbery Medal honor book, 2010

Twelve-year-old Homer, a poor but clever orphan, has extraordinary adventures after running away from his evil uncle to rescue his brother, who has been sold into service in the Civil War

"The book wouldn't be nearly as much fun without Homer's tall tales, but there are serious moments, too, and the horror of war and injustice of slavery ring clearly above the din of playful exaggerations." Publ Wkly

Zane and the hurricane; a story of Katrina. Rodman Philbrick. The Blue Sky Press, an imprint of Scholastic Inc. 2014 181 p. maps (hardback) $16.99
Grades: 5 6 7 8 **Fic**
1. Rescue work -- Fiction 2. Hurricane Katrina, 2005 -- Fiction 3. Survival -- Fiction 4. African Americans -- Fiction 5. New Orleans (La.) -- Fiction 6. Racially mixed people -- Fiction
ISBN 0545342384; 9780545342384
LC 2013025489

In this children's novel, by Rodman Philbrick, "Zane Dupree is a charismatic 12-year-old boy of mixed race visiting a relative in New Orleans when Hurricane Katrina hits. Unexpectedly separated from all family, Zane and his dog experience the terror of Katrina's wind, rain, and horrific flooding. Facing death, they are rescued from an attic air vent by a kind, elderly musician and a scrappy young girl." (Publisher's note)

"Careful attention to detail in representations of the storm, the city and local dialect give this tale a realistic feel. Zane's perspective as an outsider allows Philbrick to weave in social commentary on race, class, greed and morality, offering rich fodder for reflection and discussion." Kirkus

Pierce, Tamora

Magic steps; book one of the Circle opens quartet. Scholastic Press 2000 264p (Circle opens quartet) hardcover o.p. pa $5.99
Grades: 5 6 7 8 **Fic**
1. Fantasy fiction 2. Magic -- Fiction
ISBN 0-590-39588-2; 0-590-39605-6 pa
LC 99-31943

"Using descriptive, personable prose, Pierce combines dimensional characters, intricate details, plot twists, and alternating story lines for a gripping read. . . . There is some vivid violence." Booklist

Other titles in this series are:
Street magic (2001)
Cold fire (2002)
Shatterglass (2003)

Pierpoint, Eric

The **last** ride of Caleb O'Toole; Eric Pierpoint. Sourcebooks Jabberwocky 2013 304 p. (tp : alk. paper) $7.99
Grades: 4 5 6 7 **Fic**
1. Oregon Trail -- Fiction 2. Historical fiction 3. Orphans -- Fiction 4. Wagon trains -- Fiction 5. Bozeman Trail -- Fiction 6. Coming of age -- Fiction 7. Brothers and sisters -- Fiction 8. Adventure and adventurers -- Fiction 9. Oregon National Historic Trail -- Fiction 10. West (U.S.) -- History -- 1860-1890 -- Fiction
ISBN 1402281714; 9781402281716
LC 2013011800

In this book, it's "1877 in Great Bend, Kan., and cholera has panicked citizens and killed scores, including Caleb O'Toole's father. The story opens as 12-year-old Caleb races through town to find one of his sisters while his mother lies dying of the disease and a mob threatens to burn down their house. Caleb then witnesses a murder, and the O'Toole children escape amid an explosive gunfight, after agreeing to . . . take the Oregon Trail to their aunt's ranch in Montana Territory." (Publishers Weekly)

The **secret** mission of William Tuck; Eric Pierpoint. Sourcebooks Jabberwocky 2015 312 p. (13 : alk. paper) $7.99

Grades: 4 5 6 7 8   **Fic**
1. Spies -- Fiction 2. United States -- History -- 1775-1783,
Revolution -- Fiction
ISBN 1402281749; 9781402281747

LC 2015009887

In Eric Pierpont's novel "the whispered words of a dying soldier, and
a mysterious watch, give William all the ammunition he needs; a secret
message for the leader of the rebel army. Rebecca disguises herself as
a boy, and she and William join the American troops. They embark on
an epic journey that pulls them into a secret network of spies, pits them
against dangerous gunmen, and leads them on a quest to find General
George Washington himself." (Publisher's note)
    "Richly detailed and exhilarating." Kirkus

Pileggi, Leah
    Prisoner 88; Leah Pileggi. Charlesbridge 2013 142 p. (reinforced
for library use) $16.95
Grades: 4 5 6 7 8   **Fic**
1. Prisons -- Fiction 2. Prisoners -- Fiction 3. Prisons -- Idaho
Territory -- Fiction
ISBN 1580895603; 9781580895606; 9781607345343;
9781607346111

LC 2012024443

In this book, by Leah Pileggi, "ten-year-old Jake Evans has just received a five-year sentence for manslaughter. . . . The warden and guards
are at a bit of a loss on how to treat so young a convict, and . . . Jake's life
improves considerably in the aftermath of his conviction." But "there are
hardened criminals who would like to take Jake down just for the grim
pleasure of it, and Jake is drawn into the turmoil of an jailbreak attempt."
(Bulletin of the Center for Children's Literature)
    Prisoner Eighty-eight

Pilkey, Dav, 1966-
    The **Adventures** of Captain Underpants; Dav Pilkey, illustrated
by Jesse Garibaldi. First color edition. Scholastic 2013 136 p. $9.99
Grades: 2 3 4   **Fic**
1. Adventure fiction 2. Superheroes -- Fiction 3. School principals
-- Fiction
ISBN 0545499089; 9780545499088

LC 2013935584

Originally published 1997

This humorous children's novel, by Dav Pilkey and illustrated by
Jose Garibaldi, is the first book in the author's "Captain Underpants"
series. In it "George and Harold have created the greatest superhero in
the history of their elementary school--and now they're going to bring
him to life! Meet Captain Underpants! His true identity is so secret, even
HE doesn't know who he is!" (Publisher's note)

Captain Underpants and the sensational saga of Sir Stinks-A-Lot;
the twelfth epic novel. by Dav Pilkey. Scholastic Inc. 2015 208 p. illustrations (Captain Underpants) (hc) $9.99
Grades: 2 3 4   **Fic**
1. Brainwashing -- Fiction 2. Elementary schools -- Fiction 3.
Inventions -- Fiction 4. Supervillains -- Fiction 5. Humorous
stories 6. Schools -- Fiction
ISBN 0545504929; 9780545504928

LC 2015005667

In this middle grades book, by Dav Pilkey, "George and Harold, and
their doubles, Yesterday George and Yesterday Harold, have a good thing
going. Two of them go to school, while the other two hide in the tree
house and play video games all day -- then they switch! But when their
malicious gym teacher, Mr. Meaner, creates a method of mind-control
that turns their fellow students into attentive, obedient, perfect children,
the future of all humanity will be in their hands!" (Publisher's note)

"The series' twelfth entry finds pals George and Harold—and their
duplicates, Yesterday George and Yesterday Harold—happily taking
turns attending school and playing hooky. . . . The insane popularity of
Pilkey's Captain Underpants series hasn't ebbed with time. A new title
will send droves of kids to the shelves, so stock up!" Booklist

Captain Underpants and the tyrannical retaliation of the Turbo Toilet 2000; the eleventh epic novel. by Dav Pilkey. Scholastic Inc. 2015
224 p. (hc) $9.99
Grades: 2 3 4   **Fic**
1. Adventure fiction 2. Superheroes -- Fiction 3. Humorous stories
4. Monsters -- Fiction 5. School principals -- Fiction 6. Captain
Underpants (Fictitious character)
ISBN 0545504902; 9780545504904

LC 2014008919

In this middle grades adventure book by Dav Pilkey, "When the Incredible Robo-Plunger defeated the evil Turbo Toilet 2000, George and
Harold thought their toilet troubles were over. Unfortunately, their porcelain problems were only beginning . . . Just when you thought it was
safe to flush . . . The Turbo Toilet 2000 strikes back!" (Publisher's note)
    "The famous superhero returns to fight another villain with all the
trademark wit and humor the series is known for...Adults may roll their
eyes here and there, but youngsters will eat this up just as quickly as they
devoured every other Underpants episode. Dizzyingly silly." Kirkus
    Part of the recommended "Captain Underpants" series.

Pincus, Greg
    The **14** fibs of Gregory K; Greg Pincus. Arthur A. Levine Books
2013 240 p. (hardcover : alk. paper) $17.99
Grades: 4 5 6 7   **Fic**
1. Mathematics -- Fiction 2. Truthfulness and falsehood 3.
Honesty -- Fiction 4. Schools -- Fiction 5. 6. Middle schools --
Fiction 7. Creative writing -- Fiction 8. Fathers and sons -- Fiction
9. Brothers and sisters -- Fiction
ISBN 0439912997; 9780439912990; 9780439913003

LC 2012044117

In this book, by Greg Pincus, "Gregory K is the middle child in a
family of mathematical geniuses. But if he claimed to love math? Well,
he'd be fibbing. What he really wants most is to go to Author Camp.
But to get his parents' permission he's going to have to pass his math
class, which has a probability of 0. THAT much he can understand!"
(Publisher's note)
    Another title in this series is:
    The homework strike (2017)

Pinkney, Andrea Davis
    ★ **Bird** in a box; illustrations by Sean Qualls. Little, Brown Books
for Young Readers 2011 278p il $16.99
Grades: 4 5 6 7   **Fic**
1. Boxing -- Fiction 2. African Americans -- Fiction 3. Radio
broadcasting -- Fiction 4. Harlem (New York, N.Y.) -- Fiction 5.
Great Depression, 1929-1939 -- Fiction
ISBN 978-0-316-07403-2; 0-316-07403-9

LC 2010-22851

In 1936, three children meet at the Mercy Home for Negro Orphans
in New York State, and while not all three are orphans, they are all dealing with grief and loss which together, along with the help of a sympathetic staff member and the boxing matches of Joe Louis, they manage
to overcome.
    "Pinkney weaves quite a bit of 1930s history into her story and suc-
ceeds admirably in showing how Louis came to represent so much more
than his sport. Her detailed notes make this an accessible and inspiring
piece of historical fiction that belongs in most collections." SLJ

★ The **red** pencil; a novel told in poems, pictures, and possibilities. by Andrea Davis Pinkney; illustrated by Shane Evans. First edition Little, Brown & Co. 2014 336 p. illustrations, map (hardcover) $17
Grades: 4 5 6 7   **Fic**
1. Sudan -- Fiction 2. Refugees -- Fiction 3. Novels in verse 4. Blacks -- Sudan -- Fiction
ISBN 9780316247801; 0316247804
                                          LC 2013044753
Amelia Bloomer Project (2014)
"Amira is twelve. . . . Maybe old enough to go to school in Nyala--Amira's one true dream. But life in her peaceful Sudanese village is shattered when the Janjaweed arrive. . . . After she loses nearly everything, Amira needs . . . to make the long journey . . . to safety at a refugee camp. Her days are tough at the camp, until the gift of a simple red pencil opens her mind." (Publisher's note)
"Amira's thoughts and drawings are vividly brought to life through Pinkney's lyrical verse and Evans's lucid line illustrations, which infuse the narrative with emotional intensity." SLJ

With the might of angels; the diary of Dawnie Rae Johnson. Scholastic 2011 324p il map (Dear America) $12.99
Grades: 5 6 7 8   **Fic**
1. School stories 2. Diaries -- Fiction 3. Virginia -- Fiction 4. Family life -- Fiction 5. Race relations -- Fiction 6. African Americans -- Fiction 7. School integration -- Fiction
ISBN 0-545-29705-2; 978-0-545-29705-9
                                          LC 2011001363
In 1955 Hadley, Virginia, twelve-year-old Dawnie Rae Johnson, a tomboy who excels at baseball and at her studies, becomes the first African American student to attend the all-white Prettyman Coburn school, turning her world upside down. Includes historical notes about the period.
"Dawnie's journal is realistic, encompassing thoughts and emotions one would expect of someone so stressed. . . . The author seamlessly incorporates historical events into the child's journal. The end matter contains age-appropriate photographs, a time line, and brief biographical sketches of the people mentioned. A first purchase." SLJ

Pinkwater, Daniel Manus
Adventures of a cat-whiskered girl; illustrations by Calef Brown. Houghton Mifflin Books for Children 2010 268p il $16
Grades: 4 5 6   **Fic**
1. Science fiction 2. Cats -- Fiction 3. Extraterrestrial beings -- Fiction
ISBN 978-0-547-22324-7; 0-547-22324-2
Big Audrey, who has catlike whiskers, and her telephathic friend Molly set out on a journey to find out why flying saucers are landing behind the old stone barn in Poughkeepsie, New York, and, more importantly, to determine whether another cat-whiskered girl really exists.
"Mixing the absurd with the profound, Pinkwater's odd narration will have even the most serious readers laughing at the chaos." Booklist

The **Hoboken** chicken emergency; by Daniel Pinkwater; illustrated by Tony Auth. Atheneum Books for Young Readers 2007 101p il $16.99; pa $4.99
Grades: 3 4 5 6   **Fic**
1. Chickens -- Fiction
ISBN 978-1-4169-2809-6; 1-4169-2809-X; 978-1-4169-2810-2 pa; 1-4169-2810-3 pa
                                          LC 2006101544
First published 1977 by Simon & Schuster
Arthur goes to pick up the turkey for Thanksgiving dinner but comes back with a 266-pound chicken.

"A contemporary tall tale that will stretch middle graders' imagination, sense of humor, and enthusiasm for reading." Booklist
Other titles about Henrietta the chicken are:
The Artsy Smartsy Club (2005)
Looking for Bobowicz (2004)

Lizard music; written and illustrated by Daniel Pinkwater. New York Review of Books 2011 157p il $15.95
Grades: 4 5 6   **Fic**
1. Science fiction 2. Lizards -- Fiction 3. Extraterrestrial beings -- Fiction
ISBN 978-1-59017-387-9; 1-59017-387-2
                                          LC 2010026945
A reissue of the title first published 1976 by Dodd, Mead
When left to take care of himself, a young boy becomes involved with a community of intelligent lizards who tell him of a little known invasion from outer space.
"The book—part satire, part sci-fi/fantasy—is amusing the original. Occasional Escher-esque drawings reflect the story's peculiarities." Horn Book Guide

Mrs. Noodlekugel and four blind mice; by Daniel Pinkwater and illustrated by Adam Stower. 1st ed. Candlewick Press 2013 96 p. $14.99
Grades: 2 3 4   **Fic**
1. Mice -- Fiction 2. Blind -- Fiction 3. Humorous stories 4. Babysitters -- Fiction
ISBN 0763650544; 9780763650544
                                          LC 2012947756
In author Daniel Pinkwater's book "four farsighted mice take center stage in the second installment of the Mrs. Noodlekugel series. Along with the mice, Mrs. Noodlekugel, Mr. Fuzzface (the talking cat), and children Maxine and Nick are having tea one afternoon. When the mice make a terrible mess of their tea table, Mrs. Noodlekugel declares it's their bad eyesight. So off they go to the oculist for a fitting of mice-sized glasses." (Booklist)

Pinter, Jason
Zeke Bartholomew, superspy. Sourcebooks Jabberwocky 2011 256p pa $7.99
Grades: 4 5 6 7   **Fic**
1. Adventure fiction 2. Spies -- Fiction
ISBN 978-1-4022-5755-1; 1-4022-5755-4
Zeke Bartholomew has always dreamed of being a spy. But when a case of mistaken identity goes horribly wrong, he's thrust into a world of real-life espionage beyond his wildest dreams. Soon this 7th grade nobody finds himself hunted by the lava-powered behemoth Ragnarok, aided by a mysterious butt-kicking girl who goes only by the codename 'Sparrow.'
"Zeke's first-person narration and ample one-liners provide plenty of laughs in a novel that combines espionage, wild sci-fi, and a satiric take on the ever-growing kids-save-the-world subgenre." Booklist

Pitchford, Dean
Captain Nobody. G.P. Putnam's Sons 2009 195p $16.99; pa $6.99
Grades: 3 4 5 6   **Fic**
1. Costume -- Fiction 2. Brothers -- Fiction 3. Halloween -- Fiction
ISBN 978-0-399-25034-7; 0-399-25034-4; 978-0-14-241667-9 pa; 0-14-241667-3 pa
                                          LC 2008-27733

When ten-year-old Newton dresses up as an unusual superhero for Halloween, he decides to keep wearing the costume after the holiday to help save townspeople and eventually his injured brother.

The author "builds suspense adeptly. . . . The young narrator's earnest voice—and his raw sense of helplessness—are real and affecting." Publ Wkly

Nickel Bay Nick; Dean Pitchford. G.P. Putnam's Sons, an imprint of Penguin Group (USA) Inc. 2013 272 p. $16.99
Grades: 4 5 6   **Fic**
1. Gifts -- Fiction 2. Secrets -- Fiction 4. Behavior -- Fiction 4. Christmas -- Fiction 5. Neighbors -- Fiction 6. City and town life -- Fiction
ISBN 039925465X; 9780399254659
LC 2012048972

In this book, 11-year-old "Sam Brattle, embittered at having the lousiest Christmas ever—and with a heart transplant and extensive history of larceny behind him—is blackmailed by his mysterious neighbor into taking on the role of Nickel Bay's homegrown secret Santa, the titular Nickel Bay Nick. Wealthy Mr. Wells has stealthily been distributing $100 bills around town at Christmastime for years, boosting the spirits and fortunes of its economically discouraged citizens." (Kirkus Reviews)

Place, Francois
The **old** man mad about drawing; a tale of Hokusai. translated from the French by William Rodarmor. David R. Godine 2004 105p il $19.95
Grades: 3 4 5 6   **Fic**
1. Artists 2. Japan -- Fiction
ISBN 1-56792-260-0
LC 2003-13521

Tojiro, a young seller of rice cakes in the Japanese capital of Edo, later known as Tokyo, is amazed to discover that the grumpy and shabby old man who buys his cakes is a famous artist renowned for his sketches, prints, and paintings of flowers, animals, and landscapes.

This book "features fine reproductions of Hokusai's work, as well as . . . elegant detailed sketches of the quiet studio and crowded streets." Booklist

Platt, Chris
Astra. Peachtree 2010 144p $15.95
Grades: 5 6 7 8   **Fic**
1. Horses -- Fiction 2. Father-daughter relationship -- Fiction
ISBN 978-1-56145-541-6; 1-56145-541-5
LC 2010001654

Forbidden to ride after her mother's death in a riding accident, thirteen-year-old Lily nurses her mother's beloved horse, Astra, back to health, hoping that someday Astra will win the Tevis Cup endurance race

"Filled with information about endurance racing as well as a cast of interesting supporting characters, including the dishy new boy in town, this novel is a quick and enjoyable read." SLJ

Platt, Randall Beth
Hellie Jondoe; [by] Randall Platt. Texas Tech University Press 2009 216p pa $16.95
Grades: 5 6 7 8   **Fic**
1. Oregon -- Fiction 2. Orphans -- Fiction
ISBN 978-0-89672-663-5 pa; 0-89672-663-0 pa
LC 2009-21514

In 1918, as the Great War ends and the Spanish influenza pandemic begins, thirteen-year-old Hellie Jondoe survives on the streets of New York as a beggar and pickpocket until she boards the orphan train to Oregon, where she learns about loyalty, honesty, and the meaning of family

"This is solid historical fiction with a scrappy heroine who is genuinely tough and a true survivor. Irrepressible and irreverent." Kirkus

Poblocki, Dan
The **stone** child. Random House 2009 274p $15.99; lib bdg $18.99
Grades: 5 6 7 8   **Fic**
1. Authors -- Fiction 2. Monsters -- Fiction 3. Supernatural -- Fiction 4. Books and reading -- Fiction
ISBN 978-0-375-84254-2; 0-375-84254-3; 978-0-375-94254-9 lib bdg; 0-375-94254-8 lib bdg
LC 2008-21722

When friends Eddie, Harris, and Maggie discover that the scary adventures in their favorite author's fictional books come true, they must find a way to close the portal that allows evil creatures and witches to enter their hometown of Gatesweed.

"The creep factor is high but not graphic, and the kids act and react like real kids. . . . This briskly paced novel is sure to be popular with fans of scary stuff." SLJ

Pogue, David
Abby Carnelia's one and only magical power. Roaring Brook Press 2010 277p $15.99
Grades: 3 4 5   **Fic**
1. Camps -- Fiction 2. Magic -- Fiction 3. Connecticut -- Fiction
ISBN 978-1-59643-384-7; 1-59643-384-1
LC 2009-46619

After eleven-year-old Abby discovers that she has a completely useless magical power, she finds herself at a magic camp where her hope of finding others like herself is realized, but when a select group is taken to a different camp, a sinister plot comes to light.

"This book is a whimsical feast for children. The characters are well developed; the story is magical and reminiscent of Eva Ibbotsen's wonderful books. The chapters are short and move the plot along quickly. It is an adventure from beginning to end and a plain good story." Libr Media Connect

Polacco, Patricia
★ **January's** sparrow. Philomel Books 2009 94p il $21.99
Grades: 4 5 6   **Fic**
1. Slavery -- Fiction 2. Family life -- Fiction 3. African Americans -- Fiction 4. Underground railroad -- Fiction
ISBN 978-0-399-25077-4; 0-399-25077-8
LC 2008-52720

After a fellow slave is beaten to death, Sadie and her family flee the plantation for freedom through the Underground Railroad.

"The illustrations, which include scenes of a bloody whipping and a heavily scarred back, have an urgent, unsettled look that fully captures the sharply felt danger and terror of Sadie's experiences. . . . This moving account effectively highlights a significant instance of nonviolent community resistance to injustice." SLJ

The **junkyard** wonders. Philomel 2010 un il $17.99
Grades: 2 3 4 5   **Fic**
1. School stories 2. Teachers -- Fiction 3. Special education -- Fiction 4. Airplanes -- Models -- Fiction
ISBN 978-0-399-25078-1; 0-399-25078-6

"Looking forward to a fresh start at a new school, Trisha is crestfallen when she is assigned to a special class with children who are different. Their teacher, Mrs. Peterson, proudly calls them the junkyard and takes them to an actual junkyard, which she describes as a place of wondrous possibilities. . . . Reclaiming and rebuilding an old model plane they intend to send to the moon, Trisha's tribe manages a triumphant launch. Illustrations, rendered in pencil and marker, portray children in addle oxfords and poodle skirts brimming with energy and excitement, guided by a model teacher. Based on her own childhood, Polacco's inspiring story will touch children and teachers alike." Booklist

Just in time, Abraham Lincoln. G. P. Putnam's Sons 2011 un il $17.99
Grades: 2 3 4 5 **Fic**
1. Lawyers 2. Presidents 3. State legislators 4. Brothers -- Fiction 5. Members of Congress 6. Time travel -- Fiction 7. Grandmothers -- Fiction 8. Antietam (Md.), Battle of, 1862 -- Fiction
ISBN 0-399-25471-4; 978-0-399-25471-0
LC 2010-23200
When two brothers visit a museum in Harper's Ferry, West Virginia, with their grandmother, they find themselves in a very realistic Civil War setting where they see the Antietam battlefield and meet historical figures from the aftermath of that momentous battle. Includes author's note on the Battle of Antietam.

"Climaxed by two wordless spreads of fields covered with twisted, bloodstained victims, the illustrations convey the boys' emotional shifts from boredom to astonishment, excitement to horror. . . . Rounded off with an afterword noting where some historical details have been telescoped, the episode will take a strong grip on readers' hearts and minds both." Kirkus

Tucky Jo and Little Heart; Patricia Polacco. Simon & Schuster Books for Young Readers 2015 48 p. color illustrations (hardcover) $17.99
Grades: 2 3 4 5 **Fic**
1. Kindness -- Fiction 2. World War, 1939-1945 3. Soldiers -- Fiction 4. Philippines -- History -- Japanese occupation, 1942-1945 -- Fiction
ISBN 1481415840; 9781481415842
LC 2014004223
In this children's story, by Patricia Polacco, "Tucky Jo . . . enlisted in the army at age fifteen. Being the youngest recruit in the Pacific during World War II was tough. But he finds a friend in a little girl who helps him soothe his bug bites, and he gets to know her family and gives them some of his rations. Although the little girl doesn't speak English, Tucky Jo and Little Heart share the language of kindness." (Publisher's note)

"Once again, this talented author/illustrator brings the past to life for young listeners and introduces them to unforgettable, admirable characters in the process." Kirkus

Polonsky, Ami
Threads; Ami Polonsky. Disney-Hyperion 2016 256 p. $16.99
Grades: 4 5 6 7 **Fic**
1. Factories -- Fiction 2. Child labor -- Fiction 3. Human trafficking -- Fiction 4. China -- Social conditions -- Fiction
ISBN 9781484746905
LC 2015043621
In this book, by Ami Polonsky, "the day twelve-year-old Clara finds a desperate note in a purse in Bellman's department store, she is still reeling from the death of her adopted sister, Lola. By that day, thirteen-year-old Yuming has lost hope that the note she stashed in the purse will ever be found. She may be stuck sewing in the pale pink factory outside of Beijing forever. Clara grows more and more convinced that she was meant to find Yuming's note." (Publisher's note)

"Based on a true incident, this is an engaging offering for readers who seek to broaden their global perspective. Especially good for teachers to use as a spark for classroom conversation." SLJ

Porter, Tracey
★ **Billy** Creekmore. Joanna Cotler Books 2007 305p $16.99; lib bdg $17.89; pa $6.99
Grades: 5 6 7 8 **Fic**
1. Circus -- Fiction 2. Orphanages -- Fiction 3. West Virginia -- Fiction 4. Coal mines and mining -- Fiction
ISBN 978-0-06-077570-4; 0-06-0-77570-X; 978-0-06-077571-1 lib bdg; 0-06-077571-8 lib bdg; 978-0-06-077572-8 pa; 0-06-077572-6 pa
LC 2007-00001
In 1905, ten-year-old Billy is taken from an orphanage to live with an aunt and uncle he never knew he had, and he enjoys his first taste of family life until his work in a coal mine and involvement with a union brings trouble, then he joins a circus in hopes of finding his father.

"Porter's writing is strong, and the story, told in Billy's steadfast yet child-true voice, makes the shocking history about the lives of children at the turn of the last century come alive for today's readers." Booklist

Potter, Ellen
The **humming** room; Ellen Potter. 1st ed. Feiwel & Friends 2012 184 p. $16.99
Grades: 4 5 6 7 **Fic**
1. Children's stories 2. Family -- Fiction 3. Haunted houses -- Fiction 4. Foster children -- Fiction 5. Gardens -- Fiction 6. Islands -- Fiction 7. Orphans -- Fiction
ISBN 0312644388; 9780312644383
LC 2011033583
In this book by Ellen Potter, "[h]idden under the family trailer, Roo hears . . . the murder of her drug-dealing father. . . . [S]he is sent to live with her . . . reclusive uncle on Cough Rock, a spooky old house named for its former use as a sanitarium. . . . [The cast of characters includes a] personal assistant, a cheerful local servant, a mysterious wild boy, and a secluded boy cousin with a fearful temper who is not expected to live." (Bulletin of the Center for Children's Books)

★ The **Kneebone** boy. Feiwel and Friends 2010 282p $16.99
Grades: 3 4 5 6 **Fic**
1. Adventure fiction 2. Mothers -- Fiction 3. Siblings -- Fiction 4. Great Britain -- Fiction 5. Eccentrics and eccentricities -- Fiction
ISBN 978-0-312-37772-4; 0-312-37772-X
LC 2010012572
Otto, Lucia, and Max Hardscrabble, whose mother has been missing for many years, have unexpected and illuminating adventures in the village of Snoring-by-the-Sea after their father, who paints portraits of deposed monarchs, goes away on a business trip.

"With a dark, witty absurdity . . . Potter . . . draws readers into this compelling mystery-adventure. . . . Potter's voice is distinguished by sharp, humorous, and poignant observations. . . . Often laugh-out-loud funny." Publ Wkly

★ **Olivia** Kidney; illustrated by Peter Reynolds. Philomel Bks. 2003 155p il $15.99; pa $5.99
Grades: 3 4 5 6 **Fic**
1. New York (N.Y.) -- Fiction 2. Apartment houses -- Fiction
ISBN 0-399-23850-6; 0-14-240234-6 pa
LC 2002-3660
Twelve-year-old Olivia explores her new apartment building and finds a psychic, talking lizards, a shrunken ex-pirate, an exiled princess, ghosts, and other unusual characters

"Potter has written a first-rate novel to be enjoyed on many levels. Its plot is so tightly woven that it's difficult to separate the mystical from the fantastical. Occasional full-page illustrations add another dimension to this narrative, which is wonderful medicine for the lonely." SLJ

Other titles about Olivia Kidney are:
Olivia Kidney and the Exit Academy (2005)
Olivia Kidney and the secret beneath the city (2007)

The **sea** pony; Ellen Potter; illustrated by Qin Leng. Alfred A. Knopf 2016 128 p. illustrations (hardback) $14.99
Grades: 2 3 4 **Fic**
1. Adventure fiction 2. Horses -- Fiction 3. Islands -- Fiction
ISBN 9780553499315; 9780553499322; 9780553499339
LC 2015035219

In this book, by Ellen Potter, illustrated by Qin Leng, "Piper Green is in for another adventure when she finds an unusual whistle hidden inside the Fairy Tree in her front yard. But Piper doesn't want a whistle... she wants a pony! On a trip with her dad to check the family's lobster traps, the whistle attracts the attention of an unexpected friend. Could the fairy whistle working its magic after all?" (Publisher's note)

"Cheerful line drawings add appeal. Completely satisfying. We wish for more." Kirkus

Other titles in this series are:
Piper Green and the Fairy Tree (2015)
Too Much Luck (2015)

Slob. Philomel Books 2009 199p $16.99
Grades: 5 6 7 8 **Fic**
1. Obesity -- Fiction 2. Orphans -- Fiction 3. Siblings -- Fiction 4. Inventions -- Fiction 5. Bereavement -- Fiction 6. New York (N.Y.) -- Fiction
ISBN 978-0-399-24705-7; 0-399-24705-X
LC 2008-40476

Picked on, overweight genius Owen tries to invent a television that can see the past to find out what happened the day his parents were killed.

"An intriguingly offbeat mystery, . . . at turns humorous, suspenseful and poignant." Kirkus

Poulsen, David A.
Old Man; David A. Poulsen. Dundurn Group Ltd 2013 224 p. $12.99
Grades: 6 7 8 **Fic**
1. Automobile travel -- Fiction 2. Father-son relationship -- Fiction 3. Vietnam War, 1961-1975 -- Veterans
ISBN 1459705475; 9781459705470

In this novel, by David A. Poulsen, "Nate Huffman's plans are unexpectedly shelved for the most unlikely of reasons: the reappearance of his estranged father. . . . Nate finds himself in a pickup with a man he can't stand. His father wants to reconnect, and he wants Nate to really understand him. Larry Huffman has chosen to make this happen by taking his son into his own past, which has the Vietnam War as its centrepiece." (Publisher's note)

Pratchett, Terry
★ **Only** you can save mankind. HarperCollins 2005 207p hardcover o.p. lib bdg $16.89; pa $6.99
Grades: 5 6 7 8 **Fic**
1. War stories 2. Computer games -- Fiction
ISBN 0-06-054185-7; 0-06-054186-5 lib bdg; 0-06-054187-3 pa
First published 1992 in the United Kingdom

Twelve-year-old Johnny endures tensions between his parents, watches television coverage of the Gulf War, and plays a computer game called Only You Can Save Mankind, in which he is increasingly drawn into the reality of the alien ScreeWee

This is "a wild ride, full of Pratchett's trademark humor; digs at primitive, low-resolution games . . .; and some not-so-subtle philosophy about war and peace." Booklist

Other titles in this trilogy are:
Johnny and the dead (2006)
Johnny and the bomb (2006)

Preller, James
The **courage** test; James Preller. Feiwel & Friends 2016 224 p. (hardcover) $16.99
Grades: 4 5 6 7 **Fic**
1. Father-son relationship -- Fiction 2. Lewis and Clark Expedition (1804-1806)
ISBN 9781250093912; 9781250093929; 9781250093936
LC 2016937798

In this book, by James Preller, "Will has no choice. His father drags him along on a wilderness adventure in the footsteps of legendary explorers Lewis and Clark--whether he likes it or not. All the while, Will senses that something about this trip isn't quite right. Along the journey, Will meets fascinating strangers and experiences new thrills, including mountain cliffs, whitewater rapids, and a heart-hammering bear encounter." (Publisher's note)

"Additionally, not only does the author slip cogent historical facts and insights into his simply told narrative without disturbing its flow, he offers more detail, plus sources of information, in an afterword." Booklist

Home sweet horror; James Preller; illustrated by Iacopo Bruno Feiwel and Friends 2013 97 p. illustrations (Scary tales) (pbk.) $5.99
Grades: 3 4 5 **Fic**
1. Ghost stories 2. Horror fiction 3. Haunted houses -- Fiction 4 Horror stories 5. Ghosts -- Fiction
ISBN 1250018862; 1250018870; 9781250018861; 9781250018878
LC 2012286525

Cybil Award: Early Chapter Book (2013)

In this horror story, by James Preller and illustrated by Iacopo Bruno "Meet Liam Finn, who's just moved into a new home with his father and sister. But this old house that seems empty, isn't . . . Bloody Mary is here. Called back from the dead by a game, she's just dying to talk." (Publisher's note)

"These two horror novels for middle-grade readers cover the legend of Bloody Mary (Home) and a terrifying amusement park ride (Scream) While the writing and plot construction are nicely targeted to a young audience, there are genuinely terrifying elements in both that make these a good match only for readers who are seeking a true scare." Horn Book

Other titles in this series are:
I scream you scream (2013)
Goodnight Zombie (2013)
Nightmareland (2014)
One-eyed doll (2014)
Swamp monster (2015)

Justin Fisher declares war! Scholastic Press 2010 135p $15.99
Grades: 3 4 5 **Fic**
1. School stories 2. Teachers -- Fiction 3. Popularity -- Fiction
ISBN 978-0-545-03301-5; 0-545-03301-2
LC 2009053641

When Justin Fisher, longtime class clown, realizes that his classmates are growing tired of his misdeeds, he declares war on their fifth grade teacher, Mr. Tripp, in hopes of regaining his popularity.

"This quiet, universal story . . . will make a good classroom read Preller handles sensitive issues with dignity, and kids will identify with Justin's eagerness to be liked and his snarky jokes." SLJ

★ **Six** innings; a game in the life. Feiwel and Friends 2008 147 $16.95
Grades: 4 5 6 7 **Fic**
1. Cancer -- Fiction 2. Baseball -- Fiction
ISBN 978-0-312-36763-3; 0-312-36763-5
LC 2007-32844

Earl Grubb's Pool Supplies plays Northeast Gas & Electric in the Little League championship game, while Sam, who has cancer and is in a wheelchair, has to call the play-by-play instead of participating in the game.

"The outcome is predictable but the journey is nailbitingly tense. Kids will be nodding in agreement at the truths laid bare." Publ Wkly

Preus, Margi

★ **West** of the moon; Margi Preus. Amulet Books 2014 224 p. (alk. paper) $16.95

Grades: 5 6 7 8   **Fic**

1. Norway -- Fiction 2. Folklore -- Norway 3. Human trafficking -- Fiction 4. United States -- Immigration and emigration -- Fiction 5. Norway -- History -- 19th century -- Fiction

ISBN 1419708961; 9781419708961

LC 2013023250

Author Margi Preus "weaves original fiction with myth and folktale to tell the story of Astri, a young Norwegian girl desperate to join her father in America. After being separated from her sister and sold to a cruel goat farmer, Astri makes a daring escape. She quickly retrieves her little sister, and, armed with a troll treasure, a book of spells and curses, and a possibly magic hairbrush, they set off for America." (Publisher's note)

"In the Scandinavian fairy tale 'East of the Sun and West of the Moon,' a young girl is taken from her home to a magnificent castle by a great bear, whom she discovers is really a prince. . . . Preus (Heart of a Samurai, 2010) interweaves the mesmerizing tale of Astri's treacherous and harrowing mid-nineteenth-century immigration to America with bewitching tales of magic. A fascinating author's note only adds to the wonder." Booklist

Includes bibliographical references

Prevost, Guillaume

The **book** of time; [by] Guillaume Prévost; translated by William Rodarmor. Arthur A. Levine Books 2007 213p $16.99; pa $6.99

Grades: 5 6 7 8   **Fic**

1. Science fiction 2. Missing persons -- Fiction

ISBN 978-0-439-88375-7; 0-439-88375-X; 978-0-439-88379-5 pa; 0-439-88379-2 pa

LC 2006-38446

Original French edition 2006

Sam Faulkner travels back in time to medieval Ireland, ancient Egypt and Renaissance Bruges in search of his missing father

"The appeal of the novel . . . comes from both well-drawn characters and a swiftly moving story." Booklist

Other titles in this series are:

The gate of days (2008)

The circle of gold (2009)

Priestley, Chris

Tales of terror from the Black Ship; by Chris Priestley; illustrated by David Roberts. Bloomsbury Children's Books 2008 243p il $12.99

Grades: 5 6 7 8   **Fic**

1. Sea stories 2. Horror fiction 3. Siblings -- Fiction 4. Storytelling -- Fiction 5. Great Britain -- Fiction 6. Cornwall (England) -- Fiction

ISBN 978-1-59990-290-6; 1-59990-290-7

LC 2008-10408

One stormy night, in their family's otherwise deserted Cornwall inn, twelve-year-old Ethan and his sister Cathy shelter a mysterious guest who indulges their love of the macabre by telling horror stories of the sea

"Priestley and Roberts, whose Gorey-esque line illustrations can distill spirits from a nightmare, understand full well what kids want to read under the covers by flashlight." Bull Cent Child Books

Primavera, Elise, 1954-

Libby of High Hopes; story and pictures by Elise Primavera. Simon & Schuster Books for Young Readers 2012 185 p. (alk. paper) $14.99

Grades: 2 3 4   **Fic**

1. Horses -- Fiction 2. Sisters -- Fiction 3. Horseback riding -- Fiction 4. Horsemanship -- Fiction

ISBN 1416955429; 9781416955429

LC 2011043908

In this children's novel, Libby wants to take horseback riding lessons. "Libby's parents do indeed fork out for lessons--for Libby's older sister, Laurel. Libby does at least get the privilege of riding an old pony during Laurel's class, and she hangs around the barn and learns as much as she can, taking a special interest in a retired jumper, Princess, and getting involved in the human drama of the stable's owners." (Bulletin of the Center for Children's Books)

Prineas, Sarah

★ The **magic** thief; illustrations by Antonio Javier Caparo. HarperCollins Pubs. 2008 419p il map

Grades: 4 5 6 7   **Fic**

1. Fantasy fiction 2. Magic -- Fiction 3. Thieves -- Fiction 4. Apprentices -- Fiction

ISBN 0-06-137587-X; 0-06-137588-8 lib bdg; 0-06-137590-X pa; 978-0-06-137587-3; 978-0-06-137588-0 lib bdg; 978-0-06-137590-3 pa

LC 2007031704

Conn is a young thief who is drawn into a life of adventure after picking the pocket of the wizard Nevery Flinglas. Finglas has returned from exile to try to reverse the decline of magic in Wellmet City. "Grades five to nine." (Bull Cent Child Books)

"Conn is a thief but, through desire and inevitability, becomes a wizard . . . This evolution begins when Conn picks the pocket of the wizard Nevery. . . . What works wonderfully well here is the boy's irresistable voice." Booklist

Other titles in this series are:

Lost (2009)

Found (2010)

Pryor, Bonnie

The **iron** dragon; the courageous story of Lee Chin. Enslow Publishers 2010 160p (Historical fiction adventures) lib bdg $27.93; pa $14.95

Grades: 4 5 6   **Fic**

1. Railroads -- Fiction 2. California -- Fiction 3. Immigrants -- Fiction 4. Chinese Americans -- Fiction

ISBN 978-0-7660-3389-4 lib bdg; 0-7660-3389-9 lib bdg; 978-1-59845-215-0 pa; 1-59845-215-0 pa

LC 2009017930

In the mid-nineteenth century, teenager Lee Chin and his father leave China for California to work on the transcontinental railroad, where Lee defies his father's wishes and saves money to free his younger sister from slavery in China, then brings her to join him in beginning a new life in America. Includes historical note about the Chinese who helped build the transcontinental railroad

"Lee Chin's tale is compellingly told. . . . Historical information is accurate and honest about the period depicted." SLJ

Simon's escape; a story of the Holocaust. Enslow Publishers 2010 160p (Historical fiction adventures) lib bdg $27.93; pa $14.95

Grades: 4 5 6   **Fic**

1. Poland -- Fiction 2. Jews -- Poland -- Fiction 3. Holocaust,

1933-1945 -- Fiction 4. World War, 1939-1945 -- Fiction
ISBN 978-0-7660-3388-7 lib bdg; 0-7660-3388-0 lib bdg; 978-1-
59845-216-7 pa; 1-59845-216-9 pa
                                                    LC 2009029322
Simon, a young Polish Jew, and his family are forced by Nazis to
leave their home for the filth and hunger of the Warsaw ghetto then,
when his family is all taken away, he escapes to fight for survival in the
countryside. Includes facts about the Holocaust
This "is a compelling, informative introduction to Holocaust history." Booklist

Pullman, Philip, 1946-
★ **I** was a rat! illustrated by Kevin Hawkes. Knopf 2000 164p
il $15.95; pa $4.99
Grades: 4 5 6 7   **Fic**
1. Fantasy fiction
ISBN 0-375-80176-6; 0-440-41661-2 pa
                                                     LC 99-31806
First published 1999 in the United Kingdom with illustrations by
Peter Bailey
"Pullman tells what happens to Cinderella's rat-turned-pageboy,
who, busily sliding down banisters at the palace, misses the pumpkin-
coach ride home and gets trapped in boy form. Young readers will find
the story completely entertaining, whether or not they appreciate the
playful spoofing of sensational news stories, mob mentality, and the
royal family." Horn Book Guide

Two crafty criminals! and how they were captured by the daring
detectives of the New Cut Gang; including Thunderbolt's Waxwork &
the gas-fitters' ball. Philip Pullman. Alfred A. Knopf 2012 281 p.
(hardback) $16.99
Grades: 5 6 7 8   **Fic**
1. Mystery fiction 2. Crime -- Fiction 3. Gangs -- Fiction 4.
Humorous fiction 5. Children's stories 6. Humorous stories 7.
Mystery and detective stories 8. Adventure and adventurers --
Fiction
ISBN 9780375870293; 9780375970290; 9780375988684
                                                    LC 2011042391
This children's book by Philip Pullman was published in 1994 as two
novellas: "Thunderbolt's Waxwork" and "The Gas-Fitters' Ball," which
are set in "1894 London . . . [and] star . . . the intrepid boy and girl detec-
tives of the New Cut Gang. . . . Thunderbolt Dobney sees his own father
hauled off to jail for what he thinks must be 'coining.' . . . [H]e and the
New Cut Gang expose the real criminal. . . . In 'The Gas-Fitters' Ball,' . .
. the Gas-Fitters' Hall is burgled." (Kirkus Reviews)

Pyron, Bobbie
★ A **dog's** way home. Katherine Tegen Books 2011 321p lib
bdg $17.89; $16.99
Grades: 4 5 6 7   **Fic**
1. Dogs -- Fiction 2. North Carolina -- Fiction 3. Traffic accidents
-- Fiction
ISBN 0-06-198673-9 lib bdg; 0-06-198674-7; 978-0-06-198673-
4 lib bdg; 978-0-06-198674-1
                                                    LC 2010006960
After a car accident strands them at opposite ends of the Blue Ridge
Parkway, eleven-year-old Abby and her beloved sheltie Tam overcome
months filled with physical and emotional challenges to find their way
back to each other.
"A heartwarming, suspenseful tale. . . . With vibrant, sympathetic
characterizations, Pyron creates an inspiring portrayal of devotion and
survival against all odds." Publ Wkly

The **dogs** of winter; by Bobbie Pyron. Arthur A. Levine Books
2012 312 p. (hardcover : alk. paper) $16.99
Grades: 5 6 7 8   **Fic**
1. Wild dogs -- Fiction 2. Dogs -- Fiction 3. Abandoned children
-- Fiction 4. Wilderness survival -- Fiction 5. Gangs -- Fiction
6. Moscow (Russia) -- Fiction 7. Street children -- Fiction 8.
Homeless persons -- Fiction
ISBN 0545399300; 9780545399302; 9780545399319;
9780545469852
                                                    LC 2011051519
In this book by Bobbie Pyron "Ivan's mother disappears, [and]
he's abandoned on the streets of Moscow, with little chance to make it
through the harsh winter. But help comes in an unexpected form: Ivan is
adopted by a pack of dogs, and the dogs quickly become more than just
his street companions: They become his family. Soon Ivan, who used to
love reading fairytales, is practically living in one." But "when help is
finally offered to him, will he be able to accept it?" (Publisher's note)

Lucky strike; Bobbie Pyron. Arthur A. Levine Books, an imprint
of Scholastic Inc. 2015 262 p. hbk $16.99
Grades: 4 5 6 7   **Fic**
1. Luck -- Fiction 2. Florida -- Fiction 3. Lightning -- Fiction 4.
Grandparent-grandchild relationship -- Fiction 5. Grandparent and
child -- Fiction 6. Franklin County (Fla.) -- Fiction
ISBN 9780545592178; 0545592178; 0545592186;
9780545592185
                                                    LC 2014013764
In this book, by Bobbie Pyron, "Nate Harlow has never had a lucky
day in his life. . . . His best friend, Genesis Beam (aka Gen), believes in
science and logic, and she doesn't think for one second that there's such a
thing as luck, good or bad. But only an extremely unlucky person could
be struck by lightning on his birthday... and that person is Nate Harlow.
By some miracle, though, Nate survives, and the strike seems to have
changed his luck." (Publisher's note)
"The quirkiness of the characters and the town never goes too far, and
there is an overall cozy feeling to the book. Genesis's dad is the preacher
at The Church of the One True Redeemer and Everlasting Light, but she
is a scientist through and through, which adds complexity to the text,
including musings on destiny, fate, probability, and weather." SLJ

Quintero, Isabel
Ugly Cat & Pablo; Isabel Quintero; illustrated by Tom Knight.
Scholastic 2017 112 p. illustrations $14.99
Grades: 2 3 4 5   **Fic**
1. Cats -- Fiction 2. Mice -- Fiction 3. Friendship -- Fiction
ISBN 0545940923; 9780545940924
In this book, by Isabel Quintero, illustrated by Tom Knight, "Ugly
Cat is dying for a paleta, or ice pop, and his friend Pablo is determined to
help him get one by scaring a little girl who is enjoying a coconut paleta.
. . . [But] instead of being scared, the little girl picks Pablo up and de-
clares that he would make a great snack for her pet snake. . . . And there's
also the small problem that Ugly Cat may have inadvertently swallowed
Pablo in all of the commotion!" (Publisher's note)

Quirk, Katie
A **girl** called Problem; by Katie Quirk. Eerdmans Books for Young
Readers 2013 191 p. $8
Grades: 4 5 6   **Fic**
1. Historical fiction 2. Tanzania -- Fiction 3. Healers -- Fiction 4.
Villages -- Fiction 5. Moving, Household -- Fiction 6. Blessing
and cursing -- Fiction 7. Farm life -- Tanzania -- Fiction 8. Mothers
and daughters -- Fiction 9. Sukuma (African people) -- Fiction 10.

Tanzania -- History -- 1964- -- Fiction
ISBN 0802854044; 9780802854049

LC 2012025468

In this novel, Shida looks forward to an education when "President Nyerere asks Shida's village to become a model of ujamaa (familyhood) for the country by moving to Njia Panda and farming communally. . . . After the move, however, the cotton crop mysteriously fails overnight, the villagers' prize possessions, their cattle, escape from their pens, and Furaha dies of fever. With the help of Shida and her cousin Grace, Babu, their grandfather and the village elder, unearths the truth." (Kirkus)

Railsback, Lisa

Noonie's masterpiece; art by Sarajo Frieden. Chronicle Books 2010 208p il $18.99

Grades: 4 5 6 7 **Fic**

1. School stories 2. Artists -- Fiction 3. Family life -- Fiction 4. Father-daughter relationship -- Fiction 5. Eccentrics and eccentricities -- Fiction

ISBN 978-0-8118-6654-5; 0-8118-6654-8

LC 2008-26831

Upon learning that her deceased mother, an artist, went through a "Purple Period," ten-year-old Noonie decides to do the same, hoping that this will bring her archaeologist father home to see her win a school art contest and that the aunt, uncle, and cousin she lives with will come to understand her just a little.

"Noonie may be an unreliable and even unlikable narrator at times, but her pain and vulnerability are as evident as her belief in herself as an artist, and by the end of the story, she'll have readers in her corner. The ink-and-watercolor illustrations, appearing throughout the book, have a 1960s-retro look." Booklist

Ransom, Candice

Rebel McKenzie; Candice Ransom. Disney Hyperion 2012 270 p. $16.99

Grades: 4 5 6 7 **Fic**

1. Country life -- Fiction 2. Beauty contests -- Fiction 3. Money-making projects for children -- Fiction 4. Nephews -- Fiction 5. Virginia -- Fiction 6. Trailer camps -- Fiction 7. Loss (Psychology) -- Fiction 8. Country life -- Virginia -- Fiction

ISBN 1423145399; 9781423145394

LC 2011032729

In this novel by Candice Ransom "Rebel McKenzie wants to spend her summer attending . . . a camp where kids discover prehistoric bones, right alongside real paleontologists. But digs cost money, and Rebel is broker than four o'clock. When she finds out her annoying neighbor Bambi Lovering won five hundred dollars by playing a ukulele behind her head in a beauty contest, Rebel decides to win the Frog Level Volunteer Fire Department's beauty pageant." (Publisher's note)

Rappaport, Doreen

Freedom ship. Hyperion Books for Children 2006 un il $15.99

Grades: 3 4 5 6 **Fic**

1. Slaves 2. State legislators 3. Slavery -- Fiction 4. Members of Congress 5. African Americans -- Fiction 6. United States -- History -- 1861-1865, Civil War -- Fiction

ISBN 0-7868-0645-1

"In 1862, Robert Smalls, 23, a black wheelman on the Confederate steamship Planter, and other members of the ship's slave crew, seized the ship and delivered it to the Union Army. Five black women and three children escaped to freedom with the crew, and Rappaport uses the fictionalized viewpoint of one of the children to tell her story. . . . Though personal narrative gives the story immediacy, and the handsome illustrations show the strong child and his proud, smiling family standing tall,

Rappaport's lengthy note about Smalls is even more exciting than the fiction." Booklist

Raschka, Chris

Seriously, Norman! [by] Chris Raschka. Scholastic/di Capua 2011 342p il $17.95

Grades: 3 4 5 **Fic**

1. Teachers -- Fiction 2. Friendship -- Fiction 3. Family life -- Fiction

ISBN 978-0-545-29877-3; 0-545-29877-6

Why are grownups so insane? That's the question Leonard, Norman, Anna and Emma (the twins) try to answer with the help of Norman's new tutor, Balthazar Birdsong (who is also fairly nuts).

"Don't expect a linear plot here but rather an ode to ten-year-old humor . . . and improbable characters and situations. . . . Emellished with Raschka's spot art, this rousing tale contains strong wordplay, a little vocabulary instruction . . . and a lot of humor." Horn Book

Raskin, Ellen

Figgs & phantoms. Dutton 2011 152p $16.99; pa $6.99

Grades: 4 5 6 **Fic**

1. Family life -- Fiction

ISBN 978-0-525-42367-6; 0-525-42367-2; 978-0-14-241169-8 pa; 0-14-241169-8 pa

A reissue of the title first published 1974

Chronicles the adventures of the unusual Figg family after they left show business and settled in the town of Pineapple.

This speaks "to both head and heart . . . a most poignant exploration of grief." Horn Book Guide

The **mysterious** disappearance of Leon (I mean Noel) Dutton 2011 149p $16.99; pa $6.99

Grades: 4 5 6 **Fic**

1. Mystery fiction

ISBN 978-0-525-42369-0; 0-525-42369-9; 978-0-14-241700-3 pa; 0-14-241700-9 pa

A reissue of the title first published 1971

The disappearance of her husband is only the first of the mysteries Mrs. Carillon must solve.

Raskin welcomes "readers in as participants in solving the story's mystery. . . . [The book speaks] to both the head and heart." Horn Book Guide

The **tattooed** potato and other clues. Dutton 2011 170p $16.99; pa $6.99

Grades: 4 5 6 **Fic**

1. Mystery fiction

ISBN 978-0-525-42368-3; 0-525-42368-0; 978-0-14-241699-0 pa; 0-14-241699-1 pa

A reissue of the title first published 1975

A Greenwich Village detective posing as an artist hires a student to act as his apprentice, spy, and eyewitness to murder.

Raskin welcomes "readers in as participants in solving the story's mystery. . . . [It speaks] to both head and heart." Horn Book Guide

★ The **Westing** game. Dutton Children's Books 2003 182p $16.99; pa $5.99

Grades: 5 6 7 8 **Fic**

1. Mystery fiction

ISBN 0-525-47137-5; 0-14-240120-X pa

LC 2004-268658

First published 1978

Awarded the Newbery Medal, 1979

"The rules of the game make eight pairs of the players; each oddly matched couple is given a ten thousand dollar check and a set of clues. The result is a fascinating medley of word games, disguises, multiple aliases and subterfuges—in a demanding but rewarding book." Horn Book

Rawlings, Marjorie Kinnan

★ The **secret** river; illustrated by Leo and Diane Dillon. Atheneum Books for Young Readers 2011 un il $19.99

Grades: K 1 2 3   **Fic**

1. Dogs -- Fiction 2. Hunger -- Fiction 3. Fishing -- Fiction 4. Florida -- Fiction 5. Forest animals -- Fiction 6. Forests and forestry -- Fiction

ISBN 978-1-4169-1179-1; 1-4169-1179-0

LC 2007-33292

A newly illustrated edition of the title first published 1955 by Scribner

Young Calpurnia takes her dog, Buggy-horse, and follows her nose to a secret river in a Florida forest, where she catches enough fresh fish to feed her hungry neighbors, even after giving some to the forest creatures she meets on the way home.

"Mesmerizing patterns and colors distinguish the Dillons' spreads, which balance large, captivating panels with smaller vignettes clustered around the text. Their acrylics are a foray into magical realism . . . and their portraits are always true to Rawlings's imaginings. Not to be missed." Publ Wkly

The **yearling**; with pictures by N. C. Wyeth. Scribner 1985 400p il hardcover o.p. pa $5.95

Grades: 5 6 7 8   **Fic**

1. Deer -- Fiction 2. Florida -- Fiction

ISBN 0-684-18461-3; 0-02-044931-3 pa

LC 85-40301

Reissue of the title first published 1938; awarded Pulitzer Prize, 1939

"With its excellent descriptions of Florida scrub landscapes, its skillful use of native vernacular, its tender relation between Jody and his pet fawn, The Yearling is a simply written, picturesque story of boyhood." Time

Rawls, Wilson

★ **Where** the red fern grows; the story of two dogs and a boy. Bantam Bks. 1996 212p $16.95; pa $5.99

Grades: 4 5 6 7   **Fic**

1. Dogs -- Fiction 2. Ozark Mountains -- Fiction

ISBN 0-385-32330-1; 0-440-41267-6 pa

First published 1961 by Doubleday

"Looking back more than 50 years to his boyhood in the Ozarks, the narrator, recalls how he achieved his heart's desire in the ownership of two redbone hounds, how he taught them all the tricks of hunting, and how they won the championship coon hunt before Old Dan was killed by a mountain lion and Little Ann died of grief. Although some readers may find this novel hackneyed and entirely too sentimental, others will enjoy the fine coonhunting episodes and appreciate the author's feelings for nature." Booklist

Ray, Delia

Ghost girl; a Blue Ridge Mountain story. Clarion Bks. 2003 216p il $15

Grades: 5 6 7 8   **Fic**

1. Presidents 2. School stories 3. Philanthropists 4. Teachers -- Fiction 5. Virginia -- Fiction 6. Spouses of presidents 7. Secretaries of commerce

ISBN 0-618-33377-0

LC 2003-4115

Eleven-year-old April is delighted when President and Mrs. Hoover build a school near her Madison County, Virginia, home but her family's poverty, grief over the accidental death of her brother, and other problems may mean that April can never learn to read from the wonderful teacher, Miss Vest

"This excellent portrayal of four important years in a girl's life rises to the top. Based on a real school and teacher, this novel seamlessly incorporates historical facts into the narrative." SLJ

Here lies Linc. Alfred A. Knopf 2011 308p $16.99; lib bdg $19.99

Grades: 5 6 7 8   **Fic**

1. School stories 2. Iowa -- Fiction 3. Death -- Fiction 4. Cemeteries -- Fiction 5. Family life -- Fiction

ISBN 978-0-375-86757-6; 0-375-86757-0; 978-0-375-96756-6 lib bdg; 0-375-96756-7 lib bdg

LC 2010030004

While researching a rumored-to-be-haunted grave for a local history project, twelve-year-old Lincoln Crenshaw unearths some startling truths about his own family.

"Ray's tale, which centers around a real legend, strikes the perfect balance of humor, realistic chills and near-teen angst." Kirkus

Reeder, Carolyn

Across the lines. Atheneum Bks. for Young Readers 1997 220p hardcover o.p. pa $5.99

Grades: 5 6 7 8   **Fic**

1. Race relations -- Fiction 2. African Americans -- Fiction 3. United States -- History -- 1861-1865, Civil War -- Fiction

ISBN 0-689-81133-0; 0-380-73073-1 pa

LC 96-31068

Edward, the son of a white plantation owner, and his black house servant and friend Simon witness the siege of Petersburg during the Civil War

"Told in the alternating voices of Edward and Simon, this thoughtful Civil War story resonates with authenticity." Horn Book Guide

Reedy, Trent

Words in the dust. Arthur A. Levine Books 2011 266p $17.99

Grades: 5 6 7 8   **Fic**

1. Literacy -- Fiction 2. Sex role -- Fiction 3. Afghanistan -- Fiction 4. Birth defects -- Fiction

ISBN 0-545-26125-2; 978-0-545-26125-8

LC 2010-26160

Zulaikha, a thirteen-year-old girl in Afghanistan, faces a series of frightening but exhilarating changes in her life as she defies her father and secretly meets with an old woman who teaches her to read, her older sister gets married, and American troops offer her surgery to fix her disfiguring cleft lip.

"The evolution of key relationships presents a nuanced look at family dynamics and Afghan culture. Though unsentimental and fraught with tragedy, Reedy's narrative offers hope and will go a long way toward helping readers understand the people behind the headlines." Publ Wkly

Rees, Douglas

Uncle Pirate; illustrated by Tony Auth. Margaret K. McElderry Books 2008 100p il $15.99

Grades: 2 3 4   **Fic**

1. School stories 2. Uncles -- Fiction 3. Pirates -- Fiction 4. Penguins -- Fiction

ISBN 978-1-4169-4762-2; 1-4169-4762-0

LC 2006-39002

Wilson is one of the most bullied fourth-graders at the chaotic Very Elementary School until his long-lost uncle, Desperate Evil Wicked

Boba pirate—and his talking penguin arrive and begin making everything shipshape, one classroom at a time

"The story's goofy humor will entertain pirate fans. Lively black-and-white pen-and-ink and watercolor spot art illustrates most pages." Horn Book Guide

Another title about Uncle Pirate is:

Uncle Pirate to the rescue (2010)

Uncle Pirate to the rescue; illustrated by Tony Auth. Margaret K. McElderry Books 2010 il pa $5.99
Grades: 2 3 4   **Fic**
1. School stories 2. Uncles -- Fiction 3. Pirates -- Fiction 4. Penguins -- Fiction
ISBN 978-1-4169-7505-2; 1-4169-7505-5
                                              LC 2009009130

When Captain Desperate Evil Wicked Bob receives a plea from his former crew, he heads out to rescue them and is soon followed by his nephew Wilson, Commodore Purvis, Captain Jack, and others who fear that he needs to be rescued, as well.

"Auth's illustrations lend depth to the comedic elements and pirate analogies throughout the story. Avid and reluctant readers alike will be enchanted and hoping to find their own mutinous crew to rescue." SLJ

Reeve, Philip

No such thing as dragons. Scholastic Press 2010 186p $16.99
Grades: 4 5 6 7   **Fic**
1. Fantasy fiction 2. Dragons -- Fiction
ISBN 978-0-545-22224-2; 0-545-22224-9

A young, mute boy who is apprenticed to a dragon-slayer suspects that the winged beasts do not exist, until he—and his master—learn the truth.

"This is certainly different from anything that Reeve has done previously, but is still shot through with his trademark imagination and feel for action. It will be eagerly devoured by young readers." SLJ

Oliver and the seawigs; by Philip Reeve and Sarah McIntyre. Random House Inc 2014 208 p. (hardcover library binding) $15.99
Grades: 3 4 5   **Fic**
1. Boats and boating -- Fiction 2. Parent-child relationship -- Fiction 3. Humorous stories 4. Islands -- Fiction 5. Mermaids -- Fiction 6. Explorers -- Fiction 7. Missing persons -- Fiction 8. Adventure and adventurers -- Fiction
ISBN 0385387911; 9780385387880; 9780385387910
                                              LC 2013043653

"When Oliver's explorer parents go missing, he sets sail on a rescue mission with some new, unexpected friends: a grumpy albatross, a nearsighted mermaid . . . even a living island! But the high seas are even more exciting, unusual, and full of mischief than Oliver could have imagined." (Publisher's note)

" joyous, original new adventure series filled with quirky characters, buoyant illustrations, and plenty of laughs." Horn Book

Other titles in this series are:

Cakes in space (2015)
Pugs of the frozen north (2016)

Reh, Rusalka

Pizzicato; the abduction of the magic violin. translated by David Henry Wilson. AmazonCrossing 2011 124p pa $9.95
Grades: 4 5 6 7   **Fic**
1. Magic -- Fiction 2. Germany -- Fiction 3. Orphans -- Fiction 4. Violins -- Fiction
ISBN 978-1-6110-9004-8; 1-6110-9004-0

Darius is none too pleased to be paired with Archibald Archinola, a master violinmaker, for a school project, especially when he thinks

about his rival—fellow orphan and constant nemesis Max—being surrounded by Porsches at Auto Frederick for the same assignment. But when Darius discovers an old violin in a glass case and strikes the chords, a cut on his hand magically disappears, and suddenly studying with the violinmaker proves to be anything but dull.

This story "has an Old World European charm, from the cast of eccentric, lovable characters to the scenes of café life. Readers will delight in watching the buffoonish villains get their comeuppance, but it's Darius' wish-fulfillment . . . that will satisfy readers most." Booklist

Reiche, Dietlof

★ **I,** Freddy; book one in the golden hamster saga. translated from the German by John Brownjohn; illustrated by Joe Cepeda. Scholastic Press 2003 201p il hardcover o.p. pa $4.99
Grades: 3 4 5   **Fic**
1. Hamsters -- Fiction
ISBN 0-439-28356-6; 0-439-28357-4 pa
                                              LC 2002-6981

Freddy, a remarkably intelligent golden hamster, learns how to read and how to write on a computer and escapes captivity to become an independent and civilized creature

"Illustrated with amusing black-ink sketches, this engaging story will appeal to fans of animal fantasies." SLJ

Other titles about Freddy are:

Freddy in peril (2004)
Freddy to the rescue (2005)
The haunting of Freddy (2006)
Freddy's final quest (2007)

Reinhardt, Dana

Odessa again; Dana Reinhardt. 1st ed. Wendy Lamb Books 2013 208 p. (ebook) $47.97; (hardcover) $15.99; (library) $18.99
Grades: 4 5 6 7   **Fic**
1. Remarriage -- Fiction 2. Time travel -- Fiction
ISBN 0385739567; 9780375897887; 9780385739566; 9780385907934
                                              LC 2012008231

In this children's novel, by Dana Reinhardt, "fourth grader Odessa Green-Light lives with her mom and her toad of a little brother, Oliver. Her dad is getting remarried. . . . Meanwhile, Odessa moves into the attic room of their new house. One day [it] . . . turns out that Odessa has gone back in time a whole day! With this new power she can fix all sorts of things--embarrassing moments, big mistakes, and even help Oliver be less of a toad. Her biggest goal: reunite Mom and Dad." (Publisher's note)

"Realistically drawn, Odessa is a believable, likable kid on the brink of growing up, struggling with family changes. . . . With humor as well as depth, this is an endearing story of a spunky girl who realizes that life gets more, not less, confusing as she grows up." Kirkus

The **summer** I learned to fly. Wendy Lamb Books 2011 216p $15.99; lib bdg $18.99; e-book $15.99
Grades: 5 6 7 8   **Fic**
1. Rats -- Fiction 2. California -- Fiction 3. Family life -- Fiction 4. Retail trade -- Fiction 5. Single parent family -- Fiction
ISBN 978-0-385-73954-2; 0-385-73954-0; 978-0-385-90792-7 lib bdg; 0-385-90792-3 lib bdg; 978-0-375-89787-0 e-book; 0-375-89787-9 e-book
                                              LC 2010029412

Thirteen-year-old Drew starts the summer of 1986 helping in her mother's cheese shop and dreaming about co-worker Nick, but when her widowed mother begins dating, Drew's father's book of lists, her pet rat, and Emmett, a boy on a quest, help her cope.

"This quiet novel invites readers to share in its heroine's deepest yearnings, changing moods, and difficult realizations." Publ Wkly

Repka, Janice

The **clueless** girl's guide to being a genius. Dutton Children's Books 2011 218p $16.99

Grades: 4 5 6   **Fic**

1. School stories 2. Genius -- Fiction 3. Teachers -- Fiction 4. Friendship -- Fiction 5. Mathematics -- Fiction 6. Baton twirling -- Fiction

ISBN 978-0-525-42333-1; 0-525-42333-8

LC 2010038139

When Aphrodite Wigglesmith, a thirteen-year-old, Harvard-educated mathematics genius, returns home to teach remedial math to middle school students, both she and her students end up getting unexpected lessons.

"A lighthearted, funny and often bizarre saga of middle-school mayhem. . . . Equal parts silly and endearing." Kirkus

Resau, Laura

★ The **lightning** queen; Laura Resau. Scholastic Press 2015 336 p. $16.99

Grades: 3 4 5 6   **Fic**

1. Friendship -- Fiction 2. Romanies -- Fiction 3. Mixtec Indians -- Fiction 4. Indians of Mexico -- Fiction

ISBN 0545800846; 9780545800846; 9780545800853; 9780545800860

LC 2015016275

In this juvenile novel, by Laura Resau, "nothing exciting happens on the Hill of Dust, in the remote mountains of Mexico in the 1950s. . . . And now, without his sister and mother, eleven-year-old Teo's life feels even more barren. And then one day, the mysterious young Esma, who calls herself the Gypsy Queen of Lightning, rolls into town like a fresh burst of color. Against all odds, her caravan's Mistress of Destiny predicts that Teo and Esma will be longtime friends." (Publisher's note)

"In present-day Oaxaca, Mexico, Mateo listens to his abuelo Teo tell of his childhood in a tight-knit Mixtec community and of his foretold "lifelong friendship" with Rom girl Esma, Queen of Lightning. Teo and Esma's tale is one of true friendship, despite cultural differences and opposition from society, and of loves lost and found. Resau's sensory descriptions heighten the tale's sweeping romanticism." Horn Book

★ **Star** in the forest. Delacorte Press 2010 149p il $14.99; lib bdg $17.99

Grades: 4 5 6   **Fic**

1. Dogs -- Fiction 2. Fathers -- Fiction 3. Friendship -- Fiction 4. Illegal aliens -- Fiction 5. Mexican Americans -- Fiction

ISBN 978-0-385-73792-0; 0-385-73792-0; 978-0-385-90700-2 lib bdg; 0-385-90700-1 lib bdg

LC 2009-03898

After eleven-year-old Zitlally's father is deported to Mexico, she takes refuge in her trailer park's forest of rusted car parts, where she befriends a spunky neighbor and finds a stray dog that she nurses back to health and believes she must keep safe so that her father will return.

"Resau has woven details of immigrant life into a compelling story. . . . This is a well-told and deeply satisfying read." SLJ

★ **What** the moon saw; a novel. Delacorte Press 2006 258p $15.95; pa $5.99

Grades: 5 6 7 8   **Fic**

1. Mexico -- Fiction 2. Country life -- Fiction 3. Grandparents -- Fiction

ISBN 0-385-73343-7; 0-440-23957-5 pa

LC 2006-04571

Fourteen-year-old Clara Luna spends the summer with her grandparents in the tiny, remote village of Yucuyoo, Mexico, learning about her grandmother's life as a healer, her father's decision to leave home for the United States, and her own place in the world.

This is an "exquisitely crafted narrative. . . . The characters are well developed. . . . Resau does an exceptional job of portraying the agricultural society sympathetically and realistically." SLJ

Rex, Adam

Champions of breakfast; Adam Rex. Balzer + Bray 2014 368 p (The cold cereal saga) (hardcover bdg. : alk. paper) $16.99

Grades: 4 5 6 7   **Fic**

1. Imaginary places 2. Magic -- Fiction 3. Fairies -- Fiction 4. Cereals, Prepared -- Fiction 5. Adventure and adventurers -- Fiction

ISBN 0062060082; 9780062060082

LC 2013021387

In this book by Adam Rex, part of the Cold Cereal Saga series, "time is quickly running out before Nimue, who has been working with the corrupt Goodco Cereal Company, finds another portal and uses it to bring the mythical dragon Saxbriton into our world--and launch the terrible fairy invasion. In the end, it's up to Scott and his companions to save the fate of two worlds." (Publisher's note)

"Scott, Polly, Emily, and Erno, together with a large supporting cast, rescue the miniaturized Queen of England and quell a fairy invasion by killing the dragon Saxbriton and healing the rift between the worlds. The superabundance of characters is hard to keep track of, but for readers following the Arthurian-reimagining trilogy, action, magic, and humor combine for a whiz-bang conclusion." (Horn Book)

★ **Cold** cereal. Balzer + Bray 2012 421p il $16.99

Grades: 4 5 6 7   **Fic**

1. Adventure fiction 2. Food -- Fiction 3. Magic -- Fiction 4. Twins -- Fiction 5. Siblings -- Fiction

ISBN 978-0-06-206002-0; 0-06-206002-3

LC 2011019538

A boy who may be part changeling, twins involved in a bizarre secret experiment, and a clurichaun in a red tracksuit try to save the world from an evil cereal company whose ultimate goal is world domination.

"The author tucks in portrait illustrations and hilariously odd TV commercial storyboards, along with a hooded Secret Society, figures from Arthurian legend, magical spells and potions, a certain amount of violence, many wonderful throwaway lines. . . . All in all, it's a mad scramble that culminates in the revelation of a dastardly plot that will require sequels to foil." Kirkus

Smek for president! Adam Rex. Disney-Hyperion Books 2014 272 p. illustrations (hardback) $16.99

Grades: 5 6 7 8   **Fic**

1. Science fiction 2. Humorous fiction 3. Adventure and adventurers 4. Human-alien encounters -- Fiction 5. Extraterrestrial beings -- Fiction 6. Humorous stories 7. Interplanetary voyages -- Fiction 8. Adventure and adventurers -- Fiction

ISBN 1484709519; 9781484709511

LC 2014010764

Sequel to: The True Meaning of Smekday (2007)

In this book, by Adam Rex, "Tip and J.Lo are back for another hilarious intergalactic adventure. . . . After Tip and J.Lo banished the Gorg from Earth in a scheme involving the cloning of many, many cats, the pair is notorious--but not for their heroics. Instead, human Dan Landry has taken credit for conquering the Gorg, and the Boov blame J.Lo for ruining their colonization of the planet." (Publisher's note)

"Rex packs his sequel with loads of action and a steady spotlight on friendship; plus, he adds witty send-ups of political elections, time trav el, and even sports rules (again using cartoon panels to good effect). And his humor is, as it was in Smekday, laugh-out-loud funny." Horn Book

★ The **true** meaning of Smekday. Hyperion Books for Children 2007 423p il $16.99; pa $6.99

Grades: 5 6 7 8   **Fic**

1. Science fiction 2. End of the world -- Fiction 3. Extraterrestrial beings -- Fiction

ISBN 0-7868-4900-2; 978-0-7868-4900-0; 0-7868-4901-0 pa; 978-0-7868-4901-7 pa

When her mother is abducted by aliens on Christmas Eve (or "Smekday" Eve since the Boov invasion), 11 year-old Tip hops in the family car and heads south to find her and meets an alien Boov mechanic who agrees to help her and save the planet from disaster.

"Incorporating dozens of his weird and wonderful illustrations and fruitfully manipulating the narrative structure, Rex skewers any number of subjects." Publ Wkly

Unlucky charms; Adam Rex. Balzer + Bray 2013 400 p. (The cold cereal saga) (hardback) $16.99

Grades: 4 5 6 7   **Fic**

1. Fantasy fiction 2. Humorous fiction 3. Prepared cereals -- Fiction 4. Magic -- Fiction 5. Twins -- Fiction

ISBN 0062060058; 9780062060051

LC 2012026714

This humorous juvenile fantasy book, by Adam Rex, is part of the "Cold Cereal Saga." "In this hectic middle volume, [Adam] Rex's notably diverse crew of human, part-human and nonhuman allies splits up in hopes of scotching the schemes of the sorceress Nimue, who is out to create a worldwide army of mind-controlled 'sugar zombies' through magically enhanced breakfast cereal." (Kirkus Reviews)

Reynolds, Jason

★ **As** brave as you; Jason Reynolds. Atheneum 2016 432 p. (hardback) $16.99

Grades: 5 6 7 8   **Fic**

1. Blind -- Fiction 2. Courage -- Fiction 3. Brothers -- Fiction 4. Virginia -- Fiction 5. Grandparents -- Fiction 6. African Americans -- Fiction 7. Country life -- Virginia -- Fiction 8. People with disabilities -- Fiction

ISBN 9781481415903; 9781481415910; 1481415913; 1481415905

LC 2016007909

Kirkus Prize Winner: Young Readers' Literature (2016)

Schneider Family Book Award: Middle Grade (2017)

Coretta Scott King (Author) Honor Book (2017)

In this book, by Jason Reynolds, "Genie's summer is full of surprises. The first is that he and his big brother, Ernie, are leaving Brooklyn for the very first time to spend the summer with their grandparents all the way in Virginia--in the COUNTRY! The second surprise comes when Genie figures out that their grandfather is blind. Thunderstruck and--being a curious kid--Genie peppers Grandpop with questions about how he covers it so well." (Publisher's note)

"This pitch-perfect contemporary novel gently explores the past's repercussions on the present." Kirkus

★ **Ghost**; Jason Reynolds. Atheneum Books For Young Readers 2016 181 p. (hardback) $16.99; (ebook) $15.99

Grades: 4 5 6 7   **Fic**

1. Running -- Fiction 2. Track athletics -- Fiction 3. Self-realization -- Fiction 4. Track and field -- Fiction 5. Coaches (Athletics) --

Fiction

ISBN 1481450158; 9781481450157; 9781481450164; 9781481450171

LC 2016029678

National Book Award Finalist: Young People's Literature (2016)

In this book, by Jason Reynolds, "Ghost wants to be the fastest sprinter on his elite middle school track team, but his past is slowing him down. . . . If he can stay on track, literally and figuratively, he could be the best sprinter in the city. But Ghost has been running for the wrong reasons—it all starting with running away from his father. . . . Since then, Ghost has been the one causing problems—and running away from them—until he meets Coach." (Publisher's note)

"Reynolds has created a wonderfully dynamic character in Ghost; his first-person narrative is one with which young readers will readily identify." Horn Book

Reynolds, Peter H.

★ **Sky** color; Peter H. Reynolds. Candlewick 2012 32 p. (hardback) $14.00

Grades: PreK K 1 2   **Fic**

1. Sky -- Fiction 2. Picture books for children 3. Mural painting and decoration 4. Color -- Fiction 5. Paint -- Fiction 6. Artists -- Fiction 7. Schools -- Fiction

ISBN 0763623458; 9780763623456

LC 2011048374

In this children's picture book, "Marisol is an artist, famous at school for her art . . . . When their teacher tells her class that they are going to paint a mural in the library, . . . Marisol volunteers to paint the sky. But to her dismay, in the box of paint there is no blue." She agonizes until she realizes that the sky isn't always blue and comes up with a solution. "On a wordless double page, her classmates admire the 'sky color' she has created." (Children's Literature)

Rhodes, Jewell Parker

★ **Ninth** Ward. Little, Brown 2010 217p $15.99

Grades: 5 6 7 8   **Fic**

1. New Orleans (La.) -- Fiction 2. Extrasensory perception -- Fiction 3. Hurricane Katrina, 2005 -- Fiction

ISBN 978-0-316-04307-6; 0-316-04307-9

LC 2009-34423

Coretta Scott King Author Award honor book, 2011

In New Orleans' Ninth Ward, twelve-year-old Lanesha, who can see spirits, and her adopted grandmother have no choice but to stay and weather the storm as Hurricane Katrina bears down upon them.

"The dynamics of the diverse community enrich the survival story, and the contemporary struggle of one brave child humanizes the historic tragedy." Booklist

Sugar; Jewell Parker Rhodes. 1st ed. Little, Brown and Co. 2013 288 p. (hardcover) $16.99

Grades: 3 4 5 6 7 8   **Fic**

1. Race relations -- Fiction 2. Plantation life -- Fiction 3. Historical fiction 4. African Americans -- Fiction 5. Chinese Americans -- Fiction 6. Reconstruction (U.S. history, 1865-1877) -- Fiction

ISBN 0316043052; 9780316043052

LC 2012026218

In this historical novel, by Jewell Parker Rhodes, "ten-year-old Sugar lives on the River Road sugar plantation along the banks of the Mississippi. Slavery is over, but laboring in the fields all day doesn't make her feel very free. . . . Here's another tale of a strong, spirited young girl who rises beyond her circumstances and inspires others to work toward a brighter future." (Publisher's note)

"Sugar's clipped narration is personable and engaging, strongly evoking the novel's historical setting and myriad racial tensions, making them accessible and meaningful to beginning readers." Pub Wkly

Richards, Jasmine

The **book** of wonders. HarperCollins 2012 400p $14.99

Grades: 4 5 6 7   **Fic**

1. Fantasy fiction 2. Adventure fiction 3. Friendship -- Fiction

ISBN 978-0-06-201007-0; 0-06-201007-7

LC 2011009153

In a tale loosely based on the Arabian nights, thirteen-year-old Zardi and her best friend, Ridhan, join forces with Captain Sinbad to defeat an evil sultan and restore magic to the world of Arribitha.

"This buoyant debut offers a fresh plot, brisk pacing and engaging characters. . . . Richards deftly borrows from lesser-known tales of the 1001 Arabian Nights to enrich her complex storyline while keeping style and syntax simple and direct." Kirkus

Richards, Justin

Thunder Raker; illustrated by Jim Hansen. IPG/HarperCollins 2010 139p il (Agent Alfie) pa $6.99

Grades: 3 4 5   **Fic**

1. School stories 2. Spies -- Fiction

ISBN 978-0-00-727357-7; 0-00-727357-6

"After Alfie moves to a new town, he is enrolled by mistake at Thunder Raker Manor, a top-secret school that trains children to be future British spies. At his new school, Alfie encounters a host of eccentric teachers and swashbuckling students. Although at first Alfie seems in over his head, his good sense and practical ideas help him get the best grades in the class on his first homework assignment, and by the end of the novel, he manages to thwart agents from the evil organization SPUD. . . . The bright concept, short length, and humorous, action-packed drawings that fill each chapter should keep this in demand and leave readers eager for the series' next installment." Booklist

Richter, Jutta

Beyond the station lies the sea; translated from the German by Anna Brailovsky. Milkweed Editions 2009 81p $14

Grades: 4 5 6 7   **Fic**

1. Angels -- Fiction 2. Homeless persons -- Fiction

ISBN 978-1-57131-690-5; 1-57131-690-6

LC 2009018135

Trying to get to the beach where it is warm, two homeless boys enlist the aid of a rich woman who gives them money in exchange for a guardian angel.

"Richter presents a darkly poetic, masterfully crafted view of life on the streets." Publ Wkly

Riddell, Chris

★ **Ottoline** and the yellow cat. HarperCollinsPublishers 2008 171p il $10.99; lib bdg $14.89; pa $6.99

Grades: 2 3 4 5   **Fic**

1. Mystery fiction 2. Cats -- Fiction 3. Dogs -- Fiction

ISBN 978-0-06-144879-9; 0-06-144879-6; 978-0-06-144880-5 lib bdg; 0-06-144880-X lib bdg; 978-0-06-144881-2 pa; 0-06-144881-8 pa

"While her parents are off traveling the world collecting 'interesting things,' Ottoline Brown lives in an elaborate apartment in Big City with her best friend, guardian, and accomplice in forming clever plans. He is called Mr. Monroe and is a silent creature from Norway. . . . Ottoline solves a mystery involving a cat burglar, who is actually a cat, and the missing lapdogs of well-to-do women. The story is told through the text and the detailed line drawings that appear on each page. Done in black and white with red highlighting a quirky detail or two, the illustrations

add humor, depth, and momentum to the narrative. The quickly moving plot is grounded in real emotion." SLJ

Another title about Ottoline is:

Ottoline goes to school (2009)

Riel, Jorn

The **raiders**; written by Jørn Riel; illustrated by Helen Cann; translated by John Mason. Barefoot Books 2012 127 p. (alk. paper) $12.99

Grades: 4 5 6   **Fic**

1. Historical fiction 2. Vikings -- Fiction 3. Greenland -- History -- To 1500 -- Fiction 4. Inuit -- Greenland -- Fiction 5. Eskimos -- Greenland -- Fiction 6. Vikings -- Greenland -- Fiction 7. Greenland -- History -- To 1500 -- Fiction

ISBN 1846867444; 9781846867446

LC 2011044383

This book by Jorn Riel, part of the Inuk Quartet series, "continues the exciting adventures of Leiv, Apuluk and Narua established in 'The Shipwreck.' The story begins with our trio settled peacefully on Thor Gunnarrsson's farmstead in Greenland. When Viking raiders arrive at the farmstead, their quiet world is disturbed forever. Leiv, Apuluk and Narua must rely on their wits, their courage, and their friendship to protect their new home." (Publisher's note)

The **shipwreck**; translated from Danish by John Mason; illustrated by Helen Cann. Barefoot Books 2011 il (The Inuk quartet) pa $12.99

Grades: 4 5 6   **Fic**

1. Adventure fiction 2. Inuit -- Fiction 3. Vikings -- Fiction

ISBN 978-1-84686-335-6; 1-84686-335-X

"This beautifully illustrated epic adventure, set circa 1000 CE, begins with the shocking, retaliatory beheading of young Viking Leiv's father by Thorstein Gunnarsson. The playful boy becomes withdrawn and vows to take revenge. When Thorstein casts off from Iceland for Greenland to serve out his sentence of exile, Leiv stows away onboard but is swept into the sea during a storm. An Inuit brother and sister, Apuluk, 12, and Narua, 11, find him and care for him in secret. . . . The narrative is straightforward and well paced, with several engaging dramatic episodes. Riel skillfully interweaves information about the Inuit culture, language, and environment without being didactic. . . . Vocabulary may pose a challenge for less-advanced readers, and mention of beheadings and amputations may be unsuitable for others. But Cann's ethereal watercolor, graphite, and collage illustrations in cool blue tones and browns have a calmer mood that will enchant readers with the beauty of the Arctic landscape." SLJ

The **snowstorm**; written by Jørn Riel; illustrated by Helen Cann; translation by John Mason. Barefoot Books 2012 126 p. (alk. paper) $12.99

Grades: 4 5 6   **Fic**

1. Greenland -- Fiction 2. Inuit -- Fiction 3. Adventure fiction -- Fiction 4. Voyages and travels -- Fiction 5. Eskimos -- Fiction 6. Arctic regions -- History -- Fiction

ISBN 1846867975; 9781846867972

LC 2012009599

This book by Jørn Riel, "the third in a four-part Viking-era adventure, pits four young Greenlanders against both a howling gale and a crew of brutal pirates. . . . Leiv, his Inuit brother-and-sister companions Apuluk and Narua, and rescued serf Sølvi sled northward in search of the vanished chieftain Thorstein. . . . The explorers weather a journey highlighted by a violent . . . storm . . . [and a] battle aboard an iced-in British longship." (Kirkus Reviews)

Riley, James

Half upon a time. Aladdin 2010 385p $15.99

Grades: 5 6 7 8 **Fic**

1. Fairy tales 2. Adventure fiction
ISBN 978-1-4169-9593-7; 1-4169-9593-5

LC 2010012714

In the village of Giant's Hand Jack's grandfather has been pushing him to find a princess and get married, so when a young lady falls out of the sky wearing a shirt that says "Punk Princess," and she tells Jack that her grandmother, who looks suspiciously like the long-missing Snow White, has been kidnapped, Jack decides to help her.

"Riley does a wonderful job of combining the 21st century with the world in which fairies are alive, as well as creating characters that middle school students will relate to." Libr Media Connect

Secret origins; by James Riley. Aladdin 2017 372 p. (Story Thieves) (hardcover) $17.99

Grades: 5 6 7 8 **Fic**

1. Magic -- Fiction 2. Adventure fiction 3. Books and reading -- Fiction 4. Superheroes -- Fiction 5. Characters in literature -- Fiction 6. Adventure and adventurers -- Fiction 7. Comic books, strips, etc. -- Fiction
ISBN 1481461257; 9781481461252

LC 2016025387

In this juvenile novel, by James Riley, "[l]ife is boring when you live in the real world, instead of starring in your own book series. Owen knows that better than anyone, what with the real world's homework and chores. But everything changes the day Owen sees the impossible happen: his classmate Bethany climb out of a book in the library. It turns out Bethany's half-fictional and has been searching every book she can find for her missing father, a fictional character." (Publisher's note)

"A literary hall of mirrors, with plenty of thrills and laughs to keep 'nonfictionals' in the game" Kirkus

Other titles in this series are:
The stolen chapters (2016)
Secret origins (2017)

Riordan, Rick, 1964-

The **blood** of Olympus; Rick Riordan. 1st edition Disney-Hyperion Books 2014 528 p. (The heroes of Olympus) (hardback) $19.99

Grades: 5 6 7 8 **Fic**

1. Adventure fiction 2. Classical mythology -- Fiction 3. Mythology, Greek -- Fiction 4. Mythology, Roman -- Fiction 5. Gaia (Greek deity) -- Fiction
ISBN 1423146735; 9781423146735

LC 2014017392

In this novel by Rick Riordan, book 5 of the "The Heroes of Olympus" series, "though the Greek and Roman crewmembers of the Argo II have made progress in their many quests, they still seem no closer to defeating the earth mother, Gaea. Her giants have risen . . . and they're stronger than ever. They must be stopped before the Feast of Spes, when Gaea plans to have two demigods sacrificed in Athens." (Publisher's note)

"Readers looking forward to the battle scenes will find plenty here, but the young heroes also rely on their wits as they dupe, charm, and negotiate their way through a series of encounters with gods, goddesses, and mythological creatures." Booklist

The **hidden** oracle; Rick Riordan. Disney-Hyperion 2016 376 p. (Trials of Apollo) (hardback) $19.99

Grades: 5 6 7 8 **Fic**

1. Greek mythology -- Fiction 2. Gods and goddesses -- Fiction 3. Gods, Greek -- Fiction 4. Mythology, Greek -- Fiction
ISBN 9781484732748

LC 2015045235

In this book, by Rick Riordan, "after angering his father Zeus, the god Apollo is cast down from Olympus. Weak and disoriented, he lands in New York City as a regular teenage boy. Now, without his godly powers, the four-thousand-year-old deity must learn to survive in the modern world until he can somehow find a way to regain Zeus's favor. But Apollo has many enemies-gods, monsters, and mortals who would love to see the former Olympian permanently destroyed." (Publisher's note)

"A clash of mythic intrigues and centuries of pop culture to thrill die-hard and new fans alike." Kirkus

The **house** of Hades; Rick Riordan. Disney-Hyperion 2013 597 p. (Heroes of Olympus) (hardback) $19.99

Grades: 5 6 7 8 **Fic**

1. Hell -- Fiction 2. Gods and goddesses -- Fiction 3. Classical mythology -- Fiction 4. Camps -- Fiction 5. Giants -- Fiction 6. Mythology, Greek -- Fiction 7. Mythology, Roman -- Fiction 8. Gaia (Greek deity) -- Fiction 9. Hera (Greek deity) -- Fiction
ISBN 1423146727; 9781423146728

LC 2013015946

In this book, by Rick Riordan, "Annabeth and Percy tumble into a pit leading straight to the Underworld. The other five demigods have to put aside their grief and follow Percy's instructions to find the mortal side of the Doors of Death. If they can fight their way through the Gaea's forces, and Percy and Annabeth can survive the House of Hades, then the Seven will be able to seal the Doors from both sides and prevent the giants from raising Gaea." (Publisher's note)

"In this fourth in Riordan's series pitting Roman and Greek demigods against an awakening goddess Gaea, Percy and Annabeth trek through Tartarus to escape through the Doors of Death, while their friends fight their way to the Doors' mortal side to rescue them. The wisecracking teens reveal emotional depths while overcoming monsters and personal obstacles in this high velocity continuation of the gripping franchise." Horn Book

★ The **lightning** thief. Miramax Books/Hyperion Books for Children 2005 377p (Percy Jackson & the Olympians) pa $7.99

Grades: 5 6 7 8 9 **Fic**

1. Classical mythology -- Fiction
ISBN 0-7868-5629-7; 1-4231-3494-X pa; 978-0-6417-2344-5; 978-1-4231-3494-7 pa

LC 2005-299400

Twelve-year-old Percy Jackson learns he is a demigod, the son of a mortal woman and Poseidon, god of the sea. His mother sends him to a summer camp for demigods where he and his new friends set out on a quest to prevent a war between the gods.

"Riordan's fast-paced adventure is fresh, dangerous, and funny." Booklist

Magnus Chase and the Gods of Asgard: The Hammer of Thor; Rick Riordan. Disney-Hyperion 2016 468 p. (Magnus Chase and the gods of Asgard) $19.99

Grades: 5 6 7 8 9 **Fic**

1. Gender identity -- Fiction 2. Lost and found possessions -- Fiction 3. Mythology, Norse -- Fiction 4. Thor (Norse deity) -- Fiction 5. Adventure and adventurers -- Fiction
ISBN 9781423160922

LC 2016025920

Stonewall Book Award, Youth (2017)

In this book, by Rick Riordan, "Thor's hammer is missing again. The thunder god has a disturbing habit of misplacing his weapon--the mightiest force in the Nine Worlds. But this time the hammer isn't just lost, it has fallen into enemy hands. If Magnus Chase and his friends can't retrieve the hammer quickly, the mortal worlds will be defenseless against an onslaught of giants." (Publisher's note)

"An entertaining sequel that will whet fans' appetites for the next installment." Kirkus

The **Mark** of Athena; Rick Riordan. Disney Hyperion Books 2012 586 p. (The Heroes of Olympus) (hardback) $19.99
Grades: 5 6 7 8 **Fic**
1. Gods and goddesses -- Fiction 2. Classical mythology -- Fiction 3. Camps -- Fiction 4. Giants -- Fiction 5. Mythology, Greek -- Fiction 6. Mythology, Roman -- Fiction 7. Gaia (Greek deity) -- Fiction 8. Hera (Greek deity) -- Fiction
ISBN 9781423140603
LC 2012017264

In this book, by Rick Riordan, "the Greek and Roman demigods will have to cooperate in order to defeat the giants released by the Earth Mother, Gaea. Then they will have to sail together to the ancient land to find the Doors of Death. What exactly are the Doors of Death? Much of the prophecy remains a mystery." (Publisher's note)

"With Gaea awakening and pitting the Greek demigods against their Roman counterparts, Percy Jackson, Jason, and their companions travel to Rome so Annabeth can search for her mother Athena's statue, stolen by the Romans in antiquity. Its return might heal the rift between the camps. Riordan's likable, strong, distinct characters drive the narrative in this rousing continuation of the saga." Horn Book

★ The **maze** of bones. Scholastic 2008 220p il (The 39 clues) $12.99
Grades: 4 5 6 7 **Fic**
1. Family -- Fiction 2. Ciphers -- Fiction
ISBN 978-0-545-06039-4; 0-545-06039-7

At the reading of their grandmother's will, Dan and Amy Cahill are given the choice of receiving a million dollars or uncovering the 39 clues hidden around the world that will lead to the source of the family's power, but by taking on the clues, they end up in a dangerous race against their own family members.

"Adeptly incorporating a genuine kids' perspective, the narrative unfolds like a boulder rolling downhill and keeps readers glued to the pages. . . . The book dazzles with suspense, plot twists, and snappy humor." SLJ

Other titles in this series are:
One false note by Gordon Korman (2008)
The sword thief by Peter Lerangis (2009)
The black circle by Patrick Carman (2009)
Beyond the grave by Jude Watson (2009)
In too deep by Jude Watson (2010)
The viper's nest by Peter Lerangis (2010)
The emperor's code by Gordon Korman (2010)
Storm warning by Linda Sue Park (2010)
Into the gauntlet by Margaret Peterson Haddix (2010)

Percy Jackson's Greek Gods; Rick Riordan; illustrated by John Rocco. Disney-Hyperion 2014 336 p. color illustrations (hardback) $24.99
Grades: 5 6 7 8 **Fic**
1. Greek mythology 2. Gods and goddesses -- Fiction 3. Gods, Greek -- Fiction
ISBN 1423183649; 9781423183648
LC 2013034612

"Riordan takes the classic guide to Greek myths and makes it his own, with an introduction and narration by beloved character Percy Jackson. With 19 chapters, this oversize hardcover includes a variety of stories, from the early tales of Gaea and the Titans to individual tales of gods readers encounter in the 'Percy Jackson' series. . . , such as Ares, Apollo, and Dionysus." (School Library Journal)

"Combining the sarcasm and wit of Percy Jackson with the original Greek myths is a great way to hook tweens and teens on the stories without boring them. The beautiful illustrations by John Rocco enhance each story without taking away from the action and drama." VOYA
Includes bibliographical references and index

★ The **Red** Pyramid; Rick Riordan. Hyperion 2010 516 p. (Kane chronicles) (hardback) $17.99
Grades: 4 5 6 7 **Fic**
1. Fantasy fiction 2. Brothers and sisters -- Fiction 3. Egypt -- Fiction 4. Siblings -- Fiction 5. Secret societies -- Fiction 6. Gods and goddesses -- Fiction 7. Voyages and travels -- Fiction
ISBN 1423113381; 9781423113386
LC 2010549563

This is the first installment of the Kane chronicles. "Since their mother's death, Carter and Sadie have become near strangers. While Sadie has lived with her grandparents in London, her brother has traveled the world with their father, the brilliant Egyptologist, Dr. Julius Kane. . . . [Dr. Kane] unleashes the Egyptian god Set, who banished him to oblivion and forces the children to flee for their lives." (Publisher's note)

"The first-person narrative shifts between Carter and Sadie, giving the novel an intriguing dual perspective made more complex by their biracial heritage and the tension between the siblings. . . . This fantasy adventure delivers . . . young protagonists with previously unsuspected magical powers, a riveting story marked by headlong adventure, a complex background rooted in ancient mythology, and wry, witty twenty-first-century narration." Booklist

The **Serpent's** Shadow; Rick Riordan. Disney/Hyperion Books 2012 viii, 406 p.p (hardcover) $19.99
Grades: 4 5 6 7 **Fic**
1. Adventure fiction 2. Supernatural -- Fiction 3. Mythology -- Fiction 4. Magic -- Fiction 5. Mythology, Egyptian -- Fiction 6. Voyages and travels -- Fiction 7. Brothers and sisters -- Fiction 8. Adventure and adventurers -- Fiction
ISBN 1423140575; 9781423140573
LC 2012454979

This book by Rick Riordan is the third installment of the Kane Chronicles series. "Despite their best efforts, Carter and Sadie Kane can't seem to keep Apophis, the chaos snake, down. Now Apophis is threatening to plunge the world into eternal darkness, and the Kanes are faced with the impossible task of having to destroy him once and for all." (Publisher's note)

The **son** of Neptune. Disney/Hyperion Books 2011 521p (The heroes of Olympus) $19.99
Grades: 5 6 7 8 **Fic**
1. Camps -- Fiction 2. Monsters -- Fiction 3. Prophecies -- Fiction 4. Classical mythology -- Fiction
ISBN 978-1-4231-4059-7; 1-4231-4059-1
LC 2011017658

Demigod Percy Jackson, still with no memory, and his new friends from Camp Jupiter, Hazel and Frank, go on a quest to free Death, but their bigger task is to unite the Greek and Roman camps so that the Prophecy of Seven can be fulfilled.

The **sword** of summer; Rick Riordan. Disney-Hyperion 2015 512 p. (Magnus Chase and the gods of Asgard) $19.99
Grades: 5 6 7 8 **Fic**
1. Fantasy fiction -- Fiction 2. Norse mythology -- Fiction 3. Mythology, Norse -- Fiction
ISBN 1423160916; 9781423160915
LC 2015018467

In this juvenile novel, by Rick Riordan, "Magnus Chase has always been a troubled kid. Since his mother's mysterious death, he's lived alone on the streets of Boston, surviving by his wits. . . . One day, he's tracked down by an uncle he barely knows-a man his mother claimed was dangerous. Uncle Randolph tells him an impossible secret: Magnus is the son of a Norse god. The Viking myths are true. The gods of Asgard are preparing for war." (Publisher's note)

"There's appeal for new readers, but Percy Jackson fans will also undoubtedly snap this up, and there's even some overlap: Magnus' cousin is Annabeth Chase." Booklist

The **throne** of fire; Rick Riordan. Disney/Hyperion Books 2011 (Kane chronicles) $18.99

Grades: 4 5 6 7   Fic

    ISBN 978-1-4231-4056-6; 1-4231-4056-7; 1423140567; 9781423140566

    Sequel to: The red pyramid (2010)

Carter and Sadie, offspring of the brilliant Egyptologist Dr. Julius Kane, embark on a worldwide search for the Book of Ra, but the House of Life and the gods of chaos are determined to stop them.

"Lit by flashes of humor, this fantasy adventure is an engaging addition to the Kane Chronicles series." Booklist

Vespers rising; [by] Rick Riordan, Peter Lerangis, Gordon Korman, Jude Watson. Scholastic 2011 238p (The 39 clues) $12.99

Grades: 4 5 6 7   Fic

    1. Ciphers -- Fiction

    ISBN 978-0-545-29059-3; 0-545-32606-0

Fourteen-year-old Amy Cahill and her younger brother Dan thought they could return to their regular lives when they found the 39 clues. But the Vespers, powerful enemies, will stop at nothing to get the clues. And with the Vespers rising, the world is in jeopardy.

Rising, Janet

The **word** on the yard. Sourcebooks 2010 189p (The pony whisperer) pa $6.99

Grades: 4 5 6   Fic

    1. Horses -- Fiction

    ISBN 978-1-4022-3952-6 pa; 1-4022-3952-1 pa

    First published 2009 in the United Kingdom

Pia finally starts to feel like she belongs in her new town after people begin to hear that she can communicate with horses, but her popularity is not the only thing she has to worry about when things start to go wrong.

"This combination of magic and a quick-moving, contemporary plot woven around horse and human conflicts and friendships is a light and enjoyable read for fans of this genre." SLJ

Rivers, Karen

Finding Ruby Starling; by Karen Rivers. Arthur A. Levine Books, an imprint of Scholastic Inc. 2014 288 p. (hardcover) $17.99

Grades: 5 6 7 8   Fic

    1. Twins -- Fiction 2. Adoption -- Fiction 3. Blogs -- Fiction 4. Email -- Fiction 5. Sisters -- Fiction 6. Mothers and daughters -- Fiction

    ISBN 0545534798; 9780545534796

                    LC 2014002269

In this middle grade book by Karen Rivers, "when Ruby Starling gets a message from a Ruth Quayle proclaiming them to be long-lost twin sisters, she doesn't know what to do with it. . . . Ruth is an extroverted American girl. Ruby is a shy English one. As they investigate the truth of their birth and the circumstances of their separation, they also share lives full of friends, family, and possible romances." (Publisher's note)

"In this epistolary, dual-narrator story, Ruth, an American twelve-year-old, e-finds her identical twin, Ruby, in England. As with any novel in letters (in this case emails, handwritten notes, and the occasional Tumblr posting), voice is everything, and Ruth and Ruby have distinctive, convincing, and entertaining writing styles. Subplots abound, including the backstory of two complicated families. Hectic, highly textured, and good-natured without being soppy." Horn Book

Roberts, Laura Peyton

Green. Delacorte Press 2010 261p $16.99; lib bdg $19.99

Grades: 5 6 7 8   Fic

    1. Fantasy fiction 2. Leprechauns -- Fiction 3. Grandmothers -- Fiction

    ISBN 978-0-385-73558-2; 0-385-73558-8; 978-0-385-90543-5 lib bdg; 0-385-90543-2 lib bdg

                    LC 2008-54241

Abducted by leprechauns on her thirteenth birthday, Lilybet Green learns that there is more to her family tree—and to her bond with her late grandmother—than she ever imagined.

"A fun, fresh take on leprechaun lore that pushes well past typical depictions to embrace banking transactions, lepro-human relations, and some creative problem-solving. Lily is a credible hero, by turns scared and confident, and definitely one young readers will enjoy following." Booklist

Roberts, Willo Davis

The **one** left behind; [by] Willo Davis Roberts. Atheneum Books for Young Readers 2006 139p $16.95; pa $5.99

Grades: 5 6 7 8   Fic

    1. Twins -- Fiction 2. Sisters -- Fiction 3. Kidnapping -- Fiction 4. Bereavement -- Fiction

    ISBN 978-0-689-85075-2; 0-689-85075-1; 978-0-689-85083-7 pa; 0-689-85083-2 pa

                    LC 2005018196

"Since losing her vivacious twin sister, Angel, nearly a year ago, . . . 11-year-old [Mandy] drifts through the days, aching for her dead sister's company. But when someone breaks into the house and steals food, Mandy snaps into action and investigates what might be going on. . . . The suspense mounts to a desperate climax before all is resolved safely. An introspective page-turner." Booklist

★ The **view** from the cherry tree. Atheneum Pubs. 1975 181p hardcover o.p. pa $5.99

Grades: 5 6 7 8   Fic

    1. Mystery fiction

    ISBN 0-689-30483-8; 0-689-71784-9 pa

"Although written in a direct and unpretentious style, this is essentially a sophisticated story, solidly constructed, imbued with suspense, evenly paced, and effective in conveying the atmosphere of a household coping with the last-minute problems and pressures of a family wedding." Bull Cent Child Books

Robertson, Keith

★ **Henry** Reed, Inc. illustrated by Robert McCloskey. Viking 1958 239p il hardcover o.p. pa $4.99

Grades: 4 5 6   Fic

    ISBN 0-14-034144-7 pa

"Henry Reed, on vacation from the American School in Naples, keeps a record of his research into the American free-enterprise system, to be used as a school report on his return. With a neighbor, Midge Glass, he starts a business in pure and applied research, which results in some very free and widely enterprising experiences, all recorded deadpan in his journal. Very funny and original escapades." Hodges. Books for Elem Sch Libr

Another title about Henry Reed is:
Henry Reed's babysitting service (1966)

Robertson, M. P.

Frank n stan; M. P. Robertson. Pgw 2012 32 p. $17.99
Grades: K 1 2 3   **Fic**
1. Robots -- Fiction 2. Siblings -- Fiction 3. Friendship -- Fiction
ISBN 1847801307; 9781847801302

In author M. P. Robertson's book, "young Franklin P. Shelley often asks his mother for a younger sibling . . . Industrious Frank decides to take matters into his own hands and sets out to build one . . . [named Stan.] Frank charges up the battery, and the light in Stan's chest begins to glow . . . One day, Mum surprises Frank with a cute baby girl, and the boy begins to spend more time with his sister, Mary, and less with Stan. One snowy evening, Stan leaves. It doesn't take long for him to freeze or for the family to miss him. A big hug convinces the big mechanical lug to return." (Kirkus Reviews)

Robertson, Robbie

Hiawatha and the Peacemaker; by Robbie Robertson; illustrated by David Shannon. Abrams Books for Young Readers 2015 48 p. 48 pages $19.95
Grades: K 1 2 3 4 5   **Fic**
1. Storytelling 2. Iroquois Indians 3. Peace -- Fiction 4. Six Nations -- History -- Fiction 5. Indians of North America -- Fiction
ISBN 1419712209; 9781419712203

                   LC 2014041310

In this children's book author Robbie Robertson and illustrator David Shannon present "the story of Hiawatha and his spiritual guide, the Peacemaker, as part of the Iroquois oral tradition. Hiawatha was a strong and articulate Mohawk who was chosen to translate the Peacemaker¿s message of unity for the five warring Iroquois nations during the 14th century. This message not only succeeded in uniting the tribes but also forever changed how the Iroquois governed themselves." (Publisher's note)

"All students should know the history of the Iroquois Confederacy, and this book provides the perfect opportunity for them to do so." SLJ

Robinet, Harriette Gillem

★ **Forty** acres and maybe a mule. Atheneum Bks. for Young Readers 1998 132p hardcover o.p. pa $4.99
Grades: 4 5 6 7   **Fic**
1. African Americans -- Fiction 2. Reconstruction (1865-1876) -- Fiction 3. United States -- History -- 1865-1898 -- Fiction
ISBN 0-689-82078-X; 0-689-83317-2 pa

                   LC 97-39169

Born with a withered leg and hand, Pascal, who is about twelve years old, joins other former slaves in a search for a farm and the freedom which it promises

"Robinet skillfully balances her in-depth historical knowledge with the feelings of her characters, creating a story that moves along rapidly and comes to a bittersweet conclusion." Booklist

Walking to the bus-rider blues. Atheneum Bks. for Young Readers 2000 146p hardcover o.p. pa $4.99
Grades: 5 6 7 8   **Fic**
1. Race relations -- Fiction 2. African Americans -- Fiction
ISBN 0-689-83191-9; 0-689-83886-7 pa

                   LC 99-29054

Twelve-year-old Alfa Merryfield, his older sister, and their grandmother struggle for rent money, food, and their dignity as they participate in the Montgomery, Alabama bus boycott in the summer of 1956

"Ingredients of mystery, suspense, and humor enhance and personalize this well-constructed story that offers insight into a troubled era.' SLJ

Robinson, Barbara

★ The **best** Christmas pageant ever; pictures by Judith Gwyn Brown. Harper & Row 1972 80p il $15.99; lib bdg $16.89; pa $5.99
Grades: 4 5 6   **Fic**
1. Pageants -- Fiction 2. Christmas -- Fiction
ISBN 0-06-025043-7; 0-06-025044-5 lib bdg; 0-06-440275-4 pa

In this story the six Herdmans, "absolutely the worst kids in the history of the world," discover the meaning of Christmas when they bully their way into the leading roles of the local church nativity play

The story "romps through the festive preparations with comic relish, and if the Herdmans are so gauche as to seem exaggerated, they are still enjoyable, as are the not-so-subtle pokes at pageant-planning in general." Bull Cent Child Books

Other titles about the Herdmans are:
The best Halloween ever (2004)
The best school year ever (1994)

Robinson, Mabel L.

Bright Island; Mabel L. Robinson; with decorations by Lynd Ward 75th anniversary ed. Random House Books for Young Readers 2012 276 p. ill. (hardback) $16.99
Grades: 3 4 5   **Fic**
1. Bildungsromans 2. School stories 3. Maine -- Fiction 4. Schools -- Fiction 5. Coming of age -- Fiction 6. Boarding schools -- Fiction 7. Islands -- Maine -- Fiction
ISBN 0394809866; 9780394809861

                   LC 2012009178

Newbery Honor Book (1938)

This book by Mabel L. Robinson follows "Thankful Curtis, [who] is more like her sea captain grandfather than any of her older brothers are. Nothing suits her better than sailing and helping her father with the farm. But when her dreaded sisters-in-law suggest that Thankful get some proper schooling on the mainland . . . Thankful finds the uncharted waters of school difficult to navigate." (Publisher's note)

Robinson, Sharon

Safe at home. Scholastic Press 2006 151p $16.99; pa $5.99
Grades: 4 5 6   **Fic**
1. Baseball -- Fiction 2. New York (N.Y.) -- Fiction 3. African Americans -- Fiction
ISBN 0-439-67197-3; 0-439-67198-1 pa

                   LC 2005-5025

After the death of his father, Elijah Breeze, a ten-year-old African American boy, moves back to New York City with his mother and attends a summer baseball camp as he tries to make new friends and adapt to urban ways.

The author "has created two intriguing protagonists and a group of equally colorful secondary characters. . . . Regardless of their interest in baseball, readers will identify with these youngsters and appreciate the simple story." SLJ

Another title about Elijah Breeze is:
Slam dunk! (2007)

Slam dunk! by Sharon Robinson. 1st ed.; Scholastic Press 2007 151p $16.99
Grades: 4 5 6   **Fic**
1. Basketball -- Fiction 2. Friendship -- Fiction 3. Family life -- Fiction 4. New York (N.Y.) -- Fiction 5. African Americans

-- Fiction

ISBN 978-0-439-67199-6; 0-439-67199-X

LC 2006102462

Sequel to: Safe home (2006)

At Harlem's Langston Hughes Middle School, eleven-year-old Elijah "Jumper" Breeze and his friends complete against Nia and her girlfriends on the basketball court, in a video dance tournament, and for a Student Council seat, and, meanwhile, several of the students face issues with their fathers.

"While serious issues broached in the earlier book . . . . are given renewed attention, this is really an amiable story about friends who stay that way, a theme that translates well in any community." Booklist

Rockliff, Mara

The **case** of the missing moose; by Lewis B. Montgomery; illustrated by Amy Wummer. Kane Press 2011 96p il (Milo & Jazz mysteries) lib bdg $22.60; pa $6.95

Grades: 1 2 3 4   **Fic**

1. Mystery fiction 2. Camps -- Fiction 3. Lost and found possessions -- Fiction

ISBN 978-1-57565-331-0 lib bdg; 1-57565-331-1 lib bdg; 978-1-57565-322-8 pa; 1-57565-322-2 pa

LC 2010023478

While Milo and Jazz, detectives-in-training, are at summer camps on the same lake, the mascot built by Milo's team for the color wars disappears.

"The short, easy chapters are accompanied by playful pen-and-ink illustrations that enhance the story. This early chapter book mystery is engaging." Booklist

The **case** of the poisoned pig; llustrated by Amy Wummer. Kane Press 2009 96p il (Milo & Jazz mysteries) $22.60; pa $6.95

Grades: 1 2 3 4   **Fic**

1. Mystery fiction 2. Pigs -- Fiction

ISBN 978-1-57565-289-4; 1-57565-289-7; 978-1-57565-286-3 pa; 1-57565-286-2 pa

LC 2008027537

When Jazz's pet piglet gets sick and the veterinarian suspects it was poisoned, she and Milo use their detective skills to try to figure out who did it.

The "volume ends with additional 'brain stretchers' and mini-cases. . . . The [story is] quick and satisfying, and challenges at the back of the [book contributes] to the enjoyment. Wummer's pencil and ink illustrations add a humorous touch and are perfect for the [story]." SLJ

Rocklin, Joanne

The **five** lives of our cat Zook; by Joanne Rocklin. Amulet Books 2012 218 p.

Grades: 3 4 5 6   **Fic**

1. Cats -- Fiction 2. Siblings -- Fiction 3. Family life -- Fiction

ISBN 1419701924; 9781419701924

LC 2011041088

"In this . . . middle-grade novel, Oona and her brother, Fred, love their cat Zook (short for Zucchini), but Zook is sick. As they conspire to break him out of the vet's office, convinced he can only get better at home with them, Oona tells Fred the story of Zook's previous lives, ranging in style from fairy tale to grand epic to slice of life. Each of Zook's lives has echoes in Oona's own family life, which is going through a transition she's not yet ready to face." (Publisher's note)

★ **One** day and one amazing morning on Orange Street. Amulet Books 2011 207p $16.95

Grades: 3 4 5   **Fic**

1. Trees -- Fiction 2. Oranges -- Fiction 3. California -- Fiction 4.

Friendship -- Fiction 5. Family life -- Fiction

ISBN 0-8109-9719-3; 978-0-8109-9719-6

LC 2010-23452

The last remaining orange tree on a Southern California street brings together neighbors of all ages as they face their problems and anxieties, including the possibility that a mysterious stranger is a threat to their tree. "Grades four to six." (Bull Cent Child Books)

"Fully realized characters and setting definitely make this one morning on Orange Street amazing." Kirkus

Rockwell, Thomas

★ **How** to eat fried worms; pictures by Emily McCully. Watts 1973 115p il lib bdg $29; pa $5.99

Grades: 3 4 5 6   **Fic**

1. Worms -- Fiction

ISBN 0-531-02631-0 lib bdg; 0-440-44545-0 pa

"A hilarious story that will revolt and delight bumptious, unreachable, intermediate-grade boys and any other less particular mortals that read or listen to it." Booklist

Rodda, Emily

★ The **key** to Rondo. Scholastic Press 2008 342p $16.99; pa $6.99

Grades: 5 6 7 8   **Fic**

1. Fantasy fiction 2. Magic -- Fiction 3. Cousins -- Fiction

ISBN 0-545-03535-X; 978-0-545-03535-4; 0-545-03536-8 pa; 978-0-545-03536-1 pa

LC 2007-16873

Through an heirloom music box, Leo, a serious, responsible boy, and his badly-behaved cousin Mimi enter the magical world of Rondo to rescue Mimi's dog from a sorceress, who wishes to exchange him for the key that allows free travel between worlds.

"Rodda fills the cousins' quest with image-rich prose and compelling action." Bull Cent Child Books

Another title about Rondo is:

The Wizard of Rondo (2009)

Rowan of Rin. Greenwillow Books 2001 151p il hardcover o.p. pa $6.99

Grades: 4 5 6   **Fic**

1. Fantasy fiction

ISBN 0-06-029707-7; 0-06-056071-1 pa

LC 00-63619

First published 1993 in Australia

Because only he can read the magical map, young, weak and timid Rowan joins six other villagers to climb a mountain and try to restore their water supply, as fears of a dragon and other horrors threaten to drive them back

The author has created "a fully conceived fantasy world complete with its own flora and fauna, a well-developed back story, and fascinating characters." Booklist

Other titles about Rowan are:

Rowan and the travelers (2001)

Rowan and the Keeper of the Crystal (2002)

Rowan and the Zebak (2002)

Rowan and the Ice creepers (2003)

Rodgers, Mary

Freaky Friday. Harper & Row 1972 145p hardcover o.p. pa $5.99

Grades: 4 5 6 7   **Fic**

1. Mother-daughter relationship -- Fiction

ISBN 0-06-025048-8; 0-06-025049-6 lib bdg; 0-06-057010-5 pa

"A fresh, imaginative, and entertaining story." Bull Cent Child Books

Rodkey, Geoff

The **Tapper** twins go to war (with each other) Geoff Rodkey. Little, Brown & Co. 2015 240 p. illustrations (Tapper twins) (hardcover) $13.99

Grades: 4 5 6 7 **Fic**

1. School stories 2. Twins -- Fiction 3. New York (N.Y.) -- Fiction 4. Practical jokes -- Fiction 5. Brothers and sisters -- Fiction 6. Schools -- Fiction 7. Oral history -- Fiction 8. Internet games -- Fiction 9. Family life -- New York (State) -- New York -- Fiction

ISBN 0316297798; 9780316297790

LC 2014015918

This book, by Geoff Rodkey, is a "comedy featuring twelve-year-old fraternal twins, Claudia and Reese, who couldn't be more different... except in their determination to come out on top in a vicious prank war! But when the competition escalates into an all-out battle that's fought from the cafeteria of their New York City private school all the way to the fictional universe of an online video game, the twins have to decide if their efforts to destroy each other are worth the price." (Publisher's note)

"Through oral-history interviews, text messages, e-mails, chat-room comments, photographs, and margin notes, Claudia documents the history of the Tapper twins' war. . . . Thanks to the inclusion of various points of view, Claudia's reasonably balanced narrative offers plenty of humorous insight, and occasional doodles and photos keep it peppy." Booklist

Other titles in this series are:

The Tapper twins tear up New York (2015)

The Tapper twins run for president (2016)

Rodman, Mary Ann

★ **Jimmy's** stars. Farrar, Straus & Giroux 2008 257p $16.95

Grades: 5 6 7 8 **Fic**

1. Siblings -- Fiction 2. Soldiers -- Fiction 3. Family life -- Fiction 4. Pittsburgh (Pa.) -- Fiction 5. World War, 1939-1945 -- Fiction

ISBN 978-0-374-33703-2; 0-374-33703-9

LC 2007-05091

In 1943, eleven-year-old Ellie is her brother Jimmy's "best girl," and when he leaves Pittsburgh just before Thanksgiving to fight in World War II, he promises he will return, asks her to leave the Christmas tree up until he does, and reminds her to "let the joy out."

Rodman "finds beauty in every emotional nuance. . . . The lively spirit of working-class Pittsburgh . . . extends Ellie's personal story with a broader sense of home-front life." Booklist

Yankee girl. Farrar, Straus and Giroux 2004 219p $17; pa $7.99

Grades: 4 5 6 7 **Fic**

1. School stories 2. Mississippi -- Fiction 3. Race relations -- Fiction

ISBN 0-374-38661-7; 0-312-53576-7 pa

LC 2003-49048

When her FBI-agent father is transferred to Jackson, Mississippi, in 1964, eleven-year-old Alice wants to be popular but also wants to reach out to the one black girl in her class in a newly-integrated school.

"Rodman shows characters grappling with hard choices, sometimes courageously, sometimes willfully, sometimes inconsistently, but invariably believably." Publ Wkly

Rodowsky, Colby F.

The **next**-door dogs; [by] Colby Rodowsky; pictures by Amy June Bates. Farrar, Straus & Giroux 2005 103p il $15

Grades: 2 3 4 **Fic**

1. Dogs -- Fiction 2. Fear -- Fiction

ISBN 0-374-36410-9

LC 2004-43333

Although terrified of dogs, nine-year-old Sara forces herself to face a labrador retriever and a dalmatian when she must help her next-door neighbor, who has fallen and broken her leg

"Rodowsky makes Sara's fear palpable and her eventual recovery believable. Plentiful pencil illustrations add to the book's accessibility." Horn Book Guide

Rogan, S. Jones

The **daring** adventures of Penhaligon Brush; pictures by Christian Slade. Alfred A. Knopf 2007 230p il $15.99; pa $6.50

Grades: 4 5 6 **Fic**

1. Adventure fiction 2. Foxes -- Fiction 3. Animals -- Fiction

ISBN 978-0-375-84344-0; 0-375-84344-2; 978-0-440-42208-2 pa; 0-440-42208-6 pa

LC 2006-35566

When Penhaligon Brush the fox is summoned by his stepbrother to the seaside town of Porthleven, he finds immediately upon arrival that his brother is incarcerated in the dungeon at Ferball Manor

This is a "swift-paced, large-scale adventure. . . . Slade's halftone art . . . [represents] these robust characters in theatrical costume and with plenty of personality." Publ Wkly

Another title about Penhaligon Brush is:

The curse of the Romany wolves (2009)

Rollins, James

Jake Ransom and the Skull King's shadow. HarperCollins 2009 399p il map $16.99; lib bdg $17.89; pa $7.99

Grades: 5 6 7 8 **Fic**

1. Adventure fiction 2. Mayas -- Fiction 3. Siblings -- Fiction 4. Archeology -- Fiction

ISBN 978-0-06-147379-1; 0-06-147379-0; 978-0-06-147380-7 lib bdg; 0-06-147380-4 lib bdg; 978-0-06-147381-4 pa; 0-06-147381-2 pa

LC 2009-14570

Connecticut middle-schooler Jake and his older sister Kady are transported by a Mayan artifact to a strange world inhabited by a mix of people from long-lost civilizations who are threatened by prehistoric creatures and an evil alchemist, the Skull King.

This is an "exciting time-travel adventure. . . . Rollins . . . presents a wide range of interesting historical information while telling a rollicking good story that should please a wide range of readers." Publ Wkly

Another title about Jake Ransom is:

Jake Ransom and the howling sphinx (2011)

Root, Phyllis

Lilly and the pirates; pictures by Rob Shepperson. Boyds Mills Press 2010 116p il $16.95

Grades: 3 4 5 6 **Fic**

1. Adventure fiction 2. Pirates -- Fiction

ISBN 978-1-59078-583-6; 1-59078-583-5

LC 2009030494

Ten-year-old Lilly, a worrier who greatly fears the sea, leaves the home of her librarian great-uncle and sets out with an old woman pirate to rescue her parents, who were shipwrecked while seeking the elusive frangipani fruit fly on an uncharted island.

"Many children will relate to this rather cozy adventure story and its lovably flawed heroine. Like the story, Shepperson's many full-page illustrations are lively, engaging, and occasionally humorous." Booklist

Rose, Caroline Starr

Blue birds; Caroline Starr Rose. G. P. Putnam's Sons, an imprint of Penguin Group (USA) 2015 400 p. map (hardcover) $16.99

Grades: 4 5 6 7 **Fic**

1. Native Americans -- Fiction 2. Roanoke Island (N.C.) -- History

-- Fiction 3. Novels in verse 4. Friendship -- Fiction 5. Lumbee Indians -- Fiction 6. Roanoke Colony -- Fiction
ISBN 0399168109; 9780399168109

LC 2014012100

In this novel by Caroline Starr Rose, "it's 1587 and twelve-year-old Alis has made the long journey with her parents from England to help settle the New World. But the land, the island Roanoke, is also inhabited by the Roanoke tribe and tensions between them and the English are running high, soon turning deadly. Amid the strife, Alis meets and befriends Kimi, a Roanoke girl about her age. Though the two don't even speak the same language, these girls form a special bond." (Publisher's note)

"The use of different typefaces works well to differentiate the two voices, which occasionally appear in tandem when the girls are together. An imaginative historical novel with two sympathetic protagonists." Booklist

Includes bibliographical references

★ **May** B. a novel-in-verse. Schwartz & Wade Books 2012 $15.99; lib bdg $18.99

Grades: 4 5 6 7   **Fic**
1. Novels in verse 2. Kansas -- Fiction 3. Frontier and pioneer life -- Fiction
ISBN 978-1-58246-393-3; 1-58246-393-X; 978-1-58246-412-1 lib bdg; 1-58246-412-X lib bdg

LC 2010033222

When a failed wheat crop nearly bankrupts the Betterly family, Pa pulls twelve-year-old May from school and hires her out to a couple new to the Kansas frontier.

"If May is a brave, stubborn fighter, the short, free-verse lines are one-two punches in this Laura Ingalls Wilder-inspired ode to the human spirit." Kirkus

Rosen, Michael J.

Running with trains; a novel in poetry and two voices. Michael J. Rosen. Boyds Mills 2012 102 p. (reinforced) $15.95

Grades: 5 6 7   **Fic**
1. Locomotives 2. Novels in verse 3. Farm life -- Fiction
ISBN 159078863X; 9781590788639

Author Michael Rosen's "story begins as 13-year-old Perry makes the train trip from his grandmother's for his weekly visit with his mother. . . . He is waiting for his father, missing in action in Vietnam, to return . . . [and] for his mother to finish nursing school so they can resume the life they knew prior to his father's going to war. Watching that same train, whose tracks bisect his family's farm, is 9-year-old Steve, who feels trapped by the constancy of his doting parents and farm chores and wishes he could ride that train to exotic locales." (Kirkus Reviews)

Sailing the unknown; around the world with Captain Cook. written by Michael J. Rosen; illustrated by Maria Cristina Pritelli. Creative Editions 2012 37 p. $17.99

Grades: 3 4 5 6 7   **Fic**
1. Sea stories 2. Explorers -- Fiction 3. Voyages around the world -- Fiction 4. Diaries -- Fiction
ISBN 1568462166; 9781568462165

LC 2011040840

This children's book, by Michael J. Rosen, illustrated by Maria Cristina Pritelli, tells the story of "an 11-year-old sailor named Nicholas, . . . [who in 1768] took to the seas with British explorer James Cook on a 3-year expedition of discovery, venturing into an uncharted world filled with strange lands, mysterious peoples, and peculiar creatures." (Publisher's note)

The tale of rescue; Michael J. Rosen, Stan Fellows. Candlewick Press 2015 112 p. color illustrations $14.99

Grades: 4 5 6 7 8   **Fic**
1. Blizzards -- Fiction 2. Rescue work -- Fiction
ISBN 0763671673; 9780763671679

LC 2014949722

In this children's story, by Michael J. Rosen, illustrated by Stan Fellows, "when a blizzard traps a family outside in a whiteout, a cattle dog devises a stunning rescue. . . . They are panicked, exhausted, freezing, and stranded in waist-deep drifts. From off in the distance, the cattle dog has heard their faint, snow-drowned cries. Her inexhaustible attention turns to saving them." (Publisher's note)

"Lavishly illustrated in full-page watercolors, the book is visually beautiful and will appeal to adults looking for a feel-good dog story to share with a child." Booklist

Ross, Gary

Bartholomew Biddle and the very big wind; Gary Ross, Matthew Meyers. Candlewick Press 2012 96 p. $17.99

Grades: 1 2 3 4 5 6   **Fic**
1. Novels in verse 2. Adventure fiction 3. Voyages and travels -- Fiction
ISBN 0763649201; 9780763649203

LC 2012942303

Author Gary Ross presents an adventure story. "Bartholomew Biddle's life has always been pretty ordinary, but when a huge wind blows past his window one night, he feels the call of adventure -- and he can't resist the urge to grab his bedsheet and catch a ride. Soon he's soaring far above his little town, heading wherever the wind takes him! . . . Bart finds himself in a mysterious cove where the wind doesn't blow. Stuck, Bart is forced to face the fact that his flying days might be over. Will he ever get home again?" (Publisher's note)

Ross, Joel

The Fog diver; Joel Ross. HarperCollins 2015 336 p. (hardback) $16.99

Grades: 4 5 6 7   **Fic**
1. Aeronautics -- Fiction 2. Science fiction 3. Orphans -- Fiction 4. Survival -- Fiction 5. Recycling (Waste) -- Fiction 6. Adventure and adventurers -- Fiction 7. Environmental degradation -- Fiction
ISBN 0062352938; 9780062352934

LC 2014034154

In this juvenile novel, by Joel Ross, "living in the sky is the new reality and a few determined slum kids just might become heroes. . . . Thirteen-year-old Chess and his friends Hazel, Bea, and Swedish sail their rickety air raft over the deadly Fog, scavenging the ruins for anything they can sell to survive. But now survival isn't enough. They must risk everything to get to the miraculous city of Port Oro, the only place where their beloved Mrs. E can be cured of fogsickness." (Publisher's note)

"[A] fresh approach, convincingly delivered, with overtones reminiscent of Dickens...the only thing missing is a sequel, which readers will hope won't be far behind." Kirkus

Another title in this series is:
The Lost Compass (2016)

Rowling, J. K.

★ **Harry** Potter and the Sorcerer's Stone; illustrations by Mary Grandpré. Arthur A. Levine Bks. 1998 309p il $22.99; pa $8.99

Grades: 4 5 6 7 8 9 10   **Fic**
1. Fantasy fiction 2. Witches -- Fiction
ISBN 0-590-35340-3; 0-590-35342-X pa

LC 97-39059

First published 1997 in the United Kingdom with title: Harry Potter and the Philosopher's Stone

Rescued from the outrageous neglect of his aunt and uncle, a young boy with a great destiny proves his worth while attending Hogwarts School for Witchcraft and Wizardry.

This "is a brilliantly imagined and beautifully written fantasy." Booklist

Other titles in this series are:

Harry Potter and the Chamber of Secrets (1999)
Harry Potter and the Prisoner of Azkaban (1999)
Harry Potter and Goblet of Fire (2000)
Harry Potter and the Order of the Phoenix (2003)
Harry Potter and the Half-Blood Prince (2005)
Harry Potter and the Deathly Hallows (2007)

Roy, Carter

The **blood** guard; Carter Roy. Two Lions 2014 288 p. (trade pbk. : alk. paper) $17.99

Grades: 5 6 7 8   **Fic**

1. Fantasy fiction 2. Adventure and adventurers 3. Survival skills -- Fiction 4. Secret societies -- Fiction 5. Adventure stories 6. Kidnapping -- Fiction

ISBN 1477847251; 9781477847251

LC 2013958330

In this book, by Carter Roy, "when thirteen-year-old Ronan Truelove's . . . mom snatches him from school, then sets off on a high speed car chase, Ronan is shocked. His . . . dad has been kidnapped? And the kidnappers are after him, too? His mom, he quickly learns, is . . . a member of an ancient order of knights, the Blood Guard, a sword-wielding secret society sworn to protect the Pure-thirty-six noble souls whose safety is crucial if the world as we know it is to survive." (Publisher's note)

"As Ronan embarks on a hero's journey, familiar tropes of righting wrongs and self-discovery persist but nevertheless remain entertaining as mystery, mysticism, and action abound." Horn Book

Other titles in this series are:

The glass gauntlet (2015)
The blazing bridge (2017)

Roy, James

Max Quigley; technically not a bully. written and illustrated by James Roy. Houghton Mifflin Harcourt 2009 202p il $12.95

Grades: 4 5 6   **Fic**

1. Bullies -- Fiction 2. Friendship -- Fiction

ISBN 978-0-547-15263-9; 0-547-15263-9

LC 2008-36110

First published 2007 in Australia

After playing a prank on one of his "geeky" classmates, sixth-grader Max Quigley's punishment is to be tutored by him.

"Straightforward chronology, believable dialogue, self-contained chapters, and plenty of humor make this accessible to reluctant readers and particularly appealing to boys who may see a bit of themselves in this realistic school story." Booklist

Roy, Jennifer

Yellow star; by Jennifer Roy. Marshall Cavendish 2006 227p $16.95

Grades: 5 6 7 8   **Fic**

1. Jews -- Fiction 2. Poland -- Fiction 3. Holocaust, 1933-1945 -- Fiction

ISBN 0-7614-5277-X; 978-0-7614-5277-5

LC 2005-50788

Boston Globe-Horn Book Honor: Fiction and Poetry (2006)

From 1939, when Syvia is four and a half years old, to 1945 when she has just turned ten, a Jewish girl and her family struggle to survive in Poland's Lodz ghetto during the Nazi occupation.

"In a thoughtful, vividly descriptive, almost poetic prose, Roy retells the true story of her Aunt Syvia's experiences. . . . This book is a standout in the genre of Holocaust literature." SLJ

Rundell, Katherine

★ **Cartwheeling** in thunderstorms; Katherine Rundell. Simon & Schuster Books for Young Readers 2014 256 p. (hardcover) $16.99

Grades: 4 5 6 7 8   **Fic**

1. School stories 2. Bullies -- Fiction 3. Orphans -- Fiction 4. Boarding schools -- Fiction 5. Interpersonal relations -- Fiction 6. Zimbabweans -- England -- London -- Fiction

ISBN 1442490616; 9781442490611; 9781442490635

LC 2013021053

Boston Globe-Horn Book Award: Fiction (2015)

In this middle grade novel by Katherine Rundell, illustrated by Melissa Castrillón, "Wilhelmina Silver's world is golden. Living half-wild on an African farm with her horse, her monkey, and her best friend, every day is beautiful. But when her home is sold and Will is sent away to boarding school in England, the world becomes impossibly difficult. Lions and hyenas are nothing compared to packs of vicious schoolgirls." (Publisher's note)

"Wilhelmina, daughter of William Silver, white foreman of the Two Tree Hill Farm in Zimbabwe, leads a 'wildcat' life. Her idyll ends abruptly and tragically with her father's death from malaria, after which she's shipped off to boarding school in England. Rundell's finely drawn etchings of the people in Will's sphere and rich descriptions of African colonial farm life sprawl across the pages." Horn Book

★ **Rooftoppers**; by Katherine Rundell and illustrated by Terry Fan. Simon & Schuster Books for Young Readers 2013 288 p. (hardcover) $16.99

Grades: 4 5 6 7   **Fic**

1. Orphans -- Fiction 2. Mother-daughter relationship -- Fiction 3. Roofs -- Fiction 4. France -- Fiction 5. Paris (France) -- Fiction 6. Missing persons -- Fiction 7. Homeless persons -- Fiction 8. Guardian and ward -- Fiction

ISBN 1442490586; 9781442490581

LC 2012049469

In this book, by Katherine Rundell, "everyone thinks that Sophie is an orphan. . . . Her guardian tells her it is almost impossible that her mother is still alive. . . . When the Welfare Agency writes to her guardian, threatening to send Sophie to an orphanage, she takes matters into her own hands and flees to Paris to look for her mother. . . . She meets Matteo and his network of rooftoppers--urchins who live in the hidden spaces above the city. Together they scour the city in a search for Sophie's mother." (Publisher's note)

The **wolf** wilder; Katherine Rundell. Simon & Schuster Books for Young Readers 2015 231 p. (hardcover) $16.99

Grades: 4 5 6 7 8   **Fic**

1. Wolves -- Fiction 2. Human-animal relationship -- Fiction 3. Mother-daughter relationship -- Fiction 4. Mothers and daughters -- Fiction 5. Russia -- History -- Nicholas II, 1894-1917 -- Fiction

ISBN 1481419420; 9781481419420; 9781481419437

LC 2014048206

In this novel, by Katherine Rundell, "Feo's . . . mother trains domesticated wolves to be able to fend for themselves in the snowy wilderness of Russia, and Feo is following in her footsteps to become a wolf wilder. . . . But not everyone is enamored with the wolves, or with the fact that Feo and her mother are turning them wild. And when her mother is taken captive, Feo must travel through the cold, harsh woods to save her--and learn from her wolves how to survive." (Publisher's note)

"Her spirited, half-wild nature shines brightly on the page, even as her vulnerabilities endear her to readers' hearts. It is a wonderful thing to see Feo's quest inspire a nation to stand up and fight, and readers will cheer her on every step of the way." Booklist

Runholt, Susan

Adventure at Simba Hill. Viking 2011 273p $16.99

Grades: 5 6 7 8   **Fic**

1. Mystery fiction 2. Kenya -- Fiction 3. Africans -- Fiction 4. Smuggling -- Fiction 5. Archeology -- Fiction 6. Friendship -- Fiction

ISBN 978-0-670-01201-5; 0-670-01201-7

LC 2010024533

When fourteen-year-old best friends Kari and Lucas travel to an archaeological dig in Kenya with Kari's uncle Geoff, they help expose a smuggling ring.

"Lighthearted and yet mostly based on logic, this outing allows readers to get a taste of Africa's pleasures. . . . The cast of suspects and rapidly made friends keeps the mood frothy and the sinister actions nicely removed." Kirkus

The **mystery** of the third Lucretia. Viking Childrens Books 2008 288p $16.99; pa $6.99

Grades: 5 6 7 8   **Fic**

1. Mystery fiction 2. Art -- Fiction 3. Europe -- Fiction 4. Friendship -- Fiction

ISBN 978-0-670-06252-2; 0-670-06252-9; 978-0-14-241338-8 pa; 0-14-241338-0 pa

LC 2007-24009

While traveling in London, Paris, and Amsterdam, fourteen-year-old best friends Kari and Lucas solve an international art forgery mystery.

"There are enough artistic details for fans of art mysteries and enough spying and fleeing for fans of detective adventure." Bull Cent Child Books

Other titles about Kari and Lucas are:

Rescuing Seneca Crane (2009)

The adventure at Simba Hill (2011)

Rupp, Rebecca

After Eli; Rebecca Rupp. 1st ed. Candlewick 2012 245 p. (hardcover) $15.99; (ebook) $15.99

Grades: 4 5 6 7 8   **Fic**

1. Bildungsromans 2. Family -- Fiction 3. Brothers -- Fiction 4. Bereavement -- Fiction 5. Death -- Fiction

ISBN 0763658103; 9780763658106; 9780763661946

LC 2011048344

In this book, "Daniel, a wry and thoughtful narrator, looks back on the summer when he was 14, three years after his older brother, Eli, died in Iraq at age 22." Daniel's "memories of larger-than-life Eli and his lingering anger about his death" are interwoven with "Daniel's day-to-day challenges, including his dysfunctional family . . .; his frustrations with his . . . friends; his attraction to Isabelle, a . . . newcomer to town; and his nascent friendship with school outcast Walter." (Publishers Weekly)

★ **Octavia** Boone's big questions about life, the universe, and everything. Candlewick Press 2010 185p $15.99

Grades: 5 6 7 8   **Fic**

1. School stories 2. Vermont -- Fiction 3. Religion -- Fiction 4. Family life -- Fiction 5. Christian life -- Fiction

ISBN 978-0-7636-4491-8; 0-7636-4491-9

LC 2009-47408

Seventh-grader Octavia puzzles over life's biggest questions when her mother seems to find the answers in a conservative Christian church, while her artist father believes the writings of Henry David Thoreau hold the key.

"This hopeful novel highlights the resilience of children and the courage of those who seek truth in a complicated world." Publ Wkly

★ **Sarah** Simpson's Rules for Living. Candlewick Press 2008 84p $13.99

Grades: 4 5 6   **Fic**

1. School stories 2. Vermont -- Fiction 3. Remarriage -- Fiction 4. Family life -- Fiction

ISBN 978-0-7636-3220-5

LC 2007-34214

In a journal, twelve-year old Sarah Simpson records important lists and the daily events of her life at home and in school, beginning one year after her father moved from Vermont to California to divorce her mother and marry someone else.

"Although Sarah's tone ranges widely, from resentful to full-out funny, . . . her vulnerable yet take-charge personality comes through." Publ Wkly

Russell, Ching Yeung

★ **Tofu** quilt. Lee & Low Books 2009 125p il $16.95

Grades: 4 5 6   **Fic**

1. Novels in verse 2. Sex role -- Fiction 3. Authorship -- Fiction 4. Hong Kong (China) -- Fiction

ISBN 978-1-60060-423-2; 1-60060-423-4

LC 2009-16903

Growing up in 1960s Hong Kong, a young girl dreams of becoming a writer in spite of conventional limits placed on her by society and family.

"The story is revealed through Russell's tender poems that beautifully describe Yeung Ying's surroundings, her home life, her family, and her inner thoughts. The poems are simple, yet filled with images and language that create an atmosphere that brings the child's early years to light." SLJ

Russell, Krista

Chasing the Nightbird. Peachtree 2011 200p $15.95

Grades: 5 6 7 8   **Fic**

1. Sailors -- Fiction 2. Slavery -- Fiction 3. Abolitionists -- Fiction 4. Massachusetts -- Fiction

ISBN 1561455970; 9781561455973

LC 2011002665

In 1851 New Bedford, Massachusetts, fourteen-year-old Cape Verdean sailor Lucky Valera is kidnapped by his estranged half-brother and forced to work in a mill, but while Lucky is plotting his escape he meets a former slave and a young Quaker girl who influence his plans.

"Without slowing the story's pace, Russell gives readers plenty to think about regarding the turbulent racial dynamics of the period— Lucky, who is dark-skinned yet free, initially sees little connection between his life and the plight of slaves. Strong-willed and goodhearted, Lucky is an especially vibrant hero in this multifaceted and suspenseful historical adventure." Publ Wkly

Rutkoski, Marie

★ The **Cabinet** of Wonders; [by] Marie Rutkoski. Farrar Straus Giroux 2008 258p (The Kronos Chronicles) $16.95; pa $6.99

Grades: 5 6 7 8   **Fic**

1. Fantasy fiction 2. Romanies -- Fiction

ISBN 978-0-374-31026-4; 0-374-31026-2; 978-0-312-60239-0 pa; 0-312-60239-1 pa

LC 2007037702

Twelve-year-old Petra, accompanied by her magical tin spider, goes to Prague hoping to retrieve the enchanted eyes the Prince of Bohemia took from her father, and is aided in her quest by a Roma boy and his sister.

"Add this heady mix of history and enchantment to the season's list of astonishingly accomplished first novels. . . . Infusions of folklore (and Rutkowski's embellishments of them) don't slow the fast plot but more deeply entrance readers." Publ Wkly

Other titles in this series are:

The Celestial Globe (2009)

The Jewel of the Kalderash (2011)

Ryan, Carrie

City of thirst; Carrie Ryan and John Parke Davis; illustrated by Todd Harris. Little, Brown & Co. 2015 400 p. illustrations (hardback) $17

Grades: 4 5 6 7 **Fic**

1. Magic -- Fiction 2. Pirates -- Fiction 3. Friendship -- Fiction 4. Fantasy 5. Maps -- Fiction

ISBN 0316240842; 9780316240840

LC 2015008673

In this children's book by Carrie Ryan and John Parke Davis "when the magical waters of the Pirate Stream begin flooding Marrill's world, the only way to stop the destruction is to return to the Stream and find the source of the mysterious Iron Tide. Reunited with her best friend Fin . . . Marrill, her disbelieving babysitter, and the Enterprising Kraken crew must make the treacherous trek to the . . . world of Monerva and uncover the secrets of its long-lost wish machine." (Publisher's note)

The **map** to everywhere; by Carrie Ryan & John Parke Davis. Little, Brown & Co. 2014 448 p. illustrations (The map to everywhere) (hardcover) $17

Grades: 4 5 6 7 **Fic**

1. Fantasy fiction 2. Pirates -- Fiction 3. Maps -- Fiction 4. Magic -- Fiction 5. Wizards -- Fiction 6. Stealing -- Fiction 7. Adventure and adventurers -- Fiction

ISBN 031624077X; 9780316240772

LC 2013044752

In this juvenile novel, by Carrie Ryan and John Parke Davis, "to Master Thief Fin, an orphan from the murky pirate world of the Khaznot Quay, the Map is the key to finding his mother. To suburban school-girl Marrill, it's her only way home after getting stranded on the Pirate Stream, the magical waterway that connects every world in creation. With the help of a bumbling wizard and his crew, they must scour the many worlds of the Pirate Stream to gather the pieces of the Map to Everywhere." (Publisher's note)

Multifaceted characters, high stakes, imaginative magic, and hints of hidden twists and complexities to come add up to a memorable start to a projected four-volume voyage." Kirkus

Ryan, Pam Munoz

★ **Becoming** Naomi Leon; [by] Pam Muñoz Ryan. Scholastic Press 2004 246p $16.95; pa $6.99

Grades: 5 6 7 8 **Fic**

1. Mexico -- Fiction 2. Family life -- Fiction 3. Mexican Americans -- Fiction

ISBN 0-439-26969-5; 0-439-26997-0 pa

LC 2004-346

When Naomi's absent mother resurfaces to claim her, Naomi runs away to Mexico with her great-grandmother and younger brother in search of her father

"Ryan has written a moving book about family dynamics. . . . All of the characters are well drawn." SLJ

★ The **dreamer**; drawings by Peter Sís. Scholastic Press 2010 372p il $17.99

Grades: 4 5 6 7 **Fic**

1. Authors 2. Diplomats 3. Novelists 4. Novelist 5. Nobel laureates for peace 6. Nobel laureates for literature 7. Father-son relationship -- Fiction

ISBN 978-0-439-26970-4; 0-439-26970-9

Boston Globe-Horn Book Award honor book: Fiction (2010)

Neftali finds beauty and wonder everywhere. He loves to collect treasures, daydream, and write—pastimes his authoritarian father thinks are for fools. Against all odds, Neftali prevails against his father's cruelty and his own crippling shyness to become one of the most widely read poets in the world, Pablo Neruda.

"Ryan loads the narrative with vivid sensory details. And although it isn't poetry, it eloquently evokes the sensation of experiencing the world as someone who savors the rhythms of words and gets lost in the intricate surprises of nature. The neat squares of Sis' meticulously stippled illustrations, richly symbolic in their own right, complement and deepen the lyrical quality of the book." Booklist

★ **Esperanza** rising. Scholastic Press 2000 262p $15.95; pa $4.99

Grades: 5 6 7 8 **Fic**

1. California -- Fiction 2. Mexican Americans -- Fiction 3. Agricultural laborers -- Fiction

ISBN 0-439-12041-1; 0-439-12042-X pa

LC 00-24186

Esperanza and her mother are forced to leave their life of wealth and privilege in Mexico to go work in the labor camps of Southern California, where they must adapt to the harsh circumstances facing Mexican farm workers on the eve of the Great Depression

"Ryan writes movingly in clear, poetic language that children will sink into, and the [book] offers excellent opportunities for discussion and curriculum support." Booklist

Rylander, Chris

The **fourth** stall. Walden Pond Press 2011 314p $15.99

Grades: 4 5 6 7 **Fic**

1. School stories 2. Bullies -- Fiction 3. Friendship -- Fiction 4. Business enterprises -- Fiction

ISBN 978-0-06-199496-8; 0-06-199496-0

LC 2010016280

Sixth-graders Mac and Vince operate a business charging school mates for protection from bullies and for help to negotiate conflicts peacefully, with amazing challenges and results.

"Rylander mines a substantial amount of humor and heart from this combination hardboiled crime novel and middle-grade character piece. . . A light and enjoyable caper." Publ Wkly

Rylant, Cynthia

★ A **fine** white dust. Simon & Schuster 2000 106p $25; pa $4.99

Grades: 5 6 7 8 **Fic**

1. Religion -- Fiction 2. Friendship -- Fiction 3. Family life -- Fiction

ISBN 978-0-689-84087-6; 0-689-84087-X; 978-1-4169-2769-3 pa; 1-4169-2769-7 pa

A reissue of the title first published 1986 by Bradbury Press

A Newbery Medal honor book, 1987

The visit of the traveling Preacher Man to his small North Carolina town gives new impetus to thirteen-year-old Peter's struggle to reconcile his own deeply felt religious belief with the beliefs and non-beliefs of his family and friends

"Blending humor and intense emotion with a poetic use of language Cynthia Rylant has created a taut, finely drawn portrait of a boy's growth from seeking for belief, through seduction and betrayal, to a spiritual acceptance and a readiness 'for something whole.'" Horn Book

★ **God** got a dog; Cynthia Rylant; illustrated by Marla Frazee. 1st Beach Lane Books ed. Beach Lane Books 2013 48 p. ill. (hardcover) $17.99

Grades: 5 6 7 8   **Fic**

1. God -- Poetry 2. Picture books for children 3. Femininity of God -- Poetry 4. God -- Fiction 5. Novels in verse
ISBN 1442465182; 9781442465183

LC 2013005577

This book is an illustrated collection of poetry from Cynthia Rylant. A major theme is the multiplicity of God, which Maria Frazee's illustrations expand on, "depicting Him or Her as a black, tattooed nail artist; a middle-aged white woman eating by herself; a little dark-skinned boy on roller skates . . .; a bearded, dark-skinned dude playing poker with Gabriel; a homeless black woman. An illustration appears opposite each poem." (Kirkus Reviews)

Gooseberry Park and the Master Plan; Cynthia Rylant; illustrated by Arthur Howard. Beach Lane Books 2015 128 p. illustrations (hardcover) $16.99

Grades: 3 4 5   **Fic**

1. Parks 2. Animals -- Fiction 3. Droughts -- Fiction 4. Cooperativeness -- Fiction
ISBN 1481404490; 9781481404495; 9781481404501

LC 2013046528

In this children's book by Cynthia Rylant, illustrated by Arthur Howard, "Stumpy the Squirrel and friends team up to save the day in this charming standalone companion to the beloved 'Gooseberry Park.' There has been no rain for months, and all of the animals in Gooseberry Park are in danger. Can the gang of dear friends come up with a brilliant solution in time to save the day? Absolutely!" (Publisher's note)

"In this follow-up to Gooseberry Park (1995), the animals are living the dream. Murray the bat has a steady supply of Oreos; Gwendolyn the hermit crab periodically cruises around on the back of Kona, the chocolate lab; and Stumpy the squirrel has three bright children, though their habit of emulating Murray by hanging upside down has generated a bit of neighborhood gossip. . . . Short chapters generously peppered with Howard's endearing and often amusing illustrations make this a natural step up from beginning readers. A sweet tale of friendship and teamwork." Booklist

★ **Missing** May. Orchard Bks. 1992 89p hardcover o.p. pa $5.99

Grades: 5 6 7 8   **Fic**

1. Death -- Fiction 2. West Virginia -- Fiction
ISBN 0-531-05996-0; 0-439-61383-3 pa

LC 91-23303

Awarded the Newbery Medal, 1993

After the death of the beloved aunt who has raised her, twelve-year-old Summer and her uncle Ob leave their West Virginia trailer in search of the strength to go on living

"There is much to ponder here, from the meaning of life and death to the power of love. That it all succeeds is a tribute to a fine writer who brings to the task a natural grace of language, an earthly sense of humor, and a well-grounded sense of the spiritual." SLJ

Sachar, Louis

★ **Holes**; [by] Louis Sachar. 10th anniversary ed.; Farrar, Straus and Giroux 2008 265p $18

Grades: 5 6 7 8   **Fic**

1. Friendship -- Fiction 2. Buried treasure -- Fiction 3. Homeless persons -- Fiction 4. Juvenile delinquency -- Fiction
ISBN 978-0-374-33266-2; 0-374-33266-5

LC 2007045430

A reissue of the title first published 1998. Includes additional information about the author and his Newbery acceptance speech

Awarded the Newbery Medal, 1999

As further evidence of his family's bad fortune which they attribute to a curse on a distant relative, Stanley Yelnats is sent to a hellish correctional camp in the Texas desert where he finds his first real friend, a treasure, and a new sense of himself

"This delightfully clever story is well-crafted and thought-provoking, with a bit of a folklore thrown in for good measure." Voice Youth Advocates

Marvin Redpost, kidnapped at birth? illustrated by Neal Hughes. Random House 1992 68p il $11.99; pa $3.99

Grades: 1 2 3   **Fic**

1. Family life -- Fiction
ISBN 0-679-91946-5; 0-679-81946-0 pa

LC 91-51105

Red-haired Marvin is convinced that the reason he looks different from the rest of his family is that he is really the lost prince of Shampoon

"Written almost completely in dialogue, the story is fast paced, easy to read, and full of humor." SLJ

Other titles about Marvin Redpost are:
Marvin Redpost, a flying birthday cake (1999)
Marvin Redpost, a magic crystal (2000)
Marvin Redpost, alone in his teacher's house (1994)
Marvin Redpost, class president (1999)
Marvin Redpost, is he a girl? (1993)
Marvin Redpost, super fast, out of control (2000)
Marvin Redpost, why pick on me? (1993)

Marvin Redpost: A magic crystal? illustrated by Amy Wummer. Random House 2000 82p il $11.99; pa $3.99

Grades: 1 2 3   **Fic**

1. Magic -- Fiction 2. Wishes -- Fiction 3. Friendship -- Fiction
ISBN 0-679-99002-X; 0-679-89002-5 pa

LC 00-37300

When Marvin Redpost's new friend Casey shares with him her magic crystal that can make wishes come true, things get out of control

Marvin Redpost: is he a girl? illustrated by Barbara Sullivan. Random House 1993 69p il $11.99; pa $3.99

Grades: 1 2 3   **Fic**

1. School stories 2. Sex role -- Fiction
ISBN 0-679-91948-1; 0-679-81948-7 pa

LC 92040784

After Casey Happleton tells him that if he kisses his elbow he will turn into a girl, nine-year-old Marvin experiments and finds himself very confused about his identity.

"Sachar writes for beginning readers with a comic simplicity that is never banal. Here he gets a lot of fun out of the identity confusion." Booklist

Sideways stories from Wayside School; illustrated by Julie Brinckloe. Morrow Junior Books 1998 124p il $15.99; pa $5.99

Grades: 3 4 5 6   **Fic**

1. School stories
ISBN 0-688-16086-7; 0-380-69871-4 pa

LC 97039420

A reissue of the title first published 1978 by Follett

Humorous episodes from the classroom on the thirtieth floor of Wayside School, which was accidentally built sideways with one classroom on each story.

Sackett, Frances

The **misadventures** of the magician's dog; by Frances Sackett. Holiday House 2013 192 p. (hardcover) $16.95

Grades: 4 5 6   **Fic**
1. Dogs -- Fiction 2. Magic -- Fiction 3. Brothers and sisters
-- Fiction 4. Adventure and adventurers -- Fiction 5. Families of
military personnel -- Fiction
ISBN 0823428699; 9780823428694

                                                LC 2012041540
In this book, by Frances Sackett, "Peter Lubinsky doesn't even like
dogs and can't understand why he asked for one for his birthday. But
it turns out that this pet, whom Peter calls The Dog, can talk and do
magic—and he needs Peter's help. In return, The Dog promises to teach
Peter conjuring and to help him bring his father home from the Middle
East, where he is deployed with the air force." (Publisher's note)

"Twelve-year-old Peter adopts a talking dog that needs Peter's help:
his former master, a magician, has turned himself into a rock. If Peter
helps return the magician to his human state, "The Dog" will teach Peter
how to conjure his father, who's deployed in the Middle East. This action-packed fantasy lightly explores the impact military parents' service
has on their children." (Horn Book)

Sage, Angie
The **Magykal** papers; illustrations by Mark Zug. Katherine Tegen
Books 2009 167p il (Septimus Heap)
Grades: 5 6 7 8   **Fic**
1. Fantasy fiction 2. Magic -- Fiction 3. Princesses -- Fiction
ISBN 0-06-170416-4; 978-0-06-170416-1
                                                LC 2008027110
Purports to be a compilation of pamphlets, journals, restaurant re-
views, maps, historical information, and other never-before-published
papers from the world of the apprentice alchemist, Septimus Heap.

"Fans of Sage's saga will rejoice in the little pieces if 'magyk' collected here. Beautifully rendered in full color." SLJ

My haunted house; as told to Angie Sage; illustrated by Jimmy
Pickering. Katherine Tegen Books 2006 132p il (Araminta Spookie)
$8.99; lib bdg $14.89; pa $4.99
Grades: 3 4 5   **Fic**
1. Ghost stories
ISBN 978-0-06-077481-3; 0-06-077481-9; 978-0-06-077482-0
lib bdg; 0-06-077482-7 lib bdg; 978-0-06-077483-7 pa; 0-06-
077483-5 pa
                                                LC 2005-23815
Araminta enlists the help of several ghosts in an attempt to stop her
Aunt Tabby from selling Spook House.

This is a "humorous, fast-paced . . . caper. . . . Pickering's quirky art
adds to the kooky—and in spots somewhat spooky—fun." Publ Wkly

Other titles in this series are:
The sword in the grotto (2006)
Frognapped (2007)
Vampire brat (2007)
Ghostsitters (2008)

SandRider; Angie Sage; illustrations by Mark Zug. Katherine Tegen Books, an imprint of HarperCollinsPublishers 2015 480 p. illustrations (TodHunter Moon) (hardback) $17.99
Grades: 5 6 7   **Fic**
1. Magic -- Fiction 2. Adventure fiction 3. Friendship -- Fiction
4. Fantasy 5. Wizards -- Fiction 6. Apprentices -- Fiction 7.
Imaginary creatures -- Fiction
ISBN 0062272489; 9780062272485
                                                LC 2015005851
This novel by Angie Sage and illustrated by Mark Zug "taking place
seven years after the events of the original Septimus Heap series, Tod-
Hunter Moon tells the story of Alice TodHunter Moon, a young Path-
Finder who comes to the Castle with a Magyk all her own. In this second

book, Tod sets out for the Desert of the Singing Sands to retrieve the Egg
of the Orm--a journey that will test not only her Magykal and PathFind-
ing skills but her friendships, too." (Publisher's note)

"This exciting and accessible adventure tale rests solidly on Sage's
appreciable skills as a story spinner and is supported by Zug's chapter-
opening illustrations (final art not seen). Another great read-aloud choice
for the young set and a delight for all ages." Booklist

Sequel to "Pathfider"

StarChaser; Angie Sage; illustrations by Mark Zug. Katherine Tegen Books, an imprint of HarperCollinsPublishers 2016 496 p. illustrations (TodHunter Moon) (hardback) $17.99; (ebook) $16.99
Grades: 5 6 7   **Fic**
1. Magic -- Fiction 2. Wizards -- Fiction 3. Apprentices -- Fiction
4. Fantasy fiction
ISBN 0062272519; 9780062272515; 9780062272539
                                                LC 2016019328
In this third book in the World of Septimus Heap series by Angie
Sage, illustrated by Mark Zug, "Tod must find a replacement Egg o:
the Orm before the Castle—and all its Magyk—disappears forever. . .
Almost one year ago, Alice TodHunter Moon left her PathFinder village
to become Apprentice to ExtraOrdinary Wizard Septimus Heap. Now in
faraway lands, the Castle is in peril. . . . Can she save the Castle while
evading the fate that befell her mother?" (Publisher's note)

"Pencil drawings sprinkled throughout enhance the narrative and
substantiate the book's setting in an alternative, medieval-ish, largely
white world. A delightful ending to a Magykal ride." Kirkus

Saint-Exupery, Antoine de
★ The **little** prince; written and illustrated by Antoine de Saint-Ex-
upery; translated from the French by Richard Howard. Harcourt 2000
83p il $18; pa $12
Grades: 4 5 6 7 8 9 10 11 12 Adult   **Fic**
1. Fantasy fiction 2. Princes -- Fiction 3. Air pilots -- Fiction 4
Extraterrestrial beings -- Fiction
ISBN 0-15-202398-4; 0-15-601219-7 pa
                                                LC 99-50439
A new translation of the title first published 1943 by Reynal & Hitch
cock

"This many-dimensional fable of an airplane pilot who has crashed
in the desert is for readers of all ages. The pilot comes upon the little
prince soon after the crash. The prince tells of his adventures on different
planets and on Earth as he attempts to learn about the universe in orde:
to live peacefully on his own small planet. A spiritual quality enhances
the seemingly simple observations of the little prince." Shapiro. Fic fo:
Youth. 3d edition

The **little** prince: deluxe pop-up book; unabridged text. translated
from the French by Richard Howard. Houghton Mifflin Harcourt 2009
60p il $35
Grades: 4 5 6   **Fic**
1. Fantasy fiction 2. Pop-up books 3. Princes -- Fiction 4. Ai
pilots -- Fiction 5. Extraterrestrial beings -- Fiction
ISBN 978-0-547-26069-3; 0-547-26069-5
An aviator whose plane is forced down in the Sahara Desert encoun
ters a little prince from a small planet who relates his adventures in seek
ing the secret of what is important in life

This "volume is a beautiful piece of bookmaking that actually ex
tends the classic story. In 3-D form, the original artwork feels new, and
inventive design elements . . . add whimsy while focusing even more
attention on the images." Booklist

Salamon, Julie

Mutt's promise; Julie Salamon; illustrated by Jill Weber. Dial Books 2016 256 p. illustrations (hardback) $16.99

Grades: 3 4 5 6 **Fic**

1. Dogs -- Fiction 2. Human-animal relationships -- Fiction 3. Survival -- Fiction
ISBN 0525427783; 9780525427780

LC 2015015747

In this children's book, by Julie Salamon and illustrated by Jill Weber, "Luna is a farm puppy . . . surrounded by her mother, Mutt, and her siblings, and cared for by Gilberto, the son of farm workers. But now Gilberto and his parents have moved on, and Mr. Thomas the farmer . . . finds new homes for the puppies, not realizing that the man who took [them] does not have their best interests at heart. Luna and Chief . . . are trapped in . . . a puppy mill--until they take matters into their own paws and find a way to escape." (Publisher's note)

"Told in third person in clear language, this tender story of courage and hope will appeal to young animal-lovers. Inset illustrations add to the book's charm." Booklist

Salisbury, Graham

Calvin Coconut: hero of Hawaii; illustrated by Jacqueline Rogers. Wendy Lamb Books 2011 147p il $12.99; lib bdg $15.99

Grades: 3 4 5 **Fic**

1. Hawaii -- Fiction 2. Hurricanes -- Fiction 3. Heroes and heroines -- Fiction
ISBN 978-0-385-73962-7; 0-385-73962-1; 978-0-385-90796-5 lib bdg; 0-385-90796-6 lib bdg

LC 2010013161

When a hurricane causes the river near his Hawaiian home to flood, a boy named Calvin Coconut makes a daring rescue.

"Rogers' pen-and-ink drawings are nicely expressive, their playful feel becoming more subdued when depicting the more serious event of the flood. The ongoing strengths of the series are once again present in this volume—cultural details that emerge contextually and blend seamlessly with the narrative and an appealingly realistic depiction of Calvin's busy and sometimes stressed family." Kirkus

Calvin Coconut: kung fooey; illustrated by Jacqueline Rogers. Wendy Lamb Books 2011 131p il $12.99; lib bdg $15.99; e-book $12.99

Grades: 3 4 5 **Fic**

1. School stories 2. Hawaii -- Fiction 3. Family life -- Fiction
ISBN 978-0-385-73963-4; 0-385-90797-4; 978-0-385-90797-2 lib bdg; 0-385-90797-4 lib bdg; 978-0-375-89796-2 e-book

LC 2010029415

Fourth-grader Cal learns a lot about teasing and standing up for others when a weird new student joins his class, while Stella, the tenth-grader who lives with Cal's family to help his mother, practices for her driving test.

"The Hawaiian island setting is a subtle but appealing presence, bringing uniqueness and diversity to the narrative. Salisbury offers gentle wisdom and understanding. . . . Expressive black-and-white illustrations add humor and are generously sprinkled throughout." SLJ

Calvin Coconut: trouble magnet; illustrated by Jacqueline Rogers. Wendy Lamb Books 2009 152p il $12.99; lib bdg $15.99; pa $6.99

Grades: 3 4 5 **Fic**

1. School stories 2. Hawaii -- Fiction 3. Bullies -- Fiction 4. Family life -- Fiction
ISBN 978-0-385-73701-2; 0-385-73701-7; 978-0-385-90639-5 lib bdg; 0-385-90639-0 lib bdg; 978-0-375-84600-7 pa; 0-375-84600-X pa

LC 2008-1415

Nine-year-old Calvin catches the attention of the school bully on the day before he starts fourth grade, while at home, the unfriendly, fifteen-year-old daughter of his mother's best friend has taken over his room

"The familial relationships among Calvin and his sister, their mom and her boyfriend are touching, realistically tempered with moments of frustration. Rogers's lively ink-and-wash drawings augment the story and evoke a playful feel." Kirkus

Other titles about Calvin are:
Calvin Coconut: the zippy fix (2009)
Calvin Coconut: dog heaven (2010)
Calvin Coconut: zoo breath (2010)
Calvin Coconut: hero of Hawaii (2011)
Calvin Coconut: kung fooey (2011)

★ Night of the howling dogs; a novel. Wendy Lamb Books 2007 191p $16.99; lib bdg $19.99; pa $6.50

Grades: 5 6 7 8 **Fic**

1. Hawaii -- Fiction 2. Camping -- Fiction 3. Tsunamis -- Fiction 4. Earthquakes -- Fiction 5. Boy Scouts of America -- Fiction 6. Survival after airplane accidents, shipwrecks, etc. -- Fiction
ISBN 978-0-385-73122-5; 978-0-385-90146-8 lib bdg; 978-0-440-23839-3 pa

LC 2007-07054

In 1975, eleven Boy Scouts, their leaders, and some new friends camping at Halape, Hawaii, find their survival skills put to the test when a massive earthquake strikes, followed by a tsunami.

This is a "vivid adventure. . . . Salisbury weaves Hawaiian legend into the modern-day narrative to create a haunting, unusual novel." Booklist

Saller, Carol Fisher

Eddie's war; [by] Carol Fisher Saller. Namelos 2011 ix, 194p $18.95

Grades: 5 6 7 8 **Fic**

1. Novels in verse 2. Brothers -- Fiction 3. Farm life -- Fiction 4. World War, 1939-1945 -- Fiction
ISBN 1-60898-108-8; 1-60898-109-6 pa; 978-1-60898-108-3; 978-1-60898-109-0 pa

"When we meet him in 1934, Eddie is five, Tom ten. In the next ten years the brothers develop friendships, discover family secrets, . . . and ponder the causes of European conflict . . . as well as the virulent prejudice rife in their own farming community. Tom's enlisting in 1943 unveils the real nature of war that has inspired the boys' games. Narrated by Eddie, these seventy-six vignettes are beautifully phrased and vividly revealing of character." Horn Book

Salten, Felix

Bambi; a life in the woods. [by] Felix Salten; illustrated by Barbara Cooney. Pocket Books 1988 190p il pa $5.99

Grades: 4 5 6 **Fic**

1. Deer -- Fiction
ISBN 978-0-671-66607-1 pa; 0-671-66607-X pa

Original German edition 1923; first United States edition published 1928 by Simon & Schuster

Describes the life of a deer in the forest as he grows into a beautiful stag

Samphire, Patrick

Secrets of the dragon tomb; Patrick Samphire. Henry Holt & Co. 2016 336 p. (hardcover) $16.99

Grades: 4 5 6 7 **Fic**

1. Adventure fiction 2. Mars -- Fiction 3. Science fiction 4. Kidnapping -- Fiction 5. Family life -- Fiction 6. Eccentrics and

eccentricities -- Fiction
ISBN 9780805099065

LC 2015004517

In this juvenile novel, by Patrick Samphire, "twelve-year-old Edward Sullivan wishes his life on 19th-century British Mars were more like the adventures he reads about in his Thrilling Martian Tales magazine. . . . But before he knows it, he is tangled up in a madcap adventure. . . . It seems that Edward's father's latest invention, the water abacus, is thought to be the key to perhaps one of the last of the great dragon tombs of Mars." (School Library Journal)

"Abundant humor, intricate worldbuilding details, and precisely timed slapstick and mayhem mesh as neatly as the gears and levers of the water abacus, producing a gorgeously articulated clockwork of a novel." Pub Wkly

Samworth, Kate

Aviary Wonders Inc. Spring Catalog and Instruction Manual; renewing the world's bird supply since 2031. by Kate Samworth. Clarion Books, Houghton Mifflin Harcourt 2014 31 p.
Grades: 3 4 5 6   **Fic**
1. Birds -- Fiction 2. Automata -- Fiction 3. Mechanical toys -- Fiction 4. Environmental degradation -- Fiction
ISBN 9780547978994

LC 2013020247

This book, by Kate Samworth, is "a catalog of bird parts and instructions for making your own in a . . . possible future in which living birds have nearly disappeared. Feathers, beaks, legs and feet, bodies, tails and even flight styles can be ordered from this enterprising company, whose motto is 'Renewing the World's Bird Supply Since 2031.' . . . The author also enumerates actual bird threats: insecticides, habitat loss, the exotic pet trade and cats." (Kirkus Reviews)

"Unsettling and unforgettable, this faux-catalog purports to replace extinct bird species with build-a-bird automatons. Sub-subtitled 'Renewing the World's Bird Supply Since 2031,' . . . 'We can't replace the birds that have been lost. But we can provide you with the opportunity to create an exquisite alternative.' Samworth, making her debut, marries conventional sales language to florid multimedia illustrations of disembodied bird parts 'handcrafted and made to order by world-class artisans.' . . . A closing section on assembly, with instructions for teaching the robotic birds to fly and sing, only deepens the uncanny sense of loss. This cautionary guidebook mimes ads that fetishize wildlife." Pub Wkly.

Sanderson, Brandon

★ Alcatraz versus the evil Librarians. Scholastic Press 2007 308p $16.99; pa $6.99
Grades: 4 5 6 7   **Fic**
1. Fantasy fiction 2. Librarians -- Fiction 3. Grandfathers -- Fiction
ISBN 0-439-92550-9; 978-0-439-92550-1; 0-439-92552-5 pa; 978-0-439-92552-5 pa

LC 2006-38378

On his thirteenth birthday, foster child Alcatraz Smedry receives a bag of sand which is immediately stolen by the evil Librarians who are trying to take over the world. Soon, Alcatraz is introduced to his grandfather and his own special talent, and told that he must use it to save civilization.

"Readers whose sense of humor runs toward the subversive will be instantly captivated. . . . This nutty novel isn't for everyone, but it's also sure to win passionate fans." Publ Wkly

Other titles about Alcatraz are:
Alcatraz versus the scrivener's bones (2008)
Alcatraz versus the Knights of Crystallia (2009)
Alcatraz versus the shattered lens (2010)

The **dark** talent; Alcatraz vs. the evil librarians. Brandon Sanderson, illustrated by Hayley Lazo. Starscape, a Tom Doherty Associates Book 2016 300 p. illustrations (Alcatraz vs. the evil librarians) $16.99
Grades: 4 5 6 7   **Fic**
1. Librarians -- Fiction 2. Imaginary places -- Fiction 3. Heroes and heroines -- Fiction 4. Fantasy 5. Humorous stories 6. Heroes -- Fiction
ISBN 0765381400; 9780765381408

LC 2016288328

In this novel in the Alcatraz Versus the Evil Librarians series, by Brandon Sanderson, illustrated by Hayley Lazo, "Alcatraz Smedry has . . defeated the army of Evil Librarians and saved the kingdom of Mokia. Too bad he managed to break the Smedry Talents. . . . Even worse, his father is trying to enact a scheme that could ruin the world, and his friend, Bastille, is in a coma. To revive her, Alcatraz must infiltrate the Highbrary . . . the seat of Evil Librarian power." (Publisher's note)

"As in previous volumes, the narrative is rife with bizarre situations, thrilling seat-of-the-pants action, and metafictional musings; the ending will set readers back on their heels." Horn Book

Sands, Kevin

★ The **blackthorn** key; by Kevin Sands. Aladdin 2015 384 p. (hardcover) $17.99
Grades: 4 5 6 7 8   **Fic**
1. Friendship -- Fiction 2. Apprentices -- Fiction 3. Supernatural -- Fiction 4. London (England) -- Fiction 5. Secret societies -- Fiction 6. Great Britain -- History -- 1660-1688, Restoration -- Fiction 7. Pharmacists -- Fiction 8. London -- History -- 17th century -- Fiction
ISBN 1481446517; 9781481446518

LC 2014048032

Sequel: Mark of the Plague (2016)

This book, by Kevin Sands, presents a "tale of alchemy and dark secrets set during the late-17th-century reign of King Charles II. Fourteen-year-old orphan Christopher Rowe is lucky to be apprenticed to a kindly apothecary, Master Benedict Blackthorn. But someone--the Cult of the Archangel, it is rumored--is murdering London's apothecaries, believing that members of the Apothecary's Guild are concealing a dangerous secret." (Publishers Weekly)

"This stunning and smart mystery is made even better by well-researched historical detail, intriguing characters, and genuinely funny moments." Kirkus

Saunders, Kate

★ Beswitched. Delacorte Press 2011 244p $16.99
Grades: 4 5 6 7   **Fic**
1. School stories 2. Magic -- Fiction 3. Time travel -- Fiction 4. Great Britain -- Fiction
ISBN 978-0-385-74075-3

LC 2011000747

First published 2010 in the United Kingdom

On her way, reluctantly, to a boarding school in present-day England, Flora suddenly finds herself in 1935, the new girl at St. Winifred's having been summoned via a magic spell by her new dormitory mates.

"This absorbing novel . . . features a dimensional, delightful protagonist, whose personality and growth ring true. . . . Along with the entertaining magical elements, the universal themes of self-discovery and looking beyond appearances combine into a wholly engaging and enjoyable read." Booklist

The **curse** of the chocolate phoenix; a companion to The Whizz Pop Chocolate Shop. Kate Saunders. Delacorte Press 2015 272 p. (hc) $16.99

Grades: 5 6 7 8 **Fic**

1. Witches -- Fiction 2. Adventure and adventurers -- Fiction 3. Brothers and sisters -- Fiction 4. Cats -- Fiction 5. Magic -- Fiction 6. Twins -- Fiction 7. England -- Fiction
ISBN 9780375991837; 9780385744720

LC 2014022137

In this juvenile novel, by Kate Saunders, sequel to "The Whizz Pop Chocolate Shop," "Oz and Lily have a top-secret mission. Alba the witch has gotten her hands on a magical chocolate phoenix and is plotting to use it for some serious evil. With the help of an army of rats and an unreliable talking cat, the children must pursue her not only across London but through time itself." (Publisher's note)

"Saunders weaves the supernatural with the ordinary with ease." Booklist

The **Whizz** Pop Chocolate Shop; Kate Saunders. 1st ed. Delacorte Press 2013 293 p. (hardcover) $16.99

Grades: 5 6 7 8 **Fic**

1. Chocolate -- Fiction 2. Fantasy fiction 3. Brothers and sisters -- Fiction 4. Cats -- Fiction 5. Magic -- Fiction 6. Twins -- Fiction 7. England -- Fiction 8. Immortality -- Fiction 9. London (England) -- Fiction
ISBN 0385743017; 9780385743013

LC 2011053081

In this children's story, by Kate Saunders, "the family of eleven-year-old twins Oz and Lily have inherited [a house], together with the mysterious shop downstairs. Long ago, the shop's famous chocolate-makers . . . were clever sorcerers. Now evil villains are hunting for the secret of their greatest recipe. . . . This magic chocolate [has] the ability to destroy the world. . . . It's up to them to stop the villains and keep the magical chocolate recipe out of harm's way." (Publisher's note)

Sawyer, Ruth

★ **Roller** skates; written by Ruth Sawyer and illustrated by Valenti Angelo. Viking 1995 186p il hardcover o.p. pa $5.99

Grades: 4 5 6 **Fic**

1. New York (N.Y.) -- Fiction
ISBN 0-670-60310-4; 0-14-030358-8 pa

LC 85-43418

A reissue of the title first published 1936
Awarded the Newbery Medal, 1937

"For one never-to-be forgotten year Lucinda Wyman (ten years old) was free to explore New York on roller skates. She made friends with Patrick Gilligan and his hansom cab, with Policeman M'Gonegal, with the fruit vendor, Vittore Coppicco and his son Tony, and with many others. All Lucinda's adventures are true and happened to the author herself as is borne out by the occasional pages of Lucinda's diary which are a part of the story." Horn Book

Sazaklis, John

Royal rodent rescue; illustrated by Art Baltazar; Superman created by Jerry Siegel and Joe Shuster. Picture Window Books 2011 48p il (DC super-pets!) lib bdg $22.65; pa $4.95

Grades: 1 2 3 **Fic**

1. Cats -- Fiction 2. Superheroes -- Fiction
ISBN 978-1-4048-6307-1 lib bdg; 1-4048-6307-9 lib bdg; 978-1-4048-6622-5 pa; 1-4048-6622-1 pa

LC 2010036376

"Streaky the Super-Cat saves Queen Markela of Kardamyla's pet hamster, Prince Zouli, from the clutches of the evil cat, Rozz. . . . [The book is] full of action, including colorful graphics within the text, reminiscent of the old live-action Batman TV show. [The] title has a colorful spread in the heat of the action. [A] solid [introduction] to comic-book-style writing." SLJ

Scaletta, Kurtis

Mamba Point. Alfred A. Knopf 2010 268p il $16.99; lib bdg $19.99

Grades: 5 6 7 8 **Fic**

1. Fear -- Fiction 2. Snakes -- Fiction 3. Liberia -- Fiction
ISBN 978-0-375-86180-2; 0-375-86180-7; 978-0-375-96180-9 lib bdg; 0-375-96180-1 lib bdg

LC 2009-22084

After moving with his family to Liberia, twelve-year-old Linus discovers that he has a mystical connection with the black mamba, one of the deadliest snakes in Africa, which he is told will give him some of the snake's characteristics. Includes facts about the author's experiences as a thirteen-year-old American living in Liberia in 1982

Scaletta "has created an appealing, well-written protagonist whose everyday and extraordinary experiences . . . change his life in unexpected, positive ways. . . . The engaging first-person narrative and array of diversely drawn characters further enliven the novel." Booklist

The **winter** of the robots; Kurtis Scaletta. Alfred A. Knopf 2013 272 p. (hard cover) $16.99

Grades: 5 6 7 8 **Fic**

1. Science fiction 2. Robots -- Fiction 3. Landfills -- Fiction 4. Science projects -- Fiction
ISBN 0307931862; 9780307931863; 9780375971105

LC 2012036376

In this book, by Kurtis Scaletta, "Jim is tired of being the sidekick to his scientific genius, robot-obsessed, best friend Oliver. So this winter, when it comes time to choose partners for the science fair, Jim dumps Oliver and teams up with a girl instead. Rocky has spotted wild otters down by the river, and her idea is to study them. But . . . they discover . . . a hidden junkyard on abandoned Half Street. And as desolate as it may seem, there's something living in the junkyard." (Publisher's note)

"The probability of his temperamental dad finding out that Jim has borrowed several high-tech security cameras for a science fair project turns out to be the least of his worries in this offbeat thriller. Set up in a seedy North Minneapolis junkyard near the river in hopes of observing otters, the cameras immediately disappear after a flash of weird footage. . . . Told in a spare, matter-of-fact narrative, this packs the space between the lines with humor, drama, romantic tension, and deftly delivered insight into the characters of a diverse, well-developed cast. . . . Scaletta amps up the voltage with suspense and excitement, but he also seamlessly integrates family issues and peer dynamics and cybernetic feats that seem only slightly futuristic." Booklist

Scanlon, Liz Garton

The **great** good summer; Liz Garton Scanlon. Beach Lane Books 2015 224 p. (hardcover) $16.99

Grades: 4 5 6 7 **Fic**

1. Summer -- Fiction 2. Friendship -- Fiction 3. Runaway children -- Fiction 4. Runaways -- Fiction 5. Bus travel -- Fiction 6. Friendship -- Fiction 7. Christian life -- Fiction 8. Mothers and daughters -- Fiction
ISBN 1481411470; 9781481411479; 9781481411486

LC 2014014988

In this children's story, by Liz Garton Scanlon, "Ivy and Paul are both having a crummy summer. . . . Ivy's mama hasn't been herself since the spring, when wildfires destroyed everything. . . . Meanwhile, Paul is sad because NASA's space shuttle program is being shut down and now he will never be able to become an astronaut. . . . The two become an unlikely pair when they hatch a plan to find Mama and say goodbye to the space shuttle." (School Library Journal)

"Equal parts peculiar and poignant, Ivy's story will have readers giggling as they root for her to find everything she's looking for." Kirkus

Scattergood, Augusta

★ **Glory** be; by Augusta Scattergood. 1st ed. Scholastic Press 2012 202 p. (hardcover) $16.99; (ebook) $16.99

Grades: 4 5 6   **Fic**

1. Racism -- History 2. Blacks -- Civil rights 3. African Americans -- Southern States 4. Sisters -- Fiction 5. Segregation -- Fiction 6. Race relations -- Fiction 7. City and town life -- Mississippi -- Fiction 8. Mississippi -- History -- 20th century -- Fiction

ISBN 9780545331807; 9780545331814; 9780545452328

LC 2011028308

Author Augusta Scattergood tells a story of "a girl trying to make sense of the tumultuous era of the Civil Rights Movement. It's the summer of 1964 in a small Mississippi town, and [it's Glory's 12th birthday] . . . Her sister Jesslyn is entering high school and no longer has any time, and things have suddenly gotten awkward with Glory's best friend, Frankie. Plus, a new girl from the North has arrived, and everyone is riled up about what to do about the town's segregated pool. Whether she wants to or not, Glory has to make some big decisions." (Publisher's note)

Schlitz, Laura Amy

★ **The night** fairy; illustrated by Angela Barrett. Candlewick Press 2010 117p il lib bdg $16.99; pa $6.99

Grades: 4 5 6   **Fic**

1. Adventure fiction 2. Magic -- Fiction 3. Fairies -- Fiction 4. Friendship -- Fiction

ISBN 978-0-7636-3674-6 lib bdg; 0-7636-3674-6 lib bdg; 978-07636-5295-1 pa; 0-7636-5295-4 pa

LC 2008-27659

When Flory the night fairy's wings are accidentally broken and she cannot fly, she has to learn to do everything differently.

"Schlitz writes with strength of vision and delicate precision of word choice. . . . Beautifully composed, the artwork combines subtle use of color with a keen observation of nature. . . . This finely crafted and unusually dynamic fairy story is a natural for reading aloud." Booklist

★ **Splendors** and glooms; Laura Amy Schlitz. Candlewick 2012 384 p. (reinforced trade ed.) $17.99

Grades: 4 5 6 7   **Fic**

1. Mystery fiction 2. Orphans -- Fiction 3. Kidnapping -- Fiction 4. Puppets and puppet plays -- Fiction 5. Puppets -- Fiction 6. Witches -- Fiction 7. Blessing and cursing -- Fiction 8. London (England) -- History -- 19th century -- Fiction 9. Great Britain -- History -- Victoria, 1837-1901 -- Fiction

ISBN 0763653802; 9780763653804

LC 2011048366

John Newbery Honor Book (2013)

In this book by Laura Amy Schlitz "Clara Wintermute . . . invites . . . the master puppeteer, Gaspare Grisini, . . . to entertain at her birthday party. . . . When Clara vanishes that night, suspicion of kidnapping falls upon the puppeteer and, by association, Lizzie Rose and Parsefall. As they seek to puzzle out Clara's whereabouts, Lizzie and Parse uncover Grisini's criminal past." (Publisher's note)

Schmatz, Pat

★ **Bluefish**. Candlewick Press 2011 226p $15.99

Grades: 7 8 9 10   **Fic**

1. School stories 2. Literacy -- Fiction 3. Teachers -- Fiction

ISBN 978-0-7636-5334-7; 0-7636-5334-9

LC 2010044815

"Travis is missing his old home in the country, and he's missing his old hound, Rosco. Now there's just the cramped place he shares with his well-meaning but alcoholic grandpa, a new school, and the dreaded routine of passing when he's called on to read out loud. But that's be-

fore Travis meets Mr. McQueen, who doesn't take "pass" for an answer--a rare teacher whose savvy persistence has Travis slowly unlocking a book on the natural world. And it's before Travis is noticed by Velveeta, a girl whose wry banter and colorful scarves belie some hard secrets of her own." (Publisher's Note)

"A cast of richly developed characters peoples this work of contemporary fiction, told in the third person from Travis' point of view, with first-person vignettes from Velveeta's perspective peppered throughout. . . . A story rife with unusual honesty and hope." Kirkus

Schmidt, Gary D.

★ **Okay** for now. Clarion Books 2011 360p il $16.99

Grades: 4 5 6 7   **Fic**

1. Moving -- Fiction 2. New York (State) -- Fiction 3. City and town life -- Fiction

ISBN 978-0-547-15260-8; 0-547-15260-4

LC 2010942981

National Book Award Finalist: Young People's Literature (2011)

"It's 1968. The Vietnam War and Apollo 11 are in the background, and . . . Doug Swieteck starts a new life in tiny Marysville, N.Y. . . . He may have moved away, but his cruel father and abusive brothers are still with him. . . . This is Schmidt's best novel yet—darker than The Wednesday Wars and written with more restraint, but with the same expert attention to voice, character and big ideas." Kirkus

★ **The Wednesday** wars. Clarion Books 2007 264p pa $6.99; $16

Grades: 5 6 7 8   **Fic**

1. Poets 2. Authors 3. Dramatists 4. School stories

ISBN 054723760X; 0618724834; 9780547237602; 9780618724833

LC 2006-23660

A Newbery Medal honor book, 2008

During the 1967 school year, on Wednesday afternoons when all his classmates go to either Catechism or Hebrew school, seventh-grader Holling Hoodhound stays in Mrs. Baker's classroom where they read the plays of William Shakespeare and Holling learns something of value about the world he lives in. "Grades five to seven." (Bull Cen Child Books)

"The serious issues are leavened with ample humor, and the supporting cast . . . is fully dimensional. Best of all is the hero." Publ Wkly

Schneider, Josh

Tales for very picky eaters. Clarion Books 2011 47p il $14.99

Grades: K 1 2 3   **Fic**

1. Food -- Fiction 2. Father-son relationship -- Fiction

ISBN 978-0-547-14956-1; 0-547-14956-5

LC 2010-24767

"The comical illustrations are done in watercolor, ink, and colored pencil and are surrounded by plenty of white space. A perfect segue into chapter books, this easy reader is sure to be a crowd pleaser." SLJ

Schneider, Robyn

Knightley Academy; by Violet Haberdasher. Aladdin 2010 469p $15.99

Grades: 5 6 7 8   **Fic**

1. School stories 2. Orphans -- Fiction 3. Knights and knighthood -- Fiction

ISBN 978-1-4169-9143-4; 1-4169-9143-3

LC 2009-24443

In an alternate Victorian England, fourteen-year-old orphan Henry Grim, a maltreated servant at an exclusive school for the "sons of Gentry and Quality," begins a new life when he unexpectedly becomes the first commoner to be accepted at Knightley Academy, a prestigious boarding school for knights.

"Robyn Schneider . . . writing as the pseudonymous Haberdasher, delivers a cute novel that balances its simple plot with a solid lead character, witty dialogue, and a jaunty narrative voice. . . . The nebulous historical setting and focus on military training and chivalry are a welcome change of pace from fictional academies that revolve around magic." Publ Wkly

Followed by: The secret prince (2011)

The **secret** prince; [by] Violet Haberdasher. Aladdin 2011 503p $16.99

Grades: 5 6 7 8 **Fic**

1. School stories 2. Orphans -- Fiction 3. Secret societies -- Fiction 4. Knights and knighthood -- Fiction
ISBN 978-1-4169-9145-8; 1-4169-9145-X

LC 2010038855

Sequel to: Knightley Academy (2010)

Fourteen-year-old orphan Henry Grim's schooling at the prestigious Knightley Academy continues, as he and some friends discover an old classroom filled with forgotten weapons which lead them into a dangerous adventure.

"Though some of the past events can be gleaned from this book, it's more enjoyable for those who have read Knightley Academy. . . . The fast-moving plotline in this installment is wrapped up nicely, but enough is left hanging and the characters are interesting enough to make readers eagerly anticipate the next in the series." SLJ

Schoenberg, Jane

The **one** and only Stuey Lewis; stories from the second grade. pictures by Cambria Evans. Farrar Straus Giroux 2011 115p il $16.99

Grades: 1 2 3 **Fic**

1. School stories 2. Teachers -- Fiction 3. Family life -- Fiction
ISBN 978-0-374-37292-7; 0-374-37292-6

LC 2010-22312

Stuey Lewis makes his way through second grade facing reading problems, pulling off a great Halloween caper, joining a soccer team, and more with the help of family, friends, and a special teacher.

This is a "hilarious early chapter book. . . . Evans' trim-lined, stylized cartoonish illustrations play up the comedy in the text while offering occasional independent chuckles." Bull Cent Child Books

Stuey Lewis against all odds; stories from the third grade. Jane Schoenberg; pictures by Cambria Evans. Farrar Straus Giroux 2012 136 p.

Grades: 2 3 **Fic**

1. Boys -- Fiction 2. Field trips -- Fiction 3. School stories -- Fiction 4. Schools -- Fiction 5. Family life -- Fiction
ISBN 0374399018; 9780374399016

LC 2011008224

This book, by Jane Schoenberg, part of the Stuey Lewis series, "takes up just where the first left off, with Stuey and his friends comforted that their second-grade teacher, Ginger Curtis, is moving on to third grade with them. . . . With the school year as the frame, these four loosely joined stories show our hero facing new challenges while growing into a more independent, less worried young man." (Kirkus Reviews)

Schreiber, Joe

Game over, Pete Watson; by Joe Schreiber. Houghton Mifflin Harcourt 2014 224 p. (hardback) $16.99

Grades: 4 5 6 7 **Fic**

1. Humorous fiction 2. Spies -- Fiction 3. Video games -- Fiction

4. Father-son relationship -- Fiction 5. Humorous stories
ISBN 0544157567; 9780544157569

LC 2013024335

In this book, by Joe Schreiber, "after he sells a vintage console of his dad's to the neighborhood exterminator, [Pete's] dad gets kidnapped before his eyes. Pete discovers that his father is a CIA agent and is now trapped in the gaming system, which also doubles as a database for government secrets. Aided by his geeky ex-best friend Wesley and Wesley's attractive older sister, Pete must stop the supervillain . . . by going into the game himself." (Bulletin of the Center for Children's Books)

"With rapid-fire plot twists, slapstick comedy, and interactive illustrations complete with an 'eight-bit' Pete animated through the page turns, this light read champions video-game history and skills." Horn Book

Schroder, Monika

Saraswati's way. Farrar Straus Giroux 2010 233p $15.99

Grades: 5 6 7 8 **Fic**

1. India -- Fiction 2. Education -- Fiction 3. Mathematics -- Fiction
ISBN 978-0-374-36411-3; 0-374-36411-7

LC 2009-37286

Leaving his village in rural India to find a better education, mathematically gifted, twelve-year-old Akash ends up at the New Delhi train station, where he relies on Saraswati, the Hindu goddess of knowledge, to guide him as he negotiates life on the street, resists the temptations of easy money, and learns whom he can trust.

"With skillfully integrated cultural details . . . and a fully realized child's story, Schröder presents a view, sobering and inspiring, of remarkably resilient young people surviving poverty without losing themselves." Booklist

Schroeder, Lisa

It's Raining Cupcakes. Aladdin 2010 193p $15.99

Grades: 4 5 6 7 **Fic**

1. Baking -- Fiction 2. Oregon -- Fiction 3. Contests -- Fiction 4. Family life -- Fiction 5. Mother-daughter relationship -- Fiction
ISBN 978-1-4169-9084-0; 1-4169-9084-4

LC 2009-14812

Twelve-year-old Isabel dreams of seeing the world but has never left Oregon, and so when her best friend, Sophie, tells her of a baking contest whose winners travel to New York City, she eagerly enters despite concerns about her mother, who is opening a cupcake bakery. Includes recipes.

Followed by: Sprinkles and secrets (2011)

My secret guide to Paris; by Lisa Schroeder. First edition Scholastic Press 2015 216 p. $16.99

Grades: 4 5 6 **Fic**

1. Bereavement -- Fiction 2. Family life -- Fiction 3. Grandmothers -- Fiction 4. Paris (France) -- Fiction 5. Grandparent-grandchild relationship -- Fiction 6. Grief -- Fiction 7. France -- Fiction 8. Families -- Fiction
ISBN 9780545708081; 0545708087

LC 2014017073

In this book, by Lisa Schroeder, "Nora loves everything about Paris. . . Of course, she's never actually been there -- she's only visited through her Grandma Sylvia's stories. And just when they've finally planned a trip together, Grandma Sylvia is suddenly gone. . . . She misses her grandmother terribly, but she still wants to see the city they both loved. So when Nora finds letters and a Paris treasure map among her Grandma Sylvia's things, she dares to dream again." (Publisher's note)

"The bittersweet circumstances of the Paris trip are offset by strong elements of wish fulfillment, including gowns and a fancy fashion show.

This is a sweet, reassuring contemporary read about handling grief and reconnecting with family." Booklist

Another title in this series is:

Sealed with a secret (2016)

Schulman, Janet

★ The **nutcracker**; [by] E.T.A. Hoffmann; adapted by Janet Schulman; illustrated by Renée Graef; audio CD narrated by Claire Bloom with music by Peter Ilyich Tchaikovsky. HarperCollins Pubs. 1999 34p il $19.95

Grades: 4 5 6 7   Fic

1. Fairy tales 2. Christmas -- Fiction

ISBN 0-06-027814-5

LC 97-22346

This adaptation of the Nutcracker with illustrations by Kay Chorao was published 1979 by Dutton

One Christmas after hearing how the toy nutcracker made by her godfather got his ugly face, a little girl helps break the spell and watches him change into a handsome prince

"Graef's illustrations are floridly old-fashioned, with careful attention to period detail." Booklist

Schulz, Heidi

Hook's revenge; by Heidi Schulz; illustrations by John Hendrix. Disney-Hyperion Books 2014 304 p. $16.99

Grades: 4 5 6 7   Fic

1. Fictional characters 2. Pirates -- Fiction 3. Revenge -- Fiction 4. Fathers and daughters -- Fiction

ISBN 1423198670; 9781423198673

LC 2013045281

In this book, by Heidi Schulz, illustrated by John Hendrix, "[t]welve-year-old Jocelyn dreams of becoming every bit as daring as her infamous father, Captain James Hook. Her grandfather, on the other hand, intends to see her starched and pressed into a fine society lady. When she's sent to Miss Eliza Crumb-Biddlecomb's Finishing School for Young Ladies, Jocelyn's hopes of following in her father's fearsome footsteps are lost in a heap of dance lessons, white gloves, and way too much pink." (Publisher's note)

"A delightfully curmudgeonly narrator sets the tone for this fast-paced and witty reimagining of Barrie's Neverland. This time readers see the pirates, mermaids, cannibals, fairies, and Lost Boys through the eyes of thirteen-year-old Jocelyn, Captain Hook's unapologetically energetic daughter, who gleefully escapes finishing school and the horrors of corsets to join Smee in hunting down the infamous crocodile that finished off her father." Horn Book

The **pirate** code; by Heidi Schulz; with illustrations by John Hendrix. Disney-Hyperion 2015 339 p. illustrations (Other titles in this series: Hook's revenge (2014)) (hardback) $16.99

Grades: 5 6 7 8   Fic

1. Pirates -- Fiction 2. Kidnapping -- Fiction 3, 4. Buried treasure -- Fiction 5. Characters in literature -- Fiction

ISBN 1484717171; 9781484717172

LC 2014049766

In this children's book by Heidi Schulz, illustrated by John Hendrix, "fresh off a fearsome encounter with the Neverland crocodile, Jocelyn Hook decides the most practical plan is to hunt down her father's famous fortune. The map proves to be a bit harder to crack . . . and she's convinced that . . . Peter Pan might be the only one with the answers. He doesn't really feel like helping her, so Jocelyn . . . kidnaps his mother." (Publisher's note)

"An imaginative adventure filled with humor and heart." Kirkus

Schur, Maxine

Gullible Gus; by Maxine Rose Schur; illustrated by Andrew Glass Clarion Books 2009 45p il $16

Grades: 2 3 4 5   Fic

1. Tall tales 2. Texas 3. Cowhands -- Fiction

ISBN 978-0-618-92710-4; 0-618-92710-7

LC 2008-10477

Tired of the teasing he gets for being the most gullible man in Texas, Cowboy Gus goes to Fibrock to find the biggest liar there in hopes of hearing a tall tale that is impossible for anyone—even him—to believe.

"The stories are filled with exaggeration and alliteration. A Western twang is used to create mood. Readers will laugh out loud and share passages with friends. . . . Glass's bright oil crayon cartoons fit the exaggerated storytelling style to a tee." SLJ

Schwabach, Karen

The **storm** before Atlanta. Random House 2010 307p $16.99; lib bdg $19.99

Grades: 5 6 7 8   Fic

1. Freedom -- Fiction 2. Slavery -- Fiction 3. Soldiers -- Fiction 4. Runaway children -- Fiction 5. United States -- History -- 1861-1865, Civil War -- Fiction

ISBN 978-0-375-85866-6; 0-375-85866-0; 978-0-375-95866-3 lib bdg; 0-375-95866-5 lib bdg

LC 2010014514

In 1863 northwestern Georgia, an unlikely alliance forms between ten-year-old New York drummer boy Jeremy, fourteen-year-old Confederate Charlie, and runaway slave Dulcie as they learn truths about the Civil War, slavery, and freedom.

"Richly detailed and well paced, the story provides both well-developed characters and plenty of suspense and gore. For those who like to know the facts behind historical fiction, the author provides historical notes and selected sources. An appealing Civil War title for readers with strong stomachs." Kirkus

Schwartz, Ellen

★ **Stealing** home. Tundra Books 2006 217p pa $8.95

Grades: 5 6 7 8   Fic

1. Jews -- Fiction 2. Orphans -- Fiction 3. Family life -- Fiction 4. Racially mixed people -- Fiction

ISBN 978-0-88776-765-4 pa; 0-88776-765-6 pa

"Joey, an orphaned, mixed-race 10-year-old isn't the only one who has to make adjustments after he's taken in by Jewish relatives he never knew he had. Wondering why his mother never told him about her side of the family, Joey moves to Brooklyn—to find a warm welcome from Aunt Frieda, an instant ally in baseball-loving cousin Bobbie, and a decidedly cold shoulder from his grandfather. . . . Keenly felt internal conflicts, lightened by some sparky banter, put this more than a cut above the average." Booklist

Scieszka, Jon, 1954-

Frank Einstein & the antimatter motor; by Jon Scieszka; illustrated by Brian Biggs. Amulet Books 2014 192 p. (Frank Einstein) (hardback) $13.95

Grades: 3 4 5 6   Fic

1. Science fiction 2. Robots -- Fiction 3. Inventors -- Fiction 4. Humorous stories

ISBN 1419712187; 9781419712180

LC 2014011918

"Frank Einstein loves figuring out how the world works by creating household contraptions that are part science, part imagination, and definitely unusual. After an uneventful experiment in his garage-lab, a lightning storm and flash of electricity bring Frank's inventions--the robots Klink and Klank--to life!" (Publisher's note)

"After a freak electrical storm, boy genius Frank Einstein wakes up to find two robots--Klink (a "self-assembled artificial-intelligence entity") and Klank (a "mostly self-assembled artificial almost [intelligent]" being)--in his lab. He hopes they'll help him win a science prize and save his grandfather's repair-shop business. The book features kid-friendly humor in spades, and an impressive amount of scientific know-how." Horn Book

Frank Einstein and the antimatter motor

Other titles include:

Frank Einstein and the Electro Finger

Frank Einstein and the BrainTurbo; Jon Scieszka; illustrated by Brian Biggs. Amulet Books 2015 192 p. illustrations (Frank Einstein) (hardback) $13.95

Grades: 3 4 5 6 **Fic**

1. Science fiction 2. Humorous fiction 3. Human body -- Fiction 4. Robots -- Fiction 5. Inventors -- Fiction

ISBN 9781419716430

LC 2015004219

In this book, by Jon Scieszka, illustrated by Brian Biggs, "Science fiction meets science fact! Frank Einstein (kid-genius scientist and inventor) and his best friend Watson, along with Klink (a self-assembled artificial intelligence entity), create the BrainTurbo to power-boost the human body and help their baseball-pitching pal Jane Goodall make the team. But when Klank (a mostly self-assembled and artificial almost intelligence entity) goes missing, they must first rescue their robot pal." (Publisher's note)

"Scieszka's third joke-filled Frank Einstein adventure jam-packed with sneaky science lessons is perfect for young scientists who may prefer fact to fiction." Kirkus

Frank Einstein and the Electro-Finger; Jon Scieszka; illustrated by Brian Biggs. Amulet Books 2015 176 p. illustrations (Frank Einstein) (hardcover) $13.95

Grades: 3 4 5 6 **Fic**

1. Inventors -- Fiction 2. Scientists -- Fiction 3. Science fiction 4. Humorous stories 5. Robots -- Fiction 6. Power resources -- Fiction

ISBN 141971483X; 9781419714832

LC 2014029591

In this novel by Jon Scieszka, illustrated by Brian Biggs, "Frank Einstein (kid-genius scientist and inventor) and his best friend, Watson, along with [robots] Klink . . . and Klank . . . find themselves in competition with T. Edison, their classmate and archrival--this time in the quest to unlock the power behind the science of energy. Frank is working on a revamped version of one of Nikola Tesla's inventions, the 'Electro-Finger,' a device that can tap into energy anywhere." (Publisher's note)

"Kid genius Frank Einstein's back for a second shocking (and silly) science adventure. . . . There's so much actual information here that the story could pass as a textbook, but science and Scieszka fans won't likely mind." Kirkus

★ **Knights** of the kitchen table; illustrated by Lane Smith. Viking 1991 55p il (Time Warp Trio) $15.99; pa $4.99

Grades: 3 4 5 **Fic**

1. Fantasy fiction 2. Middle Ages -- Fiction 3. Time travel -- Fiction 4. Knights and knighthood -- Fiction

ISBN 0-670-83622-2; 0-14-240043-2 pa

LC 90-51009

"Transported to the Middle Ages, three friends save themselves from a dragon and a giant through quick thinking. The tongue-in-cheek narrative makes for laugh-out-loud enjoyment, and the easy-to-read sentences and zany dialogue perfectly suit the breathless pace." SLJ

Other titles about The Time Warp Trio are:

2095 (1995)

Da wild, da crazy, da Vinci (2004)

The good, the bad, and the goofy (1992)

Hey kid, want to buy a bridge? (2002)

It's all Greek to me (1999)

Marco? Polo! (2006)

Me oh Maya! (2003)

The not-so-jolly Roger (1991)

Oh say I can't see (2005)

Sam Samurai (2001)

See you later, gladiator (2000)

Summer reading is killing me! (1998)

Tut, tut (1996)

Viking it & liking it (2002)

Your mother was a Neanderthal (1993)

Seen Art? [by] Jon Scieszka and Lane Smith. Viking 2005 un il $16.99

Grades: 4 5 6 7 **Fic**

1. Art appreciation -- Fiction 2. Museum of Modern Art (New York, N.Y.) -- Fiction

ISBN 0-670-05986-2

While looking for his friend Art, a boy wanders through the Museum of Modern Art and is amazed by what he discovers there.

"The unusually long and narrow shape of the book and the stylized characters echo the modern-art theme while the muted background tones are an effective foil for the well-reproduced if sometimes diminutive artwork. . . . For anyone planning a trip to MoMA with a youngster, this is a provocative read." SLJ

★ **Spaceheadz**; [by] Jon Scieszka with Francesco Sedita; illustrated by Shane Prigmore. Simon & Schuster Books for Young Readers 2010 163p il (SPHDZ) $14.99

Grades: 3 4 5 **Fic**

1. School stories 2. Spies -- Fiction 3. Moving -- Fiction 4. Family life -- Fiction 5. Extraterrestrial beings -- Fiction 6. Brooklyn (New York, N.Y.) -- Fiction

ISBN 978-1-4169-7951-7; 1-4169-7951-4

LC 2010001983

On his first day at Brooklyn's P.S. 858, fifth-grader Michael K. is teamed with two very strange students, and while he gradually comes to believe they are aliens who need his help, he has trouble convincing anyone else of the truth

This is "fun enough to become the next big word-of-mouth, multi-platform attention suck." Booklist

Spaceheadz, book 2; illustrated by Shane Prigmore; sugar-free goodness by Casey Scieszka; high-fiber extras by Steven Weinberg. Simon & Schuster 2010 230p il (SPHDZ) $14.99

Grades: 3 4 5 **Fic**

1. School stories 2. Extraterrestrial beings -- Fiction

ISBN 978-1-4169-7953-1; 1-4169-7953-0

Sequel to: Spaceheadz (2010)

This "continues the adventures of fifth-grader Michael K. and the influx of aliens . . . who pose as students. The joke-filled, intentionally disjointed, post-modern narration eventually involves the Spaceheadz in a kindergarten play. . . . Lots of humor leads this multiplatform effort with links to websites that are sure to expand the series' fan base." Booklist

Spaceheadz, book 3; illustrated by Shane Prigmore. Simon & Schuster 2011 213p il (SPHDZ) $15.99

Grades: 3 4 5 **Fic**

1. School stories 2. Extraterrestrial beings -- Fiction 3. Brooklyn

(New York, N.Y.) -- Fiction

ISBN 978-1-4169-7955-5; 1-4169-7955-7

"An imperiled world once more relies on rescue from Brooklyn fifth-graders Michael K. and his friends, along with aliens who are disguised as fifth-graders. . . . Meanwhile, Agent Umber of the AAA (Anti Alien Agency) is on a nonstop campaign to thwart the Spaceheadz. Finally, a tough-talking military-type Santa recruits Michael K. into a search for a stolen brain wave. . . . With plenty of twists, lots of well-timed comic noises . . . this is sure to delight fans, while recruiting new ones." Booklist

Scotto, Michael

Postcards from Pismo; Michael Scotto; [edited by] Ashley Mortimer. Midlandia Press 2012 180 p. (paperback) $10.99

Grades: 4 5 6   **Fic**

1. Afghan War, 2001- -- Fiction 2. Filipino Americans -- Fiction 3. Military personnel -- United States -- Correspondence -- Fiction

ISBN 0983724369; 9780983724360

LC 2011943050

In this book, a "class assignment blossoms into friendship as a fourth-grade (later fifth-) Californian showers a young soldier stationed in Afghanistan with letters, e-mail messages and postcards. [Michael] Scotto supplies only chatty Felix's side of the continuing correspondence. . . . Felix queries his pen pal about what soldiers do while detailing his own interests, teachers, town, hard-working Filipino American parents (and their reactions when his restless big brother enlists)." (Kirkus)

Scrimger, Richard

Viminy Crowe's comic book; Marthe Jocelyn, Richard Scrimger. Tundra Books of Northern New York 2014 317 p. illustrations (hardcover) $17.99

Grades: 4 5 6 7   **Fic**

1. Adventure fiction 2. Comic books, strips, etc. 3. Adventure stories 4. Steampunk fiction 5. Caricatures and cartoons -- Fiction. 6. Congresses and conventions -- Fiction

ISBN 1770494790; 9781770494794; 9781770494800

LC 2013943886

"Is there a personality conflict? Oh, yes. Addy wants to go home; Wylder wants to stay and explore the world of Viminy Crowe's comic book. Do things go wrong? You bet they do, from the very start, when Addy loses her pet rat, Catnip, and almost gets shot by a Red Rider. All the while the actual comic book story is going on around them." (Publisher's note)

"A bathroom portal at ComicFest launches two kids, Wylder Wallace and Addy Crowe, into the pages of a comic book. Suspense builds as the kids' presence affects the story, their adventures shown (in interspersed comic panels) in Davila's clear, humorous illustrations. It's a clever concept that's well executed by Jocelyn and Scrimger." Horn Book

Seabrooke, Brenda

Wolf pie; illustrated by Liz Callen. Clarion Books 2010 46p il $16

Grades: 1 2 3   **Fic**

1. Pigs -- Fiction 2. Wolves -- Fiction 3. Friendship -- Fiction

ISBN 978-0-547-04403-3; 0-547-04403-8

LC 2009-15820

When Wilfong the wolf fails to blow down the house of the Pygg brothers, he stays outside their door all winter learning their games and listening to their jokes and stories, but although he claims to be reformed, the pigs are reluctant to offer friendship.

"Callen's humorous, vibrant multimedia art deftly matches the tone of Seabrooke's amusing tale, resulting in a winning collaboration for independent readers ready to move on to meatier texts." Kirkus

Sebestyen, Ouida

★ **Words** by heart. Little, Brown 1979 162p pa $5.50

Grades: 5 6 7 8   **Fic**

1. Family life -- Fiction 2. Race relations -- Fiction 3. African Americans -- Fiction

ISBN 0-440-22688-0

LC 78-27847

"It is 1910, and Lena's family is the only black family in her small Southwestern town. When Lena wins a scripture reciting contest that a white boy is supposed to win, her family is threatened. Lena's father tries to make her understand that by hating the people who did this the problems that cause their behavior are not solved. Only more hatred and violence cause Lena and the village to understand the words of her father." ALAN

Followed by: On fire (1985)

Seegert, Scott

How to grow up and rule the world; illustrated by John Martin. Egmont USA 2010 191p il (Vordak the Incomprehensible) $13.99

Grades: 3 4 5 6   **Fic**

1. Science fiction 2. Superheroes -- Fiction

ISBN 978-1-60684-013-9; 1-60684-013-4

"Evil mastermind Vordak the Incomprehensible shares his 'evilosity' with aspiring supervillains in this hilarious spoof on superheroes . . . Comical black-and-white cartoons on nearly every page extend the humor. . . . Vordak's distinctive voice, peppered with alliteration typical of the genre, remains fresh and funny throughout." SLJ

Seidler, Tor

★ **Gully's** travels; pictures by Brock Cole. Michael di Capua Books 2008 173p il $16.95

Grades: 4 5 6   **Fic**

1. Dogs -- Fiction 2. New York (N.Y.) -- Fiction 3. Voyages and travels -- Fiction

ISBN 978-0-545-02506-5; 0-545-02506-0

Gulliver leads a life of luxury with his master. But when his master falls in love with a woman who is allergic to dogs, Gulliver is sent to a new home. He finds himself with a family of raucous human beings and three mutts. But just as Gulliver begins to make a grudging peace with his new reality, he gets swept up in a harrowing new adventure.

"Gulliver is a character readers won't forget. . . . Seidler vividly evokes each setting. . . . Cole's expressive, scribbled sketches of interesting characters appear on almost every page." Booklist

Selden, George

★ **The cricket** in Times Square; illustrated by Garth Williams. Farrar, Straus & Giroux 1960 151p il $16; pa $6.99

Grades: 3 4 5 6   **Fic**

1. Cats -- Fiction 2. Mice -- Fiction 3. Crickets -- Fiction 4. New York (N.Y.) -- Fiction

ISBN 0-374-31650-3; 0-312-38003-8 pa

A Newbery Medal honor book, 1961

"A touch of magic comes to Times Square subway station with Chester, a cricket from rural Connecticut. He is introduced to the distinctive character of city life by three friends: Mario Bellini, whose parents operate a newsstand; Tucker, a glib Broadway mouse; and Harry, a sagacious cat. Chester saves the Bellinis' business by giving concerts from the newsstand, bringing to rushing commuters moments of beauty and repose. This modern fantasy shows that, in New York, anything can happen." Moorachian. What is a City?

Other titles about Chester and his friends are:

Chester Cricket's new home (1983)

Chester Cricket's pigeon ride (1981)

Harry Cat's pet puppy (1974)

Harry Kitten and Tucker Mouse (1986)
The old meadow (1987)
Tucker's countryside (1969)

Selfors, Suzanne

Smells like dog. Little, Brown 2010 360p $15.99

Grades: 4 5 6 7   **Fic**

1. Dogs -- Fiction 2. Uncles -- Fiction 3. Buried treasure -- Fiction

ISBN 978-0-316-04398-4; 0-316-04398-2

When farm boy Homer Pudding's explorer-uncle dies and leaves him a droopy dog with a mysterious coin hidden on its collar, it leads him to The City, where they meet Madame La Directeur, the conniving head of the Natural History Museum, who is trying to steal the coin and take Homer's place in a secret society of adventurers.

"Full of fantasy, fun, and humorous dialogue, this will attract dog lovers, mystery enthusiasts, adventure addicts, and reluctant readers. A thoroughly enjoyable read." Voice Youth Advocates

Another title about Homer Pudding is:
Smells like treasure (2011)

Selzer, Adam

I put a spell on you; from the files of Chrissie Woodward, spelling bee detective. Delacorte Press 2008 247p $15.99; lib bdg $18.99

Grades: 4 5 6 7   **Fic**

1. School stories 2. Mystery fiction 3. Spelling bees -- Fiction

ISBN 978-0-385-73504-9; 0-385-73504-9; 978-0-385-90498-8 lib bdg; 0-385-90498-3 lib bdg

LC 2008035673

When Gordon Liddy Community School's resident tattletale-detective, Chrissie Woodward, realizes that the adults are out to fix the big spelling bee, she transfers her loyalty to her fellow students and starts collecting evidence. Told through in-class letters, administrative memos, file notes from Chrissie's investigation, and testimony from spelling bee contestants

"The wit in this school story is directed almost entirely against the grownups in a scathingly funny indictment of a shady principal and insanely competitive parents." Horn Book

Selznick, Brian

The **Houdini** box. Atheneum Books for Young Readers 2008 un l $17.99; pa $6.99

Grades: 3 4 5   **Fic**

1. Magicians 2. Nonfiction writers 3. Magicians -- Fiction

ISBN 978-1-4169-6878-8; 1-4169-6878-4; 978-0-689-84451-5 pa; 0-689-84451-4 pa

LC 2008024693

A reissue of the title first published 1991 by Knopf

A chance encounter with Harry Houdini leaves a small boy in possession of a mysterious box—one that might hold the secrets to the greatest magic tricks ever performed.

"In this new edition, Selznick follows his intriguing tale with bonus material: a biographical note on Houdini, an illustrated magic trick, research notes on the writing of the book, and early sketches for the artwork. . . . It is sure to intrigue youngsters, particularly those interested in magic." SLJ

★ The **invention** of Hugo Cabret; a novel in words and pictures. Scholastic Press 2007 533p il $22.95

Grades: 4 5 6 7   **Fic**

1. Robots -- Fiction 2. Orphans -- Fiction 3. Motion picture directors 4. Paris (France) -- Fiction 5. Motion pictures -- Fiction

ISBN 0-439-81378-6

LC 2006-07119

National Book Award Finalist: Young People's Literature (2007)

Caldecott Medal (2008)

When twelve-year-old Hugo, an orphan living and repairing clocks within the walls of a Paris train station in 1931, meets a mysterious toyseller and his goddaughter, his undercover life and his biggest secret are jeopardized.

"With characteristic intelligence, exquisite images, and a breathtaking design, Selznick shatters conventions related to the art of bookmaking." SLJ

The **Marvels**; Brian Selznick. Scholastic Press 2015 640 p. illustrations (hard cover : alk. paper) $32.99

Grades: 5 6 7 8   **Fic**

1. Theater -- Fiction 2. Actors -- Fiction 3. Actresses -- Fiction 4. Family life -- Fiction 5. London (England) -- Fiction 6. Adventure and adventurers -- Fiction 7. Adventure stories

ISBN 0545448689; 9780545448680

LC 2015023161

In this book, author Brian Selznick presents "[t]wo seemingly unrelated stories -- one in words, the other in pictures. . . . The illustrated story begins in 1766 with Billy Marvel, the lone survivor of a shipwreck, and charts the adventures of his family of actors over five generations. The prose story opens in 1990 and follows Joseph, who has run away from school to an estranged uncle's puzzling house in London, where he, along with the reader, must piece together many mysteries." (Publisher's note)

"This brilliant journey through time in words and pictures is also a story of a theatrical family and their fortunes. This heavy tome opens to tell of one family, the Marvels, from 1766 to 1900 as their connection to the Royal Theatre in London begins and perhaps ends. In the first half of the book, all of this complex history is vividly conveyed through illustrations, with minor hints from playbills, cards, and letters that appear as part of the art. . . . Complex, entertaining, and full of gorgeous art and writing, this is a powerhouse of a book." SLJ

★ **Wonderstruck**; a novel in words and pictures. Scholastic Press 2011 637p il $29.99

Grades: 4 5 6 7   **Fic**

1. Deaf -- Fiction 2. Museums -- Fiction 3. New York (N.Y.) -- Fiction 4. Runaway children -- Fiction 5. American Museum of Natural History -- Fiction

ISBN 978-0-545-02789-2; 0-545-02789-6

LC 2011009113

"Readers know that the two stories will converge, but Selznick keeps them guessing, cutting back and forth with expert precision. . . . Both stories are equally immersive and impeccably paced. . . . Visually stunning, completely compelling." Kirkus

Sendak, Maurice

★ **Higglety** pigglety pop! or, There must be more to life. story and pictures by Maurice Sendak. HarperCollins Pubs. 1979 69p il $14.95; pa $8.95

Grades: 2 3 4   **Fic**

1. Dogs -- Fiction

ISBN 0-06-028479-X; 0-06-443021-9 pa

"The story has elements of tenderness and humor; it also has . . . typically macabre Sendak touches. . . . The illustrations are beautiful, amusing, and distinctive." Sutherland. The Best in Child Books

Sensel, Joni

The **Farwalker's** quest. Bloomsbury U.S.A Children's Books 2009 372p $16.99

Grades: 5 6 7 8 **Fic**

1. Fantasy fiction

ISBN 978-1-59990-272-2; 1-59990-272-9

LC 2008-30523

When twelve-year-old Ariel and her friend Zeke find a mysterious artifact the like of which has not been seen in a long time, it proves to be the beginning of a long and arduous journey that will untimately reveal to them their true identities.

"This is a solid and well-paced fantasy in which the journey is more important than the conclusion." SLJ

Followed by: The timekeeper's moon (2010)

Sepahban, Lois

★ **Paper** wishes; Lois Sepahban. Farrar, Straus & Giroux 2016 192 p. 2 unnumbered pages (hardback) $16.99

Grades: 4 5 6 **Fic**

1. Self-acceptance -- Fiction 2. Japanese Americans -- Evacuation and relocation, 1942-1945 -- Fiction 3. Family life -- Fiction 4. Selective mutism -- Fiction 5. Manzanar War Relocation Center -- Fiction 6. World War, 1939-1945 -- United States -- Fiction 7. Japanese Americans -- Evacuation and relocation, 1942-1945 -- Fiction

ISBN 9780374302160; 0374302162

LC 2015005786

In this children's book, by Lois Sepahban, "it's 1942, after the attack on Pearl Harbor, and Manami and her family are Japanese American, which means that the government says they must . . . join other Japanese Americans at a prison camp. Even worse is that they are going to have to give [up] her and her grandfather's dog, Yujiin. It isn't until she finds a way to let go of her guilt that Manami can reclaim the piece of herself that she left behind and accept all that has happened to her family." (Publisher's note)

"This engaging chapter book offers a personal perspective on events and reasons to care about the outcome. A fine selection for historical-fiction fans and a natural choice for readers who loved Kirby Larson's Dash (2014)." Booklist

Seredy, Kate

The **Good** Master; written and illustrated by Kate Seredy. Viking 1935 210p il hardcover o.p. pa $4.99

Grades: 4 5 6 **Fic**

1. Hungary -- Fiction 2. Farm life -- Fiction

ISBN 0-14-030133-X

A Newbery Medal honor book, 1936

Into this story of Jancsi, a ten-year-old Hungarian farm boy and his little hoyden of a cousin Kate from Budapest, is woven a description of Hungarian farm life, fairs, festivals, and folk tales. Under the tutelage of Jancsi's kind father, called by the neighbors The Good Master, Kate calms down and becomes a more docile young person

"The steady warm understanding of the wise father, the Good Master, is a shining quality throughout." Horn Book

Followed by The singing tree (1939)

The **white** stag; written and illustrated by Kate Seredy. Viking 1937 94p il hardcover o.p. pa $4.99

Grades: 4 5 6 **Fic**

1. Hungary -- Fiction

ISBN 0-14-031258-7 pa

Awarded the Newbery Medal, 1938

"Striking illustrations interpret this hero tale of the legendary founding of Hungary, when a white stag and a red eagle led the people to their promised land." Hodges. Books for Elem Sch Libr

Service, Pamela F.

Escape from planet Yastol; illustrated by Mike Gorman. Darby Creek 2011 102p il $15.95; pa $5.95

Grades: 4 5 6 **Fic**

1. Science fiction 2. Siblings -- Fiction 3. Authorship -- Fiction 4. Kidnapping -- Fiction 5. Books and reading -- Fiction 6. Extraterrestrial beings -- Fiction

ISBN 978-0-7613-7918-8; 0-7613-7918-5; 978-0-7613-7921-8 pa; 0-7613-7921-5 pa

LC 2010049235

Eleven-year-old Joshua Higgins' prize-winning science fiction novel draws the attention of sinister blue aliens who capture Josh and his sister Maggie and take them to the planet Yastol, the setting of his novel.

"Readers ready for longer chapter books will enjoy having some science fiction to choose from and welcome further adventures." Kirkus

Seuling, Barbara

Robert takes a stand; illustrated by Paul Brewer. Cricket Books 2004 168p il hardcover o.p. $15.95

Grades: 2 3 4 **Fic**

1. School stories 2. Endangered species -- Fiction

ISBN 0-8126-2712-1

LC 2003-18499

Political experience gained in a class election comes in handy when Robert and his friend Paul act on behalf of endangered animals.

"The simple text, short chapters, and quirky black-and-white charcoal drawings all contribute to making this a great choice for beginning independent readers. Equally important, most primary-grade children will relate to earnest, charming Robert, his world, his concerns, and his everyday adventures." Booklist

Other titles about Robert are:

Oh no, it's Robert (1999)

Robert and the snake escape (2001)

Robert and the attack of the giant tarantula (2001)

Robert and the great Pepperoni (2001)

Robert and the hairy disaster (2002)

Robert and the instant millionaire show (2002)

Robert and the scariest night (2002)

Robert and the sneaker snobs (2002)

Robert and the three wishes (2002)

Robert and the back-to-school special (2002)

Robert and the weird and wacky facts (2002)

Robert and the class president (2002)

Robert and the clickety-clackety teeth (2003)

Robert and the embarrassing secret (2003)

Robert and the troublesome tuba (2003)

Robert and the world's worst wristwatch (2003)

Robert and the lemming problem (2003)

Robert and the great escape (2003)

Robert and the chocolate-covered worms (2004)

Robert finds a way (2005)

Robert and the practical jokes (2006)

Robert and the happy endings (2007)

Robert goes to camp (2007)

Sewell, Anna

★ **Black** Beauty; the autobiography of a horse. by Anna Sewell; text illustrated by Fritz Eichenberg. Grosset & Dunlap 1995 301p il $17.99

Grades: 4 5 6 **Fic**

1. Horses -- Fiction 2. Great Britain -- Fiction

ISBN 0-448-40942-9

LC 9404099

First published 1877 in the United Kingdom; first United States edition, 1891

A horse in nineteenth-century England recounts his experiences with both good and bad masters.

Shahan, Sherry

Ice island. Delacorte Press 2012 $10.99; lib bdg $18.99; ebook $10.99

Grades: 4 5 6 7   **Fic**

1. Dogs -- Fiction 2. Alaska -- Fiction 3. Sled dog racing -- Fiction 4. Wilderness survival -- Fiction 5. Iditarod Trail Sled Dog Race, Alaska -- Fiction

ISBN 978-0-385-74154-5; 0-385-74154-5; 978-0-375-99009-0 lib bdg; 0-375-99009-7 lib bdg; 978-0-375-98575-1 ebook

LC 2011003838

Thirteen-year-old Tatum's dream of competing in the grueling 1,049-mile Iditerod Trail Sled Dog Race may be at an end when she becomes lost in a freak snowstorm during a training run on Alaska's remote Santa Ysabel Island.

"Riveting and atmospheric. . . . This survival adventure creates an almost otherworldly experience within a treacherous and bracingly beautiful landscape." Kirkus

Shang, Wendy Wan-Long

The **great** wall of Lucy Wu; [by] Wendy Wan-Long Shang. Scholastic Press 2011 312p $17.99

Grades: 4 5 6   **Fic**

1. School stories 2. Family life -- Fiction 3. Chinese Americans -- Fiction

ISBN 0-545-16215-7; 978-0-545-16215-9

LC 2010-13536

Eleven-year-old aspiring basketball star and interior designer Lucy Wu is excited about finally having her own bedroom, until she learns that her great-aunt is coming to visit and Lucy will have to share a room with her for several months, shattering her plans for a perfect sixth-grade year. "Grades four to six." (Bull Cent Child Books)

"Bolstered by frequent use of Chinese language and proverbs, this is a realistic and amusing portrait of family dynamics, heritage, and the challenge of feeling like an outsider—even in one's own family." Publ Wkly

The **way** home looks now; Wendy Wan-Long Shang. Scholastic Press 2015 272 p. $16.99

Grades: 4 5 6 7 8   **Fic**

1. Grief -- Fiction 2. Baseball -- Fiction 3. Pittsburgh (Pa.) -- Fiction 4. Chinese Americans -- Fiction 5. Traffic accidents -- Fiction 6. Bereavement 7. Baseball stories 8. Little League baseball -- Fiction 9. Chinese American families -- Pennsylvania -- Pittsburgh

ISBN 0545609569; 9780545609562

LC 2014028707

This book, by Wendy Wan-Long Shang, is a "story of family and loss, healing and friendship, and the great American pastime, baseball. Twelve-year-old Peter Lee and his family are baseball lovers, who bond over back lot games and talk of the Pittsburgh Pirates. But when tragedy strikes, the family flies apart and baseball no longer seems to matter. Is that true? Peter wonders if just maybe the game they love can pull them together and bring them back." (Publisher's note)

"The first-person narration is smooth and believable. This is a fine story of family, loss, growing up and learning to play baseball, raised to a higher level by gracefully incorporated themes of feminism and kindness." Kirkus

Sharmat, Marjorie Weinman

Nate the Great and the hungry book club; by Marjorie Weinman Sharmat and Mitchell Sharmat; illustrated by Jody Wheeler. Delacorte Press 2009 62p il $12.99; lib bdg $15.99

Grades: K 1 2   **Fic**

1. Mystery fiction 2. Books and reading -- Fiction

ISBN 978-0-385-73695-4; 0-385-73695-9; 978-0-385-90637-1 lib bdg; 0-385-90637-4 lib bdg

LC 2009030319

Nate and his dog Sludge help Rosamond discover who has been tearing pages out of her books.

Sharpe, Luke

Billy Sure, kid entrepreneur; Luke Sharpe. Simon & Schuster 2015 160 p. (Billy Sure, kid entrepreneur) (hardcover : alk. paper) $17.99

Grades: 3 4 5 6   **Fic**

1. Entrepreneurship 2. Inventions -- Fiction 3. Middle schools -- Fiction 4. Contests -- Fiction 5. Young businesspeople -- Fiction

ISBN 1481439480; 9781481439473; 9781481439480; 9781481439497

LC 2014949478

In this book by Luke Sharpe, illustrated by Graham Ross, "everyone is talking about Billy Sure, the twelve-year-old CEO of Sure Things, Inc. and genius inventor of the All Ball, a ball that turns into different sports balls with the push of a button. Now Billy wants to help other kids achieve their inventing dreams just like he has! So Billy is hosting an online contest for other kid-inventors to share their inventions, and the winning submission will be produced by his company." (Publisher's note)

"Billy Sure has newfound celebrity after inventing the All Ball, a ball that can change into any type of sports ball. Fame comes with its risks and challenges, however, and while trying to maintain his business, Sure Things, Inc., Billy must also protect a secret about the All Ball. An enjoyable start to a funny new series accented with comics-style doodles." Horn Book

Shaw, Susan

Tunnel vision. Margaret K. McElderry Books 2011 272p $16.99

Grades: 5 6 7 8   **Fic**

1. Crime -- Fiction 2. Homicide -- Fiction 3. Witnesses -- Fiction 4. Organized crime -- Fiction

ISBN 978-1-4424-0839-5; 1-4424-0839-1

LC 2010036306

After witnessing her mother's murder, sixteen-year-old high school student Liza Wellington and her father go into the witness protection program.

"The author creates a completely believable character in Liza, who often reverts to childlike emotions only to learn the hard way that cold reality takes precedence over even dearly held wishes. Kudos for the unexpected double ending, both illusory and realistic, giving readers a choice." Kirkus

Shefelman, Janice Jordan

Anna Maria's gift; by Janice Shefelman; illustrated by Robert Papp. Random House 2010 104p il $12.99; lib bdg $15.99

Grades: 2 3 4   **Fic**

1. Composers 2. Violinists 3. School stories 4. Italy -- Fiction 5. Orphans -- Fiction 6. Violinists -- Fiction 7. Venice (Italy) -- Fiction

ISBN 978-0-375-85881-9; 0-375-85881-4; 978-0-375-95881-6 lib bdg; 0-375-95881-9 lib bdg

LC 2009004553

In 1715 Italy, eight-year-old Anna Maria Lombardini arrives at a Venice orphanage with little but the special violin her father made for her, but when her teacher, Antonio Vivaldi, favors her over a fellow student, the beloved instrument winds up in a canal

"Strong emotions . . . lie at the heart of the story. . . . [This is a] short, appealing historical novel." Booklist

Includes glossary

Sheinmel, Courtney
All the things you are. Simon & Schuster Books for Young Readers 2011 244p $15.99

Grades: 5 6 7 8   **Fic**
1. Theft -- Fiction 2. Friendship -- Fiction 3. Family life -- Fiction 4. Stepfamilies -- Fiction 5. New York (N.Y.) -- Fiction
ISBN 978-1-4169-9717-7; 1-4169-9717-2

LC 2010010090

When Carly Wheeler's mother is arrested for embezzling, Carly's perfect life begins to fall apart as friends at her prestigious private school stop talking to her, her beloved stepfather starts worrying about finances, and her image of herself and her family changes.

"Sheinmel persuasively and sensitively conveys Carly's conflicting emotions and her attempts to make sense of what's been thrust upon her." Publ Wkly

Sherlock, Patti
Letters from Wolfie. Viking 2004 232p $16.99; pa $6.99

Grades: 5 6 7 8   **Fic**
1. Dogs -- Fiction 2. Vietnam War, 1961-1975 -- Fiction
ISBN 0-670-03694-3; 0-14-240358-X pa

LC 2003-24316

Certain that he is doing the right thing by donating his dog, Wolfie, to the Army's scout program in Vietnam, thirteen-year-old Mark begins to have second thoughts when the Army refuses to say when and if Wolfie will ever return.

"In this topnotch novel, Sherlock weaves together numerous threads of emotion, information, and plot so seamlessly that readers will be surprised by how much they've learned by the time they finish this deceptively simple story." SLJ

Sherman, Deborah
The **BEDMAS** conspiracy. Fitzhenry & Whiteside 2011 170p pa $9.95

Grades: 4 5 6 7   **Fic**
1. School stories 2. Bands (Music) -- Fiction
ISBN 978-1-55455-181-1; 1-55455-181-1

Adam's band, Sick on a Snow Day, is challenged by more than just an unusual name: Adam is mistakenly accused of cheating on a test and must maintain a clean record and B-average if he wants to stay in the band. Then his lead singer, Daniela, gets stage fright.

"Adam's academic difficulties and Daniela's stage fright are only two of the challenges thrown their way, but both are handled imaginatively and with humor. . . . A genial read." SLJ

Sherman, Delia
Changeling. Viking 2006 292p $16.99; pa $8.99

Grades: 5 6 7 8   **Fic**
1. Fantasy fiction 2. New York (N.Y.) -- Fiction
ISBN 0-670-05967-6; 0-14-241188-4 pa

"Neef is a changeling, a human baby stolen by fairies. She lives in 'New York Between,' an invisible parallel city, and she was raised under the protection of her godmother (a white rat) and the Green Lady of Central Park. . . . After breaking Fairy Law, Neef is expelled, and she must complete a heroic quest . . . in order to regain entry to her community. . . . Silly, profound, and lightning paced all at once, this novel will please adventure fans and fantasy readers alike." Bull Cent Child Books

Another title about Neef is:

The Magic Mirror of the Mermaid Queen (2009)

Sherrard, Valerie
The **glory** wind. Fitzhenry & Whiteside 2011 222p pa $12.95

Grades: 5 6 7 8   **Fic**
1. Ontario -- Fiction 2. Prejudices -- Fiction 3. Country life -- Fiction
ISBN 978-1-55455-170-5; 1-55455-170-6

Eleven-year-old Luke must come to terms with the moral prejudices of his small town in rural 1950s Ontario when he befriends Gracie, the daughter of a young widow who moves in next door.

"Luke's first person narration is fresh and emotionally true. . . . The haunting depiction of small-mindedness will leave readers wondering, as Luke comes to, about Gracie's true nature: heavenly child—or angel?" Kirkus

★ **Tumbleweed** skies. Fitzhenry & Whiteside 2010 153p pa $11.95

Grades: 3 4 5 6   **Fic**
1. Grandmothers -- Fiction 2. Saskatchewan -- Fiction
ISBN 978-1-55455-113-2; 1-55455-113-7

"In the summer of 1954, Ellie's grandma reluctantly agrees to look after 10-year-old Ellie in Saskatchewan so that her dad can take a job as a traveling salesman. Ellie's mother died on the day that Ellie was born, and Grandma blames Ellie for her death. . . . Many kids will recognize the sorrow and difficulty of living with a hostile, bitter relative. . . . The girl next door, a spoiled, bossy brat, offers some levity, but true to Ellie's viewpoint, the spare first-person narrative tells a heartbreaking family story with no mushy reconciliation." Booklist

Sherry, Maureen
Walls within walls; illustrated by Adam Stower. Katherine Tegen Books 2010 349p il $16.99

Grades: 4 5 6 7   **Fic**
1. Mystery fiction 2. Siblings -- Fiction 3. New York (N.Y.) -- Fiction
ISBN 978-0-06-176700-5; 0-06-176700-X

LC 2010-09494

When the Smithfork family moves into a lavish Manhattan apartment building, they discover clues to a decades-old mystery hidden behind the walls of their new home.

This "packs all sorts of interesting information about topics like history and architecture into a mystery that kids can (almost) solve. . . . Readers will get a real feel for the uniqueness that is New York City." Booklist

Sheth, Kashmira
Blue jasmine; [by] Kashmira Sheth. Hyperion Books for Children 2004 186p $15.99; pa $5.99

Grades: 5 6 7 8   **Fic**
1. India -- Fiction 2. Immigrants -- Fiction 3. East Indians -- Fiction
ISBN 0-7868-1855-7; 0-7868-5565-7 pa

LC 2003-50818

When twelve-year-old Seema moves to Iowa City with her parents and younger sister, she leaves friends and family behind in her native India but gradually begins to feel at home in her new country

"Seema's story, which articulates the ache for distant home and family, will resonate with fellow immigrants and enlighten their classmates." Booklist

Boys without names. Balzer & Bray 2010 316p $15.99

Grades: 4 5 6 7   **Fic**
1. India -- Fiction 2. Slavery -- Fiction 3. Child labor -- Fiction 4.

Missing persons -- Fiction
ISBN 978-0-06-185760-7; 0-06-185760-2

LC 2009-11747

Eleven-year-old Gopal and his family leave their rural Indian village for life with his uncle in Mumbai, but when they arrive his father goes missing and Gopal ends up locked in a sweatshop from which there is no escape.

"Readers quickly come to care for this clever, perceptive boy who tries hard to do the right thing. . . . The author includes more about child labor at the end of this well-told survival story with a social conscience." SLJ

Shevah, Emma

★ **Dara** Palmer's major drama; Emma Shevah. Sourcebooks Jabberwocky 2016 288 p. illustrations (alk. paper) $16.99
Grades: 4 5 6 7   **Fic**
1. Acting -- Fiction 2. Adoption -- Fiction 3. Prejudices -- Fiction 4. Self-confidence -- Fiction 5. Cambodians -- Great Britain -- Fiction
ISBN 9781492631385

LC 2015031876

In this book, by Emma Shevah, "Dara Palmer longs for stardom-but when she isn't cast in her middle school's production of The Sound of Music, she get suspicious. It can't be because she's not the best. She was born to be a famous movie star. It must because she's adopted from Cambodia and doesn't look like a typical fraulein. . . . So irrepressible Dara comes up with a genius plan to shake up the school: write a play about her own life. Then she'll have to be the star." (Publisher's note)

"Crawford-White's charming doodle illustrations along the margins reflects Dara's inner monologues throughout the book.This funny, charismatic heroine will capture her readers' hearts." Kirkus

★ **Dream** On, Amber; by Emma Shevah; illustrated by Helen Crawford-White. Sourcebooks Inc 2015 272 p. illustrations $12.99
Grades: 4 5 6   **Fic**
1. Sisters -- Fiction 2. Racially mixed people -- Fiction 3. Single-parent families -- Fiction 4. Imagination -- Fiction 5. London (England) -- Fiction
ISBN 1492622508; 9781492622505

In this book, by Emma Shevah, illustrated by Helen Crawford-White, as "a half-Japanese, half-Italian girl with a ridiculous name, Amber's not feeling [good] about making friends at her new school. But the hardest thing about being Amber is that a part of her is missing. Her dad. He left when she was little and he isn't coming back. Not for her first day of middle school and not for her little sister's birthday." (Publisher's note)

" Almost-12-year-old Amber Miyamoto hates germs, loves to draw, and can't figure out why her father left 6 years ago. She is also half Italian and half Japanese, which makes her feel "mixed up like a salad" and isn't helping with her anxiety over starting middle school. . . . While its humor and illustrations lend it Wimpy Kid appeal, its emotional depth makes it stand out from the pack. Molto bene!" Booklist

Shimko, Bonnie

★ The **private** thoughts of Amelia E. Rye. Farrar, Straus Giroux 2010 234p $16.99
Grades: 5 6 7 8   **Fic**
1. Friendship -- Fiction 2. New York (State) -- Fiction 3. Mother-daughter relationship -- Fiction
ISBN 978-0-374-36131-0; 0-374-36131-2

LC 2008048092

Growing up in a small town in upstate New York during the 1960s, 13-year-old Amelia E. Ryel, unwanted by her mother, searches for love and acceptance.

"The book is peopled with believable, multilayered characters. . . . Shimko's . . . story is original, and Amelia's distinctive voice and likable nature will have readers rooting for her in times of trouble and cheering her ultimate good fortune." Publ Wkly

Shreve, Susan Richards

★ The **flunking** of Joshua T. Bates; [by] Susan Shreve; illustrated by Diane de Groat. Knopf 1984 82p il hardcover o.p. pa $4.99
Grades: 3 4 5   **Fic**
1. School stories 2. Teachers -- Fiction 3. Family life -- Fiction
ISBN 0-679-84187-3 pa

LC 83-19636

Driving home from the beach on Labor Day, Joshua receives some shocking news from his mother: he must repeat third grade.

"In addition to the warm depiction of a teacher-pupil relationship, the story has other relationships, astutely drawn: Joshua's parents, the former classmate who teases Joshua, the best friend who stoutly defends him. The dialogue is particularly good, often contributing to characterization, just as often crisply humorous." Bull Cent Child Books

Other titles about Joshua are:
Joshua T. Bates in trouble again (1997)
Joshua T. Bates takes charge (1993)

Shulman, Mark

Ann and Nan are anagrams; a mixed-up word dilemma. by Mark Shulman; illustrated by Adam McAuley. Chronicle Books 2013 36 p. (alk. paper) $16.99
Grades: 1 2 3 4   **Fic**
1. Word games 2. Anagrams -- Fiction
ISBN 1452109141; 9781452109145

LC 2013006596

In this book, written by Mark Shulman and illustrated by Adam Mc-Cauley, "Robert (or Bert) thought he had his hands full when his mom and dad were palindromes. But now, his Grandma Reagan is in anagram danger! In fact, his sisters, Ann and Nan, and almost every other thing in his world, have become anagrams. Can Robert (or Bert) figure out the answer to his word dilemma, or is he fated to live a scrambled life?" (Publisher's note)

Treasure hunters; by James Patterson, Chris Grabenstein, and Mark Shulman and illustrated by Juliana Neufeld. Little, Brown and Company 2013 480 p. (Treasure hunters) $14.99
Grades: 3 4 5 6   **Fic**
1. Pirates -- Fiction 2. Siblings -- Fiction 3. Buried treasure -- Fiction 4. Twins -- Fiction 5. Seafaring life -- Fiction 6. Missing persons -- Fiction 7. New York (N.Y.) -- Fiction 8. Brothers and sisters -- Fiction 9. Adventure and adventurers -- Fiction
ISBN 031620756X; 9780316207560

LC 2012040968

In this book, by James Patterson, Chris Grabenstein and Mark Shulman, "the Kidd siblings have grown up diving down to shipwrecks and traveling the world, helping their famous parents recover everything from swords to gold doubloons from the bottom of the ocean. But after their parents disappear n the job, the kids are suddenly thrust into the biggest treasure hunt of their lives." (Publisher's note)

Shulman, Polly

★ The **Grimm** Legacy. G. P. Putnam's Sons 2010 325p $16.99
Grades: 5 6 7 8   **Fic**
1. Fantasy fiction 2. Magic -- Fiction 3. Libraries -- Fiction 4. New York (N.Y.) -- Fiction
ISBN 0-399-25096-4; 978-0-399-25096-5

LC 2009028919

New York high school student Elizabeth gets an after-school job as a page at the "New-York Circulating Material Repository," and when she gains coveted access to its Grimm Collection of magical objects, she and the other pages are drawn into a series of frightening adventures involving mythical creatures and stolen goods.

"This modern fantasy has intrigue, adventure, and romance, and the magical aspects of the tale are both clever and intricately woven. . . . Shulman's prose is fast paced, filled with humor, and peopled with characters who are either true to life or delightfully bizarre." SLJ

The **Poe** Estate; by Polly Shulman. Nancy Paulsen Books, an imprint of Penguin Group (USA) 2015 272 p. $16.99
Grades: 5 6 7 8   **Fic**
1. Ghost stories 2. Family -- Fiction 3. Supernatural -- Fiction 4. Haunted houses -- Fiction 5. Buried treasure -- Fiction 6. Books and reading -- Fiction 7. Ghosts -- Fiction 8. Families -- Fiction
ISBN 9780399166143
       LC 2014042105

In this book, by Polly Shulman, "Sukie's been lonely since the death of her big sister, Kitty—but Kitty's ghost is still with her. At first that was comforting, but now Kitty's terrifying anyone who gets too close. Things get even weirder when Sukie moves into her family's ancestral home, and an older, less familiar ghost challenges her to find a treasure." (Publisher's note)

"Shulman's novel stands alone and is all the richer for readers who know the backstory of the Grimm Collection, and the treasures kept in the Repository." SLJ

The **Wells** Bequest; by Polly Shulman. Nancy Paulsen Books, an imprint of Penguin Group (USA) Inc. 2013 272 p. (hardcover) $16.99
Grades: 5 6 7 8   **Fic**
1. Time travel -- Fiction 2. Fantasy fiction -- Fiction 3. Science fiction
ISBN 0399256466; 9780399256462
       LC 2012036571

This book is a companion to Polly Shulman's "The Grimm Legacy." Here, New York Circulating Material Repository page "Leo notices an object materializing on the floor. The glittering, football-sized machine has 'gears and rods and knobs and a little saddle' 'and two miniscule humans, one of whom is himself.'" He discovers that he and his fellow page Jaya must travel in time to prevent another page from misusing Nikola Tesla's death ray. (Kirkus Reviews)

Shurtliff, Liesl
Rump; the true story of Rumpelstiltskin. Liesl Shurtliff. 1st ed. Alfred A. Knopf 2013 272 p. (hardcover) $16.99
Grades: 3 4 5 6 7   **Fic**
1. Fractured fairy tales 2. Magic -- Fiction 3. Fairy tales 4. Gold -- Fiction 5. Humorous stories 6. Magic -- Fiction 7. Names, Personal -- Fiction
ISBN 0307977935; 9780307977939 trade; 9780307977946; 9780307977953; 9780307977960
       LC 2012005093

In this fractured fairy tale, by Liesl Shurtliff, "12-year-old [Rumpelstiltskin] . . . finds an old spinning wheel, . . . [and] discovers he has a gift for spinning straw into gold. His best friend, Red Riding Hood, warns him that magic is dangerous, and she's right. With each thread he spins, he weaves himself deeper into a curse. To break the spell, Rump must go on a perilous quest, fighting off pixies, trolls, poison apples, and a wickedly foolish queen." (Publisher's note)

"Debut author Shurtliff upends the traditional characterization of this fairy tale's antihero, recasting Rumpelstiltskin as a sympathetic and tragically doomed protagonist. . . . [T]he picaresque-style narrative gives

the maligned character a refreshingly plainspoken voice, while honoring the original story's hauntingly strange events." Pub Wkly

Silberberg, Alan
★ **Milo**; sticky notes and brain freeze. written and illustrated by Alan Silberberg. Aladdin 2010 275p il $15.99
Grades: 5 6 7 8   **Fic**
1. Death -- Fiction 2. Mothers -- Fiction 3. Friendship -- Fiction 4. Bereavement -- Fiction
ISBN 978-1-4169-9430-5; 1-4169-9430-0
       LC 2010012708

"This is more than just another funny story about a middle school misfit who is the new kid in the neighborhood. While Milo does struggle with all the normal tween anxieties and self-consciousness about his family, there is more. Silberberg details the daily events with Wimpy Kid-like drawings and quick-witted humor that will keep the pages turning. Milo's new friendships with classmates Marshall and Hillary and elderly neighbor Sylvia Poole allow readers to glimpse at the deeper truth–Milo's mother's death–as it emerges between laugh lines. Silberberg takes on a tough topic and always stays true to the age of the character through dialogue and artwork while maintaining that wisecracking, 12-year-old humor." SLJ

Simmons, Jane
Beryl; a pig's tale. Little, Brown Books for Young Readers 2010 216p $14.99
Grades: 2 3 4 5   **Fic**
1. Adventure fiction 2. Pigs -- Fiction 3. Family -- Fiction 4. Toleration -- Fiction
ISBN 978-0-316-04410-3; 0-316-04410-5
       LC 2009-3800

Tired of being mistreated and cooped up, Beryl the piglet escapes her farm and meets a group of wild pigs, whose settlement splits up over the decision of whether to let her stay, and with her new "family" she sets out to find a new home

"Simmons interjects humorous episodes through her colorful cast of animal characters, providing a rich contrast to the serious topics she explores. Before the hopeful ending is neatly resolved, Beryl and her cohorts face cruelty and despair. Vivid black-and-white drawings convey a range of emotion by varying shade and light. Expressive faces highlight a wealth of feeling." SLJ

Simon, Francesca
Horrid Henry; illustrated by Tony Ross. Sourcebooks 2009 90p il pa $4.99
Grades: 2 3 4   **Fic**
1. Brothers -- Fiction
ISBN 978-1-4022-1775-3; 1-4022-1775-7
First published 1994 in the United Kingdom

"Four short chapters follow Henry as he tries to have a perfect day (and upstages his brother, Perfect Peter), disrupts a dance recital with his imitation of a pterodactyl, meets his piratical match in neighbor Moody Margaret, and sabotages a family camping vacation. . . . Short, easy-to-read chapters will appeal to early readers, who will laugh at Henry's exaggerated antics and relate to his rambunctious personality. . . . Ross's comical illustrations perfectly complement the [text]." SLJ

Other titles in this series are:
Horrid Henry and the mega-mean time machine (2009)
Horrid Henry and the scary sitter (2009)
Horrid Henry tricks the tooth fairy (2009)
Horrid Henry's Christmas (2009)
Horrid Henry's stinkbomb (2009)
Horrid Henry rocks (2011)

Horrid Henry wakes the dead (2011)

Horrid Henry rocks; illustrated by Tony Ross. Sourcebooks Jabberwocky 2011 98p il pa $4.99
Grades: 2 3 4   **Fic**
  1. Bands (Music) -- Fiction
ISBN 978-1-4022-5674-5; 1-4022-5674-4
Collects four stories recounting the adventures of Horrid Henry as he torments his younger brother, ruins Moody Margaret's sleepover, irritates his teacher, and tries to trick his family into seeing his favorite band.

Horrid Henry wakes the dead; illustrated by Tony Ross. Sourcebooks Jabberwocky 2011 il pa $4.99
Grades: 2 3 4   **Fic**
  1. Magicians -- Fiction
ISBN 978-1-4022-5934-0; 1-4022-5934-4
Henry will do anything to win the grand prize at this year's talent show . . . even wake the dead! Plus three other stories.

Singh, Vandana
  ★ **Younguncle** comes to town; illustrated by B. M. Kamath. Viking 2006 153p il $14.99
Grades: 3 4 5   **Fic**
  1. India -- Fiction 2. Uncles -- Fiction
ISBN 978-0-670-06051-1; 0-670-06051-8
                                LC 2005-14146
First published 2004 in India
In a small town in northern India, three siblings await their father's youngest brother, Younguncle, who is said to be somewhat eccentric
"Singh's prose is humorous and delightfully understated." SLJ

Skelton, Matthew
  ★ **Endymion** Spring. Delacorte Press 2006 392p il $17.95; lib bdg $19.99; pa $9.99
Grades: 5 6 7 8   **Fic**
  1. Inventors 2. Printers 3. Magic -- Fiction 4. Great Britain -- Fiction 5. Books and reading -- Fiction
ISBN 0-385-73380-1; 0-385-90397-9 lib bdg; 0-385-73456-5 pa
                                LC 2006-46259
Having reluctantly accompanied his academic mother and pesky younger sister to Oxford, twelve-year-old Blake Winters is at loose ends until he stumbles upon an ancient and magical book, secretly brought to England in 1453 by Gutenberg's mute apprentice to save it from evil forces, and which now draws Blake into a dangerous and life-threatening quest
"This book is certain to reach an audience looking for a page-turner, and it just might motivate readers to explore the . . . facts behind the fiction." SLJ

  ★ The **story** of Cirrus Flux. Delacorte Press 2010 288p il $17.99; lib bdg $20.99
Grades: 4 5 6 7   **Fic**
  1. Adventure fiction 2. Orphans -- Fiction 3. Supernatural -- Fiction 4. London (England) -- Fiction 5. Great Britain -- History -- 1714-1837 -- Fiction
ISBN 978-0-385-73381-6; 0-385-73381-X; 978-0-385-90398-1 lib bdg; 0-385-90398-7 lib bdg
                                LC 2009-18987
In 1783 London, the destiny of an orphaned boy and girl becomes intertwined as the boy, Cirrus Flux, is pursued by a sinister woman mesmerist, a tiny man with an all-seeing eye, and a skull-collecting scoundrel, all of whom believe that he possesses an orb containing a divine power.

Skelton "neatly weaves touches of fantasy into a late-eighteenth century London setting. . . . His literary sensibility and grubby atmospherics are strong enough to carry the tale." Booklist

Skye, Obert
  Wonkenstein: the creature from my closet. Henry Holt and Co. 2011 224p $13.99
Grades: 4 5 6   **Fic**
  1. School stories 2. Monsters -- Fiction 3. Family life -- Fiction 4. Books and reading -- Fiction
ISBN 978-0-8050-9268-4; 0-8050-9268-4
                                LC 2011004870
Twelve-year-old Rob has stuffed his closet with old laboratory experiments, unread books, and more, and when a creature emerges from that chaos causing a great deal of trouble, Rob has to do such horrible things as visit a library and speak at a school assembly to set things right again.
"The writing is quite funny and has a lot of laugh-out-loud moments." SLJ

Slade, Arthur G.
  Jolted; Newton Starker's rules for survival. [by] Arthur Slade. Wendy Lamb Books 2009 227p $15.99; lib bdg $18.99
Grades: 5 6 7 8   **Fic**
  1. School stories 2. Lightning -- Fiction
ISBN 978-0-385-74700-4; 0-385-74700-4; 978-0-385-90944-0 lib bdg; 0-385-90944-6 lib bdg
                                LC 2008-8632
First published 2008 in Canada
Many of Newton Starker's ancestors, including his mother, have been killed by lightning strikes, so when he enrolls at the eccentric Jerry Potts Academy of Higher Learning and Survival in Moose Jaw, Saskatchewan, he tries to be a model student so that he can avoid the same fate.
"The premise will snag readers immediately [and] . . . Slade's portrayal of Newton's sweep of emotions as he deals with his perceived fate–fear, fury, dogged determination–is especially convincing." Publ Wkly

Sleator, William
  The **boxes**. Dutton Children's Bks. 1998 196p hardcover o.p. pa $4.99
Grades: 6 7 8 9   **Fic**
  1. Science fiction
ISBN 0-525-46012-8; 0-14-130810-9 pa
                                LC 98-9285
When she opens two strange boxes left in her care by her mysterious uncle, fifteen-year-old Annie discovers a swarm of telepathic creatures and unleashes a power capable of slowing down time
"Sleator has written a page-turner. . . . His writing is crisp and clean, letting the story speak for itself." Voice Youth Advocates

  Interstellar pig. Dutton 1984 197p hardcover o.p. pa $6.99
Grades: 5 6 7 8   **Fic**
  1. Science fiction
ISBN 0-14-037595-3 pa
                                LC 84-4132
Barney's boring seaside vacation suddenly becomes more interesting when the cottage next door is occupied by three exotic neighbors who are addicted to a game they call "Interstellar Pig."
The author "draws the reader in with intimations of danger and horror, but the climactic battle is more slapstick than horrific, and the victor's prize could scarcely be more ironic. Problematic as straight science fiction but great fun as a spoof on human-alien contact." Booklist

Another title about Barney is:
Parasite Pig (2002)

Sloan, Holly Goldberg

★ **Counting** by 7s; by Holly Goldberg Sloan. Dial Books for Young Readers 2012 384 p. (hardcover) $16.99

Grades: 4 5 6 7   **Fic**

1. Genius -- Fiction 2. Orphans -- Fiction 3. Alienation (Social psychology) -- Fiction 4. Schools -- Fiction 5. Gardening -- Fiction 6. High schools -- Fiction 7. Eccentrics and eccentricities -- Fiction
ISBN 0803738552; 9780803738553

LC 2012004994

This book follows "Willow Chance . . . an extremely precocious and analytical 12-year-old 'genius'. . . . Despite Willow's social difficulties, she makes an impression on everyone around her--whether it's Dell Duke, a lonely and ineffectual school district counselor, or Jairo Hernandez, the taxi driver Willow hires to drive her to her meetings with Dell. After Willow's parents die in a car crash, her new friend Mai Nguyen persuades her mother to take Willow in." (Publishers Weekly)

Short; Holly Goldberg Sloan. Dial Books for Young Readers 2017 304 p. $16.99

Grades: 4 5 6 7 8   **Fic**

1. Size -- Fiction 2. Theater -- Fiction 3. Self-acceptance -- Fiction
ISBN 9780399186219

LC 2016013964

In this book, by Holly Goldberg Sloan, "Julia is very short for her age, but by the end of the summer run of The Wizard of Oz, she'll realize how big she is inside, where it counts. She hasn't ever thought of herself as a performer, but when the wonderful director of Oz casts her as a Munchkin, she begins to see herself in a new way. Julia becomes friendly with the poised and wise Olive--one of the adults with dwarfism who've joined the production's motley crew of Munchkins." (Publisher's note)

"Her self-acceptance is inspiring, and the joy she experiences in her foray into theater is irresistible." Booklist

Slote, Alfred

★ **Finding** Buck McHenry. HarperCollins Pubs. 1991 250p pa $4.95

Grades: 4 5 6   **Fic**

1. Baseball -- Fiction 2. African Americans -- Fiction
ISBN 0-06-440469-2 pa

LC 90-39190

Eleven-year-old Jason, believing the school custodian Mack Henry to be Buck McHenry, a famous pitcher from the old Negro League, tries to enlist him as a coach for his Little League team by revealing his identity to the world

"Slote skillfully blends comedy, suspense and baseball in a highly entertaining tale." Publ Wkly

Smiley, Jane, 1949-

Gee Whiz; Jane Smiley; with illustrations by Elaine Clayton. Alfred A. Knopf 2013 272 p. (The horses of Oak Valley Ranch) (library binding) $19.99

Grades: 4 5 6 7   **Fic**

1. Ranch life -- Fiction 2. Horses -- Fiction 3. Christian life -- Fiction 4. Horses -- Training -- Fiction 5. Ranch life -- California -- Fiction 6. Family life -- California -- Fiction 7. California -- History -- 1950- -- Fiction
ISBN 0375969691; 9780375869693; 9780375969690; 9780375985331

LC 2012024370

In this book, by Jane Smiley, "Gee Whiz is a striking horse, and only part of that is because of his size. . . . When Abby is confronted with an onslaught of reminders of just how little of the world she has seen, she finds herself connecting with Gee Whiz's calm and curious nature, and his desire to know more." (Publisher's note)

★ The **Georges** and the Jewels; with illustrations by Elaine Clayton. Alfred A. Knopf 2009 232p il $16.99; lib bdg $19.99

Grades: 4 5 6 7   **Fic**

1. Horses -- Fiction 2. California -- Fiction 3. Ranch life -- Fiction 4. Christian life -- Fiction
ISBN 978-0-375-86227-4; 0-375-86227-7; 978-0-375-96227-1 lib bdg; 0-375-96227-1 lib bdg

LC 2009-06241

Seventh-grader Abby Lovitt grows up on her family's California horse ranch in the 1960s, learning to train the horses her father sells and trying to reconcile her strict religious upbringing with her own ideas about life.

"As might be expected from the skilled hands of Smiley . . . there are synchronous storylines . . . [and] many will find it difficult to say goodbye to Abby, Jack and especially to Ornery George." Publ Wkly

Other titles in this series are:
A good horse (2010)
True blue (2011)

Smith, Clete Barrett

Aliens on vacation; illustrated by Christian Slade. Hyperion 2011 251p il (The intergalactic bed & breakfast) $16.99

Grades: 4 5 6   **Fic**

1. Vacations -- Fiction 2. Hotels and motels -- Fiction 3. Extraterrestrial beings -- Fiction
ISBN 1-4231-3363-3; 978-1-4231-3363-6

Unhappy at being sent to stay with his grandmother at the inn she operates, The Intergalactic Bed & Breakfast, Scrub discovers that each room is actually a portal to space and the inn's visitors are aliens who are vacationing on Earth.

Smith "delivers a first novel about being a stranger in a strange land that many middle-schoolers will find funny and relatable. Slade adds a few goofy touches in the black-and-white spot art." Booklist

Smith, Cynthia Leitich

Indian shoes; illustrated by Jim Madsen. HarperCollins Pubs 2002 66p il $15.95

Grades: 3 4 5   **Fic**

1. Grandfathers -- Fiction 2. Native Americans -- Fiction
ISBN 0-06-029531-7

LC 2001-39510

Together with Grampa, Ray Halfmoon, a Seminole-Cherokee boy finds creative and amusing solutions to life's challenges

"The writing is warm and lively; the situations are sometimes humorous, sometimes poignant; and Ray and Grampa's loving relationship is depicted believably and without sentimentality." Horn Book Guide

Smith, Doris Buchanan

★ A **taste** of blackberries; illustrated by Charles Robinson. Crowell 1973 58p il lib bdg $14.89; pa $4.95

Grades: 4 5 6   **Fic**

1. Death -- Fiction 2. Friendship -- Fiction
ISBN 0-690-80512-8 lib bdg; 0-06-440238-4 pa

"A difficult and sensitive subject, treated with taste and honesty, is woven into a moving story about a believable little boy. The black-and-white illustrations are honest, affective, and sensitive." Horn Book

Smith, Hope Anita

★ **Keeping** the night watch; with illustrations by E.B. Lewis. Henry Holt 2008 73p il $18.95

Grades: 4 5 6 7 **Fic**

1. Novels in verse 2. Fathers -- Fiction 3. Family life -- Fiction 4. African Americans -- Fiction

ISBN 978-0-8050-7202-0; 0-8050-7202-0

LC 2007-12372

Sequel to: The way a door closes (2003)

Coretta Scott King honor book for text, 2009

A thirteen-year-old African American boy chronicles what happens to his family when his father, who temporarily left, returns home and they all must deal with their feelings of anger, hope, abandonment, and fear.

"The words are simple . . . and the beautiful watercolor pictures of the African American family have the same quiet intensity as pictures in the first book. . . . Although mainly in free verse, there's also a sonnet." Booklist

Smith, Icy

Half spoon of rice; a survival story of the Cambodian genocide. written by Icy Smith; illustrated by Sopaul Nhem. East West Discovery Press 2010 42p il

Grades: 5 6 7 8 **Fic**

1. Cambodia -- Fiction 2. Genocide -- Fiction

ISBN 0-9821675-8-X; 978-0-9821675-8-8

LC 2009002973

Nine-year-old Nat and his family are forced from their home on April 17, 1975, marched for many days, separated from each other, and forced to work in the rice fields, where Nat concentrates on survival. Includes historical notes and photographs documenting the Cambodian genocide

"Bold, impressionistic oil paintings, mainly full page but some full spreads, speak volumes, and archival photographs are appended. This powerful child's eye view of war is harsh and realistic—like its subject—though accessible and thought-provoking." SLJ

Smith, Robert Kimmel

★ **Chocolate** fever; illustrated by Gioia Fiammenghi. Putnam 1989 93p il $14.99; pa $4.99

Grades: 4 5 6 **Fic**

1. Chocolate -- Fiction

ISBN 978-0-399-24355-4; 0-399-24355-0; 978-0-14-240595-6 pa; 0-14-240595-7 pa

LC 88-23508

A reissue of the title first published 1972 by Coward-McCann

"It's all quite preposterous and lots of laughs, and so are the cartoon illustrations." Publ Wkly

Smith, Roland

Chupacabra; Roland Smith. Scholastic Press 2013 336 p. illustrations $16.99

Grades: 5 6 7 8 **Fic**

1. Cryptozoology 2. Kidnapping -- Fiction 3. Mythical animals -- Fiction 4. Father-daughter relationship -- Fiction 5. Chupacabras -- Fiction 6. Missing persons -- Fiction 7. Adventure and adventurers -- Fiction

ISBN 0545178177; 9780545178174

LC 2013404665

This book, part of the Cryptid Hunters series, by Roland Smith, "reunites Marty and his unusual uncle, cryptozoologist Travis Wolfe, as they search the world for Wolfe's daughter, Grace. Grace has been kidnapped by her grandfather, the ruthless and dangerous Noah Blackwood. . . . Now, with word that the mysterious creature known as Chupacabra has been sighted again, Wolfe is torn between his obsession

with finding cryptids and his desperate need to rescue his daughter." (Publisher's note)

"Plunging readers in where Tentacles (Scholastic, 2009) left off, this fast-paced novel opens right after Grace discovers that her twin brother, Marty, is in fact her cousin, and that her father's unscrupulous enemy, Noah Blackwood, is actually her grandfather...Though this sequel suffers in comparison to the previous books in the series, Smith adeptly adds enough new characters, dangers, and cool science to reel in reluctant readers and keep them turning pages long after their lights should have been turned off." SLJ

Other titles in the series include:

Cryptid Hunters (2005)

Mutation (2014)

Tentacles (2009)

I, Q.: book one, Independence Hall. Sleeping Bear Press 2008 302p pa $8.95

Grades: 5 6 7 8 **Fic**

1. Adventure fiction 2. Spies -- Fiction 3. Terrorism -- Fiction

ISBN 978-1-58536-325-4 pa; 1-58536-325-1 pa

In Philadelphia, Angela realizes she's being followed, and Q soon learns the secret about Angela's real mother, a former Secret Service agent

"Adventure, suspense, humor, fascinating characters, and plot twists galore will draw middle-graders to this series starter." Booklist

Followed by: I, Q.: book two, The White House (2009)

I. Q.: book two, The White House. Sleeping Bear Press 2010 pa $8.95

Grades: 5 6 7 8 **Fic**

1. Spies -- Fiction 2. Siblings -- Fiction 3. Terrorism -- Fiction 4. Remarriage -- Fiction 5. Washington (D.C.) -- Fiction 6. Philadelphia (Pa.) -- Fiction 7. White House (Washington, D.C.) -- Fiction

ISBN 978-1-58536-456-5; 1-58536-456-8

LC 2011378292

Q (Quest) and Angela make it to the White House in Washington, D.C. to find that it is even harder to determine who are the 'good' and 'bad' guys than ever before.

"This spellbinding James Bond genre espionage novel for the middle school set will leave readers breathlessly waiting for the next installment." Voice Youth Advocates

Mutation; Roland Smith. Scholastic Press 2014 352 p. (Cryptid hunters) (hardback) $16.99

Grades: 5 6 7 8 **Fic**

1. Brazil -- Fiction 2. Missing persons -- Fiction 3. Jungles -- Fiction 4. Animals, Mythical -- Fiction 5. Adventure and adventurers -- Fiction

ISBN 0545081807; 9780545081801; 9780545081818

LC 2014017169

In this book by Roland Smith "Marty and his best friend, Luther, have managed to rescue Marty's cousin Grace from the clutches of the nefarious pseudo-naturalist Noah Blackwood, but . . . Marty's parents have been missing in Brazil for months. With time running out, Marty and the Cryptos Island crew race off for Brazil -- where they discover that Noah Blackwood has twisted the natural order of things beyond their wildest, most terrifying dreams." (Publisher's note)

"Marty, Grace, and friends make their way to Brazil to continue their twofold quest: find Marty's missing parents and stop the evil Noah Blackwood from continuing his unethical genetic experiments. Action, adventure, and high-tech gadgetry all combine into an exciting but over-the-top story. Stunning revelations and other dramatic turns provide additional impetus to keep readers turning the pages." Horn Book

Storm runners. Scholastic Press 2011 143p $16.99

Grades: 5 6 7 8   **Fic**

1. Florida -- Fiction 2. Hurricanes -- Fiction 3. Father-son relationship -- Fiction

ISBN 978-0-545-08175-7; 0-545-08175-0

LC 2010-32720

Twelve-year-old Chase Masters travels the country with his father, a "storm runner," but he is tested in ways he never could have imagined when he and a new friend are caught in a hurricane near St. Petersburg, Florida.

"This is an exciting, quick read. . . . Readers will feel engaged with Chase and his friends in their struggles to survive." SLJ

Followed by: The surge (2011)

Smith, Ronald L.

★ **Hoodoo**; by Ronald L. Smith. Houghton Mifflin Harcourt 2015 224 p. (hardback) $16.99

Grades: 4 5 6 7   **Fic**

1. Magic -- Fiction 2. Alabama -- Fiction 3. Demonology -- Fiction 4. African Americans -- Fiction 5. Family life -- Alabama -- Fiction 6. Country life -- Alabama -- Fiction 7. Alabama -- History -- 20th century -- Fiction

ISBN 0544445252; 9780544445253

LC 2014046838

Coretta Scott King/John Steptoe New Talent Author Award (2016)

In this novel by Ronald L. Smith "twelve-year-old Hoodoo Hatcher was born into a family with a rich tradition of practicing folk magic: hoodoo, as most people call it. But even though his name is Hoodoo, he can't seem to cast a simple spell. When a mysterious man called the Stranger comes to town, Hoodoo starts dreaming of the dead rising from their graves. The entire town is at risk from the Stranger's black magic, and only Hoodoo can defeat him. He'll just need to learn how to conjure first." (Publisher's note)

"Folks in the insular 1930s African American community of Sardis, Alabama, believe in God and in folk magick, or hoodoo. Twelve-year-old Hoodoo Hatcher's father tried to cheat death by transporting part of his soul into Hoodoo. To free him, Hoodoo must destroy the evil Stranger. This creepy Southern Gothic ghost story is steeped in time and place; Hoodoo's folksy asides relieve tension." Horn Book

Sneve, Virginia Driving Hawk

Lana's Lakota moons. University of Nebraska Press 2007 116p pa $12.95

Grades: 3 4 5   **Fic**

1. Death -- Fiction 2. Cancer -- Fiction 3. Cousins -- Fiction 4. Teton Indians -- Fiction 5. Hmong (Asian people) -- Fiction

ISBN 978-0-8032-6028-3 pa; 0-8032-6028-8 pa

LC 2007-05469

Cousins Lori and Lana, Lakota Indians who have a close but competitive relationship, learn about their heritage and culture throughout the year, and when a Laotian-Hmong girl comes to their school, they make friends with her and "adopt" her as one of their own

This is an "unassuming yet potent chronicle. . . . This novel repays readers with its portraits of the sisters and their living heritage." Publ Wkly

Snicket, Lemony

The **bad** beginning; illustrations by Brett Helquist. HarperCollins Pubs. 1999 162p il (A series of unfortunate events) $11.99; pa $6.99

Grades: 4 5 6   **Fic**

1. Orphans -- Fiction

ISBN 0-06-440766-7; 0-06-114630-7 pa

LC 99-14750

After the sudden death of their parents, the three Baudelaire children must depend on each other and their wits when it turns out that the distant relative who is appointed their guardian is determined to use any means necessary to get their fortune

"While the misfortunes hover on the edge of being ridiculous, Snicket's energetic blend of humor, dramatic irony, and literary flair makes it all perfectly believable. . . . Excellent for reading aloud." SLJ

Other titles in this series are:

The reptile room (1999)

The wide window (2000)

The miserable mill (2000)

The austere academy (2000)

The ersatz elevator (2000)

The vile village (2001)

The hostile hospital (2001)

The carnivorous carnival (2003)

The slippery slope (2003)

The grim grotto (2004)

The penultimate peril (2005)

The end (2006)

File under: 13 suspicious incidents; by Lemony Snicket; art by Seth. Little Brown & Co 2014 259 p. (All the wrong questions) (hardback) $12

Grades: 4 5 6 7   **Fic**

1. Mystery fiction 2. Humorous fiction 3. Apprentices -- Fiction 4. City and town life -- Fiction 5. Humorous stories 6. Mystery and detective stories

ISBN 0316284033; 9780316284035

LC 2013037873

This book, by Lemony Snicket, presents "thirteen mini-mysteries. Paintings have been falling off of walls, a loud and loyal dog has gone missing, a specter has been seen walking the pier at midnight--strange things are happening all over the town of Stain'd-By-The-Sea. . . . Join the investigation and tackle the mysteries alongside Snicket, then turn to the back of the book to see the solution revealed." (Publisher's note)

"Kid-detective Lemony Snicket treats us to thirteen short mysteries (missing newt, ghostly appearance, series of break-ins) in which he leaves readers poised just before the reveal, with a chance to solve the mystery themselves before they flip to the back of the book. (It's Encyclopedia Brown for Snicket-Hipsters.) The actual puzzles are dandy, and the format is ideal for the author's comic avalanche." Horn Book

Other titles in the series include:

Who Could That be at This Hour

When Did You See Her Last

Shouldn't You Be in School

Lemony Snicket: the unauthorized autobiography. HarperCollins Pubs. 2002 212p il $11.99; pa $6.99

Grades: 4 5 6 7   **Fic**

1. Humorous fiction

ISBN 0-06-000719-2; 0-06-056225-0 pa

LC 2001-51745

"The story of the fictitious Lemony Snicket and how he has dedicated his life to the case of the orphaned Baudelaire children. . . . Snicket tells you what he cannot tell you and then tells you, but what he tells you makes no sense. . . . [A] hilarious and clever book. . . . Lemony Snicket fans will love it, and new readers will laugh so much that they will want to read the series." Voice Youth Advocates

Shouldn't you be in school? Lemony Snicket. Little, Brown & Co. 2014 325 p. illustrations (some color) (All the wrong questions) (hardcover) $16
Grades: 4 5 6 7 **Fic**
1. School stories 2. Mystery fiction 3. Arson -- Fiction 4. Humorous stories 5. Apprentices -- Fiction 6. Detective and mystery stories 7. Arson investigation -- Fiction
ISBN 0316123064; 9780316123068; 9780316225045; 9780316279703; 9780316409681
LC 2014933203

In this children's book by Lemony Snicket "Lemony Snicket must work together with his incompetent chaperone to figure out who is burning down all of the buildings in the quaint town of Stain'd-by-the-Sea. Snicket is part of a special program, the V.F.D., and spends his days sleuthing with his chaperone, Theodora, in an attempt to catch the elusive and mysterious Hangfire, who is supposedly to blame for all of the mysterious happenings." (School Library Journal)

"In his third adventure, twelve-year-old Lemony Snicket, apprentice investigator, tackles a series of arsons in the economically depressed and highly mysterious town of Stain'd-by-the-Sea. Readers already hooked by this series will be pleased to check in with heroic librarian Qwerty, investigative journalist Moxie Mallahan, and the bickering Officers Mitchum and their bullying son, Stewart...As to the actual story, clues of the gray-matter sort (such as anagrams) combine with escapes, attacks, cliffhangers, and looming bad guys, keeping the whole crazy plot buoyant. Just." Horn Book

When did you see her last? Lemony Snicket; illustrated by Seth. Little Brown & Co 2013 288 p. (All the wrong questions) (hardcover) $16
Grades: 4 5 6 7 **Fic**
1. Missing persons -- Fiction 2. Mystery fiction -- Fiction
ISBN 0316123056; 9780316123051; 9780316251952
LC 2012955921
Parents' Choice: Silver Medal Fiction (2013)

In this book, author Lemony Snicket "has a new case to solve when he and his chaperone are hired to find a missing girl. Is the girl a runaway? Or was she kidnapped? Was she seen last at the grocery store? Or could she have stopped at the diner? Is it really any of your business? These are All The Wrong Questions." (Publisher's note)

"A further adventure for the young private eye Lemony Snicket involves the disappearance of a brilliant young chemist, the only hope for rejuvenation of the town of Stain'd-by-the-Sea. In the course of Snicket's investigation he reconnects with characters from "Who Could That Be at This Hour?". This tongue-in-cheek adventure is peppered with references to classic children's books." (Horn Book)

★ **Who** could that be at this hour? by Lemony Snicket; art by Seth. Little, Brown 2012 272 p. $15.99
Grades: 4 5 6 7 **Fic**
1. Bildungsromans 2. Mystery fiction 3. Humorous fiction 4. Statues -- Fiction 5. Stealing -- Fiction 6. Apprentices -- Fiction
ISBN 0316123080; 9780316123082
LC 2012012657

This children's adventure mystery, by Lemony Snicket, begins in "Stain'd-by-the-Sea, the mostly deserted town where 12-year-old Lemony Snicket takes his first case as apprentice to chaperone S. Theodora Markson. They have been hired by Mrs. Murphy Sallis to retrieve a vastly valuable statue of the local legend, the Bombinating Beast.... With the help and/or hindrance of girls Moxie and Ellington, can Snicket keep his promises and come close to solving a mystery?" (Kirkus Reviews)

Other titles in this series are:
When did you see her last? (2013)
Shouldn't you be in school? (2014)

Why is this night different from all the other nights? (2015)

Sniegoski, Tom
Billy Hooten, Owlboy; by Thomas E. Sniegoski; illustrated by Eric Powell. Yearling 2007 242p il lib bdg $11.99; pa $5.99
Grades: 3 4 5 6 **Fic**
1. Superheroes -- Fiction 2. Cartoons and comics -- Fiction
ISBN 978-0-385-90402-5 lib bdg; 978-0-440-42180-1 pa
LC 2007001552

Unassuming twelve-year-old Billy Hooten, who loves reading superhero comic books, suddenly learns that he has been chosen to become the next Owlboy, whose destiny it is to save the inhabitants of Monstros, a city underneath the cemetery next to Billy's house

"This lively tale should be a hit, especially with reluctant readers. A few black-and-white sketches appear throughout." SLJ

Others title about Owlboy are:
Billy Hooten, Owlboy: the girl with the destructo touch (2007)
Billy Hooten, Owlboy: the flock of fury (2008)
Billy Hooten, Owlboy: tremble at the terror of Zis-boom-bah (2008)

Quest for the Spark; Book 2 written by Tom Sniegoski; illustrated by Jeff Smith; color by Steve Hamaker. Graphix 2012 234 p. (hardcover : alk. paper) $22.99
Grades: 4 5 6 7 **Fic**
1. Fantasy fiction 2. Magic -- Fiction 3. Adventure fiction 4. Dreams -- Fiction 5. Dragons -- Fiction 6. Fantasy 7. Humorous stories 8. Heroes -- Fiction 9. Adventure and adventurers -- Fiction
ISBN 9780545141031; 9780545141048
LC 2011020281

This book is set in the world of illustrator Jeff Smith's "Bone" graphic novels. Here, author Tom Sniegoski tells the story of "Tom, a Valley turnip farmer" who "receives a vision that the peaceful otherworld of the Dreaming is under attack. The evil Nacht, a renegade Dragon, seeks to control the dreamland, and through it, the Waking World as well. A mysterious forest woman tells Tom that he has been chosen to lead a quest to find the scattered pieces of the Spark--the light of creation that can drive back the dark power. When his family falls under the Nacht's corrupted sleep spell, Tom realizes that he has no choice and sets out with his best friend, a talking raccoon." (School Libr J)

Quest for the spark; book one. written by Tom Sniegoski; illustrated by Jeff Smith; color by Steve Hamaker. Graphix 2011 218p il (Bone) $22.99; pa $10.99
Grades: 4 5 6 7 **Fic**
1. Fantasy fiction 2. Adventure fiction 3. Magic -- Fiction 4. Dreams -- Fiction 5. Heroes and heroines -- Fiction
ISBN 978-0-545-14101-7; 0-545-14101-X; 978-0-545-14102-4 pa; 0-545-14102-8 pa
LC 2010017002

Twelve-year-old Tom Elm, his raccoon friend Roderick, Percival, Abbey, and Barclay Bone, warrior-priest Randolf, and forest-woman Lorimar join in a quest to find the pieces of the Spark that can save Dreaming—and the Waking World—from a Darkness created by the Nacht.

"At long last . . . we return to the Valley that was the setting for Smith's comics-landscape-changing Bone, though this adventure takes place in prose rather than panels. . . . As long as fans are not expecting a repeat of the old magic and not too disappointed that there isn't nearly enough of Smith's always excellent full-color, full-page artwork helping out, it looks as if they're in for a cheery jaunt back through a beloved world." Booklist

Snow, Maya

Sisters of the sword. HarperCollins 2008 275p (Sisters of the sword) $16.99; lib bdg $17.89; pa $6.99

Grades: 5 6 7 8   Fic

1. Japan -- Fiction 2. Samurai -- Fiction 3. Sisters -- Fiction 4. Sex role -- Fiction

ISBN 978-0-06-124387-5; 0-06-124387-6; 978-0-06-124388-2 lib bdg; 0-06-124388-4 lib bdg; 978-0-06-124389-9 pa; 0-06-124389-2 pa

LC 2007-029610

Two aristocratic sisters in ancient Japan disguise themselves as samurai warriors to take revenge on the uncle who betrayed their family.

"This rousing new series . . . . starts off with a bang, or more accurately, the silent thrust of a sword." Booklist

Other titles in this series are:

Chasing the secret (2009)

Journey through fire (2009)

Snyder, Laurel

Any which wall; drawings by LeUyen Pham. Random House 2009 242p il $16.99; lib bdg $19.99

Grades: 4 5 6 7   Fic

1. Iowa -- Fiction 2. Magic -- Fiction 3. Wishes -- Fiction 4. Siblings -- Fiction 5. Space and time -- Fiction

ISBN 978-0-375-85560-3; 0-375-85560-2; 978-0-375-95560-0 lib bdg; 0-375-95560-7 lib bdg

LC 2008-22605

In the middle of an Iowa cornfield, four children find a magic wall that enables them to travel through time and space.

"Snyder's fresh, down-to-earth voice is complemented by Pham's energetic illustrations, which seem at once retro and modern. Fantasy fans will enjoy this novel, but so will readers who like stories about ordinary kids." SLJ

Bigger than a bread box. Random House 2011 226p $16.99

Grades: 4 5 6   Fic

1. Magic -- Fiction 2. Family life -- Fiction

ISBN 978-0-375-86916-7; 0-375-86916-6

Twelve-year-old Rebecca is struggling with her parents' separation, as well as a sudden move to her Gran's house in another state. For a while, a magic bread box, discovered in the attic, makes life away from home a little easier. Then suddenly it starts to make things much, much more difficult, and Rebecca is forced to decide not just where, but who she really wants to be.

"Introspective and rich with delicate imagery. . . . The insightful, memorable, and complex characters that Snyder creates result in a story with the same qualities." Publ Wkly

★ Penny Dreadful; drawings by Abigail Halpin. Random House 2010 304p il $16.99; lib bdg $19.99

Grades: 3 4 5   Fic

1. Tennessee -- Fiction 2. Family life -- Fiction 3. Country life -- Fiction

ISBN 978-0-375-86199-4; 0-375-86199-8; 978-0-375-96199-1 lib bdg; 0-375-96199-2 lib bdg

LC 2009-32104

When her father suddenly quits his job, the almost-ten-year-old, friendless Penny and her neglectful parents leave their privileged life in the city for a ramshackle property in the eccentric town of Thrush Junction, Tennessee.

"Snyder's characters are well-developed and endearing, and the author strikes an excellent balance between the reality of the Greys' financial straits and the quiet magic that everyday life has to offer." Publ Wkly

Snyder, Zilpha Keatley

★ The Egypt game; drawings by Alton Raible. Atheneum Books for Young Readers 2007 215p il $16.99; pa $6.99

Grades: 5 6 7 8   Fic

1. Egypt -- Fiction 2. Games -- Fiction 3. Imagination -- Fiction

ISBN 978-1-4169-6065-2; 1-4169-6065-1; 978-1-4169-9051-2 pa; 1-4169-9051-8 pa

First published 1967

A Newbery Medal honor book, 1968

A group of children, entranced with the study of Egypt, play their own Egypt game, are visited by a secret oracle, become involved in a murder, and befriend the Professor before they move on to new interests, such as Gypsies.

★ The headless cupid; illustrated by Alton Raible. Atheneum Books for Young Readers 2009 219p il $16.99; pa $6.99

Grades: 5 6 7 8   Fic

1. Occultism -- Fiction

ISBN 978-1-4169-9532-6; 1-4169-9532-3; 978-1-4169-9052-9 pa; 1-4169-9052-6 pa

A reissue of the title first published 1971

A Newbery Medal honor book, 1972

Life is never quite the same again for eleven-year-old David after the arrival of his new stepsister, a student of the occult.

"The author portrays children with acute understanding, evident both in her delineation of Amanda and David and of the distinctively different younger children. Good style, good characterization, good dialogue, good story." Sutherland. The Best in Child Books

William S. and the great escape. Atheneum Books for Young Readers 2009 214p $16.99

Grades: 5 6 7 8   Fic

1. Acting -- Fiction 2. Siblings -- Fiction

ISBN 978-1-4169-6763-7; 1-4169-6763-X

LC 2008-10377

In 1938, twelve-year-old William has already decided to leave home when his younger sister informs him that she and their brother and sister are going too, and right away, but complications arise when an acquaintance decides to "help" them.

"Wit and pluck are rewarded in this quick-paced, high-drama adventure, which may also whet young appetites for Shakespeare." Publ Wkly

Followed by: William's midsummer dreams (2011)

William's midsummer dreams. Atheneum Books for Young Readers 2011 209p $16.99

Grades: 5 6 7 8   Fic

1. Aunts -- Fiction 2. Acting -- Fiction 3. Theater -- Fiction 4. Adoption -- Fiction 5. Siblings -- Fiction

ISBN 978-1-4424-1997-1; 9781442419995 e-book

LC 2010036958

Sequel to: William S. and the great escape (2009)

Now permanently settled with Aunt Fiona, who has adopted him and his siblings, thirteen-year-old William gets the chance to play Puck in a professional production of A Midsummer Night's Dream.

"An adventure story with a lot to say about identity, ambition and character." Kirkus

The witches of Worm; illustrated by Alton Raible. Atheneum Books for Young Readers 2009 183p il $16.99; pa $6.99

Grades: 5 6 7 8   Fic

1. Cats -- Fiction 2. Witchcraft -- Fiction

ISBN 978-1-4169-9531-9; 1-4169-9531-5; 978-1-4169-9053-6 pa; 1-4169-9053-4 pa

A reissue of the title first published 1972

A Newbery Medal honor book, 1973

Lonely, twelve-year-old Jessica is convinced that the cat she finds is possessed by a witch and is responsible for her own strange behavior.

"This is a haunting story of the power of mind and ritual, as well as of misunderstanding, anger, loneliness and friendship. It is written with humor, pace, a sure feeling for conversation and a warm understanding of human nature." Commonweal

Sobol, Donald J.

Encyclopedia Brown and the case of the carnival crime; illustrated by James Bernardin. Dutton Children's Books 2011 86p il $16.99
Grades: 3 4 5   **Fic**
1. Mystery fiction
ISBN 978-0-525-42211-2; 0-525-42211-0
                                                 LC 2010045854

Ten brief cases allow the reader to match wits with ten-year-old crime-buster, Encyclopedia Brown, as he investigates such cases as toys missing from a fair, music stolen from a singer-songwriter, and arrowheads that disappear during a campout.

Encyclopedia Brown and the case of the midnight visitor; illustrated by Lillian Brandi. Puffin Books 2008 96p il pa $4.99
Grades: 3 4 5   **Fic**
1. Mystery fiction
ISBN 978-0-14-241106-3; 0-14-241106-X
A reissue of the title first published 1977

As Idaville's ten-year-old star detective, Encyclopedia has an uncanny knack for trivia. With his unconventional knowledge, he solves mysteries for the neighborhood kids through his own detective agency. But his dad also happens to be the chief of the Idaville police department, and every night around the dinner table, Encyclopedia helps him solve some of the most baffling crimes.

Encyclopedia Brown and the case of the secret UFOs; illustrated by James Bernardin. Dutton Children's Books 2010 84p il $16.99
Grades: 3 4 5   **Fic**
1. Mystery fiction
ISBN 978-0-525-42210-5; 0-525-42210-2
                                                 LC 2009053287

Ten brief cases allow the reader to match wits with ten-year-old crime-buster, Encyclopedia Brown, as he investigates such cases as whether a diary of George Washington's mother is authentic, or if a UFO picture supposedly taken by the army is real.

"Young Brown remains a model for budding detectives everywhere." Kirkus

Encyclopedia Brown and the case of the treasure hunt; illustrated by Gail Owens. Morrow Junior Bks. 1988 91p il hardcover o.p. pa $5.50
Grades: 3 4 5   **Fic**
1. Mystery fiction
ISBN 0-688-06955-X; 978-0-553-15650-8 pa; 0-553-15650-0 pa
                                                 LC 87-22048
Another title in the author's series about Encyclopedia Brown

"Readers can delve into ten cases, some occuring when Encyclopedia's astute insights help out his father, the chief of police, and some when the boy opens his own detective agency in the family garage. Encyclopedia is frequently aided by his partner, Sally Kimball, whose tart observations add zest to the dialogue. It takes knowledge of a variety of subjects to guess the case solutions (given at the conclusion): math, science, and nature facts; boat terminology; and alphabet letter-switching, to name a few. Sobol's tight, logical plot construction provides junior sleuths with real stumpers." Booklist

Encyclopedia Brown cracks the case; [by] Donald J. Sobol; illustrated by James Bernardin. Dutton Children's Books 2007 90p il $15.99; pa $4.99
Grades: 3 4 5   **Fic**
1. Mystery and detective stories.
ISBN 978-0-525-47924-6; 0-525-47924-4; 978-0-14-241167-4 pa; 0-14-241167-1 pa
                                                 LC 2006-39766

Ten brief cases allow the reader to match wits with ten-year-old crime-buster, Encyclopedia Brown, as he locates stolen jewels, retrieves a stuffed tiger, and more. Solutions are included at the back of the book.

Encyclopedia Brown takes the cake! by Donald J. Sobol with Glenn Andrews; illustrations by Ib Ohlsson. Scholastic 1991 121p il pa $4.99
Grades: 3 4 5   **Fic**
1. Mystery fiction 2. Cooking -- Fiction
ISBN 978-0-590-44576-4; 0-590-44576-6
                                                 LC 2009277144

A reissue of the title first published 1983 by Four Winds Press

The ten-year-old detective solves 'The case of the Missing Garlic Bread' and other food-related mysteries. Includes menus and recipes for a Fourth-of-July party, a birthday brunch, and other occasions.

Encyclopedia Brown, boy detective; illustrated by Leonard Shortall. Dutton Children's Bks. 1963 88p il hardcover o.p. pa $4.99
Grades: 3 4 5   **Fic**
1. Mystery fiction
ISBN 978-0-14-240888-9; 0-14-240888-3
First published by Thomas Nelson

"The answers are logical; some are tricky, but there are no trick questions, and readers who like puzzles should enjoy the . . . challenge. The episodes are lightly humorous, brief, and simply written." Bull Cent Child Books

Other titles about Encyclopedia Brown are:
Encyclopedia Brown and the case of the carnival crime (2011)
Encyclopedia Brown and the case of the dead eagles (1975)
Encyclopedia Brown and the case of the disgusting sneakers (1990)
Encyclopedia Brown and the case of the jumping frogs (2003)
Encyclopedia Brown and the case of the midnight visitor (1977)
Encyclopedia Brown and the case of the mysterious handprints (1985)
Encyclopedia Brown and the case of Pablo's nose (1996)
Encyclopedia Brown and the case of the secret pitch (1965)
Encyclopedia Brown and the case of the secret UFO (2010)
Encyclopedia Brown and the case of the sleeping dog (1998)
Encyclopedia Brown and the case of the slippery salamander (1999)
Encyclopedia Brown and the case of the treasure hunt (1988)
Encyclopedia Brown and the case of the two spies (1994)
Encyclopedia Brown cracks the case (2007)
Encyclopedia Brown finds the clues (1966)
Encyclopedia Brown gets his man (1967)
Encyclopedia Brown keeps the peace (1969)
Encyclopedia Brown lends a hand (1974)
Encyclopedia Brown saves the day (1970)
Encyclopedia Brown sets the pace (1982)
Encyclopedia Brown shows the way (1972)
Encyclopedia Brown solves them all (1968)
Encyclopedia Brown: super sleuth (2009)
Encyclopedia Brown takes the cake! (1983)
Encyclopedia Brown takes the case (1973)
Encyclopedia Brown tracks them down (1971)

Encyclopedia Brown, super sleuth; illustrated by James Bernardin. Dutton Children's Books 2009 87p il $15.99

Grades: 3 4 5 **Fic**

1. Mystery fiction

ISBN 978-0-525-42100-9; 0-525-42100-9

LC 2008048983

Idaville's secret weapon against lawbreakers, ten-year-old Leroy "Encyclopedia" Brown, helps the police force solve ten new cases, the solutions to which are found in the back of the book.

"Reluctant and avid readers alike will enjoy learning new things and finding the hidden clues along with these memorable junior sleuths." SLJ

Solomons, David

My brother is a superhero; by David Solomons. Viking, published by Penguin Group 2015 304 p. $16.99

Grades: 4 5 6 **Fic**

1. Superheroes -- Fiction 2. Comic books, strips, etc. -- Fiction 3. Brothers -- Fiction 4. Cartoons and comics -- Fiction

ISBN 0451474775; 9780451474773

LC 2014030547

In this children's story, by David Solomons, "Luke Parker was just your average comic book fan until his boring, teacher's pet, helps-old-ladies-across-the-street brother Zack got turned into a superhero. Luke can't believe the unfairness of it all. . . . But when Star Guy gets into super-size trouble, it's up to Luke--and his intrepid neighbor, Lara--to rescue his big brother and, with a little luck, help him save the world." (Publisher's note)

Sonneborn, Scott

Shell shocker; written by Scott Sonneborn; illustrated by Dan Schoening, Mike DeCarlo, and Lee Loughridge. Stone Arch Books 2011 48p il (DC super heroes: The Flash) lib bdg $25.32; pa $5.95

Grades: 2 3 4 **Fic**

1. Superheroes -- Fiction

ISBN 978-1-4342-2615-0 lib bdg; 1-4342-2615-8 lib bdg; 978-1-4342-3092-8 pa; 1-4342-3092-9 pa

LC 2010025350

While deactivating an explosive for the bomb squad, the police scientist receives a call, tipping him off about a robbery across town. Luckily, Barry is secretly the fastest man alive, the Flash!

This "chapter-book [adaptation] of [a] popular comic [superhero has] great, full-page illustrations and . . . onomatopoeia. . . . [The cover is a] 3D [hologram] that will attract kids. . . . [This is] action-packed." SLJ

Includes glossary and bibliographical references

Sonnenblick, Jordan

★ **After** ever after. Scholastic Press 2010 260p $16.99

Grades: 5 6 7 8 **Fic**

1. School stories 2. Cancer -- Fiction 3. Friendship -- Fiction 4. Family life -- Fiction

ISBN 978-0-439-83706-4; 0-439-83706-5

Jeffery's cancer is in remission but the chemotherapy and radiation treatments have left him with concentration problems, and he worries about school work, his friends, his family, and a girl who likes him

"Sonnenblick imbues Jeffrey with a smooth, likable, and unaffected voice. . . . As hilarious as it is tragic, and as honest as it is hopeful . . . [this book is] irresistable reading." Booklist

Zen and the art of faking it. Scholastic Press 2007 264p $16.99; pa $7.99

Grades: 5 6 7 8 **Fic**

1. School stories 2. Pennsylvania -- Fiction 3. Zen Buddhism --

Fiction 4. Asian Americans -- Fiction

ISBN 978-0-439-83707-1; 0-439-83707-3; 978-0-439-83709-5 pa; 0-439-83709-X pa

LC 2006-28841

When thirteen-year-old San Lee moves to a new town and school for the umpteenth time, he is looking for a way to stand out when his knowledge of Zen Buddhism, gained in his previous school, provides the answer—and the need to quickly become a convincing Zen master.

The author gives readers "plenty to laugh at. . . . Mixed with more serious scenes, . . . lighter moments take a basic message about the importance of honesty and forgiveness and treat it with panache." Publ Wkly

Sonnichsen, A. L.

Red butterfly; A. L. Sonnichsen, illustrated by Amy June Bates Simon & Schuster Books for Young Readers 2015 392 p. hardcover $16.99

Grades: 4 5 6 7 **Fic**

1. China 2. Adopted children 3. Novels in verse 4. China -- Fiction 5. Adoption -- Fiction 6. Families -- Fiction 7. Foundlings -- Fiction 8. Abnormalities, Human -- Fiction 9. Intercountry adoption -- Fiction

ISBN 1481411098; 9781481411097

LC 2013050300

In this book by A. L. Sonnichsen, "Kara never met her birth mother Abandoned as an infant, she was taken in by an American woman living in China. Now eleven, Kara spends most of her time in their apartment wondering why she and Mama cannot leave the city of Tianjin and go live with Daddy in Montana. Mama tells Kara to be content with what she has. . . but what if Kara secretly wants more?" (Publisher's note)

"Sympathetic readers will appreciate that Kara learns to build trust with those who demonstrate their compassion in constructive attempts to right some of the wrongs of her difficult beginnings." Booklist

Soto, Gary

The **skirt**; illustrated by Eric Velasquez. Delacorte Press 2008 74p il $14.99; lib bdg $17.99; pa $5.99

Grades: 1 2 3 **Fic**

1. Mexican Americans -- Fiction 2. Clothing and dress -- Fiction 3. Lost and found possessions -- Fiction

ISBN 978-0-385-30665-2; 0-385-30665-2; 978-0-385-90534-3 lib bdg; 0-385-90534-3 lib bdg; 978-0-440-40924-3 pa; 0-440-40924-1 pa

A reissue of the title first published 1992

When Miata leaves on the school bus the skirt that she is to wear in a dance performance, she needs all her wits to get it back without her parents' finding out that she has lost something yet again.

"This is a light, engaging narrative that successfully combines information on Hispanic culture with familiar and recognizable childhood themes. . . . A fine read-aloud and discussion starter, this story blends cultural differences with human similarities to create both interest and understanding." SLJ

★ **Taking** sides. Harcourt Brace Jovanovich 1991 138p hardcover o.p. pa $5.95

Grades: 5 6 7 8 **Fic**

1. Basketball -- Fiction 2. Hispanic Americans -- Fiction

ISBN 0-15-284076-1; 0-15-204694-1 pa

LC 91-11082

Fourteen-year-old Lincoln Mendoza, an aspiring basketball player must come to terms with his divided loyalties when he moves from the Hispanic inner city to a white suburban neighborhood

This is a "light but appealing story. . . . Because of its subject matter and its clear, straightforward prose, it will be especially good for reluctant readers." SLJ

Includes glossary

Soup, Cuthbert

A **whole** nother story; illustrations by Jeffrey Stewart Timmins. Bloomsbury 2010 264p il $16.99

Grades: 3 4 5 6   Fic

1. Spies -- Fiction 2. Moving -- Fiction 3. Inventions -- Fiction 4. Family life -- Fiction 5. Automobile travel -- Fiction

ISBN 978-1-59990-435-1; 1-59990-435-7

LC 2009-21998

Ethan Cheeseman and his children, ages eight, twelve, and fourteen, hope to settle in a nice small town, at least long enough to complete work on a time machine, but spies and government agents have been pursuing them for two years and are about to catch up

"The storytelling, which merges deadpan narration with an absurdist sense of humor, is the real star of this fast-paced adventure." Publ Wkly

Followed by: Another whole nother story (2011)

Sovern, Megan Jean

★ The **meaning** of Maggie; by Megan Jean Sovern. Chronicle Books 2014 224 p. (alk. paper) $16.99

Grades: 4 5 6 7   Fic

1. Family life -- Fiction 2. Middle schools -- Fiction 3. Multiple sclerosis -- Fiction 4. Father-daughter relationship -- Fiction 5. Fathers and daughters -- Fiction

ISBN 1452110212; 9781452110219

LC 2013029644

In this book, by Megan Jean Sovern, "Maggie Mayfield has decided to write a memoir of the past year of her life. And what a banner year it's been! During this period she's Student of the Month on a regular basis, an official shareholder of Coca-Cola stock, and defending Science Fair champion. Most importantly, though, this is the year Maggie has to pull up her bootstraps (the family motto) and finally learn why her cool-dude dad is in a wheelchair, no matter how scary that is." (Publisher's note)

"Maggie's self-realizations come quickly, but her distinct voice, with a snarky superiority that often masks her true vulnerability, creates a character who's not easy to love but tough to forget." Horn Book

Speare, Elizabeth George

The **bronze** bow. Houghton Mifflin 1961 255p $16; pa $6.95

Grades: 6 7 8 9   Fic

1. Palestine -- Fiction 2. Christianity -- Fiction

ISBN 0-395-07113-5; 0-395-13719-5 pa

Awarded the Newbery Medal, 1962

"Daniel had sworn vengence against the Romans who had killed his parents, and he had become one of a band of outlaws. . . . Each time he saw the Rabbi Jesus, the youth was drawn to his cause; at last he resolved his own conflict by giving up his hatred and, as a follower of the Master, accepting his enemies. The story has drama and pace, fine characterization, and colorful background detail." Bull Cent Child Books

The **sign** of the beaver. Houghton Mifflin 1983 135p $16

Grades: 5 6 7 8   Fic

1. Friendship -- Fiction 2. Native Americans -- Fiction 3. Frontier and pioneer life -- Fiction

ISBN 0-395-33890-5

LC 83-118

A Newbery Medal honor book, 1984

Left alone to guard the family's wilderness home in eighteenth-century Maine, Matt is hard-pressed to survive until local Indians teach him their skills

Matt "begins to understand the Indians' ingenuity and respect for nature and the devastating impact of the encroachment of the white man. In a quiet but not unsuspenseful story . . . the author articulates historical facts along with the adventures and the thoughts, emotions, and developing insights of a young adolescent." Horn Book

★ The **witch** of Blackbird Pond. Houghton Mifflin 1958 249p $17

Grades: 6 7 8 9   Fic

1. Puritans -- Fiction 2. Witchcraft -- Fiction 3. Connecticut -- History -- 1600-1775, Colonial period -- Fiction

ISBN 0-395-07114-3

LC 58-11063

Awarded the Newbery Medal, 1959

"Headstrong and undisciplined, Barbados-bred Kit Tyler is an embarrassment to her Puritan relatives, and her sincere attempts to aid a reputed witch soon bring her to trial as a suspect." Child Books Too Good to Miss

Speck, Katie

Maybelle goes to tea; [by] Katie Speck; illustrations by Paul Ratz de Tagyos. 1st ed.; Henry Holt 2008 60p il $15.95

Grades: 2 3 4   Fic

1. Insects -- Fiction 2. Cockroaches -- Fiction

ISBN 978-0-8050-8093-3; 0-8050-8093-7

LC 2007040937

Maybelle the cockroach follows the advice of her new fly friend Maurice and tumbles into a terrifying but tasty adventure during Mrs. Peabody's Ladies' Spring Tea.

"Easy-reader graduates will delight in Maybelle's antics and enjoy her housefly pal, Maurice. . . . With humorous illustrations on nearly every spread, this is a sweet offering." SLJ

Sperry, Armstrong

Call it courage. Simon & Schuster Books for Young Readers 1968 95p il $17.99; pa $5.99

Grades: 5 6 7 8   Fic

1. Courage -- Fiction 2. Polynesia -- Fiction 3. Wilderness survival -- Fiction

ISBN 978-0-02-786030-6; 0-02-786030-2; 978-1-4169-5368-5 pa; 1-4169-5368-X pa

First published 1940 by Macmillan

Awarded the Newbery Medal, 1941

"Because he fears the ocean, a Polynesian boy is scorned by his people and must redeem himself by an act of courage. His lone journey to a sacred island and the dangers he faces there earn him the name Mafatu, 'Stout Heart.' Dramatic illustrations add atmosphere and mystery." Hodges. Books for Elem Sch Libr

Spinelli, Eileen

The **Dancing** Pancake; illustrated by Joanne Lew-Vriethoff. Alfred A. Knopf 2010 248p il $12.99; lib bdg $15.99

Grades: 3 4 5   Fic

1. Novels in verse 2. Divorce -- Fiction 3. Restaurants -- Fiction

ISBN 978-0-375-85870-3; 0-375-85870-9; 978-0-375-95870-0 lib bdg; 0-375-95870-3 lib bdg

LC 2009-22645

"Bindi's life is pretty normal. She loves to read and has good friends and a loving extended family. This normalcy ends when her parents announce that they are separating and that her father is moving to another city to look for a job. Told entirely in verse, the story relates the sixth grader's experiences, her feelings, and snippets of her daily life. . . . The poetic structure of this novel succeeds in capturing the child's voice and deepest feelings. The verse also provides sound development of secondary characters. Lew-Vriethoff's lively pen-and-ink illustrations add texture to the story and offer touches of humor." SLJ

★ **Where** I live; illustrated by Matt Phelan. Dial Books 2007 unil $16.99

Grades: 1 2 3 4 **Fic**

1. Novels in verse 2. Moving -- Fiction 3. Family life -- Fiction
ISBN 978-0-8037-3122-6; 0-8037-3122-1

LC 2006-30971

In a series of poems, Diana writes about her life, both before and after her father loses his job and she and her family move far away to live with Grandpa Joe.

"Spinelli crafts a reassuring and engaging story in verse. . . . Phelan's charming pencil drawings are a perfect complement to this heartfelt tale." SLJ

Spinelli, Jerry

Hokey Pokey; by Jerry Spinelli. Alfred A. Knopf Books for Young Readers 2013 304 p. (hard cover) $15.99

Grades: 5 6 7 8 **Fic**

1. Bildungsromans 2. Fantasy fiction 3. Imaginary places 4. Play -- Fiction 5. Growth -- Fiction
ISBN 0375831983; 9780307975706; 9780375831980; 9780375832017; 9780375931987

LC 2012004177

In this book, Jerry Spinelli "creates a surreal landscape." There are no adults in "Hokey Pokey, where boys and girls dine on flavored ice and spend their days watching cartoons, playing cowboy games, and using their bicycles as trusty steeds. Jack's bike, Scramjet, is . . . stolen by his archenemy, Jubilee. This marks the first of a series of unsettling events that give Jack, a boy on the brink of adolescence, the eerie impression that 'things have shifted.'" (Publishers Weekly)

Jake and Lily; Jerry Spinelli. 1st ed. Balzer + Bray 2012 335 p. (hardback) $15.99

Grades: 3 4 5 6 7 **Fic**

1. Twins -- Fiction 2. Bullies -- Fiction 3. Children's stories 4. Friendship -- Fiction 5. Individuality -- Fiction 6. Brothers and sisters -- Fiction
ISBN 9780060281359; 9780060281366

LC 2011053362

This book offers a "story about a pair of twins growing apart. For almost as long as they can remember, Jake and Lily have shared a 'special sense,' which they call 'goombla.' . . . Lily tries to find out who she is without her brother, but it's hard work, and most of her attempts are unsuccessful. . . . Though the twins eventually rediscover their 'goombla.' . . . [author Jerry] Spinelli doesn't suggest that the two will go back to being the people they once were." (Publishers Weekly)

Loser. HarperCollins Pubs. 2002 218p $15.99; lib bdg $16.89; pa $5.99

Grades: 4 5 6 7 **Fic**

1. School stories 2. Family life -- Fiction
ISBN 0-06-000193-3; 0-06-000483-5 lib bdg; 0-06-054074-5 pa

LC 2001-47484

Even though his classmates from first grade on have considered him strange and a loser, Daniel Zinkoff's optimism and exuberance and the support of his loving family do not allow him to feel that way about himself

"This novel is an offbeat, affectionate, colorful, and melancholy work." Voice Youth Advocates

★ **Maniac** Magee; a novel. Little, Brown 1990 184p $16.99; pa $6.99

Grades: 5 6 7 8 **Fic**

1. Orphans -- Fiction 2. Race relations -- Fiction 3. Homeless persons -- Fiction
ISBN 0-316-80722-2; 0-316-80906-3 pa

LC 89-2714

Awarded the Newbery Medal, 1991

"Orphaned at three, Jeffery Lionel Magee, after unhappy years with relatives, one day takes off running. A year later, he ends up 200 miles away in Two Mills, a highly segregated community. Part tall tale and part contemporary realistic fiction, this unusual novel magically weaves timely issues of homelessness, racial prejudice, and illiteracy into an energetic story that bursts with creativity, enthusiasm, and hope for the future. In short, it's a celebration of life." Booklist

Wringer. HarperCollins Pubs. 1997 228p $16.99; lib bdg $16.89; pa $6.50

Grades: 4 5 6 7 **Fic**

1. Courage -- Fiction 2. Pigeons -- Fiction 3. Violence -- Fiction
ISBN 0-06-024913-7; 0-06-024914-5 lib bdg; 0-06-440578-8 pa

LC 96-37897

A Newbery Medal honor book, 1998

"Palmer LaRue is running out of birthdays. For as long as he can remember, he's dreaded the day he turns ten -- the day he'll take his place beside all the other ten-year-old boys in town, the day he'll be a wringer. But Palmer doesn't want to be a wringer...Palmer can't stop himself from being a wringer just like he can't stop himself from growing one year older, just like he can't stand up to a whole town -- right?" (Publisher's note)

"During the annual pigeon shoot, it is a town tradition for 10-year old boys to break the necks of wounded birds. In this riveting story told with verve and suspense, Palmer rebels." SLJ

Spratt, R. A.

★ The **adventures** of Nanny Piggins; illustrated by Dan Santat. Little, Brown 2010 239p il $15.99

Grades: 3 4 5 6 **Fic**

1. Pigs -- Fiction 2. Nannies -- Fiction 3. Siblings -- Fiction
ISBN 978-0-316-06819-2; 0-316-06819-5

LC 200904504

When Mr. Green, a stingy widower with three children he cannot be bothered with, decides to find a nanny for his children, he winds up hiring a glamorous ex-circus pig who knows nothing about children but a lot about chocolate.

"This is smart, sly, funny, and marvelously illustrated with drawings that capture Nanny's sheer pigginess." Booklist

Other titles in this series are:
Nanny Piggins and the Pursuit of Justice (2010)
Nanny Piggins and the Wicked Plan (2012)
Nanny Piggins and the Race to Power (2013)
Nanny Piggins' Guide to Conquering Christmas (2013)
Nanny Piggins and the Runaway Lion (2014)
Nanny Piggins and the Accidental Blast-off (2015)
Nanny Piggins and the Rival Ringmaster (2015)

Friday Barnes, girl detective; by R.A. Spratt; illustrations by Phil Gosier. Roaring Brook Press 2016 272 p. illustrations (hardback) $13.99

Grades: 4 5 6 7 **Fic**

1. School stories 2. Mystery fiction 3. Genius -- Fiction 4. Private schools -- Fiction 5. Schools -- Fiction 6. Boarding schools -- Fiction 7. Mystery and detective stories
ISBN 9781626722972

LC 201500592.

In this book, by R. A. Spratt, illustrated by Phil Gosier, "When Friday Barnes, girl genius, solves a bank robbery, she uses the reward money to send herself to Highcrest Academy, the most exclusive boarding school in the country—and discovers it's a hotbed of crime! Soon she's investigating everything from disappearing homework to the terrifying Yeti haunting the school swamp. But the biggest mystery yet is Ian Wainscott." (Publisher's note)

"Delightful, highly logical, and well-informed fun." Kirkus

Other titles in this series are:

Under suspicion (2016)

Big trouble (2017)

Springer, Nancy

The **case** of the cryptic crinoline; an Enola Holmes mystery. Philomel Books 2009 160p $14.99

Grades: 5 6 7 8   **Fic**

1. Nurses 2. Mystery fiction 3. Nonfiction writers 4. Great Britain -- Fiction 5. Missing persons -- Fiction 6. London (England) -- Fiction

ISBN 978-0-399-24781-1; 0-399-24781-5

LC 2008040475

In late nineteenth-century London, fourteen-year-old Enola Holmes, much younger sister of detective Sherlock Holmes, turns to Florence Nightingale for help when her investigation into the disappearance of a Crimean War widow grows cold.

"From the riveting prologue to the satisfying conclusion, readers are hurled headlong into Enola Holmes's latest case." SLJ

The **case** of the gypsy good-bye; an Enola Holmes mystery. Philomel Books 2010 166p

Grades: 5 6 7 8   **Fic**

1. Mystery fiction 2. Missing persons -- Fiction

ISBN 0399252363; 9780399252365

This is the concluding volume in the Enola Holmes mystery series. "As Enola searches for the missing Lady Blanchefleur del Campo, she discovers that her brother Sherlock is just as diligently searching for Enola herself. . . . He is in possession of a . . . message from their long-lost mother that only Enola can decipher. Sherlock, along with their brother Mycroft, must follow Enola into the reeking tunnels of London's dark underbelly as they solve a triple mystery: What has happened to their mother? And to Lady Blanchefleur? And what does either have to do with Mycroft, who holds Enola's future in his hands?" (Publisher's note) "Intermediate, middle school." (Horn Book)

"The series that features Enola Holmes, the (much) younger sister of Sherlock, continues to be flat-out among the best mysteries being written for young people today. Not only are the mysteries sharp attention holders but the conclusions are well thought out, with i's dotted and t's crossed in true Holmesian fashion." Booklist

★ The **case** of the missing marquess; an Enola Holmes mystery. Philomel Books 2006 216p pa $6.99; $10.99

Grades: 5 6 7 8   **Fic**

1. Mystery fiction 2. Missing persons -- Fiction 3. London (England) -- Fiction

ISBN 0-14-240933-2 pa; 0-399-24304-6

Enola Holmes, much younger sister of detective Sherlock Holmes, must travel to London in disguise to unravel the disappearance of her missing mother. "Grades four to eight." (Bull Cent Child Books)

"Enola's loneliness, intelligence, sense of humor, and sheer pluck make her an extremely appealing heroine." SLJ

Other titles about Enola Holmes are:

The case of the left-handed lady (2007)

The case of the bizarre bouquets (2008)

The case of the peculiar pink fan (2008)

The case of the cryptic crinoline (2009)

The case of the gypsy good-bye (2010)

★ **Rowan** Hood, outlaw girl of Sherwood Forest. Philomel Bks. 2001 170p hardcover o.p. pa $5.99

Grades: 4 5 6 7   **Fic**

1. Adventure fiction 2. Middle Ages -- Fiction 3. Robin Hood (Legendary character) -- Fiction

ISBN 0-399-23368-7; 0-698-11972-X pa

LC 00-63694

In her quest to connect with Robin Hood, the father she has never met, thirteen-year-old Rosemary disguises herself as a boy, befriends a half-wolf, half-dog, a runaway princess, and an overgrown boy whose singing is hypnotic, and makes peace with her elfin heritage.

"This tale is a charmer, filled with exciting action, plenty of humor, engaging characters, and a nice fantasy twist." Booklist

Other titles about Rowan Hood are:

Lionclaw (2002)

Outlaw princess of Sherwood (2003)

Wild boy (2004)

Rowan Hood returns (2005)

Springstubb, Tricia

Every single second; Tricia Springstuff; [edited by] Donna Bray. Balzer + Bray 2016 368 p. illustrations, map (hardback) $16.99

Grades: 4 5 6 7 8   **Fic**

1. Death -- Fiction 2. Family -- Fiction 3. Accidents -- Fiction 4. Friendship -- Fiction

ISBN 9780062366283

LC 2015958372

This book, by Tricia Springstuff, is "about the effects of an accidental shooting on family, friendship, and community. . . . Twelve-year-old Nella Sabatini's life is changing too soon, too fast. Her best friend, Clem, doesn't seem concerned. . . . The only person who might understand how Nella feels is Angela, but the two of them have gone from being 'secret sisters' to not talking at all. Then Angela's idolized big brother makes a terrible, fatal mistake." (Publisher's note)

"The narrative structure of then and now, with short chapters devoted to the musings of a statue, sometimes intrudes upon the story, but this is rich in complex issues that include caring for the elderly, the problems of friendship, and the role of God in everyday life. Lots of plates here, but Springstubb keeps them spinning to a satisfying end." Booklist

Mo Wren, lost and found. Balzer + Bray 2011 248p $15.99

Grades: 3 4 5 6   **Fic**

1. Moving -- Fiction 2. Family life -- Fiction 3. Restaurants -- Fiction

ISBN 978-0-06-199039-7; 0-06-199039-6

LC 2011001896

Sequel to: What happened on Fox Street (2010)

When eleven-year-old Mo's mother dies in an accident and Mo's devastated father deals with the loss by moving the family to a new town and starting a new life as the owner of a sports bar, Mo must leave her much loved neighborhood on Fox Street to live in an apartment above the 'cursed' Corky's Tavern.

"Readers will feel both inspired and comforted by these indefatigable sisters, whose humanity brings out the very same qualities in others." Booklist

Moonpenny Island; Tricia Springstubb; illustrated by Gilbert Ford. Balzer + Bray, an imprint of HarperCollins Publishers 2015 292 p. map (hardcover) $16.99

Grades: 4 5 6 7   **Fic**

1. Change -- Fiction 2. Islands -- Fiction 3. Friendship -- Fiction

4. Best friends -- Fiction

ISBN 9780062112958; 0062112937; 9780062112934

LC 2014006062

In this book, by Patricia Springstubb, "Flor and her best friend Sylvie are the only eleven year-old girls on Moonpenny Island, a rocky little bit of land in the middle of one of the Great Lakes. . . . At the beginning of sixth grade Sylvie is shipped off to a boarding school on the mainland while Flor must deal with both Sylvie's absence and her own mother's, who has left the island to care for Flor's ailing grandmother." (Bulletin of the Center for Children's Books)

"While exploring familiar themes of the unavoidable changes of adolescence, the novel weaves complex layers of fresh, relatable imagery and charming characterization across education levels, cultures, and generations, beautifully teaching that our shared humanity is one thing that doesn't change." Pub Wkly

Includes bibliographical references

★ **What** happened on Fox Street. Balzer + Bray 2010 218p $15.99

Grades: 3 4 5 6   Fic

1. Ohio -- Fiction 2. Friendship -- Fiction 3. Family life -- Fiction 4. Father-daughter relationship -- Fiction

ISBN 978-0-06-198635-2; 0-06-198635-6

LC 2009053563

Fox Street means everything to Mo Wren, who is nearly eleven, and so she is very upset when a land developer offers to buy her father's house, especially since she has not yet found the fox she is sure lives in the nearby ravine.

"Springstubb creates a richly human and believable story of the conflicts of growing up and a well-paced, interesting plot with plenty of surprises that readers should find pleasurable and satisfying." SLJ

Followed by: Mo Wren, lost and found (2011)

Spyri, Johanna

★ **Heidi**; by Johanna Spyri; illustrated by Jessie Willcox Smith. Morrow/Books of Wonder 1996 383p il $24.99

Grades: 4 5 6   Fic

1. Alps -- Fiction 2. Orphans -- Fiction 3. Switzerland -- Fiction

ISBN 0-688-14519-1

First published 1880

A Swiss orphan is heartbroken when she must leave her beloved grandfather and their happy home in the mountains to go to school and to care for an invalid girl in the city.

St. Antoine, Sara, 1966-

Three bird summer; Sara St. Antoine. Candlewick Press 2014 256 p. $16.99

Grades: 5 6 7   Fic

1. Mystery fiction 2. Lakes -- Fiction 3. Summer -- Fiction 4. Neighbors -- Fiction 5. Grandmothers -- Fiction 6. Vacations -- Fiction 7. Summer resorts -- Fiction

ISBN 0763665649; 9780763665647

LC 2013946623

In this book, by Sara St. Antoine, "[f]or as long as he can remember, Adam and his parents have spent their summers at his grandmother's rustic cabin on Three Bird Lake. But this year will be different. There will be no rowdy cousins running around tormenting Adam. There will be no Uncle John or Aunt Jean. And there'll be no Dad to fight with Mom. This year, the lake will belong just to Adam. But then Adam meets Alice, the girl next door, who seems to want to become friends." (Publisher's note)

"St. Antoine's setting is remarkably palpable and lyrically described: pine trees are 'spindly giants in pointy hats.' And her characters are well

realized, with Grandma both strong-willed and fragile and loner Adam experiencing true friendship." Horn Book

St. John, Lauren

The **white** giraffe; illustrated by David Dean. Dial Books for Young Readers 2007 180p il $16.99; pa $6.99

Grades: 4 5 6 7   Fic

1. Orphans -- Fiction 2. Giraffes -- Fiction 3. South Africa -- Fiction 4. Mythical animals -- Fiction

ISBN 978-0-8037-3211-7; 0-8037-3211-2; 978-0-14-241152-0 pa; 0-14-241152-3 pa

LC 2006-21323

After a fire kills her parents, eleven-year-old Martine must leave England to live with her grandmother on a wildlife game reserve in South Africa, where she befriends a mythical white giraffe

"The story is captivating and well spun." SLJ

Other titles in this series are:

Dolphin song (2008)

Last leopard (2009)

The elephant's tale (2010)

Stadler, Alexander

Julian Rodriguez: episode two, Invasion of the relatives. Scholastic Press 131p $16.99

Grades: 2 3 4   Fic

1. Science fiction 2. Extraterrestrial beings -- Fiction

ISBN 978-0-439-91967-8; 0-439-91967-3

First Officer Julian Rodriguez, imaginary space warrior, must endure the odious and unhygienic festivities of genetically linked minibrains when members of his extended family visit over the holidays.

"This entry in the Julian Rodriguez series is even sharper and funnier than the first." Booklist

Staib, Walter

A **feast** of freedom; tasty tidbits from the City Tavern. by Walter Staib and Jennifer Fox; illustrated by Fernando Juarez. RP Kids 2010 un il map $15.95

Grades: 3 4 5 6   Fic

1. Mice -- Fiction 2. City Tavern (Philadelphia, Pa.) -- Fiction 3. United States -- History -- 1775-1783, Revolution -- Fiction

ISBN 978-0-7624-3598-2; 0-7624-3598-4

"The City Tavern, a pedigreed Philadelphia institution, bore witness to much of the behind-the-scenes wrangling and politicking of a country on the verge of independence. . . . This book's initial, chronological spreads cover the building's conception, the basic floor plans, the importance of its location to both trade and politics, and how people ate, partied, did business, and kept up with the news in the late 1700s. Later spreads describe the building's historical connections. . . . Closing pages include a recipe for corn bread, a time line, and an update on the City Tavern as it now stands. A Disneyesque mouse in a tricornered hat leads readers through the pages, adding a touch of humor with brief quips in speech bubbles. . . . Add this title for a fresh look at a requisite time in U.S. history." SLJ

Standiford, Natalie

The **secret** tree; Natalie Standiford. Scholastic Press 2012 245 p. $16.99

Grades: 4 5 6 7   Fic

1. Bildungsromans 2. Mystery fiction 3. Children's stories 4. Friendship -- Fiction

ISBN 0545334799; 9780545334792

This coming of age story combines "[m]iddle-school dynamics, pesky sibling relations, a rumored haunted house, . . . and a mystery. . . . When 10-year-old Minty discovers a hollow tree in the woods . . . [and]

find[s] a secret written on a scrap of paper stashed inside, it sets the stage for a . . . mystery. . . . [W]hile Minty tries to figure out what's going on, she . . . befriend[s] an apparently parentless kid, Raymond, who seems to live in an abandoned spec house." (Kirkus)

Switched at birthday; Natalie Standiford. Scholastic Press 2014 240 p. (jacketed hardcover) $16.99

Grades: 4 5 6 7   **Fic**

1. Change -- Fiction 2. Birthdays -- Fiction 3. Friendship -- Fiction 4. Identity (Psychology) -- Fiction 5. Magic -- Fiction 6. Schools -- Fiction 7. Identity -- Fiction 8. Middle schools -- Fiction 9. Change (Psychology) -- Fiction

ISBN 0545346509; 9780545346504

LC 2013018598

In this book, by Natalie Standiford, "Lavender and Scarlet are nothing alike. . . . There's only one thing Lavender and Scarlet know for sure they have in common: the same birthday. . . . They've never swapped presents. But this year, because of two wishes that turned all too true, they are about to swap something much bigger than presents. Because the morning after their birthdays, Lavender is going to wake up in Scarlet's body . . . and Scarlet is going to make up in Lavender's." (Publisher's note)

"While the body switch is not a new idea, Standiford uses it effectively in this engaging story. Though swiftly drawn, even the minor characters are convincing, and the two leads are memorable in their separate ways." Booklist

Staniszewski, Anna

My sort of fairy tale ending; Anna Staniszewski. Sourcebooks Jabberwocky 2013 224 p. (tp : alk. paper) $6.99

Grades: 4 5 6 7   **Fic**

1. Magic -- Fiction 2. Fairies -- Fiction 3. Rescues -- Fiction 4. Families -- Fiction 5. Adventure and adventurers -- Fiction

ISBN 1402279337; 9781402279331

LC 2013017896

Sequel to: My epic fairy tale fail

In this book, by Anna Staniszewski, "Jenny only wants to rescue her parents . . . She's certain that the Queen Fairy has captured them, but when the queen captures Jenny too, the plot becomes complex. It turns out that the Queen Fairy is more than a bit insane. . . . When Jenny actually finds her parents, she must concoct a plan to rescue them, but with no power and her friends disappearing, she faces difficulties. . . . Of course Jenny will prevail, but how?" (Kirkus Reviews)

My very unfairy tale life. Sourcebooks Jabberwocky 2011 198p pa $6.99

Grades: 4 5 6 7   **Fic**

1. Fairy tales 2. Magic -- Fiction

ISBN 978-1-4022-5946-3; 1-4022-5946-8

Jenny, a professional adventurer, would prefer spending time with her friends over helping magical kingdoms around the universe, but soon she is given the choice to return to her normal life or go into a battle she doesn't think she can win.

"An eye for imaginative detail mixes with these likable characters and a theme of empathy for others to keep the story appropriate to a younger audience, who easily will identify with Jenny. Charming." Kirkus

Stanley, Diane

★ **Bella** at midnight; illustrated by Bagram Ibatoulline. HarperCollins Pubs. 2006 278p il $15.99; lib bdg $16.89; pa $6.99

Grades: 5 6 7 8   **Fic**

1. Fairy tales 2. Knights and knighthood -- Fiction

ISBN 978-0-06-077573-5; 0-06-077573-4; 978-0-06-077574-2 lib bdg; 0-06-077574-2 lib bdg; 978-0-06-077575-9 pa; 0-06-077575-0 pa

LC 2005-05906

Raised by peasants, Bella discovers that she is actually the daughter of a knight and finds herself caught up in a terrible plot that will change her life and the kingdom forever

"What raises this above other recreated fairy tales is the quality of the writing, dotted with jeweled description and anchored by the strong values—loyalty, truth, honor." Booklist

The **chosen** prince; Diane Stanley. Harper, an imprint of HarperCollinsPublishers 2015 368 p. illustration, map $16.99

Grades: 5 6 7 8   **Fic**

1. Magic -- Fiction 2. Princes -- Fiction 3. Shipwrecks -- Fiction 4. Fate and fatalism -- Fiction

ISBN 0062248979; 9780062248978

LC 2014022042

This children's book by Diane Stanley is "based on [William] Shakespeare's 'The Tempest.' On the day of his birth, Prince Alexos is revealed to be the long-awaited champion of Athene. He grows up lonely, conscious of all that is expected of him. Alexos follows the course of his destiny through war and loss and a deadly confrontation with his enemy to its end: shipwreck on a magical, fog-shrouded island. There he meets the unforgettable Aria and faces the greatest challenge of his life." (Publisher's note)

"Stanley's newest fantasy, set in ancient Greece, is a bittersweet delight. Prince Alexos learns early that being the champion of a goddess does not make for an easy life. Alexos is destined to bring about reconciliation between battling gods, Athene and Zeus, if he can survive a childhood filled with near-impossible challenge and little joy, except for his love of running and his little brother Teo...Other characters—especially the court physician Suliman and Teo's new sister Aria—are equally well done. The language is lyrical and accessible, and the end is satisfying in the extreme." SLJ

The **cup** and the crown; Diane Stanley. Harper 2012 344 p. (hardback) $16.99

Grades: 5 6 7 8   **Fic**

1. Fantasy fiction 2. Magic -- Fiction 3. Fantasy 4. Identity -- Fiction 5. Clairvoyance -- Fiction

ISBN 0061963216; 9780061963216

LC 2012025280

In this fantasy novel by Diane Stanley "Molly has visions of a beautiful goblet: one of her grandfather's loving cups, which he filled with magic that bound people together. So it hardly surprises Molly when handsome King Alaric asks her to find a loving cup to help him win the heart of the beautiful Princess of Cortova. As Molly and her friends Winifred and Tobias journey far beyond the safe borders of Westria, a mysterious raven appears to guide their quest." (Publisher's note)

Joplin, Wishing; by Diane Stanley. Harpercollins Childrens Books 2017 272 p. $16.99

Grades: 4 5 6   **Fic**

1. Magic -- Fiction 2. Wishes -- Fiction 3. Friendship -- Fiction

ISBN 0062423703; 9780062423702

In this middle grade novel, by Diane Stanley, "while cleaning out her reclusive grandfather's house, Joplin discovers pieces of a broken platter in a cookie tin. After having the platter repaired, Joplin wishes that she could both find a friend at school, and befriend the girl pictured in the platter. The next day, Joplin befriends a boy named Barrett, and also notices a girl outside her apartment. A girl who looks remarkably like the girl in the platter." (Publisher's note)

The **mysterious** matter of I.M. Fine. HarperCollins Pubs. 2001 201p hardcover o.p. pa $5.99

Grades: 4 5 6 7   Fic

1. Mystery fiction 2. Magic -- Fiction 3. Books and reading -- Fiction

ISBN 0-688-17546-5; 0-380-73327-7 pa

LC 00-54040

Noticing that a popular series of horror novels is having a bizarre effect on the behavior of its readers, Franny and Beamer set out to find the mysterious author

"The solidly constructed mystery, well-rounded characters, and playful jab at wildly successful horror writers go down a treat." Horn Book Guide

Another title about Franny and her friends is:

The mysterious case of the Allbright Academy (2008)

★ The **princess** of Cortova; Diane Stanley. Harper, an imprint of HarperCollinsPublishers 2013 320 p. (hardback) $16.99

Grades: 5 6 7 8   Fic

1. Betrothal -- Fiction 2. Occult fiction -- Fiction 3. Alternative histories -- Fiction 4. Fantasy 5. Magic -- Fiction 6. Princesses -- Fiction 7. Clairvoyance -- Fiction 8. Courts and courtiers -- Fiction 9. Kings, queens, rulers, etc. -- Fiction

ISBN 0062047302; 9780062047304; 9780062047311

LC 2013021824

Sequel to: The cup and the crown

This book is the final one in Diane Stanley's trilogy about prescient Molly and her friends. Here, Molly and "young Kind Alaric and . . . Tobias journey from Westria to the Kingdom of Cortova in search of an alliance that will include Alaric's betrothal to Princess Elizabetta. To complicate matters, however, Alaric's cousin, the foxy Reynard, King of Austlind, has arrived with a similar goal. Who will win the hand of the fair Elizabetta?" (Booklist)

Roughing it on the Oregon Trail; illustrated by Holly Berry. HarperCollins Pubs. 2000 un il (Time-traveling twins) hardcover o.p. pa $7.99

Grades: 2 3 4   Fic

1. Oregon Trail -- Fiction 2. Frontier and pioneer life -- Fiction 3. Overland journeys to the Pacific -- Fiction

ISBN 0-06-027065-9; 0-06-449006-8 pa

LC 98-41711

Twins Liz and Lenny, along with their time-traveling grandmother, join a group of pioneers journeying west on the Oregon Trail in 1843

"An engaging trip and a painless history lesson." SLJ

Other titles in this series are:

Joining the Boston Tea Party (2001)

Thanksgiving on Plymouth Plantation (2004)

★ **Saving** Sky. Harper 2010 199p $15.99

Grades: 5 6 7 8   Fic

1. Terrorism -- Fiction 2. Immigrants -- Fiction 3. New Mexico -- Fiction 4. Prejudices -- Fiction 5. Ranch life -- Fiction 6. Family life -- Fiction

ISBN 978-0-06-123905-2; 0-06-123905-4

LC 2010-09393

In an America that has suffered continual terrorist attacks since 9/11, seventh-grader Sky stands up for what is right and helps a classmate of Middle Eastern descent, although doing so places her and her family at great risk.

"Readers will have much to discuss after finishing this beautifully written, disturbing book." Booklist

★ The **silver** bowl. Harper 2011 307p $16.99

Grades: 5 6 7 8   Fic

1. Fantasy fiction 2. Clairvoyance -- Fiction

ISBN 978-0-06-157543-3; 0-06-157543-7

"Molly is a young scullery maid in the castle of King Edmund, and like her mother before her, she sees visions and hears voices that offer glimpses of the future. But is this a blessing or a curse?. . . . The girl's choice of silence . . . is challenged when she learns that a rumored curse on the royal family is true and only by sharing her visions might they be saved. Combining carefully chosen details of setting with a richly realized fantasy premise, Stanley succeeds in creating a believable world large enough to accommodate not only menace and evil but also loyalty, enduring friendship, and love." Booklist

Starke, Ruth

Noodle pie. Kane Miller 2010 187p il $15.99

Grades: 4 5 6 7   Fic

1. Vietnam -- Fiction 2. Vietnamese -- Fiction

ISBN 978-1-935279-25-9; 1-935279-25-4

"Eleven-year-old Andy's first trip to Vietnam with his father, a 'Viet Kieu' (someone born in Vietnam who now lives overseas), exposes him to internalized prejudices about his heritage. . . . Andy distinguishes himself from his pushy relatives by emphasizing his Australian citizenship and criticizing customs that seem unfair. . . . This humorous, touching novel is a delicious cross-cultural treat, and includes an appendix of Vietnamese recipes." Publ Wkly

Starmer, Aaron

The **only** ones. Delacorte Press 2011 321p $17.99; lib bdg $20.99; e-book $17.99

Grades: 4 5 6 7   Fic

1. Supernatural -- Fiction

ISBN 978-0-385-74043-2; 0-385-74043-3; 978-0-385-90839-9 lib bdg; 0-385-90839-3 lib bdg; 978-0-375-89919-5 e-book

LC 2010040383

After setting off from the island where he has been leading a solitary existence, thirteen-year-old Martin discovers a village with other children who have been living similarly without any adults, since the grown-ups have all been spirited away.

"Both literary and engaging, this is the kind of book readers will want to return to for new discoveries." Kirkus

Stauffacher, Sue

★ **Gator** on the loose! illustrated by Priscilla Lamont. Alfred A Knopf 2010 149p il (Animal rescue team) $12.99; lib bdg $15.99

Grades: 4 5 6   Fic

1. Alligators -- Fiction 2. Family life -- Fiction 3. Racially mixed people -- Fiction

ISBN 978-0-375-85847-5; 0-375-85847-4; 978-0-375-95847-2 lib bdg; 0-375-95847-9 lib bdg

LC 2009018340

Chaos ensues when Keisha's father brings an escaped alligator home to Carter's Urban Rescue, but it gets out of the bathroom while Grandma is guarding it.

"Situational comedy, appealing spot art, and a personable protagonist will give this series broad appeal." Booklist

Other titles about Keisha and the Carter family are:

Hide and seek (2010)

Show time (2011)

Special delivery (2010)

★ **Harry** Sue. Knopf 2005 288p hardcover o.p. lib bdg $17.99; pa $6.50

Grades: 5 6 7 8   Fic

1. Prisoners -- Fiction 2. People with disabilities -- Fiction 3. Mother-daughter relationship -- Fiction

ISBN 0-375-83274-2; 0-375-93274-7 lib bdg; 0-440-42064-4 pa

LC 2004-16945

Although tough-talking Harry Sue would like to start a life of crime in order to be "sent up" and find her incarcerated mother, she must first protect the children at her neglectful grandmother's home day care center and befriend a paralyzed boy.

"This is a riveting story, dramatically and well told, with characters whom readers won't soon forget." SLJ

Stead, Rebecca

★ **Goodbye** stranger; Rebecca Stead. Wendy Lamb Books, an imprint of Random House Children's Books 2015 304 p. (trade) $16.99

Grades: 5 6 7 8 9   Fic

1. Friendship -- Fiction 2. Family life -- Fiction 3. Middle schools -- Fiction 4. New York (N.Y.) -- Fiction 5. Schools -- Fiction 6. Best friends -- Fiction

ISBN 0385743173; 9780307980861; 9780375990984; 9780385743174

LC 2014037289

Boston Globe Horn Book Fiction Honor Book (2016)

In this book, by Rebecca Stead, "Bridge is an accident survivor who's wondering why she's still alive. Emily has new curves and an almost-boyfriend who wants a certain kind of picture. Tabitha sees through everybody's games--or so she tells the world. The three girls are best friends with one rule: No fighting. Can it get them through seventh grade?" (Publisher's note)

"Ah, seventh grade! A year when your friends transform inexplicably, your own body and emotions perplex you, and the world seems fraught with questions, and the most confusing ones of all concern the nature of love. Stead focuses on Bridge Barsamian, her best girlfriends, and her newest friend Sherm—a boy who is definitely not her boyfriend (probably). . . . An immensely satisfying addition for Stead's many fans." SLJ

Liar & spy; by Rebecca Stead. Wendy Lamb Books 2012 180 p. (hardback) $15.99

Grades: 4 5 6 7 8   Fic

1. Spy stories 2. Boys -- Fiction 3. Neighbors -- Fiction 4. Friendship -- Fiction 5. Spies -- Fiction 6. Schools -- Fiction 7. Middle schools -- Fiction 8. Apartment houses -- Fiction 9. Brooklyn (New York, N.Y.) -- Fiction 10. Family life -- New York (State) -- New York -- Fiction

ISBN 0385737432; 9780375899539; 9780385737432; 9780385906654

LC 2011042674

In this book, protagonist "Georges has a lot going on. Dad was laid off so Mom has started working extra shifts at the hospital, and they had to sell their house in Brooklyn and move into an apartment. One good thing about the new building is Safer, an unusual boy who lives on the top floor. He's determined to teach Georges how to be a spy. Their main case: spy on the mysterious Mr. X in the apartment above Georges. As Georges and Safer go deeper into their Mr. X plan, the line between games, lies, and reality begin to blur." (Barnes and Noble)

★ **When** you reach me. Wendy Lamb Books 2009 199p $15.99; lib bdg $18.99

Grades: 5 6 7 8   Fic

1. Space and time -- Fiction 2. New York (N.Y.) -- Fiction

ISBN 0-385-73742-4; 0-385-90664-1 lib bdg; 978-0-385-73742-5; 978-0-385-90664-7 lib bdg

LC 2008-24998

Awarded the Newbery Medal, 2010

As her mother prepares to be a contestant on the 1980s television game show, The 20,000 Pyramid, a twelve-year-old New York City girl tries to make sense of a series of mysterious notes received from an anonymous source. "Ages nine to fourteen." (Publisher's note)

"The '70s New York setting is an honest reverberation of the era; the mental gymnastics required of readers are invigorating; and the characters . . . are honest bits of humanity." Booklist

Steele, William Owen

The **perilous** road; [by] William O. Steele; with an introduction by Jean Fritz. Harcourt 2004 156p $17; pa $5.95

Grades: 5 6 7 8   Fic

1. Tennessee -- Fiction 2. United States -- History -- 1861-1865, Civil War -- Fiction

ISBN 0-15-205203-8; 0-15-205204-6 pa

A reissue of the title first published 1958

A Newbery Medal honor book, 1959

Fourteen-year-old Chris, bitterly hating the Yankees for invading his Tennessee mountain home, learns a difficult lesson about the waste of war and the meaning of tolerance and courage when he reports the approach of a Yankee supply troop to the Confederates, only to learn that his brother is probably part of that troop.

"Mr. Steele makes the tensions and excitements of the Brother's War very real, and customs of the mountain people, the speech and setting are well integrated into the narrative." NY Times Book Rev

Steer, Dugald

The **dragon** diary; [by] Dugald A. Steer; illustrated by Douglas Carrel. Candlewick Press 2009 248p il (Dragonology chronicles) $16.99

Grades: 5 6 7 8   Fic

1. Fantasy fiction 2. Dragons -- Fiction 3. Siblings -- Fiction

ISBN 978-0-7636-3425-4; 0-7636-3425-5

LC 2009005795

Apprentice dragonologists Daniel and Beatrice Cook's mentor is called away at a crucial time, leaving the brother and sister alone to search for an ancient diary that could cure some gravely ill dragons

"This fast-paced fantasy features sibling rivalry, multitudes of dragons, and mid-air heroics." Horn Book Guide

Steig, William

★ **Abel's** island. Farrar, Straus & Giroux 1976 117p il $15; pa $5.99

Grades: 3 4 5   Fic

1. Mice -- Fiction 2. Survival after airplane accidents, shipwrecks, etc. -- Fiction

ISBN 0-374-30010-0; 0-312-37143-8 pa

A Newbery Medal honor book, 1977

Castaway on an uninhabited island, Abel, a very civilized mouse, finds his resourcefulness and endurance tested to the limit as he struggles to survive and return to his home.

"The line drawings washed with gray faithfully and delightfully record not only the rigors of Abel's experiences but the refinement of his domestic existence." Horn Book

Dominic; story and pictures by William Steig. Farrar, Straus & Giroux 1972 145p il hardcover o.p. pa $5.99

Grades: 3 4 5 **Fic**

1. Dogs -- Fiction

ISBN 0-312-37144-6 pa

Dominic, a gregarious dog, sets out on the high road one day, going no place in particular, but moving along to find whatever he can. And that turns out to be plenty, including an invalid pig who leaves Dominic his fortune; a variety of friends and adventures; and even—in the end—his life's companion

"A singular blend of naiveté and sophistication, comic commentary and philosophizing, the narrative handles situation clichés with humor and flair—perhaps because of the author's felicitous turn of phrase, his verbal cartooning, and his integration of text and illustrations. A chivalrous and optimistic tribute to gallantry and romance." Horn Book

★ The **real** thief; story and pictures by William Steig. Farrar, Straus & Giroux 1973 58p il hardcover o.p. pa $5.99

Grades: 3 4 5 **Fic**

1. Animals -- Fiction 2. Thieves -- Fiction

ISBN 0-312-37145-4 pa

"Steig's gray line-and-wash drawings provide a charming accompaniment to a wholly winning story." SLJ

Steinhofel, Andreas

An **elk** dropped in; [by] Andreas Steinhofel; pictures by Kerstin Meyer; translated by Alissa Jaffa. Front Street 2006 78p il $16.95

Grades: 2 3 4 **Fic**

1. Elk -- Fiction 2. Christmas -- Fiction 3. Santa Claus -- Fiction

ISBN 1-932425-80-2; 978-1-932425-80-2

LC 2006-00804

While on a pre-Christmas trial run for the famous man in red, an elk named Mr. Moose crashes through the roof of a house and, while recuperating from a sprain, regales Billy Wagner and his family with stories.

"Winsome watercolor illustrations, droll details, and a young narrator who relates both wild and everyday details in the same matter-of-fact tone combine to create a charming, if offbeat, Christmas fantasy." SLJ

Stephens, John

The **black** reckoning; John Stephens. Alfred A. Knopf 2015 432 p. (Books of beginning) (hardback) $17.99

Grades: 4 5 6 7 **Fic**

1. Magic -- Fiction 2. Identity -- Fiction 3. Monsters -- Fiction 4. Prophecies -- Fiction 5. Space and time -- Fiction 6. Brothers and sisters -- Fiction 7. Books and reading -- Fiction

ISBN 0375868720; 9780375868726; 9780375968723

LC 2014023538

In this novel, by John Stephens, part of the Books of Beginning series, "the adventures of siblings Kate, Michael, and Emma come to a stunning conclusion when they must find the last Book of Beginning--the Book of Death--before the Dire Magnus does, for when all three books are united, their combined power will be unstoppable." (Publisher's note)

"Heartbreaking sacrifices, joyous reunions, and poignant partings round out this rousing old-school fantasy adventure." Horn Book

Other titles in the trilogy are:

The Emerald Atlas (2011)

The Fire Chronicle (2012)

★ The **emerald** atlas. Alfred A. Knopf 2011 417p (The books of beginning) $17.99; lib bdg $20.99

Grades: 4 5 6 **Fic**

1. Magic -- Fiction 2. Monsters -- Fiction 3. Siblings -- Fiction 4. Prophecies -- Fiction 5. Space and time -- Fiction 6. Books and

reading -- Fiction

ISBN 978-0-375-86870-2; 0-375-86870-4; 978-0-375-96870-9 lib bdg; 0-375-96870-9 lib bdg

LC 2010029100

Kate, Michael, and Emma have passed from one orphanage to another in the ten years since their parents disappeared to protect them, but now they learn that they have special powers, a prophesied quest to find a magical book, and a fearsome enemy.

"This fast-paced, fully imagined fantasy is by turns frightening and funny, and the siblings are well-crafted and empathetic heroes. Highly enjoyable, it should find many readers." Publ Wkly

★ The **fire** chronicle; John Stephens. Alfred A. Knopf 2012 437 p. (hardback) $17.99

Grades: 4 5 6 **Fic**

1. Fantasy fiction 2. Adventure fiction 3. Time travel -- Fiction 4. Magic -- Fiction 5. Identity -- Fiction 6. Monsters -- Fiction 7. Prophecies -- Fiction 8. Space and time -- Fiction 9. Books and reading -- Fiction 10. Brothers and sisters -- Fiction

ISBN 0375868712; 9780375868719; 9780375899560; 9780375968716

LC 2012016139

In this novel by John Stephens, part of the Books of Beginning series, "Kate, Michael, and Emma long to continue the hunt for their missing parents. . . . A frantic chase sends Kate a hundred years into the past, to a perilous, enchanted New York City. . . . Meanwhile, Michael and Emma have set off to find the second of the Books of Beginning. A series of clues leads them into a hidden world where they must brave harsh polar storms, track down an ancient order of warriors, and confront terrible monsters." (Publisher's note)

Sternberg, Julie

Like pickle juice on a cookie; illustrations by Matthew Cordell. Amulet Books 2011 122p il $14.95

Grades: 3 4 5 **Fic**

1. Novels in verse 2. Babysitters -- Fiction 3. Loss (Psychology) -- Fiction

ISBN 0-8109-8424-5; 978-0-8109-8424-0

LC 2009-15975

When nine-year-old Eleanor's beloved babysitter Bibi moves away to take care of her ailing father, Eleanor must spend the summer adjusting to a new babysitter while mourning the loss of her old one. "Grades two to three." (Bull Cent Child Books)

"Eleanor's gradual warming to her new sitter is affectingly narrated, and Cordell's halftone cartoons convey the story's pathos and humor, as well as Eleanor's changeable moods." Publ Wkly

Secrets Out! by Julie Sternberg; illustrated by Johanna Wright. Boyds Mills Press 2015 176 p. illustrations $15.95

Grades: 3 4 5 6 **Fic**

1. Diaries -- Fiction 2. Secrets -- Fiction 3. Sisters -- Fiction 4. Grandmothers -- Fiction

ISBN 1620917777; 9781620917770

LC 2015904691

In this book, by Julie Sternberg, illustrated by Johanna Wright, "Celie's grandmother has moved in with her family, and Granny's forgetfulness is starting to worry Celie. In the meantime, she can tell her parents are keeping secrets, but she can't talk to her best friend Lula or her sister Jo, because they're both keeping secrets, too! . . . Celie turns to her diary as she tries to sort this all out, filling the pages with heartfelt and often humorous entries." (Publisher's note)

"Celie comes across with an authentic voice; Sternberg has created a three-dimensional, convincing character. Wright's illustrations provide a perfect highlight to the text. Not only will readers enjoy reading Celie's diary, they might be inspired to start one of their own." Booklist

The **top**-secret diary of Celie Valentine; friendship over. Julie Sternberg. Boyds Mills Press, an imprint of Highlights 2014 160 p. illustrations (The top-secret diary of Celie Valentine) $15.95
Grades: 3 4 5 6   **Fic**
1. Diaries -- Fiction 2. Sisters -- Fiction 3. Emotions -- Fiction 4. Friendship -- Fiction 5. Humorous stories
ISBN 1590789938; 9781590789933
LC 2014939248
In this book, by Julie Sternberg, "ten-year-old Celie's father gives her a journal and a punching bag for her birthday [and] tells her they'll help her work through her feelings. . . . Her best friend Lula isn't speaking to her, her sister Jo locks her out of their room to hang out with her new, cooler friend, and her Granny is suddenly behaving in the most perplexing manner. Good thing Celie's armed with a grape-flavored pen and a solid sense of humor." (Publisher's note)

"Ten-year-old Celie confides her worries about her ex-best friend, her maddening older sister, and her ailing grandmother in her journal. Humor and an accessible epistolary format lighten the story's heavy issues of bullying, age-related illness, and parental discord...This title has both wide appeal and substance and begins what will likely be a popular series."

Another book about Celia is:
Secrets out (2015)

Stevens, Robin
First class murder; Robin Stevens. Simon & Schuster Books for Young Readers 2017 320 p. (Wells & Wong mystery) (hardcover) $16.99
Grades: 4 5 6 7   **Fic**
1. Mystery fiction 2. Murder -- Fiction 3. Friendship -- Fiction 4. Railroad travel -- Fiction 5. Europe -- History -- 1918-1945 -- Fiction 6. Chinese -- Europe -- FIction 7. Mystery and detective stories 8. Orient Express (Express train) -- Fiction
ISBN 9781481422185; 9781481422192
LC 2015050408
In this book, by Robin Stevens, "Hazel Wong and Daisy Wells are taking a vacation across Europe on world-famous passenger train, the Orient Express—and it's clear that each of their fellow first-class travelers has something to hide. Even more intriguing: There's rumor of a spy in their midst. Then, during dinner, a bloodcurdling scream comes from inside one of the cabins. When the door is broken down, a passenger is found murdered—her stunning ruby necklace gone." (Publisher's note)

Murder is bad manners; Robin Stevens. Simon & Schuster Books for Young Readers 2015 320 p. (hardcover) $16.99
Grades: 4 5 6 7   **Fic**
1. School stories 2. Mystery fiction 3. Murder -- Fiction 4. Friendship -- Fiction 5. Boarding schools -- Fiction 6. Chinese -- England -- Fiction 7. Mystery and detective stories
ISBN 148142212X; 9781481422123; 9781481422130
LC 2014003939
"Daisy Wells and Hazel Wong are best friends at Deepdean School for Girls, and they both have a penchant for solving mysteries. . . . [T]hey form their own (secret!) detective agency. The only problem? They have nothing to investigate. But that changes once Hazel discovers the body of their science teacher, Miss Bell--and the body subsequently disappears." (Publisher's note)

"Here's a mystery import, set in the 1930s, that does justice to its British roots. Hazel Wong has come from Hong Kong to attend Deepdean boarding school. An outcast until she is accepted by upper-crust Daisy Wells, Hazel is happy to be half of a two-girl detective agency. . .

. Hazel makes a good narrator, and while the mystery plods a bit and has too many teachers--though a cast list helps--not every reader will guess the ending. Nancy Drew, meet Wells and Wong." Booklist

Poison is not polite; Robin Stevens. Simon & Schuster Books for Young Readers 2016 336 p. (A Wells & Wong mystery) (hardback) $16.99; (paperback) $7.99
Grades: 4 5 6 7   **Fic**
1. Parties -- Fiction 2. Mystery fiction 3. Murder -- Fiction 4. Friendship -- Fiction 5. Chinese -- England -- Fiction 6. Mystery and detective stories 7. Great Britain -- History -- George V, 1910-1936 -- Fiction
ISBN 1481422162; 9781481422154; 9781481422161
LC 2015015300
In this juvenile novel, by Robin Stevens, part of the "Wells & Wong Mystery" series, "schoolgirl detectives Daisy Wells and Hazel Wong are at Daisy's home . . . for the holidays. Daisy's glamorous mother is throwing a tea party for Daisy's birthday, and the whole family is invited. . . . But . . . when one of their guests falls seriously and mysteriously ill--and everything points to poison . . . , it's up to Daisy and Hazel to find out what's really going on." (Publisher's note)

"A first-rate whodunit, reminiscent of a game of Clue and terrific preparation for the works of Agatha Christie." Kirkus

Stevenson, Robert Louis, 1850-1894
Treasure Island; Robert Louis Stevenson; illustrated by John Lawrence. 1st U.S. ed. Candlewick Press 2009 269 p. col. ill. (reinforced) $24.99
Grades: 5 6 7 8 9 10 11 12 Adult   **Fic**
1. Adventure fiction 2. Pirates -- Fiction 3. Buried treasure -- Fiction
ISBN 0763644455; 9780763644451
LC 2009007338
First published in 1883.
While going through the possessions of a deceased guest who owed them money, the mistress of the inn and her son find a treasure map that leads them to a notorious pirate's fortune

"Lawrence evokes the essence of classic adventure stories with his vinyl-cut illustrations, as thick black shapes are tempered by muted tones of blue, gold and green. . . . Readers will feel they've discovered a true relic with this edition." Publ Wkly

Stevenson, Steve
The **curse** of the pharaoh; by Sir Steve Stevenson; illustrated by Stefano Turconi; translated by Siobhan Kelly; translation adapted by Maya Gold. Grosset & Dunlap, an imprint of Penguin Group (USA) Inc. 2013 144 p. (Agatha Mistery) (pbk : alk. paper) $5.99
Grades: 3 4 5   **Fic**
1. Mystery fiction -- Fiction 2. Adventure fiction -- Fiction 3. Eccentrics and eccentricities -- Fiction 4. Memory -- Fiction 5. Mystery and detective stories 6. Egypt -- Antiquities -- Fiction 7. Adventure and adventurers -- Fiction 8. Eccentrics and eccentricities -- Fiction
ISBN 0448462176; 9780448462172
LC 2012031484
This children's novel, by Steve Stevenson, illustrated by Stefano Turconi, is first in the "Agatha: Girl of Mystery" series. It features "a headstrong girl detective who jets off on exotic . . . adventures with the help of her hulking bodyguard and loyal cat named . . . Watson. . . . Rumors of a mysterious tablet unearthed in the Valley of the Kings may be just the clue that Agatha needs to unlock the secret curse of an ancient Pharaoh." (Publisher's note)

"A well-plotted mystery full of quirky details... and carefully constructed clues." Booklist

Stevermer, Caroline

Magic below stairs. Dial Books for Young Readers 2010 199p
$16.99

Grades: 4 5 6 7   **Fic**

1. Magic -- Fiction 2. Orphans -- Fiction 3. Household employees
-- Fiction 4. Great Britain -- History -- 19th century -- Fiction

ISBN 978-0-8037-3467-8; 0-8037-3467-0

LC 2009-25100

Ten-year-old Frederick, who is surreptitiously watched over by a
household elf, is plucked from a London orphanage to be a servant to a
wealthy wizard, and eventually his uncanny abilities lead him to become
the wizard's apprentice.

"A well-developed fictional world and the many concrete details of
belowstairs life make the magical events in this engaging chapter book
more believable." Booklist

Stewart, Paul

★ **Beyond** the Deepwoods; [by] Paul Stewart, Chris Riddell. David Fickling Bks. 2004 276p il (Edge chronicles) $12.95; lib bdg
$14.99; pa $6.99

Grades: 4 5 6   **Fic**

1. Fantasy fiction

ISBN 0-385-75068-4; 0-385-75069-2 lib bdg; 0-440-42087-3 pa

First published 1998 in the United Kingdom

Thirteen-year-old Twig, having always looked and felt different
from his woodtroll family, learns that he is adopted and travels out of his
Deepwoods home to find the place where he belongs

"Those with hearty appetites for adventure (and strong stomachs)
will find this a tremendously exciting fantasy. Riddell's wonderfully detailed ink drawings, on nearly every page, create a strong sense of the
believable, well-imagined otherworld and bring its strange creatures to
life." Booklist

Other titles in The Edge Chronicles series are:

Stormchaser (2004)

Midnight over Sanctaphrax (2004)

The curse of the Gloamglozer (2005)

The last of the sky pirates (2005)

Vox (2005)

Freeglader (2006)

The winter knights (2007)

Clash of the sky galleons (2007)

Immortals (2010)

The **curse** of the night wolf; [by] Paul Stewart and Chris Riddell; illustrated by Chris Riddell. David Fickling Books 2008 204p il
(Barnaby Grimes) $15.99; lib bdg $18.99

Grades: 4 5 6 7   **Fic**

1. Mystery fiction 2. Physicians -- Fiction 3. Werewolves --
Fiction 4. London (England) -- Fiction 5. Great Britain -- History
-- 19th century -- Fiction

ISBN 978-0-385-75125-4; 0-385-75125-7; 978-0-385-75126-1
lib bdg; 0-385-75126-5 lib bdg

LC 2008-01697

Soon after Victorian messenger Barnaby Grimes is attacked by a
huge beast while crossing London's rooftops, he becomes entangled in
a mystery involving patent medicine, impoverished patients, and very
expensive furs.

"Moody, highly detailed pen-and-ink drawings provide ornamentation throughout, lending a classic Victorian feel to help punctuate the
drama. . . . Possessing an easy confidence and quick wit . . . Barnaby is
an appealing character." Booklist

Other titles in this series are:

Return of the emerald skull (2009)

Legion of the Dead (2010)

★ **Fergus** Crane; [by] Paul Stewart & Chris Riddell. David Fickling Books 2006 214p (Far-flung adventures) $14.95

Grades: 3 4 5   **Fic**

1. Adventure fiction

ISBN 0-385-75088-9

LC 2005018478

Nine-year-old Fergus Crane's life is filled with classes on the school
ship Betty Jeanne, interesting neighbors, and helping with his mother's work until a mysterious box flies into his window and leads him
toward adventure

"With a simple plot, a few hints of mystery, and many intriguing details, this story will quickly hook readers. Riddell's expressive ink drawings make the fantastic elements more believable and add enormously to
the book's appeal." Booklist

Other titles in this series are:

Corby Flood (2006)

Hugo Pepper (2007)

Phantom of Blood Alley; [by] Paul Stewart & Chris Riddell; illustrated by Chris Riddell. David Fickling Books 2010 201p il (Barnaby
Grimes) $16.99

Grades: 4 5 6 7   **Fic**

1. Mystery fiction 2. Photography -- Fiction 3. Supernatural --
Fiction 4. Great Britain -- History -- 19th century -- Fiction

ISBN 978-0-385-75134-6; 0-385-75134-6

First published 2009 in the United Kingdom

Barnaby finds himself in the fiercely competitive world of early photography, where the rewards are immense but so are the risks. After an
experiment goes disastrously wrong, Barnaby is on the trail of a mad
chemist with a talent for disappearing into thin air.

Stewart, Trenton Lee

The **extraordinary** education of Nicholas Benedict; by Trenton
Lee Stewart; illustrated by Diana Sudyka. Little, Brown 2012 470 p.
$17.99

Grades: 4 5 6 7 8   **Fic**

1. Bullies -- Fiction 2. Orphans -- Fiction 3. Friendship -- Fiction
4. Narcolepsy -- Fiction 5. Orphanages -- Fiction 6. Genius
-- Fiction 7. Mystery and detective stories 8. Adventure and
adventurers -- Fiction

ISBN 9780316176194

LC 2011031690

This book tells the story of Nicholas Benedict who "is just 9 years. .
. . Small in physical stature but intellectually gifted, he has an 'unfortunate' nose . . . and a medical condition that prompts 'unpredictable sleeping episodes' that drop 'him from consciousness like a trapdoor into a
black dungeon' at the least opportune of times. . . . What has long made
him a nuisance to less intelligent adults and target practice for bullies
also makes him a curiosity for a slightly older boy who befriends him at
his new home -- the ominously named Rothschild's End. The orphanage
is housed in a two-story mansion. . . . [The book] revolves around . . . the
. . . themes . . . [of] orphans, friendship and the sorts of surrogate families
that form as a result." (LA Times)

★ The **mysterious** Benedict Society; illustrated by Carson Ellis.
Little, Brown 2007 485p il $16.99; pa $6.99

Grades: 5 6 7 8   **Fic**

1. Science fiction 2. Adventure fiction

ISBN 978-0-316-05777-6; 0-316-05777-0; 978-0-316-00395-7
pa; 0-316-00395-6 pa

LC 2006-09925

After passing a series of mind-bending tests, four children are selected for a secret mission that requires them to go undercover at the Learning Institute for the Very Enlightened, where the only rule is that there are no rules

"Stewart's unusual characters, threatening villains, and dramatic plot twists will grab and hold readers' attention." SLJ

Other titles about the Benedict Society are:
The mysterious Benedict Society and the perilous journey (2008)
The mysterious Benedict Society and the prisoner's dilemma (2009)

The **secret** keepers; Trenton Lee Stewart; illustrated by Diana Sudyka. Little, Brown & Co. 2016 512 p. illustrations (ebook) $57; (hardcover) $18.99

Grades: Adult   **Fic**
1. Magic -- Fiction 2. Adventure fiction 3. Secrets -- Fiction 4. Invisibility -- Fiction 5. Clocks and watches -- Fiction 6. Adventure and adventurers -- Fiction
ISBN 9780316319126; 9780316389556

LC 2016006406

In this book, by Trenton Lee Stewart, illustrated by Diana Sudyka, "when Reuben discovers an extraordinary antique watch, he soon learns it has a secret power and his life takes an intriguing turn. At first he is thrilled with his new treasure, but as one secret leads to another, Reuben finds himself torn between his innately honest nature and the lure to be a hero. Now he is on a dangerous adventure . . . as he races to solve the mystery before it is too late." (Publisher's note)

"This epic story filled with adventure and twists and turns is certain to keep readers' interest from beginning to end." SLJ

Stiefvater, Maggie

Hunted; Maggie Stiefvater. Scholastic Inc. 2014 192 p. map (Spirit animals) (paper-over-board) $12.99

Grades: 4 5 6 7   **Fic**
1. Fantasy fiction 2. Wolves -- Fiction 3. Human-animal relationship -- Fiction
ISBN 0545522447; 9780545522441; 9780545522564; 9780545599726

LC 2013947126

This fantasy novel by Maggie Stiefvater, part of the Spirit Animals series, describes how its "four young heroes have barely had time to come together as a team, their own spirit animal bonds are still greatly untested. But now they face a brutal confrontation against an enemy who will break any rule to defeat them." (Publisher's note)

"Stiefvater blends Mull's brilliant world building with her talent of writing memorable villains." Booklist

Stier, Catherine

The **terrible** secrets of the Tell-All Club. Albert Whitman & Co. 2009 125p $14.99

Grades: 4 5 6   **Fic**
1. School stories 2. Clubs -- Fiction 3. Friendship -- Fiction
ISBN 978-0-8075-7798-1; 0-8075-7798-7

LC 2008055704

When four fifth-grade friends complete a "tell-all" survey, tensions arise and come to a head during an overnight class trip

"Told in the four voices of the club members, the story shows the characters' insecurities and the family issues they face. Reluctant readers will find it fast paced, easy to follow, and populated with likable personalities." SLJ

Stine, R. L., 1943-

★ **It's** the first day of school--forever! Feiwel and Friends 2011 183p $15.99

Grades: 3 4 5   **Fic**
1. Horror fiction 2. School stories 3. Monsters -- Fiction
ISBN 978-0-312-64954-8; 0-312-64954-1

LC 2010050896

Everything goes wrong for eleven-year-old Artie on his first day at Ardmore Middle School, from the moment his alarm goes off until the next morning, when everything is repeated exactly the same way.

"Stine delivers the hilarity and horror that readers love, and his mastery of sustaining mood will not disappoint." SLJ

St.John, Amanda, 1982-

Bridget and Bo build a blog; by Amanda St John; illustrated by Katie McDee. Norwood House Press 2012 32 p.

Grades: K 1 2 3   **Fic**
1. Weblogs -- Fiction 2. Internet and children 3. Child authors -- Fiction 4. Online authorship 5. Language arts (Elementary)
ISBN 1599535076; 9781599535074

LC 2011039361

This children's book presents "introductions to a number of tasks young writers will eventually tackle. . . . This volume introduces nine-year-old Bo, whose recent experience blogging from a family stay in England gives him the expertise to show his friend, Bridget, how it's done. . . . Bridget's concerns are understandable: "Well, does my blog have to be as long as yours?" Bo's answers are a little my-way-or-the-highway, but nonetheless bring up good things to consider: a design template, the intended audience, and using correct terminology such as posting. They read other blogs for inspiration, which is where they learn never to gossip or use full names or personal info. The wisecracks never intrude upon the learning, and the advice can easily extend to other kinds of writing." (Booklist)

Includes bibliographical references (p. 32)

Stockton, Frank

The **bee-man** of Orn; [by] Frank R. Stockton; illustrated by P.J. Lynch. Candlewick Press 2003 un il $17.99

Grades: 2 3 4   **Fic**
1. Fairy tales
ISBN 0-7636-2239-7

LC 2003-48454

Story first published in St. Nicholas magazine 1883

When a Sorcerer tells him that he has been transformed from another sort of being, the Beeman sets out to discover what he was in his earlier incarnation. Story is accompanied by a DVD which provides a behind-the-scenes look at the illustrator at work.

"Lynch's spirited artwork, richly detailed and darkly atmospheric, provides a series of imaginative settings and creates a romantic and broadly appealing vision of this original fairy tale. . . . This edition is a read-aloud treasure for good listeners." Booklist

Stone, Phoebe

The **boy** on Cinnamon Street; by Phoebe Stone. Arthur A. Levine Books 2012 234 p. (alk. paper) $16.99

Grades: 3 4 5 6 7 8   **Fic**
1. Girls -- Psychology 2. Friendship -- Fiction 3. Grandparent-grandchild relationship 4. Memory -- Fiction 5. Schools -- Fiction 6. Best friends -- Fiction 7. Grandparents -- Fiction 8. Massachusetts -- Fiction
ISBN 0545215129; 9780545215121

LC 2011017862

This book tells the story of "seventh-grader [Louise who] lives with her grandparents in their condo and she's quit [gymnastics], . . . instead spending her time with friends Reni and her brother Henderson Elliot, whose warm and embracing family she adores. When a cute ninth-grader turns up on her doorstep delivering pizza, and she then finds a note under the mat confessing interest in Louise, she's transported into her first serious crush." (Bulletin of the Center for Children's Books)

Deep down popular; a novel. by Phoebe Stone. Arthur A. Levine Books 2008 280p $16.99; pa $4.99

Grades: 4 5 6 7 **Fic**
1. School stories 2. Virginia -- Fiction 3. Friendship -- Fiction 4. Family life -- Fiction 5. Country life -- Fiction
ISBN 978-0-439-80245-1; 0-439-80245-8; 978-0-439-80244-4 pa; 0-439-80244-X pa

LC 2007017198

In a small Virginia town, sixth-grader Jessie Lou Ferguson has a crush on the hugely popular Conrad Parker Smith, and when he suddenly develops a medical problem and the teacher asks Jessie Lou to help him, they become friends, to her surprise

"Jessie Lou tells her tale with the strong, rough-edged purity of a young poet, which she is; equally strong are the story's underpinnings, longing and laughter, and a willingness to believe in something despite the facts." Booklist

★ The **Romeo** and Juliet code. Arthur A. Levine Books 2011 300p $16.99

Grades: 4 5 6 7 **Fic**
1. Maine -- Fiction 2. Ciphers -- Fiction 3. Family life -- Fiction 4. World War, 1939-1945 -- United States -- Fiction 5. World War, 1939-1945 -- Evacuation of civilians -- Fiction
ISBN 978-0-545-21511-4; 0-545-21511-0

LC 2010-30005

During World War II, eleven-year-old Felicity is sent from London to Bottlebay, Maine, to live with her grandmother, aunt, uncle, and a reclusive boy who helps her decode mysterious letters that contain the truth about her missing parents.

Felicity "is endearingly portrayed, and the back story, so gradually revealed, provides a peek into the depths of the souls of some of the adults. The pacing is deliberately slow, yet Felicity's growing awareness of how she can help heal the troubled adults makes this an eminently satisfying read." Kirkus

Romeo blue; by Phoebe Stone. 1st ed. Arthur A. Levine Books 2013 352 p. (hardcover) $16.99

Grades: 4 5 6 7 **Fic**
1. Espionage -- Fiction 2. World War, 1939-1945 -- Children -- Fiction 3. World War, 1939-1945 -- Evacuation of civilians -- Fiction 4. Identity -- Fiction 5. Foster children -- Fiction 6. Families -- Fiction 7. Family life -- Maine -- Fiction 8. World War, 1939-1945 -- Maine -- Fiction 9. Maine -- History -- 20th century -- Fiction 10. Foster children -- Maine -- Fiction 11. World War, 1939-1945 -- Maine -- Fiction
ISBN 0545443601; 9780545443609

LC 2012038060

Parents' Choice: Silver Medal Fiction (2013)

"In this sequel to the WWII historical mystery 'The Romeo and Juliet Code,' . . . twelve-year old . . . Flissy now knows her Uncle Gideon is actually her biological father. . . . And she knows her whole family are some kind of spies, but she does not know . . . if they are still alive. And she has no idea why the creepy neighbor, Mr. Fitzwilliam, has invited her and adopted cousin Derek for tea, how he seems to know about her parents' secret activities." (Children's Literature)

Stout, Shawn K.

Fiona Finkelstein meets her match!! illustrated by Angela Martini. Aladdin 2010 146p il $14.99; pa $4.99

Grades: 2 3 4 **Fic**
1. School stories 2. Clubs -- Fiction 3. Maryland -- Fiction 4.

Family life -- Fiction
ISBN 978-1-4169-7928-9; 1-4169-7928-X; 978-1-4169-7110-8 pa; 1-4169-7110-6 pa

LC 201002682

Fiona Finkelstein does not get along with Milo, a new student in her Ordinary, Maryland, fourth-grade class, and when he starts a meteorology club she responds by trying to start a matchmaking club.

"Stout continues to develop her protagonist in this entertaining installment." Horn Book Guide

Fiona Finkelstein, big-time ballerina! illustrated by Angela Martini. Aladdin 2009 166p il $14.99; pa $4.99

Grades: 2 3 4 **Fic**
1. Worry -- Fiction 2. Ballet -- Fiction 3. Maryland -- Fiction 4. Family life -- Fiction 5. Weather forecasting -- Fiction
ISBN 978-1-4169-7927-2; 1-4169-7927-1; 978-1-4169-7109-2 pa; 1-4169-7109-2 pa

LC 200902259

Nine-year-old Marylander Fiona Finkelstein tries to deal with stage fright, missing her mother who is an actress in California, and hoping that her father, a television meteorologist, does not get in trouble when she antagonizes the anchorman.

"This novel is light and fun, with just enough wit and sass to keep young readers entertained. . . . The story maintains a fast pace throughout, and the illustrations give Fiona and company a sweet look that is simple and charming." SLJ

Another title about Fiona Finkelstein is:
Fiona Finkelstein meets her match (2010)

Streatfeild, Noel

Ballet shoes. Yearling 1999 281p il pbk 6.99

Grades: 2 3 4 5 **Fic**
1. Ballet -- Fiction 2. Orphans -- Fiction 3. Sisters -- Fiction 4. Acting -- Fiction 5. Ballet dancing -- Fiction
ISBN 9780679847595

"In the tradition of Frances Hodgson Burnett's The Little Princess come Noel Streatfeild's tales of triumph. In this story, three orphan girl vow to make a name for themselves and find their own special talents. With hard work, fame just may be in the stars! Originally published in 1937." (Publisher's Note)

Companion titles include:
Circus Shoes (2015)
Theater Shoes (1994)
White Boots (2014)

Strickland, Brad

The **sign** of the sinister sorcerer; [by] Brad Strickland. Dial Books for Young Readers 2008 168p $16.99

Grades: 4 5 6 7 **Fic**
1. Mystery fiction 2. Magic -- Fiction 3. Uncles -- Fiction 4. Orphans -- Fiction 5. Witches -- Fiction 6. Michigan -- Fiction 7. Supernatural -- Fiction
ISBN 978-0-8037-3151-6; 0-8037-3151-5

LC 200800769

In Michigan in the mid-1950s, Lewis Barnavelt is convinced that the series of accidents he and his uncle are experiencing are the result of a curse by a mysterious, hooded figure that may be part of his uncle's past

"For readers who enjoy trying to solve the mystery as they read there are abundant clues including an anagram. A quick, exciting read." SLJ

Other titles about Lewis Barnavelt by Brad Strickland are:
The beast under the wizard's bridge (2000)
The house where nobody lived (2006)
The spector from the magician's museum (1998)

The tower at the end of the world (2001)

The whistle, the grave, and the ghost (2003)

Stringer, Helen

★ **Spellbinder**. Feiwel and Friends 2009 372p $17.99

Grades: 5 6 7 8   **Fic**

1. Ghost stories 2. Dead -- Fiction 3. Great Britain -- Fiction

ISBN 978-0-312-38763-1; 0-312-38763-6

LC 2008-28552

Twelve-year-old Belladonna Johnson, who lives with the ghosts of her parents in the north of England, teams up with an always-in-trouble classmate to investigate why all of the ghosts in the world have suddenly disappeared.

"Magical creatures, amulets, and verses are all a part of this delightful tale. . . . Stringer maintains the humor and logic of preteens who are awkwardly coming into their magical destinies." SLJ

Followed by: The midnight gate (2011)

Stroud, Jonathan, 1970-

The **creeping** shadow; Jonathan Stroud; illustrations by Kate Adams. Disney-Hyperion 2016 445 p. illustrations (Lockwood & Co.) (hardback) $16.99

Grades: 4 5 6 7   **Fic**

1. Ghost stories 2. Paranormal fiction -- Fiction 3. Ghosts -- Fiction 4. England -- Fiction 5. Supernatural -- Fiction

ISBN 9781484709672

LC 2016014383

In this book in the Lockwood & Co. series, by Jonathan Stroud, Lucy has become "a freelance operative. . . . One day she is pleasantly surprised by a visit from Lockwood, who tells her . . . [that] Penelope Fittes, the leader of the giant Fittes Agency, wants them--and only them--to locate and remove the Source for the legendary Brixton Cannibal. They succeed in their very dangerous task, but tensions remain high between Lucy and the other agents." (Publisher's note)

"Stroud's scene setting and storytelling are second to none, but it's his ability to create credible, idiosyncratic characters and relationships that makes avid fans of the Lockwood & Co. series." Booklist

The **hollow** boy; Jonathan Stroud. Disney-Hyperion 2015 385 p. (Lockwood & Co.) (hardback) $16.99

Grades: 4 5 6 7   **Fic**

1. Paranormal fiction 2. Ghost stories -- Fiction 3. Mystery fiction -- Fiction 4. Ghosts -- Fiction 5. England -- Fiction 6. Supernatural -- Fiction 7. London (England) -- Fiction 8. Mystery and detective stories

ISBN 9781484709689

LC 2015015076

In this juvenile novel, by Jonathan Stroud, part of the "Lockwood & Co." series, "as a massive outbreak of supernatural Visitors baffles Scotland Yard and causes protests throughout London, Lockwood & Co. continue to demonstrate their effectiveness in exterminating spirits. Anthony Lockwood is dashing, George insightful, and Lucy dynamic, while the skull in the jar utters sardonic advice from the sidelines." (Publisher's note)

"As always, the descriptions of the hauntings are genuinely frightening, especially that of a spindly, humanoid creature that crawls on all fours and whispers Lucy's name." SLJ

★ The **screaming** staircase; by Jonathan Stroud. Disney-Hyperion 2013 400 p. (Lockwood & Co.) hbk $16.99

Grades: 4 5 6 7   **Fic**

1. Adventure fiction 2. Ghosts -- Fiction 3. England -- Fiction 4. Supernatural -- Fiction 5. Haunted houses -- Fiction 6. Psychic ability -- Fiction 7. London (England) -- Fiction

ISBN 1423164911; 9781423164913

LC 2013000352

This is the first book in Jonathan Stroud's Lockwood & Co. series. Lucy Carlyle has joined the Lockwood & Co. firm to help with England's ghost problem. "As its third member, she teams with glib, ambitious Anthony Lockwood and slovenly-but-capable scholar George Cubbins to entrap malign spirits for hire. The work is fraught with peril, not only because a ghost's merest touch is generally fatal, but also, as it turns out, as none of the three is particularly good at careful planning." (Kirkus Reviews)

The **whispering** skull; by Jonathan Stroud. Disney-Hyperion 2014 448 p. illustrations (Lockwood & Co.) (hardback) $17.99

Grades: 4 5 6 7   **Fic**

1. Mystery fiction 2. Paranormal fiction 3. Ghosts -- Fiction 4. England -- Fiction 5. Supernatural -- Fiction 6. Psychic ability -- Fiction 7. London (England) -- Fiction 8. Mystery and detective stories

ISBN 142316492X; 9781423164920

LC 2014014683

This novel, by Jonathan Stroud, is book 2 in the "Lockwood & Co." supernatural mystery series. "In the six months since Anthony, Lucy, and George survived a night in the most haunted house in England, Lockwood & Co. hasn't made much progress. . . . A new client, Mr. Saunders, hires Lockwood & Co. to be present at the excavation of Edmund Bickerstaff. . . . Saunders needs the coffin sealed with silver to prevent any supernatural trouble. All goes well-until George's curiosity attracts a horrible phantom." (Publisher's note)

Stuchner, Joan Betty

Honey cake; illustrated by Cynthia Nugent. Random House 2008 101p il $11.99; lib bdg $14.99; pa $4.99

Grades: 3 4 5   **Fic**

1. Jews -- Fiction 2. Denmark -- Fiction 3. Holocaust, 1933-1945 -- Fiction

ISBN 978-0-375-85189-6; 0-375-85189-5; 978-0-375-95189-3 lib bdg; 0-375-95189-X lib bdg; 978-0-375-85190-2 pa; 0-375-85190-9 pa

LC 2007-11501

First published 2007 in the United Kingdom and Canada

David and his family live in Denmark during the Nazi occupation, until September 1943 when their neighbors help smuggle them to Sweden to escape Hitler's orders to send the Danish Jews to concentration camps. Includes a recipe for honey cake, typically made to celebrate the Jewish New Year.

"The simply told story and black-and-white illustrations convey tension, fear, and hope." Horn Book Guide

Sullivan, Laura L.

Under the green hill. Henry Holt and Company 2010 308p $16.99

Grades: 5 6 7 8   **Fic**

1. Fantasy fiction 2. Fairies -- Fiction 3. Siblings -- Fiction 4. Supernatural -- Fiction

ISBN 978-0-8050-8984-4; 0-8050-8984-5

LC 2009-50772

While staying with distant relatives in England, Americans Rowan, Meg, Silly, and James Morgan, with their neighbors Dickie Rhys and Finn Fachan, learn that one of them must fight to the death in the Midsummer War required by the local fairies

"Sullivan draws heavily on her knowledge of Middle English folklore and creates a story rich with memorable characters and evocative language." SLJ

Followed by: Guardian of the green hill (2011)

Summers, Susan

The **greatest** gift; the story of the other Wise Man. retold by Susan Summers; illustrated by Jackie Morris. Barefoot Books 2011 il $16.99

Grades: K 1 2 3   **Fic**

1. Magi -- Fiction 2. Christmas stories 3. Middle East -- Fiction 4. Voyages and travels -- Fiction

ISBN 978-1-84686-578-7; 1-84686-578-6

LC 2011015507

Artaban, a fourth Wise Man, delays journeying with the other Magi to see the newborn Jesus, but after thirty-three years of helping others he has an unusual opportunity to meet his Savior.

"This intriguing story unfolds in flowing prose with the feeling of a folktale, conveying a subtle message in Artaban's kindness toward the needy of any religion. Morris provides handsome watercolor illustrations in a smoky palette of earth tones, with a soft focus that complements the ancient setting." Kirkus

Sutton, Kelsey

The **lonely** ones; Kelsey Sutton. Philomel Books 2016 227 p. (hardback) $16.99

Grades: 6 7 8 9   **Fic**

1. Novels in verse 2. Loneliness -- Fiction 3. Imagination -- Fiction 4. Interpersonal relations -- Fiction 5. Family problems -- Fiction

ISBN 0399172890; 9780399172892

LC 2015029562

In this book, by Kelsey Sutton, "Fain spends most of her time in a world of her own making. During the day, Fain takes solace in crafting her own fantastical adventures in writing, but in the darkness of night, these adventures come to life as Fain lives and breathes alongside a legion of imaginary creatures. Whether floating through space or under the sea, climbing mountains or traipsing through forests, Fain becomes queen beyond--and in spite of--the walls of her bedroom." (Publisher's note)

"There is no excess here. There are no distractions. Fain's story is simply a brilliantly crafted coming-of-age novel that will appeal to the hearts and minds of all readers who have ever felt alone." Kirkus

Svingen, Arne

The **Ballad** of a Broken Nose; by Arne Svingen, translated by Kari Dickson. Simon & Schuster 2016 224 p. $16.99

Grades: 5 6 7   **Fic**

1. Opera -- Fiction 2. Bullies -- Fiction 3. Friendship -- Fiction

ISBN 1481415425; 9781481415422

Batchelder Honor Book (2017)

In this book, by Arne Svingen, translated by Kari Dickson, "Bart is an eternal optimist. At thirteen years old, he's had a hard life. But Bart knows that things won't get any better if you have a negative attitude. His mother has pushed him into boxing lessons so that Bart can protect himself, but Bart already has defense mechanisms: he is relentlessly positive and he loves opera." (Publisher's note)

"An absorbing, well-paced story with a heartening conclusion." Booklist

Swinburne, Stephen R.

Wiff and Dirty George: the Z.E.B.R.A. Incident. Boyds Mills Press 2010 167p il $17.95

Grades: 4 5 6 7   **Fic**

1. Nineteen sixties -- Fiction 2. Great Britain -- Fiction

ISBN 978-1-59078-755-7; 1-59078-755-2

Witt and Dirty George give chase to the notorious Basil King, a criminal genius who is best on taking over Great Britain. "Grades four to seven." (Bull Cent Child Books)

"London in 1969 was a trippy place, no doubt, but it's made even more psychodelic with the adventures of Wiff and Dirty George, two twelve-year-olds who follow their noses into a world of trouble. While on a morning train, the boys are slightly horrified when everyone's pants fall down, but instead of worrying overmuch about their own embarrassment, they take off after the large white rabbit who seems to be the instigator of the mass humiliation. . . . The humor is more situational than verbal; the characters are all comedic straight men in a twisted, absurd world. . . . Delightfully daft 'clues' precede each chapter, and a glossary of Britishisms will help young Yanks navigate the dialect." Bull Cent Child Books

Taback, Simms

Postcards from camp. Nancy Paulsen Books 2011 un il $17.99

Grades: 1 2 3   **Fic**

1. Camps -- Fiction 2. Letters -- Fiction

ISBN 978-0-399-23973-1; 0-399-23973-1

"Taback's signature illustrative style is perfect for this brief tale. Michael's scrawl and his father's cursive share space with collaged stamps and photographs as well as illustrations that suit the correspondents ages." Kirkus

Tacang, Brian

Bully-be-gone; [by] Brian Tacang. HarperCollins 2006 216p (Misadventures of Millicent Madding) $15.99

Grades: 3 4 5 6   **Fic**

1. Bullies -- Fiction 2. Friendship -- Fiction 3. Inventions -- Fiction

ISBN 0-06-073911-8

LC 2005-07777

Budding-inventor Millicent Madding launches her latest invention to disastrous results, and she has only days to create an antidote before the local bullies wreak havoc and her dearest friendships are destroyed forever

"The book has zippy dialogue and brilliant use of alliteration. . . The eccentric characters are fun, and the silly but substantive plot will surely appeal to children." SLJ

Tak, Bibi Dumon

Soldier bear; written by Bibi Dumon Tak; illustrated by Philip Hopman; translated by Laura Watkinson. Eerdmans Books for Young Readers 2011 145p il $13

Grades: 4 5 6 7   **Fic**

1. Iran -- Fiction 2. Bears -- Fiction 3. Italy -- Fiction 4. Poland -- Fiction 5. Soldiers -- Fiction 6. World War, 1939-1945 -- Fiction

ISBN 978-0-8028-5375-2; 0-8028-5375-7

LC 2011013963

An orphaned Syrian brown bear cub is adopted by Polish soldiers during World War II and serves for five years as their mischievous mascot in Iran and Italy. Based on a true story.

"This is smoothly translated and engagingly illustrated with sketches and helpful maps. Funny, fresh and heartwarming." Kirkus

Tanner, Lian

Ice Breaker; Lian Tanner. Feiwel & Friends 2015 304 p. $16.99

Grades: 5 6 7 8   **Fic**

1. Secrets -- Fiction 2. Ocean travel -- Fiction 3. Tribes -- Fiction 4. Ships -- Fiction 5. Outcasts -- Fiction

ISBN 1250052165; 9781250052162

In Lian Tanner's novel "Petrel is an outcast on the ancient ship . . . that has been following the same course for 300 years. In that time, the ship's crew has . . . broken into three warring tribes. A mysterious boy is discovered barely alive on an iceberg, and brought onto the ship. The tribes don't trust strangers, so Petrel hides the boy. What she doesn't know is that the ship guards a secret - a secret the boy has been sent to destroy." (Publisher's note)

"Tanner (the Keepers trilogy) offers an unusual take on the post-apocalyptic genre with this chilly tale of life board a massive ship that has been traversing the frozen seas for three centuries, ever since the Anti-Machinist movement caused the collapse of society..... These interior journeys are just one part of a fast-paced adventure featuring talking rats, a rusting mazelike setting, and growing tension, which leaves things wide open for the next installment of the Hidden trilogy." PW

Museum of thieves. Delacorte Press 2010 312p (The Keepers Trilogy) $16.99; lib bdg $19.99

Grades: 5 6 7 8   **Fic**

1. Fantasy fiction 2. Adventure fiction 3. Museums -- Fiction 4. Thieves -- Fiction

ISBN 978-0-385-73905-4; 0-385-73905-2; 978-0-385-90768-2 lib bdg; 0-385-90768-0 lib bdg

LC 2009053655

Goldie, an impulsive and bold twelve-year-old, escapes the oppressive city of Jewel, where children are required to wear guardchains for their protection, and finds refuge in the extraordinary Museum of Dunt, an ever-shifting world where she discovers a useful talent for thievery and mysterious secrets that threaten her city and everyone she loves.

"Readers will be quickly caught up in the highly dramatic chases, the intriguing museum that shifts layout at will, and the nifty otherworld elements. There's depth beneath that, though. . . . [The book] may set young readers thinking about their own world's choices." Bull Cent Child Books

Followed by: City of lies (2011)

Tanquary, Kathryn

The **night** parade; Kathryn Tanquary. Sourcebooks Jabberwocky 2016 332 p. (alk. paper) $16.99

Grades: 5 6 7 8   **Fic**

1. Japan -- Fiction 2. Curses -- Fiction 3. Grandmothers -- Fiction 4. Supernatural -- Fiction 5. Blessing and cursing -- Fiction

ISBN 1492623245; 9781492623243

LC 2015022869

In this book, by Kathryn Tanquary, "The last thing Saki Yamamoto wants to do for her summer vacation is trade in exciting Tokyo for the antiquated rituals . . . of her grandmother's village. Preparing for the Obon ceremony is boring. Then the local kids [dare] Saki [to disrespect] her family's ancestral shrine. . . . But as Saki rings the sacred bell, the darkness shifts. A death curse has been invoked...and Saki has three nights to undo it." (Publisher's note)

"Vivid details and realistic situations ensure accessibility, and subtle teaching moments are wrapped in wide-eyed enchantment." Pub Wkly

Tarshis, Lauren

★ **Emma**-Jean Lazarus fell out of a tree. Dial Books for Young Readers 2007 199p $16.99

Grades: 5 6 7   **Fic**

1. School stories 2. Friendship -- Fiction

ISBN 978-0-8037-3164-6; 0-8037-3164-7

LC 2006-18428

A quirky and utterly logical seventh-grade girl named Emma-Jean Lazarus discovers some interesting results when she gets involved in the messy everyday problems of her peers.

"Readers will be fascinated by Emma-Jean's emotionless observations and her adult-level vocabulary. Tarshis pulls off a balancing act, showing the child's detachment yet making her a sympathetic character. Exceptionally fleshed-out secondary characters add warmth to the story." SLJ

Followed by: Emma-Jean Lazarus fell in love (2009)

I survived the Battle of Gettysburg, 1863; Lauren Tarshis. Scholastic 2013 89 p. (paperback) $4.99

Grades: 3 4 5 6   **Fic**

1. Fugitive slaves -- Fiction 2. Gettysburg (Pa.), Battle of, 1863 -- Fiction

ISBN 0545459362; 9780545459365

This children's book, by Lauren Tarshis, is book 7 in the "I Survived" series. "It's 1863, and Thomas and his little sister, Birdie, have fled the farm where they were born and raised as slaves. . . . They soon cross paths with a Union soldier . . . , marching with the army. But then orders come through: The men are called to battle in Pennsylvania. Thomas has made it so far . . . but does he have what it takes to survive Gettysburg?" (Publisher's note)

I survived the shark attacks of 1916; illustrated by Scott Dawson. Scholastic 2010 87p il (I survived) $16.99; pa $4.99

Grades: 3 4 5 6   **Fic**

1. Sharks -- Fiction 2. New Jersey -- Fiction

ISBN 978-0-545-20688-4; 0-545-20688-4; 978-0-545-20695-2 pa; 0-545-20695-2 pa

In the summer of 1916, ten year-old Chet Roscow is captivated by the local news: A great white shark has been attacking and killing people up and down the Atlantic coast, not far from Chet's hometown of Springfield, New Jersey.

"An absorbing story. . . . Black-and-white illustrations that resemble old photographs enhance the events of the story. Tarshis incorporates information about the real attacks and fictionalizes it, then follows the story with facts about the attacks and sharks. This is a gripping story that will hold the interest of reluctant readers." SLJ

Other titles in this series are:

I survived the sinking of the Titanic, 1912 (2010)

I survived Hurricane Katrina, 2005 (2011)

I survived the bombing of Pearl Harbor, 1941 (2011)

Tashjian, Janet

★ **My** life as a book; with cartoons by Jake Tashjian. Henry Holt 2010 211p il $16.99; pa $6.99

Grades: 4 5 6 7   **Fic**

1. Summer -- Fiction 2. Animals -- Fiction 3. Family life -- Fiction 4. Books and reading -- Fiction

ISBN 978-0-8050-8903-5; 0-8050-8903-9; 978-0-312-67289-8 pa; 0-312-67289-6 pa

LC 2009-18909

Dubbed a "reluctant reader" by his teacher, twelve-year-old Derek spends summer vacation learning important lessons even though he does not complete his summer reading list.

"The protagonist is by turns likable and irritating, but always interesting. He is sure to engage fans of Jeff Kinney's 'Diary of a Wimpy Kid' books . . . as well as those looking for a spunky, contemporary boy with a mystery to solve. Reluctant readers will appreciate the book's large print and quick-paced story." SLJ

"Another title about Derek is:

My life as a stuntboy (2011)

My life as a joke; Janet Tashjian; with cartoons by Jake Tashjian. Henry Holt and Company 2014 252 p. illustrations (hardback) $13.99

Grades: 4 5 6 7   **Fic**

1. School stories 2. Middle schools -- Fiction 3. Friendship -- Fiction 4. Maturation (Psychology) -- Fiction 5. Family life -- California -- Los Angeles -- Fiction

ISBN 080509850X; 9780805098501

LC 2013046395

In this middle grade book by Janet Tashjian, illustrated by Jake Tashjian, "Derek Fallon discovers all the angst that comes with being twelve--he just wants to feel grown up, but life gets in the way with a series of mishaps that make him look like a baby. . . . Why isn't being in middle school as great as Derek imagined?" (Publisher's note)

"In his fourth appearance, twelve-year-old Derek resolves to appear more mature, but he's constantly a laughingstock. . . . Fans will enjoy the fast plot, Derek's supportive friends, and cartoon marginalia representing Derek's ever-expanding collection of vocabulary words." Horn Book

Tate, Eleanora E.

Celeste's Harlem Renaissance. Little, Brown 2007 279p $15.99; pa $5.99

Grades: 4 5 6 7   **Fic**

1. Aunts -- Fiction 2. African Americans -- Fiction 3. Harlem Renaissance -- Fiction 4. Harlem (New York, N.Y.) -- Fiction

ISBN 978-0-316-52394-3; 978-0-316-11362-5 pa

In 1921, thirteen-year-old Celeste leaves North Carolina to stay with her glamorous Aunt Valentina in Harlem, New York, where she discovers the vibrant Harlem Renaissance in full swing, even though her aunt's life is not exactly what she was led to believe.

"Both sobering and inspiring, Tate's novel is a moving portrait of growing up black and female in 1920s America." Booklist

Tate, Lindsey

Kate Larkin, bone expert; [by] Lindsey Tate; illustrated by Diane Palmisciano. Henry Holt 2008 72p il $16.95

Grades: 1 2 3 4   **Fic**

1. Bones -- Fiction 2. Family life -- Fiction

ISBN 978-0-8050-7901-2; 0-8050-7901-7

LC 2007027588

When Kate breaks her arm, she learns all about bones, from how x-rays work to how bones heal, and by the time she gets her cast removed at the end of the summer, she is an expert. Includes related activities and glossary

"The format is appealing: large type, short chapters, and black-and-white illustrations generously dispersed throughout. . . . This is a solid choice for newly independent readers or for science-minded children looking for some fiction." SLJ

Taylor, Chloe

Ready to wear; Chloe Taylor. 1st ed. Simon Spotlight 2013 176 p. (Sew Zoey) (paperback) $5.99; (hardcover) $15.99

Grades: 3 4 5 6 7   **Fic**

1. Fashion -- Juvenile literature 2. Middle schools -- Fiction 3. School stories -- Fiction

ISBN 1442479345; 9781442479333; 9781442479340

LC 2013935204

In this children's novel, by Chloe Taylor, illustrated by Nancy Zhang, "fashion-loving Zoey Webber gets the best news ever: Her middle school is getting rid of uniforms! . . . Zoey has sketchbooks full of fashion designs, but nothing to wear! So with a little help from her best friends Kate and Priti, she learns to make her own clothes. She even begins to post her fashion design sketches online in a blog. That's how the Sew Zoey blog begins, and soon it becomes much more." (Publisher's note)

Other titles in this series are:

On Pins and Needles

Lights, Camera, Fashion!

Stitches and Stones

Cute as a Button

A Tangled Thread

Knot Too Shabby!

Swatch Out!

A Change of Lace

Bursting at the Seams

Clothes Minded

Dressed to Frill

Sewing in Circles

Cut from the Same Cloth

Taylor, Mildred D.

★ The **friendship**; pictures by Max Ginsburg. Dial Bks. for Young Readers 1987 53p il $15.99; pa $4.99

Grades: 4 5 6 7   **Fic**

1. Mississippi -- Fiction 2. Race relations -- Fiction 3. African Americans -- Fiction

ISBN 0-8037-0417-8; 0-14-038964-4 pa

LC 86-29309

Coretta Scott King Award for text

This "story about race relations in rural Mississippi during the Depression focuses on an incident between an old Black man, Mr. Tom Bee, and a white storekeeper, Mr. John Wallace. Indebted to Tom for saving his life as a young man, John had promised they would always be friends. But now, years later, John insists that Tom call him 'Mister' and shoots the old man for defiantly—and publicly—calling him by his first name. Narrator Cassie Logan and her brothers . . . are verbally abused by Wallace's villainous sons before witnessing the encounter." Bull Cen Child Books

★ The **gold** Cadillac; pictures by Michael Hays. Dial Bks. for Young Readers 1987 43p il $16.99; pa $4.99

Grades: 4 5 6 7   **Fic**

1. Prejudices -- Fiction 2. Race relations -- Fiction 3. African Americans -- Fiction

ISBN 0-8037-0342-2; 0-14-038963-6 pa

LC 86-11526

"Full-page sepia paintings effectively portray the characters, setting and mood of the story events as Hays ably demonstrates his understanding of the social and emotional environments which existed for blacks during this period." SLJ

★ **Let** the circle be unbroken. Dial Bks. for Young Readers 1981 394p $17.99; pa $7.99

Grades: 4 5 6 7   **Fic**

1. Mississippi -- Fiction 2. African Americans -- Fiction 3. Great Depression, 1929-1939 -- Fiction

ISBN 0-8037-4748-9; 0-14-034892-1 pa

LC 81-65854

Sequel to: Roll of thunder, hear my cry

The author "provides her readers with a literal sense of witnessing important American history. . . . Moreover, [she] never neglects the details of her volatile 9-year-old heroine's interior life. The daydreams, the jealousy, the incredible ardor of that age come alive." N Y Times Book Rev

★ **Mississippi** bridge; by Mildred Taylor; pictures by Max Ginsburg. Dial Bks. for Young Readers 1990 62p il hardcover o.p. pa $4.99

Grades: 4 5 6 7   **Fic**

1. Prejudices -- Fiction 2. Mississippi -- Fiction 3. Race relations -- Fiction 4. African Americans -- Fiction

ISBN 0-14-130817-6 pa

LC 89-27898

"Taylor has shaped this episode into a haunting meditation that will leave readers vividly informed about segregation practices and the unequal rights that prevailed in that era. . . . The incident and its context constitute a telling piece of social history." Booklist

★ The **road** to Memphis; by Mildred Taylor. Dial Bks. 1989 290p pa $6.99; $18.99

Grades: 4 5 6 7   **Fic**

1. Mississippi -- Fiction 2. Race relations -- Fiction 3. African Americans -- Fiction

ISBN 0-14-036077-8 pa; 0-8037-0340-6

LC 88-33654

Coretta Scott King Award for text

This is a sequel to Let the Circle Be Unbroken (BRD 1982). "The time is 1941, with the U.S. on the verge of war; Cassie {Logan} . . . is sure that nothing will stop her from college and career. When her friend Moe is humiliated and ridiculed by local bigots, he loses control and attacks three men with a crowbar. Cassie and her brothers and friends (including one white friend, Jeremy Simms) help Moe escape. . . . Grades seven to twelve." (Booklist)

"Taylor's continued smooth, easy language provides readability for all ages, with a focus on universal human pride, worthy values, and individual responsibility. This action-packed drama is highly recommended." Voice Youth Advocates

★ **Roll** of thunder, hear my cry; 25th anniversary ed; Phyllis Fogelman Books 2001 276p $17.99; pa $7.99

Grades: 4 5 6 7 8 9   **Fic**

1. Mississippi -- Fiction 2. African Americans -- Fiction

ISBN 0-8037-2647-3; 0-14-240112-9 pa

LC 00-39378

First published 1976 by Dial Press

Awarded the Newbery Medal, 1977

"The time is 1933. The place is Spokane, Mississippi where the Logans, the only black family who own their own land, wage a courageous struggle to remain independent, displeasing a white plantation owner bent on taking their land. But this suspenseful tale is also about the story's young narrator, Cassie, and her three brothers who decide to wage their own personal battles to maintain the self-dignity and pride with which they were raised. . . . Ms. Taylor's richly textured novel shows a strong, proud black family . . . resisting rather than succumbing to oppression." Child Book Rev Serv

Song of the trees; pictures by Jerry Pinkney. Dial Bks. for Young Readers 1975 48p il hardcover o.p. pa $5.99

Grades: 4 5 6 7   **Fic**

1. Mississippi -- Fiction 2. African Americans -- Fiction 3. Great Depression, 1929-1939 -- Fiction

ISBN 0-8037-5452-3; 0-14-250075-5 pa

Eight-year-old Cassie Logan tells how her family "leaving Mississippi during the Depression was cheated into selling for practically nothing valuable and beautiful giant old pines and hickories, beeches and walnuts in the forest surrounding their house." Adventuring with Books

★ The **well**; David's story. Dial Bks. for Young Readers 1995 92p hardcover o.p. pa $5.99

Grades: 4 5 6 7   **Fic**

1. Mississippi -- Fiction 2. Race relations -- Fiction 3. African Americans -- Fiction

ISBN 0-8037-1802-0; 0-14-038642-4 pa

LC 94-25360

This story "delivers an emotional wallop in a concentrated span of time and action. . . . This story reverberates in the heart long after the final paragraph is read." Horn Book

Taylor, S. S.

The **Expeditioners** and the Treasure of Drowned Man's Canyon; by S. S. Taylor; illustrated by Katherine Roy. Pgw 2012 320 p. $22

Grades: 5 6 7 8   **Fic**

1. Adventure fiction 2. Maps 4. Exploration

ISBN 1938073061; 9781938073069

In this book by S. S. Taylor, illustrated by Katherine Roy, "computers have failed, electricity is extinct, and the race to discover new lands is underway! Brilliant explorer Alexander West has just died under mysterious circumstances, but not before smuggling half of a strange map to his intrepid children--Kit the brain, M.K. the tinkerer, and Zander the brave. Why are so many government agents trying to steal the half-map? (And where is the other half?)" (Publisher's note)

Taylor, Sydney

★ **All**-of-a-kind family; illustrations by Helen John. Delacorte Press 2005 188p il hardcover o.p. pa $5.99

Grades: 4 5 6   **Fic**

1. Jews -- Fiction 2. New York (N.Y.) -- Fiction

ISBN 0-385-73295-3; 0-440-40059-7 pa

First published 1951 by Follett

"A genuine and delightful picture of a Jewish family . . . with an understanding mother and father, rich in kindness and fun though poor in money. The important part the public library played in the lives of these children is happily evident; and the Jewish holiday celebrations are particularly well described." Horn Book

Other titles about this family are:

All-of-a-kind family downtown (1957)

All-of-a-kind family uptown (1957)

Ella of all-of-a-kind family (1978)

More all-of-a-kind family (1954)

Taylor, Theodore

★ The **cay**. Delacorte Press 1987 137p $16.95; pa $5.50

Grades: 5 6 7 8   **Fic**

1. Blind -- Fiction 2. Race relations -- Fiction 3. Caribbean region -- Fiction 4. Survival after airplane accidents, shipwrecks, etc. -- Fiction

ISBN 0-385-07906-0; 0-440-22912-X pa

A reissue of the title first published 1969

When the freighter on which they are traveling is torpedoed by a German submarine during World War II, Phillip, an adolescent white boy blinded by a blow on the head, and Timothy, an old black man, are stranded on a tiny Caribbean island where the boy acquires a new kind of vision, courage, and love from his old companion

"Starkly dramatic, believable and compelling." Saturday Rev

Followed by: Timothy of the cay

Ice drift; [by] Theodore Taylor. Harcourt 2005 224p $16; pa $5.95

Grades: 4 5 6 7   **Fic**

1. Inuit -- Fiction 2. Brothers -- Fiction 3. Arctic regions -- Fiction

ISBN 0-15-205081-7; 0-15-205550-9 pa

LC 2003-27783

Two Inuit brothers must fend for themselves while stranded on an ice floe that is adrift in the Greenland Strait.

This is "a masterful and detailed look into a culture unfamiliar to most Americans, a gripping adventure, and a moving depiction of brotherly love." SLJ

★ **Teetoncey**. Harcourt 2004 208p hardcover o.p. pa $5.95

Grades: 5 6 7 8   **Fic**
1. Amnesia -- Fiction 2. North Carolina -- Fiction
ISBN 0-15-205298-4; 0-15-205294-1 pa
                                    LC 2003-67745
A reissue of the title first published 1974 by Doubleday
In this first novel of the Cape Hatteras trilogy, eleven-year-old Ben rescues an English girl from a shipwreck off the Outer Banks of North Carolina; and, though she becomes part of his family, she never speaks.
"The novel is rich with details of of local geography, history, and folklore." Horn Book
Other titles in the Cape Hatteras trilogy are:
The odyssey of Ben O'Neal (2004 c1977)
Teetoncey and Ben O'Neal (2004 c1975)

The **trouble** with Tuck. Doubleday 1981 110p hardcover o.p. pa $4.50
Grades: 5 6 7 8   **Fic**
1. Dogs -- Fiction 2. Blind -- Fiction
ISBN 0-385-17774-7; 0-440-41696-5 pa
                                      LC 81-43139
Helen trains her blind dog Tuck to follow and trust a seeing-eye companion dog
This is "a touching dog story, written with good flow, pace, and structure." Bull Cent Child Books
Another title about Helen and Tuck is:
Tuck triumphant (1991)

Teagan, Erin
The **friendship** experiment; by Erin Teagan. Houghton Mifflin Harcourt 2016 256 p. (ebook) $16.99; (hardback) $16.99
Grades: 4 5 6   **Fic**
1. Friendship -- Fiction 2. Scientists -- Fiction 3. Family life -- Fiction 4. Middle schools -- Fiction 5. Schools -- Fiction
ISBN 9780544635371; 9780544636224
                                    LC 2016009618
In this book, by Erin Teagan, "future scientist Madeline Little is dreading the start of middle school. Nothing has been right since her grandfather died and her best friend changed schools. Maddie would rather help her father in his research lab or write Standard Operating Procedures in her lab notebook than hang out with a bunch of kids who aren't even her friends." (Publisher's note)
"Highly enjoyable for aspiring scientists, budding artists, and regular kids." Kirkus

Teague, David
★ **Saving** Lucas Biggs; by Marisa de los Santos and David Teague. Harper, an imprint of HarperCollinsPublishers 2014 288 p. (hardback) $16.99
Grades: 5 6 7 8   **Fic**
1. Girls -- Fiction 2. Time travel -- Fiction 3. Detective and mystery stories
ISBN 0062274627; 9780062274625
                                    LC 2013043189
This "time-travel story from husband-and-wife team Marisa de los Santos and David Teague follows one girl's race to change the past in order to save her father's future. Thirteen-year-old Margaret knows her father is innocent, but that doesn't stop the cruel Judge Biggs from sentencing him to death. Margaret is determined to save her dad, even if it means using her family's secret--and forbidden--ability to time travel." (Publisher's note)
"The authors weave a tale of justice and family bonds with threads of historical fiction accented with the fantastical physics of time travel. The heroine begins to realize that the very stuff that makes people who they are--that combination of all their life experiences—can sometimes

shift the very fabric of history. At least that's what Margaret is hoping, because the only way to save her father is to first save corrupt Lucas Biggs from himself." SLJ

Teague, Mark
★ The **doom** machine; a novel. Blue Sky Press 2009 376p $17.99
Grades: 4 5 6 7   **Fic**
1. Science fiction 2. Space and time -- Fiction 3. Extraterrestrial beings -- Fiction
ISBN 978-0-545-15142-9; 0-545-15142-2
                                    LC 2009-14262
When a spaceship lands in the small town of Vern Hollow in 1956, juvenile delinquent Jack Creedle and prim, studious Isadora Shumway form an unexpected alliance as they try to keep a group of extraterrestrials from stealing eccentric Uncle Bud's space travel machine.
"This book is filled with humor and dramatic figurative language that makes the setting completely approachable. It is a great fit for science fiction, humor, and adventure genre fans." Voice Youth Advocates

Tellegen, Toon
Letters to anyone and everyone; stories by Toon Tellegen; illustrated by Jessica Ahlberg; translated by Martin Cleaver. Boxer Books 2010 154p il lib bdg $12.95
Grades: 2 3 4 5   **Fic**
1. Animals -- Fiction 2. Letters -- Fiction
ISBN 978-1-906250-95-9 lib bdg; 1-906250-95-2 lib bdg
"In this novel, snails, elephants, bears, and ants write letters to one another, to the Sun, and to other letter writers. . . . Every brief missive is written in a distinct voice, and the complete collection reveals Tellegen's richly imagined world in which the creatures reside. The book was originally published in Holland, and Cleaver's smooth English translation retains humor and charm." SLJ

Teplin, Scott
The **clock** without a face; a Gus Twintig mystery. [by Scott Teplin, Mac Barnett & Eli Horowitz; plus faces by Adam Rex & numbers by Anna Sheffield] McSweeney's 2010 un il $19.95
Grades: 4 5 6 7   **Fic**
1. Mystery fiction 2. Picture puzzles 3. Theft -- Fiction 4. Apartment houses -- Fiction 5. Clocks and watches -- Fiction
ISBN 978-1-934781-71-5; 1-934781-71-1
Narrator Gus Twintig and Roy Dodge "are summoned to a 13-story apartment building to investigate a string of robberies: the emerald-encrusted numbers have been stolen from a clock belonging to owner Bevel Ternky, and his 12 tenants have also been burgled. . . . The right side of each spread is an overhead cutaway view of each apartment ostensibly drawn by Twintig. Given the potential of discovering clues to where the actual bejeweled numbers . . . have been hidden, kids should be plenty motivated to pore over each scene." Publ Wkly

Testa, Maria
Almost forever. Candlewick Press 2003 69p $14.99; pa $5.99
Grades: 3 4 5   **Fic**
1. Vietnam War, 1961-1975 -- Fiction
ISBN 0-7636-1996-5; 0-7636-3366-6 pa
                                    LC 2002-34757
In free verse, a young girl describes what she, her brother, and their mother do during the year that her doctor father is serving in the Army in Vietnam
This is "sensitive and moving. . . . Testa's poems give her young speaker a believable, sympathetic voice." Publ Wkly

Thomas, Elizabeth Marshall, 1931-

Certain poor shepherds; a Christmas tale. Elizabeth Marshall Thomas; illustrated by Andrew Davidson. Simon & Schuster 1996 128 p. color illustrations $15.99

Grades: 3 4 5 6 7 **Fic**

1. Animals -- Fiction 2. Christmas stories

ISBN 0684833131; 0763670626; 9780684833132; 9780763670627

LC 96034263

This book, by Elizabeth Marshall Thomas, illustrated by Andrew Davidson and Jonathan Bartlett, presents a Nativity story told from the perspective of two animals. "A star appears behind the cedars on the eastern skyline. It is big and powerful, and it has a pure, clean scent. . . . Lila, the sheepdog, and Ima, the goat, are compelled to follow the star on a journey to a humble manger in Bethlehem, a journey beset with danger, adventure, and love." (Publisher's note)

"The story is far from sentimental, with unflinching demonstrations of the human faults listed in the prologue, including poor treatment of animals and humans. The prose is simple and elegant. Harsh elements are balanced by tenderness and gentle humor, and there is an uplifting ending for the dual protagonists. An affecting, well-spun tale that will especially resonate with animal lovers. (Historical fiction. 8-12)" Kirkus

Thomas, Scarlett

Dragon's Green; Scarlett Thomas. Simon & Schuster Books for Young Readers 2017 384 p. (Worldquake) (hardback) $17.99

Grades: 4 5 6 7 **Fic**

1. Fantasy fiction 2. Books -- Fiction 3. Magic -- Fiction 4. Friendship -- Fiction 5. Fantasy

ISBN 9781481497848; 9781481497855; 9781481497862

LC 2016035327

In this book, by Scarlett Thomas, part of the "Worldquake" series, "Effie Truelove believes in magic, as does her grandfather Griffin (although he refuses to do any magic, let alone teach Effie how to use it). After a mysterious incident leaves Griffin close to death, Effie is given an unusual silver ring and told she must look after her grandfather's library of rare and powerful books." (Publisher's note)

Thomason, Mark

Moonrunner. Kane/Miller 2009 217p $15.95

Grades: 4 5 6 7 **Fic**

1. Horses -- Fiction 2. Australia -- Fiction

ISBN 978-1-935279-03-7; 1-935279-03-3

First published 2008 in Australia

"In the 1890s, Casey and his parents immigrate to Australia, to a homestead that they inherited from his grandfather. The 12-year-old finds the change difficult. He is bullied at school, and he misses his baseball team in Montana and his horse. Then he happens upon a magnificent wild stallion, and he is determined to befriend the brumby, whom he names Moonrunner. . . . This well-paced story effectively portrays the family's struggles. Casey is a strong, engaging protagonist whose interactions with the other characters are believable and interesting." SLJ

Thompson, Colin

Good neighbors; by Colin Thompson; illustrated by Crab Scrambly. HarperCollinsPublishers 2008 214p il (The Floods) lib bdg $16.89; pa $5.99

Grades: 3 4 5 6 **Fic**

1. Magic -- Fiction 2. Witches -- Fiction

ISBN 978-0-06-113199-8 lib bdg; 0-06-113196-2 lib bdg; 978-0-06-113197-4 pa; 0-06-113197-0 pa

A family of wizards and witches living in an ordinary neighborhood in an ordinary town decides that they have had enough of the noisy family living next-door and makes them disappear.

The author "careens wildly from one extreme scenario to the next, letting the Floods get away with everything—despite their appearances, they're the good guys. Kids can enjoy the prankishness; adults can rest easy given the conventional underpinnings." Publ Wkly

Another title in this series is:

School plot (2008)

Thompson, J. E.

The girl from Felony Bay; John Thompson. Walden Pond Press, an imprint of HarperCollinsPublishers 2013 384 p. (hardcover bdg.) $16.99

Grades: 4 5 6 7 **Fic**

1. Theft -- Fiction 2. Mystery fiction -- Fiction 3. Coma -- Fiction 4. Fathers -- Fiction 5. Families -- Fiction 6. Charleston (S.C.) -- Fiction 7. Mystery and detective stories

ISBN 0062104462; 9780062104465

LC 2012025338

In this book, 12-year-old Abbey Force's "father has suffered an accident and now lies in the hospital in a coma. Meanwhile, he has been accused of stealing from a client named Miss Lydia Jenkins, and his law firm . . . has sold the Force family home, Reward Plantation, in order to repay her." Abbey makes friends with the new owners' daughter Bee and the girls "stumble upon a mystery--someone is digging holes at Felony Bay, perhaps in search of buried treasure." (Kirkus Reviews)

Thompson, Kate

Highway robbery; illustrated by Jonny Duddle and Robert Dress. Greenwillow Books 2009 118p il $15.99

Grades: 3 4 5 6 **Fic**

1. Thieves 2. Adventure fiction 3. Horses -- Fiction 4. Thieves -- Fiction 5. Great Britain -- History -- 1714-1837 -- Fiction

ISBN 978-0-06-173034-4; 0-06-173034-3

LC 2008-27720

On a cold day in eighteenth-century England, a poor young boy agrees to watch a stranger's fine horse for a golden guinea but soon finds himself in a difficult situation when the king's guard appears and wants to use him as bait in their pursuit of a notorious highwayman.

"It's a suspenseful and tautly written story as is, and Thompson's sly twist makes it all the richer." Publ Wkly

Most wanted; illustrated by Jonny Duddle. Greenwillow Books 2010 136p il $15.99

Grades: 3 4 5 **Fic**

1. Emperors 2. Horses -- Fiction 3. Slavery -- Fiction 4. Rome -- History -- Fiction

ISBN 978-0-06-173037-5; 0-06-173037-8; 978-0-06-173038-2 lib bdg; 0-06-173038-6 lib bdg

In first century Rome, in the turmoil after a rumor circulates that mad Emperor "Littleboots" is dead, young Marcus brings home a horse that the emperor had proclaimed a consul and his family decides they must treat it as an honored guest.

"This brief chapter book is nicely suited for reading aloud or for those independent readers who enjoy their adventure and history touched with humor. Marcus's voice is engaging and credible. . . . A cleverly told tale of an odd and interesting piece of history that will intrigue young readers." Publ Wkly

Thompson, Lisa

The goldfish boy; Lisa Thompson. Scholastic Press 2017 320 p. (ebook) $16.99; (hardcover) $16.99

Grades: 4 5 6 **Fic**

1. Mystery fiction 2. Guilt -- Fiction 3. Missing children -- Fiction 4. Obsessive-compulsive disorder -- Fiction 5. England -- Fiction 6. Neighbors -- Fiction 7. London (England) -- Fiction 7. Families

-- Fiction 8. Mystery and detective stories 9. Family life -- England
-- London -- Fiction
ISBN 9781338053944; 9781338053920

LC 2016037797

In this book, by Lisa Thompson, "Matthew Corbin suffers from severe obsessive-compulsive disorder. . . . He refuses to leave his bedroom. To pass the time, he observes his neighbors from his bedroom window. . . . When a toddler staying next door goes missing, it becomes apparent that Matthew was the last person to see him alive. Suddenly, Matthew finds himself at the center of a high-stakes mystery, and every one of his neighbors is a suspect." (Publisher's note)

"Though the topic is serious, the tone is fairly light and the story well-paced, considering the setting rarely changes from Matthew's home. Readers will root for Matthew. " SLJ

Thompson, Paul B.

The **devil's** door; a Salem witchcraft story. Enslow Publishers 2010 160p (Historical fiction adventures) lib bdg $27.93; pa $14.95
Grades: 4 5 6 **Fic**
1. Trials -- Fiction 2. Witchcraft -- Fiction 3. Salem (Mass.) -- Fiction
ISBN 978-0-7660-3387-0 lib bdg; 0-7660-3387-2 lib bdg; 978-1-59845-214-3 pa; 1-59845-214-2 pa

Sarah Wright and her father Ephraim move to Salem Village, Massachusetts, in 1692, where they witness the Salem witchcraft hysteria, during which Ephraim is arrested and Sarah must try to help him escape from jail.

"Factual material is incorporated into the narrative, creating a fast-paced, fascinating read." SLJ

Thomson, Melissa

Keena Ford and the second-grade mixup; pictures by Frank Morrison. Dial Books for Young Readers 2008 102p il $14.99; pa $5.99
Grades: 1 2 3 **Fic**
1. School stories 2. Diaries -- Fiction 3. African Americans -- Fiction
ISBN 978-0-8037-3263-6; 0-8037-3263-5; 978-0-14-241396-8 pa; 0-14-241396-8 pa

LC 2007-43749

Keena Ford chronicles her many mishaps as she begins second grade
"Thomson, a former teacher, skillfully zeroes in on an eight-year-old's anxieties and creates a vivid sense of Keena's world, both at school and at home. . . . Morrison's full-page pencil sketches extend both the comedy and the emotions, particularly Keena's sense that she is accepted and loved, even as she clears up mistakes with family and friends." Booklist

Other titles about Keena Ford are:
Keena Ford and the field trip mix-up (2009)
Keena Ford and the secret journal mix-up (2010)

Thor, Annika

A **faraway** island; translated from the Swedish by Linda Schenck. Delacorte Press 2009 247p map $16.99; lib bdg $19.99
Grades: 4 5 6 7 **Fic**
1. Jews -- Fiction 2. Sweden -- Fiction 3. Islands -- Fiction 4. Sisters -- Fiction 5. Refugees -- Fiction 6. World War, 1939-1945 -- Fiction
ISBN 978-0-385-73617-6; 0-385-73617-7; 978-0-385-90590-9 lib bdg; 0-385-90590-4 lib bdg

LC 2009-15420

ALA ALSC Batchelder Award (2010)
In 1939 Sweden, two Jewish sisters wait for their parents to flee the Nazis in Austria, but while eight-year-old Nellie settles in quickly, twelve-year-old Stephie feels stranded at the end of the world, with a

foster mother who is as cold and unforgiving as the island on which they live.

"Children will readily empathize with Stephie's courage. Both sisters are well-drawn, likable characters. This is the first of four books Thor has written about the two girls." SLJ

Followed by The Lily Pond
Followed by: The lily pond (2011)

Thorne, Jack, 1978-

Harry Potter and the cursed child parts one and two; the official script book of the original west end production. J.K. Rowling, John Tiffany, Jack Thorne. Arthur A. Levine Books 2016 327 p. (ebook) $44.97; (jacketed hardcover : alk. paper) $29.99
Grades: 4 5 6 7 8 9 10 **Fic**
1. Magic -- Drama 2. Time travel -- Drama 3. Good and evil -- Drama
ISBN 9781781107041; 1338099132; 9781338099133

LC 2016944764

This play by J. K. Rowling, John Tiffany, and Jack Thorne, "is the eighth story in the Harry Potter series and the first official Harry Potter story to be presented on stage. . . . While Harry grapples with a past that refuses to stay where it belongs, his youngest son Albus must struggle with the weight of a family legacy he never wanted. As past and present fuse ominously, both father and son learn the uncomfortable truth: sometimes, darkness comes from unexpected places." (Publisher's note)

"Series fans can breathe easy knowing this play has been respectfully and lovingly wrought. Tensions thrum, spells fly, and Slytherins finally have their day in the sun—but at center stage, as always in the Potterverse, is the overriding importance of love and friendship, especially in the face of danger." Booklist

Timberlake, Amy

★ **One** came home; Amy Timberlake. Alfred A. Knopf 2012 272 p. (hard cover) $16.99
Grades: 4 5 6 **Fic**
1. Missing persons -- Fiction 2. Historical fiction 3. Frontier and pioneer life -- Wisconsin -- Fiction 4. Sharpshooters -- Fiction 5 Counterfeits and counterfeiting -- Fiction 6. Wisconsin -- History -- 19th century -- Fiction
ISBN 0375869255; 9780375869259; 9780375969256; 9780375989346

LC 2011037095

Newberry Honor Book (2014)
This novel, by Amy Timberlake, is set "in the town of Placid, Wisconsin, in 1871, . . .when Georgie blurts out something she shouldn't, her older sister Agatha flees. . . . And when the sheriff returns to town with an unidentifiable body--wearing Agatha's blue-green ball gown--everyone assumes the worst. Except Georgie. Refusing to believe the facts that are laid down (and coffined) before her, Georgie sets out on a journey to find her sister." (Publisher's note)

Tingle, Tim

★ **Crossing** Bok Chitto; a Choctaw tale of friendship & freedom. illustrated by Jeanne Rorex Bridges. Cinco Puntos Press 2006 un il $17.95; pa $8.95
Grades: 2 3 4 5 **Fic**
1. Slavery -- Fiction 2. Friendship -- Fiction 3. Mississippi -- Fiction 4. Choctaw Indians -- Fiction 5. African Americans -- Fiction
ISBN 978-0-938317-77-7; 0-938317-77-6; 978-1-933693-20-0 pa; 1-933693-20-7 pa

LC 2005-23612

In the 1800s, a Choctaw girl becomes friends with a slave boy from a plantation across the great river, and when she learns that his family is in trouble, she helps them cross to freedom

The "text has the rhythm and grace of . . . oral tradition. It will be easily and effectively read aloud. The paintings are dark and solemn, and the artist has done a wonderful job of depicting all of the characters as individuals." Booklist

How I became a ghost; a Choctaw trail of tears story. by Tim Tingle. RoadRunner Press 2013 160 p. (The how I became a ghost series) (hardcover : alk. paper) $18.95

Grades: 4 5 6 7   Fic

1. Ghost stories 2. Choctaw Indians -- Fiction
ISBN 1937054535; 9781937054533; 9781937054540; 9781937054557

LC 2013935579

American Indian Youth Literature Award Winner (2014)

In this book, "a 10-year-old Choctaw boy recounts the beginnings of the forced resettlement of his people from their Mississippi-area home-lands in 1830. . . . Even as the Choctaw prepare to leave their homes, Isaac begins to have unsettling visions. . . [The] visions begin to come true, as some are burned to death by the Nahullos and others perish due to smallpox-infested blankets. . . . But the Choctaw barrier between life and death is a fluid one, and ghosts follow Isaac, providing reassurance." (Kirkus Reviews)

Tocher, Timothy

Bill Pennant, Babe Ruth, and me. Cricket Books 2009 178p $16.95

Grades: 5 6 7 8   Fic

1. Baseball players 2. Baseball managers 3. Baseball -- Fiction 4. New York Giants (Baseball team) -- Fiction 5. New York Yankees (Baseball team) -- Fiction.
ISBN 978-0-8126-2755-8; 0-8126-2755-5

LC 2008026829

In 1920, sixteen-year-old Hank finds his loyalties divided when he is assigned to care for the Giants' mascot, a wildcat named Bill Pennant, as well as keep an eye on Babe Ruth in Ruth's first season with the New York Yankees.

The author "seamlessly blends fact and fiction. He recreates the era with scrupulous attention to its syntax and slang, as well as details of daily life. Ruth, McGraw and the other historical figures come alive for readers, and the fictional Hank is a sympathetic, fully developed character." Kirkus

Toft, Di

Wolven. Scholastic 2010 322p $16.99; pa $7.99

Grades: 5 6 7 8   Fic

1. Werewolves -- Fiction 2. Supernatural -- Fiction 3. Great Britain -- Fiction
ISBN 978-0-545-17109-0; 0-545-17109-1; 978-0-545-17110-6 pa; 0-545-17110-5 pa

Twelve-year-old Nat, with help from his friends, and his "pet" Woody, a wolf that turns into a boy, must face werewolves that have been altered as part of a dastardly plan.

"Toft spins an incredible tale full of action, mystery, and suspense. This hair-raising adventure with its fresh perspective on werewolf lore is perfect for audiences not ready for some of the edgier material out there. A satisfying read with a fly-off-the-shelves cover." SLJ

Another title in this series is:
The twilight circus (2011)

Toksvig, Sandi

★ **Hitler's** canary. Roaring Brook Press 2007 191p $16.95

Grades: 5 6 7 8   Fic

1. Jews -- Fiction 2. Denmark -- Fiction 3. World War, 1939-1945 -- Fiction
ISBN 978-1-59643-247-5; 1-59643-247-0

LC 2006-16607

Ten-year-old Bamse and his Jewish friend Anton participate in the Danish Resistance during World War II.

"Though . . . suspenseful episodes will thrill readers, it is Bamse's growing courage and deepening understanding that drive the story." Booklist

Tolan, Stephanie S.

Surviving the Applewhites. HarperCollins Pubs. 2002 216p $15.99; lib bdg $17.89; pa $5.99

Grades: 5 6 7 8   Fic

1. Theater -- Fiction 2. Family life -- Fiction 3. Eccentrics and eccentricities -- Fiction
ISBN 0-06-623602-9; 0-06-623603-7 lib bdg; 0-06-441044-7 pa

LC 2002-1474

A Newbery Medal honor book, 2003

Jake, a budding juvenile delinquent, is sent for home schooling to the arty and eccentric Applewhite family's Creative Academy, where he discovers talents and interests he never knew he had

This is a "thoroughly enjoyable book with humor, well-drawn characters, and a super cover." Voice Youth Advocates

Wishworks, Inc. illustrated by Amy June Bates. Arthur A. Levine Books 2009 146p il $15.99

Grades: 3 4 5   Fic

1. Dogs -- Fiction 2. Moving -- Fiction 3. Wishes -- Fiction 4. Divorce -- Fiction 5. Friendship -- Fiction 6. Imagination -- Fiction
ISBN 978-0-545-03154-7; 0-545-03154-0

LC 2008-42694

When he is granted his wish for a dog from Wishworks, Inc., third-grader Max is disappointed to find that his new pet is nothing like the dog of his imagination.

"Tolan's vivid, clean writing is deceptively uncomplicated and the many issues touched upon are handled well." SLJ

Tolkien, J. R. R.

★ The **hobbit,** or, There and back again. Houghton Mifflin 2001 330p il $18; pa $10

Grades: 5 6 7 8 9 10 11 12 Adult   Fic

1. Fantasy fiction
ISBN 0-618-16221-6; 0-618-26030-7 pa

LC 2001276594

A reissue of the title first published 1938

"Bilbo Baggins is a hobbit who enjoys a comfortable, unambitious life, rarely traveling any farther than his pantry or cellar. But his contentment is disturbed when the wizard Gandalf and a company of dwarves arrive on his doorstep one day to whisk him away on an adventure. They have launched a plot to raid the treasure hoard guarded by Smaug the Magnificent, a large and very dangerous dragon. Bilbo reluctantly joins their quest, unaware that on his journey to the Lonely Mountain he will encounter both a magic ring and a frightening creature known as Gollum." (Publisher's note)

"This fantasy features the adventures of hobbit Bilbo Baggins, who joins a band of dwarves led by Gandalf the Wizard. Together they seek to recover the stolen treasure that is hidden in Lonely Mountain and guarded by Smaug the Dragon. This book precedes the Lord of the Rings trilogy." Shapiro. Fic for Youth. 3d edition

Followed by: The lord of the rings trilogy: The fellowship of the ring; The two towers; The return of the king

Tolkien, J. R. R. (John Ronald Reuel), 1892-1973

★ The **hobbit**; or, There and back again. illustrated by Michael Hague. Houghton Mifflin 1984 290p il $29.95

Grades: 5 6 7 8 9 10 11 12 Adult   **Fic**

1. Magic 2. Satire 3. Allegories 4. Fantasy fiction 5. Fantasies 6. Imaginary kingdoms

ISBN 0-395-36290-3

    LC 84-9023

First published 1937 in the United Kingdom; first United States edition 1938

Bilbo Baggins, a respectable, well-to-do hobbit, lives comfortably in his hobbit-hole until the day the wandering wizard Gandalf chooses him to share in an adventure from which he may never return. "Grades four to eight." (Bull Cent Child Books)

"It must be understood that this is a children's book only in the sense that the first of many readings can be undertaken in the nursery. . . . [The hobbit] will be funniest to its youngest readers, and only years later, at a tenth or twentieth reading, will they begin to realize what deft scholarship and profound reflection have gone to make everything in it so ripe, so friendly, and in its own way so true." Times Lit Suppl

Tooke, Wes

King of the mound; my summer with Satchel Paige. Simon & Schuster Books for Young Readers 2012 155p $15.99

Grades: 4 5 6   **Fic**

1. Baseball players 2. People with disabilities -- Fiction 3. Baseball -- Fiction 4. Poliomyelitis -- Fiction 5. African Americans -- Fiction 6. Father-son relationship -- Fiction

ISBN 978-1-4424-3346-5; 1-4424-3346-9

    LC 2011012740

Twelve-year-old Nick loves baseball so after a year in the hospital fighting polio and with a brace on one leg, Nick takes a job with the minor league team for which his father is catcher and gets to see the great pitcher, Satchel Paige, play during the 1935 season. Includes historical notes.

"Tooke sticks closely to historical records, with the addition of a few extra Paige exploits and aphorisms, and . . . the fictional overlay offers a comfortably predictable 'hard work brings just rewards' arc. Nourishing fare for Matt Christopher graduates." Kirkus

Tougas, Shelley

Finders keepers; Shelley Tougas. Roaring Brook Press 2015 280 p. (hardback) $16.99

Grades: 4 5 6   **Fic**

1. Adventure fiction 2. Friendship -- Fiction 3. Buried treasure -- Fiction 4. Wisconsin -- Fiction

ISBN 1596439904; 9781596439900

    LC 2015005138

In Shelley Tougas' children's novel "Christa spends every summer at . . . her family's cabin on Whitefish Lake in Wisconsin. Only her dad recently lost his job and her parents have decided to sell the cabin. But not if Christa can help it. Everyone knows there is Al Capone blood money hidden somewhere in Whitefish Lake, and her friend Alex's cranky grandpa might have the key to finding it. If she finds it, she can keep it and save her family and their beloved cabin." (Publisher's note)

"Lighter than Gennifer Choldenko's Al Capone Does My Shirts (Putnam, 2004), this is an entertaining middle grade mystery." SLJ

Towell, Ann

Grease town. Tundra Books 2010 232p $19.99

Grades: 5 6 7 8   **Fic**

1. Canada -- Fiction 2. Race relations -- Fiction

ISBN 0-88776-983-7; 978-0-88776-983-2

"When twelve-year-old Titus Sullivan decides to run away to join his Uncle Amos and older brother, Lem, he finds an alien and exciting world in Oil Springs, the first Canadian oil boomtown of the 19th century. The Enniskillen swamp is slick with oil, and it takes enterprising folk to plumb its depths. The adventurers who work there are a tough lot of individuals. In this hard world, Titus becomes friends with a young black boy, the child of slaves who came to Canada on the Underground Railroad. When tragedy strikes in the form of a race riot, Titus's loyalties are tested." (Publisher's note) "Ages ten to fourteen." (Quill Quire)

"In 1863, oil has recently been discovered in Oil Springs, Ontario, and a variety of people, black and white, and from many different walks of life, are settling there. Orphans Lem and Titus Sullivan live in their aunt's stuffy and regimented house. When 19-year-old Lem sets out for Oil Springs, 13-year-old Titus stows away in his brother's wagon. . . . Towell skillfully creates the setting of this mucky little town and its colorful inhabitants. Titus, who narrates, has a voice that is believable and uncontrived. . . . Supporting characters are equally strong and well developed. . . . Towell has created a strong narrator and a compelling plot." SLJ

Towell, Katy

Skary childrin and the carousel of sorrow. Alfred A. Knopf 2011 265p $16.99; lib bdg $19.99; ebook $16.99

Grades: 4 5 6 7   **Fic**

1. Ghost stories 2. School stories 3. Supernatural -- Fiction

ISBN 978-0-375-86859-7; 0-375-86859-3; 978-0-375-96860-0 lib bdg; 0-375-96860-1 lib bdg; 978-0-375-89931-7 e-book; 0-375-89931-6 e-book

    LC 2010-38830

In Widowsbury, an isolated village where people believe "known is good, new is bad," three outcasts from the girls' school join forces with a home-schooled boy to uncover and combat the evil that is making people disappear.

"Towell tucks violent tempests, maggoty slime, hideous transformations, nightmares, sudden terrors and like atmosphere-building elements into a rousingly melodramatic literary debut." Kirkus

Townley, Rod

The **blue** shoe; a tale of thievery, villainy, sorcery, and shoes. by Roderick Townley; illustrated by Mary GrandPré. Alfred A. Knopf 2009 254p il $16.99; lib bdg $19.99

Grades: 4 5 6 7   **Fic**

1. Fables 2. Fairy tales

ISBN 978-0-375-85600-6; 0-375-85600-5; 978-0-375-95600-3 lib bdg; 0-375-95600-X lib bdg

    LC 2008-4385

A mysterious stranger commissions a single, valuable shoe from a humble cobbler, changing the cobbler's life and the life of his young apprentice forever.

This is a "fun, whimsical fairy tale. . . . The good-versus-evil plotline, dynamic cast of characters, . . . light romance between Hap and Sophia, and copious amounts of magic and intrigue will be a hit with a wide range of readers." Booklist

The **door** in the forest; [by] Roderick Townley. Alfred A. Knopf 2011 245p $16.99; lib bdg $19.99

Grades: 4 5 6   **Fic**

1. Magic -- Fiction 2. Honesty -- Fiction 3. Soldiers -- Fiction 4. Space and time -- Fiction

ISBN 0-375-85601-3; 0-375-95601-8 lib bdg; 978-0-375-85601-3; 978-0-375-95601-0 lib bdg

    LC 2010034710

While trying to outwit the soldiers who are occupying their small town, fourteen-year-old Daniel, who cannot lie, and Emily, who discovers she has magical powers, are inexplicably drawn to a mysterious island in the heart of the forest where townsfolk have been warned never to go. "Intermediate." (Horn Book)

"Townley's fanciful story swings like a pendulum from Wild West tall tale to a vague mysticism that is enlivened by colorful imagery. . . . At its considerable best, it is quirky and engaging; sentences hurry purposefully along, deepening atmosphere, theme, and plot." Horn Book

Townsend, Wendy

★ The **sundown** rule. Namelos 2011 128p $18.95

Grades: 5 6 7 8 **Fic**

1. Aunts -- Fiction 2. Uncles -- Fiction 3. Wildlife conservation -- Fiction 4. Father-daughter relationship -- Fiction

ISBN 1-60898-099-5; 978-1-60898-099-4

Louise and her dad live an idyllic life surrounded by nature. When he gets an assignment to go to Brazil to write an article for a magazine, Louise has to go live in a suburb with her aunt and uncle, leaving her cat, Cash, behind, since Aunt Kay is allergic to animals. Her dad says that it will be for only six weeks, and that everything will be okay. But it isn't, especially when Cash gets hit by a car and dies. And when a new friend's dad shoots a crow for no reason. And when her own dad gets sick, really sick, and might not be coming home.

"Townsend builds a rich, moving story that is refreshing for its subject matter and lyrical realism." Publ Wkly

Tracy, Kristen

Bessica Lefter bites back; by Kristen Tracy. Delacorte Press 2012 263 p. $16.99

Grades: 4 5 6 7 **Fic**

1. Gifts -- Fiction 2. Mascots -- Fiction 3. Middle schools -- Fiction 4. School children -- Fiction 5. Friendship -- Fiction 6. Schools -- Fiction

ISBN 9780385740692; 0385740697

LC 2011045677

In this children's book, "[s]ixth-grader Bessica's new middle-school persona meets a host of problems, including mending a friendship damaged by mean text messages, facing a bully in her first outing as team mascot and coming to terms with her grandmother's boyfriend. . . . Rumor has it the opposing mascot in the first game will facebomb her. Neither Bessica nor readers learn what facebombing actually is in this context until after the disastrous event." (Kirkus Reviews)

★ **Camille** McPhee fell under the bus. Delacorte Press 2009 293p $16.99; lib bdg $19.99

Grades: 3 4 5 **Fic**

1. School stories 2. Idaho -- Fiction 3. Friendship -- Fiction 4. Family life -- Fiction

ISBN 978-0-385-73687-9; 0-385-73687-8; 978-0-385-90633-3 lib bdg; 0-385-90633-1 lib bdg

LC 2008-24903

Ten-year-old Camille McPhee relates the ups and downs of her fourth-grade year at her Idaho elementary school as she tries to adjust to the absence of her best friend, maintain control of her low-blood sugar, cope with the intensifying conflict between her parents, and understand the importance of honesty and fairness.

"The lively, first-person narrative moves readers through possibly banal or overly traumatic episodes with a gentleness and humor that has them rooting for Camille." SLJ

The **reinvention** of Bessica Lefter. Delacorte Press 2011 305p $15.99

Grades: 4 5 6 7 **Fic**

1. School stories 2. Idaho -- Fiction 3. Friendship -- Fiction

ISBN 978-0-385-90634-0; 0-385-90634-X

LC 2010-04844

Eleven-year-old Bessica's plans to begin North Teton Middle School as a new person begin to fall apart even before school begins.

Tracy "offers a positive and comforting message about learning to make adjustments, ending the book on a happy note, with Bessica finding her niche as school mascot." Publ Wkly

Trafton, Jennifer

★ The **rise** and fall of Mount Majestic; illustrations by Brett Helquist. Dial Books for Young Readers 2010 338p il $16.99

Grades: 4 5 6 7 **Fic**

1. Fairy tales 2. Adventure fiction 3. Giants -- Fiction

ISBN 978-0-8037-3375-6; 0-8037-3375-5

LC 2009-51659

Ten-year-old Persimmony Smudge, who longs for heroic adventures, overhears a secret that thrusts her into the middle of a dangerous mission that could destroy the island on which she lives.

"Trafton imbues her tale with a delightful sense of fun and fascinating, well-rounded characters-playful wordsmithing and flowing dialogue make this an excellent choice for bedtime read-aloud." Publ Wkly

Travers, P. L.

★ **Mary** Poppins; illustrated by Mary Shepard. rev ed; Harcourt Brace & Co. 1997 202p il $12.95; pa $6

Grades: 4 5 6 **Fic**

1. Fantasy fiction

ISBN 0-15-205810-9; 0-15-201717-8 pa

LC 97-223987

First published 1934; this is a reissue of the 1981 revised edition

An extraordinary English nanny blows in on the East Wind with her parrot-headed umbrella and magic carpetbag and introduces her charges, Jane and Michael Banks, to some delightful people and experiences

"The chapter 'Bad Tuesday,' in which Mary and the Banks children travel to the four corners of the earth and meet the inhabitants, has been criticized for portraying minorities in an unfavorable light. . . . [In] the revised edition . . . the entourage meet up with a polar bear, macaw, panda, and dolphin instead of Eskimos, Africans, Chinese, and American Indians." Booklist

Other titles about Mary Poppins are:

Mary Poppins comes back (1935)

Mary Poppins in the kitchen (1975)

Mary Poppins in the park (1952)

Mary Poppins opens the door (1943)

Trevayne, Emma

The **accidental** afterlife of Thomas Marsden; by Emma Trevayne. Simon & Schuster Books for Young Readers 2015 256 p. (hardcovers) $16.99

Grades: 5 6 7 8 **Fic**

1. Magic -- Fiction 2. Fairies -- Fiction 3. Identity -- Fiction 4. Grave robbing -- Fiction 5. Spiritualists -- Fiction 6. London (England) -- Fiction 7. Great Britain -- History -- 19th century -- Fiction 8. Changelings -- Fiction 9. London (England) -- History -- 19th century -- Fiction 10. Great Britain -- History -- Victoria, 1837-1901 -- Fiction

ISBN 144249882X; 9781442498822; 9781442498846

LC 2014032574

In this book, by Emma Trevayne, "[g]rave robbing is a messy business. . . . And for Thomas Marsden, on what was previously an unremarkable spring night in London, it becomes a very spooky business. For lying in an unmarked grave and half covered with dirt is a boy the spitting image of Thomas himself. This is only the first clue that . . . lead[s] Thomas into a strange world of spiritualists, death, and faery folk." (Publisher's note)

"Full of hidden messages, midnight graveyard escapades, unlikely friendships, magic, and deceit, it's an engaging tale of one boy's efforts to find himself and his way back home." Pub Wkly

Trevino, Elizabeth Borton de

I, Juan de Pareja. Farrar, Straus & Giroux 1965 180p $17; pa $6.99

Grades: 6 7 8 9   **Fic**

1. Slaves 2. Artists 3. Painters 4. Spain -- Fiction 5. Artists -- Fiction 6. Slavery -- Fiction
ISBN 0-374-33531-1; 0-312-38005-4 pa

LC 65-19330

Awarded the Newbery Medal, 1966

The black slave boy, Juan de Pareja, "began a new life when he was taken into the household of the Spanish painter, Velázquez. As he worked beside the great artist learning how to grind and mix colors and prepare canvases, there grew between them a warm friendship based on mutual respect and love of art. Created from meager but authentic facts, the story, told by Juan, depicts the life and character of Velázquez and the loyalty of the talented seventeenth-century slave who eventually won his freedom and the right to be an artist." Booklist

Tripp, Jenny

Pete & Fremont; [by] Jenny Tripp; with illustrations by John Manders. Harcourt 2007 180p il $16; pa $5.95

Grades: 2 3 4   **Fic**

1. Dogs -- Fiction 2. Bears -- Fiction 3. Circus -- Fiction
ISBN 978-0-15-205629-2; 0-15-205629-7; 978-0-15-206238-5 pa; 0-15-206238-6 pa

LC 2006008757

When circus owner Mike decides Pete the poodle has grown too old to continue as the starring act, Pete forms an unlikely alliance with a young grizzly bear, who only wants to go home to the woods

"Manders's busy, freewheeling illustrations add an appropriate and enticing touch to this entertaining chapter book." SLJ

Another title about Pete is:
Pete's disappearing act (2009)

Trivas, Tracy

The wish stealers. Aladdin 2010 283p $16.99

Grades: 4 5 6 7   **Fic**

1. Wishes -- Fiction
ISBN 978-1-4169-8725-3; 1-4169-8725-8

LC 2009-42742

"Wish-obsessed sixth-grader Griffin Penshine's life changes dramatically following a chance encounter with an evil old woman, who curses her with a gift of 11 Indian Head pennies. Each penny represents a wish stolen from a wishing fountain, and the curse says that the person holding the stolen wishes will never have a good wish come true (bad ones will, though)." Publ Wkly

Trueit, Trudi Strain

No girls allowed (dogs okay) [illustrated by Jim Paillot] Aladdin Paperbacks 2009 128p il (Secrets of a lab rat) $14.99; pa $4.99

Grades: 2 3 4   **Fic**

1. School stories 2. Twins -- Fiction 3. Siblings -- Fiction
ISBN 978-1-4169-7592-2; 1-4169-7592-6; 978-1-4169-6111-6 pa; 1-4169-6111-9 pa

LC 2008-22329

Fearless nine-year-old 'Scab' McNally tries to get his twin sister's help in convincing their parents to let them get a dog, but when he em-

barrasses her in school with a particularly obnoxious invention, it looks like he has lost her cooperation forever.

"Scab is a likable, freethinking boy who is full of charm and humor . . . His many tips, diagrams, and facts scattered throughout are entertaining, as are the numerous comical black-and-white illustrations." SL.

Other titles in this series are:
Mom, there's a dinosaur in Beeson's Lake (2010)
Scab for president? (2011)

Trueman, Terry

Hurricane; a novel. HarperCollins 2008 137p $15.99; lib bdg $16.89

Grades: 5 6 7   **Fic**

1. Honduras -- Fiction 2. Hurricanes -- Fiction 3. Survival after airplane accidents, shipwrecks, etc. -- Fiction
ISBN 978-0-06-000018-9; 0-06-000018-X; 978-0-06-000019-6 lib bdg; 0-06-000019-8 lib bdg

LC 2007-02990

A revised edition of Swallowing the sun, published 2004 in the United Kingdom

"Thirteen-year-old Jose lives with his family in Honduras. A hurricane hits, causing the recently clear-cut hillside adjacent to his village to become a mudslide that smothers and kills most of its fifty inhabitants. . . Jose quickly takes charge and becomes a resourceful member of his ailing community. This survival tale is concise but engaging. Trueman's descriptions of the village buried in mud and of the difficulties it creates for the survivors are vivid." Voice Youth Advocates

Tuck, Pamela M.

As fast as words could fly; by Pamela M. Tuck; illustrations by Eric Velasquez. Lee & Low Books 2013 40 p. (hardcover) $18.95

Grades: K 1 2 3   **Fic**

1. Picture books for children 2. Segregation in education -- Fiction 3. Racism -- Fiction 4. Typewriting -- Fiction 5. African Americans -- Fiction 6. School integration -- Fiction 7. Civil rights movements -- Fiction 8. Family life -- North Carolina -- Fiction 9. Greenville (N.C.) -- History -- 20th century -- Fiction
ISBN 1600603483; 9781600603488

LC 2012030983

This book by Pamela M. Tuck, which won Lee & Low's New Voices award in 2007, is based on Tuck's "father's personal experiences with school segregation in 1960s North Carolina. . . . Mason Steele helps his father's civil rights efforts by writing letters for him; when the Steeles get a manual typewriter, Mason shows a gift for typing quickly and accurately. . . . Mason's typing skills earn him the chance to represent the school at a typing competition, but his record-setting victory there is tinged by prejudice." (Publishers Weekly)

Tunis, John R.

Keystone kids; with an introduction by Bruce Brooks. 1st Odyssey Classics ed.; Harcourt 1990 239p pa $5.95

Grades: 4 5 6 7   **Fic**

1. Jews -- Fiction 2. Baseball -- Fiction 3. Brothers -- Fiction 4. Antisemitism -- Fiction 5. Brooklyn Dodgers (Baseball team) -- Fiction
ISBN 0-15-205634-3

LC 2006274518

A reissue of the title first published 1943

When two young brothers join the Brooklyn Dodgers, one becomes team manager and is faced with the task of uniting a team rife with dissension and prejudice against the new Jewish rookie catcher.

The kid from Tomkinsville; with an introduction by Bruce Brooks. Odyssey Classic/Harcourt 2006 278p pa $5.95

Grades: 4 5 6 7 **Fic**
1. Baseball -- Fiction 2. Brooklyn Dodgers (Baseball team) -- Fiction
ISBN 0-15-205641-6

LC 2006277855

A reissue of the title first published 1940
As the newest addition to the Brooklyn Dodgers, young Roy Tucker's pitching helps pull the team out of a slump; but, when a freak accident ends his career as a pitcher, he must try to find another place for himself on the team.
Other titles about Roy Tucker and the Brooklyn Dodgers are:
World series (1941)
Keystone kids (1943)
Rookie of the year (1944)
The kid comes back (1946)

Rookie of the year; with an introduction by Bruce Brooks. 1st Odyssey Classics ed.; Harcourt 1990 220p pa $5.95
Grades: 4 5 6 7 **Fic**
1. Baseball -- Fiction 2. Brooklyn Dodgers (Baseball team) -- Fiction
ISBN 978-0-15-205648-3; 0-15-205648-3

LC 2006273436

A reissue of the title first published 1944
Dodger manager Spike Russell's efforts to rally his team to a pennant victory are threatened by a scheming club secretary and the seeming irresponsibility of a star rookie pitcher.

Turnage, Sheila
★ The **ghosts** of Tupelo Landing; by Sheila Turnage. Kathy Dawson Books 2014 368 p. (hardcover) $16.99
Grades: 5 6 7 8 **Fic**
1. Ghost stories 2. Hotels and motels 3. City and town life -- Fiction 4. Ghosts -- Fiction 5. Hotels -- Fiction 6. Identity -- Fiction 7. Foundlings -- Fiction 8. Haunted places -- Fiction 9. North Carolina -- Fiction 10. Mystery and detective stories 11. Community life -- North Carolina -- Fiction
ISBN 0803736711; 9780803736719

LC 2013019376

In this book, by Sheila Turnage, "when Miss Lana makes an Accidental Bid at the Tupelo auction and winds up the mortified owner of an old inn, she doesn't realize there's a ghost in the fine print. Naturally, Desperado Detective Agency (aka Mo and Dale) opens a paranormal division to solve the mystery of the ghost's identity. But Mo and Dale start to realize . . . [p]eople can also be haunted by their own past." (Publisher's note)

The **odds** of getting even; by Sheila Turnage. Kathy Dawson Books, an imprint of Penguin Group (USA) Inc. 2015 352 p. illustration (hardback) $16.99
Grades: 5 6 7 8 **Fic**
1. Mystery fiction 2. Crime -- Fiction 3. Fathers -- Fiction 4. North Carolina -- Fiction 5. Mystery and detective stories 6. Community life -- North Carolina -- Fiction
ISBN 9780803739611

LC 2015008293

In this book, by Sheila Turnage, "Mo and Dale, aka Desperado Detectives, head to court as star witnesses against Dale's daddy--confessed kidnapper Macon Johnson. Dale's nerves are jangled, but Mo, who doesn't mind getting even with Mr. Macon for hurting her loved ones, looks forward to a slam dunk conviction--if everything goes as expected." (Publisher's note)
"The author gracefully weaves a laundry list of characters with a plot that has a lot of moving pieces, and she does it with charm and humor,

hitting the sweet spot for young readers searching for more-complex tales but not ready to leave the silly behind." Kirkus

★ **Three** times lucky; by Sheila Turnage. Dial Books for Young Readers 2012 256 p. (hardcover) $16.99
Grades: 5 6 7 8 **Fic**
1. Absent mothers -- Fiction 2. Adopted children -- Fiction 3. Abandoned children -- Fiction 4. Murder -- Fiction 5. Identity -- Fiction 6. Foundlings -- Fiction 7. Restaurants -- Fiction 8. North Carolina -- Fiction 9. Mystery and detective stories 10. Community life -- North Carolina -- Fiction
ISBN 0803736703; 9780803736702

LC 2011035027

John Newbery Honor Book (2013)
This is the story of Mo LoBeau, who washed downstream as an infant 11 years ago and who has since been in the care of the Colonel, "a stranger who can't remember anything about his own past," and "Miss Lana, owner of the Tupelo Cafe. Mo . . . loves the Colonel and Lana, but" wonders about her origins. She "send[s] messages in bottles to her 'Upstream Mother.'" Also featured are "an out-of-town detective, a dead body . . . , a long-forgotten bank robbery, and a kidnapping." (Publishers Weekly)

Twain, Mark, 1835-1910
★ The **adventures** of Tom Sawyer; illustrated by Barry Moser; afterword by Peter Glassman. Books of Wonder 1989 261p il $24.99
Grades: 5 6 7 8 **Fic**
1. Missouri -- Fiction 2. Mississippi River -- Fiction
ISBN 0-688-07510-X
First published 1876
The adventures and pranks of a mischievous boy growing up in a Mississippi River town on the early nineteenth century.

Uchida, Yoshiko
★ A **jar** of dreams. Atheneum Pubs. 1981 131p hardcover o.p. pa $4.99
Grades: 5 6 7 8 **Fic**
1. California -- Fiction 2. Prejudices -- Fiction 3. Family life -- Fiction 4. Japanese Americans -- Fiction
ISBN 0-689-50210-9; 0-689-71672-9 pa

LC 81-3480

"Rinko in her guilelessness is genuine and refreshing, and her worries and concerns seem wholly natural, honest, and convincing." Horn Book
Other titles about Rinko Tsujimura and her family are:
The best bad thing (1983)
The happiest ending (1985)

★ **Journey** to Topaz; a story of the Japanese-American evacuation. illustrated by Donald Carrick. Heyday Books 2005 149p il pa $9.95
Grades: 5 6 7 8 **Fic**
1. World War, 1939-1945 -- Fiction 2. Japanese Americans -- Evacuation and relocation, 1942-1945 -- Fiction
ISBN 978-1-890771-91-1 pa; 1-890771-91-0 pa

LC 2004-16537

First published 1971 by Scribner
After the Pearl Harbor attack an eleven-year-old Japanese-American girl and her family are forced to go to an aliens camp in Utah
Followed by: Journey home (1978)

Umansky, Kaye
Clover Twig and the magical cottage; illustrated by Johanna Wright. Roaring Brook 2009 297p il $16.99

Grades: 4 5 6 **Fic**

1. Magic -- Fiction 2. Witches -- Fiction

ISBN 978-1-59643-507-0; 1-59643-507-0

"British author Umansky's giggle-worthy characterizations and dialogue make this winsome read-aloud stand out from the pack." Kirkus

Solomon Snow and the stolen jewel. Candlewick Press 2007 245p $12.99

Grades: 5 6 7 8 **Fic**

1. Orphans -- Fiction

ISBN 978-0-7636-2793-5; 0-7636-2793-3

LC 2006-47331

Sequel to: The silver spoon of Solomon Snow (2005)

While trying to rescue Prudence's father from prison, Solomon, Prudence, the Infant Prodigy, and Mr. Skippy the rabbit find themselves caught up in the mad plans of the villainous Dr. Calimari to steal a fabulous and cursed ruby.

"Fans of Lemony Snicket will enjoy this fast-paced read. . . . Reluctant readers might find the short chapters, silly comedy, and simple characters attractive." SLJ

Updale, Eleanor

Johnny Swanson. David Fickling Books 2011 383p $16.99; lib bdg $19.99

Grades: 4 5 6 **Fic**

1. Mystery fiction 2. Fraud -- Fiction 3. Honesty -- Fiction 4. Homicide -- Fiction 5. Great Britain -- Fiction 6. Single parent family -- Fiction 7. Mother-son relationship -- Fiction

ISBN 0-385-75198-2; 0-385-75199-0 lib bdg; 978-0-385-75198-8; 978-0-385-75199-5 lib bdg

LC 2010-11762

In 1929 England, eleven-year-old Johnny Swanson helps his widowed mother by starting a newspaper advertising scam, which leads him to a real-life murder mystery. "Grades five to eight." (Bull Cent Child Books)

This is "a compelling tale. . . . Updale spins an enjoyable tale, seamlessly mixing the humor of Johnny's fraudulent ads . . . with the seriousness of medical fraud and murder, as well as painting a fascinating picture of an England that is just starting to forget the sacrifices made by WWI soldiers." Publ Wkly

Upjohn, Rebecca

The **secret** of the village fool; by Rebecca Upjohn; illustrated by Renne Benoit. Second Story Press 2012 32 p. $18.95

Grades: 5 6 7 8 **Fic**

1. World War, 1939-1945 -- Jews -- Fiction 3. World War, 1939-1945 -- Poland -- Fiction 4. World War, 1939-1945 -- Children -- Fiction

ISBN 1926920759; 9781926920757

In this children's book by Rebecca Upjohn, illustrated by Renne Benoit, "Milek and his brother Munio live in a sleepy village in Poland. . . . They reluctantly do as their mother asks when she asks them to visit their neighbor Anton, knowing that the rest of the village laughs at him because of his strange habits of speaking to animals and only eating vegetables. Things change quickly when war comes to their town in the form of Nazi soldiers searching for Jewish families like that of Milek and Munio." (Publisher's note)

Urban, Linda

★ The **center** of everything; by Linda Urban. Houghton Mifflin Harcourt 2013 208 p. $15.99

Grades: 4 5 6 7 **Fic**

1. Wishes -- Fiction 2. Bereavement -- Fiction

ISBN 0547763484; 9780547763484

LC 2012954515

In this book, "months after her grandmother's death, 12-year-old Ruby Pepperdine composes a winning essay honoring her New Hampshire town's namesake" and will get to read it to the community. But she's more concerned that "she didn't listen to her grandmother's final words before she died. Ruby thinks that maybe if she wishes hard enough, 'everything will be back to how it is supposed to be,' but making a wish the right way is a tricky business." (Publishers Weekly)

★ A **crooked** kind of perfect. Harcourt 2007 213p $16; pa $5.95

Grades: 4 5 6 **Fic**

1. School stories 2. Musicians -- Fiction 3. Family life -- Fiction 4. Organ (Musical instrument) -- Fiction

ISBN 978-0-15-206007-7; 0-15-206007-3; 978-0-15-206608-6 pa; 0-15-206608-X pa

LC 2006-100622

Ten-year-old Zoe Elias, who longs to play the piano but must resign herself to learning the organ, instead, finds that her musicianship has a positive impact on her workaholic mother, her jittery father, and her school social life.

"An impressive and poignant debut novel. . . . The refreshing writing is full of pearls of wisdom, and readers will relate to this fully developed character. The sensitive story is filled with hope and humor." SLJ

★ **Hound** dog true. Harcourt 2011 152p $15.99

Grades: 3 4 5 **Fic**

1. School stories 2. Moving -- Fiction 3. Shyness -- Fiction 4. Janitors -- Fiction 5. Friendship -- Fiction 6. Family life -- Fiction

ISBN 978-0-547-55869-1; 0-547-55869-4

LC 2011009599

Mattie, a shy fifth-grader, wants to hide out at her new school by acting as apprentice to her Uncle Potluck, the custodian, but her plan falls apart when she summons the courage to speak about what matters most and finds a true friend.

"Combining Mattie's poignant writing and interior monologue, exquisite character development and a slow, deliberate pace, Urban spins a story that rings true." Kirkus

Weekends with Max and his dad; written by Linda Urban; illustrated by Katie Kath. Houghton Mifflin Harcourt 2016 160 p. illustrations (hardback) $16.99

Grades: 1 2 3 4 **Fic**

1. Father-son relationship -- Fiction 2. Children of divorced parents -- Fiction 3. Divorce -- Fiction 4. Neighborhoods -- Fiction 5. Fathers and sons -- Fiction

ISBN 9780544598171

LC 2015014878

This juvenile novel, by Linda Urban and illustrated by Katie Kath, depicts the child of a divorced couple. "Max and his dad love their weekends together. Weekends mean pancakes, pizza, spy games, dog-walking, school projects, and surprising neighbors! Every weekend presents a small adventure as Max gets to know his dad's new neighborhood—and learns some new ways of thinking about home." (Publisher's note)

"Urban's touch is light throughout, and with likable characters, cheerful black-and-white illustrations (final art not seen), and a story just right for budding chapter-book readers, she's off to a good start." Horn Book

Ursu, Anne

★ **Breadcrumbs**; drawings by Erin McGuire. Walden Pond Press 2011 313p il $16.99

Grades: 4 5 6 7 **Fic**
1. Fairy tales 2. Magic -- Fiction 3. Friendship -- Fiction
ISBN 978-0-06-201505-1; 0-06-201505-2
LC 2010045666

"Fifth-grader Hazel embarks on a memorable journey into the Minnesota woods to find her best friend Jack, who vanishes after a shard of glass pierces his eye. . . . Hazel enters the woods to find 'an entirely different place,' populated by creatures from the pages of Hans Christian Andersen. . . . [This is a] multi-layered, artfully crafted, transforming testament to the power of friendship." Kirkus

The **Real** Boy. Harpercollins Childrens Books 2013 288 p. (hardcover) $16.99
Grades: 3 4 5 6 7 **Fic**
1. Occult fiction -- Fiction 2. Fantasy fiction -- Fiction
ISBN 0062015079; 9780062015075
LC 2013021861

In this book, "an isolated, insecure orphan living in magical Aletheia becomes a 'real boy' when his ordered world crumbles and he must rely on himself." Oscar works for the magician Caleb. "When urgent business takes Caleb away, his apprentice is murdered, and Oscar must run Caleb's shop. Lacking social skills, Oscar longs to fold 'up, like an envelope,' but he manages the shop with help from a kindhearted girl who befriends him." More things go wrong, and Oscar must help. (Kirkus Reviews)

Usher, Mark David
The **golden** ass of Lucius Apuleius; adapted from the Latin original by M.D. Usher; illustrations by T. Motley. David R. Godine 2011 85p il $17.95
Grades: 4 5 6 7 **Fic**
1. Magic -- Fiction 2. Social classes -- Fiction 3. Classical mythology -- Fiction
ISBN 978-1-56792-418-3; 1-56792-418-2
LC 2010032978

Lucius Apuleius, a young nobleman fascinated by magic, accidentally turns himself into an ass and then sets out on a journey that reveals to him the conditions of peasants and slaves in and around Thessaly and leads him to find redemption as a follower of Isis and Osiris.

"A faithful (if relatively clean) version of the world's oldest surviving complete novel. . . . Though all of the sex and most of the dissolute behavior has been excised, the lad's first transformation is milked throughout for double entendres . . . and there are plenty of silly incidents and names . . . to lighten the overall tone. Motley's elaborate illustrated initials and pen-and-ink drawings add satiric bite. . . . An entertaining romp." Kirkus

Vail, Rachel
★ **Justin** Case; school, drool, and other daily disasters. illustrated by Matthew Cordell. Feiwel and Friends 2010 245p il $16.99
Grades: 3 4 5 **Fic**
1. School stories 2. Family life -- Fiction
ISBN 978-0-312-53290-1; 0-312-53290-3

"Honest and full of heart, Justin Case is a story for an oft-ignored segment of kids: the sensitive, introverted, and observant." SLJ

Well, that was awkward; Rachel Vail. Viking 2017 320 p. (hardcover) $16.99
Grades: 5 6 7 8 **Fic**
1. Friendship -- Fiction 2. Triangles (Interpersonal relations) -- Fiction
ISBN 9780670013081
LC 2016020347

In his book, by Rachel Vail, "Gracie has never felt like this before. . . . And the reason is standing right there in front of her, all tall and weirdly good-looking: A.J. But it turns out A.J. likes not Gracie but Gracie's beautiful best friend, Sienna. Obviously Gracie is happy for Sienna. . . . She helps Sienna compose the best texts, responding to A.J.'s surprisingly funny and appealing texts. . . . Because Gracie is fine. . . . She's had lots of practice being the sidekick, second-best." (Publisher's note)

"Hilarious and heartfelt." Kirkus

Valente, Catherynne M.
The **boy** who lost Fairyland; Catherynne M. Valente; illustrated by Ana Juan. Feiwel & Friends 2015 240 p. (Fairyland) (hardback) $16.99
Grades: 5 6 7 8 **Fic**
1. Fantasy fiction 2. Trolls -- Fiction 3. Fantasy 4. Changelings -- Fiction
ISBN 1250023491; 9781250023490; 9781250073327
LC 2014042417

In this novel, by Catherynne M. Valente, illustrated by Ana Juan, "when a young troll named Hawthorn is stolen from Fairyland by the Golden Wind, he becomes a changeling--a human boy--in the strange city of Chicago. . . . Left with a human family, Hawthorn struggles with his troll nature and his changeling fate. But when he turns twelve, he stumbles upon a way back home, to a Fairyland much changed from the one he remembers." (Publisher's note)

"In this fourth book in the fantastical series, a young troll named Hawthorn is stolen away by the Golden Wind and brought to live in Chicago as a changeling. When he turns 12, he finds a way back to Fairyland, a place now much changed from the magical realm he left...While readers unfamiliar with the series can certainly jump in with this novel, most will want to start at the beginning. A phenomenal fantasy series worthy of a spot in every library collection." SLJ

Other titles in this series are:
The Girl who Soared Over Fairyland and Cut the Moon in Two (2013)
The Girl who Circumnavigated Fairyland in a Ship of her Own Making (2011)
The Girl who Fell Beneath Fairyland and Led the Revels There (2012)

★ The **girl** who circumnavigated Fairyland in a ship of her own making; [by] Catherynne M. Valente; with illustrations by Ana Juan. Feiwel and Friends 2011 247p il $16.99
Grades: 4 5 6 7 8 **Fic**
1. Fantasy fiction
ISBN 978-0-312-64961-6; 0-312-64961-4
LC 2010050895

"The book's appeal is crystal clear from the outset: this is a kind of The Wonderful Wizard of Oz by way of Alice's Adventures in Wonderland, made vivid by Juan's Tenniel-inflected illustrations. . . . Those who thrill to lovingly wrought tales of fantasy and adventure . . . will be enchanted." Publ Wkly

The **girl** who fell beneath Fairyland and led the revels there; by Catherynne M. Valente; with illustrations by Ana Juan. Feiwel and Friends 2012 258 p. $16.99
Grades: 4 5 6 7 8 **Fic**
1. Fantasy fiction 2. Magic -- Fiction 3. Fairies -- Fiction
ISBN 0312649622; 9780312649623

In this book by Catherynne M. Valente, illustrated by Ana Juan, "September has longed to return to Fairyland after her first adventure there. And when she finally does, she learns that its inhabitants have been losing their shadows--and their magic--to the world of Fairyland Below. This underworld has a new ruler: Halloween, the Hollow Queen, who is September's shadow. And Halloween does not want to give Fairyland's shadows back." (Publisher's note)

The **Girl** Who Soared over Fairyland and Cut the Moon in Two; by Catherynne M. Valente; illustrated by Ana Juan. Feiwel & Friends 2013 256 p. $16.99

Grades: 4 5 6 7 8   **Fic**

1. Moon -- Fiction 2. Fairies -- Fiction 3. Female friendship -- Fiction

ISBN 1250023505; 9781250023506

In this book, by Catherynne M. Valente, September is "tasked with delivering a package to the moon, which has begun to shudder and shake with moonquakes because a . . . yeti is trying to break it to pieces. September and her friends traverse the moon, meet their fates, encounter older and younger versions of themselves, and wonder what, exactly, makes them who they are--all while trying to find the speedy yeti and stop him from his destructive plans." (Booklist)

"In this third volume, following The Girl Who Fell Beneath Fairyland and Led the Revels There, September returns to Fairyland and finds herself on a mission to stop a vengeful yeti from destroying his Fairy abusers--and everyone else on the moon. September is now wiser and sadder, and longs for autonomy; likewise, Fairyland and its inhabitants have become darker and more adult." (Horn Book)

Valério, Geraldo

Turn on the night; by Geraldo Valério. Groundwood Books 2016 40 p. color illustrations $18.95

Grades: PreK K 1   **Fic**

1. Dreams -- Fiction

ISBN 1554988411; 9781554988419

In this book, by Geraldo Valério, "a little girl falls asleep and in her dream becomes a huge gray wolf, like the one in her bedtime story. Out the window she leaps, and a marvelous nighttime adventure unfolds. She visits the rooster in his coop, and invites him to hop upon her back and together they run through the night. A reindeer joins in the fun, until the three are suddenly stopped in their tracks by a giant dazzling star." (Publisher's note)

"Dwelling in images of sinuous animals, sweeping landscapes, and the sheer joy of running for the sake of running, Valério's paint and pencil artwork almost vibrates with the idea that not even the sky is the limit in one's dreams." Pub Wkly

Van Cleve, Kathleen

★ **Drizzle**. Dial Books for Young Readers 2010 358p il $16.99

Grades: 4 5 6   **Fic**

1. Rain -- Fiction 2. Farms -- Fiction 3. Magic -- Fiction 4. Droughts -- Fiction

ISBN 978-0-8037-3362-6; 0-8037-3362-3

                          LC 2009-23819

When a drought threatens her family's magical rhubarb farm, eleven-year-old Polly tries to find a way to make it rain again

"Van Cleve's debut is emotionally subtle and action packed with a highly memorable setting." Publ Wkly

Van Draanen, Wendelin, 1965-

Flipped. Knopf 2001 212p $14.95

Grades: 6 7 8 9   **Fic**

1. Family life 2. Conduct of life 3. Self-perception 4. Interpersonal relations

ISBN 9780375811746; 0-375-81174-5; 0-375-82544-4 pa

                          LC 2001-29238

In alternating chapters, two teenagers describe how their feelings about themselves, each other, and their families have changed over the years. "Grades six to nine." (Bull Cent Child Books)

"There's lots of laugh-out-loud egg puns and humor in this novel. There's also, however, a substantial amount of serious social commentary woven in, as well as an exploration of the importance of perspective in relationships." SLJ

★ **Sammy** Keyes and the hotel thief. Knopf 1998 163p il hardcover o.p. pa $6.50

Grades: 4 5 6 7   **Fic**

1. Mystery fiction

ISBN 978-0-679-88839-0; 0-679-89264-8 pa

                          LC 97-40776

Thirteen-year-old Sammy's penchant for speaking her mind gets her in trouble when she involves herself in the investigation of a robbery at the "seedy" hotel across the street from the seniors' building where she is living with her grandmother

"This is a breezy novel with vivid characters." Bull Cent Child Books

Other titles about Sammy Keyes are:

Sammy Keyes and the skeleton man (1998)

Sammy Keyes and the Sisters of Mercy (1999)

Sammy Keyes and the runaway elf (1999)

Sammy Keyes and the curse of Moustache Mary (2000)

Sammy Keyes and the Hollywood mummy (2001)

Sammy Keyes and the search for Snake Eyes (2002)

Sammy Keyes and the art of deception (2003)

Sammy Keyes and the psycho Kitty Queen (2004)

Sammy Keyes and the dead giveaway (2005)

Sammy Keyes and the wild things (2007)

Sammy Keyes and the cold hard cash (2008)

Sammy Keyes and the wedding crasher (2010)

Sammy Keyes and the night of skulls (2011)

Sammy Keyes and the power of Justice Jack (2012)

Sammy Keyes and the showdown in Sin City (2013)

Sammy Keyes and the killer cruise (2013)

Sammy Keyes and the kiss goodbye (2014)

Van Eekhout, Greg

The **boy** at the end of the world. Bloomsbury Children's Books 2011 212p $16.99

Grades: 4 5 6 7   **Fic**

1. Science fiction 2. Robots -- Fiction

ISBN 978-1-59990-524-2; 1-59990-524-8

                          LC 2010035741

Born half-grown in a world that is being destroyed, Fisher has instinctive knowledge of many things, including that he must avoid the robot that knows his name.

"A pleaser for readers who prefer their sf livened up with unpredictable elements and emotional complexity." Booklist

Van Leeuwen, Jean

★ **Bound** for Oregon; pictures by James Watling. Dial Bks. for Young Readers 1994 167p il map hardcover o.p. pa $5.99

Grades: 4 5 6   **Fic**

1. Oregon Trail -- Fiction 2. Overland journeys to the Pacific -- Fiction

ISBN 0-14-038319-0 pa

                          LC 93-26709

A fictionalized account of the journey made by nine-year-old Mary Ellen Todd and her family from their home in Arkansas westward over the Oregon Trail in 1852

"The appealing narrator, the forthright telling, and the concrete details of life along the Oregon Trail will draw readers into the story." Booklist

Cabin on Trouble Creek. Dial Books for Young Readers 2004
119p $16.99; pa $6.99

Grades: 4 5 6 7 **Fic**

1. Ohio -- Fiction 2. Brothers -- Fiction 3. Frontier and pioneer
life -- Fiction

ISBN 0-8037-2548-5; 0-14-241164-7 pa

LC 2003-14151

In 1803 in Ohio, two young brothers are left to finish the log cabin
and guard the land while their father goes back to Pennsylvania to fetch
their mother and younger siblings.

"Excellent pacing is what makes this novel work so well. . . . The
suspense builds consistently. The boys' struggle is portrayed realistically, without sugarcoating nature's harshness." SLJ

Van Leeuwen, Joke, 1952-

Eep! Joke van Leeuwen; translated by Bill Nagelkerke. Gecko
Press 2012 149 p. ill.

Grades: 3 4 5 **Fic**

1. Fantasy fiction 2. Birds -- Fiction 3. Girls -- Fiction 4.
Friendship -- Fiction

ISBN 1877579076; 9781877579073

In this children's book by Dutch children's author Joke van Leeuwen, "avid bird watcher Warren finds a strange creature under a bush.
'This was a bird in the shape of a little girl. Or a little girl in the shape
of a bird.' . . . He takes the bird-girl home to his reclusive wife, Tina. . .
. When Beedy flies away one day without a good-bye, Warren and Tina
. . . begin to search for their bird-girl. On their quest, they meet a host of
equally downtrodden individuals." (Kirkus Reviews)

"This original and creative work is compelling from the opening
drawing right to the end of the book." SLJ

Van Vleet, Carmella

Eliza Bing is (not) a big, fat quitter; by Carmella Van Vleet; illustrated by Karen Donnelly. Holiday House 2014 165 p. (hardcover)
$16.95

Grades: 3 4 5 6 7 **Fic**

1. Family life -- Fiction 2. Tae kwon do -- Fiction 3. Attention
deficit disorder -- Fiction 4. Martial arts -- Fiction 5. Determination
(Personality trait) -- Fiction 6. Attention-deficit hyperactivity
disorder -- Fiction

ISBN 082342944X; 9780823429448

LC 2013015279

This novel, written by Carmella Van Vleet and illustrated by Karen
Donnelly, is "about determination and the rewards of hard work[.] A
preteen girl struggling with ADHD must stick with a summer taekwondo
class to prove that she s dedicated enough to pursue her true passion:
cake decorating." (Publisher's note)

"Fast moving and humorous with chapter titles such as 'Sticky Note
to Self: Wear White Underwear on Wednesdays and Saturdays,' feisty
Eliza will have readers, especially those with ADHD, rooting for her."
SLJ

Vande Velde, Vivian

8 class pets + one squirrel ÷ one dog; illustrated by Steve Björkman.
Holiday House 2011 68p il $15.95

Grades: 2 3 4 **Fic**

1. School stories 2. Animals -- Fiction

ISBN 978-0-8234-2364-4; 0-8234-2364-6

LC 2010048153

A dog chases a squirrel into an elementary school one night, creating
monumental chaos.

This is a "fast-paced romp. . . . The action is predictably frenetic, but
the changes in voice from chapter to chapter provide a refreshing and
humorous diversion from most chapter-book fare. . . . Occasional pen-

and-ink spot illustrations add energy to an already high-octane story."
Kirkus

Frogged; Vivian Vande Velde. Houghton Mifflin Harcourt 2013
208 p. $16.99

Grades: 5 6 7 8 **Fic**

1. Fantasy fiction 2. Fractured fairy tales 3. Fairy tales 4. Frogs
-- Fiction 5. Humorous stories 6. Princesses -- Fiction 7. Self-
perception -- Fiction

ISBN 054794215X; 9780547942155

LC 2013003905

In this alternate version of "The Frog Prince," "Princess Imogene,
who is 12 and 'gawky,' is tired of falling short in her family's eyes. The
real trouble begins when a . . . frog, who tells Imogene he's a prince beset by a witch's spell, tricks her into kissing him. He returns to his human
form, but she is transformed into a frog as a result; worse, he was just the
lowly son of a wagon maker. Too kind to use that sort of deceit on someone else, Imogene searches for another solution." (Publishers Weekly)

Three good deeds. Harcourt 2005 147p $16; pa $5.95

Grades: 3 4 5 **Fic**

1. Geese -- Fiction 2. Witches -- Fiction

ISBN 0-15-205382-4; 0-15-205455-3 pa

LC 2004-29578

Caught stealing some goose eggs from a witch, Howard is cursed
for his heartlessness and turned into a goose himself, and he can only
become human again by performing three good deeds.

"With well-spaced print, plenty of dialogue, a strong dose of humor,
and more invention than many books written at this level, this goose tale
is a nicely accomplished, entertaining read." Booklist

Wizard at work; a novel in stories. Harcourt 2003 134p $16;
pa $5.95

Grades: 3 4 5 6 **Fic**

1. Magic -- Fiction 2. Princesses -- Fiction

ISBN 0-15-204559-7; 0-15-205309-3 pa

LC 2002-68665

A young wizard, who runs a school to teach wizards, looks forward
to a quiet summer off but is drawn into adventures with princesses, unicorns, and ghosts instead

"A lot of fairy-tale conventions are turned on their heads. . . . The
language sparkles with sunny good humor. . . . Lighthearted and sly."
Booklist

Vanderpool, Clare

★ **Moon** over Manifest. Delacorte Press 2010 351p $16.99; lib
bdg $19.99

Grades: 5 6 7 8 **Fic**

1. Kansas -- Fiction 2. Fathers -- Fiction 3. Great Depression,
1929-1939 -- Fiction

ISBN 978-0-385-73883-5; 0-385-73883-8; 978-0-385-90750-7
lib bdg; 0-385-90750-8 lib bdg

LC 2009-40042

Awarded the Newbery Medal, 2011

Twelve-year-old Abilene Tucker is the daughter of a drifter who, in
the summer of 1936, sends her to stay with an old friend in Manifest,
Kansas, where he grew up, and where she hopes to find out some things
about his past.

"The absolute necessity of story as a way to redemption and healing
past wounds is at the heart of this beautiful debut, and readers will cherish every word up to the heartbreaking yet hopeful and deeply gratifying
ending." Kirkus

★ **Navigating** Early; Clare Vanderpool. Delacorte Press 2013 320 p. $16.99

Grades: 5 6 7 8 **Fic**

1. Adventure fiction -- Fiction 2. Appalachian Trail -- Fiction 3. Eccentrics and eccentricities -- Fiction 4. Maine -- Fiction 5. Schools -- Fiction 6. Boarding schools -- Fiction 7. Adventure and adventurers -- Fiction

ISBN 0385742096; 9780307974129; 9780375990403; 9780385742092

LC 2012014973

Printz Honor Book (2014)

In this children's novel, by Clare Vanderpool, "Jack Baker, . . . after his mother's death, . . . [is] placed in a boy's boarding school in Maine. There, Jack encounters Early Auden. . . . Newcomer Jack feels lost yet can't help being drawn to Early. . . . When the boys find themselves unexpectedly alone at school, they embark on a quest on the Appalachian Trail in search of the great black bear. But what they are searching for is sometimes different from what they find." (Publisher's note)

Vaught, Susan

Things too huge to fix by saying sorry; Susan Vaught. Simon & Schuster Books for Young Readers 2016 352 p. (ebook) $15.99; (hardcover) $16.99

Grades: 5 6 7 8 **Fic**

1. Vendetta -- Fiction 2. Mississippi -- Fiction 3. Civil rights -- Fiction 4. Grandmothers -- Fiction 5. Race relations -- Fiction 6. Alzheimer's disease -- Fiction 7. Families -- Fiction 8. Oxford (Miss.) -- FIction 9. Civil rights movements -- Fiction 10. Oxford (Miss.) -- History -- 20th century -- Fiction

ISBN 9781481422819; 1481422790; 9781481422796

LC 2015025579

In this book, by Susan Vaught, "a mysterious note takes Dani Beans into the secrets of Ole Miss and its dark past. . . . Lately, Grandma Beans doesn't make a lot of sense. But when she tells Dani to find a secret key and envelope that she's hidden, Dani can't ignore her. So she investigates, with the help of her friend, Indri, and her not-friend, Mac." (Publisher's note)

"Combining middle-school mystery and civil rights history with reflections on dying, friendship, and the ethics of writing another's story from a racially different perspective, this novel is ambitious, thought provoking, and very readable." Booklist

Includes bibliographical references.

Vaupel, Robin

The **rules** of the universe by Austin W. Hale. Holiday House 2007 265p $16.95

Grades: 4 5 6 7 **Fic**

1. Science fiction 2. Death -- Fiction 3. Grandfathers -- Fiction

ISBN 978-0-8234-1811-4; 0-8234-1811-1

LC 2003-56751

Thirteen-year-old Austin Hale, an aspiring scientist and disciple of his grandfather, a Nobel Prize-winning molecular physicist, finds himself in control of a powerful energy force that can turn back time and turn his orbit upside down

"The captivating blend of scientific research and magic is effectively balanced against the stark realism of a boy facing his first significant losses; the overall tone is one of cautious optimism." Bull Cent Child Books

Vawter, Vince

★ **Paperboy**; Vince Vawter. 1st ed. Delacorte Press 2013 240 p. (library) $19.99; (hardcover) $16.99

Grades: 5 6 7 8 **Fic**

1. Stuttering -- Fiction 2. Race relations -- Fiction 3. Newspaper carriers -- Fiction 4. Self-esteem -- Fiction 5. Interpersonal relations -- Fiction 6. Family life -- Tennessee -- Fiction 7. Memphis (Tenn.) -- History -- 20th century -- Fiction

ISBN 0385742444; 9780307975058; 9780375990588; 9780385742443

LC 2012030546

Newbery Honor Book (2014)

In this book by Vince Vawter, "[a]fter an overthrown baseball busts his best friend's lip, 11-year-old Victor Vollmer takes over the boy's paper route. This is a particularly daunting task for the able-armed Victor as he has a prominent stutter that embarrasses him. . . . Through the paper route he meets a number of people, gains a much-needed sense of self and community, and has a life-threatening showdown with a local con man." (School Library Journal)

"Carefully crafted language, authenticity of setting and quirky characters that ring fully true all combine to make this a worthwhile read. Although Little Man's stutter holds up dialogue, that annoyance also powerfully reflects its stultifying impact on his life. An engaging and heartfelt presentation that never whitewashes the difficult time and situation as Little Man comes of age." Kirkus

Venable, Colleen A. F.

Raining cats and detectives; Colleen A.F. Venable; illustrated by Stephanie Yue. Graphic Universe 2012 46 p. col. ill. (lib. bdg. : alk paper) $27.93

Grades: 2 3 4 **Fic**

1. Cats -- Fiction 2. Detectives -- Fiction 3. Missing persons -- Fiction 4. Graphic novels 5. Humorous stories 6. Animals -- Fiction 7. Hamsters -- Fiction 8. Pet shops -- Fiction 9. Guinea pigs -- Fiction 10. Mystery and detective stories

ISBN 0761360085; 9780761360087

LC 2011021620

In author Colleen AF Venable's book, "[g]uinea pig Sasspants, her faithful, exuberantly enthusiastic sidekick, Hamisher the hamster, and all the denizens of Mr. Venezi's Pets & Stuff are still in the store . . . Then (human) Detective Pickles arrives and adopts Sasspants, so when Tummytickles, the bookstore cat next door, vanishes, there's no one to find him. Suddenly, everyone from the goldfish . . . to the snooty chinchillas are donning detective hats and well, calling themselves detectives. Will Sasspants return to save the day, or can Hamisher detect on his own?" (Kirkus)

Venkatraman, Padma

★ **Island's** end. G.P. Putnam's Sons 2011 240p $16.99

Grades: 5 6 7 8 9 **Fic**

1. India -- Fiction 2. Islands -- Fiction 3. Apprentices -- Fiction

ISBN 978-0-399-25099-6; 0-399-25099-9

LC 2010036298

"Uido's clear, intelligent, present-tense voice consistently engrosses as she pushes through doubt and loss to find the right path. The beach jungle and cliff settings are palpable. . . . There is very little information known about Andaman Islanders, making it hard to gauge the authenticity of this portrayal; the author's note indicates a respectful and diligent approach to her subject. . . . Refreshingly hopeful and beautifully written." Kirkus

Venuti, Kristin Clark

Leaving the Bellweathers. Egmont USA 2009 242p $15.99; lib bdg $18.99

Grades: 4 5 6 **Fic**

1. Authorship -- Fiction 2. Family life -- Fiction 3. Lighthouses -- Fiction 4. Household employees -- Fiction 5. Eccentrics and

eccentricities -- Fiction

ISBN 978-1-60684-006-1; 1-60684-006-1; 978-1-60684-050-4 lib bdg; 1-60684-050-9 lib bdg

LC 2009016244

In Eel-Smack-by-the-Bay, put-upon butler Tristan Benway writes a memoir of his years working for the chaotic and eccentric Bellweather family in their lighthouse, as he prepares for his long-awaited departure from indentured servitude

"Venuti's entertaining and humorous debut features an eccentric cast, absurdities, and droll details. . . . Readers will find much amusement in the quirky characters and scenarios touched with heart." Booklist

Another title about the Bellweathers is:

The butler gets a break (2010)

Verne, Jules

★ **20,000** leagues under the sea; illustrated by the Dillons; translated by Anthony Bonner. Books of Wonder 2000 394p il $21.95

Grades: 5 6 7 8 9 10 11 12 Adult **Fic**

1. Science fiction 2. Submarines -- Fiction

ISBN 0-688-10535-1

LC 00-24336

Original French edition, 1870

Retells the adventures of a French professor and his two companions as they sail above and below the world's oceans as prisoners on the fabulous electric submarine of the deranged Captain Nemo

Vernick, Audrey

Two Naomis; by Olugbemisola Rhuday-Perkovich and Audrey Vernick. Harpercollins Childrens Books 2016 208 p. $16.99; (ebook) $15.99

Grades: 4 5 6 7 **Fic**

1. Stepfamilies -- Fiction 2. Personal names -- Fiction 3. Children of divorced parents -- Fiction

ISBN 0062414259; 9780062414250; 9780062414274

This book, by Olugbemisola Rhuday-Perkovich and Audrey Vernick, is the "story of two girls, both named Naomi, whose divorced parents begin to date. . . . Other than their first names, Naomi Marie and Naomi Edith are sure they have nothing in common, and they wouldn't mind keeping it that way. . . . When Naomi Marie's mom and Naomi Edith's dad get serious about dating, each girl tries to cling to the life she knows and loves." (Publisher's note)

"A smart, endearing story about two girls who are blending families, growing up, and building a friendship." Kirkus

★ **Water** balloon. Clarion Books 2011 312p $16.99

Grades: 4 5 6 7 **Fic**

1. Dogs -- Fiction 2. Divorce -- Fiction 3. Friendship -- Fiction 4. Babysitters -- Fiction 5. Father-daughter relationship -- Fiction

ISBN 978-0-547-59554-2; 0-547-59554-9

LC 2011009847

With her best friends pulling away from her, her newly-separated parents deciding she should spend the summer at her father's new home, and a babysitting job she does not want, Marley's life is already as precarious as an overfull water balloon when a cute boy enters the picture.

"The book moves along at a pace that will keep tweens interested, and the dialogue among the characters feels real. Marley's relationships with her friends and family are complex, and even the most reluctant readers will relate to her and the choices that she makes." SLJ

Vernick, Shirley Reva

The **blood** lie; a novel. Cinco Puntos Press 2011 141p $15.95

Grades: 5 6 7 8 **Fic**

1. Love -- Fiction 2. Prejudices -- Fiction 3. Antisemitism -- Fiction 4. New York (State) -- Fiction 5. Jews -- United States

-- Fiction

ISBN 978-1-933693-84-2; 1-933693-84-3

LC 2011011429

"Based on an actual incident in Massena in 1928, the slim novel effectively mines layers of ignorance, fear, intolerance and manipulation, and it connects the incident to Henry Ford's anti-Semitic writing and to the lynching of Jewish businessman Leo Frank in 1915." Kirkus

Vernon, Ursula

Castle Hangnail; by Ursula Vernon. Dial Books for Young Readers, an imprint of Penguin Group (USA) Inc. 2015 384 p. (hardback) $16.99

Grades: 5 6 7 8 9 **Fic**

1. Humorous fiction 2. Magic -- Fiction 3. Witches -- Fiction 4. Haunted houses -- Fiction 5. Humorous stories

ISBN 0803741294; 9780803741294

LC 2014017106

In this book, by Ursula Vernon, "Molly shows up on Castle Hangnail's doorstep to fill the vacancy for a wicked witch [and] the castle's minions are understandably dubious. After all, she is twelve years old, barely five feet tall, and quite polite. . . . But the castle desperately needs a master or else the Board of Magic will decommission it, leaving all the minions without the home they love." (Publisher's note)

"Creatively drawn characters--from a Minotaur cook to a donkey-dragon to clockwork bees--enjoy mutual respect and will sacrifice whatever is needed to safeguard the castle and its master. The illustrations add whimsy to this delightful tale." Booklist

★ **Dragonbreath**: attack of the ninja frogs. Dial Books for Young Readers 2010 203p il $16

Grades: 3 4 5 **Fic**

1. Japan -- Fiction 2. Ninja -- Fiction 3. Dragons -- Fiction 4. Reptiles -- Fiction 5. Amphibians -- Fiction 6. Friendship -- Fiction

ISBN 978-0-8037-3365-7; 0-8037-3365-8

LC 2009012273

When Suki the salamander—the new foreign exchange student—is being stalked by ninja frogs, Danny, Wendell the iguana, and Suki travel to Great-grandfather Dragonbreath's home in mythical Japan to find a solution for the problem.

"The spirited illustrations, done in green and black with touches of red, capture the humor of the characters' adventures. This delightful easy chapter book could tempt reluctant readers into turning another page." SLJ

Other titles in this series are:

Dragonbreath (2009)

Dragonbreath: curse of the were-wiener (2010)

Dragonbreath: lair of the bat monster (2011)

Dragonbreath: no such thing as ghosts (2011)

Dragonbreath: curse of the were-wiener. Dial Books for Young Readers 2010 208p il $12.99

Grades: 3 4 5 6 7 **Fic**

1. School stories 2. Dragons -- Fiction 3. Iguanas -- Fiction 4. Frankfurters -- Fiction

ISBN 978-0-8037-3469-2; 0-8037-3469-7

LC 2009049358

When Danny Dragonbreath's best friend Wendell the iguana is bitten by one of the hot dogs from his school lunch, he begins to turn into a were-wiener.

"The book is just spooky enough for young readers who don't want to get too scared, and it features the return of the monster potato salad." Booklist

★ **Hamster** Princess; Harriet the invincible. by Ursula Vernon. Dial Books for Young Readers, an imprint of Penguin Group (USA) Inc. 2015 256 p. illustrations (Hamster Princess) (hardcover) $12.99

Grades: 3 4 5 **Fic**

1. Hamster -- Fiction 2. Princesses -- Fiction 3. Humorous fiction -- Fiction 4. Blessing and cursing -- Fiction 5. Humorous stories
ISBN 0803739834; 9780803739833

LC 2014034037

In this book, by Ursula Vernon, "Harriet Hamsterbone is not your typical princess. She may be quite stunning in the rodent realm (you'll have to trust her on this one), but she is not so great at trailing around the palace looking ethereal. . . . She finds the royal life rather . . . dull. One day, though, Harriet's parents tell her of the curse that a rat placed on her at birth, dooming her to prick her finger on a hamster wheel when she's twelve and fall into a deep sleep." (Publisher's note)

"Vernon deploys the same winning elements found in her Dragonbreath books, a mix of boldly drawn, two-tone cartoons, occasional speech bubbles, and a boisterously humorous text." Kirkus

Other titles in this series are:
Of mice and magic (2016)
Ratpunzel (2016)
Giant trouble (2016)

Vigilante, Danette

Trouble with half a moon. G. P. Putnam's Sons 2011 181p $16.99

Grades: 5 6 7 8 **Fic**

1. Faith -- Fiction 2. Friendship -- Fiction 3. Bereavement -- Fiction 4. Child abuse -- Fiction 5. Puerto Ricans -- Fiction 6. City and town life -- Fiction 7. Jamaican Americans -- Fiction
ISBN 978-0-399-25159-7; 0-399-25159-6

LC 2010-07377

Overwhelmed by grief and guilt over her brother's death and its impact on her mother, and at odds with her best friend, thirteen-year-old Dellie reaches out to a neglected boy in her building in the projects and learns from a new neighbor to have faith in herself and others.

"The story is told with considerable appeal and accessibility, and kids won't have to lead the same life as Dellie to recognize her travails." Bull Cent Child Books

Vining, Elizabeth Gray

Adam of the road; illustrated by Robert Lawson. Viking 1942 317p il $19.99; pa $6.99

Grades: 5 6 7 8 **Fic**

1. Minstrels -- Fiction 2. Middle Ages -- Fiction 3. Great Britain -- Fiction
ISBN 0-670-10435-3; 0-14-240659-7 pa
Awarded the Newbery Medal, 1943

Tale of a minstrel and his son Adam, who wandered through southeastern England in the thirteenth century. Adam's adventures in search of his lost dog and his beloved father led him from St. Alban's Abbey to London, and thence to Winchester, back to London, and then to Oxford where the three were at last reunited

Viorst, Judith, 1931-

Lulu's mysterious mission; Judith Viorst; illustrated by Kevin Cornell; jacket by Lane Smith. Atheneum Books for Young Readers 2014 192 p. (hardcover) $15.99

Grades: 2 3 4 5 **Fic**

1. Spies -- Fiction 2. Secrets -- Fiction 3. Babysitters -- Fiction 4. Behavior -- Fiction
ISBN 1442497467; 9781442497467; 9781442497474

LC 2013004350

In this book, by Judith Viorst, "Lulu has put her tantrum-throwing days behind her. That is, until her parents announce that they are going

on vacation—WITHOUT LULU. Not only that, but they are leaving her with the formidable Ms. Sonia Sofia Solinsky. . . . The second her parents are out of the house, Lulu tries out several elaborate schemes to bring them straight back. But just when she seems to finally be making some headway, her babysitter reveals an astonishing secret." (Publisher's note)

"Spoiled little Lulu is back in a third book to tackle a new challenge: a babysitter. Despite Lulu's objection that "babysitters sit babies, and I'm no baby," her parents head off on vacation, leaving her in the care of the intimidating Ms. Solinsky...Lulu now looks a little more like a regular girl, with a rounder nose and sneakers, but in the wide variety of diabolical facial expressions she wears, readers will recognize the same troublemaker they have come to know and love. Lulu's fans will be happy to read her next (mis)adventure." SLJ

Other titles include:
Lulu and the Brontosaurus
Lulu Walks the Dogs

Vivat, Booki

Frazzled; Everyday Disasters and Impending Doom. Booki Vivat. HarperCollins 2016 240 p. illustrations (hardcover) $12.99

Grades: 4 5 6 7 **Fic**

1. Girls -- Fiction 2. School children -- Fiction 3. Child psychology -- Fiction
ISBN 9780062398796

LC 2016936039

In this children's book by Booki Vivat, "Abbie is in crisis—and not just because she's starting middle school or because she's stuck in a family that doesn't quite get her or because everyone seems to have a Thing except her. . . . Frazzled dives right into the mind of this hilariously neurotic middle school girl as she tries to figure out who she is and where she belongs." (Publisher's note)

"Abbie's phobias and worries are charmingly depicted in this heavily illustrated hybrid novel. The humorous, doodlelike artwork makes her struggles entertaining and relatable." SLJ

Voake, Steve

Daisy Dawson is on her way! illustrated by Jessica Meserve. Candlewick Press 2008 98p il $14.99; pa $5.99

Grades: 2 3 4 **Fic**

1. Dogs -- Fiction 2. Animals -- Fiction
ISBN 978-0-7636-3740-8; 0-7636-3740-8; 978-0-7636-4294-5 pa; 0-7636-4294-0 pa

LC 2007-23150

One day when Daisy is late for school, an encounter with a butterfly leaves her suddenly able to communicate with animals, and when Boom, a stray dog, is caught by the pound, she enlists the help of a host of other animals to rescue him.

"Sprightly illustrations in a variety of shapes appear throughout. First in a series, this charmer, long on whimsy and adventure, is sure to appeal to newly independent and reluctant readers." SLJ

Other titles about Daisy Dawson are:
Daisy Dawson and the secret pond (2009)
Daisy Dawson and the big freeze (2010)
Daisy Dawson at the beach (2011)
Daisy Dawson on the farm (2012)

Voelkel, J.

The **end** of the world club; [by] J&P Voelkel. Egmont USA 2011 384p (The Jaguar stones) $16.99

Grades: 4 5 6 7 **Fic**

1. Adventure fiction 2. Mayas -- Fiction 3. Supernatural -- Fiction

4. Central America -- Fiction
ISBN 978-1-60684-072-6; 1-60684-072-X

LC 2010036641

Sequel to: Middleworld (2007)

With the end of the Mayan calendar fast approaching, fourteen-year-old Max Murphy and his friend Lola, the Maya girl who saved his life in the perilous jungle, race against time to outwit the twelve villainous Lords of Death, following the trail of the conquistadors into a forgotten land steeped in legend and superstition.

"The authors use Maya mythology and terms and add interesting facts about Spain and Spanish culture. This is a fast-paced book, and the action starts right away." SLJ

Middleworld; [by] J & P Voelkel [i.e., Jon Voelkel, Pamela Craik Voelkel] Smith and Kraus Publishers 2007 397p il (The Jaguar stones) $17.95; pa $8.99

Grades: 4 5 6 7   **Fic**

1. Adventure fiction 2. Mayas -- Fiction 3. Central America -- Fiction
ISBN 978-1-57525-561-3; 1-57525-561-8; 978-1-60684-071-9 pa; 1-60684-071-1 pa

"Suspense and intrigue, human sacrifice, smuggling, and secret doors and escape routes through pyramids ensure that the novel, the first in a projected trilogy, is likely to win legions of fans." SLJ

Followed by: The end of the world club (2010)

The river of no return; J&P Voelkel. Egmont USA 2012 348 p. ill., maps (hardcover) $16.99; (ebook) $16.99

Grades: 5 6 7 8   **Fic**

1. Mayas -- Fiction 2. Fantasy fiction 3. Supernatural -- Fiction 4. Adventure and adventurers -- Fiction 5. Indians of Central America -- Fiction
ISBN 1606840738; 9781606840733; 9781606842706

LC 2012007093

This is the third book in the Jaguar Stones series from J. and P. Voelkel. Here, "after spending the previous two books evading the disgusting and power-hungry machinations of the Death Lords of the Mayan Underworld, Max and Lola are back together again, trying to stop the same bad guys from taking over the world yet again." (School Library Journal)

Voigt, Cynthia

Dicey's song. Atheneum Pubs. 1982 196p $17.95; pa $6.99

Grades: 5 6 7 8   **Fic**

1. Siblings -- Fiction 2. Grandmothers -- Fiction
ISBN 0-689-30944-9; 0-689-86362-4 pa

LC 82-3882

Sequel to Homecoming

Awarded the Newbery Medal, 1983

"The vividness of Dicey is striking; Voigt has plumbed and probed her character inside out to fashion a memorable protagonist." Booklist

Mister Max; the book of kings. Newbery Medalist Cynthia Voigt; illustrated by Iacopo Bruno. Alfred A. Knopf 2015 352 p. illustrations (trade) $16.99

Grades: 5 6 7 8   **Fic**

1. Adventure fiction 2. Parents -- Fiction 3. Self-reliance -- Fiction 4. Missing persons -- Fiction 5. Problem solving -- Fiction 6. Adventure and adventurers -- Fiction
ISBN 0307976874; 9780307976871; 9780375971259

LC 2014017699

Sequel to: Mister Max : the book of secrets

In this book, by Cynthia Voigt, illustrated by Iacopo Bruno, Mister Max "sets off to rescue his missing parents! . . . He's solved case after case for other people in his business as 'solutioneer.' And he's puzzled out the coded messages sent by his father. He doesn't know exactly what's happened, but he knows his parents are in danger—and it's up to Max to save them." (Publisher's note)

"Fans of the first two books will be eager to see how the 'solutioneer' saves the day." SLJ

★ **Young** Fredle. Alfred A. Knopf 2011 227p il $16.99; lib bdg $19.99

Grades: 3 4 5 6   **Fic**

1. Adventure fiction 2. Cats -- Fiction 3. Dogs -- Fiction 4. Mice -- Fiction 5. Freedom -- Fiction
ISBN 978-0-375-86457-5; 0-375-86457-1; 978-0-375-96457-2 lib bdg; 0-375-96457-6 lib bdg

LC 2010-11430

"Readers will identify with the universal conflict at the heart of Fredle's journey—even as he longs for home, he enjoys the newfound freedom and experiences that contrast with the restrictive regulations of his clan. Yates's expressive cartoon spot art counters the book's darker, sadder moments with cheeriness." Publ Wkly

Vrabel, Beth

Pack of dorks; Beth Vrabel. Skyhorse Publishing, Inc. 2014 240 p. (hardback) $15.95

Grades: 4 5 6   **Fic**

1. School stories 2. Bullies -- Fiction 3. Friendship -- Fiction 4. Interpersonal relations -- Fiction 5. Schools -- Fiction 6. Bullying -- Fiction
ISBN 1629146234; 9781629146232

LC 2014021035

In this book, by Beth Vrabel, "Lucy knows that kissing Tom Lemmings behind the ball shed will make her a legend. But she doesn't count on [it] propelling her from coolest to lamest fourth grader overnight. Suddenly Lucy finds herself trapped in Dorkdom, where a diamond ring turns your finger green, where the boy you kiss hates you three days later, where your best friend laughs as you cry, where parents seem to stop liking you, and where baby sisters are born different." (Publisher's note)

"Debut author Vrabel takes three knotty, seemingly disparate problems--bullying, the plight of wolves and coping with disability--and with tact and grace knits them into an engrossing whole of despair and redemption." Kirkus

Another title in this series is:
Camp dork (2016)

Wagner, Hilary

Lords of Trillium; by Hilary Wagner; illustrated by Omar Rayyan. Holiday House 2014 224 p. (Nightshade chronicles) (hardcover) $17.95

Grades: 5 6 7 8   **Fic**

1. Fantasy fiction 2. Rats -- Fiction 3. Animal experimentation -- Fiction 4. Fantasy
ISBN 0823424138; 9780823424139

LC 2013031299

In this book, by Hilary Wagner, "when the albino rat Billycan left Trillium at the end of The White Assassin, he fled to the island of Tosca. There, here learns that a former ally, working undercover in Nightshade City, is plotting to free Killdeer's imprisoned evil generals and seize power. . . . But something even more sinister is afoot in Trillium City. . . . They discover that Prince Pharmaceuticals, the insidious corporation that tortured so many rats, is back in business." (Publisher's note)

"Wagner reveals lingering secrets, along with intrigue, rivalries, revenge, and redemption in the satisfying third book in this complex animal fantasy series." Booklist

Nightshade City; [illustrations by Omar Rayyan] Holiday House 2010 262p il $17.95

Grades: 5 6 7 8   **Fic**

1. Fantasy fiction 2. Rats -- Fiction

ISBN 978-0-8234-2285-2; 0-8234-2285-2

LC 2010-02474

Eleven years after the cruel Killdeer took over the Catacombs far beneath the human's Trillium City, Juniper Belancourt, assisted by Vincent and Victor Nightshade, leads a maverick band of rats to escape and establish their own city.

"The themes of love, loss and loyalty resonate through the novel, and the moments of darkness and violence are ultimately overpowered by hope and redemption. A good story well-told." Kirkus

Followed by: The white assassin (2011)

Waite, Michael P.

The **witches** of Dredmoore Hollow; by Riford McKenzie; with illustrations by Peter Ferguson. Marshall Cavendish Children 2008 264p il $16.99

Grades: 4 5 6 7   **Fic**

1. Aunts -- Fiction 2. Witches -- Fiction 3. New England -- Fiction

ISBN 978-0-7614-5458-8; 0-7614-5458-6

LC 2007-29781

Strange things begin happening at Elijah's New England home just before his twelfth birthday in 1927, especially after two aunts he had never met whisk him away to Moaning Marsh, where he realizes that they are witches who need something from him in order to remove a curse.

"The book has continuous action and piles of demonic atmosphere." SLJ

Walden, Mark

H.I.V.E; The Higher Institute of Villainous Education. Simon & Schuster Books for Young Readers 2007 309p $15.99; pa $6.99

Grades: 5 6 7 8   **Fic**

1. Criminals -- Fiction

ISBN 1-4169-3571-1; 978-1-4169-3571-1; 978-1-4169-3572-8 pa; 1-4169-3572-X pa

LC 2007-16205

"H.I.V.E. is operated on a volcanic island in a distant ocean by G.L.O.V.E., a shadowy organization of worldwide wickedness. And, as 13-year-old master of mischief Otto Malpense soon discovers, here the slickest of young tricksters, thieves, and hackers have been brought against their will to be trained as the next generation of supervillains. . . . [This] novel is a real page-turner; those who love superhero stories will eat it up." SLJ

Other titles about H.I.V.E. are:

H.I.V.E.: The Overlord protocol (2008)

H.I.V.E.: Escape velocity (2011)

H.I.V.E.: Dreadnought (2011)

Walker, Kate

I hate books! [by] Kate Walker; illustrated by David Cox. Cricket Books 2007 78p il $16.95

Grades: 2 3 4 5   **Fic**

1. School stories 2. Brothers -- Fiction 3. Books and reading -- Fiction

ISBN 978-0-8126-2745-9; 0-8126-2745-8

LC 2006-36492

Although he is a great storyteller and good at art, Hamish cannot read, even with remedial classes, but his brother Nathan finally comes up with a way to teach him

"This is a warm and fast-paced story. . . . Witty black-and-white line drawings enhance the narrative." SLJ

Wallace, Bill

★ **Skinny**-dipping at Monster Lake. Simon & Schuster Bks. for Young Readers 2003 212p hardcover o.p. pa $5.99

Grades: 4 5 6 7   **Fic**

ISBN 0-689-85150-2; 0-689-85151-0 pa

LC 2002-152820

When twelve-year-old Kent helps his father in a daring underwater rescue, he wins the respect he has always craved.

"This old-fashioned adventure has wide appeal, and the youngsters' games and camaraderie will hook even reluctant readers." SLJ

Wallace, Rich

The **ball** hogs; illustrated by Jimmy Holder. Alfred A. Knopf 2010 119p il (Kickers) $12.99

Grades: 2 3 4   **Fic**

1. Soccer -- Fiction

ISBN 978-0-375-85754-6; 0-375-85754-0

Nine-year-old Ben, a natural athlete and member of the Bobcats coed soccer team, wants to overcome his inexperience and prove himself on the field, but his obnoxious teammate, Mark, keeps hogging the ball.

"A good sports story for younger readers, this beginning chapter book balances bits of information about playing the game with realistic scenes on the field, at home, and at school. . . . Lively black-and-white drawings illustrate the story." Booklist

Other titles in this series are:

Fake out (2010)

Benched (2010)

Game-day jitters (2011)

Sports camp. Alfred A. Knopf 2010 149p $15.99; lib bdg $18.99

Grades: 4 5 6   **Fic**

1. Camps -- Fiction 2. Sports -- Fiction

ISBN 978-0-375-84059-3; 0-375-84059-1; 978-0-375-94059-0 lib bdg; 0-375-94059-6 lib bdg

LC 2009-04278

Eleven-year-old Riley Liston tries to fit in at Camp Olympia, a summer sports camp where he is one of the youngest boys.

Wicked cruel; Rich Wallace. Knopf Books for Young Readers 2013 208 p. (hardback) $16.99

Grades: 5 6 7 8   **Fic**

1. Ghost stories -- Fiction 2. Horror fiction 3. Schools -- Fiction 4. Halloween -- Fiction 5. Supernatural -- Fiction 6. New Hampshire -- Fiction 7. Folklore -- New Hampshire -- Fiction

ISBN 0375867481; 9780375865145; 9780375867484; 9780375967481

LC 2012042504

This book of three "ghostly stories explore urban legends--actually rural New England legends--and how they changed lives. A bullied boy moves away and dies from a brain injury, yet he is seen in a music video after his death. A team of horses drowns in a flooded brickyard, but on certain rainy nights, they run free. Five farm children die young, but one mysteriously communicates with a young boy who may be as afraid of girls as of ghosts." (Kirkus Reviews)

Wallace, Sandra Neil

Little Joe; illustrated by Mark Elliott. Alfred A. Knopf 2010 192p il $15.99; lib bdg $18.99

Grades: 3 4 5 6   **Fic**

1. Bulls -- Fiction 2. Farm life -- Fiction 3. Family life -- Fiction 4. Grandfathers -- Fiction 5. Father-son relationship -- Fiction

ISBN 978-0-375-86097-3; 0-375-86097-5; 978-0-375-96097-0 lib bdg; 0-375-96097-X lib bdg

"This is a sweet book about the relationships among three generations of farmers—Eli Stegner, his father, and his grandfather. It is also about Eli's connection to the first calf he gets to call his own. Little Joe is destined to be a winner at the county fair cattle show, but that blue ribbon will pretty much insure that he goes to the highest bidder and then to the butcher. . . . This thoughtful, tender book will appeal to those readers who are familiar with the Stegners' world, and many more will be able to identify with the highs and lows of familial love." SLJ

Walliams, David

★ The **boy** in the dress; illustrated by Quentin Blake. Razorbill 2009 231p il $15.99

Grades: 4 5 6 7   **Fic**

1. School stories 2. Soccer -- Fiction 3. Great Britain -- Fiction 4. Transvestites -- Fiction

ISBN 1-59514-299-1; 978-1-59514-299-3

"Dennis' life is boring and lonely. His mother left two years ago, his truck driver father is depressed, his brother is a bully and, worst of all, 'no hugging' is one of their household rules. But one thing Dennis does have is soccer—he's the leading scorer on his team." (Publisher's note) "Grades six to eight." (Bull Cent Child Books)

"Dennis is a bit surprised—but not terribly nonplussed—to discover that he enjoys wearing dresses. The 12-year-old does, however, realize this is not the kind of revelation he wants to share with his truck-driving dad, his older brother, or his mates on the school football team, where he is the star player. . . . Walliams . . . has written a witty, high-spirited, and, well, sensible story about cross-dressing and other real-life issues." Booklist

★ **Mr.** Stink; illustrated by Quentin Blake. Razorbill 2010 265p il pa $9.99

Grades: 4 5 6   **Fic**

1. School stories 2. Family life -- Fiction 3. Homeless persons -- Fiction

ISBN 978-1-59514-332-7 pa; 1-59514-332-7 pa

Walliams "has a gift for crafting memorable scenes and, in the person of Mr. Stink, has created a delightfully offbeat character. . . . Readers of all ages will be thrilled with the in-a-word perfect illustrations of the great Quentin Blake." Booklist

Walsh, Pat

★ The **Crowfield** curse. Chicken House 2010 326p il $16.99

Grades: 5 6 7 8   **Fic**

1. Magic -- Fiction 2. Orphans -- Fiction 3. Monasteries -- Fiction 4. Great Britain -- History -- 1154-1399, Plantagenets -- Fiction

ISBN 0-545-22922-7; 978-0-545-22922-7

LC 2009-51483

In 1347, when fourteen-year-old orphan William Paynel, an impoverished servant at Crowfield Abbey, goes into the forest to gather wood and finds a magical creature caught in a trap, he discovers he has the ability to see fays and becomes embroiled in a strange mystery involving Old Magic, a bitter feud, and ancient secrets.

"This suspenseful and spooky story will thrill readers. . . . With fascinating attention to detail and an edgy battle between evil and good, Walsh sweeps readers almost effortlessly into another time and place." SLJ

The **Crowfield** demon; Pat Walsh. Scholastic 2012 360 p. $16.99

Grades: 5 6 7 8   **Fic**

1. Fantasy fiction 2. Adventure fiction 3. Demonology -- Fiction 4. Magic -- Fiction 5. Orphans -- Fiction 6. Identity -- Fiction 7. Monasteries -- Fiction 8. Blessing and cursing -- Fiction 9. Great

Britain -- History -- 14th century -- Fiction

ISBN 054531769X; 9780545317696; 9780545373500

LC 2011029246

Sequel to: The Crowfield curse

This juvenile historical fantasy novel by Pat Walsh is the sequel to his earlier story 'The Crowfield Curse.' 'In The Crowfield Curse,' young monks' apprentice Will learned he was gifted with the Sight: able to see beyond this mortal coil into the spirit realms of Old Magic. Protected by the warrior fay Shadlok -- and befriended by the wry, wary hobgoblin called Brother Walter -- the boy is just coming into his strange powers. But now, from its very foundations, Crowfield Abbey has begun to crumble. As Will slaves to salvage the chapel, he discovers something truly terrifying. A heathen creature from a pagan past is creeping up through the rubble -- avowed to unleash havoc on holy ground!' (Publisher's note)

Walter, Mildred Pitts, 1922-

★ **Justin** and the best biscuits in the world; with illustrations by Catherine Stock. Lothrop, Lee & Shepard Bks. 1986 122p il pa $7.99; $16

Grades: 3 4 5 6   **Fic**

1. Sex role -- Fiction 2. Family life -- Fiction 3. Grandfathers -- Fiction 4. African Americans -- Fiction

ISBN 0-06-195891-3 pa; 0-688-06645-3

LC 86-7148

Coretta Scott King Award for text

Ten-year-old Justin feels that cleaning and keeping house is women's work until he spends time on his beloved grandfather's ranch." Grades three to six." (SLJ)

"The strong, well-developed characters and humorous situations in this warm family story will appeal to intermediate readers; the large print will draw slow or reluctant readers." SLJ

Walters, Eric

Catboy. Orca Book Publishers 2011 229p pa $9.95

Grades: 4 5 6 7   **Fic**

1. Boys -- Fiction 2. Cats -- Fiction 3. Canada -- Fiction

ISBN 978-1-55469-953-7 pa; 1-55469-953-3 pa

The wild cat colony Taylor has been caring for is at risk of being destroyed, and in order to save it, Taylor will need the help of all his friends.

"Walters' story . . . moves fast and is plenty appealing. . . . Solid writing, strong kid characters, caring adults, and cute animals could make this a popular choice." Booklist

The **money** pit mystery. Fitzhenry & Whiteside 2011 289p pa $9.95

Grades: 4 5 6 7   **Fic**

1. Mystery fiction 2. Islands -- Fiction 3. Family life -- Fiction 4. Buried treasure -- Fiction

ISBN 978-1-55455-123-1; 1-55455-123-4

"Sam's grandfather and mother had a fight years ago, and now Sam, his sister, and their mother are visiting him for the first time in years. When they arrive on tiny Oak Island, they are shocked to discover how rundown the man's once-immaculate house has become. To make matters worse, he isn't even there. When Sam, Beth, and their friend, Buzz, do some exploring, they are surprised by some security guards at the town's 'money pit.' Some folks believe that Captain Kidd buried treasure here. . . . This is a well-thought-out mystery with lots of suspense and a fully realized picture of a struggling family." SLJ

Ward, David

Between two ends. Amulet Books 2011 288p $16.95

Grades: 4 5 6 **Fic**

1. Fantasy fiction 2. Adventure fiction 3. Pirates -- Fiction 4. Arabian nights -- Fiction 5. Books and reading -- Fiction

ISBN 978-0-8109-9714-1; 0-8109-9714-2

LC 2010-23696

Trying to help his father deal with his long-standing depression, Yeats and his parents visit his grandmother's old and eerie house, where he discovers a pair of pirate bookends that unlock a thirty-year-old secret that Yeats must try to resolve by entering the exotic world of The Arabian Nights.

"Quickly sketching credible characters in both worlds, Ward plunges Yeats into a series of adventures. . . . Unexpected moments of humor lighten the gloomy prospect of failure and offer hope that the ending will resolve the family crisis so vividly portrayed in the opening chapters. A satisfying chapter-book fantasy." Booklist

Warner, Penny

The **secret** of the skeleton key. Egmont USA 2011 209p (The Code Busters Club) $15.99; e-book $15.99

Grades: 3 4 5 6 **Fic**

1. Mystery fiction 2. Ciphers -- Fiction 3. Cousins -- Fiction

ISBN 978-1-60684-162-4; 1-60684-162-9; 978-1-6068-4281-2 e-book

LC 2011003240

"Cody and Quinn notice their neighbor Mr. Skelton signaling from his window; later his house burns and cousins Jasper and Jezabel appear, searching for Mr. Skelton's will. By solving Mr. Skelton's coded clues, the club members manage to unearth the authentic document before his cousins can force him to sign a new one. . . . This well-crafted mystery reads smoothly; characters are well developed, clues . . . skillfully dropped, and the solution feels plausible." Booklist

Warner, Sally

EllRay Jakes is not a chicken! illustrated by Jamie Harper. Viking Children's Books 2011 108p il $14.99

Grades: 1 2 3 **Fic**

1. School stories 2. Bullies -- Fiction 3. California -- Fiction 4. Family life -- Fiction

ISBN 978-0-670-06243-0; 0-670-06243-X

LC 2010-25106

Eight-year-old EllRay's father has promised a family trip to Disneyland if EllRay can stay out of trouble for a week, but not defending himself against Jared, the class bully, proves to be a real challenge.

"Warner's clever plotting brings an unexpected and rewarding ending. EllRay's ingenuous narration and the well-observed classroom dynamics are the main draw, and Harper's cartoons, incorporated throughout, further enliven the story." Publ Wkly

Another title about EllRay is:

EllRay Jakes is a rock star! (2011)

EllRay Jakes is not a rock star; illustrated by Jamie Harper. Viking 2011 il $14.99

Grades: 1 2 3 **Fic**

1. School stories 2. Bullies -- Fiction 3. California -- Fiction 4. Family life -- Fiction 5. African Americans -- Fiction

ISBN 978-0-670-01158-2; 0-670-01158-4

LC 2011009182

Eight-year-old EllRay Jakes decides to 'borrow' his father's crystals to impress his classmates, but his plan to return the crystals before his father notices goes awry.

"The protagonist's voice is humorous, and the charming cartoon illustrations make this beginning chapter book approachable for reluctant readers." SLJ

EllRay Jakes Rocks the Holidays! by Sally Warner; illustrated by Brian Biggs. Viking, published by Penguin Group 2014 143 p. illustrations (hardcover) $14.99

Grades: 1 2 3 **Fic**

1. School stories 2. Christmas -- Fiction 3. African Americans -- Fiction 4. African American children -- Fiction 5. Schools -- Fiction 6. California -- Fiction 7. Family life -- California -- Fiction

ISBN 0451469097; 9780451469090

LC 2013048390

In this children's book, by Sally Warner, illustrated by Brian Biggs, "[i]t's almost Christmas and school is going great for EllRay. He's 'blending in' just the way he likes. So when his father tells him he should be proud to be part of the African-American 'community,' EllRay isn't so sure he wants to call attention to his differences. After all, he's only one of two boys in his class with brown skin. And then, totally by accident, he insults the other boy." (Publisher's note)

"In a holiday-themed episode, EllRay finds himself the emcee of his school's Winter Wonderland show. When he accidentally hurts a friend's feelings, it results in an exploration of friendship, values, and race perfectly pitched for middle graders. EllRay must ultimately make a difficult choice and stand up for what he knows is right. Biggs's black-and-white illustrations capture all the emotional nuances." Horn Book

Other titles in the series include:

Ellray Jakes is not a Chicken (2011)

Ellray Jakes is a Rock Star (2011)

Ellray Jakes Walks the Plank (2012)

Ellray Jakes the Dragon Slayer (2013)

Ellray Jakes and the Beanstalk (2013)

Ellray Jakes is Magic (2014)

It's only temporary; written and illustrated by Sally Warner. Viking Childrens Books 2008 182p il $15.99

Grades: 4 5 6 7 **Fic**

1. Bullies -- Fiction 2. Siblings -- Fiction 3. Grandmothers -- Fiction 4. Brain -- Wounds and injuries -- Fiction

ISBN 978-0-670-06111-2; 0-670-06111-5

LC 2007-038220

When Skye's older brother comes home after a devastating accident, she moves from Albuquerque, New Mexico, to California to live with her grandmother and attend middle school, where she somewhat reluctantly makes new friends, learns to stand up for herself and those she cares about, and begins to craft a new relationship with her changed brother.

"Warner deftly handles Skye's anger toward her brain-injured brother, also infusing her with a convincingly developed sense of compassion. Witty line art decorates some pages." Horn Book Guide

Only Emma; illustrated by Jamie Harper. Viking 2004 115p il $14.99; pa $5.99

Grades: 2 3 4 **Fic**

ISBN 0-670-05979-X; 0-14-240711-9 pa

LC 2004-12478

Third-grader Emma's peaceful life as an only child is disrupted when she has to temporarily share her tidy bedroom with four-year-old Anthony Scarpetto.

"The black-and-white illustrations are charming, and thumbnail sidebars present fun scientific facts about animals mentioned in the story. . . . Emma is a likable character whose feelings and behaviors are common to many children." SLJ

Other titles about Emma are:

Not-so-weird Emma (2005)

Super Emma (2006)

Best friend Emma (2007)

Excellent Emma (2009)

Happily ever Emma (2010)

Waters, Zack C.

Blood moon rider; [by] Zack C. Waters. Pineapple Press 2006 126p $13.95

Grades: 5 6 7 8 **Fic**

1. Florida -- Fiction 2. Ranch life -- Fiction 3. Grandfathers -- Fiction 4. World War, 1939-1945 -- Fiction

ISBN 978-1-56164-350-9; 1-56164-350-5

LC 2005030749

After his father's death in World War II, fourteen-year-old Harley Wallace tries to join the Marines but is, instead, sent to live with his grandfather in Peru Landing, Florida, where he soon joins a covert effort to stop Nazis from destroying a secret airbase on Tampa Bay

This is "an adventure filled with unexpected kindnesses and the irrepressibility of family ties, as well as a brush with espionage and a couple of suspenseful shoot'em-up scenes. A colorful cast of characters and a nod to teenage romance help make this a good choice for middle school boys." SLJ

Watkins, Yoko Kawashima

My brother, my sister, and I. Bradbury Press 1994 275p hardcover o.p. pa $5.99

Grades: 6 7 8 9 **Fic**

1. Japan -- Fiction 2. Korea -- Fiction 3. World War, 1939-1945 -- Fiction

ISBN 0-02-792526-9; 0-689-80656-6 pa

LC 93-23535

"Watkins's first-person narrative is beautifully direct and emotionally honest." Publ Wkly

★ **So** far from the bamboo grove. Lothrop, Lee & Shepard Bks. 1986 183p map hardcover o.p. pa $5.99

Grades: 6 7 8 9 **Fic**

1. Japan -- Fiction 2. Korea -- Fiction 3. World War, 1939-1945 -- Fiction

ISBN 0-688-13115-8 pa

LC 85-15939

A fictionalized autobiography in which eight-year-old Yoko escapes from Korea to Japan with her mother and sister at the end of World War II

"An admirably told and absorbing novel." Horn Book

Followed by: My brother, my sister and I

Watson, Geoff

Edison's gold. Egmont USA 2010 312p $15.99; lib bdg $18.99

Grades: 4 5 6 7 **Fic**

1. Inventors 2. Mystery fiction 3. Adventure fiction 4. Electrical engineers 5. Inventors -- Fiction 6. Secret societies -- Fiction

ISBN 978-1-60684-094-8; 1-60684-094-0; 978-1-60684-095-5 lib bdg; 1-60684-095-9 lib bdg

LC 2010-11312

Tom Edison and his friends become embroiled in a mystery involving his 'double-great' grandfather's inventions, a secret society, and a vendetta being carried out by a descendant of inventor Nikola Tesla.

This "is a fast-paced adventure filled mystery that middle schoolers will like." SLJ

Watson, Jude

The **39** clues; unstoppable: nowhere to run. Jude Watson. Scholastic 2013 272 p. (The 39 clues: unstoppable) (paper over board) $12.99

Grades: 4 5 6 7 **Fic**

1. Supernatural -- Fiction 2. Brothers and sisters -- Fiction 3. Adventure and adventurers -- Fiction

ISBN 9780545521376; 0545521378

LC 2013934701

In this book, by Jude Watson, "the Cahill family has a secret. For five hundred years, they have guarded the 39 Clues-thirty-nine ingredients in a serum that transforms whomever takes it into the most powerful person on earth. . . . Certain Cahills have always made it their mission to keep the serum safe. . . . Thirteen-year-old Dan Cahill and his older sister, Amy, are the latest guardians of the Clues. They think they've done everything right, but a tiny mistake leads to catastrophe." (Publisher's note)

"Six months after sixteen-year-old Amy and thirteen-year-old Dan defeated the vespers, the Cahill siblings set out on another quest to stop the serum their family has protected for centuries from wreaking havoc on the world. This first entry in a new spinoff series is formulaic, but the suspense and high stakes that 39 Clues fans love are front and center." (Horn Book)

Beyond the grave. Scholastic 2009 190p (The 39 clues) $12.99

Grades: 4 5 6 7 **Fic**

1. Ciphers -- Fiction 2. Orphans -- Fiction 3. Siblings -- Fiction

ISBN 978-0-545-06044-8; 0-545-06044-3

Sequel to: The sword thief by Peter Lerangis (2009)

A clue sends Amy and Dan jetting off to find out just what's behind the fierce rivalry between the Tomas and Ekaterina branches of the Cahill family. Was a Clue stolen from the Tomas branch? Where is it now? And most important, can Amy and Dan get their hands on it before their rivals do?

"Like the previous books, historical information is woven into the fast-paced adventure." SLJ

Followed by: The black circle by Patrick Carman (2009)

In too deep. Scholastic 2009 206p (The 39 clues) $12.99

Grades: 4 5 6 7 **Fic**

1. Adventure fiction 2. Ciphers -- Fiction 3. Orphans -- Fiction 4. Siblings -- Fiction

ISBN 978-0-545-09064-3; 0-545-09064-4

Sequel to: Beyond the grave by Jude Watson (2009)

"Amy and Dan fly to Australia. Attemping to trace their late parents' journey eight years earlier, they link Amelia Earhart's last flight to their own family quest. . . . The spy-versus-spy mentality will keep readers guessing. . . . The series' fans will devour the breathless action scenes in this fast-paced adventure." Booklist

Followed by: The viper's nest by Peter Lerangis (2010)

Loot; how to steal a fortune. Jude Watson. Scholastic Press 2014 272 p. (alk. paper) $16.99

Grades: 4 5 6 7 **Fic**

1. Twins -- Fiction 2. Adventure fiction 3. Jewelry -- Fiction 4. Orphans -- Fiction 5. Robbers and outlaws -- Fiction 6. Brothers and sisters -- Fiction 7. Adventure and adventurers -- Fiction

ISBN 0545468027; 9780545468022

LC 2014001218

"When master jewel thief Alfie McQuinn dies, his stashed set of clues and cryptic last words to March, his 12-year-old son and apprentice, mark the beginning of a race against time. The first clue leads March to discover his twin sister, Jules, a traveling circus acrobat. Tossed into a group home, they meet Darius, a juvenile delinquent with a soft spot for Izzy, a code-cracking hacker." (Booklist)

"Pitch-perfect characters, from scheming criminals to a twisted former cop to the twins' father, move in and out of the narrative, but it's the four young teens that drive the tale forward with enviable schemes and ingenious plans.Taut, engrossing and unstoppable." Kirkus

Watson, Renee

What Momma left me. Bloomsbury 2010 224p $15.99

Grades: 5 6 7 8 **Fic**
1. Orphans -- Fiction 2. Bereavement -- Fiction 3. Family life -- Fiction 4. Grandparents -- Fiction 5. Christian life -- Fiction 6. African Americans -- Fiction
ISBN 978-1-59990-446-7; 1-59990-446-2

LC 2009-18263

After the death of their mother, thirteen-year-old Serenity Evans and her younger brother go to live with their grandparents, who try to keep them safe from bad influences and help them come to terms with what has happened to their family.

"Serenity's struggles and insights, as she wrestles with her parents' legacy and an uncertain future, are inspiring, authentic, and told in a straighforward yet poetic style. The first-person narration is consistent, and the mystery of the painful circumstances of her mother's death—as well as additional tragedies—propels the story." Publ Wkly

Watson, Stephanie Elaine
Elvis & Olive; by Stephanie Watson. Scholastic Press 2008 230p $15.99
Grades: 3 4 5 **Fic**
1. Friendship -- Fiction
ISBN 978-0-545-03183-7; 0-545-03183-4

LC 2007023924

In spite of their differences, Natalie Wallis and Annie Beckett become friends and decide to spend their summer spying on their neighbors

This is an "accomplished first novel." Publ Wkly

Another title about Elvis & Olive is:
Elvis & Olive: super detectives (2010)

Watts, Frances
Extraordinary Ernie and Marvelous Maud; illustrated by Judy Watson. Eerdmans Books for Young Readers 2010 66p il (Ernie & Maude) pa $5.99
Grades: 2 3 4 **Fic**
1. Sheep -- Fiction 2. Superheroes -- Fiction
ISBN 978-0-8028-5363-9; 0-8028-5363-3

Ten-year-old Ernie is thrilled when he wins a contest to be trained as a superhero, and although he is disappointed that his sidekick is a talking sheep, just looking at his costume makes him feel heroic

"The action is tame . . . but the slapstick premise and banter between superhero and sidekick save the day. The brevity, spry pace, and humorous line art make Watts's . . . story a good choice for kids." Publ Wkly

Other titles about Ernie and Maud are:
The middle sheep (2010)
The greatest sheep in history (2011)

Weatherford, Carole Boston
Dear Mr. Rosenwald; by Carole Boston Weatherford; illustrated by Gregory Christie. Scholastic Press 2006 un il $16.99
Grades: 2 3 4 **Fic**
1. School stories 2. Philanthropists 3. Retail executives 4. African Americans -- Fiction 5. Segregation in education -- Fiction
ISBN 0-439-49522-9

LC 2005-27971

Young Ovella rejoices as her community comes together to raise money and build a much-needed school in the 1920s, with matching funds from Julius Rosenwald, the president of Sears, Roebuck, and Company

"Christie's gouache and colored-pencil illustrations have the variegated look and stylized layout of collage art—a good complement to the child's rough-around-the-edges narration. An afterword explains Rosenwald's impact on thousands of poor black communities. An uplifting and inspiring story." SLJ

Webb, Holly
The **case** of the stolen sixpence; written by Holly Webb; illustrated by Marion Lindsay. Houghton Mifflin Harcourt 2014 108 p. illustrations (The mysteries of Maisie Hitchins) (hardback) $14.99
Grades: 2 3 4 5 **Fic**
1. Mystery fiction 2. Detectives -- Fiction 3. London (England) -- Fiction 4. Boardinghouses -- Fiction 5. Mystery and detective stories 6. London (England) -- History -- 19th century -- Fiction 7. Great Britain -- History -- Victoria, 1837-1901 -- Fiction
ISBN 0544339282; 9780544339286

LC 2014007446

Written by Holly Webb, illustrated by Marion Lindsay, and part of The Mysteries of Maisie Hitchins series, this is a middle grade mystery story. "In 'The Case of the Stolen Sixpence,' Maisie's big chance to prove herself finally arrives when crime strikes her Victorian London neighborhood. While the grown-ups turn a blind eye to the whodunit and justice goes un-served, Maisie and her canine sidekick, Eddie, search the streets for clues to crack the case." (Publisher's note)

"Lindsay's black-line drawings add to the appeal and break up the text for younger readers. This makes a perfect choice for graduates of David A. Adler's Cam Jansen series who are not quite ready for Nancy Springer's Enola Holmes Mysteries." Booklist

Other titles in this series are:
The case of the phantom cat (2015)
The case of the vanishing emerald (2015)

Webb, Philip
Six days. Chicken House 2011 336p $17.99
Grades: 5 6 7 8 **Fic**
1. Science fiction 2. Siblings -- Fiction 3. Space and time -- Fiction 4. London (England) -- Fiction
ISBN 978-0-545-31767-2; 0-545-31767-3

LC 2010054233

Cass and her brother Wilbur scavenge in the ruins of a future London seeking an artifact for their Russian masters, but the search takes on a new urgency after the arrival of Erin and Peyto, strangers from afar who claim to hold the key to locating the mysterious object.

Webb "has created a complex and intriguing dystopia filled with devastation, clever devices . . . and lots of local color. . . . The novel's rapid pacing will hook readers and keep them turning pages." Booklist

Weber, Elka
★ The **Yankee** at the seder; illustrated by Adam Gustavson. Tricycle Press 2009 un il $16.99
Grades: 2 3 4 5 **Fic**
1. Jews -- Fiction 2. Passover -- Fiction 3. Soldiers -- Fiction 4. United States -- History -- 1861-1865, Civil War -- Fiction
ISBN 978-1-58246-256-1; 1-58246-256-9

LC 2008-11229

As a Confederate family prepares for Passover the day after the Civil War has ended, a Yankee arrives on their Virginia doorstep and is invited to share their meal, to the dismay of ten-year-old Jacob. Includes historical notes about Corporal Myer Levy, on whom the story is based, and his prominent Philadelphia family.

"With a cinematic flair and rich, realist oils, Gustavson . . . depicts how a détente between North and South is forged—albeit tenuously—by the timeless values of faith, civility and chicken soup. Basing her writing on a historical incident, Weber makes an impressive debut. . . . Sensitively written and beautifully illustrated." Publ Wkly

Wedekind, Annie
A **horse** of her own; by Annie Wedekind. Feiwel and Friends 2008 275p $16.95; pa $7.99

Grades: 5 6 7 8   **Fic**

1. Camps -- Fiction 2. Horses -- Fiction 3. Kentucky -- Fiction 4. Horsemanship -- Fiction

ISBN 978-0-312-36927-9; 0-312-36927-1; 978-0-312-58146-6 pa; 0-312-58146-7 pa

LC 2007032769

At summer camp Jane feels like an outsider among the cliquish rich girls who board their horses at Sunny Acres farm, and when the horse she has been riding is sold to another camper, she feels even worse until her teacher asks her to help train a beautiful but skittish new horse, and the experience brings out the best in her.

"Tenacious and thoughtful, Jane is an appealing protagonist who gradually recognizes that being accepted no longer matters to her. The plot . . . has enough twists, including a hint of romance, to sustain readers' interest." SLJ

Wild Blue; the story of a mustang Appaloosa. Feiwel and Friends 2009 124p (Breyer horse collection) $16.99; pa $5.99

Grades: 3 4 5   **Fic**

1. Horses -- Fiction

ISBN 978-0-312-38424-1; 0-312-38424-6; 978-0-312-59917-1 pa; 0-312-59917-X pa

LC 2008-34742

After being captured by men, Blue the Appaloosa grabs a chance at freedom and tries to find her way home.

"A modern-day adventure that reads like an exuberant nature journal, this novel will grip readers from start to finish." SLJ

Weeks, Sarah

As simple as it seems. Laura Geringer Books 2010 181p $15.99; lib bdg $16.89

Grades: 4 5 6   **Fic**

1. Ghost stories 2. Adoption -- Fiction 3. Friendship -- Fiction 4. Catskill Mountains (N.Y.) -- Fiction

ISBN 978-0-06-084663-3; 0-06-084663-1; 978-0-06-084664-0 lib bdg; 0-06-084664-X lib bdg

Eleven-year-old Verbena Polter gets through a difficult summer of turbulent emotions and the revelation of a disturbing family secret with an odd new friend who believes she is the ghost of a girl who drowned many years before.

"Weeks's characters are well rounded and her story line is engaging." Horn Book Guide

Jumping the scratch; a novel. Laura Geringer Books 2006 167p il $15.99; pa $5.99

Grades: 5 6 7 8   **Fic**

1. Aunts -- Fiction 2. Memory -- Fiction 3. Child sexual abuse -- Fiction

ISBN 978-0-06-054109-5; 0-06-054109-1; 978-0-06-054110-1 pa; 0-06-054111-3 pa

LC 2005-17776

After moving with his mother to a trailer park to care for an injured aunt, eleven-year-old Jamie Reardon struggles to cope with a deeply buried secret

"Weeks alludes to sexual abuse, but with a broad brush and no graphic details. . . . Weeks perfectly captures not only the guilt, shame, and pain of the abused boy but also the tenor of a fifth-grade classroom from the point of view of a new student who is friendless, targeted, and belittled by an insensitive teacher. Touches of humor ameliorate the pain and poignancy." SLJ

Oggie Cooder. Levithan/Scholastic Press 2008 172p il $16.99; pa $5.99

Grades: 3 4 5   **Fic**

1. School stories 2. Friendship -- Fiction 3. Eccentrics and eccentricities -- Fiction

ISBN 978-0-439-92791-8; 0-439-92791-9; 978-0-439-92794-9 pa; 0-439-92794-3 pa

LC 2007-18645

Quirky fourth-grader Oggie Cooder goes from being shunned to everyone's best friend when his uncanny ability to chew slices of cheese into the shapes of states wins him a slot on a popular television talent show, but he soon learns the perils of being a celebrity—and having a neighbor girl as his manager.

The author "delivers a funny, fast-paced story, with the likable Oggie at its center." Booklist

Followed by: Oggie Cooder, party animal (2009)

Oggie Cooder, party animal; illustrations by Doug Holgate. Scholastic Press 2009 165p il $16.99

Grades: 3 4 5   **Fic**

1. School stories 2. Parties -- Fiction 3. Birthdays -- Fiction 4. Friendship -- Fiction 5. Eccentrics and eccentricities -- Fiction

ISBN 978-0-439-92792-5; 0-439-92792-7

LC 2009024909

Neither a long list of rules, nor the inability to find the perfect gift—Cheddar Jam—nor being locked in a bathroom with a juggling bear will keep quirky fourth-grader Oggie Cooder from attending neighbor Donnica Perfecto's birthday pool party.

"A fast-paced chapter book with cheerful cartoon illustrations provided by Holgate, this can easily be read on its own and will certainly win Oggie new fans." Kirkus

★ **Pie**. Scholastic Press 2011 183p $16.99

Grades: 4 5 6 7   **Fic**

1. Cats -- Fiction 2. Pies -- Fiction 3. Aunts -- Fiction

ISBN 978-0-545-27011-3; 0-545-27011-1

In the 1950s in the small town of Ipswitch, PA, Polly Portman dies and leaves the recipe for her prize-winning piecrust to her cat Lardo, in the care of her niece Alice, but then the cat is kidnapped and the bakery is trashed.

"Weeks deftly leavens moments of hilarity with the process of grieving in this sweet coming-of-age story in which Alice learns from Aunt Polly to follow her heart and to open it as well. Readers will close the book with a satisfied sigh and may seek out an adult to help them bake a pie. Recipes included." SLJ

Save me a seat; Sarah Weeks and Gita Varadarajan. Scholastic Press 2016 240 p. (hardcover) $16.99

Grades: 3 4 5 6   **Fic**

1. School stories 2. Friendship -- Fiction 3. Schools -- Fiction 4. Bullying -- Fiction 5. Learning disabilities -- Fiction

ISBN 9780545846608

LC 2015048831

In this juvenile novel, by Sarah Weeks and Gita Varadarajan, "Joe's lived in the same town all his life, and was doing just fine until his best friends moved away and left him on his own. Ravi's family just moved to America from India. . . . Joe and Ravi don't think they have anything in common -- but soon enough they have a common enemy (the biggest bully in their class) and a common mission: to take control of their lives over the course of a single crazy week." (Publisher's note)

"Anyone who has ever felt like an outsider will appreciate and draw strength from Ravi and Joe as they strive to find the courage to improve their lives." Pub Wkly

★ **So** B. it; a novel. Laura Geringer Books 2004 245p $15.99; pa $6.99

Grades: 5 6 7 8   **Fic**

1. Mental illness -- Fiction 2. People with mental disabilities -- Fiction
ISBN 0-06-623622-3; 0-06-441047-1 pa

LC 2003-15643

After spending her life with her mentally retarded mother and agoraphobic neighbor, twelve-year-old Heidi sets out from Reno, Nevada, to New York to find out who she is.

"This is lovely writing—real, touching, and pared cleanly down to the essentials." Booklist

Weissman, Elissa Brent

Nerd camp. Atheneum Books for Young Readers 2011 261p $15.99

Grades: 4 5 6   **Fic**

1. Camps -- Fiction
ISBN 1-4424-1703-X; 978-1-4424-1703-8

LC 2010-42913

For ten-year-old Gabe, the Summer Center for Gifted Enrichment is all that he dreamed it would be, but he must work hard to write about the fun in letters to Zach, his cool future stepbrother, without revealing that it is a camp for "nerds."

This "novel features an appealing 10-year-old. . . . Weissman depicts a camp whose academic classes sound almost as fun as kayaking and color war." Booklist

The **short** seller; Elissa Brent Weissman. 1st ed. Atheneum Books for Young Readers 2013 256 p. (hardcover) $15.99

Grades: 3 4 5 6   **Fic**

1. Girls -- Fiction 2. Stocks -- Fiction 3. Friendship -- Fiction 4. Best friends -- Fiction 5. Mononucleosis -- Fiction 6. Electronic trading of securities -- Fiction
ISBN 1442452552; 9781442452558

LC 2012018632

In this middle-grade novel, by Elissa Brent Weissman, "a twelve-year-old takes on the stock market. . . . It all starts when seventh grader Lindy Sachs is granted $100 and access to her father's online trading account. . . . With trading talent and access to her parents' savings, the opportunity to make some real dough is too tempting to pass up. In fact, given how well Lindy's stocks are doing, it would be a disservice to not invest it all. . . . Right?" (Publisher's note)

The **trouble** with Mark Hopper. Dutton Children's Books 2009 227p $16.99

Grades: 5 6 7 8   **Fic**

1. School stories 2. Contests -- Fiction 3. Maryland -- Fiction 4. Identity (Psychology) -- Fiction
ISBN 978-0-525-42067-5; 0-525-42067-3

LC 2008-34211

When two eleven-year-olds with the same name, similar looks, and very different personalities go to the same Maryland middle school, confusion and bad feelings ensue, but things improve after a teacher insists that they become study partners.

"Realistic school interactions give Weissman's novel a lot of kid appeal with substance." Horn Book Guide

Welch, Sheila Kelly

Waiting to forget. Namelos 2011 170p $18.95

Grades: 5 6 7 8   **Fic**

1. Siblings -- Fiction 2. Foster home care -- Fiction
ISBN 978-1-60898-114-4; 1-60898-114-2

T.J. and his sister, Angela, learn how to move forward and be happy while in foster care.

"T.J.'s authentic voice and the multilayered presentation of his memories, shifting between the waiting room and his past, make for a poignant, realistic tale of child-survivors." Kirkus

Wells, Ken

Rascal; a dog and his boy. illustrations by Christian Slade. Alfred A. Knopf 2010 201p il $16.99; lib bdg $19.99

Grades: 4 5 6 7   **Fic**

1. Dogs -- Fiction 2. Louisiana -- Fiction
ISBN 978-0-375-86652-4; 0-375-86652-3; 978-0-375-96652-1 lib bdg; 0-375-96652-8 lib bdg

LC 2009-37606

Rascal may be the happiest beagle ever to live. He used to live on Voclain's Farm, but now he lives with his very own boy, Meely. Together they explore the Louisiana bayou. But when Meely gets stuck on a rotting bridge deep in the bayou, it's up to Rascal to save his boy from danger.

"This is a cracking good animal story of classic pedigree. . . . Characterizations of both humans and animals are sharp and distinct. . . . [The] narration sings with the same lively Cajun-flavored spice as the dialogue, and it's an easy dialect to get the hang of." Bull Cent Child Books

Wells, Kitty

Paw power; illustrated by Joanna Harrison. David Fickling Books 2011 199p il (Pocket cats) $13.99; lib bdg $16.99

Grades: 2 3 4   **Fic**

1. School stories 2. Cats -- Fiction 3. Magic -- Fiction 4. Bullies -- Fiction
ISBN 978-0-385-75201-5; 0-385-75201-6; 978-0-385-75202-2 lib bdg; 0-385-75202-4 lib bdg

LC 2010011892

"Nine-year-old Maddy Lloyd is desperate for a kitten, but younger brother Jack is allergic, so she settles for three small ceramic cats purchased at a flea market. Later, Maddy is surprised when one of the figurines, Greykin, comes to life, explaining that he has been sent to help her do a job—eventually revealed to be dealing with school-bully Sherry. . . . Newly independent readers will identify with Maddy's concerns about friendship and self-assertiveness (as well as her desire for a cat), and the inclusion of large type and frequent illustrations . . . will support those readers through the book's lengthy chapters." Booklist

Followed by: Shadow magic (2011)

Wells, Rosemary

Felix stands tall; Rosemary Wells. Candlewick Press 2015 32 p. color illustrations $14.99

Grades: PreK K 1   **Fic**

1. Guinea pigs -- Fiction 2. Bullies -- Fiction 3. Friendship -- Fiction
ISBN 0763661112; 9780763661113

LC 2013957482

"Felix has a new best friend! With take-charge Fiona, anything seems possible, and before Felix knows it, she sweeps him into singing and dancing with her as pixies in the Guinea Pig Jubilee talent show. But right after Felix's first-prize triumph, trouble waits in the wings. 'Twinkletoes!' someone taunts, and Felix crumbles. Can he pull himself together and face down the bullies?" (Publisher's note)

"With a cast of guinea pigs who correspond to instantly recognizable human types, this series opener from Max and Ruby creator Wells humorously captures the fluidity of social dynamics—and proves that it's possible to captain one's own destiny." Pub Wkly

Another book about Felix and Fiona is:
Felix's Little Lie (2016)

★ **Ivy** takes care; Rosemary Wells, illustrated by Jim LaMarche. Candlewick Press 2013 208 p. $15.99

Grades: 2 3 4   **Fic**

1. Pets -- Fiction 2. Historical fiction

ISBN 0763653527; 9780763653521

LC 2012942383

This book is "set in 1949 on a ranch near Reno, Nev., where almost-sixth-grader Ivy's parents work. Ivy's deep compassion for animals spurs her to offer herself as caretaker for pets and farm animals while their owners are away; her experiences inspire her aspirations to become a veterinarian." (Publishers Weekly)

Lincoln and his boys; illustrated by P.J. Lynch. Candlewick Press 2009 96p il $16.99

Grades: 3 4 5 6   **Fic**

1. Lawyers 2. Presidents 3. State legislators 4. Members of Congress 5. Presidents -- Fiction 6. Children of presidents 7. Father-son relationship -- Fiction

ISBN 978-0-7636-3723-1; 0-7636-3723-8

LC 2008-21418

"Inspired by a 200-word essay by Willie Lincoln, Wells offers a fictional account of Lincoln and his boys. Written first from Willie's point of view, then Tad's after Willie dies, it's a touching account of Lincoln as a patient and loving father. . . . Lynch captures the people and the warmth of their interactions in carefully researched oil paintings that reflect his mastery with light, perspective, and portraiture." SLJ

My Havana; [by] Rosemary Wells with Secundino Fernandez; illustrated by Peter Ferguson. Candlewick Press 2010 65p il $17.99

Grades: 4 5 6 7   **Fic**

1. Architects 2. Cuba -- Fiction 3. Dictators -- Fiction 4. Family life -- Fiction

ISBN 0-7636-4305-X; 978-0-7636-4305-8

LC 2009-12053

This novel relates events in the childhood of architect Secundino Fernandez, who left Havana, Cuba, with his parents, first to spend a year in Spain, and later to move to New York City. "Grades four to seven." (Bull Cent Child Books)

"Wells has chosen anecdotes wisely, and Ferguson's illustrations are atmospheric, capturing Dino's childlike enthusiasm and longing." Kirkus

★ **On** the Blue Comet; illustrated by Bagram Ibatoulline. Candlewick Press 2010 329p il $16.99

Grades: 5 6 7 8   **Fic**

1. Adventure fiction 2. Railroads -- Fiction 3. California -- Fiction 4. Space and time -- Fiction

ISBN 978-0-7636-3722-4; 0-7636-3722-X

LC 2009051358

During the Great Depression, Oscar's dad must sell their home and head west in search of work. Oscar meets a mysterious drifter and witnesses a crime so stunning it catapults Oscar on a train journey from coast to coast, from one decade to another.

"Ibatoulline's full-color, atmospheric Norman Rockwell-like vignettes enhance the nostalgic feel of this warm, cleverly crafted adventure." Kirkus

Welsh, M. L.

Heart of stone; a Verity Gallant tale. M.L. Welsh. David Fickling Books 2012 409 p. (hard cover) $16.99

Grades: 5 6 7 8   **Fic**

1. Romance fiction 2. Paranormal fiction 3. Witches -- Fiction 4. Fantasy 5. Sailing -- Fiction 6. Betrayal -- Fiction 7. Friendship

-- Fiction 8. Family life -- Fiction 9. Books and reading -- Fiction

ISBN 0385752431; 9780375899164; 9780385752428; 9780385752435

LC 2011023878

Sequel to: Mistress of the Storm

This book is a "companion novel to 'Mistress Of The Storm' . . . tell[ing] the story of heroine Verity Gallant's fight against an evil force determined to put an end to all happily-ever-after stories. . . . The evil force appears to be trying to destroy Verity's cliffside hometown of Wellow, which is rapidly being eroded by white sand gathering as if it had a single motive—to erase all the 'Original Stories' with happy endings." (Voice of Youth Advocates)

★ **Mistress** of the Storm; a Verity Gallant tale. David Fickling Books 2011 318p $16.99; lib bdg $19.99

Grades: 5 6 7 8   **Fic**

1. Fantasy fiction 2. Sailing -- Fiction 3. Witches -- Fiction 4. Friendship -- Fiction 5. Family life -- Fiction 6. Books and reading -- Fiction

ISBN 978-0-385-75244-2; 0-385-75244-X; 978-0-385-75245-9 lib bdg; 0-385-75245-8 lib bdg

LC 2010018721

First published in the United Kingdom

After a stranger gives an ancient book to unpopular, twelve-year-old Verity Gallant, she and her new-found friends, Henry and Martha, uncover secrets stirring in the harbor town of Wellow and use them to face a powerful, vengeful witch.

"Welsh's prose is lovely, her characters are well-drawn, and the atmosphere of the town is palpable. In creating a place in the world where a story read aloud can become true, Welsh offers a benediction of sorts to readers, that 'every child who is alone or out of place will find the friends they need, and the love they deserve.'" Publ Wkly

West, Jacqueline

Still life; by Jacqueline West; illustrated by Poly Bernatene. Dial Books for Young Readers, an imprint of Penguin Group (USA) Inc. 2014 330 p. (The books of Elsewhere) (hardback) $16.99

Grades: 4 5 6   **Fic**

1. Fantasy fiction 2. Magic -- Fiction 3. Dwellings -- Fiction 4. Space and time -- Fiction

ISBN 0803736916; 9780803736917

LC 2013041383

In this middle grades book by Jacqueline West, illustrated by Poly Bernatene, part of The Books of Elsewhere series, "Annabelle McMartin is gone for good, but something worse lurks just out of sight-watching, waiting, preparing to strike. Then a field trip to the local art museum reveals a shock. What Olive discovers will create a chain of events that propel her to discoveries she may not wish to uncover." (Publisher's note)

"In this series-ending fifth installment, Olive learns further secrets behind the paintings-as-portals magic of Elsewhere, its origins, and the world's creator. The magic's ability to preserve life indefinitely gets creepy, but characters with silly quirks keep the tone from becoming too dark. Illustrations are shadowy but still manage to make the heroes appear friendly." Horn Book

Other titles in the series include:

The Shadows (2010)

Spellbound (2011)

The Second Spy (2012)

The Strangers (2013)

Westera, Marleen

★ **Sheep** and Goat; by Marleen Westera; illustrations by Sylvia van Ommen; translation by Nancy Forest-Flier. Front Street 2006 99p il $16.95

Grades: 1 2 3   **Fic**

1. Goats -- Fiction 2. Sheep -- Fiction 3. Friendship -- Fiction
ISBN 978-1-932425-81-9

LC 2006000793

Follows the daily activities of Sheep and Goat who, despite often being grouchy or grumpy, are always there for one another when it counts

"Told with a subtle and consistent undercurrent of wit, these 18 short stories are pleasant bedtime reading. . . . The occasional pen-and-ink drawings are pitch perfect and more than a little extraordinary. They convey the low-key humor exquisitely." SLJ

Weston, Carol

The **diary** of Melanie Martin; or, How I survived Matt the Brat, Michelangelo, and the Leaning Tower of Pizza. Knopf 2000 144p hardcover o.p. pa $5.50

Grades: 3 4 5 6   **Fic**

1. Italy -- Fiction 2. Family life -- Fiction 3. Voyages and travels -- Fiction
ISBN 0-375-80509-5; 0-440-41667-1 pa

LC 99-53384

Fourth-grader Melanie Martin writes in her diary, describing her family's trip to Italy and all that she learned

"Sections of the book are laugh-out-loud funny and Weston's descriptions will have readers wanting to see the country for themselves. An enjoyable read." SLJ

Other titles about Melanie Martin are:
Melanie in Manhattan (2005)
Melanie Martin goes Dutch (2002)
With love from Spain, Melanie Martin (2005)

Weston, Robert Paul

Prince Puggly of Spud and the Kingdom of Spiff; Robert Paul Weston. Penguin Group USA 2013 256 p. $15.99

Grades: 2 3 4 5   **Fic**

1. Fashion -- Fiction 2. Humorous fiction
ISBN 1595145672; 9781595145673

In this "middle-grade rhyming novel . . . [by Robert Paul Weston] Prince Puggly of the . . . Kingdom of Spud . . . receives an invitation to a lavish ball in the far more chic Kingdom of Spiff. Puggly is sure that the Spiffs will take one look at him and laugh him out of their kingdom. . . . But then Puggly meets Francesca, the bookish Princess of Spiff, and together the two set out to teach Francesca's Spiffian countrymen an absurd lesson in style." (Publisher's note)

"Plot, theme, and writing style make this a terrific read-aloud." SLJ

★ **Zorgamazoo**. Razorbill 2008 281p il $15.99

Grades: 4 5 6 7   **Fic**

1. Novels in verse 2. Adventure fiction 3. Imagination -- Fiction
ISBN 978-1-59514-199-6; 1-59514-199-5

LC 2007-51682

Imaginative and adventurous Katrina eludes her maniacal guardian to help Morty, a member of a vanishing breed of zorgles, with his quest to uncover the fate of the fabled zorgles of Zorgmazoo as well as of other creatures that seem to have disappeared from the earth.

"This book is a natural descendant to the works of Dr. Seuss and Roald Dahl." Booklist

Westrick, A. B.

Brotherhood; Anne Westrick. Viking Juvenile 2013 368 p. (hardback) $17.99

Grades: 5 6 7 8 9   **Fic**

1. Historical fiction 2. Ku Klux Klan -- Fiction 3. Prejudices -- Fiction 4. Race relations -- Fiction 5. Family life -- Virginia -- Fiction 6. Ku Klux Klan (19th cent.) -- Fiction 7. Reconstruction (U.S. history, 1865-1877) -- Fiction 8. Richmond (Va.) -- History -- 19th century -- Fiction
ISBN 0670014397; 9780670014392

LC 2013008272

In this historical novel, 14-year-old Shad Weaver's "life is full of secrets. Desperate to learn to read, he begins attending a school for African-Americans. . . . He is very careful not to be seen, especially by any members of the other secret group to which he belongs, the Klan. Shad is deeply ambivalent about the brotherhood, appreciating it for the camaraderie it fosters but becoming increasingly uncomfortable with the violence it perpetuates." He must make a stand when his teacher is murdered. (Kirkus Reviews)

Wharton, Thomas

The **shadow** of Malabron. Candlewick Press 2009 382p (The perilous realm) $16.99

Grades: 5 6 7 8   **Fic**

1. Fantasy fiction
ISBN 978-0-7636-3911-2; 0-7636-3911-7

LC 2009-7768

When Will, a rebellious teen, stumbles from the present into the realm where stories come from, he learns he has a mission concerning the evil Malabron and, aided by some of the story folk, he faces a host of perils while seeking the gateless gate that will take him home.

"Lush descriptive prose, cleverly sustained suspense, a sprinkling of humor and an exciting climax will keep readers riveted to the story while those who know their folklore will be delighted by Wharton's twisting of the tropes and tales of myth and legend." Kirkus

Whelan, Gloria

★ **Homeless** bird. HarperCollins Pubs. 2000 216p hardcover o.p. pa $5.99

Grades: 6 7 8 9 10   **Fic**

1. India -- Fiction 2. Women -- India -- Fiction
ISBN 0-06-028454-4; 0-06-440819-1 pa

LC 99-33241

When thirteen-year-old Koly enters into an ill-fated arranged marriage, she must either suffer a destiny dictated by India's tradition or find the courage to oppose it.

"This beautifully told, inspiring story takes readers on a fascinating journey through modern India and the universal intricacies of a young woman's heart." Booklist

In Andal's house; written by Gloria Whelan; illustrated by Amanda Hall. Sleeping Bear Press 2013 40 p. $17.95

Grades: 2 3 4   **Fic**

1. Religious holidays 2. India -- Social conditions -- Fiction 3. India -- Fiction 4. Prejudices -- Fiction 5. Social classes -- Fiction
ISBN 158536603X; 9781585366033

LC 2012033684

In this book by Gloria Whelan, "as part of the annual Diwali celebration, Kumar is invited to the house of his classmate Andal. Andal is from a high-caste Brahmin family so Kumar is especially pleased to be included. But there in Andal's house, Kumar's two worlds collide. Instead of being welcomed as a guest, Kumar is sent away, forbidden to join the festivities. Angry and hurt, Kumar is left questioning his place in Indian society. Where does he fit in?" (Publisher's note)

★ **Listening** for lions. HarperCollins 2005 194p $15.99; lib bdg $16.89; pa $5.99

Grades: 5 6 7 8   **Fic**

1. Orphans -- Fiction 2. Physicians -- Fiction 3. East Africa -- Fiction 4. Great Britain -- Fiction

ISBN 0-06-058174-3; 0-06-058175-1 lib bdg; 0-06-058176-X pa

Left an orphan after the influenza epidemic in British East Africa in 1918, thirteen-year-old Rachel is tricked into assuming a deceased neighbor's identity to travel to England, where her only dream is to return to Africa and rebuild her parents' mission hospital.

"In a straightforward, sympathetic voice, Rachel tells an involving, episodic story." Booklist

★ The **locked** garden. HarperCollins Children's Books 2009 168p $15.99

Grades: 4 5 6 7   **Fic**

1. Michigan -- Fiction 2. Family life -- Fiction 3. Mental illness -- Fiction 4. Psychiatric hospitals -- Fiction

ISBN 0-06-079094-6; 978-0-06-079094-3

LC 2008-24637

This story is set in 1900. After their mother dies of typhoid fever, Verna and her younger sister Carlie move with their father, a psychiatrist, and stern Aunt Maude to a home on the grounds of an asylum for the mentally ill in Michigan. "Ages eight to twelve." (Publisher's note)

"Whelan establishes a strong sense of time, unusual setting and characters. . . . This convincing melodrama portrays an atypical attitude toward treating mental illness." Kirkus

White, E. B.

★ **Charlotte's** web; pictures by Garth Williams. Harper & Row 1952 184p il $16.95; lib bdg $16.89; pa $5.95

Grades: 3 4 5 6   **Fic**

1. Pigs -- Fiction 2. Spiders -- Fiction

ISBN 0-06-026385-7; 0-06-026386-5 lib bdg; 0-06-440055-7 pa

A Newbery Medal honor book, 1953

The story of a little girl who could talk to animals, but especially the story of the pig, Wilbur, and his friendship with Charlotte, the spider, who could not only talk but write as well

"Illustrated with amusing sketches . . . [this] story is a fable for adults as well as children and can be recommended to older children and parents as an amusing story and a gentle essay on friendship." Libr J

★ **Stuart** Little; pictures by Garth Williams. Harper & Row 1945 131p il $16.95; lib bdg $16.89; pa $5.95

Grades: 3 4 5 6   **Fic**

1. Mice -- Fiction

ISBN 0-06-026395-4; 0-06-026396-2 lib bdg; 0-06-440056-5 pa

This is "the story of a 'Tom Thumb'-like child born to a New York couple who is to all intents and purposes a mouse. . . . The first part of the book explores, with dead-pan humour, the advantages and disadvantages of having a mouse in one's family circle. Then Stuart sets out on a quest in search of his inamorata, a bird named Margalo, and the story ends in mid-air. The book is outstandingly funny and sometimes touching." Oxford Companion to Child Lit

★ The **trumpet** of the swan; illustrated by Fred Marcellino. HarperCollins Pubs. 2000 251p il $16.95; pa $5.95

Grades: 3 4 5 6   **Fic**

1. Swans -- Fiction

ISBN 0-06-028935-X; 0-06-440867-1 pa

LC 99-44250

A newly illustrated edition of the title first published 1970

Louis, a voiceless Trumpeter swan, finds himself far from his wilderness home when he determines to communicate by learning to play a stolen trumpet

The author "deftly blends true birdlore with fanciful adventures in a witty, captivating fantasy." Booklist

White, J. A.

The **Thickety**; a path begins. J.A. White. Katherine Tegen Books, an imprint of HarperCollinsPublishers 2014 496 p. (hardcover bdg.) $16.99

Grades: 5 6 7 8   **Fic**

1. Fantasy fiction 2. Magic -- Fiction 3. Witches -- Fiction

ISBN 0062257242; 9780062257246

LC 2013021509

This book, by J.A. White, "is the thrilling start of a new middle-grade fantasy series about a girl, a mysterious forest, and a book of untold magical powers. Kara and her brother, Taff, are shunned by their village because their mother was a witch. The villagers believe nothing is more evil than magic, except for what lurks in the nearby Thickety. But when Kara enters the forbidden forest, she discovers a strange book, a grimoire that might have belonged to her mother." (Publisher's note)

"When Kara was just a child, she was accused of witchcraft and forced to watch her mother executed for the same crime. Ever after, she and her family have lived in their isolated theocratic community as pariahs...White's persistent dark imagery, along with Offermann's eerie silhouette spot illustrations, adds to the overall dark atmosphere." Booklist

Other books in this series are:

The Whispering Trees (2015)

Well of Witches (2016)

The Last Spell (2017)

The **whispering** trees; J.A. White; illustrations by Andrea Offermann. Katherine Tegen Books, an imprint of HarperCollinsPublishers 2015 528 p. illustrations (The thickety) $16.99

Grades: 5 6 7 8   **Fic**

1. Fantasy fiction 2. Magic -- Fiction 3. Brothers and sisters -- Fiction 4. Human-animal communication -- Fiction 5. Fantasy

ISBN 0062257293; 9780062257291

LC 2014022226

In this book, by J.A. White, "[a]fter Kara Westfall's village turns on her for practicing witchcraft, she and her brother, Taff, flee to the one place they know they won't be followed: the Thickety. Only this time the Forest Demon, Sordyr, is intent on keeping them there. Sordyr is not the Thickety's only danger: unknown magic lurks behind every twist and shadow of the path." (Publisher's note)

"White has hit his stride in this follow-up to A Path Begins. . . . He's created a vivid, unsettling environment of rich magic and terrifying horrors: monsters composed of bones and teeth, tentacled creatures that feed on feelings, shadows that consume bodies, and more." Booklist

White, Ruth

★ **Belle** Prater's boy. Farrar, Straus & Giroux 1996 196p $17

Grades: 5 6 7 8   **Fic**

1. Cousins -- Fiction 2. Virginia -- Fiction 3. Appalachian region -- Fiction

ISBN 0-374-30668-0

LC 94-43625

A Newbery Medal honor book, 1997

"Gypsy and her cousin Woodrow become close friends after Woodrow's mother disappears. Both sixth-graders feel deserted by their parents—Gypsy discovers that her father committed suicide—and need to define themselves apart from these tragedies. White's prose evokes the coal mining region of Virginia and the emotional quality of her characters' transformations." Horn Book Guide

Another title about Belle Prater is:

The search for Belle Prater (2005)

★ **Little** Audrey. Farrar, Straus & Giroux 2008 145p $16
Grades: 5 6 7 8   **Fic**
1. Death -- Fiction 2. Virginia -- Fiction 3. Coal miners -- Fiction
4. Country life -- Fiction
ISBN 978-0-374-34580-8; 0-374-34580-5
                                            LC 2007-29310

In 1948, eleven-year-old Audrey lives with her father, mother, and three younger sisters in Jewell Valley, a coal mining camp in Southwest Virginia, where her mother still mourns the death of a baby, her father goes on drinking binges on paydays, and Audrey tries to recover from the scarlet fever that has left her skinny and needing to wear glasses.

"The setting is perfectly portrayed and the characterizations ring true." Voice Youth Advocates

The **treasure** of Way Down Deep; Ruth White. Margaret Ferguson Books 2013 176 p. (hardcover) $16.99
Grades: 5 6 7 8   **Fic**
1. Halloween -- Fiction 2. Buried treasure -- Fiction 3. Dogs -- Fiction 4. Orphans -- Fiction 5. Foundlings -- Fiction 6. Boardinghouses -- Fiction 7. Community life -- West Virginia -- Fiction 8. West Virginia -- History -- 1951- -- Fiction
ISBN 0374380678; 9780374377472; 9780374380670
                                            LC 2012021665

Sequel to: Way Down Deep
Parents' Choice: Silver Medal Fiction (2013)
In this book by Ruth White, "Ruby loves her life, but things start turning when her pet goat dies and Miss Arbutus feels an ill wind blowing into town. Then the local mines start closing, and everyone in Way Down Deep feels the pinch. Can Ruby help save the town? Will the special button Rita gave her as a gift be part of the solution? And can the town come together when a treasure appears?" (Booklist)

★ **Way** Down Deep. Farrar, Straus and Giroux 2007 197p $16
Grades: 5 6 7 8   **Fic**
1. Orphans -- Fiction 2. West Virginia -- Fiction
ISBN 0-374-38251-4; 978-0-374-38251-3
                                            LC 2006-46324

In the West Virginia town of Way Down Deep in the 1950s, a foundling called Ruby June is happily living with Miss Arbutus at the local boarding house when suddenly, after the arrival of a family of outsiders, the mystery of Ruby's past begins to unravel.

This is "a story as tender as a breeze and as sharp as a tack. . . . At the heart of the story are profound questions that readers will enjoy puzzling out." Booklist

You'll like it here (everybody does) Delacorte Press 2011 272p $16.99; lib bdg $19.99
Grades: 4 5 6 7   **Fic**
1. Science fiction 2. Family life -- Fiction 3. Interplanetary voyages -- Fiction 4. Extraterrestrial beings -- Fiction
ISBN 978-0-385-73998-6; 0-385-73998-2; 978-0-385-90813-9 lib bdg; 0-385-90813-X lib bdg
                                            LC 2010-32153

Although Meggie Blue seems to be an average sixth-grader she is abnormally frightened when residents of her small, North Carolina town become fixated on aliens, and soon she and her family are forced to flee, making it clear that all is not as it seems.

White's "considerable writing skills elevate a story with many familiar elements, including the importance of individuality, the pitfalls of conformity, and the tyranny of a dictatorship. Kids will like this, but it's also a fun jumping off point for serious discussion." Booklist

White, T. H.
★ The **sword** in the stone; with illustrations by Dennis Nolan. Putnam 1993 256p il $24.99
Grades: 4 5 6 7   **Fic**
1. Kings 2. Merlin (Legendary character) -- Fiction
ISBN 0-399-22502-1
                                            LC 92-24808

A newly illustrated edition of the title first published 1938 in the United Kingdom; first United States edition 1939 by G.P Putnam's Sons
"In White's classic story about the boyhood of King Arthur, Wart—unaware of his true identity—is tutored by Merlyn, who occasionally transform the young boy into various animals as part of his schooling. Contemporary children will still enjoy the text, which is both fantastical and down-to-earth." Horn Book Guide

Whittemore, Jo
Odd girl in. Simon & Schuster 2011 234p pa $6.99
Grades: 4 5 6   **Fic**
1. School stories 2. Siblings -- Fiction
ISBN 978-1-4424-1284-2; 1-4424-1284-4

"Spunky 12-year-old Alex doesn't really want friends or a social life. . . . She hates girly giggling parties and doesn't see any other girls in her middle school that she'd want to have as a friend, so she just concentrates on following in the footsteps of her prankster older twin brothers. . . . Alex's absent mother provides an element of drama in this otherwise witty, laugh-out-loud romp. Whittemore handles not only the comedy but deftly portrays Alex's and her brothers' advancement into a more mature state of mind. It should keep middle-schoolers laughing from start to finish." Kirkus

Whittenberg, Allison
Sweet Thang. Delacorte Press 2006 149p $15.95
Grades: 5 6 7 8   **Fic**
1. School stories 2. Family life -- Fiction 3. African Americans -- Fiction
ISBN 0-385-73292-9
                                            LC 2005-03809

In 1975, life is not fair for fourteen-year-old Charmaine Upshaw, who shares a room with her brother, tries to impress a handsome classmate, and acts as caretaker for a rambunctious six-year-old cousin who has taken over the family.

"Whittenberg has created a refreshing cast and a good read." SLJ
Another title about the Upshaw family is:
Hollywood & Maine (2009)

Wildavsky, Rachel
The **secret** of Rover. Amulet Books 2011 351p $16.95
Grades: 5 6 7 8   **Fic**
1. Twins -- Fiction 2. Uncles -- Fiction 3. Siblings -- Fiction 4. Inventions -- Fiction 5. Kidnapping -- Fiction 6. Washington (D.C.) -- Fiction 7. Voyages and travels -- Fiction
ISBN 0-8109-9710-X; 978-0-8109-9710-3
                                            LC 2010-23450

Twelve-year-old twins Katie and David Bowen evade foreign militants and make their way from Washington, D.C. to their uncle's Vermont home, hoping he can help rescue their parents, who were kidnapped because of their secret invention, Rover.

"Kids making the transition from series mysteries to more sophisticated thrillers will do well by this suspenseful and age-appropriate drama." Bull Cent Child Books

Wilder, Laura Ingalls
By the shores of Silver Lake; illustrated by Garth Williams. HarperCollins 1953 290p il (Little house) $16.99; pa $8.99

Grades: 4 5 6   **Fic**
  1. Family life -- Fiction 2. Frontier and pioneer life -- Fiction
ISBN 978-0-06-026416-1; 0-06-026416-0; 978-0-06-058184-8
pa; 0-06-058184-0 pa
Sequel to: On the banks of Plum Creek
A newly illustrated edition of the title first published 1939
A Newbery honor book, 1940
Ma and the girls follow Pa west by train where they make their home
at a rough railroad camp and plan for their own homestead.
  Followed by: The long winter

★ **Little** house in the big woods; illustrated by Garth Williams.
newly illustrated, uniform ed; Harper & Row 1953 237p il (Little
house) $16.95; lib bdg $16.89; pa $6.99
Grades: 4 5 6   **Fic**
  1. Wisconsin -- Fiction 2. Family life -- Fiction 3. Frontier and
pioneer life -- Fiction
ISBN 0-06-026430-6; 0-06-026431-4 lib bdg; 0-06-440001-8 pa
First published 1932
A year in the life of two young girls growing up on the Wisconsin
frontier, as they help their mother with the daily chores, enjoy their fa-
ther's stories and singing, and share special occasions when they get
together with relatives or neighbors.
  Other titles in the Little House series are:
  Farmer boy (1933)
  Little house on the prairie (1935)
  On the banks of Plum Creek (1937)
  By the shores of Silver Lake (1939)
  The long winter (1940)
  Little town on the prairie (1941)
  These happy golden years (1943)
  The first four years (1971)

Little house on the prairie; illustrated by Garth Williams. 75th an-
niversary ed.; Harper 2010 335p il $16.99
Grades: 4 5 6   **Fic**
  1. Family life -- Fiction 2. Frontier and pioneer life -- Fiction
ISBN 978-0-06-195827-4; 0-06-195827-1
Sequel to: Farmer boy
First published 1935
A family travels from the big woods of Wisconsin to a new home on
the prairie, where they build a house, meet neighboring Indians, build a
well, and fight a prairie fire.
  Followed by: On the banks of Plum Creek

The **long** winter; illustrated by Garth Williams. HarperCollins
1953 334p il (Little house) $16.99; pa $8.99
Grades: 4 5 6   **Fic**
  1. Winter -- Fiction 2. Blizzards -- Fiction 3. Family life -- Fiction
4. Frontier and pioneer life -- Fiction
ISBN 978-0-06-026460-4; 0-06-026460-8; 978-0-06-058185-5
pa; 0-06-058185-9 pa
Sequel to: By the shores of Silver Lake
A newly illustrated edition of the title first published 1940
A Newbery Medal honor book, 1941
After an October blizzard, Laura's family moves from the claim
shanty into town for the winter, a winter that an Indian has predicted will
be seven months of bad weather.
  Followed by: Little town on the prairie

On the banks of Plum Creek; illustrated by Garth Williams. HarperCollins 1953 339p il (Little house) $16.99; pa $8.99
Grades: 4 5 6   **Fic**
  1. Minnesota -- Fiction 2. Family life -- Fiction 3. Frontier and

pioneer life -- Fiction
ISBN 978-0-06-026470-3; 0-06-026470-5; 978-0-06-058183-1
pa; 0-06-058183-2 pa
Sequel to: Little house on the prairie
A newly illustrated edition of the title first published 1937
A Newbery honor book, 1938
Laura and her family move to Minnesota where they live in a dugout
until a new house is built and face misfortunes caused by flood, blizzard,
and grasshoppers.
  Followed by: By the shores of Silver Lake

Wiles, Deborah
★ The **Aurora** County All-Stars. Harcourt 2007 242p il $16;
pa $5.99
Grades: 4 5 6   **Fic**
  1. Death -- Fiction 2. Baseball -- Fiction 3. Mississippi -- Fiction
4. Race relations -- Fiction
ISBN 978-0-15-206068-8; 0-15-206068-5; 978-0-15-206626-0
pa; 0-15-206626-8 pa
                           LC 2006-102551
In a small Mississippi town, after the death of the old man to whom
twelve-year-old star pitcher House Jackson has been secretly reading for
a year, House uncovers secrets about the man and the history of baseball
in Aurora County.
  "Quotations from Walt Whitman's poetry, baseball players and Aurora County news dispatches pepper the story and add color. . . . A home
run for Wiles." Publ Wkly

★ **Countdown**. Scholastic 2010 377p il (The sixties trilogy)
$17.99
Grades: 5 6 7 8   **Fic**
  1. Cold war -- Fiction 2. Family life -- Fiction 3. Cuban Missile
Crisis, 1962 -- Fiction
ISBN 978-0-545-10605-4; 0-545-10605-2
It's 1962, and it seems everyone is living in fear. Twelve-year-old
Franny Chapman lives with her family in Washington, DC, during the
days surrounding the Cuban Missile Crisis. Amidst the pervasive threat
of nuclear war, Franny must face the tension between herself and her
younger brother, figure out where she fits in with her family, and look
beyond outward appearances.
  "Wiles skillfully keeps many balls in the air, giving readers a story
that appeals across the decades as well as offering enticing paths into the
history." Booklist

Love, Ruby Lavender. Harcourt 2001 188p il $16; pa $5.95
Grades: 4 5 6   **Fic**
  1. Mississippi -- Fiction 2. Grandparents -- Fiction
ISBN 0-15-202314-3; 0-15-205478-2 pa
                              LC 00-11159
When her quirky grandmother goes to Hawaii for the summer, nine-
year-old Ruby learns to survive on her own in Mississippi by writing
letters, befriending chickens as well as the new girl in town, and finally
coping with her grandfather's death
  "The engaging narrative . . . is witty and fast paced and the quirky,
diverse cast of human and poultry characters is colorful and spirited, if
not totally realistic." SLJ

★ **Revolution**; Deborah Wiles. First edition Scholastic 2014 495
p. illustrations, map (The sixties trilogy) $19.99
Grades: 5 6 7 8   **Fic**
  1. Family life -- Fiction 2. Nineteen sixties -- Fiction 3. United
States -- History -- Fiction 4. African Americans -- Civil rights

-- Fiction
ISBN 0545106079; 9780545106078

LC 2014935954

National Book Award Shortlist: Young People's Literature (2014)

In this book, by Deborah Wiles, "it's 1964, and Sunny's town is being invaded. Or at least that's what the adults of Greenwood, Mississippi are saying. All Sunny knows is that people from up north are coming to help people register to vote. They're calling it Freedom Summer. Meanwhile, Sunny can't help but feel like her house is being invaded, too. She has a new stepmother, a new brother, and a new sister crowding her life, giving her little room to breathe." (Publisher's note)

"Wiles does an excellent job of entwining the two plot strands and seamlessly integrating her exhaustive research, which is detailed at the book's conclusion. . . . As in Countdown, the outstanding period artwork, photographs, snippets of sayings, and songs interspersed throughout bring a troubled time close." Booklist

Williams, Alex

The **talent** thief; an extraordinary tale of an ordinary boy. Philomel Books 2010 300p $16.99

Grades: 5 6 7 8   Fic

1. Adventure fiction 2. Orphans -- Fiction

ISBN 978-0-399-25278-5; 0-399-25278-9

Orphaned Cressida, a magnificent singer, and her twelve-year-old brother Adam attend the by-invitation-only Festival of Youthful Genius, where they join forces with a former race car driver to try to stop a bizarre creature from stealing the talents of the young prodigies.

"This is a story that fantasy and adventure fans will enjoy, and the well-paced action will propel them to the end." SLJ

Williams, Laura E.

Slant; [by] Laura E. Williams. Milkweed Editions 2008 149p $16.95; pa $6.95

Grades: 5 6 7 8 9   Fic

1. Mothers -- Fiction 2. Adoption -- Fiction 3. Friendship -- Fiction 4. Prejudices -- Fiction 5. Plastic surgery -- Fiction 6. Korean Americans -- Fiction

ISBN 978-1-57131-681-3; 1-57131-681-7; 978-1-57131-682-0 pa; 1-57131-682-5 pa

LC 2008007093

Thirteen-year-old Lauren, a Korean-American adoptee, is tired of being called "slant" and "gook," and longs to have plastic surgery on her eyes, but when her father finds out about her wish—and a long-kept secret about her mother's death is revealed—Lauren starts to question some of her own assumptions

"The characters are exceptionally well drawn, and the friendship between Julie and Lauren is not only believable, featuring humor, conflict, and true wit, but also captures both girls' gains in maturity." SLJ

Williams, Maiya

The **Fizzy** Whiz kid. Amulet Books 2010 273p $16.95

Grades: 5 6 7 8   Fic

1. Moving -- Fiction 2. Advertising -- Fiction 3. Hollywood (Calif.) -- Fiction

ISBN 978-0-8109-8347-2; 0-8109-8347-8

Moving to Hollywood with his academic parents, eleven-year-old Mitch feels like an outsider in his school where everyone has connections to the powerful and famous in the entertainment industry, until he is cast in a soda commercial that launches a popular catchphrase.

"Williams' breezy tale is as addictive and bubbly as a Fizzy Whiz itself, and her experience in the entertainment industry packs real value into her descriptions of auditions, movie sets, and agent negotiations. . . . Mitchell's realization that he is a product being assembled is both goofy and poignant." Booklist

Williams, Marcia, 1945-

Archie's war; my scrapbook of the First World War, 1914-1918. Candlewick Press 2007 45p il $17.99

Grades: 3 4 5 6   Fic

1. Great Britain -- Fiction 2. World War, 1914-1918 -- Fiction

ISBN 0-7636-3532-4; 978-0-7636-3532-9

LC 2007-23012

When Archie is given a scrapbook for his tenth birthday in 1914, he chronicles the next four years of his life using documents, artifacts, and comic strips

"The large-format pages, jam-packed with tiny colored-pencil drawings with extensive captions, detailed sidebars, and pasted-in letters and postcards, flesh out the story and characters. . . . This imaginative presentation of historical fiction puts them in context and provides a highly visual experience that readers will pore over again and again." SLJ

My secret war diary, by Flossie Albright; my history of the Second World War, 1939-1945. Candlewick Press 2008 141p il lib bdg $21.99

Grades: 3 4 5 6   Fic

1. Diaries -- Fiction 2. World War, 1939-1945 -- Fiction

ISBN 978-0-7636-4111-5 lib bdg; 0-7636-4111-1 lib bdg

Marcia Williams uses her own childhood momentos to create a diary of a nine-year-old girl in Britain during World War II

"Children will quickly come to enjoy Flossie's energetic delivery and endless doodling. They will love poring over the extras-asides, sidebars, and letters found under flaps and in envelopes, that Williams has compiled to give the book the feel that one has stumbled into a real girl's private keepsake. . . . Children who enjoy history will be fascinated by Flossie and will undoubtedly be inspired to learn more about the events she describes." SLJ

Williams, Mary

Brothers in hope; the story of the Lost Boys of Sudan. illustrated by R. Gregory Christie. Lee & Low Books 2005 un il $17.95

Grades: 3 4 5   Fic

1. War stories 2. Sudan -- Fiction 3. Refugees -- Fiction

ISBN 1-58430-232-1

LC 2004-20965

Eight-year-old Garang, orphaned by a civil war in Sudan, finds the inner strength to help lead other boys as they trek hundreds of miles seeking safety in Ethiopia, then Kenya, and finally in the United States.

"Christie's distinctive acrylic illustrations, done in broad strokes of predominantly green, yellow, and burnt orange, are arresting in their combination of realism and the abstract. . . . This important profile in courage is one that belongs in most collections." SLJ

Williams, Michael

★ **Now** is the time for running. Little, Brown 2011 233p $17.99

Grades: 6 7 8 9 10   Fic

1. Soccer -- Fiction 2. Brothers -- Fiction 3. Refugees -- Fiction 4. Zimbabwe -- Fiction 5. Homeless persons -- Fiction 6. People with mental disabilities -- fiction

ISBN 978-0-316-07790-3; 0-316-07790-9

LC 2010043460

"There is plenty of material to captivate readers: fast-paced soccer matches every bit as tough as the players; the determination of Deo and his fellow refugees to survive unthinkably harsh conditions; and raw depictions of violence. . . . But it's the tender relationship between Deo and Innocent, along with some heartbreaking twists of fate, that will endure in readers' minds." Publ Wkly

Williams, Tad

The **dragons** of Ordinary Farm; by Tad Williams and Deborah Beale; pictures by Greg Swearingen. Harper 2009 412p il $16.99
Grades: 4 5 6 7 **Fic**
1. Farms -- Fiction 2. Uncles -- Fiction 3. Siblings -- Fiction 4. Supernatural -- Fiction 5. Mythical animals -- Fiction
ISBN 978-0-06-154345-6; 0-06-154345-4

LC 2008035298

When their great-uncle Gideon invites Tyler and Lucinda to his farm for the summer, they discover his animals are extremely unusual.

"Williams and Beale have created a gripping fantasy with realistic but appealing characters as well as scientific magic that explains the appearance of legendary creatures." SLJ

Williams-Garcia, Rita

★ **Clayton** Byrd goes underground; Rita Williams-Garcia, illustrated by Frank Morrison; [edited by] Rosemary Brosnan. HarperColins 2017 176 p. illustrations (hardcover) $16.99
Grades: 4 5 6 **Fic**
1. Blues music -- Fiction 2. Grandfathers -- Fiction
ISBN 9780062215918

LC 2016950351

In this book, by Rita Williams-Garcia, illustrated by Frank Morrison, "Clayton feels most alive when he's with his grandfather, Cool Papa Byrd, and the band of Bluesmen—he can't wait to join them, just as soon as he has a blues song of his own. But then the unthinkable happens. Cool Papa Byrd dies, and Clayton's mother forbids Clayton from playing the blues. And Clayton knows that's no way to live." (Publisher's note)

★ **Gone** Crazy in Alabama; by Rita Williams-Garcia. Harpercolins Childrens Books 2015 304 p. $16.99
Grades: 4 5 6 7 8 **Fic**
1. Sisters -- Fiction 2. Family secrets -- Fiction 3. African American children -- Fiction 4. Mothers -- Fiction
ISBN 0062215876; 9780062215871
Coretta Scott King Author Award (2016)

This novel by Rita Williams-Garcia "tells the story of the Gaither sisters, who are about to learn what it's like to be fish out of water as they travel from the streets of Brooklyn to the rural South for the summer of a lifetime. . . . As Delphine hears about her family history, she uncovers the surprising truth that's been keeping the sisters apart. But when tragedy strikes, Delphine discovers that the bonds of family run deeper than she ever knew possible." (Publisher's note)

"This well-crafted depiction of a close-knit community in rural Alabama works beautifully, with language that captures its humor, sorrow and resilience. Rich in all areas, Delphine and her sisters' third outing will fully satisfy the many fans of their first two." Kirkus

Previous books in the trilogy are:
One Crazy Summer (2010)
P.S. Be Eleven (2013)

★ **One** crazy summer. Amistad 2010 218p $15.99; lib bdg $16.89
Grades: 4 5 6 7 8 **Fic**
1. Poets -- Fiction 2. Mothers -- Fiction 3. Sisters -- Fiction 4. Black Panther Party -- Fiction. 5. African Americans -- Civil rights -- Fiction
ISBN 978-0-06-076088-5; 0-06-076088-5; 978-0-06-076089-2 lib bdg; 0-06-076089-3 lib bdg

LC 2009-09293

A Newbery Medal honor book, 2011
National Book Award Finalist: Young People's Literature (2010)
Coretta Scott King Author Award, 2011

In the summer of 1968, after travelling from Brooklyn to Oakland, California, to spend a month with the mother they barely know, eleven-year-old Delphine and her two younger sisters arrive to a cold welcome as they discover that their mother, a dedicated poet and printer, is resentful of the intrusion of their visit and wants them to attend a nearby Black Panther summer camp.

"Delphine's growing awareness of injustice on a personal and universal level is smoothly woven into the story in poetic language that will stimulate and move readers." Publ Wkly

★ **P.S.** Be Eleven; Rita Williams-Garcia. Harpercollins Childrens Books 2013 288 p. $16.99
Grades: 4 5 6 7 8 **Fic**
1. Historical fiction 2. African American children -- Fiction
ISBN 0061938629; 9780061938627
Sequel to: One crazy summer.
Coretta Scott King Book Award Author Winner (2014)

This book is a follow-up to Rita Williams-Garcia's Newbery Honor-winning "One Crazy Summer." Here, "Delphine and her sisters return to Brooklyn from visiting their estranged mother, Cecile, a poet . . . . Change and conflict have the Gaither household in upheaval: Pa has a new girlfriend, Uncle Darnell returns from Vietnam a damaged young man, and the sixth-grade teacher Delphine hoped to get has been replaced by a man from Zambia." (Publishers Weekly)

"...Soars as a finely drawn portrait of a family in flux and as a memorable slice of a specific time in our nation's history." Booklist

Willingham, Bill

★ **Down** the Mysterly River; illustrations by Mark Buckingham. Tor/Starscape 2011 333p il $15.99
Grades: 4 5 6 7 **Fic**
1. Fantasy fiction 2. Memory -- Fiction 3. Animals -- Fiction 4. Forests and forestry -- Fiction
ISBN 978-0-7653-2792-5; 0-7653-2792-9

LC 2011018958

Top notch Boy Scout Max "the Wolf" cannot remember how he came to be in a strange forest, but soon he and three talking animals are on the run from the Blue Cutters, hunters who will alter the foursome's very essence if they can catch them.

"Willingham roles out his themes slowly, only fully spelling them out in the final scene, but they don't interfere with the rollicking story, nasty (but fully realized) villains, and heroic camaraderie. . . . [This] is a stellar example of a novel working both as an adventure tale and as metafiction." Publ Wkly

Willner-Pardo, Gina

The **hard** kind of promise. Clarion Books/Houghton Mifflin Harcourt 2010 200p $16
Grades: 4 5 6 7 **Fic**
1. School stories 2. California -- Fiction 3. Friendship -- Fiction 4. Popularity -- Fiction
ISBN 978-0-547-24395-5; 0-547-24395-2

California seventh-graders Sarah and Marjorie made a promise in kindergarten to always be friends, but Marjorie is weird and Sarah, wanting to be at least somewhat popular, makes friends with a fellow choir member.

"Willner-Pardo's avoidance of overblown crises and dramatic climaxes creates a steadily paced, authentic story" Publ Wkly

Willocks, Tim

Doglands. Random House 2011 308p $16.99; lib bdg $19.99; ebook $16.99
Grades: 5 6 7 8 **Fic**
1. Adventure fiction 2. Dogs -- Fiction 3. Supernatural -- Fiction

4. Animal welfare -- Fiction
ISBN 978-0-375-86571-8; 0-375-86571-3; 978-0-375-96571-
5 lib bdg; 0-375-96571-8 lib bdg; 978-0-375-89604-0 ebook;
0-375-89604-X ebook
LC 2009033328

Furgal, a half-greyhound puppy, escapes a cruel dogtrack owner and
sets out in the hope of finding his father and the fabled Doglands, later
returning to try to free his mother, sisters, and the other abused dogs.

"The dogs each have distinct personalities, and the mystic lore of the
Doglands adds a secondary fantasy layer to the narrative. Humans are
only sketched in, which is fitting, since the tale is told from the dog point
of view. A riveting dog tale with a healthy serving of savagery, not all on
the part of the four-legged characters." Kirkus

Wilson, Daniel H.
A **boy** and his bot. Bloomsbury 2011 180p $16.99
Grades: 4 5 6 7   **Fic**
1. Science fiction 2. Robots -- Fiction
ISBN 978-1-59990-280-7; 1-59990-280-X
LC 2010-10635

When timid young Code falls down a hole into Mekhos, where everything is made of metal and circuitry, he must obtain the legendary
Robonomicon from evil Immortalis in order to save the robots of this
subterranean world and return home.

"Wilson ably balances Code's grief about his grandfather's fate with
his astonishment and excitement about the quest upon which he embarks; both sets of emotions feel authentic. . . . Readers who are curious about the ways robots work or about electronics in general will
find the level of detail throughout particularly interesting." Bull Cent
Child Books

Wilson, Jacqueline
Cookie; illustrated by Nick Sharratt. Roaring Brook Press 2009
320p il $16.99
Grades: 4 5 6 7   **Fic**
1. Friendship -- Fiction 2. Father-daughter relationship -- Fiction
ISBN 978-1-59643-534-6; 1-59643-534-8

Cookie is plain and shy, not the confident, popular girl her father
wanted when he named her Beauty Cookson. Her mother helps her cook
up a clever scheme to change her image—but, as usual, Dad doesn't approve, and this time his anger reaches frightening new heights

"Wilson's talent shows again in this novel with strong, compelling
characters and a plot that makes the book hard to put down." SLJ

The **illustrated** Mum; [by] Jacqueline Wilson. Delacorte Press
2005 282p hardcover o.p. pa $5.50
Grades: 5 6 7 8   **Fic**
1. Sisters -- Fiction 2. Tattooing -- Fiction 3. Manic-depressive
illness -- Fiction 4. Mother-daughter relationship -- Fiction
ISBN 0-385-73237-6; 0-440-42043-1 pa
LC 2003-70123

First published 1999 in the United Kingdom

Ten-year-old Dolphin is determined to stay with her family, no matter what, but when her sister goes to live with her newly-discovered father, sending their mother further into manic-depression, Dolphin's life
takes a turn for the better.

"Dolphin is a sympathetic character and the relationship between the
sisters is realistically portrayed, as is Marigold's mental illness." SLJ

Wilson, N. D.
★ The **dragon's** tooth; [by] N. D. Wilson. Random House 2011
485p (Ashtown burials) $16.99; lib bdg $19.99; e-book $16.99
Grades: 5 6 7 8   **Fic**
1. Fantasy fiction 2. Magic -- Fiction 3. Siblings -- Fiction 4.

Secret societies -- Fiction
ISBN 978-0-375-86439-1; 0-375-86439-3; 978-0-375-96439-8
lib bdg; 0-375-96439-8 lib bdg; 978-0-375-89572-2 e-book
LC 2009038651

"This fast-paced fantasy quickly draws readers in to its alternate reality. . . . Allusions to mythology and complex character development . .
. make Wilson's first in a proposed series a gem." Booklist

The **drowned** vault; N.D. Wilson. Random House 2012 449 p
(Ashtown burials) (lib. bdg.) $19.99
Grades: 5 6 7 8   **Fic**
1. Fantasy fiction 2. Paranormal fiction 3. Magic -- Fiction 4
Apprentices -- Fiction 5. Supernatural -- Fiction 6. Secret societies
-- Fiction
ISBN 0375964401; 9780375864407; 9780375895739;
9780375964404
LC 2011051618

This book is N.D. Wilson's sequel to "The Dragon's Tooth." "Thanks
to Cyrus and Antigone Smith, Dr. Phoenix now possesses the Dragon's
Tooth—and he's been using it to hunt and kill immortals worldwide
Phoenix has a dark agenda, but an evil alliance of immortals, Ordo Dra-
conis, also seeks the tooth's power. Worse, the Ordos have a centuries-
old vendetta against the Smith family." (School Library Journal)

Wilson, Nancy Hope
Mountain pose. Farrar, Straus & Giroux 2001 233p $17
Grades: 5 6 7 8   **Fic**
1. Diaries -- Fiction 2. Vermont -- Fiction 3. Grandmothers --
Fiction
ISBN 0-374-35078-7
LC 00-57269

When twelve-year-old Ellie inherits an old Vermont farm from her
cruel and heartless grandmother Aurelia, she reads a set of diaries written by an ancestor and discovers secrets from the past

"Beautifully written and suspenseful, this novel explores the many
emotions associated with the tragedy of spousal and child abuse." Voice
Youth Advocates

Wilson, Nathan D.
100 cupboards; [by] N. D. Wilson. Random House 2007 289p
$16.99; lib bdg $19.99; pa $6.99
Grades: 5 6 7 8   **Fic**
1. Magic -- Fiction 2. Kansas -- Fiction 3. Cousins -- Fiction
ISBN 978-0-375-83881-1; 978-0-375-93881-8 lib bdg; 978-0-
375-83882-8 pa
LC 2007-00164

After his parents are kidnapped, timid twelve-year-old Henry York
leaves his sheltered Boston life and moves to small-town Kansas, where
he and his cousin Henrietta discover and explore hidden doors in his attic room that seem to open onto other worlds

"There's an appealing blend of genuine creepiness and kindly do-
mesticity here." Bull Cent Child Books
Other titles in this series are:
Dandelion Fire (2008)
The Chestnut King (2010)

★ **Leepike** Ridge; [by] N. D. Wilson. Random House 2007 224p
$15.99; lib bdg $18.99; pa $6.99
Grades: 4 5 6 7   **Fic**
1. Adventure fiction 2. Caves -- Fiction 3. Missing persons --

Fiction 4. Mother-son relationship -- Fiction

ISBN 978-0-375-83873-6; 0-375-83873-2; 978-0-375-93873-3 lib bdg; 0-375-93873-7 lib bdg; 978-0-375-83874-3 pa; 0-375-83874-0 pa

LC 2006-13352

While his widowed mother continues to search for him, eleven-year-old Tom, presumed dead after drifting away down a river, finds himself trapped in a series of underground caves with another survivor and a dog, and pursued by murderous treasure-hunters

"While Leepike Ridge is primarily an adventure story involving murder, treachery, and betrayal, Wilson's rich imagination and his quirky characters are a true delight." SLJ

Winerip, Michael

Adam Canfield of the Slash. Candlewick Press 2005 326p $15.99; pa $6.99

Grades: 5 6 7 8   **Fic**

1. School stories 2. Journalism -- Fiction

ISBN 0-7636-2340-7; 0-7636-2794-1 pa

While serving as co-editors of their school newspaper, middle-schoolers Adam and Jennifer uncover fraud and corruption in their school and in the city's government.

"This is a deceptively fun read that somehow manages to present kids with some of the most subtle social and ethical questions currently shaping their futures." SLJ

Other titles about Adam Canfield are:

Adam Canfield, watch you back! (2007)

Adam Canfield, the last reporter (2009)

Winston, Sherri

President of the whole fifth grade. Little, Brown 2010 273p $15.99

Grades: 3 4 5   **Fic**

1. School stories 2. Baking -- Fiction 3. Elections -- Fiction 4. Friendship -- Fiction

ISBN 0-316-11432-4; 978-0-316-11432-5

LC 2010-06366

To gain leadership skills needed to run a cupcake-baking empire when she grows up, Brianna runs for president of the fifth grade—expecting little competition—until a new girl enters the race.

"The story will resonate with preteens navigating the ups, downs, and drama that come with the territory of many young girls' friendships." SLJ

Winters, Ben H.

The **mystery** of the missing everything. Harper 2011 263p $16.99

Grades: 4 5 6 7   **Fic**

1. School stories 2. Mystery fiction

ISBN 978-0-06-196544-9; 0-06-196544-8

LC 2011010167

Sequel to: The secret life of Ms. Finkleman (2010)

When a treasured trophy disappears from the display case at Mary Todd Lincoln Middle School and the principal cancels the eagerly anticipated eighth grade class trip, Bethesda Fielding has no choice but to solve the mystery.

"Featuring the same cast of eccentric teachers and eclectic students, this zany sequel offers another fast-moving middle-school puzzler, lots of pre and early teen humor and one relentless sleuth who's willing to admit when she's wrong. Fans will cheer more mystery and mayhem at Mary Todd Lincoln Middle School." Kirkus

The **secret** life of Ms. Finkleman. Harper 2010 247p $16.99

Grades: 4 5 6 7   **Fic**

1. School stories 2. Teachers -- Fiction 3. Musicians -- Fiction 4.

Rock music -- Fiction

ISBN 978-0-06-196541-8; 0-06-196541-3

LC 2010-04601

Spurred by a special project from her social studies teacher, seventh-grader Bethesda Fielding uncovers the secret identity of her music teacher, which leads to a most unusual concert performance and a tutoring assignment.

"Liberally laced with humor and featuring an upbeat heroine, unexpected friendship and rock-music trivia, this witty middle-school drama offers a lighthearted lesson in the importance of getting the facts straight." Kirkus

Another title about Bethesda Fielding is:

The mystery of missing everything (2011)

Winterson, Jeanette, 1959-

Tanglewreck. Bloomsbury Children's Books 2006 414p $16.95; pa $6.95

Grades: 5 6 7 8   **Fic**

1. Science fiction 2. Space and time -- Fiction 3. Clocks and watches -- Fiction

ISBN 978-1-58234-919-0; 1-58234-919-3; 978-1-59990-081-0 pa; 1-59990-081-5 pa

LC 2005-30630

Eleven-year-old Silver sets out to find the Timekeeper—a clock that controls time—and to protect it from falling into the hands of two people who want to use the device for their own nefarious ends

"Winterson seamlessly combines rousing adventure with time warps, quantum physics, and a few wonderfully hapless flunkies." Booklist

Winthrop, Elizabeth

Counting on Grace. Wendy Lamb Books 2006 232p $15.95; lib bdg $17.99; pa $6.99

Grades: 5 6 7 8   **Fic**

1. Photographers 2. Vermont -- Fiction 3. Factories -- Fiction 4. Child labor -- Fiction

ISBN 0-385-74644-X; 0-385-90878-4 lib bdg; 0-553-48783-3 pa

It's 1910 in Pownal, Vermont. At 12 Grace and her best friend Arthur must go to work in the mill, helping their mothers work the looms. Together Grace and Arthur write a secret letter to the Child Labor Board about underage children working in the mill. A few weeks later, Lewis Hine, a famous reformer, arrives undercover to gather evidence. Grace meets him and appears in some of his photographs. "Grades five to eight." (Bull Cent Child Books)

"Much information on early photography and the workings of the textile mills is conveyed, and history and fiction are woven seamlessly together in this beautifully written novel." SLJ

Wise, William

Christopher Mouse; the tale of a small traveler. illustrations by Patrick Benson. Bloomsbury Children's Books 2004 152p il $15.95; pa $5.95

Grades: 3 4 5   **Fic**

1. Mice -- Fiction

ISBN 1-58234-878-2; 1-58234-708-5 pa

LC 2003-56393

After being sold to an unscrupulous pet store owner, a young mouse lives with several owners and has many adventures, before ending up with an appreciative family.

"The writing is nicely mannered but very accessible, making the book not only a winner for reading aloud but also a delightful offering for children moving past beginning readers. The ink illustrations and the enticing cover will help them along." Booklist

Wiseman, David

Jeremy Visick. Houghton Mifflin 1981 170p hardcover o.p. pa $5.95

Grades: 5 6 7 8 **Fic**

1. Miners -- Fiction 2. Supernatural -- Fiction 3. Great Britain -- Fiction 4. Space and time -- Fiction

ISBN 0-618-34514-0 pa

LC 80-28116

Twelve-year-old Matthew is drawn almost against his will to help a boy his own age who was lost in a mining disaster a century before.

"This story blends the mystery and awe of the supernatural with the real terror and peril of descending the shaft of an 1850 Cornish copper mine." SLJ

Wissinger, Tamera Will

Gone camping; A Novel in Verse. by Tamera Will Wissinger; illustrated by Matthew Cordell. Houghton Mifflin Harcourt 2017 112 p. illustrations (hardcover) $15.99

Grades: 1 2 3 4 **Fic**

1. Novels in verse 2. Nature -- Fiction 3. Camping -- Fiction 4. Grandfathers -- Fiction 5. Brothers and sisters -- Fiction

ISBN 9780544638730

LC 2016014201

In this novel in verse, by Tamera Will Wissinger, illustrated by Matthew Cordell, "hiking in the great outdoors, catching fish, watching the stars come out at night-camping is fun. Until it's time to sleep. Then, Lucy wonders, what kinds of creatures lurk in the dark? With only her brother and grandpa as tent-mates, will Lucy be able to face her camping fears?" (Publisher's note)

Includes bibliographical references

Gone fishing; a novel. by Tamera Will Wissinger. Houghton Mifflin Books for Children 2013 128 p. (hardcover) $15.99

Grades: 1 2 3 4 **Fic**

1. Novels in verse 2. Fishing -- Poetry 3. Fishing -- Fiction 4. Brothers and sisters -- Fiction

ISBN 0547820119; 9780547820118

LC 2012032796

This book from Tamera Will Wissinger "offers a collection of more than 40 poems, which join to form a novel in verse about a family's fishing trip. Sam is initially distraught when his sister, Lucy, worms her way into his fishing trip with his father; as the day progresses, though, sibling rivalry turns to appreciation, especially after Sam catches a giant catfish." (Publishers Weekly)

Wittlinger, Ellen

This means war! Simon & Schuster Books for Young Readers 2010 224p $16.99

Grades: 5 6 7 8 **Fic**

1. Fear -- Fiction 2. Contests -- Fiction 3. Friendship -- Fiction

ISBN 978-1-4169-97101-6; 1-4169-7101-7

LC 2008-32586

In 1962, when her best friend Lowell begins to hang around new friends who think girls are losers, Juliet, a fearful fifth-grader, teams up with bold, brave Patsy who challenges the boys to a series of increasingly dangerous contests

"Wittlinger latches on to a poignant metaphor for war in the lively and readable tale set against the backdrop of the 1962 Cuban missile crisis." Booklist

Woelfle, Gretchen

All the world's a stage; a novel in five acts. illustrated by Thomas Cox. Holiday House 2011 163p il $16.95

Grades: 4 5 6 7 **Fic**

1. Actors -- Fiction 2. Orphans -- Fiction 3. Theater -- Fiction 4. Apprentices -- Fiction 5. Globe Theatre (London, England) -- Fiction 6. Chamberlain's Men (Theater company) -- Fiction 7. Great Britain -- History -- 1485-1603, Tudors -- Fiction

ISBN 978-0-8234-2281-4; 0-8234-2281-X

LC 2010023474

Twelve-year-old orphan Christopher "Kit" Buckles becomes a stage boy in a London theater in 1598, tries his hand at acting, and later helps build the Globe Theater for playwright William Shakespeare and the Chamberlain's Men acting troupe.

"The most compelling drama is Kit's universal search for his calling and his shifting friendships. . . . Frequent charming drawings enhance the sense of time and place." Booklist

Includes glossary and bibliographical references

Wojciechowska, Maia

Shadow of a bull; drawings by Alvin Smith. Atheneum Pubs. 1964 165p il $16; pa $5.99

Grades: 6 7 8 9 **Fic**

1. Spain -- Fiction 2. Bullfights -- Fiction

ISBN 0-689-30042-5; 1-4169-3395-6 pa

Awarded the Newbery Medal, 1965

"In spare, economical prose [the author] makes one feel, see, smell the heat, endure the hot Andalusian sun and shows one the sand and glare of the bullring. Above all, she lifts the veil and gives glimpses of the terrible loneliness in the soul of a boy. . . . Superbly illustrated." N Y Times Book Rev

Wolf, Joan M.

★ **Someone** named Eva. Clarion Books 2007 200p $16; pa $6.99

Grades: 5 6 7 8 **Fic**

1. School stories 2. National socialism -- Fiction 3. World War 1939-1945 -- Fiction 4. Europe -- History -- 1918-1945 -- Fiction

ISBN 0-618-53579-9; 0-547-23766-9 pa

LC 2006-26070

From her home in Lidice, Czechoslovakia, in 1942, eleven-year-old Milada is taken with other blond, blue-eyed children to a school in Poland to be trained as "proper Germans" for adoption by German families, but all the while she remembers her true name and history.

"This amazing, eye-opening story, masterfully written, is an essential part of World War II literature and belongs on the shelves of every library." SLJ

Wolfson, Jill

Home, and other big, fat lies. Henry Holt 2006 281p $16.95

Grades: 5 6 7 8 **Fic**

1. Nature -- Fiction 2. Foster home care -- Fiction 3. Environmental protection -- Fiction

ISBN 978-0-8050-7670-7; 0-8050-7670-0

LC 200035843

Eleven-year-old Termite, a foster child with an eye for the beauty of nature and a talent for getting into trouble, takes on the loggers in her new home town when she tries to save the biggest tree in the forest.

"Written with humor and sensitivity." Voice Youth Advocates

What I call life. Holt & Co. 2005 270p $16.95; pa $6.99

Grades: 5 6 7 8 **Fic**

1. Foster home care -- Fiction

ISBN 0-8050-7669-7; 0-312-37752-5 pa

Placed in a group foster home, eleven-year-old Cal Lavender learns how to cope with life from the four other girls who live there and from their storytelling guardian, the Knitting Lady.

"Wolfson paints her characters with delightful authenticity. Her debut novel is a treasure of quiet good humor and skillful storytelling that conveys subtle messages about kindness, compassion, and the gift of family regardless of its configuration." Booklist

Wolitzer, Meg

The **fingertips** of Duncan Dorfman. Dutton Childrens Books 2011 294p $16.99

Grades: 4 5 6 7   **Fic**

1. Contests -- Fiction 2. Individualism -- Fiction 3. Scrabble (Game) -- Fiction

ISBN 978-0-525-42304-1; 0-525-42304-4

LC 2011005228

"The novel is shot through with Scrabble words and rules in a way that is reminiscent of Louis Sachar's The Cardturner (2010). Readers will identify with and root for the characters as their tales intertwine to a satisfying if slightly too cheery close. Word wizards aren't the only ones who will enjoy this readable rumination on ethics, competition and identity." Kirkus

Wolk, Lauren

★ **Wolf** Hollow; a novel. by Lauren Wolk. Dutton Children's Books, an imprint of Penguin Random House LLC 2016 304 p. (hardback) $16.99

Grades: 4 5 6 7 8   **Fic**

1. Bullies -- Fiction 2. Veterans -- Fiction 3. Pennsylvania -- Fiction 4. Conduct of life -- Fiction 5. Homeless persons -- Fiction 6. Bullying -- Fiction 7. Family life -- Pennsylvania -- Fiction 8. Pennsylvania -- History -- 20th century -- Fiction

ISBN 9781101994825; 1101994827

LC 2015038506

Newbery Honor Book (2017)

In this book, by Lauren Wolk, "Annabelle has lived a mostly quiet, steady life in her small Pennsylvania town. Until the day new student Betty Glengarry walks into her class. Betty quickly reveals herself to be cruel and manipulative, and while her bullying seems isolated at first, things quickly escalate, and reclusive World War I veteran Toby becomes a target of her attacks. While others have always seen Toby's strangeness, Annabelle knows only kindness." (Publisher's note)

"Wolk is relentless in her message: lies and secrets, even for the most noble of reasons, have unintended consequences, as Annabelle's poignant dilemma reminds us long after the last page is turned.' Booklist

Wong, Janet S.

Me and Rolly Maloo; illustrated by Elizabeth Buttler. Charlesbridge 2010 121p il $15.95

Grades: 3 4 5   **Fic**

1. School stories 2. Honesty -- Fiction 3. Popularity -- Fiction 4. Mathematics -- Fiction

ISBN 978-1-58089-158-5; 1-58089-158-6

"The characterizations are spot-on, and Buttler's frequent graphic-novel-style artwork and dialogue balloons emphsize reactions and emotions . . . The story is one worth telling." SLJ

Minn and Jake; [by] Janet Wong; pictures by Geneviève Côté. Farrar, Straus & Giroux 2003 146p il $16; pa $6.95

Grades: 3 4 5   **Fic**

1. School stories 2. Novels in verse 3. Friendship -- Fiction

ISBN 0-374-34987-8; 978-0-374-34987-5; 978-0-374-40021-7 pa; 0-374-40021-0 pa

LC 2002-35421

Fifth-grader Minn, the tallest girl in school, begins a rocky friendship with Jake, a new student who is not only very short, but is also afraid of the worms and lizards that Minn likes to collect

"This breezy free-verse novel introduces memorable characters in recognizable situations. . . . [Côté's] b&w illustrations achieve unusual dimension. Incorporating what seem to be collage elements, her strikingly graphic compositions mirror the deceptive ease of the verse narration." Publ Wkly

Another title about Minn and Jake is:

Minn and Jake's almost terrible summer (2008)

Wood, Maryrose

The **hidden** gallery; illustrated by Jon Klassen. Balzer + Bray 2011 313p il (Incorrigible children of Ashton Place) $15.99

Grades: 4 5 6   **Fic**

1. Orphans -- Fiction 2. Great Britain -- Fiction 3. Wild children -- Fiction 4. London (England) -- Fiction

ISBN 978-0-06-179112-3; 0-06-179112-1

LC 2010-32737

Sequel to: The mysterious howling (2010)

Fifteen-year-old Miss Penelope Lumley, a governess trained at the Swanburne Academy for Poor Bright Females, takes the three Incorrigible Children of Ashton Place to London, England, and learns they are under a curse.

"Humorous antics and a climactic cliffhanger ending will keep children turning pages and clamoring for the next volume, while more sophisticated readers will take away much more. Frequent plate-sized illustrations add wit and period flair." SLJ

★ The **mysterious** howling; illustrated by Jon Klassen. Balzer & Bray 2010 267p il (The incorrigible children of Ashton Place) $15.99

Grades: 4 5 6   **Fic**

1. Orphans -- Fiction 2. Christmas -- Fiction 3. Wild children -- Fiction

ISBN 978-0-06-179105-5; 0-06-179105-9

Fifteen-year-old Miss Penelope Lumley, a recent graduate of the Swanburne Academy for Poor Bright Females, is hired as governess to three young children who have been raised by wolves and must teach them to behave in a civilized manner quickly, in preparation for a Christmas ball.

"Smartly written with a middle-grade audience in mind, this is both fun and funny and sprinkled with dollops of wisdom." Booklist

Another title in this series is:

The hidden gallery (2011)

The **unseen** guest; by Maryrose Wood; illustrated by Jon Klassen. Balzer + Bray 2012 340 p. (hardback) $15.99

Grades: 4 5 6   **Fic**

1. Mystery fiction 2. Wolves -- Fiction 3. Nannies -- Fiction 4. Wild children -- Fiction 5. Great Britain -- History -- 19th century -- Fiction 6. England -- Fiction 7. Orphans -- Fiction 8. Secrets -- Fiction 9. Governesses -- Fiction 10. Feral children -- Fiction 11. London (England) -- Fiction

ISBN 9780061791185

LC 2011053315

This young adult novel offers a "Victorian mystery [story about] teenage governess Penelope Lumley [who] takes on threats to her wolfish young charges that include a hustler after the Ashton fortune. . . . Once she meets the three feral children Penelope is charged with training up to be human, Faucet's scheme to finance the introduction of ostrich racing to the British Isles by marrying the Dowager Lady Ashton is transformed to visions of wolf racing and sideshow exhibitions. . . . Along with . . . pitching her plucky protagonist into one crisis after another . . . the author slips in a few more seemingly significant Clues to the Ashtons' curious history and Penelope's apparent involvement in it." (Kirkus)

Woodruff, Elvira

Fearless. Scholastic Press 2008 224p il $16.99; pa $6.99

Grades: 5 6 7 8   **Fic**

1. Artists 2. Engravers 3. Inventors 4. Architects 5. Adventure fiction 6. Orphans -- Fiction 7. Lighthouses -- Fiction 8. Great Britain -- History -- 1603-1714, Stuarts -- Fiction

ISBN 978-0-439-67703-5; 0-439-67703-3; 978-0-439-67704-2 pa; 0-439-67704-1 pa

LC 2006-10137

In late seventeenth-century England, eleven-year-old Digory, forced to leave his hometown after his father is lost at sea, becomes an apprentice to the architect Henry Winstanley, who built a lighthouse on the treacherous Eddystone Reef—the very rocks that sank Digory's grandfather's ship years before.

"This fascinating, well-written story is closely based on the life of the real Henry Winstanley. . . . The characters are finely drawn and the action is nonstop." SLJ

George Washington's spy; a time travel adventure. Scholastic Press 2010 229p $16.99

Grades: 4 5 6   **Fic**

1. Authors 2. Diplomats 3. Inventors 4. Statesmen 5. Scientists 6. Writers on science 7. Members of Congress 8. Time travel -- Fiction 9. Boston (Mass.) -- Fiction 10. United States -- History -- 1775-1783, Revolution -- Fiction

ISBN 978-0-545-10487-6; 0-545-10487-4

LC 2009032700

Sequel to: George Washington's socks (1991)

Ten-year-old Matt and six other children travel to 1776 Boston, living out American history as they meet Benjamin Franklin, learn about colonial medicine, and become part of a rebel spy ring

"Woodruff does an excellent job of conveying the complexities of war. . . . This is a great introduction to the Revolutionary period. . . . The story is fast paced, exciting, and informative." SLJ

The **Ravenmaster's** secret. Scholastic Press 2003 225p $15.95; pa $5.99

Grades: 5 6 7 8   **Fic**

1. Ravens -- Fiction 2. London (England) -- Fiction 3. Tower of London (England) -- Fiction 4. Great Britain -- History -- 1714-1837 -- Fiction

ISBN 0-439-28133-4; 0-439-28134-2 pa

LC 2002-15963

The eleven-year-old son of the Ravenmaster at the Tower of London befriends a Jacobite rebel being held prisoner there.

"An absorbing historical adventure with a unique and colorful setting. . . . The novel can be read for its exciting plot and sympathetic characters, but readers will also sense its underlying theme of courage." Booklist

Woods, Brenda

My name is Sally Little Song. G.P. Putnam's Sons 2006 182p $15.99; pa $5.99

Grades: 4 5 6 7   **Fic**

1. Florida -- Fiction 2. Georgia -- Fiction 3. Slavery -- Fiction 4. Seminole Indians -- Fiction 5. African Americans -- Fiction

ISBN 0-399-24312-7; 0-14-240943-X pa

LC 2005-32651

When their owner plans to sell one of them in 1802, twelve-year-old Sally and her family run away from their Georgia plantation to look for both freedom from slavery and a home in Florida with the Seminole Indians.

"Based on historical accounts, this novel provides readers with an alternative view of the realities of slavery—an escape to the South rather than North. . . . This accessible tale will prove a rich resource for study and discussion." SLJ

The **red** rose box. Putnam 2002 136p $16.99; pa $5.99

Grades: 5 6 7 8   **Fic**

1. Louisiana -- Fiction 2. African Americans -- Fiction 3. Los Angeles (Calif.) -- Fiction

ISBN 0-399-23702-X; 0-14-250151-4 pa

LC 2001-18354

In 1953, Leah Hopper dreams of leaving the poverty and segregation of her home in Sulphur, Louisiana, and when Aunt Olivia sends train tickets to Los Angeles as part of her tenth birthday present, Leah gets a first taste of freedom

"In language made musical with southern phrases, this . . . novel shapes the era and characters with both well-chosen particulars and universal emotions." Booklist

★ **Saint** Louis Armstrong Beach. Nancy Paulsen Books 2011 137p $16.99

Grades: 4 5 6   **Fic**

1. Dogs -- Fiction 2. Musicians -- Fiction 3. New Orleans (La.) -- Fiction 4. Hurricane Katrina, 2005 -- Fiction

ISBN 978-0-399-25507-6; 0-399-25507-9

Saint Louis Armstrong Beach is enjoying life in New Orleans, playing clarinet for the tourists in his spare time, accompanied by Shadow, a local stray dog. When Hurricane Katrina approaches, Saint faces unexpected challenges in trying to rescue Shadow.

This is a "gripping addition to the growing body of fiction portraying Katrina's profound effect on children and families. . . . Woods' marvelous characterizations of Saint and Miz Moran more than stand up to the vivid backdrop of the flooded, chaotic city. Shadow's credulity-straining heroics will please kids." Kirkus

Woodson, Jacqueline

★ **Feathers**. G.P. Putnam's Sons 2007 118p $15.99; pa $6.99

Grades: 4 5 6 7   **Fic**

1. Religion -- Fiction 2. Race relations -- Fiction 3. African Americans -- Fiction

ISBN 978-0-399-23989-2; 0-399-23989-8; 978-0-14-241198-8 pa; 0-14-241198-1 pa

LC 2006-24713

A Newbery Medal honor book, 2008

When a new, white student nicknamed "The Jesus Boy" joins her sixth grade class in the winter of 1971, Frannie's growing friendship with him makes her start to see some things in a new light.

"Woodson creates in Frannie a strong protagonist who thinks for herself and recognizes the value and meaning of family. The story ends with hope and thoughtfulness while speaking to those adolescents who struggle with race, faith, and prejudice." SLJ

★ **Locomotion**. Putnam 2003 100p $17.99; pa $5.99

Grades: 4 5 6 7   **Fic**

1. Novels in verse 2. Foster home care -- Fiction 3. African Americans -- Fiction

ISBN 978-0-399-23115-5; 0-399-23115-3; 978-0-14-241552-8 pa; 0-14-241552-9 pa

LC 2002-69779

National Book Award Finalist: Young People's Literature (2003)

Boston Globe-Horn Book Award Honor: Fiction (2003)

In a series of poems, eleven-year-old Lonnie writes about his life, after the death of his parents, separated from his younger sister, living in a foster home, and finding his poetic voice at school

"In a masterful use of voice, Woodson allows Lonnie's poems to tell a complex story of loss and grief and to create a gritty, urban environment. Despite the spare text, Lonnie's foster mother and the other minor characters are three-dimensional, making the boy's world a convincingly real one." SLJ

★ **Peace,** Locomotion. G.P. Putnam's Sons 2009 134p $15.99; pa $7.99

Grades: 4 5 6 7   **Fic**

1. Letters -- Fiction 2. Orphans -- Fiction 3. Siblings -- Fiction 4. Foster home care -- Fiction 5. African Americans -- Fiction

ISBN 978-0-399-24655-5; 0-399-24655-X; 978-0-14-241512-2 pa; 0-14-241512-X pa

LC 2008-18583

Through letters to his little sister, who is living in a different foster home, sixth-grader Lonnie, also known as "Locomotion," keeps a record of their lives while they are apart, describing his own foster family, including his foster brother who returns home after losing a leg in the Iraq War

"Woodson creates a full-bodied character in kind, sensitive Lonnie. Readers will understand his quest for peace, and appreciate the hard work he does to find it." Publ Wkly

Worley, Rob M.

Scratch 9; created and written by Rob M. Worley; illustrated by Jason T. Kruse. Ape Entertainment 2011 100p 1

Grades: 3 4 5   **Fic**

1. Cats -- Fiction 2. Pets -- Fiction 3. Comic books, strips, etc.

ISBN 9781936340538

In this collection of comics, named one of the Best Comics for Kids 2010 by School Library Journal, "mad science gives an ordinary cat named Scratch the ability to summon any of his nine lives. He must use his powers to save his pet friends from the CRUEL corporation." (Publisher's note) The protagonist "can summon any of his previous or future lives and fight side-by-side with them, a handy skill when you were a saber-toothed tiger, a ninja, and a minor Egyptian deity in your previous lives!" (School Libr J)

Wrede, Patricia C.

Dealing with dragons. Harcourt Brace Jovanovich 1990 212p (The Enchanted Forest Chronicles) hardcover o.p. pa $6.99

Grades: 5 6 7 8   **Fic**

1. Fairy tales 2. Magic -- Fiction 3. Dragons -- Fiction

ISBN 0-15-222900-0; 0-15-204566-X pa

LC 89-24599

Bored with traditional palace life, a princess goes off to live with a group of dragons and soon becomes involved with fighting against some disreputable wizards who want to steal away the dragons' kingdom

"A decidedly diverting novel with plenty of action and many slightly skewed fairy-tale conventions that add to the laugh-out-loud reading pleasure and give the story a wide appeal." Booklist

Other titles in this series are:

Searching for dragons (1991)

Calling on dragons (1993)

Talking to dragons (1993)

Searching for dragons. Harcourt Brace 1991 242p (The Enchanted forest chronicles) hardcover o.p. pa $6.99

Grades: 5 6 7 8   **Fic**

1. Fairy tales 2. Magic -- Fiction 3. Dragons -- Fiction

ISBN 0-15-200898-5; 0-15-204565-1 pa

LC 91-8305

Sequel to: Dealing with dragons (1990)

With the aid of King Mandanbar, Princess Cimorene rescues the dragon Kazul and saves the Enchanted Forest from a band of wicked wizards

"Wrede's tongue-in-cheek humor balances well with sweet adolescent discovery, and the result is another winning chapter in a delightful tale." SLJ

Followed by:Calling on dragons (1993)

Wright, Barbara

★ **Crow.** Random House 2012 $16.99; lib bdg $19.99; ebook $10.99

Grades: 4 5 6   **Fic**

1. Friendship -- Fiction 2. Family life -- Fiction 3. North Carolina -- Fiction 4. Race relations -- Fiction 5. African Americans -- Fiction

ISBN 978-0-375-86928-0; 0-375-86928-X; 978-0-375-96928-7 lib bdg; 0-375-96928-4; 978-0-375-98270-5 ebook

LC 2011014892

In 1898, Moses Thomas's summer vacation does not go exactly as planned as he contends with family problems and the ever-changing alliances among his friends at the same time as he is exposed to the escalating tension between the African-American and white communities of Wilmington, North Carolina.

"An intensely moving, first-person narrative of a disturbing historical footnote told from the perspective of a very likable, credible young hero." Kirkus

Wright, Betty Ren

Princess for a week; illustrated by Jacqueline Rogers. Holiday House 2006 105p il $16.95; pa $6.95

Grades: 2 3 4   **Fic**

1. Ghost stories 2. Mystery fiction

ISBN 0-8234-1945-2; 0-8234-2111-2 pa

LC 2005-50288

When a confident girl named Princess arrives to spend a week at Roddy's house, she encourages him to help her investigate the suspicious activities happening at a supposedly haunted house.

"The story moves quickly and is excellently paced. . . . The full-page illustrations add realism and depth to the story." SLJ

Wynne-Jones, Tim

★ **Rex** Zero and the end of the world. Farrar, Straus & Giroux 2007 86p $16

Grades: 4 5 6   **Fic**

1. Canada -- Fiction 2. Moving -- Fiction 3. Cold war -- Fiction 4. Family life -- Fiction

ISBN 0-374-33467-6; 978-0-374-33467-3

LC 2006-45172

Boston Globe-Horn Book Honor: Fiction (2007)

In the summer of 1962 with everyone nervous about a possible nuclear war, ten-nearly-eleven-year-old Rex, having just moved to Ottawa from Vancouver with his parents and five siblings, faces his own personal challenges as he discovers new friends and a new understanding of the world around him.

"Despite the weighty themes, Wynne-Jones writes with a light, often humorous touch and maintains a perspective true to an 11-year-old's perspective." Publ Wkly

Other titles about Rex Zero are:

Rex Zero, king of nothing (2008)

Rex Zero, the great pretender (2010)

Wyss, Thelma Hatch

Bear dancer; the story of a Ute girl. Margaret K. McElderry Books 2005 181p il $15.95

Grades: 5 6 7 8 **Fic**
1. Ute Indians -- Fiction
ISBN 1-4169-0285-6

LC 2005-40620

In late ninetenth-century Colorado, Elk Girl, sister of Ute chief Ouray, is captured by Cheyenne and Arapaho warriors, rescued by the white "enemy," and finally returned to her home. Includes historical notes.

"This fascinating story is based on a real person. . . . An excellent addition to historical-fiction collections." SLJ

Yardi, Robin
The **midnight** war of Mateo Martinez; by Robin Yardi. Carolrhoda Books 2016 184 p. (lb : alk. paper) $17.99
Grades: 4 5 6 **Fic**
1. Skunks -- Fiction 2. Mexican Americans -- Fiction 3. War -- Fiction 4. Skunks -- Fiction 5. Mexican Americans -- Fiction
ISBN 9781467783064

LC 2015016191

In this juvenile novel, by Robin Yardi, "life is confusing for Mateo Martinez. He and Johnny Ramirez don't hang out anymore, even though they used to be best friends. He and his new friend Ashwin try to act like brave, old-time knights, but it only gets them in trouble. And last night, two skunks stole Mateo's old trike." (Publisher's note)

"Mateo is an admirable character striving to live by a knight's code of honor, while struggling with a lost friendship and school bullies. His gallantry, developing relationship with Mila, and antics with the neighborhood wildlife make for quite the charming tale." Booklist

Yee, Lisa
Aloha, Kanani; illustrations by Sarah Davis. American Girl 2011 116p il (American girl) $12.95; pa $6.95
Grades: 3 4 5 **Fic**
1. Hawaii -- Fiction 2. Cousins -- Fiction 3. Racially mixed people -- Fiction
ISBN 978-1-59369-840-9; 1-59369-840-2; 978-1-59369-839-3 pa; 1-59369-839-9 pa

LC 2010046870

When the tropical paradise of Kauai, Hawaii, fails to impress her cousin from New York City, ten-year-old Kanani wonders why nothing seems to make her happy.

"In this story with an animal-rescue sub-plot, beautiful full-color illustrations and a Hawaiian glossary are included, along with several ending pages about real-life girls who have helped animals." Booklist

Another title about Kanani is:
Good job, Kanani (2011)

Bobby vs. girls (accidentally) illustrated by Dan Santat. Arthur A. Levine Books 2009 170p il $15.99; pa $5.99
Grades: 3 4 5 **Fic**
1. School stories 2. Friendship -- Fiction
ISBN 978-0-545-05592-5; 0-545-05592-X; 978-0-545-05593-2 pa; 0-545-05593-8 pa

When Bobby inadvertently gets into a fight with his best friend Holly, their disagreement develops into a boys versus girls war involving their whole fourth-grade class.

"Yee really understands children's thought processes and presents them with tact and good humor. . . . Santat's drawings manage the fine line between cartoon and realism and add dimension to the events. Readers will recognize themselves and learn some gentle lessons about relationships while they are laughing at the antics." Kirkus

Another title about Bobby is:
Bobby the brave (sometimes) (2010)

Millicent Min, girl genius. Arthur A. Levine Books 2003 248p $16.95; pa $4.99
Grades: 5 6 7 **Fic**
1. School stories 2. Gifted children -- Fiction 3. Chinese Americans -- Fiction
ISBN 0-439-42519-0; 0-439-42520-4 pa

LC 2003-3747

"At the tender age of eleven, Millicent Min has completed her junior year of high school. Summer school is Millie's idea of fun, so she is excited that her parents are allowing her to take a college poetry course . . . The tension between Millie's formal, overly intellectual way of expressing herself and her emotional immaturity makes her a very funny narrator. . . . Readers considerably older than Millicent's eleven years will enjoy this strong debut novel." Voice Youth Advocates

Other titles about Millicent Min and her friends are:
Stanford Wong flunks big-time (2005)
So totally Emily Ebers (2007)

Warp speed. Arthur A. Levine Books 2011 310p $16.99
Grades: 5 6 7 8 **Fic**
1. School stories 2. Bullies -- Fiction 3. California -- Fiction 4. Popularity -- Fiction 5. Family life -- Fiction
ISBN 978-0-545-12276-4; 0-545-12276-7

LC 2010-24228

"Entering 7th grade is no big deal for Marley Sandelski: Same old boring classes, same old boring life. The only thing he has to look forward to is the upcoming Star Trek convention. But when he inadvertently draws the attention of Digger Ronster, the biggest bully in school his life has officially moved from boring to far too dramatic . . . from invisible to center stage." (Publisher's note)

"Yee's combination of humor and sympathy works a charm here giving Marley a life of his own and a chance at success in this solid addition to her prismatic look at middle school." Kirkus

Yelchin, Eugene, 1956-
★ **Breaking** Stalin's nose; written and illustrated by Eugene Yelchin. Henry Holt and Company 2011 140p il $15.99
Grades: 4 5 6 7 **Fic**
1. Communism -- Fiction 2. Soviet Union -- Fiction 3. Father-son relationship -- Fiction
ISBN 0-8050-9216-1; 978-0-8050-9216-5

LC 2011005792

In the Stalinist era of the Soviet Union, ten-year-old Sasha idolizes his father, a devoted Communist, but when police take his father away and leave Sasha homeless, he is forced to examine his own perceptions, values, and beliefs.

"Readers will quickly pick up on the dichotomy between Sasha's ardent beliefs and the reality of life under Stalinism, and be glad for his ultimate disillusion, even as they worry for his future. An author's note concisely presents the chilling historical background and personal connection that underlie the story." Publ Wkly

The **haunting** of Falcon House; written and illustrated by Eugene Yelchin. Henry Holt & Co. 2016 320 p. illustrations (hardcover $15.99
Grades: 4 5 6 7 8 **Fic**
1. Aunts -- Fiction 2. Orphans -- Fiction 3. Haunted houses -- Fiction
ISBN 9780805098457

LC 2015049783

In this book, by Eugene Yelchin, "when twelve-year-old Prince Lev Lvov goes to live with his aunt at Falcon House, he takes his rightful place as heir to the Lvov family estate. Prince Lev dreams of becoming a hero of Russia like his great ancestors. But he'll discover that dark secrets haunt this house. Prince Lev is the only one who can set them free-will he be the hero his family needs?" (Publisher's note)

"This is a haunting tale at its very best." Booklist

Yep, Laurence, 1948-
City of fire. Tom Doherty Associates 2009 320p $15.99
Grades: 5 6 7 8   **Fic**
1. Fantasy fiction 2. Magic -- Fiction 3. Hawaii -- Fiction 4. Dragons -- Fiction
ISBN 978-0-7653-1924-1; 0-7653-1924-1
LC 2009016737
Twelve-year-old Scirye and her companions travel to Houlani, a new Hawaiian island created by magic, where they enlist the help of volcano goddess Pele in an attempt to stop an evil dragon and a mysterious man from altering the universe.

"Readers will be on tenterhooks awaiting the next episode of this exhilarating chase." Booklist

Followed by: City of ice (2011)

★ The **dragon's** child; a story of Angel Island. [by] Laurence Yep, with Kathleen S. Yep. HarperCollinsPublishers 2008 133p $15.99; lib bdg $16.89
Grades: 3 4 5 6   **Fic**
1. China -- Fiction 2. California -- Fiction 3. Immigrants -- Fiction 4. Chinese Americans -- Fiction
ISBN 978-0-06-027692-8; 0-06-027692-4; 978-0-06-027693-5 lib bdg; 0-06-027693-2 lib bdg
LC 2007-18373
"In a dramatic blend of fact and fiction, Laurence Yep and his niece draw on family stories, immigration records, and memories of Laurence's own conversations to tell his dad's story of coming to America at age 10 with his Chinese American dad. . . . With family photos, a historical note, and a long bibliography, this stirring narrative will spark readers' own search for roots." Booklist

A **dragon's** guide to making your human smarter; Laurence Yep & Joanne Ryder; illustrations by Mary GrandPré. Crown Books for Young Readers 2016 304 p. illustrations (A Dragon's Guide) (hc) $16.99
Grades: 4 5 6 7   **Fic**
1. School stories 2. Dragons -- Fiction 3. Fantasy fiction 4. Magic -- Fiction 5. Schools -- Fiction
ISBN 9780385392327; 9780385392334; 9780385392358
LC 2015010892
In this children's novel, by Laurence Yep and Joanne Ryder with illustrations by Mary GrandPré, "three-thousand-year-old [dragon] Miss Drake has arranged to send her dear pet Winnie to The Spriggs Academy, an extraordinary school for humans. . . . Winnie is particularly excited about magic class and having Sir Isaac Newton for science. . . .When a plot to snatch Winnie from her San Francisco home is uncovered, Miss Drake is ready to use all her cunning and magic to thwart it." (Publisher's note)

"Winnie's straightforward narration alternates with passages from Miss Drake, whose wry tone adds light humor to the story. An appealing black-and-white drawing opens each chapter." SLJ

A **dragon's** guide to the care and feeding of humans; Laurence Yep & Joanne Ryder; Illustrations by Mary GrandPré. Crown Books for Young Readers 2015 160 p. illustrations (hc) $15.99
Grades: 4 5 6 7   **Fic**
1. Pets -- Fiction 2. Dragons -- Fiction 3. Magic -- Fiction 4. Artists -- Fiction 5. Friendship -- Fiction 6. Imaginary creatures -- Fiction
ISBN 0385392281; 9780385392280; 9780385392297
LC 2014017803

In this novel by Laurence Yep and Joanne Ryder, "crusty dragon Miss Drake has a new pet human, precocious Winnie. Oddly enough, Winnie seems to think Miss Drake is her pet. . . . Unknown to most . . . , the City by the Bay is home to many . . . fantastic creatures. . . . And Winnie wants to draw every new creature she encounters. . . . But Winnie's sketchbook is not what it seems. Somehow, her sketchlings have been set loose on the city streets!" (Publisher's note)

"With a black-and-white spot illustration opening most chapters, an engaging narrator, and a consistently fluid writing style, this title makes a fine dragon choice for readers not yet ready for more weighty fantasy novels." SLJ

The **magic** paintbrush; drawings by Suling Wang. HarperCollins Pubs. 2000 89p il hardcover o.p. pa $5.99
Grades: 3 4 5   **Fic**
1. Magic -- Fiction 2. Chinese Americans -- Fiction
ISBN 0-06-028199-5; 0-06-440852-3 pa
LC 99-34959
A magic paintbrush transports Steve and his elderly caretakers from their drab apartment in Chinatown to a world of adventures

"Yep's crisp style keeps the pages turning, and he leavens his story with snappy dialogue, realistic characters and plenty of wise humor." Publ Wkly

★ The **star** maker. Harper 2010 100p $15.99; lib bdg $16.89
Grades: 5 6 7 8   **Fic**
1. Uncles -- Fiction 2. Family life -- Fiction 3. Chinese New Year -- Fiction 4. Chinese Americans -- Fiction 5. San Francisco (Calif.) -- Fiction
ISBN 978-0-06-025315-8; 0-06-025315-0; 978-0-06-025316-5 lib bdg; 0-06-025316-9 lib bdg
LC 2010-07856
With the help of his popular Uncle Chester, a young Chinese American boy tries hard to fulfill a promise to have firecrackers for everyone on the Chinese New Year in 1954. Includes an afterword with information about the Chinese customs portrayed in the story.

"Yep skillfully portrays the significance and emotional nature of common childhood dramas, from fears of going back on one's word to worries of losing a favorite uncle to a new girlfriend. . . . Yep has crafted other memorable characters, including Chinatown itself, which sparkle with energy and camaraderie." Publ Wkly

Includes bibliographical references

★ The **traitor**; Golden Mountain chronicles, 1885. HarperCollins Pubs. 2003 310p hardcover o.p. pa $6.99
Grades: 5 6 7 8   **Fic**
1. Friendship -- Fiction 2. Prejudices -- Fiction 3. Chinese Americans -- Fiction
ISBN 0-06-027522-7; 0-06-000831-8 pa
LC 2002-22534
Sequel to: Dragon's gate
In 1885, a lonely illegitimate American boy and a lonely Chinese American boy develop an unlikely friendship in the midst of prejudices and racial tension in their coal mining town of Rock Springs, Wyoming

"The short chapters read quickly, and readers will become involved through the first-person voices that capture each boy's feelings of being an outsider and a traitor." Booklist

When the circus came to town; drawings by Suling Wang. Harper-Collins Pubs. 2002 113p il hardcover o.p. pa $5.99
Grades: 3 4 5   **Fic**
1. Circus -- Fiction 2. Chinese New Year -- Fiction 3. Chinese

Americans -- Fiction 4. Frontier and pioneer life -- Fiction
ISBN 0-06-029325-X; 0-06-440965-1 pa

LC 2001-39290

An Asian cook and a Chinese New Year celebration help ten-year-old Ursula at a Montana stage coach station to regain her confidence after smallpox scars her face

"Yep has based his novel on a true story, and his writing is, by turns, direct, humorous, and poignant." Booklist

Ylvisaker, Anne

The **luck** of the Buttons. Candlewick Press 2011 224p $15.99

Grades: 4 5 6 **Fic**

1. Mystery fiction 2. Iowa -- Fiction 3. Chance -- Fiction 4. Friendship -- Fiction 5. Family life -- Fiction 6. Photography -- Fiction 7. Great Depression, 1929-1939 -- Fiction
ISBN 978-0-7636-5066-7; 0-7636-5066-8

LC 2010039169

In Iowa circa 1929, spunky twelve-year-old Tugs vows to turn her family's luck around, with the help of a Brownie camera and a small-town mystery that only she can solve.

"The tale has a whiff of nostalgia, . . . but the good old days are balanced by the strongly realized, immediate characters and the delicacy and originality of the writing." Horn Book

Yohalem, Eve

★ **Escape** under the forever sky; a novel. Chronicle Books 2009 220p $16.99

Grades: 4 5 6 7 **Fic**

1. Ethiopia -- Fiction 2. Kidnapping -- Fiction 3. Wilderness survival -- Fiction 4. Mother-daughter relationship -- Fiction
ISBN 978-0-8118-6653-8; 0-8118-6653-X

LC 2008-19565

As a future conservation zoologist whose mother is the United States Ambassador to Ethiopia, thirteen-year-old Lucy uses her knowledge for survival when she is kidnapped and subsequently escapes.

"Lucy's past and present are gracefully woven together, through well-integrated flashbacks, into a powerful picture of the life of a foreigner in Ethiopia. The story should appeal to all with a sense of adventure." Publ Wkly

Yolen, Jane

B.U.G. (Big Ugly Guy) by Jane Yolen and Adam Stemple. Dutton Children's Books 2013 344 p.

Grades: 4 5 6 7 8 **Fic**

1. Golem -- Fiction 2. Magic -- Fiction 3. Bullies -- Fiction 4. Friendship -- Fiction 5. Bands (Music) -- Fiction 6. Klezmer music -- Fiction 7. Jews -- United States -- Fiction
ISBN 9780525422389

LC 2012018217

A constant target for bullies, Sammy Greenburg is glad to make friends with a boy named Skink, who even agrees to "start up a Klezmer fusion garage band after Sammy introduces Skink to the unique combination of jazz and Jewish folk music. When the bullies beat up Skink, however, Sammy decides enough is enough, and, using a formula he finds in his rabbi's study, he creates a golem to take vengeance on his enemies—and fill the missing drummer spot in his new band." (Bulletin of the Center for Children's Books)

Snow in Summer. Philomel Books 2011 243p $16.99

Grades: 4 5 6 7 **Fic**

1. Fairy tales 2. Magic -- Fiction 3. Stepmothers -- Fiction 4. West Virginia -- Fiction
ISBN 0-399-25663-6; 978-0-399-25663-9

LC 2010044242

Recasts the tale of Snow White, setting it in West Virginia in the 1940s with a stepmother who is a snake-handler.

"This story is beautifully written and deliciously scary, with just enough differences from familiar versions to keep readers guessing." Publ Wkly

Trash Mountain; by Jane Yolen; illustrated by Chris Monroe. Carolrhoda Books, Inc. 2015 184 p. illustrations, map (trade hardcover) $16.99

Grades: 3 4 5 6 **Fic**

1. Animals -- Fiction 2. Squirrels -- Fiction 3. Animal behavior -- Fiction 4. Survival -- Fiction 5. Gray squirrel -- Fiction 6. Red squirrels -- Fiction 7. Introduced animals -- Fiction
ISBN 1467712345; 9781467712347

LC 201303072

This book "follows a young squirrel who finds himself alone in the world when his parents are suddenly killed. Jane Yolen has crafted a compelling array of characters, including young Nutley, wise Larie, and loyal Naw. The age-old battle between the grey squirrels and the reds is captivating and young readers will also detect subtle themes concerning species diversity and evolution." (Publisher's note)

"Yolen's clear voice is a benevolent presence, strongly felt in 'This You Should Know' paragraphs, which open each chapter. They offer scientific facts about red and gray squirrels along with whimsical speculations which encourage readers to look for meaning behind the facts." SLJ

Yoo, David

The **detention** club. Balzer + Bray 2011 299p $16.99

Grades: 5 6 7 8 **Fic**

1. School stories 2. Siblings -- Fiction 3. Popularity -- Fiction 4. Korean Americans -- Fiction
ISBN 978-0-06-178378-4; 0-06-178378-1

LC 2010-46211

Sixth-grader Peter Lee, in a desperate attempt to regain the popularity he had in elementary school, discovers that serving detention can win him important friends, much to the dismay of his over-achieving eighth-grade sister, Sunny.

"Even readers who guess the thief's identity early on will be entertained by the boys' hijinks and empathize with their desire to fit in." Publ Wkly

Young, Judy

A **book** for black-eyed Susan; written by Judy Young; illustrated by Doris Ettlinger. Sleeping Bear Press 2011 un il $16.95

Grades: 2 3 4 **Fic**

1. Oregon -- Fiction 2. Sewing -- Fiction 3. Sisters -- Fiction 4. Books and reading -- Fiction 5. Frontier and pioneer life -- Fiction 6. Overland journeys to the Pacific -- Fiction
ISBN 978-1-58536-463-3; 1-58536-463-0

LC 2010028422

While traveling along the Oregon Trail, ten-year-old Cora and her newborn baby sister suffer the loss of their mother and are separated but Cora stitches a book to tell the dark-eyed baby of their journey and family.

"The surprise ending, however unlikely, will warm readers' hearts Realistic watercolor images reveal the intricacies of pioneer life and the emotional turmoil of the characters. An engaging introduction to life during the Westward expansion." SLJ

Minnow and Rose; an Oregon trail story. written by Judy Young illustrated by Bill Farnsworth. Sleeping Bear Press 2009 un il (Tales of young Americans) $17.95

Grades: 3 4 5 **Fic**

1. Friendship -- Fiction 2. Native Americans -- Fiction 3. Frontier and pioneer life -- Fiction

ISBN 978-1-58536-421-3; 1-58536-421-5

LC 2008024768

Traveling west with her pioneer family in a wagon train, Rose meets Minnow, who lives in a native American village along the banks of a river.

"Beautiful oil paintings . . . lend additional action and understanding to the story." SLJ

Young, Karen Romano

Doodlebug; a novel in doodles. Feiwel and Friends 2010 un il $14.99

Grades: 4 5 6 7 **Fic**

1. School stories 2. Moving -- Fiction 3. California -- Fiction 4. Family life -- Fiction 5. Racially mixed people -- Fiction

ISBN 978-0-312-56156-7; 0-312-56156-3

Doreen Bussey, aka Dodo, takes the nickname Doodlebug when her family moves from Los Angeles to San Francisco and she records her experiences in a notebook with words, scribbles, and drawings.

This offers "an engaging, originial heroine, a satisfying story and lots of great pictures. . . . Some details, like the fact that the family is interracial, are shown but not stated, rewarding careful examination of the artwork. . . . Charming and thoughtful." Kirkus

Hundred percent; by Karen Romano Young. Chronicle Books 2016 256 p. (alk. paper) $16.99

Grades: 5 6 7 **Fic**

1. Girls -- Fiction 2. Nicknames -- Fiction 3. Friendship -- Fiction 4. Emotions in children -- Fiction 5. Schools -- Fiction 6. Family life -- Fiction 9. Best friends -- Fiction

ISBN 9781452138909

LC 2015047481

In this children's book by Karen Romano Young, "Christine Gouda faces change at every turn, starting with her own nickname—Tink—which just doesn't fit anymore. Readers will relate to this strong female protagonist whose voice rings with profound authenticity and absolute novelty, and her year's cringingly painful trials in normalcy—uncomfortable Halloween costumes, premature sleepover parties, crushed crushes, and changing friendships." (Publisher's note)

"Romano's characters jump off the page in a thoughtful and realistic look at what it means to be on the precipice of adolescence." Pub Wkly

Zahler, Diane

The **thirteenth** princess. Harper 2009 243p

Grades: 4 5 6 7 **Fic**

1. Fairy tales 2. Magic -- Fiction 3. Sisters -- Fiction 4. Princesses -- Fiction 5. Household employees -- Fiction 6. Father-daughter relationship -- Fiction 7. Folklore -- Germany

ISBN 0-06-182498-4; 0-06-182499-2 lib bdg; 978-0-06-182498-2; 978-0-06-182499-9 lib bdg

LC 2009-14575

Zita, cast aside by her father and raised as a kitchen maid, learns when she is nearly twelve that she is a princess and that her twelve sisters love her, and so when she discovers they are victims of an evil enchantment, she desperately tries to save them. Inspired by the Grimm fairy tale, "The twelve dancing princesses."

Zahler "deftly and thoughtfully embellishes the tale's classic elements. . . . Zahler takes a light story and gives it gratifying depth, rounding out the characters and their motivations without betraying the source material and wrapping it all together in a graceful and cohesive romantic drama." Publ Wkly

A **true** princess. Harper 2011 182p $15.99

Grades: 4 5 6 **Fic**

1. Fairy tales 2. Friendship -- Fiction 3. Princesses -- Fiction 4. Voyages and travels -- Fiction

ISBN 978-0-06-182501-9; 0-06-182501-8

LC 2010017846

Twelve-year-old Lilia goes north to seek the family she has never known, accompanied by her friends Kai and Karina and their dog Ove, on an adventure fraught with peril, especially when they become lost in Bitra Forest, the Elf King's domain. Inspired by the Hans Christian Andersen tale, The princess and the pea.

"Readers who enjoyed . . . Zahler's The Thirteenth Princess . . . will also relish this tale." SLJ

Zalben, Jane Breskin

Brenda Berman, wedding expert; illustrated by Victoria Chess. Clarion Books 2009 48p il lib bdg $16

Grades: 2 3 4 **Fic**

1. Uncles -- Fiction 2. Weddings -- Fiction 3. Friendship -- Fiction

ISBN 978-0-618-31321-1 lib bdg; 0-618-31321-4 lib bdg

LC 2006-34851

When Brenda's favorite uncle decides to marry, Brenda sees visions of a gold lame flower-girl's outfit, until Uncle Harry and his bride-to-be show up with her niece. Includes cake recipe.

"Brenda's robust personality drives the narrative as well as the art, as Chess's folksy watercolors capture the girl's expressions, which vacillate wildly between outrage and exhilaration." Publ Wkly

Zemke, Deborah

My life in pictures; Deborah Zemke. Dial Books for Young Readers 2016 144 p. illustrations (Bea Garcia) (hardcover) $14.99

Grades: 1 2 3 **Fic**

1. Drawing -- Fiction 2. Friendship -- Fiction 3. Hispanic Americans -- Fiction

ISBN 0803741545; 9780803741546

LC 2014049059

In this children's book, by Deborah Zemke, "Bea Garcia is an artist. She draws anywhere and everywhere—but mostly in her own notebook. When Bea's first and only best friend Yvonne moves to Australia, not even drawing makes Bea feel better. And things only get worse when a loud, rambunctious boy moves in next door. He's nothing at all like Yvonne! But with a little imagination and a whole lot of doodles, Bea Garcia might just make a new friend." (Publisher's note)

"Bea Garcia is an honest and funny protagonist with whom readers will identify and want to check back with regularly" SLJ

Zimmer, Tracie Vaughn

42 miles; illustrated by Elaine Clayton. Clarion Books 2008 73p il $16

Grades: 4 5 6 **Fic**

1. Novels in verse 2. Divorce -- Fiction 3. Farm life -- Fiction 4. Family life -- Fiction 5. City and town life -- Fiction

ISBN 978-0-618-61867-5; 0-618-61867-8

LC 2007-31032

As her thirteenth birthday approaches, JoEllen decides to bring together her two separate lives—one as Joey, who enjoys weekends with her father and other relatives on a farm, and another as Ellen, who lives with her mother in an apartment near her school and friends.

"Using free verse, Zimmer shows the richness in both places, while black-and-white composit illustrations bright the bits and pieces together." Booklist

The **floating** circus; by Tracie Vaughn Zimmer. Bloomsbury Children's Books 2008 198p $15.99

Grades: 4 5 6   **Fic**
1. Circus -- Fiction 2. Boats and boating -- Fiction 3. Abandoned children -- Fiction
ISBN 978-1-59990-185-5; 1-59990-185-4

                                         LC 2007038998
In 1850s Pittsburgh, thirteen-year-old Owen leaves his younger brother and sneaks aboard a circus housed in a riverboat, where he befriends a freed slave, learns to work with elephants, and finally comes to terms with the choices he has made in his difficult life
This is a "lively historical novel. Readers will be hooked from the start by the voice of the narrator. . . . Bittersweet and satisfying." Publ Wkly

Sketches from a spy tree; poems by Tracie Vaughn Zimmer; illustrated by Andrew Glass. Clarion Books 2005 63p il $16
Grades: 3 4 5 6   **Fic**
1. Twins -- Fiction 2. Divorce -- Fiction 3. Sisters -- Fiction 4. Stepfamilies -- Fiction
ISBN 0-618-23479-9

                                         LC 2003-27768
In a series of poems, narrator Anne Marie paints pictures of family life from grief to hope after her father abandons his "four girls" Anne Marie and her mother and twin and baby sister.
"The writing is lyrical yet fresh. . . . Glass's remarkable watercolors, sketches, photographs, and collages bring Anne Marie's experiences to life." SLJ

Zoehfeld, Kathleen Weidner
★ **Secrets** of the garden; food chains and the food web in our backyard. illustrated by Priscilla Lamont. Alfred A. Knopf 2012 il $16.99; lib bdg $19.99
Grades: K 1 2 3   **Fic**
1. Gardens -- Fiction 2. Gardening -- Fiction 3. Food chains (Ecology) -- Fiction
ISBN 978-0-517-70990-0; 0-517-70990-2; 978-0-517-70991-7 lib bdg; 0-517-70991-0 lib bdg; 978-0-375-98730-4 ebook

                                         LC 2011032059
This "is a wonderfully informative and enjoyable journey through one family's backyard garden, from spring planting to fall harvest. Covering a dazzling array of topics, the author still manages to hold onto a story line that will draw readers in and allow them to experience both the good and the bad right along with narrator Alice. . . . The text comes alive through Lamont's pen-and-watercolor illustrations, which reinforce the learning while entertaining at the same time." Kirkus

Zucker, Naomi Flink
★ **Callie's** rules; by Naomi Zucker. Egmont USA 2009 240p $15.99; lib bdg $18.99
Grades: 4 5 6 7   **Fic**
1. School stories 2. Halloween -- Fiction 3. New Jersey -- Fiction 4. Family life -- Fiction
ISBN 978-1-60684-027-6; 1-60684-027-4; 978-1-60684-052-8 lib bdg; 1-60684-052-5 lib bdg

                                         LC 2009-15419
Eleven-year-old Callie Jones tries to keep track of all the rules for fitting in that other middle schoolers seem to know, but when the town decides to replace Halloween with an Autumn Festival, Callie leads her large family in an unusual protest.
"Callie herself is both funny and resourceful. Worthwhile and entertaining." Kirkus
Followed by: Write on, Callie Jones (2010)

S C   STORY COLLECTIONS

Alexander, Lloyd
★ The **foundling** and other tales of Prydain; rev & expanded ed. Holt & Co. 1999 98p hardcover o.p. pa $5.99
Grades: 5 6 7 8   **S C**
1. Short stories 2. Fantasy fiction
ISBN 0-8050-6130-4; 0-8050-8053-8 pa

                                       LC 98-42807
First published 1973; this revised and expanded edition includes two additional stories Coll and his white pig and The truthful harp, first published separately 1965 and 1967 respectively
Eight short stories dealing with events that preceded the birth of Taran, the Assistant Pig-Keeper and key figure in the author's five works on the Kingdom of Prydain which began with The book of three
"The stories are written with vivid grace and humor." Chicago. Children's Book Center [review of 1973 edition]

Andersen, Hans Christian
★ **Hans** Christian Andersen's Fairy Tales; selected and illustrated by Lisbeth Zwerger; translated by Anthea Bell. Minedition 2006 104p il $19.99
Grades: 4 5 6 7   **S C**
1. Fairy tales 2. Short stories
ISBN 0-698-40035-6
A reissue of the edition first published 1991
"This collection of . . . tales includes relatively unknown stories, such as 'The Rose Tree Regiment,' along with such familiar favorites as 'The Princess & the Pea.' Bell's finesse in writing is well matched by Zwerger's delicate, understated approach in the illustrations, which are introspective rather than dramatic. Sophisticated in design, the book features fluid watercolors and wide-bordered text on tall, white pages." Booklist

Arato, Rona
On a medieval day; story voyages around the world. illustrated by Peter Ferguson. Maple Tree Press 2010 96p il $24.95; pa $15.95
Grades: 4 5 6   **S C**
1. Short stories 2. Middle Ages -- Fiction
ISBN 978-1-897349-94-6; 1-897349-94-7; 978-1-897349-95-3 pa; 1-897349-95-5 pa
"Alternating between male and female narrators, this book presents stories about nine fictional youth of the medieval period. From the Mayan Civilization in 720 to the Kingdom of Castile in 1395, with stops in Vinland in 1002, Japan in 1205, and other places and years, their tales provide readers with a worldview of the era. Each chapter follows one child or teen through a day in which a conflict or crisis for the protagonist brings in some cultural and social context of the period. . . . The fast-paced stories make for entertaining reading. Each chapter ends with a brief history of the period and includes a simple map. . . . The book is a wonderful attempt to expand the usual concept of the medieval world beyond Europe." SLJ

Avi
Strange happenings; five tales of transformation. Harcourt 2006 147p $15; pa $5.95
Grades: 5 6 7 8   **S C**
1. Short stories 2. Supernatural -- Fiction
ISBN 0-15-205790-0; 0-15-206461-3 pa

                                       LC 2004-29579
"In this short story collection, Avi offers five fantastical tales, set in both contemporary and fairy-tale lands, that explore the notion of transformation. . . . The pieces are vividly imagined and shot through with a captivating, edgy spookiness, which, along with their brevity and some

droll, crackling dialogue, makes them great choices for sharing aloud in class or as inspiration in creative-writing units." Booklist

What do fish have to do with anything? and other stories; illustrated by Tracy Mitchell. Candlewick Press 1997 202p il hardcover o.p. pa $6.99

Grades: 4 5 6 7   **S C**

1. Short stories

ISBN 0-7636-0329-5; 0-7636-2319-9 pa

         LC 97-1354

"While Avi's endings are not tidy, they are effective: each story brings its protagonist beyond childhood self-absorption to the realization that one is an integral part of a bigger picture." Horn Book

Babbitt, Natalie

The **Devil's** storybook; stories and pictures by Natalie Babbitt. Farrar, Straus & Giroux 1974 101p il hardcover o.p. pa $3.95

Grades: 4 5 6   **S C**

1. Short stories 2. Devil -- Fiction

ISBN 0-374-41708-3 pa

"Twists of plot within traditional themes and a briskly witty style distinguish this book, illustrated amusingly with black-and-white line drawings." Booklist

Bachmann, Stefan

The **Cabinet** of Curiosities; 36 Tales Brief & Sinister. by Stefan Bachmann, Katherine Catmull, Claire Legrand and Emma Trevayne; illustrated by Alexander Jansson. Harpercollins Childrens Books 2014 496 p. illustrations $16.99

Grades: 3 4 5 6 7   **S C**

1. Short stories 2. Horror fiction 3. Mystery fiction

ISBN 0062331051; 9780062331052

         LC 2013362532

This book, by Stefan Bachmann, Katherine Catmull, Claire Legrand and Emma Trevayne, is "a collection of thirty-six forty eerie, mysterious, intriguing, and very short stories. . . . The book features an introduction and commentary by the authors and black-and-white illustrations throughout." (Publisher's note)

"Many of these are moral tales in which nasty children or adults die horribly; others, though, feature perfectly nice people who meet similarly gruesome ends. Readers who enjoy their Halloween chills all year round will find this anthology a delight." Pub Wkly

★ **Baseball** crazy: ten short stories that cover all the bases; edited by Nancy E. Mercado. Dial Books for Young Readers 2008 191p $16.99; pa $6.99

Grades: 4 5 6 7   **S C**

1. Short stories 2. Baseball -- Fiction

ISBN 978-0-8037-3162-2; 0-8037-3162-0; 978-0-14-241371-5 pa; 0-14-241371-2 pa

         LC 2007-26649

"There's no shortage of great writing in this collection of 10 stories. Baseball unifies the entries, but there the similarities end. . . . Readers will be drawn in by the masterful storytelling." Publ Wkly

The **big** book of pirates; text abridged and adapted by Alissa Heyman; illustrated by Xose Tomas; [original Spanish text by by Joan and Albert Vinyoli] Sterling Pub. Co. 2011 103p il $12.95

Grades: 3 4 5 6   **S C**

1. Short stories 2. Adventure fiction 3. Pirates -- Fiction

ISBN 978-1-4027-8056-1; 1-4027-8056-7

         LC 2010015049

This "is a treasure trove of abridged yarns by the likes of Sir Arthur Conan Doyle, Joseph Conrad, Daniel Defoe, and others. Of course the

stories deal with pillaging, treachery, and all-around bad behavior on the open seas. The artwork is a dark, graphic-novel-like spin on N.C. Wyeth's illustrations for classics such as Treasure Island and Robinson Crusoe. Tomás uses a bold color palette and has given many of his characters angular faces and staring eyes, all to an appropriately menacing effect. This entertaining package will not make port on the shelves for long." SLJ

Byars, Betsy Cromer

Cat diaries; secret writings of the MEOW Society. [by] Betsy Byars, Betsy Duffey, Laurie Myers; illustrated by Erik Brooks. Henry Holt and Company 2010 80p il $15.99

Grades: 2 3 4   **S C**

1. Short stories 2. Cats -- Fiction

ISBN 978-0-8050-8717-8; 0-8050-8717-6

         LC 2009-18877

On one night every year, cats in the MEOW Society, which stands for "Memories Expressed In Our Writing," gather to read from their diaries, hearing stories of a gypsy cat, a Caribbean pirate cat, a library cat, and many others.

"This is a solid collection of stories that young readers will enjoy." Libr Media Connect

Dog diaries; secret writings of the WOOF Society. [by] Betsy Byars, Betsy Duffey, Laurie Myers; illustrated by Erik Brooks. Henry Holt 2007 72p il $15.95

Grades: 2 3 4   **S C**

1. Short stories 2. Dogs -- Fiction 3. Storytelling -- Fiction

ISBN 978-0-8050-7957-9; 0-8050-7957-2

         LC 2006011634

At the first annual meeting of WOOF—Words of Our Friends—assorted dogs preserve their heritage by sharing tales of canines throughout history, including Abu, who ruled all of Egypt except for one pesky cat, and Zippy, who simply must find the squeaky toy

"This collection of short stories combines the bedrocks of mass appeal: dogs, humor, and short chapters brimming with illustrations. . . . Expressive, energetic pencil illustrations adorn nearly every page." Booklist

★ The **chronicles** of Harris Burdick; 14 amazing authors tell the tales. Houghton Mifflin Harcourt 2011 un il $24.99

Grades: 5 6 7 8 9   **S C**

1. Short stories

ISBN 978-0-547-54810-4; 0-547-54810-9; 0547548109; 9780547548104

         LC 2011006564

"Van Allsburg's The Mysteries of Harris Burdick, published in 1984, paired foreboding sentences with cryptic, highly detailed charcoal-pencil illustrations. With mostly stimulating, sometimes conventional results, seasoned authors (and Van Allsburg himself) play the game children have for decades, incorporating the sentences and visual cues into new stories . . . that expand on the original's enigmas. The liveliest entries pick up on Van Allsburg's haunting ambiguity: Jon Scieszka ends with a cliffhanger, Gregory Maguire weaves a complex tale of magic, and M.T. Anderson concocts a chilling Halloween offering. For a lakeside picture of two children, Sherman Alexie writes a sinister narrative about exasperating twins who pretend to have a third sibling, until their creepy prank backfires. . . . This star-studded exercise in creative writing tests the wits of favorite authors and shows readers how even the big shots hone their craft." Publ Wkly

Delacre, Lulu

★ **Salsa** stories; stories and linocuts by Lulu Delacre. Scholastic Press 2000 105p il hardcover o.p. $16.99

Grades: 4 5 6   **S C**
1. Short stories 2. Latin America 3. Family life -- Fiction 4. Latin America -- Fiction
ISBN 0-590-63118-7; 0-590-63121-7 pa

LC 99-25534

A collection of stories within the story of a family celebration where the guests relate their memories of growing up in various Latin American countries. Also contains recipes

"Kids will respond to both the warmth and the anxiety of the family life described in the vivid writing, and in Delacre's nicely composed linocuts." Booklist

Flanagan, John
    The **lost** stories. Philomel 2011 422p (Ranger's apprentice) $17.99
Grades: 5 6 7 8   **S C**
1. Short stories 2. Fantasy fiction
ISBN 978-0-399-25618-9; 0-399-25618-0

This is "a collection of nine stories showing events not recorded in the books [of the Ranger's Apprentice series] and following the familiar characters during certain unrecorded times. In the framework story, set in 1896, an archaeologist discovers the fabled lost stories of the medieval Kingdom of Araluen. . . . Inspired by questions from readers, these short stories retain the adventure and the camaraderis of the novels." Booklist

Fleischman, Paul
    Graven images; three stories. by Paul Fleischman; illustrations by Bagram Ibatoulline. Candlewick Press 2006 116p il $16.99; pa $5.99
Grades: 5 6 7 8   **S C**
1. Short stories 2. Supernatural -- Fiction
ISBN 0-7636-2775-5; 0-7636-2984-7 pa

LC 2005054283

A newly illustrated edition with a new afterword of the title first published 1982 by Harper & Row
A Newbery Medal honor book, 1983
A collection of three stories about a child who reads the lips of those who whisper secrets into a statue's ear; a daydreaming shoemaker's apprentice who must find ways to make the girl he loves notice him; and a stone carver who creates a statue of a ghost.

"Readers will be delighted with the return to print of [this title] with haunting new acrylic gouache illustrations . . . evoking the spinetingling aspects of this trio of tales. . . . Via a new afterword, the author explains the stories' inspiration and describes this book's significance early in his career." Publ Wkly

Girl meets boy; edited by Kelly Milner Halls. Chronicle Books 2012 v. cm.
       S C
1. Short stories 2. Teenagers -- Fiction 3. Interpersonal relations -- Fiction 4. Short stories, American 5. Perspective (Philosophy) -- Fiction 6. Interpersonal relations -- Fiction 7. Perspective (Philosophy) -- Fiction
ISBN 9781452102641

LC 2011025405

In this book "[t]welve writers answer [editor Kelly Milner] Halls's question: 'What if a group of authors took on the challenge of perception—boys versus girls?' Together, they create a thoughtful collection of paired short stories (and one joint offering) that give two distinct perspectives on the same events. While romantically themed, the stories do not all end in love connections. In James Howe and Ellen Wittlinger's stories, a gay teen learns the person he has been chatting with online is actually a girl; meanwhile, in Sarah Ryan and Randy Powell's joint

story, 'Launchpad to Neptune,' a teen reunites with his first crush, only to find Stephanie has transitioned to Stephen." (Publishers Weekly)

★ The **Great** War; an anthology of stories inspired by objects from the first World War. illustrated by Jim Kay. Candlewick Press 2014 304 p. illustrations
Grades: 3 4 5 6 7 8   **S C**
1. World War, 1914-1918 2. War stories 3. Historical fiction
ISBN 9780763675547

LC 2013955699

In this book, illustrated by Jim Kay, "eleven internationally acclaimed writers draw on personal objects to bring the First World War to life. . . . Each author was invited to choose an object that had a connection to the war . . . and use it as the inspiration for an original short story." (Publisher's note)

"Each of the 11 original short stories in this superlative collection about WWI has been inspired by an object evoking the conflict. Thus the catalyst for contributor Almond is a soldier's writing case; for Timothée de Fombelle, it's a Victoria Cross; for Adèle Geras, a wartime butter dish; for John Boyne, a recruitment poster; and so forth...Haunting black-and-white illustrations by Kate Greenaway Medal-winning illustrator Kay reinforce the stories' somber mood and cumulative power. This book is both beautifully designed and beautifully written." Booklist

Guys Read Terrifying Tales; edited by Jon Scieszka. Harpercollins Childrens Books 2015 288 p. illustrations
Grades: 4 5 6 7 8   **S C**
1. Anthologies 2. Ghost stories 3. Horror fiction 4. Short stories
ISBN 0062385585; 9780062385581

In this anthology, part of the Guys Read series edited by Jon Scieszka, "[e]leven masters of suspense--Kelly Barnhill, Michael Buckley, Adam Gidwitz, Adele Griffin and Lisa Brown, Claire Legrand, Nikki Loftin, Daniel José Older, Dav Pilkey, R.L. Stine, and Rita Williams-Garcia -have come together to bring you a bone-chilling collection of original ghost stories with illustrations by Gris Grimly." (Publisher's note)

"The stories are well-chosen and, unlike too many collections, consistently terrific, every story indeed scary and full of surprises. Strong leads serve many stories well, pulling readers in, perhaps against their own apprehensions." Kirkus

★ **Guys** read: funny business; edited and with an introduction by Jon Scieszka; stories by Mac Barnett [et al.]; with illustrations by Adam Rex. Walden Pond Press 2010 268p il $16.99; pa $5.99
Grades: 4 5 6 7   **S C**
1. Short stories 2. Humorous fiction 3. Boys -- Fiction
ISBN 978-0-06-196374-2; 0-06-196374-7; 978-0-06-196373-5 pa; 0-06-196373-9 pa

LC 2010-08122

A collection of humorous stories featuring a teenaged mummy, a homicidal turkey, and the world's largest pool of chocolate milk.

"A must-have collection for the boys in your library—and while you're at it, get a copy for the girls too!" Booklist

★ **Guys** read: thriller. Walden Pond Press 2011 viii, 272p $16.99; pa $6.99
Grades: 5 6 7 8   **S C**
1. Short stories 2. Adventure fiction
ISBN 978-0-06-196376-6; 0-06-196376-3; 978-0-06-196375-9 pa; 0-06-196375-5 pa

"Scieszka has gathered 10 thrilling stories from stellar writers. There are ghost stories, a deeply touching tale of a wish-granting machine and one about monsters that live in storm drains. . . . This anthology is brimming with choice stuff for guys who appreciate the uncanny, the uncouth and the unput-down-able." Kirkus

★ **Half-**minute horrors; edited by Susan Rich. HarperCollinsPublishers 2009 141p il $12.99

Grades: 5 6 7 8   S C

1. Short stories 2. Horror fiction

ISBN 978-0-06-183379-3; 0-06-183379-7

LC 2009-18293

An anthology of very short, scary stories by an assortment of authors and illustrators including Chris Raschka, Joyce Carol Oates, Neil Gaiman, Jack Gantos, and Lane Smith.

"This collection of more than 70 chilling snippets is ideal for campfires and car trips. The stories—some a couple sentences, some a few pages—range from darkly humorous . . . to outright creepy. . . . These are inherently quick reads, but with enough plot and detail to encourage further imagining." Publ Wkly

Gay, Marie-Louise

Short stories for little monsters; Marie-Louise Gay. Groundwood Books 2017 48 p. color illustrations $19.95

Grades: K 1 2 3   S C

1. Children's stories 2. Short stories -- Collections

ISBN 1554988969; 9781554988969

This collection of illustrated stories, by Marie-Louise Gay, "gives us a glimpse into the things children wonder about every day. What do cats really see? What do trees talk about? Should you make funny faces on a windy day? Do worms rule the world? Do mothers always tell the truth? Do snails have nightmares?" (Publisher's note)

Hawes, Louise

Black pearls; a faerie strand. by Louise Hawes; illustrations by Rebecca Guay. Houghton Mifflin Company 2008 211p il $16

Grades: 5 6 7 8 9 10 11 12   S C

1. Fairy tales 2. Short stories

ISBN 978-0-618-74797-9; 0-618-74797-4

LC 2007-41166

"Seven gems based on traditional fairy tales make up this collection of unique short stories. . . . Each contains enough clues to guide teens back to the familiar and sometimes innuendo-laden classic fairy tales of their childhoods, and Guay's fantastical pencil drawings . . . enhance the sense of character and magic. Twisted, clever, and artfully written." Booklist

Hearne, Betsy Gould

The **canine** connection: stories about dogs and people; [by] Betsy Hearne. Margaret K. McElderry Bks. 2003 113p hardcover o.p. pa $8.95

Grades: 5 6 7 8   S C

1. Short stories 2. Dogs -- Fiction

ISBN 0-689-85258-4; 1-4169-6817-2 pa

LC 2001-58991

Twelve short stories that reflect the varied ways that dogs and humans relate

"The emotions and dialogue are pitch perfect. . . . A rewarding collection that will stay with readers." Booklist

Horse tales; collected by June Crebbin; illustrated by Inga Moore. Candlewick Press 2005 148p il $18.99

Grades: 4 5 6 7   S C

1. Short stories 2. Horses -- Fiction

ISBN 0-7636-2657-0

LC 2004-51897

In these "short stories, the remarkable nature of the horse is revealed. . . . The offerings excerpted from novels work well as short stories here and may inspire readers to look for the full-length books. . . . This is an excellently conceived and executed collection with wonderful art." SLJ

I fooled you; ten stories of tricks, jokes, and switcheroos. collected and edited by Johanna Hurwitz. Candlewick Press 2010 174p il $16.99; pa $6.99

Grades: 4 5 6   S C

1. Short stories

ISBN 978-0-7636-3789-7; 0-7636-3789-0; 978-0-7636-4877-0 pa; 0-7636-4877-9 pa

LC 2009-26017

"Hurwitz asked 10 authors to write a piece with the tagline of the title. . . . Megan McDonald uses her familiar characters, Judy Moody and Stink. . . . Douglas Florian's poem is distinctively in his style, but contains unexpected elements, nonetheless. . . . Michelle Knudsen's 'The Bridge to Highlandsville' is absolutely logical yet lacks the ending most would expect. Matthew Holm's almost wordless 'Sam and Pam' . . . adds a nice graphic-novel-style component to the package. Most readers will likely find something that they appreciate and something that they don't—which may be the best indication of the range of depth and complexity in this collection." SLJ

Ionesco, Eugène, 1912-1994

Stories 1,2,3,4; Eugene Ionesco; illustrated by Etienne Delessert. Pgw 2012 112 p. $19.95

Grades: K 1 2 3   S C

1. Children's stories 2. Picture books for children

ISBN 1936365510; 9781936365517

In this collection of stories by Eugene Ionesco, illustrated by Etienne Delessert, provides "snippets of playful conversation between Papa, Mama, their daughter Josette, and Jacqueline the maid. . . . In Story 3, the father tells Josette about an airplane journey they'll take together . . . over the Paris rooftops, and on to the moon. . . . Visual quotes (including plenty of Ionesco rhinoceri) pop up everywhere." (Publishers Weekly)

Johnson, Hal

Fearsome Creatures of the Lumberwoods; 20 Chilling Tales from the Wilderness. by Hal Johnson, illustrated by Tom Mead. Workman Pub Co. 2015 176 p. illustrations $14.95

Grades: 5 6 7 8   S C

1. Short stories 2. Horror fiction -- Fiction 3. Mythical animals -- Fiction

ISBN 0761184619; 9780761184614

This children's horror story collection, by Hal Johnson, illustrated by Tom Mead, offers "twenty bone-chilling tales about the most dangerous fantastical beasts in American folklore. Meet the Snoligoster, who feeds on the shadows of its victims. The Hodag, like a spiny-backed bull-horned rhinoceros. The Hoop Snake, which can chase prey at speeds of up to 60 miles per hour and then, with one sting of its tail, cause it to turn purple, swell up, and die." (Publisher's note)

"Look out for what's lurking around every corner. The book is told from the perspective of a cryptozoologist who focuses on the lumberwoods of North America and who recounts many painful and horrifying incidents he witnessed during his years of seeking the most bizarre creatures. . . . A captivating collection for fans of Alvin Schwartz's Scary Tales to Tell in the Dark, this is also ideal for those looking for something fresh, creative, and deliciously creepy. VERDICT Outstanding faux-lore creature tales that will blow away middle school readers." SLJ

Juster, Norton

Alberic the Wise and other journeys; illustrated by Domenico Gnoli. 2010 88p il pa $5.99

Grades: 3 4 5 6   S C

1. Short stories

ISBN 978-0-375-86699-9; 0-375-86699-X

A reissue of the title first published 1965 by Pantheon

"Three stories leave readers wondering: What happened next? The first tells of Alberic, who spent his life searching without knowing what for. In the second a modern boy steps into a Renaissance painting. The third tells of two kings who briefly exchange kingdoms. Juster's smooth storytelling weaves together action and characterization. Gnoli's striking illustrations have a medieval feeling and are in perfect harmony." Horn Book Guide

Kipling, Rudyard, 1865-1936

★ A **collection** of Rudyard Kipling's Just so stories. Candlewick Press 2004 127p il $22.99

Grades: 3 4 5 6 **S C**

1. Short stories 2. India -- Fiction 3. Animals -- Fiction

ISBN 0-7636-2629-5

LC 2004-45858

"This colorful collection of eight tales distinguishes itself with its range of artwork. Well-known children's book artists, including Peter Sis, Jane Ray, and Satoshi Kitamura, contributed the art, each one illustrating a different story. The vibrant mix of styles and materials adds new dimension to favorite stories. . . . A lively, accessible edition." Booklist

Lay-ups and long shots; an anthology of short stories. by Joseph Bruchac . . . [et al.] Darby Creek Pub. 2008 112p il $15.95

Grades: 4 5 6 **S C**

1. Short stories 2. Sports -- Fiction

ISBN 978-1-58196-078-5; 1-58196-078-6

"These nine new short stories feature tweens or teens who, despite lack of skill or other obstacles, engage in athletic pursuits. Some . . . have autobiographical elements. . . . Consistently readable and engaging, the collection should have as much appeal for geeks as it does for jocks." Booklist

Lucky dog; twelve tales of rescued dogs. [by Kirby Larson, Tui T. Sutherland, Ellen Miles, Leslie Margolis, Teddy Slater, Michael Northrop, Randi Barrow, Jane B. Mason & Sarah Hines Stephens, C. Alexander London, Marlane Kennedy, Elizabeth Cody Kimmel, Allan Woodrow] Scholastic Press 2013 192 p. $15.99

Grades: 4 5 6 7 **S C**

1. Short stories 2. Dogs -- Fiction 3. Dog rescue -- Fiction 4. Dog adoption -- Fiction

ISBN 0545554519; 9780545554510

LC 2013011309

This book is a collection of dog stories for children by authors such as Kirby Larson, Tui T. Sutherland, and Ellen Miles. "You'll meet Foxtrot, a feisty Pomeranian who can't bear the thought of leaving her best friend. And Beatrice, whose bark is definitely worse than her bite. And then there's Pumpkin, one of the 101 Chihuahuas who turn life at the center upside down." (Publisher's note)

"A dozen dog-crazy authors, 12 stories of rescued dogs, and one busy animal shelter make up this collection of short stories sure to bring out the dog lover in anyone. The stories are varied in plot, narrative style, and tone, but they all end with a dog finding its one true owner. . . . The reading level is good for independent readers who might not be ready for a full-length novel or advanced readers who need something more gentle. Pair this book with Waiting for Magic (2011) by Patricia MacLachlan for two heartwarming books about rescued dogs." Booklist

Marcantonio, Patricia Santos

Red ridin' in the hood; and other cuentos. pictures by Renato Alarcão. Farrar, Straus & Giroux 2005 181p il $16

Grades: 3 4 5 **S C**

1. Fairy tales 2. Short stories 3. Hispanic Americans -- Fiction

ISBN 0-374-36241-6

"The fractured fairy tale gets cool Latino flavor in this lively collection of 11 fresh retellings, with witty reversals of class and gender roles and powerful, full-page pictures that set the drama in venues ranging from the desert and the barrio to a skyscraper." Booklist

Marshall, James

Rats on the roof, and other stories. Dial Bks. for Young Readers 1991 79p il hardcover o.p. pa $4.99

Grades: 2 3 4 **S C**

1. Short stories 2. Animals -- Fiction

ISBN 0-8037-0835-1; 0-14-038646-7 pa

LC 90-4408

An illustrated collection of seven stories about various animals including a frog with magnificent legs, a hungry brontosaurus, and a mouse who gets married

"Marshall's fertile imagination gets lots of exercise here as does his sardonic wit, and he's included plenty of expressive illustrations, all done in his signature style." Booklist

McKissack, Pat, 1944-2017

★ The **dark**-thirty; Southern tales of the supernatural. illustrated by Brian Pinkney. Knopf 1992 122p il $18.95; lib bdg $20.99; pa $6.50

Grades: 4 5 6 7 **S C**

1. Ghost stories 2. Short stories 3. African Americans -- Fiction

ISBN 0-679-81863-4; 0-679-91853-9 lib bdg; 0-679-89006-8 pa

LC 92-302

Coretta Scott King Award for text, 1993; A Newbery honor book 1993

A collection of ghost stories with African American themes, designed to be told during the Dark Thirty—the half hour before sunset—when ghosts seem all too believable

"Strong characterizations are superbly drawn in a few words. The atmosphere of each selection is skillfully developed and sustained to the very end. Pinkney's stark scratchboard illustrations evoke an eerie mood, which heightens the suspense of each tale." SLJ

★ **Porch** lies; tales of slicksters, tricksters, and other wily characters. [by] Patricia C. McKissack; illustrated by André Carrilho. Schwartz & Wade Books 2006 146p il $18.95; lib bdg $22.99

Grades: 4 5 6 7 **S C**

1. Short stories 2. African Americans -- Fiction

ISBN 0-375-83619-5; 0-375-93619-X lib bdg

LC 2005-22048

The "original tales in this uproarious collection draw on African American oral tradition and blend history and legend with sly humor, creepy horror, villainous characters, and wild farce. McKissack based the stories on those she heard as a child while sitting on her grandparents' porch. . . . Carrilho's full-page illustrations—part cartoon, part portrait in silhouette—combine realistic characters with scary monsters." Booklist

Naidoo, Beverley

Out of bounds: seven stories of conflict and hope. HarperCollins Pubs. 2003 175p $16.99; pa $5.99

Grades: 5 6 7 8 **S C**

1. Short stories 2. South Africa -- Race relations -- Fiction

ISBN 0-06-050799-3; 0-06-050801-9 pa

LC 2002-6890

First published 2001 in the United Kingdom

Seven stories, spanning the time period from 1948 to 2000, chronicle the experiences of young people from different races and ethnic groups as they try to cope with the restrictions placed on their lives by South Africa's apartheid laws

"Naidoo's book reveals our humanity and inhumanity with starkness and precision. . . . She honors her country's past, present, and future with these brave tales." Horn Book

Other worlds; edited by Jon Scieszka, illustrated by Greg Ruth. Walden Pond Press 2013 352 p. (Guys read) (hardback) $16.99

Grades: 4 5 6 7 8 **S C**

1. Short stories 2. Science fiction 3. Fantasy fiction

ISBN 0061963801; 9780061963797; 9780061963803

LC 2013021863

This book, edited by Jon Scieszka, is the fourth Guys Read collection of science fiction short stories. It "is anchored by Ray Bradbury's 1946 'Frost and Fire,' about colonists stranded for generations on a planet so harsh that the average life span is less than two weeks." Other topics include "unsuccessful alien invasions of Earth to Tom Angleberger's tale of smart clothes in rebellion, an eerie ghost story from Kenneth Oppel and . . . a 'girl in armor' episode from Shannon Hale." (Kirkus Reviews)

"Though most of the tales here are entertaining and 'mind-expandingly fun,' Shusterman's and Bradbury's especially stand out as intriguing, suspenseful, and thought-provoking." Horn Book

Paulsen, Gary

Paintings from the cave; three novellas. Wendy Lamb Books 2011 161p $15.99; lib bdg $18.99

Grades: 4 5 6 7 **S C**

1. Short stories 2. Art -- Fiction 3. Dogs -- Fiction 4. Violence -- Fiction 5. Homeless persons -- Fiction

ISBN 978-0-385-74684-7; 978-0-385-90921-1 lib bdg; 978-0-375-89743-6 e-book

LC 2011016287

"These novellas portray an unflinching look at children who have endured neglectful and abusive homes and are surviving on their own. The atmospheric first tale, 'Man of the Iron Heads,' is narrated by Jake, a boy of about 11, who hides from the local gang until he finds the courage to outsmart its violent leader. 'Jo-Jo the Dog-Faced Girl' presents a lonely girl with three adopted dogs who finds acceptance in befriending a girl with leukemia. Finally, 'Erik's Rules' celebrates the power of art and is told by Jamie, the younger of two homeless brothers, whose unstable existence changes after a chance encounter with a friendly volunteer at the animal shelter. By incorporating the solace found in dogs, art, libraries, and new friends into these tales of heartache and redemption, Paulsen provides his readers with hope of a better life." SLJ

Pratchett, Terry, 1948-2015

Dragons at Crumbling Castle; and other tales. Terry Pratchett; illustrated by Mark Beech. Clarion Books, Houghton Mifflin Harcourt 2015 336 p. illustrations (hardback) $16.99

Grades: 3 4 5 6 **S C**

1. Short stories 2. Fantasy fiction 3. Humorous fiction 4. Humorous stories 5. Youths' writings 6. Teenagers' writings

ISBN 0544466594; 9780544466593

LC 2014024233

This book is a "never-before-published collection of fourteen . . . tales by acclaimed author Sir Terry Pratchett." (Publisher's note) "In Pratchett's tales, dragons invade a castle, having lost their caves to a stopped-up river; itty bitty people live, explore, and fight within the carpets; an odd caveman keeps inventing things that then cause disaster (a fire burning down the village); and a champion egg dancer catches a pair of thieves." (School Library Journal)

"Though these stories lack the perfectly timed wordplay of Pratchett's later work, they are a charming and funny sample of his early fictional imaginings. Accompanied by Beech's wiry Quentin Blake-like illustrations, as well as numerous typographical flourishes, this volume

will please both its intended audience and older Pratchett completists." Pub Wkly

Reichenstetter, Friederun

Andersen's fairy tales; retold by Friederun Reichenstetter; illustrated by Silke Leffler. North-South 2007 92p il $19.95

Grades: 4 5 6 **S C**

1. Authors 2. Novelists 3. Dramatists 4. Fairy tales 5. Children's authors 6. Short story writers

ISBN 0-7358-2141-0

"Thirteen tales . . . are adapted from excellent translations by Anthea Bell and H. P. Paul. . . . Leffler's often-humorous painted folk-art illustrations show cute little people with chubby line-drawn faces dressed in clothing of 18th-century style. . . . The volume . . . is quite handsome." SLJ

Root, Phyllis

Aunt Nancy and the bothersome visitors; illustrated by David Parkins. Candlewick Press 2007 57p il $16.99

Grades: 1 2 3 4 **S C**

1. Aunts -- Fiction 2. Cousins -- Fiction

ISBN 978-0-7636-3074-4; 0-7636-3074-8

LC 2007-60856

Includes two stories previously published separately in picture book format: Aunt Nancy and Old Man Trouble (1996) and Aunt Nancy and Cousin Lazybones (1998)

Clever Aunt Nancy manages to foil all those who try to get the better of her.

"Root's folksy style shines in every sentence. . . . Parkins provides full-color paintings to introduce each story, but his wit really shows itself in the droll silhouettes that milk body language for all it's worth." Horn Book

Rowling, J. K.

The **tales** of Beedle the Bard; translated from the ancient runes by Hermione Granger; commentary by Albus Dumbledore; introduction, notes, and illustrations by J.K. Rowling. Arthur A. Levine 2008 111p il $12.99

Grades: 5 6 7 8 9 10 11 12 **S C**

1. Fairy tales 2. Short stories 3. Magic -- Fiction

ISBN 978-0-545-12828-5; 0-545-12828-5

A collection of tales from the world of Harry Potter.

"The introduction is captivating . . . [and] the tales themselves are entertaining. . . . Rowling is at the top of her game as a superb storyteller, providing her legions of fans with an enchanting collection of wizard folklore." Voice Youth Advocates

San Souci, Robert

Double-dare to be scared: another thirteen chilling tales; [by] Robert D. San Souci; illustrated by David Ouimet. Cricket Books 2004 170p il $15.95

Grades: 4 5 6 7 **S C**

1. Short stories 2. Horror fiction

ISBN 0-8126-2716-4

LC 2003-26610

Companion volume to Dare to be scared (2003)

"San Souci uses elements of urban legend and folklore to weave powerful and suspenseful yet age-appropriate stories that youngsters will revisit, finding new meaning with each reading." SLJ

Haunted houses; [by] Robert D. San Souci; illustrated by Kelly Murphy and Antoine Revoy. Henry Holt 2010 276p il (Are you scared yet?) $16.99

Grades: 4 5 6 7 **S C**

1. Ghost stories 2. Short stories 3. Horror fiction
ISBN 978-0-8050-8750-5; 0-8050-8750-8

LC 2009-50763

"These 10 spooky stories include a classic Halloween scare: visitors get their admission fee of $25 back if they make it to the top floor of a haunted house—but can they? In another, the primary occupant of a dollhouse is a ghost of a child who needs help moving from one consciousness to another. . . . The stories are well paced and satisfyingly startling. . . . This book won't stay on the shelves for long. Murphy and Revoy's black-and-white illustrations heighten the fright factor, making San Souci's collection even more riveting." SLJ

Sandburg, Carl

★ **Rootabaga** stories; illustrated by Maud and Miska Petersham. Harcourt 2003 176p il hardcover o.p. pa $5.95 **S C**

1. Fairy tales 2. Short stories
ISBN 0-15-204709-3; 0-15-204714-X pa

LC 2002-191949

First published 1922; previously published as: Rootabaga stories, part one

A selection of tales from Rootabaga Country peopled with such characters as the Potato Face Blind Man, the Blue Wind Boy, and many others

★ **Shelf** life: stories by the book; edited by Gary Paulsen. Simon & Schuster Bks. for Young Readers 2003 173p $16.95
Grades: 5 6 7 8 **S C**

1. Short stories 2. Books and reading -- Fiction
ISBN 0-689-84180-9

LC 2002-66901

Ten short stories in which the lives of young people in different circumstances are changed by their encounters with books

"Covering almost every genre of fiction, including mystery, SF, fantasy and realism, these well-crafted stories by familiar authors offer sharply drawn characterizations and intriguing premises." Publ Wkly

Shusterman, Neal

Darkness creeping; twenty twisted tales. Puffin Books 2007 291p pa $7.99
Grades: 5 6 7 8 **S C**

1. Short stories 2. Horror fiction
ISBN 0-14-240721-6

"The author takes a walk on the dark side in this collection of spooky stories, some old, some new, all delightfully creepy. He knows his audience, providing enough horrific touches to appeal to the most challenging readers—those hard-to-reach middle school boys. Each story is introduced with a brief statement describing where he got the idea." Voice Youth Advocates

Singer, Isaac Bashevis

Stories for children. Farrar, Straus & Giroux 1984 337p hardcover o.p. pa $14
Grades: 4 5 6 7 **S C**

1. Short stories 2. Jews -- Fiction
ISBN 0-374-37266-7; 0-374-46489-8 pa

LC 84-13612

This collection of thirty-six stories includes "parables, beast fables, allegories and reminiscences. Some stories are silly and charming, while others are wildly fantastic, dealing with savagery and miracles in mythical, medieval Poland. Frequently they are about scary situations, but all tend to end happily, with an edifying idea. Most appealing is the Nobel Prize winner's sheer story-telling power. In this respect, he has no equal among contemporaries." N Y Times Book Rev

Soto, Gary

★ **Baseball** in April, and other stories; 10th anniversary ed; Harcourt Brace Jovanovich 2000 111p $16; pa $6
Grades: 5 6 7 8 **S C**

1. Short stories 2. California -- Fiction 3. Mexican Americans -- Fiction
ISBN 0-15-202573-1; 0-15-202567-7 pa

A reissue of the title first published 1990

A collection of eleven short stories focusing on the everyday adventures of Hispanic young people growing up in Fresno, California

Each story "gets at the heart of some aspect of growing up. The insecurities, the embarrassments, the triumphs, the inequities of it all are chronicled with wit and charm. Soto's characters ring true and his knowledge of, and affection for, their shared Mexican-American heritage is obvious and infectious." Voice Youth Advocates

Facts of life; stories. Harcourt 2008 176p $16
Grades: 5 6 7 8 **S C**

1. Short stories 2. California -- Fiction 3. Mexican Americans -- Fiction
ISBN 978-0-15-206181-4; 0-15-206181-9

LC 2007-35765

"Pivitol moments in the lives of California Latino teens and tweens provide the starting points for Soto's collection of 10 . . . stories. For Letty, it's the realization that her boyfriend loves her money more than he does her; for Hector, it's the announcement of his parents' plan to divorce. . . . Soto's affection and concern for his characters is evident throughout." Booklist

Local news. Harcourt Brace Jovanovich 1993 148p hardcover o.p. pa $5.95
Grades: 5 6 7 8 **S C**

1. Short stories 2. California -- Fiction 3. Mexican Americans -- Fiction
ISBN 0-15-248117-6; 0-15-204695-X pa

LC 92-37905

A collection of thirteen short stories about the everyday lives of Mexican American young people in California's Central Valley

"These stories resonate with integrity, verve, and compassion." Horn Book

Petty crimes. Harcourt Brace & Co. 1998 157p $16; pa $6.99
Grades: 5 6 7 8 **S C**

1. Short stories 2. Mexican Americans -- Fiction
ISBN 0-15-201658-9; 0-15-205437-5 pa

LC 97-37114

A collection of short stories about Mexican American youth growing up in California's Central Valley

"A sense of family strength relieves the under-current of sadness in these raw stories." Horn Book Guide

Spinelli, Jerry

The **library** card. Scholastic 1997 148p pa $4.99
Grades: 4 5 6 7 **S C**

1. Short stories 2. Books and reading -- Fiction
ISBN 0-590-38633-6

LC 96-18412

"A library card is the magical object common to each of these four stories in which a budding street thug, a television addict, a homeless orphan, and a lonely girl are all transformed by the power and the possibilities that await them within the walls of the public library. Spinelli's characters . . . are unusual and memorable; his writing both humorous and convincing." Horn Book Guide

The **sports** pages; edited and with an introduction by Jon Scieszka; stories by Dustin Brown, ... [et al.]; with illustrations by Dan Santat. Walden Pond Press 2012 245 p ill (Guys read) (paberback bdg.) $6.99; (hardcover bdg.) $16.99

Grades: 4 5 6 7 8   **S C**

1. Short stories 2. Sports -- Fiction

ISBN 9780061963773; 9780061963780

LC 2012012716

This book, edited and with an introduction by Jon Scieszka, "offers a smorgasbord of sportswriting--fiction and nonfiction--to appeal to every sports enthusiast. From baseball to football, ice hockey to track and mixed martial arts, there is plenty here for sports-minded readers to like, with lively action, humor and even a dose of mysticism in the form of magical grapefruit and a witch doctor." (Kirkus Reviews)

"In the third volume of his Guys Read series (the first focused on humor, and the second on thrillers), editor Scieszka turns his attention to sports, serving up 10 stories. . . . In his introduction, Scieszka wisely notes that good stories and good games are alike: Both reveal character and truths bigger than the game or the story." Booklist

Stine, R. L.

The **haunting** hour. HarperCollins Pubs. 2001 153p il $11.95; pa $5.99

Grades: 4 5 6 7   **S C**

1. Short stories 2. Horror fiction

ISBN 0-06-623604-5; 0-06-441045-5 pa

LC 2001-39142

A collection of ten short horror stories featuring a ghoulish Halloween party, a long, mysterious car trip, and a very dangerous imaginary friend. Each story includes drawings by a different illustrator

"The predictability of the stories and the unsophisticated storytelling won't keep Stine fans old and new from swallowing this down in one big gulp." Bull Cent Child Books

Tan, Shaun

★ **Lost** & found; 3 by Shaun Tan. Arthur A. Levine Books 2011 in il $21.99

Grades: 5 6 7 8   **S C**

1. Short stories

ISBN 978-0-545-22924-1; 0-545-22924-3

LC 2010030936

This book comprises three previously published stories by the Australian author-illustrator "In 'The Red Tree,' a young girl moves listlessly through her day with a sense of dreadful ennui that escalates with each page turn . . . until finally finding some hope at the end. In 'The Lost Thing,' a young boy discovers a most peculiar object and dutifully tries to find a proper home for it. . . . Finally, 'The Rabbits' (with a text by John Marsden) is a colonization fable, as rabbits invade and populate a new land, overwhelming the native animal population and severely altering the landscape. . . . Intermediate, middle school." (Horn Book)

"'The Red Tree' follows a solitary girl through a single, not very good day, exploring her feelings as they shift from disappointment and confusion to alienation and despair. The spare, lyrical text provides an anchor for Tan's large, moody, beautiful paintings. 'The Lost Thing' is a more upbeat tale of a boy who discovers an unusual object and then must decide what to do with it. Freedom and imagination are the themes in this story, and here the art includes fascinating and sometimes humorous bits of technical drawings. The prose of John Marsden's 'The Rabbits,' an allegory about imperialism, is so simple and melodic that it verges on poetry. The artist emphasizes the invasive foreignness of the rabbits by dressing them in baroque uniforms, drawing mystifying, gigantic machines and buildings for them to build and deploy in their inexorable drive to dominate." SLJ

★ **Troll's** eye view; a book of villainous tales. Viking 2009 200p $16.99; pa $7.99

Grades: 5 6 7 8   **S C**

1. Fairy tales 2. Short stories

ISBN 978-0-670-06141-9; 0-670-06141-7; 978-0-14-241673-0 pa; 0-14-241673-8 pa

Everyone thinks they know the real story behind the villains in fairy tales—evil, no two ways about it. But the villains themselves beg to differ. In this anthology for younger readers, you'll hear from the Giant's wife (from Jack and the Beanstalk), Rumpelstiltskin, the oldest of the Twelve Dancing Princesses, and more.

"A mixed bag of funny, quirky, and downright creepy entries. . . . The collection is largely accessible and very enjoyable." Booklist

Under my hat; tales from the cauldron. edited by Jonathan Strahan. Random House 2012 415 p. (trade) $16.99

Grades: 5 6 7 8   **S C**

1. Short stories 2. Witches -- Fiction 3. Children's stories 4. Witches -- Fiction

ISBN 0375868305; 9780375868047; 9780375868306; 9780375898815; 9780375968303

LC 2011031253

This book presents "eighteen short tales about witches. . . . Garth Nix's 'A Handful of Ashes' features a library and librarian. Delia Sherman's 'The Witch in the Woods' . . . [features] deer and bear shape-shifters and no small darkness. . . . Jane Yolen makes Hans Christian Andersen's life a tale itself." (Kirkus Reviews)

Under the weather; stories about climate change. edited by Tony Bradman. Frances Lincoln Children's 2009 215p pbk $8.99; $16.95

Grades: 5 6 7 8   **S C**

1. Short stories 2. Greenhouse effect -- Fiction

ISBN 9781845079444; 1-84507-930-2; 978-1-84507-930-7

"Eight stories by a variety of authors attempt to make the facts about climate change and its global ramifications relevant to today's children. The majority of the selections are about youngsters enacting change and working toward solutions in tangible ways. For example, "How to Build the Perfect Sandcastle" is about a Philippino boy who works to rebuild the coral reefs, which are dying due to the rise in ocean temperature. . . . Overall . . . this is a worthwhile effort that will appeal to children wanting to make a difference in their world as well as to teachers trying to make the scientific reality of climate change real to their students." SLJ

AUTHOR, TITLE, AND SUBJECT INDEX

This index to the books in the Classified Collection includes author, title, and subject entries; added entries for publishers' series, illustrators, joint authors, and editors of works entered under title; and name and subject cross-references; all arranged in one alphabet.

The number or symbol in bold face type at the end of each entry refers to the Dewey Decimal Classification or to the Fiction (Fic) or Story Collection (S C), or Easy Books (E) section where the main entry for the book will be found. Works classed in 92 will be found under the headings for the biographies' subject.

Cassidy, C. Indigo Blue **Fic**

ABYSSAL ZONE

Hoyt, E. Weird sea creatures **591.77**

ACADEMIC FREEDOM

See also Intellectual freedom; Toleration

ACADEMIC LIBRARIES

See also Libraries

ACADEMIC LIBRARIES -- RELATIONS WITH FACULTY AND CURRICULUM -- CASE STUDIES

Growing schools **370.71**

ACADEMY AWARDS (MOTION PICTURES)

See also Motion pictures

Acampora, Paul

Rachel Spinelli punched me in the face **Fic**

The **ACB** with Honora Lee. De Goldi, K. **Fic**

Accelerati trilogy [series]

Elfman, E. Tesla's attic **Fic**

ACCESS TO HEALTH CARE

See also Medical care

An accidental adventure [series]

London, C. A. We are not eaten by yaks **Fic**

London, C. A. We dine with cannibals **Fic**

The **accidental** adventures of India McAllister. Agell, C. **Fic**

The **accidental** afterlife of Thomas Marsden. Trevayne, E. **Fic**

ACCIDENTS -- FICTION

Every single second **Fic**

ACCLIMATIZATION *See* Adaptation (Biology); Environmental influence on humans

ACCOUNTABILITY *See* Liability (Law); Responsibility

ACCOUNTANTS

McCarthy, M. Pop! **664**

ACCULTURATION

See also Anthropology; Civilization; Culture; Ethnology

Ace it! information literacy [series]

Bullard, L. Ace your oral or multimedia presentation **808.5**

Gaines, A. Ace your Internet research **001.4**

Gaines, A. Master the library and media center **020**

Rau, D. M. Ace your creative writing project **808**

Rau, D. M. Ace your writing assignment **808**

Ace Lacewing, bug detective: the big swat. Biedrzycki, D. **E**

Ace your animal science project. Gardner, R. **590.7**

Ace your biology science project [series]

Gardner, R. Ace your animal science project **590.7**

Gardner, R. Ace your exercise and nutrition science project: great science fair ideas **613**

Gardner, R. Ace your human biology science project **612**

Gardner, R. Ace your plant science project **580.7**

Gardner, R. Ace your science project about the senses **612.8**

Ace your chemistry science project. Gardner, R. **540.7**

Ace your creative writing project. Rau, D. M. **808**

Ace your ecology and environmental science project. Gardner, R. **577**

Ace your exercise and nutrition science project: great science fair ideas. Gardner, R. **613**

Ace your food science project. Gardner, R. **664**

Ace your forces and motion science project. Gardner, R. **531**

Ace your human biology science project. Gardner, R. **612**

Ace your Internet research. Gaines, A. **001.4**

Ace your math and measuring science project. Gardner, R. **530.8**

Ace your oral or multimedia presentation. Bullard, L. **808.5**

Ace your physical science project. Gardner, R. **530**

Ace your physics science project [series]

Gardner, R. Ace your forces and motion science project **531**

Gardner, R. Ace your math and measuring science project **530.8**

Gardner, R. Ace your physical science project **530**

Goodstein, M. Ace your sports science project **507.8**

Ace your plant science project. Gardner, R. **580.7**

Ace your science project [series]

Gardner, R. Ace your chemistry science project **540.7**

Gardner, R. Ace your ecology and environmental science project **577**

Gardner, R. Ace your food science project **664**

Gardner, R. Ace your science project using chemistry magic and toys **540.7**

Ace your science project about the senses. Gardner, R. **612.8**

Ace your science project using chemistry magic and toys. Gardner, R. **540.7**

Ace your sports science project. Goodstein, M. **507.8**

Ace your writing assignment. Rau, D. M. **808**

Ace! Woods, M. **796.342**

Acedera, Kei

(il) Oliver, L. Liesl & Po **Fic**

(il) Secrets of the crown **Fic**

ACERRAS (BASEBALL TEAM)

Brothers at bat **796.357**

Aces wild. Perl, E. S. **Fic**

Achebe, Chinua

How the leopard got his claws **Fic**

ACHIEVEMENT TESTS

See also Academic achievement; Educational tests and measurements

ACID PRECIPITATION *See* Acid rain

ACID RAIN

Jakubiak, D. J. What can we do about acid rain? **363.7**

ACID RAIN

See also Rain; Water pollution

ACIDS

See also Chemicals; Chemistry

Ackerman, Karen

Song and dance man **E**

ACORNS -- FICTION

The Promise **Fic**

Acoustic Rooster and his barnyard band. Alexander, K. **E**

ACOUSTICS *See* Architectural acoustics; Hearing; Music -- Acoustics and physics; Sound

ACROBATS AND ACROBATICS

See also Circus

ACROBATS AND ACROBATICS -- FICTION

Chantler, S. Tower of treasure **741.5**

Hunt, J. Precious Little **E**

Across America on an emigrant train. Murphy, J. **385**

Gerstein, M. The man who walked between the towers **791**

AEROBICS
See also Exercise

AERODROMES *See* Airports

AERODYNAMICS
See also Air; Dynamics; Pneumatics

AERONAUTICAL ENGINEERS
Provensen, A. The glorious flight: across the Channel with Louis Bleriot, July 25, 1909 **92**
Wyckoff, E. B. Helicopter man: Igor Sikorsky and his amazing invention **92**

AERONAUTICAL SPORTS
See also Aeronautics; Sports

AERONAUTICS
Bailey, G. Flight **629.13**
Carson, M. K. The Wright Brothers for kids **629.13**
Clark, W. Planes on the move **629.133**
Hense, M. How fighter pilots use math **629.13**
Hodgkins, F. How people learned to fly **629.13**
Mercer, B. The flying machine book **745.592**
Parker, S. My first trip on an airplane **387.7**
Parker, S. By air **387.7**
Rocketry **621.43**
Skurzynski, G. This is rocket science **629.4**
Venezia, M. The Wright brothers **92**

AERONAUTICS
See also Engineering; Locomotion

AERONAUTICS -- ACCIDENTS *See* Aircraft accidents

AERONAUTICS -- FICTION
Armstrong, A. Racing the moon **Fic**
Kuhlmann, T. Lindbergh **Fic**
Ross, J. The Fog diver **Fic**

AERONAUTICS -- FLIGHTS
Brown, D. Ruth Law thrills a nation **629.13**
Grove, T. First flight around the world **910.4**
Skrypuch, M. F. Last airlift **959.704**

AERONAUTICS -- FLIGHTS
See also Voyages and travels

AERONAUTICS -- HISTORY
Borden, L. Touching the sky **629.13**
Carson, M. K. The Wright Brothers for kids **629.13**
Collins, M. Airborne: a photobiography of Wilbur and Orville Wright **92**
Freedman, R. The Wright brothers: how they invented the airplane **92**
Griffith, V. The fabulous flying machines of Alberto Santos-Dumont **92**
Hardesty, V. Epic flights **629.13**
Nahum, A. Flying machine **629.133**
O'Sullivan, R. The Wright brothers fly **92**
Wyckoff, E. B. Helicopter man: Igor Sikorsky and his amazing invention **92**
White, R. Cleared for takeoff **629.133**

AEROSPACE ENGINEERS
Skurzynski, G. This is rocket science **629.4**

AEROTHERMODYNAMICS
See also Astronautics; High speed aeronautics; Super-

sonic aerodynamics; Thermodynamics

Aesop
Hartman, B. Mr. Aesop's story shop **398.2**
Moerbeek, K. Aesop's fables: a pop-up book of classic tales **398.2**
Mouse & Lion **E**
Naidoo, B. Aesop's fables **398.2**
Waters, F. Aesop's fables **398.2**

Adaptations
Brett, J. Town mouse, country mouse **398.24**
Forest, H. The contest between the Sun and the Wind **398.2**
Morpurgo, M. The McElderry book of Aesop's fables **398.2**
Palatini, M. Lousy rotten stinkin' grapes **398.2**
Pinkney, J. The lion & the mouse **E**
Wormell, C. Mice, morals, & monkey business **398.2**
Aesop's fables. Waters, F. **398.2**
Aesop's fables. Naidoo, B. **398.2**
Aesop's fables: a pop-up book of classic tales. Moerbeek, K. **398.2**

AESTHETICS
See also Philosophy

AESTHETICS -- FICTION
Reibstein, M. Wabi Sabi **E**

AFFECTION *See* Friendship; Love

AFFLUENT PEOPLE *See* Rich

Afghan dreams. O'Brien, T. **958.1**

AFGHAN WAR, 2001-
Biden, J. Don't forget, God bless our troops **355.1**
Souter, J. War in Afghanistan and Iraq **355**

AFGHAN WAR, 2001- -- FICTION
Postcards from Pismo **Fic**
Afghanistan. Fordyce, D. **958.1**

AFGHANISTAN
Ali, S. E. Afghanistan **958.1**
Ellis, D. Off to war **303.6**
Fordyce, D. Afghanistan **958.1**
O'Brien, T. Afghan dreams **958.1**
Whitfield, S. Afghanistan **958.1**
Afghanistan. Ali, S. E. **958.1**
Afghanistan. Whitfield, S. **958.1**
Afghanistan. Bjorklund, R. **958.1**

AFGHANISTAN -- DESCRIPTION AND TRAVEL
Bjorklund, R. Afghanistan **958.1**

AFGHANISTAN -- FICTION
Clements, A. Extra credit **Fic**
King, D. I see the sun in Afghanistan **E**
Reedy, T. Words in the dust **Fic**
Waiting for the owl's call **E**
Williams, K. L. Four feet, two sandals **E**

AFGHANISTAN -- SOCIAL CONDITIONS
Winter, J. Nasreen's secret school **371.82**
Africa. Solway, A. **780.9**
Africa. Murray, J. **960**

AFRICA
A gift from childhood **92**
Mooney, C. Amazing Africa **960**
Stojic, M. Rain **E**

American archaeology uncovers the Underground Railroad. Huey, L. M. **973.7**

American archaeology uncovers the Vikings. Huey, L. M. **970.01**

American archaeology uncovers the westward movement. Huey, L. M. **978**

AMERICAN ART

Finger, B. 13 American artists children should know **709**

Heart to heart **811**

Raczka, B. The art of freedom **704.9**

AMERICAN ART

See also Art

AMERICAN ARTIFICIAL SATELLITES

See also Artificial satellites

American Association of School Librarians

Standards for the 21st-century learner in action **025.5**

AMERICAN AUTHORS

A Home for Mr. Emerson **92**

AMERICAN AUTHORS

See also Authors

AMERICAN AUTHORS -- BIOGRAPHY

Burgess, M. Enormous smallness **92**

American babies. Global Fund for Children (Organization) **E**

AMERICAN BALLADS

See also American poetry

American bison. Caper, W. **599.64**

AMERICAN BISON *See* Bison

American celebrations [series]

Craats, R. Columbus Day **394.26**

Foran, J. Martin Luther King, Jr. Day **394.26**

Hamilton, L. Presidents' Day **394.26**

Tait, L. Cinco de Mayo **394.26**

AMERICAN COOKING -- HISTORY

Eat your U.S. history homework **641.5973**

AMERICAN FICTION -- WOMEN AUTHORS

Funny Girl **Fic**

AMERICAN FLAG *See* Flags -- United States

AMERICAN FOLK ART

See also American art; Folk art

AMERICAN FOLK SONGS *See* Folk songs -- United States

American folk songs for children in home, school, and nursery school. Seeger, R. C. **782.42**

American food. Blaxland, W. **641.5**

American girl [series]

Yee, L. Aloha, Kanani **Fic**

AMERICAN GOVERNMENT *See* United States -- Politics and government

The **American** Heritage children's dictionary. **423**

The **American** Heritage Children's Thesaurus. **423**

The **American** Heritage first dictionary. **423**

The **American** Heritage picture dictionary. **423**

American Heritage Publishing Co.

(comp) The American Heritage children's dictionary **423**

(comp) The American Heritage Children's Thesaurus **423**

(comp) The American Heritage picture dictionary **423**

The **American** Heritage student thesaurus. Hellweg, P. **428**

American heroes [series]

Brimner, L. D. Booker T. Washington **92**

Brimner, L. D. Chief Crazy Horse **92**

Brimner, L. D. Pocahontas **92**

AMERICAN HISTORY *See* America -- History; United States -- History

American history [series]

Bjornlund, L. D. The Trail of Tears **970.00**

American humane pet care library [series]

Jeffrey, L. S. Dogs **636.**

AMERICAN ILLUSTRATORS *See* Illustrators -- United States

American Indian art and culture [series]

Kissock, H. Apache **970.00**

Kissock, H. Caddo **970.00**

Kissock, H. Cherokee **970.00**

Kissock, H. Comanche **970.00**

Kissock, H. Tigua **970.00**

American Indian biographies [series]

Englar, M. Chief Joseph, 1840-1904 **92**

AMERICAN INDIANS *See* Native Americans

American kids in history [series]

King, D. C. Pioneer days **978**

AMERICAN LETTERS

See also American literature; Letters

American Library Association

The Newbery and Caldecott awards **028.**

American Library Association. Office for Intellectual Freedom

(comp) Intellectual Freedom Manual **025.**

Scales, P. R. Protecting intellectual freedom in your school library **025.2**

AMERICAN LITERATURE

Sandburg, C. The Sandburg treasury **818**

AMERICAN LITERATURE

See also Literature

AMERICAN LITERATURE (SPANISH)

See also American literature

AMERICAN LITERATURE -- AFRICAN AMERICAN AUTHORS

Tate, D. Poet **92**

AMERICAN LITERATURE -- AFRICAN AMERICAN AUTHORS -- HISTORY AND CRITICISM

Bishop, R. S. Free within ourselves **028.**

Brooks, W. M. Embracing, evaluating, and examining African American children's and young adult literature **028.**

Embracing, evaluating, and examining African American children's and young adult literature **028.**

AMERICAN LITERATURE -- BLACK AUTHORS *See* American literature -- African American authors

AMERICAN LITERATURE -- INDIAN AUTHORS -- BIOGRAPHY

Ray, D. K. Paiute princess **92**

AMERICAN LOYALISTS

See also United States -- History -- 1775-1783, Revolution

American Medical Assocation boy's guide to becoming a teen. Pfeifer, K. G. **613**

Andronik, Catherine M.
Copernicus   92

Andros, Camille
Charlotte the scientist is squished   E

Andy & Sandy and the first snow. dePaola, T.   E

Andy and the lion. Daugherty, J. H.   E

Andy Shane and the barn sale mystery. Jacobson, J.   Fic

Andy Shane and the pumpkin trick. Jacobson, J.   Fic

Andy Shane and the Queen of Egypt. Jacobson, J.   Fic

Andy Shane and the very bossy Dolores Starbuckle. Jacobson, J.   Fic

Andy Shane is NOT in love. Jacobson, J.   Fic

Andy Shane, hero at last.   Fic

Andy Warhol. Rubin, S. G.   92

ANECDOTES
Belanger, J. What it's like   179

ANEMONES
Rustad, M. E. H. Clown fish and sea anemones work together   597

Ang, Joy
(il) 101 reasons why I'm not taking a bath   E
(il) Mustache baby   E

Angaramo, Roberta
(il) Gormley, G. Dog in boots   E
(il) Perry, A. The Bicklebys' birdbath   E

Angel Island.   979.4

ANGEL ISLAND (CALIF.) -- HISTORY
Angel Island   979.4

ANGEL ISLAND (CALIF.) -- HISTORY -- 20TH CENTURY -- FICTION
James, H. F. Paper son   Fic

Angel, Carl
(il) Moss, M. Sky high: the true story of Maggie Gee   92

Angela and the baby Jesus. McCourt, F.   E

Angelina Ballerina. Holabird, K.   E

Angelo, Valenti
(il) Sawyer, R. Roller skates   Fic

Angelou, Maya
Amazing peace   811

ANGELS -- FICTION
Chaikin, M. Angels sweep the desert floor   296.1
Creech, S. The unfinished angel   Fic
DePaola, T. Pascual and the kitchen angels   E
Kleven, E. The friendship wish   E
Morpurgo, M. On angel wings   Fic
Newbound, A. Ghoul strike!   Fic
Richter, J. Beyond the station lies the sea   Fic

Angels sweep the desert floor. Chaikin, M.   296.1

ANGER
Vail, R. Sometimes I'm Bombaloo   E

ANGER
See also Emotions

ANGER -- FICTION
Applesauce   E
Arnold, E. K. Far from fair   Fic
Bang, M. When Sophie gets angry--really, really angry   E
Berger, S. Crankenstein   E

Eaton, M. Two dumb ducks   E
Elliott, D. Finn throws a fit   E
Harris, R. H. The day Leo said I hate you   E
Sakai, K. Mad at Mommy   E
Urban, L. Mouse was mad   E
Vail, R. Sometimes I'm Bombaloo   E
Yolen, J. How do dinosaurs act when they're mad?   E

ANGER
Graves, S. I hate everything!   152.4

ANGER IN CHILDREN -- FICTION
McDonnell, P. A perfectly messed-up story   E

ANGINA PECTORIS
See also Heart diseases

ANGKOR (CITY)
Sobol, R. The mysteries of Angkor Wat   959.6

ANGKOR WAT (ANGKOR: ANCIENT CITY)
Sobol, R. The mysteries of Angkor Wat   959.6

Angleberger, Tom
Crankee Doodle   E
Darth Paper strikes back   Fic
Emperor Pickletine rides the bus   Fic
Fake mustache   Fic
Hemphill, M. Stonewall Hinkleman and the Battle of Bull Run   Fic
Horton Halfpott   Fic
Inspector Flytrap   Fic
Inspector Flytrap in The goat who chewed too much   Fic
Rocket and Groot   Fic
The secret of the Fortune Wookiee   Fic
The strange case of Origami Yoda   Fic
The surprise attack of Jabba the Puppett   Fic
(jt. auth) Dellinger, P. Fuzzy   Fic
(il) Princess Labelmaker to the rescue!   Fic

ANGLING *See* Fishing

Angliss, Sarah
Gold   546

ANGLO-SAXONS
See also Great Britain -- History -- 0-1066; Teutonic peoples

Angola. Sheehan, S.   967.3

ANGOLA
Sheehan, S. Angola   967.3

Angus, Jennifer
In search of Goliathus hercules   Fic

Anholt, Laurence
Cezanne and the apple boy   E
Matisse   92

ANIMAL ABUSE *See* Animal welfare

Animal aha! Swanson, D.   590

Animal architects [series]
George, L. Prairie dogs   599.3

Animal attack and defense [series]
Pryor, K. J. Amazing armor   591.4
Pryor, K. J. Clever camouflage   591.4
Pryor, K. J. Mimicry and relationships   591.4
Pryor, K. J. Tricky behavior   591.4
Pryor, K. J. Warning colors   591.4

Way Back Then	398.2
Where's the Baboon?	E
Yours sincerely, Giraffe	Fic

ANIMALS -- HUMOR

Lewis, J. P. Last laughs | 818

ANIMALS -- LANGUAGE See Animal communication

ANIMALS -- MEXICO -- FOLKLORE

Goldman, J. Whiskers, tails, and wings | 398.2

ANIMALS -- MIGRATION

Berkes, M. Going home	591.56
Carney, E. Great migrations	591.56
Catt, T. Migrating with the caribou	599.65
Catt, T. Migrating with the humpback whale	599.5
Catt, T. Migrating with the salmon	597
Catt, T. Migrating with the wildebeest	599.64
Dowson, N. North	591.56
Marsh, L. Amazing animal journeys	591.56
O'Sullivan, J. Migration Nation	591.56

ANIMALS -- MIGRATION

See also Animal behavior

ANIMALS -- MIGRATION -- FICTION

Marino, G. Following Papa's song | E

ANIMALS -- MISCELLANEA

Cooper, E. 8, an animal alphabet	513.2
Hearst, M. Unusual creatures	590
How to swallow a pig	591.5
Jenkins, S. Animals by the Numbers	590.72
Jenkins, S. Biggest, strongest, fastest	590

ANIMALS -- MISTREATMENT See Animal welfare

ANIMALS -- MOVEMENTS See Animal locomotion

ANIMALS -- NOMENCLATURE (POPULAR)

Wright, A. A tower of giraffes | 590

ANIMALS -- NORTH AMERICA

Person, S. Cougar | 599.75

ANIMALS -- PHOTOGRAPHY See Photography of animals

ANIMALS -- PICTORIAL WORKS

Carle, E. What's your favorite animal?	E
Van Hout, M. Happy	E
Wildlife of the world	591

ANIMALS -- PICTORIAL WORKS -- FICTION

Empson, J. Never Ever | E

ANIMALS -- POETRY

Beastly Verse	808.81
Forbes, R. L. Beast Friends Forever	811
Harrison, D. L. Now you see them, now you don't	591.472
Lewis, J. P. Last laughs	818
Prelutsky, J. I've lost my hippopotamus	811
Pug and other animal poems	811
Vulture verses	811
Wake up!	811.54

ANIMALS -- POETRY -- COLLECTIONS

National Geographic book of animal poetry | 808.81

ANIMALS -- POLAR REGIONS

Kainen, D. Polar | 590.911

ANIMALS -- SLEEP BEHAVIOR -- FICTION

Howatt, S. J. Sleepyheads	E
Logue, M. Sleep like a tiger	E

ANIMALS -- SONGS

Berkes, M. C. Over in Australia	782.42
Carle, E. Today is Monday	782.42
Comden, B. What's new at the zoo?	E
Dylan, B. Man gave names to all the animals	782.42
Hillenbrand, W. Down by the station	782.42
Hort, L. The seals on the bus	782.42
Langstaff, J. M. Oh, a-hunting we will go	782.42
Langstaff, J. M. Over in the meadow	782.42
Staines, B. All God's critters	782.42
Taback, S. There was an old lady who swallowed a fly	782.42

ANIMALS -- SOUNDS See Animal sounds

ANIMALS -- TEMPERATURE See Body temperature

ANIMALS -- TRAINING

Patent, D. H. The right dog for the job | 362.4

ANIMALS -- TREATMENT See Animal welfare

ANIMALS -- TREATMENT -- FICTION

Hopkinson, D. A bandit's tale	Fic
Kelly, L. Chained	Fic
Moon bear	Fic

ANIMALS -- VISION See Vision in animals

ANIMALS -- WAR USE

Grayson, R. Military | 355.4

ANIMALS -- WAR USE

See also Working animals

Animals after dark [series]

Landau, E. Big cats | 599.75

Animals alive. | 590

Animals and me. Greenwood, M. | 612

ANIMALS AND PEOPLE WITH DISABILITIES

Bozzo, L. Service dog heroes	362.4
Goldish, M. Prison puppies	362.4
Hoffman, M. A. Helping dogs	362.4
Martin, C. Helpers	362.4
Patent, D. H. The right dog for the job	362.4

Animals and their families. Nascimbeni, B. | E

Animals animals [series]

Bailer, D. Geese	598
Mara, W. Coyotes	599.77
Mara, W. Ducks	598
Otfinoski, S. Alligators	597.98
Otfinoski, S. Skunks	599.7

ANIMALS AS CARRIERS OF DISEASE

Plagues, pox, and pestilence | 614.4

Animals at work [series]

Barnes, J. Camels and llamas at work	636.2
Barnes, J. Horses at work	636.1

Animals by the Numbers. Jenkins, S. | 590.72

Animals Charles Darwin saw. Markle, S. | 92

Animals don't, so I won't! Derrick, D. G. | E

Animals home alone. Riphagen, L. | E

ANIMALS IN ART

Ames, L. J. Draw 50 endangered animals	743
Animal talk	591.59
Basseches, K. B. ABeCedarios	E
Bergin, M. How to draw pets	743
Carle, E. What's your favorite animal?	E

See also Theater

Aretha, David
Awesome African-American rock and soul musicians **781.644**
Sit-ins and freedom rides **323.1**
The story of the civil rights march on Washington for jobs and freedom in photographs **975.3**

Argent, Kerry
(il) Fox, M. Sleepy bears **E**

ARGENTINA -- HISTORY
Favor, L. J. Eva Peron **92**

ARGONAUTS (GREEK MYTHOLOGY)
Jason and the Argonauts **398.2**

ARGONAUTS (LEGENDARY CHARACTERS)
See also Legendary characters

Argueta, Jorge
A movie in my pillow **861**
Somos Como Las Nubes / We Are Like the Clouds **861.64**
Talking with Mother Earth **811**

ARGUMENTATION *See* Debates and debating; Logic

Argus. Knudsen, M. **E**

ARID REGIONS
See also Earth

Arihara, Shino
(il) Franco, B. Zero is the leaves on the tree **513**
(il) Hudes, Q. A. Welcome to my neighborhood! **E**
(il) Lord, M. A song for Cambodia **92**

Ariol. **741.5**

ARISTOCRACY
See also Political science; Upper class

ARISTOCRACY (SOCIAL CLASS) -- FICTION
Nooks & crannies **Fic**

Arithme-tickle. Lewis, J. P. **513**

ARITHMETIC
Fisher, V. How high can a dinosaur count? **513**
Lewis, J. P. Arithme-tickle **513**
Markel, M. Tyrannosaurus math **513**
Marsico, K. Football **796.332**
Marsico, K. Running **796.42**
Marsico, K. Speed skating **796.91**
Marsico, K. Tennis **796.342**
Minden, C. Swimming **797.2**

ARITHMETIC
See also Mathematics; Set theory

ARITHMETIC -- ESTIMATION *See* Approximate computation

ARITHMETIC -- FICTION
Banks, K. Max's math **E**

Arizona. Brezina, C. **979.1**
Arizona. Somervill, B. A. **979.1**
Arizona. McDaniel, M. **979.1**

ARIZONA
Somervill, B. A. Arizona **979.1**

ARIZONA -- FICTION
Broach, E. Revenge of Superstition Mountain **Fic**
The **ark** plan. **Fic**
Arkansas. Prentzas, G. S. **976.7**

ARKANSAS

Altman, L. J. Arkansas **976.7**
Levy, J. Arkansas **976.7**
Prentzas, G. S. Arkansas **976.7**
Arkansas. Levy, J. **976.7**
Arkansas. Altman, L. J. **976.7**

ARKANSAS -- FICTION
Greene, B. Philip Hall likes me, I reckon maybe **Fic**
Hilmo, T. With a name like Love **Fic**
Manley, C. Skeeter's dream **Fic**
McCrite, K. D. In front of God and everybody **Fic**

ARKANSAS -- RACE RELATIONS
Walker, P. R. Remember Little Rock **379**

Arlington. Demarest, C. L. **975.5**

ARLINGTON NATIONAL CEMETERY (VA.)
Demarest, C. L. Arlington **975.5**

Arlon, Penelope
Emergency vehicles **629.04**
Puppies and kittens **636.7**

ARM
See also Anatomy

Armadillo trail. Swinburne, S. R. **599.3**

ARMADILLOS
Markovics, J. L. My body is tough and gray **599.3**
Swinburne, S. R. Armadillo trail **599.3**

ARMADILLOS -- FICTION
Brimner, L. D. Trick or treat, Old Armadillo **E**
Fearnley, J. Milo Armadillo **E**

Armand, Glenda
Love twelve miles long **E**

Armando and the blue tarp school. Fine, E. H. **E**

ARMED FORCES
See also Military art and science

Armenia. Dhilawala, S. **947.5**

ARMENIA
Dhilawala, S. Armenia **947.5**

ARMIES -- MEDICAL CARE
See also Medical care; Military medicine

ARMOR
Arms & armor **355.8**
Kent, P. Peter Kent's big book of armor **687**

ARMOR
See also Art metalwork; Costume; Military art and science

Arms & armor. **355.8**

ARMS AND ARMOR *See* Armor; Weapons

ARMS CONTROL
See also International relations; International security; War

Armstrong & Charlie. **Fic**

Armstrong, Alan
Looking for Marco Polo **Fic**
Racing the moon **Fic**
Raleigh's page **Fic**
Whittington **Fic**

Armstrong, Jennifer
The American story **973**
Once upon a banana **E**

Away. **E**

Awesome adventures at the Smithsonian. Korrell, E. B. **069**

Awesome African-American rock and soul musicians. Aretha, D. **781.644**

Awesome animal science projects. Benbow, A. **590.7**

Awesome autumn. Goldstone, B. **E**

An awesome book! Clayton, D. **E**

Awesome forces of nature [series]
Spilsbury, L. Howling hurricanes **551.55**
Spilsbury, L. Raging floods **551.48**
Spilsbury, L. Shattering earthquakes **551.2**
Spilsbury, L. Sweeping tsunamis **551.46**
Spilsbury, L. Terrifying tornadoes **551.55**
Spilsbury, L. Violent volcanoes **551.2**

Awesome snake science. Blobaum, C. **597.96**

Axelrod, Amy
Your friend in fashion, Abby Shapiro **Fic**

Axtell, David
(il) We're going on a lion hunt **E**

Ayala, Jacqueline
Alire, C. Serving Latino communities **027.6**

Aye-aye. Aronin, M. **599.8**

AYE-AYE (ANIMAL)
Aronin, M. Aye-aye **599.8**

Ayer, Paula
(jt. auth) Banyard, A. Water wow! **553.7**

Aylesworth, Jim
The full belly bowl **E**
Goldilocks and the three bears **398.2**
Little Bitty Mousie **E**
The mitten **398.2**
My grandfather's coat **E**
Old black fly **E**
Our Abe Lincoln **92**

Ayliffe, Alex
(il) Mayo, M. Choo choo clickety-clack! **E**

Ayres, Charlie
Lives of the great artists **709**

Ayto, Russell
(il) Are the dinosaurs dead, Dad? **E**
(il) Burgess, M. Where teddy bears come from **E**
(il) Cutbill, A. The cow that laid an egg **E**

AYURVEDIC MEDICINE
See also Medicine

Azad's camel. Pal, E. **E**

Azarian, Mary
(il) Connor, L. Miss Bridie chose a shovel **E**
(il) The Hound dog's haiku **811**
(il) Martin, J. B. Snowflake Bentley **551.57**
(il) McGinty, A. B. Darwin **92**
(il) Michelson, R. Tuttle's Red Barn **630**

The Aztec empire. Apte, S. **972**

AZTEC GODS -- COMIC BOOKS, STRIPS, ETC
Camper, C. Lowriders to the center of the Earth **741.5**

The Aztecs. Heinrichs, A. **972**

AZTECS
Apte, S. The Aztec empire **972**

Cooke, T. Ancient Aztec **972**
Coulter, L. Ballplayers and bonesetters **971**
Heinrichs, A. The Aztecs **972**
Lourie, P. Hidden world of the Aztec **972**
Serrano, F. The poet king of Tezcoco **92**

AZTECS -- FOLKLORE
Bernier-Grand, C. T. Our Lady of Guadalupe **232.91**
Ollhoff, J. Mayan and Aztec mythology **972.81**
Tonatiuh, D. The princess and the warrior **398.2**

AZTECS -- RELIGION
Ollhoff, J. Mayan and Aztec mythology **972.81**

Azzi in Between. Garland, S. **Fic**

B

B is for blue planet. **550**

B. Franklin, printer. Adler, D. A. **92**

B.U.G. Yolen, J. **Fic**

Baasansuren, Bolormaa
My little round house **E**

BABA YAGA (LEGENDARY CHARACTER) -- FICTION
Marsh, K. The door by the staircase **Fic**

Baba Yaga and Vasilisa the brave. Mayer, M. **398.2**

Babbage, Charles, 1791-1871
About
Ada Lovelace, poet of science **92**
Wallmark, L. Ada Byron Lovelace and the thinking machine **B**

Babbitt, Natalie, 1932-2016
The Devil's storybook **S**
The eyes of the Amaryllis **Fic**
Jack Plank tells tales **Fic**
Kneeknock Rise **Fic**
The moon over High Street **Fic**
The search for delicious **Fic**
Tuck everlasting **Fic**
(il) Worth, V. All the small poems and fourteen more **811**

Babe. King-Smith, D. **Fic**

The Babe & I. Adler, D. A. **E**

Babe & me. Gutman, D. **Fic**

Babe conquers the world. Wallace, R. **92**

Babe Didrikson Zaharias. Freedman, R. **92**

BABIES *See* Infants

BABIES -- FICTION
The baby swap **E**
Beaton, K. King Baby **E**
Blackall, S. The baby tree **E**
Fogliano, J. Old dog baby baby **E**
Frazee, M. The bossier baby **E**
Gantos, J. The key that swallowed Joey Pigza **Fic**
Howatt, S. J. Sleepyheads **E**
Hyewon Yum The twins' little sister **E**
Katz, K. Now I'm big **E**
Leo loves baby time **E**
Look, L. Henry's first-moon birthday **E**
Mustache baby **E**
The nest **Fic**

Nichols, L. Maple | E
One special day | E
Palatini, M. No nap! yes nap! | E
Paschkis, J. Mooshka | E
Ward, L. Henry finds his word | E
Babies don't eat pizza. Danzig, D. | 649
Babies in the bayou. Arnosky, J. | E
Babies in the library! Marino, J. | 027.62
Babies on the go. | E
Baboon. Banks, K. | E
Baboons. Roumanis, A. | 599.865

BABOONS
Roumanis, A. Baboons | 599.865

BABOONS
See also Apes

BABOONS -- FICTION
Banks, K. Baboon | E
Napoli, D. J. Lights on the Nile | Fic
Baboushka and the three kings. Robbins, R. | 398.2
Babushka's doll. Polacco, P. | E
Babushka's Mother Goose. Polacco, P. | 398.8
Baby animal pop! | 590

BABY ANIMALS *See* Animal babies
Baby Australian animals [series]
Doudna, K. It's a baby kangaroo! | 599.2
Hengel, K. It's a baby Australian fur seal! | 599.79
Baby baby baby! Janovitz, M. | E
Baby Bear. Nelson, K. | E
Baby Bear sees blue. Wolff, A. | E
Baby Bear's books. Yolen, J. | E
Baby Bear, Baby Bear, what do you see? | E
Baby Beluga. Raffi | 782.42
Baby blessings. Jordan, D. | 242
Baby board books [series]
Kubler, A. Humpty Dumpty | E

BABY BOOM GENERATION
See also Population
Baby Brains. James, S. | E
Baby can. Bunting, E. | E

BABY CARE *See* Infants -- Care
Baby carnivores. Kalman, B. | 599.7
Baby danced the polka. Beaumont, K. | E
Baby Dragon. Ehrlich, A. | E
A **baby** elephant in the wild. | 599.67
Baby Flo. Schroeder, A. | 92
The **baby** goes beep. O'Connell, R. | E
The **baby** in the hat. Ahlberg, A. | E
Baby knows best. Granstrom, B. | E
Baby mammals. Kalman, B. | 591.3
Baby mammoth mummy. Sloan, C. | 569
The **baby** on the way. English, K. | E
Baby Pig Pig talks. McPhail, D. | E
Baby Pig Pig walks. McPhail, D. | E
Baby Polar. Murphy, Y. | E
Baby primates. Kalman, B. | 599.8
Baby rhyming time. Ernst, L. L. | 027.62
Baby rodents. Kalman, B. | 599.35

Baby Ruby bawled. Stanley, M. R. | E
Baby says moo! Macken, J. E. | E
Baby Seasons [series]
Broach, E. Barnyard baby | E
Baby shoes. Slater, D. | E
Baby shower. Zalben, J. B. | E
The **baby** sister. DePaola, T. | E

BABY SITTING *See* Babysitting
The **baby** swap. | E
Baby talk. Hindley, J. | E
The **baby** tree. Blackall, S. | E
Baby whale's journey. London, J. | E
Baby whales drink milk. Esbensen, B. J. | 599.5
Baby's got the blues. Shields, C. D. | E
The **Baby's** Lap Book. | 398.8
Baby, come away. Adler, V. | E
The **Baby-sitter's** Club: Kristy's great idea. Martin, A. M. | 741.5
Babyberry pie. Frederick, H. V. | E

BABYMOUSE (FICTIONAL CHARACTER)
Holm, J. L. Babymouse: queen of the world | 741.5
Babymouse: queen of the world. Holm, J. L. | 741.5
The **babysitter's** survival guide. Chasse, J. D. | 649

BABYSITTERS -- FICTION
Farrant, N. After Iris | Fic
Graff, L. Absolutely almost | Fic
Harper, C. M. Dreamer, wisher, liar | Fic
Lulu's mysterious mission | Fic
Reagan, J. How to babysit a grandma | E
Reagan, J. How to babysit a grandpa | E

BABYSITTING
Buckley, A. Be a better babysitter | 649
Chasse, J. D. The babysitter's survival guide | 649

BABYSITTING
See also Child care; Infants -- Care

BABYSITTING -- GRAPHIC NOVELS
Martin, A. M. The Baby-sitter's Club: Kristy's great idea | 741.5

Baccalario, Pierdomenico
The long-lost map | Fic

Bacchin, Matteo
Giant vs. giant | 567.9
T. rex and the great extinction | 567.9

Bach, Johann Sebastian, 1685-1750
About
Krull, K. Lives of the musicians | 920
Leonard, T. Becoming Bach | 92

Bachelet, Gilles
My cat, the silliest cat in the world | E

Bacher, Lindsay
Alia Muhammad Baker | 92

Bachmann, Stefan
The Cabinet of Curiosities | S
Back of the bus. Reynolds, A. | E
Back to bed, Ed! Braun, S. | E
Back to school Tortoise. George, L. M. | E
Back to school, Mallory. Friedman, L. B. | Fic

BACKPACKING

Barrett, Mary Brigid
Shoebox Sam — **E**

Barrett, Robert
(il) Turner, A. W. Dust for dinner — **E**
(il) Weatherford, C. B. Obama — **92**

Barrett, Ron
(il) Barrett, J. Cloudy with a chance of meatballs — **E**
(il) Weitzman, J. P. Superhero Joe — **E**

Barrett, Tracy
The 100-year-old secret — **Fic**
The Beast of Blackslope — **Fic**

Barretta, Gene
Neo Leo — **609**
Now & Ben — **609**
Timeless Thomas — **E**
(il) Zoola Palooza — **E**

Barrie, J. M. (James Matthew), 1860-1937
Peter Pan and Wendy — **Fic**

About
Yolen, J. Lost boy — **92**

BARRISTERS See Lawyers

Barron's Educational Series Inc.
(comp) Insects and spiders — **595**
Wonders of the world — **031.02**

Barron's junior rhyming Dictionary. Foster, J. — **423**

Barron's totally wild fact-packed fold-out animal atlas. — **590**

Barron, Ashley
(il) Sorting through spring — **510**

Barron, T. A.
The book of magic — **Fic**
The fires of Merlin — **Fic**
Ghost hands — **E**
The lost years of Merlin — **Fic**
The mirror of Merlin — **Fic**
The seven songs of Merlin — **Fic**
The wings of Merlin — **Fic**

Barros, Bruna
The carpenter — **E**

Barroux
(il) Bunny's lessons — **E**
(il) Lucy rescued — **E**

Barroux, Stephane
Bunny's lessons — **E**
(il) LeBlanc, A. The red piano — **92**
Owen, K. I could be, you could be — **E**
(il) Ziefert, H. My dog thinks I'm a genius — **E**

Barrow, David
Have You Seen Elephant? — **E**

Barrow, Randi G.
Saving Zasha — **Fic**

Barrows, Annie
Ivy + Bean — **Fic**
Ivy + Bean and the ghost that had to go — **Fic**
Ivy + Bean bound to be bad — **Fic**
Ivy + Bean break the fossil record — **Fic**
Ivy + Bean take care of the babysitter — **Fic**
Ivy + Bean: doomed to dance — **Fic**

Ivy + Bean: what's the big idea? — **Fic**
The magic half — **Fic**

Barry, Dave
Peter & the shadow thieves — **Fic**
Peter and the secret of Rundoon — **Fic**
Peter and the starcatchers — **Fic**
Peter and the Sword of Mercy — **Fic**
The worst class trip ever — **Fic**

Barry, Frances
Let's save the animals — **591.68**

Barshaw, Ruth McNally
(il) Leopold the Lion — **E**
Ellie McDoodle: best friends fur-ever — **Fic**
Ellie McDoodle: have pen, will travel — **Fic**
Ellie McDoodle: new kid in school — **Fic**

Barsony, Piotr
The stories of the Mona Lisa — **759.00**

Bart's king-sized book of fun. King, B. — **79.**

BARTER
See also Commerce; Economics; Money; Subsistence economy; Underground economy

BARTER -- FICTION
Swap! — **E**

Bartholdi, Frédéric Auguste, 1834-1904
About
Maestro, B. The story of the Statue of Liberty — **974.**
Mann, E. Statue of Liberty — **974.**
Shea, P. D. Liberty rising — **974.**
Yolen, J. Naming Liberty — **E**

Bartholomew and the oobleck. Seuss — **E**

Bartholomew Biddle and the very big wind. — **Fic**

Bartleby speaks! Cruise, R. — **E**

Bartlett, Alison
(il) French, V. T. Rex — **567.9**

Bartlett, Jonathan
(il) Certain poor shepherds — **Fic**

Bartlett, T. C.
Tuba lessons — **E**

Bartoletti, Susan Campbell
The boy who dared — **Fic**
Growing up in coal country — **331.**
Kids on strike! — **331.8**
Naamah and the ark at night — **E**

Barton, Bethany
Give Bees a Chance — **595.799**
(il) I'm trying to love spiders — **595.**

Barton, Byron
My bike — **E**
(il) My bus — **E**

Barton, Byron
Airplanes — **387.**
Boats — **387.2**
Bones, bones, dinosaur bones — **567.9**
Building a house — **690**
Dinosaurs, dinosaurs — **E**
The little red hen — **398.2**
Machines at work — **690**

(il) Tolan, S. S. Wishworks, Inc. **Fic**
(il) Weatherford, C. B. First pooch **973.932**
Bates, George
(il) Day, N. R. On a windy night **E**
Bates, Ivan
(il) Rylant, C. Puppies and piggies **E**
Bates, Janet Costa
Seaside dream **E**
Bates, Katharine Lee
America the beautiful **811**
Bates, Martin Van Buren, 1837-1919
About
Andreasen, D. The giant of Seville **E**
Bates, Peg Leg
About
Barasch, L. Knockin' on wood **92**
Bateson, Catherine
Being Bee **Fic**
Magenta McPhee **Fic**
Bathing. Slegers, L. **E**
The **bathing** costume, or, The worst vacation of my life. **E**
BATHROOMS -- FICTION
Elya, S. M. Oh no, gotta go! **E**
BATHROOMS -- POETRY
A funeral in the bathroom **811**
BATHS
Barner, B. Animal baths **591.5**
Ehrlich, F. Does an elephant take a bath? **E**
Fielding, B. Animal baths **591.5**
Jenkins, S. Time for a bath **591.56**
Pattison, D. Desert baths **591.754**
Sis, P. Dinosaur! **E**
BATHS
See also Cleanliness; Hygiene; Physical therapy
BATHS -- FICTION
101 reasons why I'm not taking a bath **E**
Cowpoke Clyde and Dirty Dawg **E**
The green bath **E**
Messer, C. Grumpy pants **E**
Russo, M. Little Bird takes a bath **E**
BATHTUBS -- FICTION
The green bath **E**
BATHYSCAPHE
See also Oceanography -- Research; Submersibles
BATHYSCAPHE -- HISTORY -- 20TH CENTURY
Bodden, V. To the ocean deep **551.46**
BATMAN (COMIC STRIP)
Enz, T. Batman science **600**
BATMAN (FICTIONAL CHARACTER)
Dahl, M. The man behind the mask **Fic**
Batman science. Enz, T. **600**
Batmanglij, Najmieh
Happy Nowruz **641.5**
BATON TWIRLING -- FICTION
Repka, J. The clueless girl's guide to being a genius **Fic**
Bats. Gish, M. **599.4**
Bats. Riggs, K. **599.4**

BATS
See also Mammals
BATS
Appelt, K. Bats around the clock **E**
Bekkering, A. Bats **599.4**
Berman, R. Let's look at bats **599.4**
Carney, E. Bats **599.4**
Carson, M. K. The bat scientists **599.4**
Davies, N. Bat loves the night **599.4**
Earle, A. Zipping, zapping, zooming bats **599.4**
Gibbons, G. Bats **599.4**
Gish, M. Bats **599.4**
Gonzales, D. Bats in the dark **599.4**
Lunde, D. P. Hello, bumblebee bat **599.4**
Markle, S. The case of the vanishing little brown bats **599.4**
Markovics, J. L. The bat's cave **599.4**
A place for bats **599.4**
Riggs, K. Bats **599.4**
Rodriguez, C. Bats **599.4**
Science comics **599.4**
Stewart, M. How do bats fly in the dark? **599.4**
Bats. Bekkering, A. **599.4**
Bats. Gibbons, G. **599.4**
Bats. Rodriguez, C. **599.4**
Bats. Carney, E. **599.4**
BATS -- FICTION
Berk, A. Nightsong **E**
BATS -- FOLKLORE
Riggs, K. Bats **599.4**
Bats around the clock. Appelt, K. **E**
Bats in the dark. Gonzales, D. **599.4**
Batten, John D.
(il) Jacobs, J. English fairy tales **398.2**
Batter. Glaser, J. **796.357**
Battersby, Katherine
Squish Rabbit **E**
Battle Bunny. **E**
The **battle** for Skandia. Flanagan, J. **Fic**
The **battle** for WondLa. **Fic**
The **battle** of Iwo Jima. Hama, L. **940.54**
Battle of the beasts. **Fic**
Battle of the dinosaur bones. Johnson, R. L. **560.9**
BATTLES
See also Military art and science; Military history; War
Battles & weapons: exploring history through art. Chapman, C. **355**
BATTLES -- FICTION
Nielsen, J. A. The shadow throne **Fic**
Battut, Eric
The fox and the hen **E**
Little Mouse's big secret **E**
Batty. Dyer, S. **E**
Baucom, Ian
Through the skylight **Fic**
Bauer, A. C. E.
Come Fall **Fic**
No castles here **Fic**

Bauer, Caroline Feller

Leading kids to books through crafts   **027.62**

Leading kids to books through magic   **027.62**

Leading kids to books through puppets   **027.62**

Bauer, Helen

Beethoven for kids   **92**

Bauer, Joan

Almost home   **Fic**

Close to famous   **Fic**

Soar   **Fic**

Bauer, Marion Dane

Bauer, M. D.   In like a lion, out like a lamb   **E**

A bear named Trouble   **Fic**

The blue ghost   **Fic**

In like a lion, out like a lamb   **E**

Little cat's luck   **Fic**

Little dog, lost   **Fic**

The longest night   **E**

On my honor   **Fic**

Thank you for me!   **E**

Bauer, Michael Gerard

Just a dog   **Fic**

Bauer, Stephanie

(il)   Hip hip hooray! it's Family Day!   **E**

Baum, L. Frank, 1856-1919

The Wizard of Oz   **Fic**

The wonderful Wizard of Oz   **Fic**

About

Cavallaro, M.   L. Frank Baum's The Wizard of Oz   **741.5**

Krull, K.   The road to Oz   **92**

Baum, Maxie

I have a little dreidel   **782.42**

Baumbach, Donna

Less is more   **025.2**

Bausum, Ann

Dragon bones and dinosaur eggs: a photobiography of Roy Chapman Andrews   **92**

Freedom Riders   **323.1**

Our Country's Presidents   **973.09**

Our Country's first ladies   **920**

Our Country's Presidents   **973.09**

Stubby the War Dog   **940.4**

Baviera, Rocco

(il)   Bruchac, J.   A boy called Slow: the true story of Sitting Bull   **92**

Baxter, Katherine

(il)   Adams, S.   The Kingfisher atlas of the ancient world   **930**

Baxter, Kathleen A.

From cover to cover   **028.1**

Gotcha again for guys!   **028.5**

Gotcha good!   **028.5**

Baxter, Roberta

The Bill of Rights   **342.73**

The particle model of matter   **530**

Bayer, Jane

A my name is Alice   **411**

Baylor, Byrd

When clay sings   **970.00**

Baynes, Pauline

Questionable creatures   **398.2**

Koralek, J.   The coat of many colors   **222**

(il)   Lewis, C. S.   The horse and his boy   **Fic**

(il)   Lewis, C. S.   The last battle   **Fic**

(il)   Lewis, C. S.   The lion, the witch, and the wardrobe   **Fic**

(il)   Lewis, C. S.   The magician's nephew   **Fic**

(il)   Lewis, C. S.   Prince Caspian   **Fic**

(il)   Lewis, C. S.   The silver chair   **Fic**

(il)   Lewis, C. S.   The voyage of the Dawn Treader   **Fic**

Bayrock, Fiona

Bubble homes and fish farts   **590**

Bazemore, Suzanne

Soccer: how it works   **796.334**

BC mambo.   Craddock, E.   **741.5**

Be a better babysitter.   Buckley, A.   **649**

Be glad your nose is on your face and other poems.   Prelutsky, J.   **811**

Be my neighbor.   Ajmera, M.   **307**

Be quiet!   **E**

Be quiet, Mike!   Patricelli, L.   **E**

Be water, my friend.   Mochizuki, K.   **92**

Be what you want [series]

Mattern, J.   So, you want to work in sports?   **796**

Wooster, P.   So, you want to work in fashion?   **746.9**

Bea at ballet.   Isadora, R.   **E**

Bea Garcia [series]

Zemke, D.   My life in pictures   **Fic**

Bea in The Nutcracker.   Isadora, R.   **E**

Beach.   Cooper, E.   **E**

Beach feet.   **E**

Beach party surf monkey.   **Fic**

A **beach** tail.   Williams, K. L.   **E**

Beach, Alfred E. (Alfred Ely), 1826-1896

About

Corey, S.   The secret subway   **E**

Beachcombing.   Arnosky, J.   **578.7**

BEACHES

Ehrlich, H. M.   Louie's goose   **E**

Huneck, S.   Sally goes to the beach   **E**

Lindeen, M.   At the beach   **551.4**

Spohn, K.   Turtle and Snake's day at the beach   **E**

BEACHES

See also Seashore

BEACHES -- FICTION

Atinuke (Author)   Splash! Anna hibiscus   **E**

Beach feet   **E**

Duck & Goose go to the beach   **E**

Gaiman, N.   Chu's day at the beach   **E**

Greenwald, L.   Welcome to Dog Beach   **Fic**

Grey, M.   Traction Man and the beach odyssey   **E**

Larsen, A.   The not-so-faraway adventure   **E**

Noni the pony goes to the beach   **E**

Sattler, J.   Pig kahuna pirates!   **E**

BEACHES -- POETRY

Scanlon, L. G.   All the world   **811**

Hamilton, S. L. Mauled by a bear	**599.78**
Hest, A. Kiss good night	E
Hirschi, R. Our three bears	**599.78**
Johnson, D. B. Henry hikes to Fitchburg	E
Kvatum, L. Saving Yasha	**599.78**
McAllister, I. Salmon bears	**599.78**
Milo's hat trick	E
Schwabacher, M. Bears	**599.78**
Swinburne, S. R. Black bear	**599.78**
Thompson, L. Polar bear night	E
Wallace, N. E. Seeds! Seeds! Seeds!	E
Winnie	**599.78**

BEARS -- FICTION

100 Bears	E
Banks, K. The bear in the book	E
Bear has a story to tell	E
Bear in love	E
The bear's song	E
Becker, B. A Library book for bear	E
Beebe, K. Brother Hugo and the bear	E
Berger, C. Finding spring	E
Bird, balloon, Bear	E
Bloom, S. Alone together	E
Browne, A. The little bear book	E
Bunting, E. Big Bear's big boat	E
Carnesi, M. Sleepover with Beatrice and Bear	E
Chaud, B. The bear's sea escape	E
Deep in the Woods	398.2
Doremus, G. Bear despair	E
Dunrea, O. Little Cub	E
Dyckman, A. Horrible bear!	E
Farrell, D. Stop following me Moon!	E
Gravett, E. Bear & Hare -- share!	E
Grumpy feet	E
Haughton, C. Goodnight everyone	E
Higgins, R. T. Hotel Bruce	E
Higgins, R. T. Mother Bruce	E
Hillenbrand, W. All for a dime!	E
Hillenbrand, W. Kite day	E
Hudson, K. Bear and duck	E
I promise	E
Lipan, S. Mom, there's a bear at the door	E
Litchfield, D. The bear and the piano	E
Lucas, D. A Letter for Bear	E
McGowan, J. One bear extraordinaire	E
Minor, F. If you were a panda bear	E
Moon bear	Fic
Morris, J. East of the Sun, West of the Moon	Fic
Na, I. S. Welcome home, Bear	E
Nelson, K. Baby Bear	E
The not so quiet library	E
Santa Claus and the Three Bears	Fic
Sarcone-Roach, J. The bear ate your sandwich	E
Seeger, L. V. Dog and Bear	E
Shea, B. Ballet Cat	E
Tea party rules	E
There's a Bear on My Chair	E

Three bears in a boat	E
Wolff, A. Baby Bear sees blue	E
Yoon, S. Found	E

BEARS -- FOLKLORE

Brett, J. Goldilocks and the three bears	398.2

BEARS -- GRAPHIC NOVELS

Coudray, P. Benjamin Bear in Fuzzy thinking	**741.5**
Bears on chairs. Parenteau, S.	
Bears! bears! bears! Barner, B.	599.78
The **Bearskinner.** Schlitz, L. A.	398.2
Bearwalker. Bruchac, J.	**Fic**
Beasley, Cassie	
Circus Mirandus	**Fic**
Beast Friends Forever. Forbes, R. L.	**811**
Beast friends forever [series]	
Evans, N. Meet the beast	**Fic**
The **Beast** of Blackslope. Barrett, T.	**Fic**
Beastly babies. Jackson, E.	E
Beastly Verse.	**808.81**
BEASTS *See* Animals	
The **beasts** of Clawstone Castle.	**Fic**
A **beasty** story. Martin, B.	E

BEAT GENERATION

See also American literature; Bohemianism

The **beatitudes.** Weatherford, C. B.	**323.1**
The **Beatles.** Manning, M.	**92**
Beatles	

About

Manning, M. The Beatles	**92**

Humor

Brewer, P. The Beatles were fab (and they were funny)	**782.42**
The **Beatles** were fab (and they were funny) Brewer, P.	**782.42**
Beaton, Kate	
King Baby	E
The princess and the pony	E
Beatrice doesn't want to. Numeroff, L. J.	E
Beatrice spells some lulus and learns to write a letter. Best, C.	E
Beatrice's dream. Williams, K. L.	**967.62**
Beatrice, Chris	
(il) Moerbeek, K. Aesop's fables: a pop-up book of classic tales	**398.2**
Beatrix Potter and the unfortunate tale of a borrowed guinea pig. Hopkinson, D.	**92**
Beatty, Richard	
Phosphorus	**546**
Sulfur	**546**
Serafina and the Twisted Staff	**Fic**
(ed) Exploring the world of mammals	**599**
Beaty, Andrea	
Ada Twist, scientist	E
Attack of the fluffy bunnies	**Fic**
Cicada summer	**Fic**
Doctor Ted	E
Dorko the magnificent	**Fic**
Happy Birthday, Madame Chapeau	E
Iggy Peck, architect	E

BEST BOOKS

Freeman, J. Books kids will sit still for 3 **011.6**

Garcha, R. The world of Islam in literature for youth **016**

Gates, P. Cultural Journeys **372**

Keane, N. J. 101 great, ready-to-use book lists for children **028.5**

Matthew, K. I. Neal-Schuman guide to recommended children's books and media for use with every elementary subject **011.6**

Zbaracki, M. D. Best books for boys **028.5**

BEST BOOKS

See also Books

BEST BOOKS -- UNITED STATES

Barr, C. Best books for children **011.62**

Silvey, A. Children's book-a-day almanac **011.62**

Zvirin, S. Read with me **028.5**

Best books for boys. Zbaracki, M. D. **028.5**

Best books for children. Barr, C. **011.62**

Best buds. Eaton, M. **E**

The **best** cat in the world. Newman, L. **E**

The **best** children's books of the year. Child Study Children's Book Committee at Bank Street **016**

The **best** Christmas pageant ever. Robinson, B. **Fic**

The **best** days are dog days. Meshon, A. **E**

Best Eid ever. Mobin-Uddin, A. **E**

Best friend on wheels. Shirley, D. **E**

Best friends. Kellogg, S. **E**

BEST FRIENDS -- FICTION

Ain, B. Starring Jules (in drama-rama) **Fic**

Armstrong & Charlie **Fic**

Baker, B. Digby and Kate and the beautiful day **E**

Baskin, N. R. Ruby on the outside **Fic**

Benjamin, A. The thing about jellyfish **Fic**

Berk, J. Strike three, you're dead **Fic**

Big friends **E**

Carnesi, M. Sleepover with Beatrice and Bear **E**

Catalanotto, P. More of Monkey & Robot **E**

Cerra, K. O. Just a drop of water **Fic**

Cervantes, A. Allie, first at last **Fic**

Cheng, A. The year of the book **Fic**

Cohen, M. The Inn Between **Fic**

Cotler, S. Cheesie Mack is running like crazy! **Fic**

Defelice, C. Fort **Fic**

DeStefano, L. The peculiar night of the blue heart **Fic**

Dowell, F. O. The sound of your voice, only really far away **Fic**

English, K. Nikki & Deja **Fic**

Federle, T. Five, six, seven, Nate! **Fic**

Ferry, B. Stick and Stone **E**

Goodrich, C. We forgot Brock! **E**

Green, T. Force out **Fic**

Hank's big day **E**

Harper, C. M. Just Grace gets crafty **Fic**

The imaginary **Fic**

Johnson, V. The great Greene heist **Fic**

Johnson, V. To catch a cheat **Fic**

Keating, J. How to outfox your friends when you don't have

a clue **Fic**

Kinard, K. The boy prediction **Fic**

LaFleur, S. Beautiful blue world **Fic**

Leonard, M. G. Beetle boy **Fic**

Levis, C. Ida, always **E**

Loftin, N. Wish girl **Fic**

Lundquist, M. Cat & Bunny **E**

Magaziner, L. The only thing worse than witches **Fic**

Mass, W. The last present **Fic**

Moonpenny Island **Fic**

Nyeu, T. Squid and Octopus **E**

Shea, B. Ballet Cat **E**

The someday suitcase **Fic**

Spooky friends **E**

Stead, R. Goodbye stranger **Fic**

Stone, P. The boy on Cinnamon Street **Fic**

Ten thank-yous **E**

Weissman, E. B. The short seller **Fic**

What James said **E**

Yee, W. H. Mouse and Mole, secret valentine **E**

Young, K. R. Hundred percent **Fic**

Best friends and drama queens. Cabot, M. **Fic**

Best friends forever. Patt, B. **Fic**

Best frints in the whole universe. Portis, A. **E**

Best holiday books [series]

MacMillan, D. M. Diwali--Hindu festival of lights **394.26**

The **best** horse ever. DeLaCroix, A. **Fic**

The **best** man. Peck, R. **Fic**

The **best** nest. Mueller, D. L. **398.2**

Best of the best. Green, T. **Fic**

The **best** of times. Tang, G. **513**

The **best** seat in second grade. Kenah, K. **E**

BEST SELLERS (BOOKS)

See also Books and reading

The **best** story. Spinelli, E. **E**

The **Best** Thing About Kindergarten. Lloyd, J. **E**

The **best** worst thing. Lane, K. **Fic**

Best, Cari, 1951-

Beatrice spells some lulus and learns to write a letter **E**

Easy as pie **E**

Goose's story **E**

My three best friends and me, Zulay **E**

Sally Jean, the Bicycle Queen **E**

Three cheers for Catherine the Great! **E**

What's so bad about being an only child? **E**

BEST-BOOK LISTS *See* Best books

BESTIARIES

Baynes, P. Questionable creatures **398.2**

BESTIARIES

See also Books

Beswitched. Saunders, K. **Fic**

Betancourt, Jeanne

Ava Tree and the wishes three **Fic**

Bethune, Mary Jane McLeod, 1875-1955

About

Let it shine **920**

McKissack, F. Mary McLeod Bethune **370.92**

Fischer, C. In the beginning: the art of Genesis **222**
Hanft, J. E. Miracles of the Bible **221.9**
Hodges, M. Moses **222**
Jules, J. Benjamin and the silver goblet **222**
Jules, J. Miriam in the desert **222**
Jules, J. Sarah laughs **222**
Kimmel, E. A. The story of Esther **222**
Koralek, J. The coat of many colors **222**
Koralek, J. The story of Queen Esther **222**
Lottridge, C. B. Stories from Adam and Eve to Ezekiel **220.9**
Lottridge, C. B. Stories from the life of Jesus **232.9**
Manushkin, F. Miriam's cup **222**
McKissack, P. C. Let my people go **Fic**
Osborne, M. P. The Random House book of Bible stories **220.9**
Pinsker, M. In the days of sand and stars **296.1**
Pirotta, S. Children's stories from the Bible **220.9**
Ray, J. Adam and Eve and the Garden of Eden **222**
Sasso, S. E. But God remembered **221.9**
Sasso, S. E. Cain & Abel **222**
Skevington, A. The story of Jesus **232.9**
Spier, P. Noah's ark **222**
Ward, E. M. Old Testament women **221.9**
Watts, M. The Bible for children from Good Books **220.9**
The **Bible**: Authorized King James Version. **220.5**

BIBLICAL CHARACTERS
Brett, J. On Noah's ark **E**
Chaikin, M. Angels sweep the desert floor **296.1**
Gerstein, M. The white ram **E**
Hodges, M. Moses **222**
Jules, J. Abraham's search for God **222**
Jules, J. Miriam in the desert **222**
Jules, J. Sarah laughs **222**
Kimmel, E. A. The story of Esther **222**
Koralek, J. The coat of many colors **222**
Koralek, J. The story of Queen Esther **222**
Krensky, S. Noah's bark **E**
Manushkin, F. Miriam's cup **222**
Ray, J. Adam and Eve and the Garden of Eden **222**
Sasso, S. E. Cain & Abel **222**

BIBLICAL COSMOLOGY
See also Cosmology
Biblioburro. Winter, J. **E**

BIBLIOGRAPHIC INSTRUCTION
Callison, D. The blue book on information age inquiry, instruction and literacy **028.7**
Donovan, S. Bob the Alien discovers the Dewey decimal system **025.4**
Donovan, S. Bored Bella learns about fiction and nonfiction **025.4**
LibrarySparks: library lessons **027.62**

BIBLIOGRAPHIC INSTRUCTION
See also Library services

BIBLIOGRAPHIC INSTRUCTION -- COLLEGE AND UNIVERSITY STUDENTS
Grassian, E. S. Information literacy instruction **025.5**

BIBLIOGRAPHY -- BEST BOOKS *See* Best books

BIBLIOGRAPHY -- BILINGUAL BOOKS *See* Bilingual books

Bickel, Cindy
Nagda, A. W. Chimp math **529**
The **Bicklebys'** birdbath. Perry, A. **E**
Bicycle book. Gibbons, G. **629.227**
The **bicycle** man. Say, A. **E**
The **bicycle** man. Dudley, D. L. **Fic**

BICYCLE MOTOCROSS
Adamson, T. K. BMX racing **796.622**

BICYCLE RACING
Adamson, T. K. BMX racing **796.622**
Brill, M. T. Marshall Major Taylor **92**

BICYCLE RACING
See also Cycling; Racing
The **bicycle** spy. McDonough, Y. Z. **Fic**

BICYCLE TOURING
See also Camping; Cycling; Travel
Bicycles. **629.227**

BICYCLES
See also Vehicles

BICYCLES
Bicycles **629.227**
Cyclist bikelist **796.6**
Gibbons, G. Bicycle book **629.227**
Haduch, B. Go fly a bike! **629.227**
Macy, S. Wheels of change **796.6**
Mulder, M. Pedal it! **388**

BICYCLES -- DESIGN AND CONSTRUCTION
Bicycles **629.227**

BICYCLES -- FICTION
Al-Mansour, H. The green bicycle **Fic**
Barton, B. My bike **E**
Boelts, M. A Bike Like Sergio's **E**
Hillenbrand, W. Off we go! **E**
Raschka, C. Everyone can learn to ride a bicycle **E**
McDonough, Y. Z. The bicycle spy **Fic**

BICYCLES AND BICYCLING *See* Bicycles; Cycling

BICYCLES AND BICYCLING -- FICTION
Al-Mansour, H. The green bicycle **Fic**
Barton, B. My bike **E**
Davies, M. Ben rides on **E**
Hillenbrand, W. Off we go! **E**
McDonough, Y. Z. The bicycle spy **Fic**
Mills, C. Gus and Grandpa and the two-wheeled bike **E**
Mollel, T. M. My rows and piles of coins **E**
Raschka, C. Everyone can learn to ride a bicycle **E**

BICYCLING *See* Cycling

Biddulph, Rob
Blown away **E**

Biden, Jill, 1951-
Don't forget, God bless our troops **355.1**

Bidner, Jenni
Is my cat a tiger? **636.8**
Is my dog a wolf? **636.7**

Bieber, Justin, 1994-
About

Bieber, J. Justin Bieber: first step 2 forever   92

Biedrzycki, David

   Ace Lacewing, bug detective: the big swat   **E**

   Me and my dragon   **E**

Biesty, Stephen

   Exploring Space   **520.9**

   (il) Giant vehicles   **629.04**

   (il) Into the unknown   **910.4**

   (il) The Story of buildings   **690**

Big & little. Jenkins, S.   **591.4**

The **big** adventure of the Smalls. Stephens, H.   **E**

The **big** adventures of Majoko, volume 1. Fuji, M.   **741.5**

Big Alaska. Miller, D. S.   **979.8**

Big and Bad. Delessert, E.   **E**

Big and little. Miller, M.   **153.7**

Big and small, room for all. Bogart, J. E.   **E**

Big bad Bruce. Peet, B.   **E**

Big Bad Bunny. Billingsley, F.   **E**

Big Bad Wolf. Archer, D.   **E**

The **Big** Bad Wolf and me. Perret, D.   **E**

The **Big** Bad Wolf Goes on Vacation. Perret, D.   **E**

The **big** balloon race. Coerr, E.   **E**

BIG BANG COSMOLOGY See Big bang theory

BIG BANG THEORY

   Older than the stars   **523.1**

BIG BANG THEORY

   See also Cosmology

Big bear hug. Oldland, N.   **E**

Big bear little chair. Boyd, L.   **E**

Big Bear's big boat. Bunting, E.   **E**

Big belching bog. Root, P.   **577.6**

Big blue whale. Davies, N.   **599.5**

The **big** book for toddlers.   **808.8**

The **big** book of pirates.   **S**

Big book of trains. National Railway Museum (Great Britain)   **625.1**

The **big** book of words and pictures. Könnecke, O.   **428.1**

BIG BOOKS

   See also Children's literature; Reading materials

Big brothers don't take naps. Borden, L.   **E**

Big Brown Bear's up and down day. McPhail, D. M.   **E**

Big bug.   **E**

Big cat, little cat. Cooper, E.   **E**

Big cats. Landau, E.   **599.75**

Big cats.   **599.75**

Big chickens. Helakoski, L. H.   **E**

Big city Otto: elephants never forget. Slavin, B.   **741.5**

The big day! [series]

   Barber, N. First day of school   **372**

   Barber, N. Going to the hospital   **362.1**

   Barber, N. Moving to a new house   **648**

The **Big** Dipper. Branley, F. M.   **523.8**

Big dogs. Hart, J.   **636.7**

Big Dogs, Little Dogs.   **636.7**

The **big** fat cow that goes kapow. Griffiths, A.   **E**

Big fat hen. Baker, K.   **398.8**

Big fat Little Lit.   **741.5**

BIG FOOT See Sasquatch

Big friends.   **E**

Big game. Gibbs, S.   **Fic**

Big game hunting. Peterson, J. M.   **799.2**

BIG GAME HUNTING

   See also Hunting

Big George: how a shy boy became President Washington. Rockwell, A. F.   **92**

The **big** green book of the big blue sea. Becker, H.   **577.7**

A **big** guy took my ball! Willems, M.   **E**

Big hugs, little hugs. Bond, F.   **E**

The **big** idea science book.   **500**

Big is big (and little, little) Lewis, J. P.   **E**

Big Jabe. Nolen, J.   **E**

Big kicks. Kolar, B.   **E**

Big little brother. Kling, K.   **E**

Big little mother. Kling, K.   **E**

Big Momma makes the world. Root, P.   **E**

Big Nate. Peirce, L.   **Fic**

Big Nate on a roll. Peirce, L.   **Fic**

Big Nate strikes again. Peirce, L.   **Fic**

A **big** night for salamanders.   **E**

Big Pig and Little Pig. McPhail, D. M.   **E**

Big plans. Shea, B.   **E**

Big red barn. Brown, M. W.   **E**

The **big** red horse. Scanlan, L.   **798.4**

Big red kangaroo.   **599.2**

Big red lollipop. Khan, R.   **E**

Big rig. Swenson, J. A.   **E**

Big rig bugs. Cyrus, K.   **E**

Big scary monster. Docherty, T.   **E**

Big sister now. Sheldon, A.   **306.8**

The **big** snow. Hader, B.   **E**

The **big** splash. Ferraiolo, J. D.   **Fic**

The **big** storm. Tafuri, N.   **E**

The **big** swim. Fagan, C.   **Fic**

Big talk. Fleischman, P.   **811**

The **big** test. Danneberg, J.   **E**

The **big** time. Green, T.   **Fic**

Big Top Otto. Slavin, B.   **741.5**

Big tracks, little tracks. Selsam, M. E.   **590**

The **big** wet balloon.   **741.5**

Big wheels. Rockwell, A. F.   **E**

Big wig. Krull, K.   **391**

The **big** wish. Conahan, C.   **E**

Big Wolf & Little Wolf. Brun-Cosme, N.   **E**

Big words for little people. Curtis, J. L.   **E**

Bigda, Diane

   (il) Park, L. S. Mung-mung!   **413**

BIGFOOT See Sasquatch

Bigfoot Boy [series]

   Into the woods   **741.5**

   The Sound of Thunder   **741.5**

   The unkindness of ravens   **741.5**

Bigger isn't always better. Simons, R.   **613.2**

Bigger than a bread box. Snyder, L.   **Fic**

The **biggest** bear. Ward, L. K.   **E**

Biscuit. Capucilli, A.   **E**

Biscuit's new trick. Capucilli, A.   **E**

BISEXUAL PEOPLE
> See also LGBT people

Bishop, Gavin
- (il) Cowley, J. Snake and Lizard   **Fic**
- (il) Mister Whistler   **Fic**

Bishop, Kay
- The collection program in schools   **027.8**
- Connecting libraries with classrooms   **375**

Bishop, Nic
- Butterflies   **595.7**
- (il) Chasing cheetahs   **599.75**
- Digging for bird-dinosaurs   **567.9**
- Lizards   **597.95**
- Nic Bishop butterflies and moths   **595.7**
- Nic Bishop frogs   **597.8**
- Nic Bishop marsupials   **599.2**
- Nic Bishop snakes   **597.96**
- (il) Cowley, J. Chameleon chameleon   **597.95**
- (il) Cowley, J. Red-eyed tree frog   **597.8**
- Jackson, E. B. The mysterious universe   **523.8**
- (il) Montgomery, S. Kakapo rescue   **639.9**
- (il) Montgomery, S. Quest for the tree kangaroo   **599.2**
- (il) Montgomery, S. Saving the ghost of the mountain **599.75**
- (il) Montgomery, S. The snake scientist   **597.96**
- (il) Montgomery, S. The tarantula scientist   **595.4**
- (il) Spiders   **595.4**
- (il) The tapir scientist   **599.66**

Bishop, Rudine Sims
- Free within ourselves   **028.5**

Bishop, Stephen, 1821?-1857
About
- Lift your light a little higher   **92**

BishopRoby, Joshua
- Animal kingdom   **590**

BISHOPS
- Demi The legend of Saint Nicholas   **270**

BISHOPS
> See also Clergy

Biskup, Agnieszka
- (jt. auth) Enz, T. Batman science   **600**
- Houdini   **92**
- Thunder rolling down the mountain   **92**

Bison. Gish, M.   **599.64**

BISON
> See also Mammals

BISON
- Bruchac, J. Buffalo song   **92**
- Caper, W. American bison   **599.64**
- George, J. C. The buffalo are back   **599.64**
- Gish, M. Bison   **599.64**

BISON -- FICTION
- Fern, T. E. Buffalo music   **E**
- Vernick, A. Is your buffalo ready for kindergarten?   **E**

BITCOIN
> See also Electronic funds transfers; Money

Bites and stings. Landau, E.   **617.1**

BITES AND STINGS
- Landau, E. Bites and stings   **617.1**

Bitten by a rattlesnake. Hamilton, S. L.   **597.96**

Bitterman, Albert
- Fortune cookies   **E**

Bix, Cynthia Overbeck
- Rauzon, M. J. Water, water everywhere   **551.48**

Bizarre dinosaurs. Sloan, C.   **567.9**

Bizarre science [series]
- Aaseng, N. Weird meat-eating plants   **583**
- Anderson, M. J. Bugged-out insects   **595.7**
- Knapp, R. Bloodsucking creatures   **591.5**
- Knapp, R. Mummy secrets uncovered   **393**
- Poynter, M. Doomsday rocks from space   **523.4**

Björk, Christina
- Linnea in Monet's garden   **Fic**

Bjorklund, Ruth
- Afghanistan   **958.1**
- Aikido   **796.8**
- Cerebral palsy   **616.8**
- Cystic fibrosis   **616.3**
- Epilepsy   **616.8**
- Lizards   **639.3**
- Mongolia   **951.73**
- Nebraska   **978.2**
- Rabbits   **636.9**
- Venus   **523.4**

Bjorkman, Steve
- Dinosaurs don't, dinosaurs do   **E**
- Cochran, B. My parents are divorced, my elbows have nicknames, and other facts about me   **E**
- Cox, J. Puppy power   **Fic**
- Murphy, S. J. Same old horse   **E**
- Post, P. Emily Post's table manners for kids   **395**
- Post, P. Emily's everyday manners   **395**
- Senning, C. P. Emily's new friend   **395**
- Vande Velde, V. 8 class pets + one squirrel one dog   **Fic**

Bjornlund, Lydia D.
- Alcohol   **362.292**
- The Trail of Tears   **970.004**

Blabey, Aaron
- The Bad Guys in mission unpluckable   **Fic**
- The Bad Guys   **Fic**

BLACK
- Johnson, D. Black magic   **E**

BLACK ACTORS
> See also Actors

BLACK AMERICANS See African Americans

Black and white. Macaulay, D.   **793.7**

BLACK ART
> See also Art

BLACK ART (MAGIC) See Magic; Witchcraft

BLACK ARTISTS
> See also Artists

BLACK ATHLETES
- Queen of the track   **796.42**

Black bear. Swinburne, S. R. **599.78**
BLACK BEAR
  Walker, S. M. Winnie **599.78**
Black Beauty. Sewell, A. **Fic**
The **black** book of colors. Cottin, M. **E**
The **Black** Book of Secrets. Higgins, F. E. **Fic**
BLACK BUSINESSPEOPLE
  See also Businesspeople
The **Black** Canary. Curry, J. L. **Fic**
Black cat. Myers, C. **E**
Black cat, white cat. Borando, S. **E**
The **Black** Cauldron. Alexander, L. **Fic**
BLACK CHILDREN
  See also Children
Black cowboy, wild horses. Lester, J. **E**
The **Black** Death. Ollhoff, J. **616.9**
BLACK DEATH *See* Plague
Black dog. Pinfold, L. **E**
Black Elk's vision. Nelson, S. D. **92**
Black Elk, 1863-1950
  About
  Nelson, S. D. Black Elk's vision **92**
Black hands, white sails. McKissack, P. C. **639.2**
The **black** heart crypt. Grabenstein, C. **Fic**
Black history in the pages of children's literature. Casement,
  R. **028.5**
A **black** hole is not a hole. **523.8**
BLACK HOLES (ASTRONOMY)
  A black hole is not a hole **523.8**
  Jackson, E. B. The mysterious universe **523.8**
  The universe, black holes, and the Big Bang **523.1**
  Venezia, M. Stephen Hawking **92**
  Waxman, L. H. Exploring black holes **523.8**
BLACK HOLES (ASTRONOMY)
  See also Astronomy; Astrophysics; Stars
BLACK HUMOR (LITERATURE)
  See also Fiction; Literature; Wit and humor
Black ice. Lane, A. **Fic**
Black is brown is tan. Adoff, A. **E**
Black Jack: the ballad of Jack Johnson. Smith, C. R. **92**
BLACK LIBRARIANS
  See also Librarians
BLACK LITERATURE (AMERICAN) *See* American litera-
  ture -- African American authors
Black magic. Johnson, D. **E**
BLACK MAGIC (WITCHCRAFT) *See* Magic; Witchcraft
BLACK MAMBA
  Franchino, V. Black mambas **597.96**
Black mambas. Franchino, V. **597.96**
BLACK MARKET
  See also Commerce
BLACK MUSIC
  See also Music
BLACK MUSICIANS
  See also Musicians
BLACK MUSLIM LEADERS
  Gunderson, J. X: the biography of Malcolm X **92**

Malcolm X **92**
BLACK MUSLIMS
  Gunderson, J. X: the biography of Malcolm X **92**
Black on white. Hoban, T. **E**
BLACK PANTHER PARTY -- FICTION.
  Williams-Garcia, R. One crazy summer **Fic**
Black pearls. Hawes, L. **S**
Black pioneers [series]
  Hansen, J. Home is with our family **Fic**
BLACK POETRY (AMERICAN) *See* American poetry --
  African American authors
The **Black** rabbit. **E**
Black radishes. Meyer, S. **Fic**
The **black** reckoning. Stephens, J. **Fic**
Black spiny-tailed iguana. Lunis, N. **597.95**
The **Black** Stallion. Farley, W. **Fic**
Black widows. Markle, S. **595.4**
BLACK WOMEN
  See also Women
Black, Ann N.
  Readers theatre for middle school boys **812**
Black, Holly, 1971-
  The copper gauntlet **Fic**
  Doll bones **Fic**
  The iron trial **Fic**
Black, Jess
  A year in the life of Bindi **333.72**
Black, Michael Ian
  Chicken cheeks **E**
  A pig parade is a terrible idea **E**
Black, Peter Jay
  Urban outlaws **Fic**
Black? white! day? night! Seeger, L. V. **E**
Blackaby, Susan
  Brownie Groundhog and the February fox **E**
  Cleopatra **92**
Blackall, Sophie
  (il) The 9 lives of Alexander Baddenfield **Fic**
  (il) And two boys booed **E**
  Are you awake? **E**
  The baby tree **E**
  Spinster Goose **811**
  (il) Edwin speaks up **E**
  (il) Finding Winnie **E**
  (il) Lord and Lady Bunny -- almost royalty! **Fic**
  (il) Manners mash-up: a goofy guide to good behavior **395**
  (il) The mighty Lalouche **E**
  (il) Mr. and Mrs. Bunny-- detectives extraordinaire! **Fic**
  (il) Pecan pie baby **E**
  (il) Barrows, A. Ivy + Bean **Fic**
  (il) Barrows, A. Ivy + Bean and the ghost that had to go **Fic**
  (il) Barrows, A. Ivy + Bean bound to be bad **Fic**
  (il) Barrows, A. Ivy + Bean break the fossil record **Fic**
  (il) Barrows, A. Ivy + Bean take care of the babysitter **Fic**
  (il) Barrows, A. Ivy + Bean: doomed to dance **Fic**
  (il) Barrows, A. Ivy + Bean: what's the big idea? **Fic**
  (il) Best, C. What's so bad about being an only child? **E**

(il) Bridges, S. Y. Ruby's wish   E
(il) Edwin speaks up   E
(il) Khan, R. Big red lollipop   E
(il) Pecan pie baby   E
(il) Rosoff, M. Jumpy Jack and Googily   E
(il) Rosoff, M. Meet wild boars   E

Blackbeard, 1680?-1718
About
Lewis, J. P. Blackbeard, the pirate king   811
Blackbeard, the pirate king. Lewis, J. P.   811
Blackbird fly. Kelly, E. E.   Fic
Blackburn, Lena, 1886-1968
About
Miracle mud   796.357
The **blacker** the berry. Thomas, J. C.   811
Blackford, Andy
Bill's bike   E
The hungry little monkey   E
Blackford, Cheryl
Hungry Coyote   E
Blackout. Rocco, J.   E
BLACKS -- AFRICA -- FICTION
The water princess   E
BLACKS -- BIOGRAPHY
Rockwell, A. F. Open the door to liberty!: a biography of
    Toussaint L'Ouverture   92
BLACKS -- BIOGRAPHY
See also Biography
BLACKS -- BOTSWANA -- FICTION
McCall Smith, A. The great cake mystery   Fic
BLACKS -- CANADA
Warner, J. Viola Desmond won't be budged!   92
BLACKS -- CANADA -- FICTION
Curtis, C. P. The madman of Piney Woods   Fic
BLACKS -- CIVIL RIGHTS
Scattergood, A. Glory be   Fic
BLACKS -- CIVIL RIGHTS
See also Blacks -- Political activity; Civil rights
BLACKS -- ECONOMIC CONDITIONS
See also Economic conditions
BLACKS -- FICTION
Medearis, A. S. Seven spools of thread   E
BLACKS -- FOLKLORE
See also Folklore
BLACKS -- HISTORY
Tarrant-Reid, L. Discovering Black America   973
BLACKS -- RELIGION
See also Religion
BLACKS -- SEGREGATION
Bass, H. Seeds of freedom   323.1
BLACKS -- SEGREGATION
See also Segregation
BLACKS -- SOUTH AFRICA -- FICTION
Bildner, P. The soccer fence   E
BLACKS -- SUDAN -- FICTION
The red pencil   Fic
BLACKS -- UNITED STATES *See* African Americans

BLACKS IN MOTION PICTURES
See also Minorities in motion pictures; Motion pictures
The **blacksmith.** Petersen, C.   682
BLACKSMITHING
Petersen, C. The blacksmith   682
Blackstone, Stella
My granny went to market   E
Storytime   398.2
The **blackthorn** key. Sands, K.   Fic
The Blackwell pages [series]
Marr, M. Loki's wolves   Fic
Marr, M. Odin's ravens   Fic
Blackwell, Elizabeth, 1821-1910
About
Who says women can't be doctors?   E
Blackwood, Freya
Ivy loves to give   E
(il) Gleeson, L. Clancy & Millie, and the very fine house   E
(il) Gleeson, L. Half a world away   E
(il) My two blankets   E
The treasure box   E
(il) Wild, M. Harry & Hopper   E
Blackwood, Gary L.
Curiosity   Fic
Enigmatic events   904
Legends or lies?   398.2
Mysterious messages   652
Second sight   Fic
The Shakespeare stealer   Fic
Shakespeare's scribe   Fic
Shakespeare's spy   Fic
Blackwood, Kristin
(il) Oelschlager, V. A tale of two daddies   E
Blackwood, Sage
Jinx   Fic
Jinx's fire   Fic
Jinx's magic   Fic
Miss Ellicott's school for the magically minded   Fic
Blair, Chris
(il) Clements, A. Room one   Fic
Blair, Margaret Whitman
Liberty or death   973.3
Blake, Francis
(il) Andrews, J. Rude stories   398.2
(il) Nibbling on Einstein's brain   507.2
Blake, Quentin
The boy in the dress   Fic
(il) Dahl, R. The BFG   Fic
(il) Dahl, R. Charlie and the chocolate factory   Fic
(il) Dahl, R. The enormous crocodile   Fic
(il) Dahl, R. The magic finger   Fic
Dahl, R. Matilda   Fic
(il) Dahl, R. The missing golden ticket and other splendiferous secrets   92
(il) Fleischman, S. Here comes McBroom!   Fic
(il) Fleischman, S. McBroom's wonderful one-acre farm   Fic
(il) Morpurgo, M. On angel wings   Fic

(il) Viorst, J. The tenth good thing about Barney   **E**

Bleiman, Andrew

   ZooBorns   **591.3**

Blériot, Louis, 1872-1936

About

Provensen, A. The glorious flight: across the Channel with Louis Bleriot, July 25, 1909   **92**

Bless this mouse. Lowry, L.   **Fic**

Blessen, Karen

   (il) Gilley, J. Peace one day   **303.6**

BLESSING AND CURSING -- FICTION

   Andersen, H. C. The Snow Queen   **E**

   Coville, B. Cursed   **Fic**

   Hayes, C. Mothman's curse   **Fic**

   Jacobson, A. Palace of dreams   **Fic**

   Morrison, M. Disenchanted   **Fic**

   Vernon, U. Hamster Princess   **Fic**

The **blessing** cup.   **E**

The **blessing** of the beasts. Pochocki, E.   **E**

Blessing, Charlotte

   New old shoes   **E**

Blexbolex

   People   **E**

   Seasons   **E**

Bley, Anette

   And what comes after a thousand?   **E**

Blia Xiong

   Nine-in-one, Grr! Grr!   **398.2**

BLIMPS See Airships

BLIND

   Adler, D. A. A picture book of Louis Braille   **686.2**

   Alexander, S. H. She touched the world: Laura Bridgman, deaf-blind pioneer   **92**

   Amoroso, C. Helen Keller   **92**

   Bender, L. Explaining blindness   **617.7**

   Best, C. My three best friends and me, Zulay   **E**

   Delano, M. F. Helen's eyes   **92**

   Freedman, R. Out of darkness: the story of Louis Braille   **92**

   Lawlor, L. Helen Keller: rebellious spirit   **92**

   Markle, S. Lost sight   **617.7**

   Saltypie   **92**

   Sullivan, G. Helen Keller   **92**

BLIND

   See also People with physical disabilities

BLIND -- BOOKS AND READING

   Adler, D. A. A picture book of Louis Braille   **686.2**

   Freedman, R. Out of darkness: the story of Louis Braille   **92**

   Jeffrey, L. S. All about Braille   **411**

BLIND -- BOOKS AND READING

   See also Books and reading

BLIND -- FICTION

   Pinkwater, D. M. Mrs. Noodlekugel and four blind mice   **Fic**

   Reynolds, J. As brave as you   **Fic**

   Seki, S. Yuko-chan and the Daruma doll   **E**

BLIND -- INSTITUTIONAL CARE

   See also Institutional care

BLIND TEACHERS -- FRANCE -- BIOGRAPHY

Bryant, J. Six dots   **92**

BLINDNESS

   See also Vision disorders

Blink of an eye. Superfast animals! [series]

   Lunis, N. Black spiny-tailed iguana   **597.95**

   Lunis, N. California sea lion   **599.7**

   Lunis, N. Cheetah   **599.75**

   Lunis, N. Greyhound   **636.7**

   Lunis, N. Peregrine falcon   **598**

   Lunis, N. Pronghorn   **599.6**

Bliss, Harry

   Bailey   **E**

   Luke on the loose   **741.5**

   (il) Birdsall, J. My favorite pet by Gus W. for Ms. Smolinski's class   **E**

   (il) Cronin, D. Diary of a fly   **E**

   (il) Cronin, D. Diary of a spider   **E**

   (il) Diary of a worm   **E**

   (il) DiCamillo, K. Louise   **E**

   (il) Invisible Inkling   **Fic**

   (il) McGhee, A. Mrs. Watson wants your teeth   **E**

   (il) McGhee, A. A very brave witch   **E**

Bliss, John

   Art that moves   **791.43**

   Preening, painting, and piercing   **391**

Blitt, Barry

   (il) The adventures of Mark Twain by Huckleberry Finn   **92**

   (il) The Founding Fathers   **920**

   (il) While you were napping   **E**

   (il) You never heard of Casey Stengel?!   **92**

   Kloske, G. Once upon a time, the end   **E**

Blitzed by a blizzard! Markovics, J. L.   **551.55**

Blizzard. Rocco, J.   **E**

Blizzard of glass. Walker, S. M.   **971**

BLIZZARDS

   Fleisher, P. Lightning, hurricanes, and blizzards   **551.55**

   Markovics, J. L. Blitzed by a blizzard!   **551.55**

   Stewart, M. Blizzards and winter storms   **551.55**

BLIZZARDS

   See also Storms

BLIZZARDS -- FICTION

   Rocco, J. Blizzard   **E**

   The tale of rescue   **Fic**

BLIZZARDS -- GRAPHIC NOVELS

   Wetterer, M. K. The snowshoeing adventure of Milton Daub, blizzard trekker   **741.5**

Blizzards and winter storms. Stewart, M.   **551.55**

Blobaum, Cindy

   Awesome snake science   **597.96**

   Explore Honey Bees!   **595.79**

   Explore money!   **332.4**

   Geology rocks!   **551**

   Insectigation!   **595.7**

Bloch, Serge

   Butterflies in my stomach and other school hazards   **E**

   Snowed under and other Christmas confusions   **E**

   (il) Cali, D. The enemy   **E**

(il) I dare you not to yawn   **E**

(il) I scream ice cream!   **E**

(il) Morgenstern, S. H. A book of coupons   **Fic**

(il) My snake Blake   **E**

Block city. Stevenson, R. L.   **E**

Block party surprise.   **E**

Block, Francesca Lia

House of dolls   **Fic**

Block, Ira

(il) Lange, K. E. 1607   **975.5**

Blockhead. D'Agnese, J.   **92**

Blocks. Dickson, I.   **E**

BLOGS *See* Weblogs

BLOGS -- FICTION

Rivers, K. Finding Ruby Starling   **Fic**

Blogs, wikis, podcasts, and other powerful Web tools for classrooms. Richardson, W.   **371.3**

Blom, Jen K.

Possum summer   **Fic**

BLOOD

Kyi, T. L. Seeing red   **612.1**

Newquist, H. The book of blood   **612.1**

Showers, P. A drop of blood   **612.1**

Venezia, M. Charles Drew   **92**

BLOOD

     See also Physiology

BLOOD -- CIRCULATION

Corcoran, M. K. The circulatory story   **612.1**

Yount, L. William Harvey   **92**

BLOOD -- DISEASES

     See also Diseases

BLOOD GROUPS

     See also Blood

The **blood** guard. Roy, C.   **Fic**

The **blood** lie. Vernick, S. R.   **Fic**

Blood moon rider. Waters, Z. C.   **Fic**

The **blood** of Olympus. Riordan, R.   **Fic**

Blood on the river. Carbone, E. L.   **Fic**

BLOOD PRESSURE

     See also Blood

BLOODSUCKING ANIMALS

Knapp, R. Bloodsucking creatures   **591.5**

Bloodsucking creatures. Knapp, R.   **591.5**

Bloom! Lieshout, M. v.   **E**

Bloom, Suzanne

Alone together   **E**

Feeding friendsies   **E**

(il) Bunting, E. Girls A to Z   **E**

(il) A splendid friend, indeed   **E**

Bloom, Tom

(il) While You Were Sleeping   **031.02**

Bloomability. Creech, S.   **Fic**

Bloomfield, Alan

Jennings, M. Baseball step-by-step   **796.357**

Bloomfield, Jill

Jewish holidays cookbook   **641.5**

Blos, Joan W.

A gathering of days: a New England girl's journal, 1830-32   **Fic**

Letters from the corrugated castle   **Fic**

Blount, Marcellus

(ed) African American Poetry   **811**

Blown away. Biddulph, R.   **E**

Blue 2. Carter, D. A.   **E**

Blue birds. Rose, C. S.   **Fic**

The **blue** book on information age inquiry, instruction and literacy. Callison, D.   **028.7**

Blue chameleon. Gravett, E.   **E**

Blue chicken. Freedman, D.   **E**

BLUE COLLAR WORKERS *See* Labor; Working class

Blue Ethel.   **E**

The **Blue** fairy book.   **398.2**

Blue fire. Hardy, J.   **Fic**

The **blue** ghost. Bauer, M. D.   **Fic**

Blue Goose. Tafuri, N.   **E**

The **blue** house dog. Blumenthal, D.   **E**

Blue jasmine. Sheth, K.   **Fic**

BLUE JAYS

Berendt, J. My baby blue jays   **598**

Blue like Friday. Parkinson, S.   **Fic**

Blue lipstick. Grandits, J.   **811**

The **Blue** marble. Nardo, D.   **525**

Blue Moo. Boynton, S.   **782.42**

Blue on blue.   **E**

Blue potatoes, orange tomatoes. Creasy, R.   **635**

BLUE RIDGE MOUNTAINS REGION -- FICTION

McDowell, M. T. Carolina Harmony   **Fic**

The **blue** shoe. Townley, R.   **Fic**

Blue sky. Wood, A.   **E**

Blue sky white stars.   **E**

Blue whales up close. Rake, J. S.   **599.5**

Blue willow. Gates, D.   **Fic**

Blue, Rose

Ron's big mission   **E**

Naden, C. J. James Monroe   **92**

Blue-ribbon dad. Glass, B. R.   **E**

Blueberries for Sal. McCloskey, R.   **E**

Blueberry pancakes forever. Banks, A.   **Fic**

Bluebird. Staake, B.   **E**

BLUEBIRDS

Kirby, P. F. What bluebirds do   **598**

BLUEBIRDS -- FICTION

Staake, B. Bluebird   **E**

Bluefish. Schmatz, P.   **Fic**

BLUEGRASS MUSIC

     See also Music

Bluemel Oldfield, Dawn

Apple   **634.11**

Leaping ground frogs   **597.8**

Bluemle, Elizabeth

How do you wokka-wokka?   **E**

Tap tap boom boom   **E**

Blues. Handyside, C.   **781.643**

BLUES (MUSIC) -- HISTORY AND CRITICISM

Adoff, A. Roots and blues   **811**

Blues journey. Myers, W. D.   **811**

BLUES MUSIC

Handyside, C. Blues   **781.643**

BLUES MUSIC

See also African American music; Folk music -- United
States; Popular music

BLUES MUSIC -- FICTION

Clayton Byrd goes underground   **Fic**

BLUES MUSIC -- POETRY

Adoff, A. Roots and blues   **811**

Myers, W. D. Blues journey   **811**

BLUES MUSICIANS

Boynton, S. Sandra Boynton's One shoe blues   **782.42**

The **blues** of Flats Brown. Myers, W. D.   **E**

BLUES POETRY

See also American poetry -- African American authors

BLUES SONGS *See* Blues music

Bluffton. Phelan, M.   **741.5**

Bluhm, Joe

(il) The fantastic flying books of Mr. Morris Lessmore   **E**

Blumberg, Rhoda

Commodore Perry in the land of the Shogun   **952**

Shipwrecked!: the true adventures of a Japanese boy   **92**

Blume, Judy

Are you there God?, it's me, Margaret   **Fic**

BFF*   **Fic**

Cool zone with the Pain and the Great One   **Fic**

Double Fudge   **Fic**

Freckle juice   **Fic**

Friend or fiend? with the Pain & the Great One   **Fic**

Fudge-a-mania   **Fic**

Going, going, gone! with the Pain and the Great One   **Fic**

Otherwise known as Sheila the Great   **Fic**

The Pain and the Great One   **E**

Soupy Saturdays with The Pain and The Great One   **Fic**

Starring Sally J. Freedman as herself   **Fic**

Superfudge   **Fic**

Tales of a fourth grade nothing   **Fic**

Blume, Lesley M. M.

The rising star of Rusty Nail   **Fic**

Blumenthal, Deborah

The blue house dog   **E**

Blumenthal, Karen

Let me play   **796**

Mr. Sam   **92**

Blundell, Judy

A city tossed and broken   **Fic**

Bluthenthal, Diana Cain

(il) Edwards, P. D. The neat line   **E**

(il) Viorst, J. Just in case   **E**

Bly, Nellie, 1864-1922

About

Macy, S. Bylines: a photobiography of Nellie Bly   **92**

Blythe, Gary

(il) Davies, N. Ice bear   **599.78**

(il) De Quidt, J. The toymaker   **Fic**

(il) Ehrlich, A. A treasury of princess stories   **398.2**

BMX racing. Adamson, T. K.   **796.622**

Bo at Ballard Creek. Hill, K.   **Fic**

Boake, Kathy

(il) Becker, H. Worms for Breakfast   **636**

(il) Swanson, D. You are weird   **612**

BOARD BOOKS FOR CHILDREN

Balouch, K. Feelings   **E**

Bancroft, B. W is for wombat   **E**

Basher, S. Go! go! Bobo: colors   **E**

Boynton, S. Happy Hippo, angry Duck   **E**

Brown, H. The robot book   **E**

Caterpillar Inc. My big book of trucks & diggers   **621.8**

Clifford, the big red dog board book   **E**

Dahl, M. Nap time for Kitty   **E**

Doodler, T. H. What color is Bear's underwear?   **E**

Dowdy, L. C. All kinds of kisses   **E**

DwellStudio (Firm) Good morning, toucan   **E**

DwellStudio (Firm) Goodnight, owl   **E**

Emberley, E. Where's my sweetie pie?   **E**

Endle, K. Bunny Rabbit in the sunlight   **E**

Franceschelli, C. (oliver)   **E**

Gershator, P. Who's in the forest?   **E**

Global baby girls   **E**

Global Fund for Children (Organization) American babies   **E**

Global Fund for Children (Organization) Global babies   **E**

Henkes, K. A good day   **E**

Hills, T. Duck & Goose, it's time for Christmas!   **E**

Hoban, T. Black on white   **E**

Hoban, T. White on black   **E**

Horacek, P. Choo choo   **E**

Hubbell, P. Firefighters! speeding! spraying! saving!   **E**

Isol It's useful to have a duck   **E**

Janovitz, M. Baby baby baby!   **E**

Katz, S. ABC, baby me!   **E**

Kim, S. How does a seed grow?   **581.4**

Katz, K. How Does Baby Feel?   **E**

Klinting, L. What do you want?   **E**

Kubler, A. Hop a little, jump a little!   **398.8**

Kubler, A. Humpty Dumpty   **E**

Kubler, A. Pat-a-cake   **398.8**

Laden, N. Peek-a-who?   **E**

Lakin, P. Skateboards   **796.22**

Laval, T. Colors   **E**

Light, S. Trains go   **E**

Martin, D. Christmas tree   **E**

Martin, D. Hanukkah lights   **E**

McPhail, D. Baby Pig Pig talks   **E**

McPhail, D. Baby Pig Pig walks   **E**

Moore, C. C. The night before Christmas   **811**

Newman, L. Daddy, papa, and me   **E**

Newman, L. Mommy, mama, and me   **E**

O'Connell, R. The baby goes beep   **E**

Patricelli, L. Potty   **E**

Patricelli, L. Tubby   **E**

Penn, A. A bedtime kiss for Chester Raccoon   **E**

Perrin, M. Look who's there!   **E**

Perrin, M. What do you see? — **E**
Quay, E. Good night, sleep tight — **E**
Salzano, T. One rainy day — **E**
Schindel, J. Busy gorillas — **599.8**
Slegers, L. Bathing — **E**
Taback, S. Simms Taback's farm animals — **E**
Tullet, H. The game of finger worms — **E**
Tullet, H. The game of let's go! — **E**
Tullet, H. The game of light — **E**
Tullet, H. The game of mix and match — **E**
Tullet, H. The game of mix-up art — **E**
Tullet, H. The game of patterns — **E**
Van Fleet, M. Moo — **E**
Verdick, E. Mealtime — **E**
Wildsmith, B. Brian Wildsmith's ABC — **E**
Wynne Pechter, L. Alligator, bear, crab — **E**
Yoon, S. One, two, buckle my shoe — **E**
Yoon, S. Who do I see? — **E**
Yuly, T. Night owl — **E**
Zuravicky, O. C is for city — **E**

BOARD BOOKS FOR CHILDREN
See also Picture books for children

BOARD GAMES
Mayer, B. Libraries got game — **025.2**

BOARD GAMES
See also Games

BOARD GAMES -- GRAPHIC NOVELS
Hotta, Y. Hikaru No Go, Volume 1 — **741.5**

BOARDING HOUSES *See* Hotels and motels
BOARDING SCHOOLS *See* Private schools
BOARDING SCHOOLS -- FICTION
Friday Barnes, girl detective — **Fic**
Hale, S. The storybook of legends — **Fic**
Robinson, M. L. Bright Island — **Fic**
Rundell, K. Cartwheeling in thunderstorms — **Fic**
Stevens, R. Murder is bad manners — **Fic**
Vanderpool, C. Navigating Early — **Fic**

BOARDINGHOUSES -- FICTION
The case of the stolen sixpence — **Fic**
Spinelli, E. Sophie's masterpiece — **E**
White, R. The treasure of Way Down Deep — **Fic**

BOARS -- FICTION
Rosoff, M. Meet wild boars — **E**

Boase, Susan
(il) Orr, W. Lost! A dog called Bear — **Fic**
(il) Orr, W. Missing! A cat called Buster — **Fic**
Boat of dreams. Coelho, R. — **E**

BOAT RACING
See also Boats and boating; Racing

BOATING *See* Boats and boating
Boats. Barton, B. — **387.2**
Boats. Hubbell, P. — **E**

BOATS AND BOATING
Barton, B. Boats — **387.2**
Lyon, G. E. Boats float! — **E**
Paulsen, G. Caught by the sea — **818**
Stickmen's guide to watercraft — **623.82**

BOATS AND BOATING
See also Water sports

BOATS AND BOATING -- FICTION
Along the river — **E**
Bagley, J. Boats for Papa — **E**
Biggs, B. By sea — **E**
Bunting, E. Big Bear's big boat — **E**
Coelho, R. Boat of dreams — **E**
Miyares, D. Float — **E**
Oliver and the seawigs — **Fic**
Sanabria, J. As Time Went By — **E**
Savage, S. Little Tug — **E**
Three bears in a boat — **E**
Van Allsburg, C. The wreck of the Zephyr — **E**
Boats float! Lyon, G. E. — **E**
Boats for Papa. Bagley, J. — **E**
Bob. Pearson, T. C. — **E**
Bob and Flo. Ashdown, R. — **E**
Bob and Otto. Bruel, R. O. — **E**
Bob the Alien discovers the Dewey decimal system. Donovan,
S. — **025.4**
Bob's best ever friend. Bartram, S. — **E**
Bob, not Bob! — **E**
Bobby vs. girls (accidentally) Yee, L. — **Fic**
Bobcats. Marks, J. L. — **599.75**

BOBCATS
Marks, J. L. Bobcats — **599.75**

Bobowicz, Pamela
(ed) A kid's guide to America's first ladies — **973.09**

Bobrick, Benson
A passion for victory: the story of the Olympics in ancient and early modern times — **796.4**
Fight for freedom — **973.3**

Bocanegra, Angel, 1918-
About
Nicholson, D. M. The school the Aztec Eagles built — **940.54**

Bochner, Arthur Berg
The new totally awesome business book for kids (and their parents) — **658**
Bochner, R. The new totally awesome money book for kids (and their parents) — **332.024**

Bochner, Rose
Bochner, A. B. The new totally awesome business book for kids (and their parents) — **658**
The new totally awesome money book for kids (and their parents) — **332.024**

Bockenhauer, Mark H.
Our fifty states — **973**

Bodach, Vijaya
Bar graphs — **510**

Bodden, Valerie
Cockroaches — **595.7**
Columbus reaches the New World — **970.01**
Concrete poetry — **809.1**
Crocodiles — **597.98**
Frank Gehry — **92**
Haiku — **809.1**

Levine, E. Henry's freedom box   **E**
Walker, S. M. Freedom song   **E**

Brown, Jeff

Flat Stanley   **E**

Brown, Jo

(il) Ainsworth, K. Hootenanny!   **E**

Brown, John, b. ca. 1810

About

Haskins, J. Get on board: the story of the Underground Railroad   **326**
Hendrix, J. John Brown   **92**

Brown, Jordan

(ed) Arnold, E. K. A boy called bat   **Fic**
(ed) Last day on mars   **Fic**

Brown, Jordan

Micro mania   **579**

Brown, Jordan D.

Science stunts   **530.078**

Brown, Judith Gwyn

(il) Robinson, B. The best Christmas pageant ever   **Fic**

Brown, Kathryn

(il) Fox, M. Tough Boris   **E**
(il) The house that Jane built   **92**
(il) Hyatt, P. R. The quite contrary man   **92**
(il) Moser, L. Kisses on the wind   **E**

Brown, Laaren

The Children's illustrated Jewish Bible   **220.9**

Brown, Laurene Krasny

Dinosaurs divorce   **306.89**
How to be a friend   **158.2**
What's the big secret?   **612.6**
When dinosaurs die   **155.9**

Brown, Lisa

The airport book   **387.7**
(il) Emily's blue period   **E**
Goldfish Ghost   **E**
How to be   **E**
Vampire boy's good night   **E**
(il) Gary, M. Sometimes you get what you want   **E**
(il) Snicket, L. The latke who couldn't stop screaming   **E**

Brown, Marc Tolon

Brown, L. K. Dinosaurs divorce   **306.89**
Brown, L. K. How to be a friend   **158.2**
Brown, L. K. What's the big secret?   **612.6**
Brown, L. K. When dinosaurs die   **155.9**
Arthur's eyes   **E**
Arthur's nose   **E**
D.W. all wet   **E**
(il) Craig, L. Dancing feet!   **E**
(il) Craig, L. Farmyard beat   **E**
(il) If all the animals came inside   **E**
In New York   **E**
Marc Brown's playtime rhymes   **398.8**
(il) Read-aloud rhymes for the very young   **811**
(il) Rennert, L. J. Buying, training & caring for your dinosaur   **E**
(il) Sierra, J. Born to read   **E**

(il) Sierra, J. Wild about books   **E**
(il) Wild about you!   **E**
(il) ZooZical   **E**

Brown, Marcia

Once a mouse   **398.2**
Stone soup   **398.2**
(il) Cendrars, B. Shadow   **841**
Perrault, C. Cinderella   **398.2**

Brown, Margaret Wise

Another important book   **E**
Big red barn   **E**
A Celebration of the Seasons   **E**
A child's good morning book   **E**
The Dead Bird   **E**
Doctor Squash, the doll doctor   **E**
Goodnight moon   **E**
Goodnight moon ABC   **E**
The little scarecrow boy   **E**
Nibble nibble   **811**
North, South, East, West   **E**
The runaway bunny   **E**
Sleepy ABC   **E**
Two little trains   **E**
Where have you been?   **E**
The fierce yellow pumpkin   **E**
The little island   **E**

Brown, Martin

(il) Lesser Spotted Animals   **590**

Brown, Monica

Chavela and the Magic Bubble   **E**
Lola Levine is not mean!   **E**
Pablo Neruda   **92**
Tito Puente, Mambo King   **784.4**
Waiting for the BiblioBurro   **E**

Brown, Oliver, 1918-1961

About

Rubin, S. G. Brown v. Board of Education   **344.73**

Brown, Peter, 1979-

Children make terrible pets   **E**
Chowder   **E**
(il) Creepy carrots!   **E**
The curious garden   **E**
Mr. Tiger goes wild   **E**
My teacher is a monster! (no, I am not)   **E**
The wild robot   **Fic**

Brown, Richard E.

(il) Clark, D. C. A kid's guide to Washington, D.C.   **917**

Brown, Rod

(il) Lester, J. From slave ship to freedom road   **306.3**
(il) Shange, N. Freedom's a-callin' me   **811**
(il) Shange, N. We troubled the waters   **811**

Brown, Roslind Varghese

Tunisia   **961.1**

Brown, Ruth

A dark, dark tale   **E**
Gracie the lighthouse cat   **E**

Brown, Stephanie Gwyn

Ghosts **741.5**

CALIFORNIA, NORTHERN -- FICTION
Ghosts **741.5**

Caligula, Emperor of Rome, 12-41
     About
Thompson, K. Most wanted **Fic**

CALISTHENICS See Gymnastics; Physical education

Calkhoven, Laurie
Daniel at the Siege of Boston, 1776 **Fic**
Michael at the invasion of France, 1943 **Fic**
Will at the Battle of Gettysburg, 1863 **Fic**

The **call**. Grant, M. **Fic**

Call for a new alphabet. Czekaj, J. **E**

Call it courage. Sperry, A. **Fic**

Call me tree. **E**

Call the horse Lucky. Havill, J. **E**

Call, Greg
(il) Abbott, T. Kringle **Fic**
Barry, D. Peter & the shadow thieves **Fic**
Barry, D. Peter and the secret of Rundoon **Fic**
Barry, D. Peter and the starcatchers **Fic**
Barry, D. Peter and the Sword of Mercy **Fic**
(il) Battle of the beasts **Fic**
(il) Elish, D. The attack of the frozen woodchucks **Fic**

Callan, Lyndall
Rappaport, D. Dirt on their skirts **796.357**

Callen, Liz
(il) Crawley, D. Reading, rhyming, and 'rithmetic **811**
(il) Seabrooke, B. Wolf pie **Fic**

Callery, Sean
World War II **940.53**

Callery, Sean
Ocean **577.7**
Polar lands **577.5**

Calli be gold. Hurwitz, M. W. **Fic**

Callie's rules. Zucker, N. F. **Fic**

CALLIGRAPHERS
Demi Su Dongpo **92**

CALLIGRAPHY
Hanson, A. Cool calligraphy **745.6**

CALLIGRAPHY
  See also Decorative arts; Handwriting; Writing

CALLIGRAPHY -- FICTION
Rumford, J. Silent music **E**

Calling all innovators: a career for you [series]
Mara, W. Robotics **629.8**

Callison, Daniel
The blue book on information age inquiry, instruction and literacy **028.7**

Calmenson, Stephanie
Jazzmatazz! **E**
Late for school! **E**
May I pet your dog? **636.7**
Rosie **636.7**
Cole, J. Why did the chicken cross the road? and other riddles, old and new **793.73**
(comp) The Eentsy, weentsy spider: fingerplays and action

rhymes **796.1**
(comp) Miss Mary Mack and other children's street rhymes **796.1**

Calver, Paul
Rocks, crystals, and gems **552**
(il) Insects and spiders **595**
Wonders of the world **031.02**

Calvert, Pam
Multiplying menace **E**
Princess Peepers **E**

Calvert, Patricia
The ancient Inca **985**
Vasco da Gama **92**

Calvin can't fly. Berne, J. **E**

Calvin Coconut: hero of Hawaii. Salisbury, G. **Fic**

Calvin Coconut: kung fooey. Salisbury, G. **Fic**

Calvin Coconut: trouble magnet. Salisbury, G. **Fic**

CALYPSO (MUSIC)
  See also Folk music

Cam Jansen and the mystery at the haunted house. Adler, D. A. **Fic**

Cam Jansen and the mystery of the stolen diamonds. Adler, D. A. **Fic**

Cam Jansen and the Secret Service mystery. Adler, D. A. **Fic**

Cam Jansen and the snowy day mystery. Adler, D. A. **Fic**

Cam Jansen and the Sports Day mysteries. Adler, D. A. **Fic**

Cam Jansen and the summer camp mysteries. Adler, D. A. **Fic**

Cam Jansen and the Valentine baby mystery. Adler, D. A. **Fic**

Cam Jansen and the wedding cake mystery. Adler, D. A. **Fic**

Cam Jansen, the mystery of the dinosaur bones. Adler, D. A. **Fic**

Cam Jansen, the mystery at the monkey house. Adler, D. A. **Fic**

Cam Jansen, the mystery of the Babe Ruth baseball. Adler, D. A. **Fic**

Cam Jansen, the mystery of the carnival prize. Adler, D. A. **Fic**

Cam Jansen, the mystery of the circus clown. Adler, D. A. **Fic**

Cam Jansen, the mystery of the gold coins. Adler, D. A. **Fic**

Cam Jansen, the mystery of the monster movie. Adler, D. A. **Fic**

Cam Jansen, the mystery of the stolen corn popper. Adler, D. A. **Fic**

Cam Jansen, the mystery of the U.F.O. Adler, D. A. **Fic**

Cam Jansen, the Triceratops Pops mystery. Adler, D. A. **Fic**

Camaros. Niver, H. M. **629.222**

CAMBODIA
Lord, M. A song for Cambodia **92**

CAMBODIA -- ANTIQUITIES
Sobol, R. The mysteries of Angkor Wat **959.6**

CAMBODIA -- FICTION
Half spoon of rice **Fic**

CAMBODIA -- HISTORY -- 1975-
Sonneborn, L. The Khmer Rouge **959.6**

CAMBODIANS -- GREAT BRITAIN -- FICTION
Shevah, E. Dara Palmer's major drama **Fic**

CAMELS
Barnes, J. Camels and llamas at work **636.2**

CAMELS

Carlstrom, Nancy White
It's your first day of school, Annie Claire   E
Jesse Bear, what will you wear?   E

Carluccio, Maria
I'm 3! look what I can do   E
The sounds around town   E

Carman, Patrick
The field of wacky inventions   Fic
Floors   Fic

Carmen learns English. Cox, J.   E

Carmichael, Clay
Wild things   Fic

Carmine. Sweet, M.   E

Carnation, Lily, Lily, Rose. Brewster, H.   Fic

Carnesi, Monica
Little dog lost   636.7
Sleepover with Beatrice and Bear   E

Carney, Elizabeth
Bats   599.4
Everything big cats   599.75
Frogs!   597.8
Great migrations   591.56
Mummies   393
Johns, C. Face to face with cheetahs   599.75
Nichols, M. Face to face with gorillas   599.8
Rosing, N. Face to face with polar bears   599.78

Carney, William, 1840-1908
About
Clinton, C. Hold the flag high   973.7

CARNIVAL
See also Festivals
The **carnival** of the animals. Prelutsky, J.   811

CARNIVALS
See also Amusements; Festivals

CARNIVALS -- FICTION
Almond, D. The Boy who swam with piranhas   Fic
Who stole New Year's Eve?   Fic

Carnivores. Reynolds, A.   E

CARNIVORES -- FICTION
Reynolds, A. Carnivores   E

CARNIVOROUS ANIMALS
Dixon, D. Meat-eating dinosaurs   567.9
Kalman, B. Baby carnivores   599.7

CARNIVOROUS ANIMALS
See also Animals

CARNIVOROUS PLANTS
Aaseng, N. Weird meat-eating plants   583
Gould, M. Meat-eating plants   583
Lawrence, E. Meat-eating plants   575.9

CARNIVOROUS PLANTS
See also Plants

Carole, Bonnie
Junk food, yes or no   613.2

Carolina Harmony. McDowell, M. T.   Fic

Carolinda clatter! Gerstein, M.   E

Caroline Arnold's animals [series]
Arnold, C. A bald eagle's world   598

Arnold, C. A moose's world   **599.65**
Arnold, C. A polar bear's world   **599.78**
Arnold, C. A walrus' world   **599.79**
Arnold, C. A wombat's world   **599.2**

Carolrhoda creative minds book [series]
Mitchell, B. Shoes for everyone: a story about Jan Matzeliger   92

Carolrhoda nature watch book [series]
Johnson, S. A. Crows   598

CAROLS
DePaola, T. Joy to the world   808.8
Groom, J. Silent night   E
Spirin, G. We three kings   782.28

CAROLS
See also Christmas music; Church music; Folk songs; Hymns; Songs; Vocal music

Caron, Lucille
Geometry smarts!   516

Carosella, Melissa
Founding mothers   305.4

CAROUSELS -- FICTION
Hyde, H. S. Feivel's flying horses   E

The **carpenter.**   E

The **carpenter's** gift.   E

Carpenter, Humphrey
The Oxford companion to children's literature   809

Carpenter, Nancy
(il) 11 experiments that failed   E
(il) Bunting, E. Big Bear's big boat   E
(il) Carbone, E. Heroes of the surf   E
(il) Dear Mr. Washington   Fic
(il) Emma Dilemma: big sister poems   811
A letter to my teacher   E
(il) Lucky Ducklings   E
(il) Queen Victoria's Bathing Machine   E
Fleming, C. Imogene's last stand   E
(il) Hopkinson, D. Apples to Oregon   E
Offill, J. 17 things I'm not allowed to do anymore   E
(il) White, L. I could do that!   92

Carpenter, Tad
(il) Burleigh, R. Zoom, zoom   E

CARPENTRY
See also Building

CARPENTRY -- FICTION
Shelby, A. The man who lived in a hollow tree   E

CARPENTRY TOOLS
See also Tools

CARPETBAG RULE *See* Reconstruction (1865-1876)

Carr, Jan
Greedy Apostrophe   E

Carrel, Douglas
(il) Steer, D. The dragon diary   Fic

Carrer, Chiara
(il) Otto Carrotto   E

CARRIAGE AND WAGON MAKING -- UNITED STATES -- HISTORY -- 18TH CENTURY
Petersen, C. The wheelwright   973.2

See also Bibliographic control; Documentation; Library science; Library technical processes

Cataloging correctly for kids. **025.3**

CATALOGING OF MUSIC
   See also Cataloging

CATALOGS -- FICTION
   Samworth, K. Aviary Wonders Inc. Spring Catalog and Instruction Manual **Fic**

Catanese, P. W.
   Dragon games **Fic**
   The End of Time **Fic**
   Happenstance found **Fic**

CATAPULT
   Gurstelle, W. The art of the catapult **623.4**

CATASTROPHES *See* Disasters

CATASTROPHES (GEOLOGY)
   See also Geology

The **catawampus** cat. **E**

Catboy. Walters, E. **Fic**

Catch that baby! Coffelt, N. **E**

Catch the wind, harness the sun. Caduto, M. J. **333.79**

Catch you later, traitor. Avi **Fic**

Catcher. Glaser, J. **796.357**

Catching a storyfish. Harrington, J. N. **Fic**

Catchpool, Michael
   The cloud spinner **E**

Cate, Annette LeBlanc
   Look up! **598**
   The magic rabbit **E**

Cate, Marijke ten
   (il) Heide, I. v. d. A strange day **E**

Catel, Patrick
   Surviving stunts and other amazing feats **613.6**

CATERING
   See also Cooking; Food service

Caterpillar Inc.
   My big book of trucks & diggers **621.8**

Caterpillar to butterfly. Marsh, L. **595.78**

Caterpillars. Latimer, J. P. **595.7**

CATERPILLARS
   See also Butterflies; Moths

CATERPILLARS
   Engle, M. Summer birds: the butterflies of Maria Merian **92**
   Heiligman, D. From caterpillar to butterfly **595.78**
   Latimer, J. P. Caterpillars **595.7**
   Marsh, L. Caterpillar to butterfly **595.78**
   Murawski, D. Face to face with caterpillars **595.7**
   Pasternak, C. How to raise monarch butterflies **595.78**
   Singer, M. Caterpillars **595.7**
   Trueit, T. S. Caterpillars **595.7**

Caterpillars. Trueit, T. S. **595.7**

Caterpillars. Singer, M. **595.7**

CATERPILLARS -- FICTION
   Bruel, R. O. Bob and Otto **E**
   Carle, E. The very hungry caterpillar **E**
   Elwell, P. Adios, Oscar! **E**
   Jarrett, C. Arabella Miller's tiny caterpillar **E**

Lionni, L. Inch by inch **E**
Swope, S. Gotta go! Gotta go! **E**
Ten little caterpillars **E**
The worm whisperer **Fic**

Cates, Karin
   The Secret Remedy Book **E**

CATFISH
   Gray, S. H. Walking catfish **597**

CATHEDRAL OF ST. JOHN THE DIVINE (NEW YORK, N.Y.) -- FICTION
   Me and Momma and Big John **E**

CATHEDRALS
   Macaulay, D. Building the book Cathedral **726.6**
   Macaulay, D. Built to last **729**

CATHEDRALS -- FICTION
   Me and Momma and Big John **E**

Catherine II, the Great, Empress of Russia, 1729-1796
       About
   Krull, K. Lives of extraordinary women **920**

Catherine's story. Moore, G. **E**

Catherine, called Birdy. Cushman, K. **Fic**

CATHOLIC CHURCH -- FICTION
   Durango, J. The walls of Cartagena **Fic**

CATHOLICS
   Cooper, I. Jack **92**
   Hawker, F. Christianity in Mexico **282**

CATHOLICS -- FICTION
   Fixmer, E. Saint training **Fic**
   Littlefield, H. The rooftop adventure of Minnie and Tessa, factory fire survivors **741.5**

Catmull, Katherine
   (jt. auth) Bachmann, S. The Cabinet of Curiosities **S**
   Summer and Bird **Fic**

CATNIP
   Malam, J. Grow your own cat toy **636.8**

Catrow, David
   (il) Beaumont, K. I ain't gonna paint no more! **E**
   (il) Beaumont, K. Where's my t-r-u-c-k? **E**
   (il) Berger, L. Dream dog **E**
   (il) Crow, K. The middle-child blues **E**
   Dinosaur hunt **E**
   (il) Dozens of cousins **E**
   (il) I wanna go home **E**
   (il) Mandel, P. Jackhammer Sam **E**
   (il) Mosquitoes are ruining my summer! **782.42**
   (il) Orloff, K. K. I wanna iguana **E**
   (il) Orloff, K. K. I wanna new room **E**
   (il) Simms, L. Rotten teeth **E**

Cats. Simon, S. **636.8**

CATS
   Arlon, P. Puppies and kittens **636.7**
   Barnes, J. Pet cats **636.8**
   Bidner, J. Is my cat a tiger? **636.8**
   Biniok, J. Mixed breed cats **636.8**
   Bozzo, L. My first cat **636.8**
   Cat **599.75**
   Five creatures **E**

Elliott, D. This orq. (he cave boy.)   **E**
Gerstein, M. The first drawing   **E**
Winter, J. Kali's song   **E**
CAVE ECOLOGY
    Banting, E. Caves   **577.5**
CAVE ECOLOGY
    See also Ecology
CAVE PAINTINGS *See* Cave drawings and paintings
CAVE PAINTINGS -- FICTION
    Barnett, M. Oh no! Not again!   **E**
    Gerstein, M. The first drawing   **E**
CAVE PAINTINGS -- FRANCE -- MONTIGNAC (DOR-DOGNE)
    Discovery in the cave   **944**
Cave, Kathryn
    One child, one seed   **E**
Cavern of secrets.   **Fic**
Caves. Banting, E.   **577.5**
CAVES
    Banting, E. Caves   **577.5**
    Discovery in the cave   **944**
    Lynette, R. Who lives in a deep, dark cave?   **591.7**
    Taylor, P. L. The secret of Priest's Grotto   **940.53**
CAVES -- FICTION
    Wilson, N. D. Leepike Ridge   **Fic**
CAVES -- NEPAL -- MUSTANG (DISTRICT)
    Athans, S. K. Secrets of the sky caves   **796.522**
Cavities and toothaches. Landau, E.   **617.6**
The **cay.** Taylor, T.   **Fic**
Cazet, Denys
    Minnie and Moo and the haunted sweater   **E**
    Minnie and Moo, hooves of fire   **Fic**
    Minnie and Moo, wanted dead or alive   **E**
    The octopus   **E**
    Will you read to me?   **E**
The **cazuela** that the farm maiden stirred.   **E**
CD-I TECHNOLOGY
    See also Compact discs; Optical storage devices
CD-ROMS
    See also Compact discs; Optical storage devices
CDS (COMPACT DISCS) *See* Compact discs
Ceccoli, Nicoletta
    (il) Bernheimer, K. The girl in the castle inside the museum **E**
    (il) Helgerson, J. Horns & wrinkles   **Fic**
    (il) Ogburn, J. K. A dignity of dragons   **398**
Cech, John
    Imagination and innovation   **791.43**
    Jack and the beanstalk   **398.2**
    The nutcracker   **E**
    The princess and the pea   **E**
    Puss in boots   **398.2**
    Rapunzel   **398.2**
Cecil the pet glacier. Harvey, M.   **Fic**
Cecil, Jennifer
    (il) Let's build a playground   **790.06**
Cecil, Randy
    (il) Bluemle, E. How do you wokka-wokka?   **E**

Duck   **E**
    (il) Howe, J. Brontorina   **E**
    (il) Lovabye dragon   **E**
    (il) Lucy   **Fic**
    (il) The runaway tortilla   **398.2**
    (il) Sayre, A. P. One is a snail, ten is a crab   **E**
Cecilia's year. Abraham, S. G.   **Fic**
Ceesay, Isatou
         About
    Paul, M. One plastic bag   **363.7**
Cefrey, Holly
    Researching people, places, and events   **001.4**
Celebrate Chinese New Year. Otto, C.   **394.26**
Celebrate Christmas. Mattern, J.   **394.26**
Celebrate Christmas. Heiligman, D.   **394.26**
Celebrate Cinco de Mayo. Mattern, J.   **394.26**
Celebrate Cinco de Mayo. Otto, C.   **394.26**
Celebrate Diwali. Plum-Ucci, C.   **294.5**
Celebrate Diwali. Heiligman, D.   **294.5**
Celebrate Halloween. Heiligman, D.   **394.26**
Celebrate Hanukkah. Heiligman, D.   **296.4**
Celebrate holidays [series]
    Jeffrey, L. S. Celebrate Martin Luther King, Jr., Day   **394.26**
    Jeffrey, L. S. Celebrate Ramadan   **297.3**
    Jeffrey, L. S. Celebrate Tet   **394.26**
    Mattern, J. Celebrate Christmas   **394.26**
    Mattern, J. Celebrate Cinco de Mayo   **394.26**
    Plum-Ucci, C. Celebrate Diwali   **294.5**
Celebrate Independence Day. Heiligman, D.   **394.26**
Celebrate Kwanzaa. Otto, C.   **394.26**
Celebrate Martin Luther King, Jr., Day. Jeffrey, L. S.   **394.26**
Celebrate Passover. Heiligman, D.   **296.4**
Celebrate Ramadan. Jeffrey, L. S.   **297.3**
Celebrate Ramadan & Eid al-Fitr. Heiligman, D.   **297.3**
Celebrate Rosh Hashanah and Yom Kippur. Heiligman, D.   **296.4**
Celebrate Tet. Jeffrey, L. S.   **394.26**
Celebrate Thanksgiving. Heiligman, D.   **394.26**
Celebrate the 50 states. Leedy, L.   **973**
Celebrate the states [series]
    Altman, L. J. Arkansas   **976.7**
    Baldwin, G. Wyoming   **978.7**
    Bennett, C. Montana   **978.6**
    Bennett, M. Missouri   **977.8**
    Bjorklund, R. Nebraska   **978.2**
    Dornfeld, M. Maine   **974.1**
    Elish, D. Washington, D.C.   **975.3**
    Hoffman, N. West Virginia   **975.4**
    McDaniel, M. Arizona   **979.1**
    McDaniel, M. New Mexico   **972**
    McDaniel, M. North Dakota   **978.4**
    Moragne, W. New Jersey   **974.9**
    Otfinoski, S. New Hampshire   **974.2**
    Schomp, V. New York   **974.7**
    Schuman, M. Delaware   **975.1**
    Schwabacher, M. Minnesota   **977.6**
    Schwabacher, M. Puerto Rico   **972.95**

Shirley, D. Alabama   **976.1**
Stefoff, R. Idaho   **979.6**
Stefoff, R. Nevada   **979.3**
Stefoff, R. Utah   **979.2**
Stefoff, R. Washington   **979.7**
Celebrate the USA. Kuntz, L.   **973**
Celebrate Valentine's Day. Otto, C.   **394.26**
Celebrating a Quinceanera. Hoyt-Goldsmith, D.   **395.2**
Celebrating culture in your library [series]
   Pavon 25 Latino craft projects   **027.62**
Celebrating Ramadan. Hoyt-Goldsmith, D.   **297.3**
A **Celebration** of the Seasons. Brown, M. W.   **E**
CELEBRITIES
   Alcorn, S. A gift of days   **808.88**
   Reusser, K. Celebrities giving back   **361.7**
CELEBRITIES -- DEATH
   Bragg, G. How they croaked   **920**
CELEBRITIES -- FICTION
   Daly, N. A song for Jamela   **E**
Celebrities giving back. Reusser, K.   **361.7**
Celebritrees. Preus, M.   **582.16**
Celenza, Anna Harwell
   Duke Ellington's Nutcracker suite   **E**
   Gershwin's Rhapsody in Blue   **E**
   Saint-Saens's Danse Macabre   **784.2**
CELERY
   See also Vegetables
Celeste's Harlem Renaissance. Tate, E. E.   **Fic**
Celestine, drama queen. Ives, P.   **E**
CELIBACY
   See also Clergy; Religious life
CELL PHONES *See* Cellular telephones
Cell systems. McManus, L.   **570**
CELLISTS -- FICTION
   Flowers for Sarajevo   **E**
CELLO
   See also Stringed instruments
Cells. Lee, K. F.   **571.6**
CELLS
   See also Biology; Physiology; Reproduction
CELLS
   Cohen, M. What is cell theory?   **571.6**
   Green, J. Inside animals   **571**
   Johnson, R. L. Mighty animal cells   **571.6**
   Lee, K. F. Cells   **571.6**
   McManus, L. Cell systems   **570**
   Rand, C. DNA and heredity   **572.8**
CELLULAR PHONES *See* Cellular telephones
CELLULAR TELEPHONES
   Spilsbury, R. The telephone   **621.385**
CELLULAR TELEPHONES
   See also Telephone
CELTIC ART
   See also Art
CELTIC CIVILIZATION
   Green, J. Ancient Celts   **936**
CELTIC MYTHOLOGY -- FICTION

McQuerry, M. D. Beyond the door   **Fic**
CELTS
   Green, J. Ancient Celts   **936**
CEMENT
   See also Adhesives; Building materials; Ceramics; Masonry; Plaster and plastering
CEMETERIES
   Huey, L. M. Forgotten bones   **306.**
CEMETERIES
   See also Burial; Public health; Sanitation
CEMETERIES -- FICTION
   Gaiman, N. The graveyard book graphic novel Volume 1   **741.5**
   Gaiman, N. The graveyard book graphic novel Volume 2   **741.5**
Cendrars, Blaise
   Shadow   **84**
Cendrillon. San Souci, R.   **398.**
CENSORSHIP
   Adams, H. R. Ensuring intellectual freedom and access to information in the school library media program   **027.8**
   Intellectual Freedom Manual   **025.2**
CENSORSHIP
   See also Intellectual freedom
CENSORSHIP -- FICTION
   Downey, J. S. The ninja librarians   **Fic**
   Grabenstein, C. Mr. Lemoncello's Library Olympics   **Fic**
CENSUS
   See also Population; Statistics; Vital statistics
CENSUS -- FICTION
   Davies, J. Tricking the Tallyman   **E**
CENTENARIANS
   Art from her heart: folk artist Clementine Hunter   **92**
   Bartoletti, S. C. Kids on strike!   **331.8**
   Brown, D. Far beyond the garden gate: Alexandra David Neel's journey to Lhasa   **92**
   Warren, A. Pioneer girl   **92**
The **Center** for Cartoon Studies presents Annie Sullivan and the trials of Helen Keller.   **362.4**
The **center** of everything. Urban, L.   **Fic**
Centerburg tales. McCloskey, R.   **Fic**
CENTIPEDES
   Elkin, M. 20 fun facts about centipedes   **595.6**
CENTRAL AMERICA
   Argueta, J. Somos Como Las Nubes / We Are Like the Clouds   **861.64**
CENTRAL AMERICA -- FICTION
   Colato Lainez, R. My shoes and I   **E**
   Voelkel, J. The end of the world club   **Fic**
   Voelkel, J. Middleworld   **Fic**
CENTRAL CANADA
   See also Canada
CENTRAL HIGH SCHOOL (LITTLE ROCK, ARK.)
   Walker, P. R. Remember Little Rock   **37**
CENTRAL PACIFIC RAILROAD
   Halpern, M. Railroad fever   **385**
   Perritano, J. The transcontinental railroad   **385**

Charlie's raven. George, J. C. **Fic**

Charlip, Remy
Fortunately **E**
A perfect day **E**

Charlotte in Giverny. Knight, J. **Fic**

Charlotte in London. Knight, J. **Fic**

Charlotte in New York. Knight, J. **Fic**

Charlotte in Paris. Knight, J. **Fic**

Charlotte the scientist is squished. **E**

Charlotte's web. White, E. B. **Fic**

Charlton, James
Cook, S. Hey batta batta swing! **796.357**

CHARM BRACELETS -- FICTION
Lowry, L. Gooney Bird and all her charms **Fic**

A Charmed Life/ Una Vida Con Suerte. Barbieri, G. E. **E**

CHARMS
See also Folklore; Superstition

CHARTER SCHOOLS
See also Schools

CHARTOGRAPHY *See* Maps

CHARTS, DIAGRAMS, ETC.
Jenkins, S. Animals by the Numbers **590.72**

Chase, Kit
Oliver's tree **E**

Chase, Richard
The Jack tales **398.2**
(ed) Grandfather tales **398.2**

Chasemore, Richard
(il) Reynolds, D. W. Star wars: incredible cross sections **791.43**

Chasing cheetahs. **599.75**

Chasing freedom. Grimes, N. **Fic**

Chasing Redbird. Creech, S. **Fic**

Chasing secrets. Choldenko, G. **Fic**

Chasing the Nightbird. Russell, K. **Fic**

Chasing Vermeer. Balliett, B. **Fic**

Chasse, Jill D.
The babysitter's survival guide **649**

Chast, Roz
Too busy Marco **E**
(il) Martin, S. The alphabet from A to Y with bonus letter, Z! **E**

CHATEAUX *See* Castles

Chatelain, Jeremy
May the stars drip down **E**

CHATHAM (ONT.) -- HISTORY -- 20TH CENTURY -- FICTION
Curtis, C. P. The madman of Piney Woods **Fic**

Chatterton, Martin
The Brain finds a leg **Fic**
The Brain full of holes **Fic**
(il) Kingfisher first thesaurus **423**

Chatton, Barbara
Using poetry across the curriculum **372.6**

Chatzky, Jean
Not your parents' money book **332.024**

Chau, Alina
(il) Double-happiness **E**

Chau, Tungwai
(il) Compestine, Y. C. The runaway rice cake **E**

Chaucer, Geoffrey, d. 1400
About
Cohen, B. Canterbury tales **821**
Cooney, B. Chanticleer and the fox **E**

Chaud, Benjamin
(il) Badescu, R. Pomelo begins to grow **E**
(il) Badescu, R. Pomelo explores color **E**
(il) Badescu, R. Pomelo's Opposites **E**
(il) The bear's song **E**
The bear's sea escape **E**

Chauffrey, Célia
(il) Little Red Riding Hood **E**

Chavela and the Magic Bubble. Brown, M. **E**

Chavez, Cesar, 1927-1993
About
Adler, D. A. A picture book of Cesar Chavez **92**
Bernier-Grand, C. T. Cesar **811**
Krull, K. Harvesting hope **92**

Chayka, Doug
(il) Greene, J. D. The secret shofar of Barcelona **Fic**
(il) Malaspina, A. Yasmin's hammer **Fic**
(il) Williams, K. L. Four feet, two sandals **E**

Cheaney, J. B.
My friend, the enemy **Fic**

CHEATING (EDUCATION)
See also Honesty

CHEATING -- FICTION
Johnson, V. To catch a cheat **Fic**

CHECHNYA (RUSSIA)
Robinson, A. Hamzat's journey **947**

Checkerboard how-to library. Cool recipes for your health [series]
Tuminelly, N. Cool meat-free recipes **641.5**

Checkerboard science library [series]
Wheeler, J. C. Alternative cars **629.222**

CHECKERS
See also Board games

Chedru, Delphine
Spot it again! **793.73**
Spot it! **793.73**

Chee, Cheng-khee
(il) Esbensen, B. J. Swing around the sun **811**

CHEERLEADING -- FICTION
Lester, H. Three cheers for Tacky **E**

The cheese. **E**

CHEESE
Emberley, E. Thanks, Mom! **E**
Peterson, C. Extra cheese, please! **637**

CHEESE -- MICROBIOLOGY
See also Microbiology

A cheese related mishap and other stories. Friesen, R. **741.5**

CHEESEMAKING
See also Dairying

Cheesie Mack is cool in a duel. Cotler, S. **Fic**

Chicken dance. Sauer, T. **E**

A **chicken** followed me home. Page, R. **636.5**

Chicken Little. Kellogg, S. **398.2**

Chicken Little. Emberley, E. **398.2**

Chicken pox. Glaser, J. **616.9**

CHICKEN POX *See* Chickenpox

Chicken pox. Hoffmann, G. **616.9**

The **chicken** problem. Aronson, B. **E**

Chicken said, Cluck! Grant, J. **E**

Chicken scratches. Shannon, G. **811**

The **Chicken** sisters. Numeroff, L. J. **E**

Chicken soup. Van Leeuwen, J. **E**

Chicken soup with rice. Sendak, M. **E**

The **Chicken** Squad. **E**

A Chicken Squad adventure [series]

    The Chicken Squad **E**

    Cronin, D. Into the wild **E**

Chicken Sunday. Polacco, P. **E**

The **chicken** thief. Rodriguez, B. **E**

A **chicken's** life. Dickmann, N. **636.5**

Chicken, chicken, duck! Krilanovich, N. **E**

Chicken, pig, cow and the class pet. Ohi, R. **E**

The **chicken-chasing** queen of Lamar County. Harrington, J. N. **E**

Chickenpox. Landau, E. **616.9**

CHICKENPOX

    See also Diseases; Viruses

CHICKENPOX

    Glaser, J. Chicken pox **616.9**

    Hoffmann, G. Chicken pox **616.9**

    Landau, E. Chickenpox **616.9**

CHICKENPOX -- FICTION

    Cazet, D. The octopus **E**

    Danziger, P. You can't eat your chicken pox, Amber Brown **Fic**

Chickens. Wearing, J. **636.5**

CHICKENS

    Arnold, C. Hatching chicks in room 6 **636.5**

    Asim, J. Preaching to the chickens **92**

    Dickmann, N. A chicken's life **636.5**

    Gibbons, G. Chicks & chickens **636.5**

    Kindschi, T. 4-H guide to raising chickens **636.5**

    Page, R. A chicken followed me home **636.5**

    Wearing, J. Chickens **636.5**

    Where do chicks come from? **636.5**

    Wiles, D. Love, Ruby Lavender **Fic**

CHICKENS -- FICTION

    Ada, A. F. With love, Little Red Hen **E**

    Aronson, B. The chicken problem **E**

    The Bad Guys in mission unpluckable **Fic**

    The buk buk buk festival **E**

    Chicks! **E**

    The Chicken Squad **E**

    Cronin, D. Into the wild **E**

    Davis, A. A hen for Izzy Pippik **Fic**

    I hatched! **E**

    Jones, K. Unusual chickens for the exceptional poultry farmer **Fic**

Last-but-not-least Lola and the wild chicken **Fic**

The legend of Diamond Lil **Fic**

Little Naomi, Little Chick **E**

Marko, C. Let's get cracking! **E**

Paschkis, J. P. Zonka lays an egg **E**

Peggy **E**

Pizzoli, G. Number one Sam **E**

Sam the man and the chicken plan **Fic**

Stoeke, J. M. The Loopy Coop hens **E**

Surfer Chick **E**

Wahl, P. Sonya's chickens **E**

When Aunt Mattie got her wings **E**

CHICKENS -- FOLKLORE

    Baker, K. Big fat hen **398.8**

    Barton, B. The little red hen **398.2**

    Forest, H. The little red hen **398.2**

    Galdone, P. The little red hen **398.2**

    Kimmel, E. A. Medio Pollito **398.2**

    Kimmelman, L. The Little Red Hen and the Passover matzah **398.2**

    Paye Mrs. Chicken and the hungry crocodile **398.2**

    Pinkney, J. The little red hen **398.2**

    Sturges, P. The Little Red Hen (makes a pizza) **398.2**

CHICKENS -- MINNESOTA -- ANECDOTES

    Heppermann, C. City chickens **636.5**

CHICKENS -- POETRY

    Shannon, G. Chicken scratches **811**

The **chickens** build a wall. Dumont **E**

Chickens to the rescue. Himmelman, J. **E**

Chicks & chickens. Gibbons, G. **636.5**

CHICKS

    Arnold, C. Hatching chicks in room 6 **636.5**

Chicks run wild. Bardhan-Quallen, S. **E**

Chicks! **E**

Chief Crazy Horse. Brimner, L. D. **92**

Chief Joseph, 1840-1904. Englar, M. **92**

CHIEF JUSTICES *See* Judges

Chien, Catia

    (il) A boy and a jaguar **E**

    (il) The longest night **E**

    (il) My blue is happy **E**

Chiggers. Jarrow, G. **616.9**

Chiggers. Larson, H. **741.5**

Chik Chak Shabbat. **E**

Chikwanine, Michel

About

    Child Soldier **355**

CHILD ABUSE

    Stewart, S. When Daddy hit Mommy **362.82**

CHILD ABUSE

    See also Child welfare; Domestic violence; Parent-child relationship

CHILD ABUSE -- FICTION

    Mending horses **Fic**

CHILD ACTORS

    See also Actors

CHILD ACTORS -- FICTION

CHILDREN'S POETRY

See also Children's literature; Poetry

CHILDREN'S POETRY

CHILDREN'S POETRY, AMERICAN

CHILDREN'S POETRY, DUTCH -- TRANSLATIONS INTO ENGLISH

CHILDREN'S POETRY, ENGLISH

CHILDREN'S QUESTIONS AND ANSWERS

CHILDREN'S READING *See* Children -- Books and reading; Reading

CIVIL WAR -- UNITED STATES *See* United States -- History -- 1861-1865, Civil War

The **Civil** War era, 1851-1865. McNeese, T.   **973.7**

A **Civil** War scrapbook.   **973.7**

The **Civil** War through the eyes of Abraham Lincoln. Kneib, M.   **973.7**

The **Civil** War, 1840s-1890s. Hernandez, R. E.   **973.7**

The **Civil** War: a visual history.   **973.7**

CIVILIAN EVACUATION *See* Evacuation of civilians; World War, 1939-1945 -- Evacuation of civilians

CIVILIZATION AND SCIENCE *See* Science and civilization

CIVILIZATION, ANCIENT *See* Ancient civilization

CIVILIZATION, ANCIENT

Ancient treasures   **930.1**

Barber, N. Lost cities   **930.1**

Barber, N. Tomb explorers   **930.1**

Panchyk, R. Archaeology for kids   **930.1**

CIVILIZATION, CLASSICAL *See* Classical civilization

CIVILIZATION, MEDIEVAL *See* Medieval civilization

CIVILIZATION, MEDIEVAL

Adkins, J. What if you met a knight?   **940.1**

Ashman, L. Come to the castle!   **940.1**

Durman, L. Castle life   **940.1**

Durman, L. Knights   **940.1**

Galloway, P. Archers, alchemists, and 98 other medieval jobs you might have loved or loathed   **940.1**

León, V. Outrageous women of the Middle Ages   **920.72**

CIVILIZATION, MYCENAEAN

Digging for Troy   **939**

CLAIRVOYANCE -- FICTION

Blackwood, G. L. Second sight   **Fic**

Johnston, J. A very fine line   **Fic**

Kimmel, E. C. Scaredy Kat   **Fic**

Kimmel, E. C. School spirit   **Fic**

Kimmel, E. C. Unhappy medium   **Fic**

Stanley, D. The cup and the crown   **Fic**

Stanley, D. The princess of Cortova   **Fic**

Stanley, D. The silver bowl   **Fic**

CLAMS

Metz, L. Discovering clams   **594**

Clancy & Millie, and the very fine house. Gleeson, L.   **E**

Clang-clang! Beep-beep! Burleigh, R.   **E**

CLANS

    See also Family

Clap your hands. Cauley, L. B.   **E**

Clara. McCully, E. A.   **E**

Clara Barton. Krensky, S.   **92**

Clara Barton. Somervill, B. A.   **92**

Clara Lee and the apple pie dream. Han, J.   **Fic**

Clara Schumann. Reich, S.   **92**

Clarabelle. Peterson, C.   **636.2**

Clare and Francis. Visconti, G.   **271**

Clare, Cassandra, 1973-

Black, H. The copper gauntlet   **Fic**

Black, H. The iron trial   **Fic**

Clare, of Assisi, Saint, 1194-1253

About

Visconti, G. Clare and Francis   **271**

Clarence Cochran, a human boy. Loizeaux, W.   **Fic**

Clarice Bean spells trouble. Child, L.   **Fic**

Clarice Bean, don't look now. Child, L.   **Fic**

Clark, Clara Gillow

Secrets of Greymoor   **Fic**

Clark, David

(il) Dollars and sense   **332.024**

(il) What's for dinner?   **811**

Clark, Diane C.

A kid's guide to Washington, D.C.   **917**

Clark, William, 1770-1838

About

Bodden, V. Through the American West   **978**

Myers, L. Lewis and Clark and me   **Fic**

Perritano, J. The Lewis and Clark Expedition   **978**

Schanzer, R. How we crossed the West   **917**

Clark, Willow

Planes on the move   **629.133**

Clarke, Cat

The Pants Project   **Fic**

Clarke, Ginjer L.

What's Up in the Amazon Rainforest   **577.34**

Clarke, Penny

Hippos   **599.63**

Clarkson, Karen

(il) Saltypie   **92**

Clash of the Worlds. Columbus, C.   **Fic**

Class is not dismissed! Daneshvari, G.   **Fic**

A class of their own [series]

Arato, R. Protists   **579**

Barker, D. M. Archaea   **579.3**

Levine, S. Plants   **580**

Wearing, J. Bacteria   **579.3**

Wearing, J. Fungi   **579**

CLASSES (MATHEMATICS) *See* Set theory

Classic fairy tale collection [series]

Cech, J. Puss in boots   **398.2**

Cech, J. Rapunzel   **398.2**

Classic horse stories.   **808.8**

Classic starts [series]

Namm, D. Greek myths   **398.2**

CLASSICAL ANTIQUITIES

    See also Antiquities

CLASSICAL CIVILIZATION

Helget, N. Barbarians   **940.1**

CLASSICAL MUSICIANS

Krull, K. Lives of the musicians   **920**

CLASSICAL MYTHOLOGY

Aliki The gods and goddesses of Olympus   **292**

Bryant, M. E. Oh my gods!   **292**

Bryant, M. E. She's all that!   **292**

Craft, M. Cupid and Psyche   **292.1**

Curlee, L. Mythological creatures   **292**

Gifts from the gods   **401**

Harris, J. Strong stuff   **398.2**

Keats, E. J. Over in the meadow   **E**

Kerr, J. One night in the zoo   **E**

Langstaff, J. M. Over in the meadow   **782.42**

Lee, H. V. 1, 2, 3 go!   **495.1**

Levine, A. A. Monday is one day   **E**

Ljungkvist, L. Follow the line   **E**

Lobel, A. 10 hungry rabbits   **E**

Lobel, A. One lighthouse, one moon   **E**

Lottridge, C. B. One watermelon seed   **E**

MacDonald, M. R. How many donkeys?   **398.2**

Maloney, P. One foot two feet   **E**

Mannis, C. D. One leaf rides the wind   **E**

Marshall, N. Numbers   **E**

Martin, B. Chicka chicka 1, 2, 3   **E**

Marzollo, J. Help me learn numbers 0-20   **E**

Math-terpieces   **510**

McGrath, B. B. Teddy bear counting   **E**

McKenna, V. Counting lions   **591.68**

Merriam, E. 12 ways to get to 11   **510**

Milich, Z. City 1 2 3   **E**

Moerbeek, K. Count 1 to 10   **E**

Mora, P. Uno, dos, tres: one, two, three   **E**

Morales, Y. Just a minute   **398.2**

Moss, L. Zin! zin! zin! a violin   **E**

Murphy, S. J. Leaping lizards   **E**

Murphy, S. J. Mall mania   **513**

Murray, A. One two that's my shoe!   **E**

Norman, K. Ten on the sled   **E**

Numeroff, L. J. When sheep sleep   **E**

One family   **E**

Otoshi, K. One   **E**

Otoshi, K. Zero   **E**

Pallotta, J. Ocean counting   **E**

Paul, A. W. Count on Culebra   **E**

Peters, L. W. Frankie works the night shift   **E**

Raschka, C. Five for a little one   **E**

Roop, P. Down East in the ocean   **E**

Rose, D. L. One nighttime sea   **513.2**

Rosen, M. J. Chanukah lights   **E**

Rubin, A. How many fish?   **513**

Ruzzier, S. Two mice   **E**

Sayre, A. P. One is a snail, ten is a crab   **E**

Schmandt-Besserat, D. The history of counting   **513.2**

Schwartz, D. M. On beyond a million   **513.5**

Sebe, M. Let's count to 100!   **E**

Seeger, L. V. One boy   **E**

Sendak, M. Bumble-Ardy   **E**

Sendak, M. One was Johnny   **E**

Stack the cats   **E**

Stiegemeyer, J. Seven little bunnies   **E**

Tafuri, N. The big storm   **E**

Tang, G. Math fables   **513**

Ten moonstruck piglets   **E**

Thompson, L. Little Quack   **E**

Thong, R. One is a drummer   **E**

Thornhill, J. The wildlife 1 2 3   **E**

Trapani, I. Haunted party   **E**

Tudor, T. 1 is one   **E**

Wadsworth, O. A. Over in the meadow   **E**

Wells, R. Emily's first 100 days of school   **E**

Werner, S. Bugs by the numbers   **595.**

Williams, S. Let's go visiting   **E**

Wilson, K. A frog in the bog   **E**

Winter, J. Josefina   **513.**

Yoon, S. One, two, buckle my shoe   **E**

Young, C. Ten birds   **E**

Zelinsky, P. O. Knick-knack paddywhack!   **782.4**

Zuffi, S. Art 123   **E**

COUNTING -- FICTION

5 little ducks

Cyrus, K. Billions of bricks

Happy punks 1 2 3

Medina, J. 1 big salad

Sam sorts

Savage, S. Ten orange pumpkins

Tullet, H. 10 times 10

COUNTING BOOKS *See* Counting

Counting by 7s. Sloan, H. G.   **Fi**

Counting crows. Appelt, K.

Counting lions. McKenna, V.   **591.6**

Counting on Grace. Winthrop, E.   **Fi**

Counting sheep. Kelly, J.   **Fi**

COUNTING-OUT RHYMES

Marzollo, J. Help me learn subtraction   **513.**

COUNTRIES *See* Nations

Countries in our world [series]

Brownlie, A. South Africa in our world   **968.0**

Countries of the world [series]

Croy, A. Colombia   **986.**

Croy, A. Guatemala   **972.8**

Croy, A. Spain   **94**

Croy, E. United States   **97.**

Dalal, A. K. India   **95**

Dalal, A. K. Laos   **959.**

Deckker, Z. Brazil   **98**

Deckker, Z. Poland   **943.8**

Deckker, Z. Portugal   **946.**

Giles, B. Nigeria   **966.**

Green, J. Cuba   **972.9**

Green, J. Greece   **949.**

Green, J. Jamaica   **972.9**

Green, J. Vietnam   **959.**

Gruber, B. Mexico   **972**

Jackson, B. New Zealand   **99**

Mace, V. South Africa   **968**

McQuinn, C. Ireland   **941.5**

Phillips, C. Japan   **95.**

Phillips, C. Sweden   **948.5**

Russell, H. Germany   **94.**

Samuels, C. Iraq   **956.**

Shields, S. D. Turkey   **956.**

Turner, K. Australia   **99**

Whitfield, S. Afghanistan   **958.**

Williams, B. Canada   **97**

Young, E. Israel   **956.94**

COUNTRY AND WESTERN MUSIC *See* Country music

The **country** bunny and the little gold shoes. Heyward, D. **E**

Country explorers [series]

Oluonye, M. N. Nigeria   **966.9**

Riehecky, J. China   **951**

COUNTRY LIFE

Barbour, K. Mr. Williams   **92**

Creech, S. Moo   **Fic**

Crews, D. Bigmama's   **92**

Evans, M. G. Spit and sticks   **598.7**

Guest, E. H. Iris and Walter   **E**

Waddell, M. Tiny's big adventure   **E**

COUNTRY LIFE -- ALABAMA -- FICTION

Smith, R. L. Hoodoo   **Fic**

COUNTRY LIFE -- FICTION

Blakemore, M. F. The spy catchers of Maple Hill   **Fic**

Ransom, C. Rebel McKenzie   **Fic**

COUNTRY LIFE -- ILLINOIS -- FICTION

Peck, R. A long way from Chicago   **Fic**

COUNTRY LIFE -- JAPAN

Art and life in rural Japan   **952**

COUNTRY LIFE -- VIRGINIA -- FICTION

Ransom, C. Rebel McKenzie   **Fic**

Reynolds, J. As brave as you   **Fic**

COUNTRY MUSIC

Bertholf, B. Long gone lonesome history of country music   **781.642**

George-Warren, H. Honky-tonk heroes & hillbilly angels **920**

Country road ABC. Geisert, A.   **E**

COUNTY GOVERNMENT

See also Local government

COUNTY LIBRARIES *See* Public libraries; Regional libraries

Coup, W. C., 1857-1895

About

Covert, R. Sawdust and spangles: the amazing life of W.C. Coup   **92**

A **couple** of boys have the best week ever. Frazee, M.   **E**

COUPONS (RETAIL TRADE)

See also Advertising

Courage. Pryor, K. J.   **179**

COURAGE

Belanger, J. What it's like   **179**

Pryor, K. J. Courage   **179**

Waldman, N. A land of big dreamers   **920**

Whelan, G. Homeless bird   **Fic**

COURAGE -- FICTION

Davies, N. The Lion who stole my arm   **Fic**

Gemeinhart, D. Some Kind of Courage   **Fic**

Giff, P. R. Winter sky   **Fic**

Millie Fierce Sleeps Out   **E**

Park, L. S. When my name was Keoko   **Fic**

Reynolds, J. As brave as you   **Fic**

Vere, E. Max the Brave   **E**

Courage for beginners. Harrington, K.   **Fic**

Courage has no color, the true story of the Triple Nickles.

Stone, T. L.   **940.54**

The **courage** test. Preller, J.   **Fic**

The **courageous** princess. Espinosa, R.   **741.5**

COURT LIFE *See* Courts and courtiers

COURTESY

See also Etiquette; Virtue

COURTESY -- FICTION

Watkins, R. Rude cakes   **E**

COURTIERS

Armstrong, A. Raleigh's page   **Fic**

Curry, J. L. The Black Canary   **Fic**

COURTIERS *See* Courts and courtiers

COURTS

See also Law

COURTS -- UNITED STATES

Rodger, E. What is the judicial branch?   **347.73**

COURTS AND COURTIERS

Aliki A medieval feast   **940.1**

COURTS AND COURTIERS -- FICTION

Nielsen, J. A. The false prince   **Fic**

Nielsen, J. A. The runaway king   **Fic**

Stanley, D. The princess of Cortova   **Fic**

COURTSHIP

See also Love

COURTSHIP (ANIMAL BEHAVIOR) *See* Animal courtship

COURTSHIP -- FICTION

Strega Nona does it again   **E**

COURTSHIP OF ANIMALS *See* Animal courtship

Cousens, David

(il) Gifford, C. 10 inventors who changed the world   **920**

(il) Gifford, C. 10 kings & queens who changed the world **920**

COUSINS

See also Family

COUSINS -- FICTION

The bathing costume, or, The worst vacation of my life   **E**

Dozens of cousins   **E**

Fearing, M. The great Thanksgiving escape   **E**

First snow   **E**

Legrand, C. Some kind of happiness   **Fic**

Lester's dreadful sweaters   **E**

Lisle, J. T. The art of keeping cool   **Fic**

Lulu and the hedgehog in the rain   **Fic**

Parry, R. The turn of the tide   **Fic**

Poor Doreen   **E**

Strega Nona does it again   **E**

Cousins of clouds.   **811**

Cousins, Lucy

Hooray for Birds!   **E**

Hooray for fish!   **E**

I'm the best   **E**

Maisy goes to preschool   **E**

(il) Maisy plays soccer   **E**

Yummy   **398.2**

Cousteau, Jacques Yves, 1910-1997

About

Berne, J. Manfish: a story of Jacques Cousteau   **92**

Yaccarino, D. The fantastic undersea life of Jacques Cous-

Shakespeare kids **792.9**

Cox, David
(il) Walker, K. I hate books! **Fic**

Cox, Judy
Butterfly buddies **Fic**
Carmen learns English **E**
Go to sleep, Groundhog! **E**
My family plays music **E**
Nora and the Texas terror **Fic**
One is a feast for Mouse **E**
Puppy power **Fic**
Ukulele Hayley **Fic**

Cox, Lynne
Elizabeth, queen of the seas **E**

Cox, Steve
(il) Fine, A. The diary of a killer cat **Fic**
(il) Kroll, S. Stuff! **E**
(il) Paxton, T. The marvelous toy **782.42**

Coxe, Molly
Branley, F. M. The Big Dipper **523.8**

Coxon, Michele
Termites on a stick **599.8**

Coy, John
Eyes on the goal **Fic**
Game changer **796.323**
Hoop genius **796.323**
Love of the game **Fic**
Strong to the hoop **E**
Their great gift **305.9**
Top of the order **Fic**

Coyne, Jennifer Tarr
Come look with me: discovering women artists for children **704**

Coyote. Swinburne, S. R. **599.77**

COYOTE (LEGENDARY CHARACTER)
Aardema, V. Borreguita and the coyote **398.2**
Johnston, T. The tale of Rabbit and Coyote **398.24**
McDermott, G. Coyote: a trickster tale from the American Southwest **398.2**
Stevens, J. Coyote steals the blanket **398.2**
Taylor, H. P. Coyote places the stars **398.24**
Coyote moon. Gianferrari, M. **599.77**
Coyote places the stars. Taylor, H. P. **398.24**
A **Coyote** solstice tale. King, T. **Fic**
Coyote steals the blanket. Stevens, J. **398.2**
The **coyote** under the table. Hayes, J. **398.2**
Coyote: a trickster tale from the American Southwest. McDermott, G. **398.2**
Coyotes. Mara, W. **599.77**

COYOTES
Gianferrari, M. Coyote moon **599.77**
Mara, W. Coyotes **599.77**
Read, T. C. Exploring the world of coyotes **599.77**
Swinburne, S. R. Coyote **599.77**

COYOTES -- FICTION
Appelt, K. When Otis courted Mama **E**
Blackford, C. Hungry Coyote **E**

King, T. A Coyote solstice tale **Fic**
Puttock, S. Little lost cowboy **E**
Tonatiuh, D. Pancho Rabbit and the coyote **E**

Craats, Rennay
Columbus Day **394.26**
Gecko **639.3**

Crab spiders. Markle, S. **595.4**

CRAB SPIDERS
Markle, S. Crab spiders **595.4**

Crabs. **595.386**

CRABS
Crenson, V. Horseshoe crabs and shorebirds **577.7**
Crabs **595.386**
High tide for horseshoe crabs **595.4**
Gilpin, D. Lobsters, crabs & other crustaceans **595.3**
Marsh, L. Amazing animal journeys **591.56**
Metz, L. Discovering crabs **595.3**

CRABS -- FICTION
Carle, E. A house for Hermit Crab **E**
Goodrich, C. The hermit crab **E**

Crabtree chrome [series]
Newland, S. Extinction! **576.8**

Cracker! Kadohata, C. **Fic**

Craddock, Erik
BC mambo **741.5**

CRADLE SONGS See Lullabies

CRAFT SHOWS
See also Exhibitions; Festivals

Craft, Charlotte
King Midas and the golden touch **398.209**

Craft, Kinuko
(il) Cinderella **398.2**
(il) Craft, C. King Midas and the golden touch **398.209**
Craft, M. F. Sleeping Beauty **398.2**
(il) Craft, M. Cupid and Psyche **292.1**
Mayer, M. Baba Yaga and Vasilisa the brave **398.2**
(il) Mayer, M. Pegasus **292**
(il) The twelve dancing princesses **398.2**

Craft, Mahlon F.
Sleeping Beauty **398.2**

Craft, Marie
Cupid and Psyche **292.1**

CRAFTS (ARTS) See Arts and crafts movement; Handicraft

Crafts for pampering yourself. Blake, S. **745.5**

Crafty Chloe. DiPucchio, K. S. **E**

Craig, David
(il) Hudson **92**
(il) Tanaka, S. Amelia Earhart **92**

Craig, Helen
(il) Holabird, K. Angelina Ballerina **E**
(il) Pearce, P. A finder's magic **Fic**
(il) Root, P. Thirsty Thursday **E**

Craig, Lindsey
Dancing feet! **E**
Farmyard beat **E**

Craigslist. Freese, S. M. **381**

CRAIGSLIST INC.

See also Embroidery

Crews, Donald

Bigmama's   92

Harbor   E

Night at the fair   E

Parade   E

Sail away   E

School bus   E

Shortcut   E

Ten black dots   E

Truck   E

(il) Giganti, P. Each orange had 8 slices   513.5

(il) Giganti, P. How many snails?   513

(il) Schaefer, L. M. This is the sunflower   E

(il) Shannon, G. Tomorrow's alphabet   E

About

Crews, D. Bigmama's   92

Crews, Jeanne Lee

About

Thimmesh, C. Girls think of everything   920

Crews, Kenneth D.

Copyright law for librarians and educators   346.04

Crews, Nina

Below   E

Jack and the beanstalk   398.2

The neighborhood Mother Goose   398.8

The neighborhood sing-along   782.42

Cribb, Joe

Eyewitness money   332.4

The **cricket** in Times Square. Selden, G.   Fic

Cricket song. Hunter, A.   E

CRICKETS

Berger, M. Chirping crickets   595.7

Gonzales, D. Crickets in the dark   595.7

CRICKETS

See also Insects

CRICKETS -- FICTION

Bunting, E. Christmas cricket   E

Carle, E. The very quiet cricket   E

Feldman, T. Harry Cat and Tucker Mouse: Tucker's beetle band   E

Firefly Hollow   Fic

Norac, C. Swing Cafe   E

Selden, G. The cricket in Times Square   Fic

Wheeler, L. Old Cricket   E

Crickets in the dark. Gonzales, D.   595.7

Crickwing. Cannon, J.   E

Crictor. Ungerer, T.   E

CRIME

Schroeder, A. Robbers!   364.15

Somervill, B. A. Graphing crime   364

CRIME

See also Administration of criminal justice; Social problems

CRIME -- FICTION

Pullman, P. Two crafty criminals!   Fic

Turnage, S. The odds of getting even   Fic

CRIME PREVENTION

See also Crime

CRIME PREVENTION -- TECHNOLOGICAL INNOVATIONS

Enz, T. Batman science   600

CRIME STORIES *See* Mystery fiction

Crimi, Carolyn

Dear Tabby   E

Rock 'n' roll Mole   E

CRIMINAL INVESTIGATION

Arroyo, S. L. How crime fighters use math   363.2

Fantaskey, B. Isabel Feeney   Fic

Graham, I. Forensic technology   363.2

Obstfeld, R. Stealing the game   Fic

Townsend, J. Famous forensic cases   363.2

CRIMINAL INVESTIGATION

See also Law enforcement

CRIMINALS -- BIOGRAPHY

Pizzoli, G. Tricky Vic   92

CRIMINALS -- FICTION

Anderson, J. D. Minion   Fic

Black, P. J. Urban outlaws   Fic

Durham, P. Fork-tongue charmers   Fic

Korman, G. Masterminds   Fic

The unexpected life of Oliver Cromwell Pitts   Fic

CRIMINALS -- IDENTIFICATION

See also Criminal investigation; Identification

CRIMINOLOGY *See* Crime

The **crimson** cap. Howard, E.   Fic

Crinkleroot's guide to giving back to nature. Arnosky, J.   333.95

CRIPPLED CHILDREN *See* Children with physical disabilities

CRIPPLED PEOPLE *See* People with physical disabilities

CRISIS MANAGEMENT

See also Management; Problem solving

Crisp, Dan

(il) Butler, D. H. The case of the library monster   Fic

Crispin at the edge of the world. Avi   Fic

Crispin: the cross of lead. Avi   Fic

Criss cross. Perkins, L. R.   Fic

Crist, James J.

Siblings   306.8

What to do when you're sad & lonely   158

What to do when you're scared & worried   158

Cristofori, Bartolomeo, 1655-1732

About

The music of life   92

CRITICAL THINKING

See also Decision making; Logic; Problem solving; Reasoning; Thought and thinking

CRITICISM

See also Aesthetics; Literature; Rhetoric

Critter sitter. Richards, C.   E

CRO-MAGNONS

See also Prehistoric peoples

The **Croaky** Pokey! Long, E.   E

Croatia. Cooper, R.   949.7

CROATIA

  Cooper, R. Croatia   949.7

CROCHETING

  See also Needlework

CROCKERY *See* Pottery

Crockett, Davy, 1786-1836
About
  Green, C. R. Davy Crockett   976.4

  Miller, B. Davy Crockett gets hitched   398.2

Crockett, Sally Ann Thunder Ann Whirlwind
About
  Kellogg, S. Sally Ann Thunder Ann Whirlwind Crockett   398.2

  Miller, B. Davy Crockett gets hitched   398.2

The **crocodile** blues. Polhemus, C.   E

Crocodile vs. wildebeest. Meinking, M.   597.98

Crocodiles. Bodden, V.   597.98

Crocodiles. Markle, S.   597.98

CROCODILES

  See also Reptiles

CROCODILES

  Alligators and crocodiles   597.98

  Bodden, V. Crocodiles   597.98

  Hamilton, S. L. Attacked by a crocodile   597.98

  Jackson, T. Saltwater crocodile   597.98

  Markle, S. Crocodiles   597.98

  Meinking, M. Crocodile vs. wildebeest   597.98

  Pringle, L. P. Alligators and crocodiles!   597.98

  Stewart, M. Alligator or crocodile?   597.98

CROCODILES -- FICTION

  The baby swap   E

  Chen Guji Guji   E

  Chichester-Clark, E. Melrose and Croc: an adventure to remember   E

  Dahl, R. The enormous crocodile   Fic

  Gordon, G. Herman and Rosie   E

  Greenberg, D. Crocs!   E

  John Jensen feels different   E

  The kindhearted crocodile   E

  Lewin, B. You can do it!   E

  Marcellino, F. I, crocodile   E

  O'Neill, G. Monty's magnificent mane   E

  Polhemus, C. The crocodile blues   E

  Princess Cora and the Crocodile   E

  Rayner, C. Solomon Crocodile   E

  Waber, B. The house on East 88th Street   E

  Waber, B. Lyle, Lyle, crocodile   E

  The watermelon seed   E

CROCODILES -- FOLKLORE

  Galdone, P. The monkey and the crocodile   398.2

  McDermott, G. Monkey   398.2

  Paye Mrs. Chicken and the hungry crocodile   398.2

CROCODILES AS PETS -- FICTION

  The kindhearted crocodile   E

Crocs! Greenberg, D.   E

Croft, James

  (il) Surprising Sharks   E

Croll, Carolyn

  (il) Berger, M. Switch on, switch off   537

  (il) Coerr, E. The big balloon race   E

Crompton, Samuel Willard

  The Boston Tea Party   973.3

Cronin, Doreen

  The Chicken Squad   E

  Click, clack, boo   E

  Click, clack, ho ho ho!   E

  Click, clack, moo   E

  Diary of a fly   E

  Diary of a spider   E

  Diary of a worm   E

  Duck for President   E

  Into the wild   E

  The legend of Diamond Lil   Fic

  Smick   E

  The trouble with chickens   Fic

  Wiggle   E

A **crooked** kind of perfect. Urban, L.   Fic

The **crooked** sixpence. Bell, J.   Fic

Crop circles. Helstrom, K.   001.9

CROP CIRCLES

  Helstrom, K. Crop circles   001.9

CROP ROTATION

  See also Agriculture

CROPS *See* Farm produce

Crosby, Jeff

  (il) Banting, E. England   942

  Harness horses, bucking broncos & pit ponies   636.1

  Little lions, bull baiters & hunting hounds   636.7

  Wiener wolf   E

Crosier, Mike

  (il) Climate Change   363.738

CROSS CULTURAL CONFLICT *See* Culture conflict

Cross-country cat. Calhoun, M.   E

CROSS-CULTURAL STUDIES

  See also Culture; Social sciences

CROSS-STITCH

  See also Embroidery

Crossan, Sarah

  The Weight of Water   Fic

The **crossing.** Murphy, J.   973.3

The **crossing.**   E

Crossing Bok Chitto. Tingle, T.   Fic

Crossing the wire. Hobbs, W.   Fic

Crossingham, John

  Spike it volleyball   796.325

Crossley-Holland, Kevin

  How many miles to Bethlehem?   232.9

The **crossover.** Alexander, K.   Fic

The **crossroads.** Grabenstein, C.   Fic

Crossroads America [series]

  Halpern, M. Railroad fever   385

  Rossi, A. Bright ideas   609

  Rossi, A. Freedom struggle   973.7

Curry, Tom
(il) Wojciechowski, S. A fine St. Patrick's day   **E**

The **curse** of the ancient mask and other case files. Cheshire, S.   **Fic**

The **curse** of the chocolate phoenix. Saunders, K.   **Fic**

The **curse** of the night wolf. Stewart, P.   **Fic**

The **curse** of the pharaoh.   **Fic**

Cursed. Coville, B.   **Fic**

CURSES -- FICTION
Abbott, T. The serpent's curse   **Fic**
Lloyd, N. A snicker of magic   **Fic**
Tanquary, K. The night parade   **Fic**

Curtain up! McLean, D.   **792**

Curtis, Andrea
What's for lunch?   **371.7**

Curtis, Christopher Paul
Bud, not Buddy   **Fic**
Elijah of Buxton   **Fic**

Curtis, Christopher Paul
The madman of Piney Woods   **Fic**
The mighty Miss Malone   **Fic**
The Watsons go to Birmingham--1963   **Fic**
         About
Parker-Rock, M. Christopher Paul Curtis   **92**

Curtis, Edward S.
(il) Weave little stars into my sleep   **782.42**

Curtis, Gavin
The bat boy & his violin   **E**

Curtis, Jamie Lee
Big words for little people   **E**
I'm gonna like me   **E**
Is there really a human race?   **E**
My mommy hung the moon   **E**
Tell me again about the night I was born   **E**

Curtis, Jennifer Keats
Animal helpers   **639.9**
Sanctuaries   **636.08**
Seahorses   **597**

Curtis, Stacy
(il) Knudson, M. Raymond & Graham: bases loaded   **Fic**
(il) Knudson, M. Raymond & Graham: cool campers   **Fic**
(il) Knudson, M. Raymond and Graham rule the school   **Fic**
(il) Knudson, M. Raymond and Graham, dancing dudes   **Fic**
(il) Tocher, T. Odd ball   **796.357**

Curto, Rosa M.
(il) Moore-Mallinos, J. I have asthma   **616.2**

Cushman, Doug
Christmas Eve good night   **E**
Dirk Bones and the mystery of the haunted house   **E**
Halloween goodnight   **E**
Inspector Hopper   **E**
Mystery at the Club Sandwich   **E**
Pigmares   **E**
(il) Franco, B. Double play!   **E**
(il) Hazen, L. E. The amazing trail of Seymour Snail   **Fic**
(il) Markel, M. Tyrannosaurus math   **513**
(il) Prelutsky, J. What a day it was at school!   **811**

(il) Weeks, S. Ella, of course!   **E**
(il) Williams, B. Albert's impossible toothache   **E**
(il) Wood, D. What dads can't do   **E**
(il) Yorinks, A. The invisible man   **E**

Cushman, Karen
Alchemy and Meggy Swann   **Fic**
The ballad of Lucy Whipple   **Fic**
Catherine, called Birdy   **Fic**
Matilda Bone   **Fic**
The midwife's apprentice   **Fic**
Rodzina   **Fic**
Will Sparrow's road   **Fic**

Cusick, Dawn
Animal eggs   **591.4**
Get the scoop on animal poop   **590**
Get the Scoop on Animal Snot, Spit & Slime!   **591.5**

Custer, George Armstrong, 1839-1876
         About
Anderson, P. C. George Armstrong Custer   **92**

Cut from the same cloth. San Souci, R.   **398.2**

Cutbill, Andy
The cow that laid an egg   **E**

Cutler, Jane
Guttersnipe   **E**
Leap, frog   **Fic**
Rats!   **Fic**
Rose and Riley   **E**

CUTLERY
Blaxland, W. Knives and forks   **683**

CUTLERY -- FICTION
Maclear, K. Spork   **E**

Cuts, bruises, and breaks. Royston, A.   **617.1**

Cuxart, Bernadette
Modeling clay animals   **738.1**

Cuyler, Margery
100th day worries   **E**
The bumpy little pumpkin   **E**
Hooray for Reading Day!   **E**
The little dump truck   **E**
Monster mess!   **E**
Princess Bess gets dressed   **E**
Skeleton hiccups   **E**
Tick tock clock   **E**
Guinea pigs add up   **E**

CYBERBULLYING
Myers, J. J. Responding to cyber bullying   **371.5**

CYBERBULLYING
   See also Bullies; Computer crimes

CYBERBULLYING -- PREVENTION
Bully   **371.5**

CYBERNETICS
   See also Communication; Electronics; System theory

CYBERSPACE
   See also Computer networks; Space and time

Cyborg. McKissack, P. C.   **Fic**

Cycle of rice, cycle of life. Reynolds, J.   **633.1**

CYCLES

Dale Earnhardt, Jr. Rappoport, K.   **92**

Dale, Anna
  Magical mischief   **Fic**

Dale, Penny, 1954-
  Fine, A. Jamie and Angus together   **Fic**

Dalen & Gole. Deas, M.   **741.5**

Dalena, Antonello
  (il) Salati, G. Race for the Ultrapods   **741.5**

Daley, Michael J.
  Space station rat   **Fic**

DALMATIANS -- FICTION
  Bauer, M. G. Just a dog   **Fic**

Dalton, David, 1945-
  Sikhism   **294.6**

Dalton, John, 1766-1844
About
  McLean, A. What is atomic theory?   **539.7**

Dalton, Pamela
  (il) Brother Sun, Sister Moon   **E**
  (il) Giving thanks   **394.26**

Daly, Cathleen
  Prudence wants a pet   **E**
  Emily's blue period   **E**

Daly, James
  Zuckerman, A. 2030   **600**

Daly, Jude
  (il) Brooks, J. Let there be peace   **242**
  (il) Buzzeo, T. Inside the books   **E**
  (il) Conway, D. Lila and the secret of rain   **E**
  (il) Cunnane, K. Chirchir is singing   **E**
  Sivu's six wishes   **E**
  (il) McGill, A. Way up and over everything   **398.2**

Daly, Niki
  Bettina Valentino and the Picasso Club   **Fic**
  (il) Borden, L. The greatest skating race   **Fic**
  (il) Gregorowski, C. Fly, eagle, fly!   **398.2**
  (il) Moses, S. P. Sallie Gal and the Wall-a-kee man   **Fic**
  Pretty Salma   **E**
  A song for Jamela   **E**
  Welcome to Zanzibar Road   **E**

Daly, Ruth
  Mandrills   **599.86**

Damerum, Kanako
  Horowitz, A. Stormbreaker: the graphic novel   **741.5**

Damkoehler, Katrina
  (il) Berlin, E. The potato chip puzzles   **Fic**

DAMS
  Macaulay, D. Building big   **720**

DAMS
  See also Civil engineering; Hydraulic structures; Water supply

DAMS -- DESIGN AND CONSTRUCTION
  Nagelhout, R. How do dams work?   **627.8**
  Stefoff, R. Building dams   **627.8**

Dance. Fishkin, R. L.   **793.3**

DANCE
  Collins, P. L. I am a dancer   **792.8**

Fishkin, R. L. Dance   **793.3**
Garofoli, W. Hip-hop dancing   **793.3**
Hardy, A. Dancers of the World   **E**
Marsico, K. Choreographer   **792.8**
Nathan, A. Meet the dancers   **920**
Reid, R. Shake & shout   **027.62**
Relota, A. Carla and Leo's world of dance   **792.8**
Smith, C. L. Jingle dancer   **E**
Young, A. Belinda, the ballerina   **E**

DANCE
  See also Amusements; Performing arts

DANCE -- AFRICA
  Keeler, P. A. Drumbeat in our feet   **793.3**

DANCE -- FICTION
  Capucilli, A. S. Katy Duck and the tip-top tap shoes   **E**
  Feiffer, J. Rupert Can Dance   **E**
  I got the rhythm   **E**
  Idle, M. Flora and the flamingo   **E**
  Idle, M. Flora and the peacocks   **E**
  Idle, M. Flora and the penguin   **E**
  Kinney, J. The third wheel   **Fic**
  McElmurry, J. Mario makes a move   **E**
  Mister Whistler   **Fic**
  Ray, M. L. Deer dancer   **E**
  The twelve dancing princesses   **398.2**
  Walsh, E. S. Hop Jump   **E**

DANCE -- STUDY AND TEACHING -- FICTION
  Isadora, R. Bea at ballet   **E**

Dance by the light of the moon. Ryder, J.   **E**

DANCE DIRECTORS
  Bernier-Grand, C. T. Alicia Alonso   **92**

DANCE IN ART
  Invitation to ballet   **792.8**

A **dance** like starlight.   **E**

DANCE MUSIC
  See also Music

DANCE MUSIC -- FICTION
  Engle, M. Drum dream girl   **E**

DANCE RECITALS -- FICTION
  McClintock, B. Emma and Julia love ballet   **E**

DANCE TEACHERS
  Tallchief, M. Tallchief   **92**

Dance, Nana, dance. Hayes, J.   **398.2**

DANCERS
  Ballet for Martha   **792.8**
  Barasch, L. Knockin' on wood   **92**
  Gauch, P. L. Tanya and the red shoes   **E**
  Gladstone, V. A young dancer   **792.8**
  Nathan, A. Meet the dancers   **920**
  Orgill, R. Footwork   **92**
  Powell, P. H. Josephine   **92**
  Schubert, L. Ballet of the elephants   **791.8**
  Stompin' at the Savoy   **92**
  Winter, J. Jazz age Josephine   **92**

DANCERS
  See also Entertainers

DANCERS -- FICTION

Dayrell, Elphinstone

Why the Sun and the Moon live in the sky   **398.2**

DAYS

   See also Calendars

DAYS -- FICTION

  Himmelman, J. Chickens to the rescue   **E**

  Lobel, A. One lighthouse, one moon   **E**

  Pullen, Z. Friday my Radio Flyer flew   **E**

Days of change [series]

  Bodden, V. Columbus reaches the New World   **970.01**

  Riggs, K. The French Revolution   **944.04**

Days to celebrate. Hopkins, L. B.   **051**

Daytime visions. Isol   **E**

The **Daytona** 500. Pimm, N. R.   **796.72**

Daywalt, Drew

  The day the crayons came home   **E**

  The day the crayons quit   **E**

  The legend of rock paper scissors   **E**

The **dazzle** disaster dinner party. Draper, S. M.   **Fic**

Dazzling dragonflies. Glaser, L.   **595.7**

Dazzling science projects with light and color. Gardner, R. **535**

DC super heroes. Batman [series]

  Dahl, M. The man behind the mask   **Fic**

DC super heroes: The Flash [series]

  Sonneborn, S. Shell shocker   **Fic**

DC super heroes: Green Lantern [series]

  Dahl, M. Guardian of Earth   **Fic**

DC super heroes: The ultimate pop-up book. Reinhart, M. **741.5**

DC super-pets! [series]

  Sazaklis, J. Royal rodent rescue   **Fic**

De Angeli, Marguerite Lofft

  The door in the wall   **Fic**

  Thee, Hannah!   **Fic**

De Carlo, Mike

  (il) Sonneborn, S. Shell shocker   **Fic**

De colores.   **782.42**

De colores and other Latin-American folk songs for children.   **781.62**

De Cristofano, Carolyn Cinami

  The sun and the moon   **523**

De Fombelle, Timothée, 1973-

  Toby alone   **Fic**

De Goldi, Kate

  The ACB with Honora Lee   **Fic**

De Groat, Diane

  Ants in your pants, worms in your plants!   **E**

  Brand-new pencils, brand-new books   **E**

  No more pencils, no more books, no more teacher's dirty looks!   **E**

  Trick or treat, smell my feet   **E**

  (il) Charlie the ranch dog   **E**

  (il) Fitzgerald, J. D. The Great Brain is back   **Fic**

  (il) Gilson, J. Bug in a rug   **Fic**

  (il) Shreve, S. R. The flunking of Joshua T. Bates   **Fic**

De Guzman, Michael

  Henrietta Hornbuckle's circus of life   **Fic**

De la Peña, Matt

Last stop on Market Street   **E**

A nation's hope   **92**

De las Casas, Dianne

  The gigantic sweet potato   **398.2**

  Tell along tales!   **027.62**

De Lint, Charles, 1951-

  The cats of Tanglewood Forest   **Fic**

  Seven wild sisters   **Fic**

De los Santos, Marisa

  (jt. auth) Teague, D. Saving Lucas Biggs   **Fic**

De Medeiros, Michael

  Screws   **621.8**

De Mouy, Iris

  Naptime   **E**

De Quay, John Paul

  (il) Stickmen's guide to watercraft   **623.82**

De Quidt, Jeremy

  The toymaker   **Fic**

De Regniers, Beatrice Schenk

  Little sister and the month brothers   **398.2**

  May I bring a friend?   **E**

De Roo, Elena

  The rain train   **E**

De Seve, Peter

  De Seve, R. The Duchess of Whimsy   **E**

  Helgerson, J. Crows & cards   **Fic**

De Seve, Randall

  The Duchess of Whimsy   **E**

  A fire truck named Red   **E**

  Peanut and Fifi have a ball   **E**

De Smet, Marian

  I have two homes   **E**

De Tagyos, Paul Ratz

  (il) Ferret fun   **E**

De Vries, Maggie

  Fraser bear   **599.78**

Deacon, Alexis

  I am Henry Finch   **E**

  A place to call home   **E**

  (il) Hicks, B. J. Jitterbug jam   **E**

DEAD

   See also Burial; Cremation; Death; Funeral rites and ceremonies; Obituaries

DEAD -- FICTION

  Gaiman, N. The graveyard book graphic novel Volume 2   **741.5**

  Great ball of light   **Fic**

  The key of Braha   **Fic**

The **Dead** Bird. Brown, M. W.   **E**

Dead end in Norvelt. Gantos, J.   **Fic**

The Deadlies [series]

  Lasky, K. Felix takes the stage   **Fic**

  Lasky, K. Spiders on the case   **Fic**

Deadliest animals. Stewart, M.   **591.6**

Deadly black widows. Lunis, N.   **595.4**

DEAF

  Alexander, S. H. She touched the world: Laura Bridgman,

deaf-blind pioneer   **92**
Amoroso, C. Helen Keller   **92**
Delano, M. F. Helen's eyes   **92**
Gerber, C. Annie Jump Cannon, astronomer   **92**
Lawlor, L. Helen Keller: rebellious spirit   **92**
McCully, E. A. My heart glow: Alice Cogswell, Thomas Gallaudet and the birth of American sign language   **92**
Millman, I. Moses goes to school   **E**
Sullivan, G. Helen Keller   **92**

DEAF
     See also Hearing impaired; People with physical disabilities

DEAF -- EDUCATION
Hauser, P. C. How deaf children learn   **371.91**
Wyckoff, E. B. Sign language man: Thomas H. Gallaudet and his incredible work   **92**

DEAF -- FICTION
Rosner, J. The mitten string   **E**
The sound of all things   **E**

DEAF -- INSTITUTIONAL CARE
     See also Institutional care

DEAF -- MEANS OF COMMUNICATION
Hauser, P. C. How deaf children learn   **371.91**
Wyckoff, E. B. Sign language man: Thomas H. Gallaudet and his incredible work   **92**

DEAF -- MEANS OF COMMUNICATION
     See also Communication

DEAF -- SIGN LANGUAGE *See* Sign language

DEAF ATHLETES -- BIOGRAPHY
Silent star   **796.357**

DEAF CHILDREN
Bell, C. El deafo   **741.5**
Gordon, J. M. The Gallaudet children's dictionary of American Sign Language   **419**
Hauser, P. C. How deaf children learn   **371.91**

DEAF CHILDREN -- UNITED STATES -- EDUCATION
Gordon, J. M. The Gallaudet children's dictionary of American Sign Language   **419**
The **deaf** musicians.   **E**

DEAFBLIND WOMEN -- UNITED STATES -- BIOGRAPHY
Annie and Helen   **362.4**
Rappaport, D. Helen's big world   **362.4**

DEAFNESS
Levete, S. Explaining deafness   **617.8**
Dealing with dragons. Wrede, P. C.   **Fic**

Dean, David
(il) Crane, N. Barefoot Books world atlas   **912**
(il) St. John, L. The white giraffe   **Fic**

Dean, James
(il) Litwin, E. Pete the Cat   **E**

Deans, Karen
Playing to win: the story of Althea Gibson   **92**

Dear America [series]
Pinkney, A. D. With the might of angels   **Fic**
Dear baobab. Foggo, C.   **E**
Dear Benjamin Banneker. Pinkney, A. D.   **520**

Dear dragon. Funk, J.   **E**
Dear fish. Gall, C.   **E**
Dear George Clooney. Nielsen, S.   **Fic**
Dear hot dog. Gerstein, M.   **811**
Dear hound. Murphy, J.   **Fic**
Dear Juno. Pak, S.   **E**
Dear Mr. Henshaw. Cleary, B.   **Fic**
Dear Mr. Rosenwald. Weatherford, C. B.   **Fic**
Dear Mr. Washington.   **Fic**
Dear Mrs. LaRue. Teague, M.   **E**
Dear Primo. Tonatiuh, D.   **E**
Dear Tabby. Crimi, C.   **E**
Dear teacher. Husband, A.   **E**
Dear Tyrannosaurus Rex. McClatchy, L.   **E**
Dear Vampa. Collins, R.   **E**
Dear Wandering Wildebeest. Latham, I.   **811**
Dear Yeti. Kwan, J.   **E**

Deas, Mike
Dalen & Gole   **741.5**
O'Donnell, L. Power play   **741.5**
Death. Murphy, P. J.   **155.9**

DEATH
     See also Biology; Eschatology; Life

DEATH
Bragg, G. How they croaked   **920**
Brown, L. K. When dinosaurs die   **155.9**
Demas, C. Saying goodbye to Lulu   **E**
Harris, R. H. Goodbye, Mousie   **E**
Kornblatt, M. Izzy's place   **Fic**
Krementz, J. How it feels when a parent dies   **155.9**
Murphy, P. J. Death   **155.9**
Raschka, C. The purple balloon   **155.9**
Thornhill, J. I found a dead bird   **306.9**
Wiles, D. Love, Ruby Lavender   **Fic**
The death (and further adventures) of Silas Winterbottom [series]
Giles, S. M. The body thief   **Fic**

DEATH -- FICTION
The 9 lives of Alexander Baddenfield   **Fic**
Coggin, L. The dog, Ray   **Fic**
Cry, Heart, but Never Break   **E**
Every single second   **Fic**
Hayes, G. Benny and Penny in How to say goodbye   **741.5**
Holczer, T. The secret hum of a daisy   **Fic**
Huneck, S. Sally goes to Heaven   **E**
My father's arms are a boat   **E**

DEATH -- POETRY
Smith, H. A. Mother poems   **811**

DEATH AND CHILDREN *See* Children and death
Death and disease. Woolf, A.   **610**

DEATH IN LITERATURE
Lewis, J. P. Last laughs   **818**

DEATH MASKS *See* Masks (Sculpture)
DEATH NOTICES *See* Obituaries
Death of a dreamer. Behnke, A. M.   **92**
The **Death** of the Hat. Janeczko, P. B.   **808.81**
Death of the iron horse. Goble, P.   **E**

Designing a school library media center for the future. Erikson, R. **027.8**

Desimini, Lisa
- (il) Aardema, V. Anansi does the impossible! **398.209**
- (il) Annino, J. G. She sang promise: the story of Betty Mae Jumper, Seminole tribal leader **92**
- (il) Doodle dandies **811**
- (il) The great big green **535.6**
- (il) Lewis, J. P. The snowflake sisters **E**

Desk stories. O'Malley, K. **741.5**

Desmond, Viola Irene
About
Warner, J. Viola Desmond won't be budged! **92**

The **desperate** dog writes again. Christelow, E. **E**

Desperate journey. Murphy, J. **Fic**

Despite all obstacles: La Salle and the conquest of the Mississippi. Goodman, J. E. **92**

Desrocher, Jack
- (il) Donovan, S. Keep your cool! **616.85**
- (il) Johnson, R. L. Amazing DNA **572.8**
- (il) Johnson, R. L. Mighty animal cells **571.6**

Desrosiers, Sylvie
- Hocus Pocus **E**

Dessert first. Durand, H. **Fic**

DESSERTS
- Bowers, S. Ghoulish goodies **641.5**
- Dunnington, R. Sweet eats **641.8**

DESSERTS
See also Cooking

DESSERTS -- FICTION
Bosch, P. This book is not good for you **Fic**

DeStefano, Lauren
- A curious tale of the in-between **Fic**
- The peculiar night of the blue heart **Fic**

Destination solar system [series]
Sparrow, G. Destination Uranus, Neptune, and Pluto **523.4**

Destination Uranus, Neptune, and Pluto. Sparrow, G. **523.4**

Destination: Mars. **523.43**

Destination: Rocky Mountains. Grupper, J. **978**

DESTITUTION *See* Poverty

DETECTIVE AND MYSTERY STORIES
- Jones, R. L. Wild boy and the black terror **Fic**
- Pastis, S. Timmy failure: now look what you've done **Fic**
- Teague, D. Saving Lucas Biggs **Fic**

DETECTIVE AND MYSTERY STORIES *See* Mystery fiction

Detective Dinosaur undercover. Skofield, J. **E**

DETECTIVE FICTION *See* Mystery fiction

Detective Gordon. Nilsson, U. **Fic**

Detective Gordon [series]
A Case in Any Case **Fic**

DETECTIVE STORIES *See* Mystery fiction

The **detective's** assistant. Hannigan, K. **Fic**

DETECTIVES
See also Police

DETECTIVES -- FICTION
A Case in Any Case **Fic**

The case of the stolen sixpence **Fic**

Gardner, S. Three Pickled Herrings 2 **Fic**

Grey, M. Hermelin the detective mouse **E**

Lawrence, C. P.K. Pinkerton and the pistol-packing widows **Fic**

Nilsson, U. A Complicated Case **E**

Pastis, S. Timmy failure: now look what you've done **Fic**

Venable, C. A. F. Raining cats and detectives **Fic**

DETECTOR DOGS
- Castaldo, N. F. Sniffer dogs **636.7**
- Wadsworth, G. Poop detectives **636.7**

The **detention** club. Yoo, D. **Fic**

DETENTION OF PERSONS -- FICTION
Danticat, E. Mama's nightingale **E**

DETERGENT POLLUTION OF RIVERS, LAKES, ETC.
See Water pollution

DETERMINATION (PERSONALITY TRAIT) -- FICTION
- Breen, S. Woodpecker wants waffles **E**
- Eliza Bing is (not) a big, fat quitter **Fic**
- Ishida, S. Little Kunoichi, the ninja girl **E**
- Turkey Tot **E**

Detlefsen, Lisl H.
Time for cranberries **E**

DETROIT TIGERS (BASEBALL TEAM) -- FICTION
Lupica, M. The batboy **Fic**

Detwiler, Susan
(il) Cohn, S. One wolf howls **599.77**

Deutsch, Barry
Hereville: how Mirka got her sword **741.5**

Devastated by a volcano! Person, S. **551.2**

DEVELOPING COUNTRIES
See also Economic conditions; Industrialization

DEVELOPING COUNTRIES -- COMMERCE
See also Commerce

DEVELOPMENT *See* Embryology; Evolution; Growth disorders; Modernization (Sociology)

DEVELOPMENTAL PSYCHOLOGY
See also Psychology

Devi, Dulari
About
Devi, D. Following my paint brush **92**

DEVIANT BEHAVIOR
See also Human behavior

DEVIL -- FICTION
- Babbitt, N. The Devil's storybook **S**
- Tegen, K. The story of the Jack O'Lantern **E**

The **devil's** door. Thompson, P. B. **Fic**

The **Devil's** storybook. Babbitt, N. **S**

Devlin, Jane
Hattie the bad **E**

Devorkin, David
Pluto's secret **523.49**

DEVOTION *See* Prayer; Worship

DEVOTIONAL CALENDARS
See also Calendars; Devotional literature

DEVOTIONAL THEOLOGY *See* Devotional exercises; Prayer

DISEASES AND PESTS *See* Agricultural bacteriology; Agricultural pests; Fungi; Household pests; Insect pests; Parasites; Plant diseases

DISEASES OF ANIMALS *See* Animals -- Diseases

Disenchanted. Morrison, M.   **Fic**

DISGUISE

    See also Costume; Deception

DISGUISE -- FICTION

  Hoot owl, master of disguise   **E**

  Lawrence, C. P.K. Pinkerton and the pistol-packing widows   **Fic**

  Miéville, C. The worst breakfast   **E**

Disgusting & dreadful science [series]

  Claybourne, A. Gut-wrenching gravity and other fatal forces   **531**

Disgusting critters [series]

  Gravel, É. The fly   **595.77**

Disgusting food invaders. Owen, R.   **615.9**

DISHES *See* Porcelain; Pottery; Tableware

DISHONESTY *See* Honesty

DISINFECTION AND DISINFECTANTS

    See also Hygiene; Pharmaceutical chemistry; Public health; Sanitation

Disney's Hero Squad: Ultraheroes [series]

  Salati, G. Race for the Ultrapods   **741.5**

DISSENTERS

  Atkins, J. Anne Hutchinson's way   **92**

  Krull, K. Lives of extraordinary women   **920**

The dissenters [series]

  Millet, L. The fires beneath the sea   **Fic**

DISSERTATIONS

    See also Research

Distance, area, and volume. Somervill, B. A.   **516**

DISTRICT ATTORNEYS

  Gitlin, M. Sonia Sotomayor   **92**

  McElroy, L. T. Sonia Sotomayor   **92**

  Otfinoski, S. Grover Cleveland   **92**

  Winter, J. Sonia Sotomayor   **92**

District of Columbia. Sonneborn, L.   **975.3**

Ditchfield, Christin

  Shwatsit!   **E**

  Wrestling   **796.8**

DiTerlizzi, Angela

  Some bugs   **E**

DiTerlizzi, Tony

  (il) The battle for WondLa   **Fic**

  A hero for WondLa   **Fic**

  Kenny & the dragon   **Fic**

  The search for WondLa   **Fic**

  (il) Howitt, M. B. The spider and the fly   **821**

Dith Pran, 1942-2008

    About

  Sonneborn, L. The Khmer Rouge   **959.6**

Divakaruni, Chitra Banerjee

  The conch bearer   **Fic**

  Grandma and the great gourd   **E**

DIVALI

  Heiligman, D. Celebrate Diwali   **294.5**

  MacMillan, D. M. Diwali--Hindu festival of lights   **394.26**

  Plum-Ucci, C. Celebrate Diwali   **294.5**

DIVALI -- FICTION

  Rahaman, V. Divali rose   **E**

Divali rose. Rahaman, V.   **E**

Dive into reading [series]

  Want to play?   **E**

Dive! Earle, S. A.   **551.46**

Dive! Hopkinson, D.   **940.54**

DIVERS

  Berne, J. Manfish: a story of Jacques Cousteau   **92**

  Reichard, S. E. Who on earth is Sylvia Earle?   **92**

  Yaccarino, D. The fantastic undersea life of Jacques Cousteau   **92**

  Yoo, P. Sixteen years in sixteen seconds   **92**

DIVERSITY IN THE WORKPLACE

    See also Multiculturalism; Personnel management

DIVERSITY MOVEMENT *See* Multiculturalism

DIVERSITY, BIOLOGICAL *See* Biodiversity

Divide and ride. Murphy, S. J.   **513**

DIVING

  Hoblin, P. Swimming & diving   **797.2**

  Yoo, P. Sixteen years in sixteen seconds   **92**

DIVING

    See also Swimming; Water sports

DIVING -- FICTION

  Jabari Jumps   **E**

Diving to a deep-sea volcano. Mallory, K.   **551.46**

DIVISION

  Murphy, S. J. Divide and ride   **513**

  Nagda, A. W. Cheetah math   **513**

  Perritano, J. Mummies in the library   **513.2**

DIVISION

    See also Arithmetic

DIVISION -- FICTION

  Hutchins, P. The doorbell rang   **E**

  McElligott, M. Bean thirteen   **E**

DiVito, Anna

  (il) A kid's guide to America's first ladies   **973.09**

  (il) Holub, J. Why do birds sing?   **598**

  (il) Krull, K. A kid's guide to America's Bill of Rights   **342**

DIVORCE

  Brown, L. K. Dinosaurs divorce   **306.89**

  Danziger, P. Amber Brown is green with envy   **Fic**

  Holyoke, N. A smart girl's guide to her parents' divorce **306.89**

DIVORCE

    See also Family

DIVORCE -- FICTION

  De Smet, M. I have two homes   **E**

  Klise, K. Homesick   **Fic**

  Ten   **Fic**

Diwali--Hindu festival of lights. MacMillan, D. M.   **394.26**

Dixie. Gilman, G.   **E**

Dixon, Debra Spina

  (il) Jacobs, P. D. Putting on a play   **792**

Dixon, Dougal

DOG WALKING -- FICTION

Greenwald, L. Welcome to Dog Beach **Fic**
Long, E. Pug **E**
The **dog** who belonged to no one. Hest, A. **E**
The **dog** who cried wolf. Kasza, K. **E**
Dog who saved Santa. Kelley, T. **E**
A **dog's** way home. Pyron, B. **Fic**
The **dog**, Ray. Coggin, L. **Fic**
Dogerella. Boelts, M. **E**
Doggie dreams. Herrod, M. **741.5**
Doggy slippers. Lujan, J. **811**
Doggy whys. Prap, L. **636.7**
The **doghouse.** Thomas, J. **E**
Dogku. **811**
Doglands. Willocks, T. **Fic**
Dogs. Jeffrey, L. S. **636.7**
Dogs. Simon, S. **636.7**

DOGS

See also Domestic animals; Mammals

DOGS

Arlon, P. Puppies and kittens **636.7**
Baines, B. Everything dogs **636.7**
Barnes, J. Pet dogs **636.7**
Bial, R. Rescuing Rover **636.7**
Bidner, J. Is my dog a wolf? **636.7**
Big Dogs, Little Dogs **636.7**
Biniok, J. The miniature schnauzer **636.7**
Biniok, J. The rottweiler **636.7**
Blake, R. J. Togo **798.8**
Buckley, C. Tarra & Bella **599.67**
Calmenson, S. May I pet your dog? **636.7**
Calmenson, S. Rosie **636.7**
Carnesi, M. Little dog lost **636.7**
Choldenko, G. Notes from a liar and her dog **Fic**
Coren, S. Why do dogs have wet noses? **636.7**
Crosby, J. Little lions, bull baiters & hunting hounds **636.7**
DeFelice, C. C. The ghost of Cutler Creek **Fic**
Demas, C. Saying goodbye to Lulu **E**
Dennis, B. Nubs **636.7**
DePaola, T. Meet the Barkers **E**
DiCamillo, K. Because of Winn-Dixie **Fic**
Estes, E. Ginger Pye **Fic**
Gagne, T. West Highlands, Scotties, and other terriers **636.755**
Gaines, A. Top 10 dogs for kids **636.7**
George, J. C. How to talk to your dog **636.7**
Gewirtz, E. W. The bulldog **636.7**
Gipson, F. B. Old Yeller **Fic**
Godwin, L. Happy and Honey **E**
Goldish, M. Baghdad pups **956.7**
Goodman, S. E. It's a dog's life **636.7**
Graham, B. Let's get a pup, said Kate **E**
Grogan, J. Marley **636.7**
Hardy, A. Dancers of the World **E**
Harper, D. Sit, Truman! **E**
Hart, J. Big dogs **636.7**
Hart, J. Small dogs **636.7**
Hearne, B. G. The canine connection: stories about dogs and

people **E**
Hoffman, M. A. Herding dogs **636.7**
Hoffman, M. A. Police dogs **363.2**
Houston, D. Bulu, African wonder dog **636.7**
Huneck, S. Even bad dogs go to heaven **636.7**
Huneck, S. Sally goes to the beach **E**
Jackson, E. A home for Dixie **636.7**
Jeffrey, L. S. Dogs **636.7**
Jenkins, S. Dogs and cats **636.7**
Johnson, J. Dogs and puppies **636.7**
Kate and Pippin **E**
Laidlaw, R. No shelter here **636.7**
Larson, K. Two Bobbies **636.08**
Leedy, L. Mapping Penny's world **912**
Lunis, N. Greyhound **636.7**
McDonald, M. Shoe dog **E**
Mehus-Roe, K. Dogs for kids! **636.7**
Miller, D. S. The great serum race **798.8**
Miller, S. S. Three more stories you can read to your dog **E**
Morn, S. B. The pug **636.7**
Myers, W. D. The blues of Flats Brown **E**
Newman, L. Hachiko waits **Fic**
Niven, F. L. Learning to care for a dog **636.7**
O'Connor, J. The perfect puppy for me **E**
Patent, D. H. Saving Audie **636.7**
Paulsen, G. My life in dog years **813**
Prap, L. Doggy whys **636.7**
Rockwood, L. Dogs are smart! **636.7**
Santiago stays **E**
Schweitzer, K. The beagle **636.7**
Schweitzer, K. The dachshund **636.7**
Selbert, K. War dogs **E**
Simon, S. Dogs **636.7**
Simont, M. The stray dog **E**
Staake, B. The First Pup **973.932**
Teague, M. Dear Mrs. LaRue **E**
Weatherford, C. B. First pooch **973.932**

DOGS -- BEHAVIOR

George, J. C. How to talk to your dog **636.7**
Goodman, S. E. It's a dog's life **636.7**
Rutherford, C. A dog is a dog **636.7**
Weitzman, G. How to Speak Dog **636.7**

DOGS -- BREEDING

O'Brien, A. Lara's gift **Fic**

DOGS -- EVOLUTION

Goodman, S. E. It's a dog's life **636.7**

DOGS -- FICTION

Agee, J. It's only Stanley **E**
Appelt, K. Mogie **E**
Ball **E**
Barkus **E**
Bauer, M. G. Just a dog **Fic**
Bauer, M. D. Little dog, lost **Fic**
Beaumont, K. Crybaby **E**
Berger, L. Dream dog **E**
Berry, L. Pig and Pug **E**
Bow-wow wiggle waggle **E**

DOGS -- FOLKLORE

DOGS -- GRAPHIC NOVELS

DOGS -- GREAT BRITAIN

DOGS -- HABITS AND BEHAVIOR

DOGS -- HUMOR

DOGS -- POETRY

About

Jones, C. Sarah Emma Edmonds was a great pretender **92**

Nurse, soldier, spy: the story of Sarah Edmonds, a Civil War hero **92**

EDMONTOSAURUS

See also Dinosaurs

Edmunds, Kirstie

(il) The monster who lost his mean **E**

Edmundson, Chris

Yeti, turn out the light! **E**

EDUCATION -- AUTOMATION *See* Computer-assisted instruction

EDUCATION -- DATA PROCESSING *See* Computer-assisted instruction

EDUCATION -- FICTION

Bruchac, J. Walking two worlds **Fic**

Hopkinson, D. Steamboat school **E**

EDUCATION -- INTEGRATION *See* School integration; Segregation in education

EDUCATION -- SEGREGATION *See* Segregation in education

EDUCATION -- SOCIAL ASPECTS

Stanley, J. Children of the Dust Bowl **371.9**

EDUCATION -- STATISTICS

See also Statistics

EDUCATION -- UNITED STATES -- HISTORY

Asim, J. Fifty cents and a dream **370.92**

EDUCATION AMENDMENTS OF 1972 -- TITLE IX

Blumenthal, K. Let me play **796**

EDUCATIONAL EVALUATION

Sykes, J. A. Conducting action research to evaluate your school library **027.8**

EDUCATIONAL GAMES

Bany-Winters, L. On stage **372.66**

Blobaum, C. Awesome snake science **597.96**

EDUCATIONAL TECHNOLOGY

Grover, S. Listening to learn **372.4**

Growing schools **370.71**

EDUCATIONAL TECHNOLOGY -- STUDY AND TEACHING -- CASE STUDIES

Growing schools **370.71**

EDUCATIONAL TESTS AND MEASUREMENTS

Angleberger, T. The surprise attack of Jabba the Puppett **Fic**

EDUCATORS

Ada, A. F. Under the royal palms **92**

Boomhower, R. E. Fighting for equality **92**

Bradby, M. More than anything else **E**

Brimner, L. D. Booker T. Washington **92**

Jurmain, S. The forbidden schoolhouse **92**

Let it shine **920**

Noah Webster's fighting words **92**

Parker-Rock, M. Alma Flor Ada **92**

Raven, M. Happy birthday to you! **782.42**

Edward Hopper. Rubin, S. G. **92**

Edward Hopper paints his world. Burleigh, R. **92**

Edward Lear. Lear, E. **821**

Edward Lear's The duck & the kangaroo. Lear, E. **821**

Edward V, King of England, 1470-1483

About

Haddix, M. P. Sent **Fic**

Edwardo. Burningham, J. **E**

Edwards, David

The pen that Pa built **E**

Edwards, Karl Newsom

I got a new friend **E**

Edwards, Mat

(il) Farndon, J. Megafast Trucks **629.224**

Edwards, Michelle

A hat for Mrs. Goldman **E**

Papa's latkes **E**

Edwards, Pamela Duncan

Jack and Jill's treehouse **E**

The leprechaun's gold **E**

The mixed-up rooster **E**

The neat line **E**

The old house **E**

Princess Pigtoria and the pea **E**

Some smug slug **E**

While the world is sleeping **E**

Edwards, Wallace

The cat's pajamas **428**

(il) Suzuki, D. T. You are the Earth **577**

Uncle Wally's old brown shoe **E**

Edwin speaks up. Coldiron, D. **E**

Eels. Coldiron, D. **597**

EELS

Coldiron, D. Eels **597**

Green, J. Moray eel **597.43**

Rustad, M. E. H. Moray eels and cleaner shrimp work together **597**

Wallace, K. Think of an eel **597**

EELS -- FICTION

Prosek, J. Bird, butterfly, eel **E**

The eensy weensy spider freaks out (big time!) Cummings, T. **E**

The eensy-weensy spider. Hoberman, M. A. **782.42**

The Eentsy, weentsy spider: fingerplays and action rhymes. **796.1**

Eep! **Fic**

Egan, Jill

How video game designers use math **794.8**

Egan, Kate

(jt. auth) Lane, M. The incredible twisting arm **Fic**

(jt. auth) Lane, M. The Vanishing Coin **Fic**

Egan, Tim

Dodsworth in London **E**

Dodsworth in New York **E**

Dodsworth in Paris **E**

Dodsworth in Rome **E**

The pink refrigerator **E**

Egg. **E**

EGG DECORATION

See also Decoration and ornament; Handicraft

Egg drop. Grey, M. **E**

Do you love me? **E**

Freymann, S. How are you peeling? **152.4**

Elfman, Eric

Tesla's attic **Fic**

Eli the Good. House, S. **Fic**

Eli, no! Kirk, K. **E**

Elias, Josie

Elias, M. L. Barbados **972.98**

Sheehan, S. Cameroon **967.11**

Elias, Marie Louise

Barbados **972.98**

Elijah of Buxton. Curtis, C. P. **Fic**

Eliopoulos, Chris

Okie Dokie Donuts **741.5**

Eliot Jones, midnight superhero. Cottringer, A. **E**

Eliot, T. S. (Thomas Stearns), 1888-1965

Old Possum's book of practical cats **811**

Elish, Dan

The attack of the frozen woodchucks **Fic**

The family Hitchcock **Fic**

James Madison **92**

The School for the Insanely Gifted **Fic**

Theodore Roosevelt **92**

Washington, D.C. **975.3**

ELITE (SOCIAL SCIENCES)

See also Leadership; Power (Social sciences); Social classes; Social groups

Eliza Bing is (not) a big, fat quitter. **Fic**

Eliza's cherry trees. **92**

Eliza's freedom road. Nolen, J. **Fic**

Eliza's kindergarten pet. McGinty, A. B. **E**

Eliza's kindergarten surprise. McGinty, A. B. **E**

Elizabeth I. Adams, S. **92**

Elizabeth I, Queen of England, 1533-1603

About

Adams, S. Elizabeth I **92**

Hollihan, K. L. Elizabeth I--the people's queen **942.05**

Krull, K. Lives of extraordinary women **920**

Stanley, D. Good Queen Bess: the story of Elizabeth I of England **92**

Elizabeth I--the people's queen. Hollihan, K. L. **942.05**

ELIZABETH II, 1926- (QUEEN OF GREAT BRITAIN)

See also Queens

Elizabeth leads the way: Elizabeth Cady Stanton and the right to vote. Stone, T. L. **92**

Elizabeth started all the trouble. **323.3**

Elizabeth, queen of the seas. Cox, L. **E**

Elizabeth, Queen, consort of George VI, King of Great Britain, 1900-2002

About

Hot dog! **973.91**

Elizabeti's doll. Bodeen, S. A. **E**

ELK -- FICTION

Steinhofel, A. An elk dropped in **Fic**

An **elk** dropped in. Steinhofel, A. **Fic**

Elkin, Mark

Samuel's baby **E**

Elkin, Matthew

20 fun facts about centipedes **595.6**

Ella enchanted. Levine, G. C. **Fic**

Ella Fitzgerald. Pinkney, A. D. **92**

Ella Kazoo will not brush her hair. Fox, L. **E**

Ella May and the wishing stone. **E**

Ella Sarah gets dressed. Chodos-Irvine, M. **E**

Ella the Elegant Elephant. D'Amico, C. **E**

Ella's big chance. Hughes, S. **E**

Ella, of course! Weeks, S. **E**

Ellen's broom. Lyons, K. S. **E**

Ellenbogen, Keith

(il) The Great White shark scientist **578.7**

(il) The Octopus Scientists **594**

Ellery, Amanda

If I were a jungle animal **E**

Ellery, Tom

(il) Ellery, A. If I were a jungle animal **E**

Ellie ever. Patterson, N. R. **Fic**

Ellie McDoodle: best friends fur-ever. Barshaw, R. M. **Fic**

Ellie McDoodle: have pen, will travel. Barshaw, R. M. **Fic**

Ellie McDoodle: new kid in school. Barshaw, R. M. **Fic**

Ellington was not a street. **E**

Ellington, Duke, 1899-1974

About

Celenza, A. H. Duke Ellington's Nutcracker suite **E**

Pinkney, A. D. Duke Ellington **781.65**

Stein, S. Duke Ellington **92**

Elliot and the goblin war. Nielsen, J. A. **Fic**

Elliot and the pixie plot. Nielsen, J. A. **Fic**

Elliot and the Yeti threat. Nielsen, J. A. **Fic**

Elliot, David

Henry's map **E**

(il) Jacques, B. Rakkety Tam **Fic**

Elliott, David

Finn throws a fit **E**

In the sea **811**

In the wild **811**

Knitty Kitty **E**

On the farm **E**

One little chicken **E**

This orq. (he cave boy.) **E**

What the grizzly knows **E**

Elliott, Laura

Give me liberty **Fic**

A string of hearts **E**

Elliott, Mark

Clements, A. Extra credit **Fic**

(il) Clements, A. About average **Fic**

(il) Clements, A. Lost and found **Fic**

(il) Clements, A. No talking **Fic**

(il) Clements, A. Troublemaker **Fic**

(il) Wallace, S. N. Little Joe **Fic**

Elliott, Rebecca

Just because **E**

Zoo girl **E**

Elliott, Zetta

(il) Emberley, B. Drummer Hoff   **398.8**

Emberley, B. Night's nice   **E**

Chicken Little   **398.2**

Ed Emberley's big green drawing book   **741.2**

Ed Emberley's big red drawing book   **741.2**

Ed Emberley's bye-bye, big bad bullybug!   **E**

Ed Emberley's drawing book of faces   **743**

Ed Emberley's drawing book: make a world   **741.2**

Ed Emberley's fingerprint drawing book   **741.2**

Ed Emberley's great thumbprint drawing book   **741.2**

Go away, big green monster!   **E**

The red hen   **398.2**

Thanks, Mom!   **E**

Where's my sweetie pie?   **E**

Emberley, R. If you're a monster and you know it   **E**

Emberley, R. The lion and the mice   **E**

Emberley, R. Ten little beasties   **E**

Emberley, R. There was an old monster!   **E**

Emberley, Michael

(il) Bottner, B. An annoying ABC   **E**

(il) Bottner, B. Miss Brooks' Story Nook   **E**

(il) Forget-me-nots   **811**

(il) It's perfectly normal   **613.9**

It's so amazing!   **612.6**

Priscilla gorilla   **E**

(il) You read to me, I'll read to you   **811**

Emberley, Rebecca

The ant and the grasshopper   **E**

(jt. auth) Emberley, E. Chicken Little   **398.2**

(jt. auth) Emberley, E. Mice on ice   **E**

(jt. auth) Emberley, E. The red hen   **398.2**

If you're a monster and you know it   **E**

The lion and the mice   **E**

Ten little beasties   **E**

There was an old monster!   **E**

EMBLEMS *See* Decorations of honor; Heraldry; Insignia; Mottoes; National emblems; Seals (Numismatics); Signs and symbols

EMBLEMS, NATIONAL

Bateman, T. Red, white, blue, and Uncle who?   **929.9**

Embracing, evaluating, and examining African American children's and young adult literature. Brooks, W. M.   **028.5**

Embracing, evaluating, and examining African American children's and young adult literature.   **028.5**

Embroidery. Sadler, J. A.   **746.44**

EMBROIDERY

    See also Decoration and ornament; Needlework; Sewing

EMBROIDERY

Sadler, J. A. Embroidery   **746.44**

EMBRYOLOGY

    See also Biology; Zoology

EMBRYOLOGY

Aston, D. H. An egg is quiet   **591.4**

Baines, R. What's in that egg?   **591.4**

Cole, J. How you were born   **612.6**

The **emerald** atlas. Stephens, J.   **Fic**

EMERGENCIES *See* Accidents; Disasters; First aid

Emergency at Three Mile Island. Feigenbaum, A.   **621.48**

EMERGENCY MEDICAL TECHNICIANS

Shepherd, J. A day with paramedics   **362.18**

Emergency vehicles. Arlon, P.   **629.04**

EMERGENCY VEHICLES

Arlon, P. Emergency vehicles   **629.04**

An **emerging** world power (1900-1929) Stanley, G. E.   **973.91**

Emerson, Kevin

Last day on mars   **Fic**

Emerson, Ralph Waldo, 1803-1882

          About

A Home for Mr. Emerson   **92**

Emery, William

Kodoku   **910.4**

Emi and the rhino scientist. Carson, M. K.   **599.66**

EMIGRANTS *See* Immigrants

EMIGRATION AND IMMIGRATION -- FICTION

Cohen, B. Molly's pilgrim   **E**

Danticat, E. Mama's nightingale   **E**

Diaz, A. The only road   **Fic**

James, H. F. Paper son   **Fic**

Nye, N. S. The turtle of Oman   **Fic**

Polacco, P. The keeping quilt   **E**

Teacup   **E**

Emil and Karl. Glatstein, J.   **Fic**

Emily Post's table manners for kids. Post, P.   **395**

Emily Post's The guide to good manners for kids. Post, P.   **395**

The **Emily** sonnets.   **811**

Emily Stew. Rockwell, T.   **811**

Emily's art. Catalanotto, P.   **E**

Emily's blue period.   **E**

Emily's everyday manners. Post, P.   **395**

Emily's first 100 days of school. Wells, R.   **E**

Emily's fortune. Naylor, P. R.   **Fic**

Emily's magic words. Post, P.   **395**

Emily's new friend. Senning, C. P.   **395**

Emily's out and about book. Senning, C. P.   **395**

Emily's sharing and caring book. Senning, C. P.   **395**

Emma and Julia love ballet. McClintock, B.   **E**

Emma Dilemma and the camping nanny. Hermes, P.   **Fic**

Emma Dilemma and the new nanny. Hermes, P.   **Fic**

Emma Dilemma and the soccer nanny. Hermes, P.   **Fic**

Emma Dilemma and the two nannies. Hermes, P.   **Fic**

Emma Dilemma, the nanny, and the best horse ever. Hermes, P.   **Fic**

Emma Dilemma, the nanny, and the secret ferret. Hermes, P.   **Fic**

Emma Dilemma: big sister poems.   **811**

Emma's friendwich. Murphy, S. J.   **E**

Emma's poem. Glaser, L.   **974.7**

Emma's yucky brother. Little, J.   **E**

Emma-Jean Lazarus fell out of a tree. Tarshis, L.   **Fic**

Emmaline and the bunny. Hannigan, K.   **Fic**

Emmanuel's dream. Walker   **92**

Emmet. Politi, L.   **E**

Emmett, Jonathan

See also Literature

The **epic** of Gilgamesh. **398.2**

EPIC POETRY
Laird, E. Shahnameh **891**

EPIC POETRY
See also Epic literature; Narrative poetry

Epic treks. Hagglund, B. **910.4**

Epic voyages. Mundy, R. **910.4**

EPIDEMICS
Cunningham, K. Pandemics **614.4**
Newman, P. Ebola **616.9**
Outbreak **614.4**

EPIDEMICS
See also Diseases; Public health

EPIDEMICS -- FICTION
Anderson, L. H. Fever, 1793 **Fic**
Giblin, J. The boy who saved Cleveland **Fic**
Hopkinson, D. The Great Trouble **Fic**

EPIDEMICS -- HISTORY
Plagues, pox, and pestilence **614.4**

EPIDEMICS -- UNITED STATES -- HISTORY
Jarrow, G. Red madness **616.3**

EPIDEMIOLOGY
See also Public health

EPIGRAMS
See also Wit and humor

Epilepsy. Bjorklund, R. **616.8**

EPILEPSY
Bender, L. Explaining epilepsy **616.8**
Bjorklund, R. Epilepsy **616.8**

EPIPHANY
Hoyt-Goldsmith, D. Three Kings Day **394.26**

EPISTOLARY POETRY
See also Poetry

EPITAPHS
See also Biography; Cemeteries; Inscriptions; Tombs

EPITHETS *See* Names; Nicknames

EPIZOA *See* Parasites

Epossumondas. Salley, C. **398.21**

Epossumondas saves the day. Salley, C. **E**

Epstein, Adam Jay
The familiars **Fic**
(jt. auth) Jacobson, A. Palace of dreams **Fic**
Secrets of the crown **Fic**

Epstein, Joyce Levy
Hutchins, D. J. Family reading night **372.4**

Epstein, Lori
(il) Delano, M. F. Master George's people **973.4**

EQUAL RIGHTS AMENDMENTS
See also Constitutions; Sex discrimination

EQUALITY
King, M. L. J. I have a dream **323.4**

EQUALITY
See also Political science; Sociology

EQUATIONS
See also Mathematics

EQUESTRIANISM *See* Horsemanship

ER vets. Jackson, D. M. **636.089**

Erak's ransom. Flanagan, J. **Fic**

Erandi's braids. Madrigal, A. H. **E**

Erased by a tornado! Rudolph, J. **551.55**

The **eraserheads.** Banks, K. **E**

Eratosthenes, 3rd cent. B.C.
About
The librarian who measured the earth **520**

Ercolini, David
(il) Lewis, K. Not inside this house! **E**

Erdős, Paul, 1913-1996
About
Heiligman, D. The boy who loved math **92**

Erdrich, Louise
The birchbark house **Fic**
Chickadee **Fic**
The game of silence **Fic**
The porcupine year **Fic**
(il) Makoons **Fic**

Ereth's birthday. Avi **Fic**

Erfanian, Banafsheh
A Cage Went in Search of a Bird **E**

ERGONOMICS
See also Applied psychology; Engineering; Industrial design; Psychophysiology

Eric Carle's animals, animals. Carle, E. **808.81**

Eric Carle's dragons dragons and other creatures that never were. Carle, E. **808.81**

Erickson, Justin
Alien abductions **001.9**

Ericsson, Jennifer A.
A piece of chalk **E**
Whoo goes there? **E**

The **Erie** Canal. Kendall, M. E. **386**

ERIE CANAL (N.Y.)
Harness, C. The amazing impossible Erie Canal **386**
Kendall, M. E. The Erie Canal **386**

ERIE CANAL (N.Y.) -- FICTION
Murphy, J. Desperate journey **Fic**

Erika-san. Say, A. **E**

Erikson, Rolf
Designing a school library media center for the future **027.8**

Eriksson, Eva
(il) Holmberg, B. R. A day with Dad **E**
(il) My Happy Life **Fic**
(il) My Heart Is Laughing **E**

Ering, Timothy Basil
The Almost fearless Hamilton Squidlegger **E**
(il) DiCamillo, K. The tale of Despereaux **Fic**
(il) Elliott, D. Finn throws a fit **E**
(il) Nelson, M. Snook alone **E**
The unexpected love story of Alfred Fiddleduckling **E**

Eritrea. NgCheong-Lum, R. **963.5**

ERITREA
The mangrove tree **577.6**
NgCheong-Lum, R. Eritrea **963.5**

Erlbruch, Wolf

(il) The King and the Sea   E

Ernest L. Thayer's Casey at the bat. Thayer, E. L.   811

Ernest, the moose who doesn't fit. Rayner, C.   E

Ernie & Maude [series]

   Watts, F. Extraordinary Ernie and Marvelous Maud   Fic

Ernst, Linda L.

   Baby rhyming time   027.62

Ernst, Lisa Campbell

   The Gingerbread Girl   E

   The Gingerbread Girl goes animal crackers   E

   How things work in the house   640

   How things work in the yard   578.7

   Little Red Riding Hood: a newfangled prairie tale   398.2

   Round like a ball!   E

   Sam Johnson and the blue ribbon quilt   E

   Sylvia Jean, scout supreme   E

   The turn-around upside-down alphabet book   E

   Zinnia and Dot   E

EROS (GREEK DEITY)

   Craft, M. Cupid and Psyche   292.1

EROSION

   Stewart, M. How does sand become glass?   666

ERRORS -- FICTION

   The book of mistakes   E

   Saltzberg, B. Beautiful oops!   E

Erskine, Kathryn

   The absolute value of Mike   Fic

   The badger knight   Fic

   Mockingbird   Fic

   Seeing red   Fic

Eruption! Rusch, E.   363.34

Esbaum, Jill

   Apples for everyone   634

   Everything spring   508.2

   I hatched!   E

   Seed, sprout, pumpkin, pie   635

   Stanza   E

   Teeny Tiny Toady   E

   To the big top   E

   Tom's tweet   E

Esbensen, Barbara Juster

   Baby whales drink milk   599.5

   Swing around the sun   811

The **escape.** Lasky, K.   Fic

Escape by night.   Fic

Escape from Mr. Lemoncello's library. Grabenstein, C.   Fic

Escape from planet Yastol. Service, P. F.   Fic

Escape under the forever sky. Yohalem, E.   Fic

Escape! Fleischman, S.   92

ESCAPES

   Spradlin, M. P. Daniel Boone's great escape   92

ESCAPES

   See also Adventure and adventurers; Prisons

ESCAPES -- FICTION

   Bar-el, D. Audrey (cow)   Fic

   Grifalconi, A. The village that vanished   E

   Jamieson, V. The great pet escape   741.5

ESCAPES -- IRELAND -- HISTORY -- 19TH CENTURY

   Fradin, D. B. The Irish potato famine   941.508

Escaping the tiger. Manivong, L.   Fic

ESCHERICHIA COLI

   See also Bacteria

Escoffier, Michael

   Have you seen my trumpet?   428.1

   Rabbit and the Not-So-Big-Bad Wolf   E

   Take away the A   428.1

   Where's the Baboon?   E

Escriva, Vivi

   Pio peep!   398.8

ESKIMOS *See* Inuit

ESKIMOS -- FICTION

   George, J. C. Nutik, the wolf pup   E

   Hill, K. Bo at Ballard Creek   Fic

   Hobbs, W. Never say die   Fic

   The snowstorm   Fic

ESKIMOS -- GREENLAND -- FICTION

   The raiders   Fic

Espeland, Pamela

   (ed) Fox, J. S. Get organized without losing it   371.3

Esperanza rising. Ryan, P. M.   Fic

Espinosa, Rod

   The courageous princess   741.5

ESPIONAGE

   Earnest, P. The real spy's guide to becoming a spy   327.12

   Gilbert, A. Codes and ciphers   652

   Gilbert, A. Spy school   327.12

   Janeczko, P. B. The dark game   327.12

   Mitchell, S. K. Spies and lies   327.12

   Mitchell, S. K. Spies, double agents, and traitors   327.12

   Mitchell, S. K. Spy codes and ciphers   652

   Mitchell, S. K. Spy gizmos and gadgets   327.12

   Spyology   327.12

ESPIONAGE

   See also Intelligence service; Secret service; Subversive activities

ESPIONAGE -- FICTION

   Stone, P. Romeo blue   Fic

ESPIONAGE -- HISTORY -- 20TH CENTURY

   Samuels, C. Spying and security   940.54

ESPIONAGE STORIES *See* Spy stories

ESPIONAGE, BRITISH -- GERMANY -- FICTION

   Gratz, A. Projekt 1065   Fic

ESQUIMAUX *See* Inuit

Esquivel!   92

Esquivel, Juan García

   About

   Esquivel!   92

Essakalli, Julie Klear

   (il) Alalou, A. The butter man   E

ESSAY

   See also Literature

ESSAYISTS

   Abrams, D. Gary Soto   92

   Adler, D. A. A picture book of Thomas Jefferson   92

See also Civil engineering; Tunnels

EXCAVATIONS (ARCHEOLOGY)

Aronson, M. The skull in the rock **569.9**

At home in her tomb **931**

Digging for Troy **939**

Logan, C. The 5,000-year-old puzzle **932**

Schlitz, L. A. The hero Schliemann **92**

EXCAVATIONS (ARCHEOLOGY)

See also Archeology

EXCAVATIONS (ARCHEOLOGY) -- CANADA

Huey, L. M. American archaeology uncovers the Vikings **970.01**

EXCAVATIONS (ARCHEOLOGY) -- CHINA

At home in her tomb **931**

EXCAVATIONS (ARCHEOLOGY) -- EGYPT

Logan, C. The 5,000-year-old puzzle **932**

Rubalcaba, J. Ancient Egypt **932**

EXCAVATIONS (ARCHEOLOGY) -- ENGLAND

Aronson, M. If stones could speak **936**

EXCAVATIONS (ARCHEOLOGY) -- EUROPE

Green, J. Ancient Celts **936**

EXCAVATIONS (ARCHEOLOGY) -- GREECE

McGee, M. Ancient Greece **938**

EXCAVATIONS (ARCHEOLOGY) -- INDONESIA

Goldenberg, L. Little people and a lost world **599.93**

EXCAVATIONS (ARCHEOLOGY) -- IRAQ

Gruber, B. Ancient Iraq **935**

EXCAVATIONS (ARCHEOLOGY) -- ITALY

Sonneborn, L. Pompeii **937**

EXCAVATIONS (ARCHEOLOGY) -- MEXICO

Cooke, T. Ancient Aztec **972**

Harris, N. Ancient Maya **972**

Kops, D. Palenque **972**

Lourie, P. Hidden world of the Aztec **972**

EXCAVATIONS (ARCHEOLOGY) -- PERU

Gruber, B. Ancient Inca **985**

EXCAVATIONS (ARCHEOLOGY) -- UNITED STATES

Huey, L. M. American archaeology uncovers the Dutch colonies **974.7**

Huey, L. M. American archaeology uncovers the earliest English colonies **973.2**

Huey, L. M. American archaeology uncovers the Underground Railroad **973.7**

Huey, L. M. American archaeology uncovers the Vikings **970.01**

Huey, L. M. American archaeology uncovers the westward movement **978**

Quigley, M. Mesa Verde **978.8**

Excellent Ed. McAnulty, S. **E**

Except if. Averbeck, J. **E**

Exclamation mark. **E**

EXCRETION

Cusick, D. Get the scoop on animal poop **590**

EXCUSES

See also Etiquette; Manners and customs

EXECUTIVE DEPARTMENTS -- UNITED STATES

Bow, J. What is the executive branch? **351**

EXECUTIVES

Weston, M. Honda **92**

Exercise. Schaefer, A. **613.7**

EXERCISE

See also Health; Hygiene

EXERCISE

Carlson, N. L. Get up and go! **E**

Gardner, R. Ace your exercise and nutrition science project: great science fair ideas **613**

Head, H. Keeping fit **613.7**

Hunt, J. Getting stronger, getting fit **613.7**

Mason, P. Improving endurance **613.7**

Mason, P. Improving flexibility **613.7**

Mason, P. Improving speed **613.7**

Mason, P. Improving strength & power **613.7**

Parker, S. How do my muscles get strong? **612.7**

Rockwell, L. The busy body book **612**

Royston, A. Why do I run? **613.7**

Schaefer, A. Exercise **613.7**

Schaefer, A. Staying healthy **613**

Tuminelly, N. Super simple bend & stretch **613.7**

EXERCISE -- PHYSIOLOGICAL ASPECTS

Head, H. Keeping fit **613.7**

Exner, Carol R.

Practical puppetry A-Z **791.5**

EXORCISM

See also Supernatural

EXOTIC ANIMALS

Singer, M. A strange place to call home **571.1**

EXPANDING UNIVERSE

The universe, black holes, and the Big Bang **523.1**

EXPECTATION (PSYCHOLOGY) -- FICTION

When Christmas feels like home **E**

Expecting animal babies [series]

Heos, B. What to expect when you're expecting joeys **599.2**

The **Expeditioners** and the Treasure of Drowned Man's Canyon. Taylor, S. S. **Fic**

EXPEDITIONS, SCIENTIFIC *See* Scientific expeditions

EXPERIENCES, LIFE CHANGE *See* Life change events

Experiment with science [series]

Just add water **546**

Experimenting with everyday science [series]

Tomecek, S. Art & architecture **701**

Tomecek, S. Music **781.2**

Tomecek, S. Tools and machines **621.9**

Experimenting with science [series]

Meiani, A. Light **535**

EXPERIMENTS -- FICTION

Korman, G. Masterminds **Fic**

Experiments to do on your family. Young, K. R. **507.8**

Experiments with electricity and magnetism. Woodford, C. **537**

Experiments with motion. Gray, S. H. **531**

Experiments with sound. Oxlade, C. **534**

EXPERIMENTS, SCIENTIFIC *See* Science -- Experiments

Explaining [series]

Ballard, C. Explaining food allergies **616.97**

Harper, C. M. Alien encounter   **Fic**
Harris, T. E. The perfect place   **Fic**
Henkes, K. Penny and her song   **E**
Hurwitz, M. W. The summer I saved the world-- in 65 days **Fic**
I wanna go home   **E**
Kinney, J. Diary of a wimpy kid   **Fic**
Klise, K. Homesick   **Fic**
Kulling, M. The Tweedles Go Electric!   **E**
Lanthier, J. Hurry up, Henry   **E**
Legrand, C. Some kind of happiness   **Fic**
Levy, D. A. The family Fletcher takes Rock Island **Fic**
Longstreth, G. G. Yes, let's   **E**
The Lotterys plus one   **Fic**
Lucy   **Fic**
Marshall, J. M. In the footsteps of Crazy Horse **Fic**
MacLachlan, P. Fly away   **Fic**
MacLachlan, P. Kindred souls   **Fic**
McAnulty, S. Excellent Ed   **E**
McCarty, P. Chloe   **E**
McDonough, Y. Z. The bicycle spy   **Fic**
Messner, K. The seventh wish   **Fic**
O'Leary, S. A family is a family is a family **E**
Peck, R. The best man   **Fic**
Pennypacker, S. The summer of the gypsy moths **Fic**
Perl, E. S. Aces wild   **Fic**
Player, M. Chloe, instead   **E**
Poor Louie   **E**
Rocklin, J. The five lives of our cat Zook **Fic**
Say hello, Sophie   **E**
Schroeder, L. My secret guide to Paris **Fic**
See you in the Cosmos   **Fic**
Selznick, B. The Marvels   **Fic**
Sovern, M. J. The meaning of Maggie   **Fic**
Stead, R. Goodbye stranger   **Fic**
Taro Miura The tiny king   **E**
Teagan, E. The friendship experiment   **Fic**
This would make a good story someday **Fic**
Tiger boy   **Fic**
Urban, L. Little Red Henry   **E**
Violet Mackerel's personal space   **Fic**
Violet Mackerel's possible friend   **Fic**
Wells, R. Stella's starliner   **E**
Wiles, D. Revolution   **Fic**

FAMILY LIFE -- FLORIDA -- FICTION
Blume, J. Starring Sally J. Freedman as herself **Fic**
Cerra, K. O. Just a drop of water   **Fic**

FAMILY LIFE -- FRANCE -- FICTION
McDonough, Y. Z. The bicycle spy   **Fic**

FAMILY LIFE -- FRANCE -- PARIS -- FICTION
Schroeder, L. My secret guide to Paris **Fic**

FAMILY LIFE -- GRAPHIC NOVELS
Gownley, J. Amelia rules!: the whole world's crazy! **741.5**
Trondheim, L. Monster Christmas   **741.5**
Wight, E. Frankie Pickle and the closet of doom **741.5**

FAMILY LIFE -- GREECE -- FICTION
Dumon Tak, B. Mikis and the donkey   **E**

FAMILY LIFE -- HAITI -- FICTION

Burg, A. E. Serafina's promise   **Fic**

FAMILY LIFE -- ILLINOIS -- CHICAGO -- FICTION
Balliett, B. Hold fast   **Fic**

FAMILY LIFE -- ILLINOIS -- FICTION
Clifton, L. Freaky Fast Frankie Joe   **Fic**
Hurwitz, M. W. The summer I saved the world-- in 65 days **Fic**

FAMILY LIFE -- LOUISIANA -- FICTION
Herlong, M. H. Buddy   **Fic**

FAMILY LIFE -- LOUISIANA -- NEW ORLEANS -- FICTION
Larson, K. Liberty   **Fic**
Patrick, D. L. Finding someplace   **Fic**

FAMILY LIFE -- MAINE -- FICTION
LaFleur, S. Listening for Lucca   **Fic**
Martin, A. M. Better to wish   **Fic**
Stone, P. Romeo blue   **Fic**

FAMILY LIFE -- MASSACHUSETTS -- BOSTON -- FICTION
Frazier, A. The mastermind plot   **Fic**

FAMILY LIFE -- MASSACHUSETTS -- FICTION
Birdsall, J. The Penderwicks in spring   **Fic**
Clementine and the spring trip   **Fic**

FAMILY LIFE -- MINNESOTA -- FICTION
Hattemer, K. The vigilante poets of Selwyn Academy **Fic**

FAMILY LIFE -- MISSOURI -- FICTION
Lawson, J. The actual & truthful adventures of Becky Thatcher **Fic**

FAMILY LIFE -- NEW YORK (STATE) -- NEW YORK -- FICTION
Graff, L. Absolutely almost   **Fic**
Graff, L. A tangle of knots   **Fic**
Lucky broken girl   **Fic**
Matti, T. Mister Orange   **Fic**
Rodkey, G. The Tapper twins go to war (with each other) **Fic**
Stead, R. Liar & spy   **Fic**

FAMILY LIFE -- NORTH CAROLINA -- FICTION
Tuck, P. M. As fast as words could fly   **Fic**

FAMILY LIFE -- NORTHWEST, PACIFIC -- FICTION
Harper, C. M. Alien encounter   **Fic**

FAMILY LIFE -- PENNSYLVANIA -- FICTION
Wolk, L. Wolf Hollow   **Fic**

FAMILY LIFE -- POETRY
Scanlon, L. G. All the world   **811**

FAMILY LIFE -- RHODE ISLAND -- FICTION
Johnson, P. The amazing adventures of John Smith, Jr., aka Houdini   **Fic**

FAMILY LIFE -- RUSSIA -- FICTION
O'Brien, A. Lara's gift   **Fic**

FAMILY LIFE -- TENNESSEE -- FICTION
Vawter, V. Paperboy   **Fic**

FAMILY LIFE -- TEXAS -- FICTION
Gibbs, S. Poached   **Fic**
Johnson, A. All different now   **E**
Kelly, J. Counting sheep   **Fic**
Kelly, J. The curious world of Calpurnia Tate **Fic**
Kelly, J. Skunked: Calpurnia Tate, girl vet **Fic**
Loftin, N. Wish girl   **Fic**

Fancy Nancy, aspiring artist. O'Connor, J. **E**

Fancy Nancy, stellar stargazer! O'Connor, J. **E**

Fandango stew. Davis, D. **E**

Fang, Linda

    The Ch'i-lin purse **398.209**

Fannie never flinched. Farrell, M. C. **92**

Fanny's dream. Buehner, C. **E**

FANS (DRESS ACCESSORIES)

    See also Clothing and dress; Costume; Fashion accessories

Fantasic physical science experiments [series]

    Gardner, R. Dazzling science projects with light and color **535**

FANTASIES

    The hobbit **Fic**

    Saint-Exupery, A. d. The little prince **Fic**

Fantaskey, Beth

    Isabel Feeney **Fic**

Fantastic adventures of Baron Munchausen. Janisch, H. **Fic**

Fantastic farm machines. Peterson, C. **631.3**

The **fantastic** Ferris Wheel. Kraft, B. H. **791.06**

FANTASTIC FICTION *See* Fantasy fiction

Fantastic flowers. **635.9**

The **fantastic** flying books of Mr. Morris Lessmore. **E**

The **fantastic** jungles of Henri Rousseau. **759**

Fantastic physical science experiments [series]

    Gardner, R. Energizing science projects with electricity and magnetism **537**

    Gardner, R. Jazzy science projects with sound and music **534**

    Gardner, R. Melting, freezing, and boiling science projects with matter **530.4**

    Gardner, R. Sensational science projects with simple machines **621.8**

    Gardner, R. Sizzling science projects with heat and energy **536**

The **fantastic** secret of Owen Jester. O'Connor, B. **Fic**

The **fantastic** undersea life of Jacques Cousteau. Yaccarino, D. **92**

Fantastic! wow! and unreal! Heller, R. **425**

Fantastical creatures and magical beasts. Knudsen, S. **398**

FANTASY

    See also Dreams; Imagination

Fantasy chronicles [series]

    Kerns, A. Wizards and witches **133.4**

    Knudsen, S. Fairies and elves **398**

    Knudsen, S. Fantastical creatures and magical beasts **398**

FANTASY FICTION

    The 9 lives of Alexander Baddenfield **Fic**

    Almond, D. Mouse bird snake wolf **Fic**

    Anderson, J. L. May Bird and The Ever After

    Auxier, J. Sophie Quire and the last Storyguard **Fic**

    Barnhill, K. R. The witch's boy **Fic**

    Barnhill, K. The girl who drank the moon **Fic**

    Booraem, E. Texting the underworld **Fic**

    Brodien-Jones, C. The glass puzzle **Fic**

    Cameron, A. The lightning catcher **Fic**

    Carman, P. The field of wacky inventions **Fic**

    Catmull, K. Summer and Bird **Fic**

Chilton, A. S. The goblin's puzzle **Fic**

Columbus, C. House of secrets **Fic**

De Lint, C. The cats of Tanglewood Forest **Fic**

A dragon's guide to making your human smarter **Fic**

Flanagan, J. The royal ranger **Fic**

Forest of wonders **Fic**

Jinks, C. Saving Thanehaven **Fic**

Johnson, J. The mark of the dragonfly **Fic**

Johnson-Shelton, N. The seven swords **Fic**

Knudsen, M. The princess of Trelian **Fic**

Lauren, R. Prisoner of ice and snow **Fic**

Lerangis, P. The colossus rises **Fic**

Morris, J. East of the Sun, West of the Moon **Fic**

Nielsen, J. A. The runaway king **Fic**

The Real Boy **Fic**

Rex, A. Unlucky charms **Fic**

Riordan, R. The sword of summer **Fic**

Sage, A. StarChaser **Fic**

Saunders, K. The Whizz Pop Chocolate Shop **Fic**

Schwarz, V. The Sleepwalkers **741.5**

Shulman, P. The Wells Bequest **Fic**

The spindlers **Fic**

Thomson, B. The Typewriter **E**

Voelkel, J. The river of no return **Fic**

FANTASY FICTION -- GRAPHIC NOVELS

The sand warrior **741.5**

FANTASY FICTION -- HISTORY AND CRITICISM

Colbert, D. The magical worlds of Harry Potter **823**

FANTASY FILMS

    See also Motion pictures

FANTASY FOOTBALL -- FICTION

Lupica, M. Fantasy league **Fic**

FANTASY GAMES

    See also Games; Role playing

FANTASY GRAPHIC NOVELS

Cavallaro, M. L. Frank Baum's The Wizard of Oz **741.5**

Colfer, E. Artemis Fowl: the graphic novel **741.5**

Crane, J. The clouds above **741.5**

Deutsch, B. Hereville: how Mirka got her sword **741.5**

Espinosa, R. The courageous princess **741.5**

Flight explorer **741.5**

Fuji, M. The big adventures of Majoko, volume 1 **741.5**

Kibuishi, K. Amulet, book one: The Stonekeeper **741.5**

Kovac, T. Wonderland **741.5**

Medley, L. Castle waiting **741.5**

Nykko, p. The shadow door **741.5**

Nytra, D. The secret of the stone frog **741.5**

Petersen, D. E. Mouse Guard: Fall 1152 **741.5**

Petersen, D. E. Mouse Guard: Winter 1152 **741.5**

Princess princess ever after **741.5**

Rapunzel's revenge **741.5**

Smith, J. Bone: out from Boneville **741.5**

Smith, J. Bone: Rose **741.5**

Smith, J. Bone: tall tales **741.5**

Soo, K. Jellaby: monster in the city **741.5**

Thompson, J. Magic Trixie **741.5**

FANTASY GRAPHIC NOVELS

FLIES -- POETRY

Howitt, M. B. The spider and the fly **821**

Flight. Bailey, G. **629.13**

FLIGHT

Bailey, G. Flight **629.13**

Collard, S. B. Wings **591.47**

Hodgkins, F. How people learned to fly **629.13**

Mercer, B. The flying machine book **745.592**

FLIGHT -- FICTION

Baker-Smith, G. Farther **Fic**

Biddulph, R. Blown away **E**

Judge, L. Flight school **E**

Little bird **E**

Light, S. Zephyr takes flight **E**

The Plan **E**

FLIGHT -- POETRY

Lewis, J. P. Skywriting **811**

Flight 1-2-3. Van Lieshout, M. **E**

Flight explorer. **741.5**

Flight of the honey bee. Huber, R. **595.79**

Flight school. Judge, L. **E**

FLIGHT TO THE MOON *See* Space flight to the moon

Flight: the journey of Charles Lindbergh. Burleigh, R. **629.13**

FLIGHTS AROUND THE WORLD *See* Aeronautics -- Flights

FLIGHTS AROUND THE WORLD

Grove, T. First flight around the world **910.4**

FLINT (MICH.) -- HISTORY -- 20TH CENTURY -- FICTION

Curtis, C. P. The mighty Miss Malone **Fic**

The **Flint** Heart. Paterson, J. **Fic**

Flint, Shamini, 1969-

Ten **Fic**

FLIP BOOKS

See also Toy and movable books

Flip the flaps [series]

Ganeri, A. Things that go **629**

Wilson, H. Seashore **551.4**

Flip, flap, fly! Root, P. **E**

Flip, float, fly. Macken, J. E. **581.4**

Flipped. Van Draanen, W. **Fic**

FLIPPED CLASSROOMS

See also Teaching

Float. Miyares, D. **E**

FLOATING BODIES -- FICTION

Berry, L. What floats in a moat? **E**

The **floating** circus. Zimmer, T. V. **Fic**

The **Floating** Islands. Neumeier, R. **Fic**

Floating on Mama's song. Lacamara, L. **E**

FLOATS (PARADES) *See* Parades

Floca, Brian

(il) Avi Ereth's birthday **Fic**

(il) Avi Poppy **Fic**

(il) Avi Poppy and Ereth **Fic**

(il) Avi Poppy and Rye **Fic**

(il) Avi Poppy's return **Fic**

(il) Avi Ragweed **Fic**

(il) Ballet for Martha **792.8**

(il) Cox, L. Elizabeth, queen of the seas **F**

Five trucks **E**

(il) Guys read **818**

(il) Hopkinson, D. Billy and the rebel **F**

(il) Hopkinson, D. From slave to soldier **F**

Lightship **387.2**

Locomotive **385**

(il) Marty McGuire **Fic**

(il) Marty McGuire has too many pets! **Fic**

Moonshot **629.45**

Princess Cora and the Crocodile **E**

The racecar alphabet **411**

A **flock** of shoes. **E**

Flood and fire. Diamand, E. **Fic**

FLOOD DAMAGE PREVENTION

Kenah, K. Flood warning **551.48**

Flood warning. Kenah, K. **551.48**

Flood, Joe

(il) Dinosaurs **567.9**

Flood, Nancy Bo

Cowboy up! **E**

FLOODS

Dwyer, H. Floods! **551.48**

Kenah, K. Flood warning **551.48**

Spilsbury, L. Raging floods **551.48**

The **Floods** [series]

Thompson, C. Good neighbors **Fic**

FLOODS

See also Meteorology; Natural disasters; Rain; Water

FLOODS -- FICTION

Burg, A. E. Serafina's promise **Fic**

MacLachlan, P Fly away **Fic**

Floods! Dwyer, H. **551.48**

Flook, Helen

(il) Horrocks, A. Silas' seven grandparents **E**

Floors. Carman, P. **Fic**

FLOORS

See also Architecture -- Details; Buildings

FLORA *See* Botany; Plants

Flora and the flamingo. Idle, M. **E**

Flora and the peacocks. Idle, M. **E**

Flora and the penguin. Idle, M. **E**

Flora and Ulysses. **Fic**

Flora's very windy day. Birdsall, J. **E**

Flora, James

The day the cow sneezed **E**

Florczak, Robert

(il) Hausman, G. Horses of myth **398.2**

FLORENCE (ITALY) -- FICTION

Fern, T. E. Pippo the Fool **E**

Florence Nightingale. Demi **92**

Flores-Gabis, Enrique

90 miles to Havana **Fic**

Florian, Douglas

Autumnblings **811**

Bing bang boing **811**

Three pennies **Fic**

FOSTER CHILDREN -- MAINE -- FICTION

Stone, P. Romeo blue **Fic**

FOSTER GRANDPARENTS

See also Grandparents; Volunteer work

FOSTER HOME CARE

Horvath, P. Everything on a waffle **Fic**

Stewart, S. A house between homes **362.7**

FOSTER HOME CARE -- BIBLIOGRAPHY

Meese, R. L. Family matters **011.6**

FOSTER HOME CARE -- FICTION

Booth, C. Kinda like brothers **Fic**

Three pennies **Fic**

Foster, Bruce

(il) Yarrow, P. Puff the magic dragon pop-up book **E**

Foster, Gerald L.

(il) Foster, M. Whale port **639.2**

Foster, John

Barron's junior rhyming Dictionary **423**

Foster, Karen

Atlas of Australia **994**

Atlas of North America **970**

Atlas of South America **980**

Atlas of the Poles and Oceans **998**

Foster, Mark

Whale port **639.2**

Foster, Stephen Collins, 1826-1864

About

Krull, K. Lives of the musicians **920**

Foster, Travis

(il) Comden, B. What's new at the zoo? **E**

Fotheringham, Edwin

(il) Corey, S. Mermaid Queen **92**

(il) Kerley, B. The extraordinary Mark Twain (according to Susy) **92**

(il) Kerley, B. Those rebels, John and Tom **973.4**

(il) Tony Baloney **E**

(il) What to do about Alice? **92**

FOTONOVELAS

See also Comic books, strips, etc.

Foucault, Jean Bernard Léon, 1819-1868

About

Come see the Earth turn: the story of Leon Foucault **92**

Found. Haddix, M. P. **Fic**

Found. Yoon, S. **E**

FOUND OBJECTS -- POETRY

Ashley Bryan's Puppets **811**

FOUNDATIONS

See also Architecture -- Details; Buildings; Structural engineering

The **founders.** Fradin, D. B. **920**

The **Founding** Fathers. **920**

FOUNDING FATHERS OF THE UNITED STATES

The Founding Fathers **920**

Freedman, R. Becoming Ben Franklin **92**

FOUNDING FATHERS OF THE UNITED STATES

See also Statesmen -- United States

Founding mothers. Carosella, M. **305.4**

Founding mothers. **920**

The **foundling** and other tales of Prydain. Alexander, L. **S**

FOUNDLINGS *See* Orphans

FOUNDLINGS -- FICTION

Kinsey-Warnock, N. True colors **Fic**

Red butterfly **Fic**

Turnage, S. The ghosts of Tupelo Landing **Fic**

Turnage, S. Three times lucky **Fic**

White, R. The treasure of Way Down Deep **Fic**

FOUNDRY WORKERS -- UNITED STATES

Philip Reid saves the statue of freedom **973**

Fountain, Joanna F.

(ed) Cataloging correctly for kids **025.3**

Four feet, two sandals. Williams, K. L. **E**

Four friends at Christmas. DePaola, T. **E**

Four seasons make a year. Rockwell, A. F. **E**

The **Four** Seasons of Lucy McKenzie. Murray, K. **Fic**

The **four** spheres of Earth. Larson, P. **551.1**

The **fourteenth** goldfish. Holm, J. L. **Fic**

FOURTH DIMENSION

See also Mathematics

FOURTH OF JULY

Heiligman, D. Celebrate Independence Day **394.26**

FOURTH OF JULY

See also Holidays; United States -- History -- 1775-1783, Revolution

FOURTH OF JULY -- FICTION

Red, white, and boom! **E**

The **fourth** stall. Rylander, C. **Fic**

Fourth-grade fuss. Hurwitz, J. **Fic**

Fox and his friends. Marshall, E. **E**

The **fox** and the hen. Battut, E. **E**

The **fox** in the dark. Green, A. **E**

The **Fox** went out on a chilly night. **782.42**

Fox's garden. Princesse Camcam **E**

Fox, Annie

Real friends vs. the other kind **158**

Fox, Debbie

Good-bye bully machine **302.3**

Fox, F. G.

Jean Laffite and the big ol' whale **E**

Fox, Helen

Eager **Fic**

Fox, Janet S.

Get organized without losing it **371.3**

Fox, Jennifer

Staib, W. A feast of freedom **Fic**

Fox, Karen C.

Older than the stars **523.1**

Fox, Kathleen

Plagiarism! Plagiarism! **808**

Fox, Lee

Ella Kazoo will not brush her hair **E**

Fox, Mem

The goblin and the empty chair **E**

Good night, sleep tight **E**

information in the school library media program   **027.8**

FREEDOM OF INFORMATION
See also Civil rights; Intellectual freedom

FREEDOM OF MOVEMENT
See also Civil rights; Freedom

FREEDOM OF RELIGION
See also Civil rights; Freedom; Toleration

FREEDOM OF SPEECH
See also Censorship; Civil rights; Freedom; Intellectual freedom

FREEDOM OF THE PRESS
See also Civil rights; Freedom; Intellectual freedom; Press

Freedom on the menu. Weatherford, C. B.   **E**

Freedom over me. Bryan, A.   **920**

Freedom Riders. Bausum, A.   **323.1**

Freedom ship. Rappaport, D.   **Fic**

Freedom song.   **E**

Freedom song. Walker, S. M.   **E**

Freedom stone. Kluger, J.   **Fic**

Freedom struggle. Rossi, A.   **973.7**

Freedom Summer. Rubin, S. G.   **323.11**

Freedom Summer. Wiles, D.   **E**

Freedom Summer, 1964. Mooney, C.   **323.1**

Freedom walkers. Freedman, R.   **323.1**

Freedom!   **741.5**

Freedom's a-callin' me. Shange, N.   **811**

Freeman, Don

   Corduroy   **E**

   Earl the squirrel   **E**

   Quiet! there's a canary in the library   **E**

Freeman, Elizabeth, 1744?-1829

     About

   Mumbet's Declaration of Independence   **92**

Freeman, Evelyn B.

   Temple, C. A. Children's books in children's hands   **028.5**

Freeman, Judy

   Books kids will sit still for 3   **011.6**

Freeman, Laura

   (il) English, K. Nikki & Deja   **Fic**

   (il) English, K. Nikki & Deja: birthday blues   **Fic**

   (il) English, K. Nikki & Deja: the newsy news newsletter **Fic**

   (il) English, K. Nikki and Deja: election madness   **Fic**

   (il) English, K. Skateboard party   **Fic**

Freeman, Martha

   Mrs. Wow never wanted a cow   **E**

   The trouble with cats   **Fic**

   Who is stealing the 12 days of Christmas?   **Fic**

   Who stole Grandma's million-dollar pumpkin pie?   **Fic**

   Who stole Halloween?   **Fic**

   Who stole New Year's Eve?   **Fic**

   Who stole Uncle Sam?   **Fic**

Freeman, Tor

   Olive and the big secret   **E**

Freese, Susan M.

   Craigslist   **381**

Freeze frame. Macy, S.   **796.98**

FREEZING *See* Cryobiology; Frost; Ice; Refrigeration

FREIGHT
See also Maritime law; Materials handling; Railroads; Transportation

FRENCH AMERICANS
Englar, M. French colonies in America   **970.01**

FRENCH CANADIANS
Englar, M. French colonies in America   **970.01**

FRENCH CANADIANS -- FOLKLORE
Kimmel, E. A. The flying canoe   **398.2**

French colonies in America. Englar, M.   **970.01**

FRENCH COOKERY *See* French cooking

FRENCH COOKING
Blaxland, W. French food   **641.5**

LaRoche, A. Recipe and craft guide to France   **641.5**

Locricchio, M. The cooking of France   **641.59**

Wagner, L. Cool French cooking   **641.594**

FRENCH COOKING
See also Cooking

FRENCH COOKING -- FICTION
Minette's feast   **E**

French ducks in Venice. Freymann-Weyr, G.   **Fic**

French food. Blaxland, W.   **641.5**

FRENCH LANGUAGE -- DICTIONARIES
Corbeil My first French English visual dictionary   **443**

Kudela, K. R. My first book of French words   **443**

FRENCH LANGUAGE -- DICTIONARIES -- ENGLISH
See also Encyclopedias and dictionaries

FRENCH LANGUAGE -- VOCABULARY
Russo, M. Peter is just a baby   **E**

FRENCH LITERATURE
See also Literature; Romance language literature

FRENCH PAINTING
Johnson, D. B. Magritte's marvelous hat   **E**

FRENCH POETRY
Cendrars, B. Shadow   **841**

FRENCH POETRY
See also French literature; Poetry

The **French** Revolution. Riggs, K.   **944.04**

French, Jackie

   Christmas wombat   **E**

   Diary of a baby wombat   **E**

   Diary of a wombat   **E**

   Pete the sheep-sheep   **E**

French, Martin

   (il) Stompin' at the Savoy   **92**

French, Vivian

   The Daddy Goose treasury   **E**

   Henny Penny   **398.2**

   The most wonderful thing in the world   **E**

   T. Rex   **567.9**

   Yucky worms   **E**

FRESHWATER ANIMALS
Aliki My visit to the aquarium   **639.34**

Hodge, D. Wetland animals   **591.7**

FRESHWATER ANIMALS
See also Aquatic animals

GALLIPOLI CAMPAIGN, 1915

Greenwood, M. The donkey of Gallipoli   **940.4**

Gallop! Seder, R. B.   **E**

Galloway, Priscilla

Archers, alchemists, and 98 other medieval jobs you might have loved or loathed   **940.1**

Gallup guides for youth facing persistent prejudice. Seba, J.   **306.76**

Galouchko, Annouchka Gravel

(il) Charles, V. M. The birdman   **E**

Gama, Vasco da, 1469-1524

About

Calvert, P. Vasco da Gama   **92**

Fritz, J. Around the world in a hundred years   **910.92**

Goodman, J. E. A long and uncertain journey: the 27,000 mile voyage of Vasco da Gama   **910**

GAMBIA -- FICTION

Lewis, G. Wild wings   **Fic**

GAMBLING

See also Games

GAMBLING -- FICTION

Helgerson, J. Crows & cards   **Fic**

GAME AND GAME BIRDS

See also Animals; Birds; Wildlife

Game changer. Coy, J.   **796.323**

Game day. Football [series]

Gigliotti, J. Defensive backs   **796.332**

Gigliotti, J. Linebackers   **796.332**

Gigliotti, J. Linemen   **796.332**

Gigliotti, J. Receivers   **796.332**

Kelley, K. C. Quarterbacks   **796.332**

Kelley, K. C. Running backs   **796.332**

The **game** of finger worms. Tullet, H.   **E**

The **game** of let's go! Tullet, H.   **E**

The **game** of light. Tullet, H.   **E**

The **game** of mix and match. Tullet, H.   **E**

The **game** of mix-up art. Tullet, H.   **E**

The **game** of patterns. Tullet, H.   **E**

The **game** of silence. Erdrich, L.   **Fic**

The **Game** of Sunken Places. Anderson, M. T.   **Fic**

Game on! Gallaway, B.   **025.2**

Game over, Pete Watson.   **Fic**

GAME PRESERVES *See* Game reserves

GAME PROTECTION

Jackson, D. M. The wildlife detectives   **363.2**

GAME PROTECTION

See also Game and game birds; Hunting; Wildlife conservation

GAME RESERVES

Lumry, A. Safari in South Africa   **E**

GAME RESERVES

See also Hunting; Wildlife conservation

GAME SHOWS -- FICTION

Gephart, D. Olivia Bean, trivia queen   **Fic**

GAME THEORY

See also Mathematical models; Mathematics; Probabilities

GAME WARDENS *See* Game protection

Game, set, match, champion Arthur Ashe. Hubbard, C.   **92**

GAMES

Anderson, M. T. The Game of Sunken Places   **Fic**

Anna Banana: 101 jump-rope rhymes   **398.8**

The art of stone skipping and other fun old-time games   **790.1**

Bell-Rehwoldt, S. The kids' guide to classic games   **790.1**

The best birthday parties ever!   **793.2**

The big book for toddlers   **808.8**

Conner, B. Unplugged play   **790.1**

Danks, F. Run wild!   **790.1**

Davies, H. The games book   **790.1**

Dennis, Y. W. A kid's guide to native American history   **970.004**

Gillman, C. The kids' summer fun book   **790.1**

Miss Mary Mack and other children's street rhymes   **796.1**

Onyefulu, I. Play   **E**

Regan, L. Games on the move!   **790.1**

Regan, L. Outdoor games!   **790.1**

Regan, L. Party games   **790.1**

Rose, J. Go out and play!   **796**

Rowell, V. Tag, toss & run   **790.1**

Steig, W. C D B   **793.73**

Strother, S. The adventurous book of outdoor games   **796**

Tullet, H. The game of finger worms   **E**

Tullet, H. The game of let's go!   **E**

Tullet, H. The game of light   **E**

Tullet, H. The game of mix and match   **E**

Tullet, H. The game of mix-up art   **E**

Tullet, H. The game of patterns   **E**

GAMES

See also Entertaining; Physical education; Recreation

GAMES

Unbored   **790**

GAMES -- FICTION

Benjamin, A. H. Oh No! Said Elephant   **E**

Czekaj, J. Oink-a-doodle-moo   **E**

The legend of rock paper scissors   **E**

Myers, C. H.O.R.S.E.   **Fic**

Na, I. S. Hide & seek   **E**

GAMES -- GRAPHIC NOVELS

SheHeWe   **741.5**

The **games** book. Davies, H.   **790.1**

Games handbook [series]

Regan, L. Games on the move!   **790.1**

Regan, L. Indoor games!   **793**

Regan, L. Outdoor games!   **790.1**

Regan, L. Party games   **790.1**

Games on the move! Regan, L.   **790.1**

GAMIFICATION

See also Games

Gaming safely.   **794.8**

Gaming technology. Oxlade, C.   **794.8**

Gamlin, Linda

Evolution   **576.8**

Gammell, Stephen

(il) Ackerman, K. Song and dance man   **E**

Dickens, C. A Christmas carol **Fic**
Frightlopedia **031.02**
Galdone, P. The teeny-tiny woman **398.2**
Ghosts **741.5**
Goldfish Ghost **E**
Goodhart, P. Three little ghosties **E**
Grabenstein, C. The black heart crypt **Fic**
Grabenstein, C. The crossroads **Fic**
Grabenstein, C. The Hanging Hill **Fic**
Griffin, P. R. The ghost sitter **Fic**
Guys Read Terrifying Tales **S**
Hahn, M. D. All the lovely bad ones **Fic**
Hahn, M. D. The ghost of Crutchfield Hall **Fic**
Hahn, M. D. Wait till Helen comes **Fic**
Herman, E. Hubknuckles **E**
Home sweet horror **Fic**
Ibbotson, E. Dial-a-ghost **Fic**
Irving, W. The Legend of Sleepy Hollow **Fic**
Kehret, P. The ghost's grave **Fic**
Kelley, J. The girl behind the glass **Fic**
Kelly, D. A. The pinstripe ghost **Fic**
Kimmel, E. C. Scaredy Kat **Fic**
Kimmel, E. C. School spirit **Fic**
Kimmel, E. C. Unhappy medium **Fic**
Klise, K. Dying to meet you **Fic**
Klise, K. Over my dead body **Fic**
Klise, K. Till death do us bark **Fic**
Kohara, K. Ghosts in the house! **E**
Little, K. G. Circle of secrets **Fic**
Lowery, L. The tale of La Llorona **398.2**
Martin, B. The ghost-eye tree **E**
McKissack, P. C. The dark-thirty **S**
McKissack, P. Ol' Clip-Clop **E**
Morales, Y. Just in case **E**
My first ghost **E**
Newbery, L. Lost boy **Fic**
Noel, A. Dreamland **Fic**
Noel, A. Radiance **Fic**
Noel, A. Shimmer **Fic**
Ogburn, J. K. The bake shop ghost **E**
Oliver, L. Liesl & Po **Fic**
Pearson, S. We're going on a ghost hunt **E**
The Peculiar Haunting of Thelma Bee **Fic**
Princess for a week **Fic**
Pulver, R. Never say boo! **E**
Sage, A. My haunted house **Fic**
San Souci, R. Haunted houses **S**
San Souci, R. Short & shivery **398.2**
Schwartz, A. Ghosts! **398.2**
Schwartz, A. In a dark, dark room, and other scary stories **398.2**
Schwartz, A. More scary stories to tell in the dark **398.25**
Schwartz, A. Scary stories 3 **398.25**
Schwartz, A. Scary stories to tell in the dark **398.25**
Shulman, P. The Poe Estate **Fic**
Stroud, J. The hollow boy **Fic**
Stroud, J. The screaming staircase **Fic**

Stroud, J. The whispering skull **Fic**
Stringer, H. Spellbinder **Fic**
Tingle, T. How I became a ghost **Fic**
Towell, K. Skary childrin and the carousel of sorrow **Fic**
Trapani, I. Haunted party **E**
Turnage, S. The ghosts of Tupelo Landing **Fic**
Wallace, R. Wicked cruel **Fic**
Weeks, S. As simple as it seems **Fic**

GHOST STORIES
See also Fantasy fiction; Horror fiction; Paranormal fiction
The **ghost's** grave. Kehret, P. **Fic**
The **ghost-eye** tree. Martin, B. **E**
Ghosts. **741.5**

GHOSTS
See also Apparitions; Folklore; Spirits

GHOSTS
Gee, J. Encyclopedia horrifica **001.9**
Hawes, J. Ghost hunt **133.1**
Hawes, J. Ghost hunt 2 **133.1**
McKay, H. Binny for short **Fic**

GHOSTS -- COMIC BOOKS, STRIPS, ETC
Ghosts **741.5**

GHOSTS -- FICTION See Ghost stories

GHOSTS -- FOLKLORE
Hamilton, M. The ghost catcher **398.2**

GHOSTS -- GRAPHIC NOVELS
Kochalka, J. Johnny Boo: the best little ghost in the world! **741.5**
Ghosts in the fog. Seiple, S. **940.54**
Ghosts in the house! Kohara, K. **E**
The **ghosts** of Gribblesea Pier. Abela, D. **Fic**
The **ghosts** of Tupelo Landing. Turnage, S. **Fic**
Ghosts! Schwartz, A. **398.2**
The **ghostwriter** secret. Barnett, M. **Fic**

Ghoting, Saroj Nadkarni
STEP into storytime **027.62**
Ghoul strike! Newbound, A. **Fic**
Ghoulish goodies. Bowers, S. **641.5**

Giacobbe, Beppe
(il) Burleigh, R. Clang-clang! Beep-beep! **E**
(il) Fleischman, P. Big talk **811**

Gianferrari, Maria
Coyote moon **599.77**
Giant African snail. Gray, S. H. **594**
The **giant** and how he humbugged America. Murphy, J. **974.7**
The **Giant** and the beanstalk. Stanley, D. **E**
A **giant** crush. Choldenko, G. **E**
The **giant** hug. Horning, S. **E**
The **giant** jam sandwich. Lord, J. V. **E**
The **giant** jumperee. **E**
The **giant** of Seville. Andreasen, D. **E**

GIANT PANDA
Firestone, M. Top 50 reasons to care about giant pandas **599.78**
Gish, M. Pandas **599.78**
Markle, S. How many baby pandas? **599.78**

Gigliotti, Jim
Defensive backs — **796.332**
Football — **796.332**
Linebackers — **796.332**
Linemen — **796.332**
Receivers — **796.332**
Gila monsters meet you at the airport. Sharmat, M. W. — **E**
GILA RIVER RELOCATION CENTER -- FICTION
Fitzmaurice, K. A diamond in the desert — **Fic**
Gilani-Williams, Fawsia
Nabeel's new pants — **E**
Gilbert Goldfish wants a pet. DiPucchio, K. S. — **E**
Gilbert, Adrian
Codes and ciphers — **652**
Secret agents — **327.12**
Spy school — **327.12**
Gilbert, Anne Yvonne
(il) Pirotta, S. Children's stories from the Bible — **220.9**
(il) Wargin The frog prince — **398.2**
Gilbert, W. S. (William Schwenck), 1836-1911
About
Krull, K. Lives of the musicians — **920**
Winter, J. The fabulous feud of Gilbert & Sullivan — **E**
Gilbreth, Lillian Moller, 1878-1972
About
Kulling, M. Spic-and-span! — **92**
Gilby, Nancy Benovich
FIRST robotics — **629.89**
Gilchrist, Jan Spivey
(il) Darrow, S. Yafi's family — **E**
(il) Greenfield, E. Brothers & sisters — **811**
(il) Greenfield, E. The friendly four — **Fic**
(il) Greenfield, E. The Great Migration — **811**
(il) Greenfield, E. When the horses ride by — **811**
My America — **E**
Gilda Joyce, psychic investigator. Allison, J. — **Fic**
The **Gilded** Age and Progressivism, 1891-1913. McNeese, T. — **973.8**
Giles, Bridget
Nigeria — **966.9**
Giles, Stephen M.
The body thief — **Fic**
GILGAMESH
The epic of Gilgamesh — **398.2**
Gill, Bob
(il) Reid, A. Supposing — **E**
Gill, Margery
Cooper, S. Over sea, under stone — **Fic**
Gillespie, John Thomas, 1928-
(jt. auth) Barr, C. Best books for children — **011.62**
The children's and young adult literature handbook — **011.6**
Gilley, Jeremy
Peace one day — **303.6**
Gilligan, Paul
(il) Madaras, L. On your mark, get set, grow! — **612.6**
Gilliland, Judith Heide
Heide, F. P. The day of Ahmed's secret — **E**

Heide, F. P. Sami and the time of the troubles — **E**
Gillingham, Sara
(il) Kirk, S. T is for tugboat — **623.82**
Gillman, Claire
The kids' summer fun book — **790.1**
The kids' winter fun book — **790.1**
Gilman, Grace
Dixie — **E**
Gilman, Laura Anne
Grail quest: the Camelot spell — **Fic**
Gilmore, Barry
Speaking volumes — **028.5**
Gilmore, P. S. (Patrick Sarsfield), 1829-1892
About
Potter, A. Jubilee! — **92**
Gilpin, Caroline Crosson
Abraham Lincoln — **92**
Gilpin, Daniel
Lobsters, crabs & other crustaceans — **595.3**
Planet Earth — **550**
Snails, shellfish & other mollusks — **594**
Gilpin, Stephen
(il) Boniface, W. The hero revealed — **Fic**
(il) Cronin, D. Into the wild — **E**
(il) King, M. G. Librarian on the roof! — **027.4**
(il) Lasky, K. Felix takes the stage — **Fic**
(il) Lasky, K. Spiders on the case — **Fic**
(il) Thomson, S. L. Pirates, ho! — **E**
Gilson, Jamie
Bug in a rug — **Fic**
Chess! I love it, I love it, I love it! — **Fic**
Gilton, Donna L.
Multicultural and ethnic children's literature in the United States — **028.5**
Gimme cracked corn and I will share. O'Malley, K. — **E**
Ginger and Petunia. Polacco, P. — **E**
Ginger Pye. Estes, E. — **Fic**
Gingerbread baby. Brett, J. — **398.2**
The **gingerbread** boy. Egielski, R. — **398.21**
The **gingerbread** boy. Galdone, P. — **398.2**
Gingerbread for liberty! — **92**
Gingerbread friends. Brett, J. — **E**
The **Gingerbread** Girl. Ernst, L. C. — **E**
The **Gingerbread** Girl goes animal crackers. Ernst, L. C. — **E**
The **gingerbread** man. Kimmel, E. A. — **398.21**
The **gingerbread** man loose in the school. — **E**
The **gingerbread** pirates. Kladstrup, K. — **E**
Gino, Alex
George — **Fic**
Ginsburg, David W.
(il) Heller, E. S. Menorah under the sea — **296.4**
Ginsburg, Max
(il) Taylor, M. D. The friendship — **Fic**
(il) Taylor, M. D. Mississippi bridge — **Fic**
Ginsburg, Mirra
The chick and the duckling — **E**
Clay boy — **398.2**

GORILLAS

See also Apes

Gorillas. Gibbons, G.   **599.8**

GORILLAS

Applegate, K. Ivan   **599.884**

Bustos, E. Going ape!   **599.8**

Eszterhas, S. Gorilla   **599.884**

Gibbons, G. Gorillas   **599.8**

Gish, M. Gorillas   **599.8**

Gorillas   **599.884**

Kushner, J. M. Who on earth is Dian Fossey?   **92**

Nichols, M. Face to face with gorillas   **599.8**

Riggs, K. Gorillas   **599.884**

Schindel, J. Busy gorillas   **599.8**

Social lives of gorillas   **599.884**

Gorillas. Riggs, K.   **599.884**

GORILLAS -- FICTION

Graves, K. Second banana   **E**

Look!   **E**

Mack, J. Playtime?   **E**

Gorman, Jacqueline Laks

The modern feminist movement   **305.4**

Gorman, Mike

(il) Service, P. F. Escape from planet Yastol   **Fic**

Gormley, Beatrice

Nelson Mandela   **92**

Gormley, Greg

Dog in boots   **E**

Gorrell, Gena K.

Heart and soul: the story of Florence Nightingale   **92**

In the land of the jaguar   **980**

Working like a dog   **636.7**

Gorski, Jason

(il) Murphy, P. Exploratopia   **507.8**

Gorton, Julia

(il) Cobb, V. I face the wind   **551.51**

(il) Cobb, V. I get wet   **532**

(il) Cobb, V. I see myself   **535**

Gorton, Steve

(il) Stott, C. Space exploration   **629.4**

Goscinny

Nicholas   **Fic**

Gosier, Phil

(il) Friday Barnes, girl detective   **Fic**

GOSPEL MUSIC

Igus, T. I see the rhythm of gospel   **782.25**

GOSPEL MUSIC

See also African American music; Church music; Popular music

GOSPEL MUSIC -- FICTION

Freedom song   **E**

Goss, Gary

Rotner, S. Where does food come from?   **664**

Gossie. Dunrea, O.   **E**

GOSSIP

See also Journalism; Libel and slander

GOSSIP -- FICTION

McDonald, M. Hen hears gossip   **E**

What James said   **E**

GOSSIP -- FOLKLORE

Waldman, D. A sack full of feathers   **398.2**

Got geography!   **811**

Gotcha again for guys! Baxter, K. A.   **028.5**

Gotcha good! Baxter, K. A.   **028.5**

Gothard, David

(il) Little Lola   **E**

GOTHIC ARCHITECTURE

Macaulay, D. Building the book Cathedral   **726.6**

GOTHS

Kroll, S. Barbarians!   **940.1**

GOTHS

See also Teutonic peoples

Goto, Scott

(il) O'Malley, K. Once upon a royal superbaby   **E**

Gott, Barry

(il) Dizzy dinosaurs   **811**

Gotta go! Gotta go! Swope, S.   **E**

Gottardo, Alessandro

(il) Moon bear   **Fic**

Gottfried, Maya

Our farm   **811**

Gottfried, Ted

Alcohol   **362.292**

Millard Fillmore   **92**

Gotting, Jean-Claude

Delval The Bible for young children   **220.9**

Gould, Margee

Giant plants   **580**

Meat-eating plants   **583**

Poisonous plants   **581.6**

Prickly plants   **581.4**

Gourley, Robbin

Bring me some apples and I'll make you a pie   **E**

(il) First garden   **712**

(il) Forest has a song   **E**

Govenar, Alan

(ed) Stompin' at the Savoy   **92**

GOVERNESSES -- FICTION

The unseen guest   **Fic**

GOVERNMENT *See* Political science

GOVERNMENT ACCOUNTABILITY

See also Public administration; Responsibility

GOVERNMENT AID TO LIBRARIES

See also Government aid; Libraries -- Government policy; Library finance

GOVERNMENT BUDGETS *See* Budget

GOVERNMENT BUSINESS ENTERPRISES

See also Business enterprises

GOVERNMENT EMPLOYEES

Parker-Rock, M. Christopher Paul Curtis   **92**

Government in action! [series]

Hamilton, J. How a bill becomes a law   **328**

GOVERNMENT OFFICIALS

Lourie, P. On the Texas trail of Cabeza de Vaca   **92**

Governments around the world. Giesecke, E.   **320.3**

GOVERNORS

Adler, D. A. A picture book of John Hancock   **92**

Brown, D. Teedie   **92**

Burgan, M. Ronald Reagan   **92**

Elish, D. Theodore Roosevelt   **92**

Freedman, R. Franklin Delano Roosevelt   **973.917**

Fritz, J. Bully for you, Teddy Roosevelt!   **92**

Fritz, J. Make way for Sam Houston   **92**

Fritz, J. Will you sign here, John Hancock?   **92**

Green, C. R. Sam Houston   **976.4**

Harness, C. The remarkable, rough-riding life of Theodore Roosevelt and the rise of empire America   **92**

Hines, G. Midnight forests   **92**

Hollihan, K. L. Theodore Roosevelt for kids   **92**

Keating, F. Theodore   **92**

Kimmelman, L. Mind your manners, Alice Roosevelt!   **E**

Krull, K. A boy named FDR   **92**

Marsico, K. Ronald Reagan   **92**

Marsico, K. Woodrow Wilson   **92**

Murphy, J. A savage thunder   **973.7**

Otfinoski, S. Grover Cleveland   **92**

Panchyk, R. Franklin Delano Roosevelt for kids   **92**

Smith, L. John, Paul, George & Ben   **E**

St. George, J. Make your mark, Franklin Roosevelt   **92**

St. George, J. You're on your way, Teddy Roosevelt!   **92**

Wade, M. D. Amazing president Theodore Roosevelt   **92**

Wadsworth, G. Camping with the president   **92**

GOVERNORS

See also State governments

Gow, Nancy

Ten big toes and a prince's nose   **E**

Gower, Catherine

Long-Long's New Year   **E**

Gownley, Jimmy

Amelia rules!: the whole world's crazy!   **741.5**

Grabenstein, Chris

Beach party surf monkey   **Fic**

The black heart crypt   **Fic**

The crossroads   **Fic**

Escape from Mr. Lemoncello's library   **Fic**

The Hanging Hill   **Fic**

Home sweet motel   **Fic**

House of robots   **Fic**

Mr. Lemoncello's Library Olympics   **Fic**

Treasure hunters   **Fic**

Word of mouse   **Fic**

Graber, Janet

Muktar and the camels   **E**

Grabien, Deborah

Dark's tale   **Fic**

Grace at Christmas. Hoffman, M.   **E**

Grace for president. Dipucchio, K.   **E**

Grace Hopper.   **92**

Grace, Catherine O'Neill

1621   **394.264**

Gracias.   **E**

Gracie & Grandma & the itsy, bitsy seed. Sandemose, I.   **E**

Gracie the lighthouse cat. Brown, R.   **E**

GRADING AND MARKING (EDUCATION)

See also Educational tests and measurements

Graef, Renée

(il) Bastianich, L. Nonna's birthday surprise   **E**

Schulman, J. The nutcracker   **Fic**

Graegin, Stephanie

Little fox in the forest   **E**

(il) Water in the park   **E**

Graf, Mike

How does a waterfall become electricity?   **621.31**

Grafe, Max

(il) Elliott, D. What the grizzly knows   **E**

(il) Schlitz, L. A. The Bearskinner   **398.2**

Graff, Lisa

Absolutely almost   **Fic**

Lost in the sun   **Fic**

It is not time for sleeping   **E**

Sophie Simon solves them all   **Fic**

A tangle of knots   **Fic**

The thing about Georgie   **Fic**

Umbrella summer   **Fic**

Graham, Amy

Great Smoky Mountains National Park   **976.8**

Graham, Bette Nesmith, 1924-1980

About

Thimmesh, C. Girls think of everything   **920**

Graham, Bob

April and Esme, tooth fairies   **E**

A bus called Heaven   **E**

Dimity Dumpty   **E**

(il) How the sun got to Coco's house   **E**

How to heal a broken wing   **E**

Let's get a pup, said Kate   **E**

Oscar's half birthday   **E**

(il) Rosen, M. I'm number one   **E**

The silver button   **E**

(il) Vanilla ice cream   **E**

Graham, Elspeth

Night sky dragons   **Fic**

Peet, M. Cloud Tea monkeys   **Fic**

(jt. auth) Peet, M. Mysterious traveler   **Fic**

Graham, Ian

Coppendale, J. The great big book of mighty machines   **621.8**

Aircraft   **629.133**

Fabulous bridges   **624.2**

Forensic technology   **363.2**

Microscopic scary creatures   **591.6**

Robot technology   **629.8**

You wouldn't want to live without dirt   **631.4**

Graham, Joan Bransfield

Flicker flash   **811**

Graham, Margaret Bloy

(il) Zion, G. Harry the dirty dog   **E**

Graham, Mark

(il) Collins, P. L. I am a dancer   **792.8**

Hanukkah lights   **811**

HANUKKAH -- SONGS

Baum, M. I have a little dreidel   **782.42**

Roth, S. L. Hanukkah, oh Hanukkah   **782.42**

Hanukkah around the world. Lehman-Wilzig, T.   **296.4**

Hanukkah at Valley Forge. Krensky, S.   **E**

Hanukkah haiku. Ziefert, H.   **296.4**

The **Hanukkah** hop.   **E**

Hanukkah in Alaska. Brown, B.   **E**

Hanukkah lights. Martin, D.   **E**

Hanukkah lights.   **811**

The **Hanukkah** mice. Kroll, S.   **E**

Hanukkah moon. Da Costa, D.   **E**

HANUKKAH STORIES

Baum, M. I have a little dreidel   **782.42**

Da Costa, D. Hanukkah moon   **E**

Glaser, L. Hoppy Hanukkah!   **E**

The Hanukkah hop   **E**

Jennings, S. A Chanukah Noel   **E**

Rosen, M. J. Chanukah lights   **E**

The story of Hanukkah   **296.4**

A **Hanukkah** with Mazel. Stein, J. E.   **E**

Hanukkah, oh Hanukkah. Roth, S. L.   **782.42**

Hapipi, Rafiz

Foley, E. El Salvador   **972.84**

Happenstance found. Catanese, P. W.   **Fic**

The **happiest** book ever! Shea, B.   **E**

HAPPINESS

Graves, S. I'm not happy   **152.4**

HAPPINESS

See also Emotions

HAPPINESS -- FICTION

A perfect day   **E**

Schwartz, A. 100 things that make me happy   **E**

Shea, B. The happiest book ever!   **E**

Taro Miura The tiny king   **E**

Happy. Van Hout, M.   **E**

Happy and healthy. Chancellor, D.   **646.7**

Happy and Honey. Godwin, L.   **E**

Happy bees. Yorinks, A.   **E**

Happy belly, happy smile. Isadora, R.   **E**

Happy birdday, Tacky! Lester, H.   **E**

Happy birthday Bad Kitty. Bruel, N.   **Fic**

Happy birthday to you! Raven, M.   **782.42**

Happy birthday, Hamster. Lord, C.   **E**

Happy Birthday, Madame Chapeau. Beaty, A.   **E**

Happy birthday, Mallory! Friedman, L. B.   **Fic**

Happy birthday, Martin Luther King. Marzollo, J.   **323**

Happy birthday, Moon. Asch, F.   **E**

Happy birthday, Sophie Hartley. Greene, S.   **Fic**

Happy birthday, Tree.   **E**

Happy Cat. Henry, S.   **E**

Happy dreamer.   **E**

Happy endings. Pulver, R.   **E**

Happy Halloween, Mittens. Schaefer, L. M.   **E**

Happy Hippo, angry Duck. Boynton, S.   **E**

Happy Honey [series]

Godwin, L. Happy and Honey   **E**

Happy in our skin. Manushkin, F.   **E**

Happy like soccer. Boelts, M.   **Fic**

Happy New Year, Mallory! Friedman, L. B.   **Fic**

Happy Nowruz. Batmanglij, N.   **641.5**

Happy punks 1 2 3.   **E**

Happy, happy Chinese New Year! Demi   **394.26**

Haptie, Charlotte

Otto and the flying twins   **Fic**

Haque, Jameel

Kwek, K. Pakistan   **954.91**

Harada, Violet H.

Assessing for learning   **027.8**

(ed) Growing schools   **370.71**

Hughes-Hassell, S. School reform and the school library media specialist   **027.8**

Inquiry learning through librarian-teacher partnerships   **371.1**

Harasimowicz, Ellen

(il) Burns, L. G. Beetle busters   **595.76**

(il) Burns, L. G. Citizen scientists   **590.72**

(il) Burns, L. G. Handle with care   **595.78**

(il) Burns, L. G. The hive detectives   **638**

Harasymiw, N. D.

Condors in danger   **598.9**

Harbo, Christopher L.

Easy animal origami   **736**

Easy holiday origami   **736**

Easy ocean origami   **736**

Easy origami toys   **736**

The kids' guide to paper airplanes   **745.592**

Paper airplanes: Flight school, level 1   **745.592**

Harbor. Crews, D.   **E**

HARBORS

Crews, D. Harbor   **E**

HARBORS

See also Civil engineering; Hydraulic structures; Merchant marine; Navigation; Shipping; Transportation

Harburg, E. Y.

Over the rainbow   **782.42**

The **hard** kind of promise. Willner-Pardo, G.   **Fic**

HARD-OF-HEARING *See* Hearing impaired

HARDANGER NEEDLEWORK

See also Drawn work; Embroidery; Needlework

Hardesty, Von

Epic flights   **629.13**

Hardin, Melinda

Hero dad   **E**

Hardinge, Frances

Hardinge, F. Fly trap   **Fic**

Fly by night   **Fic**

Hardinge, Frances, 1973-

Fly trap   **Fic**

The Hardy Boys: the new case files [series]

Conway, G. Crawling with zombies   **741.5**

Hardy, Aurelia

Dancers of the World   **E**

Hardy, Janice

Blue fire **Fic**

Darkfall **Fic**

Hare and tortoise. Murray, A. **E**

HARES *See* Rabbits

HARES -- FICTION

Gravett, E. Bear & Hare -- share! **E**

Hargis, Wes

(il) Jackson and Bud's bumpy ride **917**

(il) Yankovic, A. When I grow up **E**

Hargraves, Orin

Seward, P. Morocco **964**

Hariton, Anca

(il) A fruit is a suitcase for seeds **581.4**

Harker, Lesley

(il) This is my family a first look at same sex parents **306.874**

(il) Thomas, P. Do I have to go to the dentist? **617.6**

(il) Thomas, P. I think I am going to sneeze **616.97**

Harkins, Susan Sales

Design your own butterfly garden **638**

Harkins, William H.

Harkins, S. S. Design your own butterfly garden **638**

Harkrader, Lisa

The adventures of Beanboy **Fic**

Harlem. Myers, W. D. **811**

HARLEM (NEW YORK, N.Y.)

Orgill, R. Jazz Day **811.6**

HARLEM (NEW YORK, N.Y.) -- FICTION

A dance like starlight **E**

Eulberg, E. The great Shelby Holmes **Fic**

Sugar Hill **E**

HARLEM (NEW YORK, N.Y.) -- INTELLECTUAL LIFE

The book itch **E**

HARLEM (NEW YORK, N.Y.) -- POETRY

Myers, W. D. Harlem **811**

HARLEM RENAISSANCE

In her hands **92**

HARLEM RENAISSANCE

See also African American art; African American music; American literature -- African American authors

HARLEM RENAISSANCE -- FICTION

McKissack, P. C. A song for Harlem **Fic**

Tate, E. E. Celeste's Harlem Renaissance **Fic**

Harlem's little blackbird. **92**

Harley, Avis

African acrostics **811**

The monarch's progress **811**

Sea stars **811**

Harley, Bill

Dirty Joe, the pirate **E**

Harlin, Greg

Cheney, L. V. We the people **342**

(il) Krensky, S. Dangerous crossing **Fic**

(il) Krensky, S. Hanukkah at Valley Forge **E**

Harline, Leigh

When you wish upon a star **782.42**

Harmon, Dan

Minnesota **977.6**

South Carolina **975.7**

Washington **979.7**

HARMONICAS -- FICTION

McCloskey, R. Lentil **E**

HARMONY

See also Composition (Music); Music; Music -- Theory

Harness horses, bucking broncos & pit ponies. Crosby, J. **636.1**

Harness, Cheryl

(il) Cummins, J. Women daredevils **920**

Abe Lincoln goes to Washington, 1837-1865 **92**

The adventurous life of Myles Standish **92**

The amazing impossible Erie Canal **386**

George Washington **92**

The groundbreaking, chance-taking life of George Washington Carver and science & invention in America **92**

The literary adventures of Washington Irving **92**

Mary Walker wears the pants **92**

The remarkable Benjamin Franklin **92**

The remarkable, rough-riding life of Theodore Roosevelt and the rise of empire America **92**

The revolutionary John Adams **973.3**

The tragic tale of Narcissa Whitman and a faithful history of the Oregon Trail **92**

Harney, Jenn, 1972-

Hamburg, J. Hazy Bloom and the tomorrow power **E**

Harold and the purple crayon. Johnson, C. **E**

Harper, Charise Mericle

Alien encounter **Fic**

Dreamer, wisher, liar **Fic**

Gigi in the big city **E**

Henry's heart **E**

Imaginative inventions **609**

Just Grace **Fic**

(il) Just Grace and the double surprise **Fic**

Just Grace and the snack attack **Fic**

(il) Just Grace and the super sleepover **Fic**

Just Grace and the Terrible Tutu **Fic**

(il) Just Grace and the trouble with cupcakes **Fic**

Just Grace gets crafty **Fic**

Just Grace goes green **Fic**

Just Grace walks the dog **Fic**

Mimi and Lulu **E**

Pink me up **E**

The power of cute **E**

Still Just Grace **Fic**

When Randolph turned rotten **E**

Harper, Dan

Sit, Truman! **E**

Harper, Jamie

(il) Miles to the finish **E**

Miles to go **E**

(il) Warner, S. EllRay Jakes is not a chicken! **Fic**

(il) Warner, S. EllRay Jakes is not a rock star **Fic**

(il) Warner, S. Only Emma **Fic**

Harper, Jessica

Uh-oh, Cleo **Fic**

Underpants on my head **Fic**

Everett, J. H. Haunted histories **133.1**

HAUNTED PLACES -- FICTION

Cohen, M. The Inn Between **Fic**

Turnage, S. The ghosts of Tupelo Landing **Fic**

Haunted places mystery [series]

Grabenstein, C. The black heart crypt **Fic**

Grabenstein, C. The crossroads **Fic**

Grabenstein, C. The Hanging Hill **Fic**

The **haunting** hour. Stine, R. L. **S**

The **haunting** of falcon house. Yelchin, E. **Fic**

Hauser, Peter C.

How deaf children learn **371.91**

Hausman, Gerald

Horses of myth **398.2**

Hausman, Loretta

Hausman, G. Horses of myth **398.2**

Hauth, Katherine B.

What's for dinner? **811**

Have fun, Anna Hibiscus! Atinuke **Fic**

Have I got a book for you! Watt, M. **E**

Have you ever seen a hippo with sunscreen? Kaner, E. **591.4**

Have you ever seen a smack of jellyfish? Asper-Smith, S. **E**

Have you heard the nesting bird? Gray, R. **E**

Have you seen Duck? Holmes, J. A. **E**

Have You Seen Elephant? Barrow, D. **E**

Have you seen my dinosaur? Surgal, J. **E**

Have you seen my dragon? Light, S. **E**

Have you seen my duckling? Tafuri, N. **E**

Have you seen my monster? Light, S. **E**

Have you seen my new blue socks? Bunting, E. **E**

Have you seen my trumpet? **428.1**

Haven, Kendall F.

Reluctant heroes **920**

Havill, Juanita

Call the horse Lucky **E**

Just like a baby **E**

Having a hearing test. Parker, V. **617.8**

Having an eye test. Parker, V. **617.7**

Hawai'i. Kent, D. **996.9**

Hawaii. Mattern, J. **996.9**

HAWAII

Kent, D. Hawai'i **996.9**

HAWAII -- FICTION

Correa, S. Gaff **Fic**

Guback, G. Luka's quilt **E**

Kono, E. E. Hula lullaby **E**

London, J. Froggy goes to Hawaii **E**

Rattigan, J. K. Dumpling soup **E**

Salisbury, G. Calvin Coconut: hero of Hawaii **Fic**

Salisbury, G. Calvin Coconut: kung fooey **Fic**

Salisbury, G. Calvin Coconut: trouble magnet **Fic**

Salisbury, G. Night of the howling dogs **Fic**

Yee, L. Aloha, Kanani **Fic**

Yep, L. City of fire **Fic**

HAWAII -- HISTORY

Karwoski, G. Tsunami **363.34**

HAWAII -- HISTORY -- 1900-1959 -- FICTION

Georgia in Hawaii

HAWAII -- HISTORY -- FICTION

Georgia in Hawaii

HAWAII -- POETRY

Volcano wakes up! **81**

Hawass, Zahi A.

Tutankhamun **93.**

Hawcock, David

(il) Platt, R. Moon landing **629.4**

Hawes, Jason

Ghost hunt **133.**

Ghost hunt 2 **133.**

Hawes, Louise

Black pearls

Hawk & Drool. Donovan, S. **612.**

The **hawk** of the castle.

Hawker, Frances

Buddhism in Thailand **294.**

Christianity in Mexico **28**

Hinduism in Bali **294.**

Islam in Turkey **29**

Judaism in Israel **29**

Sikhism in India **294.**

Hawkes, Kevin

(il) Anderson, M. T. Handel, who knew what he liked **78**

(il) The beasts of Clawstone Castle **Fi**

(il) Black, M. I. Chicken cheeks

(il) Black, M. I. A pig parade is a terrible idea

(il) A boy had a mother who bought him a hat

(il) Cruise, R. Bartleby speaks!

(il) Fleischman, P. Sidewalk circus

(il) Fleischman, P. Weslandia

(il) Ibbotson, E. Dial-a-ghost **Fi**

(il) Ibbotson, E. The dragonfly pool **Fi**

(il) Ibbotson, E. The star of Kazan **Fi**

(il) Just behave, Pablo Picasso! **709.2**

(il) Knudsen, M. Library lion

(il) Krull, K. The road to Oz **9.**

(il) Lasky, K. Marven of the Great North Woods

(il) The librarian who measured the earth **52**

(il) A little bitty man and other poems for the very young **83**

(il) Madison, A. Velma Gratch & the way cool butterfly

(il) The man who made time travel **52**

(il) Meanwhile, back at the ranch

(il) Pullman, P. I was a rat! **Fi**

(il) Remy and Lulu

(il) Stutson, C. By the light of the Halloween moon

The wicked big toddlah

The wicked big toddlah goes to New York

Hawking, Stephen W., 1942-

About

Venezia, M. Stephen Hawking **9.**

Hawkins, Aaron R.

The year money grew on trees **Fi**

Hawkins, B. Waterhouse

About

Kerley, B. The dinosaurs of Waterhouse Hawkins **567.**

HERBS -- THERAPEUTIC USE

> *See also* Therapeutics

Hercufleas. Gayton, S.   **Fic**

Hercules. McCaughrean, G.   **292**

HERCULES (LEGENDARY CHARACTER)

Harris, J. Strong stuff   **398.2**

McCaughrean, G. Hercules   **292**

Orr, T. The monsters of Hercules   **398.2**

HERCULES (LEGENDARY CHARACTER)

> *See also* Legendary characters

Herding dogs. Hoffman, M. A.   **636.7**

Here come the Girl Scouts! Corey, S.   **369.463**

Here come the humpbacks!   **599.5**

Here comes Destructosaurus! Reynolds, A.   **E**

Here comes Grandma! Lord, J.   **E**

Here comes Jack Frost. Kohara, K.   **E**

Here comes McBroom! Fleischman, S.   **Fic**

Here comes Mother Goose. Opie, I. A.   **398.8**

Here comes Santa Cat.   **E**

Here comes the Easter Cat!   **E**

Here comes the garbage barge! Winter, J.   **E**

Here comes the strikeout. Kessler, L. P.   **E**

Here comes the Tooth Fairy Cat.   **E**

Here comes Valentine Cat.   **E**

Here I am. Kim, P.   **E**

Here lies Linc. Ray, D.   **Fic**

Here lies the librarian. Peck, R.   **Fic**

Here there be monsters. Newquist, H. P.   **594**

Here we go round the mulberry bush. Cabrera, J.   **E**

Here we go round the mulberry bush. Fatus, S.   **782.42**

Here we grow. Stewart, M.   **612.7**

Here's a little poem.   **811**

Here's looking at me. Raczka, B.   **757**

Here, kitty, kitty. Mora, P.   **E**

HEREDITY

DNA   **572.86**

Rand, C. DNA and heredity   **572.8**

Simons, R. Too many Sunday dinners   **616.3**

HEREDITY

> *See also* Biology; Breeding

HERESY

> *See also* Religion

Hereville: how Mirka got her sword. Deutsch, B.   **741.5**

Hergé, 1907-1983

The adventures of Tintin, vol. 1   **741.5**

Herlong, M.H.

Buddy   **Fic**

Herman and Rosie. Gordon, G.   **E**

Herman, Charlotte

First rain   **E**

Herman, Emily

Hubknuckles   **E**

Hermelin the detective mouse. Grey, M.   **E**

Hermes, Patricia

Emma Dilemma and the camping nanny   **Fic**

Emma Dilemma and the new nanny   **Fic**

Emma Dilemma and the soccer nanny   **Fic**

Emma Dilemma and the two nannies   **Fic**

Emma Dilemma, the nanny, and the best horse ever   **Fic**

Emma Dilemma, the nanny, and the secret ferret   **Fic**

The **hermit** crab. Goodrich, C.   **E**

HERMITS

Arnosky, J. Crinkleroot's guide to giving back to nature   **333.95**

Hernandez de la Cruz, Maria

Endredy, J. The journey of Tunuri and the Blue Deer   **398.2**

Hernandez, Leeza

(il) Eat your U.S. history homework   **641.5973**

Dog gone!   **E**

(il) Donovan, S. Bored Bella learns about fiction and nonfiction   **025.4**

(il) McCallum, A. Eat your math homework   **641.5**

Hernandez, Roger E.

The Civil War, 1840s-1890s   **973.7**

Early explorations: the 1500s   **970.01**

New Spain: 1600-1760s   **973.1**

Hernandez-Divers, Sonia

Geckos   **639.3**

Hero dad. Hardin, M.   **E**

A **hero** for WondLa. DiTerlizzi, T.   **Fic**

The **hero** of Little Street. Rogers, G.   **E**

Hero of the high seas. Cooper, M. L.   **92**

Hero on a bicycle. Hughes, S.   **Fic**

The **hero** revealed. Boniface, W.   **Fic**

The **hero** Schliemann. Schlitz, L. A.   **92**

The Hero's guide [series]

The Hero's Guide to Being an Outlaw   **Fic**

The hero's guide to storming the castle   **Fic**

The **Hero's** Guide to Being an Outlaw.   **Fic**

The **hero's** guide to saving your kingdom. Healy, C.   **Fic**

The **hero's** guide to storming the castle.   **Fic**

Heroes. Mochizuki, K.   **E**

Heroes [series]

McCaughrean, G. Hercules   **292**

McCaughrean, G. Odysseus   **292**

McCaughrean, G. Perseus   **292**

HEROES -- FICTION

The Bad Guys in mission unpluckable   **Fic**

Blabey, A. The Bad Guys   **Fic**

Clements, A. About average   **Fic**

Cottrell Boyce, F. The astounding broccoli boy   **Fic**

The dark talent   **Fic**

Donaldson, J. Superworm   **E**

Foxlee, K. Ophelia and the marvelous boy   **Fic**

Hatke, B. Legends of Zita the spacegirl   **741.5**

The hero's guide to storming the castle   **Fic**

Maberry, J. The orphan army   **Fic**

Maberry, J. Vault of shadows   **Fic**

Maximilian and the mystery of the Guardian Angel   **Fic**

Quest for the Spark   **Fic**

Rocco, J. Blizzard   **E**

The sand warrior   **741.5**

Savage, S. Supertruck   **E**

Slack, M. Elecopter   **E**

HEROES -- PAKISTAN -- BIOGRAPHY

Heuer, Karsten
Being caribou   599.65

Heur, Valerie d'
(il) Bourguignon, L. Heart in the pocket   E

Hewett, Richard
(il) Arnold, C. The ancient cliff dwellers of Mesa Verde   970.004

Hewitt Anderson's great big life. Nolen, J.   E

Hewitt, Kathryn
Bunting, E. Flower garden   E
(il) Krull, K. Lives of extraordinary women   920
(il) Krull, K. Lives of the artists   709.2
(il) Krull, K. Lives of the athletes   796
Krull, K. Lives of the musicians   920
(il) Krull, K. Lives of the presidents   920
(il) Lives of the explorers   920
(il) Lives of the scientists   509.2
(il) Lives of the writers   809

Hewitt, Sally
Hear this!   612.8
Look here!   612.8
Smell it!   612.8
Tastes good!   612.8
Touch that!   612.8
Using energy   333.79
Your food   641.3

Hey batta batta swing! Cook, S.   796.357
Hey Canada! Bowers, V.   971
Hey diddle diddle. Bunting, E.   E
Hey there, stink bug! Bulion, L.   595.7
Hey! listen to this.   028.5
Hey, Al. Yorinks, A.   E

Heyer, Carol
(il) O'Malley, K. Once upon a royal superbaby   E

Heyman, Alissa
(ed) The big book of pirates   S

Heyman, Ken
(il) Morris, A. Hats, hats, hats   391

Heyward, DuBose
The country bunny and the little gold shoes   E

Heyworth, Heather
(il) Troupe, T. K. If I were a ballerina   792.8

Hi, cat! Keats, E. J.   E
Hi, Fly Guy! Arnold, T.   E
Hi, Koo! Muth, J. J.   811
Hi-tech clothes. Spilsbury, R.   746.9

Hiaasen, Carl
Flush   Fic
Hoot   Fic
Scat   Fic

Hiawatha. Longfellow, H. W.   811
Hiawatha and the Peacemaker. Robertson, R.   Fic

HIBERNATION
Baines, R. A den is a bed for a bear   599.78

HIBERNATION
See also Animal behavior

HIBERNATION -- FICTION

Bear has a story to tell   E
Banks, K. The bear in the book   E
Hibernation station. Meadows, M.   E

HICCUPS -- FICTION
Cuyler, M. Skeleton hiccups   E

Hickory dickory dock. Baker, K.   E

Hickox, Rebecca
The golden sandal   398.2

Hicks, Barbara Jean
Jitterbug jam   E
Monsters don't eat broccoli   E

Hicks, Betty
Basketball Bats   Fic
Doubles troubles   Fic
Out of order   Fic
Scaredy-cat catcher   Fic
Swimming with Sharks   Fic
Track attack   Fic
The worm whisperer   Fic

Hicks, Faith Erin
(il) Into the woods   741.5
(il) The Sound of Thunder   741.5
(il) The unkindness of ravens   741.5

Hicks, Mark A.
(il) Kuntz, L. Celebrate the USA   973

Hicks, Terry Allan
The Chumash   970.004
Earth and the moon   525
Karate   796.8
Obesity   616.3
Saturn   523.4
Why do leaves change color?   575

Hidden. Dauvillier, L.   741.5
The **hidden** boy. Berkeley, J.   Fic
The **hidden** children. Greenfeld, H.   940.53

HIDDEN CHILDREN (HOLOCAUST)
See also Jewish children in the Holocaust

The **hidden** gallery. Wood, M.   Fic
The **hidden** life of the toad.   597.87
The **hidden** oracle. Riordan, R.   Fic

HIDDEN TREASURE *See* Buried treasure

Hidden world of the Aztec. Lourie, P.   972
Hidden worlds: looking through a scientist's microscope. Kramer, S.   502.8
Hide & seek. Na, I. S.   E
Hide and seek. Grant, K.   Fic
Hide and seek. Helman, A.   591.47
Hide and Seek. Fox, N.   E
Hide and Seek. Carter, D. A.   E
Hide and seek first words. Sirett, D.   793.73
Hide and seek fog. Tresselt, A. R.   E

HIDE-AND-SEEK -- FICTION
Barrow, D. Have You Seen Elephant?   E
Chase, K. Oliver's tree   E
Landström, L. Where is Pim?   E
Na, I. S. Hide & seek   E
Savage, S. Where's walrus? and penguin?   E

Walsh, E. S. Where is Jumper? **E**

Where's the Baboon? **E**

Hide-and-squeak. Frederick, H. V. **E**

Hiding Edith. Kacer, K. **940.53**

Hiding from the Nazis. **940.53**

HIEROGLYPHICS

Giblin, J. The riddle of the Rosetta Stone **493**

Rumford, J. Seeker of knowledge **92**

HIEROGLYPHICS

See also Inscriptions; Writing

Hierstein, Judith

(il) Garland, S. Voices of the dust bowl **973.917**

Higgins, Anne Keenan

(il) Ain, B. Starring Jules (as herself) **E**

(il) Ain, B. Starring Jules (in drama-rama) **Fic**

Higgins, F. E.

The Black Book of Secrets **Fic**

The bone magician **Fic**

Higgins, Nadia

National Geographic Kids everything Vikings **948**

Splash! Learn about water **546**

Weigh it! **530.8**

Higgins, Ryan T.

Be quiet! **E**

Hotel Bruce **E**

Mother Bruce **E**

Higgins, Simon

Moonshadow **Fic**

The nightmare ninja **Fic**

Higgledy-piggledy chicks. Joosse, B. M. **E**

Higglety pigglety pop! Sendak, M. **Fic**

HIGH DEFINITION TELEVISION

Hirschmann, K. HDTV **384.55**

High hopes. Heiligman, D. **92**

HIGH INCOME PEOPLE *See* Rich

HIGH INTEREST-LOW VOCABULARY BOOKS

Michalak, J. Joe and Sparky go to school **E**

HIGH JUMPERS

Freedman, R. Babe Didrikson Zaharias **92**

Krull, K. Lives of the athletes **796**

Van Natta, D. Wonder girl **92**

The **high** king. Alexander, L. **Fic**

HIGH RISE BUILDINGS *See* Skyscrapers

HIGH SCHOOL LIBRARIES

See also School libraries

HIGH SCHOOL STUDENTS

See also Students

HIGH SCHOOL STUDENTS -- FICTION

Dowell, F. O. The sound of your voice, only really far away **Fic**

Paulsen, G. Crush **Fic**

HIGH SCHOOLS

See also Public schools; Schools

HIGH SCHOOLS -- FICTION

Sloan, H. G. Counting by 7s **Fic**

HIGH SPEED AERONAUTICS

See also Aeronautics

HIGH TECH *See* Technology

HIGH TECHNOLOGY *See* Technology

High tide for horseshoe crabs. **595.4**

HIGH-CARBOHYDRATE DIET

See also Diet

HIGH-FIBER DIET

See also Diet

HIGH-FIDELITY SOUND SYSTEMS *See* Sound -- Recording and reproducing

High-rise private eyes [series]

Rylant, C. The case of the missing monkey **E**

The **higher** power of Lucky. Patron, S. **Fic**

Higher! higher! Patricelli, L. **E**

Hightower, Paul

The greatest mathematician **92**

HIGHWAY ACCIDENTS *See* Traffic accidents

HIGHWAY CONSTRUCTION *See* Roads

HIGHWAY ENGINEERING

See also Civil engineering; Engineering

The **Highway** Rat. Donaldson, J. **E**

Highway robbery. Thompson, K. **Fic**

HIGHWAY TRANSPORTATION

See also Transportation

Highway, Tomson

Dragonfly kites **E**

Caribou Song **E**

HIGHWAYMEN *See* Thieves

HIGHWAYS *See* Roads

Hikaru No Go, Volume 1. Hotta, Y. **741.5**

HIKING

See also Outdoor life

HIKING -- FICTION

Harper, J. Underpants on my head **Fic**

Kwan, J. Dear Yeti **E**

Leach, S. Count me in **Fic**

Hilb, Nora

(il) Nora's ark **E**

Hilb, Nora Ines

Pearson, D. Sophie's wheels **E**

Hilda and the troll. Pearson, L. **741.5**

Hildafolk [series]

Pearson, L. Hilda and the troll **741.5**

Hile, Lori

Surviving extreme sports **796**

Hill, Isabel

Building stories **E**

Hill, I. Building stories **E**

Urban animals **729**

Hill, Kirkpatrick

Bo at Ballard Creek **Fic**

The year of Miss Agnes **Fic**

Hill, Laban Carrick

Dave, the potter **92**

When the beat was born **92**

Hill, Mildred, 1859-1916

About

Raven, M. Happy birthday to you! **782.42**

Hill, Patty Smith, 1868-1946

About

Raven, M. Happy birthday to you!   **782.42**

Hill, Susan

Ruby's perfect day   E

Hill, Susanna Leonard

April Fool, Phyllis!   E

Can't sleep without sheep   E

Not yet, Rose   E

Punxsutawney Phyllis   E

Hillary Rodham Clinton. Levinson, C.   92

Hillary, Edmund, 1919-2008

About

Berne, E. C. Summiting Everest   **796.522**

Bodden, V. To the top of Mount Everest   **796.52**

Coburn, B. Triumph on Everest: a photobiography of Sir Edmund Hillary   92

Helfand, L. Conquering Everest   **741.5**

Krull, K. Lives of the athletes   **796**

HILLBILLY MUSIC *See* Country music

Hillenbrand, Will

All for a dime!   E

(il) Bear in love   E

(il) Chaconas, D. Don't slam the door!   E

Cock-a-doodle Christmas!   E

(il) Cuyler, M. The bumpy little pumpkin   E

Down by the station   **782.42**

(il) Ehrlich, A. Baby Dragon   E

(il) Hickox, R. The golden sandal   **398.2**

Kite day   E

Louie!   E

(il) Miller, B. One fine trade   **398.2**

Mother Goose picture puzzles   **398.8**

Off we go!   E

(il) Root, P. Kiss the cow   E

Spring is here!   E

(il) St. George, J. The journey of the one and only Declaration of Independence   **973.3**

(il) This little piggy   **398.8**

(il) Wilson, K. Whopper cake   E

(il) Wright, M. Sleep, Big Bear, sleep!   E

(il) Wright, M. Sneeze, Big Bear, sneeze!   E

Hillerich, Robert L.

The American Heritage picture dictionary   **423**

Hilliard, Richard

(il) Harrison, D. L. Mammoth bones and broken stones **970.01**

Hillman, Ben

How big is it?   **153.7**

How fast is it?   **531**

How strong is it?   **620.1**

How weird is it   **500**

Hills, Tad

Duck & Goose   E

(il) Duck & Goose go to the beach   E

Duck & Goose, it's time for Christmas!   E

How Rocket learned to read   E

R is for rocket   E

Rocket writes a story   E

Rocket's 100th day of school   E

Hilmo, Tess

Skies like these   Fic

With a name like Love   Fic

Hilo. Winick, J.   **741.5**

Hilo [series]

Winick, J. Hilo   **741.5**

Hilton, Marilyn

Full cicada moon   Fic

HIMALAYA MOUNTAINS -- FICTION

Cossi, O. Pemba Sherpa   F

Himler, Ronald

(il) Adler, D. A. A picture book of Dolley and James Madison   92

(il) Adler, D. A. A picture book of John and Abigail Adams   92

(il) Adler, D. A. A picture book of John Hancock   92

(il) Always with you   E

(il) Bunting, E. Fly away home   E

(il) Bunting, E. The Wall   E

(il) Coerr, E. Sadako and the thousand paper cranes   92

(il) Cohen, M. First grade takes a test   E

(il) Cohen, M. My big brother   E

(il) Cohen, M. Will I have a friend?   E

(il) DeLaCroix, A. The best horse ever   Fic

(il) Fritz, J. Why not, Lafayette?   92

(il) Garland, S. The buffalo soldier   E

(il) Lawlor, L. The school at Crooked Creek   Fic

(il) Newman, L. The best cat in the world   E

(il) Van Steenwyk, E. Prairie Christmas   E

Himmelman, John

10 little hot dogs   E

Chickens to the rescue   E

Cows to the rescue   E

Duck to the rescue   E

Frog in a bog   E

Katie loves the kittens   E

Noisy bug sing-along   **595.7**

Tales of Bunjitsu Bunny   Fic

There's a bug on my book!   **595.7**

Who's at the seashore?   **591.7**

HINDENBURG (AIRSHIP)

Benoit, P. The Hindenburg disaster   **363.1**

Surviving the Hindenburg   **363.12**

The **Hindenburg** disaster. Benoit, P.   **363.1**

Hinderliter, John

(il) Where is Mount Rushmore?   **978.3**

Hindle, James K.

(il) Hayes, C. Mothman's curse   Fic

Hindley, Judy

Baby talk   E

Hinds, Gareth, 1971-

(il) Gifts from the gods   **401**

HINDU HOLIDAYS

MacMillan, D. M. Diwali--Hindu festival of lights   **394.26**

HINDU HOLIDAYS

See also Religious holidays

HMONG (ASIAN PEOPLE)
   Cha, D. Dia's story cloth   **305.8**

HMONG (ASIAN PEOPLE) -- FICTION
   Gerdner, L. Grandfather's story cloth   **E**
   Sneve, V. D. H. Lana's Lakota moons   **Fic**

HMONG (ASIAN PEOPLE) -- FOLKLORE
   Blia Xiong Nine-in-one, Grr! Grr!   **398.2**

Ho, Minfong
   Hush!   **782.4**

Hoaxed! Isabella, J.   **500**

HOAXES See Impostors and imposture

Hoban, Lillian
   Arthur's Christmas cookies   **E**
   Silly Tilly's Thanksgiving dinner   **E**

Hoban, Russell
   Bedtime for Frances   **E**
   Rosie's magic horse   **E**

Hoban, Tana
   Black on white   **E**
   Colors everywhere   **535.6**
   Exactly the opposite   **428**
   Is it red? Is it yellow? Is it blue?   **E**
   Let's count   **513.2**
   Of colors and things   **535.6**
   Over, under & through, and other spatial concepts   **E**
   Shadows and reflections   **779**
   So many circles, so many squares   **516**
   White on black   **E**

Hobbie, Holly
   A cat named Swan   **E**
   Everything but the horse   **E**
   Gem   **E**
   (il) The night before Christmas   **811**
   Toot & Puddle   **E**
   Toot & Puddle: let it snow   **E**
   Toot & Puddle: the new friend   **E**
   Toot & Puddle: wish you were here   **E**
   Toot and Puddle: you are my sunshine   **E**

HOBBIES
   See also Amusements; Leisure; Recreation

The **hobbit.**   **Fic**
The **hobbit**, or, There and back again. Tolkien, J. R. R.   **Fic**

Hobbs, Valerie
   Defiance   **Fic**
   The last best days of summer   **Fic**
   Maggie and Oliver, or, A bone of one's own   **Fic**

Hobbs, Will
   Crossing the wire   **Fic**
   Jason's gold   **Fic**
   Never say die   **Fic**
   Take me to the river   **Fic**

Hoberman, Mary Ann
   (ed) Forget-me-nots   **811**
   I like old clothes   **E**
   The seven silly eaters   **E**
   You read to me, I'll read to you   **811**

Hoblin, Paul

Swimming & diving   **797.2**
The **Hoboken** chicken emergency. Pinkwater, D. M.   **Fic**
Hockey. Johnstone, R.   **796.962**
Hockey. McMahon, D.   **796.962**

HOCKEY
   See also Winter sports

HOCKEY
   Adams, C. Queens of the ice   **796.962**
   I'm cool!   **E**
   Johnstone, R. Hockey   **796.962**
   McClellan, R. Hockey   **796.962**
   McKinley, M. Ice time   **796.962**
   McMahon, D. Hockey   **796.962**
   Sharp, A. W. Ice hockey   **796.962**
   Stewart, M. Score!   **796.962**
   Wiseman, B. Stanley Cup   **796.96**
Hockey. McClellan, R.   **796.962**

HOCKEY PLAYERS
   Krull, K. Lives of the athletes   **796**

HOCKEY PLAYERS -- FICTION
   Gretzky, G. Great   **E**
Hocus Pocus. Desrosiers, S.   **E**

Hodge, Deborah
   Desert animals   **591.7**
   Forest animals   **591.7**
   Polar animals   **591.7**
   Rain forest animals   **591.7**
   Rescuing the children   **940.53**
   Savanna animals   **591.7**
   Up we grow!   **630**
   Watch me grow!   **630**
   Wetland animals   **591.7**

Hodges, Gary
   Chapman, G. Coffee   **641.3**

Hodges, Margaret
   Dick Whittington and his cat   **398.2**
   The kitchen knight   **398.22**
   Moses   **222**
   Saint George and the dragon   **398.2**
   The wee Christmas cabin   **E**

Hodgkins, Fran
   Amazing eggs   **591.4**
   Champions of the ocean   **920**
   How people learned to fly   **629.13**
   The whale scientists   **599.5**
   Who's been here?   **E**

Hodgkinson, Jo
   The talent show   **E**

Hodgkinson, Leigh
   Limelight Larry   **E**
   Smile!   **E**

Hodgman, Ann
      About
   Hodgman, A. The house of a million pets   **92**
   Hodgman, A. How to die of embarrassment every day   **92**

Hodson, Sally
   Granny's clan   **E**

Hoefler, Kate
Real cowboys — E

Hoena, Blake
Everything birds of prey — 598.9

Hof, Marjolijn
Against the odds — Fic
Mother number zero — Fic

Hoff, Syd
The littlest leaguer — E
Oliver — E
Sammy the seal — E
(il) Schwartz, A. I saw you in the bathtub, and other folk rhymes — 398.2

Hoffman, Lawrence A.
What you will see inside a synagogue — 296.4

Hoffman, Mary
Amazing Grace — E
The color of home — E
Grace at Christmas — E
The great big body book — 612
The great big book of families — 306.8
Guard dogs — 636.7
Helping dogs — 362.4
Herding dogs — 636.7
Police dogs — 363.2

Hoffman, Nancy
West Virginia — 975.4

Hoffmann, E. T. A.
Anderson, A. The Nutcracker — E
Jeffers, S. The Nutcracker — E
Koppe, S. The Nutcracker — Fic
Schulman, J. The nutcracker — Fic

Hoffmann, Gretchen
Chicken pox — 616.9

Hog-eye. Meddaugh, S. — E

Hogan, Jamie
(il) Arnold, C. A warmer world — 363.738
(il) Here come the humpbacks! — 599.5
(il) Perkins, M. Rickshaw girl — Fic
Seven days of Daisy — E
(il) Tiger boy — Fic

Hogan, Sophie
(il) Watters, D. Where's Mom's hair? — 616.99

Hogg, Hogg & Hog. Palatini, M. — E

Hogrogian, Nonny
(il) Come back, Moon — E
The contest — 398.2
Cool cat — E
One fine day — 398.2
(il) Leodhas, S. N. Always room for one more — 782.42

HOGS See Pigs

Hogwash. Geisert, A. — E

Hogwash. — E

HOISTING MACHINERY
See also Machinery

Hokanson, Lois
(il) Finkelstein, N. H. Remember not to forget — 940.53

Hokey Pokey. Spinelli, J. — Fic

Hokusai. Ray, D. K. — 92

Hokusai (Katsushika Hokusai), 1760-1849
About
Place, F. The old man mad about drawing — Fic
Ray, D. K. Hokusai — 92

Holabird, Katharine
Angelina Ballerina — E

Holbrook. Becker, B. — Fic

Holbrook, Sara
Zombies! — 811

Holczer, Tracy
The secret hum of a daisy — Fic

Hold fast. Balliett, B. — Fic

Hold the flag high. Clinton, C. — 973.7

Hold up the sky: and other Native American tales from Texas and the Southern Plains. Curry, J. L. — 398.2

Holden, Henry M.
The coolest job in the universe — 629.44
Danger in space — 629.45

Holder, Jimmy
(il) Wallace, R. The ball hogs — Fic

Holderness, Grizelda
(il) Koralek, J. The story of Queen Esther — 222

The hole in the middle. Budnitz, P. — E

The Hole in the Wall. Fraustino, L. R. — Fic

Hole, Stian
Garmann's summer — E

Holes. Sachar, L. — Fic

HOLES
Barnett, M. Sam and Dave dig a hole — E

Holgate, Douglas
(il) Brallier, M. The last kids on Earth — 741.5
(il) Cotler, S. Cheesie Mack is running like crazy! — Fic
(il) Weeks, S. Oggie Cooder, party animal — Fic

HOLIDAY COOKING
Bowers, S. Ghoulish goodies — 641.5
Tuminelly, N. Cool holiday food art — 641.5

HOLIDAY COOKING
See also Cooking

HOLIDAY DECORATIONS
Harbo, C. L. Easy holiday origami — 736

Holiday house reader [series]
Wallace, C. Turkeys together — E

Holiday House reader [series]
Caple, K. The friendship tree — E
Kimmelman, L. In the doghouse — E

HOLIDAYS
DeRubertis, B. Let's celebrate Constitution Day — 394.263
Dia De Los Muertos — E
Douglass, S. L. Ramadan — 297.3
Gibbons, G. Halloween is-- — 394.26
Hopkins, L. B. Days to celebrate — 051
Jones, L. Kids around the world celebrate! — 394.26
Kenney, K. L. Cool holiday parties — 793.2
Peppas, L. Cultural traditions in Mexico — 394.26
Webb, L. S. Holidays of the world cookbook for stu-

Gonzalez, C. D. Moving target — **Fic**

HOLY LAND *See* Palestine

The **holy** twins: Benedict and Scholastica. Norris, K. — **271**

Holyfield, John

(il) Belle, the last mule at Gee's Bend — **E**

(il) Bildner, P. The Hallelujah Flight — **E**

Holyoke, Nancy

Money — **332.024**

A smart girl's guide to her parents' divorce — **306.89**

Holyoke, Polly

The Neptune Project — **Fic**

Holzer, Harold

The president is shot! — **973.7**

Hom, Nancy

(il) Blia Xiong Nine-in-one, Grr! Grr! — **398.2**

Home. Baker, J. — **E**

HOME

Ashman, L. Castles, caves, and honeycombs — **E**

HOME -- FICTION

Biddulph, R. Blown away — **E**

Holczer, T. The secret hum of a daisy — **Fic**

If all the animals came inside — **E**

Na, I. S. Welcome home, Bear — **E**

Nelson, K. Baby Bear — **E**

The quiet place — **E**

Stead, P. C. A home for Bird — **E**

HOME AND SCHOOL -- FICTION

Bean, J. This is my home, this is my school — **E**

HOME ECONOMICS -- EQUIPMENT AND SUPPLIES

Ernst, L. C. How things work in the house — **640**

HOME ECONOMICS -- FICTION

Bradford, W. Why do I have to make my bed? — **E**

Huget, J. L. How to clean your room in 10 easy steps — **E**

HOME ECONOMISTS

Thimmesh, C. Girls think of everything — **920**

A **home** for Bird. Stead, P. C. — **E**

A **home** for Dixie. Jackson, E. — **636.7**

A **Home** for Mr. Emerson. — **92**

Home front. Samuels, C. — **940.53**

Home is with our family. Hansen, J. — **Fic**

HOME LIFE *See* Family life

Home of the brave. Applegate, K. — **Fic**

Home on the moon. Dyson, M. J. — **629.45**

Home on the range. Hopkinson, D. — **92**

A **home** on the tundra. Marsico, K. — **577.5**

Home run. Burleigh, R. — **811**

Home Run. Green, T. — **Fic**

Home run! Bonnet, R. L. — **530**

HOME SCHOOLING -- FICTION

Bean, J. This is my home, this is my school — **E**

Cavanaugh, N. J. This journal belongs to Ratchet — **Fic**

Home sweet horror. — **Fic**

Home sweet motel. — **Fic**

Home, and other big, fat lies. Wolfson, J. — **Fic**

HOME-BASED BUSINESS

See also Business; Self-employed; Small business

Home-field advantage. Tuck, J. — **E**

Homegrown house. Wong, J. S. — **E**

HOMELESS *See* Homeless persons; Homelessness

Homeless bird. Whelan, G. — **Fic**

HOMELESS FAMILIES -- FICTION

Balliett, B. Hold fast — **Fic**

HOMELESS GIRLS -- FICTION

Ellis, S. Outside in — **Fic**

HOMELESS PEOPLE *See* Homeless persons

HOMELESS PERSONS

Lynette, R. What to do when your family loses its home — **362.5**

HOMELESS PERSONS

See also Poor

HOMELESS PERSONS -- FICTION

Bauer, J. Almost home — **Fic**

Still a Family — **E**

Wolk, L. Wolf Hollow — **Fic**

HOMELESSNESS

See also Housing; Poverty; Social problems

HOMEOPATHY

See also Alternative medicine; Pharmacy

Homer. Cooper, E. — **E**

Homer

Ita, S. The Odyssey — **741.5**

Homer, fl. ca. 900 B.C.-ca. 801 B.C.

About

Chwast, S. The odyssey — **741.5**

Landmann, B. The fate of Achilles — **883**

Landmann, B. The incredible voyage of Ulysses — **883**

Homer Price. McCloskey, R. — **Fic**

Homer, the library cat. Lindbergh, R. — **E**

HOMES *See* Houses

HOMES (INSTITUTIONS) *See* Charities; Institutional care; Orphanages

Homesick. Klise, K. — **Fic**

Homesick: my own story. Fritz, J. — **92**

HOMESICKNESS -- FICTION

In a village by the sea — **E**

My two blankets — **E**

The quiet place — **E**

Say, A. Tea with milk — **E**

Homework. Yorinks, A. — **E**

HOMEWORK

Intner, C. F. Homework help from the library — **025.5**

Kraus, J. Annie's plan — **371.3**

HOMEWORK

See also Study skills

HOMEWORK -- FICTION

The bear report — **E**

Homework help from the library. Intner, C. F. — **025.5**

The **homework** machine. Gutman, D. — **Fic**

HOMICIDE

See also Crime; Criminal law; Offenses against the person

HOMICIDE -- FICTION

Quicksand Pond — **Fic**

HOMICIDE TRIALS *See* Trials (Homicide)

HOMING PIGEONS -- FICTION

Horace Pippin. Venezia, M.   92

Horacek, Judy
   (il) Fox, M. Good night, sleep tight   E
   (il) Fox, M. Where is the green sheep?   E

Horáček, Petr
   (il) Animal opposites   E
   Choo choo   E
   Look out, Suzy Goose   E
   One spotted giraffe   E
   Silly Suzy Goose   E
   Suzy Goose and the Christmas star   E

Hord, Colleen
   My safe community   331.7
   Need it or want it?   332.024

Horie, Ken'ichi
About
   Emery, W. Kodoku   910.4

A **horn** for Louis. Kimmel, E. A.   92

Horn, Geoffrey
   Environmental engineer   628
   Sojourner Truth   305.5

Hornaday, William Temple, 1854-1937
About
   Caper, W. American bison   599.64

Hornbooks and inkwells. Kay, V.   E

HORNBY ISLAND (B.C. : ISLAND) -- FICTION
   Mr. and Mrs. Bunny-- detectives extraordinaire!   Fic

Hornby, Hugh
   Soccer   796.334

Horne, Lena
About
   Weatherford, C. B. The legendary Miss Lena Horne   92

Hornets. Markle, S.   595.7

HORNETS AND YELLOWJACKETS
   Markle, S. Hornets   595.7

Horning, Sandra
   Chicks!   E
   The giant hug   E

Horns & wrinkles. Helgerson, J.   Fic

HOROLOGY See Clocks and watches; Sundials; Time

HOROSCOPES
   Jennings, R. W. Orwell's luck   Fic

Horowitz, Anthony
   The Falcon's Malteser   Fic
   The Greek who stole Christmas   Fic
   Public enemy number two   Fic
   South by southeast   Fic
   Stormbreaker   Fic
   Stormbreaker: the graphic novel   741.5
   The switch   Fic
   Three of diamonds   Fic

Horowitz, Dave
   Twenty-six pirates   E
   Twenty-six princesses   E

Horowitz, Eli
   Teplin, S. The clock without a face   Fic

Horrible bear! Dyckman, A.   E

Horrible Harry in room 2B. Kline, S.   Fic
Horrid Henry. Simon, F.   Fic
Horrid Henry rocks. Simon, F.   Fic
Horrid Henry wakes the dead. Simon, F.   Fic

Horrocks, Anita
   Silas' seven grandparents   E

HORROR
   See also Emotions; Fear

HORROR FICTION
   The August House book of scary stories   398.2
   Bachmann, S. The Cabinet of Curiosities   S
   Brodien-Jones, C. The glass puzzle   Fic
   Cohen, M. The Inn Between   Fic
   DeKeyser, S. The Brixen Witch   Fic
   Delaney, J. The ghost prison   Fic
   Drago, T. The Undertakers: rise of the Corpses   Fic
   Gaiman, N. Coraline   Fic
   Gidwitz, A. In a glass Grimmly   Fic
   The Grimm conclusion   Fic
   Guys Read Terrifying Tales   S
   Half-minute horrors   S
   Hayes, C. Mothman's curse   Fic
   Home sweet horror   Fic
   Johnson, H. Fearsome Creatures of the Lumberwoods   S
   Lettrick, R. The murk   Fic
   MacDonald, M. R. When the lights go out   027.62
   The nest   Fic
   Priestley, C. Tales of terror from the Black Ship   Fic
   San Souci, R. Double-dare to be scared: another thirteen chilling tales   S
   San Souci, R. Haunted houses   S
   Schwartz, A. In a dark, dark room, and other scary stories   398.2
   Schwartz, A. More scary stories to tell in the dark   398.25
   Schwartz, A. Scary stories 3   398.25
   Schwartz, A. Scary stories to tell in the dark   398.25
   Shusterman, N. Darkness creeping   S
   Stine, R. L. It's the first day of school--forever!   Fic
   Stine, R. L. The haunting hour   S
   Wallace, R. Wicked cruel   Fic

HORROR FICTION -- AUTHORSHIP
   Litwin, L. B. Write horror fiction in 5 simple steps   808.3

HORROR FILMS
   See also Motion pictures

HORROR GRAPHIC NOVELS
   Nykko, p. The shadow door   741.5

HORROR GRAPHIC NOVELS
   See also Graphic novels

HORROR NOVELS See Horror fiction

HORROR STORIES
   Auxier, J. The Night Gardener   Fic
   Beatty, R. Serafina and the Twisted Staff   Fic
   Cohen, M. The Inn Between   Fic
   Delaney, J. The ghost prison   Fic
   Hayes, C. Mothman's curse   Fic
   Home sweet horror   Fic
   Lettrick, R. The murk   Fic

How to hide a lion. Stephens, H.   **E**

How to make a bouncing egg. Shores, L.   **507.8**

How to make a cherry pie and see the U.S.A. Priceman, M. **E**

How to make a liquid rainbow. Shores, L.   **507.8**

How to make a mystery smell balloon. Shores, L.   **507.8**

How to make an apple pie and see the world. Priceman, M. **E**

How to make bubbles. Shores, L.   **530.4**

How to negotiate everything. Lutz, L.   **302.3**

How to outfox your friends when you don't have a clue. Keating, J.   **Fic**

How to raise monarch butterflies. Pasternak, C.   **595.78**

How to read a map. Waldron, M.   **912.01**

How to really fool yourself. Cobb, V.   **152.1**

How to speak cat. Whitehead, S.   **636.8**

How to Speak Dog. Weitzman, G.   **636.7**

How to steal a dog. O'Connor, B.   **Fic**

HOW TO STUDY *See* Study skills

How to survive anything. Buchholz, R.   **646.7**

How to survive in Antarctica. Bledsoe, L. J. **998**

How to survive middle school. Gephart, D.   **Fic**

How to swallow a pig.   **591.5**

How to talk to an autistic kid.   **616.85**

How to talk to your cat.   **636.8**

How to talk to your dog. George, J. C.   **636.7**

How to teach a slug to read. Pearson, S.   **E**

How to train a train. Eaton, J. C.   **E**

How to use waste energy to heat and light your home. O'Neal, C.   **621.1**

How video game designers use math. Egan, J.   **794.8**

How we crossed the West. Schanzer, R.   **917**

How we know what we know about our changing climate. Cherry, L.   **363.7**

How weird is it. Hillman, B.   **500**

How you were born. Cole, J.   **612.6**

How your body works. Stewart, D. E.   **612**

How's your health [series]

Royston, A. Allergies   **616.97**

Royston, A. Asthma   **616.2**

Royston, A. Cuts, bruises, and breaks   **617.1**

Royston, A. Head lice   **616.5**

Royston, A. Tooth decay   **617.6**

How-to-do-it manuals for librarians [series]

Alire, C. Serving Latino communities   **027.6**

Herb, S. Connecting fathers, children, and reading   **028.5**

Martin, B. S. Fundamentals of school library media management   **025.1**

How? Ripley, C.   **031.02**

Howard Thurman's great hope. Jackson Issa, K.   **92**

Howard, Arthur

(il) Byars, B. C. The SOS file   **Fic**

(il) Cuyler, M. 100th day worries   **E**

(il) Cuyler, M. Hooray for Reading Day!   **E**

(il) Gooseberry Park and the Master Plan   **Fic**

Hoodwinked   **E**

(il) Mr. Putter & Tabby drop the ball   **E**

(il) Mr. Putter & Tabby hit the slope   **E**

Mr. Putter & Tabby pour the tea   **E**

(il) Mr. Putter & Tabby ring the bell   **E**

(il) Mr. Putter & Tabby smell the roses   **E**

(il) Mr. Putter & Tabby turn the page   **E**

(il) Scanlon, L. G. Noodle & Lou   **E**

Howard, Elizabeth Fitzgerald

Aunt Flossie's hats (and crab cakes later)   **E**

Virgie goes to school with us boys   **E**

Howard, Ellen

The crimson cap   **Fic**

Howard, Paul

(il) Cooke, T. Full, full, full of love   **E**

(il) Henderson, K. Look at you!   **E**

Howarth, Craigh

(il) Mair, J. S. The perfect gift   **E**

Howarth, Daniel

(il) Glaser, L. Hoppy Hanukkah!   **E**

(il) Glaser, L. Hoppy Passover!   **E**

(il) Roth, C. Will you still love me?   **E**

Howatt, Sandra J.

Sleepyheads   **E**

Howden, Sarah

Moto and me   **599.752**

Howe, Deborah

Bunnicula   **Fic**

Howe, Ian

Jennings, M. Soccer step-by-step   **796.334**

Howe, James

Howe, D. Bunnicula   **Fic**

Howe, J. Addie on the inside   **Fic**

Howe, J. Totally Joe   **Fic**

Brontorina   **E**

Dew drop dead   **Fic**

Horace and Morris but mostly Dolores   **E**

Houndsley and Catina   **E**

Kaddish for Grandpa in Jesus' name, amen   **E**

Otter and odder   **E**

Pinky and Rex   **E**

When you go to kindergarten   **372.21**

Howe, Peter

Waggit's tale   **Fic**

Warriors of the black shroud   **Fic**

Howe, Samuel Gridley, 1801-1876

About

Alexander, S. H. She touched the world: Laura Bridgman, deaf-blind pioneer   **92**

Howe, William Howe, 5th Viscount, 1729-1814

About

Murphy, J. The crossing   **973.3**

Howell, Brian

Sports   **796**

The US Civil War and Reconstruction   **973.8**

Howell, Troy

(il) Friddell, C. Goliath   **975.2**

The dragon of Cripple Creek   **Fic**

(il) Osborne, M. P. Favorite Greek myths   **292**

Howells, Tania

(il) Button, L. Willow's whispers   **E**

Reagan, J. How to babysit a grandma — **E**

Reagan, J. How to babysit a grandpa — **E**

Reid, R. What's black and white and Reid all over? — **027.62**

Rex, A. Smek for president! — **Fic**

Rex, A. Unlucky charms — **Fic**

Shea, B. Cheetah can't lose — **E**

Small, D. Imogene's antlers — **E**

Snicket, L. Lemony Snicket: the unauthorized autobiography — **Fic**

Splat! — **E**

The terrible two get worse — **Fic**

That is not a good idea! — **E**

Thank you, Octopus — **E**

Triangle — **E**

Vernon, U. Castle Hangnail — **Fic**

Vernon, U. Hamster Princess — **Fic**

The way to the zoo — **E**

The watermelon seed — **E**

We are growing! — **E**

Weston, R. P. Prince Puggly of Spud and the Kingdom of Spiff — **Fic**

While you were napping — **E**

Who could that be at this hour? — **Fic**

HUMOROUS FICTION
See also Fiction; Wit and humor

HUMOROUS GRAPHIC NOVELS

Aguirre, J. Giants beware! — **741.5**

Alley, Z. B. There's a princess in the palace — **398.2**

Alley, Z. B. There's a wolf at the door — **398.2**

Baltazar, A. Tiny Titans: welcome to the treehouse — **741.5**

Bliss, H. Luke on the loose — **741.5**

Brallier, M. The last kids on Earth — **741.5**

Cammuso, F. Knights of the lunch table: the battling bands — **741.5**

Cammuso, F. Knights of the lunch table: the dodgeball chronicles — **741.5**

Cammuso, F. Knights of the lunch table: the dragon players — **741.5**

Coudray, P. Benjamin Bear in Fuzzy thinking — **741.5**

Davis, E. The secret science alliance and the copycat crook — **741.5**

Davis, E. Stinky — **741.5**

Flight explorer — **741.5**

Ford, C. Stickman Odyssey — **741.5**

Giarrusso, C. G-Man, volume 1: learning to fly — **741.5**

Gownley, J. Amelia rules!: the whole world's crazy! — **741.5**

Guibert, E. Sardine in outer space — **741.5**

Holm, J. L. Babymouse: queen of the world — **741.5**

Kochalka, J. Johnny Boo: the best little ghost in the world! — **741.5**

Krosoczka, J. J. Lunch Lady and the League of Librarians — **741.5**

Long Tail Kitty, come out and play — **741.5**

Lynch, J. Mo and Jo: fighting together forever — **741.5**

Mack, J. Hippo and Rabbit in three short tales — **E**

Morse, S. Magic Pickle — **741.5**

Pien, L. Long Tail Kitty — **741.5**

Rapunzel's revenge — **741.5**

Robbins, T. The drained brains caper — **741.5**

Roman, D. Astronaut Academy: Zero gravity — **741.5**

Rosenstiehl, A. Silly Lilly and the four seasons — **741.5**

Sava, S. C. Hyperactive — **741.5**

Sias, R. Zoe and Robot: let's pretend — **741.5**

Smith, J. Little Mouse gets ready — **741.5**

Sonishi, K. Leave it to PET!: the misadventures of a recycled super robot, vol. 1 — **741.5**

Spires, A. Binky the space cat — **741.5**

Thompson, J. Magic Trixie — **741.5**

Trondheim, L. Tiny Tyrant — **741.5**

Wight, E. Frankie Pickle and the closet of doom — **741.5**

HUMOROUS GRAPHIC NOVELS
See also Graphic novels

HUMOROUS PICTURES *See* Comic books, strips, etc.

HUMOROUS POETRY

Brown, C. Hallowilloween — **811**

Brown, C. Soup for breakfast — **811**

Ciardi, J. You read to me, I'll read to you — **811**

Florian, D. Laugh-eteria — **811**

For laughing out loud — **811**

Katz, A. Oops! — **811**

Katz, A. Poems I wrote when no one was looking — **811**

Levy, D. Maybe I'll sleep in the bathtub tonight — **811**

Lobel, A. Odd owls & stout pigs — **811**

Prelutsky, J. I've lost my hippopotamus — **811**

Prelutsky, J. Behold the bold umbrellaphant — **811**

Prelutsky, J. The new kid on the block: poems — **811**

Prelutsky, J. A pizza the size of the sun — **811**

Prelutsky, J. Something big has been here — **811**

Silverstein, S. Don't bump the glump and other fantasies — **811**

Silverstein, S. Every thing on it — **811**

Silverstein, S. Falling up — **811**

Silverstein, S. A light in the attic — **811**

Silverstein, S. Runny Babbit — **811**

Silverstein, S. Where the sidewalk ends — **811**

Viorst, J. If I were in charge of the world and other worries — **811**

When you're a pirate dog and other pirate poems — **811**

HUMOROUS POETRY
See also Poetry; Wit and humor

HUMOROUS POETRY, AMERICAN

Florian, D. Laugh-eteria — **811**

Prelutsky, J. I've lost my hippopotamus — **811**

HUMOROUS STOIRES

Novak, B. J. The book with no pictures — **E**

HUMOROUS STORIES *See* Humorous fiction

HUMOROUS VERSE *See* Humorous poetry

HUMPBACK WHALE -- CALIFORNIA -- SAN FRANCISCO

O'Connell, J. The eye of the whale — **599.5**

HUMPBACK WHALE -- FICTION

Marino, G. Following Papa's song — **E**

HUMPBACK WHALE

Here come the humpbacks! — **599.5**

Humpback whales up close. Rake, J. S. — **599.5**

In Andal's house. **Fic**

In business with Mallory. Friedman, L. B. **Fic**

In daddy's arms I am tall. **811**

In front of God and everybody. McCrite, K. D. **Fic**

In front of my house. Dubuc, M. **E**

In God's hands. Kushner, L. **E**

In her hands. **92**

In like a lion, out like a lamb. Bauer, M. D. **E**

In loving memory of Gorfman T. Frog. **Fic**

In New York. Brown, M. **E**

In our mothers' house. Polacco, P. **E**

In plain sight. Jackson, R. **E**

In search of Goliathus hercules. Angus, J. **Fic**

In search of Sasquatch. Halls, K. M. **001.9**

In temperate zones. Baker, S. **551.6**

In the Antarctic. Baker, S. **508**

In the Arctic. Baker, S. **971**

In the bag! Kulling, M. **E**

In the beginning: the art of Genesis. Fischer, C. **222**

In the beginning; creation stories from around the world. Hamilton, V. **201**

In the belly of an ox: the unexpected photographic adventures of Richard and Cherry Kearton. Bond, R. **92**

In the days of sand and stars. Pinsker, M. **296.1**

In the days of the Salem witchcraft trials. Roach, M. K. **133.4**

In the days of the vaqueros. Freedman, R. **636.2**

In the doghouse. Kimmelman, L. **E**

In the footsteps of Crazy Horse. Marshall, J. M. **Fic**

In the garden with Dr. Carver. Grigsby, S. **E**

In the hollow of your hand. **782.42**

In the land of the jaguar. Gorrell, G. K. **980**

In the library [series]

  Donovan, S. Bob the Alien discovers the Dewey decimal system **025.4**

  Donovan, S. Bored Bella learns about fiction and nonfiction **025.4**

  Donovan, S. Pingpong Perry experiences how a book is made **070.5**

In the meadow. Katō, Y. **E**

In the night kitchen. Sendak, M. **E**

In the picture. Micklethwait, L. **750**

In the rainforest. Duke, K. **577.34**

In the sea. Elliott, D. **811**

In the small, small pond. Fleming, D. **E**

In the tall, tall grass. Fleming, D. **E**

In the trees, honeybees! Mortensen, L. **595.7**

In the tropics. Baker, S. **508**

In the wild. Elliott, D. **811**

In the woods: who's been here? George, L. B. **591**

In the Year of the Boar and Jackie Robinson. Lord, B. B. **Fic**

In the zone [series]

  Johnstone, R. Hockey **796.962**

In too deep. Watson, J. **Fic**

In touch with basic science [series]

  Spilsbury, L. What is light? **535**

  Spilsbury, R. What are forces and motion? **531**

  Spilsbury, R. What are solids, liquids, and gases? **530.4**

  Spilsbury, R. What is energy? **621**

In, over and on the farm. Long, E. **E**

The **Inca** empire. Newman, S. **985**

INCANDESCENT LAMPS *See* Electric lamps

INCAS

  Calvert, P. The ancient Inca **985**

  Gruber, B. Ancient Inca **985**

  Newman, S. The Inca empire **985**

Inch by inch. Mallett, D. **782.42**

Inch by inch. Lionni, L. **E**

Incident at Hawk's Hill. Eckert, A. W. **Fic**

INCINERATION *See* Cremation; Refuse and refuse disposal

INCLINED PLANES

  See also Simple machines

Includes bibliographical references (page 266-268) and index. [series]

  Wallace, R. Babe conquers the world **92**

INCOME TAX

  See also Internal revenue; Taxation

An **inconvenient** truth. Gore, A. **363.7**

Incorrigible children of Ashton Place [series]

  Wood, M. The hidden gallery **Fic**

  Wood, M. The mysterious howling **Fic**

The **incredible** book eating boy. Jeffers, O. **E**

Incredible inventions. **811**

The **incredible** life of Balto. McCarthy, M. **636.7**

The **incredible** twisting arm. Lane, M. **Fic**

The **incredible** voyage of Ulysses. Landmann, B. **883**

Incredibly disgusting food [series]

  Furgang, A. Carbonated beverages **613.2**

  Furgang, A. Salty and sugary snacks **613.2**

  Johanson, P. Fake foods **613.2**

  Watson, S. Mystery meat **613.2**

INCUNABULA

  See also Books

INDEBTEDNESS *See* Debt

INDEPENDENCE DAY (UNITED STATES) *See* Fourth of July

Independence Hall. Staton, H. **974.8**

INDEPENDENCE HALL (PHILADELPHIA, PA.)

  Staton, H. Independence Hall **974.8**

Independent dames. Anderson, L. H. **973.3**

INDEPENDENT FILMS

  See also Motion pictures

Independent school libraries. **025.1**

INDEPENDENT SCHOOLS *See* Private schools

INDEPENDENT STUDY

  See also Study skills; Tutors and tutoring

INDEX LIBRORUM PROHIBITORUM *See* Books -- Censorship

Index to fairy tales. **398.2**

India. Dalal, A. K. **954**

India. Apte, S. **954**

INDIA

  Tejubehan (Singer) Drawing from the City **745**

INDIA -- FICTION

  Krishnaswami, U. Out of the way! Out of the way! **E**

Franklin, P. Library 101   **027.8**

Gaines, A. Master the library and media center   **020**

Harada, V. H. Assessing for learning   **027.8**

Martin, B. S. Fundamentals of school library media management   **025.1**

Morris, B. J. Administering the school library media center   **027.8**

Safford, B. R. Guide to reference materials for school library media centers   **011.6**

INSTRUCTIONAL MATERIALS CENTERS

  See also Libraries

INSTRUCTIONAL MATERIALS CENTERS -- DESIGN AND CONSTRUCTION

Erikson, R. Designing a school library media center for the future   **027.8**

INSTRUCTIONAL TECHNOLOGY *See* Educational technology

Instructions. Gaiman, N.   **E**

INSURGENCY -- FICTION

Nielsen, J. A. Mark of the thief   **Fic**

INTEGRATED SCHOOLS *See* School integration

INTEGRATION IN EDUCATION *See* School integration; Segregation in education

INTEGRATION, RACIAL *See* Race relations

INTELLECT

  See also Psychology

INTELLECT -- FICTION

Chatterton, M. The Brain finds a leg   **Fic**

INTELLECTUAL COOPERATION

  See also International cooperation

INTELLECTUAL FREEDOM

Intellectual Freedom Manual   **025.2**

Scales, P. R. Protecting intellectual freedom in your school library   **025.2**

INTELLECTUAL FREEDOM

  See also Freedom

Intellectual freedom front lines [series]

Scales, P. R. Protecting intellectual freedom in your school library   **025.2**

Intellectual Freedom Manual.   **025.2**

Intellectual Freedom Manual.   **025.2**

INTELLECTUAL LIFE

  See also Culture

Intelli, Nanci

  (ed) Brown, M. W. North, South, East, West   **E**

INTELLIGENCE AGENTS *See* Spies

INTELLIGENCE OF ANIMALS *See* Animal intelligence

INTELLIGENCE SERVICE

Earnest, P. The real spy's guide to becoming a spy   **327.12**

INTERCOUNTRY ADOPTION -- FICTION

Peacock, C. A. Red thread sisters   **Fic**

Red butterfly   **Fic**

INTERCULTURAL EDUCATION *See* Multicultural education

INTERDISCIPLINARY APPROACH IN EDUCATION

Hansen, D. The music and literacy connection   **780**

INTERDISCIPLINARY APPROACH IN EDUCATION

  See also Curriculum planning

INTEREST GROUPS *See* Lobbying; Political action committees

The intergalactic bed & breakfast [series]

Aliens on vacation   **Fic**

INTERGENERATIONAL RELATIONS -- FICTION

Casarosa, E. La Luna   **E**

The hula hoopin' queen   **E**

McDonald, M. Judy Moody and the bucket list   **Fic**

INTERGOVERNMENTAL TAX RELATIONS

  See also Taxation

INTERIOR DECORATION *See* Interior design

INTERIOR DESIGN

Weaver, J. It's your room   **747**

INTERIOR DESIGN

  See also Art; Decoration and ornament; Design; Home economics

Interjections.   **428**

INTERLIBRARY LOANS

  See also Library circulation; Library cooperation

INTERNATIONAL ADOPTION

Skrypuch, M. F. Last airlift   **959.704**

The **international** cookbook for kids. Locricchio, M.   **641.5**

INTERNATIONAL COOPERATION

Shoveller, H. Ryan and Jimmy   **361.7**

INTERNATIONAL SPACE STATION

The amazing International Space Station   **629**

Holden, H. M. The coolest job in the universe   **629.44**

Houran, L. H. A trip into space   **629.4**

INTERNATIONAL SPACE STATION

  See also Space stations

INTERNATIONAL STANDARD BIBLIOGRAPHIC DESCRIPTION

  See also Cataloging

INTERNATIONAL SWEETHEARTS OF RHYTHM

Nelson, M. Sweethearts of rhythm   **811**

INTERNATIONAL TRADE

  See also Commerce; International economic relations

INTERNET

Grayson, R. Managing your digital footprint   **004.6**

Popek, E. Copyright and digital ethics   **346**

Rowell, R. YouTube   **006.7**

Woog, A. YouTube   **006.7**

INTERNET (COMPUTER NETWORK) *See* Internet

INTERNET -- HOME SHOPPING SERVICES *See* Internet marketing; Internet shopping

INTERNET -- SAFETY MEASURES

Gaming safely   **794.8**

INTERNET -- SECURITY MEASURES

Schwartz, H. E. Safe social networking   **302.3**

INTERNET -- SOCIAL ASPECTS

Cornwall, P. Online etiquette and safety   **004.6**

INTERNET ADDRESSES

  See also Internet

INTERNET AND CHILDREN

Bridget and Bo build a blog   **Fic**

Gaming safely   **794.8**

Kalman, Bobbie
- Baby carnivores   **599.7**
- Baby mammals   **591.3**
- Baby primates   **599.8**
- Baby rodents   **599.35**
- The life cycle of a beaver   **599.3**
- What are opposites in nature?   **508**
- What is symmetry in nature?   **570**

Kalman, Maira
- (il) 13 words   **E**
- Fireboat   **974.7**
- Looking at Lincoln   **92**
- Thomas Jefferson   **92**

Kalz, Jill
- An A-MAZE-ing amusement park adventure   **793.73**

Kamath, B. M.
- (il) Singh, V. Younguncle comes to town   **Fic**

Kamen, Dean
> **About**
- Gilby, N. B. FIRST robotics   **629.89**

Kamishibai man. Say, A.   **E**

Kamkwamba, William, 1987-
- (jt. auth) Mealer, B. The boy who harnessed the wind   **92**
> **About**
- The boy who harnessed the wind   **92**

Kan, Katharine
- (ed) Graphic novels and comic books   **741.5**

Kandinsky, Wassily, 1866-1944
> **About**
- The noisy paint box   **92**

Kane chronicles [series]
- Collar, O. The red pyramid   **741.5**
- Riordan, R. The Red Pyramid   **Fic**
- Riordan, R. The throne of fire   **Fic**

Kanefield, Teri, 1960-
- Alexander Hamilton   **92**
- The girl from the tar paper school   **92**

Kaneko, Yuki
- (tr) Beach feet   **E**
- Hatsue Nakawaki Wait! wait!   **E**
- Into the Snow   **E**

Kaner, Etta
- And the Winner Is ...   **612.7**
- Earth-friendly buildings, bridges, and more   **720**
- Have you ever seen a hippo with sunscreen?   **591.4**
- Who likes the rain?   **551.57**
- Who likes the snow?   **551.57**
- Who likes the wind?   **551.51**

Kanevsky, Polly
- Sleepy boy   **E**

Kang, A. N.
- The very fluffy kitty, Papillon   **E**

Kang, Anna
- You are (not) small   **E**

Kang, Hildi
- Chengli and the Silk Road caravan   **Fic**

Kangaroo and crocodile. Bancroft, B.   **E**

Kangaroos. Riggs, K.   **599.2**
Kangaroos. Gish, M.   **599.2**
KANGAROOS
- Big red kangaroo   **599.2**
- Bredeson, C. Kangaroos up close   **599.2**
- Doudna, K. It's a baby kangaroo!   **599.2**
- Gish, M. Kangaroos   **599.2**
- Riggs, K. Kangaroos   **599.2**

KANGAROOS -- FICTION
- Bourguignon, L. Heart in the pocket   **E**
- Payne, E. Katy No-Pocket   **E**
- Stein, D. E. Pouch!   **E**
- Ungerer, T. Adelaide   **E**

KANGAROOS -- POETRY
- Lear, E. Edward Lear's The duck & the kangaroo   **821**

Kangaroos up close. Bredeson, C.   **599.2**

Kangas, Juli
- (comp) A child's book of prayers   **242**

Kanninen, Barbara J.
- A story with pictures

Kansas. Cannarella, D.   **978.1**
KANSAS
- Cannarella, D. Kansas   **978.1**
Kansas. Bailey, D.   **978.1**

KANSAS -- FICTION
- Kadohata, C. The thing about luck   **Fic**
- Rose, C. S. May B.   **Fic**
- Vanderpool, C. Moon over Manifest   **Fic**
- Wilson, N. D. 100 cupboards   **Fic**

KANSAS -- GRAPHIC NOVELS
- Phelan, M. The storm in the barn   **741.5**

Kantorovitz, Sylvie
- (il) Hays, A. J. Smarty Sara   **E**
- (il) Murphy, S. J. Room for Ripley   **530.8**
- (il) Schaefer, L. M. Loose tooth   **E**
- The very tiny baby   **E**
- (il) Wing, N. Go to bed, monster!   **E**

Kaplan, Bruce Eric
- Monsters eat whiny children   **E**

Kaplan, Elizabeth
- Price-Groff, C. Illinois   **977.3**

Kaplan, Michael B.
- Betty Bunny didn't do it   **E**
- Betty Bunny loves chocolate cake   **E**

Kaplowitz, Joan R.
- (jt. auth) Grassian, E. S. Information literacy instruction   **025.5**

Kaposy, Jeremy
- (il) O'Meara, S. J. Are you afraid yet? the science behind scary stuff   **500**

Karas, G. Brian
- (il) The apple orchard riddle   **E**
- (il) Applegate, K. Ivan   **599.884**
- (il) Beeler, S. B. Throw your tooth on the roof   **398**
- (il) Billingsley, F. Big Bad Bunny   **E**
- (il) Bluemle, E. Tap tap boom boom   **E**
- (il) Edwards, M. A hat for Mrs. Goldman   **E**
- (il) Elya, S. M. F is for fiesta   **E**

Kitchel, JoAnn E.
(il) Celenza, A. H. Saint-Saens's Danse Macabre **784.2**
(il) Gershwin's Rhapsody in Blue **E**
Kitchen. Burke, L. **507.8**
Kitchen dance. Manning, M. **E**
KITCHEN GARDENS See Vegetable gardening
KITCHEN GARDENS
What's in the garden? **635**
The **kitchen** knight. Hodges, M. **398.22**
KITCHEN UTENSILS
Ernst, L. C. How things work in the house **640**
KITCHEN UTENSILS
See also Household equipment and supplies
Kitchen, Bert
(il) Whoo goes there? **E**
KITCHENS
See also Houses; Rooms
KITCHENWARE See Kitchen utensils
Kite day. Hillenbrand, W. **E**
Kite flying. Lin, G. **E**
The **kite** rider. McCaughrean, G. **Fic**
KITES
Hosking, W. Asian kites **629.133**
Ichikawa, S. My pig Amarillo **E**
Lin, G. Kite flying **E**
McCaughrean, G. The kite rider **Fic**
KITES
See also Aeronautics
KITES -- FICTION
Hillenbrand, W. Kite day **E**
Khan, R. King for a day **E**
Night sky dragons **Fic**
When the wind blows **E**
Kites sail high: a book about verbs. Heller, R. **428**
A **kitten** tale. Rohmann, E. **E**
Kitten's autumn. Eugenie **E**
Kitten's first full moon. Henkes, K. **E**
Kitten's spring. Eugenie **E**
Kitten's summer. Eugenie **E**
Kitten's winter. Eugenie **E**
KITTENS See Cats
KITTENS
Arlon, P. Puppies and kittens **636.7**
KITTENS -- FICTION
Preston-Gannon, F. Pepper & Poe **E**
Kittinger, Jo S.
Rosa's bus **323.1**
Kitty cat, kitty cat, are you going to sleep? Martin, B. **E**
Kitty Cat, Kitty Cat, are you waking up? Martin, B. **E**
Kladstrup, Kristin
The gingerbread pirates **E**
Klages, Ellen
The green glass sea **Fic**
White sands, red menace **Fic**
Klass, David
Barnett, M. Extra yarn **E**
(il) Wood, M. The hidden gallery **Fic**

(il) Wood, M. The mysterious howling **Fic**
Stuck on Earth **Fic**
Stutson, C. Cats' night out **E**
Klassen, Jon
(il) Barnett, M. Sam and Dave dig a hole **E**
(il) The dark **E**
I want my hat back **E**
(il) The nest **Fic**
(il) Pax **Fic**
This is not my hat **E**
Triangle **E**
(il) The unseen guest **Fic**
We found a hat **E**
Klassen, Karen
(il) You are one **E**
You are three **E**
(il) You are two **E**
Klatt, Kathy Fling
(jt. auth) Ghoting, S. N. STEP into storytime **027.62**
Klausmeier, Jesse
Open this little book **E**
Klavan, Laurence
City of spies **741.5**
Kleber, Dori
More-igami **E**
Klee, Paul, 1879-1940

About
Paul Klee for children **759.9**
Klein, Laurie Allen
(il) Balloon trees **633.8**
(il) Solar system forecast **551.5**
Klepeis, Alicia Z.
Understanding Saudi Arabia today **953.8**
Kleven, Elisa
The apple doll **E**
(il) De colores and other Latin-American folk songs for children **781.62**
(il) Dorros, A. Abuela **E**
The friendship wish **E**
(il) Hurd, T. The weaver **E**
(il) One little chicken **E**
(il) Orozco Diez deditos. Ten little fingers & other play rhymes and action songs from Latin America **782.42**
(il) Orozco Fiestas: a year of Latin American songs of celebration **782.42**
(il) Thong, R. Wish **398**
Welcome home, Mouse **E**
KLEZMER MUSIC -- FICTION
Yolen, J. B.U.G. **Fic**
Klimley, A. Peter

About
Mallory, K. Swimming with hammerhead sharks **597.3**
Klimo, Kate
The dragon in the driveway **Fic**
The dragon in the library **Fic**
The dragon in the sock drawer **Fic**
The dragon in the volcano **Fic**

KNIGHTS AND KNIGHTHOOD

    See also Middle Ages; Nobility

KNIGHTS AND KNIGHTHOOD -- FICTION

    Kraegel, K. King Arthur's very great grandson   **E**

    Larson, M. A. Pennyroyal Academy   **Fic**

    Lewin, B. Good night, Knight   **E**

    Mull, B. Rogue Knight   **Fic**

    Sabuda, R. The dragon & the knight   **E**

KNIGHTS AND KNIGHTHOOD -- FOLKLORE

    Hodges, M. Saint George and the dragon   **398.2**

    Paterson, K. Parzival   **398.2**

KNIGHTS AND KNIGHTHOOD -- GRAPHIC NOVELS

    Chantler, S. The iron hand   **741.5**

Knights in shining armor. Gibbons, G.   **394**

Knights of the kitchen table. Scieszka, J.   **Fic**

Knights of the lunch table: the battling bands. Cammuso, F.   **741.5**

Knights of the lunch table: the dodgeball chronicles. Cammuso, F.   **741.5**

Knights of the lunch table: the dragon players. Cammuso, F.   **741.5**

KNIGHTS OF THE ROUND TABLE *See* Arthurian romances

The knights' tales [series]

    Morris, G. The adventures of Sir Lancelot the Great   **Fic**

Knit your bit.   **E**

Knit, hook, and spin. Carlson, L.   **745.5**

KNITTING

    Bradberry, S. Kids knit!   **746.43**

    Junor, B. Fun & funky knits   **746.43**

    Shall I knit you a hat?   **E**

KNITTING

    See also Needlework

KNITTING -- FICTION

    Brosgol, V. Leave me alone   **E**

    Edwards, M. A hat for Mrs. Goldman   **E**

    Knit your bit   **E**

KNITTING -- PATTERNS

    Junor, B. Fun & funky knits   **746.43**

Knitty Kitty. Elliott, D.   **E**

KNIVES

    See also Hardware; Weapons

Knives and forks. Blaxland, W.   **683**

Knock at a star.   **811**

Knock knock. Beaty, D.   **E**

Knock on wood.   **811**

Knock, knock! Freymann, S.   **817**

Knockin' on wood. Barasch, L.   **92**

KNOTS AND SPLICES

    Sadler, J. A. Knotting   **746.42**

KNOTS AND SPLICES

    See also Navigation; Rope

Knots in my yo-yo string. Spinelli, J.   **92**

Knots on a counting rope. Martin, B.   **E**

Knott, Cheryl Denise

    Laman, T. Face to face with orangutans   **599.8**

Knotting. Sadler, J. A.   **746.42**

Know your sport [series]

    Gifford, C. Golf: from tee to green   **796.352**

    Gifford, C. Tennis   **796.342**

    Gifford, C. Track athletics   **796.42**

    Mason, P. Judo   **796.815**

    Storey, R. Sailing   **797.1**

    Thorpe, Y. Canoeing and kayaking   **797.1**

Knowledge Encyclopedia.   **031**

Knowles, Laura

    (ed) Ancient treasures   **930.1**

Knowlton, Laurie Lazzaro

    A young man's dance   **E**

Knowlton, MaryLee

    Albania   **949.65**

    Macedonia   **949.7**

    Turkmenistan   **958.5**

Knox, Henry, 1750-1806

                About

    Brown, D. Henry and the cannons   **973.3**

    Henry Knox   **92**

Knucklehead. Scieszka, J.   **92**

Knudsen, Michelle

    Argus   **E**

    Bugged!   **E**

    The dragon of Trelian   **Fic**

    Library lion   **E**

    Marilyn's monster   **E**

    The princess of Trelian   **Fic**

Knudsen, Shannon

    Fairies and elves   **398**

    Fantastical creatures and magical beasts   **398**

    From egg to butterfly   **595.7**

Knudson, Mike

    Raymond & Graham: bases loaded   **Fic**

    Raymond & Graham: cool campers   **Fic**

    Raymond and Graham rule the school   **Fic**

    Raymond and Graham, dancing dudes   **Fic**

Knuffle Bunny. Willems, M.   **E**

Knuffle Bunny free. Willems, M.   **E**

Knutson, Barbara

    Love and roast chicken   **398.2**

Koala Hospital.   **599.2**

Koala Lou. Fox, M.   **E**

KOALAS

    Koala Hospital   **599.2**

    Markle, S. Finding home   **599.2**

KOALAS -- FICTION

    Ferrell, S. I don't like Koala   **E**

    Gibbs, S. Poached   **Fic**

Kobald, Irena

    My two blankets   **E**

Kobayashi, Issa, 1763-1827

    Today and today   **895.6**

                About

    Gollub, M. Cool melons--turn to frogs!: the life and poems of Issa   **92**

Kobe Bryant. Thornley, S.   **796.323**

LAKE ECOLOGY
> *See also* Ecology

LAKE ERIE -- FICTION
Markle, S. Butterfly tree   **E**

LAKES
Johansson, P. Lakes and rivers   **577.6**

LAKES
> *See also* Physical geography; Water; Waterways

LAKES -- FICTION
St. Antoine, S. Three bird summer   **Fic**

Lakes and rivers. Johansson, P.   **577.6**

Lakin, Patricia
Bicycles   **629.227**
Skateboards   **796.22**

LAKOTA INDIANS -- FICTION
Marshall, J. M. In the footsteps of Crazy Horse   **Fic**

Lakritz, Deborah
Say hello, Lily   **E**

Lala salama. MacLachlan, P.   **E**

Laman, Tim
Face to face with orangutans   **599.8**
(il) Rain Forest Colors   **591.734**

Lamanna, Paolo
Colfer, E. Artemis Fowl: the graphic novel   **741.5**

LaMarca, Luke
(il) Johnson, A. The day Ray got away   **E**

LaMarche, Jim

LaMarche, Jim
(il) The carpenter's gift   **E**
(il) The day Tiger Rose said goodbye   **E**
(il) Hanson, W. The Sea of Sleep   **E**
(il) Ivy takes care   **Fic**
(il) Johnston, T. Winter is coming   **E**
Lost and found   **E**
(il) Napoli, D. J. Albert   **E**
Pond   **E**
The raft   **E**

Lamb, Albert
Tell me the day backwards   **E**

Lamb, Braden
(il) Ghosts   **741.5**

Lamb, Susan Condie
(il) Houston, G. Miss Dorothy and her bookmobile   **E**
(il) Houston, G. My great-aunt Arizona   **371.1**

Lambert, Jonny
(il) Lach, W. I Am Not a Dinosaur!   **566**

Lambert, Sally Anne
(il) Tegen, K. The story of the leprechaun   **E**

LAMBS *See* Sheep

Laminack, Lester L.
Three hens and a peacock   **E**

Lamont, Priscilla
(il) Lulu and the dog from the sea   **Fic**
(il) Lulu and the duck in the park   **Fic**
(il) Lulu and the hedgehog in the rain   **Fic**
(il) Secrets of the garden   **Fic**
(il) Secrets of the seasons   **E**

Lamont, Priscilla
(il) Dowdy, L. C. All kinds of kisses   **E**
(il) George, J. C. Goose and Duck   **E**
(il) Stauffacher, S. Gator on the loose!   **Fic**
(il) Zoehfeld, K. W. Secrets of the garden   **Fic**

Lamorisse, Albert
The red balloon   **E**

Lamour, Sandrine
(il) My Little Handbook of Experiments   **E**

The lamp, the ice, and the boat called Fish. Martin, J. B.   **919**

Lamstein, Sarah Marwil
A big night for salamanders   **E**

Lamut, Sonja
(il) Toscano, C. Papa's pastries   **E**

Lana's Lakota moons. Sneve, V. D. H.   **Fic**

Lanan, Jessica
Out of school and into nature   **92**
(il) Schoettler, J. Good fortune in a wrapping cloth   **E**

LANCELOT (LEGENDARY CHARACTER)
> *See also* Legendary characters

LANCELOT (LEGENDARY CHARACTER) -- FICTION
Morris, G. The adventures of Sir Lancelot the Great   **Fic**

LAND DEVELOPERS -- FICTION
Appelt, K. The true blue scouts of Sugarman Swamp   **Fic**

The land is our storybook [series]
Andre We feel good out here   **970.004**
Enzoe, P. The caribou feed our soul   **970.004**
McLeod, T. The Delta is my home   **970.004**
Zoe, T. Living stories   **970.004**

A land of big dreamers. Waldman, N.   **920**

The land of forgotten girls. Kelly, E. E.   **Fic**

The Land of the Silver Apples. Farmer, N.   **Fic**

LAND SURVEYING *See* Surveying

LAND SURVEYS *See* Surveying

Landau, Elaine
Are the drums for you?   **786.9**
Beluga whales   **599.5**
Beyond Pluto   **523.4**
Big cats   **599.75**
Bites and stings   **617.1**
Broken bones   **617.1**
Bumps, bruises, and scrapes   **617.1**
Burns   **617.1**
Cavities and toothaches   **617.6**
Chickenpox   **616.9**
The common cold   **616.2**
Earaches   **617.8**
Earth   **525**
Emperor penguins   **598**
Fleeing to freedom on the Underground Railroad   **973.7**
Food allergies   **616.97**
The history of everyday life   **609**
Is singing for you?   **783**
Is the flute for you?   **788**
Is the guitar for you?   **787.87**
Is the trumpet for you?   **788**
Is the violin for you?   **787.2**

Leiper, Kate
(il) Breslin, T. An Illustrated Treasury of Scottish Mythical Creatures   **398.245**

Leitao, Julio
Keeler, P. A. Drumbeat in our feet   **793.3**

Leloup, Genevieve
(il) Reidy, J. Too purpley!   **E**

Lemaître, Pascal
(il) Heilbroner, J. A pet named Sneaker   **E**
Beaty, A. Doctor Ted   **E**
Bulldog's big day   **E**
McGhee, A. Always   **E**
Muntean, M. Do not open this book!   **E**

Lemieux, Michele
Menotti, G. C. Amahl and the night visitors   **232.9**

Lemlich, Clara, 1886-1982
About
Markel, M. Brave girl   **331.892**

LEMMINGS
Slade, S. What if there were no lemmings?   **577.5**

Lemmons, Bob
About
Lester, J. Black cowboy, wild horses   **E**

LEMONADE -- FICTION
Jenkins, E. Lemonade in winter   **E**
The **Lemonade** Club. Polacco, P.   **E**
The **lemonade** crime. Davies, J.   **Fic**
Lemonade in winter. Jenkins, E.   **E**
The **lemonade** war. Davies, J.   **Fic**
The **lemonade war series**
Davies, J. The bell bandit   **Fic**
Davies, J. Candy smash   **Fic**
Davies, J. The magic trap   **Fic**
Lemonade, and other poems squeezed from a single word. **811**

LEMONS -- FICTION
Staake, B. The red lemon   **E**
Lemons are not red. Seeger, L. V.   **E**
Lemony Snicket: the unauthorized autobiography. Snicket, L.   **Fic**
Lemur. Ganeri, A.   **599.8**

LEMURS
Aronin, M. Aye-aye   **599.8**
Ganeri, A. Lemur   **599.8**
Lena's sleep sheep. Lobel, A.   **E**

Lendroth, Susan
Calico Dorsey   **Fic**

Leng, Qin
A flock of shoes   **E**
(il) Foggo, C. Dear baobab   **E**

Lennon, John, 1940-1980
About
Behnke, A. M. Death of a dreamer   **92**
Brewer, P. The Beatles were fab (and they were funny) **782.42**
Rappaport, D. John's secret dreams   **92**
Lenny & Lucy.   **E**
Lenore finds a friend. Katz, J.   **636.73**

Lenski, Lois

(il) Lovelace, M. H. Betsy-Tacy   **Fic**

Lent, Blair
(il) Dayrell, E. Why the Sun and the Moon live in the sky   **398.2**
(il) Mosel, A. The funny little woman   **398.2**

Lentil. McCloskey, R.   **E**
Leo. Barnett, M.   **E**
Leo Geo and the cosmic crisis.   **741.5**
Leo loves baby time.   **E**
Leo the snow leopard. Hatkoff, J.   **599.75**

Leodhas, Sorche Nic
Always room for one more   **782.42**
Leon's story. Tillage, L.   **92**

León, Vicki
Outrageous women of the Middle Ages   **920.72**

Leonard, David
(il) Today on election day   **E**

Leonard, M. G.
Beetle boy   **Fic**

Leonard, Tom
Becoming Bach   **92**
(il) Brenner, B. One small place in a tree   **577.3**
(il) Who will plant a tree?   **582.16**

Leonardo da Vinci. Phillips, J.   **92**
Leonardo da Vinci. Stanley, D.   **92**
Leonardo da Vinci. Krull, K.   **92**
Leonardo's horse. Fritz, J.   **730.92**

Leonardo, da Vinci, 1452-1519
About
Barretta, G. Neo Leo   **609**
Fritz, J. Leonardo's horse   **730.92**
Krull, K. Leonardo da Vinci   **92**
Phillips, J. Leonardo da Vinci   **92**
Stanley, D. Leonardo da Vinci   **92**

Leonardo, da Vinci, 1452-1519. Mona Lisa
About
Barsony, P. The stories of the Mona Lisa   **759.06**
Knapp, R. Who stole Mona Lisa?   **E**
Leonardo, the terrible monster.   **E**

Leone, Tony
(il) Unbored   **790**
Leontyne Price.   **92**
Leopard & Silkie.   **599.79**
The **leopard** boy. Johnson, J.   **E**

LEOPARD SEAL
Snyder, E. Alarming leopard seals   **599.79**
Leopards. Gish, M.   **599.75**

LEOPARDS
Gish, M. Leopards   **599.75**
Joubert, B. Face to face with leopards   **599.75**
Markle, S. The great leopard rescue   **599.75**
Marks, J. L. Clouded leopards   **599.75**
Riggs, K. Leopards   **599.75**
Leopards. Riggs, K.   **599.75**

LEOPARDS -- FICTION
Achebe, C. How the leopard got his claws   **Fic**
Johnson, J. The leopard boy

Two little monkeys   **E**

Leopards' gold. Nimmo, J.   **Fic**

Leopold the Lion.   **E**

LEPIDOPTERA *See* Butterflies; Moths

Lepora, Nathan

  Atoms and molecules   **539.7**

  Molybdenum   **546**

Lepp, Bil

  The King of Little Things   **E**

The **leprechaun's** gold. Edwards, P. D.   **E**

LEPRECHAUNS

  Edwards, P. D. The leprechaun's gold   **E**

  Wojciechowski, S. A fine St. Patrick's day   **E**

LEPRECHAUNS -- FICTION

  Bunting, E. That's what leprechauns do   **E**

  Edwards, P. D. The leprechaun's gold   **E**

  Krensky, S. Too many leprechauns   **E**

  Roberts, L. P. Green   **Fic**

  Tegen, K. The story of the leprechaun   **E**

LEPROSY

    See also Diseases

LEPROSY -- FICTION

  Durango, J. The walls of Cartagena   **Fic**

  Ellis, D. No ordinary day   **Fic**

Lerangis, Peter

  The colossus rises   **Fic**

  Lost in babylon   **Fic**

  Riordan, R. Vespers rising   **Fic**

  Tomb of shadows   **Fic**

Lerer, Seth

  Children's literature   **028.5**

Leroy Ninker saddles up. Dicamillo, K.   **Fic**

Leroy, Jean

  A well-mannered young wolf   **E**

LESBIAN MOTHERS -- FAMILY RELATIONSHIPS

  This is my family a first look at same sex parents   **306.874**

LESBIAN MOTHERS -- FICTION

  Heather has two mommies   **Fic**

  The Pants Project   **Fic**

  This would make a good story someday   **Fic**

LESBIANS

    See also Gays; LGBT people; Women

LESBIANS -- FICTION

  Heather has two mommies   **Fic**

LESBIANS' WRITINGS

    See also Literature

Leshem, Yossi

  Vogel, C. G. The man who flies with birds   **598**

Less is more. Baumbach, D.   **025.2**

Lessac, Frané, 1954-

  Greenwood, M. The donkey of Gallipoli   **940.4**

  (il) Greenwood, M. Drummer boy of John John   **786.9**

  (il) Greenwood, M. The Mayflower   **974.4**

  Melmed, L. K. Heart of Texas   **976.4**

  Melmed, L. K. New York, New York   **974.7**

  Pomerantz, C. The chalk doll   **E**

  Rockwell, A. F. Clouds   **551.57**

Lessem, Don

  The fastest dinosaurs   **567.9**

  Flying giants of dinosaur time   **567.9**

  Sea giants of dinosaur time   **567.9**

  The smartest dinosaurs   **567.9**

  The ultimate dinopedia   **567.9**

Lesser Spotted Animals.   **590**

Lesser, Rika

  Hansel and Gretel   **398.2**

Lester's dreadful sweaters.   **E**

Lester, Alison, 1952-

  Noni the pony   **E**

  (il) Noni the pony goes to the beach   **E**

  Running with the horses   **E**

  Sophie Scott goes south   **E**

Lester, Helen

  The Loch Mess monster   **E**

  Happy birdday, Tacky!   **E**

  Hooway for Wodney Wat   **E**

  The sheep in wolf's clothing   **E**

  Tacky and the haunted igloo   **E**

  Three cheers for Tacky   **E**

  Wodney Wat's wobot   **E**

        About

  Lester, H. Author   **813**

Lester, Julius

  Black cowboy, wild horses   **E**

  From slave ship to freedom road   **306.3**

  John Henry   **398.2**

  Let's talk about race   **305.8**

  The old African   **Fic**

  Sam and the tigers   **E**

  The tales of Uncle Remus   **398.2**

  To be a slave   **326**

  Uncle Remus, the complete tales   **398.2**

Lester, Mike

  (il) Crow, K. Cool Daddy Rat   **E**

  (il) Marcus, K. Scritch-scratch a perfect match   **E**

Lesynski, Loris

  Crazy about soccer   **811**

Let it begin here! Fradin, D. B.   **973.3**

Let it begin here! Brown, D.   **973.3**

Let it shine.   **782.25**

Let it shine.   **920**

Let me play. Blumenthal, K.   **796**

Let my people go. McKissack, P. C.   **Fic**

Let the circle be unbroken. Taylor, M. D.   **Fic**

Let the whole earth sing praise. DePaola, T.   **231.7**

Let there be peace. Brooks, J.   **242**

Let there be peace on earth. Jackson, J.   **782.42**

Let your voice be heard. Silvey, A.   **92**

Let's build a playground.   **790.06**

Let's celebrate Constitution Day. DeRubertis, B.   **394.263**

Let's clap, jump, sing, and shout; dance, spin, and turn it out! McKissack, P.   **305.896**

Let's count. Hoban, T.   **513.2**

Let's count goats! Fox, M.   **E**

Prince Caspian   **Fic**
The silver chair   **Fic**
The voyage of the Dawn Treader   **Fic**
About
Ellis, S. From reader to writer   **372.62**
Lewis, E. B.
(il) Bass, H. The secret world of Walter Anderson   **92**
(il) Carbone, E. L. Night running   **E**
(il) Curtis, G. The bat boy & his violin   **E**
(il) Each kindness   **E**
(il) Grimes, N. Talkin' about Bessie: the story of aviator Elizabeth Coleman   **92**
(il) Hansen, J. Home is with our family   **Fic**
(il) Howard, E. F. Virgie goes to school with us boys   **E**
(il) Kurtz, J. Faraway home   **E**
(il) Kurtz, J. Fire on the mountain   **398.2**
(il) Michelson, R. Across the alley   **E**
(il) Mollel, T. M. My rows and piles of coins   **E**
(il) Nolen, J. Pitching in for Eubie   **E**
The other side   **E**
(il) Rappaport, D. Dirt on their skirts   **796.357**
(il) Raven, M. Circle unbroken   **E**
(il) Raven, M. Night boat to freedom   **E**
(il) Rodman, M. A. My best friend   **E**
(il) San Souci, R. Robin Hood and the golden arrow   **398.2**
(il) Slate, J. I want to be free   **E**
(il) Smith, H. A. Keeping the night watch   **Fic**
(il) Tarpley, N. Bippity Bop barbershop   **E**
(il) This little light of mine   **782.25**
(il) Wong, J. S. Homegrown house   **E**
(il) Woodson, J. Coming on home soon   **E**
Lewis, Earl B., 1956-
(il) Asim, J. Preaching to the chickens   **92**
(il) Bass, H. Seeds of freedom   **323.1**
(il) Johnson, A. All different now   **E**
(il) Kearney, M. Trouper   **E**
(il) The other side   **E**
Lewis, Edna, 1916-2006
About
Gourley, R. Bring me some apples and I'll make you a pie   **E**
Lewis, Elizabeth Foreman
Young Fu of the upper Yangtze   **Fic**
Lewis, Gill
Wild wings   **Fic**
Moon bear   **Fic**
Lewis, H. B.
(il) Kimmel, E. C. My penguin Osbert   **E**
Lewis, Ida, 1842-1911
About
Moss, M. The bravest woman in America   **92**
Lewis, J. Patrick
(jt. auth) Florian, D. Poem-mobiles   **811**
(ed) National Geographic book of animal poetry   **808.81**
(ed) National Geographic book of nature poetry   **808.81**
And the soldiers sang   **Fic**
Arithme-tickle   **513**
Big is big (and little, little)   **E**

Blackbeard, the pirate king   **811**
Countdown to summer   **811**
Doodle dandies   **811**
Edgar Allan Poe's apple pie   **811**
Face bug   **E**
The house   **811**
If you were a chocolate mustache   **811**
Last laughs   **818**
Monumental verses   **811**
Self-portrait with seven fingers   **811**
Skywriting   **811**
The snowflake sisters   **E**
Spot the plot   **811**
When thunder comes   **811**
World Rat day   **E**
The World's Greatest   **811**
Lewis, Jill
Don't read this book!   **E**
Lewis, John, 1940-
About
Asim, J. Preaching to the chickens   **92**
Bausum, A. Freedom Riders   **323.1**
Haskins, J. John Lewis in the lead   **92**
Lewis, Kevin
Not inside this house!   **E**
Lewis, Maggie
Morgy makes his move   **Fic**
Morgy's musical summer   **Fic**
Lewis, Marisa
(il) Johnson, J. The leopard boy   **E**
Lewis, Mark J.
North Dakota   **978.4**
Lewis, Meriwether, 1774-1809
About
Bodden, V. Through the American West   **978**
Myers, L. Lewis and Clark and me   **Fic**
Perritano, J. The Lewis and Clark Expedition   **978**
Schanzer, R. How we crossed the West   **917**
Lewis, Paeony
No more yawning!   **E**
Lewis, Rose A.
Every year on your birthday   **E**
I love you like crazy cakes   **E**
Lewis, Stevie
(il) Banks, A. Blueberry pancakes forever   **Fic**
(il) Banks, A. Finding Serendipity   **Fic**
(il) Banks, A. A week without Tuesday   **Fic**
Lexau, Joan M.
Who took the farmer's [hat]?   **E**
LEXICOGRAPHERS -- GREAT BRITAIN -- BIOGRAPHY
Bryant, J. The right word   **92**
LEXICOGRAPHERS -- UNITED STATES -- BIOGRAPHY
Noah Webster's fighting words   **92**
LEXICOGRAPHY
   See also Encyclopedias and dictionaries
Lexie. Couloumbis, A.   **Fic**

Lion's lunch? Tierney, F.   **E**

The **lion's** share. McElligott, M.   **E**

The **lion,** the witch, and the wardrobe. Lewis, C. S.   **Fic**

Lionni, Leo

    Alexander and the wind-up mouse   **E**

    Fish is fish   **E**

    Frederick   **E**

    Inch by inch   **E**

    Little blue and little yellow   **E**

    Six crows   **E**

    Swimmy   **E**

Lions. Schafer, S.   **599.75**

LIONS

    Bodden, V. Lions   **599.75**

    Bredeson, C. Lions up close   **599.75**

    Hague, B. Rise of the lioness   **599.757**

    Helfer, R. World's greatest lion   **E**

    Hurd, E. T. Johnny Lion's book   **E**

    Joubert, B. Face to face with lions   **599.75**

    Schafer, S. Lions   **599.75**

Lions. Bodden, V.   **599.75**

LIONS -- FICTION

    Agee, J. Lion lessons   **E**

    Cummins, L. R. A hungry lion, or, a dwindling assortment of animals   **E**

    Davies, N. The Lion who stole my arm   **Fic**

    Leopold the Lion   **E**

    The lion and the bird   **E**

    McCall Smith, A. The mystery of the missing lion   **Fic**

    McPhail, D. Pig Pig meets the lion   **E**

    O'Neill, G. Monty's magnificent mane   **E**

    Smith, A. T. Little Red and the very hungry lion   **398.2**

    Stephens, H. How to hide a lion   **E**

LIONS AS PETS -- FICTION

    Leopold the Lion   **E**

The **lions** of Little Rock. Levine, K.   **Fic**

Lions up close. Bredeson, C.   **599.75**

Lipan, Sabine

    Mom, there's a bear at the door   **E**

Lipchenko, Oleg

    Humpty Dumpty and friends   **398.8**

Lipman Pike. Michelson, R.   **92**

Lippert, Margaret H.

    Paye Head, body, legs   **398.2**

    Paye Mrs. Chicken and the hungry crocodile   **398.2**

Lippincott, Gary

    (il) Coville, B. Jennifer Murdley's toad   **Fic**

    (il) Coville, B. Jeremy Thatcher, dragon hatcher   **Fic**

    (il) Coville, B. The skull of truth   **Fic**

    (il) Yolen, J. Come to the fairies' ball   **E**

Lipson, Eden Ross

    Applesauce season   **E**

Lipsyte, Robert

    Heroes of baseball   **796.357**

    The twinning project   **Fic**

Lipton, Lenny

    Lipton, L. Puff, the magic dragon

Yarrow, P. Puff the magic dragon pop-up book   **E**

Lipton, Leonard

    Puff, the magic dragon

LIQUIDS

    Adamson, T. K. How do you measure liquids?   **530.8**

    Boothroyd, J. What is a liquid?   **530.4**

    Hurd, W. Changing states   **530.4**

LIQUIDS

    See also Fluid mechanics; Physics

LIQUOR PROBLEM *See* Alcoholism; Drinking of alcoholic beverages

LIQUORS

    See also Alcoholic beverages; Beverages

Lisker, Sonia O.

    Blume, J. Freckle juice   **Fic**

Lisle, Andria

    Plumley, A. P. Sewing school   **646.2**

Lisle, Holly

    The Ruby Key   **Fic**

    The silver door   **Fic**

Lisle, Janet Taylor

    Afternoon of the elves   **Fic**

    The art of keeping cool   **Fic**

    Quicksand Pond   **Fic**

Listen to the wind. Mortenson, G.   **371.8**

Listen, listen. Gershator, P.   **E**

Listen, Slowly. Lai, T.   **Fic**

The **listeners.** Whelan, G.   **E**

LISTENING -- FICTION

    Harrington, J. N. Catching a storyfish   **Fic**

    The Shema in the mezuzah   **E**

Listening for lions. Whelan, G.   **Fic**

Listening for Lucca. LaFleur, S.   **Fic**

Listening to learn. Grover, S.   **372.4**

The **listening** tree. Lottridge, C. B.   **Fic**

Lister, Adrian

    The Ice Age tracker's guide   **569**

Lister, Joseph, Baron, 1827-1912

         About

    Ollhoff, J. The germ detectives   **616.9**

Liston, Melba

         About

    Little Melba and her big trombone   **92**

Litchfield, David

    The bear and the piano   **E**

LITERACY -- FICTION

    Bauer, J. Close to famous   **Fic**

    Mango, Abuela, and me   **E**

    Murphy, S. J. Write on, Carlos!   **E**

    Reedy, T. Words in the dust   **Fic**

    Schmatz, P. Bluefish   **Fic**

LITERACY -- STUDY AND TEACHING -- UNITED STATES

    Grover, S. Listening to learn   **372.4**

LITERACY, VISUAL *See* Visual literacy

The **literary** adventures of Washington Irving. Harness, C. **92**

Little kids first big book of why. Shields, A.   **031.02**
Little Kunoichi, the ninja girl. Ishida, S.   **E**
LITTLE LEAGUE BASEBALL
   See also Baseball
LITTLE LEAGUE BASEBALL -- FICTION
   Northrop, M. Plunked   **Fic**
   Shang, W. The way home looks now   **Fic**
Little Leap Forward. Guo Yue   **Fic**
Little lions, bull baiters & hunting hounds. Crosby, J.   **636.7**
The **little** little girl with the big big voice.   **E**
Little Lola.   **E**
Little lost cowboy. Puttock, S.   **E**
LITTLE MAGAZINES
   See also Periodicals
Little Mama forgets. Cruise, R.   **E**
The **Little** Matador. Hector, J.   **E**
The **little** match girl. Pinkney, J.   **E**
The **little** match girl. Andersen, H. C.   **Fic**
Little Melba and her big trombone.   **92**
The **Little** Mermaid. Sabuda, R.   **E**
Little Miss Muffet counts to ten. Chichester-Clark, E.   **E**
Little Mist. McAllister, A.   **E**
The **little** moon princess. Lee, Y.   **E**
Little mouse. Murray, A.   **E**
Little Mouse gets ready. Smith, J.   **741.5**
Little Mouse's big book of fears. Gravett, E.   **E**
Little Mouse's big secret. Battut, E.   **E**
Little Naomi, Little Chick.   **E**
Little neighbors on Sunnyside Street. Spanyol, J.   **E**
Little newts. Goldish, M.   **597.8**
Little Night. Morales, Y.   **E**
The **little** old lady who was not afraid of anything.   **E**
Little One Step. James, S.   **E**
Little owl lost. Haughton, C.   **E**
Little Owl's day. Srinivasan, D.   **E**
Little Owl's night. Srinivasan, D.   **E**
Little panda. Ryder, J.   **599.74**
A **little** peace. Kerley, B.   **327.1**
Little penguins.   **E**
Little people and a lost world. Goldenberg, L.   **599.93**
The **little** piano girl. Ingalls, A.   **E**
Little Poems for Tiny Ears. Oliver, L.   **E**
The **little** prince. Sfar, J.   **741.5**
The **little** prince. Saint-Exupery, A. d.   **Fic**
The **little** prince: deluxe pop-up book. Saint-Exupery, A. d.   **Fic**
A **little** princess. Burnett, F. H.   **Fic**
Little Quack. Thompson, L.   **E**
Little Rabbit lost. Horse, H.   **E**
The **little** rabbit who liked to say moo. Allen, J.   **E**
Little Rat makes music. Bang-Campbell, M.   **E**
Little Red and the very hungry lion. Smith, A. T.   **398.2**
Little red bird. Bruel, N.   **E**
The **little** red elf. McGrath, B. B.   **E**
The **little** red hen. Pinkney, J.   **398.2**
The **little** red hen. Galdone, P.   **398.2**
The **little** red hen. Forest, H.   **398.2**
The **little** red hen. Barton, B.   **398.2**

The **Little** Red Hen (makes a pizza) Sturges, P.   **398.2**
The **Little** Red Hen and the Passover matzah. Kimmelman, L.   **398.2**
Little Red Henry. Urban, L.   **E**
The **little** red lighthouse and the great gray bridge. Swift, H. H.   **E**
The **Little** Red Pen. Crummel, S. S.   **E**
Little Red Riding Hood. Pinkney, J.   **398.2**
Little Red Riding Hood. Ziefert, H.   **398.2**
Little Red Riding Hood.   **E**
Little Red Riding Hood. Spirin, G.   **398.2**
Little Red Riding Hood. Hyman, T. S.   **398.2**
Little Red Riding Hood. Grimm, J.   **398.2**
LITTLE RED RIDING HOOD (TALE) -- ADAPTATIONS -- FICTION
   Smith, A. T. Little Red and the very hungry lion   **398.2**
Little Red Riding Hood: a newfangled prairie tale. Ernst, L. C.   **398.2**
Little Red Writing. Holub, J.   **E**
Little Robot.   **741.5**
LITTLE ROCK (ARK.) -- HISTORY -- 20TH CENTURY -- FICTION
   Levine, K. The lions of Little Rock   **Fic**
Little Roja Riding Hood. Elya, S. M.   **E**
Little Rooster's diamond button. MacDonald, M. R.   **398.2**
Little Santa. Agee, J.   **E**
The **little** scarecrow boy. Brown, M. W.   **E**
The **little** school bus. Roth, C.   **E**
The **little** ships. Foreman, M.   **E**
Little sister and the month brothers. De Regniers, B. S.   **398.2**
Little Sister is not my name. Draper, S. M.   **Fic**
The **little** snowplow. Koehler, L
LITTLE THEATER MOVEMENT
   See also Theater
Little Toot. Gramatky, H.   **E**
Little treasures. Ogburn, J. K.   **413**
Little tree. Long, L.   **E**
The **little** tree.   **E**
Little trucks with big jobs. Maass, R.   **629.224**
Little Tug. Savage, S.   **E**
Little Vampire. Sfar, J.   **741.5**
Little White Duck. Liu, N.   **741.5**
The **little** white owl. Corderoy, T.   **E**
Little white rabbit. Henkes, K.   **E**
Little wolf's first howling.   **E**
Little wolf's song. Teckentrup, B.   **E**
Little women. Alcott, L. M.   **Fic**
Little world math concepts [series]
   Mattern, J. Even or odd?   **513**
Little world social studies [series]
   Hord, C. My safe community   **331.7**
   Hord, C. Need it or want it?   **332.024**
The **little** yellow leaf. Berger, C.   **E**
Little you.   **E**
Little, Jean, 1932-
   Emma's yucky brother   **E**
                         About

Maine. Peterson, J. M.   **974.1**

MAINE

    Heinrichs, A. Maine   **974.1**

Maine. Dornfeld, M.   **974.1**

MAINE -- FICTION

    Robinson, M. L. Bright Island   **Fic**

MAINE -- GRAPHIC NOVELS

    Roop, P. The stormy adventure of Abbie Burgess, lighthouse keeper   **741.5**

MAINE -- HISTORY -- 20TH CENTURY -- FICTION

    LaFleur, S. Listening for Lucca   **Fic**

    Martin, A. M. Better to wish   **Fic**

    Robinson, M. L. Bright Island   **Fic**

    Stone, P. Romeo blue   **Fic**

The **Maine** coon's haiku. Rosen, M. J.   **811.54**

MAINTENANCE OF BIODIVERSITY *See* Biodiversity conservation

Maione, Heather Harms

    (il) Beard, D. B. Annie Glover is not a tree lover   **Fic**

    (il) Cuyler, M. Princess Bess gets dressed   **E**

    (il) Hest, A. Remembering Mrs. Rossi   **Fic**

    How Oliver Olson changed the world   **Fic**

    (il) McDonough, Y. Z. The cats in the doll shop   **Fic**

    (il) McDonough, Y. Z. The doll shop downstairs   **Fic**

    (il) Napoli, D. J. Sly the Sleuth and the pet mysteries   **Fic**

Mair, J. Samia

    The perfect gift   **E**

Maison, Jerome

    Jacquet, L. March of the penguins   **598**

Maisy first experiences [series]

    Maisy plays soccer   **E**

Maisy goes to preschool. Cousins, L.   **E**

Maisy plays soccer.   **E**

MAIZE *See* Corn

Maizel, Karen

    (il) Sheldon, A. Big sister now   **306.8**

Major Black contributions from Emancipation to civil rights [series]

    Davidson, T. African American scientists and inventors **509.2**

Major European nations [series]

    Indovino, S. C. Germany   **943**

Major inventions through history [series]

    Jango-Cohen, J. The history of food   **641.3**

    Landau, E. The history of everyday life   **609**

Mak, Kam

    My Chinatown   **E**

Make a splash! Cousteau, P.   **577.7**

Make art mistakes. Museum of Modern Art (New York, N. Y.   **701**

Make it wild. Schofield, J.   **796.5**

Make magic! do good! Clayton, D.   **811**

Make way for ducklings. McCloskey, R.   **E**

Make way for Dyamonde Daniel. Grimes, N.   **Fic**

Make way for readers.   **E**

Make way for Sam Houston. Fritz, J.   **92**

Make your mark, Franklin Roosevelt. St. George, J.   **92**

Make your own books. D'Cruz   **686**

Make your own crafts [series]

    Henry, S. Paper folding   **736**

Make your own masks. D'Cruz   **646.4**

Make your own musical instruments. D'Cruz   **784.19**

Make your own puppets. D'Cruz   **791.5**

Make your own purses and bags. D'Cruz   **646.4**

Make your own slippers and shoes. D'Cruz   **685**

MAKE-BELIEVE PLAYMATES *See* Imaginary playmates

Maker Lab. Challoner, J.   **507.8**

Makers and takers. Hooks, G.   **577.7**

MAKEUP (COSMETICS) *See* Cosmetics

MAKEUP, THEATRICAL *See* Theatrical makeup

Making a difference [series]

    Barraclough, S. Reusing things   **363.7**

Making a friend. McGhee, A.   **E**

Making amazing art. Henry, S.   **745.5**

Making choices. Parker, V.   **170**

Making friends. Rogers, F.   **158**

Making graphs [series]

    Bodach, V. Bar graphs   **510**

Making magic windows. Garza, C. L.   **745.54**

Making masks. Schwarz, R.   **646.4**

Making mischief. Maguire, G.   **741.6**

Making music. Wiseman, A. S.   **784.19**

The **making** of America. Johnston, R. D.   **973**

Making secret codes. Gregory, J.   **652**

Making shelter. Champion, N.   **613.6**

Making sounds. Guillain, C.   **534**

Making the moose out of life. Oldland, N.   **E**

Makoons.   **Fic**

Mal and Chad. McCranie, S.   **741.5**

Malala, a brave girl from Pakistan/Iqbal, a brave boy from Pakistan. Winter, J.   **920**

Malam, John

    The Egyptians   **932**

    Fairies   **398.2**

    Giants   **398.2**

    The Greeks   **938**

    Grow your own butterfly farm   **638**

    Grow your own cat toy   **636.8**

    Grow your own sandwich   **635**

    Grow your own smoothie   **634**

    Grow your own snack   **641.3**

    Grow your own soup   **635**

    Journey of a glass of milk   **637**

    Monsters   **398.2**

    Pinnipeds   **599.79**

    The Romans   **937**

    The Vikings   **948**

Maland, Nick

    (il) Davies, N. Big blue whale   **599.5**

    (il) Garlick, N. Aunt Severe and the dragons   **Fic**

    (il) McKay, H. Wishing for tomorrow   **Fic**

Malaria. Person, S.   **614.5**

MALARIA

    See also Diseases

MALARIA

super robot, vol. 1 **741.5**

MANGA

See also Graphic novels

MANGA -- STUDY AND TEACHING

Brenner, R. E. Understanding manga and anime **025.2**

Manga math mysteries [series]

Thielbar, M. The ancient formula **741.5**

Mangelsen, Thomas D.

(il) Hirschi, R. Our three bears **599.78**

Manger. **E**

Mangled by a hurricane! Aronin, M. **551.55**

A **mango** in the hand. **E**

Mango, Abuela, and me. **E**

MANGOES -- FICTION

A mango in the hand **E**

MANGROVE ECOLOGY

The mangrove tree **577.6**

The **mangrove** tree. **577.6**

MANHATTAN (NEW YORK, N.Y.)

Vila, L. Building Manhattan **974.7**

MANHATTAN PROJECT (U.S.) -- HISTORY

The secret project **355.825**

Maniac Magee. Spinelli, J. **Fic**

MANIC-DEPRESSIVE ILLNESS -- FICTION

Leal, A. H. A finders-keepers place **Fic**

Mills, C. One square inch **Fic**

Wilson, J. The illustrated Mum **Fic**

MANIPULATIVES

See also Audiovisual materials; Mathematics -- Study
and teaching; Teaching -- Aids and devices

Manivong, Laura

Escaping the tiger **Fic**

Mankiller, Wilma

About

Krull, K. Lives of extraordinary women **920**

Sonneborn, L. Wilma Mankiller **92**

Manley, Candace

Skeeter's dream **Fic**

Manley, Curtis

Shawn loves sharks **E**

The summer Nick taught his cats to read **E**

Manley, Effa, 1900-1981

About

She loved baseball: the Effa Manley story **92**

Mann, Bethany

Hines-Stephens, S. Show off **790.1**

Mann, Charles C.

Before Columbus **970.01**

Mann, Elizabeth

Hoover Dam **627**

The Parthenon **726**

The Roman Colosseum **937**

Statue of Liberty **974.7**

Taj Mahal **954**

Tikal **972.81**

Mann, Janet

About

Turner, P. S. The dolphins of Shark Bay **599.53**

Mann, Jennifer K.

Two speckled eggs **E**

(il) Turkey Tot **E**

Manna, Anthony L.

The orphan **398.2**

MANNED SPACE FLIGHT *See* Space flight

MANNED SPACE FLIGHT

Goodman, S. E. How do you burp in space? **629.45**

Holden, H. M. The coolest job in the universe **629.44**

Manners. Aliki **395**

MANNERS *See* Courtesy; Etiquette

MANNERS AND CUSTOMS -- FICTION

Leroy, J. A well-mannered young wolf **E**

Manners mash-up: a goofy guide to good behavior. **395**

Manning, Jane

(il) Jane, P. Little goblins ten **E**

(il) Katz, B. Nothing but a dog **E**

(il) Millie Fierce Sleeps Out **E**

(il) There's no place like school **811**

(il) Weeks, S. Drip, drop **E**

(il) Weeks, S. Mac and Cheese **E**

Manning, Matthew K.

Ali Baba and the forty thieves **741.5**

Manning, Maurie

Kitchen dance **E**

Laundry day **E**

Manning, Mick

(jt. auth) Granström, B. Nature adventures **508**

The Beatles **92**

Charles Dickens **92**

Tail-end Charlie **940.54**

Under your skin **612**

Woolly mammoth **569**

Manning, Peyton, 1976-

About

Rappoport, K. Peyton Manning **796.332**

Wilner, B. Peyton Manning **92**

Mannis, Celeste Davidson

Julia Morgan built a castle **92**

One leaf rides the wind **E**

Manny's cows. Becker, S. **E**

Manolessou, Katherina

T-Veg **E**

Manolito Four-Eyes. Lindo, E. **Fic**

Manolito Four-Eyes [series]

Lindo, E. Manolito Four-Eyes **Fic**

Lindo, E. Manolito Four-Eyes: the 2nd volume of the great
encyclopedia of my life **Fic**

Lindo, E. Manolito Four-Eyes: the 3rd volume of the great
encyclopedia of my life **Fic**

Manolito Four-Eyes: the 2nd volume of the great encyclopedia
of my life. Lindo, E. **Fic**

Manolito Four-Eyes: the 3rd volume of the great encyclopedia
of my life. Lindo, E. **Fic**

Mansa Musa. Burns, K. **Fic**

Manta rays. Wearing, J. **597**

Rizzo, J. Oceans | **551.46**
Rose, D. L. Ocean babies | **591.3**
Rose, D. L. One nighttime sea | **513.2**
Rubin, A. How many fish? | **513**
Shark wars | **591.77**
Sill, C. About marine mammals | **599.5**
Snyder, E. Alarming leopard seals | **599.79**
Swinburne, S. R. Ocean soup | **591.7**
Turner, P. S. Prowling the seas | **591.7**
Webb, S. Far from shore | **591.7**
Woodward, J. Under the waves | **551.46**
Young, K. R. Across the wide ocean | **623.89**

MARINE ANIMALS
See also Aquatic animals

MARINE ANIMALS -- FICTION
Siminovich, L. You are my baby | **E**

MARINE ANIMALS -- LOCOMOTION
Page, R. Flying frogs and walking fish | **591.57**

MARINE ANIMALS -- POETRY
Bulion, L. At the sea floor cafe | **811**
Elliott, D. In the sea | **811**
Harley, A. Sea stars | **811**

MARINE ANIMALS IN ART
Farrell, R. All about drawing sea creatures & animals | **743**

MARINE AQUARIUMS
Aliki My visit to the aquarium | **639.34**

MARINE AQUARIUMS
See also Aquariums

Marine biologist. Thomas, W. D. | **578.7**
Marine biologist. Somervill, B. A. | **578.7**

MARINE BIOLOGISTS
The Great White shark scientist | **578.7**
Nivola, C. A. Life in the ocean | **551.46**

MARINE BIOLOGY
Arnosky, J. Shimmer & splash | **591.77**
Beck, W. H. Glow | **591.47**
Becker, H. The big green book of the big blue sea | **577.7**
Conlan, K. Under the ice | **578.7**
Creatures of the deep | **591.77**
Eyewitness ocean | **551.46**
Fitzsimmons, D. Curious Critters | **591.77**
Green, J. Great white shark | **597.3**
Green, J. Sea otter | **599.769**
Guiberson, B. Z. The most amazing creature in the sea | **591.77**
Heller, E. S. Menorah under the sea | **296.4**
Hoyt, E. Weird sea creatures | **591.77**
Hughes, C. D. First big book of the ocean | **551.4**
Jackson, T. Green sea turtle | **597.92**
Lourie, P. The manatee scientists | **599.5**
MacQuitty, M. Shark | **597.3**
Mallory, K. Diving to a deep-sea volcano | **551.46**
Miller, S. S. Seahorses, pipefishes, and their kin | **597**
Ocean | **591.77**
Ocean sunlight | **571.4**
The Octopus Scientists | **594**
Reichard, S. E. Who on earth is Sylvia Earle? | **92**
Riggs, K. Killer whales | **599.53**

Roy, K. Neighborhood sharks | **597.**
Santoro, L. Wild oceans | **578.**
Sharks have six senses | **597.**
Somervill, B. A. Marine biologist | **578.**
Thomas, W. D. Marine biologist | **578.**
Wandering whale sharks | **597.**
Wicks, M. Coral reefs | **577.**

MARINE BIOLOGY
See also Biology; Oceanography

MARINE DEBRIS
Burns, L. G. Tracking trash | **551.4**

MARINE DISASTERS *See* Shipwrecks

MARINE ECOLOGY
Basher, S. Oceans | **551.4**
Becker, H. The big green book of the big blue sea | **577.**
Callery, S. Ocean | **577.**
Eyewitness ocean | **551.4**
Hooks, G. Makers and takers | **577.**
Jackson, K. Explore the ocean | **577.**
Slade, S. What if there were no sea otters? | **577.**
Wicks, M. Coral reefs | **577.**

MARINE ECOLOGY
See also Ecology; Marine biology

MARINE LIFE -- EFFECT OF LIGHT ON
Ocean sunlight | **571.**

MARINE MAMMALS
Malam, J. Pinnipeds | **599.7**
Sill, C. About marine mammals | **599.5**

MARINE MAMMALS
See also Mammals; Marine animals

MARINE MINERAL RESOURCES
See also Marine resources; Mines and mineral resources
Ocean bottom; Ocean engineering

MARINE PAINTING
See also Painting

MARINE PLANKTON
Kirby, R. R. Ocean drifters | **578.**

MARINE PLANTS
Parker, S. Seashore | **577.**

MARINE PLANTS
See also Marine biology; Plants

MARINE POLLUTION
Conlan, K. Under the ice | **578.**
Jakubiak, D. J. What can we do about oil spills and ocean pollution? | **363.**

MARINE POLLUTION
See also Oceanography; Water pollution

MARINE POLLUTION -- PREVENTION
Cousteau, P. Make a splash! | **577.7**

MARINE RESOURCES
See also Commercial products; Marine biology; Natural resources; Oceanography

MARINE RESOURCES CONSERVATION
The Great White shark scientist | **578.**

MARINE SALVAGE
See also International law; Maritime law; Salvage

MARINELAND (FLA.)

Marklew, Gilly
(il) Drake, S. Dragonsdale   **Fic**

Marko, Cyndi
Let's get cracking!   **E**

Markovics, Joyce L.
The bat's cave   **599.4**
Blitzed by a blizzard!   **551.55**
The honey bee's hive   **595.7**
My body is tough and gray   **599.3**
Oak tree   **583**
Sunflower   **583**
Tasmanian devil   **599.2**
Weddell seal   **599.79**

Marks, Alan
(il) High tide for horseshoe crabs   **595.4**
Markle, S. Family pack   **E**
(il) Markle, S. Finding home   **599.2**
(il) Markle, S. Hip-pocket papa   **597.8**
(il) Markle, S. A mother's journey   **598**
(il) Markle, S. Snow school   **E**
(il) Markle, S. Waiting for ice   **599.786**

Marks, Diana F.
Children's book award handbook   **028.5**

Marks, Jennifer L.
Bobcats   **599.75**
Clouded leopards   **599.75**
Jaguars   **599.75**

MARKSMEN
Wills, C. A. Annie Oakley: a photographic story of a life   **92**

Markuson, Carolyn A.
Erikson, R. Designing a school library media center for the future   **027.8**

Marley. Grogan, J.   **636.7**

Marley, Bob
        About
Medina, T. I and I   **92**

Marlow, Layn
Hurry up and slow down   **E**

MARMOTS
Gibbons, G. Groundhog day!   **394.26**

MARMOTS -- FICTION
April Fool, Phyllis!   **E**
Blackaby, S. Brownie Groundhog and the February fox   **E**
Cherry, L. How Groundhog's garden grew   **E**
Cox, J. Go to sleep, Groundhog!   **E**
Elish, D. The attack of the frozen woodchucks   **Fic**
Hill, S. L. Punxsutawney Phyllis   **E**
Mr. and Mrs. Bunny-- detectives extraordinaire!   **Fic**
Olson, J. Tickle, tickle! itch, twitch!   **E**
Swallow, P. C. Groundhog gets a say   **E**

Marooned. Kraske, R.   **92**

Marquez, Francisca
(il) Houran, L. H. A trip into space   **629.4**

Marr, Melissa, 1972-
Loki's wolves   **Fic**
Odin's ravens   **Fic**

MARRIAGE

See also Family; Sacraments

MARRIAGE -- FICTION
Buehner, C. Fanny's dream   **E**
Lyons, K. S. Ellen's broom   **E**

MARRIAGE CUSTOMS AND RITES
See also Manners and customs; Marriage; Rites and ceremonies; Weddings

MARRIED PEOPLE
See also Family; Marriage

Marrin, Albert
Marrin, A. Flesh & blood so cheap   **974.7**
Oh, rats!   **599.35**

Marrin, Albert, 1936-
Flesh & blood so cheap   **974.7**

Marriott, Pat
(il) Aiken, J. The wolves of Willoughby Chase   **Fic**

Mars. Capaccio, G.   **523.4**

MARS (PLANET)
Capaccio, G. Mars   **523.4**
Carson, M. K. Far-out guide to Mars   **523.4**
Destination: Mars   **523.43**

MARS (PLANET)
See also Planets

MARS (PLANET) -- EXPLORATION
Aldrin, B. Welcome to Mars   **523.43**
Rusch, E. The mighty Mars rovers   **523.43**

MARS (PLANET) -- EXPLORATION
See also Planets -- Exploration

MARS (PLANET) -- FICTION
Last day on Mars   **Fic**
Life on Mars   **E**
Secrets of the dragon tomb   **Fic**

MARS PROBES
Rusch, E. The mighty Mars rovers   **523.43**

MARS PROBES
See also Mars (Planet); Space probes

Marsalis, Wynton, 1961-
Jazz A-B-Z   **781.65**
Squeak! rumble! whomp! whomp! whomp!   **E**

Marschall, Ken
Inside the Titanic   **910.4**

Marschark, Marc
(jt. auth) Hauser, P. C. How deaf children learn   **371.91**

Marsden, Carolyn
The gold-threaded dress   **Fic**
Silk umbrellas   **Fic**
Take me with you   **Fic**
When heaven fell   **Fic**

Marsden, John
Tan, S. Lost & found   **S**

MARSH ECOLOGY
Johansson, P. Marshes and swamps   **577.6**
Wechsler, D. Marvels in the muck   **578.7**

MARSH ECOLOGY
See also Ecology

Marsh, Katherine
The door by the staircase   **Fic**

(il) Too many tamales   E

Martinez, Miriam G.

Temple, C. A. Children's books in children's hands   028.5

Martínez, Pedro, 1971-

About

Tavares, M. Growing up Pedro   92

Martinez, Sergio

(il) San Souci, R. Little Gold Star   398.2

Martini, Angela

(il) Stout, S. K. Fiona Finkelstein meets her match!!   Fic

(il) Stout, S. K. Fiona Finkelstein, big-time ballerina!   Fic

Martini, Helen

About

Lyon, G. E. Mother to tigers   92

Martins, George

(il) Giovanni, N. Spin a soft black song: poems for children   811

Martins, Isabel Minhós

Where do we go when we disappear?   E

My neighbor is a dog   E

The World in a Second   E

Marton, Jirina

(il) Pendziwol, J. Marja's skis   E

(il) Rivera, R. Arctic adventures   920

Marts, Doreen M.

(il) Berman, K. Easy-peasy recipes   641.5

Marty McGuire.   Fic

Marty McGuire digs worms! Messner, K.   Fic

Marty McGuire has too many pets!   Fic

MARTYRS

Hodges, M. Saint George and the dragon   398.2

MARTYRS

See also Church history; Heroes and heroines

Marvelous Cornelius. Bildner, P.   E

Marvelous math.   811

Marvelous Mattie. McCully, E. A.   92

Marvelous multiplication. Long, L.   513

The **marvelous** toy. Paxton, T.   782.42

The **Marvels**. Selznick, B.   Fic

Marvels in the muck. Wechsler, D.   578.7

Marven of the Great North Woods. Lasky, K.   E

Marvin makes music. Hamlisch, M.   E

Marvin Redpost, kidnapped at birth? Sachar, L.   Fic

Marvin Redpost: A magic crystal? Sachar, L.   Fic

Marvin Redpost: is he a girl? Sachar, L.   Fic

Marx, Trish

Borden, L. Touching the sky   629.13

Elephants and golden thrones   951

Everglades forever   577.6

Kindergarten day USA and China   371.82

Sharing our homeland   956.04

MARXISM

See also Economics; Philosophy; Political science; Sociology

Mary. Demi   232.91

MARY (BLESSED VIRGIN, SAINT)

See also Saints

Mary (Blessed Virgin, Saint)

About

Bernier-Grand, C. T. Our Lady of Guadalupe   232.91

MARY (BLESSED VIRGIN, SAINT) -- ART

See also Art; Christian art

MARY (BLESSED VIRGIN, SAINT) -- PRAYERS

See also Prayers

Mary and her little lamb. Moses, W.   E

Mary Cassatt. Harris, L. V.   92

Mary had a little glam.   E

Mary had a little lamb. Hoberman, M. A.   782.42

Mary had a little lamb. Hale, S. J.   811

Mary Mae and the gospel truth. Dutton, S.   Fic

Mary McLeod Bethune. McKissack, F.   370.92

Mary on horseback. Wells, R.   92

Mary Poppins. Travers, P. L.   Fic

Mary Walker wears the pants. Harness, C.   92

Mary Wrightly, so politely. Bridges, S. Y.   E

Mary, Blessed Virgin, Saint

About

Demi Mary   232.91

DePaola, T. The night of Las Posadas   E

Mary, Blessed Virgin, Saint (Spirit)

About

Gollogly, E. Talking Eagle and the Lady of Roses   232.91

Mary, Queen of Scots, 1542-1587

About

Cotter, C. Kids who rule   920

Maryland. Mattern, J.   975.2

Maryland. Blashfield, J. F.   975.2

MARYLAND

Blashfield, J. F. Maryland   975.2

MARYLAND -- FICTION

Mills, C. The totally made-up Civil War diary of Amanda MacLeish   Fic

Stout, S. K. Fiona Finkelstein meets her match!!   Fic

Stout, S. K. Fiona Finkelstein, big-time ballerina!   Fic

Weissman, E. B. The trouble with Mark Hopper   Fic

MARYLAND -- HISTORY

Doak, R. S. Maryland, 1634-1776   975.2

Maryland, 1634-1776. Doak, R. S.   975.2

Marzel, Pepi

(il) Groner, J. S. My first Hebrew word book   492.4

(il) Sussman, J. K. My first Yiddish word book   439

Marzollo, Jean

Happy birthday, Martin Luther King   323

Help me learn numbers 0-20   E

Help me learn subtraction   513.2

I spy a Christmas tree   793.73

I spy an egg in a nest   793.73

I spy school days   793.73

Pierre the penguin   598

Wick, W. I spy   793.73

Wick, W. I spy extreme challenger!   793.73

Wick, W. I spy fantasy   793.73

Wick, W. I spy gold challenger!   793.73

Wick, W. I spy spooky night   793.73

McGowan, Michael
Sunday is for God — E
McGrath, Barbara Barbieri
The little red elf — E
Teddy bear counting — E
McGraw, Eloise Jarvis
The moorchild — Fic
McGraw, John Joseph, 1873-1934
About
Tocher, T. Bill Pennant, Babe Ruth, and me — Fic
The **McGraw-Hill** children's dictionary. — 423
The **McGraw-Hill** children's thesaurus. — 423
McGrory, Anik
(il) Hurwitz, J. Mighty Monty — Fic
Quick, slow, mango! — E
McGuiness, Dan
Pilot & Huxley: the first adventure — 741.5
Pilot & Huxley: the next adventure — 741.5
McGuinness, Bill
(il) Bryan, A. Ashley Bryan — 92
McGuinness, Lisa
The dictionary of ordinary extraordinary animals — 590
McGuire, Erin
(il) Breadcrumbs — Fic
(il) Freymann-Weyr, G. French ducks in Venice — Fic
(il) Lord, C. Jelly Bean — Fic
(il) The Real Boy — Fic
McGuire, Robert
(il) Fleischman, S. The white elephant — Fic
(il) Myers, T. The furry-legged teapot — 398.2
McGuirk, Leslie
If rocks could sing — E
McHugh, Erin
National Parks — 333.78
McIllwain, John
DK Children's illustrated dictionary — 423
McIntosh, Iain
(il) McCall Smith, A. The great cake mystery — Fic
(il) McCall Smith, A. The Mystery of Meerkat Hill — Fic
(il) McCall Smith, A. The mystery of the missing lion — Fic
McIntyre, Sarah
(il) Lumry, A. Safari in South Africa — E
(il) Oliver and the seawigs — Fic
McIntyre, Thomas
The behavior survival guide for kids — 158
McKay, Christopher P.
About
Turner, P. S. Life on earth--and beyond — 576.8
McKay, Hilary, 1959-
Binny for short — Fic
Binny in secret — Fic
Lulu and the dog from the sea — Fic
Lulu and the duck in the park — Fic
Lulu and the hedgehog in the rain — Fic
Saffy's angel — Fic
Wishing for tomorrow — Fic
McKay, Kim

True green kids — 333.72
McKean, Dave
(il) Almond, D. Mouse bird snake wolf — Fic
(il) Almond, D. Slog's dad — Fic
(il) Gaiman, N. Crazy hair — E
(il) Gaiman, N. The graveyard book — Fic
(il) The wolves in the walls — E
McKee, David
(il) The King of Quizzical Island — E
Elmer — E
McKellar, Danica, 1975-
McKellar, D. Math doesn't suck — 510
McKendry, Joe
Beneath the streets of Boston — 625.4
(il) One Times Square — 974.7
McKenna, Virginia
Counting lions — 591.68
McKenzie, Precious
(ed) Cleland, J. Getting your zzzzs — E
McKeown, Rosalyn
Into the classroom — 370.71
McKinlay, Meg
Below — Fic
Duck for a day — Fic
McKinley, Michael
Ice time — 796.962
McKinnon, Hannah Roberts
Franny Parker — Fic
The properties of water — Fic
McKissack, Fredrick, 1939-2013
Mary McLeod Bethune — 370.92
McKissack, Fredrick, Jr.
McKissack, P. C. Black hands, white sails — 639.2
McKissack, P. C. The clone codes — Fic
McKissack, P. C. Cyborg — Fic
McKissack, P. C. Let my people go — Fic
McKissack, P. C. The royal kingdoms of Ghana, Mali, and Songhay — 966.2
McKissack, John Patrick
McKissack, P. C. The clone codes — Fic
McKissack, P. C. Cyborg — Fic
McKissack, Pat, 1944-2017
Abby takes a stand — Fic
Black hands, white sails — 639.2
The clone codes — Fic
Cyborg — Fic
The dark-thirty — S
Flossie & the fox — E
Goin' someplace special — E
Let my people go — Fic
McKissack, F. Mary McLeod Bethune — 370.92
McKissack, P. The all-I'll-ever-want Christmas doll — E
McKissack, P. Let's clap, jump, sing, and shout; dance, spin, and turn it out! — 305.896
McKissack, P. Ol' Clip-Clop — E
Mirandy and Brother Wind — E
Never forgotten — Fic

Rats   **636.9**

McNicholas, Shelagh
(il) Geras, A. Little ballet star   E
(il) Herthel, J. I am Jazz!   E

McNulty, Faith
If you decide to go to the moon   **629.45**

McPhail, David M.
(il) Byars, B. C. Little Horse   Fic
(il) Dragonwagon, C. All the awake animals are almost asleep   E
(il) Evans, L. Who loves the little lamb?   E
(il) Lamb, A. Tell me the day backwards   E
(il) Numeroff, L. J. When sheep sleep   E
(il) Rockwell, T. Emily Stew   **811**
(il) Spinelli, E. When Papa comes home tonight   E
Baby Pig Pig talks   E
Baby Pig Pig walks   E
Bad dog   E
Bella loves Bunny   E
Ben loves Bear   E
Big Brown Bear's up and down day   E
Big Pig and Little Pig   E
Boy, Bird, and Dog   E
Drawing lessons from a bear   E
I promise   E
Mole music   E
No!   E
Pig Pig meets the lion   E
Pig Pig returns   E
Pigs aplenty, pigs galore!   E
Sylvie & True   E
The teddy bear   E
Waddles   E
Water boy   E
Weezer changes the world   E

McPhee, Marc E.
Farmer, L. S. J. Neal-Schuman technology management handbook for school library media centers   **025.1**

McPherson, James M.
Fields of fury   **973.7**

McPherson, Stephanie Sammartino
Iceberg right ahead!   **910.4**

McQuerry, Maureen Doyle
Beyond the door   Fic

McQuinn, Anna
Leo loves baby time   E
Lola at the library   E
McQuinn, C. Ireland   **941.5**
My friend Jamal   E
My friend Mei Jing   E
The sleep sheep   E

McQuinn, Colm
Ireland   **941.5**

McReynolds, Linda
Eight days gone   **629.45**

McSwigan, Marie
Snow treasure   Fic

McVoy, Terra Elan
This Is All Your Fault, Cassie Parker   Fic

McWhorter, Diane
A dream of freedom   **323.1**

McWhorter, Heather
(il) Willey, M. Clever Beatrice   **398.2**

McWilliam, Howard
(il) Markle, S. What If You Had Animal Teeth?   E
(il) When a dragon moves in   E

Me . . . Jane. McDonnell, P.   **92**

Me and Meow. Gudeon, A.   E

Me and Momma and Big John.   E

Me and my dad. Morgan, S.   E

Me and my dragon. Biedrzycki, D.   E

Me and Rolly Maloo. Wong, J. S.   Fic

Me and Uncle Romie. Hartfield, C.   E

Me and you. Browne, A.   E

Me first! Pulver, R.   E

Me too! Gorbachev, V.   E

Me with you. Dempsey, K.   E

MÉTIS -- FICTION
Erdrich, L. Chickadee   Fic

Me, Frida.   E

Meachum, John B., 1789-
About
Hopkinson, D. Steamboat school   E

Mead, Alice
Junebug   Fic
Junebug in trouble   Fic

Mead, Tom
(il) Johnson, H. Fearsome Creatures of the Lumberwoods   S

Mead, Wendy
Bennett, C. Montana   **978.6**
McDaniel, M. Arizona   **979.1**
Top 10 birds for kids   **636.6**
Stefoff, R. Utah   **979.2**

Meade, Holly
(il) Bartoletti, S. C. Naamah and the ark at night   E
(il) Best, C. Goose's story   E
(il) Brenner, T. And then comes Halloween   E
(il) Elliott, D. In the sea   **811**
(il) Elliott, D. In the wild   **811**
(il) Elliott, D. On the farm   E
(il) Gershator, P. Sky sweeper   E
(il) Ho, M. Hush!   **782.4**
(il) Lindbergh, R. On morning wings   **223**
If I never forever endeavor   E
Inside, inside, inside   E
John Willy and Freddy McGee   E

Meadowlands. Yezerski, T.   **577.69**

MEADOWLANDS (N.J.)
Yezerski, T. Meadowlands   **577.69**

MEADOWS -- FICTION
Cole, H. On Meadowview Street   E
Katō, Y. In the meadow   E

MEADOWS -- POETRY
Sidman, J. Butterfly eyes and other secrets of the meadow   **811**

Johnson, R. L. Mighty animal cells   **571.6**

MICROSCOPES

Kramer, S. Hidden worlds: looking through a scientist's microscope   **502.8**

Levine, S. The ultimate guide to your microscope   **502.8**

MICROSCOPIC ANALYSIS *See* Metallography; Microscopes

MICROSCOPIC ORGANISMS *See* Microorganisms

Microscopic scary creatures. Graham, I.   **591.6**

MICROSCOPISTS

Kramer, S. Hidden worlds: looking through a scientist's microscope   **502.8**

Ollhoff, J. The germ detectives   **616.9**

MICROWAVE COMMUNICATION SYSTEMS

See also Intercommunication systems; Shortwave radio; Telecommunication

MICROWAVE COOKING

See also Cooking

Micucci, Charles

The life and times of corn   **633.1**

The life and times of the ant   **595.79**

MID-AUTUMN DAY -- FICTION

Lin, G. Thanking the moon   **E**

MIDAS (LEGENDARY CHARACTER)

Craft, C. King Midas and the golden touch   **398.209**

Demi King Midas   **398.2**

Middaugh, Dallas

The city of Ember   **741.5**

MIDDLE AGE

See also Age; Life (Biology)

The **Middle** Ages. Corbishley, M.   **940.1**

MIDDLE AGES

Arato, R. On a medieval day   **S**

Cohen, B. Canterbury tales   **821**

Corbishley, M. The Middle Ages   **940.1**

Cushman, K. Matilda Bone   **Fic**

Durman, L. Siege   **355.4**

Helget, N. Barbarians   **940.1**

Kroll, S. Barbarians!   **940.1**

León, V. Outrageous women of the Middle Ages   **920.72**

Springer, N. Rowan Hood, outlaw girl of Sherwood Forest   **Fic**

MIDDLE AGES

See also World history

MIDDLE AGES -- DRAMA

Schlitz, L. A. Good masters! Sweet ladies!   **940.1**

MIDDLE AGES -- FICTION

Beebe, K. Brother Hugo and the bear   **E**

MIDDLE AGES -- HISTORY *See* Middle Ages

MIDDLE EAST

Ollhoff, J. Middle Eastern Mythology   **398.209**

MIDDLE EAST -- BIBLIOGRAPHY

Al-Hazza, T. C. Books about the Middle East   **016**

MIDDLE EAST -- FICTION

Alexander, L. The golden dream of Carlo Chuchio   **Fic**

The greatest gift   **Fic**

Kimmel, E. A. Joha makes a wish   **E**

MIDDLE EASTERN AMERICANS -- FICTION

Faruqi, R. Lailah's lunchbox   **Fic**

MIDDLE EASTERN COOKING

Batmanglij, N. Happy Nowruz   **641.5**

Blaxland, W. Middle Eastern food   **641.5**

Middle Eastern food. Blaxland, W.   **641.5**

Middle Eastern Mythology. Ollhoff, J.   **398.209**

Middle school is worse than meatloaf. Holm, J. L.   **Fic**

Middle school, the worst years of my life.   **Fic**

MIDDLE SCHOOLS

See also Schools

MIDDLE SCHOOLS -- FICTION

Angleberger, T. The secret of the Fortune Wookiee   **Fic**

Angleberger, T. The surprise attack of Jabba the Puppett   **Fic**

Baskin, N. R. Nine, ten   **Fic**

Billy Sure, kid entrepreneur   **Fic**

Brown, G. Josh Baxter levels up   **Fic**

Brown, J. Star Wars   **741.5**

Dellinger, P. Fuzzy   **Fic**

Dowell, F. O. The second life of Abigail Walker   **Fic**

Drama   **741.5**

Gale, E. K. The Bully Book   **Fic**

Kinard, K. The boy prediction   **Fic**

Lane, K. The best worst thing   **Fic**

My life as a joke   **Fic**

Palacio, R. J. Auggie & me   **Fic**

Palacio, R. J. Wonder   **Fic**

The Pants Project   **Fic**

Perl, E. S. The capybara conspiracy   **Fic**

Posted   **Fic**

Sovern, M. J. The meaning of Maggie   **Fic**

Stead, R. Goodbye stranger   **Fic**

Taylor, C. Ready to wear   **Fic**

Teagan, E. The friendship experiment   **Fic**

Tracy, K. Bessica Lefter bites back   **Fic**

MIDDLE WEST -- HISTORY -- 20TH CENTURY

Garland, S. Voices of the dust bowl   **973.917**

MIDDLE-BORN CHILDREN -- FICTION

Pincus, G. The 14 fibs of Gregory K   **Fic**

The **middle-child** blues. Crow, K.   **E**

Middleman, Amy B.

(ed) Pfeifer, K. G. American Medical Assocation boy's guide to becoming a teen   **613**

(ed) Pfeifer, K. G. American Medical Association girl's guide to becoming a teen   **613**

Middleton, Julie

Are the dinosaurs dead, Dad?   **E**

Middleworld. Voelkel, J.   **Fic**

Midnight for Charlie Bone. Nimmo, J.   **Fic**

Midnight forests. Hines, G.   **92**

The **Midnight** Library. Kohara, K.   **E**

Midnight magic. Avi   **Fic**

The **midnight** tunnel. Frazier, A.   **Fic**

The **midnight** war of Mateo Martinez. Yardi, R.   **Fic**

The **midwife's** apprentice. Cushman, K.   **Fic**

MIDWIFERY *See* Midwives

MIDWIVES

MILITARY BASES -- FICTION

Grimes, N. Poems in the attic   **Fic**

Holmes, S. L. Operation Yes   **Fic**

MILITARY CAMPS

     See also Military art and science

MILITARY EDUCATION -- FICTION

Larson, M. A. Pennyroyal Academy   **Fic**

MILITARY ENGINEERING

     See also Civil engineering; Engineering

MILITARY GEOGRAPHY

     See also Geography

MILITARY GOVERNMENT

Donovan, S. Lethal leaders and military madmen   **920**

MILITARY HISTORY

Chapman, C. Battles & weapons: exploring history through art   **355**

Callery, S. World War II   **940.53**

McNab, C. 50 things you should know about the Vietnam War   **959.7**

Samuels, C. Home front   **940.53**

Solway, A. Graphing war and conflict   **355**

MILITARY OCCUPATION

Park, L. S. When my name was Keoko   **Fic**

MILITARY PERSONNEL -- UNITED STATES -- CORRE-SPONDENCE -- FICTION

Postcards from Pismo   **Fic**

MILITARY ROADS -- MASSACHUSETTS -- HISTORY -- 18TH CENTURY

Brown, D. Henry and the cannons   **973.3**

MILK

Aliki Milk from cow to carton   **637**

Gibbons, G. The milk makers   **637**

Malam, J. Journey of a glass of milk   **637**

MILK

     See also Dairy products; Dairying; Food

MILK -- FICTION

Alsdurf, P. It's milking time   **E**

Ross, F. Chilly Milly Moo   **E**

Milk from cow to carton. Aliki   **637**

The **milk** makers. Gibbons, G.   **637**

MILK SUPPLY

Malam, J. Journey of a glass of milk   **637**

MILK SUPPLY

     See also Food adulteration and inspection; Public health

MILKING -- FICTION

Alsdurf, P. It's milking time   **E**

MILKY WAY

Asimov, I. The Milky Way and other galaxies   **523.1**

Gifford, C. Stars, galaxies, and the Milky Way   **523.8**

Jefferis, D. Galaxies   **523.1**

MILKY WAY

     See also Galaxies

The **Milky** Way and other galaxies. Asimov, I.   **523.1**

Millar, H. R.

(il) Nesbit, E. Five children and it   **Fic**

Millard Fillmore. Gottfried, T.   **92**

Millard, Anne

A street through time   **936**

Millard, Glenda

Layla, Queen of hearts   **Fic**

The naming of Tishkin Silk   **Fic**

Millen, C. M.

The ink garden of brother Theophane   **E**

MILLENNIALS (PERSONS)

     See also Population

The **miller**. Petersen, C.   **664**

Miller, Bobbi

Davy Crockett gets hitched   **398.2**

One fine trade   **398.2**

Miller, Brandon Marie

Benjamin Franklin, American genius   **92**

Declaring independence   **973.3**

George Washington for kids   **92**

Thomas Jefferson for kids   **92**

Miller, Debbie S.

Arctic lights, arctic nights   **591.4**

Big Alaska   **979.8**

The great serum race   **798.8**

Survival at 40 below   **591.7**

Survival at 120 above   **591.7**

Miller, Donalyn

The book whisperer   **372.6**

Miller, Edward, 1964-

(il) Adler, D. A. Fractions, decimals, and percents   **513**

(il) Adler, D. A. Millions, billions & trillions   **513**

(il) Adler, D. A. Money madness   **332.4**

(il) Adler, D. A. Mystery math   **512**

(il) Adler, D. A. Perimeter, area, and volume   **516**

(il) Adler, D. A. Place value   **513.2**

(il) Adler, D. A. Time zones   **389**

(il) Adler, D. A. Triangles   **516.15**

(il) Bardhan-Quallen, S. Nature science experiments   **508**

Branley, F. M. The sun, our nearest star   **523.7**

Fireboy to the rescue!   **613.6**

The monster health book   **613**

Recycling day   **363.728**

The tooth book   **617.6**

(il) Showers, P. A drop of blood   **612.1**

(il) Showers, P. What happens to a hamburger?   **612.3**

Miller, Heather

Smoking   **616.86**

Subway ride   **388.4**

This is your life cycle   **595.7**

Miller, Jeanne

Food science   **641.3**

Miller, Kirsten

Kiki Strike   **Fic**

Miller, Lee

Roanoke   **975.6**

Miller, Linda L.

Baumbach, D. Less is more   **025.2**

Miller, Maggie

My first ghost   **E**

Miller, Marcia

MINISTERS (DIPLOMATIC AGENTS) *See* Diplomats

MINISTERS OF THE GOSPEL *See* Clergy

Minkel, Walter

How to do The three bears with two hands ... **791.5**

Minn and Jake. Wong, J. S. ... **Fic**

Minnesota. Harmon, D. ... **977.6**

Minnesota. Schwabacher, M. ... **977.6**

MINNESOTA

Harmon, D. Minnesota ... **977.6**

Root, P. Big belching bog ... **577.6**

Schwabacher, M. Minnesota ... **977.6**

MINNESOTA -- FICTION

Applegate, K. Home of the brave ... **Fic**

Blume, L. M. M. The rising star of Rusty Nail ... **Fic**

Friend, C. Barn boot blues ... **Fic**

Hattemer, K. The vigilante poets of Selwyn Academy ... **Fic**

Lasky, K. Marven of the Great North Woods ... **E**

Lovelace, M. H. Betsy-Tacy ... **Fic**

Paulsen, G. The winter room ... **Fic**

Wilder, L. I. On the banks of Plum Creek ... **Fic**

MINNESOTA -- HISTORY -- 20TH CENTURY -- FICTION

Hayles, M. Breathing room ... **Fic**

Minnie and Moo and the haunted sweater. Cazet, D. ... **E**

Minnie and Moo, hooves of fire. Cazet, D. ... **Fic**

Minnie and Moo, wanted dead or alive. Cazet, D. ... **E**

Minnie's Diner. Dodds, D. A. ... **E**

Minnow and Rose. Young, J. ... **Fic**

MINNOWS -- FICTION

Sauer, T. Nugget and Fang ... **E**

MINOR ARTS *See* Decorative arts

MINOR LEAGUE BASEBALL

See also Baseball

MINOR PLANETS *See* Asteroids

Minor, Florence

If you were a panda bear ... **E**

Minor, Wendell

Aldrin, B. Reaching for the moon ... **92**

(il) Aldrin, B. Look to the stars ... **629.4**

Ben's Revolution ... **Fic**

(il) Brown, M. W. Nibble nibble ... **811**

(il) Burleigh, R. Abraham Lincoln comes home ... **92**

(il) Burleigh, R. Edward Hopper paints his world ... **92**

Burleigh, R. Night flight ... **629.13**

(il) Ehrlich, A. Rachel ... **92**

(il) George, J. C. The buffalo are back ... **599.64**

(il) George, J. C. Everglades ... **975.9**

(il) George, J. C. Luck ... **E**

(il) George, J. C. Morning, noon, and night ... **E**

(il) George, J. C. The wolves are back ... **599.77**

Henry Knox ... **92**

(il) Minor, F. If you were a panda bear ... **E**

Minor, W. My farm friends ... **E**

(il) Titcomb, G. The last train ... **E**

(il) Turner, A. W. Abe Lincoln remembers ... **973.7**

(il) Turner, A. W. Sitting Bull remembers ... **92**

Yankee Doodle America ... **973.3**

MINORITIES -- UNITED STATES -- HISTORY

Stefoff, R. A different mirror for young people ... **305.8**

MINORITIES IN ENGINEERING

See also Engineering

MINORITIES IN LITERATURE

Gilton, D. L. Multicultural and ethnic children's literature in the United States ... **028.5**

MINSTRELS -- FICTION

Vining, E. G. Adam of the road ... **Fic**

Minter, Daniel

(il) Bowman, D. J. Step right up ... **92**

(il) Lyons, K. S. Ellen's broom ... **E**

(il) Medearis, A. S. Seven spools of thread ... **E**

(il) Reynolds, S. The first marathon: the legend of Pheidippides ... **938**

MINTS

See also Money

Minty: a story of young Harriet Tubman. Schroeder, A. ... **305.5**

Mira's Diary. Moss, M. ... **Fic**

Miracle man. Hendrix, J. ... **232.9**

Miracle mud. ... **796.357**

Miracle on 133rd Street. Manzano, S. ... **E**

MIRACLES

Hanft, J. E. Miracles of the Bible ... **221.9**

MIRACLES -- FICTION

Arnold, E. K. The question of miracles ... **Fic**

MIRACLES -- FOLKLORE

DePaola, T. The clown of God ... **398.2**

The **miracles** of Passover. ... **296.4**

Miracles of the Bible. Hanft, J. E. ... **221.9**

The **miraculous** journey of Edward Tulane. DiCamillo, K. ... **Fic**

Mirallès, 1959-

(il) Waluk ... **741.5**

Miranda Cosgrove. Yasuda, A. ... **92**

Miranda's beach day. Keller, H. ... **E**

Miranda, Anne

To market, to market ... **E**

Mirandy and Brother Wind. McKissack, P. C. ... **E**

Mirette on the high wire. McCully, E. A. ... **E**

Miriam (Biblical figure)

About

Jules, J. Miriam in the desert ... **222**

Manushkin, F. Miriam's cup ... **222**

Miriam in the desert. Jules, J. ... **222**

Miriam's cup. Manushkin, F. ... **222**

Miron, Marie-Charlotte

My Little Handbook of Experiments ... **E**

Mirpuri, Gouri

(jt. auth) Cooper, R. Indonesia ... **959.8**

Mirror. Morpurgo, M. ... **E**

Mirror. Baker, J. ... **E**

Mirror mirror. Singer, M. ... **811**

The **mirror** of Merlin. Barron, T. A. ... **Fic**

A **mirror** to nature. Yolen, J. ... **811**

MIRRORS

Cobb, V. I see myself ... **535**

MIRRORS -- FICTION

Morpurgo, M. Mirror ... **E**

The **misadventures** of Maude March. Couloumbis, A. **Fic**

Misadventures of Millicent Madding [series]

  Tacang, B. Bully-be-gone **Fic**

The **Misadventures** of Salem Hyde. Cammuso, F. **Fic**

The **misadventures** of the family Fletcher. Levy, D. A. **Fic**

The **misadventures** of the magician's dog. Sackett, F. **Fic**

MISCARRIAGE

  See also Pregnancy

MISCELLANEA *See* Books of lists; Curiosities and wonders

MISCELLANEOUS FACTS *See* Books of lists; Curiosities and wonders

Miss Bindergarten celebrates the 100th day of kindergarten. Slate, J. **E**

Miss Bridie chose a shovel. Connor, L. **E**

Miss Brooks loves books (and I don't) Bottner, B. **E**

Miss Brooks' Story Nook. Bottner, B. **E**

Miss Dorothy and her bookmobile. Houston, G. **E**

Miss Ellicott's school for the magically minded. **Fic**

Miss Etta and Dr. Claribel. Fillion, S. **92**

Miss Fox's class goes green. Spinelli, E. **E**

Miss Lina's ballerinas. **E**

Miss Lina's ballerinas and the prince. **E**

Miss Little's gift. Wood, D. **E**

Miss Malarkey leaves no reader behind. Finchler, J. **E**

Miss Mary Mack. Hoberman, M. A. **398.8**

Miss Mary Mack and other children's street rhymes. **796.1**

Miss Mary Reporting. Macy, S. **92**

Miss Moore thought otherwise. **020**

Miss Nelson is missing! Allard, H. **E**

Miss Tutu's star. Newman, L. **E**

Missile Mouse [series]

  Parker, J. Missile Mouse: the star crusher **741.5**

Missile Mouse: rescue on Tankium3. Parker, J. **741.5**

Missile Mouse: the star crusher. Parker, J. **741.5**

The Missing [series]

  Haddix, M. P. Caught **Fic**

  Haddix, M. P. Risked **Fic**

  Haddix, M. P. Found **Fic**

  Haddix, M. P. Sabotaged **Fic**

  Haddix, M. P. Sent **Fic**

  Haddix, M. P. Torn **Fic**

The **missing** chick. Gorbachev, V. **E**

MISSING CHILDREN

  See also Children; Missing persons

MISSING CHILDREN -- FICTION

  Fitzgerald, S. M. The apple tart of hope **Fic**

  The goldfish boy **Fic**

  Hello universe **Fic**

The **missing** golden ticket and other splendiferous secrets. Dahl, R. **92**

MISSING IN ACTION

  See also Prisoners of war; Soldiers

The **missing** manatee. DeFelice, C. C. **Fic**

Missing May. Rylant, C. **Fic**

The **missing** mitten mystery. Kellogg, S. **E**

Missing mommy. **E**

Missing on Superstition Mountain. Broach, E. **Fic**

MISSING PERSONS

  Burleigh, R. Night flight **629.13**

  Fleming, C. Amelia lost: the life and disappearance of Amelia Earhart **92**

  A picture book of Amelia Earhart **629.13**

  Tanaka, S. Amelia Earhart **92**

MISSING PERSONS

  See also Criminal investigation

MISSING PERSONS -- FICTION

  Leonard, M. G. Beetle boy **Fic**

  Miss Ellicott's school for the magically minded **Fic**

  Moss, M. Mira's Diary **Fic**

  Thompson, C. Space dumplins **741.5**

  Timberlake, A. One came home **Fic**

  When did you see her last? **Fic**

Missing! A cat called Buster. Orr, W. **Fic**

Mission control, this is Apollo. Chaikin, A. **629.45**

Mission to Mars. Hartman, E. **629.45**

Mission to Mars. Branley, F. M. **629.45**

Mission to Pluto. Carson, M. K. **629.43**

Mission to the moon. Dyer, A. **629.45**

Mission unstoppable. Gutman, D. **Fic**

Mission: back to school. Hood, S. **E**

Mission: planet Earth. Ride, S. K. **525**

Mission: save the planet. Ride, S. K. **333.72**

Mission: science [series]

  BishopRoby, J. Animal kingdom **590**

  Cregan, E. R. The atom **539.7**

  Cregan, E. R. Marie Curie **92**

  Fuoco, G. D. Earth **333.72**

  Herweck, D. Robert Fulton **92**

  Housel, D. J. Ecologists **920**

  Housel, D. J. Ecosystems **577**

  Jankowski, C. Astronomers **920**

  Lee, K. F. Cells **571.6**

  Van Gorp, L. Elements **540**

  Van Gorp, L. Gregor Mendel **92**

  Weir, J. Matter **530**

  Weir, J. Max Planck **92**

  Zamosky, L. Louis Pasteur **92**

  Zamosky, L. Simple organisms **579**

MISSIONARIES

  DePaola, T. Patrick: patron saint of Ireland **92**

  Harness, C. The tragic tale of Narcissa Whitman and a faithful history of the Oregon Trail **92**

MISSIONARIES, MEDICAL -- AFRICA, SOUTHERN -- BIOGRAPHY

  Bodden, V. To the heart of Africa **916**

MISSIONS

  Perritano, J. Spanish missions **266**

MISSIONS -- FICTION

  Politi, L. Song of the swallows **E**

Mississippi. Casil, A. S. **976.2**

Mississippi. Dell, P. **976.2**

MISSISSIPPI

  Dell, P. Mississippi **976.2**

MISSISSIPPI -- FICTION

(il) Marrin, A. Oh, rats! **599.35**

(il) Silent movie **E**

Morden, Daniel

Lupton, H. The adventures of Odysseus **292**

More about Boy. Dahl, R. **92**

More bears! Nesbitt, K. **E**

More bones. Olson, A. N. **398.2**

More bullies in more books. Bott, C. J. **371.5**

More family storytimes. Reid, R. **027.62**

More life-size zoo. Komiya, T. **590**

More more more said the baby. Williams, V. B. **E**

More of Monkey & Robot. Catalanotto, P. **E**

A **more** perfect union. Maestro, B. **342**

More scary stories to tell in the dark. Schwartz, A. **398.25**

More simple science fair projects, grades 3-5. Tocci, S. **507.8**

More stories to solve. Shannon, G. **398.2**

More storytime action! Bromann, J. **027.62**

More than anything else. Bradby, M. **E**

More than meets the eye. Raczka, B. **750**

More-igami. **E**

Moreillon, Judi

Collaborative strategies for teaching reading comprehension **372.4**

Moreno, Rene King

(il) Goldman, J. Uncle monarch and the Day of the Dead **E**

(il) Guy, G. F. Fiesta! **E**

(il) Stanton, K. Papi's gift **E**

Morey, Walt

Gentle Ben **Fic**

MORGAN LE FAY (LEGENDARY CHARACTER)

See also Legendary characters

Morgan, Garrett A., 1877-1963

About

Kulling, M. To the rescue! **92**

Morgan, Jody

Elephant rescue **599.67**

Morgan, Julia

About

Mannis, C. D. Julia Morgan built a castle **92**

Morgan, Pierr

The children's garden **E**

(il) Schaefer, C. L. Dragon dancing **E**

Morgan, Sally

Me and my dad **E**

Pollution **363.7**

Waste and recycling **363.7**

Morgenstern, Susie Hoch

A book of coupons **Fic**

Morgy makes his move. Lewis, M. **Fic**

Morgy's musical summer. Lewis, M. **Fic**

Moriarty, Chris

The inquisitor's apprentice **Fic**

The watcher in the shadows **Fic**

Morin, Paul

(il) Mollel, T. M. The orphan boy **398.21**

Moriuchi, Mique

(il) Fisher, A. L. The story goes on **E**

My village **808.8**

(il) Piper, S. Prayers for a better world **24.**

(il) Rivett, R. I imagine **24.**

Moriya, Kwanchai

(il) Ocean animals from head to tail **591.7**

Morley, Agnes, 1874-1958

About

Basketball belles **796.32**

Morley, Taia

(il) De Cristofano, C. C. The sun and the moon **52.**

Morlock, Lisa

Track that scat! **591.4**

MORMON CHURCH *See* Church of Jesus Christ of Latter day Saints

MORMONS

Bial, R. Nauvoo **289.**

George, C. What makes me a Mormon? **289.**

Hailstone, R. The white ox **9**

Morn, September B.

The pug **636.**

MORNING -- FICTION

Brown, M. W. A child's good morning book

DwellStudio (Firm) Good morning, toucan

Judge, L. Good morning to me!

Krauss, R. The backward day

Lobel, A. Hello, day!

Morning Girl. Dorris, M. **Fi**

A **morning** with grandpa.

Morning, noon, and night. George, J. C.

Morocco. Seward, P. **96**

MOROCCO

Seward, P. Morocco **96**

MOROCCO -- FICTION

Alalou, A. The butter man

Baker, J. Mirror

Ichikawa, S. My father's shop

Turk, E. The storyteller

Morpurgo, Michael

Beowulf **398.**

Hansel and Gretel **398.**

Kensuke's kingdom **Fi**

The McElderry book of Aesop's fables **398.**

Mirror

On angel wings **Fi**

The Pied Piper of Hamelin **398.**

Sir Gawain and the Green Knight **398.**

Waiting for Anya **Fi**

Wave

Morris and Boris at the circus. Wiseman, B.

Morris Micklewhite and the Tangerine Dress. Baldacchino C.

Morris's disappearing bag. Wells, R.

Morris, Ann

Hats, hats, hats **39**

Shoes, shoes, shoes **39**

Tsunami **959.**

Morris, Betty J.

(il) Harper, D. Sit, Truman!   E

Moser, Lisa

Cowboy Boyd and Mighty Calliope   E

Kisses on the wind   E

Railroad Hank   E

Squirrel's world   E

Moses. Hodges, M.   222

Moses. Weatherford, C. B.   92

Moses (Biblical figure)

About

Chaikin, M. Angels sweep the desert floor   296.1

Hodges, M. Moses   222

Moses goes to school. Millman, I.   E

Moses, Shelia P.

Sallie Gal and the Wall-a-kee man   Fic

Moses, Will

Mary and her little lamb   E

Raining cats and dogs   428

Will Moses Mother Goose   398.8

MOSLEMS *See* Muslims

Mosque. Macaulay, D.   726

MOSQUE OFFICERS

See also Muslims

MOSQUES

Khan, A. K. What you will see inside a mosque   297.3

MOSQUES

See also Islamic architecture; Religious institutions; Temples

MOSQUES -- DESIGN AND CONSTRUCTION

Macaulay, D. Built to last   729

Macaulay, D. Mosque   726

Mosquito bite. Siy, A.   595.7

Mosquitoes. Webster, C.   595.7

MOSQUITOES

Siy, A. Mosquito bite   595.7

Webster, C. Mosquitoes   595.7

MOSQUITOES

See also Insects

MOSQUITOES -- FICTION

Knudsen, M. Bugged!   E

MOSQUITOES -- FOLKLORE

Aardema, V. Why mosquitoes buzz in people's ears   398.2

Mosquitoes are ruining my summer!   782.42

Moss, Cynthia

About

A passion for elephants   599.67

Moss, Lloyd

Zin! zin! zin! a violin   E

Moss, Marissa

Alien Eraser to the rescue   Fic

Amelia writes again   Fic

Amelia's 6th-grade notebook   Fic

Amelia's notebook   Fic

Barbed wire baseball   796.357

Brave Harriet   92

The bravest woman in America   92

Mira's Diary   Fic

Nurse, soldier, spy: the story of Sarah Edmonds, a Civil War hero   92

(il) Schwartz, D. M. G is for googol   510

Sky high: the true story of Maggie Gee   92

Moss, Miriam

This is the mountain   577.5

Moss, Onawumi Jean

McKissack, P. C. Precious and the Boo Hag   E

Moss, Peggy

One of us   E

Moss, Sue

Hunt, J. Precious Little   E

Moss, Wendy

Being me   158

MOSSES

Plants without seeds   586

MOSSES

See also Plants

Mossflower. Jacques, B.   Fic

The **most** amazing creature in the sea. Guiberson, B. Z.   591.77

The **most** amazing hide-and-seek alphabet book. Crowther, R.   E

The **most** amazing hide-and-seek numbers book. Crowther, R.   E

The **most** beautiful roof in the world. Lasky, K.   577.3

The **most** explosive science book in the universe. Watts, C.   500

The **most** famous pirates. Jenson-Elliott, C.   910.4

The **Most** Important Thing. Avi   Fic

Most loved in all the world. Hegamin, T.   E

The **Most** Magnificent Thing. Spires, A.   E

The **most** perfect spot. Goode, D.   E

Most wanted. Thompson, K.   Fic

The **most** wonderful thing in the world.   E

Most, Bernard

ABC T-Rex   E

Whatever happened to the dinosaurs?   E

The mostly miserable life of April Sinclair [series]

Friedman, L. B. Too good to be true   Fic

Mostly Monty. Hurwitz, J.   Fic

The **mostly** true adventures of Homer P. Figg. Philbrick, W. R.   Fic

The **mostly** true story of Jack. Barnhill, K. R.   Fic

Mosz, Gosia

(il) Da Costa, D. Hanukkah moon   E

MOTELS *See* Hotels and motels

MOTHER AND CHILD *See* Mother-child relationship

MOTHER AND CHILD

Hughes, L. Lullaby (for a Black mother)   811

MOTHER AND CHILD -- FICTION

Asper-Smith, S. I would tuck you in   E

Bagley, J. Boats for Papa   E

Bob, not Bob!   E

Cub's big world   E

Derrick, D. G. Animals don't, so I won't!   E

Fox, M. Sleepy bears   E

Galindo, R. My new mom and me   E

Hyewon Yum The twins' little sister   E

MURAL PAINTING AND DECORATION
Reynolds, P. H. Sky color **Fic**
Rubin, S. G. Diego Rivera **759.9**
Murasaki Shikibu
About
Lives of the writers **809**
Murawski, Darlyne
Face to face with butterflies **595.7**
Face to face with caterpillars **595.7**
Spiders and their webs **595.4**
MURDER -- FICTION
Anderson, R. J. A pocket full of murder **Fic**
First class murder **Fic**
Gonzalez, C. D. Moving target **Fic**
Stevens, R. Murder is bad manners **Fic**
MURDER -- NEW YORK (STATE) -- NEW YORK
Behnke, A. M. Death of a dreamer **92**
Murder afloat. Conly, J. L. **Fic**
Murder is bad manners. Stevens, R. **Fic**
MURDER MYSTERIES *See* Mystery and detective plays;
  Mystery fiction; Mystery films; Mystery radio programs;
  Mystery television programs
MURDER TRIALS *See* Trials (Homicide)
MURDER VICTIMS
D'Adamo, F. Iqbal **Fic**
Kushner, J. M. Who on earth is Dian Fossey? **92**
MURDERERS
Coleman, W. Racism on trial **345**
MURDERERS--ENGLAND--LONDON
Jones, R. L. Wild boy and the black terror **Fic**
Murdoch, David Hamilton
North American Indian **970.004**
Muriel's red sweater. Dokas, D. **E**
The **murk.** Lettrick, R. **Fic**
Murphy in the city. Provensen, A. **E**
Murphy, Chris
(il) Haduch, B. Go fly a bite! **629.227**
Murphy, Claire Rudolf
Marching with Aunt Susan **E**
Murphy, Glenn
How loud can you burp? **502**
Why is snot green **500**
Murphy, Jill
Dear hound **Fic**
Murphy, Jim
Across America on an emigrant train **385**
An American plague **614.5**
The boys' war **973.7**
Breakthrough! **617**
The crossing **973.3**
Desperate journey **Fic**
The giant and how he humbugged America **974.7**
The great fire **977.3**
Invincible microbe **616.9**
The long road to Gettysburg **973.7**
A savage thunder **973.7**
Truce **940.4**

A young patriot **973.3**
Murphy, Kelly
(il) Appelt, K. Brand-new baby blues **E**
(il) Ashburn, B. Over at the castle **E**
(il) Yolen, J. Creepy monsters, sleepy monsters **E**
(il) Broach, E. James to the rescue **Fic**
(il) Broach, E. Masterpiece **Fic**
(il) Broach, E. The miniature world of Marvin & James **Fic**
(il) La Fevers, R. L. The unicorn's tale **Fic**
(il) Lewis, J. P. Face bug **E**
(il) Marsh, K. The door by the staircase **Fic**
(il) The mouse with the question mark tail **Fic**
(il) San Souci, R. Haunted houses **S**
(il) Secrets at sea **Fic**
Murphy, Liz
ABC doctor **610**
Murphy, Lizzie, 1894-1964
About
McCully, E. A. Queen of the diamond **92**
Murphy, Mary
Good night, sleep tight, like this **E**
I kissed the baby **E**
A Kiss like this **E**
Say hello like this **E**
Murphy, Pat
Exploratopia **507.8**
Murphy, Patricia J.
Death **155.9**
Illness **616**
Murphy, Rita
Bird **Fic**
Murphy, Roxane
(il) MacDonald, M. R. Look back and see **027.62**
(il) MacDonald, M. R. When the lights go out **027.62**
Murphy, Sally
Pearl verses the world **Fic**
Murphy, Stuart J.
Beep beep, vroom vroom! **515**
Divide and ride **513**
Emma's friendwich **E**
Freda is found **E**
It's about time! **529**
Leaping lizards **E**
Mall mania **513**
Mighty Maddie **389**
Polly's pen pal **516**
Room for Ripley **530.8**
Same old horse **E**
The sundae scoop **511**
Write on, Carlos! **E**
Murphy, Yannick
Baby Polar **E**
Murray, Alison
Apple pie ABC **E**
Hare and tortoise **E**
The house that Zack built **E**
Little mouse **E**

Finding the music | **E**
Greene, J. D. The secret shofar of Barcelona | **Fic**
Isadora, R. Ben's trumpet | **E**
Kraegel, K. The song of Delphine | **E**
Lewis, M. Morgy's musical summer | **Fic**
MacLachlan, P. The facts and fictions of Minna Pratt | **Fic**
Patricelli, L. Be quiet, Mike! | **E**
Pinfold, L. The Django | **E**
Urban, L. A crooked kind of perfect | **Fic**
Winters, B. H. The secret life of Ms. Finkleman | **Fic**
Woods, B. Saint Louis Armstrong Beach | **Fic**
Zoola Palooza | **E**

MUSICIANS -- FOLKLORE
Huling, J. Ol' Bloo's boogie-woogie band and blues ensemble | **398.2**
Shepard, A. The sea king's daughter | **398.2**

MUSICIANS -- TRINIDAD AND TOBAGO -- BIOGRAPHY
Greenwood, M. Drummer boy of John John | **786.9**
The **musicians** of Bremen. Puttapipat, N. | **398.2**

MUSICOLOGISTS
Hopkinson, D. Home on the range | **92**

MUSICOLOGY
See also Research

MUSKRATS -- FICTION
Chaconas, D. Cork & Fuzz | **E**

MUSLIM ART *See* Islamic art
MUSLIM CIVILIZATION *See* Islamic civilization
MUSLIM WOMEN
See also Muslims; Women

MUSLIMS
Brown, T. Salaam | **297.3**
Bullard, L. Rashad's Ramadan and Eid al-Fitr | **297.3**
Ruelle, K. G. The grand mosque of Paris | **940.53**

MUSLIMS -- FICTION
Amina's voice | **Fic**
Faruqi, R. Lailah's lunchbox | **Fic**

Mustache baby. | **E**
Mustache! | **E**

MUSTACHES -- FICTION
Angleberger, T. Fake mustache | **Fic**
Clanton, B. Mo's mustache | **E**
Mustache baby | **E**

MUSTANG (NEPAL : DISTRICT) -- DISCOVERY AND EXPLORATION
Athans, S. K. Secrets of the sky caves | **796.522**

Mutation. Smith, R. C. | **Fic**
MUTATION (BIOLOGY) *See* Evolution; Variation (Biology)

MUTE PERSONS -- FICTION
LaFleur, S. Listening for Lucca | **Fic**

Muth, Jon J.
City Dog, Country Frog | **E**
(il) A family of poems | **808.81**
(il) Hesse, K. Come on, rain! | **E**
(il) Hest, A. Mr. George Baker | **E**
Hi, Koo! | **811**

(il) Kimmel, E. A. Gershon's monster | **398.**
(il) Poems to learn by heart | **821.00**
Stone soup | **398.**
(il) Thompson, L. The Christmas magic | ▶
Zen ghosts | ▶
Zen shorts | ▶
Mutt dog! King, S. M. | ▶
Mutt's promise. Salamon, J. | **Fi**
MUTUAL FUNDS
See also Investments
MUTUALISM (BIOLOGY) *See* Symbiosis
Muhammad, d. 632
About
Demi Muhammad | **29**
My 1st graphic novel [series]
Meister, C. Clues in the attic | **741.**
My abuelita. Johnston, T. | ▶
My achy body. Fromer, L. | **61**
My America. Gilchrist, J. S. | ▶
My America. | **81**
My American government [series]
Thomas, W. D. What are citizens' basic rights? | **32.**
Thomas, W. D. What is a constitution? | **34.**
My art book. | **745.**
My autumn book. Yee, W. H. | ▶
My baby blue jays. Berendt, J. | **59**
My baseball book. Gibbons, G. | **796.35**
My basketball book. Gibbons, G. | **796.32**
My basmati bat mitzvah. Freedman, P. J. | **Fi**
My bear Griz. McGinness, S. | ▶
My beautiful birds. | ▶
My best friend. Rodman, M. A. | ▶
My best friend is as sharp as a pencil. Piven, H. | ▶
My Bibi always remembers. Buzzeo, T. | ▶
My big book of trucks & diggers. Caterpillar Inc. | **621.**
My big brother. Cohen, M. | ▶
My big brother. Fisher, V. | ▶
My bike. Barton, B. | ▶
My blue is happy. | ▶
My body [series]
Korb, R. My brain | **612.**
Korb, R. My mouth | **612.**
Korb, R. My muscles | **612.**
Korb, R. My nose | **612.**
Korb, R. My spine | **612.**
Korb, R. My stomach | **612.**
My body is tough and gray. Markovics, J. L. | **599.**
My brain. Korb, R. | **612.**
My brother. Browne, A. | ▶
My brother Bert. Hughes, T. | ▶
My brother Charlie. | ▶
My brother is a superhero. Solomons, D. | **Fi**
My brother Martin. Farris, C. | **9**
My brother Sam is dead. Collier, J. L. | **Fi**
My brother's book. Sendak, M. | **81**
My brother, my sister, and I. Watkins, Y. K. | **Fi**
My bus. | ▶

DeFelice, C. C. The ghost of Cutler Creek **Fic**
Dionne, E. Ollie and the science of treasure hunting **Fic**
Draanen, W. v. Sammy Keyes and the hotel thief **Fic**
Edge, C. Twelve minutes to midnight **Fic**
Eulberg, E. The great Shelby Holmes **Fic**
Fairlie, E. The lost treasure of Tuckernuck **Fic**
Fantaskey, B. Isabel Feeney **Fic**
File under: 13 suspicious incidents **Fic**
First class murder **Fic**
Fitzgerald, L. M. The gallery **Fic**
Fitzgerald, L. M. Under the egg **Fic**
Frazier, A. The mastermind plot **Fic**
Friday Barnes, girl detective **Fic**
Gantos, J. From Norvelt to nowhere **Fic**
Gibbs, S. Big game **Fic**
Gibbs, S. Poached **Fic**
Gibbs, S. Space case **Fic**
The goldfish boy **Fic**
Gonzalez, C. D. Moving target **Fic**
Hale, S. Princess Academy **Fic**
Home sweet motel **Fic**
Inspector Flytrap in The goat who chewed too much **Fic**
Lacey, J. Island of Thieves **Fic**
Lane, A. Black ice **Fic**
Lane, A. Rebel fire **Fic**
Larwood, K. Freaks **Fic**
Lawrence, C. The case of the deadly desperados **Fic**
Lawrence, C. P.K. Pinkerton and the petrified man **Fic**
Lawrence, C. P.K. Pinkerton and the pistol-packing widows **Fic**
The legend of Diamond Lil **Fic**
Leonard, M. G. Beetle boy **Fic**
The magician's bird **Fic**
McCall Smith, A. The great cake mystery **Fic**
McCall Smith, A. The Mystery of Meerkat Hill **Fic**
McCall Smith, A. The mystery of the missing lion **Fic**
Milford, K. Greenglass House **Fic**
Mr. and Mrs. Bunny-- detectives extraordinaire! **Fic**
Nooks & crannies **Fic**
Obstfeld, R. Stealing the game **Fic**
Panda-monium **Fic**
Patron, S. Behind the masks **Fic**
Pullman, P. Two crafty criminals! **Fic**
Rylant, C. The case of the missing monkey **E**
Seagulls don't eat pickles **Fic**
Sobol, D. J. Encyclopedia Brown cracks the case **Fic**
Stanley, D. The mysterious matter of I.M. Fine **Fic**
Stevens, R. Murder is bad manners **Fic**
Stevens, R. Poison is not polite **Fic**
Stewart, T. L. The extraordinary education of Nicholas Benedict **Fic**
Stroud, J. The hollow boy **Fic**
Stroud, J. The whispering skull **Fic**
Thompson, J. E. The girl from Felony Bay **Fic**
Turnage, S. The ghosts of Tupelo Landing **Fic**
Turnage, S. The odds of getting even **Fic**
Turnage, S. Three times lucky **Fic**

Venable, C. A. F. Raining cats and detectives **Fic**

MYSTERY AND DETECTIVE STORIES *See* Mystery fiction

Mystery at the Club Sandwich. Cushman, D. **E**

MYSTERY COMIC BOOKS, STRIPS, ETC.
See also Comic books, strips, etc.

MYSTERY FICTION

Adler, D. A. Cam Jansen and the mystery at the haunted house **Fic**
Adler, D. A. Cam Jansen and the mystery of the stolen diamonds **Fic**
Adler, D. A. Cam Jansen and the Secret Service mystery **Fic**
Adler, D. A. Cam Jansen and the snowy day mystery **Fic**
Adler, D. A. Cam Jansen and the Sports Day mysteries **Fic**
Adler, D. A. Cam Jansen and the summer camp mysteries **Fic**
Adler, D. A. Cam Jansen and the Valentine baby mystery **Fic**
Adler, D. A. Cam Jansen and the wedding cake mystery **Fic**
Adler, D. A. Cam Jansen, the mystery of the dinosaur bones **Fic**
Adler, D. A. Cam Jansen, the mystery at the monkey house **Fic**
Adler, D. A. Cam Jansen, the mystery of the Babe Ruth baseball **Fic**
Adler, D. A. Cam Jansen, the mystery of the carnival prize **Fic**
Adler, D. A. Cam Jansen, the mystery of the circus clown **Fic**
Adler, D. A. Cam Jansen, the mystery of the gold coins **Fic**
Adler, D. A. Cam Jansen, the mystery of the monster movie **Fic**
Adler, D. A. Cam Jansen, the mystery of the stolen corn popper **Fic**
Adler, D. A. Cam Jansen, the mystery of the U.F.O. **Fic**
Adler, D. A. Cam Jansen, the Triceratops Pops mystery **Fic**
Adler, D. A. Young Cam Jansen and the 100th day of school mystery **E**
Adler, D. A. Young Cam Jansen and the dinosaur game **E**
Allison, J. Gilda Joyce, psychic investigator **Fic**
Amato, M. Edgar Allan's official crime investigation notebook **Fic**
Anderson, R. J. A pocket full of murder **Fic**
Angleberger, T. Horton Halfpott **Fic**
Angleberger, T. Inspector Flytrap **Fic**
Aronson, S. Beyond lucky **Fic**
Avi Catch you later, traitor **Fic**
Avi City of orphans **Fic**
Baccalario, P. The long-lost map **Fic**
Bachmann, S. The Cabinet of Curiosities **S**
Balliett, B. The Calder game **Fic**
Balliett, B. Chasing Vermeer **Fic**
Balliett, B. Hold fast **Fic**
Balliett, B. Pieces and players **Fic**
Balliett, B. The Wright 3 **Fic**
Barden, S. The super secret mystery **Fic**
Barnett, M. The case of the case of mistaken identity **Fic**
Barnett, M. The ghostwriter secret **Fic**
Barnett, M. It happened on a train **Fic**
Barnholdt, L. Girl meets ghost **Fic**
Barrett, T. The 100-year-old secret **Fic**
Barrett, T. The Beast of Blackslope **Fic**

hearts	**Fic**	Sherry, M. Walls within walls	**Fi**
Kennedy, E. Wilma Tenderfoot: the case of the putrid poison	**Fic**	Shouldn't you be in school?	**Fi**
		Simont, M. Nate the Great and the stolen base	**Fi**
Konigsburg, E. L. Up from Jericho Tel	**Fic**	Skofield, J. Detective Dinosaur undercover	**Fi**
Lane, A. Black ice	**Fic**	Snicket, L. The composer is dead	**Fi**
Lane, A. Rebel fire	**Fic**	Sobol, D. J. Encyclopedia Brown and the case of the carnival	
Larwood, K. Freaks	**Fic**	crime	**Fi**
Lasky, K. Spiders on the case	**Fic**	Sobol, D. J. Encyclopedia Brown and the case of the midnight	
Lawrence, C. The case of the deadly desperados	**Fic**	visitor	**Fi**
Lawrence, C. P.K. Pinkerton and the petrified man	**Fic**	Sobol, D. J. Encyclopedia Brown and the case of the secret	
Lawrence, C. P.K. Pinkerton and the pistol-packing widows	**Fic**	UFOs	**Fi**
		Sobol, D. J. Encyclopedia Brown and the case of the treasure	
Leck, J. The adventures of Jack Lime	**Fic**	hunt	**Fi**
The legend of Diamond Lil	**Fic**	Sobol, D. J. Encyclopedia Brown takes the cake!	**Fi**
Levine, G. C. A tale of Two Castles	**Fic**	Sobol, D. J. Encyclopedia Brown, boy detective	**Fi**
Little, K. G. The time of the fireflies	**Fic**	Sobol, D. J. Encyclopedia Brown, super sleuth	**Fi**
Lloyd Jones, R. Wild boy	**Fic**	Springer, N. The case of the cryptic crinoline	**Fi**
MacDonald, B. The secret of the sealed room	**Fic**	Springer, N. The case of the gypsy good-bye	**Fi**
MacDonald, B. Wicked Will	**Fic**	Springer, N. The case of the missing marquess	**Fi**
Mack, T. The fall of the Amazing Zalindas	**Fic**	St. Antoine, S. Three bird summer	**Fi**
Mack, T. The mystery of the conjured man	**Fic**	Standiford, N. The secret tree	**Fi**
Margolis, L. Girl's best friend	**Fic**	Stanley, D. The mysterious matter of I.M. Fine	**Fi**
McCall Smith, A. The great cake mystery	**Fic**	Stevens, R. Murder is bad manners	**Fi**
McCall Smith, A. The mystery of the missing lion	**Fic**	Stevens, R. Poison is not polite	**Fi**
McCall Smith, A. The Mystery of Meerkat Hill	**Fic**	Stewart, P. The curse of the night wolf	**Fi**
McDonald, M. Judy Moody, girl detective	**Fic**	Stewart, P. Phantom of Blood Alley	**Fi**
Milford, K. Greenglass House	**Fic**	Strickland, B. The sign of the sinister sorcerer	**Fi**
Mills, R. Charlie's key	**Fic**	Stroud, J. The hollow boy	**Fi**
Montgomery, L. B. The case of the stinky socks	**Fic**	Stroud, J. The whispering skull	**Fi**
Mr. and Mrs. Bunny-- detectives extraordinaire!	**Fic**	Teplin, S. The clock without a face	**Fi**
Napoli, D. J. Sly the Sleuth and the pet mysteries	**Fic**	Thompson, J. E. The girl from Felony Bay	**Fi**
Newbery, L. Lost boy	**Fic**	The trouble with chickens	**Fi**
Newman, R. The case of the missing carrot cake	**E**	Turnage, S. The odds of getting even	**Fi**
Nilsson, U. Detective Gordon	**Fic**	The unseen guest	**Fi**
Nooks & crannies	**Fic**	Updale, E. Johnny Swanson	**Fi**
Odyssey, S. T. The Wizard of Dark Street	**Fic**	Walters, E. The money pit mystery	**Fi**
Panda-monium	**Fic**	Warner, P. The secret of the skeleton key	**Fi**
Park, L. S. Trust no one	**Fic**	The watcher in the shadows	**Fi**
Patron, S. Behind the masks	**Fic**	Watson, G. Edison's gold	**Fi**
Princess for a week	**Fic**	When did you see her last?	**Fi**
Pullman, P. Two crafty criminals!	**Fic**	Who could that be at this hour?	**Fi**
Raskin, E. The mysterious disappearance of Leon (I mean Noel)	**Fic**	Who stole New Year's Eve?	**Fi**
		Winters, B. H. The mystery of the missing everything	**Fi**
Raskin, E. The tattooed potato and other clues	**Fic**	Ylvisaker, A. The luck of the Buttons	**Fi**
Raskin, E. The Westing game	**Fic**	**MYSTERY FILMS**	
Riddell, C. Ottoline and the yellow cat	**Fic**	*See also* Motion pictures	
Roberts, W. D. The view from the cherry tree	**Fic**	**MYSTERY GRAPHIC NOVELS**	
Rockliff, M. The case of the July 4th jinx	**E**	Collicutt, P. City in peril!	**741.**
Rockliff, M. The case of the missing moose	**Fic**	Conway, G. Crawling with zombies	**741.**
Rockliff, M. The case of the poisoned pig	**Fic**	Explorer	**741.**
Runholt, S. Adventure at Simba Hill	**Fic**	Kibuishi, K. Amulet, book one: The Stonekeeper	**741.**
Runholt, S. The mystery of the third Lucretia	**Fic**	Meister, C. Clues in the attic	**741.**
Rylant, C. The case of the missing monkey	**E**	O'Donnell, L. Power play	**741.**
Schlitz, L. A. Splendors and glooms	**Fic**	Pastis, S. Timmy failure	**Fi**
Selzer, A. I put a spell on you	**Fic**	Renier, A. Spiral-bound	**741.**
Sharmat, M. W. Nate the Great	**E**	Reynolds, A. Joey Fly, private eye in big hairy drama	**741.**
Sharmat, M. W. Nate the Great and the hungry book club	**Fic**	Reynolds, A. Joey Fly, private eye in Creepy crawly	

NATIONAL PARKS AND RESERVES
    See also Parks; Public lands

NATIONAL PARKS AND RESERVES -- UNITED STATES
    The camping trip that changed America   **979.4**
    Carson, M. K. The park scientists   **333.78**
    National Parks   **333.78**

NATIONAL PARKS AND RESERVES -- UNITED STATES
-- GUIDEBOOKS
    National Geographic kids national parks guide U.S.A. **917.3**

NATIONAL PARKS AND RESERVES -- UNITED STATES
-- HISTORY
    The camping trip that changed America   **979.4**

NATIONAL PEACE JUBILEE AND MUSICAL FESTI-
VAL (1869 : BOSTON, MASS.)
    Potter, A. Jubilee!   **92**

National Railway Museum (Great Britain)
    Big book of trains   **625.1**

NATIONAL RESOURCES *See* Economic conditions; Natu-
    ral resources; United States -- Economic conditions

NATIONAL SERVICE
    See also Public welfare

NATIONAL SOCIALISM -- FICTION
    Bartoletti, S. C. The boy who dared   **Fic**
    Wolf, J. M. Someone named Eva   **Fic**

NATIONAL SONGS
    National anthems of the world   **782.42**

NATIONAL SONGS
    See also Songs

NATIONAL SYMBOLS *See* National emblems

NATIONALISM
    See also International relations; Political science

NATIONALITY (CITIZENSHIP) *See* Citizenship

NATIONS
    Wojtanik, A. The National Geographic Bee ultimate fact
    book   **910**

NATIONS
    See also Political science

NATIVE AMERICAN ARCHITECTURE
    See also Architecture

NATIVE AMERICAN ART
    Baylor, B. When clay sings   **970.004**

NATIVE AMERICAN ART
    See also Art

NATIVE AMERICAN AUTHORS
    See also Authors

NATIVE AMERICAN CHILDREN
    Not my girl   **E**

NATIVE AMERICAN CHILDREN
    See also Children

NATIVE AMERICAN COSTUME
    See also Costume

NATIVE AMERICAN DANCE -- FICTION
    Smith, C. L. Jingle dancer   **E**

NATIVE AMERICAN DRAMA
    Bruchac, J. Pushing up the sky: seven Native American plays
    for children   **812**

NATIVE AMERICAN GAMES

    See also Games; Native Americans -- Social life and
    customs

NATIVE AMERICAN LITERATURE
    Weave little stars into my sleep   **782.42**

NATIVE AMERICAN LITERATURE
    See also Literature

NATIVE AMERICAN MEDICINE
    See also Medicine

NATIVE AMERICAN MUSIC
    See also Music

NATIVE AMERICAN MYTHOLOGY
    Goldman, J. Whiskers, tails, and wings   **398.2**

NATIVE AMERICAN NAMES
    See also Names

NATIVE AMERICAN SIGN LANGUAGE
    See also Sign language

NATIVE AMERICAN WOMEN
    Nelson, M. The life of Sacagawea   **92**
    Ray, D. K. Paiute princess   **92**
    Tallchief, M. Tallchief   **92**

NATIVE AMERICAN WOMEN
    See also Women

NATIVE AMERICANS
    A Braid of lives   **970.004**
    Dennis, Y. W. Children of native America today   **970.004**
    Goble, P. All our relatives   **970.004**
    King, D. C. First people   **970.004**
    McNeese, T. The fascinating history of American Indi-
    ans   **970.004**
    Murdoch, D. H. North American Indian   **970.004**
    Perritano, J. Spanish missions   **266**
    Swamp, J. Giving thanks   **299.7**
    Weber, E. N. R. Rattlesnake Mesa   **92**

NATIVE AMERICANS -- AGRICULTURE
    See also Agriculture

NATIVE AMERICANS -- ANTIQUITIES
    Quigley, M. Mesa Verde   **978.8**

NATIVE AMERICANS -- ANTIQUITIES
    See also Antiquities

NATIVE AMERICANS -- BIOGRAPHY
    Nelson, M. The life of Sacagawea   **92**

NATIVE AMERICANS -- CANADA
    Andre We feel good out here   **970.004**
    Fatty legs   **92**
    Jordan-Fenton, C. A stranger at home   **92**
    McLeod, T. The Delta is my home   **970.004**
    Zoe, T. Living stories   **970.004**

NATIVE AMERICANS -- CAPTIVITIES
    See also Frontier and pioneer life

NATIVE AMERICANS -- CHILDREN *See* Native Ameri-
    can children

NATIVE AMERICANS -- ECONOMIC CONDITIONS
    See also Economic conditions

NATIVE AMERICANS -- FICTION
    Alexie, S. Thunder Boy Jr.   **E**
    Bruchac, J. Talking leaves   **Fic**
    Bruchac, J. Walking two worlds   **Fic**

Frost, H. Salt **Fic**
Rose, C. S. Blue birds **Fic**
NATIVE AMERICANS -- FOLKLORE
Bruchac, J. The girl who helped thunder and other Native American folktales **398.2**
Bruchac, J. Between earth & sky **398.2**
Bruchac, J. How Chipmunk got his stripes **398.2**
Bruchac, J. Thirteen moons on a turtle's back **398.2**
Caduto, M. J. Keepers of the night **398.2**
Curry, J. L. Hold up the sky: and other Native American tales from Texas and the Southern Plains **398.2**
Delacre, L. Golden tales **398.2**
Dembicki, M. Trickster: Native American tales **398.2**
DePaola, T. The legend of the Indian paintbrush **398.2**
Goble, P. The girl who loved wild horses **398.2**
Goble, P. The legend of the White Buffalo Woman **398.2**
Goble, P. The woman who lived with wolves, & other stories from the tipi **398.2**
James, E. The woman who married a bear **398.2**
Larson, J. C. Hummingbirds **598**
Longfellow, H. W. Hiawatha **811**
McDermott, G. Coyote: a trickster tale from the American Southwest **398.2**
McDermott, G. Jabuti the tortoise **398.2**
McDermott, G. Raven **398.2**
Steptoe, J. The story of Jumping Mouse **398.2**
Taylor, C. J. Spirits, fairies, and merpeople **398.2**
Zoe, T. Living stories **970.004**
NATIVE AMERICANS -- FOLKLORE
See also Folklore
NATIVE AMERICANS -- FOLKLORE -- MEXICO
Goldman, J. Whiskers, tails, and wings **398.2**
NATIVE AMERICANS -- GREAT PLAINS
The horse and the Plains Indians **978**
NATIVE AMERICANS -- HISTORY
Connolly, S. The Americas and the Pacific **970.004**
Dennis, Y. W. A kid's guide to native American history **970.004**
Mann, C. C. Before Columbus **970.01**
NATIVE AMERICANS -- HUNTING
See also Hunting
NATIVE AMERICANS -- MEDICAL CARE
See also Medical care
NATIVE AMERICANS -- NORTH AMERICA
Cooper, S. Ghost Hawk **Fic**
NATIVE AMERICANS -- NORTHWEST COAST OF NORTH AMERICA
Proud to be Inuvialuit **970.004**
NATIVE AMERICANS -- ORIGIN
Mann, C. C. Before Columbus **970.01**
NATIVE AMERICANS -- PERU
Krebs, L. Up and down the Andes **985**
NATIVE AMERICANS -- POETRY
Bruchac, J. Thirteen moons on a turtle's back **398.2**
Dancing teepees: poems of American Indian youth **897**
Longfellow, H. W. Hiawatha **811**

NATIVE AMERICANS -- POLITICS AND GOVERNMENT
See also Politics
NATIVE AMERICANS -- RELATIONS WITH EARLY SETTLERS
Cooper, S. Ghost Hawk **Fi**
NATIVE AMERICANS -- RELIGION
See also Religion
NATIVE AMERICANS -- RELOCATION
Bjornlund, L. D. The Trail of Tears **970.00**
Bruchac, J. The Trail of Tears **970.00**
NATIVE AMERICANS -- RITES AND CEREMONIES
Ancona, G. Powwow **394.2**
NATIVE AMERICANS -- RITES AND CEREMONIES
See also Rites and ceremonies
NATIVE AMERICANS -- SOUTH AMERICA -- FOLKLORE
Knutson, B. Love and roast chicken **398.**
NATIVE AMERICANS -- SOUTHWESTERN STATES
Baylor, B. When clay sings **970.00**
NATIVE AMERICANS -- UNITED STATES
Green, C. R. Sacagawea **92**
NATIVE AMERICANS -- WARS
Anderson, P. C. George Armstrong Custer **92**
Zimmerman, D. J. Saga of the Sioux **970.00**
NATIVE AMERICANS -- WOMEN *See* Native American women
NATIVE PLANTS
See also Plants
Natterson, Cara
The care & keeping of you 2 **61.**
Natti, Susanna
(il) Adler, D. A. Cam Jansen and the mystery at the haunted house **Fi**
(il) Adler, D. A. Cam Jansen and the mystery of the stolen diamonds **Fi**
(il) Adler, D. A. Cam Jansen and the Secret Service mystery **Fi**
(il) Adler, D. A. Cam Jansen and the snowy day mystery **Fi**
(il) Adler, D. A. Cam Jansen and the Valentine baby mystery **Fi**
(il) Adler, D. A. Cam Jansen, the mystery of the dinosaur bones **Fi**
(il) Adler, D. A. Cam Jansen, the mystery at the monkey house **Fi**
(il) Adler, D. A. Cam Jansen, the mystery of the carnival prize **Fi**
(il) Adler, D. A. Cam Jansen, the mystery of the circus clown **Fi**
(il) Adler, D. A. Cam Jansen, the mystery of the gold coins **Fi**
(il) Adler, D. A. Cam Jansen, the mystery of the monster movie **Fi**
(il) Adler, D. A. Cam Jansen, the mystery of the stolen corn popper **Fi**
(il) Adler, D. A. Cam Jansen, the mystery of the U.F.O. **Fi**
(il) Adler, D. A. Cam Jansen, the Triceratops Pops mystery **Fi**

Granström, B. Nature adventures **508**

Lee, D. Biomimicry **608**

Potter, J. Nature in a nutshell for kids **508**

Schwartz, D. M. What in the wild? **508**

NATURE STUDY

See also Education; Science -- Study and teaching

NATURE STUDY -- FICTION

Yee, W. H. My autumn book **E**

NATURE TELEVISION PROGRAMS

See also Television programs

Nature's green umbrella. Gibbons, G. **577.3**

Nature's miracles [series]

Heneghan, J. Once there was a seed **581.4**

Nature's paintbox. Thomas, P. **811**

Nature's patchwork quilt. Miché, M. **E**

Nature's wonders [series]

Heinrichs, A. The Nile **962**

Kras, S. L. The Galapagos Islands **986.6**

Kummer, P. K. The Great Lakes **977**

Nature: a child's eye view [series]

Fujiwara, Y. Honey **638**

NATURECRAFT *See* Nature craft

NATUROPATHY

See also Alternative medicine; Therapeutics

Naujokaitis, Pranas T.

The totally awesome epic quest of the brave boy knight **741.5**

NAUTICAL ALMANACS

See also Almanacs; Navigation

NAUTICAL ASTRONOMY

See also Astronomy

NAUTICAL CHARTS

See also Maps; Navigation

Nauvoo. Bial, R. **289.3**

NAVAHO INDIANS *See* Navajo Indians

The **Navajo.** Cunningham, K. **970.004**

NAVAJO CHILDREN

See also Native American children; Navajo Indians

NAVAJO INDIANS

Cunningham, K. The Navajo **970.004**

Flood, N. B. Cowboy up! **E**

Roessel, M. Songs from the loom **746.1**

NAVAJO INDIANS -- FICTION

Miles, M. Annie and the Old One **Fic**

O'Dell, S. Sing down the moon **Fic**

NAVAJO WOMEN

See also Native American women; Navajo Indians

NAVAL AIR BASES *See* Air bases

NAVAL ARCHITECTURE

See also Architecture

NAVAL ART AND SCIENCE -- GRAPHIC NOVELS

Weigel, J. Thunder from the sea **741.5**

NAVAL OFFICERS

Berne, J. Manfish: a story of Jacques Cousteau **92**

Blumberg, R. Commodore Perry in the land of the Shogun **952**

Cooper, M. L. Hero of the high seas **92**

Yaccarino, D. The fantastic undersea life of Jacques Cous-

teau **92**

NAVAL PERSONNEL *See* Sailors

Navigating Early. Vanderpool, C. **Fic**

NAVIGATION

Borden, L. Sea clocks **526**

Fern, T. Dare the wind **92**

Kirk, S. T is for tugboat **623.82**

The man who made time travel **526**

Young, K. R. Across the wide ocean **623.89**

NAVIGATION (AERONAUTICS)

See also Aeronautics

NAVIGATION (ASTRONAUTICS)

See also Astrodynamics; Astronautics

NAVIGATORS *See* Explorers; Sailors

Navigators [series]

Smith, M. Ancient Egypt **932**

Naylor, Phyllis Reynolds

Alice in rapture, sort of **Fic**

Alice in-between **Fic**

Alice the brave **Fic**

All but Alice **Fic**

Emily's fortune **Fic**

Faith, hope, and Ivy June **Fic**

Outrageously Alice **Fic**

Roxie and the Hooligans **Fic**

Shiloh **Fic**

A Shiloh Christmas **Fic**

Starting with Alice **Fic**

NAZI HUNTERS

Rubin, S. G. The Anne Frank Case: Simon Wiesenthal's search for the truth **92**

Nazoa, Aquiles

A small Nativity **E**

NBA FINALS (BASKETBALL)

See also Basketball; Sports tournaments

NCAA Basketball. Bekkering, A. **796.323**

A Neal Porter book [series]

Lewin, T. How to babysit a leopard **910.4**

Neal, Christopher Silas

(il) Messner, K. Up in the garden and down in the dirt **635**

(il) Messner, K. Over and under the snow **591.4**

Over and under the pond **577.636**

Neal-Schuman guide to recommended children's books and media for use with every elementary subject. Matthew, K. I. **011.6**

Neal-Schuman technology management handbook for school library media centers. Farmer, L. S. J. **025.1**

NEANDERTHALS

See also Fossil hominids

NEAR EAST *See* Middle East

Near, Far. Borando, S. **E**

NEAR-DEATH EXPERIENCES

See also Death

NEAR-EARTH OBJECTS

See also Solar system

A **nearer** moon. Crowder, M. **Fic**

Nearly nonsense. Singh, R. **398.2**

Nelson, James

(il) Christopher, N. On the Shoulder of a Giant **Fic**

Nelson, Jessie

(jt. auth) Hopkins, K. L. Labracadabra **Fic**

Nelson, Jon

Cassino, M. The story of snow **551.57**

Nelson, Kadir

(il) Abe's honest words **92**

(il) Allen, D. Dancing in the wings **E**

Baby Bear **E**

Blue sky white stars **E**

(il) Coretta Scott **92**

(il) De la Peña, M. A nation's hope **92**

(il) Ellington was not a street **E**

(il) Grifalconi, A. The village that vanished **E**

Heart and soul **305.8**

He's got the whole world in his hands **782.25**

(il) Jordan, D. Salt in his shoes **E**

(il) King, M. L. J. I have a dream **323.4**

(il) Levine, E. Henry's freedom box **E**

(il) Napoli, D. J. Mama Miti: Wangari Maathai and the trees of Kenya **92**

Nelson Mandela **968.06**

(il) Nolen, J. Big Jabe **E**

(il) Nolen, J. Hewitt Anderson's great big life **E**

(il) Nolen, J. Thunder Rose **E**

(il) Staines, B. All God's critters **782.42**

(il) Testing the ice: a true story about Jackie Robinson **92**

We are the ship **796.357**

(il) Weatherford, C. B. Moses **92**

Nelson, Kristin L.

Monster trucks on the move **796.7**

Nelson, Maria

20 fun facts about dragonflies **595.7**

The life of Sacagawea **92**

Nelson, Marilyn

Beautiful ballerina **792.8**

Snook alone **E**

Sweethearts of rhythm **811**

Nelson, Nina

Bringing the boy home **Fic**

Nelson, Robin

(jt. auth) Donovan, S. Getting elected **324.7**

Nelson, S. D.

Bruchac, J. Crazy Horse's vision **E**

Black Elk's vision **92**

Digging a hole to heaven **Fic**

Sitting Bull **92**

Nelson, Scott Reynolds

Ain't nothing but a man **92**

Nelson, Vaunda Micheaux

Bad news for outlaws **92**

The book itch **E**

Juneteenth **394.26**

Who will I be, Lord? **E**

Neo Leo. Barretta, G. **609**

NEO-IMPRESSIONISM (ART) *See* Impressionism (Art)

NEON GENESIS EVANGELION

See also Fictional robots; Manga; Mecha

NEOPAGANISM

See also Religions

NEPAL -- DESCRIPTION AND TRAVEL

Athans, S. K. Secrets of the sky caves **796.522**

NEPAL -- FICTION

Cohn, D. Namaste! **E**

Tenzing Norbu Secret of the snow leopard **E**

NEPHEWS -- FICTION

Ransom, C. Rebel McKenzie **Fic**

NEPHILA MACULATA

Stronger Than Steel **595.4**

Neptune. Sherman, J. **523.4**

Neptune. Landau, E. **523.4**

NEPTUNE (PLANET)

Carson, M. K. Far-out guide to Neptune **523.4**

Landau, E. Neptune **523.4**

Sherman, J. Neptune **523.4**

Sparrow, G. Destination Uranus, Neptune, and Pluto **523.4**

NEPTUNE (PLANET)

See also Planets

The **Neptune** Project. Holyoke, P. **Fic**

Nerd camp. Weissman, E. B. **Fic**

Nerdy Birdy. **E**

Neri, Greg

Chess rumble **Fic**

Neri, G. Ghetto cowboy **Fic**

Neruda, Pablo, 1904-1973

About

Brown, M. Pablo Neruda **92**

Ryan, P. M. The dreamer **Fic**

NERVES

See also Nervous system

Nervous system. Tieck, S. **612.8**

NERVOUS SYSTEM

Berger, M. Why I sneeze, shiver, hiccup, and yawn **612.7**

Gold, M. V. Learning about the nervous system **612.8**

Rotner, S. Body actions **612**

Simon, S. The brain **612.8**

Stewart, M. You've got nerve! **612.8**

Tieck, S. Nervous system **612.8**

NERVOUS SYSTEM

See also Anatomy; Physiology

NERVOUS SYSTEM -- DISEASES

See also Diseases

Nesbet, Anne

Cloud and Wallfish **Fic**

Nesbit, E.

The enchanted castle **Fic**

Five children and it **Fic**

Jack and the beanstalk **398.2**

Nesbitt, Kenn

(ed) One minute till bedtime **821.008**

More bears! **E**

Nesbø, Jo

Doctor Proctor's fart powder **Fic**

See also Ability grouping in education; Education -- Experimental methods; Schools

Noni the pony. Lester, A.   **E**

Noni the pony goes to the beach.   **E**

NONINDIGENOUS PESTS

Burns, L. G. Beetle busters   **595.76**

Drake, J. Alien invaders   **578.6**

Jackson, C. Alien invasion   **578.6**

Metz, L. What can we do about invasive species?   **578.6**

NONINDIGENOUS PESTS

See also Biological invasions; Pests

NONLINGUISTIC COMMUNICATION *See* Nonverbal communication

Nonna's birthday surprise. Bastianich, L.   **E**

NONOBJECTIVE ART *See* Abstract art

NONPUBLIC SCHOOLS *See* Church schools; Private schools

The **Nonsense** Show. Carle, E.   **E**

NONSENSE VERSES

Doyen, D. Once upon a twice   **E**

Florian, D. Bing bang boing   **811**

His shoes were far too tight   **821**

Lear, E. The complete verse and other nonsense   **821**

Lear, E. Edward Lear   **821**

Lear, E. Edward Lear's The duck & the kangaroo   **821**

Lear, E. The owl and the pussycat   **821**

Prelutsky, J. The frogs wore red suspenders   **811**

Prelutsky, J. Ride a purple pelican   **811**

Prelutsky, J. Scranimals   **811**

Silverstein, S. Every thing on it   **811**

Silverstein, S. Falling up   **811**

Silverstein, S. A light in the attic   **811**

Silverstein, S. Where the sidewalk ends   **811**

Willard, N. A visit to William Blake's inn   **811**

NONSENSE VERSES

See also Children's poetry; Humorous poetry; Wit and humor

NONVERBAL COMMUNICATION

Jackson, D. M. Every body's talking   **153.6**

NONVERBAL COMMUNICATION

See also Communication

NONVIOLENT NONCOOPERATION *See* Passive resistance

NONWORD STORIES *See* Stories without words

Noodle & Lou. Scanlon, L. G.   **E**

Noodle pie. Starke, R.   **Fic**

Noodle's knitting. Webster, S.   **E**

Noodlehead nightmares.   **741.5**

Noodleheads [series]

Noodleheads see the future   **E**

Noodleheads see the future.   **E**

Nooks & crannies.   **Fic**

Noon, Steve

Millard, A. A street through time   **936**

Noonie's masterpiece. Railsback, L.   **Fic**

Noordeman, Arjen

(il) Hearst, M. Unusual creatures   **590**

Noordeman, Jelmer

(il) Hearst, M. Unusual creatures   **590**

Nora and the Texas terror. Cox, J.   **Fic**

The **Nora** notebooks [series]

The trouble with ants   **Fic**

The trouble with babies   **Fic**

Nora's ark. Kinsey-Warnock, N.   **E**

Nora's ark.   **E**

Norac, Carl

Swing Cafe   **E**

Norcliffe, James

The boy who could fly   **Fic**

NORDIC PEOPLES *See* Teutonic peoples

Nordling, Lee

SheHeWe   **741.5**

Nordqvist, Sven

Tomtes' Christmas porridge   **E**

Norling, Beth

(il) Herrick, S. Naked bunyip dancing   **Fic**

Norman Rockwell. Gherman, B.   **759.13**

Norman, Kimberly

I know a wee piggy   **E**

Ten on the sled   **E**

Norris, Kathleen

The holy twins: Benedict and Scholastica   **271**

NORSE LEGENDS

Treasury of Norse mythology   **398.209**

NORSE LEGENDS

See also Legends

NORSE MYTHOLOGY

Explore Norse Myths!   **293**

Fisher, L. E. Gods and goddesses of the ancient Norse   **293**

Lunge-Larsen, L. The adventures of Thor the Thunder God   **293**

Treasury of Norse mythology   **398.209**

NORSE MYTHOLOGY

See also Mythology

NORSE MYTHOLOGY -- FICTION

Marr, M. Loki's wolves   **Fic**

Marr, M. Odin's ravens   **Fic**

Riordan, R. The sword of summer   **Fic**

NORSEMEN *See* Vikings

Norstrand, Torstein

(il) Lerangis, P. The colossus rises   **Fic**

(il) Lerangis, P. Lost in Babylon   **Fic**

(il) Lerangis, P. Tomb of shadows   **Fic**

North. Dowson, N.   **591.56**

NORTH AMERICA

Foster, K. Atlas of North America   **970**

NORTH AMERICA -- ANTIQUITIES

Harrison, D. L. Mammoth bones and broken stones   **970.01**

NORTH AMERICA -- HISTORY -- FICTION

Lasky, K. The escape   **Fic**

North American Indian. Murdoch, D. H.   **970.004**

NORTH BUXTON (ONT.) -- HISTORY -- 20TH CENTURY -- FICTION

Curtis, C. P. The madman of Piney Woods   **Fic**

Odin's ravens. Marr, M. **Fic**

The **odious** Ogre. Juster, N. **E**

Odriozola, Elena

(il) Wolff, F. The story blanket **E**

Odysseus. McCaughrean, G. **292**

ODYSSEUS (GREEK MYTHOLOGY)

Chwast, S. The odyssey **741.5**

Lupton, H. The adventures of Odysseus **292**

McCaughrean, G. Odysseus **292**

The **Odyssey.** Ita, S. **741.5**

The **odyssey.** Chwast, S. **741.5**

Odyssey, Shawn Thomas

The Wizard of Dark Street **Fic**

OEDIPUS (LEGENDARY CHARACTER)

See also Legendary characters

Oelschlager, Vanita

I came from the water **972.94**

A tale of two daddies **E**

Oeming, Michael

(il) Bendis, B. M. Takio, vol. 1 **741.5**

Oertel, Andreas

The Archaeolojesters **Fic**

Of colors and things. Hoban, T. **535.6**

Of numbers and stars. Love, D. A. **92**

Of thee I sing. **179**

Ofanansky, Allison

Harvest of light **E**

The patchwork Torah **E**

What's the buzz? **E**

Off like the wind! Spradlin, M. P. **383**

Off to class. Hughes, S. **371**

Off to first grade. Borden, L. **E**

Off to war. Ellis, D. **303.6**

Off we go! Hillenbrand, W. **E**

OFFENSES AGAINST PROPERTY

See also Crime; Criminal law

OFFENSES AGAINST PUBLIC SAFETY

See also Crime; Criminal law

OFFENSES AGAINST THE PERSON

See also Crime; Criminal law

Offermann, Andrea

Milford, K. The Boneshaker **Fic**

(il) Milford, K. The Broken Lands **Fic**

(il) The Thickety **Fic**

(il) The whispering trees **Fic**

OFFICE BUILDINGS

See also Buildings

OFFICE EQUIPMENT AND SUPPLIES -- FICTION

Crummel, S. S. The Little Red Pen **E**

OFFICE SUPPLY INDUSTRY EXECUTIVES

Thimmesh, C. Girls think of everything **920**

Officer Buckle and Gloria. Rathmann, P. **E**

Offill, Jenny

11 experiments that failed **E**

17 things I'm not allowed to do anymore **E**

Sparky **E**

While you were napping **E**

OFFSET PRINTING

See also Lithography; Printing

OFFSHORE WATER POLLUTION See Marine pollution

Ogburn, Jacqueline K.

The bake shop ghost **E**

A dignity of dragons **398**

Little treasures **413**

The magic nesting doll **E**

Oggie Cooder. Weeks, S. **Fic**

Oggie Cooder, party animal. Weeks, S. **Fic**

OGLALA INDIANS

Freedman, R. The life and death of Crazy Horse **978**

Nelson, S. D. Black Elk's vision **92**

OGLALA INDIANS -- FICTION

Bruchac, J. Crazy Horse's vision **E**

The **Ogre** of Oglefort. Ibbotson, E. **Fic**

Oh my baby, little one. Appelt, K. **E**

Oh my gods! Bryant, M. E. **292**

Oh no! Not again! Barnett, M. **E**

Oh No! Said Elephant. Benjamin, A. H. **E**

Oh no! Time to go! Doughty, R. **E**

Oh no!, or, How my science project destroyed the world. Barnett, M. **E**

Oh no, gotta go! Elya, S. M. **E**

Oh no, monster tomato! Helmore, J. **E**

Oh, a-hunting we will go. Langstaff, J. M. **782.42**

Oh, brother! Grimes, N. **E**

Oh, Daddy! Shea, B. **E**

Oh, Ellen

(ed) Flying lessons & other stories **Fic**

Oh, Harry! Kumin, M. **E**

Oh, how Sylvester can pester! Kinerk, R. **811**

Oh, look! Polacco, P. **E**

Oh, no! Fleming, C. **E**

Oh, rats! Marrin, A. **599.35**

Oh, the places you'll go! Seuss, D. **158**

Oh, yuck! Masoff, J. **031.02**

Ohi, Debbie Ridpath

(il) Where are my books? **E**

Ohi, Ruth

Chicken, pig, cow and the class pet **E**

Kenta and the big wave **E**

Ohio. Stille, D. R. **977.1**

Ohio. Lew, K. **977.1**

OHIO

Stille, D. R. Ohio **977.1**

OHIO -- FICTION

Clements, A. Lost and found **Fic**

Cook, K. Nuts **Fic**

DeFelice, C. C. Weasel **Fic**

Dutton, S. Mary Mae and the gospel truth **Fic**

Giblin, J. The boy who saved Cleveland **Fic**

Hamilton, V. The house of Dies Drear **Fic**

Hayes, C. Mothman's curse **Fic**

Kuhlman, E. The last invisible boy **Fic**

McCloskey, R. Lentil **E**

Springstubb, T. What happened on Fox Street **Fic**

OMAN -- DESCRIPTION AND TRAVEL
Ejaz, K. We visit Oman **953.53**

OMAN -- FICTION
Nye, N. S. The turtle of Oman **Fic**

Omega City. Peterfreund, D. **Fic**

Ommen, Sylvia van
(il) Westera, M. Sheep and Goat **Fic**

Omololu, Cynthia Jaynes
When it's six o'clock in San Francisco **E**

On a beam of light. Berne, J. **92**

On a medieval day. Arato, R. **S**

On a road in Africa. Doner, K. **636.08**

On a windy night. Day, N. R. **E**

On angel wings. Morpurgo, M. **Fic**

On beyond a million. Schwartz, D. M. **513.5**

On Bird Hill. **E**

On Earth. Karas, G. B. **525**

On Market Street. Lobel, A. **E**

On Meadowview Street. Cole, H. **E**

On morning wings. Lindbergh, R. **223**

On Mother's lap. Scott, A. H. **E**

On my honor. Bauer, M. D. **Fic**

On my own biography [series]
Lowery, L. Aunt Clara Brown **978.8**

On my own folklore [series]
Krensky, S. Anansi and the box of stories **398.2**
Krensky, S. John Henry **398.2**
Krensky, S. Paul Bunyan **398.2**
Krensky, S. Pecos Bill **398.2**
Lowery, L. The tale of La Llorona **398.2**
Schram, P. The magic pomegranate **398.2**
Wang Ping The dragon emperor **398.2**

On my own history [series]
Figley, M. R. Prisoner for liberty **92**

On my own holidays [series]
Douglass, S. L. Ramadan **297.3**
Jango-Cohen, J. Chinese New Year **394.26**
Nelson, V. M. Juneteenth **394.26**

On My Street. **E**

On my way. DePaola, T. **92**

On my way to buy eggs. Chen **E**

On Noah's ark. Brett, J. **E**

On our way home. Braun, S. **E**

On parade. Laidlaw, R. **791.8**

On Sand Island. Martin, J. B. **E**

On stage. Bany-Winters, L. **372.66**

On the ball. Pinkney, J. B. **E**

On the banks of Plum Creek. Wilder, L. I. **Fic**

On the Blue Comet. Wells, R. **Fic**

On the day you were born. Frasier, D. **E**

On the farm. Elliott, D. **E**

On the night you were born. Tillman, N. **E**

On the radar: sports [series]
Eason, S. Free running **613.7**

On the road. Cooper, W. **629.2**

On the road. Nolan, L. A. **Fic**

On the road to Mr. Mineo's. O'Connor, B. **Fic**

On the scale. Cleary, B. P. **530.8**

On the seabed. Woodward, J. **551.46**

On the Shoulder of a Giant. Christopher, N. **Fic**

On the Texas trail of Cabeza de Vaca. Lourie, P. **92**

On the town. Caseley, J. **E**

On the verge of extinction: crisis in the environment [series]
Leathers, D. Polar bears on the Hudson Bay **599.78**
Whiting, J. Threat to ancient Egyptian treasures **93.**

On the way to the beach. Cole, H. **E**

On the wings of heroes. Peck, R. **Fic**

On time. Skurzynski, G. **52.**

On top of spaghetti. Johnson, P. B. **E**

On your mark, get set, grow! Madaras, L. **612.6**

Onassis, Jacqueline Kennedy, 1929-1994
About
Axelrod, A. Your friend in fashion, Abby Shapiro **Fic**
When Jackie saved Grand Central **720.97.**

Once a mouse. Brown, M. **398.2**

Once I ate a pie. MacLachlan, P. **811**

Once I knew a spider. Dewey, J. **E**

Once there was a seed. Heneghan, J. **581.**

Once upon a baby brother. Sullivan, S. **E**

Once upon a banana. Armstrong, J. **E**

Once upon a bathtime. Hughes, V. **E**

Once upon a crime. Buckley, M. **Fic**

Once upon a Marigold. Ferris, J. **Fic**

Once upon a royal superbaby. O'Malley, K. **E**

Once upon a starry night. Mitton, J. **523.8**

Once upon a time. Heitman, J. **372.6**

Once upon a time, the end. Kloske, G. **E**

Once upon a twice. Doyen, D. **E**

Once upon an alphabet. Jeffers, O. **E**

Once upon MacDonald's farm. Gammell, S. **E**

One. Otoshi, K. **E**

The **one** and only Ivan. Applegate, K. **Fic**

The **one** and only Marigold. Heide, F. P. **E**

The **one** and only Stuey Lewis. **Fic**

One bean. Rockwell, A. F. **635**

One bear extraordinaire. McGowan, J. **E**

One beetle too many: the extraordinary adventures of Charles Darwin. Lasky, K. **92**

One boy. Seeger, L. V. **E**

One busy day. **E**

One came home. Timberlake, A. **Fic**

One candle. Bunting, E. **E**

One child, one seed. Cave, K. **E**

One city, two brothers. Smith, C. **398.2**

One cool friend. Buzzeo, T. **E**

One crazy summer. Williams-Garcia, R. **Fic**

One day and one amazing morning on Orange Street. Rocklin, J. **Fic**

One day in the eucalyptus, eucalyptus tree. Bernstrom, D. **E**

One day, the end. Dotlich, R. K. **E**

One dog and his boy. Ibbotson, E. **Fic**

One family. **E**

One fine day. Hogrogian, N. **398.2**

One fine trade. Miller, B. **398.2**

One foot two feet. Maloney, P.   E

One for the Murphys. Hunt, L. M.   **Fic**

One giant leap. Burleigh, R.   **629.45**

One gorilla. Browne, A.   **513.2**

One green apple. Bunting, E.   E

One half from the east.   **Fic**

One hen. Milway, K. S.   E

One Hundred Bones.   E

One is a drummer. Thong, R.   E

One is a feast for Mouse. Cox, J.   E

One is a snail, ten is a crab. Sayre, A. P.   E

One last word.   **811.54**

One leaf rides the wind. Mannis, C. D.   E

The one left behind. Roberts, W. D.   **Fic**

One lighthouse, one moon. Lobel, A.   E

One little chicken.   E

One little chicken. Elliott, D.   E

One million things [series]

    Woodward, J. Planet Earth   **550**

One minute till bedtime.   **821.008**

One moon, two cats. Godwin, L.   E

One more hug for Madison. Church, C.   E

One night in the Coral Sea. Collard, S. B.   **593.6**

One night in the Everglades. Larsen, L.   **577**

One night in the zoo. Kerr, J.   E

One nighttime sea. Rose, D. L.   **513.2**

One of us. Moss, P.   E

ONE PARENT FAMILY See Single-parent families

One peace. Wilson, J.   **305.23**

One plastic bag. Paul, M.   **363.7**

One potato, two potato. DeFelice, C. C.   E

One rainy day. Salzano, T.   E

One red apple. Ziefert, H.   **634**

One red dot. Carter, D. A.   E

One Saturday evening. Baker, B.   E

One small place in a tree. Brenner, B.   **577.3**

One special day.   E

One spooky night. Stone, K.   E

One spotted giraffe. Horáček, P.   E

One square inch. Mills, C.   **Fic**

One starry night.   E

One Ted falls out of bed. Donaldson, J.   E

One Times Square.   **974.7**

One Today. Blanco, R.   **811**

One true bear. Dewan, T.   E

One two that's my shoe! Murray, A.   E

One was Johnny. Sendak, M.   E

One watermelon seed. Lottridge, C. B.   E

One well. Strauss, R.   **553.7**

One wolf howls. Cohn, S.   **599.77**

One word from Sophia. Averbeck, J.   E

One world kids cookbook. Mendez, S.   **641.59**

One world kids cookbook. Mendez, S.   **641.5**

One world, many religions. Osborne, M. P.   **200**

One world, one day. Kerley, B.   **305.23**

One year in Beijing. Wang Xiaohong   E

One, two, buckle my shoe. Yoon, S.   E

One, two, buckle my shoe. Cabrera, J.   E

One-handed catch. Auch, M. J.   **Fic**

One-of-a-kind stamps and crafts. Ross, K.   **761**

Ones and twos. Jocelyn, M.   E

Ong, Jacqueline

    Sheehan, P. Cote d'Ivoire   **966.68**

Ong, Wilson

    (il) James, H. F. Paper son   **Fic**

Onion John. Krumgold, J.   **Fic**

Onion juice, poop, and other surprising sources of alternative energy. Weakland, M.   **333.79**

ONLINE AUTHORSHIP

    Bridget and Bo build a blog   **Fic**

ONLINE CHAT GROUPS

    See also Conversation

Online etiquette and safety. Cornwall, P.   **004.6**

ONLINE JOURNALISM

    See also Journalism

ONLINE MARKETING See Internet marketing

ONLINE SELLING See Internet marketing

ONLINE SOCIAL NETWORKS

    Freese, S. M. Craigslist   **381**

    Richardson, W. Blogs, wikis, podcasts, and other powerful Web tools for classrooms   **371.3**

    Schwartz, H. E. Safe social networking   **302.3**

ONLINE SOCIAL NETWORKS -- FICTION

    Baskin, N. R. Runt   **Fic**

ONLINE SOCIAL NETWORKS -- SECURITY MEA-SURES

    Schwartz, H. E. Safe social networking   **302.3**

Only a witch can fly. McGhee, A.   E

The only child. Guojing   **741.5**

ONLY CHILD

    See also Children; Family size

ONLY CHILD -- FICTION

    Adderson, C. Jasper John Dooley   **Fic**

    Best, C. What's so bad about being an only child?   E

Only Emma. Warner, S.   **Fic**

The only game. Lupica, M.   **Fic**

Only one neighborhood. Harshman, M.   E

Only one year.   **Fic**

The only ones. Starmer, A.   **Fic**

Only passing through: the story of Sojourner Truth. Rockwell, A. F.   **92**

The only road. Diaz, A.   **Fic**

Only the mountains do not move. Reynolds, J.   **305.8**

The only thing worse than witches. Magaziner, L.   **Fic**

Only you can save mankind. Pratchett, T.   **Fic**

Onoda, Yuta

    (il) Lewis, G. Wild wings   **Fic**

ONTARIO

    Greenwood, B. A pioneer sampler   **971**

ONTARIO -- FICTION

    Sherrard, V. The glory wind   **Fic**

ONTOLOGY

    See also Philosophy

Onward. Johnson, D.   **92**

flight

OUTER SPACE -- EXPLORATION -- FICTION

Cottrell Boyce, F. Cosmic — **Fic**

Greenberg, D. Enchanted lions — **E**

The three little aliens and the big bad robot — **E**

OUTER SPACE -- EXPLORATION -- HISTORY

Arnold, T. Fly guy presents — **E**

OUTER SPACE -- FICTION

Anderson, M. T. He laughed with his other mouths — **Fic**

Baldacchino, C. Morris Micklewhite and the Tangerine Dress — **E**

Brawer, M. Archie takes flight — **Fic**

Brown, J. Star Wars — **741.5**

Ganz-Schmitt, S. Planet Kindergarten — **E**

Hatke, B. The Return of Zita the Spacegirl — **741.5**

Interstellar Cinderella — **E**

Viva, F. A long way away — **E**

OUTER SPACE -- POETRY

Out of this world — **811**

Whitman, W. When I heard the learn'd astronomer — **E**

Outfielders. Glaser, J. — **796.357**

The **outlandish** adventures of Liberty Aimes. Easton, K. — **Fic**

OUTLAWS See Criminals; Thieves

Outrageous women of the Middle Ages. León, V. — **920.72**

Outrageously Alice. Naylor, P. R. — **Fic**

Outside and inside dinosaurs. Markle, S. — **567.9**

Outside and inside mummies. Markle, S. — **393**

Outside and inside rats and mice. Markle, S. — **599.35**

Outside and inside woolly mammoths. Markle, S. — **569**

Outside beauty. Kadohata, C. — **Fic**

Outside in. Ellis, S. — **Fic**

Outside over there. Sendak, M. — **E**

Outside the box. — **811.6**

Outside your window. Davies, N. — **E**

OUTSIDER ART

The fantastic jungles of Henri Rousseau — **759**

OUTSIDER ART

See also Art

Outstanding in the rain. — **E**

Outstanding library service to children. Cerny, R. — **027.62**

Over and under the pond. — **577.636**

Over and under the snow. Messner, K. — **591.4**

Over at the castle. Ashburn, B. — **E**

Over in Australia. Berkes, M. C. — **782.42**

Over in the forest. Berkes, M. — **E**

Over in the hollow. Dickinson, R. — **E**

Over in the meadow. Keats, E. J. — **E**

Over in the meadow. Wadsworth, O. A. — **E**

Over in the meadow. Langstaff, J. M. — **782.42**

Over my dead body. Klise, K. — **Fic**

Over sea, under stone. Cooper, S. — **Fic**

Over the hills and far away. — **398.8**

Over the moon. Aronica-Buck, B. — **811**

Over the ocean. Gomi, T. — **E**

Over the rainbow. Harburg, E. Y. — **782.42**

Over the river and through the wood. Child, L. M. F. — **811**

Over under. Jocelyn, M. — **E**

Over, under & through, and other spatial concepts. Hoban, T.

OVERLAND JOURNEYS TO THE PACIFIC

Calabro, M. The perilous journey of the Donner Party — **979.**

Friedman, M. The Oregon Trail — **97**

Harness, C. The tragic tale of Narcissa Whitman and a faithf history of the Oregon Trail — **9**

How to get rich on the Oregon Trail — **97**

Todras, E. H. Wagon trains and settlers — **973.**

OVERLAND JOURNEYS TO THE PACIFIC

See also Frontier and pioneer life; Voyages and travels

OVERLAND JOURNEYS TO THE PACIFIC -- FICTION

Applegate, K. The buffalo storm

Coerr, E. The Josefina story quilt

The crossing

Hopkinson, D. Apples to Oregon

Kay, V. Covered wagons, bumpy trails

Lawlor, L. He will go fearless — **Fi**

Stanley, D. Roughing it on the Oregon Trail — **Fi**

Van Leeuwen, J. Bound for Oregon — **Fi**

Wagons ho!

Young, J. A book for black-eyed Susan — **Fi**

OVERPOPULATION

See also Population

OVERUSE INJURIES

See also Wounds and injuries

OVERWEIGHT See Obesity

OVERWEIGHT PERSONS -- FICTION

Dowell, F. O. The second life of Abigail Walker — **Fi**

Owen. Henkes, K.

Owen & Mzee. Hatkoff, I. — **599.6**

Owen & Mzee: the language of friendship. Hatkoff, I. — **599.6**

Owen Foote, frontiersman. Greene, S. — **Fi**

Owen Foote, mighty scientist. Greene, S. — **Fi**

Owen Foote, money man. Greene, S. — **Fi**

Owen, Cheryl

Gifts for kids to make — **745.**

Owen, Karen

I could be, you could be

Owen, Ruth

Creepy backyard invaders — **578.**

Disgusting food invaders — **615.**

Gross body invaders — **578.**

Icky house invaders — **578.**

Valentine's Day origami — **73**

Woods, M. Ace! — **796.34**

Woods, M. Goal! — **796.33**

Woods, M. Xtreme! Extreme sports facts and stats — **79**

Owens, Gail

(il) Hurwitz, J. The adventures of Ali Baba Bernstein — **Fi**

(il) Sobol, D. J. Encyclopedia Brown and the case of th treasure hunt — **Fi**

Owens, Jesse, 1913-1980

About

Adler, D. A. A picture book of Jesse Owens — **796.4**

Krull, K. Lives of the athletes — **79**

Owens, L. L.

The life cycle of a snail — **59**

Higher! higher!   E
Potty   E
Tubby   E
Patricia von Pleasantsquirrel. Proimos, J.   E
Patrick in A teddy bear's picnic and other stories. Hayes, G.   **741.5**
Patrick's dinosaurs. Carrick, C.   E
Patrick, Denise Lewis
Finding someplace   **Fic**
Patrick, Saint, 373?-463?
About
DePaola, T. Patrick: patron saint of Ireland   **92**
Patrick: patron saint of Ireland. DePaola, T.   **92**
PATRIOTIC POETRY
See also Poetry
PATRIOTIC SONGS *See* National songs
PATRIOTISM
Park, L. S. When my name was Keoko   **Fic**
PATRIOTISM
See also Citizenship; Human behavior; Loyalty
PATRIOTISM -- FICTION
Blue sky white stars   E
Patrol. Myers, W. D.   E
Patron, Susan
Behind the masks   **Fic**
The higher power of Lucky   **Fic**
Maybe yes, maybe no, maybe maybe   **Fic**
PATRONS OF THE ARTS
Fritz, J. Leonardo's horse   **730.92**
Patt, Beverly
Best friends forever   **Fic**
Patten, E. J.
Return to Exile   **Fic**
PATTERN PERCEPTION
Cleary, B. P. A-B-A-B-A--a book of pattern play   **515**
Goldstone, B. I see a pattern here   **152.14**
Spotty, stripy, swirly   **152.14**
PATTERN PERCEPTION
See also Perception
PATTERN RECOGNITION *See* Pattern perception
PATTERNMAKING
See also Models and modelmaking
PATTERNS (MATHEMATICS)
Cleary, B. P. A-B-A-B-A--a book of pattern play   **515**
Murphy, S. J. Beep beep, vroom vroom!   **515**
PATTERNS (MATHEMATICS)
See also Mathematics
Patterson, Annie
(il) Arnold, C. Too hot? too cold?   **612**
(il) Sayre, A. P. Turtle, turtle, watch out!   E
Patterson, James, 1947-
(jt. auth) Grabenstein, C. House of robots   **Fic**
(jt. auth) Grabenstein, C. Word of mouse   **Fic**
Middle school, the worst years of my life   **Fic**
Treasure hunters   **Fic**
Patterson, Nancy Ruth
Ellie ever   **Fic**

Pattison, Darcy
Desert baths   **591.754**
The journey of Oliver K. Woodman   E
Pattison, D. Prairie storms   **577.4**
Prairie storms   **577.4**
Patton, Julia
(il) Chernesky, F. S. From Apple Trees to Cider, Please!
Paul & Antoinette. Kerascoët (Illustrator)   E
Paul Bunyan. Kellogg, S.   **398.2**
Paul Bunyan. Krensky, S.   **398.2**
Paul Cezanne. Burleigh, R.   **92**
Paul Klee for children.   **759.9**
Paul Revere's ride. Mortensen, L.   **92**
Paul Robeson. Greenfield, E.   **92**
Paul Thurlby's alphabet. Thurlby, P.   E
Paul Thurlby's wildlife. Thurlby, P.   **591**
Paul, Alice
About
Wishinsky, F. Freedom heroines   **920**
Paul, Alison
The Plan   E
Paul, Ann Whitford
Fiesta fiasco   E
Count on Culebra   E
Snail's good night   E
Word builder   E
Paul, Greg
(il) Scaly spotted feathered frilled   **567.9**
Paul, Les, 1915-2009
About
Wyckoff, E. B. Electric guitar man: the genius of Les Paul   92
Paul, Miranda
One plastic bag   **363.7**
Whose hands are these?   **331.7**
Water is water   **551.48**
Paula Bunyan. Root, P.   E
Paulsen, Gary
Crush   **Fic**
Flat broke   **Fic**
How Angel Peterson got his name   **813**
Lawn Boy   **Fic**
The legend of Bass Reeves   **Fic**
Liar, liar   **Fic**
Masters of disaster   **Fic**
Mudshark   **Fic**
Notes from the dog   **Fic**
Paintings from the cave   **S**
Road trip   **Fic**
(ed) Shelf life: stories by the book   **S**
Vote   **Fic**
The winter room   **Fic**
About
Paulsen, G. Caught by the sea   **818**
Paulsen, G. How Angel Peterson got his name   **813**
Paulsen, G. My life in dog years   **813**
This side of wild   **92**
Paulsen, Jim

Pearl verses the world. Murphy, S. **Fic**

Pearl's new skates. Keller, H. **E**

Pearle, Ida

A child's day **E**

The moon is going to Addy's house **E**

Pearlman, Robb

Groundhog's day off **E**

Pearls of Lutra. Jacques, B. **Fic**

Pearsall, Shelley

All of the above **Fic**

The seventh most important thing **Fic**

Pearson, Debora

Sophie's wheels **E**

Pearson, Kit

About

Ellis, S. From reader to writer **372.62**

Pearson, Luke

Hilda and the troll **741.5**

Pearson, Mike Parker

About

Aronson, M. If stones could speak **936**

Pearson, Ridley

Barry, D. Peter & the shadow thieves **Fic**

Barry, D. Peter and the secret of Rundoon **Fic**

Barry, D. Peter and the starcatchers **Fic**

Barry, D. Peter and the Sword of Mercy **Fic**

Pearson, Susan

How to teach a slug to read **E**

We're going on a ghost hunt **E**

Pearson, Tracey Campbell

(il) Cutler, J. Rats! **Fic**

(il) Guinea pigs add up **E**

(il) Hughes, T. My brother Bert **E**

Bob **E**

(il) Stevenson, R. L. The moon **E**

Peary, Marie Ahnighito, 1893-1978

About

Kirkpatrick, K. Snow baby **92**

Peary, Robert Edwin, 1856-1920

About

Kirkpatrick, K. Snow baby **92**

PEASANT ART See Folk art

Pebble plus: Amphibians [series]

Kolpin, M. Salamanders **597.8**

Sweeney, A. Toads **597.8**

Pebble Plus: animals working together [series]

Rustad, M. E. H. Ants and aphids work together **595.7**

Rustad, M. E. H. Clown fish and sea anemones work together **597**

Rustad, M. E. H. Moray eels and cleaner shrimp work together **597**

Rustad, M. E. H. Zebras and oxpeckers work together **599.66**

Pebble plus: Asian animals [series]

Mattern, J. Orangutans **599.8**

Sirota, L. A. Giant pandas **599.78**

Pebble plus: Healthy teeth [series]

Schuh, M. C. All about teeth **617.6**

Pebble plus: physical science [series]

Auch, A. All about temperature **536**

Conrad, D. Gravity all around **531**

Waters, J. All kinds of motion **531**

Pebble plus: Wildcats [series]

Marks, J. L. Bobcats **599.75**

Marks, J. L. Clouded leopards **599.75**

Marks, J. L. Jaguars **599.75**

Shores, E. L. Canada lynx **599.75**

Shores, E. L. Mountain lions **599.75**

Shores, E. L. Snow leopards **599.75**

Pecan pie baby. **E**

Peck, Beth

(il) Bunting, E. How many days to America? **E**

(il) Johnson, A. Just like Josh Gibson **E**

Peck, Penny

Crash course in storytime fundamentals **027.62**

Readers' advisory for children and 'tweens **025.5**

Peck, Richard

The best man **Fic**

Here lies the librarian **Fic**

The mouse with the question mark tail **Fic**

On the wings of heroes **Fic**

Peck, R. A long way from Chicago **Fic**

A season of gifts **Fic**

Secrets at sea **Fic**

A year down yonder **Fic**

Peck, Richard, 1934-

Pecos Bill. Kellogg, S. **398.2**

Pecos Bill. Krensky, S. **398.2**

PECOS BILL (LEGENDARY CHARACTER)

Kellogg, S. Pecos Bill **398.2**

Krensky, S. Pecos Bill **398.2**

The Peculiar Haunting of Thelma Bee. **Fic**

The peculiar night of the blue heart. DeStefano, L. **Fic**

Peculiar pets [series]

Lunis, N. Furry ferrets **636.9**

Lunis, N. Green iguanas **639.3**

Lunis, N. Miniature horses **636.1**

PEDAGOGY See Education; Education -- Study and teaching; Teaching

Pedal it! Mulder, M. **388**

PEDDLARS -- FICTION

Mending horses **Fic**

PEDDLERS AND PEDDLING -- FICTION

Slobodkina, E. Caps for sale **E**

PEDDLERS AND PEDDLING -- FOLKLORE

Miller, B. One fine trade **398.2**

Pedersen, Janet

(il) In loving memory of Gorfman T. Frog **Fic**

(il) Jackson, A. Thea's tree **E**

PEDIATRICIANS

Bogacki, T. The champion of children **92**

PEDICULOSIS -- FICTION

Shannon, D. Bugs in My Hair! **E**

PEDIGREES See Genealogy; Heraldry

Pedler, Caroline

PHYSICS

Adams, T. Feel the force!	**530**
Claybourne, A. Gut-wrenching gravity and other fatal forces	**531**
Gardner, R. Ace your physical science project	**530**
Gardner, R. Slam dunk! science projects with basketball	**530**
Goodstein, M. Ace your sports science project	**507.8**
Goodstein, M. Wheels!	**530**
Green, D. Physics	**530**
Lee, C. The great motion mission	**530**
Macdonald, W. Galileo's leaning tower experiment	**531**
Space and time	**530.11**
Taylor-Butler, C. Think like a scientist in the gym	**530**

PHYSICS -- EXPERIMENTS

Austin, J. Labcraft wizards	**507.8**
Brown, J. D. Science stunts	**530.078**
Mercer, B. Junk drawer physics	**530**

PHYSIOGNOMY

See also Psychology

PHYSIOLOGISTS

Saunders, B. R. Ivan Pavlov	**92**
Yount, L. William Harvey	**92**

PHYSIOLOGY

Bassington, C. Your bones	**612.7**
Bassington, C. Your brain	**612.8**
Bassington, C. Your heart	**612.1**
Buchanan, S. C. Animal senses	**573.8**
Cole, J. The magic school bus inside the human body	**612**
Fittleworth, G. Your muscles	**612.7**
Goddard, J. Inside the human body	**612**
The great big body book	**612**
Green, J. Inside animals	**571**
Greenwood, M. Animals and me	**612**
Lew, K. Farts, vomit, and other functions that help your body	**612**
Rockwell, L. The busy body book	**612**
Silverstein, A. Snot, poop, vomit, and more	**612**

PHYSIOLOGY

See also Biology; Medicine; Science

PI

Ball, J. Why pi	**530.8**
Pi in the sky. Mass, W.	**Fic**

PIANISTS

Celenza, A. H. Duke Ellington's Nutcracker suite	**E**
Hopkinson, D. A band of angels	**E**
Ingalls, A. The little piano girl	**E**
Krull, K. Lives of the musicians	**920**
LeBlanc, A. The red piano	**92**
Parker, R. A. Piano starts here: the young Art Tatum	**92**
Raven, M. Happy birthday to you!	**782.42**
Reich, S. Clara Schumann	**92**

PIANISTS -- FICTION

Blume, L. M. M. The rising star of Rusty Nail	**Fic**
Cheng, A. Where do you stay?	**Fic**
Hamlisch, M. Marvin makes music	**E**
Ingalls, A. The little piano girl	**E**
Ketzel, the cat who composed	**E**

McGhee, A. Song of middle C

PIANO MAKERS -- ITALY -- BIOGRAPHY

The music of life 9

PIANO MUSIC

See also Instrumental music; Music

PIANO MUSIC -- FICTION

Litchfield, D. The bear and the piano

Piano starts here: the young Art Tatum. Parker, R. A. 9

PIANOS

See also Percussion instruments

PIANOS -- FICTION

Litchfield, D. The bear and the piano	
Perkins, L. R. The cardboard piano	
Pianos and Keyboards. Ganeri, A.	**786.**

PICARESQUE LITERATURE

See also Fiction; Literature

Picasso. Jacobson, R. 9

Picasso, Pablo, 1881-1973

About

Jacobson, R. Picasso	9
Just behave, Pablo Picasso!	**709.**
Niepold, M. Oooh! Picasso	**730.**
Penrose, A. The boy who bit Picasso	9
Serres, A. And Picasso painted Guernica	75
Yolleck, J. Paris in the spring with Picasso	

Piccard, Jacques

About

Bodden, V. To the ocean deep **551.4**

PICCOLO -- FICTION

Draper, S. M. The silver secret F

Pichon, Liz

The three horrid little pigs

Pick a pup. Chall, M. W.

Pick, pull, snap! Schaefer, L. M. 58

Pickering, Jimmy

(il) Prelutsky, J. The swamps of Sleethe	81
(il) Sage, A. My haunted house	F
(il) Shivery Shades of Halloween	

PICKETING *See* Strikes

Pickett, Bill, ca. 1860-1932

About

Bill Pickett, rodeo-ridin' cowboy 9

PICKLES -- FICTION

Isadora, R. I hear a pickle

Picnic. Burningham, J.

PICNICS

See also Dining; Dinners; Luncheons; Outdoor recreation

PICNICS -- FICTION

Burningham, J. Picnic	
Mack, J. Good news, bad news	
Pig & Goose and the first day of spring	
Picture a tree. Reid, B.	
A **picture** book of Amelia Earhart.	**629.1**
A **picture** book of Cesar Chavez. Adler, D. A.	9
A **picture** book of Dolley and James Madison. Adler, D. A.	9
A **picture** book of Harriet Beecher Stowe. Adler, D. A.	9

PICTURE BOOKS FOR CHILDREN

Ryan, C. The map to everywhere **Fic**

Seagulls don't eat pickles **Fic**

Stinky Spike the Pirate Dog **E**

Swap! **E**

Treasure hunters **Fic**

PIRATES -- POETRY

Florian, D. Shiver me timbers **E**

When you're a pirate dog and other pirate poems **811**

Pirates go to school. Demas, C. **E**

The **pirates** of Crocodile Swamp. Arnosky, J. **Fic**

Pirates' tools for life at sea. Jenson-Elliott, C. **910.4**

Pirates, ho! Thomson, S. L. **E**

Pirner, Connie White

Even little kids get diabetes **616.4**

Pirotta, Saviour

Children's stories from the Bible **220.9**

Firebird **398.2**

The McElderry book of Grimms' fairy tales **398.2**

Pistoia, Sara

Fractions **513.2**

Pitamic, Maja

(jt. auth) Laidlaw, J. Modern art adventures **709.04**

Pitcairn, Ansel

(il) Bolden, T. Portraits of African-American heroes **920**

Pitcher. Glaser, J. **796.357**

Pitcher, Molly, 1754-1832

About

Rockwell, A. F. They called her Molly Pitcher **973.3**

Pitchford, Dean

Captain Nobody **Fic**

Nickel Bay Nick **Fic**

Pitching in for Eubie. Nolen, J. **E**

Pitman, Gayle E.

This day in June **E**

Pittau, Francesco

(jt. auth) Gervais, B. Out of sight **590**

PITTSBURGH (PA.) -- FICTION

Shang, W. The way home looks now **Fic**

PITTSBURGH PIRATES (BASEBALL TEAM)

Yolen, J. All star! **92**

Piven, Hanoch

My best friend is as sharp as a pencil **E**

My dog is as smelly as dirty socks **E**

PIZZA -- FICTION

Fusco Castaldo, N. Pizza for the queen **E**

Wellington, M. Pizza at Sally's **E**

Pizza at Sally's. Wellington, M. **E**

Pizza for Sam. Labatt, M. **E**

Pizza for the queen. Fusco Castaldo, N. **E**

A **pizza** the size of the sun. Prelutsky, J. **811**

Pizza, pigs, and poetry. Prelutsky, J. **808.1**

Pizzicato. Reh, R. **Fic**

Pizzoli, Greg

(il) Brendler, C. Not very scary **E**

(il) Brown, M. W. North, South, East, West **E**

(il) Dipucchio, K. Dragon was terrible **E**

(il) Good night Owl **E**

Number one Sam **E**

Tricky Vic **92**

(il) The watermelon seed **E**

PJF easy-to-read [series]

Van Leeuwen, J. Amanda Pig and the awful, scary monster **E**

A **place** for bats. **599.4**

A **place** for birds. **598**

A **place** for fish. Stewart, M. **597**

A **place** for frogs. Stewart, M. **597.8**

The **Place** my words are looking for. **811**

A **place** to call home. Deacon, A. **E**

Place value. Adler, D. A. **513.2**

PLACE VALUE (MATHEMATICS)

Adler, D. A. Place value **513.2**

A **place** where hurricanes happen. Watson, R. **E**

A **place** where sunflowers grow. **E**

Place, Francois

Fombelle, T. d. Toby and the secrets of the tree **Fic**

L'Homme, E. Tales of a lost kingdom **398.2**

The old man mad about drawing **Fic**

Toby alone **Fic**

Places in time. Leacock, E. **911**

PLAGIARISM

Fox, K. Plagiarism! Plagiarism! **808**

PLAGIARISM

See also Authorship; Offenses against property

Plagiarism! Plagiarism! Fox, K. **808**

PLAGUE

Jarrow, G. Bubonic panic **614.5**

Ollhoff, J. The Black Death **616.9**

Person, S. Bubonic plague **614.5**

PLAGUE

See also Communicable diseases; Epidemics

PLAGUE -- FICTION

Choldenko, G. Chasing secrets **Fic**

Plagues, pox, and pestilence. **614.4**

Plain, Nancy

This strange wilderness **92**

Plaisted, Caroline

Boy talk **612.6**

Girl talk **612.6**

The **Plan.** **E**

Planck, Max, 1858-1947

About

Weir, J. Max Planck **92**

PLANE CRASHES *See* Aircraft accidents

PLANE GEOMETRY

See also Geometry

PLANE GEOMETRY

Brocket, J. Circles, stars, and squares **516**

A **plane** goes ka-zoom! London, J. **E**

Planes fly! Lyon, G. E. **E**

Planes go. Light, S. **E**

Planes on the move. Clark, W. **629.133**

Planet Earth. Gilpin, D. **550**

Planet Earth. Reilly, K. M. **333.72**

Planet Earth. Richards, J. **910**

The keeping quilt   E
The Lemonade Club   E
Luba and the wren   398.2
Mr. Lincoln's way   E
Mr. Wayne's masterpiece   E
Mrs. Katz and Tush   E
My rotten redheaded older brother   E
Oh, look!   E
Pink and Say   E
Rechenka's eggs   E
Someone for Mr. Sussman   E
Thank you, Mr. Falker   E
The trees of the dancing goats   E
Tucky Jo and Little Heart   Fic
When lightning comes in a jar   E
Poland. Deckker, Z.   943.8
Poland. Docalavich, H.   943.8
POLAND
   Docalavich, H. Poland   943.8
   Mara, W. Poland   943.8
Poland. Mara, W.   943.8
POLAND -- FICTION
   Hesse, K. The cats in Krasinski Square   E
   Pryor, B. Simon's escape   Fic
   Roy, J. Yellow star   Fic
   Tak, B. D. Soldier bear   Fic
Polar. Kainen, D.   590.911
Polar animals. Hodge, D.   591.7
Polar bear night. Thompson, L.   E
The **polar** bear son. Dabcovich, L.   398.2
Polar bear vs. seal. Meinking, M.   599.75
A **polar** bear's world. Arnold, C.   599.78
Polar bear, polar bear, what do you hear? Martin, B.   E
Polar bear, why is your world melting? Wells, R. E.   363.7
Polar bears. Newman, M.   599.78
Polar bears. Bodden, V.   599.78
Polar bears. Marsh, L.   599.78
Polar bears. Rosing, N.   599.78
POLAR BEARS
   Arnold, C. A polar bear's world   599.78
   Bodden, V. Polar bears   599.78
   Davies, N. Ice bear   599.78
   Guiberson, B. Z. Ice bears   599.78
   Hirsch, R. E. Top 50 reasons to care about polar bears   599.78
   Leathers, D. Polar bears on the Hudson Bay   599.78
   Markle, S. Waiting for ice   599.786
   Marsh, L. Polar bears   599.78
   Meinking, M. Polar bear vs. seal   599.75
   Newman, M. Polar bears   599.78
   Olson, G. M. Polar bears' search for ice   599.78
   Rosing, N. Face to face with polar bears   599.78
   Rosing, N. Polar bears   599.78
   Ryder, J. A pair of polar bears   599.78
   Thompson, L. Polar bear night   E
   Thomson, S. L. Where do polar bears live?   599.78
POLAR BEARS -- EFFECT OF GLOBAL WARMING ON
   Markle, S. Waiting for ice   599.786

POLAR BEARS -- FICTION
   Levis, C. Ida, always   E
   Pastis, S. Timmy failure   **Fic**
   Pastis, S. Timmy failure : now look what you've done   **Fic**
   The bear report   E
   Cub's big world   E
   Kimmel, E. A. Simon and the bear   E
   Tolman, M. The island   398.209
   Waluk   741.5
   Winter, J. Nanuk the ice bear   E
POLAR BEARS -- FOLKLORE
   Dabcovich, L. The polar bear son   398.2
Polar bears on the Hudson Bay. Leathers, D.   599.78
Polar bears' search for ice. Olson, G. M.   599.78
POLAR EXPEDITIONS *See* Antarctica -- Exploration; Arctic regions -- Exploration; Scientific expeditions
The **Polar** Express. Van Allsburg, C.   E
Polar lands. Callery, S.   577.5
Polar opposites. Brooks, E.   E
POLAR REGIONS
   Kainen, D. Polar   590.911
POLAR REGIONS -- PICTORIAL WORKS
   Kainen, D. Polar   590.911
Polar worlds. Wade, R.   998
POLARITY *See* Opposites
POLARITY -- FICTION
   Boyd, L. Big bear little chair   E
   Na, I. S. The opposite zoo   E
Polenghi, Evan
   Singer, M. I'm your bus   E
Polhemus, Coleman
   The crocodile blues   E
Police. Mezzanotte, J.   363.2
POLICE
   See also Administration of criminal justice; Law enforcement
POLICE
   Kenney, K. L. Police officers at work   363.2
POLICE -- FICTION
   Barnett, M. The case of the case of mistaken identity   **Fic**
   Bug patrol   E
   Hamilton, K. R. Police officers on patrol   E
   Hubbell, P. Police: hurrying! helping! saving!   E
   Nilsson, U. A Complicated Case   E
POLICE -- GRAPHIC NOVELS
   Dog man unleashed   741.5
POLICE -- HISTORY -- 20TH CENTURY
   Samuels, C. Spying and security   940.54
POLICE -- SAFETY MEASURES
   Spilsbury, L. Robots in law enforcement   629.8
POLICE BRUTALITY
   See also Police
POLICE CORRUPTION
   See also Misconduct in office; Police
Police dog heroes. Bozzo, L.   363.2
Police dogs. Hoffman, M. A.   363.2
POLICE OFFICERS *See* Police

Harrison, D. L. Mammoth bones and broken stones **970.01**

PREHISTORIC PEOPLES

See also Antiquities; Archeology; Human beings

PREHISTORIC PEOPLES -- FICTION

Beckhorn, S. W. The wolf's boy — **Fic**

Winter, J. Kali's song — **E**

Prehistoric skies. Dixon, D. — **567.9**

PREHISTORY *See* Archeology; Fossil hominids; Prehistoric peoples

PREJUDICE *See* Prejudices

PREJUDICE-MOTIVATED CRIMES *See* Hate crimes

PREJUDICES

Haptie, C. Otto and the flying twins — **Fic**

Hesse, K. Witness — **Fic**

Lester, J. Let's talk about race — **305.8**

Marsden, C. The gold-threaded dress — **Fic**

Polacco, P. Mr. Lincoln's way — **E**

Schwartz, J. Short — **612.6**

Yep, L. The traitor — **Fic**

PREJUDICES

See also Attitude (Psychology); Emotions; Interpersonal relations

PREJUDICES -- FICTION

Mending horses — **Fic**

Naylor, P. R. A Shiloh Christmas — **Fic**

Shevah, E. Dara Palmer's major drama — **Fic**

Preller, James

The courage test — **Fic**

Home sweet horror — **Fic**

Justin Fisher declares war! — **Fic**

A pirate's guide to first grade — **E**

Six innings — **Fic**

Prelutsky, Jack

(comp) The 20th century children's poetry treasury — **811**

(comp) For laughing out loud — **811**

Be glad your nose is on your face and other poems — **811**

Behold the bold umbrellaphant — **811**

The carnival of the animals — **811**

The dragons are singing tonight — **811**

The frogs wore red suspenders — **811**

Good sports — **811**

The Headless Horseman rides tonight — **811**

If not for the cat — **811**

It's Christmas! — **811**

It's snowing! it's snowing! — **811**

It's Thanksgiving! — **811**

It's Valentine's Day — **811**

I've lost my hippopotamus — **811**

My dog may be a genius — **811**

The new kid on the block: poems — **811**

Nightmares: poems to trouble your sleep — **811**

A pizza the size of the sun — **811**

Pizza, pigs, and poetry — **808.1**

Ride a purple pelican — **811**

Scranimals — **811**

Something big has been here — **811**

Stardines swim high across the sky and other poems — **811**

The swamps of Sleethe — 81

Tyrannosaurus was a beast — 81

What a day it was at school! — 81

(ed) The Random House book of poetry for children — 81

(comp) Read a rhyme, write a rhyme — 81

(comp) Read-aloud rhymes for the very young — 81

Seuss Hooray for Diffendoofer Day! — 81

(ed) There's no place like school — 81

PREMATURE BABIES -- FICTION

Kantorovitz, S. The very tiny baby

PREMENSTRUAL SYNDROME

See also Menstruation; Syndromes

PRENATAL CARE

See also Pregnancy

Prendergast, Maggie

(jt. auth) Proujansky, A. Go photo! — 77

Prentzas, G. S.

Arkansas — 976.

Georgia — 975.

Wyoming — 978.

PREPARATION GUIDES FOR EXAMINATIONS *See* Examinations -- Study guides

PREPARATORY SCHOOLS -- FICTION

Hood, S. Mission: back to school

PREPARED CEREALS

See also Breakfasts; Food

PREPARED CEREALS -- FICTION

Rex, A. Unlucky charms — F

Prepositions. Heinrichs, A. — 42

PREPRIMERS *See* Easy reading materials

PRESCHOOL CHILDREN *See* Children

PRESCHOOL CHILDREN -- BOOKS AND READING

Zvirin, S. Read with me — 028.

Preschool favorites. Briggs, D. — 372.

PRESCHOOL READING MATERIALS *See* Easy reading materials

Presenting Buffalo Bill. Fleming, C. — 978.0

PRESENTS *See* Gifts

Presents through the window. Gomi, T.

Preserve our planet [series]

Delano, M. F. Earth in the hot seat — 363.

President George Washington. Allen, K. — 9

The president is shot! Holzer, H. — 973.

President of the whole fifth grade. Winston, S. — F

President Pennybaker. Feiffer, K.

President taft is stuck in the bath. Barnett, M.

PRESIDENTIAL ADVISERS

Let it shine — 92

PRESIDENTIAL CANDIDATES

Bardhan-Quallen, S. Ballots for Belva — 9

Krull, K. The brothers Kennedy — 92

Krull, K. A woman for president — 9

Let it shine — 92

Murphy, J. A savage thunder — 973.

Raatma, L. Shirley Chisholm — 9

Presidential pets. — 97

PRESIDENTS

PRESIDENTS -- FICTION

PRESIDENTS -- SOUTH AFRICA -- BIOGRAPHY

PRESIDENTS -- SUCCESSION -- UNITED STATES -- HISTORY -- 20TH CENTURY

PRESIDENTS -- UNITED STATES

Jakubiak, D. J. What can we do about toxins in the environment? **615.9**

Metz, L. What can we do about invasive species? **578.6**

PROTECTIVE COLORATION (BIOLOGY)

Harrison, D. L. Now you see them, now you don't **591.472**

PROTEINS

See also Biochemistry; Nutrition

PROTEST MARCHES AND RALLIES See Demonstrations

PROTEST MOVEMENTS

Scandiffio, L. People who said no **303.48**

PROTEST MOVEMENTS -- FICTION

Violet Mackerel's pocket protest **Fic**

Protists. Arato, R. **579**

PROTISTS

Arato, R. Protists **579**

The **protoctist** kingdom. Zabludoff, M. **579**

PROTOCTISTA

Zabludoff, M. The protoctist kingdom **579**

PROTONS

See also Atoms; Particles (Nuclear physics)

PROTOPLASM

See also Biology; Life (Biology)

Protopopescu, Orel

Thelonious Mouse **E**

PROTOZOA

Arato, R. Protists **579**

Graham, I. Microscopic scary creatures **591.6**

PROTOZOA

See also Microorganisms

Proud as a peacock, brave as a lion. Barclay, J. **E**

A **proud** taste for scarlet and miniver. Konigsburg, E. L. **Fic**

Proud to be Inuvialuit. **970.004**

Proujansky, Alice

Go photo! **770**

Prove it! Glass, S. **507**

Provensen, Alice

The buck stops here **973**

A day in the life of Murphy **E**

The glorious flight: across the Channel with Louis Bleriot, July 25, 1909 **92**

Murphy in the city **E**

(il) Willard, N. A visit to William Blake's inn **811**

Provensen, Martin

Provensen, A. The glorious flight: across the Channel with Louis Bleriot, July 25, 1909 **92**

(il) Willard, N. A visit to William Blake's inn **811**

PROVERBS

The Night has ears **398.9**

PROVERBS

See also Folklore; Quotations

PROVERBS -- FICTION

Gregorich, B. Waltur paints himself into a corner and other stories **E**

A mango in the hand **E**

PROVIDENCE (R.I.) -- FICTION

Johnson, P. The amazing adventures of John Smith, Jr., aka Houdini **Fic**

PROVIDENCE AND GOVERNMENT OF GOD

See also God

Prowling the seas. Turner, P. S. **591.7**

Proxy. London, A. **Fic**

Prudence wants a pet. Daly, C. **E**

Pruessen, Linda

Saving Eyesight **362.19**

PRUNING

See also Forests and forestry; Fruit culture; Gardening; Trees

Pryor, Bonnie

The iron dragon **Fic**

Simon's escape **Fic**

Pryor, Kimberley Jane

Amazing armor **591.47**

Clever camouflage **591.47**

Cooperation **177**

Courage **179**

Honesty **177**

Kindness **177**

Mimicry and relationships **591.47**

Respect **177**

Tolerance **177**

Tricky behavior **591.47**

Warning colors **591.47**

PRZEWALSKI'S HORSE

Riggs, K. Wild horses **599.665**

The **PS** brothers. Boelts, M. **Fic**

Psalm 23. Moser, B. **223**

Psalms for young children. Delval **223**

PSEUDONYMS

See also Names; Personal names

PSI (PARAPSYCHOLOGY) See Parapsychology

Pssst! Rex, A. **E**

PSYCHE (GREEK DEITY)

Craft, M. Cupid and Psyche **292.1**

PSYCHE (GREEK DEITY)

See also Gods and goddesses

PSYCHIATRIC HOSPITALS

See also Hospitals

PSYCHIATRIC HOSPITALS -- FICTION

Edge, C. Twelve minutes to midnight **Fic**

PSYCHIATRY

See also Medicine

PSYCHIC ABILITY -- FICTION

The creeping shadow **Fic**

Hello universe **Fic**

PSYCHOLOGY

Totally human **612**

Winston, R. M. L. What goes on in my head? **612.8**

Young, K. R. Experiments to do on your family **507.8**

PSYCHOLOGY

See also Brain; Philosophy; Soul

PSYCHOLOGY, PATHOLOGICAL

Ouch! **616**

PSYCHOTHERAPY

Rashkin, R. Feeling better **616.89**

Shea, B. Cheetah can't lose   E
Racing against the odds. Weatherford, C. B.   **92**
Racing the moon. Armstrong, A.   **Fic**
RACISM
Brimner, L. D. Birmingham Sunday   **323.1**
Lester, J. Let's talk about race   **305.8**
RACISM
   See also Attitude (Psychology); Prejudices; Race awareness; Race relations
RACISM -- FICTION
Bruchac, J. Walking two worlds   **Fic**
Kidd, R. Night on Fire   **Fic**
RACISM -- HISTORY
Scattergood, A. Glory be   **Fic**
RACISM -- POETRY
Argueta, J. Talking with Mother Earth   **811**
Racism on trial. Coleman, W.   **345**
RACKETEERING
   See also Crime; Organized crime
Rackham, Arthur
(il) Grimm, J. Grimm's fairy tales   **398.2**
(il) Irving, W. Washington Irving's Rip van Winkle   **Fic**
RACQUETBALL
   See also Ball games; Sports
Racz, Michael
(il) Mann, E. The Roman Colosseum   **937**
Raczka, Bob
3-D ABC   **730**
Action figures   **704.9**
The art of freedom   **704.9**
Artful reading   **750**
Before they were famous   **704**
Fall mixed up   **E**
Guyku   **811**
Here's looking at me   **757**
Lemonade, and other poems squeezed from a single word **811**
More than meets the eye   **750**
Name that style   **709**
Niko draws a feeling   **E**
Santa Clauses   **811.6**
Snowy, blowy winter   **E**
(ed) Speaking of art   **700**
Spring things   **E**
Unlikely pairs   **750**
The Vermeer interviews   **759.9**
Wet cement   **811.6**
Who loves the fall?   **E**
RADAR
   See also Navigation; Radio; Remote sensing
Rader, Laura
(il) Mayr, D. Run, Turkey run   **E**
Radiance. Noel, A.   **Fic**
Radiant child.   **92**
RADIO BROADCASTING -- FICTION
Pinkney, A. D. Bird in a box   **Fic**
RADIO BROADCASTING OF SPORTS
Smith, C. R. Stars in the shadows   **796.357**

RADIOACTIVE WASTE DISPOSAL
Jakubiak, D. J. What can we do about nuclear waste?   **363.7**
RADIOACTIVE WASTE DISPOSAL
   See also Nuclear engineering; Nuclear power plants -- Environmental aspects; Radioactivity; Refuse and refuse disposal
RADIOACTIVITY
Jerome, K. B. Atomic universe   **539.7**
Radunsky, Vladimir
(il) Berne, J. On a beam of light   **92**
(il) Fox, M. Where the giant sleeps   **E**
(il) Hip hop dog   **E**
What does peace feel like?   **E**
You?   **E**
Raf. Vries, A. d.   **E**
Raff, Anna
(il) Adler, D. A. Things that float and things that don't   **532**
(il) Lewis, J. P. World Rat day   **E**
Raffi
Aruego, J. Five little ducks   **782.42**
Baby Beluga   **782.42**
Down by the bay   **782.42**
Raffi songs to read [series]
Aruego, J. Five little ducks   **782.42**
Raffi Baby Beluga   **782.42**
Raffi Down by the bay   **782.42**
The **raft.** LaMarche, J.   **E**
RAFTING (SPORTS) -- FICTION
LaMarche, J. The raft   **E**
RAGE *See* Anger
Raggin', jazzin', rockin' VanHecke, S.   **784.19**
Raging floods. Spilsbury, L.   **551.48**
Raglin, Tim
(il) Coville, B. William Shakespeare's Twelfth night   **822.3**
(il) Elya, S. M. Cowboy Jose   **E**
Ragweed. Avi   **Fic**
Ragweed's farm dog handbook. Kennedy, A. V.   **E**
Rah, rah, radishes! Sayre, A. P.   **641.3**
Rahaman, Vashanti
Divali rose   **E**
Raible, Alton
(il) Snyder, Z. K. The Egypt game   **Fic**
(il) Snyder, Z. K. The headless cupid   **Fic**
(il) Snyder, Z. K. The witches of Worm   **Fic**
The **raiders.**   **Fic**
Raiders' ransom. Diamand, E.   **Fic**
Raiders' ransom [series]
Diamand, E. Flood and fire   **Fic**
RAILROAD ACCIDENTS
   See also Accidents; Disasters
RAILROAD ENGINEERING
   See also Civil engineering; Engineering; Railroads
Railroad fever. Halpern, M.   **385**
Railroad Hank.   **E**
RAILROAD STATIONS
Low, W. Old Penn Station   **725**

Thomson, S. L. What Lincoln said **92**

(il) Wolff, F. It is the wind **E**

(il) Woodson, J. Visiting day **E**

Ranson, Claire

(ed) Sally go round the stars **398.8**

Rao, Sandhya

My mother's sari **E**

Rap a tap tap. Dillon, L. **792.7**

RAP MUSIC

Alexander, K. The crossover **Fic**

Harris, A. R. Tupac Shakur **92**

RAP MUSIC

See also African American music; Popular music

RAP MUSIC -- FICTION

Czekaj, J. Hip & Hop, don't stop **E**

Hip hop dog **E**

RAP MUSICIANS

Spilsbury, R. Jay-Z **92**

RAP MUSICIANS -- UNITED STATES -- BIOGRAPHY

Hill, L. C. When the beat was born **92**

Spilsbury, R. Jay-Z **92**

RAP SONGS *See* Rap music

Rapp, Valerie

Protecting Earth's air quality **363.7**

Rappaport, Doreen, 1939-

Abe's honest words **92**

Dirt on their skirts **796.357**

Eleanor, quiet no more **92**

Elizabeth started all the trouble **323.3**

Frederick's journey **92**

Free at last! **305.8**

Freedom ship **Fic**

Helen's big world **362.4**

Jack's path of courage **92**

John's secret dreams **92**

Lady Liberty **974.7**

Martin's big words: the life of Dr. Martin Luther King, Jr. **92**

Nobody gonna turn me 'round **323.1**

The secret seder **E**

To dare mighty things **92**

We are the many **920**

RAPPING (MUSIC) *See* Rap music

Rappoport, Ken

Dale Earnhardt, Jr. **92**

David Wright **92**

Peyton Manning **796.332**

Raptor. Henry, M. **567.9**

RAPTOREX

See also Dinosaurs

Rapunzel. Zelinsky, P. O. **398.22**

Rapunzel. Isadora, R. **398.2**

Rapunzel. Sage, A. **398.2**

Rapunzel. Cech, J. **398.2**

Rapunzel's revenge. **741.5**

RARE AMPHIBIANS

Reptiles and amphibians **333.95**

RARE ANIMALS

Lasky, K. Interrupted journey **639.9**

RARE ANIMALS

See also Animals

RARE BIRDS

Gish, M. Falcons **598.96**

RARE BOOKS

See also Books

RARE MAMMALS

Meerkats **599.742**

RARE MAMMALS -- SOUTH AMERICA

The search for Olinguito **599.763**

RARE PLANTS

See also Plants

RARE REPTILES

Iguanas **597.95**

Reptiles and amphibians **333.95**

Rare treasure: Mary Anning and her remarkable discoveries. Brown, D. **560**

Rasamandala Das

Hinduism **294.5**

Rascal. Wells, K. **Fic**

Raschka, Christopher

A ball for Daisy **E**

(il) Bitterman, A. Fortune cookies **E**

(il) Brown, M. W. Another important book **E**

The Cosmobiography of sun ra **781.65**

(il) Daisy gets lost **E**

Everyone can learn to ride a bicycle **E**

Farmy farm **E**

Five for a little one **E**

(il) Fogliano, J. Old dog baby baby **E**

(il) A foot in the mouth **808.81**

(il) Giovanni, N. The grasshopper's song **E**

(il) Granny Torrelli makes soup **Fic**

Hip hop dog **E**

(il) Hooks, B. Grump groan growl **E**

(il) Howe, J. Otter and odder **E**

(il) If you were a dog **E**

(il) Janeczko, P. B. The Death of the Hat **808.81**

John Coltrane's Giant steps **E**

(il) Juster, N. The hello, goodbye window **E**

(il) A kick in the head **811**

Little black crow **E**

New York is English, Chattanooga is Creek **E**

Ogburn, J. K. Little treasures **413**

Peter and the wolf **E**

(il) A Poke in the I **811**

(il) Prelutsky, J. Good sports **811**

The purple balloon **155.9**

Raschka, C. Seriously, Norman! **Fic**

Seriously, Norman! **Fic**

A song about myself **811**

(il) Thomas, D. A child's Christmas in Wales **828**

Yo! Yes? **E**

Rash, Andy

(il) Game over, Pete Watson **Fic**

(il) Reynolds, A. Superhero School **E**

REFERENCE BOOKS
See also Bibliography; Books; Books and reading

REFERENCE BOOKS -- BIBLIOGRAPHY

REFERENCE SERVICES (LIBRARIES)

REFERENCE SERVICES (LIBRARIES)
See also Information services; Library services

Reference shelf [series]

REFERENCE WORK (LIBRARIES) *See* Reference services (Libraries)

REFERENDUM
See also Constitutional law; Democracy; Elections

REFLEXES

REFORESTATION
See also Forests and forestry

REFORM, SOCIAL *See* Social problems

REFORMATION
See also Christianity; Church history -- 1500- , Modern period

REFORMERS

REFRACTION
See also Light; Optics

REFRIGERATION

REFRIGERATION AND REFRIGERATING MACHINERY *See* Refrigeration

REFRIGERATORS *See* Refrigeration

Refugee diary [series]

REFUGEES

REFUGEES
See also Homeless persons; Immigration and emigration; Noncitizens

REFUGEES -- FICTION

REFUSE AND REFUSE DISPOSAL

REFUSE AND REFUSE DISPOSAL
See also Municipal engineering; Pollution control industry; Public health; Sanitary engineering; Sanitation

REFUSE AND REFUSE DISPOSAL -- FICTION

REFUSE COLLECTION VEHICLES -- FICTION

REFUSE COLLECTORS -- FICTION

Regan, Laura

Regan, Lisa

Betsy Ross **92**

Ross, Fiona
Chilly Milly Moo **E**

Ross, Gary
Bartholomew Biddle and the very big wind **Fic**

Ross, Graham
(il) Billy Sure, kid entrepreneur **Fic**

Ross, Heather
(il) DiPucchio, K. S. Crafty Chloe **E**

Ross, Joel
The Fog diver **Fic**

Ross, Kathy
The best birthday parties ever! **793.2**
Beautiful beads **745.58**
One-of-a-kind stamps and crafts **761**

Ross, Michael Elsohn
Mama's milk **E**

Ross, Pat
(il) Hafner, M. M & M and the bad news babies **E**
Meet M & M **E**

Ross, Stewart
Into the unknown **910.4**
Moon: science, history, and mystery **629.45**
Sports technology **688.7**

Ross, Tony
(il) Coville, B. Amber Brown is tickled pink **Fic**
(il) Danziger, P. Amber Brown goes fourth **Fic**
(il) Danziger, P. Amber Brown is feeling blue **Fic**
(il) Danziger, P. Amber Brown is green with envy **Fic**
(il) Danziger, P. Amber Brown is not a crayon **Fic**
(il) Danziger, P. Amber Brown sees red **Fic**
(il) Danziger, P. Amber Brown wants extra credit **Fic**
(il) Danziger, P. Forever Amber Brown **Fic**
(il) Danziger, P. I, Amber Brown **Fic**
(il) Danziger, P. It's Justin Time, Amber Brown **E**
(il) Danziger, P. You can't eat your chicken pox, Amber Brown **Fic**
I want a party! **E**
I want my light on! **E**
Three little kittens and other favorite nursery rhymes **398.8**
(il) Shields, C. D. English, fresh squeezed! **811**
Simon, F. Horrid Henry **Fic**
(il) Simon, F. Horrid Henry rocks **Fic**
(il) Simon, F. Horrid Henry wakes the dead **Fic**
(il) Willis, J. Gorilla! Gorilla! **E**
Willis, J. Susan laughs **E**

Rossell, Judith
(il) Oliver **E**
(il) Parker, M. You are a star! **E**

Rossi, Ann
Bright ideas **609**
Freedom struggle **973.7**

Rostoker-Gruber, Karen
Farmer Kobi's Hanukkah match **E**
Ferret fun **E**
Bandit **E**

Roten, Lindsay Grace

Webb, L. S. Holidays of the world cookbook for students **641.5**

Roth, Carol
The little school bus **E**
Will you still love me? **E**

Roth, R. G.
(il) Ehrhardt, K. This Jazz man **E**

Roth, Rita
The story road to literacy **372.6**

Roth, Robert
Ehrhardt, K. This Jazz man **E**
(il) Michelson, R. Busing Brewster **E**
Staub, L. Everybody gets the blues **E**

Roth, Roger
(il) Armstrong, J. The American story **973**
(il) Friedman, D. Star of the Week **E**
(il) Gauch, S. Voyage to the Pharos **E**

Roth, Stephanie
Greene, S. Princess Posey and the first grade parade **Fic**
Nagda, A. W. The perfect cat-sitter **Fic**

Roth, Susan
(il) Aston, D. H. Dream something big **E**
(il) Abouraya, K. L. Hands around the library **962.05**
(il) The mangrove tree **577.6**
(il) Parrots over Puerto Rico **597**
(il) Prairie dog song **599.36**
(il) The mangrove tree **577.6**
(il) Mortenson, G. Listen to the wind **371.82**
Hanukkah, oh Hanukkah **782.42**
(il) Tillage, L. Leon's story **92**

Roth, Terri
About
Carson, M. K. Emi and the rhino scientist **599.66**

Rothenberg, Joani Keller
(il) Sasso, S. E. Cain & Abel **222**
(il) The Shema in the mezuzah **E**

Rothman, Michael
(il) Collard, S. B. Forest in the clouds **577.3**

Rothschild, Lionel Walter Rothschild, Baron, 1868-1937
About
Judge, L. Strange creatures **92**

Rotner, Shelley
Body actions **612**
(il) Families **306.85**
(il) Glaser, L. Garbage helps our garden grow **631.8**
Grow! Raise! Catch! **641.3**
Hello spring! **508.2**
I'm adopted! **362.7**
(il) Kelly, S. M. Yummy! **E**
Senses at the seashore **E**
Senses in the city **E**
Shades of people **E**
Where does food come from? **664**

Rotten pumpkin. **577**
Rotten Ralph. Gantos, J. **E**
Rotten Ralph feels rotten. Gantos, J. **E**
Rotten Ralph's rotten family. Gantos, J. **E**
Rotten teeth. Simms, L. **E**

See also Cooking; Diet

Salten, Felix

Bambi **Fic**

Saltwater crocodile. Jackson, T. **597.98**

SALTWATER FISHING

See also Fishing

Salty and sugary snacks. Furgang, A. **613.2**

Saltypie. **92**

Saltz, Gail

Amazing you **612.6**

Changing you! **612.6**

Saltzberg, Barney

Beautiful oops! **E**

Chengdu could not, would not, fall asleep **E**

I want a dog! **E**

Stanley and the class pet **E**

SALUTATIONS *See* Etiquette

Salvadori, Mario George

Levy, M. Earthquakes, volcanoes, and tsunamis **551.2**

SALVAGE

Alter, A. What can you do with an old red shoe? **745.5**

Sirrine, C. Cool crafts with old CDs **745.58**

Sirrine, C. Cool crafts with old t-shirts **745.5**

Sirrine, C. Cool crafts with old wrappers, cans and bottles **745.5**

SALVAGE (WASTE, ETC.) *See* Salvage

Salzano, Tammi

One rainy day **E**

Sam and Dave dig a hole. Barnett, M. **E**

Sam and the lucky money. Chinn, K. **E**

Sam and the tigers. Lester, J. **E**

Sam Houston. Green, C. R. **976.4**

Sam Johnson and the blue ribbon quilt. Ernst, L. C. **E**

Sam Patch. Cummins, J. **92**

Sam sorts. **E**

Sam the man and the chicken plan. **Fic**

Sam who never forgets. Rice, E. **E**

Sam, Bangs & Moonshine. Ness, E. **E**

Samantha on a roll. Ashman, L. **E**

Same old horse. Murphy, S. J. **E**

Same same. Jocelyn, M. **E**

The **same** stuff as stars. Paterson, K. **Fic**

Same, same, but different. Kostecki-Shaw, J. S. **E**

SAME-SEX MARRIAGE -- FICTION

This is my family a first look at same sex parents **306.874**

Sami and the time of the troubles. Heide, F. P. **E**

Sammy in the sky. Walsh, B. **E**

Sammy Keyes and the hotel thief. Draanen, W. v. **Fic**

Sammy the seal. Hoff, S. **E**

Samphire, Patrick

Secrets of the dragon tomb **Fic**

SAMPLERS

See also Needlework

SAMPLING (STATISTICS)

See also Probabilities; Statistics

Sampson, Michael

(ed) The Bill Martin Jr. Big book of poetry **811**

Sampson, Michael R.

Martin, B. Chicka chicka 1, 2, 3

Martin, B. Kitty cat, kitty cat, are you going to sleep?

Martin, B. Kitty Cat, Kitty Cat, are you waking up?

Martin, B. Trick or treat?

Samuel de Champlain. MacLeod, E. **9**

Samuel's baby. Elkin, M.

Samuels, Barbara

The trucker

Samuels, Charlie

Home front **940.5**

Life under occupation **940.5**

Propaganda **940.5**

Soldiers **940.5**

Spying and security **940.5**

Iraq **956.**

Samurai. Murrell, D. J. **35**

SAMURAI

Murrell, D. J. Samurai **35**

Riggs, K. Samurai **95**

Samurai. Riggs, K. **95**

SAMURAI -- FICTION

Bradford, C. Young samurai: the way of the sword **Fi**

Bradford, C. Young samurai: the way of the warrior **Fi**

Snow, M. Sisters of the sword **Fi**

Samworth, Kate

Aviary Wonders Inc. Spring Catalog and Instruction Manual **Fi**

SAN ANTONIO (TEX.) -- FICTION

Lopez, D. Ask my mood ring how I feel **Fi**

SAN FRANCISCO (CALIF.) -- FICTION

Choldenko, G. Chasing secrets **Fi**

SAN FRANCISCO (CALIF.) -- HISTORY

Hopkinson, D. Into the firestorm **Fi**

Krensky, S. Lizzie Newton and the San Francisco earthquake **979.**

SAN FRANCISCO (CALIF.) -- HISTORY -- 20TH CENTURY -- FICTION

Blundell, J. A city tossed and broken **Fi**

Choldenko, G. Chasing secrets **Fi**

SAN FRANCISCO (CALIF.) -- HISTORY -- FICTION

Blundell, J. A city tossed and broken **Fi**

SAN FRANCISCO BAY AREA (CALIF.) -- EMIGRATION AND IMMIGRATION -- HISTORY

Angel Island **979.**

SAN FRANCISCO EARTHQUAKE AND FIRE, CALIF. 1906 -- FICTION

Blundell, J. A city tossed and broken **Fi**

SAN JOSÉ MINE ACCIDENT, CHILE, 2010

Scott, E. Buried alive! **363.**

SAN NICOLAS ISLAND (CALIF.) -- FICTION

O'Dell, S. Island of the Blue Dolphins **Fi**

San Souci, Daniel

Kimmel, E. A. The flying canoe **398.**

(il) San Souci, R. As luck would have it **398.**

(il) San Souci, R. Sister tricksters **398.**

(il) Yosemite's songster

SANTA CLAUS -- POETRY

The night before Christmas ... **811**

Santa Claus and the Three Bears. ... **Fic**

Santa Claus, the world's number one toy expert. Frazee, M. **E**

Santa Clauses. ... **811.6**

Santa Duck. Milgrim, D. ... **E**

Santa Duck and his merry helpers. Milgrim, D. ... **E**

SANTA FE (N.M.) -- FICTION

DePaola, T. The night of Las Posadas ... **E**

Santa from Cincinnati. Barrett, J. ... **E**

SANTA MARIA DEL FIORE (CATHEDRAL: FLORENCE, ITALY) -- FICTION

Fern, T. E. Pippo the Fool ... **E**

Santat, Dan

The adventures of Beekle ... **E**

(il) Are we there yet? ... **E**

(il) Barnett, M. Oh no! Not again! ... **E**

(il) Barnett, M. Oh no!, or, How my science project destroyed the world ... **E**

(il) Beaty, A. Attack of the fluffy bunnies ... **Fic**

(il) Berger, S. Crankenstein ... **E**

(il) Buckley, M. Kel Gilligan's daredevil stunt show ... **E**

(il) Choldenko, G. Dad and the dinosaur ... **E**

(il) Elya, S. M. Fire! Fuego! Brave bomberos ... **E**

(il) Going, K. L. Dog in charge ... **E**

(il) Gutman, D. The Christmas genie ... **Fic**

(il) Manners mash-up: a goofy guide to good behavior ... **395**

(il) Reynolds, A. Carnivores ... **E**

(il) The sports pages ... **S**

(il) The three ninja pigs ... **E**

(il) Sauer, T. Chicken dance ... **E**

Sidekicks ... **741.5**

Spratt, R. A. The adventures of Nanny Piggins ... **Fic**

(il) Yee, L. Bobby vs. girls (accidentally) ... **Fic**

Santella, Andrew

Kentucky ... **976.9**

The Korean War ... **951.9**

SANTERIA

See also Religion

Santiago stays. ... **E**

Santillan, Jorge

(il) Gassman, J. You can't spike your serves ... **Fic**

Santore, Charles

(il) Baum, L. F. The Wizard of Oz ... **Fic**

(il) Grimm, J. Snow White ... **398.2**

(il) Moore, C. C. The night before Christmas ... **811**

Santorelli, Dina

(ed) Bully ... **371.5**

Santoro, Christopher

(il) Brown, S. G. Bang! Boom! Roar! ... **E**

Santoro, Lucio

Wild oceans ... **578.7**

Santoro, Meera

Santoro, L. Wild oceans ... **578.7**

Santos-Dumont, Alberto, 1873-1932

About

Griffith, V. The fabulous flying machines of Alberto Santos-Dumont

Santoso, Charles

(il) Arnold, E. K. A boy called bat ... **Fi**

(il) Ferrell, S. I don't like Koala ... **[**

(il) Ferrell, S. The Snurtch ... **[**

(il) Levis, C. Ida, always ... **[**

Sapin, Mathieu

(il) Abouet, M. Akissi ... **[**

Sarah (Biblical figure)

About

Jules, J. Sarah laughs ... **22**

Sarah Emma Edmonds was a great pretender. Jones, C. ... **9**

Sarah gives thanks. Allegra, M. ... **[**

Sarah laughs. Jules, J. ... **22**

Sarah Morton's day. Waters, K. ... **974.**

Sarah Simpson's Rules for Living. Rupp, R. ... **Fi**

Sarah, Linda

Big friends ... **[**

Sarah, plain and tall. MacLachlan, P. ... **Fi**

SARAJEVO (BOSNIA AND HERCEGOVINA)

Halilbegovich, N. My childhood under fire ... **949.**

SARAJEVO (BOSNIA AND HERCEGOVINA) -- FICTION

Flowers for Sarajevo ... **[**

SARAJEVO (BOSNIA AND HERZEGOVINA) -- HISTORY -- SIEGE, 1992-1996 -- FICTION

Flowers for Sarajevo

Saraswati's way. Schroder, M. ... **Fi**

Sarcone-Roach, Julia

The bear ate your sandwich ... **[**

(il) Incredible inventions ... **81**

(il) McAnulty, S. Excellent Ed ... **[**

Subway story ... **[**

SARCOSUCHUS IMPERATOR

See also Dinosaurs

Sardine in outer space. Guibert, E. ... **741.**

Sarg, Tony, 1882-1942

About

Sweet, M. Balloons over Broadway ... **9**

Sargent, John Singer, 1856-1925

About

Brewster, H. Carnation, Lily, Lily, Rose ... **Fi**

Saroff, Phyllis V.

(il) Collard, S. B. Teeth ... **591.4**

(il) Johnson, R. L. A walk in the boreal forest ... **577.**

(il) Johnson, R. L. A walk in the deciduous forest ... **577.**

(il) Johnson, R. L. A walk in the desert ... **577.5**

(il) Johnson, R. L. A walk in the prairie ... **577.**

(il) Johnson, R. L. A walk in the tundra ... **577.**

Sarrazin, Marisol

(il) Labatt, M. Pizza for Sam ... **[**

Sartell, Debra

Time for bed, baby Ted ... **[**

Sartore, Joel

Face to face with grizzlies ... **599.7**

Sasaki, Sadako, 1943-1955

About

Savage, Stephen
Little Tug   **E**
Mouse   **599.35**
Rat   **599.35**
Supertruck   **E**
Ten orange pumpkins   **E**
(il) Thompson, L. Polar bear night   **E**
Where's Walrus?   **E**
Where's walrus? and penguin?   **E**
Savanna animals. Hodge, D.   **591.7**
Save Earth's animals! [series]
Allgor, M. Endangered desert animals   **591.68**
Save me a seat. Weeks, S.   **Fic**
Save the planet [series]
Barker, D. Compost it   **631.8**
Farrell, C. Keeping water clean   **363.7**
Farrell, C. Using alternative energies   **333.79**
Hirsch, R. E. Growing your own garden   **635**
Hirsch, R. E. Protecting our natural resources   **333.72**
Minden, C. Reduce, reuse, and recycle   **363.7**
Vogel, J. Local farms and sustainable foods   **630**
Saving. Morrison, J.   **332.024**
SAVING AND INVESTMENT
Morrison, J. Saving   **332.024**
SAVING AND INVESTMENT
   See also Capital; Economics; Personal finance; Wealth
SAVING AND INVESTMENT -- FICTION
Williams, V. B. A chair for my mother   **E**
SAVING AND THRIFT *See* Saving and investment
Saving animals from oil spills. Person, S.   **628.1**
Saving ARM PIT. Hyde, N.   **Fic**
Saving Audie. Patent, D. H.   **636.7**
Saving birds. Salmansohn, P.   **333.95**
Saving Eyesight. Pruessen, L.   **362.19**
Saving lives & changing hearts. Laidlaw, R.   **333.95**
Saving Lucas Biggs. Teague, D.   **Fic**
Saving Mr. Terupt. Buyea, R.   **Fic**
Saving our living Earth [series]
Rapp, V. Protecting Earth's air quality   **363.7**
Welsbacher, A. Earth-friendly design   **745.2**
Welsbacher, A. Protecting Earth's rain forests   **577.34**
Saving Sky. Stanley, D.   **Fic**
Saving Sweetness. Stanley, D.   **E**
Saving Thanehaven. Jinks, C.   **Fic**
Saving the Baghdad Zoo. Halls, K. M.   **636.088**
Saving the ghost of the mountain. Montgomery, S.   **599.75**
Saving Yasha. Kvatum, L.   **599.78**
Saving Zasha. Barrow, R. G.   **Fic**
SAVINGS AND LOAN ASSOCIATIONS
   See also Banks and banking; Cooperation; Cooperative
   societies; Investments; Loans; Personal loans; Saving
   and investment
Savitz, Harriet May
Wolff, F. The story blanket   **E**
Savvy. Law, I.   **Fic**
Savvy. Fashion origami [series]
Everyday origami   **736**

Sawa, Maureen
The library book   **02**
Sawdust and spangles: the amazing life of W.C. Coup. Cover
R.   **9.**
SAWS
   See also Carpentry tools; Tools
Sawyer, Ruth
Hodges, M. The wee Christmas cabin ▶
Roller skates   **Fi**
The way of the storyteller   **372.**
Sawyer, Sarah
Florida   **975.**
Saxby Smart, private detective [series]
Cheshire, S. The curse of the ancient mask and other cas
files   **Fi**
Cheshire, S. The pirate's blood and other case files   **Fi**
Cheshire, S. The treasure of Dead Man's Lane and other cas
files   **Fi**
Saxby, Claire
Big red kangaroo   **599.**
Emu   **598.5.**
SAXONS
Farmer, N. The Sea of Trolls   **Fi**
SAXOPHONISTS
Before John was a jazz giant: a song of John Coltrane   **9**
SAXOPHONISTS -- UNITED STATES -- BIOGRAPHY
Golio, G. Spirit seeker   **788.**
Say hello. Foreman, J. ▶
Say hello like this. Murphy, M. ▶
Say hello to Zorro! Goodrich, C. ▶
Say hello! Isadora, R. ▶
Say hello, Lily. Lakritz, D. ▶
Say hello, Sophie. ▶
Say something, Perico. Harris, T. ▶
Say, Allen
Allison ▶
The bicycle man ▶
Boy in the garden ▶
Drawing from memory   **741.**
Erika-san ▶
The favorite daughter ▶
(il) Friedman, I. R. How my parents learned to eat ▶
Grandfather's journey ▶
Kamishibai man ▶
(il) Snyder, D. The boy of the three-year nap   **398.**
Tea with milk ▶
Tree of cranes ▶

              About
Say, A. Drawing from memory   **741.**
Sayago, Mauricio Trenard
(il) Hayes, J. Dance, Nana, dance   **398.**
Saying goodbye to Lulu. Demas, C. ▶
SAYINGS *See* Epigrams; Proverbs; Quotations
Sayles, Elizabeth
(il) Kohuth, J. Anne Frank's chestnut tree ▶
(il) Krilanovich, N. Moon child ▶
Sayre, April Pulley

School library management. 025.1

SCHOOL LIFE *See* Students

SCHOOL LIFE -- GRAPHIC NOVELS

Roman, D. Astronaut Academy: Zero gravity 741.5

SCHOOL LIFE -- FICTION

Perl, E. S. The capybara conspiracy Fic

A school like mine. 370

SCHOOL MUSIC -- INSTRUCTION AND STUDY

Hansen, D. The music and literacy connection 780

SCHOOL NURSES

    See also Nurses

School of Fear. Daneshvari, G. Fic

SCHOOL PLAYGROUNDS *See* Playgrounds

SCHOOL PLAYS *See* Children's plays; College and school drama

SCHOOL PRINCIPALS -- FICTION

The Adventures of Captain Underpants Fic

Pilkey, D. Captain Underpants and the tyrannical retaliation of the Turbo Toilet 2000 Fic

The terrible two get worse Fic

SCHOOL PROSE *See* Children's writings

School reform and the school library media specialist. Hughes-Hassell, S. 027.8

School spirit. Kimmel, E. C. Fic

SCHOOL SPORTS

    See also Sports; Student activities

SCHOOL SPORTS -- FICTION

Abdul-Jabbar, K. Sasquatch in the paint Fic

SCHOOL STORIES

Abbott, T. Firegirl Fic

Adler, D. A. Cam Jansen and the Sports Day mysteries Fic

Adler, D. A. Cam Jansen, the mystery of the carnival prize Fic

Adler, D. A. Young Cam Jansen and the 100th day of school mystery E

Ain, B. Starring Jules (in drama-rama) Fic

Alexander, M. G. Max and the dumb flower picture E

Aliki Painted words: Marianthe's story one E

Allard, H. Miss Nelson is missing! E

Allen, C. Spirit week showdown Fic

Amato, M. Edgar Allan's official crime investigation notebook Fic

Amato, M. Snarf attack, underfoodle, and the secret of life Fic

Amelia Bedelia's first Valentine E

Andrews, J. The very fairy princess E

Angleberger, T. Darth Paper strikes back Fic

Angleberger, T. The strange case of Origami Yoda Fic

Angleberger, T. Emperor Pickletine rides the bus Fic

Armstrong & Charlie Fic

Ashdown, R. Bob and Flo E

Auch, M. J. I was a third grade science project Fic

Baldacchino, C. Morris Micklewhite and the Tangerine Dress E

Balliett, B. The Wright 3 Fic

Barden, S. Cinderella Smith Fic

Barnett, M. Billy Twitters and his big blue whale problem E

Barnholdt, L. Girl meets ghost Fic

Barrows, A. Ivy + Bean and the ghost that had to go Fic

Barrows, A. Ivy + Bean: what's the big idea? Fic

Barshaw, R. M. Ellie McDoodle: best friends fur-ever Fic

Barshaw, R. M. Ellie McDoodle: new kid in school Fic

Baskin, N. R. Anything but typical Fic

Baskin, N. R. Runt Fic

Bauer, A. C. E. Come Fall Fic

Becker, B. The magical Ms. Plum Fic

Beil, M. D. The Red Blazer Girls: the ring of Rocamadour Fic

Beil, M. The Red Blazer Girls: the mistaken masterpiece Fic

Bergman, M. Lively Elizabeth! what happens when you push E

Bertrand, D. G. Adelita and the veggie cousins E

Birney, B. G. Adventure according to Humphrey Fic

Birney, B. G. Friendship according to Humphrey Fic

Birney, B. G. Surprises according to Humphrey Fic

Birney, B. G. Trouble according to Humphrey Fic

Birney, B. G. The world according to Humphrey Fic

Bliss, H. Bailey E

Bloch, S. Butterflies in my stomach and other school hazards E

Blume, J. Cool zone with the Pain and the Great One Fic

Blume, J. Freckle juice Fic

Blume, J. Friend or fiend? with the Pain & the Great One Fic

Blume, J. Going, going, gone! with the Pain and the Great One Fic

Boie, K. The princess trap Fic

Booraem, E. Texting the underworld Fic

Borden, L. The A+ custodian E

Borden, L. The last day of school Fic

Borden, L. The lost-and-found tooth Fic

Borden, L. Off to first grade E

Bottner, B. An annoying ABC E

Bottner, B. Miss Brooks loves books (and I don't) E

The boy in the dress Fic

Brand-new pencils, brand-new books E

Brennan, E. Dirtball Pete E

Brezenoff, S. The burglar who bit the Big Apple Fic

Brezenoff, S. The painting that wasn't there Fic

Brezenoff, S. The zombie who visited New Orleans Fic

Brisson, P. I remember Miss Perry E

Bromley, A. C. The lunch thief Fic

Brown, J. Star Wars 741.5

Brown, M. Lola Levine is not mean! E

Bugs in my hair?! E

Bunting, E. Cheyenne again E

Bunting, E. One green apple E

Burnett, F. H. A little princess Fic

Burningham, J. John Patrick Norman McHennessy E

Butler, D. H. The case of the fire alarm Fic

Butler, D. H. The case of the library monster Fic

Butler, D. H. The truth about Truman School Fic

Buyea, R. Because of Mr. Terupt Fic

Buyea, R. Mr. Terupt falls again Fic

Buyea, R. Saving Mr. Terupt Fic

Byars, B. C. The SOS file Fic

Cabot, M. Allie Finkle's rules for girls: book two; The new girl Fic

Cabot, M. Best friends and drama queens **Fic**

Cabot, M. Blast from the past **Fic**

Cabot, M.   From the notebooks of a middle school princess **Fic**

Cabot, M. Moving day **Fic**

Cabot, M. Stage fright **Fic**

Calmenson, S. Late for school! **E**

Cammuso, F. The Misadventures of Salem Hyde **Fic**

Carlson, N. L. Henry and the Valentine surprise **E**

Carlstrom, N. W. It's your first day of school, Annie Claire **E**

Catalanotto, P. No more pumpkins **Fic**

Catalanotto, P. The secret lunch special **Fic**

Cerra, K. O. Just a drop of water **Fic**

Chatterton, M. The Brain finds a leg **Fic**

Cheng, A. Where the steps were **Fic**

Cheng, A. The year of the book **Fic**

Cheshire, S. The pirate's blood and other case files **Fic**

Child, L. Clarice Bean, don't look now **Fic**

Child, L. I am too absolutely small for school **E**

Child, L. Utterly me, Clarice Bean **Fic**

Chodos-Irvine, M. Best best friends **E**

Choldenko, G. A giant crush **E**

Clark, C. G. Secrets of Greymoor **Fic**

Cleary, B. Dear Mr. Henshaw **Fic**

Cleary, B. Henry Huggins **Fic**

Cleary, B. Muggie Maggie **Fic**

Cleary, B. Ramona forever **Fic**

Cleary, B. Ramona Quimby, age 8 **Fic**

Cleary, B. Ramona the brave **Fic**

Cleary, B. Ramona the pest **Fic**

Cleary, B. Ramona's world **Fic**

Clementine **Fic**

Clementine and the spring trip **Fic**

Clements, A. About average **Fic**

Clements, A. No talking **Fic**

Clements, A. The report card **Fic**

Clements, A. Fear itself **Fic**

Clements, A. Frindle **Fic**

Clements, A. Lost and found **Fic**

Clements, A. Lunch money **Fic**

Clements, A. Room one **Fic**

Clements, A. We the children **Fic**

Cody, M. Powerless **Fic**

Cohen, B. Molly's pilgrim **E**

Cohen, M. First grade takes a test **E**

Cohen, M. Will I have a friend? **E**

Comerford, L. B. Rissa Bartholomew's declaration of independence **Fic**

Comics Squad **741.5**

Cooper, A. Sticks & stones **Fic**

Cornwell, N. Christophe's story **Fic**

Cottrell Boyce, F. The astounding broccoli boy **Fic**

Cousins, L. Maisy goes to preschool **E**

Cox, J. Butterfly buddies **Fic**

Cox, J. Carmen learns English **E**

Cox, J. Nora and the Texas terror **Fic**

Cox, J. Puppy power **Fic**

Coy, J. Love of the game **Fic**

Coy, J. Top of the order **Fic**

Cox, J. Ukulele Hayley **Fic**

Creech, S. Bloomability **Fic**

Creech, S. Hate that cat **Fic**

Creech, S. Love that dog **Fic**

Crews, D. School bus **E**

Crossan, S. The Weight of Water **Fic**

Crummel, S. S. The Little Red Pen **E**

Cuyler, M. 100th day worries **E**

Cuyler, M. Hooray for Reading Day! **E**

Dahl, R. Matilda **Fic**

Daly, N. Bettina Valentino and the Picasso Club **Fic**

D'Amico, C. Ella the Elegant Elephant **E**

Daneshvari, G. Class is not dismissed! **Fic**

Daneshvari, G. School of Fear **Fic**

Danneberg, J. The big test **E**

Danziger, P. Amber Brown is not a crayon **Fic**

Danziger, P. Amber Brown sees red **Fic**

Danziger, P. Amber Brown wants extra credit **Fic**

Davies, J. Candy smash **Fic**

Davies, J. The lemonade crime **Fic**

Davis, E.   The secret science alliance and the copycat crook **741.5**

De Groat, D. Ants in your pants, worms in your plants! **E**

De Groat, D. No more pencils, no more books, no more teacher's dirty looks! **E**

DeGross, M. Donavan's double trouble **Fic**

DeJong, M. The wheel on the school **Fic**

Demas, C. Pirates go to school **E**

DePaola, T. Meet the Barkers **E**

dePaola, T. Stagestruck **E**

Diesen, D. The pout-pout fish goes to school **E**

DiSalvo, D. The sloppy copy slipup **E**

Dodds, D. A. Teacher's pets **E**

Dory and the real true friend **Fic**

Dotty **E**

Dowell, F. O. The kind of friends we used to be **Fic**

Dowell, F. O. Phineas L. MacGuire . . . blasts off! **Fic**

Dowell, F. O. Phineas L. MacGuire . . . gets slimed! **Fic**

Dowell, F. O. Phineas L. Macguire erupts! **Fic**

Dowell, F. O. The secret language of girls **Fic**

A dragon's guide to making your human smarter **Fic**

Drama **741.5**

Draper, S. M. The dazzle disaster dinner party **Fic**

Dunston, M. The magic of giving **Fic**

Durand, H. Dessert first **Fic**

Durand, H. Just Desserts **Fic**

Durand, H. No room for Dessert **Fic**

Dutton, S. Mary Mae and the gospel truth **Fic**

Elish, D. The School for the Insanely Gifted **Fic**

Elkin, M. Samuel's baby **Fic**

EllRay Jakes Rocks the Holidays! **Fic**

English, K. Nikki & Deja **Fic**

English, K. Nikki & Deja: birthday blues **Fic**

English, K. Nikki & Deja: the newsy news newsletter **Fic**

English, K. Nikki and Deja: election madness **Fic**

Robinson, M. L. Bright Island	**Fic**	the school bus	
Rockwell, A. F. First day of school	**E**	The terrible two	**Fi**
Rockwell, A. F. My preschool	**E**	Thomson, M. Keena Ford and the second-grade mixup	**Fi**
Rodkey, G. The Tapper twins go to war (with each other)	**Fic**	Torrey, R. Ally-Saurus & the First Day of School	**Fi**
Rodman, M. A. First grade stinks	**E**	Towell, K. Skary childrin and the carousel of sorrow	**Fi**
Rodman, M. A. Yankee girl	**Fic**	Tracy, K. Camille McPhee fell under the bus	**Fi**
Rosen, M. Totally wonderful Miss Plumberry	**E**	Tracy, K. The reinvention of Bessica Lefter	**Fi**
Rundell, K. Cartwheeling in thunderstorms	**Fic**	The trouble with ants	**Fi**
Rupp, R. Octavia Boone's big questions about life, the universe, and everything	**Fic**	Trueit, T. S. No girls allowed (dogs okay)	**Fi**
		Underwood, D. A balloon for Isabel	
Rupp, R. Sarah Simpson's Rules for Living	**Fic**	Urban, L. A crooked kind of perfect	**Fi**
Rylander, C. The fourth stall	**Fic**	Urban, L. Hound dog true	**Fi**
Sachar, L. Marvin Redpost: is he a girl?	**Fic**	Urdahl, C. Polka-dot fixes kindergarten	
Sachar, L. Sideways stories from Wayside School	**Fic**	Vail, R. Justin Case	**Fi**
Salisbury, G. Calvin Coconut: kung fooey	**Fic**	Vande Velde, V. 8 class pets + one squirrel ÷ one dog	**Fi**
Salisbury, G. Calvin Coconut: trouble magnet	**Fic**	Vernick, A. Is your buffalo ready for kindergarten?	
Saltzberg, B. Stanley and the class pet	**E**	Vernon, U. Dragonbreath: curse of the were-wiener	**Fi**
Saunders, K. Beswitched	**Fic**	Vrabel, B. Pack of dorks	**Fi**
Schachner, J. Skippyjon Jones class action	**E**	Walker, K. I hate books!	
Schaefer, C. L. Dragon dancing	**E**	Wallace, N. E. Ready! Set! 100th day!	
Schmatz, P. Bluefish	**Fic**	Walliams, D. Mr. Stink	**Fi**
Schmid, P. Hugs from Pearl	**E**	Warner, S. EllRay Jakes is not a chicken!	**Fi**
Schmidt, G. D. The Wednesday wars	**Fic**	Warner, S. EllRay Jakes is not a rock star	**Fi**
Schneider, R. Knightley Academy	**Fic**	Waylon!	**Fi**
Schneider, R. The secret prince	**Fic**	Weatherford, C. B. Dear Mr. Rosenwald	**Fi**
Schotter, R. Doo-Wop Pop	**E**	Weeks, S. Oggie Cooder	**Fi**
Scieszka, J. Spaceheadz, book 2	**Fic**	Weeks, S. Oggie Cooder, party animal	**Fi**
Scieszka, J. Spaceheadz, book 3	**Fic**	Weeks, S. Save me a seat	**Fi**
Scotton, R. Splat the cat	**E**	Weissman, E. B. The trouble with Mark Hopper	**Fi**
Selzer, A. I put a spell on you	**Fic**	Wells, K. Paw power	**Fi**
Seuling, B. Robert takes a stand	**Fic**	Wells, R. Emily's first 100 days of school	**Fi**
Seuss Hooray for Diffendoofer Day!	**E**	Wells, R. Hands off, Harry!	
Shang, W. The great wall of Lucy Wu	**Fic**	Wells, R. Otto runs for President	
Shea, B. Big plans	**E**	Wells, R. Yoko	
Shefelman, J. J. Anna Maria's gift	**Fic**	Whitaker, Z. Kali and the rat snake	
Sherman, D. The BEDMAS conspiracy	**Fic**	Whiting, S. The firefighters	
Shouldn't you be in school?	**Fic**	Whittemore, J. Odd girl in	**Fi**
Shreve, S. R. The flunking of Joshua T. Bates	**Fic**	Whittenberg, A. Sweet Thang	**Fi**
Simms, L. Rotten teeth	**E**	Willner-Pardo, G. The hard kind of promise	**Fi**
Skye, O. Wonkenstein: the creature from my closet	**Fic**	Winerip, M. Adam Canfield of the Slash	**Fi**
Slade, A. G. Jolted	**Fic**	Winston, S. President of the whole fifth grade	**Fi**
Sonnenblick, J. After ever after	**Fic**	Winters, B. H. The mystery of the missing everything	**Fi**
Sonnenblick, J. Zen and the art of faking it	**Fic**	Winters, B. H. The secret life of Ms. Finkleman	**Fi**
Spaceheadz	**Fic**	Winters, K. This school year will be the best!	
Spinelli, E. Miss Fox's class goes green	**E**	Wolf, J. M. Someone named Eva	**Fi**
Spinelli, J. Loser	**Fic**	Wong, J. S. Me and Rolly Maloo	**Fi**
Stevens, R. Murder is bad manners	**Fic**	Wong, J. S. Minn and Jake	**Fi**
Stier, C. The terrible secrets of the Tell-All Club	**Fic**	Wortche, A. Rosie Sprout's time to shine	
Stine, R. L. It's the first day of school--forever!	**Fic**	Yamashita, H. Seven little mice go to school	
Stone, P. Deep down popular	**Fic**	Yankovic, A. When I grow up	
Stout, S. K. Fiona Finkelstein meets her match!!	**Fic**	Yee, L. Bobby vs. girls (accidentally)	**Fi**
Stuey Lewis against all odds	**Fic**	Yee, L. Millicent Min, girl genius	**Fi**
Tallulah's Nutcracker	**E**	Yee, L. Warp speed	**Fi**
Tallulah's solo	**E**	Yoo, D. The detention club	**Fi**
Tarshis, L. Emma-Jean Lazarus fell out of a tree	**Fic**	Young, K. R. Doodlebug	**Fi**
Taylor, C. Ready to wear	**Fic**	You're wearing that to school?!	**Fi**
Ten rules you absolutely must not break if you want to survive		Zucker, N. F. Callie's rules	**F**

Black, H. The copper gauntlet **Fic**
Jung, M. Geeks, girls, and secret identities **Fic**
Lowry, L. Son **Fic**
McDonough, Y. Z. The bicycle spy **Fic**
Secret agents. Gilbert, A. **327.12**
The **secret** bay. **577.7**
The **secret** box. Lehman, B. **E**
The **secret** cave. McCully, E. A. **E**
Secret coders. **741.5**
Secret coders [series]
  Secret coders **741.5**
The **secret** garden. Burnett, F. H. **Fic**
Secret history of mermaids and creatures of the deep. Berk,
  A. **398**
The **secret** hum of a daisy. Holczer, T. **Fic**
The **secret** keepers. Stewart, T. L. **Fic**
The **secret** kingdom. Nimmo, J. **Fic**
The **secret** language of girls. Dowell, F. O. **Fic**
The **secret** legacy. Menchu, R. **398.2**
The **secret** life of a snowflake. Libbrecht, K. G. **551.57**
The **secret** life of Ms. Finkleman. Winters, B. H. **Fic**
The **secret** life of the red fox. **599.775**
Secret lives [series]
  Miller, S. S. Secret lives of burrowing beasts **591.7**
  Miller, S. S. Secret lives of cave creatures **591.7**
  Miller, S. S. Secret lives of deep-sea creatures **591.7**
  Miller, S. S. Secret lives of seashell dwellers **594**
  Miller, S. S. Secret lives of soil creatures **591.7**
Secret lives of burrowing beasts. Miller, S. S. **591.7**
Secret lives of cave creatures. Miller, S. S. **591.7**
Secret lives of deep-sea creatures. Miller, S. S. **591.7**
Secret lives of seashell dwellers. Miller, S. S. **594**
Secret lives of soil creatures. Miller, S. S. **591.7**
The **secret** lunch special. Catalanotto, P. **Fic**
The **secret** mission of William Tuck. Pierpoint, E. **Fic**
The **secret** of Dreadwillow Carse. Farrey, B. **Fic**
The **secret** of platform 13. Ibbotson, E. **Fic**
The **secret** of Priest's Grotto. Taylor, P. L. **940.53**
The **secret** of Rover. Wildavsky, R. **Fic**
The **secret** of the Fortune Wookiee. Angleberger, T. **Fic**
Secret of the plant-killing ants . . . and more! Rodriguez, A.
  M. **595.7**
The **secret** of the sealed room. MacDonald, B. **Fic**
The **secret** of the skeleton key. Warner, P. **Fic**
Secret of the snow leopard. Tenzing Norbu **E**
The **secret** of the stone frog. Nytra, D. **741.5**
Secret of the suffocating slime trap . . . and more! Rodriguez,
  A. M. **597**
The **secret** of the village fool. **Fic**
The **secret** of zoom. Jonell, L. **Fic**
Secret origins. Riley, J. **Fic**
The **secret** pool. **577.63**
The **secret** prince. Schneider, R. **Fic**
The **secret** project. **355.825**
The **Secret** Remedy Book. **E**
The **secret** river. Rawlings, M. K. **Fic**
The **secret** science alliance and the copycat crook. Davis,

E. **741.**
The **secret** seder. Rappaport, D.
SECRET SERVICE
  Gilbert, A. Secret agents **327.1**
SECRET SERVICE
  See also Police
The **secret** shofar of Barcelona. Greene, J. D. **Fi**
SECRET SOCIETIES
  See also Rites and ceremonies; Societies
SECRET SOCIETIES -- FICTION
  Abbott, T. The forbidden stone **Fi**
  The door in the alley **Fi**
  Durham, P. The luck uglies **Fi**
  Farrey, B. The Shadowhand Covenant **Fi**
  Gonzalez, C. D. Moving target **Fi**
  Roy, C. The blood guard **Fi**
  Sands, K. The blackthorn key **Fi**
The **secret** subway. Corey, S.
The **secret** tree. Standiford, N. **Fi**
Secret tree fort. Farley, B.
The secret world of spies [series]
  Mitchell, S. K. Spies and lies **327.1**
  Mitchell, S. K. Spies, double agents, and traitors **327.1**
  Mitchell, S. K. Spy codes and ciphers **65**
  Mitchell, S. K. Spy gizmos and gadgets **327.1**
The **secret** world of Walter Anderson. Bass, H. **9**
The **secret** world of whales. Baker, M. **599.**
SECRET WRITING *See* Cryptography
The **secret** zoo. Chick, B. **Fi**
The **secret** zoo: riddles and danger. Chick, B. **Fi**
The **secret** zoo: secrets and shadows. Chick, B. **Fi**
The **secret-keeper.** Coombs, K.
SECRETARIES OF COMMERCE
  Ray, D. Ghost girl **Fi**
SECRETARIES OF STATE
  Adler, D. A. A picture book of Dolley and James Madison **9**
  Burgan, M. James Buchanan **9**
  Elish, D. James Madison **9**
  Fritz, J. The great little Madison **9**
  Krensky, S. Dangerous crossing **Fi**
  Naden, C. J. James Monroe **9**
SECRETARIES OF THE TREASURY
  Duel! **973.**
  Fritz, J. Alexander Hamilton **9**
SECRETS -- FICTION
  Black, H. The copper gauntlet **Fi**
  Davies, J. Candy smash **Fi**
  Harrison, M. 13 secrets **Fi**
  Legrand, C. Some kind of happiness **Fi**
  Lulu's mysterious mission **Fi**
  McDonough, Y. Z. The bicycle spy **Fi**
  Secrets I know **Fi**
  Sternberg, J. Secrets Out! **Fi**
  Shea, B. Ballet Cat **Fi**
  Stewart, T. L. The secret keepers **Fi**
  The stowaways **Fi**
  Tanner, L. Ice Breaker **Fi**

he **sheep** in wolf's clothing. Lester, H.　　　**E**

HEET MUSIC
　　See also Music

hefelman, Janice Jordan
Anna Maria's gift　　　**Fic**
I, Vivaldi　　　**92**

hefelman, Tom
(il) Shefelman, J. J. I, Vivaldi　　　**92**

hefrin, Sima Elizabeth
(il) Hughes, V. Once upon a bathtime　　　**E**
(il) Jewish fairy tale feasts　　　**641.5**

heHeWe.　　　**741.5**

heila Rae, the brave. Henkes, K.　　　**E**

heinkin, Steve
Bomb　　　**623.4**
King George: what was his problem?　　　**973.3**
Lincoln's Grave Robbers　　　**973.7**
The Port Chicago 50　　　**940.54**
Two miserable presidents　　　**973.7**
Which way to the wild West?　　　**978**

heinmel, Courtney
All the things you are　　　**Fic**

helby, Anne
The adventures of Molly Whuppie and other Appalachian
　folktales　　　**398.2**
The man who lived in a hollow tree　　　**E**

heldon, Annette
Big sister now　　　**306.8**

heldon, David
Into the deep　　　**92**

helf life: stories by the book.　　　**S**

helf-esteem. Kitain, S.　　　**028.5**

hell shocker. Sonneborn, S.　　　**Fic**

helley Rotner's early childhood library [series]
Rotner, S. Senses in the city　　　**E**

helley, John
(il) Danneberg, J. Family reminders　　　**Fic**

HELLFISH
　　See also Aquatic animals

HELLFISH
Gilpin, D. Snails, shellfish & other mollusks　　　**594**

HELLS
Ripley, C. How?　　　**031.02**
Zoehfeld, K. W. What lives in a shell?　　　**591.4**

HELLS -- FICTION
Slate, J. Marcel the Shell with shoes on　　　**E**

helly, Jeff
(il) Fisher, D. All about drawing dinosaurs & reptiles　　**743**

helton, Paula Young
Child of the civil rights movement　　　**323.1**

he **Shema** in the mezuzah.　　　**E**

hepard, Aaron
The princess mouse　　　**398.2**
The sea king's daughter　　　**398.2**
Stories on stage　　　**812**

hepard, Ernest H. (Ernest Howard), 1879-1976
(il) Grahame, K. The reluctant dragon　　　**Fic**

(il) Grahame, K. The wind in the willows　　　**Fic**
(il) Milne, A. A. The House at Pooh Corner　　　**Fic**
(il) Milne, A. A. Now we are six　　　**821**
(il) Milne, A. A. When we were very young　　　**821**
(il) Milne, A. A. Winnie-the-Pooh　　　**Fic**

Shepard, Mary Eleanor
(il) Travers, P. L. Mary Poppins　　　**Fic**

The **shepherd's** trail. Urbigkit, C.　　　**636.3**

Shepherd, Jodie
A day with paramedics　　　**362.18**

Shepherd, Keith D.
(il) Walking home to Rosie Lee　　　**E**

SHEPHERDS
Urbigkit, C. The shepherd's trail　　　**636.3**
Urbigkit, C. A young shepherd　　　**636.3**

SHEPHERDS -- FICTION
Johnson, J. The leopard boy　　　**E**
Levine, G. C. Betsy who cried wolf　　　**E**
Morpurgo, M. On angel wings　　　**Fic**

Shepperson, Rob
Coman, C. The Memory Bank　　　**Fic**
(il) Coman, C. Sneaking suspicions　　　**Fic**
(il) Mills, C. Cody Harmon, king of pets　　　**Fic**
(il) Mills, C. Kelsey Green, reading queen　　　**Fic**
(il) Root, P. Lilly and the pirates　　　**Fic**

Sher, Emil
Away　　　**E**
Levine, K. Hana's suitcase on stage　　　**812**

Sheridan, Sara
I'm me!　　　**E**

SHERIFFS
Alter, J. John Barclay Armstrong　　　**92**
Bad news for outlaws　　　**92**

SHERIFFS -- FICTION
McGhee, A. The case of the missing donut　　　**E**
Paulsen, G. The legend of Bass Reeves　　　**Fic**
Shea, B. Kid sheriff and the terrible Toads　　　**E**

The Sherlock files [series]
Barrett, T. The 100-year-old secret　　　**Fic**

Sherlock Holmes and the Baker Street Irregulars [series]
Mack, T. The fall of the Amazing Zalindas　　　**Fic**
Mack, T. The mystery of the conjured man　　　**Fic**

SHERLOCK HOLMES FILMS
　　See also Motion pictures; Mystery films

Sherlock Holmes. The legend begins [series]
Lane, A. Black ice　　　**Fic**
Lane, A. Rebel fire　　　**Fic**

Sherlock, Patti
Letters from Wolfie　　　**Fic**

Sherman, Casey
The finest hours　　　**910.4**

Sherman, Deborah
The BEDMAS conspiracy　　　**Fic**

Sherman, Delia
Changeling　　　**Fic**

Sherman, Josepha
Asteroids, meteors, and comets　　　**523.4**

Greenwood, M. The donkey of Gallipoli **940.4**

Gunderson, J. Conquistadors **970.01**

Hodges, M. Saint George and the dragon **398.2**

Hopkinson, D. From slave to soldier **E**

Janisch, H. Fantastic adventures of Baron Munchausen **Fic**

Murphy, J. A young patriot **973.3**

Myers, W. D. Patrol **E**

Park, L. The Spartan hoplites **938**

Rockwell, A. F. They called her Molly Pitcher **973.3**

Samuels, C. Soldiers **940.54**

Tallec, O. Waterloo & trafalgar **E**

SOLDIERS -- FAMILY RELATIONSHIPS -- UNITED STATES

Biden, J. Don't forget, God bless our troops **355.1**

SOLDIERS -- FICTION

Anderson, L. H. Forge **Fic**

Cali, D. The enemy **E**

Cohen, M. My big brother **E**

Dowell, F. O. Shooting the moon **Fic**

Finding Winnie **E**

Hardin, M. Hero dad **E**

Hartnett, S. The silver donkey **Fic**

Hendrix, J. Shooting at the stars **E**

Lewis, J. P. And the soldiers sang **Fic**

Lynch, C. The right fight **Fic**

Madison, A. 100 days and 99 nights **Fic**

Polacco, P. Tucky Jo and Little Heart **Fic**

Rodman, M. A. Jimmy's stars **Fic**

Ruth, G. Coming Home **E**

Schwabach, K. The storm before Atlanta **Fic**

Tak, B. D. Soldier bear **Fic**

Townley, R. The door in the forest **Fic**

Ungerer, T. Otto **E**

Weber, E. The Yankee at the seder **Fic**

SOLDIERS -- HISTORY -- 20TH CENTURY

Samuels, C. Soldiers **940.54**

SOLDIERS -- ROME

Beller, S. P. Roman legions on the march **937**

SOLDIERS -- SPAIN -- HISTORY

Gunderson, J. Conquistadors **970.01**

SOLDIERS -- TEXAS -- BIOGRAPHY

Chemerka, W. R. Juan Seguin **976.4**

SOLDIERS -- UNITED STATES

Beller, S. P. Billy Yank and Johnny Reb **973.7**

Beller, S. P. The doughboys over there **940.4**

Jones, C. Sarah Emma Edmonds was a great pretender **92**

Nurse, soldier, spy: the story of Sarah Edmonds, a Civil War hero **92**

Soldiers on the battlefront [series]

Beller, S. P. Billy Yank and Johnny Reb **973.7**

Beller, S. P. The doughboys over there **940.4**

Beller, S. P. Roman legions on the march **937**

SOLDIERS' LIFE See Soldiers

Solheim, James

Born yesterday **E**

SOLICITORS See Lawyers

SOLICITORS GENERAL

Adler, D. A. A picture book of Thurgood Marshall **34**

SOLID GEOMETRY

See also Geometry

SOLID GEOMETRY

Round **516.**

SOLID WASTE DISPOSAL See Refuse and refuse disposa

SOLIDS

Boothroyd, J. What is a solid? **530**

Hurd, W. Changing states **530**

SOLIDS

See also Physical chemistry; Physics

SOLILOQUIES

See also Drama; Monologues

SOLITUDE

Crist, J. J. What to do when you're sad & lonely **15**

SOLITUDE -- FICTION

Brosgol, V. Leave me alone

Frazee, M. Boot & Shoe

Solomon and the ant. Oberman, S. **398**

Solomon Crocodile. Rayner, C.

Solomon Snow and the stolen jewel. Umansky, K. **F**

Solomon, Heather

(il) Coombs, K. The secret-keeper

(il) Wheeler, L. Ugly Pie

(il) Willey, M. The 3 bears and Goldilocks **398**

(il) Willey, M. A Clever Beatrice Christmas

Solomons, David

My brother is a superhero **F**

SOLPUGIDA

Markle, S. Wind scorpions **595.**

Soltis, Sue

Nothing like a puffin

Solve that crime! [series]

Spilsbury, R. Bones speak! **61**

Spilsbury, R. Counterfeit! **363.**

SOLVENT ABUSE

See also Social problems; Substance abuse

Solving the puzzle under the sea. Burleigh, R. **9**

Solway, Andrew

Africa **780.**

Castle under siege! **621.**

Communication **303.**

Graphing immigration **32**

Graphing war and conflict **35**

Inventions and investigations **60**

Latin America and the Caribbean **780.**

Understanding cycles and systems **55**

Why is there life on Earth? **576.**

SOMALI AMERICANS -- FICTION

Hoffman, M. The color of home

O'Brien, A. S. I'm new here

Somalia. Hassig, S. M. **967.7**

SOMALIA

Hassig, S. M. Somalia **967.7**

SOMALIA -- FICTION

Hoffman, M. The color of home

Soman, David

Berger, M. Spinning spiders   **595.4**

Dewey, J. Once I knew a spider   **E**

'm trying to love spiders   **595.4**

Insects and spiders   **595**

Spiders   **595.4**

Stronger Than Steel   **595.4**

Johnson, J. Simon & Schuster children's guide to insects and
spiders   **595.7**

Lomberg, M. Spider   **639**

Lunis, N. Deadly black widows   **595.4**

Markle, S. Black widows   **595.4**

Markle, S. Crab spiders   **595.4**

Markle, S. Fishing spiders   **595.4**

Markle, S. Harvestmen   **595.4**

Markle, S. Jumping spiders   **595.4**

Markle, S. Orb weavers   **595.4**

Markle, S. Sneaky, spinning, baby spiders   **595.4**

Markle, S. Wolf spiders   **595.4**

Murawski, D. Spiders and their webs   **595.4**

Silk & venom   **595.4**

Simon, S. Spiders   **595.4**

Stewart, M. Insect or spider?   **595.7**

Tait, N. Insects & spiders   **595.7**

Wadsworth, G. Up, up, and away   **595.4**

▶iders.   **595.4**

▶IDERS -- FICTION

Carle, E. The very busy spider   **E**

Cronin, D. Diary of a spider   **E**

Cummings, T. The eensy weensy spider freaks out (big
time!)   **E**

Dewey, J. Once I knew a spider   **E**

Dodd, E. I love bugs   **E**

Lasky, K. Felix takes the stage   **Fic**

Lasky, K. Spiders on the case   **Fic**

Spinelli, E. Sophie's masterpiece   **E**

Urgency emergecy! Itsy bitsy spider   **E**

White, E. B. Charlotte's web   **Fic**

▶IDERS -- FOLKLORE

Kimmel, E. A. Anansi and the moss-covered rock   **398.2**

Kimmel, E. A. Anansi's party time   **398.2**

Kimmel, E. A. The spider's gift   **398.2**

▶IDERS -- POETRY

Bug off!   **811**

▶IDERS -- SONGS

Hoberman, M. A. The eensy-weensy spider   **782.42**

▶iders and their webs. Murawski, D.   **595.4**

▶iders on the case. Lasky, K.   **Fic**

▶iegel, Beth

(il) Bunting, E. Will it be a baby brother?   **E**

(il) Rodman, M. A. First grade stinks   **E**

▶iegel, Carol

Book by book   **011.6**

▶iegelman, Art, 1948-

(ed) Big fat Little Lit   **741.5**

Jack and the box   **E**

(ed) The TOON treasury of classic children's comics   **741.5**

▶ielman, Gloria

Marcel Marceau   **92**

Spier, Peter

(il) The Fox went out on a chilly night   **782.42**

Noah's ark   **222**

SPIES

Earnest, P. The real spy's guide to becoming a spy   **327.12**

Gilbert, A. Secret agents   **327.12**

Gilbert, A. Spy school   **327.12**

Horowitz, A. Stormbreaker   **Fic**

Jones, C. Sarah Emma Edmonds was a great pretender   **92**

Mitchell, S. K. Spies and lies   **327.12**

Mitchell, S. K. Spies, double agents, and traitors   **327.12**

Mitchell, S. K. Spy codes and ciphers   **652**

Nurse, soldier, spy: the story of Sarah Edmonds, a Civil War
hero   **92**

Shea, P. D. Patience Wright   **92**

Spyology   **327.12**

SPIES

See also Espionage; Subversive activities

SPIES -- FICTION

Daneshvari, G. The League of Unexceptional Children   **Fic**

Game over, Pete Watson   **Fic**

Gibbs, S. Spy camp   **Fic**

Gibbs, S. Spy ski school   **Fic**

Lulu's mysterious mission   **Fic**

Pierpoint, E. The secret mission of William Tuck   **Fic**

SPIES -- GRAPHIC NOVELS

City of spies   **741.5**

Horowitz, A. Stormbreaker: the graphic novel   **741.5**

SPIES -- HISTORY -- 20TH CENTURY

Samuels, C. Spying and security   **940.54**

Spies and lies. Mitchell, S. K.   **327.12**

Spies, double agents, and traitors. Mitchell, S. K.   **327.12**

Spike it volleyball. Crossingham, J.   **796.325**

Spiky, slimy, smooth. Brocket, J.   **612.8**

Spilling ink. Mazer, A.   **808.3**

Spilling, Jo-Ann

(jt. auth) Foo Yuk Yee   Malaysia   **959.5**

(jt. auth) Layton, L.   Singapore   **959.57**

Cooper, R.   Bahrain   **953.6**

Hestler, A.   Wales   **942.9**

Hestler, A.   Yemen   **953.3**

Spilling, M.   Cyprus   **956.93**

Spilling, Michael

(jt. auth) Cooper, R.   Indonesia   **959.8**

Brown, R. V.   Tunisia   **961.1**

Cooper, R.   Croatia   **949.7**

McGaffey, L.   Honduras   **972.83**

O'Shea, M.   Kuwait   **953.67**

Sioras, E.   Czech Republic   **943.7**

Cyprus   **956.93**

Estonia   **947.98**

Yoga step-by-step   **613.7**

Spilsbury, Louise

Dolphin   **599.5**

Howling hurricanes   **551.55**

Jellyfish   **593.5**

Yolen, J. Naming Liberty   E

TATUES *See* Monuments; Sculpture

TATUES -- FICTION

Who could that be at this hour?   Fic

TATUTES *See* Law

taub, Leslie

(il) Danticat, E. Mama's nightingale   E

(il) Lives: poems about famous Americans   811

Everybody gets the blues   E

tauffacher, Sue

Tillie the terrible Swede   92

tauffacher, Sue

Gator on the loose!   Fic

Harry Sue   Fic

Nothing but trouble   92

Tillie the terrible Swede   92

tay! Lowry, L.   Fic

taying healthy. Schaefer, A.   613

taying safe. Schaefer, A.   613.6

tead, Erin E., 1982-

(il) Bear has a story to tell   E

(il) Cuevas, M. The uncorker of ocean bottles   E

(il) Fogliano, J. And then it's spring   E

(il) Fogliano, J. If you want to see a whale   E

(il) Galing, E. Tony   E

(il) Lenny & Lucy   E

(il) Stead, P. C. A sick day for Amos McGee   E

tead, Judy

(il) Raczka, B. Snowy, blowy winter   E

(il) Raczka, B. Spring things   E

(il) Raczka, B. Who loves the fall?   E

Shirley, D. Best friend on wheels   E

tead, Philip C.

(il) Ideas are all around   E

(il) Sebastian and the balloon   E

Bear has a story to tell   E

Hello, my name is Ruby   E

A home for Bird   E

Jonathan and the big blue boat   E

Lenny & Lucy   E

A sick day for Amos McGee   E

Special delivery   E

tead, Rebecca

Goodbye stranger   Fic

Liar & spy   Fic

When you reach me   Fic

teady hands. Zimmer, T. V.   811

TEALING -- FICTION

Davies, M. Ben rides on   E

Ryan, C. The map to everywhere   Fic

Who could that be at this hour?   Fic

tealing home. Schwartz, E.   Fic

tealing home. Burleigh, R.   92

tealing the game. Obstfeld, R.   Fic

TEAM

See also Heat; Power (Mechanics); Water

TEAM ENGINEERING

See also Engineering

STEAM ENGINES

Zimmermann, K. R. Steam locomotives   385

STEAM ENGINES

See also Engines; Steam engineering

Steam locomotives. Zimmermann, K. R.   385

STEAM LOCOMOTIVES

See also Locomotives

STEAM LOCOMOTIVES

The Stourbridge Lion   625.26

STEAM NAVIGATION

See also Navigation; Steam engineering; Transportation

Steam train, dream train.   E

STEAM TURBINES

See also Steam engines; Steam navigation; Turbines

STEAM-SHOVELS -- FICTION

Burton, V. L. Mike Mulligan and his steam shovel   E

Zimmerman, A. G. Digger man   E

Steamboat school. Hopkinson, D.   E

STEAMBOATS

Herweck, D. Robert Fulton   92

STEAMBOATS

See also Boats and boating; Naval architecture; Ocean travel; Shipbuilding; Ships

STEAMPUNK FICTION

Gratz, A. The League of Seven   Fic

Lloyd Jones, R. Wild boy   Fic

STEAMPUNK FICTION

See also Science fiction

STEAMSHIPS *See* Steamboats

Stearman, Kaye

Women of today   305.4

Stearn, Ted

(il) Jackson, D. M. The name game   929.9

Stearns, Megan

(il) Mooney, C. Amazing Africa   960

Stearns, Precious McKenzie

Manatees   599.5

Whooping cranes   598

STEEL

See also Iron; Metalwork

STEEL CONSTRUCTION

See also Building; Structural engineering

STEEL CONSTRUCTION -- FICTION

Kirk, C. A. Sky dancers   E

STEEL DRUM (MUSICAL INSTRUMENT) -- FICTION

Bootman, C. Steel pan man of Harlem   E

STEEL DRUM (MUSICAL INSTRUMENT)

Greenwood, M. Drummer boy of John John   786.9

STEEL INDUSTRY -- FICTION

Winter, J. Steel Town   E

STEEL INDUSTRY -- TECHNOLOGICAL INNOVATIONS

See also Technological innovations

Steel pan man of Harlem. Bootman, C.   E

Steel Town. Winter, J.   E

Steele, Christy

Cauley, L. B. Clap your hands	E
Chaconas, D. Don't slam the door!	E
Chall, M. W. Pick a pup	E
Charlip, R. A perfect day	E
Chichester-Clark, E. Little Miss Muffet counts to ten	E
Christian, C. Witches	E
City shapes	E
Clayton, D. An awesome book!	E
Cleary, B. The hullabaloo ABC	E
Clements, A. The handiest things in the world	E
Cleminson, K. Cuddle up, goodnight	E
Cohn, S. One wolf howls	599.77
Copp, J. Jim Copp, will you tell me a story?	E
Cordsen, C. F. Market day	E
Cotten, C. Rain play	E
Cotten, C. This is the stable	E
Craig, L. Dancing feet!	E
Craig, L. Farmyard beat	E
Crews, D. Ten black dots	E
Cronin, D. Wiggle	E
Crow, K. Cool Daddy Rat	E
Crow, K. The middle-child blues	E
Crowley, N. Nanook & Pryce	E
Cummings, P. Harvey Moon, museum boy	E
Curtis, J. L. Big words for little people	E
Curtis, J. L. I'm gonna like me	E
Curtis, J. L. Is there really a human race?	E
Curtis, J. L. My mommy hung the moon	E
Cushman, D. Christmas Eve good night	E
Cuyler, M. The little dump truck	E
Cuyler, M. Monster mess!	E
Cuyler, M. Princess Bess gets dressed	E
Cuyler, M. Tick tock clock	E
Cyrus, K. Big rig bugs	E
Cyrus, K. Tadpole Rex	E
Cyrus, K. The voyage of Turtle Rex	E
Davies, J. The night is singing	E
The day the babies crawled away	E
Day, N. R. On a windy night	E
Degen, B. Jamberry	E
Degman, L. 1 zany zoo	E
Demas, C. Pirates go to school	E
Dempsey, K. Me with you	E
Dempsey, K. Mini racer	E
Dewdney, A. Llama, llama red pajama	E
Dewdney, A. Nobunny's perfect	E
Dewdney, A. Roly Poly pangolin	E
Dickinson, R. Over in the hollow	E
Diesen, D. The pout-pout fish	E
Dillon, L. Rap a tap tap	792.7
DiTerlizzi, A. Some bugs	E
Dobbins, J. Driving my tractor	E
Dodd, E. Meow said the cow	E
Dodd, E. No matter what	E
Dodds, D. A. Full house	513
Dodds, D. A. Minnie's Diner	E
Dodds, D. A. The prince won't go to bed	E

Donaldson, J. Superworm	
Donaldson, J. The fish who cried wolf	
Donaldson, J. One Ted falls out of bed	
Donaldson, J. Stick Man	
Donaldson, J. Tyrannosaurus Drip	
Donaldson, J. What the ladybug heard	
Doner, K. On a road in Africa	636.0
Doodler, T. H. What color is Bear's underwear?	
Double-happiness	
Doughty, R. Oh no! Time to go!	
Dowdy, L. C. All kinds of kisses	
Doyen, D. Once upon a twice	
Doyle, M. Get happy	
Dubosarsky, U. The terrible plop	
Dunrea, O. Ollie's Halloween	
Durango, J. Cha-cha chimps	
Edwards, D. The pen that Pa built	
Edwards, P. D. While the world is sleeping	
Ehlert, L. Rain fish	
Ehlert, L. Boo to you!	
Ehlert, L. Feathers for lunch	
Ehlert, L. Market day	
Ehlert, L. Nuts to you!	
Ehlert, L. Oodles of animals	
Ehlert, L. Top cat	
Ehlert, L. Wag a tail	
Ehlert, L. Waiting for wings	595.7
Ehrhardt, K. This Jazz man	
Elffers, J. Do you love me?	
Elliott, D. What the grizzly knows	
Elya, S. M. Fire! Fuego! Brave bomberos	
Elya, S. M. Little Roja Riding Hood	
Elya, S. M. Rubia and the three osos	398.
Elya, S. M. Adios, tricycle	
Elya, S. M. Bebe goes shopping	
Elya, S. M. Cowboy Jose	
Elya, S. M. F is for fiesta	
Elya, S. M. Fairy trails	
Elya, S. M. N is for Navidad	
Elya, S. M. No more, por favor	
Elya, S. M. Oh no, gotta go!	
Emberley, E. Where's my sweetie pie?	
Engle, M. Orangutanka	
Esbaum, J. Stanza	
Eugenie Kitten's autumn	
Eugenie Kitten's spring	
Eugenie Kitten's summer	
Eugenie Kitten's winter	
Evans, L. Who loves the little lamb?	
Everywhere babies	
Ewart, C. Fossil	
Fall mixed up	
Falwell, C. Gobble, gobble	
Falwell, C. Scoot!	
Falwell, C. Shape capers	
Falwell, C. Turtle splash!	
Fenton, J. What's under the bed?	

Katz, K. Ten tiny babies	E	Martin, B. Brown bear, brown bear what do you see?	
Kay, V. Covered wagons, bumpy trails	E	Martin, B. Chicka chicka 1, 2, 3	
Kay, V. Hornbooks and inkwells	E	Martin, B. Chicka chicka boom boom	
Kelley, E. A. My life as a chicken	E	Martin, B. Kitty cat, kitty cat, are you going to sleep?	
Kerr, J. One night in the zoo	E	Martin, B. Kitty Cat, Kitty Cat, are you waking up?	
Ketteman, H. Goodnight, Little Monster	E	Martin, B. Panda bear, panda bear, what do you see?	
Ketteman, H. Swamp song	E	Martin, B. Polar bear, polar bear, what do you hear?	
Kimmelman, L. Everybody bonjours!	E	Martin, D. Peep and Ducky	
Kinerk, R. Clorinda	E	Martin, E. W. Dream animals	
The King of Quizzical Island	E	Martin, S. The alphabet from A to Y with bonus letter, Z!	
King, T. A Coyote solstice tale	Fic	McCanna, T. Watersong	
Kirk, D. Honk honk! Beep beep!	E	McGhee, A. Only a witch can fly	
Kirk, D. Keisha Ann can!	E	McGrath, B. B. Teddy bear counting	
Kohuth, J. Duck sock hop	E	McPhail, D. M. Pigs aplenty, pigs galore!	
Kohuth, J. Ducks go vroom	E	Meadows, M. Hibernation station	
Kraus, R. Whose mouse are you?	E	Meadows, M. Piggies in the kitchen	
Krebs, L. The Beeman	E	Melmed, L. K. Hurry! Hurry! Have you heard?	
Kroll, V. L. Everybody has a teddy	E	Meltzer, L. The construction crew	
Krull, K. Fartiste	Fic	Metaxas, E. It's time to sleep, my love (a lullabye)	
Kumin, M. Oh, Harry!	E	Meyers, S. Bear in the air	
Kuskin, K. Green as a bean	E	Mighty, mighty construction site	
Laden, N. Peek-a-who?	E	Millen, C. M. The ink garden of brother Theophane	
Le Guin, U. K. Cat dreams	E	Minor, F. If you were a panda bear	
A leaf can be	E	Minor, W. My farm friends	
Lester, A. Noni the pony	E	Miranda, A. To market, to market	
Levine, A. A. Monday is one day	E	Miss Lina's ballerinas	
Lewin, B. Where is Tippy Toes?	E	Modarressi, M. Taking care of Mama	
Lewis, J. P. The snowflake sisters	E	Montes, M. Los gatos black on Halloween	
Lewis, K. Not inside this house!	E	Moonlight	
Lindbergh, R. Homer, the library cat	E	Mora, P. Uno, dos, tres: one, two, three	
Lithgow, J. Micawber	E	Morales, M. Jam & honey	
Lobel, A. On Market Street	E	Mortiz, D. Hush little beachcomber	
London, J. I'm a truck driver	E	Moss, L. Zin! zin! zin! a violin	
The longest night	E	Murphy, S. J. Leaping lizards	
Longstreth, G. G. Yes, let's	E	Murray, A. The house that Zack built	
Lord, J. V. The giant jam sandwich	E	Murray, A. One two that's my shoe!	
Lund, D. Monsters on machines	E	Murray, M. D. Halloween night	
Lyon, G. E. Boats float!	E	Neitzel, S. The jacket I wear in the snow	64
Lyon, G. E. Trucks roll!	E	Nelson, K. Nelson Mandela	968.0
MacHale, D. J. The monster princess	E	Neubecker, R. What little boys are made of	
Mack, J. Hush little polar bear	E	Nevius, C. Building with Dad	
Mackall, D. D. First day	E	Nevius, C. Karate hour	
Macken, J. E. Baby says moo!	E	Nevius, C. Soccer hour	
Macken, J. E. Waiting out the storm	E	Newbery, L. Posy!	
MacLachlan, P. The Poet's Dog	E	Newman, J. Hand book	
Mahy, M. 17 kings and 42 elephants	E	Newman, L. Donovan's big day	
Mahy, M. Bubble trouble	E	Niemann, C. Subway	
Make way for readers	E	Norman, K. Ten on the sled	
Mama's kisses	E	Numeroff, L. J. When sheep sleep	
Mandel, P. Jackhammer Sam	E	Nutt, R. Amy's light	
Manushkin, F. The belly book	E	Odanaka, B. Crazy day at the Critter Cafe	
Marciano, J. B. Madeline at the White House	E	O'Hair, M. My kitten	
Marcus, K. Scritch-scratch a perfect match	E	O'Hair, M. My pup	
Mariconda, B. Ten for me	E	On Bird Hill	
Markes, J. Shhhhh! Everybody's sleeping	E	One starry night	
Martin, B. Barn dance!	E	Ormerod, J. If you're happy and you know it!	
Martin, B. A beasty story	E	Owen, K. I could be, you could be	

STORIES WITHOUT WORDS

Drawing 741.2
TEMPLES
Sobol, R. The mysteries of Angkor Wat 959.6
TEMPLES
See also Buildings; Religious institutions
Ten. Fic
Ten. Myracle, L. Fic
Ten big toes and a prince's nose. Gow, N. E
Ten birds. Young, C. E
Ten black dots. Crews, D. E
TEN COMMANDMENTS -- FICTION
Sadie and the big mountain E
Ten days and nine nights. Heo, Y. E
Ten for me. Mariconda, B. E
Ten little beasties. Emberley, R. E
Ten little caterpillars. E
Ten little fingers and ten little toes. Fox, M. E
Ten little puppies. Ada, A. F. 398.8
Ten moonstruck piglets. E
Ten on the sled. Norman, K. E
Ten orange pumpkins. Savage, S. E
Ten red apples. Hutchins, P. E
Ten rules for living with my sister. Martin, A. M. Fic
Ten rules you absolutely must not break if you want to survive the school bus. E
Ten thank-yous. E
Ten tiny babies. Katz, K. E
Ten, nine, eight. Bang, M. 513
Ten-Gallon Bart beats the heat. Crummel, S. S. E
TENBY (WALES) -- FICTION
Brodien-Jones, C. The glass puzzle Fic
Tenderini, Emanuele
Chwast, S. The odyssey 741.5
Tenement. Bial, R. 974.7
TENEMENT HOUSES -- FICTION
Manning, M. J. Laundry day E
TenNapel, Doug
Cardboard 741.5
Tenner, Suzanne
(il) McDonald, M. Judy Moody goes to Hollywood 791.43
Tennessee. Somervill, B. A. 976.8
TENNESSEE
Somervill, B. A. Tennessee 976.8
TENNESSEE -- FICTION
Isaacs, A. Swamp Angel E
Lloyd, N. A snicker of magic Fic
McKissack, P. C. Abby takes a stand Fic
McKissack, P. C. Goin' someplace special E
McKissack, P. C. Tippy Lemmey Fic
Snyder, L. Penny Dreadful Fic
Steele, W. O. The perilous road Fic
Tenniel, John, 1820-1914
(il) Carroll, L. Alice's adventures in Wonderland Fic
Tennis. Wendorff, A. 796.342
TENNIS
Bow, P. Tennis science 796.342
Gifford, C. Tennis 796.342

Marsico, K. Tennis 796.3
Wendorff, A. Tennis 796.3
Woods, M. Ace! 796.3
Tennis. Gifford, C. 796.3
TENNIS
See also Sports
Tennis. Marsico, K. 796.3
TENNIS -- BIOGRAPHY
Deans, K. Playing to win: the story of Althea Gibson
Hubbard, C. Game, set, match, champion Arthur Ashe
Stauffacher, S. Nothing but trouble
TENNIS -- FICTION
Hicks, B. Doubles troubles F
TENNIS -- TOURNAMENTS
See also Sports tournaments
TENNIS PLAYERS
Deans, K. Playing to win: the story of Althea Gibson
Hubbard, C. Game, set, match, champion Arthur Ashe
Krull, K. Lives of the athletes 7
Stauffacher, S. Nothing but trouble
TENNIS PLAYERS -- BIOGRAPHY
Martina & Chrissie 796.3
Tennis science. Bow, P. 796.3
TENSION (PSYCHOLOGY) *See* Stress (Psychology)
Tentacles! Redmond 5
Tenth book of junior authors and illustrators. Rockman, C. 920.0
The tenth good thing about Barney. Viorst, J.
TENTS
See also Camping
Tenzing Norbu
Secret of the snow leopard
Tenzing Norgay, 1914-1986
About
Berne, E. C. Summiting Everest 796.5
Bodden, V. To the top of Mount Everest 796.
Burleigh, R. Tiger of the snows
Helfand, L. Conquering Everest 741
Teplin, Scott
The clock without a face F
TEPOZTLÁN (MEXICO) -- HISTORY -- 20TH CENTUR
Nicholson, D. M. The school the Aztec Eagles built 940.5
Terban, Marvin
Mad as a wet hen! and other funny idioms 4
Scholastic dictionary of idioms 4
Scholastic dictionary of spelling 4
Scholastic guide to grammar 4
TEREZÍN (CZECH REPUBLIC: CONCENTRATIO CAMP)
Thomson, R. Terezin 940.
Terezin. Thomson, R. 940.
TEREZIN (CZECHOSLOVAKIA: CONCENTRATIO CAMP)
Volavkova, H. --I never saw another butterfly-- 741
TEREZIN (CZECHOSLOVAKIA: CONCENTRATIO CAMP)
See also Concentration camps

U

U'Ren, Andrea
  (il) DeFelice, C. C. One potato, two potato   E
  (il) Kimmel, E. A. Stormy's hat   E
  (il) Moss, M. The bravest woman in America   92
  (il) Schubert, L. Feeding the sheep   E

U.S. FISH AND WILDLIFE SERVICE -- FORENSICS LABORATORY
  Jackson, D. M. The wildlife detectives   363.2

UAVS (UNMANNED AERIAL VEHICLES) *See* Drone aircraft

Ubiquitous.   811

Uchida, Yoshiko
  The bracelet   E
  A jar of dreams   Fic
  Journey to Topaz   Fic

Udry, Janice May
  The moon jumpers   E
  A tree is nice   E

Uegaki, Chieri
  Rosie and Buttercup   E
  Suki's kimono   E

Uff, Caroline
  (il) Doyle, M. Get happy   E

UFOS *See* Unidentified flying objects

Uganda. Barlas, R.   967.61

UGANDA
  Barlas, R. Uganda   967.61
  Shoveller, H. Ryan and Jimmy   361.7

Ugliano, Natascia
  (il) Gellman, E. B. Netta and her plant   E
  (il) Jules, J. Abraham's search for God   222
  (il) Jules, J. Benjamin and the silver goblet   222
  (il) Jules, J. Miriam in the desert   222
  (il) Jules, J. Sarah laughs   222

Ugly Cat & Pablo.   Fic
The ugly dinosaur. Bardoe, C.   E
The ugly duckling. Andersen, H. C.   E
The ugly duckling. Pinkney, J.   E
The ugly duckling. Watts, B.   E
The ugly duckling. Braun, S.   E
The ugly duckling. Mitchell, S.   E
The ugly dumpling. Campisi, S.   E
Ugly Pie. Wheeler, L.   E

Uh-oh Cleo [series]
  Harper, J. Underpants on my head   Fic

Uh-oh! DePalma, M. N.   E
Uh-oh, Cleo. Harper, J.   Fic
Uh-oh, dodo!   E

Uhlberg, Myron
  Dad, Jackie, and me   E
  The sound of all things   E
  A storm called Katrina   E

Uhlman, Tom
  (il) Carson, M. K. The bat scientists   599.4
  (il) Carson, M. K. Emi and the rhino scientist   599.66

  (il) Carson, M. K. Mission to Pluto   629.4
  (il) Carson, M. K. The park scientists   333.7
  (il) Rusch, E. Eruption!   363.3

UIGHUR (TURKIC PEOPLE) -- FICTION
  La Valley, J. The Vine basket   F

Ukraine. Bassis, V.   947

UKRAINE
  Bassis, V. Ukraine   947

UKULELE -- FICTION
  Cox, J. Ukulele Hayley   F

Ukulele Hayley. Cox, J.   F

Ulrich, George
  (il) Murphy, S. J. Divide and ride   51

The ultimate 10. Natural disasters [series]
  Stewart, M. Blizzards and winter storms   551.5

The ultimate dinopedia. Lessem, D.   567
Ultimate fighting. Wiseman, B.   796

ULTIMATE FIGHTING CHAMPIONSHIP (ORGANIZATION)
  Wiseman, B. Ultimate fighting   796

Ultimate guide to baseball. Buckley, J.   796.35
Ultimate guide to football. Buckley, J.   796.33
The ultimate guide to grandmas and grandpas. Jones, S. L.
The ultimate guide to your microscope. Levine, S.   502
The ultimate indoor games book. Gunter, V. A.   79
Ultimate trains. McMahon, P.   38

ULTRASONIC WAVES
  See also Sound waves; Ultrasonics

ULTRASONICS
  See also Sound

Uluru, Australia's Aboriginal heart. Arnold, C.   99

ULURU-KATA TJUTA NATIONAL PARK (AUSTRALIA
  Arnold, C. Uluru, Australia's Aboriginal heart   9

Ulysses Moore [series]
  Baccalario, P. The long-lost map   F

Uman, Jennifer
  (il) Jemmy button

Umansky, Kaye
  Clover Twig and the magical cottage   F
  Solomon Snow and the stolen jewel   F

The umbrella. Schubert, I.
Umbrella. Iwamatsu, A. J.
The Umbrella Queen. Bridges, S. Y.
Umbrella summer. Graff, L.   F

UMBRELLAS AND PARASOLS
  See also Clothing and dress

UMBRELLAS AND PARASOLS -- FICTION
  Bridges, S. Y. The Umbrella Queen
  Franson, S. E. Un-brella
  Iwamatsu, A. J. Umbrella
  Na, I. S. The thingamabob
  Schubert, I. The umbrella

Un-brella. Franson, S. E.
The un-forgotten coat. Cottrell Boyce, F.   F
UnBEElievables. Florian, D.   8
Unbored.   79

UNBORN CHILD *See* Fetus

ncle Andy's. Warhola, J. **E**
ncle Bobby's wedding. Brannen, S. S. **E**
ncle Elephant. Lobel, A. **E**
ncle Jed's barbershop. Mitchell, M. K. **E**
ncle monarch and the Day of the Dead. Goldman, J. **E**
ncle Nacho's hat. Rohmer, H. **398.2**
ncle Peter's amazing Chinese wedding. Look, L. **E**
ncle Pirate. Rees, D. **Fic**
ncle Pirate to the rescue. Rees, D. **Fic**
ncle Rain Cloud. Johnston, T. **E**
ncle Remus, the complete tales. Lester, J. **398.2**
ncle Wally's old brown shoe. Edwards, W. **E**
ncle Willie and the soup kitchen. DiSalvo, D. **E**

NCLES
Hartfield, C. Me and Uncle Romie **E**
Henkes, K. The birthday room **Fic**
Horvath, P. Everything on a waffle **Fic**
Johnston, T. Uncle Rain Cloud **E**

NCLES
See also Family

NCLES -- FICTION
Applesauce weather **Fic**
Lacey, J. Island of Thieves **Fic**
Schwartz, A. Willie and Uncle Bill **E**

ncommon animals [series]
Aronin, M. Aye-aye **599.8**
Goldish, M. Fossa **599.74**
Markovics, J. L. Tasmanian devil **599.2**
Markovics, J. L. Weddell seal **599.79**
Person, S. Arctic fox **599.77**

ncommoners [series]
Bell, J. The crooked sixpence **Fic**
he **uncorker** of ocean bottles. Cuevas, M. **E**
ncovering Earth's crust. Storad, C. J. **551.1**
nder my hat. **S**
nder the egg. Fitzgerald, L. M. **Fic**
nder the freedom tree. **811.54**
nder the green hill. Sullivan, L. L. **Fic**
nder the hood. Merlin, C. **E**
nder the ice. Conlan, K. **578.7**
nder the mambo moon. **811**
nder the Ramadan moon. Whitman, S. **297.3**
nder the royal palms. Ada, A. F. **92**
nder the snow. Stewart, M. **591.7**
nder the spell of the moon. **741.6**
nder the waves. Woodward, J. **551.46**
nder the weather. **S**
nder their skin. Haddix, M. P. **Fic**
nder Wildwood. **Fic**
nder your skin. Manning, M. **612**

NDERACHIEVERS
See also Students
nderground. Macaulay, D. **624**
nderground. Fleming, D. **E**
nderground. Evans, S. W. **973.7**
he **underground** abductor. Hale, N. **741.5**
nderground animals. Racanelli, M. **591.5**

UNDERGROUND ARCHITECTURE
See also Architecture
UNDERGROUND AREAS -- FICTION
Fleming, D. Underground **E**
UNDERGROUND CONSTRUCTION
Stefoff, R. Building tunnels **624.1**
UNDERGROUND ECONOMY
See also Economics; Small business
UNDERGROUND LEADERS
Bartoletti, S. C. The boy who dared **Fic**
The **Underground** Railroad. Heinrichs, A. **326**
The **Underground** Railroad. Bial, R. **326**
The **Underground** Railroad. Raatma, L. **973.7**
The **Underground** Railroad. Williams, C. **973.7**
UNDERGROUND RAILROAD
Adler, D. A. A picture book of Harriet Tubman **305.5**
Adler, D. A. Harriet Tubman and the Underground Railroad **973.7**
Bial, R. The Underground Railroad **326**
Evans, S. W. Underground **973.7**
Hamilton, V. Many thousand gone **326**
Haskins, J. Get on board: the story of the Underground Railroad **326**
Heinrichs, A. The Underground Railroad **326**
Huey, L. M. American archaeology uncovers the Underground Railroad **973.7**
Landau, E. Fleeing to freedom on the Underground Railroad **973.7**
Morrow, B. O. A good night for freedom **E**
Raatma, L. The Underground Railroad **973.7**
Weatherford, C. B. Moses **92**
Williams, C. The Underground Railroad **973.7**
UNDERGROUND RAILROAD -- COMIC BOOKS, STRIPS, ETC.
Hale, N. The underground abductor **741.5**
UNDERGROUND RAILROAD -- FICTION
Cole, H. Unspoken **E**
Freedom song **E**
Grifalconi, A. Ain't nobody a stranger to me **E**
Grimes, N. Chasing freedom **Fic**
Levine, E. Henry's freedom box **E**
Monjo, F. N. The drinking gourd **E**
Morrow, B. O. A good night for freedom **E**
Nolen, J. Eliza's freedom road **Fic**
Polacco, P. January's sparrow **Fic**
Raven, M. Night boat to freedom **E**
Stroud, B. The patchwork path **E**
Walker, S. M. Freedom song **E**
Winter, J. Follow the drinking gourd **E**
UNDERGROUND RAILROAD -- OHIO -- HISTORY
Fradin, D. B. The price of freedom **973.7**
UNDERGROUND RAILROAD -- POETRY
Lawrence, J. Harriet and the Promised Land **811**
Shange, N. Freedom's a-callin' me **811**
UNDERGROUND RAILROADS *See* Subways
Underground towns, treetops, and other animal hiding places. Halpern, M. **591.47**

Carbone, E. Heroes of the surf   **E**

UNITED STATES. NAVY

Llanas, S. G. Women of the U.S. Navy   **359**

Lunis, N. The takedown of Osama bin Laden   **958.104**

Sheinkin, S. The Port Chicago 50   **940.54**

UNITED STATES. NAVY -- BIOGRAPHY

   See also Biography

UNITED STATES. NAVY. FICTION

Holt, K. W. Piper Reed gets a job   **Fic**

Holt, K. W. Piper Reed, the great gypsy   **Fic**

UNITED STATES. NAVY. SEALS

Lunis, N. The takedown of Osama bin Laden   **958.104**

UNITED STATES. PUBLIC HEALTH SERVICE -- HISTORY

Jarrow, G. Red madness   **616.3**

UNITED STATES. SUPREME COURT

Adler, D. A. A picture book of Thurgood Marshall   **347**

UNITED STATES. SUPREME COURT -- BIOGRAPHY

   See also Biography

UNITED STATES. WHITE HOUSE OFFICE

White House kids   **973.09**

The United States: past and present [series]

Bailey, D. Kansas   **978.1**

Brezina, C. Arizona   **979.1**

Brezina, C. Indiana   **977.2**

Brezina, C. New Mexico   **978.9**

Bringle, J. Nebraska   **978.2**

Byers, A. West Virginia   **975.4**

Byers, A. Wyoming   **978.7**

Casil, A. S. Mississippi   **976.2**

Ching, J. Utah   **979.2**

Ciarleglio, L. New Hampshire   **974.2**

Cook, C. Kentucky   **976.9**

DaSilva-Gordon, M. Puerto Rico   **972.95**

Dorman, R. L. Oklahoma   **976.6**

Freedman, J. Iowa   **977.7**

Freedman, J. Louisiana   **976.3**

Freedman, J. Massachusetts   **974.4**

Furgang, A. Rhode Island   **974.5**

Harmon, D. Minnesota   **977.6**

Harmon, D. South Carolina   **975.7**

Harmon, D. Washington   **979.7**

Hasan, H. Pennsylvania   **974.8**

Heos, B. Alabama   **976.1**

Heos, B. Colorado   **978.8**

Heos, B. Wisconsin   **977.5**

La Bella, L. California   **979.4**

La Bella, L. Connecticut   **974.6**

Levy, J. Arkansas   **976.7**

Levy, J. Michigan   **977.4**

Lew, K. North Carolina   **975.6**

Lew, K. Ohio   **977.1**

Lewis, M. J. North Dakota   **978.4**

Mattern, J. Alaska   **979.8**

Mattern, J. Hawaii   **996.9**

Mattern, J. Illinois   **977.3**

Mattern, J. Maryland   **975.2**

Mattern, J. New Jersey   **974.**

Mills, J. E. New York   **974.**

Nagle, J. Texas   **976.**

Petersen, C. South Dakota   **978.**

Peterson, J. M. Maine   **974.**

Porterfield, J. Montana   **978.**

Porterfield, J. Virginia   **975.**

Roza, G. Missouri   **977.**

Roza, G. Nevada   **979.**

Roza, G. Oregon   **979.**

Sawyer, S. Florida   **975.**

Sommers, M. Vermont   **974.**

Sonneborn, L. District of Columbia   **975.**

Stanley, J. Idaho   **979**

Watson, S. Georgia   **975**

Wolny, P. Delaware   **975**

The **United** States: past and present [series]   **97**

UNITED STEELWORKERS OF AMERICA

   See also Labor unions

United tweets of America. Talbott, H.   **97**

UNIVERSAL HISTORY *See* World history

Universe.   **523**

UNIVERSE

A black hole is not a hole   **523**

Universe   **523**

The universe, black holes, and the Big Bang   **523**

UNIVERSE -- FICTION

Mass, W. Pi in the sky   **F**

The **universe,** black holes, and the Big Bang.   **523**

UNIVERSITÄT MÜNCHEN -- RIOT, 1943

Freedman, R. We will not be silent   **9**

UNIVERSITY OF WASHINGTON -- ROWING -- HISTORY

Brown, D. J. The boys in the boat   **797.**

The **unkindness** of ravens.   **741**

Unlikely pairs. Raczka, B.   **7**

Unlucky charms. Rex, A.   **F**

UNMANNED AERIAL VEHICLES *See* Drone aircraft

UNMARRIED FATHERS

   See also Fathers; Single parents

UNMARRIED MOTHERS

   See also Mothers; Single parents

Uno, dos, tres: one, two, three. Mora, P.

The **unofficial** LEGO builder's guide. Bedford, A.   **688**

The **unofficial** Narnia cookbook. Bucholz, D.   **641.5**

Unplugged play. Conner, B.   **790**

The **unseen** guest.   **F**

The unseen world of Poppy Malone [series]

Harper, S. A gaggle of goblins   **F**

The **Unsinkable** Walker Bean. Renier, A.   **741**

Unsolved history [series]

Blackwood, G. L. Enigmatic events   **9**

Blackwood, G. L. Legends or lies?   **398**

Unspoken. Cole, H.

Untamed. Silvey, A.

Unusual chickens for the exceptional poultry farmer. Jon K.   **F**

VETERINARIANS -- FICTION
Arnold, E. K. A boy called bat   **Fic**
Bruel, N. Bad kitty goes to the vet   **E**
Kelly, J. Counting sheep   **Fic**
Kelly, J. Skunked: Calpurnia Tate, girl vet   **Fic**
VETERINARY MEDICINE
Jackson, D. M. ER vets   **636.089**
VETERINARY MEDICINE
See also Medicine
Vetter, Jennifer Riggs
Down by the station   **782.42**
VIADUCTS *See* Bridges
VIBRATION
See also Mechanics; Sound
VICE
See also Conduct of life; Ethics; Human behavior
VICE-PRESIDENTS
Adler, D. A. A picture book of John and Abigail Adams **92**
Adler, D. A. A picture book of Thomas Jefferson   **92**
Aronson, B. Richard M. Nixon   **92**
Bradley, K. B. Jefferson's sons   **Fic**
Brown, D. Teedie   **92**
Duel!   **973.4**
Elish, D. Theodore Roosevelt   **92**
Fleming, C. The hatmaker's sign   **E**
Fritz, J. Bully for you, Teddy Roosevelt!   **92**
Gold, S. D. Lyndon B. Johnson   **92**
Gottfried, T. Millard Fillmore   **92**
Harness, C. The remarkable, rough-riding life of Theodore
    Roosevelt and the rise of empire America   **92**
Harness, C. The revolutionary John Adams   **973.3**
Hollihan, K. L. Theodore Roosevelt for kids   **92**
Jurmain, S. The worst of friends   **973.4**
Keating, F. Theodore   **92**
Kerley, B. Those rebels, John and Tom   **973.4**
Kimmelman, L. Mind your manners, Alice Roosevelt! **E**
Krensky, S. Dangerous crossing   **Fic**
Miller, B. M. Thomas Jefferson for kids   **92**
Smith, L. John, Paul, George & Ben   **E**
St. George, J. You're on your way, Teddy Roosevelt! **92**
Wade, M. D. Amazing president Theodore Roosevelt   **92**
Wadsworth, G. Camping with the president   **92**
VICE-PRESIDENTS
See also Presidents
VICE-PRESIDENTS -- FICTION
Daneshvari, G. The League of Unexceptional Children **Fic**
Vick, Michael, 1980-
About
Patent, D. H. Saving Audie   **636.7**
VICTIMS OF ATOMIC BOMBINGS *See* Atomic bomb
    victims
VICTIMS OF CRIMES
See also Crime
Victoria, Queen of Great Britain, 1819-1901
About
Deedy, C. A. The Cheshire Cheese cat   **Fic**
Krull, K. Lives of extraordinary women   **920**

The mouse with the question mark tail
Queen Victoria's Bathing Machine
Victory. Cooper, S.
Vidal, Beatriz
(il) Aardema, V. Bringing the rain to Kapiti Plain **398**
(il) Alvarez, J. A gift of gracias
Vidal, Oriol
(il) Dahl, M. Nap time for Kitty
Vidali, Valerio
(il) Jemmy button
Video game developer. Jozefowicz, C.   **794**
VIDEO GAMES
Bedell, J. So, you want to be a coder?   **00**
Egan, J. How video game designers use math   **794**
Gallaway, B. Game on!   **02**
Jozefowicz, C. Video game developer   **794**
Oxlade, C. Gaming technology   **794**
VIDEO GAMES
See also Electronic toys; Games
VIDEO GAMES -- FICTION
Brown, G. Josh Baxter levels up
Game over, Pete Watson
VIDEO GAMES AND CHILDREN
Gallaway, B. Game on!   **02**
VIDEO GAMES AND TEENAGERS
Gallaway, B. Game on!   **02**
VIDEO RECORDINGS -- PRODUCTION AND DIRE
TION -- FICTION
Farrant, N. After Iris
VIDEO TELEPHONE
See also Data transmission systems; Telephone; Tele
    sion
Viegas, Jennifer
Beethoven's world
VIENNA (AUSTRIA) -- FICTION
Glatstein, J. Emil and Karl
Ibbotson, E. The star of Kazan
VIENNNA (AUSTRIA) -- HISTORY -- 19TH CENTU
-- FICTION
A gift for Mama
Vietnam. Green, J.   **959**
VIETNAM
Green, J. Vietnam   **95**
Guile, M. Culture in Vietnam   **95**
VIETNAM -- FICTION
In a village by the sea
Lai, T. Listen, Slowly
VIETNAM VETERANS MEMORIAL (WASHINGTO
D.C.) -- FICTION
Bunting, E. The Wall
VIETNAM WAR, 1961-1975
Collins, S. Year of the jungle
McNab, C. 50 things you should know about the Vietn
    War   **95**
VIETNAM WAR, 1961-1975 -- CHILDREN
Skrypuch, M. F. Last airlift   **959.7**
VIETNAM WAR, 1961-1975 -- FICTION

AITING (PHILOSOPHY) -- FICTION

Henkes, K. Waiting   E

'aiting for Anya. Morpurgo, M.   Fic

'aiting for Augusta. Lawson, J.   Fic

'aiting for ice. Markle, S.   599.786

'aiting for normal. Connor, L.   Fic

'aiting for Pumpsie.   E

'aiting for the BiblioBurro. Brown, M.   E

'aiting for the magic. MacLachlan, P.   Fic

'aiting for the owl's call.   E

'aiting for wings. Ehlert, L.   595.78

'aiting for winter. Meschenmoser, S.   E

'aiting is not easy!   E

'aiting out the storm. Macken, J. E.   E

'aiting to forget. Welch, S. K.   Fic

AKA

Engle, M. Orangutanka   E

ake up!   811.54

akefield, Ruth

About

Thimmesh, C. Girls think of everything   920

aking up is hard to do. Sedaka, N.   782.42

AL-MART STORES, INC.

Blumenthal, K. Mr. Sam   92

ald, Christina

(il) Gerber, C. Annie Jump Cannon, astronomer   92

alden then & now. McCurdy, M.   818

alden, Katherine

Meerkats   599.74

Rhinoceroses   599.66

Warthogs   599.63

Wildebeests   599.64

alden, Mark

H.I.V.E   Fic

aldman, Debby

Clever Rachel   398.2

A sack full of feathers   398.2

aldman, Neil, 1947-

(il) Schecter, E. The family Haggadah   296.4

A land of big dreamers   920

Out of the shadows   92

The snowflake   551.48

About

Waldman, N. Out of the shadows   92

aldman, Stuart

The last river   978

ALDORF-ASTORIA HOTEL (NEW YORK, N.Y.) -- FIC-TION.

Avi City of orphans   Fic

aldrep, Richard

(il) Crowe, E. Surfer of the century   92

aldron, K.

(il) Rosen, M. Tiny Little Fly   E

aldron, Kevin

Mr. Peek and the misunderstanding at the zoo   E

aldron, Melanie

How to read a map   912.01

Wales. Hestler, A.   942.9

WALES

Hestler, A. Wales   942.9

WALES -- FICTION

Bond, N. A string in the harp   Fic

Brodien-Jones, C. The glass puzzle   Fic

Cooper, S. The grey king   Fic

Cooper, S. Silver on the tree   Fic

Newbery, L. Lost boy   Fic

Nimmo, J. The snow spider   Fic

WALES -- HISTORY -- 1063-1284 -- FICTION

Brodien-Jones, C. The glass puzzle   Fic

A walk in London. Rubbino, S.   942

A walk in New York. Rubbino, S.   917

A Walk in Paris. Rubbino, S.   944

A walk in the boreal forest. Johnson, R. L.   577.3

A walk in the deciduous forest. Johnson, R. L.   577.3

A walk in the desert. Johnson, R. L.   577.54

A walk in the forest.   E

A walk in the prairie. Johnson, R. L.   577.4

A walk in the tundra. Johnson, R. L.   577.5

Walk on! Frazee, M.   E

Walk two moons. Creech, S.   Fic

Walk With Me.   E

Walker, Alice

There is a flower at the tip of my nose smelling me   811

Why war is never a good idea   811

Walker, Anna

(il) Peggy   E

(il) Quay, E. Good night, sleep tight   E

I love Christmas   E

Walker, Barbara Muhs

The Little House cookbook   641.5

Walker, C. J., Madame, 1867-1919

About

Lasky, K. Vision of beauty: the story of Sarah Breedlove Walker   92

Walker, David

(il) Adler, V. Baby, come away   E

(il) Bennett, K. Your daddy was just like you   E

(il) Bennett, K. Your mommy was just like you   E

(il) Boelts, M. Before you were mine   E

(il) Elya, S. M. No more, por favor   E

(il) Gershator, P. Time for a hug   E

(il) Macken, J. E. Baby says moo!   E

(il) Martin, D. Peep and Ducky   E

(il) Parenteau, S. Bears on chairs   E

(il) Root, P. Flip, flap, fly!   E

Walker, Ida

(jt. auth) Indovino, S. C. Belgium   949.304

(jt. auth) Indovino, S. C. Germany   943

Walker, Kate

I hate books!   Fic

Walker, Mary Edwards, 1832-1919

About

Harness, C. Mary Walker wears the pants   92

Walker, Niki

Evolution revolution **576.8**
Life as we know it **570**
What goes on in my head? **612.8**
Winston, Sam
(il) A child of books **E**
Winston, Sherri
President of the whole fifth grade **Fic**
Winter. Schnur, S. **E**
WINTER
Anderson, M. Explore winter! **508.2**
Bancroft, H. Animals in winter **591.56**
Carlson-Voiles, P. Someone walks by **591.7**
Freedman, C. Gooseberry Goose **E**
Gerber, C. Winter trees **582.16**
Gillman, C. The kids' winter fun book **790.1**
Glaser, L. Not a buzz to be found **595.7**
The grasshopper & the ants **E**
Hansen, A. S. Bugs and bugsicles **595.7**
Messner, K. Over and under the snow **591.4**
Rustad, M. E. H. Animals in fall **578.4**
Schnur, S. Winter **E**
Schuette, S. L. Let's look at winter **508.2**
Smith, S. Winter **508.2**
Stewart, M. Under the snow **591.7**
Twelve kinds of ice **Fic**
WINTER
See also Seasons
Winter. Smith, S. **508.2**
WINTER -- FICTION
Brenner, T. And then comes Christmas **E**
Cold snap **E**
Doyle, E. Sleep tight, farm **E**
Johnston, T. Winter is coming **E**
Little penguins **E**
Mr. Putter & Tabby hit the slope **E**
WINTER -- FOLKLORE
Aylesworth, J. The mitten **398.2**
WINTER -- PICTORIAL WORKS
Wonderful winter **508.2**
WINTER -- POETRY
Alarcon, F. X. Iguanas in the snow and other winter poems **811**
Florian, D. Winter eyes **811**
Hines, A. G. Winter lights **811**
Prelutsky, J. It's snowing! it's snowing! **811**
Winter Bees & Other Poems of the Cold **811.54**
Winter Bees & Other Poems of the Cold. **811.54**
Winter eyes. Florian, D. **811**
WINTER GARDENING
See also Gardening
Winter is coming. Johnston, T. **E**
Winter is the warmest season. Stringer, L. **E**
Winter lights. Hines, A. G. **811**
The **winter** of the robots. Scaletta, K. **Fic**
The **winter** room. Paulsen, G. **Fic**
Winter sky. Giff, P. R. **Fic**
WINTER SOLSTICE

Pfeffer, W. The shortest day **394.**
WINTER SOLSTICE -- FICTION
King, T. A Coyote solstice tale
WINTER SPORTS
Macy, S. Freeze frame **796.**
WINTER SPORTS
See also Sports
Winter trees. Gerber, C. **582.**
The **winter** visitors. Hayes, K.
Winter's tail. Hatkoff, J. **63**
Winter, Jeanette
(il) Johnston, T. Day of the Dead **39**
Biblioburro
Calavera abecedario
Follow the drinking gourd
Henri's scissors
Josefina **513**
Kali's song
The librarian of Basra
Malala, a brave girl from Pakistan/Iqbal, a brave boy from Pakistan **9**
Mama
My name is Georgia
Nanuk the ice bear
Nasreen's secret school **371.**
(il) The secret project **355.8**
Wangari's trees of peace
The watcher: Jane Goodall's life with the chimps
Winter, Jonah
Born and bred in the Great Depression **97(**
The fabulous feud of Gilbert & Sullivan
Frida
The Founding Fathers
Gertrude is Gertrude is Gertrude is Gertrude
Here comes the garbage barge!
Jazz age Josephine
Joltin' Joe DiMaggio
Just behave, Pablo Picasso! **70**
Lillian's right to vote
Mickey Mantle
Peaceful heroes **9**
Roberto Clemente
The secret project **355.8**
Sonia Sotomayor
Steel Town
Wild women of the Wild West **9**
You never heard of Casey Stengel?!
You never heard of Sandy Koufax!?
You never heard of Willie Mays?!
Winterberg, Jenna
Light and its effects **5**
Winterberries and apple blossoms. Forler, N. **8**
Winterbottom, Julie
Frightlopedia **031.**
Winters, Ben H.
The mystery of the missing everything **F**
The secret life of Ms. Finkleman

OK COOKING
See also Cooking

olcott, Dyanna
  il) Kuskin, K. I am me   **E**

olf brother. Paver, M.   **Fic**

olf camp. Zuill, A.   **E**

OLF CHILDREN *See* Wild children

olf Hollow. Wolk, L.   **Fic**

olf in the snow. Cordell, M.   **E**

olf island. Godkin, C.   **577**

e **wolf** keepers. Broach, E.   **Fic**

olf pie. Seabrooke, B.   **Fic**

olf song. Bevis, M. E.   **E**

olf spiders. Markle, S.   **595.4**

e **wolf** wilder. Rundell, K.   **Fic**

olf won't bite! Gravett, E.   **E**

olf! wolf! Rocco, J.   **E**

e **wolf's** boy. Beckhorn, S. W.   **Fic**

e **wolf's** chicken stew. Kasza, K.   **E**

olf's coming! Kulka, J.   **E**

olf, Gita
Devi, D. Following my paint brush   **92**
The Enduring Ark   **222**
Gobble You Up!   **398.2**

olf, Joan M.
Someone named Eva   **Fic**

olf, Laurie Goldrich
Recyclo-gami   **745.5**

olf, Sallie
The robin makes a laughing sound   **598**
Truck stuck   **E**

olf, Shelby A.
(ed) Handbook of research on children's and young adult literature   **028.5**

e **Wolf-birds.** Dawson, W.   **E**

olfe, Gillian
Look! Drawing the line in art   **750.1**
Look! Seeing the light in art   **750.1**

olff, Ashley
(il) Edwards, D. The pen that Pa built   **E**
(il) Raffi Baby Beluga   **782.42**
(il) Ross, M. E. Mama's milk   **E**
(il) Ryder, J. Each living thing   **E**
(il) Siddals, M. M. Compost stew   **E**
(il) Slate, J. Miss Bindergarten celebrates the 100th day of kindergarten   **E**
Baby Bear sees blue   **E**

olff, Ferida
It is the wind   **E**
The story blanket   **E**

olfgang Amadeus Mozart. Riggs, K.   **92**

olfie the bunny. Dyckman, A.   **E**

olfram
Paterson, K. Parzival   **398.2**

olfsgruber, Linda
(il) Lottridge, C. B. Stories from the life of Jesus   **232.9**

olfsnail. Campbell, S. C.   **594**

Wolfson, Jill
Home, and other big, fat lies   **Fic**
What I call life   **Fic**

Wolfson, Ron
Hoffman, L. A. What you will see inside a synagogue   **296.4**

Wolitzer, Meg
The fingertips of Duncan Dorfman   **Fic**

Wolk, Lauren
Wolf Hollow   **Fic**

Wolk-Stanley, Jessica
(il) Cobb, V. How to really fool yourself   **152.1**

Wolny, Philip
Delaware   **975.1**
Waterfowl   **799.2**

WOLOF (AFRICAN PEOPLE)
Paul, M. One plastic bag   **363.7**

Wolven. Toft, D.   **Fic**

WOLVERINES
Jacques, B. Rakkety Tam   **Fic**

Wolves. Gravett, E.   **E**

WOLVES
Bidner, J. Is my dog a wolf?   **636.7**
Brandenburg, J. Face to face with wolves   **599.77**
Cohn, S. One wolf howls   **599.77**
Dawson, W. The Wolf-birds   **E**
George, J. C. The wolves are back   **599.77**
Gibbons, G. Wolves   **599.74**
Goldish, M. Red wolves   **599.77**
Markle, S. Wolves   **599.77**
Marshall, J. Swine Lake   **E**
McAllister, I. The sea wolves   **599.77**
Patent, D. H. When the wolves returned   **599.77**
Read, T. C. Exploring the world of wolves   **599.77**
Riggs, K. Wolves   **599.77**
Rutherford, C. A dog is a dog   **636.7**
Slade, S. What if there were no gray wolves?   **577.3**
Whatley, B. Wait! No paint!   **E**
Wolves. Riggs, K.   **599.77**
Wolves. Gibbons, G.   **599.74**
Wolves. Markle, S.   **599.77**

WOLVES -- FICTION
Archer, D. Big Bad Wolf   **E**
Beckhorn, S. W. The wolf's boy   **Fic**
Black, H. The copper gauntlet   **Fic**
Broach, E. The wolf keepers   **Fic**
Cordell, M. Wolf in the snow   **E**
Dyckman, A. Wolfie the bunny   **E**
Gliori, D. What's the time, Mr. Wolf?   **E**
Gravett, E. Wolf won't bite!   **E**
Leroy, J. A well-mannered young wolf   **E**
Little Red Riding Hood   **E**
Little wolf's first howling   **E**
Rundell, K. The wolf wilder   **Fic**
Stiefvater, M. Hunted   **Fic**
Ts'o, P. Whispers of the wolf   **E**
The unseen guest   **Fic**
Virginia Wolf   **Fic**

O'Neal, C. We visit Yemen — 953.3

Yep, Kathleen S.

Yep, L. The dragon's child — Fic

Yep, Laurence, 1948-

Auntie Tiger — E
City of fire — Fic
The dragon's child — Fic
A dragon's guide to making your human smarter — Fic
A dragon's guide to the care and feeding of humans — Fic
The lost garden — 979.4
The magic paintbrush — Fic
The star maker — Fic
The traitor — Fic
When the circus came to town — Fic

About

Yep, L. The lost garden — 979.4

Yertle the turtle and other stories. Seuss — E
Yes Day! Rosenthal, A. K. — E
Yes she can! Stout, G. — 920
Yes, let's. Longstreth, G. G. — E
Yesterday I had the blues. Frame, J. A. — E

YETI

See also Monsters; Mythical animals

YETI -- FICTION

Edmundson, C. Yeti, turn out the light! — E
Harper, C. M. Alien encounter — Fic
Kwan, J. Dear Yeti — E
Magoon, S. The boy who cried Bigfoot! — E
Yeti, turn out the light! Edmundson, C. — E

Yezerski, Thomas

(il) Cutler, J. Rose and Riley — E
Meadowlands — 577.69

YIDDISH LANGUAGE

Sussman, J. K. My first Yiddish word book — 439

YIDDISH LANGUAGE -- VOCABULARY

Pinkwater, D. M. Beautiful Yetta — E
Yikes-lice! Caffey, D. — 616.5

Yin

Coolies — E

Ying-Hwa Hu

(il) Schroeder, A. Baby Flo — 92

Ylvisaker, Anne

The luck of the Buttons — Fic
Yo! Yes? Raschka, C. — E

Yockteng, Rafael

(il) Jimmy the greatest! — E
(il) Two White Rabbits — E
(il) Messengers of rain and other poems from Latin America — 861
Walk With Me — E

YOGA

Birkemoe, K. Strike a pose — 613.7
I am yoga — E
Spilling, M. Yoga step-by-step — 613.7

YOGA

See also Hindu philosophy; Hinduism; Theosophy

YOGA -- FICTION

A morning with grandpa

YOGA -- POETRY

Wong, J. S. Twist — 8
Yoga step-by-step. Spilling, M. — 613

Yogi, Stan

Fred Korematsu speaks up —

Yohalem, Eve

Escape under the forever sky — F

Yoko. Wells, R.

Yokota, Junko

Temple, C. A. Children's books in children's hands — 028

Yolen, Jane

(ed) Switching on the moon — 8
(ed) This little piggy — 398
All star! —
Apple for the teacher — 782.
Baby Bear's books —
Birds of a feather — 8
Bug off! — 8
B.U.G. —
Come to the fairies' ball —
Commander Toad and the voyage home —
Creepy monsters, sleepy monsters —
The day Tiger Rose said goodbye —
Elsie's bird —
The Emily sonnets — 8
Fairy tale feasts — 641
(ed) Here's a little poem — 8
How do dinosaurs act when they're mad? —
How do dinosaurs say goodnight? —
Jewish fairy tale feasts — 641
Johnny Appleseed —
(jt. auth) Lewis, J. P. Last laughs — 8
Lewis, J. P. Self-portrait with seven fingers — 8
Lost boy —
A mirror to nature — 8
My father knows the names of things —
Naming Liberty —
Not all princesses dress in pink —
Not one damsel in distress — 398.
On Bird Hill —
Owl moon —
Pretty princess pig —
Sea queens — 9
Sing a season song —
Sister Bear — 398
Sleep, black bear, sleep —
Snow in Summer — F
(ed) Switching on the moon — 8
Touch magic — 028
Trash Mountain — F

Yolleck, Joan

Paris in the spring with Picasso —
Yolonda's genius. Fenner, C. — F

YOM KIPPUR

Heiligman, D. Celebrate Rosh Hashanah and Yom Kippur — 296

APPENDIX

APPENDIX

The following charts list Caldecott and Newbery medalists in the collection and their locations in the Classified Collection. Caldecott titles with both an author and illustrator are listed under the illustrator's name with a reference to the author's name, under which the book's entry can be found.

Caldecott Medal titles

Author/Illustrator	Title	Dewey Location
Azarian, Mary See Martin, J. B.	Snowflake Bentley (biography of Wilson Alwyn Bentley)	551.57
Blackall, Sophie See Mattick, L.	Finding Winnie	E
Brown, Marcia	Once a mouse	398.2
Brown, Marcia	Stone soup	398.2
Brown, Marcia See Cendrars, B.	Shadow	841
Brown, Marcia See Perrault, C.	Cinderella	398.2
Burton, Virginia Lee	The little house	E
Cooney, Barbara	Chanticleer and the fox	E
Cooney, Barbara See Hall, D.	Ox-cart man	E
Diaz, David See Bunting, E.	Smoky night	E
Dillon, L. and Dillon D. See Musgrove, M.	Ashanti to Zulu: African traditions	960
Dillon, Leo See Aardema, V.	Why mosquitos buzz in people's ears	398.2
Duvoisin, Roger See Tresselt, A. R.	White snow, bright snow	E
Egielski, Richard See Yorinks, A.	Hey, Al	E
Emberley, Ed See Emberley B.	Drummer Hoff	398.8
Floca, Brian	Locomotive	385
Gammell, Stephen See Ackerman, K.	Song and dance man	E
Gerstein, Mordicai	The man who walked between the towers	E
Goble, Paul	The girl who loved wild horses	398.2
Hader, Berta	The big snow	E
Haley, Gail E.	A story, a story	398.2
Henkes, Kevin	Kitten's first full moon	E
Hogrogian, Nonny	One fine day	398.2
Hogrogian, Nonny See Leodhas, S. N.	Always room for one more	782.42
Hyman, Trina Schart See Hodges, M.	Saint George and the dragon	398.2
Jones, Elizabeth Orton See Field, R.	Prayer for a child	242
Keats, Ezra Jack	The snowy day	E
Klassen, Jon	This is not my hat	E
Lathrop, Dorothy P. See Fish, H. D.	Animals of the Bible	220.8
Lent, Blair See Mosel, A.	The funny little woman	398.2
Lobel, Arnold	Fables	Fic
Macaulay, David	Black and white	E
McCloskey, Robert	Make way for ducklings	E
McCloskey, Robert	Time of wonder	E
McCully, Emily A.	Mirette on the high wire	E
McDermott, Gerald	Arrow to the sun	398.2

Monresor, Beni See De Regniers, B. S.	*May I bring a friend?*	**E**
Ness, Evaline	*Sam, Bangs & Moonshine*	**E**
Pinkney, Jerry	*The lion and the mouse*	**E**
Politi, Leo	*Song of the swallows*	**E**
Provensen, A. and Provensen M. See Provensen, A.	*The glorious flight: across the Channel with Louis Blériot, July 25, 1909*	**92**
Raschka, Christopher See Juster, N.	*The hello, goodbye window*	**E**
Raschka, Christopher	*A ball for Daisy*	**E**
Rathmann, Peggy	*Officer Buckle and Gloria*	**E**
Rohmann, Eric	*My friend Rabbit*	**E**
Rojankovsky, Feodor See Langstaff, J. M.	*Frog went a-courtin'*	**782.42**
Santat, Dan	*The adventures of Beekle*	**E**
Say, Allen	*Grandfather's journey*	**E**
Selznick, Brian	*The invention of Hugo Cabret*	**Fic**
Sendak, Maurice	*Where the wild things are*	**E**
Sidjakov, Nicolas See Robbins, R.	*Baboushka and the three kings*	**398.2**
Simont, Marc See Udry, J. M.	*A tree is nice*	**E**
Slobodkin, Louis See Thurber, J.	*Many moons*	**E**
Spier, Peter	*Noah's ark*	**222**
Stead, Erin E See Stead, P. C.	*A sick day for Amos McGee*	**E**
Steig, William	*Sylvester and the magic pebble*	**E**
Steptoe, Javaka	*Radiant Child*	**92**
Taback, Simms	*Joseph had a little overcoat*	**E**
Van Allsburg, Chris	*Jumanji*	**E**
Van Allsburg, Chris	*The Polar Express*	**E**
Ward, Lyn Kendall	*The biggest bear*	**E**
Weisgard, L. See Brown, M. W.	*The little island*	**E**
Wiesner, David	*Flotsam*	**E**
Wisniewski, David	*Golem*	**398.2**
Young, Ed	*Lon Po Po*	**398.2**
Zelinsky, Paul O.	*Rapunzel*	**398.2**

Newbery Medal titles

Author/Illustrator	Title	Dewey Location
Alexander, K.	*The crossover*	Fic
Applegate, K.	*The one and only Ivan*	Fic
Armstrong, W. H.	*Sounder*	Fic
Avi.	*Crispin: the cross of lead*	Fic
Barnhill, K.	*The girl who drank the moon*	Fic
Blos, J. W.	*A gathering of days: a New England girl's journal, 1830-32*	Fic
Brink, C. R.	*Caddie Woodlawn*	Fic
Cleary, B.	*Dear Mr. Henshaw*	Fic
Coatsworth, E. J.	*The cat who went to heaven*	Fic
Cooper, S.	*The grey king*	Fic
Creech, S.	*Walk two moons*	Fic
Curtis, C. P.	*Bud, not Buddy*	Fic
Cushman, K.	*The midwife's apprentice*	Fic
De Angeli, M. L.	*The door in the wall*	Fic
De la Peña, M.	*Last stop on Market Street*	E
DeJong, M.	*The wheel on the school*	Fic
DiCamillo, K.	*Flora and Ulysses*	Fic
DiCamillo, K.	*The tale of Despereaux*	Fic
Du Bois, W. P.	*The twenty-one balloons*	Fic
Estes, E.	*Ginger Pye*	Fic
Field, R.	*Hitty: her first hundred years*	Fic
Fleischman, P.	*Joyful noise: poems for two voices*	811
Fleischman, S.	*The whipping boy*	Fic
Freedman, R.	*Lincoln: a photobiography*	92
Gaiman, N.	*The graveyard book*	Fic
Gantos, J.	*Dead end in Norvelt*	Fic
Hamilton, V.	*M.C. Higgins, the great*	Fic
Henry, M.	*King of the wind*	Fic
Hesse, K.	*Out of the dust*	Fic
Kadohata, C.	*Kira-Kira*	Fic
Keith, H.	*Rifles for Watie*	Fic
Konigsburg, E. L.	*From the mixed-up files of Mrs. Basil E. Frankweiler*	Fic
Konigsburg, E. L.	*The view from Saturday*	Fic
Krumgold, J.	*Onion John*	Fic
Lawson, R.	*Rabbit Hill*	Fic
L'Engle, M.	*A wrinkle in time*	Fic
Lowry, L.	*The giver*	Fic
Lowry, L.	*Number the stars*	Fic
MacLachlan, P.	*Sarah, plain and tall*	Fic
Naylor, P. R.	*Shiloh*	Fic
Neville, E. C.	*It's like this, Cat*	Fic

O'Brien, R. C.	Mrs. Frisby and the rats of NIMH	Fic
O'Dell, S.	Island of the Blue Dolphins	Fic
Park, L. S.	A single shard	Fic
Paterson, K.	Bridge to Terabithia	Fic
Patron, S.	The higher power of Lucky	Fic
Peck, R.	A year down yonder	Fic
Perkins, L. R.	Criss cross	Fic
Raskin, E.	The Westing game	Fic
Rylant, C.	Missing May	Fic
Sachar, L.	Holes	Fic
Sawyer, R.	Roller skates	Fic
Schlitz, L. A.	Good masters! Sweet ladies!	940.1
Seredy, K.	The white stag	Fic
Speare, E. G.	The bronze bow	Fic
Speare, E. G.	The witch of Blackbird Pond	Fic
Sperry, A.	Call it courage	Fic
Spinelli, J.	Maniac Magee	Fic
Stead, R.	When you reach me	Fic
Taylor, M. D.	Roll of thunder, hear my cry	Fic
Treviño, E. B. d.	I, Juan de Pareja	Fic
Vanderpool, C.	Moon over Manifest	Fic
Vining, E. G.	Adam of the road	Fic
Voigt, C.	Dicey's song	Fic
Willard, N.	A visit to William Blake's inn	811
Wojciechowska, M.	Shadow of a bull	Fic